WHO WAS WHO

VOLUME II

1916 – 1928

WHO'S WHO

An annual biographical dictionary
first published in 1849

WHO WAS WHO

VOL. I	1897–1915
VOL. II	1916–1928
VOL. III	1929–1940
VOL. IV	1941–1950
VOL. V	1951–1960
VOL. VI	1961–1970
VOL. VII	1971–1980
VOL. VIII	1981–1990

A CUMULATED INDEX 1897–1990

Published by
A & C BLACK

WHO WAS WHO VOLUME II

WHO WAS WHO

1916–1928

A COMPANION TO

WHO'S WHO

CONTAINING THE BIOGRAPHIES
OF THOSE WHO DIED DURING
THE PERIOD 1916–1928

A & C BLACK

LONDON

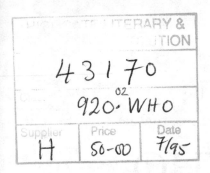
FIRST PUBLISHED 1929
SECOND EDITION 1947
THIRD EDITION 1962
FOURTH EDITION 1967
FIFTH EDITION 1992

A & C BLACK (PUBLISHERS) LIMITED
35 BEDFORD ROW LONDON WC1R 4JH

COPYRIGHT © 1992 A & C BLACK (PUBLISHERS) LTD

ISBN 0-7136-3143-0

Typeset by OTS (Typesetting) Limited, Caterham, Surrey,
printed in Great Britain by BPCC Wheatons Ltd, Exeter

PREFACE

The first edition of *Who's Who* in its present, biographical form, was published in 1897, and in 1920 Volume I of *Who Was Who* appeared, listing the entries removed from *Who's Who* on account of death between 1897 and 1915.

Who Was Who Volume II, containing the biographies of those who died between 1916 and 1928, followed in 1929. Since then it has been reprinted with corrections, but this fifth edition is the first to have been completely reset, making it possible to carry out extensive revision. The style of the entries has been brought into line with that of the current *Who's Who*, and each entry has been checked and, where necessary, corrected, using many contemporary sources of reference. It has not always been possible to reconcile conflicting information, for example on dates of birth; in such cases the details printed have been checked against those originally given by each individual at the time of his or her inclusion.

In preparing this new edition all the original material has been retained – even when, as with some references and abbreviations, its meaning is obscure. The only amendments made have been additions, principally of such items as the dates of decorations and honours, and family details of holders of hereditary titles. In a few instances, records of careers have been extended to include information that might not readily be available elsewhere. Thus the entries which appear in *Who Was Who* Volume II have been rendered more accurate and more accessible, whilst remaining true to the autobiographical nature of *Who's Who*.

ADAM AND CHARLES BLACK

CONTENTS

ABBREVIATIONS USED IN THIS BOOK

Some of the designatory letters in this list are used merely for economy of
space and do not necessarily imply any professional or other qualification.

A

A1 — First Rate (at Lloyd's)
AA&QMG — Assistant Adjutant and Quarter-Master General
AAG — Assistant Adjutant-General
AB — Bachelor of Arts; able-bodied seaman
Abp — Archbishop
AC — *Ante Christum* (before Christ)
ACA — Associate, Institute of Chartered Accountants
Acad. — Academy
ACGI — Associate, City and Guilds of London Institute
ACIS — Associate, Chartered Institute of Secretaries
ACP — Associate, College of Preceptors
ACS — Additional Curates Society
AD — *Anno Domini*
ADC — Aide-de-camp
Ad eund. — *Ad eundem gradum* (admitted to the same degree)
ADGO — Assistant Director General of Ordnance
Adj. or Adjt — Adjutant
Ad lib. — *Ad libitum* (at discretion)
Adm. — Admiral
ADMS — Assistant Director of Medical Supplies/Services
ADOS — Assistant Director of Ordnance Stores
ADST — Assistant Director of Supplies and Transport
Adv. — Advocate
ADVS — Assistant Director of Veterinary Services
Advt — Advertisement
aeg. — *aegrotat* (being ill)
Æt., Ætat. — *Ætatis* (aged)
Aft. — Afternoon
AG — Attorney-General; Adjutant-General
AGI — Associate, Institute of Certificated Grocers
AICE — Associate, Institution of Civil Engineers
AIChemE — Associate, Institute of Chemical Engineers
AIF — Australian Imperial Forces
AIG — Adjutant-Inspector-General
AKC — Associate of King's College, London
Ala — Alabama (US)
Alta — Alberta (Canada)
ALI — Argyll Light Infantry
AM — *Ante Meridiem* (before mid-day); *Anno Mundi* (in the year of the world); Master of Arts; Alpes Maritimes
AMC — Army Medical Corps; Association of Municipal Corporations
AMD — Army Medical Department
AMICE — Associate Member, Institution of Civil Engineers
AMIEE — Associate Member, Institution of Electrical Engineers
AMIMechE — Associate Member, Institution of Mechanical Engineers
AMS — Army Medical Staff; Army Medical Service; Assistant Military Secretary
ANA — Associate National Academician (America)
Anat. — Anatomy; Anatomical
Anon. — Anonymously
AOD — Army Ordnance Department
AP — Anti-Parnellite
APD — Army Pay Department
APS — Aborigines Protection Society
AQMG — Assistant Quartermaster-General
ARA — Associate, Royal Academy
Ar. Agt — Army Agent
ARAM — Associate, Royal Academy of Music
ARBC — Associate, Royal British Colonial Society of Artists
ARCA — Associate, Royal Cambrian Academy
ARCE — Academical Rank of Civil Engineers
Archt — Architect
ARCO — Associate, Royal College of Organists
ARCS — Associate, Royal College of Science
ARE — Associate, Royal Society of Painter Etchers
ARHA — Associate, Royal Hibernian Academy of Painting, Sculpture and Architecture
ARIBA — Associate, Royal Institute of British Architects
Ark — Arkansas (US)
ARMS — Associate, Royal Society of Miniature Painters
ARSA — Associate, Royal Scottish Academy
ARSM — Associate, Royal School of Mines
Art — Artist
ARWS — Associate, Royal Society of Painters in Water-Colours
AS — Anglo-Saxon
ASAM — Associate, Society of Art Masters
ASC — Army Service Corps
ASO — Assistant Staff Officer
Asst Commiss. Gen. — Assistant-Commissary-General
Assoc. Sc. — Associate in Science
Asst — Assistant
Astr. — Astronomy
Ath. — Athabasca (Canada)
AUC — *Anno urbis conditæ* (from the foundation of the city) (Rome)
AV — Authorised Version
Av. — Avenue
AVD — Army Veterinary Department
Avoird. — Avoirdupois

B

B — Baron
b — born; brother
BA — Bachelor of Arts
BAI — Bachelor of Engineering
BAO — Bachelor of Obstetrics
Bar. — Barometer
Barr. — Barrister
Bart — Baronet
Batt. or Batn — Battalion
BB&CIR — Bombay, Baroda and Central India Railway
BBKA — British Bee Keepers' Association
BC — Before Christ; British Columbia
BCA — British Central Africa
BChir — Bachelor of Surgery
BCL — Bachelor of Civil Law
BCS — Bengal Civil Service
BD — Bachelor of Divinity
Bd — Board
BE — Bachelor of Engineering
BEA — British East Africa
Beds — Bedfordshire
BEF — British Expeditionary Force
BEI — Bachelor of Engineering
Berks — Berkshire
BFBS — British and Foreign Bible Society
BI — Bengal Infantry
BISN — British India Steam Navigation Co.
BL — Bachelor of Law
BLI — Bengal Light Infantry
BLitt — Bachelor of Letters
BMA — British Medical Association
BMJ — British Medical Journal
BNA — British North America
BNC — Brasenose College, Oxford
BNI — Bengal Native Infantry
BomCS — Bombay Civil Service; Bombay Staff Corps
BoT — Board of Trade
Bot. — Botany, Botanical
BOU — British Ornithologists' Union
BP — British Public
Bp — Bishop
Brev. — Brevet
Brig. — Brigade; Brigadier
BS — Bachelor of Surgery
BSA — British South Africa
BSC — Bengal Staff Corps
BSc — Bachelor of Science
BScA — Bachelor of Science in Agriculture
Bt — Baronet; Brevet
BTh — Bachelor of Theology
BVM — Blessed Virgin Mary
Bucks — Buckinghamshire

C

(C) — Conservative; 100
c — cents; centimes; child
CA — County Alderman; Chartered Accountant (Scotland)
Cal. or Calif — California (US)
Cambs — Cambridgeshire
CAMC — Canadian Army Medical Corps
Cantab — of Cambridge
Cantuar — of Canterbury

Capt.	Captain
Cav.	Cavalry
CB	Companion of the Order of the Bath; Confined to Barracks; Cape Breton (Canada)
CBE	Commander of the Order of the British Empire
CBSA	Clay Bird Shooting Association
CC	County Councillor; County Council; Cricket Club; Cycling Club; County Court
CCC	Corpus Christi College
CCCS	Colonial and Continental Church Society
CCS	Ceylon Civil Service; Casualty Clearing Station
CE	Civil Engineer
CEF	Canadian Expeditionary Force
CEMS	Church of England Men's Society
CETS	Church of England Temperance Society
CEZMS	Church of England Zenana Missionary Society
CF	Chaplain to the Forces
Cf	*confer* (compare)
CFA	Canadian Field Artillery
CGH	Cape of Good Hope
CH	Companion of Honour
Ch.	Chief
Chanc.	Chancellor; Chancery
Chap.	Chaplain
ChB	Bachelor of Surgery
Ch. Ch.	Christ Church
Ch. Coll.	Christ's College
ChM	Master of Surgery
Chm.	Chairman
CI	Imperial Order of the Crown of India
CID	Criminal Investigation Department
CIE	Companion of the Order of the Indian Empire
Cir.	Circus
Circ.	*Circa* (about)
CIV	City of London Imperial Volunteers
Civ.	Civil
CJ	Chief Justice
CL	Commander of the Order of Leopold
Cl.	Class
CM	Church Missionary; Master in Surgery; Certificated Master
CMF	Central Mediterranean Force
CMG	Companion of the Order of St Michael and St George
CMR	Cape Mounted Riflemen
CMS	Church Missionary Society
CMZS	Corresponding Member, Zoological Society
CO	Commanding Officer; Colonial Office
Co.	County; Company
Col.	Colony; Colonel
CoL	Coalition Liberal
CoLab	Coalition Labour
Coll.	College, Collegiate
Colo	Colorado (US)
Col.-Sergt	Colour-Sergeant
Comdg	Commanding
Comdt	Commandant
Com.-in-Chf	Commander-in-Chief
Comm.	Commander
Comr	Commissioner
Comy-Gen.	Commissary-General
Conn	Connecticut (US)
cons.	consecrated
Corp.	Corporal
Corr. Mem. or Fell.	Corresponding Member or Fellow
COS	Charity Organization Society
CoU, Coal.U	Coalition Unionist
CP	Central Provinces; Captain of the Parish (IOM)
CPA	Church Pastoral Aid
CPR	Canadian Pacific Railway
Cr.	Crown
cr	created
CRA	Commander, Royal Artillery
CRE	Commander, Royal Engineers
Cres.	Crescent
CS	Civil Service
CSA	Confederate States Army; Confederate States of America
CSB	Bachelor of Christian Science
CSC	Conspicuous Service Cross
CSI	Companion of the Order of the Star of India
CSO	Chief Staff Officer
CSSR	Congregation of the Most Holy Redeemer (Redemptorist Order)
CTC	Cyclists' Touring Club
CTF	Chaplain to the Territorial Forces
CU	Cambridge University; Conservation Unionist
CUAC	Cambridge University Athletic Club
CUBC	Cambridge University Boating Club
CUCC	Cambridge University Cricket Club
CUFC	Cambridge University Football Club
CVO	Commander of the Royal Victorian Order
Cwt	Hundredweight

D

D	Duke; 500
d	pence; died; daughter
DAA&QMG	Deputy Assistant Adjutant and Quartermaster General
DAAG	Deputy-Assistant-Adjutant-General
DACG	Deputy Assistant Commissary-General
DADQ	Deputy Assistant Director of Quartering
DAG	Deputy-Adjutant-General
DAQMG	Deputy-Assistant-Quartermaster-General
DBE	Dame Commander of the Order of the British Empire
DBot	Doctor of Botany
DC	District of Columbia (US)
DCL	Doctor of Civil Law
DCO	Duke of Connaught's Own; Duke of Cambridge's Own
DCS	Doctor of Commercial Sciences
DD	Doctor of Divinity
DDMS	Deputy Director of Medical Supplies
DDS	Doctor of Dental Surgery
deg.	degree
Del.	Delaware (US)
del.	*delineavit* (he drew)
Dele. or d.	Cancel
DEng	Doctor of Engineering
DEO	Duke of Edinburgh's Own
DEOVR	Duke of Edinburgh's Own Volunteer Rifles
Dep.	Deputy
Dept	Department
DFC	Distinguished Flying Cross
DG	*Dei Gratia* (by the grace of God); Dragoon Guards
DGM	Deputy Grand Master (Masonic)
DGMW	Director-General of Military Works
Dio.	Diocese; Diocesan
Diplo.	Diplomatic
DistR	District Railway
Ditto or do	(It.) the same
Div.	Division; Divorced
DJur	Doctor of Jurisprudence
DL	Deputy Lieutenant
DLI	Durham Light Infantry
DLit or DLitt	Doctor of Literature
DMRE	Diploma in Medical Radiology and Electrology
DMS	Director of Medical Supplies
Do. or $	Dollar
DŒc	Doctor of Economics
DOM	Deo Optimo Maximo
Dom.	*Dominus*
Dow.	Dowager
DPAS	Discharged Prisoners' Aid Society
DPh	Doctor of Philosophy
DPH	Diploma in Public Health
DQMG	Deputy Quartermaster General
Dr	Doctor; Debtor
dr.	drachm
Dr Univ. Par.	Doctor of University of Paris
DSc	Doctor of Science
DSO	Companion of the Distinguished Service Order
dsp	*decessit sine prole* (died without issue)
DTheol	Doctor of Theology
Dunelm	*Dunelmensis* (of Durham)
DV	*Deo volente* (God willing)
DVH	Diploma in Veterinary Hygiene
dwt	pennyweight
DYO	Duke of York's Own
12mo	duodecimo (folded in 12)

E

E	East; Earl
E&WLR	East and West London Railway
Ebor	*Eboracensis* (of York)
EC	East Central (postal district); Episcopal Church
Eccl	Ecclesiastical
ECU	English Church Union
Ed	Editor
Edin.	Edinburgh
Educ	Educated

Edw.	Edward
EE	Early English
EETS	Early English Text Society
eg	*exempli gratia* (for example)
EI	East Indian
EIC	East India Company
EICS	East India Company's Service
Ency Brit.	Encyclopædia Britannica
Eng.	England; Engineer
ER	East Riding
esp.	especially
EsqOStJ	Esquire, Order of St John of Jerusalem
Ext	Extinct

F

f	fathoms
FA	Football Association
FAAAS	Fellow, American Association for the Advancement of Science
FAGS	Fellow, American Geographical Society
Fahr.	Fahrenheit
FAI	Fellow, Auctioneers' Institute
FASB	Fellow, Asiatic Soc. of Bengal
FBA	Fellow of the British Academy
FBOU	Fellow, British Ornithologists' Union
FC	Free Church (Scotland)
FCA	Fellow, Institute of Chartered Accountants
FCGI	Fellow, City and Guilds of London Institute
FCH	Fellow, Cooper's Hill College
FCIS	Fellow, Institute of Chartered Secretaries
Fcp	Foolscap
FCP	Fellow, College of Preceptors
FCS	Fellow, Chemical Society
FCTB	Fellow, College of Teachers of the Blind
FEIS	Fellow, Educational Institute of Scotland
FES	Fellow, Entomological Society
FF	Field Force
FFA	Fellow, Faculty of Actuaries
FFPS	Fellow, Royal Faculty of Physicians and Surgeons (Glasgow)
FGI	Fellow, Institute of Certificated Grocers
FGS	Fellow, Geological Society
FGSA	Fellow, Geological Society of America
FHAS	Fellow, Highland and Agricultural Society of Scotland
FIA	Fellow, Institute of Actuaries
FIB	Fellow, Institute of Bankers
FIBD	Fellow, Institute of British Decorators
FIC	Fellow, Institute of Chemistry
FID	Fellow, Institute of Directors
FIInst	Fellow, Imperial Institute
FInstP	Fellow, Institute of Physics
FJI	Fellow, Institute of Journalists
FKC	Fellow of King's College, London
Fla	Florida (US)
FLS	Fellow of Linnean Society
FM	Field-Marshal
FMRS	Foreign Member, Royal Society
FMS	Federated Malay States
FMU	Fellow of Madras University
Fo or Fol.	Folio (a sheet of paper folded once)
FO	Foreign Office; Field Officer
fob	free on board
fol.	folio
FP	Fire-plug
FPhysS	Fellow, Physical Society
FPS	Fellow of Philosophical Society; also of Philharmonic Society
FRAeS	Fellow, Royal Aeronautical Society
FRAI	Fellow, Royal Anthropological Institute
FRAM	Fellow, Royal Academy of Music
FRAS	Fellow, Royal Astronomical Society
FRBS	Fellow, Royal Botanic Society
FRCI	Fellow, Royal Colonial Institute
FRCO	Fellow, Royal College of Organists
FRCP	Fellow, Royal College of Physicians
FRCPE	Fellow, Royal College of Physicians of Edinburgh
FRCPI	Fellow, Royal College of Physicians of Ireland
FRCS	Fellow, Royal College of Surgeons
FRCScI	Fellow, Royal College of Science of Ireland
FRCSE or FRCSEd	Fellow, Royal College of Surgeons of Edinburgh
FRCSI	Fellow, Royal College of Surgeons of Ireland
FRCVS	Fellow, Royal College of Veterinary Surgeons
FREconS	Fellow, Royal Economic Society
FRFPS	Fellow, Royal Faculty of Physicians and Surgeons
FRFPSG	Fellow, Royal Faculty of Physicians and Surgeons, Glasgow

FRGS	Fellow, Royal Geographical Society
FRGSA	Fellow, Royal Geographical Society of Australia
FRHistS	Fellow, Royal Historical Society
FRHortS	Fellow, Royal Horticultural Society
FRIAI	Fellow, Royal Institute of Architects of Ireland
FRIBA	Fellow, Royal Institute of British Architects
FRIPH	Fellow, Royal Institute of Public Health
FRMS	Fellow, Royal Microscopical Society
FRMetS	Fellow, Royal Meteorological Society
FRNSA	Fellow, Royal School of Naval Architecture
FRPS	Fellow, Royal Photographic Society
FRPSE	Fellow, Royal Physical Society of Edinburgh
FRS	Fellow of the Royal Society
FRSA	Fellow, Royal Society of Arts
FRSAI	Fellow, Royal Society of Antiquaries of Ireland
FRSanI	Fellow, Royal Sanitary Institute
FRSC	Fellow, Royal Society of Canada
FRSE	Fellow, Royal Society of Edinburgh
FRSGS	Fellow, Royal Scottish Geographical Society
FRSL	Fellow, Royal Society of Literature
FRSM	Fellow, Royal Society of Medicine
FRSNA	Fellow, Royal School of Naval Architecture
FRSS	Fellow, Royal Statistical Society
FRSSAf	Fellow, Royal Society of South Africa
FRUI	Fellow, Royal University of Ireland
FSA	Fellow, Society of Antiquaries
FSAA	Fellow, Society of Accountants and Auditors
FSAS or FSAScot	Fellow, Society of Antiquaries of Scotland
FSI	Fellow, Surveyors' Institution
FSS	Fellow, Royal Statistical Society
FSScA	Fellow, Society of Science and Art of London
FTCD	Fellow of Trinity College, Dublin
FZS	Fellow, Zoological Society
FZSScot	Fellow, Zoological Society of Scotland

G

Ga	Georgia (US)
Gal.	Gallon
GAR	Grand Army of the Republic
GBE	Knight or Dame Grand Cross of the Order of the British Empire
g c	grandchild
GCB	Knight Grand Cross of the Order of the Bath
GCH	Knight Grand Cross of the Hanoverian Order
GCIE	Knight Grand Commander of the Order of the Indian Empire
GCMG	Knight Grand Cross of the Order of St Michael and St George
GCO-in-C	General Officer Commanding-in-Chief
GCR	Great Central Railway
GCSG	Knight Grand Cross, Order of St Gregory the Great
GCSI	Knight Grand Commander of the Order of the Star of India
GCVO	Knight Grand Cross of the Royal Victorian Order
g d	granddaughter
Gdns	Gardens
Gen.	General
gen.	genus=kind
GER	Great Eastern Railway
ges.	gesellschaft
g f	grandfather
GFS	Girls' Friendly Society
g g f	great-grandfather
Gib.	Gibraltar
GIP	Great Indian Peninsular Railway
GL	Grand Lodge; Gladstonian Liberal
Glos	Gloucestershire
GNR	Great Northern Railway
GOC	General Officer Commanding
GOC-in-C	General Officer Commanding-in-Chief
Goth.	Gothic
Gov.	Governor
Govt	Government
GPO	General Post Office
Gr.	Greek
Gram. Sch	Grammar School
g s	grandson
GS(M)	Good Service (Medal)
GSP	Good Service Pension
GWR	Great Western Railway

H

HAC	Honourable Artillery Company
Hants	Hampshire
Harv.	Harvard

HBC   Hudson's Bay Company
HBM   His (or Her) Britannic Majesty
hc   *honoris causa*
HCS   Home Civil Service
HE   His (or Her) Excellency
HEIC   Honourable East India Company
HEICS   Honourable East India Company's Service
Heir app.   Heir apparent
Heir pres.   Heir-presumptive
Herts   Hertfordshire
HFARA   Honorary Foreign Associate of the Royal Academy
HFRA   Honorary Foreign Member of the Royal Academy
HH   His (or Her) Highness
HIH   His (or Her) Imperial Highness
HIM   His (or Her) Imperial Majesty
HLI   Highland Light Infantry
HM   His (or Her) Majesty
HMC   His (or Her) Majesty's Customs
HMI   His (or Her) Majesty's Inspector
HMIS   His (or Her) Majesty's Inspector of Schools
HMS   His (or Her) Majesty's Ship; His (or Her) Majesty's Service
Hon.   Honourable; Honorary
Hons   Honours
h–p   half-pay
hp   horse-power
HQ   Headquarters
(HR)   Home Ruler
HRCA   Honorary Royal Cambrian Academician
HRH   His (or Her) Royal Highness
HRHA   Honorary Member of the Royal Hibernian Academy
HRSA   Honorary Member of the Royal Scottish Academy
HSH   His (or Her) Serene Highness
Hum.   Humanity, Humanities (Classics)
Hunts   Huntingdonshire

I

Ia   Iowa (US)
IA   Indian Army
IAHM   Incorporated Association of Headmasters
ib. or ibid.   *ibidem* (in the same place)
ICA   Institute of Chartered Accountants in England and Wales
Icel.   Icelandic
ICS   Indian Civil Service
Id   Idaho (US)
id.   *idem* (the same)
IDB   illicit diamond buying
ie   *id est* (that is)
IEF   Indian Expeditionary Force
IGC   Inspector General of Communications
IGF   Inspector General of Fortifications
ign.   *ignotus* (unknown)
IHS   *Jesus Hominum Salvator* (Jesus the Saviour of Men), more correctly
            IHΣ, the first three letters of the name of Jesus in Greek
ILH   Imperial Light Horse
Ill   Illinois (US)
ILP   Independent Labour Party
IMA   Indian Mountain Artillery
IMD   Indian Medical Department
Imp.   Imperial
IMS   Indian Medical Service
(IN)   Irish Nationalist
INA   Institution of Naval Architects
Incog.   *Incognito* (in secret)
Ind.   Independent; Indiana (US)
Insp.   Inspector
Inst.   Instant; Institute
Instn   Institution
I of M   Isle of Man
IOGT   International Order of Good Templars
IOOF   Independent Order of Oddfellows
IOP   Institute of Painters in Oil Colours
IOU   I owe you
ipi   *in partibus infidelium* (in the regions of unbelievers)
ISC   Indian Staff Corps
ISO   Companion of the Imperial Service Order
IT   Indian Territory (US)
Ital. or It.   Italian
ital.   italics
IW   Isle of Wight
IY   Imperial Yeomanry
IZ   I Zingari (Cricket Club)

J

JA   Judge-Advocate
Jas   James
Jes.   Jesus
Joh. or Jno   John
JP   Justice of the Peace
Jun.   Junior
Jun. Opt.   Junior Optime

K

K   King
Kans   Kansas (US)
KBE   Knight Commander of the Order of the British Empire
KC   King's Counsel
KCB   Knight Commander of the Order of the Bath
KCC   Commander of the Order of the Crown, Belgium and
            Congo Free State
KCH   Knight Commander of the Hanoverian Order
KCHS   Knight Commander, Order of the Holy Sepulchre
KCIE   Knight Commander of the Order of the Indian Empire
KCL   King's College London
KCMG   Knight Commander of the Order of St Michael and St George
KCSG   Knight Commander of the Order of St Gregory the Great
KCSI   Knight Commander of the Order of the Star of India
KCVO   Knight Commander of the Royal Victorian Order
KDG   King's Dragoon Guards
Keb.   Keble College, Oxford
KEO   King Edward's Own
KG   Knight of the Order of the Garter
KGO   King George's Own
KGStJ   Knight of Grace, Order of St John of Jerusalem
KH   Knight of the Hanoverian Order
KHC   Hon. Chaplain to the King
KHP   Hon. Physician to the King
KHS   Hon. Surgeon to the King; Knight of the Holy Sepulchre
K-i-H   Kaisar-i-Hind
Kil.   Kilometre
Kilo.   Kilogramme
KJStJ   Knight of Justice, Order of St John of Jerusalem
KL   Knight of the Order of Leopold
KLH   Knight of the Legion of Honour
KLS   Knight of the Lion and the Sun (Persia)
KO   King's Own
KOLI   King's Own Light Infantry
KOSB   King's Own Scottish Borderers
KOYLI   King's Own Yorkshire Light Infantry
KP   Knight of the Order of St Patrick
KPM   King's Police Medal
KRR   King's Royal Rifles
KRRC   King's Royal Rifle Corps
KS   King's Scholar
KSF   Knight of San Fernando
KSG   Knight of the Order of St Gregory the Great
KT   Knight of the Order of the Thistle
Kt   Knight
KTS   Knight of the Order of the Tower and Sword (Portugal)
Ky   Kentucky (US)

L

(L)   Liberal; 50
£   pounds (sterling)
l   left
LA   Literate in Arts; Liverpool Academy
La   Louisiana (US)
(Lab)   Labour
LAC   London Athletic Club
LAH   Licentiate, Apothecaries' Hall (Dublin)
L–Corp. or Lance- Corp.   Lance-Corporal
Lancs   Lancashire
L&NWR   London and North-Western Railway
L&SWR   London and South-Western Railway
L&YR   Lancashire and Yorkshire Railway
Lat.   Latin
lat.   latitude
LB   Bachelor of Letters
lb   pound (weight)
LB&SCR   London, Brighton and South Coast Railway
LC   Lower Canada
LC&DR   London, Chatham and Dover Railway

LCC	London County Council
LCE	Licentiate of Civil Engineering
LCh	Licentiate in Surgery
LCJ	Lord Chief Justice
LCP	Licentiate, College of Preceptors
LDiv	Licentiate in Divinity
LDS	Licentiate in Dental Surgery
LFPS	Licentiate, Faculty of Physicians and Surgeons
LGB	Local Government Board
LHD	*Literarum Humaniorum Doctor* (Doctor of Literature)
LI	Light Infantry; Long Island
Lic.	Licentiate
LicMed	Licentiate in Medicine
Lieut	Lieutenant
Linc. or Lincs	Lincolnshire
Lit.	Literature, Literary
lit.	literally
Lit.Hum.	*Literae Humaniores* (Classics)
LittD	Doctor of Letters
LJ	Lord Justice
LKQCPI	Licentiate, King and Queen's College of Physicians of Ireland (now LRCPI)
LL	Lord Lieutenant
LLA	Lady Literate in Arts
LLB	Bachelor of Laws
LLD	Doctor of Laws
LLM	Master of Laws
LM	Licentiate in Midwifery
LMSSA	Licentiate in Medicine and Surgery, Society of Apothecaries
L of C	Lines of Communication
long.	longitude
Loq.	*Loquitur* (speaks)
LRCP	Licentiate, Royal College of Physicians
LRCPE	Licentiate, Royal College of Physicians, Edinburgh
LRCPI	Licentiate, Royal College of Physicians of Ireland
LRCS	Licentiate, Royal College of Surgeons
LRCSE	Licentiate, Royal College of Surgeons, Edinburgh
LRCSI	Licentiate, Royal College of Surgeons of Ireland
LRCVS	Licentiate, Royal College of Veterinary Surgeons
LRFPSG	Licentiate, Royal Faculty of Physicians and Surgeons of Glasgow
LSA	Licentiate, Society of Apothecaries
LSB	London School Board
£sd	pounds, shillings, and pence; money
Lt	Light (*eg* Light Infantry)
Lt or Lieut	Lieutenant
Lt-Col	Lieutenant-Colonel
Lt-Gen.	Lieutenant-General
LTh	Licentiate in Theology
(LU)	Liberal Unionist
LUOTC	London University Officers' Training Corps
LXX	Septuagint

M

M	Marquess; Member; Militia; Monsieur; motor car registration number; 1000
m	married
MA	Master of Arts
MABYS	Metropolitan Association for Befriending Young Servants
Mag.	Magnetism; Magazine
Magd.	Magdalen; Magdalene
MAI	*Magister in Arte Ingeniaria* (Master of Engineering)
MAIEE	Member, American Institute of Electrical Engineers
Maj.-Gen.	Major-General
Man	Manitoba (Canada)
MAO	Master of Obstetric Art
Marq.	Marquess
MASCE	Member, American Society of Civil Engineers
Mass	Massachusetts (US)
Math.	Mathematics, Mathematical
MB	Bachelor of Medicine
MBE	Member of the Order of the British Empire
MBOU	Member, British Ornithologists' Union
MC	Military Cross; Member of Congress
MCanSocCE	Member, Canadian Society of Civil Engineers
MCC	Marylebone Cricket Club
MCE	Master of Civil Engineering
MCh	Master in Surgery
MCMES	Member, Civil and Mechanical Engineers' Society
MCom	Master of Commerce
MCS	Madras Civil Service
MD	Doctor of Medicine
Md	Maryland (US)

ME	Mining Engineer; Methodist Episcopal
Me	Maine (US)
MEC	Member of Executive Council
Mech.	Mechanics
Med.	Medical
MEF	Middle East Force
Mem	Memorundum; Member
MEng	Master of Engineering
MetR	Metropolitan Railway
MFH	Master of Foxhounds
MGI	Member, Institute of Certificated Grocers
Mgr	Monsignor
MHA	Member of House of Assembly
MHR	Member of House of Representatives
MI	Madras Infantry; Mounted Infantry
MICE	Member, Institution of Civil Engineers
Mich	Michigan (US)
MIEE	Member, Institute of Electrical Engineers
MIES	Member, Institution of Engineers & Shipbuilders in Scotland
MJI	Member, Institute of Journalists
Mil.	Military
MIM	Member, Institution of Metallurgists
MIME	Member, Institute of Mining Engineers
MIMechE	Member, Institution of Mechanical Engineers
MIMM	Member, Institute of Mining and Metallurgy
Min.	Minister; Ministry
Minn	Minnesota (US)
MInstCE	Member, Institution of Civil Engineers
MInstME	Member, Institution of Mining Engineers
MInstT	Member, Institute of Transport
MINA	Member, Institution of Naval Architects
MInstWE	Member, Institution of Water Engineers
Miss	Mississippi (US)
MIStructE	Member, Institution of Structural Engineers
MJI	Member, Institute of Journalists
MJS	Member, Japan Society
ML	Licentiate in Medicine
MLA	Member of Legislative Assembly
MLC	Member of Legislative Council
Mlle	*Mademoiselle* (Miss)
MLSB	Member, London School Board
Mme	Madame
MMS	Member of Council, Institution of Mining Engineers
Mngr	Monsignor
MNI	Madras Native Infantry
MO	Medical Officer
Mo	Missouri (US)
Mods	Moderations (Oxford)
MOH	Master of Otter Hounds; Medical Officer of Health
Mon	Montana (US); Monmouthshire
Most Rev.	Most Reverend
MP	Member of Parliament
MPC	Member of Provincial Council (South Africa)
MPP	Member of Provincial Parliament
MR	Master of the Rolls; Midland Railway; Municipal Reform
MRAC	Member, Royal Agricultural College
MRAS	Member, Royal Asiatic Society
MRCP	Member, Royal College of Physicians
MRCPE	Member, Royal College of Physicians of Edinburgh
MRCS	Member, Royal College of Surgeons
MRCSE	Member, Royal College of Surgeons of Edinburgh
MRCVS	Member, Royal College of Veterinary Surgeons
MRI	Member, Royal Institution
MRIA	Member, Royal Irish Academy
MRPS	Member, Royal Photographic Society
MRUSI	Member, Royal United Service Institution
MRZSI	Member, Royal Zoological Society of Ireland
MS	Master of Surgery
MS, MSS	Manuscript, Manuscripts
MSA	Member, Society of Architects
MS&LR	Manchester, Sheffield and Lincoln Railway
MSC	Madras Staff Corps
MSc	Master of Science
MScTech	Master of Technical Science
MSH	Master of Stag-hounds
MSI	Member, Sanitary Institute
Mt	Mount; Mountain
MusB	Bachelor of Music
MusD	Doctor of Music
MusM	Master of Music
MVO	Member of the Royal Victorian Order

N

(N)	Nationalist
N	North
n	noun; nephew
NA	North Atlantic; National Academician (USA)
Nat.Sci.	Natural Sciences
NB	North Britain; *Nota Bene* (notice); New Brunswick
NBA	North British Academy
NBR	North British Railway
NC	North Carolina (US)
NCU	National Cyclists' Union
ND	No date
NDak	North Dakota (US)
NE	North-east
NEAC	New English Art Club
Neb	Nebraska (US)
nem.con.	*nemine contradicente* (no one contradicting; unanimously)
NER	North Eastern Railway
net, nett	(It.) *Netto* (free from all deductions)
Nev	Nevada (US)
New M	New Mexico (US)
NGSNY	National Guard, State of New York
NH	New Hampshire (US)
NI	Native Infantry
NJ	New Jersey (US)
NL	National Liberal
NLF	National Liberal Federation
NNE	North-north-east
NNW	North-north-west
non seq.	*non sequitur* (it does not follow)
Northants	Northamptonshire
Notts	Nottinghamshire
NP	Notary Public
NR	North Riding
NRA	National Rifle Association
NRS	Navy Records Society; National Rose Society
NS	Nova Scotia; New Style in the Calendar (in Great Britain since 1752); National Society
NSA	National Skating Association
NSPCC	National Society for Prevention of Cruelty to Children
NSW	New South Wales
NT	New Testament; Northern Territory of South Australia
NUT	National Union of Teachers
NUTN	National Union of Trained Nurses
NUWW	National Union of Women Workers
NW	North-west
NWFP	North-West Frontier Province
NWMP	North-West Mounted Police (Canada)
NWP	North-West Province
NWT	North-Western Territories
NY	New York—City or State
NYC	New York City
NZ	New Zealand

O

O	Ohio (US)
o	only
O&O	Oriental and Occidental (Steamship Co.)
ob	*obiit* (died)
OBE	Officer of the Order of the British Empire
o c	only child
OC	Officer Commanding
OD	Ordinary seaman
o d	only daughter
OFM	Order of Friars Minor
OFS	Orange Free State
OHMS	On His (or Her) Majesty's Service
OL	Officer of the Order of Leopold
OM	Order of Merit
OMI	Oblate of Mary Immaculate
Ont	Ontario
OP	*Ordinis Praedicatorum* (of the Order of Preachers, Dominican ecclesiastical title)
op	opposite prompter
ORC	Orange River Colony
Ore	Oregon (US)
OS	Old Style in the Calendar (in Great Britain before 1752)
o s	only son
OSA	Ontario Society of Artists; Order of St Augustine
OSB	Order of St Benedict
OSFC	Franciscan (Capuchin) Order

OSM	Order of the Servants of Mary (Servites)
OSNC	Orient Steam Navigation Co.
OT	Old Testament
OU	Oxford University
OUAC	Oxford University Athletic Club
OUBC	Oxford University Boating Club
OUCC	Oxford University Cricket Club
OUFC	Oxford University Football Club
Oxon	Oxfordshire; of Oxford
oz	ounces
8vo	*Octavo* (folded in eight)

P

(P)	Parnellite
P	Prince
Pa	Pennsylvania (US)
PA	Protonotary Apostolic
pac	passed Advanced Class (at Military College of Science)
P&OSNCo	Peninsular and Oriental Steam Navigation Co.
PAO	Prince Arthur's Own
Parl.Agt	Parliamentary Agent
PASI	Professional Associate, Surveyors' Institution
PC	Privy Counsellor; Police Constable; Perpetual Curate
pc	*per centum* (in the hundred); post card
PCMO	Principal Colonial Medical Officer
PCS	Principal Clerk of Session
PDG	President, Dudley Gallery
PE(Ch)	Protestant Episcopal (Church)
PEI	Prince Edward Island
Penn	Pennsylvania
PF	Procurator-Fiscal
PFF	Punjab Frontier Force
PGD	Past Grand Deacon (Masonic)
PhB	Bachelor of Philosophy
PhD	Doctor of Philosophy
Phil.	Philology, Philological; Philosophy, Philosophical
PhNatD	Doctor of Natural Philosophy
Phys.	Physical
PI	Punjab Infantry
PICE	President, Institution of Civil Engineers
PIEE	President, Institution of Electrical Engineers
pinx.	(he) painted it
Pl.	Place; Plural
Plen.	Plenipotentiary
PM	*Post Meridiem* (after mid-day); Pacific Mail; Past Master
PMG	Postmaster-General; Pall Mall Gazette
PMO	Principal Medical Officer
PMS	President, Miniature Society
PNI	Punjab Native Infantry
P&O	Peninsular and Oriental Steamship Co.
PO	Post Office; Postal Order
POO	Post Office Order
Pop.	Population
PP	Parish Priest; Past President
Pp	Pages
PPC	Fr. *Pour prendre congé* (To take leave)
PPGW	Past Provincial Grand Warden (Masonic)
PQ	Province of Quebec
PR	Prize ring (The)
PRA	President of the Royal Academy
PRBC	President, Royal British Colonial Society of Artists
PRE	President, Royal Society of Painter Etchers
Preb.	Prebendary
Pres.	President
PRHA	President, Royal Hibernian Academy
PRI	President, Royal Institute of Painters in Water Colours
Prin.	Principal
Proc.	Proctor; Proceedings
Prof.	Professor
Pro tem.	*Pro tempore* (for the time being)
Prov.	Provost; Province, Provincial
Prox.	*Proximo* (next)
prox. acc.	*proxime accessit* (next in order of merit to the winner)
PRS	President of the Royal Society
PRSA	President, Royal Scottish Academy
PS	*Postscriptum* (postscript); prompt side
ps	passed School of Instruction (of Officers)
psc	passed Staff College
PSI	President, Surveyors' Institution
PSNC	Pacific Steam Navigation Co.
Pt	Pint
Pte	Private (soldier)
PTO	Please turn over

PVO	Principal Veterinary Officer
PWD	Public Works Department (roads, buildings, Gov. railways, telegraphs, etc.)
PWO	Prince of Wales's Own

Q

Q	Queen
QC	Queen's Counsel
QCPI	Queen's College of Physicians of Ireland
QED	*Quod erat demonstradum* (which was to be demonstrated), applied to a theorem
QEF	*Quod erat faciendum* (which was to be done), applied to a problem
QHC	Queen's Honorary Chaplain
QHP	Queen's Honorary Physician
QM	Quartermaster
QMG	Quartermaster-General
Qr	Quarter
QS	Queen's Scholar
Qt	Quart
Qto	Quarto (folded in four)
Queensl.	Queensland
QUB	Queen's University, Belfast
QUI	Queen's University in Ireland
qv	*quod vide* (which see)
QVO	Queen Victoria's Own

R

(R)	Radical
R	Rector
r	right
RA	Royal Academician; Royal Artillery
RAC	Royal Agricultural College
RAM	Royal Academy of Music
RAMC	Royal Army Medical Corps
RAS	Royal Astronomical or Asiatic Society
RB	Rifle Brigade
RBA	Member, Royal Society of British Artists
RBC	Royal British Colonial Society of Artists
RBS	Royal Society of British Sculptors
RC	Roman Catholic
RCA	Member, Royal Cambrian Academy; Royal Canadian Artillery; Royal Canadian Academy
RCI	Royal Colonial Institute
RCM	Royal College of Music
RCO	Royal College of Organists
RCPSI	Royal College of Physicians and Surgeons of Ireland
RCS	Royal College of Surgeons of England
RCSI	Royal College of Surgeons of Ireland
RCVS	Royal College of Veterinary Surgeons
RD	Rural Dean; Royal Naval Reserve Decoration
Rd	Road
RE	Royal Engineers; Fellow, Royal Society of Painter-Etchers and Engravers
rem.	remainder
REng	Royal Engineers
Rear-Adm.	Rear-Admiral
Rect.	Rector
Reg. Prof.	Regius Professor
Regt	Regiment
Res.	Resigned; Reserve
Rev.	Reverend
RFA	Royal Field Artillery
RFC	Royal Flying Corps
RGA	Royal Garrison Artillery
RGS	Royal Geographical Society
RHA	Royal Hibernian Academy; Royal Horse Artillery
RHG	Royal Horse Guards
RHMS	Royal Hibernian Military School
RHS	Royal Humane Society
RI	Member, Royal Institute of Painters in Water Colours; Rhode Island
RIBA	Royal Institute of British Architects
RIE	Royal Indian Engineering (College)
RIM	Royal Indian Marines
RIP	*Requiescat in pace* (May he or she rest in peace)
RM	Royal Marines; Resident Magistrate
RMA	Royal Marine Artillery; Royal Military Academy, Woolwich
RMC	Royal Military College, Sandhurst
RMLI	Royal Marine Light Infantry
RMO	Resident Medical Officer

RMS	Royal Microscopical Society; Royal Mail Steamer; Royal Society of Miniature Painters
RN	Royal Navy
RNAS	Royal Naval Air Service
RNAV	Royal Naval Artillery Volunteers
RNR	Royal Naval Reserve
RO	Reserve of Officers
Rock, The	Gibraltar
ROI	Member, Royal Institute of Oil Painters
Roy.	Royal
RR	Rail Road
RRC	Royal Red Cross
Rs	Rupees
RSA	Royal Scottish Academician
RSC	Royal Society of Canada
RSE	Royal Society of Edinburgh
RSF	Royal Scots Fusiliers
RSL	Royal Society of Literature
RSO	Railway Sub-Office
RSPCA	Royal Society for the Prevention of Cruelty to Animals
RSSA	Royal Scottish Society of Advocates
RSVP	Fr. *Répondez s'il vous plaît* (Please answer)
RSW	Royal Scottish Water Colour Society
Rt. Hon.	Right Honourable
Rt. Rev.	Right Reverend
RTS	Religious Tract Society; Royal Toxophilite Society
RU	Rugby Union
RUI	Royal University of Ireland
RUSI	Royal United Service Institution
RV	Revised Version; Rifle Volunteers
RVC	Rifle Volunteer Corps
RWA	Member, Royal West of England Academy
RWF	Royal Welch Fusiliers
RWS	Royal Society of Painters in Water Colours
RYS	Royal Yacht Squadron

S

(S)	Socialist
S	succeeded; South; Saint
s	son; shillings
SA	South Australia; South Africa
SAC	South African Constabulary
SALH	South Africa Light Horse
Salop	Shropshire
SAMC	South Africa(n) Medical Corps
SAR	Son Altesse Royale; Sons of the American Revolution
Sarum	Salisbury
SB	Bachelor of/in Science
SC	South Carolina (US)
sc	Student at the Staff College
SCAPA	Society for Checking the Abuses of Public Advertising
ScD	Doctor of Science
Sch.	School
Schol.	Scholar
SCL	Student in Civil Law
scr.	scruple
sculps.	*sculpsit* (he engraved)
Sculpt.	Sculptor
SD	Doctor of/in Science
SDak	South Dakota (US)
SDF	Social Democratic Federation
SE	South-east
Sec.	Secretary
Selw.	Selwyn College, Cambridge
Sen. Opt.	Senior Optime
SER	South-Eastern Railway
Serjt	Serjeant
SF	Sherwood Foresters; Sinn Fein
SG	Solicitor-General
SGW	Senior Grand Warden (Masonic)
SJ	Society of Jesus (Jesuits)
SJAB	St John Ambulance Brigade
SL	Serjeant-at-Law
SM	Society of Mary; Society of Miniaturists
SME	School of Military Engineering
SMO	Sovereign Military Order; Senior Medical Officer
SO	Sub Office; Staff Officer
Soc.	Society
Sovs	Sovereigns
sp	*sine prole* (without issue)
SPCA	Society for the Prevention of Cruelty to Animals
SPCC	Society for the Prevention of Cruelty to Children
SPCK	Society for Promoting Christian Knowledge

SPG	Society for the Propagation of the Gospel
SPQR	*Senatus Populusque Romanus* (The Senate and People of Rome)
SPR	Society for Psychical Research
SPRC	Society for Prevention and Relief of Cancer
Sq.	Square
sqq	*et sequentes* (and those that follow)
SS	Steamship; Saints; Straits Settlements
SSC	Solicitor before Supreme Court (Scotland)
SSM	Society of the Sacred Mission
SSP	Pious Society of St Paul
St	Street; Saint
STB	Bachelor of Sacred Theology
STD	*Sacræ Theologiæ Doctor*
St Edm. Hall	St Edmund Hall
stg	sterling
Stip.	Stipend, Stipendiary
stip. cond.	stipendiis condonatis
STL	*Sacræ Theologiæ Lector* (Reader or a Professor of Sacred Theology)
STM	*Sacræ Theologiæ Magister* (Master of Sacred Theology)
STP	*Sacræ Theologiæ Professor* (Professor of Divinity, old form of DD)
suppl.	supplement
Supt	Superintendent
Surg.	Surgeon
Surv.	Surviving
SW	South-west
SWB	South Wales Borderers
SY	Steam Yacht
Syn.	Synonymous, synonym

T

(T)	Temporary
T	Telephone
TA	Telegraphic Address
T&AVR	Territorial and Army Volunteer Reserve
Tas	Tasmania
TCD	Trinity College, Dublin
TD	Territorial Decoration
TF	Territorial Force
Theol.	Theology
TRH	Their Royal Highnesses
Temp.	Temperature; Temporary; *tempore* (in the time of)
Tenn	Tennessee (US)
Ter. or Terr.	Terrace
Tex	Texas (US)
Theol.	Theology
Tn	Ton
TO	Turn over; Telegraph Office
tr.	transpose
Trans	Transactions
TRC	Thames Rowing Club; Tithes Rent Charge
Trin.	Trinity
TYC	Thames Yacht Club; Two-Year-Old Course

U

(U)	Unionist
u	Uncle
UC	University College; Upper Canada
UF or UFC	United Free Church
UK	United Kingdom
(UL)	Unionist Liberal
Ult.	*Ultimo* (last)
UMCA	Universities Mission to Central Africa
Univ.	University
UP	United Presbyterian; United Provinces
US	United States; United Service; Unemployed Supernumerary
USA	United States of America
USV	United States Volunteers

V

V	Version; Vicar; Viscount; Vice; 5
v	*versus* (against)
v or vid.	*vide* (see)
VA	Victoria and Albert; Royal Order of Victoria and Albert
Va	Virginia (US)
VB	Volunteer Battalion
VC	Victoria Cross
VD	Volunteer Officers' Decoration; Volunteer Division
Ven.	Venerable
Very Rev.	Very Reverend
Vet.	Veterinary
VG	Vicar General
VI	Vancouver Island
Vice-Adm.	Vice-Admiral
Vict.	Victoria
Visc.	Viscount
viz.	*videlicet* (namely)
VL	Vice-Lieutenant
VMH	Victoria Medal of Honour (Royal Horticultural Society)
Vol.	Volume; Volunteers
VP	Vice-President
VPCS	Vice-Pres., Chemical Society
VPSA	Vice-Pres., Society of Antiquaries
VR	*Victoria Regina* (Queen Victoria); Volunteer Reserve
VR et I	*Victoria Regina et Imperatrix* (Victoria Queen and Empress)
Vt	Vermont (US)
VTC	Volunteer Training Corps

W

W	West
WA	Western Australia
Wadh.	Wadham College, Oxford
Wash.	Washington State (US)
WhSc	Whitworth Scholar
WI	West Indies
Wilts	Wiltshire
Wis	Wisconsin (US)
WLF	Women's Liberal Federation
Wm	William
WMC	Working Men's College
WMS	Wesleyan Missionary Society
WO	War Office
WR	West Riding
WS	Writer to the Signet
WSPU	Women's Social and Political Union
WVa	West Virginia (US)
Wyo	Wyoming (US)

X

X	10
Xmas	Christmas

Y

YC	Yeomanry Cavalry
yds	yards
Yeo.	Yeomanry
YMCA	Young Men's Christian Association
Yorks	Yorkshire
YRA	Yacht Racing Association
yrs	years
YWCA	Young Women's Christian Association

A

ABBAY, Rev. Richard, MA; Hon. Canon of Norwich since 1906; Rector of Earl Soham, Suffolk, 1880–1912; *b* Aldborough, Yorkshire, 11 Feb. 1844; *m* 1880, Janet Norman, *d* of Canon C. F. Norman, Mistley Place, Essex; two *s* three *d. Educ:* St Peter's School, York; Exeter College, Oxford. (Scholar); 1st class Math. Mods 1865; 1st class final Math. School, 1867; Lecturer and Demonstrator in Physics, King's College, London, 1868; Fellow of Wadham College, Oxford, 1869; member of Eclipse Expedition, S Spain, 1870; S India, 1871; member of French Transit of Venus Expedition, New Caledonia, 1874; chaplain, Kandyan Province, 1872–74; Rector of Little Bromley, Essex, 1878; Rural Dean of Loes, 1893; County Council, East Suffolk, 1900; Alderman, 1911. *Publications:* papers in the Royal Astronomical, Geological, Physical, Linnean Societies' Journals; Castle of Knaresburgh, a tale in verse of the Civil War; Life, a Mode of Motion, in verse. *Recreation:* cricket. *Address:* Earl Soham, Framlingham.   *Died 11 Dec. 1924.*

ABBE, Prof. Cleveland, AM, LLD; FRAS, FRMetS; Member, US National Acad. of Science; Professor of Meteorology, US Weather Bureau, since 1871; Lecturer on Meteorology, Johns Hopkins University, since 1895; *b* New York City, 3 Dec. 1838; *s* of George Waldo Abbe and Charlotte Colgate, and descended from purely English families; *m* 1st, 1870, Frances Martha, *d* of David Neal and Calista Lane; three *s*; 2nd, 1909, Margaret Augusta, *d* of W. Geo. Halman Percival of St Kitts, WI. *Educ:* College of the City of New York, 1851–57; University of the State of Michigan, 1858–60; Harvard University, 1860–64; Central Nicolas Observatory, Poulkova, near St Petersburg, Russia, 1864–66. Instructor in Mathematics, Trinity Parish School, New York, 1857–58; in Engineering, Michigan State Agricultural College, 1859; and in University of the State of Michigan, Ann Arbor, 1859–60; Aid in US Coast Survey (under B. A. Gould), 1860–64; Resident at the Central Nicholas Observatory, 1864–66; Aid at the US Naval Observatory, 1867–68; Director of Cincinnati Observatory, 1868–73; started the reform in standards of civil time reckoning by even hours of longitude from Greenwich, 1875; conducted the Harrison expedition to observe the solar eclipse of August 1869 at Sioux Falls City, Dakota and the Signal Service expedition to observe the solar eclipse of July 1878 from Pike's Peak; Signal Service Delegate First Forestry Congress, Cincinnati, 1872, and US Electrical Conference, 1884, where he moved the formation of the American Institute of Electrical Engineers; US Delegate International Congress on Standard Meridian and Time, Washington, 1884; Meteorologist to the US Scientific Expedition to the west coast of Africa, 1889–90; US delegate to the International Meteorological Congress, Munich, 1891; associate-editor of the American Meteorological Journal, 1891–94, and of the Beiträge zur Physik der freien Atmosphäre, 1905; founder and editor of Monthly Weather Review, 1893–1909 and since 1914, and of Bulletin, Mt Weather Research Observatory, 1908–13; Professor of Meteorology, George Washington University, Washington, 1885–1910; Adviser in Meteorology to the Carnegie Institution of Washington; Founder of the Abbe Meteorological Library of the Johns Hopkins University; delegate to the Kelvin Jubilee, 1896; to the Benjamin Franklin Bicentenary, 1906; Symons' medallist RMetS, 1912. *Publications:* numerous writings in Astronomy and Meteorology, since 1859. *Recreations:* none. *Address:* US Weather Bureau, Washington. *TA:* Clevabbe, Washington.
                                Died Oct. 1916.

ABBOTT, Rev. Edwin Abbott, MA, DD; FBA 1913; student and author; Hon. Fellow of St John's College, Cambridge, 1912; *b* London, 20 Dec. 1838; *s* of Edwin Abbott, Headmaster, Philological School, London; *m* 1863, Mary Elizabeth Rangeley (*d* 1919); one *s* one *d. Educ:* City of London School; St John's College, Cambridge. Senior Classic; Chancellor's Classical Medallist, Cambridge, 1861; Fellow of St John's College, Cambridge, 1862; Assistant Master King Edward's School, Birmingham, 1862–64; Clifton College, 1865; Headmaster of City of London School, 1865–89; Hulsean Lecturer, Cambridge, 1876; Select Preacher, Oxford, 1877. *Publications:* Bible Lessons, 1872; Cambridge Sermons, 1875; Through Nature to Christ, 1877; Oxford Sermons, 1879; article on "Gospels" in 9th edn of Encyclopædia Britannica; The Common Tradition of the Synoptic Gospels (with Mr W. G. Rushbrooke), 1884; Shakespearian Grammar, 1870; English Lessons for English People (with Prof. J. R. Seeley), 1871; How to Write Clearly, 1872; Latin Prose through English Idiom, 1873; The Good Voices, or A Child's Guide to the Bible, and Parables for Children, 1875; How to Tell the Parts of Speech, and How to Parse, 1875; edition of Bacon's Essays, 1876; Bacon and Essex, 1877; Philochristus, 1878; Via Latina, 1880; Hints on Home Teaching, 1883; Francis Bacon, an Account of his Life and Works, 1885; The Latin Gate, 1889; Onesimus, 1882; Flatland, or A Romance of Many Dimensions, 1884; The Kernel and the Husk, 1886; Philomythus, 1891; The Anglican Career of Cardinal Newman, 1892; The Spirit on the Waters, 1897; St Thomas of Canterbury, his Death and Miracles, 1898; Clue, a Guide through Greek to Hebrew Scripture, 1900; Corrections of Mark adopted by Matthew and Luke, 1901; From Letter to Spirit, 1903; Paradosis, or, In the Night in which He was (?) Betrayed, 1904; Johannine Vocabulary, A Comparison of the Words of the Fourth Gospel with those of the Three, 1905; Johannine Grammar, 1906; Silanus the Christian, 1906; Apologia, 1907; Notes on New Testament Criticism, 1907; Indices to Diatessarica, 1908; The Message of the Son of Man, 1909; The Son of Man, Contributions to the Study of the Thoughts of Jesus, 1910; Light on the Gospel from an Ancient Poet, 1912; The Fourfold Gospel, Introduction, 1913; Miscellanea Evangelica (I), 1913; The Fourfold Gospel, The Beginning, 1914; The Fourfold Gospel, The Proclamation of the New Kingdom, 1915; Miscellanea Evangelica (II), Christ's Miracles of Feeding, 1915; The Fourfold Gospel, The Law of the New Kingdom, 1916; The Fourfold Gospel, The Founding of the New Kingdom, 1917. *Address:* Wellside, Well Walk, Hampstead, NW3.   *Died 12 Oct. 1926.*

ABBOTT, Frank Frost, AB, PhD, AM(Hon.); Kennedy Professor of the Latin Language, Princeton University; Trustee American Academy in Rome; ex-President American Phil. Association; *b* 27 March 1860; *s* of Thaddeus Marvin Abbott and Mary Jane Frost; *m* Jane Harrison, New Haven, Conn. *Publications:* Roman Political Institutions; A Short History of Rome; The Toledo Manuscript of the Germania of Tacitus; Society and Politics in Ancient Rome; The Common People of Ancient Rome; Selected Letters of Cicero; Roman Politics; The Spanish Pleas of Alberico Gentili, 2 vols. *Recreation:* fishing. *Address:* Princeton University, Princeton, New Jersey, USA.   *Died 23 July 1924.*

ABBOTT, Brig.-Gen. Henry Alexius, CB 1898; Indian Army, 15th Sikhs; *b* Allahabad, 22 Jan. 1849; 4th *s* of late Maj.-Gen. Augustus Abbott, CB, Bengal Artillery; *m* 1883, Isabella Agnes, 2nd *d* of Robert Laing of Kinder, Kirkcudbrightshire, and Queensborough Terrace, Hyde Park, W. *Educ:* King William's Coll., Isle of Man. Joined 37th Foot, 1868; Indian Staff Corps (15th Sikhs), 1870; Afghan War, 1878–80; actions of Ahmed Khel, Urzoo, and Kandahar; General Roberts' march Cabul to Kandahar (despatches, medal, 2 clasps, bronze star); Soudan, 1885; actions of Hasheen, Tofrek, and Tamai (despatches, medal, 2 clasps, bronze star, brevet of Major); 2nd

Miranzai Expedition, 1891 (despatches, medal and clasp); operations of Flying Column in Kurrum Valley, 1897; Tirah, 1897–98; actions of Chagru Kotal and Dargai, capture of Sampagha and Arhanga Passes, Saransar and Waran Valley, and action of 16th Nov., twice severely wounded (despatches, medal with 3 clasps, CB); Colonel 15th Sikhs, 1913. *Address:* H. S. King and Co., 9 Pall Mall, SW.

Died 26 June 1924.

ABBOTT, Rev. Lyman, DD, LLD, LHD; editor-in-chief of The Outlook since 1893; *b* Roxbury, Mass, 18 Dec. 1835; *s* of Jacob and Harriet Vaughan Abbott; *m* 1857, Abby Frances Hamlin (*d* 1907); four *s* two *d. Educ:* New York Univ. Entered Bar, 1856, New York; after three years' practice left the law for the ministry; and from the spring of 1860 engaged in ministerial, literary, and editorial work; Pastor, Plymouth Church, Brooklyn, NY, 1888–99. *Publications:* Jesus of Nazareth; A Layman's Story; Illustrated Commentary on the New Testament, 1875; In Aid of Faith, 1891; Life of Christ, 1894; Evolution of Christianity, 1896; Christianity and Social Problems, 1897; The Theology of an Evolutionist, 1897; The Life and Letters of Paul, 1898; The Life and Literature of the Ancient Hebrews, 1900; The Rights of Man, 1901; Henry Ward Beecher, 1903; The Great Companion, 1904, 1905; The Other Room, 1904; Christian Ministry, 1905; Personality of God, 1905; The Home Builder, 1908; The Temple, 1909; The Spirit of Democracy, 1910; My Four Anchors, 1911; America in the Making, 1911; Letters to Unknown Friends, 1913; Reminiscences, 1915; The Twentieth-Century Crusade, 1918; What Christianity Means to Me, 1921. *Recreations:* driving, walking, travel. *Address:* Cornwall on Hudson, New York; The Outlook, 381 Fourth Avenue, NY City. *Clubs:* Century, National Arts, Union League, Aldine Association, Post-Graduate, NY City.

Died 22 Oct. 1922.

ABBOTT, Rt. Rev. Robert Crowther; *b* 1869; *s* of Rev. A. R. Abbott, late Vicar of Gorleston. *Educ:* Marlborough College; Trinity College, Cambridge (Scholar). 7th Wrangler, 1891; Assistant Master Marlborough College, 1892, 1907; Chaplain, 1904–7; Principal of Salisbury Theological College and Canon in Salisbury Cathedral, 1907–13; Vicar of Great St Mary's with St Michael's, Cambridge, 1913–14; of Holy Trinity, Weymouth, 1914–16; of Gillingham, Dorset, 1916–25; Chaplain to Bishop of Salisbury, 1912; Canon in Salisbury Cathedral, 1917; Examining Chaplain, 1918; Bishop of Sherborne, 1925–27. *Died 25 Nov. 1927.*

ABBOTT, Thomas Charles; JP for the City of Manchester, and Alderman; *b* Blackburn; *m* Anna Pye of Fulwood, Preston; one *s* one *d.* President Library Association, 1921–22; Chairman Manchester Public Libraries Committee; Governor of the John Rylands Library; Member of Lancashire Asylums Board and Chairman of Mental Defectives Committee; Member of Board of Overseers, township of Manchester; Vice-President Manchester and Salford Sanitary Association; Vice-President Manchester Playgoers' Club; Member of Council, Workers' Educational Association; lectures for Working Men's Clubs Association; Organiser and Lecturer, Altrincham centre, Oxford University Extension Lectures; Commander of the Order of George I (Greece). *Publications:* contributed many articles to periodicals, etc, some of which have been reprinted. *Recreations:* golf, music. *Address:* 20 Pall Mall, Manchester. *Clubs:* Royal Societies; Clarendon, Manchester. *Died 26 Jan. 1927.*

ABDY, Captain Sir Anthony (Charles Sykes), 3rd Bt *cr* 1850; *b* 19 Sept. 1848; 2nd *s* of Sir Thomas Neville Abdy, 1st Bt and Hariot, *d* of Rowland Alston, Pishiobury, Herts; *S* brother, 1910; *m* 1886, Hon. Alexandrina Victoria Macdonald, *d* of 4th Baron Macdonald; three *d.* Late Captain 2nd Life Guards; Military Attaché, Vienna, 1885; served Egyptian Expedition, 1882 (medal with clasp, bronze star). *Heir: b* Henry Beadon Abdy [*b* 13 June 1853; *m* 1891, Anna Adele Coronna; one *s* one *d*]. *Address:* 100 Eaton Square, SW. *T:* Victoria 5969; Albyns, Romford, Essex; Foss House, Pitlochry, Perthshire. *Died 1921.*

ABDY, Brig.-Gen. Anthony John, CB 1911; CBE 1918; *b* 26 April 1856; *s* of J. T. Abdy, Regius Professor of Civil Laws, Cambridge, and Marian, 2nd *d* of J. H. Hollway; *m* 1888, Laura, *d* of J. Bonham-Carter, of Adhurst, Petersfield; one *s* one *d. Educ:* Charterhouse; RMA Woolwich. Entered RA, 1876; Captain, 1884; Major, 1892; Lt-Col, 1901; Col, 1904; Secretary RA Institution, 1891–98; served S Africa, 1899–1900 (slightly wounded, despatches, brevet Lt-Col, Queen's medal with clasp); commanded RHA and RFA South Africa, 1908–12; AMS Southern Command, 1916–18; retired. *Recreations:* cricket, travel, fishing. *Address:* Woodbridge, Suffolk. *Club:* Naval and Military. *Died 4 July 1924.*

ABDY, Sir Henry Beadon, 4th Bt, *cr* 1850; *b* 13 June 1853; *s* of 1st Bt and Hariot, *d* of Rowland Alston of Pishiobury, Herts; *S* brother 1921; *m* 1891, Anna Adele Coronna; one *s* one *d. Heir: s* Robert Henry Edward Abdy, *b* 11 Sept. 1896. *Address:* 100 Eaton Square, SW. *T:* Victoria 5969; Albyns, Romford, Essex; Foss House, Pitlochry, Perthshire. *Died 1 Dec. 1921.*

A'BECKETT, Hon. Sir Thomas, Kt 1909; Puisne Judge of the Supreme Court of Victoria since 1886; *b* London, 31 Aug. 1837; *e s* of Hon. Thomas Turner A'Beckett; *m* 1875, Isabella, *d* of Sir Archibald Michie, KCMG, QC. *Educ:* King's College. Called to Bar after winning the Law Studentship of the Hon. Society of Lincoln's Inn; member of the Council of the Melbourne University, 1887. *Recreation:* travelling. *Address:* Karbarok, Orrong Road, Armidale, Melbourne. *Club:* Melbourne. *Died 24 June 1919.*

ABEL-SMITH, Geoffrey Samuel, CMG 1917; DSO 1915; *b* 1871; 3rd *s* of late Rev. Albert Smith, of Wendover, Bucks; *m* 1st, 1915, Marjorie (*d* 1918), *d* of Rev. Chas Garnett, Rector of Ardtrea, Co. Tyrone, and Lady Ella, 3rd *d* of 4th Earl Castlestewart; 2nd, 1923, Lilias, *d* of Major M. A. Close; one *d*; added Abel to surname by deed-poll, 1922. Served South African War, 1902, and World War, 1914–18, Lt-Col New Zealand Imperial Forces. *Address:* 44 Stanford Road, Kensington Court, W8. *T:* Western 3896.

Died 17 Sept. 1926.

ABERCROMBIE, Capt. Alexander Ralph, DSO 1916; MC; 1st Battalion. The Queen's (Royal West Surrey) Regiment; *b* 14 Oct. 1896. *Educ:* Haileybury; Sandhurst. Entered Army, 1914; served European War in France, 1914–18, including engagements of Hill 60, Belgium, 19–21 April 1915 (wounded, Military Cross); Hohenzollern Redoubt, 13 Oct. 1915 (DSO); Vimy (Bois-en-Hache), April 1917; Locon (Battle of Lys), 9–16 April 1918. *Address:* 34 Gloucester Terrace, Hyde Park, W.

Died 31 Dec. 1918.

ABERCROMBY, 4th Baron, *cr* 1801; **George Ralph Campbell Abercromby;** *b* 23 Sept. 1838; *S* father 1852; *m* 1858, Lady Julia Janet Georgina Duncan, VA (*d* 1915), *d* of 2nd Earl of Camperdown. Owned about 16,000 acres. *Heir: b* Hon. John Abercromby, *b* 15 Jan. 1841. *Address:* 41 Brompton Square, SW. *T:* Western 3601; Tullibody Castle, Clackmannan. *Club:* Turf.

Died 30 Oct. 1917.

ABERCROMBY, 5th Baron, *cr* 1801; **John Abercromby,** LLD; FRSE; *b* 15 Jan. 1841; 2nd *s* of 3rd Baron Abercromby and Louisa Penuel, *d* of Lord Medwyn; *S* brother 1917; *m* 1876, Adele Wilhemine Marika (marr diss 1879), *d* of Chevalier Charles von Heidenstam; one *d.* Entered Army, 1858; retired as Lieut Rifle Brigade, 1870; Vice-President, Folklore Society; ex-President, Society of Antiquaries of Scotland; Hon. Member, Finno-Ougrian Society of Helsingfors, and of Finnish Archæological Society. *Publications:* A Trip through the Eastern Caucasus; Pre- and Proto-Historic Finns (2 vols); Bronze Age Pottery of Great Britain and Ireland (2 vols), 1912. *Heir:* none. *Address:* 62 Palmerston Place, Edinburgh. *Clubs:* Athenæum; New, Edinburgh. *Died 7 Oct. 1924 (ext).*

ABERGAVENNY, 2nd Marquess of, *cr* 1876; **Reginald William Bransby Nevill,** JP; Baron Abergavenny, 1450; Earl of Abergavenny and Viscount Nevill, 1784; Earl of Lewes, 1876; *b* 4 March 1853; *s* of 1st Marquess and Caroline, *d* of Sir John Vanden-Bempde-Johnstone, 2nd Bt; *S* father 1915. *Educ:* Eton. Conservative. Owned about 50,000 acres. *Heir: b* Lord Henry Nevill, *b* 2 Sept. 1854. *Address:* 7A Eaton Square, SW. *T:* Victoria 2324; Eridge Castle, Tunbridge Wells. *Died 13 Oct. 1927.*

ABINASH CHANDRA SEN, Rai Bahadur, CIE 1921; *b* Oct. 1870; *s* of late Rao Bahadur Sansar Chandra Sen, CIE, MVO; *m* 1886. *Educ:* Jaipur; Bombay. Assistant in the office of Private Secretary, 1901–6; Assistant Private Secretary, 1906–12; Private Secretary to the Maharaja, 1912–18; Member of the State Council, 1918, and of the Cabinet, 1920; title of Rai Bahadur, 1916; an estate holder and one of the First-class nobles. *Address:* Huthroi Villa, Jaipur, Rajputana, India. *Died Dec. 1922.*

ABINGDON, 7th Earl of, *cr* 1682; **Montagu Arthur Bertie;** Baron, 1572; *b* 13 May 1836; *S* father 1884; *m* 1st, 1858, Caroline (*d* 1873), *d* of Charles Towneley; two *d*; 2nd, 1883, Gwendeline, *d* of Lieut-Gen. Hon. Sir J. C. Dormer, and *sister* of 13th Baron Dormer; two *s* two *d. Educ:* Eton. *Heir: g s* Lord Norreys, *b* 3 Oct. 1860. *Address:* Oaken Holt, Oxford. *Club:* Travellers'.

Died 10 March 1928.

ABINGER, 5th Baron, *cr* 1835; **Shelley Leopold Lawrence Scarlett,** JP; late Captain 3rd Battalion, Bedfords Regiment; *b* 1 April 1872; *s* of late Lieut-Col L. J. Y. C. Scarlett, *g s* of 1st Baron Abinger, and Bessie Florence, *d* of Edward Gibson of Spring Vale, Isle of Wight, and *niece* and adopted *d* of Sir Percy F. Shelley, 3rd Bt, and Lady Shelley; *S* cousin 1904; *m* 1899, Lila Lucy Catherine, *o d* of late Rt Hon. Sir William White, GCB, GCMG, sometime British Ambassador in Constantinople, and *widow* of late Kammerherr C. E. de Geijer, of the Swedish Diplomatic Service. Appointed Hon. Attaché to HBM's Legation at Berne, 1894, transferred to Stockholm, 1897. Owned about 41,000 acres. *Heir: b* Hon. Robert Brooke Campbell Scarlett, *b* 8 Jan. 1876. *Address:* Rownhams House, Rownhams. *M:* 342. *Clubs:* Carlton, Junior United Service, Wellington, Garrick, Marlborough; RYS, Cowes.

Died 23 May 1917.

ABINGER, 6th Baron, *cr* 1835; **Robert Brooke Campbell Scarlett;** Barrister, Inner Temple; Assistant Paymaster RNR; Lieut RNVR; *b* 8 Jan. 1876; *s* of late Lieut-Col L. J. Y. C. Scarlett, *g s* of 1st Baron Abinger, and Bessie Florence, *d* of Edward Gibson of Spring Vale, Isle of Wight, and *niece* and adopted *d* of Sir Percy F. Shelley, 3rd Bt, and Lady Shelley; *S* brother 1917; *m* 1917, Jean Marguerite, *d* of late Edouard Japy and *widow* of M. Steinheil, Paris. *Educ:* Wellington. *Heir: b* Major Hon. Hugh Richard Scarlett, *b* 25 Nov. 1878. *Address:* Brookehurst, Ewhurst, Surrey; Inverlochy Castle, Inverness-shire. *Club:* Conservative.

Died 10 June 1927.

ABNEY, Sir William de Wiveleslie, KCB 1900 (CB 1888); DSc, DCL; FRS 1876; Adviser to the Board of Education (Science Department) since 1903; Member of the Advisory Council for Education to the War Office, 1903; *b* Derby, 24 July 1843; *e s* of Rev. Canon Edward Henry Abney; *m* 1st, 1864, Agnes Mathilda (*d* 1888), *d* of E. W. Smith of Tickton Hall, Yorks; one *s* two *d*; 2nd, 1890, Mary Louisa, *d* of late Rev. E. N. Meade, DD, of St Mary's Knoll, Scarborough on Hudson, USA; one *d*. *Educ:* Rossall. Lieut RE 1861; Capt. 1873. President, Royal Astronomical Society, 1893–95; President, Physical Society, 1895–97; Chairman, Society of Arts, 1904. Principal Assistant Secretary, Board of Education, South Kensington, 1899–1903. *Publications:* Instruction in Photography, 1870; Treatise on Photography, 1875; Colour Vision, Colour Measurement and Mixture, 1893; Thebes and its Five Great Temples, 1876; The Pioneers of the Alps (with C. D. Cunningham), 1888; Trichromatic Theory of Colour, 1914. *Recreations:* painting, golf, shooting. *Address:* Measham Hall, Leicestershire. *T:* Measham 7; Rathmore Lodge, South Bolton Gardens, SW. *T:* Western 4203. *M:* AY 3060. *Club:* Athenæum.

Died 2 Dec. 1921.

ABRAHAM, Phineas Simon, MA, MD, BSc; FRCSI; Associate Royal College of Science, Ireland; Consulting Dermatologist, West London Hospital; late Lecturer on Dermatology to West London Post Graduate College; President W London Medico-Chirurgical Society, 1910–11; President Derm. Section, BMA London Meeting, 1910; Ex-President, Irish Medical Schools and Graduates' Association, and of the New London Dermatological Society; Fellow Royal Society of Medicine; *b* Falmouth, Jamaica; *s* of late Phineas Abraham, JP, formerly of that island; *m* Ellen, 2nd *d* of late Wm Chard of Longford, Middlesex; one *d*. *Educ:* University College, London (First Honours, BSc); Royal College of Science, Dublin (Royal Exhibitioner and Prizeman); Trinity College, Dublin (First Senior Moderator and Large Gold Medallist in Natural Science, Erasmus Smith Scholar, and MA Stip. Con. Hon. Causa); St Bartholomew's Hospital; Ecole de Médicine, Paris; Clausthal in Germany. Qualified as a chemical and mining engineer; obtained the Science Exhibition and the 1st Scholarship of the year, St Bartholomew's Hospital, 1876; Curator of the Museums of the Royal College of Surgeons, Dublin, 1879, and subsequently Member of Court of Examiners; Lecturer on Physiology and Histology, Westminster Hospital Medical School, 1885; Medical Secretary of the National Leprosy Fund, 1889; represented this country at the International Lepra Conference, Berlin, 1897; one of the principal founders of the Royal Academy of Medicine of Ireland, and of the Dermatological Society of Great Britain and Ireland; member of Council, Royal Drawing Society; PGD in Masonry. *Publications:* The Journal of the Leprosy Investigation Committee; articles on Leprosy and various Diseases of the Skin in Professor Clifford Allbutt's System of Medicine; Skin Affections in Syphilis (Oxford System); numerous papers on pathological and dermatological subjects in the Transactions of various learned Societies. *Recreations:* motoring, gardening. *Address:* 66 Harley Street, W1. *T:* Mayfair 522. *M:* LN 8468. *Clubs:* Savage, Royal Automobile, Wigwam.

Died 23 Feb. 1921.

ABRAHAM, Rt. Hon. William, PC 1911; LLD; MP (R) Glamorganshire (Rhondda Valley), 1885–1918, Rhondda, West Division, 1918–20; *b* 1842; *s* of a working miner; *m* 1860, Sarah Williams (*d* 1900); three *s* three *d*. *Educ:* Carnarvon National School. Known as "Mabon"; Miners' agent from 1873; Ex-President South Wales Miners' Federation. *Address:* Bryn-y-Bedw, Pentre, Pontypridd. *TA:* Mabon, Pentre. *T:* PO Pentre 35.

Died 14 May 1922.

ABRAHAMS, Israel; author and lecturer; reader in Talmudic and Rabbinic Literature in University of Cambridge; formerly Senior Tutor at Jews' College, London; first President of the Union of Jewish Literary Societies; President, Jewish Historical Society of England, 1905; Hon. President, Univ. of Glasgow Theological Society, 1907; first Lewisohn Lecturer, New York, 1912; President Society of Historical Theology, Oxford, 1921; *b* London, 26 Nov. 1858; *m* Frederica, *o d* of late Rev. S. Singer, minister of New West End Synagogue; two *d*. *Educ:* Jews' Coll., London; University Coll., London; MA London and Cambridge; LitD Western Pennsylvania; DD Hebrew Union College, Cincinnati. *Publications:* The Jewish Quarterly Review from 1889 till 1908; Aspects of Judaism, 1895; Jewish Life in the Middle Ages, 1896; Chapters on Jewish Literature, 1899; contributions to Encyclopædia Biblica, 1900; Hebrew Lessons, 1903; Maimonides, 1903; Festival Studies, 1905; A Short History of Jewish Literature, 1906; Judaism, 1907; edited Literary Remains of S. Singer, 3 vols, 1908; Macaulay on Jewish Disabilities, 1909; Rabbinic Aids to Exegesis, 1910; Jews and other articles in Encyclopædia Britannica, 1911; The Book of Delight, 1913; Annotated Hebrew Prayer Book, 1914; Jews, in Hutchinson's History of the Nations, 1915; contributions to Encyclopædia of Religion, 1916; Studies in Pharisaism, 1917; Essays on the Future of Palestine, 1918; By-paths in Hebraic Bookland, 1920; Poetry and Religion 1921; Permanent Values, 1923; Studies in Pharisaism, 2nd series, 1924. *Recreation:* photography. *Address:* Christ's College, Cambridge.

Died 6 Oct. 1925.

ABRAHAMS, Sir Lionel, KCB 1915 (CB 1908); *b* London, 9 Dec. 1869; *o s* of M. Abrahams; *m* 1896, Lucy, *d* of N. S. Joseph; one *s*. *Educ:* City of London School; Balliol College, Oxford (Scholar, 1888–92; Exhibitioner, 1892–96; Arnold Prize, 1894). Entered India Office, 1893; Assistant Secretary to Indian Currency Committee, 1898; Assistant Financial Secretary, 1901; Financial Secretary, 1902–11; Member of Departmental Committees on Indian Railway Administration and Finance, 1907–8, and West African Currency, 1912, and of the Indian Wheat Committee, 1915; Assistant Under-Secretary of State, India Office, 1911–17. *Publications:* The Expulsion of the Jews from England in 1290; contributions to the Dictionary of Political Economy. *Address:* 18 Porchester Terrace, W. *T:* Paddington 3854. *Club:* Athenæum.

Died 30 Nov. 1919.

ABRAHAMS, Louis Barnett; Order of Mercy; *b* Swansea, 3 Oct. 1839; *s* of Rev. Barnett Abrahams, minister of the Jewish community of that town; *m* Fannie, *e d* of late Ephraim Moseley of London; one *d*. *Educ:* Jews' School, London; Univ. Coll.; BA London. Principal assistant master, vice-master, and headmaster of Jews' Free School, Spitalfields, E; editor for three years of the Jewish Record; one of the founders of the Jewish Education Board; vice-president of the League of Mercy; Hon. Captain, Jewish Lads' Brigade; member of various Care Committees of the LCC. *Publications:* Chronological History of England; Manual of Scripture History; translator of the Standard Hebrew Prayer Book. *Recreations:* literary pursuits. *Address:* 3 Seaforth Road, Westcliff-on-Sea. *Clubs:* University of London, Maccabæans. *Died 3 June 1913.*

ABRAM, Sir George Stewart, Kt 1922; BA, MB, BChir (Cantab); MRCS, LRCP; JP; Physician Royal Berks Hospital; Major RAMC (T); *b* 18 March 1866; *m* 1893, Ethel May, *d* of late T. F. Rider, MVO; one *s* two *d*. *Educ:* Merchant Taylors' School; Cambridge; University College Hospital, London. Mayor of Reading, 1919–20. *Publications:* medical in Lancet. *Recreations:* golf, lawn tennis. *Address:* 106 London Road, Reading. *T:* 268. *M:* DP 2926.

Died 24 Oct. 1928.

ACHESON, Maj.-Gen. Hon. Edward Archibald Brabazon; late Coldstream Guards; *b* 22 May 1844; *brother* of 4th Earl of Gosford; *m* 1869, Clementina, *d* of late Gen. Sir J. Gaspard le Marchant, GCSI, KCB; four *d*. *Educ:* Harrow. Served Egypt, 1882 (medal with clasp, Khedive's Star). *Clubs:* Travellers', Guards'.

Died 3 July 1921.

ACHURCH, Janet, (Janet Achurch Sharp); *b* Lancashire; *m* Charles Charrington. First appeared in London with Genevieve Ward; toured in provinces, playing over a hundred parts; played in Harbour Lights; and with Mr Beerbohm Tree through run of three pieces; appeared as Nora Helmer in A Doll's House, 1889; first English actress to visit Khedivial theatre, Cairo; toured with own company in Australia, India, and America; played Rita Allmees in Little Eyolf, Cleopatra in special Manchester production afterwards given at matinées in London; and Candida in play of that name; also original Lady Cicely in Captain Brassbound's Conversion; Merete Beyer in The Witch, Anna Redvers in A Secret Woman, Mrs Alving in Ghosts. *Publications:* several short stories. *Recreations:* travelling, seeing new places and people. *Address:* c/o The Stage, 16 York Street, WC.

Died 11 Sept. 1916.

ACKLAND, Robert Craig, CBE 1920; MRCS, LRCP, LDS; Dental Surgeon to St Bartholomew's Hospital; Medical Officer in Charge of the Red Cross Hospital for Facial Injuries, 78 Brook Street, W, and 24 Norfolk Street, W; *s* of late Robert Ackland, Exeter; *m* Ruth, *d* of late Edmund Macrory, KC; two *d*. *Educ:* Torquay; Charing Cross Hospital. *Publications:* Diseases of the Teeth, Quain's Dictionary of Medicine, etc. *Recreations:* shooting, golf, etc. *Address:* 54 Brook Street, W1. *T:* Mayfair 2433; The Hill, Winterton, Norfolk. *M:* T 512. *Clubs:* Bath; Denham Golf; Great Yarmouth Golf.

Died 6 Aug. 1923.

ACKLOM, Major (Temp. Lieut-Col) Spencer, DSO 1917; MC; 1st Battalion The Highland Light Infantry; Commanding 22nd Northumberland Fusiliers (3rd Tyneside Scottish); *m* 1909, Lucie, *e d* of Mountford Spencer, The Hill, Teignmouth, Devon. *Educ:* RMC, Sandhurst. Joined 2nd Batt. HLI 1902; transferred to 1st Batt. 1905; adjutant of the 9th (TF) Battalion HLI (The Glasgow Highlanders), 1913; proceeded to France with that battalion on 4 Nov. 1914; posted to 22nd NF (3rd Tyneside Scottish) as second in command, May 1916, and appointed to command that battalion with temporary rank of Lieut-Col, 2 July 1916 (despatches thrice, DSO, MC). *Recreations:* golf, polo, racquets, etc. *Club:* Junior Naval and Military. *Died 30 March 1918.*

ACLAND, Rt. Hon. Sir Arthur Herbert Dyke, 13th Bt, *cr* 1644; PC 1892; MA; Hon. LLD (Leeds); *b* 13 Oct. 1847; 2nd *s* of Rt Hon. Sir Thomas Dyke Acland, 11th Bt, and first wife, Mary, *d* of Sir Charles Mordaunt, 8th Bt; *S* brother 1919; *m* 1873, Alice Sophia, *e d* of Rev. Francis Cunningham; one *s* one *d*. *Educ:* Rugby; Christ Church, Oxford. Formerly Steward and Senior Student of Christ Church; was Senior Bursar, and later Honorary Fellow of Balliol; Vice-President, Committee of Council on Education, 1892–95; MP (L) Rotherham, Yorks, 1885–99; late Chairman Executive Committee, Imperial College of Science and Technology. *Publications:* Handbook of Political History of England; Working Men Co-operators; Patriotic Poetry of William Wordsworth, 1915. *Heir: s* Rt Hon. Francis Dyke Acland, *b* 7 March 1874. *Address:* 85 Onslow Square, SW7. *Club:* Athenæum.

Died 9 Oct. 1926.

ACLAND, Sir (Charles) Thomas Dyke, 12th Bt, *cr* 1644; MA; JP, DL, Somerset, Devon, Cornwall, etc; *b* 16 July 1842; *e s* of Rt Hon. Sir Thomas Dyke Acland, 11th Bt; *S* father 1898; *m* 1879, Gertrude, 3rd *d* of Sir John Walrond, 1st Bt, and *sister* of 1st Baron Waleran. *Educ:* Bradfield; Eton; Christ Church, Oxford. 3rd class Classics, 1866. Lieut-Col late Devon Yeomanry Cavalry; Deputy Warden of the Stanneries; Barrister; MP (L) East Cornwall, 1882–85; NE Cornwall, 1885–92; Parliamentary Secretary to Board of Trade and Ecclesiastical Commissioner, 1886; County Alderman, Devon; Chairman of Technical Education Committee of Devon County Council from its commencement, 1890 till 1910; VP Bath and West of England and Southern Counties Agricultural Society, in which Society for some years chairman, or acting-chairman, of the Journal Committee, Experiments Committee, and Dairy Committee; Sheriff of Devon, 1903–4. *Heir: brother* Rt Hon. Arthur Herbert Dyke Acland, MP, *b* 13 Oct. 1847. *Address:* Killerton, Exeter; Holnicote, Taunton. *Clubs:* Athenæum, Travellers', Cavendish, Cobden; Devon and Exeter, Exeter; Somerset County, Taunton.

Died 18 Feb. 1919.

ACLAND, Sir Reginald Brodie Dyke, Kt 1914; KC 1904; Recorder of Oxford since 1903; Judge-Advocate of the Fleet, 1904; *b* 18 May 1856; 6th *s* of Sir Henry Wentworth Acland, 1st Bt, KCB, MD, sometime Regius Professor of Medicine in the University of Oxford; *m* 1885, Helen, *d* of Rev. Thomas Fox, Rector of Temple Combe, Somerset; two *s* two *d*. *Educ:* Winchester; University College, Oxford. Called to the Bar, 1881; Junior Counsel to the Admiralty, 1897–1904;

Counsel for Great Britain, North Sea Enquiry, 1905; formerly for many years Member of the General Council of the Bar; late Treasurer, Barristers' Benevolent Association; has taken interest in hospital work in London; Chairman Hospital Saturday Fund, 1890–98; Recorder of Shrewsbury, 1901–3; JP Berks; Chairman Quarter Sessions. *Recreations:* gardening, all country pursuits. *Address:* 2 Hare Court, Temple, EC4. *T:* Central 2722; Cold Ash, Newbury. *Club:* United University. *Died 18 Feb. 1924.*

ACLAND, Admiral Sir William Alison Dyke, 2nd Bt, *cr* 1890; CVO 1903; JP Oxfordshire and Devon; *b* Oxford, 18 Dec. 1847; *e s* of Sir Henry W. Acland, 1st Bt; *S* father 1900; *m* 1887, Hon. Emily Anna, author of several novels, *d* of late Viscountess Hambleden and late Rt Hon. William Henry Smith; two *s*. *Educ:* private schools. Entered HMS Britannia as Cadet, 1861; Lieut 1868; Comdr 1879; Capt. 1885; attached to 1st Brigade Chilian Army in campaign against Peru, 1881 (medal, two clasps); Deputy Commissioner Western Pacific; ADC to the Queen, 1896–99; Jubilee Medal, 1897; Captain of Dockyard Reserve at Devonport, 1897–99; Rear-Admiral, 1899; 2nd in command Channel Squadron, 1901–2; Superintendent, Gibraltar Dockyard, 1902–4; Vice-Admiral, 1904; Admiral, 1908; retired, 1911. *Recreations:* fishing, boat-sailing. *Heir: s* William Henry Dyke Acland [*b* 16 May 1888; *m* 1916, Margaret Emily, *d* of late Theodore Barclay of Fanshaws, Herts; two *d*. Capt. Devon Yeomanry and late Major RAF; served European war (MC, AFC, 4th Class Order of St George). *Address:* Barnes Wood, Welwyn. *Clubs:* Bath, Athenæum]. *Address:* Wilmead, Torquay. *T:* Torquay 695. *M:* T289. *Club:* United Service. *Died 26 Nov. 1924.*

ACTON, 2nd Baron, *cr* 1869; **Richard Maximilian Dalberg-Acton,** KCVO 1916 (MVO 1901); Bt 1643; *b* 7 Aug. 1870; *s* of 1st Baron and Countess Marie Arco-Valley, of Munich; *S* father 1902; *m* 1904, Dorothy (*d* 1923), *d* of late T. H. Lyon, of Appleton Hall, Cheshire; two *s* seven *d*. *Educ:* Magdalen Coll., Oxford. Entered Foreign Office, 1894; 3rd Secretary Diplomatic Service, Berlin, 1896; 2nd Secretary, 1900; 2nd Secretary, Vienna, 1902; Berne, 1903; Madrid, 1906; The Hague, 1907; Lord in Waiting to HM, 1905–15; 1st Secretary Diplomatic Service; Chargé d'Affaires, Darmstadt, 1911–14; Councillor of Embassy, 1914; Consul-General, Zurich, 1917–19; Envoy to Finland, 1919–20. *Heir: s* Hon. John Emerich Henry Dalberg-Acton, *b* 15 Dec. 1907. *Address:* Aldenham Park, Bridgnorth. *Club:* Athenæum. *Died 16 June 1924.*

ACTON, Fitzmaurice, CMG 1918; *b* Feb. 1874; *s* of Colonel and Mrs Hampden Acton, of Chalet Lucia, Pau, France; *m* 1910, Ruby, *widow* of Lieut P. Crabtree, RN; one *s*. Joined Britannia, 1887; Commander, 1908; Naval Attaché, Paris, 1915–17; Naval Attaché, Tokyo, since 1918; Acting Captain, 1915; Officer Legion of Honour, Order of the Rising Sun 3rd class. *Recreations:* fishing, shooting. *Address:* Rathmullen, Donegal. *Club:* United Service.

Died 7 Aug. 1921.

ACWORTH, Sir William Mitchell, KCSI 1922; Kt 1921; barrister; *b* 22 Nov. 1850; 3rd *s* of Rev. W. Acworth of the Hall, South Stoke, Bath; *m* 1st, 1878, Elizabeth Louisa Oswald (*d* 1904), *e d* of James Brown of Orangefield, Ayrshire; 2nd, 1923, Elizabeth Learmonth, *yr d* of late Thomas Wotherspoon, Hundleshope, Peebles. *Educ:* Uppingham; Christ Church, Oxford; MA 1875. Member London County Council, 1889–92; Unionist Candidate for Keighley Division of West Riding, 1906, 1910, 1911; member of many Royal Commissions and Committees on British Railways; Royal Commission of Enquiry into Canadian Railways, 1916; S Rhodesian Railways, 1918; Chairman of Committee on Indian Railways, 1921; reported on Austrian Railways for the League of Nations, 1923; on German Railways for the Reparations Commission, 1924; member of Council of the Royal Economic Society and of the Institute of Transport; Director of the Underground Electric Railways of London, Limited, and other companies. *Publications:* Railways of England, 1889; Railways of Scotland, 1890; Railways and the Traders, 1891; Railway Economics, 1905; State Railway Ownership, 1920. *Address:* The Albany, Piccadilly, W1. *T:* Regent 696; Underwood, Ide, Exeter. *Clubs:* Brooks's, Reform. *Died 2 April 1925.*

ADAIR, Admiral Charles Henry; *b* 2 July 1851; 2nd *s* of General Sir Charles W. Adair, KCB, RMLI; *m* 1893, Annette C., *d* of W. H. Wilson of Nortonsea, Waterloo, Lancashire; two *s* one *d*. Entered Royal Navy, 1864; Lieut, 1874; Commander, 1886; Captain, 1893; Rear-Admiral, 1905; Vice-Admiral, 1909; Admiral, 1913; served continuously at sea in all parts of the world; Suakim, 1884 (Egyptian medal and star); retired, 1913. *Address:* Hendon, Regents Park, Southampton. *Club:* United Service.

Died 9 March 1920.

ADAIR, Mrs Cornelia; *e d* of Gen. Wadsworth (*d* 1864), of New York and Mary, *d* of late William Wharton; *m* 1st, 1858, Col Montgomery Ritchie (*d* 1864); 2nd, 1867, John George Adair (*d* 1885), of Rathdaire. *Address:* 11 Portman Square, W. *T:* Mayfair 4760; Glenveagh Castle, Churchill, Co. Donegal.   *Died 22 Sept. 1922.*

ADAIR, Rear-Admiral Thomas Benjamin Stratton; Head of the Ordnance Department of W. Beardmore & Co. Ltd, Parkhead Steelworks, Glasgow; *b* Nov. 1861; *s* of late Gen. Sir Charles William Adair, KCB. Entered Navy, 1874; retired, 1906; Member of the Ordnance Committee, 1900–2; MP (CU) Shettleston Division of Glasgow, Dec. 1918–Oct. 1922. *Address:* 45 St George's Road, SW1. *T:* Victoria 5802. *Club:* United Service.   *Died 12 Aug. 1928.*

ADAM, Sir Charles Elphinstone, 1st Bt, *cr* 1882; DL, JP Kinross and Fife; Barrister Inner Temple and Lincoln's Inn, 1885; Convener Kinross-shire, 1893–1910; Chairman Kinross Territorial Association, 1908; Lord-Lieutenant Kinross-shire, and President Territorial Association, 1909–11; *b* 7 Aug. 1859; *s* of late Rt Hon. William Patrick Adam, CIE, Governor of Madras, and Emily Eliza, *d* of Gen. Sir William Wyllie, GCB; *m* 1912, Edith, *d* of late W. Dobson, Victoria, British Columbia. *Educ:* Eton; Christ Church, Oxford. Private Sec. to Parliamentary Secretary of Treasury, Lord Privy Seal and Chancellor of Duchy of Lancaster (Lord Tweedmouth), 1892–95; Volunteer Long Service Medal, 1904; served with RNVR (AAC Gun Stations), June 1915–Dec. 1916; Lieut in Army, and Train Conducting Officer (France), 1916–18. Owned 4,250 acres. *Heir:* none. *Publication:* editor of Political State of Scotland in the Last Century, 1887. *Address:* Blair-Adam, Kinross-shire; 5 New Square, Lincoln's Inn, WC. *Clubs:* Brooks's, United University, National Liberal.   *Died 6 Dec. 1922 (ext.)*

ADAM, Rev. David Stow, MA, DD; Professor of Systematic Theology and Church History at Ormond College, University of Melbourne, since 1908; *b* Langside, near Glasgow, 9 Feb. 1859; *s* of George Adam, teacher in Glasgow Normal Seminary, and Jane Constable of Perth; *m* 1892, Mary Grace, *d* of John Paterson, Skirling Mains, Biggar; four *s* one *d*. *Educ:* Langside Academy; Glasgow University; Free Church College; Erlangen University. MA with first-class Honours in Mental Philosophy, 1881; BD, 1884; DD, 1912; Scott Scholar, Glasgow University, 1881; Eglinton Fellow and Lecturer in Logic and Mental Philosophy, Glasgow University, 1882–83; Stevenson Scholar, Freeman Fellow, and Hebrew Tutor, Glasgow Free Church Theological Hall, 1882–86; Minister at Banchory, Deeside, 1886–90; Kelso, 1890–95; St Andrews, Greenock, 1895–1907; President of Council of Churches, Victoria, 1910; Chairman of Church-Union Committee of Australia since 1916. *Publications:* Cardinal Elements of the Christian Faith, 1911; various articles in Hastings' Dictionaries. *Recreations:* golf, fishing. *Address:* Ormond College, Melbourne. *T:* Cent. 6419.   *Died 31 Jan. 1925.*

ADAM, Eric Graham Forbes, CMG 1923; 1st Secretary in the Foreign Office; *b* Bombay, 3 Oct. 1888; 2nd *s* of Sir Frank Forbes Adam, 1st Bt; *m* 1918, Agatha Perrin, *e d* of Dr R. W. Macan; one *s*. *Educ:* Eton (KS); King's College, Cambridge (Scholar). First class in Parts I and II of the History Tripos; passed first into the Foreign Office, 1913; 3rd Secretary in British Peace Delegation, Paris, 1919; London and San Remo Conferences, 1920; 1st Secretary, 1922; 1st Secretary in British Delegation, Lausanne Conference, 1922–23. *Address:* c/o British Embassy, Constantinople. *Club:* 1917.   *Died 7 July 1925.*

ADAM, Sir Frank Forbes, 1st Bt, *cr* 1917; Kt 1890; CB 1919; CIE 1888; LLD Vict.; JP, DL; *b* 17 June 1846; *m* 1883, Rose Frances, *d* of C. G. Kemball, late Judge High Court, Bombay; two *s* one *d* (and one *s* decd). *Educ:* Loretto. Went to India 1872 as a merchant; President Bank of Bombay; President Chamber of Commerce; Member of Port Trust; Member of Legislative Council; returned to England 1890; President of Manchester Chamber of Commerce, 1894 and 1903–5; Chairman of Council of Manchester University; Chairman of Manchester Royal Infirmary Board, 1900–2; Chairman of St Mary's Hospitals Board; Chairman, Territorial Force Association since 1914; Chairman Manchester and County Bank; Member Commercial Intelligence Committee. *Recreation:* golf. *Heir:* s Col Ronald Forbes Adam, *b* 30 Oct. 1885. *Address:* The Palace Hotel, Buxton. *TA:* Wilmslow. *Club:* Union.   *Died 22 Dec. 1926.*

ADAM, Maj.-Gen. Frederick Archibald, CB 1913; *b* 8 Aug. 1860; *s* of Archibald MacIndoe Adam, of Glasgow, and Sophia Catherine Gillespie; *m* 1884, Florence, *d* of late Maj.-Gen. Thomas James Watson, Bengal Cavalry; two *d*. *Educ:* Fettes College, Edinburgh; Royal Military College, Sandhurst. Joined 40th Regiment in India, 1880; served S Africa, 1900–2; commanded 1st Batt. South Lancashire Regt, 1901 (despatches twice, Brevet Lt-Col); 2nd South Lancashire Regt, 1906–10; North Lancashire Infantry Brigade (TF), 1910–13; Infantry Brigade, Malta, 1913–14. *Recreations:* shooting, cricket, music, natural history. *Address:* Dunain, Inverness.   *Died 5 March 1924.*

ADAM, Capt. Herbert Algernon, CBE 1919; RN; Captain for Coastguard Duties on Staff of C-in-C Nore; *b* 3 Jan. 1872; *s* of late Rev. B. W. Adams, DD, Rector of Santry, Co. Dublin; assumed original name of Adam by Deed Poll, 1901; *m* 1898, Emily Banner Clough, *d* of Captain S. J. Johnstone, RN; one *s*. *Educ:* HMS Britannia; Royal Naval College, Greenwich. Served in Witu Expedition, 1890 (medal and clasp); Egyptian Waters during Dongola Expedition (medals, British and Egyptian); was in command of HMS Barham at Messina Earthquake (medal and Chevalier of the Order of St Maurice and St Lazarus for services) and at Somaliland Blockade, 1909; Flag Captain to Admiral Sir Cecil Thursby in command of HMS Queen at the Dardanelles, and landed the Anzac Division at Gallipoli, Easter Sunday, 1915; PNTO at Salonica, and in command of HMS Cornwall on North Atlantic Convoy work and employed bringing over US Troops (despatches). *Recreations:* riding, driving, motoring, gardening, poultry-rearing. *Address:* The Chillies, Uckfield, Sussex. *T:* Crowborough 211. *Clubs:* United Service; Union, Malta.   *Died 27 Sept. 1920.*

ADAMI, John George, CBE 1919; FRS 1905; MA, MD (Camb.); FRCP, FRCS, FRSS Edin. 1898, Canada 1902; MA, MD (ad eundem), McGill, 1899; MD (Hon.) Belfast, 1921; LLD (New Brunswick), 1900; (Toronto), 1912; (Manchester), 1923; ScD (TCD), 1912; Vice-Chancellor of the University of Liverpool since 1919; . *b* Manchester, 12 Jan. 1862; *s* of late John George Adami of Manchester and Ashton-upon-Mersey, Cheshire, and Sarah Ann Ellis, *d* of Thomas Leech of Urmston, Lancs; *m* 1st, 1894, Mary Stuart (*d* 1916), *d* of James Alexander Cantlie and Eleonora Stephen of Montreal; one *s* one *d*; 2nd, 1922, Marie, *er d* of Rev. T. W. Wilkinson, The Vicarage, Litherland, Lancs. *Educ:* Owens College, Manchester; Christ's College, Cambridge (Scholar); Breslau and Paris. 1st cl. 1st pt Natural Science Tripos, 1882; 1st cl. 2nd pt 1884; Darwin Prizeman, 1885; House Physician, Manchester Royal Infirmary, and Demonstrator of Pathology, Univ. of Camb., 1887; John Lucas Walker Student of Pathology, 1890; Fellow of Jesus Coll., 1891; President Association American Physicians, 1911–12; Canadian Association Prevention of Tuberculosis, 1909–12; Montreal City Improvement League, 1909–16; Montreal Child Welfare Exhibition, 1912; Colonel CAMC; Medical Historical Recorder, Canadian Expeditionary Force, ADMS; Strathcona Professor of Pathology and Bacteriology, McGill University, Montreal, 1892–1919; Fothergillian Medallist, Medical Society, London, 1914; Hon. Fellow of Christ's College and Jesus College, Camb., 1920; Member Consultative Committee of Minister of Education. *Publications:* The Principles of Pathology, 1908; Medical Contributions to the Study of Evolution, 1918; Charles White of Manchester, and the Prevention of Puerperal Fever, 1922; numerous papers upon pathological subjects in journals and transactions; articles on Inflammation, Allbutt's System of Medicine. *Address:* The University, Liverpool. *Clubs:* Athenæum; University, Exchange, Athenæum, Conservative, Reform, Liverpool.   *Died 29 Aug. 1926.*

ADAMS, Rev. Arthur; Hon. Canon of Truro since 1912; Vicar of Crowan since 1904; *b* 11 Oct. 1852; *s* of William Adams, Bridge House, East Molesey. *Educ:* Sherborne; St John's College, Cambridge; Cuddesdon Theological College. Ordained, 1875; Curate of Camborne, 1875–81; Vicar of St Colan, 1881–83; of Tuckingmill, 1883–1904. *Address:* Crowan Vicarage, Praze, Cornwall.   *Died 13 Feb. 1926.*

ADAMS, Brooks; *b* Quincy, Massachusetts, 24 June 1848; *y s* of Charles Francis Adams; *g s* of John Quincy Adams; *m* 1889, Evelyn Davis. *Educ:* Harvard; graduated class of 1870. Lawyer and literary. *Publications:* Emancipation of Massachusetts, 1887; Law of Civilisation and Decay, 1895 (translated into French and German); The Gold Standard, 1894; America's Economic Supremacy, 1900 (translated into German); The New Empire, 1902 (translated into German and Russian); two chapters in Centralisation and the Law, 1906; Railway as Public Agents, 1910; Theory of Social Revolutions, 1913; The Degradation of the Democratic Dogma (with Henry Adams), 1919; numerous addresses, etc. *Address:* 84 State Street, Boston, Mass.   *Died 13 Feb. 1927.*

ADAMS, George Burton, PhD, LittD, LLD; Professor of History in Yale University since 1888; *b* Fairfield, Vermont, 8 June 1851; *s* of Rev. Calvin Carlton and Emeline Nelson Adams; *m* 1878, Ida, *d* of Mills de Forest Clarke. *Educ:* Beloit Coll.; Yale and Leipzig Universities. Professor of History in Drury College, 1877–88; president of the American Historical Association, 1907–8; one of the editors of the American Historical Review, 1895–1913; member of the American Antiquarian Society; Corresponding Member Royal Historical Society, Massachusetts Colonial Society, and Massachusetts and Vermont Historical Societies, etc. *Publications:* Civilisation during the Middle Ages; The Growth of the French Nation; European History; Vol. II in Hunt and Poole's Political History of England; The Origin of the English Constitution; Outline of English Constitutional History; The British Empire; Constitutional History of England; editor of Duruy's Middle Ages; Bémont and Monod's Medieval Europe; and with Prof. H. Morse Stephens of Select Documents of English Constitutional History; and author of many articles and addresses. *Recreations:* fishing, boat sailing. *Address:* 57 Edgehill Road, New Haven, Conn. *Clubs:* Graduates, Elizabethan, New Haven. *Died 26 May 1925.*

ADAMS, George Francis, CBE 1919; MInstCE; Chief Inspector of Mines in India since 1910; *b* 6 May 1870; *s* of late George Frederick Adams, MInstCE, Cardiff; *m* 1904, Margaret Elizabeth, *d* of late Cornelius O'Connor, London; one *d*. *Educ:* Harrow; Bedford. HM Asst-Inspector of Mines, South Wales District, 1894–1902; Inspector of Mines in India, 1902–10. *Publications:* various reports on Mining and Mining Education. *Recreation:* golf. *Address:* Hirapur House, Dhambad, India. *TA:* Mines, Dhambad. *Clubs:* Sports; Bengal United Service, Calcutta. *Died 10 Jan. 1921.*

ADAMS, Henry Carter, PhD, LLD; Professor of Political Economy and Finance, University of Michigan, since 1887; Associate Editor International Journal of Ethics; *b* Davenport, Iowa, 31 Dec. 1851; *m* 1890, Bertha H. Wright, Port Huron, Michigan. *Educ:* Iowa College; Johns Hopkins University; Heidelberg; Berlin; Paris; Andover Theological Seminary. *Publications:* Outline of Lectures on Political Economy, 1881, 1886; State in Relation to Industrial Action, 1887; Taxation in the United States, 1787–1816, 1884; Public Debts, 1887; The Science of Finance, 1888; Statistics of Railways, 1888–1910; Economics and Jurisprudence, 1897; Description of Industry, 1918; American Railway Accounting, 1918. *Address:* Ann Arbor, Michigan, USA. *Died 11 Aug. 1921.*

ADAMS, Capt. Joseph Ebenezer; RAMC(T); Surgeon to St Thomas' Hospital; Senior Surgeon East London Hospital for Children; *b* 7 Feb. 1878; 5th *s* of William Adams, merchant in City of London; *m* 1913, Muriel Emma, *y d* of late Harry Webb, of Southlaund, Chislehurst. *Educ:* City of London School; St Thomas' Hospital (Entrance Scholarship); qualified MRCS, LRCP, 1902. House Surgeon, Clinical Asst in Throat Department; MB, BS London, 1904; FRCS, 1904; Beaney scholar in Surgery and Surgical Pathology, St Thomas' Hospital, 1904; Surgical Registrar and Resident Assistant Surgeon, 1905–9; Hunterian Professor, Royal College of Surgeons, 1913; same year appointed Surgeon in charge of out-patients at St Thomas'; besides above appointments, conducting research in abdominal surgery. *Publications:* Acute Abdominal Diseases; Peritoneal Adhesions, Lancet, 1913; Intestinal Obstruction, Practitioner, 1918; Observations on Operations for Appendicitis, Practitioner, April 1917; many other publications in Medical Journals. *Recreations:* golf, lawn tennis. *Address:* 19 Harley Street, W1. *T:* Langham 2108; Holt's Crest, Fordcombe, Kent. *T:* Fordcombe 19. *M:* XA 3528.
Died 22 Dec. 1926.

ADAMS, Joseph Robert George; General Secretary, Public Library, Museum, and Art Gallery of South Australia since 1909; *b* Melbourne, Victoria, 17 May 1859; *e s* of late Joseph Adams, Hawthorn, Victoria; *m* 1884, Alice, *y d* of late Robert Downing, Melbourne; one *s* four *d*. *Educ:* Scotch College, Melbourne, Victoria. Assistant Librarian of the South Australian Institute, 1879; Assistant Librarian of the new Institution, 1884, when the South Australian Institute developed into the Public Library, Museum, and Art Gallery of South Australia; Librarian, 1896; Principal Librarian and Secretary, 1904. *Publications:* articles in Library Record of Australasia and Proceedings of Library Association of Australasia; ed Proceedings of Library Association of Australasia for 1900. *Recreations:* angling, walking, gardening. *Address:* Public Library, Adelaide, South Australia.
Died 16 Aug. 1919.

ADAMS, Rev. Reginald Samuel; Hon. Canon of Chester, 1913. *Educ:* Gonville and Caius Coll., Cambridge. Ordained deacon 1862, priest 1863. Curate, Christ Church, Carlisle, 1862–65; Lectr, St

Cuthbert, Carlisle, 1863; Rector, Sebergham, 1865–76; Vicar, Marple, Stockport, 1876–1918. *Address:* 222 Hale Road, Hale.
Died 6 July 1928.

ADAMS, Maj.-Gen. Sir Robert Bellew, VC 1897; KCB 1912 (CB 1898); *b* 26 July 1856; *s* of late Major R. Adams, ISC. Entered army, 1876; Captain, 1887; Major, 1896; Bt Lt-Col 1896; Bt Col 1901; Lt-Col 1902; Col 1904; Brig.-Gen. 1904; Maj.-Gen. 1906; served Afghan War, 1879–80, including operations round Kabul, engagement at Charasieh (medal with clasp); Chitral Relief Force, in command Queen's Own Corps of Guides, cavalry, 1895 (despatches, Brevet Lieut-Col, medal with clasp); North-West Frontier, 1897 (despatches, VC); operations Bajaur (despatches); commanded troops Rustam and Persai in Buner Expedition (despatches, CB, two clasps); Brig. Commander Commanding Derajat Brigade, 1906–9; commanded Corps of Guides, Mardan; retired, 1911. *Decorated* for rescue (with others) of Lieut Greaves under heavy fire, 17 Aug. 1897, Upper Swat. *Club:* East India United Service.
Died 13 Feb. 1928.

ADAMS, William Henry, ISO 1902; late First Clerk, Teachers' Pension Office, Treasury Remembrancer's Department, Dublin Castle; *b* July 1844; *s* of William Henry Adams, Dublin; *m* 1st, 1866, Barbara (*d* 1892), *d* of William Greene; 2nd, 1893, Jane C., *d* of John F. Ruthven, Dublin; two *s* three *d*. *Educ:* private schools. Entered office of Commissioners of National Education, 1858; transferred to Teachers' Pension Office, 1879. *Recreations:* cycling, photography. *Address:* 143 Tritonville Road, Sandymount, Dublin.
Died 30 Oct. 1928.

ADAMSON, John, RBA; *b* Aug. 1865; *s* of Sir William Adamson. *Educ:* Sherborne; Royal Academy of Arts. *Address:* 3 Steele's Studios, Haverstock Hill, NW. *Died 12 Dec. 1918.*

ADAMSON, Sir William, Kt 1907; CMG 1897; merchant; *b* 1832; *s* of Ebenezer Adamson of Glasgow; *m* 1859, Margaret, *d* of Andrew Hamilton. A merchant of the Straits Settlements, and for many years a resident at Singapore; on several occasions a member of the Legislative Council of the Colony; a director of the Peninsular and Oriental Steam Navigation Company. *Decorated* for public services in connection with the Colony. *Address:* Rothbury, Avenue Road, Highgate, N. *T:* Hornsey 85. *Died 11 March 1917.*

ADCOCK, Sir Hugh, Kt 1901; CMG 1897; late Persian Consul, Florence; first-class Star of Lion and Sun with cordon, 1897; first-class Gold Star from Imperial College, Teheran, presented by the late Shah, Nasr-e-Din, 1893, for services during the severe cholera epidemic, 1892; consulting physician-in-chief to HIM the Shah of Persia; *b* London, 1847; 4th *s* of Christopher Adcock, surgeon, and Catherine Elizabeth of Church Hill House, Hunstanton, Norfolk, and of London; *m* 1st, 1866, Elizabeth, *d* of William Watkin of New Town, Wales; 2nd, 1908, Florence Beatrice (*d* 1911), *d* of Lt-Colonel J. S. G. Manera, Indian Army, retired; two *s*. *Educ:* privately, London and Cambridge. LSA; LRCPE; LMEd, 1869; MRCS, 1872. In private practice at Heacham, Norfolk, 1870–72; London, 1872–88; chief physician to HIH Mouzaffer-e-Din, Vali-ahd, at Tabreez, Persia, 1889–97, when Mouzaffer-e-Din ascended the Persian throne. *Decorations:* Legion of Honour, 4th class, France; Iron Crown, 2nd class, Austria; Medjidie, 1st class, Turkey; Orders of Civil Merit—1st class, Bulgaria; St Sava, 1st class, Servia; Leopold, 2nd class, Belgium; Orange, 2nd class, Holland. *Recreations:* hunting, shooting. *Address:* Nymet House, Nymet Rowland, N Devon. *Club:* Royal Societies.
Died 13 April 1920.

ADDIS, Rev. William Edward, MA; Vicar of All Saints, Ennismore Gardens, SW, since 1910; *b* Edinburgh, 9 May 1844; *s* of FC minister there; *m* 1888, Miss Flood, Sydenham; one *s* one *d*. *Educ:* Merchiston Castle School, Edin.; Glasgow Coll.; Balliol Coll., Oxford. Snell Exhibitioner; 1st class in Class. Mods and Final Classical Schools. Became RC 1866; joined London Oratory, 1868; ordained priest, 1872; parish priest of Sydenham, 1878–88; returned to Church of England, 1901; permission to officiate as priest in Church of England granted by Primate, 1907; Curate of St Martin and All Saints, Oxford, 1909; Professor of Old Testament Criticism, Manchester College, Oxford, 1898–1910; Master of Addis Hall, 1900–10. *Publications:* Catholic Dictionary in conjunction with Thomas Arnold (fourth edn), 1884; Documents of Hexateuch (2 vols), 1893–98; Christianity and the Roman Empire, 1893; Hebrew Religion and the Rise of Judaism under Ezra, 1906; various pamphlets, reviews, articles in Encyclopædia Biblica, Ency. Brit., etc. *Recreations:* walking, study of Gothic architecture. *Address:* 34 Rutland Gate, SW.
Died 20 Feb. 1917.

ADENEY, Walter Frederick, MA London; DD St Andrews; *b* Ealing, Middlesex, 14 March 1849; *s* of late Rev. G. J. Adeney, of Reigate; *m d* of late W. Hampton, Reigate; four *s* four *d*. *Educ:* New Coll., London. Seventeen years Congregational Minister at Acton; fourteen years Professor of New Testament Exegesis and Church History at New Coll., London, and Lecturer at Hackney Coll., London; Principal, Lancashire Independent College and Lecturer in History of Doctrine at the University of Manchester, 1903–13; Chairman of Congregational Union, 1912. *Publications:* The Hebrew Utopia; From Christ to Constantine; From Constantine to Charles the Great; Theology of the New Testament, which has been translated into Japanese (Theological Educator); Ezra, Nehemiah, and Esther; Canticles and Lamentations (Expositor's Bible); Women of the New Testament; How to Read the Bible (translated into Welsh); A Century's Progress; St Luke, and Galatians and Thessalonians (Century Bible); History of the Greek and Eastern Churches (International Theological Library); The New Testament Doctrine of Christ; The Christian Conception of God; Faith To-Day; joint author of The Bible Story and also of Biblical Introduction; Editor of Century Bible. *Recreation:* gardening. *Address:* The Croft, Southover, Lewes.
Died 1 Sept. 1920.

ADKINS, Sir (William) Ryland Dent, Kt 1911; KC 1920; MP (L) Middleton Division Lancs (SE), 1906–23; Recorder of Birmingham since 1920; *b* 11 May 1862; *o* surv. *s* of late William Adkins, JP, of Springfield, Northampton, and Harriet, *y d* of John Dent, Manor House, Milton, Northampton. *Educ:* Mill Hill School; University Coll. London; Balliol Coll., Oxford (Exhibitioner). Called to Bar, 1890; Recorder of Nottingham, 1911–20; Chairman Northants CC since 1920; Vice-Chairman Northants Territorial Force Association; Chairman Executive Council of County Councils Association; DL Northants; JP Northants and Northampton. *Recreations:* shooting, gardening, history, literature. *Address:* 5 Paper Buildings, EC4. *T:* Central 507; Springfield, Northampton. *Clubs:* Athenæum, Reform, Bath.
Died 30 Jan. 1925.

ADRIAN, Alfred Douglas, CB 1895; KC 1904; *b* 1845; *s* of late E. Adrian of Local Government Board; *m* 1885, Flora, *d* of Charles Howard Barton; one *s*. *Educ:* London University. Late Assistant Secretary Local Government Board, 1883; Legal Adviser to Local Government Board, 1899–1910. *Address:* 40 Elsworthy Road, Hampstead, NW.
Died 18 April 1922.

ADY, Mrs Henry, (Julia Cartwright); *b* Edgcote, Northamptonshire; 2nd *d* of Aubrey Cartwright and Hon. Mrs Cartwright, *d* of Lord Cottesloe; *m* 1880, Rev. W. H. Ady (*d* 1915), Rector of Ockham; one *d*. *Educ:* home. *Publications:* The Pilgrims' Way, 1892; Sacharissa, 1895; Madame: the Life and Letters of Henrietta, Duchess of Orleans, 1894; Life and Work of Sir Edward Burne-Jones, 1894; Raphael in Rome, 1895; J. F. Millet: his Life and Letters, 1896; Life and Work of G. F. Watts, 1896; Bastien-Lepage, 1895; Christ and His Mother in Italian Art, 1897; Beatrice d'Este, Duchess of Milan, 1899; The Painters of Florence, 1901; Isabella d'Este, a Study of the Renaissance, 1903; Sandro Botticelli, 1904; Raphael, 1905; The Perfect Courtier; Life and Letters of Count B. Castiglione, 1908; Hampton Court, 1909; Christina of Denmark, 1913; Italian Gardens of the Renaissance, 1914; The Journals of Lady Knightley of Fawsley, 1915; besides many volumes of fiction and magazine articles. *Recreations:* travelling, motoring. *Address:* 40 St Margaret's Road, Oxford.
Died 28 April 1924.

AFFLECK, Sir James Ormiston, Kt 1911; FRSE; LLD Edin; MD, MB, CM; FRCPE, FRCSE; Consulting Physician Royal Infirmary, Edinburgh; Physician, Royal Edinburgh Hospital for Incurables. *Address:* 38 Heriot Row, Edinburgh.
Died 24 Sept. 1922.

AFFLECK, Sir Robert, 7th Bt, *cr* 1782; JP, DL, Suffolk; *b* 4 March 1852; *S* father 1882; *m* 1886, Julia Georgina (who *div.* him 1914), *d* of John Sampson Prince. *Educ:* Eton; Oxford. Owned about 4,000 acres. *Heir: cousin* Frederick Danby James Affleck, *b* 3 Feb. 1856.
Died 4 Dec. 1919.

AFLALO, Frederick George, FRGS; Editor of the Encyclopædia of Sport, the Angler's Library, The Cost of Sport, the Young Naturalists' Library, Sport in Europe, Sports of the World, The Sportsman's Handbook for India, Half a Century of Sport in Hampshire, Fishermen's Weather, The Call of the Sea (a prose anthology), A Book of Fishing Stories; *b* London, 17 Aug. 1870; *m* 1895; one *d*. *Educ:* Clifton College; Rostock University, Mecklenburg. In 1891 studied in Italy; founded the British Sea Anglers' Society (subseq. 1,000 strong), 1893; travelled in Australia, particularly in Queensland, 1895,

and in Morocco and the Atlas, 1899; visited every important fishing port on the English coast from Berwick-on-Tweed round to the Solway Firth, 1903; Madeira and Porto Santo, 1905; Florida and West Indies, 1906; California and Canada, 1908; Near East, Holy Land and Caucasus, 1909; Cape Breton Island and Nova Scotia, 1910; Russia, 1911; British East Africa, Uganda, and Sudan, 1913–14; India, 1915; War Service (Red Cross) in Volknyia, 1916; British Vice Consul at Bale, 1917. *Publications:* Sea-Fishing on the English Coast, 1891; Hints and Wrinkles on Sea-Fishing, 1894; A Sketch of the Natural History of Australia, 1896; A Sketch of the Natural History (Vertebrates) of the British Islands, 1897; Sea Fish, 1897; Types of British Animals, 1899; A Walk through the Zoological Gardens, 1900; Sea and Coast Fishing, 1901; Fifty Leaders of Sport, 1904; The Sea Fishing Industry of England and Wales, 1904; Saltwater Fishes (Woburn Library), 1904; The Salt of My Life, 1905; Sunshine and Sport in Florida and the West Indies, 1907; Sunset Playgrounds, 1909; Regilding the Crescent, 1910; An Idler in the Near East, 1910; A Fisherman's Summer in Canada, 1911; Behind The Ranges, 1911; Our Agreeable Friends, 1911; A Book of the Jungle and Wilderness, 1912. *Recreation:* fishing. *Address:* Teignmouth. *Clubs:* Sports; East Devon and Teignmouth, Teignmouth.
Died 7 Dec. 1918.

AGNEW, Sir Andrew Noel, 9th Bt, *cr* 1629; *b* 14 Aug. 1850; *s* of 8th Baronet and Lady Louisa, *d* of 1st Earl of Gainsborough; *S* father 1892; *m* 1889, Gertrude, *d* of Hon. Gowron Charles Vernon, and *g d* of 1st Baron Lyveden. *Educ:* Harrow; Trinity Coll., Camb. Barrister, Inner Temple, 1874. Vice-Lieut Wigtowns; MP (LU) South Edinburgh, 1900–6; late Captain 1st Ayrshire and Galloway Volunteer Artillery; Member of Royal Company of Archers (King's Body Guard for Scotland); former President Royal Scottish Arboricultural Society. *Publications:* An Introduction to Forestry; A Guide to Wigtownshire. *Heir: brother* Major Charles Hamlyn Agnew [*b* 21 June 1859; *m* 1897, Lilian Ann (whom he divorced, 1908), *d* of Lt-Gen. Sir J. Wolfe Murray; one *s*. Late 4th Hussars. *Clubs:* Naval and Military, Brooks's, Cavalry]. *Recreations:* shooting, forestry, golf. *Address:* Lochnaw Castle, Stranraer, Wigtownshire. *Clubs:* Brooks's; New, Edinburgh.
Died 14 July 1928.

AGNEW, Sir Patrick Dalreagle, KBE 1920 (CBE 1918); Knight of Grace of the Order of St John of Jerusalem; MA (Hon.) Oxford; *b* Victoria, Australia, 26 April 1868; *s* of William Henry and Janet Moubray Agnew; *m* 1897, Elizabeth Frances Seaton, *d* of Lt-Col C. F. Massy, Indian Army, of Granstown Tipperary; one *d*. *Educ:* Bedford Grammar School; Balliol College, Oxford. Joined Indian Civil Service in 1889; Assistant Commissioner in the Punjab till 1898; Deputy Commissioner, 1898; Divisional Judge, 1910; Officiating Judge, Chief Court, 1913; retired, 1914; Managing Director and Vice-Chairman Central Prisoners of War Committee, 1916–19. *Recreation:* golf. *Address:* 8 Northmoor Road, Oxford. *Club:* East Indian United Service.
Died 5 Sept. 1925.

AGNEW, Sir Stair, KCB 1895 (CB 1885); FRSE; *b* 6 Dec. 1831; 5th *s* of Sir Andrew Agnew of Lochnaw, 7th Bt; *m* 1870, Georgina, *d* of George M. Nisbett; two *s* three *d*. *Educ:* Trinity Coll., Camb. (BA 1855; MA 1858). Late Lieut 9th Regt; Scotch Barrister 1860; Legal Secretary to Lord Advocate, 1861–66, 1868–70; Queen's Remembrancer for Scotland, 1870–81; Registrar-General for Scotland, and Keeper of Records, Scotland, 1881–1909. *Recreation:* rowed in Oxford and Cambridge boat race, 1854. *Address:* 22 Buckingham Terrace, Edinburgh. *Clubs:* Reform; New, Edinburgh.
Died 12 July 1916.

AGNEW, William Lockett, JP; Head of Thomas Agnew and Sons; *b* 1858; *s* of Thomas Agnew, Manchester; *m* 1884, Augusta, *d* of late F. Sheil of Bearforest, Mallow. *Address:* 10 Chesterfield Street, Mayfair, W. *T:* Mayfair 1124; Hallingbury Place, Bishops Stortford.
Died 15 Feb. 1918.

AGOSTINI, L. E., KC; late Attorney-General, Trinidad and Tobago, West Indies; *b* 1858. *Educ:* Stonyhurst College; Downside College; University College London. Called to Bar, Lincoln's Inn, 1874. *Address:* Port of Spain, Trinidad, West Indies.
Died 7 Aug. 1918.

AGUET, Gustave Charles, CBE; Chairman Nestlé and Anglo-Swiss Condensed Milk Co. *Educ:* University of Lausanne. *Recreations:* golf, shooting, fishing. *Address:* 42A Great Cumberland Place, W1; Kiln Cottage, Holmwood, Surrey. *Clubs:* Reform, Ranelagh.
Died 19 Feb. 1927.

AHMAD, Hon. Ahsanuddin, ISO 1915; CS; Commissioner of Excise and Salt, Inspector-General of Registration, Registrar-General of

Births, Deaths, and Marriages, and Registrar of Joint Stock Companies, Bihar and Orissa; Additional Member, Bihar and Orissa Legislative Council; President, Bihar and Orissa Provincial Haj Committee; *b* Calcutta, 16 Aug. 1859; 3rd *s* of late Nawab Amir Ali Khan Bahadur, CIE; *m* 1881; three *s*. *Educ:* Balliol, Oxford; Doveton College, Calcutta. Barrister, Inner Temple; nominated to Bengal Covenanted Civil Service; Assistant Magistrate and Collector at Monghyr, Bengal; Joint Magistrate; acted for 6 or 7 years as District and Sessions Judge; elected Executive branch of the Service; acted as Collector and Magistrate in different districts; Fishery Commissioner for Bengal; Durbar Medal. *Recreations:* racquets, tennis, golf, auction bridge. *Address:* Ranchi, BNR, India. *Clubs:* Calcutta, Calcutta; Ranchi, Ranchi; Bankipur, Bankipur.

Died 3 July 1918.

AICARD, Jean; Membre de l'Académie Française; président d'honneur de la Société des Gens de Lettres; président de l'Union Française; poète, romancier, auteur dramatique; Officer of the Legion of Honour; *b* Toulon, 1848. *Educ:* Lycée de Mâcon; Lycée de Nîmes. *Publications: Poèmes:* Les Jeunes Croyances; Rébellions et Apaisements; Poèmes de Provence, 1873; Chanson de l'enfant; Miette et Noré; Visite en Hollande, 1879; Le Dieu dans l'homme, 1885; Le Livre des petits, 1886; Le Livre d'heures de l'amour, 1887; Au bord du désert, 1888; Jésus; Don Juan, 1889; Le Jardin des enfants, 1913; Le Témoin, 1915; Le Sang du sacrifice, 1917. *Romans:* Roi de Camargue; Pavé d'amour; Fleur d'abîme; Melita; L'Ibis bleu; Diamant noir; Notre Dame d'amour; Tata; Arlette des Mayons; Gaspard de Besse; L'Âme d'un enfant; Maurin des Maures and L'Illustre Maurin (traduit en anglais). *Critique:* Alfred de Vigny; La Vénus de Milo. *Divers:* Des Cris dans la mêlée. *Théâtre:* Le Père Lebonnard; Smilis; La Légende du cœur; Le Manteau du roi; La Milésienne, Gaspard de Besse. *Address:* Paris, 40 rue Guynemer; La Garde, Var, Villa les Lauriers-roses; Solliès-le-Vieux, Var, France.

Died May 1921.

AIKMAN, Sir Robert (Smith), Kt 1910; MA; Hon. LLD, St Andrews; *b* 13 July 1844; *s* of A. Aikman, St Andrews; *m* 1st, 1877, Mary (*d* 1914), *e d* of late J. Craig, JP, Three Crofts, Kirkcudbrightshire; three *d*; 2nd, 1916, Catherine Maud, *d* of Mr Richards, Burton-on-Trent. *Educ:* Madras College, St Andrews; St Andrews and Edinburgh Universities. Entered Indian Civil Service, 1867; retired 1909; for fifteen years Puisne Judge of the High Court of the North-Western Provinces; for three years Vice-Chancellor of the Allahabad University. *Address:* c/o H. S. King and Co., 9 Pall Mall, SW.   *Died 6 April 1917.*

AILWYN, 1st Baron, *cr* 1921, of Honingham, Norfolk; **Ailwyn Edward Fellowes,** PC 1905; KBE 1917; KCVO 1911; DL, JP Norfolk; *b* 10 Nov. 1855; 2nd *s* of 1st Baron de Ramsey; *m* 1886, Hon. Agatha Eleanor Augusta Joliffe, *d* of 2nd Baron Hylton; three *s* (and one *s* decd). *Educ:* Eton; Trinity Hall, Camb. Vice-Chamberlain of Queen Victoria's Household, 1895–1900; a Junior Lord of the Treasury, 1900–5; President Board of Agriculture, 1905–6; MP (C) Hunts, Ramsey, 1887–1906; Chairman of Norfolk County Council; late Chairman of Agricultural Wages Board; Deputy-Chairman GE Railway. Owned 4,500 acres. *Heir: s* Major Hon. Ronald T. Fellowes, *b* 7 Dec. 1886. *Address:* Honingham, Norwich. *T:* Honingham 2. *Club:* Carlton.   *Died 23 Sept. 1924.*

AINGER, Arthur Campbell, MVO 1908; MA; *b* 4 July 1841; *s* of Rev. Thomas Ainger, Prebendary of St Paul's and Incumbent of Hampstead, Middlesex; unmarried. *Educ:* Eton; Trinity College, Cambridge. First class Classics, 1864; Assistant Master at Eton, 1864–1901; Hon. Secretary Old Etonian Association, 1900; Eton Memorial Buildings, 1902. *Publications:* Eton Songs (including Carmen Etonense, Vale, etc); various school books (Clivus, English Latin Verse Dictionary, with H. G. Wintle, MA, etc); Eton, an Anthology in Prose and Verse, 1910; Memories of Eton Sixty Years Ago, 1917; sundry Hymns (including "God is working His purpose out," etc). *Address:* Mustians, Eton, Bucks. *Club:* United University.

Died 26 Oct. 1919.

AINSLIE, Rev. Richard Montague, TD 1912; MA; Vicar of Childwall since 1903; Hon. Canon of Liverpool; *b* 23 Jan. 1858; *m* 1st, 1887, Mabel Bower Forwood (*d* 1893); 2nd, 1895, Euphemia Brown Fortune; one *s* four *d*. *Educ:* St Peter's School, York; Pembroke College, Cambridge. Deacon, 1884; Priest, 1885; Curate of Witton, Northwich, 1884–87; Vicar of St Saviour's, Liverpool, 1887–1903; Chaplain of 1st Batt. King's Liverpool Regt 1890; Chaplain 5th Batt. KLR 1908; Secretary of Liverpool Hospital Sunday Fund since 1893; Secretary of Liverpool Diocesan Church Building Society since 1902; Secretary of Diocesan Conference since 1893; Member of Liverpool

Cathedral Committee. *Recreations:* shooting, fishing. *Address:* Childwall Vicarage, Liverpool. *TA:* Vicarage, Broad Green. *T:* Gateacre 69. *Club:* Athenæum, Liverpool.

Died 23 Dec. 1924.

AINSWORTH, Sir John (Stirling), 1st Bt, *cr* 1916; DL; JP; *b* 30 Jan. 1844; *s* of late Thomas Ainsworth of The Flosh, Cleator, Cumberland, and Mary Laurie, *d* of John Stirling, DD, of Craigie, Ayrshire; *m* 1879, Margaret Catherine (*d* 1918), *d* of Robert Reid Macredie; one *s* two *d*. *Educ:* University College School and University College, London; MA, LLB. Sheriff of the county of Cumberland, 1891; commanded the 3rd Volunteer Batt. Border Regt, 1898–1902; contested Barrow-in-Furness, 1886; Argyllshire, 1900; MP (L) Argyllshire, 1903–18. *Heir: s* Thomas Ainsworth, Lieut 11th Hussars [*b* 8 Feb. 1886; *m* 1911, Lady Edina Dorothy Hope, 4th *d* of 4th Marquess Conyngham; one *s* one *d*]. *Address:* Ardanaiseig, Loch Awe, Argyllshire; Harecroft, Gosforth, Cumberland. *Club:* Reform.

Died 24 May 1923.

AIREY, Paymaster Rear-Adm. Frederick W. I., CB 1920; RN; *b* 3 June 1861; *s* of late Rev. John A. L. Airey, MA, Rector of St Helen's Church, Bishopsgate Street, EC, and Mary Lumb; *m* 1899, Katherine Mary, *yr d* of William Parham, Bath; no *c*. *Educ:* Merchant Taylors' School, London. Joined Royal Navy, 1877; served in Egyptian Campaign of 1882; Soudan Campaign, 1884–85; Boxer Insurrection in China, 1900; European War, 1914–18; retired from Royal Navy, 1919. *Publications:* Pidjin Inglis Tails, and others. *Recreations:* tennis, golf. *Address:* c/o Admiralty, SW1. *Club:* Royal Dorset Yacht, Weymouth.

Died 18 Aug. 1922.

AIRY, Rev. Basil Reginald, TD; MA; Prebendary of Exeter Cathedral; Vicar of St John's, Torquay, since 1886; *b* Keysoe, 20 April 1845; *s* of Rev. William Airy, MA, Vicar of Keysoe, Beds, and *nephew* of Sir George Biddell Airy, KCB, late Astronomer Royal; *m* 1874, Emma, *d* of Shepley Watson, of York; two *s* two *d*. *Educ:* King Edward's School, Birmingham; Trinity College, Cambridge. Deacon, 1868; Priest, 1869; Curate of Wisbech St Mary, 1868; Stretham, nr Ely, 1870; Kirkby Misperton, 1871; Vicar of Whitwell, Yorks, 1873; Chaplain to Devon and Somerset Engineers (Vol.), and to Devon Royal Engineers (Territorial) for 24 years; Chaplain to High Sheriff of Yorkshire, 1890. *Address:* St John's Vicarage, Torquay.

Died 15 Jan. 1924.

AIRY, Osmund, LLD St Andrews, 1899; MA; JP Berks; *b* Royal Observatory, Greenwich, 29 Oct. 1845; *y s* of late Sir George Biddell Airy, KCB, Astronomer-Royal, and Richarda Smith, *e d* of Rev. C. Smith, Edensor, Derbyshire; *m* 1873, Emily Josephine, *d* of late Canon Miller, DD; one *s* three *d*. *Educ:* Blackheath Proprietary School; Trinity Coll., Cambridge. 27th Wrangler, 1868. Asst Master Blackheath Proprietary School, 1868; Asst Master Wellington College, 1868–76; HM Inspector of Schools, 1876; Divisional Inspector, and Inspector of Training Colls, 1904; retired, 1910. *Publications:* Treatise on Geometrical Optics, 1870; Selections from Addison's Spectator, 1874; historical and other articles in various Reviews, Encyclopædia Britannica, and Dict. of Nat. Biog.; Louis XIV and the English Restoration (Epochs of Modern History), 1888; edited Lauderdale Papers, 3 vols (Camden Society), 1884, 1885; Essex Papers (Camden Soc.), 1890; Text Book of English History, 1893; Burnet's History of His Own Time (Charles II), 2 vols, 1897–99; Biography of Charles II (Goupil), 1901. *Address:* Crowthorne, Berks.

Died 30 Nov. 1928.

AIRY, Wilfrid, BA; MICE. *Publications:* Levelling and Geodesy; Weighing Machines. *Address:* White House, Croom's Hill, Greenwich, SE.   *Died 8 Oct. 1925.*

AITCHISON, Gen. Charles Terrington, CB 1875; *b* 28 May 1825; *m* 1854, Annie, *d* of Alexander Colquhoun. Entered army, 1842; Captain, 1855; Major, 1858; Lieut-Col, 1864; Colonel, 1869; Major-Gen., 1881; Lieut-Gen., 1884; General, 1888; retired; served South Mahratta country, 1844–45 (wounded, despatches); Persian Expeditionary Force, 1856–57 (despatches, thanks of Governor-General, medal with clasp, brevet of major); Southern Mahratta country during Mutiny, 1857–58 (medal). *Address:* 48 Duke Street, St James's, SW.   *Died 5 Jan. 1919.*

AITKEN, George Atherton, MVO 1911; Assistant Secretary, Home Office; *b* Barkingside, Essex, 19 March 1860; *o s* of late John Aitken and Mary Ann Elizabeth, *d* of William Salmon; *m* 1903, Emma, *d* of John Cawthorne. *Educ:* King's Coll. School; University Coll. London. Entered the Secretary's Office, General Post Office, 1883;

private secretary to the Permanent Secretary, Sir Arthur Blackwood, KCB, 1890; transferred to the Home Office, 1892; Secretary to Reformatory and Industrial Schools Departmental Committee, 1895, and to Inebriate Reformatories Committee, 1898; private secretary to Sir Kenelm Digby, KCB, Permanent Under Secretary of State, 1896–1901; member of Home Office Committee on grants to Reformatory and Industrial Schools, 1905; Chairman of Committee on Superannuation of Officers of Reformatory and Industrial Schools, 1914; British Delegate at International Conferences at Paris on White Slave Traffic, etc, 1910, and at International Congress at Brussels on the Protection of Child Life, 1913; Life Governor of University College, 1902. *Publications:* Life of Richard Steele, 2 vols, 1889; Life and Works of Dr John Arbuthnot, 1892; editions of Marvell, 1892; Burns, 1893; Steele's Plays, 1893; Defoe's Romances and Narratives, 16 vols, 1896; Spectator, 8 vols, 1898; Tatler, 4 vols, 1899; Swift's Journal to Stella, 1901; contributions to Dictionary of National Biography and Cambridge History of English Literature. *Recreations:* walking, book-collecting. *Address:* 21 Church Row, Hampstead, NW. *Club:* Athenæum. *Died 16 Nov. 1917.*

AITKEN, Hon. J. G. W., MLC; Moderator, Presbyterian Church, New Zealand, 1917. *Address:* Wellington, New Zealand.
Died Aug. 1921.

AITKEN, John, LLD; FRS, FRSE; 4th s of late Henry Aitken, Darroch, Falkirk. *Educ:* Grammar School, Falkirk; Glasgow University. Served apprenticeship as marine engineer in the works of R. Napier and Sons, Lancefield, Glasgow. Has invented instruments for counting the dust particles in the atmosphere, chromomictors and the koniscope. *Publications:* has investigated and written papers in the publications of the Royal Society, London, and Royal Society of Edinburgh, on Colour and Colour Sensation; Rigidity produced by Centrifugal Force; Dust Fogs and Clouds; Colour of Water; Dew; Apparatus for Counting the Dust Particles in the Air; Observations of the Number of Dust Particles in the Atmosphere of Different Places in Europe; Hazing Effect of Atmospheric Dust; Cloud Particles; Cyclones and Anticyclones; The Sun as a Fog-Producer, etc. *Recreations:* trout and salmon fishing, photography, gardening, wood and metal work. *Address:* Ardenlea, Falkirk, NB.
Died 13 Nov. 1919.

AITKEN, John Hobson, ISO 1916; b 28 March 1851; s of late Richard Aitken, formerly of Aberdeen; unmarried. In Government Office, Isle of Man, 1870; retired as Chief Clerk, 1914; Private Secretary to successive Lieut-Governors; Secretary to Local Government Board of Isle of Man, 20 July 1894 to 31 Dec. 1894; acted as Insular Registrar General, two months, 1910. *Address:* Farnley, Beverley Mount, Douglas, Isle of Man. *Died 21 March 1923.*

AITKEN, Sir Robert, Kt 1918; Managing Governor, Imperial Bank of India; b 13 May 1863; s of John Aitken of West Linton, Peeblesshire; m Carolina Mary, d of Theophilus Lobb, Ex-Engineer, PWD, India; two s one d. *Address:* Kinellan, Malabar Hill, Bombay. *Club:* Oriental.
Died 18 April 1924.

AITKEN, Colonel William, CB 1896; ADC to HM, 1900–3; b 24 Feb. 1846; 4th s of late James Aitken of Gartcow's, Falkirk, NB; m 1894, Susan Elizabeth, y d of George A. Coventry, Shanwell, Kinross-shire, NB; one s one d. *Educ:* Edinburgh Academy; Heidelberg. Entered RA 1867; Captain, 1878; Major, 1884; Brevet Lieut-Col, 1887; Bt Col, 1897; served Afghan War, 1878–80 (despatches, medal); Mahsud Waziri Expedition, 1881; Burmah Expedition, 1885–87 (despatches, Bt Lieut-Col); Chitral Relief Force, 1895 (despatches, CB); ADC to Queen Victoria, 1897; Malakand Field Force, Mohmand and Buner Expeditions, 1897–98; commanded Mountain Artillery, Rawal Pindi, Punjab, to 1899; Col on Staff commanding RA Scottish District, 1899–1903; retired, 1903. *Recreations:* shooting, golf. *Address:* Kemback, Cupar, Fife. *Clubs:* Army and Navy; New, Edinburgh; Royal and Ancient Golf, St Andrews.
Died 11 Jan. 1917.

AITKEN, Rev. William Hay Macdowall Hunter, MA; Canon Residentiary of Norwich Cathedral since 1900; General Superintendent of the Church Parochial Mission Society since 1876; b Grove Street, Liverpool, 21 Sept. 1841; y s of late Rev. Robert Aitken, Vicar of Pendeen, Cornwall, and his second wife, Wilhelmina Day Macdowall Grant, of Arndilly, Banffshire, NB; m 1867, Eleanor Marian Barnes of Arkley, Barnet; two s four d. *Educ:* at home; Wadham Coll., Oxford. Second Class Lit.Hum., BA 1865, MA 1867. Ordained 1865 to curacy of St Jude's, Mildmay, N; took prominent part in Twelve Days' Mission, 1869; Incumbent of Christ Church, Great Homer Street, Liverpool, 1871; resigned to be a Mission-

Preacher 1875; was the means of founding Church Parochial Mission Society, 1876 (originally the Aitken Memorial Fund, being a memorial to his father); visited the United States on a Mission Tour 1886, and again 1895–6, when he worked also in Canada, the tour extending over six months; was invited by the Bishop of London to take part in the Fulham Conference on the subject of the Confessional, January 1902. *Publications:* Mission Sermons, 3 Series; Newness of Life; What is your Life?; The School of Grace; God's Everlasting Yea; The Glory of the Gospel; The Highway of Holiness; Around the Cross; The Revealer Revealed; Temptation and Toil; Eastertide; The Love of the Father; The Romance of Christian Work and Experience; Soul-Difficulties; The Doctrine of Baptism; The Divine Ordinance of Prayer; The Mechanical Versus the Spiritual; Apostolical Succession; Life, Light, and Love—Thoughts on the First Epistle of St John. *Address:* The Close, Norwich. *TA:* Canon Aitken, Norwich.
Died 28 Oct. 1927.

AKELEY, Carl Ethan; taxidermist, inventor, sculptor; b Orleans Co., NY, 19 May 1864; s of Daniel Webster Akeley and Julia M. Glidden. *Educ:* State Normal School, Brockport, NY. With Field Museum, Chicago, 1895–1909; American Museum of Natural History, New York, since 1909. Served as Consulting Engineer, Division of Investigation, Research and Development, Engineering Department, United States Army; also as Special Assistant, Concrete Department, Emergency Fleet Corporation. Inventor of Cement-gun, Akeley camera, etc; medallist Franklin Inst.; big-game hunter; made four trips to Africa for study and collection of big game. *Publication:* In Brightest Africa. *Address:* American Museum of Natural History, 77th Street and Central Park W, New York. *Clubs:* Century, Boone and Crockett, Explorers, African Big Game, Camp Fire of America, Wilderness, Ends of the Earth, New York; Camp Fire, Adventurers, Chicago. *Died 29 Nov. 1926.*

ALBEE, Ernest; Professor of Philosophy in Cornell University; b Langdon, NH, 8 Aug. 1865; s of Solon Albee and Ellen Lucillia Eames; m 1911, Emily Humphreys Manly. *Educ:* University of Vermont (AB 1887); Clark University; Cornell University (PhD 1894). Fellow in Psychology, Clark University, 1891; Fellow in Philosophy, Cornell Univ., 1892; Teacher of Philosophy in Cornell Univ. since 1892; co-editor of the Philosophical Review, 1903–8. *Publications:* A History of English Utilitarianism, 1902; articles on philosophical subjects. *Recreations:* golf, walking. *Address:* 207 Kelvin Place, Ithaca, New York, USA. *Clubs:* Authors'; City, New York.
Died May 1927.

ALCOCK, Capt. Sir John William, KBE 1919; DSO 1919; DSC 1917; late RAF; b 6 Nov. 1892; e s of John and Mary Alcock, Manchester. Apprentice, Empress motor works, Manchester, 1909; aviator's cert. 1912; joined RNAS, 1914, commissioned 1915; retd from RAF 1919; decorated for first crossing the Atlantic in an aeroplane (Vickers-Vimy Atlantic), Newfoundland to Clifden, Ireland, 4.28PM June 14–8.40AM June 15, 1919.
Died 18 Dec. 1919.

ALDEN, Henry Mills, AM, LLD; Editor, Harper's Magazine, since 1869; b Mt Tabor, near Danby, Vermont, USA, 11 Nov. 1836; m 1st, 1861, Susan Frye Foster of North Andover, Mass; 2nd, 1900, Ada Foster Murray of Norfolk, Va. *Educ:* graduated at William's Coll. 1857; Andover Theological Seminary, 1860. Lecturer before Lowell Institute, 1863–64, subject "The Structure of Paganism"; Managing Editor, Harper's Weekly, 1863–69. *Publications:* God in His World, 1890; A Study of Death, 1895; Magazine Writing and the New Literature, 1908. *Address:* Metuchen, New Jersey. *Club:* Authors', New York. *Died 7 Oct. 1919.*

ALDERSON, Lt.-Gen. Sir Edwin Alfred Hervey, KCB 1916 (CB 1900); b 8 April 1859; o s of late Edward Mott Alderson, Poyle House, Ipswich; m 1886, Alice Mary, 2nd d of late Rev. Oswald P. Sergeant, Vicar of Chesterton, Oxon. Entered Royal West Kent Regiment, 1878; Capt. 1886; Major, 1896; Bt Lt-Col 1897; Bt Col 1900; Col 1903; Maj.-Gen. 1906; Lt-Gen. 1914; Adjutant, Mounted Infantry, 1887–91; Royal West Kent Regt, 1890–94; DAAG and commanding MI Aldershot, 1897–99; Brigadier-General Commanding 2nd Infantry Brigade, Aldershot, 1903–7; commanded 6th (Poona) Division, S Army, India, 1903–12; served with MI, Boer War, 1881; Egyptian War, with MI, 1882, including Kassassin (both actions) and Tel-el-Kebir (medal with clasp, Khedive's star); Nile Expedition, with MI Camel Regt, 1884–85 (two clasps); South Africa, 1896; in command of MI and expedition which relieved Salisbury, and finally in command of troops in Mashonaland, 1896 (despatches, brevet of Lt-Col, medal); commanded Mounted Infantry in South Africa, 1900–1; Inspector-Gen. MI, S Africa, 1900–2, rank Br.-Gen.

(despatches three times, two medals with seven clasps, ADC to the King, brevet of Col, CB); served European War, 1914–18, commanding 1st Canadian Division and subsequently the Canadian Army Corps (despatches, KCB, Commander Legion of Honour); awarded bronze medal of Royal Humane Society, 1885; ADC to Queen Victoria and King Edward VII, 1900–6. *Publications:* With the Mounted Infantry and Mashonaland Field Force, 1896; Pink and Scarlet, or Hunting as a School for Soldiering, 1900; Lessons from 100 Notes made in Peace and War. *Recreations:* hunted the Shorncliffe Drag Hounds, 1891–93; the Staff College Drag Hounds, 1894–95; Cape Jackal Hounds and Salisbury Hounds, 1896; Alderson's Hounds, Pretoria, 1902; Poona and Kirkee Hounds, 1910; S Shropshire Foxhounds, 1914–23; owned several racing and other yachts. *Clubs:* Marlborough, Naval and Military; Royal Norfolk and Suffolk Yacht; Royal Canoe.   *Died 14 Dec. 1927.*

ALDERSON, Sir George Beeton, KBE 1922; engineer; *b* 8 Jan. 1844; *s* of Frederic Henry Alderson, of Ingham House, Ipswich, Suffolk; *m* 1st, 1869, Ellen Owen Wells; 2nd, 1906, Helen, *d* of Dr Andrew Pouzetta. Resided in Egypt for over 50 yrs. Helped Army of Occupation with engineering works in 1882; built Sailors' Home, Alexandria, 1885, Ramleh Church, 1890, Victoria Coll., Ramleh, 1906, Mosque at Aboukir, 1907. *Address:* Norland House, Ramleh, Egypt. *Club:* Union, Alexandria.
                 Died 2 Dec. 1926.

ALDINGTON, Charles, CBE 1918; General Manager, Great Western Railway, 1919–21; late Superintendent of the Line; *b* 20 Dec. 1862. *Address:* 53 Eastbourne Terrace, W2.
                 Died 15 Oct. 1922.

ALDRICH-BLAKE, Dame Louisa Brandreth, DBE 1925; MS, MD, MB (1st class hons), BS (1st class hons); Dean, London School of Medicine for Women, since 1914; Senior Surgeon, Elizabeth Garrett Anderson Hospital, Euston Road; Consulting Surgeon with beds, Royal Free Hospital, Gray's Inn Road; Fellow, Royal Society of Medicine; late Anaesthetist and Surgical Registrar, Royal Free Hospital; *b* 15 Aug. 1865; *d* of Rev. Frederick Aldrich-Blake, Rector of Chingford. *Educ:* St Hilda's Coll., Cheltenham; London Sch. of Med. for Women; MB 1892; MD 1894; MS 1895. *Publication:* Abdomino-Perineal Excision of the Rectum by a New Method. *Address:* 17 Nottingham Place, W1. *T:* Mayfair 371. *Clubs:* University Women's, London University.
                 Died 28 Dec. 1925.

ALDRIDGE, Very Rev. John Mullings; Dean of Clonfert since 1907; Rector of Donanaughta, 1898–1906 and since 1911; Canon of St Patrick's, Dublin, 1914. *Educ:* Trinity College, Dublin (MA). Ordained 1870; Incumbent of Donanaughta, 1871–86; Rector of St John, Forfar, 1886–92; West Bridgford, 1892–94; Charton, 1894–95; Meyseyhampton, 1895–98; Rector of Creagh, 1906–11. *Address:* Rectory, Eyre Court, Co. Galway.
                 Died 18 March 1920.

ALEXANDER, Alexander, FRGS; *b* Liverpool, 14 May 1849; 2nd *s* of W. C. Alexander of Glanmire and Liverpool; *m* Emily Adelaide, *d* of late John and Mary Smith of Ranelagh, Dublin; one *s*. *Educ:* Liverpool College and Liverpool Institute. Apprenticed to John Hulley, gymnasiarch, 1862; trained by James Mace (Champion of England), André Durbec (Paris), and J. Beckton (Cumberland); Public Demonstrator of Physical Training at Liverpool Gymnasium, 1864; took to the road, 1870, and as a pioneer of physical training gave lectures and demonstrations at the various public schools and military stations throughout the United Kingdom; Prof. of Gymnastics at Trinity College, Dublin, 1875; Director of the Liverpool Gymnasium, 1880; invented and patented (which was not renewed) bent handles for cycles; founded with Lord Gladstone the National Physical Recreation Society, 1886; at the invitation of King Oscar of Sweden he took over a team of English athletes to Stockholm to introduce athletic sports, 1896; in same year, at request of HM Government, visited the principal colleges and military stations of Europe with the view of ascertaining the relative values of the various systems of physical training in vogue; about the same period his advice in physical training was sought by the French, South African, Canadian, and Australian Governments; Vice-President of International Board of Education, USA; holder of many prizes, including Military Gymnastic Championship, National Physical Recreation Societies Challenge Shield, and first prize for activity and strength, Stockholm 1896. *Publications:* Musical Drill, 1882; Modern Gymnastic Exercises, 1884; Advanced Gymnastics, 1888; Physical Training at Home, 1890; Physical Training of all Nations, 1896; British Physical Education, 1903; A Holiday Romance, 1904; Robin Hood, 1908; Pirates' Hoard,

1908; A Wayfarer's Log, 1919; A Wayfarer's Caravan, 1921. *Recreations:* chess, draughts, reading, music, walking. *Address:* Innisfallen, Birkdale, Lancs.
                 Died 23 May 1928.

ALEXANDER, Col Aubrey de Vere, DSO 1903; retired; late Officiating Colonel on Staff, Rawal Pindi; *b* 28 May 1849; *s* of late G. H. M. Alexander, ICS; *m* 1875, Mary Georgina Carter, *d* of late General Sir James Brind, GCB. *Educ:* Wellington College. Entered army, 1869; Captain, 1881; Major, 1889; Lieut-Col, 1895; Bt-Col, 1899; served with Khyber Field Force in Afghan War, 1879–80 (medal); China Field Force, 1900–1 (despatches, DSO); European War, 1914–19, Intelligence Department, War Office. *Address:* c/o Cox & Co., Charing Cross, SW1.
                 Died 11 Sept. 1923.

ALEXANDER, Lt-Col Boyd Francis; late Rifle Brigade; *b* 17 April 1834; 3rd *s* of Boyd Alexander of Ballochmyle, Ayrshire, and Sophia, 3rd *d* of Sir Benjamin Hobhouse, 1st Bt; *m* 1865, Mary, *d* of D. Wilson; two *s* one *d*. *Educ:* Harrow. Served with the Rifle Brigade in Turkey, 1854; Indian Mutiny, 1857–58; Battle of Cawnpore; siege and capture of Lucknow; Oudh campaign; action at Nawabgunge; commanded storming party at attack on Fort Birwah (twice wounded, despatches, Bt Major, medal and clasp); in Canada, Fenian Raid, 1870 (medal). *Address:* Swifts Place, Cranbrook. *TA:* Alexander, Swifts, Cranbrook. *Club:* Carlton.
                 Died 19 Aug. 1917.

ALEXANDER, Charles McCallon, MA; Evangelist; *b* 24 Oct. 1867; *e s* of late John D. Alexander of Maryville, Tennessee, USA; *m* 1904, Helen, *d* of late Richard Cadbury of Birmingham. Engaged in evangelistic work, singing, organising and conducting large chorus choirs for 8 years; made an evangelistic tour of the world with Rev. R. A. Torrey, 1902–6; made the Glory Song famous throughout the world at this time; second tour of the world with his wife, 1906–7; conducted the largest evangelistic choir ever organised (4,000 members) for two months daily in the Royal Albert Hall, London; compiler of Alexander's hymns; worked with Dr J. Wilbur Chapman of New York in evangelistic work, 1908–18, conducting united missions in Australia, Philippine Islands, China, Japan and Korea; also in America and Great Britain. *Address:* Tennessee, Moor Green Lane, Birmingham; 158 Fifth Avenue, New York City, USA. *TA:* Bible, Moseley. *T:* South 310.   *Died 13 Oct. 1920.*

ALEXANDER, Conel W. O'D. L., MSc, BE, AMICE; Professor of Civil Engineering, University College, Cork, since 1906; *b* Imlick, Co. Donegal, 6 June 1879; *s* of Joseph Alexander, JP; *m* 1907, Hilda Barbara Bennett; two *s* one *d*. *Educ:* Foyle College, Derry; Friars School, Bangor; Queen's University, Belfast; Birmingham University. Graduated in Royal University, 1901, and in Birmingham University, 1905; Engineer-Assistant to City Engineer of Birmingham, 1902–6; won James Forrest Medal, Miller Scholarship, and Birmingham Students' Medal, Institution of Civil Engineers, 1904, Heslop Medal, Birmingham University, 1906, and Mullins Medal, Institution of Civil Engineers of Ireland, 1913; Dean of Faculty of Engineering of National University of Ireland since 1909; Examiner to National University, to Institution of Civil Engineers, and to the Civil Service Commissioners; President, Irish Rugby Football Union, 1909–10, and member of Committee since 1909. *Publications:* Fluid Friction in Pipe Bends; Reinforced Concrete; Hydraulic Diagrams; and several technical papers. *Recreations:* Rugby football, cricket, gardening. *Address:* Tyrconel, Perrott Avenue, Cork.
                 Died 17 Dec. 1920.

ALEXANDER, David Lindo, KC; JP; *b* 1842; *s* of J. Alexander; *m* Hester (*d* 1913), *e d* of S. J. Joseph. *Educ:* Trinity Hall, Cambridge (BA). Called to Bar, Lincoln's Inn, 1866; Bencher, 1895; QC 1892. President of Jewish Board of Deputies. *Address:* 11 York Gate, Regent's Park, NW1. *T:* Mayfair 592.
                 Died 29 April 1922.

ALEXANDER, Edwin, RSA 1918; RWS; artist; *b* Edinburgh, 1870; *s* of late Robert Alexander, RSA; father Scotch, mother English; *m* 1904. *Educ:* Edinburgh. Studied in the Edinburgh School of Art, at the Royal Scottish Academy's life class, and in Paris; has exhibited chiefly in the Royal Scottish Academy, and the RWS. *Address:* Links Lodge, Musselburgh, Midlothian. *Club:* Scottish Arts, Edinburgh.
                 Died April 1926.

ALEXANDER, Sir George, Kt 1911; JP; (Hon.) LLD; actor and manager, St James's Theatre; *b* Reading, 19 June 1858; *o s* of William Murray Samson and Mary Ann Hine Samson; *m* 1882, Florence

Théleur. *Educ:* Dr Benham's, Clifton; Relton's, Ealing; High School, Stirling. Started in the City, but being an enthusiastic amateur actor, soon took to the stage. Theatre Royal, Nottingham, in 1879; then on tour with Robertsonian Comedy, till, in 1881, joined Mr Irving at the Lyceum; played there and at other leading theatres. He opened own management with Dr Bill, at Avenue Theatre, 1890, and migrated to the St James's Theatre in 1891. Represented South St Pancras in London County Council, 1907–13; president of Royal General Theatrical Fund; vice-president and active associate of Actors' Benevolent Fund; admitted Freeman of Turners' Company, 1908. *Recreations:* riding, bicycling, golfing. *Address:* 57 Pont Street, SW; Little Court, Chorleywood, Herts. *TA:* Ruritania, London. *Clubs:* Carlton, Garrick, Beefsteak, Green Room.

Died 16 March 1918.

ALEXANDER, Colonel John Donald, CBE 1919; DSO; MB, BCh; AMS (retired); *b* 11 April 1867; *e s* of Very Rev. John Alexander, Dean of Ferns; *m* 1906, Georgina Eleanor, *d* of Alexander Going of Altavilla, Cahir; no *c*. *Educ:* St Columba's College; Trinity College, Dublin. Gazetted to the Army Medical Service, 1892, serving till 1920; served South African War, 1899–1902 (despatches twice, 2 medals and 7 clasps); Tirah and NW Frontier of India, 1907–8 (despatches, medal and 2 clasps); European War on Western Front, 1914–18 (despatches four times, DSO, CBE, Chevalier de l'Ordre de Leopold, 4 British medals, Croix de Guerre, France and Belgium). *Address:* Landcross Grange, Bideford. *TA:* Landcross, Bideford. *T:* Bideford 2X2. *M:* XF 4691. *Club:* University, Dublin.

Died 9 July 1922.

ALEXANDER, Joseph Gundry, LLB Lond.; JP, Kent; retired barrister; Hon. Secretary of Society for the Suppression of the Opium Trade, since 1894; Member of Permanent International Peace Society, Berne; *b* Bath, 1848; *s* of Samuel Alexander and Sarah Gundry; *m* 1881, Josephine Crosfield; four *s*. *Educ:* private Friends' Schools, Brighton and Weston-super-Mare. Business at Leominster, 1863–71; called to Lincoln's Inn, 1874; practised as an equity draftsman and conveyancer till 1890; Hon. General Secretary of International Law Association, 1883–1905; Secretary of Society for the Suppression of the Opium Trade, 1890; accompanied the Royal Opium Commission to India and Burma, 1893–94, afterwards visiting China; Chairman of International Peace Congress, London, 1908. *Address:* 3 Mayfield Road, Tunbridge Wells. *T:* Tunbridge Wells 950. *Club:* National Liberal.

Died 16 Feb. 1918.

ALEXANDER, Reginald Gervase, MA Cantab, MD; FLS; JP Yorks; Consulting Physician to the Royal Infirmaries of Bradford and Halifax; *s* of late Wm Alexander, MD, FRCP, JP Yorks; *m* Alicia Mary, *o* surv. *d* of late John Greenwood, Castle Hall, Mytholmroyd, Yorks; two *s* two *d*. *Educ:* Cambridge; King's College, London; Edinburgh University. A pioneer in the advocacy of open-air treatment of phthisis and other complaints. [Declared by House of Lords 23 July 1912 co-heir of the ancient baronies of Burgh (1529) and Cobham of Kent (1313); also claimant to the Peerage of Strathbolgie.] Late Senior Physician Bradford Fever Hospital. *Publications:* The Art of Prolonging Life; various medical contributions. *Address:* Blackwall Lodge, Halifax; Manningham Lane, Bradford.

Died 14 Feb. 1916.

ALEXANDER, Robert, RSA. *Address:* Hailes Cottage, Slateford, W Edinburgh.   *Died Aug. 1923.*

ALEXANDER, William, CIE 1917; Traffic Dept, Great Indian Peninsula Railway, Bombay. *Address:* Wadi Bunder, Bombay.

Died 6 March 1921.

ALEXANDER, William Cleverly; *b* 1840; *y s* of late George William Alexander, of Woodhatch, Surrey; *m* 1861, Rachel Agnes, *d* of Jeffery Lucas of Hitchin, Herts; one *s* six *d*. *Address:* Heathfield Park, Sussex; Aubrey House, Kensington, W. *Club:* Burlington Fine Arts.

Died 17 April 1916.

ALFORD, Rev. Henry Powell; Rector of Worthen, Shrewsbury; Prebendary of Hereford; 3rd *s* of late Richard Alford, FRCS; *m* Amy, *d* of Major Joseph Rimington, Indian Army. *Educ:* Clifton College; New College, Oxford. Vicar of Woodbury Salterton; Rural Dean of Aylesbeare; Rural Dean of Montgomery. *Address:* Worthen Rectory, Shrewsbury.   *Died 18 Jan. 1921.*

ALFORD, Rev. Josiah George, CBE 1919; VD; TD; MA; Canon Residentiary and Sub-Dean of Bristol; Hon. Chaplain to Bishop of Bristol; Personal Chaplain to late Bishop; *b* 1 Jan. 1847; 2nd *s* of late Charles Richard Alford, DD, Bishop of Victoria; *m* Catherine Mary,

d of late Colonel Leslie, CB; one *s* three *d*. *Educ:* King's College, London; Corpus Christi College, Cambridge. Graduated, 1869; ordained 1870, as Curate of St Leonards-on-Sea; Assistant to Archbishop's Inspector of Training Colleges, 1872–75; Minor Canon of Bristol Cathedral, 1873; Vicar of St Nicholas, Bristol, 1880; Vicar of Stoke Bishop, 1895; Hon. Canon, 1897; Rural Dean, 1905; Bishop's Commissioner since 1882; Governor under the Colston Trust since 1887; Chaplain to the Lord Mayor of Bristol, 1893; Chaplain (1st class, ranking as Colonel); Territorial Force; mobilised, 1914–19, SCF Bristol; later SCF No 2 Area, Southern Command; Surrogate for the Diocese, and Diocesan Trustee; Member of the Education Committee for Bristol, 1903–13; Proctor in Convocation, 1919–21; Member of the Royal United Service Institution. *Address:* 5 Richmond Hill, Clifton, Bristol; Park Cottage, Cleeve, near Bristol.

Died 12 Jan. 1924.

ALINGTON, 2nd Baron, *cr* 1876; **Humphrey Napier Sturt,** KCVO 1908 (CVO 1905); JP, DL; *b* 20 Aug. 1859; *o s* of 1st Baron Alington and Lady Augusta Bingham, *d* of 3rd Earl of Lucan; *S* father 1904; *m* 1883, Lady Feodorowna Yorke, *d* of 5th Earl of Hardwicke; two *s* two *d* (and one *s* one *d* decd). *Educ:* Eton; Christ Church, Oxford. Formerly Lieut Dorset Yeomanry; MP (C) Dorset E, 1891–1904. Owned about 18,000 acres. *Heir: s* Hon. Gerard Philip Montagu Napier Sturt, *b* 9 April 1893. *Address:* Crichel, Wimborne; 38 Portman Square, W. *T:* Paddington 389. *Clubs:* Carlton, Turf, Marlborough, White's.   *Died 30 July 1919.*

ALINGTON, Admiral Arthur Hildebrand, JP, Lindsey, Lincs; Lord of the Manor of Swinhope; Patron of Livings of Swinhope and Stenigot, Lincs; *b* 1889; 3rd *s* of late George Marmaduke Alington, DL, JP, of Swinhope, Lincs; *m* 1870, Charlotte Mary (*d* 1913), *d* of Rev. Charles Moore, of Garlenick, Cornwall; two *s* one *d*. *Educ:* Dr Lovell's, Winslow Hall, Bucks. Entered Royal Navy, 1852; served throughout Russian war in Baltic and Black Sea, 1854–56; Lieut commanding HMS Britomart on Lake Erie during Fenian troubles, 1866–68; Commander of HMS Boxer on West Coast Africa; Niger Expedition; Captain of Conqueror, Dreadnought, and Superb battleships; 2nd in command Channel Fleet, 1895–96; flagships Empress of India and Magnificent; retired, 1899. *Recreations:* fishing, shooting, cycling, motoring. *Address:* Swinhope House, near North Thoresby, Lincs. *TA:* Swinhope, Binbrook. *M:* BE 419. *Club:* United Service.   *Died 7 Dec. 1925.*

ALISON, Sir Archibald, 3rd Bt, *cr* 1852; *b* 20 May 1862; *s* of Sir Archibald Alison, 2nd Bt, and Jane, *d* of late James Black, Dalmonach; *S* father 1907; *m* 1888, Georgina, *y d* of late J. Bond Cabbell of Cromer Hall, Norfolk; two *s* (and one *s* decd). *Educ:* Eton; Sandhurst. Capt. 5th Batt. Rifle Brigade, 1885–95; Colonial Secretary, Bermuda, 1888–1900. *Heir: s* Archibald Alison, Lieut-Commander, RN [*b* 5 Nov. 1888; *m* 1919, Isa Margery Tyrrell, *d* of C. Tyrrell Giles]. *Address:* Possil, Budleigh Salterton, Devon. *Club:* Boodle's.

Died 7 Nov. 1921.

ALLAN, Arthur Percy, MD, BS (Lond. Univ.); medical practitioner; for five years Editor of the General Practitioner; *b* Chislehurst, 1868; 7th *s* of late John Allan; *m* Margaret, *d* of late Richard Clark, Amersham. *Educ:* private schools, Hanover; Birkbeck College; Guy's Hospital, London. Formerly Clinical Assistant, Assistant House Physician and House Physician, Guy's Hospital; Vice-President University of London Graduates' Association. *Publications:* contributions to Times, Kent Messenger, Lancet, British Medical Journal, British Journal of Children's Diseases, General Practitioner, Clinical Journal. *Recreations:* walking, gardening, billiards. *Address:* Crogdene, Croham Road, Croydon. *T:* Croydon 1369. *TA:* Dr Allan, South Croydon.   *Died 2 Sept. 1927.*

ALLAN, Maj.-Gen. William; Colonel, Welsh Regiment, since 1904; *b* 22 June 1832; *s* of Alex. Allan, of Hillside, Edinburgh; *m* 1st, 1870, Anne Campbell Penney (*d* 1876), *d* of Lord Kinloch; 2nd, Jane Husey, *d* of Rev. James Senior, afterwards Husey-Hunt. Entered army, 1850; Maj.-Gen. 1889; retired, 1894; served Crimea with the 41st, The Welsh Regt, at the battles of the Alma and Inkerman, both assaults on the Redan, siege and fall of Sevastopol, 1854–56 (medal with three clasps, Knight of Legion of Honour, Turkish medal); Brig.-Gen. commanding troops, Cyprus, 1890–94. *Address:* Hillside, Bidborough, Kent. *Clubs:* Army and Navy; New, Edinburgh.

Died 12 July 1918.

ALLANBY, Ven. Christopher Gibson; *b* Flimby Park, Sorell, Tasmania; 5th *s* of John William Allanby, formerly of Cross Canonby, Cumberland, England; *m* Alice Mary, 2nd *d* of Sidney James Fletcher of Moreland Road, Croydon, England; two *d*. *Educ:* Moore College,

New South Wales. Ordained Deacon, 1862; Priest, 1864, by the Bishop of Melbourne (Dr Perry); appointed Curate of St Paul's, Ballarat, 1862; Archdeacon of the Wimmera, 1885; Archdeacon of the Loddon, 1894; Incumbent of Brown Hill, Ballarat, 1866–1914; Archdeacon to the Bishop of Ballarat, 1902–14; retired 1914. *Address:* 55 Morland Road, Croydon, Surrey.

Died 13 Jan. 1917.

ALLBON, Charles F., ARE 1886; watercolour painter, black and white artist and etcher; *b* 1856; *s* of C. F. Allbon. *Educ:* Mr Hudson's Academy. Joined School of Art, Croydon, 1870; all his art studentship free—won by scholarships; came to London, 1880; elected a member of the Langham, 1885; exhibited Old Post Office, Beddington, Suffolk Street, and engraved in Pictorial World, 1874. *Publications:* The Seasons; Castle Elly in the Olden Time; Breezy Weather; Old Chrome and Chepstow Castle; Evening in Hertfordshire. *Recreations:* reading, chess, backgammon, cards. *Address:* Cheshunt Cottage, Chingford Green, Essex. *Died 14 June 1926.*

ALLBUTT, Rt. Hon. Sir (Thomas) Clifford, PC 1920; KCB 1907; MA, MD; FRS 1880; FLS, FSA; DL; Fellow of Caius College; Regius Professor of Physic, Cambridge University, since 1892; Hon. Colonel Eastern Division, RAMC; *b* 20 July 1836; *s* of Rev. Thomas Allbutt; *m* Susan, *d* of late Thomas England of Headingley. *Educ:* St Peter's, York; Caius Coll., Cambridge. 1st class Natural Science Tripos, 1860. Consulting Physician Leeds General Infirmary, Belgrave Hospital for Children, and King Edward VII Sanatorium, Midhurst; Physician Addenbrooke's Hospital, Cambridge; Commissioner in Lunacy, 1889–92; Member of Council of Royal Society, 1896–98 and 1914–16; Vice-President, 1914–16; Hon. Fellow Royal Society of Medicine; Member of Committee of Home Office on Trade Diseases, Nat. Med. Research, and other Government and Royal Society Committees; Hon. Member American Association of Physicians; Foreign Hon. Member American Academy of Arts and Sciences. Hon. LLD Cantab, Hon. DSc Oxon, Hon. MD, Hon. LLD. Inventor of Short Clinical Thermometer. *Publications:* The Ophthalmoscope in Medicine, 1871; Goulstonian Lectures (On Visceral Neuroses), 1884; On Scrofula, 1885; The Lane Lectures on Diseases of the Heart, 1896; Science and Medieval Thought, 1901; The Historical Relations of Medicine and Surgery, 1905; editor of Systems of Medicine and Gynæcology, 1896–99–1907; Fitzpatrick Lectures on Greek Medicine in Rome, 1909–10; Greco-Roman Medicine and other historical essays, 1921; Diseases of the Arteries and Angina Pectoris, 1915; Science in the School, 1917; Notes on Composition of Scientific Papers, 3rd edn, 1923. *Recreations:* Alpine Club, cycling. *Address:* St Radegund's, Cambridge. *T:* Cambridge 307. *Clubs:* Athenæum, Alpine. *Died 22 Feb. 1925.*

ALLCOCK, Rev. Arthur Edmund, MA; Headmaster of Highgate School, 1893–1908; *b* Harborne, Staffs, 16 Feb. 1851; *s* of late Thomas Allcock. *Educ:* King Edward's School, Birmingham; Emmanuel Coll., Camb. Assistant Master, King Edward's School, Birmingham, 1874–80; Wellington Coll., 1880–93; ordained 1889. *Recreations:* cricket, fives, golf. *Address:* 46 Carpenter Road, Edgbaston, Birmingham. *Died 23 Dec. 1924.*

ALLDRIDGE, Thomas Joshua, ISO 1905; FRGS, FRCI, FZS; District Commissioner of Sherbro, West Coast of Africa (retired); *b* 1847; *y s* of late R. W. Alldridge, Old Charlton. *Educ:* City of London School; Blackheath Proprietary School. FRGS and awarded the Cuthbert Peek grant (1900) for geographical work in the interior of the colony of Sierra Leone, West Coast Africa; presented with the Life Fellowship of the Zoological Society, London, 1884; Acting United States Consular Agent at Sierra Leone, 1871–72; travelling commissioner for that colony, 1889; Hon. Inspector Police; Justice of the Peace; Commissioner of the Court of Requests; Coroner, etc; Pioneer into Upper Mendi, Bandi, and Bundi countries, and made numerous treaties on behalf of the British Government with the paramount chiefs; sent on special mission by the Government to Robari, and succeeded in stopping war and making peace between the Timinis and Yonnis; convened meeting of 3,000 chiefs and people at Bandasuma, Barri country, to meet the Governor, Sir Francis Fleming, KCMG, by direction of Secretary of State; as topographical and astronomical observer accompanied His Excellency Sir Frederic Cardew, KCMG, 1894, upon his first interior tour of 617 miles, occupying 52 days; special mission to Sama country, 1894; through the Mendi Rising, 1898 (medal and clasp). *Publications:* The Sherbro and its Hinterland, 1901; A Transformed Colony (Sierra Leone), 1910. *Address:* Oak Mount, Bagshot, Surrey. *Club:* Royal Societies.

Died 28 June 1916.

ALLEN, Col Sir Charles, Kt 1908; VD; JP; *b* 1852; widower. Late Col Commanding 3rd Brigade West Riding RFA, and 2/5th North London Brigade, RFA; Chairman of Sir Henry Bessemer and Co.; Chairman Ebbw Vale Steel, Iron, and Coal Co., Ltd; Local President, London City and Midland Bank Ltd, Sheffield. *Address:* 10 Gladstone Road, Fulwood Road, Sheffield. *Club:* Junior Carlton.

Died 13 April 1920.

ALLEN, Charles Francis Egerton, JP; *b* 14 Oct. 1847; *s* of Charles Allen of Tenby and Mary, *d* of James Allen of Freestone, parish of Carew, County of Pembroke; *m* 1891, Elizabeth Georgina, *d* of William Wilcox of Whitburn, near Sunderland; no *c*. *Educ:* Eton; St John's College, Cambridge; Senior Optime, Mathematical Tripos, 1870. Called to Bar, Inner Temple, 1871; joined the Northern Circuit, afterwards the North Eastern; went to India, 1873; practised in Calcutta and Rangoon; law lecturer, Presidency College; Judge in Calcutta Court of Small Causes; went to Rangoon as Government Advocate, 1877; officiated as Recorder of Rangoon; returned, 1888; retired from practice; MP (L) Pembroke and Haverfordwest District Borough, 1892–95; lived at Tenby; served as Borough Magistrate, 1896–1905; served for a time on the Town Council and as Guardian on the Pembroke Union Board. *Recreations:* wasting his time dabbling in heraldry, genealogy, local history, local politics. *Address:* Norton House, Tenby. *Clubs:* Tenby and County; Pembrokeshire County, Haverfordwest. *Died 31 Dec. 1927.*

ALLEN, George Berney; *b* 11 Sept. 1862; *e s* of late Sir George Allen, KCIE, founder of the Indian Pioneer newspaper. *Educ:* Clifton College. Head of Allen Bros & Co., East India Agents, London, and connected with other businesses in India; Managing Proprietor of The Near East and The Indiaman, weekly newspapers. *Address:* Freechase, Warninglid, Sussex. *Club:* White's.

Died 19 June 1917.

ALLEN, Sir Harry Brookes, Kt 1914; Professor of Pathology, 1906–24, and Dean of Faculty of Medicine, University of Melbourne; Pathologist Melbourne Hospital; Chairman, Executive and Finance Committee, Australian Red Cross Society (BRCS); *b* 13 June 1854; 2nd *s* of late Thomas Watts Allen, Geelong, Victoria; *m* 1891, Ada, *e d* of late Henry Mason, HM Customs, Liverpool; three *d*. *Educ:* Flinders' School, Geelong; Church of England Grammar School, Melbourne; Melbourne University; MB 1876; MD 1878; BS 1879; Hon. LLD Edin. 1912; LLD Adel. 1914. Demonstrator of Anatomy, Melbourne University, and Pathologist, Melbourne Hospital, 1876; Lecturer, 1881, Professor, 1882, of Anatomy and Pathology; President, Professorial Board, 1895–97; Editor, Australian Medical Journal, 1879–83; Hon. Secretary, Medical Society of Victoria, 1879–87; Member Tuberculosis in Cattle Board, 1883–84, and joint author of report; Member of Central Board of Health, 1883–84; drafted Model Bye-Laws for Local Boards, etc; advised meat-preserving companies to revolutionise construction of freezing chambers, 1883; created Museum of Pathology in Melbourne University; President, Royal Commission on Sanitary state of Melbourne, and of Intercolonial Rabbit Commission, 1888–89; Gen. Secretary, Intercolonial Medical Congress, 1889; visited Europe and obtained recognition of Melbourne Medical Degrees, 1890; drafted Deed of Union of Medical Societies of Victoria under British Medical Association; President, Old Melburnians, 1897; Member of Council, Melbourne University, 1898; President, Australasian Medical Congress, 1908; Member Executive Committee International Medical Congress, 1913. *Publications:* Typhoid Fever and Milk Supply, 1889; Reports to Victoria Government on Hospital Construction, Sewerage Works, Tuberculin, etc, 1891; Address as President of Medical Society of Victoria, 1892; Medical Periodicals in Melbourne, 1893; Tumours of Kidney, 1896; Address on Cancer and Cancer Statistics in Australasia, 1902; Tumours, 1903; Tubercle of Joints, 1904; Address as first Pres. of United Medical Societies of Victoria, 1908; Specific Disease, 1908; Address as Pres. of Australasian Med. Cong., and various papers, 1908; Address on Vaccines, Aust. Med. Cong., 1911; Report to Commonwealth Government on Health Conditions at Panama, 1913; on Risks of Middle Age and Specific Diseases, 1916; Pathology, Lectures and Demonstrations, 1920. *Address:* The University, Melbourne.

Died 28 March 1926.

ALLEN, Henry Seymour, JP, CC, DL; *b* 30 Aug. 1847; *s* of late Seymour Philipps Allen and Lady Catherine, 2nd *d* of 4th Earl of Portsmouth; unmarried. *Educ:* Harrow. Late Lieut, 1st Life Guards. High Sheriff, Pembs, 1873. *Recreations:* hunting, shooting, cycling, skating. *Address:* Cresselly House, Cresselly, Begelly, Pembrokeshire. *Clubs:* Brooks's, Naval and Military, Eighty.

Died 25 Feb. 1928.

ALLEN, James Lane; American author; *b* Kentucky, 1849. *Educ:* Transylvania Univ. *Publications:* A Kentucky Cardinal; The Choir Invisible; A Summer in Arcady; Flute and Violin; The Blue Grass Region of Kentucky; The Increasing Purpose; Aftermath: second part of A Kentucky Cardinal; The Mettle of the Pasture, 1903; The Bride of the Mistletoe, 1909; The Doctor's Christmas Eve, 1910; A Heroine in Bronze, 1912; The Sword of Youth, 1915; A Cathedral Singer, 1916; The Emblems of Fidelity, 1917; The Kentucky Warbler, 1918. *Address:* 66 5th Avenue, New York. *Died 18 Feb. 1925.*

ALLEN, Richard William, MA (NZ); MD (London); Captain, New Zealand Medical Corps; *b* Auckland, New Zealand, 28 Nov. 1876; *s* of James and Jessie Balfour Allen; *m* 1909, Beatrice Mary Harston; one *s* two *d*. *Educ:* Auckland College and Grammar School; University College, Auckland; Guy's Hospital, London. Junior and Senior University Scholar, and Master of Arts; 1st class honours of University of New Zealand; entrance Science Scholar Guy's Hospital, 1899; Wooldrige Memorial Scholar in Physiology, 1902; gold medallist in Materia Medica University of London, 1902; MB, BS 1st class honours in medicine, 1905; Gull student in pathology, 1904; late Pathologist to Royal Eye Hospital; late Director of Vaccine Therapy Department, Mount Vernon Hospital for diseases of chest; Fellow of Royal Society of Medicine. *Publications:* late editor Journal of Vaccine Therapy; Practical Vaccine Treatment for the General Practitioner; Vaccine Therapy (4th edition); Bacterial Diseases of Respiration; numerous monographs in chemical and medical sciences. *Recreations:* football, cricket, running, fishing, yachting. *Address:* 128 Harley Street, W1. *T:* Mayfair 3086; 2 Carlton Houses, Westgate-on-Sea.
Died 28 Aug. 1921.

ALLEN, Col Robert Franklin, DSO 1905; Royal Engineers; *b* 21 Feb. 1860; *s* of late Major R. Austen Allen, MD, AMS; *m* 1886, Alice Gordon, *d* of late Surgeon-General Inkson; one *s*. Entered army, 1879; Captain, 1889; Major, 1897; served Manipur, 1891 (despatches, medal with clasp); East Africa, 1904 (despatches, medal with two clasps, DSO); retired, 1909. *Address:* c/o Cox and Co., Charing Cross, SW.
Died 20 Nov. 1916.

ALLEN, Very Rev. Thomas, AM, TCD; Rector of Killoran and Kilvarnet, Diocese of Achonry, since 1904; Canon of St Patrick's Cathedral, Dublin, since 1904; Dean of Achonry since 1916; member of the Diocesan Council of Killala and Achonry; Examining Chaplain to Bishop of Tuam, 1923; Diocesan Secretary for Temperance; *b* 2 Nov. 1873; *e s* of William Allen, Camp Hill House, Ballymena, Co. Antrim. *Educ:* Model School, and Collegiate and Intermediate School, Ballymena; Trinity College, Dublin. 1st class exhibitioner—Junior Grade Intermediate Educ. Board; 1st class Divinity Testimonium, TCD; Ryan Prizeman, TCD; BA 1897, MA 1900, of TCD. Curate of Maryborough, Queen's Co., 1897–1900; senior curate of Galway, 1900–4; Diocesan Inspector of Religious Education, Tuam, 1903–4. *Address:* The Rectory, Coolaney, Co. Sligo.
Died 16 May 1927.

ALLEN, Thomas Carleton, LLB, DCL; KC; Registrar, Supreme Court of New Brunswick, Deputy Attorney-General, and Clerk of the Crown; *b* Fredericton, NB, 9 Nov. 1852; *s* of Sir John Campbell Allen; *m* Louisa L. Wetmore; two *s* one *d*. Mayor of Fredericton, 1890–93. *Recreations:* golf, tennis, hunting. *Address:* Fredericton, NB.
Died Sept. 1927.

ALLEN, Wilfred Baugh; JP Pembrokeshire and Nottinghamshire; late County Court Judge, Nottingham, resigned Dec. 1917; *b* 14 Nov. 1849; 2nd *s* of George Baugh Allen of Cilrhiw, Co. Pembroke; *m* 1883, Anne Sophia, *d* of late Rev. Robt Wedgewood of Dumbleton, Glos; one *s*. *Educ:* Rugby; Trinity Coll., Camb. Called to Bar, Inner Temple, 1882; Member of SE Circuit. *Publications:* (joint) Forms of Endorsement of Writs of Summons and Pleadings in Queen's Bench Division; Criminal Evidence Act. *Address:* Cilrhiw, Narberth, Pembrokeshire; Rosemount, Tenby. *Club:* Notts County, Nottingham.
Died 10 June 1922.

ALLEN, William Henry, DL, JP; Bedfordshire High Sheriff, 1904–5; Member of the Territorial Association; Chairman of W. H. Allen, Sons & Co. Ltd, Bedford; *b* 1844; *s* of late William George Allen of Cardiff; *m* 1st, Annie Mary Pemberton, *d* of Richard Thomas Howell of Bryn-Caeran Castle, Carmarthenshire; six *s* four *d*; 2nd, Madeline, *d* of W. J. Fedden, Clifton, Bristol; one *d*. *Educ:* under John Elwell, Wallescote House, Weston-super-Mare. Educated as an engineer; founded The Queen's Engineering Works, Bedford. Member of Royal Institution, of Institution of Civil Engineers; Vice-President, Institution of Mechanical Engineers; Member of Council of Institute of Metals. *Publication:* paper read before Institution of Civil Engineers on Auxiliary Machines for large steamships. *Recreations:* all games, including hunting and shooting, gardening, farming, organ-playing. *Address:* Bromham House, Bromham, near Bedford. *M:* MB 27. *Club:* Athenæum. *Died 3 Sept. 1926.*

ALLENDALE, 1st Viscount, *cr* 1911; **Wentworth Canning Blackett Beaumont;** Baron 1906; DL; MA; MP (L) Hexham Division of Northumberland, 1895–1907; Vice-Chamberlain of HM's Household, 1905–7; Captain of HM's Bodyguard of the Yeomen of the Guard, 1907–11; Lord-in-Waiting to HM, 1911–16; Chairman, Territorial Force Association, Northumberland, 1908–19; *b* Bywell Hall, Northumberland, 2 Dec. 1860; *e s* of 1st Baron Allendale and Margaret, 4th *d* of 1st Marquess of Clanricarde; *S* father 1907; *m* 1889, Lady Alexandrina Louisa Maud (Aline) Vane-Tempest, *d* of 5th Marquess of Londonderry; two *s* three *d* (and one *d* decd). *Educ:* Eton; Trinity College, Cambridge. *Heir: s* Capt. Hon. Wentworth Henry Canning Beaumont, *b* 6 Aug. 1890. *Recreation:* hunting. *Address:* 144 Piccadilly, W1; Bywell Hall, Stocksfield-on-Tyne; Bretton Park, Wakefield. *Clubs:* Brooks's, Travellers', Turf.
Died 12 Dec. 1923.

ALLERTON, 1st Baron, *cr* 1902, of Chapel Allerton; **William Lawies Jackson,** PC 1890; FRS 1891; JP; Chairman of Great Northern Railway Co.; *b* 16 Feb. 1840; *s* of late W. Jackson, Leeds; *m* 1860, Grace (*d* 1901), *d* of G. Tempest; two *s* five *d*. Contested Leeds, 1876; MP (C) Leeds N, 1880–1902; Financial Secretary to Treasury, 1885–86, 1886–91; Chief Secretary for Ireland, 1891–92. *Heir: s* Hon. George Herbert Jackson, *b* 20 Jan. 1867. *Address:* 41 Cadogan Square, SW. *T:* Kensington 310; Allerton Hall, Chapel Allerton, Leeds. *Clubs:* Carlton, Athenæum. *Died 4 April 1917.*

ALLERTON, 2nd Baron, *cr* 1902, of Chapel Allerton; **George Herbert Jackson;** *b* 20 Jan. 1867; *e s* of 1st Baron Allerton and Grace, *d* of G. Tempest; *S* father 1917; *m* 1899, Katherine Louisa, *y d* of W. W. Wickham, JP, of Chestnut Grove, Boston Spa; one *s* one *d*. *Educ:* Rugby. *Heir: s* George William Lawies Jackson, *b* 23 July 1903.
Died 29 Jan. 1925.

ALLETSON, Major G. C., DSO 1917; Remount Service; *s* of G. H. Alletson, Ewloe Wood, Northop, Flintshire; *m* 1902, Norah, *g c* of late Charles Trevor Roper, Plas Teg, Flintshire; one *s* one *d*. *Educ:* privately. Served in South African War, Denbighshire Yeomanry; then Lieut in Prince of Wales Light Horse, and finally Capt. Remount Service, 1900–2; Adjutant, Flintshire National Reserve, 1912–14; Capt. in Remount Service, France and Italy, Oct. 1914; Major, May 1915 (DSO, despatches). *Recreations:* shooting, fishing. *Address:* Clun, Lee-on-Solent, Hants. *Died 14 May 1928.*

ALLGEYER, Bishop Emile Auguste; Bishop of Ticelia and Apostolic Vicar of Zanzibar and British East Africa, 1906–13; *b* Rixheim, Alsace, near Mulhouse, 14 April 1856; *s* of Benoit Allgeyer and Genevieva Haby. *Educ:* at home; Blackrock College, Dublin; Bretagne; Philosophy and Theology in Paris. Priest, 1885; Professor at St Mary's College, Port-of-Spain, Trinidad, W Indies, 1885; Parish Priest at Newton, Port-of-Spain, 1890–96; St Andrews, Grenada, 1896–97; Bishop of German and British East Africa, 1897–1906; erected a Cathedral in Zanzibar; founded seven new centres of mission in German East Africa; four convents for the education of Negro girls; and in British East Africa six new missions and an English high boarding school at St Austin's Mission, near Nairobi. *Recreations:* has been thrice in Europe on business and twice in Natal for his health. *Address:* Kilana, Tang Territory, East Africa.
Died 9 April 1924.

ALLHUSEN, (Augustus) Henry (Eden), JP, DL; *b* 20 Aug. 1867; *s* of late Henry Christian Allhusen and Alice, *d* of late Thos Eden, Norton Hall, Gloucestershire; *g s* of Christian Allhusen, JP, DL, Stoke Court, Bucks, chemical manufacturer, Newcastle-on-Tyne; *m* 1896, Dorothy Stanley, *d* of Lady St Helier and her 1st husband, Col Hon. John Stanley, Grenadier Guards, 2nd *s* of 2nd Baron Stanley of Alderley; two *d* (one *s* decd). *Educ:* Cheltenham Coll.; Trinity Coll., Camb. (BA 1890). Formerly Lieut Bucks Yeomanry; MP (C) Salisbury, 1897–1900; Central Hackney, 1900–6; High Sheriff, Bucks, 1913; Chairman of Magistrates and Guardians at Slough. *Address:* Stoke Court, Stoke Poges, Bucks. *T:* Farnham Common 68. *Clubs:* Carlton, White's, Boodle's. *Died 2 May 1925.*

ALLHUSEN, Beatrice May; *d* of late Col Thomas Bromhead Butt, 79th Highlanders; *m* 1876, William Hutt Allhusen. *Publications:* Miss Molly; Ingelheim; An Episode on a Desert Island; The Great Reconciler. *Address:* 15 Kensington Palace Gardens, W. *Clubs:* Ladies' Athenæum, Writers'. *Died 29 July 1918.*

ALLHUSEN, William Hutt; b 16 Sept. 1845; s of late Christian Allhusen of Stoke Court; m 1876, Beatrice May (d 1918), d of late Col T. Bromhead Butt, 79th Highlanders. *Educ:* Cheltenham College; Carlsruhe; Magdalen College, Cambridge. *Recreation:* motoring. *Address:* 15 Kensington Palace Gardens, W; Lemoenfontein, Beaufort West, Cape Colony. *Clubs:* Wellington, Royal Automobile; Civil Service, Royal Automobile, Cape Town.

Died 25 Aug. 1923.

ALLIES, Mary H. A.; b 2 Feb. 1852; e d of Thomas William Allies, KCSG, and Eliza Hall, 2nd d of Thos Harding Newman of Nelmes, Essex. *Educ:* The Convent of the Holy Child, St Leonard's-on-Sea; Visitation Convent, rue d'Enfer, Paris. Published her first book in 1875 under the guidance of her father, who formed and directed both her studies and her pen. *Publications:* Life of Pope Pius VII, 1875; Three Catholic Reformers of the 15th Century, 1878; Leaves from St Augustine, 1886; Leaves from St John Chrysostom, 1889; Letters of St Augustine, 1890; History of the Church in England, 2 vols, 1892–97; The Heiress of Cronenstein, adapted from the German of Countess Hahn-Hahn, 1900; Treatise on Holy Images (Greek, St John Damascene), 1898; Thomas William Allies, 1907; How to help the Dead (de Cura gerenda pro Mortuis), 1914; Thomas William Allies, *secundo*, 1924; numerous articles, notably for the Catholic World and Dublin Review, occasionally in French. *Address:* Berkeley Lodge, 7 Melina Place, St John's Wood, NW.

Died 27 Jan. 1927.

ALLINGHAM, Helen, (Mrs William Allingham), RWS 1890; water-colour painter; b 26 Sept. 1848; d of A. Henry Paterson, MD; m 1874, William Allingham, the Irish poet; two s one d. *Educ:* Royal Academy Schools. Drew in black and white for Graphic, Cornhill; ARWS 1875. Occasional exhibitions of English cottage and rural subjects, in the Fine Art Society's rooms. *Publications:* Happy England, 1903 (with M. B. Huish); The Homes of Tennyson (with Arthur Paterson), 1905; The Cottage Homes of England (with Stewart Dick), 1909; (edited) William Allingham, a Diary; Letters to William Allingham; By the Way, by William Allingham. *Recreations:* country walks and drives. *Address:* Eldon House, Lyndhurst Road, Hampstead, NW.

Died 28 Sept. 1926.

ALLISON, Sir Robert Andrew, Kt 1910; JP, DL; b 5 March 1838; m 1st, 1867, Laura Alicia (d 1892), d of J. M. Atkinson of Thorp Arch, Yorks; two s two d; 2nd, 1897, Sara Eudora, d of Canon Slater, Branksome Park, Bournemouth. *Educ:* Rugby; Trinity College, Cambridge. MP (R) North Cumberland, 1885–1900. *Publications:* Essays and Addresses, 1913; Five Plays of Piautus, 1914 (translated); Belgium in History, 1914; Cicero on Old Age, in verse, 1916; Lucretius on the Nature of Things, translated, 1919; translations mainly from the Greek Anthology. *Address:* Scaleby Hall, Carlisle. *TA:* Kirklinton. *Club:* County, Carlisle.

Died 15 Jan. 1926.

ALLISON, William; The Special Commissioner, The Sportsman; Barrister-at-Law; Managing Director of The International Horse Agency and Exchange, Ltd (Lessees of the Cobham Stud, Cobham, Surrey); b 30 April 1851; s of late J. P. Allison, Kilvington, Thirsk, Yorkshire, and Maria, d of late William Whytehead; m 1876, Frances, d of late James Leslie Walker; one s one d. *Educ:* Rugby; Balliol College, Oxford (MA). *Career:* The Law, Inner Temple and NE Circuit, and Sporting Journalism. *Publications:* Blair Athol; A Tory Lordling; The Parson and the Painter (illustrated by Phil May); The British Thoroughbred Horse; My Kingdom for a Horse; Blairmount, Memories of Men and Horses, 1922, etc. *Recreation:* golf. *Address:* 50 Harrington Gardens, SW7; 46A Pall Mall, SW1; Cobham Stud, Cobham, Surrey. *TA:* Ciliary, London. *T:* Regent 49. *Club:* Sports.

Died 15 July 1925.

ALLIX, Charles Peter, JP, DL; MA; landed proprietor; b 21 Feb. 1842; s of late Col Charles Allix, Grenadier Guards, and Mary C. E., his cousin, d of late Chas Allix of Willoughby Hall, Lincolnshire; m 1866, Laura A. W., d of R. L. Bevan, Brixworth Hall, Northants; two s three d. *Educ:* Harrow; Trinity College, Cambridge. Appointed JP 1864, and served continuously; Vice-Chairman of the Cambridgeshire Quarter Sessions; Chairman of the Bottisham Petty Sessional Division; Chairman of the Swaffham and Bottisham Fen Drainage District Commissioners; served as a representative of the diocese of Ely in the Canterbury House of Laymen, 1889–96; also Deputy Chairman of the Ely and Bury St Edmunds Light Railway Company authorised by Act of Parliament in 1875, in which capacity he promoted the construction of the Cambridge and Mildenhall Railway, subsequently constructed by the Great Eastern Railway Company in 1884. *Publications:* papers read before the Cambridge Archæological Society:

St Mary's Church, Swaffham-Prior; A Primitive Neolithic Dwelling discovered on the estate; The Escape of Allix the Huguenot from France in 1685. *Recreations:* shooting, fishing, landscape gardening, carving, carpenters' work, archæology, geology. *Address:* Swaffham-Prior House, near Cambridge. *Clubs:* Junior Carlton; Cambridge County, Cambridge.

Died 10 June 1920.

ALLMAN, Robert, CMG 1901; LRCSI, LRCPI; Principal Medical Officer Oil Rivers Protectorate (later Southern Nigeria) since 1891, and organised Medical Department; b 11 Sept. 1854; s of late Rev. William Allman, MA, MD, of Lurgy Vale, Kilmacrenan, Ireland; m 1893, Constance Maude, 2nd d of late Edmund Murphy, JP; one s three d. PMO Cross River, Eket, Okrika Expeditions, 1895–96; PMO Protectorate troops, Benin City Expedition, 1897 (despatches, medal and clasp, thanks of Sec. of State); PMO Oron, 1897; Ekuri, 1897–98 (despatches); Ubium and Ishan, 1899 Expeditions; Aro Expedition, 1901–2 (medal and clasp); Member of Committee at Colonial Office for Reorganisation of the West African Medical Staff, 1901 (thanks of Sec. of State). *Address:* 2 Cowper Villas, Palmerston Park, Dublin.

Died 16 Nov. 1917.

ALLNUTT, Rev. George Herbert, RD; Rector of St Paul's, Cobbitty, and St Thomas, Narellan, since 1883; Rural Dean of Liverpool and Camden, since 1904; Hon. Canon of St Andrew's Cathedral, 1911; b London, 1843; e s of late Rev. Thos Allnutt, BD, Rector of Stibbard, Norfolk; m o d of late John Cash Neild, MD, ChD, Sydney; one s two d. *Educ:* Queen Elizabeth's Grammar School, Ipswich. Third Master of Chesterfield Grammar School, 1862; emigrated to Queensland, 1864; engaged for some years in station work, and sugar making, Queensland and NSW; Catechist at St Paul's, Sydney, 1874; entered Moore Theological College, 1875 (1st class and prizeman); ordained, 1876; incumbent of Milchester and Charters Towers, N Queensland, 1876–78; Rector of Mulgoa, NSW, 1878–83. *Address:* The Rectory, Cobbity, NSW.

Died 28 July 1919.

ALLSOPP, Hon. Frederic Ernest; b 21 Sept. 1857; e surv. s of 1st Baron Hindlip. Late Capt. RA; served Afghan War, 1879–81 (despatches, medal and two clasps); Suakin Campaign, 1885 (medal and clasp); Burma Campaign, 1886–87 (despatches, medal and clasp).

Died Dec. 1928.

ALLSOPP, Capt. Hon. Herbert Tongue; late 10th Hussars; e surv. s of 1st Baron Hindlip; b 5 Dec. 1855; m 1891, Edith Mary, d of late H. C. Akroyd; one d. Served Afghan War, 1878–80 (medal with clasp); Egypt, 1884 (medal with clasp, bronze star). *Address:* Walton-Bury, Stafford.

Died 31 Jan. 1920.

ALLSUP, Major Edward Saunders, DSO 1917; RA; Commanding 8th Field Battery RA, Edinburgh; b 27 Nov. 1879; s of late William James Allsup; unmarried. *Educ:* Monkton Combe School, Bath. First Commission, 1900; Captain, 1913; Major, 1915; served North-West Frontier, India, Mohmand Field Force, 1908 (medal and clasp); European War, 1914–18 (DSO, 1914 Star). *Address:* Lloyds Bank Ltd, Cox's Branch, 6 Pall Mall, SW. *Club:* Junior United Service.

Died 22 Feb. 1928.

ALLWORK, Rev. Robert Long, MA; Vicar of Epping since 1906; Hon. Canon of Chelmsford; Rural Dean of Chigwell; Surrogate for the Diocese of Chelmsford; Chaplain to the Epping Union; b 1863; y s of late C. L. Allwork, Surgeon, of Maidstone; m Helen Margaretta, d of late C. W. Chaldecott, Surgeon, of Dorking; one d. *Educ:* Tonbridge; Corpus Christi College, Cambridge. Curate of S Botolph, Bishopsgate, 1886–87; S Ann, Stamford Hill, 1887–97; S Mary's, Southampton, 1897–1900; Vicar of S Saviour's, Walthamstow, 1900–6. *Recreations:* music, mechanics. *Address:* The Vicarage, Epping, Essex.

Died 15 March 1919.

ALMOND, W. Douglas, RI; Member of the Artists' Society and the Langham Sketching Club; Member of the Royal Institute of Oil Painters. *Address:* 188 Regent's Park Road, NW. *Club:* Savage.

Died 12 March 1916.

ALSOP, James Willcox, OBE; Hon. LLD Liverpool; Solicitor, practising in Liverpool; Pro-Chancellor of University of Liverpool since 1909; Chairman of Liverpool Education Committee (member since 1903); Deputy Chairman, London and Lancashire Insurance Co., Ltd; b Birmingham, 6 June 1846; e s of Rev. James Alsop, and Mary, d of William Willcox, Birmingham; m 1886, Constance, 2nd d of Charles Grey Mott, JP of Harrow Weald, Middlesex; no c. *Educ:* Hope St British Schools, Liverpool; Liverpool Institute; Queen's College, Liverpool. BA (London) 1867, with 1st class Honours in

English Language and Literature (University Exhibition), and in Logic and Mental and Moral Philosophy; President of Liverpool Incorporated Law Society, 1892–93; Life Governor of University College, Liverpool, from its Incorporation, 1882; Life Governor of University of Liverpool from its Incorporation, 1903; Vice-President of University Council, 1903–9; President, 1909–18; Member of Liverpool City Council since 1899. *Publications:* various papers and addresses. *Recreations:* golf, travel. *Address:* Ulverscroft, Bidston Road, Birkenhead; 14 Castle Street, Liverpool. *TA:* Jurist, Liverpool. *T:* Birkenhead 835; Liverpool Bank 865. *Clubs:* Reform; University, Exchange, Liverpool.   *Died 19 May 1921.*

ALTON, Sir Francis (Cooke), KBE 1919; CB 1902; CMG 1917; Paymaster Rear-Admiral; retired; *b* 24 Aug. 1856; *s* of late Francis Cooke Alton, Chief Inspector of Machinery, RN; *m* 1884, Lina (*d* 1919), *d* of Ernest Barclay; one *s* one *d*. Secretary to Admiral Seymour, Commander-in-Chief, China, 1898–1901; took part in Naval Expedition for relief of Legations at Pekin during Boxer outbreak in China, 1900 (promoted Fleet Paymaster); Secretary to Admiral of the Fleet Sir Edward Seymour when British Representative at Hudson Fulton Celebration, New York, 1909; served as Secretary to several Naval Commanders-in-Chief; retired, 1914; served European War as Secretary to Principal Naval Transport Office, France, 1914–17 (despatches).   *Died 27 March 1926.*

ALVORD, Clarence Walworth; historian; *b* Greenfield, Mass, 21 May 1868; *s* of Daniel Wells Alvord and Caroline Betts Dewey; *m* 1st, 1893, Jennie Kettell Blanchard (*née* Parrott) (*d* 1911); 2nd, 1913, Idress Head, St Louis. *Educ:* Williams College; University of Berlin; University of Chicago; PhD, University of Illinois, 1908. Instructor Milton (Mass) Academy, 1891–93; Instructor Preparatory School, University of Illinois, 1897–1901; Instructor in History, 1901–6; Associate, 1906–7; Assistant Professor, 1907–9; Associate Professor, 1909–13; Professor, 1913–20; Professor Univ. of Minn, 1920–23; Gen. Editor Illinois Historical Collections, 1906–20; President Mississippi Valley Historical Association, 1908–9; Member American Historical Association, Massachusetts Historical Society (Hon.), Missouri Historical Society of St Louis (Hon.), American Antiquarian Society (Hon.); Corresponding Member Missouri State Historical Society, Nebraska Historical Society, Chicago Historical Society, Minnesota Historical Society (life); Fellow Royal Historical Society; Managing Editor Mississippi Valley Historical Review, 1914–23; Editor-in-chief, Illinois Centennial History; Unitarian. *Publications:* Mississippi Valley in British Politics (2 vols), 1917 (Loubat prize, 1917); The Illinois Country, 1919; Lord Shelburne and the Founding of British-American Goodwill, the Raleigh Lecture on History, 1925; contributions to Historical periodicals; Editor of Cahokia Records (Illinois Historical Collections), 1906; Invitation Sérieuse aux Habitants des Illinois (with Dr C. E. Carter), 1908; Governors' Letter-Books (with Dr E. B. Greene) (Illinois Historical Collections), 1909; Kaskaskia Records (Illinois Historical Collections), 1909; Early Explorations of the Virginians in the Trans-Alleghany Region (with Lee Bidgood), 1912; (with C. E. Carter), The British Series, vols i, ii, iii (Illinois Historical Collections), 1915–25. *Recreations:* golf, gardening. *Address:* American University Union, 50 Russell Square, WC1; 56 Clarence Avenue, Minneapolis, Minn, USA.   *Died 25 Jan. 1928.*

AMEER-ALI, Rt. Hon. (Syed), PC 1909; CIE 1887; Hon. LLD Cambridge; DL (Calcutta Univ.); DLitt (Aligarh Univ.); Member of the Judicial Committee of the Privy Council; *b* 6 April 1849; 4th *s* of late (Syed) Saâdut Ali of Mohan, Oudh; *m* Isabelle Ida, 2nd *d* of late H. Konstam, 64 Gloucester Place, Portman Square, W; two *s. Educ:* Hooghly College. Called to Bar, Inner Temple, 1873; Lecturer on Mahommedan Law at the Presidency College, 1873–78; President of the Committee of Management of the Mohsin Endowment, Bengal, 1876–1904; Member of the Commission to enquire into the affairs of the ex-King of Oude, 1879; Magistrate and Chief Magistrate of Calcutta, 1878–81; Member of the Bengal Legislative Council, 1878–83; Tagore Law Professor, 1884; President of the Faculty of Law, Calcutta University, 1891–92; Member of the Imperial Legislative Council of India, 1883–85; a Judge of His Majesty's High Court of Judicature at Fort William in Bengal, 1890–1904. *Decorated* for services in the Imperial Legislative Council of India. *Publications:* Critical Examination of the Life and Teachings of Mohammed; Spirit of Islam; Ethics of Islam; A Short History of the Saracens; Personal Law of the Mahomedans; Mahommedan Law, in 2 vols; Student's Handbook of Mahommedan Law; joint author of The Law of Evidence Applicable to British India; of a Commentary on the Bengal Tenancy Act; The Code of Civil Procedure, etc. *Recreations:* riding, shooting. *Address:* 2 Cadogan Place,

SW1. *T:* Sloane 4430; Pollingfold Manor, near Rudgwick, Sussex. *TA:* Ameer-Ali, London. *Club:* Reform.
                                    Died 3 Aug. 1928.

AMES, Frederick; *b* 1836; *s* of G. H. Ames, Cote House, Gloucestershire; *m* Letitia, *d* of Geo. Fillingham of Syerston, Nottinghamshire. *Educ:* Brighton Coll. Late Rifle Brigade. *Recreation:* hunting. *Address:* Hawford Lodge, Worcester. *TA:* Fernhill Heath, Worcester. *Club:* Junior United Service.
                                    Died 3 June 1918.

AMES, Lt-Col Oswald Henry, JP Norfolk; *b* 3 January 1862; *s* of Lionel Ames, of The Hyde, Bedfords; *m* 1901, Violet, 2nd *d* of late Lord Francis Cecil of Stocken Hall, Rutland; one *s* one *d. Educ:* Charterhouse. Entered Herts Militia, 1881, and 2nd Life Guards, 1884; retired, 1906; rejoined Aug. 1914. *Address:* Durfold Hall, Dunsfold, Surrey. *T:* Dunsfold 19. *Club:* Guards.
                                    Died 6 Nov. 1927.

AMES, Percy W., LLD; FSA; Secretary of Royal Society of Literature, 1890–1917; lecturer on literary and scientific subjects; *b* Kirkstall, Yorks, 1853; *y s* of late John William Ames, schoolmaster; *m* 1879, Isabella, *d* of late George Neville Turner of Croydon, and *g d* of late William Rushton of Liverpool; two *s* three *d*. Hon. LLD Wilberforce University. *Publications:* Obituary—Sir Patrick Colquhoun, The Eagle, Camb. 1891; edited, with Introductory Address, Afternoon Lectures on English Literature, 1893; Papers in Transactions RSL: Positivism in Literature, vol. xvii, 1894; Supposed Source of The Vicar of Wakefield, vol. xix, 1897; Racial and Individual Temperaments, vol. xx, 1898; Edmund Spenser, vol. xxv, 1904; edited, with Historical Sketch of the Princess Elizabeth and Margaret of Navarre, The Mirror of the Sinful Soul, 1897; edited, with Introduction and one lecture, Chaucer Memorial Lectures, 1900; edited, with Introduction, Milton Memorial Lectures, 1908; various articles and addresses uncollected. *Address:* 77 Primrose Mansions, Battersea Park, SW11. *Club:* Authors'.
                                    Died 11 Feb. 1919.

AMHERST, 4th Earl, *cr* 1826; **Hugh Amherst;** Baron Amherst of Montreal, 1788; Viscount Holmesdale, 1826; *b* 30 Jan. 1856; 6th *s* of 2nd Earl; *S* brother 1910; *m* 1896, Hon. Eleanor Clementina St Aubyn, *d* of 1st Baron St Levan; two *s* two *d*. Joined Coldstream Guards, 1875; Captain, 1887; served Nile, 1884–85, with Guards' Camel Regiment (medal with two clasps, Khedive's star). Heir: *s* Viscount Holmesdale, *b* 13 Dec. 1896. *Address:* 1 Wilton Crescent, SW1. *Clubs:* Carlton, Travellers'.
                                    Died 7 March 1927.

AMHERST OF HACKNEY, Baroness (2nd in line) *cr* 1892; **Mary Rothes Margaret Cecil,** OBE; *b* 25 April 1857; *d* of 1st Baron and Margaret Susan, *o c* of Admiral Robert Mitford; *S* father 1909; *m* 1885, Lord William Cecil; Lady of Justice, St John of Jerusalem. Owned about 10,000 acres. Heir: *g s* William Alexander Evering Cecil, *b* 31 May 1912. *Address:* Stow Langtoft Hall, Bury St Edmunds.   *Died 27 Dec. 1919.*

AMHERST, Hon. Sybil Margaret; 2nd *d* of 1st Baron Amherst of Hackney. Lady of Justice, St John of Jerusalem. *Address:* Foulden Hall, Brandon, Norfolk. *Club:* Ladies' Automobile.
                                    Died 21 June 1926.

AMOS, Major Herbert Gilbert Maclachlan, DSO 1900; KOSB; *b* 28 April 1866; *s* of Rev. James Amos of St Ibbs, Hitchin, Herts; *m* 1893, *d* of Gen. Stratton; one *d*. Entered army, 1890; Adjutant, 1898; Captain, 1900; served South Africa (despatches twice, DSO); European War, 1914–17. *Address:* St Ibbs, Hitchin, Herts. *T:* Hitchin 145. *Club:* Junior United Service.
                                    Died 30 June 1924.

AMPHLETT, Major Charles Grove, DSO 1900; JP Salop and Staffordshire; Reserve of Officers, North Staffs Regiment; *b* 8 March 1862. Entered army, 1884; Capt. 1893; Major, 1901; commanded the 1st Mounted Infantry Regt in the S African Campaign. *Address:* Four Ashes Hall, near Stourbridge. *Club:* Naval and Military.
                                    Died 18 Aug. 1921.

AMPHLETT, His Honour Richard Holmden, JP; Judge of County Court of Birmingham since 1908; *b* 24 April 1847; *e s* of late Samuel Holmden Amphlett and Mary Georgiana, *d* of George Edward Male; *nephew* of late Rt Hon. Sir Richard P. Amphlett of Wychbold Hall; *m* 1877, Sophy Emily, 2nd *d* of John Shapter, QC; three *d. Educ:* Eton; Trinity Coll., Camb.; MA 1873. Called to Bar at Lincoln's Inn, 1871; Bencher, 1903; QC 1896; Vice-Chairman of Quarter Sessions;

Recorder of Worcester, 1891–1908. *Address:* Wychbold Hall, Droitwich. *Died 23 Nov. 1925.*

AMUNDSEN, Captain Roald; Leader of the Norwegian Polar Expedition which reached the South Pole; *b* Borge, Smaalenene, 16 July 1872; *s* of Jens Amundsen, shipowner (*d* 1886). *Educ:* Christiania. Student, 1890; two years study medicine; went to sea; Examen 1st officer at the Christiania public sailors' school; Mate with the Belgica, Capt. de Gerlache, 1897–99; ice navigation in the north, 1901–2; first voyage with the Gjoa, hunting and making deep-water observations, Spitzberg-Greenland; 2nd Gjoa Expedition, North Magnetic pole and North-West Passage, 1903–6; Norwegian Antarctic Expedition on the Fram, 1910–12; Maud Expedition, North-East Passage, 1918–21; Airplane Flight to 87° 44′ N latitude, 1925; Transpolar Flight from Spitzbergen to Teller, Alaska, over the North Pole, 1926. *Publications:* The North-West Passage; The South Pole; The North-East Passage; The First Flight Across the Polar Sea; My Life as an Explorer, 1927. *Address:* Oslo, Norway. *T:* 1911. *Died June 1928.*

AMYAND, Arthur; *see* Haggard, Major E. A.

ANDERSON, Maj.-Gen. Alexander Dingwall, RA; *b* 19 March 1843. Entered army, 1859; Maj.-Gen., 1897; retired, 1897; served Afghan War, 1878–79 (medal). *Died 13 March 1916.*

ANDERSON, Sir Arthur Robert, Kt 1918; CIE 1915; CBE 1917; *b* 28 July 1860; *s* of late James Anderson, Auchendarroch, Argyllshire; *m* 1891, Gertrude (decd), *d* of late J. D. Fraser, JP, Tiverton; one *s* one *d. Educ:* Glasgow Academy and University. Educated as a Civil Engineer; Chief Engineer Madras and Southern Mahratta Railway, 1897–1908; General Manager, 1908–14; Member Railway Board, Government of India, 1914–17; President, 1919–20; Member of Indian Railways Committee to enquire and report on working of Indian Railways, 1921; retired 1921; Director Madras and Southern Mahratta Railway, 1921. *Address:* Roffey Place, Faygate, Horsham. *Club:* Caledonian. *Died 24 Sept. 1924.*

ANDERSON, Lt-Col Barton Edward, DSO 1916; 59th Royal Scinde Rifles, FF; *b* 15 Sept. 1881; *s* of Beresford Anderson, late Chief Engineer, Madras Railway, and Dora, *d* of late Michael O'Shaughnessy, QC. Served NW Frontier, Bazaar Valley, and Mohmand Expedition, 1908 (despatches); European War, 1914–18 (despatches three times, Bt of Major, DSO); 3rd Afghan War, 1919; Mesopotamia Rebellion, 1920; Waziristan, 1920–22 (despatches). *Club:* United Service. *Died 23 May 1927.*

ANDERSON, Daniel Elie, MD Lond. and Paris; BA, BSc Lond.; MRCS, LRCP, LSA; FRSE, FRGS; Lecturer and Research Scholar to the Honyman Gillespie Trust in London in Tropical Diseases; *b* Mauritius; 4th *s* of John Anderson, Glasgow, and Euphémie Elie Bourelly; *m* Marion, *d* of D. Munro Drysdale, Liverpool; one *s* two *d. Educ:* Royal College of Mauritius; University College and Hospital, London; Examiner of Recruits and Assessor of Pensions during the War; Paris University; School of Tropical Medicine, London. Late Physician Assistant, University College Hospital, and Obstetric Assistant; late Deputy Medical Officer Parish of Hampstead; Liston Gold Medal, University College Hospital; late Superintendent of McAll Medical Mission, Paris, 1886–89; Physician, Hertford British Hospital, Paris, and practised in Paris for 22 years; returned to London, 1908; went on scientific mission to Mauritius; to Chile and West Indies, 1913; travelled extensively; Fellow of the Royal Medical Society; Fellow of the Royal Tropical Society of Medicine; Member of the British Medical Association. *Publications:* Fever after Operations (in French); Epidemics of Mauritius; Notes on Tropical Disease; Atlas of Venomous Snakes; Atlas of Fly Carriers of Diseases; Scientific Mission to Chile, Peru, Panama, and the West Indian British Possessions; Sunday Stories for Children; contributions to medical and scientific journals. *Recreation:* travelling abroad. *Address:* 3 North Grove, Hampstead Lane, Highgate, N6. *T:* Hornsey 734; 26 Harley Street, W1. *T:* Paddington 2192; Cannes, France (Jan. to April). *Died 23 Jan. 1928.*

ANDERSON, Dr Elizabeth Garrett, MD (Paris); Mayor of Aldeburgh, 1908; *b* 9 June 1836; *d* of Newson Garrett of Aldeburgh, Suffolk; *m* 1871, J. G. S. Anderson, JP (*d* 1907), shipowner and managing director of Orient Line of Royal Mail steamers; one *s* one *d. Educ:* privately. Began to study medicine in 1860; Colleges of Surgeons and Physicians refused to admit her to their examinations; was admitted to the examinations of the Society of Apothecaries and obtained its licence to practise in 1865; passed the medical

examinations of University of Paris and received MD degree, 1870; elected to first School Board for London, 1870; Senior Physician to New Hospital for Women, 1866–90; Dean of the London Sch. of Medicine for Women, 1883–1903; Lecturer on Medicine ditto, 1876–98; President of East Anglian Branch of British Medical Association, 1896–97; first woman elected as mayor in England; Hon. Sec. Imp. Vaccination League. *Recreations:* travelling, gardening. *Address:* Alde House, Aldeburgh, Suffolk. *Died 17 Dec. 1917.*

ANDERSON, Lt-Col Francis, DSO 1917; MC; Royal Highlanders; *b* 1888; *m*; one *s* one *d.* Served European War, 1914–18 (despatches, DSO, MC). *Address:* Diana Lodge, Sandhurst. *Died 17 May 1925.*

ANDERSON, Brig.-Gen. Sir Francis James, KBE 1919; CB 1917; Chairman, Army Sanitary Committee, and attached General Staff; 3rd surv. *s* of late Dep. Inspector-General of Hospitals, Robert Carew Anderson; *m* 1886, Frances Alice, *e d* of late Major Purcell O'Gorman, MP for Waterford; one *s* one *d. Educ:* privately; RMA, Woolwich. Has served as Colonial Engineer and Member of Executive and Legislative Councils of the Straits Settlements; commanded Queen Victoria's Own Sappers and Miners; served as Assistant Director at the War Office. *Recreations:* yachting, shooting, fishing. *Address:* 4 Trebovir Road, Earl's Court, SW5. *Died 6 March 1920.*

ANDERSON, Sir George, Kt 1905; Treasurer of the Bank of Scotland, 1898–1917; *b* Fraserburgh, Aberdeenshire, 26 March 1845; *s* of John Anderson, who resided there; *m* 1870, Mary, *y d* of Alexander Anderson, London. *Educ:* Fraserburgh. Entered service of North of Scotland Bank as apprentice at the Fraserburgh Branch, 1857; Accountant, 1860; Accountant at Banff Branch, 1863; Elgin Branch, 1866; Peterhead Branch, 1868; Agent at Huntly Branch, 1873; Dundee Branch, 1879; Assistant-Manager at Head Office, Aberdeen, 1888; General Manager, 1889; Convener and Chairman of the Scottish Bank Managers, 1898–1917; President of Institute of Bankers in Scotland, 1903–7; JP Aberdeenshire and Midlothian; attended Coronations 1902 and 1911, Courts at Holyrood 1903 and 1911 as Deputy-Usher of White Rod of Scotland; a Director of Scottish Widows' Fund; a Governor of Donaldson's Hospital; and one of Walker Trustees. *Address:* Beechmount, Murrayfield, Midlothian. *T:* Edinburgh Central 7817. *Died 1 Dec. 1923.*

ANDERSON, Gen. Harry Cortlandt, CB 1907; Hon. Colonel 4th Rajputs, Indian Army, since 1904; *b* 28 May 1826; *m* Alice Forbes (*d* 1911). Entered army, 1842; Gen., 1894; US List, 1886; served Sutlej campaign, 1846 (medal with clasp); Indian Mutiny, 1857–58 (despatches, medal, Brevet-Major). *Address:* Harrington Road, S Kensington, W. *Died 20 Sept. 1921.*

ANDERSON, Major Henry Graeme, MBE 1919; MD, ChB; FRCS; Consulting Surgeon to the Royal Air Force; Surgeon to St Mark's Hospital for Diseases of the Rectum; Senior Assistant Surgeon to the Belgrave Hospital for Children; *b* Scotland, 1882; *yr s* of Nicol Anderson; *m* 1921, Gladys, *er d* of Charles Hood; one *d. Educ:* Glasgow University; King's College; London Hospital. Fellow of Royal Society of Medicine; House Surgeon, St Mark's Hospital, 1907–8; Surgical Registrar to Metropolitan Hospital, Cancer Hospital, and to Royal National Orthopædic Hospital, 1909–12; joined Royal Navy as Surgeon-Lieutenant, Aug. 1914; attached as Surgeon to original RN Air Service Expeditionary Force; served at Antwerp, Ypres, and Belgian and Northern France Coasts (1914 Star); attached RN Air Station, Eastbourne, and RN Airship Station, Polegate, 1916; gained Aviator's certificate, No 3758, of Royal Aero Club, 26 Oct. 1916; at Eastbourne on Maurice Farman; Surgeon to British Flying School, Vendome, France, 1917; Surgeon to Central RAF Hospital, 1918–19; transferred from Royal Navy to Royal Air Force as Major RAFMS. *Publications:* The Medical and Surgical Aspects of Aviation; The Rectum—Encylopædia of Surgery; Combined Operations for Excision of Rectum—System of Operative Surgery; Operative Treatment of Hæmorrhoids—British Medical Journal; Aeroplane Accidents—Journal RN Medical Service; numerous articles on surgery, and aviation. *Recreations:* aviation, tennis, dancing. *Address:* 75 Harley Street, W1. *T:* Langham 2772. *M:* RI 7703. *Clubs:* Royal Air Force, Royal Aero. *Died 28 June 1925.*

ANDERSON, Sir Hugh Kerr, Kt 1922; MA, MD; FRCP; FRS 1907; Master of Gonville and Caius College, Cambridge, since 1912; *b* Hampstead, 6 July 1865; *yr s* of James Anderson and Eliza, *d* of Surgeon-General John Murray; *m* Jessie, *d* of Surgeon-General F. W. Innes, CB; one *s* one *d. Educ:* Harrow (Sayer Scholar); Gonville and Caius

College, Cambridge (Scholar); St Bartholomew's Hospital. Fellow of Gonville and Caius College, 1897–1912; member of Royal Commission on Oxford and Cambridge Universities, 1919, and of the University of Cambridge Statutory Commission, 1922; a Governor of Harrow School. *Publications:* papers on physiological subjects. *Recreations:* fishing, gardening. *Address:* The Lodge, Gonville and Caius College, Cambridge. *T:* Cambridge 860. *Club:* Athenæum.
Died 2 Nov. 1928.

ANDERSON, James Drummond, MA, LittD; University Lecturer on Bengali, Cambridge; *b* Fort William, Calcutta, 11 Nov. 1852; *s* of James Anderson, MD, and Ellen Garstin; *m* Frances Louisa, *d* of Captain S. Cordue; five *s* one *d. Educ:* Cheltenham College; Rugby. Was in the Indian Civil Service, 1875–1900; served mostly in Assam. *Publications:* Kachari Folk Tales, a collection of Chittagong Proverbs, and other works on languages of NE India; The Peoples of India (Cambridge Manuals); Indira and Other Stories (translation from B. C. Chatterjee); A Manual of the Bengali Language; papers on linguistic subjects in Journal Royal Asiatic Society and elsewhere. *Address:* Mostyn House, Brooklands Avenue, Cambridge.
Died 24 Nov. 1920.

ANDERSON, James Maitland, Hon. LLD (St And.) 1912; Librarian, University of St Andrews and Hon. Keeper of the University and College Records since 1924; *b* Rossie, Fifeshire, 22 Oct. 1852; *e s* of James Anderson, gardener to Capt. James Maitland, RN; *m* 1880, Margaret Elizabeth, *e d* of John Bain, Brisbane, Queensland; two *d. Educ:* Free Church School, Giffordtown; Parish School, Auchtermuchty; private study. Began life as a cow-herd, thereafter gradually drifted, through business occupations, into journalism; reported for various newspapers; contributed to several minor periodicals in English and German; edited the Phonographic Standard, 1872–74; appointed assistant librarian, University of St Andrews, 1874; was also Secretary of the University, 1878–99; Quæstor, 1881–92; Registrar and Secretary of the General Council, 1881–99. *Publications:* Historical Sketch of the University of St Andrews, 1878; Heraldry of the University, 1895; Register of Students at St Andrews 1747–1897, 1905; Handbook to the City and University of St Andrews, 1911; Writings and Portraits of George Buchanan, 1906; Matriculation and Graduation Rolls of St Andrews University 1413–1579, 1926; articles in Cyclopædias, etc; editor of the St Andrews University Calendar, 1882–99, and of the Library Bulletin, 1901–24. *Recreations:* reading and walking daily; antiquarian rambles at home or abroad, occasionally; collector of books on academical and local history. *Address:* Kinnessbank East, St Andrews.
Died 25 Aug. 1927.

ANDERSON, James Wallace, MD; FRFPSG; Physician; Hon. Associate of the Order of St John of Jerusalem in England; *b* Glasgow, 20 Oct. 1848; *e s* of Hugh Locke Anderson and Helen Willox, Glasgow; *m* 1886, Mary (*d* 1916), *d* of late James Ramsay Orr, Montreal; no *c. Educ:* Langside Academy; Glasgow University; Dublin; Berlin. Connected with the Glasgow Royal Infirmary as Student, Resident Physician, Physician, Hon. Consulting Physician, and Manager since 1866; late Lecturer on the Practice of Medicine, Queen Margaret College, University of Glasgow. *Publications:* Medical Nursing; Home Nursing and Hygiene (joint author); The Power of Nature in Disease; Four Chiefs of the GRI, and various medical papers. *Recreation:* music. *Address:* 41 Falkland Mansions, Hyndland, Glasgow.

ANDERSON, Sir John, GCMG 1909 (KCMG 1901; CMG 1898); KCB 1913; Hon. LLD Edin. 1911; Governor and Commander-in-Chief of Ceylon since 1916; *b* Gartly, Aberdeenshire, 23 January 1858; *o s* of John Anderson, Supt Gordon Mission, Aberdeen; married. *Educ:* Aberdeen University. MA, 1st class honours in Mathematics; gold medal as most distinguished graduate of year; Hon. LLD 1907; 2nd class clerk Colonial Office, 1879; Bacon scholar, Gray's Inn, 1887; Inns of Court studentship, 1888; private secretary to late Hon. Sir R. Meade (Under-Secretary of State), 1892; attached to staff for the Behring Sea Arbitration in London and Paris, 1892–93; 1st class clerk, 1896; principal clerk, 1897; secretary to Conference of Colonial Premiers with Mr Chamberlain, June and July 1897, and to Conference of 1902; with Prince of Wales on Colonial Tour; Governor Straits Settlements and High Commissioner Federated Malay States, 1904–11; High Commissioner, State of Brunei, 1906–11; Permanent Under-Secretary of State for the Colonies, 1911–16. *Publications:* editor of Colonial Office List, 1885–97. *Address:* Queen's House, Colombo, Ceylon.
Died 24 March 1918.

ANDERSON, Sir John, Kt 1912; attorney of Guthrie & Co., Ltd, East India merchants; *b* Rothesay, March 1852 *m* 1901, Winifred Ethel

Dunbar-Pope. *Educ:* Raffles Institution, Singapore. Arrived Singapore, 1859; in Government Service at Singapore till 1871, when commenced mercantile career; Siamese Consul-general for Singapore, 1880–1910; Member Legislative Council, Straits Settlements, 1886–88 and 1905–8. *Address:* 5 Whittington Avenue, EC; Eastcote Place, near Pinner. *Clubs:* Bath, City Carlton.
Died 18 Dec. 1924.

ANDERSON, John William Stewart, CB 1918; MVO 1911; an Assistant Secretary, Secretary's Department, Admiralty, since 1917; *b* 22 April 1874. *Address:* 28 Argyll Road, Kensington, W. *T:* Park 3641.
Died 28 May 1920.

ANDERSON, Joseph, LLD; Keeper of the National Museum of Antiquities, Edinburgh, 1870–1913, and Assistant-Secretary of the Society of Antiquaries of Scotland; *b* Arbroath, Forfarshire, 1832; *m* Jessie Dempster (*d* 1913). *Educ:* St Vigeans Parish School; Educational Institution, Arbroath. Teacher in East Free School, Arbroath, 1852–56; in English School, Hasskioy, Constantinople, 1856–59; editor of John O'Groat Journal, Wick, Caithness, 1860–69. Edited The Orkneyinga Saga, 1873; The Oliphants in Scotland, 1879; Drummond's Ancient Scottish Weapons, 1881. Was Rhind Lecturer in Archæology to the Society of Antiquaries of Scotland, 1879–82, the subject of the four courses of lectures being Scotland in Early Christian and in Pagan Times, subsequently published in 4 vols, 1881–86; again Rhind Lecturer in 1892, the subject being The Early Christian Monuments of Scotland, published by the Society, with an illustrated descriptive list of the Monuments, by J. Romilly Allen, 1903. Honorary Member of the Royal Society of Northern Antiquaries, Copenhagen; of the Society of Antiquaries, Stockholm; of the Royal Irish Academy; and Honorary Professor of Antiquities to the Royal Scottish Academy. *Publications:* numerous papers in the Proceedings of the Society. *Address:* 8 Great King Street, Edinburgh.
Died 27 Sept. 1916.

ANDERSON, Rev. K. C., DD; retired Minister; *b* Jedburgh, Roxburghshire; *s* of George Anderson and Isabella Cranston; *m* Robina Fisher; one *s* one *d. Educ:* Jedburgh Grammar School; Middlebury College, Vermont, USA; Yale Theological Seminary. Congregational Minister at Fairhaven, Vermont, USA; Milwaukee, Wis; Oskkosh, Wis; Troy, NY; Bradford, Yorkshire; Dundee, Scotland; DD Union College, Schenectady. *Publications:* The Larger Faith; The New Theology.

ANDERSON, Peter John, MA, LLB; Librarian to the University of Aberdeen since 1894; Clerk of the General Council since 1907; Registrar since 1918; *s* of Peter Anderson, solicitor, Inverness. *Educ:* Inverness Royal Academy; Universities of Aberdeen and Edinburgh. Held various posts in connection with the University of Aberdeen. *Publications:* Fasti Academiæ Mariscallanæ, 3 vols, 1889–98; Charters and other Writs illustrating the History of the Royal Burgh of Aberdeen, 1890; Inventories of Ecclesiastical Records in the NE Synods of Scotland, 1890; Historical Notes on the Libraries of the Universities of Aberdeen, 1893; Officers and Graduates of King's College, Aberdeen, 1893; Aurora Borealis Academica, 1899; Records of Aberdeen Universities Commission of 1716–17, 1900; Roll of Alumni of King's College, Aberdeen, 1900; Rectorial Addresses at the Universities of Aberdeen, 1902; Studies in the History of the University, 1906; Record of Quatercentenary, 1907; Bibliography of the University, 1907; Aberdeen Friars, 1909; Bibliography of Inverness-shire, 1917. *Address:* The University, Aberdeen.
Died 12 May 1926.

ANDERSON, Sir Robert, 1st Bt, *cr* 1911; Kt 1903; *b* 1 Dec. 1837; *s* of James Anderson of Ballybay, Co. Monaghan, and Elizabeth, *d* of Andrew Ker of Newbliss; *m* 1890, Wilhelmina, *d* of Rev. Andrew Long, MA, of Monreagh, Co. Donegal. Chairman of Anderson and M'Auley Ltd, Arnott & Co. Ltd, Vulcanite Ltd, City Estates Ltd, Milfort Weaving and Finishing Co. Ltd, William Ross & Co. Ltd, Spinners, Baltic Firewood Co. Ltd; Alderman and JP City of Belfast; High Sheriff of Belfast, 1903; Lord Mayor, 1907–8-9; retired from Corporation, 1918; High Sheriff Co. Monaghan, 1911; JP Co. Antrim. *Heir:* none. *Address:* Parkmount, Belfast; Mullaghmore, Co. Monaghan.
Died 16 July 1921 (ext.)

ANDERSON, Sir Robert, KCB 1901 (CB 1896); JP for London; LLD; Barrister-at-law (Dublin and Middle Temple); *b* 29 May 1841; *s* of Matthew Anderson, Crown Solicitor, Dublin; *m* 1873, Lady Agnes A. Moore, *sister* of 9th Earl of Drogheda; three *s* one *d. Educ:* Trinity Coll., Dublin; BA 1862; LLD 1875. Home Office as adviser in matters relating to political crime from 1868; late Assistant Commissioner of Police of the Metropolis, and Head of Criminal

Investigation Department from 1888, resigned 1901. *Publications:* The Coming Prince; Human Destiny; The Gospel and its Ministry; Daniel in the Critics' Den; The Silence of God, 1897; The Buddha of Christendom, 1899; The Bible and Modern Criticism, 1902; Pseudo-criticism, 1904; For Us Men, 1905; The Way, 1905; Sidelights on the Home Rule Movement, 1906; In Defence: a Plea for the Faith; Criminals and Crime, 1907; The Bible or the Church?, 1908; The Lord from Heaven, 1910; The Lighter Side of my Official Life, 1910; The Hebrews Epistle, 1911; The Honour of His Name, 1912; Forgotten Truths, 1913; The Entail of the Covenant, 1914; Misunderstood Texts of the New Testament, 1916. *Address:* 39 Linden Gardens, W. *Club:* National.

Died 15 Nov. 1918.

ANDERSON, Sir Robert Rowand, Kt 1902; LLD; FRSE, HRSA, FRIBA; architect; *b* 1834; *s* of James Anderson, solicitor, Edinburgh, and Margaret Rowand; *m* 1863, Mary, *d* of Henry Ross of Kinnahaird, Co. Ross. *Educ:* Edinburgh. *Address:* 16 Rutland Square, Edinburgh; Allermuir House, Colinton, Midlothian. *Clubs:* Royal Societies; Conservative, Edinburgh. *Died 1 June 1921.*

ANDERSON, Thomas, ISO; late Superintendent of Registry, Board of Trade; retired, 1910; *b* 24 Feb. 1844. *Address:* The Châlet, Gipsy Lane, Putney, SW15. *Died 28 March 1926.*

ANDERSON, Thomas Scott, MD; JP; MFH; *b* 1853; *s* of Thomas Anderson, MD, Selkirk, and Joan M'Laurin; *m* 1876, Joan A., *d* of Thomas Shaw, Wooriwyrite, Australia. *Educ:* Merchiston Castle School; Edinburgh University; Ecole de Médecine, Paris. Practised profession for a short while in Australia, and afterwards travelled, forming a collection of Australian birds. Returned home and took to sheep-farming. *Publications:* Holloas from the Hills; Hound and Horn in Jedforest, 1909; a book of hunting verses and other contributions to sporting magazines over the signature of Teviotdale. *Recreations:* fox-hunting, shooting, natural history. *Address:* Ettrick Shaws, Selkirk, NB. *Clubs:* Nimrod; Scottish Conservative, Edinburgh. *Died June 1919.*

ANDERSON, Col William Campbell, DSO 1900; FRGS; late Lt-Col 3rd Cameronians (Scottish Rifles); *b* 14 Dec. 1868; *m* 1894, Elizabeth, *d* of late Edward Barnes. *Educ:* Harrow. Formerly Capt. 15th Hussars; served S Africa 5th Batt. Imperial Yeomanry (despatches twice, 2 medals and clasps); served Gold Coast and Nigeria (W African medal and clasp). *Club:* Naval and Military.

Died 21 Dec. 1926.

ANDERSON, William Crawford; MP (Lab) Attercliffe Division of Sheffield, 1914–18; *b* 1877; *m* 1911, Mary R. Macarthur (Secretary, Women's Trade Union League and National Federation of Women Workers); one *d*. Apprenticed to a manufacturing chemist, 1893; organiser, Shop Assistants' Union, 1903–7; Member National Administrative Council Independent Labour Party; Chairman, Independent Labour Party, 1911–13, National Labour Party, 1914–15; contested Parliamentary Elections, Hyde, 1910; Keighley, 1911. *Recreation:* reading. *Address:* 7 Mecklenburgh Square, WC. *T:* Holborn 2485. *Died 25 Feb. 1919.*

ANDERSON, Colonel William Patrick, CMG 1913; *b* Levis, Quebec, 4 Sept. 1851; *e s* of late Thomas Anderson, Edmonton, Alberta; *m* 1876, Dorothea Susannah, *e d* of late Henry Beaumont Small; four *s* one *d*. *Educ:* University of Lennoxville; University of Manitoba. Entered Civil Service of Canada as Assistant Engineer, Department of Marine and Fisheries, 1874; Chief Engineer, 1880; superannuated, 1919; erected over 900 lighthouses and 80 fog-alarm installations; a Past President of the Engineering Institute of Canada, a member of the Institution of Civil Engineers, and FRGS; Chairman of the Geographic Board of Canada, and a member of the Lighthouse Board of Canada; was in command of the 43rd Regt Canadian Militia up to 1892 (Fenian raid medal, with two clasps, VD); and has been in command of the Canadian Bisley Team; represented Canada at the International Congress of Navigation, 1912; and at the National Waterways Congress, Washington, 1913. Established in 1885, and for two years edited, Canadian Militia Gazette; contributor to Encyclopædia Britannica, etc. *Recreations:* golf, curling. *Address:* 64 Cooper Street, Ottawa. *T:* Queen 1910. *Clubs:* Royal Ottawa Golf, Rideau Curling, Governor-General's Curling, Ottawa.

Died Feb. 1927.

ANDERSON-MORSHEAD, Acting Lt-Col Rupert Henry, DSO 1918; 2nd Battalion, Devonshire Regiment; *s* of John Y. Anderson-Morshead, Barrister, Salcombe Regis, Sidmouth; *m* 1914, Lucy Helen, *d* of William Carstares-Dunlop, Gairbraid, Scotland. *Educ:* Wellington

College; Royal Military College, Sandhurst. Served European War, 1914–18 (DSO). *Recreations:* cricket, tennis, fishing, shooting. *Address:* Wayside, Lingfield, Surrey. *TA:* Wayside, Dormansland, Surrey. *T:* Longfield 8X. *Club:* Junior Army and Navy.

Died 27 May 1918.

ANDREWES, Major (Acting Lt-Col) Francis Edward, DSO 1916; RA; *b* 8 May 1878; *s* of Rev. Nesfield Andrewes and Katherine Phillipps; *m* 1905, Margaret Agnes Malden; four *s* one *d*. *Educ:* Bradfield College. Served South African War, 1899–1902 (Queen's and King's medals, 5 clasps), European War, 1914–16 (DSO); Brevet Lt-Col, Jan. 1919. *Address:* 15 Mount Avenue, Ealing, W. *Club:* United Services. *Died 29 March 1920.*

ANDREWES, Rev. John Brereton, MA; Canon of Chelmsford, 1916. *Address:* The Vicarage, Harlow, Essex.

Died 1 April 1920.

ANDREWS, Charles William, BA, DSc; FRS 1906; Assistant-Keeper in the Geological Department of the British Museum (Natural History); *b* Hampstead, 1866. *Educ:* private school. BA (Lond.) 1837; BSc (Lond.) Hons in Zoology, 1890; DSc (Lond.) and Sherbrooke Scholarship, 1900; member of the staff of the Geological Department, British Museum, 1892; awarded Lyell Fund of Geological Society, 1896; Lyell Medal, 1916; visited Christmas Island and Cocos-Keeling Islands on a collecting expedition, 1897–98; made several expeditions to the Fayûm, Egypt, collecting fossil vertebrates, 1900–6; made a second expedition to Christmas Island, 1908. *Publications:* A Descriptive Catalogue of the Tertiary Vertebrata of the Fayûm, Egypt; part author of A Monograph of Christmas Island (Indian Ocean); Catalogue of the Marine Reptiles of the Oxford Clay, vols i and ii; numerous papers on fossil vertebrates. *Recreations:* walking, reading. *Address:* Natural History Museum, SW7. *Clubs:* Athenæum, Savage.

Died 25 May 1924.

ANDREWS, Edward Gordon, ISO 1909; Treasurer, Kingston, Jamaica. *Address:* Kingston, Jamaica.

Died 11 Nov. 1915.

ANDREWS, Hon. Elisha Benjamin, PhD, DD, LLD; Chancellor Emeritus, University of Nebraska since 1909; *b* Hinsdale, NH, 10 Jan. 1844; *s* of Erastus and Almira Bartlett; *m* 1870, Ella Anna Allen. *Educ:* Brown Univ.; University of Berlin; University of Munich; Newton, Mass, Theological Institution. Private, Corporal, Sergeant, and Lieutenant in First Conn Heavy Artillery in Civil War, 1861–64; student in Brown University, 1866–70; ordained Baptist ministry, 1874; pastor, Beverly, Mass, 1874–75; President Denison University, Ohio, 1875–79; Professor in Newton Theological Institution, 1879–82; Prof. of History and Political Economy in Brown University, 1882–88; Professor of Political Econ. and Finance in Cornell University, 1888–89; President Brown University, 1889–98; Supt Chicago Public Schools, 1898–1900; Chancellor University of Nebraska, 1900–8; member Loyal Legion, Grand Army of the Republic, American Economic Association; member International Monetary Conference, Brussels, 1892; member Gen. Educ. Board until 1912. *Publications:* Institutes of Constitutional History, English and American; Institutes of General History; Institutes of Economics; History of the United States; History of Last Quarter Century in United States; History of the United States in our Own Time; Outlines of the Principles of History (translated); Eternal Words (sermons); Wealth and Moral Law; An Honest Dollar; The Problem of Cosmology (translated); The Call of the Land. *Address:* Interlachen, Fla, USA. *Died 30 Oct. 1917.*

ANDREWS, Rev. Prof. Herbert T., DD; Professor of New Testament Exegesis and Criticism, New and Hackney Colleges, University of London, since 1903; *b* Oxford, 22 Dec. 1864; *m* 1st, 1891, Edith Mary Birt; one *s* one *d*; 2nd, 1915, Jessie Caroline, *o d* of late Rev. Dr Forsyth. *Educ:* Oxford High School; Magdalen (Classical Demy) and Mansfield Colleges, Oxford; 1st Class Honours Classical Moderations, 1885; 2nd Class Literæ Humaniores, 1887; Senior Septuagint (Hall-Houghton) Prize, 1889; Ellerton Essay Prize, 1889; Denyer and Johnson Scholarship, 1890. Entered Congregational ministry at Chingford, Essex, 1890; removed to Swansea, 1892; Professor of Church History and Historical Theology at Cheshunt College, 1895. *Publications:* Commentary on Acts in the Westminster New Testament, 1908; Century Bible Handbook on Apocrypha Books, 1908; The Value of the Theology of St Paul, 1915; contributed an article on the Social Principles and Effects of the Reformation to Christ and Civilisation, and articles for the 11th edition of the Encyclopædia Britannica, Chambers's Encyclopædia, and the Universal Encyclopædia, etc; edited the Epistle of Aristeas for the

Oxford Apocrypha and Pseudepigrapha, 1913; contributed several sections in Peake's Commentary on the Bible, 1920, also articles for Contemporary Review, Expositor, etc. *Recreation:* golf. *Address:* 283 Willesden Lane, NW. *Club:* Neasden Golf.

Died 1 Jan. 1928.

ANDREWS, Hugh, JP; *s* of late Hugh Andrews of Fortview; *m* Isabel, *e d* of late John Sowerby of Benwell Tower, Northumberland. High Sheriff, Northumberland, 1891–92. *Address:* 18 Rutland Court, Rutland Gardens, SW; Toddington Manor, Winchcombe, RSO, Gloucestershire. *TA:* Andrews, Toddington, Winchcombe. *T:* Toddington 1. *Clubs:* White's, Aero, Royal Automobile; Royal Yacht Squadron, Cowes. *Died 25 May 1926.*

ANDREWS, James Frank, ISO 1913; JP; late Secretary to New Zealand Cabinet, Clerk of the Executive Council, and Secretary to the Prime Minister, Dominion of New Zealand; *b* Plymouth, 26 June 1848; *s* of late Henry John Andrews, surgeon HEICS; widower; one *s. Educ:* Church of England Grammar School, Auckland (scholarship). Six years in Customs Department, nine in Telegraph Department; Private Secretary to late Hon. John Ballance, Prime Minister; thirteen years Private Secretary to late Rt Hon. R. J. Seddon, and three years to Rt Hon. Sir J. G. Ward, Prime Minister. *Address:* 35 Bidwell Street, Wellington, New Zealand. *T:* 927 and 913 A.

Died 10 Dec. 1922.

ANDREWS, Rt. Hon. Thomas, PC (Ire.) 1903; DL, Co. Down; flax spinner; *b* Comber, 26 Feb. 1843; 4th *s* of late John Andrews, JP, of Comber, and Sarah, *o d* of late Dr William Drennan of Cabin Hill, Co. Down; *m* 1870, Lizzie, *o d* of late James A. Pirrie of Little Clandeboye, Co. Down; three *s* one *d. Educ:* Royal Academical Institution and Queen's College, Belfast. President Ulster Liberal Unionist Association since 1892; one of promoters of Great Ulster Convention, 1892; member of Ulster Defence Union, 1893; member of Recess Committee, 1895; chairman of Belfast and Co. Down Railway Company since 1895; member of Appeal Commission under Local Government (Ireland) Act, 1898; chairman Co. Down County Council since 1902; member of Arterial Drainage Commission, Ireland, 1905; High Sheriff of Down, 1912. *Address:* Ardara, Comber, County Down, Ireland. *TA:* Andrews, Ardara, Comber. *T:* 1 Comber. *Clubs:* Ulster Reform, Ulster, Belfast; County, Downpatrick.

Died 16 Sept. 1916.

ANDREWS, Rt. Hon. William Drennan, PC (Ireland) 1897; *b* 24 Jan. 1832; 2nd *s* of late John Andrews, Comber, Co. Down; *m* 1857, Eliza (*d* 1901), *d* of late John Galloway, Monkstown, Co. Dublin. *Educ:* Royal Belfast Academical Institution; Trinity Coll., Dublin. LLD 1860; a senior gold medallist in Ethics and Logic. Barrister, Ireland, 1855; QC 1872; Hon. Bencher, King's Inns, Dublin, 1910; Judge in the Exchequer Division of the High Court of Justice, Ireland (since merged in the King's Bench Division), 1882–1910. *Address:* 51 Lower Leeson Street, Dublin. *Died 3 Dec. 1924.*

ANGELL, Col Frederick John, CBE 1918; late Assistant Director of Ordnance Services Southern Command; late Colonel Royal Irish Fusiliers; *b* 1861. Served Egyptian Expedition, 1884; Bechuanaland Expedition, 1884–85; retired pay, 1921.

Died Jan. 1922.

ANGELL, James Burrill, LLD; President of the University of Michigan 1871, President Emeritus, 1909; *b* Scituate, Rhode Island, 7 Jan. 1829; *m* 1855, Sarah S., *d* of President Caswell, of Brown University; two *s* one *d. Educ:* Brown University and in Europe. Professor of Modern Languages, Brown University, 1853–60; editor Providence Journal, 1860–66; President Univ. of Vermont, 1866–71; Minister of United States to China, 1880–81; member of Fisheries Commission of US and Great Britain, 1887; member of Deep Waterways Commission, Canada and US, 1896; United States Minister to Turkey, 1897–98. *Publications:* Reminiscences; Selected Addresses; numerous articles in leading American Reviews. *Address:* Ann Arbor, Michigan, USA. *TA:* Ann Arbor. *T:* 40.

Died 1 April 1916.

ANGERS, Hon. Sir Auguste Réal, Kt 1913; PC; KC; LLD: Knight Grand Cross of St Gregory the Great; *b* Quebec, 3 Oct. 1837; *s* of François Réal Angers, Quebec, Barrister; *m* 1st, Julia Marguerite (*d* 1879), *d* of late Senator Chinic; 2nd, 1890, Emilie, *d* of late Alexander Le Moine, Notary. *Educ:* College of Nicolet and Laval University. Barrister; admitted at Bar, 1860; Member of Legislative Assembly, 1874, and Leader of House until 1878; elected a member of the House of Commons of Canada; appointed one of the Justices of the High Court of the Province of Quebec; resigned in 1887 to accept

Lieutenant-Governorship of the Province; at the expiration of term entered Sir John Thompson's administration, Ottawa, and continued in office under Sir MacKenzie Bowell; in 1896 entered Sir Charles Tupper's administration; was defeated at the general election of June 1896, and retired from office. *Address:* City of Westmount, near Montreal; 35 St James Street, Montreal.

Died April 1919.

ANGST, Sir Henry, KCMG 1906 (CMG 1902); HBM Consul-General in Switzerland (unpaid) 1896, resigned 31 March 1916; Hon. FSA; *b* Regensberg (Zurich), 18 October 1847; widower. *Educ:* Zurich at the Gymnasium; Federal Polytechnic School. Doctor Philosophiæ, honoris causa, University of Zurich; Hon. LLD Harvard. Vice-Consul, Zurich, 1886; Consul for German and Italian speaking Cantons of Switzerland, 1886; Director of Swiss National Museum, Zurich, 1892–1903. *Publications:* Annual Illustrated Museum's Reports, and various publications on ancient Swiss art. *Address:* Regensberg (Canton of Zurich). *Club:* Athenæum.

Died 14 May 1922.

ANGUS, Henry Brunton, MB, MS Durh.; FRCS; Honorary Surgeon, Royal Victoria Infirmary, Newcastle-on-Tyne; Professor of Surgery, University of Durham; *b* Dec. 1867; *s* of J. Acworth Angus, MRCS, LSA; *m* Marian, *d* of late J. Arnison, Sandyford, Newcastle-on-Tyne; two *d. Educ:* University of Durham; St Bartholomew's Hospital. House Surgeon, Royal Infirmary, Newcastle-on-Tyne; Southport Infirmary, Lancashire; Resident Medical Officer, Newcastle-on-Tyne Dispensary; Hon. Assistant Surgeon, Royal Infirmary, and Hon. Surgeon, Royal Victoria Infirmary, Newcastle-on-Tyne; Professor of Surgery, University of Durham College of Medicine. *Publications:* A Method of treating Damaged Intestine without Resection; Case of Subcortical Cerebral Tumour, tuberculous in nature, removed by operation, recovery, The Lancet, 8 March 1913. *Recreations:* fishing, shooting, golf. *Address:* 5 Eslington Road, Newcastle-on-Tyne. *T:* 373 Jesmond. *Died 4 Oct. 1927.*

ANGUS, Richard Bladworth; Director, Bank of Montreal and Canadian Pacific Railway; *b* 28 May 1831. Went to Canada, 1857; General Manager, Bank of Montreal, 1869–79. *Address:* 240 Drummond Street, Montreal. *Died 17 Sept. 1922.*

ANNALY, 3rd Baron, *cr* 1863; **Luke White;** GCVO 1917 (KCVO 1912; CVO 1908); DL; Hon. Colonel, Northants Yeomanry; MFH Pytchley, 1902–14; *b* 25 Feb. 1857; *S* father 1888; *m* 1884, Hon. Lilah Georgiana Augusta Constance Agar-Ellis, *d* of 3rd Viscount Clifden; one *s* two *d.* Formerly Capt. Scots Guards; Permanent Lord-in-Waiting to the King; served in Egyptian Campaign, 1882. *Heir: s* Hon. Luke Henry White, *b* 7 Aug. 1885. *Address:* 43 Berkeley Square, W. *T:* Gerrard 3768; Holdenby House, Northampton. *Clubs:* Turf, Marlborough. *Died 15 Dec. 1922.*

ANNANDALE, (Thomas) Nelson, CIE 1923; BA (Oxon), DSc (Edin.); FLS; corresponding member of the Zoological Society of London, and the Natural History Society of Saratow; Fellow of the Asiatic Society of Bengal; Director of the Zoological Survey of India, 1916; Superintendent of the Indian Museum and Secretary to the Trustees 1906–16; President, Asiatic Society of Bengal; *b* 15 June 1876; *e s* of late Prof. Thomas Annandale, FRCS; unmarried. *Educ:* Rugby; Edinburgh University; Balliol College, Oxford. Travelled in the Malay Peninsula, 1899, 1901–2, and 1916; Research Fellow in Anthropology in the University of Edinburgh, 1902–4; Deputy Superintendent of the Indian Museum, 1904; investigated the fauna of the Sea of Galilee, 1912. *Publications:* The Faroes and Iceland: Studies in Island Life, 1905; with other authors, Fasciculi Malayenses, Zoology and Anthropology, 1903; many papers on zoological and anthropological subjects in scientific periodicals; edited the Records and the Memoirs of the Indian Museum since their foundation in 1907, and also The Indian Museum: 1814–1914, 1914. *Recreations:* travelling, Official Correspondence. *Address:* Indian Museum, Calcutta. *Clubs:* Royal Societies; Bengal United Service, Calcutta.

Died 10 April 1924.

ANNESLEY, Lt-Col James Howard Adolphus, CMG 1917; DSO 1900; *b* 3 March 1868; *s* of Capt. F. C. Annesley, 28th Regt; *cousin* of 5th Earl Annesley; *m* 1900, Hélène Marie, *d* of late C. E. Johnston. *Educ:* Eastman's Royal Naval Academy. Joined 18th Hussars, 1893; served as ADC to GOC Tirah Field Force through the expedition, 1897–98 (despatches, medal with two clasps); Adjutant of Bethune's Mounted Infantry from beginning of Boer War, 1899 (DSO), and on the Staff (despatches, Queen's medal and six clasps, King's medal and two clasps). *Clubs:* Army and Navy, Cavalry.

Died 22 April 1919.

ANNINGSON, Bushell, MD, MA; MRCS; Lecturer in Medical Jurisprudence, Cambridge University, since 1884; Medical Officer of Health for Districts in Cambridgeshire, Herts, and Hunts; Examiner in Sanitary Science, Birmingham and Cambridge; Fellow and Member of Council, Royal Sanitary Institute. *Educ:* King's College, London; Caius College, Cambridge. *Publications:* Evolution of Human Communities in Relation to Disease; Origin and Progress of Sanitary Endeavour; etc. *Address:* Walt-hamsall, Barton Road, Cambridge. *T:* 0393.   *Died 19 July 1916.*

ANSCOMB, Major Allen-Mellers, ISO 1911; VD 1898; Government (India) Civil pensioner; Municipal Commissioner, Quetta; Commandant of the Baluchistan Rifles, Indian Defence Force; *b* 27 Feb. 1849; *s* of late John Anscomb, of Appleby, Derbyshire; *m* 1885, Alice, *d* of late Alfred Booth, of Horninglow, Staffordshire. *Educ:* Appleby Grammar School. Joined Indian Uncovenanted Civil Service, 1875; served in Baluchistan from 1881; raised the Baluchistan Volunteer Rifle Corps, 1883, and was its Commandant for more than 20 years; Kaisar-i-Hind Medal, 1904; Treasury Officer at Quetta, 1892–96; and City Magistrate, Quetta, 1896–1911; selected to represent the Baluchistan Volunteers at Coronation of King George V in London, 1911. *Address:* Quetta, Baluchistan. *Club:* Junior Army and Navy.

ANSELL, William James David, ISO 1907; Chief Collector of Customs and Excise and Superintendent of Ports, Cyprus, since 1898; *b* 19 May 1858. *Educ:* St Martin's, Jersey. Assistant Superintendent Larnaca Port, Cyprus, 1880–81; Deputy Harbourmaster, 1881–2; Government and Municipal Inspector Weights and Measures, 1892–98; Assistant Collector Customs and Excise, 1894–96; passed examination in Modern Greek. *Address:* Larnaca, Cyprus.   *Died 16 June 1920.*

ANSON, Maj.-Gen. Sir Archibald Edward Harbord, KCMG 1882; JP Sussex; RA, retired; *b* London, 16 April 1826; *s* of Gen. Sir William Anson, 1st Bt, KCB; *m* 1st, 1851, Elizabeth (*d* 1891), *d* of Richard Bourchier; one *s* one *d* (and one *s* decd); 2nd, 1906, Isabelle Jane (*d* 1923), *d* of Robert Armistead of Dunscar, Lancs. RA 1844; RHA 1848; employed in right and left siege trains in Crimea in the bombardments of 6 and 18 June 1855; Inspector-General of Police, Mauritius, 1858–67; employed Mission to the King of Madagascar, 1862; Lieut-Governor, Penang, 1867; Administrator of Government of the Straits Settlements, 1871–72, 1877, 1879; had charge of Expedition in Sungie Ujong, and Negri Sambilan, Malay Peninsula, 1875–76. *Publication:* About Others and Myself, 1745–1920, 1920. *Recreations:* horticulture, carpentry, and other works. *Address:* Southfield, Silverhill, St Leonards-on-Sea.

            Died 26 Feb. 1925.

ANSON, Hon. Frederic (William), JP; *b* 4 Feb. 1862; 4th *s* of 2nd Earl of Lichfield; *m* 1st, 1886, Florence Louisa Jane (*d* 1908), *d* of Lieut-Col John Henry Bagot Lane of Kings Bromley, Staffordshire; two *s* three *d*; 2nd, 1915, Edith, *d* of E. S. Rowland, Bramlyns, Horsham. Director London and South-Western Bank, Ltd. *Address:* 8 Pall Mall, SW. *T:* Gerrard 3652; Cell Barnes, St Albans. *Club:* Arthur's.   *Died 2 April 1917.*

ANSON, Sir John Henry Algernon, 5th Bt, *cr* 1831; Sub-Lieutenant RN; *b* 13 Jan. 1897; *s* of late Rear-Adm. Algernon Horatio Anson, 4th *s* of 2nd Bt, and Hon. Adela Vernon, *d* of 6th Baron Vernon; *S* cousin 1914. *Heir: b* Edward Reynell Anson, *b* 31 Jan. 1902.   *Died 10 March 1918.*

ANSTEY, Percy, BSc (Econ.) London; Principal of the Sydenham College of Commerce and Economics, Bombay, since 1914; *b* Paris, 25 Feb. 1876; *s* of Captain Adolph Page, 2nd Queen's Regiment, and Mary, *e d* of Alexander Anstey, whose name he took by deed-poll; *m* 1913, Vera, *d* of James Powell, Reigate; two *s* one *d*. *Educ:* Felsted; St Paul's School; Vienna University; London School of Economics. After studying abroad, joined the stage in 1898, and acted till 1906 with Forbes Robertson, the German Theatre in London, Tree, Martin Harvey, etc; studied at London School of Economics, 1906–10; a Lecturer on Economics, Sheffield University, 1910–11; Head of Economics Department, Bristol University, 1911–14; elected first Chairman of the Indian Economic Association, 1914. *Publication:* The Abuse of the Psychological Method in Sociology. *Recreations:* tennis, mountaineering. *Address:* Dungarsi Road, Malabar Hill, Bombay. *Clubs:* Bombay Yacht, Orient, Bombay.

            Died 23 Nov. 1920.

ANSTICE, Lieut-Col and Hon. Col Sir Robert Henry, KCB 1910 (CB 1902); *b* 17 Aug. 1843; *s* of late J. Anstice, Madeley Wood Hall,

Shropshire. *Educ:* Rugby; St Leonards-on-Sea; Oxford (MA). Ensign 29th Regt, 1866; Lieut, 1869; Captain, 1879; exchanged to 55th (2nd Batt. Border Regt), 1881; Major, half-pay, 1885; Adjutant, 1st Aberdeenshire Royal Engineers (Volunteers), 1884; placed on retired pay, 1889; Commanding 1st Aberdeenshire Royal Engineers (Volunteers), 1891–1904; Hon. Colonel, Highland Division, RE (Terr.), 1914. *Address:* Norfolk Hotel, Brighton. *Clubs:* Junior United Service, Junior Army and Navy.

            Died 9 April 1922.

ANSTIE, James, KC; *b* 1836; *m* 1867, Sarah, *d* of Lindsey Winterbotham. Called to Bar, Lincoln's Inn, 1859, Bencher; QC 1882; Certificate of Honour. *Address:* Millandreath, 87 Southbourne Road, Stourwood, Bournemouth.

            Died Oct. 1924.

ANSTRUTHER, Colonel Charles Frederick St Clair, DSO 1900; MVO 1905; JP, DL Fife; Officer of Légion d'Honneur; Knight Commander of the Sword of Sweden; Knight Commander of Isabel la Católica; Esquire of St John of Jerusalem; *b* 6 May 1855; *e* surv. *s* of John Anstruther-Thomson of Charleton, Fife; *m* 1882, Agnes, 3rd *d* of late James A. Guthrie of Craigie; one *d*. Entered army, 1874; Major, 1895; served South Africa, 1899–1900 (despatches, medals, 6 clasps, DSO); commanded 2nd Life Guards; retired, 1907. *Address:* Charleton, Fife; Rutland House, Rutland Gardens, SW7. *T:* Kensington 3152. *Clubs:* Bachelors', Travellers'; New, Edinburgh.   *Died 21 Oct. 1925.*

ANSTRUTHER, Henry Torrens; JP Co. Bucks and Co. Fife; member of the Administrative Council Suez Canal Co. since 1903; Alderman, LCC, 1905–10; *b* 27 Nov. 1860; 2nd *s* of Sir Robert Anstruther, 5th Bt, MP (Director of the North British Railway Co., 1900–23); *m* 1889, Hon. Eva I. H. Hanbury-Tracy; one *s* one *d*. *Educ:* Eton; Edinburgh University. Advocate, Edinburgh, 1884; MP (LU) St Andrews District, 1886–1903; a Lord of the Treasury, 1895–1903. *Address:* Old Court House, Whitchurch, Aylesbury. *Club:* Brooks's.   *Died 5 April 1926.*

ANSTRUTHER, Sir Windham Frederick Carmichael-, 10th Bt, *cr* 1700 and 1798; Hereditary Carver to Royal Household in Scotland; one of the Hereditary Masters of the Household for Scotland; *b* 30 April 1902; *s* of 10th Bt and Sylvia, *d* of late Rt Hon. Sir Frederick Darley, GCMG, PC [she married 2nd, 1905, Major Hon. A. H. C. Hanbury-Tracy (decd)]; *S* father 1903; *m* 1925, Katharine Mary, *d* of late D. A. Neilson, of Westbridge House, Pontefract, Yorks. *Heir: c* Windham Eric Francis Carmichael-Anstruther, *b* 29 May 1900. *Address:* Carmichael House, Thankerton RSO, Scotland; 66 Upper Berkeley Street, W1.   *Died 29 Nov. 1928.*

ANTHONISZ, James Oliver, CMG 1914; retired from Civil Service, Straits Settlements, 1914; *b* Galle, Ceylon, 15 Jan. 1860; 2nd *s* of late James Edmund and Eliza Sarah Caroline Anthonisz; *m* 1894, Florence Lowndes; three *d*. *Educ:* Ceylon; St John's College, Cambridge; BA Math. Tripos, 1882. Cadet, Straits Settlements Civil Service, 1883; Magistrate, Singapore; Official Assignee, SS; District Judge, Singapore; President, Singapore Municipality; Colonial Treasurer, Straits Settlements; Acting Resident Councillor, Penang; Acting British Resident, Selangor; the currency of the Colony was placed on a gold basis during tenure of office as Treasurer; President of a Commission to enquire into the working of the Municipalities of the Colony, 1910. *Recreation:* golf. *Address:* The Cottage, Dynevor Road, Richmond.   *Died 28 May 1921.*

ANTRIM, 11th Earl of, *cr* 1620; **William Randal M'Donnell,** Viscount Dunluce, 1785; *b* 8 Jan. 1851; *S* father 1869; *m* 1875, Louisa Jane, VA, *d* of late Gen. Hon. Charles Grey, and Lady of the Bedchamber to the Queen; two *s* one *d*. Owned about 35,000 acres. *Heir: s* Viscount Dunluce, *b* 10 Dec. 1878. *Address:* Glenarn Castle, Larne, Antrim.   *Died 19 July 1918.*

ANTROBUS, John Coutts, JP; *b* 1829; *e s* of Gibbs Crawfurd Antrobus and 1st wife Jane, 2nd *d* of Sir Coutts Trotter, 1st Bt; *m* 1st, 1855, Frances (*d* 1863), 2nd *d* of late Clement Swetenham, of Somerford Booths, Cheshire; one *s* three *d*; 2nd, 1865, Mary Caroline (*d* 1872), *d* of late Geoffrey Joseph Shakerley; three *s* one *d*; 3rd, 1875, Mary Egidia, *y d* of late Gen. Hon. Sir James Lindsay, KCMG; four *s* one *d*. *Educ:* Eton; St John's College, Cambridge; MA. Called to Bar, Lincoln's Inn, 1857; High Sheriff, Cheshire, 1868; patron of two livings; Hon. Lieut-Col retired, Earl of Chester's Yeomanry Cavalry. *Address:* Eaton Hall, Congleton. *Club:* United University.   *Died 19 Dec. 1916.*

APLIN, Col Philip John Hanham, DSO 1904; *b* 18 Dec. 1858; *m* 1st, 1905, Mary Bertha, *d* of Brig.-Surg. C. F. Oldham of The Lodge, Gt Bealings; one *s* one *d*; 2nd, 1920, Martha Lyon, *d* of late George Edward Barnard. *Educ:* Sherborne School. Entered army, 1878; Capt., 1889; Major, 1898; Lt-Col, 1904; served Afghanistan, 1879–80 (medal); Burmah, 1885–89 (medal with two claps); East Africa, 1904 (despatches, DSO); retired, 1919.

Died 10 May 1927.

APPERLEY, Newton Wynne, MVO 1903; JP Co. Durham; Private Secretary to successive Marquises of Londonderry since 1879, including three years' service as Assistant Private Secretary to the 6th Marquis as Lord-Lieutenant of Ireland, 1886–89; Chairman Durham (County) Petty Sessional Division, and Chairman of Visiting Justices; Member of Standing Joint Committee; *b* Australia, 29 July 1846; 4th *s* of Col W. W. Apperley, 4th Bengal Cavalry, of Morben, Machynlleth, Montgomeryshire, N Wales, and of Esther, *d* of Brig.-Gen. Wallace, killed at Ferozeshah; *m* 1880, Mary, *o d* of A. W. Hutchinson of Hollingside, Durham; two *s* three *d*. *Educ:* Dr Huntingford's School, Eagle House, Hammersmith; Rev. F. Faithfull's, Headley Rectory, near Epsom. Cornet in the Montgomeryshire Yeomanry Cavalry, 1868; served in it twenty years, and retired with the rank of Major. *Publications:* The Nimrod Game Book; Sport in Wales Thirty Years Ago; An Old Coaching Road; Various Hunting Diaries, etc. *Recreations:* hunting, shooting. *Address:* South End, Durham. *TA:* Durham. *T:* Durham 284. *Clubs:* Junior Constitutional; County, Durham.

Died 21 Jan. 1925.

APPLEGARTH, Robert, MIEE; retired from business after an interesting career as a Trade Unionist, and as Agent for Submarine and Mining Engineers; *b* Kingston-on-Hull, 26 Jan. 1834; *s* of a mariner, who afterwards went as quartermaster on the "Terror" to the North Polar regions. Received but a scanty education; at 19 was in Sheffield, the next year, 1854, went to the USA, and spent some time at Galesburg, Knox County, Illinois; his spare time, both in the USA and afterwards in Manchester and Sheffield, was spent in self-education; led early to study economic and industrial questions, with special regard to the condition of workmen in those days. Member of the Amalgamated Society of Carpenters and Joiners from the first; General Secretary, 1862–71; member of the Sheffield No 1 Branch of the ASC and Joiners; politician and reformer, and promoter of popular education; took up electric lighting; was member of the Royal Commission of Inquiry into the CD Acts, the first workman so appointed; member of the Reform League, of the London General Council of the International Working Men's Association of the London Chamber of Commerce, and a delegate to the International Congress at Basle in 1869; was war correspondent in the Franco-Prussian War, 1870 (Sheffield Independent, the Scotsman, and the New York World). *Publications:* Letters to the Sheffield Independent in 1869, on Schools in Switzerland. *Recreation:* work, more work, and still again more. *Address:* 23 Parchmore Road, Thornton Heath, Surrey. *Club:* National Liberal.

Died 13 July 1924.

ARBER, Edward Alexander Newell, MA, ScD; FLS, FGS; Demonstrator in Palæobotany in the University of Cambridge since 1899; Hon. Member New Zealand Institute; *b* 5 Aug. 1870; *e s* of late Professor Edward Arber, DLitt; *m* 1909, Agnes, *d* of H. R. Robertson; one *d*. *Educ:* King Edward's High School, Birmingham; Trinity College, Cambridge. *Publications:* Monograph of the Glossopteris Flora (British Museum Catalogue); Plant Life in Alpine Switzerland; The Natural History of Coal; The Coast Scenery of North Devon; author or joint-author of numerous botanical papers contributed to various scientific journals. *Recreations:* gardening, music, photography. *Address:* The Sedgwick Museum, and 52 Huntingdon Road, Cambridge. *Died 14 June 1918.*

ARBUTHNOT, Charles George, MA; Director of Bank of England; *b* Oct. 1846; *s* of John Alves Arbuthnot, of Coworth Park, Berks. *Educ:* Eton; Merton College, Oxford. After leaving Oxford, travelled abroad, and afterwards mainly occupied in banking house of Messrs Arbuthnot, Latham & Co., of which a partner for many years. *Address:* 69 Eaton Square, SW1. *T:* Victoria 2933. *Clubs:* Athenæum, Carlton, Wellington, Burlington Fine Arts.

Died 27 Sept. 1928.

ARBUTHNOT, Ven. George, DD; Archdeacon of Coventry since 1908; *b* 24 May 1846; *s* of George Clerk Arbuthnot of Mavisbank, Midlothian; *m* 1885, Margaret Evelyn, *e d* of Very Rev. H. M. Luckock, late Dean of Lichfield. *Educ:* Eton; Christ Church, Oxford (MA). Read with Dr Vaughan at the Temple; ordained to the Curacy

of Arundel, Sussex, 1872; Vicar, 1873; Vicar of Stratford-on-Avon, 1879; Surrogate for the Diocese of Worcester, 1883; Proctor for the Clergy in Convocation, 1906. *Publications:* The Passion of Christ; A Plain Guide to Holy Communion; Sermons on Disestablishment, etc; Editor, Shakespeare Sermons. *Recreation:* travelling. *Address:* Comyn House, Leamington. *T:* 121 Leamington. *Club:* United University.

Died 9 Nov. 1922.

ARBUTHNOT, Gerald Archibald; *b* 19 Dec. 1872; *o s* of late Major-General William Arbuthnot, 14th Hussars, and Selina, 7th *d* of Sir Thomas Moncreiffe, 7th Bt of Moncreiffe; *m* 1894, Dulce Johanna, *d* of late Charles Oppenheim, 40 Great Cumberland Place, W; three *d*. *Educ:* privately; HMS Britannia. Left Navy, 1892; Private Secretary to Rt Hon. Walter H. Long, MP, 1894; served in that capacity during Unionist governments of 1895 and 1900 at the Board of Agriculture, Local Government Board, and Irish Office; contested Burnley, 1906; Vice-Chairman Budget Protest League, 1909; Chairman of the Lancashire and Cheshire Federation of Junior Unionist Associations; MP (U) Burnley, 1910; Vice-Chancellor, Primrose League, 1912. *Publications:* various magazine and newspaper articles. *Recreations:* mountaineering, golf. *Address:* 43 Princes Gardens, SW. *T:* 60 Western. *Club:* Carlton. *Died Sept. 1916.*

ARBUTHNOT, Maj.-Gen. Henry Thomas, CB 1907; Royal Artillery, retired; *b* 16 Oct. 1834; *s* of George Arbuthnot, Asst Secretary HM's Treasury; *m* 1862, Anna Jane (*d* 1909), *d* of B. H. Mowbray of Surbiton, Surrey; one *s*. *Educ:* Royal Military Academy, Woolwich. Joined Royal Regiment of Artillery as 2nd Lieut, 1853; served Crimean War, 1854–56, including affair of Mackenzie Farm, Repulse of Sortie, 26 Oct. 1854, Battles of Alma and Inkerman and Siege and Fall of Sebastopol (medal and clasps for Alma, Inkerman, and Sebastopol, Knight of Legion of Honour, Turkish medal); Indian Mutiny, 1857–59, Action of Secundra, Siege and Capture of Lucknow, Capture of forts Rehara and Koorlee (despatches, medal and clasp for Lucknow, Brevet-Major); Assistant Superintendent Royal Small Arms Factory, Enfield and Birmingham, 1862–72; Captain of the Company of Gentlemen Cadets, Royal Military Academy, Woolwich, 1875–79; Superintendent Royal Small Arms Factory, Enfield, 1880–87; retired with rank of Major-General, 1887; Chairman of the Aerial League of the British Empire, 1912; JP borough of Sutton Coldfield. *Publications:* articles on Military Subjects in Chambers's Encyclopædia. *Address:* Ramsay House, Shooters Hill, SE18. *Club:* United Service. *Died 3 May 1919.*

ARBUTHNOT, James Woodgate; *b* 1848; *e surv. s* of late George Arbuthnot and Maria, *d* of James Thomas, Madras Civil Service; *m* 1877, Anne Susan Charlotte, *d* of Sir Charles Jackson, Judge of the High Court of Calcutta. *Educ:* Eton. Formerly a banker in Madras; retired, 1884; JP Surrey. *Address:* Elderslie, near Dorking. *Club:* Athenæum. *Died 21 Oct. 1927.*

ARBUTHNOT, Robert Edward Vaughan, CSI 1922; Indian Civil Service; Financial Commissioner, Burma, since 1919; *b* 15 Jan. 1871; *s* of late Rev. Robert Keith Arbuthnot, Vicar of St James, Ratcliff, E; *m* 1899, Ethel Mary, *d* of late Major Charles Wyndham, Bengal Cavalry; one *d*. *Educ:* Merchant Taylors' School; St John's College, Oxford (Scholar). Appointed ICS 1892, and posted to Burma; Acting Secretary to Burma Govt, 1899; Under Secretary to Govt of India in Revenue and Agricultural Dept, 1900–4; Revenue Secretary to Burma Govt, 1905–7, and 1910–13; Acting Chief Secretary to Burma Govt, 1913–14; Member Imperial Legislative Council, 1914–15; Commissioner of Settlements, Burma, 1915–19; Member Burma Reforms Committee, 1921. *Publication:* Settlement Report of the Hanthawaddy District, 1910. *Address:* Rangoon; 20 Via de Bardi, Florence, Italy. *Clubs:* Athenæum, East India United Service.

Died 22 Oct. 1922.

ARBUTHNOT, Rear-Adm. Sir Robert Keith, 4th Bt, *cr* 1882; MVO 1904; RN; *b* 23 March 1864; *S* father 1889; *m* 1897, Lina, *d* of Col A. C. Macleay, CB; one *d*. Entered Navy, 1877; Commander, 1897; Captain, 1902; Rear-Admiral, 1912; Rear-Admiral 2nd Battle Squadron, 1913–14. *Heir:* *b* Major Dalrymple Arbuthnot, RFA, *b* 1 April 1867. *Recreations:* motor-cycling, cricket. *Address:* 51 Elsworthy Road, Hampstead, NW. *Clubs:* Travellers', Royal Automobile.

Died 31 May 1916.

ARBUTHNOTT, 12th Viscount of, *cr* 1641; **William Arbuthnott;** Baron Inverbervie, 1641; *b* 24 Oct. 1849; 4th *s* of 9th Viscount and Lady Jean Graham Drummond Ogilvy, *d* of 6th Earl of Airlie; *S* brother 1914. *Heir:* *cousin* Lt-Col Walter Charles Warner Arbuthnott, *b* 2 Oct. 1847. *Address:* Arbuthnott House, Fordoun, Kincardineshire.

Died 8 Nov. 1917.

ARBUTHNOTT, 13th Viscount of, *cr* 1641; **Walter Charles Warner Arbuthnott;** Baron Inverbervie, 1641; *b* 2 Oct. 1847; *g s* of 8th Viscount; *S* cousin 1917; *m* 1878, Emma Marion Hall, *d* of Rev. J. H. Parlby; two *s* two *d*. *Heir: s* Hon. John Ogilvy, Master of Arbuthnott [*b* 15 Sept. 1882; *m* 1914, Dorothy, *d* of Adm. Charles L. Oxley, The Hall, Ripon. *Address:* Spotted Lake Ranche, Alberta]. *Address:* Arbuthnott House, Fordoun, Kincardineshire.

Died 9 Aug. 1920.

ARBUTHNOTT, John Campbell, CIE 1898; ICS, retired; President, Assam Legislative Council since 1921; *b* 6 April 1858; *s* of late Lieut-Col Hon. Hugh Arbuthnott, 3rd *s* of 8th Viscount Arbuthnott; *m* 1887, Jeannie, *d* of Robert Hamilton of Elmhirst, Kent; one *s* three *d*. Entered Indian Civil Service, 1879; served in Bengal as Assistant-Magistrate and Collector; transferred to Assam, 1883; Deputy Commissioner, 1890; Commissioner, Surma Valley and Hill Districts, Eastern Bengal and Assam, 1905-14; retired 1914; Member of the Legislative Council, Eastern Bengal and Assam; Additional Member, Imperial Legislative Council, 1913-14. *Publication:* Report on the Conditions of Tea Garden Labour in the Duars of Bengal, Madras, and Ceylon. *Address:* Shillong, Assam, India.

Died 20 May 1923.

ARCH, Joseph; *b* 10 Nov. 1826; *s* of a labourer; widower. Worked in fields for living; self-educated by reading; founded National Agricultural Union, 1872; after an unsuccessful contest, MP (R) NW Norfolk, 1885-86, 1892, 1895-1900. *Address:* The Cottage, Barford, Warwick. *Died 12 Feb. 1919.*

ARCHAMBEAULT, Hon. Sir Horace, Kt 1914; KC; LLD; Chief-Justice of the Court of King's Bench of the Province of Quebec since 1911; Puisne-Judge of same court since 1908; Professor of Commercial and Maritime Law at Laval University, Montreal, since 1881; *b* 6 March 1857; *m* 1882, Elizabeth, *d* of Roger Lelievre, Quebec. *Educ:* L'Assomption College; studied law at Laval University, Quebec (LLL (Summa Cum Laude) 1878, LLD 1886). Called to Bar 1878, and practised his profession in Montreal. Called to Legislative Council, 1888; Member of Council of Public Instruction, 1890; Batonnier General of the Bar, Province of Quebec, 1901-2; Attorney-General, Quebec, 1897-1905; and Speaker of the Legislative Council, 1897-1908. Roman Catholic; Liberal. *Address:* Quebec.

Died 26 Aug. 1918.

ARCHDALE, Rt. Hon. Edward, PC 1913; JP; HM Lieutenant for Co. Tyrone; head of the Archdale family; landowner; *b* 22 March 1850; *s* of Rev. Henry Montgomery Archdale and Sarah, *d* of Blackwood Price of Saintfield House, Co. Down; *m* 1908, Elizabeth, *d* of late Nicholas Harwood, HM Dockyard, Pembroke, and *widow* of Captain Wingfield Clark, Leicestershire Regiment; no *c. Educ:* Marlborough College; Keble College, Oxford; BA 1871. Civil Engineer; engaged in submarine cable laying in various parts of the world up to 1880; succeeded his uncle the late William H. Mervyn Archdale, 1899; High Sheriff, Co. Fermanagh, 1902; Co. Tyrone, 1906; Foreman of Co. Fermanagh Grand Jury; a Liberal in politics. *Recreations:* riding, yachting, shooting, motoring, croquet, billiards, golf. *Address:* Castle Archdale, Irvinestown. *M:* IL 122. *Clubs:* Fermanagh Co.; Tyrone Co.

Died 4 July 1916.

ARCHDALE, Brig.-Gen. Hugh James, CB 1902; CMG 1918; Royal Welsh Fusiliers and Lincolnshire Regiment; *b* 15 Jan. 1854; 2nd *s* of late Capt. Mervyn Edward Archdale, of Castle Archdale, Co. Fermanagh; *m* 1st, Minnie (*d* 1888), *e d* of Capt. Hugh Montgomery Archdale, late 52nd Light Infantry; 2nd, 1894, Helen Evelyn Trevor, *e d* of Captain B. T. Griffith Boscawen of Trevalyn Hall, Rossett, N Wales; one *d. Educ:* Cheltenham College. Entered army, 1875; Captain, 1885; Major, 1892; Lieut-Col, 1900; Col, 1904; served Soudan, 1884-85 (medal with clasp, Khedive's star); Burmah, 1886-87, with 1st Batt. Royal Welsh Fusiliers (medal with clasp); Crete, 1897-98, with 2nd Batt. Royal Welsh Fusiliers; South Africa (despatches, Queen's medal, 5 clasps, King's medal, 2 clasps, CB), 1899-1902; Commandant, Imperial Yeomanry Discharge Depot, Aldershot, 1908; Commanding a Division, 1907-11; retired, 1911. *Club:* Naval and Military. *Died 31 Aug. 1921.*

ARCHDALE, Major Theodore Montgomery, DSO 1900; RFA; *b* 24 Sept. 1873; *y s* of late Nicholas Montgomery Archdale of Crock na Crieve, Co. Fermanagh; *m* 1901, Helen Alexander, *d* of late Alexander Russel. Entered RA, 1894; served South Africa (despatches, DSO); European War, 1914-15 (despatches, wounded). *Address:* c/o Cox and Co., Charing Cross, SW. *Club:* Army and Navy.

Died 10 Oct. 1918.

ARCHDALE, Rev. Thomas Hewan; Hon. Canon of Durham. *Address:* Tanfield Vicarage, Tantobie, Durham.

Died 23 June 1924.

ARCHER, Major Henry, DSO 1917; RFA; Brigade-Major, Royal Artillery, 51st Division, BEF; *b* 17 April 1883; *s* of H. C. Archer, Cenis Lodge, Wimbledon, SW; *m* Sybil Mary, *d* of late Rev. A. H. Cooke of Quethiock; one *d. Educ:* Oundle; Royal Military Academy, Woolwich. Commissioned, 1902; 1st Lieut, 1905; Captain, 1914; Major, 1916; joined 128th Battery RFA on first Commission; served in 128th Battery six years; Adjutant 4th East Lancs Brigade RFA, 1909-13; joined 126th Battery RFA on outbreak of war; commanded 125th Battery RFA, Sept. 1915-Feb. 1917; served continuously in France from Aug. 1914 (DSO). *Recreations:* hunting, golf. *Address:* Cox & Co., 16 Charing Cross, SW1. *Club:* Junior Army and Navy.

Died 17 Dec. 1917.

ARCHER, Walter E., CB 1911; FRSE; Assistant Secretary, Board of Agriculture and Fisheries, 1903-12; *b* 4 July 1855; *s* of late Captain Clement R. Archer, 4th Dragoon Guards; *m* 1878, Alice Lina, *d* of late Robert Hay Murray, Spinfield, Bucks; three *s* three *d. Educ:* Eton. Engaged in salmon research, 1884-92; for this purpose acquired entire control of two rivers and intervening sea-coast in Norway; publicly thanked in 1890 for improvement effected in economic condition of the Norwegian fishermen in the county of Stavanger; Inspector of Salmon Fisheries for Scotland, 1892-98; Chief Inspector of Fisheries to the Board of Trade, 1898-1903; British Delegate to the International Conference for the Investigation of the Sea, 1899; Member of the Royal Commission appointed to inquire into the Salmon Fisheries of Great Britain, 1900-2; Member of the Tethyological Research Committee, 1901; British Delegate to the International Council for the study of the sea since 1904; President of that Council since 1908; Fellow, Statistical Society, London. *Publications:* Salmon Fishery Reports of the Fishery Board for Scotland, 1892-98; Sea and Salmon Fishery Reports of England and Wales since 1898. *Recreations:* fishing, yachting. *Address:* 17 Sloane Court, SW. *T:* 3592 Vic; Sand, Stavanger, Norway. *Club:* Union.

Died 19 Aug. 1917.

ARCHER, William; *b* Perth, Scotland, 23 Sept. 1856; *s* of Thomas Archer, CMG, of Gracemere, Queensland, formerly Agent-General for Queensland in London. *Educ:* Edinburgh University (MA). Barrister, Middle Temple, 1883; journalism, in Edinburgh, 1875; travelled in Australia, 1876-77; came to London, 1878; dramatic critic of London Figaro, 1879-81; travelled in Italy, 1881-82; dramatic critic of World, 1884-1905; afterwards of the Tribune, the Nation, and of the Star. *Publications:* edited Ibsen's Prose Dramas, 5 vols, and Collected Works of Ibsen, 11 vols; translated with his brother, Lt-Col Charles Archer, Ibsen's Peer Gynt; wrote Life of Macready; Masks or Faces: a Study in the Psychology of Acting; The Theatrical World, 1893-97, 5 vols; Study and Stage, a Yearbook of Criticism, 1899; America To-day, 1900; Poets of the Younger Generation, 1901; Real Conversations, 1904; Through Afro-America, 1910; The Life, Trial, and Death of Francisco Ferrer, 1911; Play-making, 1912; The Great Analysis, 1912; The Thirteen Days, 1915; 501 Gems of German Thought, 1917; God and Mr Wells, 1917; India and the Future, 1917; The Peace President, 1918; War is War (a drama), 1919; The Green Goddess (a drama), 1921; The Old Drama and the New, 1928; with H. Granville Barker, A National Theatre Scheme and Estimates, 1907. *Address:* 27 Fitzroy Square, W1. *T:* Museum 664. *Club:* Reform.

Died 27 Dec. 1924.

ARCHIBALD, Very Rev. John, MA; Canon of Inverness Cathedral since 1894; Rector of Trinity Episcopal Church, Keith, 1876-1912; *b* Musselburgh, Midlothian; *m* Miss Boyd, of Peterhead. *Educ:* University of Aberdeen; Trinity College, Glenalmond. Ordained Deacon, 1870; Priest, 1871; Curate, St John's Church, Darwen, Lancs; Incumbent, St John's Church, Wick; Dean of the United Diocese of Moray, Ross, and Caithness, 1902-12; Synod Clerk Moray Diocese. *Publications:* History of the Episcopal Church at Keith in 17th, 18th and 19th Centuries, 1889; Historic Episcopate in Columbian Church and Diocese of Moray, 1892; A Ten Years' Conflict, 1907. *Address:* Northfield, Worcestershire.

Died 10 Sept. 1916.

ARCHIBALD, Sir William Frederick Alphonse, Kt 1917; MA; FSS; Barrister-at-Law; *b* 1846; *g s* of late Hon. S. G. W. Archibald, LLD, Master of the Rolls and Speaker of the House of Assembly, Nova Scotia, and *s* of late Hon. Sir Thomas Dickson Archibald, one of the Judges of the Court of Queen's Bench and afterwards of the Common Pleas Division of the High Court; *m* 1873, Florence, *d* of late C. W. H. Wallroth of Lee, Kent; four *s* three *d. Educ:* Repton

School; St John's College, Oxford (Fereday Fellow). Civil Engineer; was AICE; Underground Surveyor of the Metropolitan Board of Works, employed on the Drainage of London; called to the Bar, 1874; Master of the Supreme Court, King's Bench Division, 1890–1916; Chairman of the Royal National Mission to Deep Sea Fishermen; late Hon. Treasurer of the Religious Tract Society, etc; late Chairman of the Scrivenery Board, RCJ; late Chairman of the London Prescribed Officers under the Poor Persons Rules, 1914; Board of Trade nominated member of the Committee of the Seamen's National Insurance Society. *Publications:* Practice at Judge's Chambers; The Country Solicitor's Practice; Joint-Author of Archibald's Metropolitan Police Guide issued by the Home Office and Editor of Broom's Common Law; Editor of Articles on Courts and Interpleader in the Laws of England. *Address:* Moorside, Hindhead, Surrey. *T:* Hindhead 53; Royal Courts of Justice, WC. *TA:* Courts Justice, London. *Club:* Oxford and Cambridge. *Died 31 March 1922.*

ARDEN, Lt-Col John Henry Morris, DSO 1915; Worcester Regiment (Reserve of Officers); Commandant, No 2 RFC Cadet Wing; *b* 2 Feb. 1875; *s* of late Rev. A. H. Arden. Entered army, 1897; Captain, 1900; retired 1912; Bt Major, 1915; served South Africa, 1899–1902 (Queen's medal 3 clasps, King's medal 2 clasps); Sudan, 1912 (medal and clasp, 2nd Class Osmanieh); European War, 1914–16 (DSO, despatches twice). *Club:* Royal Automobile. *Died Aug. 1918.*

ARDRON, John, CB 1906; AIEE; *b* 1843; *s* of John Ardron of Queniborough, Leics; *m* 1873, *d* of J. J. Ridge, MD, Gravesend. Retired Assistant Secretary, GPO. Identified with the progress and organisation of the telegraph service of the country since it was taken over from the private electric telegraph companies, 1870; also with telephone and wireless telegraph services; Vice-Chairman, International Telegraph Conference, 1903; Commander of the Danish Order of the Dannebrog. *Address:* "Nordra", Stanmore. *Club:* Stanmore Golf. *Died 4 Dec. 1919.*

ARENBERG, Auguste Louis Alberic, Prince D'; Member of the Institute; *b* 15 Sept. 1837. President of the Suez Canal Company; Vice-Pres. of the Paris-Orleans Railway Company; Chef des Battalions during War of 1870–71. *Address:* Rue de la Ville-l'Evêque 20, Paris VIIIᵉ; Menetou-Salon, Cher. *Club:* Jockey, Paris. *Died 24 Jan. 1924.*

ARGLES, Rev. Canon George Marsham; Rector of St Clement's, York, 1871–1919; *b* 1841; *s* of late Dr Argles, Dean of Peterborough; *m* 1870, Mary Ann, *d* of Thos Harrison of Singleton Park, Kendal; three *s* four *d*. *Educ:* Harrow; Balliol Coll., Oxford. 2nd class Final Classical School; Denyer and Johnson Univ. theological scholar. Curate of Christ Church, Doncaster, 1865–71; Canon of York, 1888; Proctor in Convocation for the Archdeaconry of York, 1896; Examining Chaplain to the Bishop of Peterborough, 1897. *Publication:* Instructions for Confirmation. *Address:* The Old Residence, York. *TA:* York. *T:* 595 York; Hawbarrow, Milnthorpe, Westmorland. *M:* EC 6 and EC 74. *Died 22 Feb. 1920.*

ARKWRIGHT, Frederic Charles, JP; Vice-Lieutenant of Derbyshire; Hon. Lt-Col Volunteer Force, 1918; *b* 7 Nov. 1853; *o s* of late Frederic Arkwright of Willersley; *m* 1883, Rebecca Olton, 3rd *d* of late Sir John G. N. Alleyne, 3rd Bt; one *s* one *d*. *Educ:* Eton; Christ Church, Oxford. Sheriff, 1887; Capt. 2nd Derbyshire RV, 1882–87; contested (C) West Derbyshire, 1885. *Address:* Willersley, Matlock. *TA:* Cromford. *T:* Matlock 75. *Club:* United University. *Died 18 July 1923.*

ARKWRIGHT, Richard; *b* 1835; *m* 1862, Lady Mary Caroline Charlotte Byng, *d* of 2nd Earl of Strafford. *Educ:* Harrow; Cambridge (MA). Barrister, Oxford Circuit; Revising Barrister for Monmouthshire, Gloucester, and Cheltenham, 1865; MP (C) Leominster, 1866–75; DL Herefordshire. *Publications:* Queen Anne's Gate Mystery; Driven Home. *Address:* Herne House, Windsor. *Club:* Carlton. *Died 14 Nov. 1918.*

ARKWRIGHT, William; *b* 21 April 1857; *o s* of late Major William Arkwright, 6th Dragoons, and Fanny Susan, 2nd *d* of Edward Thornewill, of Dovecliff, Co. Stafford; *m* 1884, Agnes Mary, *e d* of Hon. John J. T. Somers-Cocks. *Educ:* Eton; Christ Church, Oxford. High Sheriff, Co. Derby, 1890. *Publications:* The Pointer and his Predecessors; Knowledge and Life; The Trend; Utinam. *Address:* Thorn, Knighton, SO, Plymouth; 28 Brompton Square, SW. *Club:* White's. *Died 19 Feb. 1925.*

ARMAGHDALE, 1st Baron, *cr* 1918; **John Brownlee Lonsdale;** 1st Bt, 1911; Lord Lieutenant, Co. Armagh, since 1920; *b* Armagh, 23 March 1850; *s* of James Lonsdale, DL, of Armagh, and Jane, *d* of William Brownlee; *m* 1887, Florence, *d* of William Rumney of Stubbins House, Lancashire. High Sheriff, 1895; MP (C) Mid Armagh, 1900–18; Hon. Secretary and Whip of the Irish Unionist Party, 1901–16; Chairman until 1918; a Conservative. *Heir:* none. *Address:* 13 Prince's Gardens, SW7. *T:* Kensington 44; The Dunes, Sandwich. *Clubs:* Carlton, Bachelors'. *Died 8 June 1924 (ext).*

ARMITAGE-SMITH, George, DLit, MA (Lond.); Principal of Birkbeck College, 1896–1918, and Lecturer on Economics and Mental Science; Dean of the Faculty of Economics, University of London, 1904–8; Fellow of the Royal Statistical Society; Member of the Council of the Royal Economic Society. *Publications:* The Citizen of England, 1895; The Free Trade Movement, 1898; Principles and Methods of Taxation, 1906; and numerous articles and reviews on social and economic subjects in magazines, journals, encyclopædias. *Address:* 3 Albert Terrace, Regent's Park, NW. *Died 10 Jan. 1923.*

ARMITSTEAD, Rev. John Richard; Vicar of Sandbach, Cheshire, since 1865; Hon. Canon of Chester; *b* 11 May 1829; *e s* of Rev. John Armitstead, Vicar of Sandbach; *m* 1866, Frances Mary, *e d* of W. H. Hornby, MP for Blackburn; five *s* two *d*. *Educ:* Westminster; Christ Church, Oxford. Formerly Incumbent of Goostrey, Cheshire; afterwards Rector of Wendlebury, Oxfordshire; Member of Cheshire County Council since 1895; Alderman, Cheshire County Council, 1912. *Recreations:* fond of farming, and outdoor sports generally. *Address:* The Vicarage, Sandbach, Cheshire. *TA:* Sandbach. *Died 19 Sept. 1918.*

ARMOUR, Rev. James Brown, MA; Minister, Trinity Church, Ballymoney, 1869–1925; *b* 31 Jan. 1842; *m* 1883, Jennie Staveley Hamilton, *d* of Rev. A. M. Staveley, St John, Canada; three *s*. *Educ:* Royal Academical Institution; Queen's Colleges, Belfast and Cork. Took active part in Land, Home Rule and Catholic University controversies; long interested in primary, secondary and university education; sometime Senator, Queen's University, Belfast; Lecturer in Classics, Magee College, Londonderry; Carey Lecturer; Hon. Chaplain to Lord-Lieutenant of Ireland, 1906–15. *Publications:* articles, including A Presbyterian View, in the New Irish Constitution. *Recreation:* formerly golf. *Address:* Ballymoney, Co. Antrim, Ireland. *Died Feb. 1928.*

ARMOUR, Jonathan Ogden; President, Corporation of Armour & Co., packers; *b* Milwaukee, 11 Nov. 1863; *s* of late Philip Danforth Armour; *m* Lolita Sheldon; one *d*. *Educ:* Yale. *Publication:* The Packers and the People, 1906. *Address:* 3724 Michigan Avenue, Chicago. *Died 16 Aug. 1927.*

ARMOUR-HANNAY, Samuel Beveridge; Sheriff-Substitute of Fifeshire since 1898; *b* 4 March 1856; *s* of John Armour of Kirktonfield, Renfrewshire; *m* 1899, Robina Anne Marjory, *o d* of Colonel George Hannay of Kingsmuir and Dalgairn, Fifeshire; assumed name of Hannay on wife succeeding to the estate of Kingsmuir. *Educ:* Madras College, St Andrews; Edinburgh Academy and University (MA 1877). Passed for Scottish Bar, 1880; appointed Sheriff-Substitute of Caithness, Orkney, and Zetland, 1887. *Publication:* Valuation of Property for Rating in Scotland, 1892 (Second Edition, 1912). *Recreations:* golf, shooting, yachting. *Address:* Dalgairn, Cupar, Fife. *Died 30 March 1919.*

ARMSTRONG, Sir Andrew Harvey, 3rd Bt, *cr* 1841; *b* 23 May 1866; *s* of 2nd Bt and Alice, *d* of W. W. Fisher; *S* father 1899. Formerly Capt. 3rd Batt. Leinster Regt (Royal Canadians); served with Imperial Yeomanry in South Africa; joined 5th Service Batt. The Connaught Rangers, 19 Sept. 1914. *Heir:* *b* Nesbitt William Armstrong [*b* 3 July 1875; *m* 1910, Clarice Amy, *d* of John Carter Hodgkinson, Maryborough, Victoria, Australia; one *s* one *d*]. *Address:* Gallen Priory, Ferbane, King's County. *Died 3 June 1922.*

ARMSTRONG, Edmund Clarence Richard, MRIA; FSA; Keeper of Irish Antiquities Collections, National Museum, Dublin, since 1914; *b* 1879; *e s* of Captain Andrew Charles Armstrong, 2nd Queen's and 3rd Batt. Leinster Regiment, an Inspector of Factories, 3rd *s* of Sir Andrew Armstrong, 1st Bt, of Gallen Priory, and Alice Maria, *y d* of Sir T. W. C. Murdoch, KCMG, sometime Chief Secretary for Canada; *m* 1906, Mary Frances, 2nd *d* of late Sir Francis R. Cruise, MD, DL; two *s* one *d*. For a short time in business, afterwards temporary assistant to Mr George Coffey, Keeper of Irish Antiquities, in the National Museum, Dublin; permanent Assistant for Irish Antiquities, 1907; an Honorary General Secretary, Royal Society of Antiquaries of Ireland, 1909–15; Vice-President, 1915–19, and since 1921; Honorary Treasurer, 1919–21; Margaret Stokes Lecturer, Alexandra College, 1921; External Examiner in Archaeology, National University of Ireland, 1922; inherited property in Galway and Limerick, which was sold under the Wyndham Act. *Publications:* numerous papers on Irish Archaeological subjects in Proceedings Royal Irish Academy, and Journal Royal Society of Antiquaries of Ireland, etc. *Address:* 73 Park Avenue, Sydney Parade, Dublin. *Club:* Kildare Street, Dublin. *Died 29 March 1923.*

ARMSTRONG, Edward, MA; FBA 1905; Fellow, Queen's College, Oxford; Hon. Fellow of Exeter College; *b* 3 March 1846; *s* of John Armstrong, DD, first Bishop of Grahamstown, South Africa, and Frances Whitmore; *m* 1st, Mabel (*d* 1920), *d* of J. W. Watson, DSc; 2nd, 1921, Geraldine Prynne, 3rd *d* of late Rev. J. A. Harriss. *Educ:* Grahamstown; Bradfield; Exeter College, Oxford (scholar); first, Class. Mods, 1866; first, Final Lit.Hum., 1869. Fellow, Queen's College, 1869; tutor, 1870; assistant master Rugby School, 1871–73; at Queen's College from 1875 (Bursar, 1878–1911); Pro Provost, 1911–22; Warden of Bradfield College, 1910–25; Lecturer to the University in Foreign History, 1902–4; for the Dante sexcentenary, 1921; Serena Medal, British Academy, 1926. *Publications:* Elisabeth Farnese; The French Wars of Religion; Lorenzo de' Medici; The Emperor Charles V, 2 vols; contributed to Cambridge Modern History, Edinburgh Quarterly, Church Quarterly, English Historical Reviews, History, and other periodicals. *Recreations:* gardening, travelling. *Address:* Queen's College and The Red House, Oxford. *T:* Oxford 1158. *M:* FC 8005. *Club:* Athenæum.

Died 14 April 1928.

ARMSTRONG, Maj.-Gen. Edward Francis Hunter; *b* 1834; *m* 1st, Matilda, *d* of late Major James Fitzgerald, Indian Army; 2nd, Florence (*d* 1890), *d* of late Henry Colbeck, Indian Army. Late 11th Madras Native Infantry and Deputy Commissioner, Mysore. *Address:* 31 Clarendon Villas, Hove. *Died 2 Jan. 1917.*

ARMSTRONG, F. A. W. T., RBA 1895; RWA; landscape painter; *b* Malmesbury, 15 Feb. 1849; *e s* of Francis Armstrong of Cannobie, Dumfriesshire, and Elizabeth Ann Leonard of Stonehill, Malmesbury, Wiltshire. *Educ:* privately. Exhibitor at Paris (Salon), Berlin, Düsseldorf, etc. *Publications:* assisted in illustrating the Edition de Luxe of Mr Blackmore's Lorna Doone; also Art Journal, Portfolio, etc. *Recreation:* fly fishing. *Address:* 42 St Michael's Hill, Bristol. *Died 1 Dec. 1920.*

ARMSTRONG, Francis Edwin, MSc, AMICE; Mining Engineer; Professor of Mining at the University of Sheffield since 1913; *b* Nottingham, 1879; *s* of late Rev. R. A. Armstrong, Liverpool; unmarried. *Educ:* Giggleswick Grammar School; University College, Liverpool. Articled pupil to Arnold Lupton, MICE, at Tinsley Park Colliery, Sheffield; held several positions as assistant at Midland Collieries; Engineer to the Askern Coal and Iron Co., Ltd, Doncaster, 1910–13; Head of Labour and Wages Section, Coal Mines Dept, Board of Trade, 1917–18; Member of Home Office Committee on Miners' Safety Lamps, 1919. *Address:* 40 Elmore Road, Sheffield. *T:* 4705 Central. *M:* LU 6695.

Died 28 Oct. 1921.

ARMSTRONG, Rev. James; Incumbent of Castle Rock since 1868; Canon of Derry since 1900. *Educ:* Trinity Coll., Dublin. Ordained 1865. *Address:* Castle Rock, Co. Derry.

Died 30 April 1928.

ARMSTRONG, Surgeon-Dentist John Alexander, CMG 1918; CBE 1919; *b* 26 Nov. 1862; *s* of Thomas Armstrong and Jane Beatty; *m* 1890, Ida G. Spittal (*d* 1904); one *s*. *Educ:* Ottawa Collegiate Institute, Ottawa; Royal College of Dental Surgeons and Toronto University, Toronto. Captain, 43rd DCOR, Canada; Chairman Ottawa Public School Board; Member of Ottawa, Canada, Public School Board for ten years; organised the Canadian Army Dental Corps in May 1915, and brought the Corps overseas, June 1915; first Army Dental Corps ever organised; Director of Dental Services, Overseas Military Forces of Canada, 1915–19. *Publications:* several papers at Dental Conventions and in Dental Magazines. *Recreations:* member of several athletic, rowing, and football clubs in Canada; Chairman 43rd DCOR Rifle Association, 1907–14. *Address:* 102 James Street, Ottawa, Canada. *T:* Queen 7940. *Clubs:* Overseas Officers, National Liberal, Sports; Laurentian, Wellington, Canadian, Ottawa.

Died 2 Nov. 1928.

ARMSTRONG, Thomas Mandeville Emerson; Barrister-at-Law, Lincoln's Inn; *b* 1869; 4th *s* of late Edward Armstrong and Emma Saunderson of Tanderagee, Co. Armagh; *m* 1904, Jean, *d* of Robert M. Young, JP, Rathvarna, Belfast, and *g d* of Rt Hon. Robert Young, PC; four *s* two *d*. President, Insurance Institute of London, 1916; General Manager Commercial Union Assurance Co. since 1920; formerly Manager Ocean Accident Insurance Company Ltd. *Address:* Limpsfield, Surrey. *T:* Oxted 5. *Clubs:* Union; Addington and Littlestone Golf. *Died 21 Aug. 1922.*

ARMSTRONG, Sir Walter, Kt 1899; JP; Hon. RHA; BA Oxon; *b* Roxburghshire, 7 Feb. 1850; *s* of Walter Armstrong, of Ennismore Gardens; *m* 1873, Emily Rose, *d* of C. C. Ferard, JP, of Ascot Place, Berks; two *s* three *d*. *Educ:* Harrow; Exeter Coll., Oxford. Art critic on staffs of Pall Mall Gazette, St James's Gazette, Manchester Guardian, Guardian, Manchester Examiner, 1880–92; Director National Gallery of Ireland, 1892–1914. *Publications:* Life of Alfred Stevens; Life of Peter de Wint; Life of Thos Gainsborough; Life of Velazquez; Notes on the Nat. Gallery; Scottish Painters; co-editor of Bryan's Dictionary of Painters; Gainsborough and his Place in English Art, 1898; Sir Joshua Reynolds, 1900; J. M. W. Turner, 1901; Sir Henry Raeburn, 1901; Art in Great Britain and Ireland, 1909; Life of Sir Thos Lawrence, 1913. *Recreations:* photography, golf, etc. *Address:* 63 Carlisle Mansions, SW. *T:* Victoria 2206. *Clubs:* Junior Athenæum, Burlington Fine Arts, Cosmopolitan.

Died 8 Aug. 1918.

ARMYTAGE, Sir George John, 6th Bt, *cr* 1738; DL; FSA; High Sheriff of Yorkshire, 1907–8; Chairman, Lancashire and Yorkshire Railway; *b* 26 April 1842; *s* of 5th Bt and Eliza Matilda Mary, *d* of Sir Joseph Radcliffe, Bt, Rudding Park, Yorks; *S* father 1899; *m* 1st, 1871, Ellen (*d* 1890), *d* of Rev. A. Fawkes of Farnley Hall, Yorkshire; two *s* one *d*; 2nd, 1893, Mary Georgiana, *d* of late Henry A. Littledale, of Bolton Hall, Yorkshire. Chairman of Council and one of founders of Harleian Society. Owned about 3,500 acres. *Publications:* edited several volumes of Harleian Society's publications. *Heir:* *s* Brig.-Gen. George Ayscough Armytage [*b* 2 March 1872; *m* 1892, Aimée, *d* of Sir L. M. Swinnerton-Pilkington, 11th Bt; two *s* one *d*. *Club:* Carlton]. *Recreations:* shooting, golf. *Address:* Kirklees Park, Brighouse, Yorks; 27 Cambridge Square, W. *TA:* Armytage, Brighouse; Armytage, Edge, London. *T:* Brighouse 16; Paddington 1391. *Club:* Windham. *Died 8 Nov. 1918.*

ARNAUD, Emile; President of the Ligue Internationale de la Paix et de la Liberté since 1891; Vice-Président du Bureau international permanent de la Paix, de Berne; *b* La Chape (Isère), France, 1864. Active speaker and writer on behalf of Peace; editor of Les États-Unis d'Europe; President of the 12th International Peace Congress, Rouen, 1903. Attended the series of Congresses which began in 1889. Notaire, Président de la Chambre des Notaires de Luzarches, plusieurs fois Vice-Président du Congrès des Notaires de France, Vice-Président de la Caisse de Retraites des Notaires de France et d'Algérie; Capitaine Commandant une Compagnie du Génie pendant la guerre, 1914–17. *Address:* Luzarches, Seine et Oise, France. *T:* 5.

Died 11 Dec. 1921.

ARNHEIM, Edward Henry Silberstein Von, ISO 1911; late Deputy Master, Royal Mint, Sydney. *Club:* Union, Sydney.

Died 25 Nov. 1925.

ARNOLD, Edward Vernon, LittD; late Fellow of Trinity College, Cambridge; Professor of Latin at the University College of North Wales, 1884–1924; *b* 18 July 1857; *s* of late Rev. C. M. Arnold, MA, Vicar of St Mark's, South Norwood; *m* 1894, Violet, *d* of late Lieut-Col R. D. Osborn; three *s* two *d*. *Educ:* Westminster School; Trinity College, Cambridge; University of Tübingen. 1st class Classical and Mathematical Triposes, 1879. *Publications:* Historical Vedic Grammar, 1897; Forum Latinum, a first Latin reading-book, 1899; The Rigveda, in D. Nutt's Popular Studies in Folk-lore and Mythology, 1900; Vedic Metre, 1905; Aeneae facts, a Stepping-stone to Virgil, 1907; Cothurnulus, 1907; Basis Latina, 1908; Roman Stoicism, 1910; (with J. W. E. Pearce) Cornelia, 1912; War-Time Lectures, 1916; The Ferment of Revolution, 1917. *Address:* Bryn Seiriol, Bangor.

Died 19 Sept. 1926.

ARNOLD, George Frederick, CIE 1912; ICS; Deputy Commissioner, 1st grade, Burma; *s* of Dr G. B. Arnold, MusDoc (Oxon), of the Close, Winchester; unmarried. *Educ:* Merchant Taylors' School; Queen's College, Oxford (open scholarship); 2nd class in Moderations and 1st class in Literæ Humaniores, 1892. Entered Indian Civil Service, 1893; was Assistant Secretary and Under Revenue Secretary to Government of Burma, Sessions Judge in

Burma, and officiating Deputy Secretary to Government of India Legislative Department, 1906; Revenue Secretary to the Government of Burma, 1906-11; Member of the Burma Legislative Council, 1909-11. *Publication:* Psychology applied to Legal Evidence and other Constructions of Law. *Recreation:* lawn tennis (champion of Burma, 1910 and 1911). *Address:* 47 Southgate Street, Winchester. *Clubs:* East India United Service; United Service, Simla; Pegu, Rangoon.

Died 3 April 1917.

ARNOLD, Henry Fraser James Coape-; Commissioner of Land Tax, Warwickshire; MA and member of the Senate of the University of Cambridge; *b* 27 Feb. 1846; *s* of James Coape, JP, of Mirables, Isle of Wight, and Georgeana, *o d* and *heiress* of G. H. Arnold, JP, of Ashby St Ledgers, Northamptonshire, and Wolvey Hall, Warwickshire; *m* Mary G., *e d* of Rev. C. J. Cummings, Rector of Cheadle, Cheshire; five *s* five *d*. *Educ:* St John's College, Cambridge. A co-heir of the abeyant Baronies of de Morley, *cr* 1299; Marshal, 1309; and Monteagle, 1514. *Address:* Wolvey Hall, near Hinckley. *TA:* Wolvey Hall, Bulkington.

Died July 1923.

ARNOLD, Rev. Henry James Lawes, MA; Rector of North Creake since 1911; Hon. Canon of Norwich; *b* 20 May 1854; *s* of Walter Brown Arnold; *m* 1892, Nora, *d* of Charles Hope of Shorestone Hall, Northumberland. *Educ:* Pembroke College, Cambridge. Mathematical Honours, 1877; Assistant Master at Walton Lodge School; ordained to Tarporley, Cheshire, 1881; curate in charge St James', Yarmouth, 1887-88; Vicar of Dereham, 1888-1911. *Recreations:* rowed in College Boat and played in College Eleven. *Address:* North Creake Rectory, Fakenham. *Club:* Alpine.

Died 13 June 1928.

ARRHENIUS, Professor Svante August, Dr phil. juris et med.; Director of the Physico-Chemical Department of the Nobel Institute since 1905; *b* Wijk, near Upsala, Sweden, 19 Feb. 1859; *s* of the engineer Svante Gustaf Arrhenius and Carolina Thunberg; *m* 1st, 1894, Sophia, *d* of Colonel-Lieutenant Carl Rudbeck; 2nd, 1905, Maria, *d* of Curate Johansson; two *s* two *d*. *Educ:* Cathedral School and University, Upsala. Dr phil. at Upsala University, 1884; Privatdocent, 1884; Teacher of Physics, University, Stockholm, 1891; Professor of Physics at the same University, 1895; Rector, 1897-1902; Director of the Nobel Institute, subordinate to the Academy of Sciences, 1905; Davy Medal, 1902; Nobel Prize, 1903; Faraday Medal, 1914; Dr med. hon. causa, Heidelberg, 1903; Groningen, 1914; Dr sc. hon. causa, Oslo, 1904, Oxford and Cambridge, 1908; Dr ph. hon. causa, Leipzig, 1909; Hon. LLD, Birmingham, 1913; Hon. Member of Chemical and of Physical Societies of London, of Royal Society and Royal Institution; Member of a great number of academies and learned societies in Europe and America; originator of the theory of electrolytic dissociation, 1884 and 1887, whereby the chemical processes are explained as dependent on the electric conductivity of the reacting solutions. *Publications:* Lehrbuch d. kosm. Physik, 1908; Electrochemistry, trans. by M'Crae, 1901; Immunochemistry, 1906; Theories of Chemistry, 1906; Worlds in the Making, 1908; Life of the Universe, 1909; Quantitative Laws in Biological Chemistry, 1915; The Destinies of the Stars, 1918; Chemistry and Modern Life, 1919; all originally written in Swedish, and translated into different languages. *Address:* Nobel Institute, Experimentalfältet, near Stockholm.

Died 2 Oct. 1927.

ARTHUR, Sir Allan, Kt 1900; merchant, Calcutta; member of the Viceroy's Legislative Council, 1898-1902; *b* 3 April 1857; *s* of Allan Arthur, of Henry Monteith & Co., Glasgow, and Margaret Hamilton Thomson, Hawick; unmarried. *Educ:* Glasgow Academy; Merchiston Castle School, Edinburgh. President of the Bengal Chamber of Commerce, 1894-95, 1896-97, part of 1898, 1899-1900; Sheriff of Calcutta, 1898. *Recreations:* fishing, shooting, polo, golf. *Clubs:* Oriental; Western, Glasgow; Bengal, Calcutta.

Died 9 Oct. 1923.

ARTSIBASHEV, Michel Petrovitch; *b* 18 Oct. 1878; his great-grandfather on the maternal side was Kosciusko. *Educ:* grammar school; school of art. *Publications:* Millionen und andere Novellen; Sanine, 1909; Tales of the Revolution, 1917; Jealousy, 1914; The Millionaire, 1915; Breaking-Point, 1915; War, 1918.

Died 3 March 1927.

ARUNACHALAM, Sir Ponnambalam, Kt 1914; JP; *b* Colombo, Ceylon, 14 Sept. 1853; 3rd *s* of A. Ponnambalam, Mudaliyar of the King's Gate, and Sellachchi, *d* of A. Coomara Swamy, Mudaliyar of the King's Gate and MLC; *nephew* of Sir Mutu Coomara Swamy, MLC; *m* Svarnam, *d* of S. Namasivayam, Mudaliyar; two *s* four *d*.

Educ: Colombo Academy (later Royal College); Christ's Coll., Cambridge (Foundation Scholar and Ceylon Government Scholar); BA 1875; MA 1879. Called to Bar, Lincoln's Inn, 1875; entered Ceylon Civil Service, 1875; held various judicial and administrative offices; for many years Registrar-General of Ceylon; received thanks of the Government for reorganising the Registrar-General's Department and for organising and reporting on Ceylon Decennial Census of 1901; Victoria Diamond Jubilee Gold Medal, 1897; MLC 1906-13; member of the Executive Council, Jan. 1912; retired from Civil Service, July 1913; served on various Ceylon Commissions; author of various Consolidating Statutes subseq. in force; President of the Royal Asiatic Society (Ceylon Branch) since 1917; President of the Ceylon University Association, 1906-13, of the Ceylon Social Service League, 1915-17, Ceylon Reform League, 1917-19, Ceylon Saiva Paripalana Sabha and Sen Tamil Paripalana Sabha (societies for the advancement of the Hindu religion and of Tamil Literature); President of the Ceylon National Congress, 1919-20, and of the Ceylon Workers' Federation, 1920-21; Vice-President, Ceylon Agricultural Society, 1904-21; member of various learned societies in England, France, and Germany. *Publications:* Codification of the Ceylon Civil Law; Decennial Census of Ceylon, 1901; Ceylon Vital Statistics; Ceylon History and Antiquities; Indian Religions and Philosophies. *Recreations:* literature, agriculture. *Address:* Ponklar, Colombo; Brindabana, Waga, Kelani Valley; Tillai, Walahapitiya, Chilaw—all in Ceylon.

Died Feb. 1924.

ARUNDELL OF WARDOUR, 14th Baron, *cr* 1605; **Edgar Clifford Arundell;** Count of the Holy Roman Empire, 1595; *b* 20 Dec. 1859; *S* cousin 1907; descended in the fifth generation from the 6th Baron; *m* 1895, Ellen, *widow* of Melbourne Evans. Conservative. Family has never ceased to be Roman Catholic since mediæval times. *Property:* about 500 acres sold since the last "Domesday" Survey. Cornish property sold, with reservation of Manors of Lanherne, Treloy, Tresithney, and Bossuen. A picture gallery; but several valuable pictures sold, and gone out of the country, since passing of Finance Act of 1894; mediæval deeds and MSS; the old castle a ruin. *Heir:* *b* Gerald Arthur Arundell, *b* 11 Dec. 1861. *Address:* Wardour Castle, Tisbury, Wiltshire.

Died 8 Dec. 1921.

ARUR SINGH, Sir Sardar Bahadur Sardar, KCIE 1921 (CIE 1913); Member Amritsar Municipality, Vice-Chairman Amritsar District Board; Hon. Magistrate, 1st Class, and Civil Judge; *b* 25 April 1863; *s* of late Sardar Harnam Singh; *m* four times; two *s* one *d*. Manager, Golden Temple, Amritsar, 18 years. *Address:* Naushera Nangli, Amritsar, Punjab.

Died 21 March 1926.

ASCROFT, Sir William, Kt 1908; JP; County Borough of Preston and County of Westmorland; Solicitor; Chairman of the Harris Orphanage, Preston; *b* Preston, 24 Aug. 1832; *e s* of Robert Ascroft of Preston, Solicitor, and Town Clerk of Preston, and Isabella Noble; *m* 1858, Christiana (*d* 1907), *d* of Charles Walker of Whitley Lower, Yorkshire, and Christiana Fawell; two *s* four *d*. *Educ:* The Grammar School, Preston. Admitted a Solicitor, 1855; since practised at Preston in partnership with his father, afterwards with his brother, Alfred Edward Ascroft, JP, and later with his sons, Robert Walker Ascroft, MA, BCL, JP, and William Fawell Ascroft, MA. *Recreations:* reading, enjoyment of the Lake District scenery. *Address:* Overleigh House, Preston. *T:* 579 Preston; The Wyke, Grasmere. *T:* 7 Grasmere. *Clubs:* Winckley, Preston; Westmorland County, Kendal.

Died 29 Sept. 1916.

ASH, Major William Claudius Casson, DSO 1916; 1st Battalion Middlesex Regiment; Temp. Lieut-Colonel 23rd Battalion; *b* 6 Feb. 1870; *e s* of W. H. Ash, of 51 Hamilton Terrace, NW, and of Heathfield, Sussex; *m* 1894, Edith Learoyd, 2nd *d* of late Edward W. Barnett, Sketty Oak, Worcestershire; two *d*. *Educ:* Westminster School. Played cricket for Westminster School; entered Army, 1892; Captain, 1900; Adjt Middlesex Regiment, 1902-7; Major, 1909; served South African War (Queen's medal 3 clasps); European War, 1914-16 (despatches, DSO). *Recreations:* cricket, rackets, music. *Address:* Rock House, Aldershot. *Clubs:* Army and Navy, MCC; Union, Malta.

Died 29 Sept. 1916.

ASHBROOK, 8th Viscount, *cr* 1751; **Robert Thomas Flower;** Baron of Castle Durrow, 1773; *b* 1 April 1836; 3rd *s* of 5th, and *b* of 6th Viscount Ashbrook; *S* brother 1906; *m* 1866, Gertrude Sophia (*d* 1911), *y d* of Rev. S. Hamilton; two *s* three *d*. Formerly Hon. Lieut-Col 4th Batt. Prince of Wales's Leinster Regt (Royal Canadians). Owned about 23,000 acres. *Heir:* *s* Hon. Llowarch Robert Flower, *b* 9 July 1870. *Address:* Castle Durrow, Co. Kilkenny.

Died 9 March 1919.

ASHBURNER, Lt-Col Lionel Forbes, DSO 1900; MVO; 1st Battalion Royal Fusiliers; Brig.-Major, Nasirabad, 1909–14; b 18 Sept. 1874; m 1907, Ethel Hermione, 2nd d of Sir Charles Bayley. Educ: Cheltenham College. Joined Durham Light Infantry 1895; served South Africa (despatches, DSO); European War, 1914–15 (despatches five times, Bt Lt-Col). Club: Army and Navy.

Died 19 Jan. 1923.

ASHBURNHAM, 6th Earl of, cr 1730; **Thomas Ashburnham;** Baron of Ashburnham, 1689; Viscount St Asaph, 1730; late 7th Hussars; b 8 April 1855; 5th s of 4th Earl of Ashburnham and Katherine Charlotte, d of George Baillie of Jerviswood, Co. Lanark; S brother 1913; m 1903, Maria Elizabeth, 2nd d of W. H. Anderson, Fredericton, NB. Knight of the Medjidie; was ADC to Lord-Lieut of Ireland; served Egypt, 1882; retired, 1889; extra ADC to Lords Carnarvon and Aberdeen, Viceroys of Ireland. Owned about 24,000 acres. Heir: none. Address: Ashburnham Place, Battle; Barking Hall, Needham Market, Suffolk; Pembrey, Carmarthenshire.

Died 12 May 1924 (ext).

ASHBURNHAM, Sir Cromer, KCB 1882 (CB 1881); Colonel Commandant KRRC; b Guestling, Sussex, 13 Sept. 1831; s of Rev. Sir John Ashburnham, 7th Bt, of Broomham, Sussex, Chancellor and Prebendary of Chichester; m 1864, Urith, d of Capt. G. B. Martin, CB, RN; one s two d (and one s decd). Served in Mutiny Campaign, 1857–58, medal and clasp; in Afghanistan Campaign, 1878–80, medal and clasp; commanded 2nd Batt. Rifles; commanded 3rd Batt. Rifles throughout Boer War, 1881; ADC to Queen Victoria; commanded 3rd Batt. Rifles in Egyptian Campaign, 1882; commanded a brigade, Tel-el-Kebir; medal and clasp, bronze star and 3rd class of the Medjidie; commanded 3rd Batt. Rifles in campaign in Eastern Soudan, 1884, 2 clasps; appointed Governor of Suakim, 1884. Recreation: shooting. Address: 165 Coleherne Court, SW.

Died 25 Feb. 1917.

ASHBY-STERRY, Joseph; b London; o s of late Henry Sterry, Moss Grange, Sydenham Hill; unmarried. Educ: privately. First ambition to be a painter; at 19 he was painting life-size oil portraits and drawing on the wood for Punch and other papers; drifted into journalism, and eventually abandoned the pencil for the pen; was the versatile Lazy Minstrel of Punch and at one time a constant contributor to its pages; originated the popular Bystander column in the Graphic, and wrote it over eighteen years (till 1909); art-critic Daily Graphic, 1891–1907. Publications: Shuttlecock Papers, Tiny Travels, Boudoir Ballads, Snailway Guides, Cucumber Chronicles, The Lazy Minstrel (a book of perpetual new editions), Nutshell Novels, A Naughty Girl, A Tale of the Thames, The Bystander, or Leaves for the Lazy (1900), and the popular edition of A Tale of the Thames, with much additional matter and numerous fresh Sketches in Song (1903); The River Rhymer, 1913. Recreations: rowing or sailing in little dinghey "The Shuttlecock" on the Thames, which stream he closely studied from his childhood, and was said to know every inch of it from the source in Trewsbury Mead to the Buoy at the Nore. His knowledge of London "extensive and peculiar", and one of his favourite recreations was the minute explorations that he made of all parts of it, old and new. Address: 8 St Martin's Place, Trafalgar Square. Clubs: Garrick, Beefsteak.

Died 1 June 1917.

ASHCOMBE, 1st Baron, cr 1892; **George Cubitt,** PC 1880; b 4 June 1828; m 1853, Laura (d 1904), d of Rev. James Joyce, Vicar of Dorking; one s five d (and two s one d decd). Educ: Trinity Coll., Camb. (MA 1854). MP (C) W Surrey, 1860–85; Mid-Surrey, 1885–92; 2nd Church Estates Commissioner, 1874–79; a member of the Council of Selwyn College; and Hon. Col 2nd VB Queen's Royal West Surrey Regiment. Heir: y surv. s Hon. Henry Cubitt, b 14 March 1867. Address: 17 Prince's Gate, SW; Fallapit, East Allington, S Devon. Club: Carlton.

Died 26 Feb. 1917.

ASHDOWN, Sir George Henry, KBE 1920 (CBE 1918); ISO 1915; Legion of Honour, 1919; DSO (USA), 1919; Director of Stores, Admiralty, 1918–20; b 1857; m 1884, Edith, d of William Haines. Address: Waratah, Effingham Road, Surbiton.

Died 3 Dec. 1924.

ASHFORD, Hon. William George; Minister for Lands and Forests, New South Wales, 1915–20; b 9 Aug. 1874; m 1904; four s. Educ: State Public Schools. Engaged all life in rural pursuits; elected State Parliament, 1910; Minister for Agriculture, 1914. Recreations: cricket, rifle-shooting, tennis. Address: Ruby Street, Mosman, New South Wales.

Died 24 March 1925.

ASHLEY, Lt-Col Frank, CBE 1918; British Red Cross Commissioner Malta (Croix de Guerre); b 1870; m 1903, Cecilia, d of F. C. Walker Educ: Clifton College.

Died 16 Oct. 1923

ASHLEY, Sir William (James), Kt 1917; PhD, MA, MCom; b London, 25 Feb. 1860; m 1888, Margaret (d 1922), d of Geo. Birkbeck Hill, DCL; one s two d. Educ: St Olave's School, Southwark; History Scholar of Balliol College, Oxford; 1st class History, 1881; Lothian prize, 1882. Fellow and Lecturer of Lincoln College, Oxford 1885–88; Professor of Political Economy, Toronto University 1888–92; Professor of Economic History, Harvard, 1892–1901 Professor of Commerce, Birmingham University, 1901–25, subseq Emeritus Professor; Vice Principal, 1918–25; a Vice-President Royal Economic Society; Corresponding Mem. Mass Hist. Society and Assoc. Acad. Roy. Belg.; Examiner in History, Economics, or Commerce, 1899–1920, in the Universities of Cambridge, London Durham, Wales, and Ireland; Pres. Econ. Section Brit. Assoc. 1907 1924; President Econ. Hist. Section of International Historical Congress, 1913; Ball Lecturer at Oxford, 1922; Member Committee on Coal Prices, 1915; Huth Jackson Committee, 1916; Food Prices Committee, 1917; Consumers' Council, 1918; Cost of Living Committee, 1918; Royal Commission on Agriculture, 1919 Glassware Committee, 1921; Agricultural Tribunal, 1923; Tariff Advisory Committee, 1923; Committee on Industry and Trade, 1924 Publications: Introduction to English Economic History and Theory pt i The Middle Ages, 1888; pt ii The End of the Middle Ages, 1893 (trans. into German, French, and Japanese); Surveys, Historic and Economic, 1900; Adjustment of Wages, 1903; The Tariff Problem 1903 (4th edn enlarged, 1920); Progress of the German Working Classes, 1904 (trans. into German); The Rise in Prices, 1912 (trans into German and Swedish); Gold and Prices, 1912; Economic Organisation of England, 1914 (trans. into French); The Christian Outlook, 1925; (ed) Economic Classics, and translated therein Turgot Reflections, and Schmoller, Mercantile System; (ed) British Industries 1903, British Dominions, 1911, and Mill's Political Economy, 1909 joint author of Report of Unionist Social Reform Committee or Industrial Unrest, 1914. Address: 3 St Stephen's Road, Canterbury Club: Authors'.

Died 23 July 1927

ASHLIN, George C., RHA, FRIBA; ex-President, Royal Institute of Architects of Ireland; b Carrigrenane House, County Cork, 1837 3rd s of J. M. Ashlin, JP, Rush Hill, Surrey; m d of late Augustus Welby Pugin; one d. Educ: College of St Servais, Liège; Oscott College, near Birmingham; student of Royal Academy, London, 1858; pupil of the late E. Welby Pugin, 1856–60. Practised as an architect in Ireland in partnership with the late E. W. Pugin, 1860–70, afterward independently; principal buildings—SS Peter and Paul's Church Cork, Queenstown Cathedral, and about 50 other churches in Ireland gained many competitions, including Portrane Asylum, which cost about £300,000. Recreations: sketching, cycling, golf. Address: St George's, Killiney, Co. Dublin; 7 Dawson Street, Dublin. Club Stephen's Green, Dublin.

Died 10 Dec. 1922

ASHMAN, Sir Frederick Herbert, 2nd Bt, cr 1907; b 16 Jan. 1875 s of Sir Herbert Ashman, 1st Bt and Lizzie, d of Frederick George Lorenzen; S father 1914; m 1898, Alice Ethel, d of late William Ansel Todd, JP, Portishead, Somersetshire. Heir: none. Address: Clarence Croft, Weston-super-Mare, Somerset.

Died 22 Dec. 1916

ASHTON, Arthur Jacob, KC 1906; Judge of Appeal, Isle of Man since 1921; b 4 Feb. 1855; e s of late Walter Ashton of Warrington Lancashire; m 1890, Emma, d of Dr Thomas Burnie of Nottingham one s two d. Educ: Manchester Grammar School; Balliol College Oxford (Classical Scholar; first class in Classical Moderations and Final Schools; BA 1878). Called to Bar, Inner Temple, 1881; Bencher 1914; Recorder of Manchester, 1914. Address: 43 Montagu Square W1. T: Paddington 3873; 2 Mitre Court Buildings, Temple, EC T: City 99; Lavender Walk, Rye, Sussex. Clubs: Garrick, Reform

Died 23 March 1925

ASHTON, Sir Ralph Percy, Kt 1911; Major (retired); partner, Kilburn Brown & Co., London, and Kilburn & Co., Calcutta; b Darwen, 1860 s of late Ralph Shorrock Ashton, JP; m 1900, Emma, d of late Robert Francis Rendell, of Kingston House, Staverton; one s. Educ Uppingham; Owens College. Additional Member of Legislative Council of India, 1901–2; has been Trustee for Port of Calcutta, for Victoria Memorial of India, and for Indian Museum; President Mining and Geological Institute of India, 1911. Address: Beechwood, Reigate T: 360; Orient House, New Broad Street, EC. T: City 20.

Died 28 Jan. 1921

SHTON, Rt. Hon. Thomas, PC 1917; JP City of Manchester; Miners' General Secretary, 1881–1918; *b* Openshaw, Manchester, 1844; father a coalminer and mother daughter of a miner; *m* 1865; two *s* four *d. Educ:* self-educated. Commenced working in the pit at an early age; Branch Secretary for the Bradford and Clayton Miners, 1865; left the pit to commence check-weighing on the pit bank, 1873; Secretary Ashton-under-Lyne and Oldham Miners' Association, 1879; General Secretary of the Lancashire and Cheshire Miners' Federation, 1881; General Secretary of the Miners' Federation of Great Britain, 1889–1919; Joint Secretary of the International Miners' Federation, 1890–1902; then General Secretary; Joint Secretary with Sir Thomas Ratcliffe Ellis of the Conciliation Board for the English and North Wales Federated Area since its formation, 1894. *Address:* Almas House, Droylsden Road, Droylsden, Manchester.

Died 13 Oct. 1927.

SHWORTH, Philip Arthur, LLD, MA; *b* 1853; *e s* of late Rev. John A. Ashworth, MA, Rector of Didcot, Berks; *m* 1879, Emma, Baroness von Estorff. *Educ:* Sherborne School; New College, Oxford (Honours Classics and Law, 1875); Universities of Bonn and Leipzig (LLD with honours, University of Würzburg); barrister-at-law, Inner Temple, 1881; Advocate of the Cyprus Courts. *Publications:* Editor of 5th, 6th, and 7th editions of Taswell Langmead's Constitutional History of England; translator, from the German, of Rudolph von Gneist's History of the English Constitution; Leopold von Ranke's History of the Latin and Teutonic Nations; Baron von der Goltz's Nation in Arms; Rudolph von Ihering's Battle for Right; author of Das Witthum (Dower) im englischen Recht; contributor of various articles to the Encyclopædia Britannica (10th and 11th editions). *Recreations:* walking, foreign travel. *Died Nov. 1921.*

SKEW, Claude Arthur Cary; 2nd *s* of late Rev. John Askew, MA; *m* 1900, Alice, *o* surv. *d* of late Col Henry Leake, 44th and 70th Regiments; one *s* one *d. Educ:* Eton; Continent. Took up a literary career after his marriage; wrote only in collaboration with Mrs Askew; their first book, The Shulamite, was published in 1904, and in 1906 this novel was dramatised by Mr Claude Askew and Mr Edward Knoblauch and produced at the Savoy Theatre by Miss Lena Ashwell. *Publications:* The Shulamite; Eve and the Law; The Premier's Daughter; Anna of the Plains; Jennifer Pontefract; The Etonian; The Baxter Family; The Love Stone; Lucy Gort; The Plains of Silence; The Path of Lies; The Orchard Close; Not Proven; Felix Stone; Testimony; The Sporting Chance; The Rod of Justice; The Woman Deborah; Destiny; The Englishwoman; The King's Signature; Through Folly's Mill; Freedom; Trespass; The Stricken Land, 1916; serial and short stories in many periodicals. *Club:* Union.

Died 5 Oct. 1917.

SLETT, Alfred; *b* York, 3 July 1847; *s* of Alfred Aslett, late District Superintendent, Great Northern Railway; *m* 1877, Emma Mary, *o d* of late Edward Francis Rimbault, LLD. *Educ:* York and Peterborough Grammar Schools. In service of Great Northern Railway Company, 1862–81; Manager of the Eastern and Midlands Railway, 1884–91, later the joint Midland and Great Northern; Secretary and General Manager of the Cambrian Railways, 1891–95; Secretary and General Manager of the Furness Railway, 1895–1918. JP Borough of Barrow-in-Furness; ex-Pres. Barrow-in-Furness Chamber of Commerce; PPG Warden for West Lancashire (Masonic). *Recreations:* golf, tennis. *Address:* Stanyan Lodge, Ulverston, Lancs. *TA:* Aslett, Ulverston. *T:* 18 Ulverston. *M:* B 231. *Clubs:* National Liberal; County, Barrow-in-Furness; North Lonsdale, Ulverston. *Died 28 April 1928.*

PINALL, Lt-Col Robert Lowndes, DSO 1900; Commanding 11th Battalion Yorkshire Regiment; late Captain 15th Hussars; *b* 3 March 1869; *s* of late Robert Augustus Aspinall. *Educ:* Eton; Sandhurst. Served as ADC to Sir John French in South Africa, 1900–2 (despatches, Queen's medal, 5 clasps, King's medal, DSO). *Recreations:* coaching, hunting, etc. *Address:* 37 Greycoat Gardens, SW. *Club:* Army and Navy, *Died 2 July 1916.*

QUITH, Raymond; Lieutenant Grenadier Guards, 1915; *b* 6 Nov. 1878; *e s* of Rt Hon. Herbert Asquith and Helen, *d* of Frederick Melland of Rusholme; *m* 1907, Katharine, *d* of Sir John Horner, KCVO, of Mells Park, Somerset; two *d. Educ:* Winchester College (Scholar); Balliol College, Oxford (Scholar). 1st Class Classical Moderations, 1899; 1st Class Lit. Hum. 1901; 1st Class Jurisprudence, 1902; Craven, Ireland, Derby and Eldon Scholarships; President Oxford Union; Fellow of All Souls, 1902. Called to Bar, Inner Temple, 1904; Junior Counsel for Great Britain in North Atlantic Fisheries Arbitration at the Hague, 1911; Junior Counsel to the Inland Revenue, 1914; 2nd Lieut 3/16th County of London Regt, 1914.

Recreations: shooting, golf, tennis. *Address:* 49 Bedford Square, WC. *T:* Museum 783. *Clubs:* Brooks's, Athenæum; Hampshire County; Prince's Tennis. *Died 18 Sept. 1916.*

ASTBURY, Rev. George, MA; Hon. Canon, Birmingham, 1906; *m. Educ:* Christ's College, Cambridge. Curate of Redditch, 1873–84; Perpetual Curate of Smethwick since 1884. *Address:* Old Church Vicarage, Smethwick, Staffs.

Died 23 April 1926.

ASTELL, Captain Somerset Charles Godfrey Fairfax, DSO 1900; JP for Transvaal and Dorset; late North Staffords Regiment; retired; *b* West Lodge, Piddlehinton, Dorset, 15 July 1866; *s* of late Maj.-Gen. Charles Edward Astell and H. D., *d* of F. Spaight, Derry Castle, Tipperary; *g s* of W. Astell, MP; *m* 1903, Fredericka Beatrice, *o c* of James F. Roberts. *Educ:* St Columba College, Dublin. Joined service, 1887; promoted, 1895; Soudan (Dongola), 1896 (two medals—Queen's and Khedive's); South Africa, 1900; Intelligence Officer, Wakkerstroom, April 1901; in charge of Johannesburg Criminal Investigation Department, 6 June 1900–25 Feb. 1901 (DSO); Adjutant 4th North Staffords quarters Lichfield, 1902–3. *Recreations:* hunting, shooting, fishing. *Address:* West Lodge, Dorchester, Dorset. *TA:* Piddlehinton. *Died 24 March 1917.*

ASTLEY, Hubert Delaval, JP; MBOU, FZS; *b* 14 July 1860; 2nd *s* of late Francis Le Strange Astley, Lieut-Col Norfolk Artillery, and late Mrs Frankland Russell Astley of Chequers Court, Bucks; *m* 1895, Constance, *d* of late Sir Vincent Rowland Corbet, 3rd Bt, and *widow* of Sir Richard F. Sutton, 5th Bt; one *s* one *d. Educ:* Eton; Christ Church, Oxford (MA). *Recreations:* ornithology, gardening, sketching, etc. *Publication:* My Birds in Freedom and Captivity. *Address:* Brinsop Court, Herefordshire. *T:* Burghill 10.

Died 26 May 1925.

ASTOR, 1st Viscount, *cr* 1917, of Hever Castle; William Waldorf; Baron, 1916; *b* New York, 31 March 1848; *o c* of John Jacob Astor and Charlotte Augusta Gibbes; *m* 1878, Mary Dahlgren (*d* 1894), *d* of James W. Paul, Philadelphia, Penn, USA; two *s* one *d. Educ:* private tutors. Barrister 1875; Legislature of State of New York, 1878, 1881; United States Minister to Italy, 1882–85. Naturalised British subject, 1899. *Publications:* Valentino, 1886; Sforza, 1889; Pharaoh's Daughter, and Other Stories, 1900. *Heir: s* Hon. Waldorf Astor, *b* 19 May 1879. *Address:* Hever Castle, Kent. *Clubs:* Marlborough, Carlton.

Died 18 Oct. 1919.

ATCHISON, Major Charles Ernest, DSO 1915; Shropshire Light Infantry, attached 3rd Battalion; *b* 12 May 1875. Entered army, 1895; Captain, 1902; served South Africa, 1899–1902 (Queen's medal, 3 clasps, King's medal, 2 clasps); European War, 1914–15 (DSO).

Died 24 Aug. 1917.

ATCHLEY, Chewton, CMG 1911; ISO 1902; *b* 23 Feb. 1850; *s* of Wm Henry Atchley, formerly of HM's Treasury; *m* 1879, Alice, *d* of Henry Whitehouse, of Highgate, N; one *s* one *d. Educ:* privately. Entered Colonial Office, 1868; Librarian, 1880–1915; retired, 1915. *Publications:* Lucas's Historical Geography of the British Colonies, vol. ii, West Indies, second edition; numerous articles in Supplement to Dictionary of National Biography. *Recreations:* interested in most forms of sport except golf and bridge.

Died 29 Dec. 1922.

ATHERTON, Colonel Thomas James, CB 1900; CMG 1918; retired; late 12th (the Prince of Wales's Royal) Lancers; *b* 19 Aug. 1856; *s* of late Sir William Atherton, MP, Attorney-General; *m* 1892, Mabel Louisa (*d* 1919), 3rd *d* of Sir Edward Dean-Paul, 4th Bt; one *s. Educ:* Charterhouse; Cambridge. Entered army, 1880; Captain, 1887; Major, 1893; Lieut-Col 1900; Colonel, 1894. Served South Africa, 1899–1902 (despatches); European War, 1914–18 (CMG). *Club:* Naval and Military. *Died 27 Sept. 1920.*

ATHILL, Charles Harold, MVO 1911; FSA; Clarenceux King of Arms, 1919; *m* Catherine Mildred, *d* of late Ven. B. F. Smith, Archdeacon of Maidstone, and Canon of Canterbury Cathedral. Entered College of Arms as Bluemantle Pursuivant of Arms, 1882; Richmond Herald, 1889–1919; Norroy King of Arms, Jan.–Sept., 1919; Registrar of the College of Arms, 1911–19. *Address:* College of Arms, Queen Victoria Street, EC; The Firs, Sevenoaks, Kent.

Died 27 Nov. 1922.

ATHOLL, 7th Duke of, *cr* 1703; John James Hugh Henry Stewart-Murray, KT; Lord Murray of Tullibardine, 1604; Earl of Tullibardine, Lord Gask and Balquhidder, 1606; Earl of Atholl, 1629;

Marquess of Atholl, Viscount Balquhidder, Lord Balvenie, 1676; Marquess of Tullibardine, Earl of Strathtay, Earl of Strathardle, Viscount Glenalmond, Viscount Glenlyon, 1703—all in the Peerage of Scotland; Lord Strange of Knockyn (England), 1628; Lord Percy (by writ), 1722; Earl Strange and Lord Murray of Stanley, 1768,—all in the Peerage of Great Britain; Lord Glenlyon of Glenlyon (UK); Lord-Lieutenant of county of Perth since 1878; Hon. Colonel 3rd Battalion The Black Watch, 1903; Chancellor of the Order of the Thistle, 1913; *b* 6 Aug. 1840; *o s* of 6th Duke of Atholl, KT and Anne, *d* of Henry Home Drummond; *S* father 1864; *m* 1863, Louisa (*d* 1902), *d* of Sir Thos Moncreiffe, 7th Bt; three *s* three *d. Educ:* Eton. Late Lieut and Capt. Scots Fusilier Guards. Owned about 202,000 acres. *Heir: s* Marquess of Tullibardine. *Address:* Blair Castle, Blair Atholl; Dunkeld, Perthshire; 84 Eaton Place, SW. *T:* Victoria 3282. *Clubs:* Carlton, Marlborough, Guards, Bachelors'.

Died 20 Jan. 1917.

ATKINS, Maj.-Gen. Sir Alban Randell Crofton, KCB 1919 (CB 1917); CMG 1915; *b* 29 June 1870. Entered army, 1889; Captain, 1898; Major, 1905; Bt Lt-Col, 1913; Bt-Col, 1915; Deputy Assistant Director War Office, 1911–14; Assistant Director of Transport, 1914; served Ashanti, 1895–96 (star); Sierra Leone, 1899–1900 (despatches, Bt Major, Queen's medal 2 clasps); European War, 1914–18 (CMG, prom. Maj.-Gen.); retired pay, 1920; 3rd Class Order of White Eagle, Serbia. *Club:* United Service.

Died 29 April 1926.

ATKINSON, Hon. Cecil Thomas, KC 1913; a Puisne Judge of the High Court of Behar and Orissa since 1915; *b* 23 Oct. 1876; *e s* of Baron Atkinson; *m* 1903, Florence, *d* of Godfrey Lovelace Taylor of Grangeville, Co. Wexford; one *s* two *d. Educ:* Trinity College, Dublin, BA. Called to the Irish Bar, 1901. *Recreations:* golf, riding, shooting. *Address:* Patna, India.

Died 20 Nov. 1919.

ATKINSON, Charles Milner, MA, LLM; Stipendiary Magistrate for Leeds since 1894; *b* 6 Nov. 1854; *e s* of late J. G. Atkinson, MD, of The Grange, near Rotherham; *m* Mary Josephine (*d* 1915). *Educ:* Clare Coll., Cambridge (scholar and exhibitioner; Sixteenth Wrangler, 1877; MA, LLM). Barrister, Inner Temple, 1878; went NE Circuit and West Riding Sessions; appointed by Lord Macnaghten to act as his registrar under the Portsea Island Building Society's Act, 1893; JP for West Riding of Yorks. *Publications:* The Magistrate's Practice, 13th edn 1916; Jeremy Bentham: his life and work, 1905; Translation of Dumont's Traités de Législation, 1914. *Address:* 47 Frognal, Hampstead, NW; Town Hall, Leeds. *Club:* New University.

Died 5 Dec. 1920.

ATKINSON, Major Edward William, DSO 1915; 1st Battalion Royal Inniskilling Fusiliers; *b* 12 Aug. 1873; *e s* of Edward Atkinson, Ashfield, Moynalty, Kells, Co. Meath; *m* 1907, Louise H. S., *y d* of John Power Oliver, Indian Medical Service; no *c. Educ:* Trinity College, Dublin; BA. Served in 3rd Batt. Royal Inniskilling Fusiliers (Fermanagh Militia) 1893–96; entered army, 1896; Captain, 1902; Major, 1915; Adjutant, 6th Batt. Notts and Derby Regt, 1906–11; Hythe (Extra), 1898; Signalling Cert. Instructor, 1906; Provisional Course, 1911; served South Africa, 1900–2 (Queen's medal, 3 clasps, King's medal, 2 clasps); in Dardanelles, European War, 1914–15 (despatches, DSO). *Club:* Army and Navy.

Died 27 July 1920.

ATKINSON, Rev. Canon Henry Sadgrove, MA; Surrogate; Canon of York and Prebendary of Givendale since 1903; Rural Dean of Pontefract, 1900–23; Vicar of Darrington since 1892; *o s* of Henry Hayes Atkinson, late of Brixton, Surrey; *m* 8 Nov. 1871, Elizabeth Frances, *e d* of Dr Owen Daly, FRCP, of Hull; three *s* one *d. Educ:* Jesus College, Cambridge. Curate of the Parish Church, Hull, 1870–74; Vicar of Royston, Yorks, 1874–92. *Address:* Darrington Vicarage, Pontefract. *T:* Pontefract 230 Y2. *M:* DN 440.

Died 25 May 1927.

ATKINSON, His Honour Judge Henry Tindal; Judge of Courts; Courts Assessor since 1901; *s* of late Henry Tindal Atkinson, Serjeant-at-Law and County Court Judge; *m* 1873, Marian, *e d* of H. Hale Lewin, of Holly Hill, Wanstead; one *s* four *d.* Called to Bar, Middle Temple, 1865; Bencher, 1896; JP Hertfordshire. *Address:* 3 Clanricarde Gardens, W; 3 Dr Johnson's Buildings, Temple, EC. *Club:* Reform. *Died 14 March 1918.*

ATKINSON, John Mitford, MB (Lond.), DPH Cambridge, etc; *b* 3 Dec. 1856; *s* of late Rev. Samuel Atkinson, MA; *m* 1898, Clara, *e d* of James Eastmond, of Puddington, Devon; two *s. Educ:* Queen's

College, Taunton; London Hospital. Resident Medical Officer, Mary Abbot's Infirmary, Kensington, 1878–85; Superintenden Government Civil Hospital, Hong-Kong; Medical Officer to Sma pox Hospital and the Government Lunatic Asylums, 1887; JP 189 received thanks of Secretary of State for services during plague, 189 Member Executive Council, Hong-Kong, 1903–12; Principal Ci Medical Officer, Hong-Kong, 1897–1912. Fellow Royal Sanita Institute, Colonial Institute and Society of Tropical Medicir *Publications:* contributions to Lancet and British Medical Journ *Recreations:* cricket, tennis, golf. *Address:* 37 Welbeck Street, W. Mayfair 1094; 107 Comeragh Road, West Kensington, W. Hammersmith 797. *Clubs:* Thatched House, Queen's.

Died 23 May 191

ATKINSON, Maj.-Gen. John Richard Breeks; Indian Army; *b* April 1844; 2nd *s* of Rev. John Breeks Atkinson, Rector of Kingstc IoW, and Vicar of Cowes, and Jane Isabella Atkinson; *m* 188 Margaret Augusta, *d* of J. L. Turner and Mrs Turner, Coombe Hou Backwell, Somerset. Went to India from Addiscombe College, 18 retired, 1895; served in 1st Punjab Cavalry, Punjab Frontier Forc 1866–94; Maj.-Gen.; served Afghan War, 1878–80 (despatcl thrice, medal with clasp, Brevet Major and Lieut-Col). *Address:* E House, Rodwell, Weymouth. *T:* Weymouth 247. *Club:* Royal Do Yacht, Weymouth. *Died 27 Nov. 192*

ATKINSON-WILLES, Adm. Sir George (Lambart), KCB 190 Commander-in-Chief, East Indies, 1903–6; *b* 13 July 1847; 2nd su *s* of late Rev. Thomas Atkinson, Rector of Kirby Sigston, Yorkshi and Henrietta J., *d* of Capt. George W. Willes, RN; took the additio surname of Willes in compliance with the will of his uncle, Adm Sir George Willes, GCB; *m* Alice, *y d* of late Thomas Sutcliffe M of Greenoakes, Darling Point, Sydney; one *s* three *d. Ed* Leamington College; RN Academy, Gosport. Entered Navy, 18 Captain, 1886; Admiral, 1901; served Abyssinian War in Na Brigade, including action of Arogee and storming of Magdala, 18 (despatches, promoted to Lieut, medal); as commodore commanc Training Squadron, 1895–97; Dockyard Reserve, Chatha 1898–1900; ADC to HM Queen Victoria, 1899–1901, and to K Edward until promoted Rear-Adm.; Rear-Admiral in comma Home Squadron and second in command of Home Fleet, 1902 Commander-in-Chief, East Indies, 1903; directed the operations a mixed naval and military force which captured the Derv stronghold of Illig, 1904; as Commander-in-Chief was present Somali Coast, 1904, during the operations against the Mullah; retii 1912. *Address:* The Stroud, Haslemere. *Clubs:* United Servi Travellers'. *Died 25 Dec. 19*

ATTERBURY, Sir Frederick, KCB 1917 (CB 1910); Barrister-law; Controller of HM Stationery Office, and King's Printer of A of Parliament since 1913; *b* 19 Oct. 1853; 2nd *s* of Benjamin Jo Atterbury, Hampstead; *m* 1889, Charlotte, *e d* of Thomas Lawrei Forbes, Hampstead; one *s. Educ:* North London Collegiate Schc First place in open competition for Civil Service, 1872; Inla Revenue, Accountant and Comptroller-General's Office, 18 Secretary's Office, 1875; Comptroller of Stamps and Taxes for Irela 1901–3; Secretary to Board of Inland Revenue, Controller of Stam and Registrar of Joint Stock Companies, 1909–13. *Publications:* arti on taxation, etc, in Dictionary of Political Economy. *Recreation:* g *Address:* 2 Upper Terrace, Hampstead Heath, NW. *T:* 6746 Hampstead. *Club:* Union. *Died 10 Feb. 19*

ATTHILL, Major Anthony William Maunsell, MVO 1907; O 1919; Chairman, Royal Norfolk Veterans' Association; *b* 10 A 1861; *e s* of Henry Maunsell Atthill; *m*; two *s* two *d. Educ:* K Edward VI School, Norwich. Founded Royal Norfolk Vetera Association, 1898; Recruiting Officer 9th Regimental District, 19 served with 2nd Battalion Norfolk Regiment in South African W 1901–2; operations in the NW Transvaal (medal with 5 clas Captain Reserve of Officers, 1902; decorated by King Edward at Sandringham, May 1907, for services in connection with Veterans of Norfolk; Capt. ASC 1914; Major, 1915; served w British Force in Egypt and Mediterranean Expeditionary Force Gallipoli (despatches, OBE, 1914–15 Star, and medals). *Publicat* From Norwich to Lichtenburg via Pretoria, 1910. *Address:* Hillcr Bourne Hall Road, Bushey, Herts.

Died 28 Feb. 19

AUBREY, William Hickman Smith, LLD; MJI; author journalist; *b* London, 9 Dec. 1858. *Educ:* privately. LLD Univer of the City of New York and Rutgers Coll., New Brunswick. S editor and then leader-writer on Morning Advertiser; editor, Bar Daily and Weekly Times; editor, Capital and Labour, 1873–82;

leader staff and reviewer, Daily News; descriptive and social articles, Illustrated London News; vice-president, London Institution, Finsbury Circus; trustee of Croydon Charities; Chairman, Croydon Board of Guardians; Chairman, Surrey Joint Poor Law Committee for the Mentally Defective; London letter on politics, literature, art and society to syndicate of American papers; contributed numerous articles on literary, social, and economic subjects to reviews and magazines; visited US and Canada seven times on lecturing tours; contested (L) North Hackney, 1886; Honiton Division, Devonshire, 1892. *Publications:* The National and Domestic History of England, three editions, 3 vols, 1886–90; London's Roll of Fame, 1884; The Rise and Growth of the English Nation, four editions and eight American and Colonial editions, 3 vols, 1896–1912. *Recreations:* collection of literary "ana" and historical portraits; incessant work, varied by change of subject. *Address:* 13 Canterbury Road, Croydon. *Club:* National Liberal.   *Died 11 Feb. 1916.*

·UCKLAND, 5th Baron *cr* Irish barony, 1789; British, 1793; **William Morton Eden;** *b* 27 March 1859; *s* of 4th Baron and Lucy Walbanke, *y d* of John Walbanke Childers of Cantley, Co. York; *S* father, 1890; *m* 1891, Sybil, *d* of late Col G. M. Hutton, CB; one *s* (and one *s* decd). Late Capt. 2nd Batt. Dorset Regt. *Heir:* s Hon. Frederick Colvin George Eden, *b* 21 Feb. 1895. *Recreations:* shooting, fishing. *Clubs:* Carlton, Naval and Military.

     Died 31 July 1917.

·UDEN, Rev. Thomas, MA; FSA; *b* 1836; *s* of William Auden, of Rowley Regis, Co. Stafford; *m* 1861, Anne (*d* 1905), 2nd *d* of William Hopkins of Dunstall, Co. Stafford; four *s* three *d*. *Educ:* St John's College, Cambridge. BA 1858; MA 1861; Deacon, 1859; Priest, 1860. Headmaster of Wellingborough Grammar School, 1863–69; Vicar of Ford, Salop, 1869–79; St Julian's, Shrewsbury, 1879–92; Condover, Salop, 1892–1908; Prebendary of Lichfield, 1905; Rural Dean of Condover, 1906; Proctor in Convocation for the Diocese of Hereford, 1908–10 and 1911–16; one of Secretaries of Church Congress at Shrewsbury, 1896; Chairman of Atcham Board of Guardians, 1905–10; Vice-Chairman of Education Committee of Salop County Council; Chairman of Council of Shropshire Archæological Society. *Publications:* Shrewsbury, School History of Shropshire, and other books and papers on local history. *Address:* Alderdene, Church Stretton, Salop. *Clubs:* Royal Societies; Shropshire.   *Died 11 Nov. 1920.*

·ULARD, Alphonse; Professeur honoraire à l'Université de Paris; président de la Société de l'Histoire de la Révolution; *b* Montbron (Charente), 19 juillet 1849. *Educ:* collège de Lons-le-Saunier; lycée Louis-le-Grand et Ecole normale supérieure. Professeur aux lycées de Nîmes et de Nice; aux Facultés d'Aix, Montpellier, Dijon, Poitiers; au lycée Janson de Sailly; à la Sorbonne. *Publications:* Les idées et l'inspiration de Leopardi; Les Orateurs de la Révolution; Le culte de la Raison et le culte de l'être suprème; La Société des Jacobins; Paris sous le Directoire, le Consulat et l'Empire; Etudes et leçons sur la Révolution; Recueil des actes du Comité de salut public; Histoire politique de la Révolution Française; Taine historien de la Révolution Française; Napoléon 1ᵉʳ et le monopole universitaire; La guerre actuelle commentée par l'histoire; La Révolution française et le Régime féodal; Le patriotisme français de la Renaissance à la Révolution; Le Christianisme et la Révolution française. *Address:* Place de l'Ecole, No 1, Paris 1ᵉʳ area.

     Died Oct. 1928.

·UMONIER, Stacy; author; *b* 1887; *s* of William Aumonier, architectural sculptor; *m* Gertrude Peppercorn; one *s*. *Educ:* Cranleigh. Began career as a decorative designer and landscape painter; exhibited frequently at the RA, the RI, and the International; in 1908 became a Society Entertainer, giving many recitals of his own original character sketches, and performing at the Comedy, the Criterion, and other theatres; began writing in 1913, and has contributed a great number of short stories to all the leading magazines of England and America; during the war served as a private in the APC, and afterwards as a maker of charts at the Ministry of National Service. *Publications:* novels—Olga Bardel; Just Outside; The Querrils; One after Another; Heartbeat, 1922; volumes of short stories—Three Bars' Interval; The Love-a-duck; Miss Bracegirdle and Others; Odd Fish; Overheard; The Baby Grand, 1926. *Recreation:* gardening. *Address:* 35 Marlborough Hill, St John's Wood, NW8. *T:* Primrose Hill 1089. *Clubs:* Savage, St John's Wood Arts, Pen.

     Died 21 Dec. 1928.

·UNG, Maung Myat Tun, CIE 1911; Deputy Commissioner, Provincial Civil Service, since 1908. *Address:* Kyaukpyu, Burma.

     Died 1920.

AUSTEN-LEIGH, Charles Edward; *b* 1833; 2nd *s* of Rev. James Edward Austen of Tring. *Educ:* Harrow; Balliol Coll., Oxford. Principal Clerk of Committees, House of Commons, 1892–97. *Recreations:* shooting, fishing, stalking, golf. *Address:* Frog Firle, Berwick Station, Sussex. *Club:* Oriental.

     Died 3 April 1916.

AUSTIN, Hon. Austin Albert; Member, South-Western Province Legislative Council of Victoria; *b* 23 Nov. 1855; *s* of Thomas and Elizabeth Philips Austin; *m* Winifred Cameron of Morgiana, Hamilton, Victoria; two *s* three *d*. *Educ:* Church of England Grammar School, Geelong. Captain of School cricket and football teams, 1872–73. *Address:* Larundel, Elaine, Victoria, Australia. *Club:* Geelong.   *Died 29 July 1925.*

AUSTIN, Michael; Member of late Royal Commission on Labour; *b* 1855; *s* of late J. Austin, Cork; *m* 1885, Jane, 2nd *d* of Peter Moriarty, The View, Orrery Hill, Cork. *Educ:* Christian Brothers' School, Cork. Apprenticed a compositor, 1869. Took a keen interest in industrial matters; MP (N) Co. Limerick, W, 1892–1900.

     Died 18 Feb. 1916.

AVERY, Sir William Eric Thomas, 2nd Bt, *cr* 1905; MC; Captain (Temp. Major) Army Service Corps, SR; *b* 16 March 1890; *s* of 1st Bt and Anna Louisa, 4th *d* of Francis Bell; *S* father 1908. *Educ:* Winchester; University College, Oxford. Served European War, 1914–18 (MC). *Heir:* none. *Recreations:* rowing, motoring. *Address:* University College, Oxford. *Club:* Conservative.

     Died 20 Nov. 1918.

AVES, Ernest, MA; FSS; Chairman of Trade Boards; *b* Cambridge, 1857; *y s* of late William Owen Aves; *m* 1897, Eva, *y d* of late Frederick Maitland; two *d*. *Educ:* private schools; Trinity Coll., Cambridge. First class Moral Sciences Tripos, 1883. Fellow of the Royal Statistical Society since 1893; Member of the Council of the Royal Economic Society since 1897. Resident at Toynbee Hall, 1886–97; Secretary to the Council of the Universities' Settlement Association, 1889–1901; acting sub-warden of Toynbee Hall, 1890–97. Commissioner (Home Office) to investigate and report on Wages Boards, Industrial Conciliation and Arbitration Acts, etc, of Australia and New Zealand 1907–8; Special Enquiries (Board of Trade), 1909–11. *Publications:* contributed several chapters to vols iv, v and ix of Mr Charles Booth's inquiry into the Life and Labour of the People; Co-operative Industry; has written articles on Wages and Hours of Labour in Ency. Brit. (new vols) and various papers on Economics and Sociology, mostly for the Economic Journal. *Recreations:* fond of mountaineering, golf, cycling, walking, etc. *Address:* 12 Thurlow Road, Hampstead, NW. *T:* Hampstead 5366. *Clubs:* Alpine, Royal Societies.

     Died 29 April 1917.

AWDRY, Sir Richard Davis, KCB 1902 (CB 1894); *b* 1843; *s* of Rev. Charles R. E. Awdry; *m* 1st, 1868, Annie Martha (*d* 1900), *d* of T. Allgood; 2nd, 1901, Katherine Louise James, adopted *d* of Herbert Worthington, late of Brithdir Hall, Berriew, Montgomery; two *s* one *d*. *Educ:* Marlborough. Accountant-General of the Royal Navy, 1896–1904. *Address:* 63 Victoria Road, Kensington, W. *TA:* 4315 Western. *Club:* St Stephen's.

     Died 4 Oct. 1916.

AYLESFORD, 8th Earl of, *cr* 1714; **Charles Wightwick Finch;** Baron of Guernsey, 1703; *b* 7 June 1851; *s* of 6th Earl and Jane Wightwick, *o c* of J. W. Knightley; *S* brother, 1885; *m* 1st, 1873, Georgiana (*d* 1874), *d* of 3rd Baron Bagot; 2nd, 1879, Ella Victoria, *d* of John Ross, Benena, and *widow* of Captain James Wingfired Linton of Hemingford Abbots, Hunts; two *s* two *d* (and one *s* decd). *Educ:* Eton. Owned about 9,000 acres. *Heir: g s* Lord Guernsey, *b* 31 Oct. 1908. *Address:* Packington Hall, Coventry; Diddington Hall, Coventry; The Friars, Aylesford. *Clubs:* Carlton, Marlborough, Cavalry.

     Died 16 Sept. 1924.

AYLMER, 8th Baron, *cr* 1718; **Matthew Aylmer;** Bt 1662; President, Kootenay Gold Mines Ltd; *b* 28 March 1842; *s* of 7th Baron and Mary, *d* of Edward Journeaux; *S* father, 1901; *m* 1875, Amy Gertrude, *d* of Hon. John Young; three *s* two *d*. Lieut 7th Royal Fus. 1864; served Fenian Raids (medal, 2 clasps, general service medal); entered Canadian Militia; served as District Paymaster AAG, etc; in command of Canadian Contingent, Queen Victoria's Diamond Jubilee; Hon. Col 11th Hussars, 1903; Inspector-General, 1904; retired, Major-General, 1907. *Heir: s* Hon. John Frederick Whitworth Aylmer, *b* 23 April 1880. *Address:* Queen's Bay, Kootenay, BC.

     Died 11 June 1923.

AYLMER, Sir Arthur Percy Fitzgerald, 12th Bt, *cr* 1622; *b* 2 March 1858; *e s* of late Fenton John Aylmer, 97th Regt, and Isabella Elinor, *e d* of late George Darling, Fowberry Tower, Northumberland; *S* grandfather, Sir Arthur Percy Aylmer, 12th Bt, 1885; *m* 1st, 1878, Annie (*d* 1884), *d* of John Sanger; 2nd, 1885, Anne (who obtained a divorce, 1886), *d* of J. Douglas Reid of New York, and divorced wife of George Stelle, Chicago. *Recreations:* music, gardening, travelling. *Heir: b* Sir Fenton John Aylmer, VC, KCB, *b* 5 April 1862.
Died 5 Dec. 1928.

AYRTON, Hertha; the only woman member of the Institution of Electrical Engineers; *b* Portsea; *d* of Levi and Alice Marks; *m* 1885, Prof. W. E. Ayrton (*d* 1908); one *d. Educ:* private school; Girton College, Cambridge. Invented and constructed a line divider; assisted in the completion of a series of experiments on the electric arc for Prof. Ayrton during his absence in America, 1893; carried out several series of experiments on the same subject; discovered the connection between current length and pressure in the arc, the cause and laws of hissing in it, etc; carried out various researches connected with the motion of water, and discovered causes and process of formation of sand-ripples on the sea-shore; invented in 1915 and presented to the War Office for the duration of the War, Anti-Gas Fan, of which over a hundred thousand were used at the Front. Nominated for Fellowship of Royal Society, 1902, but, on counsel's opinion, the Council had no power to elect a woman; Hughes medal awarded by the Royal Society, 1906. *Publications:* The Electric Arc, 1902; twelve papers on the Electric Arc in The Electrician, 1896; papers before the British Association, 1895, 1897, 1898; the Institution of Electrical Engineers, 1899; the International Electrical Congress, 1900; La Société Française de Physique, 1911; The Royal Society, 1901, 1904, 1908, 1911, 1915, 1919; Afternoon Lecture before British Association, 1904. *Recreations:* novel reading, sketching. *Address:* 41 Norfolk Square, W2. *T:* Paddington 3109.
Died 26 Aug. 1923.

AYSCOUGH, John; *see* Bickerstaffe-Drew, Rt Rev. Mgr Count F.B.D.

AYSCOUGH, Rev. Thomas Ayscough; Prebendary of Hereford; *b* 11 Sept. 1830; *s* of Ayscough Smith, Leesthorpe Hall, Melton Mowbray; *m* 1858, Ethel Anna, *d* of J. P. Fearon, Ockenden, Cuckfield. *Educ:* Rugby; Trinity College, Cambridge (BA 1853, MA 1856). Curate of Skipsea, dio. York, 1854-56; Loughborough, 1856-60; Vicar of Tenbury, 1860-92; Rector of Cradley, near Malvern, 1892-1917. *Address:* Pinehurst, Evesham Road, Cheltenham.
Died 18 April 1920.

AZOPARDI, Sir Vincent Frendo, Kt 1912; CMG 1908; LLD; Chief Justice and President of HM's Court of Appeal, and Vice-President of the Council of Government of Malta, 1915; *b* 6 Jan. 1865; *s* of Pasquale Frendo Azopardi, LLD; *m* 1892, Caterina, *d* of late M. A. De Giorgio, LLD. LLD Malta Univ.; Bar Malta, 1887; Advocate for the Poor, Malta, 1895; Professor of Law, Malta University, 1899-1905; Magistrate of Judicial Police, 1900; Assistant Crown Advocate, 1903; Crown Advocate and Govt Legal Adviser to Naval and Military Authorities (with seat in Executive and Legislative Councils), 1905. *Address:* Valetta, Malta.
Died June 1919.

B

BABBAGE, Maj.-Gen. Henry Prevost; retired; *b* 1824; *y s* of late Charles Babbage, FRS; *m* Mary, *d* of late Colonel P. W. A. Bradshawe; two *d. Educ:* University College School and University College, London. East India Company's Bengal Army, 1843; passed Interpreters' Examination, 1845; served in Sutlege Campaign, 1846; services placed at disposal of the Bengal Government for employment in Assam, 1847; resigned, 1849; commanded expedition against the Abor tribe, 1848; Adjutant and acting 2nd in command Shekhawatte Battalion, 1850; furlough to England, 1854-57; interpreter to his regiment, Mutiny, 1857; Assistant Commissioner in the Punjab, 1857; JP Punjab, 1859; Member of the Senate, Lahore University; resigned the Service, 1874, with rank of Major-General; served at Bromley,

in Kent, six years on the Bromley Town Council, and three years as Guardian of the Poor; Elective Auditor at Cheltenham, 1904-5; Member of Royal Asiatic and the Royal Statistical Societies; Calculating Machine, British-Japan Exhibition 1910, Coronation Exhibition 1911, Science Museum, South Kensington, 1912. *Publications:* On Mechanical Notation, British Association, 1856; Magistrates' Handbook of Special Laws, Post Office, Railways, Excise, etc, etc, 1863, in India; Occulting Lights, 1889; Babbage's Calculating Machines, 1889; Scheme of Accounts for Municipal Boroughs, 1900; Thoughts on Income Tax by C. Babbage, 4th edn, 1907. *Address:* Mayfield, Lansdown Place, Cheltenham. *Club:* New, Cheltenham.
Died 29 Jan. 1918.

BABTIE, Lt-Gen. Sir William, VC 1899; KCB 1919 (CB 1912); KCMG 1916 (CMG 1899); Hon. Surgeon to His Majesty, 1914-19; a Knight of Grace of the Order of St John of Jerusalem in England; *b* 7 May 1859; *e s* of late John Babtie, JP, of Dunbarton; *m* 1902, Edith Mary, *d* of late W. H. Barry, JP, of Ballyadam, Co. Cork, and widow of Major P. A. Hayes; one *d. Educ:* Univ. of Glasgow; MV 1880; LLD 1919. Entered Army Medical Service, 1881; Assistant Director-General, 1901-6; Asst Med. Officer, Eastern Command 1906-7; Inspector of Medical Services, 1907-10; Deputy-Director General Army Medical Service, 1910-14; Director, Medical Service in India, 1914-15; served during international occupation of Crete as senior medical officer, 1897-98 (CMG); in South Africa on Staff of Natal army, present at all the actions for the relief of Ladysmith and subsequent operations in Natal and Eastern Transvaal, 1899-1900 (despatches, promoted Lieut-Col, medal with five clasps, VC); served European War, Principal Director, Medical Services, Mediterranean during operations in Gallipoli, Egypt, and Salonika, 1915-16 (despatches, KCMG); Director and later Inspector Medical Services, War Office, 1916-19 (KCB). *Address:* 7 Campden Hill Gardens, W. *Club:* Junior United Service.
Died 11 Sept. 1920.

BACK, Ven. Hugh Cairns Alexander; Rector of Hampton-Lucy since 1924; Archdeacon of Warwick since 1923; Hon. Canon of Coventry; Proctor in Convocation, 1919; Rural Dean; *b* 20 Aug. 1863; *m* Maud E., *d* of Colonel and Lady Harriet Fletcher of Kenward, Kent; one *s* one *d. Educ:* Trinity College, Cambridge (MA). Deacon 1887; Priest, 1888; Curate of Ulverston, 1887-89; Kidderminster 1889-92; Rector of Brandiston, 1892-97; Vicar of Rostherne 1897-1903; Rector of Berkswell, 1903-24. *Address:* Hampton-Lucy Rectory, Warwick.
Died 27 Dec. 1928.

BACKHOUSE, Sir Jonathan Edmund, 1st Bt, *cr* 1901; JP, DL; Director of Barclay and Co. Ltd; *b* 15 Nov. 1849; *e s* of late James Backhouse, MP, and Juliet Mary, *d* of Charles Fox; *m* 1871, Florence (*d* 1902), *d* of Sir John S. Trelawny, 9th Bt; four *s* (incl. twins) one *d* (and one *s* decd). *Educ:* Rugby School; Trinity Hall, Cambridge. *Heir: s* Edmund Trelawny Backhouse, *b* 20 Oct. 1873. *Address:* The Rookery, Middleton Tyas, Yorks.
Died 27 July 1918.

BACON, Edwin Munroe, MA; editor of Time and the Hour 1892-1900; *b* Providence, Rhode Island, 20 Oct. 1844. Formerly Editor successively of Boston Globe, Boston Advertiser, and Boston Post. *Publications:* Boston Illustrated; Bacon's Dictionary of Boston; Walks and Rides in the Country round about Boston; Historic Pilgrimages in New England; Literary Pilgrimages in New England; Boston: a Guide Book; The Connecticut River and the Valley of the Connecticut; English Voyages of Adventure and Discovery (retold from Hakluyt); The Boy's Drake; Manual of Ship Subsidies; Manual of Navigation Laws; Direct Elections and Law-Making by Popular Vote: The Initiative—The Referendum—The Recall—Commission Government for Cities—Preferential Voting (latter in association with Morrill Wyman). *Address:* 36 Pinckney Street, Boston, USA.
Died 24 March 1916.

BACOT, Arthur William, FES; Entomologist to the Lister Institute of Preventive Medicine; Hon. Entomologist to War Office; Member War Office Sanitary Committee; *b* London, 1866; *s* of Edmund Alexander Bacot; unmarried. *Educ:* Birkbeck School. Student of Entomology for many years; worked in Sierra Leone for Yellow Fever Commission. *Publications:* numerous contributions concerning Lepidoptera to Entomological Magazine and Tutt's British Lepidoptera; many papers dealing with Insects and Disease in Journal of Hygiene, Parasitology; report of Yellow Fever Commission, British Medical Journal, etc. *Recreations:* gardening, cycling, skating. *Address:* 19 York Hill, Loughton, Essex.
Died 12 April 1922.

BADCOCK, Brig.-Gen. Francis Frederick, DSO 1892; late Commandant 2nd Battalion 6th Ghoorka Rifles; *b* 13 Sept. 1867; *s* of late General Sir Alexander Badcock, KCB, CSI; *m* 1896, Eleanor Sara Austen, *d* of late Rev. G. F. de Gex; one *s* one *d*. *Educ:* Wellington College. Entered army, 1886; Captain, 1897; served Hazara Expedition, 1891 (despatches, clasp); Miranzai Expedition, 1891 (clasp); Hunza-Nagar, 1891–92 (wounded, despatches, DSO, clasp); Waziristan Field Force, 1894–95 (clasp); Tirah Expeditionary Force (severely wounded, medal with two clasps); NW Frontier of India, Zakka Khel Expedition (medal with clasp); retired, 1920.
Died 9 July 1926.

BADCOCK, Jasper Capper, CB 1899; *b* 2 Sept. 1840; *e s* of late John Badcock of Chelsea; *m* 1864, Mary, *d* of E. G. Burton. *Educ:* private school. Appointed clerk in General Post Office, 1858; Asst-Controller, London Postal Service, 1882; Vice-Controller, 1887; Controller, London Postal Service, 1892–1905; retired, 1905. *Address:* Springfield, 37 Brodrick Road, Upper Tooting, SW17.
Died 25 May 1924.

BADDELEY, Col Charles Edward, CB 1919; CMG 1916; RE; *b* 27 July 1861; *s* of late Col W. H. C. Baddeley; *m* Kathleen, *d* of Rev. M. Chaplin. Served Burmese Expedition, 1885–87 (despatches, medal with clasp); NW Frontier, India, 1897–98 (despatches, medal with clasp); Tirah, 1897–98; capture of Sampagha and Arhanga Passes; Operations in Bazar Valley (clasp); European War, 1914–18 (CMG, CB).
Died 28 April 1923.

BADDELEY, Sir John James, 1st Bt, *cr* 1922; Kt 1909; JP; Alderman, Farringdon Within; Member of the Common Council since 1886; Chairman of Cripplegate Foundation, 1902, and of many Committees; *b* 22 Dec. 1842; *e s* of John Baddeley, Hackney; *m* 1st, 1868, Mary, *d* of William Locks, Hackney; five *s* four *d*; 2nd, 1912, Florence, *d* of J. Douglass Mathews. Sheriff of the City of London, 1908–9; Lord Mayor of London, 1921–22. Commander Swedish Order of Wasa, of Russian Order of St Anne, and Crown of Belgium. *Publications:* A History of St Giles's Church, Cripplegate; A History of the Guildhall; The Aldermen of the Cripplegate Ward from 1275; Cripplegate Ward, 1921. *Recreation:* fishing. *Heir: e s* John William Baddeley [*b* 24 Aug. 1869; *m* 1892, Kate, *d* of John Shaw, Clapton]. *Address:* Lakefield, 32 Woodberry Down, Stoke Newington, N4. *T:* Clissold 1343.
Died 28 June 1926.

BADEN-POWELL, (Henry) Warington (Smyth), KC; Lieutenant, Royal Naval Reserve; *b* 3 Feb. 1847; *s* of Rev. Baden Powell, FRS, sometime Vicar of Plumstead, Kent, and Savilian Prof. of Geometry, Oxford Univ., and Henrietta, *d* of Vice-Adm. W. H. Smyth, FRS; assumed additional surname of Baden, by Royal Licence, 1902; *m* 1913, Cicely Hilda Farmer. Went to sea and served in various parts of the world, 1860–73; Barrister Inner Temple; QC 1897; practised in Admiralty Court, Wreck Court, and Northern Circuit. *Recreations:* yachting, canoeing, salmon fishing, shooting. *Address:* 1 Chelsea Court, Chelsea Embankment, SW. *Clubs:* Athenæum, Royal Thames Yacht.
Died 24 April 1921.

BAGGALLAY, Rev. Frederick; *b* 16 May 1855; *s* of Rt Hon. Sir Richard Baggallay, Lord Justice of Appeal; *m* 1885, Emily Cecile (*d* 1920), *e d* of Wilson Fox, MD, FRS, Physician in Ordinary to Queen Victoria; one *s*. *Educ:* Rugby; Gonville and Caius Coll., Camb. (Scholar). Ordained, 1880; Curate of Great Yarmouth; Clerk in Orders at St George's, Hanover Square, 1883; Vicar of St Peter, Mancroft, Norwich, 1884; Holy Trinity, Weymouth, 1890; Oakham, 1894; Hon. Canon of Peterborough, 1903–5; Rural Dean of Rutland, 1897; Rector of Pulborough, 1904–21; Prebendary of Ferring in Chichester Cathedral, 1915–21; Proctor in Convocation for Diocese of Chichester, 1918–21; Licensed Preacher, Diocese of Rochester, 1921. *Address:* The Vicarage, Bickley, Kent. *T:* Ravensbourne 1001. *Club:* Overseas.
Died 3 Dec. 1928.

BAGGE, Sir Alfred Thomas, 3rd Bt, *cr* 1867; Captain RN (retired 1893); *b* 5 July 1843; 2nd *s* of 1st Bt and Frances, *d* of Sir Thomas Preston, Bt; *S* brother 1881; *m* 1872, Millicent, *d* of J. Grant Morris, Allerton Priory, Liverpool; three *s* one *d*. Entered RN 1857; served throughout China War, 1857–61. *Heir: s* Alfred William Francis Bagge [*b* 14 Sept. 1875. *Educ:* Eton; King's Coll., Camb.; BA, LLB. *Address:* St Faith's Lane, Norwich; 4 Temple Gardens, EC. *Club:* Oxford and Cambridge]. *Address:* Stradsett Hall, Downham Market, Norfolk. *TA:* Fincham.
Died 16 Feb. 1916.

BAGHOT DE LA BERE, Stephen; *b* Dec. 1877; *s* of Kinard Baghot de la Bere of Burbage Hall, Leicestershire, and Catherine Leahy; unmarried. *Educ:* Ilkley College, Yorkshire. Studied in London and

France; Exhibitor RA, Paris, Madrid, etc; illustrated various books; black and white work for leading magazines and periodicals. 2nd Lieut RGA (SR); served in France, 1917. *Recreations:* golf, motoring, fishing, etc. *Address:* 52 Sydney Building, Bath. *Clubs:* Chelsea Arts, London Sketch.
Died 29 July 1927.

BAGNALL-WILD, Ralph Bagnall, JP, CC; MA; *b* 1845; 2nd *s* of William Kirkby; assumed the surnames of Bagnall-Wild by Royal Licence, 1868, on succeeding to estates of late Samuel Bagnall-Wild; *m* 1871, Alice, *d* of R. A. Pfeil of Guildford; one *s* one *d*. *Educ:* Ruabon School; Gonville and Caius College, Cambridge. Senior Open Scholarship, 1864; rowed in college boat; 18th Wrangler, 1868; BA 1868; MA 1871. A pupil of Arthur Cohen, KC, PC, and of late Thos Lewin; called to Bar, Inner Temple, 1870; practised Northern Circuit and Liverpool Sessions; in the Lawn Tennis world he was known for introducing the system of "draw" in matches known as the "Bagnall-Wild" system; JP Co. Notts. *Address:* Manor House, Costock, Loughborough. *TA:* Bagnall-Wild, East Leake.
Died 11 Oct. 1925.

BAGOT, Sir Alan Desmond, 1st Bt, *cr* 1913; Lieutenant Royal Horse Guards; *b* 20 Feb. 1896; *s* of Lt-Col Josceline Fitzroy Bagot (nominated a Baronet, 1913) and Lady Theodosia Bagot, *d* of Sir John Leslie, 1st Bt. *Heir:* none. *Address:* 71A Duke Street, Grosvenor Square, W1. *T:* Mayfair 5394; Levens Hall, Milnthorpe, Westmorland. *Clubs:* Bachelors', Wells.
Died 11 Jan. 1920 (ext).

BAGOT, Richard; novelist; *b* 8 Nov. 1860; 2nd surv. *s* of late Col Charles Bagot, Grenadier Guards, and Sophy Louisa, *d* of Admiral Hon. Josceline Percy, *s* of the Earl of Beverley, and *brother* of 5th Duke of Northumberland; succeeded to the Levens and Kilburn estates on death of his nephew, Sir Alan Bagot, 1st Bt, of Levens, 1920. *Educ:* privately. Private Secretary to the late Sir Frederick Napier Broome, when Governor of Western Australia, 1882–83; member of Royal Institution; hon. member of Società Leonardo da Vinci, Florence. Was presented in 1917 with an Illuminated Address from the Italian nation, signed by the Members of the Government, Senate, and Chamber, and by the leading representatives of Italian Science, Literature, Art, and Industries, and Mayors of the chief cities, as a tribute to his literary, international and other services to Italy. Grand Officer and Commendatore of the Order of the Crown of Italy; a Knight of Honour of the Sovereign Order of Malta. *Publications:* A Roman Mystery, 1899; Casting of Nets, 1901; The Just and the Unjust, 1902; Donna Diana, 1903; Love's Proxy, 1904; The Passport, 1905; Temptation, 1907; The Lakes of Northern Italy, 1907; Anthony Cuthbert, 1908; The House of Serravalle, 1910; My Italian Year, 1911; The Italians of To-day, 1912; Darneley Place, 1912; The Gods Decide, 1918; articles in reviews (British and Italian) on political and literary subjects. *Recreations:* fishing, travelling, etc. *Address:* Levens Hall, Westmorland; Tripalle, Crespina, Italy. *Clubs:* Travellers', Bachelors', Authors', Athenæum, Royal Automobile.
Died 11 Dec. 1921.

BAGOT, Major Hon. Walter Lewis, DSO 1900; General Manager, The Victoria Falls and Transvaal Power Company, Ltd, and Chairman of Rand Mines Power Supply Co. Ltd (Johannesburg); *b* Blithfield, Rugeley, 22 April 1864; *s* of 3rd and *heir-pres.* of 4th Baron Bagot; *m* 1892, Margaret Jane Caroline, *d* of Hon. F. W. Cadogan, *s* of 3rd Earl Cadogan; one *d* (one *s* decd). *Educ:* Eton; RMC, Sandhurst. Entered Grenadier Guards, 1884; ADC to Governor of S Australia, 1890; served Soudan, 1898 (British medal, Khedive's medal and clasp); retired 1898; recalled as DAAG Imperial Yeomanry, 1900; South Africa (despatches, Queen's medal three clasps, King's medal two clasps, Brevet Major, DSO); served on staff of GOC 4th Army Corps in France, Nov. 1914–June 1915, and as a Director in Ministry of Munitions of War, June 1915–Jan. 1916. *Address:* PO Box 2671, Johannesburg. *Club:* Travellers'.
Died 26 May 1927.

BAGSTER, Robert, FSA; FZS; Chairman and Managing Director, Samuel Bagster & Sons Ltd; *b* 1847; *s* of head of Bagster & Sons, Publishers; *m* C. J. Toms, Chard; one *d*. *Educ:* Brighton. Printer and Publisher; Freeman of City of London; Ambulance Section during War; Treasurer British Archæological Association, etc. *Address:* 15 Paternoster Row, EC4. *TA:* Bagster Cent. London. *T:* Central 3172. *M:* XP 2669. *Clubs:* Constitutional; Conservative, Edinburgh.
Died 20 Nov. 1924.

BAGWELL, Richard, JP and DL Co. Tipperary; JP Co. Waterford; Commissioner of National Education since 1905; *b* 9 Dec. 1840; *e s* of John Bagwell, MP, Clonmel, 1857–74; *m* 1873, Harriet, *d* of P. J. Newton, Dunleckney; one *s* three *d*. *Educ:* Harrow; Christ

Church, Oxford. Called to Bar, Inner Temple; Special Local Government Commissioner, 1898–1903. Hon. LittD, Dublin University; Oxford University, 1917; a Unionist and has been an active speaker and writer for that cause. *Publications:* Ireland under the Tudors, 3 vols; Ireland under the Stuarts, 3 vols. *Address:* Marlfield, Clonmel. *Clubs:* Brook's, Athenæum, Oxford and Cambridge; Kildare Street, Dublin.   *Died 4 Dec. 1918.*

BAIKIE, Brig.-Gen. Sir Hugh Archie Dundas Simpson-, KCMG 1919; CB 1915; late RA; *b* 18 March 1871; *s* of F. Simpson-Baikie; *m* 1907, Marion Evelyn, *d* of C. Miller; one *d*. Served Nile Expedition, 1899 (despatches, 4th Class Medjidie, Egyptian medal, 2 clasps); S Africa, 1900–1902 (despatches twice, Queen's medal, 4 clasps, King's medal, 2 clasps); France, 1914–15; Dardanelles, 1915 (despatches, CB, Officer Legion of Honour); France, 1916 (despatches); Salonica, 1917 (Bt Colonel, despatches); Egypt and Palestine, 1917–18 (KCMG, despatches 4 times). *Club:* Army and Navy.

Died 6 March 1924.

BAILEY, Captain Arthur Harold, DSO 1900; late South Lancs Regiment; *b* 24 Aug. 1873; *s* of W. H. Bailey. Entered army, 1894; Adjutant, 1899; served Matabeleland, 1896; South Africa, 1900 (despatches twice, Queen's medal, five clasps, Queen's medal, two clasps, DSO).   *Died 17 Feb. 1925.*

BAILEY, Lt-Col Edmund Wyndham-Grevis, JP Co. Kent; late commanding 3rd Battalion, Royal West Kent Regiment; *b* 1858; *e s* of Rev. James Sandford Bailey and Lavinia Margaret, *d* of late Demetrius Grevis-James; *m* 1885, Alberta, *o d* of Capt. Jas Evelyn, Grenadier Guards; one *s*. *Educ:* privately. Joined the West Kent Militia, 1876; served in Malta with the Regt during the S African War, 1900; the Regt being the first to leave England and volunteer for service; Lord of the Manors of Ightham, Wrotham, and Stansted. *Recreations:* shooting, hunting. *Address:* Ightham Court, Kent. *Clubs:* Junior United Service; Kent County, Maidstone.

Died 1920.

BAILEY, Rt. Hon. William Frederick, PC (Ireland) 1909; CB 1906; BA; FRGS, MRIA; Estates Commissioner under the Irish Land Act, 1903, and one of the Irish Land Commissioners; Governor of the National Gallery; *b* Castletown Conyers, Co. Limerick, 1857; *e s* of W. Bailey, MD, RN. *Educ:* Trinity College, Dublin; a first senior moderatorship and large gold medal in History and Political Science; was auditor and gold medallist in oratory of the College Historical Society. Called to Irish Bar and joined the Munster Circuit, 1881; was Barrington Lecturer in Political Economy; examiner in English under the Intermediate Education Board; appointed one of the Secretaries to the Royal Commission on Irish Public Works, 1886; became a Legal Assistant Commissioner under the Irish Land Acts, 1887; for many years Secretary of the Statistical and Social Inquiry Society of Ireland, and was elected President of the Society, 1902. *Publications:* The Slavs of the War Zone, 1916; The Law of Franchise and Registration in Ireland; Local and Centralised Government in Ireland; Ireland Since the Famine; Report on the Condition of Peasant Purchasers in Ireland; editions of Gray's Poems, Coleridge's Ancient Mariner, etc, and various papers in Reviews, etc, and in the Irish Statistical Society's Journal. *Recreations:* golf, cycling, motoring, photography, travel (has been in every European country, and has travelled extensively in North, Central and South America, North and South Africa, India, Transcaucasia, and Palestine). *Address:* 3 Earlsfort Terrace, Dublin. *Clubs:* Reform, Royal Automobile; University, Dublin.   *Died 16 April 1917.*

BAILEY, William Henry, ISO 1905; *b* 10 July 1855; *s* of Wm R. Bailey of Barbados; *m* 1882, Isabella, *d* of late I. K. Brown, Comptroller of Customs; four *s* two *d*. 3rd Clerk, Customs Department, 1875; 2nd Clerk, 1876; Chief Clerk, Colonial Secretary's Department, 1882; acted Auditor-General on several occasions; Registrar of the Courts, 1898; Colonial Postmaster, 1900; acted as a member of the Legislative Council, 1912–13 and 1919; Manager Savings Bank, Aug. 1919; Auditor-General, Feb. 1920; resigned, May 1920. *Address:* Bridgetown, Barbados.

BAILHACHE, Hon. Sir Clement Meacher, Kt 1912; KC 1908; LLB; Judge of the High Court since 1912; *b* Leeds, 2 Nov. 1856; *s* of a Baptist minister; *m* 1881, Fanny Elizabeth, *d* of Herman Liebstein; two *d*. *Educ:* City of London School; London University. Practised for some years as a Solicitor; Bar, Middle Temple, 1889; joined South Wales and Chester Circuit. *Address:* Trevanion, Totteridge, Herts.   *Died 8 Sept. 1924.*

BAILIE, Maj.-Gen. Thomas Maubourg, JP; *b* 16 Aug. 1844; *m* 1886, Amy, *d* of Sir William Miller, 1st Bt, of Manderston. Entered army, 1862; Maj.-Gen. 1893; retired, 1896. *Address:* 54 Sloane Street, SW; Caldecot House, Abingdon. *Club:* Naval and Military.

Died 5 April 1918.

BAILLIE, Sir Duncan (Colvin), KCSI 1914 (CSI 1910); ICS; retired; *b* Inverness, 27 Nov. 1856; *s* of late Peter Baillie, ship-owner, Inverness; *m* 1887, Julia Luisa, *d* of late Rev. Henry Stern, Rector of Brampton, Norwich; one *s* one *d*. *Educ:* Inverness Academy; Glasgow Academy; Edinburgh University. Entered ICS 1879; Asst Settlement Officer, 1886–89; Superintendent of Provincial Census, 1890–92; Dep.-Commissioner and Settlement Officer of Rai Bareli, 1892; Director of Land Records and Agriculture, 1895; Magistrate and Collector, 1896; Secretary to Board of Revenue, 1896; Opium Agent, Benares, 1899; Commissioner, Benares, 1903; has been officiating and subsequently permanent member of the Board of Revenue since 1907 except whilst employed in the Punjab as Member and subsequently President of a Committee on the Canal Colony Administration, 1907–8; Member, Lt-Governor's Council, 1909; officiated as Lieut-Governor, UP, in 1913; retired 1914. *Publication:* Census Report of 1891. *Recreation:* golf. *Address:* 89 Queen's Gate, SW. *T:* Kensington 6422. *Club:* East India United Service.

Died 30 Aug. 1919.

BAILLIE, Sir Frank, KBE 1918; President, Bankers Investments Ltd, and Burlington Steel Co. Ltd; *b* Toronto, 9 Aug. 1875; *s* of John Baillie and Marian Wilton; *m* 1900, Edith Julia, *d* of late Aubrey White, CMG, Deputy Minister of Lands and Mines for Ontario; three *s* two *d*. Commenced business career as clerk with the Central Canada Loan & Savings Co., Toronto; became private secretary to the late Senator George A. Cox; accountant, Central Canada Loan & Savings Co. 1896; Secretary, 1898; Assistant Manager, 1901; General Manager, Metropolitan Bank, Toronto, 1902; formed the firm of Baillie, Wood & Croft, members of Toronto Stock Exchange, 1903; organised the Burlington Steel Co. Ltd, Hamilton, 1910, the Bankers Bond Co. Ltd, Toronto, 1912, and Dominion Steel Foundry Co. Ltd, Hamilton, 1912; shortly after the commencement of the European War in 1914, organised the Canadian Cartridge Co. Ltd, Hamilton, to manufacture brass cartridge cases for the British Government and later Anti-Aircraft Cases for USA Government; Director of Aviation for Canada, Imperial Munitions Board, Dec. 1916, same month acting for the British Government, organised and became President of Canadian Aeroplanes Ltd, which Company manufactured aeroplanes for the Royal Air Force in Canada, and flying boats for the American Government. Anglican. Independent (Politics). *Recreations:* golf, motoring, curling, yachting. *Address:* Lisonally Farm, Oakville, Ontario, Canada. *Clubs:* Albany, Lambton Golf and Country, Mississauga Golf, National, Royal Canadian Yacht, Toronto; Victoria, Hamilton, Hamilton Golf, Hamilton, Ontario; Los Angelos, Country, Beverley Hills, Cal.   *Died 2 Jan. 1921.*

BAILLIE, Gen. James Cadogan Parkison; Bengal Infantry; *b* 8 Sept. 1835. Entered army, 1852; General, 1894; served Indian Mutiny, 1857–59 (twice wounded, once severely, medal). *Club:* East India United Service.   *Died 31 March 1928.*

BAILLIE-GROHMAN, William A., JP; author; *b* 1 April 1851; *m* 1887, Florence, *d* of T. Nickalls, Patteson Court, Nutfield, Surrey; one *s* one *d*. *Educ:* Austria, England, France. JP, BC, Canada. Since Majuba Hill disclosures, strong advocate of improved National rifle training; started with Lord Bryce, Sir Martin Conway, and others, the Tyrolese Relief Fund. *Publications:* Tyrol and the Tyrolese, 1875; Gaddings with a Primitive People; Camps in the Rockies; Sport in the Alps; Fifteen Years' Sport and Life in Western America; Das Jagdbuch Kaiser Maximilian I; edited with his wife and Theodore Roosevelt, the Master of Game, the oldest English Book on Hunting, by Edward, 2nd Duke of York; The Land in the Mountains, 1907; Tyrol, 1908; Sport in Art, 1913; contributor to Badminton Library Big Game Vols, Sport in Europe, Quarterly, Nineteenth Century Reviews, and other principal magazines of England and America. *Recreations:* big game shooting in the Alps and Rocky Mountains; rifle shooting (winner of upwards of seventy prizes on the Continent, England, and America); historical researches concerning history of the chase, and collecting books and prints relating to this subject, collection consisting of more than 4,000. *Address:* (temp.) Boxley Abbey, Maidstone; Schloss Matzen, Brixlegg, Tyrol. *Clubs:* Alpine, Royal Societies.   *Died 27 Nov. 1921.*

BAILLIE-HAMILTON, Sir William Alexander, KCMG 1897 (CMG 1887); CB 1892; Officer of Arms, Order of St Michael and St George, 1901; Gentleman Usher of the Blue Rod, 1911; Chief

Clerk of the Colonial Office, 1896–1909; Lieutenant-Colonel and Hon. Colonel (retired) Lothians and Berwickshire Imperial Yeomanry; *b* 6 Sept. 1844; *s* of the late Adm. W. A. Baillie-Hamilton and Lady Harriet, *o sister* of 1st Duke of Abercorn, KG; *m* 1871, Mary Aynscombe, *d* of late Rev. John Mossop; two *s*. Barrister, Inner Temple, 1871; Sec. to Colonial Conference, 1887; Private Secretary to Secretaries of State for Colonies, 1886–92. *Recreations:* hunting, shooting, fencing, field sports generally. *Address:* 55 Sloane Street, SW. *Clubs:* Carlton; Scottish Conservative, Edinburgh.

Died 6 July 1920.

BAINBRIDGE, Francis Arthur, MA, MD, DSc; FRCP, FRS; Professor of Physiology, University of London; *b* Stockton-on-Tees, 1874; *s* of R. R. Bainbridge; *m* 1905, Hilda Winifred, *d* of Rev. Thornton Smith; one *d. Educ:* The Leys, Cambridge; Trinity College, Cambridge (Scholar); St Bartholomew's Hospital, London. 1st Class Natural Sciences Tripos, Part I (1895) and Part II (1897), and Horton Smith Prize (1904), Cambridge; Shuter Scholarship, House Physician and Casualty Physician, St Bartholomew's Hospital; Demonstrator in Physiology and Pharmacology, St Bartholomew's Hospital; Gordon Lecturer in Pathology, Guy's Hospital; Assistant Bacteriologist, Lister Institute of Preventive Medicine; Arris and Gale Lecturer, Royal College of Surgeons, 1908; Milroy Lecturer, Royal College of Physicians, 1912. *Publications:* numerous papers on physiological and bacteriological subjects. *Recreations:* walking, tennis. *Address:* St Bartholomew's Hospital, EC. *Club:* Reform.

Died 27 Oct. 1921.

BAINBRIGGE, Rev. Philip Thomas, MA; Prebendary of Reculversland in St Paul's Cathedral, 1918; Vicar of St Thomas, Regent Street, W, since 1883; *o s* of Major-Gen. Bainbrigge, RE; *m* 1st, 1884, Helen Jane (*d* 1904), *d* of Alexander Gillespie of Biggar Park, Lanarkshire; one *d*; 2nd, 1905, Beatrice Eleanora, *d* of Francis Borthwick of Haslieburn, Peeblesshire; one *s. Educ:* Haileybury; Pembroke College, Oxford. Six years in business in the City, between School and College; 2nd Class Theol. Schs 1874; Curate of Oakham, 1875–78; St Peter's, Leicester, 1878–80; St Philip's, Regent Street, 1880–83. *Publications:* The Day Dawn from on High; The Use and Abuse of the Word Protestant; The Credulity of Unbelief, and other pamphlets. *Recreations:* golf, chess. *Address:* 12 Kingly Street, W1. *Clubs:* Athenæum; Walton Heath Golf.

Died 1 Nov. 1919.

BAINES, Lieut-Colonel J. C., DSO, TD; ARIBA; practising architect; *b* 8 Sept. 1876; *s* of S. C. Baines of Leicester; *m* E. S. Britten, *d* of Vicar of Somerby; two *s*. Served S African War in Volunteer Service Co. 1st Leicester Regt; European War, commanded 2/5 Sherwood Foresters and 14th Leicester Regt (badly wounded, despatches 3 times). *Address:* Barn Close, Oadby, near Leicester. *T:* Oadby 141. *M:* NR 6486 and BC 6893. *Club:* Leicestershire, Leicester.

Died 26 Jan. 1928.

BAINES, Sir Jervoise Athelstane, Kt 1905; CSI 1894; Indian Civil Service, retired; Alderman, LCC, 1892–1902; Councillor, Oxon CC, 1917–22; President (Gold Medallist), Royal Statistical Society, 1909–10; *b* Bluntisham, Hunts, 17 Oct. 1847; *s* of Rev. Edward Baines and Catherine Eularia Baines, *d* of John Baines of Eltham; *m* 1874, Constance, *d* of late Henry Pyne, barrister; one *s* one *d. Educ:* Rugby; Trinity Coll., Cambridge. India Civil Service, Bombay, 1870–89; Census Commissioner under Government of India, 1889–93; employed at India Office and as Secretary to Royal Commission on Opium, 1894–95; retired 1895. *Decorated* for Census Administration. *Publications:* Official Reports on Provincial Administration, on Indian Census Operations, 1881–91; on Indian Progress (Parliamentary), 1894; many papers, ethnographic and statistical, for London Societies. *Address:* Home Close, Kidlington, Oxon. *M:* BW 323. *Clubs:* Reform, Unionist.

Died 26 Nov. 1925.

BAINES, Matthew Talbot, MA; JP; late agent for the Marquess of Lansdowne, KG; formerly Senior Small Holdings Commissioner for the Board of Agriculture and Fisheries; *b* 1863; *e s* of late L. T. Baines, of Westbrook, Horsham; *m* 1892, Eveleigh, *e d* of W. R. Holden, of Victoria Park, Dover; two *s. Educ:* Harrow; Trinity Hall, Cambridge. Land agent since 1886. *Recreations:* cricket, lawn tennis, shooting, fishing. *Address:* Westbrooke Hall, Horsham, Sussex. *Club:* New University.

Died 6 May 1925.

BAINES, William; composer of music; *b* Horbury, near Wakefield, 26 March 1899. At the age of seventeen had written a symphony, a string quartette, two pianoforte trios, sonatas, etc; later his works were chiefly for the pianoforte. *Publications:* for piano—Paradise Gardens; Seven Preludes; Silverpoints; Milestones; Tides; Four

Poems; Coloured Leaves. *Address:* 91 Albemarle Road, The Mount, York.

Died 6 Nov. 1922.

BAIRD, Sir Alexander, 1st Bt *cr* 1897; Lord-Lieutenant of Kincardineshire since 1889; *b* Scotland, 22 Oct. 1849; *e s* of John Baird, of Lochwood and Urie; *m* 1873, Hon. Annette Palk, *d* of 1st Baron Haldon (*d* 1884); two *s* three *d* (and two *d* decd). *Educ:* Harrow. Sent to Upper Egypt to relieve the famine in the provinces of Girgeh, Kenneh, and Esneh, 1879. *Heir: s* John Lawrence Baird, *b* 27 April 1874. *Address:* Urie, Stonehaven, NB. *M:* SU 30. *Clubs:* Carlton, Turf.

Died 21 June 1920.

BAIRD, Edith Elina Helen, "Queen of Chess"; *o* surv. *d* of late T. Winter Wood, of Hareston, Devon; *m* Deputy-Inspector-General W. J. Baird, MD, RN (decd); one *d. Educ:* privately. From early childhood displayed more taste for the intellectual side of life than for the social. At the age of five she was taken to the Crystal Palace by her parents to put together puzzles purposely cut by an expert, which she did in a given time in the presence of numerous spectators. Her taste for chess developed when she was very young, inheriting it from her parents, who were known chess-players. She has composed and published upwards of a thousand problems, and with them has won many prizes; invented and introduced the Twentieth Century Retractor, 1902. *Publications:* Seven Hundred Chess Problems; The Twentieth Century Retractor and Chess Novelties, 1907. *Recreations:* archery, painting. *Address:* Hareston, Paignton, S Devon.

Died 1 Feb. 1924.

BAIRD, Rear-Adm. Sir George Henry, KCB 1924 (CB 1918); RN; Commanding the Destroyer Flotillas of the Atlantic Fleet since 1923; *b* 1871; *e s* of Alexander Baird, JP, of The Willows, Wickhambreaux, Canterbury; *m* 1908, Frances Josephine Sharp; three *d*. Entered Britannia naval cadets training ship at Dartmouth, 1885; midshipman, 1887; passed first in the examination of all midshipmen afloat, 1889; Lieutenant for meritorious examinations, 1892; Commander, 1903; Captain, 1909; Commodore, 1st class, 1918; Rear-Admiral, 1920. Served European War, 1914–19 (despatches, CB, Legion of Honour, Rising Sun, Crown of Italy); Director of Mobilisation Department, Admiralty, 1921–23. *Address:* Littlebourne Court, near Canterbury. *M:* XN 7222. *Club:* United Service.

Died 22 Oct. 1924.

BAIRD, Hon. George Thomas; Senator of Dominion of Canada since 1895; *b* Andover, Victoria Co., New Brunswick, 3 Nov. 1847; of Scotch descent; *m* 1879, Ida J., *d* of Capt. D. W. Sadler; two *s* one *d. Educ:* Carleton Co. Grammar School. Began life, after having spent his boyhood on a farm, by teaching; taught at a superior school in Andover, NB, 1870–74; moved to Perth, NB, where he carried on lumber and general store business, 1874; represented Victoria County in the Local Legislature at Fredericton, 1884–95; appointed to Legislative Council, 1891; voted to abolish the Council, which was done in 1892, when he was again elected and sat until 1895. Episcopalian; Conservative. *Address:* Andover, New Brunswick, Canada.

Died 21 April 1917.

BAIRD, John George Alexander, DL; *b* Rosemount, Ayrshire, 31 May 1854; 3rd *s* of William Baird, Gartsherrie, and Janet Johnston; *m* 1880, Susan Georgiana, *e d* of Rt Hon. Sir James Fergusson, 6th Bt, GCSI, KCMG, CIE; two *d. Educ:* Eton; Christ Church, Oxford. Joined 6th Dragoon Guards, 1877, and 16th Lancers six months afterwards; left army, 1882; MP (C) Central Division, Glasgow, 1886–1900 and 1900–6. *Publication:* The Private Letters of the Marquis of Dalhousie, 1910. *Address:* 89 Eaton Square, SW; Wellwood, Muirkirk, NB. *Clubs:* Carlton, Naval and Military.

Died 6 April 1917.

BAIRD, William, JP, DL; *b* 1848; *e s* of late William Baird of Elie; *m* 1883, Caroline Muriel, *d* of late John Alex. Burn Callander of Preston Hall, Midlothian; one *s* two *d*. Hon. Col, late Lieut-Col and Hon. Col Commanding Fife RGA Militia. *Address:* Deanscroft, Oakham, Rutland. *Clubs:* Carlton, Turf, Conservative.

Died 29 June 1918.

BAIRD, Sir William James Gardiner, 8th Bt, *cr* 1695, of Saughton Hall, Midlothian; *b* 23 Feb. 1854; *S* father, 1896; *m* 1879, Hon. Arabella Rose Evelyn Hozier (*d* 1916), *d* of 1st Baron Newlands; one *s* one *d* (and one *s* one *d* decd). Late Lieut 7th Hussars; JP for Mid and East Lothian; Lieut-Col and Hon. Col, retired, Lothians and Berwickshire Yeomanry Cavalry. *Heir: s* James Hozier Gardiner Baird [*b* 25 Nov. 1883. Capt. 4th Batt. Argyll and Sutherland Highlanders; retired; rejoined the army as Captain 4th Bedfordshire Regiment, 1914 (wounded at Neuve Chapelle, despatches, Military Cross)]. *Address:*

Glendalough, North Berwick, NB. *T:* 55 North Berwick. *Clubs:* Carlton; New, Edinburgh.
Died 19 April 1921.

BAKER, Major Arthur Brander, DSO 1900; Brigade Major, Commonwealth Military Forces; *b* 4 Aug. 1868; *s* of late Capt. Arthur Baker, RN, Secretary Vancouver Club, British Columbia. Entered army 1st Battalion The Royal Sussex Regt, 1887; served Hazara, 1888 (medal and clasp); South Africa, 1899–1902, with New South Wales Bushmen and raised and commanded Colonial Light Horse (DSO, despatches, Queen's medal with five clasps, and King's medal with two clasps); European War, 1914–16 (wounded).
Died 23 Sept. 1918.

BAKER, Sir Augustine FitzGerald, Kt 1903; MA Trinity College, Dublin; admitted Solicitor in Ireland, 1878; President of the Incorporated Law Society of Ireland, 1903; *b* 1851; *y s* of Hugh Baker, of Lismacue, Tipperary. *Address:* 56 Merrion Square, Dublin. *Clubs:* Constitutional; University, Dublin; Royal Irish Yacht.
Died 7 Oct. 1922.

BAKER, Vice-Adm. Casper Joseph; retired; *b* 8 May 1852; 3rd *s* of Admiral James Vashon Baker; *m* 1886, Harriet Penuel, *y d* of Professor John Hutton Balfour of Edinburgh; two *s* three *d.* *Educ:* Clifton College. Entered Britannia as Naval Cadet, 1865; Sub-Lieut 1872; Lieut 1875; Commander, 1891; Capt. 1898; retired, 1907; Rear-Admiral, 1908; Vice-Admiral, retired list, 1913; when First-Lieut of Egeria, at anchor in the Friendly Islands, a seaman fell overboard and was stunned, he and Quartermaster Bulloch jumped overboard and rescued him; served as Commander in Persian Gulf for three years in command of HMS Sphinx; served as Capt. in Blake; Astraea (China Station); Flora (Pacific); Edgar and Ramillies. *Address:* Oaklands, South Petherton, Somerset.
Died 3 Aug. 1918.

BAKER, Lieut-Col Edward Mervyn, DSO 1916; *b* 1875. Entered Royal Fusiliers (City of London Regt), 1897; Capt., Manchester Regt, 1901; Major, Royal Fusiliers, 1915; Bt Lt-Col, 1917; served S Africa, 1899–1901 (despatches, Queen's medal with five clasps); Yola Expedition, 1901 (despatches, medal with clasp); Kontagora Expedition, 1902 (medal with clasp); European War, 1914–17 (despatches, DSO, Bt Lt-Col, Order of Redeemer of Greece); retired. *Address:* Neatham Grange, Alton, Hants.
Died 19 Oct. 1925.

BAKER, His Honour Sir George Sherston, 4th Bt, *cr* 1796; County Court Judge, Circuit 17, since 1901; Recorder of Barnstaple and Bideford since 1889; JP Lincs, City of Lincoln, Great Grimsby, Boston, Barnstaple, and Bideford; *b* London, 19 May 1846; *s* of Henry Sherston Baker, barrister and Maria, *d* of John Burke, York; *S* cousin 1877; *m* 1st, 1871, Jane Mary (*d* 1909), *d* of late F. J. Fegen, CB, RN, Ballinlonty, Tipperary; two *s* three *d* (and one *s* one *d* decd); 2nd, 1912, Mary Josephine (*d* 1977) of The Manor House, Lillington, Warwickshire, *y d* of late Henry Bacchus; 3rd, 1920, Emmeline, *d* of James Andrews, MICE, Dublin. Barrister, Lincoln's Inn and Middle Temple; Examiner to Inns of Court, 1895–1901; Examiner in Equity to Birkbeck Institute, 1889–97; Standing Counsel to Hon. Society of the Baronetage, 1898–1901. *Publications:* Hallock's International Law, 2nd edn 1878, 3rd 1893, 4th 1908; The Laws relating to Quarantine, 1879; The Office of Vice-Admiral of the Coast, 1884; Law Reports, Digest of Cases, 1881–85; editor of Law Magazine and Review, 1895–98; Archbold's Quarter Sessions, 5th edn 1898; First Steps in International Law, 1899; many magazine articles and reviews. *Recreation:* late Inns of Court RV. *Heir: s* Col Dodington George Richard Sherston Baker, IMS [*b* 22 July 1877; *m* 1906, Irene Roper, *y d* of Sir Roper Parkington; one *s* one *d*]. *Address:* Castle Moat House, Lincoln. *Club:* Devonshire.
Died 15 March 1923.

BAKER, James, FRGS, FRHistS; Corresponding Member, Royal Academy of Arts Madrid, 1911; Hon. Secretary British International Association Journalists since 1906, and International Press Conference, 1909; *b* 1 Jan. 1847; *s* of James Baker; *m* Agnes Anne, *d* of J. Hallett, Swell Court, Somerset; three *s* three *d.* *Educ:* by his father. Has travelled in Greece, Russia, Lapland, Egypt, etc; made a special study of Bohemia, was voted Great Silver Medal of Prague by Senate for literary work; in 1899 travelled in Tunis and Sicily and studied technical and commercial education in Prussia, Poland, Galicia, and Bohemia, to write a report thereon for the Education Department, published 1900; travelled in Georgia and Palestine, 1903; Bohemia, 1905; Spain, 1906–9; Bosnia, 1907; Bukovina, 1911; Guest of City of Prague at Palacky and Sokol Commemoration, 1912; lectured throughout Britain on the War, Bohemia, Roumania, 1914–18; to Army on Front, 1919. Kt of Imperial Order of Francis Joseph, 1908.

Publications: Quiet War Scenes; Poems and Translations, 1879; Days Afoot and European Sketches, 1881; John Westacott, 1886; By the Western Sea, 1889; Our Foreign Competitors, 1892; Mark Tillotson, 1892; A Forgotten Great Englishman, 1894; Pictures from Bohemia, 1894; The Gleaming Dawn, 1896; The Cardinal's Page, 1898; A Double Choice, 1901; A National Education to National Advancement, 1904; The Inseparables, 1905; A plea for power for the Church of England, 1906, Anglicanus; The Harrogate Tourist centre, 1906; Literary and Biographical Studies, 1908; Austria: her People and their Homelands, 1912; Reminiscent Gossip of Men and Matters, 1913; Bohemia and her People: a Buffer State against Berlin, 1917; A Leader of Men (Mayor S. Harold Baker), 1919; has written for the principal magazines. *Recreations:* foreign travel, music, glee-singing, archaeology. *Address:* Sewelle Villa, Clifton. *Clubs:* Savage, Authors'; University, Musical, Bristol.
Died 24 June 1920.

BAKER, James H., MA, LLD; President University of Colorado, 1892–1914, President-Emeritus since 1914; *b* Harmony, Maine, 13 Oct. 1848; *m* 1882, Jennie V. Hilton; one *s* one *d.* *Educ:* Bates College, Lewiston, Maine. Principal of Yarmouth High School, 1873–75; Principal of Denver High School, 1875–92; President, National Council of Education, 1892; President of National Association of State Universities, 1907; author of movement that resulted in national investigation of "Committee of Ten" on secondary schools; chairman of NEA Committee on Economy of Time in Education (Report published by US Government); member of NEA Committee on A National University and of National Association of State Universities Committee on The Standards of American Universities; Fellow, American Association for the Advancement of Science. *Publications:* Elementary Psychology; Education and Life; American Problems; Educational Aims and Civic Needs; American University Progress and College Reform relative to School and Society; After the War— What?; Of Himself and Other Things. *Clubs:* University, Denver; Colorado Mountain.
Died 10 Sept. 1925.

BAKER, John Gilbert, FRS, FLS; MRIA 1902; *b* Guisbro', Yorks, 13 Jan. 1834; *m* 1860, Hannah Unthank; one *s* one *d.* *Educ:* public schools of Society of Friends, Ackworth and York. First assistant, Herbarium of Royal Gardens, Kew, 1866; Keeper, 1890–99; Victoria Medallist of the Royal Horticultural Society, 1897; Gold Medallist of the Linnean Society, 1899; Veitch Gold Medal for Horticulture, 1907. *Publications:* North Yorkshire; Flora of English Lake District; Synopsis Filicum (with Sir W. J. Hooker); Flora of Mauritius; Handbooks of Fern Allies, Irideæ, Amaryllideæ, and Bromeliaceæ. *Recreations:* walking, botanising. *Address:* 3 Cumberland Road, Kew.
Died Aug. 1920.

BAKER, Joseph Allen; MP (L) East Finsbury since 1905; Member, LCC, 1895–1906; Chairman, Baker and Sons Ltd, Willesden; *b* Canada, 1852; *m* 1878, Eliz. B. Moscrip of Roxburghshire, NB; three *s* four *d.* *Educ:* Trenton High School. Entered his father's business (engineering) in 1876, came over to London, establishing his business here. Has been prominently connected with tramway extension in the LCC; published special reports on tramway traction and recommended the conduit system for London; acted as Chairman of Highway Committee; contested (L) East Finsbury, 1900; initiated and organized interchange of visits between representatives of the Christian churches of Great Britain and Germany in the interests of international peace and closer friendship; Chairman, Executive Committee of British Council of the Associated Councils of Churches in the British and German Empires for Fostering Friendly Relations; Chairman, Executive Committee British Group of the World Alliance of Churches for Promoting International Friendship. *Address:* Donnington, Harlesden, NW. *TA:* Bakers, London. *T:* 1138 Willesden. *M:* A 3. *Club:* National Liberal.
Died 3 July 1918.

BAKER, Lawrence James; *b* 1827; *e s* of Capt. John Law Baker and Caroline Brown; *m* 1st, 1857, Ellen Catherine Thompson; 2nd, 1871, Susan Taylor. MP (L) Somerset (Frome Div.), 1885–86; High Sheriff of Surrey, 1898. *Address:* Brambridge Park, Eastleigh, Hants. *Club:* Reform.
Died 10 June 1921.

BAKER, Sir Thomas, KBE 1920; ex-Mayor of Plymouth; Freeman of the Borough of Plymouth; JP Plymouth, 1919. *Address:* The Crossways, Yelverton, S Devon. *T:* Yelverton 37.
Died 17 Dec 1926.

BAKER, William, MA, LLB; FRHS; Hon. Director and Chairman of Council of Dr Barnardo's Homes: National Incorporated Association; *b* 23 April 1849; 3rd *s* of late Hugh Baker of Lismacue,

Bansha, Co. Tipperary, Ireland; m 1882, Annie Austin (d 1901). *Educ:* Trinity College, Dublin. Called to Bar, 1875; practised at the Chancery Bar; joined Dr Barnardo's Committee, 1887; became Honorary Director on the death of Dr Barnardo in 1905. *Address:* 18-26 Stepney Causeway, E. *TA:* Waifdom, Step, London.
Died 17 Nov. 1920.

BAKER, Ven. William George; Vicar of Brightwater since 1894; Archdeacon of Waimea since 1909; m. Ordained, 1872; Curate of Stalbridge, Dorset, 1882-84; St John, Wakefield, New Zealand, 1884-91; Holy Trinity, Richmond, New Zealand, 1891-94. *Address:* Brightwater, New Zealand.
Died 4 Oct. 1923.

BAKST, Léon; artiste peintre; b St Petersbourg, 1868; m 1903, Mademoiselle Trétiakoff, fille du maire de Moscou; one s. *Educ:* Collège de Pétrograd, puis École des Beaux Arts à Pétrograd. En 1897 délégué par l'Etat russe pour assister et peindre "L'Arrivée de l'Amiral Avellan à Paris" (tableau au musée de la Marine à Petrograd); en 1900 participé à la fondation de la société artistique "Mir Iskousstva"; en 1905 Sociétaire du Salon d'Automne à Paris; en 1907 Chevalier de la Légion d'Honneur; en 1909 peint les ballets "Schéhérasade" et "Cléopatre"; en 1910 première médaille d'or de la section russe à l'Exposition Universelle à Bruxelles; exposition pavillon Marsan en 1911 à Paris (musée du Louvre); en 1912 peint ballets "L'Après-midi d'un Faune" et "Hélène de Sparte", de Verhaeren; puis "St Sébastien" de d'Annunzio; en 1913 peint "La Pisanella" de d'Annunzio et en juillet 1913, en 1920 "Dames de bonne humeur", en 1923 "La Nuit ensorcellée" à l'Opéra de Paris, 1923 Exposition Knoedler New York, 4 tableaux acquis Albert et Victoria Museum 1922; et 3 tableaux acquis 1923 Metropolitan Museum New York. Membre de l'Académie Impériale russe de Beaux Arts, 1916; Membre de l'Académie Royale de Bruxelles. Par ligne directe descendant des familles Scheryra (d'Espagne) du sang du roi David de Judée. *Publications:* article "Les Problèmes de l'art nouveau", Nouvelle Revue 1910, Paris, à Londres et à Paris en 1913 édition d'art: "L'Art décoratif de Léon Bakst", par Arsène Alexandre; La Vie de Léon Bakst, monographie par A. Levinson; L'Œuvre de Léon Bakst pour La belle au bois dormant. *Recreations:* escrime, gymnastique. *Address:* 112 boulevard Malesherbes, Paris.
Died 27 Dec. 1924.

BALDWIN, Hon. Simeon Eben, AM (Yale), LLD (Harvard, Columbia, Wesleyan, and Yale); Professor of Law, Yale University, since 1872; Governor of Connecticut, 1911-15; b 5 Feb. 1840; s of Hon. Roger Sherman Baldwin, LLD, Governor of Connecticut and US Senator; g s of Hon. Simeon Baldwin, Judge of the Supreme Court of Errors; m 1865, Susan Winchester of Boston. *Educ:* Hopkins Grammar School of New Haven; Yale College; Yale and Harvard Law Schools. Member of State Commissions to revise Education Laws, 1872; General Statutes, 1873-74; Civil Procedure Laws, 1878-79; Taxation, 1885-87 and 1915-17; Associate Justice, Supreme Court of Errors, Connecticut, 1893-1907; Chief Justice, 1907-10; Director, Bureau of Comparative Law of the American Bar Association, 1909-19; Member of the American Antiquarian Society, the American Philosophical Society, and of the National Institute of Arts and Letters; Corresponding Member of the Massachusetts Historical Society, the Colonial Society of Massachusetts, and of the Institut de Droit Comparé, of Brussels; Fellow of the American Academy of Arts and Sciences, and of the American Association for the Advancement of Science; Associate of the Institut de Droit International. *Publications:* Baldwin's Connecticut Digest; Modern Political Institutions; Baldwin's Illustrative Cases on Railroad Law; American Railroad Law; The American Judiciary; The Relations of Education to Citizenship; The Young Man and the Law; co-author of Two Centuries' Growth of American Law. *Address:* 44 Wall Street, New Haven, Conn, USA. *Clubs:* Yale, New York City; Graduates', New Haven.
Died 30 Jan. 1927.

BALE, Edwin, RI 1877; Art Director, Cassell and Co. Ltd, 1882-1907; Secretary, Artists' Committee for Promoting Art Copyright Bill; b London, 1838; m 1878, Julia Dalton (d 1901). *Educ:* South Kensington Schools; the Academy of Arts, Florence. 1st Chairman Imperial Arts League, 1909-12; Editor of the Journal of the League, 1910-19. *Publications:* contributed articles to Ency. Brit. on Artistic Copyright and Process. *Recreations:* painting, gardening. *Address:* 11 Grove End Road, St John's Wood, NW. *Club:* Arts.
Died 9 April 1923.

BALFOUR OF BURLEIGH, 6th Baron, cr 1607; **Alexander Hugh Bruce,** KT; PC; GCMG 1911; GCVO 1917; b Kennet, Alloa, NB, 13 Jan. 1849; s of Robert Bruce, Kennet, sometime MP for Co. Clackmannan; title attainted 1716 for rising of 1715, and only restored in 1869; m 1876, Lady Katherine Hamilton-Gordon, y d of 5th and

sister of 7th Earl of Aberdeen; one s three d (and one s decd). *Educ:* Loretto; Eton; Oriel Coll., Oxford. BA with honours, 1871; MA 1872. Member Factory Commission, 1874-75; Member Endowed Institution Scotland Commission, 1878-79; Chairman Educational Endowments Commission, 1882-89; Chairman Welsh Sunday Closing Commission, 1889; Chairman Metropolitan Water Supply Commission, 1893-94; Chairman Rating Commission, 1896; Lord-in-Waiting to the Queen, 1888-89; Parliamentary Secretary to Board of Trade, 1889-92; Lord Rector, Edinburgh University, 1896-99; Sec. for Scotland (in the Cabinet), 1895-1903; Chancellor of St Andrews University, 1900; Chairman Royal Commission on Food Supply in Time of War, 1903; Chairman Royal Commission on Closer Trade Relations between Canada and West Indies, 1909; Chairman of Committee on Commercial and Industrial Policy after the War, 1916-17; Lord Warden of the Stannaries since 1904. DCL 1904; LLD, Universities of St Andrews, Aberdeen, Glasgow, and Edinburgh, and of the Welsh University. Church of Scotland. Conservative. Owned about 3,000 acres. *Heir:* s Major Hon. George Bruce, b 18 Oct. 1883. *Address:* Kennet, Alloa, NB; 47 Cadogan Square, SW. *T:* Kensington 800. *Clubs:* Carlton, Athenæum; New Conservative, Edinburgh; Western, Glasgow.
Died 6 July 1921.

BALFOUR, Ven. Andrew Jackson, MA, DCL; Archdeacon of Quebec since 1906; b Waterloo, Quebec, 25 Dec. 1845; m 1910, Edith Marina, d of late Alexander Marling. *Educ:* Bishops' University, Lennoxville. Ordained, 1869; Curate at Levis, PQ, 1869-72; Incumbent of Hatley, 1872-81; Rector of Richmond, 1881-88; Rector of St Peter's, Quebec, 1888-1906; Canon of Quebec Cathedral, 1902-6; Archdeacon of St Francis, 1906-9. *Address:* Church House, 2 Donnacona Street, Quebec, Canada.
Died 6 Oct. 1923.

BALFOUR, Charles Barrington, CB 1919; Lord-Lieutenant, Berwickshire, 1917; JP Roxburghshire and Berwickshire; County Councillor, Berwickshire, and Chairman of Finance Committee; President and Chairman, Berwickshire Territorial Force Association, and Chairman Berwickshire National Health Insurance Committee; Director, Barclay's Bank and Scottish Widows' Fund Life Assurance Society; b 20 Feb. 1862; s of Charles Balfour of Balgonie and Newton Don, and Hon. Adelaide, 5th d of 6th Viscount Barrington; m 1888, Lady Nina McDonnell, d of 5th Earl of Antrim; four s. Formerly Lieutenant, Scots Guards, 1881-90; Captain, Royal Guards Reserve Regt, 1900-1; served Egyptian Campaign, 1882; contested Roxburghshire, 1885; Berwickshire, 1892, 1894, 1895; Southport Division of Lancashire, 1899; MP (C) Hornsey Div. of Middlesex, 1900-7; President of National Union of Conservative Associations for Scotland, 1894-95. *Address:* Newton Don, Kelso, Scotland. *T:* Kelso 21; 14 Grosvenor Crescent, SW1. *T:* Gerrard 1307. *Clubs:* Carlton, Guards, Bachelors', Royal Automobile; New, Edinburgh.
Died 31 Aug. 1921.

BALFOUR, Edward, JP, DL; b 23 Jan. 1849; e surv. s of late Col John Balfour, Balbirnie, and Lady Georgiana Isabella, 2nd d of 1st Earl of Cawdor; m 1879, Isabella Weyman Hooper, Boston, USA; one s two d. *Address:* 2 Grosvenor Crescent, SW1. *T:* Sloane 4270; Balbirnie, Markinch, NB. *Clubs:* Turf, Marlborough; New, Edinburgh.
Died 10 Sept. 1927.

BALFOUR, Rt. Rev. Francis Richard Townley; Assistant Bishop of Bloemfontein since 1910; b Sorrento, 21 June 1846; s of late Blayney Townley Balfour and Elizabeth Catherine Reynell, Townley Hall, Co. Lough, Ireland. *Educ:* Harrow; Trinity College, Cambridge; Cuddesdon Theological College, Oxon. BA 1869, 3rd class Classical Tripos; MA 1872; Deacon, 1872; Curate of Buckingham; Priest, 1874; chaplain to the Bishop of Bloemfontein, 1876; missionary in Basutoland; Canon of Bloemfontein, 1884; chaplain to the British South Africa Company's Police on the Pioneering Expedition from Bechuanaland to Mashonaland, 1890; missionary in Mashonaland, 1890-92; director of the Mission at Sekubu, Basutoland, 1894-98; Archdeacon of Bloemfontein, 1901-6; of Basutoland, 1907-22. *Address:* Mafeteng, Basutoland, S Africa.
Died 3 Feb. 1924.

BALFOUR, Sir Isaac Bayley, KBE 1920; MD, DSc, LLD, MA; FRS 1884; b Edinburgh, 31 March 1853; s of John Hutton Balfour, Professor of Botany, University of Edinburgh, 1845-79; m 1884, Agnes, d of late Robert Balloch, Glasgow; one d (one s decd). *Educ:* Edinburgh Academy; Universities of Edinburgh, Strasburg, and Würzburg. Transit of Venus Expedition to Rodriguez, 1874; Regius Professor of Botany, University of Glasgow, 1879-84; explored Island of Socotra, 1880; Sherardian Professor of Botany, University of

Oxford, and Fellow of Magdalen College, 1884–88; King's Botanist in Scotland, Regius Keeper of Royal Botanic Garden, Edinburgh, and Professor of Botany, University of Edinburgh, 1888–1922. *Publications:* botanical. *Address:* Courts Hill, Haslemere. *T:* Haslemere 113. *Club:* Athenæum.   *Died 30 Nov. 1922.*

BALL, Sir Charles Bent, 1st Bt, *cr* 1911; Kt 1902; MD, MCh; FRCSI; Hon. FRCS; Regius Professor of Surgery, University of Dublin, and Surgeon, Sir Patrick Duns Hospital; Consulting Surgeon, Steevens, Monkstown and Orthopædic Hospitals; Hon. Surgeon to the King in Ireland; Member of General Medical Council; *b* 21 Feb. 1851; *y s* of late Robert Ball, LLD, Dublin; *m* 1874, Annie Julia, *e d* of late Daniel Kinahan, JP, Roebuck Park, Dublin; three *s* four *d*. *Educ:* Trinity Coll., Dublin. Medical Scholarship, senior Moderatorship, and gold medal Natural Science; Surgical Travelling Prize, University of Dublin; Lane Lecturer at San Francisco, 1902; late Member of Advisory Board for Army Medical Service; Erasmus Wilson Lecturer, Royal College of Surgeons of England, 1903; Lord Chancellor's Consulting Visitor in Lunacy; Medical Referee under Workmen's Compensation Act; late Commissioner for Education, Ireland; Temp. Lt-Col RAMC 1914. *Publications:* various surgical works. *Heir:* s Charles Arthur Kinahan Ball, MD [*b* 29 March 1877; *m* 1907, Elizabeth, *d* of Joseph S. Wilson, Berkeley, California; no *c*. *Address:* 22 Lower Fitzwilliam Street, Dublin]. *Address:* 24 Merrion Square, Dublin; White House, Killybegs, Co. Donegal. *T:* 1076. *Clubs:* Constitutional; Kildare Street, University, Dublin.

          Died 17 March 1916.

BALL, Rev. Charles Richard, MA; late Vicar of All Saints, Peterborough; Hon. Canon of Peterborough; Rural Dean of Peterborough, No 1 Deanery; *b* Clifton, Bristol; *s* of Joseph and Rebecca Ball; *m* Mary Eliza, 3rd *d* of Very Rev. A. P. Saunders, DD, late Dean of Peterborough, and formerly Headmaster of the Charter House; one *s* four *d*. *Educ:* Christ's Coll., Camb. Curate of Trentham, Staffordshire; Belgrave, Leicestershire; St John's, Leicester; St Andrew's, Leicester; appointed to the Vicarage of St Paul's, Peterborough, and to an Hon. Canonry in the Cathedral by Bishop Magee; Rural Dean of Peterborough, 1st Deanery, by Bishop Creighton; elected one of the Proctors in Convocation for the Diocese of Peterborough. *Publications:* Lessons on our Lord's Life and Ministry; The Promised Seed; The Apostle of the Gentiles; The Dispensation of the Spirit; Plain Instructions on the Church Catechism; The Blankthorpe Papers; Plain Thoughts on a Great Subject (Salvation); The Faith in Outline; Confirmation Before and After; Character: its Signification and its Outcome; The Chosen People and the Promised Christ; Preliminary Studies on the Books of the New Testament in the probable order of their writing; The Holy Communion in Substance and Shadow; The Voyage of Life. *Address:* Madeley House, Peterborough.

          Died 20 May 1918.

BALL, Ernest. *Publications:* (songs) Mother Machree, When Irish Eyes are Smiling, Love Me and the World is Mine, Till the Sands of the Desert Grow Cold, Will you Love me in December as you did in May?, A Little Bit of Heaven, Down the Trail to Home, Sweet Home, Let the Rest of the World Go By, Ten Thousand Years from Now, Saloon.   *Died May 1927.*

BALL, James Barry, MD; FRCP; Consulting Physician, Department for Diseases of Throat, Nose, and Ear, West London Hospital; Consulting Physician for Diseases of Throat and Ear, SS John and Elizabeth Hospital; formerly Lecturer on Diseases of Throat, Nose, and Ear, West London Post-Graduate College; Ex-President, Laryngological Society of London; *m* Clare, *d* of Joseph Weld. *Publications:* Hand-book of Diseases of the Nose and Pharynx; Intubation of the Larynx; various contributions to medical journals and Transactions of Societies. *Address:* 12 Upper Wimpole Street, W1. *T:* Paddington 826; 65 Stert Street, Abingdon, Berks.

          Died 2 Oct. 1926.

BALL, Sir James Benjamin, Kt 1918; MInstCE, MInstME; civil engineer; Past President, Permanent Way Institution; Major, Engineer and Railway Staff Corps; *b* 9 March 1867; *m* 1st, Emily Frances Alexandra, *d* of late Edward Spencer Shapley, Torquay; three *d*; 2nd, Julia, *widow* of late Robert Hill, Melbourne; one *s*. *Educ:* privately. Entered service Great Northern Railway, 1890; Engineer Lancashire, Derbyshire, and East Coast Railway, 1899; New Works Engineer, Great Central Railway, 1907; Engineer-in-Chief, Great Central Railway, 1912; London, Brighton, and South Coast Railway, 1917; services lent to Government in May 1917 by LB and SC Company and appointed by President of the Board of Trade as Controller of Timber Supplies; has been responsible for design and carrying out

of heavy railway and dock works involving large expenditure; Telford Gold Medal, Instn Civil Engineers. *Publications:* several technical papers presented to the Institution of Civil Engineers. *Club:* Reform.

          Died 16 Sept. 1920.

BALL, James Dyer, ISO 1908; MRAS and MRAS (China Br.); Hong-Kong Civil Service (retired); Director LMS; Editor, Friend of China, 1915–17; *b* Canton, 4 Dec. 1847; *s* of Rev. Dyer Ball, MA, MD, and Isabella Ball; *m* 1885, Gertrude Jane, *d* of Rev. Samuel Joseph Smith; two *s* one *d*. *Educ:* home; King's College, London; University College, Liverpool. Thirty-five years in the Hong-Kong Civil Service as Chief Interpreter, Sheriff, Registrar-General and Protector of Chinese; Member of Civil Service Board of Examiners; Commissioner for Oaths; JP; Editor China Review, 1900–1; Member Oxford Local Board of Examiners, Hong-Kong, etc; literary work for the Admiralty, 1916–18; work for the WO, 1917–18. On Committee SSU; on Committee Anti-Opium Society. *Publications:* Things Chinese; The Chinese at Home; The Religious Aspect in China; The Pith of the Classics; The Cantonese made Easy Series; Hakka made Easy; How to Write Chinese; Macao; and articles in Encyclopædia of Religion and Ethics, etc. *Recreations:* numismatics, philately. *Address:* Belstone, Alexandra Grove, North Finchley, N12.

          Died 21 Feb. 1919.

BALL, Thomas, CMG 1901; *b* Hull, 12 Dec. 1846; *m* 1st, 1869, Emily Joanna, *d* of John Dunkley; 2nd, 1890, Louise, *d* of John Wilson, and *widow* of Oscar Branmuller; three *s* two *d*. Mayor of Cape Town, 1898, 1899, 1900; President Mayoral Congress, South Africa, 1899, 1900, 1901, 1902, 1903, 1904 and 1905. *Address:* Rondebosch, Cape Town.   *Died 16 March 1922.*

BALL, Very Rev. Thomas Isaac, LLD; Examining Chaplain to Bishops of Argyll since 1884; Provost of Cathedral Chapter and College, Cumbrae, since 1891; Rector of St Andrew, Millport, since 1892. Ordained 1865; served in the Diocese of Brechin till 1874; Domestic Chaplain to late Earl of Kinnoull, 1874–76; served in the diocese of Edinburgh from 1876; Rector of St Michael's, Edinburgh, 1888–91; LLD degree conferred *honoris causa* by St John's College, Annapolis, Maryland. *Publications:* A Plea for Simplicity in Eucharistic Teaching; The Royal Supremacy over the Church of France in 1789; English Catholic's Vade Mecum (compiled); A Pastoral Bishop: Memoir of Bishop Chinnery-Haldane; numerous articles and literary contributions in various periodicals; translations of Latin hymns; compiler and translator, or co-compiler of many works of liturgical interest. *Address:* Millport, RSO, Buteshire, Scotland. *TA:* College, Millport.   *Died 4 Aug. 1916.*

BALL, Walter William Rouse, MA; Barrister; Fellow of Trinity College, Cambridge, and University College, London; *b* 1850; *m* 1885, Alice Mary Ball (*d* 1919). *Educ:* University College, London; Trinity College, Cambridge. Honours in Philosophy and Mathematics, University of London; Second Wrangler and First Smith's Prizeman, University of Cambridge. Deputy Professor for J. K. Clifford, London, 1877; Lecturer, Trinity College, Cambridge, 1878; Director of Mathematical Studies of College, 1891; Senior Tutor and Chairman of College Education Committee, 1898; Representative of University of Cambridge on Borough Council, 1905; member of Governing Bodies of Westminster School and the Cambridge Perse School; has examined on various occasions in the Tripos and other examinations, and has served on numerous Boards and Syndicates; owner of the largest collection in Great Britain of portraits of mathematicians. *Publications:* A History of Mathematics, and a Primer of the same subject; Mathematical Recreations and Essays; The Genesis and History of Newton's Principia; History of Mathematics at Cambridge; Text-Book on Algebra; A Guide to the Bar; History of Trinity College, Cambridge; A History of the First Trinity Boat Club; Records of Admission to Trinity College, 1546–1900, etc; and various memoirs in mathematical journals. *Address:* Trinity College and Elmside, Grange Road, Cambridge. *Clubs:* New University, Junior Constitutional.

          Died 4 April 1925.

BALL, Wilfrid, RE; painter in watercolours and etcher; Member of Council, Royal Society of Painter Etchers; *b* London, 4 Jan. 1853; *m* 1895, Florence, *d* of H. Brock-Hollinshead. *Educ:* Grammar School, Hackney. Began life as public accountant in London; studied art at Heatherley's School; exhibited in RA since 1876; bronze medal, Paris Exhibition 1900, for etching. *Publications:* Paper on Mezzotint Engraving; Sussex; Hampshire. *Recreations:* holder of London Athletic Club challenge cup for walking, 1876; rowing. *Address:* Sunnerset, Lymington, Hants. *Club:* Arts.

          Died 14 Feb. 1917.

BALLANTYNE, John William, MD, CM; FRCPE; FRSE; Extra Physician, Royal Maternity Hospital, Edinburgh (in charge of Antenatal Department); Lecturer on Midwifery and Gynaecology (to women students) in the University of Edinburgh and in the Edinburgh Post-Graduate Courses in Medicine; Hon. Librarian Royal College of Physicians, Edinburgh; obstetric physician and gynaecologist in private practice; *b* Eskbank, Dalkeith, 4 June 1861; *o s* of late John Ballantyne, nursery and seedsman, of Dalkeith and Birkdale, Windermere, and Helen Pringle, *o d* of Walter Mercer, Silk-Mercer, Edinburgh; *m* 1889, Emily Rosa (*d* 1914), 2nd *d* of late George Mathew, of Worsted Lodge, Cambridgeshire; no *c*. *Educ:* Bonnington Park School, Peebles; George Watson's College, Edinburgh; Edinburgh University. MB, CM Edin., 1883, with Buchanan Scholarship in Midwifery and Gynaecology; MD 1889, with gold medal and Gunning Simpson Prize in Obstetrics; Cullen Prize, RCPE, 1902. Senior Assistant to the Professor of Midwifery in the University of Edinburgh, 1885–90; Lecturer on Midwifery and Gynaecology, School of Medicine of the Royal Colleges and School of Medicine for Women, Edinburgh, 1890–1916; Examiner in Midwifery in the Universities of Aberdeen, 1895–99, Edinburgh, 1901–5, Glasgow and Liverpool; Edinburgh University Lecturer in Antenatal Pathology and Teratology, 1899–1900, and Lecturer on Midwifery to Women Students, 1916; President, Edinburgh Obstetrical Society, 1906–7; President, Edinburgh Medical Missionary Society, 1907–12. Hon. Fellow Glasgow Obstetrical and Gynaecological Society; Hon. Fellow American Association of Obstetricians and Gynaecologists; Hon. Member American Child Hygiene Association; Socio Honorario Soc. Scientifica Protectora da Infancia (Brazil).*Publications:* Diseases of Foetus, 2 vols, 1892–95; Teratogenesis, 1897; Manual of Antenatal Pathology and Hygiene, 1902–4; Diseases of Infancy, 1891; Essentials of Obstetrics, 1904; Essentials of Gynaecology, 1905; Expectant Motherhood, 1914; editor of Teratologia, 1894–95, of two issues of Green's Encyclopedia and Dictionary of Medicine, of second edition of Encyclopaedia Medica, and of Quinquennium of Medicine and Surgery; sub-editor for Scotland of the International Clinics; over four hundred articles. *Recreations:* literary research in medicine, addressing brotherhood meetings. *Address:* 19 Rothesay Terrace, Edinburgh. *TA:* Antenatal, Edinburgh. *T:* Central 2235.
Died 23 Jan. 1923.

BALLARD, Henry, CMG 1901; Port Captain, Durban, 1884–1904; *b* 1840; *s* of Henry James Ballard, of Southampton; *m* 1st, 1868, Harriet E. J. Richardson; 2nd, 1877, Sarah Eugenie Wroe, 3rd *d* of James Wroe of London. *Educ:* Southampton. Went to sea, 1854; made first voyage to Black Sea during Crimean War; served 25 years in the Union Steamship Company, Cape Mail Service; last ship command SS Mexican. *Address:* Inchanga, Howard Road, Southampton.
Died 30 Jan. 1919.

BALRAMPUR, Maharaja Bahadur of, Sir Bhagwati Prasad Singh, KCIE 1906; KBE 1918; Member of the Legislative Council of the UP of Agra and Oudh; Hon. Fellow of the University of Allahabad for life; Chairman Municipal Board, Balrampur; Special Magistrate; *b* 19 July 1879; *S* 1893. *Educ:* European and Indian tutors. Contributed large sums towards objects of charity and public utility in War Funds; invested about 30 lacs in War Loans; fond of sports; motorist, possessing nine cars of different makes; owning over a hundred elephants. *Address:* District Gonda, Oudh.
Died 25 May 1921.

BALZANI, Count Ugo; President of the Reale Società Romana di Storia Patria; Member of the Reale Accademia dei Lincei, and of the Instituto Storico Italiano; Hon. LittD Oxford; Corresponding Fellow of the British Academy; *b* Rome, 6 Nov. 1847; *s* of Count Andrea Balzani; *m* Mary Augusta Simon Agnew (decd), of Kilwaughter Castle, Ireland. *Educ:* University of Rome. *Publications:* Le Cronache Italiane nel Medio Evo; Il Regesto di Farfa di Gregorio di Catino; The Popes and the Hohenstaufen; Il "Chronicon Farfense"; Sisto V; besides many contributions to the transactions of the various institutions, Italian and foreign, of which he was a member. *Recreations:* walking, climbing. *Address:* 9 Via Po, Rome. *Club:* Athenæum.
Died 27 Feb. 1916.

BAMBER, Capt. Wyndham Lerrier, CBE 1919; RN; was Drafting Commander and Assistant Director Mobilisation Division, Admiralty, during European War (CBE). *Address:* 23 Vineyard Hill Road, SW19. *T:* Wimbledon 1438. *Club:* Junior United Service.
Died 14 Jan. 1924.

BAMBRIDGE, Rev. Joseph John, MA; MRAS; Vicar of St Mary Bredin, Canterbury, since 1895; Rural Dean of Canterbury, 1909–19; Hon. Canon of Canterbury Cathedral; *m;* one *d. Educ:* Durham University. CMS Missionary in Sindh, India; Fellow of and Examiner in the University of Bombay, 1881–91. *Address:* St Mary Bredin Vicarage, Canterbury.
Died 28 April 1923.

BAMFORD, Major Edward, VC 1918; DSO 1916; RM; Instructor of Small Arms, Hong-Kong, since 1926; *b* 28 May 1887; *s* of late Rev. Robert Bamford and Mrs Myers; unmarried. *Educ:* Sherborne School. 2nd Lieut Royal Marine Light Infantry, 1905; Lieut, 1906; served in HMS Bulwark, Magnificent, Britannia, Chester, Royal Sovereign and Highflyer; temp. Captain, 2 May 1916; Captain, 1 Sept. 1916; present at Battle of Jutland and operations at Zeebrugge, 23 April 1918 (DSO, VC, Bt-Major). *Recreations:* golf, hockey, lawn-tennis, boat-sailing, fishing. *Address:* Hong-Kong.
Died 29 Sept. 1928.

BANBURY, Brig.-Gen. Walter Edward, CMG 1916; Indian Army; retired; *b* 25 Dec. 1863. Served Burma, 1885–87 (medal with clasp); NW Frontier, India, 1897–98 (despatches, medal with clasp); European War, 1914–17 (despatches, CMG, Bt-Col). *Address:* St Cuthbert's, Ledbury. *T:* Ledbury 61. *Club:* East India United Service.
Died 2 Dec. 1927.

BANCROFT, Claude Keith; Assistant-Director of Science and Agriculture, and Government Botanist, British Guiana, since 1918; *b* 1885; *s* of Joseph Richard and Helena Blanche Bancroft; *m* 1909, Irene Mary, *d* of George Ernest Boorman, Faversham, Kent; two *s. Educ:* Harrison College, Barbados (scholar); Trinity College, Cambridge (major scholar, prizeman); First Class Natural Sciences Tripos, 1908. For some time research student in mycology, Royal Gardens, Kew; Mycologist and Botanist, Federated Malay States, 1910–13; Deputy-Chairman, Board of Agriculture, British Guiana, 1913. *Publications:* various, dealing with botany, mycology, and agricultural subjects in the Annals of Botany, Journal of Board of Agriculture, England, Kew Bulletin, and publications of tropical departments of agriculture. *Recreation:* cricket. *Address:* Botanic Gardens, Georgetown, British Guiana. *Club:* West India.
Died Jan. 1919.

BANCROFT, Edgar Addison; American Ambassador to Japan since 1924; *b* Galesburg, Ill, USA, 20 Nov. 1857; *m* 1896, Margaret Healy (*d* 1923), Brooklyn, NY. AB Knox College, 1878; LLD 1882; LLB Columbia University, 1880. Solicitor for Ill. of AT and SFRR Co., 1892–95; VP and general solicitor Chicago and Western Ind. RR Co. and the Belt RR Co., 1895–1904; member law firm Scott, Bancroft, Martin & McLeish, 1904–24; General Counsel International Harvester Co., 1907–20; Pres., Ill. State Bar Assoc., 1910; ex-Pres. of Law Club and of Chicago Bar Assoc.; orator on numerous patriotic, academic and festive occasions; gave the main addresses of welcome to various World-War Commissioners and heroes from Europe visiting Chicago at different times. *Publications:* The Chicago Strike of 1894; The Moral Sentiment of the People the Foundation of National Greatness; Destruction or Regulation of Trusts; The Mission of America; Belgium; Why we are in the War; Marshal Foch, and other War-time Addresses; Chairman of the Commission that published The Negro in Chicago: a Study of Race Relations and a Race Riot, 1922. *Recreations:* golf, hunting. *Address:* 134 S La Salle Street, Chicago, Ill.; American Embassy, Tokio, Japan. *Clubs:* Chicago, Union League (Pres. 1904–5), University, Literary, Merchants (Pres. 1899), Commercial (Pres. 1919–20), City, Cliff Dwellers, Onwentsia, Old Elm.
Died 28 July 1925.

BANCROFT, Elias, RCA. *Address:* 10 Acomb Street, Manchester.
Died 22 April 1924.

BANCROFT, Hubert Howe; historian; *b* Granville, Ohio, 5 May 1832; *s* of Ashley Bancroft, Massachusetts, and Lucy Howe, Vermont; *m* 1876, Matilda Griffing (*d* 1910), New Haven, Conn; three *s* one *d.* Entered book-store of his brother-in-law, Geo. H. Derby, Buffalo, NY, 1848; went to establish a branch in San Francisco, 1852; collected as materials for Pacific coast history a library of 60,000 vols (later in possession of California University), and with aid of a staff of collaborators, has written and published an historical series of 39 vols, covering the western part of N America, comprising the Native Races of the Pacific States, History of Central America, History of Mexico, and of various other districts. *Publications* include: Popular Tribunals, Essays, and Miscellany, Literary Industries; other works: The Book of the Fair, The Book of Wealth, Resources of Mexico, The New Pacific and Retrospection, etc. *Address:* 2898 Jackson Street, San Francisco. *T:* West 904.
Died 3 March 1918.

BANCROFT, Marie Effie, (Lady Bancroft); actress; *b* 12 Jan. 1839; *d* of late Robert Pleydell Wilton, a member of one of the oldest

Gloucestershire families, who left home to become an actor; *m* 1867, Squire (later Sir Squire) Bancroft; one *s*. After acting as a child in provinces, first appeared in London in Sept. 1856, as the boy in Belphegor; then chiefly at Strand Theatre until 1865, when the memorable management of the old Prince of Wales's Theatre began with production of the Robertson Comedies; migrated to Haymarket in 1880; retired from an exceptional career of successful management in 1885; has only occasionally acted since. *Publications:* joint-author of Mr and Mrs Bancroft On and Off the Stage, 1888; sole author of A Riverside Story, 1890; My Daughter, 1892; A Dream, 1903; The Shadow of Neeme, 1912. *Address:* A1 The Albany, W; Underlea, Sandgate.   *Died 22 May 1921.*

BANCROFT, Sir Squire Bancroft, Kt 1897; Hon. LLD; *b* London, 14 May 1841; *er s* of Secundus Bancroft White Butterfield and Julia, *d* of Thos Anthony Wright; adopted surname of Bancroft, 1867; *m* 1867, Marie Effie Wilton, the famous actress (*d* 1921); one *s* [*b* 1868; *m* 1893, Effie Lucy, *d* of late Sir John Hare]. *Educ:* private schools, England and France. First appeared on the stage at Birmingham in 1861; acted afterwards at leading provincial theatres with all the prominent "stars" of the stage; twenty years manager old Prince of Wales's and Haymarket Theatres, during which modern revival of stage was started; retired from an exceptional career of successful management, 1885; acted afterwards with Irving, but rarely since; was knighted by Queen Victoria for notable services to his profession; has devoted much time to "Readings" for hospitals throughout the country, and by which he raised £20,000; President of the Royal Academy of Dramatic Art; a member of the Lord Chamberlain's Advisory Board for the Licensing of Plays. *Publications:* joint-author of Mr and Mrs Bancroft On and Off the Stage: written by themselves, 1888; The Bancroft Recollections of Sixty Years, 1909; Empty Chairs, 1925. *Address:* A1 The Albany, W1. *T:* Gerrard 3206. *Clubs:* Athenæum, Garrick, Green Room (Pres.).

Died 19 April 1926.

BANDON, 4th Earl of, *cr* 1880; **James Francis Bernard,** KP; Baron Bandon, 1793; Viscount Bandon, 1795; Viscount Bernard, 1800; Irish Representative Peer; HM's Lieutenant of Co. Cork since 1874; *b* 12 Sept. 1850; *o s* of 3rd Earl and Catherine Mary, *e d* of Thomas Whitmore, Apley, Salop; *S* father 1877; *m* 1876, Hon. Georgiana Dorothea Harriet Evans-Freake, CBE 1920, *o c* of 7th Baron Carbery. *Educ:* Eton. Owned about 41,000 acres. *Heir: cousin* Percy Ronald Gardner Bernard, *b* 30 Aug. 1904. *Address:* Castle Bernard, Bandon; Durras Court, Bantry, Co. Cork. *Club:* Carlton.

Died 18 May 1924.

BANERJEA, Sir Surendranath, Kt 1921; BA; editor of The Bengalee; Professor of English Literature, Ripon College; *b* 10 Nov. 1848; 2nd *s* of late Dr Durga Churn Banerjea, physician; *m* 1867; one *s* five *d*. *Educ:* Doveton College, Calcutta; University College, London. Entered ICS, 1871; left the service, 1874; Professor of English Literature, Metropolitan Institution of Calcutta, 1875; founded Indian Association, 1876; founded Ripon College, Calcutta, 1882; was twice President of the Indian National Congress; for eight successive years was a Member of the Bengal Legislative Council; again elected, 1913; Member of the Imperial Legislative Council, 1913–20; President of the Moderate Conference, 1918; appointed a Member of the Franchise Committee in connection with Montagu-Chelmsford Scheme of Reforms for India, 1918; went to England and gave evidence before the Joint Parliamentary Committee of both Houses on Indian Reforms, 1919; Member of the Bengal Legislative Council under the Reforms Scheme, 1921; appointed Minister to the Government of Bengal in charge of Local Self-Government and Public Health. *Recreation:* gardening. *Address:* Bengalee Office, Calcutta.   *Died 6 Aug. 1925.*

BANERJEE, Sir Gooroo Dass, Kt 1904; MA, DL, PhD; retired High Court Judge; *b* Narikeldanga, Calcutta, Jan. 1844; *e s* of late Babu Ram Chandra Banerjee; *m* 1861, 3rd *d* of Pandit Pitambar Tarkapanchanan; four *s* two *d*. *Educ:* Hare School; Presidency College, Calcutta. Junior, Senior, and Burdwan Scholarships; BA 1864; Gold Medal for Mathematics; BL Gold Medallist, 1866; Vakil of the Calcutta High Court, 1866; Assistant Lecturer in Mathematics, Presidency College, 1865; Law Lecturer in the Berhampur College, 1866–72; Tagore Law Lecturer, 1878; Fellow of Calcutta University, 1878; Vice-Chancellor, 1889–91; Municipal Commissioner for the Suburbs of Calcutta, 1886; Presidency Magistrate, 1887; Member of the Bengal Legislative Council, 1888; Judge of the Calcutta High Court, 1889–1903; President of the Central Text-Book Committee, 1896–99; Member of the Indian Universities Commission, 1902. Hon. PhD 1908. *Publications:* The Elements of Arithmetic, 1879; The Tagore Law Lectures on the Hindu Law of Marriage and Stridhans,

1879; A Note on the Devanagari Alphabet, 1893; A Few Thoughts on Education, 1904; Elementary Geometry, 1907; The Education Problem in India, 1914; in Bengali— Siksha; Juan O Karma, 1910; Saral Patiganit, 1914; Saral Vijarganit, 1914; Saral Jyamiti, 1914. *Address:* 28 Sastitala Road, Narikeldanga, Calcutta.

Died 1919.

BANFIELD, Col Rees John Francis, CB 1900; late The Welsh Regiment; passed Staff College; *b* 10 Oct. 1850; *e s* of late Rees Silvanus Price Banfield of Chiswick, W; *m* 1877, Marie Louise, *d* of late J. G. Upton, Esq., of the East India Company; three *s* one *d*. Entered army, 1871; Capt. 1881; Major 1886; Lieut-Col 1896; served S Africa, 1899–1900 (severely wounded, despatches, medal with 5 clasps, CB); AAG, Chief Staff Officer, and Brig.-Gen. in charge of Administration, Gibraltar; commanded South Wales Territorial Brigade, 1906–10; retired, 1910. *Address:* Park View, Poole Road, Bournemouth.

Died 15 Jan. 1926.

BANGS, John Kendrick; author; *b* Yonkers, New York, 27 May 1862. *Educ:* Columbia University, New York. Managing Editor, Life, 1884–88; Editorial Staff, Harpers' Magazine, 1888–1900; Editor of Harpers' Weekly, 1900–2; Vice-President, Board of Education, Yonkers, NY, 1895; President, Halstead School, Yonkers, 1895–1903; Candidate for Mayor of Yonkers, 1894. *Publications:* Coffee and Repartee; A House-Boat-on-Styx; Mr Bonaparte of Corsica; Ghosts I Have Met; Mollie and the Unwise Man; Alice in Municipaland; and about thirty other books. *Recreations:* golf, gardening, travel. *Address:* Ogunquit, Maine; 7 West 43rd Street, New York City. *Clubs:* Century, Players, New York.

Died 21 Jan. 1922.

BANISTER, Col Fitzgerald Muirson, CMG 1917; retired pay, RFA; *b* 17 Sept. 1853; 3rd *s* of late Surg.-Gen. G. Banister, IMS; *m* 1888, Caroline Margaret (*d* 1921), *d* of Gen. R. E. Hamilton, RE. *Educ:* Wellington College; RMA. Entered Army, 1872; Lt-Col, 1897; Bt Col, 1901; retired, 1904; served Afghan War, 1879 (medal); rejoined, 1914; BEF, 1915–17 (despatches twice, CMG). *Address:* 58 Westbourne Terrace, W2. *T:* Paddington 2738.

Died 28 June 1928.

BANISTER, Rt. Rev. William, DD; *b* Walton le Dale, Lancashire, 31 May 1855; *m* Alice, *d* of T. Grime, Preston, Lancashire. *Educ:* privately; CMS College, Islington. Ordained deacon, 1879, priest, 1880, by Bishop of London; Curate, Balderstone, Blackburn, Lancashire, 1879–80; CMS Missionary, Foochow and Ku Cheng, Fuh-Kien Mission, 1880–93; Principal, CMS Theological College, Foochow, 1893–96; Secretary, CMS Hong-Kong, 1897; Archdeacon of Hong-Kong, 1902–9; Commissary to Archbishop of Canterbury during vacancy in See of Victoria, Hong-Kong, 1906–7; Bishop of Kwangsi-Hunan, China, 1909–23; retired. *Publications:* Scripture Catechism for the Young, in Chinese; Notes on 1st Corinthians, in Chinese. *Address:* c/o Church Missionary Society, Salisbury Square, EC.   *Died 26 Feb. 1928.*

BANKES, Ralph Vincent, KC 1910; Metropolitan Police Magistrate, S Western Police Court, since 1917; *b* 1867; *y s* of late J. Scott Bankes, Soughton Hall, Flint; *m* Ethel Georgina, 2nd *d* of late W. G. Mount, Wasing Place, Berks, many years MP for Newbury Division, Berks; two *s*. *Educ:* Winchester; University College, Oxford. Called Inner Temple, 1890. *Address:* 39 St George's Square, SW. *T:* Victoria 2134. *Club:* Oxford and Cambridge.

Died 25 Oct. 1921.

BANKS, Rev. John Shaw, DD Edin. 1903; Professor of Theology, Leeds, 1880–1910, then Emeritus; *b* Sheffield, 8 Oct. 1835; *m* Charity A. Hill, Plymouth; two *s* two *d*. *Educ:* King Edward's Branch School, Birmingham. Missionary in South India, 1856–64; laboured in Plymouth, Dewsbury, London, Manchester, Glasgow, 1865–80. President of the Wesleyan Conference, 1902. *Publications:* Manual of Christian Doctrine; Science of Religion (Fernley Lecture); Development of Christian Doctrine, 2 vols; Tendencies of Modern Theology; Central Questions of Faith; The New Testament Books; Translations from German of works by Philippi, Dorner, Monrad, Delitzsch, etc. *Address:* 3 Richmond Road, Leeds.

Died 17 March 1917.

BANNATYNE, Rev. Prof. Colin A., MA; Professor of Church History and Principles, College of the Free Church of Scotland, Edinburgh, since 1905; *b* 5 June 1849; *s* of late Rev. Archibald Bannatyne, Oban; unmarried. *Educ:* Edinburgh University and New College. Graduated at Edinburgh University; ordained minister Culter Free Church, 1876; Moderator of Free Church, 1900 and 1906. Took

leading part in famous law case, Bannatyne *v* Overtoun, appealed to and twice heard before House of Lords, decided in favour of the Free Church of Scotland, 1904. *Address:* 11 Bright's Crescent, Edinburgh.
Died 23 Nov. 1920.

BANNERMAN, Maj.-Gen. William Burney, CSI 1911; MD, DSc; FRSE; KHP 1913; IMS (ret.); *b* 6 July 1858; *s* of late Rev. James Bannerman, DD, Abernyte, Perthshire, Professor of Theology, New College, Edinburgh, and D. A. Douglas; *m* 1889, Helen, *d* of late Rev. R. Boog Watson, LLD, late Chaplain HM Forces; two *s* two *d. Educ:* Edinburgh Academy and University. MB, CM, Edinburgh, 1881. Entered IMS 1883; in military employ till 1891; Burmese Campaign, 1886–89 (medal, two clasps); in civil employ since 1891; Deputy Sanitary Commissioner, Madras; Superintendent, Plague Research Laboratory; Director, Bombay Bacteriological Laboratory, Parel; Surgeon-General, Madras, 1911–18; Associate Fellow College of Physicians, Philadelphia; corresponding member, American Society Tropical Medicine. *Publications:* Serum Therapy of Plague in India; Production of Alkali by Plague Bacillus in Liquid Media; Scientific Memoirs of Government of India; various papers on Plague in Journal of Hygiene; Treatment of Snake-Bite with Potassium Permanganate, Indian Journal of Medical Research, 1914–15, etc. *Recreations:* motoring, golf. *Address:* 11 Strathearn Place, Edinburgh. *Club:* University, Edinburgh. *Died 3 Feb. 1924.*

BANNISTER, Rev. Henry Marriott, MA, DLitt; Acting Sub-Librarian of the Bodleian; *b* 18 March 1854; *s* of Henry Powell Bannister, MRCS, and Hannah Maria Marriott; unmarried. *Educ:* Epsom College; Pembroke College, Oxford; 2nd Class Classical Moderations, 1875; 2nd Class Theology, 1877. Deacon, 1877; Priest, 1878; Assistant Curate of St Mary-Charterhouse, 1877–83; Mission Priest of St John the Baptist, Newport, Mon, 1883–84; Vicar of Winterbourne Down, Bristol, 1884–87. *Publications:* Editor of Analecta Hymnica Medii Aevi, vol. xl; co-editor of vols xlvii, liii, liv; Editor of Missale Gothicum, Henry Bradshaw Society, vol. lii; author of Catalogo sommario della Esposizione Gregoriana, Rome, 1904; Introduction to Ye Solace of Pilgrims, London, 1911; Monumenti Vaticani di Paleografia Musicale, 1918; contributor to English Historical Review, Journal of Theological Studies, Rassegna Gregoriana. *Address:* 205 Woodstock Road, Oxford. *T:* Oxford 69. *Clubs:* Union, Deal; Union, Rome; Oxford and County, Oxford.
Died 16 Feb. 1919.

BARBÉ, Louis A., B-ès-L Univ. Gall.; Officier d'Académie; Professor of Modern Languages (retired) and author; on the editorial staff of Blackie & Son; reviewer on the Glasgow Herald since 1887; *b* 15 Nov. 1845; *s* of Charles Barbé, Commissaire de Marine, Cherbourg; *m* 1880, Alice Rosa, *d* of John George Allen, Guernsey; one *s. Educ:* France. Began his scholastic career as Professor of English at the Collège Jean-Bart, Dunkerque; for six years tutor to the Princes of Schaumburg-Lippe; Headmaster of the Modern Languages department in the Glasgow Academy, 1884–1918; additional Examiner in French, University of Edinburgh, 1901; and in Modern Languages to the Faculty of Advocates. *Publications:* The Tragedy of Gowrie House, 1887; Kircaldy of Grange, and Viscount Dundee (Famous Scots Series); The Bass Rock and its Story (with his son, the late Lieut Adrien E. Barbé, RAF); In Byways of Scottish History, 1912; Margaret of Scotland and the Dauphin Louis, 1917; Sidelights on the Political, Social, and Industrial History of Scotland, 1919; has contributed many articles to various magazines and journals. *Address:* May View, Dunbar, Haddingtonshire.
Died Sept. 1926.

BARBENSON, Nicholas Peter Le Cocq; Ex-Judge and President of the States of Alderney; *b* 2 May 1838; *e s* of Thomas Nicholas Barbenson, late Judge of Alderney, and Margaret Le Cocq; *m* 1869, Elizabeth Isabella Charlotte, *e d* of Commissary-General David Gibbons; two *s* two *d. Educ:* Queen Elizabeth College, Guernsey; studied Law subsequently at Caen in the University of France (diploma of Bachelor of Law and Licentiate at Law in 1857–59). Called to Alderney Bar, 1860; Attorney-General, 1878. *Recreation:* yachting. *Address:* 7 Banister Road, Southampton.
Died 3 Aug. 1928.

BARBER, Ohio C.; Chairman, Board of Directors, Diamond Match Co. since 1881; *b* Middlebury, Ohio, 20 April 1841; *s* of George Barber and Eliza Smith; *m* 1866, Laura L. (decd), *d* of Daniel Brown of Akron, Ohio, lineal descendant of Cotton Mather; *m* 1915, Mary, *d* of Wilbur Orr, Akron, Ohio. *Educ:* Akron, Ohio, common schools, until 16 years of age, then began selling matches for his father (who was a match manufacturer), travelling in Ohio, Indiana, Michigan, and Pa. When he became of age, had entire management of the

business; in 1881 he arranged consolidation of a number of leading match manufacturers, and formed Diamond Match Co.; built up and developed Barberton, later a town of fully 18,000 population; interested in various large corporations. Director of Babcock & Wilcox Co. and Bryant & May Co. Ltd, President and Director of American Steam Board Co. Interested in many other manufacturing industries. *Address:* Barberton, Ohio, USA.
Died 4 Feb. 1920.

BARBER, William Charles, MB, MD, CM; Superintendent and Managing Director of Simcoe Hall Sanatorium, Barrie, Ont, Canada; Canadian-Irish parentage; *m* 1896, Susan C. Graham, Toronto. *Educ:* private tuition; Toronto Collegiate Institute, University of Toronto. After serving 21 months as Senior House Surgeon, Toronto General Hospital, entered service of Ontario Government Hospital for Insane; 10½ years Assistant Superintendent Mimico Hospital; 9½ years Rockwood Hospital, Kingston. *Recreations:* fishing, shooting. *Address:* Simcoe Hall Ltd, Barrie, Ont, Canada. *T:* 441. *Club:* Albany, Toronto.
Died 13 Dec. 1921.

BARBER, Sir (William) Henry, 1st Bt, *cr* 1924; *b* 9 Nov. 1860; *s* of late William Henry Barber, Edgbaston; *m* 1893, Martha Constance, *o c* of Simon Onions, Bourne Bank, Earls Croom, Worcestershire. A Life Governor of Birmingham University. *Heir:* none. *Address:* Culham Court, Remenham, Berks. *Clubs:* Boodle's; Union, Brighton.
Died 2 July 1927 (ext).

BARBER-STARKEY, William Joseph Starkey, JP; *b* 1847; *o s* of late Rev. Wm Henry Barber, of Darley Dale, Derbyshire, and Mary, 3rd *d* of late John Starkey, of Wheat House, Yorkshire; *m* 1873, Margaret Aimée, 3rd *d* of Sir George Kinloch, 1st Bt, of Kinloch, Perthshire; three *s* four *d. Educ:* Rugby; Trinity College, Cambridge. Called to the Bar, Inner Temple, 1877. *Address:* Knockshannoch, Glen Isla, Forfarshire; Aldenham Park, Bridgnorth, Shropshire. *Clubs:* Athenæum, Royal Automobile.
Died 10 July 1924.

BARBIER, Paul; officier d'Académie; officier de l'Instruction publique, Univ. Gall.; Professor of French language and literature, University of Wales, Cardiff; *b* Colombier Chatelot, Doubs, France; 2nd *s* of late Pasteur G. Barbier, French Protestant Church, London; *m* Euphémie, *e d* of Prof. Bornet, Aubonne, Lausanne. *Educ:* Ecole de la Confession d'Augsbourg, Paris. Read for the ministry; appointed French master at Felstead Grammar School, then in the Manchester Grammar School; permanent lectureship in French language and literature, 1883, which was raised to the status of a professorship in the University College of South Wales and Monmouthshire, Cardiff; past examiner-in-chief, University of London, etc; has taken a leading rôle in bringing the Keltic branch of France and the Welsh together; has been, by a singular literary coincidence, identified with the Paul Barbier of Mrs Humphry Ward's novel David Grieve. *Publications:* school editions of French classics. *Address:* University College, Cardiff.
Died 24 Sept. 1921.

BARBOUR, A. H. Freeland, MA, BSc, MD, LLD; FRCPE, FRSE; JP; Hon. Gynæcological Physician, Royal Infirmary; Consulting Physician, Royal Maternity Hospital, Edinburgh; *b* 7 Jan. 1856; *s* of G. F. Barbour of Bonskeid and Gryffe; *m* 1889, Margaret Nelson, *e d* of Hon. George Brown of Toronto; two *s* three *d. Publications:* (with Dr Berry Hart) Manual of Gynaecology; Spinal Deformity in its Relation to Obstetrics; Atlas of the Sectional Anatomy of Labour; The Sectional Anatomy of Labour, and its Bearing on Clinical Work; (with Professor Watson) Gynaecological Diagnosis and Pathology; Gynaecological Treatment. *Address:* 4 Charlotte Square, Edinburgh. *T:* 2414. *Died 11 June 1927.*

BARBOUR, Sir David Miller, KCSI 1889; KCMG 1899; *b* 1841; *s* of late Miller Barbour of Calkill, Ireland; *m* 1883, Katherine Constance, *d* of late Thomas Gribble; three *s* one *d.* Member of Royal Commission on Gold and Silver, 1886; Financial Member of Council of Governor-General of India, 1887–93; Member of Royal Commission on Financial Relations of Great Britain and Ireland, 1893; Member of Royal Commission on Sugar-Growing Colonies of the West Indies, 1897; of Indian Currency Committee, 1898; Commissioner to inquire into the finances of Jamaica; Chairman of Committee on the Currency of the West African Colonies, 1899; Special Commissioner to inquire into the finances of the Orange River Colony and the Transvaal, 1900; Chairman of the Committee on the Currency of the Straits Settlements, 1902; Chairman of the Royal Commission on London Traffic, 1903; Member of the Royal Commission on Shipping Rings, 1907. *Publications:* The Theory of Bimetallism; The Standard of Value; The Influence of the Gold Supply on Prices and Profits. *Address:* Tiltwood, Crawley Down, Sussex. *Clubs:* Athenæum, East India United Service.

Died 12 Feb. 1928.

BARBOUR, George, MA; JP, DL; *b* 1841; *o s* of late Robert Barbour and Janet Andrew, *d* of late William Fleming, of Sawmillfield, Glasgow; *m* 1869, Caroline Easton, *d* of late Robert Andrew Macfie, of Dreghorn Castle, Midlothian; one *s* six *d. Educ:* Harrow; Trinity College, Cambridge. Called to Bar, Inner Temple, 1865; High Sheriff, Cheshire, 1890; Patron of one living. Hon. Major, late Earl of Chester's Yeomanry Cavalry. *Address:* Bolesworth Castle, near Chester. *Clubs:* Carlton, New University.

Died 3 Nov. 1919.

BARBOUR, Major Robert, TD; MA; JP, DL; *b* 1876; *o s* of late George Barbour and Caroline Easton, *d* of late Robert Andrew Macfie, of Dreghorn Castle, Midlothian; *m* 1909, Ida Lavington, *o d* of Arthur Lavington Payne; three *s. Educ:* Harrow; Trinity College, Cambridge. Major, Earl of Chester's Yeomanry; High Sheriff, Cheshire, 1925; served South African War, 1900–1; European War, 1914–18. *Address:* Bolesworth Castle, near Chester. *Clubs:* Carlton, Junior Carlton.

Died 3 Sept. 1928.

BARCLAY, Florence Louisa; *b* 2 Dec. 1862; *d* of Rev. Charlesworth; *m* 1881, Rev. Charles W. Barclay; two *s* six *d. Publications:* (as Brandon Roy) Guy Mervyn, 1891; The Wheels of Time, 1908; The Rosary, 1909; The Mistress of Shenstone, 1910; The Following of the Star, 1911; Through the Postern Gate, 1912; The Upas Tree, 1912; The Broken Halo, 1913; The Wall of Partition, 1914; My Heart's Right There, 1914; In Hoc Vince, 1915; The White Ladies of Worcester, 1917; Returned Empty, 1920. *Address:* Little Amwell Vicarage, Hertford Heath, Hertford, Herts. *TA:* Hertfordheath; The Corner House, Overstrand, Norfolk. *M:* AR 2230.

Died 10 March 1920.

BARCLAY, Sir George Head, KCSI 1913; KCMG 1908; CVO 1906; HM Minister at Bucharest since 1912; *b* 23 March 1862; 3rd *s* of late Henry Ford Barclay of Monkhams, Woodford; *m* 1891, Beatrix Mary Jay, *d* of late Henry G. Chapman of New York; one *d. Educ:* Eton; Trinity College, Camb. Attaché, 1886; appointed to Washington, 1888; to Rome as 3rd Secretary, 1891; transferred to Madrid, 1894, where he was acting Chargé d'Affaires, 1897 and 1898; transferred to Constantinople, 1898; First Secretary of Legation at Tokyo, 1902–5; Councillor of Embassy, 1905; and again Constantinople, 1906; Minister at Constantinople, April–July 1908, and at Tehran, 1908–12. *Address:* British Legation, Bucharest. *Clubs:* Travellers', St James's.

Died 26 Jan. 1921.

BARCLAY, Rev. James, DD; Minister of St Paul's Church, Montreal, 1883–1910; *b* Paisley, 19 June 1844; 3rd *s* of late James Barclay of Edinburgh; *m* 1873, Marian Simpson of Dumfries. *Educ:* Paisley Grammar School; Merchiston Castle, Edinburgh; Glasgow University. Minister at Dalbeattie, 1870; Canonbie, 1874; Linlithgow, 1876; St Cuthbert's, Edinburgh, 1878. *Clubs:* St James's University, Montreal.

Died 18 May 1920.

BARCLAY, Robert Buchanan, ISO 1902; General Superintendent of Poor, Local Government Board for Scotland (retired); *b* 24 Feb. 1843; *s* of Hugh Barclay, LLD, Sheriff-Substitute of Perthshire; *m* 1875, Margaret, *d* of Bailie Binnie of Glasgow. *Educ:* Perth Academy. *Address:* 17 Inverleith Gardens, Edinburgh.

Died 26 Dec. 1919.

BARCLAY, Sir Thomas, Kt 1908; JP for Birmingham, Warwickshire, Worcestershire; *b* Sunderland, 30 Aug. 1839; 2nd *s* of James and Margaret Barclay of Felling, Co. Durham; *m* 1st, 1861, Mary Anne (*d* 1891), 2nd *d* of late Robert Jaques, MRCS; 2nd, Mary Dingley, 2nd *d* of late Edward D. Pethybridge, JP, banker, Launceston, Cornwall; two *s* five *d. Educ:* private tuition. Was the first Managing Director of Southall Bros & Barclay Ltd, Birmingham, which position he continued to hold; was for 8 years member King's Norton School Board, and 9 years member of the Birmingham City Council, during that time he was a member of the Water Committee and one of the pioneers of the scheme for bringing the Welsh water to Birmingham; represented British Pharmacists at the International Congress, 1881; after several years' agitation, commencing 1877, succeeded in abolishing the compulsory collection of Income Tax, Land Tax Grants, by unwilling collectors; was the Founder of the Chemists' and Druggists' Trade Association of Great Britain, 1876. *Publications:* The Future Water Supply of Birmingham (3 editions); The Class Leader at Work. *Recreations:* golf, travelling. *Address:* The Uplands, Blackwell, near Bromsgrove. *TA:* Uplands, Bromsgrove. *T:* 20 Barnt

Green. *M:* AB 640 and AB 4260. *Club:* National Liberal.

Died 23 Dec. 1921.

BARDSLEY, Rev. Joseph Udell Norman, MA; Vicar and Rural Dean of Lancaster; *b* 13 Dec. 1868; *s* of Rev. S. Bardsley, MA, Rector of Finchley; *m* 1895, Annie Mabel Killick, Beech Mount, Aigburth, Liverpool; two *s* four *d. Educ:* St Paul's School; Gonville and Caius College, Cambridge. Ordained 1892; Curate of St Leonard's, Bootle; St Anne, Aigburth; St Philip, Litherland; Rector of Ulverston, 1896; Vicar of Lancaster and Chaplain to the Bowerham Barracks, 1909; Proctor in Convocation, 1907–10; Rural Dean, 1911; Proctor in Convocation, 1919; Hon. Canon of Blackburn, 1927. *Publication:* The Church of England and her Endowments, 1912. *Recreation:* golf. *Address:* The Vicarage, Lancaster. *T:* Lancaster 87.

Died 8 July 1928.

BARE, Captain Arnold Edwin, MVO 1916; 1st Artists' Rifles; *b* 1880; *s* of Thomas Edwin Bare, Past President, Quantity Surveyors' Association; *m* 1906, Janie H. Stormont; one *s* two *d. Educ:* Emanuel School. Quantity Surveyor; member of firm, Bare, Leaning & Bare; Fellow of The Surveyors' Institution; enrolled in Artists' Rifle Volunteers, 1897; to France with BEF Oct. 1914. *Address:* Rokra, Bushey Grove Road, Bushey, Herts. *T:* Holborn 5675.

Died 30 Oct. 1917.

BAREFOOT, Lt-Col George Henry, CB 1916; CMG 1915; late RAMC; *b* 29 Nov. 1864. Entered army, 1886; Major 1898; Lt-Col 1906; served Hazara Expedition, 1888 (despatches, medal with clasp): European War, 1914–18 (despatches, CMG, CB); retired pay, 1919.

Died 15 Sept. 1924.

BARFF, Henry Ebenezer, CMG 1923; MA; Warden and Registrar, University of Sydney, since 1914; *b* Tahaa, Society Islands, 9 July 1857; *s* of Rev. John Barff, of LMS; *m* 1899, Jane Foss, *d* of H. C. Russell, CMG, BA, FRS, Govt Astronomer of NSW; one *d. Educ:* Camden College School; Sydney University. BA 1876; MA 1882; Master of Studies, University of Sydney, 1880; Acting Registrar, 1880; Registrar, 1882. *Publication:* A Short Historical Account of the University of Sydney. *Recreation:* golf. *Address:* Cotham, Newcastle Street, Rose Bay, Sydney, NSW. *T:* Sydney F7017. *Clubs:* University, Royal Sydney Golf, Sydney.

Died 2 May 1925.

BARFF, Rev. Henry Tootal, MA; Canon of Gilbraltar since 1894; *b* Wakefield, 1834; *m* Mary, *d* of Rev. J. Matthews, Vicar of Sherburn; two *s* one *d. Educ:* Trinity Hall, Camb.; 2nd Class Classical Tripos. Ordained 1858; Incumbent of Hawkley, Hants, 1862–65; Curate of Holy Trinity, Maidstone, 1868–70; Hythe, Kent, 1870–71; Assistant Chaplain, Nice, 1872–75; Chaplain at Naples, 1875–1904. *Address:* Nailsea House, Nailsea, Somersetshire. *TA:* Nailsea.

Died 4 April 1917.

BARING, Major Hon. Guy Victor; Reserve of Officers; MP (C) Winchester since 1906; *b* 26 Feb. 1873; 4th *s* of 4th Lord Ashburton; *m* 1903, Olive, *y d* of Hugh C. Smith, Mount Clare, Roehampton; four *s* one *d. Educ:* Eton; Sandhurst. Joined Coldstream Guards, 1893; served with 2nd Batt., S Africa, 1899–1900 (medal, three clasps); present with the Imperial Representative Corps at the Inauguration of the Australian Commonwealth, Sydney, 1901; served with Ogaden Punitive Force, 1901 (medal, clasp). *Recreation:* travel. *Address:* 16 Cadogan Square, SW; St Cross Mill, Winchester. *Clubs:* Carlton, Guards.

Died 16 Sept. 1916.

BARING, Harold Herman John, MBE 1920; landowner; *b* 4 March 1869; *e s* of late Thomas Charles Baring, MP, and Susan Carter, *d* of Robert Bowne Minturn, of New York; *m* 1898, Mary, *d* of John Augustus Churchill, New York. *Address:* High Beech, Loughton, Essex. *T:* Loughton 102.

Died 10 Dec. 1927.

BARING, Hon. Windham; Managing Director of Baring Brothers & Co. Ltd, and Director of The Buenos Ayres Great Southern Railway Co. Ltd; *b* 29 Sept. 1880; 2nd *s* of 1st and *brother* of 2nd Earl of Cromer; *m* 1913, Lady Gweneth Frida Ponsonby, *y d* of 8th Earl of Bessborough; three *s. Educ:* Eton; Christ Church, Oxford. Served in European War as Lieut RNVR. *Recreations:* shooting, golf. *Address:* 57 Portland Place, W. *T:* Mayfair 2627; Woodcock, Little Berkhampstead, Hertford. *T:* Essendon 16. *Clubs:* Turf, Brooks's, Bath.

Died 28 Dec. 1922.

BARING-GOULD, Sabine, MA; JP; Hon. Fellow of Clare College, Cambridge; Rector, Lew-Trenchard, Devon; *b* Exeter, 28 Jan. 1834; *e s* of Edward Baring-Gould, Lew-Trenchard, and Charlotte Sophia, *d* of Admiral F. Godolphin Bond, RN; *m* 1868, Grace (*d* 1916), *d*

of Joseph Taylor, Horbury, Yorkshire. *Educ:* Clare College, Cambridge. Travelled in Iceland, 1861; various parts of Europe; Curate, Horbury, Yorkshire, 1864; Vicar, Dalton, Yorkshire, 1866; Rector of East Mersea, Essex, 1871; inherited family estates, Lew-Trenchard, 1872, on death of father; presented himself to Rectory of Lew-Trenchard on death of his uncle, 1881. Owned 3,000 acres.

Publications: The Path of the Just, 1854; Iceland, its Scenes and Sagas, 1862; Post-Mediæval Preachers, 1865; Book of Were-Wolves, 1865; Curious Myths of the Middle Ages, 1866, 1868; The Origin and Development of Religious Belief, 1869–70; The Golden Gate, 1870; The Silver Store, 1870, 1883; In Exitu Israel, 1870; Legendary Lives of Old Testament Characters, 1871; One Hundred Sermon Sketches for Extempore Preachers, 1872; Secular *v* Religious Education, 1872; Lives of the Saints, 1872–77; Village Conferences on the Creed, 1873; The Lost and Hostile Gospels, 1874; Some Modern Difficulties, 1875; Village Sermons for a Year, 1875; The Mystery of Suffering, 1877; Mehalah, 1880, 1885; John Herring, 1883–86; Court Royal, 1886–88; Red Spider, 1887–88; The Gaverocks, 1887–88; Richard Cable, 1888; Eve, 1888; The Sacristy, a Quarterly Review of Ecclesiastical Art and Literature, 1871–73; Germany, Present and Past, 1879, 1883; Sermons to Children, 1879; The Preacher's Pocket, 1880; The Village Pulpit, 1881, 1887; Village Preaching for a Year, 1884; Church Songs, 1884; The Seven Last Words, 1884; The Passion of Jesus, 1885, 1886, 1887; The Nativity, 1885; Germany (Story of the Nations Series), 1886; Our Parish Church, 1886; The Resurrection, 1888; Our Inheritance, a History of the Holy Eucharist in the First Three Centuries, 1888; The Pennycomequicks, 1889; Arminell, 1889; Historic Oddities and Strange Events, 1889–91; Old Country Life, 1889; History of the Church in Germany, 1891; Urith, 1890; In Troubadours' Land, 1890; Conscience and Sin, 1890; Songs of the West, 1891; In the Roar of the Sea, 1892; The Tragedy of the Cæsars, 1892; Curious Survivals, 1892; Mrs Curgenven, 1893; Cheap Jack Zita, 1893; The Deserts of Southern France, 1894; The Queen of Love, 1894; A Garland of Country Song, 1894; Old Fairy Tales Retold, 1894; Noémi, 1895; The Old English Fairy Tales, 1895; Napoleon Bonaparte, 1896; The Broom Squire, 1896; A Study of St Paul, 1897; Guavas the Tinner, 1897; Bladys, 1897; The Sunday Round, sermons, 1898; Domitia, 1898; Pabo the Priest, 1899; A Book of the West, 1899; Furze-Bloom, 1899; The Crock of Gold, 1899; Winefred, 1900; A Book of Dartmoor, 1900; In a Quiet Village, 1900; Virgin Saints and Martyrs, 1900; The Frobishers; A Book of Brittany; Royal Georgie, 1901; Miss Quillet; Nebo the Nailer, 1902; Brittany, 1902; A Book of N Wales, 1903; Chris of All Sorts, 1903; A Book of Ghosts, 1904; In Dewisland, 1905; A Book of S Wales, 1905; A Book of the Riviera, 1905; A Memorial of Nelson, 1905; A Book of the Rhine, 1906; A Book of the Pyrenees, 1907; The Restitution of all Things, 1907; A Book of the Cevennes, 1908; Devonshire Characters, 1908; Cornish Characters, 1909; Family Names, 1910; The Land of Teck, 1911; Cliff Castles and Cave Dwellings, 1911; The Church Revival, 1914; The Evangelical Revival, 1920; Early Reminiscences (1834–1864), 1923. *Address:* Lew-Trenchard House, N Devon. *TA:* Lew Down.
Died 2 Jan. 1924.

BARKER, Arthur Edward James; Professor of Surgery, University College, since 1893; Surgeon, University College Hospital, London, since 1885; Consulting Surgeon to the Queen Alexandra Military Hospital, Millbank, SW; Consulting Surgeon to Osborne Convalescent Home for Officers RN and Army; Lieutenant-Colonel, RAMC; Consulting Surgeon to the Southern Command; *m* 1880, Emilie Blanche, *d* of Julius Delmege of Rathkeale, Co. Limerick; one *s* four *d*. *Publications:* Manual of Operative Surgery, 1887; Diseases of Joints (Treves's System of Surgery), 1896; Address in Surgery, British Medical Association, 1909; Operations for Hernia in System of Operative Surgery, edited by F. F. Burghard, 1909. *Recreations:* yachting, cricket, lawn-tennis, golf. *Address:* 144 Harley Street, W. *T:* 1547 Paddington.
Died 8 April 1916.

BARKER, Col Charles William Panton, CBE 1920; VD; Solicitor, Clerk to Justices; Notary Public; *b* 15 Sept. 1857; *m* 1884, Mary (*d* 1922), 2nd *d* of John Carr Tone, Grange House, Sunderland; two *s* two *d*. *Educ:* Crow Tree House, Sunderland. Law Society's Prizeman, 1878; Durham RGA (T), 1877–1910; 160th RFA (Wearside) Brigade 1915. *Address:* The Hawthorns, Sunderland. *T:* Sunderland 363, 974. *Club:* Sunderland.
Died 21 March 1926.

BARKER, Edward Harrison; British Vice-Consul for Tréport and Eu, France, since 1904; *b* 19 Feb. 1851; *s* of Benjamin Barker, *g s* of Thomas Barker, painter of The Woodman, etc; *m* 1876, Mary Isabel, *d* of late Captain Kitching, EICS, Inspecting Commander of HM Coastguard; two *s* two *d*. *Educ:* Bath Grammar School. Editor of Bath Argus at age of 21; subsequently on editorial staff of Galignani's

Messenger and Paris Correspondent of London and other newspapers; contributed frequently to Temple Bar and various magazines; British Vice-Consul at Pauillac, 1900. *Publications:* Wayfaring in France; Wanderings by Southern Waters; Two Summers in Guyenne; France of the French; A British Dog in France, etc. *Recreation:* natural history. *Address:* Le Tréport, Seine Inférieure, France.
Died 31 Oct. 1919.

BARKER, Sir Francis (Henry), Kt 1917; Director, Vickers, Ltd; *b* 18 June 1865; 2nd *s* of late Alfred Barker of Constantinople and Elmfield, Esher; *m* 1897, Aimée, *e d* of late Arthur de Vere; two *s*. *Educ:* private tutors; Clifton College. Vice-Chairman of Metropolitan-Vickers Electrical Co. Ltd; President of British Russia Club; Chairman of Executive Council of Russo-British Chamber of Commerce; travelled all over Europe and Asia Minor. *Recreations:* shooting, riding. *Address:* Lowndes House, Lowndes Place, Belgrave Square, SW. *T:* Victoria 6354; Burnt Stub, Chessington, Surrey. *T:* Esher 227. *TA:* Barkonia, London. *Clubs:* Marlborough, St James's, Royal Automobile.
Died 28 Jan. 1922.

BARKER, Colonel Sir Francis (William James), Kt 1906; RA, retired; *b* 29 April 1841; *e s* of late William Barker, FRCPI, ex-President of Royal College of Physicians, Ireland; *m* 1873, C. Jessie, *o d* of late John Foster; four *s* two *d*. *Educ:* Trinity College, Dublin; Royal Military Academy, Woolwich. Entered RA 1863; Major, 1883; Lt-Col, 1890; Col, 1896; retired from Army, 1898; served Abyssinian Expedition, 1867–68, including assault and capture of Magdala (medal); Instructor in Gunnery, 1873–76; Inspector of Warlike Stores, 1878–84; Assistant Superintendent, Royal Gunpowder Factory, 1885–92; Acting Superintendent, 1892; Superintendent, Royal Small Arms Factory, Birmingham, 1892. *Recreations:* yachting, boating, fishing. *Address:* 1 Westbourne Mansions, Folkestone. *Club:* Radnor, Folkestone.
Died 3 March 1924.

BARKER, Hon. Sir Frederic Eustace, Kt 1913; Chief Justice of the Supreme Court of New Brunswick, 1908–14; *b* 27 Dec. 1838; *s* of Enoch Barker of Sheffield, county of Sunbury; *m* 1st, Julia (*d* 1874), *d* of Edward Lloyd, RE Civil Staff; 2nd, Mary Ann, *d* of late B. E. Black of Halifax; one *s* four *d*. *Educ:* Sunbury Grammar School; University of New Brunswick. BA with honours, 1856; MA 1858; BCL 1861; DCL 1866. Called to Bar, 1860; QC 1873; Judge of the Supreme Court of New Brunswick, 1893; member House of Commons for City of St John, 1885; Administrator of the Government during absence of Lieutenant-Governor Fraser, 1896; some years a member of the University Senate; one of the Commissioners to revise the Provincial Statutes, 1866; Chairman of the St John School Board, etc. *Recreation:* fishing. *Address:* The Cedars, Mount Pleasant, St John, NB. *Club:* Union.
Died 15 Dec. 1916.

BARKER, Maj.-Gen. John Stewart Scott, CB 1903; RA; commanding Royal Artillery, Malta since 1912; *b* 13 Sept. 1853; *s* of Sir George Barker; *m* 1885, Agnes Mary, *y d* of late Major Peel of Aylesmore, Glos. Entered army, 1872; Captain, 1882; Major, 1889; Lt-Col, 1898; Col, 1902; served S Africa, 1901–2 (despatches twice; medals with 5 clasps, Brevet-Col); Brig.-Gen. commanding Jhansi Brigade, 1907–12. *Address:* Malta.
Died 20 April 1918.

BARKER, Very Rev. Joseph, DD; *b* 23 Oct. 1834; *s* of John Perkins Barker; *m* 1st, 1853, Elizabeth Annie White (*d* 1869), Huntley, Gloucestershire; six *d*; 2nd, 1870, Isabel S. Fannin; one *s* one *d*. *Educ:* Kidderminster Diocesan School; private tuition as Pupil Teacher, St Mary's National School; in 4th year, acting Master during vacancy. Arrived in Natal, 1853; ordained, 1857; Curate of Ladysmith, 1857–61; Canon of St Saviour's Cathedral, Maritzburg; Incumbent of St Patrick's, Umzinto, 1861–87; Archdeacon of Durban, 1878–87; Vicar of Ladysmith, 1887–1906; Archdeacon of Maritzburg, 1887–1908; Dean of Maritzburg and Archdeacon, city of Maritzburg 1906; Vicar of St Saviour's, Maritzburg, 1913; retired on pension, 1915. *Address:* The Deanery, Maritzburg, Natal.
Died 25 June 1924.

BARKER, Lt-Col Randle Barnett-, DSO 1916; Commanding 22nd Battalion Royal Fusiliers; *b* 1870; *e s* of late Major J. B. Barnett-Barker, 5th Fusiliers; *m* 1897, Ellinor Gertrude, *e d* of Richard Hobson, JP, DL, The Marfords, Bromborough, Cheshire; two *s*. *Educ:* privately. Joined Royal Welsh Fusiliers, 1891; Brigade Major, Cheshire Brigade, 1907–12; retired from Army; Commandant prisoners of war, Aug. 1914; raised the 22nd Batt. Royal Fusiliers in Kensington, Sept. 1914; afterwards commanded them when they embarked for France (despatches 4 times, Brevet Majority, June 1917); DSO (immediate reward) for gallantry on the Somme, Bar to DSO (immediate reward for gallantry at Arras, 1917); in following actions: Vimy Ridge, 1916; Delville Wood, 1916; Beaumont-Hamel, 1916; Ancre advance and Miraumont battle, 1917; Arras, April 1917. *Recreations:* shooting, fishing; won many point-to-point races. *Address:* Cae Kenby, Abergavenny. *Club:* Naval and Military.

Died 24 March 1918.

BARKER, Rev. Rowland Vectis; Hon. Canon of St Edmundsbury and Ipswich; Hon. Chaplain to the Bishop; Proctor in Convocation for Archdeaconry of Suffolk, 1906–19; *b* 1846; *y s* of John Barker, JP, DL, of Albrighton Hall, Shifnal, and Cleveland House, Wolverhampton; *m* 1883, Elizabeth, *d* of late Sir R. H. Inglis Palgrave, FRS; three *s* one *d. Educ:* Shrewsbury School; Christchurch, Oxford, MA. Ordained, 1871; Curate of Gt Yarmouth, 1871–75; Nantwich, 1877–79; Vicar of St Paul's, Preston, 1879–85; Vicar of St Mark, Lakenham, Norwich, 1885–94; Vicar of Bramford with Burstall, Suffolk, 1894–1904; Rector of Henstead, Suffolk, 1904–18; Organising Secretary SPG for Archdeacon of Suffolk, 1898–99; Rural Dean of Bosmere, 1898–1904. *Address:* The Lodge, Woodbridge, Suffolk. *TA:* Woodbridge. *M:* DX 2240.

Died 8 Nov. 1926.

BARKER, Very Rev. William, DD, Oxford; Dean of Carlisle since 1908; Hon. Chaplain to the King; Prebendary of St Paul's; Rural Dean, 1905; *b* London, 1 Dec. 1838; *s* of Joseph Charles Barker; *m o d* of Adm. Sir James Ross, Arctic explorer; two *s* one *d. Educ:* private tutors; Worcester Coll., Oxford. BA 1861, MA 1863; ordained Deacon, 1862; Priest, by Bishop of London, Dr Tait, 1863; Curate of Hanover Chapel, Regent Street (the church has since been pulled down), 1862–68; Chaplain to Royal Ophthalmic Hospital, Moorfields; Assistant Minister, Curzon Chapel, 1867–70; Organising Secretary of Curates' Augmentation Fund, 1870–73; Vicar of St Mary's, West Cowes, 1873–82; Chaplain to the Queen, 1876–99; member of London School Board, 1882–88; Rector of St Marylebone to 1908; Chaplain to the "Foresters"; Hon. Chaplain in ordinary to the King, 1902. *Publications:* no book; writings chiefly articles; once sub-editor of the old English Churchman. *Recreations:* fishing, golf, foreign travelling. *Address:* The Deanery, Carlisle. *TA:* Deanery, Carlisle. *T:* 427. *M:* LB 9094. *Club:* Felixstowe Golf.

Died 28 Jan. 1917.

BARKER, Lt-Col William Arthur John, DSO 1916; late Commanding 8th South Staffordshire Regiment; *b* 22 Aug. 1879; 2nd *s* of Col Sir Francis Barker. Entered South Staffordshire Regt, 1899; served South Africa, 1900–2 (Queen's medal, 3 clasps; King's medal, 2 clasps); European War, 1914–16 (wounded three times, despatches thrice, DSO, Croix de Guerre with palms); resigned, 1909; rejoined, 1915. *Address:* 1 Westbourne Mansions, Folkestone.

Died 25 Aug. 1924.

BARLOW, Adm. Charles James, DSO 1887; RN; *b* 11 Aug. 1848; *m* 1892, Elizabeth Hume, *d* of Arthur Dight of Queensland and NSW, Australia. Entered navy, 1862; Capt. 1889; served Egypt, First Lieut HMS Inflexible, bombardment of Alexandria and ashore, 1882 (medal, Alexandria clasp, Khedive's star, 4th class Osmanieh); Burmah, 2nd in command Naval Brigade, 1885–86 (despatches, DSO, India medal, clasp); 2nd in command Channel Fleet, 1905; 2nd in command Home Fleet, 1904; Admiral Superintendent Devonport Dockyard, 1906–8; retired, 1911. *Died 25 Aug. 1921.*

BARLOW, George Thomas, CIE 1915; Chief Engineer and Secretary, Government Irrigation Branch, UP, India; *b* 11 March 1865; *s* of Rev. J. M. Barlow, Ewhurst Rectory, Guildford; *m* 1891, A. S. Anthony; two *s* two *d. Educ:* Haileybury; RIE College. Appointed PWD, India, 1886; after a year's practical course in England went to India as Irrigation Engineer; employed at various posts on Ganges Canal till 1901; Executive Engineer, 1897; Superintending Engineer, 1911; from 1901 worked in the trans-Jumna Tract, UP, known as Bundel-Khund, or prospecting on the Survey and on the construction of numerous reservoirs and large masonry dams and canals. *Publications:* a few text-books. *Recreations:* tennis, big game shooting. *Address:* Allahabad, UP, India.

Died 9 April 1919.

BARLOW, Jane, Hon. DLitt Dublin; *b* Clontarf, Co. Dublin, 1857; *e d* of Rev. J. W. Barlow, late Vice-Provost, TCD. *Educ:* at home. *Publications:* Bogland Studies, 1892; Irish Idylls, 1892; Kerrigan's Quality, 1893; The End of Elfintown, 1894; The Battle of the Frogs and Mice, 1894; Maureen's Fairing, 1895; Strangers at Lisconnel, 1895; Mrs Martin's Company, 1896; Creel of Irish Stories, 1897; From the East unto the West, 1898; From the Land of the Shamrock, 1900;

Ghost-Bereft, 1901; The Founding of Fortunes, 1902; By Beach and Bog Land, 1905; Irish Neighbours, 1907; The Mockers, 1908; Irish Ways, 1909; Mac's Adventures, 1911; Flaws, 1911; Doings and Dealings, 1913. *Recreation:* music. *Address:* The Cottage, Raheny, Co. Dublin. *TA:* Barlow, Raheny. *T:* 47 Clontarf.

Died 17 April 1917.

BARLOW, Col John, MVO 1909; VD 1910; Vice-President, National Rifle Association. Late 5th VB Manchester Regt, Hon. Col 8 (Ardwick) Batt., 1906. *Address:* NRA School of Musketry, Bisley Camp. *Died 30 Sept. 1924.*

BARNARD, 9th Baron, *cr* 1698; Henry de Vere Vane, FSA; JP, DL; Hon. DCL Durham; Provincial Grand Master Durham Freemasons since 1900; Hon. Colonel 4th (Special Reserve) Battalion Durham Light Infantry; Chairman Tees Fishery Board; a Governor of Shrewsbury School; *b* 10 May 1854; *s* of Sir Henry Morgan Vane; *S* kinsman, 4th and last Duke of Cleveland, in Barony of Barnard, 1891; *m* 1881, Lady Catharine Sarah Cecil (*d* 1918), *d* of 3rd Marquess of Exeter; two *s* (and one *s* decd). *Educ:* Eton; Brasenose College, Oxford (BA 1876). Barrister 1879; Northamptonshire Militia, 1876–84; served in Charity Commission, 1881–91; Private Secretary to Chief Commissioner, 1885–90. *Heir: er* surv. *s* Hon. Christopher William Vane, MC, Capt. Westmorland and Cumberland Yeomanry; [*b* 28 Oct. 1888. Served European War (wounded)]. *Address:* 20 Belgrave Square, SW; Raby Castle, Darlington. *Clubs:* Brooks's, Oxford and Cambridge. *Died 28 Dec. 1918.*

BARNARD, Andrew Bigoe, CIE 1911; Deputy Director of Criminal Intelligence with the Government of India, 1905–14; retired, 1914; *b* 26 July 1862; 2nd *s* of late Colonel W. A. M. Barnard, Grenadier Guards and 96th Regt; *m* 1903, Florence Anne, *e d* of James Worrall, JP, of Westwell, Tenterden, Kent; one *s* two *d. Educ:* Bedford School. Entered Bengal Police as Assistant-Superintendent, 1881; Deputy Commissioner of Police, Calcutta, 1889; Assistant Inspector-General, Government Railway Police, 1897; Deputy Inspector-General of Police, 1906; Commandant, Prisoner of War Camp, with rank of Major, 1916. *Address:* Withersdane Hall, Wye, Kent. *T:* Wye 12. *Club:* Windham. *Died 16 Feb. 1928.*

BARNARD, Rev. Charles William; Rector and Rural Dean of Sutton Coldfield since 1909; Hon. Canon of Birmingham; Proctor of Convocation, 1905–19. *Educ:* Oriel College, Oxford (MA). Ordained, 1879; Curate of St George, Barrow-in-Furness, 1879–82; St Mary's, Beverley, 1882–85; Vicar of Rowley Regis, Staffs, 1885–88; Rector of Churchill, Worcester, 1888–93; Hon. Canon, Worcester, 1904–5; Vicar of Kings Norton, 1893–9; Rural Dean of Kings Norton, 1907–9; Deputy Provincial Grand Master and Grand Superintendent of Freemasonry in Warwickshire. *Address:* Merlewood, Leamington Spa. *Club:* Fly Fishers'. *Died 18 Aug. 1928.*

BARNARD, Sir Herbert, Kt 1898; JP London, Middlesex, and Surrey; late Chairman of Public Works Loan Commission; *b* 1 Oct. 1831; *s* of John Barnard, Cornhill, London, banker; *m* 1854, Ellen, *d* of William Wyndham of Dinton, Wilts, MP; three *s* nine *d. Educ:* Eton. *Address:* 23 Portland Place, W. *Club:* Union.

Died 30 June 1920.

BARNARD, Maj.-Gen. William Osborne; *b* 1838; 3rd *s* of late George Barnard, who was *g s* of Sir Frederick Augusta Barnard; *m* 1872, Isabella, *d* of late Francis Tucker, Bengal Civil Service. *Educ:* Charterhouse. Joined 96th Regiment, 1856; Captain, 1859; Major, 1878; Lieut-Col, 1881; commanded, 1882–86; commanded 53rd Regimental District, 1887–88; Brig.-Gen. commanding Nerbudda District, 1888–93; Maj.-Gen. commanding Mauritius, 1895–96; Maj.-Gen. 1896; Maj.-Gen. commanding 2nd Infantry Brigade, Aldershot, 1896–99; retired, 1899; Col the Manchester Regt, 1904. *Recreations:* ordinary. *Address:* 5 Montagu Mansions, W. *T:* Paddington 4493. *Clubs:* Army and Navy, United Service; Union, Brighton.

Died 15 Jan. 1920.

BARNARD, William Tyndall, KC 1905; Registrar of the Divorce Court; *b* 1855; *e s* of W. T. Barnard, Barrister, and Charlotte Jane, *g d* of Richard Jeune; *m*; one *s*. Student, Gray's Inn, 1875. Called to Bar, 1879. *Address:* 13 King's Bench Walk, Temple, EC; Somerset Lodge, The Manor Way, Blackheath.

Died 30 Sept. 1923.

BARNARDISTON, Col Nathaniel, JP Essex and Suffolk; DL Suffolk; County Councillor, West Suffolk (Chairman), 1889–99; Chairman, Quarter Sessions, 1876–1909; *b* 24 April 1832; *s* of N. C. Barnardiston; *m* 1858, Lady Florence Legge, 5th *d* of 4th Earl of

Dartmouth; four s five d. *Educ:* Harrow. Entered 27th Inniskilling Regt 1851; served in India; Brigadier-General Commanding Harwich Volunteer Brigade, 1890–1900. *Address:* The Ryes, Sudbury, Suffolk.

Died 12 Feb. 1916.

BARNARDISTON, Maj.-Gen. Nathaniel Walter, CB 1918; MVO 1904; JP; Commanded HBM's Forces in North China, 1914–15; *b* 29 Nov. 1858; *e s* of late Col Nathaniel Barnardiston of The Ryes, Sudbury, Suffolk, and Lady Florence Legge (*d* 1917), *d* of 4th Earl of Dartmouth; *m* 1892, Sarah Hall, *d* of late Hon. D. R. Floyd-Jones, of Fort Neck House, Massapequa, Long Island, USA, sometime Secretary of State and Lieut-Governor of New York; one *d*. *Educ:* privately; Merton College, Oxford (matriculated 1877). Joined 77th (Duke of Cambridge's Own) Regiment from West Suffolk Militia, 1878; was Adjutant 2nd Batt. Middlesex Regiment, 1882–86; passed Staff College, 1888; ADC to Governor of Bermuda (Sir E. N. Newdegate, KCB), 1889; DAAG Eastern District, 1894–97; Staff Captain Intelligence Division, War Office, 1898–99; DAAG, 1899–1901; served in South African campaign as second in command 2nd Batt. Middlesex Regiment, 1901–2 (South African medal with 4 clasps); commanded British Troops at capture of Tsingtao, 1914 (prom. Maj.-Gen.); commanded a Division, 1915–16; Chief of British Military Mission to Portugal, 1916; Military Attaché, Brussels and The Hague, 1902, and to the Scandinavian Courts, 1904; Assistant-Commandant, Royal Military College, Sandhurst, 1906–10; Assistant-Director of military training and Substantive Col, War Office, 1910–14; coronation medals, 1902 and 1911; 2nd class of the Order of the Rising Sun, conferred upon him by the Emperor of Japan for his services in the Tsingtao Expedition, and 1st class of the Order of Aviz; Commander of the Orders of the Osmanieh, Dannebrog, Sword, Leopold, and St Olaf. *Recreations:* shooting, hunting, tennis, golf. *Address:* The Ryes, Sudbury, Suffolk. *Club:* Naval and Military.

Died 18 Aug. 1919.

BARNARDISTON, Lt-Col Samuel John Barrington, DSO 1900; the Suffolk Regiment; *b* 19 Aug. 1875; 5th *s* of late Nathaniel Barnardiston of The Ryes; *m* 1919, Mlle van Riemsdyk. *Educ:* Haileybury. Entered army, 1897, from 3rd Batt. Suffolk Regt; Adjutant, 1900; served South Africa (despatches); served in European War, 1914. *Club:* Junior United Service.

Died 31 Jan. 1924.

BARNE, Major Miles, DSO 1917; Suffolk Yeomanry; *b* 15 March 1874; *e s* of late Frederick St John Newdegate Barne and late Lady Constance Adelaide Seymour, 5th *d* of 5th Marquess of Hertford; *m* 1904, Violet Ella, *e d* of Sir Archibald Orr-Ewing, 3rd Bt; three *s* one *d*. Late Capt. Scots Guards; served South Africa, 1900–2; seconded July 1915 from Suffolk Yeomanry to Scots Guards; European War, 1914–17 (DSO). *Address:* Grey Friars, Dunwich; Sotterley Hall, Wangford, Suffolk; May Place, Cragford, Kent. *Clubs:* Carlton, Guards.

Died 17 Sept. 1917.

BARNES, Alexander, ISO 1915; *b* 1855; *m* 1st, 1885, Ellen Nevison (*d* 1914), *d* of Rev. E. Hammond; one *s*; 2nd, 1915, Ella Mary, *d* of Thomas Holland; two *s* one *d*. *Educ:* Wells Grammar School. Entered Board of Trade, 1873; Accountant, 1909; Accountant-General, 1915–19. *Address:* 22 Park Hill, Ealing, W5. *T:* Ealing 145. *Clubs:* National Liberal, Alpine; W Middlesex Golf.

Died 2 March 1924.

BARNES, Capt. Charles Roper Gorell, DSO 1915; MC; Rifle Brigade; General Staff Officer, 3rd grade, June 1917; *b* 1 July 1896; *e s* of Sir Frederic Gorell Barnes. *Educ:* Stubbington House, Fareham; RNC Osborne and Dartmouth; Pembroke College, Cambridge (Scholar). Joined Lord Kitchener's 1st Army, and served with 14th Division in the European War, May 1915–Sept. 1916; 2nd Lieut, 1914; Lieut, 1915; Adjutant, 1915 (despatches twice, DSO, Military Cross). *Address:* Eyot Wood, Shiplake, Oxon.

Died 17 April 1918.

BARNES, Henry, OBE 1918; MD, LLD; FRSE, Fellow Royal Society of Medicine; *b* 20 July 1842; 3rd *s* of Joseph Barnes, Aikton, Cumberland; *m* 1873, Emily Mary, *d* of Thomas Barnes, Bolton, Lancs; one *s* one *d*. *Educ:* St Bees School, Cumberland; Edinburgh University, graduating with first-class honours in 1864. Practised as a physician in Carlisle from 1866; consulting physician to the Cumberland Infirmary, Cumberland and Westmorland Convalescent Institution, and Border Counties Home for Incurables; President, Border Counties Home for Incurables; Vice-President, Cumberland Infirmary; Vice-President of the British Medical Association, and was President, 1896–97; has been twice President of the Border Counties branch of the Association; Vice-President of Cumberland and

Westmorland Antiquarian and Archæological Association; Vice-President, Royal Society of Medicine (History of Medicine section); Vice-President, Royal Medical Benevolent Fund; Hon. Sec. and Treasurer, Cumberland Br., British Red Cross Soc., 1907–19. JP for Carlisle and Cumberland, and Chairman of Cumberland Ward Justices, 1904. *Publications:* The Medical History of Carlisle; On Roman Medical Inscriptions found in Britain; various papers and addresses on medical and archæological subjects. *Recreations:* walking, hill climbing, travel. *Address:* 6 Portland Square, Carlisle. *T:* 240. *Club:* County, Carlisle.

Died 12 April 1921.

BARNES, John Frederick Evelyn, CMG 1901; *b* Innistiogue, Co. Kilkenny, 1851; *s* of late Frederick Piers Barnes, Firgrove, Co. Kilkenny, and Matilda, *d* of late Rev. George Armstrong, Listerlin, Co. Kilkenny; *m* 1879, Mary Sanbach, *d* of E. E. Graves; one *d*. *Educ:* Trinity Coll., Dublin. MInstCE 1889. Practised as civil engineer in Ireland; engineer and surveyor, Duke of Abercorn's estates for several years prior to 1879; went to Natal, 1880; Govt surveyor until 1882, then borough engineer, Durban; carried out waterworks and many municipal improvements; in Government Public Works Department, 1888, till retirement, 1910; Acting Colonial Engineer for periods totalling 3 years with seats on Executive and Legislative Councils; on the establishment of Responsible Government in Natal, 1893, became chief engineer PWD; during the war assisted the military engineering and other departments in many directions (CMG, despatches several times); Commissioner for Natal at the St Louis Exposition of 1904; Major on Sup. Staff, 1907; formed Natal Engr Corps, Feb. 1910; resigned with rank of Major, July 1912; took up dairy farming and wattle planting, 1911; Assessor, Court of Income Tax Appeal, 1915; practising as Consulting Engineer; Member for Ward No 1, Municipality of Pietermaritzburg, 1911; Hon. Secretary South African Party, Natal Province, 1917–21; Member, Natal Mental Hospital Board and Water Court, 1918; Member, Rents Board, Natal. *T:* 821. *Club:* Victoria, Maritzburg.

Died 24 June 1925.

BARNES, Rev. Peter; Vicar of St Columba's, Wanstead Slip, since 1890; Hon. Canon of Chelmsford, 1919; *b* 1856; *y s* of late Rev. E. B. Barnes, RN; *m* 1919, Ellen Grace, *e d* of late Rev. C. Matheson, headmaster, Clergy Orphan School, Canterbury. *Educ:* Bedford Grammar School; Salisbury Theological Coll. Eleven years with Corrie & Co., colonial brokers; ordained 1883; Assistant Curate of Rampisham, Dorset, 1883; of All Hallows, East India Docks, 1885. *Address:* St Columba Vicarage, Stratford, E15.

Died 15 Dec. 1921.

BARNES-LAWRENCE, Herbert Cecil, MA; *b* Bridlington, 9 Dec. 1852; 2nd *s* of Rev. Canon H. F. Barnes-Lawrence; widower. *Educ:* King's School, Canterbury; Durham Grammar School; Trinity and Lincoln (Scholar) Colleges, Oxford. Assistant-Master Manchester Grammar School, 1876–81; Giggleswick Grammar School, 1881–83; Headmaster, Perse Grammar School, Cambridge, 1884–1901; Weymouth College, 1902–17. *Recreations:* golf, cycling. *Address:* Melfort House, Crowborough, Sussex. *Club:* National.

Died 7 June 1921.

BARNETT, Harry Villiers; *b* Bristol, 1 Oct. 1858; *s* of late Henry N. Barnett, editor of Sunday Times. Virtually self-taught, but was at Newcastle-on-Tyne Grammar School for a year. Assistant Editor, Graphic, 1877–82; then literary and pictorial free-lance; articles and sketches, Graphic, Black and White Magazine of Art, of which last was art critic under W. E. Henley; frequent contributor, St James's Gazette, and, occasionally, Saturday Review, Athenæum, etc; founded, 1904, and owned and edited, the Continental Weekly; Riviera Correspondent of The Times since 1920. *Publications:* authorised English versions of the Prince of Monaco's La Carrière d'un Navigateur, 1909, and Massenet's Mes Souvenirs; Portus Heraklis Monoëki: a Vision of the Story of Monaco, 1909 (3rd edition, revised and illustrated); nouvelle version française de Merlin; 1ᵉʳ drame de la Trilogie King Arthur, by Francis Coutts and I. Albeniz, 1914; Les Persans à Monaco; Etude sur l'Origine du Nom de lieu Gaumatâ, 1916; Beauvallon and the Pays des Maures; Olivula: a Mystery of the Maritime Alps, 1920; The Revelation of Walter Rummel, 1922. *Recreations:* painting, singing. *Address:* Villa Mer et Mont, Monte Carlo, France, AM.

Died 13 May 1928.

BARNETT, John Francis, FRAM; Professor, Royal College of Music and Guildhall School of Music; Examiner for the Associated Board; Member of the Philharmonic Society; *b* London, 16 Oct. 1837; *e s* of late Joseph Alfred Barnett and Emma, *d* of late William Hudson; *m* 1st, 1875, Alice Dora Booth (*d* 1882); 2nd, 1891, Mary Emily Tussaud. *Educ:* Royal Academy of Music and Leipsic Conservatoire.

Gained King's Scholarship at RAM, 1850; performed Concerto D minor Mendelssohn, at New Philharmonic Concert, 1852; played at Gewandhaus Concert, Leipsic, 1861; and at Philharmonic Society, London, 1863; composed Cantata Ancient Mariner for Birmingham Festival, 1867; Paradise and the Peri, produced at Birmingham Festival, 1870; The Raising of Lazarus, Hereford Festival, 1876; The Building of the Ship, Leeds Festival, 1880; The Wishing Bell, Norwich Festival, 1893; The Eve of St Agnes, London Choral Society, 1914. Works for orchestra: Lay of the Last Minstrel, Liverpool Festival, 1873; Pastoral Suite, Philharmonic Society, 1890; Liebeslied im alten Styl, Crystal Palace Concerts, 1895. *Publications:* The Vocal Scores of the above-mentioned Cantatas; Pianoforte Solos—Home Scenes, Musical Landscapes, Wayside Sketches, The Flowing Tide, Valse Brillante, The Dream Maiden, etc; songs—A Pair of Sabots, Bird of Happiness, Give me thy Love; book—Musical Reminiscences and Impressions, etc. *Recreation:* sketching from nature. *Address:* St Ann's Villa, 56 Acacia Road, NW.

Died 24 Nov. 1916.

BARNETT-CLARKE, Very Rev. Charles William; Dean and Rector of St George's Cathedral, Cape Town, since 1881. *Educ:* Worcester College, Oxford. MA. Ordained 1854; Curate of Lambourn, 1854–58; Vicar of Toot-Oaldon, Oxon, 1858–60; Curate of Fenny Stratford, 1860–64; Vicar of Cadmore End, Bucks, 1868–71. *Address:* Deanery, Cape Town.

Died 24 Feb. 1916.

BARNEWALL, Hon. Reginald Nicholas Francis; b 24 Sept. 1897; e s and heir of 18th Baron Trimlestown. 2nd Lieut 5th Batt. Leinster Regt. *Died 24 March 1918.*

BARNSLEY, Brig.-Gen. Sir John, Kt 1914; VD; JP, DL; Governor, King Edward VI School; Military Member, Warwickshire County Association; b 17 Nov. 1858; m 1882, Ellen Rutherford, d of late Robert Davis, JP; three s one d. *Educ:* King Edward VI's School, Birmingham. Wesleyan. Lt-Col comdg 5th Batt. Royal Warwicks Regt, 1908–14; Lt-Col, TF Reserve, 1914, Hon. Col 1917. DL Warwicks; JP Warwicks and Birmingham. *Recreations:* golf, shooting. *Address:* Earlsfield, Edgbaston, Birmingham. *T:* Edgbaston 187. *M:* LF 4566. *Clubs:* Clef, Liberal, Birmingham.

Died 19 Jan. 1926.

BARON, Sir Barclay Josiah, Kt 1918; MB, CM; Lord Mayor of Bristol; Consulting Physician for Diseases of Throat and Nose, Bristol General Hospital. *Educ:* Edinburgh; Berlin; Strasburg; Vienna. Late Lecturer on Pathology and Morbid Anatomy, Bristol Medical School, and Assistant to Professor of Pathology, Edinburgh University. *Address:* 16 Whiteladies Road, Clifton, Bristol. *T:* 1445.

Died 7 June 1919.

BARR, Amelia Edith; novelist; b Ulverston, Lancashire, 29 March 1831; d of William Henry Huddleston; m 1850, at 19, Robert Barr (d 1867), merchant, Glasgow, s of Rev. John Barr. Left widow, with three daughters, at 35, in Texas; came to New York; began writing for Rev. Henry Ward Beecher's paper, and other papers and magazines; at 50 began novel-writing; published 47 in America and England; many German and French translations. *Publications:* Jan Vedder's Wife, 1885; Bow of Orange Ribbon, 1888; Friend Olivia, 1890; A Daughter of Fife, 1886; The Squire of Sandal-Side, 1887; A Border Shepherdess, 1887; Paul and Christina, 1887; The Last of the Macallisters, 1890; Between Two Loves, 1886; Feet of Clay, 1889; Bernicia, A Knight of the Nets, The Lone House, 1894; The Hallam Succession, 1885; She Loved a Sailor, 1891; Love for an Hour is Love Forever, 1892; A Sister to Esau, 1891; Cluny M'Pherson, 1894; Remember the Alamo; Prisoners of Conscience, 1897; I, Thou, and the Other One, Trinity Bells, 1899; The Maid of Maiden Lane, 1900; The Lion's Whelp; A Song of a Single Note; Thyra Varrick; Black Shilling; The Measure of a Man, 1915. *Recreations:* music (the organ), the cultivation of flowers. *Address:* 436 Greenwood Avenue, Richmond Hill, Long Island, New York.

Died 11 March 1919.

BARR, Lieut-Col Sir David William Keith, KCSI 1902; Indian Army; b 29 Nov. 1846; e s of late Lt-Gen H. J. Barr; m 1871, Constance, d of late Maj.-Gen. J. Guillum Scott; three s one d. *Educ:* private school; Royal Military Coll. Sandhurst. Ensign, 44th Regt, 1864; served with 33rd (Duke of Wellington's) Regt, Abyssinia, 1868 (medal); entered the Political Department, Government of India, 1869; First Asst-Agent, Gov.-Gen. for Central India, 1874; Political Agent, Jodhpore, 1880; Political Agent and Superintendent, Rewah, 1881–87; Resident at Gwalior, 1887–92; Resident in Kashmir, 1892–94; Agent to the Governor-General in Central India, 1894–1900; Resident at Hyderabad, 1900–5; retired 1905; member of Council of India, 1905–15. *Address:* 92 Onslow Gardens, SW. *Club:* United Service.

Died 22 Nov. 1916.

BARR, James (Angus Evan Abbot); b Wallacetown, Ontario, Canada, 1862; 5th s of Robert Barr, Windsor, Ontario, Canada, an Jane, d of William Watson, West Glen, Kilmalcolm, Scotland; Elizabeth Sabel (d 1909), d of A. C. Wylie, Brook Green, London three s three d. *Educ:* Canadian Public Schools. From 16 to 21 newspaper man in America; since then a journalist in London *Publications:* The Gods Give My Donkey Wings; The Gods Gave M Donkey Wings; Under the Eaves of Night; The Great Frozen North The Witchery of the Serpent; Laughing through a Wilderness; Th Grey Bat; Jarl Armstrong. *Recreations:* cricket, lacrosse, billiards. *Clubs* London Sketch, Authors'.

Died March 1923

BARR, Thomas, MD, FFPS; Lecturer on Diseases of the Ear, Glasgow University, since 1895; Aural Surgeon, Glasgow Western Infirmary Hon. Aurist, Glasgow Sick Children's Hospital; Senior Surgeon Glasgow Hospital for Diseases of the Ear, Nose, and Throat; Elderslie, Renfrewshire, 1846. *Educ:* University of Glasgow; Vienna London. Graduated MB, CM, with highest honours, Glasgow University, 1868; MD, Glasgow, 1870. Appointed to Glasgow Western Infirmary, 1877; Lecturer in Anderson's College, 1879–95 President of the Otological Section of the British Medical Association 1888; President of the Glasgow Pathological and Clinical Society 1899–1900; President of the Otological Society of the Unite Kingdom, 1904–5. *Publications:* Manual of Diseases of the Ear including those of the Nose and Throat in relation to the Ear (thre editions); Effects upon the Hearing of those who Work amid Nois Surroundings; Investigation into the Hearing of School Children Giddiness and Staggering in Ear Diseases; Traumatic Affections c the Ear; The Operative Treatment of Intra-Cranial Condition dependent upon Purulent Diseases of the Ear, etc. *Recreations:* walking golfing. *Address:* 13 Woodside Place, Charing Cross, Glasgow. *T:* 161 Central, Glasgow.

Died 14 Dec. 1916

BARRATT, Reginald, RWS; FRGS; artist; b London, 25 July 1861 s of late Dr J. G. Barratt, FRCS. *Educ:* King's Coll. and by late Dean Plumptre. Studied architecture under R. Norman Shaw, RA, an painting under Lefevre and Bouguereau, Paris; worked for Graphi and Daily Graphic; exhibited at Royal Academy, Royal Society o Painters in Water Colours; painted twice for Queen Victoria and Kin Edward; travelled in Italy, Spain, Morocco, Algeria, Tunis, Egyp India, Persia, Asia Minor, etc; worked chiefly at Oriental life an architecture, such as Abu Simbel for late Khedive, The Moole Ahmadee, and Courtyard of Ducal Palace, Venice, in Mancheste Corporation Gallery; has published drawings in colour, Venice, Egyp etc. *T:* Regent 6400. *Club:* Athenæum.

Died 8 Feb. 1917

BARRAUD, Francis; s of late Henry Barraud, artist; nephew of George Rose, dramatist, novelist, and journalist as Arthur Sketchley. *Educ* Ushaw; St Edmund's College, Ware. Studied at the Royal Academy Schools (silver medal for drawing from life); Heatherley's, the Beau Arts, Antwerp; painter of portraits and genre subjects; frequen exhibitor at the RA, Institute of Painters in Oil Colours, and mos other art exhibitions. *Works:* An Encore too Many, exhibited at the Walker Art Gallery, Liverpool, 1887, and purchased by th Corporation for the permanent Art Gallery; His Master's Voice purchased by the Gramophone Co. and reproduced as a advertisement; Portraits: Cardinal Bourne, Admiral the Hon. Sir H Keppel, Prof. M'Coll of Glasgow, etc. *Recreations:* billiards, walking *Address:* 28 Finchley Road, NW8. *Clubs:* St John's Wood Arts, Arts

Died 29 Aug. 1924

BARRES, Maurice; Député de Paris; Member of French Academy b Charmes-sur-Moselle, 17 Aug. 1862. Studied law, but preferre to devote himself to literature; elected Deputy, 1889. *Publications* Sous l'œil des Barbares, 1888; Huit jours chez Monsieur Renan, 1888 Un homme libre, 1889; Le Jardin de Berenice; Les Déracinés; Lewi Figures; Au Service de l'Allemagne; Colette Baudoche; L'Ennem des lois; Du Sang, de la Volupté et de la Mort; Les Amitiés françaises Le Voyage de Sparte; Amori et Dolori Sacrum (La mort de Venise) Trois stations de Psychothérapie; Toute licence sauf contre l'amour Une journée parlementaire (comédie de mœurs en 3 actes); La Collin Inspirée; L'Ame française et la Guerre; L'Union Sacrée; Les Saint de la France; La Croix de Guerre; L'Amitié des Tranchées; Le Voyages de Lorraine et d'Artois; Pour les Mutilés; Sur le Chemin de l'Asie; Le Suffrage des Morts; Pendant le Bataille de Verdun; Le Familles spirituelles de la France; Les Traits eternels de la France; E regardant au fond des crevasses; L'Appel du Rhin; La Minute Sacrée

Un jardin sur l'Oronte, 1922. *Address:* Boulevard Maillot 100, Neuilly, Paris. *Died 4 Dec. 1923.*

BARRETT, Field Marshal Sir Arthur (Arnold), GCB 1918 (KCB 1908; CB 1903); GCSI 1920 (KCSI 1915); KCVO 1912; *b* 3 June 1857; 3rd *s* of late Rev. Alfred Barrett, DD; *m* 1st, 1894, Mary (*d* 1897), *d* of James Haye of Fowey, Cornwall; 2nd, 1907, Ella (*d* 1917), *d* of H. Lafone, 59 Onslow Square, SW. Entered army, 1875; Captain, 1886; Major, 1895; Lieutenant-Colonel, 1901; Major-General, 1907; Lieut-Gen., 1911; General, 1917; retired 1920; Field Marshal, 1921; Brig. Com. Nowshera, 1907-9; Adjt-Gen. in India, 1909-12; Divisional Commander, Poona, 1912-14; Northern Command, India, 1916-20; served Afghan War, 1879-80; march to Candahar and battle of Candahar (medal with two clasps, bronze decoration); Hazara, 1888 (medal with clasp); 2nd Miranzai Expedition, 1891 (clasp); Hunza-Nagar Expedition, 1891 (clasp); NWF India, 1897-98 (despatches, brevet Lt-Col, medal with two clasps); NW Frontier, India, 1908; Bazar Valley Expedition (despatches); Mohmand Expedition (despatches, KCB, medal with clasp); Mesopotamia, 1914-15 (despatches, KCSI); Afghan War, 1919 (despatches, GCSI). *Address:* Sharnbrook, Beds. *Club:* United Service.
Died 20 Oct. 1926.

BARRETT, Rev. Daniel William, MA; Rector of Holdenby since 1910; Hon. Canon, St Albans since 1905. *Educ:* Trinity Coll., Dublin. Curate of Waltham, Leicester, 1873-76; Chaplain, Bishop of Peterbro's railway mission, 1873-79; Vicar of Nassington, 1879-87; Rural Dean, Oundle, 1881-87; Rector of Chipping Barnet, 1887-1910; Rural Dean of Barnet, 1893-1910. *Publications:* Life and Work among the Navvies, 4th edn 1885; Sketches of Church Life, 1902; Hymns; Diocesan Charts for Peterborough and St Albans; The Royal Prisoner of Holdenby; King Charles I at Holmby House. *Address:* The Rectory, Holdenby, Northampton.
Died 10 Sept. 1925.

BARRETT, Francis E. H. Joyce; Musical Editor and Chief Musical Critic of the Morning Post; *y s* of late William Alexander Barrett, Musical Critic of the Morning Post, 1865-91; *m* 1891, Marie Louise Eugénie, *d* of Louis Pineau Bertin of Paris; no *c. Educ:* Dulwich and Durham. Attached to the Morning Post since 1890; worked in all branches of journalism since 1887; pupil of Manuel Garcia (singing), John Tiplady Carrodus (violin), Edward Howell (violoncello), Henry Gadsby and W. A. Barrett (composition). *Publications:* Daily Criticisms. *Recreations:* yesterday's concerts. *Address:* Boitakhana, Endymion Terrace, Finsbury Park, N4. *T:* Hornsey 2608.
Died 19 Jan. 1925.

BARRETT, Frank; novelist, inventor, scientist; *b* 1848; *m* Joan Barrett, novelist; one *d* (an artist). Began journalism at eighteen as literary and dramatic critic; took to pottery; potter's help, modeller, and then sculptor; became partner in a pottery; kiln fell in, destroying the work of two years; there ended that branch of career; returned to literature, and so fell into the groove in which he ran thereafter. *Publications:* fifty-two novels and bound volumes of stories; contributions to magazines, journals, and other ephemera; three plays. *Recreations:* modelling, chess, mechanical invention. *Address:* Rocky Close, St Ives, Cornwall. *Died 21 May 1926.*

BARRETT, Rev. George Slatyer; former Pastor of Princes Street Congregational Church, Norwich; *b* Jamaica, 16 Sept. 1839; father was a missionary; *m* 1868, Catharine Lance Bower (*d* 1910), *g d* of late George Lance; three *d. Educ:* University College, London; Independent College, Manchester. BA of London University; DD of St Andrews University; Chairman of the Congregational Union of England and Wales, 1894. *Publications:* The Temptation of Christ; The Earliest Christian Hymn; The Intermediate State; Religion in Daily Life; Family Prayers; The Bible and its Inspiration; The Seven Words from the Cross; The Whole Armour of God; Commentary 1st Epistle of St John; Editor of The Congregational Church Hymnal; The Mission Hymnal; Sunday School Hymnal. *Recreation:* walking. *Address:* 4 Grove Avenue, Norwich. *T:* 803 Norwich.
Died 24 April 1916.

BARRETT, Sir William Fletcher, Kt 1912; FRS, Lond., Edin., and Dublin; MIEE, MRIA, FPSL; JP Co. Dublin; *b* 10 Feb. 1844; *s* of Rev. W. G. Barrett; *m* 1916, Dr Florence Willey, CBE, MD. *Educ:* Old Trafford Grammar School, Manchester, and private study. Assistant to Professor Tyndall, 1863; Science Master, International Coll., 1867; Lecturer on Physics, Royal School of Naval Architecture, 1869; Professor of Physics, Royal College of Science, Dublin, 1873-1910. Ex-President of the Society for Psychical Research, of which he was chief founder. *Publications:* Original Investigations

published in the Transactions and Proceedings of the Royal Dublin Society, Philosophical Magazine and elsewhere; editor of Lessons in Science, 1880; of Early Chapters in Science, 1899; joint author of Introduction to Practical Physics, 1892; On the Threshold of a New World of Thought, 1908; On Creative Thought, 1910; On Swedenborg, 1912; On Psychical Research, Home University Library, 1911; On the Threshold of the Unseen, 1917; Monograph on so-called Divining Rod, vol. i, 1897, vol. ii, 1900; Discovery of and Papers on Sensitive Flames, 1867; ditto, Recalescence, 1873 *et seq.*; Shortening of Nickel by Magnetisation, 1882; Thought-Transference, 1882 *et seq.*; Researches on the Electric and Magnetic Properties of Alloys of Iron, 1895 *et seq.*, including the discovery, in 1899, of the remarkable magnetic and electrical properties of the silicon-iron alloy, subseq. known as *Stallory*, which has been of immense value in electrical engineering for the construction of transformers, dynamos, etc; Researches on Entoptic Vision, 1905-7, leading to the invention of the Entoptiscope and a new Optometer. *Recreations:* gardening; interested in temperance and philanthropic work. *Address:* 31 Devonshire Place, W1. *T:* Langham 1691.
Died 26 May 1925.

BARRETT, Sir William Scott, Kt 1913; JP, DL Lancs; Constable of Lancaster Castle since 1916; *b* 28 Nov. 1843; *s* of late J. C. Barrett of Leeds; *m* 1869, Julia L., *d* of late Rev. A. A. Colvile; four *s* three *d*. Alderman and Chairman of Lancashire County Council and of Quarter Sessions. *Address:* Abbotsgate, Blundellsands, Lancs.
Died 5 June 1921.

BARRIE, Sir Charles, Kt 1919; JP, DL; Charles Barrie & Sons, Shipowners; *b* 10 Feb. 1840; *m* Jane, *d* of Alexander Cathro, Arbroath; two *s* one *d*. Lord Provost of Dundee, 1902-5. *Address:* Airlie Park, Broughty Ferry. *Clubs:* National Liberal; Eastern, Dundee.
Died 28 Feb. 1921.

BARRIE, Rt. Hon. Hugh Thom, PC (Ireland) 1920; DL, JP; MP (C) North Londonderry since 1906; High Sheriff, Derry, 1918; Vice-President, Department of Agriculture and Technical Education (Ireland), 1919-21; *b* Glasgow, 1860; *m* 1892, Katherine, *e d* of Rev. W. H. Quarry. *Address:* The Manor House, Coleraine. *Clubs:* Carlton, St Stephen's Constitutional; Ulster, Belfast.
Died 18 April 1922.

BARRINGTON, Hon. Sir (Bernard) Eric (Edward), KCB 1902 (CB 1889); *b* London, 5 June 1847; *y s* of 6th Viscount Barrington and Jane, *d* of 1st Baron Ravensworth; *m* 1879, Christina, *y d* of late William Graham. *Educ:* Eton. Entered Foreign Office, 1867; Private Secretary to Parliamentary Under-Secretaries of State for Foreign Affairs (A. J. Otway and Viscount Enfield), 1869-74; précis writer to Foreign Secretary (Earl of Derby), 1874-78; to Marquis of Salisbury, 1878-80; Private Secretary to Earl of Iddesleigh, 1885-86; to Marquis of Salisbury, 1887-92, and 1895-1900; to Marquis of Lansdowne, 1900-5; Assistant Under Secretary of State for Foreign Affairs, 1906; retired from Foreign Office, 1907; attached to Special Mission to Berlin, 1878. *Address:* The Old Lodge, Wimbledon Common, SW. *T:* Wimbledon 780. *TA:* Esoteric, London. *Club:* Travellers'.
Died 24 Feb. 1918.

BARRINGTON, Hon. Sir William Augustus Curzon, KCMG 1901; *b* Beckett, Shrivenham, Berks, 28 Jan. 1842; 3rd *s* of 6th Viscount Barrington and Jane Elizabeth, *d* of 1st Baron Ravensworth; unmarried. *Educ:* private schools at Cheam and Woolwich; Mannheim and Bonn, Germany. Entered Diplomatic Service, 1860; Secretary of Legation, Buenos Aires, 1883; Acting Chargé d'Affaires and Consul-General, Lima, 1884; Consul-General, Hungary, Budapest, 1885; Chargé d'Affaires, Belgrade, 1886; Secretary of Embassy, Madrid, 1888; Vienna, 1892; Envoy to the Argentine Republic and Minister in Paraguay, 1896-1902; HM's Envoy Extraordinary and Minister Plenipotentiary to Sweden and Norway, 1902-4; Councillor for Borough of St Marylebone (Ward 5) since 1912. *Address:* 17B Great Cumberland Place, W. *TA:* Linnet Phone, London. *T:* Paddington 2215. *Clubs:* Bachelors', St James's, Turf, Pratt's, Travellers', Prince's, Lord's.
Died 23 Feb. 1922.

BARRINGTON-FLEET, George Rutland; actor; *b* Penge, 15 Jan. 1853; 4th *s* of John George and Esther Faithfull Fleet; *nephew* of Emily Faithfull; married. *Educ:* private tutor; Merchant Taylors' School. From age of 14 to 21 in the City; then made first appearance on stage at Olympic Theatre under Henry Neville; later joined the Gilbert-Sullivan-Carte management, and played in all their operas except Yeoman of the Guard, during run of which took a lease of St James's Theatre; relinquished management and returned to Savoy for a time.

Publications: Thirty-Five Years on the Stage, 1908; produced one play and numerous short pieces and duologues, magazine articles and songs, and at one time a regular contributor to Punch; adapted Kingsley's Water-Babies for the stage (Garrick Theatre), Xmas 1902. *Recreations:* golf, painting.   *Died 31 May 1922.*

BARRINGTON-KENNETT, Lt-Col Brackley Herbert Barrington, JP; Royal Bodyguard since 1895; *b* 1846; 2nd *s* of late Captain Vincent F. Kennett, Manor House, Dorchester-on-Thame, and Arabella Henrietta, last surv. *d* of Sir J. Barrington, KC, Judge of Admiralty, and *widow* of Edward, Baron Calabella; *m* 1884, Ellinor Frances, *d* of F. L. Austen of Brightwell Park, Oxfordshire and *g d* of Sir H. Austen, DL, of Shalford Park, Surrey; one *s. Educ:* Rugby; Trinity College, Cambridge (BA). Served with British National Aid to wounded in Franco-German War (2 French orders), 1871, also Carlist War in Spain; Affridi Campaign, 1877 (medal); Afghan War, 1878 (despatches, medal, wounded); Afghan War, 1879–80; Lieut-Col, 1885. *Address:* 19 Cheyne Gardens, Chelsea Embankment, SW3. *Clubs:* Army and Navy; Leander.

Died 12 March 1919.

BARRINGTON-WARD, Rev. Mark James, MA, SCL, DD; FLS; Rector of Duloe, Cornwall, since 1909; Hon. Canon of Truro Cathedral, 1921; *b* Belfast; *m* 1879, Caroline Pearson; five *s* four *d. Educ:* Royal Belfast Academical Institution; Royal School, Dungannon; Queen's College, Belfast; Worcester and Hertford (Scholar) Colleges, Oxford; 1st class, Natural Science, 1869; BA, SCL, 1869; MA, 1872; BD and DD, 1919, Oxford. Assistant Master, Clifton College, 1869–72; HM Inspector of Schools, 1872–1907; ordained, 1907; curate of The Tything, Worcester, 1907–9. *Publications:* several geographical works. *Recreations:* gardening, botany. *Address:* The Rectory, Duloe SO, Cornwall. *M:* LY 6770. *Club:* United University.

Died 4 Feb. 1924.

BARRON, Maj.-Gen. Sir Harry, KCMG 1909; CVO 1907; Knight of Grace St John of Jerusalem; *b* 11 Aug. 1847; *s* of Charles Barron, Denmark Hill, Surrey; *m* 1877, Clara Emily, *d* of Maj.-Gen. T. Conyngham Kelly, CB; one *d. Educ:* Rev. W. Foster, Stubbington; Rev. R. Fowler, Tonbridge Wells; Woolwich. Lieut Royal Artillery, 1867; Capt. 1879; Major 1884; Lieut-Col 1894; Col 1898; Maj.-Gen. 1904; Adjutant 1st Forfar Artillery Volunteers, 1880–84; Chief Instructor, School of Gunnery, Shoeburyness, 1897–1900; Commanding RA, Thames District, 1900–4; Malta, 1904–8; retired, 1909; Governor of Tasmania, 1909–13; Governor of Western Australia, 1913–17; Col Commandant, Royal Artillery, 1920. *Address:* Swiss Cottage, Weybridge. *T:* Weybridge 31. *Club:* Naval and Military.   *Died 27 March 1921.*

BARRON, James; Editor and Proprietor of Inverness Courier; *b* Corshelloch, Edinkillie, Forres, 1847; *m* 1875, Isabella (*d* 1912), *d* of late Evan Macleod, Inverness; one *s* two *d. Educ:* Relugas and Rafford Schools. Served business apprenticeship in Nairn, where he had opportunities of private study; joined staff of Inverness Courier in his nineteenth year. JP; Hon. Sheriff-Substitute; FSAScot; member Inverness Gaelic Society and Inverness Scientific Society and Field Club; twice president of latter society, and has edited seven volumes of its transactions; engaged on a work illustrating the history of the Northern Highlands in 19th century, of which he has published three volumes. *Address:* Ravelrig, Abertarff Road, Inverness. *TA:* Courier, Inverness. *T:* 59 Inverness. *Club:* Highland, Inverness.

Died 13 Feb. 1919.

BARROW, Alderman Sir Alfred, Kt 1922; OBE 1918; DL; *b* 1850. Mayor of Barrow-in-Furness, 1913–19. *Address:* Ulverscroft, Barrow-in-Furness.   *Died 3 Feb. 1928.*

BARROW, Sir Reuben Vincent, Kt 1912; FRGS; JP; *b* 27 April 1838; *s* of John Barrow, Grange, Bermondsey, SE; *m* 1859, Mary (*d* 1917), *d* of Edward Aggett, Adelaide; one *d.* MP (L) Bermondsey Division of Southwark, 1892–95; an Alderman of Croydon, Mayor 1885. *Address:* Engadine, 9 Park Hill Road, Croydon. *T:* Croydon 250. *Club:* Reform.   *Died 13 Feb. 1918.*

BARRY, Charles David, KC; 2nd *s* of late Rt Hon. Charles Robert Barry. *Educ:* Bassett's; Dublin University (Moderatorship and Prizeman). Served Local Government Board; Arbitrator Board of Trade (Tramways and Railways Act); Ministry of Labour (Trade Boards). *Recreations:* Captain University Eleven; won Rackets Cup three years; won Irish Lawn Tennis Championship; rode winner Point to Point Barristers *v* Solicitors, 1888; scratch Royal Dublin and Royal Portrush Golf Clubs. *Clubs:* Athenæum; Royal Irish Yacht, Kingstown.   *Died Feb. 1928.*

BARRY, Edward, JP Co. Cork; farmer; *b* 1852; *m* 1882, Marian, of late Timothy Sullivan. *Educ:* St Vincent's College, Castleknoc. MP (N) S Cork Co., 1892–1910. *Address:* Rathbarry, Rosscarber Cork.   *Died 7 Dec. 192*

BARRY, Hon. Lt-Col James, CMG 1918; Remount Service. Serve Zulu Campaign, 1879 (medal and clasp); South African Wa 1899–1902 (Queen's medal, three clasps; King's medal, two clasps
Died 12 June 192

BARRY, Sir John Edmond, Kt 1899; *b* 6 Feb. 1828; *e s* of late Joh Barry, merchant, of Middle Abbey Street, Dublin, and Catharin *d* of late Thos Browne of Wexford; *m* 1849, Teresa (*d* 1909), *d* late John Keefe of Iffernock, Co. Meath. *Educ:* private schools, Dubl and Wexford. President, Dublin Chamber of Commerce, 1897–9 Member of Dublin Port and Docks Board, 1867–97; re-elected, 189 retired, 1903; Ex-Chairman of Board of Superintendence of Dubl Hospitals; ex-Governor of Royal Hibernian Military School. *Addre* 12 Mountjoy Square, Dublin.

Died 12 March 191.

BARRY, Sir John Wolfe Wolfe-, KCB 1897 (CB 1894); VD; LLI FRS; DL County of London; Colonel, Engineer and Railwa Volunteer Staff Corps; Past President, Institution of Civil Engineer Vice-President of Institution of Mechanical Engineers; late Chairmai Society of Arts; late Representative of Great Britain on Internation Technical Commission for Suez Canal; member of the Army Railwa Council; Chairman of Westminster Hospital; Chairman of the Easter and Eastern Extension and Western Telegraph Companies; *b* Londoi 7 Dec. 1836; *y s* of Sir Charles Barry, RA; assumed additional nam of Wolfe by Royal licence in 1898; *m* 1874, Rosalind Grace, *y d* o Rev. E. E. Rowsell, Rector of Hambledon, Surrey; four *s* three *Educ:* Trinity Coll., Glenalmond; King's Coll., London. Consultin Engineer to following Companies: Caledonian; London, Chatham and Dover; Lanarkshire and Ayrshire and Barry Railway Companie and to the Underground Electric Railways Co. of London; Consultin Engineer to Bridge House Estates Committee of Corporation o London, to Commissioners of River Tyne, to the Surrey Commerci Docks, to the Alexandra Dock, Newport Company, to the Reger Canal and Dock Co., to Bengal Nagpur Rly, to Bombay Port Trus and to the Kowloon Railway for the Government of Hong-Kon and to the Shanghai and Nankin, and other Chinese Railway Engineer of Tower Bridge, Blackfriars railway arched bridge, Barr Dock and Railways, Kew Bridge, Grangemouth Dock, Surre Commercial Dock, Middlesbrough Dock Extension, Hull Joint Docl Immingham Dock, New Alexandra Docks, Newport, Natal Harbou and other important works; Royal Commissioner, Irish Public Work Government Commissions, 1886–90; Highlands and Islands o Scotland, 1889–90; Estuary of Ribble, 1889–91, and Lower Thame Navigation, 1894–96; National Physical Laboratory, 1897–98; Roy Commissioner on Accidents to Railway Servants, 1899–1900 Vibration on Tube Railways, 1901–2; Royal Commissioner on th Port of London, 1900–2; Royal Commissioner on London Traffic 1903–5; Member of Court of Arbitration under the Metropolis Wate Act, 1902. Late member of Senate of University of London; Governo of Imperial College of Science and Technology; Chairman o Delegacy, City and Guilds Engineering College, South Kensington Member of Council, King's College, London; Chairman, Executiv Committee, City and Guilds of London Technical Institute and Britis Engineering Standards Committee; Member of Executive Committe of National Physical Laboratory. *Publications:* Railway Appliance 1874–92; Lectures on Railways and Locomotives, 1882; The Towe Bridge, 1894; Barry Genealogy in England and Wales. *Recreation* riding, fishing. *Address:* Delahay House, 15 Chelsea Embankmen SW. *TA:* Chelbank, Sloane, London. *T:* Kensington 201. *M:* LC 8103. *Clubs:* Athenæum, Reform.

Died 22 Jan. 1918

BARRY, Ralph Brereton, KC; County Court Judge of the counti of Kildare, Carlow, Wicklow, and Wexford; *b* 7 June 1856; *e s* o James Barry, Solicitor, Limerick, and Elizabeth, *d* of Ralph Westrop Brereton of Ballyadams, Queen's Co.; *m* 1884, Claire, *y d* of William Roche, Crown Solicitor for City and County of Limerick, 7. Harcourt Street, Dublin; three *s. Educ:* Baylis House, Slough Clongoweswood Coll.; Trinity Coll., Dublin, BA; Senior Moderato and gold medallist, 1878; first Senior Scholar, Middle Templ London, Common and Criminal Law, 1879. Called to Irish Bai Michaelmas Term, 1880; joined the Munster Circuit, 1881; appointe Professor of Law, Queen's College, Cork, 1884; Professor of Rea Property, Incorporated Law Society of Ireland, 1891–96; Professo of Equity and Practice, King's Inns, Dublin, 1895–98; sometim Examiner in Law at the Royal University of Ireland. *Address:* Langara

Glenageary, Co. Dublin. *Club:* Royal St George, Kingstown.
Died 16 March 1920.

BARRY, Richard Fitzwilliam; late Crown Solicitor, King's County; *b* 18 Sept. 1861; *o* surv. *s* of late Capt. William Fitzjames Barry, JP, Resident Magistrate, and Annette Thelaire, *o d* of Edmond Hore, Liverpool; *m* 1890, Catherine Frances, *d* of late Frederick Augustus White, County Inspector, Royal Irish Constabulary; five *s* four *d*. *Educ:* Trinity Coll., Dublin. BA 1883; LLB 1891; claimant to dormant title of Viscount Buttevant, to which his grandfather, James Redmond Barry, lodged a claim, the hearing of which was adjourned, before the Committee of Privileges of the House of Lords, 1825. *Address:* Johns Place, Birr, King's County; Glandore, Co. Cork. *Clubs:* University, Dublin; King's County and Ormond, Birr.
Died 16 June 1916.

BARRY, Rt. Rev. Thomas Francis, DD; Bishop of Chatham since 1902; *b* Poke Mouche, NB, 3 March 1841. *Educ:* St John Coll.; Montreal Coll.; Grand Seminary, Montreal. Was Rector of Cathedral, Chatham; Pastor of St Basil; of Caraquae, and of Bathurst; Coadjutor Bishop, 1900. *Address:* Bishop's Palace, Chatham, New Brunswick.
Died 19 Jan. 1920.

BARRYMORE, 1st Baron, *cr* 1902; **Arthur Hugh Smith-Barry;** PC 1896; JP, DL; *b* 17 Jan. 1843; *m* 1st, 1868, Lady Mary Frances Wyndham-Quin (*d* 1884), *d* of 3rd Earl of Dunraven; one *d* (one *s* decd); 2nd, 1889, Elizabeth, *widow* of Arthur Post, of New York and *d* of Gen. Wadsworth, Geneseo, USA; one *d*. *Educ:* Eton; Christ Church, Oxford. MP Co. Cork, 1867-74; Vice-Pres. of Irish Landowners Convention; MP (C) South Huntingdonshire, 1886-1900. *Recreation:* Admiral, Royal Cork Yacht Club. *Heir:* none. *Address:* 20 Hill Street, Berkeley Square, W1. *T:* Grosvenor 2667; Fota Island, Co. Cork; Marbury Hall, Northwich, Cheshire. *Clubs:* Carlton, Travellers'; Royal Yacht Squadron, Cowes.
Died 22 Feb. 1925 (ext).

BARTER, Sir Richard, Kt 1911; JP; *b* 19 Nov. 1837; *e s* of late Dr Richard Barter; *m* 1873, Anna Madelene Jameson. *Educ:* Flynn's, Hartcourt Street, Dublin. Farming, stock breeding, especially Kerry cattle; pedigree large York pigs; Chairman Cork Muskerry Railway Co.; also was Chairman, Agricultural Section, Cork Exhibition, Co. Cork Agricultural Society. *Publications:* several papers on agricultural subjects. *Recreations:* yachting, hunting, fishing, shooting. *Address:* St Ann's Hill, Cork. *Clubs:* Cork, Royal Cork.
Died 16 Aug. 1916.

BARTHOLOMÉ, Albert; peintre et sculpteur; Hon. RA 1921; Commandeur de la Légion d'Honneur; Président de la Société Nationale des Beaux-Arts; Grande Croix d'Isabella la Catholique; Grand Officier de Léopold de Belgique et du Trésor Sacré du Japon; engagé volontaire de 1870; membre des Académies des Beaux-Arts d'Ecosse, d'Angleterre, de Belgique, de Saxe, de Milan, de Madrid; *b* Thiverval, 29 août 1848; *m* Florence Letessier. *Educ:* Lycée de Versailles. *Œuvres dans les Musées:* Pau, près des blés, pastel; Luxembourg, Paris, Tête de paysanne, pastel; Petite fille pleurant, bronze; Buste de Mme Bartholomé, marbre; Femme pleurant appuyé sur une stèle, marbre; Dresde, Jeune fille se coiffant, marbre; Moulage du Monument aux morts, plâtre; Arts décoratifs Paris, Petite fontaine, marbre; Bruxelles, L'adieu, pierre; Vienne, Femme sortant du bain, pierre; Krefeld, Le baiser, marbre; Mulhouse, Jeune fille pleurant, pierre; Aix-la-Chapelle, Baigneuse, plâtre; Budapest, Moulage du Monument aux morts, plâtre; Copenhague, Petite fille en pleurs, pierre; Au bord de l'eau, pierre; Santiago du Chili, Jeune fille à sa toilette, bronze; Rome, L'union dans l'au-delà, marbre; Reims, Baigneuse, marbre, etc. *Grands Monuments:* Le tombeau du cimetière de Bouillant; Le monument aux morts au Père-Lachaise, Paris; Le tombeau Pam et le tombeau Meilhac, cimetière Montmartre; Le tombeau Dubufe, cimetière du Père-Lachaise; Le monument aux victimes du Pluviôse; Le Chénois, Belfort; Le tombeau de J.-J. Rousseau au Panthéon, Paris; Le monument de Sardou pour Paris; Le monument aux auteurs et compositeurs dramatiques morts pour la patrie; Le monument du sénateur aviateur Reymond à Montbrison; Le Monument à Paris 1914-18, place du Carrousel; Aux avocats morts pour la patrie, Palais de Justice; 1874, embrasse l'epée de 1918 à Cognac. *Recreation:* les voyages. *Address:* 1 rue Raffet, Paris.
Died Oct. 1928.

BARTHOLOMEW, John George, LLD (Edin.); FRGS, FRSE; geographer and cartographer to the King; head of the Edinburgh Geographical Institute; *b* Edinburgh, 22 March 1860; *s* of John Bartholomew, cartographer; *m* 1889, Jennie, *d* of late A. Sinclair Macdonald of Cyder Hall, Dornoch; two *s* two *d*. *Educ:* Edinburgh

High School and University. One of founders of Royal Scottish Geographical Society, and Hon. Secretary since its foundation in 1884; Secretary of Section E, British Association, 1892; Victoria Research Gold Medallist, Royal Geographical Society, 1905; Council of Royal Society, Edinburgh, 1909-12; introduced layer system of contour colouring for topographical maps; Hon. Member of Geographical Societies of Paris, St Petersburgh and Chicago. *Publications:* Survey Atlas of Scotland, 1895-1912; Citizen's Atlas, 1898-1912; Atlas of Meteorology, 1899; Survey Gazetteer of British Isles, 1904; Survey Atlas of England and Wales, 1903; Atlas of World's Commerce, 1907; Imperial Indian Gazetteer Atlas, 1908; Atlas of Zoogeography, 1911; numerous educational atlases and special maps. *Recreations:* fishing, travel. *Address:* The Geographical Institute, Edinburgh. *TA:* Bartholomew, Edinburgh. *T:* 2737 Central. *M:* S 1053. *Club:* Royal Societies.
Died 16 April 1920.

BARTLEET, Rev. Samuel Edwin, MA; FSA 1890; Hon. Canon of Gloucester, 1907; Vice-President, Bristol and Gloucestershire Archæological Society; *b* 24 Feb. 1835; *s* of Edwin Bartleet, of Birmingham, and Henrietta, *d* of Samuel Hiron, of Chipping Campden; *m* 1874, Henrietta (*d* 1915), *d* of Henry Gurney, Torquay. *Educ:* King Edward's School, Birmingham; Trinity College, Cambridge. Curate of Hallow, Worcestershire, 1858-60; Prestwich, Lancs, 1861-66; Vicar of Crompton (or Shaw), 1866-75, and 1877-78; Perpetual Curate of Ringley, 1875-77; Vicar of Brockworth, Glos, 1878-85; St Mark's, Gloucester, 1885-89; Rector of Dursley, 1899-1910; Rural Dean of Dursley, 1907-10. *Publications:* History of the Manor and Advowson of Brockworth; History of the Borough and Manor of Chipping Campden; The Leper Hospital of St Margaret, Gloucester; The Priory of St Guthlac, Hereford, in Transactions of Bristol and Gloucestershire Archæological Society; History of the Priory of St Mary, Bromfield, in Gloucester Cathedral Records. *Recreation:* the study of archæology. *Address:* Glenmore Lodge, Pittville, Cheltenham. *TA:* Cheltenham.
Died 27 Oct. 1924.

BARTLEMAN, Maj.-Gen. Woodburn Francis; Indian Army; *b* 26 April 1840. Entered army, 1857; Maj.-Gen., 1893; Unemployed Supernumerary List, 1895; served Indian Mutiny, 1858 (medal); Cossyah and Jyntiah Hills Campaign, 1862-63. *Address:* 19 Belmont Drive, Newnham Park, Liverpool.
Died 18 July 1924.

BARTLETT, Ven. Arthur Robert; Archdeacon of Goulburn, and Canon and Precentor of St Saviour's Cathedral since 1902; Incumbent of St Saviour's Cathedral Parish since 1904; *b* London, 1851; *s* of John and Harriet Huddlestone Bartlett; *m* 1887, Mary, 3rd *d* of Charles H. Humphrey, JP, of Luscombe, Burwood, NSW. *Educ:* Merchant Taylors' School; Wadham College, Oxford. Matriculated at Wadham Coll., Oxford, 1870; Death's Exhibitioner at School and College, also Goodridge Exhibitioner at College; took Honours in the Theological School, 1874; BA, 1874; MA, 1880. Deacon, 1874; Priest, 1875; served as Curate of Great Risington, Berkeley, West Hackney; appointed Minor Canon of Sydney; Examining Chaplain to the Bishop of Bathurst; Vicar of St Paul's, Burwood, for nine years; made Hon. Canon of Brisbane and Rural Dean and Rector of Ipswich. *Publications:* tracts; sermons; Story of the Temptation; Story of the Incarnation; Story of the Ascension (in verse). *Recreations:* chess (President of Ipswich club), cricket. *Address:* St Saviour's Cathedral, Goulburn, New South Wales. *Club:* Broughton, Sydney.
Died 14 April 1923.

BARTLETT, Sir Herbert Fogelstrom, Kt 1911; ISO 1903; a Commissioner of Inland Revenue, 1909-13; *b* 24 Nov. 1847; *s* of E. T. Bartlett, Plymouth; *m* 1876, Frances, *d* of R. Linwood, Bath. Assistant Secretary to Board of Inland Revenue, 1897-1908; Controller of Stamps and Registrar of Joint Stock Companies, 1903-9. *Address:* 49 Salisbury Road, Southsea. *Club:* Royal Albert Yacht, Southsea.
Died Nov. 1923.

BARTLETT, Sir Herbert Henry, 1st Bt, *cr* 1913; Partner in Perry and Co., Contractors; *b* 30 April 1842; *s* of late Robert Bartlett, of Hardington, Somerset, and Anne Guppy; *m* 1874, Ada Charlotte, *d* of Joseph Barr; four *s* three *d* (and two *s* decd). *Heir: g s* Basil Hardington Bartlett, *b* 15 Sept. 1905. *Address:* 54 Cornwall Gardens, SW. *T:* Western 2480. *Clubs:* St Stephen's, City Carlton, Constitutional, Royal London Yacht (Commodore), Royal Thames Yacht, Royal Temple Yacht.
Died 28 June 1921.

BARTLETT, Paul Wayland; sculptor; *b* New Haven, 1865; *s* of Truman Howe and Mary Ann White. *Educ:* New Haven and Boston.

Began sculpture under the instruction of Frémiet; exhibited in Salon at the age of 14; entered Ecole des Beaux Arts, 1880; received recompense at Salon for the group, The Bear Tamer (later in Met. Mus. of New York), 1887; represented US on International Jury of Awards for Sculpture, Paris Exposition, 1900; Chevalier, Legion of Honour, France, 1895; Officer, 1908. *Principal Works:* Statue of Gen. Joseph Warren, Boston; equestrian statue of Lafayette in the Square of the Louvre, Paris (gift to France from the school children of the US); statues of Columbus and Michelangelo; six statues on the front of the New York Public Library; pediment over House wing of the Capitol, Washington, DC; statue of Benjamin Franklin. *Address:* 229 E 20th Street, New York.   *Died Sept. 1925.*

BARTON, Major Charles Gerard, DSO 1900; The King's Own (retired); *b* 26 April 1860; *s* of Rev. J. Barton; *m* Mabel Eleanour, *widow* of Captain Maurice W. Kirk. *Educ:* Tonbridge School; Sherborne. Entered army, 1881; Capt. 1889; Maj. 1900; served South Africa, 1899–1902; Relief of Ladysmith (despatches, Queen's medal with two clasps, King's medal, DSO). *Recreation:* has played cricket for Hampshire. *Address:* Hatfield Bury, Witham, Essex.
Died 3 Nov. 1919.

BARTON, Rt. Hon. Sir Edmund, GCMG 1902; PC 1901; Order of Rising Sun (Japan) First Class, 1903; MA; Hon. DCL Oxon, Hon. LLD Cantab and Edin.; Fellow of Senate, University of Sydney; Senior Puisne Judge, High Court of Australia, since 1903; *b* Glebe, Sydney, 18 Jan. 1849; *m* 1877, Jean Mason, *d* of David Ross; four *s* two *d*. *Educ:* Public School, Fort Street; Sydney Grammar School; Univ., Sydney. Barrister, 1871; KC; MLA Sydney Univ., 1879–80; Wellington, 1880–82; East Sydney, 1882–87 and 1891–94; and Hastings-Macleay, 1898–99; Speaker, Legislative Assembly, NSW, 1883–87; MLC 1887–91, 1897–98; Attorney-General, NSW, 1889, and again 1891–93; Member, Federal Convention, Sydney, 1891; Senior Representative, NSW, to Federal Convention, 1897; Leader of Federal Convention, Adelaide, Sydney, Melbourne, 1897–98; Leader, NSW Opposition, 1898–99; Leader of Delegation to London with Australian Commonwealth Bill, 1900; Prime Minister and Minister for External Affairs, first Australian Federal Cabinet, 1901–3. Hon. Bencher Gray's Inn, 1902; received freedom of City of Edinburgh, 1902. *Recreation:* literature. *Address:* Avenel, Darling Point, Sydney, NSW.   *Died 6 Jan. 1920.*

BARTON, Edwin Henry, DSc; FRS, FRSE, FPSL, FInstP; Professor of Experimental Physics, University College, Nottingham, since 1905; *b* 23 Oct. 1858; 3rd *s* of John Barton, Nottingham, and Eliza Lake, Nottingham; *m* 1894, Mary, 6th *d* of late Wm Stafford, Newark; two *s*. *Educ:* People's College and University College, Nottingham; Imperial College of Science, London; University of Bonn. Engaged for a number of years in engineering works at Nottingham as draughtsman and in other positions; joined the staff of the physical department of University College, Nottingham, 1893; senior lecturer and demonstrator, 1895. *Publications:* A Text-Book of Sound, 1908 (revised reprints, 1914, 1919, and 1922); Analytical Mechanics, 1911 (2nd edn 1924); An Introduction to the Mechanics of Fluids, 1915; jointly with late Capt. T. P. Black, MSc, PhD, Practical Physics for Colleges and Schools, 1912 (revised, 1918 and 1919); sole or joint author of over forty papers giving the results of original researches in magnetism, electrical waves, acoustics, etc, published in the Philosophical Magazine, Physical Society's Proceedings, and Royal Societies of London and Edinburgh, 1894–1924; contributor to Physical Abstracts and Science Abstracts since 1894; author of article on Sound in the Dictionary of Applied Physics, vol. iv, 1923. *Recreations:* cycling, boating, mountaineering, gardening. *Address:* University College, Nottingham. *T:* 776.
Died 23 Sept. 1925.

BARTON, Maj.-Gen. Sir Geoffry, KCVO 1906; CB 1889; CMG 1900; Colonel Royal Fusiliers; JP Dumfriesshire; Knight of Grace of the Order of St John of Jerusalem; *b* 22 Feb. 1844; *s* of late C. C. Barton of Rownhams, Hants; *m* 1890, Beryl, *d* of Col Mackenzie, of Auchenskeoch, Kirkcudbrightshire; one *s* one *d*. *Educ:* Eton. Entered army, 1862; Major-General, 1898; served Ashanti War, 1873–74 (wounded, despatches, promoted Captain, medal with clasp); ADC Aldershot, 1874–77; Zulu War, 1879 (despatches, brevet of Major, medal with clasp); Deputy Assistant Adjutant-General with Expeditionary Force to Egypt, 1882; present at Kassassin and Tel-el-Kebir (despatches, medal with clasp, 4th class Osmanieh, Khedive's star, brevet of Lieut-Col); Asst Mil. Sec., China, 1884–85; Military Secretary, Expeditionary Force to Suakin, 1885 (clasp); AAG Thames District, 1895–97; AAG North-West District, 1895–98; commanded Fusilier Brigade, South Africa Field Force, 1899 (wounded Ladysmith, despatches twice); later commanded Krugersdorp and Pretoria

Districts till end of war, 1902 (despatches). *Address:* Craigs, Dumfries, NB. *Clubs:* United Service, Wellington; Dumfries and Galloway.
Died 6 July 1922.

BARTON, George Alexander Heaton, MD; LRCP, MRCS, LSA; Anæsthetist, Hampstead General and Royal National Orthopædic Hospitals; *b* Hongkong, 1865; *s* of Z. Barton, merchant; *m* 1889, Mary Matilda, *d* of Francis Goold, Madras army; four *s* one *d*. *Educ:* De Aston School. Matriculated London University (1st div.), 1882; St Mary's Hospital (Prizeman, Prosector and Clinical Assistant to Out-patients); qualified, 1886; Surgeon in Royal Mail and Blue Funnel Lines, and practised in Devonshire till 1901; Fellow, Royal Society of Medicine; Member, British Medical Association and Harveian Society (late Hon. Secretary and Vice-President); formerly Anæsthetist to the Throat Hospital, Golden Square, the Female Lock Hospital, the National Dental Hospital, King George Hospital, and (acting) St Mary's Hospital. *Publications:* A Guide to the Administration of Ethyl Chloride; Backwaters of Lethe; Prolonged Anæsthesia by Ethyl Chloride in Operations on the Nose and Throat (Lancet); the CE-Ethyl Chloride-Chloroform Sequence (Pract.); The Open Method of Ether Administration with some modifications (Pract.); Alkaloids in Anæsthesia (Pract.); the Eye in Anæsthesia (Clin. Jl); Ether, some simple Methods and Musings (Clin. Jl). *Address:* 15 Talbot Road, W2. *T:* Park 953; 7 Devonshire Street, W1. *T:* Langham 1916.
Died 13 Jan. 1924.

BARTON, Richard, ISO 1911; late Superintendent of Demands, Stationery Office (retired, 1913); *b* 25 May 1850; *e s* of Alfred Barton, Winslow, Bucks; *m* 1884, Frances, 3rd *d* of John J. Youlin, MD, Jersey City, USA. *Educ:* Cowley School, Oxford. *Address:* Old Rectory, Pitchcott, Aylesbury, Bucks.
Died 1 Sept. 1927.

BARTON, William Henry; pioneer of the popular journalism and the Penny Press in Burma (retired, 1927); *b* 6 May 1869; *e s* of late Daniel Barton, of Downend, Isle of Wight, and Southampton; *m* Jane Caroline (decd), *y d* of late Alex. Ritchie, of Aberdeen and London; two *d*. *Educ:* British School, Southampton; King's College, London. Editor, Queenstown Free Press (South Africa), 1890; proprietor and editor, London Associated Press, 1900; editor, Rangoon Daily Times, 1905; sole proprietor and editor-in-chief since 1908 of Burma Pictorial Press, Daily Times of Burma, Moulmein Daily News, Weekly Times of Burma, and Burma Sunday Times. *Publications:* Thirty Days in the Jungle; Wild Life in Beautiful Burma; Modern Politics in Ancient India; The Indian Reforms and Diarchy; The Parish and District Councils Act; Holidays; The Book of the Home. *Address:* Park View, Tovil, Maidstone.
Died 20 Sept. 1928.

BARTRAM, Sir Robert Appleby, Kt 1922; JP; *b* 23 March 1835; *e s* of late George Bartram of South Hylton, near Sunderland, and Margaret Appleby, of Newcastle-on-Tyne; *m* 1859, Ann, *d* of William Naizby, of South Hylton. *Educ:* privately. Chairman of Bartram & Sons Ltd, Shipbuilders, Sunderland; Chairman of Samuel Tyzack & Co. Ltd, Steel Manufacturers, Sunderland; Director of Sunderland and South Shields Water Co. Ltd. Has always taken a great interest in education; was ten years President, Sunderland Chamber of Commerce, three times chosen Chairman of the Sunderland School Board. *Address:* Thornhill Park, Sunderland. *TA:* Bartram, Sunderland. *T:* National 308.
Died 8 Aug. 1925.

BARTTELOT, Major Sir Walter Balfour, 3rd Bt, *cr* 1875; DSO 1916; Coldstream Guards; *b* 22 March 1880; *s* of 2nd Bt and Georgiana Mary, *d* of George E. Balfour, of Sidmouth Manor, Devon; *S* father, 1900; *m* 1903, Gladys St Aubyn, *y d* of W. C. Angove; two *s*. *Educ:* Eton; Sandhurst. Contested (U) Saffron Walden Division of Essex, 1906. Served South Africa, 1899–1902 (Queen's medal, 6 clasps; King's medal, 2 clasps); Military Secretary to Lord Denman, Gov.-General of Australia, 1911–14; served France, 1914 (wounded); Gallipoli, 1915; GSO 3 (Croix de Guerre); Mesopotamia Brigade, 1916–17; Major 13th Division (despatches, DSO). *Heir:* *s* Walter de Stopham Barttelot, *b* 27 Oct. 1904. *Address:* Stopham House, Pulborough, Sussex. *Clubs:* Guards, Carlton, Boodle's.
Died 23 Oct. 1918.

BARZELLOTTI, Giacomo, Dottore in Lettere e Filosofia; Decorato di Ordini cavallereschi italiani e Cav. della Legione d'Onore di Francia; Professore ordinario di Storia della Filosofia nella Regia Università di Roma; Senatore del Regno; *b* Firenze, 7 Luglio 1844; *s* of Gaspero Barzellotti, medico, and Teresa Benvenuti, *d* of Pietro Benvenuti, insigne pittore di Arezzo; *m* Antonietta Tabarrini, *d* of Marco, Presidente del Consiglio di Stato e Senatore del Regno; two *s. Educ:* Firenze. Prese la doppia Laurea di Dottore in Lettere e in Filosofia all' Università di Pisa nell' anno 1866; Professore di Filosofia nel Regia Liceo Dante in Firenze, 1867–77; Libero docente all' Università di Roma nell' anno scolastico 1879–80; vinse il concorso per professore ordinario alla cattedra di Filosofia morale nelle Regia Università di Pavia, ove insegnò 1881–83; dopo una rinunzia volontaria all' insegnamento, 1884–85, fu incaricato dell' insegnamento della Filosofia della Storia nell' Università di Roma, 1886; chiamato dalla Facoltà di Lettere e di Filosofia dell' Università di Napoli, vi riprese l'insegnamento della Filosofia morale, 1887; per voto favorevole della Facoltà di Filosofia e Lettere dell' Università di Roma assunse, nel 1897, in questa Università l'insegnamento della Storia della Filosofia, che tiene tuttora. Membro Nazionale della Regia Accademia dei Lincei di Roma. *Publications:* Delle dottrine filosofiche nei libri di Cicerone, 1867; La Morale nella Filosofia positiva, 1871, tradotto in inglese col titolo The Ethics of Positivism, 1878; David Lazzaretti di Arcidosso, detto il Santo, i suoi seguaci, la sua leggenda, 1885; Santi, Solitari e Filosofi, 1886; Studi e Ritratti, 1893; Ippolito Taine; La Philosophie de H. Taine, traduzione francese e seconda ediz. della stessa opera, 1900; Dal Rinascimento al Risorgimento (con un discorso su G. Carducci), 2nd edn, 1909; Monte Amiata e il suo Profeta (David Lazzaretti), terza e nuova edizione dell' opera sopra citata, con introduzione, aggiunte e illustrazioni, 1910. *Address:* Roma, Via Borgognona, 12. *Died 18 Sept. 1917.*

BASHFORD, Ernest Francis, OBE 1919; late RAMC, TC; MD; *b* Bowdon, Cheshire, 1873; *e s of* Wm Taylor Bashford and Elizabeth Booth; *m* 1902, Elisabeth, *e d of* Felix Alfermann, Frankfurt-on-Main; one *d. Educ:* Universities of Edinburgh and Berlin, Frankfurt-on-Main; MB, ChB Edin., 1899; MD (Gold Medal), 1902. Vans Dunlop Scholar in Anatomy, Chemistry, Zoology, and Botany; Mackenzie Bursar in Practical Anatomy; Prosector to Sir Wm Turner; Whitman Prizeman in Clinical Medicine; Houldsworth Research Scholarship in Experimental Pharmacology; Stark Scholarship in Clinical Medicine and Pathology; Pattison Prizeman in Clinical Surgery; on graduating was awarded the M'Cosh Graduate's Scholarship for Study and Research in the Medical Schools of Europe, and proceeded to Germany; studied bacteriology and pharmacology in the University of Berlin; later worked with Ehrlich at the Royal Prussian Institute for Experimental Therapeutics, Frankfurt-on-Main; also studied there under Weigert-Grocers Research Scholar, 1900–2; Milner Fothergill Gold Medal in Therapeutics, University Edinburgh, 1901. Assistant to Director of Pharmacological Institute, Berlin, 1901; Assistant to Professor of Materia Medica, Pharmacology and Clin. Med., Univ. of Edin., 1902; founded the modern experimental investigation of cancer in this country, and placed the statistical and biological investigation of cancer on a comparative basis; General Superintendent of Research, 1902–14, and Director of the Laboratories of the Imperial Cancer Research Fund, 1903–14. Honorary President, First International Cancer Congress, Heidelberg, 1906; awarded 1911 the Walker Prize for the quinquennial period, 1905–10; Ingleby Lecturer, Univ. of Birmingham, 1911; Middleton Goldschmidt Lecturer, New York, 1912; Von Leyden Memorial Lecturer, Berlin, 1912. Served MEF 1915–16, BEF 1916–19, Germany, 1919 (despatches, OBE). *Publications:* editor and part author of Scientific Reports on the Investigations of the Imperial Cancer Research Fund, i–v; numerous papers on pharmacology, immunity, biochemistry, cancer, and pathology of wounds; successfully opposed from 1906 the efforts of the German Cancer Committee, Berlin, to gather all Cancer Research under its control. *Recreation:* fishing. *Address:* c/o Holt & Co., Whitehall Place, SW1. *Died 23 Aug. 1923.*

BASHFORD, Rt. Rev. James W., DD, LLD, PhD; Bishop, Methodist Episcopal Church since 1904; *b* Fayette, Wisconsin, 29 May 1849; *s of* Rev. Samuel Bashford and Mary Ann M'Kee; *m* 1878, Jane M. of Madison, Wis, *d of* Hon. W. W. Field. *Educ:* classical course, University of Wisconsin, AB 1873; theological course at Boston University, STB 1876; School of Oratory, Boston University, 1878; course in all sciences of Boston University; PhD 1881. Pastor of Methodist Episcopal Churches in Boston, Mass, Newton, Mass, Portland, Maine, and Buffalo, NY, 1878–89; President, Ohio Wesleyan University, 1889–1904; visited Europe, 1881; again, and especially the German Universities, 1887; Italy, Greece, Egypt, Palestine, etc, 1896–97; revisited England, 1907, 1910; in former year visiting also India; and in latter year re-visiting Germany and Russia; Representative of Methodist Episcopal Church on World Commission on Faith and Order, and on Continuation Committee for China. DD, *pro honore,* from North-Western University, Evanston, Ill, 1890; LLD Wesleyan University of Middletown, Conn, 1903; University of Wisconsin, 1912; Ohio Wesleyan University, 1912. *Publications:* Outlines of the Science of Religion, for class use; Wesley and Goethe, 1903; The Awakening of China; China and Methodism,

1906; God's Missionary Plan for the World, 1907. *Address:* Peking, China. *Died 18 March 1919.*

BASHFORD, Major (Radcliffe James) Lindsay, OBE 1919; RAOC; *b* London, 6 Feb. 1881; *s of* late Frederick Bashford; *m* 1919, Catherine, *y d of* late Joseph W. Lovibond, JP, Lake House, Wilts. *Educ:* Bedford; Germany; Edinburgh University; the College of Political Science, Paris. Lecturer in English Literature at the University of Bordeaux, 1902–3; Private Sec. to Hon. Joseph Pulitzer, proprietor of the New York World, 1903; London Evening News, 1906; Literary Editor of The Daily Mail, 1908; took a commission in the Army Ordnance Department, 1914; served in Gallipoli, Egypt, and Palestine, 1915–19 (despatches thrice); special correspondent of the Daily Mail in France, Germany, Poland, and on the Baltic, 1919–20; contributor on political subjects to reviews. *Publications:* Everybody's Boy, 1912; Splendrum, 1914; Cupid in the Car, 1914. *Recreations:* music, yachting. *Club:* Devonshire. *Died 20 Aug. 1921.*

BASING, 2nd Baron, *cr* 1887; **George Limbrey Sclater-Booth,** CB 1902; DL, JP, CC; Colonel in army; *b* 1 Jan. 1860; *S* father, 1894; *m* 1889, Mary (*d* 1904), *d of* John Hargreaves, Maiden Erlegh, Berks, and Whalley Abbey, Lancashire; one *s* two *d. Educ:* Eton; Balliol Coll., Oxford. Late Lieut-Col 1st Dragoons. Served South Africa, 1899–1901 (despatches, Brevet Lieut-Col); retired, 1906. *Heir: s* Hon. John Limbrey Robert Sclater-Booth, *b* 3 Dec. 1890. *Address:* Hoddington House, Upton Grey, Hants. *Clubs:* Arthur's, Naval and Military. *Died 8 April 1919.*

BASKERVILLE, Rev. Charles Gardiner, MA; Hon. Canon of Rochester; Surrogate; *b* 20 Oct. 1830; *m* 1858, Ellen Spencer Parsons (*d* 1919); two *s* two *d. Educ:* Bishops' College, Clifton. Curate of Bath Abbey; Curate of St Thomas', Wells; Vicar of St Silas, Lozells, Birmingham; Vicar of St Stephen, Walthamstow, and Vicar of Tonbridge. *Publications:* Abba Father; Sidelights on Ephesians and on Philippians; Hints to Sunday School Teachers. *Address:* 3 Park Road, Southborough Kent. *Died 28 Feb. 1921.*

BASKERVILLE, Ralph Hopton, JP; *b* 13 Feb. 1883; *s of* late Walter Thomas Mynors Baskerville and Bertha Maria, *o c* and *heiress of* late John Hopton, of Canon-ffrome Court, Co. Hereford, and of Kemerton Court, Gloucestershire. Late Lieutenant 1st Royal Dragoons. *Address:* Clyro Court, Hay, Co. Radnor. *Died 9 April 1918.*

BASSETT, John Spencer, PhD, LLD; Professor of American History, Smith College, Mass, since 1906; Head of History Department, 1914–21; *b* Tarborough, NC (USA), 10 Sept. 1867; *s of* Richard Baxter Bassett and Mary J. Wilson; *m* 1892, Jessie Lewellin; one *s* one *d. Educ:* Trinity Coll. (NC), AB 1888; Johns Hopkins Univ., PhD 1894. Teacher in Durham (NC) Public School, 1888–90; Headmaster of High School in connection with Trinity College (NC), 1890–91; Student in History and Economics at Johns Hopkins Univ., 1891–94; Fellow in History at Johns Hopkins Univ., 1893–94; founded the South Atlantic Quarterly at Durham (NC), 1902, and continued its editor till 1905; Professor of History, Trinity Coll., North Carolina, 1893–1906; Lecturer in History, Yale University, 1907; NY University, 1908–10; Columbia University, 1909–13. Secretary American Historical Society since 1919; Fellow of the Royal Historical Society; Member of the American Historical Association, the Massachusetts Historical Society, the American Antiquarian Society (Worcester, Mass), the American Academy for Arts and Sciences (Boston), and the National Institute of Arts and Letters. *Publications:* Constitutional Beginnings of North Carolina; Slavery and Servitude in North Carolina; Anti-Slavery Leaders of North Carolina; Slavery in the State of North Carolina; The Regulators of North Carolina; The Federalist System, 1789–1801; The Life of Andrew Jackson, 1911; A Short History of the United States, 1913; The Plain Story of American History, 1915; The Middle Group of American Historians, 1917; The Lost Fruits of Waterloo, 1918, revised edition, 1919; Our War with Germany, 1919; The Plantation Overseer as Shown in his Letters, 1925; Expansion and Reform, 1926; The State of History Writing (in Jusserand, Report on the Writing of History), 1926; Martin Van Buren (in Lives of the Secretaries of State), 1926; edited new edition of the writings of Colonel William Byrd of Westover; The Correspondence of Andrew Jackson, vol. i, 1926; Joint Editor of the Smith College Studies in History, 1915–25. *Recreation:* gardening. *Address:* Northampton, Mass, USA. *Clubs:* English-Speaking Union; Century, New York; Cosmos, Washington; Northampton. *Died 27 Jan. 1928.*

BASSETT-SMITH, Surgeon-Rear-Admiral Sir Percy William, KCB 1921 (CB 1911); CMG 1918; FRCS, FRCP; DTM & H Camb.;

President, Royal Society of Tropical Medicine and Hygiene; *b* St Albans, 1861; *s* of William Bassett-Smith; *m* Constance Brightman, MBE (*d* 1925), *d* of Rev. F. Hastings; two *d*. *Educ:* St John's College, Hurstpierpoint. House Physician, Middlesex Hospital, London; entered Royal Navy, 1883; served Egyptian Expedition (medal and Khedive star, special promotion to Fleet Surgeon); Gilbert Blane Gold Medal; London School Trop. Medicine, 1899; Cragg's Prize, 1906; Lecturer on Tropical Medicine and Bacteriology, RN Medical School, Haslar, 1900–12; late Professor of Pathology and Lecturer Tropical Medicine, Medical School, RN College, Greenwich; Physician to Out-Patients Disease of Chest Hospital, Victoria Park, and St John's Hospital, Lewisham; Consultant Tropical Diseases, 23 Harley Street, W1. *Publications:* Snake Bites and Poisonous Fishes, Ency. Med. vol xi; many medical scientific papers on undulant fever, typhoid, syphilis, etc; sub-editor, Tropical Disease Bulletins. *Recreations:* golf, natural history. *Address:* 3 Aberdeen Terrace, Blackheath, SE3. *T:* Lee Green 368. *Club:* Royal Societies.   *Died 29 Dec. 1927.*

BASU, Bhupendra Nath, MA, BL; Member, Council of Secretary of State for India, 1917–23; Member of Executive Council of Governor of Bengal since 1924; Vice-Chancellor, Calcutta University; *b* Calcutta, Jan. 1859. *Educ:* Presidency College, Calcutta. Was member, Bengal Legislative Council, also Viceroy's Legislative Council; President of the Indian National Congress held in Madras, 1914; Representative of the Government of India at the International Labour Conference at Geneva, 1922; Member, Royal Commission on Indian Public Services, 1923. *Address:* Temple Chambers, Calcutta. *Clubs:* National Liberal; Calcutta, Calcutta.

                                                                Died 16 Sept. 1924.

BATCHELOR, Ferdinand Campion; Professor of Surgery, Otago University; Lieutenant-Colonel, Expeditionary Force of New Zealand. *Educ:* Guy's Hospital. *Address:* Otago University, New Zealand.   *Died 31 Aug. 1916.*

BATE, Col Albert Louis Frederick, CMG 1916; LRCSI, LM and LKQCPI, LM, Rotunda Hospital; Fellow Royal Institute of Public Health, London; FRGS, FRCI; *b* 5 Oct. 1862; *s* of Henry Alexander Bate, Dublin; *m* 1896, Emily Florence Wilson, *d* of Henry West, Hampton on Thames; four *s*. *Educ:* Methodist College, Belfast; Wesley College, Dublin. Royal Army Medical Corps, 1886; Major, 1898; Lt-Col, 1906; Col, 1915; served Sikkim Expedition, 1888; South African War, 1899–1902, as SMO Zululand, Secretary and Registrar PMO, Maritzburg, Natal, and later OC No 21 Stationary Hospital, Machadodorp, Transvaal (Queen's medal, 2 clasps, King's medal, 2 clasps); European War, 1914–19 (despatches twice, CMG, Mons star and clasp, Victory medal and General Service medal, with 2 laurel leaves); started and organised a Convalescent Hospital; materially assisted in the efficient organisation of similar smaller establishments at every divisional headquarters. French Médaille d'Honneur de l'Assistance Publique. *Address:* c/o Holt & Co., 3 Whitehall Place, SW.   *Died 20 Feb. 1924.*

BATE, Sir Henry Newel, Kt 1910; Chairman of the Ottawa Improvement Commission; *b* Truro, 9 April 1828; *m* 1853, Catherine (*d* 1906), *d* of Allan Cameron; four *s*. *Educ:* St Catharine's, Ontario, Canada. Has resided in Ottawa since 1854; first Chairman of the Ottawa Improvement Commission on its formation, 1899; President of the Beechwood Cemetery, Ottawa and Aylmer Road Company, the Russell Company, Limited; Director of the Bank of Ottawa, etc. *Recreations:* Member of the Hunt Club, St Patrick's Golf Club, Green Lake Fish and Game Club. *Address:* Treuwick House, Chapel Street, Ottawa, Canada. *Clubs:* Rideau, Country, Ottawa.

                                                                Died 8 April 1917.

BATE, John Pawley, JP; Barrister-at-Law; Reader to Inns of Court in Roman and International Law since 1897; has been Examiner in these subjects in the Universities of Oxford and London; *b* 1857; *e s* of late Rev. George Osborn Bate; *m* Mary, *widow* of Sir Charles Wathen of Cook's Folly, Clifton; one *d*. *Educ:* Woodhouse Grove School; Peterhouse, Camb. Obtained Members' Prize for English Essay, 1884; LLD 1893. For some years Fellow and Law Lecturer of Trinity Hall; Professor of Jurisprudence in Univ. Coll. London, 1894–1901; has contributed articles on International Law to the Quarterly Review; British legal representative on the staff of the League of Nations, 1919–20. *Publications:* Notes on the Doctrine of Renvoi; Declaration of London; Translations of works on International Law by Ayala, Victoria, Rachel, Textor, etc. *Address:* Lambpark, Honiton. *T:* Honiton 26; 8 Stone Buildings, Lincoln's Inn, WC. *Club:* Athenæum.

                                                                Died 10 Feb. 1921.

BATEMAN, Alys; soprano singer; *d* of late Robert Bateman and Marian Moore, relative of Hannah Moore; *m* 1st, Malcolm Colin, *s* of Francis Simon Dring, of Simonstown, Co. Cork; 2nd, John Starkie Gardner. *Educ:* Bodleian College; Trinity College of Music. Début concert in England at St James' Hall, 1903; initiated Union Jack Club Concerts; toured Canada twice, 1906 and 1907; sang to King and Queen of Spain at Welbeck; organised Requiem Concert in aid of Prince Francis of Teck Memorial Fund, 1911; toured England, 1913, with Sapelnikoff; gave first recitals ever held in London of Russian music, 1914 and 1915; organised five concerts of Russian music, Grand Duke Michael's Fund, 1915; concerts for Belgian Relief Fund, Polish Victims' Relief Fund, Red Cross Fund, and Polish Flag Day, 1915; eight concerts of Russian music, Oct. 1915–June 1916; raised fund for Berkshire room, Star and Garter; gave concert in Queen's Hall for Queen Charlotte's Hospital, 1917; proprietor of the metal works of J. Starkie Gardner. *Recreations:* riding, punting, gardening. *Address:* 20 Elvaston Place, SW7. *T:* Kensington 7315; 2A Merivale Road, Putney, SW15. *Club:* Ladies' Athenæum.

                                                                Died 7 Nov. 1924.

BATEMAN, Francis John Harvey, MA (Camb.), MD, CM (Edin.); FZS; JP County of London; Civil Surgeon, Lewisham Military Hospital; Senior Medical Officer, Blackheath and Charlton Hospital; Hon. Medical Officer, Belmont Home for Ladies, Lewisham, Dartmouth Home for Crippled Boys, Blackheath, and St Dunstan's Annexe for Blinded Soldiers, Blackheath; Medical Adviser, Blackheath High School; *b* Norwich; *s* of late Sir Frederic Bateman, MD, LLD, FRCP, and Emma Brownfield, *d* of John Gooderson of Heigham Fields, Norwich; *m* 1902, Bertha Isabel, *d* of late Hugh Roberts, Llanrwst, N Wales; three *s*. *Educ:* Norwich School; Pembroke Coll., Cambridge; medical schools of Edinburgh, Dublin, and Paris; Prizeman in Public Health Edinburgh School of Medicine. After graduating MB, CM, was appointed Resident Physician to the Royal Infirmary, Edinburgh, and Resident Surgeon to the Leith Hospital; after holding the post of Assistant Medical Officer to the West Riding Asylum, Wakefield, went to Paris as Resident Medical Officer to the Hertford British Hospital, 1900; worked at the Pasteur Institute and at the French Hospitals; Vice-President of Medical Society, London, and Fellow of Obstetrical Society, Edinburgh; Member d'Alliance Franco Britannique; has contributed to medical journals. *Recreations:* golf, fishing, shooting. *Address:* Heath End, Blackheath. *T:* Lee Green 294. *M:* LK 8664. *Clubs:* Oxford and Cambridge; Magistrates'.   *Died 2 Aug. 1920.*

BATEMAN, Rev. William Fairbairn La Trobe-, MA; Hon. Canon of Christ Church Cathedral, Oxford, 1922; *b* 8 Jan. 1845; *s* of late John Frederic La Trobe-Bateman, FRS, of Moor Park, Surrey, and Anne, *o d* of Sir William Fairbairn, 1st Bt; *m* 1870, Mildred Jane (*d* 1878), 2nd *d* of Rev. Robert Sumner, and *g d* of Bishop Sumner of Winchester; one *s* two *d*. *Educ:* Cheam; Harrow; Trinity College, Cambridge. Deacon, 1868; Priest, 1870; Curate of Alverstoke, 1868–69; Castle Rising, 1869–71; Christ Church, St Pancras, 1871–74; Vicar of St John Evangelist, Norwood, 1875–1900; Rector of Ascot, 1900–17; Diocesan Chaplain to Bishop of Oxford, 1917–19. *Publications:* Our Companion by the Way; The Pattern Life; Problems and Issues of the Spiritual Life, 1915. *Address:* Streatley, near Reading. *Club:* Athenæum.   *Died 3 Oct. 1926.*

BATEMAN, Rev. William Henry Fraser; Canon of York, 1912–21; Surrogate, 1901–21; Proctor in Convocation, 1913–19; Synodal Secretary of Convocation of York, 1917–21; *b* Manchester, 1855; *s* of R. D. Bateman, Manchester; *m* 1883, Jane Thomas (*d* 1911), Glam, South Wales; one *s* one *d*. *Educ:* Chorlton High School, Manchester; Christ's College, Cambridge (MA). Curate at St Lawrence's, York, 1883–90; Rector, Holy Trinity, York, 1890–95; Vicar of Mexborough, 1895–1914; Vicar of Wistow, 1914–21. *Publication:* Editor Parish Register, Holy Trinity, Micklegate, York, 1903. *Recreation:* cycling. *Address:* Cartref, Clifton Park Road, Caversham, Oxon.   *Died 6 Aug. 1923.*

BATEMAN-HANBURY, Rev. Hon. Arthur Allen; Rector of Shobdon; Prebendary of Hereford; *b* 13 March 1829; *e surv s* of 1st Baron Bateman; *m* 1858, Mary Ward (*d* 1895), *e d* of John Davenport of Foxley, Herefords; one *s* four *d*. *Educ:* Eton; Christ Church, Oxford. Ordained 1853. *Address:* Shobdon Rectory, Kingsland, Herefordshire.   *Died 5 March 1919.*

BATES, Arlo, SB, AB, AM, LitD; Professor of English, Massachusetts Institute of Technology, Boston, Mass, USA, 1893–1915; *b* East Machias, Maine, 16 Dec. 1850; *s* of Dr Niran Bates and Susan Thaxter Bates; *m* 1882, Harriet L. Vose; one *s*. *Educ:* Washington Academy; Bowdoin College, class 1876. Editor, Broadside, 1878–79; Boston

Courier, 1880–93; correspondent, Providence Journal, Chicago Tribune, Book Buyer, etc; lecturer on literary subjects before societies, clubs, etc; member Phi Beta Kappa, American Academy Arts and Sciences, National Institute of Arts and Letters, etc. *Publications:* Patty's Perversities; The Pagans; The Philistines; The Puritans; Mr Jacobs; F. Seymour Hayden and Engraving; Albrecht; A Lad's Love; Book of Nine Tales; In the Bundle of Time; Talks on Writing English, First and Second Series; Talks on the Study of Literature; Love in a Cloud; The Diary of a Saint; Talks on Teaching Literature; The Intoxicated Ghost and Other Stories; Counsels of a Worldly Godmother (anon.); with Mrs Bates, Prince Vance. *Poems:* Berries of the Brier; Sonnets in Shadow; The Poet and His Self; The Torch-bearers; Told in the Gate; Under the Beech-Tree. *Recreations:* yachting, whist, digging in Indian shell-middens, collecting book-plates. *Address:* 4 Otis Place, Boston, Mass, USA. *Club:* Tavern, Boston. *Died Sept. 1918.*

BATES, Henry Montague; late Principal Clerk, Public Health Department, Corporation of London; *b* 17 March 1849; *s* of Robert M. Bates and Charlotte Emily Taylor; *m o d* of Colonel Francis Chancellor Rybot, 1st Bombay Lancers, and *widow* of Lt-Col A Gammell, 12th Lancers; one *s. Educ:* Bell Burrows and Johnson's Naval Establishment, Southsea, etc. Private Secretary to Rt Hon. Edward Horsman, MP, for four years; Assistant Clerk to Commissioners of Sewers of City of London, 1875; Clerk of the Commission, 1895; Commission amalgamated with Corporation of London, 1898, by the City of London Sewers Act, 1897, and the municipal work of the City carried on by the Public Health Department created for the purpose; PG Steward, Grand Lodge, Freemasons; twice Master of Lodge of Regularity; Member of Council of London Cart Horse Parade Society; Director of Kent and East Sussex Railway Company, The Selsey Tramway Company, and Snailbeach District Railways; Chairman of North Devon and Cornwall Junction Light Railway Company; Chairman, Committee of Control of Eccentric Club Hostels for Limbless Sailors and Soldiers; Liveryman, Spectacle-Makers' Company. King's Coronation Medal, 1911. *Publication:* Origin, Statutory Powers, and Duties of the Commissioners of Sewers of the City of London. *Address:* 33 Colville Square Mansions, Bayswater, W; Manaccan, St Martin RSO, Cornwall. *Club:* Eccentric. *Died 30 Dec. 1928.*

BATES, Oric, MA; FRGS; Curator of African Archaeology and Ethnology, Peabody Museum (Harvard University); Editor of Harvard African Studies; *b* Boston, Mass, 5 Dec. 1883; *s* of Arlo Bates; *m* 1913, Natica, *d* of John Chester Inches, Boston; two *s. Educ:* private school; Harvard University; Berlin University. Assistant in charge Egyptian Department, Museum of Fine Arts, Boston, 1906–7; Berlin University, 1907–8; Nubian Archaeological Survey, 1908–9; Harvard Palestinian Expedition; Harvard Univ. Museum of Fine Arts Egyptian Expedition; Exploration in Cyrenaica, 1909–10; Exploration in Libyan Desert; studied in Cairo, 1910–11; Excavation in Anglo-Egyptian Sudan, 1911–12; Excavation in Marmarica, 1913–14; Excavation in Anglo-Egyptian Sudan, 1915; National Service US Shipping Board, 1917–18. *Publications:* contributions to Harvard African Studies and to various scientific journals; The Eastern Libyans, 1914. *Recreation:* shooting. *Address:* 37 Chestnut Street, Boston, Mass, USA. *Died 10 Oct. 1918.*

BATESON, William, MA, Hon. DSc Sheffield; FRS 1894; Director John Innes Horticultural Institution, Merton Park, Surrey, since 1910; Trustee of the British Museum since 1922; *b* Whitby, 8 Aug. 1861; *s* of Rev. W. H. Bateson, DD, Master of St John's College, Cambridge; *m* 1896, Beatrice, *d* of late Arthur Durham, Senior Surgeon to Guy's Hospital; one *s. Educ:* Rugby School; St John's College, Cambridge. Balfour Student, 1887–90; Fellow, St John's College, Cambridge, 1885–1910; Hon. Fellow of St John's College, Cambridge; Silliman Lecturer, Yale University, 1907; Professor of Biology, Cambridge, 1908–9; Fullerian Prof. of Physiology, Royal Institution, 1912–14; President, British Association for Advancement in Science, Australia, 1914. Foreign Member, National Academy of Science, Washington; Royal Danish Academy; Royal Academy, Belgium; NY Academy of Science; Academy of Sciences, Leningrad; Soc. Helv. Sci. Nat.; Videnskabs Selskabet Christiania, etc; Darwin Medal, Royal Society, 1904; Royal Medal, 1920. *Publications:* Materials for the Study of Variation, 1894; Mendel's Principles of Heredity, 1902; Problems of Genetics, 1913; various papers on biological subjects. *Address:* The Manor House, Merton, SW20. *T:* Wimbledon 972. *Clubs:* Athenæum, Burlington Fine Arts. *Died 8 Feb. 1926.*

BATH, Engineer-Rear-Admiral George Clark, MVO 1908; RN, retired; *b* 19 Sept. 1862; *m* 1889, Maria, *o d* of late Hector John Davidson, Devonport. Assistant Engineer, 1883; Chief Engineer, 1896; Engineer-Commander, 1900; Engineer-Captain, 1912. *Address:* 14 Whitwell Road, Southsea, Hants. *Died 5 May 1925.*

BATTEN, Adm. Alexander William Chisholm, MVO 1903; DSO 1917; JP, Mid-Lothian; *b* 28 Sept. 1851; 2nd *s* of E. Chisholm Batten, Thornfalcon, Somerset; *m* Brittie Ellen Wood; one *s* two *d. Educ:* Eagle House. Joined RN 1865; Member War Office Committees Coast Defence; employed suppression slave trade; present Bangkok during French Blockade; Ordnance Department, Admiralty; in conjunction with Sir N. Lockyer read paper before Royal Society on Solar Eclipse Expedition; ADC to King, 1905; retired, 1907; served afloat as Captain RNR, 1915–17 (DSO). *Address:* Thorncote, Murrayfield Gardens, Edinburgh. *Club:* Caledonian United Service, Edinburgh. *Died 2 Nov. 1925.*

BATTEN, Frederick Eustace, MD; FRCP; Physician to the National Hospital for the Paralysed and Epileptic, Queen Square, and to the Children's Hospital, Great Ormond Street; *b* Plymouth, 1865; 3rd *s* of late John Winterbotham Batten, KC, and Sarah, *d* of Samuel Derry, MRCS; *m* Jean Evelyn, *d* of John J. Stevenson. *Educ:* Westminster; Trinity College, Cambridge; St Bartholomew's Hospital. *Publications:* scientific papers on the nervous system. *Address:* 22 Harley Street, W. *T:* Mayfair 769. *Died 27 July 1918.*

BATTEN, Col Herbert Cary George, OBE 1919; BA; JP, DL; Hon. Colonel 3rd Battalion Dorset Regiment; Director of Westminster Bank Ltd; *b* 1849; 3rd *s* of John Batten, FSA, DL, JP (*d* 1900), of Aldon, Somerset; *m* 1st, 1878, Frances Eleanor, *d* of John Beardmore, of Uplands, Fareham, Hants; 2nd, 1898, Isabel Frances, *d* of late Gen. Sir Robert Bright, GCB; two *s* one *d. Educ:* Cheltenham College; Trinity Hall, Cambridge. Called to Bar, Inner Temple, 1874; practised for some years on the Western Circuit; Lt-Col commanding 3rd Batt. Dorset Regt, 1901–9. *Recreations:* hunting, shooting. *Address:* Keyford, Yeovil. *M:* Y709. *Club:* New University. *Died 26 Nov. 1926.*

BATTEN, Col John Mount, CB 1903; HM Lieutenant for Dorset and Poole; JP, Somerset and Dorset; late The King's (Liverpool) Regiment); *b* 7 April 1843; *e s* of late John Batten, JP, FSA, of Aldon, Somerset, and Grace Eleanor, *d* of John White of Upcerne; *m* 1st, 1873, Margaret Annie (*d* 1893), *e d* of Rev. John Brooks; 2nd, 1895, Mary Edith, *e d* of J. Sant, RA, and *widow* of H. F. Nalder; one *s* four *d. Educ:* Winchester. High Sheriff of Dorset, 1903, and Alderman of CC of Dorset. Patron of two livings. *Address:* Mornington Lodge, West Kensington, W; Upcerne, Cerne Abbas, Dorset. *Club:* Army and Navy. *Died 5 March 1916.*

BATTERSBY, Maj.-Gen. John Prevost; retired; *b* 16 Oct. 1826; *s* of Lt-Col Francis Battersby, CB, and Eliza Jane Rotheram; *m* 1857, Louisa Wilhelmina, *d* of Sir William Dillon, 4th Bt; one *s* two *d. Educ:* Portora Royal School, Enniskillen. Joined the 1st Batt. 60th King's Royal Rifles, 1844; served as ADC to Brig.-Gen. Lord Melville and to Sir Arthur Lawrence, Inspector-General of Infantry; Brigade Major, Dover; Assistant Adjutant-General, Secunderabad; Commandant, Royal Military Asylum, Chelsea; Assistant Director of Military Education, War Office. *Recreations:* tennis, hockey. *Address:* Lyncroft, Weybridge. *Died 12 Jan. 1917.*

BATTISCOMBE, Rear-Adm. Albert Henry William; retired; *b* 14 April 1831; 2nd *s* of late Rev. Richard Battiscombe of Hacton, Essex; *m* Lucy, *d* of late Sir Henry Robinson, DL, JP, of Knapton House, Norfolk, formerly Lieut Commanding HM Body Guard of Gentlemen-at-Arms; one *s* one *d. Educ:* Stoke Poges; Eton College. Cadet, Royal Navy, 1846; appointed to the Ringdove and took part in the operations against Bruni Borneo, 1846; midshipman, Medea, 1850, which in that year captured a fleet of piratical junks in Miro Bay, Cochin China; Sub-Lieut 1852; Lieut 1854; appointed to the Hecla and was present at the bombardment of Bomarsund, and subsequently at the capture of this fortress; as a lieutenant in the Cornwallis was engaged at the bombardment of Sveaborg (Battle Medal); as Gunnery and 1st Lieut in the Naval Brigade in 1858; in New Zealand under Commodore Beauchamp Seymour in 1860, part of the time acted as Assistant Engineer under Colonel Commanding Royal Engineers (despatches, promoted to Commander, 1861); served as Commander of the Snipe on the West Coast of Africa, and subsequently in the Coastguard; as Commander of the Victory, 1868, and Royal Naval Reserve ship at Bristol; Captain, 1870; retired 1873; Rear-Admiral, retired list, 1887. *Address:* Eastwood, Weston-super-Mare. *Died 16 Sept. 1918.*

BATTISTINI, Mattia; Barone di Poggio Casalino; Kamessinger; e decorazioni di quasi tute le nazioni; decorazioni altissime; baritone; *b* Rome, 27 Feb. 1858; vedovo della nobile donna Dolores Figuera della famiglia del Conte di Romanones, Duca di Cosa e Duca di Villamejor di Spagne. *Educ:* Roma; Nobile Collegio Bandinello. Dal 1879 la piu gloriose delle carriere artistiche Russia, Italia, Spagna, Portogallo, Germania, Austria, Ungheria, Polonia, Londres, Boemia, Francia, America del Sud. *Publications:* qualche romanze di salone e marcia. *Address:* Contigliano, Italia Sabina.

Died Nov. 1928.

BATTY, Herbert; Hon. Mr Justice Batty, MA; Barrister-at-law, Lincoln's Inn; *b* 1849. *Educ:* Christ's Coll., Cambridge. Entered ICS 1868; Prof. of Logic and Moral Philosophy, Deccan College, Poona, 1872–75, and Assistant Judge and Sessions Judge; Under-Secretary to Government, Bombay, 1885; Remembrancer of Legal Affairs, 1892; Acting Chief Secretary to Government Political Departments, 1896; Acting Judicial Commissioner in Sind, 1899; Acting Judge, High Court, Bombay, 1900; Judicial Commissioner, Sind, 1901; Judge of High Court of Judicature, Bombay, 1902–8.

Died March 1923.

BATTY-SMITH, Henry; late Proprietor and Editor of The Sportsman newspaper; retired, 1924; *m* Lilian, *d* of late G. Kent of Farnborough; three *s* one *d*. *Educ:* privately and abroad (France and Germany). Well known in the world of sport, having taken an active part in nearly all sports and games. *Recreations:* golf, shooting, racing; formerly cricket, football, rowing, tennis, etc. *Address:* Shinfield Grove, Berks. *T:* Reading 1693. *Clubs:* Sports, MCC; Sunningdale Golf; Thames Rowing, etc. *Died 21 May 1927.*

BATTYE, Lt-Col Clinton Wynyard, DSO 1900; 85th King's Light Infantry; Lieutenant-Colonel, 1/4th East Lancashire Regiment in France; *b* 24 May 1874; 3rd *s* of late Major Montagu Battye, HM's Hon. Corps of Gentlemen-at-Arms. *Educ:* Wellington College. Entered army, 1894; served South Africa, 1899–1902, with 1st Batt. Mounted Infantry (Queen's medal, 4 clasps, King's medal, 2 clasps, despatches); Mohmand operations, 1908 (medal and clasp); European War, 1914–17 (wounded). *Club:* Army and Navy.

Died 25 Nov. 1917.

BAUGH, Captain George Johnstone, DSO 1917; RIM; Marine Superintendent and Harbour Master, London & North-Western Railway, Fleetwood, since 1907; *b* 1862; *s* of Henry Bempde Baugh, Colonel, Bengal Staff Corps, of Barnstaple, Devon; *m* 1903, Grace Geraldine, *e d* of Edward Franks, India Office, Whitehall; two *s*. *Educ:* Westward Ho! College. Entered RIM 1882; Lieut, 1884; Commander, 1894; Captain, 1920; appointments held: Transport Officer, Upper Burmah; Staff Officer, Government Dock Yards, Bombay; Officiating Assistant Director RIM, Conservator Port of Madras, and Presidency Port Officer, Madras (retired 1907); served Burmah Campaign, 1885–88 (two clasps), South Africa, China and Somaliland; Royal Humane Society's bronze medal, 1891; posted to Liverpool, 1914, as Divisional Sea Transport Officer under Railway Executive Committee; granted temporary commission as Major, Jan. 1915, and posted to War Office as Deputy Assistant Director of Movements, responsible for the organisation and supervision of building of self-propelled craft in Britain for the inland Water Transport, Royal Engineers, for service on the canals of France and Belgium; service in France as Assistant Director and Deputy Director, Inland Water Transport, RE, 1915–17, with rank of Colonel (despatches twice). *Recreations:* shooting, fishing, golf. *Address:* Warrenhurst Park, Fleetwood, Lancs. *T:* 41. *Club:* Sports.

Died 3 May 1924.

BAX, Ernest Belfort; Barrister-at-Law, Middle Temple; author; *b* Leamington, 23 July 1854; *m* 1st, 1877 (*d* 1893); 2nd, 1897; four *s* two *d*. *Educ:* privately in London; Germany. Studied music, especially theory and composition; also later, philosophy, more particularly the German movement from Kant to Hegel; practised journalism as foreign correspondent, 1880–81; returning to England, was one of the founders of the English Socialist movement; in 1885 helped to start the Socialist League in conjunction with late William Morris, and for some time co-edited with him the weekly journal Commonweal; subsequently resigned from League, and again became connected with the Social Democratic Federation, co-operating on, and for a time editing, its organ Justice; delegate of the SDF to various international congresses. *Publications:* Jean-Paul Marat, 1878; Kant's Prolegomena, etc, with Biography and Introduction, 1882; Handbook to the History of Philosophy, 1884; Religion of Socialism, 1886; Ethics of Socialism, 1889; French Revolution, 1890; Outlooks from the New Standpoint, 1891; The Problem of Reality, 1893; German Society

at the Close of the Middle Ages, 1894; Socialism, its Growth and Outcome (in conjunction with the late William Morris), 1894; Outspoken Essays on Social Subjects, 1897; The Peasants' War in Germany, 1899, etc; a new Life of Marat (2nd edn), 1901; Rise and Fall of the Anabaptists, 1903; Essays in Socialism, New and Old, 1906; The Roots of Reality, 1907; The Last Episode of the French Revolution, 1911; Problems of Men, Mind, and Morals, 1912; German Culture, Past and Present, 1915; Reminiscences and Reflections, 1918; The Real, The Rational, and the Alogical, 1920; contributed to Professor Muirhead's Contemporary British Philosophy, 1925; also edited the monthlies Time and Today. *Recreations:* no special sports. *Clubs:* National Liberal, Authors'.

Died 26 Nov. 1926.

BAXTER, Sir George Washington, 1st Bt, *cr* 1918; Kt 1904; JP, DL; *b* 20 Nov. 1853; *y s* of late Rt Hon. W. E. Baxter of Kincaldrum, Forfarshire, and Janet, *d* of John Home Scott; *m* 1889, Edith, OBE, *e d* of Major-General J. L. Fagan. *Educ:* High School, Dundee; St Andrews and Edinburgh Universities; Hon. LLD St Andrews. Chairman of Dundee and District Liberal Unionist Association, 1886–1910; Chairman of Dundee Unionist Association, 1910–19; President, Scottish Unionist Association, 1919; President of University College, Dundee; Chairman of Territorial Force Association, Dundee, for some years; contested Montrose Burghs, 1895; Dundee, 1908, and Dec. 1910; DL, JP Dundee; JP Forfarshire. *Heir:* none. *Address:* Invereighty, Forfarshire. *TA:* Invereighty, Kincaldrum. *Clubs:* Carlton; Eastern, Dundee.

Died 26 Nov. 1926 (ext).

BAXTER, Sir William James, Kt 1907; JP, DL, Co. Londonderry; *b* Tattykeel, Cookstown, Co. Tyrone, 1845; *s* of Samuel Baxter and Sarah, *e d* of John Beatty, Mullinahunch House, Co. Tyrone; *m* 1892, Mary, 2nd *d* of Rev. Robert Wallace, Beresford Villas, Coleraine; three *d*. *Educ:* Ballymena Academy; Carmichael College, Dublin. First place in two examinations of Pharmaceutical Society of Ireland; elected by co-option on Council of this Society, 20 years on the Council, President, 1910–11–12–13; Chairman Coleraine Town Commissioners, 1897, 1898 and 1899, being last Chairman of old Commissioners and first Chairman of new Urban Council; President of Coleraine Agricultural and Industrial Association; President, Coleraine Savings Bank; Vice-President, Congress of Health, Dublin, 1898. Contested (L) North Antrim, 1910. *Address:* Avondale, Coleraine. *TA:* Baxter, Chemist. Coleraine. *T:* 27.

Died 19 Dec. 1918.

BAXTER, Wynne Edwin, FGS, FRMS; JP, DL; Coroner for East London and the Tower of London; clerk to two of the City Guilds; Treasurer of the Royal Microscopical Society; *b* 1844; *e s* of William Edwin Baxter of Lewes (*d* 1871); *m* 1868, Kate Bliss (*d* 1915), *d* of F. H. Parker, Mayor of Northampton, 1849–51; three *s* one *d*. *Educ:* Lewes Grammar School; Rev. P. Frost, Sussex Square, Brighton. Admitted a solicitor, 1867; Under-Sheriff of London and Middlesex, 1876–79, 1885–86; High Constable of Lewes, 1877–81; first Mayor of Lewes, 1881–82; Coroner for Sussex, 1879–87; Vice-President of the Provincial Newspaper Society, 1871–76. *Publications:* Baxter's Judicature Acts and Rules (5th edn); Doomsday Book of Sussex, Surrey, Kent, and Middlesex; Van Heurck's Microscope; The Diatomaceæ. *Recreations:* the Diatomaceæ, Bibliography, Miltoniana. *Address:* 170 Church Street, Stoke Newington, W; The Granvilles, Stroud, Gloucestershire. *TA:* Inquest, London. *T:* 550 Dalston; 93 Lewes; 68 Stroud; 642 Bank. *Club:* Constitutional.

Died 1 Oct. 1920.

BAYARD, Brig.-Gen. Reginald, DSO 1902; late the Buffs; retired pay; *b* 11 Sept. 1860; *s* of Robertson Bayard, BL of St Louis, New Brunswick; *m* Edith (*d* 1916), *d* of late John Quain, JP Co. Dublin; one *d*. *Educ:* privately. Entered service, 1881; Captain, 1893; Major, 1900; served S Africa, 1899–1902 (despatches twice, medal, DSO); Southern Arabia, 1903–4; Lieut-Colonel, 1907. *Recreations:* hunting, polo, cricket, golf, skating. *Died 23 July 1925.*

BAYFIELD, Rev. Matthew Albert, MA; Rector of Hertingfordbury, Hertford; *b* Edgbaston, Birmingham, 17 June 1852; *s* of L. A. Bayfield, chartered accountant, Birmingham; *m* Helen Campbell, *d* of late John Boyes; one *s* one *d*. *Educ:* King Edward's School, Birmingham; Clare Coll., Camb. (Scholar). 1st class Classical Tripos, 1875. Assistant Master, Blackheath School, 1875–79; Marlborough Coll., 1879–81; Headmaster's Assistant, Malvern Coll., 1881–90; Headmaster, Christ Coll., Brecon, 1890–95; Headmaster, Eastbourne College, 1895–1900. Member of Council of Society for Psychical Research. *Publications:* editor of Ion, Alcestis, and Medea of Euripides; Electra and Antigone of Sophocles; Septem contra Thebas (with Dr Verrall);

Iliad (with Dr Leaf); Latin Prose for Lower Forms; Memoir of A. W. Verrall, 1913; Our Traditional Prosody and an Alternative (in Modern Language Review, 1918); The Measures of the Poets: a new system of English Prosody, 1919; Shakespeare's Versification with an inquiry into the Trustworthiness of the Early Texts, 1920; articles on Shakespeare's Versification and Handwriting, Spenser's Versification, etc, in Times Literary Supplement; various contributions to Proceedings of SPR. *Address:* The Rectory, Hertingfordbury. *T:* Hertford 113. *Club:* Alpine.

Died 2 Aug. 1922.

BAYFORD, Robert Augustus, JP for Hants; KC; retired from the Bar; Bencher of the Hon. Society of Inner Temple, Treasurer, 1912; *b* Albury, Surrey, 13 March 1838; *o s* of late A. F. Bayford, LLD, formerly Chancellor of the Diocese of Manchester and Principal Registrar of HM Ct of Probate, and Julia, *d* of late Robert Ballard; *m* 1868, Emily Jane (*d* 1922), *d* of late John Deverell of Purbrook Park, Hants. *Educ:* Kensington School; Trinity Hall, Camb. (scholar); Kensington exhibitioner; Wrangler; 1st class Law Tripos; Law student Trinity Hall. Rowed head of the river, 1859; University Eleven, 1857–59; captain, 1859. Barrister, 1863; QC 1885; Bencher, 1891; retired, 1897. *Address:* Netley Hill, Botley, Hants. *Club:* Oxford and Cambridge.   *Died 24 Aug. 1922.*

BAYLEY, Charles Butterworth, CVO 1912 (MVO 1906); Government of Bengal, Public Works Department (retired); *b* 7 Sept. 1876; 4th *s* of late Sir Steuart C. Bayley, GCSI; *m* 1913, Violet, *d* of late Digby Templeton Brett. Special correspondent for Tibet mission, Daily Telegraph and Pioneer (Allahabad), 1903–4; for Mohmund expedn, Daily Mail, 1908; Private Sec. to Lt-Gov. of Bihar and Orissa, 1912–16; Asst Sec., Govt of Bengal. *Address:* 83 Middle Road, Barrackpore, India. *Clubs:* Junior Carlton; Bengal, Calcutta.

Died 30 Sept. 1926.

BAYLEY, Charles Clive; HBM Consul-General at New York since 1915; *b* 20 Nov. 1864; *s* of late Sir Edward Clive Bayley, KCSI, CIE, *m* 1910, Constance Evelina, *d* of Francis Ricardo of The Friary, Old Windsor. *Educ:* Harrow; Trinity College, Cambridge. Colonial Audit Department, 1888–93; Treasurer, Niger Coast Protectorate, 1894–97; served Benin Campaign, 1897; HM's Consul New York, 1899–1908; Warsaw, 1908–13; Visiting Consular Officer for Russia; Consul-General at Moscow, 1913–15. *Address:* British Consulate General, New York. *Clubs:* Athenæum, Wellington.

Died 20 Jan. 1923.

BAYLEY, Lt-Col Edward Charles, CIE 1911; OBE 1919; Indian Army, retired; *b* 13 Dec. 1867; 4th *s* of late George Bayley, WS, Edinburgh; unmarried. *Educ:* privately; Sandhurst. Joined 2nd Batt. Scottish Rifles, 1887; transferred to 15th Lancers (Cureton's Multanis), 1890; Private Secretary to the Lieutenant-Governor North-West Provinces and Oudh, 1899–1901; and to the Lieut-Governor, Punjab, 1907–20; served with the Somaliland Field Force, 1903–4; retired 1920. Received Kaisar-i-Hind Medal, 1910. *Recreations:* shooting, golf. *Club:* United Service.   *Died 26 April 1924.*

BAYLEY, Sir Steuart Colvin, GCSI 1911 (KCSI 1878; CSI 1874); CIE 1882; *b* 26 Nov. 1836; *m* 1860, Anna, *d* of R. N. Farquharson, Bengal CS; four *s* three *d*. *Educ:* Eton; Haileybury. Commissioner of Patna, 1873–74; Secretary to Government of Bengal, 1877; Lieut-Gov. of Bengal, 1887–90; Secretary, Political Department, India Office, 1890–1905; member of Indian Council, 1895–1905. *Address:* 2 Cathcart Road, SW10. *T:* Kensington 4042. *Club:* Athenæum.

Died 3 June 1925.

BAYLISS, Sir William Maddock, Kt 1922; MA, DSc (Oxon); LLD (Hon.) Aberdeen and St Andrews; FRS 1903; Professor of General Physiology in University College, London, 1912; Member of Council, Royal Society, 1913–15; President, Physiological Section, British Association, 1915; *b* 2 May 1860; *s* of Moses Bayliss, manufacturer; *m* 1893, Gertrude E., *d* of Matthew Henry Starling, late Clerk of the Crown, Bombay; three *s* one *d*. *Educ:* private school in Wolverhampton; University College, London; Wadham College, Oxford. Fellow of University College, London; engaged in research from 1888; with Prof. E. H. Starling, FRS, discovered secretin, 1902; Acting Professor of Physiology in University College, 1910–11. Treasurer of the Physiological Society; Editor of Physiological Abstracts and (with Professor Harden) of the Biochemical Journal; Chairman, Shock Committee of Medical Research Council, and of Committee on the Biological Action of Light; Member of Chemical Warfare Medical Committee and of Research Committee of Food Investigation Board. Hon. Fellow, Wadham College, Oxford; Croonian Lecturer, Royal Society, 1904; Royal Medal, 1911; Copley

Medal, 1919; Baly Medal, Royal College of Physicians, 1917; Oliver-Sharpey Lecturer, 1918; Silvanus Thompson Lecturer, 1919; Herter Lecturer, 1922. Corresponding Member of Soc. de Biologie, Paris; Assoc. Member of Royal Society of Brussels and Belgian Society of Biology; Foreign Member Danish Acad. Sci. *Publications:* Principles of General Physiology, 3rd edn 1920; The Nature of Enzyme Action, 1908, 4th edn 1919; The Physiology of Food and of Economy in Diet, 1917; Intravenous Injection in Wound-Shock, 1919; Introduction to General Physiology, and others; numerous articles in the Journal of Physiology and elsewhere, chiefly on the Vasomotor Nervous System and on Secretion; Physical Chemistry of Enzyme-action; Properties of Colloidal Systems. *Recreations:* lawn-tennis, music, photography. *Address:* St Cuthbert's, West Heath Road, NW3. *TA:* Child's Hill, NW. *T:* Speedwell 2267. *Club:* Athenæum.

Died 27 Aug. 1924.

BAYLY, Maj.-Gen. Sir Alfred William Lambart, KCB 1911 (CB 1900); KCMG 1917; CSI 1909; DSO 1887; *b* Paisley, 18 Feb. 1856; *y s* of late Major George Bayly and Eliza, *d* of Lieut-Gen. Savage, RE; *m* 1st, 1877, Ada Margaret (*d* 1880), *d* of late Maj.-Gen. S. Thacker, Bombay Staff Corps; 2nd, 1889, Eva, *d* of late John Naylor, Leighton Hall, Montgomeryshire; one *s*. *Educ:* Wellington College. Joined 108th Regt, 1874; Bombay Staff Corps, 1879; passed through Staff College, 1893; officiating DAQMG, Bombay, 1885–86; DAA and QMG, Burma Expedition, 1886–87; DAAG, Mhow District, 1887–92; commanded 26th Bombay (Baluchistan Regt), Infantry, 1896; Afghan War, 1880–81; defence and battle of Kandahar, 1880 (medal and clasp); Soudan, 1885; Suakin (medal and clasp, bronze star); Burma, 1886–87 (despatches, medal and two clasps, DSO); South Africa, 1899–1900, as DAAG (despatches, medal and five clasps, CB); ADC to the King, 1902–6; AAG, District, India, 1896–1903; AQMG, Headquarters, India, 1903–4; DAG, Northern Command, 1904–5; Commandant, Indian Staff College, 1905–6; Col, 126th Baluchistan Infantry, later 2/10th Baluch Regt; Secretary to the Government of India, Army Department, 1906–9; retired, 1912; special duty War Office, 1914–18; Inspector of Temporary Non-Effectives, 1915–18 (despatches, KCMG). *Address:* c/o Thomas Cook & Sons, Berkeley Street, W1. *Club:* United Service.

Died 27 June 1928.

BAYNE, William; Lecturer in English, Training College, Dundee, since 1906. *Educ:* Madras College and University, St Andrews. Rector's Prize for an English Essay, Chancellor's Prize and two Gray Prizes for distinction in theological subjects. Literary work in London, 1885–92, contributed many articles to the literary supplement of the Daily Chronicle; occupied in literary work in Edinburgh, 1892–1900; assistant to the Professor of English Literature, 1900–6, and Lecturer in German in St Andrew's University, 1900–2; Examiner in English, St Andrew's University, 1914–18. *Publications:* A Summary of the Legends in the Early South English Legendary, published by the Early English Text Society; library, college, and school editions of Stormonth's Etymological English Dictionary; James Thomson in the Famous Scots Series; an edition of Poems by James Thomson (Canterbury Poets); Sir David Wilkie, RA (Makers of British Art), etc. *Recreations:* walking, cycling, golf. *Address:* Radernie, Cupar, Fife.

Died 10 Nov. 1922.

BAYNES, Frederick, JP, DL; *b* 1848; *m* Anna Adelaide, 3rd *d* of Thomas Simpson of Church. *Educ:* Rugby; Cambridge. High Sheriff of Lancashire, 1900; Director L&NW Railway Co.; Member of Tariff Commission; Chairman of Cotton Trade Tariff Reform Association. *Address:* Summerhill, Kidderminster. *Clubs:* Junior Carlton, Constitutional.   *Died 12 Nov. 1917.*

BAYNES, Hon. Joseph, CMG 1902; JP; owner of Nel's Rust, near Pietermaritzburg, where he has resided and farmed since 1862; senior member for the Ixopo since 1890; *b* near Settle, Yorkshire, England, 2 March 1842; *s* of Richard Baynes; *m* 1st, 1874, Maria H., 2nd *d* of Paul Hermanus Zietsman; 2nd, Sarah A., *d* of late Edward Tomlinson of Maritzburg. Minister of Lands and Works, 1903–4; former MLC; Chairman (1902) of the Indian Immigration Trust Board, and member of the Board, 1887–1904; Fellow of the Royal Colonial Institute since 1885; and JP for the County of Pietermaritzburg. *Address:* 289 Chapel Street, Pietermaritzburg, Natal, SA. *Club:* Victoria, Pietermaritzburg.

Died July 1925.

BAYNES, Robert Edward; Student and Tutor of Christ Church, Oxford, and Dr Lee's Reader in Physics; *b* Blackburn, Lancashire, 27 Sept. 1849; 5th *s* of John Baynes, JP, DL, Co. Lancaster, and Major in 5th Lancashire Artillery Volunteers, of Claremont, Blackburn; *m* 1887, Thomasine Anne, *e d* of Thomas Hutton of Ormskirk, Lancs;

one *s. Educ:* Rugby; Wadham College, Oxford (Scholar); 1st class Mathematical Mods, 1870; 1st class Final Mathematics, 1871; 1st class Natural Science, 1872. Student of Christ Church, 1873, Censor, 1884–87, Steward, 1895–1902, junior proctor, 1886; examiner in Natural Science Honours at Oxford, 1878–79, 1881–82, 1891–92, 1897–98, 1912–14, 1916–18; examiner in Electricity and Magnetism at South Kensington, 1893–1900. Deputy Provincial Grand Master of Oxfordshire Freemasons, 1915; formerly Captain in the 3rd Lancashire Artillery Volunteers. *Publications:* The Book of Heat, 1878; Lessons on Thermodynamics, 1878. *Recreations:* boating, masonry. *Address:* 2 Norham Gardens, and Christ Church, Oxford.

Died 9 Sept. 1921.

BAZELEY, Rev. William, MA Cantab; Rector of Matson, Gloucestershire, 1875–1925; Hon. Canon of Gloucester Cathedral, 1901; *b* St Ives, Cornwall, 1843; *s* of William Bazeley; *m* 1879, Henrietta, *d* of late Rev. E. J. Selwyn, Rector of Pluckley, Kent; three *s* three *d. Educ:* Cheltenham College; Christ's College, Cambridge. Assistant Master, Cheltenham Coll., 1864–68; deacon, 1867; priest, 1868; Curate of Charlton Kings, 1867–70; Hornsey, 1870–75. Bristol and Gloucestershire Archæological Society, Hon. Gen. Sec., 1879–1906, President, 1908–9, President of Council, 1908–17; Hon. Sec., Gloucester Diocesan Conference, 1892–1907; Hon. Local Sec., Society of Antiquaries of London; Hon. Librarian of Gloucester Cathedral. *Publications:* Records of Matson and the Selwyns; Matson in Tudor and Early Stuart Times; The Bibliographer's Manual of Gloucestershire Literature (Joint Author); Battle of Tewkesbury, and many contributions to the Transactions of Bristol and Glos Archæol Soc. *Recreations:* rifle shooting, shot in University VR match, 1863; Queen's Sixty, Wimbledon, 1863; travel, archæological research, numismatics, philately, mediæval stained glass, autographs, etc. *Address:* Gowan Lea, Charlton Kings, Cheltenham.

Died 12 July 1925.

BAZLEY, Sir Thomas Sebastian, 2nd Bt, *cr* 1869; MA; JP, DL; *b* 30 April 1829; *s* of Sir Thomas Bazley, 1st Bt and Mary, *d* of Sebastian Nash, Clayton, Lancs; *S* father 1885; *m* 1855, Elizabeth (*d* 1890), *d* of Robert Gardner of Chaseley, Manchester; five *d* (one *s* decd). *Educ:* Trinity Coll., Cambridge. High Sheriff, Glos, 1874; DL Glos, JP Glos and Ches. *Heir: g s* Thomas Stafford Bazley, *b* 5 Oct. 1907. *Publications:* Charts of the Stars; books on Geometric Turning. *Address:* Kilmorie, Torquay.

Died 6 Jan. 1919.

BAZLEY-WHITE, John, JP, DL, Kent; Director, John Bazley White and Brothers Ltd, manufacturers of Portland cement; *b* 1847; *e* surv. *s* of J. Bazley-White, JP, of Swanscombe, Kent, and Mary, *d* of late William Leedham; assumed additional surname of Bazley, 1887; *m* 1876, Lady Grace, *y d* of Countess of Rothes and Capt. Haworth-Leslie, late 60th Rifles; two *s* five *d.* MP (C) Gravesend, 1885–92; late Hon. Colonel 3rd Volunteer Brigade, Cinque Ports Division, RA. *Clubs:* Carlton, Arthur's, Constitutional.

Died 9 Feb. 1927.

BEACHCROFT, Sir Charles Porten, Kt 1922; *b* 13 March 1871; 4th *s* of late Francis Porten Beachcroft, Bengal Civil Service; *m* Elizabeth, *d* of late A. E. Ryles. *Educ:* Rugby; Clare College, Cambridge. Passed Indian Civil Service, 1890; Assistant Magistrate and Collector, Bengal, 1892; Officiating District and Sessions Judge, 1900; District and Sessions Judge, 1906; Officiating Judge, High Court, Calcutta, 1912; Additional Judge, 1913–15; Puisne Judge, High Court, Calcutta, 1915–21; retired, 1921. *Recreation:* golf. *Address:* Montjoie, Camberley. *T:* Camberley 80. *Club:* East India United Service.

Died 15 May 1927.

BEACHCROFT, Sir (Richard) Melvill, Kt 1904; *b* 22 Jan. 1846; *e s* of Richard Beachcroft and Henrietta, *e d* of late Sir James Cosmo Melvill, KCB, of Tandridge, 1877, Charlotte, *d* of late Robert M. Bonnor-Maurice, Bodynfoel Hall, Montgomeryshire. *Educ:* Harrow. Admitted Solicitor, London, 1868; partner in Beachcroft, Thompson & Co., 29 Bedford Square, WC; Solicitor to Christ's Hospital since 1873; Master of the Clothworkers' Co., 1913–14, with which Co. his name has been associated for six generations, his ancestor, Sir Robert Beachcroft, Lord Mayor of London in 1711, having been a member and master of the Guild; an original member of the LCC, representing North Paddington in 1st Council; South Paddington, 1907; Alderman, 1892; Deputy Chairman, 1896; Vice-Chairman, 1897; Chairman, 1909–10; first Chairman, Metropolitan Water Board, 1903–8; an old member of the Alpine Club, having served on its committee. *Address:* Littlemount, Cookham Dean; 29 Bedford Square, WC1. *Club:* Conservative.

Died 11 Jan. 1926.

BEADON, Bt-Col Lancelot Richmond, DSO 1918; CMG 1919; Assistant Director of Transport, War Office; *b* 1875; *y s* of late Sir Cecil Beadon, KCSI; *m* 1904, Hilda Marian, *o d* of late Maj.-Gen. A. G. Raper, CVO; one *d. Educ:* Winchester; Sandhurst. Served West Africa, 1897–98 (clasp); Sierra Leone, 1898–99 (clasp); First Commission, West India Regt, 1896; Garrison Adjutant, Jamaica, 1901; transferred to Royal Army Service Corps, 1902; ADC to Major-Gen., Inf. Brigade, Gibraltar, 1903; Instructor, RMC Sandhurst, 1910; Comdt, Training Establishment, RASC, 1914; AQMG, GHQ, Dardanelles, 1915; AQMG, Northern Army Home Defence, 1916; AQMG, GHQ, France, 1917; Deputy Director of Transport, War Office, 1919; European War, 1914–18 (despatches thrice, DSO, Legion of Honour). *Address:* Mayfield, Addlestone, Surrey.

Died 31 July 1922.

BEAL, Charles, FZS; late Senior Registrar, Supreme Court (Chancery Division); retired, 1912; *b* 16 Sept. 1841; *s* of Henry Ridley Beal, Solicitor, London. *Educ:* King's College School. Admitted a Solicitor, 1863; appointed to Chancery Registrars' Office, 1864. *Recreations:* shooting, fishing. *Address:* 14 Pall Mall, SW. *Clubs:* Junior Carlton, Garrick, Thatched House.

Died 23 Jan. 1921.

BEALE, Sir William Phipson, 1st Bt, *cr* 1912; FGS, FCS; KC; MP (L) S Ayrshire, 1906–18; *b* 29 Oct. 1839; *e s* of William John Beale, Bryntirion, Merionethshire; *m* 1869, Mary, *e d* of William Thompson, late of Sydney, New South Wales. *Educ:* Heidelberg and Paris. Bar, Lincoln's Inn, 1867; QC 1888; Bencher, 1892. *Heir:* none. *Address:* 6 Stone Buildings, Lincoln's Inn, WC; Drumlamford, Barrhill, Ayrshire. *Clubs:* Savile, Reform, Albemarle.

Died 13 April 1922 (ext).

BEALL, Captain George, ISO 1903; FRGS; *b* 17 Nov. 1840; *s* of late George Beall, Kingston-on-Thames, late Inland Revenue; *m* 1866, Annie Robinson Grace (*d* 1915). Went to sea, East India service, 1857; joined John Bibby & Co.; first command, 1865; several years Examiner in Navigation and Nautical Astronomy to HM's training ship Conway; inventor of Deviascope for magnetic work (Gold Medal and Diploma, Liverpool International Exhibition, 1886); Younger Brother of Trinity House; late Principal Examiner of Masters and Mates to Board of Trade; retired 1903. *Publication:* Handbook to Deviascope, with short treatise on magnetism. *Recreations:* golf, croquet, etc. *Address:* London County and Westminster Bank Ltd, Eastbourne, Sussex.

Died 28 June 1918.

BEAMAN, Sir Frank (Clement Offley), Kt 1917; philosophical writer; *b* 27 Nov. 1858; *s* of late Surg.-Gen. A. H. Beaman; *m* 1st, 1881, Caroline Emily Banks; one *s* two *d*; 2nd, 1926, Mrs Wilson-Dickson. *Educ:* Bedford Grammar School; Queen's College, Oxford. Entered ICS, 1879; Asst Judge, 1885; Special Settlement Officer, Baroda, 1886, 1887; Judicial Asst to Political Agent, Kathiawar, 1891; Judge and Sessions Judge, 1896; Judicial Commissioner and Judge of Sadar Court in Sind, 1904–6; a Puisne Judge, High Court, Bombay, 1906–18. *Address:* 18 Palace Gardens Terrace, Kensington, W8. *T:* Park 6062. *Club:* Savile.

Died 12 Aug. 1928.

BEAN, Alderman Sir George, Kt 1919; Chairman of Birmingham and Midland Hospital; Trustee for RU Dudley's Homes for the Poor of Dudley; *b* 27 April 1855; *m d* of John Harper, Dudley; one *s* two *d.* Three times Mayor of Dudley; Alderman of the Town Council; Chairman of A. Harper, Son & Bean, Dudley, Motor Manufacturers, also Allen Everitt & Sons, Smethwick, and Manning, Wardle & Co. Ltd, Locomotive Manufacturers, Leeds. *Address:* Oakham Lodge, Dudley.

Died 23 Jan. 1924.

BEANLANDS, Rev. Arthur John, MA; FSA; *b* 1857; *s* of Arthur Beanlands, MA, JP, late Treasurer of Durham University; *m* 1st, 1884, Laura Maud, *e d* of Walter A. Hills, MA, barrister; 2nd, 1905, Sophia Theresa (artist and exhibitor), 2nd *d* of Joseph Despard Pemberton, MA, 1st Surveyor-General of Vancouver Island; one *s* two *d. Educ:* Durham School and University. After serving curacies in the Durham and Oxford dioceses was appointed Sub-Dean, Christ Church Cathedral, Victoria, BC, 1884; instrumental in establishing the Provincial Museum, and Natural History Society of BC, of which he served as President, also the Yorkshire Society of BC; wrote several pamphlets for the Government on the condition and prospects of the Province, and addressed the Royal Colonial Institute, 1892, on the same; instrumental in the passing of the Habitual Drunkards Bill, one of the earliest efforts of legislation in that direction; Rector of the Cathedral, 1892; Canon Residentiary, 1891; Hon. Canon 1909; Hon. Chaplain to Gov.-Gen. of the Dominion, 1895; was a member of the Diocesan Synod, elected continuously 1884–1909; a member of the 1st, 2nd, and 3rd General Synods of the C of E in Canada;

resigned and returned to England, 1909. *Recreations:* archæology, heraldry, genealogy. *Address:* Wickhurst Manor, Weald, Sevenoaks. *TA:* Weald. *T:* Sevenoaks 247.

Died 26 Sept. 1917.

BEARD, Charles Thomas, CB 1917; ISO 1903; Secretary to the Irish Land Commission, Dublin; *b* 18 Oct. 1858; *s* of late C. T. Beard, Horfield, Glos; *m* 1st, Alice C. (*d* 1886), *d* of J. Mackay; 2nd, Gertrude A. M., *d* of E. J. Figgis, JP. *Educ:* privately; Trinity College, Dublin; BA, 1st Senior Moderator and Gold Medallist, Wray Prizeman, etc. Entered Civil Sevice, 1877; Private Secretary to the Chief Secretary and to successive Under Secretaries for Ireland, and Chief Clerk at the Irish Office, Westminster, SW. *Recreation:* golf. *Address:* Falmore, Shankill, Co. Dublin. *Clubs:* Royal Societies; University, Dublin.

Died 26 May 1918.

BEARD, Lt-Col George John Allen, DSO 1916; Union Defence Force, S Africa; *b* Gloucester, England; *m* E. M. Myers, Potchefstroom, Transvaal; one *s* one *d*. *Educ:* Sir Thomas Rich's School, Gloucester (winner of open scholarship); Borough Road College, London; matriculated London University, 1898. Served SA Rebellion as Captain 11th Mounted Regiment, Oct. 1914; Major and DAQMG 4th Mounted Brigade in German South-West African campaign; Lt-Col and AA and QMG 2nd Division in German East Africa campaign (DSO, despatches). *Recreations:* all-round sportsman, played in representative football and cricket, keen oarsman, President Potchefstroom Rugby FC, winner several home boxing competitions. *Address:* Cymry, Maré Street, Potchefstroom. *T:* Potchefstroom 102. *Club:* Potchefstroom.

Died 16 Aug. 1922.

BEARE, John Isaac, MA; Fellow and Senior Tutor, Trinity College, Dublin; late Regius Professor of Greek (sometime Professor of Moral Philosophy), University of Dublin. *Publications:* Editor of Select Satires of Horace, 2nd edn, 1887; Greek Theories of Elementary Cognition, from Alcmæon to Aristotle, 1906; translation (with notes) of Aristotle, de Sensu, de Memoria, de Somno, de Somniis, and de Divinatione per Somnum, 1908; articles in newer edition of Smith's Dictionary of Classical Antiquities; articles and reviews in Mind and the International Journal of Ethics on philosophical subjects; papers in the Classical Review and in Hermathena on subjects of classical and philosophical criticism. *Address:* Carisbrooke, 14 Bushy Park Road, Dublin. *Club:* University, Dublin.

Died 13 Nov. 1918.

BEARNE, Catherine Mary; *e d* of late Thomas Broughton Charlton of Chilwell Hall, Notts; *m* 1882, E. H. Bearne (decd). *Publications:* Lives of the Early Valois Queens; Pictures of the Old French Court; The Cross of Pearls; A Leader of Society at Napoleon's Court; A Queen of Napoleon's Court; Heroines of French Society; A Sister of Marie Antoinette; A Royal Quartette; Four Fascinating Frenchwomen; A Court Painter and his Circle. *Address:* 26 The Parks, Minehead, Somerset. *Died 9 May 1923.*

BEARSTED, 1st Viscount, *cr* 1925, of Maidstone; **Marcus Samuel;** Bt 1903; Baron, 1921; Kt 1898; LLD Sheffield, 1924; LLD Cambridge (Hon.), 1925; DL of City; JP Kent; *b* 5 Nov. 1853; 2nd *s* of late Marcus Samuel; *m* 1881, Fanny Elizabeth, *o d* of late Benjamin Benjamin; one *s* two *d*. *Educ:* privately. Travelled widely in Far East and Japan; introduced transport of petroleum in bulk through Suez Canal; knighted for services rendered to HMS "Victorious," 1898; developed large oilfields in the Far East and received official vote of thanks from Lord Commissioner of the Admiralty in May 1915, for "services of the utmost importance to the fighting forces at the present time"; Peerage bestowed for eminent public and national services; Alderman of City of London, 1891–1900; Lord Mayor of London, 1902–3; Sheriff, 1894–95; Lord of Manor Mote; Commander of Order of Leopold of Belgium; Grand Officer, Legion of Honour; Freeman of city of Sheffield and town of Maidstone; Knight Commander Order of Rising Sun, Japan; 2nd Class Sacred Treasure, Japan. Owned about 2,000 acres. *Recreations:* fishing, literature. *Heir:* s Capt. Hon. Walter Horace Samuel, *b* 13 March 1882. *Address:* 3 Hamilton Place, W1. *T:* Grosvenor 2652; The Mote, Kent. *T:* Maidstone 411. *Club:* Carlton. *Died 17 Jan. 1927.*

BEATTIE, Rt. Hon. Sir Andrew, Kt 1920; PC (Ireland), 1921; DL, JP; FID; a Senator of Southern Ireland; *b* Rathfriland, Co. Down, 6 Aug. 1860; *m* 1885, Rachel, MBE, JP, *d* of late Thomas Brien, Lanistown House, Co. Dublin; four *s*. *Educ:* privately. Civic and Social Worker; contested seat for Parliament on three occasions (West Down, Ireland); member of the Governing Body, University College, Dublin; Commissioner of National Education, Ireland; High Sheriff of Dublin, 1918; member of the College of Nursing; Royal Dublin

Society; Royal Zoological Society of Ireland; member of the General Council of County Councils of Ireland; member of the Board of Agriculture and Technical Instruction, Ireland; member of the Statistical and Social Inquiry Society of Ireland; member of the Corporation of Dublin for over 25 years; as Alderman and Councillor has been Chairman of most of the important Committees. *Recreations:* riding, driving, motoring. *Address:* 46 Fitzwilliam Square, Dublin. *TA:* Beattie, Dublin. *T:* Dublin 162. *Club:* National Liberal.

Died 1923.

BEATTY, Major Charles Harold Longfield, DSO 1900; Staff, 1st Canadian Division; late 6th Battalion Royal Warwickshire Regiment; *b* 16 Jan. 1870; *e s* of Capt. D. L. Beatty (late 4th Hussars) of Borodale, Co. Wexford, Ireland; *m* 1905, Lucy Alice, *widow* of J. S. Langlands, Major 43rd Light Infantry; one *s*. Served South Africa (despatches twice, medal, 5 clasps); European War, 1914–15 (despatches). *Address:* Oakfield Atherstone, Borodale, Co. Wexford. *Club:* Junior United Service. *Died 17 May 1917.*

BEATTY, Haslitt Michael, CMG 1902; Ex-Chief Locomotive Superintendent, Cape Government Railways, South Africa. *Address:* Rosclare, Rouwkoop Road, Rondebosch, Cape Town. *Club:* Senior Civil Service, Cape Town. *Died 13 June 1916.*

BEATTY, Wallace, MD Univ. Dublin; FRCPI; Physician to the Adelaide Hospital, Dublin; Hon. Professor of Dermatology, Trinity College, Dublin; *b* Halifax, Nova Scotia, 13 Nov. 1853; *s* of James Beatty (*d* 1856), Engineer-in-Chief of the Balaklava Railway during the Crimean War, and Sarah Jane (*d* 1888), *d* of Rev. Henry Anthony Burke; *m* Frances Eleanor (*d* 1908), *d* of late Samuel Edge, MD, Grantstown, Queen's Co.; three *s*. *Educ:* Royal School, Dungannon; Trinity College, Dublin (Royal Scholarship, 1872; Classical Scholarship, 1875; Medical Scholarship, 1877). BA 1876; MB, BCh 1879; MD 1886; FRCPI 1887. *Publications:* Lectures on Diseases of the Skin, 1922; various articles in medical journals, the majority on dermatological subjects. *Recreations:* no special recreations; when a student in Trinity College was a footballer. *Address:* 38 Merrion Square, Dublin. *T:* Dublin 1273.

Died 8 Nov. 1923.

BEAUCHAMP, Sir Edward, 1st Bt, *cr* 1911; MP (L) Lowestoft, Northern Division of Suffolk, 1906–10, and 1910–22; *b* 12 April 1849; *s* of late Rev. William Henry Beauchamp, Rector of Chedgrave, Norfolk, and *g s* of Admiral Sir William Beauchamp-Proctor, 3rd Bt; *m* 1st, 1875, Frances Mary (*d* 1886), *d* of His Honour Judge Stephen, LLD, Newport House, Lincoln; 2nd, 1890, Betty Campbell, *d* of late Archibald Woods, Columbus, Ohio, USA; one *s* (and one *s* decd). *Educ:* privately, and in Royal Navy. Served as midshipman in Royal Navy; retired, 1867. Member of Lloyds since 1873; Deputy Chairman, 1900; Chairman, 1905 and 1913. *Heir:* s Brograve Campbell Beauchamp [*b* 5 May 1897; *m* 1923, Lady Evelyn Leonora Almina Herbert, *e d* of 5th Earl of Carnarvon]. *Address:* 26 Grosvenor Place, SW1. *T:* Victoria 3899.

Died 1 Feb. 1925.

BEAUCHAMP, Sir Sydney, Kt 1920; MB, BChir Cantab; MA; Physician; *b* 18 May 1861; *s* of late Henry Herron Beauchamp of Bexley, Kent; *m*; one *s* one *d*. *Educ:* Lausanne; University College School; Caius College, Cambridge. Medical Officer-in-charge West Park Military Hospital, 1914–16; Physician to Officers' Families' Fund Lying-in Hospital; Resident Medical Officer to British Delegation during Peace Conference in Paris; Visiteur medical des Hôpitaux Croix Rouge Française. *Address:* 8 William Street, Lowndes Square, SW1. *T:* Kensington 514; Salter's Meadow, Penn, Bucks. *Club:* United University. *Died 22 Nov. 1921.*

BEAUFORT, 9th Duke of, *cr* 1682; **Henry Adalbert Wellington FitzRoy Somerset,** JP, DL; Baron Botetourt, 1305, confirmed, 1803; Baron Herbert of Raglan, Chepstow, and Gower, 1506; Earl of Worcester, 1514; Marquess of Worcester, 1642; Hon. Colonel Royal Gloucestershire Hussars; MFH Badminton Hunt; *b* 19 May 1847; *e s* of 8th Duke and Lady Georgiana Charlotte Curzon, *d* of 1st Earl Howe; *S* father, 1899; *m* 1895, Louise Emily, *d* of William H. Harford of Oldown, Almondsbury, Gloucestershire, and *widow* of Baron Carlo de Tuyll; one *s* two *d*. Captain Royal Horse Guards, 1865–78. Owned about 52,000 acres. *Heir:* s Marquess of Worcester, *b* 4 April 1900. *Address:* Badminton, RSO Gloucestershire. *TA:* Badminton. *T:* PO Badminton. *M:* AD 195.

Died 27 Nov. 1924.

BEAUFORT, Sir Leicester Paul, Kt 1919; MA, BCL; barrister-at-law; *b* Warburton, Cheshire, 13 Dec. 1853; 2nd *s* of late Rev. D.

A. Beaufort and Emily Nowell, *d* of Sir John Davis, 1st Bt, KCB, DCL; *m* 1883, Edith Mary, *d* of late Rev. C. H. Griffith, BA, FRMS, of Strathfield Turgis, Hants. *Educ:* Westminster; Oxford. Barrister, Inner Temple, 1879. Member of the London School Board, 1888. Gov. Sec. and Judicial Commissioner, British N Borneo, 1889; received the Jubilee Medal; Gov. and Commander-in-Chief of the Colony of Labuan, and of the State of N Borneo, 1895–1900; Chief Justice, Northern Rhodesia, 1901–18; retired. *Recreations:* shooting, fishing, golf. *Address:* Sandown, Wynberg, Cape Colony, Africa.
Died 12 Aug. 1926.

BEAUFOY, Mark Hanbury, JP; *b* 1854; *o s* of late George Beaufoy; *m* 1884, Mildred Scott, *d* of Robert Tait; three *s* one *d*. *Educ:* Eton; Trinity Hall, Cambridge. MP (L) Kennington, 1889–95. *Address:* Coombe House, Shaftesbury. *Clubs:* Kennel, New University.
Died 10 Nov. 1922.

BEAUMONT, Hon. Hubert; *b* 6 April 1864; 3rd *s* of 1st Baron Allendale; *m* 1900, Elisa Mercedes (*d* 1917), *e d* of M. P. Grace; one *s*. *Educ:* Eton; Cheltenham; Balliol College, Oxford. Contested (R) King's Lynn, 1895; North Bucks, 1900; Barnard Castle, 1903; MP (R) Eastbourne Division of Sussex, 1906–10. *Address:* 16 Dorset Square, NW1. *T:* Paddington 5496; Wotton House, Aylesbury. *T:* Aylesbury 130. *Clubs:* Brooks's, Garrick, Reform.
Died 14 Aug. 1922.

BEAUMONT, Admiral Sir Lewis Anthony, GCB 1911 (KCB 1904); KCMG 1901; FRGS; Grand Officer, Legion of Honour; *b* 19 May 1847; *m* 1889, Mary Eleanor (*d* 1907), *d* of Charles C. Perkins of Boston, USA. Entered RN 1860; Rear-Admiral, 1897; Admiral, 1906. Served Arctic Expedition, 1875–76 (promoted, Arctic medal); Naval Attaché for Europe, 1882; Private Secretary to the Earl of Northbrook, 1883–85, as First Lord of Admiralty and High Commissioner to Egypt, 1894; Director of Naval Intelligence, 1894–99; ADC to Queen, 1895–97; Commander-in-Chief, Pacific, 1899–1900; Commander-in-Chief, Australia, 1901–3; Commissioner on the Paris Court of Enquiry, 1904; Commander-in-Chief, Devonport, 1905–8; First and Principal Naval ADC to the King, 1911; retired, 1912. *Address:* St Georges, Hurstpierpoint, Sussex. *Club:* United Service.
Died 19 June 1922.

BEAUMONT, Roberts, MSc, MIMechE; Professor of Textile Industries, Leeds University, 1889–1913; founder of the Departments of Woollen and Worsted Yarn Manufacture (English and Continental Systems), of the Clothworkers' Museums, and of the Textile Research and Analytical Laboratories, also reorganiser of the Departments of Textile Design, Manufacture, and Fabric Finishing; *b* 1862; 3rd *s* of late Prof. John Beaumont; *m* Annie, 2nd *d* of late E. J. Rawlins, principal of the firm of the Leeds Colour Works; two *s*. Inspector of Textile Insts City and Guilds of London Inst., 1892–1916; Vice-Pres., International Jury on Textile Machinery, Paris Exhibition, 1900; Dir, Expert and Adv. Dept, Textile Interests Ltd. Silver medal, Society of Arts; special medal awarded by City and Guilds of London Institute for services as Examiner in Woollen and Worsted Weaving and Designing, 1892–1906. *Publications:* Woollen and Worsted; Colour in Woven Design; Wool Manufacture (Fabrication pratique des lainages); Standard Cloths: Structure and Manufacture; Finishing of Textile Fabrics (Apprêt des tissus); Union Textile Fabrication; Woven Fabrics at the World's Fair, Chicago; articles on Woollen and Worsted Manufacturing and Textiles in Chambers's Encyclopædia, and Newnes' Technological and Scientific Dictionary; on Textile Educational Preparedness; British Dyes—Technical Research, etc. *Address:* 1 Grosvenor Terrace, Headingley, Leeds; 5 Cheapside, Bradford.

BEAUMONT, Somerset Archibald, DL; *b* 1836; 3rd *s* of late T. Wentworth Beaumont, MP, Bretton, Yorks. *Educ:* Harrow; Trinity College, Cambridge. MP (L) Newcastle, 1860–65; Wakefield, 1868–74; promoted Commercial Treaty by inquiring into Austrian Tariff, 1865; one of the founders (with Messrs Glyn and Co.) of the Anglo-Austrian Bank. *Address:* Skere, Guildford. *Clubs:* Travellers', St James's, Burlington Fine Arts.
Died 8 Dec. 1921.

BEAZLEY, Patrick Langford; Editor of the Catholic Times since 1884; *b* 1859; *s* of James Beazley, Aghadoe, Killarney; *m* 1880, Nannie H., *d* of P. E. Hickey, Newcastle West, Co. Limerick; two *s*. *Educ:* St Brendan's Seminary, Killarney; Paris. A journalist for thirty-five years. *Publications:* stories, biographies, poems, etc. *Recreations:* walking, boating. *Address:* Glengariff, Rudgrave Square, Egremont, Cheshire.
Died 30 Nov. 1923.

BECK, Col Hon. Sir Adam, Kt 1914; LLD; Member, Legislative Assembly, Province of Ontario, Canada, 1905–19; Chairman of the Hydro-Electric Power Commission since 1906; President, London Health Association since 1910; gazetted Colonel of the Canadian Militia, 1912; MFH of the London Hunt, London, Ontario; *b* Baden, Ontario, 20 June 1857; *s* of George Beck and Charlotte, *d* of George Hespeler; *m* 1898, Lilian (*d* 1921), *o c* of late C. J. Ottaway; one *d*. *Educ:* Galt. Mayor of London, Ont, 1902, 1903, 1904. Episcopalian; manufacturer. *Address:* Headley, London, Ontario, Canada. *Clubs:* Albany, Toronto; London.
Died Aug. 1925.

BECK, Edward Anthony; Master of Trinity Hall, Cambridge, since 1902; *b* 21 March 1848; *s* of late John Redin Beck, of Castle Rising, Norfolk; *m* 1874, E. M., *d* of late James Clark, of Winchmore Hill; two *s* three *d*. *Educ:* Bishop Stortford Grammar School; Trinity Hall, Cambridge (Scholar, 1867; 1st Class in Classical Tripos, 1871; Fellow, 1871). Chancellor's English Medallist, 1868 and 1870; Seatonian Prizeman, 1874; Assistant Tutor, 1875; Deputy Esquire Bedell, 1876; Junior Tutor, 1885; Senior Tutor, 1887; served as one of the Proctors or Pro-Proctors for six years between 1881 and 1888; eight years member Council of Senate; Vice-Chancellor, 1904–5 and 1905–6. *Publication:* (ed) Euripides' Heracleidæ, 1881. *Address:* The Lodge, Trinity Hall, Cambridge.
Died 12 April 1916.

BECK, Rev. Edward Josselyn; Hon. Canon of Southwark Cathedral; *b* 1832; *s* of Henry Beck of Needham Market, Suffolk; *m* 1865, Mary Coleridge, *d* of Charles Bradshaw Stutfield, JP. *Educ:* Ipswich School. Formerly Curate of Christ Church, St Pancras, NW; Fellow and Dean of Clare College, Cambridge; Rector of Rotherhithe, SE, 1867–1907. *Publication:* History of the Parish of St Mary, Rotherhithe, 1907. *Address:* 4 Scroope Terrace, Cambridge.
Died 17 Oct. 1924.

BECK, Rev. Frederick John; Precentor and Hon. Canon of Llandaff, 1903. *Educ:* Trinity Coll., Oxford. Ordained deacon 1876, priest 1877. Curate, Roath, Cardiff, 1879–83, Vicar, 1883. *Address:* Honiton.
Died 10 June 1922.

BECK, Hon. Sir Johannes Henricus Meiring, Kt 1911; MD; FRSE; JP; Minister of Posts and Telegraphs, Union of South Africa, since 1916; Senator since 1910, and Chairman of Committees of Senate; *b* Worcester, Cape Province, 1855; *s* of late C. Beck, JP, of Worcester (Cape); *m* 1855, Mary Emily, *d* of W. C. Kuijs of Napier (Cape); three *d*. *Educ:* Worcester Public School; S African College; University of Edinburgh; Berlin, and Vienna. Graduated in medicine, Edinburgh University, 1879 (First Cl. Honours and Beavey Scholarship); MLA Worcester (Cape), 1898–10; one of the delegates from Cape of Good Hope to S African National Convention; Member of Council, University, Cape of Good Hope, 1888–1912; ex-President, Cape Medical Council. *Publications:* numerous contributions on hygienic and medical subjects to British and S African medical and scientific journals. *Recreations:* horticultural farming, music. *Address:* De Oude' Brostdii, Tulbagh, S Africa. *Club:* Civil Service, Capetown.
Died May 1919.

BECK, Hon. Nicholas Du Bois Dominic; Puisne Judge of the Supreme Court of Alberta since 1907; one of the Justices of the Appellate Division since 1921; *b* Cobourg, Ontario, 4 May 1857; *s* of Rev. J. W. R. Beck, MA, for many years Anglican Rector of Peterborough, Ontario, and Georgina Boulton; *m* 1st, Mary Ethel Lloyd; two *s* two *d*; 2nd, Louisa Teefy. *Educ:* private schools; Peterborough Collegiate Institute; LLB University of Toronto. Admitted to Ontario Bar, 1879; Manitoba, 1883; Bar of North-West Territories, 1889; QC, Dominion, 1893. Member and Chairman of the Territorial Educational Council till the formation of the Provinces of Alberta and Saskatchewan, 1905, and since then of Educational Council of Alberta; Member of the Senate and Vice-Chancellor of the University of Alberta; Editor of the Territorial Law Reports, published by the Territorial Law Society, which has now ceased to exist; one of the Board of Management of the Catholic Extension Society of Canada; a member of the Board of Governors of St Joseph's (Catholic) College, affiliated to the University of Alberta; became a Catholic, 1883. *Publications:* Edited for some years the Catholic North-West Review. *Recreations:* reading, bridge, golf. *Address:* Edmonton, Alberta, Canada. *T:* 82349. *Clubs:* Edmonton, Edmonton Golf and Country.
Died 14 May 1928.

BECKER, Sir Walter (Frederick), KBE 1918; Consul-General, Province of Piemonte, for the King of Siam; Chairman of Board of Governors of the British Institute of Florence; Knight Commander of the Order of the Crown of Siam; *b* 9 March 1855; *s* of late Frederick Becker; *m* 1895, Delphine Thérèse, *d* of late Alphonse de Martelly;

no *c. Educ:* Falmouth Classical and Grammar School. Engaged in ship-owning in various countries, since 1880 in Sicily and Italy; founded, maintained, and acted as Chairman of Maternity and Rescue Home, Turin; founded, maintained, and directed a hospital in Turin for British Expeditionary Force in Italy; war work of various kinds for British sailors and soldiers; local war propaganda work. *Recreations:* study, golf, tennis, sailing, motoring. *Address:* Val Salice, near Turin; Villa Delphine, Roquebrune, Cap-Martin, France. *Clubs:* Royal Automobile; Royal Cornwall Yacht; Royal Automobile of Italy, Union, Rome. *Died 1 May 1927.*

BECKETT, Brig.-Gen. Charles Edward, CB 1898; JP Dorset; *b* 11 June 1849; *s* of late Charles William Beckett, Thorne, Yorks; *m* 1st, Louisa Augusta (*d* 1900), *y d* of late Field-Marshal Sir John Michel, GCB; one *d*; 2nd, Mary Philippa, *d* of late J. A. Farrell, DL, JP, Moynalty, Co. Meath, and *widow* of M. Kenneth Angelo, Culachy, Fort Augustus. *Educ:* privately. Joined 7th Dragoon Guards, 1869; Adjutant, 1872–77; Brigade-Major, Egypt, 1882–83; Asst Military Secretary, Ireland, 1886–88; DAAG Ireland, 1888–91; commanded 2nd Dragoon Guards, 1892–95; commanded 3rd Hussars, 1895–98; ADGO, War Office, 1898–99; AAG, Natal, 1899–1901; AQMG, War Office, 1901–3; served in Egyptian Campaign, 1882; Nile Expedition, 1884–85; South Africa, 1899–1900 (wounded Dundee, despatches); Chief Staff Officer, Malta, 1904–6; Brig.-General in charge Administration, Malta, 1905–6; retired 1906; Command of 2nd SW Mounted Brigade, 1908–12, and of 2/1st East Lancashire Division, 1914–15. *Recreations:* hunting, shooting. *Address:* Culachy, Fort Augustus. *Died 17 Sept. 1925.*

BECKETT, Lt-Col John Douglas Mortimer, DSO 1915; 1st Battalion Hampshire Regiment; *b* 12 May 1881; *s* of late Col Beckett, Royal Fusiliers; *m* 1915, Wilmet Rose, *d* of Col Lumley Peyton, Rosslyn, Winchester. Entered army, 1901; Lieut Hants Regiment, 1903; Captain, 1907; Major, 1916; Lt-Col, 1916; served South Africa, 1901–2 (Queen's medal, 5 clasps); European War, 1914–17 (DSO, Bt Lt-Col). *Address:* Bramerton, Norfolk.
Died 9 Feb. 1918.

BECKETT, Colonel Stephen, CB 1885; retired ISC; *b* 1840; 5th *s* of late Captain J. O. Beckett, HEICS; *m* 1st, 1875, Cecilia (*d* 1889), *d* of P. Griffith; 2nd, 1894, Ida Maud, *d* of John Macfarlane; two *s*. *Educ:* private school and Edinburgh Academy. Ensign, HEICS, 1857; attached 54th Regt, 1857–58; Punjab Frontier Force, 1858–69; Asst Political Agent and Supt, Bahawalpur, 1869–79; Commissariat Dept, 1879–81; 31st Punjab Infantry, 1881–82; Commissariat and Transport Dept, 1882–87; commanded 38th Bengal Infantry, 1887–89; served in Indian Mutiny (despatches, dangerously wounded, medal); Umbeylah campaign, 1863–64 (despatches twice, medal with clasp); commanded Bahawalpur contingent on Dera Ghazi Khan Frontier during 1st Kabul campaign, 1879; Suakin, 1885, as Director of Indian Transport with British troops (despatches, medal with clasp, Khedive's star, CB). *Died 19 Nov. 1921.*

BECKETT, Walter Ralph Durie, CMG 1909; FRGS; Consul-General, Dutch East Indies, since 1913; *b* Agra, NWP, India, 24 Aug. 1864; *s* of Col W. H. Beckett; *m* 1911, Ivy Nina, *d* of H. R. Goring. *Educ:* Tonbridge School. Passed a competitive examination, 1886; student interpreter, Siam, 1886; 2nd Assistant, 1888; 1st Asst, 1891; HM Vice-Consul at Bangkok, 1893; Acting Consul 11 April–22 Oct. 1894; acted as Chargé d'Affaires, 23 Oct.–6 Nov. 1894; Acting Consul, 1894–95, when he was again in charge of the Legation; HM Consul for territories of Chiengmai, Lampun, Lakhon, Phré, Nan, etc (Northern Siam), 1897; HM Consul at Bangkok, 1903, and granted local rank of First Secretary, 1904; Chargé d'Affaires during 1904, 1906, 1907, 1908, 1909, 1910, 1911, 1912, and 1913; HBM Consul-General, Bangkok, Siam, 1913. *Recreations:* cricket, polo, tennis, golf, etc. *Address:* HBM Consulate-General, Batavia, Java. *Clubs:* Oriental, Queen's. *Died 18 Sept. 1917.*

BECTIVE, Countess of; Alice Maria; *d* of 4th Marquess of Downshire; *m* 1867, Thomas, Earl of Bective (*d* 1893), *er s* of 3rd Marquess of Headfort; one *d* (and one *d* decd). *Address:* 29 Eaton Place, SW; Lunefield, Kirkby Lonsdale, Westmorland.
Died 25 Feb. 1928.

BEDALE, Rev. Frederick; Vicar of St Mary's, Nuneaton, since 1903; Canon of Coventry Cathedral, 1920; *s* of late John Bedale, Streatham; *m* Mary, *d* of Staff Commander R. A. Burstal, RN; two *s* four *d*. *Educ:* Worcester College, Oxford. Curate of Christ Church, Luton, 1891–96; Vicar of Pirton, Herts, 1896–1903. *Address:* St Mary's Vicarage, Nuneaton, Warwickshire.
Died 8 Nov. 1924.

BEDDARD, Frank Evers, MA, DSc; FRS 1892; Prosector of Zoological Society, 1884–1915 and formerly Lecturer on Biology at Guy's Hospital; has been Examiner in Zoology and Comparative Anatomy, University of London, and of Morphology at Oxford, and in the University of New Zealand; *b* Dudley, 19 June 1858; *s* of late John Beddard. *Educ:* Harrow; New College, Oxford. Naturalist to "Challenger" Expedition Commission, 1882–84. *Publications:* Animal Coloration, 1892; Text-book of Zoogeography, 1895; A Monograph of the Oligochæta, 1895; Structure and Classification of Birds, 1898; many papers in the Transactions of Royal Societies of London and Edinburgh, of the Zoological Society, and the Quarterly Journal of Microscopic Science, etc. *Recreation:* conversation at clubs. *Address:* Zoological Society's Gardens, Regent's Park, NW. *Clubs:* United University, Royal Societies.
Died 14 July 1925.

BEDFORD, Maj.-Gen. Sir Walter George Augustus, KCMG 1918 (CMG 1900); CB 1916; (Hon.) DCL Dunelm; MB; *b* 24 Oct. 1858; *s* of Vice-Admiral G. A. Bedford; *m* 1880, Harriette Adelaide, *d* of Rev. D. J. Drakeford, MA; one *d*. *Educ:* St Bartholomew's Hospital; University of Durham. Headquarters, War Office, 1894–99; Staff Officer to the Surgeon-General, Army Headquarters, S African Field Force, 1899–1901 (despatches, CMG); PMO, South China, 1908–11; Deputy-Director of Medical Services, London District, 1912; Deputy-Director of Medical Services, South Africa, 1914; Deputy Director of Medical Services, Southern Command, 1914–15; Director of Medical Services, Mediterranean, and Egyptian Expeditionary Forces, 1915–16 (despatches, CB); Deputy Director of Medical Services, Northern Command, 1916–19. *Address:* The Holt, Eynsham, Oxon. *Club:* Junior United Service.
Died 8 Jan. 1922.

BEDFORD, Rev. William Campbell Riland, MA; *b* 29 May 1852; *s* of late Rev. W. K. Riland Bedford, late Rector of Sutton Coldfield; *m* 1877, Eleanor Phœbe, *d* of Sir James Chance, 1st Bt; one *s* three *d*. *Educ:* Westminster; Clare College, Cambridge. Curate of St Michael's, Coventry, 1875–77; All Saints, Leamington, 1878; Vicar of Little Aston, 1878–81; Curate of Sutton Coldfield, 1882–87; Vicar of Knowle, Warwickshire, 1889–92; late Rural Dean of Sutton Coldfield; Hon. Canon of Birmingham; Rector of Sutton Coldfield, Warwickshire, 1892–1908. Grand Chaplain of England (Masonic), 1902; PPSW, Warwickshire; PM, Warden Lodge, 794. *Recreation:* archery. *Address:* Cotswold, Leamington. *T:* 487.
Died 15 Aug. 1922.

BEDWELL, Rev. Francis, BD; late Hon. Canon of Llandaff. *Educ:* Corpus Christi College, Oxford. BA 1860; BD 1874. Curate of St Woolos, Newport, Mon, 1861–72; Rector of Holy Trinity, Pillgwenily, 1872–85; Vicar of Caerleon, Mon, 1885–1906; Rector of Down Hatherley, 1907–12. *Address:* Oakdene, Churchdown, Gloucester. *Died 18 Aug. 1925.*

BEECHAM, Sir Joseph, 1st Bt, *cr* 1914; Kt 1911; JP; manufacturer and philanthropist; *b* 8 June 1848; *m* 1873, Josephine, *d* of William Burnett, London; two *s* five *d*. Mayor of St Helens, 1899–1900, 1910–11 and 1911–12; proprietor of Aldwych Theatre. Knight of the Order of St Stanislaus (Russia). *Heir: s* Sir Thomas Beecham, *b* 29 April 1879. *Address:* 9 Arkwright Road, Hampstead, NW. *T:* Hampstead 1653; Ewanville, Huyton, Liverpool. *Club:* Devonshire.
Died 23 Oct. 1916.

BEECHING, Maj.-Gen. Frank; Indian Army; *b* 23 July 1839; *m* 1870, Marianne, *d* of P. Mathews. Entered army, 1857; Maj.-Gen. 1894; Unemployed Supernumerary List, 1894. *Address:* 13 Highland Road, Norwood, SE. *Died 1 Sept. 1916.*

BEECHING, Very Rev. Henry Charles, DD, Hon. DLitt Durham; Dean of Norwich since 1911; Canon of Westminster Abbey, 1902–11; Preacher to the Hon. Society of Lincoln's Inn, 1904–12; Examining Chaplain to the Bishop of Carlisle, 1905–11; *b* 15 May 1859; 2nd *s* of late James P. G. Beeching, of Bexhill, Sussex, and Harriet Skaife; *m* 1891, Mary, *e d* of late Rev. A. J. Plow; three *d*. *Educ:* City of London School; Balliol College, Oxford (Classical Exhibitioner). Curate of Mossley Hill Church, Liverpool, 1882–85; Rector of Yattendon, Berks, 1885–1900; Oxford Sacred Poem, 1896; Select Preacher Oxford University, 1896–97, 1912–13; Cambridge, 1903–9–12; Dublin, 1905; Clark Lecturer at Trinity Coll., Camb., 1900; Prof. of Pastoral Theology, King's Coll. London, 1900–3; Chaplain of Lincoln's Inn, 1900–3. *Publications:* Faith (eleven sermons with a Preface), 1892; Seven Sermons to Schoolboys, 1894; In a Garden, and other poems, 1895; Pages from a Private Diary, 1898; Conferences on Books and Men, 1900; Two Lectures on Poetry;

Inns of Court Sermons, 1901; Religio Laici, 1902; The Apostles' Creed; The Grace of Episcopacy, 1906; Provincial Letters; Lectures on the Atonement, 1907; Lectures on the Doctrine of Sacraments, 1908; Francis Atterbury, 1909; Revision of the Prayer Book, 1910; Inspiration, 1914; The Library of the Cathedral Church of Norwich, 1915; Editor of A Paradise of English Poetry, 1892; Lyra Sacra, 1894; Milton's Poetical Works, 1900; Shakespeare's Sonnets, 1904; Ainger's Lectures and Sermons, 1906; Essays and Studies by Members of the English Association, vol ii, 1911; Herbert's Country Parson, Vaughan's Poems, Tennyson's In Memoriam, Shakespeare's Julius Cæsar, Poems of Daniel and Drayton, Lyra Apostolica, etc. *Address:* The Deanery, Norwich. *T:* 1090 Norwich. *Club:* Athenæum.

Died 25 Feb. 1919.

BEER, Col James Henry Elias, CIE 1909; VD; Commandant Mussoorie Rifles; *b* 1848. *Address:* Mussoorie, India.

Died 1 Nov. 1925.

BEER BIKRAM SINGH, Rajkumar, CIE 1898; Hon. Lieutenant-Colonel; ADC to Viceroy, 1906; Officer commanding Sirmour Imperial Service Sappers and Miners; also attached to 1st PWO Sappers and Miners. Served in command of his corps in the Tirah expedition, 1897–98; was Acting ADC to Field-Marshal Earl Roberts during the Coronation and rode in procession, August 1902; also rode on the staff of the Prince of Wales at the march past at Rawal Pindi. *Address:* Sirmour State, Punjab. *Died 13 Aug. 1923.*

BEESTON, Col the Hon. Joseph Livesley, CMG 1915; MD; Army Medical Corps, Australian Imperial Force; *b* 19 Sept. 1859; *s* of late J. L. Beeston; *m* 1882, Anna Maria, *d* of William Read. Served Dardanelles, 1914–15 (despatches, CMG). *Address:* New Lambton, New South Wales. *Died March 1921.*

BEET, Rev. Joseph Agar, DD; theological writer and lecturer; *b* Sheffield, 27 Sept. 1840; *s* of W. J. Beet, manufacturer; *m* Sarah Elizabeth, *d* of S. T. Baugh, JP, Wrexham; three *s* one *d.* *Educ:* Wesley College, Sheffield; Wesleyan College, Richmond. Theological Tutor, Wesleyan College, Richmond, 1885–1905; one of the original Members of the Faculty of Theology, University of London; Hon. DD of the Univ. of Glasgow; Fernley Lecturer, 1889; Lecturer at University of Chicago and at Chautauqua and Ocean Grove (USA) Summer Schools, 1896. *Publications:* Commentaries on St Paul's Epistles; Credentials of the Gospel, 1889; The Last Things, 1897; A Manual of Theology, 1906; Church, Churches, and Sacraments, 1907; Shorter Manual of Theology, 1908; The New Testament, its Authorship, Date, and Worth, 1909; Holiness, Symbolic and Real, 1910; The Old Testament, its Contents, Truth, and Worth, 1912; A Theologian's Workshop, Tools, and Method, 1914. *Address:* 11 Dynevor Road, Richmond, Surrey. *Died 25 May 1924.*

BEEVOR, Lt-Col Walter Calverley, CB 1916; CMG 1900; *b* 8 Oct. 1858; *m* 1890, Ella Beatrice, *e d* of late Charles Taylor, DL, JP, Horton Manor, Slough; one *s* one *d.* *Educ:* Edinburgh University. Served Soudan Campaign, 1885 (medal with clasp, Khedive's star); Ashantee, 1895–96 (despatches, promoted Surgeon-Major, Star); North-West Frontier, India, 1897–98 (despatches, medal with two clasps); South Africa, 1899–1902 (despatches, medal with six clasps, King's medal); European War, 1914–19 (despatches, CB); served on Personal Staff of Duke of Connaught to Durbar, Nov. 1902–April 1903; on Personal Staff of Lord Northcote, Governor-General of Bombay, 1903. *Clubs:* Guards, Naval and Military. *Died 6 Feb. 1927.*

BEGBIE, Colonel Francis Warburton, CBE 1919; Army Medical Service; Knight of Grace, Order of St John of Jerusalem; *b* 13 June 1864; *s* of James Warburton Begbie, MD, LLD, late of Edinburgh; *m* Mary, *d* of Walter Reynolds, JP, late High Sheriff of Herts. Served Indian Frontier Chitral Campaign (medal with clasp); South African War, 1899–1902 (Queen's medal with six clasps, King's medal with two clasps, despatches twice); European War, 1914–19; OC Base Hospital, Mesopotamia Field Forces, Commandant RAMC Training Battalion, OC No VI General Hospital, Rouen, ADMS, Le Trepat, Dieppe and Dunkerque (despatches four times, 1915 star, War medal, Victory medal, CBE). *Address:* Holt & Co., 3 Whitehall Place, SW1. *Club:* Junior Naval and Military.

Died 25 April 1922.

BEGG, Col Charles Mackie, CB 1918; CMG 1915; MD; FRCP, FRCSEd; NZ Army Medical Service; Hon. Physician Wellington Hospital; Hon. Surgeon Wellington Children's Hospital. Served Dardanelles, 1914–18 (despatches, CMG, CB). *Publications:* medical papers. *Address:* 148 Willis Street, Wellington, NZ.

Died Feb. 1919.

BEGG, Ferdinand Faithfull, FRSE; *b* Edinburgh, 27 Dec. 1847; *s* of late Rev. James Begg, DD, and Maria, *d* of Rev. Ferdinand Faithfull, Rector of Headley, Epsom; *m* 1873, Jessie Maria (*d* 1925), *d* of F. A. Cargill, Dunedin, New Zealand. *Educ:* privately. Emigrated to New Zealand, 1863; returned to Scotland, 1872; became a stockbroker, and was chairman of the Edinburgh Stock Exchange 1885; established himself on the London Stock Exchange, 1887; retired, 1913. Contested (C) Kennington Division of Lambeth, 1892; MP (C) St Rollox Division of Glasgow, 1895–1900; chairman of London Chamber of Commerce, 1912–15. *Recreations:* golf, yachting, heraldry. *Address:* 46 St Aubyns, Hove, Sussex. *Club:* Union, Brighton.

Died 4 Dec. 1926

BEGIN, HE Most Rev. Louis Nazaire, DD; RC Archbishop of Quebec since 1898; *b* Levis, Quebec, 10 Jan. 1840; *s* of Charles Begin, a farmer, and Luce Paradis. *Educ:* Levis Model School; Commercial College, St Michel; Seminary of Quebec, 1857–62. BA at Laval, and Prince of Wales Prize, Grand Seminary of Quebec; Professor at Laval left for Rome, 1863; ordained, 1865; Professor, Faculty of Theology Laval University, 1868–84; Principal of the Normal School until Oct 1888; Bishop of Chicoutimi, 1888; Coadjutor of Cardinal Taschereau, 1891; Administrator, Archdiocese of Quebec, 1894; Cardinal, 1914. *Publications:* La primauté et l'infaillibilité des souverains pontifes; La sainte écriture et la règle de foi, 1874; Le culte catholique, 1875; Aide-mémoire, ou chronologie de l'histoire du Canada, 1886; Chronologie de l'Histoire des Etats-Unis d'Amérique, 1895; Catéchisme de Controverse, 1902. *Address:* Archbishop's Palace, Quebec. *T:* 989.

Died 19 July 1925

BEHR, Fritz Bernhard, AMICE; Engineer to the Manchester and Liverpool Electric Express Railway; Consulting Engineer Railway Co (Tampico-Panuco Valley), and several important oil companies in Mexico and elsewhere; *b* Berlin, 9 Oct. 1842; *s* of Dr Bernhard Behr, of the University of Berlin. *Educ:* Paris; afterwards pupil to Mr Wentworth Shields and Sir John Fowler. Employed on a great many railway works in England and abroad; went through the Franco-German War, 1870–71; administering a portion of the conquered territory for the German Government. Became a naturalised Englishman, 1876, and has devoted himself specially to the development of mono-rail lines since 1885; invented practically the mono-rail, later known as the High-Speed Mono-Rail System, and obtained two Acts of Parliament for the construction of the Manchester and Liverpool Electric Express Railway in 1901 and 1902, to be worked at an average speed of 110 miles an hour. Was decorated during the German War. *Publications:* a number of pamphlets and lectures in English, French, and German on high-speed mono-rails; the principal one published in 1893, entitled Lightning Express Railway Service, 120 to 150 Miles an Hour. *Recreation:* motoring. *Address:* 3 Alexandra Court, 171 Queen's Gate, SW7; Villa Violet, Roquebrune, AM, France. *TA:* Syndigef, London. *T:* Kensington 5844. *Club:* Orleans. *Died 25 Feb. 1927*

BEHRENS, Sir Charles, Kt 1912; JP; Member of Sir Jacob Behrens & Sons, of Manchester, Bradford, Glasgow, London and Calcutta; *b* 5 Aug. 1848; *s* of late Sir Jacob Behrens, Bradford; *m* 1883, Emily Milnes, *d* of late Samuel Shaw, JP, of Brooklands, near Halifax; three *d.* *Educ:* Bradford Grammar School and High School. Lord Mayor of Manchester, 1909–10 and 1910–11; Director of Manchester Ship Canal Co.; Local Director of Commercial Union Assurance Co., also of the Ocean Accident and Guarantee Corporation Ltd; Governor of the Manchester Grammar School; Member of Court of Victoria University, Manchester, of Board of Manchester Royal Infirmary, and of many other philanthropic institutions. *Address:* Holm-Acre, Altrincham, Cheshire. *Clubs:* Reform; Clarendon, Reform, Manchester. *Died 25 Sept. 1925*

BEHRENS, Walter, Knight of Legion of Honour; *b* Manchester, 1856; *s* of late Louis Behrens, of West Hill, Bowdon, Cheshire; *m* 1st, 1894, Evelyn (*d* 1910), *d* of S. H. Beddington, 21 Hyde Park Square, W; two *s*; 2nd, 1914, Mme Gomez-Vaëz, Paris. *Educ:* Grammar School and Owens College, Manchester; Polytechnic Institute, Carlsruhe. Engineer; has taken an active part in the movement for Anglo-French Postal and Telegraphic Reform, and the reciprocal protection of British and French merchandise marks; an advocate of the Channel Tunnel scheme between England and France, and has written many articles on the subject in the daily papers; has been instrumental in promoting the use of British machinery in France, especially the linotype machine, and the locomotives of the North British Locomotive Co.; President, British Chamber of Commerce, Paris, 1908–9; official agent of the Commercial Committee of the House of Commons in Paris. *Recreations:* golf, musical composition, violin. *Address:* 48 Avenue Henri-Martin, Paris. *T:* Passy 42.00. *TA:* Walbe

Paris. *Clubs:* Reform, Royal Automobile, Isthmian; Automobile, Aero, Interallié, Bois de Boulogne, Paris.

Died 27 April 1922.

BEILBY, Sir George Thomas, Kt 1916; JP; FRS; LLD Glasgow and Birmingham, DSc Durham; FIC, FCS, AIChemE; Member of Advisory Council on Scientific and Industrial Research; Chairman of the Royal Technical College, Glasgow, 1907–23; *b* 17 Nov. 1850; *s* of G. T. Beilby, MD, of Edinburgh; *m* 1877, Emma Clarke, *e d* of Rev. S. Newnam; one *s* one *d. Educ:* private schools; University of Edinburgh. Inventor of processes in use in several departments of industry; specially studied fuel economy and smoke prevention in connection with the coal consumption of Great Britain, and reported to the Royal Commission on Coal Supplies, 1903; Member of the Royal Commission on Fuel and Engines for the Navy, 1912; Director of Fuel Research, 1917–23. President of Society of Chemical Industry, 1899; of Chemical Section of British Association at S African Meeting, 1905; of Institute of Chemistry, 1909–12; and of the Inst. of Metals, 1916–18; has devoted much time to chemical and microscopical research. *Publications:* Aggregation and Flow of Solids, 1921; Scientific and technical papers in Proceedings of Royal Society, Proceedings of Chemical Society, BA Reports, Soc. Chem. Ind. Jl., and Phil. Mag., etc. *Address:* 29 Kidderpore Avenue, Hampstead, NW3. *Club:* Athenæum. *Died 1 Aug. 1924.*

BEITH, Hon. Robert; *b* Fairfield Farm, Darlington, Durham, Ontario, 17 May 1843; unmarried. Senator since 1907; stock-breeder and importer; MP (L) W Durham, 1891–96 and 1902. *Address:* Waverley Farm, Bowmanville, Ontario. *Died Jan. 1922.*

BELCHER, Lt-Col Harold Thomas, DSO 1900; *b* 17 March 1875; *s* of Rev. T. H. Belcher. Entered RA 1895; served South Africa (severely wounded, medal with five clasps); European War, 1914–16 (despatches, wounded); Lt-Col, 1915. *Address:* Bramley Rectory, Basingstoke. *Died 8 July 1917.*

BELCHER, Major Robert, CMG 1900; *b* 23 April 1849; *s* of Robert Tovey Belcher and Elizabeth Bounford; *m* 1880, Maggie, *d* of Donald M'Leod; three *s* four *d. Educ:* Byron House, Ealing. 9th Lancers, 1868–73; North-West Mounted Police of Canada, 1873–1908; through North-West Rebellion, 1885; served in Yukon, 1897–99; attended the Queen's Diamond Jubilee with NWMP, 1897; served South Africa, 1900–1 with Strathcona's Horse (despatches, CMG). *Address:* Edmonton, Alberta, Canada.

Died 13 Feb. 1919.

BELFIELD, Sir Henry Conway, KCMG 1914 (CMG 1909); *b* 29 Nov. 1855; *e s* of late John Belfield, JP, Primley Hill, South Devon, and Eliza Conway, *o d* of Captain George Bridges, RN; *m* 1884, Florence, CBE, 4th *d* of late Rev. James Rathbone; one *s* two *d. Educ:* Rugby; Oriel College, Oxford, BA. Barrister-at-law, Inner Temple, 1880, and practised on the Western Circuit and at the Devon and Exeter Sessions; entered Selangor Civil Service as Magistrate, 1884; Chief Magistrate, Selangor, 1888; Senior Magistrate, Perak, 1892; on the federation of the Malay States in 1896 was appointed to be the First Commissioner of Lands and Mines; also chief examiner in the Malay language; acted as British Resident, Selangor on frequent occasions, 1897–1901; British Resident, Negri Sembilan, 1901; British Resident of Selangor, Federated Malay States, 1902–12; Acting British Resident, Perak, 1904; special mission to Labuan and Brunei, 1905; Acting Resident-General, Federated Malay States, May 1908; British Resident, Perak, 1911; Special Mission to Gold Coast and Ashanti to report on Land Tenure, 1912; Governor of East Africa Protectorate, 1912; also High Commissioner of Zanzibar, 1914; retired, 1918. JP Devonshire. *Publication:* The Handbook of the Federated Malay States. *Recreations:* shooting, fishing, reading. *Address:* 4 Roxburghe Mansion, Kensington Court, W8. *T:* Western 3565. *Clubs:* Junior Carlton, Bachelors', Ranelagh. *Died 8 Jan. 1923.*

BELFIELD, Major William Seymour, CMG 1919; *s* of late T. D. Belfield, Torquay; *m* 1924, Doris Evelyn, *d* of Rev. George Thompson, Rector of North Bovey, South Devon. Served European War, 1914–19 (despatches, CMG). *Address:* c/o Lloyds Bank, Cox and King's Branch, 6 Pall Mall, SW1.

Died 3 Nov. 1924.

BELHAVEN and STENTON, 10th Lord, *cr* 1647; **Alexander Charles Hamilton;** Scottish Representative Peer, 1900; JP, DL; *b* Tunbridge Wells, 3 July 1840; *s* of William John Hamilton, FRS, MP and Margaret Frances, *d* of 13th Lord Dillon; *S* kinsman, 1893; *m* 1880, Georgiana, *d* of Legh Richmond; one *s* decd. *Educ:* Woolwich. Church of England. Conservative. Entered RE 1857;

served in Zulu War, 1879; retired 1888, with rank of Colonel; commanded Surrey Vol. Brigade, 1888–1902; Territorial Decoration. On Council Royal Geographical Society. Owned 2,200 acres in Lanarkshire. *Heir: nephew* Lt-Col Robert Edward Archibald Hamilton, *b* 8 April 1871. *Address:* Wishaw House, Wishaw, NB; 41 Lennox Gardens, SW. *Club:* United Service. *Died 31 Oct. 1920.*

BELHAVEN, Master of; Hon. Ralph Gerard Alexander Hamilton; Major, Royal Field Artillery (formerly 3rd Hussars); *b* 22 Feb. 1883; *o s* of 10th Baron Belhaven and Stenton; *m* 1904, Lady Grizel Cochrane, *d* of 12th Earl of Dundonald. *Educ:* Eton; RM College, Sandhurst. Hon. Attaché to British Legation at Darmstadt, 1913 and 1914. *Address:* 1 St James's Terrace, Regent's Park, NW; Wishaw House, Wishaw, NB. *Club:* United Service.

Died 31 March 1918.

BELL, Capt. Adolphus Edmund, CBE 1919; *b* 1850. An Elder Brother of the Trinity House. *Address:* 23 Down Street, W1. *T:* Mayfair 4947. *Club:* Junior Athenæum.

Died 11 Sept. 1927.

BELL, Alexander Graham, LLD, PhD, DSc, MD; *b* Edinburgh, 3 March 1847; *s* of late Alexander Melville Bell and Eliza Grace, *d* of Dr Samuel Symonds, Surgeon, RN; *m* 1877, Mabel Gardiner, *d* of G. G. Hubbard; two *d. Educ:* Royal High School, Edinburgh; Edinburgh University; University College, London; Matriculated London University, 1867. Went to Canada, 1870; became Professor of Vocal Physiology, Boston Univ.; patented invention of telephone, 1876; invented also photophone, induction balance, and telephone probe, and (with C. A. Bell and Sumner Tainter) graphophone; has investigated laws of flight and studied education of the deaf. Founder and endower and late President, American Association to Promote Teaching of Speech to the Deaf; late President National Geographic Society; Regent Smithsonian Institution since 1898; received freedom of city of Edinburgh, 1920; awarded Volta Prix by French Govt, 1881; officier of French Legion of Honour; Prince Albert Medal (London Society of Fine Arts), 1902; Hughes Medal of Royal Society, 1913; Founder and endower Volta Bureau; Member National Academy of Sciences; and many foreign and American Societies. *Publications:* many scientific and educational monographs, including Memoir on the formation of Deaf Variety in the Human Race; Census Report on the Deaf of the United States, 1906; Lectures on the Mechanism of Speech, 1906. *Address:* 1331 Connecticut Avenue, Washington, DC, USA. *T:* Franklin 58; Beinn Bhreagh, near Baddeck, Nova Scotia. *Club:* Cosmos. *Died 2 Aug. 1922.*

BELL, Arthur George, RI, ROI; *b* parish of St Dunstan's, City of London; *s* of George Bell, publisher; *m* 1882, Nancy Meugens (writer, as N. D'Anvers); two *s* one *d. Educ:* Slade School; Ecole des Beaux Arts, Paris, under Gerôme. *Publications:* Nuremberg; Picturesque Brittany; Skirts of the Great City; The Royal Manor of Richmond; From Harbour to Harbour; etc. *Address:* York House, Portugal Street, WC; Rastgarth, Southbourne-on-Sea, Hants.

Died 24 Sept. 1916.

BELL, Edward, MA; FSA; Chairman of G. Bell & Sons, Ltd, publishers; *b* 1844; *e s* of late George Bell; *m* 1873, Alice (*d* 1917), 2nd *d* of Rev. J. W. van Rees Hoets, MA, formerly Vicar of Mowbray, Cape Colony; one *s* three *d. Educ:* St Paul's School; Trinity Coll., Cambridge. President Publishers Association, 1906–09; a Commissioner of Income and Land Tax. *Publications:* translator and editor of Goethe's Early Letters, Wilhelm Meister's Travels, and the Nibelungenlied; author of Architecture of Ancient Egypt; Prehellenic Architecture in the Ægean; Hellenic Architecture, Architecture of Western Asia, and of various papers on literature and art. *Recreations:* sketching, photography. *Address:* The Mount, Hampstead, NW; York House, Portugal Street, WC. *Clubs:* New University, Bath.

Died 8 Nov. 1926.

BELL, Francis Jeffrey; Emeritus Professor and Fellow of King's College, London; Assistant, British Museum, 1878–1919; since when he has been working for unemployed ex-officers. *Educ:* Magdalen College, Oxford (MA).Corr. Member Linnean Soc., New South Wales. *Publications:* Manual of Comparative Anatomy and Physiology; Catalogue of British Echinoderms in British Museum; editor of Catalogue of Madreporaria in British Museum, and of Natural History Reports of Voyage of the Discovery; Memoirs in Trans and Proc. Zool. Soc., Journal Linnean Society, etc. *Club:* Athenæum.

Died 1 April 1924.

BELL, Hon. George Alexander; late Provincial Treasurer and Minister of Telephones in the Government of Saskatchewan; *b* Brant

County, Ont., 3 Aug. 1856; 2nd *s* of David and Agnes Bell (Scotch); *m* 1883, Elizabeth Smith; four *s* three *d. Educ:* Public School No 1, Colborne Township, Huron County, Ontario. On farm till 20 years of age; blacksmith for 12 years; in the farm implement business; left Ontario for Western Canada, 1880. Clerk of County Court, Dominion Homestead Inspector; elected to Legislative Assembly, 1908; re-elected, 1912 and 1917; sworn in a member of the Executive Council of Saskatchewan, 1912; resigned seat in Leg. Assembly and Executive Council, June 1918; Chairman Local Government Board, June 1918. *Recreation:* golf. *Address:* Regina, Saskatchewan, Canada. *T:* 3021. *Club:* Regina Golf. *Died Sept. 1927.*

BELL, Gertrude Margaret Lowthian, CBE 1917; Oriental Secretary to the High Commissioner of the Iraq, Baghdad, since 1920; *b* 14 July 1868; *e d* of Sir Hugh Bell, 2nd Bt. *Educ:* Queen's College, London; Lady Margaret Hall, Oxford (1st Class History 1887). FRGS; Founder's Medal, 1918. Attached to Military Intelligence Dept, Cairo, 1915; liaison officer of Arab bureau in Iraq, 1916; Assistant Political Officer, Baghdad, 1917 (despatches four times). *Publications:* Safar Nameh, 1894; Poems from the Divan of Hafiz, 1897; The Desert and the Sown, 1907; The Thousand and One Churches, 1909 (in collaboration with Sir William M. Ramsay); Amurath to Amurath, 1911; Palace and Mosque at Ukhaider, 1914; Review of the Civil Administration of Mesopotamia, 1921. *Address:* Rounton Grange, Northallerton; 95 Sloane Street, SW1; Baghdad. *Died 12 July 1926.*

BELL, Rev. Henry; Hon. Canon of Carlisle; retired; *b* 1838; *s* of John Bell, Vicar of Rothwell, Yorkshire, Hon. Canon of Ripon, and Isabella Elizabeth, *d* of Sir Charles Loraine, 5th Bt, Kirkharle, Northumberland; *m* 1873, Katherine, *d* of Sir Peter FitzGerald, Knight of Kerry, 1st Bt; three *s* three *d. Educ:* Marlborough College; University College, Durham. Deacon, 1861; Priest, 1864; Hon. Canon of Carlisle, 1883; Proctor in Convocation, 1896; Assistant Master in Marlborough College, 1861–73; Vicar of Muncaster, Cumberland, 1873–1907; Chaplain to Lord Muncaster, 1873–1907; Rural Dean of Gosforth, 1878–1907, and Surrogate. *Recreation:* in the eleven which played the first match *v* Rugby at Lord's in 1855, was captain of eleven in 1856. *Address:* Eskilenca, St Jean de Luz, Basses-Pyrénées, France. *Died 11 June 1919.*

BELL, Rev. James, MA; Canon of Lincoln; *m* Eliza Mary, *d* of late Henry Peake. *Educ:* Corpus Christi College, Cambridge. Curate of New Sleaford, 1871–83; Dorrington, Lincs, 1883–85; Vicar of N Somercotes, Lincs, 1885–93; Rector of Kettlethorpe, 1893–1910; Rector of Risholme, 1913–15. *Address:* The Grove, Lincoln. *Died 3 April 1918.*

BELL, Maj.-Gen. Sir James Alexander, KCVO 1911; *b* 28 Jan. 1856; *s* of late Col James Giberne Bell; *m* 1880, Edith, *d* of late Colonel James Elphinston Robertson, 21st RS Fusiliers and Royal Warwicks; two *s* one *d. Educ:* Harrow. Joined 44th E Essex Regt, 1875; Indian Army, 1879; Commandant 42nd Deoli Regiment, 1889–99; Assistant Adjutant General Poona Division, 1899–1902; Bombay Command, 1902; Commandant School of Musketry, Satara, 1906–8; general officer commanding Belgaum and Lucknow Brigades, 1908–10; General Officer Commanding and Political Resident, Aden, 1910–19; retired, April 1919. *Recreations:* racquets, fishing, shooting. *Address:* The Wilderness, Sherborne, Dorsetshire. *M:* 6472. *Died 10 Nov. 1926.*

BELL, Alderman Sir John Charles, 1st Bt, *cr* 1908; Kt 1902; High Sheriff County of Bucks; Sheriff of the City of London, 1902; Lord Mayor, 1907–8; *b* 1844; *m* 1st, 1868, Caroline Elizabeth (*d* 1912), *e d* of Thomas Clare, Enfield; one *d*; 2nd, 1914, Ellen, *d* of late John James, Burgess Hill, Sussex. Joined the Court of Common Council as a representative of the ward of Coleman Street, 1882; elected by the ward of Coleman Street to represent them in the Court of Aldermen, 1894; on the court of the Haberdashers' Company; Master of Haberdashers', 1912–13; a past-master of Glovers' and Fanmakers' Companies, and on livery of Innholders', Loriners', and Spectacle-makers' Companies. JP, Bucks; Chairman of E Section of Commissioner for Income Tax for City; one of HM's Lieutenants for the City of London. Grand Officer of Legion of Honour; Commander of Prussian Order of Red Eagle (2nd class with star); received Coronation Medal, 1902; member of the No 1 Grand Master's Lodge, and also a member of the Grand Master Chapter in Royal Archmasonry; Past Grand Warden of Freemasons. *Heir:* none. *Address:* Framewood, Stoke Poges, Bucks; 165–167 Moorgate, EC. *Clubs:* City Carlton, Junior Carlton. *Died 2 Feb. 1924 (ext).*

BELL, John Keble, (pen-name "Keble Howard"); writer; *b* 8 Jun 1875; 3rd *s* of Rev. G. E. Bell, late Vicar of Henley-in-Arden Warwickshire. *Educ:* Worcester Coll., Oxford. Joined Sketch a assistant editor, 1899; editor of The Sketch, 1902–4; dramatic criti Daily Mail, 1904–8; founded Croydon Repertory Theatre, 1913 temporary commission in Royal Air Force, 1917; seconded to Ministr of Information, 1918. *Plays:* Compromising Martha, 1906; Marth Plays the Fairy, 1907; Charles, His Friend, 1907; The Dramatist a Home, 1909; Come Michaelmas, 1909; The Girl Who Couldn't Lie 1911; The Embarrassed Butler, 1912; Dropping the Pilot, 1913; The Cheerful Knave, 1914; The Green Flag, 1915; The Test Kiss, 1918 Lazy Lubin (America), 1920; Sweet William, 1921; The Smiths o Surbiton, 1922; Puss in the Corner, 1923; An Order to View, 1923 All in Train, 1924; Lord Babs, 1925. *Publications:* The Chicot Papers 1901; Letters to Dolly, 1902; Love and a Cottage, 1903; The Go in the Garden, 1904; Love in June, 1905; The Smiths of Surbiton 1906; The Whip Hand, 1906; The Bachelor Girls, 1907; Miss Charity 1908; The Smiths of Valley View, 1909; Potted Brains, 1909; The Cheerful Knave, 1910; The Happy Vanners, 1911; Chicot in America 1911; One of the Family, 1911; London Voices, 1913; Lord London 1913; So the World Wags, 1914; Merry-Andrew, 1915; Forke Lightning, 1916; Chin Music; The Gay Life, 1917; The Smiths in War-Time, 1918; The Adorable Lad, 1918; The Comedy of It; Tak One at Night; An Author in Wonderland; The Peculiar Major, 1919 Puck and Mr Purley, 1920; The Purleys of Wimbledon; King of the Castle, 1922; The Fast Lady, 1925; Chicot Calling, 1925; The Chico Club; Paradise Island, 1926; Lord Babs; My Motley Life, 1927 *Address:* 2 Brunswick Place, Hove. *T:* Hove 3256; Little Quay, Potte Heigham, Norfolk. *M:* PM 5198. *Clubs:* Constitutional; Susse County Cricket; Royal Norfolk and Suffolk Yacht; Yarmouth Yacht *Died 29 March 1928*

BELL, Ven. John White, MA; Archdeacon of Emly, 1918; Incumbent of Cappamore, 1878; Rural Dean, Doone, 1894. *Educ:* Trinit College, Dublin. Canon and Treasurer of Cashel Cathedral, 1900 retired, 1920. *Address:* 10 Summer Hill, Kingstown, Co. Dublin. *Died July 1928*

BELL, Lt-Col John William, CMG 1900; VD; JP; *b* Edinburgh, Oct. 1844; *s* of William Bell, native of Dumfries, Scotland (Bells o Blacket House), late of Grahamstown, South Africa, advocate; *m* 1873 Eliza Jane Bradfield, 4th *d* of Edward Mortimer Turvey, one of Britis settlers of 1820; two *s* two *d. Educ:* High School, Edinburgh. Solicitor practised at Queenstown, South Africa; mem. of Queenstown Rifl Volunteers since formation of corps in 1873; in command since 1881 S African war medal, 1877–78; was granted long service medal, 1898 volunteer officer's decoration (20 years' commissioned service); South African Campaign, 1899–1900 (despatches, medal and three clasps) Master of the Supreme Court of the Transvaal, 1901–6. *Address* Nairobi, British East Africa. *Died 27 May 1928*

BELL, Louis, PhD; MAIEE; Consulting Engineer; *b* New Hampshire 1864; *s* of late Gen. Louis Bell, USA. *Educ:* Dartmouth Coll.; John Hopkins University. Past Manager, AIEE; Fellow and Membe Rumford Committee, American Academy of Arts and Sciences; Pas Pres., Illuminating Engineering Society; Member, National Electric Light Association, American Astronomical Society, Nationa Geographical Society, American Association for the Advancemen of Science; President, Massachusetts Rifle Association; Technica Officer, Volunteer Electrical Corps, 1898; Lecturer, Mass Institute of Technology, 1895–1905; Lecturer, Harvard Univ., 1914–18 Mem., International Electrotechnical Commission; Internationa Illumination Commission; Advisory Commission Council of Nationa Defence. *Publications:* The Elements of Practical Electricity; Powe Distribution for Electric Railroads; Electrical Power Transmission The Art of Illumination; The Telescope. *Address:* 120 Boylston Street Boston, Mass; 32 Sylvan Avenue, West Newton, Mass. *Clubs* Examiner, Engineers', Boston. *Died 14 June 1923*

BELL, Lt-Col Matthew Gerald Edward; Lieutenant-Colonel Specia Reserve, 6th Battalion Rifle Brigade; *b* 24 July 1871; *s* of Captain M J. Bell, *e s* of Matthew Bell of Bourne Park, and Kathleen Matilda *d* of John Reilly and Augusta, *d* of 1st Lord St Leonards; *m* 1905, Hon Mary (Maid of Honour to Queen Alexandra), *d* of Rt Hon. Si William Dyke, 7th Bt; one *s. Educ:* Eton. Joined Rifle Brigade, 1893 served Indian Frontier, Tochi Valley, Signalling Officer 1st Brigade (medal and clasp); Somaliland Field Force (despatches, medal and clasp); retired from regular army, 1909; Staff, Aug. 1914–Sept. 1919 *Recreations:* shooting, fishing, tennis, golf. *Address:* Bourne Park Canterbury, Kent. *T:* Bridge 11. *TA:* Bridge. *Clubs:* Marlborough Princes Racquet; St Georges, Sandwich. *Died 8 May 1926*

BELL, Robert, ISO 1903; DSc (Cantab and M'Gill); MD, CM (M'Gill); LLD (Queen's); FGS (L and A), FRSC, FRS, 1897; late Director and Chief Geologist Geological Survey of Canada; *b* Toronto, 3 June 1841; *s* of late Rev. Andrew Bell and *g s* of late Rev. William Bell, both of Church of Scotland; *m* Agnes, *d* of late Alex. Smith of Westbourne, Glasgow, and Auchentroig, Stirlingshire; one *s* three *d. Educ:* Grammar School of the county of Prescott; M'Gill and Edinburgh Universities. FCS, 1865; member of American Institute of Mining Engineers, 1881; hon. member Medico-Chirurgical Society, Montreal, and of Ottawa; FAAAS; one of foundation Fellows of Royal Society of Canada; Member of Government Geographical Board. Joined Geological Survey of Canada, 1857; has made very extensive topographical and geological surveys in nearly all parts of the Dominion since 1857; the Bell River or W branch of the Nottaway, which he surveyed in 1895, is officially named after him; was medical officer, naturalist, and geologist of "Neptune" expedition in 1884, and of "Alert" expedition in 1885 to Hudson's Strait and Bay; was also geologist on the "Diana" expedition in 1897, when he surveyed the south coast of Baffinland and penetrated to the great lakes of its interior; among the rivers he has surveyed are the Athabasca, Slave, Peace, Churchill, Nelson, Hayes and branches, the Winnipeg, English, Albany, Kenogami, Nipigon, Moose and its numerous branches, the Harricanaw, Broadback, Nottaway and its branches, the upper Gatineau and most of the rivers of northern Ontario; also the first surveys of some of largest lakes of Canada, including Great Slave, Nipigon, Seul, Osnaburgh, Timagami, and parts of Athabasca, Winnipeg, and Lake of the Woods. Delegate from the Dominion Government and the Royal Society of Canada to the Internat. Geol. Congress, Vienna, 1903; has been Canadian cor. of the Royal Scottish Geographical Soc. from its foundation; Canadian cor. of la Société de Géographie; Fellow of the Royal Ast. Soc. of Canada; was a Royal Comdr on the Mineral Resources of Ontario, 1888–89; Professor of Chemistry and Natural Science in Queen's Univ. Kingston, 1863–67; Hon. Chief of Algonquin Indians of Grand Lake; Pres. International Congress of Americanists, 1906; King's or Patron's gold medal of the Royal Geographical Society of London, 1906; Cullum gold medal of the Am. Geographical Society, 1906. *Publications:* over 200 reports and papers, mostly on geology, biology, geography, and folk-lore. *Recreations:* study of the forests and mammals of Canada, and folk-lore and archæology of the North American Indians. *Address:* 136 Maclaren Street, Ottawa, Canada. *TA:* Geologist, Ottawa. *T:* Queen 2139. *Club:* Rideau, Ottawa.   *Died 20 June 1917.*

BELL, Robert, MD, MB; FRFPS, etc; Consulting Physician; Vice-President of International Cancer Research Society; Superintendent of Cancer Research, Battersea Hospital; *b* 6 Jan. 1845; *s* of William Bell, Alnwick, and Annie Turnbull, Alnwick; *m* Clara Ellen, *d* of late George Sims; one *s* two *d. Educ:* Alnwick Grammar School; Glasgow University; Paris. Commenced practice in Glasgow, 1868; Senior Physician to Glasgow Hospital for Women, 1876–97; Consulting Physician, which ceased on departing to take up consulting work in London, 1904. *Publications:* Cancer, its Cause and Treatment without Operation; Prevention of Cancer; Conquest of Cancer; Reminiscences of an Old Physician; several brochures on Dietetics; contributions to Lancet, British Med. Jl. and Med. Times, also to American Medical Journals. *Recreations:* fishing, shooting. *Address:* 15 Half Moon Street, W1. *T:* Grosvenor 1201; 10 Thorney Court, W8. *T:* Kensington 6491. *TA:* Bell, Thorneydom, London. *Club:* Devonshire.   *Died 20 Jan. 1926.*

BELL, Robert Stanley Warren; author; *b* 1871; *e s* of G. E. Bell, late Vicar of Henley-in-Arden, Warwickshire; *m* 1905, Edithe M. Barry. *Educ:* St John's, Leatherhead. Editor of The Captain, 1899–1910. *Publications:* The Cub in Love, 1897; The Papa Papers, 1898; Bachelorland, 1899; Tales of Greyhouse; Love the Laggard, 1901; J. O. Jones, 1903; Jim Mortimer, 1904; The Duffer, 1905; Cox's Cough-Drops, 1906; Green at Greyhouse, 1908; Company for George, 1911; Black Evans, 1912; Mystery of Markham, 1913; Dormitory Eight, 1914; The Secret Seven, Smith's Week, 1915; Young Couples, The Three Prefects, Greyhouse Days, 1918; Happy Beginnings, 1919; Comedy: Company for George (Kingsway Theatre), 1910. *Address:* 4 Cranley Avenue, Westcliff-on-Sea. *Club:* Press.   *Died 26 Sept. 1921.*

BELL, Very Rev. Thomas; Dean of Guernsey since 1892; Hon. Canon of Winchester; Rector of the Vale, Guernsey, 1859–1914; *b* 1820; *m. Educ:* Exeter Coll., Oxford (MA). Ordained, 1845; Curate of Finstock, Oxford, 1845–48; St Mathew, City Road, 1848–51; Burston, Norfolk, 1851–53; The Vale, Guernsey, 1853–59; Vice-Dean of Guernsey, 1880–92. *Address:* Guernsey.
     Died 31 Oct. 1917.

BELL, Rev. William; Vicar of Cranbrook, Kent, since 1898; Hon. Canon of Canterbury Cathedral since 1904; Rural Dean of West Charing, 1901; *s* of William Bell, Highberries, Cumberland; widower; one *s* one *d. Educ:* St Bees' School; Christ's College, Cambridge (Scholar); Second Class Classical Tripos, 1866. Assistant Master, Royal Grammar School, and Curate of Christ Church, Lancaster, 1866–71; first Head Master of Dover College, 1871; Vicar of Parish Church, Sittingbourne, 1892–98; Rural Dean of Sittingbourne, 1897–98; Assessor under Clergy Discipline Act, 1906: Hon Secretary of Diocesan Board of Education, 1899–1913. *Address:* Cranbrook Vicarage, Kent. *TA:* Cranbrook.
     Died 10 Dec. 1918.

BELL, William Abraham; *b* 26 April 1841; *o s* of late William Bell, MD, and Margaret, *d* of Abraham Grubb, of Merlin, Clonmel; *m* 1872, Cara Georgina Whitmore, *d* and *co-heir* of Whitmore Scovell, of Waddon, Surrey; one *s* three *d. Educ:* Ipswich Grammar School; Trinity Hall, Cambridge (MA, 1865; MB, 1866). *Address:* Pendell Court, Blechingley; 8 Park Street, W.
     Died 6 June 1920.

BELL-IRVING, John, JP; *b* 2 Feb. 1846; *e s* of late John Bell-Irving and Mary, *d* of David Jardine of Muirhousehead, Dumfries; *m* 1884, Isabella, *d* of Henry Thornton; one *s* two *d.* Late MLC Hong-Kong; formerly a partner in the firm of Jardine Matheson and Co. of Hong Kong and China. *Address:* White Hill, Lockerbie; Milkbank, Lockerbie. *TA:* Kettleholm. *M:* GA 818, GA 5999. *Club:* Dumfries and Galloway, Dumfries.   *Died 30 July 1925.*

BELL-SMITH, Frederick Marlett, RCA; artist; Member of Council of the Royal Canadian Academy of Arts; Life Member Ontario Society of Artists, 1904–8; *b* London, 26 Sept. 1846; *s* of late John Bell Smith, artist; *m* 1871, Annie Myra Dyde; one *s. Educ:* London. Studied drawing at South Kensington; went to Canada, 1867; charter member Society of Canadian Artists, 1867; Member Royal British Colonial Society of Artists, London, since its formation; served in Volunteers in suppressing Fenian invasion, 1870 (medal); Director of Fine Arts, Alma College, since 1881; teacher of drawing, public schools, London, Ontario, 1882–89; Director Toronto Art School, 1889–91; lecturer and writer on Art subjects. *Principal pictures:* Queen Victoria's Tribute to Canada (for which Her Majesty gave personal sittings); Landing of the Blenheim, National Collection, Ottawa; Whitehead, Diploma work, Nat. Coll.; Lights of a City Street, Ontario Collection; has exhibited at Royal Academy and other principal exhibitions. *Recreations:* annual visits to Rocky Mountains of Canada, and has made some ascents; member of Canadian Alpine Club. *Address:* 336 Jarvis Street, Toronto, Ontario, Canada. *Clubs:* Arts and Letters, Palette, Canadian, Toronto.   *Died 23 June 1923.*

BELL-SMYTH, Brig.-Gen. John Ambard, CB 1919; CMG 1916; late 1st Dragoon Guards; *b* 1868; *m* 1921, Dorothy, *d* of late Dr Charles Sharp Smith, Canford Cliffs, Bournemouth. *Educ:* Oratory School. Served S Africa, 1899–1900 (despatches, Bt Major, Queen's medal, 6 clasps); European War, 1914–18 (despatches, CB, CMG, Bt Col); retired, 1920.   *Died 24 March 1922.*

BELLAMY, Sir Joseph Arthur, Kt 1904; JP; Mayor of Plymouth, 1901–2; *b* 6 Sept. 1845; *m* 1868, Susan Mill (*d* 1908), *d* of William Saul Wills of Plymouth; one *s* two *d.* Past Chairman, Chamber of Commerce; Chairman, Plymouth Gas Co. and Sutton Harbour Co. *Address:* Yalta, Mannamead, Plymouth.
     Died 1 March 1918.

BELLAMY, Lt-Col Robert, DSO 1900; late Royal Sussex Regiment; *b* 29 Nov. 1871; *s* of late Col P. L. Bellamy, Border Regiment; *m* 1903, Constance Gwendoline, *e d* of late Col Alfred Borton, Welsh Regt; two *s.* Entered Army, 1894; Adjutant, 1900; Captain, 1902; Lt-Col 1920; served South Africa, 1899–1902; European War, 1914–18; retired pay, 1925.   *Died 29 April 1927.*

BELLASIS, Edward, JP; Lancaster Herald, 1882; *b* 1852; 2nd *s* of Mr Serjeant Bellasis and Eliza Jane, *d* of William Garnett of Quernmore Park, Lancashire. *Educ:* Oratory School, Edgbaston. Barrister-at-law, 1873. Bluemantle Pursuivant, 1873; Secretary to the Garter Missions to Spain, 1881; Saxony, 1882; Registrar of College of Arms, 1894–99; Unionist; Catholic. *Publications:* Cherubini: Memorials Illustrative of his Life, 1874–1912; Laws of Arms, Chiefly in Connection with Changes of Name, 1879; Westmorland Church Notes (2 vols), 1888–89; Memorials of Mr Serjeant Bellasis, 1893–95; Money Jar of Plautus, 1885; New Terence, etc; Facsimile edn Gerontius; Coram Cardinali, 1917. *Recreations:* music, church history, cycling. *Address:* 90 Hagley Road, Edgbaston.   *Died 17 March 1922.*

BELLINGHAM, Sir (Alan) Henry, 4th Bt (2nd creation) *cr* 1796; MA, SCL Oxford, LLD Dublin; JP; HM's Lieutenant, Louth; *b* 23 Aug. 1846; *er s* of Sir Alan Edward Bellingham, 3rd Bt and Elizabeth Clarke, W Skirbeck House, Lincs; *S* father 1889; *m* 1st, 1874, Lady Constance Julia Eleanor Georgiana Noel (*d* 1891), *d* of 2nd Earl of Gainsborough; two *s* two *d*; 2nd 1895, Hon. Lelgarde Clifton, *d* of 23rd Baroness Grey de Ruthyn. *Educ:* Harrow; Exeter College, Oxford. Barrister, 1876; Captain, 5th Battalion Royal Irish Rifles; Commissioner of National Education, Ireland; MP Co. Louth, 1880; Private Chamberlain, Pius IX, Leo XIII and Pius X; Senator of the Royal University. Owned about 6,000 acres. *Publications:* Social Aspects: Catholicism *v* Protestantism, 1878; articles in Dublin Review, Month, Catholic World, and CTS. *Recreation:* gardening. *Heir: s* Brig.-Gen. Edward Henry Charles Bellingham, *b* 26 Jan. 1879. *Address:* Castle Bellingham, Co. Louth, Ireland. *Clubs:* United University, Junior Travellers'; United Service, Dublin.
Died 9 June 1921.

BELLOT, Hugh Hale Leigh, MA, DCL; Barrister-at-law; Membre de l'Institut de Droit International; *b* 19 Oct. 1860; *o surv. s* of William Henry Bellot, MD, FRCS, 3rd Batt. Cheshire Regiment, and Frances Leigh, *d* of John Egerton Killer, late of Millgate Hall, Stockport; *m* 1888, Beatrice Violette (*d* 1927), *y d* of Charles Clarke, late of Chorlton-cum-Hardy; one *s*. *Educ:* Leamington Coll.; Trinity Coll., Oxford. Called to Bar, Inner Temple, 1890; Hon. Sec. International Law Association and Grotius Society; formerly Acting Professor of Constitutional Law, University of London; Secretary, Breaches of the Laws of War Committee. *Publications:* Ireland and Canada; Unconscionable Bargains with Moneylenders; The Inner and Middle Temple; The Miner's Guide; Bargains with Moneylenders; Commerce in War; Law of Children and Young Persons; The Pharmacy Acts; Pitt Cobbett's Leading Cases on Int. Law, 4th edn; Permanent Court of International Justice; The Temple; Foot's Private Int. Law, 5th edn; Gray's Inn and Lincoln's Inn; La Théorie Anglo-Saxonne des conflits de lois; Thomas's Leading Cases in Constitutional Law, 6th edn; contributor to Reviews, etc. *Address:* 10 Gray's Inn Place, WC; The Mill, High Ham, Somerset; 2 King's Bench Walk, Temple, EC. *T:* City 1066. *TA:* Temple 41.
Died 11 Aug. 1928.

BELMONT, August; banker; *b* New York, 18 Feb. 1853; *s* of late August Belmont; *m* 1910, Eleanor Robson. *Educ:* Harvard. Head of August Belmont & Co. *Address:* 45 Cedar Street, New York.
Died 10 Dec. 1924.

BELSHAW, Edward, ISO 1904; *m* 1st, Mary Ann (*d* 1909), *e d* of late James Couchman of Kensington; 2nd, Gertrude, *widow* of Rev. M. B. O'Connor of Fulneck, Leeds. Late Chief Clerk, Board of Education, South Kensington. *Address:* 49 Lee Terrace, Blackheath, SE. *T:* 1249 Lee Green.
Died 29 Jan. 1916.

BENBOW, Sir Henry, KCB 1902; DSO 1891; Chief Inspector of Machinery, RN; retired 1893; *b* 5 Sept. 1888; 5th *s* of late James Benbow, of Thornton Heath, Surrey, and Caroline, *d* of late Benjamin Parrey; *m* 1892, Elizabeth Jean, *o d* of late Henry Bird, Uxbridge, Middlesex; one *d*. *Educ:* private school. Entered RN as Asst Engineer, 1861; became Chief Engineer, 1879; promoted (for gallantry in Action) to Inspector of Machinery, 1885; and Chief Inspector Machinery, 1888; served with Naval Brigade in Nile Expedition, 1884–85 (medal, bronze star), and repaired under heavy fire from the enemy the boiler of the "Safia", when disabled from a shot from Fort Wad Habeshi; specially mentioned in despatches. *Decorated* for services with Nile Expedition. *Address:* Osborne House, Eastbourne.
Died 20 Oct. 1916.

BENCKENDORFF, Count de, (Alexandre); Russian Ambassador in London since 1903; *b* Berlin, 1 Aug. 1849; *s* of Constantin, Comte de Benckendorff, and Louise, Princesse de Croÿ-Dülmen; *m* 1879, Sophie, Comtesse Schouvaloff; one *s* one *d*. *Educ:* France; Germany. Entered diplomatic service, 1869; hon. attaché Rome and Vienna; left diplomatic service, 1876; re-entered it as 1st Secretary at Vienna, 1886; Russian Minister at Copenhagen, 1897–1903. *Address:* Chesham House, Chesham Place, SW. *Clubs:* Turf, St James's, Marlborough, Travellers', Beefsteak.
Died 11 Jan. 1917.

BENDALL, Ernest Alfred, MVO 1917; late Joint Examiner of Plays, St James's Palace, 1912–20; *b* 31 Aug. 1846; *s* of late Alfred Bendall of Shortlands, Kent; *m* 1868, Agnes (*d* 1918), *d* of late William Chatterley; no *c*. *Educ:* Edinburgh Academy; City of London School. Clerk in Paymaster-General's Office, 1866; retired 1896. Began journalism on London Figaro when in succession to Clement Scott and as predecessor to William Archer he wrote as Almaviva about

the theatres, till in 1874, Edward Dicey, CB, made him Dramatic Critic of the Observer. This position, together with a similar one on the Daily Mail, he was holding till he resigned both on his appointment in February 1912 as Joint-Examiner of Plays in the Lord Chamberlain's Office. He was Dramatic Critic to the St James's Gazette during the whole of late Frederick Greenwood's editorship, has from time to time done similar work for the Morning Post, the Standard and the Daily News, and may be regarded, if any one regards dramatic critics, as having been the *doyen* of his craft. *Recreations:* billiards, travel. *Address:* Queen Anne's Mansions SW.
Died 12 July 1924.

BENEDITE, Leonce; Conservator Musée du Luxembourge, et du Musée Rodin, Paris; Président, Société des Peintres Graveurs des Lithographes et des Peintres Orientalistes. Hon. Member, The Senefelder Club; Officier de la Légion d'honneur. Many publications of modern art.
Died May 1925.

BENGOUGH, Maj.-Gen. Sir Harcourt Mortimer, KCB 1908 (CB 1886); *b* 25 Nov. 1837; *s* of George Bengough of The Ridge, Gloucester; *m* 1876, Christina, *d* of H. Maybery. *Educ:* Rugby. Entered 77th Regt 1855; Maj.-Gen., 1894; retired, 1898. Served Crimea, 1855; the Zulu Campaign, 1878–79 (despatches, medal with clasp, Brevet Lt-Col); Burma expedition, 1885–86 (despatches, medal with clasp); AAG, Madras, 1882–86; commanded 2nd class district, Madras, 1886–91; troops in Jamaica, 1893–94; 1st Infantry Brigade, Aldershot, 1894–97. *Publications:* Preparatory Battle Formations, 2nd edn 1900; Notes on Boer War, 1901; Night Fighting, from the Russian; Memories of a Soldier's Life, 1913. *Address:* Hyde Brae, Chalford, Gloucester.
Died 30 March 1922.

BENN, Alfred William, BA London; Member of the Society for the Promotion of Hellenic Studies; *b* Moylescar Rectory, Westmeath, Ireland, 1843; *y s* of late Rev. Wm Benn, BD, and Mary, *d* of the Rev. Wm Dunn, Rector of Charleville, Co. Cork, Ireland; *m* 1886, Edith Maude, BA London, *y d* of late Edward Thomson of Tunbridge Wells. *Educ:* chiefly at home. 1st class Classical Honours, and 3rd class Honours in Logic and Moral Philosophy at the second BA Examination, University of London. Matriculated at the University of London, 1864; graduated BA 1865. Left England, 1866, and lived abroad ever since, chiefly in Italy and Switzerland; on the staff of the Academy, 1885–97; represented London University at the Philosophical Congress, Bologna, 1911. *Publications:* The Greek Philosophers, 2 vols 1882, 2nd edn revised and partly rewritten, 1914; The Philosophy of Greece, 1898; The History of English Rationalism in the Nineteenth Century, 2 vols, 1906; Modern England, 2 vols, 1908; A Primer of Early Greek Philosophy, 1908; Revaluations, 1909; History of Ancient Philosophy; History of Modern Philosophy (History of Science Series), 1912. *Recreations:* astronomy, book-collecting, cycling. *Address:* Il Ciliegio, Via del Palmerino, Florence, Italy. *Clubs:* Royal Societies, Authors', London University.
Died 16 Sept. 1916.

BENN, Sir John (Williams), 1st Bt, *cr* 1914; Kt 1906; JP, DL; Chairman, LCC, 1904; *b* Hyde, Cheshire, 13 Nov. 1850; *e s* of Rev. Julius Benn and Ann, *d* of William Taylor of Gerrards, Cheshire; *m* Lily, 4th *d* of late John Pickstone of Silver Hill, Hyde, Cheshire; four *s* two *d*. MP (L) St George's, E, 1892–95; contested Deptford, 1897; Bermondsey, 1900; member of LCC since its creation 1889; chairman, 1904–5; MP (L) Devonport, 1904–10; contested Clapham, 1910; late chairman of the General Purposes and of the Highways Committee. *Recreations:* sketching, golf. *Heir: s* Ernest John Benn [*b* 25 June 1875; *m* 1903, Gwendoline Dorothy, *y d* of Frederick M. Andrews, of Edgbaston]. *Address:* Stone Wall, Limpsfield, Surrey. *T:* Oxted 161.
Died 10 April 1922.

BENNETT, Alfred Rosling, MIEE; Past Vice-President, Institution of Locomotive Engineers; *b* London, 1850; unmarried. *Educ:* Bellevue Academy. General Manager and Chief Engineer for Scotland and North of England to the National Telephone Co., 1883–90; subsequently General Manager and Chief Engineer to the Mutual Telephone Co. and the New Telephone Co.; Engineer to the Municipal Telephone Exchange systems at Glasgow, Guernsey, Portsmouth, Hull, Brighton, and Swansea; Vice-Chairman Executive Council, Edinburgh International Exhibition, 1890; Inventor of the Telephonic Translator, 1880; the Caustic Alkali and Iron Battery, 1881; and Convection Mill, 1896. *Publications:* A Cheap Form of Voltaic Battery, 1882; An Electrical Parcels Exchange, 1892; Telephone Systems of Continental Europe, 1895; A Convection-Scope and Calorimeter, 1897; Proposals for London Improvements, 1904; Historic Locomotives, 1906; The First Railway in London, 1912; A Saga of Guernsey, 1918; London and Londoners in the 1850s and 1860s, 1924; and numerous pamphlets on telephonic subjects and papers contributed to scientific societies. *Recreations:* travel, research. *Club:* Engineers.   *Died 24 May 1928.*

BENNETT, George Lovett, MA Cambridge; Headmaster of Sutton Valence School, 1883–1910; *b* 28 March 1846; *s* of late Edmund Bennett of Florence, 3rd *s* of late George Bennett, QC, of Grange, King's County, and Merrion Square, Dublin; *m* 1874, Emma Lucretia, *d* of Joseph Sheridan Le Fanu, of Merrion Square, Dublin; two *d.* *Educ:* Rugby School; St John's Coll., Cambridge (Scholar). Second Class Classical Tripos, 1869; Assistant Master Rugby School, 1875; Headmaster Plymouth College, 1877. *Publications:* Easy Latin Stories; First and Second Latin Writers; Second Latin Reader; Viri Illustres; Selections from Cæsar; Selections from Virgil. *Recreations:* riding, cycling, shooting, fishing. *Address:* East Sutton, near Maidstone. *Club:* Constitutional.   *Died 30 Nov. 1916.*

BENNETT, George Wheatley, ISO 1903; *b* 22 Aug. 1845; *s* of Richard Wheatley Bennett, Demerara and London; *m* 1875, Kathleen, *d* of Charles Glenton; one *s.* Entered the Civil Service as a clerk in the Customs, 1863; Accountant and Comptroller-General of Customs, 1902; retired 1906. *Recreations:* mainly literary. *Address:* 82 Milton Park, Highgate, N6. *Club:* Constitutional.
                                                          Died 12 Nov. 1921.

BENNETT, James Gordon; Proprietor of the New York Herald; *b* 10 May 1841; *m* 1914, Baroness de Reuter. Commissioned the late Sir Henry Morton Stanley "to find Livingstone." Owned yacht "Namouna." *Address:* 28 West 21st Street, New York; 120 Avenue des Champs Elysées, Paris. *T:* 524, 49. *Clubs:* Automobile, Polo, Yacht.   *Died 14 May 1918.*

BENNETT, Engineer Rear-Adm. James Martin Cameron, MVO 1902. Assistant Engineer, 1871; Chief Engineer, 1887; Engineer Captain, 1892; served Perak Expedition, 1885–86 (medal and clasp); Engineer Captain HM Yacht Victoria and Albert, 1903. *Address:* Boldrewood, Winn Road, Southampton.
                                                                  Died 1922.

BENNETT, Sir Thomas Jewell, Kt 1921; CIE 1903; JP, Kent; MP (U) Sevenoaks Division of Kent, 1918–23; Principal Proprietor of the Times of India; *b* 1852; *s* of late J. T. Bennett, of Wisbech, Cambridgeshire; *m* 1917, Elena, 2nd *d* of late Thomas Brooke-Jones. Took to journalism early in life; was for some years assistant editor of the Western Daily Press at Bristol; joined the leader-writing staff of the Standard; proceeded to Bombay, 1884; for eight years associate-editor of the Bombay Gazette; succeeded to the editorship and the principal proprietary interest in the Times of India; when he left India in 1901, he was presented by 3,000 of the agriculturists of Guzerat with an address thanking him for the successful persistency with which he had brought the grievances of the cultivating class to the notice of Government; awarded the silver medal of the Society of Arts for a paper on the British connection with the Persian Gulf, 1902; nominated by the Bombay Government a Fellow of the Bombay Univ. Contested (U) Brigg Div. of Lincolnshire 1910; a representative of Rochester Diocese in the National Assembly of the Church of England. *Address:* 38 Ham Place, SW. *T:* Kensington 306; Harwarton House, Speldhurst, Tunbridge Wells. *T:* Tunbridge Wells 779. *Clubs:* Carlton, Oriental; Byculla, Royal Yacht, Bombay.
                                                               Died 16 Jan. 1925.

BENNETT, William H., KC; Senator, Canada, Nov. 1917; *b* Barrie, 23 Dec. 1859; *m* 1905, Margaret A., *d* of Henry Cargill, MP. *Educ:* Barrie High School. MP for East Simcoe, 1892–1917. *Address:* Midland, Ontario, Canada.
                                                             Died 15 March 1925.

BENNETT, William Hart, CMG 1909; FRCI; Governor of British Honduras since 1918; *b* 4 June 1861; *s* of Hart Bennett, CE; *m* 1899, Ella Mary (*d* 1914), *y d* of late Charles Tuck, JP, of Norwich; no *c.* Entered Colonial Office, 1878; chief clerk, Chief Secretary's Office, Cyprus, 1884–1900; Acting Comr, Paphos, 1894; Asst Secretary to Govt, 1895; Colonial Secretary, Falklands, 1900–5; acted as Governor of the Falklands and Bahamas on many occasions; Member of the West India Committee; Colonial Secretary, Bahamas, 1905–17. *Address:* Government House, British Honduras. *Club:* Royal Societies.
                                                              Died 4 Sept. 1918.

BENNETT-GOLDNEY, Francis, FSA; MP (C), since 1910, and Mayor of the City and County of Canterbury; *b* Moseley, near Birmingham, 1865; 2nd *s* of late Sebastian Evans, MA, LLD, author, artist, and journalist, and *nephew* of late Sir John Evans, KCB, FRS.

Educ: privately Bournemouth, Paris. Assumed mother's name of Goldney, 1892. Post of Hon. Director of the Royal Museum at Canterbury; Hon. Freeman and Alderman of the City; Governor of the Kent and Canterbury Hospital, and of the Simon Langton Schools; formerly Captain 6th Militia Batt. the Middlesex Regiment; Member Territorial Association for the County of Kent. *Recreations:* writing, riding, fencing, swimming. *Address:* Abbott Barton, Canterbury; Devonshire Terrace, Sandgate.   *Died 27 July 1918.*

BENNING, Captain Charles Stuart, DSO 1916; RN; *b* 28 Nov. 1884; 2nd *s* of Crichton S. Benning, The Limes, Dunstable, Beds: *m* 1908, Effie, 2nd *d* of R. Byrth Rowson, Warrington; two *d* one *s. Educ:* Dunstable. Joined HMS Britannia, 1899; passed out as Midshipman; passed examination for Lieutenant with five firsts, receiving Admiralty prize for meritorious examination; Lieut, 1905; joined submarine service, 1905; appointed E5, 1914; present at Battle of Heligoland Bight, 28 Aug. (despatches); Commander, June 1915; Captain, 1920; awarded DSO for services in submarines in enemy's waters, Oct. 1916; in command of British Submarines in the Mediterranean, 1918 (despatches, Order of Crown of Italy). *Address:* c/o Admiralty, SW1.   *Died 7 March 1924.*

BENSON, Arthur Christopher, CVO 1907; LLD (Hon.) Cambridge, 1915; MA; FRHistS, FRSL; Master of Magdalene College, Cambridge, since 1915; Member of the Academic Committee; Member of the Court of the Fishmongers' Company; Governor of Gresham's School, Holt; *b* 24 April 1862; *s* of late Archbishop of Canterbury, Most Rev. Edward White Benson and Mary Sidgwick; unmarried. *Educ:* Eton; King's College, Cambridge (Scholar). First class Classics, 1884; Master at Eton College, 1885–1903; Fellow of Magdalene College, Cambridge, 1904–15. *Publications:* Memoirs of Arthur Hamilton, 1886; Archbishop Laud: a study, 1887; Men of Might (with Mr H. F. W. Tatham), 1890; Poems, 1893; Lyrics, 1895; Essays, 1896; Lord Vyet and other Poems, 1896; Fasti Etonenses (a Biographical History of Eton College), 1899; Life of Archbishop Benson, 1899; The Professor, and other poems, 1900; The Schoolmaster, 1902; The House of Quiet, 1903; Tennyson (Little Biographies Series); Selections from Whittier, 1903; The Hill of Trouble, 1903; The Isles of Sunset, 1904; Rossetti, English Men of Letters Series, 1904; Peace and other Poems, 1905; Edward FitzGerald, English Men of Letters Series, 1905; The Upton Letters, 1905; The Thread of Gold, 1906; Walter Pater, English Men of Letters Series 1906; From a College Window, 1906; The Gate of Death, 1906; Beside Still Waters, 1907; The Altar Fire, 1907; Selections from the Correspondence of Queen Victoria (edited, with Viscount Esher), 1907; At Large, 1908; Poems (Collected), 1909; The Silent Isle, 1910; Ruskin: a Study in Personality, 1911; The Leaves of the Tree, 1911; The Child of the Dawn, 1912; Thy Rod and Thy Staff, 1912; Along the Road; Joyous Gard; Watersprings, 1913; Where No Fear Was; The Orchard Pavilion, 1914; Hugh: Memoirs of a Brother; Escape and Other Essays, 1915; Father Payne, 1916; Life and Letters of Maggie Benson, 1917; The Reed of Pan, Selections from Ruskin, A Little History of Magdalene College, The Trefoil 1923; Memories and Friends, 1924. *Recreations:* football till 1889; Alpine Club, 1894; bicycling, etc. *Address:* The Old Lodge, Magdalene College, Cambridge; Lamb House, Rye. *Clubs:* Alpine, Royal Societies, Athenæum.   *Died 17 June 1925*

BENSON, Maj.-Gen. Sir Frederick William, KCB 1910 (CB 1901); retired; Colonel, 21st Lancers; Hon. Colonel, 19th St Catharine's Regiment, Canadian Militia; *b* St Catharine's, Canada, 2 August 1849; 3rd *s* of late Hon. J. R. Benson, of the Canadian Senate, and Marianne, *d* of late Charles Ingersoll, of Ingersoll, Canada; *m* 1881, Caroline, *d* of late Sir George Couper, 2nd Bt, KCSI. *Educ:* Upper Canada College, Toronto; RMC, Sandhurst. Served as Volunteer during Fenian raids in Canada, 1866 (medal with clasp); joined 21st Hussars, 1869; exchanged to 12th Royal Lancers, 1876; passed Staff College 1880; Captain, 5th Dragoon Guards, 1880; exchanged to 17th Lancers, 1881; ADC to Lieut-Governor, North-West Provinces, India, 1877; Brigade-Major, Poona, 1882–84; Garrison Instructor, Bengal, 1884–90; commanded Egyptian cavalry, 1892–94; DAAG (Instruction) Dublin, 1895–98; Assistant Adjutant-General, Chief Staff Officer, South-Eastern District, 1898–1900; special service S Africa, AAG 6th division SA Field Force, 1900–1 (despatches, medal, three clasps, CB); Headquarters, 1901–3; Inspector-General of Remounts, 1903–4; Director of Transport and Remounts, 1904–7; Maj.-Gen. in charge of Administration, 1907–9. *Address:* Dahinda, 5 Hartfield Road, Eastbourne. *Club:* Army and Navy.
                                                              Died 19 Aug. 1916.

BENSON, Sir Ralph (Sillery), Kt 1906; ICS, retired; *b* 1851; *s* of Charles Benson, President, Royal College of Surgeons, Dublin, and

Maria, *d* of Maunsell Andrews, JP; *m* 1876, Fanny Catharine Alice (Kaiser-i-Hind gold medal), *d* of Rev. W. Gilbert-Cooper, MA, formerly of the Indian Ecclesiastical Establishment; one *s*. *Educ:* Trinity College, Dublin (MA, LLB). Entered ICS 1873; Barrister, Middle Temple, 1887; Registrar, High Court, Madras, 1885; Under-Secretary to Government, Madras, 1887; Secretary to Board of Revenue, 1888; District and Sessions Judge, 1888–95; Puisne Judge, High Court, Madras, 1896–1913 (twice Acting Chief Justice); Vice-Chancellor, Madras University, 1905. *Recreations:* travel, shooting, golf. *Address:* Roebuck Grove, Donnybrook, Dublin. *T:* Ballsbridge 296. *Club:* University, Dublin.   *Died 19 Oct. 1920.*

BENSON, Vice-Adm. Robert Edmund Ross, CB 1916; RN; *b* 1864; *m* 1897, Williama Margaret (*d* 1924). Served as midshipman at Bombardment of Alexandria, 1882; Egyptian War (medal, clasp, bronze star); European War, 1914–16 (CB); Inspecting Captain of Mechanical Training Establishments, 1912–14; Rear-Adm. retired, 1918; Vice-Adm. 1923. *Address:* Snail Creep, Houghton, Stockbridge, Hants.   *Died 3 Feb. 1927.*

BENSON, Ven. Thomas M.; Archdeacon of Connor since 1914; Rector of Ballymoney since 1880; Rural Dean of Coleraine since 1898; member of Diocesan Council since 1898; member of General Synod of The Church of Ireland since 1903; *b* London; *s* of late George Benson, MusB Cantab, Professor Royal Academy of Music, Lay Vicar of Westminster Abbey, and Gentleman of Her Majesty's Chapel Royal; *m* 1871, Jane Gardner, *e d* of Rev. James Orr, Newmills, Co. Down; five *s* four *d*. *Educ:* King's College School, London; private tuition in South of France. Deacon 1874; Priest, 1875; Curate of Donaghcloney, Diocese of Dromore, 1874–78; Vicar of Scarva, 1878–80; Chaplain of Ballymoney Union; Rural Dean of Balleymena, 1893–98; Prebendary of Cairncastle, 1898–1908; Chancellor of Connor, 1908. *Address:* The Rectory, Ballymoney, Co. Antrim.
                                                                    Died 16 Nov. 1921.

BENSON, William Arthur Smith; Architect and Designer in Metal-Work; *b* 1854; *s* of William Benson, JP, of Alresford, Hants; *m* 1886, Venetia, *d* of Alfred W. Hunt, RWS. *Educ:* Winchester; New College, Oxford. Was a pupil of Basil Champneys; started the business which bore his name, 1880; was one of the originators of the Arts and Crafts Exhibition Society, and of the Home Arts and Industries Association; has lectured on decorative design for the University Extension. *Publication:* Elements of Handicraft and Design, 1893. *Address:* 18 Hereford Square, SW7. *Clubs:* Royal Societies, Burlington Fine Arts.
                                                                    Died 5 July 1924.

BENSON, His Honour Judge William Denman, LLD; JP Glamorganshire; Judge of County Courts, Circuit 13, since 1907; *b* 21 March 1848; 2nd *s* of Gen. Henry Roxly Benson, CB, and Mary Henrietta, *d* of late Mr Justice Wightman; *m* 1876, Jane, 2nd *d* of late Thos Penrice, DL, of Kilvrough, Glamorganshire; two *s* one *d*. *Educ:* Eton; Balliol College, Oxford. Called to Bar, 1874; joined South Wales and Chester Circuit; Revising Barrister and Counsel to the Post Office. *Recreations:* shooting; Pres. OUBC, 1870–71, rowed Oxford and Cambridge Boat Race, 1868–69–70. *Address:* 10 William Street, Lowndes Square, SW. *Clubs:* Reform, National Liberal, MCC; Leander; Sheffield.   *Died 19 Feb. 1919.*

BENTLEY, Alfred, RE, ARCA Lond.; artist; *y s* of late Capt. W. E. Bentley, FRGS; unmarried. *Educ:* Royal College of Art, London. Exhibited in all the principal Galleries in England and abroad; joined Artists' Rifles, April 1915; gazetted to Norfolk Regt and served in France (MC). *Recreation:* music. *Address:* 15 Radcliffe Square, SW.
                                                                    Died 18 Feb. 1923.

BENTON, Sir John, KCIE 1911 (CIE 1902); late India Public Works Department; Chief Engineer and Secretary to Government, Panjab Irrigation Branch; *b* 5 Aug. 1850; *s* of late John Benton of Sherrifhaugh; *m* 1885, Margaret Forsyth, *d* of Provost Dick of Rothes, NB; two *d*. *Educ:* Aberdeen University; Edinburgh University; Royal Indian Engineering College, Coopers Hill (Fellow). Appointed Assistant Engineer, 1873; Executive Engineer, 1881; Superintending Engineer, 1897; Chief Engineer, 1900; Inspector-General of Irrigation, 1905; retired, 1912. *Address:* Westcroft, Silverdale Road, Eastbourne. *T:* Eastbourne 1386.
                                                                    Died 29 Aug. 1927.

BERENS, Alexander Augustus; country gentleman; JP Northamptonshire; *b* 1842; *o s* of Otto Berens, Raleigh Hall, Brixton; *m* 1st, 1865, Mary Shaw Hellier; 2nd, 1886, Louise Winifred, *d* of Rev Edward Stewart; one *s* three *d*. *Educ:* Trinity Hall, Cambridge

(BA, MA). Major (retired) 3rd Batt. Northamptonshire Regiment. *Address:* 30 Chester Square, SW1. *T:* Victoria 1648.
                                                                    Died 31 May 1926.

BERESFORD, 1st Baron, *cr* 1916, of Metemmeh and of Curraghmore; **Admiral Charles William de la Poer Beresford,** GCB 1911 (KCB 1903); GCVO 1906; *b* Ireland, 10 Feb. 1846; 2nd *s* of Rev. John, 4th Marquess of Waterford; *m* 1878, Mina, *d* of late Richard Gardner, MP Leicester; two *d*. *Educ:* Bayford School; Rev. Mr Foster's, Stubbington, Fareham, Hants. Entered "Britannia" as cadet, 1859; Sub-Lieut 1866; Lieut 1868; Commander, 1875; Capt. 1882; Rear-Admiral, 1897; Naval ADC to HM the Queen, 1896–97; Naval ADC to HRH Prince of Wales on his visit to India, 1875–76; MP (C) Waterford, 1874–80; East Division of Marylebone, 1885–89; MP York, 1897–1900; commanded "Condor", bombardment Alexandria, 1882 (medal with clasp, bronze star, 3rd class Medjidieh, and specially mentioned in despatches for gallantry); landed at Alexandria after bombardment and instituted regular police system; served on Lord Wolseley's staff, Nile Expedition, 1884–85; and subsequently in command of naval brigade at battles of Abu Klea, Abu Kru, and Metemmeh (mentioned for gallantry); in command of expedition which rescued Sir Charles Wilson's party in "Safia", when boiler was repaired under fire; specially mentioned in despatches for gallantry, and in the speeches of both Houses in the vote of thanks for operations in the Soudan; a Lord Commissioner of the Admiralty, 1886; resigned 1888, on question of strength of fleet; while Capt. of "Undaunted" rendered assistance on the occasion of the grounding of the "Seignalay", for which received thanks of French Government; in command of steam reserve at Chatham, 1893–96; visited China on a special mission, at request of Associated Chambers of Commerce of Great Britain, 1898–99; Rear-Admiral, Mediterranean, 1900-2; MP (C) Woolwich, 1902; Commanded Channel Squadron, 1903–5; Admiral, 1906; Commander-in-Chief, Mediterranean Fleet, 1905–7, Channel Fleet, 1907–9; retired 1911; MP (U) Portsmouth, 1910–16. Three medals for saving life. *Publications:* Nelson and his Times; numerous essays and articles on naval matters and Egypt; The break-up of China, 1899; The Betrayal, 1912; Memories, 1914. *Recreations:* turning, carpentering, cycling, hunting, or any sport. *Heir:* none. *Address:* 1 Great Cumberland Place, W. *Clubs:* Athenæum, Carlton, Turf, United Service, Savage, Marlborough.
                                                                    Died 6 Sept. 1919 (ext).

BERESFORD, Col Charles Edward de la Poer; *b* Corfu, 23 Oct. 1850; *m* 1882, Solita Henrietta, *d* and *co-heiress* of Henry Coburn Milne Ximénes de Cisneros, Bear Place, Berks. *Educ:* Versailles; Rev. Mr Foster's, Stubbington, Fareham; RMC, Sandhurst, psc. Interpreter, French, etc. Entered HM 46th Regt 1869 as Ensign, without purchase; DAAG Jamaica, 1890; Chief Staff Officer Jamaica, 1891; DAAG Western District, 1893; Lieut-Colonel, 1898; Military Attaché, British Embassy, St Petersburg, 1898–1903; Colonel, 1902; Knight Commander of Order of St Anne of Russia, 1903; retired 1904; rejoined for Active Service, 1914; appointed Commandant School of Instruction, N District; retired for age, March 1916; King's Badge, June 1916. *Publications:* The Conquest of Oran; A Historical Account of the Beresford Family, etc; contributor to various periodicals; corresp. The Times, siege of Port Arthur, 1903. *Recreation:* change. *Address:* Old Place, Boveney, Windsor.
                                                                    Died 22 Aug. 1921.

BERESFORD, Rev. John, MA; Vicar of Wells, 1870–1916; Prebendary of Combe, the 9th in Wells Cathedral, since 1883; *b* 1839; *m* 1865, Maria Emelia (*d* 1918), *o d* of Quintin Jamieson, MD, late Madras Horse Artillery; six *s* two *d*. *Educ:* Priory School, Norwich; Emmanuel Coll., Cambridge. BA 1861; MA 1865. Curate of St Margaret's, Ipswich, 1862–64; senior Curate of Walcot, Bath, 1864–70; Curate of St Stephen, Lansdown, Bath, 1870; Rural Dean of Shepton Mallet, 1898–1916. *Publication:* Sermons, 1863. *Recreation:* riding. *Address:* 6 St Ann Street, Salisbury.
                                                                    Died Dec. 1918.

BERESFORD, Maj.-Gen. John Beresford; retired; Bengal Staff Corps; *b* Oct. 1828; *m* 1866, Emma E.A., 3rd *d* of Rev. B. Savile; five *s* five *d*. *Educ:* Lucan School, Co. Dublin. Entered EI Company's service by director's nomination, 1845; posted to 29th Regt Bengal Infantry; passed Interpreter's Exam. and served as Interpreter and Quartermaster, 1850–56; served in second Punjab campaign (medal) and on Punjab Frontier during Mutiny, 1857–58, passed as Interpreter in Punjabi language; two years British Resident in Cashmere; retired on colonel's pension, 1877, with hon. rank of Major-General. *Address:* Craig Dhu Varren House, Portrush; Glenamoyle Lodge, Co. Londonderry. *M:* IW 64.

BERESFORD, John Stuart, CIE 1900; *b* 11 Feb. 1845; *s* of late Thomas Beresford; *m* 1872, Elizabeth (*d* 1919), *d* of late William Quinton; three *d*. Appointed to Public Works Department, India, 1867; Chief Engineer and Secretary to Government NW Provinces and Oudh, 1892; Chief Engineer and Sec. to Chief Commissioner, Central Provinces, 1893–96; Chief Engineer and Secretary to Government of Punjab, Irrigation Branch, 1896–1900; Member of Punjab Legislative Council, 1897–1900; Secretary to the Government of India and Inspector General of Irrigation, 1898; retired from the Indian Service, 1900; ME Queen's University, Ireland; Member of the Institution of Civil Engineers; Fellow of Allahabad University. *Publications:* several monographs and reports on engineering subjects. *Address:* Maythorne, Ealing, W. *T:* Ealing 768. *Club:* East India, United Service. *Died 1 May 1926.*

BERESFORD, Lord Marcus de la Poer, KCVO 1918 (CVO 1909; MVO 1901); Extra Equerry and Manager of HM's thoroughbreds; *b* Christmas Day, 1848; *s* of 4th Marquis of Waterford; *m* 1895, Louisa Catherine (*d* 1920), *e d* of late Maj.-Gen. C. W. Ridley, CB. *Educ:* Harrow. Entered 7th Hussars; ADC to Lord Lieut of Ireland, 1874–76; starter for Jockey Club, 1885–90; manager Sandringham Stud. *Died 16 Dec. 1922.*

BERESFORD, Hon. Seton Robert de la Poer Horsley; Shipper (Managing Director of two Shipping Associations); *b* 25 July 1868; 3rd *s* of 3rd Baron Decies; *m* 1st, 1899, Delia Dorothy (who obtained a divorce, 1909), *d* of late Daniel John O'Sullivan of the Grange, Killarney, Co. Kerry; 2nd, 1915, Rosemary, *e d* of Rear-Admiral Sir Charles Graves Sawle, MVO, of Penrice, Cornwall. *Educ:* Eton; Cambridge. Acted for Central News, SA Campaign; first to enter Kimberley, 4 hours ahead of Gen. French; notified Cecil Rhodes of approach of relief force; associated with The Tribune during its 8 years' life; went into business in US, 1909; carried through negotiations with Peruvian Govt whereby the Peruvian Irrigation and Colonisation Scheme was sanctioned by Pres. Beuvenides; joined Archer H. Brown, New York, 1914; organised assembly and despatch of 25,000 horses to France and formulated a co-operative shipping plan subsequently in operation between N and S America; an authority on the relationship between Capital and Labour, on which subject he has written articles especially dealing with profit-sharing plans and co-partnership between employers and employed. *Recreations:* shooting, fishing, hunting, skating, boxing, cricket, etc; played cricket for Middlesex; played for Old Niagara ice hockey, unbeaten team, and also for All England Team, 1897–98; held the World's Championship, Monte Carlo (trap shooting), 1901–4; won (representing Ireland) International Championship, San Sebastian, Spain; swam Cap Martin to Monaco Bay, 3 hrs 7 mins; won Atherstone Hunt, point-to-point steeplechase. *Address:* 2 Wall Street, New York. *TA:* Bereschilli, New York. *Club:* Wellington. *Died 28 May 1928.*

BERESFORD-PEIRSE, Sir Henry Monson de la Poer, 3rd Bt, *cr* 1814; *b* 25 Sept. 1850; *s* of Henry William de la Poer Beresford-Peirse, 2nd *s* of 1st Bt, and Henrietta, *o d* of Hon. and Rev. Thomas J. Monson; *S* uncle, 1873; *m* 1st, 1873, Lady Adelaide Bernard (*d* 1884), *d* of 3rd Earl of Banon; five *s* (two *d* decd); 2nd, 1886, Henrietta, OBE, *o d* of Sir Matthew Smith-Dodsworth, 4th Bt; one *d*. *Educ:* Eton; Trinity Coll., Camb. Owned over 3,000 acres. *Heir:* *s* Henry Bernard de la Poer Beresford-Peirse, *b* 9 Jan. 1875. *Address:* The Hall, Bedale, Yorkshire. *Club:* Carlton. *Died 8 July 1926.*

BERGH, Rt. Rev. Frederick Thomas; Benedictine Abbot; visitor of certain Benedictine Monasteries in England; Chaplain to nuns; *b* Brixham, Devon, 9 Oct. 1840, of Danish family settled in England in eighteenth century. *Educ:* England and France; university course in Rome. Priest, 1869; Teacher of Philosophy and Mathematics in Rome; Superior of Ramsgate Monastery, 1877; appointed Abbot by Papal Decree, 1896. *Publications:* compiling and editing liturgical books, articles in Catholic periodicals. *Address:* The Convent, Carshalton House, Carshalton. *T:* Sutton 287. *Died 12 Aug. 1924.*

BERGHOLT, Ernest George Binckes, MA; author and journalist; Indoor Pastimes Editor of The Queen since 1908; Cards Editor of Field since 1915; Member of Council and Fellow of Chartered Institute of Secretaries, 1904–21; *b* Worcester, 14 Feb. 1856; *m* 1892, Florence Woodland. *Educ:* Christ's Hospital; Cambridge. Senior Optime, Mathematical Tripos, 1879. Entered Civil Service, First Class, by competitive Examination; Chief Modern Side Master, Bradfield College, 1880–81; Army Coach, 1882–86; on staff of Dramatic Review, 1886; on Court and Society Review and Editor of Musical Standard, 1888; at invitation of Cavendish contributed regularly to Field on Whist, etc, 1898; Bridge Editor of Onlooker, 1901–7, when he first introduced journalistic Bridge Tournaments; organized Daily Mirror Bridge Competition, 1903–4; wrote the Auction Bridge Column (under name of Yarborough) in Sunday Times, 1915–24; specialist on all indoor games. *Publications:* Principles and Practice of Whist, 1902; Double Dummy Bridge Problems, 1905; edited Hoyle's Games Modernized, 1909; First and Second New Book of Patience Games, 1914; Royal Auction Bridge, 1917; Rover Bridge; Outlaw Bridge; Compendium of Poker; Compendium of Dominoes; Contract Bridge; Translations into Latin Elegiac Verse, 1918; Complete Handbook of Solitaire, 1920; Bergholt's Modern Auction, 1925. *Recreations:* music, private theatricals, *Address:* Wethermel, Letchworth Garden City. *Died 18 Nov 1925.*

BERINGER, Oscar; Director of Philharmonic Society; Examiner, Royal Academy of Music; Royal College of Music; *b* Baden, Germany, 14 July 1844. *Educ:* Conservatoire, Leipzig; Tausig's School, Berlin. First appearance, Saturday Concerts, Crystal Palace, 1860. *Recreations:* no time to indulge in hobbies. *Address:* 40 Wigmore Street, W. *Club:* Arts. *Died 21 Feb 1922.*

BERKELEY, Sir Henry Spencer, Kt 1896; JP; KC (Hong Kong) 1906; *b* 6 Sept. 1851; *m* 1878, Katharine, *d* of F. S. Cassin, of Antigua, West Indies; two *s* three *d*. Barrister, Inner Temple, 1873; Solicitor-General, Leeward Islands, 1878; Attorney-General, Fiji, 1885–89; Chief-Justice, 1889–1902; Attorney-General, Hong-Kong, 1902–6; administered the Government of Fiji and acted as High Commissioner for the Western Pacific on several occasions while Chief Justice of Fiji; Member of West Suffolk County Council, 1913; JP, West Suffolk, 1916. *Address:* Bures, Suffolk. *Club:* Junior Carlton. *Died 20 Sept. 1918.*

BERKELEY, Maj.-Gen. James Cavan, CIE 1888; *b* Clifton, 23 Jan. 1839; *s* of late General Sackville Hamilton Berkeley; *m* 1st, 1860, Anna Sophia (*d* 1886), *d* of Capt. G. Middlecoat, Madras Artillery; 2nd, 1892, Maud, *y d* of W. Tomlinson, FRAS, of York and Sandown, Isle of Wight; three *s* five *d*. *Educ:* King's Coll., London, Fellow. Joined Indian Army, 1857; entered Political Service under Government of India, 1862; and, after holding many minor posts, was successively British Resident at Gwalior, Kashmir and Nepal Courts, and Agent to the Governor-General at Baroda. *Decorated* for political services in India. *Address:* 12 Rosemount Road, Bournemouth, W. *Died 12 Oct. 1926.*

BERNAL, Frederic, CMG 1891; retired; *b* London, 8 Feb. 1828; *y s* of late Ralph Bernal, Chairman of Committee of the House of Commons; *m* 1850, Charlotte Augusta (*d* 1903), *d* of J. Brewster Cozens, Woodham Mortimer Lodge, Maldon, Essex; one *s* one *d*. *Educ:* Eton. Supernumerary Committee Clerk of the House of Commons, 1847–48; HM's Consul at Madrid, 1854; Carthagena (New Granada), 1858; Baltimore, 1861; Havre, 1866; Consul-General, Havre, 1883. *Decorated* for his services under the Foreign Office, 1891. *Address:* 94 Cheriton Road, Folkestone. *Club:* Royal Yacht Squadron, Cowes (Hon. Mem.). *Died 10 June 1924.*

BERNAL, Lt-Col Greville Hugh Woodlee, DSO 1900; 4th Battalion, Nottinghamshire and Derbyshire Regiment; *o s* of Augustus Woodley Bernal; *m* 1905, Florence Mary Fyers, *d* of late David Kent. *Educ:* Marlborough. Served S Africa, 1899–1900 (despatches, Queen's medal, three clasps, King's medal, two clasps, DSO). *Died 6 March 1922.*

BERNARD, Rev. Edward Russell; Canon of Salisbury Cathedral; Chaplain in Ordinary to the King; *b* 12 July 1842; *e s* of Rev T. D. Bernard, Chancellor and Canon of Wells Cathedral; *m* 4 Sept. 1878, Ellen, *e d* of William Nicholson, of Basing Park, Hants; three *d*. *Educ:* Harrow; Exeter Coll., Oxford; Hertford University Scholar, 1863; Craven University Scholar, 1866. Fellow of Magdalen Coll., Oxford, 1866–76; Vicar of Selborne, 1876–89; Canon Residentiary of Salisbury, 1889–1909. *Address:* High Hall, Wimborne. *T:* Wimborne 42. *Died 22 April 1921.*

BERNARD, Most Rev. and Rt. Hon. John Henry, PC (Ireland) 1919; DD; Archbishop of Dublin, 1915–19; Provost of Trinity College, Dublin, since 1919; *b* India, 27 July 1860; *e s* of late Robert Bernard, MD, RN, Deputy Inspector-General of Hospitals and Fleets; *m* 1885, Maud Nannie, *d* of Robert Bernard, MD, RN; one *s* two *d* (and one *s* decd). *Educ:* private school; Trinity College, Dublin (Scholar), 1879; Senior Moderator in Mathematics and in Philosophy,

1880; Wray prize, 1880; M'Cullagh prize, 1883; Madden prize, 1883; MA 1883; BD 1888; DD 1892. Fellow and Tutor, Trinity College, 1884; ordained 1886; chaplain to Lord Lieut of Ireland, 1886–1902; Abp King's Lecturer in Divinity (Dublin), 1888–1911; Treasurer of St Patrick's Cathedral, 1897–1902; Dean of St Patrick's, 1902–11; Bishop of Ossory, Ferns and Leighlin, 1911–15; Examining Chaplain to Bishop (Reeves) of Down, 1889; member of University Council, 1892; select preacher, Oxford, 1893–95, 1912, 1919–20; Cambridge, 1898, 1901, 1904, 1917, 1923; Warden, Alexandra College, Dublin, for higher education of women, 1903–11; President of Royal Irish Academy, 1916–21; member of General Synod of Church of Ireland, 1894; Representative Church Body, 1897; Commissioner of National Education, Ireland, 1897–1903; Commissioner of Intermediate Education, Ireland, 1917; sometime Visitor of Queen's College, Galway; Hon. DCL (Oxford) 1920 and (Durham), 1905; Hon. DD (Aberdeen), 1906; Hon. Fellow of Queen's College, Oxford, 1919; Hon. Fellow, Royal College of Physicians (Ireland), 1921. *Publications:* editor (in conjunction with Professor Mahaffy) Kant's Critical Philosophy for English Readers, 2 vols 1889; translator Kant's Critique of Judgment, 1892, 2nd edn 1915; From Faith to Faith, University Sermons, 1895; Via Domini, Cathedral Sermons, 1898; The Prayer of the Kingdom, 1904; St Patrick's Cathedral, a Handbook and a History, 1904; Archbishop Benson in Ireland, 1896; (in conjunction with Prof. Atkinson) The Irish Liber Hymnorum, 2 vols, 1898; editor The Pigrimage of St Silvia of Aquitania, 1893; The Pastoral Epistles of St Paul, 1899; The Second Epistle to the Corinthians, 1903; The Works of Bishop Butler, 2 vols, 1900; The Psalter in Latin and English, 1911; The Odes of Solomon, 1912; Christmas Thoughts, 1913; Verba Crucis, 1915; Easter Hope, 1916; Studia Sacra, 1917; In War Time, 1917; author of various memoirs in the Transactions of the Royal Irish Academy, etc. *Address:* Provost's House, Trinity College, Dublin. *TA:* Provost, Trinity, Dublin. *Clubs:* Athenæum; University, Dublin.
Died 29 Aug. 1927.

BERNARD, Lt-Col Ronald Percy Hamilton; *b* 18 March 1875; *s* of Percy Brodrick Bernard, *g s* of 2nd Earl of Bandon, and Isabel, *d* of John Newton Lane, Kings Bromley Manor, Staffs; *cousin and heir pres.* to 4th Earl of Bandon; *m* 1904, Lettice Mina, *y d* of Gerald C. S. Paget; two *s* one *d.* Captain, late Rifle Brigade. *Address:* Bury Greens, Cheshunt, Herts.
Died 2 Feb. 1921.

BERNAYS, Acting-Commander Leopold Arthur, CMG 1916; DSO 1917; RN. Served European War, 1914–17 (CMG, DSO); 4th Class Order of St Vladimir, with swords, 1915.
Died Nov. 1917.

BERNERS, Baroness (7th in line) *cr* 1455; **Emma Harriet Tyrwhitt;** *b* 18 Nov. 1835; *o surv c* of late Hon. Rev. Robert Wilson, *o brother* of 6th Baron Berners; *S* uncle, 1871; *m* 1853, Sir Henry Tyrwhitt, 3rd Bt (*d* 1894); six *s* three *d* (and three *s* decd). Distinctly Protestant. *Heir: s* Sir Raymond Tyrwhitt-Wilson, 4th Bt, *b* 22 July 1855. *Address:* Ashwell, Thorpe, Norwich. *TA:* Tacolneston.
Died 18 Aug. 1917.

BERNERS, 8th Baron, *cr* 1455; **Raymond Robert Tyrwhitt-Wilson;** Bt 1808; *b* 22 July 1855; *e s* of 7th Baroness Berners and Sir Henry Tyrwhitt, 3rd Bt; assumed additional name of Wilson, 1892; *S* father 1894, and mother 1917. *Educ:* Trinity College, Cambridge. Owned about 12,000 acres. *Heir: nephew* Gerald Hugh Tyrwhitt, *b* 18 Sept. 1883. *Address:* 4 Down Street, W; Stanley Hall, Bridgnorth; Ashwellthorpe, Norwich.
Died 5 Sept. 1918.

BERNHARDT, Sarah; French actress and manager of the Théâtre Sarah Bernhardt in Paris; *b* Paris, 23 Oct. 1845; widow of M. Jacques Damala. *Educ:* Grandchamp Catholic Convent near Paris. Prize of the Conservatory of Paris, 1862; entrée à la Comédie Française—partie de la Comédie Française—entrée à l' Odéon puis de nouveau à la Comédie Française en 1872; quitté la Comédie Française en 1880, et fait de nombreux voyages en Amérique, en Europe, devint directrice du Théâtre de la Renaissance en 1893; et fondé le Théâtre Sarah Bernhardt en 1899. Cross of Legion of Honour, 1913; Officier, 1921. *Sculpture:* many busts, groups, marbles; bronzes, Exhibition, 1900, silver medal. *Painting:* several tableaux, some prized in Paris Salon. *Publications:* several books and plays, represented in Paris; novels in divers papers. *Recreations:* sculpture, painting, etc; in summer at her country house, fishing, boating, lawn-tennis, etc. *Address:* 56 Boulevard Pereire, and Théâtre Sarah Bernhardt, Paris; Manoir de Pen Hoët, Belle-Ile en Mer, Sauzon, Morbihan, France.
Died 26 March 1923.

BERNIER, Hon. Michel Esdras, PC Canada; Deputy Chief Commissioner of Railways, Canada, since 1904; *b* 27 Sept. 1841; *s*

of Etienne Bernier, farmer, and Julie Lussier; *m* 1865, Alida Marchesseault. *Educ:* St Hyacinthe Seminary. Notary by profession, also engaged in farming, manufactures, and financial institutions; MP, County of St Hyacinthe, 1882–1904; Minister of Inland Revenue, Canada, 1900–4. *Club:* Garrison, Quebec.
Died 30 July 1921.

BERRANGÉ, Major Christian Anthony Lawson, CMG 1902; JP; Cape Police; *b* 28 Oct. 1864; *s* of late Christian Berrangé, of Graaff Reinet, Cape Colony; *m* 1897, *d* of John M. Lang. Served Bechuanaland, 1896–97 (despatches several times); South African War (despatches frequently, CMG).
Died 3 Aug. 1922.

BERRIDGE, Sir Thomas Henry Devereux, KBE 1920; Kt 1912; *b* 6 July 1857; *s* of Rev. W. Berridge, formerly Headmaster of Upholland Grammar School, Lancashire, and Vicar of Lowton St Mary's, Lancashire; *m* 1887, Agnes (*d* 1909), *d* of Frederick Campion of Frenches, Redhill; one *s* one *d. Educ:* Upholland Grammar School; privately. Articled to Maskell Peace of Wigan, Solicitor to Mining Association of Great Britain; admitted Solicitor, 1878; member of firm of Burn and Berridge, Solicitors to Government of Newfoundland, 1882; Past-master City of London Solicitors' Company; MP (L) Warwick and Leamington, 1906–10; contested same Division, 1910; Chairman, Executive Committee, Royal Flying Corps Voluntary Hospitals, 1916–19. *Recreations:* golf, farming. *Address:* 6 Austin Friars, EC. *T:* London Wall 1475; 11 and 12 Southampton Street, Bloomsbury, WC. *T:* Museum 5298; 29 Elm Park Gardens, SW10. *T:* Kensington 4263; Greenwood, Alkham, near Dover. *T:* Kearsney 5Y3. *TA:* Bees, London. *Clubs:* Reform, Royal Automobile, National Liberal, Eighty.
Died 24 Oct. 1924.

BERROW, William Lewis, OBE 1918; ISO 1911; an Assistant in Librarians Department, Foreign Office, since 1920; *b* 12 Dec. 1862; *s* of late John Berrow of Newport, Salop, and Worcester; *m* Henrietta Adeline (*d* 1911), *d* of late Henry Alexander Scott; one *s* two *d. Educ:* Newport (Salop) Grammar School. Registrar, Foreign Office, 1906–20; Joint-Editor of Hertslet's Commercial Treaties since 1914. *Address:* Foreign Office, SW1. *Club:* North Surrey Golf.
Died 13 Feb. 1928.

BERRY, Henry Fitz-Patrick, ISO 1903; MA; MRIA: Barrister-at-law; Assistant Keeper of the Public Records in Ireland since 1899; *b* 12 May 1847; *e s* of Parsons Berry, MB, Mallow, Co. Cork; *m* 1895, S. Elizabeth Letitia, *d* of Hastings Twiss, JP, Birdhill House, Co. Tipperary. *Educ:* privately; Trinity College, Dublin; Honourman in Classis; First Honourman History and English Literature; First Junior Moderator in History, Political Science, English Literature, and Law. Entered the Public Record Office, 1868. A Vice-President, Royal Irish Academy; Fellow Royal Society of Antiquaries of Ireland, and member of Council of that Society. *Publications:* edited Early Statutes and Ordinances of Ireland, John to Henry V (Irish Record Office Series), 1907, and for Royal Society of Antiquaries of Ireland a Register of Wills and Inventories, Dio. Dublin, 1457–83, from a MS in the Library, Trinity College, Dublin; The Water Supply of Ancient Dublin; Histories of some of the old Dublin City Guilds, and numerous other papers in the Journal RSAI; also Notes on an Unpublished MS Inquisition, AD 1258, as to the Dublin City Watercourse and History of St Anne's Religious Guild, Dublin, 1430–1740, in the Proceedings Royal Irish Academy. *Address:* 51 Waterloo Road, Dublin. *Club:* Dublin University.

BERRY, Hon. Sir William Bisset-, Kt 1900; MA, MD, LLD 1911; *b* Aberdeen, Scotland, July 1839; *m* 1864, Marion (*d* 1884), *d* of William Beale. *Educ:* public schools; University, Aberdeen. Member of the Council of University of Cape of Good Hope; settled at Queenstown, Cape of Good Hope, in 1864, and practised medicine there; took keen interest in municipal and educational needs of his town, bringing several important undertakings to successful termination; returned to Parliament for Queenstown, 1894, 1898, and 1904; Speaker of the House of Assembly of Cape of Good Hope, 1989–1907; elected to Parliament of Union, 1910, as MLA for Queenstown. *Publications:* contributions at various times to medical and other journals. *Address:* Ebden Street, Queenstown, Cape of Good Hope.
Died June 1922.

BERRY, William Grinton, MA; Editor of the Sunday at Home since 1909, and of the Tract and Booklet Publications of the Religious Tract Society since 1918; *b* Edinburgh, 14 Aug. 1873; *m* Alice Maud, *d* of late Captain George Morrison, RE; one *s* one *d. Educ:* George Heriot's School and Edinburgh University. Sub-Editor of Southern

Report, Selkirk, 1894–95; on the staff of the British Weekly, 1895–98; editor of the publications of the National Council of the Evangelical Free Churches, 1898–1902; on the editorial staff of the Amalgamated Press, 1902–4; on the editorial staff of the RTS since 1904. *Publications:* Scotland's Struggles for Religious Liberty; a monograph on Milton; France since Waterloo; edited the autobiography of Gipsy Smith, Heroes and Pioneers, The Life of Bishop Hannington, Men of Grit, Men of Faith and Daring, etc. *Recreation:* educational lecturing. *Address:* 4 Bouverie Street, EC4. *TA:* Tracts, London. *T:* Central 8428-9. *Club:* 9 Vesta Road, Brockley, SE4.

Died 12 March 1926.

BERTIE OF THAME, 1st Viscount, *cr* 1918; **Francis Leveson Bertie;** Baron, 1915; GCB 1908 (KCB 1902); GCMG 1904; GCVO 1903; PC 1903; *b* 17 Aug. 1844; 2nd *s* of 6th Earl of Abingdon; *m* 1874, Lady Feodorowna Cecilia Wellesley, *d* of 1st Earl Cowley; one *s. Educ:* Eton. Entered Foreign Office, 1863; Private Secretary to Hon. R. Bourke, afterwards Lord Connemara (Parliamentary Under-Secretary of State), 1874–80; attached to Special Embassy to Berlin, 1878; Secretary to Duke of Fife's mission to invest King of Saxony with Order of Garter, 1881; Assistant Under-Secretary of State for Foreign Affairs, 1894; Chairman of Uganda Railway Committee, 1896–1903; British Ambassador at Rome, 1903; at Paris, 1905–18. Coronation Medals, 1902 and 1911; Grand Cross Order of St Maurice and St Lazarus; Grand Cross Legion of Honour, 1918. *Heir: s* Hon. Vere Frederick Bertie, *b* 20 Oct. 1878. *Address:* 22 Bryanston Square, W1. *T:* Paddington 6710. *Clubs:* Turf, Brooks's, St James's, Travellers'.

Died 26 Sept. 1919.

BERTIE, Rev. Hon. Alberic Edward, MA; Rector of Gedling, Notts, 1887–1923; *b* 14 Nov. 1846; 3rd *s* of 6th Earl of Abingdon; *m* 1881, Lady Caroline Elizabeth M'Donnell, *e d* of 5th Earl of Antrim; three *s* three *d* (and one *s* decd). *Educ:* Merton College, Oxford. Ordained deacon 1870, priest 1871. Curate, St Paul's, Middlesbrough, 1870–73; Curate in charge, All Saints, Middlesbrough, 1873–78, Vicar, 1878–79; Rector, Albury, Oxon, 1879–86; Staveley, Derbys, 1886–87. *Address:* 86 Woodstock Road, Oxford. *Club:* United University.

Died 20 March 1928.

BERTIE, Lieut-Col Hon. George Aubrey Vere; late Coldstream Guards; *b* 2 May 1850; 4th *s* of 6th Earl of Abingdon; *m* 1885, Harriet Blanche Elizabeth (*d* 1923), *d* of Sir Walter Farquhar, 3rd Bt; two *d* (one *s* decd). Served Zulu War, 1879 (medal with clasp). *Clubs:* Guards; Royal Yacht Squadron, Cowes.

Died 8 Nov. 1926.

BERTRAM, Brig.-Gen. Sir Alexander, Kt 1916; *b* Dundas, Ontario, 18 Feb. 1853; *m* 1869, *d* of Hugh T. Smith; three *s* one *d. Educ:* Dundas High School. Appointed to command 3rd Infantry Brigade, West Ontario Command, 1905; Col 1910; commanded Bisley team, 1909; Deputy-Chairman, Canadian Imperial Munitions Board. *Address:* Dundas, Ont; Canadian Military Institute, Toronto.

Died April 1926.

BERUETE Y MORET, Aureliano de; Directeur du Musée du Prado since 1918; *b* 1878; *s* of late Aureliano Beruete; *m* 1921, Isabel Regoyos; one *s. Educ:* Madrid. Docteur en Philosophie et Lettres; écrivain, critique d'art; membre de l'Académie Royale de l'Histoire; owner of a picture gallery. *Publication:* Goya as a portrait painter. *Address:* Celle Genova 19, Madrid. *T:* 1546–T. *M:* 3049 M. *Clubs:* Athénié, Caviar de Madrid, Gran Pèna, Madrid.

Died 10 June 1922.

BESANT, William Henry, MA, ScD; FRS; Fellow, St John's College, Cambridge, 1851–59, re-elected 1889; *b* Portsmouth, 1 Nov. 1828; *s* of a merchant of Portsmouth; *b* of late Sir Walter Besant; *m* 1861, Margaret Elizabeth (*d* 1911), *d* of late Rev. R. Willis, Jacksonian Professor in the University of Cambridge; two *s* one *d. Educ:* Grammar School, Portsea; a Proprietary School at Southsea; St John's Coll., Camb.; graduated BA as Senior Wrangler and 1st Smith's Prizeman, 1850. In 1883 received degree of Doctor of Science, being the first ScD created by the University of Cambridge. Lecturer of St John's Coll. for thirty-five years; Moderator for Mathematical Tripos 1856 and 1885; one of the Examiners for the University of London, 1859–64; very active and successful as private tutor; College Lecturer and Examiner in Cambridge and elsewhere. *Publications:* Treatises on Hydro-Mechanics, Geometrical Conics, Dynamics, Roulettes and Glissettes, and various papers in the Quarterly Journal of Mathematics, the Messenger of Mathematics, and the Educational Times. *Address:* 4 Harvey Road, Cambridge. *Died 2 June 1917.*

BESSBOROUGH, 8th Earl of, *cr* 1739; **Edward Ponsonby;** Baron of Bessborough; Viscount Duncannon, 1723; Baron Ponsonby, 1749; Baron Duncannon (UK), 1834; KP 1915; CB 1895; CVO 1902; JP Middlesex and Co. Carlow; DL, JP, and CC Co. Kilkenny; Knight of Grace, St John of Jerusalem; Legion of Honour; *b* 1 March 1851; *e s* of 7th Earl of Bessborough and Lady Louisa Susan Cornwallis Eliot, *o d* of 3rd Earl of St Germans; *S* father, 1906; *m* 1875, Blanche Vere, CBE (*d* 1919), *d* of Sir John Guest, 1st Bt; two *s* three *d* (and one *s* decd). Lieut RN; retired 1874; Barrister, 1879; Secretary to Speaker of House of Commons (Peel), 1884–95; Secretary to the Caledonian Canal Commissioners, 1896–99; Chairman, Brighton and South Coast Railway, and of Guest, Keen and Nettlefold. *Heir: s* Viscount Duncannon, *b* 27 Oct. 1880. *Address:* 17 Cavendish Square, W; Bessborough, Piltown, Kilkenny. *Club:* Brooks's.

Died 1 Dec. 1920.

BETHELL, Hon. (Albert) Victor, *b* 8 Jan. 1864; *s* of 2nd Baron Westbury and Mary Florence, *d* of Rev. A. Fownes-Luttrell; *m* 1918, Eleanor Violet, *d* of late Stephen Egan, *widow* of Charles Brett, Coldstream Guards. *Educ:* Eton. *Publications:* Ten Days at Monte Carlo, 1898; Monte Carlo Anecdotes, 1901; Bridge Reflections, 1908. *Recreations:* shooting, travelling, bridge. *Address:* 4 Knightsbridge Mansions, SW3. *T:* Kensington 738. *Clubs:* Baldwin, MCC, Royal Automobile.

Died 20 July 1927.

BETHELL, George Richard; Captain RN retired; *b* 23 March 1849; 2nd *s* of W. F. Bethell, of Rise, Hull. *Educ:* Laleham; Gosport; "Britannia". Entered navy, 1862; served as Mid. in "Sutlej"; Sub-Lieut in Mediterranean and Gulf of Suez surveys; Lieut in "Challenger" and "Minotaur"—attached to Sir C. Warren's expedition to Bechuanaland, 1884; MP (C) Holderness Div. Yorks, 1885–1900; contested same Division, 1910. *Address:* Sigglesthorne, Hull. *Clubs:* Naval and Military, Arthur's, Yorkshire.

Died 3 Dec. 1919.

BETHELL, William, JP, DL; *b* 11 Aug. 1847; *e s* of late W. F. Bethell and Elizabeth, 2nd *d* of Sir Edmund Beckett, Bt; *m* 1880, Hon. Maria Myrtle Willoughby (*d* 1900), 5th *d* of 8th Lord Middleton; one *s* one *d. Address:* Rise Park, near Hull; Watton Abbey, near Beverley. *Clubs:* Carlton, Yorkshire.

Died 13 Aug. 1926.

BETJEMANN, Gilbert H., Hon. RAM; LRAM; Member of the Royal Philharmonic Society; Musician in Ordinary to Queen Victoria and King Edward VII; Examiner for Royal Academy of Music, Associated Board RAM and RCM; late Conductor of Italian Opera, Her Majesty's Theatre, and English Opera, Covent Garden Theatre; *b* London, 17 Nov. 1840. Violinist at Italian Opera, Covent Garden, 1858; First Violin and Répétiteur with Pyne and Harrison Co. at Covent Garden, 1860; Conductor of the Ballet and Leader of the Second Violins at the Opera until the death of Mr Carrodus, then became principal First Violin; resigned this appointment in 1898; many years Conductor and Stage Director with the Carl Rosa Opera Co.; Principal and Solo Violin Norwich Musical Festival; many years Director of the Operatic Class RAM, and Conductor of the Oxford Philharmonic Society; Conductor of the Highbury Philharmonic Society (London), 1884–1907; Director of Ensemble-playing, Oxford University Musical Union, 1886–1911. Member of the Court of Assistants of the Royal Society of Musicians. *Recreations:* painting, making working models of engines, billiards. *Address:* Ivy Bank, 14 Hillmarton Road, Camden Road, N7. *T:* North 2674.

Died 26 Nov. 1921.

BEVAN, Francis Augustus; late Chairman, Barclay and Company; *b* 17 Jan. 1840; 2nd *s* of late Robert Cooper Lee Bevan of Fosbury and of Trent Park, and 1st wife, Lady Agneta Elizabeth, *d* of 4th Earl of Hardwicke; *m* 1st, 1862, Elizabeth Marianne (*d* 1863), *d* of Lord Charles James Fox Russell; one *s*; 2nd, 1866, Constance (*d* 1872), *d* of Sir James Weir Hogg, 1st Bt; five *s*; 3rd, 1876, Maria (*d* 1903), *d* of late John Trotter of Dyrham Park, Barnet; three *d. Educ:* Harrow. A Lieutenant for the City of London; High Sheriff of Middlesex, 1899. *Address:* 1 Tilney Street, Park Lane, W. *Clubs:* Union, National, City.

Died 31 Aug. 1919.

BEVAN, Captain George Parker, CMG 1918; DSO 1916; RN; *b* 23 June 1878; 2nd *s* of late James Frederick Bevan of Stanwell Moor, Middlesex; *m* 1911, Lilian, *y d* of J. Williams Daw of Walreddon Manor, South Devon. Served European War, 1914–19; Dardanelles, did patrol work and carried out valuable feints at landing in Gulf of Xeros and Suvla; Commodore 2nd Class, 1917–19 (despatches, DSO, Albert Medal, Officier of Legion of Honour, France, 1914–15 Star, Order of St Anne, 2nd Class, Russia). *Club:* United Service.

Died 14 Jan. 1920.

BEVAN, Major the Rev. Llewelyn David, BA, LLB (London), DD (Princeton); Principal, Parkin College, Adelaide, since 1910; *b* Llanelly, Caermarthenshire, 11 Sept. 1842; *s* of Hopkin and Eliza Bevan; *m* 1870, Louisa Jane, *d* of John Willett, MD, Bishops Lavington, Wilts; three *s* four *d*. *Educ:* University College School; New and University Colleges, London. Colleague of Rev. T. Binney, King's Weigh House Chapel, London, 1865; Minister of Tottenham Court Road Chapel, London, 1869; Member of London School Board for Marylebone, 1873-76; Lecturer on English Language and Literature, New College, London, and Dean of Faculty, 1871-76; Member of Council, Working Men's College, Great Ormond Street, London, 1866-76; Minister of Old Brick Presbyterian Church, New York, 1876-82; Minister of Highbury Quadrant Church, London, 1882-86; Minister of Collins Street Independent Church, Melbourne, 1886-1910; Professor of Systematic Theology, Congregational College of Victoria; Chaplain of the Forces, Victoria; Chairman of Jury on Education of the Melbourne International Exhibition, and was made by the French Government Officier d'Instruction publique de la République Française, 1888; Vice-President of International Congregational Council, London, 1891; Vice-President of International Congregational Council, Boston, 1899; President, Parliamentary Commission on Inebriety, 1901; Chairman, Congregational Union of Victoria, 1888 and 1898; Chairman of Congregational Union of Australasia, 1910-13; Past Grand Chaplain of the Grand Lodge of Victoria. *Publications:* various sermons, lectures, and addresses; Sermons to Students, 1881-82; Christ and the Age, 1885; Presidential Addresses, 1888-1889-1898; articles, in magazines etc, 1865-1915. *Recreations:* travel, swimming, boating; book and curio collecting in later years, "far niente in villéggiatura". *Address:* Parkin College, Adelaide.   *Died 9 Aug. 1918.*

BEVENOT, Prof. Clovis, MA Oxon; *b* near Cambrai; *m* Flavie Bevenot; three *s* one *d*. *Educ:* Cambrai; Universities of Göttingen, Naples and Oxford (Balliol Coll.); Classical Honours, Exhibitioner, Lecturer, and Examiner, Oxford. For six years on Staff of Clifton College; Examiner or past Examiner in the Romance Languages, including Roumanian, to Cambridge, London, Victoria, Liverpool, St Andrews, National of Ireland, Birmingham, etc, Universities; LCC Technical Education Board; ICS; Interpreter to the Treasury, etc; interim Prof. of German, Lecturer in Spanish and Italian, Professor of French Language, Literature, History, and Philology, University of Birmingham, 1889-1909; subsequently pensioned. Cross and medal, Mentana campaign. *Publications:* edited various: Cervantes, French and German Poets, etc; collaborated in Moncalm's L'Origine de la pensée et de la parole; the Spanish Grammar (Parallel Series); Ralph Thomas' Swimming; Report on Physical Education in English Schools for the Education Congress at the Paris Exhibition, etc. *Recreations:* coaching in Russian, Spanish, etc after-war pioneers to-be. *Address:* St Florence, Tor Vale, Torquay.

Died 21 Feb. 1925.

BEVERIDGE, Erskine, LLD; FRSE; JP; manufacturer; *b* Dec. 1851; *m*. *Educ:* private schools; Edinburgh University. *Publications:* Churchyard Memorials of Crail, 1893; A Bibliography of Dunfermline and West Fife, 1901; Coll and Tiree, their Prehistoric Forts and Ecclesiastical Antiquities, 1903; North Uist, its Archæology and Topography, 1911; The Burgh Records of Dunfermline, 1488-1584 (edited), 1917. *Recreations:* archæology (especially Hebridean), photography, fishing. *Address:* St Leonard's Hill, Dunfermline; Vallay, North Uist. *Club:* Scottish Conservative.

Died 10 Aug. 1920.

BEVES, Brig.-Gen. Percival Scott, CMG 1917; South Africa Defence Force; late Captain Royal Inniskilling Fusiliers; *b* 25 Jan. 1868; 4th *s* of late Edward Beves, JP, Brighton. *Educ:* Leys School, Cambridge. Served Tirah, 1897-98; South Africa, 1899-1902; German SW Africa, 1914-15; German East Africa, 1916-17.

Died 26 Sept. 1924.

BEVILLE, Lt-Col Francis Granville, CSI 1921; CIE 1908; Agent to the Governor General in Central India; *b* 24 March 1867. Lieutenant, N Staffs Regt, 1886; Indian Staff Corps, 1888; Capt. Indian Army, 1897; Major, 1904; Lt-Col, 1912; Acting Consul, Muscat, 1896; Consul, 1896-97; Political Agent, Bundelkhand, 1900-4; Bhopawar, 1905-12; Resident, Gwalior, 1914. *Address:* Indore, Central India.   *Died 21 April 1923.*

BEWERUNGE, Rev. Henry; Professor of Church Music, St Patrick's College, Maynooth, since 1888; *b* Letmathe, Westphalia, 7 Dec. 1862. *Educ:* Düsseldorf; Würzburg; Eichstätt; Ratisbon. Ordained priest at Eichstätt, 1885. *Publications:* six five-part motets by Palestrina, arranged for five male voices; The Vatican Edition of Plain-Chant: A Critical

Study, 1906; Die vatikanische Choralausgabe, 1906; Die vatikanischen Choralausgabe zweiter Teil, 1907; articles in the Catholic Encyclopedia and English and German periodicals. *Address:* St Patrick's College, Maynooth. *TA:* Bewerunge, Maynooth.

BEWES, Lt-Col Arthur Edward, CMG 1916; RMLI; *b* 7 Jan. 1871; 2nd *s* of late Capt. F. D. Bewes, Newton Abbot; *m* 1898, Ethel, *d* of Rev. T. S. Treanor, Deal; one *d*. *Educ:* Newton College; Blundell's School, Tiverton. Joined the Royal Marines, 1890; Capt., 1898; Major, 1909; served European War, 1914-16; present at Antwerp, Kum Kale, and at first landing at Gallipoli (wounded, despatches twice, CMG). *Address:* 6 The Beach, Walmer, Kent.

Died 17 Jan. 1922.

BEWICKE-COPLEY, Brig.-Gen. Sir Robert Calverley Allington Bewicke, KBE 1919; CB 1900; DL, JP; late Commanding West Riding (Yorkshire) Volunteers; *b* Shotton Hall, Durham, 8 April 1855; *e s* of Robert Calverley Bewicke Bewicke, Coulby Manor, Yorkshire; *m* 1886, Selina Frances, *d* of Sir Chas Watson, 3rd Bt; one *s* two *d*. *Educ:* Rugby; Merton Coll., Oxford. Sub-Lieut Royals, 1876; trans. 60th Rifles, 1877; ADC to Lieut Governor, Bengal, 1879; DAAG Nile Expedition, 1885 (medal and Khedive's star); DAAG Barbados, 1890; DAAG Headquarters, Ireland, 1892; Military Attaché, special mission, Morocco, 1894; Chitral, 1895 (medal); AMS Bengal, 1896; DAQMG Intelligence, Kuram-Kohat, 1897; AAG 2nd Division, Tirah Expeditionary Force, 1898 (2 clasps, despatches); commanding 3rd Batt. King's Royal Rifles, South African War, 1899; commanding Mobile Columns, South Africa, 1900-2 (despatches, Queen's medal, 6 clasps, King's medal, 2 clasps, CB); late Brig.-Gen. Commanding 17th Infantry Brigade, Cork; late Colonel, General Staff, Northern Command; retired 1912. *Address:* Sprotborough Hall, Doncaster. *TA:* Sprotbro, Doncaster. *Clubs:* Carlton, Naval and Military; Yorkshire, York.   *Died 23 June 1923.*

BHANDARI, Rai Bahadur Sir Gopal Das, Kt 1923; CIE 1921; MBE 1919; *b* Amritsar, June 1860. *Educ:* Government College and Law School, Lahore. Pleader, 1880; President, Bar Association, Amritsar; Member, Municipal Council for the last forty years; Rai Bahadur, 1907; Punjabis' Representative to the All India Sanitary Conferences, Madras, Simla, and Lucknow; Special Delegate, All India Malaria Conference, 1907; The Kaiser-i-Hind Medal 1st Class, 1915; specially enrolled Advocate, High Court of Judicature, Lahore, 1917; Special Commissioner, Lahore Conspiracy Case, 1917; First non-official President, Municipal Council since 1921; President, Hindu Sahha; member of the Punjab Legislative Council, 1923; President, Board of Directors Punjab National Bank (Amritsar Branch). *Publications:* Malaria; Milk Supply; Town Planning; Insanitary Conditions of Boys' and Girls' Schools in Cities, etc. *Address:* Amritsar, Punjab.

Died Feb. 1927.

BHANDARKAR, Sir Ramkrishna Gopal, KCIE 1911 (CIE 1889); MA; Hon. LLD, Bombay and Edinburgh; Hon. PhD Göttingen and Calcutta; Professor of Oriental Languages, Deccan College, Poona, 1882-93; *b* 1837; *m*; two *s* one *d*. *Educ:* Ratnagiri Government English School; Elphinstone College, Bombay, 1847-58. Headmaster of High Schools, 1864-68; Professor of Sanskrit, Elphinstone College, Bombay, 1869-1881. Fellow, and for two years Vice-Chancellor, Bombay University; Fellow of Calcutta University; nominated to membership of Viceroy's Legislative Council in connection with Lord Curzon's Educational Reforms, 1903; member of Bombay Legislative Council, 1904-8; a leader of Hindu social and religious reform movements; Dakshina Fellow, 1859-64. *Publications:* First and Second Books of Sanskrit; Early History of the Deccan; Sanskrit and Derived Languages; Vaisnavism, Saivism, and Minor Religious Systems. *Address:* Poona, Deccan.

Died Aug. 1925.

BHAVNAGAR, HH Maharaja of, Sir Bhavsinhji Takhtasinhji, KCSI; Hon. Lieutenant-Colonel in Army; *b* 26 April 1875; *s* of Sir Takhtasinhji Jaswatsinhji, GCSI; *S* father, 1896; *m* 1905, HH Maharani Nandkunorrba, CI; two *s* one *d*. The State, which ranked high for the efficiency of its administration—the Chief having fully maintained his father's progressive policy—had an area of 2,860 square miles and a population of 441,367. The State came in close and intimate connection with the British Government in the eighteenth century, when it co-operated with them in the extirpation of piracy from the Kathiawar coast; it was the pioneer of railway enterprise in Kathiawar, maintaining a line of about 250 miles, and had large projects of extension in hand; had an excellent and sheltered harbour, open to ocean-going steamers; maintained a body of Imperial Service Lancers, the largest in the province. Salute, 15 guns. *Recreations:* a keen sportsman and an excellent shot, keeping several hunting cheetahs

whom he trained personally. *Address:* Bhavanagar, Kathiawar.
Died 11 July 1919.

BHUTAN, Maharajah of, Sir Ugyen Wungchuk, GCIE 1921 (KCIE 1905); KCSI 1911; *b* 1861. Had a salute of 15 guns. *Address:* Bhutan. *Died Aug. 1926.*

BIAGI, Dott. Comm. Guido; Grande Ufficiale dell' Ordine dei SS Maurizio e Lazzaro e dell' Ordine della Corona d' Italia; Hon. OBE; formerly Director of the Biblioteca Medicea-Laurenziana, and of the Biblioteca Riccardiana, in Florence, since 1895; Bibliographical Superintendent of Umbria and the Marches; *b* Florence, 29 Jan. 1855; *s* of Prof. Luigi Biagi, a painter, and Emilia Costetti, of Bologna, Superintendent of the Town Schools of Florence; *m* Amelia, *d* of avv. Piroli, member of the Italian Senate and Vice-President of the State Council; one *s* one *d*. *Educ:* Instituto Superiore di Perfezionamento, Florence; DLit 1878. Assistant Librarian, 1880; Vice-Librarian, 1882; Librarian of the Vittorio Emanuale Library in Rome, and Chief of the Cabinet of the Under-Secretary of Public Education, 1884–86; Librarian of the Marucelliana Library in Florence, 1885; Prefetto of the Medicea-Laurenziana Library in Florence, 1885; Chief of the Cabinet of the Ministry of Public Instruction, 1892–93; General Inspector of the Ministry of Education, 1893–95; Resident Member of the Academy Della Crusca since 1913; Hon. Treasurer of the Societa Dantesca Italiana since 1899; Member of the History Deputation of Tuscany; representative of the Italian Government at the International Librarians' Conference of London, 1897, St Louis, 1904, and Brussels, 1908; member of different academies and of the Royal Society of Literature. Knight of the Polar Star of Sweden. *Publications:* The Private Life of the Florentines; Men and Manners of Old Florence; The Last Days of Shelley; Napoleon inconnu; Le Novelle antiche; Vita di Giuseppe Giusti; Aneddoti letterari; Vocabolario italiano di Niccolo Tommaseo compendiato e rifatto; Indice del Mare Magnum di F. Marucelli, etc; Passatisti (Biographies of leading Italian men); La Divina Commedia nella figurazione artistica e nel secolare commento; Rivista delle biblioteche e degli archivi. *Recreation:* making plans. *Address:* Florence, 18 Via Pier Capponi; in summer, Castiglioncello (Pisa). *T:* 1360 (Private). *Club:* Soc. Leonardo da Vinci, Firenze.

Died 6 Jan. 1925.

BIBBY, Frank, CBE 1920; JP, DL; *b* 4 Jan. 1857; *o surv. s* of late James Jenkinson Bibby, and Sarah, *d* of Thomas Cook, Dewsbury; *m* 1890, Edith, *e d* of Maj.-Gen. Sir Stanley de Astel Calvert Clarke; one *s* two *d*. *Educ:* Eton. High Sheriff of Shropshire, 1900; Lord of the Manor of Hadnall. *Address:* 39 Hill Street, W1. *T:* Grosvenor 2165; Hardwicke Grange, Sansaw, near Shrewsbury. *Clubs:* Carlton; Royal Yacht Squadron, Cowes. *Died 12 Feb. 1923.*

BICE, Hon. Sir John George, KCMG 1923; MLC; Chief Secretary and Minister of Marine since 1919; *b* Callington, Cornwall, 1853; *s* of Samuel S. Bice, late of Moonta, Wallaroo, and Port Augusta; *m* 1897, Elizabeth J., 2nd *d* of late John Trewenack; one *s* two *d*. *Educ:* village school in Cornwall, night school at Moonta. For some time Mayor of Port Augusta; represented the Northern District in the Legislative Council since 1894; Honorary Minister, 1908–9; Chief Secretary, 1909–10, 1912–15. *Address:* Ruthven Lodge, Bishopsplace, Kensington, South Australia. *T:* Norwood 1582. *Club:* Liberal. *Died Nov. 1923.*

BICKERSTAFFE-DREW, Rt. Rev. Monsignor Count Francis Browning Drew, CBE 1919; KHS; LLD; *b* Headingly, Leeds, 11 Feb. 1858; *s* of late Rev. Harry Lloyd Bickerstaffe and Mona Brougham, *d* of Rev. Pierce William Drew, of Heathfield Towers, Youghal; assumed 1879 additional surname of Drew. *Educ:* King Edward VI School, Lichfield; St Chad's Coll., Denstone (ASNC 1st Class Honours); Oxford; subsequently at St Thomas's Seminary, Hammersmith. Ordained Priest, 1884, by Bishop Wethers; Assistant Priest of Pro-Cathedral, Kensington, 1884–86; Acting Chaplain to the Forces, Plymouth, 1892–99; Senior RC Chaplain, Malta, 1899–1905, and 1909; Salisbury Plain, 1905–9 and 1916; Private Chamberlain of His late Holiness Pope Leo XIII, 1891; decorated with Cross of Leo XIII, Pro Ecclesia et Pontifice, 1901; an Examiner in, and Member of the Special Council of the Pontifical Chamber of Malta since 1900; Private Chamberlain of Pope Pious X, 1903; created Domestic Prelate of His Holiness, 1904; Knight of the Sacred Military Order of the Holy Sepulchre and Count, 1909; also special Jubilee Medal from His Holiness; Protonotary Apostolic, 1912; Foreign Member and Delegate of the Société Archéologique de France, 1913; served European War, 1914–15 (despatches twice, and Secretary of State's Special Despatch, Mons Medal, 2 roses, Victory Medal, General Service Medal, CBE); Hon. LLD University of Notre Dame, Indiana, and of Marquette University, Wisconsin, 1917; Assistant Principal RC Chaplain, 1918; retired, 1919. *Publications:* (as John Ayscough) Rosemary; Mezzogiorne; Marotz; Dromina; San Celestino; Hurdcott; Admonition; Mr Beke of the Blacks; A Roman Tragedy; Outsiders and In; Faustula; Levia Ponders; Gracechurch; Monksbridge; French Windows; The Tideway; Jacqueline; Fernando; A Prince in Petto; Abbotscourt; The Foundress; First Impressions in America; Pages from the Past, 1922; Mariquita, etc; an essayist and contributor to magazines and reviews. *Recreations:* books and writing them. *Died 3 July 1928.*

BICKERSTETH, Robert Alexander, MA, MB (Cantab); FRCS; retired; Consulting Surgeon, late Hon. Surgeon, Liverpool Royal Infirmary; *b* 4 Sept. 1862; *s* of late E. R. Bickersteth, FRCS, Liverpool; *m* Ellen Constance, *d* of Charles Bowman Wilson, MRCS, Liverpool; three *s* two *d*. *Educ:* Eton; Trinity College, Cambridge; St Bartholomew's Hospital. Late Lecturer and Examiner in Clinical Surgery in the University of Liverpool; Fellow Royal Society of Medicine; Membre Correspondent de l'Association Française d'Urologie. *Publications:* occasional contributions to medical journals. *Recreations:* shooting, fishing. *Address:* Borwick Lodge, Outgate, Hawkshead. *Clubs:* Athenæum, University, Liverpool.
Died 29 Feb. 1924.

BICKFORD, Admiral Andrew Kennedy, CMG 1885; *b* India, 16 July 1844; 2nd *s* of W. Bickford, of Newport House, South Devon; *m* 1868, Louisa (*d* 1910), *d* of J. D. Dore, MD; four *s* two *d*. *Educ:* South Devon Collegiate School; Foster's, Stubbington. Entered Navy, 1858; served in China as sub-Lieut during operations in Japan; taking of Forts at Simonosaki, etc; was senior and gunnery Lieut of Amethyst during actions with Peruvian rebel ironclad Huascar; as commander, in charge of naval transport arrangements at Alexandria during war; negotiated release of captured crew of Nisero in Acheen; CMG for this service as Capt., senior officer of combined French and English and German and English squadrons at various operations in South Pacific; at Samoa received surrender of Mactafa and chiefs, putting a stop to civil war on that occasion; received thanks of Government, etc; commanded Resolution in Channel squadron; Capt. of Fleet Reserve at Portsmouth; Superintendent of Sheerness Dockyard, 1898–99; Commander-in-Chief Pacific, 1901–4; Egyptian medal, Khedive Star, Medjidie 3rd Class, Jubilee Medal; ADC to Queen, 1896–99; JP and Land Tax Commissioner for County of Sussex. *Address:* 33 Selborne Road, Hove, Sussex. *Club:* United Service.
Died 9 Oct. 1927.

BICKFORD, Major Arthur Louis, CIE 1911; 56th Rifles, Frontier Force, Indian Army; DAAG, 1st (Peshawar) Division, since 1914; *b* 1870; *s* of Admiral A. K. Bickford; unmarried. *Educ:* Stonyhurst; Sandhurst. Entered 2nd Queen's Regiment, 1892; Captain Indian Army, 1901; Brevet Major, 1908; Substantive Major, 1910; served Tirah Expedition, 1897–98 (medal with two clasps); Bazar Valley Expedition, 1908 (despatches, Brevet of Major, medal with one clasp); Commandant Khyber Rifles, 1910–13. Durbar medal, 1911. *Recreations:* tennis, golf. *Address:* c/o H. S. King and Co., 9 Pall Mall, SW. *M:* P 3. *Club:* East India United Service.
Died 18 March 1916.

BIDDLE, Major Fred Leslie, DSO 1916; Officer Commanding 4th Battery Australian Field Artillery, Australian Imperial Forces; *b* Melbourne, Australia, 27 Oct. 1885; parents, English born; unmarried. *Educ:* Hawthorn College, Melbourne. Matriculated, Melbourne University, 1901; Business Career, Wholesale Warehouseman (soft goods); joined Australian Field Artillery (Militia), 1904; joined AIF for service abroad, and seconded from AFA 1914; landed to evacuation, Anzac, 1915; Major, 1916. *Recreations:* football (Australian rules), field artillery. *Address:* 92 Vale Street East, Melbourne, Victoria, Australia. *Clubs:* Naval and Military; United Service Institution, Melbourne. *Died Aug. 1917.*

BIDDULPH, 1st Baron, *cr* 1903, **Michael Biddulph;** DL, JP; partner in the banking firm of Cocks, Biddulph, and Co.; *b* 17 Feb. 1834; *e s* of Robert Biddulph, Ledbury; *m* 1st, 1864, Adelaide Georgiana (*d* 1872), *y d* of Rt Hon. Gen. Jonathan Peel; two *s* two *d* (and one *d* decd); 2nd, 1877, Lady Elizabeth Yorke, VA (*d* 1916), *d* of 4th Earl of Hardwicke, and *widow* of Henry Adeane, MP [Lady Biddulph was author of Charles Philip Yorke, Fourth Earl of Hardwicke]. *Educ:* Harrow. MP (L) Herefordshire, 1865–85; South Herefordshire, 1885–86; MP (LU) Ross Division Herefordshire, 1886–1900. *Heir:* *s* Hon. John Michael Gordon Biddulph, *b* 9 Nov. 1869. *Address:* Ledbury, Herefordshire; Kemble House, Cirencester. *Clubs:* Brooks's, Reform. *Died 6 April 1923.*

BIDDULPH, Assheton; Master of Fox Hounds, King's Co. Hunt; *b* 1850; 2nd surv. *s* of late Francis Marsh Wellesley Biddulph, JP, Rathrobin, King's Co.; *m* 1880, Florence Caroline, *y d* of late Rev. Cunningham Boothby, Holwell Vicarage, Oxfordshire; one *s* four *d*. Entered 57th Regt as Ensign, 1869; retired, 1873; became MFH, 1884, hunting the Ormond and King's County till 1897, when the country was divided, and after 1897 continued Master of King's Co. Hunt, himself hunting his hounds all the time. *Recreations:* field sports in general; fox-hunting particularly. *Address:* Moneyguyneen, Birr, King's Co. *Club:* Junior United Service.

Died 17 Jan. 1916.

BIDDULPH, General Sir Robert, GCB 1899 (KCB 1896; CB 1877); GCMG 1886 (KCMG 1880); *b* London, 26 Aug. 1835; *s* of Robert Biddulph, MP, Ledbury; *m* 1864, Sophia (*d* 1905), *d* of Rev. A. L. Lambert, Rector of Chilbolton, and *widow* of R. S. Palmer; four *s* six *d*. Royal Artillery, 1853; Captain 1860; Major 1861; Lieut-Col 1864; Col 1872; Maj.-Gen. 1883; Lieut-Gen. 1887; Gen. 1892; served in Crimean War, 1854–56; Indian Mutiny Campaign, 1857–59; China War, 1860; Assistant Boundary Commissioner for Reform Act, 1867; private secretary to Mr Cardwell when Secretary of State for War, 1871–73; AAG War Office, 1873–78; HM Commissioner, Constantinople, 1879; High Commissioner for Cyprus, 1879–86; Inspector-General of Recruiting, 1886–88; Director-General of Military Education, 1888–93; Quartermaster-Gen. to the Forces, Jan. 1893; Governor and Commander-in-Chief, Gibraltar, 1893–1900; retired 1902; Army Purchase Commissioner, 1904; Master Gunner of St James's Park, 1914. *Publication:* Lord Cardwell at the War Office, 1904. *Address:* 83 Cornwall Gardens, SW. *Club:* United Service.

Died 18 Nov. 1918.

BIDDULPH, Thomas Stillingfleet, CIE 1907; late Accountant-General, India; *b* 25 Nov. 1846; *s* of Rev. Francis John Biddulph, formerly of Amroth Castle, Pembrokeshire; *m* 1878, Lydia Beatrice, *d* of late Col S. Becher, Indian Army. *Educ:* Lancing. Joined Financial Department, Government of India, 1871; Deputy Auditor-General, and latterly Accountant-General; specially deputed to reorganise the finances of the Mysore State, and subsequently Patiala State, in connection with which received the thanks of Government on several occasions; Captain in Indian Volunteers, services specially brought to notice of Government of India by GOC Secunderabad, 1886; PM Masonic Lodge; retired 1905. *Address:* Biddulph, Rawlins and Co., 7 Nicholas Lane, Lombard Street, EC. *T:* City 4261. *Club:* East India United Service.

Died 24 April 1919.

BIGELOW, Melville Madison, PhD, LLD; *b* 2 Aug. 1846; *o s* of Rev. Wm E. and Daphne F. Bigelow; *m* 1898, Alice Bradford, *d* of Dr George S. and Jane G. Woodman. *Educ:* Univ. of Michigan; Harvard University. Lawyer, author, and teacher of law. Mem. Mass Historical Soc.; Fellow American Academy of Arts and Sciences; Harvard Chap. Phi Beta Kappa, and other learned societies. *Publications:* Law of Estoppel (6 editions); Leading Cases in Law of Torts; Law of Torts (8 American and 3 English editions); Placita Anglo-Normannica; History of English Procedure; Law of Fraudulent Conveyances (2 editions); Law of Bills, Notes, and Cheques (2 editions); Law of Wills; Chaps vi and viii of Cambridge Modern History, vol. 7; A False Equation—The Problem of the Great Trust; Papers on the Legal History of Government. *Address:* 200 Brattle Street, Cambridge, Mass, USA.

Died 4 May 1921.

BIGGAR, Maj.-Gen. James Lyons, CMG 1918; VD; *b* 16 July 1856; 3rd *s* of James Lyons Biggar, MP East Northumberland, and Isabel Hodgins; *m* 1882, Mary Scott, *e d* of R. W. Elliot, Toronto; two *s* one *d*. *Educ:* Upper Canada College, Toronto. Argyll Light Infantry, 1881–1901; Camp Quartermaster District Staff, 1891–1900; on Staff Canadian Contingent Queen Victoria's Diamond Jubilee (Jubilee medal); South Africa, 1899–1901; Staff-Officer for Overseas Colonials at chief Base and Lines of Communication; also acted as Canadian Red Cross Commissioner for seven months (Queen's medal with 4 clasps, Hon. Associate Order of St John of Jerusalem); appointed to Headquarters Staff as DAG for ASC and organised the CASC; Staff-Officer for Colonials at King Edward's Coronation, 1902 (Coronation medal); Director General Supplies and Transport, 1904; Quartermaster-General, 1917; retired 1920. Order of St Saba, 1918; Order of Leopold II, 1918; Officer Légion d'Honneur, 1919. *Publications:* Hints to Quartermasters and ASC Manual. *Recreations:* lawn bowling, curling. *Address:* The Roxborough 49, Ottawa. *TA:* Biggar, Ottawa. *Clubs:* Rideau, Country, Ottawa.

Died 19 Feb. 1922.

BIGGE, Sir William Egelric, Kt 1909; MA, Hon. DCL Durham; Chairman, Associated Board of Royal College and Royal Academy

of Music; *b* 18 Oct. 1850; 4th *s* of late Rev. John Frederick Bigge, Vicar of Stamfordham, and *brother* of 1st Baron Stamfordham. *Educ:* New College, Oxford. First Judge of Small Cause Court, Rangoon, 1886; officiating Judge, Moulmein, 1892; officiating Recorder, Rangoon, 1898; Judge, Chief Court, Lower Burma, 1900–8. *Address:* Queen Anne's Mansions, SW. *Clubs:* Oxford and Cambridge, Brooks's; Northern Counties, Newcastle.

Died 24 Dec. 1916.

BIGGS, Sir Arthur Worthington, Kt 1906; Major (retired) VI Lancashire Artillery Volunteers; *b* 2 March 1846; 4th *s* of late Wm Biggs, JP, of Leicester, formerly MP for Newport (Isle of Wight); *m* 1872, Lillian (*d* 1891), 3rd *d* of late Charles Holland, JP, Liscard, Cheshire; five *s* one *d*. *Educ:* privately, and in Paris. Has taken active interest in the Volunteer movement; an active Liberal; contested South Worcestershire, 1906. *Club:* National Liberal (a Vice-President).

Died 6 Dec. 1928.

BIGGS, George Nixon, MB, BS; Consulting Aural Surgeon to the Evelina Hospital for Sick Children; Surgeon-in-Charge of the Ear and Throat Department, Waterloo Hospital for Women and Children; Surgeon in charge Ear and Throat Department, Dreadnought Hospital, at Greenwich, and Hospital for Paralysis and Epilepsy, Maida Vale; Teacher of Otology, Laryngology, and Rhinology at the London School of Clinical Medicine; *b* 28 March 1881; *s* of M. G. Biggs, MD. *Educ:* Westminster School; St Thomas' Hospital. Late House Surgeon, Clinical Assistant and Senior Clinical Assistant, Royal Ear Hospital; Senior Clinical Assistant and Registrar, Metropolitan Ear, Nose, and Throat Hospital; Surgeon-in-Charge of the Ear and Throat Dept, Evelina Hospital; Lt-Col, RAMC(T); Lt-Col RAF; late Consulting Aurist and Laryngologist, Boulogne Base, BEF, and to RAF. *Publications:* A Text-Book of Diseases of the Ear, Nose, and Throat; articles in the various medical journals. *Address:* 31 Wimpole Street, W1. *T:* Langham 1872.

Died 10 Nov. 1922.

BIGGS, Colonel Henry Vero, DSO 1898; Royal Engineers; *b* Belgaum, 9 May 1860; 3rd *s* of late Col T. Biggs, RA, and Mary, *d* of late Rev. W. Beynon; *m* 1887, Frances Kate, *e d* of late Col C. H. Ewart, BSC; one *s*. *Educ:* private school at Clifton. Passed into RMA, Woolwich, 1877; joined RE, 1879; embarked for India, 1882, where joined the Bombay S and M; spent nearly three years on Afghan frontier (including the 1884 Zhob Valley Expedition); in the 3rd Burmese War, 1885–87 (medal with clasp); joined the Military Works from the S and M, 1887; promoted Captain, 1889; Adjutant, RE, Tirah Expeditionary Force, 1897–98; operations on North-West Frontier, 1897; operations in the Kurram and on the Samana, the Chagru Kotal; capture of the Sampaga Pass, and operations in the Khyber (despatches, medal with 3 clasps, and DSO); Major, 1898; Lieut-Col 1905; Bt-Col 1908; Col 1910; Commanding Royal Engineers, 2nd (Rawalpindi) Division, 1901–12; retired, 1912; re-employed for war, 1914 (despatches); retired, 1919. *Recreations:* shooting, riding, rowing. *Address:* c/o Cox's Branch, 6 Pall Mall, SW1.

Died 28 Feb. 1925.

BIGGS, Hermann M., MD, LLD, ScD Harvard; Professor of Medicine, University and Bellevue Hospital Medical College; Consulting Physician Bellevue, Willard Parker, and St Vincent's Hospitals; late Chief Medical Officer, Health Department, New York City; Commissioner of Health, and Chairman Public Health Council, for New York State; Member of International Health Board and War Relief Commission, Rockefeller Foundation and Medical Section—Council of National Defence; *b* Trumansburg, New York, 29 Sept. 1859; *s* of Joseph H. and Melissa P. Biggs; *m* 1898, Frances Richardson; one *s* one *d*. *Educ:* Cornell University; Bellevue Hospital Medical College; Universities of Berlin, and Greifswald, Germany. Fellow NY Academy of Medicine; President Association American Physicians, British Medical Association; Member Board of Directors Rockefeller Institute for Medical Research. Established Bacteriological Laboratories of New York Health Department, 1892, the first municipal Bacteriological Laboratories in the world; devised the methods of bacteriological diagnosis in diphtheria, tuberculosis, etc, as applied to municipal laboratories; introduced methods for sanitary supervision of tuberculosis, beginning in 1887; member of Medical Faculty of Bellevue of Bellevue Hospital Med. College and New York University since 1885; Hon. Fellow Sanitary Inst. Great Britain; Hon. Fellow Royal College Physicians, Edinburgh; Medical Director-General, League of Red Cross Societies, Geneva, Switzerland, 1920. Knight, Order of Isabella the Catholic of Spain. *Publications:* numerous contributions to current medical literature. *Address:* 39 West 56th Street, New York. *T:* Circle 137. *Clubs:* University, Century, Psi Upsilon, Automobile of America.

Died 28 June 1923.

BIGLAND, Percy, RP; artist; *s* of Edwin and Adelaide Bigland, Birkenhead; *m* Edith McHanbury Aggs; one *s* one *d*. *Educ:* Sidcot, Somerset. Seven years Art Student in Munich; 1st Medal, Royal Academy, Munich, 1880; Original Member Royal Society of Portrait Painters, London. *Recreations:* golf, motoring. *Address:* Stone Dean, Beaconsfield, Bucks. *T:* 2Y Chalfont St Giles. *Clubs:* Arts; Beaconsfield Golf; Berrow Golf.
Died 8 April 1926.

BIGWOOD, James, MA; JP, DL; Middlesex County Alderman, Chairman of its Parliamentary Committee, and representative for County upon the Thames Conservancy; Partner, Champion and Co., London; *b* 1839; *s* of James Bigwood, Clifton, Gloucestershire; *m* 1862, Marian, *o d* of Edward Webb, Torquay. *Educ:* St John's Coll., Camb. MP (C) East Finsbury, 1885–86; Brentford Division, Middlesex, 1886–1906. *Recreations:* golf, cricket, tennis, cycling. *Address:* The Lawn, Twickenham. *Club:* Carlton.
Died 6 Dec. 1919.

BILGRAMI, Syed Hossain, Nawab, Imadul Mulk, Bahadur; CSI 1908; *b* Gya, 18 Oct. 1842; *s* of Syed Zainuddin Hossain Khan Bahadur of the Uncovenanted Civil Service, Bengal; *m* 1st, 1864, wife died 1897; *m* 2nd, Edith Boardman, LSA (Lond.), MD; four *s* one *d*. *Educ:* Presidency College, Calcutta. Professor of Arabic, Canning College, Lucknow, 1866–73; Private Secretary to HE Sir Salas Jung till his death; Private Secretary to HH the Nizam; Director of Public Instruction for HH the Nizam's Dominions; Member of the Legislative Council, Member of the Universities Commission, 1901–2; retired on good service pension, 1907; 1st Indian Member of Council of Secretary of State for India, 1907–9; Chief Adviser to the Prime Minister, 1912–13. *Publications:* Life of Sir Salas Jung; Lectures and Addresses; (in collaboration) Historical and Descriptive Sketch of His Highness the Nizam's Dominions, 2 vols. *Club:* Secunderabad, Secunderabad.
Died June 1926.

BILIOTTI, Sir Alfred, KCMG 1896 (CMG 1886); CB 1890; *b* 14 July 1833; *s* of late Charles Biliotti, Vice-Consul; *m* 1889. Vice-Consul at Rhodes, 1856–73; at Trebizond, 1873; Consul, 1879; Trebizond and Sivas, 1883–85; Crete, 1885–99; Consul-General, 1899; Consul-General at Salonica; retired 1903. *Address:* Island of Rhodes, Turkey.
Died 1 Feb. 1915.

BILLE, Frank Ernest, Hon. GCVO; Grand Cross of the Order of Dannebrog; Chamberlain to HM the King of Denmark; *b* Copenhagen, 14 Feb. 1832; 2nd *s* of Vice-Admiral Sten Andersen Bille and Caroline Bülow; *m* 1869, Sarah Augusta, *d* of O. Zabriskie, Chancellor of the State of New Jersey, US; two *s* one *d*. *Educ:* Copenhagen. The Danish Army, 1851–65; Royal Engineers and General Staff (Headquarters) during the Danish-German War, 1864; Diplomatic Service; Peace Negotiations in Vienna, 1864; Secretary of Legation in Paris, 1865–67; Minister resident in Washington, 1868–72; Envoy extraordinary in Stockholm, 1872–90; Delegate to the Hague Peace Conference, 1899; Danish Envoy Extraordinary and Minister Plenipotentiary to the Court of St James, 1890–1908. *Address:* 24 Pont Street, SW. *T:* Kensington 4833. *Clubs:* Travellers', Bachelors'.
Died 10 June 1918.

BILLINGTON, Mary Frances; newspaper special correspondent; *b* Chalbury Rectory, Wimborne, Dorset; *d* of late Rev. G. H. Billington, MA Cantab, and Frances Anne, *d* of late Rev. T. Barber, BD, Rector of Houghton Conquest, Beds. *Educ:* home. Began journalistic career on the Echo, going subsequently to the Daily Graphic for some few years; exclusively attached since 1897 to the permanent staff of the Daily Telegraph; an occasional contributor to magazines; President, Society of Women Journalists, 1913–19; represented Society as only overseas woman delegate invited to Imperial Press Conference, Ottawa, 1920; paid two long visits of investigation to India; travelled upon North-West Frontier and in Nepal. *Publications:* Woman in India, 1895; edited Marriage, and A Mule-driver at the Front (by her brother), 1900; Women in Journalism, 1903; The Red Cross in War for Daily Telegraph Series of War Books, 1914; The Roll-Call of Serving Women, 1915. *Recreations:* horses, travel. *Address:* 23 Warwick Square, Belgrave Road, SW1. *Club:* Cowdray.
Died 27 Aug. 1925.

BILSLAND, Sir William, 1st Bt, *cr* 1907; LLD; Lord Provost of Glasgow and Lord Lieutenant of County of City of Glasgow, 1905–8; *b* Ballat, 17 March 1847; *s* of late James Bilsland, Ballat, Stirlingshire; *m* 1885, Agnes Anne, 3rd *d* of late Alexander Steven of Provanside, Glasgow; one *s* two *d*. *Educ:* Dalmonach School, Vale of Leven. Bread Manufacturer; Chairman of Bilsland Brothers Ltd, Glasgow; member of Town Council of Glasgow, 1886–1908; Extraordinary Director,

Royal Bank of Scotland; Knight Commander of Royal Norwegian Order of St Olaf, 1906; Imperial Japanese Order of Sacred Treasure (third class), 1907; Hon. LLD, Glasgow, 1907; FSAScot; DL and JP Counties of Lanark and City of Glasgow. *Heir: s* Alexander Steven Bilsland, MC, Director of Bilsland Bros Ltd, and a partner of Gray, Dunn & Co., Biscuit Manufacturers; late Captain, 8th Scottish Rifles [*b* 13 Sept. 1892]. *Address:* 28 Park Circus, Glasgow. *Clubs:* Western, Art, Liberal, Glasgow.
Died 27 Aug. 1921.

BINGHAM, Lionel John; late Dramatic Editor and Critic, Standard, Evening Standard and St James's Gazette; formerly Music Critic of these papers and Daily Express; and musical contributor to Standard of Empire; *b* Alfreton, Derbyshire, 15 March 1878; *s* of J. J. Bingham, MD, and K. L. Robinson; *m* 1908, Margaret Sarah Clarkson, Highgate, N; one *s* one *d*. *Educ:* home and London. Fond of art and music as a child; studied painting when a boy, music later; came to London at about eighteen years of age and entered the Royal Academy of Music; remained there three years studying pianoforte, violin, organ, and harmony; joined the music and dramatic staffs of the papers above mentioned in 1905. *Publications:* chiefly magazine articles, including Choral Singing in England To-day and Behind the Scenes at the Opera. *Recreations:* art, sailing, London Chamber Concert Society. *Address:* Trent House, Oxford Road, Gunnersbury, W4.
Died 30 Oct. 1919.

BINGHAM, Rear-Adm. Hon. Richard, RN; *b* 6 Jan. 1847; 2nd *s* of 3rd Earl of Lucan; *m* 1st, 1877, Mary Elizabeth (*d* 1908), *y d* of Edward H. Cole of Stoke Lyme; two *d*; 2nd, 1914, Ida Louisa, *d* of late Charles Galton, late ICS, and Mrs Galton. *Address:* 5 Palmeira Court, Hove. *Club:* Union, Brighton.
Died 12 Nov. 1924.

BINNEY, Rev. William Hibbert, TD 1911; DD; FRGS; Hon. Canon of Chester, 1907–13; Residentiary Canon since 1913; Vicar of Northwich, Cheshire, 1886–1913; Rural Dean; *b* 21 Jan. 1857; *s* of Rt Rev. Hibbert Binney, DD, Bishop of Nova Scotia, 1851–87; unmarried. *Educ:* Winchester; New College, Oxford; Leeds Clergy School. BA degree, 2nd Class Modern History, 1879; MA, 1882; Hon. DD Windsor, Nova Scotia, 1905. Commissary to Bishops of Nova Scotia since 1885; Rural Dean of Middlewich, 1888; Chaplain 3rd VB Cheshire Regt, 1889; 1st Class Chaplain Territorial Force, to 1913; Member of Education Committee Cheshire County Council since 1903; Proctor in Convocation for Archdeaconry of Chester since 1904; Vice-President Society for the Propagation of the Gospel, 1909. *Address:* Witton House, Northwich. *TA:* Northwich.
Died 4 May 1916.

BINNIE, Sir Alexander Richardson, Kt 1897; FGS; MInstME; FRMS and MRI; Member of Council of Institution of Civil Engineers; *b* London, 26 March 1839; *m* 1865, Mary (*d* 1901), *d* of Dr Eames, Londonderry, Ireland. *Educ:* private schools. Pupil of late J. F. Bateman, FRS, President Instn CE; engaged on Welsh railways, 1862–66; in the Indian Public Works Dept, 1868–74; Chief Engineer LCC, 1890–1901; Engineer, City of Bradford, 1875–90; works constructed—Nagpore Water Works; Blackwall Tunnel; Bradford Water Works; Barking Road Bridge, etc. *Publications:* various papers and reports on professional subjects; lectures on waterworks; papers on rainfall, etc. *Recreations:* scientific. *Address:* 77 Ladbroke Grove, W.
Died 18 May 1917.

BINNIE, Rev. Alfred Jonathan, MA; Vicar of Nuthurst-cum-Hockley Heath; Canon of Cathedral Church, Birmingham, 1913. *Educ:* King's College School; Bruce Castle, Tottenham; Corpus Christi College, Cambridge. Deacon, 1874; Priest, 1875; Curate of St Andrew's, Leeds, 1874–77; St George's, Campden Hill, 1877–78; PC St Silas, Leeds, 1878–79; Curate of Kenilworth, 1880–82; St Andrew's, Plymouth, 1882–84; Vicar of Kenilworth, 1884–91; St Asaph's, Birmingham, 1891–1917. *Address:* The Vicarage, Nuthurst-cum-Hockley Heath.
Died 14 Feb. 1926.

BINNING, Col Lord George Baillie-Hamilton, CB 1904; MVO 1902; commanding Lothian and Border Horse since 1905; Lord-Lieutenant Co. Berwick; Deputy Governor, Bank of Scotland; DL Co. Haddington; *b* 24 Dec. 1856; *e s* of 11th Earl of Haddington; *m* 1892, Katherine Millicent, *o c* of W. Severin Salting; two *s* one *d*. *Educ:* Eton; Trinity College, Cambridge, BA. Joined Royal Horse Guards, 1880; served in Egyptian Campaign, 1882, present at Kassassin, Tel-el-Kebir, and capture of Cairo (medal and clasp); Nile Expedition, 1884–85, present at Abu Klea, El Gobat, and Metemmeh (two clasps); Hazara Campaign, 1889 (despatches, medal, and clasp); commanded Royal Horse Guards, 1899–1903; retired 1907; ADC to Viceroy of India, 1888–89. *Address:* Mellerstain, Gordon, NB.

Clubs: Carlton, Turf, Naval and Military; New, Edinburgh.
Died 12 Jan. 1917.

BINNS, Percy, KC; Resident Chief Magistrate, Durban; *s* of late Sir Henry Binns, Premier of Natal; *m* 1897, Ethel Laura, *d* of William Hayes Accutt; two *s* three *d. Educ:* Bishop's College, Maritzburg; Diocesan College, Rondebosch. Attorney, Supreme Court, Natal, 1885; Notary, 1888; Advocate, 1893. *Address:* Durban, Natal. *Club:* Durban. *Died 8 Jan. 1920.*

BINNY, Major Steuart Scott, DSO 1902; 19th Hussars; *b* 1 July 1871; *m* 1911, Marjorie, 3rd *d* of Henry Champion, Sibdon Castle, Salop. Entered army, 1894; served South Africa, 1899–1901 (despatches, DSO); retired, 1914. *Died 5 March 1916.*

BINSTEAD, Mary; Hon. Secretary of the Femina Vie Heureuse and Bookman Prizes Committee; *d* of late J. A. Openshaw, Kendal, Westmorland; *m* Edward Arthur Binstead. *Educ:* privately; The Manor House, Brondesbury Park. Hon. Secretary of the Society of Women Journalists, 1917–27. *Publications:* historic novels: The Loser Pays; The Cross of Honour; Little Grey Girl; Madam Lucifer; modern novels: Laughter Street, London, etc, under the name of Mary Openshaw; contributor to daily and weekly papers. *Recreations:* motoring, reading, the theatre. *Address:* 136 Cromwell Road, SW7. *T:* Western 5282. *Club:* Lyceum. *Died 28 Sept. 1928.*

BIRCH, Henry William; *b* 1854; 2nd *s* of late John William Birch and Julia, *e d* of late Joseph Arden, of Rickmansworth Park, Herts; *m* 1897, Kate Hazeltine, *d* of R. Anson Yates, of San Francisco. Inherited Loudwater under will of maternal grandfather, and The Grove, Old Windsor, under will of Miss Thackeray, 1879. *Club:* Garrick. *Died 15 Dec. 1927.*

BIRCH, Rev. John George, MRIA; Senior Moderator, TCD; Canon of Killaloe; Incumbent of Kilfinaghty, Diocese of Killaloe, 1885–1918; *b* 22 Feb. 1839; *e* surv. *s* of late W. H. Birch, The Hills, Roscrea, Co. Tip. *Educ:* Trinity College, Dublin. Ordained for curacy of Mullingar, Co. Meath, during incumbency of Rev. Dr Reichel, afterwards Bishop of Meath; then curate in England for several years. *Publications:* a paper entitled Numerical Factors in the Messenger of Mathematics, etc. *Address:* The Hills, Roscrea, Co. Tipperary.

BIRCH, Walter de Gray, FSA; Librarian and Curator to Marquess of Bute, 1902–14; *b* 1 Jan. 1842; *s* of Dr Samuel Birch the Egyptologist, and of Charlotte F. Gray, *sister* of Dr J. E. Gray; *m* 1st, Maria Carolina (*d* 1877), *d* of Colonel J. A. Figueiroa Freitas de Albuquerque, Madeira; 2nd, Florence (*d* 1920), *d* of Isaac Brown; four *s* three *d. Educ:* Charterhouse; Trinity Coll., Cambridge. Entered MSS Department in British Museum, 1864, where he was continuously employed in the study and arrangement of the MSS charters and seals; Senior Assistant, 1865–1902; made an especial study of the Anglo-Saxon, mediæval Latin, Portuguese, and Spanish languages; a specialist in matters relating to literary and record research, printing, book-binding, and disputed handwriting. Vice-President of the British Archæological Association and the St Paul's Ecclesiological Society; for many years Hon. Secretary, Editor, and Treasurer, Brit. Archæological Assoc. Hon. LLD Glasgow University; Hon. Corr. Member of the Royal Academies of Seville and Turin; Hon. Member of the Hispanic Society of America. *Publications:* The Commentaries of Afonso d'Albuquerque; the Cartularium Saxonicum; edited the Journal of the British Archæological Association for twenty-two years; author of History of Margam Abbey; History of Neath Abbey; Memorials of the See and Cathedral of Llandaff; The Register of Hyde Abbey, Winchester; the Nunnaminster MS; Catalogues of the Margam and Penrice MSS; The History of the Domesday Book; History of Scottish Seals, 2 vols; Catalogue of the Seals in the Dept of MSS of British Museum, 6 vols; Ordinale Conventus Vallis Caulium; Sermones Fratris Adæ, Ordinis Præmonstratensis; The Royal Charters of the City of London; The Royal Charters of the City of Lincoln; Catalogue of Saxon Abbots; Memorials of St Guthlac. *Address:* Belgrave Lodge, Harvard Road, Chiswick, W4.
Died 8 March 1924.

BIRCHAM, Major Humphry Francis William, DSO 1915; KRRC; *b* 20 March 1875. Entered army, 1896; Adjutant, 1899; Captain, 1901; Major, 1914; Adjutant, TF, 1908–11; served South Africa, 1901–2 (despatches, Queen's medal 3 clasps); European War, 1914–15 (DSO).
Died 21 July 1916.

BIRD, Sir Alfred (Frederick), Kt 1920; DL; JP; MP (C) Wolverhampton (West) since 1910; *b* Birmingham, 27 July 1849; *s* of Alfred Bird, FCS; *m* 1875, Eleanor Frances, *e d* of Robert Lloyd

Evans; four *s* two *d. Educ:* King Edward's School, Birmingham. Manufacturer; retired 1905; contested Wednesbury, 1906. *Recreations:* mountaineering—member Alpine Club, all matters pertaining to art, travelling all over the world, cycling, motoring. *Address:* Artillery Mansions, SW; Tudor Grange, Solihull, Warwickshire. *TA:* Bird, Solihull. *T:* Solihull 81. *Clubs:* Carlton, Junior Carlton, Royal Automobile; Automobile de France, Paris.
Died 7 Feb. 1922.

BIRD, Hon. Bolton Stafford, CMG 1920; late MLC Huon, Tasmania, and Member Executive Council of the State; *b* near Newcastle, 30 Jan. 1840; *s* of Thomas Bird and Ann Stafford; *m* 1867, Helen, *d* of Robert Chisholm, Hope Park, Auckland, NZ; one *s* two *d. Educ:* private academy. Went to Australia, 1853; entered Wesleyan Ministry, 1865; Congregational Minister in Victoria, Australia, and in Tasmania, 1867–79; farmer and fruit-grower, 1879–94 and 1904–19; MHA Franklin, 1882–1903, and South Hobart, 1904–9; Treasurer, Postmaster-General, and Minister of Education, 1887–92 and 1899–1903; Speaker, House of Assembly, 1894–96; MLC, 1909–24; Chairman of Committees in Legislative Council, 1919–22. *Address:* Bruni Vale, Lunawanua, South Bruny, Tasmania.
Died Dec. 1924.

BIRD, Christopher John, CMG 1901; *b* Pietermaritzburg, Natal, 1855; *s* of late John Bird, CMG, of the Natal Civil Service; *m* 1887, Edith, *d* of late William Armstrong, MRCSE; five *s* three *d. Educ:* High School, Pietermaritzburg. Entered the Natal Civil Service, 1874, and was appointed to be Principal Under-Secretary of the Colony on the establishment of Responsible Government in Natal in 1893; JP for the Colony, and Chairman of the Civil Service Board; on the establishment of the Union of the South African Colonies, on 31 May 1910, acted as Under-Secretary for the Interior in Natal up to the date of his retirement on pension, 1 Sept. 1911; served as a member of the Higher Education Commission, 1911. *Address:* Pietermaritzburg. *Died 17 Nov. 1922.*

BIRD, Captain Frederic Godfrey, CMG 1918; DSO 1916; RN; Commanding Drifter Patrol, Dover; *b* 3 Nov. 1868; *s* of late Colonel Frederic Vincent Godfrey Bird, RMLI, and Anne Narcisse Elise Wood; *m* 1908, Elizabeth, *d* of late Charles Evans Whitlock of Richmond, Virginia, USA; four *s* one *d. Educ:* Stubbington House, Fareham; HMS Britannia. Midshipman, 1884; Sub-Lieut, 1888; Lieut, 1890; Commander, 1903; Commanded HMS Perseus in operations against Afghan gun-runners (Naval General Service Medal, Persian Gulf Clasp); retired, 1911; County Councillor, Norfolk, 1913 and 1919; mobilised for European War, Aug. 1914 (DSO, Commander of Swedish Order of Swords of 2nd Class, 1916, Officier Légion d'Honneur). *Recreations:* cricket, shooting. *Address:* Hethel Hall, Norwich. *Clubs:* United Service; Norfolk, Norwich.
Died 29 Dec. 1919.

BIRD, Sir James, Kt 1918; Clerk of the London County Council since 1915; *b* 1 July 1863; *s* of late George Bird; *m* 1891, Jane, *d* of late Henry Riley; no *c.* On staff of Metropolitan Board of Works, 1881; became an officer of London County Council, 1889; Deputy Clerk, 1905. *Address:* County Hall, Spring Gardens, SW; Oakfield, Oakcroft Road, Blackheath, SE. *Club:* National.
Died 12 Feb. 1925.

BIRD, Rev. James Grant; Vicar of Christ Church, Dukinfield; Hon. Canon of Chester Cathedral; Rural Dean of Mottram; *s* of Rev. Charles Robinson Bird, Vicar of Castle Eden, Co. Durham, and Rural Dean of Easington, Chaplain (Lt-Col) 6th Batt. Cheshire Regt, PG Chaplain Lodge of Cheshire; *g s* of Robert Merttius Bird, of Taplow Hill, Maidenhead, and Barton, Warwickshire; *m* Hannah Broome, *d* of Thomas Bulloch, Rock House, Macclesfield. *Educ:* Repton; privately. Ordained, 1875; Assistant Curate of St George's, Macclesfield, 1875–77; Chairman of the (late) Stalybridge School Board; an Alderman of Cheshire County Council; Chairman of Cheshire County Higher Education Committee and of County Training College; Chairman of the Ashton-under-Lyne Board of Guardians; a Governor of Ashton-under-Lyne Infirmary; Hon. Governor of the British and Foreign Bible Society; President of the Stalybridge Harmonic Society, of the District Branch of the NSPCC, and of the District Blind and Deaf and Dumb Societies; a Governor of Manchester Grammar School; a member of the Court of Manchester University, etc. *Recreation:* travel in Europe and the near East. *Address:* Albion House, Stalybridge. *T:* Ashton-under-Lyne 719.
Died 16 Dec. 1920.

BIRD, Lieut-Col Robert, CIE 1905; MVO 1912; VHS 1916; MD, MS (Lond.); FRCS, DPH (Camb.); IMS; Surgeon to the Viceroy,

1904; Professor of Surgery, Medical College, Calcutta, since 1908; *b* 12 Dec. 1866; *m* 1909, Harriet Ellen, *d* of late Lt-Col Dewar, Royal Artillery. *Address:* 2 Upper Wood Street, Calcutta; c/o Grindlay & Co., Parliament Street, SW. *Clubs:* East India United Service; Bengal United Service, Calcutta.

Died 30 March 1918.

BIRD, Rev. Samuel William Elderfield; Prebendary of Exeter, 1903. *Educ:* Oriel Coll., Oxford. Deacon 1862, priest 1863. Asst Master, Felsted Sch., 1861–64; Curate, St James, Plymouth, 1864–72; St David, Exeter, 1872–74, 1878–80; Vicar, All Saints, Plymouth, 1875–78; Launceston, 1880–83; Veryan, 1883–87; Rector, St Sidwell, Exeter, 1887–1916. *Address:* 31 Raleigh Road, Exeter.

Died 27 June 1926.

BIRD, Col Spencer Godfrey, DSO 1900; Royal Dublin Fusiliers (retired); *b* 5 Jan. 1854; *s* of late Rev. Godfrey Bird; *m* 1880, Mary Katherine, *e d* of late W. C. Macready; one *s* one *d*. Entered Army, 1874; Captain, 1881; Major, 1892; Lieut-Colonel, 1902; Brevet-Col 1905; served South Africa, 1899–1902 (despatches three times, Queen's medal, four clasps, King's medal, two clasps); served as Colonel in Command of 15th Royal Fusiliers (Kitchener's Army), 1914–16. *Address:* c/o Cox & Co., 6 Pall Mall, SW1.

Died 12 Dec. 1926.

BIRD, William Seymour, KC; *b* 22 May 1846; *e s* of John James Bird, MD, FRCSI, of Banagher, King's Co., and Hannah Maria, *d* of Garrett Moore, of Annaghbeg, Co. Galway, Capt. 88th (The Connaught Rangers). *Educ:* Trinity Coll., Dublin; Senior Moderator and Gold Medallist in History and English Literature, BA, MA. Called to the Bar, 1870; QC 1889; County Court Judge, and Chairman of the Quarter Sessions, Co. Cork (West Riding), 1892–1915; resigned Sept. 1915. *Recreations:* shooting, gardening. *Address:* Churchtown House, Dundrum, Co. Dublin. *Club:* University, Dublin.

Died June 1919.

BIRDWOOD, Sir George (Christopher Molesworth), KCIE 1887; Kt 1881; CSI 1877; MD Edin., LLD Camb.; *b* Belgaum, Bombay, 8 Dec. 1832; *s* of late General Christopher Birdwood and Lydia Juliana, *d* of Rev. Joseph Taylor, agent of the London Missionary Society, Belgaum; *m* 1856, Frances Anne, *e d* of late Edward Tolcher, RN, and Mary Brodrick Birdwood, Harewood House, Plympton St Mary, Devonshire; three *s* two *d*. *Educ:* Plymouth New Grammar School; Dollar Academy; Watt Institute (Mechanic), and University, Edinburgh. Bombay Medical Staff, 1854; served in the Persian Expedition, 1856–57; Professor of Anatomy and Physiology, and of Materia Medica and Botany, Grant Medical Coll., Bombay; Registrar and Fellow, Univ. of Bombay; Curator, Government Museum; Secretary, Asiatic Society and Agric. Hort. Society, Bombay; in co-operation with Dr Bhau Daji, and the leading Indians of Western India, established the Victoria and Albert Museum and the Victoria Gardens, Bombay; JP, and Sheriff of Bombay, 1864; held leading positions at all the principal exhibitions since 1851, and as a Royal Commissioner for the Indian and Colonial Exhibition, 1886, the Chicago Exhibition, 1893, the Paris Exhibition, 1900; with assistance of late Prof. Chenery, Mr Demetrius Boulger and others, founded Primrose Day; special service, Revenue and Statistics Dept, India Office, 1871–1902. Knight of Grace, St John of Jerusalem; Officer Legion of Honour; Laureate of French Academy. *Publications:* Economic Vegetable Products of the Bombay Presidency, 1868: Handbook, British Indian Section, Paris Exhibition, 1878; The Industrial Arts of India, 1888; The Genus "Boswellia," Transactions Linnæan Society, vol. xxvii; the article Incense, Ency. Brit.; Report on Old Records of the India Office, 3rd edn 1890; Report on Cultivation of Spanish Chestnuts, 1892; Report on Cultivation of Carrots in India, 1897–98; First Letter Book of East India Company, 1895; Appendix on the Aryan Fauna and Flora to Max Müller's Biography of Words, 1888; botanical Foot-notes to Markham's translation of Garcias ab Horto, 1914; Introductions to—Sir Lewis Pelly's Miracle Play of Hasan and Hasain; Steven's Dawn of British Trade to the East; Vincent Robinson's Eastern Carpets; Count Goblet d'Alviella's Migrations of Symbols; Charles Lamb's Adventures of Ulysses, 1899; Mrs Aynsley's Symbolism of the East and West; and S. M. Mitra's Indian Problems, 1908; Preface to—Miss Gabrielle Festing's From the Land of Princes, 1904; The Genealogy of the Naosari Parsi Priests; and Grigg's Relics of the Honourable East India Company, 1909; Appendix to the Life of John Hungerfold Pollen, by Anne Pollen, 1912; Monograph on the Antiquity of Carpets in work on Oriental Carpets, published by Austrian Government; Sva, 1915; numerous contributions to reviews, etc. *Recreation:* gardening. *Address:* 5 Windsor Road, Ealing, W. *Club:* Northbrook.

Died 28 June 1917.

BIRKBECK, William John, MA; FSA; JP, DL; landowner; a member of House of Laymen, Province of Canterbury; *b* 13 Feb. 1859; *o s* of late W. Birkbeck, JP; *m* 1883, Rose K., *d* of Sir Somerville Gurney; two *s* one *d*. *Educ:* Eton; Magdalen College, Oxford. Owned about 4,000 acres; High Sheriff, 1910; travelled in various foreign countries, more especially Russia; attended the Bishop of Peterborough, Dr Creighton, at the Coronation of the Emperor Nicholas II at Moscow, 1896; the Archbishop of Finland at Queen Victoria's Diamond Jubilee, 1897; member of the Speaker's Anglo-Russian Deputation, 1912; appointed to Ilchester Lectureship, Oxford, 1895; Birkbeck Lectureship in Ecclesiastical History, Trinity College, Cambridge, 1914–16. *Publications:* Russia and the English Church, 1895; various pamphlets, articles, and reviews on ecclesiastical, historical, and musical subjects. *Recreations:* ecclesiastical and historical studies, music, shooting. *Address:* Stratton Strawless Hall, Norwich. *TA:* Buxton-Norfolk. *T:* Coltishall 6. *M:* AH 711. *Clubs:* Athenæum, United University, Junior Carlton.

Died 9 June 1916.

BIRKIN, Sir Thomas Isaac, 1st Bt, *cr* 1905; JP, DL; *b* 15 Feb. 1831; 2nd *s* of late Richard Birkin of Apsley Hall, Notts, and Mary Ann, *d* of late Thomas Walker of Trowell, Notts; *m* 1856, Harriet (*d* 1921), *d* of Matthew Tebbutt of Bluntisham; six *s* three *d*. Dir, GNR and Mercantile Steamship Co.; late Capt., 3rd VB Notts and Derbys Regt (Robin Hood Rifles), of which he was one of the original officers on its formation in 1859. High Sheriff of Notts, 1892. *Heir: s* Thomas Stanley Birkin [*b* 18 Oct. 1857; *m* 1894, Hon. Margaret Diana Hopetoun, *y d* of late Capt. Hon. Henry Weyland Chetwynd, RN, and *sister* of 8th Viscount Chetwynd; two *s* one *d*. *Address:* Park House, Nottingham]. *Address:* Ruddington Grange, Nottingham.

Died 16 Jan. 1922.

BISCOE, Lt-Gen. William Walters, CB 1896; retired; *b* Donnington, Hereford, 12 Aug. 1841; 2nd *s* of late Rev. W. Biscoe. *Educ:* Winchester College. Joined 1st Bengal European Light Cavalry, 1860; appointed to Fane's Horse (later 19th Lancers), 1862; Asst Adjt-Gen., Umballa Division, 1882–85; commanded 19th Bengal Lancers, 1885–92; Colonel on Staff, Multan, 1892–95; commanded Bandelkand District, Agra, during 1895; served in Bezoti Expedition, 1869; throughout Afghan Campaigns of 1878–80 (medal and Brevet of Lieut-Colonel); commanded Cavalry Brigade in Miranzai Expedition, 1891 (medal, CB). *Recreations:* hunting, shooting, polo, cricket, racquets. *Club:* United Service.

Died 27 April 1920.

BISGOOD, Joseph John, BA; JP; *b* Glastonbury, 6 Jan. 1861. *Educ:* Prior Park, Bath; University of London. Editor and Proprietor, Insurance Record; author various works on Insurance; Editor, Pitman's Life Assurance Dictionary; contributor to various journals on Assurance matters; late Secretary in London-Edinburgh Assurance Company, Ltd; President, Chartered Institute of Secretaries, 1918–19; Chairman, London Safety First Council, 1924–26; Member of Surrey County Council and Surrey Education Committee; Member of Richmond Town Council (Alderman-Mayor, 1912–13); Member Richmond Education Committee; Member of Council, London Chamber of Commerce; President of various local societies at Richmond; Director, Vauxhall Motors Ltd, and other public companies. *Recreations:* amateur acting, motoring. *Address:* Lindores, Kew Gardens. *T:* Richmond 0460. *Club:* Gresham.

Died 10 Feb. 1927.

BISHOP, Joseph Bucklin, LittD; Secretary, Isthmian Canal Commission, 1905–14; *b* 5 Sept. 1847; *m* 1872, Harriet Hartwell (*d* 1917), Providence; one *s*. *Educ:* Brown University (AB); LittD 1923. Member, National Institute of Arts and Letters; on Editorial Staff, New York Tribune, 1870–83; Editorial Writer, New York Evening Post, 1883–1900; Chief of Editorial Staff, New York Globe, 1900–5. *Publications:* Cheap Money Experiments, 1892; Our Political Drama, 1904; Issues of a New Epoch, 1904; The Panama Gateway, 1913; Recent Tariff Developments in England; Presidential Nominations and Elections, 1916; A Chronicle of One Hundred and Fifty Years, 1918; Theodore Roosevelt's Letters to his Children, 1919; Theodore Roosevelt and his Time—shown in his Letters (2 vols), 1920; Life of Charles Joseph Bonaparte, 1922; Life of A. Barton Hepburn, 1923. *Club:* University, New York.

Died 13 Dec. 1928.

BISPHAM, David, BA, LLD; Mus. Doc.; Baritone, Royal Opera, Covent Garden; Metropolitan Opera House, New York; *b* Philadelphia, USA, 5 Jan. 1857; *o s* of William D. Bispham and Jane Lippincott Scull; *m* 1885, Caroline, *d* of late Gen. Charles S. Russell, US army. *Educ:* Haverford Coll., near Philadelphia. Début as the Duc de Longueville in The Basoche, Royal English Opera, Nov. 1891;

later with the Royal Opera, Covent Garden, and the Metropolitan Opera Co. of New York, singing the principal roles in German, French, and Italian; founder, American Singers; Opera Comique Co., New York, 1917. *Publications:* autobiography, A Quaker Singer's Recollections; magazine articles. *Recreations:* swimming, cycling. *Clubs:* Players', Century, New York; University, Philadelphia.

Died Oct. 1921.

BISSET, Colonel Sir William Sinclair Smith, KCIE 1897 (CIE 1888); *b* 13 Nov. 1843; *s* of late Rev. James Bisset, DD; *m* 1888, Henrietta Mary, *d* of Lt-Gen. W. P. La Touche, Indian Army; one *s* two *d*. Entered Royal Engineers, 1863; Colonel, 1895; served Afghan War, 1878–80 (medal, Bt Maj.); Deputy Consulting Engineer for Railways, 1872–75; Manager, Rajputana Malwa State Railways, 1875–84; Agent for Bombay, Baroda, and Central India Railway System, 1884–93; Secretary to Government of India in Public Works Department, 1893–97; Government Director of Indian Railways, 1897–1901. *Address:* Hill House, Stoke Poges. *Club:* United Service.

Died 30 July 1916.

BISSETT-SMITH, George Tulloch, FSS; (*pen-name* George Bizet); Civil Servant; Registration Examiner; Travelling Officer, Department of the Registrar-General for Scotland; Member of Council, Franco-Scottish Society and of League of Nations Union for Scotland; Vice-Chairman, Whitley Departmental Council; Founder of the Bizet Correspondence College of Authorship and Journalism; *b* Aberdeen, 11 Jan. 1863; *o c* of late Captain George Bisset-Smith and Christian, *d* of Theodore Morison, Bognie, Aberdeenshire; *m* 1900, Elise, *e d* of James Morison, Glasgow; three *d*. *Educ:* Old Aberdeen Grammar School; Edinburgh University (Prizeman in English Literature and Composition). Entered Civil Service, 1882; office of Registrar-General for Scotland, 1886; HM Registration Examiner for East of Scotland, 1899–1922; Southern District, 1922; Member of Sociological Society, of Society of Scottish Economists, and of the Incorporated Society of Authors. *Publications:* Vital Registration: a Manual of the Law and Practice concerning the Registration of Births, Deaths, and Marriages in Scotland, new edition, 1922; Some Eminent Scotsmen; Leira: a Love Story; Early Part of an Honest Autobiography; The British Constitution compared with Modern Republics; Marriage and Registration, 4th edn, 1921; An Outline of a Philosophy of Population; The Census, and some of its Uses, 1921; Population, and Problems of Sex, 1922; The Census and Social Progress; Industrial Welfare and the League; Hints to Beginners in Literature, 1923. *Recreations:* literature, lawn tennis, sociology. *Address:* 11 Carlton Terrace, Edinburgh. *T:* Central 7985.

Died 21 Oct. 1922.

BIZET, George; *see* Bissett-Smith, G. T.

BLACK, Andrew, RSW 1884; *b* 11 May 1850; *s* of Andrew Black, merchant, and Isabella Jackson; unmarried. *Educ:* Glasgow; Paris. In business as designer for 11 years, and became a professional artist, 1877; exhibitor occasionally at Royal Academy, Paris Salon, Munich, Prague, Edinburgh, and 42 years in Glasgow. *Recreations:* reading, boating. *Address:* 69 St Vincent Street, Glasgow. *Club:* Glasgow Art.

Died 16 July 1916.

BLACK, Prof. Ebenezer Charlton, LLD; Professor of English Literature, Boston University, USA, since 1900; *b* United Presbyterian Manse, Liddesdale, Scotland, 18 June 1861; *y s* of Rev. John Black and Mary Beattie; *m* 1893, Agnes Knox; one *s* one *d*. *Educ:* Edinburgh University. Medallist in Rhetoric and English Literature; Lecturer on English Literature, Harvard University, 1891–93; Principal of Language and Literature Department, New England Conservatory of Music, Boston, 1893–1900; Lecturer on Literature, Emerson College, since 1903; New England University Extension Commission since 1910. LLD, Glasgow University, 1902; Hon. Member Phi Beta Kappa Society, 1905; Member Royal Society of Arts, Scottish Text Society; Pres. New England Association of Teachers of English; Pres. Emerson College Endowment Association; authority and lecturer on educational and literary subjects. *Publications:* Early Songs and Lyrics, 1886; Introduction to Shakespeare, 1913; University Addresses, 1913; contributor to reviews and magazines; editor of the New Hudson Shakespeare (school edition and library edition). *Address:* 50 Kirkland Street, Cambridge, Mass. *Clubs:* Authors'; Twentieth Century, Boston.

Died 11 July 1927.

BLACK, James Watt, MA, Aberdeen; MD, Edin.; FRCP, London; Consulting Obstetric Physician to Charing Cross Hospital, London; *b* 1840; 2nd *s* of James Black, JP, a Commissioner of Supply for the County of Banff, of Knock, Banffshire, and Margaret, *d* of John Watt of Ordens, Banffshire; *m* 1869, Mary Wedderburn, *d* of Captain James

Cox, 92nd (Gordon) Highlanders, and Mary, *d* of Major Archibald Douglas. *Educ:* Aberdeen, Edinburgh, Paris, Vienna, and Berlin. Private Assistant to the late Sir James Y. Simpson, Bt, Edinburgh 1862–67; Obstetric Physician and Lecturer at Charing Cross Hospital London, 1869–98; President of the Obstetrical Society of London 1891–92; has been Examiner in Obstetrics and Gynæcology to the University of Oxford, and to the Royal College of Physicians of London. *Publications:* Editor of Selected Obstetrical and Gynæcological Works of the late Sir James Y. Simpson. *Address:* Crockham Hill Place Edenbridge, Kent. *Club:* Athenæum.

Died 2 Feb. 1918

BLACK, John Sutherland, FRSE; author and editor; *b* Kirkcaldy, NB, 4 July 1846; *e s* of late Rev. James Black, AM (Aberd.), Minister of the Free Church at Dunnikier, Kirkcaldy. *Educ:* at home; Burgh School of Kirkcaldy; Edinburgh University and New College Edinburgh; Tübingen; Göttingen. MA Edin., Hon. LLD Edin. Asst editor of ninth edition of Encyclopædia Britannica, 1878–89; joint editor of Enclopædia Biblica, 1894–1903; joint author and editor of Life and Lectures of William Robertson Smith, 1912. *Address:* 125 St James' Court, Buckingham Gate, SW. *Clubs:* Athenæum, Savile

Died 20 Feb. 1923.

BLACK, Sir Robert James, 1st Bt, *cr* 1922; Director of the Mercantile Bank of India and other companies; *b* 19 July 1860; 3rd *s* of late Robert John Black, London; *m* 1890, Ellen Cecilia, 2nd *d* of late General W. P. La Touche, Indian Army; one *s* four *d*. *Educ:* privately. Went to India, 1878; left 1900; retired from Best & Co. Ltd, Madras, 1918; sometime President, Bank of Madras and member of Port Trust of Madras, and since connected with finance and commerce of India and the further East. *Recreations:* hunting, shooting, fishing. *Heir: s* Robert Andrew Stransham Black, *b* 17 Jan. 1902. *Address:* Midgham Park, Berks. *T:* Woolhampton 5. *Clubs:* Oriental, Ranelagh.

Died 28 Sept. 1925.

BLACKADER, Maj.-Gen. Charles Guinand, CB 1917; DSO 1900; (temp. Major-General) Leicester Regiment; ADC to the King, 1916; *b* 20 Sept. 1869; *s* of C. G. Blackader; *m* 1888, Marian Ethel, *d* of late George Melbourne; two *d*. Entered army, 1888; Captain, 1895; Major, 1904; Lt-Col, 1912; served West Africa, 1897–98 (despatches, medal 2 clasps); South Africa, 1899–1902 (despatches twice, Queen's medal with four clasps, King's medal with two clasps, DSO); European War, 1914–18 (despatches twice, brevet Colonel, promoted Maj.-Gen.). *Club:* Naval and Military.

Died 2 April 1921.

BLACKBURN, Colonel John Edward, CB 1917; late RE, retired pay; *b* 1851; *s* of late R. B. Blackburn, Sheriff of Stirlingshire. *Educ:* Trinity College, Glenalmond; Eton. Entered Army, 1871; Capt. 1883; Major, 1890; Lieut-Colonel, 1898; Colonel, 1902; retired pay, 1903; served in Egypt, 1882–83 and 1884–85 (medal with 3 clasps and large bronze star, despatches); European War, 1915–16 (CB). *Clubs:* United Service; New, Edinburgh.

Died 29 Sept. 1927.

BLACKBURNE, Lt-Col Charles Harold, DSO 1902; 5th Dragoon Guards; *b* 20 May 1876; *s* of late C. E. Blackburne of Oldham; *m* 1903, Emily Beatrice, *d* of Canon H. D. Jones; one *s* one *d*. *Educ:* Tonbridge. Served South Africa with 11th Batt. Imperial Yeomanry, 1900–2 (King's and Queen's Medals, despatches, DSO); European War, 1914–17 (wounded, despatches, brevet Major and Lt-Col); Assistant Secretary for Transvaal Repatriation Department, 1902; General Manager of Transvaal Government Stud, 1902–6. *Address:* Tyddyn, Mold, N Wales. *Club:* Cavalry.

Died 10 Oct. 1918.

BLACKBURNE, Joseph Henry; British Chess Champion; *b* Chorlton-on-Medlock, Manchester, 10 Dec. 1841; *m*; wife died 1922. *Educ:* Manchester. *Address:* 45 Sandrock Road, Lewisham, SE. *Club:* City of London Chess. *Died 1 Sept. 1924.*

BLACKWELL, Major Francis Victor, CBE 1920; MC 1916; publicist and journalist; *s* of John Blackwell, Shipley, Yorks. *Educ:* Belle Vue; privately. Studied banking, law, and journalism; served in Duke of Wellington's West Riding Regt (MC); wounded, 1916; invalided home; attached Northumbrian Reserve Brigade; sent with British Military Mission to America, Oct. 1917; commanded group of British Officers, Camp Dodge, Iowa; attached British War Mission, Crewe House, and afterwards Canadian Mission in London; Assistant Director of Publicity, Victory Loan, 1919; Press Adviser, Russian Famine Relief Fund, 1921; Publicity Adviser, Dept of Overseas Trade, Pageant of Empire, British Empire Exhibition, 1924; Brighter London

Campaign, 1922; Director of Publicity, Torchlight and Searchlight Tattoo; also responsible for many political, financial, and industrial campaigns. *Address:* 1 Lancaster Gate, W2. *T:* Paddington 3567. *Clubs:* Devonshire, Royal Automobile.

Died 12 March 1928.

BLACKWOOD, Lieut-Col Albemarle Price, DSO 1918; The Border Regiment; *b* 4 Nov. 1881; *s* of Major Price Frederick Blackwood; *m* 1920, Kyra, *d* of late Albert Llewellyn Hughes. *Educ:* Sandhurst. 2nd Lieut, The Border Regt, 1901; served S African War, 1901–2; European War, 1914–18 (Bt Lt-Col, DSO, 2nd Class Vladimir, Star of Roumania). *Address:* c/o Cox & Co., 16 Charing Cross, SW1. *M:* LW 5009. *Club:* Naval and Military.

Died Oct. 1921.

BLACKWOOD, Sir Francis, 4th Bt, *cr* 1814; Captain RN, retired 1886; *b* Stonehouse, 11 Nov. 1838; *s* of Sir Henry Blackwood, 2nd Bt and Harriet, *d* of J. M. Bulkeley; *S* brother, 1854; *m* 1st, 1861, Laura Olivia (*d* 1865), *d* of R. S. Palmer of Great Torrington; one *d* (one *s* decd); 2nd, 1874, Dorothy (*d* 1919), *d* of Rev. E. H. Quicke, Newton St Cyres, Devon; two *s* one *d* (and one *s* decd). *Heir: g s* Henry Palmer Temple Blackwood, *b* 12 May 1896. *Club:* United Service.

Died 20 June 1924.

BLACKWOOD, Captain Frederick Herbert, DSO 1914; Lincolnshire Regiment; Inspector-General of Police and Commandant Local Forces, British Guiana since 1924; *b* 9 Nov. 1885; *m* 1915, Nora, *d* of Dr Ponsonby Widdup; one *s* one *d*. Entered Army from Militia, 1906; served European War, 1914–15 (DSO); Bimbashi, 13th Sudanese, Egyptian Army, 1916; Commandant Military School, Khartoum, 1916; Kaimakam, commanding 14th Sudanese, 1920. *Address:* Eve Leary Barracks, Georgetown, Demerara.

Died Aug. 1926.

BLACKWOOD, Lord (Ian) Basil (Gawaine Temple); Private Secretary to Lord-Lieutenant of Ireland; *b* Clandeboye, Ireland, 4 Nov. 1870; 3rd *s* of 1st and *brother and heir-pres.* of 2nd Marquess of Dufferin and Ava. *Educ:* Harrow; Balliol Coll., Oxford. Barrister, 1896; Dep. Judge Advocate, South Africa, 1900–1; Asst Colonial Secretary, Orange River Colony to 1907; Colonial Secretary, Barbados, 1907–9; Intelligence Corps (attached 9th Lancers), Aug. 1914; Grenadier Guards, June 1915; served Eurpean War, 1914–16 (wounded). Illustrated the Bad Child's Book of Beasts, More Beasts, and the Modern Traveller, under the initials B. T. B., 1898. *Address:* Clandeboye, Co. Down, Ireland. *Clubs:* White's, Pratt's.

Died 3 July 1917.

BLAGDEN, Rev. Henry; Hon. Canon, Christ Church, Oxford, 1892; *b* 25 Oct. 1832; *m* 1864; three *s* four *d*. *Educ:* Trinity Coll., Cambridge (Scholar, MA). Curate of St Neots, 1855–57 and 1859–62; St Mark, Torquay, 1858; Westbury, 1859; Christ Church, St Leonards, 1862–65; Newbury, 1865–69; Vicar of Hughenden, 1869–93. *Address:* 27 Kensington Court Mansions, SW8.

Died 16 Dec. 1922.

BLAGROVE, Col Henry John, CB 1900; CBE 1919; retired; *b* 30 July 1854; *s* of H. J. Blagrove of Gloucester Place, Hyde Park, and Cardiff Hall and Orange Valley estates in Island of Jamaica; *m* 1st, 1884, Alice Evelyn, *d* of late Rev. E. Boothby of Whitwell, Derbyshire; 2nd, 1904, Violet, *d* of F. Walton, of Cwmllecoedfog, Montgomeryshire; three *s* (and one *s* decd). *Educ:* Eton; Magdalen Coll., Oxford. Entered 13th Hussars, 1875; Capt. 1883; Major, 1890; Lt-Col, 1896; Bt Col, 1900; served Afghanistan, 1879–80; Egyptian Expedn 1882; Battles of Kassassin and Tel-el-Kebir, and march to Cairo (medal with clasp and bronze star); S Africa, 1899–1901 (despatches, CB); commanded 13th Hussars, 1896–1901; Commandant, Prisoners of War Camp, Leigh, 1915–17. *Address:* Dowdeswell Court, Glos. *Club:* Cavalry.

Died 29 Nov. 1925.

BLAIKIE, Walter Biggar, LLD; FRSE; JP, DL; Chairman of T. & A. Constable Ltd, University Press, Edinburgh; *b* Edinburgh, 1847; 2nd *s* of late Rev. Prof. William Garden Blaikie, DD, LLD, Edinburgh; *m* 1873, Janet Marshall, *o d* of John Macfie, Edinburgh; five *d*. *Educ:* Edinburgh Academy; Brussels; Edinburgh University. Went to India in 1870; served in Department of Public Works; retired 1879, when Executive Engineer, Military Works; entered his present firm, 1879; Chairman, Edinburgh Chamber of Commerce, 1903–6; formerly a Member of Council, Scottish History Society and Royal Scottish Geographical Society; a Manager of the Edinburgh Royal Infirmary, 1900–20. Hon. LLD University of Edinburgh, 1913. *Publications:* The Itinerary of Prince Charles Edward, 1896; Origins

of the Forty-five, 1916; Edinburgh at the Time of the Occupation of Prince Charles, 1910; numerous contributions to magazines, etc, dealing with the Jacobite period of Scottish history; Monthly Star Maps, an annual series, 1898–1920. *Address:* Bridgend, Colinton, Midlothian. *TA:* Blaikie, Colinton. *T:* Colinton 45. *Clubs:* Savile, Athenæum; University, United Service, Edinburgh.

Died 3 May 1928.

BLAIR, Colonel James Molesworth, CMG 1919; DSO 1917; Military Attaché at Belgrade since 1921 and Belgrade and Prague since 1923; *b* near Ardrishaig, Argyllshire, 15 July 1880; *s* of Charles Blair, DL, JP, of Glenfoot, Tillicoultry; *m* 1909, Lilian Louise Archer, *e d* of Maj.-Gen. Sir O. R. A. Julian of Broomhill, near Ivybridge, S Devon; one *s*. *Educ:* Winchester; Magdalen College, Oxford. Served in S African War as Lieut, 1st Volunteer Battalion Hampshire Regt (Queen's medal and 5 clasps); nominated by C-in-C S Africa for Commission as 2nd Lieut in the Black Watch, 1901; Adjutant of Black Watch in India as Orderly Officer to GOC; served in Mohmand Expedition of 1908 (medal with clasp); Captain in Gordon Highlanders, 1911; passed staff college, 1913; Assistant Military Attaché Petrograd, Aug. 1914; served during World War in Russia and France (despatches twice, DSO, Legion of Honour, 2nd Class Order of Stanislaus, 4th Class Vladimir, both with swords, 1914 Star, General Service and Victory medals); with British Military Mission in Siberia, first as Chief Staff Officer, then as Chief Mission, 1918–20 (CMG, Czech War Cross, 2nd Class Order of Sacred Treasure); Colonel, 1923. *Recreations:* fishing, shooting, golf. *Address:* British Legation, Belgrade, Yugoslavia.

Died 8 June 1925.

BLAIR, Rt. Rev. Laurence Frederick Devayne, DD. *Educ:* Pembroke College, Cambridge; Ridley Hall, Cambridge. Ordained, 1892; Curate of Portman Chapel, 1892–95; Rector of Chalgrave and Vicar of Langley, 1895–1902; Chaplain of Bellary, Madras, 1902–3; Sangor, 1903–4; Army Chaplain in England, 1904–5; Church Parochial Mission Society, 1906–10; Bishop of the Falkland Islands, 1910–14. *Address:* The Church House, Westminster, SW1.

Died 18 Nov. 1925.

BLAIR, Very Rev. William, VD; MA, DD; FSAScot; Minister of Leighton Church, Dunblane; *b* Cluny, Fifeshire, 13 Jan. 1830; 9th *s* of George Blair and Elspeth Welch; *m* 1858, Elizabeth Allan (*d* 1904), 2nd *d* of David Corsar, flaxspinner, Arbroath; five *s* four *d*. *Educ:* Auchterderran Parish School; Univ. of St Andrews. 1st class honours in Greek, 1847, 1850; MA 1850; DD 1879. Ordained, 1856; Chaplain to 6th Perthshire Rifle Volunteer Corps, 1864; and Acting Chaplain to 4th Perthshire Vol. Batt. The Black Watch (Royal Highlanders), 1892; Hon. Chaplain, Territorial Force, 1911; Clerk to the UP Synod, 1884; Chairman of Dunblane School Board, 1885–1909; Parish Councillor, 1896; Moderator of UP Synod, 1898–99; one of principal clerks of United Free Church General Assembly, 1900–7; member of Univ. Court, St Andrews, 1903–11. *Publications:* Chronicles of Aberbrothec; Rambling Recollections of Scenes Worth Seeing; History and Principles of the United Presbyterian Church; Life of Rev. George Jacque; Life of Archbishop Leighton; Log of "The Hersilia"; editor of M'Kelvie's Annals of the United Presbyterian Church; of Jubilee Memorial Volume; Robert Leighton; Kildermoch, etc. *Recreation:* golf. *Address:* Leighton Manse, Dunblane, Perthshire, NB.

Died 11 Aug. 1916.

BLAIS, Rt. Rev. Andrew Albert; Bishop of Rimouski since 1891; *b* Quebec, 26 Aug. 1842. *Educ:* Quebec Seminary. Titular Bishop of Germanicopolis; Coadjutor of Rimouski with future succession, 1890. *Address:* Bishop's Palace, Rimouski, Canada.

Died Jan. 1919.

BLAKE, Col Arthur Maurice, CB 1897; JP, DL; Colonel 1st Volunteer Battalion Bedfordshire Regiment; *b* Glasgow, 11 Sept. 1852; *o s* of Col F. R. Blake, CB, 33rd Duke of Wellington's Regt, and Henrietta, *d* of G. S. Marten; *m* 1881, Isabella, 2nd *d* of J. S. Crawley of Stockwood, Luton; two *s*. *Educ:* Eton. Joined Grenadier Guards, 1870; retired 1877; Major, 1st Herts Vols 1878; Lt-Col of 1st VB Beds. Regt, 1880. *Recreations:* cricket, shooting. *Clubs:* Arthur's, Junior Carlton.

BLAKE, Sir Ernest Edward, KCMG 1901; Crown Agent for the Colonies, 1881–1909; *b* 1845; *s* of Rev. Edmund Blake, of Bramerton, Norfolk; *m* 1874, Catharine Isabella (*d* 1902), *d* of Alfred Blyth; two *s* one *d*. Entered Colonial Office, 1863; Assistant Private Secretary to Earl of Kimberley, 1872, Private Secretary, 1874; 1st class Clerk and Head of Gen. Dept, 1879. *Address:* Woolcombe St Mary's, Uplyme, Devon.

Died 30 Nov. 1920.

BLAKE, Sir Henry Arthur, GCMG 1897 (KCMG 1888; CMG 1887); FRGS; FRCI; FID; JP, DL; Knight of Justice of Order of St John of Jerusalem; Hon. Colonel Ceylon Mounted Rifles; District Grand Master, Ceylon Freemasons; Member of the Council, Royal Dublin Society; Hon. Member, Zoological Society, London; *b* Limerick, 18 Jan. 1840; *s* of late Peter Blake, County Inspector of Irish Constabulary; *m* 1st, 1862, Jeannie (*d* 1866), *d* of Andrew Irwin of Ballymore, Boyle; 2nd, 1874, Edith, *e d* and *co-heir* of Ralph Bernal Osborne of Newtown Anner, Clonmel; two *s* one *d.* Cadet, Irish Constabulary, 1859; Resident Magistrate, 1876; Special Resident Magistrate, 1882; Governor of Bahamas, 1884–87; Newfoundland, 1887–88; appointed to Queensland, 1888, but resigned without entering upon the administration; Capt.-Gen. and Gov.-in-Chief, Jamaica, 1889–97; at request of Legislature and public bodies of the Island his term was extended in 1894, and again in 1896; Governor of Hong-Kong, 1897–1903; Governor of Ceylon, 1903–7. *Publications:* Pictures from Ireland, by Terence M'Grath; China, 1909. *Recreations:* riding, shooting. *Address:* Myrtle Grove, Youghal, Co. Cork. *Clubs:* Marlborough, Brooks's; Kildare Street, Dublin.

Died 23 Feb. 1918.

BLAKE, Capt. Sir (Herbert) Acton, KCMG 1918; KCVO, 1914; FRGS; JP; Deputy Master, Trinity House, EC; *b* 19 Oct. 1857; *o s* of John George Blake of Winchester; *m* 1897, Lucy Grace, *e d* of James Tine, London. *Educ:* privately. Mariner; some years in command in the British India Steam Navigation Company and the African Royal Mail Company; Captain (retired) RNR; Elder Brother of Trinity House, 1901; Member of Departmental Committee of Board of Trade on Mercantile Marine, and also on Committee on Tonnage; Member of Port of London Authority, 1906–7; a British Delegate on International Committee for Safety of Life at Sea, 1913; Chairman, Advisory Committee of Pilotage to Board of Trade; Chairman, Dock and Harbour Dues Claims Commission. *Address:* 48 Kensington Mansions, SW5. *T:* Western 225; Puck's Croft, Rusper, Sussex. *T:* Rusper 16. *Club:* United Service.

Died 7 March 1926.

BLAKE, Col Maurice Charles Joseph, CB 1897; retired 1897; JP Cos Mayo and Galway; DL Co. Mayo; *b* 20 July 1837; *e s* of late Valentine O. C. Blake and Hon. Margaret, *d* of 3rd Baron ffrench; *m* 1863, Jeannette, *d* of Richard P. O'Reilly of Sans Souci, Booterstown, Co. Dublin, and Castle Wilder, Co. Longford; two *s* three *d. Educ:* Stonyhurst. Joined North Mayo Militia, 1861, which afterwards became 6th Batt. Connaught Rangers; Major, 1884; Lieut-Col commanding, 1885; granted Hon. rank of Col, 1886; High Sheriff for Co. Mayo, 1864. *Recreations:* shooting, farming, county gentleman's amusements. *Address:* Tower Hill, Ballyglass, Co. Mayo, Ireland. *Club:* United Service, Dublin.

Died 5 Feb. 1917.

BLAKE, Major Napoleon Joseph Rodolph, DSO 1900; retired, 1901; DCO Middlesex Regiment; *b* 1853; *s* of late Captain Maurice L. Blake; *m* 1888, Alice, *d* of late R. H. Page-Henderson of Oswaldkirk, Yorks; one *d.* Entered Army, 1873; Captain, 1881; Major, 1890; served Zulu War, 1879 (medal with clasp); South Africa, 1899–1901 (despatches, medal with 7 clasps, DSO). *Address:* Skirsgill, Camberley. *T:* Camberley 32.

Died 21 Oct. 1926.

BLAKE, Lt-Col Terence Joseph Edward, DSO 1918; Stock Exchange; *b* 1886; *m* 1910, Ethel Maud Moore; two *s. Educ:* Owens School. Joined 2/1st Queen's Westminster Rifles in the ranks, Aug. 1914; Commissioned Dec. 1914, and gazetted to 13th Royal Fusiliers; served European War, 1914–19 (wounded thrice, despatches thrice, DSO). *Address:* 18 Glenmore Road, Hampstead, NW3. *T:* Hampstead 5825.

Died 15 Dec. 1921.

BLAKE, Sir Thomas Patrick Ulick John Harvey, 15th Bt, *cr* 1622; *b* 18 March 1870; *s* of 14th Bt and Camilla, *y d* of Harvey Combe, late MCS: *S* father, 1912; *m* 1903, Evelyn Winifred, *y d* of L. G. Stewart, late Liet, RE; one *s.* JP Co. Galway; late Capt. RGA. *Heir: s* Ulick Temple Blake, *b* 6 Aug. 1904. *Address:* Menlough, Co. Galway. *Clubs:* Junior Carlton; Co. Galway.

Died 15 Dec. 1925.

BLAKER, Sir John George, 1st Bt, *cr* 1919; Kt 1897; OBE 1918; Mayor of Brighton, 1895–98; *b* 15 Oct. 1854; *s* of J. G. Blaker; *m* 1890, Lily, *d* of Samuel Cowell; one *s* one *d. Educ:* private schools, Sandgate and Brighton. Elected Councillor, Brighton, 1886; Alderman, 1893; Chief Mil. Rep., Brighton Area, 1914–18. *Heir: s* Reginald Blaker, *b* 27 April 1900. *Address:* The Romans, Stanford Avenue, Brighton.

Died 11 June 1926.

BLAKEWAY, Ven. Charles Edward, DD; Archdeacon of Stafford, since 1911; Canon of Lichfield since 1914; *b* 1868; *s* of Roger Charles and Emily Brassey Blakeway; *m* Ophelia Martha Antisdel, Chicago; two *s* one *d. Educ:* Shrewsbury School; Christ Church, Oxford. Ordained, 1897; Assistant Master, Malvern College, 1894–1902; Curate of Great Malvern, 1900–2; Vicar of Dunston, Stafford, 1902–14; Prebendary of Lichfield Cathedral, 1912; Examining Chaplain to Bishop of Lichfield, 1913. *Publication:* Claims of Modern Thought upon the Clergy. *Address:* The Close, Lichfield.   *Died 7 June 1922.*

BLAKISTON-HOUSTON, John, JP, DL; *b* 11 Sept. 1829; *e s* of late Richard Bayley Blakiston-Houston and Mary Isabella, *d* of John Holmes Houston (whose name he assumed by Royal Licence in 1843); *m* 1859, Marion (*d* 1890), *d* of Richard Shuttleworth Streatfeild, of Uckfield, Sussex; five *s* seven *d.* Held a commission in South Down Militia; High Sheriff of Co. Down, 1860; MP (C) North Down, 1898–1900. *Address:* Orangefield, Belfast; Roddens, Co. Down. *Club:* Carlton.

Died 27 Feb. 1920.

BLANC, Edmond; *b* 1861; *s* of François Blanc; *brother of* Princess Constantine Radziwill and late Princess Roland Bonaparte; *uncle* of SAR la Princesse Georges de Grèce. Membre du Comité des Courses et du Conseil; Supérieur des Haras au Ministère de l'Agriculture; late Member of the French Parliament. Officier de la Légion d'Honneur; Grand Officier de l'Ordre de Saint Stanislas de Russie. *Address:* Château de la Chataignerie, La Celle, St Cloud; 42 Avenue Gabriel, Paris. *T:* 572-95.

Died 12 Dec. 1920.

BLANC, Hippolyte Jean, RSA 1896 (ARSA 1892); FRIBA, 1901; FSAScot; JP; architect; *b* Edinburgh, 18 Aug. 1844; *y s* of Victor Blanc, Privas, France, who became a naturalised British subject in 1849, and Sara Bauress, of French parentage, Dublin; *m d* of Thomas Shield, London; one *s. Educ:* Edinburgh. Pupil of David Rhind, Architect; National Medallist, Science and Art Department School, 1866; Chief Assistant, HM Office of Works, 1877–78; President, Edinburgh Architectural Association, 1871–72, 1872–73, 1888–89, 1889–90, 1906–7, 1907–8; Vice-President, Royal Scottish Society of Arts, 1889–90; President, Edinburgh Photographic Society, 1892–96; Hon. President since 1896; Treasurer, RSA; Medallist for design, Paris, 1889; and Edinburgh, 1886. Designed and erected, among others, Thomas Coats Memorial Church, Paisley; St Cuthbert's Church, Edinburgh; extensive restorations of Edinburgh Castle; Architect for the new Edinburgh Village Asylum, Bangour; Gymnasium at Dunfermline and Forfar; a Royal Commissioner for the International Exhibitions at Brussels, Rome, and Turin, 1910–11. *Publications:* numerous contributions upon Architectural Art, and Archæological subjects. *Recreations:* sketching, architectural photography, golfing. *Address:* 25 Rutland Square, and The Neuk, Strathearn Place, Edinburgh. *TA:* Blanc, Edinburgh. *T:* 2497 and 504. *Clubs:* Scottish Conservative, Scottish Arts.

Died 12 March 1917.

BLANCHE, Rt. Rev. Gustave, CJM; DD; Vicar Apostolic of Gulf of St Lawrence since 1905; *b* Josselin, Vannes, 1848. Sent to Eudist Missions in Canada, 1890; Superior of the Eudist College, Versailles, 1899–1903; Provincial in Canada, 1903–5; Bishop of Sicca-Veneria, 1905. *Address:* Seven Islands, Saguenay Co., Quebec.

Died 8 July 1916.

BLANE, Commander Sir Charles Rodney, 4th Bt, *cr* 1812; RN; *b* 28 Oct. 1879; *s* of late Captain Arthur Rodney Blane, RN, 2nd *s* of 2nd Bt, and Mary Georgina, 2nd *d* of J. Pitcairn Campbell; *S* uncle, 1911; *m* 1912, Amy, *e d* of Col G. F. Leverson; one *d.* Entered Navy, 1893; Lieut, 1900; Commander, 1912; served Benin Expedition, 1897 (General Africa medal, Benin clasp); received the Italian Order of St Maurice and St Lazarus for services rendered at the time of the Messina Earthquake, 1911. *Heir: brother* James Pitcairn Blane, *b* 27 May 1883. *Address:* 44 Montpelier Street, SW. *Club:* Naval and Military.

Died 31 May 1916.

BLANE, Gilbert Gordon, JP; *b* 1851; *e surv. s* of Gilbert James Blane (*d* 1881), and Harriet Stewart, *d* of Rev. Gordon Forbes, Dyce, Aberdeen; *m* 1888, Mabel Augusta, 8th *d* of late Admiral Hon. Keith Stewart, CB; three *d. Educ:* Eton. Was Captain Scots Guards. *Address:* Alltan Donn, Nairn, Scotland. *T:* Nairn 45X4. *Club:* Wellington.

Died 24 Nov. 1928.

BLASERNA, Pietro, Hon. LLD; Professor of Experimental Physics, University of Rome; Director of the Institute of Physics; Member and Vice-President of the Senate of Italy. *Publications:* Treatises on the Conservation of Force, the Dynamic Theory of Heat, the Theory of Sound in Relation to Music, etc. *Address:* University, Rome.

Died 26 Feb. 1918.

BLAYLOCK, Colonel Harry Woodburn, CBE 1918; DCL; *b* 1878; *s* of late Rev. Thos Blaylock, MA, Quebec; *m* 1905, Agnes Georgina, *d* of Dr Jas Mills, Dominion Railway Commissioner, Ottawa; one *s*. *Educ:* Bishops' College School, Bishops' University; McGill University (Macdonald Scholarship). Studied International Law at Paris University, 1903–4; engaged in commercial undertakings until outbreak of war; served with Canadian Forces; Assistant Commissioner, Canadian Red Cross Society in France, 1915–18; after that Chief Commissioner Overseas (despatches). Knight of Grace of the Order of St John of Jerusalem, Officer of the Legion of Honour, Commander of the Order of the Crown of Italy, Commander of the Order of St Sava of Serbia, Cross of Regina Maria of Roumania; Hon. DCL, Bishop's University. *Address:* Chelsea Place, Montreal. *Clubs:* Junior Carlton; St James's, Montreal. *Died Jan. 1928.*

BLECK, Edward Charles, CMG 1910; Consul-General at Genoa since 1918; *b* 26 July 1861; *s* of late Joseph Edward Bleck, sometime of Dulwich, Surrey, and Georgiana Henrietta, *d* of W. L. Reynolds, late HM Colonial and Consular Services; *m* 1895, Helen Laura Ogilvy, *d* of late Captain David Steuart Ogilvy of Corrimony, NB; two *s* three *d*. *Educ:* Dulwich College. Entered public service, 1883; Chargé d'Affaires at Sofia, 1891 and 1892; Archivist of HM Embassy at Constantinople, 1894–1906; Consul for Palestine, 1906–9; Consul-General at Port Said, 1909–14; Librarian and Keeper of the Papers at the Foreign Office, 1914–18. *Address:* British Consulate-General, Genoa; Downe Lodge, Richmond Hill, Surrey. *Died 2 March 1919.*

BLENCOWE, Rev. Alfred James; Canon Residentiary of Chester Cathedral, 1886–1927; Proctor in Convocation, 1908–21; 3rd *s* of John Jackson Blencowe, of Marston House, Marston St Lawrence, Northants; *m* Sophia Louisa, *d* of Rev. John Walcot of Bitterley Court, Shropshire; six *s* one *d*. *Educ:* St John's College, Oxford. BA 1870, MA 1874. Ordained, 1874; Curate of Applethwaite, 1874–76; Vicar of Witton, Northwich, 1876–86; Christ Church, Chester, 1887–89; Rector of West Kirby, 1889–1920. *Address:* Dee Hills Park, Chester. *Died 25 March 1928.*

BLENKIN, Very Rev. George Wilfrid, DD; Dean of St Albans since 1914; *b* 16 Feb. 1861; *s* of Canon G. B. Blenkin, Vicar of Boston; *m* Katharine Anne, *d* of Owen March, Solicitor, Rochdale; two *s* one *d*. *Educ:* Harrow (Scholar); Trinity College, Cambridge (Exhibitioner and Scholar); Bell University Scholar; Bachelor's Carus Greek Testament Prize; 1st Class Classical Tripos. Ordained, 1886; Chaplain of Emmanuel College, Cambridge, 1886–91; Trinity College, 1891–99; Fellow and Junior Dean, 1899–1906; Fellow of Corpus Christi College, 1899; Examining Chaplain to Bishop of Lincoln, 1892–1910; to Bishop of St Albans since 1915; Prebendary of Lincoln, 1903–14; Vicar of Brading, 1906–13; Hitchin, 1913–14. *Publication:* 1st Epistle of St Peter, Cambridge Greek Test. *Address:* The Deanery, St Albans. *T:* 106. *Died 24 Sept. 1924.*

BLENNERHASSETT, Col Blennerhassett Montgomerie, CMG 1896; FRCSI; *b* 18 Nov. 1849; *m* Gertrude Harcourt, *d* of Captain Willcox, RN. Entered army, 1872; Lt-Col 1896; Col 1902; served Ashanti Expedition, 1895–96 (CMG, Queen's Star, despatches); retired, 1906. *Club:* Naval and Military. *Died 24 May 1926.*

BLEWETT, Francis Richard, KC 1908; Practising law at Straford, Ont, Canada; Barrister, Solicitor, Notary Public, etc; *b* Napanee, Ont, Canada, 11 May 1869; *s* of John Blewett and Eliza Getty; unmarried. *Educ:* Napanee Public High Schools; Osgoode Hall, Toronto; Law School. Called to Ontario Bar, 1891; moved to Stratford, 1911, and has been practising alone in said city since; Vice-President, North Perth Liberal-Conservative Association; Anglican; Conservative. *Publications:* articles in Oddfellows Review, St Paul, Minn; The Talisman, Indianapolis; and other papers. *Recreations:* long-distance walking, whist, etc. *Address:* Stratford, Ont, Canada. *Club:* Stratford Country and Crescent.

BLIND, Rudolf; artist and translator; *b* Brussels, 1850; *s* of Karl and Frederica Blind; *m* 1871, Sarah Annie Parsoné; three *s*. *Educ:* University College School (all available prizes two years following), and Royal Academy. Assisted with the decorations of the Opera House at Vienna; enlisted as a volunteer with the German Army in the Franco-German War of 1870–71, and was at the siege of Strasburg in the ambulance service; has painted many well-known pictures, including the Golden Gates, Christ the Consoler, the World's Desire, Love's Extasy, and the Throne of Grace. *Recreations:* walking, fishing, talking, rowing. *Address:* 20 Queen Anne's Grove, Bedford Park, W. *Died 3 Feb. 1916.*

BLISS, 4th Baron; Henry Edward Ernest Victor Bliss, JP; *b* 16 Feb. 1869; *s* of 3rd Baron; *S* father, 1890; *m* 1891, Ethel Wolton. *Educ:* Cheltenham. *Recreations:* fishing, yachting. *Address:* Yacht Sea King, Nassau, NP, Bahamas. *Club:* Royal Yacht Squadron, Cowes. *Died 9 March 1926.*

BLISS, Sir Henry (William), KCIE 1897 (CIE 1889); JP Co. Berks; *b* 1840; *s* of late Rev. J. Bliss, Rector of Manningford Bruce, Wilts, and Mary, *d* of Rear-Adm. Sir Thomas Fellowes; *m* 1st, 1863, Mary (*d* 1876), *d* of late Edmund Rendel, MD, Plymouth; (*s* Major Charles Bliss, CIE, *d* 1914); 2nd, 1879, Edith (*d* 1898), *d* of late James Wheeler, Great Cumberland Place; 3rd, 1900, Florence (*d* 1919), *d* of Sir Frederick Bramwell, 1st Bt. *Educ:* Merton Coll., Oxford (MA). Entered Indian Civil Service, 1863, and filled various appointments; Member of Council, Madras, 1893–98; LCC Holborn, 1901–7. *Address:* The Abbey, Abingdon. *Died 28 Oct. 1919.*

BLISS, Rev. Howard S., DD; President of the Syrian Protestant College, Beyrout, Syria, since 1902; *b* on Mt Lebanon, 6 Dec. 1860; *s* of Daniel Bliss and Abby Wood Bliss; *m* 1889, Amy Blatchford of Chicago; two *s* three *d*. *Educ:* fitted for college at Beyrout; entered Amherst College, USA, 1878; BA 1882; taught two years at Washburn College, Topeka, Kansas; studied theology at Union Theological Seminary, New York City; secured Travelling Fellowship, and studied at Oxford University and Mansfield College, Oxford, 1887–88; Göttingen University and Berlin University, 1888–89. Assistant Pastor of Plymouth Church, Brooklyn, 1889–94; ordained in the Congregational Ministry, 1890; Pastor Christian Union Congregational Church, Upper Montclair, NJ, 1894–1902; received degree of DD from New York University, 1902; from Amherst College, 1902; from Princeton University, 1913. *Recreations:* golf, tennis, etc. *Address:* Beyrout, Syria. *TA:* Beyrout. *Club:* Century, New York. *Died May 1920.*

BLISS, Rev. John Worthington; Rector of Betteshanger with Ham since 1876; Hon. Canon, Canterbury, 1888; Rural Dean of Sandwich, 1881; *b* Halifax, NS, 1832; *s* of late Hon. Mr Justice Bliss, Judge of Supreme Court, NS; *m* 1858, Maria, *d* of late Rev. Henry Lindsay, Rector of Sundridge, Kent. *Educ:* Harrow; Trinity College, Cambridge. Curate of Ide Hill, 1857–58; Speldhurst, 1858–63; Betteshanger, 1865. *Recreations:* travelling, golf. *Address:* Betteshanger, Eastry SO, Kent. *TA:* Eastry. *Club:* Union. *Died 20 April 1917.*

BLISS, Rev. William Henry, MA 1870; MusB Oxon 1863; Hon. Chaplain to the King; *b* 1834; *m* 1st, 1864, Sara, 2nd *d* of T. H. Pyle, MRCS, Earsdon, Northumberland; 2nd, 1900, Margaret Isabella, *e d* of late James Ellison, MD, Surgeon to HM Household, Windsor. *Educ:* private schools; Exeter Coll., Oxford. BA 1862. Deacon, 1862; Priest, 1863; Assistant Master at King's School, Sherborne, 1864–67; Minor Canon of St George's Chapel, Windsor Castle, 1867–74; Rector of West Isley, Berks, 1873–81; Curate in Charge of Wexham, Bucks, 1882–85; Vicar of Kew cum Petersham, 1885–90; Hon. Chaplain to Queen Victoria, 1874; Chaplain-in-Ordinary, 1876–1901; Vicar of Kew, 1885–1915. *Publications:* various sermons; sacred music; anthems; chant Communion Office; chant Te Deums, etc; Kew Supplement of Hymns and Tunes, 1909. *Address:* Eversleigh, Frances Road, Windsor. *Died 15 Feb. 1919.*

BLOMEFIELD, Sir Thomas Wilmot Peregrine, 4th Bt, *cr* 1807; CB 1903; late Assistant Secretary, Finance Department of the Board of Trade; *b* Winchester, 31 Dec. 1848; *s* of Rev. Sir Thomas Blomefield, 3rd Bt and Georgina, *d* of Gen. Sir Peregrine Maitland, GCB; *S* father, 1878; *m* 1874, Lilias, *d* of Major the Hon. Charles Napier, Woodlands, Taunton; one *s* two *d* (and two *s* decd). *Educ:* Repton. *Heir: g s* Thomas Edward Peregrine Blomefield, *b* 31 May 1907. *Address:* Windmill House, Lichfield, Staffordshire. *Died 20 July 1928.*

BLOMFIELD, Maj.-Gen. Charles James, CB 1904; DSO 1898; retired 1917; JP; *b* Bow, Devonshire, 26 May 1855; 2nd *s* of Rev. George J. Blomfield and Isabel, *d* of late Charles James Blomfield, Bishop of London; *m* 1881, Henrietta, *d* of late Major E. Briscoe, 20th Foot; two *s*. *Educ:* Haileybury; Sandhurst. Sub-Lieut 20th Foot, 1875; Lieut 1875. Captain, Lancashire Fusiliers, 1881; Major, 1890; Lt-Col 1898; Bt-Col 1900; Adjt Lancs Fusiliers, 1880–88; Acting Military Secretary to HE Commander-in-Chief, Bombay Army, 1891; DAAG Poona, 1892–97; AAG Bombay, 1897; Soudan Expedition, 1898; Battle of Khartoum (despatches, DSO, Egyptian medal with clasp, Queen's medal); S African War, 1899–1902; with Ladysmith relief force (severely wounded at Spion

Kop, despatches twice, brevet of Colonel, Queen's medal four clasps, King's medal two clasps); Colonel on Staff to Command District, 1900, and in command of columns in SE Transvaal and on Zululand border; commanded Harrismith and Natal Sub-District, 1902–6; Wessex Division, TF, 1909–10; Mhow Division, India, 1911–12; Peshawar Division, India, 1913–15. *Address:* Frampton Lodge, Frampton-on-Severn, Glos. *Club:* Army and Navy.

Died 3 March 1928.

BLOMFIELD, Rear-Admiral Sir Richard Massie, KCMG 1904 (CMG 1903); *b* 3 March 1835; 3rd *s* of late Rev. G. B. Blomfield, Rector of Stevenage, Herts, and Canon of Chester Cathedral; *m* 1877, Rosamund Selina, *d* of late Rt Rev. Charles Graves, Bishop of Limerick; one *s*. *Educ:* Stevenage Grammar School. Served throughout Crimean Campaign as Mid., Mate, and Lieutenant of Agamemnon and Royal Albert, flagships of Sir E. Lyons (Crimean and Turkish medals, 2 clasps); Lieut of HMS Hero conveying HRH The Prince of Wales to the British American colonies and back, 1860; selected as Commander of Admiralty flagship in command of Channel Fleet and Reserve Squadron, 1869; Member of Admiralty Confidential Torpedo Committee, 1873–76; Comptroller of Port of Alexandria from the institution of that Office in 1879; present by invitation of Commander-in-Chief on board his flagship during bombardment of Alexandria, 1882; received thanks of British Government for services rendered during the war (medal with clasp and Khedive's Star); Deputy Controller-General of Egyptian Ports and Lighthouses, 1887; Controller-General, 1901; Director-General, 1905–7; retired, 1908. Medjidieh, 1st class, and Osmanieh, 3rd class. *Publications:* papers in Alexandria Archæological Society's Bulletins. *Recreations:* natural history, archæology. *Address:* 35 Holland Park Avenue, W. *Died 26 June 1921.*

BLOOMFIELD, Maurice; Professor of Sanskrit and Comparative Philology, Johns Hopkins University; *b* Bielitz, Austria, 23 Feb. 1855; *m* 1885, Rosa Zeisler. *Educ:* Chicago University; Furman University, South Carolina (MA 1879); Yale University; Johns Hopkins University (PhD 1879). Vice-President and President of the American Oriental Society 1905–10; President of the Linguistic Society of America; Member of the American Philological Association; German Oriental Society; Member and Councillor of the American Philosophical Society; Member of the Committee on International Congresses for the History of Religions; Advisory Council of American Spelling Reform Association; National Institute of Social Sciences; Fellow of the American Academy of Arts and Sciences; Foreign Member of the Royal Bohemian Society of Prague; Hon. Member Finno-Ugrian Society of Helsingsfors; Hardy prize of the Royal Bavarian Academy of Munich, 1908. Hon. LLD of Princeton University, 1896; Furman University, 1898; Doctor of Humane Letters, University of Chicago, 1916; Hon. Doctor, University of Padua, 1922. *Publications:* edited for the first time from the original Sanskrit manuscripts, the Grihyasamgraha of Gobhilaputra (Leipsic, 1881), and the Sûtra of Kâuçika (New Haven, 1890); translated the Atharva-Veda in the Sacred Books of the East (edited by Max Müller); author of the Atharva-Veda and the Gopatha-Brâhmana (Strassburg, 1899); joint-editor (with Professor Richard Garbe of the University of Tübingen) of the chromo-photographic reproduction of The Kashmirian Atharva-Veda, the so-called Paippalâda, 1900; author of Cerberus, The Dog of Hades, 1905; A Concordance of the Vedas (Harvard Oriental Series), 1907; Religion of the Veda, 1907; Rig-Veda Repetitions (Harvard Oriental Series; two volumes), 1916; The Life and Stories of the Jaina Savior, Pârçvanatha, 1919; contributor to numerous learned journals and reviews on subjects connected with the history, religions, mythology, and literature of Ancient India; on Sanskrit, Greek, Latin, and Comparative Grammar; on Ethnology and Science of Religions. *Address:* 861 Park Avenue, Baltimore, USA. *T:* Mount Vernon 4560 W. *Clubs:* University; Johns Hopkins, Baltimore. *Died 13 June 1928.*

BLORE, Rev. George John, DD; Hon. Canon of Canterbury since 1887; *b* 5 May 1835; *s* of Edward Blore, DCL, FRS, FSA; *m* Mary, *d* of T. Alleh, Headington, Oxfordshire; five *s* one *d*. *Educ:* Charterhouse; Christ Church, Oxford. Senior Student and Tutor of Christ Church, Oxford, 1861–67; Headmaster of King Edward's School, Bromsgrove, 1868–73; Headmaster of King's School, Canterbury, 1873–86; Examining Chaplain to the Archbishop of Canterbury, 1894. *Address:* St Stephen's House, Canterbury.

Died 6 Feb. 1916.

BLOUNDELLE-BURTON, John Edward; novelist; *m* Frances (*d* 1910), 2nd *d* of late Charles W. Churchman, Philadelphia. *Educ:* for Army. Travelled and lived in Canada, United States, and principal countries of Europe; was a naval correspondent and special correspondent of The Standard. *Publications:* The Silent Shore, 1886; His own Enemy, 1887; The Desert Ship, 1890; The Hispaniola Plate, 1894; A Gentleman Adventurer, 1895; In the Day of Adversity, 1896; Denounced, 1896; The Clash of Arms, 1897; Across the Salt Seas, 1898; The Scourge of God, 1898; Fortune's my Foe; A Bitter Heritage, 1899; The Seafarers; Servants of Sin, 1900; A Vanished Rival, 1901; The Year One, 1901; The Fate of Valsec, 1902; A Branded Name, 1903; The Intriguer's Way, 1903; A Dead Reckoning, 1904; The Sword of Gideon, 1905; Traitor and True, 1906; Knighthood's Flower, 1906; A Woman from the Sea, 1907; The Last of her Race, 1908; Within Four Walls; The King's Mignon, 1909; A Fair Martyr, 1910; The Fate of Henry of Navarre (historical work); Under the Salamander, 1911; The Right Hand, 1911; The Sea Devils, 1912; Fortune's Frown, 1913; Love lies Bleeding, 1915. *Recreations:* riding, cycling, rowing, sailing. *Address:* 385 Upper Richmond Road, Putney, SW. *Clubs:* Constitutional, Yorick.

Died 11 Dec. 1917.

BLOXAM, John Astley, FRCS; JP; Consulting Surgeon to Charing Cross Hospital and Lock Hospital. *Address:* The Old Malt House, Bourne End, Bucks. *Died 12 Jan. 1926.*

BLUMHARDT, J. F., MA; formerly Professor of Hindustani, and Reader of Hindi and Bengali, University College, London; and Teacher of Bengali at Oxford University. *Publications:* a series of Catalogues of Printed Books and Manuscripts in the North-Indian Languages and Dialects, in the British Museum and India Office Libraries. *Address:* Woodlands, Gerrard's Cross, Bucks.

Died 10 Dec. 1922.

BLUNDEN, Sir John, 5th Bt, *cr* 1776; *b* 26 Feb. 1880; *er s* of Sir William Blunden, 4th Bt, and Florence, *d* of Henry Shuttleworth, of New Zealand; *S* father, 1923; *m* 1918, Phyllis Dorothy, *d* of P. C. Creaghe, of Shankill, Co. Dublin; two *s*. *Heir: s* William Blunden, *b* 26 April 1919. *Died 28 Oct. 1923.*

BLUNDEN, Sir William, 4th Bt, *cr* 1776; BA, BM Dublin; LRCS Ireland; LM and LKQCPI; *b* 25 July 1840; *s* of Sir John Blunden, 3rd Bt, Barrister, and Elizabeth, *d* of John Knox, Castlerea, Co. Mayo; *S* father, 1890; *m* 1879, Florence, *d* of Henry Shuttleworth of New Zealand; two *s* one *d*. *Heir: s* John Blunden, *b* 26 Feb. 1880. *Address:* Castle Blunden, Kilkenny. *Died 25 Oct. 1923.*

BLUNT, Rev. Alexander Colvin; Hon. Canon of Winchester, 1889; Rural Dean, Kingsclere, 1890; *m* 1875, Lady Susanna (*d* 1900), *d* of 2nd Earl Nelson. *Educ:* Christ Church, Oxford (MA). Curate of Alverstoke, 1855–66; Rector of Millbrook, 1866–89; Burghclere, 1889–1915; Rural Dean, Southampton, 1876–89. *Address:* 9 Kingsgate Street, Winchester. *Died 1 April 1920.*

BLUNT, Sir John Elijah, Kt 1902; CB 1878; *b* 14 Oct. 1832; *s* of Charles Blunt, late HM Consul at Smyrna, and Caroline, *d* of A. Vitalis, late HM Consul at Tinos; *m* 1858, Fanny Janet, *d* of Donald Sandison, late HM Consul at Brussa. *Educ:* Dr Greig's Private School, Walthamstow; Kensington Grammar School. Has been connected with His Majesty's Consular Service since 1850, and after holding various Consular appointments in Turkey, was promoted Consul-General for the Vilayets of Salonica, Cossova, Janina, and Monastir, 1878; served as Chief Interpreter to the Cavalry Division under Gen. Lord Lucan in the Crimea, and acted as his Lordship's Secretary; present at battles of the Alma, Balaclava, and Inkerman; has also acted temporarily as French Vice-Consul, twice at Volo and twice at Monastir; as German Consul and twice as Belgian Consul at Salonica; Her Majesty's Consul-General for Salonica, 1879–99; HBM Consul (with rank of Consul-Gen.) at Boston, 1899–1902. Received in 1862 and 1868 the thanks of the President of the United States for services rendered to American citizens in the province of Adrianople, and was nominated in 1868 US Consul for Roumelia, but was not permitted to accept the appointment. *Decorated:* Crimean medal with clasps for Alma, Balaclava, and Inkerman; Turkish Crimean medal, 1855; Turkish Imtiaz medal in silver, 1890, and in gold, 1898; Jubilee medal, 1897. *Recreations:* shooting, lawn tennis, cricket, bridge. *Address:* Floriana, Malta. *Club:* Athenæum.

Died 19 June 1916.

BLUNT, Captain Sir John Harvey, 8th Bt, *cr* 1720; late 1st Battalion Royal Dublin Fusiliers, retired; *b* 1 Jan. 1839; *s* of William Blunt, BCS, 3rd *s* of 3rd Bt, and Eliza, *d* of Gen. Goddard Richards; *S* brother, 1902; *m* 1869, Susan (*d* 1917), *d* of P. Hoad; four *s* one *d* (and one *d* decd). Served with 1st Batt. Royal Welsh Fusiliers through Indian Mutiny, including taking of Futteghur, operations on the Ramgunga, siege and capture of Lucknow, besides several minor engagements (medal and clasp). *Heir: e s* John Harvey Blunt [*b* 30 July 1872; *m* 1906, Maud Julia, *e d* of Sir David Lionel Goldsmid-Stern-Salomons, 2nd Bt, of Broomhill, Tunbridge Wells; two *s* two *d. Educ:* Beaumont College, Windsor. Capt. Natal Border Police; served South African War (three medals, eight clasps); European War. *Recreations:* hunting, shooting. *Address:* Huntleys, Tunbridge Wells. *T:* 966. *Club:* Royal Automobile]. *Address:* East House, St George's Terrace, Herne Bay.

Died 26 Jan. 1922.

BLUNT, Wilfrid Scawen; poet and author; *b* Petworth House, 17 Aug. 1840; *s* of F. S. Blunt, of Crabbet Park; *m* 1869, Lady Anne Noel (later Baroness Wentworth (15th in line), *d* 1917), *d* of 1st Earl of Lovelace; one *d. Educ:* Stonyhurst; Oscott. Diplomatic Service, 1858–70; travelled in Arabia, Syria, Persia, Mesopotamia, etc, 1877–81; took part in Egyptian National Movement, 1881–82; travelled in India, 1883–84; stood for Camberwell, Tory Home Ruler, 1885; Kidderminster, Liberal Home Ruler, 1886; arrested in Ireland for calling meeting in a proclaimed district, Oct. 1887; imprisoned two months in Galway and Kilmainham Gaols, 1888. Owned about 2,000 acres; succeeded to Crabbet estates on death of elder brother, 1872. *Publications:* Love Sonnets of Proteus, 1880; Future of Islam, 1882; The Wind and the Whirlwind, 1883; Ideas about India, 1885; In Vinculis, 1889; A New Pilgrimage, 1889; Esther, 1892; Stealing of the Mare, 1892; Griselda, 1893; Satan Absolved, 1899; Seven Golden Odes of Pagan Arabia, 1903; Secret History of the English Occupation of Egypt, 1907; India under Ripon, 1909; Gordon at Khartoum, 1911; The Land War in Ireland, 1912; Poetical Works, complete edition, 1914; My Diaries, 1919; My Diaries, Pt 2, 1920. *Recreation:* breeder of Arab horses. *Address:* Newbuildings, Horsham, Sussex. *Club:* Sussex.   *Died 10 Sept. 1922.*

BLUNT, Rear-Adm. William Frederick, CBE 1919; DSO 1914; *b* 3 March 1870; 3rd *s* of late F. W. Blunt of Culcheth Hall, Teddington; *m* 1896, Laura, *o d* of late Maj.-Gen. Henry Way Mawbey, RMA; two *s*. Was midshipman of HMS Garnet during blockade of Zanzibar coast, 1888–89; Lieut in command HMS Dragon during operations at Crete, 1897–98; Lieut in command HMS Esk, China 1900–1 (medal); European War, 1914–15: in command of HMS Fearless at the action in Heligoland Bight, 18 Aug. 1914 (DSO); and at the Cuxhaven Raid, Christmas Day, 1914; Captain in command of 1st Destroyer Flotilla, 1913–15; HMS Jupiter, 1915–16; operations at Aden and in Suez Canal; Capt. HMS Gloucester at the Battle of Jutland, 31 May 1916 (despatches, commended); HMS Berwick and HMS Achilles, 1916–19, Atlantic Convoy Service (CBE); retired list, 1917; Rear-Adm. retired, 1922. *Address:* Baharini, Lake Solai, Kenya Colony. *Club:* United Service.

Died 5 July 1928.

BLYTH, 1st Baron, *cr* 1907; **James Blyth;** Bt, 1895; JP Essex and Herts; Director of W. and A. Gilbey Ltd, Partner 1863; *b* 10 Sept. 1841; *s* of James Blyth, Chelmsford, and Caroline, *d* of Henry Gilbey, Bishops Stortford; *m* 1865, Eliza (*d* 1894), *d* of William Mooney, Clontarf, Co. Dublin; two *s* four *d*. Vice-President, British Empire League; Treasurer, Homes for Little Boys, Farningham and Swanley; Treasurer, Empire Parliamentary Association, and Treasurer of the Byron Centenary Commemoration; Vice-President, governor or member of many agricultural and other Societies; a Manager of the Royal Institution of Great Britain; governor, or member of: British Dairy Farmers' Association, Shire Horse Soc., Royal Agricultural Soc., English Jersey Soc.; Chairman, Organising Committee Franco-British Exhibition, 1908; Japan-British Exhibition, 1910. Imperial Order of Leopold; Order of the Medjidie; a Knight Commander and Grand Cross of Civil Order of Merito Agricola of Portugal; The Order of the Sacred Treasure of Japan. *Publications:* has written on viticultural and agricultural questions, also on the fiscal and commercial policy of the Empire, cheap postal and telegraphic communication, an Anglo-French Commercial Alliance, etc. *Heir: s* Hon. Herbert William Blyth, *b* 1 March 1868. *Address:* 33 Portland Place, W1. *T:* Langham 2176; Blythwood, Stansted, Essex. *T:* Stansted 10. *TA:* Brigador London. *Clubs:* Athenæum, British Empire, Devonshire.

Died 8 Feb. 1925.

BLYTH, Alexander Wynter, MRCS; FCS; Public Analyst for St Marylebone and County of Devon; Registrar of Sanitary Institute; past President of Incorporated Society of Medical Officers of Health; Barrister at Law (Lincoln's Inn); *s* of Alex. Blyth, Surgeon, Woolwich; *m* Anne Eliz. Morgan (decd), Monmouthshire. *Educ:* King's College, London. Associate King's College, London. Member Soc. Française d'Hygiène and Italian Soc. Hygiene, Milan. *Publications:* Dictionary of Hygiene and Public Health; Foods, their Composition and Analysis, 3rd edn 1895; Poisons, their Effects and Detection, 4th edn 1906; Diet in Relation to Health and Work, 1884; A Manual of Public Health, 1890; Lectures on Sanitary Law, 1893; and numerous scientific communications to the Royal Society, Chemical Society, Sanitary Institute, and the Society of Medical Officers of Health. *Address:* Halfway Manor House, Kintbury, Berks; 3 Upper Gloucester Place, NW1. *T:* Paddington 3146.

Died 30 March 1921.

BLYTH, Benjamin Hall, MA; FRSE; a civil engineer in Edinburgh; *b* Edinburgh, 25 May 1849; *s* of Benjamin Hall Blyth, civil engineer, and Mary Dudgeon Wright; *m* 1872, Millicent, *y d* of Thomas Edward Taylor of Dodworth, Yorkshire, JP, DL; one *d. Educ:* Merchiston Castle School; Edinburgh University. Consulting engineer to the North British and Great North of Scotland Railway Companies; constructed many railways, docks, bridges, and other works; contested (U) East Lothian, Jan. and Dec. 1910, and April 1911; Lieut-Col in the Engineer and Railway Staff Corps; member of the Royal Company of Archers, King's Body Guard for Scotland; President of the Institution of Civil Engineers. *Recreations:* shooting, golfing, curling. *Address:* 17 Palmerston Place, Edinburgh; Kaimend, North Berwick. *Clubs:* Carlton, Conservative; Western, Glasgow; University, Conservative, Edinburgh.   *Died 12 May 1917.*

BLYTH, Lt-Col James, CBE 1919; *b* 1869; *m* 1896, Ethel, *e d* of late C. J. Gibb, MD, of Sandyford Park, Newcastle-on-Tyne; one *s. Educ:* Eton. Contested (U) Barnsley Division of Yorkshire, 1897; Director of the Law Land Co. and the Warner Estate; commanded the 3rd Bn Oxford and Buckinghamshire Light Infantry during the war (CBE). *Recreations:* shooting, fishing. *Address:* Iver Grove, Iver, Bucks. *Clubs:* Bachelors', Wellington, Garrick.

Died 9 July, 1925.

BLYTHSWOOD, 2nd Baron, *cr* 1892; **Rev. Sholto Douglas Campbell,** MA; DD (Glasgow); JP Lanarks; *b* 28 June 1839; 2nd *s* of late Archibald Douglas, of Mains, Co. Dumbarton (who assumed surname of Campbell on inheriting Blythswood in 1838), and Caroline Agnes, *d* of late M. Dick, of Pitkerro, Co. Fife; S brother, 1908; *m* 1889, Violet (*d* 1908), *d* of late Lord Alfred Paget, CB. *Educ:* Cheam; Trinity Coll., Camb.; MA. Curate, Nuneaton, Warwickshire, 1866–67; St Mary's, Gateshead, 1867–70; Vicar of Nonington, Kent, 1870–72; All Saints, Derby, 1872–79; Rector of All Souls, St Marylebone, 1879–86; St Silas, Glasgow, 1887–99. *Publications:* Order of Events in Our Lord's Second Coming; The Anti-Christ. *Heir: brother* Maj.-Gen. Sir Barrington Bulkeley Douglas Campbell-Douglas, KCB, CVO, *b* 18 Feb. 1845. *Address:* Blythswood, Renfrew, NB; Balmacara House, Loch Alsh, NB. *Clubs:* Carlton, National; Conservative, Western, Glasgow; New, Edinburgh.   *Died 30 Sept. 1916.*

BLYTHSWOOD, 3rd Baron, *cr* 1892; **Barrington Bulkeley Douglas Campbell-Douglas,** KCB (CB 1900); CVO 1902 (MVO 1897); retired; *b* 18 Feb. 1845: *s* of Archibald Campbell of Blythswood, Renfrewshire, formerly Douglas of Mains, Dumbartonshire; S brother, 1916; assumed additional name Douglas on succeeding to Douglas Support; *m* 1869, Mildred Catherine (*d* 1902), *d* of Sir Joseph Hawley, 3rd Bt; three *s. Educ:* Eton. Entered army, Scots Guards, 1864; commanded 1st Scots Guards, 1892–96; commanded Scots Guards and South London Brigade, 1896–98; Major-General, 1898; Egyptian War, 1882 (1st Batt. Scots Guards), including El Magfar, Tel-el-Mahuta, Kassassin, and Tel-el-Kebir (medal with clasp, Khedive's star); commanded 16th Brigade Aldershot and South Africa, Jan. 1900–July 1902; actions Orange River Colony, including battle Biddulphsberg, Prinsloe's surrender, actions in Transvaal and Natal; commanding Ficksberg, Brandwater, Bethlehem district (Queen's medal, three clasps, King's medal, two clasps, despatches twice); DL and JP Renfrewshire; DL Lanarkshire; Lieut-Governor and commanding-in-chief, Guernsey, 1903–8. *Heir: s* Capt. Hon. Archibald Campbell-Douglas [*b* 25 April 1870; *m* 1895, Evelyn, 3rd *d* of late John Fletcher of Saltoun; one *d. Educ:* Eton. Late Lieut Scots Guards. *Address:* 55 Montagu Square, W. *Clubs:* Guards, Travellers', Naval and Military; New, Edinburgh]. *Address:* Blythswood, Renfrew; Douglas Support, Coatbridge, Lanarkshire. *T:* Coatbridge 225; 13 Manchester Square, W. *T:* Mayfair 4329. *M:* LK 8839. *Clubs:* Carlton, Turf, Marlborough, Guards; New, Edinburgh; Conservative, Glasgow.

Died 11 March 1918.

BOARDMAN, Admiral Frederick Ross, CB 1885; RN, retired; *b* 1843; *e s* of late Frederick Boardman, Liverpool; *m* 1881, Sophia Almon, *d* of Hon. Jas Cogswell of Halifax, Nova Scotia; one *s* two *d*. Commander of Salamis during Egyptian War, 1882; as captain commanded Nile flotilla, Gordon Relief Expedition, 1884–85. Specially mentioned in despatches; Egyptian medal and clasp;

Khedive's bronze star; Royal Victorian medal and captain's good service pension for Nile flotilla services. *Recreations:* boating, fishing, riding, reading. *Address:* Landsdowne Park Road, Lewes. *Club:* United Service.   *Died 24 Sept. 1927.*

BOCQUET, (Roland) Roscoe (Charles), CIE 1878; *b* 9 April 1839; *s* of Frances S. Bocquet of Liverpool; *m* 1863, Edith (*d* 1902), *d* of John Bampton. Engineer, then Gen. Manager, on Scinde-Delhi Railway at Lahore, 1860–85; Engineer for 12 years on South American Rlys, Buenos Ayres. *Decorated* for services in connection with Madras famine, 1876. *Address:* St Leonard's, Springvale, Ryde, Isle of Wight.
                                                Died 13 Nov. 1920.

BODDAM-WHETHAM, Major Sydney A., DSO 1917; MC; RFA; *b* 4 May 1885; *e* surv. *s* of late J. W. Boddam-Whetham of Kirklington Hall, Notts; *m* 1916, E. Sybil, *d* of J. L. Brinkley, Allershaw, Folkestone and Fortlands, Ireland; one *s* two *d*. *Educ:* Oundle; RMA, Woolwich. Joined RFA 1903; ADC and Private Secretary to Governor of Bahamas, 1907–12; served European War continuously with 7th Division in Belgium, France, and Italy, Oct. 1914–March 1918; then transferred to a Corps (despatches six times, DSO, MC, Belgian Croix de Guerre). *Recreations:* tennis, football, hockey. *Address:* RA Mess, Nasirabad, Rajputana, India.
                                                Died 9 Dec. 1925.

BODDINGTON, Rev. Edward Henry; Hon. Canon of Coventry. *Educ:* Brasenose Coll., Oxford. Deacon 1875, priest 1877. Curate, Newbold-on-Stour, Worcs, 1875–88; Vicar of Honington, 1889. *Address:* Honington Vicarage, Shipston-on-Stour.
                                                Died 28 Feb. 1920.

BODINGTON, Rev. Charles; Canon Residentiary since 1888, and Precentor of Lichfield Cathedral, 1894–96; *b* 28 Nov. 1836. Deacon 1863, priest 1864. Curate, St James, Wednesbury, 1865–67; Vicar of St Anne, Willenhall, 1867–70; St Andrew, 1870–79; Rector, St James, Wednesbury, 1879–83; Vicar, Christ Church, Lichfield, 1883–89. *Educ:* King's Coll., London (Fellow). *Publications:* Books of Devotion; Devotional Life in the Nineteenth Century; The Life of Grace; Notes on Prayer; Jesus the Christ; Lichfield Cathedral; The Twelve Gates of the Holy City; Devotions for Every Day of the Week; Wesley; Devotion; A Gospel of Miracle; The Doctrine of Confession and Absolution in the Church of England. *Address:* The Close, Lichfield.   *Died 23 Nov. 1918.*

BODLE, Brig.-Gen. William, CMG 1900; *b* 5 July 1855; *s* of C. Bodle, Alfriston, Sussex. Served Basuto War under Sir F. Carrington (medal and clasp); Matabele War, 1893 (medal); Matabele Rebellion, 1896 (clasp); South African War, 1899–1902 (despatches, Queen's medal three clasps, King's medal two clasps); retired with rank of Colonel, Oct. 1909; European War, 1914–18, commanded a Brigade. *Address:* c/o BSA Co., London Wall Buildings, EC.
                                                Died 9 July 1924.

BODLEY, John Edward Courtenay, MA; *b* 6 June 1853; *e s* of late Edward Fisher Bodley, JP, of Dane Bank House, Cheshire, and Mary, *d* of Joseph Ridgway; *m* 1st, 1891, Evelyn Frances (whom he div. 1908), *e d* of John Bell, of Rushpool Hall, Yorks; 2nd, 1920, Phyllis Helen, *d* of late Rev. H. J. Lomax of Stoke Golding. *Educ:* Balliol College, Oxford; BA 1877; MA 1879. Barrister, Inner Temple, 1874; private secretary to President of Local Government Board, 1882–85; Secretary to Royal Commission on Housing of the Working Classes, 1884–85, and author of the three Reports on England, Scotland, and Ireland. Corresponding Member of the French Institute (Académie des Sciences Morales et Politiques), 1902. *Publications:* France: Vol. I, The Revolution and Modern France, Vol. II, The Parliamentary System, 1898 (7th Eng. edn 1907), (French edns trans. by author, 1901–4); L'Anglomanie et les traditions françaises, Paris, 1899; The Coronation of Edward VII, a Chapter of European and Imperial History (by His Majesty's commmand), 1903 (2nd edn 1911); Introduction to English edn of Emile Boutmy's Psychology of the English People, 1904; The Church in France, 1906; two articles in Ency. Brit. on the History of the Third Republic, 1900 and 1910; Cardinal Manning, and other Essays, 1912; L'Age mécanique et le déclin de l'idéalisme en France (discours prononcé à l'Institut de France), 1913; Introduction to English edition of National History of France, 1916; The Romance of the Battle-line in France, 1920. *Address:* Hatchlands, Cuckfield, Sussex.   *Died 28 May 1925.*

BOEHM BOTELER, Sir Edgar Collins; *see* Boteler.

BOEVEY, Sir Francis (Hyde) Crawley-, 6th Bt, *cr* 1784; JP; Verderer of the Forest of Dean; *b* 25 April 1868; *s* of Sir Thomas Crawley-

Boevey, 5th Bt and Frances Elizabeth, *d* of Rev. Thomas Peters; *S* father, 1912; *m* 1896, Eliza Barbara, *o d* of Valentine Blake McGrath, late of Hope Hall, Manchester; one *s*. *Educ:* Winchester; Christ Church, Oxford. BA 1891. *Heir:* *s* Launcelot Valentine Hyde Crawley-Boevey [*b* 26 April 1900; *m* 1927, Elizabeth G., *d* of Herbert d'Auvergne Innes, Moorend Park Lawn, Cheltenham]. *Recreations:* painting, shooting, lawn tennis (Capt. of OULTC, 1891), etc. *Address:* Flaxley Abbey, near Newnham, Glos. *T:* Westbury on Severn 10.
                                                Died 6 Oct. 1928.

BOGERT, Ven. James John; Archdeacon of Ottawa since 1897; *b* 2 Aug. 1835; *s* of John Bogert, Barrister, and Mary Radcliffe; *m* 1860; four *s* four *d*. *Educ:* Trinity Coll., Toronto (MA, DCL). Ordained 1858; Priest, 1859; Curate of Brampton, 1858; Prescott, 1859–61; Rector of Napanee, 1862–81; Rector of St Alban's Church, Ottawa, 1881–1914; Rural Dean, Carleton, Ontario, 1891–97. *Address:* 196 Asgoode Street, Ottawa, Canada.
                                                Died 10 Feb. 1920.

BOGLE-SMITH, Colonel Steuart, CB 1902; CBE 1919; late Lieutenant-Colonel commanding 1st Dragoon Guards; *b* 11 July 1859; *m* 1895, Julia Katharine, *y d* of C. H. Berners, of Woolverstone Park, Ipswich; one *s*. Entered army, 1882; Captain, 1892; Major, 1896; Lieut-Col 1902; Col 1905; AAG Irish Command, 1910–14; served South Africa, 1901–2 (despatches, medal with 5 clasps, CB). *Club:* Naval and Military.   *Died 6 Jan. 1921.*

BOITO, Arrigo; poet, composer, librettist; *b* Padua, 24 Feb. 1842. *Educ:* Milan Conservatory; MusD Cantab 1893. *Opera:* Mefistofele, 1868; *cantatas:* le 4 Juin, 1860; La Sorella d'Italia; *libretti:* Otello; Falstaff; La Gioconda; Amleto; Ero e Leandre; Nero. *Publications:* Libro dei versi, 1877; Re Orso (epic poem); L'Alfier Meno (novel). *Address:* Milan.   *Died 10 June 1918.*

BOLAND, Harry; MP (S Fein) for N Roscommon since Dec. 1918. TD (Sinn Fein) for S Roscommon until 1921 and Anti-Treaty mem., 1921–22; Private Sec. and Press Agent to Eamonn de Valera.
                                                Died 1 Aug. 1922.

BOLE, Hon. W. Norman; retired; Local Judge of the Supreme Court, New Westminster, BC; *b* Castlebar, 6 Dec. 1846; *e s* of late John Bole of Lakefield, Mayo, Ireland, and Elizabeth Jane Campbell; *m* 1881, Florence Blanchard, *o d* of Major John Haning Coulthard, JP; two *s* one *d*. Went to New Westminster, 1877; called to British Columbia Bar, 1877; QC 1887; MPP New Westminster, 1886–89; Captain No 1 Battery, BC Brigade Artillery, 1884–89; Hon. Colonel First Regiment Imperial Canadian Reserve; Fellow Royal Colonial Institute. *Recreations:* shooting, yachting, magazine writing. *Address:* Ardagh, Royal Avenue, New Westminster, BC. *T:* 795. *Clubs:* Westminster, Royal Vancouver Yacht, Vancouver.
                                                Died 7 April 1923.

BOLINGBROKE, Leonard George; solicitor; Registrar of the Diocese of Norwich; Chapter Clerk; *b* 27 May 1859; *y s* of Charles Nathaniel Bolingbroke; *m* Alice Laura, *d* of William Thomas Bensly, LLD, FSA; three *s* two *d*. *Educ:* Forest School, Walthamstow. *Recreations:* archæology, yachting. *Address:* Ferryside, Norwich.
                                                Died 9 Aug. 1927.

BOLITHO, Thomas Robins; banker and landowner; *b* 13 Sept. 1840; *e s* of Thos S. Bolitho, of Trengwainton; *m* 1870, Augusta Jane, *d* of R. B. Wilson, of Cliffe Hall, Yorks. *Educ:* Harrow; Corpus Christi College, Oxford. Engaged throughout life in banking in the county of Cornwall; formerly Bolitho and Co., later Barclay and Co.; and interested in the industries of the county, mining and agriculture; an original member of Cornwall County Council; Sheriff of County, 1890. *Recreation:* Joint Master of Western Fox Hounds since 1864. *Address:* Trengwainton, Hea Moor, Cornwall. *TA:* Heamoor. *Club:* Athenæum.   *Died 28 Sept. 1925.*

BOLITHO, Lt-Col William Edward Thomas, DSO 1900; Lieutenant-Colonel commanding 2/1st Royal Devon Yeomanry; MFH Western; *b* 2 July 1862; *s* of late William Bolitho of Polwithen; *m* 1888, Ethel Grace, *d* of Aeneás Bruce Macleod of Cadboll; one *d*. Served with 7th Battalion Imperial Yeomanry, South Africa, 1899–1900 (wounded, despatches, DSO); European War (Bt Lt-Col). *Address:* York House, Penzance; Hannaford, Ashburton, S Devon. *Club:* Carlton.   *Died 21 Feb. 1919.*

BOLLARD, Hon. R. F; Minister of Internal Affairs, New Zealand. *Address:* Department of Internal Affairs, Wellington, New Zealand.
                                                Died 24 Aug. 1927.

BOLSTER, Rev. Canon Robert Crofts; Canon of Cloyne since 1870. *Educ:* Trinity College, Dublin (MA). Ordained 1868; Curate of Castlemartyr, Co. Cork, 1868–70; Incumbent, 1870–1904. *Address:* Bedford.   *Died 9 Feb. 1918.*

BOLTON, 4th Baron, *cr* 1797; **William Thomas Orde-Powlett,** TD; JP, DL; Alderman, North Riding of Yorkshire; late Hon. Colonel Commanding Yorkshire (APWO) Hussars Imperial Yeomanry; Hon. Colonel of the Regiment; *b* 31 Jan. 1845; *s* of 3rd Baron and Letitia, *y d* of Col Crawford, Newfield, Ayrshire; *S* father, 1895; *m* 1868, Lady Algitha Frederica Mary Lumley (*d* 1919), *d* of 9th Earl of Scarbrough; one *s* one *d*. *Educ:* Eton; Trinity Coll., Camb. *Heir: s* Lt-Col Hon. William George Algar Orde-Powlett, *b* 21 Aug. 1869. *Address:* Bolton Hall, Leyburn, Yorkshire; Hackwood Park, Basingstoke. *Clubs:* Carlton, Junior Carlton; Yorkshire, York.
                                              Died 14 Aug. 1922.

BOLTON, Rev. Charles Nelson, MA; Vicar of St Mary's, Lichfield, since 1895; Prebendary of Dassett Parva in Lichfield Cathedral; *b* 7 Nov. 1844; *s* of Charles Bolton, Commander, Royal Navy; *m* 1872, Catherine Ann, *d* of John Norman of Botcherby, Carlisle; two *s* seven *d*. *Educ:* Rossall; New College, Oxford. Curate, St John the Evangelist, Carlisle, 1868–72; Vicar, All Saints, Darlaston, 1872–81; Vicar, Cannock, 1881–95; Rural Dean of Lichfield. *Address:* St Mary's Vicarage, Lichfield.   *Died 10 March 1918.*

BOLTON, Charles Walter, CSI 1897; *b* 1850; *s* of Dr J. Bolton; *m* 1st, 1882, Alice Emma Wilford (*d* 1895), *d* of R. R. Wilford Brett, 2nd Bombay Cavalry; 2nd, 1898, Jessie Laura (*d* 1905), *d* of late Maj.-Gen. James Templeton Brett; 3rd, 1909, Violet, *d* of R. J. Graham of Edmond Castle, Cumberland; two *s*. *Educ:* University College School; Royal College, Mauritius; King's College, London. Entered ICS 1872; Under Secretary Government, Bengal, 1879; Magistrate and Collector, 1885; Secretary to Board of Revenue, 1891; Chief Secretary to Government, Bengal, 1896; member, Board of Revenue, Bengal, 1900; additional member, Governor-General's Council, 1900; officiating Chief Commissioner of Assam, 1903; retired 1905. JP, Eastbourne; Mayor, 1912–15. *Address:* Avonmore, Eastbourne.
                                              Died 27 Dec. 1919.

BOLTON, Sir Frederic, Kt 1908; *b* 7 March 1851; 2nd *s* of late William Treacher Bolton; *m* 1876, Ann Haycroft (*d* 1915), *e d* of late William Pearse of Plymouth; one *s* two *d*. *Educ:* privately. Underwriter; sometime Chairman of Lloyd's; Insurance Broker; Shipowner. *Address:* Westridge, Prince Arthur Road, Hampstead, NW3. *T:* Hampstead 3385. *Clubs:* Reform, City of London.
                                              Died 23 Jan. 1920.

BOLTON, Gambier; *s* of late Rev. James Jay Bolton, Kilburn; *m* Georgiana Maria, 4th *d* of late Col Evelegh, CB. *Educ:* private schools; Corpus Christi College, Cambridge. Public lecturer and writer on (popular) Natural History; travelled in Europe, America, Canada, Hawaian Islands, Japan, China, Java, Malay Peninsula, Burmah, India, South Africa; accompanied the Duke of Newcastle on his tour round the world, 1893–94. *Publications:* A Book of Beasts and Birds; The Animals of the Bible; Psychic Force; has published a large series of animal photographs from life, collected from most parts of the world. *Recreation:* motoring (car and motor boat). *Club:* Royal Southampton Yacht.   *Died 29 July 1928.*

BOLTON, Thomas Henry; a Master in the Supreme Court; Taxing Master in Chancery since January 1896; *b* Feb. 1841; *s* of Thomas Bolton, Canonbury; *m* 1861, Elizabeth Ann (*d* 1907), *d* of William Wegg. Admitted Solicitor, 1869; MP (L) N St Pancras, 1885–86, and (LU), 1890–95. *Address:* Royal Courts, Strand, WC. *Club:* Garrick.
                                              Died 24 Sept. 1916.

BONAPARTE, Hon. Charles Joseph; *b* Baltimore, 9 June 1851; *s* of Jerome Napoleon Bonaparte and Susan May Williams; *m* 1875, Ellen Channing Day, of Newport, RI. Secretary of the Navy, 1905–6; Attorney-General, 1906–1909. *Address:* Glen Arm, Maryland, USA; 601 Park Avenue, Baltimore, USA.
                                              Died 28 June 1921.

BONAPARTE, HIH Prince Roland; *b* Paris, 19 May 1858; *s* of Prince Pierre-Napoléon, 3rd *s* of Prince Lucien, *brother* of Napoleon I, and Mlle Ruffin; *m* Mlle Felix Blanc (*decd*); one *d* (Marie, who *m* 1907, Prince George of Greece). *Educ:* Lycée St Louis; St Cyr; Hon. DSc Upsala and Cambridge. Member of the Institute; twice President of the French Geographical Society; much interested in travel and scientific research. *Publications:* Les Habitans de Suriname, 1883; Le Théâtre javanais, 1885; Premiers Voyages; Derniers Voyages; Récents

Voyages des Néerlandais à la Nouvelle Guinée; Les Lapps de Finmarck; Le Fleuve Augusta; Le Golfe Huon; La Pêchewa à la baleine sur les côtes de Norvège; Une Excursion en Corse; Les Idées géographiques à travers l'histoire; Notes Stéridologiques, Vols I à VIII. *Address:* 10 avenue d'Iéna, Paris.
                                              Died 14 April 1924.

BONAVIA, Hon. Edgar, CMG 1917; ISO 1926; Permanent Secretary to Head of Ministry under Malta Home Rule Constitution, 1919; *b* 22 Feb. 1896; *m* 1st, Camilla, *d* of late Paolo Vassallo; two *s*; 2nd, Maria, *d* of late Robert Casolani; four *s* one *d*. *Educ:* St Ignatius College and Malta University. Entered Malta Civil Service, 1886; Deputy Assistant Secretary to Government, 1911; Assistant Secretary, 1912; visited Tunis to report on Malta Charities in the Regency, 1912; acted as Lieutenant Governor on several occasions; Assistant Secretary to Government of Malta, with seat as official member in Executive and Legislative Councils, 1914; Commissioner for Malta, Baden Powell Boy Scouts, 1916 (Silver Wolf, Jamboree, 1920); Hon. Vice-President, St John's Ambulance Association, Malta Branch, 1916. *Address:* 146 Strada Ittorri, Sliema, Malta.
                                              Died 2 March 1927.

BOND, Rev. Charles Watson, VD; Canon and Prebendary of Chichester Cathedral since 1903; *b* 19 June 1839; *s* of William and Maria Bond, Alrewas, Staffordshire; *m* 1863, Eliza Vines, of Warwick Gardens, Kensington; four *s* two *d*. *Educ:* private school; Cheltenham College; Christ's College, Cambridge. Scholar; Bishop of Porteus Gold Medallist, 1862; BA 1862; MA 1866. Deacon, 1862; Priest, 1863; Curate of Waltham Abbey, 1862–65; St John's, Birkenhead, 1865–69; Perpetual Curate of Hanley, Staffs, 1869–76; Vicar of Haddenham, Cambs, 1876–82; All Souls, Brighton, 1882–88; St Nicholas, Brighton, 1888–1910; Pevensey, 1910–18; Surrogate, 1888. *Publications:* sundry sermons. *Address:* Lyndhurst, Henfield, Sussex. *TA:* Henfield.   *Died 20 Aug. 1922.*

BOND, Edward, MA; Chairman, East End Dwellings Co.; *b* London, Oct. 1844; *e s* of late Edward Bond, of Elm Bank, Hampstead; unmarried. *Educ:* Merchant Taylors' School; St John's Coll., Oxford. Fellow, Queen's Coll., Oxford, 1869. Barrister, 1871; Assistant Charity Commissioner, 1884–91; LCC, Hampstead, 1895–1901; contested West Southwark, 1892; MP (C) East Nottingham, 1895–1906; Chairman of Governing Body of the Cholmeley School, Highgate and of the Buss Foundation Schools for Girls. *Recreations:* bridge, book-collecting. *Address:* 43 Thurloe Square, SW. *T:* Kensington 6861. *Clubs:* Albemarle, Athenæum, Burlington Fine Arts.   *Died 18 Aug. 1920.*

BOND, Francis, MA; FGS; Hon. ARIBA; *m*. *Publications:* Gothic Architecture in England; Cathedrals of England and Wales; Screens and Galleries; Stalls and Tabernacle Work; Misericords; Fonts and Font Covers; Westminster Abbey; Introduction to English Church Architecture; Dedications of English Churches; English Chancel. *Recreation:* golf. *Address:* Stafford House, Croydon.
                                              Died 1918.

BOND, Rt. Hon. Sir Robert, KCMG 1901; PC 1902; Hon. LLD Edin.; *b* 25 Feb. 1857; *s* of late John Bond of Torquay; descended from an old Devonshire family; his father, the late John Bond, a native of Torquay, for more than half a century conducted an extensive mercantile business in St John's, Newfoundland, under the style of William Hounsell & Co., a branch of the well-known Bridport (Dorsetshire) firm of that name; not married. *Educ:* for the Bar but entered politics before being called thereto. Entered the Legislature, 1882; elected Speaker of the House of Assembly, 1884; an executive councillor, with portfolio of Colonial Secretary, 1889–97; appointed a delegate to Her Majesty's Government by the Government of this colony on the French Treaties question, 1890; in the same year Her Majesty's Government appointed him to assist Lord Pauncefote in negotiating a Reciprocity Treaty with the United States, and he was mainly instrumental in completing what is known as the Bond-Blain Convention; one of the delegates appointed by the Government to meet Sir John Thompson, Sir Mackenzie Bowell, and Sir Adolph Chapleau at Halifax on the Newfoundland Fisheries question, 1892; appointed chairman of the deputation sent by the Government to the "Ottawa Conference", 1895; Premier and Colonial Sec. Newfoundland, 1900–9; special delegate to Conference on French Treaties in Downing Street, 1901; recipient of the Freedom of the City of Edinburgh, 1902; in the same year was authorised by His Majesty's Government to reopen negotiations with the United States for reciprocal trade between that country and Newfoundland, and succeeded in concluding a treaty with that country known as the Hay-Bond Treaty; assisted in drafting regulations for carrying out Anglo-

French Convention, 1904; Freedom of City of London, Bristol, and Manchester, 1907; resigned seat in the House of Assembly, and retired from public life in 1913. *Address:* St John's, and The Grange, Whitbourne, Newfoundland.   *Died 16 March 1927.*

BOND, Maj.-Gen. William Dunn, CB 1886; *b* 5 Nov. 1836; *s* of late Robert Bond of Dullerton House, Tyrone. Entered army, 1855; Maj.-Gen. 1890; served Zulu War, 1879 (severely wounded, despatches, brevets of Lieut-Col and Col, medal with clasp); Boer War, 1881. *Address:* Dullerton, Londonderry. *TA:* Dullerton, Londonderry. *Club:* Army and Navy.   *Died 30 Nov. 1919.*

BONE, Rev. Frederic James; Vicar of Lanhydrock, Cornwall, 1903-15; *b* 1844; *s* of Allan Belfield Bone, solicitor, and Jane Anne, *d* of John Scobell, of Holwell, Tavistock. *Educ:* Cheltenham Coll.; Trinity Coll., Cambridge (Scholar, BA, MA); 22nd Wrangler. Assistant Curate of Stratton, Cornwall, 1870; Vicar, 1873; St Newlyn, Cornwall, 1892; Hon. Canon of Truro, 1898-1915. *Address:* Betworth, Exmouth.   *Died 31 Dec. 1917.*

BONET MAURY, Amy-Gaston, Knight of Legion of Honour; DD of Paris, Glasgow, and Aberdeen Univs; LLD, St Andrews; Emeritus Professor of Protestant School of Divinity of Paris, etc; *b* 2 Jan. 1842; *s* of Lieut-General Bonet, late head of Polytechnical School, Paris; *m* 1868, Isabelle Maury; two *s* two *d. Educ:* Lycée Henry IV, Paris; Schools of Divinity, Geneva and Strassburg. Served as Presbyterian Minister in the Walloon Churches of Netherland, 1868-72; called back to France after the disasters of his country in 1870-71, he served as Protestant minister at Beauvais, where he erected the first church, and at St Denis; lecturer in Church history at Protestant School of Divinity of Paris, 1879; for twenty years took a large share in all endeavours made to improve in France primary education as librarian of the Musée Pédagogique, and to advance the knowledge of the history of the Huguenots. French delegate at Congress of Health and Education, London, 1884; the Parliament of Religions, Chicago, 1893; the Congress of Religious Sciences at Stockholm 1897, and of Free Religious Thinkers at Paris 1900, London 1901, Basel 1903, Boston 1907, Berlin, 1910; corresponding member Institut de France, 1908; contributor to Revue politique et littéraire, du protestantisme français, etc. *Publications:* Revue des deux mondes, Bulletin d'Histoire, Gérard de Groote, 1878; Des origines du Christianisme unitaire chez les Anglais, 1881; Arnauld de Brescia, 1881; G. A. Bürger ou les Origines anglaises de la ballade littéraire en Allemagne, 1890; Lettres et déclarations de Dœllinger au sujet des décrets du Vatican, 1893; Le Congrès des religions à Chicago en 1893-1895; Histoire de la liberté de conscience depuis l'Edit de Nantes jusqu'à la Séparation de l'Etat et des Eglises, 1905; Les Précurseurs de la Réforme et de la liberté de conscience dans les pays latins du XIIᵉ au XVᵉ siècle, 1904; Edgar Quinet, son œuvre religieuse et son caractère moral, 1903; L'Islamisme et le Christianisme en Afrique, 1906; France, Christianisme et Civilisation, 1907; L'Unité morale des religions, 1913. *Address:* 32 Rue du Bac, Paris VIIᵉᵐᵉ.
                                                  Died 20 June 1919.

BONHAM, Sir George (Francis), 2nd Bt, *cr* 1852; MA; JP; *b* 28 Aug. 1847; *s* of Sir S. G. Bonham, 1st Bt, KCB, and Ellen E., *d* of Thomas Barnard, Bombay Civil Service; *S* father, 1863; *m* 1871, Louisa (*d* 1923), 3rd *d* of Rt Hon. Sir Andrew Buchanan, 1st Bt, GCB; one *s* three *d* (and two *s* decd). *Educ:* Eton; Exeter Coll., Oxford. Joined Diplomatic Service, 1869; Attaché at St Petersburg, 1870; at Vienna, 1872; 3rd Secretary at Vienna, 1873; at Rome, 1875; 2nd Secretary at Lisbon, 1876; at Madrid, 1878; at Paris, 1884; First Secretary at Lisbon, 1886; at The Hague, 1890; Secretary of Embassy at Madrid, 1893-97; Secretary of Embassy at Rome, 1897-1900; Minister at Belgrade, 1900-3; Envoy Extraordinary and Minister Plenipotentiary, Swiss Confederation, 1905-9; retired from Diplomatic Service, 1909. *Heir: s* Eric Henry Bonham, CVO, *b* 3 July 1875. *Address:* Knowle Park, Cranleigh, Surrey. *Club:* Travellers'.
                                                  Died 31 July 1927.

BONHAM, Col John, CB 1906; JP; *b* July 1834; 2nd *s* of late Rev. John Bonham, JP, of Ballintaggart, and Barbarina, 3rd *d* of late John Norris, of Hughenden House, Bucks; *m* 1870, Mary (*d* 1891), 2nd *d* of Philip Wroughton, of Woolley Park, Berks; two *s* one *d. Educ:* Addiscombe. Col Royal Artillery; retired. Served Indian Mutiny, 1857, including defence of Lucknow (despatches, three times wounded, medal with clasp, brevet of Major). *Club:* Kildare Street, Dublin.   *Died 18 May 1928.*

BONHAM-CARTER, Arthur Thomas; Judge of HM High Court of East Africa since 1906; Member of the Court of Appeal for Eastern Africa; *b* 1869; *s* of John Bonham-Carter, Adhurst St Mary, Petersfield;

unmarried. *Educ:* Winchester; Trinity College, Cambridge. Called to Bar, Inner Temple, and Western Circuit, 1894; Lieutenant (temporary) The Hampshire Regiment, 1900; served South African War (Queen's Medal and 4 Clasps); Assistant Resident Magistrate, Transvaal, 1902; Magistrate, East Africa Protectorate, 1905. *Address:* Mombasa, East Africa Protectorate. *Clubs:* Oxford and Cambridge; Royal Southern Yacht; Mombasa; Nyanza; Jubaland.
                                                  Died 1 July 1916.

BONI, Comm. Giacomo, Hon. LLD Camb.; Director of the excavations in the Roman Forum and on the Palatine; Member of the Superior Council of Antiquities and Fine Arts; *b* Venice, 25 April 1859. *Educ:* Venice; Pisa; Austria; Germany. Student journeys in most of the ancient provinces of the Roman Empire; Royal Academy of Fine Arts, Venice (Sup. School of Architecture); DLitt (Oxon); HM Inspector of Antiquities, Minister of Public Instruction; Royal Commissioner for the Monuments of Rome. *Publications:* Aedes Vestae; Fons Tuturnae; Prisco-Latin and Romulean Sepulcretum in the Roman Forum; Methods of Archæological Excavations; Hibernica; Forum Ulpium; Trajanic Legends and Column of Trajan; Dalle Origini; Bimbi Romulei; Porta Capena; Terra Mater; Mura Urbane; Flora Palatina; The Tower of St Mark, Venice, etc; Official Reports published by the R. Academia dei Lincei; illustrated articles by the review Nuova Antologia. *Recreation:* gardening. *Address:* Rome, Palatino.   *Died 7 July 1925.*

BONNAT, Leon, Hon. RA; President Société des Artistes Français; Grand Cross Legion of Honour; Member of the Institute; Member of Council of Legion of Honour. *Address:* Rue de Bassano 48, VIIIᵉ, Paris.   *Died 7 Sept. 1922.*

BONNER, Captain Singleton, DSO 1915; 1st Battalion the South Staffordshire Regiment; *b* 7 July 1879; *s* of late John Bonner of Liverpool; *m* 1904, Sisely Alexander, *o d* of late Ebenezer Park of Edinburgh; no *c. Educ:* Harrow. Entered army, 1900; Captain, 1908; Adjutant, 1913; Adjutant Volunteers, 1906; served South Africa, 1899-1902 (Queen's medal, 3 clasps, King's medal, 2 clasps); European War, 1914-15 (DSO, twice wounded).   *Died 1 May 1917.*

BONNEY, Rev. Thomas George, DSc Cambridge; Hon. LLD Montreal; Hon. DSc Dublin and Sheffield; FRS; Emeritus Professor of Geology, University College, London; Hon. Canon of Manchester; Fellow of St John's College, Cambridge; *b* Rugeley, 27 July 1833; *e s* of late Rev. Thomas Bonney. *Educ:* Uppingham; St John's Coll., Camb. Ordained 1857; Fellow, 1859, and Tutor, St John's Coll., Camb., 1868-76; Yates-Goldsmid Prof. of Geology, UCL, 1877-1901; Whitehall Preacher, 1876-78; Hulsean Lecturer (Camb.), 1884; President, Geological Society, 1884-86; Boyle Lecturer, 1890-92; Rede Lecturer (Camb.), 1892; Vice-President of Royal Society, 1899; President of British Association, 1910-11. *Publications:* Outline Sketches in the High Alps of Dauphiné, 1865; The Alpine Regions, 1868; The Story of our Planet, 1893; Charles Lyell and Modern Geology, 1895; Ice-Work, 1896; Volcanoes, 1898; The Building of the Alps, 1912; The Present Relations of Science and Religion, 1913; Text to Anderson's Volcanic Studies, 1917; Memories of a Long Life, 1922; four volumes of sermons and numerous contributions to scientific periodicals. *Recreation:* Alpine travel; ex-President Alpine Club. *Address:* 9 Scroope Terrace, Cambridge. *Club:* Alpine.   *Died 10 Dec. 1923.*

BONSALL, Arthur Charles; newspaper proprietor and editor since 1880; *b* 1859; *y s* of Isaac Bonsall, Dole Hall, Aberystwith; *m* 1880, Jane, *e d* of J. R. Swift, Lincoln's Inn. *Educ:* private school and tutor. Proprietor, Burlington Publishing Company. *Recreations:* shooting, fishing, golfing, motoring. *Address:* Kennet Lodge, Theale, Berks. *M:* BL 7076.   *Died April 1924.*

BONSALL, Major Hugh Edward, JP, Cardiganshire and Montgomeryshire; retired Major, late Cardigan Artillery; *b* 1863; 2nd *s* of John George William Bonsall of Fronfraith, Cardiganshire; *m* 1896, Gertrude E., *d* of late J. T. Morgan of Nantcaerio, Cardiganshire, MBE, JP. *Address:* Fronfraith, Aberystwyth. *TA:* Galltyllan, Machynlleth. *Club:* Junior Constitutional.
                                                  Died 18 March 1928.

BONSEY, His Honour Henry Dawes; Judge of County Court No 2 since 1911; Recorder of Bedford, 1910-12; 3rd *s* of late William Henry Bonsey, Slough, Bucks; *m* 1898, Helen Jane, *d* of late Archibald Dymock, Louth. *Educ:* St John's College, Cambridge; BA. Called to Bar, Inner Temple, 1875; went Midland Circuit. *Address:* 9 Windsor Crescent, Newcastle-on-Tyne. *Club:* Oxford and Cambridge.   *Died 12 May 1919.*

BONUS, Maj.-Gen. Joseph; late Royal Engineers; *b* 1836; 5th *s* of John Bonus; *m* 1st, Frances Mary, *d* of William Hart, ICS; 2nd, Marion Sophia, *d* of R. Stuart Poole, British Museum; three *s* one *d. Educ:* privately; Addiscombe. Served Indian Mutiny (medal and clasp); Afghan War, 1878–80 (medal); Engineer-in-Chief, Scindiah State Railway, Punjab Northern Railway; Joint Secretary to Government of Bombay Railways; retired, 1886; JP Midlesex. *Address:* Newlands, Stanstead Abbotts, Herts. *T:* Stanstead Abbotts 9. *TA:* Stanstead Abbotts. *M:* NK 4736. *Club:* United Service.
Died 11 June 1926.

BOOKEY, Col John Trench Brownrigg, CB 1900; Indian Medical Service; late Surgeon to the Viceroy; retired 1902; *b* Carnew, Co. Wicklow, Ireland, 10 Dec. 1847; *s* of Dr Bookey; *m* 1892. *Educ:* Trinity College, Dublin. LRCP Edin; LRCSI. Entered IMS, 1872; served with the Punjab Frontier Force, 1873–1900; appointed PMO Presidency Dist, May 1900; Colonel same date; served in the following Expeditions—Jowaki Afridi, 1877–78; Mahsud Waziri, 1881; Burmah, 1886–87 (despatches); Hazara Black Mountain, 1888 (despatches); Miranzai, 1891 (despatches); Mahsud Waziri, 1894–95 (despatches); Malakand Field Force, 1897 (despatches); Tirah, 1897–98; China Expeditionary Force, 1900. *Address:* c/o Grindlay & Co., 54 Parliament Street, SW. *Club:* East India United Service.
Died 19 Nov. 1921.

BOON, Quartermaster and Hon. Capt. George, DSO 1900; The Buffs; retired; *b* 9 Sept. 1846; *s* of Charles Boon; *m* 1871, Sarah, *d* of James T. Easter. Served South Africa, 1899–1900 (despatches, Queen's medal four clasps, King's medal two clasps, DSO).
Died 8 Oct. 1927.

BOON, John, FIJ; member of the Editorial Staff of The Times; editor of the Exchange Telegraph Co. Ltd, 1894–1914; *b* Clontarf, Dublin, 8 June 1859; *e s* of Andrew Boon, near Coollagh, Co. Dublin, and Sophie Léon. *Educ:* Lycée de Bordeaux; Sorbonne, Paris; Rome; Madrid. Commenced to contribute to English-French Press, 1880; travelled in Algeria and Egypt; spent 3 years in Rome; joined literary staff of Central News; in 1883 acted as foreign editor and special correspondent; in 1886 became special correspondent of the Exchange Telegraph Co., and representative of that Co. in Lobby of House of Commons during the eventful years of 1885–92; acted as special correspondent throughout the three kingdoms and in most parts of Continent; has twice visited Morocco and seen much adventure in Spain; contributed largely to the old Pall Mall Gazette and the Westminster Gazette; acted as Special Correspondent of The Times in France and Flanders during the early stages of the War, and in 1916 as Special Correspondent in Spain and Portugal. Knight Commander of the Royal Spanish Order of Isabel the Catholic. *Recreations:* fencing, riding, mountaineering. *Address:* 46 Upper Park Road, Hampstead, N. *Club:* National Liberal. *Died 26 June 1928.*

BOORD, Sir (William) Arthur, 2nd Bt, *cr* 1896; FRGS; *b* 24 May 1862; *e s* of Sir William Boord, 1st Bt and Margaret D'Almaine, *d* of Thomas G. Mackinlay, FSA; *S* father, 1912; unmarried. *Educ:* Harrow; Germany and France. Travelled extensively. *Publications:* several books of verse. *Recreations:* photography, travel, chess. *Heir:* nephew Richard William Boord, *b* 9 Nov. 1907. *Club:* Junior Carlton.
Died 26 May 1928.

BOOT, William Henry James, RI; Vice-President, Royal Society of British Artists, 1895–1914; Member Japan Society, etc; *b* Nottingham. Studied at Derby School of Art. Contributed drawings to Picturesque Europe, British Battles, Our Village, Our Own Country, British Ballads, Royal River, Rivers of England, Greater London, Picturesque Mediterranean, Art Journal, Magazine of Art, Graphic, Illustrated London News, Strand Magazine, etc, 1869–92; art editor, Strand Magazine, 1891–1910. *Exhibitor:* RA 1874–84, and at intervals since; also at RBA, RI, and most of the principal exhibitions in the provinces. *Publication:* Trees and How to Paint Them, 1888. *Recreation:* travel. *Address:* 1 Cannon Place, Hampstead, NW. *Club:* Arts.
Died 8 Sept. 1918.

BOOTH, Rt. Hon. Charles, PC 1904; DSc (hon.), Camb.; DCL (hon.), Oxford; LLD Liverpool; FRS 1899; Chairman of Alfred Booth & Co. Ltd, Liverpool; Director of Booth Steamship Co.; *b* Liverpool, 30 March 1840; *m* 1871, Mary, *d* of Charles Zachary Macaulay; three *s* four *d. Educ:* Royal Inst. Sch., Liverpool. President, Royal Statistical Society, 1892–94; Member of Tariff Commission, 1904. *Publications:* Life and Labour of the People in London (Poverty, 1891; Industry, 1897; The Religious Influences of London, 1903; Summary, 1903); Pauperism: a Picture, 1892; The Endowment of Old Age, 1892; The Aged Poor: Condition, 1894; Old Age Pensions, 1899. *Address:* 28

Campden House Court, Kensington, W. *Clubs:* Reform, Athenæum.
Died 23 Nov. 1916.

BOOTH, Very Rev. Lancelot Parker; Dean of St John's, Cape Colony, 1900–12; *s* of Lancelot Parker Booth of Bishop Auckland, Co. Durham; *m* 1st, 1884, Olive (*d* 1888), *d* of Dr Hugh Stott, Blackheath; 2nd, 1894, Annie Sophia, *d* of J. R. Grimes of St Leonard's. MD Durham Univ.; DD Trinity Coll., Toronto. Natal Govt Medical Service and Indian Immigration Dept, 1876–83; ordained, 1883; Diocesan Supt of Indian Missions and Canon of Maritzburg, Natal, 1889; Natal Indian Ambulance MO, 1899–1900 (medal, 2 clasps); Vicar-General of St John's, 1900–1; Vicar and Sub-Dean of St George's Cathedral, Capetown, 1912–13; Rector of St Barnabas', Capetown, 1913; Captain RAMC, BEF, France, 1916. *Address:* St Barnabas' Rectory, Capetown.
Died 28 March 1925.

BOOTH, Leonard William, CMG 1913; Colonial Secretary, Ceylon (Acting); *b* 10 June 1856; 2nd *s* of George Booth, Solicitor, and Margaret Emily, *d* of William Shipton Browning; *m* 1883, Mary Emily, *d* of H. R. von Dadelszen, Coffee Planter, Ceylon; two *s* four *d. Educ:* Lancing College. Cadet, Ceylon Civil Service, 1878; Class I, 1906; Police Magistrate; District Judge; Forest Settlement Officer; Government Agent North Central, Sabaragamawa, Uva, North-Western, Southern, Central, and Western Provinces; acted as Principal Collector of Customs, Colonial Treasurer, Controller of Revenue, and Colonial Secretary. *Address:* c/o Crown Agents for the Colonies, Millbank, Westminster, SW. *Died 20 Nov. 1923.*

BOOTH, S. Lawson, RCA; JP. *Address:* 172 Roe Lane, Southport.
Died 25 Aug. 1928.

BOOTHBY, Sir Charles Francis, 12th Bt *cr* 1660; *b* 22 June 1858; 2nd *s* of Rev. Sir Brooke Boothby, 10th Bt and Martha Serena, *d* of Rev. Charles Boothby, Vicar of Sutterton, Lincs; *S* brother, 1913. *Educ:* Harrow. *Heir:* brother Rev. Herbert Cecil Boothby, *b* 8 Dec. 1863. *Died 4 April 1926.*

BOOTHBY, Josiah, CMG 1878; *b* 1837; *m* 1861, Susannah, *d* of W. G. Lawrence, Adelaide. Entered Colonial Secretary's Office, South Australia, 1853; Permanent Under-Secretary, South Australia, 1868–80; Commissioner, Paris Exhibition, 1878. *Address:* 158 Barnard Street, North Adelaide, South Australia.
Died 19 June 1916.

BORASTON, Sir John, Kt 1916; JP; Principal Unionist Agent since 1912; *b* 1851; *m* 1876; one *s* (Major J. H. Boraston, OBE). *Address:* Ringwood, 31 Southend Road, Beckenham; 1 Sanctuary Buildings, Great Smith Street, Westminster, SW1. *Club:* Carlton.
Died 18 April 1920.

BORDEN, Hon. Sir Frederick William, KCMG 1902; PC (Canada) 1896; Knight of Grace, Order of St John of Jerusalem, 1902; BA, MD, DCL, LLD; Minister of Militia Defence, 1896–1911; *b* 14 May 1847; *s* of Dr J. and Maria F. Borden; *m* 1st, 1873, Julia M. Clarke (*d* 1880); 2nd, 1884, Bessie B. Clarke; two *d. Educ:* University of King's College, Windsor, Nova Scotia, BA; Harvard Medical School, Boston, Mass, MD. Began practice of medicine, 1868; appointed Asst Surgeon 68th Batt. King's County (Militia), 1869; subseq. Surg. Lt-Col and Hon. Col of Canadian Army Medical Corps; Hon Surgeon-General in the Imperial Army, 1911; first elected to House of Commons, 1874; since then represented same Riding (King's NS) continuously to 1911 except during the years 1883–86, having been elected ten times and defeated once. *Recreations:* walking, fishing, music. *Address:* Canning, Nova Scotia; 17 Blackburn Avenue, Ottawa, Ont. *Clubs:* Rideau, Ottawa; Halifax, Halifax, NS.
Died 6 Jan. 1917.

BORRADAILE, Col George William, CB 1882; *b* Poona, Bombay, 13 June 1838; 3rd *s* of Harry Borradaile, Bombay CS; *m* 1864, Catherine Cornelia (*d* 1912); 4th *d* of late Surgeon-General Charles Doyle Straker, Bombay Medical Service. *Educ:* private school; Cheltenham College, 1854–55. Passed out of Addiscombe as a Bombay artillery cadet, 1857; transferred to Royal Artillery; served in India, 1858–71; England, 1872–83; India, 1883–94, when retired on pension after 38 years; 3rd Class Order of the Medjidie, medal and clasp for Tel-el-Kebir, Bronze Star, Egypt, 1882 (despatches); JP Bucks. *Address:* c/o Lloyds Bank Ltd, Cox & Co.'s Branch (GI Section), 6 Pall Mall, SW1. *Died 3 Feb. 1927.*

BORRETT, Major-General Herbert Charles, CB 1902; *b* Great Yarmouth, Norfolk, 23 Sept. 1841; *y s* of Thomas Borrett of Cransford

Hall, Suffolk; *m* 1867, Annie, *e d* of Major John Bennett, 1st Bombay Fusiliers; four *s* three *d*. *Educ:* Radley College. Ensign 4th Foot, 1858; Adjutant, 1869 and 1870; Colonel, 1885; commanded 49th Royal Berkshire Regimental District, 1890-95; AAG for Recruiting, Headquarters Staff, 1895-98; Major-General, 1898; Inspector-General of Recruiting, Headquarters Staff, 1899-1903; served with the 4th Foot throughout the Abyssinian Expedition, 1867-68; present at action of Arogee and capture of Magdala (medal). *Address:* Lancaster Lodge, Bath Road, Reading, Berks. *Club:* United Service.

Died 4 April 1919.

BORROWES, Lieut-Col Sir Kildare Dixon, 10th Bt, *cr* 1646; JP, DL; *b* 21 Sept. 1852; *s* of Sir Erasmus Dixon Borrowes, 9th Bt and Frederica, *e d* of Brig.-Gen. Hutchinson; *S* father, 1898; *m* 1886, Julia Aline, *d* of late Wm Holden of Palace House, Lancashire. *Educ:* Cheltenham College. Retired Lt-Col; late Major 11th Hussars. High Sheriff, Co. Kildare, 1902; served in France throughout European War (1914-15 Star, War and Victory Medals); served in the South Irish Horse; formerly ADC to Duke of Marlborough, Lord Lieut of Ireland. Owned 11,000 acres. *Heir-pres.: brother* Eustace Borrowes [*b* 31 Dec. 1866; *m* 1899 (Louisa Margaret) Winifred (Mary), *d* of John Macdonald Royse. *Address:* 49 Rathdown Road, Dublin]. *Address:* Beechborough Park, near Folkestone. *Clubs:* Brooks's, United Service, MCC; Kildare Street, Dublin.

Died 21 Oct. 1924.

BORTHWICK, William Henry; *b* 28 Nov. 1832; 3rd *s* of late John Borthwick and 1st wife, Anne, *e d* of late Rt Hon. Robert Dundas, of Arniston, Midlothian; *m* 1864, Rebecca (*d* 1887), *o d* of late Robert Cathcart; three *s*. *Address:* Crookston House, Heriot, Midlothian.

Died 8 Oct. 1928.

BORTON, Colonel Charles Edward, CB 1902; retired; *b* 3 June 1857; *y s* of late General Sir Arthur Borton, GCB, GCMG; *m* 1893, Amy Louisa, *y d* of late Richard Cotton Lewin, ICS; one *s*. *Educ:* Wellington. Entered army, 1878; Capt. 1885; Maj. 1896; Lt-Col 1901; served Afghan War, 1879-80 (medal with clasp); Burmese Expedition, 1887-89 (medal with clasp); South Africa, 1900-2 (despatches, CB); European War, Aug. 1914-Jan. 1918 (despatches). *Address:* Ruthaven, Horley, Surrey. *Club:* Naval and Military.

Died 23 March 1924.

BORWICK, Leonard; pianist; *b* 26 Feb. 1868. *Educ:* Hoch Conservatoire, Frankfort-on-the-Main. Appeared first at Frankfort, 1889; London Philharmonic and Richter Concerts, 1890. *Recreations:* travel, chess. *Address:* 14 Brunswick Square, WC1. *T:* Museum 6386.

Died 15 Sept. 1925.

BOSANQUET, Bernard, MA Oxon, LLD Glasgow, DCL Durham; FBA; Fellow of University College, Oxford, 1870-81; past President of Aristotelian Society; *b* 14 June 1848; *s* of Rev. R. W. Bosanquet of Rock Hall, Alnwick; *m* 1895, Helen Dendy. *Educ:* Harrow; Balliol College, Oxford (scholar). First class in Moderations and Literae Humaniores. Lecturer at Univ. Coll., Oxford, 1871-81; in London occupied with authorship and Univ. Extension lecturing and social work, especially in connection with Charity Organisation Society, 1881-97; then went to live in country; Professor of Moral Philosophy, St Andrews, 1903-8; Gifford Lecturer (Edinburgh), 1911-12. *Publications:* Knowledge and Reality, 1885; Logic, or Morphology of Knowledge, 1888; History of Aesthetic, 1892; Essays and Addresses; Civilisation of Christendom; Essentials of Logic, 1895; Aspects of Social Problem; Companion to Plato's Republic for English Readers, 1895; Psychology of Moral Self, 1897; Education of the Young in Plato's Republic; Philosophical Theory of the State, 1899; Three Lectures on Aesthetic, Social and Internal Ideals; Implication and Linear Influences, 1919; The Meeting of Extremes in Contemporary Philosophy, 1921. *Address:* The Heath Cottage, Oxshott, Surrey.

Died 8 Feb. 1923.

BOSANQUET, Admiral Sir Day Hort, GCMG 1914; GCVO 1907; KCB 1905; JP, DL, Hereford; Governor of South Australia, 1909-14; *b* 22 March 1843; *m* 1881, Mary, *d* of late Col T. Bromhead Butt, Cameron Highlanders; two *d*. Entered RN 1857; Commander, 1874; Captain, 1882; Rear-Admiral, 1897; Vice-Admiral, 1902; was Commander-in-Chief, East Indies, 1899-1902; Commander-in-Chief, North America and West Indies, 1904-7; Commander-in-Chief, Portsmouth, 1907-8. *Decoration:* Grand Cross of Swords of Sweden, 1906. *Address:* Old Vicarage, Newbury. *Club:* United Service.

Died 28 June 1923.

BOSANQUET, Sir (Frederick) Albert, Kt 1907; KC; an additional Judge of the Central Criminal Court since 1917; *b* 8 Feb. 1837; *s*

of S. R. Bosanquet, Dingestow Court, Monmouth; *m* 1st, 1871, Albinia Mary (*d* 1882), *d* of J. Curtis-Hayward; two *s* two *d*; 2nd, 1885, Philippa, *d* of W. Bence Jones; one *s* one *d*. *Educ:* Eton; King's College, Cambridge. 1st Class Classics and Senior Optime, 1860; Fellow of King's Coll., Camb. Barrister, 1863; QC 1882; Bencher of Inner Temple, 1889; Recorder of Worcester, 1879; Recorder of Wolverhampton, 1891-1900; Common Serjeant of London, 1900-17; Chairman of E Sussex Quarter Sessions, 1912-21; Chairman of Council of Law Reporting, 1909-17. *Address:* 12 Grenville Place, S Kensington, SW7. *T:* Western 3983.

Died 2 Nov. 1923.

BOSANQUET, Helen, LLD St Andrews; *b* 10 Feb. 1860; *d* of Rev. John Dendy; *m* 1895, Bernard Bosanquet, FBA (*d* 1923); no *c*. *Educ:* Newnham College, Cambridge; First Class Honours Moral Sciences Tripos. District Secretary to the Charity Organisation Society; University Extension Lecturer; Member of Royal Commission on Poor Laws, 1905; Writer on Social Subjects. *Publications:* Rich and Poor; The Standard of Life; The Strength of the People; The Family; The Poor Law Report of 1909 (Summary); Social Work in London, etc. *Address:* 13 Heathgate, Golders Green, NW11.

Died 7 April 1925.

BOSCAWEN, Major Hon. George Edward, DSO 1914; Royal Field Artillery; *b* 6 Dec. 1888; 2nd *s* of 7th Viscount Falmouth. Entered army, 1907; served European War, 1914-16 (despatches, DSO, Bt Major, for gallantly fighting his section of guns in front of La Bassée). *Address:* Tregothnan, Truro.

Died 27 May 1918.

BOSE, Sir Kailas Chandra, Rai Bahadur, Kt 1916; CIE 1910; OBE 1918; Kaiser-i-Hind Gold Medal, 1909. Fellow, Calcutta Univ.; Vice-President, Indian Medical Congress; Fellow, Royal Institute of Public Health; Member, British Association; Hon. Presidency Magistrate; Member of Governing Body, State Medical Faculty of Bengal; Presidency Magistrate and Ex-officio JP; Municipal Commissioner; President of Calcutta Medical Club; Member of Plague Commission; Bengal Delegate at All India Sanitary Conference, etc. *Address:* 1 Sukeos Street, Calcutta. *T:* 1993. *M:* 741.

Died Feb. 1927.

BOSTOCK, Henry; Chairman, Lotus Ltd, boot manufacturers, Stafford; Vik Heels Ltd, Stafford, and Sutor Ltd, Northampton. *Address:* The Oaklands, Stafford. *T:* 7.

Died 11 Oct. 1923.

BOSWELL, Arthur Radcliffe, KC; *b* Cobourg, Ont, 3 Jan. 1838; *s* of late Judge Boswell and Susan Radcliffe; *m* Ella, *d* of M. D. Cruso, late of Cobourg, Ont; no *c*. *Educ:* Brockville, Ont; UC Coll., Toronto. Alderman of Toronto several years; Mayor of Toronto, 1883 and 1884; Commodore, Royal Canadian Yacht Club for 14 years; President, Canadian Association Amateur Oarsmen for 9 years; passed Royal Military School, 1864; a Freemason; an Anglican, and a delegate to Synod for many years. *Recreations:* yachting, golf. *Clubs:* York, Royal Canadian Yacht, M. Golf, Toronto.

BOSWORTH, Colonel William John; Founder and Principal of the Military College, Roehampton; *b* Stoke, Devonport, 1858; *m* (wife *d* 1916). *Educ:* King Edward VI Grammar School, Birmingham; Caius and Downing Colleges, Cambridge. Founded the Military College, Roehampton, 1884, and transferred it to Earl's Court, 1910; during South African Campaign commanded the 2nd Provisional Battalion, Aldershot; greatly interested in aviation and motoring as applied to military uses; one of the founders and first Chairman of the Automobile Association; a founder, and Chairman for three years, of the Motor Club; Chairman of the first International Rubber Exhibition and other International Exhibitions. *Publications:* contributions to the military publications on technical subjects. *Recreations:* big game shooting, motoring, golf, bulldog breeding. *Address:* 65 Earl's Court Square, SW5. *T:* Kensington 217. *Clubs:* Savage, Royal Temple Yacht.

Died 28 Nov. 1923.

BOTELER, Sir Edgar Collins Boehm, 2nd Bt, *cr* 1889; FRGS; *b* 1 Oct. 1869; *o s* of Sir Edgar Joseph Boehm, 1st Bt, RA, and Louisa Frances Boteler, of West Derby, Lancs; *S* father, 1890; assumed surname of Boehm Boteler by deed poll, 1918. *Educ:* Eton. Late Lieut, Royal Garrison Artillery. *Publications:* Over the World; The Persian Gulf and South Sea Isles, 1904. *Recreation:* sport. *Heir:* none. *Address:* Craufurd, Maidenhead, Berkshire. *M:* L 9046. *Clubs:* Badminton, Royal Automobile, New Oxford and Cambridge.

Died 23 May 1928 (ext).

BOTHA, Rt. Hon. Louis, PC; LLD Edin., Oxon and Cantab; Premier and Minister of Native Affairs, Union of S Africa; Hon. General in British Army; MLA Losberg; *b* Greytown, Natal, 1863. Was a member of first Volksraad of Transvaal, in which he represented Vryheid; acted as veldt-cornet for that district at the beginning of the Anglo-Boer War; succeeded General Joubert as Commander-in-Chief of the Boer forces, which he commanded at the battle of Colenso and during the rest of the war; visited England, 1902, 1907, and 1911; Premier of Transvaal, 1907–10; commanded the Union Forces in South-West Africa, 1914–15, and achieved complete success, receiving surrender of the German army. *Address:* Pretoria, Transvaal.
Died 27 Aug. 1919.

BOTHAMLEY, Rev. Hilton, MA. *Educ:* Harrow; Trinity Coll., Cambridge. Ordained, 1861; Curate of St John, Weymouth, 1867–73; Rector of Peperharow, Surrey, 1873–79; Curate of St Stephen, Lansdown, Bath, 1880–81; Vicar, 1881–1909; Prebendary of Wells, 1892–1913; Archdeacon of Bath, 1895–1909. *Address:* Richmond Lodge, Bath.
Died 1 July 1919.

BOTTOMLEY, Col Herbert, CMG 1900; Imperial Light Horse; *b* Natal, 18 July 1866; parents both from Yorkshire, England; *m* 1902, Helena Emma, *d* of late Captain Barnes, RN, and *widow* of Mr Graham. *Educ:* Diocesan College, Rondebosch, Cape Town. Matriculated, 1884. Entered the law, 1885, and threw it up, 1886; proceeded to Barberton, and spent 3 years prospecting for gold; proceeded to Johannesburg in 1890, and took up gold-mining; was mine manager of Village Main Reef; joined the ILH 1889, as lieutenant; attained rank of colonel, 1901; served South African War, 1899–1902 (CMG); Deputy Inspector of Mines, Transvaal, 1902; commanded 12th SAI, German East Campaign, 1916 (despatches). *Club:* Rand, Johannesburg.
Died 20 Sept. 1926.

BOTTOMLEY, James Thomson, MA, DSc, Hon. LLD (Glasgow); FRS; electrical engineer; *b* 10 Jan. 1845; *s* of late William Bottomley, JP, Belfast; *nephew* of Lord Kelvin; *m* 1st, Annie Elizabeth, *d* of late W. W. Heap, Manchester; one *s*; 2nd, Eliza Jennet (*d* 1913), *d* of late Chas R. Blandy, Madeira. *Educ:* Queen's College, Belfast; Trinity Coll., Dublin. Gold medallist at degrees of BA and MA. Assistant to late Professor Thomas Andrews, FRS, Belfast; Demonstrator, 1st, of Chemistry; 2nd, of Physics, King's Coll., London; for 29 years occupied the position of Arnott and Thomson Demonstrator in the University of Glasgow, and acted as deputy for Lord Kelvin; resigned 1899, when Lord Kelvin resigned the Professorship of Natural Philosophy. *Publications:* elementary books on Dynamics and Hydrostatics; Mathematical Tables; original papers contributed to Royal Society, etc. *Recreations:* swimming, rowing, climbing, cycling, motoring. *Address:* Netherhall, Largs, Ayrshire; 13 University Gardens, Glasgow. *T:* 35 Western, Glasgow. *M:* G 5007, G 9341. *Clubs:* Athenæum, Royal Automobile, British Empire League; Western, Royal Scottish Automobile, Glasgow; Brooklands.
Died 16 May 1926.

BOTTOMLEY, William Beecroft, MA (Camb.), PhD; FLS, FCS; Fellow, King's College, London; Professor of Botany, King's College, London, 1893–1921; Professor of Biology, Royal Veterinary College, London, since 1891; *b* Apperley Bridge, Leeds, 1863; *o s* of J. Bottomley, Fern Cliffe, Morecambe; *m* 1891. *Educ:* Royal Grammar School, Lancaster; King's Coll., Camb. Science Tutor and Lecturer on Biology, St Mary's Hospital Medical School, 1886–91; Camb. University Extension Lecturer, 1891–94; interested in Agricultural Co-operation; founder of South-Eastern Co-operative Agricultural Society; Hon. Sec., Agricultural Banks Association; Hon. Sec., English Land Colonisation Society. *Recreations:* photography, cycling. *Address:* Botanical Laboratory, King's College, WC.
Died 24 March 1922.

BOUCAUT, Hon. Sir James Penn, KCMG 1898; *b* near Falmouth, 29 Oct. 1831; *m* 1864, Janet, *d* of Alexander M'Culloch of Yongala, SA; six *s* one *d*. Went to South Australia, 1846; Barrister, 1855; MLA 1861; Attorney-General, 1865; Premier, 1866, 1875, 1877; Deputy-Governor, 1885–86, 1888, 1890; Administrator of the Government, 1890 and 1891; Judge of the Supreme Court of the State of South Australia, 1878–1905; retired. *Publications:* The Arab: the Horse of the Future, 1905; Letters to My Boys, 1906; The Arab Horse, The Thoroughbred, and the Turf, 1912. *Recreation:* breeding pure Arab horses. *Address:* Glenelg, South Australia.
Died 1 Feb. 1916.

BOUCHE-LECLERCQ, August; Professeur d'Histoire Ancienne à l'Université de Paris; *b* Francières (Oise), 30 Juillet 1842; *s* of Thomas Bouché et Joséphine Leclercq; *m* 1876, Julie Guillaume; three *s* one *d*. *Educ:* Petit-Séminaire de Noyon (Oise). Chargé de cours, puis professeur à la Faculté des Lettres de Montpellier, 1873–78; professeur suppléant, 1879, puis titulaire, 1887, honoraire 1918, à la Faculté des Lettres de Paris; Membre de l'Institut (Académie des Inscriptions et Belles-Lettres), 1898; Officier de l'Instruction Publique. Officier de la Légion d'Honneur; Officier de SS Maurizio e Lazzaro. *Publications:* Les Pontifes de l'ancienne Rome, 1871; Placita Graecorum de origine generis humani, 1871; Giacomo Leopardi, sa vie et ses œuvres, 1874; Histoire de la Divination dans l'antiquité, 4 vols, 1879–82; Manuel des Institutions romaines, 1886; L'Astrologie grecque, 1899; Leçons d'Histoire grecque, 1900; Histoire des Lagides, 4 vols, 1903–7; Leçons d'Histoire romaine, 1909; L'Intolérance religieuse et la politique, 1911; Histoire des Sélencides, 2 vols, 1913–14; a publié, de 1880 à 1890, onze volumes de traductions des ouvrages de E. Curtius, J. G. Droysen, G. F. Hertzberg, concernant l'histoire de la Grèce, et un Atlas pour servir à l'Histoire Grecque de E. Curtius, 1883. *Address:* Nogent-sur-Marne (Seine), 26 Avenue de la Source.
Died 17 July 1923.

BOUCHER, Lt-Col Benjamin Hamilton, DSO 1900; retired; *b* 20 Feb. 1864; *e s* of late B. Boucher, of the Croft, Wiveliscombe, Somerset; *m* 1st, 1896, Helen (*d* 1904), *e d* of late C. Boucher, JP, of Eaglemont, Klimington, Devon, and of Lambcroft, Lincolnshire; three *s*; 2nd, 1907, Dorothy (*d* 1916), *d* of late Engledue Prideaux, of Luson, Wellington, Somerset. *Educ:* Marlborough. Entered Army, 1885; Captain, 1892; Station Staff Officer, Bengal, 1893–95; Adjutant, 1st Batt. Hampshire Regiment, 1896–1900; Adjutant, 4th Vol. Batt., 1900–4; served Burmese Expedition, 1887–89 (medal with clasp); Chitral Relief Force, 1895; South Africa, 1899–1900 (despatches, DSO, medal with 3 clasps). *Club:* Junior Army and Navy.
Died 8 Jan. 1928.

BOUGHEY, Sir Francis, 8th Bt, *cr* 1798; *b* 2 April 1848; *s* of 3rd Bt and Louisa Paulina, *y d* of Thomas Giffard of Chillington; *S* brother, 1921. *Heir: cousin* George Menteth Boughey, OBE, ICS [*b* 28 March 1879; *m* 1913, Noel Evelyn, *d* of late J. G. H. Glass, CIE; two *s* three *d*. *Educ:* Wellington]. *Address:* The Derwen, Oswestry.
Died 6 March 1927.

BOUGHEY, Col George Fletcher Ottley, CSI 1896; RE; a Light Railway Commissioner; *b* 23 Jan. 1844; *m* 1872, Harriet Rose Amy, *d* of late Lieut-Col W. Stuart Menteth; one *s* three *d*. Entered army, 1862; Col 1895; served Bhutan Expedition, 1865–66 (medal with clasp); Afghan War, 1878–80 (medal). *Address:* 60 Courtfield Gardens, SW.
Died 17 Jan. 1918.

BOUGHEY, Rev. Sir Robert, 7th Bt, *cr* 1798; Vicar of Betley, Crewe, since 1876; *b* 21 March 1843; *s* of Sir Thomas Boughey, 3rd Bt and Louisa Paulina, *y d* of Thomas Giffard of Chillington; *S* brother, 1912. *Educ:* Christ Church, Oxford (BA). Ordained, 1867; Curate, Stoke-on-Trent, 1866–76. *Heir: b* Francis Boughey [*b* 2 April 1848. *Address:* The Derwen, Oswestry]. *Address:* Betley Vicarage, Crewe.
Died 22 May 1921.

BOULDEN, Rev. Alfred William, MA; Hon. Canon of Rochester, 1919; Rural Dean of Dartford, 1916; Vicar of Christ Church, Erith, Kent, since 1891; *b* 23 April 1849; *e s* of Joseph and Elizabeth Boulden; unmarried. *Educ:* Dane Hill House, Margate; Corpus Christi College, Cambridge (Mawson Scholar). Manners Scholar and Prizeman in Divinity, 1870; Prizeman in Greek Testament, Hebrew, and English Literature, 1871; Deacon, 1872, Priest, 1873; Headmaster of Dane Hill House School, Margate, and Hon. Curate of Holy Trinity, Margate, 1872–88; Curate of St Paul's, Cliftonville, Margate, 1888–90. *Address:* Christ Church Vicarage, Erith, Kent. *TA:* Boulden, Erith.
Died 10 Feb. 1920.

BOULGER, Demetrius Charles; Chevalier of the Order of Leopold II; *b* 14 July 1853. *Educ:* Kensington Grammar School; and private tuition. Has contributed to all the leading journals on questions connected with our Indian Empire, China, Egypt, and Turkey, since 1876; has also closely studied military questions, especially those connected with the French frontiers and the position of Belgium; founded, in conjunction with Sir Lepel Griffin, the Asiatic Quarterly Review, 1885, and edited it during the first four and half years of its existence. *Publications:* Life of Yakoob Beg of Kashgar, 1878; England and Russia in Central Asia; Central Asian Portraits; The History of China; General Gordon's Letters from the Crimea; Armies of the Native States of India; Central Asian Questions; Lord William Bentinck; Short History of China; Life of Gordon; Story of India; Life of Sir Stamford Raffles, 1897; The Congo State, 1898; The Belgians at Waterloo; India in the 19th Century, 1901; History of

Belgium, Part I, 1902, Part II, 1909; Belgian Life in Town and Country, 1904; The Life of Sir Haliday Macartney, 1908; Belgium of the Belgians, 1911; The Battle of the Boyne and the Formation of the Irish Brigade, 1912; Holland of the Dutch, 1913; England's Arch-Enemy, 1914; Reign of Leopold II, 1925. *Recreation:* travelling. *Address:* 12 Bloomsbury Square, WC1.

Died 15 Dec. 1928.

BOULGER, Dorothy Henrietta, (Theo. Gift); novelist; *b* 30 May 1847; 2nd *d* of Thomas Havers of Thelton Hall, Norfolk, and Ellen, *d* of late Rogers Ruding; *m* 1879, Professor George S. Boulger (*d* 1922). *Educ:* home. Went to the Falkland Islands, 1854, her father having received the appointment of Colonial Manager; removed to Uruguay, 1861, and resided in Monte Video, till her father's death in 1870 brought her and her brothers and sisters to England; began to publish, 1871, in Once a Week, and Cassell's (London), and Galaxy (New York); worked for ten years on All the Year Round under Charles Dickens, Jun., and for two on Cassell's under G. Manville Fenn. *Publications:* True to her Trust; Pretty Miss Bellew; Maid Ellice; A Matter-of-Fact Girl; Visited on the Children; Victims; Lil Lorimer; An Innocent Maiden; A Garden of Girls; Not for the Night-time; Dishonoured; Wrecked at the Outset; An Island Princess; Women who Work; Cape Town Dicky; The Little Colonists; Fairy Tales from the Far East; The Case of a Man with His Wife, etc. *Address:* 12 Lancaster Park, Richmond, Surrey. *Died 22 July 1923.*

BOULGER, George Simonds, FLS, FGS, FRHS; Vice-President, Selborne Society, Essex Field Club, South-Eastern Union of Scientific Societies, etc; Lecturer on Botany and Geology, City of London College, since 1884; Imperial Institute, 1917; *b* Blechingley, Surrey, 5 March 1853; *s* of Edward Boulger, MD; *m* Dorothy. *Educ:* Wellington and Epsom Colleges; Middle Temple. Professor of Natural History, Royal Agricultural College, Cirencester, 1876; Hon. Professor, 1906. *Publications:* Familiar Trees, 1886–89, 2nd edn 1906-7; The Uses of Plants, 1889; Biographical Index of British and Irish Botanists, with J. Britten, 1893; The Country Month by Month, with J. A. Owen, 1894–95, 5th edn 1914; Elementary Geology, 1896; Flowers of the Field, 1900, 33rd edn 1911; Wood, 1902, 2nd edn 1908; Botany, 1912; Plant-geography, 1912; British Flowering Plants, with Mrs Henry Perrin, 4 vols, 1914. *Recreation:* ecclesiology. *Address:* 12 Lancaster Park, Richmond, Surrey.

Died 4 May 1922.

BOULTER, Stanley Carr, JP for Surrey; Chairman of Law Debenture Corporation, Ltd, and Director of other important financial companies; Barrister-at-Law; formerly editor of the Times Law Reports; *b* 29 May 1852; *s* of late John Boulter; *m* 1st, Edith, *d* of James Anderson; 2nd, Helen (*d* 1913), widow of Richard D'Oyly Carte; three *s* four *d*. *Educ:* Cambridge University. Contested (U) Spen Valley Division, West Riding of Yorks, 1886; four times Unionist candidate for London County Council. *Address:* 3 Essex Court, Temple, EC. *Clubs:* Oxford and Cambridge, City of London.

Died 5 Jan. 1917.

BOULTON, Major Charles Percy, DSO 1902; Member of Lloyd's; *b* 1 Sept. 1867; *s* of Charles G. Boulton, JP. *Educ:* Haileybury; Magdalen College, Oxford. BA 1890. Gazetted to 4th Bedfordshire Militia, 1888; served South African War, 1900–1902; commanded Regiment from Nov. 1900 to June 1902; Camp Commandant, Mafeking; operations in Transvaal west of Pretoria to Sept. 1900; operations in Cape Colony south of Orange River, 1900; operations in Cape Colony north of Orange River; operations in the Transvaal and Orange River Colony, Sept. 1901 to April 1902; temporarily Commandant Bloemhof sub-district; operations in Cape Colony, Dec. 1900 to Sept. 1901 (despatches, Queen's Medal with three clasps, King's Medal with two clasps). *Recreations:* shooting, fishing, golf. *Address:* The Cottage, Stanmore. *Clubs:* Junior United Service, Constitutional. *Died 24 Feb. 1916.*

BOULTON, Sir Samuel Bagster, 1st Bt, *cr* 1905; Knight of Grace of Order of St John of Jerusalem in England; FRGS, AICE; Lord of the Manor of Totteridge; JP Hertfordshire, Middlesex, and borough of West Ham; Chairman of the Barnet Bench; DL Hertfordshire; *b* 12 July 1830; *m* 1855, Sophia Louisa (*d* 1900), *d* of Thomas Cooper; two *s* five *d*. Chairman of Burt, Boulton, and Haywood, Ltd, of London, Paris, Riga, Selzaette (Belgium), and Bilbao; in conjunction with late H. P. Burt established this firm more than fifty years ago; Chairman of the Dominion Tar and Chemical Company, Ltd, and of the British Australian Timber Company, Ltd; has been active in promoting the application of scientific methods to chemical and other industries, and has been a contributor to scientific literature in that connection; received the Telford Medal of the Institution of Civil

Engineers, 1884; Chairman of London Labour Conciliation and Arbitration Board 1889–1913; he was instrumental in its foundation in 1889, and has, *inter alia*, presided at settlement of more than 50 cases of labour disputes; member of Tariff Commission; in 1898–99 he successfully conducted, on behalf of the London Chamber of Commerce and under the auspices of the British Foreign Office, a series of negotiations with the French Customs Administration with respect to grievances of British Importers; a member of the Council of the London Chamber of Commerce; Vice-President, 1893–98; President of the West Ham Chamber of Commerce, 1893–1902; President, Federation of Working Men's Social Clubs for two periods of service. *Publications:* The Russian Empire, its Origin and Development; a contributor to periodical literature, and has written numerous pamphlets, and given lectures on social and economic subjects. *Heir: s* Harold Edwin Boulton, *b* 7 Aug. 1859. *Address:* Copped Hall, Totteridge, Herts. *T:* Barnet 142. *TA:* Boultridge, London; 64 Cannon Street, EC. *Clubs:* Carlton, Bath, Royal Societies, British Empire. *Died 27 April 1918.*

BOURCARD, Gustave (Amaury René); *b* Rennes (Ille-et-Vilaine), 12 Oct. 1846; writer on art; originaire de Bâle (Suisse) de la grande et vieille famille Christophe Burckhardt 1494, dont il possèdait le grand arbre généalogique; il était le dernier Bourcard de la branche française. Président d'Honneur de la Société des Amis des Arts de Nantes; Membre d'Honneur de la Société des Peintres-Graveurs Français; Membre d'Honneur de la Société des Peintres Lithographes; Honorary Foreign Fellow of the Royal Society of Painter-Etchers and Engravers; a fait la campagne 1870–71 dans l'armée de Paris. *Publications:* Les Estampes du XVIII siècle, 1885; Les Françaises du XVIII siècle, portraits gravés, en collaboration du marquis de Granges de Surgères, 1887; Dessins gouaches estampes et tableaux du XVIII siècle, 1893; Felix Buhot, catalogue descriptif de son œuvre gravé, 1899; A travers cinq siècles de gravures, 1903; Graveurs et gravures, essai de bibliographie, 1910; La Cotes des Estampes, 1912. *Address:* 24 rue Crébillon, Nantes (Loire-Inférieure), France.

Died 17 June 1925.

BOURCHIER, Arthur, MA; Actor-Manager; *b* Speen, Berkshire, 22 June 1864; *o s* of Capt. Charles John Bourchier, late 8th Hussars; *m* 1st, 1894, Violet Augusta Mary, (Violet Vanburgh) (marr. diss. 1917), *er d* of Rev. R. H. Barnes; one *d*; 2nd, 1918, Kyrle Bellew. *Educ:* Eton; Christ Church, Oxford. Obtained permission and co-operation of late Professor Jowett—then Vice-Chancellor—to found University Dramatic Society and build theatre at Oxford, where he played Shylock, Hotspur, Falstaff, Brutus, Feste, and Thanatos (in Alcestis); member of the Old Stagers and Windsor Strollers; first professional appearance at Wolverhampton, as Jaques in As You Like It, Sept. 1889; played Joseph Surface and Charles Courtly with Charles Wyndham; joined late Augustus Daly as leading man; joined Mr Wyndham in partnership at the Criterion, where they produced His Excellency the Governor, Lady Huntworth's Experiment, The Noble Lord, and Mamma; also at Garrick, The Wedding Guest, The Man who Stole the Castle, and Shockheaded Peter; a revival of Peril, Iris, Pilkerton's Peerage; The Bishop's Move; My Lady Virtue, Water Babies, Whitewashing Julia, The Golden Silence, The Cricket on the Hearth, The Arm of the Law, The Fairy's Dilemma, A Lesson in Harmony, The Walls of Jericho, Shylock, and The Fascinating Mr Vanderveldt, a Lancashire Lout in the Third Time of Asking; the Old Costermonger in Down our Alley, Macbeth, Mr Sheridan, Father Daniel in The Duel; and the title-part in Simple Simon, Her Father, John Glayde's Honour, 1908; The Outsider, Samson, 1909; Making a Gentleman; The Knife; The Tenth Man; Parasites; Glass Houses; also King Henry VIII, Brutus, Bottom, Sir Toby Belch, and Ford, 1910–11; The Firescreen, Proper Peter, Find the Woman, Trust the People, The Greatest Wish, Crœsus, The Double Mystery, the Green Flag, Mrs Pretty and the Premier, Stand and Deliver, The Fourth of August, The Sacrament of Judas, Pistols for Two, created Old Bill in the Bairnsfather war play, The Better 'Ole, and Stillbottle, the Broker's Man in Tilly of Bloomsbury; took over long lease of Strand Theatre in 1919, produced The Crimson Alibi, Tiger, Tiger!, At the Villa Rose, The Storm, the Safety Match, and created Long John Silver in James Bernard Fagan's adaptation of Robert Louis Stevenson's Treasure Island. *Publications:* adapter Femmes qui pleurent; Jean-Marie; Der Rabenvater; Monsieur le Directeur (The Chili Widow); Mr Richards; The Cricket on the Hearth; La Robe Rouge (The Arm of the Law); Down our Alley (Crainquebille); The Duel. *Recreations:* driving, golf, tennis, motoring. *Address:* 2 King's Gardens, Hove. *Clubs:* White's, St James's, Garrick, Beefsteak, Lord's, I Zingari.

Died 14 Sept. 1927.

BOURCHIER, James David, MA; FRGS; 4th *s* of late John Bourchier, JP of Baggotstown, Co. Limerick, and Maidenhall, Co.

Cork. *Educ:* Cambridge (Scholar of King's College, and 1st class Classical Tripos); previously Scholar and Classical Gold Medallist of Trinity College, Dublin. Was for some years Assistant Master at Eton; in 1888 acted as special correspondent of the Times in Roumania and Bulgaria, and has subsequently represented that journal in South-Eastern Europe; in 1895 investigated the atrocities at Dospat in Macedonia, and prepared a report for the British Government; in 1896 received the thanks of the Cretan Assembly for his services in promoting the arrangement with Turkey in that year; in 1898 accompanied the Emperor William's pilgrimage to Jerusalem; 1911–12 played an important part in the foundation of the Balkan League. Grand Officer of the Order of Prince Danilo of Montenegro and Commander of the Orders of the Saviour of Greece, Crown of Roumania, and Officer of the Order of St Alexander of Bulgaria. *Publications:* numerous contributions to the Fortnightly and other reviews, and the articles Athens, Albania, Bulgaria, Crete, Greece, Macedonia, Montenegro, etc, in Encyclopædia Britannica. *Recreations:* most outdoor sports and games, music, chess. *Address:* La Rive, Castlecomer, Co. Kilkenny. *Clubs:* Athenæum, St James's, New University; Athenian, Athens; Union, Sofia.

Died 30 Dec. 1920.

BOURCHIER, Very Rev. William Chadwick, MA; Dean of Cashel, since 1916; *b* 28 Feb. 1852; 5th *s* of late John Bourchier, JP, of Baggotstown, Co. Limerick; *m* 1889, Katharine Christian, *y d* of Cathcart Thomson, JP, Nova Scotia, and *g d* of Hon. Joseph Howe, Lt-Governor of Nova Scotia. *Educ:* Portora Royal School, Enniskillen; Trinity College, Dublin; Scholar and Silver Medallist in classics. Curate of Wellingborough, 1878; Domestic Chaplain to the Marquess Camden at Bayham Abbey, 1879; Curate of S Mary the Virgin, Dover, 1883; Chaplain, RN, 1885–1909; Chaplain of the RN Dockyards of Sheerness and Chatham; Rector of Aney, Co. Limerick, 1919. *Address:* The Deanery, Cashel, Co. Tipperary.

Died 24 June 1924.

BOURDILLON, Francis William, MA; *b* 22 March 1852; *s* of late Rev. F. Bourdillon (author of *Bedside Readings,* etc); *m* 1882, Agnes, *y d* of late R. Watson Smyth, JP, of Wadhurst, Sussex; two *s* one *d.* *Educ:* Haileybury, under Dr A. G. Butler and the late Dr E. H. Bradby; Worcester College, Oxford (Scholar). From 1876 to 1879 resident tutor to the two sons of TRH Prince and Princess Christian at Cumberland Lodge; then for some years took private pupils for the universities, at Eastbourne. *Publications:* Among the Flowers and other Poems, 1878; Aucassin and Nicolette (edited and translated), 1887; Ailes d'Alouette, 1890; A Lost God, 1891; Sursum Corda, 1893; Nephelé, 1896; Minuscula, 1897; Through the Gateway, 1902; early editions of the Roman de la Rose, 1906; Preludes and Romances, 1908, etc. *Address:* Buddington, near Midhurst, Sussex. *Clubs:* Athenæum, Alpine.   *Died 13 Jan. 1921.*

BOURGEOIS, Léon Victor Auguste; President of the Senate, 1920; Délégué de la France au Conseil de la Société des Nations; Ministre d'Etat, 1915; Nobel Peace Prize, 1920; *b* Paris, 29 May 1851. *Educ:* L'Institution Massin; Lycée Charlemagne. Faculté de Droit de Paris; Docteur en Droit; Secrétaire de la Conférence des Avocats; Secrétaire Général du département de la Marne, 1877; Sous-Préfet de Reims, 1880; Préfet du Tarn, 1882; Secrétaire Général de la Préfecture de la Seine, 1883; Préfet de la Haute-Garonne, 1885; Directeur des Affaires Communales et Départementales au Ministère de l'Intérieur, 1886; Préfet de Police, 1887; élu Député de la Marne, 1888; Sous-Secrétaire d'Etat au Ministère de l'Intérieur, 1889–89; Ministre de l'Instruction Publique, 1890–92; Ministre de la Justice, 1892–93; Président du Conseil, Ministre de l'Intérieur, 1895–96; Ministre des Affaires Etrangéres, 1896; Ministre de l'Instruction Publique, 1898; Premier Délégué de la France à la Conférence de La Haye, 1809; Président de la Chambre des Députés, 1902–3; Membre de la Cour permanente d'arbitrage de La Haye, réélu Député en 1889, 1893, 1898 et en 1902; élu Sénateur, 1905 et 1906; Ministre des Affaires Etrangères, 1906; Premier Délégué de la France à la Conférence de la Haye, 1907; Ministre du Travail et de la Prévoyance sociale 1912–13, 1917; Président de la Société d'Education sociale; Président de l'Alliance d'Hygiène sociale. *Publications:* Solidarité, 1894; Education de la Démocratie, 1897; Philosophie de la Solidarité, 1902; La Déclaration des Droits, 1903; Pour la Société des Nations, 1910; La Politique de la Prévoyance Sociale, 1914; Le Pacte de 1919 et la Société des Nations, 1920; Le Traité de Versailles, 1920. *Address:* Paris, 3 rue Palatine VIe; et au Palais du Petit Luxembourg.

Died 20 Sept. 1925.

BOURKE, Hon. Algernon Henry; *b* 31 Dec. 1854; *b* and *heir-pres.* of 7th Earl of Mayo; *m* 1887, Gwendoline, *d* of Hans Sloane Stanley,

Paultons, Southampton; one *d.* Formerly Member of Stock Exchange. *Address:* 7 Church Row, Fulham, SW.

Died 7 April 1922.

BOURKE, Lt-Col Henry Beresford, DSO 1894; 3rd Battalion West India Regiment; retired; serving as Draft Conducting Officer; *b* 12 June 1855; *s* of Rev. John Bourke, *g s* of 3rd Earl of Mayo. *Educ:* Sherborne School. Entered Army, 1878; served West Coast Africa, 1892; Jambaba Expedition, capture of Jambi (medal and clasp); Sofa Expedition, 1893–94 (despatches, DSO, clasp); Sierra Leone Rebellion, 1898–99 (clasp). *Club:* United Service.

Died 1 Nov. 1921.

BOURKE, Hon. Terence Theobald, OBE 1920; Consul, Bizerta, since 1917; *b* 2 April 1865; *b* and *heir-pres.* of 7th Earl of Mayo; *m* 1896, Eveline Constance (*d* 1917), *d* of late Col T. W. Haines of Haskerton Manor, Suffolk; two *d.* *Educ:* Eton. Was Consular Agent at Bizerta, 1891; Vice-Consul, 1898; acted as Representative of the Ministry of Shipping at Bizerta during the war; Director of London and Greenwich Railway. *Address:* HBM Consulate, Bizerta; Pekes, Hellingly, Sussex. *Clubs:* Carlton, White's, Pratt's.

Died 13 May 1923.

BOURNE, Rev. Charles William, MA; Rector of Staplehurst, Kent, 1913–20; Fellow of King's College, London, and member of Council; Fellow of Physical Society; *b* Atherstone, 2 June 1846; *m* Ada, *d* of the late J. M'Minn, 1875. *Educ:* Atherstone Grammar School; St John's Coll., Cambridge (Exhibitioner and Foundation Scholar); 26th Wrangler and 2nd class in Classics in 1868. Asst Master Marlborough College, 1868–74; Headmaster Bedford County School, 1875–80; Headmaster Inverness Coll., 1881–89; ordained Deacon by Bishop of Rochester, 1898; Priest, 1899; Headmaster of King's College School, 1889–1906; Rector of Frating, 1906–13; Rural Dean of West Charing, 1919. *Publications:* Key to Tod-Hunter's Conic Sections, and numerous contributions to educational periodicals. *Address:* 15 Ridgway Place, Wimbledon.

Died 10 Dec. 1927.

BOURNE, Rev. George Hugh, DCL; Canon and Treasurer of Salisbury. *Address:* The College, Salisbury.

Died 1 Dec. 1925.

BOURNS, Newcome Whitelaw; anæsthetist, retired; *b* Hatley, Carrick-on-Shannon, Ireland. *Educ:* private tutor. After hospital career went into general practice. *Publications:* papers on medical subjects in Lancet and Medical Annual. *Recreations:* shooting, fishing, golf. *Address:* Churchfield, Wincanton, Somerset.

Died 2 Oct. 1927.

BOUTROUX, Emile; membre de l'Institut de France, 1898, et de l'Académie française, 1912; Professeur Université de Paris depuis 1888; Directeur Fondation Thiers depuis 1902; *b* Montrouge (Seine), 28 July 1845; *s* of Louis Adrien Boutroux and Suzanne Hortense Blanchard; *m* Aline Catherine Eugénie, *d* of Léon Poincaré, Prof. Fac. de Médecine, Nancy; one *s* two *d.* *Educ:* Paris, Lycée Henri IV, École Normale sup^re.; étudiant à l'Université de Heidelberg, 1869–70; Docteur ès Lettres, 1874. Prof. de Philosophie Univ. de Montpellier, 1874; Nancy, 1876; Maître de Conférences à l'Ecole normale supérieure, 1877; R. Instituto Lombardo di Scienze e Lettere, Milano; Institut génévois; R. Accademia dei Lincei, Roma; British Academy; National Education Association, USA; Académie Royal de Danemark; Académie hongroise, Budapest; Accademia delle Scienze morali et politiche, Napoli; Académie des sciences de Pétrograd. *Publications:* De la contingence des lois de la nature, 1874; Trad. française de la 1re partie de Die Philos. der Griechen v. Ed. Zeller, 1877–82; Leibniz, La Monadologie, 1880; De l'idée de loi naturelle dans la science et dans la philos., 1895; Questions de morale et d'éducation, 1895; Du devoir militaire, in L'Armée à travers les âges, 1899; Pascal, 1900 (English, 1902); Etudes d'histoire de la philosophie, 1901 (English, 1912); Science et religion dans la philosophie contemporaine, 1908 (English, 1909); William James, 1911 (English, 1912); The Beyond that is Within, 1912; Philosophy and War, 1916. *Address:* Paris, XVI, rond-point Bugeaud 5. *T:* Passy 53–82.   *Died 22 Nov. 1921.*

BOVELL, John Redman, ISO 1908; JP; Director of Agriculture, Barbados, BWI, 1919; retired under age limit, 31 March 1925; *b* 31 Dec. 1855; *s* of late John Bovell, Barbados; *m* 1897, Annie Louisa, *d* of late Benjamin T. Bovell, Barbados; one *s.* *Educ:* private schools; Lodge School and Harrison College, Barbados. Trained as a sugar planter; Superintendent Botanical Station, 1886; went to Antigua, 1890, to start Skerrett's Training School; Vice-President, Windward

District Agricultural Society, 1890; Member of Commission to inquire into sugar-cane borers, 1893; Chairman Emigration Committee, 1895; Superintendent of Agriculture, Barbados, BWI, 1898; went to Antigua and St Kitts to start sugar-cane experiments, 1899; one of the Barbados representatives at the various agricultural conferences held by Imperial Commissioner of Agriculture; sent to St Vincent to report on damage done in Carib country by volcanic eruptions of 1902–3, 1907; went to Porto Rico, 1909, to report on sugar cane diseases occurring on a number of sugar plantations; went to Saint Croix in 1910 at the request of the Governor of that island to formulate a scheme for a Department of Agriculture; went to Guadeloupe and Martinique in 1917 at the request of the Governors of those Colonies and with the consent of the Governor of Barbados to report on the sugar industry of those two islands; went to Santo Domingo with consent of the Governor of Barbados, to report on a large sugar estate, 1924. *Publications:* reports and papers in connection with the agriculture of Barbados. *Recreation:* reading. *Address:* Paradise House, Tacarigua, Trinidad, BWI.

Died 23 Nov. 1928.

BOVILL, Charles Harry; 2nd Lieutenant Coldstream Guards, 1916; author; *b* Coonoor, India, 1878; *o s* of Major Charles Edward Bovill, Royal Inniskilling Fusiliers, and Ellen Maria Lang; *m* 1907, Ethel Rachel, *d* of Edwin Kay; two *s. Educ:* Bedford Grammar School. Was in the Civil Service, 1899–1912; author of Empire Revues—Everybody's Doing It (with George Grossmith), All the Winners, The Gay Lothario, Nuts and Wine; of the Alhambra Revues—5064 Gerrard, and Now's the Time (with C. G. Lennox); of the London Pavilion Revues—Honi Soit and Pick-a-dilly; part-author of Mr Manhattan and Half-Past Eight, and of Drury Lane Pantomime, The Sleeping Beauty. *Publications:* The Spur of Love; numerous short stories in The Strand, The Grand, Pearson's The London, and other magazines. *Address:* 94 Prince of Wales Mansions, SW. *T:* Battersea 1267; The Knowle, Barcombe, Sussex.

Died 21 March 1918.

BOWATER, Sir Frederick William, KBE 1920; Paper-maker; *b* 8 June 1867; *s* of late William Vansittart Bowater of Bury Hall, Enfield, Middlesex; *m* 1890, Alice Emily, *d* of Joseph Sharp, Bognor, Sussex; one *s* three *d. Educ:* privately. *Recreation:* golf. *Address:* 181 Queen's Gate, SW7. *T:* Kensington 4120; Copley Dene, Walton Heath, Surrey. *T:* Burgh Heath 368. *Clubs:* Constitutional, Ranelagh; Walton Heath Golf; Chislehurst Golf; Gullane Golf, Luffness.

Died 16 May 1924.

BOWDEN, Sir Frank, 1st Bt, *cr* 1915; JP Nottingham; FRGS; *b* 30 Jan. 1848; *s* of late William Bowden, Bristol, manufacturer; *m* 1879, Amelia Frances, *d* of late Colonel Alexander Houston of San Francisco; one *s* four *d* (and one *s* decd). *Educ:* privately. Founder and sole owner, with son, of The Raleigh Cycle Co., Ltd, principally engaged since the commencement of the war in making munitions; founder, chairman, managing director and principal owner of Sturmey-Archer Gears, Ltd. *Publications:* Cycling for Health; articles upon his travels and other subjects. *Recreations:* oriental studies, travelling, cycling, etc. *Heir: s* Harold Bowden [*b* 9 July 1880; *m* 1st, 1908, Vera (marr. diss. 1919), *d* of Joseph Whitaker; one *s* one *d*; 2nd, 1920, Mrs Muriel Smythe, *d* of late William Ker-Douglas of Dalry, Ayrshire]. *Address:* Bestwood Lodge, Arnold, Notts. *T:* Arnold 47. *Died 25 April 1921.*

BOWDEN, Major George Robert Harland; MP (U) North-East Derbyshire, 1914–18; *b* 1873. Major commanding 1st Herts Battery RFA(T); retired, Feb. 1914; Lt-Col commanding 17th Batt. Royal Fusiliers, 1914–15; Member Institute Mechanical Engineers and Iron and Steel Institute. *Address:* 17 Victoria Street, SW1. *TA:* Harbowdeco, Vic., London. *T:* Victoria 5076; Hazeldene, St Albans. *Clubs;* Carlton, Junior Army and Navy.

Died 10 Oct. 1927.

BOWDEN, Walter, DSO 1894; RN; Deputy Inspector-General, 1908; *b* London, 10 June 1859; *s* of late Wm Bowden of Hilldrop Crescent, Camden Road, N, and Jane, *d* of James Beer; *m* 1900, Alithea M., 2nd *d* of James Ogilvie, JP, The Grove, Rushbrooke, Queenstown, Ireland; two *s* one *d.* MRCS, LRCP. Entered Royal Navy Medical Service, 1887; Staff Surg., 1899; Fleet Surg., 1903; retired, 1908; served River Gambia, 1894 (despatches); bombardment and occupation of Gunjur, 1894 (DSO, general Africa Medal, Gambia Clasp). *Address:* Bantry, Kirtleton Avenue, Weymouth, Dorset. *Club:* Junior United Service. *Died 13 Nov. 1919.*

BOWDEN-SMITH, Admiral Sir Nathaniel, KCB 1897; *b* Careys, Brockenhurst, Hants, 21 Jan. 1838; *s* of Nathaniel Bowden-Smith,

Careys, Brockenhurst, and Emily Mary, *d* of John Richard Ripley, merchant, London; *m* 1864, Emily Cecilia, *d* of George Glas Sandeman, Westfield, Hayling Island, Hants; three *d.* Entered RN 1852; Commander, 1866; Capt. 1872; Rear-Admiral, 1888; Vice-Admiral, 1894; Admiral, 1899; served in Burmah war (medal and Pegu clasp), 1852–53; Baltic, during the Russian War (medal), 1854–1855; China war, 1856–59; boat actions in Escape Creek, and at Fatshan; and at capture of the Ta Ku forts (medal, Fatshan and Ta Ku clasps), severely wounded June 1859; Royal Humane Society's medal for saving life at sea; served as Flag-Capt. successively in a detached squadron and on the Mediterranean and East Indian Stations; Sen. Officer, SE Coast of America, and commanded the "Britannia," 1883–86; one of the British representatives at the International Maritime Conference, Washington, 1889; Commander-in-Chief, Australian Station, 1892–95; at the Nore, 1899–1900. *Address:* 16 Queen's Gate Terrace, SW7. *T:* Kensington 6111. *Clubs:* United Service, Ranelagh. *Died 28 April 1921.*

BOWDLER, Colonel Cyril William Bowdler, CB 1902; late 8th Hussars; *b* 28 Sept. 1839. Entered army, 1864; Captain, 1876; Major, 1881; Lt-Col 1883; Col 1887; retired, 1891. Knight of Justice and Hon. Commander Order St John of Jerusalem. *Club:* Army and Navy. *Died 7 Nov. 1918.*

BOWELL, Hon. Sir Mackenzie, KCMG 1895; Premier of Canadian Parliament, 1894–95; *b* Rickinghall, Suffolk, 27 Dec. 1823; *s* of late John Bowell; *m* 1847, Harriet (*d* 1884), *e d* of late J. G. Moore. Emigrated to Canada 1833 and became a journalist. Entered Canadian Parliament, 1867; Minister of Customs, 1878–91; of Defence, 1891; of Trade and Commerce, 1892–94; President of Privy Council, 1895–96; called to the Senate, 1892. *Address:* Belleville, Ont, Canada. *Clubs:* Rideau, Ottawa; Albany, Toronto.

Died 11 Dec. 1917.

BOWEN, Sir Albert Edward, 1st Bt, *cr* 1921, of Colworth, Bedfordshire; Chairman, Buenos Aires Great Southern Railway Ltd; Chairman, Wilson Sons and Co. Ltd, etc; *b* Hanley, Staffs, 1 Nov. 1858; *e s* of Edward Bowen of Hanley; *m* 1884, Alice Anita, *d* of Frederick Crowther of Buenos Aires; two *s* three *d. Educ:* Upper Canada College, Toronto. Merchant in Buenos Aires, 1879–95; Director of public companies in London since 1896; High Sheriff of Bedfordshire, 1910–11; during the war served on many government committees. *Recreations:* racing, fishing, etc. *Heir: s* Major Edward Crowther Bowen, MC, Inniskilling Dragoons, *b* 11 March 1885. *Address:* 5 Queen's Gate Place, SW7. *T:* Western 32; Colworth, Beds. *T:* Sharnbrook 3; Eskdale, Beauly, Scotland. *T:* Beauly 13. *TA:* Bowenical, London. *M:* BM 100. *Club:* Junior Carlton.

Died 19 Sept. 1924.

BOWEN, Lt-Col Alfred John Hamilton, DSO 1915; 2nd Battalion the Monmouthshire Regiment, Territorial Force; solicitor; *b* 15 Dec. 1885; *e s* of Alfred E. Bowen, Usk; *m* 1916, Jean Gertrude, *d* of Henry Wilton, Winnipeg. *Educ:* Marlborough College; Merton College, Oxford. Served European War, 1914–16 (DSO).

Died 2 March 1917.

BOWEN, Hon. Sir Charles Christopher, KCMG 1914; Kt 1910; MLC; FRGS; late Speaker of Legislative Council, New Zealand; Vice-Chancellor of Senate of New Zealand University; *b* 29 Aug. 1830; *s* of Charles Bowen, 3rd *s* of Christopher Bowen, of Milford, Co. Mayo, Ireland; *m* 1861, Georgina Elizabeth, *d* of Rev. David Markham, Canon of Windsor; four *s* three *d. Educ:* Rugby; Cambridge. Left Cambridge after first year to join founders of Canterbury, New Zealand, 1850; Private Secretary to Mr Godley, agent of Canterbury Association, 1851–52; Provincial Treasurer and Member Provincial Government, 1854–59; went to England, 1859; returned, 1862; Resident Magistrate, Christchurch, 1864–74; Member House of Representatives, 1874; Minister of Justice and Education, 1875–77; carried National Education Act, 1877; Member of Royal Commission on Federation, 1901. *Publications:* Visit to Peru in Notes of Travel, 1860; occasional articles in periodicals. *Address:* Middleton Grange, Upper Riccarton, Christchurch, New Zealand.

Died 14 Dec. 1917.

BOWEN, Rev. David; Prebendary of St Davids. *Address:* Monkton, Pembroke. *Died 6 Nov. 1928.*

BOWER, George Spencer, KC 1903; Barrister-at-law (Midland Circuit); *b* 12 Oct. 1854; *s* of late George Bower, St Neots, Huntingdonshire; *m* 1885, Minnie Blanche, *d* of late Sir Charles Wyndham. *Educ:* Winchester College (Scholar), 1866–73; Senior Prefect, 1872–73; Goddard Scholar, 1872; Queen's Gold and Silver

Medals, 1873; New College, Oxford (Scholar). First Class Honours Moderations, 1874; First Class Honours Greats, 1877; Gaisford (Greek Prose), 1876; Chancellor's (English Essay), 1878. Called to Bar, 1880; Bencher of the Inner Temple, 1912. *Publications:* Hartley and James Mill, 1880; A Study of the Prologue and Epilogue in English Literature from Shakespeare to Dryden, 1884; A Code of the Law of Actionable Defamation, 1909, 2nd edition, 1923; The Law of Actionable Misrepresentation, 1911, 2nd edition, 1927; The Law of Actionable Non-Disclosure, and other Breaches of Duty in Relations of Confidence and Influence, 1914; The Law of Estoppel by Representation, 1923; The Doctrine of Res Judicata, 1924. *Address:* 45 Finchley Road, NW8. *T:* Primrose Hill 3534; 2 Hare Court, Temple, EC4. *T:* Central 1777.
Died 4 Sept. 1928.

OWERLEY, Amelia M., ARE; Member Ridley Art Club; Royal Water Colour Art Club; Women's Guild of Arts; *b* London. *Educ:* Notting Hill High School and abroad. Studied at South Kensington and Slade School of Art and at Munich and Italy; etching under Sir Frank Short; anatomy at Women's School of Medicine, London. *Publications:* Black and white and other drawings for numerous books and magazines, including the Sphere, Graphic, Windsor Magazine, the Yellow Book; numerous etchings, including A Boy of Teneriffe, Spanish Children, Goblin Market, Orpheus, Pan, The Sphinx; exhibited pictures at Royal Academy; Paris Salon; International Exhibs, Franco-British, St Louis and Christ Church, etc; Exhibitions at Dowdeswell Gallery—When the World was Young. *Address:* 59 Craven Park, NW. *Club:* Ladies' University.
Died 5 Feb. 1916.

OWERS, Rt. Rev. John Phillips Allcot; Archdeacon of Lynn since 1903; Canon Residentiary of Norwich, 1910; Select Preacher before the University of Cambridge, 1905 and 1911; *b* 15 May 1854; *e s* of J. Bowers of Glenlui, Southampton; *m* 1879, Mary, *e d* of late J. Beaumont, of The Lawn, Coggeshall, and 33 Chancery Lane, London; one *s* one *d*. *Educ:* Magdalen School; St John's Coll., Cambridge (MA, DD Hon. Causa, 1903). Canon Residentiary and Canon Missioner of the Diocese of Gloucester, 1885–1902; Archdeacon of Gloucester, 1902–1903; examining and domestic chaplain to Bishop of Gloucester, 1882–1903; Rector of North Creak, 1903–10; Provincial Grand Master of Norfolk, 1920; Past Grand Chaplain of England, 1898; Suffragan Bishop of Thetford, 1903–26. *Address:* The Close, Norwich. *T:* Norwich 969. *Club:* Norfolk County, Norwich.
Died 6 Jan. 1926.

OWERS, Ven. Percy Harris; Archdeacon of Loughborough since 1921; Warden of the Mission Clergy of the Diocese of Peterborough; *b* 1856; *yr s* of James Bowers, Warren Hall, Flintshire; *m* Annie, *d* of A. E. Lloyd, Worsley, Lancashire; one *s* three *d*. *Educ:* The Forest School; St John's, Cambridge. *Address:* The Rectory, Market Bosworth, Nuneaton.
Died 15 Nov. 1922.

OWLES, Thomas Gibson; *b* 1844; *m* 1876, Jessica (*d* 1887), *d* of General Evans Gordon; two *s* two *d*. *Educ:* King's College, London. Was in Inland Revenue Office; MP (C) King's Lynn, 1892–1906; and (L) 1910; contested same division, 1910; Southern Division, Leicester, 1916. *Publications:* The Defence of Paris; Maritime Warfare, 1878; Flotsam and Jetsam, 1882; Log of the Nereid, 1889; The Declaration of Paris of 1856, 1900; Sea Law and Sea Power, 1910, etc. *Address:* 25 Lowndes Square, SW1. *T:* Victoria 3062. *Club:* Carlton.
Died 12 Jan. 1922.

OWLING, Paymaster-in-Chief Thomas Henry Lovelace, CB 1907; *b* June 1839; *s* of Thomas Bowling of Ramsgate; unmarried. *Educ:* privately. Entered navy, 1855; Assistant Paymaster, 1860; Paymaster, 1866; Fleet Paymaster, 1886; Paymaster-in-Chief (retired), 1898; served China, 1857 (medal); Indian Mutiny, 1857–59 despatches thrice, medal, promoted); Abyssinia, 1868 (medal); Secretary to various Admirals, 1869–85. *Address:* 47 Central Hill, Upper Norwood, SE. *Club:* Royal Navy, Portsmouth.
Died 18 Jan. 1922.

OWMAN, Sir William Paget, 2nd Bt, *cr* 1884; MA; *b* 25 Sept. 1845; of Sir William Bowman, 1st Bt and Harriet, *d* of Thomas Paget, Leicester; *S* father 1892; *m* 1870, Emily, *d* of late Capt. W. Swabey; two *s* one *d*. *Educ:* Eton; University Coll. Oxford. Barrister 1870. Registrar of the Sons of the Clergy and Treasurer Cholmondeley Charities. *Heir: s* Rev. Paget Mervyn, Vicar of St Luke, Woodside, Norwood [*b* 1 Sept. 1873; *m* 1901, Rachel Katherine, *d* of late James Manning of Kilcrone, Co. Cork; one *s* one *d*]. *Address:* Corporation House, Bloomsbury Place, WC; Joldwynds, Dorking. *Club:* Athenæum.
Died 7 Jan. 1917.

BOWN, Rev. George Herbert; Priest in charge of St Alban's, Charles Street, Oxford, since July 1918; *b* 11 Nov. 1871; *s* of George Bown, Carlton Villa, Bromsgrove. *Educ:* Bromsgrove School; Trinity College and St Stephen's House, Oxford. Deacon, 1895; Priest, 1896; Assistant Curate at St Andrew's, Taunton, 1895–1903; Principal of St Stephen's House, Oxford, 1903–17; Assistant Priest at St Barnabas', Oxford, 1917–18. *Address:* St Alban's Presbytery, Percy Street, Oxford.
Died 21 Nov. 1918.

BOWRING, Sir William Benjamin, 1st Bt, *cr* 1907; Shipowner; *b* 13 Feb. 1837; *e s* of C. T. Bowring of Liverpool; *m* 1863, Isabel M'Lean, *d* of E. L. Jarves, St John's, Newfoundland; no *c*. *Heir:* none. Lord Mayor, Liverpool, 1893–94; presented Roby Hall Estate to the City. *Address:* Beechwood, Aigburth, Liverpool.
Died 20 Oct. 1916 (ext).

BOWRON, Sir Edward, Kt 1913; Chairman of Joseph Travers and Sons, Ltd; Director Société Privilégiée, Athens; *b* 5 Sept. 1857; *s* of John Bowron, Cotherstone; *m* 1887, Maude Mary, *d* of W. F. Morgan, Sevenoaks. *Address:* Bramley Oaks, Bramley Hill, Croydon. *T:* Croydon 1591. *Club:* Reform.
Died 10 Dec. 1923.

BOWSER, Rev. Sidney W., BA; *b* Old Mansion House, Cheapside, London, 2 Oct. 1853; *s* of late Mr Alfred T. Bowser, a well-known layman in the Baptist denomination; *m* 1883, Mary Edwards, of Hackney; one *s* two *d*. *Educ:* Priory House School, Clapton; University College, London (prizes and honours, and President of the Debating Society); Regent's Park College. Assistant minister to late Rev. F. Bosworth, MA, at South Street Baptist Church, Exeter, 1879–80; Minister of Grange Road Baptist Church, Birkenhead, 1881–99; Principal Midland Baptist Coll., Nottingham, 1899–1913; for many years honorary secretary Lancashire and Cheshire Association of Baptist Churches; Moderator, 1894; President of Birkenhead Free Church Council, 1898; Founder of Liverpool Guild of Bible Study; for many years President Birkenhead Working Men's Total Abstinence Society; President of the Nottingham Peace and Arbitration Society, 1905–13. President of the East Midland Baptist Association, 1909–10; Minister of the Baptist Church, Long Buckby, 1914–19; Lecturer at the Loughborough College (Literary Department) since 1920. *Publications:* occasional Addresses, etc. *Address:* 107 Ashby Road, Loughborough. *Club:* University of London.
Died 19 May 1928.

BOWSTEAD, Rev. Canon Christopher J. K.; Canon of St Ninian's Cathedral, 1899; Priest in charge of Kilmaveonaig, Blair-Atholl; resigned 1912; *b* 1844; *s* of John Bowstead, Vicar of Messingham, Lincolnshire, and Eliza, *e d* of John Kaye, Bishop of Lincoln. *Educ:* Durham University. MA, Theol. Exhibitioner. Ordained deacon, 1872; Priest, 1874; Curate of Grantham, 1872; Riseholme, 1874; St Andrew's Croydon, 1875; Felpham, 1882; Domestic Chaplain to Earl of Strathmore, 1890; Rector of Holy Trinity, Pitlochry, 1891–99. *Publication:* Facts and Fancies about Kilmaveonaig. *Address:* St Gabriel's Bield, Elie, Fife.
Died 11 May 1924.

BOXALL, Sir Alleyne Alfred, 1st Bt, *cr* 1919; *b* Belle Vue Hall, Brighton, 11 Oct. 1855; *s* of William Percival Boxall, JP Brighton, and Caroline, *d* and co-heir of late William Money; *m* 1881, Mary Elizabeth, *e d* of J. H. Lermitte, JP, of Knightons; one *s*. *Educ:* Eton; University College, Oxford. *Heir: s* Lt-Col Alleyne Percival Boxall, RFA (TD), *b* 14 Sept. 1882. *Address:* 14 Cambridge Square, W2.
Died 5 May 1927.

BOYD, Charles Walter, CMG 1904; *b* 11 April 1869; 4th *s* of Very Rev. A. K. H. Boyd (*d* 1899), St Andrews, and Margaret, *d* of late Captain Kirk, 77th Regiment. *Educ:* Fettes College, Edinburgh; Edinburgh University for Scottish Bar. Sometime occupied in journalism; as, under Mr Henley on old National Observer; and Saturday Review, from editorship of Mr W. H. Pollock, and subsequently; an occasional contributor Times, Morning Post, Athenæum, Daily Chronicle, Spectator, etc; private secretary successively to Right Hon. George Wyndham, MP, and Dr, now Sir Starr, Jameson, CB; Political Secretary to late Right Hon. Cecil Rhodes, 1898–1902; Joint-Secretary Rhodes Trust, 1902; Secretary, 1904–8, when sent to Rhodesia on special service; member Education Committee Victoria League, etc. *Publications:* George Wyndham, 1913; edited The Nation and the Empire, speeches and addresses of Lord Milner, 1913; and Mr Chamberlain's speeches, 2 vols, 1914; occasional contributor reviews etc. *Address:* 2 Down Street, Piccadilly, W. *Clubs:* St James's, Garrick, Savile, National, Pilgrims; New, Edinburgh.
Died 1 Aug. 1919.

BOYD, Francis Darby, CB 1919; CMG 1901; MD, FRCPEd; Professor of Clinical Medicine, University of Edinburgh; Physician to the Royal Infirmary, Edinburgh; Consulting Physician to the Deaconess Hospital, Edinburgh; Lecturer on Materia Medica and Therapeutics, School of Medicine of the Royal Colleges, Edinburgh; *b* 19 Oct. 1866; *s* of John Boyd of Edinburgh; *m* 1904, Clara Constance, *e d* of Alfred J. A. Lepper; two *d.* Served as physician with Edinburgh Hospital in South Africa (despatches, CMG); served as Colonel AMS, Consultant to British Army in Egypt (despatches, CB); formerly Member of Board of Examiners for Entrance to the Indian Medical Service. *Address:* 22 Manor Place, Edinburgh. *T:* 2462. *Club:* University, Edinburgh.   *Died 4 April 1922.*

BOYD, Rev. Francis Leith, MA; Vicar of St Paul's Knightsbridge, SW, since 1908; *b* 1856; *e s* of George John Boyd, Toronto, Canada; *m* 1905, Elizabeth Archdale, *o c* of T. Hastings Harris, formerly of Ashfort, Co. Armagh, Ireland; one *d. Educ:* University College, Toronto (Classical Silver Medal); Gonville and Caius College, Cambridge (Scholar), 1876. BA 1879; MA 1884. Deacon, 1879; Priest, 1880; Curate of St Peter's, Eaton Square, 1879–84; Vicar of Teddington, Middlesex, 1884–1908; Vicar of the Annunciation, St Marylebone, 1908; Select Preacher at Cambridge, 1885 and 1907; Oxford, 1923; Golden Lecturer at St Margaret's Lothbury, 1911 and 1917; Prebendary of Ealdland in St Paul's Cathedral, 1914. *Publications:* Law and Love, 1909; Tasks and Visions; articles in Nineteenth Century. *Address:* St Paul's Vicarage, Wilton Place, SW1. *T:* Victoria 3599. *Club:* Oxford and Cambridge.

Died 13 Dec. 1927.

BOYD, Henry, DD; Principal of Hertford College, Oxford, since 1877; late Fellow; Vice-Chancellor, 1890–94; *b* 26 Feb. 1831; *s* of William Clark Boyd. *Educ:* Hackney Sch.; Exeter Coll., Oxford. Ellerton Essay, 1853; Denyer Essay, 1856–57. Ordained 1854; Curate of Bellean, Lincs, 1854, Probus, Cornwall, 1856; PC, St Mark's, Victoria Docks, 1862. Master, Drapers' Co., 1896–97. *Address:* Hertford College, Oxford.   *Died 4 March 1922.*

BOYD, Hon. Sir John Alexander, KCMG 1901; Kt 1899; Chancellor of High Court Province of Ontario; Governor of M'Master University; *b* Toronto, 23 April 1837; *s* of J. Boyd, late Principal of Bay St Acad., Toronto; *m* 1863, Elizabeth, *d* of David Buchan. *Educ:* UC Coll. and Toronto Univ.; scholarship, gold medal for modern languages; MA degree. Called to the Bar 1863; Master in Chancery; QC, by Dominion patent, 1880; Chancellor, 1881; President of High Court, 1887; Arbitrator for Dominion Government, 1888–89; Hon. LLD of Toronto Univ., 1889; Arbitrator for Ontario, 1893. *Publication:* Summary of Canadian History. *Address:* 119 Bloor Street, Toronto, Ontario.

Died 23 Nov. 1916.

BOYD, Maj.-Gen. Julius Middleton; Indian Army; *b* 4 Oct. 1837; *m* 1867, *d* of Captain Blennerhassett, RN. Entered army, 1854; Maj.-Gen. 1894; unemployed list, 1896; served Indian Mutiny, 1858; Abyssinian Expedition, 1868 (despatches, medal); Afghan War, 1879–80 (despatches, medal). *Address:* Upton Dene, 56 Coombe Road, Croydon.   *Died 17 Dec. 1919.*

BOYD, Ven. Robert Wallace; Archdeacon of Ardagh since 1915; Vicar of Kilronan since 1896. *Educ:* Queen's University, Belfast; Edinburgh. 1st Class Honours Biological Science; ordained 1887; Curate of Maryborough, 1887–89; Templemichael, 1889–96; Registrar, Ardagh, 1891; Prebendary and Canon of St Patrick's Cathedral, 1904. *Address:* Kilronan Vicarage, Keadue, Carrick-on-Shannon, Ireland.   *Died 10 Nov. 1921.*

BOYD, Rt. Hon. Sir Walter, 1st Bt, *cr* 1916; PC Ire. 1916; LLD; JP; a Justice of the High Court of Justice in Ireland, 1897–1916; *b* Dublin, 28 Jan. 1833; *m* 1862, Annie Catherine, *d* of Matthew Anderson, Dublin; two *s. Educ:* Portora, Enniskillen; Trinity College, Dublin. Barrister, Ireland, 1856; QC 1877; Queen's Advocate for Ireland, 1878; Judge of Court of Bankruptcy, Ireland, 1885–97. *Publication:* Law and Practice of the Court of Admiralty in Ireland. *Recreations:* yachting, shooting, photography. *Heir: s* Walter Herbert Boyd, barrister [*b* 31 March 1867. *Address:* 13 Upper Mount Street, Dublin]. *Address:* 66 Merrion Square, Dublin; Howth House, Howth, Co. Dublin. *Clubs:* Kildare Street, Dublin; Royal St George's Yacht; Royal Alfred Yacht.   *Died 25 June 1918.*

BOYD-CARPENTER, Henry John; *b* 1865; *e s* of late Right Rev. William Boyd-Carpenter, Bishop of Ripon; *m* 1902, Ethel, *y d* of Sir Francis Ley, 1st Bt; one *s* one *d. Educ:* Westminster; King's College, Cambridge. Called to Bar; HMI Board of Education; Chief Inspector,

Ministry of Education, Egypt. *Publications:* various educational repo Recreation: gardening. *Address:* Riversea, Kingswear. *Clubs:* Ro Societies; Royal Dart Yacht.   *Died 1 June 19*

BOYD CARPENTER, Rt. Rev. William, KCVO 1912; DD; H Fellow of St Catharine's College, Cambridge; Hon. DD Glasgc Hon. DCL Oxon; Hon. DCL Durham, and Hon. Mem University College; Hon. DD Aberdeen; Hon. DLitt Leeds; L M'Gill; FRSL; Knight of the Order of the Royal Crown, Prussia; Cl of the Closet since 1903; Sub-Dean and Canon of Westminster si 1911; Hon. Chaplain to the Forces (13th County of London, Liverpool, 26 March 1841; *s* of Rev. Henry Carpenter, incumb of St Michael's, Liverpool, and Hester, *d* of Archibald Bo Londonderry, Ireland; *m* 1st, 1864, Harriet Charlotte, *o d* of R J. W. Peers, of Chislehampton, Oxon; 2nd, 1883, Annie Maudc 1915), *d* of W. W. Gardner; four *s* six *d. Educ:* Royal Institut School, Liverpool; St Cath. Coll. Camb. (Scholar). Senior Optir 1864; Hulsean Lecturer, Cambridge, 1878; Bampton Lectu Oxford, 1887; Pastoral Lecturer on Theology, Cambridge, 18 Noble Lecturer (Harvard) 1904 and 1913; Donnellan Lectu Dublin, 1914–15 and 1915–16. Curate of All Saints, Maidsto 1864–66; St Paul's, Clapham, 1866–67; Holy Trinity, Lee, 1867– Vicar of St James's, Holloway, 1870–79; Vicar of Christ Chur Lancaster Gate, 1879–84; Canon of Windsor, 1882–84; hon. chap to the Queen, 1879–83; chaplain-in-ordinary, 1883–84; Bishop Ripon, 1884–1911. *Publications:* Commentary on Revelation, 18 Thoughts on Prayer, 1871; Witness of Heart to Christ (Huls Lectures), 1879; Permanent Elements of Religion (Bramp Lectures), 1889; Lectures on Preaching, 1895; Christian Reuni 1895; The Great Charter of Christ, 1895; District Visite Companion, 1881; My Bible, 1884; Truth in Tale, 1884; Twili Dreams, 1894; A Popular History of the Church of England, 19 The Religious Spirit in the Poets, 1900; The Wisdom of James Just, 1902; Introduction to Study of the Bible, 1902; Witness to Influence of Christ, 1905; Some Pages of my Life, 1911; The Spiri Message of Dante, 1914; The Witness of Religious Experience, 19 Further Pages of my Life, 1916. *Recreation:* a good collection of Da literature. *Address:* 6 Little Cloisters, Westminster Abbey, W Riversea, Kingswear. *Clubs:* Athenæum, Authors'.

Died 26 Oct. 19

BOYER, Hon. Arthur; *b* 9 Feb. 1851; *m* 1875, Ernestine, *d* of P. Galarneau, Montreal. *Educ:* St Mary's College. MP (L) Jacques Cari 1884–92; member of Cabinet without Portfolio, 1891–92; Sena since 1909. *Address:* 210 Drummond Street, Montreal. *Clubs:* Natic Liberal; Forest and Stream, Montreal; Rideau, Ottawa.

Died 24 Jan. 19

BOYES, Charles Edward, CBE 1919; Deputy Resid Commissioner, Basutoland; *b* King William's Town, 1866; *s* of Major James Fichat Boyes; *m* 2nd *d* of E. J. Turner, Will Brook, Na two *s* two *d. Educ:* Bishops College, Rondebosch; St Andre College, Grahamstown. Joined the Basutoland Service in 1888 which served since. *Recreations:* cricket, polo, tennis, golf. *Add* Maseru, Basutoland.   *Died 12 July 19*

BOYLE, Sir Cavendish, KCMG 1897 (CMG 1888); *b* 29 May 18 *y s* of late Captain Cavendish Spencer Boyle, 72nd Highlanders 1914, Louise, *y d* of late Reuben Sassoon, MVO. *Educ:* Charterhou Magistrate, etc, Leeward Islands, 1879; Colonial Secretary, Bermu 1882–88; Gibraltar, 1888–94; Government Sec., British Guia 1894–1901, during which period administered the Government several occasions, and was Chairman of the British Guiana B 1896–97; delegate for British Guiana and Bermuda in recipro negotiations with the USA, 1899; Governor of Newfoundla 1901–4; Mauritius, 1904–11; retired on a pension, 1911. Al Author of Newfoundland, adopted as the National Ode of the Isla and other Poems. *Address:* 6 Third Avenue, Hove, Sussex. Cl Marlborough, Badminton, Beefsteak.

Died 17 Sept. 19

BOYLE, Daniel; MP (N) North Mayo, 1910–18; JP; *b* Kilc Fermanagh, 10 Jan. 1859; *y s* of late Donal Boyle, farmer; *m* 18 Annie (*d* 1921), 2nd *d* of late Patrick Gardiner, Sligo; two *d. E* National School. Qualified as teacher, 1877; settled in Manches 1877, adopting journalism as a profession; elected to Manchester C Council, 1894; Alderman, 1908–1917, then resigned; Chairr Tramways Committee, 1898–1906; member Executive Cou United Irish League of Great Britain; and leader of Nationalist P in Manchester; founded an Irish Friendly Society in Manchester, 18 Visited USA with Mr John Edward Redmond, autumn of 1910. the famous "dollar" mission.   *Died 19*

BOYLE, Commander Edward Louis Dairymple, CMG 1917; RN (ret.); *b* 1864; *m* 1st, 1889, Theodosia Isabella (*d* 1910), 3rd *d* of late E. D. S. Ogilvie, NSW; one *s* one *d*; 2nd, 1912, Sybil Mary, *d* of late Berkeley Paget. Served Egyptian War, 1882 (medal, bronze star); Sudan, 1884 (two clasps); Naval Attaché at Rio de Janeiro, 1914–19. *Address:* 40 Cranley Gardens, SW7.

Died 15 Dec. 1923.

BOYLE, Colonel Lionel Richard Cavendish, CMG 1918; MVO 1903; *b* 24 Nov. 1851; *s* of Charles John Boyle; *m* 1883, Alice Pulteney; one *s* three *d*. Entered Royal Navy, 1865; retired, 1875; joined Honourable Artillery Company of London, 1886; retired, 1903; commanded Battalion, 1897–1903; raised and commanded 2nd Batt. HAC, Aug. 1914. *Recreations:* golf, foreign travel. *Address:* 6 Mulberry Walk, Chelsea, SW3. *T:* Kensington 5786. *Clubs:* Army and Navy, Naval and Military.

Died 2 Jan. 1920.

BOYLE, Vice-Adm. Hon. Robert Francis, MVO; RN; *b* 12 Dec. 1863; 3rd *s* of 5th (and *uncle* and *heir-pres.* to 8th) Earl of Shannon and 1st wife, Lady Blanche Emma Lascelles, 3rd *d* of 3rd Earl of Harewood; *m* 1899, Cerise, 2nd *d* of Sir Claude Champion de Crespigny, 4th Bt; two *s* two *d*. Entered Navy, 1877; Lieut 1886; Commander, 1897; Captain, 1903; Vice-Adm. retired, 1919; served Egypt, 1882 (medal, Khedive's bronze star); West Africa, 1894 (wounded, despatches, medal, clasp); European War, 1915–1919. *Address:* Fairthorne, Catisfield, Fareham. *TA:* Titchfield. *T:* Titchfield 12. *Club:* Naval and Military.

Died 11 Sept. 1922.

BOYLE, William Lewis; MP (U) Mid-Norfolk since 1910; in Ministry of National Service (unpaid); *b* 27 May 1859; *s* of Charles John Boyle and Zacyntha, *d* of late General Sir Lorenzo Moore; *g s* of late Vice-Admiral Hon. Sir Courtenay Boyle, 3rd *s* of 7th Earl of Cork and Orrery; *m* 1887, Charlotte Mary, *d* of late Charles Lloyd Norman; one *s* one *d*. *Address:* Tuddenham Lodge, Honingham, Norfolk. *Clubs:* Carlton, Constitutional.

Died 2 Oct. 1918.

BOYSON, Sir John Alexander, Kt 1914; Director of Binny & Co., Madras; *b* 1846; *o s* of John Robert Boyson and Matilda Margaret, *d* of late Col Alexander Adam; *m* 1885, Mary Josephine, *o d* of late Col Charles Bowen, RE; two *s* two *d*. *Educ:* Harrow. *Address:* 9 Hornton Street, W8. *T:* Park 2502.

Died 15 March 1926.

BOYTON, Sir James, Kt 1918; member of firm Elliott, Son and Boyton, estate agents, since 1878; *b* 1855; *m* 1881, Emma, *d* of Peter Middleton. Member LCC, 1907–10; MP (U) East Marylebone, 1910–18; Fellow of the Surveyors' Institution; Fellow of the Auctioneers' and Estate Agents' Institute (President, 1905–6); JP County of London. *Address:* 2 Park Square West, NW1. *T:* Langham 1952. *Clubs:* Carlton, Constitutional.

Died 16 May 1926.

BRABAZON, Maj.-Gen. Sir John Palmer, KCB, 1911 (CB 1893); CVO 1901; *b* 13 Feb. 1843; *s* of late Major Hugh Brabazon, Brabazon Park, Co. Mayo, late 15th King's Hussars, and Eleanor Ambrosia, *d* of late Sir William Henry Palmer, 3rd Bt, Kenure Park, Co. Dublin, and Palmerstown, Co. Mayo; unmarried. Served in Grenadier Guards; 10th Prince of Wales' Own Hussars; commanded 4th Queen's Own Hussars; Colonel of the 18th (Queen Mary's Own) Hussars, 1913; served in Ashanti Campaign, 1873–74, Afghan Campaign, 1878–79; 2nd Afghan Campaign as Brigade Major, Cavalry Division, 1879–80, including march Kabul to Kandahar; Soudan Campaign at Suakim, 1884 (wounded at El Teb); and the Nile Campaign for the relief of Gordon, 1884–1885; commanded 2nd Cavalry Brigade, South Africa Field Force, 1899–1900, and Imperial Yeomanry in South Africa, Feb. to Dec. 1900 (despatches, medal with five clasps); in receipt of pension for distinguished services in the field; ADC to Viceroy of India, 1878–80; ADC to Queen Victoria, 1889–1901; Gentleman Usher to King Edward VII; Chevalier (1st class) of the order of the Dannebrog (Denmark); had a property in Co. Mayo, and another in Co. Galway. *Address:* 10 Wilton Crescent, SW1; Brabazon Park, Swinford, Co. Mayo; Glen Corrib, Headfort, Co. Galway. *Clubs:* Marlborough, Turf, Guards, Pratt's, Carlton.

Died 20 Sept. 1922.

BRACKEN, Clio Hinton; sculptor; *b* Rhinebeck, NY; *d* of Howard Hinton and Lucy Bronson; *m* 1st, 1892, James Huneker; 2nd, 1900, William Barrie Bracken, both of New York; two *s* one *d*. Studied at Arts Students' League, NY City, and with St Gaudens and Macmonnies, Paris, France. Exhibited at Paris Salon, Academy of Design (New York), Panama P. L. Expn, San Francisco, 1915. *Principal Works:* Rubaiat Punch Bowl; portrait of Paderewski, etc. *Address:* 140 East 22nd Street, New York. *T:* Gramercy 5441.

Died 12 Feb. 1925.

BRACKENBURY, Col Henry Langton, JP; *b* Colchester, 26 April 1868; *o s* of late Major Henry Brackenbury, HM Bodyguard; *m* 1898, Florence, *d* of late Edgar Mills, California; two *s* three *d*. *Educ:* Corpus Christi College, Oxford. Called to Bar, Inner Temple, 1893; MP (U) Louth Division, Lincoln, 1910 and since 1918; High Steward of the Borough of Louth; Captain, 3rd Lincolnshire Regiment. *Address:* Thorpe Hall, Louth, Lincs. *Clubs:* Oxford and Cambridge, Carlton.

Died 28 April 1920.

BRACKENBURY, Admiral John William, CB 1887; CMG 1879; retired; *b* 1842; *s* of late William Congreve C. Brackenbury; *m* 1880, Frances Mary, *d* of late Colonel Gilbert Francklyn. Commanded "Shah's" Naval Brigade Zulu War, 1879; promoted captain for services on West Coast of Africa, 1881; captain of "Thalia," Egypt, 1882; captain of "Turquoise" during operations on East Coast of Africa, 1887–91; Rear-Admiral second in command Channel Squadron, 1898–99. *Address:* 8 Belsize Square, Hampstead, NW. *Club:* Junior United Service.

Died 15 March 1918.

BRADDELL, Octavius Henry, ISO 1903; late Accountant Board of Public Works, Ireland; *b* 26 Dec. 1843; *e s* of late John Revell Braddell, Raheengrany, Co. Wicklow, and Maria, *née* Donovan; *m* 1866, Theresa Louisa (*d* 1911), 2nd *d* of Francis Abbott Payn, Le Colombier, Jersey; one *s* one *d*. *Educ:* Marlborough College. Entered Board of Works, 1862; retired, 1906. *Address:* Lower Bullingate, Carnew, Co. Wicklow.

Died 23 Oct. 1921.

BRADDELL, Sir Thomas de Multon Lee, Kt 1914; Chief Judicial Commissioner, Federated Malay States, 1912; retired 1917; *b* 25 Nov. 1856; *e s* of late Thomas Braddell, CMG, FRGS, FES (Attorney-General of the Straits Settlements, 1867–82), of Raheengrany, Co. Wicklow, and Anne Lee; *m* 1879, Ida Violet Nassau, 2nd *d* of John Roberts Kirby, JP, formerly of St Osyth's Priory, Essex; four *s* two *d*. *Educ:* Brighton College; Worcester College, Oxford. Called to Bar, Inner Temple, 1879; proceeded to Singapore, where he practised at the Bar of the Straits Settlements; acted as Attorney-General of the Straits Settlements, 1897 and 1908; a Puisne Judge of the Straits Settlements, 1907; Attorney-General of the Straits Settlements, 1911. *Recreations:* yachting, swimming, and all sports connected with the sea or river. *Address:* 32 Westbourne Gardens, Folkestone. *Club:* Reform.

Died 31 Jan. 1927.

BRADFIELD, William Walter, CBE 1918; Director since 1918, and Joint General Manager since 1919, Marconi Wireless Telegraph Co. Ltd; *b* London, 18 March 1879; *m* 1906, Jessica Whitcomb. *Educ:* Parmiter's School; City and Guilds of London Engineering College. *Address:* 1 St James's Place, SW1. *Clubs:* Junior Constitutional, Royal Automobile.

Died 17 March 1925.

BRADFORD, Temp. Lt-Col Roland Boys, VC 1916; Durham Light Infantry; *b* 23 Feb. 1892. Joined Durham LI 1912; Adjt TF 1915; served European War, 1914–17 (despatches, VC, MC).

Died Nov. 1917.

BRADLEY, Francis Herbert, OM 1924; Fellow of Merton College, Oxford, since 1870; writer on philosophy; *b* 30 Jan. 1846; *s* of Rev. Charles Bradley, Vicar of Glasbury, and *half-b* of late Very Rev. George Granville Bradley, Dean of Westminster. *Educ:* Cheltenham; Marlborough; University Coll., Oxford. BA; MA. Hon. FBA 1923. *Publications:* The Presuppositions of Critical History, 1874; Ethical Studies, 1876; The Principles of Logic, 1883; Appearance and Reality, 1893; Essays on Truth and Reality, 1914; The Principles of Logic revised, with Commentary and Terminal Essays, 1922. *Address:* Merton College, Oxford.

Died 18 Sept. 1924.

BRADLEY, Henry, FBA 1907; joint-editor of the Oxford English Dictionary since 1889 (subseq. senior editor); *b* Manchester, 3 Dec. 1845; *s* of John Bradley and Mary Spencer; *m* 1872, Eleanor Kate Hides; one *s* four *d*. *Educ:* Chesterfield Grammar School. Hon. MA Oxford, 1891 (MA by decree, 1916); Hon. DLitt Oxford, 1914; Hon. PhD Heidelberg, 1903; DLitt Durham, 1913; LittD Sheffield, 1913; Fellow of Magdalen College, Oxford, 1916; Hon. Member of Netherlands Society of Arts, Science, and Literature, and of the Royal Flemish Academy. In early life engaged in private teaching; afterwards (till 1884) employed as commercial clerk and foreign correspondent at Sheffield; removed to London, 1884; contributor to the Academy,

Athenæum, etc; temporary editor of Academy, 1884–85; President, Philological Society, 1891–93, 1900–3 and 1909–10; President, Oxford Philological Society, 1921. *Publications:* The Story of the Goths, 1888; The Making of English, 1904; articles in the Dictionary of National Biography, Encyclopædia Britannica, Chambers's Encyclopædia, the Cambridge History of English Literature, etc; Revised Edition of Stratmann's Middle-English Dictionary, 1891; revised editions of Morris's Elementary Lessons in Historical English Grammar and Primer of English Grammar, 1897; editions of Caxton's Dialogues (Early English Text Society) and of Gammer Gurton's Needle (in Professor Gayley's Representative English Comedies); edited the portions of the Oxford English Dictionary comprising E, F, G, L, M, and S, and engaged on W. *Recreation:* walking. *Address:* 173 Woodstock Road, Oxford.

Died 23 May 1923.

BRADLEY, Herbert, CSI 1906; *b* 29 Jan. 1856; *s* of R. H. Bradley of Blackheath; *m* 1891, Lillias Sarah, *d* of Rev. Dr M'Culloch. *Educ:* Winchester. Entered ICS 1876; posted to Madras, 1878; Assistant Collector and Magistrate, special duty, 1885–87; Secretary to the Board of Revenue, 1887; Collector, 1891; Member of the Board of Revenue, 1900; President of the Salt Committee, 1904; Member of the Legislative Council, 1900; Chief Secretary, 1905–8; Temporary Member of Council, 1908; retired, 1909. Barrister, Middle Temple, 1878; JP Dorset. *Address:* c/o Grindlay & Co., 54 Parliament Street, SW1. *Clubs:* East India United Service; Royal and Ancient Golf, St Andrews. *Died 3 June 1923.*

BRADSHAW, Surg.-Maj.-Gen. Sir Alexander Frederick, KCB 1912 (CB 1891); MRCP, MRCS and LSA; FRGS; Member Royal Society of Medicine; Hon. Physician to Queen Victoria, King Edward VII, and King George V; MA Oxon (*hon.,* 1900; by decree, 1910); AMS (retired); *b* 1834; *m* 1864, Ellen C., *d* of Col R. S. Ewart, Bengal Army; two *s* five *d.* *Educ:* private school, Cambridge; St Bartholomew's Hospital, London; Worcester College, Oxford, 1897–1900. Entered Army Medical Department, 1857, and appointed to Rifle Brigade; served with 2nd Battalion during Indian Mutiny; present at siege of Lucknow, 1858 (medal and clasp); Garrison and Brigade Surgeon, Delhi, 1863–64; appointed to Chestnut Troop, Royal Horse Artillery, 1866; on personal staff of three Commanders-in-Chief in India, Sir William Mansfield (afterwards Lord Sandhurst), Lord Napier of Magdala, and Sir Frederick Haines, 1869–81; went with last to Afghanistan, 1879, during the war; principal medical officer of the Quetta District, Baluchistan, 1884–86; of the Zhob Valley Expeditionary Force, 1884 (despatches); of the Frontier Field Force, Assuan, Egypt, 1886–87; of the Northern District, England, 1887; of the Rawal Pindi District, Punjab, 1887–92; of the Hazara (Black Mountain) Field Force, 1891 (despatches, medal and clasp, CB); Hon. Surgeon to Viceroys of India, Lords Lansdowne and Elgin, 1891–95; principal medical officer, HM's Forces in India, 1892–95; served 35 years in India; retired, 1895; received King's Coronation Medals, 1902 and 1911; received Reward for Distinguished Service, 1914; Member for five years from Dec. 1907 of the Honorary Consulting Staff of the Queen Alexandra's Military Hospital, London; Hon. Consulting Physician to the Military Hospitals in Oxford and Neighbourhood, 1916–19. *Publication:* Edited Memoir of Catherine G. Loch, Senior Lady Superintendent, Queen Alexandra's Military Nursing Service for India. *Address:* 111 Banbury Road, Oxford. *Clubs:* United Service; Oxford and County, Oxford.

Died 27 Sept. 1923.

BRADSHAW, Octavius; *b* 1845; *e s* of late William Bradshaw, Barrister-at-law, and Mary Anne, *d* of Joseph Horsley; *m* 1871, Emily Sarah, *d* of Thomas Ferguson, of Greenville, Co. Down, and *widow* of Hon. Fleetwood John Pellew, Canonteign, Exeter. JP and DL Devon; High Sheriff, 1884; was Major 1st Royal Devon Yeomanry Cavalry. *Club:* Wellington. *Died 16 Jan. 1928.*

BRADSHAW, Thomas R., MD Dublin; FRCP; Consulting Physician at Liverpool Royal Infirmary; Major à la suite, RAMC (TF); *b* Leamington, 1857; *s* of John W. Bradshaw, solicitor, Dublin, and Sarah Houghton Waters; *m* 1904, Rose Mary, *d* of Professor T. R. Glynn, MD, FRCP, Liverpool; no *c. Educ:* Rathmines School, Dublin; Trinity College, Dublin; University College Hospital, London. Held resident posts in Royal Infirmary and Northern Hospital; then Hon. Physician, Liverpool Stanley Hospital, and Hon. Physician, Royal Infirmary; Physician, Samaritan Hospital for Women; Hon. Examining Physician, Queen Alexandra's Sanatorium, Davos; sometime Examiner in Medicine, University of London; President of the Liverpool Medical Institution, 1910–11. *Publications:* various contributions to Medical Transactions and Periodicals. *Recreations:*

travel, photography, motoring. *Address:* The Tower, Mold, Flintshire N Wales. *T:* Mold 51. *M:* DM 1983. *Club:* Athenæum, Liverpool

Died 25 Jan. 1927

BRADSHAW, William, JP; *b* 1844; *s* of late James E. Bradshaw of Darcy Lever Hall, Lancaster, and Fair Oak Park, Hants; *m* 1st, 1869 Floretta (*d* 1889), *o c* of John Chandless; 2nd, 1892, Maud Hamilton 2nd *d* of late Charles George Barclay of Dura, Cupar, Fife. *Address* 43 Cadogan Place, SW. *Clubs:* Boodle's; Royal Yacht Squadron Cowes. *Died 18 Jan. 1927*

BRADSTREET, Sir Edward Simon Victor, 7th Bt, *cr* 1759; *b* 1856 *s* of Sir Edmund Simon Bradstreet, 6th Bt and Emily Matilda *d* o General de Gaja, of Las Courtines, Castelnaudary, France, and *g* of Lord Robert Fitzgerald, *y s* of 1st Duke of Leinster; *S* father, 1905 *m* 1888, Fiorina Mary, *y d* of Felix Fiori de Lerichi of Bougie, Algeria three *d* (one *s* decd). *Educ:* Trinity College, Dublin. A Civil Engineer *Heir:* none. *Address:* St Jean de Luz, France.

Died 13 Jan. 1924 (ext,

BRADY, George Stewardson, MD, MRCS; DSc, LLD; FRS CMZS; Professor (Hon.) Natural History, Armstrong College Newcastle-on-Tyne; Consulting Physician to Sunderland Infirmary *b* Gateshead, 18 April 1832; *e s* of Henry Brady, Surgeon; *m* 1859 Ellen, *d* of Robt Wright, Chesterfield; one *s* three *d. Educ:* Friends School, Ackworth; Tulketh Hall, Preston; Univ. of Durham Coll of Medicine. Practised Medicine in Sunderland since 1857; Prof. Nat Hist. Armstrong Coll., 1875–1906. *Publications:* on th Ostracoda and Copepoda of the Challenger Expedition; *A* Monograph of the Free and Semi-parasitic Copepoda of the Britis Islands (Ray Soc.); jointly, a Monograph of the Ostracoda of the Nort Atlantic and North-Western Europe; and numerous othe contributions to scientific literature. *Recreations:* gardening photography. *Address:* Park Hurst, Endcliffe, Sheffield.

Died 25 Dec. 1921

BRADY, Major Sir William Longfield, 4th Bt, *cr* 1869; *b* 16 Jul 1864; *s* of late Maziere John Brady, 2nd *s* of Sir Maziere Brady, 1s Bt and Elizabeth, *d* of Rev. Robert Longfield; *S* brother, 1909; *r* 1891, Caroline Florence, *d* of Alfred M'Clintock, MD; one *d. Hei* none. *Address:* Glenart Avenue, Blackrock, Co. Dublin.

Died 7 April 1927 (ext,

BRAGGE, Rev. Charles Albert; Vicar of Thorncombe since 187! Canon of Ilfracombe, Salisbury Cathedral. *Educ:* Trinity College Cambridge, MA. Deacon, 1864; priest, 1864; Curate of Huntspil 1863–5; Burstock, 1865–1870; Vicar of Hatton, 1870–75. *Address* Thorncombe Vicarage, Chard.

Died 16 Dec. 1923

BRAIN, Sir Francis William Thomas, Kt 1913; Chairman Chepstov Water Co. and Cinderford Gas Co.; *b* 28 Oct. 1855; *o s* of Corneliu Brain, *s* of Cornelius Brain of Ruardean, and Ann Tummy, *d* o Thomas Brain of The Hawthorns, Drybrook; *m* 1884, Dorothy, *d* of late Rev. Lewis Roberts; two *d. Educ:* Monmouth Gramma School. Member Institute Civil Engineers and Institute Minin Engineers; Fellow Surveyors Institution; Past President Minin Association of Great Britain; Past President National Association c Colliery Managers; JP Gloucestershire; Verderer of the Forest of Dear pioneer of Electric Blasting in Mines and of Electricity applied t Mines; Vice-Chairman of the Board for Mining Examinations unde Coal Mines Act. *Publications:* various papers to Mining and othe Associations; paper on Electricity applied to Mining, Britis Association Meeting at Bath, 1886. *Recreation:* foreign travel. *Address* Huntworth, Stoke Bishop, Bristol. *T:* Stoke Bishop 80. *TA* Rockleaze, Bristol. *M:* AE 4604. *Clubs:* Royal Automobile; County Gloucester. *Died 31 Aug. 192*

BRAITHWAITE, Robert, MD; FLS, FRMS; *b* Ruswarp, nea Whitby, Yorks, 10 May 1824; *e s* of Robert Braithwaite, Shipowner *m* 1869, Charlotte Elizabeth Ward, *d* of N. B. Ward, FRS, of Claphan Rise. Retired from practice, 1899. *Publications:* Sphagnaceæ of Europe The British Moss-Flora; various papers in scientific journals. *Addres* 26 Endymion Road, Brixton Hill, SW.

Died 20 Oct. 1917

BRAITHWAITE, William Charles, JP; BA, LLB; Barrister-at-lav (Lincoln's Inn); Local Director, Barclays Bank Limited; Autho President, Woodbrooke Settlement, Birmingham; Chairmar National Council of Adult School Unions; *b* 1862; 3rd *s* of J. Beva Braithwaite, London, and Martha Gillett; *m* 1896, Janet, *d* of Charle C. Morland, Croydon; three *s* one *d. Educ:* Oliver's Mount Schoo

Scarborough; University College, London. Practised as a barrister till 1896; then became a partner in Gillett & Co., Bankers, Banbury and Oxford, and on their amalgamation in 1919 a Local Director in Barclays Bank Ltd; Swarthmore Lecturer, 1909; Treasurer of Friends' Ambulance Unit during the war. *Publications:* Red Letter Days; a Verse Calendar, 1907; The Beginnings of Quakerism, 1912; Foundations of National Greatness, 1915; The Second Period of Quakerism, 1919; various papers on Education, Biblical criticism, Quaker history and religious subjects. *Address:* Castle House, Banbury.

Died 28 Jan. 1922.

BRAMELD, Rev. William Arthur, MA; Prebendary of North Kelsey in Lincoln Cathedral since 1888; *e s* of late Rev. A. J. Brameld, vicar of New Wortley, Leeds; *m* 1st, 1882, Mary (*d* 1920), *e d* of Henry John Grieveson, JP, of Startforth Hall, Barnard Castle; one *s* four *d*; 2nd, 1921, Margaret Isabel, *y d* of Charles E. Bousfield, of Leeds and Ilkley. *Educ:* Leeds Grammar School; Keble College, Oxford. Deacon, 1876; Priest, 1877; was Curate of Kintbury, Berks; and afterwards of Lee, Kent; Principal of St Paul's Missionary College, Burgh, 1883–90; Vicar of Wortley, Leeds, 1890–97; Vicar of St Stephen's, Lewisham, 1897–1904; Commissary to the Bishop of St John's, Kaffraria, 1897–1914; Vicar of Chapel Allerton, Leeds, 1904–14. *Publications:* In Type and Shadow, 1892, 2nd edn.; The Marriage Service, with Notes and Prayers, 1904. *Address:* 11 Marine Parade, Folkestone.

Died 16 Nov. 1922.

BRAMLEY, Fred; Secretary, British Trades Union Congress since 1923; *b* Peel, near Otley, Yorks, 27 Sept. 1874; *s* of journeyman engineer; *m* 1898; one *s* one *d*. *Educ:* practically self-educated. Served apprenticeship as cabinetmaker; became lecturer on Social and Economic Questions; employed by Clarion newspaper for five years as lecturer; appointed Organising Secretary, Furnishing Trade Association; three times elected to Parliamentary Committee, Trades Union Congress; subsequently appointed Assistant Secretary. *Publications:* special articles on Economic and Social Questions in magazines and newspapers. *Recreations:* no special recreation except walking. *Address:* 32 Eccleston Square, SW1. *T:* Victoria 6410.

Died 10 Oct. 1925.

BRAMLEY, Rev. Henry Ramsden; *b* 4 June 1833; unmarried. *Educ:* Blackheath School; Oriel and University Colleges, Oxford. Fellow Magdalen Coll. Oxford, 1857; Tutor, 1858–68; 1871–83; Precentor and Canon of Lincoln, 1892–1901. *Recreations:* riding, walking. *Address:* Nettleham Hall, Lincoln. *TA:* Nettleham, Lincoln.

Died 28 Jan. 1917.

BRAMLEY-MOORE, Rev. William, MA (Cantab); *b* 1831; *e s* of John Bramley-Moore (*d* 1886), of Langley Lodge, Gerrard's Cross, Bucks, formerly of Aigburth, Liverpool, Chairman of the Liverpool Docks, after whom the Bramley-Moore Dock was named, late MP for Maldon and Lincoln, JP, DL; *m* 1865, Ella, 3rd *d* of Swinfen Jordan, of Clifton; six *s* four *d*. Vicar of Gerrard's Cross, 1859–69. *Publications:* Six Sisters of the Valleys; Great Oblation; Marturia; The Church's Forgotton Hope; Ancient Tyre and Modern England, etc; edited Cassell's Foxe's Book of Martyrs. *Recreations:* travelling, writing, authorship. *Address:* 26 Russell Square, WC.

Died Oct. 1918.

RAMSTON, Sir John, GCMG 1900 (KCMG 1897); CB 1896; DCL Oxford; Assistant Under-Secretary of State for the Colonies, 1876–97; *b* Skreens, Essex, 14 Nov. 1832; *s* of Thomas William Bramston, MP for S Essex, 1835–66, and Eliza, *d* of Admiral Sir Eliab Harvey, GCB, who commanded the "Temeraire" at Trafalgar; *m* 1872, Eliza Isabella (*d* 1920), *d* of Rev. Harry Vane Russell. *Educ:* Winchester; Balliol College, Oxford. Fellow of All Souls College, Oxford, 1855; Barrister, Middle Temple, 1857; Member Legislative Council, Queensland, 1863–69; Legislative Assembly, 1871–73; Executive Council, 1863–66, 1870–73; Attorney-Gen. Queensland, 1870–73; Hong Kong, 1874–76; Royal Commissioner in Newfoundland, 1898. *Address:* 18 Berkeley Place, Wimbledon.

Died 13 Sept. 1921.

RAMWELL, John Milne, MB, CM; consulting physician; *b* Perth, 11 May 1852; *y s* of late James Paton Bramwell, MD, of Perth; *m* 1st, 1875, Mary, *d* of late Capt. Reynolds, Indian Army; two *d*; 2nd, 1914, Katharine Mary Chisholm, *widow* of Henry Valentine Corrie. *Educ:* Perth Grammar School; Edinburgh University. Took degrees at Edinburgh in 1873; travelled for a year, and then settled in private practice at Goole, Yorks; commenced hypnotic researches in 1889; settled in London in 1892. *Publications:* On Imperative Ideas; James Braid, Surgeon and Hypnotist; On the Evolution of Hypnotic Theory; Hypnotic Anæsthesia; Hypnotic and Post-hypnotic Appreciation of Time; Secondary and Multiplex Personalities; Suggestion, its Place

in Medicine and Scientific Research; Hypnotism in the Treatment of Insanity and Allied Disorders; Dipsomania and its Treatment—by Suggestion; "Hypnotism" in Encyclopædia Medica, 1901; Hypnotism, its History, Practice, and Theory, 1903; Hypnotism and Treatment by Suggestion, 1909, etc. *Recreations:* yachting, fishing. *Address:* The Hove, Torquay, S Devon. *T:* Torquay 877. *Club:* Royal Torbay Yacht, Torquay.

Died 16 Jan. 1925.

BRANCH, James, JP; boot manufacturer, Bethnal Green and Kingsthorpe, Northampton; Member LCC, 1889–1907; *b* Bethnal Green, 27 Feb. 1845. MP (L) Enfield Div. Middlesex, 1906–10; contested same division, 1910. *Address:* Canford, 43 Etchingham Park Road, Finchley, NW3.

Died 16 Nov. 1918.

BRAND, Hon. Arthur George, JP, DL; *b* 1 May 1853; *s* of 1st Viscount Hampden and Eliza, *d* of Gen. Robert Ellice; *m* 1886, Edith (*d* 1903), *d* of late Joseph Ingram of Brooklands, Cheshire; one *s*. *Educ:* Rugby. Assistant Clerk in House of Commons; MP (L) Wisbech Division of Cambs., 1891–95, and 1900–6; Treasurer in HM Household, 1894–95. *Address:* 101 Mount Street, W. *Clubs:* Turf, Bachelors', Garrick.

Died 9 Jan. 1917.

BRAND, Ferdinand, ISO 1902; *b* 28 March 1846; 4th *s* of late Captain W. H. Brand, RN, who as a Midshipman served in HMS "Revenge" at the battle of Trafalgar, and Christina Cecilia, 2nd *d* of J. Greig, Procurator-Fiscal of Shetland; *m* 1875, Edith Mary, *d* of late W. F. Hartley, JP, of Simpson Hill House, Heywood, Lancashire; one *s* two *d*. *Educ:* Royal Naval School, New Cross. Entered Admiralty, 1867; retired 1908; edited Navy List, 1880–98; Admiralty Librarian, 1898–1908. *Recreations:* natural history, naval history, gardening. *Address:* Heywood Lodge, Cumberland Road, Kew.

Died 19 April 1922.

BRAND, Rear-Admiral Hon. Thomas Seymour, JP; Alderman CC, East Sussex; *b* 20 Sept. 1847; 2nd *s* of 1st Viscount Hampden; *m* 1879, Blanche, *y d* of late Henry Lomax Gaskell, Kiddington Hall, Woodstock; one *s* one *d*. *Educ:* at sea. Flag-Lieut to late Lord Alcester, 1874–77; commanded "Bittern," Bombardment of Alexandria, 1882; contested (L) Hastings, 1886; Eastbourne Division of Sussex, 1892, 1895, and 1900. *Address:* Glynde Place, Lewes. *TA:* Glynde. *Club:* United Service.

Died 12 Nov. 1916.

BRANDES, George, LLD St Andrews; Athens; *b* Copenhagen, 4 February 1842. *Educ:* University of Copenhagen. Lived in France and Italy, 1866–67, 1870–71; Berlin, 1877–82; Poland, Russia, 1886–87; Italy, 1898–1913; France, every year; England, 1913; United States, 1914. Member American Academy of Arts and Sciences, Free Trade Association, Thomas Paine Association, New York, of the Rationalist Press Association, the Royal Society of Literature, the Polyglot Club, the Rationalist Peace Society, the Garrick Club, Institute of British Poetry, London. *Publications:* 33 Volumes of history, of literature, and criticism. Principal works: Main Currents of the Literature of the 19th Century, 6 vols; Ludvig Holberg; Sören Kierkegaard; Danish Poets; Impressions of Poland; Impressions of Russia; Berlin; Ferdinand Lassalle; Lord Beaconsfield; William Shakespeare; Men and Works; Men of the Modern Revival; A Study of Ibsen; Poems, 1896; Complete Works, 21 vols, 1910; Goethe, 2 vols; Julius Cæsar, 2 vols; The Jesus Myth, 1925; Hellas, 1925; Petrus, 1926; English: Main Currents, 6 vols; Shakespeare; Beaconsfield; Poland; Creative Spirits; Ibsen and Björnson; Recollections of my Childhood and Youth; Ferdinand Lassalle; The World at War; Voltaire; Cæsar, 2 vols; Goethe, 2 vols; Michel Angelo, 2 vols. *Address:* Copenhagen.

Died 19 Feb. 1927.

BRANNER, Prof. John Casper, PhD, LLD; DSc (Chicago); President Emeritus of Stanford University since 1916; Associate Editor Journal of Geology; *b* New Market, Tennessee, of American parents, 4 July 1850; *m* 1883, Susan Kennedy; two *s* one *d*. *Educ:* Cornell University, NY. Imperial Geological Commission, Brazil, 1875–77; Agent US Department of Agriculture in Brazil, 1882–83; Geological Survey of Penn, 1883–85; Prof. of Geology, University of Indiana, 1885–91; State Geologist of Arkansas, 1887–93; Prof. of Geology since 1891, and Vice-President of Stanford University, 1899–1913; President, 1913–1916; Director of the Branner-Agassiz Expedition to Brazil, 1899; Geologist of the US Geological Survey until 1906; Fellow of Geological Societies of London and Belgium and Société Géologique of France; Pres. Geological Society of America, 1904; Member of the National Academy of Sciences, Washington; Member American Philosophical Society, Instituto Historico do Brasil, Academia Brasileira, etc. *Publications:* numerous works on the geology of Brazil and Arkansas. *Address:* Stanford University, California.

Died 1 March 1922.

BRASSEY, 1st Earl, *cr* 1911; **Thomas Brassey;** Baron Brassey 1886; GCB 1906 (KCB 1881); DL, JP; DCL Oxford; LLD Dublin; Younger Brother Trinity House; Hon. Colonel 2nd Home Counties Brigade, Royal Field Artillery, Territorial Force; Military Member, Sussex Territorial Force Association; Hon. Captain RNR, June 1914; Board of Trade (yacht-owner's) Master's Certificate, by examination, 1872; Commander of Legion of Honour, 1896; late Lord Warden of Cinque Ports; Grand Cross of Order of Crown of Italy; *b* 11 Feb. 1836; *e s* of late Thomas Brassey and Maria Farrington, *d* of T. Harrison; *m* 1st, 1860, Anna (*d* 1887), *o c* of John Allnutt of Charles Street, W; *one s* three *d* (and one *d* decd); 2nd, 1890, Sybil de Vere, *d* of Viscount Malden; one *d*. *Educ:* Rugby; University College, Oxford, BA Honours History School. Liberal. MP (GL) Devonport, 1865; Hastings, 1868–85; President Statistical Society, 1879–80; Civil Lord of Admiralty, 1880–84; Secretary to Admiralty, 1884–85; served on Royal Commissions on Unseaworthy Ships, Defence of Coaling Stations, Relief of Aged Poor, Opium (Chairman), Canals and Inland Navigation; Lord-in-Waiting, 1894; President, Institute of Naval Architects, 1893–95; Governor of Victoria, 1895–1900. Owned yacht "Sunbeam" (presented to Government of India as hospital-ship, 1916), in which he covered over 400,000 nautical miles. *Publications:* Work and Wages, 1872; British Wages, 5 vols 1881; Foreign Work and British Wages, 1879; Sixty Years of Progress, 1904; founder and first editor of the Naval Annual. *Heir: s* Viscount Hythe, *b* 7 March 1863. *Address:* 24 Park Lane, W. *T:* Mayfair 6803; Chapelwood Manor, Nutley, Sussex. *Clubs:* Athenæum, Brooks's; Royal Yacht Squadron, Cowes. *Died 23 Feb. 1918.*

BRASSEY, 2nd Earl, *cr* 1911; **Thomas Allnutt Brassey;** Baron Brassey 1886; DCL, MA; JP; Lieutenant-Colonel West Kent Yeomanry; retired 1 May 1914, with thanks of Army Council for services; raised and commanded 2nd West Kent Yeomanry, Sept. to Dec. 1914; *b* 7 March 1863; *o s* of 1st Earl Brassey and Anna (*d* 1887), *o c* of John Allnutt of Charles Street, W; *S* father 1918; *m* 1889, Lady Idina Nevill, Lady of Justice of Order of St John of Jerusalem in England, *d* of 1st Marquis of Abergavenny; no *c*. *Educ:* Eton; Balliol College, Oxford; DCL, Oxford; Hon. Fellow of Balliol. Editor Naval Annual, since 1890; Assistant Private Secretary to Earl Spencer when First Lord of the Admiralty; Assistant Secretary to Royal Commission on Opium, 1894; contested Epsom Division, Surrey, 1892; Christchurch, 1895 and 1900; Devonport, 1902; raised 69th Sussex Company Imperial Yeomanry; First Acting Civil Commissioner of Pretoria, 1900; initiated Oxford University Endowment Fund; served on Archbishop's Committee on Church Finance, 1910–11; Chairman Executive Central Board of Finance; Managing Director of Mining and Lead Smelting business in Italy and Sardinia; Master's certificate for yacht owners; Commander of Crown of Italy; Knight of Grace of Order of St John of Jerusalem. *Publications:* Problems of Empire; The Case for Devolution, 1913. *Heir:* none. *Recreations:* hunting, deerstalking, shooting. *Address:* Normanhurst, Battle, Sussex. *Clubs:* Brooks's; Royal Yacht Squadron, Cowes.

Died 12 Nov. 1919 (ext).

BRASSEY, Albert, MA; JP; Master of Heythrop Hounds since 1873; *b* Rouen, 22 Feb. 1844; *s* of late Thomas Brassey and Maria Farrington, *d* of T. Harrison; *m* 1871, Hon. Matilda, *d* of 4th Lord Clanmorris; one *s* five *d*. *Educ:* Eton; Univ. Coll. Oxford. 14th Hussars, 1867–71; Oxfordshire Yeomanry, 1871–94; Colonel 1893–94; High Sheriff of Oxfordshire, 1878; MP (C) Banbury Div. Oxon, 1895–1906. Owned about 5,000 acres. *Recreation:* Member Royal Yacht Squadron since 1879. *Address:* Heythrop, Chipping Norton; 29 Berkeley Square, W. *T:* Gerrard 2424. *Clubs:* Carlton, Oxford and Cambridge, Army and Navy, Naval and Military, Cavalry; Royal Yacht Squadron, Cowes. *Died 7 Jan. 1918.*

BRASSEY, Capt. Harold Ernest; Royal Horse Guards; *b* 29 March 1877; 3rd *s* of late Henry Arthur Brassey, of Preston Hall; *m* 1906, Lady Norah Hely-Hutchinson, *y d* of 5th Earl of Donoughmore; two *d*. *Address:* 40 Hill Street, Berkeley Square, W.

Died July 1916.

BRAY, His Honour Judge Sir Edward, Kt 1919; County Court Judge, Bloomsbury and Brentford; *b* 19 Aug. 1849; *s* of Reginald Bray of Shere, Surrey, and Frances, *d* of Thomas N. Longman; *m* 1873, Edith Louisa, *d* of Rev. Thomas Hubbard, Newbury; three *s* one *d*. *Educ:* Westminster School (Captain of); Trinity College, Cambridge. Called to Bar, 1875; South Eastern Circuit; County Court Judge, Birmingham, 1905–7; London, 1908–11. *Publications:* Bray on Discovery; Bray's Digest of Discovery. *Recreations:* Westminster Cricket Eleven, 1864–68; Cambridge University Cricket Eleven, 1871–72; also played for Surrey; shooting, lawn tennis. *Address:* 26 Queen's Gate Gardens, SW7. *T:* Western 2307. *Club:* United University. *Died 19 June 1926.*

BRAY, Sir Reginald More, Kt 1904; DL; **Hon. Mr Justice Bray;** Judge of King's Bench Division since 1904; Recorder of Guildford, 1891; Bencher of the Inner Temple since 1891; *b* 26 Sept. 1842; *s* of Reginald Bray of Shere, Surrey, and Frances, *d* of Thomas N. Longman; *m* 1868, Emily Octavia, 4th *d* of Arthur Kett Barclay of Bury Hill, Dorking; four *s* two *d*. *Educ:* Harrow; Trinity College, Cambridge (scholar, 12th wrangler). Called to the Bar, 1868. *Recreation:* shooting. *Address:* The Manor House, Shere, Guildford; 17 The Boltons, SW10. *T:* Kensington 2823. *Club:* Athenæum. *Died 22 March 1923.*

BRAY, Brig.-Gen. Robert Napier, CMG 1919; DSO 1916; *b* 7 Dec. 1872; *s* of Major-General G. F. C. Bray; *m* 1907, Ruth Ellinor Boys; two *s*. *Educ:* United Services College, Westward Ho. Gazetted to the 1st Batt. Duke of Wellington's Regt, 1894; served in China; present at the Relief of Pekin, 1900; served in France (DSO, CMG, Bt Lt-Col). *Died 23 Oct. 1921.*

BRAYE, 5th Baron, *cr* 1529; **Alfred Thomas Townshend Verney-Cave,** DL, JP; Hon. Colonel in Army, late Lieutenant-Colonel and Hon. Colonel 3rd Battalion (Militia) Leicestershire Regiment (S African medal and clasp); *b* 23 July 1849; *s* of Edgell Wyatt-Edgell and Henrietta, Baroness Braye; *S* mother, 1879; *m* 1873, Cecilia, *d* of William Gerard Walmesley, of Westwood House, Wigan; one *s* two *d* (and one *s* one *d* decd). *Educ:* Eton; Christ Church, Oxford. *Publication:* Fewness of My Days: A Life in Two Centuries, 1927. *Heir: s* Hon. Adrian Verney Verney-Cave, *b* 11 Oct. 1874.

Died 1 July 1928.

BREADALBANE, 1st Marquis of, *cr* 1885; **Gavin Campbell,** KG 1894; PC; JP, DL; Bt of Nova Scotia, 1625; Earl of Breadalbane; Earl of Holland; Viscount of Tay and Paintland; Lord Glenorchy, Benederaloch, Ormelie, and Weik, 1677; Baron Breadalbane (UK), 1873; Earl of Ormelie, 1885; CC for Perthshire and Argyllshire; Lord Lieutenant of Argyllshire since 1914; Keeper of the Privy Seal of Scotland since 1907; Knight of the Order of the Seraphim; awarded silver medal Royal Humane Society; Knight of Order of St John of Jerusalem; ADC to the King; late Colonel Highland Cyclist Battalion; Hon. Colonel Highland Cyclist Battalion; Brigadier-General Royal Company of Archers; *b* 9 April 1851; *s* of 6th Earl of Breadalbane and Mary Theresa, *o d* of J. F. Edwards; *S* father as 7th Earl, 1871; *m* 1872, Lady Alma Imogen Carlotta Leonore Graham, Lady of Grace of the Order of St John of Jerusalem, *y d* of 4th Duke of Montrose. *Educ:* St Andrews. Lieut 4th Batt. Argyll and Sutherland Highlanders, and Captain Shropshire Yeomanry Cavalry, 1873–74; Lord-in-Waiting to the Queen; Treasurer Queen's Household, 1880–85; Lord Steward, 1892–95; Lord High Commissioner General Assembly Church of Scotland, 1893–95. Member of Fishery Board for Scotland. Owned about 200,000 acres. *Heir:* to earldom: *n* Iain Edward Herbert Campbell, *b* 14 June 1885. *Address:* 68 Ennismore Gardens, SW7. *TA:* Breadalbane, London. *T:* Kensington 114; Craig Dalmally, Argyllshire. *Clubs:* Reform, Brooks's, National Liberal; Royal Yacht Squadron, Cowes. *Died 19 Oct. 1922 (ext).*

BREADALBANE, 8th Earl of, *cr* 1677; **Iain Edward Herbert Campbell;** Earl of Holland; Viscount of Tay and Paintland; Lord Glenorchy, Benederaloch, Ormelie and Weik, 1677; Baronet of Nova Scotia; *b* 14 June 1885; *s* of Capt. Hon. Ivan Campbell, 2nd *s* of 6th Earl of Breadalbane; *S* uncle, 1st Marquis of Breadalbane, 1922. *Heir: cousin* Capt. Charles William Campbell, *b* 11 June 1889.

Died 10 May 1923.

BREBNER, Arthur, MRCS, LRCP; late Lieutenant RAMC; *b* 5 June 1870; 3rd *s* of late James Brebner, Manager of National Provincial Bank of England, Piccadilly; *m* 1905, Alice Rose Ewing, *e d* of Alexander Steven, MD, of St Kilda, Melbourne. *Educ:* Merchant Taylors' School and University College, London. Has travelled in China, Japan, East Indies, Australia, etc. *Publications:* Patches and Pomander; John Saint; Stories in Temple Bar, Argosy, Royal, London, Queen, Argus, Age, Queenslander, etc. *Address:* 5 S Kilda Villas, Buckhurst Hill, Essex. *Died 28 July 1922.*

BREBNER, Percy James, (Christian Lys); *b* 24 March 1864; *e s* of late James Brebner, Manager of National Provincial Bank of England, Piccadilly; *m* 1892, Adelaide, *e d* of late Rev. R. Taylor, Vicar of St Faith's, Wandsworth; one *s*. *Educ:* King's College School. Formerly in Share and Loan Department of Stock Exchange; subsequently engaged in editorial work. *Publications:* The Gate of Temptation; A Gallant Lady; The Turbulent Duchess; The Little Grey Shoe; The White Gauntlet; The Brown Mask; A Gentleman of Virginia; A Royal Ward; Vayenne; Princess Maritza; The Crucible of Circumstance; Mr Quixley of the Gate House; The Mystery of Ladyplace; The

Fortress of Yadasara; The Hepsworth Millions; Market Sefton; The Doctor's Idol; The Dunthorpes of Westleigh; Suspicion; The Black Card, etc; Christopher Quarles, 1921; special articles on Hospitals and their work. *Recreations:* music, tennis, golf. *Address:* 122 Upper Richmond Road, East Sheen, SW14. *Clubs:* Authors', Roehampton.
Died 31 July 1922.

BREDON, Sir Robert Edward, KCMG 1904 (CMG 1903); MA (Dublin); MB, CM; Deputy Inspector-General Imperial Maritime Customs, China, 1898–1908; Acting Inspector-General of Customs with rank of Provincial Lieutenant-Governor, 1908–10; *b* Portadown, Ireland, 4 Feb. 1846; *e s* of late Alexander Bredon, MD, and Katherine, *d* of late Joseph Breadon, RN, Stanstead, Canada; *m* 1879, Lily Virginia, *y d* of Thomas Crane Banks, San Francisco, Cal., USA; one *d. Educ:* Royal School, Dungannon; Trinity Coll. Dublin. Honourman in Mathematics and Classics; passed for Army Medical Staff (1st place), 1867; passed out of Netley (1st place), 1867; appointed 97th Regiment, 1867; retired, 1873; joined Chinese Customs Service, 1873; retired, 1897, and rejoined same year; appointed to Chinese Board of Customs, 1910, but retired in deference to wishes of British Government; war medal and clasp (Defence of Legations), China, 1900. 2nd Div. 2nd class Double Dragon of China; Officer Legion of Honour, France; Commander 1st Class of St Olaf, Norway; 2nd Class Sacred Treasure, Japan; Grand Cross Order of St Stanislas, Russia; 2nd Class Crown of Prussia, with star; 2nd Class Rising Sun, Japan; Grand Cross Order of Francis Joseph of Austria; Commander, First Class, Polar Star of Sweden; Commander, First Class, Dannebrog of Denmark; Civil rank, First Class, with red button, in China. *Address:* Chuan Pan Hutung, Peking, China. *Club:* Junior United Service.
Died 3 July 1918.

BREE, Ven. William, DD; Rector and Patron of Allesley since 1863; *b* 19 Nov. 1822; *o s* of Rev. W. T. Bree, MA, Rector of Allesley; *m* 1st, 1853, Mary, *d* of Rev. E. Duke, MA, FAS, FLS, of Lake House, Co. Wilts; 2nd, 1889, Sophy Adèle, *d* of Rev. G. Hesketh Biggs, MA, Vicar of Ettington, Co. Warwick. *Educ:* Bridgnorth School; Merton College, Oxford. Rector of Polebrook, Co. Northampton, 1862; Archdeacon of Coventry, 1887–1908. *Recreation:* natural history. *Address:* Allesley Rectory, Coventry. *TA:* Allesley.
Died 29 Jan. 1917.

BREEKS, Brig.-Gen. Richard William, CB 1918; DL; RA; *b* 1863; *s* of late James Wilkinson Breeks, HEICS, and Susan Maria, *e d* of Sir W. Y. Denison, KCB; *m* 1893, Olive, 2nd *d* of late Henry Arthur Blyth of Stansted House, Essex. Entered RA, 1863. Served South African War, 1900 (medal, three clasps); European War (CB); Col RHA, Mons to Aisne, 1914; Brig.-Gen. Gallipoli, 1915; DOAGC, 1916–18; CO Woolwich, 1918–19. *Address:* Helbeck Hall, Brough, Westmorland.
Died 2 May 1920.

BREMA, Marie, (*née* Minny Fehrman); opera singer; *b* Liverpool, 1856. First appeared in Popular Concerts, 1891; engaged to sing at Covent Garden for Royal Opera, 1892; first English singer invited by Wagner to sing at Bayreuth festival; has also appeared in many other operas and at musical festivals. *Address:* Royal College of Music, Manchester.
Died 22 March 1925.

BREMER, Prof. Walther Erich Emanuel Friedrich, DrPhil; Curator of Irish Antiquities in the National Museum, Dublin, since 1925; *b* Wismar, Mecklenburg, Germany, 8 June 1887; *m* 1922, Friede Berta Busse; one *d. Educ:* Wismar, Rostock; Universities Marburg, München, Rostock, Giessen. Dr Phil Giessen, 1910. Asst of the Romano–German Central Museum at Mainz, 1911–12; travelled through Central and South Eastern Europe, 1913–14; Excavations in Greece; Privatdozent of Prehistoric Archæology in the University of Marburg, 1920; Professor extraordinary, Marburg, 1922; Corresponding Member of the German Archæological Institute; MRIA, FRSAI. *Publications:* Die Haartracht des Mannes in Arch. griech Zeit, 1911; Eberstadt, steinzeitl, Dorf der Nordwetterau, 1913. *Address:* 34 Fitzwilliam Square, Dublin.
Died Nov. 1926.

BRENAN, Byron, CMG 1894; FRCI 1907; *b* France, 27 Dec. 1847; *s* of Col E. F. Brenan; *m* 1st, Matilda Susan (*d* 1899), *d* of late General T. C. Kelly, CB; 2nd, 1901, Emily, *d* of Robert Gore of Raveagh, Co. Tyrone. *Educ:* private. Student Interpreter, China, 1866; 3rd Assistant, 1868; Acting Interpreter, Canton, 1871–72; 2nd Class Assistant, 1872; Acting Interpreter, Shanghai, 1873; 1st Class Assistant, 1874; Acting Interpreter, Hankow, 1875; Acting Assistant Chinese Secretary, Pekin, 1875, and 1877–78; Acting Chinese Secretary, 1878–80; Consul at Wuhu, 1880; Acting Consul at Tien-tsin, 1882–1883; Chefoo, 1883; Tientsin and Pekin, 1885; British

Representative on Opium Mixed Commission at Hong Kong, 1886; Consul, Canton, 1893; was instructed to visit officially the principal Treaty Ports of China, Japan, and Corea, to report on the subject of British Trade, 1895; HBM Consul-General, Shanghai, China, 1898–1901. Retired on pension, 1901. *Address:* 30 Bramham Gardens, SW5. *Clubs:* Royal Societies, Hurlingham.
Died 28 Feb. 1927.

BRENNAN, Very Rev. Nicholas J.; President of Blackrock College, Dublin, 1910–16; *b* 1854. *Educ:* Blackrock College, Dublin; Paris. Ordained Priest, 1879; Professor and Dean, Blackrock, 1880–94; President of St Mary's College, Trinidad, and of Rockwell College, Cashel, 1894–1905; Member of Council, Classical Association, Ireland. *Address:* Blackrock College, Dublin. *TA:* and T: Blackrock 27.
Died 4 Oct. 1928.

BRERETON, Alfred, CSI 1903; *b* 26 Aug. 1849; *s* of Rev. Charles David Brereton, Rector of Framingham Earl, Norfolk; *m* 1st, 1894, Haidée (*d* 1902), *e d* of Col Shaw of Heathburn Hall, Co. Cork; 2nd, 1908, Frances, *d* of late D. Stewart of Ealing; one *s. Educ:* Norwich Grammar School. Entered railway branch of the Indian Public Works Dept, 1873; Executive Engineer, 1880; Assistant Director, NW Railway, 1887; District Traffic Superintendent, 1888; Deputy Manager, 1891; Officiating Manager, Eastern Bengal State Railway, 1893; Manager and Engineer in Chief, East Coast Railway, 1893; Director of Railway Traffic and Deputy Secretary to the Government of India (Railway Dept), 1897; Secretary, 1901–1904; retired, 1904; Govt Director, Guaranteed Railway Companies, 1905; retired, 1914. *Recreations:* a successful gentleman rider both across country and on the flat; good at most games. *Address:* c/o Grindlay and Co., 54 Parliament Street, SW1. *Club:* Oriental.
Died 1 May 1926.

BRERETON, Austin; journalist; *b* Liverpool, 13 July 1862. Writer of Dramatis Personæ in The Observer. Came to London, 1881; dramatic critic of The Stage, editor of Dramatic Notes, assistant editor of The Theatre, etc, 1881–87; dramatic and art critic, Sydney (NSW) Morning Herald, 1889–91; dramatic critic and assistant editor of The Illustrated American (New York), 1893–94; dramatic critic of The Sphere, 1901–1906. *Publications:* Henry Irving, a Biographical Sketch, 1883; Some Famous Hamlets, a Record of all the Chief Actors of Hamlet from Burbage to Fechter, 1884; Dramatic Notes, an Illustrated Critical Record of the London Stage from 1880 to 1886; Shakesperean Scenes and Characters, Descriptive Notes on the Plays and on the Principal Shakesperean Players from Betterton to Irving, 1886; Romeo and Juliet on the Stage, 1890; Sarah Bernhardt, an Illustrated Memoir, 1891; Gallery of Players (New York), 1894; A Short History of the Strand Theatre, 1899; Cheltenham, 1899; A Short History of She Stoops to Conquer, The Rivals, and The School for Scandal, 1900; By The Silent Highway, 1900; The Criterion, Past and Present, 1900; Shakespeare (arranged the illustrations, on a novel plan, for the complete works), 1900; new and extended edition of the same, 1902; Peg Woffington, On and Off the Stage, 1901; The Well of St Ann (Buxton), 1901; A Ramble in Bath, 1901; The Lyceum and Henry Irving, 1903; Henry Irving, 1905; At Home and Abroad; Ellen Terry, a Biographical Sketch, 1906; The Literary History of the Adelphi and its Neighbourhood, 1907; 2nd ed., 1908; The Life of Henry Irving, 1908; The Story of Old Whitehall; Cyril Maude, a Memoir, 1913; The Story of Drury Lane, 1918; A Walk down Bond Street; Whitehall Court and Scotland, 1921; The Hotel Cecil; A Glimpse of Old London and the New, 1921; H. B. and Laurence Irving. *Address:* 19 York Buildings, Adelphi, WC2.
Died 20 Nov. 1922.

BRERETON, William Westropp, MRCPI, MRCSI; Professor of Surgery, Queens' College, Galway, since 1888; member of staff, Galway Hospital; *b* Dublin, 1845; *s* of late William Westropp Brereton, QC, of Fitzwilliam Square, Dublin; *m* 1871, Helen, *y d* of J. Doig, Oughterard House, Surgeon, Hon. East India Company; three *s* one *d. Educ:* Trinity College and College of Surgeons. Pupil of John Morgan, Professor of Anatomy, College of Surgeons; qualified, 1865; Demonstrator of Anatomy, 1866, under Prof. Clelland in Galway; Medical Officer, Oughterard Union, 1868–88. *Publication:* Local Fixation during Operations. *Address:* University College, Galway, Ireland.
Died Feb. 1924.

BRETEUIL, Henri Charles Joseph, Marquis de, GCVO 1912 (KCVO 1905); *b* 17 Sept. 1848; *m* 1891, Miss Garner, New York; two *s. Educ:* Paris. Officier de Cavalerie, 5ᵉ huissards démissionnaire, 1876; député des Hautes-Pyrénées, 1877–92; Chevalier de la Légion d'Honneur; Chevalier de Malte (Hérédité). *Heir: s* François Breteuil. *Address:* 2 rue Rude, Paris; Château de Bevilliers, Breteuil (Seine-et-

Oise). *Clubs:* Jockey, Cercle de la Rue Royale, du Bois de Boulogne, Paris.   *Died 5 Nov. 1916.*

BRETT, Sir Charles Henry, Kt 1906; LLD; solicitor; *b* Grey Abbey, Co. Down, 16 July 1839; *e s* of Rev. Wills Hill Brett; *m* 1863, Margaret, *d* of Robert Neill, Belfast; two *s* three *d*. *Educ:* privately. *Recreations:* music, gardening. *Address:* Gretton, Malone, Belfast. *Club:* National Liberal.   *Died 17 July 1926.*

BRETT, Sir Henry, Kt 1926; principal proprietor, Auckland Star; *b* Hastings, England, 1843. Arrived in Auckland, 1862; with Mr McCullough Reed, started the Auckland Star, 1870; started the New Zealand Graphic, 1890; Mayor of Auckland, 1877–78; represented New Zealand as Commissioner at Paris Exhibition, 1889. *Publications:* Early History of New Zealand; Brett's Colonist's Guide; Life and Times of Sir George Grey, etc. *Address:* Promenade, Takapuna, Auckland, New Zealand.   *Died 29 Jan. 1927.*

BREUN, J. E., RBA, 1895; Portrait Painter; *b* 27 Nov. 1862; 2nd *s* of late John Needham Breun. *Educ:* Private school, London. Bronze medal, South Kensington, for drawing from the nude figure; 1st silver medal for portrait painting in the Royal Academy Schools, 1881; 1st silver medal for the second best drawing from the nude, RA Schools, 1882; 1st prize of £50 for the best set of 6 drawings from the nude figure at the RA Schools, 1883; 1st silver medal for the best drawing of a figure from the life, RA, 1884; extra silver medal for the painting of the nude, RA, 1884; 1st silver medal for the best copy of an oil painting, RA, 1881; gold medal for a picture at the Paris Salon, 1892, called Cold Steel. *Principal Portraits:* Princess Victoria of Wales; Adelina Patti; Princess of Pless; Countess of Londesborough; Countess of Carnarvon; Marquise d'Hautpoul; Lady Victoria Plunket; Earl of Carnarvon; Gen. Sir Redvers Buller; Maj.-General Sir E. Hutton; Gen. Sir Percy Feilding; Dr W. G. Grace; Field-Marshal Lord W. Paulet; Earl of Stamford, etc. *Recreations:* boating, lawn tennis, billiards. *Address:* Studio, 4 Greek Street, Soho Square, W. *Club:* Junior Constitutional.   *Died 8 July 1921.*

BREWER, Sir (Alfred) Herbert, Kt 1926; MusD Cantuar 1905; MusB Dublin, 1897; FRCO 1897; Hon. RAM 1906; Organist and Master of Choristers, Gloucester Cathedral, since 1896; Conductor Gloucester Festivals, 1898, 1901, 1904, 1907, 1910, 1913, 1922, 1925; *b* Gloucester, 21 June 1865; *e s* of late Alfred Brewer, Gloucester; *m* 1894, Ethel Mary, 2nd *d* of late Henry WilliamBruton, Gloucester; two *s* one *d*. *Educ:* Cathedral School, Gloucester; Exeter College, Oxford. Chorister, Gloucester Cathedral, 1877–80; Organist, St Catharine's Church, Gloucester, 1881; Organist, St Mary de Crypt, 1881; Organist, St Giles Church, Oxford, 1882–85; First Organ Scholar, Royal College of Music, 1883; Organ Scholar of Exeter College, Oxford, 1883; Organist of Bristol Cathedral, 1885; Organist of St Michael's Church, Coventry, 1886–92; Organist and Music Master, Tonbridge School, 1892–97; Conductor, Bristol Choral Society, Gloucestershire Orchestral Society, Gloucester Choral Society; Examiner in Music, Birmingham University, 1924–26; Examiner for RCO and Associated Board RAM and RCM; High Sheriff, City of Gloucester, 1922–23. *Publications:* chief compositions—Orchestral Service in C (Gloucester Festival, 1895); 98th Psalm (Gloucester Festival, 1898); Emmaus (Gloucester Festival, 1901); Dedication Ode (Worcester Festival, 1902); The Holy Innocents (Gloucester Festival, 1904); A Song of Eden (Worcester Festival, 1905); Three Elizabethan Pastorals (Hereford Festival, 1906); Sir Patrick Spens (Cardiff Festival, 1907); In Springtime (Leeds Festival, 1907); England, my England (Worcester Festival, 1908); Age and Youth (Promenade Concerts, Queen's Hall, 1908); Summer Sports (Gloucester Festival, 1910); Jillian of Berry, Pastorals (Hereford Festival, 1921); Millers Green (Hereford Festival, 1924); A Sprig of Shamrock (Gloucester Festival, 1925); For Your Delight (song cycle), Hereford Festival, 1927; Idyl for orchestra. *Recreation:* motoring. *Address:* Millers Green, Gloucester. *T:* 3283. *M:* FH 4466.
                                    Died 1 March 1928.

BREWER, Rev. Edward, MA; Vicar of Holy Trinity, Old Hill, 1888–1920; Hon. Canon of Worcester; *m* Mary Jane (*d* 1920). *Educ:* St John's College, Cambridge. Ordained, 1872; Curate of Broadwater, 1872–74; London Diocesan Home Missionary, St John's, N, 1874–78; Vicar of St Thomas, Islington, 1878–88. *Address:* Wilton Lodge, Malvern.   *Died 31 May 1922.*

BREWER, Rt. Rev. Leigh Richmond, STD; Bishop of Montana since 1880; *b* Berkshire, Vermont, 20 Jan. 1839; *m* 1866, Henrietta W. Foote; one *d*. *Educ:* Hobart College; General Theological Seminary, New York. Ordained, 1866; in charge of Grace Church,

Carthage, NY, 1866–72; Rector, Trinity Church, Watertown, 1872–80; DD, 1881. *Address:* Helena, Montana, USA.
                                    Died 28 Aug. 1916.

BREWILL, Lt-Col Arthur William, DSO 1916; *b* 17 May 1861; *s* of late W. R. Brewill, Nottingham; *m* 1884, Clementine K. Thornley; three *s* two *d*. *Educ:* University School; private tutor. Fellow of the Royal Institute of British Architects, and for 20 years Surveyor to the Diocese of Southwell; Lieutenant in The Robin Hoods, 1881 (subseq. the 7th (Robin Hood) Batt. Sherwood Foresters), taking over the command of the Battalion, 31 July 1915, on the OC being wounded; commanded the Battalion at Hooge, 31 July 1915, when they were ordered to dig a new trench, and connect the British trench line where it had been captured by the Germans; commanded the Battalion at the attack on the Hohenzollern Redoubt, 13 Oct. 1915 (despatches, DSO). *Address:* Edwalton Valley, Notts.
                                    Died 18 Feb. 1923.

BREWIS, Nathaniel Thomas, MB, CM; FRCS, FRCPE; Gynaecologist to the Royal Infirmary of Edinburgh; Lecturer on Gynaecology, Royal Infirmary, Edinburgh; *b* Eshott Hall, Northumberland; 2nd *s* of Thomas Brewis of Eshott; *m* Annie Eliza, *e d* of R. S. Douglas of Acton Hall, Northumberland; one *s* one *d*. *Educ:* Edinburgh Institution and Edinburgh University. President Scottish Rugby Football Union; President Edinburgh Obstetrical Society; Examiner in Gynaecology, Edinburgh University; Obstetrician and Gynaecologist, Edinburgh New Town Dispensary; Gynaecologist in Leith Hospital. *Publications:* Outlines of Gynaecological Diagnosis; A Series of Abdominal Sections; Displacements of the Uterus; Endometritis, etc. *Recreations:* riding, fishing, golf. *Address:* 6 Drumsheugh Gardens, Edinburgh. *T:* Central 2248. *Club:* Caledonian United Service, Edinburgh.
                                    Died 21 Oct. 1924.

BRICE, Arthur John Hallam Montefiore; Barrister-at-law; of the Middle Temple and the Oxford Circuit; JP; FRGS; Hon. ARIBA; Recorder of Tewkesbury since 1923; *s* of Rev. Thomas Law Montefiore, MA, Rector of Catherston, Dorset, and Rural Dean, and Katherine, *o c* of Rev. Edward Cowell Brice, MA, Winterbourne Manor and Newnham, Glos; *m* 1st, 1886, Sybil (*d* 1895), *d* of E. L. Osbaldeston Mitford of Mitford Castle, Northumberland, and Hunmanby Hall, Yorkshire; 2nd, 1902, Sybil Constance, *e d* of late Major H. Reveley Mitford (51st KOLI); one *s*. Major in the Army, attached Staff, 1914–19; Judicial Officer in Ireland, 1920–22. Travelled in earlier years about Asia, North and South America, Oceania, and the Arctic regions. *Publications:* David Livingstone; Geographical Methods, 1895; The Great Frozen Land (editor), 1895; The Law relating to the Architect; the Law of Misrepresentation; numerous scientific and legal papers. *Recreation:* fly-fishing. *Address:* 2 Hare Court, Temple, EC4. *TA:* 5 Temple. *T:* Central 1777. *Club:* Reform.
                                    Died 6 Jan. 1927.

BRIDGE, Brig.-Gen. Sir Charles Henry, KCMG 1916 (CMG 1900); CB 1897; Inspector Remount Department since 1906; 1st Army Corps, 1903; *b* 16 June 1852; 4th *s* of late Ven. T. F. H. Bridge, Archdeacon of St John's, Newfoundland, and Sarah Christianna, *d* of J. Dunscombe; *m* 1885, Elizabeth Dorcas, *d* of late Sir Edward Morris, KCB; one *s*. *Educ:* Canterbury; Jesus College, Cambridge. Joined Control Department, 1872; Egyptian Campaign, 1882 (medal and star); DAQMG, Headquarters War Office, 1886–91; command of ASC, Aldershot, 1892–96; campaign in Rhodesia, 1896, on staff of Sir Frederick Carrington (medal and CB); brevet of Colonel; Headquarters Staff, Colchester, 1897–99; Director of Transport, South Africa Field Force, 1899–1900; AAG Aldershot, 1900–2 (medal 3 clasps, despatches, CMG); Director of Transport, 1903; Inspector of Remounts, 1903; Brig.-Gen. 1914; retired, 1918. *Club:* Junior United Service.   *Died 18 July 1926.*

BRIDGE, Admiral Sir Cyprian Arthur George, GCB 1903 (KCB 1899); *b* 15 March 1839; *s* of late Ven. T. F. H. Bridge, Archdeacon of St John's, Newfoundland; *m* 1877, Eleanor, *d* of George Thornhill, CSI. Entered Navy, 1853; Rear-Admiral, 1892; Vice-Admiral, 1898; Admiral, 1903; served White Sea, 1854; Bay of Bengal during Indian Mutiny; and with Naval Brigade in Burma; member of Committee on Heavy Guns, 1878; of War Office Committee on Explosives; also on Armour Plates and Projectiles, 1879; of Ordnance Committee, 1881; Director of Naval Intelligence, 1889–94; Commander-in-Chief Australian station, 1895–98; Commander-in-Chief China station, 1901–4; retired 1904; presided, North Sea Enquiry Commission, 1904; Admiralty Representative on Royal Patriotic Fund Corporation, 1906–12; Member of Statutory Mesopotamia Commission, 1916–17. *Publications:* The Art of Naval Warfare; Sea-Power and Other Studies,

1910; Some Recollections, 1918. *Address:* Coombe Pines, Coombe Warren. *T:* Kingston 1746.

Died 16 Aug. 1924.

BRIDGE, Sir Frederick, Kt 1897; CVO 1911 (MVO 1902); MA; MusD Oxon; FRCO; Fellow, Royal College of Music, 1921; King Edward Professor of Music, London University, since 1902; Organist Westminster Abbey, 1875–1918; retired with title Emeritus-Organist of Wesminster Abbey; Gresham Professor of Music from 1890; Conductor Royal Choral Society, 1896–1922; *b* Oldbury, Worcestershire, 5 Dec. 1844; *s* of John Bridge and Rebecca Cox; *m* 1st, 1872, Constance Ellen (*d* 1879), *d* of S. L. Moore; one *s* one *d*; 2nd, 1883, Helen Mary Flora (*d* 1905), *d* of E. Amphlett; one *d*; 3rd, 1914, Marjory Wedgwood, *d* of Reginald N. Wood, of Bignall End, Staffordshire. *Educ:* Cathedral School, Rochester. Chorister, Rochester Cathedral, 1850–59; Assistant Organist, 1865; Organist Trinity Church, Windsor, 1865–69; Organist Manchester Cathedral, 1869–75. *Publications:* Cantatas; Oratorios; Theoretical Works; Church Music; Shakespeare and Music Birthday Book; Samuel Pepys; Lover of Music, 1904; A Westminster Pilgrim, 1919; Twelve good Musicians, 1920; The Old Cryes of London, 1921, Shakesperean Music (In the Plays and early Operas), 1923, etc. *Recreations:* fishing, shooting. *Address:* Cloisters, Westminster Abbey, SW1. *T:* Victoria 3384; Cairnborrow Lodge, Glass, Scotland. *Club:* Athenæum.

Died 18 March 1924.

BRIDGEMAN, Brig.-Gen. Hon. Francis (Charles), JP Salop and Staffordshire; *b* 4 July 1846; *s* of 3rd Earl of Bradford and Selina Louisa, *y d* of 1st Lord Forester; *m* 1st, 1883, Gertrude (*d* 1911), *e d* of George Hanbury, of Blythewood, Bucks; four *s* one *d*; 2nd, 1913, Agnes Florence, *d* of late Richard Holt Briscoe. *Educ:* Harrow. Entered Scots Guards, 1865; Lieut and Capt. 1869; Capt. and Lieut-Col 1877; Colonel, 1887; retired on half-pay, 1889; retired from the Army, 1894, on retired pay; ADC to General Officer commanding Home District, 1875–76; appointed to Special Embassy to Madrid to marriage of Alphonso XII; Knight of Isabel la Catolica of Spain; served in Soudan campaign of 1885 (medal with clasp and Khedive's star). Contested (C) Stafford, 1874; Tamworth, 1878; Bolton, 1880. MP (C) for Bolton at General Elections, 1885–95. Brig.-Gen. commanding Staffordshire Volunteer Infantry Brigade, 1892–99; commanded Central London Vol. Group of Co. of London Vol. Regt, 1915. *Address:* 59 Ennismore Gardens, SW. *T:* Western 3308; The Priory, Beech Hill, Reading. *Clubs:* Carlton, Wellington.

Died 14 Sept. 1917.

BRIDGES, John Henry, MA; JP for Surrey and Co. Aberdeen; *b* 26 March 1852; *o s* of late Rev. Alexander Henry Bridges, Hon. Canon of Winchester and Rector of Beddington, Surrey, and Caroline Matilda, *d* of C. Hodgson, Treasurer of Queen Anne's Bounty; *m* 1st, 1879, Edith Isabella (*d* 1907), *y d* of late Henry Tritton, banker, 54 Lombard Street; six *s* three *d*; 2nd, 1909, Dorothy Mary, *e d* of R. B. Jacomb of 4 Wetherby Gardens, SW. *Educ:* Winchester; Oriel College, Oxford. High Sheriff of Surrey, 1919–20. Breeder of Aberdeen-Angus Cattle; Captain Oxford Univ. Assoc. Football XI, 1874–5; played in winning XI for Oxford in Association Challenge Cup; Champion Archer, 1905; has represented Surrey in cricket; Member of Royal Company of Archers, King's Body Guard for Scotland. *Recreations:* agriculture, shooting, archery. *Address:* The Court, Eastbourne; *TA:* Court, Eastbourne. *T:* Eastbourne 62; Fedderate, Aberdeenshire. *Clubs:* United University; Sussex, Eastbourne.

Died 12 Feb. 1925.

BRIDGES, Rear-Admiral Walter Bogue, FRGS, FRCI; *b* 1843; *s* of John William and Harriet Bridges of Birch, Essex, and London; *m* 1880, Annie Caroline, *d* of John and Anna Wilson of Woodlands, Victoria, Australia; one *s* four *d*. Entered Navy, 1856, as naval cadet on board the Royal Albert, flagship of Admiral Lord Lyons, Commander-in-Chief in the Black Sea and Mediterranean; afterwards served in the English Channel and North Sea, West Indies, and North America, West Coast of Africa and Australian stations, and Pacific Islands; captain, 1884; Rear-Admiral on the retired list, 1899; Fellow Royal United Service Institution. *Address:* Trawalla, Victoria, Australia. *Clubs:* United Service, London; Melbourne, Melbourne; Union, Sydney.

Died 27 Dec. 1917.

BRIERLEY, Edgar, OBE 1918; Stipendiary Magistrate for the City of Manchester since 1903; *b* 1858; 5th *s* of James Brierley, Rochdale; *m* Catharine, *d* of J. H. Lancashire, Rochdale; one *s* one *d*. *Educ:* Rugby School; University College, Oxford. Called to the Bar, 1882; Northern Circuit; Member Royal Commission on Divorce, 1909–12; Chairman Manchester Tribunal, 1915–18. *Address:* Sandfield, Rochdale.

Died 25 Jan. 1927.

BRIGGS, Hon. Sir Henry, Kt 1916; President Legislative Council, Western Australia, since 1906; *b* Kettering, 17 March 1844; *s* of George Briggs. *Educ:* Kettering; St Mark's College, Chelsea. Master in Practising School, 1865–67; Headmaster of Mottram Grammar School, 1868; founded Fremantle Grammar School, 1882; Member for West Province, 1896; Chairman of Committees, Legislative Council, 1900; President, 1906; Delegate, Australian Federal Convention, 1897–98; Past Master and PZ in Freemasonry: Member of WA Museum, Library and Art Gallery Boards; Territorial Magistrate for WA. *Address:* Fremantle, W Australia. *Club:* Freemasons', WA.

BRIGHT, James Franck, DD; *b* London, 29 May 1832; *s* of Richard Bright, MD; *m* 1864, Emmeline Theresa, *d* of Rev. E. D. Wickham, Vicar of Holmwood; four *d*. *Educ:* Rugby; University Coll., Oxford. Master at Marlborough Coll.; Head of Modern Dept there for 16 years; returned to Oxford, 1872, as History Tutor in Balliol New College and University; Fellow and Dean of University College, 1874; Hon. Fellow of Balliol, 1878; Master of University College, Oxford, 1881–1906. Lord of the Manor of Brockbury, Colwall, Hereford. *Publications:* History of England to 1900; Lives of Maria Theresa and Joseph II, 1897. *Recreations:* fishing, sketching. *Address:* Hollow Hill, Ditchingham, Norfolk. *Club:* Athenæum.

Died Oct. 1920.

BRIGHT, John Albert; *b* 1848; *e s* of late Rt Hon. John Bright and late Margaret Elizabeth, *d* of late William Leatham of Heath, Wakefield; *m* 1883, Edith Eckersley, *d* of late W. T. Shawcross of Foxholes, Rochdale; one *s* one *d*. *Educ:* Grove House School, Tottenham; University Coll., London. MP (LU) Central Birmingham, 1889–95, and (L) Oldham, 1906–10. *Address:* One Ash, Rochdale. *T:* Rochdale 541; Bright's Farm, Christian Malford, Wilts; Monkshill, Monkton Combe, Somerset. *Club:* Reform.

Died 11 Nov. 1924.

BRIGHT, Sir Joseph, Kt 1906; Alderman of the City of Nottingham, since 1896; *b* 1849; *s* of Joseph Bright of Nottingham; *m* 1879, Frances Ellen (*d* 1906), *d* of Nathaniel Dickinson of Nottingham; two *s* two *d*. *Educ:* Sherwood House School, Nottingham. Solicitor, 1871; Sheriff of Nottingham, 1892; Mayor, 1894, 1895 and 1904; JP 1896; Chairman Nottingham University College, 1895–1911. *Recreation:* golf. *Address:* Park, Nottingham. *T:* 646. *Club:* National Liberal.

Died 3 July 1918.

BRIGHTMORE, A. W., DSc; MInstCE; Engineering Inspector, Ministry of Health, Whitehall; *b* 9 May 1864; *s* of late Henry Brightmore of Bowdon; *m* 1894, Fanny Alexandra, *y d* of late J. McM. Cannon, of Rock Ferry, Cheshire. *Educ:* The Owens College, Manchester. Resident Engineer for late Dr G. F. Deacon on part of the Liverpool (Vyrnwy) Waterworks; afterwards Resident Engineer for late James Mansergh, FRS, on part of the Birmingham (Elan) Water Supply; Professor of Structural Engineering, Royal Indian Engineering College, Coopers Hill, Staines, 1899–1907. *Publications:* Waterworks Engineering, with J. H. T. Tudsbery, DSc, MInstCE, 1893; Structural Engineering, 1908. *Address:* Egham Hill, Surrey.

Died 20 April 1927.

BRINDLE, Rt. Rev. Robert, DSO; Provost of Westminster Cathedral, since 1901; *b* 1837. Consecrated March 1899 as Bishop Auxiliary to Cardinal Vaughan, Archbishop of Westminster; retired Army Chaplain; DSO conferred for services in Egypt and Soudan, including battles of Atbara and Khartoum; recipient of many medals and clasps, and many times mentioned in despatches. RC Bishop of Nottingham, 1901–16. *Address:* Bishop's House, Nottingham.

Died 27 June 1916.

BRINKLEY, Captain John Turner, OBE 1925; Chief Constable of Warwickshire; *b* 1855; *e s* of late Walter Stephens Brinkley, of Knockmaroon House, Co. Dublin; *m* Mary (*d* 1923), *d* of late General Henry Alexander Carleton, CB, of Clare, Co. Tipperary; one *d*. *Educ:* Clifton; Pembroke College, Cambridge. Captain North Staffordshire Regt. *Address:* Wasperton House, near Warwick. *Club:* Naval and Military.

Died 14 Dec. 1928.

BRINSON, J. Paul, RBA; landscape painter. Exhibitor at the Royal Academy, International Society, Royal Institute of Painters in Water-Colours, etc; Secretary of the British Water-Colour Society. *Address:* West Woodlands, Reading.

Died 21 Dec. 1927.

BRISCO, Sir Hylton Ralph, 5th Bt, *cr* 1782; *b* 24 Sept. 1871; *s* of 4th Bt and Mary, *d* of Sir W. H. Feilden, 2nd Bt; *S* father, 1909;

m 1904, Lilian Mabel (who div. him, 1915), *d* of James King and *niece* of Lucy, Countess of Egmont; 2nd, 1916, Grace (whom he divorced, 1921), *d* of late Henry Vaughan. Owned about 4,000 acres. *Heir: cousin* Aubrey Hylton Brisco, *b* 11 Dec. 1873. *Address:* Coghurst Hall, Hastings, Sussex. *Clubs:* Junior Carlton, Wellington.

Died 29 Jan. 1922.

BRISCOE, Sir Alfred Leigh, 2nd Bt, *cr* 1910; JP; Barrister; *b* 26 April 1870; *s* of Sir John James Briscoe, 1st Bt and Ellen (*d* 1910), *o d* of A. Charlton, Oak House, Altrincham; *S* father, 1919; *m* 1910, Margaret Mackie, *d* of late Thomas Sinclair of Conyair, Harray, Orkney; no *c. Educ:* Corpus Christi College, Oxford. *Heir: brother* Dr John Charlton Briscoe, *b* 8 April 1874. *Address:* 26 Buckingham Mansions, West Hampstead, NW; 8 Old Square, Lincoln's Inn, WC2. *T:* Holborn 899. *Died 13 May 1921.*

BRISCOE, Major Edward William; Royal Artillery (retired); *b* 29 Sept. 1857; 2nd and *e* surv. *s* of late Henry Briscoe, MD, RA; *m* 1887, Helen Mary, *d* of late Surg.-Colonel Edmund Greswold McDowell, CB. *Educ:* Royal Military Academy, Woolwich. Lieut Royal Artillery, 1877; retired as Major, 1895; appointed to the Prison Service, 1895; and served as Deputy-Governor of Portland Prison, and afterwards as Governor of Lincoln, Borstal, and Portland prisons; Inspector of Prisons, 1907; Commissioner, 1916; retired, 1921; a Member of the Home Office Committee for the Employment of Conscientious Objectors, 1916–19; Member of Advisory Committee to Home Secretary at HM Preventive Detention Prison at Camp Hill, IW. *Club:* Junior United Service. *Died 27 Nov. 1928.*

BRISCOE, Sir John James, 1st Bt, *cr* 1910; JP, DL; *b* 6 Dec. 1836; *s* of John and Elizabeth Briscoe; *m* 1863, Ellen (*d* 1910), *o d* of A. Charlton, Oak House, Altrincham; four *s* three *d.* Sheriff of Cambridgeshire and Hunts, 1888. *Heir: s* Alfred Leigh Briscoe, JP, Barrister [*b* 26 April 1870; *m* 1910, Margaret Mackie, *d* of late Thomas Sinclair of Conyair, Harray, Orkney. *Address:* 26 Buckingham Mansions, West Hampstead, NW; 8 Old Square, Lincoln's Inn]. *Address:* Bourn Hall, Cambridgeshire. *Club:* National.

Died 1 May 1919.

BRISCOE, John Potter, FRSL, FRHistS, Hon. FLA; City Librarian of Nottingham, 1869–1916; Consulting City Librarian, 1917; Vice-President of Library Association, 1891–1920, of which he was an original member; *b* Lever Bridge, near Bolton, 20 July 1848; *e s* of late John Daly Briscoe; *m* 1st, Elizabeth Baxter, Bolton; 2nd, Sophia Wallis, Nottingham; one *s. Educ:* Bolton; by father. Engaged in tuition at Bolton, 1862–66; Assistant Borough Librarian at Bolton, 1866–69; Member of Council of Thoroton Society. *Publications:* Curiosities of the Belfry; Bypaths of Nottinghamshire History; Chapters of Nottinghamshire History; Gleanings from God's Acre; Nottinghamshire Facts and Fictions, two series; Sonnets and Songs of Robert Millhouse; Old Nottinghamshire, 2 vols; Stories about the Midlands; Nottinghamshire and Derbyshire at the Dawn of the 20th Century; A Great Masonic Writer (Dr Oliver), and other Masonic publications; Editor of The Bibelots series, 29 vols; Sportsman's Classics, 3 vols; Nottinghamshire and Derbyshire Notes and Queries, 6 vols; Tudor and Stuart Love Songs; Mitford's Stories of Village and Town Life; Antiquarian Editor of Nottinghamshire Guardian for twenty-one years. *Recreations:* literary work, gardening, snapshotting. *Address:* 38 Addison Street, Nottingham.

Died 7 Jan. 1926.

BRISSON, Adolphe; Commandeur Légion d'Honneur; Président d'honneur de la Critique; late Dramatic Critic of Le Temps; Directeur des Annales politiques et Littéraires; *m* Madeleine Sarcey; four *c. Educ:* Ecole Monge; Lycée Condorcet. *Publications:* Portraits intimes; Florise Bonheur; L'Envers de la gloire; Paris intime; Coindu Parnasse; Le Théâtre et les mœurs; Nos humoristes; Pointes sèches; La Comédie littéraire; Les Prophêtes; Le Théâtre contemporain (9 vols) *Address:* 5 rue la Bruyère, Paris. *Died 28 Aug. 1925.*

BRISTOL, Hon. Edmund, PC (Canada) 1921; KC 1908; Member House of Commons of Canada for Centre Toronto since 1905; *b* 4 Sept. 1861; *m* 1889, Dorothy, *d* of late Hon. Chief Justice Armour. *Educ:* Toronto University (BA). Barrister, 1886; Director Dubilier Condenser and Radio Corporation; Associate Counsel with legal firm of Bain, Bicknell, Macdonnell & Gordon; Cabinet Minister of the Government of the Dominion of Canada, without portfolio, 1921. *Recreations:* yachting, hunting, golf. *Address:* 179 Beverley Street, Toronto. *Clubs:* Constitutional; York, Toronto, Albany, Hunt, Royal Canadian Yacht, Toronto; Mount Royal, Montreal; Rideau, Ottawa. *Died 14 July 1927.*

BRITTAIN, William Henry, JP; FRGS, FLA; Member of the Sheffield City Council since 1871 (the senior member); *b* 2 April 1835; *s* of late W. Swann Brittain of Sheffield and Mary, *d* of Rev. T. Bosher of Brightwell, Berks; *m* 1871, Fanny, *o d* of late J. J. Mellor of Prestbury, Cheshire; two *s* two *d.* Chairman of the Town Trustees, Sheffield; Mayor, 1883–84 and 1884–85; entertained Prince Albert Victor at Storth Oaks on his first public visit, 1885; The Master Cutler of Sheffield, 1878 and 1879; President of the Chamber of Commerce, 1892–95; British Commissioner to Antwerp Exhibition, 1894, and to Brussels Exhibition, 1897; Chairman Dore and Chinley Railway Company; Member of the Archæological Association; Member of the General Committee of the British Association since 1878; Past President of the Museums Association, and of the Public Libraries Association; Past Master of many lodges; Past Grand Warden, W Yorks, and Past GSB (England). *Recreations:* literature, music, collecting objects of arts and antiquity. *Address:* Storth Oaks, near Sheffield. *TA:* Alma Sheffield. *T:* Broomhill 16, Sheffield. *M:* LN 3544. *Clubs:* Royal Societies; Sheffield.

Died 29 June 1922.

BRITTEN, James; Vice-President Catholic Truth Society (Hon. Secretary, 1884–1922); *b* Chelsea, 3 May 1846. *Educ:* private schools. Assistant in Kew Herbarium, 1869; in Department of Botany, British Museum, 1871–1909; created Knight of St Gregory by Leo XIII, 1897, and Knight Commander, con placca, 1917; Fellow of Linnean Society, 1870; original member of Folklore, English Dialect, Bibliographical and Catholic Record Societies. *Publications:* Dictionary of English Plant-Names (with R. Holland), 1878–86; European Ferns, 1879–81; Old Country and Farming Words, 1880; Biographical Dictionary of English and Irish Botanists (with G. S. Boulger), 1893; Protestant Fiction, 1896, 1899; Illustrations of Australian Plants collected by Banks and Solander, 1900–1905; edited Aubrey's Remaines of Gentilisme, 1880; Turner's Names of Herbes, 1881; editor League of Cross Magazine, 1884–87; Nature Notes, 1890–97; Journal of Botany since 1880; Catholic Book-Notes, 1898–1922; numerous pamphlets and contributions to religious, literary and scientific journals. *Recreations:* editing, music, pictures. *Address:* 41 Boston Road, Brentford, Middlesex. *Club:* Reform.

Died 8 Oct. 1924.

BRITTON, Hon. Byron Moffat, KC; Justice of the Supreme Court of Judicature, Ontario; Judge of King's Bench Division, High Court of Justice; *b* Gananoque, County of Leeds, 3 Sept. 1833; *m* 1863, Mary Eliza, *d* of late Hon. L. H. Holton; one *s* six *d. Educ:* Victoria University. Barrister; KC; Mayor of Kingston; Chairman Public School Board; County Crown Attorney; Kingston Bencher of Law Society of Upper Canada; Drainage Referee of Ontario; Member House of Commons for Kingston; Director of National Trust Company. *Address:* Osgoode Hall, Toronto. *Clubs:* Frontenac, Kingston; York, Toronto. *Died 14 Jan. 1921.*

BROADBENT, A., RBS. *Address:* 436 Fulham Road, SW6. *Died Sept. 1919.*

BROADBENT, Benjamin, CBE 1918; JP; MA, LLD; Freeman of the Borough of Huddersfield, 1918; Fellow of King's College, London; Hon. Member American Child Welfare Association; *b* 7 May 1850; 6th *s* of John Broadbent, Longwood Edge, Huddersfield; *m* 1880, Louisa Ann, *d* of William Keighley, Huddersfield; one *s. Educ:* Huddersfield College; King's College, London; Queen's College, Oxford. Member of Huddersfield Corporation, 1886–1913; Chairman of Health Committee; Mayor of Huddersfield, 1904–5 and 1905–6; succeeded to business of Woollen Merchant, established by grandfather before 1796, with younger brother as partner; Millowner and Director of Parkwood Mills Co., Ltd; Longwood Finishing Co., Ltd; Longwood Engineering Co., Ltd. *Publications:* various articles and papers connected with public health administration, and in particular with the prevention of infantile mortality and the promotion of the welfare of mothers and children. *Recreations:* reading, gardening, walking. *Address:* Gatesgarth, Lindley, Huddersfield. *TA:* Gatesgarth, Lindley. *T:* 1286. *Clubs:* Cavendish, Overseas; Huddersfield.

Died 25 June 1925.

BROADFOOT, Col Archibald, CB 1894; *b* 15 Jan. 1843; 2nd *s* of late Alexander Broadfoot, Amberley, New Zealand, and Margaret, *d* of William Douglas. *Educ:* Royal Academy, Woolwich. Lieut RA 1864; Lieut RHA 1875; Captain RA 1877; Captain RHA 1881; Brevet Major, 1881; Major RA 1884; Major RHA 1886; Lieut-Colonel RA 1892; Lieut-Col RHA 1893; Colonel, 1896; retired, 1898; served Bhootan, 1865–66 (medal with clasp); Abyssinia, 1868 (medal); Afghanistan, 1878–79–80 (medal with three clasps, Brevet Major); Mahsoud Waziri Expedition, 1881; Annexation of Upper Burmah,

1885–86 (clasp). *Recreations:* riding, fishing, shooting. *Address:* Duncree, Newton Stewart, NB.

Died 15 March 1926.

BROADFOOT, Major William; Royal Engineers (retired); *b* 1841; *e s* of the late Alexander Broadfoot, and late Margaret, *d* of late William Douglas; *m* 1870, Esther Sutherland, *d* of late Dr A. Broadfoot; no *c. Educ:* privately; Addiscombe College. Lieutenant, RE, 1860; Captain, 1874; Major, on retirement, 1881; served with the Hazara Field Force (Black Mountain) 1868 (medal with clasp); served in civil capacity in Irrigation Department of Punjab, 1864–68; Assistant Secretary to Punjab Government, 1868–78; since retirement engaged chiefly in literary work, scientific geography, the study of small arms, ammunition, and bullet wounds, municipal management and public health; was Councillor, Borough of Paddington, 1902; referee of Royal Geographical Society on Afghanistan, Baluchistan, and India. *Publications:* The Career of Major George Broadfoot, CB, 1888; Billiards, 1896, revised 1906, in Badminton Library; paper on Pests of the Ghilzi Country, Afghanistan; articles in Quarterly, National, and Historical Reviews; in Blackwood's and Badminton Magazines; in Athenæum, Times, Encyclopædia Britannica, etc. *Recreations:* sport, travel, rowing, landscape painting in watercolour, billiards. *Address:* 103 Gloucester Terrace, W2. *Club:* Naval and Military.

Died 8 April, 1922.

BROADHURST, Sir Edward Tootal, 1st Bt, *cr* 1918; DL, JP; *b* 19 Aug. 1858; 2nd *s* of Henry Tootal Broadhurst, of Woodhill, Prestwich, Manchester; *m* 1887, Charlotte Jane, *y d* of Thomas Ashton of Ford Bank, Didsbury, Manchester; no *c. Educ:* Dr Huntingford's Eagle House, Wimbledon; Winchester. In business in Manchester since 1876; President Manchester Athenæum; President Warehousemen and Clerks' Orphan Schools; Chairman Manchester and Liverpool District Bank; Director London and North Western Railway; High Sheriff of Lancs, 1906–7. *Heir:* none. *Address:* The Manor House, North Rode, Congleton. *Clubs:* Conservative, Garrick.

Died 2 Feb. 1922 (ext).

BROADHURST, Mary Adelaide, MA (London); President of National Political League since its organisation in 1911; *d* of late William Broadhurst, CC, Manchester. *Educ:* London University; MA degree in Mental and Moral Science. One of the first to organise Physical Science Laboratories in Girls' Secondary Schools, and other educational movements; founder of the National Political League in association with Miss Margaret Milne Farquharson; on the outbreak of war in 1914 was the originator of the Women's Land Army, and pioneered its work during the war, when it was the means of sending over 30,000 women as workers on the land, and developing food production centres, etc; as President of the League promoted the formation of the American Women's Land Army; was leader in organising the political work of the National Political League after the war, in particular the National Campaign to rouse the spirit of the nation to an understanding of the Communist forces that menaced it, and in defence of its own ideals of national freedom; organised also the movement in England for the promotion of Anglo-Arab friendship and Arab development; took an active part in work for the protection of British Empire interests and against Bolshevist intrigues in the Middle East. *Address:* Bank Buildings, 16 St James's Street, SW1; 22 Hornton Court, Kensington, W8. *T:* Gerrard 0334; Regent 2944. *Died 8 Dec. 1928.*

BROADLEY, Alexander Meyrick; lawyer, author, journalist, and collector; *b* 19 July 1847; *e s* of late Rev. A. Broadley, Canon of Salisbury, and late Frances Jane, *y d* of late Thomas Meyrick, of Bush, Pembrokeshire. *Educ:* Warminster and Marlborough Grammar Schools; Switzerland. Called to Bar, Lincoln's Inn, 1869; began to practise as an advocate in Tunis, 1873; represented the Bey of Tunis in his differences with the French Republic, 1880–81; special correspondent of Times in Tunis, 1881, and Egypt, 1882; Senior Counsel of Arabi Pacha and the other state-prisoners at Cairo, Dec. 1882; made an Advocate of the French Bar by decree of President of Republic, 1883; for many years held the appointment of Standing Counsel to the ex-Khedive Ismail Pacha of Egypt. *Publications:* History of Freemasonry in Malta and Tunis, 1880; Tunis Past and Present, 2 vols, 1882; How we defended Arabi, 1883; (joint) The Three Dorset Captains at Trafalgar, 1906; The Boyhood of a Great King, 1906; The History of Freemasonry in West Dorset, 1907; (joint) Napoleon and the Invasion of England, 1907, 2 vols; (joint) Nelson's Hardy, 1907; (joint) Dumouriez and the Defence of England against Napoleon, 1908; (joint) Doctor Johnson and Mrs Thrale, 1909; (joint) Bath Pageant, 1909; (joint) The War in Wexford, 1910; Chats on Autographs, 1910; Napoleon in Caricature, 2 vols, 1910; West Dorset Pageant, 1911; History of Garrards, 1731–1911, 1911; The Royal

Miracle, 1912; (joint) The Romance of an Elderly Poet; (joint) The Beautiful Lady Craven, 2 vols; The Journal of a British Chaplain in Paris during the Peace Negotiations of 1801–2; The Ship Beautiful, Art and the Aquitania, 1914; contributions to numerous reviews and newspapers, etc. *Recreations:* collections of portraits, prints, medals, and MSS relating to Napoleon, Nelson, Dorset history, Freemasonry, Bath, the drama, caricature, Boscobel, cricket, aviation, and many other subjects; extra-illustrated some fifty volumes. *Address:* The Knapp, Bradpole, Bridport, Dorset. *Club:* Junior Conservative.

Died 16 April 1916.

BROADWOOD, Brig.-Gen. Arthur, CVO 1905; *b* 1849; *s* of late Henry Broadwood, MP for Bridgwater; *m* 1873, Mary Frances (*d* 1925), *d* of the late Edward Richard Meade. *Educ:* Trinity Hall, Cambridge. Entered Scots Guards, 1869; Captain, 1871; Lieut-Col, 1881; Col, 1902 (retired, 1906); Hon. Brig.-Gen., 1912; served with Soudan Expedition, 1885 (medal with clasp, bronze star); Commandant at School of Instruction for Auxiliary Forces, Wellington Barracks, 1884–86, and at School of Instruction for Mil. and Vol. there, 1900; in command of Royal Guards Reserve Regt, 1900–1, and of 1st Regt Dist, 1901–5; Brig.-Gen. commanding Lowland Grouped Regt Dist, Scottish Command, 1905–6; in command of a Vol. Infantry Brigade, 1906–8; East Midland TF Brigade, 1908–11; specially employed on Home Defence, 1914–16. *Address:* 52 Wilbury Road, Hove. *Club:* Carlton.

Died 2 Jan. 1928.

BROADWOOD, Lt-Gen. Robert George, CB 1900; retired; late commanding troops in South China, 1906; Brigadier-General commanding Orange River Colony District, 1904–6; Aide-de-camp to the King; *b* 14 March 1862; *s* of late Thomas Broadwood of Holmbush Park, Surrey. Entered army, 12th Lancers, 1881; Lt-Col 1897; served Dongola Expeditionary Force, 1896 (despatches, brevet of Lieut-Col, British medal, Khedive's medal with two clasps); Egyptian War, 1898, including Atbara (despatches) and Khartoum (despatches, brevet of Col, Osmanieh, British medal, three clasps to Khedive's medal); served South Africa, 1899–1902 (despatches twice, Queen's medal and six clasps, King's medal and two clasps); commanding troops in Natal, 1903–4. *Address:* 94 Piccadilly, W.

Died 21 June 1917.

BROCK, Sir Thomas, KCB 1911; RA 1891 (ARA 1883); RSA (hon. 1910); ARIBA (hon. 1908); DCL Oxford; sculptor; Membre d'honneur de la Société des Artistes français; *b* 1847; *s* of William Brock, Worcester; *m* 1869, Mary Hannah, *o c* of late Richard Sumner of Nottingham. *Educ:* under Foley. *Works:* The Moment of Peril; The Genius of Poverty; Eve; Edward the Black Prince; busts of Queen Victoria and Lord Leighton; statues of Sir Richard Owen and Dr Philpott, Bishop of Worcester; sepulchral monument to Lord Leighton in St Paul's; memorial statues of Queen Victoria; designer and sculptor the Queen Victoria Memorial, Buckingham Palace. *Address:* 30 Osnaburgh Street, Regent's Park, NW; Merrieweathers, Mayfield, Sussex. *Club:* Athenæum.

Died 22 Aug. 1922.

BROCKLEBANK, Thomas, JP, DL; *b* 1841; 2nd *s* of late Ralph Brocklebank, JP and DL, Lancashire, and Eliza Ann, *d* of Richard Moon of Liverpool; *m* 1867, Mary Petrena, *d* of Henry Royds of Elm House, Wavertree, JP, Lancashire; five *s. Educ:* Sir R. Cholmeley's School, Highgate. High Sheriff, Cheshire, 1901; patron of four livings. *Address:* Wateringbury Place, Kent; Villa San Leonardo, Florence, Italy. *M:* LD 7648. *Clubs:* Conservative, Constitutional, Ranelagh, Burlington Fine Arts.

Died 16 Feb. 1919.

BROCKWELL, Rev. Canon John Cornthwaite, MA; Vicar of Thorpe Salvin, Worksop, 1917–24; Canon of Sheffield Cathedral, 1914; *b* 25 March 1843; *s* of Josiah Brockwell, a London merchant; *m* 1868, Clara Walter, *d* of Walter Brodie, and *g g d* of John Walter; four *s* three *d. Educ:* University College School, London; Christchurch, Oxford. Formerly Curate to Dr Llewelyn Davies at Christchurch, St Marylebone, 1866; also Curate of St Mary Magdalen's, Paddington, 1867, and of Honiton, Devon, 1868; Vicar of Owston, Yorkshire, 1869. *Recreations:* rowing, cycling. *Address:* Ivy House, Norton, Doncaster.

Died 25 Nov. 1927.

BRODEUR, Hon. Louis Philippe, LLD Laval; PC; a Judge of the Supreme Court of Canada since 1911; *b* Beloeil, Province of Quebec, 21 Aug. 1862; *s* of Toussaint Brodeur, a patriot of 1837, and of Justine Lambert; *m* 1887, Emma, *d* of J. R. Brillon, Notary, of Beloeil; four *s* one *d. Educ:* College of St Hyacinthe and Laval University. Called to Bar, 1884; KC 1899; editor of Le Soir, 1896; elected to House of Commons for Rouville, 1891, 1896, 1900, 1904, 1908; Deputy-Speaker of the House of Commons, 1896–1900; Speaker, 1900–4; Minister of Inland Revenue, 1904–6; Minister of Marine and Fisheries, Dominion Government, 1906–11; introduced a Bill against the American Tobacco Trust, and this legislation had the desired effect of putting an end to the American methods which the Tobacco Company wanted to establish in Canada; a member of the Imperial Conferences of 1907 and 1911, and one of the Ministers who negotiated the Franco-Canadian Treaty of 1907; represented Canada at the Imperial Defence Conference of 1909; author of the first Naval Bill introduced in the Canadian Parliament (1910), and when the Department of the Naval Service was organised he was put in charge of it; Canada's representative at the Washington Conference held in pursuance of the decision of the Hague Tribunal on the North Atlantic fisheries; took keen interest in navigation in all Canadian waters, and by establishment of innumerable aids to navigation along the St Lawrence made that river navigable under all conditions, whether during night or day or in foggy weather. *Address:* Ottawa, Canada. *Clubs:* Hunt, Rideau, Rivermead, Ottawa; Country, Winchester, Montreal.   *Died 2 Jan. 1924.*

BRODIE, George Bernard, MD; Physician to Queen Charlotte's Hospital; Consulting Physician Accoucheur to St George's Hanover Square Dispensary; *b* 6 Aug. 1839; *s* of late Charles George Brodie, Salisbury; *m* 1893, Mary, *d* of late James Maxwell, Petrograd; three *s* one *d. Address:* 65 Princes Gate, SW; Woodbury, Farley Hill, Reading. *Club:* Athenæum.

Died 27 May 1919.

BRODIE, Thomas Gregor, FRS 1904; FRSC; Professor of Physiology, Toronto University, since 1908; Captain, Canadian Army Medical Corps, No 4 Canadian General Hospital; *b* Northampton, 8 Feb. 1866; 2nd *s* of late Rev. Alexander Brodie, Vicar of Grandborough; *m*; three *s. Educ:* King's College School, London; St John's College, Cambridge; King's College, London. Demonstrator of Physiology, King's College, London, 1890; Senior Demonstrator of Physiology, London Hosp. Med. School, 1894; Lecturer on Physiology, St Thomas's Hosp. Med. School, 1895; Director of the Research Laboratories of the Royal Colleges of Physicians and Surgeons, London, 1899; Fellow of King's College, London; Professor-Superintendent, Brown Animal Sanatory Institution, University of London, 1903–9; Professor of Physiology, Royal Veterinary Coll., London, 1903–9; Lecturer on Physiology, London School of Medicine for Women, 1899–1909; Croonian Lecturer, Royal Society. *Publications:* Essentials of Experimental Physiology; and numerous papers in scientific journals. *Recreation:* golf. *Address:* The University, Toronto. *Club:* Devonshire.

Died 20 Aug. 1916.

BRODIE, Brevet Major (Acting Lt-Col) Walter Lorrain, VC 1914; MC; 2nd Battalion Highland Light Infantry; *b* 28 July 1884. Entered army, 1904; served European War, 1914–17 (VC, MC); Brevet Major, 1918. *Address:* 23 Belgrave Crescent, Edinburgh.

Died 23 Aug. 1918.

BRODRICK, Sir Thomas, Kt 1922; late Secretary and Chief Accountant, Co-operative Wholesale Society, Ltd; *b* Scarborough, Yorks, March 1856; *s* of Patrick Brodrick and Bessie Donlon; *m* 1884, Margaret Kelly; two *s* two *d. Educ:* Private School, Scarborough. Commenced with Co-operative Wholesale Society Ltd as Junior Clerk, 1872; retired, 1923; Member of Committees on Post Office Wages and Food Prices. *Address:* Woodlands, Victoria Crescent, Eccles. *T:* Eccles 8.   *Died 26 Oct. 1925.*

BROMFIELD, Rev. George Henry Worth, MA; Vicar, St Mary, Princes Road, Lambeth, 1873–1919; Rural Dean of Lambeth, 1881–1912; Hon. Canon of Southwark Cathedral; *b* 29 May 1842; *s* of Henry Jenkins Bromfield, Causton, Dunchurch, Warwickshire. *Educ:* Rugby; University Coll., Oxford. Ordained to the curacy of St Mary, Lambeth, 1867. *Address:* St Botolph's Road, Worthing.

Died 4 July 1920.

BROMFIELD, Major Harry Hickman, DSO 1900; of Newnham Hall, Northamptonshire; Chief Constable Radnorshire; *b* 29 Jan. 1869; *e s* of Henry Bromfield (*d* 1888), of Newnham Hall and Mary Elizabeth, *e d* of late John Colthurst of Chew Court, Somersetshire; *m* 1906, Ethel Philippa, *e d* of Sir Charles Philipps, 1st Bt; one *s. Educ:* Malvern; Hertford College, Oxford. Capt. and Hon. Major 3rd Batt. S Wales Borderers; served with 2nd S Wales Borderers in S Africa, 1900–1 (despatches, DSO); afterwards served with 3rd S Wales Borderers, 1901–2; rejoined 9th Service Batt. S Wales Borderers,

1915, and transferred to the 1st Batt. Welsh Guards, 1915. *Address:* The Lee, Knighton; County Constabulary Headquarters, Llandrindod Wells, Radnorshire. *Clubs:* Guards, Junior Carlton.

Died Sept. 1916.

BROMHEAD, Col Charles James, CB 1893; *b* 15 Sept. 1840; *s* of Sir Edmund de Gonville Bromhead, 3rd Bt; *m* 1876, Alice Marie, *d* of late Thomas Freckleton; one *s.* Served in Ashanti, Zulu, and Burmese Wars; in command of the 24th Regimental District, 1892–97; JP Denbighshire. *Address:* Plâs Drâw, Ruthin.

Died 24 Dec. 1922.

BROOK, Edward Jonas, JP, County of Dumfries; *b* 13 March 1865; *e s* of Edward Brook and Emma Brooke; *m* 1905, Jessie Elizabeth, *y d* of late John Bell-Irving of White Hill. *Educ:* Radley; Jesus College, Cambridge. Director Glasgow and South-Western Railway. *Recreations:* hunting, shooting, fishing. *Address:* Hoddom Castle, Ecclefechan, NB. *Clubs:* Boodle's, Carlton.

Died 17 July 1924.

BROOK, Herbert Arthur, ISO 1905; JP; *b* 31 Jan. 1855; *s* of late Joshua Anderson Brook and Eliza Beresford Wylly; *m* 1883, Mary Elizabeth Brace; one *s. Educ:* Nassau Grammar School, New Providence, Bahamas. Librarian, Nassau Public Library, 1875–79; Clerk to Police Office, 1879–83; Chief Clerk in Colonial Secretary's Department, Bahamas, Clerk to Board of Public Works, 1883–87; Registrar of Records, Bahamas, 1887–1911; retired 1911; superintended Bahamas Census, 1891 and 1901; sometime Army Dist Paymaster, Bahamas. *Address:* 34 Queen Street, Nassau, New Providence, Bahamas.

Died 25 Jan. 1925.

BROOKE, Emma Frances; novelist; *b* Cheshire; descended from old yeoman family on the mother's side, and on the father's side an old Yorkshire family; unmarried. *Educ:* Newnham Coll., Cambridge. Came to London, 1879; belonged to the Fabian Society since its beginning and formerly a student of London School of Economics. *Publications:* A Superfluous Woman, 1894; Transition, 1895; Life the Accuser, 1896; The Confession of Stephen Whapshare, 1898; A Tabulation of European Factory Acts, in so far as they relate to the hours of labour, and special regulations for women and children, 1898; The Engrafted Rose, 1900; The Poet's Child; Twins of Skirlaugh Hall, 1903; Susan Wooed and Susan Won, 1905; Sir Elyot of the Woods, 1907; The Story of Hauksgarth Farm, 1909; The House of Robershaye, 1912. *Recreations:* walking, the study of bird life, sitting over the fire with a friend or a book, hearing clever people talk.

Died 28 Nov. 1926.

BROOKE, Rt. Rev. Francis Key, DD; Missionary Bishop of Oklahoma since 1893; *b* Gambier, Ohio, 2 Nov. 1852; *s* of Rev. J. T. Brooke, DD, and Louisa R. Hunter; *m* 1881, Mildred R. Baldwin; four *d. Educ:* Kenyon Coll., Gambier, Ohio, USA. Deacon, 1875; Priest, 1877; Clerical Charges at College Hill, Portsmouth, Piqua and Sandusky in Ohio, also in St Louis, Mo, and Atchison, Kans. *Publications:* official reports, charges, etc, and a few sermons. *Address:* 427 N 9th Street, Oklahoma City, Oklahoma, USA.

Died 22 Oct. 1918.

BROOKE, Rt. Hon. Frank, PC; DL; JP; Chairman Dublin and South-Eastern Railway; Chairman Irish Branch of Norwich Union Society, National Bank; Commissioner of Irish Lights; Steward of Turf Club; *b* 1851; *y s* of George Brooke and the Lady A. Brooke of Ashbrooke, Brookbore, Co. Fermanagh; *m* Alice Mary (*d* 1909), *d* of Very Rev. W. Ogle Moore, Dean of Clogher; two *s* one *d. Educ:* private school. Joined Royal Navy, 1865; retired as Lieutenant, 1877; contested S Fermanagh twice in Unionist interest; Land Agent of Fitzwilliam Estates in Ireland. *Recreations:* shooting, hunting. *Address:* Ardeen, Shillelagh, Co. Wicklow. *Clubs:* Bachelors'; Kildare Street, Dublin; Royal St George Yacht, Kingstown.

Died 30 July 1920.

BROOKE, Temp. Lt-Col George Frank, DSO 1917; retired list; late Connaught Rangers; *b* 30 Oct. 1878; *e s* of Rt Hon. Frank Brooke, RN, and Alice Mary, *d* of Very Rev. W. Ogle Moore, Dean of Clogher; *m* 1907, Theodora Olivia, *d* of Richard Meredith Jackson, Natal; two *s.* Served S Africa, 1899–1900 (severely wounded, medal with clasp); European War (despatches thrice, DSO); ADC to GOC Dublin, and to GOC Cape Colony. *Address:* Saxenberg, Kuils River, Cape Province, S Africa. *Club:* Army and Navy.

BROOKE, Sir George Frederick, 1st Bt, *cr* 1903; DL; *b* 13 Aug. 1849; *s* of late Francis R. Brooke of Summerton, and Hon. Henrietta (*d* 1911), *d* of 3rd Viscount Monck; *m* 1st, 1875, Annie (*d* 1877), *d* of

Geoffrey J. Shakerley (one *s* one *d* decd); 2nd, 1881, Emily Alma (*d* 1910), *d* of Augustine H. Barton; seven *s* two *d*. *Educ:* Eton; Trinity Coll., Camb. DL City Dublin; JP Co. Wexford; High Sheriff, 1882; JP Co. Dublin; High Sheriff, 1898; Director (Governor, 1904–6) of Bank of Ireland since 1891. Protestant (Church of Ireland). Owned 6,500 acres. *Heir: s* Francis Hugh Brooke, Capt. South Irish Horse, late 60th King's Regt Rifles [*b* 10 Nov. 1882; *m* 1915, Mabel, *y d* of late Sir John Arnott, 1st Bt, and Lady FitzGerald Arnott]. *Address:* Pickering, Celbridge, Co. Kildare. *Clubs:* Carlton; Kildare Street, Sackville Street, Dublin.   *Died 21 Aug. 1926.*

BROOKE, Captain Sir Harry Vesey, KBE 1920; JP; DL; *b* 23 Sept. 1845; 2nd *s* of late Sir Arthur Brinsley Brooke, 2nd Bt, MP of Colebrooke, Co. Fermanagh, Ireland, and Hon. Henrietta Julia Anson, Maid of Honour to HM Queen Victoria, 1839–42; *m* 1879, Patricia, *o c* of late J. G. Moir Byres of Tonley, Aberdeenshire; one *s* two *d* (and four *s* decd). *Educ:* Sandhurst. Served in 92nd Gordon Highlanders, 1864–79. *Recreations:* shooting, fishing, golfing, etc. *Address:* Fairley, Countess-walls, Aberdeenshire. *Clubs:* Naval and Military; Royal Northern, Aberdeen.
                                     Died 11 June 1921.

BROOKE, Rev. James Mark Saurin, MA; FRGS, FRBS; Rector of St Mary Woolnoth, and St Mary Woolchurch Haw, Lombard Street; *b* Warrenpoint, 23 April 1842; 2nd *s* of Canon Brooke and Lucy, *d* of Rt Rev. James Saurin, Bishop of Dromore; *m* Amy, *o c* of John Stanford, Bridge Place, Suffolk; one *s* four *d*. *Educ:* Leicester; Trin. Coll., Dublin. Received 1st class certificate extra at School of Musketry, Fleetwood, 1865. Served in 1st Batt. 17th Foot of which was Assistant and Acting Instructor of Musketry in 1865; took Holy Orders, 1867; travelled in Europe, Asia Minor, Palestine, Egypt, North of Africa, West Indies, Bahamas, etc; Fellow of Sion College; Fellow of Royal Botanic Society; patron of one living; Lord of the Manors of Bressingham, Norfolk, of Badingham Hall, Colston Hall, Peasenhall, Southolt, Ufford, Woodbridge, etc, Suffolk; Hon. Chaplain to Worshipful Company of Makers of Playing Cards. *Publications:* Heart be Still, 1879; Transcript of Registers of St Mary Woolnoth, with History of Church, 1886; Under the Lantern, 1888; Opus Consummavi, 1891; A Stirlingshire Pastoral; Hymns for Special Occasions, 1894; Do we believe?; Unity and Wisdom, 1908; numerous articles, reviews, poems. *Recreations:* botany, fishing. *Address:* 20 Gledhow Gardens, SW. *T:* Kensington 1702. *Club:* United Service.   *Died 20 Feb. 1918.*

BROOKE, Sir John Arthur, 1st Bt, *cr* 1919; JP West Riding, Yorks, and Co. Ross; *b* 22 March 1844; 4th *s* of late Thomas Brooke; *m* 1873, Blanche, *d* of Major Weston, Morvich; one *s* two *d* (and one *s* decd). *Heir: s* Robert Weston Brooke, *b* 10 Aug. 1885. *Address:* Fenay Hall, Huddersfield.   *Died 12 July 1920.*

BROOKE, Ven. Richard; Rector of Kalk Bay since 1901; Canon of St George's Cathedral, Cape Town, since 1887; Archdeacon of the Cape, 1905; resigned, 1925; made Archdeacon Emeritus. *Educ:* University of the Cape, BA. Ordained 1864; Tutor Diocesan College, Cape Town, 1861–66; Rector of Phillipolis, 1866–68; Clanwilliam, 1868–78; Claremont, 1878–87; Warden Diocesan College School, 1886–87; Principal Diocesan College, Rondebosch, 1887–1901; JP. *Address:* Rondebosch (P), Cape Town.
                                     Died 4 April 1926.

BROOKE, Sir Richard Marcus, 8th Bt, *cr* 1662; JP; DL; *b* 26 Oct. 1850; *s* of Sir Richard Brooke, 7th Bt and Lady Louisa Duff, *d* of 5th Earl of Fife; *S* father, 1888; *m* 1883, Alice, *d* of J. S. Crawley, Stockhood Park, Luton; one *s*. *Educ:* Eton. Formerly Lieut 1st Life Guards. Owned about 6,500 acres. *Heir s* Richard Christopher Brooke [*b* 8 Aug. 1888; *m* 1912, Marian Dorothea, *o d* of Arthur Charles Innes of Dromantine, County Down]. *Address:* Norton Priory, Runcorn. *Club:* Travellers'.   *Died 9 Oct. 1920.*

BROOKE, Rev. Stopford Augustus, MA, LLD; man of letters; *b* Letterkenny, Donegal, Ireland, 1832; *e s* of Richard Sinclair Brooke and Anna, *d* of Rev. T. Stopford, DD; *m* 1858, Emma Diana, *d* of Thomas Wentworth Beaumont, MP, Bretton Park, Yorkshire. *Educ:* Kidderminster; Kingstown; Trin. Coll., Dublin. Downe's Divinity Prize and Vice-Chancellor's Prize for English Verse. Ordained, June 1857; Curate of St Matthew's, Marylebone, 1857–59; of Kensington Church, 1860–63; Chaplain to Princess Royal, Berlin, 1863–65; Minister of St James's Chapel, York Street, 1866–75; Hon. Chaplain to the Queen; Minister of Bedford Chapel, 1876–94; seceded from the Church of England, 1880. *Publications:* Life and Letters of the late Frederick W. Robertson, 1865; Sermons, 1868–77; Freedom in the Church of England, 1871; Theology in the English Poets, 1874;

Primer of English Literature, 1876; A Fight of Faith, 1877; Riquet of the Tuft, a Love Drama, 1880; Spirit of the Christian Life, 1881; Unity of God and Man, 1886; The Early Life of Jesus, 1887; Poems, 1888; Dove Cottage, 1890; History of Early English Literature, 1892; Short Sermons, 1892; History of English Literature, 1894; Study of Tennyson, 1894; God and Christ, 1894; Jesus and Modern Thought, 1894; Old Testament and Modern Life, 1896; Life and Writings of Milton (Primers of English Literature); The Gospel of Joy, 1898; Poetry of R. Browning, 1902; Ten Plays of Shakespeare, 1905; Studies in Poetry, 1907; Four Poets, 1908. *Address:* The Four Winds, Ewhurst, Surrey. *Club:* Athenæum.
                                     Died 18 March 1916.

BROOKE, Sir William Robert, KCIE 1895 (CIE 1894); *b* 12 March 1842; *s* of Thomas Britannicus Brooke, EICS; *m* 1870, Evelyn, *d* of John Simons. Entered Indian Telegraph Department, 1857; Superintendent Bombay, 1866–69; Punjab, 1869–71; Director 1883; Deputy Director-General, 1886–87; Director-Gen. of Telegraphs in India, 1887; retired 1895. *Address:* Albert Gate Mansions, 219 Knightsbridge, SW. *Club:* Oriental.
                                     Died 8 July 1924.

BROOKE-HITCHING, Sir Thomas Henry, Kt 1902; *b* 1858; *s* of John Walter Hitching, Halifax, Yorks; adopted surname of Brooke-Hitching by Royal licence; *m* 1878, Sarah Kussuth, *d* of David Brooke of Stannary; two *s*. Sheriff of London, 1902–3; one of His Majesty's Lieutenants for the City of London; ex-member London County Council; Common Councilman, and ex-Mayor of Marylebone Borough Council; one of the prime movers in the creation of separate municipalities for the Metropolis; contested Elland Division (Yorks), 1906. *Orders:* Coronation Silver Medal; Officer of the Legion of Honour, France; Officer of Leopold II, Belgium; Grand Cross of St Saba, Servia; Grand Cross Danillo, Montenegro. *Address:* 8 Hereford Gardens, W1. *TA:* Brooke-Hitching, London. *T:* Mayfair 7029; Corston House, Ryde, Isle of Wight. *Clubs:* Royal Thames Yacht, Pilgrims.   *Died 4 Feb. 1926.*

BROOKMAN, Sir George, KBE 1920; JP; late Chairman Repatriation Department for South Australia; Member of War Council of South Australia during the War; Chairman War Savings' Council during the War; Member of Royal Red Cross Society, South Australian Division; one of the Founders and Deputy-Chairman of the South Australian Soldiers' Fund; elected twice as Member of the Legislative Council; *b* Glasgow, 1853; *m* 1878, Eliza Martha, *d* of Alfred Marshall, Melbourne. Member of Council of University of Adelaide; Life Governor Children's Hospital; Chairman of Adelaide Electric Supply Company; organised the original Syndicate which discovered and proved the famous Golden Mile at Kalgoorlie in 1893; Chairman of Bank of Adelaide; assisted to establish School of Mines in 1898. *Address:* Brookman Buildings, Grenfell Street, Adelaide. *T:* 497. *TA:* Brookman, Adelaide. *Club:* Junior Constitutional.
                                     Died 20 June 1927.

BROOKS, Herbert, JP, Surrey; one of HM Lieutenants for the City of London; Director of Bank of England; *b* 1842; *m* Alice, *d* of Rev. Richard Buller of Lanreath, Cornwall. *Educ:* Harrow. High Sheriff for the County of London, 1910. *Address:* 17 Princes Gardens, SW. *T:* Western 2682. *Clubs:* Carlton, Conservative.
                                     Died 10 Oct. 1918.

BROOKSBY; *see* Elmhirst, Capt. E. P.

BROOME, Viscount; Henry Franklin Chevallier Kitchener; Captain retired, Royal Navy; *b* 17 Oct. 1878; *o s* of 2nd Earl Kitchener; *m* 1916, (cousin) Adela Mary Evelyn, *e d* of late J. H. Monins, Ringwould House, near Dover; two *s* one *d*. Specialised in gunnery; Intelligence Division, Admiralty War Staff, 1912; served China, 1900; European War, 1914–18. *Heir: s* Hon. Henry Herbert Kitchener, *b* 24 Feb. 1919. *Address:* Broome Park, Canterbury.
                                     Died 13 June 1928.

BROS, James Reader White, JP; Police Magistrate, Clerkenwell, 1888–1921; *b* 1841; *s* of Thomas Bros, barrister; *m* 1871, Emily Spearman (*d* 1921), *d* of A. Wilkinson, of Coxhoe Hall, Co. Durham. Barrister Inner Temple, 1866. *Address:* 31 Elm Park Gardens, SW. *Club:* Athenæum.   *Died 2 Oct. 1923.*

BROUGH, Charles Allan La Touche, JP; LLB, MB, BS; FRCS; Barrister-at-Law; Mayor of Suva, Fiji (3 times); President Fijian Society; Corresponding Secretary Royal Colonial Institute; *s* of Hon. Secker Brough, Judge of Court of Probate, Toronto, Canada, and Mary Austwick de Bohun, Midhurst; *m* Mary Golightly, Durham;

two *d. Educ:* Upper Canada College; University of Toronto; University of Durham. Private Secretary to Sir Oliver Mowat, Premier of Ontario; Stipendiary Magistrate and Medical Officer, New Guinea, 1898; Stipendiary Magistrate, Fiji, 1904; Governor's Commissioner and Magistrate, 1907; Chief Police Magistrate, Suva, Fiji, 1908; Acting Attorney-General, Fiji, 1908; Member of the Executive and Legislative Councils of Fiji, 1908; served through the Fenian and Red River Expeditions in Canada. *Publications:* Law of Parliamentary Elections; The Monroe Doctrine; Anchylostomiasis; various scientific papers. *Address:* Suva, Fiji. *TA:* Brough, Fiji. *T:* Suva 71 and 94. *Clubs:* Royal Societies, Constitutional, Authors', Corona.
Died 5 May 1925.

BROUGH, Major John, CMG 1916; MVO 1911; Royal Marine Artillery. Assistant to Professor of Fortification, RN College, Greenwich, 1901; Officer of Company of Gentleman Cadets, RM College, Sandhurst, 1903–7; psc; Staff-Captain, War Office, 1910; Coronation medal, 1911; Staff-Officer to Insp.-Gen. W African Field Force, 1911–14; served European War (Cameroons), 1914–16 (despatches, CMG). *Club:* United Service.
Died 29 July 1917.

BROUGH, Joseph, BA, MSc, LLD: External Examiner to University of London, 1919–23; *b* 16 March 1852; *s* of William Brough of Rosemary Hill, near Newcastle-under-Lyme; unmarried. *Educ:* Grammar School, Newcastle-under-Lyme; Wesleyan Collegiate Institution, Taunton; Downing College, Camb. (1st Class in Moral Sciences Tripos, 1880, and in Law Tripos, 1881; Cobden Prize, 1883). Articled to Joseph Knight, solicitor, Newcastle-under-Lyme, 1870; admitted as a solicitor, 1875; lectured on Logic, Political Economy, and Jurisprudence, 1881–83; Professor of Logic and Philosophy, University College of Wales, Aberystwith, 1883–1911; Lecturer at Bedford College for Women, London, 1912; Emeritus Lecturer, 1922. *Publications:* The Study of Mental Science, 1902; articles in Encyclopædias of Religion and Education; reviews and occasional papers in Mind, Proceedings of Aristotelian Society, and other journals, etc. *Recreations:* music, dramatics. *Address:* 12 Carlingford Road, Hampstead, NW3. *Died 7 Dec. 1925.*

BROUGHAM AND VAUX, 3rd Baron, *cr* 1860; **Henry Charles Brougham,** KCVO 1905; DL, JP; MA; *b* 2 Sept. 1836; *s* of 2nd Baron and Frances, *d* of Sir Charles Wm Taylor, 1st Bt; *S* father, 1886; *m* 1882, Adora Frances Olga, *d* of Peter Wells, Windsor Forest, and *widow* of Sir Richard Musgrave, 11th Bt; one *d* (one *s* decd). *Educ:* Eton; Trin. Coll., Camb. Clerk in House of Lords, 1857–86. Owned about 5,000 acres. *Heir: g s* Victor Henry Peter Brougham, *b* 23 Oct. 1909. *Address:* 36 Chesham Place, SW1. *T:* Victoria 3953; Brougham Hall, Penrith; Château Eléonore, Cannes. *Clubs:* Marlborough, Arthur's, Brooks's, Bachelors', Garrick. *Died 24 May 1927.*

BROUGHAM, Captain Hon. Henry; Coldstream Guards, SR; *b* 26 May 1883; *o s* and *heir* of 3rd Baron Brougham and Vaux; *m* 1st, 1908, Hon. Diana Sturt (who obtained a divorce, 1919), *o d* of 2nd Baron Alington; two *s* one *d*; 2nd, 1923, Baroness Hengelmüller, *d* of late Austro-Hungarian Ambassador in Washington. Knight of Grace of St John of Jerusalem. *Clubs:* Carlton, Pratt's, White's, St James's.
Died 4 May 1927.

BROUGHAM, James Rigg; *b* 1826; 4th *s* of J. W. Brougham, Edinburgh; *m* 1854, Isabella Eliza, *d* of late J. Cropper of Dingle Bank, Liverpool. Registrar in Bankruptcy, 1848–91; Senior Registrar, 1891; retired, 1917. *Address:* Beathwaite, Milnthorpe, Westmorland.
Died 5 March 1919.

BROUGHTON, Rev. Henry Ellis, MA; Vicar of Hugglescote since 1889; Hon. Canon, Peterborough, 1903; Rural Dean South Akley, 1893. *Educ:* Harrow; Caius College, Cambridge. Curate of Polebrook, Northants, 1872–75. *Address:* Hugglescote Vicarage, Leicester.
Died 29 Dec. 1924.

BROUGHTON, Miss Rhoda; novelist; *b* North Wales, 29 Nov. 1840. *Publications:* Cometh up as a Flower, 1867; Not Wisely but Too Well, 1867; Red as a Rose is She, 1870; Goodbye, Sweetheart, Goodbye, 1872; Nancy, 1873; Joan, 1876; Second Thoughts, 1880; Belinda, 1883; Dr Cupid, 1886; Alas, 1890; Mrs Bligh, 1892; A Beginner, 1894; Scylla or Charybdis?, 1895; Dear Faustina, 1897; The Game and the Candle, 1899; Foes in Law, 1901; Lavinia, 1902; The Devil and the Deep Sea, 1910; Between Two Stools, 1912.
Died 5 June 1920.

BROUN, Sir William, 10th Bt, *cr* 1686; *b* 18 Dec. 1848; *s* of 9th Bt and Elizabeth, *d* of John Smith, Drongan, Ayrshire; *S* father, 1882;

m 1871, Alice, *d* of late J. C. Peters, Hope House, Manly Beach, Sydney; four *s* three *d. Heir: s* James Lionel Broun, *b* 1875. *Address:* Colstoun, Gunnedah, NSW. *T:* Gunnedah 72; Coonimbia, Coonamble, NSW. *TA:* Gunnedah and Coonamble. *T:* Coonamble 813. *M:* 1425. *Died 23 Oct. 1918.*

BROUNGER, Richard Ernest, MInstCE; late Agent-General for Orange River Colony in London; *b* 5 Dec. 1849; *m*; three *s* one *d. Educ:* King's College, London. Engaged for about thirty years in the survey, construction, maintenance, and management of railways in South Africa; constructed the main line of railway across the Orange Free State for the Cape Government, and was Director-General of the Orange Free State Government Railways. *Address:* Eden Lodge, Tilford, near Farnham, Surrey. *Club:* National Liberal.
Died 19 Jan. 1922.

BROUSSON, Louis Maurice; editor and manager of London Citizen newspaper since 1895; writer of the financial article, From Moses Moss to Benjamin Boss; also city editor of provincial daily papers, including the Belfast News Letter, Liverpool Daily Courier, Yorkshire Observer, Sheffield Daily Independent, Bristol Daily Times, and The East Anglian Daily Times; of a Huguenot family; *m* 1870, Clara Emily, 2nd *d* of Robert Mace Habgood, of Perth, Western Australia; four *s*. For many years connected with financial press; editor, La Cité, French daily financial paper in London and of The City, 1880–83; editor of Invention, 1884–90; city editor of Truth, 1883–1902; city editor, Financial News, 1890–1904. *Address:* 31 Belsize Avenue, NW3. *T:* Hampstead 6800; 2 Copthall Buildings, EC. *T:* Wall 4984.
Died 1 Jan. 1920.

BROWN, Adrian John, MSc; FRS 1911; FIC; Professor of Biology and Chemistry of Fermentation, and Director of School of Brewing, University of Birmingham, since 1899; late Examiner in Biological Chemistry, Institute of Chemistry; *b* Burton-on-Trent, 27 April 1852; *s* of Edwin Brown, FGS, Burton-on-Trent; *m* Helen F., *d* of John Hutchison, Glasgow; two *s* two *d. Educ:* Burton-on-Trent Grammar School; Royal School of Mines. Asst to Dr Russell, FRS, St Bartholomew's Hosp.; Chemist to T. Salt and Co., Burton-on-Trent. *Publications:* Laboratory Studies for Brewing Students; numerous papers published in Journal of Chemical Society and other journals. *Recreations:* fishing, geology, botany. *Address:* University, Birmingham; Rimside, Northfield. *Died 2 July 1919.*

BROWN, Hon. Alexander, JP; MLC; Consul for Italy and Belgium; Managing Director, Dalgety & Co., Ltd; *b* NSW, 1851; *s* of W. Brown, MD; *m* 1872. *Educ:* High School, West Maitland. Studied for the Law; admitted a Solicitor of the Supreme Court of NSW in 1873; abandoned Law for Commerce; entered Parliament Popular Branch; was defeated later on, and afterwards called to the Legislative Council; created Chevalier, Ordre de Léopold for Consular Service, 1902. *Recreations:* reading, walking. *Address:* Cumberland Hall, East Maitland, NSW. *Club:* Warrigal, Sydney.

Died 28 March 1926.

BROWN, Alexander Crum, MA, MD, Edinburgh; DSc London; FRS; FRSE; FRCPE; FCS; FIC; *b* Edinburgh, 26 March 1838; *s* of Rev. John Brown, DD; *m* Jane Bailie (*d* 1910), *d* of Rev. James Porter, Drumlee, Co. Down. *Educ:* Royal High School, Edinburgh; Mill Hill School; Universities of Edinburgh, Heidelberg, Marburg. Extra-academical Lecturer on Chemistry, Edinburgh, 1863–69; President Chemical Society of London, 1892–93; Professor of Chemistry, Edinburgh University, 1869–1908. LLD Aberdeen, Glasgow, Edinburgh, and St Andrews. *Address:* 8 Belgrave Crescent, Edinburgh.
Died 28 Oct. 1922.

BROWN, Sir Alexander Hargreaves, 1st Bt, *cr* 1903; VD; *b* 11 April 1844; *g s* of Sir William Brown, 1st Bt, Liverpool; *m* 1876, Henrietta Agnes Terrell (*d* 1921), *d* of C. R. Blandy, Madeira; one *s* two *d* (and one *s* decd). JP Lancashire and Surrey; late partner in Brown, Shipley and Co., Founders Court, Lothbury, EC; MP (U) for Wenlock, 1868–85; Wellington Division Shropshire, 1885–1906. *Heir: g s* John Hargreaves Brown [*b* 16 Aug. 1913. *Address:* Bearehurst, Holmwood, Surrey]. *Address:* Broome Hall, Holmwood, Surrey. *Clubs:* Reform, Brooks's. *Died 12 March 1922.*

BROWN, Alexander Kellock, RSA; RBC, RSW, RI; landscape painter; *b* 11 Feb. 1849; *s* of Robert Brown and Margaret Kellock; *m* 1881, Mary Frew; one *s* one *d. Educ:* Glasgow Normal Seminary; Glasgow School of Art; Heatherley's London. *Works:* Frost in the Air; A Dagger Day; September in Arran; Winter Morn; A Spring Day; Winter Twilight; 'Twixt March and April; Autumn at the Clachan. *Recreation:* a little cycling. *Address:* 152 Renfrew Street,

Glasgow. *T:* Douglas 2216. *Club:* Glasgow Art.
Died 9 May 1922.

BROWN, Rev. Archibald Geikie; *b* 18 July 1844; *s* of late John Wm Brown, Clapham Park. *Educ:* C. H. Spurgeon's College. Founded Baptist Church, Bromley, Kent, 1863; Pastor at Stepney Green Tabernacle, 1866; built East London Tabernacle, opened 1872; President of London Baptist Association, 1877; withdrew from Baptist Union in company with C. H. Spurgeon, owing to "Down Grade Controversy," 1887; Pastor of Baptist Church, Chatsworth Road, West Norwood, SE, 1897–1907; Pastor of Metropolitan-Tabernacle, 1907–10. *Publications:* several volumes of sermons, and the protest The Devil's Mission of Amusement. *Recreation:* fishing. *Address:* 45 Endlesham Road, Balham, SW. *Died 2 April 1922.*

BROWN, Major Cecil, MA; RBS; *b* Ayr, 1867. *Educ:* Harrow; Oxford. Studied in Florence and Paris; exhibited at Royal Academy etc, since 1895; designed medal for International Medical Congress, London, 1913; enlisted Aug. 1914; Major, Sept. 1917; demobilised March 1919; designed Memorial to Imperial Camel Corps. *Publication:* The Horse in Art and Nature. *Recreations:* hunting, rowing, golf. *Club:* Arts.

BROWN, Rev. Prof. Francis, MA 1873; PhD 1884; DD 1884, 1894, 1901, 1908, 1909; DLitt 1901; LLD 1901; Davenport Professor of Hebrew and the Cognate Languages, Union Theological Seminary, New York, since 1890; President of the Faculty, Union Theological Seminary, since 1908; *b* 26 Dec. 1849; *s* of Rev. Prof. Samuel Gilman Brown, DD, LLD, and Sarah Van Vechten; *m* 1879, Louise F. M. Reiss, Berlin; one *s* two *d. Educ:* Phillips Academy, Andover, Mass; Dartmouth College, Hanover, New Hampshire; Union Theological Seminary, New York, USA; University of Berlin, Germany. Asst-Master, Ayers' Latin School, Pittsburg, Pa, 1870–72; Tutor in Greek, Dartmouth College, 1872–74; Fellow of Union Theological Seminary, 1877–79; Instructor in Biblical Philology, Union Theological Seminary, 1879–81; Associate Professor of Biblical Philology, Union Theological Seminary, 1881–90. *Publications:* editor of Lenormant's Beginnings of History (English trans. of Les Origines de l'Histoire I), New York, 1882; of The Teachings of the Twelve Apostles (with Rev. Prof. R. D. Hitchcock, DD), 1884, revised and enlarged edn 1885; author of Assyriology: its Use and Abuse, 1885; The Christian Point of View (with Rev. Profs George Wm Knox, DD, and Arthur C. McGiffert, DD), 1902; A Hebrew and English Lexicon of the Old Testament (with Rev. Profs S. R. Driver, DD, and C. A. Briggs, DD), thirteen parts, 1891–1906; also many articles and reviews. *Recreations:* walking, rowing. *Address:* 80 Claremont Avenue, New York, USA. *TA:* Brown, Kissamchar, New York. *T:* Morningside, 1491 New York. *Club:* Century, New York.
Died 15 Oct. 1916.

BROWN, George, MRCS 1874; LSA 1873; Hon. Surgeon, Exeter Dispensary; General Secretary of Imperial Medical Reform Union; Vice-President, Tariff Reform League; Chairman, General Apothecaries' Co., Ltd, and Native Guano Co., Ltd; Founder and Editor of Medical Times and Hospital Gazette and Founder of General Practitioner; *b* Callington, Cornwall, 16 Jan. 1844; *s* of late Thomas Brown; *m* 1898, Edith Kate, *o d* of Maj.-Gen. Joseph Reay, Bengal Staff Corps; one *s. Educ:* private schools; Charing Cross Hospital School of Medicine, London. Golding Scholar, 1871; Llewellyn Scholar, 1872; Gold Medal, 1873. House Surgeon at Charing Cross Hospital, 1873; Resident Medical Officer at the North-Eastern Hospital for Children, 1874; Prosector of Anatomy at the Royal College of Surgeons of England, 1874; Demonstrator of Anatomy at the Westminster Hospital Medical School, 1873–74; Advocate of Fiscal Reform; Direct Representative for England and Wales on General Medical Council, 1897–1907. *Publications:* Aids to Anatomy, 1875; Aids to Surgery, 1876; The Fiscal Problem, 1903; contributions to the Times, Lancet, British Medical Journal, General Practitioner, etc. *Recreations:* shooting, bowls, horticulture. *Address:* Mount Lodge, Silver Valley, Callington, Cornwall; 38 Southernhay East, Exeter. *Club:* Liberal Union.

BROWN, Hon. George William; Second Lieutenant-Governor of Province of Saskatchewan since 1910; *b* Holstein, Ont, 30 May 1860; *m* 1895, Annie Gardiner, *d* of James Barr, Norwich, Ont. *Educ:* Toronto University. Studied law, and was admitted to the Bar of North-West Territories, 1892; member of North-West Legislative Assembly, 1894–1905. *Address:* Regina, Sask, Canada.
Died 17 Feb. 1919.

BROWN, Major Harold, DSO 1915; 5th Battalion Yorkshire Regiment (Territorial Force). Entered army, 1914; late Captain, 4th

Vol. Batt. Suffolk Regt; served European War, 1914–15 (DSO, Bt Major); made successful and daring reconnaissances, especially near Hooge. *Died 23 March 1918.*

BROWN, Horace T., FRS; LLD (Hon.) Edinburgh; *b* Burton-on-Trent, 20 July 1848; *m* 1874, Annie (*d* 1915), *d* of Paul J. Fearon; one *s* two *d. Educ:* Burton-on-Trent and Atherstone Grammar Schools; Royal College of Chemistry. Entered brewing business at Burton-on-Trent, 1866; retired, 1893; Longstaff Medal of Chemical Society, 1894; President of Chemical Section of British Association, 1899; Royal Medal of the Royal Society, 1903; Member of Royal Commission on Whiskey, 1908; Copley Medal of the Royal Society, 1920; Governor of the Imperial College of Science and Technology, S Kensington. *Publications:* numerous papers on chemical, biological, and geological subjects, etc. *Address:* 5 Evelyn Gardens, SW7. *T:* Kensington 5665. *Club:* Athenæum.
Died 6 Feb. 1925.

BROWN, Horatio Robert Forbes, JP; LLD; *b* Nice, 16 Feb. 1854; *e s* of late Hugh Horatio Brown of Newhall and Carlops, and late Gulielmina, *d* of Colonel Ranaldson Macdonell of Glengarry. *Educ:* Clifton College; New College, Oxford (Exhibitioner); 2nd class, Classical Greats. Taylorian Lecturer, 1895; Hon. LLD Edinburgh, 1900; gold medal of the British Academy Serena Foundation, 1923; Member of the Ateneo Veneto; Honorary Member of the Regio Istituto Veneto di Scienze, Lettere ed Arti; Corresponding Member of the Regie Deputazioni, Veneta e Toscana, di Storia Patria. The following manuscripts burned: Life on the Lagoons, at Kegan Paul's, 1883; A Study in the Venetian Inquisition, by fire in a mail car, Switzerland, 1886; Calendar of State Papers, at Spottiswoode's, 1892; Studies in Archæology, at Mr Cecil Rhodes' house, Rondebosch, Capetown, 1895. *Publications:* Life on the Lagoons, 1884, 5th edition, 1909; Venetian Studies, 1887; The Venetian Printing Press, 1891; Venice, an Historical Sketch, 1893, 2nd edition, 1895; John Addington Symonds, a Biography, 1895, 2nd edition, 1903; Calendar of State Papers (Venetian): 1581–1591, 1895; 1592–1603, 1897; 1603–1607, 1900; 1607–1610, 1904; 1610–1613, 1905; Drift: Verses, 1900; Temple Primer, The Venetian Republic, 1902; Cambridge Modern History: vol i, chapter on Venice, 1902; vol iv, chapter on The Valtelline, 1905; In and Around Venice, 1905; Pensieri persi, a contribution to Die Festschrift des Herren Prälat Schneider, 1906; translation of Molmenti's Venice, vols i, ii, iii and iv; Studies in the History of Venice, 1907; Introduction to the Poems of T. E. Brown, Golden Treasury series; translation of Molmenti's Venice, vols v and vi, 1908; Letters and Papers of John Addington Symonds, 1923; Cambridge Medieval History, vol. vi Chapter xiii, 1923; Dalmatia, 1925. *Address:* 560 Campiello Incurabili, Zattere, Venice. *Clubs:* Athenæum; New, Edinburgh.
Died 19 Aug. 1926.

BROWN, James Clifton, JP; *b* 13 Feb. 1841; 2nd *s* of late Alexander Brown (*e s* of 1st Bt of Beilby Grange, Co. York), and Sarah Benedict, *d* of James Brown; *m* 1866, Amelia, *d* of Charles Rowe; five *s* four *d. Educ:* Trin. Hall, Camb.; MA. High Sheriff, Sussex, 1888; patron of one living; Col late Lancashire Artillery, S Div. RA; formerly Lieut-Col 1st Lancashire Artillery Volunteers; MP (L) Horsham, 1876–80. *Address:* 32 Ennismore Gardens, SW; Holmbush, near Horsham. *Clubs:* Reform, New University.
Died 5 Jan. 1917.

BROWN, Hon. James Drysdale; MLC Nelson Province since 1904; Minister of Mines, Forests, and Public Health, Victoria, 1913–15; Attorney-General and Solicitor-General, 1909–13; *b* 21 April 1850. *Address:* Public Offices, Royal Chambers, Collins Street, Melbourne.
Died 5 April 1922.

BROWN, Rev. (James) Wilson (Davy), BA; Hon. Canon of Ely Cathedral; *b* 25 Aug. 1839; *s* of late Rev. Thomas Brown, JP, Rector of Hemingstone, Suffolk; *m* 1st, *d* of late Rev. Charles Bridges, Rector of Hinton Martell, Dorset; 2nd, *e d* (*d* 1918) of late Col F. Maitland Wilson, MP, of Stowlangtoft Hall, Suffolk. *Educ:* The Collegiate School, Leicester; Gonville and Caius College, Cambridge. Ordained, 1862; Curate of All Saints, Northampton, 1862–65; Curate in charge of Hinton Martell, Dorset, 1865–69; Brockworth, Gloucestershire, 1869–70; Stoke-by-Nayland, Suffolk, 1870–77; Vicar of Assington, Suffolk, 1877–93; Rector of Stowlangtoft, Suffolk, 1893–1920. *Address:* St Mary's Square, Bury St Edmunds. *Club:* County, Bury St Edmunds. *Died 27 May 1922.*

BROWN, Sir John, Kt 1920; JP; landed proprietor; Member of Kincardineshire County Council; Chairman of the Aberdeen Coal and Shipping Co. Ltd. *Died 28 April 1928.*

BROWN, Very Rev. Dr John, DD, MA; Moderator, General Assembly, Church of Scotland, 1916; Minister of Bellahouston, Glasgow, since 1887; *b* Irvine, 5 April 1850; *e s* of John Brown and Janet Sandilands; *m* 1882, Margaret Romanes, *e d* of Very Rev. John Rankine, DD, Sorn, Ayrshire; one *s* three *d*. *Educ:* Irvine; Edinburgh University. Ordained, 1876, to Parish of Galston, Ayrshire. *Publications:* Imperialism and Church Union, 1916, and other addresses and papers. *Recreations:* golf, fishing. *Address:* The Manse, Bellahouston, Glasgow. *T:* Ibrox 221.

Died 20 Feb. 1919.

BROWN, Dr John, BA; DD; retired Congregational Minister; *b* 19 June 1830; *e s* of William Brown, Bolton, Lancashire; *m* 1859, Ada Haydon, 2nd *d* of Rev. D. E. Ford, of Manchester; three *s* three *d*. *Educ:* private school; Owens Coll., Manchester; Lancashire Independent Coll., Manchester. Graduated BA at London University, 1853; received hon. degree of DD from Yale University, USA, 1887; Minister of Park Chapel, Manchester, 1855; Bunyan Church at Bedford, 1864-1903; was Chairman of the Congregational Union of England and Wales, 1891; was Congregational Union Lecturer, 1898; Lyman Beecher Lecturer at Yale University, USA, 1899. *Publications:* Lectures on the Book of Revelation, 1866; God's Book for Man's Life, 1882; John Bunyan, his Life, Times, and Work, 1885; The Pilgrim Fathers of New England, 1895; Apostolical Succession in the Light of History and Fact, 1898; Puritan Preaching in England, etc, 1900; From the Restoration to the Revolution, 1904; Commonwealth England, 1904; The English Puritans, 1910; History of the English Bible, 1911. *Address:* 10 Upper Park Road, Hampstead, NW3. *T:* Hampstead 8562.

Died 16 Jan. 1922.

BROWN, John James Graham, MD; FRCPE, FRSE; late President Royal College of Physicians of Edinburgh; in practice as a Physician in Edinburgh since 1880; Lecturer in Clinical Medicine in Edinburgh University and in School of Medicine of the Royal Colleges, Edinburgh; *s* of Rev. Thomas Brown, DD; *m* Jane Pasley Hay Thorburn; three *s* one *d*. *Educ:* Edinburgh Academy; Universities of Edinburgh, Berlin, Vienna, and Prague. Sometime Senior President of the Royal Medical Society; House Physician and Surgeon to Royal Infirmary, Edinburgh, and in the Chalmers Hospital, Edinburgh; late Lecturer on Neurology, Edinburgh University; Morison Lecturer to the Royal College of Physicians of Edinburgh, 1912 and 1918. *Publications:* Medical Diagnosis, 4th edn 1897; Treatment of Nervous Diseases, 1905; various contributions to medical journals. *Address:* 3 Chester Street, Edinburgh. *T:* Central 313. *Clubs:* Royal Societies; University, Edinburgh.

Died 28 Feb. 1925.

BROWN, Sir John McLeavy, Kt 1906; CMG 1898; LLD; Head of the Customs and Controller of Finance, Korea, 1898-1906; *b* 1842; *m* Maria (*d* 1911). Student-Interpreter in China, 1861; Asst Chinese Sec., 1864; in charge of the Legation, 1867; Secretary to Chinese Mission to Europe, 1868; Acting Chinese Secretary at Pekin, 1871-72; resigned, 1872; Commissioner in the Chinese Customs; first-class Sacred Treasure of Japan, and first-class Order of Tai-Kuk, Korea. *Address:* 49 Portland Place, W1.

Died 6 April 1926.

BROWN, Very Rev. John Pierce; Dean of Down, 1912-24; *b* 23 July 1843; *m* Sarah Price (*d* 1907), *d* of Rev. W. Ferrier Jex-Blake; no *c*. *Educ:* Trinity College, Dublin, MA. Ordained 1868; Curate of Kilmore, 1868-70; Rector of Loughinisland, 1870-1911; Archdeacon of Down, 1899-1911. *Address:* Newcastle, Co. Down. *TA:* Clough, Down. *M:* IJ 272. *Club:* Ulster, Belfast.

Died 15 March 1925.

BROWN, Sir Joseph, Kt 1914; President of the Legislative Council of the Bahamas. *Address:* Nassau, Bahama Islands.

Died 19 Aug. 1919.

BROWN, Peter Hume, MA; LLD Edin. and St Andrews; DD Geneva; member British Academy; Historiographer-Royal for Scotland since 1908; Professor of Ancient (Scottish) History and Palæography, Edinburgh (Sir William Fraser Chair) since 1901; Ford Lecturer, 1913-14; author; *b* Haddingtonshire, Scotland, 17 Dec. 1850. *Educ:* various schools in Scotland and England; Edinburgh University. Originally meant to enter the Church; but took to teaching instead and eventually to authorship; appointed Editor of the Register of the Privy Council of Scotland (1898). *Publications:* George Buchanan, Humanist and Reformer, 1890; Early Travellers in Scotland, 1891; Scotland before 1700, from Contemporary Documents, 1893; John Knox: a Biography, 1895; History of Scotland, vol. i 1898, vol. ii 1902, vol. iii 1909; Scotland in the time

of Queen Mary—being the Rhind Lectures for 1903, 1904; A Short History of Scotland, 1909; The Youth of Goethe, 1913; Ford Lectures—The Legislative Union of England and Scotland, 1914. *Address:* 20 Corrennie Gardens, Edinburgh.

Died 30 Nov. 1918.

BROWN, Sir Robert Charles, Kt 1919; MB; FRCP, FRCS; Consulting Medical Officer, Preston Royal Infirmary; *b* 27 Winckley Square, Preston, 2 Oct. 1836; *s* of late Alderman Brown, FRCS, Preston. *Educ:* King's College, London; Edinburgh and Dublin. Admitted a member of the Royal College of Surgeons of England and a Licentiate of the Society of Apothecaries, 1858; MB London, 1861; FRCS 1862; a Fellow of the Royal College of Physicians, 1908; Associate of King's College, London; Esquire of the Order of St John of Jerusalem; three times President of the Lancashire and Cheshire Branch of the British Medical Association; MA (hon.), Cambridge, 1912; presented with the Freedom of the borough of Preston, 1910. *Address:* 27 Winckley Square, Preston.

Died 23 Nov. 1925.

BROWN, Major Sir Robert Hanbury, KCMG 1902 (CMG 1898); late Inspector-General of Irrigation, Egypt; *b* Brixton Hill, 13 Jan. 1849; 2nd *s* of the late Robert Brown, surgeon; *m* 1878, Marian, MBE, *e d* of Rev. Edwin Meyrick; one *s* one *d*. *Educ:* Marlborough Coll.; RMA, Woolwich. Joined RE 1870; went to India, 1872; Irrigation Department of Public Works, Bengal, 1873; served in Afghan War, 1879-80 (despatches, medal); Egypt, Irrigation Department, 1884-1903. *Decorated* for service in the Irrigation Dept, Egypt (2nd class Osmanieh and 1st class Medjidie). *Publications:* The Fayum and Lake Moeris; History of the Barrage; The Land of Goshen and the Exodus; The Delta Barrage; Irrigation. *Recreations:* photography, wireless. *Address:* Newlands, Crawley Down, Sussex. *TA:* Hanbury Brown, Copthorne. *Died 4 May 1926.*

BROWN, Lt-Col Robert Tilbury, CMG 1918; DSO 1916; MD; Royal Army Medical Corps (retired); *b* 26 June 1873; *s* of Surg. Lieut-Colonel Robert Ross Brown, VD, JP, LRCP, etc, of Strood, Kent; *m* 1904, Pauline, *d* of F. Normandy, Barrister-at-law. *Educ:* King's School, Rochester; Guy's Hospital; Durham University Medical School. MRCS, LRCP 1896; MB, BS Durham 1899; MD (Gold Medal) 1904; DPH, RCPSI, 1902. 1st Kent Artillery Vol., Lieut-Capt., 1894-1900; general practice and Deputy MOH Strood, 1896-1900; Lieut Royal Army Medical Corps, 1900, Lieut-Col 1917; Specialist in charge laboratory, Lucknow, 1903-6; Sanitary Officer, East Command and Burma Division, 1906-13; DADMS (Sanitation), GHQ, and Officer Commanding Indian Sanitary Section, the forces in East Africa, 1914-15; DADMS, GHQ, 1916; ADMS, 1917-19 (despatches four times, DSO, CMG, Chevalier Ordre de Léopold); Officer Commanding Royal Herbert Hospital, Woolwich, 1919-21; SMO, Ceylon Command, 1922-24; SMO, Bordon, 1925-26; retired pay, 1926. *Publications:* The Bacteriology of Asylum Dysentery, Jl RAMC, 1903; Camp Sanitation, ib. 1908; Examination of Water on Field Service; Camping Arrangements for Sanitary Officers, ib. 1909; Sanitary Reports of Manœuvres, Eastern Command and Burma Division, ib. 1910-12; Training and Working of an Indian Sanitary Section, ib. 1912. *Recreations:* shooting, fishing. *Address:* Lambert, Hatherleigh, N Devon. *Died 21 Jan. 1928.*

BROWN, T. Austen, ARSA; *b* Edinburgh; *m* Elizabeth Christie Macrae. *Educ:* Edinburgh. Member of the National Portrait Society, London; Associate of the Société Nationale des Beaux Arts, Paris; Corresponding Member of the Société Royale des Beaux Arts, Brussels; Member of the Royal British Colonial Society of Artists; Hon. Member of South Wales Art Society; Member of Society of Graver Printers in Colour; represented in the Pinakotheck, Munich; National Galleries of Dresden, Budapest, and Corporation Galleries of Aberdeen, Glasgow, Mannheim, Exeter, and Leeds; Santiago, Chile; National Gallery, Brussels; Art Musée, Liège; National Gallery of Canada, Ottawa; Art Museum, Toronto; National Gallery, Wellington, New Zealand; Walker Art Gallery, Liverpool; Corporation Gallery, Bath; Victoria and Albert Museum, South Kensington; medal of the 1st class, Munich, 1896; medals of the 2nd class, Munich, Dresden, and Barcelona, 1911; grand gold medal, Budapest; silver medal, Barcelona. *Address:* 16 Fulham Road, Chelsea, SW3. *Died 9 June 1924.*

BROWN, Lt-Col Walter Henry, CB 1916; DSO 1919; late 103rd Mahratta Light Infantry; *b* 27 Jan. 1867; *s* of Major Francis Brown, Carabineers; *m* Edith, *d* of late Col D. Stewart, Ceylon Rifles; three *d*. *Educ:* Lancing College; RMC, Sandhurst. Entered Royal West Kent Regiment, 1886; Capt., Indian Army, 1897; Major, 1904; Lt-Col 1912; Adjutant, Indian Volunteers, 1900-2; served European War,

Mesopotamia, 1914–18 (wounded—prisoner, CB, DSO, despatches four times); retired, 1919. *Address:* Trevena, The Down, Bexhill-on-Sea. *T:* 162.   *Died 8 March 1928.*

BROWN, William Henry; late Partner in firm of Messrs Speyer Bros, American bankers; *b* Highworth, Wiltshire, 1845; *s* of Samuel Brown and Jemima, *d* of Samuel Jones, Stratton St Margaret's; *m* Jane, *d* of late Ralph Thorne, Wanborough, Wiltshire; three *s* two *d*. *Educ:* The Grammar School, Highworth. Late Director of Metropolitan District Railway Company and Investment Trust Corporation; Chairman of London Congregational Union, 1901; Chairman of London Congregational Union Missions Committee. *Recreation:* farming. *Address:* Harts, Woodford Green, Essex; Crimplesham Hall, Norfolk. *TA:* Harts, Woodford Green. *T:* 536 Woodford. *Club:* City Reform.   *Died June 1918.*

BROWN, Very Rev. William Henry; Incumbent of Monivea since 1890; Provost of Tuam since 1898. *Educ:* Trinity Coll., Dublin, MA. Ordained, 1869; Curate of Ballinrobe, 1867–71; Monivea, 1872–76; Incumbent of Ballyconree, 1876–90. *Address:* Monivea, Athenry, Ireland.   *Died 24 Aug. 1924.*

BROWN, His Honour William Herbert, JP (Co. Londonderry); BSc (London); MA, LLB (RUI); KC 1911; *b* Limavady, Co. Londonderry; 2nd *s* of late Rev. N. M. Brown, DD, LLD, Ex-Moderator of the Presbyterian Church in Ireland; *m* 1892, Elizabeth Rose, *d* of late Captain Sandes, JP, of Clontarf, Dublin, and Carrigafoyle, Co. Kerry; one *s* two d. *Educ:* Coleraine Academical Institution; Queen's Colleges, Galway and Belfast; private study. Mathematical, Law, and Natural Philosophy Scholar; and Classical Exhibitioner; Peel Exhibitioner and 1st Honorman (QUI); 1st Honorman (RUI); King's Inns Exhibitioner, 1886. Called to Bar, 1887; went NE Circuit; Crown Counsel, County of Louth, 1896–1903; Crown Counsel, County of Down, 1903–14; Revising Barrister, Borough of Cork, 1896–1905; Borough of Dublin, 1909; County of Dublin, 1910–13; Counsel to the Post Office, NE Circuit, 1913–14; contested (L) North Derry, Dec. 1910; County Court Judge and Chairman of Quarter Sessions for the Counties of Leitrim and Cavan, 1914; retired 1924, on abolition of office of County Court Judge in the Irish Free State. *Publications:* The Present Position of the Law of Lake and River Fishery (Law Magazine and Review); Town Tenants and Landlords; A Popular Explanation of the Town Tenants (Ireland) Act, 1906. *Address:* Glenfern, Blackrock, Co. Dublin. *T:* Blackrock, 132.   *Died 7 Feb. 1927.*

BROWN, Col Sir William James, KCB 1907 (CB 1897); *b* 1832; *s* of late Thomas Brown; *m* 1856, *y d* of late William Silverthorne. Hon. Col 19th Batt. County of London Territorial Regiment (late North Middlesex Rifles). *Address:* Gloster Lodge, Argyle Road, West Ealing.   *Died 8 Feb. 1918.*

BROWN, Sir William Slater, Kt 1911; *b* Edinburgh, 14 Jan. 1845; 2nd *s* of Henry Raeburn Brown, Edinburgh, and Helen, *d* of James Clyde, Edinburgh; *m* 1865, Margaret (*d* 1912), *d* of George Dods, Duns, Berwickshire; four *s* two *d*. *Educ:* St Stephen's School, Edinburgh. JP of Co. of the City of Edinburgh; ex-Lord Provost of Edinburgh and Deputy Lord Lieutenant of the County of the City of Edinburgh; head of the firm of W. S. Brown and Sons, furnishers. *Address:* 5 Corrennie Gardens, Edinburgh. *T:* 6478 Central.   *Died 19 April 1917.*

BROWNE, Hon. Sir Albert, KBE 1920 (CBE 1919; OBE 1918); CMG 1911; ISO 1903; *b* Bury St Edmunds, 1860; *s* of J. C. Browne; *m* Mabel, *d* of Dr Lawrence of Cape Colony. *Educ:* Guildhall School, Bury St Edmunds; King's College, London. Clerk Colonial Office, 1877; on duty in Cyprus, 1880–83; Assistant Imperial Secretary and Accountant in South Africa, 1891; Acting Imperial Secretary, January to March 1895, and March to August 1896; Financial Adviser to Military Governor, Bloemfontein, 1900; Auditor-General, 1901; Colonial Treasurer, 1901–7, and Member of Executive and Legislative Councils of the Orange River Colony; member of the South African Convention for the formation of Union, 1908; Union Delegate to England, 1909; Joint Hon. Sec. Governor-Generals Fund, 1915–19. *Club:* Civil Service, Cape Town.   *Died 20 Dec. 1923.*

BROWNE, Maj.-Gen. Andrew Smythe Montague, JP, DL; Colonel Royal Scots Greys since 1905; *b* 12 June 1836; *m* 1872, Alice Jane, *o c* of Col Fergusson; one *s* five *d*. *Educ:* Cheltenham; Sandhurst. Entered army 1853; Major-Gen. 1893; retired, 1897; served Crimea, 1855–56 (medal with clasp, Turkish medal); Colonel 3rd Dragoon Guards, 1903–5; Commanded 49th Berkshire Regimental District;

High Sheriff, Co. Down, 1905. *Address:* St John's Point, Killough, Co. Down. *Club:* Army and Navy.   *Died 10 March 1916.*

BROWNE, Sir Benjamin Chapman, Kt 1887; DL, JP; DCL; MInstCE, MINA, MIME; Director of R. and W. Hawthorn, Leslie, and Co., Newcastle-on-Tyne, engineers and shipbuilders; *b* 26 Aug. 1839; *s* of Col B. C. Browne, 9th Lancers, of Stouts Hill, Gloucestershire; *m* 1861, Annie, *d* of R. T. Atkinson, CE; three *s* four *d*. *Educ:* Westminster; King's College, London. Apprenticed as an engineer to Lord Armstrong, Elswick Works, 1856; Mayor of Newcastle, 1885–87. *Recreation:* social economic questions. *Address:* Westacres. Newcastle-on-Tyne. *T:* National 17.   *Died 1 March 1917.*

BROWNE, Sir Edmond, Kt 1918; Standing Counsel to a number of Trades Unions; *b* 1857; *m* 1907; one *d*. Called to Bar, Middle Temple, 1894. *Address:* 2 Pump Court, Temple, EC4. *T:* City 68.   *Died 9 March 1928.*

BROWNE, Edward Granville, MA, MB; MRCS; FRCP 1911; FBA 1903; Lecturer in Persian, 1888–1902; Sir Thomas Adams Professor of Arabic since 1902; Fellow of Pembroke College, Cambridge, since 1887; *b* Uley, near Dursley, 7 Feb. 1862; *s* of late Sir Benjamin C. Browne, of R. and W. H. Hawthorn, Leslie, and Co., engineers and shipbuilders, Newcastle-on-Tyne; *m* 1906, Alice Caroline Blackburne Daniell (*d* 1925); two *s*. *Educ:* Glenalmond; Eton; Pembroke College, Cambridge; St Bartholomew's Hospital. Graduated at Cambridge in Natural Sciences Tripos, 1882; Indian Languages Tripos, 1884; Beatson Scholar Pembroke Coll., Camb., 1884; studied Medicine and Oriental Languages in Cambridge, 1879–84; London, 1884–87; but never practised as a doctor; travelled in Persia, 1887–88. *Publications:* A Traveller's Narrative, written to illustrate the Episode of the Báb, Persian text and English translation, with notes, 1891; A Year amongst the Persians, 1893; The New History of Mírzá Alí Muhammad the Báb, translated from the Persian, 1893; Catalogue of Persian MSS in Cambridge University Library, 1896; Hand-list of the Muhammadan MSS in the same library, 1900; supplement to same, 1922; critical edition of Dawlatsháh's Tadhkira, 1901; ditto of Awfí's Lubábu'l-Albáb, 1903; Literary History of Persia until the time of Firdawsi, 1902; continuation of same until the Mongol Invasion, 1906; continuation of same to rise of Safawi Dynasty, 1920; continuation of same until the present day, 1924; abridged translation of Ibu Isfandiyar's History of Tabaristán; Short Account of Recent Events in Persia, 1909; History of the Persian Revolution (1905–9), 1910; The Press and Poetry in Modern Persia, 1914; Materials for the Study of the Bábí Religion, 1918; translation of Chahár Maqála, with notes, 1921; Arabian Medicine, 1921; besides numerous papers in the Journal of the Royal Asiatic Society since 1889. *Recreations:* fishing, bicycling. *Address:* Pembroke College, Cambridge; Firwood, Cambridge. *T:* Cambridge 245; Westacres, Benwell, Newcastle-on-Tyne. *M:* ER 2490. *Club:* Royal Societies.

                 Died 5 Jan. 1926.

BROWNE, George, CMG 1917; ISO 1903; Hon. Private Secretary to Governor of Tasmania. Entered Tasmanian Civil Service, 1862; was Clerk of the Peace, Deputy Sheriff, Registrar of Insolvency, and Registrar of the Court of Requests, Launceston; Associate to the Judges of the Supreme Court of Tasmania; Registrar of the Supreme Court in Bankruptcy, Curator of Intestate Estates, etc; JP; Private Secretary to the following Governors: Sir C. Du Cane, Sir F. Weld (and in the Straits Settlements, 1881–84), Sir G. Strahan, Sir Robert Hamilton, Vicount Gormanston, Sir Arthur Havelock, Sir Gerald Strickland, Sir Harry Barron, Rt Hon. Sir William G. Ellison-Macartney, and Sir Francis A. Newdegate; also to Sir V. Fleming, Sir F. Smith, and Sir L. Dobson, Administrators of the Government. *Address:* Hobart, Australia. *Club:* Tasmanian, Hobart.

                 Died 15 Dec. 1919.

BROWNE, Rev. George Rickards, MA Oxon; Rector of Iron Acton since 1889; Rural Dean of Bitton since 1910; and Hon. Canon of Bristol since 1912; *b* 20 Feb. 1854; *s* of Thomas Briarly Browne, MA, TCD, and Mary Ann Rickards; *m* 1883, Jessie Frances Pearce; two *s*. *Educ:* St John's Foundation School, Hereford Cathedral School and Brasenose College, Oxford (Somerset Scholar, Philpott Exhibitioner and Hulme Exhibitioner; First Class in Classical Mods, 1875; BA (Second Class in Modern History), 1877; MA 1880). Deacon, 1878; Priest, 1879; Curate of East Acklam, Yorks, 1878–80; Chaplain of Christ Church, Oxford, 1879–89; Chaplain of New College, 1880–90. *Publication:* National Service. *Address:* Iron Acton Rectory, Bristol. *TA:* Iron Acton.   *Died Sept. 1921.*

BROWNE, Harold Carlyon Gore, MA; Chancellor, Diocese of Winchester to 1914; *b* Wales, 11 June 1844; *e s* of late Bishop of Ely and Winchester. *Educ:* Rugby; Emmanuel Coll., Camb. Barrister Lincoln's Inn. *Recreations:* golf; member of Alpine Club. *Address:* 15 Kingsgate Street, Winchester. *Clubs:* Athenæum, Savile.
Died 22 May 1919.

BROWNE, Gen. Henry Ralph, CB 1905; Colonel Norfolk Regiment since 1903; *b* 29 Dec. 1828; *m* 1852, Frances M. A., *o d* of late Admiral R. W. Parsons. Entered army, 1846; Lt-Gen. 1885; retired, 1885; served Crimea, 1854 (despatches, medal with clasp, Knight of Legion of Honour, 5th class Medjidieh, Turkish medal, brevet of Major); Afghanistan, 1879–80 (medal). *Club:* United Service.
Died 23 Dec. 1917.

BROWNE, Henry William Langley, OBE 1920; JP Co. Stafford; MD, BS, LLD; FRCSE; Consulting Surgeon, West Bromwich Hospital; *b* Bishop Auckland, Co. Durham, 26 Nov. 1848; *e s* of Dr Benjamin S. Browne; *m* Gertrude, *d* of Richard Heckels, Sunderland; one *d. Educ:* Edgbaston; Sydenham College; Birmingham Hospital. Commenced practice at West Bromwich, 1870; retired, 1920; Hon. Surgeon to the West Bromwich and District Hospital, 1871–1904; elected to represent the Midland Counties Branch of the British Medical Association on the London Council, 1893; Chairman, 1906–8; President of the Branch, BMA, 1894; Midland Medical Society, 1902; Association Factory Surgeons, 1905; at the election of English Representatives in the General Medical Council 1906, was returned at the head of the poll, and again at the next election, 1911; retired 1920; Life-Member of Court of Governors, Birmingham University; Fellow of the Royal Society of Medicine. *Publications:* many articles in the medical papers. *Address:* 196 Hagley Road, Edgbaston, Birmingham. *T:* Edgbaston 1356.
Died 7 March 1928.

BROWNE, Maj.-Gen. James; *b* 9 Nov. 1840; *m* Evelyn Elizabeth, *y d* of late Archdeacon Badnall, DD, and *widow* of Major F. L. Northcott. Entered army, 1859; Maj.-Gen. 1896; retired 1898; served Zulu War, 1879–81 (despatches, medal with clasp); Transvaal Campaign, 1881. *Address:* The Wilderness, Worthing, Sussex.
Died 13 June 1917.

BROWNE, John Hutton Balfour-, LLD; JP, DL; KC 1885; *b* Scotland, 13 Sept. 1845; *s* of Dr W. A. F. Browne; *m* 1874, Caroline, *d* of Lord Justice Lush; two *s* one *d. Educ:* Edinburgh University. Barrister 1870; Bencher Middle Temple, 1890; Registrar and Secretary to Railway Commission, 1874; contested Dumfriesshire (C), 1906; East Bradford, 1910. Owned 500 acres. *Publications:* Medical Jurisprudence of Insanity, 1871; Law of Carriers, 1873; Law of Rating, 1874; Law of Usages and Customs, 1875; Law of Railways, 1880; Law of Compensation, 1896; South Africa, 1905; Essays, Critical and Political, 1907; War Problems, 1914; Forty Years at the Bar, 1916; Recollections Literary and Political, 1917. *Address:* 28 Eaton Square, SW1. *T:* Victoria 6169; Goldielea, near Dumfries. *Clubs:* Athenæum, Carlton; Dumfries and Galloway, Dumfries.
Died 27 Sept. 1921.

BROWNE, Sir John Walton, Kt 1921; DL County of Belfast; BA, MD, LLD; Hon. MRCS; Consulting Surgeon, Belfast Royal Hospital; Surgeon, Belfast Ophthalmic Hospital; Senator, Queen's University of Belfast; late Medical Officer, Belfast Post Office; *b* 5 Oct. 1845; *e s* of late Dr S. Browne, RN, formerly Mayor of Belfast; *m* 1st, Fanny, *d* of David Anderson, Strandtown, Belfast; 2nd, Matilda, *d* of Rev. Francis B. Grant, MA, Barbados; one *d. Educ:* Belfast, Dublin, London, and Vienna. Ex-President Ulster Medical Society; Ex-President North of Ireland Branch British Medical Association; Ex-President Ophthalmological Section Annual Meeting British Medical Association; Lecturer Clinical Surgery Ophthalmology, Belfast Medical School; Member of Ophthalmological Society; Medical Referee, Workman's Compensation Act. *Publications:* various papers to Lancet, British Medical Journal, and Transactions of Ulster Medical Society. *Recreation:* travelling. *Address:* Lismore, Windsor Avenue, Belfast. *T:* Malone 187. *Clubs:* Ulster, Royal Ulster Yacht, Belfast.
Died 19 Dec. 1923.

BROWNE, William, MVO 1902; ISO 1903; late HM Office of Works; *b* 17 Feb. 1838; *m* 1872. For 30 years Supt of Central London Parks. *Address:* Ravenswood, 210 Preston Road, Preston, Brighton.
Died 21 Nov. 1924.

BROWNE, Rev. (William) Bevil; Prebendary of Exeter; Licensed Preacher in the Diocese; *b* Standish Vicarage, near Gloucester, 7 June 1845; 5th *s* of Rev. T. Murray Browne and Catherine, *d* of T. Lloyd

Baker of Hardwicke Court, Gloucester; *m* 1871, Mary, *d* of T. Nelson Waterfield, Indian Office; one *s. Educ:* Wellington College; Trinity College, Cambridge.
Died 26 July 1928.

BROWNE, Surgeon-General William Richard, CIE 1906; MD; retired, 1908; *b* 23 May 1850. Joined IMS, 1873; served Rumpa, 1879–80; served on jail duty, Madras; Professor of Pathology, Medical College, 1883–90, of Surgery, 1890; Fellow Madras University, 1892; Principal Medical College, 1901; PMO Madras District, 1903; Hon. Surgeon to Viceroy, 1905.
Died 16 Sept. 1924.

BROWNELL, William Crary, LHD (Amherst College, 1896), LittD (Columbia University, 1910), LLD (Amherst College, 1916); Member of the American Academy of Arts and Letters; author, editor, and literary adviser, with Charles Scribner's Sons, publishers, since 1888; *b* New York City, 30 Aug. 1851; *s* of Isaac Wilbour Brownell and Lucia Emilie Brown; *m* 1st, 1878, Virginia Shields Swinburne (*d* 1911) of Newport, Rhode Island; no *c*; 2nd, 1921, Anna Gertrude Hall of New York. *Educ:* Amherst College, Amherst. On staff of The World, 1871–79; The Nation, 1879–81; resided in Paris and travelled in Europe, 1881–84; on staff of The Philadelphia Press, 1885–86; contributor to various literary and art journals since 1875. *Publications:* French Traits: an Essay in Comparative Criticism, 1889; French Art: Classic and Contemporary Painting and Sculpture, 1892, Newport, 1896; Victorian Prose Masters: Thackeray, Carlyle, George Eliot, Matthew Arnold, Ruskin, George Meredith, 1901; American Prose Masters: Cooper, Hawthorne, Emerson, Poe, Lowell, Henry James, 1909; Criticism, 1914; Standards, 1916; The Genius of Style, 1924. *Address:* 597 Fifth Avenue, New York. *Clubs:* Century, Barnard, New York.
Died 22 July 1928.

BROWNING, Oscar, CBE 1923; MA; Fellow King's College, Cambridge, 1859; University Lecturer in History and Principal of Cambridge University Day Training College, 1891–1909; *b* London, 17 Jan. 1837; *s* of William Shipton Browning and Mariana Margaret Bridge; unmarried. *Educ:* Eton; King's College, Cambridge; President of the Union; 4th in Classical Tripos, 1860. Master at Eton, 1860–75; College and University work at Cambridge, 1876–1909; Examiner, University of London, 1899; Officier d'Académie, 1889; Officier de l'Instruction Publique, 1898; Fellow of the Arcadia Academy, Rome, 1918; Trustee and Chairman British Academy of Arts, Rome, 1921; candidate for Parliament, Norwood, 1886; East Worcestershire, 1892; West Derby, 1895. *Publications:* Cornelius Nepos, 1868; Modern England, 1879; Modern France, 1880; History of Educational Theories, 1881 (translated into Hungarian and Servian); Milton's Tractate on Education, 1883; Political Memoranda of the Duke of Leeds, 1884; Earl Gower's Despatches, 1885; True Stories from English History, 1886; England and Napoleon in 1803, 1887; Aspects of Education, 1888; History of England, in 4 vols, 1890; Life of George Eliot, 1890; Dante: Life and Works, 1891; Goethe: Life and Works, 1891; The Life of Bartolommeo Colleoni, 1891; The Flight to Varennes and other Historical Essays, 1892; The Citizen: his Rights and Responsibilities, 1893; Guelphs and Ghibellines, 1894; The Age of the Condottieri, 1895; Journal of Sir George Rooke, 1897; Life of Peter the Great, 1898; Charles XII of Sweden, 1898; Wars of the Nineteenth Century, 1899; Preface to President Woodrow Wilson's book The State; History of Europe, 1814–1843, 1901; Impressions of Indian Travel, 1903; Napoleon: the first phase, 1905; The Fall of Napoleon, 1907; Memories of Sixty Years, 1910; Despatches from Paris, vols i and ii 1784–91, 1911; History of the Modern World, 1815–1910, 2 vols, 1912, popular edition in one vol., 1916; General History of the World, 1913; History of Medieval Italy, 568–1530 1914; General History of Italy, 1915; Memories of Later Years, 1923; many contributions to Quarterly, Edinburgh, and other reviews. *Recreations:* music, mountaineering, cycling, swimming, golf. *Address:* Palazzo Simonetti, 12 Via Pietro Cavallini, Rome. *Clubs:* Athenæum Bath, Alpine; Royal & Ancient Golf, St Andrews; Circolo Roma, Rome.
Died 6 Oct. 1923.

BROWNING, Sidney, CMG. Assistant District Commissioner Nyasaland Protectorate, 1894; Assistant District Commissioner Uganda Protectorate, 1900; District Commissioner, 1904; Provincial Commissioner, 1914; retired, 1921. *Club:* Sports.
Died 27 Oct. 1928.

BROWNLOW, 3rd Earl, *cr* 1815; **Adelbert Wellington Brownlow Cust,** PC 1887; Bt 1677; Baron Brownlow, 1776; Viscount Alford 1815; Lord-Lieutenant of Lincolnshire, since 1867; Ecclesiastical Commissioner for England; Trustee of the National Gallery, 1897; Aide-de-camp to the King; Hon. Colonel Lincolnshire Imperial Yeomanry; *b* London, 19 Aug. 1844; *s* of Viscount Alford (*e s* of 2nd

Baron and 1st Earl Brownlow) and Lady Marian Margaret Compton, *d* of 2nd Marquess of Northampton; *S* brother 1867; *m* 1868, Lady Adelaide Talbot (*d* 1917), *d* of 18th Earl of Shrewsbury and Talbot. Grenadier Guards, 1863–66; MP (C) N Shropshire, 1866–67; Parliamentary Secretary to Local Government Board, 1885–86; Paymaster-General, 1887–89; Under Secretary of State for War, 1889. Owned about 58,400 acres. *Heir to Barony: kinsman* Major Adelbert Salusbury Cockayne Cust, *b* 14 Sept. 1867. *Address:* 8 Carlton House Terrace, SW1. *T:* Regent 3894; Ashridge Park, Berkhampstead, Herts; Belton House, Grantham, Lincolnshire. *Club:* Carlton.

Died 17 March 1921.

BROWNLOW, 5th Baron, *cr* 1776; **Major Adelbert Salusbury Cockayne Cust;** Bt 1677; *b* 14 Sept. 1867; *y* and *o* surv. *s* of late Major Henry Francis Cockayne Cust of Cockayne Hatley, Beds; *S* 3rd Earl Brownlow to Brownlow Barony, 1921; *m* 1895, Maud, *d* of late Capt. S. Buckle, RE; one *s* one *d. Educ:* Eton. Entered Army, 1888; served in Somerset Light Infantry; retired, 1908; served European War, 1914–18, France and Belgium; JP, DL, Lincolnshire; Hon. Col 4th Bn Lincolnshire Regt; employed in Board of Agriculture and Fisheries, 1918–20; Director Hand in Hand Branch Commercial Insurance Company; ADC and Private Secretary to late Sir Frederick Napier Broome, KCMG, Governor and Commander-in-Chief, Trinidad, WI, 1894–95; Adjt 2nd Vol. Batt. Lincolnshire Regt, 1899–1904; Mayor of Grantham, 1924–25; was Organising Secretary, Royal National Lifeboat Institution. *Heir: s* Hon. Peregrine Francis Adelbert Cust, JP, Lieut and Adjutant Grenadier Guards [*b* 1899. *Educ:* Eton; Royal Military College, Sandhurst. Served European War, 1918]. *Address:* Belton House, Grantham. *Clubs:* United Service, Royal Automobile.

Died 19 April 1927.

BROWNLOW, Lt-Col Celadon Charles, CB 1900; Indian Staff Corps (retired); *b* 20 Nov. 1843; *s* of late Henry B. Brownlow, HEICS; *m* 1888, Rosalie, *d* of late Rev. J. R. Munn. Entered army, 1861; Col 1891; served North-West Frontier, India, and Afghanistan (two medals, despatches, brevet of Col, three clasps). *Address:* Stoatley Copse, Farnham Lane, Haslemere, Surrey.

Died 9 March 1925.

BROWNLOW, Field-Marshal Sir Charles Henry, GCB 1887 (KCB 1872; CB 1864); *b* 12 Dec. 1831; *o s* of Col George A. Brownlow (*brother* of 1st Baron Lurgan); *m* 1890, Georgiana (*d* 1912), *d* of W. C. King, of Warfield Hall, Berks. Punjab Campaigns, 1848; medal, Hazara, 1852–53; expedition against Momund tribes, 1854 (severely wounded); Bozdar Expedition, 1857; Eusofzai Expedition, 1858 (medal with clasp); China War, 1860; action of Sinho, Taku Forts, occupation of Pekin (medal with two clasps); Ambeyla Campaign, 1863, CB; Hazara Campaign, 1868; commanded column Looshai Expedition, 1871–72, KCB; ADC to the Queen, 1869–81; Assistant Military Secretary at Horse Guards, 1879–89. *Recreation:* horse-breeding. *Address:* Warfield Hall, Bracknell, Berks. *Clubs:* United Service, Arthur's.

Died 5 April 1916.

BROWNLOW, Col Charles William, CMG 1919; CBE 1919; DSO 1918; *s* of late Capt. H. R. Brownlow, Royal (late Bengal) Artillery; *b* 1862; *m* 1895, Ethel Mary, *y d* of late W. H. Preston of Minstead Lodge, Hampshire; one *s* one *d. Educ:* Cheltenham College; Royal Military Academy, Woolwich. Served Zhob Valley Expedition, 1890; Burma Expedition, 1891–92 (medal and clasp); NW Frontier of India, 1897–98 (medal and clasp); Tirah Expedition, 1897–98 (clasp); European War, 1914–18 (despatches, DSO, CMG, CBE); retired from Army 1919. *Address:* Kingston Lodge, Dartmouth.

Died 30 April 1924.

BROWNLOW, Maj.-Gen. William Vesey, CB 1887; Colonel 1st King's Dragoon Guards, 1908; *o* surv. *s* of William and Charlotte Brownlow, Knapton House, Queen's Co.; *b* 14 June 1841; *m* 1st, 1881, Lady Anne Henrietta (*d* 1898), 3rd *d* of 10th Earl of Stair; 2nd, 1904, Lady Kathleen Bligh, 2nd *d* of 6th Earl of Darnley. *Educ:* private school. With 1st Dragoon Guards in Zulu War, 1879 (brevet of Major); in command of a mounted force in Boer War, 1880–81 (brevet of Lt-Col); Assistant Commandant cavalry depot, 1882–88; Col commanding a regimental district, 1889–94; Major-General, 1898; retired, 1901; High Sheriff, Co. Monaghan, 1907; JP Hampshire. *Decorated:* 1st Boer War. *Recreations:* hunting, shooting. *Address:* Eveley, Bordon, Hants. *Clubs:* Army and Navy; Kildare Street, Dublin.

Died 15 March 1926.

BROWNRIGG, Rt. Rev. Abraham; RC Bishop of Ossory since 1884; *b* Kildavin, Co. Carlow, 23 Dec. 1836. *Educ:* St Peter's College, Wexford; Maynooth Coll., 1856; read a course of Philosophy, Sacred Scripture, and Theology. Ordained priest, 1861; appointed Professor at St Peter's Coll., Wexford, 1861; member of a Diocesan missionary community established at Enniscorthy, Co. Wexford, 1866; Rector of same community, 1876, *Address:* Kilkenny.

Died 1 Oct. 1928.

BROWNRIGG, Colonel Metcalfe Studholme, JP London County; late Commanding Wiltshire and Dorset Brigade, 30/47 Regimental District and Oxfordshire Light Infantry; *b* 1845; 3rd *s* of General Brownrigg, CB; *m* 1869, Emily, *d* of Sir Edward Borough, Bt, and Lady Elizabeth Borough; two *d. Educ:* Eton. Entered army, 1863; was first ADC to Lord-Lieutenant of Ireland; Gold Stick Staff Officer at Coronation; Jubilee and Coronation medals. *Address:* 20 Onslow Square, SW7. *T:* Western 2630. *Clubs:* Travellers', United Service.

Died 28 Feb. 1924.

BRUCE, Alexander, KC 1885; head of law firm of Bruce, Bruce and Counsell, Hamilton, Ontario; *b* 23 Nov. 1836; 3rd *s* of William and Isabella Bruce, Longside, Aberdeenshire, Scotland; *m* 1863, Agnes, *d* of Rev. Ralph Robb; two *s* three *d. Educ:* Longside Parish School; Grammar School, Aberdeen; Marischal College, Aberdeen, MA. Student of and for some years partner of the late Chief Justice Sir George Burton; called to the Bar of the Law Society of Upper Canada, 1861; practised profession in Hamilton, Ontario, to 1905, when removed to Toronto; a Bencher of the Law Society of Upper Canada since 1886; a member of the Corporation of Trinity University, Toronto; a Director of the Canada Life Assurance Company and National Trust Company, Limited, both of Toronto; President of Calydor Sanatorium, Ltd (for Tuberculosis), Gravenhurst, Ontario. *Recreations:* walking, travelling. *Address:* 91 Bedford Road, Toronto. *TA:* Bruce, Canlife, Toronto. *T:* Hillerest 2290. *Clubs:* Toronto, Royal Canadian Yacht, Toronto; Hamilton, Hamilton; Caledon Mountain Trout.

Died 20 Aug. 1920.

BRUCE, Sir Alexander Carmichael, Kt 1903; JP; Assistant Commissioner Metropolitan Police, 1884–1914; *b* 1850; 4th *s* of late Rev. Canon David Bruce; *m* 1876, Helen (*d* 1915), *d* of John Fletcher, DL. *Educ:* Brasenose College, Oxford. Called to Bar, Lincoln's Inn, 1875; went North-Eastern Circuit. *Address:* 25 Egerton Terrace, SW3. *T:* Kensington 3670.

Died 25 Oct. 1926.

BRUCE, Col Andrew Macrae, CB 1900; *b* 5 Jan. 1842; *s* of late William Bruce of Symbister, Shetland, and Agnes Macrae; *m* 1889, Margaret, *d* of late Charles Hay, Edinburgh; one *d* (one *s*, Lieut 59th Scind Rifles, Frontier Force; killed in a German trench when in charge of a bombing party at Givenchy near La Bassee, 19 Dec. 1914). Joined the Indian Army as Ensign, 1860; served with the 2nd Bengal Fusiliers, 1860–61; with the 1st Gurkhas, 1861–65; with the 4th Regt Punjab Infantry, Punjab Frontier Force, 1865–94; British Agent in Gilgit, 1893–94; Colonel on the Staff, Ferozepore, 1896–97; Brig.-General commanding at Bangalore, 1897–98; at Lahore and Rohilkund, 1898; served NE Frontier of India, Bhutan, 1865–66 (medal and clasp); NW Frontier of India, Besoti-Afridi Affair, 1869 (received special thanks of Government of India); NW Frontier of India, Miranzi, 1869; NW Frontier of India, Jowaki, 1877–87 (clasp); Afghanistan, 1879–80 (medal); NW Frontier of India, Mahsud Waziri, 1881 (despatches, brought specially to notice of C-in-C); NW Frontier of India, Tukht-i-Suliman, 1881 (despatches); NW Frontier of India, Zhob Valley, 1884; NW Frontier of India, Hazara, 1888 (clasp); (1st) Miranzai, 1891; commanded 1st column (despatches); Good Service Pension, 1899. *Address:* La Fontaine, Pontac, Jersey, CI. *Club:* East India United Service.

Died 6 April 1920.

BRUCE, Sir Charles, GCMG 1901 (KCMG 1889; CMG 1881); JP, DL; *b* 1836; *m* 1868, Clara (*d* 1916), *d* of J. Lucas; two *s. Educ:* Harrow; Yale University; Germany. Professor of Sanscrit, King's College, 1865; Rector, Royal College, Mauritius, 1868; Director of Public Instruction, Ceylon, 1878; Colonial Secretary, Mauritius, 1882; Lieut-Gov. of British Guiana, 1885–93; Governor of the Windward Isles, 1893–97; Governor of Mauritius, 1897–1904. *Publications:* Die Geschichte von Nala (Imperial Academy of Petrograd), 1862; Poems, 1865; The Broad Stone of Empire, 1910; The True Temper of Empire, 1912; Milestones on my Long Journey, 1917; and numerous contributions to English and foreign reviews. *Address:* Arnot Tower, Leslie, NB. *Clubs:* Carlton; New, Edinburgh.

Died 13 Dec. 1920.

BRUCE, Sir Hervey Juckes Lloyd, 4th Bt, *cr* 1804; late Lieutenant-Colonel Coldstream Guards; *b* 5 Oct. 1843; *s* of 3rd Bt and Marianne, *d* of Sir J. G. Juckes Clifton, 8th Bt; *S* father, 1907; *m* 1872, Ellen Maud (OBE), *d* of Percy Ricardo of Bramley Park, Guildford; four *s. Educ:* Eton College. Entered army, 1862; retired 1878. Owned about 22,000 acres. *Heir: s* Hervey Ronald Bruce, Capt., late Irish Guards [*b* 9 Dec. 1872; *m* 1st, 1903, Ruth Isabel (*d* 1915), 3rd *d* of late H. C. Okeover; 2nd, 1916, Margaret Florence, *d* of Rev. Robert Jackson, Rector of Little Thurlow, Newmarket; one *d*]. *Address:* Downhill, Londonderry; Clifton Hall, Nottingham. *TA:* Clifton, Nottingham. *T:* Nottingham 5140. *Clubs:* Turf, Guards.

Died 8 May 1919.

BRUCE, Sir Hervey Ronald, 5th Bt, *cr* 1804; late Major, Royal Irish Rifles; *b* 9 Dec. 1872; *s* of 4th Bt and Ellen Maud (OBE), *d* of Percy Ricardo of Bramley Park, Guildford; *S* father 1919; *m* 1st, 1903, Ruth Isabel (*d* 1915), 3rd *d* of late H. C. Okeover; 2nd, 1916, Margaret Florence, *d* of Rev. Robert Jackson, Rector of Little Thurlow, Newmarket; two *s* one *d*. Served S Africa, 1899–1902 (Queen's Medal and five clasps, King's Medal and two clasps); JP, DL, Co. Londonderry. Owned about 22,000 acres. *Heir: s* Hervey John William Bruce, *b* 29 June 1919. *Address:* Downhill, Londonderry; Clifton Hall, Nottingham. *TA:* Clifton, Nottingham. *T:* Nottingham 5140. *Club:* Guards. *Died 18 May 1924.*

BRUCE, Admiral Sir James Andrew Thomas, KCMG 1900; *b* 15 July 1846; *yr s* of Rt Hon. Sir Hervey Bruce, 3rd Bt; *m* 1877, Catherine Mary Philippa, *d* of Col Edwin Wodehouse, CB. Entered RN 1859; Rear-Admiral, 1898; served Niger River, 1876; ADC to the Queen, 1895–98; Senior Officer, Gibraltar, 1895–98; 2nd in command China Station, 1900–1; Admiral, 1907. *Address:* 3 Montagu Square, W1. *T:* Mayfair 3252. *Club:* United Service.

Died 25 May 1921.

BRUCE, Richard Isaac, CIE 1881; Commissioner, Punjab, Indian Provincial Civil Service; retired 1896; *b* 1840; *s* of Jonathan Bruce of Miltown Castle, Co. Cork; *m* 1871, Lilla (*d* 1912), *d* of Rev. J. Beavor Webb, Rector of Dunderrow, Kinsale, Co. Cork. Served Afghanistan, 1878–79 (despatches, medal); North-West Frontier of India; Zhob Valley Expedition, affair at Dowlatzai, 1884; Zhob Valley Expedition, 1890 (despatches); received special thanks and commendation of HM's Secretary of State for India for distinguished services in connection with the opening of the Gomal Pass, 1890; appointed British Commissioner of the Afghan-Waziristan Delimitation Commission, 1894; action at Wano, 1894; Waziristan, 1894–95 (despatches, medal with clasp); received on several occasions thanks of Government of India for distinguished frontier services. *Publications:* A Gazetteer of Dera Ghazi Khan District; A Manual of the Beluchi Language; A History of the Marri-Beluch Tribe; The Forward Policy, and its Results. *Address:* Quetta, Fairfax Road, Teddington. *Club:* East India United Service.

Died 29 Jan. 1924.

BRUCE, William, AM, MD, LLD (Hon.) Aberdeen; Medical Officer of Health for the County of Ross and Cromarty; Direct Representative for Scotland in the General Medical Council, 1887–1907; *s* of Alexander Bruce, Keig, Aberdeenshire; *m* Agnes, *d* of William Ironside; two *s* four *d*. *Educ:* Aberdeen Grammar School, and King's College and University. After practising twelve years in Aberdeenshire, and holding the post of Examiner in Medicine at Aberdeen University, settled in Dingwall, 1870, and practised there and in Strathpeffer till 1890; since then Consulting Physician; Governor of Highlands and Islands Educational Trust, 1900–15; Chairman of Ross-shire Advisory Committee of Aberdeen Agricultural College, and of the Parish Council of Dingwall. *Publications:* Sciatica, a fresh Study; and to the newspapers on educational subjects. *Recreations:* gardening, golfing. *Address:* The Castle, Dingwall, NB. *T:* Dingwall Exchange XI; Strathpeffer 13.

Died 24 Oct. 1920.

BRUCE, Ven. William Conybeare; Rector of Rogiet, near Newport, 1901. *Educ:* Rugby; University Coll., Oxford (MA). Rector of St Nicholas, near Cardiff, 1871–82; Vicar of St Woolos, Newport, 1882–1901; Canon of Llandaff, 1885; Archdeacon of Monmouth, 1885–1914. *Address:* Rogiet Rectory, Newport, Monmouthshire; Canonry, Llandaff.

Died 12 Feb. 1919.

BRUCE, William Ironside, MD, DPH; Physician in Charge of the X-Ray Departments, Charing Cross Hospital, the Hospital for Sick Children, Great Ormond Street, etc; *s* of William Bruce, MD, of Dingwall, and Agnes Ironside; *m* Violet, *d* of late N. Randle of Bombay, India; no *c*. *Educ:* Edinburgh Academy; Aberdeen University. Served as Civil Surgeon in South Africa, and later returned to Aberdeen, obtaining the degrees of MD, DPH; began practice in London shortly afterwards at Charing Cross Hospital. *Publications:* A System of Radiography with an Atlas of the Normal; X-Ray Examination; Choyce's System of Surgery; X-Ray Treatment;

Churchill's System of Treatment; many papers on subjects connected with X-Rays. *Recreations:* motoring, golf. *Address:* 10 Chandos Street, Cavendish Square, W1. *T:* 3985; Mayfair 3984. *M:* LA 8057.

Died 21 March 1921.

BRUCE, William Speirs, LLD Aberdeen; FRSE, etc; *b* 1 Aug. 1867; *s* of Samuel Noble Bruce, MRCS, of Edinburgh; *m* 1901, Jessie, *d* of late Alexander Mackenzie, Nigg, Ross-shire; one *s* one *d*. *Educ:* Univ. of Edinburgh. Lecturer on Geography, Heriot-Watt College, 1899–1901 and since 1917, and Church of Scotland Training College, Edinburgh, 1899–1901; George Heriot Research Fellow, Univ. of Edinburgh, 1900–1; Director of Scottish Oceanographical Laboratory, Edinburgh; Assistant in Challenger Expedition Commission; also in Zoology at the School of Medicine of the Royal Colleges, Edinburgh; Naturalist, Scottish Antarctic Expedition, 1892–93; in charge of Ben Nevis Observatory, 1895 and 1896; Zoologist, Jackson-Harmsworth Polar Expedition, 1896 and 1897; Naturalist Major Andrew Coats' Expedition to Novaya Zemlya, Wiche Islands, and Barents Sea, 1898; Naturalist, HSH the Prince of Monaco's Expedition, Spitsbergen, 1898, 1899, and 1906; Leader of Scottish National Antarctic Expedition (SY "Scotia"), 1902–4; discovered 150 miles of the Coast Line of Antarctica, naming it Coats' Land; bathymetrically surveyed the South Atlantic Ocean and Weddell Sea to 74° 1' S and between 60° W and 20° E; explored and surveyed Prince Charles Foreland and other parts of Spitsbergen, 1906, 1907, 1909, 1912, 1914, 1919, and 1920. Gold Medallist of the Royal Scottish Geographical Society, 1904; Royal Gold Medal (Paton's) of Royal Geographical Society, 1910; Hon. Member, Gesellschaft für Erdkunde zu Berlin; Neill Prize and Gold Medallist of Royal Society of Edinburgh, 1911–13; Livingstone Gold Medal of American Geographical Society, 1920; Membre de Comité de Perfectionnement de l'Institut Oceanographique, Paris; Honorary Member New Zealand Institute. *Publications:* Scientific Results of the Voyage of SY "Scotia," 1902–4; Polar Exploration; author and joint author of papers and contributions to the Royal Society of Edinburgh and other learned societies and journals. *Recreations:* gardening, walking, photography. *Address:* 22 George Street, Edinburgh. *Club:* Royal Eastern Yacht, Edinburgh.

Died 31 Oct. 1921.

BRUCE-JOY, Albert, RHA, FRGS; sculptor; *b* Dublin; *e s* of Dr W. Bruce Joy, and *b* of George W. Joy, painter. *Educ:* Becker's School, Offenbach; tutor, Paris; King's Coll., London; S Kensington and Royal Acad. Schools of Art. Pupil of Foley; studied in Rome three years. Public statues, chiefly colossal: Gladstone (in front Bow Church), Lord Frederick Cavendish (Barrow-in-Furness), John Bright (Manchester), Bright (Birmingham), Harvey Tercentenary Memorial (Folkestone), Chief Just. Whiteside (St Patrick's Cath.), Sir Mathew Wilson (Skipton), Alexander Balfour (Liverpool), Christopher Bushell (University, Liverpool), Graves (Royal Coll. of Physicians, Ireland), Oliver Heywood (Manchester), Laird (Birkenhead), Whitley (Liverpool), Berkeley, Bishop (Cloyne Cath.), Lord Kelvin (Belfast), Hornby (Blackburn), Lord Justice FitzGibbon (St Patrick's Cathedral), Cranmer Memorial (Cambridge), the John Bright statue (House of Commons), The Provost, George Salmon, DD, Memorial (St Patrick's Cathedral), the Memorial Dean Farrar (Canterbury Cathedral); bust Viscount Morley (India); busts King Edward VII—in University, Manchester, Paris Chamber of Commerce, Norwich Memorial Hospital, Peace Palace (Hague), Genoa Chamber of Commerce, Royal Chelsea Hospital, Indian Memorial (Mayo Hospital, Lahore), and Belfast Memorial Hospital, etc; King George V (Public Park, Amod, India); Queen Victoria (colossal), for Victoria, BC; bust Lord Salisbury (Mansion House), Matthew Arnold (Westminster Abbey), Adams (astronomer) Memorial and Russel Wallace (Westminster Abbey), Archbishop of Canterbury (Benson), Lord Farnborough (House of Commons), Codrington Memorial (St Paul's), Montgomery (St Paul's), Sir R. Montgomery (India Office), Lord Cairns Memorial (Lincoln's Inn), and bust (Royal Law Courts), Mark Firth (Firth Coll., Sheffield), Pratt Memorial (School Chapel, Harrow), Archbishop Benson Memorial (Rugby School Chapel); the Maharajah of Nepal; bust Mary Anderson (Stratford-on-Avon); in America—the Ayer Colossal Lion (Lowell, Boston), Chauncey Depew bust (Lotus Club, New York), Hon. Loudon Snowden (Philadelphia); ideal works—The Young Apollo, The Forsaken, The First Flight, The Little Visitor, The Fairy Tale, Moses and Brazen Serpent, Faith (Christian Knowledge Society's Building), Thetis and Achilles, The Pets, Beatrice, Sunshine, The Cricketer (C. B. Fry), The Fencer (Seligman), Tennis (E. Miles), The Boy Scout. *Recreations:* boating, riding, skating, music. *Address:* 2 Whitehall Court, SW1; Chase Lodge, near Hindhead, Haslemere. *Clubs:* Athenæum, Arts, Authors'.

Died 22 July 1924.

BRUNGER, Captain Robert, DSO 1916; 4th Suffolk Regiment; *b* Framlingham, 25 May 1893; *s* of W. T. Brunger of Framlingham

College, Suffolk; unmarried. *Educ:* Framlingham College. Second Lieut 4th Suffolk Regt, 1911; proceeded to New Zealand in 1913 and was engaged in sheep-farming, during which time he became attached to the 3rd Auckland Infantry Batt. (allied regiment to the Suffolks); recalled to rejoin his regiment in England on the outbreak of war; Captain, Jan. 1915; served in France; wounded May 1916, and returned to England (despatches, DSO). *Address:* College House, Framlingham, Suffolk.   *Died 8 Oct. 1918.*

BRUNNER, Ernst August, JP; Life Member Royal Colonial Institute; general merchant; *b* Oude Wetering, Holland; *s* of Rev. E. A. Brunner and M. J. Rademaker; *m* 1879, Cornelie Louise Colenbrander; no *c. Educ:* Leiden. Arrived in Natal, 1872; found employment at sugar and coffee estates, and finally settled down at a small trading station in the Lower Tugela valley where he engaged in trade with the natives and few Europeans in the district, running at the same time a ferry, a butchery, and a bakery; went through the Zulu War as a volunteer, being a member of the Stanger Mounted Rifles; attached himself to the Natal Guides under Major Barrow, and connected with his Mounted Infantry with Col Pearson's column (medal and clasp); at termination of war was appointed a magistrate under Chief John Dunn, who sent him home in 1881 to interview authorities in Downing Street with regard to the proposed return of Cetywayo to Zululand; the mission proved futile, and upon the return of the exiled King settled at what became the township of Eshowe, of which he was the originator, since he built the first house there, 1883, and the town grew around him; passed through the rebellion of 1885 and 1888, the last Boer war, and the rebellions of 1906 and 1908; represented Zululand in the Natal House of Assembly, 1899–1910; Colonial Treasurer, 1906–7; Union medal, presented at time Union was consummated "to those who rendered special service in connection with the establishment of the Union". *Recreations:* music, crayon drawing. *Address:* Samarang, Eshowe, Zululand. *Clubs:* Victoria, Pietermaritzburg.   *Died 13 Jan. 1920.*

BRUNNER, Rt. Hon. Sir John Tomlinson, 1st Bt, *cr* 1895; PC 1906; DL; MP (L) Northwich, 1885–86, and 1887–1909; Pro-Chancellor Liverpool University, 1909; Chairman, Brunner, Mond and Co., Ltd, alkali manufacturers; *b* Everton, Liverpool, 8 Feb. 1842; *s* of Rev. John Brunner, of Canton Zürich, Switzerland, schoolmaster at Everton; *m* 1st, 1864, Salome (*d* 1874), *d* of James Davies of Liverpool; two *s* three *d* (and one *s* decd); 2nd, 1875, Jane (*d* 1910), *d* of Dr Wyman of Kettering; two *d* (and one *d* decd). *Educ:* his father's school. Entered mercantile life at Liverpool, 1857; served John Hutchinson and Co., alkali manufacturers of Widnes, 1861–72; in company with Ludwig Mond, FRS, he established (1873) the Alkali Works at Northwich, which became the largest in the world. Presented Northwich with a public library; Runcorn and Winsford with Guildhalls for the use of Trade Unions, Friendly and other Societies; benefactor to Liverpool University (endowed three chairs; Hon. LLD); Sir John Deane's Grammar School, Witton, Northwich, and several public libraries; Member of Royal Commission for Paris Exhibition, 1900; of Civil List Committee, 1901; of Royal Commission on Canals and Waterways, 1906; Vice-President Cheshire Football Association. *Publications:* Handbooks on Public Education in Cheshire, 1891 and 1896; Eight Hours Question. *Recreation:* golf (Sunningdale and Cannes Golf Clubs). *Heir: s* John Fowler Leece Brunner, *b* 24 May 1865. *Address:* Silverlands, Chertsey. *T:* Chertsey 23. *M:* LB 7197, P 6845. *Clubs:* Reform, National Liberal, Ranelagh.   *Died 1 July 1919.*

BRUNNER, Roscoe, DL; JP; *b* 22 Jan. 1871; 3rd *s* of late Rt Hon. Sir John Tomlinson Brunner, 1st Bt, and Salome, *d* of James Davies, Liverpool; *m* 1898, Ethel (author of Celia and her Friends, Celia Once Again, Celia's Fantastic Voyage, etc), *e d* of late Arthur Houston, KC; two *s* one *d. Educ:* Cheltenham; Cambridge. Called to Bar, Inner Temple, 1895; Director of Brunner, Mond & Co. Ltd. *Club:* Bath.   *Died 3 Nov. 1926.*

BRUNSKILL, Gerald FitzGibbon, KC Ireland, 1914; *b* 4 April 1866; 2nd *s* of late Thomas R. Brunskill, 58 Upper Mount Street, Dublin; *m* 1896, Annie, *d* of late Archibald Robinson, Taxing Master in Chancery, High Court of Justice in Ireland; one *s* one *d. Educ:* Trinity College, Dublin, BA (1887), MA (1891). Gold Medallist in Oratory and Composition, University Philosophical Society; Silver Medallist in Oratory and Composition, College Historical Society; auditor of College Historical Society, 1889; called to Irish Bar, 1888; admitted a Solicitor, 1900; recalled to Bar, 1901; a Director of the City of Dublin Steam Packet Co.; MP (C) Mid-Tyrone, 1910; contested same Division, 1910. *Recreation:* golf. *Address:* 35 Leeson Park, Dublin. *T:* Ballsbridge 471. *Clubs:* Constitutional; Dublin University.   *Died 4 Oct. 1918.*

BRUNTON, Sir (Thomas) Lauder, 1st Bt, *cr* 1908; Kt 1900; MD, ScD, LLD (Hon.) (Edin.); LLD (Hon.) (Aberdeen); MD RUI (Hon.); FRCP; FRS (Vice-President, 1906); Consulting Physician to St Bartholomew's Hospital; late Surgeon Lieutenant-Colonel and Chief Medical Officer, 1st City of London Cadet Brigade; *b* 14 March 1844; *s* of James Brunton of Hiltonshill, Roxburghshire; *m* 1879, Louisa Jane (*d* 1909), *d* of late Ven. Edward A. Stopford, Archdeacon of Meath; one *s* two *d. Publications:* The Bible and Science, 1881; Text-Book of Pharmacology; Modern Therapeutics, 1892; Lectures on the Action of Medicines, 1897; on Disorders of Assimilation, 1901; collected papers on Circulation and Respiration, 1st Series, 1907, 2nd Series, 1916; Therapeutics of the Circulation, 1908. *Heir: s* Capt. James Stopford Lauder Brunton [*b* 11 Oct. 1884; *m* 1915, Elizabeth, *o d* of Prof. J. Bonsall Porter, Instructional Staff, Canadian Army]. *Address:* 1 De Walden Court, New Cavendish Street, W. *TA:* Lauder Brunton, Wesdo, London. *T:* Mayfair 1627. *Club:* Athenæum.   *Died 16 Sept. 1916.*

BRUYNE, Pieter Louis de, CVO (hon.) 1904 (MVO (hon.) 1897); retired British Vice-Consul; *b* 11 Feb. 1845; *m*; three *s. Address:* Middelburg, Holland. *TA:* debruyne, Middelburg. *T:* 251.   *Died 1 April 1917.*

BRYAN, Prof. George Hartley, ScD; FRS; *b* Cambridge, 1 March 1864; *o s* of late Robert Purdie Bryan; *m* 1906, Mabel Williams; one *d. Educ:* Peterhouse, Cambridge. Fellow, 1889–95; Smith's Prize, 1889; Hon. Fellow, 1915; Hopkins Prize, 1920; Gold Medal Inst. Naval Architects, 1901; Gold Medal Royal Aeronautical Society, 1914 (both medals stolen); Silver Medal Prestito Littorio, 1926–27; awarded special grant from Research Department, 1917–20; Past President Cambridge Entomological Society, Postal Microscopical Society, Mathematical Association, Inst. Aeronaut. Engineers; Hon. Member Calcutta Mathematical Society. *Publications:* chiefly on aeroplane rigid dynamics; Stability in Aviation; Reports on Compressible Fluids, Acoustics of Airscrews and Canonical Forms (Aeronautics); text books, Briggs and Bryan series; Thermodynamics; Mathematical Tables; illustrations in Things seen in Italian Lakes and Riviera. *Recreations:* natural history, photography, cutting rolls for player piano. *Address:* Le Lucciole, Bordighera, Italy. *TA:* Lucciole, Bordighera. *Club:* Touring Club Italiano.   *Died 13 Oct. 1928.*

BRYAN, William Jennings; late editor and proprietor of The Commoner; *b* Salem, Illinois, 19 March 1860; *m* 1884, Mary E. Baird, of Perry, Ill; one *s* two *d. Educ:* Illinois Coll.; Union College of Law, Chicago; degrees from many colleges and universities. Practised at Jacksonville, Ill, 1883–87; afterwards at Lincoln, Neb; Editor Omaha World-Herald, 1894–96; Delegate to National Democratic Convention, 1896; nominated for President, 1896, 1900, and 1908; advocated free coinage of silver, and opposed Trusts and Imperialism; made tour round world, 1905–6; Secretary of State, 1913–15. Presbyterian. *Publications:* The First Battle; The Old World and its Ways; In His Image; Famous Figures of the Old Testament; Shall Christianity remain Christian?; Heart to Heart Appeals; many articles in magazines and newspapers. *Address:* Miami, Florida, USA.   *Died 26 July 1925.*

BRYANT, Frederick Beadon, CSI 1911; *b* 20 March 1858; *m* 1885, Mary, *d* of Alfred Lund. Assistant Conservator, 1881; Deputy Conservator, 1890; Conservator, 1901; Chief Conservator, Burma, 1905; Inspector-General of Forests, Government of India, 1908–13; retired, 1913. *Address:* Ryders, Walton-on-Thames. *Club:* East India United Service.   *Died 28 Nov. 1922.*

BRYANT, Sophie, DSc (London); LittD Dublin (hon.); *b* Dublin, 1850; *d* of late Rev. W. A. Willock, DD; *m* at 19, Dr William Hicks Bryant (decd), of Plymouth. *Educ:* privately; Bedford College, London (graduated with Mathematical and Moral Science honours, 1881; took degree of Doctor of Science in the Moral Science branch, 1884, being the first woman to take that degree). Childhood spent chiefly in Co. Fermanagh, Ireland, where her father played a prominent part in the Irish national education movement; after removing to London, she gained an Arnott scholarship at Bedford Coll.; after husband's death, a year later resumed her work as a student, and became mathematical mistress at the North London Collegiate School for Girls; succeeded Miss Buss as head mistress of the school, 1895; retired 1918; appointed to serve upon Royal Commission on Secondary Education, 1894; a member of the Consultative Committee of the Board of Education, 1900–11; of the Senate of the University of London, 1900–7; and of the London Education Committee, 1908–14; Ex-President Head Mistresses' Association. *Publications:* Educational Ends; Celtic Ireland; Studies in Character; The Teaching of Morality in the Family and the School; The Teaching of Christ on Life and Conduct; The Genius of the Gael; How to read the Bible in the Twentieth Century; Moral and Religious Education; Liberty, Order and Law under Native Irish Rule, A Study in the Book of the Ancient Laws of Ireland; and other educational, philosophical, and scientific articles. *Recreations:* cycling, boating, mountaineering. *Address:* North London Collegiate School for Girls, Sandall Road, NW. *Club:* University of London.

Died 14 Aug. 1922.

BRYCE, 1st Viscount, *cr* 1914, of Dechmont, Lanarks; **James Bryce**, OM 1907; GCVO 1917; PC 1892; DCL, LLD; FRS 1893; FBA 1902; *b* 10 May 1838; *e s* of James Bryce (*d* 1877), LLD, of Glasgow and Margaret, *e d* of James Young, Abbeyville, Co. Antrim; *m* 1889, Elizabeth Marion, *d* of Thomas Ashton, Fordbank, near Manchester. *Educ:* High School and University of Glasgow; Scholar of Trin. Coll. Oxford (BA 1862, DCL 1870); Fellow of Oriel Coll., 1862; at Heidelberg University, 1863. Barrister Lincoln's Inn, 1867; practised till 1882; Regius Professor of Civil Law at Oxford, 1870; resigned that office, 1893; MP for Tower Hamlets, 1880; MP (L) Aberdeen, S, 1885–1907; Under-Secretary of State for Foreign Affairs, 1886; Chancellor of Duchy of Lancaster (with seat in Cabinet), 1892; President of Board of Trade, 1894; Chief Secretary for Ireland, 1905–7; HM Ambassador Extraordinary and Plenipotentiary at Washington, 1907–13; Chairman of Royal Commission on Secondary Education, 1894; member of Senate of London University, 1893; corresponding member of Institute of France, 1891 (foreign member, 1904); foreign member of Royal Academies of Turin and Brussels, 1896, of Naples, 1903, St Petersburg and Stockholm; corresponding member of Società Romana di Storia Patria, 1885; member of Reale Accademia dei Lincei, Rome, 1904; one of the British members of the International Tribunal at the Hague. Hon. LLD of Edinburgh University, 1883; Glasgow University, 1886; Michigan University, 1887; St Andrews, 1902; Aberdeen, 1906; Jena, 1908; California and Leipzig, 1909; Buenos Aires, 1910; Adelaide and Brisbane, 1912; Belfast, 1919; Doctor of Political Science of Royal Hungarian University of Buda Pest, 1896; LittD Victoria University, 1897; Cambridge, 1898; Oxford, 1914; TCD, 1920; DCL Trinity University, Toronto, 1897; Harvard and Princeton University, 1907; Hon. Fellow of Trinity and Oriel Colleges, Oxford; Pres. of the Alpine Club, 1899–1901; Hon. Member Faculty of Law University of Santiago; ex-Pres. British Academy; a trustee of the National Portrait Gallery; Hon. Fellow of the Royal Geographical Society. *Publications:* The Flora of the Island of Aran, 1859; The Holy Roman Empire, 1862; Report on the Condition of Education in Lancashire, 1867; The Trade Marks Registration Act, with Introduction and Notes on Trade Mark Law, 1877; Transcaucasia and Ararat, 1877; The American Commonwealth, 1888; Impressions of South Africa, 1897; Studies in History and Jurisprudence, 1901; Studies in Contemporary Biography, 1903; The Hindrances to Good Citizenship, 1909; South America: Observations and Impressions, 1912; University and Historical Addresses, 1913; Essays and Addresses on War, June 1918; Modern Democracies, 1921. *Recreations:* mountain-climbing, angling. *Heir:* none. *Address:* Hindleap, Forest Row, Susex; 3 Buckingham Gate, SW. *Club:* Athenæum.

Died 22 Jan. 1922 (ext).

BRYCE, John Annan, JP Island of Bombay; MP (L) Inverness Burghs, 1906–18; *b* 1844; *s* of James Bryce, LLD, of Glasgow, and Margaret, *d* of James Young, of Abbeyville, Belfast; *brother* of Viscount Bryce; *m* 1888, Violet, *d* of Captain Champagné L'Estrange, RA; one *s* two *d*. *Educ:* High School and Univ. of Glasgow (MA); Edinburgh Univ.; Balliol College, Oxford (Brackenbury History Scholar), BA. First Class Hons, Final Classical School; Hons in History School; was Secretary, Treasurer, and Pres., Oxford Union Society; formerly East India Merchant, was Chairman Rangoon Chamber of Commerce, Member of Legislative Council of Burma; made extensive explorations in unknown parts of Upper Burma before the war, and in Upper Siam; Director, London County and Westminster Bank; English Scottish and Australian Bank; Atlas Assurance Co.; Bombay Baroda Railway Co.; and Burma Railway Co.; Chairman of British Westinghouse Co.; twice Member of Council of Royal Geographical Society; Member of Royal Commission on Congestion in Ireland, 1906–8. *Address:* 35 Bryanston Square, W1. *T:* Paddington 400. *Clubs:* Alpine, Savile.

Died 25 June 1923.

BRYMER, Ven. Frederick Augustus, MA; Archdeacon of Wells since 1899; Rector of Charlton Mackrell, Somerset, since 1876; 3rd surv. *s* of late John Brymer of Islington House, Dorchester; *m* 1882, Mary, *d* of late Preb. W. F. Neville, of Butleigh Vicarage, Somerset; one *s* one *d*. *Educ:* Radley; Christ Church, Oxford. Curate of Wargrave, 1874–76; Assistant Diocesan Inspector of Schools for Cary Deanery, 1880–88; Hon. Secretary, Bath and Wells Diocesan Societies, 1887–1902; Prebendary of Wiveliscombe, 1891; Secretary, Bath and Wells Diocesan School Association, 1897; Proctor in Convocation for Bath and Wells, 1898; Prebendary of Huish and Brent, in right of the Archdeaconry, 1899. *Address:* The Rectory, Charlton Mackrell, Somerset. *TA:* Charlton Mackrell. *Club:* Oxford and Cambridge.

Died 1 May 1917.

BUCHANAN, Lt-Col Arthur Louis Hamilton; late Gordon Highlanders; MP (CU) Coatbridge Division of Lanarkshire, 1918–22; *b* 1866; *e s* of D. W. R. Carrick-Buchanan of Drumpellier and Carswall; *m* 1903, Adeline Musgave, *e d* of late Richard Harvey; three *s* four *d*. *Educ:* Newton College, Devon. Served twenty-five years Gordon Highlanders; served South African War (despatches); commanded a Base Depot, L of C, European War, 1914–19 (despatches); JP and DL, Lanarkshire. *Address:* Drumpellier, Coatbridge, Scotland. *Clubs:* Carlton; New, Edinburgh.

Died 15 Feb. 1925.

BUCHANAN, Sir Eric Alexander, 3rd Bt, *cr* 1878; *b* 19 Aug. 1848; *s* of 1st Bt and Frances Mellish, *d* of the Dean of Hereford; *S* brother, 1901; *m* 1898, Constance (*d* 1914), *d* of late Comdr Tennant, RN; one *s* one *d*. *Educ:* Wellington. *Heir:* *s* Charles James Buchanan, Lieut Highland LI, *b* 16 April 1899. *Died 29 July 1928.*

BUCHANAN, Rt. Hon. Sir George (William), GCB 1915 (CB 1900); GCMG 1913 (KCMG 1909); GCVO 1909 (KCVO 1905; CVO 1900); PC 1910; LLD Birmingham, 1918; *b* Copenhagen, 25 Nov. 1854; *s* of Sir Andrew Buchanan, 1st Bt, GCB; *m* 1885, Lady Georgiana Bathurst (*d* 1922), *d* of 6th Earl Bathurst; one *d*. *Educ:* Wellington College. Attaché, 1876; 3rd Secretary, Rome, 1878; 2nd Secretary, Tokio, 1879; Vienna, 1882; Berne, 1889, where he acted as Chargé d'Affaires several times; Secretary of Legation, 1893; Chargé d'Affaires, Darmstadt, 1893–1900; British Agent to the Venezuelan Arbitration Tribunal, 1898; Secretary of Embassy at Rome, 1900; Berlin, 1901–3; Minister Plenipotentiary at Sofia, 1903–8; Minister at The Hague, 1908–10; Ambassador to Petrograd, 1910–18; Freedom of the City of Moscow, 1916; Hon. Member of the Universities of Moscow and Petrograd, 1917; Ambassador to Rome, 1919–21; retired from the Diplomatic Service, Nov. 1921. *Publication:* My Mission to Russia, and other Diplomatic Memories, 1923. *Address:* 15 Lennox Gardens, SW1. *T:* Kensington 1727. *Club:* Marlborough.

Died 20 Dec. 1924.

BUCHANAN, John Lee, AM, LLD; President of the University of Arkansas, Fayetteville, Arkansas, 1894–1902; *b* Smyth County, Virginia, 19 June 1831; 2nd *s* of Patrick C. Buchanan and Margaret, *d* of Major Samuel Graham; *m* 1859, Frances Elizabeth, *d* of Dr E. E. Wiley. *Educ:* Emory and Henry College, Virginia. Professor in Emory and Henry College, 1856–78; Professor of Latin, Vanderbilt University, 1878–79; President of Emory and Henry College, 1879–80; President Virginia Agricultural and Mechanical College, 1880–82; Joint Principal, Martha Washington College, 1882–86; State Superintendent of Public Instruction of Virginia, 1886–90; Professor of Latin, Randolph Macon College, 1890–94. *Publications:* Educational Reports of Virginia from 1886–90. *Recreations:* hunting, fishing, chess. *Address:* Fayetteville, Arkansas. *Clubs:* American Institute of Civics; Southern Educational Association. *Died 19 Feb. 1922.*

BUCHANAN, John Young, MA; FRS; chemist; *b* Scotland, 20 Feb. 1844; *s* of John Buchanan of Dowanhill. *Educ:* Glasgow High School and University; Universities of Marburg, Leipzig, and Bonn; Ecole de Médecine, Paris. Chemist and Physicist of the "Challenger" Expedition; later, Lecturer in Geography, University of Cambridge; Vice-Président du Conseil de Perfectionnement de l'Institut océanographique de Paris; Croix du Commandeur de l'Ordre de Saint Charles de Monaco: Hon. Member of the Gesellschaft für Erdkunde, Berlin; and the Société Helvétique des Sciences Naturelles; awarded Keith Medal, Royal Society, Edinburgh, and Gold Medal, Royal Scottish Geographical Society. *Recreation:* travelling. *Club:* Athenæum.

Died 16 Oct. 1925.

BUCHANAN, Robert J. M., MD; FRCP, MRCS; Captain Royal Army Medical Corps (T); Professor of Forensic Medicine, University of Liverpool. *Educ:* University, Liverpool. Hon. Physician Royal Infirmary, Liverpool; was Hon. Physician, Stanley Hospital, and Assistant Hon. Physician, Hospital for Consumption and Diseases of the Chest, Liverpool; Demonstrator of Pathology, University College, Liverpool. *Publications:* Rabies and Hydrophobia; Textbook of Forensic Medicine and Toxicology; The Blood in Health and Disease, etc. *Recreations:* painting, fishing. *Address:* 6 Rodney Street, Liverpool. *T:* Royal 2356, Liverpool. *Club:* Athenæum, Liverpool.

Died April 1925.

BUCHANAN, Ven. Thomas Boughton, MA; *b* 1833; *m* Laura Maria (*d* 1915), *d* of late George Richmond, RA. *Educ:* Exeter Coll., Oxford (1st Class Mods). Ordained 1857; Curate of Wilton, 1857–59; Chaplain to Lord Herbert of Lea, 1859–60; Rector of Wishford Magna, Wilts, 1863–71; Chaplain to Bishop of Salisbury, 1870–85; Vicar of Potterne, Wilts, 1871–91; Rector of Poulshot, 1891–1905; Archdeacon of Wilts, 1874–1911; Residentiary Canon of Salisbury, 1895–1915. *Address:* The Close, Salisbury.
Died 28 June 1924.

BUCHANAN, Hon. Sir Walter Clarke, Kt 1913; MLC since 1915; *b* Argyllshire, 1838. *Educ:* Parish School, Greenock. Went to Melbourne, 1857; New Zealand a few years later; one of the founders and a Director of Wellington Meat Export Co.; Member House of Representatives for Wairarapa South, 1881–87; Wairarapa, 1887–91, 1902–5 and 1908–14. *Address:* Alexandra Street, Masterton, NZ.
Died 19 July 1924.

BUCHANAN, Sir Walter James, KCIE 1918 (CIE 1913); MD; Lieutenant-Colonel Indian Medical Service, retired; Editor of the Indian Medical Gazette, Calcutta, 1899–1919; Inspector-General of Prisons, Bengal Presidency, 1902–19; *b* Londonderry, 12 Nov. 1861; *e s* of late Robert Buchanan of Fintona, County Tyrone; *m* Lilian Edith (*d* 1916), *d* of late E. Simpson-Byrne; one *s*. *Educ:* Foyle College, Londonderry; Trinity College, Dublin; Vienna. BA, MD, BCh; Diplomate in State Medicine, Univ. Dublin; University Travelling Prizeman in Medicine, 1887. Entered IMS, 1887; took part in Hazara Expedition, 1888; Lushai Expedition, 1890; Manipur Field Force, 1891 (medal and clasp); entered Civil Medical employ, Bengal, 1892; Delhi Durbar coronation medals, 1903 and 1911; as Member Indian Prisons Commission visited USA, Japan, China, etc. *Publications:* Manual of Jail Hygiene, 2nd edn 1900; Tours in Sikkim, 1917. *Recreation:* golf. *Address:* 56 Leeson Park, Dublin. *Clubs:* East India United Service; University, Dublin.
Died 23 March 1924.

BUCK, Sir Edward Charles, KCSI 1897 (CSI 1892); Kt 1886; Hon. Fellow of Clare College, 1898; *b* 1838; *s* of Z. Buck, of Norwich. *Educ:* Norwich and Oakham Schools; Clare College, Cambridge (LB 1861; LLD 1886). Bengal Civil Service; represented Indian Government at Colonial Exhibition, 1886; Sec., Government of India, 1882–97; retired. *Club:* East India United Service.
Died 6 July 1916.

BUCKELL, Sir Robert, Kt 1907; *b* 22 Sept. 1841; *m* 1863, Ann Ellen, *d* of James Goold of Oxford; one *s*. Hon. MA Oxford University; Alderman of City of Oxford and JP; six times mayor of the city. *Address:* 4 Staverton Road, Oxford. *Died 1 June 1925.*

BUCKHAM, Sir George Thomas, Kt 1917; Chief Ordnance Designer and a Director, firm of Vickers, Ltd; Member of the Shipbuilding and Armaments Board; Director of the Electrode Co. of Sheffield; Member of Council of Sheffield Chamber of Commerce; Member of Grand Council of Federation of British Industries; *b* Newcastle, 1863; *s* of late John Buckham; *m* Selina Elizabeth (*d* 1919), 3rd *d* of late M. Langley, Newcastle; one *s* one *d*. *Educ:* Newcastle. Trained as an Ordnance Engineer at the Elswick Works of Sir W. G. Armstrong, Whitworth & Co. Ltd; joined staff of Vickers, Ltd in 1895; member of the Institute of Mechanical Engineers; Third Class of the Order of the Rising Sun (Japan). *Address:* Springfield House, Sandygate, Sheffield. *T:* Broomhill 236. *Club:* Sheffield.
Died 9 May 1928.

BUCKLAND, 1st Baron, *cr* 1926, of Bwlch; Henry Seymour Berry; JP County of Breconshire and Borough of Merthyr Tydfil; *b* 1877; *e s* of late Alderman John Mathias Berry, JP; *m* 1907, Gwladys Mary, *e d* of Simon Sandbrook, JP; five *d*. *Educ:* privately. Coalowner; Chairman, Guest, Keen & Nettlefolds, Ltd; closely identified with his native town of Merthyr Tydfil, to which he gave a new wing for the Merthyr General Hospital, Public Swimming Baths, and many other gifts; Freeman of the Borough of Merthyr Tydfil. *Address:* Buckland, Bwlch, Breconshire; 3 Whitehall Court, SW1. *Club:* Carlton. *Died 23 May 1928 (ext).*

BUCKLE, Commander Archibald Walter, DSO 1918; RNVR; Headmaster, Rotherhithe New Road Nautical School; *m* Elsie; two *s*. Served European War, 1914–18 (wounded thrice, DSO and 3 bars, despatches five times). *Address:* Tower House, Crescent Way, Brockley. *Died 6 May 1927.*

BUCKLE, Lt-Col Arthur William Bentley-, CMG 1915; Army Pay Department; *b* 13 Aug. 1860; *s* of late Capt. George Bentley-Buckle,

40th Regt, and *g s* of late Archdeacon Buckle; *m* Mary Bunbury, 2nd *d* of late Bishop of Limerick; one *s* two *d*. *Educ:* Wellington College. Entered army, 1881; Lieut West Riding Regt 1881; Adjutant, 1885–89; Captain, 1888; Major, 1902; Lieut-Col 1908; Adjutant Militia, 1889–94; Paymaster, 1895–1903; Staff Paymaster, 1903; 1st Class Asst Accountant, 1905–9; served S Africa, 1899–1902 (Queen's medal with clasp; King's medal, 2 clasps); European War, 1914–18 (CMG, Chevalier Légion d'Honneur).
Died 21 Jan. 1923.

BUCKLE, Maj.-Gen. Charles Randolph; *b* 29 Oct. 1835. Served thirty years in the Royal Artillery; served in the Garibaldian campaign of 1860; afterwards with the Sardinian Artillery at the siege of Gaeta (wounded); killed the largest elephant ever known in Travancore, which had killed over thirty people. *Recreations:* shooting, travelling. *Clubs:* Army and Navy, United Service.
Died 14 Nov. 1920.

BUCKLE, John, JP; MP (Lab) Eccles, 1922–24; *b* Leeds, 1867. Travelling organizer, Boot and Shoe Operatives Soc. Mem. Leeds City Council; first Lab Alderman, Leeds. JP Leeds.
Died 8 Nov. 1925.

BUCKLEY, Sir Edmund, 2nd Bt, *cr* 1868; JP; *b* 7 May 1861; *s* of 1st Bt and Sarah, *e d* of W. Rees of Tonn, County Carmarthen; *m* 1885, Harriet Olivia Louisa, *d* of Rev. Maurice Lloyd. Owned about 11,800 acres. *Heir:* none. *Address:* The Plas, Dinas Mawddwy, N Wales; Aberturnant Hall, Bala. *Club:* New Oxford and Cambridge.
Died 20 Jan. 1919 (ext).

BUCKLEY, Rev. James Monroe, DD, LLD; Editor of The Christian Advocate, New York, 1880–1912; *b* Rahway, New Jersey, 16 Dec. 1836; *s* of Rev. John Buckley, native of Lancashire, and Abby, *d* of Judge C. Monroe, Mount Holly, New Jersey. *Educ:* Pennington Seminary, New Jersey; Wesleyan Univ., Middletown, Connecticut; studied theology, Exeter, New Hampshire. Entered ministry, Methodist Episcopal Church, 1858; spent 1863 in Europe; returning, settled Detroit, Mich; removed to Brooklyn, NY, 1866; continued in ministry till 1880; DD Wesleyan University; LLD Emory and Henry College, Virginia; LHD Syracuse University; Hon. Member American Medico-Psychological Society. *Publications:* Supposed Miracles; Midnight Sun; Czar and Nihilist; Faith Healing; Christian Science and Kindred Phenomena; Travels in Three Continents; History of Methodism in the United States; Extemporaneous Oratory; The Fundamentals of Religion and their Contrasts; Wrong and Peril of Woman Suffrage; Constitutional and Parliamentary History of the Methodist Episcopal Church. *Recreations:* President Board of Managers, Seney Methodist Episcopal Hospital, Brooklyn, and President of the Board of Managers of the State Hospital for the Insane at Morris Plains, NJ; Vice-President Society for Prevention of Vice. *Address:* 150 Fifth Avenue, New York.
Died 8 Feb. 1920.

BUCKLEY, Ven. James Rice, BD; Archdeacon of Llandaff since 1913; Vicar of Llandaff, 1878–1913; Chaplain to the Lord Bishop of Llandaff since 1905; *b* 28 Jan. 1849; *m* Catherine, *d* of late James Kempthorne, solicitor, Neath; four *s* three *d*. *Educ:* Carmarthen Grammar School; Manilla Hall, Clifton; St David's College, Lampeter. Graduated in Honours, 1872; Curate of Neath, 1872; Surrogate for the Diocese of Llandaff; Rural Dean of Llandaff; Proctor for the Clergy, 1906; Hon. Canon of St Cross in Llandaff Cathedral; Chairman of the Cardiff Board of Guardians and of the Llandaff Diocesan Branch of the Church in Wales Temperance Society. *Recreations:* no special recreation, chiefly change of work. *Address:* The Vicarage, Llandaff. *TA:* Llandaff Post Office.
Died 8 Sept. 1924.

BUCKLEY, Rev. Jonathan Charles; Hon. Canon, St Albans, 1895. *Educ:* Hatfield Hall, Durham. Curate of Rotherham, 1870; Holy Trinity, Brompton, 1872–75; St James', Newhampton, 1875–78; Hackney, 1878–82; Vicar of St Luke's, Victoria Docks, 1882–1918; Surrogate of S Alban's Diocese, 1918. *Address:* Thornville, Hemel Hempstead. *Died 28 Dec. 1927.*

BUCKLEY, Robert Burton, CSI 1901; *b* Brighton, 23 August 1847; *s* of Rev. John Wall Buckley, Vicar of St Mary's, Paddington; *m* 1880, Ada Marion, *d* of late Major B. K. Finnimore, RA; one *s* three *d*. *Educ:* Merchant Taylors' School. Whitworth Scholar Mechanical Science, 1869; went to India as an Assistant Engineer in the Public Works Department, 1869; rose through various grades to rank of Chief Engineer, 1st class; Member Instn of Civil Engineers, 1880; was chiefly connected with works of irrigation. *Publications:* three books on irrigation in India and several pamphlets on engineering subjects. *Address:* 44 Clanricarde Gardens, Bayswater, W.

Died 19 Dec. 1927.

BUCKNILL, His Honour Sir John Alexander Strachey, Kt 1916; KC; Puisne Judge of the Patna High Court since 1920; *b* Clifton, 14 Sept. 1873; *m* 1901, Alice, *y d* of Admiral Sir George Richards, KCB, FRS; two *d. Educ:* Charterhouse; Keble College, Oxford. MA (Oxon), FZS, MBOU. Barrister-at-law, Inner Temple, 1896; Midland Circuit; Commissioner of Patents, Transvaal, 1902; MLC Transvaal, 1904; Chairman of Committees Legislative Council, Transvaal, 1906; a Legal adviser to Transvaal, 1907; Sole Commissioner to enquire into immorality amongst Chinese labourers in Transvaal, 1906; Member of Legislative and Executive Councils of Cyprus, 1907; acted Chief Secretary, 1908; King's Advocate of Cyprus, 1907–12; Attorney-General of Hong-Kong, 1912–14; Chief Justice, Straits Settlements, 1914–20; Chairman, Singapore Military Service Advisory Committee, 1916; President, Commission of Investigation into Administration of State of Trengganu, 1918; President, Straits Settlements, Kedah and Johore Military Service Tribunals, 1918; President, Malayan Public Services Salaries Commission, 1918–19; President, Raffles Centenary Memorial Committee, 1920; Chairman, Raffles Museum and Library Committee, 1920; President, Children's Aid Society, Singapore, 1920; President, Patna Museum Committee, 1921; President, Patna Law College, 1921; President, Numismatic Society of India, 1923. *Publications:* The Birds of Surrey, 1901; The Ornithology of Cyprus, 1910; The Imperial Ottoman Penal Code, 1914; late editor of the South African Ornithologists' Journal. *Recreations:* ornithology, numismatics, shooting, fishing. *Address:* King George's Avenue, Patna, India. *Club:* Athenæum. *Died 5 Oct. 1926.*

BUCKSTON, Rev. Henry, MA; *b* 1834; *e s* of late Rev. Henry Thomas Buckston and Mary Goodwin, *d* of late John Goodwin-Johnson; *m* 1875, Eliza Amy, *d* of William John Marrow; one *s. Educ:* St John's College, Cambridge. Lord of the Manors of Mapleton and Ash; patron of one living. *Address:* Sutton-on-the-Hill, Derby; Bradborne Hall, Ashbourne; The Ash, Etwall, Derby; The Callow, Ashbourne. *Died 22 Nov. 1916.*

BUDD, Alfred, MVO 1908; British Vice-Consul San Sebastian, 1907–15; Consul since 1915. *Address:* British Consulate, San Sebastian, Spain. *Died June 1927.*

BUDD, John Wreford, MA Cambridge; Senior Partner of the firm of Budd, Johnson, Jecks & Colclough, solicitors; *b* 10 Dec. 1838; *e s* of John Wreford Budd, Plymouth; *m* 1866, Lucy Isabella, *y d* of Rev. George Skinner, MA, formerly Fellow and Tutor of Jesus College, Cambridge; three *d. Educ:* home; Pembroke College, Cambridge (Fellow 1861). Thirteenth Wrangler in the Mathematical Tripos, and 2nd Class Classical Tripos; admitted a Solicitor, 1865; a Member of the Council of the Law Society since 1881; President, 1895–96; for many years a member of the Statutory Discipline Committee under the Acts of 1888 and 1919, and Chairman of the Legal Education Committee of the Law Society; Member of the Council of Law Reporting; Member of Senate, University of London; Member of Court of University of Bristol; a Life Governor of the London Hospital. *Recreations:* hunting, fishing, shooting, as opportunity occurred. *Address:* 21 Craven Hill Gardens, Hyde Park, W2. *T:* Paddington 3946; Combe Park, Lynton, N Devon. *Clubs:* New University, City of London.

Died 18 Dec. 1922.

BUDWORTH, Maj.-Gen. Charles Edward Dutton, CB 1916; CMG 1917; MVO 1903; Royal Horse Artillery; *b* 3 Oct. 1869; 3rd *s* of late P. J. Budworth, JP, DL, of Greensted Hall, Ongar, Essex; *m* 1st, Winifred (*d* 1914), *d* of late Sir Patteson Nickalls; no *c*; 2nd, 1918, Helen, *o d* of Maj.-Gen. W. E. Blewitt; two *s. Educ:* RMA, Woolwich. Joined the Royal Artillery, 1889; served South African War (despatches, Bt Major); European War, 1914–17 (despatches ten times, CB, CMG, Bt Col, Major-Gen.); formerly Adjutant of the Honourable Artillery Company and Chief Instructor of the Royal Horse and Field School of Gunnery; Commander of the Legion of Honour; Croix de Guerre; Order of St Stanislaus. *Publications:* various military pamphlets. *Recreations:* shooting, fishing. *M:* AB 903. *Club:* Army and Navy. *Died 15 July 1921.*

BULLEN, Arthur Henry; *b* London, 9 Feb. 1857; *s* of late Dr George Bullen, CB; *m* 1879, Edith, *d* of W. J. Goodwin; two *s* three *d. Educ:* Worcester College, Oxford. Set up as publisher, 1889; established in 1904 The Shakespeare Head Press, Stratford-on-Avon. *Publications:* edited the works of John Day, 1881; Collection of Old English Plays, 1882–84; Selections from Poems of Michael Drayton, 1883; the Works of Christopher Marlowe, Thomas Middleton, John Marston, George Peele, Thomas Campion; Lyrics from the Song Books of Elizabethan Age, 1886; More Lyrics, 1887; England's Helicon, 1887. *Address:* Stratford-on-Avon.

Died 29 Feb. 1920.

BULLER, Arthur Tremayne, JP; landowner; *b* 19 March 1850; 5th *s* of late James Wentworth Buller, JP, DL, MP, DCL, of Downes, and Charlotte Juliana Jane, 3rd *d* of Lord Henry Thomas Molyneux Howard; *m* Elinor Louisa, *d* of Francis Leyborne Popham of Littlecote; three *s* three *d. Educ:* Harrow; Trinity College, Cambridge. JP Devon. *Address:* Downes, Crediton. *Club:* Arthurs'.

Died 28 Jan. 1917.

BULLER, Charles William Dunbar-; *b* 2 Oct. 1847; *e s* of late Rev. William Buller of Pelynt and Trenant, Cornwall; assumed by Royal Licence the surname of Dunbar before that of Buller; *m* 1890, Georgiana Anne Elizabeth Dunbar (*d* 1920), *o surv. c* of late George Dunbar, MP, and *sister* and *heiress* of late Capt. John George Dunbar, 1st Life Guards. *Educ:* Eton; Christ Church, Oxford. Was Fellow of All Souls College, Oxford; DL, JP, Co. Down, and DL Norfolk; High Sheriff, Co. Down, 1894; patron of the living; contested (U) South Molton Division of Devonshire, 1891, and South Belfast, 1902. *Address:* Woburn, Donaghadee, Co. Down; 15 Upper Grosvenor Street, W. *Clubs:* Brooks's, St James's; Devon and Exeter, Exeter; Ulster, Belfast. *Died 29 April 1924.*

BULLER, Major Herbert Cecil, DSO 1915; Rifle Brigade; attached Princess Patricia's Canadian Light Infantry; *b* 2 Jan. 1882. Entered army, 1900; Captain, 1910; Adjutant, 1907–10; ADC to Governor-General, Canada, 1911–14; Adjutant Canadian Light Infantry, 1914; served European War, 1914–15 (DSO). *Address:* Erle Hall, Plympton, S Devon. *Died 3 June 1916.*

BULLOCK, Lt-Gen. Sir George Mackworth, KCB 1911 (CB 1900); *b* Warangol, India, 15 August 1851; *s* of Thomas Henry Bullock, Deputy Commissioner, Berar; *m* 1884, Amy Isabel, OBE, *d* of Colonel J. Thomson, DL; one *d. Educ:* Cheltenham; University College, Oxford; Sandhurst. Entered 1st Batt. 11th Foot, 1872; passed Staff College, 1880; Brigade Major at Shorncliffe, 1882–87; DAAG India, 1889–94; won Gold Medal, United Service Institution, India, 1892; in command of 2nd Devonshire Regt South Africa, 1899; Colonel on Staff commanding Volksrust Sub Dist; Brig.-General commanding a column (despatches, Brevet Colonel, CB); Chief Staff Officer, Egypt, 1902–4; Brigadier-General commanding Alexandria, 1904–5; Major-General commanding in Egypt, 1905–8; commanded West Riding Territorial Division, 1910–11; Governor and Commander-in-Chief, Bermuda, 1912–17; Colonel, Devonshire Regiment; retired. *Address:* 3 Carlton Hill, NSW. *Club:* Junior United Service. *Died 28 Jan. 1926.*

BULLOCK, Rev. Richard, VD; MA; Prebendary of Lincoln, 1875; Member of Convocation for Chapter of Lincoln; *b* London, 23 May 1889; *s* of late Edward Bullock, Common Serjeant, City of London, and Katharine, *d* of J. Cripps, MP, Cirencester; *m* Ada, *d* of T. H. Whipham, barrister-at-law; two *s* two *d. Educ:* Oriel Coll., Oxford. Curate of Barton-on-Humber, 1863–66; Vicar and Wray Lectr of Barrow-on-Humber, 1866–78; Rector of Welton-le-Wold, Lincs, 1878–82; Vicar of Holy Trinity, Leeds, 1882–1900; Rural Dean of W Elloe, 1900; Vicar of Spalding, Lincolnshire, 1900–13, of Shurdington, Gloucestershire, 1913–17; late Dep. Prov. Grand Master of Freemasons, Lincolnshire. *Address:* Park Grange, Charlton Kings, Cheltenham. *Died 13 Sept. 1918.*

BULLOCK, Samuel, ISO 1902; late Superintendent for Wrecks and Loss of Life at Sea, Board of Trade; *b* 1844; *s* of late Thomas Bullock, Teemore, Fermanagh; *m* Fanny Sarah, *d* of Edmund Hartley of Banbury; two *s* two *d. Educ:* Portora Royal School, Enniskillen. Secretary of the Committee on the Manning of Merchant Ships, 1904–6, and of other official committees. *Recreations:* fishing, billiards, golf. *Address:* Holly Nook, Burwood Park Road, Walton-on-Thames. *Died 20 May 1922.*

BULMAN, Henry Herbert, RBA; *b* 9 Nov. 1871; *s* of Jonathan and Elizabeth Bulman, Carlisle; *m* 1896, Beatrice Elizabeth, *d* of W. A. Boone, ARCS, Ramsgate; two *s* one *d. Educ:* Carlisle; Antwerp; London. Portraits in home surroundings, landscape, flowers; drawing in South Kensington Museum; drawings and paintings in colonial and various collections. *Address:* 51 Oakhill Road, Putney, SW15. *T:* Putney 3390. *Club:* Chelsea Arts.

Died 11 Dec. 1928.

BULYEA, His Honour George Hedley Vicars, LLD; Chairman of the Board of Public Utilities Commissioners for the Province of Alberta since 1915; *b* Gagetown, Queen's County, New Brunswick, 17 Feb. 1859; *s* of James Albert Bulyea of NE, Loyalist; *m* 1885, Annie Blanche, 2nd *d* of R. T. Babbit, Registrar of Queen's Co., NB. *Educ:* Grammar School, Queen, NB; graduated at University of New Brunswick, 1878. Principal of Sunbury Grammar School, 1878–82; came to Winnipeg, 1882, and to Qu'appelle, 1883; engaged there in general business, which was disposed of in 1898 to accept position as Territorial Commissioner in Yukon Territory; candidate for Territorial Assembly, for Electoral District of South Qu'appelle, 1891, but defeated; elected 1894, 1896, 1898, and 1902; Territorial Secretary and Minister of Agriculture, 1899–1903; Commissioner of Public Works, 1903–5; 1st Lieut-Governor of the Province of Alberta, 1905–15. *Address:* Edmonton, Alberta.

Died 23 July 1928.

BUN BEHARI KAPUR, Raja Bahadur, CSI 1903; *b* 11 Nov. 1853. A scion of Burdwan family, he was appointed Dewan-i-Raj of the zamindari in 1877; joint manager, 1885; and sole manager, on behalf of his natural son, the present Mahraja of Burdwan, 1891–1903, when Maharaja received full charge; has served on Bengal Legislative Council (three times nominated), and for many years, as hon. magistrate; Kaiser-i-Hind gold medal, 1914; *Address:* The Bonabas, Burdwan.

Died 4 June 1924.

BUNBURY, Maj.-Gen. Sir Herbert Napier, KCB 1911 (CB 1906); *b* 15 Feb. 1851; *s* of late Capt. R. H. Bunbury, RN, and *g s* of late Sir Henry Bunbury, 7th Bt, KCB; *m* 1878, Mary Louisa, *d* of Major D. P. Campbell, of Balliveolen, Argyllshire, late 92nd Highlanders; two *s* (and one *s* decd). Educ: Marlborough. Lieut RA 1871; Captain, 1881; Major, 1887; ASC 1889; Lieut-Col 1894; Col 1901; AAG Cork, 1901–2; Director of Transport, 3rd Army Corps, 1902–3; of Supplies and Transport, Irish Command, 1903; served S Africa, 1899–1900 (Queen's medal, three clasps); Brig.-Gen. in command of Administration at Gibraltar, 1906; in charge of Administration in Irish Command, 1907–11; retired, 1913; a Commissioner of Chelsea Hospital. *Address:* 85 St George's Road, SW. *Club:* United Service.

Died 18 Jan. 1922.

BUNBURY, Maj.-Gen. William Edwin, CB 1911; Indian Army, retired; *b* Clonfert, 5 April 1858; *s* of late Bishop of Limerick; *m* 1893, Eva Mary, *d* of Francis Gale, Cheltenham; one *s*. Educ: St Columba's College, Rathfarnham. Entered Army, 1878; Captain ISC, 1889; Major, Indian Army, 1898; Lieut-Col 1904; Col 1908; Major-General, 1912; passed Staff College; DAAG Bengal, 1894–97; DAQMG, 1897–1900; DAG Northern Army, India, 1908; Brig.-General, General Staff Northern Army, 1909–12; served Afghan War, 1880 (medal); Mahsud-Waziree Expedition, 1881; Isazai Expedition, 1892; Chitral, 1895 (despatches, medal and clasp); Waziristan, 1901, 1902 (despatches, clasp); commanded 14th PWO Sikhs, 1902–8; Commanded Kohat Brigade, May to Nov. 1912; Quartermaster-General in India, 1912–16; commanded Rawal Pindi Division, May 1916 to Oct. 1917. *Address:* Chope Barton, Northam, N Devon. *T:* Northam 84.

Died 31 Oct. 1925.

BUNDI, HH Maharao Raja, Sir Raghubir Singhji Sahib Bahadur, GCSI 1919 (KCSI 1897); GCIE 1909; GCVO 1912; *b* 1869; *S* 1889. The State had an area of 2,220 square miles and a population of 187,068. *Address:* Bundi, Rajputana, India.

Died 28 July 1927.

BUNDY, Edgar, ARA 1915; RI, ROI, RBC. *Address:* 3 Acacia Road, St John's Wood, NW8. *T:* Hampstead 7190.

Died 10 Jan. 1922.

BUNE, John; journalist; Chief of the Parliamentary Staff of The Times; *b* Clatford; 2nd *s* of late F. J. Bune, paper manufacturer, Clatford, Andover; *m* Lucy Catherine, *d* of Henry Bennett; three *s* one *d*. Formerly on the staffs of the Echo and Daily Telegraph; joined The Times staff in 1883; chief sub-editor, 1890–1908; news editor, 1908–14. *Recreations:* golf, gardening. *Address:* The Nook, Oakhill Road, Beckenham, Kent.

Died 13 Feb. 1925.

BUNTINE, James Robertson; Sheriff-Substitute of Stirlingshire, etc, at Stirling since 1876; resigned 1906, and appointed Hon. Sheriff-Substitute; President of the Sheriff-Substitutes' Association, 1905–6; *b* 10 Nov. 1841; *e s* of William Buntine, HEICS, of Ayr; *m* 1st, 1874, Jane (*d* 1883), *d* of David Sandeman of Glasgow; 2nd, Jean, *d* of Archibald Finnie of Springhill and Grange, Ayrshire. *Educ:* Ayr and Edinburgh Academies, and Edinburgh University. MA 1862. Called to Scotch Bar, 1865. *Recreations:* golf, shooting, etc. *Address:* Torbrex

House, Stirling, NB. *Clubs:* Junior Carlton, Conservative; University, New, Edinburgh.

Died 10 Aug. 1920.

BURBANK, Luther; owner and manager of Burbank Experiment Farms; *b* Lancaster, Mass, 7 March 1849; *s* of Samuel Walton Burbank of Lancaster, Mass, and Olive Ross of Sterling, Mass; *m* 1916, Elizabeth Waters. *Educ:* Lancaster Academy. Naturalist and originator of new fruits and flowers; always devoted to study of nature, especially plant life; moved to Santa Rosa, Calif, 1875; originator of many improved thornless cacti; Gold, Wickson, Apple, October Purple, Santa Rosa, America, Climax, and Beauty plums; Giant, Splendor, and Sugar prunes; Peachblow, Burbank, Santa Rosa and other roses; giant and fragrant callas; and numerous new apples, peaches, nuts, berries, and other valuable trees, fruits, flowers, grasses, grains, and vegetables. Fellow of American Association for Advancement of Science; Hon. Member of American Plant and Animal Breeders Association; Special Lecturer, Stanford University; Hon. Member Californian Academy of Science, Swedish Botanical Society, Royal Agricultural Society of Italy, American Eugenic Society; Fellow Royal Horticultural Society; Doctor of Science, Tufts College, 1905. *Publications:* Training of the Human Plant; New Creations in Fruits and Flowers; Fundamental Principles of Plant Breeding; Luther Burbank: his Methods and Discoveries, 12 vols, 1913; How Plants are Trained to Work for Man, 8 vols, 1921; numerous magazine articles on scientific and humanitarian subjects. *Recreations:* botanizing, music. *Address:* Santa Rosa, Sonoma Co., Calif. *TA:* Burbank, Santarosa. *T:* Main 389. *M:* 44,286.

Died 11 April 1926.

BURBIDGE, Sir Richard, 1st Bt, *cr* 1916; JP for the County of London; Chairman of Committee on Royal Aircraft Factory; Managing Director Harrod's Stores since 1890; Member of Advisory Board of the Ministry of Munitions; Trustee of the Crystal Palace; President, Society of Wiltshiremen in London; *b* South Wraxall, Wilts, March 1847; 4th *s* of George Bishop Burbidge; *m* 1st, Emily (*d* 1905), *y d* of late J. Woodman of Melksham, Wilts; two *s* four *d*; 2nd, 1910, Lilian, *y d* of late J. A. Preece of Bartestree Court, Herefordshire. Sat on the Committee on Post Office Wages; Director Hudson's Bay Co.; Chairman, Dickins & Jones, Ltd; Hon. Treasurer Tariff Commission; was member of the Garrison and Regimental Institutes Committee dealing with Canteens; was also Member of Board of Control of Regimental Institutes and on the General Purposes Committee of this Board. *Recreations:* hackney breeding, horticulture. *Heir:* *s* Richard Woodman Burbidge [*b* 7 Dec. 1872; *m* Catherine Jemima, *d* of H. Grant, Sodbury House, Great Clacton, Essex]. *Address:* 51 Hans Mansions, SW; Littleton Park, Shepperton, Middlesex; Osborne Cottage, Whippingham, Isle of Wight. *T:* Western 1; Weybridge 25. *M:* LC 8560; LB 5388.

Died 31 May 1917.

BURD, Rev. Prebendary John, MA; Vicar of Chirbury, Shropshire, 1863–1912; *b* 1828; *s* of Henry Edward Burd; unmarried. *Educ:* Shrewsbury School; Christ Church, Oxford (Fell Exhibitioner). 3rd class Lit. Hum.; BA 1850; MA 1853. Deacon, 1852; priest, 1853; Curate of Parham, Hacheston, 1852; Myddle Salop, 1855; Surrogate, Diocese of Hereford; Prebendary in Hereford Cathedral, 1888; Rural Dean of Montgomery, 1906. *Address:* Clawdd-y-dre, Montgomery.

Died 2 April 1918.

BURDETT, Sir Henry, KCB 1897; KCVO 1908; author and statist; founder and editor of The Hospital; *b* 18 March 1847; *s* of Rev. Halford Burdett, MA, of Gilmorton, Co. Leicester, and Alsina, *d* of T. Brailsford, DL of Barkwith, and Toft Grange, Lincolnshire; *m* 1875, Helen (*d* 1919), *d* of Gay Shute, FRCS; two *s* two *d*. Late Superintendent of the Queen's Hospital, Birmingham, and of the Seaman's Hospital, Greenwich; late Secretary Share and Loan Department, London Stock Exchange. *Publications:* Burdett's Official Intelligence of British, American, and Foreign Securities (17 volumes); The National Debt; The Sinking Funds of the National Debt; National Debts of the World; Local Taxation in England and Wales; London Water Companies; Light Railways; Municipal, County, and Indian Finance; Colonial Loans, Finance, and Development; Seventeen Years of Securities; The Patriotic Fund; The Admiralty and the Country; Hospitals and Asylums of the World (4 volumes and portfolio of plans); Cottage Hospitals; Pay Hospitals of the World; The Relative Mortality of Large and Small Hospitals; Burdett's Hospitals and Charities; A Year-book of Philanthropy; The Uniform System of Accounts for Hospitals and Institutions; Hospitals and the State; Unhealthiness of Public Institutions; Architects, Hospitals, and Asylums; A History of the Hospital Saturday and Sunday Funds; The National Pension Fund for Nurses and Officials; A National Pension Fund for Workers among the Sick in the United States; A Practical Scheme for Old Age Pensions; Nurses' Food, Work, and Recreation;

The Registration of Nurses; How to become a Nurse; The Nursing Profession, How and Where to Train; Housing of the Poor; Dwellings of the Middle Classes; Helps in Sickness and to Health; Burdett's Official Nursing Directory; The Future of the Hospitals, a Scheme of Co-operation between the Patients, the Hospitals, and the State. *Address:* The Lodge, 13 Porchester Square, W2. *T:* Park 873. *Clubs:* Marlborough, City of London, Ranelagh, Roehampton.

Died 29 April 1920.

BURDETT-COUTTS, Rt. Hon. William Lehman Ashmead Bartlett-, PC 1921; MP (C) Westminster since 1885; *b* USA, 1851; 2nd *s* of late Ellis Bartlett of Plymouth, New England, and Sophia, *d* of John King Ashmead of Philadelphia; grandparents on both sides British subjects; *m* 1881, Baroness Burdett-Coutts (*d* 1906), whose name he assumed. *Educ:* privately; Keble Coll., Oxford (Scholar; MA 1876). The Baroness Burdett-Coutts having originated the Turkish Compassionate Fund, he volunteered to proceed to the Russo-Turkish war as Special Commissioner, 1877 (Star and 2nd class of the Medjidie); one of the originators of the Fisheries Exhibition; interested himself in the question of the food supply of the poor of London; re-opened Columbia Market for the sale of fish and vegetables, and obtained parliamentary powers for railway access, but was unable to make satisfactory arrangements with the Railway Companies; visited Ireland to assist in organising relief in the distressed districts, 1879–80; subsequently largely developed the Baroness's scheme for benefiting the Irish fishermen; founder and owner of the Brookfield Stud; Trustee of the Baltimore Fishery School; Governor of Christ's Hospital; twice Master of the Turners' Company (1888 and 1889); one of the founders of the British East African Possessions; Mr Burdett-Coutts carried the Hampstead Heath Act, 1885 (adding Parliament Hill and 300 acres as public recreation ground), Police Enfranchisement, and Metropolitan Management Amendment Acts, 1887, and also the Advertisement Rating Act, 1889; proceeded to S Africa as Times Correspondent with regard to the sick and wounded, 1900, and thus led to the appointment of a Royal Commission of Inquiry; after the publication of its Report the Government promised a "drastic reform" of the Army Medical Service (Session 1901), and a complete reform followed; since 1902, a prominent advocate of railway reform, including better loading, co-operation, and a fuller system of statistics as a guide to efficient working, and for the information of Parliament; this led to the appointment by the Board of Trade of a Committee of Inquiry, as a result of which the Government introduced the Railway (Accounts and Returns) Bill, 1910. *Publications:* volume on Russo-Turkish War; Lest we Forget (on S African Hospitals); many articles, etc. *Address:* 1 Stratton Street, W1; Holly Lodge, Highgate, N6. *T:* Gerard 3643; Hornsey 496. *Club:* Carlton. *Died 28 July 1921.*

BURGE, Sir Charles Henry, Kt 1918; JP; FIC; *b* Devon, 4 June 1846; *s* of late John Burge; *m* 1870, Amelia, *d* of late Joseph Woodcock; two *s* two *d. Educ:* Crediton Grammar School; private tuition; Royal College of Chemistry. Somerset House, 1867; became Deputy Principal of the Government Laboratory, and retired 1907; Surrey County Council, 1913; Kingston-on-Thames Town Councillor, 1907; Mayor, 1912–18; Alderman since 1914; Chairman and Treasurer of War Relief Fund; Chairman of the following—Kingston Branch of Red Cross Society, Food Control and Food Savings Committee, Education Committee; Director of various industrial companies. *Address:* Iddesleigh, Crescent Road, Kingston-on-Thames.

Died 21 Dec. 1921.

BURGE, Rt. Rev. Hubert Murray, MA, DD; *b* 9 Aug. 1862; *s* of Rev. M. R. Burge, of Fort-William, Calcutta; *m* 1898, Evelyn, *y d* of late Rev. Dr J. F. Bright. *Educ:* Bedford Grammar School; Marlborough; University Coll., Oxford (scholar, 1882–86). Hon. Mods I; Lit. Hum. II; Sixth form master at Wellington College, 1887–90; Fellow and Tutor of University College, Oxford, 1890; Dean, 1895; Headmaster of Repton School, 1900; Headmaster of Winchester, 1901–11; Hon. Fellow of University College, Oxford, 1908; Bishop of Southwark, 1911–19; Bishop of Oxford, 1919–25. Select Preacher, Oxford, 1899–1902, 1920–21; Chaplain of the Order of St John of Jerusalem in England, 1909; Sub-Prelate, 1911; Chancellor of the Most Noble Order of the Garter; Clerk to the Closet, 1919. *Publications:* contributor to Essays on Secondary Education. *Address:* Bishop's House, Cuddesdon, Oxford. *Clubs:* MCC, Free Foresters, I Zingari.

Died 11 June 1925.

BURGER, Schalk William; formerly a member of the Executive Raad, and Acting President of the South African Republic; *b* Lydenburg, East Transvaal. *Address:* Pretoria, Transvaal.

Died 18 Dec. 1918.

BURGES, Ven. Ernest Travers; Archdeacon of Maritzburg; Vicar of Richmond cum Byrne, Natal; late Superintendent of Native Missions; *b* 14 Aug. 1851; *s* of Daniel and Eliza Mary Burges; *m* Janet, *d* of William Webb, Sea View, Verulam, Natal; three *s* two *d. Educ:* Shrewsbury School; St John's College, Cambridge (MA). For 25 years Vicar of Karkloof Parish, Natal; Representative to Provincial Synod; Chairman of Advisory Board to Native Education Department, Colony of Natal; twice appointed to Special Committees by Government of Natal; acted as RM; formerly Chairman of Hilton College, Natal. *Publications:* several short stories. *Recreations:* fishing, shooting, riding, driving. *Address:* Vicarage, Richmond, Natal.

Died 19 June 1921.

BURGESS, Charles, (Cathal Brugha); MP (Sinn Fein) Waterford County since Dec. 1918; a candle manufacturer; *b* 8 July 1874. *Educ:* Belvedere Coll. TD Co. Waterford until 1921 and E Tipperary and City and Co. Waterford, 1921–22; Chm. of Dail, 1919; Minister of Defence, 1921–22. *Address:* 5 Fitzwilliam Terrace, Upper Rathmines, Dublin. *Died 7 July 1922.*

BURGESS, Duncan, MA, MB Cantab; FRCP; Senior Physician, Sheffield Royal Hospital; Ex-Professor of Medicine, Sheffield University; *b* 1850; unmarried. *Educ:* Aberdeen University; Cambridge. 13th Wrangler, 1875; Fellow of Corpus Christi College; Lt-Col RAMC (T). *Recreation:* golf. *Address:* 442 Glossop Road, Sheffield. *T:* Sheffield 1408. *Club:* Sheffield, Sheffield.

Died 17 Jan. 1917.

BURGESS, Rt. Rev. Frederick, DD; LLD (Cantab); Bishop of Long Island since 1902; *b* Providence, 6 Oct. 1853; *m* 1881, Caroline (deceased); four *s. Educ:* Brown University, Providence; General Theological Seminary; Europe. Rector, Grace Church, Amherst, Mass, 1878–83; Christ Church, Pomfret, Conn, 1883–89; Church of St Asaph, Bala, 1889–96; Christ Church, Detroit, Mich, 1896–98; Grace Church, Brooklyn, 1898–1902. *Address:* See House, Garden City, Long Island, New York. *Club:* Hamilton, Brooklyn.

Died 15 Oct. 1925.

BURGESS, James, CIE 1885; Hon. LLD Edin. 1881; FRSE, Hon. ARIBA, FRGS, MRAS; *b* Kirkmahoe, Dumfriesshire, 14 Aug. 1832; *m* 1855; four *s* three *d.* Engaged in educational work in Calcutta, 1856, and Bombay, 1861; Secretary Bombay Geographical Society, 1868–73; Head of Archæological Survey, Western India, 1873, and of S India, 1881; Director-General of the Archæological Surveys in India, 1886–89. Member, Soc. Asiatique, Paris; Hon. Member, Imp. Russian Archæol Soc.; Amer. Oriental Soc.; Royal Phil Soc., Glasgow; Hon. Associate, Finno-Ugrian Soc.; Hon. Corr. Member, Ethnol Soc., Berlin; Batavian Soc. of Arts and Sciences. *Publications:* The Temples of Shatrunjaya, 1869; The Rock Temples of Elephanta, 1871; Temples of Somanath, Junagadh, and Girnar, 1870; Scenery and Architecture in Gujarat and Rajputana, 1873; Notes on Ajanta Paintings, 1879; The Cave Temples of India (conjointly with late James Fergusson), 1880; Indian Antiquary, 1872–84; Archæological Survey of W India, 9 vols, 1874–1905; Buddhist Stupas of Amaravati, etc, 1887; Antiquities of Dabhoi, 1888; The Sharqi Architecture of Jaunpur (edited), 1889; Archæological Research in India, 1890; Epigraphia Indica, 2 vols, 1889–94; On Hindu Astronomy, 1893; Constable's Hand-Gazetteer of India 1898; Hypsometry by Boiling-point, 1858 and 1863; Transliteration of Indian Place-names, 1868, 1891, 1894–95; On the Error-function Definite Integral, 1898 (awarded the Keith medal, RSE); The Ancient Monuments, Temples, and Sculptures of India illustrated in a series of photographs, 1897–1910; Grünwedel's Buddhist Art in India (enlarged translation), 1901; The Indian Sect of the Jainas (translated and edited), 1903; Fergusson's Indian Architecture, enlarged edn, 2 vols, 1910; Chronology of Modern India, 1494 to 1894, 1913; etc. *Address:* 22 Seton Place, Edinburgh. *Died 5 Oct. 1916.*

BURGESS, James John Haldane, MA; author and private teacher; blind since 1887; *b* Lerwick, Shetland Isles, 28 May 1862. *Educ:* Anderson Institute, Lerwick. Entered Edinburgh University 1886; graduated 1889. *Publications:* A Nicht in Tammy Scolla's But-End and Laama Deep, 1885; Shetland Sketches and Poems, 1886; Rasmie's Buddie—Poems in the Shetlandic, 1891, 2nd edn 1892, 3rd edn 1913; The Viking Path—a Tale of the White Christ, 1894; Lowra Biglan's Mutch, 1896; Tang—A Shetland Story, 1898; Some Shetland Folk, 1902; The Treasure of Don Andres—A Shetland Romance of the Spanish Armada, 1903; Dr Robertson: Memorial Lines, 1914; Rasmie's Smaa Murr, 1916; short stories, articles, and poems, from time to time, in various periodicals. *Recreations:* free gymnastics, gardening, conversation, dipping into foreign languages. *Address:* Lerwick, Shetland. *Died 16 Jan. 1927.*

BURGESS, Thomas Joseph Workman, MD, FRSC; late Medical Superintendent, Protestant Hospital for Insane; Professor of Mental Diseases, McGill University, Montreal, since 1893; *b* Toronto, Canada, 11 March 1849; *y s* of Thomas Burgess and Jane Rigg, both natives of Carlisle, Cumberland; *m* 1875, Jessie, 2nd *d* of late Lieut-Col Alexander Macpherson, of Whitby, Ontario; three *d*. *Educ:* Upper Canada Coll. and Toronto Univ. Graduated in medicine as Starr gold medallist and 1st Univ. silver medallist, 1870; appointed surgeon to HM's British North American Boundary Commission, 1872, and served as such until the close of the work, being thanked by HM's Government for the efficient way in which he had carried out the duties; took up the study of mental diseases and became assistant physician of the London Asylum for Insane, 1875; assistant superintendent of Hamilton Asylum, 1887; medical superintendent of the Protestant Hospital for the Insane, Montreal, 1890; FRS Canada, 1885, and President of the Geological and Biological Section 1898; Fellow of the American Association for the Advancement of Science, 1886; hon. secretary for the Dominion of Canada of the Pan-American Medical Congress, Mexico, 1896; President American Medico-Psychological Association, 1904–5. *Publications:* The Beneficent and Toxic Effects of the Various Species of Rhus; A Botanical Holiday in Nova Scotia; Canadian Filiciniæ; Recent Additions to Canadian Filiciniæ; How to study Botany; Orchids; Notes on the Flora of the 49th Parallel; The Lake Erie Shore as a Botanising Ground; Art in the Sick Room; Ophioglossaceae and Filices; A Historical Sketch of Canadian Institutions for the Insane; The Insane in Canada; (Joint) Institutional Care of the Insane in the United States and Canada, 4 vols; numerous hospital reports, etc. *Recreations:* botany, golf, cricket, philately. *Address:* Suite 91 Laurentian Apts, 29 Cote des Neiges Road, Montreal, Quebec, Canada. *T:* Montreal 7403. *Clubs:* Authors'; University, Pen and Pencil, Montreal.   *Died 18 Jan. 1926.*

BURGESS, Hon. William Henry, JP; merchant, Hobart; *b* Hobart, 1847; *m* 1869, *y d* of John Turner, Hobart. *Educ:* Horton College. Alderman of Hobart, 1876–81; Mayor of Hobart, 1879–80; Member of Executive Council, 1884; entered Tasmanian Parliament, 1881; Treasurer, Minister of Defence, and Postmaster General, 1884–87; represented Tasmania at Sydney Federation Convention, 1891; commissioned as Captain in Tasmanian Defence Force (unattached), late STV Artillery; Master Warden, Marine Board; Vice-Consul for France; Officier d'Académie Française. *Address:* Milliara, Hobart, Tasmania. *TA:* Burgess, Hobart. *T:* Private, 95; Business, 166. *Clubs:* Athenæum, Civic, Hobart.   *Died 1 May 1917.*

BURGH, 5th Baron, *cr* 1529 (called out of abeyance, 1916); **Lt-Col Alexander Henry Leith,** JP, DL, Aberdeenshire and Isle of Wight; Lieutenant-Colonel late Commanding 3rd Battalion Gordon Highlanders; Commanding Garrison and Coast Defences, Aberdeen, during European War; *b* 27 July 1866; *e s* of late Gen. R. W. Disney Leith, CB, of Glenkindie and Westhall, Aberdeenshire, and Mary Charlotte Julia (*d* 1926) of North Court, Isle of Wight, *o c* of Sir Henry Percy Gordon, 2nd Bt (*ext*), and the Lady Mary Ashburnham (*d* of 3rd Earl of Ashburnham); in 1912 proved his claim as senior co-heir to the ancient Baronies of Burgh and Cobham, and in 1914 to ancient Barony of Strathbogie as senior co-heir; *m* 1st, 1893, Mildred Katherine (*d* 1894), *d* of Gen. Stuart James Nicholson, CB, one *d*; 2nd, 1902, Phyllis, *y d* of Col Mark Goldie, CRE; two *s* one *d*. Late Lieut the Welsh Regiment; served in Soudan Campaigns, 1888–89. *Recreations:* polo, hunting, golf, tennis, shooting, sailing. *Heir: s* Hon. Alexander Leigh Henry Leith, *b* 16 May 1906. *Address:* Glenkindie and Freefield, Aberdeenshire; Northcourt, Isle of Wight. *Clubs:* Army and Navy; Royal Victoria Yacht, Cowes.

Died 19 Aug. 1926.

BURGHCLERE, 1st Baron, *cr* 1895; **Herbert Coulstoun Gardner,** PC; DL; MA; Director of Peninsular and Oriental Steamship Company; President of Board of Agriculture, 1892–95; an Ecclesiastical Commissioner; Chairman of Royal Commission on Historical Monuments; *b* 9 June 1846; *m* 1890, Lady Winifred Henrietta Christina Herbert (author of George Villiers, 2nd Duke of Buckingham; Life of James, First Duke of Ormone, 1610–1688, 1912), *e d* of 4th Earl of Carnarvon, and *widow* of Capt. Hon. Alfred Byng; four *d*. *Educ:* Harrow; Trinity Hall, Cambridge. Member (L) for N Essex, 1885–95. *Publication:* The Georgics of Virgil, translated into English Verse, 1904. *Heir:* none. *Address:* 48 Charles Street, W1. *T:* Mayfair 2747. *Clubs:* Athenæum, Brooks's, St James's.

Died 6 May 1921 (ext).

BURGOYNE, Col Sir John Montagu, 10th Bt, *cr* 1641; Grenadier Guards, retired 1861; *b* 23 Oct. 1832; *s* of 9th Bt and Mary Harriet, *e d* of William Gore-Langton, MP; *S* father 1858; *m* 1st, 1856, Amy

(*d* 1895), *d* of Captain H. N. Smith, RE; 2nd, 1903, Kate, *e d* of late John Gretton of Stapleford Park, Leicestershire. *Educ:* Eton. Entered army, 1850. Owned about 2,400 acres. *Heir:* none. *Address:* Sutton Park, Sandy, Beds. *Clubs:* Carlton; Royal Yacht Squadron, Cowes.

Died 19 March 1921.

BURKE, Rt. Rev. Mgr. Alfred Edward, PA; DD, LLD; *b* Georgetown, Prince Edward Island, 8 Sept. 1862; *s* of James Burke and Mary Moar. *Educ:* St Dunstan's College, Charlottetown; Laval University, Quebec. Priest, 1885; Pastor of Alberton, PEI, 1888; called by the Apostolic Delegate Mgr Sbarretti to found the Catholic Church Extension Society of Canada, 1908; President, 1909–15; Catholic Chaplain in Canadian Contingents with rank of Major; Lieut-Colonel, 1916; served European War, 1914–17; Mexico, 1919–20, secured return of Bishops and re-opening of churches from Carranza. *Publications:* Editor-in-Chief, Catholic Register Extension; author innumerable monographs, religious and secular. *Recreations:* billiards, English croquet, boating, swimming. *Address:* 119 Wellington Street, W, Toronto, Canada.   *Died 1927.*

BURKE, Major Charles James, DSO 1915; Royal Irish Regiment; Commandant Central Flying School since 1916; *b* 9 March 1852; *s* of Michael Charles Christopher Burke of Ballinahore House, Armagh; *m* Beatrice Osborn, 3rd *d* of W. Shakspeare, 42 Prince's Gardens, SW, and Yateley, Hants. Entered army, 1903; Captain, 1909; Major, 1913; with W African Frontier Force, 1905–9; at Aeroplanes and Balloon School, 1910–11; Air Batt., 1911–12; Royal Flying Corps, 1912; served S African War, 1899–1902 (Queen's medal, five clasps); European War, 1914–15 (DSO); injured in aeroplane accidents on Jan. 7, 1911, and Jan. 8, 1912; member Royal United Service Institution and Meterological Society; Associate Fellow of Aeronautical Society. *Address:* Central Flying School, Upavon, Salisbury Plain. *Clubs:* Army and Navy, Royal Aero.

Died 9 April 1917.

BURKE, Henry Lardner, KC 1898; MA (Oxford), LLB (Cape); Solicitor-General for the Cape Colony, 1903–11; *b* Dublin, 3 May 1850; *e s* of late Rev. John Lardner Burke, LLD, of Rutland Square, Dublin, and Marian, *y d* of late Rev. Henry Tweedy, MA; *m* Frances Charlotte, *e d* of Samuel Bain, late of Port Elizabeth, Cape Colony; five *s* one *d*. *Educ:* Lincoln College, Oxford (scholar); 2nd class Classical Mods 1871; 3rd class Final Classical School, 1873. Admitted as Advocate of Eastern Districts Court, 1880; Crown Prosecutor in High Court of Griqualand, 1897–1902; acted as one of the judges of Supreme Court, Cape Colony, July–Sept. 1904, and Nov.–Dec. 1905. *Recreations:* walking, travel, literature. *Address:* c/o The Standard Bank of S Africa, Adderley Street, Cape Town, S. Africa.

Died Aug. 1927.

BURKE, Sir John, Kt 1921; DL; JP; ship-broker. *Address:* Ravensdale, Strandtown, Belfast.   *Died 14 March 1922.*

BURKE, Rt. Rev. Maurice Francis; Roman Catholic Bishop of St Joseph, Missouri, since 1893; *b* Ireland, 5 May 1845. *Educ:* St Mary's, Chicago; Notre Dame, Indiana; American College, Rome. Went to United States with his parents at the age of four; was educated in lower branches in United States; spent nine years at the American College in Rome, studying for the church, and was ordained there, 1875; Curate at St Mary's Church, Chicago two years; Pastor of St Mary's Church, Joliet, Ill, nine years, where he built a church and two schools; Bishop of Cheyenne, Wyoming, 1887. *Recreations:* reading Dante, studying the languages. *Address:* 718 North 7th Street, St Joseph, Missouri, USA.

Died 17 March 1923.

BURLINGAME, Edward Livermore; Editor of Scribner's Magazine, 1886–1914, and since 1879 on the editorial staff of Charles Scribner's Sons, New York; on board of directors since 1904; *b* Boston, Massachusetts, 30 May 1848; *e s* of Anson Burlingame; *m* 1871, Ella F. Badger. *Educ:* Harvard (hon. MA 1901) and Heidelberg (PhD). Hon. LittD Columbia, 1914. On staff New York Tribune, 1871; American Cyclopædia, 1872–76. *Address:* 440 West End Avenue, New York. *Clubs:* Century, Harvard, NY.

Died 15 Nov. 1922.

BURLS, Sir Edwin Grant, Kt 1909; CSI 1902; *b* 25 April 1844; *e s* of late Charles Burls; *m* 1875, Edith Louisa, *d* of late James Williams; one *s* one *d*. *Educ:* Denmark Hill Grammar School. Entered India Office, 1863; Junior Clerk, Store Dept, 1865; Senior Clerk, 1875; Assistant to Director-General of Stores, 1891; Deputy Director-General, 1895; Director-General of Stores, India Office, 1896–1909; Member of Ordnance Council, 1896–1909; late Major 1st Surrey

Artillery Volunteer Corps, having held commission, 1868–82; Director of John I. Thornycroft & Co. Ltd, and of Vulcan Foundry, Ltd; Member of Committees of National Hospital for Paralysed and Epileptic, of Evelina Hospital, the Evangelical Church Schools, and of The Missions to Seamen. *Address:* Shortlands, Kent. *TA:* Burls, Shortlands. *T:* Ravensbourne 0668. *M:* XN 1964. *Clubs:* East India United Service, St Stephen's.

Died 10 Sept. 1926.

BURN, Very Rev. Andrew Ewbank, DD; Dean of Salisbury since 1920; *b* Bareilly, India, 17 Jan. 1864; *s* of late Rev. T. H. Burn, Chaplain at Bareilly; *m* C. M., *d* of E. Richardson; one *s* three *d. Educ:* Clifton Coll.; Charterhouse; Trinity Coll., Camb. (3rd class Class. Tripos, MA 1889, BD 1898, DD 1904). Student with Bishop Lightfoot of Durham at Auckland Castle; Curate of St Cuthbert, Bensham, 1897–91; St Andrew, Auckland, 1891–93; Rector of Kynnersley, 1893; Rural Dean of Edgmond; Prebendary of Lichfield, 1903; Rector of Handsworth, 1904; Rural Dean of Handsworth; Special Preacher, Oxford, 1906; Vicar of Halifax, 1909–20; Chaplain to the King; Hon. Canon of Wakefield; Examining Chaplain to Bishops of Lichfield and Wakefield; Rural Dean, Halifax, 1914. *Publications:* The Athanasian Creed and its early Commentaries; An Introduction to the Creeds and the Te Deum; Niceta of Remesiana, His Life and Works; The Crown of Thorns; The Council of Nicaea; The Te Deum and its Author, 1926. *Address:* The Deanery, Salisbury. *Club:* Authors'. *Died 28 Nov. 1927.*

BURN, Lt-Col Charles Pelham Maitland; Lieutenant-Colonel retired, Seaforth Highlanders; *b* 6 Feb. 1880; *s* of late Charles Maitland Pelham Burn and Isabella Romanes, *d* and *co-heiress* of James Russel of Blackbraes, Stirlingshire; *m* 1908, Mabel (*d* 1912), *d* of Sir John Arthur Fowler, 2nd Bt, of Braemore; one *s. Address:* The Lodge, Craigellachie, Banffshire. *T:* Craigellachie 11. *Club:* New, Edinburgh. *Died 15 Aug. 1925.*

BURNABY, Lt-Col Eustace Beaumont; *b* 4 April 1842; *s* of late T. F. A. Burnaby, Brampton Manor, Hunts; *m* 1879, Alice Caroline, *d* of Beaumont Hotham, late Grenadier Guards. Served nearly 18 years in 2nd Lincoln Regt; late Senior Major, Hon. Lieut-Col, 4th Lincoln Regiment (Militia); City Marshal of London, 1886–89; Common Cryer and Sergeant-at-Arms, City of London, 1889–1901. Jubilee medals of 1887 and 1897. *Address:* 28 Wellington Square, Chelsea, SW. *T:* Kensington 3950. *Club:* United Service. *Died 20 Oct. 1916.*

BURNABY, Lt-Col Hugo Beaumont, DSO 1902; Captain 15th Durham Light Infantry, 1914; Lieutenant-Colonel commanding 11th (S) Battalion The Queens (Royal West Surrey Regiment), 1915; *b* 5 May 1874; *y s* of Sherrard Beaumont Burnaby, late Vicar of Hampstead, NW; *m* 1906, Evelyn Violet, *y d* of late Maj.-Gen. C. H. Smith, CB, RHA; one *s* two *d. Educ:* Uppingham. Engaged in ranching in British Columbia, 1893–99; served in S Africa, 1900–2; first in the ranks; commission, March 1901; Captain, June 1901, 1st Batt. Imperial Yeomanry (despatches, medal, DSO). *Recreation:* shooting. *Address:* Wendover, Bucks. *TA:* Rocketer, Wendover. *Died 8 Sept. 1916.*

BURNABY-ATKINS, Thomas Frederick, JP, DL, Kent; *b* 13 March 1836; 2nd *s* of late Thomas Fowke Andrew Burnaby of Brampton Manor, Hunts, and Emily, 11th *d* of late Rupert Chawner, MD; inherited Halstead Place and estate, 1872, under the will of J. P. Atkins, whose name he assumed in addition to that of Burnaby by Royal Licence; *m* 1868, Elizabeth, *d* of late John Francklin, Gonalston Hall, Notts; one *s* six *d. Educ:* Eton; Trinity Hall, Cambridge (MA). On the Roll for High Sheriff of Kent for 1902. *Address:* Hamptons, Tonbridge, Kent. *TA:* Hadlow, Kent. *T:* Plaxtole 14. *Club:* Carlton. *Died 28 Sept. 1918.*

BURNAND, Sir Francis Cowley, Kt 1902; barrister, Lincoln's Inn; editor of Punch, 1862–1906; dramatic author, light literature; *b* 29 Nov. 1836; descended on father's side from old Savoyard family; great-great-grandfather was partner in Minet and Co., silk merchants; mother, Emma Cowley, *d* of Christian Cowley, direct descendant of Hannah Cowley, authoress; *m* 1st, 1860, Cecilia Victoria (*d* 1870), *d* of James Ranoe; five *s* two *d*; 2nd, 1874, Rosina, *widow* of P. Jones; two *s* four *d. Educ:* Eton (where at fifteen he wrote a farce played at Cookesley's house, also at Theatre Royal, Worthing); Trinity College, Cambridge. Founded the Amateur Dramatic Club, where his earliest pieces were produced; studied for English Church at Cuddesdon under Canon Liddon; became a Roman Catholic; read for Bar at Bourdillon's Chambers; called; practised occasionally; commenced writing; introduced by George Meredith to Once a

Week; by Lacy, theatrical bookseller, to Charles Young, actor, who successfully produced Dido at St James's Theatre under management of Chatterton and Willert; with Montagu Williams, wrote for Robson, then alone for Robson, Buckstone, and several theatres; comedies, burlesques, for Strand; his burlesque Black-Eyed Susan ran 800 nights at Royalty Theatre, Soho, was played for years provincially and in America, and was twice revived in London; when about 26, wrote for Fun, but on its proprietor refusing his burlesque novelette, Mokeanna, he brought it to Mark Lemon, who accepted it for Punch; on its staff from that date, succeeding Mark Lemon, Shirley Books, Tom Taylor, as editor, 1880. Wrote over a hundred and twenty plays, chiefly burlesques and light comedies; among the latter The Colonel, which satirised the æsthetic craze of that period; adapted several farcical comedies for Augustine Daly, New York; wrote two light operas (Contrabandista and The Chieftain) with Sir Arthur Sullivan, with whom he wrote musical version of Morton's old farce, "Box and Cox," entitled, perversely, "Cox and Box"; "His Majesty," an opera, with R. C. Lehmann. *Publications:* Happy Thoughts, 1866; the Happy Thought Series; Modern Sandford and Merton, New Light on Darkest Africa, Strapmore, Ride to Khiva; eccentric Guide to Isle of Thanet, illustrated by Phil May; Amateur Dramatic Club Reminiscences, 1880; Records and Reminiscences, 1904. *Recreations:* riding, sea-boating. *Address:* 18 Royal Crescent, Ramsgate. *Club:* Garrick. *Died 21 April 1917.*

BURNE, Brig.-Gen. Rainald Owen, CBE 1919; *b* 3 Jan. 1871; 5th *s* of Newdigate Burne, Barrister-at-law, and Hon. Mrs Burne, *d* of 2nd Viscount Sidmouth; *m* 1897, Sybil Mary, *d* of David Owen, Senior Registrar of HM Court of Probate; *no c. Educ:* St Lawrence College, Ramsgate; Bedford Grammar School; Royal Military College, Sandhurst. 2nd Lieut Royal Fusiliers, 1891; transferred to Royal Army Service Corps, 1895; served South African War, 1899–1902 (Queen's medal and 3 clasps, King's medal and 2 clasps); on Staff, War Office, 1908–11; European War, 1914–18; served on Staff; wounded 1st Battle Ypres (despatches, Brevet of Colonel, CBE, 1914 Star, Allies medal and Victory medal); Brig.-General and Commandant Mechanical Transport Reception and Training Area, RASC, 1917; retired, 1920. *Recreations:* fishing, cricket. *Club:* United Service. *Died 4 May 1923.*

BURNE-JONES, Sir Philip, 2nd Bt, *cr* 1894; painter; *b* 2 Oct. 1861; *s* of Sir Edward Coley Burne Burne-Jones, 1st Bt, and Georgiana, *d* of Rev. George Macdonald; *S* father, 1898. *Educ:* Marlborough College; University College, Oxford. *Heir:* none. *Address:* 41 Egerton Terrace, SW3. *T:* 607 Western. *Club:* Bath. *Died 21 June 1926 (ext).*

BURNET, Rev. Amos; Secretary, Wesleyan Methodist Missionary Society; President of Wesleyan Methodist Conference, 1924; *b* Little Steeping, Lincolnshire, 5 Aug. 1857; *m* Esther Ann Dring of Brinkhill, Lincolnshire; five *d. Educ:* Wesleyan College, Richmond. Spent eleven years as a missionary in Bangalore, South India; then nine years in Nottingham; went to South Africa at the end of the Boer War as General Superintendent of Wesleyan Missions in the Transvaal and Swaziland District, and remained in that post for seventeen years; appointed General Secretary of the Wesleyan Missionary Society in 1919. *Publication:* A Mission to the Transvaal. *Address:* 24 Bishopsgate, EC2. *TA:* Wesleystock, London.

Died 1 Aug. 1926.

BURNET, John, MA (Oxon); LLD Edin.; Hon. PhD Prague; LLD California, 1926; St Andrews, 1927; FBA; Emeritus Professor of Greek, St Andrews University; Officier de l'Instruction Publique, 1911; Associate of the Royal Academy of Belgium, 1919; Hon. Fellow, Educational Institute of Scotland, 1919; *b* Edinburgh, 9 Dec. 1863; *s* of John Burnet, advocate; *m* 1894, Mary, *d* of late John Farmer; one *d. Educ:* Royal High School and University, Edinburgh; Balliol College (Scholar). 1st class in Moderations and in Lit. Hum. Oxford; Taylorian Scholar. Master at Harrow, 1888; Fellow of Merton College, Oxford, 1890; Hon. Fellow, 1915; Professor of Greek, St Andrews, 1892–1926; Examiner in Literæ Humaniores, Oxford, 1901–3, 1911, and 1915, and in Classical Tripos (Part II), Cambridge, 1908–9; Romanes Lecturer, 1923; Hon. Fellow of Balliol, 1925; Sather Professor in Classical Literature, California, 1925. *Publications:* Early Greek Philosophy, 1892 (2nd edn 1908; 3rd edn 1920; German translation, 1913; French translation, 1919); Greek Rudiments, 1897; The Nicomachean Ethics of Aristotle, 1899; Aristotle on Education, 1903; Platonis Opera (5 vols), 1899–1907; Plato's Phaedo, 1911; Euthyphro, Apology and Crito, 1924; Greek Philosophy, Part I, Thales to Plato, 1914; Higher Education and the War, 1917. *Address:* Balfour House, St Andrews. *Club:* Athenæum.

Died 26 May 1928.

BURNETT, Sir (Edward) Napier, KBE 1919; JP; MD Glas., FRCSE, FRCPE; Consulting Surgeon; Chairman Economical Committee Army Medical Department, War Office; Director of Hospital Service, British Red Cross Society; a Knight of Grace of the Order of St John of Jerusalem; *b* 12 July 1872; *y s* of late James Burnett, Fraserburgh; *m* 1903. *Educ:* Glasgow University; Edinburgh; Dublin. *Publications:* Lectures on Hospital Administration; various papers in medical journals. *Address:* 16 Frognall Lane, Hampstead, NW3. *T:* Hampstead 7073. *Club:* Reform.   *Died 25 Dec. 1923.*

BURNETT, Mrs Frances (Eliza)Hodgson; novelist and dramatist; *b* Manchester, 24 Nov. 1849; went with her parents to Knoxville, Tennessee, USA, 1865; *m* 1st, 1873, Dr Swan M. Burnett, Washington, USA; obtained a divorce, 1898; one *s* (and one *s* decd); 2nd, 1900, Stephen Townesend, surgeon, lecturer and author (marr. diss.; he *d* 1914). Began to publish 1867; her name began to be known with That Lass o' Lowrie's, Scribner's Magazine and book form, 1877; Little Lord Fauntleroy, which she dramatised, brought its author over £20,000; other plays— Phyllis, The Showman's Daughter, The First Gentleman of Europe, Esmeralda (which ran for three years in America), and in collaboration with Mr Townesend, Nixie and A Lady of Quality. *Publications:* Surly Tim and other Stories, 1877; Haworth's, 1879; Louisiana, 1880; A Fair Barbarian, 1881; Through One Administration, 1883; Little Lord Fauntleroy, 1886; Sara Crewe, 1888; Little Saint Elizabeth, 1889; The Pretty Sister of José; A Lady of Quality, 1896; His Grace of Ormonde, 1897; The Captain's Youngest, 1898; In Connection with the De Willoughby Claim, 1899; The Making of a Marchioness, 1901; The Little Unfairy Princess, 1902; The Dawn of a Tomorrow, 1907; The Secret Garden, 1911; Tembarom, 1913; The Head of the House of Coombe, 1922; Robin, 1922. *Recreation:* improving the lot of children. *Address:* Maytham Hall, Rolvenden, Kent.

Died 29 Oct. 1924.

BURNETT of Leys, Sir Thomas, 12th Bt, *cr* 1626; late Colonel Royal Horse Artillery 1890; Lord Lieutenant; *b* 27 Nov. 1840; *s* of 10th Bt and Lauderdale, *d* of Sir Alexander Ramsay, Bt, of Balmain, and *widow* of David Duncan of Rosemount, Forfar; *S* half-brother, 1894; *m* 1875, Mary Elizabeth, *e d* of J. Cumine of Rattray, Aberdeenshire; two *s* one *d* (and one *d* decd). Owned about 12,300 acres. *Heir: s* Col James Lauderdale Gilbert Burnett, *b* 1 April 1880. *Address:* Crathes Castle, Aberdeen.   *Died 25 Jan. 1926.*

BURNEY, Rev. Charles Fox, MA, DLitt; Hon. DD (Durham); Oriel Professor of Interpretation of Holy Scripture, Oxford University, since 1914; Canon of Rochester Cathedral; Fellow, Oriel and St John's Colleges; Examining Chaplain to the Bishop of Rochester; *b* 4 Nov. 1868; *o s* of Charles George Burney, Paymaster-in-Chief, RN, and of Eleanor Agnes, *d* of Rev. William Addington Norton, MA, Rector of Alderton and Eyke, Suffolk; *m* 1913, Ethel Wordsworth, *e d* of Falconer Madan; two *s* one *d*. *Educ:* Merchant Taylors' School; St John's College, Oxford. Exhibitioner, 1887; Senior Scholar, 1893; Lecturer in Hebrew, 1893; Librarian, 1897–1908; Fellow, 1899; Vice-President, 1900, 1906, 1910, 1911; BA 1890, MA 1894, DLitt 1903. Deacon, 1893; Priest, 1894; Curate of All Saints, Oxford, 1893–95. Obtained the following University distinctions:—1st class in Final Honour School of Theology, 1890; 1st class in Final Honour School of Semitic Studies, 1892; Pusey and Ellerton Scholar, 1887; Junior Kennicott Scholar, 1890; Houghton Syriac Prize, 1891; Hall-Houghton Septuagint Prizes, junior 1892, senior 1894; Denyer and Johnson Scholar, 1893; Senior Kennicott Scholar, 1895; Examiner Final Honour Schools of Theology, 1901–3; Oriental Studies, 1904, 1906, 1907, 1916; Examiner, University of London, 1898–1903; Examining Chaplain to the Bishop of Southwell, 1904–15; Grinfield Lecturer on the Septuagint in the University of Oxford, 1911–15. *Publications:* Outlines of Old Testament Theology, Oxford Church Text-Books, 1899, 3rd edn 1906; Notes on the Hebrew Text of the Books of Kings, 1903; Israel's Hope of Immortality, 1909; Israel's Settlement in Canaan (Schweich Lecturers, 1917), 1918, 3rd edn 1921; The Book of Judges with Introduction and Notes, 1918, 2nd edn 1920; The New Lessons explained, Part 1, 1920; The Gospel in the Old Testament, 1920; The Aramaic Origin of the Fourth Gospel, 1922; contributor to Contentio Veritatis, 1902; articles in Hastings' Bible Dictionary, Encyclopædia Biblica, Journal of Theological Studies, etc. *Recreations:* breeding horses, riding, gardening; formerly running. *Address:* 34 St Giles', Oxford; The Precinct, Rochester.   *Died 15 April 1925.*

BURNHAM, 1st Baron, *cr* 1903; **Edward Levy Lawson;** Bt 1892; KCVO 1904; DL, JP, Co. Bucks; principal proprietor of the Daily Telegraph; Lieutenant for the City of London; *b* London, 28 Dec. 1833; *e s* of J. M. Levy and Esther, his wife, both deceased; under the will of his uncle, Mr Lionel Lawson, assumed the name of Lawson in 1875 by Royal licence; *m* 1862, Harriette Georgiana (*d* 1897), *o d* of B. N. Webster; two *s* one *d*. *Educ:* University College, London. High Sheriff for Bucks, 1886; President Royal Institute of Journalists, 1892–93; late Alderman, Bucks CC. Owned about 4,000 acres. *Recreations:* golf, shooting, riding. *Heir: s* Hon. Harry Lawson Webster Lawson, *b* 18 Dec. 1862. *Address:* 20 Norfolk Street, Park Lane, W; Hall Barn, Beaconsfield, Bucks. *T:* 12 Bourne End. *Clubs:* Marlborough, Garrick, Beefsteak.

Died 9 Jan. 1916.

BURNLEY, James; author and journalist; *b* Shipley, Yorkshire. *Educ:* privately. On staff of Yorkshire Observer, 1871–82; Editor of The Yorkshireman, 1875–85. *Publications:* Idonia, 1870; Phases of Bradford Life, 1871; West Riding Sketches, 1873; Two Sides of the Atlantic, 1878; Looking for the Dawn, 1880; Yorkshire Stories Re-told, 1884; Sir Titus Salt and George Moore (World's Workers Series), 1885; Fortunes made in Business, 1887; The Romance of Life Preservation, 1888; The Romance of Modern Industry, 1889; History of Wool and Wool-combing, 1891; Romance of Invention, 1892; Desert London, 1895; Industries and Resources of America, 1896; Colorado's Golden Glories, 1900; Millionaires and Kings of Enterprise, 1901; Summits of Success, 1901; Studies in Millionaires, 1901; The Story of British Trade, 1904; Nets of Gold, 1908; In the Trail of a Crime, 1909; contributor to the Encyclopædia Britannica, Dictionary of National Biography, Chambers's Encyclopædia, etc; author of several plays, including Fetters, Moneysworth, and The Shadow of the Mill; editor of Pears' Cyclopædia and Pears' Annual. *Address:* The Croft, Chesham, Bucks; 71–75 New Oxford Street, WC. *Club:* National Liberal.   *Died 29 Dec. 1919.*

BURNS, Col Hon. Sir James, KCMG 1917; MLC since 1908; Chairman and Managing Director of Burns, Philp & Co.; *b* near Edinburgh, 10 Feb. 1846; *s* of David Burns, retired Colonial merchant; *m* twice; widower; two *s* three *d*. *Educ:* Edinburgh High School. Went to Australia, 1862; engaged in pastoral pursuits four years; began commercial career, 1866; the company had 30 branches in Australasia, Pacific, Java, etc; owned fleet of steamers trading to Java and Singapore; also interested in cattle and sheep properties in Queensland; commanded NSW Lancer Regt 14 years; later Brig.-Col 1st Australian Mounted Brigade; retired, 1907; Director of 20 Australian companies and institutions; President of the Highland Society of New South Wales. *Address:* Gowan Brae, near Parramatta, NSW. *Clubs:* Union, Australian, Sydney.   *Died 21 Aug. 1923.*

BURNS-BEGG, Col Robert; KC 1906; *b* 10 March 1872; *s* of Robert Burns-Begg, Kinross; *m* Ethel, *o d* of C. H. Tapply, Tregenna, Sutton, Surrey; no *c*. *Educ:* privately; Edinburgh University. Called to Scotch Bar, 1895; Bar of Southern Rhodesia, 1898; on active service as Lieut and Capt. South African Mounted Irregular Forces, 1899–1902 (Queen's Medal, 5 clasps; King's Medal, 2 clasps); temporarily attached to Intelligence Dept, War Office, 1902–3; Legal Adviser to Transvaal Govt 1903; called to Transvaal Bar, 1903; commanding Northern Mounted Rifles, 1904–7; member of Committee on Re-organisation of Police Forces of the Colony, 1908; Commissioner, Transvaal Police, 1908–10; Commandant General and Resident Commissioner, Northern and Southern Rhodesia, 1911–15; Temp. Col in the Army, 1915. *Recreations:* golf, shooting. *Address:* Tregenna, Sutton, Surrey. *Club:* Windham.   *Died 9 Jan. 1918.*

BURNSIDE, Helen Marion; artist and poet; *b* Bromley Hall, 1844; *e d* of late John Fullerton Burnside. *Educ:* at home. Exhibited at Royal Academy, 1863; Columbian Exposition (honourable mention), 1895; Society of Lady Artists, 1897; designer to Royal School of Art Needlework, 1880–89; editor to Messrs Raphael Tuck and Co., 1889–95. *Publications:* first book of poems, Blithe Tweed, 1897; Her Highland Laddie, 1897; The Little VC; The Lost Letter; Tales for Children, 1897; The Deaf Girl next Door, 1899; compiled R. N. Carey Birthday Book; A Girl without a Penny, 1907; numberless songs (published with music), magazine poems and tales, card verses, etc. *Recreations:* reading, gardening, walking. *Address:* Up Down House, Windlesham, Surrey.

Died 5 Dec. 1923.

BURNSIDE, William, MA, DSc (Dublin), LLD (Edin.); FRS 1893; Hon. Fellow of Pembroke College, Cambridge; Professor of Mathematics, Royal Naval College, Greenwich, 1885–1919; *b* 2 July 1852; *m* 1886, Alexandrina, *d* of Kenneth Urquhart; two *s* three *d*. *Educ:* Pembroke Coll., Camb.; 2nd Wrangler, 1st Smith's Prizeman, 1875. Pres., London Mathematical Soc., 1906–8. *Publication:* Theory of Groups, 1897. *Address:* Cotleigh, West Wickham.

Died 21 Aug. 1927.

BURNSIDE, William Snow, MA, DSc; Senior Fellow and Member of Governing Body, Trinity College, Dublin; Erasmus Smith's Professor of Mathematics, Dublin University, 1879–1914. *Publications:* (with the late A. W. Panton): Theory of Equations; some mathematical papers in the Quarterly Journal of Mathematics with some contributions to Salmon's Conic Sections. *Address:* Trinity College, and 35 Raglan Road, Dublin. *Club:* University, Dublin. *Died 11 March 1920.*

BURNYEAT, William John Dalzell, JP; MA; MP (L) Whitehaven, 1906–10; *b* 13 March 1874; *e s* of William and Sarah Frances Burnyeat, of Millgrove, Moresby, Cumberland; *m* 1908, Hildegard, *d* of Col Retzlaff of Friedenaw, Berlin. *Educ:* Rugby; Corpus Christi College, Oxford (Exhibitioner). Called to Bar, Inner Temple, 1899; has travelled. *Address:* Moresby House, Moresby, Cumberland. *T:* Whitehaven 90. *M:* AO 737. *Club:* Reform. *Died 8 May 1916.*

BURR, Rear-Adm. John Leslie, CMG 1899; MVO 1904; JP; RN, retired; Captain of the Port Holyhead since 1902; *b* 14 Aug. 1847; *s* of Charles Burr of Luton House, Luton, Beds. Entered Navy, 1861; Capt. 1894; served Ashanti War, 1873–74 (despatches twice, medal); West Coast Africa, 1879 (thanks of Foreign Office, Admiralty, and Government at Sierra Leone); in command of HMS Pioneer, went 700 miles up the Niger with presents for the Emir of Nupi (thanks of Governor of Gold Coast and Secretary of Foreign Office); appointed to take the Commissioners for the Behring Sea Commission, 1894. *Decorated* for distinguished services in Central America by putting an end to the revolutions in Nicaragua and Honduras. *Address:* Government House, Holyhead. *Clubs:* United Service; Naval, Portsmouth *Died 3 Nov. 1917.*

BURRINGTON, Arthur, RI. *Address:* c/o Cole Bros, 2 Percy Street, W1. *Died 10 Oct. 1924.*

BURROUGHS, John; *b* Roxbury, NY, 3 April 1837; *s* of C. A. Burroughs, farmer; *m*; one *s*. *Educ:* Ashland and Cooperstown Seminaries. Teacher, clerk in Treasury Department, bank examiner, author, farmer; Doctor of Literature, Yale; Doctor of Humane Letters, Colgate University; Member of American Academy of Arts and Letters. *Publications:* Walt Whitman, Poet and Person, 1867; Wake-Robin, 1871; Winter Sunshine, 1875; Birds and Poets, 1877; Locusts and Wild Honey, 1879; Pepacton, 1881; Fresh Fields, 1884; Signs and Seasons, 1886; Indoor Studies, 1889; Riverby, 1894; Whitman, 1896; The Light of Day, 1900; Literary Values, 1902; Far and Near, 1904; Ways of Nature, 1905; Bird and Bough (Poems), 1906; Camping and Tramping with Roosevelt, 1907; Leaf and Tendril, 1908; Time and Change, 1912; The Summit of the Years, 1913; The Breath of Life, 1915; Under the Apple Trees, 1916. *Recreations:* sauntering, automobiling, fishing. *Address:* West Park, New York. *Died 29 March 1921.*

BURROWES, Lt-Col Algernon St Leger, CB 1911; Royal Marine Light Infantry (retired); *b* 1847; 2nd *s* of late Rev. J. R. Burrowes, formerly Rector of Hutton, Somerset; *m* Fanny Henrietta, *e d* of late W. Barry Hoard, JP of Monkstown, Co. Cork; two *d*. Entered Royal Marine Light Infantry, 1866; served HMS Ariadne, 1868–69; Special Service to convey Prince and Princess of Wales to the East; served in HMS Serapis, 1875–76, with Guard of Honour of Royal Marines, during cruise of Prince of Wales to India; served Egyptian Campaign, 1882; as Adjutant of the Batt. RMLI present at the actions of Tel-el-Mahuta, Masamah, Kassassin (horse shot), and storming of Tel-el-Kebir; served Eastern Soudan, 1884–85; as Adjutant of the Batt. RMLI during the defence of Suakin, and afterwards in the Mounted Infantry to the close of the campaign; present at the actions of Handoub, Hasheen, Tamai, Thakeol, and attacks on the convoys (despatches, brevet Major); served in HMS Imperieuse, Flagship on the China Station, 1893–94; served as Recruiting Staff Officer, 1916–18 (special mention). *Address:* Moorside, Budleigh Salterton, Devon. *Died 18 Dec. 1925.*

BURROWES, Thomas Cosby; *b* 1856; *s* of late James Edward Burrowes and Mary Anne, *y d* of John Nesbitt of Lismore; *m* 1885, Anna Frances Maxwell, *sister* of 10th Baron Farnham; two *d*. JP Co. Cavan; High Sheriff, 1888. *Address:* Lismore, Cavan. *Died 20 Feb. 1925.*

BURROWES, William Henry Aglionby, ISO 1911; Commissary of Taxation, British Guiana. *Address:* Georgetown, British Guiana. *Died 4 Nov. 1922.*

BURROWS, Colonel Edmund Augustine, CMG 1900; CBE 1919; Royal Artillery (retired); *b* 19 March 1855; *s* of late Canon Burrows

of Rochester; *m* 1891, Mary Claudine, *d* of late William Coode of Trevarna, St Austell; one *s*. Entered Army, 1875; Captain, 1884; Major, 1892; Lieut-Col 1900; served Burmah, 1885–86 (medal with clasp); South Africa, 1900 (medal with 6 clasps and CMG); re-employed Oct. 1914. JP Bucks. *Address:* Manor House, Long Crendon, Thame. *Died 19 May 1927.*

BURROWS, Sir Ernest Pennington, 3rd Bt, *cr* 1874; *b* 11 July 1851; *s* of Sir George Burrows, 1st Bt, FRS and Elinor, *d* of late John Abernethy, FRS; *S* brother 1904. *Heir:* none. *Address:* 21 Connaught Square, W. *Club:* Oriental.
Died 4 Aug. 1917 (ext).

BURROWS, Rev. Francis Henry, MA; Hon. Canon of Manchester since 1916; *b* Atherton, 28 Nov. 1857; *s* of Abraham Burrows, JP, CA, Atherton; *m* Margaret Nelson, *d* of Richard Curtis, JP, Bowdon; three *s* one *d*. *Educ:* Christ's College, Cambridge; BA 1878, MA 1881. Curate of S Mary, Stoke, Ipswich, 1880–82; Assistant Diocesan Inspector, Manchester, 1882–89; Diocesan Inspector, Manchester, 1889–96; Vicar of Christ Church, Ashton-under-Lyne, 1896–1919; Rural Dean, 1909–19; CTF, 1909–19. *Recreation:* golf. *Address:* The Glen, Linden Chase, Sevenoaks. *T:* Sevenoaks 168. *Club:* Oxford and Cambridge. *Died 20 July 1928.*

BURROWS, General George Reynolds Scott; Bombay Infantry; *b* 18 Feb. 1827; *m* 1st, 1851, Emilie, *d* of General Goodfellow, RE; 2nd, 1871, Dorothea, *d* of J. J. Ellis, Escrick, Yorks. Entered Army, 1844; General, 1890; retired list, 1886; served Afghan War, 1880 (despatches four times, medal with clasp). *Address:* 4 Cavendish Crescent, Bath. *Died July 1917.*

BURROWS, Ronald Montagu; Principal, King's College, London, since 1913; *b* Rugby, 16 Aug. 1867; *y s* of late Rev. L. F. Burrows, and Mary, *d* of Captain Vicars, RE; *m* 1892, Una Geraldine, *d* of Rt Rev. C. J. Ridgeway, Bishop of Chichester. *Educ:* Charterhouse; Christ Church, Oxford. Scholar; 1st Class Classical Moderations, 1888; 1st Class Lit. Hum. 1890; DLitt, Oxford, 1910; Hon. PhD Athens, 1914; Fellow of King's College, London, 1914. Assistant to Professor of Greek, University of Glasgow, 1891–97; Professor of Greek in University Coll., Cardiff, 1898–1908; Professor of Greek in the University of Manchester, 1908–13; Acting Chairman Anglo-Hellenic League; Member of Council, Hellenic Society, Serbian Society, Serbian Relief Fund, United Russia Societies Association, British-Italian League, Anglo-Roumanian Society, Anglo-Spanish Society; Hon. Member of Archæological Society of Athens; Grand Commander Order of King George of Greece; Commander Order of the Saviour; Order of St Sava (3rd Class). *Publications:* various articles in the classical journals, especially on Pylos Sphacteria, Rhitsóna, and Kothons in the Journal of Hellenic Studies, vols xvi, xviii, xxviii, xxix, and xxxi, and Delium and Rhitsóna in the Annual of the British School at Athens, vols xi and xiv; (with Prof. W. F. Walters) Florilegium Tironis Graecum, 1904; The Discoveries in Crete, 1907; also articles on social and educational reform and modern Greece. *Address:* King's College, Strand, WC. *T:* Gerrard 207. *Club:* Athenæum.
Died 14 May 1920.

BURT, Sir John Mowlem, Kt 1902; JP; Lieutenant of the City of London; *b* 2 Feb. 1845; *e s* of late George Burt, Sheriff of the City of London, 1878–79; *g n* of John Mowlem of Swanage, founder of John Mowlem & Co.; *m* 1st, 1869, Marion (*d* 1903), *d* of R. K. Aitchison; 2nd, 1904, Grace Emma, *o d* of Joseph Blackstone. *Educ:* private schools; Marischal Coll., Aberdeen. Entered John Mowlem & Co. 1862; partner, 1875; senior partner, 1888; Vice-Chairman, Swanage Urban District Council, 1899–1902; represented Swanage in Dorset County Council. *Recreation:* yachting. *Address:* Durlston, Elsworthy Road, NW. *Died 20 Feb. 1918.*

BURT, Hon. Septimus, KC; *b* St Kitts, 25 Oct. 1847; 7th *s* of Sir A. P. Burt; *m* 1872, Louisa Fanny, *d* of G. E. C. Hare; four *s* four *d*. *Educ:* Shaw House School, Melksham, Wilts, England; Bishop's School, Perth, WA. Barrister West Australia, 1870; member of Legislative Council, 1874–1900; first acted as Attorney-Gen. 1886; QC 1887; Delegate, Colonial Conference (Lond.), 1887; 1st Attorney-Gen. of West Australia, 1890–97, under responsible Government; Acting Agent-Gen. West Australia in London, 1891; returned to WA 1891. *Address:* Strawberry Hill, Perth, West Australia. *TA:* Minderoo. *T:* 4083. *Club:* Weld, Perth.
Died 15 May 1919.

BURT, Rt. Hon. Thomas, PC 1906; DCL Durham University; MP (L) Morpeth, 1874–1918; *b* Northumberland, 12 Nov. 1837; *s* of Peter Burt, miner; *m* 1860, Mary, *d* of Thomas Weatherburn, engineman;

three *s* one *d*. *Educ:* village schools (two years' attendance in all) and by half a century of continuous reading and intercourse with men. Commenced working in the coal mines at ten years of age; continued at various kinds of underground work for eighteen years; Secretary of Northumberland Miners' Mutual Confident Association, 1865–1913; one of British Representatives to Berlin Labour Conference, convened by the Emperor of Germany, 1890; President Trades Union Congress, Newcastle, 1891; took part in the International Miners' Conferences; Parliamentary Secretary of Board of Trade from 1892–95. *Publications:* articles for Nineteenth Century, Contemporary, Fortnightly. *Recreations:* walking, cycling. *Address:* 20 Burdon Terrace, Newcastle. *Clubs:* Reform, National Liberal, Eighty.

Died 13 April 1922.

BURTCHAELL, George Dames, KC; MA, LLB; MRIA; Peerage Counsel; Athlone Pursuivant of Arms, 1908; Registrar of the Office of Arms, Ireland; Deputy Ulster King of Arms, 1910–11 and since 1915; JP Counties Kilkenny and Carlow; *b* 12 June 1853; *e s* of Peter Burtchaell, CE, and Maria Isabella, *d* of Lundy Edward Foot, barrister. *Educ:* Kilkenny College; Trinity College, Dublin. Barrister King's Inns, 1879; KC 1918; Fellow Royal Society of Antiquaries of Ireland; Assistant Secretary and Treasurer, 1891–99; Hon. Secretary, 1907–9; Vice-President, 1909–14 and 1919; Inspector of Historical MSS, 1899–1903; Member of Council of Royal Irish Academy, 1915–18. *Publications:* Genealogical Memoirs of the Members of Parliament for Kilkenny, 1888; A Complete List of Knights Bachelor dubbed in Ireland, incorporated with The Knights of England, by W. A. Shaw, DLitt, 1906; numerous papers on genealogical and heraldic subjects published in the Journal of the Royal Society of Antiquaries of Ireland and other periodicals. *Recreations:* walking, genealogical research. *Address:* The Office of Arms, Dublin Castle; 44 Morehampton Road, Dublin. *Club:* Royal Societies.

Died 18 Aug. 1921.

BURTON, Maj.-Gen. Benjamin, CB 1900; CMG 1917; Royal Artillery; *b* 10 March 1855; *s* of Rev. Benjamin Burton. *Educ:* RMA, Woolwich. Entered Army, 1874; Lieut Colonel, 1900; served South Africa, 1900–1 (despatches, medal with five clasps, CB). *Clubs:* Naval and Military, Cavalry; Kildare Street, Dublin.

Died 6 Aug. 1921.

BURTON, Rev. Canon Edwin Hubert, DD; FRHistS; Procurator-Fiscal of RC diocese of Westminster; *b* 12 Aug. 1870; *s* of Major Edwin Burton, late 4th Batt. Royal Fusiliers, and Sarah Mary, *d* of Thomas Mosdell Smith, late of Vimeira House, Hammersmith. *Educ:* St Edmund's College, Old Hall; St Mary's College, Oscott. Solicitor, 1893; priest, 1898; Vice-President, St Edmund's College, Old Hall, 1902–16; President, 1916–18; Canon of Westminster Cathedral, 1917; Treasurer to Westminster Chapter, 1918; Archivist of Westminster Diocese, 1919; Catholic Rector at Hampton Hill, 1920–24. *Publications:* Life and Times of Bishop Challoner, 1909; London Streets and Catholic Memories, 1925; Yesterday Papers, printed privately; joint-editor of Kirk's Biographies of English Catholics, 1909; editor of some volumes of Catholic Record Society; various pamphlets; contributor to Dublin Review, Tablet, Universe, etc. *Recreation:* reading. *Address:* Convent Lodge, Sudbury Hill, Harrow, Middlesex. *Club:* Authors'. *Died 13 Dec. 1925.*

BURTON, Rev. Ernest De Witt, DD; Professor of New Testament Interpretation (and Head of New Testament Department), University of Chicago, USA, since 1892; Acting President, University of Chicago since 1923; *b* Granville, Ohio, 4 Feb. 1856; *s* of Rev. Nathan Smith Burton, DD, and Sarah J. Fairfield; *m* 1883, Frances Mary Townson; one *d*. *Educ:* Denison Univ., Granville, Ohio (BA 1876); Rochester Theological Seminary, 1879–82; Univ. of Leipzig, 1887; Univ. of Berlin, 1894. Teacher, public and private schools, 1876–79; Instructor in Rochester Theological Seminary, 1882–83; Associate-Prof., 1883–86, Prof., 1886–92, of New Testament Interpretation in the Newton Theological Institution; Associate-Editor of the Biblical World, 1892–1906, 1913; Editor-in-Chief, 1906–12; Editor (with others) of the American Journal of Theology, 1897–1920; Univ. of Chicago Commissioner for Oriental Educational Investigation, 1908–9; Chairman of China Educational Commission, 1921–22. *Publications:* Syntax of the Moods and Tenses in New Testament Greek, 1893; Harmony of the Gospels for Historical Study (with W. A. Stevens), 1884, revised edn 1904; Records and Letters of the Apostolic Age, 1895; Constructive Studies in the Life of Christ (with S. Mathews), 1901; Principles and Ideals for the Sunday School (with S. Mathews), 1903; A Short Introduction to the Gospels, 1904; Principles of Literary Criticism and their Application to the Synoptic Problem, 1904; Studies in the Gospel of Mark, 1904; Biblical Ideas of Atonement: their History and Significance (with J. M. P. Smith

and G. B. Smith), 1909; Harmony of the Synoptic Gospels in English (with E. J. Goodspeed), 1917; Spirit, Soul, and Flesh, 1918; Commentary on the Epistle to the Galatians, 1920; Harmony of the Synoptic Gospels in Greek (with E. J. Goodspeed), 1920; A Source Book for the Study of the Teaching of Jesus in its Historical Relationships, 1923; various essays, chiefly in Amer. Journal of Theol. *Address:* 5525 Woodlawn Avenue, Chicago; University of Chicago, Chicago, Ill, USA. *Clubs:* Quadrangle, University, Chicago.

Died 26 May 1925.

BURTON, Rev. John James, MA; Vicar of Inkberrow, Worcestershire, 1896–1924; Hon. Canon of Worcester Cathedral; Rural Dean of Feckenham Deanery, 1901–24; *b* 3 Jan. 1849; *e s* of late John Daniel Burton of Alderley Edge, Cheshire; *m* 1880, Lilian Maria, 2nd *d* of late Rev. Thomas Pownall Boultbee, LLD, Prebendary of St Paul's; no *c*. *Educ:* Trinity College, Cambridge; BA 1870; MA 1874. Member of Lincoln's Inn, 1870; called to Bar, 1873; Deacon, 1875; Priest, 1876; Curate of Holbrook, Suffolk, 1875–80; Vicar of Eridge Green, Sussex, 1880–91; Vicar of Milton Ernest, Beds, 1891–96; Chaplain to the Marquess of Abergavenny. *Address:* Elborough Cottage, Charlton Kings, Cheltenham.

Died 14 Feb. 1927.

BURWASH, Rev. Nathanael; *b* Argenteuil, Quebec, 25 July 1839; *s* of Adam Burwash, UEL, descended from Burghersh family, Sussex, England, and Anne Taylor of Killean, Argyllshire; *m* 1868, Margaret Proctor of Sarnia, Ontario. *Educ:* Victoria College, Cobourg; Yale University, New Haven; Carrett Biblical Insitutute. Entered Methodist Ministry, 1860; professor in Victoria College, 1866; Dean of Faculty of Theology, 1873; and President and Chancellor of Victoria University, 1887; resigned official position in Victoria College, 1913; secretary of education for the Methodist Church in Canada, 1874–86; president of Conference, 1889–90; member of the several general conferences since 1874; member of Senate and Council of University of Toronto, and of Council of Education for province of Ontario; FRS Can. 1902. *Publications:* Memorials of Edward and Lydia Jackson, 1874; Wesley's Doctrinal Standards, 1881; Handbook on the Epistle to the Romans, 1887; Inductive Studies in Theology, 1896; Manual of Christian Theology, 1900; Life and Times of Egerton Ryerson, 1902; The Development of the University of Toronto as a Provincial Institution, 1905. *Recreations:* canoeing and fishing in Muskoka. *Address:* 26 Aloin Avenue, Toronto, Canada.

Died March 1918.

BURY, Francis George, CBE 1918; Hon. Treasurer, King George's Club for the Overseas Forces; Barrister; *m*; three *s*. *Educ:* Eton; Trinity College, Cambridge. *Address:* 8 Cheniston Gardens, W8. *T:* Western 3478. *Club:* United University.

Died 3 Jan. 1926.

BURY, George Wyman; explorer and naturalist; *b* 3 Jan. 1874; *s* of late Henry Charles Bury, Mancetter Manor House, near Atherstone; *m* 1913, Florence Ann Marshall; no *c*. *Educ:* Atherstone Grammar School; Army Crammers. Commission 3rd Batt. Royal Warwicks, 1894; joined one of the rebel tribes in S Morocco, 1895; Aden littoral desert, 1896; engaged in archæology, natural history, and intelligence survey among the mountaineers of the Aden hinterland and penetrated into the Great Red Desert, 1897–1901; with the Aden Boundary Commission, 1902; political officer in the Aden Protectorate during military operations of 1903–4; Zoological Expedition in Somaliland, 1905–6; South Arabian Exploration, 1908–9; Yemen highlands, 1912–13; special service in Egypt, Aug. 1914; intelligence staff on the canal front, Feb.–March 1915; political officer to the Red Sea Northern Patrol with rank of Lieut. RNVR 1915; took part in naval operations on Arabian coast in first half of 1916, and was closely connected with successful Arab revolt headed by the Sherif of Mecca (later King of Hedjaz) against Turkish rule. *Publications:* The Land of Uz, 1911; Arabia Infelix, 1915; Pan-Islam, 1919. *Recreations:* psychical research, pistol-shooting. Lived abroad.

Died 23 Sept. 1920.

BURY, John Bagnell, MA; Hon. LittD of Oxford, Durham, and Dublin, and Hon. LLD of Edinburgh, Glasgow, and Aberdeen Universities; Regius Professor of Modern History, Cambridge University, since 1902; Fellow King's College, Cambridge; Hon. Fellow Oriel College, Oxford; Fellow of the British Academy; Corresponding Member of the Imperial Academy of Sciences of Petrograd, the Hungarian Academy of Science, the Roumanian Academy, the Massachusetts Historical Society, and the Russian Archæological Institute at Constantinople; Romanes Lecturer, 1911; Fellow of Trinity College, Dublin, 1885–1903; Professor of Modern History in Dublin University, 1893–1902; Regius Professor of Greek,

1898; *b* 16 Oct. 1861; *s* of Rev. E. J. Bury, Canon of Clogher and Anna, *d* of Henry Rogers, Monaghan; *m* 1885, Jane, *d* of J. C. Bury; one *s*. *Educ:* Trinity Coll., Dublin. *Publications:* History of the Later Roman Empire from Arcadius to Irene, 1889; Student's History of the Roman Empire from Augustus to Marcus Aurelius, 1893; History of Greece to Death of Alexander the Great, 1900 (library edn in 2 vols 1902); The Science of History (Inaugural lecture), 1903; Life of St Patrick and his place in History, 1905; The Ancient Greek Historians (Harvard Lectures), 1908; The Constitution of the Later Roman Empire (Creighton Memorial Lecture), 1909; Imperial Administration in the Ninth Century, 1911; Romances of Chivalry on Greek Soil (Romanes Lecture), 1911; History of the Eastern Roman Empire (from 802 to 867), 1912; History of Freedom of Thought, 1913; The Idea of Progress, 1920; History of the Later Roman Empire (395-565), 2 vols 1922; ed. of Pindar's Nemean Odes, 1890; Pindar's Isthmian Odes, 1892; Freeman's History of Federal Government in Greece and Italy, 1893; Gibbon's Decline and Fall, vols i and ii 1896, iii and iv 1897, v and vi 1898; vii 1900; Freeman's Historical Geography of Europe, 1903. *Address:* King's College, Cambridge; Limne Cottage, Southwold. *Club:* Athenæum.

Died 1 June 1927.

BURY, Rev. William, MA; Residentiary Canon of Peterborough since 1908; Rector of Ickenham, Uxbridge, since 1907; *b* Radcliffe-on-Trent, Notts, 1839; *s* of Rev. W. Bury, then Rector of Radcliffe-on-Trent; *m* Eliz. A. Foljambe, *d* of Geo. Saville Foljambe of Osberton, Notts; one *d*. *Educ:* Trinity Coll., Cambridge (sen. opt., 1861). In the "Varsity" eleven, played twice against Oxford; and for two years for his county (Notts). Ordained by Archbishop of York; 1st Curacy, Tickhill, Yorks; six months sole charge of Handley, Dorset; travelled three months; Rector of Fifehead Neville, Dorset, 1866-67; Hazelbeach, Northants, 1867; Guardian for Hazelbeach, 1868, and made Poor Law his subject, commencing in 1872 a reform in the union to which he belonged (Brixworth), which resulted in reducing the number of outdoor paupers from 1062 in 1872 to 16 in 1894, without increasing indoor pauperism; his policy upset by Local Government Act, 1894, ceased to be chairman; but in 1899 was elected chairman of the DC, retired 1905; established a co-operative public house in Harleston; all the grocery and general business of the village on same principle and under same management; Rector of Harleston, 1882-1907. *Publications:* pamphlets, Charity and the Poor Law; Outdoor Relief, or A more Excellent Way; and a few sermons on kindred subjects. *Address:* Ickenham, Uxbridge.

Died 1 April 1920.

BUSH, Rev. Thomas Cromwell; of Cheshunt Park, Herts; *e s* of late Paul Bush, Rector of Duloe and Canon of Truro, and Avarilla Oliveria Cromwell, *o d* of Thomas A. Russell of Cheshunt Park, Herts; *m* 1st, 1887, Gertrude Julia (*d* 1888), *d* of G. Coles of Stratham; 2nd, 1892, Barbara Christiana (*d* 1914), *d* of late David Horndon, DL, and JP, of Pencrebar, Cornwall; two *s*. *Educ:* Rugby; Hertford College, Oxford. Represented Oxford in mile. Ordained 1878. Curate, Thornbury, Glos, 1878-80; St Mary, Redcliffe, 1881-83; Chaplain to Earl of Home, 1883-86; Curate, Fairford, 1886-87; Vicar, Queen Camel, Som, 1887-95; Rector, Micheldean, Glos, 1895-97; Hornblotton W Alford, 1897-1904; Burwarton with Cleobury N, Salop, 1904-8; was Hon. Chaplain to North Somerset Imperial Yeomanry. *Address:* Cheshunt Park, Herts; Cample Haye, Tavistock. *M:* FB 376. *Club:* RW Yacht.

Died 4 March 1919.

BUSHBY, Thomas, MB, CM (Edinburgh), MRCP; Hon. Physician to the David Lewis Northern Hospital; Consulting Physician, Liverpool School for the Blind; *m* Mary Bowring Wimble; one *s* one *d*. *Educ:* Marlborough College; Edinburgh University. Assistant Physician, Liverpool Consumption Hospital; Lecturer in Clinical Medicine to the University of Liverpool; Examiner in Clinical Medicine, University of Liverpool. *Address:* 43 Catharine Street, Liverpool. *T:* 2404 Royal, Liverpool.

Died 1 Jan. 1916.

BUSHE, Robert Gervase, CMG 1911; Auditor-General Trinidad and Tobago, 1903-23; retired, 1923; *b* 1851; *s* of late John Scott Bushe, CMG, Colonial Secretary, Trinidad; *m* 1880, Violet, *d* of A. R. Gray, Trinidad. *Educ:* Clifton College; Queen's Collegiate School, Trinidad; King's College, Cambridge (scholar), 27th Wrangler, 1875; BA; Master Queen's Royal College, Trinidad, 1878; Inspector of Schools, 1891; acted as Colonial Secretary, 1906, 1908-9, 1911, 1913, and 1914-15. *Address:* Port of Spain, Trinidad.

Died 13 July 1927.

BUSHE, Seymour Coghill Hort, KC; *b* 5 April 1853; *s* of late Rev. Charles Bushe of Castlehaven, Co. Cork; *g s* of late Rt Hon. Chief-

Justice Bushe of Kilmurry, Co. Kilkenny; *m* 1886, Lady Kathleen Maude, *d* of 1st Earl De Montalt. *Educ:* Rathmines School, Dublin; Trinity College, Dublin (BA); scholar (classics); senior moderator and Berkeley gold medallist; gold medallist in oratory of the College Historical Society. Called to Irish Bar, 1879; QC 1892; Bencher of King's Inns, 1896; senior Crown Prosecutor for county and city of Dublin, 1901; called to English Bar, 1899; KC 1904; JP, Co. Cork, travelled in Australasia and Central America, etc. *Recreations:* fishing, cycling, travel. *Address:* 49 Drayton Gardens, SW. *Clubs:* Union; Dublin University; Cork County.

Died 27 Jan. 1922.

BUSHE-FOX, Loftus Henry Kendal, MA, LLM; Fellow, Tutor, and Lecturer, St John's College, Cambridge; *b* Hampstead, 6 Dec. 1863; *s* of Major Luke Loftus Bushey-Fox, and Marian, *d* of Benjamin Brown; *m* 1906, Theodora, *y d* of late H. W. Willoughby; one *s*. *Educ:* Charterhouse; St John's Coll., Cambridge. Herschel Prizeman, 1884; Twelfth Wrangler, 1885; Law Tripos, 1886; MacMahon Law Student, 1886; called to Bar, Inner Temple, 1890; Fellow and Junior Dean of St John's College, 1903; Tutor, 1905. *Recreations:* rowing (Camb. Univ. pairs and trial eights), lawn tennis, shooting, sailing. *Address:* St John's College, and 15 Madingley Road, Cambridge; Cordara, Lanesborough, Co. Longford.

Died 21 March 1916.

BUSHELL, Rev. William Done, VD 1887; MA; FSA (Bardic Appellation, Hwysivr Pyr); *b* Bristol, 10 Nov. 1838; *s* of William Done Bushell, Resident Director at Cardiff of the Taff Vale Railway, and *g s* of William Bushell, Bristol Merchant; *m* 1866, Mary, *e d* of Charles Lestourgeon, MB, of Howes' Close, Cambridge; four *s* four *d*. *Educ:* Cheltenham College; St John's College, Cambridge (Scholar and Fellow); MA; Seventh Wrangler and 2nd Class Classical Tripos. Deacon, 1864; Priest, 1866; Fellow of St John's, 1862; Assistant Master Clifton College, 1865-66; Assistant Master Harrow School, 1866-99; Hon. Assistant Chaplain, Harrow School, 1899-1917; Original member of the Cambridge University Volunteers, 1860; Capt., 1861-65; Hon. Capt. Harrow School Corps, 1884-91; Chaplain local Volunteers, 1870-1908; Lord of the Manor of Caldey Island. *Publications:* Church Life on Harrow Hill 767-1600; antiquarian articles in Archæologia Cambrensis and various other journals; sermons. *Recreations:* Alpine Club, 1863 onwards; Champion Racquet Player, St John's College, medal (twice); golf, Northwood and other Clubs. *Address:* The Hermitage, Harrow-on-the-Hill; Caldey Priory, Tenby. *TA:* Harrow. *T:* 395. *M:* DE 119. *Clubs:* Athenæum, Alpine; Tenby and County, Tenby.

Died 27 Aug. 1917.

BUSK, Sir Edward Henry, Kt 1901; MA, LLB; Commissioner by London University Commission Act, 1898, under University College, London, Transfer Act, 1905, and King's College, London, Transfer Act, 1908; *b* London, 10 Feb. 1844; *o s* of Henry William Busk, barrister, and Mary Anne, *d* of Rev. Philip Le Breton; *m* 1880, Marian, *y d* of Lewis Balfour. *Educ:* University College School and University Coll., London. BA with 1st Class Honours, 1863; MA, 1864; LLB with 1st Class Honours and University Law Scholarship, 1866; Joseph Hume Scholar and Fellow of University College, London; solicitor, 1868-99; Reader in Elementary Law to the Incorporated Law Society, 1879-92; past Vice-Chancellor and Chairman of Convocation of Univ. of London; Fellow of that University, 1892; Major (retired) of the Artists' Corps of Volunteers; Member of the Kent Education Committee, 1903-9; Governor of Dulwich College, and of the Ladies' College, Cheltenham; Chairman of the Governors of Holt School, Norfolk, and of the Central Foundation Schools, London; Member of the Governing Body of the Imperial Coll. of Science and Technology; Chairman of Executive Committee and Vice-President of the City and Guilds Institute; Member of the Court of the Fishmongers' Company; Corresponding Member of the Educational Association of America; President of the National Sea Fisheries Protection Association, and President and Treasurer of the Oyster Merchants' and Planters' Association; Chairman of the London Board of the London and Lancashire Insurance Co. *Address:* Heath End, Checkendon, Oxon. *Clubs:* Athenæum, Albemarle.

Died 29 Oct. 1926.

BUSONI, Ferruccio Benvenuto; Hon. Member of Royal Academy of Music, Bologna; *b* Empoli, near Florence, 1 April 1866; father and mother musicians; *m* 1890, Gerda Sjostrand, *d* of a Finnish sculptor. *Educ:* Austria. Eight years before public; has composed much chamber music, orchestral scores, piano; teacher at Helsingfors, 1888-89; Professor at the Moscow Imperial Conservatory, 1890; at the Boston (New England) Conservatory, 1891; first Rubinstein prize, 1890. *Recreations:* walking, smoking, billiards, collecting and reading books, writing about music.

Died 27 July 1924.

BUSZARD, Marston Clarke, KC 1877; MA; LLM; Leader of Midland Circuit; JP and Deputy Chairman, Quarter Sessions, Leicestershire; Recorder of Leicester since 1899; *b* Lutterworth, 13 July 1837; *s* of Marston Buszard, MD; *m* 1st, 1864, Louisa (*d* 1895), *d* of John Mayor Threlfall, of Salford; 2nd, 1898, Annie Violet, *e d* of E. R. Whitwell of the Friarage, Yarm-on-Tees; three *d*. *Educ:* Rugby; Trinity Coll., Camb. Chancellor's Gold Medallist for Legal Studies, 1863. Barrister 1862. Bencher Inner Temple, 1880; Treasurer, 1903. Contested Stamford (L) 1874; MP Stamford, 1880–85, when the borough was disfranchised; joined Liberal Unionist Party, and unsuccessfully contested Rugby, 1886; Recorder of Derby, 1890–99. *Address:* 25 Pembridge Square, W2. *T:* 4663 Park; 5 Crown Office Row, Temple, EC4. *TA:* 63 Temple. *T:* (Temple) 807 Central. *Clubs:* Reform, Brooks's.

Died 11 Sept. 1921.

BUTCHER, William Deane, MRCS, FPS; Consulting Surgeon, London Skin Hospital; formerly Editor Archives of the Röntgen Ray; *b* 17 Oct. 1846; *s* of William Butcher of Red House, Rudgwick, and Rachel, *d* of Isaac Deane of Wambrook, Somerset; *m* 1877, Fanny, *d* of Col C. Y. Bazett, 9th Bengal Cavalry, HEICS; three *s* two *d*. *Educ:* Grammar School, Maidstone; London University; St Bartholomew's Hospital. Senior Scholar; House Surgeon to St James Paget, 1868; practised in Port of Calcutta, 1870–74; Reading and Windsor; Surgeon on SS "Gothic," 1894; introduced the first Röntgen installation in England for dermatological work at London Skin Hospital, 1898; represented the Electrotherapeutic Society at the Congress of Physiotherapy at Liège, 1905, and at the Berlin Röntgen Congress, 1906; represented the Röntgen Society at the International Congress of Electrology and Radiology, Amsterdam, 1908; represented the Electrotherapeutic Section of Royal Society of Medicine at the Congress of Physiotherapy, Paris, 1910; President of Röntgen Society, 1908–9; President of Electrotherapeutic Section of Royal Society of Medicine, 1909–10; President of the Ealing Scientific and Microscopic Society. *Publications:* Papers and Lectures on Radium, X-rays, Osmotic Growth, and Physical Basis of Education; Translation of Belot's Radiotherapy in Skin Diseases, Guilleminot's Medical Electricity, and Leduc's Mechanism of Life. *Recreations:* science, chess, wood-carving. *Address:* Holyrood, Cleveland Road, Ealing, W.

Died 10 Jan. 1919.

BUTLER, Rev. Alexander Douglas; Superintendent Minister of Whitefields Central Mission, Tottenham Court Road, since 1925; *b* Brighton; *m* 1919, Eva M. Pearce of Woolwich, SE; one *s* one *d*. *Educ:* Brighton; Moody Bible College; Chicago Theological Seminary (Chicago University). Minister of Ware Independent Church, 1910–12; Rectory Place Congregational Church, Woolwich, 1912–17; Queen's Park Congregational Church, Paddington, 1917–25; Editor of The London Signal; writer and lecturer on Psychology and related subjects. *Recreations:* golf, trout-fishing, all out-of-door sport. *Address:* 15 Kingswood Avenue, Brondesbury, NW6. *T:* Willesden 4300.

Died 27 July 1926.

BUTLER, Arthur Gardiner, PhD; FLS, FZS, FES; MBOU; CMAOU; retired Civil Servant; *b* Chelsea, 27 June 1844; 3rd *s* of Thomas Butler, late Assistant Secretary at the British Museum; *m* Mary, *e d* of George Tonge of Sittingbourne, Kent; one *s*. *Educ:* St Paul's School. Entered S Kensington Art School, 1861; received bronze medal for Outlines from Nature, 1862; entered Zoological branch of the British Museum, 1863; Assistant Keeper with special charge of the Arthropods, 1879; retired 1901. *Publications:* Catalogue of Diurnal Lepidoptera of the family Satyridæ in the British Museum, 1868; Catalogue of Diurnal Lepidoptera described by Fabricius in the British Museum, 1869; Lepidoptera Exotica, 1869; Typical Specimens of Lepidoptera Heterocera in the Collection of the British Museum, 1877–89; British Birds' Eggs, 1886; Foreign Finches in Captivity, 1895–96; the first volumes of British Birds with their Nests and Eggs, 1897–98; Foreign Bird-Keeping, 1899–1900; Birds' Eggs of the British Isles, 1901; Hints on Cage-Birds, British and Foreign, 1903; How to sex Cage-Birds, 1907; Birds of Great Britain and Ireland, Order Passeres, 1907–8; Foreign Birds for Cage and Aviary, 1908 and 1910; monographs and other articles dealing with all Orders of Insects, Spiders, Myriopods, and with Cage-Birds. *Recreations:* aviculture, floriculture, reading, writing, and entertaining friends—with an excellent cabinet gramophone. *Address:* 124 Beckenham Road, Beckenham, Kent.

Died 28 May 1925.

BUTLER, Arthur Stanley, MA; Professor of Natural Philosophy, St Andrews University, 1880–1922; *b* 17 May 1854; 2nd *s* of late George Butler, DD, Canon of Winchester, and Josephine, *d* of John Grey, Dilston, Northumberland; *m* Edith, *d* of Jasper Bolton, Ballykisteen, Tipperary; one *s* one *d*. *Educ:* Cheltenham College; Exeter College,

Oxford (1st class Math. Mods; 1st class Final School). *Address:* c/o University, St Andrews. *Clubs:* Royal Societies; Royal and Ancient Golf, St Andrews.

Died 2 March 1923.

BUTLER, Rev. Dugald, MA, DD; *b* Glasgow, 1862; *m* 1893, Catherine, *d* of late Sir James Marwick. *Educ:* High School and University of Glasgow. Minister of Abernethy, Perthshire, 1890–1902; Tron Parish, Edinburgh, 1902–7; Galashiels, 1907–19 (retired); Hon. DD Glasgow University, 1907. *Publications:* Ancient Church and Parish of Abernethy, 1897; John Wesley and George Whitefield in Scotland, 1898; Henry Scougal and the Oxford Methodists, 1899; Scottish Cathedrals and Abbeys, 1900; Life and Letters of Archbishop Leighton, 1903; Eternal Elements in the Christian Faith, 1905; The Tron Kirk of Edinburgh, 1906; Thomas à Kempis, a Religious Study, 1908; Gothic Architecture, its Christian Origin and Inspiration, 1910; Archbishop Leighton's Practice of the Presence of God, with introduction, 1911; Unity, Peace, and Charity: a Tercentenary Lecture on Archbishop Leighton, 1912; Woman and the Church in Scottish History, 1912; George Fox in Scotland: an Appreciation of the Society of Friends and its Founders, 1913; Life of St Cuthbert, 1913; Life of St Giles, 1914; Lindean and Galashiels, or Abbeys, Church, Manor and Town, 1915; Prayer in Experience, 1922; Jottings of an Invalid, 1924. *Address:* 16 Dreghorn Loan, Colinton, Midlothian.

Died 9 Jan. 1926.

BUTLER, Capt. Hon. Francis Almeric; late Hampshire Yeomanry; *b* 17 May 1872; 3rd *s* of 6th Earl of Lanesborough and Anne Elizabeth, *d* of Rev. John Dixon Clark; *m* 1902, Madeline, *d* of late Richard Birkett Gibbs; one *s* one *d*. *Address:* Belmore Cottage, Upham, Hants. *Clubs:* Cavalry, Royal Automobile, Roehampton.

Died 8 May 1925.

BUTLER, Frank Hedges, FRGS; *b* 17 Dec. 1855; *s* of late James Butler, Hollywood, Wimbledon Park, and Frances, *d* of late William Hedges; *m* 1880, Ada (*d* 1905), *d* of J. B. Tickle, London and Sydney; one *d*. Director, Hedges & Butler, Ltd, Regent Street, W1; Orchestral Member, 1st violin, Handel Festival, 1874; Royal Amateur Orchestral Society, 1875; Wandering Minstrels, 1876; Royal Albert Hall Choral Society, 1877; Founder of the Lyric Club Orchestra, 1889; Founder and Chairman of the Imperial Institute Orchestral Society, 1894; first Hon. Treasurer, Royal Automobile Club, 1897–1902; suggested first motor car run of the Automobile Club, 1898; obtained permission from Sandown Park to allow motor cars on course, Eclipse Stakes, 1898; inaugurated first concert at the Automobile Club, Whitehall Court, 1898; obtained sanction to allow motor cars on Ascot course, 1900; introduced motor car races and gymkana at Ranelagh Club, 1900, and balloon ascents, 1902; proposed the first ball (Durbar) at the Royal Automobile Club, 1911; presented challenge shield to the Royal Automobile Club to form a golfing society, 1910; took part in 1,000 miles trial of the Royal Automobile Club, 1900; founder of Royal Aero Club, 1901; winner and pilot of the first three Royal Aero Club balloon races, 1906 and 1907; has made over a hundred free balloon ascents, including record of longest distance in England done alone in a balloon, 1902, and record of the world for the longest cross Channel sea voyage from London to Caen in Normandy, 1905; Commemorative medal Aero Club of France, 1905; pioneer of the dirigible balloon, 1907, and aeroplane, 1908; Life-Fellow Royal Geographical Society in 1877; travelled in India, China, Japan, Korea, Burmah, Russia, Lapland, North and South America, Africa, Asia Minor, South Sea Islands, Falkland Islands, Java, Australia and New Zealand. *Publications:* Five Thousand Miles in a Balloon, 1907; Across Lapland with Reindeer and Skis, 1917; Fifty Years of Travel by Land, Water, and Air, 1920; Round the World, 1925; Wine and the Wine Lands of the World, 1926. *Recreations:* big-game shooting, golf, yachting, music. *Address:* 1 St James's Street, SW1. *T:* Gerrard 6131. *Clubs:* Royal Thames Yacht, Royal Automobile, Ranelagh, Royal Motor Yacht; Aero Club of France; East Brighton Golf.

Died 27 Nov. 1928.

BUTLER, Sir George Beresford, Kt 1921; senior resident magistrate, Ireland, to 1921; *b* 31 Jan. 1857; *o s* of Capt. A. S. Butler, CB, late 7th Dragoon Guards, and May, *d* of Rev. George de la Poer Beresford; *m* 1896, Georgina Rose Mary, *o d* of Capt. Charles Walker, 21st Fusiliers. *Educ:* Marlborough. *Address:* Tullamore, Ireland. *Club:* Hibernian United Service, Dublin.

Died 1 Sept. 1924.

BUTLER, Rev. Henry Montagu, DD; DCL Oxford; LLD Glasgow and St Andrews; Commendatore della Corona d'Italia, 1871; Master of Trinity College, Cambridge, from 1886; Chaplain in Ordinary to the King, 1912; *b* Gayton Rectory, Northants, 2 July 1833; 4th *s* of George Butler, DD [Senior Wrangler, 1794; Headmaster of

Harrow, 1805–1829; Rector of Gayton, 1814–53; Dean of Peterborough, 1842–53] and Sarah Maria, *d* of John Gray, of Wembley Park, Middlesex; *m* 1st, 1861, Georgina Isabella Elliot, *g d* of Rt Hon. Hugh Elliot, sometime Minister at Court of Frederick the Great; 2nd, 1888, Agnata Frances Ramsay, *d* of Sir James Ramsay of Bamff, 10th Bt; four *s* two *d*. *Educ:* Harrow; Trinity Coll., Cambridge. Fellow of Trinity, 1855; Priv. Sec. to Rt Hon. W. F. Cowper (Lord Mount Temple), 1856–57; Headmaster of Harrow, 1859–85; Hon. Chaplain to the Queen, 1875–77; Chaplain in Ordinary, 1877–85; Examining Chaplain to Archbishops Tait and Benson, 1879–83; Select Preacher at Oxford, 1877, 1878, 1882, 1899; at Cambridge, 1879, 1885, 1887, 1889, 1890, 1895, 1896, 1897, 1898, 1903, 1906, 1913; Preb. of Holborn in St Paul's Cathedral, 1882–85; Dean of Gloucester, 1885–86; Hon. Canon of Ely, 1897; Bell Univ. Scholar, 1852; Battie Univ. Sch. and Greek Ode, 1853; Greek Ode, Camden Medal, Porsion Prize, Latin Essay Prize, 1854; Senior Classic, 1855; Vice-Chancellor, 1889, 1890. *Publications:* Sermons preached in the Chapel of Harrow School, 1861; Second Series, 1866; Belief in Christ and other Sermons, 1898; Words of Good Cheer for the Holy Communion, 1898; University and other Sermons, Historical and Biographical, 1899; Ten Great and Good Men, 1909; Romanes Lecture, Lord Chatham as an Orator, 1912; Presidential Address of Classical Association, 1913; Lift up your Hearts, 1898 and 1914; Some Leisure Hours of a Long Life, 1914. *Recreations:* Harrow Cricket Eleven, 1851; ascended Monte Rosa, 1856, Parnassus, 1857, Sinai, 1858. *Address:* Trinity Lodge, Cambridge.

Died 14 Jan. 1918.

BUTLER, Rev. Hercules Scott; Rector of Mareham le Fen; *b* 1850; *m;* three *s. Educ:* Loretto; Rossall; Brasenose College, Oxford. Curate of Leeds, 1875–83; Vicar of St Barnabas, Holbeck, 1883–94; Farnworth, 1894–1900; Preston, 1900–20. *Address:* The Rectory, Mareham le Fen, Boston. *T:* Horncastle 20 Y1. *TA:* Mareham le Fen. *M:* OM 832. *Died 27 Jan. 1928.*

BUTLER, Capt. John Fitshardinge Paul, VC 1915; KRRC; attached Pioneer Company, Gold Coast Regiment, West African Frontier Force; *b* 20 Dec. 1888. Entered Army, 1907; served with West African Frontier Force, European War, 1914–15.

Died 4 Sept. 1916.

BUTLER, Hon. Sir Richard, Kt 1913; Speaker of House of Assembly, South Australia, 1921–24; *b* England, 3 Dec. 1850; *s* of Richard Butler, pastoralist, SA; *m* 1st, 1878, Helena Kate, *d* of Edward Wills Lagton, Sydney; 2nd, 1894, Ethel Pauline, *d* of late Thomas Dixie Finey; four *s* seven *d. Educ:* St Peter's Coll., Adelaide. Went South Australia, 1854; MHA, Yatala, 1890–1902; Minister of Education and Agriculture, 1901–5; Commissioner of Crown Lands and Minister of Mines, 1902–5; Premier and Treasurer, 1905; Treasurer and Minister controlling Northern Territory, 1909–10; Commissioner of Public Works, Minister of Mines, and of Marine, South Australia, 1912–15. *Recreation:* work. *Address:* Northcote Road, Mitintie, near Adelaide.

Died 28 April 1925.

BUTLER, Richard William; *b* London, 21 May 1844. *Educ:* City of London School. Proof-reader on Daily Telegraph, 1871–77; sub-editor of The Referee, 1877–91; editor, 1891–1921. Contributor to several other journals; many years dramatic critic; part author of several farces, burlesques, melodramas, and comediettas. *Address:* c/o Referee Office, 17 Tudor Street, EC4.

Died 21 Dec. 1928.

BUTLER, Slade; Recorder of Rye since 1911. MA of Christ Church, Oxford; Barrister of the Middle Temple and South-Eastern Circuit. *Address:* 2 Middle Temple Lane, Temple, EC. *Club:* Reform.

Died 6 Dec. 1923.

BUTLIN, Sir Henry Guy Trentham, 2nd Bt, *cr* 1911; *b* 7 Jan. 1893; *s* of Sir Henry Trentham Butlin, 1st Bt and Annie, *e d* of late Henry Balderson; *S* father 1912. Heir: none. *Educ:* Harrow; Trinity College, Cambridge. *Address:* 22 Harcourt Terrace, SW. *T:* Western 2951.

Died 16 Sept. 1916 (ext).

BUTLIN, Sir William, Kt 1921; BA Cantab; Hon. Member Real Sociedad Economica (Madrid); Chairman, Louis Cassier Co., Ltd; *b* Northampton, 26 April 1851; *s* of William Butlin, CE, of Spratton, Northampton; unmarried. *Educ:* Abington House School, Northampton; Cambridge University. Studied Chemistry, Geology, Metallurgy under Associate of Royal School of Mines, London, in relation to Iron Smelting at Irthlingborough Iron Works, Wellingborough, Northants; Chairman and Managing Director of T. Butlin & Co., Ltd, for 24 years; improved quality of British pig-

iron and castings; entertained American Institute of Mining Engineers at Wellingborough, also Royal Geological Society; was Hon. Treasurer of British Iron Trade Association; visited United States with Iron and Steel Institute; speciality, direct castings by scientific method; also for tube railways, etc; 20 years Spanish Vice-Consul Northampton; Chairman of Banquet Ibero-American Benevolent Society, Member of Committee, and a Governor of the Foundation; Cross of Isabel la Catolica of Spain; Member of Imperial Air-Fleet Committee. *Publications:* Evolution or Revolution, by Ironicus; Northampton Iron Ore Industry, Proceedings Iron and Steel Inst London; Direct Castings, Cassiers Engineering Magazine; Civil Engineering, Iron Age, New York; contributions to the Press, some foreign Strikes, Anarchy, International Arbitration, Criminal Law Powers and Physical Force, etc. *Recreations:* reading, writing, antiques walking, boating, travel, billiards, etc. *Address:* The Grove, Tiptree Essex. *TA:* Tiptree, Kelvedon, Essex. *M:* HK 9739. *Club:* Authors'

Died 13 May 1923

BUTTER, Archibald Edward, CMG 1903; FRGS, FZS; sportsman Captain in Scottish Horse Imperial Yeomanry; *b* 29 March 1874; of Lt-Col Butter, who served in Mutiny and Crimea, and Julie Macpherson, *e d* of Brewster Macpherson of Belleville; *g s* of Archibald Butter of Faskally, who married Miss Menzies of Castle Menzies; *m* 1910, Helen Ciceley, 3rd *d* of late Charles W. R. Kerr; two *s. Educ* Eton. *Decorated* for Survey of country to N of E Africa Protectorate for purpose of proposing a frontier between British E Africa and Abyssinia. *Address:* Riddell, Lilliesleaf, Roxburghshire. *Clubs:* Carlton Turf.

Died 6 Jan. 1928

BUTTERWORTH, Arthur Reginald; Barrister-at-law; Fellow of the Royal Colonial Institute; Hon. Member of the Institute of Bankers of New South Wales; *b* 22 July 1850; 3rd *s* of late Rev. Joseph Henry Butterworth and Mary Eliza Alexandrina, *d* of late Captain William Atkins Bowen, HEIC; *m* Margaret (*d* 1913), *y d* of late John Patterson of Craigdarragh, Belfast; one *s. Educ:* Marlborough College. Travelled in Australia, India, Egypt, and Europe, 1869–74; called to the Bar Inner Temple, 1877; admitted to the Bar of New South Wales, 1883; practised in Sydney, 1883–95; one of the Crown Prosecutors for New South Wales, 1887–91; practised in the Privy Council and High Court, 1896–1914; then lived abroad; Member of the Western Circuit since 1878. *Publications:* (Joint) Treatise on Maximum Railway Rates and Charges, 1896; Treatise on the Criminal Evidence Act, 1898; The Privy Council and Australian Appeals, 1901; Bankers' Advances on Mercantile Securities, 1902; The Creation of Peers as a Constitutional Question (articles republished from The Times), 1911; joint-editor of Benjamin on the Sale of Personal Property, 5th edn 1906; many articles and lectures on Constitutional and Banking Law *Address:* 7 Fig Tree Court, The Temple, EC. *Club:* Montreux Territet.

Died 30 Dec. 1924

BUTTERWORTH, Comdr Henry; RN, retd; Captain Superintendent, Training Ship Indefatigable, Rock Ferry, Birkenhead, since 1911; *b* Southport, 23 May 1866; *y c* of Henry Butterworth and Mary Jane Schofield, of Rochdale; *m* 1899, Mary, *d* of Rev. Joseph Chamney, of Dromiskin, Ireland; no *c. Educ:* Torquay College; Elizabeth College, Guernsey; HMS Worcester. Midshipman RNR 1883; joined Messrs Shaw Savill's Clipper Ship, 1884–87; joined British India Steam Navigation Co. 1887; serving in Royal Navy 1891–93; joined RN as Supplementary Lieut 1895; took part in HMS Arethusa in suppressing Boxer rebellion, 1900; King's Harbour Master, Hong-Kong, 1906–10; retired with rank of Commander 1911. *Recreations:* reading, walking, billiards, photography. *Address* Training Ship Indefatigable, Rock Ferry, Birkenhead. *Club* Conservative, Liverpool. *Died 28 May 1926*

BUXTON, Alfred St Clair, FRCSE; consulting surgeon, and formerly senior active surgeon to the Western Ophthalmic Hospital, London *b* Taden, France, 14 Nov. 1854; 2nd *s* of late Alfred Isaac Buxton *Educ:* Dinan; Guy's Hospital. *Publications:* several contributions to ophthalmic surgery; inventor of the Telechrome test for colour blindness. *Address:* 32 Weymouth Street, W1. *T:* Mayfair 1818.

Died 19 Dec. 1920

BUXTON, Commander Bernard, DSO 1917; RN; *b* 21 Oct. 1882 *s* of Geoffrey F. Buxton of Hoveton Hall, Norwich; *m* 1904, Lady Hermione Grimston, *d* of 3rd Earl of Verulam; three *s* one *d. Educ* Cheam School; HMS Britannia. Mediterranean (Crete), 1898; Naval Staff College, 1913; North Sea, 1914 and 1915; Mesopotamia, 1916 and 1917; Admiralty, 1918; Staff College, Camberley, 1921. *Clubs* Bath; Royal Yacht Squadron, Cowes (Hon.).

Died 29 Dec. 1923

BUXTON, Edward North, JP, DL; late Chairman of Quarter Sessions, Essex; Alderman Essex County Council; a Director, Truman, Hanbury, Buxton and Co.; *b* 1 Sept. 1840; 3rd *s* of Sir Edward North Buxton, 2nd Bt and Catherine, *d* of Samuel Gurney; *m* 1862, Emily, 3rd *d* of Hon. and Rev. R. H. Digby; two *s* five *d* (of whom one *s* one *d* twins) (and two *s* decd). *Educ:* Trinity Coll., Cambridge. Engaged in public work as a member, vice-chairman, and chairman of the London School Board, 1871–88; as a magistrate, alderman of Essex County Council; MP (L) Walthamstow Division, 1885–86; a verderer of Epping Forest for 42 years; Vice-President of the Commons Preservation Society, member since 1866; for many years a promoter of public open spaces. *Publications:* Short Stalks; Short Stalks, second series; Two African Trips; Epping Forest. *Recreations:* a keen follower of big game in four continents; fond of travelling for its own sake; Epping Forest owes much to him. *Address:* Knighton, Buckhurst Hill. *T:* Woodford 550. *Club:* Athenæum.

Died 9 Jan. 1924.

BUXTON, Sir (Thomas Fowell) Victor, 4th Bt, *cr* 1840; MA; JP; FRGS, FZS; *b* 8 April 1865; *s* of Sir Thomas Fowell Buxton, 3rd Bt and Lady Victoria Noel, *d* of 1st Earl of Gainsborough; *S* father 1915; *m* 1888, Anne Louisa Matilda, 2nd *d* of Rev. H. T. O'Rorke; five *s* one *d* (and one *s* decd). *Educ:* Harrow; Trinity College, Cambridge. High Sheriff of Essex, 1905; Member of Essex TF Assoc.; Commandant 1/2nd Batt. Essex Vol. Regt; President, Anti-Slavery and Aborigines Protection Society; Treasurer, CMS. *Publications:* articles on Christian Industrial Missions, African native questions, etc. *Recreations:* travel (has travelled extensively in Africa), shooting, fishing. *Heir: s* Thomas Fowell Buxton, *b* 8 Nov. 1889. *Address:* Warlies, Waltham Abbey; Colne House, Cromer. *TA:* Upshire. *Club:* Athenæum.

Died 31 May 1919.

BUZACOTT, Charles Hardie; *b* 3 Aug. 1835; *s* of James Buzacott, Great Torrington, Devon; *m* 1857, Louisa, *d* of Rev. George Whiteford, Sydney. *Educ:* Great Torrington. Arrived Sydney, 1852; left for Queensland, 1860; started Maryborough Chronicle, Peak Downs Telegram, converted Rockhampton Bulletin into daily; returned to Legislative Assembly (Brisbane), 1873; Postmaster-General 1879–80; originated scheme British-India Mail Service (London to Brisbane) 1880, Divisional Boards Acts 1879–81, and signed Proclamation in Government Gazette establishing 74 local authorities; acquired one-third interest and managed Brisbane Courier and Queenslander, 1880–94; started Brisbane Daily Mail, 1903; late senior leader-writer. *Address:* Banea View, Garden Street, Stanthorpe, Queensland. *T:* Stanthorpe 61. *Died 19 July 1918.*

BUZZARD, Thomas, MD; FRCP; (retired) Consulting Physician, National Hospital for the Paralysed and Epileptic, Queen Square; Fellow Royal Society of Medicine; late representative of King's College on Senate of University of London; *b* London, 24 Aug. 1831; *s* of late G. Buzzard, solicitor; *m* Isabel (*d* 1901), *d* of late Joseph Wass, The Green, Lea, Derbyshire; four *s* two *d*. *Educ:* King's College School, and College, London. University Medical Scholar and Gold Medal (University London); Fellow King's College, London; Vice-President, King's College Hospital. During Crimean War surgeon British Medical Staff, Ottoman Army, attached to headquarters of HH Omer Pasha; was present at the siege of Sebastopol; with the second expedition to Kertch; and at the battle of the Tchernam; after the fall of Sebastopol accompanied the Turkish army to the Caucasus, and took part in the establishment and conduct of a base hospital at Trebezonde in Asia Minor; Crimean medal (clasp for Sebastopol), Order of Medjidie, Turkish war medal. Ex-president Clinical, Neurological, and Harveian Societies; Foreign Corresponding Member, Société de Neurologie, Paris. *Publications:* numerous works on diseases of the nervous system, and contributions to medical and other journals; With the Turkish Army in the Crimea and Asia Minor, 1915. *Recreations:* sketching, reading. *Address:* 74 Grosvenor Street, W. *T:* 64 Mayfair. *Clubs:* Athenæum, Arts.

Died 1 Jan. 1919.

BYERS, Sir John William, Kt 1906; MA, MD, MAO (hon. causa), RUI; Professor of Midwifery and of Diseases of Women and Children, The Queen's University of Belfast; Consulting Physician for Diseases of Women to the Royal Victoria Hospital, Belfast, and Chairman (1915–18) of the Medical Staff; Physician to the Belfast Maternity Hospital; Consulting Physician to the Belfast Hospital for Sick Children; to the Belfast Hospital for Nervous Diseases and to the Hilden Convalescent Hospital, Belfast; ex-Examiner in Obstetric Medicine to Royal University of Ireland; Member of Central Midwives Board for Ireland (elected by medical practitioners resident in Ireland); Member of Medical Advisory Board, Babies of the Empire Society; Member of Executive Committee of the National Association for Prevention of Infant Mortality; *b* Shanghai, China; *o c* of late Rev. John Byers, MA (Glas.), missionary to China, and Margaret Byers, LLD University, Dublin, Founder and late Principal of Victoria College, Belfast, *d* of Andrew Morrow, Windsor Hill, Rathfriland; *m* 1902, Fanny, *d* of late James Reid, Netherleigh, Belfast; three *s*. *Educ:* Royal Academical Institution; Queen's College, Belfast (Senior Scholar in Natural Science and Senior Scholar in Medicine, Midwifery, and Medical Jurisprudence); Dublin; London; Gold Medallist and 1st class Honours at BA and MA degrees of Queen's University of Ireland; Honours at MD, Honorary MAO (Master of Obstetrics) of Royal Univ. of Ireland. Beginning practice in Belfast 1879, was first appointed to the Children's Hosp.; in 1882 organised the department for Diseases of Women at the Royal Victoria Hosp.; Hon. President of International Congress of Obstetrics and Gynecology, 1896; Vice-President Obstetrical Society of London, 1899–1901; President Ulster Medical Society, 1893–94; North of Ireland Branch of British Medical Association, 1900–1; Belfast Branch of Irish Medical Association, 1903–9; Section of Obstetric Medicine and Gynecology, British Med. Assoc. Cheltenham, 1901; Section of Physical Education and Training in Personal Hygiene, International Congress on School Hygiene, London, 1907. President, Belfast Literary Society, 1885–86 and 1915–16; Belfast Natural History and Philosophical Society, 1908–11; Conference on Hygiene of Childhood, Royal Sanitary Congress, Belfast, 1911. President, Belfast County Borough Medical Committee, 1912–13; member of Council of British Medical Association, 1902–6; Fellow Royal Society of Medicine; Governor and Vice-Chairman of Campbell College, Belfast. *Publications:* Antiseptic Midwifery; The Prevention of Puerperal Fever in Private Practice; A Plea for the Early Recognition and Treatment of Puerperal Fever; Puerperal Fever, its Nature, Prevention, and Treatment; Puerperal Eclampsia; The Tendon-Reflex Phenomenon; The Jaundice of Infants; The Relationship of Chorea to Rheumatism; Rötheln (German Measles), its Symptoms and Nosological Position; The Prevention and Treatment of Post-Partum-Hæmorrhage; Nineteenth-Century Progress in Obstetrics and Gynæcology; The Early Treatment of Acute Puerperal Infection; The Address in Obstetric Medicine, Belfast Meeting of British Medical Association, 1909; The Evolution of Obstetric Medicine, 1912; Tetragenus Septicæmia (with Dr Houston), 1913; on The Dialect and Folk-lore of Ulster; numerous other papers. *Recreations:* literature, folk-lore. *Address:* Dreenagh House, Lower Crescent, Belfast. *T:* 1340. *M:* 0I 1800.

Died 20 Sept. 1920.

BYLES, William Hounsom; late Lieutenant (Horse Transport) Army Service Corps; *b* 19 Feb. 1872. *Educ:* St John's Wood Art School; Royal Academy. Gained the medal for figure painting, and the second prize in the Armitage Sketching Competition at RA Schools, 1893; first exhibited at Royal Academy, 1894; New Gallery, 1896; black-and-white work for most of the London magazines and illustrated papers; exhibition of sketches of Morocco, Teneriffe, and Madeira at Messrs Clifford's, 1901; painted chiefly figure pictures, horses and portraits; photogravures of his works have been published; went to New Zealand, 1906; returned to England, 1910; joined 2nd Batt. Artists' Rifles; served in France and N Russia. *Address:* The Cottage, Westerton, Sussex. *Club:* Langham Sketching.

Died 12 Feb. 1928.

BYLES, Sir William Pollard, Kt 1911; MP (R) N Salford since 1906; *b* Bradford, 13 Feb. 1839; *s* of William Byles, founder of Bradford Observer; *m* 1865, Sarah Anne, *o d* of late Stephen Unwin, Colchester. *Educ:* private schools. MP (R) Yorkshire (Shipley Division), 1892–95; strong Radical and Social Reformer. *Address:* 8 Chalcot Gardens, Hampstead, NW. *Clubs:* National Liberal; Reform, Manchester.

Died 15 Oct. 1917.

BYNG, Col Hon. Charles Cavendish George; Colonel, retired pay; JP Cornwall, Devon, Hants; *b* 9 Feb. 1849; *s* of 2nd Earl of Strafford; unmarried. *Educ:* Eton. 1st Life Guards, 1867–93; retired pay, 1898; ADC to GOC Southern District, 1878–82; served in Sudan Expedition, 1884–85 (despatches; Brevet Lt-Col); Cornwall CC, 1898–1904; Cornwall CA, 1904–10. *Club:* Cavalry.

Died 16 May 1918.

BYNG, Hon. Sydney; *b* 9 April 1844; *s* of late Major Hon. Robert Barlow Palmer Byng, 3rd *s* of 6th Viscount Torrington, and Elizabeth Maria Lowther, *d* of Col J. Gwatkin; *uncle* and *heir-pres.* of 9th Viscount Torrington; *m* 1871, Annie, *d* of late Henry Chellingworth of Park Attwood, Worcester; three *s* four *d*. *Address:* Branksome, Hampton Hill, Middlesex.

Died 27 Feb. 1920.

BYRDE, Ven. Louis; Archdeacon of Kwangsi (Diocese of Kwangsi and Hunan, China), since 1914; *s* of late Rev. F. L. Byrde, chaplain of Brislington House, Brislington, Bristol; *g s* of Col Henry Byrde, JP, of Goytrey House, Pontypool; *m* Emma Constance, *d* of Major George Croft; one *s* three *d*. *Educ:* De Aston School, Market Rasen; Bedford Grammar School; Corpus Christi College, Cambridge (Spencer scholar); Ridley Hall, Cambridge. BA. Ordained, 1893; curate of St Peter's, Islington, 1893–94; SPG missionary, Kohala, Hawaii, 1894–98; CMS missionary, diocese Victoria, S China, 1898–1907; to Chinese students at Tokio, 1907–9; Yungehow, 1909–13; at Siangtan, 1913–14; at Yungehow since 1914. *Publication:* Editor of The Newsletter of the Kwangsi and Hunan Mission (quarterly). *Recreations:* photography, carpentry, gardening. *Address:* Yungehow, Hunan, China; 10 Oakland Road, Bedford.

Died 11 Dec. 1917.

BYRNE, Donn, (Brian Oswald Donn-Byrne); Irish novelist; *b* 20 Nov. 1889; *s* of Thomas and Jane McFarland Donn-Byrne, of Forkhill, Co. Armagh; *m* Dorothea Mary, *o d* of Anthony Cadogan, Waterford; two *s* two *d*. *Educ:* privately; Dublin and Leipsic. *Publications:* Stories without Women; The Strangers' Banquet; The Foolish Matrons; Messer Marco Polo; The Wind Bloweth; Blind Raftery; An Untitled Story (in America as O'Malley of Shanganagh); Changeling; Hangman's House; Brother Saul. *Recreations:* racing, hunting, golf. *Address:* Coolmain Castle, Co. Cork. *Clubs:* Badminton, Savage; Worplesdon Golf; Sandown Park.

Died 18 June 1928.

BYRNE, Rt. Rev. Mgr. Frederick; Vicar-General of Adelaide, South Australia, since 1874; *b* Dublin, 22 Feb. 1834. *Educ:* Subiaco, Italy; Jesuit College, Sevenhill, SA. Went to Italy at the age of eighteen, and entered the Benedictine monastery at Subiaco with the intention of becoming a monk; failure of health after two years obliged him to return home; stayed a short time in Dublin, and went to West Australia, where he conducted the Catholic School of Perth; from West he went to South Australia, and entered the Jesuit College at Sevenhill; ordained Adelaide, 1860; for four years did parochial duty in that city, and was then sent to do pioneer work in the outlying districts; STD by Brief, 1880; became Administrator of the Archdiocese, 1893; created Urban Prelate by Brief, 1902. *Publications:* history of Catholic Church in South Australia from landing of first emigrants in 1836 to death of second bishop in 1864; translated Vera Sapientia, a work of Thomas à Kempis. *Address:* Goodwood, South Australia.

BYRNE, Lieut-Col John Dillon, DSO 1917; RA; *b* 1875; *s* of late W. H. Byrne, Dublin; *m* 1919, Lena, *widow* of Capt. C. J. C. Barrett, Royal Scots Fusiliers. *Educ:* Beaumont College, Windsor. Entered Army, 1900; served India, 1901–14; saw service on Indian Frontier, 1908 (Frontier medal with clasp); went to France with Brigade of Artillery from India, 1914; present at battles Neuve Chapelle, Aubers Ridge, Festubert, Loos, Somme, and Paschendaele; operations in Egypt, 1915; and Palestine, 1918 (wounded at Festubert, Loos, and Ypres); on Staff, Aug. 1915–March 1917 (despatches three times, Bt Lt-Col, DSO, Russian Order of St Stanislas with Swords). *Address:* 77 Cadogan Place, SW. *Club:* United Service.

Died 17 Feb. 1925.

BYRNE, Louis Campbell, DSO 1919; MC; Lieutenant, The Royal Dublin Fusiliers; *s* of Dr B. Byrne, Rocquaine, New Malden, Surrey; unmarried. *Educ:* Mount St Mary's College, Chesterfield; Sandhurst. Served with the 2nd Battalion The Royal Dublin Fusiliers in France from May 1915 until the cessation of hostilities in November 1918 (despatches, DSO, MC and bar). *Recreations:* hockey, golf, tennis, swimming, the drama. *Address:* Rocquaine, New Malden, Surrey. *T:* Malden 109. *Clubs:* Junior Army and Navy, Carlyle.

Died 27 June 1923.

BYRNE, Rev. Peter, CM, LLD; *b* 1840; *s* of William Byrne, JP, Glenconnor, Clonmel. *Educ:* Castleknock, Dublin; Jesuit College, Rue des Postes, Paris. Vice-President of Castleknock College, 1869–82; Principal St Patrick's Training College, Drumcondra, Dublin, 1883–1911; Hon. LLD, RUI, 1909, for his educational services in Ireland; Commissioner of Education, Ireland, Endowed Schools. *Publications:* articles in the press. *Address:* St Patrick's Training College, Drumcondra, Dublin.

BYRON, 9th Baron, *cr* 1643; **George Frederick William Byron;** *b* 27 Dec. 1855; *s* of Frederick Byron, 2nd *s* of 7th Baron, and Mary Jane, *d* of Rev. W. Wescombe, Rector of Langford, Essex; *S* uncle 1870; *m* 1901, Lucy, *d* of late Thomas Radmall, formerly married to Sir Theodore Brinckman, 3rd Bt, whom she divorced. *Educ:* Harrow; Christ Church, Oxon. Late Lieut West Essex Militia. *Heir:* *b* Rev. Hon. Frederick Ernest Charles Byron, *b* 26 March 1861.

Address: Langford Grove, Maldon, Essex; Byron Cottage, Hampstead Heath, NW. *T:* Hampstead 584. *Clubs:* Carlton, Bachelors'.

Died 30 March 1917.

BYRON, Edmund, JP for Surrey; *b* 5 Oct. 1843; *e s* of Thomas and Julia Byron; *m* Charlotte Emily, *o d* of late Gen. E. R. Jeffreys, of Seafield House, Ryde, I of W. *Educ:* Eton; Christ Church, Oxford. *Address:* Coulsdon Court, Surrey. *Club:* United University.

Died 30 April 1921.

C

CABLE, 1st Baron, *cr* 1921, of Ideford, Devon; **Ernest Cable,** Kt 1906; senior partner Bird & Co., Calcutta, and Bird & Co., London, and F. W. Heilgers & Co., Calcutta, and F. W. Heilgers & Co., London; *b* 1 Dec. 1859; *s* of late G. H. Cable and Emily Pickersgill; *m* 1888, Lilian S. Sparkes; two *d*. *Educ:* privately. Career mercantile; ex-Sheriff of Calcutta; former member Viceroy's Council; ex-President Bengal Chamber of Commerce; ex-High Sheriff of Devonshire; Member The Indian Finance and Currency Commission. *Heir:* none. *Address:* 44 Grosvenor Square, W1. *T:* Mayfair 5528; Lindridge, Bishopsteignton, S Devon. *TA:* Cablesque. *Clubs:* Carlton, Brooks's, Wellington, Ranelagh, City of London; Bengal, Calcutta.

Died 28 March 1927 (ext).

CABLE, George Washington; author; *b* New Orleans, La, 12 Oct. 1844; *s* of George W. Cable, a Virginian, and Rebecca Boardman, Indiana; *m* 1st, 1869, Louise S. Bartlett; six *d*; 2nd, 1906, Eva C. Stevenson. *Educ:* New Orleans Public Schools. AM (hon.), Doctor in Letters (hon.) Yale Univ.; Doctor in Letters (hon.) Washington and Lee University (Virginia) and Bowdoin Coll. (Maine). Member American Academy of Arts and Letters. At the age of fourteen was required, by the death of his father, to assist in the support of the family; went into commercial employment; at nineteen (1863) he entered the Confederate Army in Gen. Wirt Adams' Brigade, 4th Mississippi Cavalry, where he served until the close of the Civil War 1865; he returned to New Orleans, re-entered counting-room employment, and with the exception of one summer spent with a State surveying party, and one season's work on the reportorial staff of the New Orleans Picayune, remained in it continuously for fourteen years, serving as accountant and cashier of a firm of cotton factors, and acting at the same time as secretary of the Finance Committee of the New Orleans Cotton Exchange; he was writing in the meantime, and in 1879 formally entered upon a literary career; in 1884 removed to New England. *Publications:* Old Creole Days, 1879; The Grandissimes, 1880; Madame Delphine, 1881; The Creoles of Louisiana, 1883; Dr Sevier, 1884; The Silent South, 1884; Bonaventure, 1888; The Negro Question, 1888; Strange True Stories of Louisiana, 1888; John March, 1894; Strong Hearts, 1899; The Cavalier, 1901; Bylow Hill, 1902; Kincaid's Battery, 1908; Gideon's Band, 1914; The Amateur Garden, 1914; The Flower of the Chapdelaines, 1918; Lovers of Louisiana, 1918. *Recreations:* landscape gardening; chief interest outside of profession, The Northampton People's Institute, founded by him in 1887. *Address:* Northampton, Massachusetts, USA. *TA:* Northampton. *T:* 1200. *Clubs:* Authors, New York.

Died 31 Jan. 1925.

CABORNE, Capt. Warren Frederick, CB 1897; RD; RNR; *b* 5 July 1849; *o s* of late Warren Caborne; *m* 1897, Mary Lilian, *e d* of S. (Thomas) William Boord, 1st Bt; one *s*. *Educ:* private schools. Entered Mercantile Marine, 1865; joined Royal Naval Reserve as Sub-Lieut 1879; Lieut 1882; retired with rank of Commander, 1894; Captain (ret.) for War Services, 1918; commanded a transport during the Burmah Expedition of 1885–86; was subsequently in the Egyptian Coast Guard Service; Assessor for Formal Investigations into Shipping Casualties, 1898–1914; Nautical Assessor to HM Court of Appeal, Supreme Court of Judicature, 1903–8; Nautical Assessor to HM Privy Council; British Nautical Assessor to Canadian Royal Commission of Inquiry into loss of Empress of Ireland, 1914; Member of Council of Royal United Service Institution since 1900, and Chairman of its Museum Committee; Deputy Chairman of Shipwrecked Mariners' Soc., 1906–20; Hon. Treasurer of St Andrew's Waterside Church Mission, to Sailors; Member of Council of the Curates' Augmentation Fund; Director of the Sailors' Home, London Docks; Hon. Commandant, British Red Cross, VAD, London 35; Fellow of Royal Astronomical and Royal Geographical Societies, and Fellow, ex-Secretary, and ex-Vice-President of Royal Meteorological Society. Served Naval Ordnance Department during the War. *Publications:* lectures and magazine articles upon naval reserve, mercantile marine, historical, and other subjects. *Address:* Loppington Hall, near Wem, Salop; The Royal United Service Institution, Whitehall, SW1. *Club:* Malta Union. *Died 14 June 1924.*

ADBURY, George, JP; Chairman of Cadbury Brothers, Limited; Founder of Bournville Model Village; *b* Edgbaston, 19 Sept. 1839; father and mother both of the Society of Friends; *m* 1st, 1871, Mary (*d* 1887), *d* of Charles Tylor, London; three *s* two *d*; 2nd, Elsie Mary, *d* of John Taylor, London; three *s* three *d*. *Address:* Manor House, Northfield, Birmingham; Winds Point, Malvern. *TA:* Manorial, Birmingham. *Died 24 Oct. 1922.*

ADELL, Alan, CSI 1895; Indian Civil Service (retired); *b* Edinburgh, 25 July 1841; *y s* of late John Cadell of Tranent, East Lothian; *m* 1872, Florence Margaret (*d* 1917), *d* of late W. J. Wallace of Bally Courcy, Co. Wexford; two *s* three *d*. *Educ:* Edin. Academy and Univ.; (BA) Germany. Passed into Bengal Civil Service and went to India 1862; was successively Assistant and Joint Magistrate, Assistant Settlement Officer, Settlement Officer, Magistrate and Collector; officiated as Commissioner of Excise, and as Opium Agent; was Commissioner of Agra and Rohilkhand; member of the Board of Revenue, United Provinces; member of the Legislative Council, UP; acted as Lieut-Governor, UP, Jan.–Nov. 1895; member of the Council of HE the Viceroy, Feb.–May 1896; was member of the Legislative Council of the Viceroy for two years prior to retirement in Oct. 1897. *Address:* 36 Rosary Gardens, SW7. *T:* Kensington 4166. *Club:* East India United Service. *Died 14 June 1921.*

ADELL, Colonel Thomas, VC 1857; CB 1906; Indian Army; *b* 5 Sept. 1835; *y s* of late Hew Francis Cadell, Cockenzie, Haddingtonshire; *m* 1867, Anna Catherine, *d* of late Patrick C. Dalmahoy, Boorhouse, Haddingtonshire; two *s* two *d*. *Educ:* Edin. Academy; Grange, Sunderland; abroad. Served with 2nd European Bengal Fusiliers (later Royal Munster Fusiliers) at siege of Delhi and subsequent operations, and with 3rd Bengal Cavalry in the Oude Campaign (mentioned in despatches); commanded a Flying Column in Bundelkhand, for which received thanks of Governor-Gen. in Council; entered the Political Department, and held various political appointments in Central India and Rajputana; Governor of the Andaman and Nicobar Islands, 1879–92. VC for saving life on two occasions at the siege of Delhi, 1857; CB for services during the Indian Mutiny. *Address:* Cockenzie House, Prestonpans, NB. *TA:* Cockenzie. *Clubs:* New, United Service, Edinburgh. *Died 6 April 1919.*

ADENHEAD, James, RSA 1921 (ARSA 1902); RSW; FSAScot; artist; *b* 1858; *s* of late George Cadenhead, advocate in Aberdeen; *m* 1891, Wilhelmina, *d* of late John Wilson, South Bantaskine, Falkirk. *Educ:* Aberdeen Grammar School and University. National Gold Medallist, 1879; student of Royal Scottish Academy, and of M. Carolus-Duran, in Paris; exhibitor of landscape, and occasionally of portraits, chiefly in Scottish Exhibitions; member Society of Scottish Artists and of Royal Scottish Society of Painters in Water-colours. *Address:* 15 Inverleith Terrace, Edinburgh. *Club:* Scottish Arts. *Died 22 Jan. 1927.*

AFE, T. Watt, RBA 1896; FPS 1890; FRGS 1901; artist; *b* London, 1856; *e s* of T. Cafe and Euphemia, *e d* of J. B. Watt, SSC, of Edinburgh. *Educ:* King's College, London; student of Royal Academy. First exhibited at RA 1876; later exhibited Wreaths of Welcome, Nydia, The Favourite, Summer Idleness, The Gift, Laurels for the Victor, An Eastern Singer (water colour), Theonoe (water colour), Hence thou lingering Light, The Valley of the Shadow, besides other works; for some time a member of the Dudley and Cabinet Picture Society; interested in all philanthropic work; St John's Ambulance medallion; active in boys' clubs and associations; a Licensed Lay Reader in the Diocese of London. *Publications:* occasional articles on art subjects in daily press. *Address:* 46 Clifton Hill, St John's Wood, NW. *Club:* Arts. *Died April 1925.*

AFFYN, Kathleen Mannington; novelist (*pseudonym* Iota); *b* Waterloo House, Co. Tipperary; *d* of William de Vere Hunt and Louisa Going; *m* 1879, Stephen Mannington Caffyn (*d* 1896), surgeon, writer, and inventor; one *s*. *Educ:* at home by English and German governesses. Lived in country until about twenty. Then was trained

at St Thomas's Hospital for a year for National and Metropolitan Nursing Association; after marriage went to Australia; lived there several years and wrote occasionally for papers. *Publications:* A Yellow Aster, 1894; Children of Circumstances, 1894; A Comedy in Spasms, 1895; A Quaker Grandmother, 1896; Poor Max, 1898; Anne Mauleverer, 1899; The Minx, 1900; The Happiness of Jill, 1901; He for God Only, 1903; Patricia; a Mother, 1905; Smoke in the Flame, 1907; The Magic of May, 1908; Whoso breaketh an Hedge, 1909; Mary Mirrielees, 1916; some short stories. *Recreations:* riding, hunting, watching polo matches. *Died 6 Feb. 1926.*

CAIN, Georges; homme de lettres; directeur du Musée Carnavalet et des Collections historiques de la ville de Paris; officier de la Légion d'honneur. *Educ:* Lycée Louis le Grand, Paris. Ancienmarin artiste-peintre (hors concours). *Publications:* Promenades dans Paris; Les Pierres de Paris, etc; Chroniques au Figaro, au Temps, au Journal. *Recreation:* automobile. *Address:* 15 Quai Voltaire, Paris. *Club:* Union artistique, Paris. *Died 4 March 1919.*

CAIN, John Cannell, DSc (Manchester), DSc (Tübingen); FIC; Editor of Chemical Society's publications since 1906; *b* 28 Sept. 1871; *e s* of Rev. Thomas Cain of Stubbins, Lancashire. *Educ:* Owens College, Manchester; Tübingen and Heidelberg Universities. Chemist to Levinstein, Limited, Manchester, 1895–1901; head of Chemistry and Physics Department, Municipal Technical School, Bury, Lancashire, 1901–4; manager and head chemist to Brooke, Simpson, and Spiller, Ltd, London, 1904–6; Chief Chemist to British Dyes, Limited, Dalton Works, Huddersfield, 1916–17. *Publications:* (Joint) The Synthetic Dyestuffs and the Intermediate Products from which they are derived, 1905 (4th edn 1918); Joint Editor of Jubilee of the Discovery of Mauve and of the Foundation of the Coal-Tar Colour Industry by Sir William Henry Perkin; The Chemistry and Technology of the Diazo-Compounds, 1908 (2nd edn 1920); The Manufacture of Intermediate Products for Dyes, 1918 (2nd edn 1919); numerous scientific papers. *Address:* 24 Aylestone Avenue, Brondesbury Park, NW6. *T:* Willesden 931. *M:* LP 4111. *Club:* Royal Societies. *Died 31 Jan. 1921.*

CAIN, Sir William Ernest, 1st Bt, *cr* 1920; Kt 1917; JP Berks; *b* 7 May 1864; *e surv. s* of late Robert Cain; *m* 1886, Florence *d* of Joseph Oakes Roberts; one *s* one *d*. *Educ:* Winwick Priory. *Recreations:* yachting, motoring. *Heir:* *s* Ernest Cain, *b* 25 Sept. 1891. *Address:* Wargrave Manor, Wargrave, Berks. *TA:* Wargrave, Berks. *T:* Wargrave 44. *Clubs:* Carlton, Constitutional, Royal Thames Yacht, Royal Automobile. *Died 5 May 1924.*

CAINE, William; author; *b* Liverpool, 28 Aug. 1873; *s* of William Sproston Caine and Alice, *d* of Rev. Hugh Stowell Brown; *m* Gordon, *d* of Farmer R. Walker of Boston, Mass, USA; no *c*. *Educ:* Manor House School, Clapham; Westminster School; St Andrews University; Balliol College, Oxford. Called to Bar on leaving Oxford; abandoned it for writing after seven years. *Publications:* Pilkington; The Confectioners (with John Fairbairn); The Pursuit of the President; The Victim and the Votery; Boom; a Prisoner in Spain; The Revolt at Roskelly's; Old Enough to Know Better; The Devil in Solution; Save us from Our Friends; An Angler at Large; The New Foresters; Hoffman's Chance; The Irresistible Intruder; But She Meant Well; Bildad the Quill-Driver; Great Snakes; The Fan and other Stories; Drones; The Wife who came Alive; The Strangeness of Noel Carton; Mendoza and a Little Lady; The Author of Trixie; The Brave Little Tailor (with George Calderon); Lady Sheba's Last Stunt. *Recreations:* trout-fishing, sketching. *Address:* 16 The Pryors, East Heath Road, NW3. *T:* Hampstead 5221. *Club:* Reform. *Died 1 Sept. 1925.*

CAIRD, Francis M., LLD, MB; FRCSEd; Emeritus Professor of Clinical Surgery, Edinburgh; Consulting Surgeon to the Royal Infirmary. *Educ:* Edinburgh; Strasburg, etc. Late Consulting Surgeon-Col AMS, BEF. *Publications:* (with Mr Cathcart) Student's Atlas of Bones and Ligaments; and a surgical handbook; contributions to medical journals. *Address:* 39 Royal Terrace, Edinburgh. *T:* 2128. *Died 1 Nov. 1926.*

CAIRD, Sir James Key, 1st Bt, *cr* 1913; FZS; LLD (St Andrews); *b* 7 Jan. 1837; *m* 1873, Sophie (*d* 1882), *d* of George Gray, Perth. *Heir:* none. *Address:* 8 Roseangle, Dundee; Belmont Castle, Meigle, Perthshire. *Club:* Royal Thames Yacht. *Died 9 March 1916 (ext).*

CAIRNES, William Plunket; Chairman, Great Northern Railway (Ireland); Director of the Bank of Ireland; *b* 1857; *s* of late Thomas Plunket Cairnes; *m* 1886; two *s*. *Educ:* Cheltenham College; Trinity

Hall, Cambridge. *Address:* Stameen, Drogheda. *Club:* Kildare Street, Dublin. *Died 18 Dec. 1925.*

CAIRNS, John, MBE 1918; MP (Lab) Morpeth, since December 1918; Financial Secretary of the Northumberland Miners' Association; Secretary of the Men's side of the Joint Committee in the Northumberland Coal Trade, and President of the Northumberland Aged Mine-Workers' Homes Association; Primitive Methodist; *b* 1859; *m* 1901, Annie Dixon. *Publications:* Money; Economics of Industry, etc. *Address:* The Drive, Gosforth, Newcastle-on-Tyne. *Died 23 May 1923.*

CALDECOTT, Lt-Col Ernest Lawrence, DSO 1916; RGA; retired; *b* 31 Aug. 1874; unmarried. *Educ:* Rugby; Oriel College, Oxford. Entered army, 1900; Captain, 1913; Major, 1915; ADC and subsequently Private Secretary to Lt-Governor of Burma, 1907-12; served Tibet, 1903-4 (medal); European War, 1914-19 (despatches four times, DSO). *Club:* Junior Naval and Military. *Died 17 Jan. 1927.*

CALDECOTT, Maj.-Gen. Francis James, CB 1894; retired list Royal Artillery; *b* 29 April 1842; *s* of late C. M. Caldecott, JP and DL, of Holbrook Grange, Warwickshire; *m* 1st, 1866, Georgina (*d* 1901), *d* of Hugh Watson of Keillor, Perthshire; 2nd, 1906, Jennie Beatrice (*d* 1920), *d* of late R. G. Clarke, formerly of Coldharbour, Wallingford. *Educ:* Cheltenham Coll. Lieut Bombay Artillery, 1860; Capt. Royal Artillery, 1872; Major, 1880; Brevet Lt-Col 1881; Col 1885; Maj.-Gen. 1894; retired, 1897. Served Abyssinian Expedition, 1867-68 (despatches, medal); Afghan War, 1879-80 (despatches, medal with clasp, Brevet Lieut-Col); many years superintendent of Indian Government Gunpowder and Experimental Explosives Factory at Kirkee, and the inventor of many improvements in the manufacture of gunpowder and its ingredients. *Recreations:* cricketer and Rugby footballer in England in the sixties, then a leading cricketer in India for many years, also sculler. *Address:* c/o Lloyd's Bank Ltd, 6 Pall Mall, SW1. *Died 30 Jan. 1926.*

CALDER, Ven. William; Archdeacon of Auckland, New Zealand, since 1901; *b* 1848; *s* of Rev. F. Calder, late Headmaster Chesterfield Grammar School; *m* Lucy, 3rd *d* of Thomas Shipton. *Educ:* Chesterfield Grammar School; private coach. Missionary, Honolulu, 1873; Incumbent, Hamilton, Waikato, 1875; Thames, 1881; Vicar, All Saints, Auckland, 1883-1918; Canon, 1894; Bishop's Commissary, 1902-16; Commissary for Melanesia, 1904. *Recreation:* travelling. *Address:* 17 Wairer Road, Auckland, NZ.

Died 10 Aug. 1923.

CALDWELL, Rt. Hon. James, PC 1910; JP; MP (GL) Lanarkshire, Midlothian, 1894-1910; Deputy Chairman Ways and Means, and Deputy Speaker, 1906-10; *b* 1839; *s* of Findley Caldwell, Glasgow. *Educ:* Glasgow and Edinburgh Universities. MP (LU) Glasgow (St Rollox Division), 1886-92; Member of the Faculty of Procurators, Glasgow. *Address:* 12 Grosvenor Terrace, Glasgow; 107 Holland Road, Kensington, W. *Clubs:* Reform, National Liberal. *Died 25 April 1925.*

CALLAGHAN, Admiral of the Fleet Sir George Astley, GCB 1916 (KCB 1910; CB 1900); GCVO 1912 (KCVO 1909; CVO 1907); First and Principal Naval ADC to the King, since 1914; *b* 21 Dec. 1852; *s* of late Frederic M. Callaghan, JP, Co. Cork; *m* 1876, Edith Saumarez, *d* of Rev. Frederick Grosvenor; one *s* three *d*. Captain, 1894; Adm. of the Fleet, 1917; commanded Hermione, Endymion, Edgar, Cæsar, Prince of Wales; commanded Naval Brigade, China, for relief of Legations, Peking, 1900; was a Naval ADC to King Edward VII; Naval Adviser to Insp.-Gen. of Fortifications, 1894-97; Rear-Admiral Channel Fleet, 1906; commanded 5th Cruiser Squadron, 1907-8; 2nd in command Mediterranean Fleet, 1908-10; commanded 2nd Division Home Fleet, 1910-11; commander-in-chief Home Fleet, 1911-14; the Nore, 1915-18; grand officer of the Crown of Italy; Grand Officer of the Legion of Honour. Bath King of Arms, 1919. *Address:* Avonstone House, Bathampton, Somerset. *Club:* United Service. *Died 23 Nov. 1920.*

CALLANDER, George Frederick William, JP, DL; *b* 28 July 1848; *e s* of James Henry Callander (*d* 1851) and 2nd wife, Charlotte Edith Eleanora, *o d* of John George Campbell, *y s* of Campbell of Islay; *m* 1876, Alice Louisa, *e d* and heiress of Col J. C. Craigie Halkett (*d* 1912) of Cramond, Midlothian, and Harthill, Lanarkshire. *Educ:* Eton. Formerly Lieut 78th Seaforth Highlanders. *Address:* Ardkinglas, Inveraray, Argyllshire; Cramond House, Midlothian; 24 Ovington Square, SW. *T:* Kensington 1938. *Died 20 Nov. 1916.*

CALLCOTT, F. T., RBS. *Address:* 17 Woodstock Road, Golder's Green, NW. *Died May 1923.*

CALLWELL, Maj.-Gen. Sir Charles Edward, KCB 1917 (CB 1907); *b* London, 2 April 1859; *s* of Henry Callwell of Lismeyne, Co. Antrim, and Maud, *d* of James Martin of Ross, Co. Galway. *Educ:* Haileybury College; Royal Military Academy. Joined the Royal Artillery, 1878; passed Staff College, 1886; Colonel, 1904; held appointments of Staff Captain, DAAG, DAQMG, and Colonel of General Staff at Headquarters, and of Brigade Major; served Afghan War, 1880 (medal); Boer War, 1881; South African War, 1899-1902, actions of Vaal Krantz, Pieters Hill, Relief of Ladysmith, Laing's Nek, and Bergendal, commanded a mobile column in 1901-2 (two medals eight clasps, despatches twice, brevet of lieut-colonel); was with Greek forces in Turko-Greek war, 1897; gold medallist and Chesney Memorial Medallist Royal United Service Institution; retired, 1909; Director of Military Operations at the War Office, with temporary rank of Major-General during the first seventeen months of European War, afterwards on special service in connection with the Allies (KCB, Commander of the Legion of Honour, of the Italian and Belgian Orders of the Crown, and of the Redeemer, Order of the Rising Sun, 2nd Class, Order of the White Eagle, 2nd Class, Grand Officer of the Crown of Roumania, Grand Cross of St Stanislas); Hon. Major-General, 1916. *Publications:* Small Wars; Tactics of To-day; Military Operations and Maritime Preponderance; The Tactics of Home Defence; Tirah, 1897; Service Yarns and Memories; The Dardanelles; The Life of Sir Stanley Maude, 1920; The Experiences of a Dug-Out, 1920; Stray Recollections, 1923; contributions to Encylopædia Britannica, etc. *Recreations:* fishing, golf. *Address:* 24 Campden House Chambers, Campden Hill, W. *Club:* United Service. *Died 16 May 1928.*

CALTHROP, Sir Calthrop Guy Spencer, 1st Bt, *cr* 1918; General Manager, London & North-Western Railway, since 1914; Coal Controller of Coal Mines, since 1917; *b* Uppingham, 26 March 1870; *y s* of late Everard Calthrop of The Grange, Sutton, Isle of Ely; *m* 1901, Gertrude Margaret, *d* of late James Morten. Joined L&NWR 1886; Assistant to General Manager, 1901; General Supt Caledonian Rly, 1902; General Manager, 1908; General Manager of Buenos Ayres and Pacific Rly, 1910; Lieut-Col Railway and Engineer Staff Corps; Lieut of the City of London; JP for the County of Lanark. *Recreation:* golf. *Heir:* none. *Address:* Croxley House, Croxley Green, Herts. *Clubs:* Conservative; Royal and Ancient, St Andrews; Jockey, Buenos Aires. *Died 23 Feb. 1919 (ext).*

CALVERT, Mrs Charles; *b* Loughborough, 1836; *d* of James Biddles, actor; *m* 1856, Charles A. Calvert; four *s* two *d*. Played as a child actress at the age of seven with Mr and Mrs Chas Kean; was leading lady at Theatre Royal, Southampton, in 1854, then two years' engagement at the Boston Theatre, United States; during her husband's twelve years' management of The Prince's Theatre, Manchester, she appeared in his fine Shakespearean productions as Miranda, Cleopatra, Hermione, Katharine of Arragon (with Mr Phelps as Wolsey), The Queen in Richard the Third, and Chorus in Henry the Fifth; after the death of her husband she toured with Madame Ristori and Mrs Langtry, and was then engaged for an American tour with Edwin Booth; other American tours were with Mrs Langtry and Mary Anderson; in 1894 she appeared at the Avenue in Bernard Shaw's Arms and the Man, and then in the following 16 years fulfilled the following engagements: The Comedy (8), Haymarket (7), Garrick (2), Criterion (2), Royalty (2), Court (1), His Majesty's (2); her final appearance was as an old lady in Sir Herbert Tree's magnificent production of Henry the Eighth, 13 July 1911. *Publications:* Sixty-eight Years on the Stage; various contributions to the Daily Mail, Sporting and Dramatic, etc. *Address:* 22 York Mansions, Battersea Park, SW. *Died 20 Sept. 1921.*

CAMBAGE, Richard Hind, CBE 1925; FLS; retired; *b* Milton, NSW, 1859; *s* of late J. F. Cambage; *m* 1881, Fanny (*d* 1897), *d* of late Henry Skillman, of Booral, NSW; two *s* two *d*. *Educ:* public and private schools. Passed the examination for Licensed Surveyors, 1882; was a Mining Surveyor in NSW, 1885-1902; Chief Mining Surveyor 1902-15; Under Secretary for Mines, NSW, 1916-24; President Institution Surveyors, NSW, 1907-9; President of Royal Society, NSW, 1912 and 1923, and Hon. Sec. for twelve years; President Linnean Society, NSW, 1924; President Australian National Research Council, Australasian Association Advancement of Science, Queen Victoria Homes for Consumptives, and Trustee Australian Museum, Sydney. *Publications:* Captain Cook's Pigeon House and Early South Coast Exploration, Sydney, 1916; Exploration beyond the Upper Nepean, Sydney, 1920; Exploration between the Wingecarribee Shoalhaven, Macquarie and Murrumbidgee Rivers, Sydney, 1921 contributed about fifty botanical papers to scientific societies dealing largely with the native flora and the geological formation upon which it grows, also on Acacia seedlings. *Recreations:* botanical and historical investigations. *Address:* 49 Park Road, Burwood, Sydney, NSW. *T:* UJ 4355. *Died 28 Nov. 1928.*

CAMBER-WILLIAMS, Rev. Robert, MA; Vicar of Lampeter, 1908; Canon Residentiary of St David's Cathedral, 1899; Examining Chaplain to Bishop of St David's, 1897; *b* 30 March 1860; *s* of late John Williams, Madryn Villa, Chwilog, Carnarvonshire; *m* 1888, Catherine, *d* of late Isaiah Davies of Llandudno. *Educ:* Keble College, Oxford (BA), First Class Hon. School of Theology, 1884; Ely Theological College, 1884–85. Deacon, 1885; priest, 1886; Curate of Bangor, 1885–86; Llandudno, 1886–87; Vicar of Dolwyddelan, 1887–96; Diocesan Lecturer in Church History, 1890–91; Lecturer in Theology and Parochialia at St David's College, Lampeter, 1896–99; St David's Diocesan Missioner, 1899–1908. *Publications:* History of the Church in Wales; sermons and pamphlets. *Recreation:* climbing. *Died 13 March 1924.*

CAMBON, Paul, DCL, LLD Cantab, Oxon, Edin.; Hon. GCB 1917; Hon. GCVO 1903; French Ambassador to Court of St James's, 1898–1920; *b* 20 Jan. 1843. Private Sec. to M. Jules Ferry; Sec. of Prefecture, Alpes-Maritimes, and Bouches-du-Rhône; Prefect of the Aube; Prefect of the Doubs; Prefect of the Nord; Minister Plenipotentiary; Resident-General to Tunis; Ambassador at Madrid and at Constantinople. Grand Cross of the Legion d'Honneur; Member of Institut Académie des sciences, morales et politiques. *Address:* 146 Boulevard Haussmann, Paris. *Died 29 May 1924.*

CAMBRIDGE, 1st Marquess of, *cr* 1917; **Lt-Col Adolphus Charles Alexander Albert Edward George Philip Louis Ladislaus Cambridge;** Earl of Eltham, 1917; Viscount Northallerton, 1917; GCB 1911; GCVO 1901 (KCVO 1897); CMG 1909; Personal ADC to the King, 1910; Governor and Constable of Windsor Castle, since 1914; *b* Kensington Palace, 13 Aug. 1868; *e s* of late Duke of Teck and Princess Mary Adelaide (*d* 1897), *d* of 1st Duke of Cambridge; *S* father, 1900; *m* 1894, Lady Margaret Evelyn Grosvenor, 3rd *d* of 1st Duke of Westminster; two *s* two *d*. *Educ:* Wellington; RMC, Sandhurst. Joined 17th (DCO) Lancers, 1888; Captain 1st Life Guards, 1895; Major, 1906; Lt-Col 1910; Commanding with BEF, 1914–15; Transport Officer of Household Cavalry Regiment in South Africa, 1899–1900 (Brevet Major, Queen's medal 6 clasps); Military Attaché, Vienna, 1904–9; Assistant Military Secretary GHQ early part of 1916; Commandeur Legion of Honour and Grand Cordon of Leopold. DL, JP Salop. *Heir: s* Earl of Eltham, *b* 11 Oct. 1895. *Address:* Shotton Hall, Shrewsbury. *Clubs:* Guards, Bachelors'. *Died 24 Oct. 1927.*

CAMBRIDGE, Ada, (Mrs George Frederick Cross); novelist; *b* Wiggenhall St Germains, Norfolk, 21 Nov. 1844; *m* 1870, Rev. G. F. Cross (*d* 1917); one *s* one *d*. *Educ:* home. Lived in Norfolk and Cambridgeshire until her marriage, when she sailed for Australia with her husband, after which she resided in colony of Victoria, mainly in bush districts; resided in Williamstown, a port of Melbourne, 1893–1912. *Publications:* My Guardian, 1877; In Two Years' Time, 1879; A Mere Chance, 1882; A Marked Man, 1891; The Three Miss Kings, 1891; Not All in Vain, 1892; A Little Minx, 1893; A Marriage Ceremony, 1894; Fidelis, 1895; A Humble Enterprise, 1896; At Midnight, 1897; Materfamilias, 1898; Path and Goal, 1900; The Devastators, 1901; Thirty Years in Australia, 1903; Sisters, 1904; A Platonic Friendship, 1905; A Happy Marriage, 1906; The Eternal Feminine, 1907; The Retrospect, 1912; The Hand in the Dark, 1913. *Recreations:* chiefly reading. *Club:* Lyceum, Melbourne. *Died 20 July 1926.*

CAMERON, (Caroline) Emily, (Mrs Lovett Cameron); novelist; *b* Walthamstow; *née* Sharp; *m* 1874, H. Lovett Cameron; two *s. Educ:* Paris; boarding-school at Putney. *Publications:* Juliet's Guardian, 1877; Deceivers Ever, 1878; Vera Nevill, 1880; Pure Gold, 1885; A North Country Maid, 1885; In a Grass Country, 1885; Jack's Secret; This Wicked World, 1889; A Sister's Sin, 1893; A Bad Lot, 1895; A Soul Astray; The Craze of Christina; Bitter Fruit; Devil's Apples, 1898; A Passing Fancy; Midsummer Madness, etc, besides numerous serials and contributions to magazines and illustrated periodicals. *Recreations:* motoring, devoted to dogs. *Address:* Millbrook House, Shepperton. *T:* Weybridge 303. *M:* BL 2476. *Club:* Sesame. *Died 4 Aug. 1921.*

CAMERON, Major Cecil Aylmer, CBE 1920; DSO 1916; Royal Field Artillery; *b* 17 Sept. 1883; *s* of Colonel Aylmer Cameron, VC,

CB, late 72nd Highlanders and *g s* of Colonel William Neville Cameron, Knight of Hanover, late Grenadier Guards, and Arabella Piercy, *d* of Piercy Henderson of Perthshire; *m* 1909, Ruby Mary, *d* of J. E. Shawe, late Manager Imperial Bank of India; one *s. Educ:* Eastman's RN Academy; Bath College; RN Academy, Woolwich. Commission in Royal Field Artillery, 1901; was a General Staff Officer, France, 1914–18 (CBE, DSO, Chevalier de la Légion d'Honneur, Chevalier de Leopold, officer of Rising Sun, despatches four times); at War Office, 1918; served as GSO Chief Intelligence Officer with General Knox's military mission to Siberia, to assist Admiral Koltchak, 1918–20; General Staff Officer at War Office, military operations Directorate, 1920; served under Irish Office. *Publications:* articles and reviews on Russian Affairs, etc, of which language he was a 1st Class Interpreter. *Recreations:* hunting, shooting, games, travelling. *Address:* 7 St James Court, Buckingham Gate, SW1. *T:* Victoria 2360. *Club:* Union. *Died 19 Aug. 1924.*

CAMERON, Sir Charles, 1st Bt, *cr* 1893; MD, MA, LLD; JP Glasgow, Lanarkshire and Renfrewshire; *b* Dublin, 18 Dec. 1841; *s* of John Cameron, newspaper proprietor, Glasgow and Dublin, and Ellen, *d* of Alexander Galloway; *m* 1st, 1869, Frances Caroline (*d* 1899), *d* of William Macauley, MD; one *d*; 2nd, 1900, Blanche, *d* of late Arthur Perman; one *s* one *d. Educ:* Madras Coll., St Andrews; Trinity Coll., Dublin; Medical Schools, Paris, Berlin, and Vienna. 1st Senior Moderator and Gold Medallist, 1862; MB (1st place-man), and CM (1st place-man), 1862. Edited NB Daily Mail, 1864–74; MP (R) Glasgow, 1874–85; Coll. Div., Glasgow, 1885–95; Bridgeton Division Glasgow, 1897–1900; carried in House of Commons resolution which led to adoption of sixpenny telegrams; introduced and carried the Inebriates Acts; Acts abolishing imprisonment for debt in Scotland; conferring the Municipal Franchise on women in Scotland; securing various reforms of the Scottish Liquor Licensing Laws; Chairman of Departmental Committee on Transit of Cattle Coastwise, 1893; Chairman of Departmental Committee on Habitual Offenders, etc (Scotland), 1894; member of Royal Commission on Liquor Licensing Laws, 1895. *Publications:* pamphlets on medical, social, and political subjects. *Recreations:* travelling, motoring. *Heir: s* John Cameron, *b* 26 Nov. 1903. *Address:* Braeside, Englefield Green, Surrey. *T:* 173 Egham. *M:* P 171. *Club:* National Liberal. *Died 2 Oct. 1924.*

CAMERON, Sir Charles Alexander, Kt 1885; CB 1899; MD, DPH (Cantab), PhD; FRCPI; ex-President and Professor of Hygiene and Chemistry, RCSI; Past President, Irish Medical Graduates and Schools Association; the Royal Institute of Public Health, the Society of Public Analysts, Leinster Branch, BMA; Irish Medical Association, Engineering and Scientific Association, Vice-President, Royal Dublin Society; Chief Medical Officer of Health and Public Analyst, Dublin; Hon. Member of many foreign societies; Harben Gold Medallist (1902); *b* Dublin, 16 July 1830; *s* of Captain Ewen Cameron, Lochaber; *m* 1862, Lucie (*d* 1883), *d* of late John Macnamara; one *s* two *d. Educ:* Dublin; Guernsey; Germany. *Publications:* Chemistry of Agriculture, 1857; Stockfeeders' Manual, 1868; Lectures on Public Health, 1868; Handy Book on Health, 1870; Handy Book on Food and Diet, 1871; Manual of Hygiene, 1874; Poems translated from the German, 1876; History of the Royal College of Surgeons, Ireland, and of Irish Medical Institutions, 1886 and 1916; Elementary Chemistry and Geology, 1896 and 1898; Reminiscences, 1913. *Recreations:* spent holidays attending medical and other congresses, and few leisure hours in reading light literature, and attendance at musical and Masonic dinners; President of the Corinthian Club, which resembles the London Savage Club. *Address:* 27 Raglan Road, Dublin. *Clubs:* Savage; Friendly Brothers', Dublin. *T:* 254. *Died 27 Feb. 1921.*

CAMERON, Maj.-Gen. Donald Roderick, CMG 1877; late Lieutenant-Colonel RA; *b* 25 April 1834; *m* 1869, Emma, *d* of Rt Hon. Sir Charles Tupper, 1st Bt. Entered army, 1856; Major-General, 1887; retired; Bhootan Expedition, 1864–65 (despatches, medal with clasp); owned bronze medal of Royal Humane Society for having swum out to a canoe in the canal at Ottawa, and righted it, thus saving the life of its occupant, 1871; superintended Boundary Commission Rocky Mountains, 1872–76. *Address:* Beaufort Cottage, Dingwall, Ross-shire. *Died 23 Dec. 1921.*

CAMERON, His Honour Sir Douglas Colin, KCMG 1914; Lieutenant-Governor of Manitoba, since 1911; *b* Hawkesbury, Ontario, 11 June 1854; *s* of Colin Cameron and Annie McLaurin; *m* 1880, Margaret, *d* of William Fergusson and Janet Candlish; two *s* one *d. Educ:* High School, Vanleek, Ontario; Ottawa Business College. Represented Rainy River in Ontario Legislature, 1902–3;

President Rat Portage Lumber Company, Maple Leaf Milling Company, and 11 other companies. *Recreation:* horses. *Address:* Government House, Winnipeg. *T:* Main 707. *M:* Manitoba 1004. *Clubs:* Manitoba, Toronto, Winnipeg Hunt, St Charles, Winnipeg.

Died 28 Nov. 1921.

CAMERON, Sir Hector Clare, Kt 1900; CBE 1918; Emeritus Professor of Clinical Surgery in the University of Glasgow; Dean of Faculties in the University of Glasgow, 1921; *b* Demerara, 30 Sept. 1843; *s* of Donald Cameron, Plantation Zeelugt, Demerara, sugar-planter; *m* 1872, Frances (*d* 1879), *d* of William Hamilton Macdonald; two *s* one *d*. *Educ:* St Andrews, Edinburgh, and Glasgow Universities, MB CM Glasgow, 1866; MD 1868; LLD St Andrews, 1911, Glasgow, 1912. Formerly President of the Faculty of Physicians and Surgeons of Glasgow, and Representative of the Faculty at the General Medical Council. *Address:* 18 Woodside Crescent, Glasgow.

Died 22 Nov. 1928.

CAMERON, Hugh, RSA 1869; RSW 1878; painter of figure subjects and portraits; *b* Edinburgh, 1835; *s* of John Cameron and Isabel Armstrong; *m* Jessie (*d* 1895), *d* of late Alexander Anderson, manufacturer, Glasgow, and *widow* of Alexander Allan, jun., shipowner, Glasgow; one *s* three *d*. Studied art at Trustees' Academy under Robert Scott Lauder. ARSA 1860. *Pictures:* Maternal Care, Age and Infancy, A Lonely Life, The Village Well, Rummaging, Crossing the Burn, Haymakers Resting, Children of the Riviera, Funeral of a Little Girl on the Riviera, The Rivals, Pleasures of the Sea, The Timid Bather. *Recreation:* golf. *Address:* 45 George Square, Edinburgh. *Clubs:* Scottish Conservative, Scottish Arts, Edinburgh.

Died 15 July 1918.

CAMERON, James Spottiswoode, MD, CM, BScEd; MRCSEng; Medical Officer of Health, City of Leeds, 1889-1915; Professor of Public Health, University of Leeds; Consulting Physician, Huddersfield Infirmary; *b* Dumfries, where father a Congregational minister, mother *d* of late William Spottiswoode of Glenfernate; *m* Ruth, 2nd *d* of William Nield, Leeds; two *s* one *d*. *Educ:* Huddersfield College; Edinburgh University. On graduating held resident appointments at Children's Hospital and Royal Infirmary, Edinburgh, and Bradford Infirmary; practised in Huddersfield; became Physician to the Infirmary; Medical Officer of Health, 1877, and Physician to Fever Hospital; President Royal Medical Society of Edinburgh; President of Literary and Scientific Society five years in Huddersfield; Secretary and President of Huddersfield Medical Society; President Leeds and West Riding Medicochirurgical Society; of Yorks Branch of British Medical Association; President Yorks Branch of Society of MOHS, later (1902) President of whole Society. *Publications:* Such Stuff as Dreams are made of; Is my House Healthy?; Editor of Leeds Health Manuals; Various Reports on the Health of Huddersfield and Leeds, and articles in Medical and Sanitary journals. *Address:* 25 Regent Park Terrace, Headingly, Leeds.

Died 30 Jan. 1918.

CAMERON, Hon. John Donald; Judge of the Court of Appeal, since 1910; *b* 18 Sept. 1858; unmarried. *Educ:* Woodstock College; Toronto University. Barrister, 1882; MP (L), S Winnipeg, 1892-99; Provincial Secretary, 1892-96; Attorney-General, 1896; Judge of the King's Bench, 1908. *Address:* Winnipeg. *Club:* Manitoba, Winnipeg.

Died 26 March 1923.

CAMERON, Malcolm Graeme, KC 1902; *b* Goderich, Ontario, 24 Feb. 1857; *s* of M. C. Cameron, Lt-Governor, NW Territories; *m* Flora, *d* of A. B. McLean, Smiths Falls, Ontario; one *d*. *Educ:* Goderich Grammar School; Galt Collegiate Inst. Pres. of Goderich Board of Trade for three years, and an unsuccessful candidate for the House of Commons for West Huron at the General Election of 1911. Called to Ontario Bar, 1879; elected to Ontario Legislature for West Huron, 1902-4; Mayor of Goderich for several years. *Publication:* A Treatise on the Law of Dower. *Address:* Goderich, Ontario, Canada. *T:* 27. *Club:* Ontario Reform.

Died 10 Aug. 1925.

CAMERON-HEAD, James; Deputy-Chairman, Union Castle Line; Director of Royal Mail Steam Packet Co., Pacific Steam Navigation Co., and Nelson Lines; *b* 25 April 1851; 4th *s* of Sir Francis Somerville Head, 2nd Bt (*d* 1887) and *g s* of Rt Hon. Sir Francis Bond Head, 1st Bt, KCH, PC, formerly Governor of Upper Canada; *m* 1888, Christian Helen Jane, *e d* and *heiress* of Duncan Cameron of Inverailort, Inverness-shire, Black Watch (*d* 1874) and *g d* of Sir Alex. Cameron, KCB, KCH, Rifle Brigade of Inverailort; one *s* one *d*. Assumed additional name of Cameron by Royal Licence, 1910. JP Inverness-shire. *Educ:* Marlborough College. Formerly Captain Middlesex Yeomanry Cavalry and also Captain 3rd Battalion "Buffs". *Recreations:*

stalking, fishing, golf, shooting. *Address:* Inverailort Castle, Inverness-shire; 40 Lowndes Square, SW1; *T:* 3078 Gerrard. *M:* LH 3288. *Club:* Carlton.

Died 10 Dec. 1922.

CAMILLERI, Rt. Rev. Giovanni M.; OSA; Adviser to the Sacred Congregation of Bishops and Regulars (Rome); gia Vescovo di Gozo, ora Titolare di Modona, Prelato Domestico, Assistente al Soglio Pont. Conte; *b* Valetta, Malta, 15 March 1843. *Educ:* Government Elementary Schools, private tuition, and Lyceum, Valetta. Entered the Augustinian Order, 1861; elevated to sacerdotal dignity, 1867; Lecturer and subsequently Regent of Studies; Doctor in Theology; Provincial at Malta and Gozo, 1880; recalled to Rome to teach Theology at the International College of the Order, 1883. *Publications:* Giudizi dello storico Rohrbacher sopra alcuni punti della dottrina di S Agostino; 8 vol. di omilie (in Maltese) nelle feste dell' Epifania, di Pasqua, di Pentecoste, della Visitazione di M.SS, del' Assunz. di M.SS; di tutti i Santi, del Natale di NSQC, ecc; 1st Diocesan Synod, 1904. *Address:* Conv. di S Agostino, Notabile, Malta.

CAMPBELL, Sir Archibald Augustus Ava, 4th Bt, *cr* 1831; *s* of Sir Archibald Ava Campbell, 3rd Bt and Henrietta Ellen, *d* of Rev. Eusebius H. Uthwatt; *b* 5 Dec. 1879; *S* father, 1913. *Heir: b* William Andrews Ava Campbell, *b* 11 Dec. 1880. *Address:* Gibliston, Colinsburgh, Fife.

Died 10 May 1916.

CAMPBELL, Lady Archibald, (Janey Sevilla); *d* of late James Callander of Ardkinglas and Craigforth, and of late Hon. Mrs Callander (whose portrait hangs in the King of Bavaria's Gallery of Beauty at Munich); ward of George, 8th Duke of Argyll; *m* 1869, Lord Archibald Campbell (*d* 1913), 2nd *s* of 8th Duke of Argyll; one *s* (10th Duke) one *d*. Originator of Pastoral Plays in Europe—As You Like It, 1884-85 (played part of Orlando); Faithful Shepherdesse, 1885 (played Shepherd Perigot); produced 1886, Fair Rosamund, specially adapted for her from Becket by the late E. W. Godwin, FSA (played Rosamund); 1887, played Oberon to Miss Kate Vaughan's Titania (Midsummer Night's Dream) in garden of Pope's villa, Twickenham; played the Pierrot in Le Baiser de Théodore de Banville, set as a pastoral by herself, 1889; author and manager of Tam Lin, Scottish Ballad play, produced at Theatre Royal, Edinburgh, 1899, appearing herself in title-rôle; dramatised Cap and Bells, poem by W. B. Yeats, staged it and played it as a monologue at Berkeley Theatre, Glasgow, in aid of the Highland Fair, Oct. 1907. *Publications:* Rainbow Music, treating of philosophy of harmony in colour-grouping; and several articles in leading periodicals on the Drama, West Highland Lore and Occultism, etc. *Recreations:* bicycling, skating. *Address:* Coombe Hill Farm, Norbiton, Kingston-on-Thames. *T:* Kingston 538.

Died July 1923.

CAMPBELL, Maj.-Gen. Archibald Edwards; Indian Army; *b* 18 March 1834; *m* 1860, Lucy (*d* 1915), *d* of Capt. Cardew, RE. Entered army, 1851; Maj.-Gen, 1892; retired list, 1892; served Santhal Rebellion, 1855-56; Indian Mutiny, 1857-58 (severely wounded, medal with clasp). *Address:* Poltair, Seymour Avenue, Mannamead, Plymouth.

Died 9 April 1921.

CAMPBELL, Rt. Rev. Archibald Ean, DD; Bishop of Glasgow and Galloway since 1904; *b* 1 June 1856; *s* of Col Walter Campbell of Skipness, Argyll (author of The Old Forest Ranger), and Anna Henrietta, *d* of Col Robert Loring; *m* 1885, Hon. Helen Anna, *d* of 8th Viscount Midleton; one *s* three *d*. *Educ:* King William's Coll., Isle of Man; Clare Coll., Cambridge (Foundation Scholar); sen. optime Mathematical Tripos; BA 1880; MA 1883; DD 1904; DCL 1910; Cuddesdon College, 1880-81. Curate of Aberdare, South Wales, 1881-85; Rector of Castle Rising, Norfolk, 1885-91; Vicar of All Souls (Hook Memorial), Leeds, 1891-1901; Acting Chaplain, Leeds Rifles; Provost of St Ninian's Cathedral, Perth, 1901-4. Commissary to Bishop, St John's, Kaffraria, 1902-4; Mission of Help to South Africa, 1903; Select Preacher, Cambridge, 1908; Church Commissioner to South Africa, 1919. *Address:* Bishop's House, Woodside Terrace, Glasgow. *T:* Charing 2.

Died 18 April 1921.

CAMPBELL, Lt-Col Charles Lionel Kirwan, CMG 1917; 16th Lancers; Brigadier-General Commanding 5th Cavalry Brigade since Oct. 1915; *b* 1 Nov. 1873. *Educ:* Cheam School; Eton; Cheltenham College; Sandhurst. Entered Army, 1895; Capt. 1900; Major, 1909. NW Frontier, India, 1897-98 (medal with clasp); Tirah, 1897-98 (clasp); S Africa, 1900-1 (despatches, Queen's medal, 1 clasp); served European War, 1914-17 (despatches twice, Bt Lt-Col, CMG). *Recreations:* hunting, shooting, fishing, polo. *Clubs:* Cavalry, United Service.

Died 31 March 1918.

CAMPBELL, Lt-Col Charles Ferguson, CIE 1906; OBE 1920; 11th King Edward's Own Lancers, Probyn's Horse; *b* 23 Nov. 1863; *s* of J. Scarlett Campbell; *m* 1908, Mrs Muirhead Gould of Bredisholm, Lanarkshire, *d* of R. P. Steuart-Muirhead and *widow* of Colonel Arthur Gould (Queen's Bays). *Educ:* Haileybury; Sandhurst. Served NW Frontier of India, 1897–98; operations on the Samana, in the Kurram Valley, 1898 (medal with two clasps); Tirah, 1897–98; operations against the Khani-Khel Chamkannis (clasp); with Indian Officers' escort, Diamond Jubilee; ADC to Prince of Wales during Indian tour, 1905–6; Extra Equerry to Prince of Wales, 1906; Extra Equerry to the King, 1910; Member of The Honourable Corps of Gentlemen-at-Arms, 1912; Clerk of the Cheque and Adjutant, 1923. *Address:* Littlebourne, Twyford, Winchester, Hants. *T:* Twyford 18; 24 St Edmund's Terrace, NW8. *T:* Hampstead 9042; Engine Court, St James's Palace, SW1. *T:* Gerrard 4739. *Club:* Naval and Military.
Died 1 Aug. 1925.

CAMPBELL, Sir Charles Ralph, 11th Bt, *cr* 1628; *b* 24 Sept. 1850; *s* of Sir John Eyton, 8th Bt and Charlotte, *d* of Louis Henry Ferrier; *S* brother 1901; *m* 1878, Sara, *d* of Hon. William Robinson, of Cheviot Hills, NZ; three *s* (and three *s* decd). *Educ:* Edinburgh Academy. Went to New Zealand, 1874; engaged in sheep-farming. *Heir: s* Captain Charles Ralph Campbell, Lieut 2nd Life Guards [*b* 14 Dec. 1881; *m* 1915, Nancy Sarah, *o d* of late Edward Chapman, Canterbury, New Zealand]. *Address:* Cheviot Hills, New Zealand. *Clubs:* Conservative, Bath.
Died 4 Oct. 1919.

CAMPBELL, Charles Sandwith, KC 1899; *b* 15 Nov. 1858. Advocate, 1884; retired 1901 as head of Campbell, Meredith, MacPherson, Hague & Holden, law firm, Montreal. *Address:* 205 St James Street, Montreal.
Died 12 June 1923.

CAMPBELL, Charles William, CMG 1901; FSS; FRGS; *b* 21 Oct. 1861; *m* 1903, Violet Gertrude, *y d* of Mrs Coutts of Well House, Banstead; one *s* five *d*. Student Interpreter, China, 1884; 2nd Class Assistant, 1891; 1st Class, 1897; HM's Vice-Consul, Shanghai, 1899–1900; attached to Admiral Seymour's force in China (despatches); Acting Consul-General, Tientsin, 1900–1; Acting Chinese Secretary, Pekin, 1901–2, and 1905–6; Acting Consul-General, Canton, 1903–4; Cheng-Tu, 1905; Consul at Wuchow, 1900–6; Chinese Secretary, Pekin, 1906–11. *Club:* Oriental.
Died 27 May 1927.

CAMPBELL, Capt. Claude Henry, DSO 1915; Queen's Own Cameron Highlanders; *b* 4 Dec. 1878. Entered army, 1899; Captain, 1907; Adjutant Volunteers, 1908; TF 1908; served European War, 1914–15 (DSO).
Died 15 March 1916.

CAMPBELL, Ven. Colin Arthur Fitzgerald, MA; Archdeacon of Wisbech, since 1915; Rector of Feltwell, Norfolk, since 1912; *b* Woolwich, 17 June 1863; 6th *s* of Col Sir Edward Campbell, 2nd Bt, and Georgiana Charlotte Theophila, 2nd *d* of Sir Theophilus Metcalfe, 4th Bt. *Educ:* Ashbocking, Tonbridge School; Clare College, Cambridge. Read theology at Llandaff with Dean Vaughan; Assistant-master, Spondon School, 1885–9; Private Secretary to Governor of South Australia (Earl of Kintore), 1889–1902; Clerk of the Executive Council, South Australia, 1890–1902; Senior Domestic Chaplain to Archbishop (Benson) of Canterbury, 1894; Private Chaplain to Lord Henniker, Governor of the Isle of Man, 1896; Curate of Hartlebury, Worcester, 1893–4; Rector of Thornham, Magna-cum-Parva, 1895–1902; Street, Somerset, 1902–8; Worlingworth, 1908–12; Rural Dean of Hoxne, 1909–12. *Recreations:* cricket, music. *Address:* The Rectory, Feltwell, Norfolk. *Club:* Royal Societies.
Died 6 Jan. 1916.

CAMPBELL, Douglas Graham, CMG 1912; British Adviser to Government of Johore; *b* 1867; *y s* of late John Campbell; *m* 1st, Ethel Mary (*d* 1903), *d* of late Villiars Taylor, ICS; 2nd, Mary Abinda, *d* of late C. E. Spooner, CMG; two *d*. Joined Malay States Government Service, 1883; Land Officer, 1885; District Officer, 1890; secretary to Resident, 1901; Resident of Negri Sembilan, 1904; Special Mission to Brunei, 1905; General Adviser, Johore, 1910. *Recreation:* motoring. *Address:* Johore, *via* Singapore. *Clubs:* Junior Carlton, Sports.
Died 25 June 1918.

CAMPBELL, Sir Duncan Alexander Dundas, 3rd Bt, *cr* 1831 of Barcaldine; CVO 1909; JP; FSA Scot, FRGS; Hereditary Keeper of Barcaldine Castle, which ancient Baronial Castle he restored; also the Parish Church of Bowers Gifford and its ancient bells (1399–1413); *b* 4 Dec. 1856; *S* father, 1880. Gentleman Usher of the Green Rod, 1884–95; Secretary to the Order of the Thistle, 1895; Carrick Pursuivant of Arms, 1909. Formerly Capt. 3rd Batt. Black Watch;

3rd and 4th Batts Highland Light Infantry; retired as Hon. Major; member of Royal Company of Archers, King's Bodyguard of Scotland; Queen Victoria's Diamond Jubilee Medal, 1897; walked officially in Procession in Westminster Abbey at Coronation of King Edward VII and Queen Alexandra, 9 Aug. 1902; silver Coronation Medal; also at the Coronation of King George V and Queen Mary, 22 June 1911; silver Coronation Medal. *Publications:* revised and reprinted the Statutes of the Order of the Thistle, 1905, and additional Statutes, 1914; assisted Dr Shaw in his The Knights of England, 2 vols 1905; The Clan Campbell, Extracts relating to Campbells in Sheriff Court Books of Argyll at Inveraray, 1689–1784, 1913; Abstracts relating to Clan Campbell in Sheriff Court Books of Perthshire, vol. ii of Series, 1914; Abstracts relating to Campbells in Sheriff Court Books of Argyll, vol. iii of Series, 1915; vol. iv, 1916; Ducal House of Argyll, Houses, Cadets, etc. vol. v, 1917; Unprinted Records of Ayrshire, relating to Clan Campbell, vol. vi, 1918; vol. vii, 1920; Campbells in some Parish Registers of Counties Argyll and Perth; vol. viii. Books of Council and Session Acts and Decrets, 1500–1650, 1922; vol. ix, Records of Clan Campbell in the Military Service of the HEICS, 1600–1858, 1924. *Recreations:* visiting scenes of historical and antiquarian interest, churches, etc. *Heir: first cousin* Alexander William Dennistoun Campbell, Lieut-Col (retired) Indian Staff Corps, *b* 8 Sept. 1848. *Address:* 16 Ridgway Place, Wimbledon, SW. *Clubs:* Junior United Service; Royal Highland Yacht, Oban.
Died 27 May 1926.

CAMPBELL, Capt. Duncan Frederick, DSO 1900; Lancashire Fusiliers; transferred to Black Watch, 1908; retired, 1910; Captain 3rd Battalion (Reserve) Black Watch, since 1910; MP (U) North Ayr, since 1911; *b* Toronto, 28 April 1876; *s* of Archibald Campbell and Helen, *d* of Col F. W. Cumberland; *m* 1902, Louise, *d* of J. E. O'Reilly. *Educ:* Trinity Sch., Port Hope; Trinity Univ., Toronto (BA). Served South Africa, 1899–1901 (wounded, despatches, Queen's medal, six clasps, DSO); European War, 1914–15 (despatches). Contested (C) Mid-Lanark, 1906; Paisley, 1910; North Ayrshire, Dec. 1910. *Address:* Wardhead House, Stewarton, Ayrshire.
Died 4 Sept. 1916.

CAMPBELL, Capt. Duncan Lorn, DSO 1901; late 3rd Battalion Welsh Regiment; *b* 12 June 1881; *s* of late Maj.-Gen. Lorn Campbell, CB. *Educ:* United Service College, Westward Ho! Served South Africa, 1900–1 (despatches, DSO). *Decorated* for defence of train at Alkmaar with four men against fifty Boers at close quarters; served European War, 1914–17.
Died 1 Feb. 1923.

CAMPBELL, Major Hon. Eric Octavius, DSO 1915; Seaforth Highlanders (Ross-shire Buffs); Brigade Major; *b* 3 Dec. 1885; 6th *s* of 3rd Earl Cawdor and Edith Georgiana, *d* of Christopher Turnor of Stoke Rochford; unmarried. *Educ:* Eton. Entered army, 1905; Captain, 1914; served European War, 1914–15 (wounded, despatches, DSO). *Address:* c/o Edith, Lady Cawdor, Golden Grove, Carmarthenshire, RSO.
Died 4 June 1918.

CAMPBELL, Colonel Frederick, CB 1902; VD; JP; late Colonel and Hon. Colonel 1st Argyll and Bute Royal Garrison Artillery (Volunteers); *b* 15 June 1843; 4th *s* of Sir John Campbell, 8th Bt and Hannah Elizabeth, *d* of James Macleod, Rasay; *m* 1869, Emilie, *e d* of late Donald Maclaine of Lochbuie, NB; seven *s* two *d* (and three *s* three *d* decd). Served New Zealand (medal and clasp). *Address:* Airds, Sydenham Hill, SE. *Club:* Naval and Military.
Died 13 Sept. 1926.

CAMPBELL, Brig.-Gen. George Polding, CIE 1920; CBE 1919; late Royal Engineers; retired list; *b* 1864; *s* of late Edward Campbell, JP, of Wanstead and Granbalang, New South Wales; *m* 1891, Frances Georgina, *d* of Rev. C. B. Fendal of Woodcote House, Windlesham, Surrey; four *s* four *d*. *Educ:* Sydney University (BA); SME, Chatham. Lieut RE, 1886; Captain, 1896; Major, 1904; Lieut-Col 1913; Brevet Col 1916; Substantive-Colonel, 1918; retired as Brig-Gen., 1921; served NWF, India, 1897–98 (medal and clasp); European War, 1914–19 (despatches 3 times, Brevet-Col, CBE); Afghan War, 1919; Waziristan Expedition, 1919–20 (despatches, CIE). *Publications:* The Engineer's Share in the Bacteriological Treatment of Sewage; many articles in newspapers, etc. *Recreations:* lawn-tennis, golf. *Address:* Home Cottage, Old Farnham Lane, Farnham. *T:* Farnham 390. *Club:* Junior Army and Navy.
Died 8 Sept. 1928.

CAMPBELL, General Gunning Morehead, CB 1919; Commandant Royal Marine Artillery; *s* of Capt. George John Gunning Campbell, Madras Horse Artillery; *m* 1887, Charlotte Sophia, *y d* of Rev. G. P. Viner; one *s*. *Educ:* Wellington; Royal Naval College, Greenwich. Joined RM Artillery, 1880; Captain, 1891; Major, 1898; Lt-Col, 1905;

2nd Commandant, 1914; Colonel Commandant, 1917; Adjutant, RMA, 1889-94; Forfar and Kincardine Artillery, 1897-1901; Inspector RN and RM Recruiting, 1914-17; served Soudan, 1884 (medal and clasp and Khedive's Bronze Star, King Edward VII Coronation medal); served Ostend and Dunkirk, 1914 (1914 Star, Victory and Allied medals); Brig.-Gen., May 1916; ADC to the King, Sept. 1917; GSP, 1917. *Recreation:* shooting. *Address:* Whitehaugh, Bishopstoke, Hants. *Club:* Caledonian.

Died 29 Nov. 1920.

CAMPBELL, Lt-Col Harry La Trobe, DSO 1916; MIME; Commander, Division of Royal Engineers; Hon. Lieutenant in Army; *b* July 1881; *s* of late Henry Hunter Campbell, St Helen's; *m* 1906, Daisy Louise, *d* of late Samuel Iles (Councillor), Cotham Lawn, Bristol; one *s* two *d*. *Educ:* Chester. Served South African War in RE, 1901-2 (Queen's medal, 4 clasps); joined 2nd Lancs (Vols) RE, 1899; Adjutant to West Lancs Div. RE, 1913-14; served European War, 1914-18 (despatches, DSO, Bt Lt-Col). Mining Engineer and Surveyor; senior partner in firm of Campbell & Son, 11 Old Hall Street, Liverpool. *Address:* Cotham, Huyton, near Liverpool.

CAMPBELL, Sir Henry, Kt 1921; Town Clerk of Dublin; *b* 1856; *m* 1st, 1879, Jenny (*d* 1906), *d* of R. Brewis; 2nd, Alice Harbottle, *d* of late R. Fogan. *Address:* Greenwood Park, Newry, Co. Down.

Died 6 March 1924.

CAMPBELL, Hon. Capt. Hon. Ivan, DL; General Staff Officer, 3rd grade; *b* 17 Nov. 1859; 2nd *s* of 6th Earl of Breadalbane and *heir pres.* to 1st Marquess of Breadalbane; *m* 1884, Lady Margaret Elizabeth Diana Agar, *d* of 3rd Earl of Normanton; one *s*. *Educ:* Eton. Late 3rd Batt. Royal Scots and Queen's Own Cameron Highlanders; served Egypt, 1882, including Tel-el-Kebir; S Africa, 1900-1; one of HM's Hon. Corps of Gentlemen-at-Arms. *Clubs:* Naval and Military, Wellington; Royal Dorset Yacht.

Died 16 March 1917.

CAMPBELL, Sir James, Kt 1918; JP, DL; LLD (Aberdeen), 1903; a Governor of Technical College, Aberdeen; Member of Aberdeen Provincial Committee for Training of Teachers; Member of General Committee of Church of Scotland; *b* 21 April 1842; *y s* of Donald Campbell and Catherine M'Laren; *m* 1st, 1873, Charlotte Rose (*d* 1898), *y d* of Capt. Alex. Robertson, 33rd Regiment; 2nd, 1906, Grace Campbell, *y d* of Ewan Campbell Cameron of Garrows, Perthshire. *Educ:* Perth Academy; Edinburgh. Trained as civil engineer; appointed land agent for Sir John Heron Maxwell of Springkell, 1873; for H. G. Murray Stewart of Cally and Broughton, 1877; and for Seafield Estates at Cullen House, 1888; gave £4000 to build Infectious Diseases Hosp. at Portsoy, 1903; £1000 to provide Parish Home for Poor of Cullen, 1912; and £3000 to establish Agricultural Bursaries at University of Aberdeen, 1914; Convener of the County of Banff, 1896-1913; Chairman of the County of Banff Road Board, 1890-1913; of County Finance Committee, 1896-1913; Chairman of North of Scotland College of Agriculture, 1911-23; Governor of the Dick Bequest Trust for Higher Education in the Counties of Aberdeen, Banff, and Moray, 1892-1923; Coronation medals, 1902 and 1911; Freeman of Royal Burgh of Cullen, 1912. *Recreations:* travelling, shooting, curling. *Address:* 14 Douglas Crescent, Edinburgh. *T:* Central, Edinburgh, 4848; Garrows, Dunkeld. *Clubs:* Conservative, Edinburgh; University, Aberdeen.

Died 14 Jan. 1925.

CAMPBELL, Lieut-Col John, DL; JP; 8th Argyll and Sutherland Highlanders (TF), retired; granted rank, on retirement from TF Reserve, 1922, of Lt-Col Regular Army Reserve; *b* 1872; *e s* of late John Campbell and Margaret, *o d* of late Thomas Lloyd, Leghorn, Italy; *m* 1913, Marion Isabel, *e d* of Lt-Col Sir Edward Durand, 1st Bt, CB; one *d*. *Educ:* Harrow; Sandhurst. Capt. retired, late Argyll and Sutherland Highlanders. *Address:* Kilberry, Argyllshire. *Clubs:* Naval and Military; New, Edinburgh.

Died 7 Feb. 1928.

CAMPBELL, John Edward, MA; FRS; Hon. DSc Queen's University of Belfast; Fellow and Tutor, Hertford College; Lecturer, Merton College; *b* 1862; *s* of late John Campbell, MD, of Lisburn, Co. Antrim; *m* Sarah, *d* of Joseph Hardman. *Educ:* Methodist College, Belfast; Queen's College, Belfast; Hertford College, Oxford. *Publications:* Introductory Treatise on Lie's Theory of Continuous Groups; various contributions to mathematical journals and societies. *Address:* Hertford College, Oxford.

Died 1 Oct. 1924.

CAMPBELL, Brig.-Gen. John Hasluck, CVO 1909. *Educ:* Trinity College, Glenalmond; Edinburgh University; Sandhurst. Joined 93rd

Sutherland Highlanders, 1876; served NW Frontier of India, 1897-98 (medal with clasp); commanded 2nd Battalion Argyll and Sutherland Highlanders, 1899-1903; commanded Eastern Co's Grouped Regimental District, 1906, and the East Anglian Division Territorial Force from 1908, with the rank of Brigadier-General; retired from the Army, 1910. *Address:* Inverardoch, Doune, Perthshire. *Clubs:* Naval and Military, Wellington; New, Edinburgh.

Died 29 Jan. 1921.

CAMPBELL, Sir John (Stratheden), KCSI 1918 (CSI 1909); CIE 1907; *b* 1863; *m* 1st, 1884, Honor (*d* 1922), *o d* of late Maj.-Gen. Sir Oliver R. Newmarch, KCSI; 2nd, 1923, Helen Colquhoun, *widow* of C. T. B. King. *Educ:* Rugby; Balliol Coll., Oxford. Entered ICS, 1881; Joint Magistrate, 1890; Deputy Commissioner, 1896; Magistrate and Collector, 1898; Commissioner United Provinces, India, 1906; Board of Revenue, UP, 1913; retired, 1918. *Address:* 92 Regent's Park Road, NW1. *Club:* Oriental.

Died 16 Aug. 1928.

CAMPBELL, Senator Hon. Sir Marshall, Kt 1916; JP; Natal Senator Union Parliament; *b* 10 July 1849; *s* of late William Campbell (sugar planter), Muckle Neuk, Victoria County, Natal; *m* Ellen, *d* of John C. Blamey, Mt Prospect, Natal; two *s* two *d*. *Educ:* privately, Natal. Sugar planter; managing director of Natal Estates Co., Ltd, etc, and director of many other companies; was MLC when Natal was Crown Colony; nominated Legislative Council under Responsible Government; appointed Natal Commissioner in the Natal-Transvaal Boundary Delimitation Commission after Boer War; one of two Natal Commissioners on Lord Milner South African Native Affairs Commission. *Recreations:* shooting, fishing, travel. *Address:* Muckle Neuk, Marriott Road, Berea, Durban. *Clubs:* Durban, Natal; Royal Yacht.

Died 9 Dec. 1918.

CAMPBELL, Lt-Col Montagu Douglas, DSO 1901; JP County Renfrew; 4th Battalion Argyll and Sutherland Highlanders; *b* 16 Oct. 1852; *y s* of Archibald Campbell of Mains and Blythswood. Served South Africa (despatches, Queen's medal, four clasps, DSO). *Address:* 34 Abercromby Place, Edinburgh. *Clubs:* Boodle's, Bachelors'; New, Edinburgh.

Died 12 Feb. 1916.

CAMPBELL, Richard Hamilton, CIE 1912; late Indian Civil Service; Lt-Col Bangalore Rifle Volunteers; Private Secretary to HH the Maharajah of Mysore, 1909-13; *b* 26 Nov. 1865; *s* of late Major-General John Peter William Campbell, Indian Staff Corps; *g s* of late Sir Duncan Campbell, 1st Bt; *m* 1889, Ellen Emily Harington, *d* of Henry Gompartz, Madras; two *s* one *d*. *Educ:* Cheltenham College. Assistant Collector and Magistrate, 1891-92; Under Secretary to the Government of Madras, 1891-92; Joint Magistrate, 1893-96; Private Secretary to the Governor of Madras, 1902; District Magistrate, 1896-1909; retired, 1913. *Recreations:* cricket, racquets, lawn tennis, riding, volunteering. *Clubs:* East India United Service; Madras.

Died 19 March 1923.

CAMPBELL, Maj.-Gen. Robert Dallas; Indian Army; *b* 27 June 1832. Entered army, 1850; Maj.-Gen., 1891; unemployed list, 1890; served Sonthal Rebellion, 1855-56; Indian Mutiny, 1857 (medal); Bhootan Expedition, 1865-66 (medal with clasp); Afghan War, 1879-80 (despatches, medal); Mahsud Waziri Expedition, 1881 (despatches).

Died 12 Feb. 1916.

CAMPBELL, Colonel Sir Robert Neil, KCMG 1917; CB 1912; CIE 1909; MB; Indian Medical Service, retired; Kaiser-i-Hind Medal, 1900; Knight of Grace of St John of Jerusalem, 1914; Inspector-General Civil Hospitals and Prisons, Assam, 1912-14; retired, 1914; *b* 24 Sept. 1854; *m* 1881, Ethel Bensley; two *d*. *Educ:* Edinburgh Institution; Edin. University. Served Naga Hills Expedition, 1879-80 (despatches, medal with clasp); Akha, 1883-84 (despatches); Officer Commanding Pavilion Military Hospital, and York Place Hospital, Brighton. *Address:* 29 Medina Villas, Hove, Sussex.

Died 18 Feb. 1928.

CAMPBELL, Samuel George, CMG 1924; JP; *b* 1861; *s* of late William Campbell, Cardonagh, Donegal; *m* Margaret Wylie, *d* of late James Dunnachie, Glenboig, Scotland. *Educ:* Bishop's College, Natal; Edinburgh University. MD, CM, Honours; MRCS, FRCSE; DPH Berlin and Vienna Universities. Medical Officer of Health Durban, 1891-99; President of South African Medical-Conference, 1919; served S Africa, 1899-1902; Zululand Native Rebellion, 1906 (despatches). *Address:* 28 Musgrave Road, Durban, S Africa. *Club:* Durban.

Died 13 March 1926.

CAMPBELL, Rev. Canon Stephen; Canon Residentiary Jerusalem since 1909. *Educ:* Trinity College, Dublin. Ordained, 1867; Curate of Scissett, Yorks, 1867–69; St Paul, Clapham, 1869–73; Rector of All Saints, Eglantine, Lisburne, 1873–82; Minor Canon of Down, 1882–85; Prebendary of Dunsford, 1885–89; Rector of Hollymount, 1882–89; Vicar of St John, Enfield, 1889–91. *Address:* Maydore Mattock Lane, Ealing, W.

Died 31 March 1918.

CAMPBELL, Capt. Sir Walter Douglas Somerset, KCVO 1910 (CVO 1901); late Deputy Ranger, Windsor Park, resigned 1916; Groom-in-Waiting to the King, since 1901; *b* 1853; *s* of Walter Frederick Campbell of Islay; *m* 1881, Marie Louise, *d* of J. Guild; one *s* one *d. Educ:* Charterhouse. Groom-in-Waiting to Queen Victoria, 1880–1901; to King Edward, 1901–10; and to King George V, 1910. Grand Cross Order of Franz Josef. *Address:* 64 Belgrave Road, SW. *Clubs:* Naval and Military, Travellers'.

Died 17 April 1919.

CAMPBELL, Col William Kentigern Hamilton, DSO 1902; late Officer Commanding 6th Imperial Yeomanry South Africa, 1900–2; *b* 30 Sept. 1865; *e s* of late C. V. Hamilton-Campbell, and Mary, *o d* of Samuel Randall, of Orford, Suffolk; *m* 1908, Edith Agnes, *d* of Robert Angus, Ladykirk, Markton, Ayrshire; one *s* two *d.* Lt-Col commanding Ayrshire Yeo.; Hon. Lt-Col in the army; JP and DL for Ayrshire; CC for Mauchline. *Address:* Netherplace, Mauchline, NB. *Died 22 Nov. 1917.*

CAMPBELL, General Sir William, KCB 1911 (CB 1904); *b* 7 Feb. 1847; *m* 1887, Frances Maria, *e d* of Capt. W. Butler Fellowes; two *s* one *d.* Ashanti War, 1873–74 (medal); Egyptian War, 1882 (medal, clasp, Khedive's star, despatches, Bt-Maj.); Jubilee medal, 1897; Coronation medal, 1901; ADC to Queen Victoria, 1893–1901; to King Edward VII, 1901–4; Col Comdt Royal Marine Artillery, 1902; Provincial Grand Master of Freemasonry, Worcestershire; JP. *Address:* Marchwood, Malvern. *Club:* United Service.

Died 5 July 1918.

CAMPBELL, Rev. William, DD of Knox College, Toronto; admitted to the Order of the Rising Sun and the Order of the Sacred Treasure (appointments confirmed by His Britannic Majesty); FRGS, MRAS; Corr. Mem. of the Japan Society; For. Mem. of the Royal Institute for study of the Languages, Topography, and Folklore of Netherlands-India; *b* 17 April 1841; *m* 1880, Janet H. Alston, *g d* of John Alston (who produced the first complete version of the Bible in any language for blind people); one *s* two *d. Educ:* University and Free Church College, Glasgow; ordained missionary to Formosa by the Presbyterian Church of England, 19 July 1871; arrived there 10 Dec.; did some research work during first furlough (1879) when travelling alone through Gilead and from Beersheba to Damascus; withdrew from office in the Mission owing to failing health, 1918. *Publications:* Formosa under the Dutch, with a Bibliography; Handbook of the South Formosa Mission; Dictionary of the Amoy vernacular spoken in Formosa; Sketches from Formosa; revised edition of several 17th-century volumes in the Malay aboriginal dialects of the island. Began work among the Chinese blind fully thirty years ago and continued to use his alphabetic adaptation of Braille for printing Christian literature on both sides of every sheet from movable types. *Address:* 50 St Michael's Road, Bournemouth.

Died 7 Sept. 1921.

CAMPBELL, Brig.-Gen. William MacLaren, CBE 1919; MVO 1906; *b* 6 March 1864; *s* of late Archibald Campbell of Glendaruel, Argyllshire; *m* 1914, Dorothy Clothilda, *d* of Rev. R. Lang, Vicar of Old Warden, and *widow* of Col F. Shuttleworth of Old Warden Park. Joined Black Watch, 1885; Captain, 1893; Major, 1903; Lt-Col commanding 2nd Black Watch, 1911–15; Colonel, 1914; Brig.-Gen. 1916; served Burmah War, 1890–92; South African War with Scottish Horse, 1902; European War. *Clubs:* Naval and Military; New, Edinburgh.

Died 7 June 1924.

CAMPBELL, William Middleton; of Colgrain, Dumbartonshire; JP, DL of Dumbartonshire, and on the Commission of Lieutenancy for the City of London; Deputy-Governor Bank of England, 1905–7; Governor, 1907–9; Director since 1886; Director, Commercial Union Assurance Co. Ltd; member Curtis, Campbell, and Co., Rood Lane, EC; *b* 15 Aug. 1849; *m* 1878, Edith Agneta, *d* of R. C. L. Bevan, of Fosbury and Trent Park; four *s* one *d. Address:* Fen Place, Turner's Hill, Sussex. *Clubs:* Oriental; Western, Glasgow.

Died 18 May 1919.

CAMPBELL-COLQUHOUN, William Erskine; *b* 1866; *s* of late Rev. J. E. Campbell-Colquhoun, MA, DL, JP, of Garscadden, and Killermont, Dumbartonshire, and Chartwell, Westerham, Kent;

unmarried. *Educ:* Harrow; Trinity College, Oxford. *Address:* Knockearn, Crieff, Perthshire. *Club:* Western, Glasgow.

Died 15 June 1922.

CAMPERDOWN, 3rd Earl of, *cr* 1831; **Robert Adam Philips Haldane-Duncan,** DL, JP; BA; LLD St Andrews; Viscount and Baron Duncan, 1797; *b* London, 28 May 1841; *S* father 1867. *Educ:* Eton; Balliol Coll., Oxford; 1st class in Classics, 1861. Lord-in-Waiting, 1868–70; Lord of the Admiralty, 1870–74. Owned about 14,000 acres. *Publication:* Admiral Duncan, 1898. *Heir:* brother Hon. George Alexander Philips Haldane-Duncan, *b* 9 May 1845. *Address:* 39 Charles Street, W; Camperdown, Dundee; Gleneagles House, Perth. *Club:* Brooks's. *Died 5 June 1918.*

CAMPION, George; Sheriff-Substitute Dumfries and Galloway 1890–1925; *b* 1846; *m* Mary Janet, *d* of Thomas Lorimer of Larkfield, Dumfries. *Educ:* Edinburgh Academy; Oxford. Advocate, 1872; Sheriff-Substitute of Argyllshire at Inveraray, 1880. *Recreation:* golf. *Address:* Larkfield, Dumfries. *Clubs:* University, Edinburgh; Dumfries and Galloway, Dumfries. *Died 1 Nov. 1926.*

CAMPION, Col William Henry, CB 1902; JP; Lieutenant-Colonel and Hon. Colonel 2nd Volunteer Battalion Royal Sussex Regiment; *b* 1 April 1836; *e s* of W. J. Campion and Harriet, *d* of late T. R. Kemp; *m* 1869, Hon. Gertrude Brand, 2nd *d* of 1st Viscount Hampden; two *s* three *d. Educ:* Eton. 72nd Highlanders, 1854–61; 53rd Regiment, 1861–63; served Crimea and Indian Mutiny with 72nd, subseq. Seaforth Highlanders. *Address:* Danny Park, Hassocks, Sussex. *Club:* Arthur's. *Died 3 Dec. 1923.*

CANDLER, Edmund, CBE 1920; author and traveller; *b* 27 Jan. 1874; *s* of John Candler, MRCS, and Anne Candler, Harleston, Norfolk; *m* 1902, Olive Mary Tooth; one *s* one *d. Educ:* Repton; Emmanuel College, Cambridge (BA 1895). Travelled widely in the East; Special Correspondent of the Daily Mail, Tibet Expedition, 1904 (severely wounded in engagement at Tuna); Correspondent in France for The Times and Daily Mail, 1914–15; Official Eye-witness, Mesopotamia, 1915–18 (despatches); Times Correspondent Middle East, 1918–19; Director of Publicity, Punjab Government, 1920–21. *Publications:* A Vagabond in Asia, 1899; The Unveiling of Lhasa, 1905; The Paraphrase of Poetry, 1905; The Mantle of the East, 1910; The General Plan, 1911; Siri Ram Revolutionist, 1912; The Year of Chivalry, 1916; The Long Road to Baghdad, 1919; On the Edge of the World, 1919; The Sepoy, 1919; Abdication, 1922; Youth and the East, 1924. *Recreations:* riding, travel, etc. *Address:* Villa Ichas Mendy, Hendaye, Basses Pyrénées, France. *Club:* Savage.

Died 4 Jan. 1926.

CANE, Lucy Mary, (Mrs Arthur Beresford Cane), CBE 1919; 2nd *d* of late E. W. O'Brien of Cahirmoyle, Co. Limerick; *m* 1894, Arthur Beresford Cane, CBE, Barrister; two *d. Educ:* at home. Member of a Voluntary Aid Detachment for four years before the war; on the Headquarters of the VAD Department at Devonshire House, 1914–17; Assistant-Director, Women's Royal Naval Service, 1917–19. *Address:* 66 Elm Park Gardens, SW10. *T:* Kensington 667.

Died 23 April 1926.

CANNAN, Charles, MA; Secretary to the Delegates of the University Press, Oxford, since 1898; sometime Fellow and Tutor of Trinity College, Oxford; *b* 1858; *m* 1891, Mary Wedderburn, *d* of late A. Wedderburn Maxwell, of Glenlair, NB; three *d. Educ:* Clifton College; Corpus Christi College, Oxford (Scholar). *Address:* Magdalen Gate House, Oxford. *T:* Oxford 348. *Club:* Alpine.

Died 15 Dec. 1919.

CANNING, Hon. Albert Stratford George, DL and JP for Cos Down and Derry; *b* 24 Aug. 1832; 2nd *s* of 1st Baron Garvagh. Owned about 4000 acres. *Publications:* Christian Toleration, 1874; Intolerance among Christians, 1876; Political Progress of Christianity, 1877; Religious Strife in British History, 1878; Philosophy of the Waverley Novels, 1879; Philosophy of Charles Dickens, 1880; Baldearg O'Donnell, 1881; Macaulay, Essayist and Historian, 1882, enlarged and revised edn, 1913; Thoughts on Shakespeare's Historical Plays, 1884; Revolted Ireland, 1886; The Divided Irish, 1888; Literary Influence in British History, 1889; Thoughts on Religious History, 1891; Words on Existing Religions, 1893; Religious Development, 1896; History in Fact and Fiction, 1897; British Rule and Modern Politics, 1898; British Power and Thought, 1901; Shakespeare studied in eight Plays, 1903; History in Scott's Novels, 1905; History in Scott's Novels, 2nd edition, 1908; Shakespeare studied in Six Plays, 1906; British Writers on Classic Lands, 1907; Shakespeare studied in Three Plays, 1908; Sir Walter Scott studied in Eight Novels, 1910; Dickens and Thackeray studied in Three Novels, 1911; Dickens studied in Six Novels, 1912; Thoughts on Christian History, 1914. *Recreations:* acclimatising foreign birds and animals, reading. *Address:* The Lodge, Rostrevor, Co. Down. *Club:* Carlton.

Died 22 April 1916.

CANNING, Hon. Conway Stratford George; *b* 15 Dec. 1854; 2nd *s* of 2nd Baron Garvagh; unmarried. Entered army (King's Royal Rifle corps), 1875; retired, 1894; served Egyptian Expedition, 1884, battles of Teb and Tamai (medal with clasp, bronze star); Hazara Expedition, 1891 (medal with clasp); Miranzai, 1891 (clasp); Isazai Expedition, 1892; South Africa, 1902 (medal with 2 clasps); Major (retired pay). *Recreations:* formerly polo and rifle-shooting; golf, fishing, reading. *Address:* 2 Ryder Street, St James's, SW. *Clubs:* Army and Navy, Royal Automobile. *Died 19 Feb. 1926.*

CANNING, Hugh; Professor of Comparative Philology, Dublin. *Address:* The University, Dublin. *Died 23 Dec. 1927.*

CANNON, Hon. Lawrence John; Puisne Justice, Superior Court, Province of Quebec, since 1905; *b* Quebec, 18 Nov. 1852; *s* of L. A. Cannon, City Clerk of Quebec; *m* 1876, Aurelie Dumoulin; five *s* three *d*. *Educ:* Quebec Seminary and Laval University; LLB and LLL Quebec. Admitted to the Bar of the Province of Quebec, 1874; practised law at Arthabaskaville, PQ, 1875–91; Assistant Attorney-Gen. and Law Clerk, Quebec, 1891; Liberal candidate for Drummond and Arthabaska at general elections of 1882 for Dominion Parliament; QC 1897; acted as Counsel for the Province of Quebec in the Fisheries Case before the Judicial Committee of the Privy Council, 1897. *Address:* 5 Collins Street, Quebec.

Died 30 Jan. 1921.

CANTAN, Major Henry Thomas, CMG 1915; Duke of Cornwall's Light Infantry; *b* 11 Jan. 1868. Served six years in ranks; Lieut army, 1892; Captain, 1900; Major, 1908; Superintendent of Gymnasia, Dublin, 1896–99; Curragh, 1902–6; South Africa, 1901–14; employed with SA Constabulary, 1900–2; served S Africa, 1899–1902 (Queen's medal, 4 clasps; King's medal, 2 clasps); European War, 1914–15 (CMG). *Address:* Tullow Lodge, Tullow, Co. Carlow, Ireland.

Died 20 April 1916.

CANTERBURY, 5th Viscount, *cr* 1835; **Henry Frederick Walpole Manners-Sutton,** DL; Baron Bottesford, 1835; *b* 8 April 1879; *s* of 4th Viscount and Amy, *o d* of Hon. Frederick Walpole, MP; *S* father, 1914. Owned about 5200 acres. *Heir: c* Capt. Charles Graham Manners-Sutton, *b* 23 Jan. 1872. *Club:* St James's.

Died 22 Oct. 1918.

CANTLIE, Sir James, KBE 1918; Consulting Surgeon, Seamen's Hospital Society; Founder and President (1921–22–23) Royal Society Tropical Medicine and Hygiene; Founder and co-Editor Journal Tropical Medicine; *b* Keithmore, Dufftown, Banffshire, Scotland, 17 Jan. 1851; *s* of Wm Cantlie, banker and farmer; *m* 1884, Mabel Barclay, OBE (*d* 1921), *d* of Robert Barclay Brown; four *s*. *Educ:* Milne's Institution, Fochabers; Aberdeen University; Charing Cross Hospital. MA Aberdeen, Natural Science Honours; MB, CM, Honours in Surgery; FRCS England; DPH London; LLD Aberdeen, 1919; Knight of Grace, Order of St John of Jerusalem; Imperial Order Osmanich (4th class). Came to London to finish medical education, 1871; Demonstrator of Anatomy at Charing Cross Hospital, 1872–87; Assistant Surgeon, 1877; Surgeon, 1887; Examiner, Univ. of Aberdeen; went to Egypt, cholera expedition, 1883, Surgeon-Commandant VMSC, London, 1885–88; went to China, 1887; Dean of College of Medicine for Chinese, 1889–96; Plague Officer for London County Council; Consulting Surgeon in London, North Eastern Railway Co.; President Caledonian Society, London, 1902–3; Honorary Colonel, RAMC (T) 1st London Division; Comdt, No 1 VAD, London, 1909–22; Member of Council, Red Cross Society. *Publications:* Naked Eye Anatomy, text-book; Ulcers, Veins, etc, Quain's Dictionary; Ligature of Arteries, etc, Heath's Dictionary; Gunshot Injuries, etc, Treves' Surgery; author of Beri-beri; Tropical Surgery, Gould and Warren's Surgery; Tropical Diseases, Allchin's Medicine; Plague; Degeneration amongst Londoners, 1885; Physical Efficiency, 1906. *Recreations:* farming, fishing, shooting; travel — from China went to India, visited medical schools and places of interest, 1891; Japan, Annam, Pekin, Great Wall, Corea, Vladivostock, United States and Canada. *Address:* 37 Harley Street, W1; The Kennels, Cottered, Buntingford, Herts. *T:* Langham 1519.

Died 28 May 1926.

CANTON, William; *b* Isle of Chusan, 27 Oct. 1845. *Educ:* France. For many years sub-editor and leader-writer on the Glasgow Herald;

sub-editor of the Contemporary Review, and manager of Isbister & Co., Ltd, 1891–1901. *Publications:* A Lost Epic and Other Poems, 1887; The Invisible Playmate, 1894; W. V., Her Book; and Various Verses, 1896; The Invisible Playmate, and W. V., Her Book (with final chapter), 1897; A Child's Book of Saints, 1898; Children's Sayings, 1900; In Memory of W.V., 1901; The Comrades, Poems Old and New, 1902; The History of the British and Foreign Bible Society, vols i–ii 1903, vols iii–v 1910; The Story of the Bible Society, 1904; A Child's Book of Warriors, 1912; The Story of St Elizabeth of Hungary, 1912; The Bible and the Anglo-Saxon People, 1914; The Bible Story, 1915; Dawn in Palestine, 1918; The Five Colours, 1924. *Address:* Inglewood, 119 Audley Road, Hendon, NW4.

Died 2 May 1926.

CAPELLINI, Prof. Giovanni; Professor of Geology and Paleontology, Bologna University, since 1860; Senatore del Regno; *b* Spezia, 23 Aug. 1833; *m* Marchioness Niccolini Beatrix; two *s*. *Educ:* Collegio, Spezia; University of Pisa. Was Professor in the College of Genoa, and Rector of the University of Bologna. *Address:* Bologna, Italy.

CAPES, Bernard. *Publications:* The Lake of Wine, 1898; The Adventures of the Comte de la Muette, 1898; Our Lady of Darkness; At a Winter's Fire, 1899; From Door to Door, 1900; Joan Brotherhood, 1900; Love like a Gipsy, 1901; A Castle in Spain, 1903; The Secret in the Hill, 1903; The Extraordinary Confessions of Diana Please, 1904; A Jay of Italy, 1905; The Story of Lohengrin, 1905; A Rogue's Tragedy, 1906; The Green Parrot, 1908; Amaranthus, a Book of Little Songs, 1908; The Love Story of St Bel, 1909; Jemmy Abercraw, 1910; Historical Vignettes, 1910; The House of Many Voices, 1911; Jessie Bazley, 1912; The Pot of Basil, 1913; The Story of Fifine, 1914; The Fabulists, 1915; Moll Davis, 1916; If Age Could, 1916; Where England sets her Feet, 1918. *Address:* 1 Southgate Road, Winchester.

Died 2 Nov. 1918.

CAPPEL, Sir Albert James Leppoc, KCIE 1887; *b* 1836; *m* 1873, Fanny Gibbon (*d* 1907), *d* of Gen. Sir Frank Turner, KCB, RA; one *s* two *d*. Served Crimea, 1855–56; entered Indian Telegraph Service, 1857; Director-Gen. of Indian Telegraphs, 1883–89. *Address:* 27 Kensington Court Gardens, W8. *T:* Western 855.

Died 20 April 1924.

CAPPER, Alfred Octavius; demonstrator of thought transmission and other mysterious phenomena; *s* of late Octavius Capper of Southampton; *m* 1913, Bettina Maud, *d* of late W. B. Partridge, JP, and *widow* of late H. R. Trafford, JP, of Michaelchurch Court, Herefordshire. *Educ:* Springhill School, Southampton. For 30 years presented his drawing-room entertainment and thought-reading-séance in most towns of the United Kingdom, also in France, Switzerland, and Italy; appeared by royal command at Windsor Castle and Marlborough House, and personally "experimented" in thought-reading with King George V and Duke of Connaught, also with Madame Sarah Bernhardt at her residence in Paris; also appeared at 500 public and preparatory schools; his various performances yielded over £60,000 to charitable institutions. During 1912 travelled 50,000 miles and gave 200 séances throughout India, Burma, Malaya, and Ceylon; his entertainment realised £5000 for War Charities and was witnessed by 600,000 soldiers in England, France, and Germany. *Publication:* A Rambler's Recollections and Reflections. *Recreations:* sport generally. *Address:* 15 Egerton Gardens, SW; Michaelchurch Court, Hereford. *Died 11 March 1921.*

CAPPER, David Sing, MA, MInstCE, MIMechE; Professor of Engineering, University of London, King's College, 1902–21; and Member of Senate, 1905–7; Fellow, King's College, London, 1907; *y s* of late Jasper John Capper (*d* 1895); *m* 1893, Lillian Grace, *y d* of late Dr A. R. Shaw, St Leonards-on-Sea (*d* 1899); one *s*. *Educ:* Royal High School, Edinburgh; Edinburgh University; University College, London. Messrs R. & W. Hawthorns; Messrs Humphrys, Tennant and Co., Deptford. Asst to Mr R. Humphrys, 1888–90. One of the Governors of Sir Roger Cholmeley's School, Highgate, 1905–20; member of governing body of Imperial College of Science and Technology, South Kensington, 1908–9; Member of Delegacy of University of London, King's College, 1910–14; Lt-Col Commanding University of London Contingent of Officers' Training Corps to 1915; Major, 2/5 Royal Warwicks, BEF. *Publications:* various professional papers in Proceedings of Engineering Institutions, Royal Agricultural Society, etc. *Recreations:* gardening, philately. *Address:* 38 West Heath Drive, Hampstead, NW8. *T:* Hampstead 2350. *Clubs:* Athenæum; St Stephen's. *Died 12 Feb. 1926.*

CAPPER, Stewart Henbest, MA (Edin. and Manc.); ARIBA 1891; RCA 1899 (ARCA 1897); FSA; Temporary Egyptian Government

Official; *b* 15 Dec. 1859; 3rd *s* of late Jasper John Capper, Upper Clapton, and Harriet Millington Jackson, Douglas, Isle of Man; unmarried. *Educ:* Royal High School, and University, Edinburgh; Heidelberg University; Ecole des Beaux Arts, Paris. Medallist and "Dux", Royal High School, 1875; MA with first class honours (classics), 1880. Private tutor and (for part of the time) acting private secretary in household of the late Sir R. B. D. Morier, Lisbon and Madrid, 1879–83; examiner in Art History and Archæology, Edinburgh University, 1895 and 1904; Macdonald Professor of Architecture, McGill University, Montreal, 1896–1903; Professor of Architecture, Victoria University, Manchester, 1903–12; late Capt. and Bt Major, 1/6th Batt. Manchester Regt, which he accompanied to Egypt on active service; Military Censor, Port Said, 1914–16, Alexandria, 1916–17, Cairo, 1917–18; Intelligence Corps, EEF, 1918; GSO, EEF, 1919 (despatches twice, TD); Chief Press Censor, Ministry of the Interior, Cairo, 1920–21; Major (local), commanding Manchester University Contingent Officers' Training Corps, 1908–12; formerly Captain Canadian Field Artillery (3rd Field Battery, Montreal). *Publications:* occasional papers. *Recreations:* member Royal St Lawrence Yacht Club; RNSYC. *Address:* European Dept, Ministry of the Interior, Cairo; St Michael's, Reigate, Surrey. *Club:* Athenæum.

Died 8 Jan. 1925.

CAPUS, (Vincent Marie) Alfred; man of letters; Officer Legion of Honour; Member French Academy; *b* 25 Nov. 1858; widower. *Educ:* Aix-en-Provence; Lycée Condorcet, Paris. Late Editor Figaro. *Publications:* Qui perd gagne; Monsieur Veut rire; Années d'aventures; Notre époque et le théâtre. *Plays:* La Veine; Tout s'arrange; L'Institut de Beauté, etc. *Address:* Vernon sur Brenne, Indre et Loire, France. *T:* 220-82.

Died 1 Nov. 1922.

CARADOS; *see* Edwards, G. Spencer.

CARBONELL, Rev. Canon Francis Rohde, MA; Vicar of Fairford, 1888–1918, and Rural Dean, 1900–18; Hon. Canon of Gloucester Cathedral since 1911; Proctor in Convocation since 1910; Subwarden Society of Sacred Study, since 1904; *b* Manor House, Westbourne Green, 4 June 1849; *s* of William Charles and Sarah Mary Carbonell; *m* 1874, Katharine Dorinda, *d* of Rev. Arthur Rainey Ludlow of Dimlands Castle, Cowbridge; two *d*. *Educ:* Kidderminster Grammar School; Merton College, Oxford (First Class, Natural Science School). Deacon 1873; Priest 1875; Curate of Kinver, Staffs, 1873–76; Rector of Littleton on Severn, Glos, 1876–84; Curate of Tewkesbury (Abbey), 1884–87; Vicar of Kingston, Somerset, 1887–88; *Publications:* pamphlets. *Recreations:* violoncello, music generally, fishing. *Address:* Worcester House, Pittville, Circus Road, Cheltenham.

Died 27 May 1919.

CARDEW, Colonel Sir Frederic, KCMG 1897 (CMG 1894); Consul for Republic of Liberia, since 1896; *b* 27 Sept. 1839; *m* 1st, 1865, Clara, *d* of J. D. Newton, West Hoe, Plymouth (*d* 1881); 2nd, 1887, Katharine, *d* of late J. Savill and *widow* of Col Kent Jones; three *s*. *Educ:* Sandhurst. Entered Bengal Army, 1858, 104th and 82nd Regts; Colonel, 1887; retired 1890; served NW Frontier of India, 1863 (despatches); Zulu War, 1879–81 (despatches), Brevet-Major; Transvaal, 1880–81; AA and QMG Natal Field Force; DAQMG Aldershot, 1873–78; South Africa, 1879–80; Assistant Military Secretary, China, 1882–83; AAG South Africa, 1890; Sub-Commissioner, Zululand, 1884–86; Resident Commissioner, 1890; Governor and Commander-in-Chief of Sierra Leone, 1894–1900. *Address:* Tudor Cottage, Whitchurch, Oxon. *TA:* Whitchurch, Oxon. *Club:* United Service.

Died 6 July 1921.

CARDIN, James Joseph, CB 1897; *b* 1839; *s* of late Joseph Cardin, of Lincoln's Inn; *m* 1870, Mary (*d* 1875), *d* of late Herbert Smith of Baverstock. Receiver and Accountant-General, General Post Office, 1886–97; Comptroller and Accountant-General, 1897–1901; late Lt-Col Prince of Wales's Own 12th Middlesex RV. *Address:* 28 Tierney Road, Streatham Hill, SW. *Club:* Junior Athenæum.

Died 3 May 1917.

CARDOT, Rt. Rev. Alexander; Bishop of Limyra and Vicar Apostolic of the Mission of Southern Burma, since 1894; *b* Fresse, Haute-Saône, France, 10 Jan. 1857. *Educ:* Luxeuil, Vesoul, and Paris. Priest, 1879; sent to Southern Burma, 1879; Coadjutor Bishop to Bishop Bigandes, 1893; built in Rangoon a cathedral; attended the Eucharistic Congress in London, 1908. *Address:* Rangoon. *TA:* Adexteros.

Died 18 Oct. 1925.

CARDWELL, Rev. John Henry, MA; Prebendary of St Paul's since 1911; *b* Sheffield, 20 June 1842; *s* of William Cardwell, colliery owner; *m* 1869, Elizabeth Barnes, *d* of John Barnes, JP, Reedley Hall, Lancashire; four *s* three *d*. *Educ:* Burnley Grammar School; Lindow Grove School; Caius College, Cambridge. Ordained 1865; Incumbent, St Andrew's, Fulham, 1868–91; Rector, St Anne's, Soho, 1891–1914. During twenty-three years in Fulham chiefly engaged in Church Building, and forming new ecclesiastical districts. Three churches (St Andrew's, St Peter's, St Clement's) built during incumbency, and eight churches, school churches, and mission rooms. Carried out restoration of St Anne's Church, and remodelling of the parochial schools. Built new Parish Hall and Clergy House for St Anne's, 1911. Progressive in municipal politics; led the way in strong measures against disorderly houses in St Anne's, brought about through the Strand Board of Works, conversion of St Anne's churchyard into a public garden. *Publications:* Story of a Charity School; joint author Two Centuries of Soho: its Institutions, Firms and Amusements; Men and Women of Soho, Famous and Infamous; Twenty Years in Soho, 1891–1911. *Recreations:* cycling, walking. *Address:* Chapel House, Ealing, W5. *T:* Ealing 682.

Died 17 April 1921.

CAREW, 3rd Baron (UK), *cr* 1838; **Robert Shapland George Julian Carew,** DL; Baron Carew (Ireland), 1834; *b* 15 June 1860; *s* of 2nd Baron and Emily, *d* of Sir George Richard Philips, 2nd Bt; *S* father, 1881; *m* 1888, Julia, *d* of the late Albert Lethbridge, and *g d* of Sir John Lethbridge, 3rd Bt, Sandhill Park, Taunton. *Educ:* Trinity College, Cambridge (BA). *Heir:* *b* Hon. George Patrick John Carew, *b* 1 Feb. 1863. *Address:* 28 Belgrave Square, SW1. *T:* Victoria 709. *Clubs:* Bachelors', Brooks's.

Died 29 April 1923.

CAREW, 4th Baron (UK), *cr* 1838; **George Patrick John Carew;** Baron Carew (Ireland), 1834; *b* 1 Feb. 1863; *s* of 2nd Baron and Emily, *d* of Sir George Richard Philips, 2nd Bt; *S* brother, 1923; *m* 1888, Maud Beatrice, *d* of late John Ramsay. *Educ:* Eton; Magdalene College, Cambridge. *Recreation:* philately. *Heir:* *c* Gerald Shapland Carew, *b* 26 April 1860. *Address:* Rostrevor, 6 Grassington Road, Eastbourne. *Club:* Badminton.

Died 21 April 1926.

CAREW, 5th Baron (UK), *cr* 1838; **Gerald Shapland Carew;** Baron Carew (Ireland), 1834; *b* 26 April 1860; *s* of late Hon. Shapland Francis Carew, *s* of 1st Baron, and Lady Hester Georgiana Browne, *d* of 2nd Marquess of Sligo; *S* cousin, 1926; *m* 1904, Catherine, *o d* of late Thomas Conolly, MP; three *s*. *Educ:* Eton; abroad. *Heir:* *s* William Francis Carew, Duke of Cornwall's LI, India, *b* 23 April 1905. *Address:* 13 Tedworth Square, SW.

Died 3 Oct. 1927.

CAREW, Lt-Gen. Sir Reginald Pole, KCB 1900 (CB 1887); CVO 1901; DL; JP of Antony; *b* Antony, Cornwall, 1 May 1849; *e s* of late W. H. Pole Carew, of Antony, and Frances Anne, *d* of John Buller, of Morval; *m* 1901, Lady Beatrice Butler, *e d* of 3rd Marquis of Ormonde; two *s* two *d*. *Educ:* Eton; Christ Church, Oxford. Served in Coldstream Guards, 1869–99; private secretary to Sir Hercules Robinson, Governor New South Wales, 1876–77; ADC to Lord Lytton, Viceroy of India, 1878–79; to Sir Frederick Roberts, Afghan War, 1879–80; to Sir Frederick Roberts, South Africa, 1881; to Duke of Connaught, Egypt, 1882; Mil. Sec. to Sir Frederick Roberts, Madras, 1884–85; Mil. Sec. to Sir Frederick Roberts, Comdr-in-Chief, India, 1885–90; commanded 2nd Batt. Coldstream Guards, 1895–99. Commanded consecutively 9th Brigade and Guards' Brigade, and 11th Division South Africa (despatches twice, promoted Major-General, KCB). *Decorated:* Afghan War, 1879–80, three clasps; march to Kandahar; Egypt, 1882 (Medjidie, 4th class, Khedive's star); Burma, 1886; Jubilee medal, 1897; S Africa, five clasps; Coronation medal, 1902; Commanding 8th Division 3rd Army Corps, 1903–5; retired, with rank of Lieut-General, 1906. Contested Pembroke Boroughs (C), 1906; Bodmin Division, 1910. MP (U) Bodmin Division, Cornwall, 1910–16; Inspector-General of Territorials, 1914. *Recreations:* hunting, shooting, etc. *Address:* Antony, Cornwall. *Clubs:* Guards, Turf, Travellers', Pratt's.

Died 19 Sept. 1924.

CAREY, Sir Bertram Sausmarez, KCIE 1918 (CIE 1893); CSI 1914; VD; Commissioner of a District, Burma, since 1909; *b* 1864; *s* of late Rev. Alfred H. Carey; *m* Mary, *e d* of late I. D. Chepmell. *Educ:* Bedford Grammar School. Appointed to Burma Police, 1886; to the Burma Commission, 1887; Political Officer in Chin Hills, 1889–95; Deputy Commissioner, 1900. *Address:* Rangoon, Burma.

Died 11 July 1919.

CAREY, Frank Stanton, MA; late Professor of Mathematics in the University of Liverpool; *b* Easton-in-Gordano, Somersetshire, 14 June 1860; *m* 1894, Jessie Mein; two *s* two *d*. *Educ:* The Grammar School,

Bristol; Trinity Coll., Cambridge. Third Wrangler, 1882, and placed in Division I, Part II, of the Mathematical Tripos, 1882; elected to a Fellowship at Trinity College, Camb., 1884; to a Professorship at University College, Liverpool, 1886. *Publications:* Solid Geometry; Infinitesimal Calculus; Papers on Mathematics; (with J. Proudman) Elements of Mechanics, 1925. *Address:* c/o The University, Liverpool.

Died 26 July 1928.

CARINGTON, Herbert Hanbury Smith-, JP; *b* Worcester, 1851; *e s* of late R. Smith-Carington, of Ashby Folville Manor, Leicestershire; *m* 1876, Elizabeth P., 2nd *d* of Josiah Stallard, of The Blanquettes, Worcs; three *s* one *d*. *Educ:* Worcester; King's College, London. Lord of the Manor of Ashby Folville; High Sheriff for Leicestershire, 1910; Director of Sir W. G. Armstrong, Whitworth, and Co., Ltd; the Norwich Union Life Insurance Soc; Deputy Chairman of St Mary's Hospitals; on the Board of the Manchester Royal Infirmary; Member of the Court of Governors and of the Council of the Victoria University of Manchester, of Council of the Manchester Royal College of Music; Governor of the Manchester Whitworth Institute; Fellow of the Royal Historical Society; Member of the Committee of Manchester Steam Users Association, of Council and Past President of the Shire Horse Society; Knight of the Royal Order of the Northern Star (Sweden); Member of the 4th class of the Order of the Rising Sun (Japan); Patron and Trustee of 2 livings. *Recreations:* shooting, farming, and shire horse-breeding. *Address:* Grangethorpe, Rusholme, Manchester. *T:* 5 Rusholme; Ashby Folville, Melton Mowbray. *Clubs:* Carlton, National, Constitutional; Union, Manchester; County, Leicester.

Died 4 March 1917.

CARLETON, Hon. Brig.-Gen. Frank Robert Crofton, CB 1916; retired; late Director of Organisation, War Office; *b* 8 Sept. 1856. Served S Africa, 1899–1902 (Queen's medal, 4 clasps, King's medal, 2 clasps). *Died 9 June 1924.*

CARLETON, Brig.-Gen. Frederick Montgomerie, DSO 1900; *b* 21 July 1867; *y s* of late Gen. Hy Carleton, CB, Royal Artillery; *m* 1899, Gwendolen, *e d* of late S. Lloyd of the Priory, Warwick, and Dolobran, Montgomeryshire; two *s* one *d*. *Educ:* Military Coll. Oxford. Joined King's Own Regt 1888; served with Dongola Expedition, 1896 (medal and two clasps); Nile Expedition, 1897 (medal); with Mendiland, Karene, and Protectorate Expeditions, Sierra Leone, 1898–99 (medal, clasp, DSO, and despatch); ADC S Africa, 1899–1902 (despatches thrice, Brevet-Major, medal and six clasps, King's medal and two clasps); passed Staff College, 1902; retired, 1909. *Recreations:* hunting, shooting, polo. *Address:* 6 Broad Street Place, EC3. *Club:* United Service. *Died 15 May 1922.*

CARLETON, Rev. James George, DD; Treasurer of St Patrick's Cathedral, Dublin, since 1913; Deputy for the Regius Professor of Divinity, University of Dublin, since 1916; *b* Blackrock, Co. Dublin, 1848; *s* of late Cornelius Carleton of Dublin and Lisburn; *m* 1872, Margaret, *d* of late George Dundas, Manager, Head Office Belfast Banking Company; two *s* one *d*. *Educ:* Rathmines School; Trinity College, Dublin; Scholar, 1868; Senior Moderator in Classics, 1869; Ecclesiastical History Prize (1st) and Abp King's Divinity Prize (2nd), 1870; Theological Exhibition (1st), 1871; Elrington Theological Prize, 1872; BD, 1877; DD, 1902. Ordained, 1870, for curacy of St John's Limerick; Curate of Kilmallock, 1875; of Holy Trinity, Rathmines, 1877; of St Peter's Dublin, 1883; of St Stephen's Dublin, 1897; Lecturer in Divinity, University of Dublin, 1888; Prebendary of Rathmichael and Canon of St Patrick's Cathedral, Dublin, 1904. *Publications:* The Bible of our Lord and His Apostles; the LXX considered in relation to the Gospel, etc, 1888; The Part of Rheims in the making of the English Bible, 1902; the Prayer Book Psalter, with introduction and marginal notes, 1909; articles in the Encyclopaedia of Religion and Ethics. *Address:* 17 Harrington Street, Dublin. *Died 1918.*

CARLILE, Sir Edward, Kt 1913; KC; JP; *b* London, 26 April 1845; *s* of John Carlile of Honston, Scotland; *m* 1878, Isabella Sophia, *y d* of Robert Hunter Young, WS, Edinburgh; two *s* three *d*. *Educ:* private schools; University of Melbourne (Law Gold Medallist, 1868). Entered public service, Victoria, 1861; Registrar-General's Office, 1862; Crown Law Offices, 1865; called to Bar, 1871; Parliamentary and Professional Assistant to Crown Law Offices, 1873; Parliamentary Draughtsman, 1881, retired 1910; QC 1900; a Trustee and Treasurer of the National Gallery, Museums, and Public Library of Victoria; Government Representative on the Faculty of Veterinary Science of the University of Melbourne; on Committee of Management of Melbourne Hospital. *Address:* South Yarra, Melbourne.

Died 15 Nov. 1917.

CARLIN, Gaston; Swiss Envoy Extraordinary and Minister Plenipotentiary at The Hague since 1920; Member of the Permanent Court of Arbitration; *b* Delémont, Berne; *m* 1887. *Educ:* Delémont, Berne (gymnasium and university, doctor juris.); Leipzig; Paris. Attaché, Rome, 1882; Secretary, Vienna, 1884; Councillor, 1887; Secretary, Political Division, Foreign Office, Berne, 1891; Envoy Extraordinary and Minister Plenipotentiary, Rome, 1895–1902; London, 1902–20; first Swiss Delegate, Venice International Sanitary Conference, 1897; Rome International Anti-Anarchic Conference, 1898; Second International Peace Conference, The Hague, 1907; Conferences on Bills of Exchange, The Hague, 1910 and 1912; 3rd Opium Conference, The Hague, 1914; Conference between Switzerland, the Scandinavian States and the Netherlands for the elaboration of a uniform scheme for the International Court of Justice, The Hague, 1920; and Communications and Transit Conference, Barcelona, 1921. *Publications:* In French or German—On the Possession and Property of Personal Estate; On the Acquisition and Loss of the Swiss Nationality; On the Transitory Dispositions of the Swiss Federal Code of Obligations; Biography of his Father; Travelling Notes, etc. *Recreations:* climbing, shooting, collecting (china, majolica, old silver, Swiss stained-glass panels, tapestries). *Address:* Swiss Legation, The Hague. *Died 13 June 1922.*

CARLINE, George, RBA; Painter in Oil and Water-Colour—chiefly portraits; *b* Lincoln, 1855; *s* of Richard Carline, Solicitor; *m* 1884, Annie, *d* of late John Smith of Buckhurst Hill; three *s* one *d*. *Educ:* privately; Lincoln Grammar School; studied at Heatherlies, London, Antwerp, and Paris. First picture, Spelling out the List, on the line at Royal Academy, 1886; among subsequent works, In the Garden of Hollyhocks, Faith, The Harvest Moon, The Blind Sister, The View of London from Hampstead Heath, Portraits of Mrs Duff, Lady Mary Stewart, Mrs Duigan, Mrs Eccles Williams, Beauchamp Tyrwhitt, Nat Gould, Presentation portrait of Colonel Dimmock, MD, Miss Heberden, sister of the Principal of Brasenose College, Daughters of Sir William Schlich, Children of Rev. E. H. Alington, Dr Collier, Professor Vinogradoff, Professor Sir Charles Oman, MP, etc; an Exhibition at The Dowdeswell Galleries, Bond Street, in 1896, of 59 works entitled The Home of our English Wild Flowers. *Publications:* Illustrations to Maud Müller, 1886; Aquarelle graveur of Snowdrop, 1895; Water-colour illustrations to Andrew Lang's Oxford, 1915; a coloured reproduction of a water-colour of King's College Chapel, Cambridge, 1920. *Address:* 47 Downshire Hill, Hampstead, NW. *Died Dec. 1920.*

CARLISLE, Rt. Hon. Alexander Montgomery, PC 1907; *b* Ballymena, Co. Antrim, 8 July 1854; *e s* of late John Carlisle, MA, Headmaster of Royal Academical Institution, Belfast; *m* Edith Wooster of San Francisco; one *s* two *d*. *Educ:* Royal Academical Institution, Belfast. Career business, shipbuilder and engineer, having joined Harland and Wolff, where apprenticeship was served in 1870; rose to be General Manager and Chairman of Managing Directors; retired, 1910; Member of Departmental Committee on Accidents in Factories and Workshops, 1908; contested West Belfast as Independent, 1906; one of the Merchant Shipping Advisory Committee in making report to the Board of Trade on Life-Saving Appliances, 1911; gave evidence at the Admiralty before Committee appointed to report on the organisation of the Royal Corps of Constructors and other cognate questions; on 9 August 1920, when Coercion Bill on Ireland was just going to be passed, he made a protest from the throne of thirteen words (My Lords, if you pass this Bill you may kill England, not Ireland). *Address:* 7 Orme Square, W2. *M:* LH 3997. *Clubs:* Royal Thames Yacht; Phyllis Court, Henley-on-Thames.

Died 5 March 1926.

CARMICHAEL, 1st Baron, *cr* 1912, of Skirling; **Thomas David Gibson-Carmichael,** Bt 1628; GCSI 1917; GCIE 1911; KCMG 1908; MA; DL; *b* Edinburgh, 18 March 1859; *e s* of Rev. Sir William Henry Gibson-Carmichael, 10th Bt and Eleanora Anne, *d* of David Anderson, St Germains, NB; *S* father as 11th Bt, 1891; *m* 1886, Mary Helen Elizabeth, *d* of late Albert Nugent; no *c*. *Educ:* St John's College, Cambridge. Private Secretary to Sir George Trevelyan and Lord Dalhousie, when Secretaries for Scotland; Chairman, Scottish Board of Lunacy, 1894–97; contested (L) Peebles and Selkirk, 1892; MP (L) Midlothian, 1895–1900, succeeding Mr Gladstone; a Trustee of the National Portrait Gallery, 1904–8, and of National Gallery, 1906–8, and since 1923; Governor of Victoria, Australia, 1908–11; Madras, 1911–12; Bengal, 1912–17; Lord Lieutenant of Peebleshire. *Heir* (to baronetcy): *c* Sir Henry Thomas Gibson-Craig, 5th Bt, *b* 5 Jan. 1885. *Address:* Skirling House, Biggar; 13 Portman Street, W1. *T:* Mayfair 6462. *Clubs:* Brooks's; New, Edinburgh.

Died 16 Jan. 1926 (ext).

CARMICHAEL, Sir Duncan, Kt 1917; MLC; partner in firm of Mackinnon, Mackenzie & Co., Calcutta, Bombay, and Karachee; a director Anderson, Green & Co., Ltd; *b* 1866; *s* of Dugald Carmichael, Greenock. *Address:* 122 Leadenhall Street, EC3.
Died 22 June 1923.

CARMICHAEL, Rev. Frederic Falkiner, LLD; Chancellor of the Cathedral of Christ Church, Dublin; Chaplain to His Excellency the Lord Lieutenant of Ireland; member of the council of the Royal Dublin Society and of the council of the Alexandra College; *b* 1831; *e s* of late James Carmichael, Clerk of the Crown of the County of Tipperary, and Elizabeth Murray, *d* of Singleton Maynard Walker and Anne Kennedy Thorpe; *m* 1855, Elizabeth Turton Cotton, *d* of Francis Bulkeley Turton Cotton of Allenton, County Dublin, and Susan Lucas, *d* of Minchin Lucas of Woodtown, County Dublin; one *s* two *d*. *Educ:* private tuition. AB, TCD and Div. Test, 1857; MA, 1868; LLB and LLD Stip. Con., 1877; select preacher, TCD, 1875, 1878, 1881; select preacher, Cambridge, 1877; Donnellan Lecturer TCD, 1875–76, and 1890–91. Deacon, 1857; Priest, 1858; Curate, St Werburgh, Dublin, 1857; St Bride's, 1860; Chaplain of the Magdalen, 1865; Canon of Christ Church, 1886; Professor of History, Alexandra College, 1880. *Publications:* Jesus Christ, the Way, the Truth, and the Life; Donnellan Lectures, TCD 1876; The Responsibilities of God, and other sermons, 2nd edn; The Ghost of Samuel, and other sermons on different subjects; Honour the King, a sermon, 6th edn; The War, a sermon, 5th edn; All Men shall at length be Saved, 2nd edn; sermons on different subjects. *Recreation:* heraldry. *Address:* 10 Sallymount Avenue, Leeson Park, Dublin.
Died 1 Aug. 1919.

CARMICHAEL, James, JP; *b* 1846; *e s* of late James Drummond of Ailly-sur-Somme, France, and Helen, *d* of Robert Stewart, and *n* of late Peter Carmichael of Arthurstone; *m* 1874, Margaret, *d* of Alexander Geekie, of Baldowrie, Co. Forfar. *Address:* Arthurstone, Meigle, Perthshire. *Club:* New, Edinburgh.
Died 14 April 1927.

CARMICHAEL-FERRALL, John, JP, DL Co. Tyrone; *b* 8 Nov 1855; *o s* of Captain Carmichael-Ferrall, RN, and Margaret, 6th *d* of Sir John Nugent Humble, 1st Bt of Clonkoscoran, Co. Waterford; *m* 1899, Elizabeth Emily, 3rd *d* of late Rev. David Henry Elrington, Vicar of Swords, and Matilda Rowena, *d* of late Rev. Pierce Wm Drew, Rector of Youghal. *Educ:* Harrow; Trinity College, Dublin. Barrister-at-law; High Sheriff, County Tyrone, 1907; Member of Council, Royal Ulster Agricultural Society. *Publications:* A Reply to Mr Hine's Identification of the British Nation with the Lost Tribes of Israel; Ireland and the Irish; The Principality of Orange and its Protestant Exiles. *Address:* Augher Castle, Augher. *TA:* Augher, Co. Tyrone. *M:* OI 4330. *Club:* Tyrone County.
Died 13 May 1923.

CARNARVON, 5th Earl of, *cr* 1793; **George Edward Stanhope Molyneux Herbert,** DL, JP; Baron Porchester, 1780; High Steward of Newbury; *b* 26 June 1866; *s* of 4th Earl and Evelyn, *d* of 6th Earl of Chesterfield; *S* father, 1890; *m* 1895, Almina, *d* of late Frederick Charles Wombwell; one *s* one *d*. *Educ:* Eton; Trinity Coll., Cambridge. Owned about 36,000 acres. *Heir: s* Lord Porchester, *b* 7 Nov. 1898. *Address:* 1 Seamore Place, W1. *T:* Gerrard 3609; Highclere Castle, Newbury; Bretby Park, Burton-on-Trent; Pixton Park, Dulverton, Somersetshire. *Clubs:* Bachelors', St James's; Royal Yacht Squadron, Cowes.
Died 5 April 1923.

CARNEGIE, Andrew; philanthropist; manufacturer; *b* Dunfermline, 15 Nov. 1835; *m* 1887, Louise Whitfield of New York; one *d*. Went with family to America (Pittsburgh), 1848; first work was as weaver's assistant in cotton factory, Allegheny, Pa; became telegraph messenger boy in Pittsburgh office of Ohio Telegraph Co., 1851; learned telegraphy, entered employ Pennsylvania Railroad Co., and became telegraph operator, advancing by promotions until he became Supt, Pittsburgh Div., Pa System; joined Mr Woodruff, inventor of the sleeping car, in organising Woodruff Sleeping Car Co., gaining through it nucleus of his fortune; careful investments in oil lands increased his means. During Civil War served as Supt Mil. Rlys and Govt Telegraph Lines in the East; after war developed ironworks of various kinds, and established at Pittsburgh Keystone Bridge Works and Union Ironworks; introduced Bessemer process of making steel, 1868; was principal owner a few years later of Homestead and Edgar Thomson Steel Works, and other large plants, as head of firms of Carnegie, Phipps, and Co., and Carnegie Bros and Co.; interests were consolidated, 1889, in the Carnegie Steel Co., which in 1901 was merged in the United States Steel Corporation, when he retired from business; gave libraries to many towns and cities in the US and Great Britain, and large sums in other benefactions; a life trustee of Carnegie Corporation of New York foundation to carry on various works in which he was engaged; Hon. Mem. AIA; Mem. Exec. Com. Nat. Civic Federation; Mem. Am. Philos. Soc.; Life Mem. Lotos Club; Mem. Indian Harbour Yacht Club; Mem. Riding Club; Life Mem. St Andrews Club; Mem. Chamber of Commerce, etc. Comdr Legion of Honour, France, 1907; Grand Cross, Order of Orange Nassau; Grand Cross, Order of Danebrog; received the freedom of fifty-three cities in Great Britain and Ireland; Lord Rector St Andrews University, 1903–7; Aberdeen University, 1912–14. *Publications:* An American Four-in-Hand in Britain, 1883; Round the World, 1884; Triumphant Democracy, 1886 (new edition 1893); The Gospel of Wealth, 1900; The Empire of Business, 1902 (translated into eight languages); Life of James Watt, 1906; Problems of To-day, 1908. *Address:* 2 East 91st Street, New York; Skibo Castle, Sutherland, NB. *TA:* Clashmore, Sutherland.
Died 11 Aug. 1919.

CARNEGY, Col Charles Gilbert, MVO 1911; *b* 29 June 1864; *s* of late General Alexander Carnegy, CB, cadet of family of Northesk; *m* 1892, Evelyn Mary, *d* of late Charles John Collins Prichard, of Pwllywrach, Co. Glamorganshire; one *s*. *Educ:* Clifton College; Sandhurst. Gazetted as Lieut to 2nd E York Regiment, 1884; joined Indian Army, 1886; served in Burmah Campaign, 1886–87 (medal and two clasps); King George V Coronation Durbar at Delhi (medal); European War, 1914–18 (Bt-Col, medal); 2nd Class Order of St Stanislas; ADC to Gen. Sir Stanley Edwardes, KCB, 1887–89; Captain, 1895; Major, 1902; Lt-Col, 1909; Bt Col, 1917. *Recreation:* golf. *Address:* The Grove, Stutton, near Ipswich, Suffolk.
Died 23 April 1928.

CARNEGY, Maj.-Gen. Sir Philip Mainwaring, KCB 1921 (CB 1911); *b* 12 Dec. 1858; *s* of late Maj.-Gen. P. A. Carnegy and Catherine Chitty; *m* 1897, Jessie Pyne, *d* of late Maj.-Gen. J. S. Rawlins, Indian Army; no *c*. *Educ:* Dollar Academy; Cheltenham College; Royal Military College, Sandhurst. Entered Army, 67th Regt 1878; Capt ISC 1889; Major Indian Army, 1898; Lieut-Col 1904; Col 1907; Maj.-Gen. 1912; AAG and AQMG India, 1909–10; Brigade Commander, Abbottabad Brigade, 1910–12; Jullundur Brigade, 1912–15; Indian Army, 1915; Indian Army, Retired List, 1919; served Afghan War, 1878–80 (despatches, medal with two clasps); Burma, 1885–86 (severely wounded, despatches, medal with clasp); Chin-Lushai Expedition, 1888–90 (clasp); Burma, 1889 (clasp); Manipur, 1891 (severely wounded, despatches, clasp); Chitral, 1895 (medal with clasp); Tirah, 1897–98 (despatches, clasp); China, 1900 (medal); European War, 1914–15 (despatches, Bronze Star 1914 with clasp); British Gen. Service and Victory Medals; Delhi Durbar Medal, 1911. *Recreation:* sport in moderation. *Address:* New Court, Tenbury, Worcestershire. *T:* Tenbury 34.
Died 8 Dec. 1927.

CARNOCK, 1st Baron, *cr* 1916, of Carnock; **Arthur Nicolson,** Bt 1637; GCB 1907 (KCB 1901); GCMG 1906 (CMG 1886); GCVO 1905 (KCVO 1903); KCIE 1888; PC 1905; Permanent Under-Secretary for Foreign Affairs, 1910; retired, 1916; *b* 19 Sept. 1849; *s* of Sir Frederick Nicolson, 10th Bt and Mary, *d* of James Loch of Drylaw; *S* father as 11th Bt, 1899; *m* 1882, Mary Katherine, *d* of Capt. Archibald Rowan Hamilton, Killyleagh Castle, Co. Down; three *s* one *d*. *Educ:* Rugby; Brasenose College, Oxford; left before taking degree. Foreign Office, 1870–74; Assistant Private Secretary to Earl Granville, 1872–74; 3rd Sec. Embassy at Berlin, 1874–76; 2nd Sec. Legation at Pekin, 1876–78; Berlin, 1878–79; 2nd Sec. at Constantinople, 1879–84; Chargé d'Affaires, Athens, 1884–85; 1st Sec. and Chargé d'Affaires, Teheran, 1885–88; Consul-Gen. Budapest, 1888–93; Sec. of Embassy, Constantinople, 1894; Agent in Bulgaria, 1894–95; Minister in Morocco, 1895–1904; HM's Ambassador Extraordinary and Plenipotentiary at Madrid, 1904–5; Ambassador to Russia, 1905–10. Hon. Fellow Brasenose College. Grand Cross, Legion of Honour; Grand Cross, Carlos III of Spain; Grand Cross, Alexander Nevsky. *Publication:* History of the German Constitution, 1873. *Recreations:* riding, tennis, sailing. *Heir: s* Hon. Frederick Archibald Nicolson, *b* 9 Jan. 1883. *Address:* 53 Cadogan Gardens, SW3. *T:* Victoria 4141. *Club:* Travellers'.
Died 5 Nov. 1928.

CAROLUS-DURAN, Emile Auguste; painter; *b* Lille, 1838; *m* Pauline Marie Croizette, herself an artist; one *s* two *d*. Studied under Souchon. *Educ:* Académie de Lille, Paris. Gained Wicar travelling scholarship and went to Italy. Resided in Spain. Works—La Prière du Soir, 1863; L'Assassine, 1866; St Francis of Assisi, 1868; The Lady with the Glove. Portraits of Emile Gerardin, Mlle Sophia Croizette, Queen Maria Pia of Portugal, Countess de Pourtales, Countess of Warwick, Countess de Vandal, Princess de Wagram, Duchess of

Marlborough. Commander of the Legion of Honour, 1889, Grand Officier; Commander of Order of Leopold; Grand Officier de St Maurice et Lazare; Grand Croix d'Isabelle la Catholique (Espagne); Commandeur Charles III (Espagne); Commandeur Christ de Portugal; Médaille de Sauvetage, etc; Président d'Honneur de la Société Nationale des Beaux-Arts; Membre de l'Institut; Directeur honoraire de l'Académie de France à Rome (Villa Médicis). *Address:* 11 Passage Stanislas, Paris. *Died 18 Feb. 1917.*

CARPENTER, Capt. Alfred, DSO 1887; AM; RN; FRMetSoc, FZS; retired; *b* Brighton, 2 Aug. 1847; *s* of Commander Charles Carpenter, RN; *m* 1st, 1879, Henrietta, *d* of G. A. F. Shadwell; one *s* one *d*; 2nd, 1891, Etheldreda, *d* of Judge Homersham Cox of Tonbridge. *Educ:* Brighton College. Entered Royal Navy, 1861; Lieut. 1870; Commander, 1883; retired Capt. 1895; served in "Challenger" Scientific Expedition (Albert medal 2nd class for saving life); Soudan Expedition, 1884, in command of "Myrmidon" (medal and thanks of Admiralty); and whilst in charge of Marine Survey of India piloted the war flotilla under fire to Mandalay and Bhamo, 1885 (specially mentioned in despatches, Burma medal and DSO); nine years in command of surveying vessels; last service, HM Coastguards at Cowes. *Publication:* Nature Notes for Ocean Voyagers. *Recreations:* billiards, golf; interested in collections of corals, and in astronomy. *Address:* The Red House, Sanderstead, Surrey. *TA:* Sanderstead. *Club:* Authors'. *Died 30 April 1925.*

CARPENTER, Rev. J. Estlin, Hon. DD Glas., DTheol Jena and Geneva; *b* 1844; 2nd *s* of William B. Carpenter, CB, MD, FRS; *m* 1878. *Educ:* University College School, London; University and Manchester New Colleges. MA Lond, DLitt and DD Oxford. Minister Oakfield Road Church, Clifton, 1866–69; Mill Hill Chapel, Leeds, 1869–75; Lecturer in Manchester College London and Oxford, 1875–1906; Principal, 1906–15; Wilde Lecturer, Oxford, 1914. *Publications:* Editor of Ewald's History of Israel, vols iii–v; translator of Tiele's Outlines of the History of Religion; author of the Life and Work of Mary Carpenter; Life in Palestine; The First Three Gospels, their Origin and Relations; The Bible in the Nineteenth Century; James Martineau, Theologian and Teacher; Phases of Early Christianity; Theism in Medieval India, 1921; joint-editor with Prof. Rhys Davids of the Dīgha Nikāya, and the Sumangala Vilāsinī; Buddhism and Christianity, 1923; joint-editor with Rev. G. Harford-Battersby of The Hexateuch according to the Revised Version; joint-author (with Rev. P. H. Wicksteed) of Studies in Theology; and other works. *Address:* 11 Marston Ferry Road, Oxford. *Died 2 June 1927.*

CARPENTER-GARNIER, John; *b* 28 Feb. 1839; *o s* of late John Carpenter, of Mount Tavy, Tavistock, Devon (*d* 1842), and Lucy, *d* of Rev. William and Lady Harriett Garnier, of Rookesbury Park, Fareham, Hants; succeeded to Devon property on coming of age, 1860; and to Rookesbury Park on the death of his uncle, William Garnier; under whose will he assumed the name of Garnier in addition to Carpenter; *m* 1868, Hon. Mary Louisa (*d* 1903), 2nd *d* of 19th Baron Clinton; three *s* three *d*. *Educ:* Harrow; Christ Church, Oxford. BA 1860; MA 1863 (was in the Harrow and Oxford Cricket Elevens). Contested South Hants as a Conservative, 1868; MP South Devon, 1873–84; Sheriff for Hants, 1890–91; JP and DL for Hants and Devon. *Address:* Rookesbury Park, Fareham, Hants. *TA:* Wickham, Hants. *Died 5 Oct. 1926.*

CARR, David; artist; *b* London, 1847; *m* Helen, *d* of James Wrigley of Netherton, Yorks; one *d*. *Educ:* Bruce Castle School, Tottenham. Applied Science Dept of King's Coll., London. Was articled as a pupil to W. H. Barlow, CE, Consulting Engineer to the Midland Rly, and for a time followed the profession of a Civil Engineer; relinquishing this, entered as an art student for three years at the Slade Schools, London University, under Prof. Legros, going later to Paris for further study; a continuous exhibitor at the Grosvenor Gallery from its commencement and afterwards at the New Gallery; also at the Royal Academy Institute, Munich, Melbourne, Sydney, etc; wrote and illustrated articles in the Pall Mall Gazette and Illustrated Magazines, and having added the profession of architecture to that of painting, designed country houses, including houses at Beer, Budleigh Salterton, Crewkerne, Exmouth, Frimley and London, etc. *Recreations:* fly-fishing, boating. *Address:* Beer Haven, Beer, S Devon. *TA:* Beer, Devon. *Died 25 Dec. 1920.*

CARR, Rev. Edmund; inherited from his cousin, the late Sir T. W. Evans, Bt, of Allestree Hall, Derbyshire, his estates in Holbrooke, Derbyshire, and at Boscobel, Shropshire; *b* 1 June 1826; *o surv. s* of Rev. J. E. Carr of The Outwoods, Derbyshire; *m* 1st, 1858, Emma Anne, *y d* of late R. Stileman of The Friars, Winchelsea, Sussex; 2nd,

1873, Mary Fanny, *o d* of late Lt-Col Thomas Salkeld of Holm H[ill] Cumberland; 3rd, 1881, Mary (*d* 1904), *e surv. d* of late Rev. Willia[m] Leeke, Vicar of Holbrooke, Derbyshire; three *s* two *d*. *Educ:* King[s] Coll., London; St John's Coll., Cambridge; BA (32nd Wrangler) 184[?] MA 1851. Ordained Deacon, 1849; Priest, 1850; Curate of Barfo[rd] St Martin, Wilts, 1849–56; Rector of Bonchurch, Isle of Wigh[t] 1856–61; Perpetual Curate of Casterton, Westmoreland, 1861–6[?] Vicar of Dalston, Cumberland, 1866–83; Vicar of Holbrook[e] Derbyshire, 1883–1907; Hon. Canon of Carlisle since 18[?] Examining Chaplain to the late Bishop (Waldegrave) of Carlis[le] 1863–69; Proctor in York Convocation for the Archdeaconry [of] Carlisle, 1874–86; Rural Dean of Wigton, Cumberland, 1880–8[?] Rural of Dean of Duffield, Derbyshire, 1894–1900. *Addres[s]* Holbrooke Hall, near Derby. *TA:* Holbrooke, Derbyshire. *Died 12 May 191[?]*

CARR, Col Edward Elliott, CB 1900; CBE 1919; Colonel in char[ge] of Records, Lowland Group of Regimental Districts, Scotland; retire[d] 1909; *b* 31 May 1854; *s* of Dep. Surg.-Gen. J. K. Carr, MD, R[?] *m* 1883, Rosa Elizabeth, *e d* of Rev. A. Hall; one *s*. *Educ:* tuto[r] Entered Army, 1873; Captain, 1883; Major, 1891; Lt-Col 189[?] employed on Staff NE District, 1893–96; served in Tirah Campaig[n] 1897 (medal with two clasps); SA Campaign, 1899–1901 (wounde[d] CB, despatches, Queen's medal four clasps, King's medal two clasp[s] A Staff Lowland Division, 1914; Inspector L of C Home, 1914–1[?] Commanding Base Depot, France, 1915–16; Reinforcement[s] 1916–18 (despatches twice, CBE). *Recreations:* hunting, crick[et] *Address:* Hilton, Sidmouth, Devon. *Clubs:* Army and Navy, Bat[h] *Died 18 May 192[6]*

CARR, J. W. Comyns; critic and dramatist; *b* 1 March 1849; *m* Mi[ss] Strettell. *Educ:* London Univ. Barrister, Inner Temple, 1869. A[rt] Critic on the Pall Mall Gazette; English editor of L'Art, 1875; Directo[r] and one of the founders of the New Gallery. *Publications:* Drawing[s] by the Old Masters, 1877; The Abbey Church of St Albans, 187[8] Examples of Contemporary Art 1878; Essays on Art; Papers on Ar[t] Founder and late Editor of The English Illustrated Magazine; join[t-] author of Called Back, Dark Days, Boys Together, In the Days [of] the Duke, and The Beauty Stone; author of A Fireside Hamlet, Th[e] United Pair, The Naturalist, The Friar, Forgiveness, King Arthu[r] Oliver Twist and Tristram and Iseult; Some Eminent Victorian[s] Coasting Bohemia, 1914. *Address:* 12 Northwick Terrace, St John'[s] Wood, NW. *Club:* Garrick. *Died 12 Dec. 191[6]*

CARR, Most Rev. Thomas Joseph, DD; RC Archbishop [of] Melbourne and Metropolitan of Victoria since 1886; *b* Co. Galway[,] 1839. *Educ:* St Jarlath's, Tuam; Maynooth. Priest, 1866; parish wor[k] at Westport; Professor at St Jarlath, Tuam; was Professor of Theology[,] Dean and Vice-President of Maynooth; Editor Irish Ecclesiastica[l] Record, 1880–83; Bishop of Galway and Kilmacduagh, and Apostoli[c] Administrator of Kilfenora, 1883–86. *Publications:* A Commentar[y] on the Constitution; Apostolicae Sedis Moderationi, 1879; a serie[s] of Lectures and Replies in connection with a polemical attack by the Anglican Bishops of Melbourne and Ballarat, 1895; The Blesse[d] Eucharist; Belief of the Early English Church, 1912. *Address[,]* Melbourne, Australia. *Died 6 May 1917*

CARR, Sir William St John, Kt 1905; *b* 21 Feb. 1848; *s* of Captain John Carr of The Lodge, Clonmel, Ireland; *m* 1878, Sarah, *d* of E[?] Slater of Port Elizabeth; one *s* one *d*. *Educ:* privately; French College Blackrock; matriculated at Catholic University of Dublin[.] Commenced life as midshipman in mercantile service, visiting New Zealand, Australia, China, Cochin China, Japan, Siam, etc[;] subsequently in 1869 went to India, and was on the Great Indian Peninsula Railway till 1874; then went to South Africa and entered the service of the Cape Government Railways; in 1887 went to Johannesburg, where he was, after some experience of the early days of the goldfields, eventually a director of some mining and other companies, and was first Chairman of the Hospital Board; was prominent member of the National Union, a political organisation started in the Transvaal about 1891; later was a member of the Reform Committee, and was imprisoned at Pretoria at the time of the Jameson Raid, being one of those sentenced to two years' imprisonment; at the commencement of the Boer War joined the Imperial Light Horse, was in the siege of Ladysmith, and served with his regiment till appointed deputy-Chairman of the Town Council of Johannesburg[,] in May 1901; was thereafter acting Chairman till his election as first Mayor of Johannesburg in 1903; Chairman of the Rand Water Board, 1904–7; created Knight of Saint Gregory by Pius X, 1907; JP. *Club:* Rand, Johannesburg. *Died 23 June 1928.*

CARR-GOMM, Francis Culling, VD; *b* 1834; 2nd *s* of late Rev. T. W. Carr of Southborough, Kent; *m* 1st, Jeanie (*d* 1869), *d* of Maj. E. Francklyn; three *s* one *d*; 2nd, 1876, Emily Blanche (*d* 1909), *d* of late A. Morton Carr, Barrister-at-law, and niece of FM Sir W. M. Gomm, GCB, Constable of the Tower of London; Mrs Carr-Gomm was Lady of the Manor of Rotherhithe; they assumed by Royal Licence the surname and arms of Gomm, 1878; two *s* one *d*. *Educ:* Cheam School; HEIC's College, Haileybury. Madras CS, retired; for many years District Judge of Tinnevelly, South India; Barrister, Inner Temple, 1869; JP, DL, Bucks; High Sheriff, 1894; late chairman London Hospital; late Hon. Col 3rd VB The Queen's RW Surrey. Liberal. *Publications:* Life of Sir William Gomm; Handbook of Administrations of Nineteenth Century; Records of the Parish of Farnham Royal. *Address:* The Chase, Farnham Royal, Bucks. *TA:* Carr-Gomm, Farnham-Common. *T:* 37 Farnham Common. *Club:* East India United Service.   *Died 12 Jan. 1919.*

CARRICK-BUCHANAN, David William Ramsay; of Drumpellier, etc; *b* 9 March 1834; *e s* of Andrew Buchanan (2nd *s* of D. Carrick-Buchanan, of Drumpellier) and Bethia, *d* of late William Ramsay; *m* 1863, Lady Kathleen Alicia Hely-Hutchinson (*d* 1892), *e d* of 3rd Earl of Donoughmore, KP; one *s* two *d*. *Educ:* Rugby; Edinburgh University. Was Captain 2nd R. Lanark Regiment, and Sec. of Commissions in the Court of Chancery. *Address:* Corsewall, Stranraer, NB. *TA:* Kirkolm. *Clubs:* Junior Carlton; New, Edinburgh.   *Died 4 May 1925.*

CARROLL, Hon. Sir James, KCMG 1911; MLC New Zealand, since 1921; Native Minister and Commissioner of Stamp Duties, 1900–12; Member of House of Representatives for Waiapu, 1893–1908, and for Gisborne, 1908–19; *b* Wairoa, Hawkes Bay, NZ, 20 Aug. 1857; *m* Heni Materoa, OBE. Native Interpreter to the House of Representatives, 1879–83; Member of the House of Representatives for the Eastern Maori Electoral Dist, 1887–93; became a member of the Executive Council representing the native race in the Ballance Govt 1892, and continued to hold same office in Seddon Govt; became Commissioner of Stamp Duties, 1896; assumed the portfolio of Native Minister, 1900 (the first of his race to hold that position); was acting Premier of NZ on occasion of Coronation of King George V. *Address:* Kahutia Road, Gisborne, NZ.

     Died 18 Oct. 1926.

CARROLL, Brig.-Gen. John William Vincent, CMG 1916; DSO 1919; *b* 12 July 1869; *e s* of late Frederick Maxwell Carroll, JP, of Moone Abbey, Co. Kildare; *m* 1901, Barbara Mary, *y d* of late James Tisdall Woodroffe, CSI; two *s* two *d*. *Educ:* Woburn; Oratory School. 2nd Lieut Norfolk Regt 1891; served in W Africa, Northern Nigeria, 1895–99 (2 medals and 6 clasps, despatches, Bt-Major); served in S African War in Mounted Infantry, 1899–1901 (Queen's medal and 3 clasps); Commandant Mounted Infantry, Egypt, 1909; Lt-Col Commanding Mounted Infantry, South Africa, 1910; Lt-Col Commanding 7th (Service) Batt. Norfolk Regt 1914–15; served European War (despatches, CMG); Commanded the Russian Force at Morjegorskaia, Mar. 1919 (DSO, St George's Cross, 4th Class, St Vladimir 4th Class). *Recreations:* steeplechase riding, polo, cricket, hunting. *Club:* Naval and Military.

     Died 16 Jan. 1927.

CARRUTHERS, William, PhD; FRS, FLS, FGS; *b* Moffat, 1830; *s* of Samuel Carruthers, merchant; *m* 1865, Jeanie, *e d* of Wm Moffatt, architect, Edinburgh; one *s*. *Educ:* Edin. Univ. and New Coll. Late Keeper of the Botanical Department, British Museum; Pres. Linn. Soc. 1886–90; Pres. Royal Micros. Soc., 1900–1; Consulting Botanist, Royal Agricultural Society, England, 1871–1910; Member of the Lawes Agricultural Trust Committee; author of many papers on Systematic, Palæontological, and Agricultural Botany; pursued as a by-study the history and literature of Puritan England and formed a considerable collection of works thereon. *Publications:* a facsimile edition of the Shorter Catechism, with full bibliography; editor of the Annals and Magazine of Natural History and of Children's Messenger, Presbyterian Church of England. *Address:* 44 Central Hill, Norwood, SE. *T:* 117 Sydenham.

     Died 2 June 1922.

CARSON, Maj.-Gen. Sir John Wallace, Kt 1917; CB 1916; Reserve of Officers, Canadian Militia Force; Canadian Expeditionary Force; Director, Union Bank of Canada; Vice-President, Crown Trust Company; Director, Crown Reserve Mining Co. and Associated Co.; Lake of the Woods Milling Co.; *b* 13 Oct. 1864; *s* of late William and Mary Johnston Carson; *m* 1885, Mary A. R., *d* of late Henry Coran of St John's, PQ; two *d*. *Educ:* Public and High Schools, Montreal. Served in Canadian Militia for a total period of 39 years; served

European War, 1914–18 (despatches, CB, Order of St Stanislas of Russia). *Address:* 4113 Sherbrooke Street, Westmount, Montreal.   *Died 13 Oct. 1922.*

CARSON, Murray; actor-dramatist; *b* 17 March 1865; *m* Mary Eleanor Stirling, *y d* of J. S. Donald, late of Australia. Made first appearance on stage, 1882; visited America, 1906. *Plays* produced in collaboration: David Gudgeons: The Blue Boar; Spell-bound Garden; Rosemary; Change Alley; The Jest; The Fly on the Wheel; A Man Himself; When a Man's Married; The Trifler; The Bishop's Move; Simple Simon, etc. *Recreations:* golf, billiards, travelling. *Address:* 7 Cowley Street, Westminster Abbey, SW. *T:* 3598 Westminster. *Clubs:* National Liberal, Royal Automobile.   *Died 20 April 1917.*

CARSON, Thomas Henry, KC 1901; *b* 24 Nov. 1843; *s* of Rev. Joseph Carson, DD, late Vice-Provost of Trinity College, Dublin; *m* 1st, 1876, Mary Sophia, 3rd *d* of late Rev. Comyns Tucker; 2nd, 1887, Marie Louise Emma, *d* of Albert Bernouilli Barlow of Le Havre, France; one *s*. *Educ:* Marlborough Coll.; Trinity College, Dublin. Scholar, 1863; Berkeley Medallist; Wray Prize; BA 1866, as first Gold Medallist in classics, first Gold Medallist in philosophy, and obtaining a Univ. studentship; MA 1867. Barrister, Lincoln's Inn, 1869; Bencher of Lincoln's Inn, 1907. *Publications:* Lectures on Prescription and Custom; joint-editor of Carson's Real Property Statutes; Tudor's Leading Cases and Real Property and Conveyancing; and of the Equity articles in Lord Halsbury's Laws of England; editor of Gale on Easements, 9th edn. *Recreations:* member of the Alpine Club and of English and French cycling clubs. *Address:* 4 Vicarage Gardens, W. *T:* 1360 Park; 6 New Square, Lincoln's Inn, WC. *T:* 8251 City. *Club:* Athenæum.   *Died 30 June 1917.*

CARTER, Alfred Henry, MD; MSc; FRCP; Consulting Physician (retired); *b* Pewsey, Wilts, 1849; *s* of C. H. Carter, FRCS; *m* 1st, 1885, Constance Mary, *d* of Albert C. Goode, The Glebe, Moseley, Birmingham; one *s*; 2nd, 1890, Elizabeth Marian, *d* of W. H. King, Solicitor, Pedmore House, Stourbridge; one *s* one *d*. *Educ:* Epsom College; University College London. Emeritus Professor of Medicine, Birmingham University, 1892–1913; Consulting Physician, Queen's Hospital, Birmingham; Emeritus Professor of Physiology, Queen's Hospital, Birmingham; Emeritus Professor of Physiology, Queen's College, Birmingham; late Examiner in Medicine for London University; JP, Worcester. *Publications:* Elements of Practical Medicine, 10th edn, 1906; Text-Book of Physical Exercises for Elementary Schools, 1896; and various contributions to medical journals. *Address:* The Lindens, Abingdon, Berks. *Club:* Oxford and County.   *Died 4 April 1918.*

CARTER, Hon. Arthur John; Member of Legislative Council of Queensland since 1901; merchant; Consul for Norway; Consular Agent for France; *b* St Ives, Hunts, 27 Sept. 1847; *s* of Rev. Charles and Margaret Carter. *Educ:* Woodhouse Grove, Yorks; Harpur Schools, Bedford; King's College, London. Entered Lloyd's Underwriting Room, London, 1863; left England for Queensland, 1870; since followed mercantile pursuits; Pres. Chamber Commerce, Brisbane, 1898, 1899, 1901, 1902, 1906; nominated Marine Board, 1899; Chairman of Queensland Board of Directors, Atlas Assurance Co., Ltd, London; and of Directors, Queensland Trustees, Ltd, Millaquin Sugar Co., Ltd, E. Rich & Co., Ltd, John Hicks & Co., Ltd; Director of Dath Henderson & Co., Ltd, and Jacques Leutenegger, Ltd; Officier d'Académie (France); Chevalier de 1ère classe de l'ordre de St Olav (Norway). *Publications:* journalistic contributions to local press on Russo-Turkish war, bimetallism, and Australian national defences. *Recreations:* fishing, literature. *Address:* Queen Street and Nunnington, Main Street, Brisbane. *Clubs:* Queensland, Johnsonian.   *Died 4 Nov. 1917.*

CARTER, Maj.-Gen. Beresford Cecil Molyneux, CB 1916; CMG 1915; late Commanding South African Military Command, Capetown, SA; *b* 12 Aug. 1872; *s* of late Col H. M. Carter, CB; *m* Bertha Isabel Ada, *e d* of late Col E. Baines; three *s* two *d*. *Educ:* Marlborough College; Gold Medallist United Service Institute (India), 1912. Entered Lancashire Fusiliers, 1891; Captain, 1898; Major, 1904; Liverpool Regt 1908; Lt-Col 1914; employed with Egyptian army, 1900–7; served Nile Expedition, 1898 (Egyptian medal with clasp; medal); Sudan, 1905 (despatches, Egyptian medal with clasp, 4th class Osmanieh); European War, 1914–18 (CB, CMG, Bt-Col); retired pay, 1922. *Recreations:* big game shooting (fine collection of heads), fishing. *Address:* Ganderbal, Newbury, Berks. *T:* Newbury 244. *Club:* Junior United Service.   *Died 23 July 1923.*

CARTER, Franklin, PhD, LLD; President, Clarke School for the Deaf, 1896–1917; *b* Waterbury, Conn. 30 Sept. 1837; *s* of Preserve W.

Carter, manufacturer, and Ruth Holmes Carter; *m* 1st, 1863, Sarah L. (*d* 1905), *d* of Chas D. Kingsbury, Waterbury; three *s* one *d*; 2nd, 1908, Mrs Frederic Leake, *d* of late H. L. Sabin, MD, of Williamstown, Mass. *Educ:* Phillips Academy, Andover, Mass; Yale and Williams Coll.; Berlin Univ. Professor in Williams College, 1865–72; in Yale University, 1872–81; President of Williams College, 1881–1901; Member of Massachusetts State Board of Education, 1897–1901. *Publications:* Goethe's Iphigenie, 1877; Life of Mark Hopkins, 1892; various addresses and magazine articles. *Recreations:* riding, fishing, golf. *Address:* Williams College, Williamstown, Mass. *Clubs:* Williams, New York.

Died 22 Nov. 1919.

CARTER, Sir George (John), KBE 1917; JP; MICE, MINA, MIME; Managing Director of Cammell Laird and Co. Limited, Birkenhead; Director of Coventry Ordnance Works, Ltd; President of the Shipbuilding Employers' Federation; was Chairman of the Merchant Shipbuilding Advisory Committee to the Controller of Shipping, and later a Member of the Shipbuilding Council; Member of Council of Institute of Naval Architects, Federation of British Industries; Member of Committee, Lloyd's Register; Member of the Mersey Docks and Harbour Board; Deputy Chairman of Liverpool Munitions Committee; *b* 1860; *m* 1894, Edith Harriet, *d* of late J. S. Vaux, Sunderland; two *s*. *Educ:* privately. *Recreation:* motoring. *Address:* Brackenwood, near Bebington, Cheshire. *T:* Rock Ferry 38; Dinbren Hall, Llangollen, North Wales. *T:* Llangollen 56. *Clubs:* Constitutional, Royal Societies, Royal Automobile.

Died 9 Feb. 1922.

CARTER, Capt. Herbert Augustine, VC 1904; The 101st Grenadiers; *b* 26 May 1874; *s* of Rev. C. R. D. Carter; *m* 1911, Helen Lilian, *d* of Rev. Canon Wilmot-Ware. Served North-West Frontier, India, 1897–98 (medal with 2 clasps); Somaliland, 1902–4 (despatches, medal with 2 clasps); Somaliland, 1908–10 (despatches, clasp). *Clubs:* United Service, Sports, Royal Aero.

Died 13 Jan. 1916.

CARTER, Hugh Hoyles, KC 1904; *e surv. s* of late Hon. Sir Frederic Bowker Terrington Carter, KCMG, Chief Justice of Newfoundland. *Educ:* Bishop Field College. Clerk to Legislative Council, Newfoundland, since 1875; called to Bar, Newfoundland, 1876; Bencher of Law Society, 1902. *Recreations:* fishing and shooting. *Address:* St John's, Newfoundland.

Died 19 Feb. 1919.

CARTER, John Corrie; Barrister, Inner Temple; Recorder of Stamford, 1881–1912; Chairman of Quarter Sessions for Radnorshire, 1895–1913; *b* 1839; *s* of late S. Carter, MP; *m* Amy Josephine Lonsdale. *Educ:* Trinity College, Cambridge. West Midland Circuit; Director of Midland Railway, 1896–1910. *Publications:* editor of three editions of Rogers on Elections, and of 10th edition of Ronald's Fly Fisher's Entomology. *Recreations:* fishing, shooting, golf; steered winning boat of the four chief races at Henley in 1862, 1st Trinity, Cambridge. *Address:* 65 Sussex Gardens, W2; Cefnfaes, Rhayader, Radnorshire. *Club:* Albemarle.

Died 5 June 1927.

CARTER, John Hilton, MVO; in Masonry—Past Grand Deacon of England (PGD); Manager and Secretary of the Royal Albert Hall since 1901; *s* of late James Carter of Mansfield, Notts; *m* Alice Ann, *d* of late Samuel Robinson of Daybrook, Notts, and *niece* of Sir John Robinson of Worksop Manor, Notts; one *s* one *d*. *Educ:* Nottingham High School. A commercial education in Nottingham, afterwards Secretary respectively of the Hampstead Conservatoire, the London Organ School, the Guildhall School of Music; founder of the London Nottinghamshire Society; originator and a founder of the Royal Albert Hall Lodge (No. 2986); holder of the Coronation medals of late King Edward VII and King George V. *Recreations:* music, gardening, freemasonry. *Address:* Corona, 43 Mapesbury Road, Brondesbury, NW2. *T:* Willesden 425. *Died 9 April 1926.*

CARTER, Robert Brudenell, FRCS England; Consulting Ophthalmic Surgeon, St George's Hospital, 1893–1903; *b* Little Wittenham, Berks, 2 Oct. 1828; *s* of Thomas Carter, Maj. RM, and 2nd wife, Louisa, *d* of Richard Jeffreys of Basingstoke and Silchester; [11th in descent from Thomas Carter, a gentleman in bearing arms, who was settled at Higham, Co. Beds., in the reign of Edward IV]; *m* 1st, Helen Ann Beauchamp, *d* of John Becher; 2nd, Rachel Elizabeth, *d* of Stephen Hallpike, and *widow* of late Walter Browne; four *s*. *Educ:* London Hospital. Staff-Surgeon during Crimean War (English and Turkish medals); settled in London as Ophthalmic Surgeon, 1868; Ophthalmic Surgeon to St George's Hospital, 1870;

member General Medical Council, 1887–1900; Hunterian Professor of Pathology and Surgery, Royal College of Surgeons, 1881–82; Lumleian lecturer, Orator, Past Pres., and Hon. Fellow Med. Soc. of London; Knight of Justice and Hon. Commander Order of St John of Jerusalem. *Publications:* books on Hysteria, Education, Diseases of the Eye; articles on Eye Disease in Quain's Dictionary of Medicine and Holmes's System of Surgery; Doctors and their Work, 1903; translator of Zander on the Ophthalmoscope and of Scheffler's Optical Defects of the Eye. *Address:* 76 South Side, Clapham Common, SW.

Died 24 Oct. 1918.

CARTER-CAMPBELL, Colonel George Tupper Campbell, CB 1919; DSO 1915; 2nd Battalion Cameronians; *b* 2 April 1869; *o surv. s* of late Col Carter Campbell, Possil, Lanarks and Ardrisbaig, Argyllshire; *m* 1908, Frances Elizabeth, *d* of late Col David Ward, RE; one *s* one *d*. Entered army, 1889; Captain, 1897; Adjutant, 1899–1903; Major, 1907; Adjutant Volunteers, 1904–7; served South Africa, 1899–1902 (despatches twice; Bt Major; Queen's medal, 4 clasps; King's medal, 2 clasps); European War, 1914–17 (Bt Lt-Col and Col, DSO, CB); Temp. Brig.-Gen., Sept. 1915; Temp. Major-General, March 1918. *Club:* Army and Navy.

Died 19 Dec. 1921.

CARTER-COTTON, Francis, LLD; Baron of the Duchy of Saxe-Coburg and Gotha, 1912; First Chancellor of the University of British Columbia; Chairman of Vancouver Harbour Commission; *b* 1847; *m* Maria Emily, *d* of late Thomas Little; two *s* one *d*. Member of Legislature of British Columbia, 1890–1900, 1903–16; Finance Minister, 1898–1900; President of Council, 1904–10. *Clubs:* Vancouver, Vancouver; Union, Victoria.

Died 20 Nov. 1919.

CARTMELL, Sir Harry, Kt 1920; JP Lancashire; Mayor of Preston 1913–19; *b* 1857; *s* of James Cartmell, Manchester; *m* 1880, Annie *d* of Thomas Dewell Scott. Chairman, Preston Education Committee *Address:* 9 Victoria Road, St Annes-on-Sea. *T:* 221.

Died 11 May 1923.

CARTMELL, James Austen-; Barrister-at-Law, Lincoln's Inn; Junior Equity Counsel to Treasury and Board of Trade since 1913; *b* 12 Aug. 1862; *o s* of late Rev. James Cartmell, DD, formerly Master of Christ's College, Cambridge, and Chaplain in Ordinary to Her late Majesty and Frances Eliza, *o d* of late Rev. John Thomas Austen, formerly Rector of West Wickham and Honorary Canon of Canterbury; *m* 1st, 1886, Mary Affleck (*d* 1906), *y d* of late W. H. Peacock of Greatford Hall, Stamford; one *d*; 2nd, 1919, Constance, *d* of late James Petrie of Dufftown, Scotland. *Educ:* Rugby; Christ's College, Cambridge (Scholar, 1881–1885; First Class Classical Tripos, Part I 1884; Second Class Classical Tripos, Part II, 1885). Called to Bar, Lincoln's Inn, 1889; has throughout practised at the Chancery Bar Junior Equity Counsel to Board of Inland Revenue, and other Government Departments, 1908–13; Bencher, Lincoln's Inn, 1913. *Publications:* Abstract of Trade Mark Cases, 1892; Finance Act 1894 (Death Duties, England), 1st edn 1894, 5th edn 1912. *Address:* 2 Campden House Court, Campden Hill, W8. *T:* Park 5336. *M:* LC 412. *Clubs:* Athenæum, Brooks's, United University.

Died 28 May 1921.

CARTON, R. C.; dramatist; *s* of late George Critchett, FRCS; *m* Miss Compton; one *d*. *Publications:* Sunlight and Shadow, Liberty Hall Robin Goodfellow, The Home Secretary, A White Elephant, The Tree of Knowledge, Lord and Lady Algy, Wheels within Wheels Lady Huntworth's Experiment, The Undercurrent, A Clean Slate The Rich Mrs Repton, Mr Hopkinson, Public Opinion, Mr Preedy and the Countess; Lorrimer Sabiston, Dramatist; Eccentric Lord Comberdene; The Bear-Leaders; A Busy Day; The Off-Chance Other People's Worries, One too Many, 1922. *Address:* The Red Lodge, Acton, W3. *T:* Chiswick 1200.

Died 1 April 1928.

CARTWRIGHT, Rt. Hon. Sir Fairfax (Leighton), PC 1908 GCMG 1914 (KCMG 1908); GCVO 1909 (CVO 1906; MVO 1903); JP Oxfordshire; *b* 20 July 1857; *o surv. s* of late William Cornwallis Cartwright of Aynho; *m* 1898, Maria, *d* of Marchese Chigi Zondodari; one *s*. Attaché, 1881; 3rd Sec. 1883; 2nd Sec. 1887; h served at Berlin, Stockholm, Teheran, Madrid, Vienna, Rome; Fir Secretary, Mexico, 1899–1902; Lisbon, 1902–6; Minister-Resident at Munich, 1906–8; Ambassador to Austro-Hungary, 1908–13 retired, 1913. *Publication:* The Mystic Rose from the Garden of the King, 1925. *Address:* Aynho Park, Banbury.

Died 9 Jan. 1924.

CARTWRIGHT, Brig.-Gen. Garnier Norton, CMG 1917; DSO 1915; late RFA; *b* 7 May 1868; *s* of R. N. Cartwright, Ixworth Abbey, Suffolk; *m* 1909, Isabel, *d* of late T. J. Masters, Llanelly Hall, Llantrisant. Entered army, 1888; Captain, 1898; Major, 1903; Lt-Col, 1914; served European War, 1914–17 (despatches, DSO, CMG); retired pay, 1922. *Club:* Naval and Military.

Died 9 April 1924.

CARTWRIGHT, J. R.; KC; Deputy Attorney-General, Ontario. *Educ:* Rugby; Queen's College, Oxford; BA 1866. *Address:* Toronto, Ontario. *Died 11 Sept. 1919.*

CARTWRIGHT, Thomas Robert Brook Leslie-Melville, JP, DL; *b* 1830; 2nd *s* of late Sir Thomas Cartwright, GCH, of Aynhoe, Co. Northampton, and Maria Elizabeth Augusta, *d* of Count Von Sandizell, of Bavaria; *m* 1858, Lady Elizabeth Jane (*d* 1892), *e d* of 8th Earl of Leven and 7th Earl of Melville; four *d*. *Educ:* Merton College, Oxford. *Address:* Newbottle Manor, Banbury. *Club:* Carlton.

Died 23 Jan. 1921.

CARUS, Dr Paul; editor of the Monist and the Open Court; *b* Ilsenburg, Germany, 18 July 1852; *s* of Gustave Carus, Superintendent-General of Prussian State Church of Eastern and Western Prussia; *m* 1888, Mary Hegeler; four *s* two *d*. *Educ:* Stettin Gymnasium; Universities of Strasburg and Tübingen. *Publications:* The Ethical Problem; Fundamental Problems; The Soul of Man; Primer of Philosophy; Truth in Fiction; Monism and Meliorism; The Religion of Science; The Philosophy of the Tool; Our Need of Philosophy; Science, a Religious Revelation; The Gospel of Buddha; Karma; Nirvana; Lao-tze's Tao Teh King; Homilies of Science; The Idea of God; Buddhism and its Christian Critics; The History of the Devil; Whence and Whither; Eros and Psyche; Goethe and Schiller's Xenions; The Crown of Thorns; The Chief's Daughter; Godward; Sacred Tunes for the Consecration of Life; Kant's Prolegomena; Our Children; Das Evangelium Buddhas; The Surd of Metaphysics; La Conscience du Moi; The Nature of the State; The Dawn of a New Era; Friedrich Schiller; Kan Ying Pien; Yin Chih Wen; Chinese Life and Customs; Chinese Thought; The Rise of Man; The Story of Samson; The Bridge of Christ; God, An Enquiry and a Solution; The Foundations of Mathematics; Angelus Silesius; Edward's Dream (Busch); Christianity as the Pleroma; The Philosopher's Martyrdom; Truth on Trial; Personality; The Oracle of Yahveh; The Philosophy of Form; The Buddha (a drama); Hymns; The Principle of Relativity; The Mechanistic Principle and the Non-Mechanical; Nietzsche; Truth and other Poems; Goethe: the Man and his Philosophy; K'ung Fu Tze, a dramatic poem on the life of Confucious; The Venus of Milo; The New Morn (a dramatic poem); The Canon of Reason and Virtue (rev. edn of Tao Teh King). *Recreation:* photography. *Address:* La Salle, Illinois, USA. *TA:* Carus. *T:* 106. *Clubs:* Authors', New York; Press, University, Cliff-dwellers', Deutsche Studenten, Chicago. *Died 11 Feb. 1919.*

CARUSO, Enrico, MVO 1907; *b* Naples, 27 Feb. 1873; *m* 2nd, 1918, Dorothy, *d* of Park Benjamin, patent lawyer, New York. No special musical education. *Principal rôles:* Edgardo in Lucia; Des Grieux in Manon Lescaut; Pagliaccia; the Duke in Rigoletto; Lohengrin, etc. *Address:* Villa alle Panche, Porta San Gallo, Florence.

Died 2 Aug. 1921.

CARVILL, Patrick George Hamilton, JP; late Member of the Court of Referees in the House of Commons; *b* 1839; *s* of late Francis Carvill of Newry and Rosstrevor, Co. Down; *m* 1869, Frances Mary, *d* of Thomas McEvoy Gartlan. *Educ:* London University. English Barrister 1888 (Northern Circuit); JP Cos Down and Armagh; Sheriff Co. Armagh, 1878; MP (N) Newry, 1892–1906. *Address:* 5 King's Bench Walk, Temple, EC; 105 Pall Mall, SW; Ballyvourney, Co. Cork. *Clubs:* Reform, Ranelagh. *Died 10 Jan. 1924.*

CARYLL, Ivan; was musical director, Gaiety and Lyric Theatres; *b* Liége; *m* Maud Hill. *Educ:* Liége Conservatoire; Paris. Came to England, 1882. Composer of a large number of musical comedies, including The Earl and the Girl, The Circus Girl, The Toreador, The Spring Chicken, Our Miss Gibbs, The Lucky Star, The Duchess of Dantzic, The Little Cherub, The New Aladdin, Nelly Neil, The Girls of Gottenburg, The Pink Lady. *Address:* c/o Chappell & Co. Ltd, 50 New Bond Street, W1.

Died 29 Nov. 1921.

CASARTELLI, Rt. Rev. Louis Charles; RC Bishop of Salford since 1903; Professor of Zend and Pehlevi, Louvain, 1900–1903; Lecturer on Iranian Languages, University of Manchester, 1903–20; *b* Manchester, 14 Nov. 1852; *s* of Jos. L. Casartelli, native of Como,

Italy. *Educ:* Ushaw Coll., Durham; University of Louvain, Belgium. MA London, 1873; Dr of Oriental Literature, Louvain, 1884; Hon. DD Louvain, 1909. Ordained priest (by late Cardinal Vaughan) 1876; Master at St Bede's College, Manchester, 1877–91; Rector of St Bede's College, 1891–1903. President Manchester Statistical Society, 1898–1900; Officer of the Order of Leopold (Belgium), 1903, Commander of the Order of Leopold II (Belgium), 1919; President of the Manchester Dante Society since 1906; Member of the Court of Manchester University, 1907–20; Pres. of Manchester Egyptian Assoc. 1909–11; President of Manchester Egyptian and Oriental Society, 1917–18; Chairman of Universities Catholic Education Board, 1915–23. *Publications:* Lectures on Commercial Geography, 1884; La Philosophie religieuse du Mazdéisme sous les Sassanides, 1884; Traité de médecine Mazdéenne, traduit du Pehlevi, 1886; Sketches in History, chiefly Ecclesiastical, 1906; Moods and Tenses (verses), 1906; Leaves from my Eastern Garden (translations from Sanskrit and Avestan), 1908; The Popes in the Divina Commedia of Dante, 1921; articles, chiefly on Oriental subjects, in Le Muséon, Babylonian and Oriental Record, Dublin Review, American Catholic Encyclopædia, Hastings' Encyclopædia of Religion and Ethics, and proceedings of various Congresses of Orientalists; also in proceedings of the Manchester Statistical and Geographical Societies. *Address:* St Bede's College, Manchester, SW. *T:* Chorlton 241.

Died 18 Jan. 1925.

CASE, Thomas, MA; President of Corpus Christi College, Oxford, 1904–24; *m* 1870, Elizabeth Donn, *e d* of late Sir William Sterndale Bennett; one *s*. *Educ:* Rugby; Balliol College, Oxford. Formerly Fellow of Brasenose, Tutor of Balliol, Lecturer at Christ Church, Fellow and Tutor of Corpus Christi College, Oxford; Waynflete Professor of Moral and Metaphysical Philosophy, Oxford, 1889–1910; Hon. Fellow, Magdalen College. *Publications:* Materials for History of Athenian Democracy from Solon to Pericles, 1874; Realism in Morals, 1877; Physical Realism, 1888; St Mary's Clusters, 1893; articles on Aristotle, Logic, and Metaphysics in the Encyclopædia Britannica, 1902, 1910; contributor to Lectures on the Method of Science, 1906; Preface to Bacon's Advancement of Learning, 1907; Twelve Songs, 1918; Three Songs, 1924. *Recreation:* Oxford Univ. Eleven, 1864–67. *Address:* Corpus Christi College, Oxford. *Club:* MCC. *Died 31 Oct. 1925.*

CASGRAIN, Rt. Hon. Thomas Chase, PC; KC; LLD; Postmaster-General of Canada since 1914; *b* Detroit, 28 July 1852; *s* of Hon. Charles Eugene Casgrain, MD, CM; *m* 1st, 1878, Marie Louise (*d* 1914), *d* of late Alexander Le Moine, Quebec, one *s*; 2nd, Madame René Masson, Paris. *Educ:* Quebec Seminary; Laval University. Called to Bar, 1877; Professor of Criminal Law, Laval University, 1883; junior Counsel for the Crown at trial of Louis Riel; elected to Legislative Assembly, 1886; Attorney General, Province of Quebec, 1891–96; Member of House of Commons, 1896–1904; Batonnier General of Quebec Bar, 1903–5. *Address:* Ottawa. *Clubs:* Constitutional; Mount Royal, St James, St Denis, Montreal; Forest and Stream, Jockey, Montreal; Rideau, Ottawa; Garrison, Quebec.

Died 29 Dec. 1916.

CASHIN, Hon. Sir Michael Patrick, KBE 1918; Member House of Assembly for Ferryland District since 1893, being longest unbroken record in history of Colony; *b* Cape Broyle, 29 Sept. 1864; *s* of Richard Cashin; *m* 1888, Gertrude C., *d* of Capt. P. Mullowney, of Witless Bay; four *s* one *d*. *Educ:* St Bonaventure's College, St John's, NF. Trained for mercantile career at St John's; engaged in business of a fishery merchant at Cape Broyle, 1885, on attaining his majority; has continued same since; entered political life in Colonial General Election, 1893; joined Liberal party in 1895; remained with said party until 1905, when broke from Liberal ranks; led Independent party in Assembly until 1908, when joined with Sir Edward Morris; Minister of Finance and Customs of Newfoundland, 1909–19; Prime Minister, 1919; Leader Opposition, 1920–23; represented colony before Imperial Royal Commission on West India trade at Jamaica, Jan. 1910; Acting Prime Minister, Acting Minister of Militia, Acting Minister of Shipping, 1918; as Minister of Finance raised the first successful Victory Loan in the Colony in 1917–18; active war worker, having been Vice-Chairman of Newfoundland Patriotic Fund, and War Finance Committee; member various Committees of Patriotic Association which conducted all Colony's war activities (KBE). *Address:* Sea View, Cape Broyle, Newfoundland; Cambroil, Circular Road, St John's, Newfoundland. *TA:* Cashin, St John's.

Died 30 Aug. 1926.

CASSAL, Colonel Charles Edward, VD; FIC, FCS, FRSanI; Public Analyst for St George's, Hanover Square, 1886–1901, for the City of Westminster since 1901, the Royal Borough of Kensington since

1885, the Metropolitan Borough of Battersea since 1888, and the County of Lincoln (Administrative Counties of Kesteven and Holland) since 1890; Editor of The British Food Journal, 1899–1914; late Lt-Col (Hon. Col) Commanding The London Brigade, RGA (TF), 1908–14; *b* London, 6 Aug. 1858; *e s* of late Professor Charles Cassal, LLD, of University College, London, and the Royal Naval College, Greenwich; *m* 1880, Mary Louisa (*d* 1884), *o d* of late F. B. Pearse, FRCS; one *s* one *d*. *Educ:* University College School and University College, London (Medallist in Chemistry and in Practical Chemistry, Univ. Coll., Honours in Chemistry, University of London). Chief Demonstrator, Laboratory of Dept. of Hygiene and Public Health, Univ. Coll., 1879–88; Censor, Institute of Chemistry of Gt Brit. and Ireland, 1892–93; joined the late 1st London Royal Engineers (Vols), 1885; Lt-Col Commanding, 1902–8; PS School of Military Engineering, Chatham, 1886–87; President, Institution of Chemical Technologists, 1914–18. *Publications:* various scientific contributions and official and other Reports relating to Water-supply, Sewage Treatment and Disposal, and to the Analysis of Food and Water; The Hygienic Examination of Drinking Water (Address as Hon. President, Section VII. International Congress of Hygiene, Budapest, 1894); Records of Water Enquiries; etc. *Recreations:* riding, cycling. *Address:* 56 Oxford Gardens, Kensington, W10. *T:* Park 3815.
Died 22 Dec. 1921.

CASSARDESAIN, 9th Marquess; Richard George Eugene Rhenier de Branchefort Cassar De Sain; *b* 27 Jan. 1850; *S* 1906; *m* 1905, Mary, *d* of late James Turnbull; two *s* one *d*. *Educ:* St Ignatius College, Malta. Hereditary Knight of the Holy Roman Empire; Hon. Secretary to Committee of Privileges, Maltese Nobility. *Address:* 137 Strada Forni, Valetta, Malta; Bowyer House, Tarxien, Malta; St Paul's Bay, Malta.
Died 1927.

CASSEL, Rt. Hon. Sir Ernest Joseph, GCB 1909; GCMG 1905 (KCMG 1899); GCVO 1906 (KCVO 1901); PC 1902; *b* Cologne, 3 March 1852; *s* of Jacob Cassel, banker, Cologne; *m* 1878, Annette (*d* 1881), *d* of R. T. Maxwell; one *d* decd. *Educ:* Cologne. Rendered important services to industrial enterprises in Sweden and Great Britain. A benefactor of many charitable and philanthropic works. Commander of the Légion d'Honneur; Commander of Royal Order of Wasa of Sweden; Grand Cordon of Polar Star of Sweden; Grand Cordon Osmanieh; Order of the Rising Sun of Japan (1st Class). *Recreations:* racing and shooting. *Address:* Brook House, Park Lane, W1. *T:* Mayfair 3690; Moulton Paddocks, Newmarket; Branksome Dene, Bournemouth. *TA:* Ploughboy, London. *Clubs:* Carlton, Conservative, Garrick.
Died 21 Sept. 1921.

CASSELS, Hon. Sir Walter, Kt 1917; Judge of the Exchequer Court of Canada since 1908; *b* Quebec City, 14 Aug. 1845; *s* of Robert Cassels, General Manager Bank Upper Canada; *m* Susan, *d* of Robert Hamilton, Hamwood, Quebec. *Educ:* Quebec High School; University of Toronto (BA). Was a member of the firm of Blake, Lash, and Cassels, Toronto; called to Bar of Ontario, 1872; QC 1883. *Address:* Ottawa. *Clubs:* Toronto, Toronto Golf, Toronto; Rideau, Ottawa Country, Golf, Ottawa; Halifax; Matane Fishing.
Died 1 March 1923.

CASSELS, Rt. Rev. William Wharton; Bishop of Western China since 1895; *b* Oporto, Portugal, 11 March 1858; *s* of late John Cassels; *m* 1887; two *s* four *d*. *Educ:* Repton School; St John's Coll., Cambridge (BA 1882). Ordained 1881; Curate of All Saints, S Lambeth, 1882–85; missionary to China, 1885. *Address:* Paoning, *via* Wanhsien, Western China. *TA:* Cassels, Pao-ning, China.
Died 7 Nov. 1925.

CASTENSKIOLD, H. Grevenkop, Hon. GCVO 1913; Danish envoy extraordinary and minister plenipotentiary for the Court of St James since 1912; Chamberlain to HM the King of Denmark; *b* 28 Aug. 1862; 3rd *s* of late J. M. Grevenkop Castenskiold, of Hoerby, Denmark, and Thecla Mathilde Hochschild; *m* 1st, 1910, Anne Margrethe (Daisy) (*d* 1917), 3rd *d* of Count Frijs of Frijsenborg, Denmark; 2nd, Elisabeth Ahlefeldt Laurvig, 2nd *d* of Count W. Ahlefeldt Laurvig, of Eriksholm, Denmark. *Educ:* Roskilde and Copenhagen. Entered diplomatic service, 1888; secretary of Legation, St Petersburg, 1890–91; and again 1893–94; Berlin, 1894–1900; London, 1901–5; Envoy extraordinary and Minister plenipotentiary Christiania, 1905–10; Vienna and Rome, 1910–12. *Address:* 1 Cadogan Square, SW1. *TA:* Legadane, London. *T:* Kensington 4834. *Clubs:* Travellers', Turf, Bachelors'.
Died 28 Aug. 1921.

CASTLE, Agnes; author; *d* of Michael Sweetman, Lamberton Park, Queen's Co., Ireland; *m* Egerton Castle (*d* 1920); one *d*. *Publications:*

My Little Lady Anne, 1896; many others in collaboration with lat Egerton Castle. *Address;* Anthony Place, Hindhead, Surrey; 49 Sloar Gardens, SW1.
Died April 192.

CASTLE, Egerton, MA; FSA; author; late Chairman Egerton Smi and Co. (the Liverpool Mercury); and since amalgamation with Dai Post, a Director of Liverpool Daily Post, Mercury, and Echo, Lt was on staff of Saturday Review, 1885–94; member of the Counc and, until 1901, of the Managing Committee of the Society Authors; a Vice-President of the Navy League; *b* 12 March 185 *o s* of M. A. Castle, 2 Chapel Street (subseq. Aldford Street), Pa Lane, London; *g s* of Egerton Smith, founder of the Liverpoo Mercury; *m* Agnes, *y d* of Michael Sweetman, Lamberton Par Queen's Co. Ireland; one *d*. *Educ:* Universities of Paris and Glasgov Exhibitioner, Trinity Coll. Cambridge (Nat. Science Trip.); Inn Temple; Sandhurst. Lieut 2nd W India Regt; Capt. Royal Engine Militia (Portsmouth Div. Submarine Miners); passed through courses of submarine mining at Chatham and Gosport. *Publicatio and plays:* Schools and Masters of Fence, 1884; Bibliothe Dimicatoria, 1891; The Story of Swordsmanship, an illustrated lectu first delivered at the Lyceum Theatre by request of Henry Irvir and repeated, by command, for the Prince of Wales, 189 Consequences, a Novel, 1891; La Bella and Others, 1892; Engli Book-Plates, 1892; Saviolo, a play written for Sir Henry Irving (wi W. H. Pollock), 1893; The Light of Scarthey, a Romance, 1895; Roman du Prince Othon, a rendering in French of R. L. Stevenson Prince Otto, 1896; The Jerningham Letters, 1896; The Pride Jennico, 1898, the same, dramatised and first produced at Lyceu Theatre, New York; The Bath Comedy, the same, dramatised wi David Belasco as Sweet Kitty Bellairs (these last two novels with Agn Castle), 1899; Desperate Remedies, a play written for Richa Mansfield, of New York; Young April, a romance, 1899; Marshfie the Observer; The Secret Orchard, 1900; the same dramatised f Mr and Mrs Kendal, 1901; The House of Romance, re-collected sho stories, 1901 (published in America only); The Star-Dreamer, 19C Incomparable Bellairs, 1904; Rose of the World, 1904; French Na 1904; If Youth but Knew, 1905; My Merry Rockhurst, 1907; Flow o' the Orange, 1908; Wroth, 1908; Diamond Cut Paste, 190 Panther's Cub, 1910; The Lost Iphigenia, 1911; Love Guilds the Sce and Women Guide the Plot; The Grip of Life, 1912; Chance t Piper; The Golden Barrier, 1913; The Ways of Miss Barbara, 191 Our Sentimental Garden, 1914; Forlorn Adventures, 1915; The Ho of the House, 1915; A Little House in War Time, 1915; Wind's W 1916; Count Raven, 1916; The Black Office, 1917; Wolf Lure, 191 The Third Year in the Little House; Minniglen, 1918; The Charter Adventurer; New Wine, 1919 (the greater number with Agr Castle); etc. *Recreations:* swordsmanship (was captain of the British ep and sabre teams at the Olympic Games, 1908); rifle and pistol shootin cycling, rambling in country scenery and old towns. *Address:* Antho Place, Hindhead, Surrey; 49 Sloane Gardens, SW1. *T:* Victoria 153 *Clubs:* Athenæum, Garrick, London Fencing, Authors'.
Died 16 Sept. 192

CASTLE, Marcellus Purnell, MVO 1911; JP; *b* 28 Oct. 1849; *s* late H. Castle of Southfields, Surrey; *m* 1st, 1873, Florence (*d* 187 *d* of S. Mason, JP; 2nd, 1906, Helene, *d* of Jean Kübler, Gene *Address:* Oakhill House, Sevenoaks. *Club:* Conservative.
Died 21 March 191

CASTLE, Walter Frances Raphael, DSC; MD Cambridge, MRC London; Physician in charge of skin departments, Queen's Hosp for Children, West End Hospital for nervous diseases, Kensingtc Chelsea and Fulham General Hospital; *b* London, 1892; *s* of L. Castle; *m* 1921, Kathleen, *d* of C. D. Seligman; one *s* one *d*. *Ec* Wellington College; Trinity College, Cambridge; London Hospi Honours, Natural Sciences, Cambridge; temp. Surgeon, Royal Nav 1914–19; Archangel Expedition, 1919. *Publications:* many scient medical papers, including The Ætiology of Scleroder Epidermolysis bullosa, Erythomélie. *Recreations:* golf, cricket, fishi ice hockey. *Address:* 10 Upper Berkeley Street, W1; 43 Queen An Street, W1. *T:* Paddington 303. *M:* XY 5996.
Died 1 July 192

CASTLESTEWART, 6th Earl, *cr* 1800; **Andrew John Stua** Viscount Stuart 1793; Barony, 1619; Baronetcy, 1628; *b* 21 Dec. 18 *s* of late Rev. the Hon. Andrew Godfrey Stuart and Hon. Cathern Anne Wingfield, *d* of 5th Viscount Powerscourt; *S* cousin, 1914 1876, Emma Georgiana, *d* of General Arthur Stevens; two *s* on (and two *s* decd). Late Madras Civil Service. Owned 36,000 acr *Heir:* *s* Viscount Stuart, *b* 6 Aug. 1889. *Address:* Stuart H Stewartstown, SO, Co. Tyrone.
Died 7 Nov. 19.

CATHCART, 5th Earl, *cr* 1814; **George Cathcart;** Viscount Cathcart, 1807; Baron Greenock (United Kingdom), and 14th Baron Cathcart (Scotland), 1447; *b* 26 June 1862; 3rd *s* of 3rd Earl Cathcart and Elizabeth Mary (*d* 1902), *e d* and *heir* of Sir Samuel Crompton, Bt (extinct); *S* brother, 1911; *m* 1919, Vera (whom he divorced, 1922), *d* of late John Fraser, of Cape Town, and *widow* of Captain de Grey Warter, 4th Dragoon Guards; one *s*. Late Lieut 4th Batt. PWO Yorks Regt. *Heir: s* Lord Greenock, *b* 22 Aug. 1919. *Address:* 39 Bryanston Square, W1. *Clubs:* Bachelors', Carlton.

Died 19 Nov. 1927.

CATHCART, Sir Reginald Archibald Edward, 6th Bt, *cr* 1703; DL; Captain Coldstream Guards, 1863 (retired); *b* 1838; *s* of Sir John Andrew Cathcart, 7th Bt and Lady Eleanor Kennedy, *d* of Archibald, Earl of Cassilis; *S* father 1878; *m* 1880, Emily, *d* of John Robert Pringle, and *g d* of Sir John Pringle, 5th Bt, of Stichill, and *widow* of late John Gordon of Cluny, Aberdeenshire. *Educ:* Harrow. Owned about 18,000 acres. *Heir:* none. *Address:* 43 Brook Street, W; Titness Park, Sunninghill; Killochan, Maybole, NB. *Clubs:* Carlton, Guards'.

Died 14 May 1916 (ext).

CATHELS, Rt. Rev. David, MA, DD (Edin); Minister of parish of Hawick since 1892; Moderator of the General Assembly of the Church of Scotland, 1924–25; *b* Arbroath, Forfarshire, 1853; *m* 1st, Mildred Margaret, *d* of Peter Gardner of Grange Academy, Edinburgh; 2nd, Margaret Agnes, *d* of John Hewat, Bank of Scotland, Edinburgh; two *s* three *d*. *Educ:* Edinburgh University. Minister of Kirkton, Roxburghshire, 1882–92; Delegate from Foreign Mission Committee of Church of Scotland to Missions in China, especially in Yangtse Valley, 1913–14; Officiating minister to the troops throughout World War; widely interested in educational and social matters throughout the Borders; Associate of Society for Psychical Research. *Publications:* pamphlets and numerous articles on educational and social subjects. *Recreations:* cycling, golf. *Address:* The Manse, Hawick, Roxburghshire. *T:* Hawick 217.

Died 16 June 1925.

CATLING, Thomas; ex-President British International Association of Journalists; *b* Cambridge, 23 Sept. 1838; 3rd *s* of Edward Catling, florist; *m* 1860; four *s* five *d*. *Educ:* private schools in Cambridge; Working Men's Coll. London. Worked for twelve years in the composing-room of Lloyd's Weekly London News; news editor, 1866; editor, 1884; retired, 1907. Travelled through America to the Pacific and Canada, 1893; Holy Land and Syria, 1898; up the Nile to Khartoum, 1900; Algeria and Kabylia, 1901; Egyptian Desert and Spain, 1903; Corsica, 1904; Cairo, 1905; Austria, 1906; Dalmatia, Bosnia, and Herzegovina, 1907; Delegate to Conference of the International Association of Journalists at Berlin, 1908; North Cape for Midnight Sun, 1909; Portugal, 1910; Southern France, 1911; Helonan, 1912; France in time of war. *Publications:* mainly journalistic—had sole charge of literary reviews for Daily Chronicle, 1878–90; edited The Press Album in aid of Journalists' Orphan Fund, 1909; Autobiography, 1910. *Recreation:* travel. *Address:* Heronville, St James's Road, Brixton, SW. *Clubs:* Savage, Whitefriars.

Died 25 Dec. 1920.

CATON, Richard, CBE 1920; MD, LLD Edin., Padua, and Liverpool; FRCP; JP; Ex-Pro-Chancellor and Emeritus Professor in University of Liverpool; ex-President and Consulting Physician Liverpool Royal Infirmary; ex-Lord Mayor of Liverpool; family came from Heysham and Caton, Lancashire; *m* Annie, *d* of William Ivory, of St Roque, Edinburgh; two *d*. *Educ:* Scarborough Grammar School; Univ. of Edinburgh. Member General Medical Council since 1904; Harveian Orator, and late Member Council Royal College of Physicians; Vice-Chairman Liverpool Cathedral Executive Committee; late Chairman of Liverpool Committee for Housing of Poor; late Chairman Secondary Education Committee; ex-Vice-Pres. of University Council; late Chairman Liverpool branch of Classical Association; Member of Hellenic Society, and Vice-Chairman of Liverpool School of Tropical Medicine; late President Liverpool Medical Institution; late Hon. Col West Lancs Div., RAMC (Territorials); Chairman West Lancashire Territorial Nursing Service Committee. *Publications:* Temples and Ritual of Asklepios; Prevention of Valvular Disease of the Heart; Iemhotep and Ancient Egyptian Medicine; How to Live; etc. *Recreations:* travel, mountain climbing, sketching. *Address:* 7 Sunnyside, Princes Park, Liverpool. *T:* Royal 5168. *M:* S 7008. *Clubs:* Athenæum, University, Liverpool.

Died 2 Jan. 1926.

CATOR, Rev. William Lumley Bertie; Hon. Canon of Southwell. *Educ:* Trinity Coll., Cambridge. Ordained priest, 1860. Curate, Salisbury, Leics, Yorks, 1858–72; Incumbent, E Hardwick, Pontefract, 1872–77; Rector, Eakring, Newark, 1877–; RD of Southwell, 1887–92. *Address:* Eakring, Newark.

Died 1918.

CAULFEILD, Colonel Gordon Napier, DSO 1893; Indian army, retired; *b* 27 Jan. 1862; *s* of late Col Robert Caulfeild; *m* 1902, Mildred, *y d* of Philip O'Reilly, DL; two *d*. Served Burmese Expedition, 1885–89 (medal with two clasps); Wontho Expedition, 1891 (clasp); Northern Chin Hills, 1892–93 (DSO clasp); commanded 17th (Reserve) Batt. Durham Light Infantry, 1914.

Died 17 March 1922.

CAULFEILD, Brig.-Gen. James Edward Wilmot Smyth, CMG 1917; *b* 4 Sept. 1850; *s* of Rev. Wm Caulfeild; *m* 1876, Sophia Morley, *d* of W. A. Parker, formerly Chief Justice of British Honduras; two *s* four *d*. *Educ:* Trinity College, Dublin, BA 1872. 2nd Lieut 2nd West India Regiment, 1873; served Ashanti campaign, 1873–74 (medal and clasp); commanded Battalion, 1892–98; West Africa (clasp, 1898); Brev.-Col, 1896; commanding Troops, West Africa, 1895–98; Colonel on Staff, West Africa, 1899–1902; Brig.-Gen. commanding, Jamaica District, 1902–6; retired, 1907; recalled, 1914; commanding 96th Infantry Brigade, 1914; commanding 8th Reserve Infantry Brigade, 1915–16 (medal). *Publication:* One Hundred Years History, 2nd West India Regiment. *Address:* 2 Douro Terrace, Jersey. *Clubs:* United Service; Victoria, Jersey.

Died 19 Sept. 1925.

CAVAYE, Maj.-Gen. William Frederick; London County Councillor; twice Mayor, Royal Borough of Kensington; *e s* of late Gen. W. Cavaye; *m*, 1882, Ada Mary, *y d* of late Col The Right Hon. Sir Walter Barttelot, 1st Bt, PC, MP, of Stopham, Pulborough, Sussex. *Educ:* Edin. Acad.; Old Charlton, Kent; RMC, Sandhurst. Commanded 2nd Royal Sussex Regt; Mil. Sec. to General HRH the Duke of Connaught, KG, when Commander-in-Chief, Bombay, etc; AA General and Chief of Staff, Southern District England; commanded 35th Regimental District, Sussex; specially employed in Zulu War, 1879 (medal and clasp); and during the South African War, 1900–1–2 (medal with clasp, King's medal with two clasps); commanding 2nd East Anglian Division; Special Service, BEF France, 1917–19 (two war medals, despatches). *Address:* 6 Neville Terrace, SW7. *T:* 6086 Kensington; Birchen Bridge, Horsham, Sussex. *Clubs:* United Service; Conservative, Edinburgh.

Died 30 Jan. 1926.

CAVE, 1st Viscount, *cr* 1918; **George Cave,** GCMG 1920; Kt 1915; PC 1915; JP for Surrey, 1891; DL 1897; Chancellor of Oxford University, since 1925; Lord Chancellor, 1922–24 and since Nov. 1924; *b* London, 23 Feb. 1856; 2nd *s* of late Thomas Cave, MP, and Elizabeth (*d* 1925), *d* of Jasper Shallcrass, Banstead, Surrey; *m* 1885, Estella Penfold, *d* of late William W. Mathews, of North Cadbury and Crewkerne, Somerset. *Educ:* Merchant Taylors' School; St John's College, Oxford (Scholar; Hon. Fellow, 1916). Taylorian Exhibitioner; first class in Moderations and the Final Classical School; BA 1878; MA 1912. Hon. DCL 1924; Inner Temple Scholar in Real Property Law; Barrister Inner Temple, 1880; KC 1904; Master of the Bench, 1913; practised at Chancery Bar; special, 1913; CC for Surrey, 1889; County Alderman, 1892; Deputy-chairman of Quarter Sessions, 1893; Chairman of Quarter Sessions, 1894–1910; Recorder of Guildford, 1904–15; Standing Counsel to Oxford University, 1913–15; Attorney-General to Prince of Wales, 1914–15; Hon. Lt-Col; was Hon. Commandant of 2nd VB, East Surrey Regt; Member of Royal Commission of Land Transfer, 1908–9; Chairman of Southern Rhodesia Commission, 1919–20; Chairman of Munitions Enquiry Tribunal, 1921; Chairman of Committee on Voluntary Hospitals, 1921; Chairman of Committee on Trade Boards, 1921–22; Chairman of British Empire Cancer Campaign, 1924; Chairman of Home Office Advisory Committee on Cruelty to Animals Acts, 1924; MP (U) Kingston Div. of Surrey, 1906–18; Solicitor-General, 1915–16; Home Secretary, 1916–19; a Lord of Appeal, 1919–22. *Publications:* editor of some legal treatises. *Recreations:* riding, rowing, golf. *Heir:* none. *Address:* House of Lords, SW1; Wardrobe Court, Richmond, Surrey. *T:* Richmond 159; St Ann's, Burnham, Somerset. *Clubs:* Athenæum, Carlton.

Died 29 March 1928 (ext).

CAVE, Sir Charles Daniel, 1st Bt, *cr* 1896; JP, DL, Gloucestershire and Devonshire; Local Director of Union Bank of London; *b* 17 Sept. 1832; 3rd *s* of Daniel Cave, Sidbury Manor, Devonshire, and Cleve Hill, Gloucestershire; *m* 1859, Edith Harriet (*d* 1912), *d* of John Addington Symonds, MD, of Clifton; three *s* one *d* (and one *s* decd). *Educ:* Exeter College, Oxford (MA). High Sheriff of Bristol, 1863; High Sheriff of Devonshire, 1898. *Heir: s* Charles Henry Cave, *b* 17 March 1861. *Address:* Stoneleigh House, Clifton Park, Bristol.

Died 29 Oct. 1922.

CAVE-BROWNE-CAVE, Sir Thomas, Kt 1911; CB 1907; Special Commissioner, Royal Hospital, Chelsea, since 1899; *b* 11 April 1835; 3rd *s* of late Thomas Cave-Browne-Cave of Cliff Hall, Warwickshire; *m* 1870, Blanche Matilda Mary Anne, *d* of late Sir John Milton; two *s* three *d*. *Educ:* Repton. Entered War Office, 1853; retired as Deputy Accountant-General of the Army, 1900. *Address:* Burnage, Streatham Common, SW16.   *Died 9 Dec. 1924.*

CAWLEY, George; Consulting Engineer to the Japanese Imperial Railways for twenty years, covering rapid extension; *b* Sankey, Lancashire, 29 July 1848; *e s* of Thomas Cawley of Aston Grange, Cheshire. In Japanese Government service, as one of the original staff of the Imperial College of Engineering, Tokyo, 1873–78; travelled in United States to visit leading mining centres, 1878; engaged in work connected with gas and hydraulic engineering, the promotion of steam engine economy, and the insurance of work-people, 1879–85; editor-in-chief of Industries, 1886–93; in general consulting practice since 1893. *Address:* Nippon, Cedar Road, Sutton, Surrey. *T:* Sutton 692. *Club:* Savage.   *Died 3 March 1927.*

CAWLEY, Hon. Oswald; MP (L) Prestwich Division of Lancashire since Feb. 1918; *b* 7 Oct. 1882; 2nd surv. *s* of 1st Baron Cawley. *Educ:* Rugby. Lieut Yeomanry; served European War. *Address:* Brooklands, Prestwich.   *Died 22 Aug. 1918.*

CAWSTON, Sir John Westerman, KCB 1919 (CB 1912); Deputy Master and Comptroller of the Royal Mint, 1917; retired 1921; *b* 1859; *e s* of late Rev. J. Cawston, DD, RN, Chaplain of the Fleet, and Hon. Chaplain to Queen Victoria; *m* 1888, Beatrice F. L., *d* of late Rev. J. Montague, of Wimbish; two *d*. *Educ:* Clifton College (head of school); New College, Oxford (open scholar); 1st class Classical Mods; 2nd class Final Classical Schools, 1882. Entered War Office, 1883; transferred to Treasury, 1889; Private Secretary to Parliamentary Secretary, 1895–1902; Principal Clerk, 1904–11; Assistant Comptroller and Auditor of the Exchequer, 1911–17. *Recreations:* golf; has also illustrated a few books. *Address:* Gulpher, Felixstowe, Suffolk. *T:* Felixstowe 68.   *Died 21 April 1927.*

CAYLEY, Sir George Everard Arthur, 9th Bt, *cr* 1661; JP, DL; *b* 8 July 1861; *e s* of Sir George Allanson Cayley, 8th Bt and Catherine Louisa, 2nd *d* of Sir William Worsley, 1st Bt; *S* father 1895; *m* 1884, Lady Mary Susan, *d* of Hon. Francis Dudley Montagu-Stuart-Wortley, and *sister* of 2nd Earl of Wharncliffe; one *s* three *d* (and one *s* decd). Late Capt. 3rd Batt. Royal Welsh Fusiliers. *Heir: s* Kenelm Henry Ernest Cayley, Lieut 3rd Batt. Suffolk Regt; *b* 24 Sept. 1896. *Address:* Tempe, Woodbridge, Suffolk. *Club:* Junior Carlton.   *Died 15 Nov. 1917.*

CAYLEY, William, MD; FRCP; Consulting Physician Middlesex Hospital; North-Eastern Hospital for Children; London Fever Hospital; *b* 1836. *Educ:* King's Coll. London; Vienna. *Publications:* Croonian Lectures on Typhoid Fever; editor of 3rd edition of Murchison on Continued Fever. *Address:* 120 Queen's Road, Richmond, Surrey.   *Died 17 Dec. 1916.*

CAYZER, Sir Charles (William), 1st Bt, *cr* 1904; Kt 1897; JP; shipowner; *b* London, 15 July 1843; *s* of Charles William Cayzer, Plymouth; *m* 1868, Agnes Elizabeth, *o d* of William Trickey of Clifton, Bristol; four *s* three *d* (and two *s* decd). Head of the firm of Cayzer, Irvine and Co., Ltd, Steamship Owners, London, Liverpool, Manchester, and Glasgow; Hon. Colonel 3rd Lowland Brigade, RFA; MP Barrow-in-Furness, 1892–1906; first Conservative elected for Barrow; contested Monmouth District (C), 1910. *Heir: s* Charles William Cayzer, *b* 19 July 1869. *Address:* St Lawrence Hall, Isle of Wight; Gartmore, Perthshire; Kinpurnie Castle, Forfarshire. *Clubs:* Carlton, City of London.   *Died 28 Sept. 1916.*

CAYZER, Sir Charles William, 2nd Bt, *cr* 1904; *b* Bombay, 19 July 1869; *e s* of Sir Charles Cayzer, 1st Bt; *m* 1893, Annie Mabel, *d* of late Thomas Jennings White, Frogmore Lodge, St Albans; one *s* four *d* (and one *s* decd). *Educ:* Rugby; Christ Church, Oxford (MA). A partner in the firm of Cayzer, Irvine and Co.; Director of the Clan Line Steamers, Ltd, 1890–1911; retired 1911. *Publications:* Ad Astra, 1900; Songs and Lyrics, 1900; David and Bathsheba, 1903; Songs of Summer, 1904; For Greater Britain, 1904; Donna Marina, 1905; Poems and Plays, 1905; The Skaith of Guillardun, 1907; Undine, 1908; By the Way of the Gate, 1911. *Heir: s* Charles William Cayzer, *b* 6 Jan. 1896. *Address:* 22 Lewes Crescent, Brighton. *TA:* Cayzer, Brighton. *T:* Kemp Town 6912, Brighton. *Clubs:* Constitutional, Authors', City of London.   *Died 20 July 1917.*

CAZALET, Edward Alexander; Founder and President of the Anglo Russian Literary Society; linguist; examiner in Russian, etc, for th Civil Service Commissioners and War Office; *s* of Alexander Cazalo and Baroness Charlotte de Bode; descendant of Huguenot famil which settled in England at the Revocation of the Edict of Nante *m* Mary Emma, *d* of late Gen. E. A. B. Travers of Indian Army an Secretary for Indian Affairs to late Duke of Cambridge; one *s* tw *d*. *Educ:* private tutors; Windlesham House, Brighton; Hig Commercial School, Petrograd (first medal). Late of A. Cazalet an Sons at Petrograd, and of the Russian Steam Navigation and Tradir Co. at Odessa, 1864–68; travelled repeatedly in Russia, Transcaucasi Persia, Turkey, etc. *Publications:* John Howard, the Prison Reforme written in Russian with the object of creating better Anglo-Russia relations (received medal from Jury of the Prison Congress Petrograd). *Address:* Imperial Institute, SW; Neva, Westgate-on-Se   *Died 13 Dec. 192*

CECIL, Colonel Lord Edward (Herbert), KCMG 1913; DSO 189 Financial Adviser to the Egyptian Government since 1912; *b* 12 Ju 1867; 4th *s* of 3rd Marquis of Salisbury; *m* 1894, Violet Georgin *d* of late Admiral Maxse; one *d* (one *s* decd). *Educ:* Eton. Entere Grenadier Guards, 1887; Major, 1898; served Dongola Expedition Force, 1896 (despatches, Bt Major, 4th class Medjidie; British med Khedive's medal, two clasps); accompanied special mission to Kir Menelik of Abyssinia, 1897; Egyptian campaign, 1898, includir Atbara (despatches); Khartoum (despatches, DSO and two clasp South Africa, 1899–1901 (despatches, Brevet Lieut-Col Queer medal, two clasps); Agent-General Sudan Government and Direct of Intelligence, Cairo; subsequently appointed Under Secretary War and Under Secretary of Finance; Grand Cordon, Order of th Nile, 1915. *Address:* Ghezireh, Cairo.   *Died 13 Dec. 191*

CECIL, Lord Eustace Brownlow Henry; JP Middlesex, Essex, ar Dorset; County Alderman, Dorset; Chairman of Foreign an Colonial, American, Foreign and General, and Alliance Tru Companies; Director Great Eastern Railway; *b* 24 April 1834; 2 *s* of 2nd Marquess of Salisbury; *m* 1860, Lady Gertrude Louisa Sco (*d* 1919), 4th *d* of 2nd Earl of Eldon; two *s* one *d*. *Educ:* Harro Sandhurst. Served with 43rd Light Infantry at the Cape and in Ind was nine months in the Crimean War with Coldstream Guar Captain and Lt-Col Coldstream Guards, 1861; retired, 186 Surveyor-General of the Ordnance, 1874–80; MP (C) South Ess 1865–68; West Essex, 1868–85. *Address:* Lytchett Heath, Poo Dorset; 111 Eaton Square, W. *Clubs:* Athenæum, Carlton.   *Died 3 July 192*

CHADWICK, Edward Marion; KC; Barrister-at-Law; Major, retir from 2nd Regiment the Queen's Own Rifles of Canada; amate Armorist and Genealogist; *b* 22 Sept. 1840; *s* of John Crav Chadwick, of Guelph, Canada, and *g s* of John Craven Chadwi of Ballinard; Tipperary, Ireland; *m* 1st, Ellen Byrne (*d* 1865), *d* James Beatty; 2nd, Maria Martha, *d* of Alexander Fisher; five *s* o *d*. Lay Canon and Treasurer of St Alban's Cathedral, Toronto; H Genealogist to the United Empire Loyalists' Association; by adopti of the Chiefs in Council an honorary Chief of the Six Nations, the Anowara or Turtle Clan of the Kanienga or Mohawks, by name of Shagotyohgwisaks. *Publications:* Ontarian Families; T People of the Longhouse; articles on heraldic subjects to magazin etc. *Address:* 107 Howland Avenue, Toronto.   *Died 15 Dec. 19.*

CHADWICK, Rt. Rev. George Alexander, DD; *b* 10 Oct. 18 *m* 1st, 1864, Emma, *d* of J. F. Browning, Ealing; 2nd, 1911, Hel *sister* of Rev. Canon E. T. Crozier. *Educ:* Trinity College, Dub Ordained 1863; Rector of Armagh, 1872–96; Dean of Arma 1886–96; Bishop of Derry and Raphoe, 1896–1915. *Publications:* Ch bearing Witness to Himself (Donnellan Lectures), 1879; As He t Serveth, 1880; My Devotional Life, 1882; Exodus and St Mark the Expositor's Bible; Pilate's Gift and other Sermons, 1899; Poer Chiefly Sacred, 1900; The Intellect and the Heart, and other Serme 1905. *Address:* 37 St Mary's Road, Dublin.   *Died Dec. 19*

CHADWICK, Rev. Canon Robert; Rector of Caldecote, n Nuneaton, since 1922; Hon. Canon Worcester, 1915; *m* 1887, Em (*d* 1924). *Educ:* St John's College, Cambridge. Ordained, 1882; Cu of St Matthew, Brixton, 1882–86; Middle Claydon, Bucks, 1886– Vicar of Chilvers-Coton, 1887–1914; Rural Dean of Athersto 1907–14; Vicar of Christ Church, Malvern, 1914–22. *Addr* Caldecote Rectory, near Nuneaton.   *Died 15 Feb. 19*

CHADWYCK-HEALEY, Sir Charles Edward Heley, 1st Bt, *cr* 1919; KCB 1909 (CB 1905); KC; Chancellor of Diocese of Exeter; formerly Chancellor of the Dioceses of Salisbury and Bath and Wells; *b* 26 Aug. 1845; *o s* of E. C. Healey, of Wyphurst, Cranley, Surrey; *m* 1st, 1872, Rosa (*d* 1880), *d* of John Close; one *s*; 2nd, 1884, Frances Katharine (*d* 1909), *d* of W. K. Wait, formerly MP Gloucester; two *s* one *d*. Called to Bar, Lincoln's Inn, 1872; QC 1891; Commander (Hon.) Royal Naval Reserve; Captain, 1914; Chairman of the Admiralty Volunteer Committee, 1903–14; Admiralty Transport Arbitration Board, 1914–18; commanding Hospital Ship No 15, Queen Alexandra, 1915–18; Fellow of the Society of Antiquaries; Bencher of Lincoln's Inn; DL; County Alderman and Chairman, Quarter Sessions, Somerset; High Sheriff of Somerset, 1911–12; JP Surrey and Somerset; served on Royal Commission on Care and Control of the Feeble-minded, 1905–9. *Heir: s* Gerald Edward Chadwyck-Healey, Lieut RNVR, *b* 16 May 1873. *Address:* Wyphurst, Cranleigh, Surrey; New Place, Porlock, Taunton. *Clubs:* Athenæum, Carlton, Savile, Garrick. *Died 5 Oct. 1919.*

CHAFFEY, Colonel Ralph Anderson, CBE 1918; VD; Retired List, NZ Forces; *b* Keinton Mandeville, Somerset, 1856; *s* of late Major E. Chaffey, 25th Somerset RV, and Isabella Anderson, Dalhousie Grange, near Edinburgh; *m* 1st, 1887, Emilie Lecren (*d* 1889), Timaru, NZ; 2nd, 1897, Agnes Rosa, *d* of late Dr Webster of Balruddery, NZ, Army Medical; three *s* one *d*. *Educ:* Sherborne. Educated for Army; owing to health came to NZ 1878; sheep farming; managed Taipo and Kauroo Estates for late W. H. Teschemaker, 1881–97; Highfield Estate for late Hy Wharton, 1897–1903; farming own account since 1903; joined Otepopo Rifles as Lieut 1882; raised and commanded as Capt., North Otago Hussars, 1887–97; raised and commanded Amuri Mt Rifles, 1900; Major 2nd Batt. North Canterbury Mt Rifles, 1901; Lt-Col 1905; Colonel, 1911; Brigadier commanding Canterbury Mt Rifle Brigade, 1911–14; attached to NZ Staff Corps and commanded Canterbury Military District, 1914–19. *Recreations:* cricket, 1st XI Sherborne, West Kent and Oamaru (NZ) CC; football, 1st XV Sherborne and North Canterbury, NZ. *Address:* Keintoncombe, Waiau, Amuri, NZ. *TA:* Waiau. *T:* 38M Waiau. *M:* 3601. *Club:* Christchurch, Christchurch. *Died 8 Nov. 1925.*

CHAINE, Lt-Col William, MVO 1901; late 10th Hussars; *b* 1 Jan 1838; *m* 1872, Maria Henrietta Sophia, *d* of Hon. Sir Charles Beaumont Phipps, KCB. Entered Army, 1856; Captain, 1864; retired, 1881; was Marshal, 1881–87 and Assistant Master, 1887–1901 of Ceremonies to Queen Victoria. *Address:* Kensington Palace, W. *Died 3 July 1916.*

CHALMERS, Albert John, MD; FRCS, DPH, FLS, FZS, FRGS; Director Wellcome Tropical Research Laboratories, Khartoum; Member Sudan Government Sleeping Sickness Commission; Central Sanitary Board; and Archaelogical Committee; *b* Manchester, 28 March 1870; *s* of late Rev. James Chalmers, MA, Aberdeen, and Mary, *d* of late Captain Martin, Peterhead, NB; *m* 1898, Alice, 2nd *d* of late Edwin Cannington, JP, Waterloo, Lancashire; no *c*. *Educ:* Manchester Grammar School; University Colleges, Liverpool and London. MD; Gold Medal, West African and Ceylon services, 1897–1911; Pellagra Field Commission, 1911–12; late Major Ceylon Volunteer Medical Corps; served Ashanti Field Force (despatches, medal and clasp); Ceylon Coronation Contingent (medal, Order of the Nile, 3rd Class); Membre Correspondant Societé de Pathologie Exotique, Paris; collaborating Editor Journal of Tropical Medicine and Hygiene. *Publications:* joint-author Castellani and Chalmers' Manual of Tropical Medicine; works, First-Aid, Physiological Chemistry, Simple Medical Directions; papers connected with Tropical Medicine, Hygiene, and Parasitology. *Recreations:* travel, shooting. *Address:* Balfour House, Khartoum. *TA:* Maamal, Khartoum. *Clubs:* Savile, National; Sudan, Khartoum. *Died 5 April 1920.*

CHALMERS, Sir Charles, Kt 1918; VD; JP, DL; MA Edinburgh; Convener of County Council of West Lothian; *b* 17 Feb. 1861; *e s* of late Thomas Chalmers, of Longcroft, and Jean Menzies, *e d* of late Charles Cowan, of Loganhouse; *m* 1900, Elizabeth, 2nd *d* of John Graham; one *d*. *Educ:* Merchiston Castle, and University, Edinburgh. Chairman of Directors of the Royal Scottish Institution, Larbert. *Address:* Cathlaw, Bathgate. *T:* Bathgate 69. *Club:* New, Edinburgh. *Died 27 Aug. 1924.*

CHALMERS, Sir Mackenzie Dalzell, KCB 1906 (CB 1904); CSI 1899; JP; MA; Barrister-at-law; *b* 7 Feb. 1847; *s* of Rev. F. Chalmers, DD, and Matilda, *d* of Rev. W. Marsh, DD, Hon. Canon of Worcester. *Educ:* King's College, London and Trinity College,

Oxford. Indian Civil Service, 1869–72; barrister 1869; revising barrister, 1881; counsel to Board of Trade, 1882; judge of County Courts, 1884; acting Chief Justice, Gibraltar, 1893; Commissioner of Assize, 1895; law member of the Viceroy's Council in India; retired, 1899; Asst Parliamentary Counsel, 1899; First Parliamentary Counsel to Treasury, 1902–3; Perm. Under-Secretary of State for Home Department, 1903–8; member of the Statute Law Committee, Royal Commission on Vivisection, and of Royal Commission on the affairs of Malta; member of Royal Commission on the Rebellion in Ireland; Chairman, South Nigeria Liquor Inquiry; Home Office Committee on Coroners and Deaths under Anæsthetics; a British Delegate The Hague Conferences on Unification of Law of Bills of Exchange, etc; member of the Sleeping Sickness Committee, of the Lord Chancellor's Committees on Criminal Law, and of the Advisory Committee on Egyptian Laws; Vice-President London Fever Hospital; Chairman of Belgian Commission in England on Violation of Laws of War; member of War Risks Insurance Committees (marine and aircraft), Aerial Transport Committee; Chairman of the Committee on Standardization of Biological Drugs, and member of Council of Royal Aeronautical Society; Knight of Grace and member of the Council and Chapter of the Order of St John, and Joint Committee of Red Cross and St John; Commander of the Order of the Crown (Belgium). *Publications:* contributions to Dictionary of Political Economy and Encyclopædia Britannica; Digest of the Law of Bills of Exchange; Digest of the Law of Sale, etc. *Recreation:* golf. *Address:* 5 Lauriston Road, Wimbledon, SW19. *Clubs:* Athenæum, Ranelagh, MCC. *Died 22 Dec. 1927.*

CHALMERS, P(eter) MacGregor, Hon. LLD Glas; FSAScot; *b* Glasgow 1859; *s* of George Chalmers and Jane M'Gregor; *m* Barbara Greig Steel. *Educ:* Secular School, Glasgow. Began business as architect, 1887; carried out church work at Cardonald, Jedburgh, Crailing, Partick, Govan, Glasgow, Kilmun, Carnoustie, Ardwell, Leven, Steps, St Andrews, Dunfermline, Edinburgh, Elgin, Ardrossan, Kirn, Carriden, Newlands, Corstorphine; carried out restorations at Whithorn, Glenluce Abbey, Inverkeithing, South Queensferry, St Monans, Town Church St Andrews, Melrose Abbey, Iona Cathedral, the Abbey of Paisley, Dalmeny Church, and Symington Church, Ayrshire; architect for the restoration of St Salvator's Chapel, St Andrews University, and for the Cathedral Church of St Anne, Belfast; was architect for the Marine Biological Station, Millport, the Glasgow Golf Club, Dargavel House, Renfrewshire, Kinnaird House, Perthshire, and other domestic work; past-President, Glasgow Architectural Association, and the Architectural Section of the Royal Philosophical Society. *Publications:* St Ninian's Candida Casa; a Scots Mediæval Architect; Art in Our City, Glasgow; Glasgow Cathedral, a Historical Sketch; The Govan Sarcophagus, The Shrine of St Constantine; The Shrines of St Margaret and St Kentigern; Dalmeny Kirk; the History of Glasgow Cathedral. *Recreations:* the study of ecclesiastical antiquities, sketching, photography. *Address:* 95 Bath Street, Glasgow. *Died 15 March 1922.*

CHAMBA, HH Raja Sir Bhuri Singh, Raja of, KCSI 1906; KCIE 1918 (CIE 1901); *b* 1869; widower; two *s* two *d*. Situated in the Himalayas, on the frontiers of Kashmir, the State is 3216 square miles in extent, and has a population of 135,989, HH receiving a salute of 11 guns; *S* brother, 1904 on abdication through ill health; Prime Minister 1897–1904. He is a Rajput, whose family has ruled there from very remote times. *Address:* Chamba, Punjab. *Died 6 Oct. 1919.*

CHAMBERLAIN, Houston Stewart; *b* Southsea, 9 Sept. 1855; *s* of late Rear-Admiral William Charles Chamberlain and Eliza Jane, *d* of Capt. Basil Hall, RN; *m* 1st, 1878, Anna Horst; 2nd, 1908, Eva Wagner, *o d* of the poet and composer, Richard Wagner; no *c*. *Educ:* Lycée Imperial, Versailles; Cheltenham College; private tutor. Intended to enter British Army; much troubled by illness during childhood and youth; incapable of standing English climate; studied Natural Sciences at University of Geneva, 1879–84; Bachelier ès Sciences physiques et naturelles; moved to Dresden, 1885; studied music, philosophy, history; lived in Vienna, 1889–1908; began writing, 1892; continued doing so thereafter. *Publications:* Das Drama Richard Wagners, 1892; Richard Wagner, 1896; Recherches sur la sève ascendante, 1897; Die Grundlagen des XIX Jahrhunderts, 1899; Parsifal-Märchen, 1900; Worte Christi, 1901; Drei Bühnendichtungen, 1902; Arische Weltanschauung, 1911; Immanuel Kant, 1909; Goethe, 1912. *Address:* Haus Wahnfried, Bayreuth, Bavaria. *Died 9 Jan. 1927.*

CHAMBERLAIN, Ven. Thomas; Archdeacon of Kokstad since 1891; Priest in charge of Clydesdale, Kaffraria, since 1894; *b* 21 April 1854; *s* of Theodore and Margaret Chamberlain; *m* 1882, Edith, *y*

d of late Rev. J. F. May; three *s* three *d*. *Educ:* Diocesan Grammar School, King William's Town; Christ's College, Cambridge (MA); Cape University. Ordained 1880; Curate of Harrow Green, Essex, 1880-81; of Weston, Herts, 1881-82; Rector of Alice, 1882-83; Rector and Chaplain of Wolesley Settlement, St John, East London, 1885-91; Canon of St John's Cathedral, Umtata, 1893. *Recreations:* astronomy, photography. *Address:* Kaffraria, South Africa.

CHAMBERLAYNE, Tankerville, JP; Lord of the Manors of Hound, North Baddesley, Woolston and Barton Peveril, Hants, and East Norton, Leicestershire; Patron of three livings; *b* 9 Aug. 1843; *o* surv. *s* of Thomas Chamberlayne of Cranbury Park; *m* 1886, Edith, *d* of late S. J. Ashley; one *s* four *d*. *Educ:* Eton; Magdalen College, Oxford. BA 1865. MP (C) Southampton, 1892-96, 1900-6; Hon. Lt RNR. *Recreations:* a well-known yachtsman and patron of cricket and all athletic sports. *Address:* Cranbury Park, near Winchester; Baddesley Manor, Romsey. *Clubs:* Carlton, Junior Carlton, St Stephen's, Royal Thames Yacht, Primrose. *Died 17 May 1924.*

CHAMBERLIN, Arthur George, ISO 1903; late Senior District Auditor Local Government Board. *Address:* Glen House, Highfield Street, Leicester. *Died 19 Feb. 1925.*

CHAMBERLIN, Edson J.; President Grand Trunk and Grand Trunk Pacific Railways, 1912-17; for twenty years General Manager of the Canada Atlantic Railway. *Address:* 333 Metcalfe Street, Ottawa, Ontario. *Died 27 Aug. 1924.*

CHAMBERLIN, Sir George, Kt 1919; DL Norfolk; JP Norwich; Mayor of Norwich, 1891; Lord Mayor, 1916 and 1918; High Sheriff of Norfolk, 1926-27; *b* 16 Feb. 1846; *m* 1876, Emily Mary (*d* 1923), *d* of A. F. C. Bolingbroke, Norwich. *Recreation:* shooting. *Address:* St Catherine's Close, Norwich. *Clubs:* Carlton; Norfolk County, Norwich. *Died 12 Aug. 1928.*

CHAMBERS, Rev. Arthur; Vicar of Brockenhurst, Hants, since 1899. Curate of Bow, Middlesex, 1888-89; Holy Trinity, Stepney, 1890-92; St Mark's, Battersea, 1892-99. *Publications:* Our Life after Death; Man and the Spiritual World; Thoughts of the Spiritual; Problems of the Spiritual. *Address:* The Vicarage, Brockenhurst, Hants. *Died 16 March 1918.*

CHAMBERS, Charles Haddon; playwright; *b* Stanmore, Sydney, NSW, 22 April 1860; *s* of John Ritchie Chambers, NSW Civil Service, formerly of Ulster, and Frances, *e* *d* of William Kellett, Waterford, Ireland. *Educ:* Marrickville and Fort Street Public Schools, Sydney, and privately. Entered NSW Civil Service, 1875; two years later became stockrider, etc, in the Bush; visited England and Ireland, 1880; returned to England, 1882; became journalist, story writer, and subsequently dramatic author. *Publications:* Captain Swift; The Idler; The Honourable Herbert; The Old Lady; John a Dreams; The Tyranny of Tears; The Awakening; The Golden Silence; Sir Anthony; Passers-by; The Impossible Woman; The Saving Grace; part-author of The Fatal Card, Boys Together, and The Days of the Duke. *Recreations:* swimming, boat-sailing, riding, driving, shooting, boxing, fencing. *Address:* 4 Aldford Street, Park Lane, W1. *T:* Mayfair 2206. *Clubs:* Bath, Green Room, National, Dramatists; Travellers', Paris. *Died 28 March 1921.*

CHAMBERS, James, KC Ireland 1902; MP (U) South Belfast since 1910; *b* 1863; *s* of Joseph Chambers. *Educ:* Royal Academical Inst.; Queen's Coll., Belfast. Called to Irish Bar, 1886. Solicitor-Gen. for Ireland, 1917. *Address:* Grove House, Foxrock, Co. Dublin. *Club:* Constitutional. *Died 11 June 1917.*

CHAMBERS, Julius, FRGS; author, newspaper man; *b* Bellefontaine, Ohio, 21 Nov. 1850; *s* of Joseph and Sarabella Chambers; *m* 1899, Margaret Belvin. *Educ:* Ohio Wesleyan University; Cornell University (Phi Beta Kappa and Delta Kappa Epsilon). Entered service of NY Tribune; joined staff NY Herald, 1873; City Editor, 1876-77; fitted out expedition to headwaters of Mississippi, 1872; discovered Elk Lake, Minn., June 9, now recognised as source of great river; served NY Herald over fifteen years in London, Paris, Havana, Madrid, and Washington; Managing Editor, 1886-89; started Paris edition of Herald, 1887; managing editor of NY World, 1889-91; since then engaged in literature and travel. *Publications:* A Mad World; On a Margin, a Wall Street Story; Lovers Four and Maidens Five; Missing, a Romance of the Sargasso Sea; The Rascal Club; The Destiny of Doris; The Mississippi River and its Wonderful Valley; Forty Years' Recollections of New York Journalism; The Joy of Living; Jack Sturgeon of Fiskkill; edited an edition of Balzac; author of a farce produced in NY, 1903, and of a comedy produced in NY, 1904;

published 200 short stories and numerous travel books, writer of Walks and Talks, a daily letter since 1904. *Recreations:* work, travel. *Clubs:* Lotos, Authors', American Dramatists', New York. *Died 12 Feb. 1920.*

CHAMBERS, Sir Newman Pitts-, Kt 1897; JP, DL, Donegal; knighted for services during his official career in Londonderry; 2nd *s* of late Thomas Chambers, Aberfoyle, Londonderry, and Mary Anna, *d* of late Captain Robert Newman, HM 56th Regt; *m* 1880, Inez Alexa (*d* 1914), *y* *d* of late Alex. T. Young, Coolkuragh House, Co. Londonderry, and Drumkeen, Co. Donegal; one *s* one *d*. *Address:* Carrig Cnoc, Co. Donegal; Lough Ash House, Co. Tyrone. *Clubs:* Constitutional, Northern Counties, Londonderry. *Died 18 Aug. 1922.*

CHAMBERS, Maj.-Gen. Robert Macdonald; Bombay Infantry; *b* 7 June 1833; *m* 1867, Lucy Edith, 3rd *d* of A. Baird, MD, Dover; six *d*. Entered army, 1858; Maj.-Gen., 1891; retired, 1891; served Indian Mutiny, 1860; China War (medal); Afghan War, 1880 (medal). *Address:* Springfield, Guildford. *Died 1924.*

CHAMIER, Maj.-Gen. Francis Edward Archibald, CB 1907; CIE 1902; Supernumerary List, Indian Staff Corps; *b* 13 May 1833; *s* of late Henry Chamier, Madras Civil Service; *m* 1st, Annie Maria Caroline, *d* of late Dr James Johnstone, IMS; 2nd, Amy Macdonell, *d* of late W. C. Capper, BCS; nine *s* three *d*. *Educ:* Cheltenham. Interpreter 34, BNI; Adjutant Calcutta Volunteers, 1857; ADC and Persian Interpreter to Gen. Sir James Outram, 1st Bt, in first relief defence, siege, and capture of Lucknow (despatches, medal and two clasps, Brevet majority); in command of HH Raja of Kapurthala's contingent during its service in Oudh, 1858. *Address:* 55 Warwick Road, SW5. *Died 3 May 1923.*

CHAMIER, Brig.-Gen. George Daniel, CMG 1900; RA; Inspector RGA and Coast Defences in India; *b* 24 Sept. 1860; *s* of late Lt-Gen. S. Chamier, CB; *m* 1903, Amy St Leger, *widow* of Hon. James Buchanan; two *d*. *Educ:* Cheltenham; Woolwich. Has served in Royal Horse Artillery, Royal Field Artillery, and Royal Garrison Artillery Boer War, 1899-1902; commanded the artillery during the defence of Kimberley (despatches); Schweizer Renike during its investment 1900; a mobile column in the operations against De Wet, 1901 (despatches); commandant and special commissioner, Bloemhof District, 1902 (South African War medal with three clasps, King's medal with two clasps). *Recreations:* hunting, cricket, golf. *Address:* Brook House, Camberley, Surrey. *Club:* United Service. *Died 3 May 1920.*

CHAMPION, Henry Hyde; *b* 22 Jan. 1859; *e* *s* of Maj.-Gen. J. H. Champion and Henrietta, *d* of Beauchamp Colclough Urquhart, of Meldrum and Byth; *m* Elsie Belle, *d* of Lt-Col Goldstein. *Educ:* Marlborough College; RMA, Woolwich. Served in RA during the Afghan War (medal), and as Adjutant at Portsmouth; resigned to become first Hon. Secretary of Social Democratic Federation; published first editions of Ibsen, Bernard Shaw, etc; tried for sedition after Trafalgar Square riots in 1886; defended himself and was acquitted; won the London Dock Strike in 1889; foretold failure of Australasian Strike in 1890; Assistant Editor, Nineteenth Century for two years; first Independent Labour Candidate (Aberdeen, 997 votes); went to Melbourne again in 1893 for good; leader writer on The Age; founded Book-Lovers' Library and Australasian Authors Agency. *Address:* 239 Collins Street, Melbourne. *TA:* Litaribus, Melbourne. *Died 30 April 1928.*

CHAMPNESS, Henry Robert, MVO 1902; *b* 18 June 1852; *e* *s* of late Henry Champness, Admiralty timber inspector; *m* 1880, Susan Augusta, *e* *d* of late Charles Rowett Quiller and Mary Augusta Quiller of Chelsea; three *s* two *d*. *Educ:* Old Brompton, Kent; Chatham Dockyard School; School of Naval Architecture, South Kensington; Royal Naval College, Greenwich. Passed out RN College, 1874; Chatham Dockyard until 1875, when ordered to Admiralty; returning to Chatham, 1875; Admiralty, 1877-85; 2nd class Asst Constructor 1883, on establishment of the Royal Corps of Naval Constructors, overseer of Admiralty Shipbuilding at Barrow-in-Furness, 1884; Portsmouth yard, 1886; 1st class Asst Constructor at Portsmouth, 1887; Constructor, 1889; Chief Constructor, Malta, 1895; Chief Constructor, Devonport Dockyard, 1897-1902; Asst-Director Naval Construction, Admiralty, 1903-13; Member of Royal Corps of Naval Constructors; several times received thanks of Lords Commissioners of the Admiralty. *Publication:* a paper, The Launch of a Battleship *Address:* 16 Evelyn Mansions, Carlisle Place, Westminster, SW. *Died 22 Feb. 1927.*

CHAMPTALOUP, Sydney Taylor; Professor of Bacteriology and Public Health, Otago University, since 1911; Government Bacteriologist, Dunedin, since 1910; *b* Auckland, 10 Aug. 1880; *m* 1909; two *d. Educ:* Auckland; Edinburgh University. MB, ChB, 1906, with 1st class honours; BSc in Public Health, 1909 (Edin); DPH, *(ad eundem)* (NZ), 1914; House Physician, Cardiff Infirmary; Chalmers' Hospital, Edinburgh; Junior Assistant Surgical Department, University, Edinburgh; Assistant Medical Waiting Room, Royal Infirmary, Edinburgh; Assistant to Professor Public Health, University, Edinburgh, and Pathologist, Chalmers' Hospital, Edinburgh; Lecturer, Bacteriology and Public Health, Otago University, and Government Medical Officer of Health, New Zealand. *Publications:* various in NZ Medical Journal, British Medical Journal, 1910–16, etc. *Address:* Dunedin, New Zealand. *Club:* Fernhill, Dunedin.
Died 11 Dec. 1921.

CHANCE, Sir Arthur, Kt 1905; FRCSI, FRCPI (Hon.), FRCS Edin (Hon.), etc; President Royal Academy of Medicine in Ireland, 1921–24; Member of Council Royal College of Surgeons, Ireland; Surgeon Mater Misericordiæ Hospital, 1886–1926; Consulting Surgeon Doctor Steevens Hospital, Orthopædic Hospital of Ireland, Dental Hospital of Ireland, and St Michael's Hospital; Hon. Consulting Surgeon in Orthopædic Surgery, Ministry of Pensions in Ireland, south region; Member of General Medical Council; Medical Visitor in Lunacy under the High Court; *b* 15 June 1859; *s* of Albert Chance and Elizabeth Fleming; *m* 1st, 1886, Martha (*d* 1891), *d* of late Daniel Rooney, Belfast; 2nd, 1900, Eileen, *d* of late William Murphy, Dartry; eight *s* five *d. Educ:* University College, Dublin. President Royal College of Surgeons in Ireland, 1904–6; Surgeon to Jervis Street Hospital, 1884–86; Examiner in Surgery, RCSI, 1893–95, 1896–99; Surgeon in Ordinary to the Lord Lieutenant of Ireland, 1892–95 and 1906–15; President Dublin Division British Medical Association, 1903–4; Univ. Examiner in Clinical Surgery Dublin Univ., 1905 and 1906; Member Senate of National University of Ireland, 1914; Col AMS: Inspector Special Military Surgical Hospitals, Irish Command, 1917–20; Chairman Irish Nursing Board; Member first General Nursing Council for Ireland, 1919–24. *Publications:* Operative Treatment of Enlarged Prostate; The Surgical Treatment of Empyema; Trans. RAMI; Choledochotomy, Dublin Medical Journ.; etc. *Address:* 42 Merrion Square East, Dublin.
Died 26 July 1926.

CHANDAVARKAR, Sir Narayen Ganesh, Kt 1910; BA, LLB; President of the Bombay Legislature since 1921; *b* 1855. *Educ:* Elphinstone College, Bombay, being appointed junior Dakshina Fellow. Became pleader of Bombay High Court, and for a time English editor of Indu Prakash; General Secretary of the Indian National Social Conferences; Vice-Chancellor University of Bombay, 1909–12; officiated as Chief-Justice, June 1909 and June 1912; Judge of the Bombay High Court, 1901–13; Chief Minister to HH the Maharajah Holkar, Indore, Central India, 1913–14. *Address:* Pedder Road, Bombay.
Died 14 May 1923.

CHANDLER, Alfred, CBE 1918; *b* 11 Nov. 1853; 3rd *s* of Captain James Henry Chandler; *m* 1880, Kate, 2nd *d* of late Robert Williams, Liverpool; three *s* two *d. Educ:* Liverpool Institute. Assistant-Secretary, Mersey Docks and Harbour Board for about 20 years; General Manager and Secretary for about 9 years; retired. *Recreations:* shooting and golf. *Address:* Broadlands, Alexandra Drive, Liverpool. *T:* Lark Lane Liverpool 545. *Club:* Exchange, Liverpool.
Died 7 March 1923.

CHANNELL, Rt. Hon. Sir Arthur (Moseley), Kt 1897; PC 1914; *b* London, 13 Nov. 1838; *s* of late Sir William Fry Channell, Baron of Exchequer; *m* 1st, 1865, Beatrice Ernestine (*d* 1871), *d* of late A. W. Wyndham of West Lodge, Blandford; 2nd, 1877, Constance Helena, *o d* of Walter B. Trevelyan; three *s* one *d. Educ:* Harrow; Trinity College, Cambridge. Wrangler and 2nd class Classical Tripos, 1861. Barrister, 1863; QC 1885; Vice-Chairman of General Council of the Bar, 1895; Recorder of Rochester, 1888–97; Judge of the Queen's Bench Division of the High Courts of Justice, 1897–1914; sat as a member of the Judicial Committee of the Privy Council on Prize Court Appeals, 1916–21; sat as a temporary Judge of the King's Bench Division, 1921. *Recreations:* rowing (winner of Colquhoun Sculls, 1860; University Pair Oars, 1861; Henley Grand Challenge and Ladies' Plate (in First Trinity Crew), 1861); yachting (yacht owner since 1876). *Address:* Hillside, Falmouth. *Clubs:* Athenæum, and several yacht clubs.
Died 4 Oct. 1928.

CHANNER, Col Bernard, DSO 1886; Indian Army; retired; *b* 20 Sept. 1846. Served Afghanistan, 1879–80 (medal); Burmah, 1885–87 (despatches, medal with clasp, DSO); Lushai, 1889 (clasp); NW Frontier, 1897–98 (medal with clasp).
Died 4 Dec. 1916.

CHANNING OF WELLINGBOROUGH, 1st Baron, *cr* 1912; **Francis Allston Channing,** Bt 1906; JP; MA; *b* United States, 21 March 1841; *s* of Rev. W. H. Channing; *m* 1869, Elizabeth, *d* of Henry Bryant of Boston; two *d* (and one *s* one *d* decd). *Educ:* Exeter College, Oxford. Has taken active part in promoting agricultural, educational, and labour reforms; Member of Royal Commission on Agricultural Depression, 1893–96; Chairman of Central and Associated Chambers of Agriculture, 1894; Member of the Rural Education Conference under the Boards of Agriculture and Education, and of the Rural Education Sub-Committee of the County Councils Association; MP (L) E Northamptonshire, 1885–1910. Sometime Fellow, Tutor, and Lecturer in Philosophy, University College, Oxford; Barrister, Lincoln's Inn; JP Northamptonshire. *Publications:* Instinct; The Greek Orators as Historical Authorities; The Second Ballot; The Truth about Agricultural Depression; Memories of Midland Politics, 1917, etc. *Recreations:* fishing, hunting, cycling. *Heir:* none. *Address:* 40 Eaton Place, SW1. *T:* Victoria 4274. *Clubs:* Oxford and Cambridge, Reform, National Liberal.
Died 20 Feb. 1926 (ext).

CHANT, Mrs Laura Ormiston; preacher (undenominational), lecturer, composer, and writer; *b* Chepstow, 1848; *d* of F. W. Dibbin, CE, and Sophia Ormiston; *m* 1876, Thomas Chant, MRCS (*d* 1913); one *s* three *d. Educ:* at home, in Kensington, W Associate of Arts, Apothecaries' Hall. Taught in schools; nursed in hospitals; was Sister Sophia in London Hospital; assistant manager of private lunatic asylum; married, and took up public advocacy of Women's Suffrage, Temperance, Purity, and Liberal Politics; became lecturer on literary and social subjects; led crusade against Empire Music Hall; took relief to Armenian refugees in Bulgaria; took out nurses to Greek frontier and Crete, for which she received the Red Cross from Queen Victoria on behalf of the then King and Queen of Greece. *Publications:* Sellcuts' Manager (novel); The Prodigal (sermonettes); Verona and other Poems; Short Stories; various pamphlets on temperance, poor law, politics, and purity; many hymns; a song, Ode to Skylark (words by Shelley); Golden Boat Action Songs; Sea-shell Songs; Toddlekins' Songs; May-time Action Songs; Daisies and Breezes Action Songs; Thistledown Action Songs; To and Fro Action Songs; Galloping Horses Action Songs; Under One Sky Action Songs; The Dragonfly Action Songs; The Wise Owl Action Songs. *Recreations:* games, especially billiards. *Address:* The Homestead, Pinvin, Pershore. *Clubs:* hon. member of New England Women's; Women's, Chicago.
Died 16 Feb. 1923.

CHAPIN, Capt. Sidney H., DSO 1900; Lieutenant, Special Reserve, 4th (Royal Irish) Dragoon Guards, since 1914; late Assistant Commissioner of Police to the Gold Coast, West Africa; *b* 23 Feb. 1875. Served with Col Plumer in Matabeleland, 1896 (medal); Boer War with South African Light Horse (DSO medal, six clasps, King's medal, two clasps); attached to the CID of the South African Government RRs, 1902–4; Director-General of Hygiene to the Republic of Guatemala, 1904–6.
Died 25 Sept. 1918.

CHAPLEAU, Samuel Edmour St Onge; ex-Captain and Brevet-Major US Army; *b* Syracuse, State of New York, 1839; *m* Caroline K., 3rd *d* of Lt-Col Geo. W. Patten, US Army; one *s. Educ:* College of Terrebonne. Went to US 1860; entered regular army, 1861. Received brevet rank of Capt. for gallant and meritorious services at battle of Murfreesboro, Tenn, and that of Brevet-Major for gallant services during Atlanta campaign and at battle of Jonesboro', Ga; was also at battle of Shiloh, Tenn, the siege of Corinth, Miss, and battles of Chickamauga and Chattanooga, Tenn; sent to Memphis during the riots in that city, 1866; in command of the troops at Augusta, Ga, during the riots, 1868. Retired from US Army, 1871; entered Civil Service of Canada, 1873; was successively Secretary of Department of Public Works, Sheriff of North-west Territories, Clerk of the Crown in Chancery, and Clerk of the Senate and of the Parliament of Canada; retired from active service, 1917. *Address:* Hotel del Coronado, California, United States.
Died Jan. 1921.

CHAPLIN, 1st Viscount, *cr* 1916, of St Oswalds, Blankney, in the county of Lincoln; **Henry Chaplin,** PC 1885; JP, DL; *b* 22 Dec. 1840; *e s* of late Rev. Henry Chaplin and Caroline Horatia, *d* of William Ellice; *m* 1876, Florence (*d* 1881), *d* of 3rd Duke of Sutherland; one *s* two *d. Educ:* Harrow; Christ Church, Oxford. Hon. LLD, Edinburgh, 1890. MP (C) Mid Lincolnshire, afterwards the Sleaford Division of Lincolnshire, 1868–1906; Chancellor of Duchy

of Lancaster, 1885–86; President of Board of Agriculture, 1886–92; President of Local Government Board, 1895–1900; Member of Royal Commission on Agriculture, 1881 and 1893; Member of Royal Commission on Horse Breeding, 1887; Member of Royal Commission on Gold and Silver, 1889; Member of Royal Commission on Supply of Food and Raw Material in Time of War, 1903; Member of Tariff Commission, and Chairman of its Agricultural Committee, 1904; MP (U) Wimbledon Div. Surrey, 1907–16. *Recreations:* sport of all kinds—hunting, racing, deerstalking, shooting. *Heir: s* Hon. Eric Chaplin, *b* 27 Sept. 1877. *Address:* 6 Charles Street, Berkeley Square, W1. *T:* Gerrard 7184; Hall Farm, Brixworth, Northants. *Clubs:* Athenæum, Carlton, Marlborough, Turf, Jockey.
Died 29 May 1923.

CHAPLIN, Col John Worthy, VC 1860; CB 1887; *b* 23 July 1840; *s* of late W. J. Chaplin; *m. Educ:* Harrow. Entered army, 1858; Col, 1883; served Chinese campaign, 1860 (medal with two clasps, VC); Afghan War, 1879–80 (medal). *Decorated* for distinguished gallantry North Taku Fort, China. *Address:* 7 Southwick Crescent, Hyde Park, W2.
Died 19 Aug. 1920.

CHAPMAN, Sir Arthur, Kt 1909; HBM Consul-General, Rio de Janeiro, 1901–9; *b* 26 Aug. 1851; *s* of late W. G. Chapman, Paul's Cray Hill, Kent; *m* 1881, Ellen Laura, *e d* of Robert Still, Lincoln's Inn. Vice-Consul Valparaiso, 1875; Bogota, 1882; Guatemala, 1885; Vera Cruz, 1891; several times Acting Consul-General; was twice in charge of the Legation in Bogota, and acted as Chargé d'Affaires in Guatemala. *Address:* 6 Hilltop Road, West Hampstead, NW.
Died 13 Oct. 1918.

CHAPMAN, Sir Arthur Wakefield, Kt 1915; JP, DL, Surrey; Chairman Surrey County Council, 1911–17; *b* 8 Aug. 1849; *s* of Henry Chapman of Wanstead, Essex; *m* 1876, Agnes (*d* 1906), *d* of late Capt. Mangles, Poyle Park, Tongham, Surrey; two *s. Educ:* Tonbridge School; private tutors. Partner in Pigott, Chapman & Co., Calcutta, 1875–1902; contested (L) Guildford Division, 1900; Alderman of Surrey CC, 1903; Chairman of Surrey Educational Committee, 1904–11; nominated Licensing Commissioner by Liberal Government under Bill of 1908; Chairman County Council Association. *Recreations:* golf, hunting. *Address:* 3 Palmer Street, St James's Park, SW1. *T:* Victoria 2500. *Club:* Reform.
Died 25 March 1926.

CHAPMAN, Hon. Sir Austin, KCMG 1924; MP; Minister for Trade and Customs, Australia, 1907–8 and 1923–24, also for Health, 1923–24; Member for Eden Monaro House of Representatives since 1901; *b* Bowral, NSW, 10 July 1864; *s* of Richard Chapman; *m* Catherine Josephine, *d* of James O'Brien, Bellevue Station, Braidwood; two *s* two *d. Educ:* Marulan. MLA, Braidwood, in NSW Parliament, 1891–1901; was Member NSW Commission for the World's Columbian Exposition, Chicago, 1893; JP NSW, 1894; was first Government Whip in Federal Parliament; attended by invitation the Coronation of King Edward VII, 1902; was Minister for Defence, 1903–4; was Chairman of Federal Royal Commission on Old Age Pensions, 1905–6; Postmaster-General of Australia, 1905–7; represented Australia, New Zealand, and Fiji at the Postal Union Convention held in Rome, 1906, advocating voting for universal penny post; proposed universal penny postage in Australian Parliament, 1906; introduced penny and toll telephone system in Australia and bush telephone scheme, 1906; also uniform telegraph rates and postal orders throughout the Commonwealth, 1906; was Member Commission New Zealand Exhibition, 1906–7. Introduced the "Chapman Wheat Sack" in Australia. *Recreations:* general athletics, reading. *Address:* The Outlook, Woollahra Point, Sydney, Australia.
Died Jan. 1926.

CHAPMAN, Rev. C., MA, LLD; Principal Emeritus Western College, Bristol, since 1910; *b* St Neot's, Hunts, 1828; *s* of late Thomas Chapman, brewer; *m* Mary Isabella, *d* of late Rev. Richard Knill, formerly of St Petersburg, Russia; five *s. Educ:* private school, St Neot's. Entered Western College (Congregational), late of Plymouth, subseq. of Bristol, 1851; graduated London University MA 1856. Pastor of Church at Chester, 1857–64; Pastor of Percy Church, Bath, till 1871; Pastor of Church and Professor of Congregational College, Montreal, 1871–76; received Diploma of LLD at the University in Montreal; Principal Western College, 1876–1910; President of the Devon Association of Science, 1881, and of the Plymouth Institution, 1883–89. *Publications:* Life of Matthew Henry; The Monodologie of Leibnitz; Homiletics of Books of Samuel, Pulpit Commentary, 2 vols; Pre-Organic Evolution and the Biblical Idea of God; The Emergence of Life and Consciousness. *Recreation:* travelling. *Address:* Crofton, Bronshill Road, Torquay.
Died July 1922.

CHAPMAN, General Sir Edward Francis, KCB 1906 (CB 188 RA; Colonel Commandant Royal Regiment Artillery; Master Gunr St James' Park; *b* 14 Nov. 1840; *m* 1886, Georgiana, 3rd *d* of Edward Clive Bayley, KCSI. Entered army, 1858; General, 18 served Abyssinia, 1867–68 (despatches, medal); Afghan War, 1878– (despatches twice, brevet of Lieut-Col, CB, medal with two clas bronze decoration); ADC to the Queen, 1881; brevet of Col 18 Burmese Expedition, 1885–86 (medal with clasp); Quartermast General in India, 1885–89; Director of Military Intelligence, 1891– commanded Scottish District 1896–1901. Was Secretary to Douglas Forsyth's Mission to Yarkand, 1874; a Fellow of the Ro Geographical Society, and an Esquire of the Order of St John Jerusalem. *Address:* Strathmore, Limpsfield, Surrey.
Died 12 May 19.

CHAPMAN, Rev. Edward William, MA; Hon. Canon of Carli assisting at Dean Vaughan Memorial Church, St Martin's, Kensal R NW; *b* 1841; *s* of William Greenwood Chapman of Pauls Cray H *m* 1872, Hon. Theodosia Spring Rice, *d* of 1st Lord Monteagle; *c s* three *d. Educ:* Eton; Trinity College, Cambridge. Vicar of Lanerc Cumberland, 1873–79; Penrith, Cumberland, 1879–88. *Address:* P. Cray Hill, St Pauls Cray, Kent. *TA:* Canon Chapman, St Mary C. *T:* Cray 5–7.
Died 1 Feb. 19.

CHAPMAN, Ven. Frank Robert, MA. *Educ:* Exeter Coll., Oxfo Vicar of St James's, Bury St Edmunds, 1865–73; Rector of To Langtoft, Suffolk, 1878–81; Archdeacon of Sudbury, 1869–19 Canon of Ely, 1879–1909. *Address:* Coombe Nevile, Warren Ro Kingston, Surrey.
Died 18 March 19.

CHAPMAN, Colonel Frederic Hamilton, MVO 1910; I commanding 2nd Battalion Duke of Cornwall's Light Infantry Chertsey, 9 Feb. 1863; *s* of late Frederick Chapman, publisher; 1894, Violet Campbell, *d* of late Capt. Pearson Campbell Johnsto RN; two *d. Educ:* Radley; Sandhurst. Gazetted, 1884; served N Frontier of India, 1897–98 (medal with 2 clasps); S African W 1899–1902 (despatches, Brev. Lieut-Col, Queen's medal with clasps); France, 1914–18; Brevet Colonel, 1908; medal of Union S Africa, 1910; twice acted as Administrator to Colony of Bermu served in Malta, India, Burma, Gibraltar, Bermuda, and S Africa; v Editor of Gibraltar Chronicle, 1906. *Recreations:* natural histo growing roses and apples; goats, poultry, rabbits, Japanese art. *Addr* Burston, Diss, Norfolk.
Died 5 Dec. 19.

CHAPMAN, Maj.-Gen. Hamilton; Hon. Colonel 8th Cava Indian Army, since 1903; *b* 11 Oct. 1835; *m* Adeline (*d* 1923); *c s* two *d* (by second wife, who died 1904). Entered army, 1856; M. Gen. 1893; unemployed list, 1895; served Indian Mutiny, 1857– (despatches, medal); Afghan War, 1878–80 (despatches, medal, bre Lieut-Col). *Address:* 25 Wilbury Road, Hove, Sussex.
Died 6 Oct. 19.

CHAPMAN, Edmund Pelly; *b* Calcutta, 16 August 1867; *s* of R. Chapman, CSI, formerly Secretary Finance Departme Government of India; *m* Mary Tupper, *d* of late Major-General R. Cameron, CMG; one *s* two *d. Educ:* Clifton College; Emman College, Cambridge (Exhibitioner and Scholar), 1st Class, Ind. Language Tripos. Served in Bengal; Assistant Secretary, Forei Department, Govt of India; Registrar High Court, Calcut Superintendent Legal Affairs and Secretary Judicial Departme Government of Bengal; Judge High Court, Calcutta, 1914–15; Pat 1915–19. *Recreation:* golf. *Club:* United Service, Calcutta.
Died 31 Jan. 19.

CHAPMAN, Martin, KC; Senior King's Counsel for New Zealar *b* Karori, near Wellington, 26 March 1846; 3rd *s* of late Mr Justi Henry Samuel Chapman, of the Supreme Court of New Zealar unmarried. *Educ:* Church of England Grammar School, Melbourr Called to Bar, Inner Temple, 1871; New Zealand Bar, 1875; practis in Wellington during his whole career; retired; was Secretary to t Judicature Commission which produced in 1882 the Code of Ci Procedure now in force; for many years editor of the New Zeala Law Reports and a member, and for a time President, of the La Society; has also, as a member of the Council, taken an active p in the proceedings of the New Zealand Institute, having several tim had the office of President, and has been interested in other scienti bodies; an advanced mathematician; as a young man he took a leadi and scientific part in yachting and other forms of recreation. *Addre* 28 Golders Hill, Wellington, New Zealand. *Clubs:* Wellingto Dunedin.
Died 192

CHAPMAN, Thomas Algernon, MD (Hon.) Glas.; FRS 1918; FES, FZS; *b* 2 June 1842. *Educ:* Glasgow University. Late Superintendent Hereford C and C Asylum. *Publications:* Papers in Journal of Mental Science; Transactions Entomological Society, and various societies, magazines, etc. *Recreation:* natural history, especially entomology. *Address:* Betula, Reigate.   *Died 17 Dec. 1921.*

CHAPMAN, Sir Thomas Robert Tighe, 7th Bt, *cr* 1782; JP; *b* 6 Nov. 1846; *s* of late William Chapman, *s* of Sir Thomas Chapman, 2nd Bt, and Louisa, *d* of Col Vansittart, of Shottesbrook; *S* cousin, 1914; *m* 1873, Edith Sarah Hamilton, *d* of G. A. Rochfort-Boyd, JP, DL, Middleton Park, Westmeath; four *d*. Heir: none.
                                    Died 8 April 1919 (ext).

CHAPMAN, William Arthur, ISO 1902; Clerk, Admiralty; *b* 1849; *s* of late Samuel Chapman, Deputy-Marshal of the Queen's Bench Prison; *m* 1873, Florence Juliet (*d* 1914), *d* of late William Kerrison; one *d*. *Educ:* St Omer, France; Sydney College, Bath. Entered the Admiralty, 1867; appointed Head of the Record Office, 1899. *Publications:* Plays and Lyrics. *Address:* 62 Lancaster Gate, W. *Club:* Authors'.   *Died 15 Feb. 1917.*

CHAPPEL, Rev. William Haighton, MA; Sub Dean and Vicar of St Michael's Cathedral Church of Coventry; Rural Dean of Coventry and Vicar of Stivichdale (in plurality), 1919; Examining Chaplain to Bishop of Coventry and Commissary, 1921; Head Master, King's School, Worcester, 1896–1918; Hon. Canon of Worcester Cathedral since 1907; Proctor Convocation, 1921; *b* 22 May 1860; *s* of late Rev. Canon Chappel, Rector of Camborne, Cornwall; *m* 1892, M. G. Carnsew, Flexbury, Cornwall; two *s* four *d*. *Educ:* Marlborough Coll. (Foundation Scholar); Worcester College, Oxford (Classical Scholar). First Class Classical Moderations, 1881; Second Class Classical Greats, 1883, BA; First Class Honour Theology, 1884; MA 1887. Assistant Master, Marlborough College, 1884–96; Chaplain to the Household, 1892–96; Hon. Captain OCMC Cadet Corps, 1890–94; Examining Chaplain to the Bishop of Worcester, 1902–5; to the Bishop of Birmingham, 1905–9. *Publication:* Progress in the Future Life, pamphlet, 1907. *Recreations:* golf and cycling. *Address:* The Sub-Deanery, Coventry.   *Died 11 July 1922.*

CHAPPLE, Frederic, CMG 1915; BA, BSc, London University; Headmaster of Prince Alfred College, Adelaide, 1876–1915; Warden of the Senate of the University since 1883; *b* London, 12 Oct. 1845; *s* of John and Louisa Chapple; *m* Elizabeth Sarah Hunter of Hackney; four *s* four *d*. *Educ:* Westminster Training College; King's College, London; Royal Science School, South Kensington. Tutor, Westminster Training College, 1870–75; Member of Council of University of Adelaide since 1897; President YMCA, Adelaide. *Publication:* The Boy's Own Grammar. *Recreations:* tennis, walking. *Address:* 26 Parade, Norwood, South Australia. *T:* Central 2840. *Clubs:* Overseas; Commonwealth.
                                    Died 29 Feb. 1924.

CHAPPLE, Paymaster Rear-Adm. Sir John Henry George, KCB 1918 (CB 1911); CVO 1916 (MVO 1901); Deputy Keeper of the Privy Purse since 1922; Assistant Treasurer to the King, 1920; Secretary HM Privy Purse, 1918–22; served on HM Yacht Victoria and Albert; *b* 4 Dec. 1859; *m* 1893, Edith Blanche, *d* of Rev. William Dyson. Clerk of Shah during engagement with Peruvian turret-ship Huascar, 1877; served Zulu War, 1879 (medal and clasp); Egyptian War, 1882 (medal, clasp, Khedive's bronze star, 5th class Medjidie); Souakim, 1884 (clasp); European War, 1914–17 (KCB). *Club:* Army and Navy.   *Died 5 March 1925.*

CHARBONNEAU, Hon. Napoleon; Puisne Judge, Quebec, since 1903; *b* 12 Feb. 1853; *m* 2nd, Mlle Lemieux. *Educ:* Montreal College. Advocate, 1879; KC, 1899; MP (L), Jacques Cartier, 1895. *Address:* 36 Simpson Street, Montreal.
                                    Died 31 Aug. 1916.

CHARLES, Rt. Hon. Sir Arthur, Kt 1887; PC 1903; *b* 1839; *y s* of Robert Charles, London and Carisbrooke; *m* 1866, Rachel Christian, *d* of T. D. Newton, Plymouth; three *s* one *d*. *Educ:* Univ. Coll. School and Univ. Coll. London. Matriculated Univ. of London, 1855; BA with Mathematical honours, 1858. Hon. MA Cantuar, 1884; Hon. DCL Durham, 1884. Barrister (1st class certificate of honour) Inner Temple, Jan. 1862; QC 1877; Bencher, 1880; Recorder of Bath, 1878–87; Chancellor of Southwell Diocese, 1884–87; Commissary of Westminster, 1884–87; Chief Commissioner of Canterbury Election Commission, 1880; Royal Commissioner to inquire into constitution of Ecclesiastical Courts, 1881–83; formerly for many years member of Councils of Law Reporting, of Legal Education, and of Univ. Coll. London; examiner in Common Law at Lond. Univ., 1877–82; President of Senate of Univ. Coll., 1889–96; contested London Univ. (C), 1880; Judge of High Court of Justice, Queen's Bench Division, 1887–97, and of the Arches Court of Canterbury and Chancery Court of York, 1899–1903. *Address:* Woodlands, Sevenoaks, Kent. *Club:* Athenæum.
                                    Died 20 Nov. 1921.

CHARLES, Commodore Sir James Thomas Walter, KBE 1920 (CBE 1919); CB 1911; RD; RNR; commanding the Cunard Line RMS Aquitania; Commodore of the Cunard Co's Fleet since 1921; *b* Hursley, 2 Aug. 1865; 2nd *s* of late James Charles; *m* 1893, Eleanor Mary, *e d* of Rev. T. Macfarlane, of Clyro Vicarage, Radnorshire; no *c*. *Educ:* privately. Went to sea in Mercantile Marine, 1880; Sub-Lieut RNR, 1891; Lieut 1895; Commander, 1907; Capt., 1914; Commodore, retired, 1921; Member Departmental Committee on Boats and Davits, 1912–13; Nautical Adviser to the British Delegation, International Conference on Safety of Life at Sea, 1913–14. *Address:* 21 Winn Road, Southampton.
                                    Died 15 July 1928.

CHARLESWORTH, Colonel Henry, CMG 1902; MRCS (Eng), LM (Lond), etc; RAMC, retired 1902; *b* 6 July 1851; *s* of M. Charlesworth, Heath House, Longnor, Staffordshire; *m* 1st, 1890, Lilian (*d* 1897), *o d* of W. Armstrong, York; 2nd, 1921, Constance Katherine, *d* of late George Bennett, 44 Holland Park, and Barnes. *Educ:* Ockbrook College, Derby. Entered the Army Medical Service, 1875; served Afghan War, 1879–80 (medal); accompanied as medical officer British mission to Sultan of Morocco, 1885, and again, 1890–91, under Sir Kirby Green, KCMG; served European War, 1914 (mentioned and thanked, Bt Col). *Recreations:* all out-door amusements. *Address:* c/o Holt & Co., 3 Whitehall Place, SW1. *Club:* Constitutional.   *Died 5 June 1926.*

CHARLTON, John, ROI, RPS, RBC; artist; *b* Bamburgh, Northumberland; *e s* of late Samuel Charlton; *m* 1882, Kate (*d* 1893), *d* of Thomas Vaughan, JP, DL, Ugthorp Lodge, Cleveland. *Educ:* Newcastle-on-Tyne; studied at Newcastle School of Arts and S Kensington; exhibited at RA 1870–73 and regularly since. *Paintings:* A Winter's Day; The Hall Fire; Rescue; Huntsman Courtship; Gone Away; Stag at Bay; British Artillery entering Enemy's Lines at Tel-el-Kebir; Ulundi; Reynard's Requiem; Bad News from the Front; Incident in the Charge of the Light Brigade, etc; the Procession of Royal Princes passing through Trafalgar Square to Westminster Abbey, 1887, painted for the Queen; also by command of HM the Queen the official picture of the thanksgiving service in front of St Paul's Cathedral on the occasion of the Royal Diamond Jubilee, entitled "God Save the Queen", and The Funeral of Queen Victoria; also a great many military, sporting, and other subjects to Graphic. *Address:* 6 William Street, Albert Gate, SW; Newcastle-on-Tyne, Northumberland. *Club:* Arts.
                                    Died 5 Nov. 1917.

CHARLTON-MEYRICK, Colonel Sir Thomas, 1st Bt, *cr* 1880; KCB 1910 (CB 1897); JP, DL; *b* 14 March 1837; 2nd *s* of late St J. C. Charlton, Apley Castle, Salop, and Jane, *o d* and *heiress* of late Thomas Meyrick, of Bush; *m* 1860, Mary Rhoda, *d* of Col F. Hill, and niece of 2nd Viscount Hill; three *s* four *d* (and two *s* decd). *Educ:* Eton. Col and Hon. Col 3rd Batt. Shropshire Regt; MP (C) Pembroke, 1868–74. Heir: *s* Brig.-Gen. Frederick Charlton-Meyrick, *b* 7 July 1862. *Address:* Bush, Pembroke; Apley Castle, Shropshire. *Clubs:* Boodle's, Windham.
                                    Died 31 July 1921.

CHARMES, Francis; Manager since 1907, and Editor since 1893, of the Revue des Deux Mondes; Officer Legion of Honour; Senator; Member of French Academy; *b* Aurillac, 21 April 1848. *Educ:* Collège d'Aurillac; Lycées of Clermont-Ferrand and Poitiers. Editor Journal des Débats, 1872–80 and 1889–1907; Deputy for Cantal, 1881–85 and 1891–98. *Publications:* many literary and political articles. *Address:* 17 Rue Bonaparte, Paris.   *Died 4 Jan. 1916.*

CHARRINGTON, Captain Eric, DSO 1900; RN retired; *b* 30 April 1872; *y s* of late Spencer Charrington, MP; *m* 1905, Rose Evelyn, *y d* of Lt-Col St J. Daubeney; one *s*. *Educ:* Brighton; Portsmouth. Obtained 4 First Classes at College as Sub-Lieut. Entered Navy, 1885; served Zanzibar, 1896; Benin, 1897 (medal, clasp); China, 1900 (medal, DSO); with storming party, capture of Taku Forts; relief of and operations round Tientsin. Decorated for services in attack and capture of Taku Forts. *Address:* Wormstall, Newbury. *TA:* Wickham, Berks. *Club:* Junior United Service.
                                    Died 15 Sept. 1927.

CHARRINGTON, Lieut-Col and Hon. Col Francis, CMG 1900; *b* 17 Nov. 1858; *s* of late Spencer Charrington, MP; *m* 1885, Alice Maud, *d* of late Walter Leith, JP; one *s* three *d*. *Educ:* Winchester. Commanded 4th South Staffordshire Regt in S Africa, 1900–1; present at actions Warrenton, Lindley, Bethlehem, and Winburg (despatches, medal with three clasps, CMG). *Address:* Pishiobury, Sawbridgeworth, Herts. *Died 3 July 1921.*

CHART, Edwin, MVO 1913; late HM Civil Service; *b* 11 May 1848; *e s* of Edwin Chart of Clarendon House, Mitcham, Surrey; *m* 1871, Martha, *e d* of William Godson of Addiscombe Road, Croydon; two *s* three *d*. *Educ:* Dr Fontaine's Private School, Sutton, Surrey. Entered HM Office of Works, 1866; Resident Architect, Hampton Court Palace and District, 1877; retired, 1913. *Address:* Banavie, Brambletye Park, Redhill, Surrey. *Died 10 Sept. 1926.*

CHASE, Rt. Rev. Frederic H., DD; *b* 21 Feb. 1853; *s* of late Rev. C. F. Chase, MA, Rector of St Andrew by the Wardrobe and St Anne, Blackfriars; *m* 1877, Charlotte Elizabeth, *e d* of late Rev. G. Armitage, Vicar of St Luke's, Gloucester; three *s* one *d*. *Educ:* King's College School, London; Christ's College, Cambridge, Scholar; Powis Medal (Latin verse), 1875; BA Classical Tripos (8th in First Class), 1876; Kaye Prize, 1884; MA 1879; BD 1891; DD 1894. Hulsean Lecturer, 1900; Hon. Fellow of Christ's Coll., 1904; Hon. Fellow of Queens' Coll., 1906; Curate of Sherborne, Dorset, 1876–79; Curate of St Michael's, Cambridge, 1879–84; Lecturer in Theology, Pemb. College, Cambridge, 1881–90; Lecturer in Theology, Christ's Coll. Camb., 1893–1901; Tutor of Clergy Training School, Cambridge, 1884–87; Principal of same, 1887–1901; Examining Chaplain to Archbishop of York, 1894–1905; President of Queens' College, Camb., 1901–6; Norrisian Prof. of Divinity, Cambridge, 1901–5; Bishop of Ely, 1905–24. *Publications:* Chrysostom, 1887; The Lord's Prayer in the Early Church (Texts and Studies, I iii) 1891; Old Syriac Element in Codex Bezae, 1895; Syro-Latin Text of the Gospels, 1897; Clement of Alexandria (a lecture), 1897; Articles on St Peter and I Peter and II Peter in Hastings' Dict. of Bible, 1900; Credibility of the Book of the Acts, 1901; Essay on the Gospels in the Light of Historical Criticism in Cambridge Theological Essays, 1905, republished separately with Preface, 1914; Confirmation in the Apostolic Age, 1909; Belief and Creed, 1918; The Creed and the New Testament, 1920; What did Christ teach about Divorce? 1921; Edited Commentary on I Peter by the late Rev. F. J. A. Hort, DD. *Address:* St Etheldreda's, 5 Constitution Hill, Woking, Surrey. *Died 23 Sept. 1925.*

CHATER, Sir Catchick Paul, Kt 1902; CMG 1897; JP; Member of Executive Council, Hong-Kong; *b* 1846; *s* of Chater Paul Chater of Calcutta. MLA 1887–1906. *Address:* Marble Hall, Conduit Road, Hong-Kong. *Club:* Hong-Kong. *Died 27 May 1926.*

CHATER, Colonel Vernor, MVO 1919; retired pay; *b* 1842; *s* of George Chater, of Langely, Bucks; *m* 1902, Edith Mary (*d* 1928), *d* of John Oliver Hanson. *Educ:* privately; Rugby. Joined the 91st Highlanders, subseq. 1st Batt. Argyll and Sutherland Highlanders, 1864; served in that Regt for 29 years; was Adjutant and Lt-Col; served in 2nd Batt. 93rd for a short time; ADC to General Officer in Scotland, 1877, and later to the Marquis of Lorne, Governor-General of Canada; commanded 25th Regimental District, King's Own Scottish Borderers, 1895–99; retired for age; served in India, Canada, South Africa (Zulu Campaign, despatches, medal and clasp), Ceylon and China; European War, served (at home) on Travelling Medical Board, 1915–17; later as acting Equerry to Princess Louise, Duchess of Argyll. *Recreations:* fishing, yachting, manly exercise. *Address:* 24 Walton Street, SW3. *T:* Western 4595. *Clubs:* Naval and Military, Garrick, Beefsteak, MCC; Royal Southern Yacht. *Died 3 Oct. 1928.*

CHATFEILD-CLARKE, Sir Edgar, Kt 1913; DL; MP (L) Isle of Wight, 1922–23, retiring owing to ill-health; *b* 17 Feb. 1863; *s* of Thomas Chatfeild-Clarke, FRIBA, FSI; *cousin* of late Rt Hon. Joseph Chamberlain, MP; unmarried. *Educ:* King's College School; Dresden. Member of the Isle of Wight County Council since 1900; JP; member of IW Education Committee; member of IW Advisory Committee *re* appointment of Magistrates. *Recreations:* yachting, Continental travel. *Address:* Wootton, Isle of Wight. *T:* Wootton 9. *Clubs:* Reform; Isle of Wight County. *Died 16 April 1925.*

CHATTERJI, Sir Protul Chandra, Kt 1909; CIE; DL; MA, LLD; Rai Bahadur; retired Judge, Chief Court, Punjab; Advocate Chief Court; *b* 8 Oct. 1848; *s* of Nabo Chandra Chatterji; *m* 1st, Nitumbini Devi, *d* of Woomachasan Banerji, Calcutta; 2nd, Basant Kumari Devi,

d of Srinath Mukerji, Landholder, Kanchrapora, Bengal; five *s* three *d*. *Educ:* General Assembly's College, Calcutta; Presidency Coll., Calcutta, Law Department; enrolled as a vakil, High Court, Calcutta, 1870; removed to Lahore, 1870; Municipal Commr, Lahore, 1887–95; Offg Judge Chief Court, 1889; Judge Chief Court, 1894–1908; Vice-Chancellor Punjab University, 1904 and 1907–9; President Public Library, Lahore. *Address:* 168 Cornwallis Street, Calcutta; Chatterji Road, Lahore. *Clubs:* India, Calcutta; Punjab Association, Lahore. *Died 17 Aug. 1917.*

CHATTERTON, Colonel Frank William, CIE 1894; unemployed list, India; *b* 1 June 1839; 3rd *s* of John Balsir Chatterton, harpist to Queen Victoria; *m* 1863, Susie (*d* 1923), *e d* of Major-Gen. J. F. Richardson, CB. *Educ:* Christ's Hospital, Mill Hill. Entered Indian Army, 1859; Adjutant 14th Sikhs; Umbeyla campaign, 1863 (frontier medal); Adjutant 29th Punjab Infantry; Bhootan campaign, 1865 (wounded, clasp); commanded Calcutta Volunteers, 1886–97; Chief Commissioner Andaman Islands, 1897. *Recreation:* cycling. *Address:* Central Lodge, Norwood, SE19. *T:* Sydenham 1839. *Club:* Junior Constitutional. *Died 4 March 1924.*

CHAUDHURI, Hon. Mr Justice Asutosh, Kt 1917; BA (Cantab), MA (Calcutta University); Barrister-at-Law; Judge of the Calcutta High Court; *b* Bengali, Brahmin, 1860; *e s* of Durgadas Chaudhuri Zemindar of Rajshye, a member of one of the oldest families of that district, the title "Chaudhuri" having been bestowed upon them by the Emperors of Delhi; *m* Prativa Devi, of the Tagore family of Calcutta, *g d* by son of Maharashi Devendranath Tagore; four *s* one *d*. *Educ:* St John's College, Cambridge; Presidency College, Calcutta. After graduating in Calcutta went to Cambridge and studied mathematics, taking 3rd Class Honours in the Mathematical Tripos, 1834; admitted as an Advocate of the Calcutta High Court, 1886; President of the Bengal National Conference; founded the Bengal Landholders' Association in Calcutta, of which he was the Honorary Secretary for years; was one of the founders of the Calcutta National College, and always took a prominent part in reform movements in Bengal; first time a Hindu member of the Calcutta Bar had been appointed Judge of the Court; later the Senior Judge on the original side of the Calcutta High Court; President of the Bengal Literary Conference, and President of the Calcutta Club. *Publications:* Elements of Trigonometry; some other works for school use. *Recreation:* walking. *Address:* 47 Old Ballygunge, Calcutta. *TA:* Baratlaw, Calcutta. *Clubs:* National Liberal, Calcutta, Calcutta. *Died May 1924.*

CHAVASSE, Rt. Rev. Francis James; *b* 27 Sept. 1846; *s* of Thomas Chavasse, FRCS, Wylde Green House, Sutton Coldfield; *m* 1881, Edith (*d* 1927), *y d* of Canon Maude, Vicar of Chirk; four *s* three *d*. *Educ:* Oxford; first-class law and history; MA, 1872; DD, 1900. Hon LLD Camb. 1908; Hon LLD Liverpool, 1920; Curate, St Paul's, Preston, 1870–73; Vicar, St Paul's, Upper Holloway, 1873–78; Rector, St Peter-le-Bailey, Oxford, 1878–89; Principal of Wycliffe Hall, Oxford, 1889–1900; Bishop of Liverpool, 1900–23. *Address:* St Peter's House, Oxford. *Died 11 March 1928.*

CHEAPE, Lt-Col Hugh Annesley Gray-, DSO 1917; JP Co. Worcester; Commissioner of Supply for Forfarshire; joint-master and huntsman of the Berwickshire Foxhounds; *b* 15 Nov. 1878; *e s* of late Col George Clerk Cheape of Wellfield, Fife, and Mrs Cheape of Bentley Manor, Worcestershire; on marriage took additional name and arms of Gray; *m* 1906, Carsina Gordon, *o d* of late Charles William Gray of Carse Gray, Forfar; one *s* three *d*. *Educ:* Glenalmond; Mulgrave Castle; Trinity Hall, Cambridge. Joined Queen's Own Worcestershire Hussars (Yeomanry), 1897; commanded Worcester Squadron Imperial Yeomanry in S Africa, 1901–2; retired with rank of Hon. Capt. in army; joined 4th Argyll and Sutherland Highlanders with rank of Capt. 1903; retired with rank of Hon. Major, 1912; while at Cambridge hunted the Cambridgeshire Harriers, and afterwards his mother's harriers in Worcestershire; joined Queen's Own Worcestershire Hussars, with rank of Major, 1914; served European War, 1915–17 (DSO); Lt-Col Warwickshire Yeomanry, 1916. *Recreation:* hunting. *Address:* Carse Gray, Forfar. *T:* Forfar 82. *M:* SR 199. *Clubs:* Cavalry; New, Edinburgh. *Died June 1918.*

CHECKLEY, Frank S., ISO 1911; Comptroller, School Lands Branch, Department of Interior, Canada. *Address:* 2 Cloverdale Road, Rockcliffe Park, Ottawa, Canada. *Died 31 March 1918.*

CHEETHAM, Rt. Hon. John Frederick, PC 1911; *b* 1835; *e s* of late John Cheetham of Eastwood, Cheshire (MP South Lancashire,

1852–59; Salford 1865–68); *m* 1887, Beatrice Emma, *y d* of late Francis Dukinfield Palmer Astley, DL, of Dukinfield, Cheshire, and Arisaig, Inverness-shire. *Educ:* University College, London; graduate BA in honours, University of London. MP (N) Derbyshire, 1880–85; Staleybridge, 1905–9; contested High Peak Div. 1885 and 1892; Bury (Lancs), 1895; Staleybridge, 1900; JP Cos Chester and Lancaster; Alderman of the Cheshire County Council; Governor of the Victoria University of Manchester; Director Manchester and Liverpool District Bank; received honorary freedom of Staleybridge, 1897, on presenting that borough with Jubilee Memorial gift of a Public Free Library. *Address:* Eastwood, Staleybridge. *Clubs:* Athenæum, Brooks's, Alpine.
Died 25 Feb. 1916.

CHENEY, E. John, CB 1915; MA (Cantab); MRAC, Haygarth Gold Medallist, FSI; Joint Secretary, HM Office of Woods, Forests and Land Revenues, 1919; *b* 1862; *s* of late E. Cheney, Brooks Hall, Ipswich; *m* Lilla Norman, *d* of late Rev. Frederick Lawson Hayward, Tunstall Rectory, Suffolk; one *s* one *d*. *Educ:* privately; Jesus College, Cambridge; Royal Agricultural College, Cirencester. Assistant Secretary Board of Agriculture and Fisheries, 1911–14; Chief Agricultural Adviser, 1914–18. *Address:* Heather Lodge, Sunningdale. *T:* Ascot 144. *Club:* Union.
Died 12 Oct. 1921.

CHERRY, Rt. Hon. Richard Robert, PC (Ireland) 1905; KC; LLD; *b* near Waterford, 19 March 1859; *y s* of Robert W. Cherry, Solicitor, and Susan, *d* of John Briscoe, MD; *m* 1886, Mary Wilhelmina, *d* of Robert Cooper of Collinstown House, Leixlip. *Educ:* Trinity Coll., Dublin; BA 1879; Double Gold Medallist in Mental Science and History and Political Science; Student in Jurisprudence and Roman Law at Inns of Court examination, London, 1880; First Scholar in International Law, Middle Temple, London. Called to Irish Bar, 1881; QC 1896; Examiner in Political Economy for Indian Civil Service, 1885–89; Professor of Constitutional and Criminal Law in University of Dublin, 1889–94; contested Kirkdale Division of Liverpool (L) 1900; Attorney-General for Ireland, 1905–9; MP (L) Exchange Div., Liverpool, 1906–9; a Lord Justice of Appeal for Ireland, 1909–14; Lord Chief Justice of Ireland, 1914–16. *Publications:* The Irish Land Law and Land Purchase Acts, 1888 (3rd edn, 1903); Lectures on the Growth of Criminal Law in Early Communities, 1890; An Outline of Criminal Law, 1892. *Address:* 92 St Stephen's Green, Dublin; Killincarrig House, Greystones, Co. Wicklow.
Died 10 Feb. 1923.

CHESNEY, Col Harold Frank, CMG 1918; retired pay RE; *b* 7 March 1859. Entered Army, 1878; retired 1911, having been CRE India; served Hazara Expedition, 1888 (despatches, medal and clasp); NW Frontier, Tochi Field Force, 1897 (medal and clasp).
Died 21 March 1920.

CHESTER-MASTER, Lt-Col (temp.) Richard, DSO 1917; Chief Constable, Gloucestershire, since 1910; *b* 29 Aug. 1870; *e s* of late Col T. W. Chester-Master, JP, of The Abbey, Cirencester, and Knole Park, Almondsbury, Gloucestershire; *m* 1901, Geraldine M. R., *e d* of late John H. Arkwright of Hampton Court, Herefordshire; two *s*. *Educ:* Harrow; Christ Church, Oxford. Captain and Brevet-Major, King's Royal Rifle Corps; retired pay, 1910; ADC to Viscount Milner (High Commissioner for South Africa), 1898–1901; served South African War, 1899–1902 (despatches, Queen's medal and 4 clasps, King's medal and 2 clasps); Commandant-General British South Africa Police (with local rank Lieut-Col), Rhodesia, 1901–5; Resident Commissioner and Commandant-General Southern Rhodesia, 1905–8; served European War, commanding 13th Batt. King's Royal Rifle Corps, 1915 (despatches, DSO and Bar). *Recreations:* all field sports. *Address:* St Clair, The Park, Cheltenham. *TA:* Cheltenham. *T:* Cheltenham 790. *Clubs:* Army and Navy, Carlton.
Died 30 Aug. 1917.

CHESTERTON, Cecil Edward; Highland Light Infantry; *b* Kensington, 12 Nov. 1879; *s* of Edward and Marie Louise Chesterton; *m* 1917, A. E. Jones (John Keith Prothero). *Educ:* St Paul's School. Entered journalism, 1901, writing first for the Outlook, and afterwards for a large number of journals and magazines; Member of the Executive of the Fabian Society, 1906–7; abandoned Fabian Socialism and began to attack the Party System, 1910; sub-editor of the Eyewitness, 1911–12; editor, 1912; founder and editor of the New Witness, 1912; commenced the attack on the Marconi Contract, August 1912; his energies mainly devoted to the exposure of the corruption of professional politics; lectured in America during the winter of 1914–15; editor of the New Witness, 1912–16; served European War, 1917. *Publications:* Gladstonian Ghosts, 1905; The People's Drink, 1909; Party and People, 1910; The Party System (with

Mr Belloc), 1911; Nell Gwynne, 1911; The Prussian hath said in his Heart, 1914; The Perils of Peace, 1916. *Recreation:* smoking. *Address:* 11 Warwick Gardens, Kensington, W; 21 Essex Street, Strand, WC. *TA:* New Witness, Estrand, London. *T:* City 1978. *Club:* Savage.
Died 7 Dec. 1918.

CHETWYND, Sir George, 4th Bt, *cr* 1795; *b* 31 May 1849; *s* of Sir George Chetwynd, 3rd Bt and Lady Charlotte Augusta Hill, *e d* of 3rd Marquess of Downshire; *S* father 1869; *m* 1870, Lady Florence Cecilia Paget (*d* 1907), *y d* of 2nd Marquess of Anglesey, and widow of 4th Marquess of Hastings; one *s* two *d* (and one *d* decd). High Sheriff, Warwickshire, 1870. Owned about 6700 acres. *Heir: s* George Guy Chetwynd [*b* 6 Dec. 1874; *m* 1902, Rosamund, who divorced him, 1909, *y d* of late Charles Secor, USA; one *s*]. *Address:* 23 Cork Street, W. *Club:* Turf.
Died 10 March 1917.

CHETWYND-STAPYLTON, Rev. William, MA; Hon. Canon of Rochester; *b* 15 May 1825; *s* of Major Henry Richard Chetwynd-Stapylton, 10th Hussars, and Margaret *d* of George Hammond, *sister* of late Lord Hammond; his grandfather, *s* of 4th Viscount Chetwynd, *m* the heiress of Wighill, Yorkshire, and by royal licence took name of Chetwynd-Stapylton; descended from Sir Brian Stapilton, one of the first Knights of the Garter, who purchased Wighill in the 14th century; *m* 1st, 1852, Elizabeth Biscoe (*d* 1893), *d* of Rev. Robert B. Tritton; two *s* one *d* (and one *s* decd); 2nd, 1898, Mary Elizabeth, *o d* of late Fred. Johnson. *Educ:* Eton. 2nd Captain of Boats, won sculling, double-sculling, and pair-oar races, the latter 3 times; Merton College, Oxford (Scholar); Fellow, 1847; won gold challenge cups for eights and for fours both at Thames and Henley Regattas, 1844. Rector of Old Malden, Surrey, 1850–94; Hallaton, Leicestershire, 1894–1907. *Address:* 21 Ferndale, Tunbridge Wells.
Died 4 March 1919.

CHEVALIER, Albert; comedian; *b* 21 March 1861; Italian, French, and Welsh blood in his veins; *m* 1895, Florence, *d* of George Leybourne. First appearance in public as a child eight years old; as an actor on the legitimate stage was for many years associated with Mr and Mrs Kendal, John Hare, A. W. Pinero, T. W. Robertson, Mr and Mrs Bancroft, John Clayton, etc; was for four years connected with music-halls, making first London appearance at London Pavilion, 1891; then toured with his own entertainment in England and America, and gave 1000 Chevalier recitals at Queen's Hall, London; author of over 100 sketches, monologues, plays. *Publication:* Before I Forget, 1901. *Address:* 38 Woodberry Down, N4. *T:* Dalston 743.
Died 10 July 1923.

CHEYLESMORE, 3rd Baron (UK), *cr* 1887; **Herbert Francis Eaton,** KCMG 1919; KCVO 1909; Major-General; retired Chairman National Rifle Association; Chairman LCC; *b* 25 Jan. 1848; 3rd *s* of 1st Lord Cheylesmore; *S* brother, 1902; *m* 1892, Elizabeth Richardson, *d* of late F. O. French, of New York; two *s*. *Educ:* Eton; passed into army direct from there. Joined Gren. Guards 1867; commanded 2nd Batt. Gren. Guards when sent to Bermuda, 1890; and the Regiment, 1899; contested Coventry, 1887, on elevation of his father to the Peerage, beaten by 16 votes. Owned Manor of Cheylesmore, Coventry, formerly possessed by Edward the Black Prince; White's Club. *Publication:* Naval and Military Medals of Great Britain. *Recreations:* rowing, shooting, rifle-shooting, coaching, etc. *Heir: s* Hon. Francis Ormond Henry Eaton, *b* 19 June 1893. *Address:* 16 Princes Gate, SW7. *T:* Western 715. *Clubs:* Guards, Travellers', Carlton, Marlborough, Turf, Bachelors', Pratts', Beefsteak, United Service, Four-in-Hand.
Died 29 July 1925.

CHICHESTER, 6th Earl of, *cr* 1801; **Jocelyn Brudenell Pelham,** Bt 1611; Baron Pelham of Stanmer, 1762; OBE 1918; DL, JP Sussex; Public Works Loan Commissioner; late Brevet Lieutenant-Colonel Royal Sussex Regiment; *b* 21 May 1871; *e s* of 5th Earl of Chichester and Hon. Alice Carr Glyn, *d* of 1st Baron Wolverton; *S* father, 1905; *m* 1898, Ruth, *e d* of late F. W. Buxton; two *s* two *d*. *Heir: s* Lord Pelham, *b* 23 March 1905. *Address:* Stanmer, Lewes, Sussex. *Clubs:* Brooks's, Bath, Beefsteak.
Died 14 Nov. 1926.

CHICHESTER, 7th Earl of, *cr* 1801; **Francis Godolphin Henry Pelham,** Bt 1611; Baron Pelham of Stanmer, 1762; *b* 23 March 1905; *e s* of 6th Earl; *S* father, 1926. *Educ:* Eton; Trinity College, Oxford. *Recreation:* shooting. *Heir: b* Hon. John Buxton Pelham, *b* 12 June 1912. *Address:* Stanmer, Lewes, Sussex. *T:* Preston, Brighton 74.
Died 23 Nov. 1926.

CHICHESTER, Rev. Edward Arthur, MA; Hon. Canon of Winchester, 1906; Rural Dean, 1891–1920; Vicar of Dorking, 1885–1921; *b* 23 Feb. 1849; *s* of late Rev. George Vaughan Chichester,

Vicar of Wotton, Surrey, *y b* of 1st Baron O'Neill, and Harriett, *d* of Hugh Lyle, of Co. Antrim; *m* 1884, Hon. Mary Agnes Cubitt, 2nd *d* of 1st Baron Ashcombe; one *s* two *d. Educ:* Cambridge (MA). Curate, Farncombe, Surrey, 1875–77; Vicar of Okewood, 1877–85. *Publications:* Ad Clerium, Foreword by Bishop Talbot, 1914; Solemn Reminder. *Address:* Ashleigh, Dorking. *T:* Dorking 210. *Club:* Royal Societies. *Died 30 Sept. 1925.*

CHICHESTER, Lord Henry Fitzwarrine; *b* 11 Sept. 1834; 2nd *s* of 4th Marquess of Donegall; *m* 1860, Elizabeth Julia (*d* 1902), *o c* and *heiress* of Samuel Amy Severne of Poslingford, and *g d* of T. A. Severne, of Wollop, Shropshire, and Thenford, Banbury, Northamptonshire; two *s* four *d* (and one *s* one *d* decd). *Clubs:* Carlton, Isthmian, Prince's, Hurlingham, Thatched House, Sandown. *Died 7 Nov. 1928.*

CHICHESTER, Colonel Robert Peel Dawson Spencer; late commanding 14th Service Battalion Royal Irish Rifles; late Captain Irish Guards; *b* 13 Aug. 1873; *e s* of late Rt Hon. Lord Adolphus John Spencer Chichester of Moyola Park, Castledawson, Co. Londonderry, and Droish, Co. Donegal; *m* 1901, Dehra, *o c* and *heiress* of late James Ker-Fisher of the Manor House, Kilrea, Co. Londonderry, and of Chicago, USA; one *s* one *d*. Served in Central Africa, 1897–99 (medals and clasps), with Central African Rifles, now King's African Regt; an Asst Commissioner and in command of the combined escorts to the Anglo-German Boundary Commission, Myassa and Tanjanika, 1908; served South Africa, 1899 and 1900; commanded 6th Batt. (The Duke of Cambridge's Own) Middlesex Regt, 1904–13. DL Co. Londonderry; JP Cos Antrim, Donegal, and Londonderry; High Sheriff Co. Londonderry, 1904–5; Co. Antrim, 1907. *Recreations:* Master of the Killultagh, Old Rock, and Chichester Harriers since 1905; fishing, shooting, and coursing (a Waterloo Cup nominator), cricket. *Address:* Moyola Park, Castledawson, Co. Londonderry; Eden Lodge, Dungiven, Co. Londonderry. *Clubs:* Guards, White's, Junior United Service; Ulster, Belfast; Union, Brighton. *Died 10 Dec. 1921.*

CHIENE, John, CB 1900; LLD, DSc, MD; FRCS; FRS (Edin); Professor of Surgery, Edinburgh University, 1882–1909; *b* 25 Feb. 1843; *s* of George Todd Chiene of Edinburgh; *m* 1869, Elizabeth Mary, *d* of David Lyall of Calcutta; two *s* one *d*. *Educ:* Edinburgh; Paris. Late President Royal Medical Society and College of Surgeons, Edinburgh; late Consulting Surgeon to HM's Forces in South Africa, 1900 (despatches, medal, CB). Member Royal Medical and Surgical Society, Edin.; Hon. Fellow Surg. Assoc. America, Paris, and Finland. *Publications:* Lectures on Surgical Anatomy, 1878; Principles of Surgery, 1882. *Recreations:* golf, fishing. *Address:* Aithernie, Davidson's Mains. *T:* Davidson's Mains 42. *Club:* University, Edinburgh. *Died 29 May 1923.*

CHILDE-PEMBERTON, William Shakespear; *b* Millichope, 1859; *s* of late C. O. Childe-Pemberton, DL, of Millichope Park, Shropshire; *m* 1894, Lady Constance, *y d* of 6th Earl of Darnley; one *s*. *Educ:* Harrow. Became representative of the family of Childe (of Kinlet) on the death of his elder brother, Major Childe, killed in the action of Bastion Hill, Natal, Jan. 1900; hereditary governor of Childe's Coll. Cleobury Mortimer (founded by Sir Lacon Childe); co-heir to several baronies derived from Plantagenets. *Publications:* Elizabeth Blount and Henry VIII; The Romance of Princess Amelia; Life of Lord Norton; Memoirs of Baroness de Bode, 1775–1803. *Recreations:* musical composition, sketching, travelling. *Address:* 12 Portman Street, W. *Club:* Bachelors'. *Died 5 Jan. 1924.*

CHILDERS, Col Edmund Spencer Eardley, CB 1900; *b* 11 Jan. 1854; *s* of late Rt Hon. Hugh Childers, MP; *m* 1883, Florence, 3rd *d* of late William Leslie, MP, Warthill, Aberdeenshire; two *s* one *d*. *Educ:* Eton; Cheltenham; RMA, Woolwich. Entered Royal Engineers, 1873; served Afghan War, 1878–80; advance on Candahar, 1878; the operations round Cabul, 1879; march from Cabul to the relief of Candahar under Sir Frederick Roberts in 1880; assistant private secretary to the Secretary of State for War, 1880–81; ADC to the Inspector-General of Fortifications, 1883–84; served in Egyptian Expedition of 1882 as ADC to Sir Garnet Wolseley; present at Tel-el-Kebir, and in the Nile Expedition of 1884–85 in a similar capacity; was Military Secretary in Ireland to Field-Marshal Viscount Wolseley, 1890–95; served on a special commission to inquire into and report on the organisation of the local forces in Cape Colony, 1897; Commanding Royal Engineer, Weymouth, 1900–5; Chief Engineer, London District, 1906–10; Deputy Chief Engineer, Southern Command, 1914–17. *Publication:* The Life and Correspondence of Rt Hon. Hugh Culling Eardley Childers, 1901. *Club:* Brooks's. *Died 18 March 1919.*

CHILDERS, Lt-Comdr (Robert) Erskine, DSC; RNVR; *b* 25 June 1870; *s* of Robert C. Childers and Anna Mary Henrietta, *d* of Thomas Johnston Barton; *m* 1904, Mary Alden Osgood; two *s*. *Educ:* Haileybury; Trinity College, Cambridge. Served European War with RNAS Jan.–May 1916 (DSC). *Publications:* In the Ranks of the CIV, 1900; The Riddle of the Sands, 1903; Vol. V of the Times History of the South African War, 1907; War and the Arme Blanche, 1910; German Influence on British Cavalry, 1911; The Framework of Home Rule, 1911. *Died 24 Nov. 1922.*

CHILSTON, 1st Viscount, *cr* 1911, of Boughton Malherbe; **Aretas Akers-Douglas;** Baron Douglas, 1911; GBE 1920; PC 1891; DL; MP (C) St Augustine's Division of Kent, 1880–1911; *b* 21 Oct. 1851; *o s* of Rev. Aretas Akers, Malling Abbey, Kent and Frances Maria, *d* of Francis Holles Brandram; *m* 1875, Adeline, *e d* of H. Austen Smith, Hayes Court, Kent; two *s* five *d*. *Educ:* Eton; Univ. Coll., Oxford. Barrister, Inner Temple, 1875. Late Capt. E. Kent, Yeomanry Cavalry; Whip to Conservative Party, 1883–95; Parliamentary Secretary to Treasury, 1885–86, 1886–92, and for short time, 1895; First Commissioner of Works, with seat in Cabinet, 1895–1902; Secretary of State, Home Department, 1902–6. *Heir: s* Hon. Aretas Akers-Douglas, *b* 17 Feb. 1876. *Address:* Chilston Park, Maidstone; 34 Lower Belgrave Street, W. *Clubs:* Carlton, Junior Carlton. *Died 15 Jan. 1926.*

CHISHOLM, Rt. Rev. Æneas; RC Bishop of Aberdeen since 1899; *b* Inverness, 26 June 1836; 4th *s* of Colin Chisholm, solicitor. *Educ:* St Mary's College, Blairs, Aberdeen; Gregorian University, Rome. LLD, Aberdeen University. Served as priest in Aberdeen Diocese from 1860 in Glenlivet, Beauly, Aberdeen, Glengairn, Banff; appointed Rector of Blairs College, 1890; made a Domestic Prelate to His Holiness, 1898. *Address:* 19 Golden Square, Aberdeen, NB. *Club:* University, Aberdeen. *Died 13 Jan. 1918.*

CHISHOLM, Hugh; Editor of the Encyclopædia Britannica (10th, 11th and 12th editions); *b* London, 22 Feb. 1866; *o s* of late Henry Williams Chisholm, Warden of the Standards, formerly Chief Clerk of HM's Exchequer; *m* 1893, Eliza Beatrix, *d* of late Henry Harrison, Holywood House, and Ardkeen, Co. Down; three *s*. *Educ:* Felsted School (exhibitioner); Corpus Christi College, Oxford (scholar), 1st class Classical Mods. 1886; 1st class Lit. Hum. 1888; MA. Barrister Middle Temple, 1892. Assistant-editor (1892–97), and editor (1897–1900) of the St James's Gazette; leader-writer for Standard (1900) and subsequently The Times; co-editor (with Sir Donald M. Wallace and President A. T. Hadley of Yale) of the supplementary vols (10th edition, 1902) of the Encyclopædia Britannica (for The Times), 1900–3; editor-in-chief of the 11th edition (Cambridge), 1911, and the New Vols, 1922, forming with it the 12th Edition; director of The Times Publishing Co., 1913–16; Financial Editor of The Times, 1913–20. *Publications:* articles on public finance, politics, and literature in Encyclopædia Britannica, Fortnightly Review, National Review, etc. *Recreations:* golf, music, bridge, billiards. *Address:* 3 Ellerdale Road, Hampstead, NW3. *T:* Hampstead 2706. *Clubs:* Athenæum, Constitutional, United, Cecil; Crowborough Beacon Golf; Lotus, New York. *Died 29 Sept. 1924.*

CHISHOLM, Sir Samuel, 1st Bt, *cr* 1902; JP, DL County of City of Glasgow and County of Lanark; LLD Glasgow, 1901; Lord Provost of Glasgow; Lord Lieutenant of the County of the City of Glasgow; Chairman of the Clyde Navigation Trustees; Member of the Carnegie Education Trust, 1899–1902; Chairman of the Executive Council of the Glasgow International Exhibiton 1901; Chairman of Housing Commission; Hon. Pres. of Glasgow Foundry Boys Religious Society; Chairman of Glasgow and West of Scotland College of Domestic Science; *b* Dalkeith, 23 Sept. 1836; *s* of John Chisholm and Isabilla, *d* of George Wilson; *m* 1st, 1866, Charlotte (*d* 1900), *d* of Rev. J. B. Thompson, Holywell; 2nd, 1903, Agnes Gibson (*d* 1921), *d* of Andrew Carnduff, The Anchorage, Cathcart, and *widow* of Thomas Henderson, founder of the Anchor Line of steamships. *Educ:* Dalkeith. Entered Town Council of Glasgow, 1888; Bailie of the Burgh, 1892–97; Senior Magistrate, 1897; Convener of City Improvement Trust, 1892–1902; was a member of the Government Commission on Glanders, and of Royal Commission on Registration of Title in Scotland; contested Camlachie Divison of Glasgow, 1897; member, Natural History Society of Glasgow, Royal Philosophical Society of Glasgow, and Glasgow Art Club. *Recreations:* walking, swimming, motoring. *Heir:* none. *Address:* 20 Belhaven Terrace, Glasgow. *T:* PO 2401. *Clubs:* Liberal, Scottish Automobile, Glasgow; Scottish Liberal, Edinburgh. *Died 27 Sept. 1923 (ext)*

CHOATE, Joseph Hodges; a Trustee of the Metropolitan Museum of Art and of the American Museum of Natural History since the foundation of each; a Governor of New York Hospital since 1877; a member (and chairman of its Committee of Elections) of the original Committee of Seventy, which in 1871 overthrew the Tweed Ring and expelled from the Bench its corrupt judges; Hon. Bencher Middle Temple; *b* Salem, Mass, 24 Jan. 1832; *m* 1861, Caroline, *d* of Frederick A. Sterling of Cleveland, Ohio; two *s* one *d*. *Educ:* Harvard and Harvard Law School. LLD Amherst, 1887; Harvard, 1888; Edinburgh and Cambridge, 1900; Yale, 1901; St Andrews, 1902; Glasgow, 1904; Williams, 1905; Univ. of Pennsylvania, 1908; Union, 1909; McGill, 1913; Toronto, 1915; Columbia, 1916; DCL Oxford, 1902; Bar (Mass), 1855; New York, 1856; for many years president of Union League Club, Harvard Club, and New England Society of New York; also of New York City Bar Association, New York State Bar Association, American Bar Association, and Harvard Law School Association; President New York State Constitutional Convention, 1894; trustee and chairman of the Peabody Education Fund, and president of the New York Association for the Blind; engaged for more than 30 years in many of the most important causes in the Courts of New York, and in the Supreme Court of the United States; United States Ambassador to Great Britain, 1899–1905; member, American Philosophical Society, 1906; Foreign Hon. Fellow Royal Society of Literature; Ambassador and First Delegate of the United States to the International Peace Conference at The Hague, 1907. *Publications:* The Two Hague Conferences; Abraham Lincoln, 1910; American Addresses, 1911; Admiral Farragut, Rufus Choate, The Supreme Court of the US, and many other subjects. *Address:* 60 Wall Street, New York; Stockbridge, Mass. USA.

Died 14 May 1917.

CHOLMONDELEY, 4th Marquess of, *cr* 1815; **George Henry Hugh Cholmondeley,** DL; Bt 1611; Viscount Cholmondeley, 1661; Baron Cholmondeley (Eng.), 1689; Earl of Cholmondeley, Viscount Malpas, 1706; Baron Newburgh (Ire.), 1715; Baron Newburgh (Gt Brit.), 1716; late Lord Great Chamberlain of England; *b* 3 July 1858; *s* of Charles George, *e s* of 3rd Marquess, and Susan Caroline, *d* of Sir George Dashwood, 4th Bt; *S* grandfather, 1884; *m* 1879, Winifred Ida, OBE, *y d* of late Col Sir Nigel Kingscote, KCB, and *g d* of 1st Earl Howe; two *s* one *d*. Owned about 34,000 acres. *Heir: s* Earl of Rocksavage, *b* 19 May 1883. *Address:* Cholmondeley Castle, Malpas, Cheshire. *Club:* Turf.

Died 15 March 1923.

CHOLMONDELEY, Mary; *b* 1859; *e d* of late Rev. R. H. Cholmondeley, late Rector of Hodnet, and formerly of Condover Hall, Shropshire, and Emily, *sister* of H. R. Beaumont of Whitley Beaumont, Yorks; grandmother was Mary Heber, *sister* of Bishop Heber, the hymn-writer. *Publications:* The Danvers Jewels, 1887; Sir Charles Danvers, 1889; Diana Tempest, 1893; A Devotee; Red Pottage, 1899; and Moth and Rust, 1902; Prisoners, 1906; The Lowest Rung, 1908; Notwithstanding, 1913; Under one Roof, 1918; The Romance of his Life, 1921. *Address:* 4 Argyll Road, Kensington, W8; The Cottage, Ufford, Suffolk.

Died 15 July 1925.

CHOUINARD, Honoré Julien Jean Baptiste, CMG 1908; City Clerk Quebec since 1889; *b* 1850; *s* of late Honoré Julien Chouinard, Barrister, Quebec; *m* 1884, Marie Louise Juchereau Duchesnay, *y d* of Hon. Elzear H. Juchereau Duchesnay, Senator of Canada; two *s* one *d*. *Educ:* St Ann's College, Quebec Seminary (LB); Laval University (LLB). Called to Bar, Quebec, 1873; was President of l'Institut Canadien of Quebec (literary); of Quebec Geographical Society; twice of National French-Canadian St Jean Baptiste Society; of Cartier Club (political), 1882; Past Director and Vice-President of Quebec and Lake St John Railway; sat as alderman in Quebec City Council, 1880–89; contested County of l'Islet, general elections, 1882; elected for County of Dorchester in 1887; sat in Canadian Commons, 1888–90; was one of the chief promoters of the Quebec Tercentenary Celebration (CMG); FRS Can. 1917; LD Laval University. *Publications:* several literary and historical works (including Annals of St Jean Baptiste Society). *Address:* Quebec.

Died 27 Nov. 1928.

CHOWN, Maj.-Gen. Ernest Edward, CB 1917; late RMLI; *b* 14 Feb. 1864. Lt RM 1883; Capt. 1893; Major, 1900; Lt-Col 1908; Col 1914; Superintendent Gymnasium, Malta, 1909–14; retired, 1917.

Died 24 Sept. 1922.

CHOWN, John; *b* Bradford; *s* of Rev. J. P. Chown, Baptist Minister; *m* Emma Emily, *d* of Rev. Thos Rees; three *s* one *d*. *Educ:* private school at Bradford. Spent six years in Bradford Warehouse; came to London as Agent; afterwards becoming a member of the Stock Exchange; President of the Baptist Union, 1922–23; Vice-President

of the British and Foreign Bible Society; President of the Willesden Liberal Association. *Recreations:* music, cycling. *Address:* 17 Brondesbury Park, NW6. *T:* Willesden 51. *Club:* National Liberal.

Died 11 Aug. 1922.

CHREE, Charles, MA, ScD (Cambridge) 1896; LLD (Aberdeen), 1898; FRS 1897; *b* Lintrathen, Forfarshire, 5 May 1860; 2nd *s* of Rev. Charles Chree, DD, and Agnes, *d* of W. Bain; unmarried. *Educ:* Grammar School, Old Aberdeen; Universities of Aberdeen and Cambridge. Graduated Aberdeen, 1879; obtaining gold medal awarded to the most distinguished graduate in Arts of the year; graduated Cambridge, 1883; 6th Wrangler, 1883; 1st division Mathematical Tripos, Part III; 1st class Natural Sciences Tripos, Part II; Fellow of King's College, 1885; re-elected as Research Fellow, 1890; Superintendent Kew Observatory, 1893–1925; awarded James Watt Medal, Institution of Civil Engineers, 1905; and Hughes Medal, Royal Society, 1919; Past President Royal Meteorological Society; Past President, Physical Society of London. *Recreations:* fishing, golf, cycling. *Address:* 75 Church Road, Richmond, Surrey.

Died 12 Aug. 1928.

CHRISTIAN, Admiral Arthur Henry, CB 1916; MVO 1910; *b* 31 Aug. 1863; 4th *s* of late George Christian and Mrs Christian, 13 Lowndes Square, SW; *m* 1911, Geraldine Diana, *d* of late Lt-Col Bolton Monsell; one *s* two *d*. *Educ:* HMS Britannia. Midshipman, HMS Bacchante, 1879–82; Lieut, 1885; specially promoted to commander, 1896, for services on East and West Coast of Africa; commander of HMS Blake and Excellent; Captain, 1901; Vice-Admiral, 1917; served HMS Highflyer as Flag-Capt. to Admiral Sir Charles Drury, East Indies, 1902, and in command of HMS Juno and Duke of Edinburgh, RN College, Osborne, and HMS Temeraire; commanded 3rd Division Home Fleet, 1912–14; served European War, 1914; hoisted flag on Euryalus, Aug. 1914, in command of a special force of cruisers, destroyers, and submarines operating in southern part of North Sea; took part in action off Heligoland, 28 Aug. 1914; Rear-Admiral in Eastern Mediterranean, 1915–17; took part in operations at the Dardanelles, commanded Naval Forces at landing at Suvla Bay, and subsequent operations up to and including evacuation of Gallipoli; wounded at Suvla Bay (despatches, CB); Adm. retired, 1919. *Recreations:* golf, riding, shooting. *Address:* 3 Sloane Gardens, SW1. *Club:* United Service.

Died 20 Aug. 1926.

CHRISTIAN, Admiral Henry, MVO 1909; Chief Constable of Gloucestershire, 1865–1910; *b* 29 Oct. 1828; *s* of Samuel Christian, Malta; *m* 1865, *d* of James Moore, Liverpool. Entered Navy, 1841; Lieut, 1849; Commander, 1858; Captain, 1863; retired Captain, 1870; retired Rear-Admiral, 1878; Vice-Admiral, 1884; Admiral, 1889; served in suppression of slave trade; Commander of HMS Euryalus, 1858–61; Commander of Royal Yacht Victoria and Albert, 1861–63. *Address:* Heighthorne, The Park, Cheltenham. *Club:* Army and Navy.

Died 10 June 1916.

CHRISTIE, Herbert Bertram, DSO 1900; NSW Bushmen Contingent; *b* 1863; *s* of late Marshall Christie. Served South Africa, 1900 (despatches, DSO). *Address:* Braemar, Casino, New South Wales.

Died 9 Dec. 1916.

CHRISTIE, Sir William Henry Mahoney, KCB 1904 (CB 1897); MA; FRS 1881; FRAS; Hon. DSc Oxon; Astronomer-Royal 1881–1910; *b* 1 Oct. 1845; *s* of late Professor Samuel Hunter Christie, FRS; *m* 1881, Mary Violette (*d* 1884), *d* of late Sir Alfred Hickman, 1st Bt; one *s* (and one *s* decd). *Educ:* King's Coll. School, London; Trinity Coll., Cambridge (Fellow). Chief Assistant Royal Observatory, Greenwich, 1870. *Publications:* Manual of Elementary Astronomy, 1875; and various scientific papers. *Address:* The Tower House, Downe, Kent. *Club:* Savile.

Died 22 Jan. 1922.

CHRISTISON, Sir Alexander, 2nd Bt, *cr* 1871; MD; Surgeon-General IMS (retired); *b* 26 Aug. 1828; *s* of Sir Robert Christison, 1st Bt; *S* father, 1882; *m* 1st, 1854, Jemima Anne (*d* 1876), *d* of James Cowley Brown, BCS; one *s* three *d*; 2nd, 1892, Florence, *d* of F. T. Elworthy, Foxdown, Wellington, Somerset; one *s* three *d* (and one *s* decd). *Educ:* Edin. Univ. Served in 2nd Burmese War and Indian Mutiny. *Heir: s* Major Robert Alexander Christison [RGA (militia); retired; *b* 23 Feb. 1870; *m* 1900, Mary Russell, *d* of A. R. Gilzean]. *Address:* 40 Moray Place, Edinburgh.

Died 14 Oct. 1918.

CHRISTMAS, E. W., RBA 1909; *b* South Australia; *s* of late John J. Christmas, JP; unmarried. *Educ:* Adelaide; artistically, Adelaide,

Sydney, and London. Exhibited Royal Glasgow Institute, 1901; exhibited, 1909, Royal Institute, Royal Oil Institute, London, Leeds Art Gallery, and Hull by special invitation; two pictures hung in Royal Academy, 1910; same year exhibited Royal Oil Institute; two pictures hung in Royal Academy, 1911; also RBA and Corporation galleries of provinces; went to South America, 1910, to paint the Andes and mountains from Argentine to Chile; went Southern Andes, 1911, and painted lakes and mountains of that interior of the far south; represented in seven National and Corporation Galleries of the Colonies of Australasia. *Club:* Langham Sketch.

Died 30 July 1918.

CHRISTOPHER, Maj.-Gen. Leonard William, CB 1898; *b* 22 Jan. 1848; *e s* of Maj.-Gen. L. R. Christopher; *m* 1878, Florence, 4th *d* of Maj.-Gen. Charles Stuart Lane, CB; one *s.* Entered 75th Regt (present 1st Gordon Highlanders), 1867; Col Bengal Staff Corps, 1897; Maj.-Gen., 1902; served Afghan War, 1878–80 (despatches, medal); Egyptian Expedition, 1882 (medal, bronze star); Tirah Expedition, 1897–98 (despatches, CB); Director-General of Supply and Transport, India, 1900–5; retired, 1908.

Died 25 Aug. 1927.

CHURCH, Robert William, CIE 1921; *b* 2 April 1882; *e s* of W. J. Church, Durham City; *m* 1919, Winifred Florence, *e d* of G. E. Platt, Hungerford, Berks; two *d. Educ:* privately; Armstrong College, Newcastle-on-Tyne. BSc University of Durham. FGS 1907; MInst ME 1907. In charge Bokero-Ramgur Coalfield Survey, 1908–10; Mining Engineer Railway Board Government of India, 1910–21. *Club:* Oriental.

Died 16 Nov. 1923.

CHURCH, Maj.-Gen. Thomas Ross, CIE 1883; unemployed list Indian Staff Corps; *b* 5 Jan. 1831; 2nd *s* of late Thomas Church, BCS; *m* 1854, Florence, 4th *d* of late Capt. Frederick Marryat, RN, CB. *Educ:* privately; Addiscombe Coll. Served in various staff appointments in India, and commanded the Madras Volunteer Guards for 14 years. *Recreations:* shooting, fishing.

Died 29 Oct. 1926.

CHURCH, Sir William Selby, 1st Bt, *cr* 1901; KCB 1902; MD, DSc Oxon; LLD Glasgow, ScD Victoria, DCL Durham Universities; late President Royal Society of Medicine; President Royal College of Physicians, 1899–1905; Consulting Physician St Bartholomew's Hospital, the City of London Hospital for Diseases of the Chest, and the Royal General Dispensary; Hon. Fellow University College, Oxford; JP Herts; *b* 4 Dec. 1837; *o* surv. *s* of John Church, of Woodside, Hatfield, Herts, and Isabella, *d* of George Selby, of Twizell House, Northumberland; *m* 1875, Sybil Constance (*d* 1913), *d* of C. J. Bigge, of Linden, Northumberland; one *s* one *d* (and one *s* decd). *Educ:* Harrow; University Coll., Oxford, 1st Class Natural Science School, 1860; representative for University in General Medical Council, 1889–99. Formerly Lee's Reader in Anatomy at Christ Church, Oxford; Lecturer on Comparative Anatomy, St Bartholomew's Medical School; member of Royal Commission on the Care and Treatment of the Sick and Wounded during the South African Campaign, 1900, and of the Royal Commission on Arsenical Poisoning, 1901, and of the Royal Commission on Vivisection, 1906; Trustee of Hunterian Museum, Royal Coll. of Surgeons of England. *Heir: s* Geoffrey Selby Church [*b* 11 Jan. 1887; *m* 1st, 1913, Doris Louise Cleghorn (*d* 1917), *d* of Sir William Somerville; *m* 2nd, 1920, Helene Trayner. *Educ:* Winchester]. *Publications:* papers in St Bartholomew's Hospital Reports; Allbutt's System of Medicine, and various Medical Journals, etc. *Recreations:* outdoor sports. *Address:* Woodside, Hatfield, Herts. *TA:* Bell Bar. *T:* Hatfield 44. *M:* NK 3870. *Club:* Athenæum. *Died 27 April 1928.*

CHURCHILL, Surg.-Gen. Alexander Ferrier, MB, LRCSI; *b* 1839; *m* 1869, Ellen Louisa Phayre; one *s* one *d. Educ:* Trinity College; Royal College of Surgeons, Dublin. Entered Army, 1862; retired, 1899; served Soudan Expedition, 1884–85 (medal with clasp, bronze star). *Address:* Tirley, Brentwood, Essex. *T:* 329.

Died 10 Oct. 1928.

CHURCHILL, Harry Lionel, CMG 1915; FRGS; HBM Consul-Gen. for Compartimenti di Liguria and Emilia, with the exception of Provinces of Ferrara, Bologna, Ravenna, and Forti, to reside at Genoa, since 1922; *b* 12 Sept. 1860; *s* of H. A. Churchill, CB, Diplomatic and Consular Services; *m* 1892, *d* of late Sir Joseph Tholozau, KCMG, who was for 40 years Physician-in-Chief to late Nasr ed Din, Shah of Persia; two *s* three *d. Educ:* privately. Acting Consul at Resht, Persia, 1878; employed in British Legation on probation, 1880–83; Translator and Clerk, 1883; passed examination, 1883; Vice-Consul, Tehran, 1883; Vice-Consul in the dominions

of the Sultan of Zanzibar, 1885; was in attendance on Special Envoy sent by the Shah of Persia on the occasion of Queen Victoria's Jubilee 1887 (Jubilee medal); Consul at Resht, Persia, 1891; was in attendance on the Special Envoy sent by the Shah of Persia on the occasion of Queen Victoria's Diamond Jubilee (clasp of the Jubilee medal), 1897 transferred to Trieste, 1899; Lisbon, 1905; Havre, 1907. *Address:* Via Marcello, Durazzo, Genoa. *TA:* British Consul, Genoa. *Clubs* Royal Societies, Junior Constitutional; Union, Genoa.

Died 5 Nov. 1924

CHURCHILL, Lady Randolph Spencer, (Jennie Spencer), C 1885; RRC 1902; Lady of Grace of St John of Jerusalem, 1901; wa proprietor and Editor of the Anglo-Saxon Review; *d* of late Leonare Jerome, New York; *m* 1st, 1874, Rt Hon. Lord Randolph Henr Spencer Churchill, 3rd *s* of 7th Duke of Marlborough (*d* 1895); tw *s;* 2nd, 1900, George Cornwallis-West (whom she divorced 1913) 3rd, 1918, Montagu Porch. Had charge of hospital-ship Maine, Sout Africa. *Publications:* The Reminiscences of Lady Randolph Churchill 1908; (play) His Borrowed Plumes, 1909; (play) The Bill, 1912 (essays) Small Talks on Big Subjects, 1916. *Address:* 8 Westbourn Street, Hyde Park, W2. *Clubs:* Ladies' Athenæum, Ladies Automobile. *Died 29 June 1921*

CHURCHILL, Sidney John Alexander, MVO 1906; Consul General Campania, Basilicata and the Calabric since, 1912; *b* 1 Marc 1862; *s* of late Henry Adrian Chuchill, CB; *m* 1908, Stella, *y d* c George Myers; one *s* one *d. Educ:* privately. Entered service of th Government of India, 1880, in the Persian Telegraph Dept of th Indian Govt Telegraph; Oriental 2nd Sec. Legation of Teheran, 1886 in attendance on the Shah of Persia during HM's visit to Englanc 1889; Consul for Dutch Guiana and also for French Guiana, 1894 transferred to Palermo for the Island of Sicily, 1898; in charge of th Consulate of Naples, 1 July–6 Oct. 1900. *Publications:* Monograp on the Present Condition of the Persian Carpet Industry in the grea Oriental Carpet Book, published by the Austrian Govt Ministry c Commerce and Public Instruction; various monographs in the Roy Asiatic Society's Journal; Bibliografia Celliniana (Florence Olschk 1907), 2nd edition, 1909, in Cust's Life of Cellini; The Goldsmith of Rome under the Papal Authority (in Papers of the British Schoo at Rome, 1907); Bibliografia Vasariana (Florence, 1912), and othe publications on art. *Recreations:* from 1880–94 collected Persiar Arabic, Turkish, and Hebrew MSS for the British Museum, vol. of the Persian Catalogue of MSS being almost entirely devoted t the Churchill MSS; under the late Gen. Sir R. M. Smith, RE, KCMC collected art objects for the South Kensington Museum in Persi engaged on researches for a history of gold and silver work in Ital *Address:* Palazzo Capomazza, Arco Mirelli, Naples. *TA:* Britis Consul, Naples. *Died 11 Jan. 192*

CHURCHILL, William; Officier de l'Ordre de Leopold II, 1920; Brooklyn, New York, 1859; *e s* of William Churchill and Sarah, of Rev. John Starkweather; married; no *c. Educ:* Yale Universit United States Consul-General for Samoa, 1896; Judge of Consul Court with exclusive jurisdiction over American citizens; Senic Member of the Consular Board in execution of the Berlin Gener Act; acted jointly with British and German Consuls as adviser t Malietoa Laupepa, King of Samoa; Receiver and Custodian Revenues of Samoa; President of the Municipality of Api commission extended as Consul-General for Tonga at Nukualof 1897; Division of Visé of Federal Committee of Public Informatio 1917; special agent Department of State, 1918; Correspondir Member Hawaiian Historical Society, 1898; Corresponding Memb Polynesian Society, 1899; Member American Philological Associatio 1910; Fellow Royal Anthropological Institute, 1912; Hon. Memb Polynesian Society, 1913; Corresponding Member America Geographical Society, Member Association American Geographer 1914; Member Institut Suisse, d'Anthropologie Générale, 191 Member American Association for the Advancement of Scienc 1916; Member American Ethnological Society, 1916; Memb Archæological Institute of America, 1916; Research Associate i Primitive Philology of the Carnegie Institution of Washington, 191 Associate of the Carnegie Institution, 1917; National Geograph Society, 1920; Honorary Consulting Ethnologist, Bishop Museur Honolulu and Dominick Pacific Exploration Fund, 1920. *Publicatio* A Princess of Fiji, 1892; The Polynesian Wanderings, Tracks of th Migration deduced from an Examination of the Proto-Samoa Content of Efaté and other Languages of Melanesia, 1910; Beach-l Mar, the Jargon or Trade Speech of the Western Pacific, 1911; East Island, Rapanui Speech and the Peopling of South-east Polynesi 1912; The Subanu, Studies of a Sub-Visayan Mountain Folk Mindanao (with Colonel John Park Finley, United States Army 1913; Sissano, Movements of Migration within and throug

Melanesia; Samoan Kava Custom, 1916; Club Types of Nuclear Polynesia, 1917; editor Malayo-Polynesian section Standard Dictionary, 1913; editorial contributor New International Encyclopædia, 1914; many monographs on ethnological and philological topics. *Clubs:* Cosmos, Washington; Yale, New York.
Died 9 June 1920.

CHURCHWARD, Percy Albert, CIE 1917; KIH; Managing Director, Bank of Rangoon, Ltd, Burma; *b* 27 May 1862; *s* of late Benjamin Hannaford Churchward; *m* 1895, Margaret Helena Madden, Balbriggan, Ireland; no *c. Educ:* Royal Naval School, New Cross, SE. Banker since 1877. *Club:* Pegu, Rangoon.
Died 17 May 1924.

CHURCHWARD, William Brown; *b* 24 Dec. 1844; 2nd *s* of J. G. Churchward, formerly of Kearsney Manor, Dover; *m* 1889, Mary Lees, 2nd *d* of late Wm Nassau Peyton, Inspector Gen. HM Customs. *Educ:* private schools in England; Lycée Impériale, Paris. Entered 14th Regiment, 1863; served through Maori war; left army in 1872; after interim of diamond digging in South Africa, and sheep farming in Tasmania, was acting Consul at Samoa and Deputy Commissioner for the Western Pacific, 1882–85; Vice-Consul at Kustendji, Roumania, 1889; removed to Ibraila, 1890; Consul, Porto Rico, USA, 1899–1912; retired, 1912; New Zealand and Coronation Medals. *Publications:* Jim Peterkin's Daughter; Blackbirding; My Consulate in Samoa; stories, sketches, etc, in magazines, English and foreign. *Recreations:* all English sports. *Club:* Junior United Service.
Died 26 Sept. 1920.

CLANCY, John Joseph, MA; KC 1906; *b* Galway, 15 July 1847; *s* of William Clancy, Carragh Lodge, Clare-Galway, Co. Galway; *m* Margaret Louise, *d* of P. J. Hickie of Newcastle West; three *s* three *d. Educ:* Summer Hill Coll., Athlone; Queen's Coll., Galway; MA Queen's (later National), University of Ireland, with Honours in Ancient Classics. Classical Master, Holy Cross School, Tralee, 1867–70; assistant-editor of The Nation (Dublin), 1870–85; editor of the Irish Press Agency in England, 1886–90; member of editorial staff of Irish Daily Independent, 1891–1902; Irish Bar, 1887; MP (HR) North Dublin, 1885–1918. *Publications:* various political pamphlets and addresses and legal publications; essays in Nineteenth Century, Fortnightly Review, Contemporary Review, etc. *Address:* Holmleigh, Kenilworth Park, Dublin.
Died 25 Nov. 1928.

CLANMORRIS, 5th Baron (Ireland), *cr* 1800; **John George Barry Bingham**, DL, JP; *b* Seamount, Galway, 27 August 1852; *s* of 4th Baron and Sarah Selina, 4th *d* of Burton Persse of Moyode Castle, Galway; *S* father, 1876; *m* 1878, Matilda, *o c* and *heiress* of late Robert Edward Ward, Bangor Castle, Co. Down; six *s* three *d* (and one *s* decd). *Educ:* Eton. Lieut 1st Batt. Rifle Brigade, 1874–78; ADC to Duke of Marlborough, Viceroy of Ireland, 1876–78; Master of Co. Galway Foxhounds (the Blazers), 1891–95. Protestant. Conservative. Owned 18,000 acres; salmon fisheries, shootings; pictures of ancestors and predecessors by old masters; also original oil painting of Sir Richard Bingham, three-quarter-life size. *Recreations:* hunting, yachting, shooting, fishing. *Heir: s* Hon. Arthur Maurice Robert Bingham, *b* 22 June 1879. *Address:* Creg Clare, Ardrahan, Co. Galway; Bangor Castle, Belfast. *TA:* Bangor, Down. *Clubs:* Carlton; Kildare Street, Dublin; Co. Galway, Galway; Ulster, Belfast; Royal Ulster Yacht, Bangor.
Died 4 Nov. 1916.

CLANRICARDE, 2nd Marquis of, *cr* 1825; **Hubert George de Burgh Canning;** Earl of Clanricarde, Baron Dunkellin, 1543; Viscount Burke, 1629; Marquis of Clanricarde, 1825; Baron Somerhill (UK), 1826; *b* 30 Nov. 1832; *s* of 1st Marquis and Harriet, only sister of 1st Earl Canning; *S* father, 1874. *Educ:* Harrow. Attaché, Turin, 1852; 2nd Secretary there, 1862; MP for Co. Galway, 1867–71. Owned about 57,000 acres. *Heir:* (to Earldom of Clanricarde), *kinsman,* 6th Marquis of Sligo, *b* 1 Sept. 1856. *Address:* 13 Hanover Square, WC; Portumna Castle, Galway. *Clubs:* Travellers', Reform.
Died 13 April 1916.

CLARE, Sir Harcourt Everard, Kt 1916; Clerk of the Peace for Lancashire, Clerk of the County Council, etc; *b* 1854; *s* of late William Harcourt Clare of Twycross, Leicestershire; *m* 1883, Clara Theodora (*d* 1918), *y d* of late Thomas Bateman of Middleton Hall, Youlgreave, Derbyshire; one *d. Educ:* Repton. Formerly Town Clerk of Liverpool and was a member of several Royal Commissions. *Address:* Bank Hall, Tarleton, Preston; County Offices, Preston, Lancs. *T:* 1 Longton, Preston.
Died 1 March 1922.

CLARE, Henry Lewis, MD, BCh Dublin; DPH Ireland; Surgeon-General and Chief Medical Officer of Health, Trinidad and Tobago,

1907–17; *b* Dublin, 1858; *o s* of late Lewis Clare, solicitor, Dublin; *m* 1883, Lucy, 4th *d* of Robert Hampson, Stockport, Cheshire; one *s. Educ:* Rathmines School; Trinity College, Dublin. Jun. Resident Medical Officer, Public Hospital, Kingston, Jamaica, 1881; various appointments in Jamaica Medical Service; District Medical Officer, Kingston, 1896; Member Central Board of Health; Pres. Jamaica Branch British Medical Association, Acting Superintending Medical Officer, Jamaica, 1906; representative of Trinidad at Conference, on Quarantine, Barbados, 1908 and 1912; President First West Indian Inter-Colonial Conference on Tuberculosis, Trinidad, 1913; Delegate from Trinidad to International Congress on Infant Mortality, London, 1913; FRSanI, FRIPH. *Publications:* various reports. *Recreations:* gardening, walking, bridge. *Address:* c/o London County & Westminster, and Parr's Bank, Blackheath, SE. *Clubs:* West Indian, Royal Societies.
Died 24 Jan. 1920.

CLARINA, 5th Baron, *cr* 1800; **Lionel Edward Massey,** DL for Co. Limerick; late Lieutenant-Colonel Scots Guards (retired 1870); *b* 20 April 1837; 3rd *s* of 3rd Baron and Susan, *y d* of Hugh Barton of Straffan; *S* brother, 1897; *m* 1st, 1877, Elizabeth Ellen, *d* of Alexander Bannatyne, Woodstown, Co. Limerick; one *s* one *d*; 2nd, 1887, Sophia Mary (*d* 1912), *d* of James Butler, DL, of Castle Crine, Co. Clare; four *d.* Served in 4th West York Militia; 82nd Regiment; Scots Fusilier Guards; High Sheriff, 1896. Owned about 2000 acres. *Heir: s* Hon. Eyre Massey, *b* 8 Feb. 1880. *Address:* Elm Park, Clarina. Limerick. *TA:* Clarina.
Died 13 Oct. 1922.

CLARK, Rt. Rev. Bernard T.; Vicar Apostolic of Seychelles. *Address:* Seychelles Islands.
Died 1916.

CLARK, Vice-Admiral Sir Bouverie Francis, KCB 1900; *b* 19 March 1842; *s* of late Rear-Admiral William Clark; *m* 1868, Catherine Colburn (*d* 1902), *d* of Capt. Wm Colburn Mayne, late 5th Fusiliers. Entered Navy, 1854; Lieut 1862; Commander, 1875; Capt., 1884; retired, 1897; Rear-Adm. (retired), 1899; Director of Transports, the Admiralty, 1896–1901. *Decorated:* Baltic, 1855; New Zealand, 1863–65; Italian medal, Al Valor di Marina, 1891; 2nd class, Saxe Ernestine Order, 1893. *Address:* Victoria Lodge, Francis Street, SW. *Clubs:* United Service, Naval and Military.
Died 20 Nov. 1922.

CLARK, Edwin Charles, LLD; FSA; Barrister; Regius Professor of Civil Law, Cambridge, 1872–1914; *b* 5 Nov. 1835; *s* of Edwin Clark, Ellinthorp Hall, Boroughbridge, Yorkshire. *Educ:* Richmond (Yorks); Shrewsbury School; Trinity College, Cambridge. Seventh Senior Optime Mathematical Tripos, Camb.; Senior Classic and 1st Chancellor's Medallist, 1858; Browne Medallist for Epigrams; formerly Scholar and Fellow of Trinity; late Professorial Fellow of St John's. Practised for a short time as a conveyancer in London. *Publications:* Early Roman Law: Regal Period, 1872; Analysis of Criminal Liability, 1880; Practical Jurisprudence: a Comment on Austin, 1883; Cambridge Legal Studies, 1888; History of Roman Private Law: Part I, Sources, 1906, Part II, Jurisprudence. *Recreations:* coin collecting, study of archæology and architecture. *Address:* Newnham House, Cambridge. *Club:* Royal Societies.
Died 20 July 1917.

CLARK, Rev. Francis E., AB, AM, DD, LLD; President, World's Christian Endeavour Union, since 1895; President, United Society of Christian Endeavour, 1887–1925; later President Emeritus; editor in chief of the Christian Endeavour World, 1886–1921, then hon. editor; *b* Aylmer, Province Quebec, Canada; *m* Harriet E. Abbott, Andover, Mass, USA, 1876; three *s* one *d. Educ:* Kimball Union Academy; Dartmouth College, NH, USA; Andover Theolog. Seminary; AB at Graduation, 1873; AM in course; DD Dartmouth College, 1887; LLD Iowa College. Graduated at Dartmouth Coll. 1873; at Andover Theol. Sem. 1876; Pastor of Williston Church, Portland, Me, 1876; Founded Christian Endeavour Soc. 1881; Pastor of Phillips Church, Boston, 1883; five times around the world, etc; Preacher at Cornell and other universities; Trustee of Church Peace Union; Director or Vice-President of several national organizations. *Publications:* The Holy Land of Asia Minor; Following Christ through His Own Country; The Charm of Scandinavia (with Sydney A. Clark); Old Homes of New Americans; Similes and Figures from Alexander Maclaren; Continent of Opportunity; Christian Endeavour in All Lands; Ways and Means; The Children and the Church; Young People's Prayer Meetings; Our Journey Around the World; World-Wide Christian Endeavour; The Great Secret; Fellow Travellers; A New Way around an Old World; Old Lanterns for New Paths; Training the Church of the Future; Christian Endeavour Manual; The Gospel in Latin Lands; (jointly with Mrs Clark) Christ and the Young People; In the Footsteps of St Paul; Our Italian Fellow-

Citizens; The Gospel of Out of Doors; Memories of Many Men in Many Lands, an Autobiography. *Recreations:* fishing, farming. *Address:* Christian Endeavour House, 41 Mt Vernon Street, Boston, Mass, USA; Sagamore Beach, Mass, USA. *TA:* Endeavour, Boston. *T:* Haymarket, Boston, 264. *Clubs:* Boston Authors, Twentieth Century, Winthrop, Monday, Boston City, Boston.

Died May 1927.

CLARK, George Ernest, FRGS; Founder and Governing Director of Clark's Civil Service and Commercial College, Chancery Lane, WC2; Hon. Director of Commercial Instruction, Queen Mary's Convalescent Auxiliary Hospitals for Wounded Soldiers, 1916; Freeman of the City of London; Member of Guild of Freeman of City of London; Member of Horner's Company. *Address:* The Beeches, Bromley, Kent; Willoughby, Sidmouth, Devon. *Clubs:* Constitutional, Eccentric, Aldwych.

Died 1 Nov. 1919.

CLARK, James Robert, CB 1902; Chief Naval Instructor, RN (retired); *b* 1844; *s* of James Richard Clark of Anderton, Cornwall. Served Egypt, 1882 (medal, Khedive's star). *Address:* 1 Chesham Terrace, Brighton.   *Died 30 Dec. 1919.*

CLARK, James William, KC 1904; *b* 30 May 1851; *e s* of late James Clark, formerly Secretary of the Colonial Bank, London; unmarried. *Educ:* Brentwood Grammar School, Essex; Trinity Hall, Cambridge. BA 1st class in Classical Tripos; Fellow, 1874; Classical Lecturer, 1874–76; MA 1877. Barrister, Lincoln's Inn, 1879; was Conveyancing Counsel to HM Office of Woods and Forests, 1894–95; Counsel to the Attorney-Gen. in charity matters, 1894–95; Legal Adviser to the Board of Agriculture and Fisheries, 1895–1915. *Publications:* joint-author of Elphinstone, Norton, and Clark on Interpretation of Deeds, and of Elphinstone and Clark on Searches; joint-editor of 3rd and 4th editions of Goodeve's Real Property and 2nd edn of Goodeve's Personal Property, and of Elphinstone's Introduction to Conveyancing; author of Student's Conveyancing Precedents. *Recreations:* rowed in Trinity Hall boats, and was in Trinity Hall cricket eleven; cycling. *Address:* High Croft, Winchmore Hill, N. *Club:* Reform.   *Died 21 July 1921.*

CLARK, Sir John Maurice, 2nd Bt, *cr* 1886; MBE 1919; VD; head of the publishing firm of T. & T. Clark, Edinburgh; DL for County of Midlothian; JP for the County of the City of Edinburgh; Colonel, formerly commanding officer, 7th Battalion Royal Scots (the Royal Regiment); Vice-Chairman Midlothian County Association Territorial Force; National Service Representative for the County of Midlothian; late Master of the Edinburgh Merchant Company; Extraordinary Director of the British Linen Bank; Chairman of the Scottish Life Assurance Company; *b* 7 March 1859; *s* of Sir Thomas Clark, 1st Bt and Eliza Maule, *d* of Rev. G. R. Davidson, DD; *S* father, 1900; *m* 1885, Helen, *d* of Rev. H. M. Douglas; three *s* one *d*. *Educ:* Edinburgh Academy and University. *Recreations:* riding, motoring, fishing. *Heir:* *s* Thomas Clark [*b* 30 March 1886; *m* 1914, Ellen Mercy, *o d* of late Francis Drake]. *Address:* 17 Rothesay Terrace, Edinburgh. *TA:* Dictionary, Edinburgh. *T:* Central, Edinburgh, 6870. *Club:* University, Edinburgh.   *Died 27 May 1924.*

CLARK, Joseph; Member of Institute of Oil Painters; *b* Cerne Abbas, Dorsetshire, 4 July 1834; *m* 1868, *d* of John Jones, Winchester; one *s* three *d*. *Educ:* Dorchester, by Rev. William Barnes, "The Dorset Poet". Came to London at the age of 18; commenced study at gallery of late J. M. Leigh in Newman Street; then became a student at Royal Academy; first picture at RA was The Sick Child, 1857; exhibited at Academy with few exceptions from 1857; several of his pictures were engraved—The Return of the Runaway, Three Little Kittens, Hagar and Ishmael, etc; two pictures bought by Chantrey Bequest and now in Tate Gallery; hon. member of the Royal Oil Institute; liberal in politics; a member of the New Church, known as the Swedenborgian religion. *Recreations:* formerly cricket and tennis, later gardening. *Address:* 95 Hereson Road, Ramsgate.

Died 4 July 1926.

CLARK, William Andrews; *b* near Connellsville, Pa, 8 Jan. 1839; *m* 1st, 1869, Kate L. Stauffer (*d* 1893); two *s* two *d*; 2nd, 1901, Anna E. La-Chapelle; one *d*. *Educ:* Laurel Hill Academy; studied law, Mount Pleasant, Ia, University. Taught school, Mo, 1859–60; went to Colorado, 1862; Montana, 1863; owned railways of Butte, Ana Miner newspaper; President, United Verde Copper Co. of Arizona; State Orator, representing Montana at Centennial Exposition, 1876; Grand Master Masons, Mont., 1877; Major Butte Battalion, leading it in Nez Perce campaign, 1878; President Constitutional Conventions, 1884 and 1889; Commissioner from Mont. to New

Orleans Exposition, 1884; Democrat candidate for delega┐ Congress, 1888; United States Senator, 1901–1907. *Address:* ┌ Montana; 111 Broadway, New York.

Died 2 March 1┐

CLARK, Sir William Mortimer, Kt 1907; WS, KC; ┐ Lieutenant-Governor of Ontario, 1903–8; Chairman, Knox Col┐ Toronto, since 1880; *b* Aberdeen, Scotland, 24 May 1836; *s* of Clark, manager, Aberdeen Insurance Company; *m* 1866, Hel┐ of Gilbert Gordon, Caithness; two *d*. *Educ:* Grammar School┐ Marischal Coll. Aberdeen; Univ. of Edinburgh; Life Memb┐ General Council of latter University. Admitted WS, 1859; se┐ in Toronto, Ontario, same year; called to Bar of Ontario, 1869; ┐ 1890; for fifteen years Senator of University of Toronto; ┐ Toronto, 1902, Queen's University, Kingston, 1903; Pres┐ Toronto Mortgage Company; Director Gas Company, Can┐ General Electric Company, Toronto General Trust Company┐ Norwich United Insurance Company; solicitor for various p┐ companies and charities; President, St Andrew's Society, for two┐ for five years Secretary, Canadian Institute; for two years Presi┐ County of York Law Association. *Publications:* numerous contribu┐ to Toronto press on public, educational, and literary ques┐ *Recreations:* travelled largely on American Continent, in Africa, and almost every country in Europe. *Address:* 28 Avenue ┌ Toronto.   *Died 11 Aug. ┐*

CLARK, Rt. Rev. William Reid; Bishop of Niagara, since 1911. Trinity College, Toronto (MA). Deacon, 1874; Priest, ┐ Missioner at Eganville, 1874–75; Principal, High School, Uxb┐ 1875–76; Incumbent, Palmerston, 1877–78; Curate of St ┐ Burlington, 1878–79; Vicar of St John, Ancaster, 1879–93; R┐ of Barton, 1893–96; Rector, Ancaster, Ont, 1896–1902; Secre┐ Treasurer of the Diocese since 1903; Registrar of the Diocese┐ 1902; Secretary of Lower House of the Provincial Synod of Ca┐ 1901–4, and of the General Synod of Canada, 1908–11; DD Bis┐ College, Lennoxville, and DCL Trinity College, Tor┐ Archdeacon of Niagara, 1902–11. *Address:* See House, Ham┐ Ont, Canada.   *Died April ┐*

CLARKE, Lt-Col Albert Edward Stanley, DSO 1917; MVO ┐ Lieutenant-Colonel, Reserve of Officers; *b* 19 Jan. 1879; *o s* c┐ Maj.-Gen. Sir Stanley de A. C. Clarke, GCVO; *m* 1907, Eve┐ *d* of Sir Alexander Baird, 1st Bt; one *s* one *d*. *Educ:* Eton; Sand┐ Page of Honour to Queen Victoria; Scots Guards, 1898–1910; s┐ S Africa at Belmont, Graspan, Modder River, Magersfontein; se┐ under FO in Macedonian gendarmerie, 1904–7; Private Secr┐ to Gen. Sir John French, 1907–10; contested (C) SW Norfolk, ┐ served European War, 1914–18 (DSO). *Address:* 28 Draycott ┐ SW3. *T:* Kensington 5663. *Clubs:* Carlton, Marlborough.

Died 8 June ┐

CLARKE, Vice-Adm. Arthur Calvert, CMG 1902; CBE ┐ DSO 1917; RN; *b* 9 Aug. 1848; *m* 1895, Margaret Macgregor┐ J. L. Adams, USA. Entered Navy, 1861; Lieut, 1872; Comma┐ 1883; Captain, 1891; Rear-Admiral, 1904; retired, 1903; ┐ Admiral, 1908; served Abyssinia 1868 (medal); China, 1901 (n┐ CMG); commanded for over 3 years an armed yacht in Eur┐ War (medals); Officer of Legion of Honour. *Club:* United Se┐

Died 9 Nov. ┐

CLARKE, Bt-Col (Charles Henry Geoffrey) Mansfield, ┐ 1907; *b* 26 March 1873; *e s* and *heir* of Sir Charles Mansfield C┐ 3rd Bt; *m* 1915, Linda Blanche Douglas-Pennant, *e d* of 3rd ┐ Penrhyn; one *d*. Entered Army, 1893; Captain, 1900; retired, ┐ served Nile Expedition, 1898 (Egyptian medal, medal); S Africa, ┐ (Queen's medal, 3 clasps). *Address:* 33 Lennox Gardens, SW. ┌ Marlborough, Army and Navy.

Died 27 July ┐

CLARKE, Charles Kirk, MD, LLD; Dean of Medical Fac┐ University of Toronto, 1907–20; Professor of Psychiatry, Univ┐ of Toronto; Superintendent Toronto General Hospital, 1911; M┐ Director of Canadian National Committee for Mental Hygiene┐ 1918; *b* Canada, 16 Feb. 1857; *s* of Hon. Charles Clarke and E┐ Kent; *m* 1st, 1880, Emma De Veber Andrews (*d* 1902); 2nd, ┐ Theresa Gallagher; four *s* two *d*. *Educ:* Grammar School, ┐ University of Toronto. Began medical career under the tutela┐ Joseph Workman, MD; became Assistant Superintendent of Har┐ and Rockwood Hospitals for Insane, then Superintende┐ Rockwood Hospital for Insane, and eventually Superintende┐ Toronto Hospital for Insane until 1911; did a great deal of me┐ legal work in Canada; one of the authorities on psychiatric m┐

in the Dominion. *Publications:* many brochures on psychiatric and medico-legal subjects; also many articles on ornithology; editor of The University of Toronto Medical Bulletin; one of the editors of the Journal of Insanity, Johns Hopkins Press, Baltimore, also of the Canadian Journal of Mental Hygiene. *Recreations:* golf, music, etc. *Clubs:* York, Toronto; Rosedale Golf, Western Golf.
Died Jan. 1924.

ARKE, Hon. Sir Charles Pitcher, Kt 1922; KC; *b* 26 June 1857; *m* 1883, Theresa Matilda, *d* of late Albert Kohl, London; one *s* one *d*. Member, House of Assembly, since 1893; Solicitor-General, 1907; Attorney-General, Barbados, 1913. *Address:* Blythswood, Worthing, Barbados. *Died 16 Dec. 1926.*

ARKE, Edith, MBE 1918; Principal of the National Training School of Cookery and Domestic Subjects, 1875-1919; *b* Shrewsbury House, Shooters Hill, Kent, 27 Oct. 1844; *d* of Lt Edward Nicolls, RN, *e* sister of General Sir Edward Nicolls, KCB, RMLI, and *g d* of Thomas Love Peacock, Chief Examiner East India Company; *m* 1876, Charles Clarke, Civil Servant, India Office; three *d*. *Educ:* at home and at private school; the pioneer of Domestic Subjects Training. Church of England. *Publications:* Plain and High-Class Cookery Book; Workhouse Cookery; Life of her grandfather, Thomas Love Peacock. *Address:* 6 Kensington Mansions, Earl's Court, SW5.
Died 20 Aug. 1926.

ARKE, Lt-Col Sir Edward Henry St Lawrence, 4th Bt, *cr* 1804; CMG 1919; DSO 1917; late Worcestershire Regiment; *b* 17 April 1857; *s* of late Rev. John William Clarke and Elizabeth, *d* of Edward Smyth of Macclesfield; *S* cousin, Sir Guy Clarke-Travers, 3rd Bt, 1905; *m* 1884, Susan Douglas (*d* 1913), *d* of Charles Langton of Barkhill, Liverpool; one *d* (and two *s* one *d* decd). Served European War, 1914-18 (DSO, CMG). *Heir:* none. *Address:* The Hyde, Bridport. *Died 7 May 1926 (ext).*

ARKE, Edward Lionel Alexander, BA; Master of the Supreme Court (Chancery Division), 1880-1912; *b* Great Yeldham, Essex, 21 April 1837; *o s* of late Rev. Edward William Clarke, Rector of Great Yeldham; *m* 1867, Lorina Alice (*d* 1911), 2nd *d* of Rev. William Fletcher, DD; two *s*. *Educ:* Wimborne Grammar School, Pembroke College, Cambridge (Scholar). BA 1860 (3rd Sen. Opt.). Solicitor, 1863-80. *Address:* 5 Ladbroke Square, W. *T:* 1753 Park; Lewens, Wimborne, Dorset. *Died 10 Dec. 1917.*

ARKE, Sir Ernest, Kt 1898; *b* Bury St Edmunds, 21 Feb. 1856; *s* of late J. J. Clarke, Bury St Edmunds; *m* 1880, Marguerite (*d* 1918), 2nd *d* of late James Prevost, Leghorn. Clerk in Medical Department Local Government Board, 1872-81; Assistant Secretary, Share and Loan Department, Stock Exchange, 1881-87; Secretary of Royal Agricultural Society of England, 1887-1905; Hon. MA Cambridge, 1894 (St John's College). First Lecturer on Agricultural History at Cambridge University, 1896-99. Fellow Society Antiquaries; Vice-President of Council of Bibliographical and other Societies; Chevalier of French Order of Mérite Agricole, 1889; Hon. member of Académie d'Agriculture de France, and of the National Agricultural Societies of England, Scotland, Italy, Moravia, and the Argentine; President of Sette of Odd Volumes, 1898-99, and Treasurer, 1908-19; Chairman Committee London Society of East Anglians, 1899-1900; Master of the Worshipful Company of Glovers, 1904-5; Member of Court of Worshipful Company of Musicians; Chairman of Committee, Folk Song Society; President, Chartered Institute of Secretaries, 1910-11. *Publications:* edited The Chronicle of Jocelin of Brakelond, 1903, 3rd edn 1907; Bury Chronicles of the Thirteenth Century, 1905; articles in Dictionary of National Biography, Nineteenth Century and other publications. *Recreations:* books, music. *Address:* 31 Tavistock Square, WC1. *T:* Museum 6619.
Died 4 March 1923.

ARKE, His Honour Sir Fielding, Kt 1894; LLB; FRGS; JP; *b* 23 Feb. 1851; *m* 1888, Mary Milward, *d* of J. Timbrell Pierce, DL, of Frettons, Danbury. *Educ:* King's Coll., London. Barrister, Middle Temple, 1876; Chief Justice of Fiji, 1881; Judge, Hong-Kong, 1889; Chief Justice, 1892-95; Chief Justice of Jamaica, 1895-1911. *Address:* Coppid Hall, Stifford, Grays, Essex. *Club:* Oriental.
Died 30 July 1928.

ARKE, Sir Frederick William Alfred, Kt 1917; CB 1922; late Accountant and Comptroller-General, HM Customs and Excise; *b* 2 May 1857; *s* of F. W. Clarke, HM Civil Service; *m* 1893, Josephine Fitzgerald Moylan; two *s*. *Educ:* private schools. Entered Civil Service, 1874; appointed to Exchequer and Audit Department; went on official tour of inspection to Hong Kong, Bermuda, etc, 1908. *Recreation:*

golf. *Address:* Beverley, The Park, Sidcup, Kent. *T:* Sidcup 488. *Club:* Royal Automobile. *Died 18 Feb. 1927.*

CLARKE, George Johnson, KC 1907; LLD; Premier and Minister of Lands and Mines of the Province of New Brunswick; *b* St Andrews, New Brunswick; *s* of Nelson and Mary Clarke; *m* Bessie C., *d* of Rev. Hezekiah and Elizabeth McKeown; two *d*. *Educ:* St Andrews and Fredericton, NB. Admitted to Bar of New Brunswick, 1886; practised law in St Stephen from time of admission to bar; contested Canadian House of Commons, 1891, and Legislative Assembly of Province of New Brunswick, 1899; Mayor of the town of St Stephen, 1898 and 1899; Warden of the Municipality of Charlotte, 1899; elected to Legislative Assembly, 1903; re-elected 1908 and 1912; Speaker of the Assembly, 1909; Attorney-General of Province, Jan.-Dec. 1914. *Address:* St Stephen, NB. *T:* 160. *M:* 950. *Club:* Union, St John. *Died 26 Feb. 1917.*

CLARKE, Most Rev. Henry Lowther, DD, DCL; *b* 23 Nov. 1850; *s* of late Rev. W. Clarke, MA, of Firbank, Westmorland; *m* 1876, Alice Lovell (*d* 1918), *d* of Rev. Canon Kemp; two *s* one *d*. *Educ:* Sedbergh; St John's College, Cambridge (scholar, 7th wrangler). Episcopal Canon of St George's, Jerusalem. Ordained, 1874; Curate St John's, Hull; Vicar of Hedon, Yorks, 1876-83; Assistant Master, St Peter's School, York, 1883-84; Vicar of St Martin's, Coney Street, York, 1884-90; Chaplain to North Riding Asylum, 1885-90; Vicar of Dewsbury, 1890-1901; Hon. Canon Wakefield Cathedral, 1893-1902; Rural Dean Dewsbury, 1898-1901; of Huddersfield, 1901-2; Vicar of Huddersfield, 1901-2; Proctor in York Convocation, 1902; Bishop of Melbourne, 1902-5; Archbishop, 1905-20. *Publications:* Addresses to Men; Addresses delivered in England and Australia; Synod Addresses (18); Synodical Government, 1920; Studies in the English Reformation, 1912; Constitutional Church Government in the Dominions beyond the Seas, 1924; History of Sedbergh School, 1925; Death and the Hereafter, 1925. *Recreation:* literary work. *Address:* Melbourne House, Lymington, Hants. *Clubs:* Royal Societies, Authors'.
Died 23 June 1926.

CLARKE, Herbert, JP Surrey; editor and proprietor of The Christian World; *b* 16 Jan. 1863; *y s* of the late James Clarke, editor and proprietor of The Christian World; *m* Sarah, *e d* of John Durrant of Stowmarket. *Educ:* Mill Hill School. *Recreations:* turning, carpentry. *Address:* 13-14 Fleet Street, EC; Northfield, Caterham. *T:* Central 646. *Club:* National Liberal.
Died 22 Jan. 1925.

CLARKE, Rev. John; Vicar of Killead since 1882; Canon of Conner. *Educ:* Queen's University, Ireland (scholar). Ordained 1873; Curate of Billy, 1872-75; Drumtullah, 1875-82; Rural Dean of Antrim, 1902. *Address:* Killead Rectory, British, Co. Antrim.
Died June 1923.

CLARKE, Rev. John Erskine, MA; Hon. Canon of Southwark, 1905; Hon. Chaplain to the King, 1901; founder of Bolingbroke Hospital, Wandsworth Common, 1880; *b* 1827. *Educ:* Wadham College, Oxford. 3rd class Lit. Hum. 1850; holder of Oxford Univ. sculls, 1849-50. Curate, St Mary, Low Harrogate, 1851; St Mary, Lichfield, 1856; Vicar of St Michael, Derby, 1856-66; of St Andrew, Litchurch, Derby, 1866-72; Prebendary of Lichfield, 1869-72; Vicar of Battersea, 1872-1909; Rural Dean, 1879-1913; Vicar of St Luke, Battersea, 1901-14; Chaplain-in-Ordinary to Queen Victoria, 1895-1901; to King Edward VII, 1901-10; to King George V, 1910; Hon. Canon of Winchester, 1875-1905; Proctor in Convocation for the Diocese of Rochester, 1888-1905. *Publications:* Heart Music, 1857; Commonlife Sermons, 1861; originator of Parish Magazines, and Editor of the Parish Magazine, 1859-95; editor of Chatterbox, 1867-1901; editor of Church Bells, 1871-96. *Address:* St Luke's Vicarage, Ramsden Road, Balham.
Died 3 Feb. 1920.

CLARKE, John Mason, PhD, ScD, LLD; State Geologist of New York since 1904; Director Department of Science and State Museum; Professor of Geology, Rensselaer Polytechnic Institute; *b* 15 April 1857; *s* of Noah Turner Clarke and Laura Mason Merrill; *m* 1887; one *s*. *Educ:* Amherst; Goettingen. After teaching in the schools of New York and colleges of Massachusetts, came to Albany, NY, 1886, as assistant to the State Geologist; in the execution of this work issued a large number of reports and special scientific papers and also did much scientific work in the Province of Quebec; made extensive reports to the Geological Service of Brazil, and of Argentina and wrote on the geology of the Falkland Islands; a member of the National Academy (ex-Chairman of the geology section) and of about forty scientific and historical societies in America and Europe; President of the Albany Institute (founded 1791); Vice-President National Parks Association; Member National Council Boy Scouts; Past President Geological Society of America and of the Paleontological Society; Chairman War Committee on Geology, National Research Council; Foreign Member, Geological Society, London; received the Hayden gold medal of the Philadelphia Academy, the gold medal of the Wild Life Protection Fund, and the Spindiaroff prize of the International Geological Congress. *Publications:* Heart of Gaspé; The Magdalen Islands; The Origin of Disease, etc; L'Ile Percée. *Recreations:* collection and study of early English lustres, Local Histories of Canada. *Address:* Albany, NY.   *Died May 1925.*

CLARKE, Col Lancelot Fox, DSO 1901; commanding 91st Infantry (Tasmanian Rangers), Commonwealth Military Forces; *b* 15 June 1858; *m* 1889, Marion (*d* 1906), *d* of John Young, and *widow* of Arthur Gilbert. Served S Africa, 1900-2 with Victorian Imperial Regiment (despatches twice, Queen's medal 4 clasps, King's medal 2 clasps, DSO). Decorated for able command in operations against De Wet. *Address:* Devonport, Tasmania.
                                Died 25 April 1925.

CLARKE, His Honour Lionel H.; Lieutenant-Governor of the Province of Ontario, Canada, since 1919; *b* Guelph, 1859; *s* of Dr Clarke, TCD; *m* Miss Small, Kincardine, Ont; three *s* one *d*. *Educ:* privately; Trinity College, Port Hope; Edinburgh. Early in life entered business and became heavily interested in the grain trade; Pres. of the Canadian Malting Co. Ltd, and a director of Financial and Commercial Companies; was a member of the Board of Grain Supervisors; President of the Toronto Board of Trade; a member of the York Highways Commission; of the Queen Victoria Niagara Falls Parks Commission; Chairman of the Toronto Harbour Commission under Statute. *Recreations:* golf, riding, driving, fishing, shooting; a keen patron of outdoor sports. *Address:* Government House, Toronto, Canada. *Clubs:* York, Toronto, Hunt, Toronto.
                                Died 29 Aug. 1922.

CLARKE, Sir Rupert (Turner Havelock), 2nd Bt, *cr* 1882; late Member Legislative Council, Victoria; *b* 16 March 1865; *s* of Hon. Sir William John Clarke, 1st Bt, and Mary, *d* of late Hon. John Walker, MLC, Tasmania; *S* father, 1897; *m* 1st, 1886, Aimée Mary (who divorced him, 1909; she *m* 2nd, 1910, Sir Philip Grey-Egerton, 12th Bt), *d* of Hon. Thomas Cumming; two *d*; 2nd, 1918, Elsie Florence, *d* of James Partridge Tucker of Marrickville, Sydney, late of Devonshire; two *s* one *d*. *Heir: s* Rupert William John Clarke, *b* 5 Nov. 1919. *Club:* Melbourne, Melbourne.
                                Died 25 Dec. 1926.

CLARKE, Somers, FSA; Architect retired, resident in Egypt; *b* 22 July 1841; *o s* of Somers Clarke, Solicitor, Brighton. *Educ:* privately. After five years' unwilling servitude in the law, entered Sir G. Gilbert Scott's office, 1864; repaired many ancient churches in connection with his partner, Mr. J. T. Micklethwaite; amongst the largest of his churches is St Martin's, Brighton; St John the Divine, Gainsborough, Lincolnshire; doubled the size of Parish church, Brighton; elected Surveyor to the Fabric, St Paul's Cathedral, London, 1897; designed electric lighting, gift of Mr J. Pierpont Morgan; co-operated with Sir W. B. Richmond in internal decorations; suggested in The Times and effected the removal of Alfred Stevens' Monument to the Duke of Wellington from SW Chapel to the place in the Cathedral it was designed to fill; designed the stalls in the SW Chapel for the order of SS Michael and George; architect to the Dean and Chapter of Chichester Cathedral, 1900; retired, 1922; Fellow of Society of Antiquaries, 1881; served on the Council; Hon. Member of the Comité de Conservation des Monuments de l'Art Arabe, Cairo; assisted in repairs of several ancient temples in Egypt. *Publications:* Christian Antiquities in the Nile Valley; Contributions to Proceedings, Soc. Antiquaries, Journal of Egyptian Archæology, etc. *Recreations:* music, walking, sketching. *Address:* Helmia, Zeitun, Egypt. *Club:* Burlington Fine Arts.   *Died 31 Aug. 1926.*

CLARKE, William, ISO 1906; Governor, Duke Street Prison, Glasgow, 1903-8; native of Perthshire; *b* 1842; *m* 1870, Helen, *d* of late James Craik, Castle Douglas, Kirkcudbrightshire; one *s* two *d*. *Educ:* Perth. Entered Prison Service, 1862, and was Governor of the prisons of Greenock, Dundee, Perth General. *Recreations:* reading, walking. *Address:* Magdalen Bank, Craigie, Perth.
                                Died 27 Jan. 1918.

CLAUGHTON, Sir Gilbert Henry, 1st Bt, *cr* 1912; JP; Chairman of London and North Western Railway; *b* 21 Feb. 1856; *s* of late Bishop of St Albans, Rt Rev. Thomas Legh Claughton, and Julia Susannah, *sister* of 1st Earl of Dudley; unmarried. *Educ:* Eton. twenty years chief mineral agent to the Earl of Dudley; Director Barclay's Bank, Ltd; North British and Mercantile Insura Company; South Staffordshire Water Works Company; Se Staffordshire Mond Gas Company; Alderman of Staffordshire Cou Council. *Heir:* none. *Address:* The Priory, Dudley. *T:* 20 Tipton. Priory, Dudley; 5 Lygon Place, SW1. *TA:* Technique, Lond Chairman, Euston. *T:* Victoria 1851; Museum 2826. *Clubs:* Carl Windham.   *Died 27 June 1921 (*

CLAUS, Emile; *b* Vive St Eloi, Belgique, 27 Sept. 1849. E Académie Royale d'Anvers. Représenté dans les musées à Bruxe Anvers, Gand, Liège, Dresde, Berlin, au Luxembourg, à Par Venise, Namur, Port Adelaide; Officier de l'Ordre de Leopol Chevalier de la Légion d'Honneur; member of the Senefelder C *Publications:* articles in The Studio and The Artist.
                                Died 6 June 1

CLAUSON, Major Sir John Eugene, KCMG 1913 (CMG 19 CVO 1912; late RE; High Commissioner and Commander-in-Ch Cyprus, since 1914; *b* 13 Nov. 1866; *e s* of Charles Clauson and Ju *d* of Rev. J. W. Buckley; *m* 1890, Mary Elisabeth, *e d* of Sir Wil Thomas Makins, 1st Bt; three *s*. *Educ:* Merchant Taylors' Sch Clifton College; RMA Woolwich. Entered RE, 1885; BA (h London, 1887; designed army pontoon, 1889; passed Staff Col (1st place), 1893; Army Headquarters Staff, 1895-1900; admi Inner Temple, 1897; Secretary Army Railway Council, 1 Secretary Mobilisation Committee, 1898; Sec. Colonial Defe Cttee and Assistant Secretary Committee of Imperial Defe 1900-6; Chief Sec. to Govt of Cyprus, 1906-11; Lieut-Gover Malta, 1911-14. *Address:* Government House, Cyprus. C Athenæum, Army and Navy, Savage.
                                Died 31 Dec. 1

CLAY, Sir Arthur Temple Felix, 4th Bt, *cr* 1841; artist; *b* Lon 9 Dec. 1842; 3rd *s* of Sir William Clay, 1st Bt; *S* brother, 187 1869, Margaret (*d* 1915), 5th *d* of A. K. Barclay of Bury Hill, Dork one *s* (and one *s* decd). *Educ:* Trinity Coll., Cambridge; BA. For y exhibited regularly at the Royal Academy, New Gallery, and o Exhibitions. *Works:* The Court of Criminal Appeal at the Law Co The Royal Bodyguard at the War Office, The Yeoman of the G at the London Museum, Portraits in several public buildi *Publications:* Abridgement of Collectivism, by P. Leroy-Beaul 1908; Syndicalism and Labour, 1911; and various pamphlets contributions to magazines on social subjects. *Recreations:* fish shooting. *Heir: s* George Felix Neville Clay, *b* 24 Nov. 1871. Add 19 Hyde Park Gate, SW7. *T:* 209 Western.
                                Died 18 March 1

CLAY, Rev. John Harden, MA; Hon. Canon of Bristol, since 1* *s* of Rev. John Clay, Vicar of Stapenhill, and Jessie Harden; *m* 1* Alice Spencer, *d* of Maj.-Gen. M. E. Bagnold, HEICS; three *s* se *d*. *Educ:* Repton; Trinity College, Cambridge (Scholar). Cura Maidstone, 1872-75; Vicar of All Saint's Child's Hill, NW, 1875 Rector of St Michael, Bristol, 1893-1918. *Address:* Miller Bri Ambleside.   *Died 31 Oct. 1*

CLAY, William Henry; Barrister-at-Law; Recorder of Stoke-Trent, since 1910; *b* Uxbridge, 1841; *o s* of late William Clay, Ski Street, EC, and afterwards of West Ford, Droitwich, and Ellen *d* of late Joseph Rutter, Hillingdon Heath; *m* 1875, Charlotte, *d* of James Christy, Boynton Hall, Roxwall. *Educ:* Chelten Grammar School. Called to Bar, Middle Temple, 1868; (Benc 1907) and joined the Oxford Circuit; Recorder of Hanley, 1900 *Address:* 4 Whitehall Court, SW. *Club:* Reform.
                                Died 4 June 1

CLAY, Rev. William Leslie, BA, DD; Minister St Andrew's Chu Presbyterian Church in Canada, Victoria, BC, since 1894; *b* Bede Prince Edward Island, 14 Nov. 1863; *s* of John Clay, Provincial I Surveyor, and Jane Townsend Cousins; *m* 1890, Florence Nightir Leitch, Stanhope, PEI; one *s* four *d*. *Educ:* Public and High Sch Summerside; Prince of Wales College, Charlottetown, PEI; M University and Presbyterian College, Montreal. Minister at M Jaw, NWT, 1890-94; Director Protestants' Orphan Ho Children's Aid Society; Member Victoria Library Board Chairman for three years; President Canadian Club, Victoria, years; Convener of Presbytery's Committee on Home Mission over thirty years, and of Synod's Committee for over twenty y Chairman of Commission appointed by the Government of Br Columbia to adjust property interests between the United Ch of Canada and the Presbyterian Church in Canada, under the Un

Church of Canada Act; twice Moderator of the Synod of BC; Moderator of the General Assembly of the Presbyterian Church in Canada, 1927–28. *Publications:* occasional articles in newspapers and magazines. *Recreations:* golf and summering with family by a mountain lake. *Address:* 821 Linden Avenue, Victoria, BC, Canada. *T:* home 863, church 1943. *Clubs:* Canadian, Victoria Golf, Victoria.

Died 3 Feb. 1928.

AYTON, Major Edward Francis; *b* 1864; 2nd *s* of late Nathaniel George Clayton and Isabel, 4th *d* of late Rev. Edward Chaloner Ogle, of Kirkley Hall, Northumberland; *m* 1900, Jeanne Marie Rénée, *o d* of Baron de Fougeres; one *s*. *Educ:* Harrow. Formerly a Major, Scots Guards; Lord of the Manor of Charlwood, Surrey; member of the Jockey Club, 1919. *Address:* Chesters, near Humshaugh, Northumberland. *Clubs:* Guards, Turf.

Died 19 April 1922.

AYTON, Major Sir Edward Gilbert, Kt 1908; CB 1905; RE; formerly Inspector of Prisons and Secretary to the Prison Commission; *b* 16 July 1841; *e s* of late Major-General Henry Clayton and Jean Henrietta, *d* of Sir Robert Blair, KCB; *m* 1864, Georgine Elizabeth Sykes, *d* and *heiress* of late Sykes Clayton of the Manor House, Rufforth, Yorks; two *s* four *d*. *Educ:* Brighton College; East India Military College, Addiscombe. Formerly in Royal Engineers; Captain, 1872; retired with hon. rank of Major, 1880; JP Surrey. *Address:* Kingswood, Woking. *Died 5 March 1917.*

AYTON, Rev. Horace Evelyn, MA; Vicar of St Mary Magdalen, Oxford, since 1884; Rural Dean of Oxford, 1914; Hon. Canon of Christ Church, Oxford, since 1903; Fellows' Chaplain of Magdalen College, Oxford, since 1887; *b* Farnborough Rectory, 3 April 1853; *y s* of late Rev. John Henry Clayton, MA, sometime Rector of Farnborough; unmarried. *Educ:* Marlborough Grammar School; Brasenose College, Oxford. Somerset Scholar, 1871; Hulme Exhibitioner, 1876; 3rd Class Mods (Classical); 2nd Class Theological School, 1875; BA 1875; MA 1878; Senior Hall Greek Testament Prize, 1877; Denyer and Johnson Scholar, 1878; Deacon, 1876; Priest, 1877; Curate of St Mary Magdalen, Oxford, 1876–80; Chaplain of New College, Oxford, 1879–85; Magdalen Coll., 1879; Lecturer in Divinity, 1884–93; Member of the Oxford School Board, 1888–1903; Member of the Oxford City Education Committee since 1907. *Recreations:* music, foreign travel, architecture. *Address:* Magdalen College, Oxford. *Died 5 Nov. 1916.*

AYTON, Rt. Rev. Lewis, DD; Assistant Bishop to Bishop of Peterborough, since 1912; *b* London, 8 June 1838; *s* of late John Clayton, solicitor; *m* 1872, Katharine, *d* of Thomas Hare of Gosbury Hill, Hook, Surrey; three *s* one *d*. *Educ:* King's College School; Emmanuel Coll., Cambridge (MA). Ordained 1861; Vicar of St James's, Dallington, 1873–75; of St Margaret's, Leicester, 1875–88; Rural Dean, 1884–88; Proctor in Convocation for Chapter of Peterborough, 1892; Canon of Peterborough, 1887; Bishop of Leicester, 1903–13. *Address:* Canonry House, Peterborough.

Died 25 June 1917.

AYTON-GREENE, William Henry, CBE 1919; MB, BCh (Cantab); FRCS (Eng.); Surgeon to St Mary's Hospital, and King Edward VII Hospital for Officers; *m* 1915, May, *o d* of Captain W. H. Guy, RNR. *Educ:* Oundle; Rossall; Cambridge. University and Kerslake Scholar at St Mary's Medical School; late lecturer on anatomy, and Dean of the Medical School; Examiner to the Conjoint Board and Society of Apothecaries; late Surgeon to the Hampstead General Hospital and King George Hospital; Chevalier de la Légion d'Honneur; examiner in surgery to the University of Cambridge and in anatomy for the Fellowship of the College of Surgeons of England; Consulting surgeon to the Richmond Hospital. *Publications:* Pye's Surgical Handicraft; articles in Cassel's Surgery, Wright's Index of Treatment, etc. *Recreation:* golf. *Address:* 86 Brook Street, W1. *T:* Mayfair 5000. *M:* LD 762. *Clubs:* Devonshire; Deal.

Died 29 June 1926.

EARY, Ven. Robert; Rector of Galbally, since 1879; Archdeacon of Emly, since 1904. *Educ:* Trinity College, Dublin. Ordained 1874; Curate of Cappoquin, 1874–76; Acting Incumbent, 1876–79; Canon of Cashel, 1898–1904; Rural Dean of Duntryleague, 1892–1912. *Publication:* Analysis of Locke's Essay, 1870. *Address:* Galbally Rectory, Tipperary. *Died 1919.*

EAVE, John, ISO 1903; *b* 9 Nov. 1837; *s* of Alderman Thomas Cleave of New Windsor, Berks; *m* 1860, Martha (*d* 1910), *d* of Mr Benjamin Wyld, Curzon Street, Mayfair; three *s* one *d*. *Educ:* private schools. Clerk in HM Customs, 1854; supplementary clerk in Treasury (after competition), 1856; 1st class Assistant in the British Museum, 1858; subsequently designated Accountant there, and retained office till close of 1904; Speaker of first Battersea Local Parliament. *Address:* 28 Vardens Road, New Wandsworth, SW11.

Died 8 April 1928.

CLEEVE, Maj.-Gen. William Frederick, CB 1916; late RA; JP; *b* 1853; *s* of late Charles Ker Cleeve; *m* 1894, Gladys Elizabeth, *e d* of F. J. Mitchell, JP, DL, of Llanfrechfa Grange, Monmouthshire; four *s* one *d*. *Educ:* RMA, Woolwich. Lieut RA, 1873; Colonel, 1904; retired, 1910; Brig.-Gen. 1914; Maj.-Gen. (Hon.), 1918; service—home, India, and South Africa; Afghan War, 1880 (medal); was a Chief Instructor in Gunnery, 1901–4; Commandant Royal Military Academy, Woolwich, 1914–18. *Address:* Llanfrechfa, Mon. *Club:* Naval and Military. *Died 31 Jan. 1922.*

CLEGHORN, Isabel, LLA, MA *hon. causa,* Welsh University and Sheffield University; late Head Mistress of Heeley Bank Council School, Sheffield; *b* Rochester, Kent, but lived for many years in Sheffield. *Educ:* Elementary School, North Shields (Scotch Church); pupil teacher in Elementary School, South Shields; Stockwell Training College. Late President Sheffield Teachers' Association, and Sheffield Head Teachers' Association; for three years Chairman Page Hall Orphanage House Committee; for 24 years on Executive of National Union of Teachers, and President of the NUT, 1911–12; on Consultative Committee, Board of Education; on Teachers' Registration Council; member of Council of the National Council of Women; member of Sheffield Education Committee since 1903; member of Ecclesall, Sheffield, Board of Guardians, 1922. *Address:* 89 Moersbrook Park Road, Sheffield.

Died 5 Dec. 1922.

CLEGHORN, Surg.-Gen. James, CSI 1897; Indian Medical Service (retired, 1898); Hon. Surgeon to King; Fellow of Allahabad University; *b* Wick, 1841; 3rd *s* of John Cleghorn; *m* 1877, 2nd *d* of Gen. de S. Barrow. *Educ:* local school; Edinburgh Univ.; Royal College of Surgeons, Edinburgh. MD St Andrews; LRCS Edinburgh. Entered Indian Medical Service, 1865; appointed Director General, Indian Medical Service, and Sanitary Commissioner with Government of India, 1895; Government of India delegate to Venice Plague Conference, 1897; Bhotan Campaign, 1865 (medal). *Publications:* various papers to medical journals. *Recreations:* fishing, etc. *Address:* Weysprings, Haslemere, Surrey.

Died 14 June 1920.

CLELAND, John, MD, LRCSE, LLD (St Andrews, Edinburgh, and Glasgow), DSc; FRS; *b* Perth, 15 June 1835; *m* 1888, Ada Marion Spottiswoode (*d* 1918), *d* of late Dr Balfour, Professor of Botany, Edinburgh; one *s*. *Educ:* High School and University of Edinburgh. Professor of Anatomy and Physiology, Queen's Coll., Galway, 1863–77; Regius Professor of Anatomy, University of Glasgow, 1877–1909. *Publications:* numerous memoirs, anatomical and other; The Mechanism of the Gubernaculum, 1856; Animal Physiology, 1874; Directory for Dissection, 1876; volume of essays entitled, Evolution, Expression, and Sensation, Cell Life and Pathology, 1881; Scala Naturae and other Poems, 1887; joint-editor of 7th edn of Quain's Anatomy, 1867; joint-author of Memoirs and Memoranda in Anatomy, 1889 and of Cleland and Mackay's Human Anatomy, 1896; lectures, addresses, etc. *Recreation:* sketching from nature. *Address:* Drumelog, Crewkerne, Somerset.

Died 5 March 1924.

CLERK, Col John, CSI 1889; CVO 1896; *s* of late Sir George Russell Clerk, GCSI, KCB. Served Crimea, with Rifle Brigade, 1854–55 (medal with two clasps, Turkish medal); subsequently exchanging into 4th Dragoon Guards; was guardian to HH the Nizam, 1874–76; was Extra Equerry to Queen Victoria and late Duke of Saxe-Coburg; Comptroller and Treasurer to Princess Henry of Battenberg, 1885–99. *Address:* 33 Elm Park Gardens, SW. *Club:* Carlton.

Died March 1919.

CLERMONT-GANNEAU, Charles Simon; *b* Paris, 19 Feb. 1846. *Educ:* Ecole des Langues Orientales. Was dragoman to Consulate at Jerusalem and Embassy at Constantinople; discovered the Stele of Mesha and the Stele of the Temple, 1870; employed by British Government to take charge of archæological expedition to Palestine, 1874; by French Government to Syria, Tripolitana, Cyrenaica, Elephantina, and Red Sea; Chevalier of the Légion of Honour, 1875; Vice-Consul, Jaffa, 1880; Premier Secrétaire-Interprète for Oriental Languages, Paris, 1882; Consul of the First Class, 1886; Consul General, 1896; Minister Plenipotentiary 1906; Director at the Ecole des Hautes Etudes and Professor of Semitic epigraphy and antiquities at the Collège de France; elected Member of the Académie des Inscriptions et Belles-Lettres, 1889; LLD, FRSL; Member correspondent de l'Académie Impériale de Petrograd; was principally instrumental in exposing the forgeries of the Moabite pottery, of Shapira's manuscripts, and of the tiara of Saitapharnes. *Publications:* Palestine Inconnue, 1886; Etudes d'Archéologie Orientale, 1880; Les Fraudes Archéologiques, 1885; Recueil d'Archéologie Orientale, 1885–1905, seven volumes; Archæological Researches in Palestine, 1896–99; Album d'Antiquités Orientales, 1897, etc. *Address:* 1 avenue George V, Paris.

CLERY, Lieut.-Gen. Sir Francis, KCMG 1900; KCB 1899 (CB 1884); *b* 13 Feb. 1838. Entered army 1858; Maj.-Gen. 1894; retired, 1901; Professor of Tactics, RM Coll. Sandhurst, 1872–75; Dep.-Asst-Adjt-Gen. Headquarters, Ireland, 1875–77; Aldershot, 1877–78; Chief Staff Officer, Flying Column, Zulu War, 1878–79 (despatches, brevet of Lieut-Colonel, medal with clasp); Egyptian War, 1882 (medal and Khedive's star); Chief of Staff, Suakim Expedition, 1884 (despatches twice, brevet of Col, CB, two clasps); Deputy Adjt-Gen. Nile Expedition, 1884–85 (clasp); Chief of Staff, Egypt, 1886–88; Commandant of Staff College, 1888–93; commanded 3rd Infantry Brigade, Aldershot, 1895–96; Deputy Adjt-Gen. to the Forces 1896–1900; Commanded 2nd Division, South African Field Force, 1899–1900 (despatches). *Publication:* Minor Tactics, 1875. *Address:* 4 Whitehall Court, SW. *Club:* United Service.

Died 25 June 1926.

CLERY, Surg.-Gen. James Albert, CB 1900; MB; RAMC; retired 1906; Surgeon-General, South Africa; *b* 21 Dec. 1846; *s* of late Thomas Clery of Ballinahinch, Limerick; *m* 1890, Isabel, *d* of W. E. Kirby, Newcastle-on-Tyne; one *s*. *Educ:* Stonyhurst College; Trinity College, Dublin. Entered army, 1871; Colonel, 1899; served Nile Expedition, 1884–85 (medal with clasp, Khedive's star); Soudan, 1898 (despatches, British medal, Khedive's medal); South Africa, 1899–1902 (despatches twice, Queen's medal, 6 clasps, King's medal, 2 clasps). *Address:* 13 St John's Park, Blackheath, SE. *Club:* Junior Constitutional. *Died 10 Feb. 1920.*

CLEVELAND, Adm. Henry Forster; retired; *b* 28 April 1834; *s* of Rev. H. Cleveland, Rector of Romaldkirk, Darlington; *m* 1863; no *c*. *Educ:* Grantham College. Entered Royal Navy, 1848; retired, 1895. *Address:* 37 Carlisle Road, Eastbourne.

Died 26 Jan. 1924.

CLEVERLY, Charles F. M., JP; *b* Hong Kong, China; father Mem. of Council there, and for over 20 years held the Government appointment of Surveyor-General; *m* May, *e d* of J. B. Somers; two *s* two d. *Educ:* Clifton Coll.; Jesus Coll., Cambridge (BA). Articled to G. Aitchison, RA, and afterwards worked in the office of G. Bodley, RA; took up church painting and decorative work generally; decorated the chancel of Bexley Church (Kent); the chapel of the Seamen's Hospital, Greenwich; St Paul's, Avenue Road, NW, etc; several altar-pieces, among them the triptych, Great Massingham Church. *Address:* Dunsborough House, Ripley, Surrey. *Clubs:* Arts; County, Guildford. *Died 9 March 1921.*

CLIFFE, Anthony Loftus, JP, DL; *b* 4 June 1861; *e s* of late Anthony John Cliffe, and Amy, *d* of Sir John Howley; *m* 1904, Frances Emma, *d* of Capt. Henry Segrave of Cabra and *widow* of Sir John Talbot Power, 3rd Bt; no *c*. Late Capt. 3rd Batt. Royal Irish Regt; High Sheriff, Co. Wexford, 1897. *Address:* Bellevue, Wexford. *Clubs:* Carlton, Boodle's; Sackville Street, Dublin.

Died Jan. 1922.

CLIFFORD OF CHUDLEIGH, 9th Baron, *cr* 1672; **Lewis Henry Hugh Clifford,** BA, DL; Barrister; ADC; Count of the Holy Roman Empire; *b* 24 Aug. 1851; *s* of 8th Baron and Hon. Agnes Catherine, *y d* of 11th Baron Petre; *S* father, 1880; *m* 1890, Mabel, *d* of Col John Towneley of Towneley, Lancashire. *Educ:* Stonyhurst. Owned about 8000 acres. *Heir:* *b* Hon. William Hugh Clifford, *b* 17 Dec. 1858. *Address:* Ugbrooke Park, Chudleigh; Court House, Cannington, Somersetshire. *Clubs:* Bachelors', Brooks's.

Died 19 July 1916.

CLIFFORD, Brig.-Gen. Henry Frederick Hugh, DSO 1915; the Suffolk Regiment; *b* 13 Aug. 1867; 2nd *s* of late Maj.-Gen. Hon. Sir Henry Clifford, VC, KCMG, CB. Entered army, 1888; Captain, 1897; Major, 1910; Lt-Col, 1914; ADC to Lt-Gen. Sir William Butler, KCB, 1899 and 1902–5; served S African War, 1899–1902 (Queen's medal, 3 clasps; King's medal, 2 clasps); European War, 1914–15 (DSO, prom. Col). *Club:* Naval and Military.

Died 16 Sept. 1916.

CLIFFORD, Rev. John, CH 1921; MA, DD, BSc; *b* Sav Derbyshire, 16 Oct. 1836; *m* 1862, Rebecca (*d* 1919), *d* of Dr C of Newbury, Berks; four *s* two d. *Educ:* Baptist College, Nottingh University College, London; Royal School of Mines. MA 1864; with honours, 1866; BSc, with honours, 1862, London; DD I University of Chicago, etc; LLD Colgate University New York, I LLD Macmaster University, Canada, 1910. President, London B: Association, 1879; Baptist Union, 1888 and 1899; General B: Association, 1872 and 1891; National Council of Free Evange Churches, 1898–99; British Chautauqua, 1899–1900; Baptist W Alliance, 1905–11; Baptist European Congress, 1913; Minist Praed Street and Westbourne Park Church, 1858–1915; Presic Baptist World Alliance, 1905–11; made tour round the world, 1 President, National Brotherhood Council, 1916–19; President W Federation of Brotherhoods, 1919–20. *Publications:* editor, Ge Baptist Magazine, 1870–83; Familiar Talks with the Young, 1 George Mostyn, 1874; Is Life Worth Living? 1880; Daily Stre for Daily Living, 1885; The Dawn of Manhood, 1886; co-ed Review of the Churches, 1891; The Inspiration and Authority o Bible, 1892; The Christian Certainties, 1893; Typical Chri Leaders, 1898; Social Worship an Everlasting Necessity; God's Gre Britain, 1899; The Fight for Education: what is at stake; Clerica in British Politics, 1902; The Secret of Jesus, 1904; The Ultin Problems of Christianity, 1906; The Carey Lecture, 1912; The Go of Gladness, 1912; Temperance Reform and the Ideal State; Lee Raper Memorial Lecture, 1913; Brotherhood in Ideal and in Ac 1916; State Education after the War, 1916; The Spirit of Man in 1 1917; Our Fight for Belgium and what it means, 1918; Saving Soul of The World in 1917, 1918; The League of Free Nations; Fa the Facts, 1919; Darkness and Dawn in 1918, 1919; The Emerge of the International Mind in 1919, 1920; World Brotherh according to Jesus, the John Clifford Lecture, 1920. *Address* Waldeck Road, West Ealing, W13. *Clubs:* National Liberal, Eig

Died 20 Nov. 1

CLIFFORD, Julian; General Entertainments Manager and Mu Director, Hastings Corporation; Musical Director, Harro Corporation; Conductor of the London Symphony Orchestra fo London Ballad Concerts Season, 1921–22; conductor, solo pia and composer; *b* 28 Sept. 1877; *s* of late Thomas Clifford, of Dr Park, Tonbridge, Kent; *m* 1902, Alice Margaret, *e d* of 5th I Henniker; one *s* one d. *Educ:* Ardingly College; Tonbridge Sch Leipzig Conservatorium; Royal College of Music. Organist Choirmaster, English Church, Leipzig, 1892; King Charles Martyr, Tunbridge Wells, 1894; played as Solo Pianist at the Que Hall Promenade Concerts, Chappell Ballad Concerts, Sco Orchestra, Norwich Philharmonic, and all principal London Provincial Concerts; conducted the following orchestras— London Symphony, The Hallé, The Leeds Symphony, Brad Permanent, Birmingham Symphony, The Harrogate Municipa years), Hastings Municipal; conducted British Musical Festival a Liége Exhibition, 1906; founded the Yorkshire Permanent Orche 1909; late conductor of the Westminster Orchestral Society, V London Choral, Leeds Philharmonic; conducted his o compositions throughout England and Belgium, and did muc further the interests of British Music. *Compositions:* Concerto for P and Orchestra in E Minor; Ode to the New Year for Solo Quart Chorus and Orchestra; Orchestral Ballad in D; Suite de Concert; T Poem Lights Out; Song Cycle The Dream of Flowers, and nume pianoforte solos, songs, etc. *Recreations:* golf, billiards, church ringing. *Address:* The Royal Hall, Harrogate. *TA:* Clifford, Harro T: 49. *Clubs:* Royal Automobile; Harrogate Conservative.

Died 27 Dec. 1

CLIFFORD, Major Wigram, DSO 1900; Northumberland Fusi *b* 20 Feb. 1876; *o s* of late Maj.-Gen. R. M. Clifford; *m* 1903, *y d* of late Major T. G. Miles. *Educ:* US College, Westward I RMC Sandhurst. Joined Loyal North Lancashire Regiment; se in South Africa, 1899–1901 (slightly wounded, despatches, D. served NW Frontier, India, 1908; Mohmand Expedition (medal clasp); European War, 1914–16.

Died 20 May 1

CLIFT, Hon. James Augustus, CBE 1918; KC 1904; a Per Commissioner for Newfoundland; *b* 1857; married. Barr Newfoundland, 1884; Parliament, 1889; retired, 1919. *Addres* Johns, Newfoundland. *Died 8 Feb. 1*

CLIFTON, John Talbot, FRGS, FZS; *b* 1 Dec. 1868; *e s* of Thomas Henry Clifton, MP, and Madeline Diana Elizabeth, e Sir Andrew Noel Agnew, 8th Bt; *m* 1907, Violet Mary (auth of Pilgrims to the Isles of Penance and The Islands of Qu

Wilhelmina), *d* of late W. Nelthorpe Beauclerk, British Minister Plenipotentiary and Extraordinary in Peru, Ecuador, and Bolivia; two *s* three *d*. *Educ:* Eton; Magdalene College, Cambridge. Explored in Africa, discovering new route between Ujiji and Victoria Nyanza; first Englishman on Lena River, Siberia, and discovered on Arctic Ocean new species of wild sheep named in British Museum Ovis Cliftonii; lived alone among Esquimaux far north of Hudson's Bay; in early part of the war carried despatches to the King of the Belgians, and afterwards served as Lieut RNVR. Owned 12,500 acres in Lancashire, some by grant of William Rufus, and 17,000 acres in the Isle of Islay; Lord of the Manor of Lytham. *Publication:* Fortune Telling by Japanese Swords. *Recreations:* music, golf, sport. *Address:* Lytham Hall, Lytham, Lancs; Kildalton Castle, Port Ellen, Islay, Scotland. *Clubs:* Carlton, Pratt's. *Died 23 March 1928.*

CLIFTON, Robert Bellamy, MA; FRS; Hon. Fellow of Wadham College; formerly Fellow of Merton College, Oxford, and of St John's College, Cambridge; *b* 1836; *m* 1862, Catherine Elizabeth Butler (*d* 1917). *Educ:* Univ. Coll. London; St John's Coll., Camb. (BA) 6th Wrangler, 1859; 2nd Smith's Prizeman; Professor of Natural Philosophy, Owens Coll. Manchester, 1860–65; Professor of Experimental Philosophy, Oxford, 1865–1915; member of Royal Commission on Accidents in Mines, 1879–86; President of Physical Society, 1882–84. *Recreation:* work. *Address:* 3 Bardwell Road, Banbury Road, Oxford. *Club:* Athenæum.
Died 22 Feb. 1921.

CLINCH, George, FGS, FSAScot; Librarian to the Society of Antiquaries of London; Vice-President of the Association of Men of Kent and Kentish Men; *b* Borden, Kent, 1860; *m*; two *d*. *Educ:* privately. *Publications:* Antiquarian Jottings relating to Bromley, Hayes, Keston, and West Wickham, in Kent, 1889; Bloomsbury and St Giles's: Past and Present, 1890; Marylebone and St Pancras: their History, Celebrities, Buildings, and Institutions, 1890; Mayfair and Belgravia: being an Historical Account of the Parish of St George, Hanover Square, 1892; Bromley and the Bromley District, 1902; Little Guide to Kent, 1903; Little Guide to the Isle of Wight, 1904; Little Guide to St Paul's Cathedral, 1906; Old English Churches, 1st edition, 1900, 2nd edition, 1903; Handbook of English Antiquities, 1905; English Costume, 1909; Little Guide to London, 1912; English Coast Defences, 1915; editor of Dr E. F. Rimbault's Soho and its Associations, 1895, etc. *Recreations:* walking, photography. *Address:* 3 Meadowcroft, Sutton, Surrey. *Died 2 Feb. 1921.*

CLINTON, Ven. Thomas William; Rector of Donaghpatrick, since 1917. *Educ:* Trinity College, Dublin. MA 1894; Divinity Testimonium, 1900; ordained 1890; Curate of Muckno, Co. Monaghan, 1890; Incumbent of Augher, 1893–94; Rector of Aghavea, Fermanagh, 1894–1901; Moka, Mauritius, 1901–4; Moka cum Quatre Bornes since 1904; Principal, Theological College, Mauritius, 1901–7; Archdeacon and Hon. Canon, Mauritius, 1907–12. *Address:* Donaghpatrick Rectory, Navan, Co. Meath.
Died 18 March 1926.

CLIPPERTON, Sir Charles (Bell Child), KBE 1924; CMG 1916; *b* Kertch (Crimea), 1864; *s* of late Capt. R. C. Clipperton, HM's Consul; *m* 1896, Ella E., *d* of late M. Ehret of Philadelphia, USA. *Educ:* Wellington College. Vice-Consul at Baltimore, 1892; Philadelphia, 1894; was in charge of the Consulate at Boston in 1902; transferred to Rouen, 1904; given the personal rank of Consul-General and also charged with the duties of a Visiting Consular Officer, 1913; appointed a Sub-Commissioner of the Joint British Red Cross and Order of St John Commission in France, 1915–16 (despatches); an Hon. Associate of the Order of the Hospital of St John of Jerusalem in England, 1918; employed in the Foreign Office since 26 March 1918; Inspector-General of Consulates and given the rank of Acting Counsellor of Embassy in HM Diplomatic Service while so employed, 26 Nov. 1918; in charge of the Consulate-General at Antwerp, 16 Dec. 1918–3 Feb. 1919. *Recreation:* motoring. *Address:* c/o Foreign Office, SW1. *Club:* Royal Automobile.
Died 18 June 1927.

CLISSOLD, Major Harry, DSO 1916; MA; RE, TF; Assistant Master in Clifton College; Major, South Midland Field Company RE (T); *e s* of late W. G. Clissold, JP, of Chestnut Hill, Nailsworth, Glos; unmarried. *Educ:* Clifton College; Trinity College, Cambridge (Scholar), 1890; BA Mathematics (Aegrotat), 1892; 1st Class Science Tripos, 1903; Assistant Physics Master at Marlborough College, 1893–94; Clifton, 1894–1914; House Master, 1912; Commanded Cadet Corps, 1906–1912; served European War, 1914–16 (DSO). *Recreations:* fives, tennis. *Address:* Clifton College, Bristol. *T:* 3443. *Died 28 Sept. 1917.*

CLIVE, Viscount; Percy Robert Herbert; *b* 2 Dec. 1892; *e s* and heir of 4th Earl of Powis. *Educ:* Eton. Entered army, Scots Guards, 1914; Lieut Welsh Guards, 1915; served European War, 1914–15.
Died 13 Oct. 1916.

CLIVE, Gen. Edward Henry; *b* 23 Sept. 1837; *s* of G. Clive, Perrystone Court, Herefordshire; *m* 1867, Isabel, *e d* of Daniel Hale Webb, Wykham Park, Oxon; four *s* four *d*. *Educ:* Harrow. Joined Grenadier Guards, 1854; served Crimea, 1856; Lieut-Col commanding Regt, 1880–85; Commandant, St College, 1885–88; Governor, RM College, 1888–93; retired, 1898; Colonel 8th King's Liverpool Regiment, 1907; MP (L) Hereford City, 1869–71; JP Herefordshire and Mayo; DL Co. Mayo. *Address:* 25 Ennismore Gardens, SW; Perrystone Court, Ross; Ballycroy, Co. Mayo. *Clubs:* United Service, Travellers'.
Died 1 March 1916.

CLIVE, Capt. Percy Archer; MP (U) South Hereford since 1908; *b* 1873; *e s* of Charles Meysey Bolton Clive and Lady Katherine Fielding, *y d* of 7th Earl of Denbigh; *m* 1905, Alice Muriel, *y d* of late Col G. F. Dallas; two *s* three *d*. Entered Grenadier Guards, 1891; Captain, 1899; served W Africa, 1898; South Africa, 1899–1901; MP (LU) South Herefordshire, 1900–6; late Parliamentary Private Sec. (hon.) to Mr Austen Chamberlain when Chancellor of Exchequer; rejoined Grenadier Guards on outbreak of War; commanded 7th Batt. E York Regt since May 1916 (despatches, Legion of Honour, twice wounded). *Address:* Whitfield, Allensmore, Herefordshire. *T:* Wormbridge 2. *Clubs:* Guards, Travellers', Carlton.
Died 5 April 1918.

CLOETE, Hendrik, CMG 1897; barrister-at-law; *b* 10 Aug. 1851; *e* surv. *s* of late Dirk Cloete of Alphen, Cape Colony; *m* 1893, *e d* of late Rev. Van Warmelo. *Educ:* private school and Diocesan College, Rondebosch, Cape Colony. Barrister, Inner Temple, 1877; advocate to Supreme Court Bar of the Cape Colony, 1878, and to High Court, Transvaal Bar, 1879; served as lieut and adjutant of volunteers, and was present at the various engagements around Pretoria in the Transvaal War, 1880–81; British agent in the S African Republic after the Jameson raid, succeeding Sir Jacobus de Wet, during 1896. Decorated for service as HM acting agent in the S A Republic. *Recreations:* cricket, tennis, rowing, shooting. *Address:* Alphen Wynberg, Cape Colony. *Clubs:* Civil Service, Cape Town; Pretoria, Rand, Transvaal. *Died 18 May 1920.*

CLONBROCK, 4th Baron, *cr* 1790; **Luke Gerald Dillon,** PC; KP; JP; Representative Peer for Ireland since 1895; HM's Lieutenant Galway since 1892; *b* 10 March 1834; *s* of 3rd Baron and Caroline, *d* of 1st Lord Churchill; *S* father, 1893; *m* 1866, Augusta, *o d* of 2nd Lord Crofton; one *s* three *d*. *Educ:* Eton; Balliol College, Oxon. 2nd class Law and Modern History, 1855. Church of Ireland. Conservative. Attaché, Berlin, 1856; Paid Attaché, Vienna, 1859; 2nd Secretary at Vienna, 1862; Private Secretary to Lord-Lieutenant of Ireland, 1866–68 and 1874–76. Owned 28,246 acres. Heir: *s* Hon. Robert Edward Dillon, *b* 21 May 1869. *Address:* Clonbrock, Ahascragh, Co. Galway. *Clubs:* Travellers', Kildare Street, Dublin; County, Galway. *Died 12 May 1917.*

CLONBROCK, 5th Baron, *cr* 1790; **Robert Edward Dillon,** DL Co. Galway; *b* 21 May 1869; *s* of 4th Baron and Augusta, *o d* of 2nd Baron Crofton; *S* father, 1917. *Educ:* Eton; University of Neuchatel; University of Göttingen. Elected member of the Royal Irish Academy, Member of Royal Society of Antiquaries of Ireland, 1916. Heir: none. *Recreations:* natural history and science, forestry, gardening, reading, fishing, shooting. *Address:* Clonbrock, Ahascragh, Co. Galway. *Clubs:* Wellington, MCC; Kildare Street, Dublin; County, Galway.
Died 1 Nov. 1926 (ext).

CLONCURRY, 4th Baron, *cr* 1789; **Valentine Frederick Lawless;** Baron (UK) 1831; Bt 1776; *b* Lyons, Co. Kildare, 2 Nov. 1840; *s* of 3rd Baron and Elizabeth, *o d* of John Kirwan; *S* father, 1869; *m* 1883, Hon. Laura Winn (*d* 1891), *e d* of 1st Baron St Oswald; one *d* (and one *d* decd). *Educ:* Eton; Balliol Coll., Oxford (BA). Owned 12,000 acres. Protestant. Conservative. Heir: *b* Hon. Frederick Lawless, *b* 20 April 1847. *Address:* Lyons, Co. Kildare. *Clubs:* Carlton, Constitutional; Royal St George Yacht, Kingstown; Kildare Street, Dublin. *Died 12 Feb. 1928.*

CLONMELL, 7th Earl of, *cr* 1703; **Rupert Charles Scott;** Baron Earlsfort, 1793; Viscount Clonmell, 1789; Captain, Warwickshire RHA (TF) (1914 decoration); *b* 10 Nov. 1877; *o c* of 6th Earl and Lucy Maria, *d* of Anthony Willson, MP, Rauceby Hall, Sleaford; *S* father, 1898; *m* 1901, Rachel Estelle, *d* of Samuel Berridge, Toft Hill,

Rugby; two *d*. Contested (L) Rugby, 1910. *Heir: u* Hon. Dudley Alexander Charles Scott, *b* 26 May 1853. *Address:* 20 Hertford Street, W1; *T:* Mayfair 3944; Eathorpe Hall, Leamington; The Little House, Mermaid Street, Rye. *Clubs:* White's, Garrick, National Liberal, Bath; Kildare Street, Dublin; Royal St George's Yacht, Kingstown.

Died 18 Nov. 1928.

CLORAN, Hon. Henry Joseph, BCL; KC; *b* Montreal, 8 May 1855; *s* of Joseph Cloran and Ann Kennedy, both natives of Ireland; *m* 1st, 1882, Agnes M. Donovan (*d* 1896), 2nd, 1906, N. Inez, *d* of George Goodwin, Ottawa; three *s* two *d. Educ:* Montreal College, St Sulpice Seminary, Paris; McGill and Laval University, Montreal (BCL). Contested Montreal Centre 1887, and Prescott Co., Ont., 1896 and 1900; editor of Montreal Post and True Witness, 1882–87; was President Press Association of Province of Quebec; Crown Prosecutor, 1889–92; Attorney of Provincial Revenue, 1897–1908; KC 1899; Reeve and Mayor of Hawkesbury, 1894–1901; called to Senate, 1903. Roman Catholic. Liberal. *Address:* Montreal, Quebec.

Died 8 Feb. 1928.

CLOSE, Admiral Francis Arden; late High Sheriff of Bristol; *b* 1829; *s* of Dean Close, Carlisle Deanery; *m* 1st, 1851, M. H. Hebden of Gothenburg, Sweden; 2nd, Paulina Krantler of Strasburg; no *c. Educ:* Cheltenham College. Entered RN, 1842; promoted Lieutenant for exemplary examinations at Naval College, 1850; Commander for service at Bomarsund, Baltic, Russian War, 1854; Captain for service on W Coast Africa, 1861. *Address:* Trafalgar, Clifton Down, Bristol. *Club:* United Service. *Died 25 Aug. 1918.*

CLOSE, Colonel Lewis Henry, CMG 1916; Royal Engineers; Chief Engineer, Western Command, India (Quetta); *b* 4 Sept. 1869; *s* of late Maj.-Gen. Frederick Close, RA; *m* 1910, Alys Dora, 3rd *d* of late Maj.-Gen. William Creagh, Bombay Staff Corps; no *c. Educ:* United Services College, Westward Ho! Commission RE, 1888; ordered to India, 1890; served Miranzai Expedition, 1891, as Asst Field Engineer, and Waziristan Expedition, 1895, as Company Officer, No. 2 Co. Bengal Sappers and Miners; thanked by Government of Bengal for services on famine work in Behar, 1896; reverted to Imperial Establishment, 1900; Division Officer for Reconstruction, South Aldershot, 1900–5; in the Military Works Services in India, 1905–14; Assistant Director of Works, Mediterranean Expeditionary Force, Feb. 1915; served at Mudros and in Egypt (despatches four times, CMG, 3rd Class Order of the Nile); Secretary in the PWD to the Hon. the AGG in Baluchistan. *Recreations:* polo, racquets, tennis, small and big-game shooting. *Address:* c/o Cox's Branch, 6 Pall Mall, SW1. *Club:* Junior Army and Navy. *Died 11 Nov. 1924.*

CLOSE, S. P., ARHA. *Address:* Fodeen, Eden Road, Carrickfergus.

CLOUGH, Sir John, Kt 1914; JP; *b* 1836; *s* of John Clough; *m* 1862, Thamar, *d* of Prince Smith, Keighley. *Address:* Haincliffe, Ingrow, Keighley, Yorks; 25 Royal Cresent, Bath.

Died 31 May 1922.

CLOUGH, Walter Owen, JP for Middlesex; one of HM's Lieutenants of the City of London; Arbitrator of the London Chamber of Arbitration; Fellow of Institute of Chartered Accountants; MP (L) Portsmouth, 1892–1900; CC Corporation of London, 1891–1905; *b* 15 Sept. 1846; *s* of late John Clough, Huddersfield; *m* 1871, Hannah (*d* 1917), *d* of George Marshall, of Newark; three *s. Educ:* Huddersfield. Practised as a Chartered Accountant, London. *Address:* 54 Gresham Street, EC2. *T:* Central 5924.

Died 17 April 1922.

CLOWES, Frank, DSc Lond; FIC; FCS; MRI; Emeritus Professor of Chemistry and Metallurgy, University College, Nottingham; Governor of Dulwich College; Expert Adviser in Gas Supply to the Corporation of London; *b* Bradford, Yorkshire, 1848; *s* of Francis Clowes, Norfolk, and Mary Low, London; *m* 1877, Mabel H. Waters. *Educ:* City of London School; Royal School of Mines, London; Royal Coll. of Science, Dublin; University of Würzburg; Lecturer on Chemistry and Physics with laboratory, Queenwood College, Hants; Professor of Chemistry, Univ. Coll., Nottingham, 1881–97, and first Principal; Chemical Adviser to the London County Council, and Director of the Council's Chemical Staff and Laboratories, 1897–1913; President of the Society of Chemical Industry, 1897–98; member of the Senate, University of London, 1901–3; Vice-President of the Institute of Chemistry, 1901–3, 1911–13; Vice-President Chemical Section Brit. Assoc., 1893, 1914; Forrest Lecturer, Institution of Civil Engineers, 1901; visitor to the Royal Inst., 1903–4 and 1919–20; Pres. of Sect. III, Congress of Sanitary Institute,

Glasgow, 1904; Hon. Member of the Midland Counties Institutic of Engineers, and of the Chester (Kingsley) Society of Scienc *Publications:* Text-book of Qualitative Analysis, 1874 (9th edn); Tex book of Quantitative Analysis, 1891 (12th edn); Elementary Practic Chemistry, 1896, Part I (7th edn); Part II (9th edn); The Detectic and Estimation of Inflammable Gases and Vapours in the Air, 189〈 Experimental Bacterial Treatment of London Sewage, 1904; ar many original papers to the Royal Society, the Chemical Society, th Society of Chemical Industry, the Federated Institution of Minir Engineers, and Roy. Inst. of Brit. Architects. *Recreation:* golf. *Addre〉* The Grange, College Road, Dulwich, SE21. *T:* 1457 Sydenhar *Club:* Athenæum. *Died 18 Dec. 192.*

CLOWES, Lieut-Col Peter Legh, CB 1900; JP, DL Herefordshir〈 *b* 30 Aug. 1853; *e s* of late John Clowes; *m* 1895, Edith, *y d* of C Warren. *Educ:* Eton; Trinity Coll., Cambridge. Joined 8th Hussar 1875; served with the regt in India (Afghanistan, 1879–80, meda] Major, 1885; commanded 8th Hussars, 1897–1901; served Sou〈 Africa, 1900–1 (medal 6 clasps); High Sheriff, Herefordshire, 192 *Address:* Burton Court, Leominster, Herefordshire. *T:* Eardisland . *TA:* Eardisland. *Clubs:* Arthur's, Naval and Military.

Died 23 Feb. 192.

CLOWES, Samuel, JP; MP (Lab) Hanley Division of Stoke-on-Tre〈 since 1924; General Secretary, National Society of Pottery Worker member Stoke-on-Trent Town Council; *b* 1864; *s* of James Clowe Stoke-on-Trent. President of the National Pottery Council. *Addre〉* 5 Hill Street, Hanley. *Died 25 March 192〈*

CLUTE, Hon. Roger Conger; Judge, High Court of Justice, Ontari〈 since 1905; *b* 18 Aug. 1848; *m* 1873, Rosa, *d* of late Henry Corb〉 Belleville, Ont; one *s* one *d. Educ:* Grammar School, Stirling; Albe College, Belleville. Barrister, 1873; QC 1890; Royal Commissio〈 to enquire into Labour troubles in British Columbia, 1899; Chairma of Royal Commission on Oriental immigration into Canada, 1900– *Address:* 19 Walmer Road, Toronto. *Club:* Toronto.

Died 12 Sept. 192〈

CLUTTON-BROCK, Arthur, BA; Art Critic of The Times; *b* 2〈 March 1868; *s* of John Alan Clutton-Brock of Oakfield, Weybridg〈 and Mary Alice Clutton-Brock; *m* 1903, Evelyn Alice Vernor Harcourt; three *s. Educ:* Eton; New College, Oxford. Called to Ba 1893; practised as a Barrister until 1903; became a journalist; Litera〈 Editor of the Speaker, 1904–6; Art Critic of the Tribune during i existence; then, for a short time, of the Morning Post; on the sta of The Times since 1908. *Publications:* Shelley, the Man and the Poe 1909; William Morris (Home University Series), 1914; Thoughts c the War, 1914; More Thoughts on the War, 1915; Simpson's Choic an Essay on the Future Life, 1916; The Ultimate Belief, 1916; Studie in Christianity, 1918; What is the Kingdom of Heaven? 1919; Essay on Art, 1919; Essays on Books, 1920; 2nd series, 1921; Shakespeare Hamlet, 1922. *Recreation:* gardening. *Address:* The Red Hous〈 Godalming. *T:* Godalming 87. *Clubs:* Reform, Burlington Fine Art

Died 8 Jan. 192〈

COAPE-SMITH, Maj.-Gen. Henry; Indian Army; *b* 24 Sept. 182〈 Entered army, 1848; Maj.-Gen., 1890; unemployed list, 1887; serve NW Frontier of India Campaign, 1854–55 (despatches, medal wit clasp). *Died 13 Dec. 192〉*

COATES, Abraham George, MVO 1906; *b* 6 April 1861. Vic Consul Havana, 1890–91; Philadelphia, 1892; Baltimore, 189〉 Messina, 1905; Consul for Iceland and Faroe Islands, 1907–16; fc Faroe Islands, 1916–19; HM's Consul-General for the States c Maryland, Virginia, and West Virginia 1919–21; retired, 1921.

Died 17 Aug. 192〈

COATES, Major Sir Edward (Feetham), 1st Bt, *cr* 1911; DL, J] MP (U) Lewisham, 1903–18, West Division, Lewisham, since 191〈 Member of Coates, Son, and Co., Stockbrokers; County Alderma for Surrey; Chairman Surrey CC, 1904–9; Member of the 73 Surre Territorial Force Association Council; one of the Trustees of th Crystal Palace; *b* 28 Feb. 1853; *e s* of late James Coates, JP and DI North Riding, Yorks, of Helperby Hall, York, and Elizabeth, *o d c* William Sayer, of Yarm, York; *m* 1878, Edith, *e d* of Captain Phili Woolley of Gravenhurst, Sussex; one *s* one *d. Educ:* Marlborougl Late 3rd Batt. Duke of Wellington's (West Riding Regiment); on of HM's Lieutenants, 1900, City of London; DL, JP Surrey and Nort Riding of Yorkshire; contested Elland Division, York, 1900; on Ro for High Sheriff, Surrey, 1906; Patron of one Living. *Heir: o s* Cap〈 Edward Clive Coates, 15th Hussars, Military Secretary to the Lord Lieut of Ireland [*b* 21 May 1879; *m* 1906, Lady Celia Crewe Milne〈

2nd *d* of 1st Marquis of Crewe, two *s* two *d*]. *Address:* Tayle's Hill, Ewell, Surrey; Queen Anne's Lodge, Queen Anne's Gate, SW1; Helperby Hall, York. *Clubs:* Carlton, Junior United Service; Yorkshire, York; Royal Yacht Squadron, Cowes.

Died 14 Aug. 1921.

COATES, Florence Earle; author; *b* Philadelphia; *d* of George H. Earle and Ellen Frances van Leer; *m* 1879, Edward Hornor Coates, President Pennsylvania Academy of the Fine Arts; one *d*. *Educ:* private school in New England; Convent of Sacred Heart, France. President, Browning Society of Philadelphia, 1895–1903 and 1907–8; a founder of the Contemporary Club, 1886, and of the Transatlantic Society of America; Member Society of Mayflower Descendants and Colonial Dames of America; President of the Contemporary Club, 1918–19; chosen poet laureate of Pennsylvania by State Federation of Women's Clubs, 1919. *Publications:* Matthew Arnold, an Essay, 1894; *poems:* Poems, 1898; Mine and Thine, 1904; Lyrics of Life, 1909; Ode on the Coronation of George V, 1911; The Unconquered Air, 1912; Poems, 2 vols, 1916; Pro Patria, 1917; contributor to Harper's Magazine, Scribner's, Atlantic Monthly, Century, and The Athenæum, London. *Recreations:* music, dramatic recitation, walking, canoeing. *Address:* 2024 Spruce Street, Philadelphia, USA. *Clubs:* Lyceum; Women's Literary, Baltimore (Hon.); New Century (Hon.); Society of Arts and Letters (Hon.), Philadelphia.

Died 16 April 1927.

COATES, Rev. Percy, MA (Oxon); Canon of Bradford; Rector of Bentham, since 1893; Rural Dean of Ewecross; County and District Councillor; Governor of the Royal Infirmary, Lancaster; Member of the Lunesdale Fishery Board; *b* Willow House, Raskelf, 1855; *o s* of Richard Coates of Helperby, uncle of Maj. Sir Edward Feetham Coates, 1st Bt, MP; *m* Margaret, *d* of James Dey, Aberdeen; five *s* one *d*. *Educ:* St Edward's School and St John's College, Oxford. BA 1882. Ordained to St Paul's, Leamington, 1883–89; Senior Curate of Kegworth, Leicestershire, 1889–93; Chaplain to the High Sheriff of Durham, 1913; President of the Royal Lancaster Infirmary, 1923. *Publications:* War-songs and other Poems. *Recreations:* all-round sportsman, golf, fishing, shooting, riding, rowing, football, cricket. *Address:* Bentham Rectory, near Lancaster.

Died 18 Nov. 1925.

COATS, Colonel George Henry Brook, CB 1909; *b* 30 Sept. 1852; *s* of late Colonel John Wilson Coats, MSC; *m* 1887, May Stella (*d* 1910), *d* of Alexander Chisholm; one *s* two *d*. Entered army, 1871; Captain, ISC (later Indian Army) 1883; Major, 1891; Lieut-Col, 1897; Bt-Col, 1901; District Staff Officer and DAAG Bengal, 1886–91; served Afghan War, 1878–80; present at actions of Taif-u-din, battle of Ahmed Khel, action of Urzu, march from Kabul to Kandahar and battle of Kandahar (medal, 2 clasps, bronze star); Isazai Expedition, 1892; Relief of Chitral, 1895 (medal with clasp); Tochi Expedition, 1897–98 (despatches, clasp). *Address:* 5 Powis Square, Brighton.

Died 18 May 1919.

COATS, Rev. Jervis, MA, DD; Principal of the Baptist Theological College of Scotland, since 1914, retaining position of Minister Emeritus of the Govan Church; *b* 7 June 1844; *s* of William and Mary Coats, Paisley; *m* 1880, Marion Wark Wyllie (*d* 1906); two *s* two *d*. *Educ:* Paisley; Glasgow and Göttingen Universities. Entered, when a lad, the Union Bank of Scotland, continuing there for eight years; in 1867 matriculated at Glasgow University, where obtained a high position in the classes; graduated MA 1872; called to a church which was being formed at Govan, Glasgow, 1872; Minister of Govan Baptist Church, 1872–1914; President of Baptist Theological College of Scotland, 1903; engaged for many years in the training of students for the Christian ministry; received the hon. degree of DD from University of Glasgow, 1898. *Publications:* The Master's Watchward—an essay recalling attention to some fundamental principles of the Christian religion, 1897; lectures and magazine articles. *Recreations:* golf, music. *Address:* 8 Dalkeith Avenue, Dumbreck, Glasgow. *T:* Ibrox 189, Glasgow. *Clubs:* Liberal, Glasgow Golf.

Died 15 Nov. 1921.

COATS, William Hodge, DL and JP County of Renfrew; JP County of Glasgow; Chairman J. and P. Coats, Ltd; *b* March 1866; *s* of Archibald Coats and Elizabeth Hodge; *m* Mrs B. E. M. Kerr; no *c*. *Educ:* Marlborough College; Continent. *Recreations:* shooting, fishing, golf, yachting, etc. *Address:* Woodside, Paisley. *Clubs:* Carlton; Western, Glasgow.

Died 21 Aug. 1928.

COBBETT, Pitt, MA, DCL (Oxon); Emeritus Professor of Law in the University of Sydney, NSW; *e s* of late Rev. Pitt Cobbett, formerly Vicar of Crofton, Hants. *Educ:* Dulwich College; University College,

Oxford. *Publication:* Cases and Opinions on International Law, 3rd edn. *Address:* Holebrook, Holebrook Place, Hobart, Tasmania; 44 The Temple, EC. *Club:* Tasmanian, Hobart.

Died 15 Nov. 1919.

COBBETT, Sir William, Kt 1909; Solicitor; *b* 20 May 1846; *e s* of Richard Baverstock Brown Cobbett, Solicitor, of Oversley, Wilmslow, Cheshire, *y s* of William Cobbett, MP for Oldham, 1832–35, author of the Political Register and other works; *m* 1868, Fanny Constantia (*d* 1923), *e d* of George Fox, late of Elmshurst Hall, Lichfield, High Sheriff, Staffs, JP, DL; four *s* four *d*. *Educ:* Hawthorn Hall School, Wilmslow. Admitted a Solicitor, 1868; President, Manchester Law Society, 1891 and 1906; Under-Sheriff for Staffs, 1887–88 and 1890–91; member Lord Chancellor's Judicature Committee, 1907–8; Chairman Board of Management Manchester Royal Infirmary since 1904. *Recreations:* hunting, shooting. *Address:* Woodlands, Wilmslow, Cheshire; 49 Spring Gardens, Manchester. *TA:* Cobbetts, Manchester. *T:* City 5235. *Club:* Union, Manchester.

Died 26 Nov. 1926.

COBHAM, 8th Viscount, *cr* 1718; **Charles George Lyttelton;** Baron Lyttelton, 1756 (renewed 1794); Baron Westcote, 1776; Bt 1618; Chairman, Royal Commission on agricultural depression, 1896–97; Member Royal Commission on London Traffic, 1903–5; Fellow of Eton, 1891–1918; late Trustee, National Portrait Gallery; *b* 27 Oct. 1842; *S* father as Baron Lyttelton, 1876, and kinsman, 3rd Duke of Buckingham as Viscount, 1889; *m* 1878, Hon. Mary Susan Caroline Cavendish, *d* of 2nd Baron Chesham; four *s* two *d* (and one *d* decd). *Educ:* Eton; Trinity Coll., Cambridge. 2nd class in Classical Tripos; 1st class in Law Tripos. Liberal MP E Worcestershire, 1868–74; Land Commissioner, 1881–89; Deputy Chairman GW Railway, 1890–91; Railway Commissioner, 1891–1905. Owned about 6000 acres. Hagley Hall Picture Gallery. Pictures by Vandyck, Mirevelt, Lely, Van Somer, Reynolds, etc. *Recreations:* a well-known cricketer to 1866; played in all Gentlemen and Players' matches, 1861–66. *Heir: s* Hon. John Cavendish Lyttelton, *b* 23 Oct. 1881. *Address:* Hagley Hall, Stourbridge. *Club:* Brooks's.

Died 9 June 1922.

COCHIN, Henry Denys Benoit Marie; *b* Paris, 31 Jan. 1854; *s* of Augustin Cochin, membre de l'Institut, d'une ancienne famille parisienne et Adeline, fille du Comte Benoist d'Azy; *m* 1883, Mlle Arnaud-Jeanti; one *s* two *d*. *Educ:* Lycée Louis-le-Grand, Paris. Licencié ès Lettres et Licencié en droit; engagé volontaire au 17e bataillon de la Garde nationale (Guerre 1870–1871); Attaché au Ministère de l'Intérieur, 1877; élu député 1893, et sans cesse réélu depuis, s'est retiré en 1914 en faveur de son fils; Conseiller Général du Nord pendant quatre ans. *Publications:* Giulietta et Roméo, 1878; Le Manuscrit de M. Larsonnier (roman), 1880; Boccace, 1890; Un Ami de Pétrarque, 1892; Chronologie du Canzonière de Pétrarque, 1898; Le Frère de Pétrarque, 1903; Le bienheureux Fra Angelico de Fiesole, 1906; sixième édition en 1920; La Vita Nuova de Dante traduite et commentée, 1908, 2e édition en 1916; Tableaux flamands, 1909; Jubilés d'Italie, 1910; Lamartine et la Flandre, 1912; Les deux Guerres, 1916; L'Œuvre de guerre du peintre Albert Besnard, 1918; François Pétrarque (collection Les cent Chefs-œuvre étrangers) 1920. *Address:* Château de Mousseau, Evry Petit Bourg (Seine-et-Oise), France.

Died 24 March 1922.

COCHRANE, Vice-Admiral Basil Edward; *b* 1841; *m* 1873, Cornelia, *y d* of Captain John J. Robinson Owen, RN, of Campbellbello and Windlesham House, Surrey. Entered Navy, 1854; Commander, 1872; Captain, 1884; Rear-Adm. retired, 1899; Vice-Adm. retired, 1904; served Russian War, 1854 (Baltic medal); E Soudan, 1884 (despatches, Egyptian medal, bronze star). *Address:* Windlesham House, Windlesham, Surrey. *Club:* United Service.

Died 4 May 1922.

COCHRANE, Hon. Francis; Minister of Railways and Canals, Canada; *b* Clarenceville, Quebec, 18 Nov. 1852; *m* 1882, Alice Levina Dunlop; one *s* one *d*. Minister of Lands and Mines, 1905; MP Sudbury, 1908. *Address:* 15 Maple Avenue, Rosedale, Toronto. *Club:* National, Toronto.

Died 22 Sept. 1919.

COCHRANE, Col William Francis Dundonald, CB 1898; retired; late Chief Staff Officer, Belfast District; *b* Cosham, Wilts, 7 Aug. 1847; *s* of late Col William Marshall Cochrane, who was nephew of Admiral 10th Earl of Dundonald; *m* 1893, Maria Carola, *d* of Henrique Theodora Möller of Valparaiso, Chili; one *d*. *Educ:* Kensington School; Military Coll. Sandhurst. Served in 32nd Light Infantry (DCLI), 1866–93, being adjutant for nine years; Chief Staff-Officer Cape Colony Colonial Forces, 1879–82, during Basuto War; DAA and QMG China and Straits Settlements, 1883–87; Headquarters Staff in Ireland, 1887–88; Asst-Military Secretary in South Africa, 1890–92; commanded infantry brigade in Egyptian army, 1893–96; on lines of communication in Dongola and Soudan Expedition, 1896–98. *Decorations:* Zulu War, Egypt, 1882, Soudan 1896–98 (5 war medals, 3rd class Medjidie, CB). *Recreations:* shooting, hunting, fishing, golf. *Club:* Naval and Military. *Died 23 Oct. 1928.*

COCK, Henry, MVO 1899; retired Chief Constructor from HM Dockyard, Pembroke Dock; *b* 1842; *s* of Thomas Cock, of Torpoint, Cornwall; *m;* eight *s* one *d. Educ:* private; Devonport Dockyard School. Shipwright apprentice, and subsequently Draughtsman; Foreman of the yard; Constructor, and Chief Constructor; retired, 1902. *Address:* 48 Durnford Street, Stonehouse, Plymouth. *Died 19 Aug. 1922.*

COCKBURN, Col George, CBE 1919; DSO 1898; Rifle Brigade; retired 1905; late commanding 3rd Battalion, Rifle Brigade; *b* 9 Jan. 1856; *s* of Admiral J. H. Cockburn; *m* 1905, Alice Lindsay, *d* of Hasell Rodwell of Tower House, Ipswich, and *widow* of Charles Reginald Orde, Rifle Brigade. *Educ:* Eton. Joined Rifle Brigade, 1876; Adjutant, 1884–89; Major, 1894; served in India, 1889–94; Staff, Eastern Command, 1896–97; Soudan, 1898, including Khartoum (despatches, DSO, British medal, Khedive's medal with clasp); Crete, (1898–99; Transvaal, 1899–1901 (despatches, medal, 4 clasps, Brevet Lieut-Col); Col 1904; AA and QMG, 1st London Territorial Division on Mobilization, 1914; Brigadier General commanding 43rd Brigade, 14th Division, Oct. 1914; France, 1915; 18th Reserve Brigade, 1915–16; Commanded Ripon Camp and Tay Defences, 1916; retired Nov. 1916; NACB 1917–20; Hon. Brigadier-General, 1917. *Recreations:* cricket, racquets, shooting, etc. *Club:* Naval and Military. *Died 9 Dec. 1925.*

COCKBURN, Sir George Jack, Kt 1910; JP; *b* 2 Sept. 1848; 2nd *s* of late John Cockburn, Stirlingshire, and Margaret Jack, Aberdeenshire; *m* 1st, 1871, Emily (*d* 1883), *e d* of D. I. Roebuck, Leeds; 2nd, 1886, Clara, 3rd *d* of William Nield, Huddersfield and Leeds; three *s* four *d. Educ:* Private schools. Was an East India merchant, but retired many years ago and became exclusively engaged in varied forms of public service; several years Chairman Leeds Poor Law Board, and founder of the Yorkshire Annual Poor Law Conferences; for 21 years, up to extinction of School Boards, was leader and Chairman Leeds School Board and Vice-President School Board Association of England and Wales; was pioneer of Higher Grade Board School system; Royal Commissioner on Secondary Education in England and Wales, 1893–95; Education Commissioner to Canada and United States, 1903; member of West Riding Education Committee; member Court and Council University of Leeds; formerly member National Liberal Federation Executive; President North Leeds Liberal Association. *Recreation:* golf. *Address:* North Grange Road, Headingley, Leeds. *TA:* Headingley, Leeds. *T:* Headingley 128. *Club:* Leeds and County Liberal, Leeds. *Died 1 Jan. 1927.*

COCKBURN, Henry, CB 1899; *b* 2 March 1859; *s* of late Francis Jeffrey Cockburn, BCS; *m* 1899, Elizabeth Gordon, *d* of Colonel James Francis Stevenson. *Educ:* Edinburgh. Entered consular service, China, 1880; Chinese Secretary to the British Legation at Pekin, 1896–1906; HBM Consul-General, Korea, 1906–9; retired, 1909. *Club:* Caledonian. *Died 19 March 1927.*

COCKBURN, General Henry Alexander, JP Midlothian; *b* 1831; *s* of John Cockburn; *m* 1862, Lucy (*d* 1916), *d* of General Auchmuty Tucker, CB, Bengal Cavalry; one *s* one *d. Educ:* Edinburgh Academy; Edinburgh 73 Military Academy; Addiscombe College. Joined 53rd Bengal Native Infantry, 1851; Adjutant 1st Cavalry Gwalior Contingent Force, 1854; commanded in several minor engagements in the Doab in May and June 1857, and present at the actions near Agra in July and October 1857; Second in Command of Meade's (Central India) Horse, November 1857; commanded that regiment and the Sipri Field Force, 1859–61; held various appointments under the Government of India from 1862; was thanked by the Government NW Provinces on four occasions, and mentioned in despatches; twice wounded—once severely; one horse killed and one wounded; medal and clasp for Central India. *Recreations:* painting, riding, etc. *Address:* Eskgrove, Inveresk, Midlothian. *TA:* Eskgrove, Musselburgh. *Clubs:* Cavalry; New, Edinburgh. *Died 20 Aug. 1922.*

COCKBURN, Nathaniel Clayton, JP, DL; FRGS; Major; MFH Blankney Hounds, 1895–1904; *b* 1866; *s* of William Yates Cockburn, DL, JP. *Educ:* Eton; Christ Church, Oxford. Served with Lincolnshire Yeomanry in Egypt and Palestine, 1916–17. *Address:* Harmston Hall, Lincoln. *Club:* Cavalry. *Died 2 Jan. 1924.*

COCKIN, Ven. John Irwin Browne, MA; Vicar of Milton Lilbourne since 1908; *b* 20 May 1850; *s* of late Rev. Canon Cockin; *m* Frances Charlotte, *d* of J. B. Moxon; one *d. Educ:* King Edward's School, Birmingham; Richmond School, Yorks; Queen's College, Oxford; 2nd Class Theological Schol. 1873; MA 1880. Deacon 1874, priest 1875. Curate, Brigg; St Mary's, Nottingham; Vicar, Esholt; Rector, St Martin's, Colchester; Chaplain, Howrah, Dacca, Saugor, Lucknow, Ranikhet, Meerut, Cathedral Allahabad, Mussoorie, Naini Tal; Archdeacon of Lucknow, 1902–5; Examining Chaplain to the Bishop of Lucknow; Chaplain on HM Bengal Establishment 1880–1905; Rector, Barnwell, 1905–8. *Publication:* The Church of England in the True Church. *Address:* Milton Lilbourne Vicarage, Marlborough, Wilts. *Died 14 April 1924.*

COCKRAN, William Bourke; lawyer; *b* Ireland, 28 Feb. 1854; *m* 1906, *d* of Hon. Henry C. Ide, formerly Governor-General of the Philippine Islands and Chief Justice of Samoa. *Educ:* Ireland and France. Went to United States, 1871; taught in private academy; later principal of a public school in Westchester Co., New York; admitted to Bar, 1876; elected to Congress, 1886; became prominent in New York City Politics; Member of Congress, 1891–95 and 1904–9; Democrat; became advocate of the gold standard and campaigned for M'Kinley, 1896; in Dec. 1896 delivered first speech by any American public man favouring intervention by the US to end barbarities in Cuba, but strongly opposed annexation of the Philippines, delivering first speech in opposition to it at the Academy of Music in 1898. *Address:* 100 Broadway, New York City. *Died 1 March 1923.*

COCOTO, Spiridon George, CMG 1913; MVO 1906; *b* 1843; *s* of George Cocoto; *m* 1869, Elizabeth, *d* of late James Duff. Pro-Consul at Brindisi, 1878; Vice-Consul, 1889; Consul there for the Province of Lecce, 1889; Consul for the Provinces of Apulia, 1912; resigned, 1913; *Address:* Palazzo Cocoto, Brindisi, Italy. *Died 14 Oct. 1916.*

CODDINGTON, Sir William, 1st Bt, *cr* 1896; JP, DL; cotton spinner and manufacturer; Director of Midland Railway; *b* 12 Dec. 1830; *s* of late William Dudley Coddington; *m* 1st, 1864, Sarah (*d* 1911), *d* of late William Thomas Hall; one *d;* 2nd, 1913, Aimée Josephine, *d* of W. J. S. Barber-Starkey, of Darley Dale, Derbyshire. MP (C) Blackburn, 1880–1906. *Heir:* none. *Address:* Wycollar, Blackburn; 143 Piccadilly, W. *Club:* Carlton. *Died 15 Feb. 1918 (ext).*

CODRINGTON, Rev. Robert Henry, DD; Prebendary of Wightring in Chichester Cathedral, 1895–1921, and Theological Lecturer until 1921; *b* Wroughton, Wilts, 15 Sept. 1830; *s* of Rev. T. S. Codrington. *Educ:* Charterhouse; Wadham College, Oxford. Scholar, 1849; Fellow, 1855; 3rd class Lit. Hum. 1852; BA 1852. Deacon, 1855; Priest, 1857; Nelson, NZ, 1860; Melanesian Mission, 1866; head of the Mission, 1871–77; DD Oxford, *honoris causa*, 1855. Vicar of Wadhurst, Sussex, 1888–93; Prebendary of Sidlesham, 1888; Examining Chaplain to Bishop of Chichester, 1894–1901. *Publications:* The Melanesian Languages, 1855; The Melanesians, etc, 1891; Dictionary of the Mota Language 1896; translations of great part of the Bible into Mota. *Address:* St Richard's Walk, Chichester. *Died 11 Sept. 1922.*

COFFEY, George, MRIA; Keeper of Irish Antiquities, National Museum, Dublin, 1896–1914; *b* Dublin, 1857; *o surv. s* of late James Charles Coffey, Co. Court Judge of Co. Londonderry; *m* Jane Sophia Frances, *d* of Sir George L'Estrange; one *s. Educ:* Trinity College, Dublin, AIB, BL. For short time practised at the Irish Bar; was for some time one of the secretaries of the Irish National League; Hon. Member of the Royal Hibernian Academy. *Publications:* Celtic Antiquities of the Christian Period, 1st edition 1909; 2nd edition 1910; New Grange, influence of Crete and Ægean in West of Europe; The Bronze Age in Ireland; numerous papers on Archæological subjects. *Address:* 5 Harcourt Terrace, Dublin. *Died 29 Aug. 1916.*

COFFIN, Walter Harris, FCS, Fellow Royal Society of Medicine; late Editor (13 years), British Dental Journal; *b* Portland, Maine, USA, 1853; *e s* of late Dr C. R. Coffin, South Kensington; *m* Sophia Lydia, *e d* of late T. R. Carey Walters of Hereford; (authoress of A Dreamer's Sketch Book, Lostara, etc). *Educ:* Royal College of Science (Medallist); University College and St Thomas' Hospital. Student at Royal School of Mines and Royal Dental Hospital; Fellow Physical Society of London; Life Member of Committee British Association; Past President Metropolitan Branch British Dental Association; late Lecturer and Examiner National Dental Hospital; Editor Transactions

Odontological Society; Original Member and Founder of Society for Psychical Research; Fabian Society; Stage Society, etc, and Hon. and Corresponding Member of several American and foreign scientific bodies; Inventor and Patentee of Electric Endoscopic Surgical Lamps. *Publications:* papers to Trans International Medical Congress, 1881, on A Generalized Treatment of Irregularities, The Use of Peroxide of Hydrogen; Gutta Percha Impressions in Orthodontia, etc; to Nature, Chemical News, etc, on Primary Batteries; Contributor to American Journal of Science; Journal of the Franklin Institute; Transactions of the Anthropological Institute, etc. *Recreations:* music, books, sociology. *Address:* 30 York Street, Portman Square, W. *T:* 4624 Paddington. *Club:* National Liberal.

Died 10 April 1916.

COGHILL, Douglas Harry, MA; Barrister, Inner Temple; *b* Newcastle-under-Lyme, 6 Aug. 1855; *s* of Harry Coghill, JP; *m* 1890, Catherine Edith, 2nd *d* of Charles Orton, MD, Newcastle-under-Lyme. *Educ:* Cheltenham; Corpus Christi Coll., Oxford. MP for Newcastle-under-Lyme, 1886–92; defeated, 1892; MP (C) Stoke-on-Trent, 1895–1906. *Address:* 14 Stanhope Gardens, SW7. *T:* Kensington 3686; Crowham Manor, Battle. *Club:* Carlton.

Died 13 Dec. 1928.

COGHILL, Sir Egerton Bushe, 5th Bt, *cr* 1778; *b* 7 Feb. 1853; 2nd *s* of Sir John Joscelyn Coghill, 4th Bt, and Katherine, 2nd *d* of 3rd Baron Plunket (*d* 1881); *S* father, 1905; *m* 1893, Elizabeth Hildegarde Augusta, *d* of late Col Thomas Henry Somerville of Drishane, Skibbereen; three *s* one *d. Educ:* Haileybury; studied art Düsseldorf and Paris. *Heir: s* Marmaduke Nevill Patrick Somerville Coghill, *b* 17 March 1896. *Recreations:* yachting, painting. *Address:* Glen Barrahane, Castletownshend, Co. Cork. *TA:* Castletownshend.

Died 9 Oct. 1921.

COGHILL, Colonel Kendal Josiah William, CB 1882; JP; *b* near Dublin, 21 Aug. 1832; *s* of Adm. Sir Josiah Coghill, 3rd Bt, and Anna Maria, *d* of Rt Hon. Chief Justice Charles Kendal Bushe. *Educ:* Cheltenham Coll. Joined 2nd European Bengal Fusiliers, India, 1851; served Burmah, 1853–55; Adjutant of Regt during Indian Mutiny, 1857–58; present at Battle of Badlee-ka-Serai, and storming heights of Delhi, 8 June 1857; throughout siege of Delhi, and at all the actions in front of the city; was with the storming column over the breach in Cashmere bastion, and during final capture of city and palace from 14 to 21 Sept.; served with General Shower's pursuing column, 1857–58; present at taking the forts of Rewarrie, Jujjher Kanoude, Furrucknugger, Bullubghur, and storming heights of Sonah; Brigade-Major of Cawnpore and Barrackpore; Station Interpreter; Assistant Adjut-Gen. Lucknow and Calcutta; Assist QMG Presidency Division, 1861–70; exchanged to 19th Hussars, 1863; which commanded in Egyptian Campaign, 1882; present at battles of Mahuta, Kassassin, and storming of Tel-el-Kebir and taking of Cairo (despatches; medals for India, and bar for Delhi; medal for Egypt, and bar for Tel-el-Kebir; 3rd class order of Medjidie; Khedivial bronze star). *Recreations:* hunting, shooting, sailing. *Address:* Castle Townshend, near Skibbereen, Co. Cork. *Clubs:* Cavalry, Hurlingham, Cork County.

Died 15 July 1919.

COGHLAN, Colonel Charles, CB 1909; VD 1894; JP, DL; late Colonel 1st West Riding Brigade RFA (TF); Ironmaster; Chairman of the Coghlan Steel & Iron Co. Ltd, Hunslet Forge, Leeds; *b* 21 Feb. 1852; *s* of late William Austen Coghlan of Grosvenor House, Leeds; *m* 1887, Josephine Mary, *y d* of Rev. J. Kenworthy, Rector of Ackworth, Yorkshire; two *s* three *d. Educ:* Ratcliffe College, near Leicester; Maison de Melle lez Grand, Belgique. Joined the 1st WRBW Artillery, 1874; was given the command, 1896, and had five extensions; appointed to the Hon. Colonelcy of the Brigade, 1914; Member of the Iron and Steel Institute; a Roman Catholic and Life Member of the Catholic Union of Great Britain and Ireland. *Recreations:* nothing special, unless being a keen Territorial soldier can be deemed a recreation. *Address:* Ashfield, Headingley Hill, Leeds, Yorkshire. *TA:* Coghlan, Leeds. *T:* 211 Headingley, Leeds. *M:* 664 U. *Clubs:* Junior Army and Navy; Leeds, County Conservative, Leeds.

Died 14 Oct. 1921.

COGHLAN, Hon. Sir Charles Patrick John, KCMG 1925; Kt 1910; solicitor; MLA Southern Rhodesia: First Premier and Minister of Native Affairs of Southern Rhodesia since 1923; *b* Cape Colony, 24 June 1863; *m* 1899, Gertrude, *d* of late Col Schermbrucker, MLA; one *c. Educ:* St Aidan's College, Grahamstown; S African College, Cape Town. Served as Captain in Kimberley Town Guard (medal and clasp). *Address:* 22 Agency Buildings, Buluwayo.

Died 23 Aug. 1927.

COGHLAN, Hon. Sir Timothy Augustine, KCMG 1918; Kt 1914; ISO 1903; Agent-General for New South Wales, 1905–15, 1916–17, and 1920–25; Representative of Commonwealth of Australia on the Pacific Cable Board; *b* 1857; 2nd *s* of late Thomas Coghlan; *m* 1897, Helen, 3rd *d* of D. C. Donnelly, MLA, NS Wales; one *s* one *d. Educ:* Sydney Grammar School. Asst Engineer, Harbours and Rivers, 1884; Government Statistician, New South Wales, 1886–1905; Registrar of Friendly Societies, 1892–1905; Chairman Board of Old Age Pensions, 1901–5; Member of Public Service Board, 1896–1900; Royal Commissioner to divide NSW into electoral districts; Royal Commissioner to divide NSW local government areas; Member various other Royal Commissions; supervised NSW Censuses of 1891 and 1901; Hon. Fellow of Royal Statistical Society, 1893; President of Conference of Australian and New Zealand Statisticians to determine number of Representatives in each State in Federal Parliament, and arrange for uniformity in Census of 1901; President of Australasian Association for the Advancement of Science (Section G, Economics and Statistics), 1902; Member of Actuarial Soc. of New South Wales, 1902; Corresponding Member of Royal Society, Tasmania, 1902; Member of Council of Royal Statistical Society; Member International Institute of Statistics; Order St Sava, Serbia, 1919. *Publications:* Wealth and Progress of New South Wales; Picturesque New South Wales; The Seven Colonies of Australasia; Discharge of Streams in Relation to Rainfall; Childbirth: a Study in Statistics; Notes on the Financial Aspect of Federation; Report on the Eleventh Census of New South Wales; Deaths of Women in Childbirth; Child Measurement; Decline in the Birthrate of Australia and New Zealand; Statistical Account of Australia and New Zealand; A History of Labour and Industry in Australia, 4 vols. *Address:* 21 Lennox Gardens, SW1.

Died 30 April 1926.

COGSWELL, Rev. Canon William H. L., MA Oxon; Hon DD, Windsor, NS; Rector of Wallasey since 1896; Rural Dean of Wallasey since 1906; Canon Residentiary of Chester since 1914; *b* Halifax, Nova Scotia, 11 Dec. 1845; *s* of Rev. William Cogswell and Eleanor Belcher; *m* 1868, Alicia Heriot, *d* of Andrew Mitchell-Uniacke, of Clarges Street, Mayfair, London; one *s* two *d. Educ:* King's Coll., Windsor; Wadham College, Oxford. Curate of Stevenage, 1868–71; Vicar of S Hinksey with Wootton, Berks, 1871–79; Chaplain of Magdalen College, 1873–79; Vicar of S Oswald's, Chester, 1879–90; Warden, Special Service Clergy; Organising Secretary CETS and Diocesan Missioner, 1890–95; Rural Dean of Birkenhead, 1900–5. *Publications:* Explanatory Readings on the Visitation of the Sick. *Recreations:* canoeing, fishing, sketching, lawn tennis, cricket, golf. *Address:* The Residence, Chester; Riverscote, Boughton, Chester. *T:* 423. *Club:* Wallasey Golf.

Died 28 May 1917.

COHEN, Mrs Nathaniel Louis; President of the Union of Jewish Women; *d* of Professor Waley, MA, Conveyancing Council to the Court of Chancery; *widow* of late Nathaniel Louis Cohen, LCC; three *s* two *d. Educ:* Queen's College, London. Social and Educational worker. *Publications:* Children's Psalm Book; Infant Bible Reader. *Address:* 10 Sussex Square, W. *T:* 790 Paddington.

Died Dec. 1917.

COKE, Charlotte, (Mrs Talbot Coke); *b* 1843; *e d* of late Major FitzGerald, Maperton, Somerset; *m* 1867, late Major-General John Talbot Coke; three *s* four *d.* Began to write on Home Decoration and other artistic subjects in the Queen paper, 1887, and in the Ladies Field. *Publications:* The Gentlewoman at Home, Holy Matrimony, The Mills of God, and other stories. *Address:* Craven Lodge, Horsham, Sussex.

Died Aug. 1922.

COKE, Brig.-Gen. Edward Beresford, CVO 1904; retired; *b* 5 May 1850; *y s* of late Colonel Edward Thomas Coke, JP and DL, of Trusley Manor, Derbyshire, and Debdale Hall, Notts; *m,* 1877, Ada Beatrice, 7th *d* of W. H. Dawes of The Hall, Kenilworth. *Educ:* Royal Naval Academy, Gosport; Royal Military Academy, Woolwich. Received HM's Commission, 1870; served on the Staff, Afghan War, 1879–80 (medal); commanded the Royal Horse Artillery at Ipswich and Aldershot, 1896–1901; Commandant of the practice camp, Trawsfynydd, Wales, 1903; Colonel on the Staff Royal Artillery at Woolwich, 1903; commanded Woolwich District, 1903–7; Inspector of Remounts, 1915–16. *Address:* Villa St Agnes, Mentone, France. *Club:* United Service.

Died 30 Dec. 1924.

COKE, Hon. Henry John, JP; *b* 3 Jan. 1827; 3rd *s* of 1st Earl of Leicester and 2nd wife, Lady Anne Amelia, *d* of 4th Earl of Albemarle; *m* 1861, Lady Katharine Grey Egerton, *d* of 2nd Earl of Wilton, a Lady in Waiting to late Duchess of Teck, and Woman of the Bedchamber to HM the Queen; one *s* one *d* (and one *s* decd). Was in Royal Navy; served China War, 1840–42. *Publications:* A Ride over the Rocky Mountains; Creeds of the Day; Tracks of a Rolling Stone, 1905; The Domain of Belief, 1910. *Address:* 64 Victoria Street, SW; Longford Hall, Derby. *Club:* Athenæum.

Died 12 Nov. 1916.

COLBORNE, Col Hon. Francis (Lionel Lydstone), MVO 1913; DL Suffolk; Major (retired) Royal Irish Rifles; *b* 29 July 1855; 2nd *s* of late Maj.-Gen. Lord Seaton and Charlotte, *d* of late General Lord Downes; *heir-pres.* to the Barony of Seaton; *m* 1906, Alice Matilda, *d* of late Capt. William Robert Gamul Farmer (formerly Grenadier Guards), JP, DL of Nonsuch and Lagham, Surrey, and Denham, Suffolk. *Educ:* Winchester; Oxford; Sandhurst. Served on the Scinde Frontier, 1878; relief of Kandahar in Afghan Campaign, 1880; with Natal Field Force in South African Campaign, 1881; in the Nile Expedition for relief of Khartoum, 1884–85 (despatches, Brevet of Maj.); Soudan Frontier Field Force, 1886; on the Staff of North Irish District, 1887; South-Eastern District, 1888; served Boer War in South Africa, 1900; European War, 1914–17; Administrative Commandant in III Army Area; Commandant 8th Batt. City of London Regiment, 1901–10; Hon. Col 1908; Order Merito Militar of Spain and Royal Victorian; Exon, King's Body Guard, since 1892; Equerry-in-Waiting to Princess Beatrice since 1898; Director of the Royal Insurance Company (West End Branch); Member of Lloyds. *Address:* Nonsuch Park, Surrey; Denham, Suffolk. *Clubs:* Carlton, Bachelors', Wellington.   *Died 8 Sept. 1924.*

COLCHESTER, 3rd Baron, *cr* 1817; **Reginald Charles Edward Abbot,** MA; FSA, FRGS; DL, JP; barrister; *b* London 13 Feb. 1842; *s* of 2nd Baron and Hon. Elizabeth Susan Law, *d* of 1st Lord Ellenborough; *S* father, 1867; *m* 1869, Lady Isabella Grace (Maude), *e d* of 1st Earl de Montalt. *Educ:* Eton; Christ Church, Oxon. 1st class Classics, Law and Modern History, 1863; Stanhope Historical Essay Prize, 1861; Fellow of All Souls, 1864; Examiner in Law and History, Oxford, 1869. Contested (C) E Sussex, 1865; Devonport, 1866; Member of Standards Commission, 1868–70; Charity Commissioner, 1880–83; London School Board, 1891–94. Church of England and Conservative. *Publications:* edited Political Diaries of Lord Ellenborough in 1828–30, and Letters relating to Indian Administration of Lord Ellenborough. *Heir:* none. *Address:* Forest Row, E Grinstead. *Clubs:* Carlton, Constitutional, Athenæum.

Died 26 Feb. 1919 (ext).

COLDRIDGE, Ward, KC 1912; *b* 1864; *o s* of C. S. Coldridge; *m* Amy, *o d* of late John Norwood, of Beckenham. *Educ:* Exeter Grammar School; Emmanuel College, Cambridge; Natural Science Tripos, Parts I and II. Bencher, Lincoln's Inn, 1917. *Publication:* Law of Gambling (joint). *Address:* 2 New Square, Lincoln's Inn, WC2; 18 Landsdowne Road, Holland Park, W11. *T:* Park 2045.

Died 3 April 1926.

COLDWELL, Hon. George Robson, KC; late Minister of Education, Manitoba; *b* Township Clarke, Co. Durham, Ontario, 4 July 1858; *s* of William Edward Coldwell and Mary Robson; *m* Ann Anderson; four *s* one *d*. *Educ:* Clinton Grammar School; Trinity College School, Port Hope; Trinity College, Toronto. Practised law in Brandon from 1883. *Address:* 122 Eighteenth Street, Brandon, Manitoba.   *Died Jan. 1924.*

COLE, Alfred Clayton, MA; Director of the Bank of England; Governor, 1911; Lieutenant for the City of London; *b* London, 17 Dec. 1854; *y s* of late William Henry Cole, Pulham, Norfolk, and West Woodhay, Berks; *m* 1907, *d* of Col Arthur T. H. Williams, Canada, and *widow* of Herbert Chamberlain. *Educ:* Eton; Trinity Coll., Cambridge. Captain of Oppidans at Eton, 1874; after leaving Cambridge, spent some time abroad. Barrister, 1880. Owned about 4500 acres in Norfolk and Berkshire. *Recreations:* shooting, tennis, golf. *Address:* 64 Portland Place, W1. *T:* Gerrard 5342; West Woodhay House, Newbury, Berks. *Clubs:* Athenæum, Carlton, St James's, Beefsteak.   *Died 5 June 1920.*

COLE, Rev. Edward Pattinson, MA; Hon. Canon of Bristol Cathedral; *s* of Thomas Bulman Cole, Somerset; *m* 1873, Edith Rhoda (*d* 1925), *d* of Col G. E. Thorold, Black Watch; two *s*. *Educ:* Exeter College, Oxford. Curate formerly of St John's, Brighton; St Paul's, Brighton; Old Shoreham, Sussex; and Midhurst, Sussex; Rector of Christ Church with S Ewen's, Bristol; Patron of two livings. *Address:* 23 Great George Street, Park Street, Brisol.

Died 26 Oct. 1926.

COLE, Grenville Arthur James, FRS 1917; Professor of Geology, Royal College of Science for Ireland, since 1890; Director of the Geological Survey of Ireland since 1905; *b* London, 21 Oct. 1859;

s of J. J. Cole, Architect; *m* Blanche, *d* of J. E. Vernon; one *s*. *Educ:* City of London School; Royal School of Mines. Examined at London, Cambridge, Oxford, and other Universities; Murchison Medal, Geological Society, 1909; President, Geological Section, British Association, 1915; President Geographical Association, 1919; and of Irish Geographical Association, 1919–22. *Publications:* Aids in Practical Geology, 1891; 7th edn 1918; The Gypsy Road, 1894; Open-air Studies, 1895; 2nd edn, 1902; The Changeful Earth, 1911; Rocks and their Origins, 1912; 2nd edn, 1922; Outlines of Mineralogy for Geological Students, 1913; The Growth of Europe, 1914; Ireland, the Land and the Landscape, 1915; section on Europe, in The World we Live in, 1917; Ireland the Outpost, 1919; Common Stones, 1921; Memoir and Map of Irish mineral localities (Geol Survey), 1922; with Blanche Cole, As We Ride, 1902; and scientific papers. *Recreation:* formerly cycling, especially as a means of travel. *Address:* Orahova, Carrickmines, Co. Dublin. *T:* Foxrock 85.

Died 20 April 1924.

COLE, Rev. John Francis; Head-master, French school since 1885; Canon of Kildare since 1908; Incumbent of Portarlington since 1885. *Educ:* St Bees. Ordained 1880; Curate Mountrath, 1880–83; Arklow, 1883–85; Rural Dean, 1907; Member of General Synod, 1907; Diocesan Representative of Glebes; Director of Irish Land Finance Co., Ltd; Director of Portarlington Electric Lighting and Power Co., Ltd. *Address:* Portarlington.

Died 29 Dec. 1921.

COLE, Rev. Robert Eden George, MA, JP; Canon and Prebendary of Lincoln Cathedral; *e s* of Lieut-Col Robert Cole of the 85th and 48th Regts, and of Mary Eden, *d* of Col G. R. P. Jarvis of Doddington Hall, Co. Lincoln; *m* 1858, Frances Elizabeth Christiana, *e d* of James Dawn, 2nd Dragoon Guards. *Educ:* Rugby; University College, Oxford. Rector of Doddington, Lincoln, 1861–1909; Chairman of Branston District Council since 1898. *Publications:* History of Doddington; Glossary of South-West Lincolnshire, etc. *Address:* 3 Pottergate, Lincoln.   *Died 9 Jan. 1921.*

COLE, Robert Henry, MD (Lond.); FRCP (Lond.); Physician for Mental Diseases to St Mary's Hospital; Lecturer on Mental Diseases at St Mary's Hospital Medical School and at Bethlem Royal Hospital; Examiner in Mental Diseases and Psychology, University of London; Home Office Visitor to the State Inebriate Reformatory, Aylesbury; Visitor to the Institutions for the Mentally Deficient, Middlesex; *b* 13 Nov. 1866; *e s* of late R. C. Cole of Ealing; *m* Mabel Effie, *e d* of late N. Randle of Bombay, and *widow* of A. T. White, MRCS, of Egypt; one *s* one *d*. *Educ:* Ealing; St Mary's Hospital. Was a clerk in the India Office before entering the medical profession; Chairman of the Parliamentary Committee of the Medico-Psychological Association; Vice-President of the Section of Psychiatry of the Royal Society of Medicine; late Resident Physician Moorcroft Asylum. *Publication:* Mental Diseases, a Textbook of Psychiatry. *Address:* 25 Upper Berkeley Street, Portman Square, W1. *T:* Paddington 4270. *M:* XA 1849. *Club:* Oriental.

Died 10 Aug. 1926.

COLE, Robert Langton, FRIBA; Architect to Royal Albert Hall since 1907; National Hospital, Queen Square, since 1892; Metropolitan Association for Improving Dwellings, since 1892; *b* 11 Jan. 1858; *s* of John Jenkins Cole (Architect to the Stock Exchange) and Josephine, *d* of Joseph Smith of Kempsey, Worcester; *m* 1885, Edith (*d* 1925), *d* of John Shepherd; five *d*. *Educ:* City of London School under Dr E. A. Abbott. Apprenticed to J. J. Cole and entered his office, 1874; partnership E. Perrott, 1858–90; Architect to the Stock Exchange, 1890–1925; Works: Convalescent Home, Finchley, 1897; Acland Home, Oxford, 1904–26; Royal Albert Hall alterations; Warneford Place, Wilts, 1904; S Ex-Rifle Club, 1904; Radley College extensions, 1909; Dartford Hospital, 1904; alterations and extensions to Stock Exchange, 1893–1925; 26 Austin Friars, 1901; residences in Sutton, Dorking, Sherborne, Oxford, etc; factory extensions for Stafford, Allen & Co.; Rubber Exchange, 1924 and 1927. *Publications:* Reviews on Architecture and Engineering for Stationer's Almanac, 1893–95; articles in RIBA Journal on Hospital Construction. *Recreation:* rifle shooting; member NRA. *Address:* Loughrigg, Sutton, Surrey; Abbey House, SW. *T:* Victoria 6678.

Died 27 May 1928.

COLEMAN, Lieut-Colonel George Burdett, DSO 1917; Royal Army Service Corps; *b* Hampstead; *s* of late F. W. S. Coleman of Bitteswell Hall, Leicestershire; *m* 1908, Claire, *d* of E. Donajowski, London; one *s*. *Educ:* tutor. Through South African War with Scottish Horse and 3rd Batt. King's Own Royal Lancaster Regt, 1899–1902 (Queen's and King's medals); appointed to Royal Garrison Regt, 1902;

transferred to Royal Army Service Corps, 1906; Adjutant of Territorial Royal Army Service Corps, 1912–14; Instructor and Adjutant at Royal Army Service Corps Training Establishment, Aldershot, 1914–15; DAQMG of an Infantry Division of New Army, and proceeded to France, 1915; AQMG of an Army Corps, 1917 (DSO); Mesopotamian Campaign, 1919–21; Bronze Medal of the Order of St John of Jerusalem; Bt Lt-Col 1918; 1914–15 Star; L'Ordre de la Couronne (Officier) and Croix de Guerre (Belgian); Croix de Guerre (avec palme) (French). *Recreations:* riding, gardening. *Club:* Army and Navy. *Died 3 July 1923.*

COLENBRANDER, Col Johann William, CB 1902; *b* Pinetown, Natal, 1859; of Dutch extraction; *m* 1st, Maria (*d* 1901), 2nd *d* of John Mullins; 2nd, 1902, Yvonne Winifred (*d* 1904), *y d* of Capt. Loftus Nunn, late 99th Lanark Rgt; 3rd, Kathleen, 2nd *d* of James Gloster of Clonmelan, Co. Kerry. Interpreter to Matabele Envoys in England, 1889; service with the Natal Guides and in thick of battle of Enyamadhloon; one of the best Zulu linguists in South Africa; friend of Lo Bengula; accompanied his envoys to England, 1890; held several responsible positions under Chartered Co. 1895; selected by Cecil Rhodes to remain with Lo Bengula while Pioneer Force of Chartered Company passed through Matabeleland; organised and officered "Colenbrander's Boys", 1896; raised and took command of Kitchener's Fighting Scouts in 1901 (despatches, CB). *Address:* Box 123, Buluwayo, Rhodesia, South Africa. *Died 8 Feb. 1918.*

COLERIDGE, 2nd Baron, *cr* 1873; **Bernard John Seymour Coleridge;** Judge of High Court of Justice (King's Bench Division), 1907–23; Commissioner of Assize, Midland Circuit, 1907–8; *b* 19 Aug. 1851; *s* of 1st Baron and Jane Fortescue, *d* of Rev. George Turner Seymour; *S* father, 1894; *m* 1876, Mary, *e d* of late John F. Mackarness, DD Bishop of Oxford; one *s* one *d* (and one *d* decd). *Educ:* Eton; Trinity Coll., Oxford (Hon. Fellow). QC 1892; Bencher of Middle Temple, 1894; Treasurer, 1919; JP and Chairman Devon Quarter Sessions; MP (GL) Sheffield (Attercliffe), 1885–94; Chairman of the Coal Conciliation Board of the Federated Trades, 1912–18; Fellow of the Royal Society of Literature, 1916. *Publications:* The Story of a Devonshire House, 1905; This for Remembrance, 1925. *Heir:* s Hon. Geoffrey Duke Coleridge, *b* 23 July 1877. *Address:* The Chanter's House, Ottery St Mary, Devon. *T:* Ottery St Mary 5. *Club:* Athenæum. *Died 4 Sept. 1927.*

COLERIDGE, Christabel Rose; Editor of Friendly Leaves; novelist; *b* Chelsea, 1843; *d* of Rev. Derwent Coleridge, *s* of Samuel Taylor Coleridge. *Publications:* Lady Betty, 1869; Hanbury Mills, 1872; Hugh Crichton's Romance, 1873; The Face of Carlyon, and other stories, 1875; The Constant Prince, 1878; Kingsworth, 1881; An English Squire, 1881; The Girls of Flaxby, 1882; A Near Relation, 1886; A Plunge into Troubled Waters, 1888; Reuben Everett, 1888; Amethyst, 1891; Waynflete, 1893; The Tender Mercies of the Good, 1895; The Main Chance, 1897; The Thought Rope, 1898; Tricks and Trials, 1899; The Winds of Cathrigg, 1901; Charlotte Mary Yonge, 1903; Miss Brent of Mead; Miss Lucy. *Address:* Cheyne, Torquay. *Died 14 Nov. 1921.*

COLERIDGE, Ernest Hartley; *b* 8 Dec. 1846; *s* of Rev. Derwent Coleridge, first Principal St Mark's College, Chelsea, and *s* of Samuel Taylor Coleridge, and Mary Simpson, *d* of John Drake Pridham, Plymouth, banker; *m* 1876, Sarah Mary (*d* 1917), *d* of William Bradford, Newton Abbot; two *s* two *d*. *Educ:* Sherborne School, 1862–66; Balliol College, Oxford, 1866–70; MA. Hon. Fellow, Royal Society of Literature; Tutor, 1872–93; secretary to the Lord Chief Justice of England, Jan. to June, 1894. *Publications:* edited Letters of Samuel Taylor Coleridge, 2 vols, 1895; edited Anima Poetae, selections from unpublished notebooks of Samuel Taylor Coleridge, 1895; edited Poetical Works of Lord Byron, vols i. ii. iii. iv. v. vi. vii, 1898–1903; Life and Correspondence of John Duke, Lord Coleridge, 2 vols, 1904; Poetical Works of Lord Byron, 1905; Christabel, by S. T. Coleridge, 1907; Poems of Coleridge, illustrated by G. Metcalfe, 1907; Poets' Country, ed. by A. Lang; Complete Poetical Works of S. T. Coleridge, 1912. *Address:* Rickford's Hill, Aylesbury. *Died 19 Feb. 1920.*

COLERIDGE, Lt-Col Hugh Portescue, CBE 1919; DSO 1900; late commanding 1st Battalion, Loyal North Lancs Regiment; *b* 11 Jan. 1859; *s* of Rev. F. J. Coleridge of Cadbury, Thorverton; *m* 1906, Kathleen, *e d* of late Rear-Adm. J. H. Bainbridge and of Mrs Bainbridge of Elfordleigh, Plympton; five *s*. Entered army, 1879; Captain, 1887; Major, 1899; served South Africa, 1899–1902 (despatches, Queen's medal 4 clasps, King's medal 2 clasps); European War, 1914–18; JP Devon. *Address:* Langstone, Tavistock. *Died 17 April 1928.*

COLES, Charles, Pasha, CMG 1900; Director-General of Egyptian Prisons, 1897–1915; *b* 17 Nov. 1853; *s* of late Maj.-Gen. Gordon Coles of Bath; *m* 1881, Mary Emma Isabelle, *d* of late Crewe Alston, of Odell, Beds; two *s* two *d*. India Police Dept, 1873; lent to Egyptian Government, 1883; Deputy Inspector-General Police, 1884. *Publication:* Recollections and Reflections, 1919; Occupational Franchise, 1922; Indian Principalities and other Problems, 1922. *Clubs:* County, Taunton; British, Biarritz. *Died 12 Nov. 1926.*

COLES, John, JP; Chairman, Clerical, Medical, and General Life Assurance Society. *Address:* 4 Kensington Park Gardens, W11. *T:* Park 406. *Died 18 Oct. 1919.*

COLEY, Frederic Collins, MD; MRCS; JP; Visiting Physician to the Sanatorium at Barrasford; Physician to the Northern Counties Hospital for Diseases of the Chest; Consulting Physician to the Hospital for Sick Children, Newcastle. *Educ:* Guy's Hospital. *Publications:* The Turkish Bath: its History and Uses; article, published in English Review for March 1927, on Trade Unionism, Old and New. *Address:* 21 Eldon Square, Newcastle. *T:* 2066. *M:* X 7737. *Died 13 Dec. 1928.*

COLLARD, Allan Ovenden, FRIBA; *b* 24 Jan. 1861; 6th *s* of John Collard, Herne Bay; *m* 1892, Lilian Clara Brockelbank; one *s* two *d*. *Educ:* Rock House School, Ramsgate; Queen Elizabeth's Grammar School, Faversham. Articled pupil to Thomas Blashill, FRIBA, 1878; assistant to Geo. Vulliamy, FRIBA, Metropolitan Board of Works, 1882; private practice, 1887; Architect to Earl's Court Exhibition, 1894–1925; past Chairman, Vice-President, and Hon. Secretary of the Association of Men of Kent and Kentish Men; Officer in Metropolitan Special Constabulary, 1914–21; Member of Selection Board, The Treasury, Whitehall; Member of Kent Migration Committee. *Publication:* The Oyster and Dredgers of Whitstable. *Address:* 1 Rutland Road, Hammersmith, W6. *T:* Riverside 2466. *Died 1 July 1928.*

COLLARD, Sir George, Kt 1903; *b* 3 July 1840; *s* of G. Plomer Collard of Canterbury, HEICS; *m* 1874, Ann (*d* 1905), *d* of Thomas Ash. Ten times Mayor of Canterbury. *Address:* The Gables, Barton Fields, Canterbury. *Died 19 June 1921.*

COLLCUTT, Thomas Edward, FRIBA; *b* 16 March 1840; widower; one *s* two *d*. *Educ:* Oxford Diocesan School, Cowley. Articled to R. W. Armstrong, London; afterwards with G. E. Street, RA, as assistant; President of Royal Institute of British Architects, 1906–8; Hon. Member of Société Centrale d'Architecture de Belgique; Corresponding Member of the Société des Artistes Français; Grand Prix for Architecture, Paris Exhibition, 1889; King's Gold Medal of the Royal Institute of British Architects, 1902; Member of the British Legion. *Professional work:* Architect of Wakefield Town Hall, the Imperial Institute, Savoy Hotel, Lloyd's Registry, etc. *Publication:* The Future of London. *Recreation:* honorary work. *Address:* Totteridge, Herts. *Club:* Arts. *Died 7 Oct. 1924.*

COLLES, Ramsay, FRHistS; JP Dublin; author; *b* Gyah, India, 1862; *s* of late Richard Colles, CE, India Civil Service; *m* Annie, *e d* of Rev. P. F. Sweeny, MA, Rector of Annascaul, Co. Kerry; one *s*. *Educ:* Bective College and Wesley College, Dublin; private tutors. Proprietor and Editor for four years of Irish Figaro; founded and edited Irish Masonry Illustrated; editor Chic, 1904; Madame, 1905–11. Member Royal Irish Academy; FRSA, Ireland. *Publications:* A Forgotten Poet: Ebenezer Jones; A Study of Swinburne; Nature as Interpreted in Poems of George Meredith; Edgar Saltus: Publicist; In Castle and Court House, 1911; History of Ulster, 1914; edited, with Introductions, the Poetical Works of Beddoes, Darley, Hartley Coleridge. *Address:* c/o Blighty, 40 Fleet Street, EC4. *Club:* Conservative, Dublin. *Died 1919.*

COLLES, William Morris, BA; FRGS, FGS; *o s* of late Rev. William Morris Colles, DD, STP, Vicar of Melton Mowbray. *Educ:* Oakham; Emmanuel College, Cambridge. Barrister Inner Temple, 1880; Founder and Managing Director of Authors' Syndicate, 1890; member of Council, Society of Authors, 1890, and of Copyright Association. *Publications:* Literature and the Pension List; The State's Eminent Domain; Playright and Copyright in all Countries (part author); Success in Literature (part author). *Recreations:* golf, fishing. *Address:* 3–7 Southampton Street, Strand, WC2. *TA:* Another, Rand, London. *T:* Gerrard 44. *Clubs:* Royal Societies, Savage. *Died 11 Oct. 1926.*

COLLETTE, Charles; *b* London, 29 July 1842; *m* Blanche Wilton, sister of Lady Bancroft. Served with 3rd Dragoon Guards, 1861–68;

first appearance on the stage at Prince of Wales Theatre under the Bancrofts, 1868; has also been an entertainer, and appeared at music halls. *Club:* Savage.   *Died 10 Feb. 1924.*

COLLIER, Frederick William, ISO 1907; retired; *b* 6 March 1851; *s* of Henry Collier, Abingdon, Berks, and Georgetown, Br. Guiana; *m* 1st, 1884, Susan Georgina (*d* 1913), 2nd *d* of late Geo. Fetherstonhaugh, Westmeath, Ireland; three *s*; 2nd, 1915, Marion Emily, 4th *d* of the same. *Educ:* Richmond House School, Reading. Entered Service of Govt, British Guiana, 1869; served in Govt Secretariat as clerk, Asst Govt Sec., Sec. Quarantine Board; Postmaster-General, 1888; established PO Savings Banks and considerably extended postal and electrical services in Colony; served also as Comptroller of Customs and Official Member of Legislature. *Recreation:* gardening. *Address:* 457 Lansdowne Avenue, Westmount, Prov. Quebec, Canada. *T:* 0139 Westmount.

Died 27 Feb. 1925.

COLLIER, James; *b* Dunfermline, Scotland, 1846; *m* 1905, Florence, *d* of Sir William Durrant, 5th Bt. *Educ:* Universities of St Andrews and Edinburgh, 1863–68. Assistant to Herbert Spencer, 1871–80. *Publications:* joint author, with Spencer, of Descriptive Sociology, and with Prof. Royce, Harvard, of volume on Spencer; author of Sir George Grey: an Historical Biography; The Pastoral Age in Australasia; The Evolution of Colonies, etc; editor of Collins's English Colony in NS Wales, and Wakefield's Art of Colonization; etc. *Address:* St Helena, Manly, Sydney, Australia.   *Died 1925.*

COLLIER, Rev. Samuel Francis; Superintendent of Manchester and Salford Wesleyan Mission since 1886; *b* Runcorn, 3 Oct. 1855; *e s* of Samuel and Mary Collier, of Runcorn; *m* Ettie Collin, of Manchester; four *s*. *Educ:* Bickerton House School, Southport. Entered Wesleyan Ministry, 1877; Didsbury College, 1877–81; Kent and London Circuits, 1881–85; began ministry in Manchester, 1885; inaugurated the first of the great Wesleyan City Missions, and still in charge of twelve centres of evangelistic and social work; organised a system of rescue, relief, and preventive work; extended property of Mission to estimated value of £300,000; elected member of Wesleyan Methodist "Legal Hundred", 1902; British Representative to the Canadian Conference, 1906; British Representative to Australian Methodist Church, 1920; President of the Wesleyan Methodist Conference for 1913–14. *Address:* The Olives, Anson Road, Victoria Park, Manchester. *T:* Rusholme 149, Manchester.

Died 2 June 1921.

COLLINGRIDGE, William, JP; MA, MD, LLM; DPH Camb; MRCS; Barrister-at-law, Gray's Inn; *b* Islington, 1854; *s* of late W. H. Collingridge, City Press; *m* Ada Thomsett. *Educ:* Clewer House, Windsor; Christ's College, Cambridge; St Bartholomew's Hospital. Formerly Examiner in State Medicine, University of Cambridge; Examiner State Medicine, London University; Milroy Lecturer Royal College of Physicians, 1897; served as Volunteer Surgeon in Servian Army during Turko-Servian War, 1875; private practice two years; Medical Officer of Health, Port of London, 1880–1901; Medical Officer of Health, City of London, 1901–13; Delegate University of Cambridge at International Congress of Hygiene, Paris, 1900; Knight of Grace of the Order of St John of Jerusalem in England. *Publications:* Hæmorrhage in Typhoid Fever; Scurvy in Mercantile Marine; Water and Filtration; Quarantine in England; Plague Prevention; Sanitary Reports, Port of London; Health Reports, City of London. *Recreations:* 10 years Honourable Artillery Co., F Battery; 4 years Cambridge Univ. Rifle Corps; 7 years in Volunteer Medical Staff Corps; 8 years in command of Militia Medical Staff Corps (Lieut Col); Hon. Colonel RAMC (Vol.) Woolwich Division; Lieut-Col Territorial Force; MO i/c Auxiliary Military Hospital 122 Kent 1914–19. *Address:* Yarrell Croft, Pennington, Lymington, Hants.

Died 29 April 1927.

COLLINGS, Rt. Hon. Jesse, PC 1892; MP (U) Bordesley (Birmingham), 1886, retired, 1918; *b* 1831; *s* of Thomas Collings, Littleham-cum-Exmouth, Devon; *m* 1859, Emily, *d* of Edward Oxenbould; one *d*. Was Head of Collings and Wallis, merchants, Birmingham; retired 1879. Mayor of Birmingham, 1878–79; MP (R) Ipswich, 1880–86; Parliamentary Secretary Local Government Board, 1886; magistrate for Birmingham; founder and president of the Rural League; was chairman Free Libraries Commission, and governor of King Edward's Grammar School; one of the founders and Hon. Sec. of the National Education League; and one of the founders of the Devon and Exeter Boys Industrial School; moved and carried the Small Holdings Amendment to the address which caused the resignation of Lord Salisbury's Government, Jan. 1886; Under-Secretary of State for Home Office, 1895–1902. *Publications:* Land

Reform; The Colonization of Rural Britain, 1914; The Great War: its Lessons and its Warnings. *Address:* Edgbaston, Birmingham.

Died 20 Nov. 1920.

COLLINGWOOD, Surg. Rear-Adm. George Trevor, CB 1919; MVO 1910; LRCP Lond., MRCS Eng., 1886; retired; *b* 22 Sept. 1863. *Educ:* London Hospital. Entered Navy, 1887; Surgeon of Widgeon; served in three expeditions on west coast of Africa, Gambia River, 1894 (despatches); Benin River, 1894; Brass River, 1895 (landed as senior medical officer in charge), (general Africa medal and three clasps); served at Dardanelles in Naval Hospital Ship Soudan, 1915; Fellow of the Society of Tropical Medicine and Hygiene; awarded Sir Gilbert Blane Gold Medal, 1909. *Publications:* papers on The Mosquito and Naval Recruits.

Died 2 Sept. 1922.

COLLINGWOOD, Harry; *see* Lancaster, W. J. C.

COLLINGWOOD, Sir William, KBE 1917; JP; MICE; Managing Director, The Vulcan Foundry, Limited, since 1892; *b* London, 18 Aug. 1855; *e s* of late George Collingwood, HEIC Home Establishment; *m* 1887, Maria Elizabeth, *d* of Rev. Gerald Thomson Lermit, LLD; two *s* three *d*. *Educ:* Dedham Grammar School. District Locomotive Superintendent East Indian Railway, 1880–92; Member Lancashire County Council, 1911–13; Member Engineering Standards Committee; President Manchester Engineering Employers' Federation, 1913; Chairman Manchester and District Armament Output Committee, 1914–18. *Address:* Dedham Grove, near Colchester. *TA:* Collingwood, Dedham. *T:* Dedham 4. *M:* YF 9941; NO 7407; PU 7968. *Clubs:* St Stephen's, Constitutional.

Died 2 Nov. 1928.

COLLINS, Arthur Ernest, CMG 1911; *b* 11 June 1871; 7th *s* of late Samuel Collins, Salisbury; unmarried. *Educ:* City of London School; Trinity College, Cambridge (Scholar). First Class Classical Tripos, 1893; BA 1893; MA 1899. Clerk, Colonial Office, 1894; Private Secretary to Sir Edward Wingfield, Permanent Under-Secretary of State, 1897; Assistant Private Secretary to Mr Chamberlain, Secretary of State, 1898; 1st Class Clerk, 1898; Principal Clerk, 1907; Assistant Secretary, 1920; Secretary to Straits Settlements Currency Committee, 1902–3; Head of West Indian Department, 1907–9; Eastern Department, 1909–19; Far Eastern Department, 1920; Member of West African Currency Board in London. *Publication:* Joint Editor of Colonial Office List since 1898. *Recreations:* music, walking, billiards. *Address:* Colonial Office, SW.

Died 5 Feb. 1926.

COLLINS, Charles, ARCA. *Address:* 20 Horsham Road, Dorking.

Died 28 Sept. 1921.

COLLINS, Hon. George Thomas, CMG 1919; *b* 10 May 1839; *s* of William and Martha Matilda Collins; *m* Ursula Flora, *d* of late Captain Robert M'Eachern; three *s* four *d*. *Educ:* Launceston Church Grammar School. Barrister, etc; Chief Secretary and Minister of Agriculture, Tasmania, 1899–1903; Minister of Defence prior to Federation, 1899–1903; Colonel, VD (reserve); late Commanding Officer Launceston Artillery, and late Senior Commanding Officer, Northern Division of Tasmania; for over thirty-five years Chairman Launceston General Hospital Board of Management; President of Central Board of Health, 1900–3; Member for Tamar, 1895–1919; first Chairman Technical School Board, Launceston; member of the firm of Douglas & Collins, barristers and solicitors, Launceston; Chairman Northern Division, Tasmania British Red Cross Society, 1914–23. *Recreations:* yachting, bowling, music. *Address:* Ila House, Launceston, Tasmania. *T:* No. 11. *Clubs:* Tasmanian, Hobart; Launceston, Launceston.

Died 25 Aug. 1926.

COLLINS, Michael, MP (Sinn Fein) South Division, Co. Cork, since Dec. 1918.   *Died 22 Aug. 1922.*

COLLINS, Rt. Rev. Richard, RC Bishop of Hexham and Newcastle; *b* Newbury, Berks, 1857. *Educ:* St Cuthbert's College, Ushaw. Priest at Wolsingham, Co. Durham; St Andrew's, Newcastle-on-Tyne; Canon of St Mary's Cathedral, Newcastle-on-Tyne. *Address:* St Mary's Cathedral, Newcastle-on-Tyne.

Died 9 Feb. 1924.

COLLINS, Col Robert Joseph, CMG 1911; ISO 1909; VD 1902; JP; *b* Cavan, County Cavan, Ireland, 28 July 1848; *s* of late Captain Robert Collins, New Zealand Militia, formerly 57th Regt; *m* Annie, *d* of Richard and Eleanor Cock of New Plymouth, NZ; three *s* one *d*. *Educ:* Ireland; India; New Zealand. Served in Taranaki Volunteer

Militia, 1863–65; joined New Zealand Government service as clerk at New Plymouth, 1865; Sub-storekeeper Public Works, 1867; transferred to Store Audit, Wellington, 1877; clerk in the Treasury Department, 1878; First Clerk, Paymaster-General's Branch, 1879; took over charge of combined offices of Pay and Revenue as Clerk-in-Charge, 1885; Accountant to the Treasury, 1890; Assistant Secretary, 1903; Secretary to the Treasury, Receiver-General, and Paymaster-General, 1906; Controller and Auditor-General of New Zealand, 1910–21; finance member of Council of Defence, 1906; Member War Pensions Board, New Zealand, 1916; officer commanding 1st Batt. Wellington Rifles, 1898; Lt-Col New Zealand Militia, for services rendered in connection with the enrolment and training of the contingents sent to South Africa from Wellington, 1902; Colonel, 1907, on retirement from command of Wellington Rifle Battalion after thirty-four years' service; ADC to Governor-General of NZ, 1911–21; actively identified with rifle-shooting in the Dominion since 1867; elected to Council of NZ Rifle Association, 1879; Statistical Officer, 1886; Chief Executive Officer of Dominion Rifle Association, 1904–21, subseq. President National Rifle Association of New Zealand; had command of the team sent to the Commonwealth meeting at Sydney in 1901, and Commandant of the New Zealand Rifle team to Bisley in 1904 (winners of the Kolapore Cup); Colonial medal for long service, 1893; voluntarily retired after being over fifty-six years in the New Zealand public service. *Recreations:* bowling, shooting. *Address:* Collina, Park Terrace, Wellington, NZ. *Club:* Wellington, Wellington, NZ.
Died 1 Dec. 1924.

COLLINS, Sir Robert Muirhead, Kt 1919; CMG 1904, Official Secretary for Commonwealth of Australia to 1918; retired Lieutenant-Commander RN, and retired Captain Australian Naval Forces; Secretary of the Department of Defence, Commonwealth of Australia, 1900–6; *b* 20 Sept. 1852; *s* of Charles H. Collins, Chew Magna, Somerset; *m* 1886, Elizabeth, *d* of Samuel Brush, Pastoralist, Australia; one *s*. *Educ:* Taunton; HMS Britannia. Entered Royal Navy, 1866; Lt 1876; retired, 1877; engaged by Government of Victoria for employment in Victoria Naval Forces; sent to England to assist in bringing out gunboats, and took command of gunboat Albert for voyage to Australia; Commander, 1884; Secretary for Defence for Victoria, 1886, and placed on retired list with rank of Captain; Secretary for Defence, Commonwealth of Australia on establishment of that Government, temporarily represented the Commonwealth of Australia in London, 1906–10, when he was appointed official Secretary in Great Britain of Commonwealth of Australia; acted Member of Royal Commission on Shipping Rings; Delegate for the Commonwealth Government at International Conference Life-Saving at Sea, London, 1913. *Recreations:* tennis, shooting. *Address:* 10 Sydney Place, Bath. *Died 19 April 1927.*

COLLINS, Sir Stephen, Kt 1913; MP (L) Kennington Division Lambeth, 1906–18; JP County of London; *b* 9 Oct. 1847; *s* of William Collins of Swanage, Dorset; *m* 1st, 1872, Frances Ann Webber (decd); 2nd, 1901, Jane, *d* of William Russell of Marsworth, Herts. *Educ:* Swanage. Was a County Councillor for Kennington Division of Lambeth; a member of Wandsworth District Board, and afterwards Alderman of Lambeth; a Congregationalist and a life abstainer; a member of Committee of the National Temperance League, a Good Templar and member of the Rechabite Order, and greatly interested in the Band of Hope movement and the cause of temperance generally. *Recreations:* reading, walking. *Address:* Elm House, Tring, Herts. *Club:* National Liberal. *Died 12 March 1925.*

COLLINS, Most Rev. Thomas Gibson George, DD; Bishop of Meath since 1926; *b* Dublin, 2 April 1873; *e s* of Rev. T. R. S. Collins, BD; *m* 1920, Kathleen Lily Bell, *d* of John Hollwey, Cabinteely House, Co. Dublin; two *s*. *Educ:* Rathmines School; Trinity College, Dublin. Ordained for Curacy of Maralin, 1896; Rector of Rathfriland and Ballyrony, 1902; Rector of Warrenpoint, 1904; Rector of St James' Parish, Belfast, 1910; Vicar of Belfast and Dean of St Anne's Cathedral, 1919. *Recreations:* golf, motoring. *Address:* Bishopscourt, Navan, Co. Meath. *T:* Navan 46. *M:* IR 1050. *Clubs:* Ulster, Belfast; University, Dublin. *Died 3 July 1927.*

COLLINSON, Alfred Howe, CBE 1917; Officer Legion of Honour, 1919; MInstCE; late Director-General of Inspection of Munitions of War; *b* 1866; *m* 1891, Isabel Douglas Creighton; two *s* one *d*. *Address:* 1 Down Street, W1; Westfield Lodge, Hayling Island, Hants. *Clubs:* Junior Athenæum; Shanghai, Shanghai; Bengal, Calcutta. *Died 28 June 1927.*

COLLINSON, Thomas Henry, MusB Oxon; Hon FRCO; Organist and Choirmaster of St Mary's Cathedral, Edinburgh, since 1878; *b*

Alnwick, 24 April 1858; 3rd *s* of Thos Collinson, late Master of Duke of Northumberland's School; *m* 1891, Annie Wyness Scott; three *s* one *d*. *Educ:* Duke's School, Alnwick. Articled Pupil of the late Professor Armes, Organist of Durham Cathedral. Organist of St Oswald's Parish Church, Durham, 1876; Lecturer in Church Music to the Theological College of Scots Episcopal Church; Conductor of Edinburgh Royal Choral Union, 1883–1913; Conductor of the Edinburgh Amateur Orchestral Society 1900–19; received a Cathedral and Diocesan Presentation of £250 on completion of 25th year of Organistship; also a presentation and address at the Jubilee of the Royal Choral Union in 1908, and an Hon. Director's badge in gold at resignation in 1913. *Publications:* Te Deum in F, anthems, responses, etc. *Recreations:* golf, sketching. *Address:* 17 Torphichen Street, Edinburgh. *Died 18 Feb. 1928.*

COLLISON, Ven. William Henry; Archdeacon of Caledonia, British Columbia; Commissary to the Bishop of Caledonia, and CMS Missionary to Nishka, Zimshean, and Haida tribes of Indians, NW Coast and Islands, British Columbia; *b* 12 Nov. 1847; *s* of J. and M. Maxwell Collison, Armagh, Ireland; *m* 1873, Marion M. Goodwin; five *s* three *d*. *Educ:* Church of Ireland Normal College; Church Missionary College, Islington. Superintendent of Industrial School, Cork; Missionary to Zimshean Indians, 1873; volunteered as first Missionary to the Haidas of Queen Charlotte's Islands, who were known then as the "Pirates of the North Pacific Coast", being the finest and fiercest of the Coast Indians, 1876; opened the Inland Mission to Gitikshans, 1880; Secretary to the North British Columbia Mission of CMS, and Bishop's Commissary, 1893–94. *Publications:* translated prayers, hymns, etc into Zimshean, Haida, and Nishka languages; History of the British Columbian Mission; In the Wake of the War Canoe. *Address:* Kincolith, North-West Coast, British Columbia. *Died Jan. 1922.*

COLLISSON, Rev. William Alexander Houston; *b* Dublin, 20 May 1865; *s* of William Houston Collisson and Elizabeth O'Callaghan. *Educ:* Trinity College, Dublin. MusB 1884; MusD 1890; BA 1897; MA 1911. Licentiate in Music, Trinity Coll. London; Organist and Master of the Choir, St Patrick's, Trim, 1881; then held appointments at Bray, Rathfarnham, Tallaght, St George's, Dublin; started Dublin Popular Concerts, 1885; also Belfast and London Popular Concerts; ordained, 1898; Assistant Priest, St Tudy's, Cornwall, 1899–1901; St Saviour's, Walton Street, 1901–6; St Mary's, Seymour Street, NW, 1907–8; St Stephen's, E Twickenham, 1908–10; Christ Church, Chelsea, 1911; All Saints, Twickenham, 1912; St Alban's, Teddington, 1914; St Andrew's, West Kensington, W14, 1916; St John's, Great Marlborough Street, W, 1919. *Compositions:* Comedy Operas—The Knight of the Road; Strongbow; Midsummer Madness; Cantatas—St Patrick; The Game of Chess; Samhain; Irish Suite—Rosaleen; Operetta—Noah's Ark; Songs—The Mountains of Mourne, The Pride of Petravore, Are ye right there, Michael? Maguire's Motorbike, etc. *Publication:* Dr Collisson in and on Ireland. *Recreation:* singing humorous songs. *Address:* 63 Tregunter Road, SW10. *T:* Kensington 3136. *Died 1 Feb. 1920.*

COLLYER, Ven. Daniel; retired; *b* 1848; *s* of John Collyer, Barrister, of Hackford Hall, Norfolk, and Georgina, *d* of Sir William Johnston of that ilk, 7th Bt; *m* Helen Augusta Preston (*d* 1924). *Educ:* Rugby; Clare College, Cambridge. Formerly Vicar of Wymondham, Norfolk; Chaplain of Christ Church, Cannes; Archdeacon of Malta, 1903–5. *Address:* Octagon House, Dedham, Essex. *Died 25 July 1924.*

COLLYER, William Robert, ISO 1903; *b* 11 Jan. 1842; 2nd *s* of John Collyer of Hackford Hall, Norfolk and Georgina Frances Amy, *e d* of late Sir William Johnston of that ilk, 7th Bt. *Educ:* Rugby; Caius Coll., Cambridge (Scholar, 1861); 2nd Class Classical Tripos, 1865. Assistant Master at Clifton College, 1865–67; called to the Bar, Inner Temple, 1869; went first Norfolk, and afterwards Midland Circuit; Acting Chief-Justice, Sierra Leone, 1879; Acting Puisne Judge, Gold Coast Colony, 1880; Acting Attorney-General, Gold Coast, 1880; Queen's Advocate, Cyprus, 1881; Puisne Judge, Straits Settlements, 1892; Attorney-General, 1903; retired, 1906; JP Co. Norfolk. *Address:* Hackford Hall, Norwich. *Died 27 Oct. 1928.*

COLMORE, Thomas Milnes, JP; Recorder of Warwick since 1882; Deputy-Chairman of Warwickshire Quarter Sessions since 1907; *b* Sheldon House, Warwickshire, 13 Jan. 1845; *e s* of late Thomas Colmore; *m* 1878, Clara, 2nd *d* of John Dugdale of 9 Hyde Park Gardens, W. *Educ:* Rugby School; Brasenose College, Oxford. Barrister, 1869; Midland Circuit; Stipendiary Magistrate, City of Birmingham, 1888–1905. *Recreations:* hunting, shooting. *Address:* The Warren, Knowle, Warwickshire. *Club:* Windham.
Died 25 April 1916.

COLQUHOUN, Ven. William. *Educ:* Trinity College, Dublin (MA, BD). Curate of Desertmartin, 1868–72; Incumbent of Drumaul, 1872–82; Curate of St James's, Bristol, 1882; Incumbent, Aghadowey, 1883–93; Archdeacon of Derry, 1897; Incumbent of Glendermot, 1893; retired 1914. *Address:* 69 Lansdowne Road, Dublin.

Died 1920.

COLTHURST, Sir George St John, 6th Bt, *cr* 1744; *b* 1850; *s* of Sir George Conway Colthurst, 5th Bt and Louisa Jane, *d* of St John Jeffryes; *S* father, 1878; *m* 1881, Edith, *d* of late Captain (The Royals) J. Morris, Dunkettle, Co. Cork; two *s* (and one *d* decd). *Educ:* Harrow. Late Lieut 43rd Foot. Owned about 31,300 acres. *Heir: s* George Oliver Colthurst, late Capt. South Irish Horse, *b* 24 Aug. 1882. *Recreation:* golf. *Address:* Blarney Castle, near Cork. *TA:* Blarney. *T:* Blarney 1. *Clubs:* Carlton, Naval and Military.

Died 25 Dec. 1925.

COLTON, William Robert, RA 1919 (ARA 1903); sculptor; Member of Standing Committee of Advice for Education in Art, Board of Education; Principal Examiner for the Board of Education in modelling and sculpture; *b* Paris, 1867; *m* 1902, Mignon, *d* of George Kroll de Laporte; two *d*. *Educ:* Paris and London. Commenced a sculptor's career at the age of 20; studied at Lambeth, S Kensington, and Royal Academy Art Schools; also in Paris; exhibited at Royal Academy Exhibition and at Salon at the age of 22; bought by Chantrey Fund, 1899 and 1903; silver medal and mention honourable, Paris; executed statues of King Edward at King's Lynn, war memorial at Worcester, drinking fountain, Hyde Park, Tangye Memorial, Birmingham, Selons Memorial Natural History Museum, and Royal Artillery war memorial in the Mall, St James's Park, several statues in India, and Angas Memorial, Adelaide; Professor of Sculpture, Royal Academy, 1907–10, 1911–12; formerly Visitor in Sculpture, Royal College of Art; President Royal Society of British Sculptors. *Address:* 5 St Mary Abbotts Place, Kensington, W. *T:* Western 6563. *Clubs:* Royal Academy, Arts.

Died 13 Nov. 1921.

COLVILE, Lieut.-Gen. Sir Fiennes Middleton, KCB 1906 (CB 1866); retired; *b* 4 April 1832; *s* of Frederick C. A. Colvile and Mary, *sister* of 1st Baron Leigh; *m* 1862, Helen (*d* 1910), *d* of Major Hugh Stafford Northcote; two *s* two *d*. *Educ:* Sandhurst. Joined 43rd LI 1850; served Indian Mutiny (medal); New Zealand War, 1863–66 (very severely wounded, Bt Lt-Col, CB, medal); commanded Shrewsbury Regt District, 1876–81; Welsh Border Brigade, 1886–91; Colonel of Oxfordshire and Bucks Light Infantry. *Recreations:* shooting, gardening. *Address:* St Mildred's, Guildford. *Club:* United Service.

Died 29 March 1917.

COLVILLE OF CULROSS, 2nd Viscount, *cr* 1902; **Charles Robert William Colville;** Baron (Scot.) 1604; Baron (UK) 1885; *b* 26 April 1854; *s* of 1st Viscount and Hon. Cecile Catherine Mary Carington, *e d* of 2nd Lord Carington; *S* father, 1903; *m* 1885 Ruby, *d* of late Col Henry D. Streatfeild, Chiddingstone, Kent; two *s* two *d*. *Educ:* Harrow. Late Maj. Grenadier Guards; served in Zulu War, 1879 (despatches); ADC to Commander-in-Chief, Bombay, 1881–83; Military Secretary to Gov.-Gen. of Canada, 1888–92; Lt-Col Territorial Force Reserve, 1915, attached to Staff of London District Command. *Heir: s* Master of Colville, *b* 26 May 1888. *Address:* Danegate House, Eridge Green, Sussex. *Club:* Carlton.

Died 25 March 1928.

COLVIN, Sir Sidney, Kt 1911; MA; DLitt Hon. Oxon; LLD Hon. St Andrews; Corresponding Member of the Institute of France and the Royal Academy of Belgium; Hon. Fellow Royal Society of Painter-Etchers; Vice-President, Library Association; Member of Council Hellenic Society, School of Athens, National Trust, National Art Collections Fund; President Art for Schools Association, Vasari Society; *b* Norwood, 18 June 1845; 3rd *s* of Bazett David Colvin, of Crawford, Colvin, & Co., and of The Grove, Little Bealings, Suffolk, and Mary Steuart, *d* of late William Butterworth Bayley; *m* 1903, Frances (*d* 1924), *d* of late Cuthbert Fetherstonhaugh, and *widow* of late Rev. A. H. Sitwell. *Educ:* home; Trinity College, Cambridge (Fellow 1868). Slade Professor of Fine Art, Cambridge 1873–85; Director, Fitzwilliam Museum, 1876–84; Keeper of the Prints and Drawings, British Museum, 1884–1912. *Publications:* numerous contributions, chiefly on history and criticism of Fine Art, to periodical literature, especially Pall Mall Gazette, 1868–73, Fortnightly Review, Portfolio, Cornhill Magazine, Nineteenth Century, Edinburgh Review, Encyclopædia Britannica, Dictionary of National Biography, etc; Lives of Landor (1881) and Keats (1887) in Morley's English Men of Letter Series; A Florentine Picture-Chronicle, 1898; Early Engraving and Engravers in England, 1906; Drawings by Old Masters at Oxford, 1902–8; John Keats, His Life and Poetry, etc, 1917;

Memories and Notes, 1921; has edited Selections from Landor in Golden Treasury Series, 1882; Letters of Keats in Eversley Series, 1887; Edinburgh edition of R. L. Stevenson's works, 1894–97, and Letters of R. L. Stevenson, 1899 and 1911. *Address:* 35 Palace Gardens Terrace, Kensington, WS. *T:* Park 4675. *Clubs:* Athenæum, Savile, Burlington Fine Arts.

Died 11 May 1927.

COMBE, Maj.-Gen. Boyce Albert, CB 1889; Colonel 14th Hussars since 1904; *b* 28 Aug. 1841; *m* 1871, Helen Edith (*d* 1892), *d* of Maj.-Gen. L. Barrow, CB. Entered army, 1860; Maj.-Gen. 1896; served Abyssinian Campaign (medal); Afghan War, 1878–80 (despatches frequently, brevets of Major and Lieut-Col, medal with four clasps, bronze decoration); commanded Sind District, Bombay, 1888–94; Cavalry Brigade at Aldershot, 1895–96; Curragh District, 1896–99; Rawal Pindi District, 1899–1903. *Club:* Naval and Military.

Died 3 June 1920.

COMBE, Charles, JP, DL, Surrey; *b* 13 Nov. 1836; *e s* of Charles James Fox Combe; *m* 1st, 1861, Marianne (*d* 1900), *o d* of Captain Inglis, RN; eight *s* six *d*; 2nd, 1906, Ethel, *widow* of A. Cushny, Pains Hill, Cobham, *o d* of J. W. Leonard, CMG. High Sheriff for Surrey, 1885; formerly in Bombay Cavalry; served in Persia and Indian Mutiny. *Address:* Pains Hill, Cobham, Surrey. *Club:* Royal Yacht Squadron, Cowes.

Died 28 June 1920.

COMBE, Harvey Trewythen Brabazon, JP Sussex and Co. Mayo; FRGS; *b* 1852; *e s* of late Boyce Harvey Combe and Anne, *o d* of late Hercules Sharpe of Oaklands, Sedlescombe, Battle, Sussex, and Ann Mary, *e d* of Sir Anthony Brabazon, Bt of Brabazon Park, Swinford, Co. Mayo; *m* 1882, Florence Amy, *d* of Alexander Lambert, JP, DL, of Brook Hill, Claremorris, Co Mayo; one *s*. Was Captain and Hon. Major late 3rd Batt. Royal Sussex Regt. *Address:* Oaklands, Sedlescombe, Battle, Sussex. *TA:* Sedlescombe. *T:* Battle, 1x6. *Club:* White's.

Died 18 Dec. 1923.

COMBES, Emile, Hon. GCVO 1903; *b* Roquecourbe, Tarn, 6 Sept. 1839. Docteurès-lettres, docteur en médecine; Président du Conseil Général de la Charente-Inférieure; élu Senateur, 1885; Vice-Président du Senat, 1893–95; Ministre de l'Instruction publique, des Beaux-Arts et des Cultes, 1891–96; Président du Conseil des Ministres, 1902–5; Ministre d'Etat, 1915–16. *Publication:* Psychology of Thomas Aquinas. *Address:* Rue Claude Bernard, 45 Vᵉ, Paris.

Died May 1921.

COMINS, Ven. Richard Blundell, DD; Corresponding Secretary of the Melanesian Mission since 1912. *Educ:* Hatfield Hall, Durham. Ordained 1873; Curate of Grantham, 1873–76; Missionary, Solomon Islands, 1876–94; Head of St Luke's Siota, 1894–1901; Priest in Charge, Florida, Solomon Islands, 1901–3; Archdeacon of Northern Melanesia, 1900–10; Chaplain of Norfolk Islands, 1904–12. *Address:* 31 Woodside Road, Mount Eden, Auckland, NZ.

Died 11 March 1919.

COMMINS, Andrew, AM, LLD London; *b* 1829; *s* of late John Commins; *m* 1885, Jane, *d* of J. Neville. *Educ:* Queen's Univ. Ireland, AE (RUE); London Univ. Barrister, Lincoln's Inn, 1860; Northern Circuit. MP (N) Roscommon, 1880–85; South Div. 1885–92; MP (N) Co. Cork, SE 1892–1900. *Address:* The Grange, W Derby; Eldon Chambers, Liverpool.

Died 7 Jan. 1916.

COMPARETTI, Prof. Domenico, Hon. DCL Oxon; Senator of the Kingdom of Italy; Member of the Academy of the Lincei; Corresponding Fellow of the British Academy; *b* Rome, 1835. *Publications:* Virgilio nel medio evo, 1873, 2nd edn 1896; Text and Translation of the Gothic War of Procopius, 1895; The Traditional Poetry of the Finns, English translation, 1898; Le Leggi di Gortyna, 1893; papers on papyri, inscriptions, etc. *Address:* Via Lamarmora, Florence.

Died 1927.

COMPTON-RICKETT, Rt. Hon. Sir Joseph, Kt 1907; PC 1911; DL; Paymaster-General since 1916; Charity Commissioner, 1917; MP (L) Osgoldcross Division, Yorks, 1906–18, West Riding of Yorkshire, Pontefract, since 1918; *b* London, 13 Feb. 1847; *e s* of late Joseph Rickett, East Hoathly; assumed by Royal licence additional surname of Compton, 1908; *m* 1868, Catharine Sarah, *d* of late Rev. Henry John Gamble of Upper Clapton; four *s* four *d*. *Educ:* King Edward VI School, Bath; privately. MP (L) Scarborough, 1895–1906; interested in various commercial undertakings; retired from the chairmanship of several companies in the coal trade, 1902; President of the National Council of Evangelical Free Churches, 1915; Chairman, Congregational Union of England and Wales, 1907. *Publications:* The Christ that is to be, a latter-day romance; The

Quickening of Caliban, a modern story of evolution; Origins and Faith; and other works; frequently contributes to current journalism. *Address:* Wingfield, Bournemouth. *TA:* Compton-Rickett, Wingfield, Bournemouth. *T:* Bournemouth 657. *Clubs:* Reform, National Liberal.
Died 30 July 1919.

CONCANON, Colonel Henry, OBE 1918; TD; JP; Director Oceanic Steam Navigation Co. Ltd; International Navigation Co. Ltd; George Thompson & Co. Ltd, and Liverpool Overhead Railway Company; Joint-Manager Oceanic Steam Navigation Co. (White Star Line) and International Navigation Co. Member of the Mersey Docks and Harbour Board; Member of Liverpool Committee, Lloyd's Register of Shipping; Chairman Liverpool Steamship Owners' Association, 1920–21; *b* 1861; *m* 1891, Isabel, *d* of Joseph Ion Wharton of Soulby. Formerly commanded 7th Batt. King's Liverpool Regiment; retired with rank of Colonel in the TFR; British Empire, Territorial, Coronation (King Edward), Italian Merit, and Messina decorations. *Address:* Beechside, Allerton, Liverpool. *Clubs:* Junior Constitutional; Exchange, Racquet, Liverpool.
Died Sept. 1926.

CONGDON, Colonel Arthur Edward Osmond, CMG 1918; late commanding 1st Royal Munster Fusiliers, retired; *s* of T. O. B. Congdon of Clifton and Glen Ridge, New Jersey, USA; *m* 1905, Ann B. G., *d* of Rev. J. H. Sutton Moxly, CF of the Royal Hospital, Chelsea; one *s* one *d. Educ:* Clifton College. Entered Army, 1882; served Burmah Expedition, 1885–88; S African War, 1901–2 (Queen's medal and four clasps); NW Frontier, India 1908 (medal and clasp); European War, 1914–18 (despatches twice, CMG, Officer Legion of Honour). *Recreations:* fishing, painting. *Address:* 60 Brompton Square, SW3. *T:* Kensington 761. *Club:* Army and Navy.
Died 17 Sept. 1924.

CONGREVE, General Sir Walter Norris, VC 1899; KCB 1917 (CB 1911); MVO 1903; DL; Governor and Commander-in-Chief, Malta, since 1924; *b* 20 Nov. 1862; *s* of late Wm Congreve, JP, DL, of Congreve, Staffs, and Burton Hall, Cheshire, and Fanny Emma, *d* of Lee Porcher Townshend of Wincham Hall, Chester; *m* 1890, Celia, *d* of late Captain C. B. La Touche; two *s. Educ:* Harrow. Entered Rifle Brigade, 1885; Captain, 1893; Major, 1901; Lt-Col 1901; Col 1908; Maj.-Gen. 1915; Lt-Gen. 1918; General 1922; served South Africa, 1899–1902 (wounded, despatches twice, VC, Queen's medal 7 clasps, King's medal 2 clasps, Brevet Lt-Col); European War, 1914–18 (despatches, KCB, Lt-Gen.); Com. School of Musketry, Hythe; GOC Troops in Egypt and Palestine; Commander-in-Chief, Southern Command, 1923–24; Commander, Legion of Honour; 1st Class St Anne of Russia and Crown of Rumania. *Address:* Chartley Castle, Staffordshire.
Died 28 Feb. 1927.

CONLAY, William Lance, CBE 1924; Deputy Agent, Federated Malay States Government Agency, EC4; *b* 21 June 1869; *m* 1902, Georgiana Maud, *y d* of Ralph Skene Archbold, Shortlands, Kent. Malay States Civil Service, 1893–1924; British Agent, Trengganu, 1909–10; Commissioner of Police, Federated Malay States, 1916–24. *Address:* Red House, Hythe, Kent. *Clubs:* Authors', Sports.
Died 2 Jan. 1927.

CONNELL, Rev. Alexander, MA, BD; Minister of Sefton Park Presbyterian Church, Liverpool, since 1906; *b* Portapin, 1866; *m* 1902, Jessie Murdoch, *d* of late Sir Henry Robson; two *s* one *d. Educ:* Edinburgh University; Theological College of Free Church of Scotland. Ordained, 1891; Convener of Foreign Missions, 1897; went mission tour, 1898; Minister of Regent Square Church, 1893–1906; President National Free Church Council, 1913–14. *Publication:* The Endless Quest, vol. of sermons. *Address:* Sefton Park Church, Liverpool. *T:* 256 Lark Lane. *Club:* University, Liverpool.
Died 17 Nov. 1920.

CONNER, Henry Daniel, KC; JP, Co. Cork; MA; Circuit Court Judge for Dublin City and County since 1924; *b* 1859; *o s* of Daniel Conner of Manch, Co. Cork, and Patience, *d* of Henry Longfield of Waterloo, Co. Cork; *m* 1st, 1881, Anne (*d* 1917), *d* of Rev. Goodwin Purcell of Charlesworth, Derbyshire; two *s* one *d*; 2nd, 1918, Mary Leonora, *widow* of Richard Dowse. *Educ:* Stratford-on-Avon; Trinity College, Dublin (Senior Exhibitioner and Gold Medallist). Barrister, 1882; QC 1899; Bencher King's Inns, 1910; contested (U) St Stephen's Green Division of Dublin, 1910. *Publications:* The Fishery Laws of Ireland, 1892; 2nd edn 1907; Joint Editor for Ireland of The English and Empire Digest. *Recreations:* shooting, fishing. *Address:* 16 Fitzwilliam Place, Dublin; Manch House, Ballineen, Co. Cork. *Clubs:* University, Dublin; Cork County.
Died 24 July 1925.

CONNOLLY, Col Benjamin Bloomfield, CB 1900; physician; *b* 10 Sept. 1845; *s* of Rev. J. C. Connolly, late Chaplain, RN, and Vicar of Brook, Norwich; *m* 1881, Olivia Frances, 2nd *d* of late William Potts, JP, of New Court, Athlone; two *s* two *d. Educ:* Merchant Taylors' School; Gonville and Caius College, Cambridge (BA, MA, MD, formerly Tancred Student in Physic); Guy's Hospital, London. FRCS; Colonel, Army Medical Staff; served Franco-German War, 1870–71 (German war medal); against Jowaki Afreedees, 1877–78 (medal and clasp); Zulu War (medal); Egyptian War, Tel-el-Kebir (medal and clasp, promoted); Eastern Soudan, El Teb, Tamai (despatches, clasp, 4th class Osmanieh); Nile Expedition, 1884–85, Commander of Camel Bearer Company, and present attack on wounded convoy (despatches twice, clasp); promoted Colonel for services rendered during operations in South Africa, 1899–1902; European War, ADMS Sussex. *Recreation:* won 100 yards, Cambridge University, 1866. *Address:* Kingsclere, Harrington Road, Brighton. *Clubs:* New Oxford and Cambridge; Union, Brighton.
Died 20 June 1924.

CONRAD, Joseph; author; Master in the Merchant Service; *b* 6 Dec. 1857, of Polish parentage; *m* 1896, Jessie, *d* of Alfred Henry George; two *s. Publications:* Almayer's Folly, 1895; An Outcast of the Islands, 1896; The Nigger of the Narcissus, 1897; Tales of Unrest, 1898; Lord Jim, 1900; Youth, and other tales, 1902; Typhoon, 1903; The Inheritors, 1901, and Romance, 1903 (with F. M. Hueffer); Nostromo, A tale of the Seaboard, 1904; One Day More (Play), 1905; The Mirror of the Sea, 1906; The Secret Agent, 1907 (dramatised, 1922); A Set of Six, 1908; Under Western Eyes, 1911; Some Reminiscences, 1912; 'Twixt Land and Sea, Tales, 1912; Chance, 1914; Within the Tides, 1915; Victory, 1915; The Shadow-Line, 1917; The Arrow of Gold, 1919; Rescue, 1920; Notes on Life and Letters, 1921; The Rover, 1923. *Address:* c/o J. B. Pinker & Son, Talbot House, Arundel Street, WC2. *Club:* Athenæum.
Died 3 Aug. 1924

CONSTABLE, Hon. Lord; Andrew Henderson Briggs Constable, CBE 1920; KC 1908; LLD (Edin.); FRSE; one of the Senators of the College of Justice in Scotland since 1922; Member University Court of Edinburgh University; Assessor to the Lord Rector; Vice-Chairman, Edinburgh Council of Social Service; Chairman of Executive, Association for the Preservation of Rural Scotland; *b* 3 March 1865; *y s* of late W. Briggs Constable of Benarty, Fife; *m* 1895, Elizabeth, *y d* of late James Simpson of Mawcarse, Kinross; two *s. Educ:* Dollar; Edinburgh University; Vans Dunlop Scholar in Political Economy. Advocate, 1889; Sheriff of Caithness, etc, 1917–20; Adviser to the Scottish Office in connection with Military Tribunals in Scotland, 1917–18; Sheriff of Argyll, Feb.–May 1920; Dean of the Faculty of Advocates, 1920–22; Solicitor-General for Scotland, Mar.–June 1922; contested (U) E Fife, 1900; Kirkcaldy Burghs, 1905; Montrose Burghs, 1908; Blackfriars Glasgow, 1910. *Publications:* Treatise on Provisional Orders, 1900. *Address:* 23 Royal Circus, Edinburgh. *Clubs:* Wellington; New University, Edinburgh.
Died 4 Nov. 1928.

CONYBEARE, Charles Augustus Vansittart, BA; Barrister; *b* Kew, 1 June 1853; *e s* of late John Charles Conybeare; *m* 1896, Florence Annie (*d* 1916), *e d* of Gustave Strauss, 2 West Bolton Gardens, SW. *Educ:* Tonbridge; Christ Church, Oxford; 1st class Classical Moderations, 1874; 3rd Litt. Hum. 1876; Lothian Prizeman (English Essay), 1877. MP (L) Camborne, NW Division of Cornwall, 1885–95; imprisoned for three months in 1889 in Derry Gaol under the Coercion Act, 1887, for assisting the tenantry on the Olphert Estate at Falcarragh, Donegal; member London School Board (Finsbury), 1888–90; member of Geographical Society, Lisbon, 1895. *Publications:* Treatises on Married Women's Property Act, 2nd edn 1883; The Corrupt and Illegal Practices Acts, 2nd edn 1892. *Recreations:* boating, cycling. *Address:* Bradbourne House, Bexley, Kent. *Clubs:* National Liberal, Eighty, International Women's Franchise.
Died 18 Feb. 1919.

CONYBEARE, Charles Frederick Pringle, KC; Barrister; *b* Little Sutton, Middlesex, 19 May 1860; *s* of Henry Conybeare, the eminent engineer; *g s* of Dean William Daniel Conybeare, the geologist; *m* 1890, Ida, *d* of Lieut-Col P. H. Attwood, Canadian Militia; one *s* two *d. Educ:* Westminster. Entered merchant service as midshipman, 1875; retired 1880, and went to Canada, where he commenced study of Law in Winnipeg, Manitoba; called to Bar, 1885; removed to Lethbridge, Alberta, and commenced practice on his own account; Crown Prosecutor for Southern Alberta, 1888–1900; QC 1894; on the formation of the Law Society of the North-West Territories in 1897, elected one of the Benchers; Vice-President Alberta Law Society, 1907; President, 1926; Chancellor of the Diocese of Calgary,

1904; DCL Bishop's College, Lennoxville, 1907; University of Alberta, 1908; elected on the Council of Dominion Bar Association, 1914; elected President of the Alberta Moderation League, 1919; re-elected 1923, and led the fight on the plebiscite taken in that year which resulted in a sweeping victory for the Moderationists and the repeal of existing Prohibition legislation. *Publications:* Vahnfried, a poetical romance; Lyrics from the West. *Address:* Riverview, Lethbridge, Alberta. *TA:* Lethbridge, Canada. *T:* 3711 and 2201.
Died 13 July 1927.

CONYBEARE, Frederick Cornwallis, FBA 1903; *b* 1856; 3rd *s* of John Charles Conybeare and Mary Catharine (Vansittart); *m* 1st, 1883, Mary Emily Max Müller (*d* 1886); 2nd, 1888, Jane MacDowell; one *s* one *d. Educ:* Tonbridge School; University College, Oxford. Scholar, 1875; Fellow and Praelector, 1881; Hon. Fellow, 1913; MA Oxon, 1883. Officier d'Académie, 1906; Hon. Doctor Theologiae, Giessen, 1907; Hon. LLD St Andrews, 1913; Member of the Armenian Academy of Venice. *Publications:* The Ancient Armenian Texts of Aristotle, 1892; Philo about the Contemplative Life, 1895; The Apology and Acts of Apollonius, 1894; Key of Truth, a Manual of the Paulician Church of Armenia, 1898; The Dialogues of Athanasius, etc, 1898; The Story of Ahikar, (with J. Rendel Harris and Mrs Lewis), 1898, 2nd edn 1913; The Dreyfus Case, 1898; The Roman Catholic Church in International Politics, 1901; Rituale Armenorum, 1905; Letters and Exercises of the Elizabethan Schoolmaster, John Conybeare, 1905; Old Armenian Texts of Revelation, 1906; Myth, Magic, and Morals, 1909; The Ring of Pope Xystus, 1910; A History of NT criticism, 1910; Catalogue of the Armenian MSS of the British Museum, 1912, of those in Bodleian Library, 1918; English Translations of Philostratus, Life of Apollonius, 1912, of Heliodorus, Ethiopica and of other Greek Romances; The Historicity of Christ, 1914; History of Russian Dissent, 1921; Old Armenian Liturgies, in Patrologia Orientalis, 1922; contributor to the learned journal of England, America, France, and Germany. *Recreation:* travel. *Address:* University College, Oxford; 21 Trinity Gardens, Folkestone. *Died 9 Jan. 1924.*

COOCH, Colonel Charles, MVO 1911; *b* 1829; *e s* of late Charles Cooch of Woodlands, near Ryde; *m* 1858, Charlotte Hyacinth, *e d* of late Lieut-Col A. H. Kirwan of Cheltenham. Served Crimea, 1854-56; Town Major in Sebastopol, 1855-56; late Major 62nd Foot; Knight Legion of Honour; 5th Class Medjidie; one of HM's Hon. Corps of Gentlemen-at-Arms since 1877. *Address:* St James's Palace, SW; 1 Cambridge Villas, Cheltenham. *Club:* New, Cheltenham.
Died 30 April 1917.

COOCH BEHAR, Maharaja Bhup Bahadur of, Sir Jitendra, KCSI 1917; *b* 20 Dec. 1886; *s* of Maharaja Nripendra and Maharani Sunity Deire (*née* Sen); *S* brother, 1913; *m* 1913, *d* of Gaekwar of Baroda; two *s* two *d. Educ:* Eton; Imperial Cadet Corps. Area of State is 1307 square miles. The Maharaja is entitled to a salute of 13 guns. *Recreations:* sport, games of all kinds. *Address:* Cooch Behar, Bengal. *Clubs:* Princes', Royal Automobile, Automobile Association, Motor; Calcutta, Orient, Royal Calcutta Turf, Calcutta; etc.
Died 20 Dec. 1922.

COO-EE; *see* Walker, William Sylvester.

COOK, Albert Stanburrough, MA, PhD, LittD, LLD; Professor of the English Language and Literature, Yale University, since 1889, Emeritus since 1921; *b* Montville, New Jersey, USA, 6 March 1853; *s* of Frederick Weissenfels and Sarah Cook; *m* 1st, 1886, Emily Chamberlain, of Berkeley, California; 2nd, 1911, Elizabeth Merrill, of Cincinnati, Ohio; one *s* one *d. Educ:* Rutgers College, New Brunswick, New Jersey; Göttingen; Leipsic; London (with Henry Sweet); Jena (PhD, 1882). Tutor in mathematics, Rutgers College, 1872-73; teacher in Freehold (New Jersey) Institute, 1873-77; Associate in English, Johns Hopkins University, 1879-81; Professor of the English Language and Literature, University of California, 1882-89; President of the Modern Language Association of America, 1897; Founder of the Concordance Society, 1906, and President ever since; Member of the Netherlandish Society of Letters (Leyden); Fellow of the Mediæval Academy of America. *Publications:* Translation of Sievers' Old English Grammar, 1885; edition of the Old English Judith, 1888, 1904; edition of Sidney's Defense of Poesy, 1890; The Art of Poetry, 1892; First Book in Old English, 1894; Glossary of the Old Northumbrian Gospels, 1894; The Artistic Ordering of Life, 1898; Biblical Quotations in Old English Prose Writers, 1898, 1903; edition of Cynewulf's Christ, 1900; Select Translations from Old English Poetry (with C. B. Tinker), 1902; edition of The Dream of the Rood, 1905; The Higher Study of English, 1906; The Authorised Version of the Bible and its Influence, 1910; Concordance to Beowulf,

1911; The Date of the Ruthwell and Bewcastle Crosses, 1912; Some Accounts of the Bewcastle Cross, 1914; A Literary Middle English Reader, 1915; The Historical Background of Chaucer's Knight, 1916; The Last months of Chaucer's Earliest Patron, 1916; edition of Elene, Phœnix, and Physiologus, 1919; Theodore of Tarsus and Gislenus of Athens, 1923; Beowulfian and Odyssean Voyages, 1926, etc; editor of Yale Studies in English (73 volumes). *Recreations:* reading, walking. *Address:* 219 Bishop Street, New Haven, Conn.; Greensboro, Vermont, USA. *T:* 514. *Clubs:* Phi Beta Kappa, Pioneer.
Died 1 Sept. 1927.

COOK, Arthur Kemball; *b* 1851; 3rd *s* of S. Kemball Cook; *m* 1884, Lucy Frances Richardson; one *d. Educ:* Winchester College; New College, Oxford. Assistant Master of Winchester College, 1875-1911. *Publications:* About Winchester College, 1917; A Commentary on the Ring and the Book, 1920. *Address:* Colebrook House, Winchester; Emerald Bank, Stair, Keswick. *M:* XU 1298.
Died 21 Nov. 1928.

COOK, Sir Edward Tyas, KBE 1917; Kt 1912; MA; *b* Brighton, 12 May 1857; *y s* of late S. Kemball Cook; *m* 1884, Emily (*d* 1903), *d* of late John Forster Baird, Bowmont Hill, Northumberland. *Educ:* Winchester; New Coll. Oxford. President of the Union and Palmerston Clubs, Oxford. Graduated (1st Class Classics), 1880; Secretary London Society for Extension of University Teaching, 1882-85; contributed to Pall Mall Gazette under Mr John Morley's editorship; succeeded Mr (later Lord) Milner as assistant editor to Mr William Stead; on Mr Stead's resignation became editor, 1890-92; on sale of paper to Mr Astor, resigned; invited by Mr (Sir George) Newnes to edit Westminster Gazette; editor thereof, 1893-96; editor of the Daily News, 1896-1901; Fellow of Winchester College, 1903; Vice-Chairman, Advisory Council, Victoria and Albert Museum, 1913; Joint Director, Official Press Bureau, 1915; Deputy President, Victoria League, 1917. *Publications:* Popular Handbook to the National Gallery, 8th edition, 1912; Studies in Ruskin, 2nd edition, 1891; Popular Handbook to the Tate Gallery, 1898; The Rights and Wrongs of the Transvaal War, 4th edn 1902; Popular Handbook to the Greek and Roman Antiquities in the British Museum, 1903; editor of Ruskin's Works, 1903-11; Memoir of Edmund Garrett, 1909; Life of Ruskin, 1911; Homes and Haunts of John Ruskin, 1912; The Life of Florence Nightingale, 1913; Catalogue of Dulwich Picture Gallery, 1914; Delane, of the Times, 1915; Literary Recreations, 1918. *Address:* Southstoke, Oxon. *Clubs:* Athenæum, National Liberal.
Died 30 Sept. 1919.

COOK, Sir Frederick Lucas, 2nd Bt, *cr* 1886; Viscount Monserrate in Portugal; DL; Lieutenant for City of London; Head of Cook, Son and Co., warehousemen, St Paul's; *b* London, 21 Nov. 1844; *e s* of Sir Francis Cook, 1st Bt and Emily, *d* of late Robert Lucas, of Lisbon. *S* father, 1901; *m* 1868, Mary (*d* 1913), *d* of Richard Payne Cotton, MD; one *s* two *d. Educ:* Harrow. MP (C) Kennington, 1895-1906. *Recreations:* member of committee Coaching Club, golf, tennis. *Heir s* Herbert Frederick Cook, *b* 18 Nov. 1868. *Address:* Doughty House, Richmond, Surrey; Monserrate, Cintra, Portugal. *Clubs:* Carlton, Prince's, Queen's, Hurlingham, Ranelagh, Sandown.
Died 21 May 1920.

COOK, Lt-Col George Trevor-Roper, DSO 1915; 20th Hussars; *b* 11 Aug. 1877; *s* of George Ward Cook, of Hoylake; *m* 1902, Alice, *y d* of A. J. Dorman, JP, of Nunthorpe, Yorkshire; one *s* four, *y d* of A. J. Dorman, JP, of Nunthorpe, Yorkshire; one *s* four, Entered army (3rd Dragoon Guards), 1897; Captain, 1900; Major, 1911; Major, 20th Hussars, 1913; Lt-Col 1915; Adjutant, TF 1908-11; served S African War, 1899-1902 (Queen's medal, 4 clasps); European War, 1914-15 (despatches twice, DSO). *Address:* Greenham, Hoylake, Cheshire. *Club:* Cavalry. *Died March 1916.*

COOK, Sir Henry, Kt 1904; senior partner of the firm of W. & J. Cook, Writers to the Signet; Secretary of the King's Bodyguard for Scotland (Royal Company of Archers); *b* 28 July 1840; *e* surv. *s* of late John Cook, WS, Edinburgh; *m* 1879, Margaret (*d* 1905), *e d* of late John Patten, Edinburgh; three *s* one *d. Educ:* Edinburgh Academy; St Andrews University, MA, 1866. Passed Writer to the Signet, and partner in the firm of W. & J. Cook, 1871; appointed Joint Secretary of the King's Bodyguard for Scotland (Royal Company of Archers); 1879; DL of the City of Edinburgh; a Director Royal Bank of Scotland and Scottish Widows' Fund Life Assurance Society. *Recreations:* golf, shooting, fishing. *Address:* 22 Eglinton Crescent, Edinburgh. *Clubs:* Caledonian, University, Edinburgh.
Died 9 March 1924.

COOK, Ven. Henry Lucas, MA; Archdeacon of Craven since 1913; Rector of Skipton 1890-1922; Hon. Canon of Bradford; *s* of

Lumley Cook of Hull; *m* Eleanor Gertrude, *d* of Welbury Kendall of Skipton. *Educ:* King's School, Canterbury; Brasenose College, Oxford. Curate of All Saints, Bradford, 1877–81; Vicar of St Mark's, Low Moor, 1881–89. *Recreations:* fond of cricket and tennis. *Address:* Woodlands, Crosshills, Keighley. *T:* Crosshills 111. *TA:* Crosshills. *Club:* Union, Bradford.   *Died 16 May 1928.*

OOK, Maj.-Gen. James, CB 1899; retired, 1900; *b* 22 March 1844. Entered army (ISC), 1861; served North-West Frontier, 1863 (medal with clasp); Afghan War, 1878–80 (despatches, brevet of Major, medal with clasp); Soudan, 1885 (despatches, brevet of Lieut-Col, medal with two clasps, Khedive's star). *Address:* 59 St Mary's Mansions, W2.   *Died 18 Feb. 1928.*

OOK, Mrs Keningale, (Mabel Collins); *b* Guernsey, 1851; *o c* of Mortimer Collins; *m* 1871, Keningale Cook (decd). *Educ:* at home, according to her father's special ideas about education. *Publications:* Light on the Path; The Idyll of the White Lotus; Through the Gates of Gold; The Crucible; Our Glorious Future; many other works on occult subjects. *Address:* Cintra Lawn, Cheltenham.
                    Died 31 Mach 1927.

OOK, Sir Theodore Andrea, Kt 1916; Editor-in-Chief of the Field since 1910; *b* Exmouth, Devonshire, 28 March 1867; *s* of Henry Cook and Jane Elizabeth Robins; *m* 1898, Elizabeth Wilhelmina Link. *Educ:* King Alfred's Grammar School, Wantage; Carr's School, Exmouth; Radley (Sewell entrance scholarship, head of the school and captain of football and boats); Wadham Coll., Oxford (open classical scholar, 2nd class in Honour Moderations and Classical Greats); rowed 3 in Oxford crew of 1889. Captain, English Fencing Team, Paris, 1903, and Athens, 1906; Member of Board of Trade Committee for the Vienna Exhibition, 1910; Editor of St James's Gazette, 1900; joined staff of Daily Telegraph, 1901. *Publications:* Old Touraine; Rouen; A History of the English Turf; An Anthology of Humorous Verse; Turner's Water-Colours in the National Gallery; Old Provence; Eclipse and O'Kelly; Thomas Doggett, Deceased (Part I); Henley Races; The Curves of Life; Twenty-five Great Houses of France; The Mark of the Beast; The Art and Science of the Oar; Leonardo da Vinci, Sculptor; The Sunlit Hours, an Autobiography, 1926; Character and Sportsmanship, 1927; contributor to Quarterly Review, Nineteenth Century, etc. *Recreation:* writing on sport. *Address:* 54 Oakley Street, Chelsea, SW3. *Clubs:* Oxford and Cambridge, Savile; Leander.   *Died 16 Sept. 1928.*

OOK, Thomas Reginald Hague, JP; *b* 1866; *s* of late Thomas Hague Cook, of Hall Croft, Mirfield, Yorks; *m* 1893, Sarah Taylor, *e d* of late Sir George Elliot, 2nd Bt. *Clubs:* Boodle's, White's; Royal Yacht Squadron, Cowes.   *Died 7 Aug. 1925.*

OOK, Rt. Rev. Thomas William, MA Oxon.; Suffragan Bishop of Lewes since 1926; Archdeacon of Hastings since 1922; *b* 2 Dec. 1866; *s* of Thomas Cook, Solicitor, Wellingborough; *m* 1895, Fanny (*d* 1927), *d* of John Best, Aldborough, Yorks; two *d*. *Educ:* Lancing College, Sussex; Hertford College, Oxford (Exhibitioner of); Cuddesdon College. Curate of Parish Church, Warrington, 1890–94; Vice-Principal and Assistant-Chaplain, Diocesan Training College, Chester, 1894–95; Second House Master, 1895–1911, Chaplain, 1902–11, Lancing College, Sussex; Vicar of Holy Trinity, Hastings, 1911–26; Rural Dean of Hastings, 1913-22; Examining Chaplain to Bishop of Chichester, 1915; Canon and Prebendary of Bracklesham in Chichester Cathedral, 1917; Proctor in Convocation for Archdeaconries of Lewes and Hastings, 1919; Canon and Prebendary of Wittering in Chichester Cathedral, 1921; Proctor for Diocese of Chichester, 1922. *Recreations:* Capt. of School Football, Cricket, Fives; Victor Ludorum, 1885; OUAFC, 1886–89; Corinthians FC. *Address:* The White House, Bexhill. *T:* Bexhill 163.
                    Died 16 Oct. 1928.

OOKE, Charles John Bowen, CBE 1918; JP and CC Cheshire; MInstCE, MInstME; Major, Engineer and Railway Staff Corps; Chief Mechanical Engineer, London and North Western Railway Company; *b* Orton Longueville, Huntingdonshire, 11 Jan. 1859; *s* of late Rev. C. J. R. Cooke, MA, Exhibitioner, Oriel College, Oxford, and *y d* of Capt. T. Bowen of Johnstone, Pembrokeshire; *m* Annie, *d* of late W. Smith, Nuneaton; one *s* four *d*. *Educ:* Cheltenham College Preparatory School; King's College School, London; on the Continent. Apprentice and pupil, Crewe Works, under late F. W. Webb, MInstCE; on completion of pupilage appointed Assistant Running Superintendent of the Southern Division of the L&NW Rly, afterwards Assistant to Geo. Whale, the Chief Mechanical Engineer. *Publications:* British Locomotives; Locomotive Development; various papers. *Recreations:* golf, yachting, campanology. *Address:* Chester Place,

Crewe, Cheshire. *TA:* Bowen Cooke, Crewe. *T:* Crewe 122; St Mawes, Cornwall. *M:* M 7655; M 5713. *Club:* St Stephen's.
                    Died 18 Oct. 1920.

COOKE, Conrad William, MInstEE; Officier de l'Instruction Publique; was head of Whieldon & Cooke, Engineers, Lambeth; *b* Barnes, Surrey, 23 Dec. 1843; *s* of late E. W. Cooke, RA, FRS, FSA, and Jane, *d* of late George Loddiges, the botanist; *m* 1st, 1871, Fanny (*d* 1906), *d* of late Rev. R. F. B. Rickards, Vicar of Constantine, Cornwall; five *s* one *d*; 2nd, 1912, Sophie Augusta, *d* of August C. B. Bonnevie, late Chief Advocate of the Norwegian Supreme Court, Christiania, Norway. Pupil in the works of John Penn & Sons, marine engineers, Greenwich; surveyed and laid out the first Isle of Wight Railway; assistant to late Sir Joseph Whitworth, Manchester, 1871; removed to London, 1872; introduced the Gramme Electrical Machine (Dynamo), 1883; installed the signal light on Clock Tower of House of Commons; a pioneer of electricity and incandescent gas lighting; a member of the juries of nearly all the International Exhibitions; with late Silvanus Thompson founded the Gilbert Club, 1889; acted as special Astronomical Correspondent for the Morning Post in the Total Solar Eclipse Expeditions of 1896, Norway; 1900, Algeria; and 1905, Spain. *Publications:* Hot Air Engines, 1873; The Loud Speaking Telephone (Society of Arts), 1897; Electric Illumination, 2 vols 1882 and 1885; Electrical Industries, 1901; Automata Old and New (issued by the Sette of Odd Volumes), 1893; contributions to many scientific societies and magazines. *Recreations:* travelling, angling, experimental physics, and collecting of books and instruments, illustration of the history and development of physical and mechanical science. *Address:* The Pines, Langland Gardens, Hampstead, NW3. *T:* Hampstead 7030. *Clubs:* Athenæum, Savage (Trustee), Sette of Odd Volumes, Wigwam (Trustee).
                    Died 9 Jan. 1926.

COOKE, Isaac; landscape painter; *b* Warrington, 1846; *m* 1st, 1873; two *s* one *d*; 2nd, 1902. The Liverpool Corporation purchased his water-colour of Passing Showers over Langdale Pikes from Blea Tarn, and in 1884 they purchased an oil painting, Golden Moments; twice on the Hanging Committee of the Walker Art Gallery Autumn Exhibitions, and was for 7 years Hon. Treasurer of the Liverpool Water-Colour Society; member of Liverpool Academy, 1884; exhibited in Royal Academy since 1879, and Royal Institute of Painters in Water-Colours since 1881; a member of the RBA, 1896–1915. *Recreations:* natural history, collections of entomology, botany, and oology, etc; golf. *Address:* 19 Glebe Road, Wallasey, Cheshire. *Club:* Liverpool Artists'.   *Died 22 April 1922.*

COOKE, Temple, JP Surrey; Barrister; Recorder of Southampton 1899–1924; *b* 14 Nov. 1851; *e s* of William Major Cooke, Metropolitan Police Magistrate; *m* Margaretta, *o d* of late George Beaufoy, RN. *Educ:* Cheltenham Coll. Called to Bar, 1874; Western Circuit; Counsel to Admiralty on Circuit, 1889. *Recreations:* all outdoor sports. *Address:* Edmondscote, Frimley, Surrey; 2 Dr Johnson's Buildings, Temple, EC. *Clubs:* Reform; Hampshire County.
                    Died 13 Oct. 1925.

COOKE, William Henry, BA; Secretary of the Chamber of Shipping of the United Kingdom and of the General Shipowners' Society, London, 1880–1910; of the Shipowners' Parliamentary Committee, 1893–1910, and of the Advisory Committee to the Board of Trade upon New Lighthouse Works, 1900–10; *b* 18 Jan. 1843; *y s* of late Rev. John Hall Cooke of Gomersal; *m* 1873, Emily Amelia, *d* of late D. Davison, of the Woodlands, Maldon, Essex; one *s* three *d*. *Educ:* Royal Grammar School and Dr Bruce's School, Newcastle-on-Tyne; BA University of London, 1866. Called to Bar, Middle Temple, 1867; went the Northern Circuit, 1867–71. Has contributed largely to newspapers and magazines. Was London Correspondent of the Indian Daily News, Calcutta, 1870–93; and an original Member of the Institute of Journalists. Has visited Japan, China, India, Australia, New Zealand, Ceylon, West Indies (twice), USA, Canada, N and S Africa, S America, Egypt, Palestine (twice), Syria, Iceland, and nearly every country in Europe. Went round the world in 1914 outwards by Cape of Good Hope to Australia and homewards from New Zealand by Cape Horn. *Publication:* joint-author with late Sir Wemyss Reid of Briefs and Papers: Sketches of the Bar and the Press by Two Idle Apprentices, 1872. *Recreations:* reading, travel. *Address:* Burnmoor, Sutton, Surrey. *Clubs:* Savile, University of London.
                    Died 5 Jan. 1921.

COOKE-TAYLOR, Richard Whately, JP; FSS, FRHistS; *b* 1842; *s* of William Cooke-Taylor, LLD; *m* 1880, Mary, *d* of John Haslam, JP of Bolton; one *s*. *Educ:* Kilkenny College; Trinity College, Dublin. Entered Office of Paymaster of Civil Services, Dublin Castle, 1859;

Paymaster-General's Office, London, 1861; HM Inspector of Factories, 1869; HM Superintending Inspector for Scotland and Ireland, 1895; HM Senior Superintending Inspector, London, 1902; retired, 1905. *Publications:* Introduction to a History of the Factory System, 1886; The Modern Factory System, 1891; The Factory System and the Factory Acts, 1894; contributor to the Westminster, Fortnightly, and Contemporary Reviews, Temple Bar Magazine, and many other periodicals; also to Dictionary of Political Economy, the Transactions of the British Association, and many other learned societies; has written plays. *Recreations:* fishing, walking. *Address:* High Trees, Chepstow. *Clubs:* Albemarle, National Liberal.

Died 12 Aug. 1918.

COOKSON, Charles Lisle Stirling, JP; *b* 1855; *o s* of late Charles Edward Cookson of Hermitage, Co. Durham, and Sarah Turnbull, *e d* of late Capt. Robert Lisle Coulson, RN, Houndwood; *m* 1st, 1885, Mary Eleanor (*d* 1898), *e d* of Sir Samuel Home Stirling, 7th Bt of Glorat and Renton; 2nd, 1902, May Elizabeth, *o d* of late John Napier of Merchiston, Renfrewshire. Formerly Capt. 2nd Brigade Scottish Div. RA. *Address:* Renton House, Grantshouse, Berwickshire. *Club:* New, Edinburgh.   *Died 17 Oct. 1919.*

COOKSON, Colonel Philip Blencowe, CMG 1915; OBE 1919; late Northumberland (Hussars) Yeomanry (Territorial Force); High Sheriff, Northumberland, 1924–25; *b* 30 Oct. 1871; *s* of late Col John Blencowe Cookson and Constance Jane, 2nd *d* of late George Fenwick; *m* 1902, Gwendoline, 5th *d* of late H. A. Brassey; two *s* one *d*. *Educ:* Eton. Entered Army, 1st Life Guards, 1894; Major, 1909; retired, 1911; served NW Frontier of India, 1897–98; S African War, 1899–1900; European War, 1914–17 (despatches, CMG). *Address:* Meldon Park, Morpeth. *T:* Hartburn 3. *Club:* White's.

Died 27 Feb. 1928.

COOLIDGE, Archibald Cary; Professor of History at Harvard University since 1908, and Director of the University Library since 1911; AB (Harvard) 1887, PhD (Freiburg, Germany) 1892; LLD (hon.) Harvard, 1916; *b* Boston, 6 March 1866; *s* of Joseph Randolph Coolidge and Julia, *d* of John Lowell Gardner; unmarried. *Educ:* Harvard; University of Berlin; Ecole des Science Politiques, Paris; Freiburg University; foreign travel. Acting secretary, Legation, St Petersburg, 1890–91; private secretary to Minister to France, 1892; secretary, Legation, Vienna, 1893; instructor history, Harvard, 1893; asst prof. 1899; Lowell Lecturer (Boston), 1902–3, 1914–15, and 1919–20; lecturer at the Sorbonne and other French Universities, 1906–7; exchange professor University of Berlin, 1913–14; Inquiry Commission to prepare for Peace Conference, 1917–18; special assistant of Dept of State and War Trade Board, Sweden and North Russia, 1918; Chief of American Mission to Vienna, 1919; special representative of American Commission to negotiate peace, Paris, 1919; with American Relief Administration in Moscow, winter of 1921–22; Editor of Foreign Affairs, an American Quarterly Review, 1922. Mem. Mass Hist. Soc., Va Hist. Soc., Amer. Acad. Polit. and Social Science, Amer. Ant. Soc., Royal Geog. Soc., Marseilles Geog. Soc. (hon.). *Publications:* The United States as a World Power, 1908; The Origins of the Triple Alliance, 1917, second edition, 1926; editor of English edition of The Secret Treaties of Austria-Hungary, 1879–1914, by Alfred Franzis Pribram, 1920; Ten Years of War and Peace, 1927; contributions American Historical Review, Foreign Affairs, etc. *Address:* Harvard University, Cambridge, USA. *Clubs:* Somerset, etc, Boston; Century, Harvard, New York.

Died Jan. 1928.

COOLIDGE, William Augustus Brevoort; Life Fellow of Magdalen College, Oxford, since 1875; *b* 28 Aug. 1850, near New York; *e s* of Frederic William Skinner Coolidge and Elisabeth Neville Brevoort; unmarried (as Fellowship dates from before 1881). *Educ:* St Paul's School, Concord, New Hampshire (USA); Elizabeth Coll., Guernsey; Exeter Coll., Oxford (Taylorian University Scholar for French, 1871; 1st class Modern History, 1873; 2nd class Jurisprudence, 1874; BA, 1874; MA, 1876). Hon. Dr Philos. (University of Bern), 1908. Deacon, 1882; Priest, 1883; Prof. English History, St David's College, Lampeter, 1880–81; Modern History Tutor Magdalen Coll. Oxford, 1881–85; Hon. curate of S Hinksey, 1883–95. FRGS 1890–1913; member English Alpine Club, 1870–99, hon. member, 1904–10; Swiss Alpine Club, 1895–1905; hon. member of the French and the Italian Alpine Clubs, 1898; of American Alpine Club, 1911; corresponding member of the Swiss Hist. Society, 1891, hon. member 1908; hon. member Bernese Historical Society, 1905; silver medallist Paris Geographical Society, 1905; hon. member Maurienne Historical Society, 1905; hon. member Lyons Section, French Alpine Club, 1910–17, and Grindelwald Section, Swiss Alpine Club, 1912; Co-founder and Hon. Member of the Société d'Histoire du Valais

Romand, 1916. *Publications:* Climbers' Guide to the Ber Oberland, new edition of vol. i, 2 Parts, 1909–10, and vol. ii 1 Josias Simler et les Origines de l'Alpinisme jusqu'en 1600, 1904; Alps in Nature and History, 1908; Die Petronella-Kapell Grindelwald, 1911; A List of my Writings (1868–1912) relati the Alps or Switzerland, 1912; Alpine Studies, 1912; Die ä Schutzhütte im Berner Oberland, 1915; Johann Madutz, 1917. Ed Alpine Journal, 1880–89; The late Aubrey Moore's Lectures Papers on the History of the Reformation, 1890; Murray's Handl for Switzerland, 18th edn 1891 and 19th edn 1904; Editor Pioneer in the High Alps, Alpine Diaries and Letters of F. F. Tuc 1856–1894, 1920. *Recreations:* Swiss history, history of the (formerly) mountaineering. *Address:* Chalet Montana, Grindelv Switzerland; Magdalen College, Oxford.

Died 8 May 1

COOMBES, Very Rev. George Frederick; Dean of Ruperts and Professor of Ecclesiastical History, St John's College, Manit since 1905; Professor of Classics, University of Manitoba, since 1 *b* 1856; 2nd *s* of late Rev. J. Coombes, Vicar of Portwood, Ches *m* 1885, Mary Elizabeth, *d* of Henry Eagles, of Walsall; three s *d. Educ:* Manchester Grammar School; St John's Coll., Cambr (Foundation Scholar, Classical Tripos, MA); DD (*honoris ca* Manitoba University. Ordained 1880; Curate of Portwood, Ches and Classical Master Manchester Grammar School, 1880–83; Ca of St John's Cathedral, Winnipeg, 1883–1905. *Recreations:* golf, *Address:* The Deanery, Winnipeg. *Club:* Manitoba, Winnipeg

Died 22 Sept. 1

COOP, Rev. James Ogden, DSO 1918; TD; MA; Chaplain to King, 1926; Hon. Canon of Liverpool, 1920; Senior Chaplain to Forces, W Command, 1923; Proctor in Convocation; Membe National Assembly, 1921; Member of Governing Body, St C College, Durham, 1925; Vicar of St Margaret's, Anfield, Liver since 1920; *b* Ashton-under-Lyne, 1869; *e s* of John Hague and S Coop, Albemarle, Ashton-under-Lyne; *m* Ethel, *d* of late (Wolstenholme, Headingley, Leeds; five *d. Educ:* Manch Grammar School; Exeter College, Oxford. 3rd class Modern His Fellow of the Royal Historical Society, 1892. Ordained 1892; C of All Hallows, Leeds, 1892–95, West Derby (priest), 1895–1 St Agnes, with charge of St Pancras, Sefton Park, Liverpool, 190 Vicar of St Catherine's, Abercromby Square, Liverpool, 1905 Chaplain 1st class TF, 1913; Senior Chaplain C/E, 55th (' Lancashire) Division, 1914–19 (despatches twice, DSO). *Publica* The Story of the 55th Division; Guide to the Battlefields, 1 various articles in the Prayer Book Dictionary, 1912. *Recrea* riding, rowing, etc. *Address:* St Margaret's Vicarage, An Liverpool. *T:* Anfield 108.   *Died 2 June 1*

COOPE, Edward Jesser, JP; *b* 1849; *o s* of late O. E. Coope, of Rochetts and Berechurch Hall, Essex; *m* 1872, Pleasance S of Rev. T. L. Fellowes. Formerly Captain Suffolk Yeomanry. C Royal Yacht Squadron, Cowes.   *Died 26 Nov. 1*

COOPER, Sir Alfred, Kt 1901; JP Surrey; Chairman, Ridgways, *b* 1846; *s* of late Henry Cooper of London; *m* 1st, 1873, Mar (*d* 1874), *d* of James Gilmore Winn; 2nd, 1883, Marion, *d* of Charles Nicholson of Dublin. *Educ:* King's Coll., London. Knig in recognition of services during S African war in maintaining a pr military hospital at Surbiton as an adjunct to the Princess of Wa hospital ship. *Recreations:* yachting, motoring. *Address:* Ossen Manor, near Christchurch, Hants.   *Died 21 Jan. 1*

COOPER, Rev. Alfred William Francis; Rector of Killanne s 1898; Canon of Ferns since 1903. *Educ:* Trinity College, Dublin; I DD Univ. of Manitoba. Ordained 1873; Curate of Stradt 1873–77; Tipperary, 1877–78; Booterstown, 1878–80; Recto Glenely, 1880–85; Priest (SPG), NW Canada, 1885–87; Recto Pro-Cathedral of the Redeemer, Calgary, 1887–98; Archdeaco Calgary, 1895–98. *Address:* Killanne Rectory, Enniscorthy.

Died 14 Nov. 1

COOPER, Alice J.; tutor and lecturer in education, Ox 1897–1914; Occasional Inspector of Secondary Schools under Board of Education, 1901; 5th *d* of late Rev. J. T. Cooper, Diss. I private tuition. Assistant mistress, Notting Hill High School; 1 mistress, Edgbaston High School for girls, 1876–95; vice-presi Head Mistresses' Association, 1887–95; sat on many educational other committees. *Publications:* lectures, addresses, and occasi papers, mostly on educational subjects. *Address:* Steyning, Beac field, Bucks. *Club:* Lyceum.

Died 17 June 1

COOPER, Charles Alfred, FRSE; Hon. LLD Edin.; editor of the Scotsman, 1876–1906; b Hull, 16 Sept. 1829; e s of Charles Cooper, architect; m 1852, Susannah (d 1887), e d of Thomas Towers, Hull; one s. Educ: Hull Grammar School. Sub-editor and manager Hull Advertiser; went to London to be reporter in Gallery of House of Commons for Morning Star, 1861; sub-editor, 1862; left London in 1868 to become assistant to Alexander Russel, editor of Scotsman; shortly after his death became editor of that paper; retired, 1906. Publications: Letters on Egypt with title of Seeking the Sun, 1891; Letters on South Africa, 1895; An Editor's Retrospect, 1896. Recreation: books. Address: 41 Drumsheugh Gardens, Edinburgh.
Died 15 April 1916.

COOPER, Sir Edward Ernest, 1st Bt, cr 1920; Kt 1913; Head of James Hartley Cooper & Co., Underwriters, Jerusalem Chambers; b Windsor, 1848; m 1876, Leonora, OBE, d of Thomas Crampton. Sheriff of London, 1912–13; Lord Mayor, 1919–20; Lieutenant of City of London; Grand Officer Legion of Honour; Officer Order of the Crown of Belgium; Order of St Sava 1st class; Chairman of Committee of Royal Academy of Music. Heir: none. Address: Berrydown Court, Overton, Hampshire. Clubs: Garrick, Oriental, Junior Carlton; Royal Thames Yacht.
Died 12 Feb. 1922 (ext).

COOPER, Col Harry, CMG 1900; CBE 1919; retired; JP, DL Essex; b London, 14 April 1847; e s of Henry Cooper and Catherine, d of late S. Lovegrove; m 1894, Emily C. E., d of late Commodore Henry Caldwell, CB, ADC, RN; one s one d. Educ: Brentwood Grammar School; Blackheath Proprietary School; Royal Military College, Sandhurst; Staff College. Ensign 98th Foot, 1865; 47th Foot, 1866; served in Canada, West Indies, Ireland, England, and East Indies; Special Service, Ashanti, 1873–74; Vice-Consul in Bosnia, 1877–78; in Asia Minor, 1879–80; with Mounted Infantry in South Africa in 1881; ADC to Viceroy, India, 1884–88; Chief Staff Officer, Army of Occupation, Egypt, 1896–98; ADC to the Sovereign, 1898–1904; Assistant-Adjutant-General, Western District, 1899; Colonel on Staff, Cape Colony, 1899–1902; Col Commanding Essex Volunteer and Territorial Infantry Brigade, 1906–11; Vice-Chairman Essex Territorial Force Association, 1908–14; served Canada, 1866 (medal with clasp); Ashanti, 1873–74 (medal); Burma, 1885–86 (medal with clasp); Sudan, 1896 (medal); South Africa, 1899–1902 (Queen's medal and clasp, King's medal 2 clasps); GHQ Expeditionary Force, France, 1914–15 (star, 2 medals); Commanding No 3 District, 1915–17. Address: Pakenham Lodge, Bury St Edmunds. Club: United Service.
Died 8 Oct. 1928.

COOPER, Rt. Rev. Henry Edward, DD; Bishop of Armidale since 1914; b 15 Oct. 1845; m 1879, d of Dr Holthouse, Ballarat. Educ: Trinity Coll., Dublin (MA 1876). Ordained 1872; Archdeacon and Vicar of Hamilton, Victoria, 1884–93; Archdeacon of Ballarat, 1894–95; Bishop Coadjutor of Ballarat, 1895; Bishop of Grafton and Armidale, 1901–14. Address: Bishopscourt, Armidale, New South Wales.
Died 1 July 1916.

COOPER, Henry St John, novelist; b London, 3 Nov. 1869; s of Charles Frederick Cooper, and g s of Henry Russell, composer of Cheer, Boys, Cheer, etc; m 1st, Laura Ethel Thwaites (d 1924); 2nd, 1925, Anne S. McGlashan; three s. Educ: privately, in France and England. Educated originally as an artist, but gave art up for literature; for some years was employed in an editorial and sub-editorial capacity in weekly journalism; has written a vast number of serial stories, a great many of which have been published in book form under the names of Henry St John Cooper and Mabel St John; several produced in film form. Publications: Life of Henry Russell (Cheer, Boys, Cheer); The Voyage of the Avenger; Sunny Ducrow; James Bevanwood; Garden of Memories; The Imaginary Marriage; Carniss & Co.; The Fortunes of Sally Luck; The Golconda Necklace; The Gallant Lover; five books on the British Bulldog. Recreations: painting, photography, making model reproductions of antique ships and furniture, judging English and Dutch paintings, inventing mechanical devices, breeding and judging bulldogs. Address: The Ivy House, Sunbury-on-Thames. TA: St John Cooper, Sunbury. T: Sunbury 33. M: AP 1929. Clubs: National Liberal, Press.
Died 9 Sept. 1926.

COOPER, Very Rev. James, VD 1899; DD; Professor of Church History, University of Glasgow, 1899–1922; b Elgin, 13 Feb. 1846; e s of late John Alexander Cooper, Spynie, Elgin, and Ann d of late James Stephen, Old Keith; m 1912, Margaret, e d of late George Williamson, Shempston. Educ: Elgin Academy; Univ. of Aberdeen. MA; DD Aberdeen, 1892; Oxford, 1920; LittD (Hon.), Trinity College, Dublin, 1909; DCL Durham, 1910. Serbian Order of St Sava, 4th Class; Olaus Petri Lecturer, University of Upsala; Member

of the Ancient Monuments Board, Scotland, 1919; Minister of St Stephen's, Broughty Ferry, 1873–81; of East Parish of St Nicholas, Aberdeen, 1881–98; Joint-Secretary, Scottish Church Society; Founder of the Scottish Ecclesiological Society, and President 1903, 1911, 1916, and 1921; deeply interested in reunion of the Church; to Glasgow University Officers' Training Corps, 1909; Moderator of the General Assembly, Church of Scotland, 1917. Publications: Cartularium Ecclesiæ S Nicolai Aberdonensis (2 vols); Bethlehem, a volume of Advent Sermons; Soldiers of the Bible; Our Sacred Heritage (Closing Address as Moderator), 1917; Reunion, A Voice from Scotland, 1918; has edited Scottish Liturgy of 1637, and, in conjunction with the Rt Rev. Bishop MacLean, an English translation of Testamentum Domini; etc. Address: Brae, Moriston, Elgin.
Died 27 Dec. 1922.

COOPER, Margaret; singer of popular songs; m Capt. Arthur Maughan Humble-Crofts (d 1918), 4th s of Prebendary Humble-Crofts, Waldron, Sussex. Address: Framba, 103 Dartmouth Road, Willesden Green, NW2. T: Willesden 1283.
Died 28 Dec. 1922.

COOPER, Hon. Sir Pope (Alexander), KCMG 1908; Kt 1904; Chief Justice, Queensland, 1903–22; b Willeroo, Lake George, 12 May 1848; 5th s of late Francis Cooper; m 1878, Alice Frener (d 1900), d of late James Cooper; one s two d. Educ: Sydney University; London University. Called to Bar, Middle Temple, 1872; returned to Australia, 1874; MLA, Bowen, 1880–83; Attorney-General, 1883; Judge of Supreme Court, N District, 1880–83. Address: Hawstead, Brisbane, Queensland. Clubs: Junior Carlton, Union, Sports; Queensland, Brisbane.
Died Aug. 1923.

COOPER, Hon. Sir Theophilus, Kt 1921; one of the Judges of the Supreme Court of New Zealand, and of the Court of Appeal of New Zealand, 1901–21; b London, 15 November 1850; s of late Theophilus Cooper and Susanna Bugby; m 1878, Bessie, y d of A. A. Alexander of Auckland; two s three d (and one s killed in action in France, June 1916). Educ: privately. Emigrated to New Zealand with parents as one of the party of Nonconformists who established the Albertland Settlements in the North of Auckland, 1862; was there for 3 years and then returned to the city of Auckland; was employed for some years in the Daily Southern Cross Newspaper Office, Auckland, and then read for the Bar; admitted to New Zealand Bar, 1878; was leader of the Auckland Bar and one of the leaders of the New Zealand Bar for some years; for three years President of the Court of Arbitration of New Zealand; was for nearly 20 years a member of the Board of Education, and a Governor of the Auckland College and Grammar School, and for 15 years as honorary Inspector of Lunatic Asylums in New Zealand. Recreation: farming. Address: Eltham, Taranaki, New Zealand. Clubs: Northern, Auckland; Dunedin, Dunedin.
Died May 1925.

COOPER, Rev. Vincent King, MA; Rector of St Mary le Bow, Durham, since 1910; b 19 April 1849; 6th s of Edward Miles Cooper, of Pendleton, Manchester; four s one d. Educ: Bradfield; Brasenose College, Oxford. Assistant Master, Bradfield College, 1873–75; Head Master, St Michael's College, Tenbury, 1875; Curate of St Oswalds, Durham, 1876–87; Minor Canon of Durham, 1876–1910; Sacrist, 1885–87; Precentor, 1887–1905; Hon. Fellow St Michael's College, Tenbury, 1887; Assistant Diocesan Inspector of Schools, Durham, 1887; Hon. Secretary and Treasurer, Durham County Hospital, 1884–1902; Hon. Canon of Durham, 1910; Rural Dean of Durham, 1910–17; Censor of Unattached Students in University of Durham, 1912–17. Publication: Tales from Euripides. Address: 16 South Bailey, Durham. TA: Durham.
Died 18 May 1922.

COOPER, Sir William Charles, 3rd Bt, cr 1863; b 22 Oct. 1851; 2nd s of Sir Daniel Cooper, 1st Bt and Elizabeth, d of William Hill; S brother, 1909; m 1876, Alice Helen, 3rd d of George Hill of Surrey Hills, Sydney, NSW; three s one d. Heir: s William George Daniel [b 14 Dec. 1877; m 1904, Lettice Margaret, y d of 1st Viscount Long; two s one d (incl. twin s and d); late Lieut 7th Hussars. Address: 15 Ennismore Gardens, SW. Clubs: Orleans, Bachelors']. Address: 18 Park Street, W1. T: Mayfair 2499. Clubs: Turf, Orleans.
Died 2 Sept. 1925.

COOPER, Lt-Col Sir William Earnshaw, Kt 1903; CIE 1897; Hon. Colonel, Cawnpore Volunteer Rifle Corps; Chairman, Cooper, Allen and Co. Ltd, Cawnpore, India; b 1843; m 1911, Gleadowe, widow of Walter de Castro; two d. Commanded 5th Administrative Batt. NWP Volunteers for several years; President Upper India Chamber of Commerce, 1889–99; Member of the Legislative Council, NWP and Oudh, 1893–1900. Publications: The Murder of Agriculture;

Socialism and its Perils, 1908; Britain for the Briton, 1909; England's Need, 1910; Spiritual Science, 1911; England's Fatal Land Policy; The Blood-Guiltiness of Christendom, 1922, etc. *Address:* Hume Towers, Bournemouth. *Died 2 July 1924.*

COOPER, William Ranson; Consulting Engineer; Editor of Science Abstracts, 1899–1901, and again since 1922; Editor of the Electrician, 1906–19; *b* 1868; *s* of late William Cooper and Jane Susanna, *d* of Col Coke; *m* Sophia Mary, *d* of late Major Cross; two *s* one *d. Educ:* privately; Central Technical College and King's College, London. MA, BSc, National University of Ireland; Fellow of City and Guilds of London Institute; Fellow of the Institute of Physics; Associate of Institute of Chemistry. Joined staff of Mr James Swinburne in his consulting practice, 1895; was a member of Advisory Panel, Ministry of Munitions; member of the Electro-Culture Committee of the Board of Agriculture; served on the Councils of the Institution of Electrical Engineers, of the Institute of Physics, and of the Faraday Society; Hon. Treasurer and for 12 years one of the Honorary Secretaries of the Physical Society; Member of the Board of Studies in Electrical Engineering of the University of London. *Publications:* Primary Batteries; Electro-Chemistry related to Engineering; The Claims of Labour and of Capital; edited 2nd edn of the Electrician Primers; revised 4th edn of Macmillan's Electro-Metallurgy; *papers—* various, including Electric Traction (Inst. Mining Engineers, 1902); Electric Traction on Tramways (Inst. Civil Engineers, 1902, Telford Premium awarded); Problems of Electric Railways (with J. Swinburne, FRS, Inst. Electrical Engineers, 1902); Alternate Current Electrolysis (Faraday Society, 1905); Electricity Supply (Inst. EE 1908); Dust Prevention (Automobile Club, 1905, 1909); Heat Tests of Electrical Machines (British Association, 1913); Electric Cooking (Inst. Electrical Engineers, 1915); Electro-chemical Effects by Superimposing Alternating Currents (Faraday Society, 1922). *Recreations:* tennis, photography. *Address:* 82 Victoria Street, SW1. *T:* Vic. 1225; 113 Tulse Hill, SW2. *T:* Brixton 615. *Clubs:* Athenæum, Royal Automobile. *Died 15 March 1926.*

COOTE, Sir Algernon (Charles Plumptre), 12th Bt, *cr* 1621; Premier Baronet of Ireland; HM Lieutenant, Queen's Co. since 1900; *b* 14 Dec. 1847; *s* of Rev. Sir Algernon Coote, 11th Bt and Cecilia, *o d* of J. P. Plumptre, Fredville, Kent; *S* father, 1899; *m* 1st, Jean (*d* 1880), *d* of Capt. John Trotter; three *s* one *d*; 2nd, 1882, Ellen Melesina, *d* of Philip Chenevix-Trench of Botley Hill, Hants; three *s* one *d* (and one *d* decd). *Educ:* Eton; Cambridge; MA 1875. Owned about 45,000 acres. *Recreations:* golf, farming. *Heir: s* Ralph Algernon Coote, late Capt. 17th Lancers [*b* 22 Sept. 1874; *m* 1904, Alice, *y d* of late Thomas Webber of Kellyville, Queen's Co.; two *s*]. *Address:* Ballyfin, Mountrath, Ireland. *TA:* Ballyfin. *M:* CI 29. *Clubs:* National, Church Imperial; Kildare Street, Dublin.
Died 22 Oct. 1920.

COOTE, Sir Eyre, Kt 1903; JP, DL; Sheriff for the Queen's County in 1887, for Co. Dublin, 1903; *b* 31 Dec. 1857; *s* of Eyre Coote of West Park, Hants, and Jessie Mary, *d* of Lieut-General Henry Lechmere-Worrall, and *g-gs* of General Sir Eyre Coote, GCB (kinsman of Sir Charles Coote of Ballyfin); *m* 1892, Evelyn Mary, *d* of Rev. E. Cadogan, Rector of Wicken, Northamptonshire. *Educ:* Eton. Owned about 11,000 acres. *Recreations:* shooting, estate work, travel. *Address:* West Park, Damerham, Salisbury. *Clubs:* Carlton, Windham, Bath; Kildare Street, Dublin.
Died 6 May 1925.

COOTE, William; MP (U) South Tyrone, 1916–22; *b* 10 Dec. 1863; *s* of William Coote, Killevalley, Ballyjamesduff, Co. Cavan, and Sarah Wilson, Ahikist, Ballybay, Co. Monaghan; *m* 1889, Letitia A. Allen (*d* 1923), of Castleblayney, Co. Monaghan; four *s* one *d. Educ:* local primary school and local private classical academy. Apprenticed to the provision trade; at twenty years started and successfully carried on a business in his native district; removed to Newry, Co. Down, 1891; and from thence to Clogher, Co. Tyrone, 1893, where he built up a business as auctioneer and stock-owner; rented a large mill premises at Ballygawley idle for 35 years, where he started and developed the manufacture of woollen yarns, 1900, subsequently forming this into a private limited Company of which he became the Managing Director; removed business to Clogher, Co. Tyrone, 1918. JP, Co. Tyrone, 1901; a County Councillor, Co. Tyrone, 1903. *Recreation:* gardening. *Address:* Carrick House, Clogher, Co. Tyrone. *TA:* Coote, Clogher, Tyrone. *Clubs:* Constitutional; Ulster Reform, Belfast. *Died 14 Dec. 1924.*

COOTE, William Alexander, OBE 1918; Secretary of National Vigilance Association since 1885; *b* 24 Dec. 1842; 27th *c* of W. Coote, Queen's County. *Educ:* private. Apprenticed to a compositor; deeply

interested in labour questions, and in 1870 led movement for short hours; official delegate to five Trade Union Congresses; Labou Candidate for North Camberwell, 1883; for many years Member Camberwell Vestry and Borough Council; organised the Municip Employees Union (7000 members from the unskilled labourers London Vestries obtained shorter hours and higher wages); h organised National Committees for Suppression of White Slave Traff in all the European capitals, in Egypt, Canada, the United States, Sou America, and South Africa; in recognition of his National Vigilano Association work, Chevalier of the Legion of Honour of France, an the Royal and Most Distinguished Order of Charles III of Spai *Publications:* A Vision and its Fulfilment; pamphlets on Social Puri A Romance of Philanthropy; Commercialised Vice. *Address:* Grosvenor Mansions, 76 Victoria Street, SW.
Died 26 Oct. 191

COPE, Sir Thomas, 1st Bt, *cr* 1918; DL, JP; MA; for 26 years Chairma of Leicestershire County Council, of Leicestershire Quarter Sessio and of the Leicestershire Appeal Tribunal; *b* 22 Aug. 1840; *e s* Thomas Cope of Osbaston Hall; *m* 1879, Alice Kate (*d* 1916), *d* George Walker, Walthamstow; one *s* one *d. Educ:* Rugby; Trinit College, Cambridge. Called to Bar, Lincoln's Inn, 1866; practise at the Chancery Bar till 1879; has been actively engaged in Count work; contested (U) Bosworth Division, 1895. *Recreations:* joined th Cambridge University Volunteers and shot in their team again Oxford at the first Wimbledon meeting; cricket, shooting, fishin *Heir: s* Lt-Col Thomas George Cope, *b* 10 Feb. 1884. *Addres* Osbaston Hall, Nuneaton. *M:* 3050. *Club:* New University.
Died 17 Oct. 192

COPLAND, William Wallace, MVO 1912; MICE; Civil Enginee Gibraltar; *b* 1853; *s* of James Copland of Dumfries; *m* 1st, Mary 1887), *d* of Joseph Pritchard; 2nd, Caroline, *d* of Joseph R. Bre *Address:* Gibraltar. *Clubs:* Junior Constitutional; Mediterranea Gibraltar. *Died 9 June 192*

COPLAND-SPARKES, Rear-Admiral Robert, CMG 1901; RN *b* 20 Nov. 1851; 2nd *s* of late John Sparkes, of Green Place, Woners Surrey; *m* 1902, Alice Maud, 2nd *d* of late Charles Jackson, Newcastle-on-Tyne. Served Egypt, 1882 (medal, Khedive's star Borneo Expedition, 1898; Gambia Expedition, 1900; Boer Wa 1901–2. *Address:* Woodhill, Shamley Green, Surrey. *Club:* Naval an Military. *Died 10 July 192*

COPLESTON, Most Rev. Reginald Stephen, MA; Hon. D Oxon; Hon. DLitt Oxon; Hon. DCL Durham; Hon. LL Cambridge; Hon. Fellow of St John's College, Oxford; lately Cano of St George in Jerusalem; *b* 26 Dec. 1845; *s* of Rev. R. E. Coplesto *m* 1882, Edith, *d* of Archbishop Trench, Dublin; one *s* two *d. Edu* Merchant Taylors'; Merton Coll., Oxford. 2nd Class Lit.Hum. 186 Fellow and Tutor St John's Coll., Oxford, 1869–75; Bishop Colombo, 1875–1902; of Calcutta, and Metropolitan of Indi 1902–13. *Publications:* Buddhism: Primitive and Present, 1894; et *Address:* 25 St John's Road, Putney, SW.
Died 19 April 192.

COPLEY, Very Rev. John Robert; Dean since 1886, and Incumber of Kilfenora since 1873. Ordained, 1870; Curate of Kilnabo 1870–73; Precentor of Kilfenora, 1884–86. *Address:* Worthing.
Died 192.

CORBAN, Maj.-Gen. William Watts; *b* 26 Nov. 1829; *e s* of W Corban, of Grange, Francestown, Co. Cork; *m* Alice, *d* of H. F Peard, of Coole Abbey, Co. Cork. Entered army, 1850; Lieut-Cc 1878; retired, 1883; served Crimea, 1854–55 (mentioned in gener orders, medal, 3 clasps, Turkish medal); Egyptian Expedition, 188 (medal, bronze star, 3rd class Medjidieh); Distinguished Servic Reward, 1905. *Address:* Bettyville, Fermoy, Co. Cork.
Died 29 Jan. 191

CORBET, Maj.-Gen. Arthur Domville, CB 1894; Royal Marin Light Infantry; retired; *b* West Felton, Shropshire, 7 Feb. 1847; *y* of late V. R. Corbet, JP for Salop, and Maria, *d* of late P. Humbersto The Friars, Chester; *m* 1888, Louisa Marie, *d* of late H. Huish, Park Lodge, Stoke Damerel, and *widow* of R. Rundle; two *d. Edu* Leamington College. Joined Royal Marines, 1865; expeditionar force, Egypt, 1882; Gambia Expedition, 1894 (despatches, medal wit clasp, promoted Lieut-Colonel, CB). *Decorated* for operations again Fodi Silah on Gambia, 1894 (meritorious service in the field *Recreations:* fishing, archæology. *Club:* United Service.
Died 26 May 1918

CORBET, Eustace Kynaston, CMG 1905; *b* South Willingham Rectory, Lincolnshire, 22 June 1854; 7th and *y s* of late Rev. Andrew Corbett (2nd *s* of William Thompson Corbett, of Darnhall, Cheshire, and Elsham, Lincs; of a younger branch of the Corbets of Acton Reynold) and Marianne, 3rd *d* of Sir Matthew White Ridley, 3rd Bt, of Blagdon, Northumberland; unmarried. *Educ:* Cheltenham; Balliol College, Oxford. English Secretary to late Khedive Tewtik, 1885–91; Judge in Native Court of Appeal, Cairo, 1891–97; Procureur-Général, Native Courts, Egypt, 1897–1908; Director of the Egyptian Educational Mission in England, 1908–13; Grand Cordon of Medjidieh, and second class Osmanieh. *Publications:* verse translation of Lessing's Nathan der Weise, with introductory essay, 1883. *Address:* Rock House, Boughton Monchelsea, Kent. *Club:* New University.
Died 21 March 1920.

CORBET, Hon. Frederick Hugh Mackenzie; HM's Advocate-General for the Presidency of Madras since 1912; *b* Barcelona, 17 July 1862; 2nd *s* of Reginald John Corbet, JP, MLC, Ceylon; and *g s* of Sir Andrew Corbet, 2nd Bt, of Moreton-Corbet; *m* 1893, Eila, *e d* of Sir George W. R. Campbell, KCMG; one *d* (and two *s* decd). *Educ:* Ceylon; privately; special attention to law and modern languages. Was granted Letters Patent of Venia Ætatis, 1879; Private Secretary to Hon. Mr Justice Lawrie, 1885, 1886, and 1888; Librarian of Colombo Museum, 1886–93; Acting Secretary of Central Irrigation Board, Ceylon, 1890–91; resigned salaried Government employment (services acknowledged by Secretary of State for the Colonies), 1893; Hon. Executive Officer and Home Agent of the Government of Ceylon at the Imperial Institute, 1893–1904; Secretary of the Royal Commission on the Church of England and other Religious Bodies in Wales and Monmouthshire, 1909–11; Hon. Secretary of Ceylon General Committee for Paris Exposition, 1889; Member of Council, and successively Hon. Sec. and Hon. Treas. of Ceylon Branch, Royal Asiatic Society, 1887–93; Delegate to International Congress of Orientalists, London, 1891. Barrister-at-Law, Gray's Inn, 1897; practised in England, mainly before the Privy Council, until 1912; Chairman and Director of several South African and other Companies, 1895–1912; Member of Committee or Council of several Societies; President of Hardwicke Society, 1902–3; Jubilee Gold Medal of Ceylon, 1897. *Publications:* various official Reports, etc; Introduction to Ceylon portion of The Golden Book of India, 1900; The Laws of the Empire, 1901. *Address:* College Bridge House, Egmore, Madras; 5 Pump Court, Temple, EC. *T:* City 8870.
Died 1 Dec. 1916.

CORBETT, Edward, JP; *b* 1843; *e s* of late Lieut-Col Edward Corbett, of Longnor Bank and of Aldershaw, Staffordshire, and Elizabeth Ann Teresa, *d* of late Robert Scholl; *m* 1871, Louisa Mary, *e d* of Sir Charles Isham, 10th Bt; one *s. Educ:* Cheltenham; RMC, Sandhurst. Formerly Lieut 17th Lancers, and Captain, Shropshire YC; Patron of 1 living. *Address:* Longnor Bank, Shrewsbury. *Club:* Junior Carlton.
Died 1918.

CORBETT, Rev. Frederick St John, MA; FRSL; Rector of St George in the East and Vicar of St Matthew's Pell Street, since 1903; Founder of Church of England Guild of Sponsors, 1911; *b* Dublin, 1862; 2nd *s* of John Corbett, MA, LLD, member of the Senate of Trinity College, Dublin, and Susanna Jane, *d* of William Richard Manderson of Dublin; *m* Elsie Lucy Victoire, *e d* of Rev. Edmund A. Askew, MA, Trinity College, Cambridge, Rector of Greystoke, Cumberland, and Hon. Canon of Carlisle Cathedral; two *s* two *d. Educ:* Trinity College, Dublin; BA 1884; MA 1887. Deacon, 1885; Priest, 1887; Curate of Hunslet, Leeds, 1885–91; Chaplain to the Leeds Rifles, 1886–93; Curate of St Michael's, Chester Square, 1891–96; Rector of Long Marton, 1896–1903; Chaplain to the High Sheriff of Westmorland, 1901; Dean of Sion College and Lord of the Manor of Bradwell in Essex, 1917; a Freemason—nominated Assistant Grand Chaplain of Cumberland and Westmorland, 1903; Governor East London Hospital for Children, 1905; Chairman of Managers, LCC Schools (St George's Group), 1905–9; Representative Manager for Church Schools and Member of Advisory Committee, 1916; Surrogate for the Diocese of London, and the Master of the Faculties, and the Vicar-General of the Province of Canterbury, 1909; Chaplain to the Territorial Force, 1911 (Hon. Lt-Col 1917); Commissary in England to the Bishop of the Falkland Isles, 1913–15; Pioneer of Church Finance Reform. Fellow of the Royal Society of Literature, 1903; Member of the Council, 1904–11; Fellow of the Royal Historical Society, 1904–13. *Publications:* The Preacher's Year; Sermon Outlines; Echoes of the Sanctuary; The Problem of Life, Led by a Little Child, 1906; Two Men and a Girl; A Thousand Things to Say in Sermons, 1906; Life: from a Parson's Point of View; A History of British Poetry from the Earliest Times to the Beginning of the Twentieth Century; The Communicants' Little Book; The

Poet of the Church of England: a Tribute to George Herbert; Church Finance Reform, Its Need and Possibilities; A Thousand Thoughts for Practical Preachers; Editor: The Service of Perfect Freedom, etc. *Recreations:* cycling, boating, swimming. *Address:* The Rectory, St George in the East, E1; Elm Grove, Ruislip. *TA:* Rector, Cannon Street Road.
Died March 1919.

CORBETT, Rev. John Reginald; Rector of Wanstead, Essex, since 1907; Hon. Canon of St Albans since 1897, of Chelmsford, 1914; *b* New Ross, Co. Wexford, 1844; *s* of Rev. John Corbett, MA, Dublin. *Educ:* King's School, Canterbury; Magdalen Hall, Oxford (Scholar). Curate of Barking, Essex; Vicar of St Botolph's, Colchester, 1870–1907; Rural Dean of Colchester, 1897–1907; Rural Dean of Wanstead and Woodford, 1919. *Address:* The Rectory, Wanstead, E11. *T:* Wanstead 417.
Died 28 Nov. 1920.

CORBETT, Sir Julian Stafford, Kt 1917; LLM; FSA; Barrister-at-law; Hon. Fellow of Trinity College, Cambridge; Director of Historical Section, Committee of Imperial Defence; *b* 12 Nov. 1854; 2nd *s* of late Chas J. Corbett, FRAS, Imber Court, Surrey; *m* 1899, Edith, *o d* of George Alexander; one *s* one *d. Educ:* Marlborough; Trinity College, Cambridge. 1st class Law Tripos, 1876; Barrister (Middle Temple), 1877; practised till 1882; special correspondent to Pall Mall Gazette, Dongola Expedition, 1896; Ford Lecturer in English History (Oxford), 1903; Lecturer in History to the Naval War College; Chesney Gold Medal, 1914. *Publications:* Romances—The Fall of Asgard; For God and Gold; Kophetua XIII; A Business in Great Waters, etc: monographs on Monk and Drake (English Men of Action): Drake and the Tudor Navy; The Successors of Drake; England in the Mediterranean; Fighting Instructions, 1530–1816; England in the Seven Years' War; Signals and Instructions, 1778–94; The Campaign of Trafalgar, 1910; Some Principles of Maritime Strategy, 1911; The Spencer Papers (1794–1801), 1913–14; Official History of the Great War Naval Operations, 1920. *Recreations:* sport, travel. *Address:* 3 Hans Crescent, SW. *T:* Victoria 42. *Clubs:* Athenæum, Ranelagh.
Died 21 Sept. 1922.

CORBY, Henry, BA, MD; Professor of Obstetrics and Gynæcology, University College, Cork; Member of Council British Medical Association; Consulting Physician, Cork Maternity Hospital; Surgeon, South Infirmary and County Hospital. *Educ:* Queen's College, Cork. High Sheriff, Cork, 1904; ex-President Incorporated Medical Practitioners' Assoc., and Cork Medical and Surgical Society; ex-Vice-President Cork Scientific Society; ex-Member of Council Cork Literary and Scientific Society; ex-Vice-President School Section Royal Institute of Public Health. *Publications:* Some Experiences of a House Surgeon; Healthy Homes; Industry and Ability; Technical Education; Bacteria the Foes and Friends of Man; Some Medical Aspects of School Life. *Address:* 19 St Patrick's Place, Cork. *TA:* Cork. *T:* X 26.
Died April 1917.

CORDER, Lt-Col Arthur Annerley, CMG 1916; OBE 1919; attached RAOC. Served European War, 1914–18 (despatches four times, CMG, OBE). *Address:* Glendoon, Havant, Hants.
Died 4 April 1923.

CORELLI, Marie; novelist; *b* 1855; of mingled Italian and Scotch (Highland) parentage and connections; adopted in infancy by Charles Mackay, the well-known song-writer and *littérateur*, and brought up during childhood in England. Afterwards sent to France and educated in a convent, where she received, with other instruction, a first-class musical training. Her first book, A Romance of Two Worlds, was an instant success, and from that time she devoted herself entirely to literature. *Recreations:* reading, music. *Publications:* A Romance of Two Worlds, 1886; Vendetta, 1886; Thelma, 1887; Ardath, 1889; Soul of Lilith, 1892; Barabbas, 1893; The Sorrows of Satan, 1895; Mighty Atom, 1896; The Murder of Delicia, 1896; Ziska: the Problem of a Wicked Soul, 1897; Jane, 1897; Boy, 1900; The Master Christian, 1900; Temporal Power, A Study in Supremacy, 1902; God's Good Man, 1904; Free Opinions, 1905; The Treasure of Heaven, 1906; Holy Orders, 1908; The Devil's Motor, 1910; The Life Everlasting, 1911; Innocent, Her Fancy and His Fact, 1914; The Young Diana, 1917; My Little Bit, a Record of War Work, 1919; The Love of Long Ago, 1920; The Secret Power, 1921. *Address:* Mason Croft, Stratford-on-Avon.
Died 21 April 1924.

CORFE, Rt. Rev. Charles John, DD; *b* 1843; *s* of C. W. Corfe, MusD Oxford; unmarried. *Educ:* All Souls Coll., Oxford (MA 1869). Ordained 1866; Chaplain RN 1867–89; Bishop of Church of England in Corea, 1889–1904; resigned, 1904. Served HMS "Victor Emanuel", Ashanti War, 1874 (medal). *Address:* Church House, Westminster, SW.
Died 30 June 1921.

CORFIELD, Rev. Claud Evelyn Lacey, MA; Rector of Heanor, 1886–1911; Prebendary of Wells Cathedral, 1919; Vicar of Taunton since 1911; *s* of Rev. Frederick Corfield, JP, Domestic Chaplain to Lord Claremont; *m* 1906, Hon. Mary Hay Burns, 3rd *d* of 1st Baron Inverclyde, *widow* of the Rev. E. Murray Robinson, and patroness of Merton, Surrey; one *d. Educ:* Trent College, Derbyshire; St Catharine's College, Cambridge (BA 1877; 1st Class Theology, MA, 1881). Ordained, 1880; Curate at Parish Church, Plymouth; Senior Curate, Rotherham Parish Church; Vicar of Shirley, Derbyshire, 1883. Hon. Canon of Southwell, 1910–11; Proctor in Convocation for Diocese of Bath and Wells, 1925. *Address:* The Vicarage, Taunton.
Died 3 June 1926.

CORK and ORRERY, 10th Earl of, *cr* 1620; **Charles Spencer Canning Boyle;** Baron Boyle of Youghall, 1616; Viscount Dungarvan, 1620; Viscount Kinalmeaky, Baron Broghill and Bandon Bridge (Ireland), 1628; Earl of Orrery, 1660; Baron Boyle of Marston, 1711; DL; *b* 24 Nov. 1861; *e s* of 9th Earl of Cork and Emily, 2nd *d* of 1st Marquis of Clanricarde; *S* father, 1904; *m* 1918, Rosalie, *d* of late William Waterman de Villiers of Romsey, Hants. Lt–Col North Somerset Yeomanry; served South Africa, 1900–1. Protestant. Unionist. Possessed the historical Orrery Jewel, connected with the accession of James I. *Heir: b* Hon. Robert Lascelles Boyle, *b* 8 Nov. 1864. *Address:* 56 Pont Street, SW1. *T:* Kensington 3891. *Clubs:* White's, Garrick, Beefsteak; Royal Yacht Squadron, Cowes.
Died 25 March 1925.

CORKE, Sir John Henry, Kt 1916; KLH; JP; four times Mayor of Portsmouth. Took an active part in recruiting, and raised three battalions for the Hampshire Regt. *Address:* 6 Alhambra Road, Southsea.
Died 3 Jan. 1927.

CORKRAN, Alice; journalist, etc; *b* Paris; *d* of J. Frazer Corkran, journalist and man of letters. *Educ:* home, especially in Paris. Sometime Editor, Girl's Realm, and The Bairn's Annual. *Publications:* Bessie Lang, 1876; Latheby Towers, 1879; Down the Snow Stairs; Marjery Merton's Girlhood, 1887; Mag's Friend; Young Philistine; Life of Lord Leighton; The Romance of Woman's Influence; The National Gallery; The Dawn of British History, etc. *Recreations:* chess, sketching from nature. *Address:* 47 Walpole Road, Boscombe, Hants.
Died 2 Feb. 1916.

CORNABY, Rev. William Arthur; China Missionary; *b* 1860; *m* 1st, Margaret (*d* 1915), *d* of late George Baker; three *s* one *d*; 2nd, Emma, *d* of late G. Foggitt; one *s. Educ:* Sydenham Grammar School; School of Mines, SW; Wesleyan Coll., Richmond. Assistant teacher of chemistry, Clifton Coll., 1881–83; Wesleyan Mission, Hankow, 1885–1903; on the editorial staff of the Christian Literature Society since 1899; resident in Shanghai, 1904–11; founding and editing the Ta Tung Pao magazine for Chinese officials and scholars; Wesleyan Mission, Hupeh, 1912. *Publications:* A String of Chinese Peach-Stones, 1898; China under the Searchlight, 1901; In Touch with Reality, 1905; China and its People (Madras), Let us Pray, The Call of Cathay, 1910; Prayer and the Human Problem, 1912; Chinese Letter-writing (Shanghai), 1914; also ten works in Chinese. *Recreations:* music, photography, drawing, gardening. *Address:* Hanyang, China.
Died 11 March 1921.

CORNEY, Bolton Glanvill, ISO 1904; MRCS (Eng.), FRGS; late Member Legislative Council and Chief Medical Officer, Fiji; *b* Barnes, Surrey, 1851; *s* of Bolton Corney, MRSL, and Henrietta Mary, *d* of Vice-Admiral Pridham, RN. *Educ:* privately, in France, England, and Germany; St Thomas's Hospital. Fellow of the Royal Society of Medicine and Royal Colonial Institute; Member of Council of the Royal Geographical Society, that of the Hakluyt Society; and that of the Society for Nautical Research; Surgeon Superintendent of Melanesian immigrants, Fiji, 1876; Colonial Surgeon, Fiji, 1877; Acting Chief Medical Officer, 1882–83; appointed Official Delegate from Fiji on Australasian Sanitary Conference, Sydney, 1884; Acting Agent-General of Immigration, 1885–87; Member Native Regulation Board, Member Legislative Council, 1885; Chief Medical Officer, 1887; Superintendent Public Lunatic Asylum, 1887–1903; Acting Receiver-General, 1892, and Member Executive Council; a Commissioner to inquire into decrease of native population; Chairman of same Commission, and joint author of Report, 1893; Commissioner to investigate misgovernment of Tailevu province by native Chief, 1895; a Commissioner of Customs; Pres. of Board of Health (Fiji); Governor's Deputy to visit the Leper Asylum; retired, 1908. *Publications:* Hakluyt Society's vols xiii, xxxii, xxxvi, xliii (Series II); in Transactions of the Epidemiological Society of London—(On Epidemic Diseases in Polynesia, 1884; On Epidemic Cerebro-Spinal Meningitis; On Dengue; Folk Lore Society—On Leprosy Stones,

1896; contributions to the Lancet, Geographical Journal, etc. *Address:* c/o Coutts & Co., 440 Strand, WC2.
Died 29 Sept. 1924.

CORNFORD, Leslie Cope; *s* of Rev. James Cornford and Emily, *d* of C. W. Cope, RA; *m* Christabel, 7th *d* of Philip Henry Lawrence; two *s. Educ:* privately. Naval Correspondent to the Morning Post during European War. *Publications:* R. L. Stevenson, 1899; English Composition, 1900; Essay-writing for Schools, 1903; Parson Brand, 1906; Troubled Waters, 1911; W. E. Henley, 1913; editor Memoirs Admiral Lord Charles Beresford, 1914; Echoes from the Fleet; Lord High Admiral, 1915; Secret of Consolation, 1915; The Merchant Seaman in War, 1918; The British Navy: the Navy Vigilant, 1918; The Paravane Adventure, 1919; Interpretations, 1926. *Address:* 9 Stone Buildings, Lincoln's Inn, WC.
Died 4 Aug. 1927.

CORNISH, Rev. Ebenezer Darrel; President of the United Methodist Free Churches, 1898; Chapel Secretary, United Methodist Church, 1910; *b* Exeter, 7 March 1849; *s* of John Lawrence Cornish of Launceston; *m* Charlotte Screen, Exeter; three *d. Educ:* Hele's School, Exeter. Assistant Master Hele's School; then engaged in business in London; entered the Ministry, 1869; Secretary of Conference, 1895–98; elected President, 1898; elected Chapel Secretary, 1902. *Publications:* sundry articles in various magazines. *Recreation:* chess. *Address:* 7 Northumberland Street, Higher Broughton, Manchester.
Died 26 Oct. 1922.

CORNISH, Francis Warre, MA; Vice-Provost of Eton College, 1893–1916; *b* 8 May 1839; *s* of Rev. H. K. Cornish, Fellow of Exeter Coll., Oxford, Vicar of Bakewell, and Louisa, *d* of Rev. F. Warre, DCL, Rector of Cheddon Fitzpaine, Somerset, and Hemyock, Devon; *m* 1866, Blanche, *d* of late Hon. W. Ritchie, Legal Member of Council in India. *Educ:* Foundation, Eton College; King's College, Cambridge (Fellow). Battie University Scholarship; 3rd in 1st class of Classical Tripos, 1861. Asst master at Eton College, 1861–93. *Publications:* Life of Oliver Cromwell; Sunningwell; Darwell Stories; Dr Ashford, etc; Chivalry; articles in periodicals. *Address:* Cloisters, Eton College. *Club:* Athenæum.
Died 28 Aug. 1916.

CORNISH, Rt. Rev. John Rundle, DD; Bishop of St Germans since 1905 (Suffragan to Truro); Archdeacon of Cornwall, 1888–1916; *b* Tavistock, 7 Oct. 1837; *m* 1874, Constance Eliza, *d* of C. Barham, MD, of Truro; one *s* one *d. Educ:* Bideford Grammar School; Sidney Sussex College, Cambridge; Fellow, Dean, and Taylor Lecturer of Sidney Sussex College; 14th Wrangler in 1859. Vicar of St John's, Kenwyn, of Veryan, and of Kenwyn; Principal Truro Training College; Examining Chaplain to Bishops Benson, Wilkinson, Gott, Stubbs, and Burrows; Select Preacher at Cambridge, 1894–1907; Vicar of Kenwyn, 1883–1916. *Address:* Truro. *TA:* Truro.
Died 20 April 1918.

CORRIE, Major Alfred Wynne, JP, DL; *b* 1856; 4th *s* of late John Malcolm Corrie, of Itchen Abbas, Hants, and Fanny, *d* of late William Wynne of Itchen Abbas; *m* 1st, 1886, Charlotte Anne (*d* 1913), *o d* and *heiress* of late Jacob Fletcher-Fletcher, of Peel Hall, Lancashire; 2nd, 1916, Mary Constance, *e d* of George Butler Lloyd; one *s. Educ:* Charterhouse. High Sheriff, Shropshire, 1909; Major, Assistant Commandant, Royal Defence Corps, Western Command; Major Shropshire Imperial Yeomanry, 1901; Mayor of Oswestry, 1889–93 (freedom of Borough). *Address:* Park Hall, Oswestry; Swan Hill House, Shrewsbury. *Clubs:* Marlborough, Carlton.
Died 4 April 1919.

CORRY, Sir William, 2nd Bt, *cr* 1885; Director Cunard Line, and Commonwealth and Dominion-Line, Ltd; *b* 20 March 1859; *s* of Sir James Porter Corry, 1st Bt and Margaret, *d* of William Service, Glasgow; *S* father, 1891; *m* 1889, Charlotte (*d* 1896), *d* of late J. Collins; two *s* one *d. Heir: s* James Perowne Ivo Myles Corry [*b* 10 June 1892; *m* 1921, Molly Irene, *y d* of Major O. J. Bell. *Educ:* Eton; Trinity Coll., Cambridge]. *Recreations:* yachting, billiards, golf. *Address:* 118 Eaton Square, SW1. *T:* Victoria 6297; Claremont, Esher. *Club:* Junior Carlton.
Died 9 June 1926.

CORSTORPHINE, George Steuart; *b* 1868; *e s* of John Corstorphine, Edinburgh; *m* 1896, Clara Ursula, 2nd *d* of George Hoffmann, Munich; one *d. Educ:* Universities of Edinburgh and Munich. Baxter Scholar in Natural Science, Edinburgh University, 1892; Falconer Fellow in Geology and Palæontology, 1892–95; Assistant to Dr James Geikie, Murchisonian Professor of Geology, Edinburgh, 1892–94; appointed Professor of Geology and Mineralogy, South African College, and Keeper of Geological Department, South African Museum, Cape Town, 1895; Director Geological Survey of the Cape Colony, 1896–1902; Consulting Geologist, Consolidated Gold Fields of South Africa, Ltd, 1902–8; in private practice, 1908–12; Principal, South African School of Mines and Technology, 1913; President, Geological Society of South Africa, 1906, Hon. Sec., 1910–15. *Publications:* Dissertation; Die Massengesteine des südlichen Teiles der Insel Arran, Wien, 1895; Annual Reports of Geological Survey of Cape Colony for 1896–1901; Papers in Trans. Geol. Society South Africa; also in Rep. South African Association Advancement of Science, 1904; co-author with Dr F. H. Hatch of The Geology of South Africa, 1905. *Address:* Box 1758 and Ravensworth, Yeo Street, Johannesburg. *TA:* University. *T:* (Office) 2318; (Residence) Yeoville 1096. *Club:* Rand, Johannesburg.

Died 25 Jan. 1919.

CORTIE, Rev. Father Aloysius Laurence, SJ; FRAS, FInstP; Dr Univ. Padua; FRMetS; Director of the Stonyhurst College Observatory; *b* London, 22 April 1859. *Educ:* Stonyhurst Coll.; St Beuno's Coll., N Wales. Entered novitiate SJ, 1878; priest, 1892; studied astronomy under the late Father Perry, SJ, FRS, and attached to Stonyhurst Observatory since 1881; FRAS 1891, and served for many years on the Council; Director of the Solar Section British Astronomical Association, 1900–10; President Manchester Astronomical Society since 1911; directed an expedition to observe total solar eclipse at Vinaroz, Spain, 1905; and the Government expeditions to the Tonga Islands, S Pacific, 1911, and to Hernösand, Sweden, 1914; distinguished in solar and stellar physics and in terrestrial magnetism; taught physics and mathematics at Stonyhurst for twenty-seven years, and director of music for nineteen years; a Gilchrist lecturer. *Publications:* numerous memoirs and papers on astrophysics and terrestrial magnetism; Memoirs and Monthly Notices RAS, the Astrophysical Journal; Memoirs and Journal, BAA, Reports of British Association. *Recreations:* music, golf. *Address:* Stonyhurst College, Blackburn. *TA:* Stonyhurst.

Died 16 May 1925.

CORYNDON, Sir Robert (Thorne), KCMG 1919 (CMG 1911); Governor and Commander-in-Chief, Kenya, and High Commissioner of Zanzibar since 1922; *b* Queenstown, Cape Colony, 2 April, 1870; *s* of Selby Coryndon of Plymouth; *m* 1909, Phyllis Mary, *d* of late J. C. Worthington; three *s* one *d. Educ:* Cheltenham College. Joined Bechuanaland Border Police, under BSA Co., 9 Nov. 1889, and the Pioneer force for the occupation of Mashonaland, June 1890–91; private Secretary to the Rt Hon. C. J. Rhodes, 1896–97, and during Parliamentary Inquiry into Jameson Raid; served in Matabele War, 1893, and Matabele rebellion, 1896 (medal and clasp); British Resident with Lewanika, and BSA Co's Representative in Barotseland, June 1897; took expedn to Lealui, Upper Zambesi river, 1897; Administrator of North-Western Rhodesia, Sept. 1900; Resident Commissioner for Swaziland 1907–16; Basutoland, 1916; Governor and Comdr-in-Chief, Uganda, 1917–22; Chairman of the S Rhodesia Native Reserves Commission, 1914–15. Commander, Crown of Belgium. *Address:* Government House, Nairobi, Kenya. *Clubs:* Travellers', Athenæum.

Died 10 Feb. 1925.

CORYTON, Frederick, JP; MFH; Joint-Master of the Hampshire pack, 1888–1909; Lord of the Manor of Greatham; *b* 1 March 1850; *s* of late George Edward Coryton, JP, of Liss Place, Hants; *m* 1888, Augusta, *d* of late Richard Manders of Shanganagh, Co. Dublin; one *s* two *d. Educ:* Harrow. *Address:* The Manor House, Greatham, Liss, Hants.

Died 12 Nov. 1924.

CORYTON, William; JP, DL, Cornwall; country gentleman, landowner; Master of Dartmoor Foxhounds, 1889–1916; Sheriff of Cornwall, 1902; *b* Hampshire, 30 Oct. 1847; *e s* of George Edward Coryton of Liss Place, Hants (*d* 1886), and of Mary Louisa Phillott, *d* of Rev. Phillott (*d* 1884); *m* 1887, E. A. Parker, *d* of Admiral Parker, Delamore, South Devon; three *s* three *d. Educ:* private school and tutors. Paid much attention to farming; had a very large dairy farm; took his pack of beagles from Hampshire to Cornwall in 1868; substituted harriers and eventually foxhounds in 1875, hunting the E Cornwall country at his own expense for fourteen years. *Address:* Pentillie Castle, St Mellion, RSO, E Cornwall. *M:* AF 460 and 912. *Clubs:* Boodle's; Royal Western Yacht.

Died 27 Aug. 1919.

COSBY, Dudley Sydney Ashworth, DL; FRAS; *b* 12 Jan. 1862; *o surv. s* of late Col R. A. G. Cosby and Alice Sophia Elizabeth (*d* 1878), *o d* of Sir George Edward Pocock, 2nd Bt; *m* 1895, Emily Mabel (*d* 1918), *o c* of Lt-Gen. James Gubbins, CB; three *s* two *d. Educ:* Eton. Late Lieut of the Rifle Brigade, and Capt. 4th Scottish Rifles; served European War on the Cable Censorship—Military Intelligence

Department, 13 March 1916–22 May 1918. *Publications:* The Irish Land Problem, and How to Solve it, 1901; The Menace of Socialism (two editions); Why England needs an Upper Chamber: A Defence of the House of Lords, 1908; Fair Trade *v* Free Trade: Cobden's Unrealised Ideal, 1909; King Edward VII: the Passing of a Great Ruler, 1910; The Governance of Empire: Forward but Not Too Fast, 1911; German Kultur: What Is It?; Towards Universal Peace, 1915; many articles to reviews and letters to the Press. *Address:* Stradbally Hall, Queen's Co.; Westcliff Lodge, West Bournemouth. *Club:* Naval and Military.

Died 23 Dec. 1923.

COSBY, Col Robert Ashworth Godolphin, JP, DL; head of Cosby family; *b* 1837; *o s* of late Sydney Cosby, and Emily, *d* of late Robert Ashworth; *m* 1st, 1859, Alice Sophia Elizabeth (*d* 1878), *o d* of Sir George Edward Pocock, 2nd Bt; 2nd, 1885, Eliza (*d* 1920), *d* of Rev. Capel Molyneux, and *widow* of Sir Charles Goring, 11th Bt. *Educ:* Eton. Vice-Lieut of Queen's Co.; High Sheriff, 1863; Hon. Col 3rd Batt. Leinster Regt; late Lieut 6th Dragoons. *Address:* Stradbally Hall, Queen's Co. *Clubs:* Wellington, Army and Navy; Kildare Street, Dublin.

Died 29 Aug. 1920.

COSGRAVE, MacDowel, MD Dublin; MRIA; late Physician in Ordinary to Lord Lieutenant of Ireland; Knight of Grace, Order of St John of Jerusalem; Professor of Biology, Royal College of Surgeons; Physician to Drumcondra and Simpson's Hospitals; *s* of late Wm A. Cosgrave, Corrstown House, Co. Dublin, Clerk of the Peace for County Longford; *m* Anna (*d* 1920), *d* of late Rev. Wm Crofts Bullen, Ballythomas, Co. Cork; (she was author of "Life Studies in Palmistry" and of papers on Poor Law Reform). *Educ:* Kingstown School; Dublin University. Practised first at Huddersfield, then at Colchester, where founded a branch of the SII Ambulance Association; returning to Dublin joined the College of Physicians, being President 1914–16, during which time was one of founders of Dublin Castle Red Cross Hospital and Chairman of Irish Medical War Committee; was Hon. Sec. to Dublin Sanitary Association, and member of Council, Royal Society of Antiquaries of Ireland, of which was elected Fellow in 1908; was for eight years Hon. Treasurer Royal Zoological Society of Ireland; founded the Georgian Society, 1909–13, and acted as Hon. Secretary and member of Editorial Committee. *Publications:* Hints and Helps for Home Nursing and Hygiene; The Student's Botany; Photography and Architecture; The Illustrated Dictionary of Dublin; Dublin and the Co. Dublin in the Nineteenth Century; Catalogue of Engravings of Dublin; Alcohol and Longevity; The Role of Alcohol; Book-plates of Irish Medical Men; edited Commonsense, 1893–1901. *Recreations:* photography; collecting Dublin prints and book-plates. *Address:* 5 Gardiner Row, Dublin. *T:* Dublin 2191. *M:* RI 8850.

Died 16 Feb. 1925.

COSTIGAN, Captain Charles Telford, DSO 1915; 10th Battalion Canadian 1st Division; *s* of Thomas John Costigan; unmarried. *Educ:* Halbrake College. Came over to Europe with 1st Canadian Division, 1914; Field Cashier; transferred to 10th Batt., 1915; 64th Regt Canadian Militia; served European War, 1914–16 (despatches, DSO); led a bombing party at Messines. *Address:* Calgary, Alberta, Canada.

Died Nov. 1917.

COSTIGAN, Senator Hon. John, PC; MP Victoria, New Brunswick; *b* St Nicholas, Province of Quebec, 1 Feb. 1835, of Irish parentage; *m* 1855, Harriet S. Ryan of Victoria, NB; one *s* two *d. Educ:* provincial schools; St Anne's College, Province of Quebec. Appointed Registrar of Deeds and Wills for Victoria County, New Brunswick, 1858; resigned 1861, to accept the candidature for that county in the general elections for the Legislature of New Brunswick; was elected and continued to represent Victoria in the NB Legislature until the election just previous to the Confederation, when, though duly elected by a majority, he authorised the Returning Officer to declare his opponent elected, to prevent a grave and serious riot; in 1867, at the first general election for the Federal House of Commons was elected to represent the said County of Victoria, NB, and elected at every general election since, the only member of the House of Commons that held his seat continuously from confederation; Minister of Inland Revenue, 1882–92; Secretary of State, 1892–94; Minister of Marine and Fisheries, 1894–96; called to the Senate, 1907. *Recreations:* for the last forty-eight years spent from four to ten weeks each year in the Canadian forests, which contributed to his good health and enabled him to acquire valuable information regarding the interior of Canada. *Address:* 152 Carling Ave, Ottawa, Ontario.

Died 1 Oct. 1916.

COTES, Sir Merton Russell, Kt 1909; JP; FRGS; art connoisseur and collector; *b* Tettenhall, near Wolverhampton, 8 May 1835; *m* 1860, Annie Nelson (*d* 1920), *o d* of John King Clark, WS, Glasgow; one

s. Educ: Old College, High Street, Glasgow. Resided in Bournemouth since 1876, and took an active part in developing the town, mainly responsible for the construction of the Undercliff Drive and Promenade, the Sanitary Hospital, etc; projected the idea of the direct line between Christchurch and Brockenhurst on the L&SWR; Member of the local Board of Improvement Commissioners prior to the incorporation of Bournemouth, 1890, when he presented the mace—a replica of that presented to Wolverhampton by Queen Elizabeth; invited to fill the Mayoral Chair in 1892 and 1893, but declined on account of ill-health; Mayor of Bournemouth, 1894–95; during his Mayoralty the Meyrick Park was opened, also two free libraries, and the two first schools of art in the borough; for upwards of thirty-five years his loan collection of about 250 pictures was exhibited in the Corporation Art Galleries of Liverpool, Leeds, Sheffield, Bradford, Nottingham, Derby, Glasgow, Bath, Oldham, Burnley, and other cities, and many of his pictures were borrowed for exhibition in Chicago Exhibition, the Guildhall (London), the People's Palace (Whitechapel), the Grafton Gallery; through Mr Choate (when American Ambassador to England) he presented to the American people an original black basalt bust of Washington made by Josiah Wedgwood, which is now in the Congressional Library, Washington; travelled with his wife in many parts of the world, including South America, Australia, New Zealand, Canada, United States of America, South and North Africa, West Indies, China, Japan, Egypt, Palestine, Syria, Turkey, Russia, Sweden and Norway, Finland, Spain, and generally the European continent; explored and wrote a paper on the volcano of Mauna Loa and the great crater of Kilauea, Hawaii; explored the Pink and White Terraces, etc, New Zealand; in conjunction with his wife gave to the Borough of Bournemouth their residence East Cliff Hall and its art treasures, to become the Russell-Cotes Art Gallery and Museum, in recognition of which they were presented with the honorary freedom of the borough, 15 July 1908. *Recreations*: art, music, foreign travel, exploration. *Address:* East Cliff Hall, Bournemouth. *Clubs:* United Empire, Constitutional.
Died 27 Jan. 1921.

COTES, Sara Jeannette, (Mrs Everard Cotes); *b* Brantford, Canada, 1861; *d* of Charles Duncan, merchant; *m* 1891, Everard Cotes. *Educ:* Brantford chiefly. Began literary work as a correspondent, and later joined the editorial staff of the Washington Post; afterwards became attached to the Toronto Globe and Week, and later to the Montreal Star as writer of special articles, which included the letters from Japan and the East, afterwards rewritten for A Social Departure. *Publications:* A Social Departure, 1890; An American Girl in London, 1891; The Simple Adventures of a Memsahib, 1893; Vernon's Aunt; The Story of Sonny Sahib; A Daughter of To-Day, 1894; His Honour and a Lady, 1896; A Voyage of Consolation, 1898; The Path of a Star, 1899; On the Other Side of the Latch, 1901; Those Delightful Americans, 1902; The Pool in the Desert, 1903; The Imperialist, 1904; Set in Authority, 1906; Cinderella of Canada, 1908; The Burnt Offering, 1909; The Consort, 1912; His Royal Happiness, 1915. *Address:* 17 Paultons Square, Chelsea, SW3. *Club:* Ladies' Empire.
Died 22 July 1922.

COTMAN, Frederic George, RI; *b* 14 Aug. 1850; *s* of Henry Cotman; *y b* of John Sell Cotman; *m* 1875, *d* of late B. Grahame of Morphie, Kincardineshire; three *s* three *d*. *Educ:* Ipswich; admitted student Royal Academy, 1868; gold medal for historical painting, 1873. *Recreation:* boating. *Address:* Whitegates, Felixstowe.
Died 16 July 1920.

COTTELL, Col Reginald James Cope, CBE 1919; late RAMC; *b* 1858; 4th *s* of late Major James W. Cottell, HEICS, and Elizabeth Ann, *e d* of late Rev. Edward Warren Caulfeild, MA; *m* 1899, Edith Clementina, *d* of James Ruthven; three *d*. Entered Army, 1886; Major, 1898; Lt-Col 1906; retired, 1913; served in Gibraltar, 1888–94; S Africa, 1897–1902; during the S African War was in medical charge of the 2nd Royal Berkshire Regt and secondly of the Medical Division of No 7 General Hospital, Pretoria (Queen's medal three clasps, King's medal two clasps, officially thanked for war services by the Commander-in-Chief); subsequently was medical officer to the Royal Military Academy, Woolwich, and afterwards was physician and surgeon for seven years to the Royal Hospital, Chelsea; volunteered for service and rejoined Army 5 Aug. 1914; was officer commanding the King George Hospital, Stamford Street, SE, Aug. 1915–Sept. 1919 (mentioned for valuable medical services 1917; promoted Brevet-Colonel, 1918, CBE). Knight of Grace of the Order of St John of Jerusalem. *Address:* 7 Phillimore Terrace, Kensington, WS.
Died 7 Aug. 1924.

COTTENHAM, 4th Earl of, *cr* 1850; **Kenelm Charles Edward Pepys;** Bt 1784 and 1801; Baron Cottenham (UK), 1836; Viscount

Crowhurst, 1850; late MFH Bicester and Warden Hill; *b* 18 May 1874; *s* of 3rd Earl and Theodosia Selina, *o d* of Sir Robert E. Dallas, 2nd Bt; *S* father, 1881; *m* 1st, 1899, Lady Rose Nevill (*d* 1913), *d* of 1st Marquess of Abergavenny; three *s*; 2nd, 1916, Patricia, *d* of late John Humphrey Burke, California. *Educ:* Eton; Oxford. Owned about 6,000 acres. *Heir:* *s* Viscount Crowhurst, *b* 13 May 1901. *Address:* Clare Priory, Suffolk. *Clubs:* Carlton, Marlborough.
Died 22 April 1919.

COTTENHAM, 5th Earl of, *cr* 1850; **Kenelm Charles Francis Pepys;** Bt 1784 and 1801; Baron Cottenham (UK) 1836; Viscount Crowhurst, 1850; *b* 13 May 1901; *s* of 4th Earl and Lady Rose Nevill (*d* 1913), *d* of 1st Marquess of Abergavenny; *S* father, 1919. *Educ:* Eton; Oxford. Owned about 6,000 acres. *Heir:* *b* Hon. Mark Everard Pepys, *b* 29 May 1903. *Address:* 2 Southwell Gardens, SW7.
Died 29 Dec. 1922.

COTTER, Maj.-Gen. Francis Gibson; *b* 12 June 1857; *s* of late Maj. J. Cotter; *m* 1891, Rose, *d* of Rev. Anson Cartwright; one *d*. Entered Royal Marines, 1876; Captain, 1885; Major, 1893; Lt-Col 1900; Col 1908; served Soudan, 1884–85.
Died 24 Sept. 1928.

COTTER, Lt-Col Harry John, CIE 1918; DSO 1916; RA; *b* 10 May 1871; *s* of Major John Cotter, the Buffs; *m* Alice Elizabeth, *d* of Rev. G. Armitage; one *s*. *Educ:* Kelly College, Tavistock; RMA Woolwich. Served Isazai Expedition, 1892; Chitral, 1895 (medal and clasp); China, 1900 (medal); European War (CIE, DSO). Serbian Order of the White Eagle, 4th class.
Died July 1921.

COTTER, Sir James Laurence, 5th Bt, *cr* 1763; FRHS, FNCS; NRS; *b* 11 July 1887; *s* of late James Lombard Cotter, 2nd *s* of 4th Bt, and Clara Mary, *d* of late Capt. Thomas Segrave [she *m* 2nd, John Francis O'Connor]; *S* grandfather, 1902; *m* 1908, Ethel Lucy (who obtained a divorce, 1924), *d* of Alfred Wheeler, 98 Buckingham Gate, SW; two *s* one *d*. *Educ:* Bradfield College, Berks. Author, journalist and artist; published various works on agricultural and horticultural matters. *Heir:* *s* Delaval James Alfred Cotter, *b* 29 April 1911. *Address:* c/o Cox's RA Branch, 6 Pall Mall, SW1.
Died 22 Aug. 1924.

COTTERILL, James Henry, MA Cantab 1866; FRS 1878; Hon. Vice President, Institution of Naval Architects, 1905; *b* Norfolk, 2 Nov. 1836; *y s* of late Rev. Joseph Cotterill, Blakeney; unmarried. *Educ:* Brighton Coll.; apprenticed to Messrs Fairbairn and Co., engineers; subsequently at St John's Coll., Cambridge. Lecturer (1866) and Vice-Principal (1870) of the former Royal School of Naval Architecture, South Kensington; Professor of Applied Mechanics at Royal Naval Coll. Greenwich, 1873; retired Sept. 1897. *Publications:* Steam Engine considered as a Thermodynamic Machine, 1878, 2nd edn 1890, 3rd edn 1895; Applied Mechanics, 1884, 5th edn 1900, reprinted, 1909. *Address:* Hill Crest, Parkstone, Dorset.
Died 8 Jan. 1922.

COTTESLOE, 2nd Baron (UK), *cr* 1874; **Thomas Francis Fremantle,** MA; DL, JP; Bt 1821; Baron of Austrian Empire, *cr* 1816; Director London, Brighton and South Coast Railway Co.; *b* 30 Jan. 1830; *s* of 1st Baron and Louisa Elizabeth, *d* of Sir George Nugent, 1st Bt; *S* father, 1890; *m* 1859, Lady Augusta Henrietta Scott (*d* 1906), 2nd *d* of 2nd Earl of Eldon; four *s* one *d* (and one *d* decd). *Educ:* Eton; Balliol Coll., Oxford. BA 1st class Classics, 1852. MP Bucks, 1876–85. Owned about 3,000 acres. *Heir:* *s* Hon. Thomas Francis Fremantle, *b* 5 Feb. 1862. *Address:* 43 Eaton Square, SW; Swanbourne, Winslow, Bucks. *Clubs:* Carlton, Travellers'.
Died 13 April 1918.

COTTET, Charles; Artiste-peintre; sociétaire de la Société Nationale des Beaux-Arts, Paris, des orientalistes français, des peintres graveurs, des peintres lithographes, de la Société Nouvelle; de l'International Society of Painters, Gravers, and Sculptors, London; Secessions, Vienne, Berlin; *b* Puy, Hte-Loire. *Educ:* Evian-les-bains. Peintre et graveur. Principaux ouvrages: série au Pays de la Mer, consacré à la Bretagne, les côtes et ses habitants; série de tableaux Égyptiens, vénitiens, algériens, espagnols; vues de montagnes de la Savoie; quelques portraits nus et nature morte; quelques paysages d'Islande. Principaux tableaux dans les musées de Paris, Luxembourg, "et ville de Paris", Bordeaux, Lille, Saint-Etienne, Trieste, Rome, Padoue, Barcelone, Dusseldorf, Münich, Venise, Carlsruhe, Moscon, Helsingfors, Gothensburg, Vienne, Strasbourg, Buenos Ayres, Philadelphie, Cincinnati, Buffalo, Providence. Officier de la Légion d'Honneur; médaille d'or Exposition Universelle, Paris, 1900; Venise, Münich, Dresden, Barcelone. *Address:* 10 rue Cassini, Paris.
Died Sept. 1925.

COTTIER, Sir Charles Edward, Kt 1924; Solicitor; Hon. Treasurer of Empire Industries Association; *b* 13 Jan. 1869; *s* of late Francis Cottier, Co. Cork, and Plymouth; *m* 1889, Lydia Jane Avent, Plymouth; two *s* two *d. Address:* Swyncombe, Oxfordshire. *Clubs:* Carlton, American. *Died 22 Aug. 1928.*

COTTON, Lt-Col Arthur Egerton, DSO 1917; late Rifle Brigade; *b* 1876; 3rd *s* (twin) of late C. C. Cotton; *m* 1909, Beryl Marie, *d* of late H. J. Cumming; three *d.* Served European War, 1914–19 (wounded twice, despatches thrice, DSO, 1914–15 star). *Address:* 7 Seymour Place, W1. *T:* Paddington 4530. *Clubs:* Wellington, Royal Automobile. *Died 10 June 1922.*

COTTON, Rev. Henry Aldrich; Priest in Ordinary to the King; *b* Ellesmere, Salop, 12 July 1835; *e s* of William Aldrich Cotton. *Educ:* Bedford Grammar School; Exeter College, Oxford. BA 1858; MA 1860. Curate of Holy Trinity, Bedford, 1859; Curate of St Michael's, Tenbury, 1861; 2nd master of Eagle House School, Wimbledon, 1862–69; Vicar of Haynes, Beds, 1869–78; Minor Canon of Westminster, 1876–92; Priest in Ordinary to Queen Victoria, 1878–1901; Vicar of Stanford-in-the-Vale, 1892–15. *Address:* Stanford-in-the-Vale, Faringdon, Berks. *Club:* Junior Conservative. *Died 3 Feb. 1927.*

COTTON, James Sutherland, MA; editor revised edition Imperial Gazetteer of India; Hon. Secretary Egypt Exploration Fund; late editor of The Academy; *b* Coonoor, Madras, 17 July 1847; *s* of J. J. Cotton, HEICS; *m* 1873, Isabella, *d* of John Carter, Clifton, Bristol. *Educ:* Magdalen Coll. School; Brighton Coll.; Winchester Coll.; Trinity Coll., Oxford. Scholar of Trinity Coll.; Fellow and Lecturer of Queen's Coll. Oxford; 1st class Classical Moderations; 1st class Final Classical School. Barrister. *Publications:* Decennial Report on the Moral and Material Progress of India, 1885; India, Citizen Series, 1883; Elphinstone, Rulers of India Series, 1892; Quinquennial Report on Education in India, 1898; editor of Paterson's Practical Statutes. *Address:* 13 Warwick Mansions, Cromwell Crescent, SW. *Club:* Savile. *Died 9 July 1918.*

COTTON, William Francis, DL, JP; MP (N) Dublin Co. South, since 1911; Alderman; First Secretary and Chairman Alliance Gas Co., Dublin; *b* Dublin, 1847. Sheriff of Dublin City, 1901. *Address:* Hollywood, Roebuck, Dundrum, Co. Dublin.

Died 8 June 1917.

COTTON-JODRELL, Colonel Sir Edward Thomas Davenant, KCB 1911 (CB 1902); DL, JP; County Director, Cheshire Branch, British Red Cross Society, since Aug. 1914; *b* Rugby, 29 June 1847; *s* of G. E. L. Cotton, late Bishop of Calcutta; *m* 1878, Mary, *d* of W. R. Coleridge, Salston, Ottery St Mary; two *d. Educ:* Rugby; Marlborough. Passed first in Artillery Commissions in June 1868, from Woolwich; entered RA 1868; retired 1881. MP (C) Wirral Div. Cheshire, 1885–1900; Lt-Col and Hon. Col 2nd Cheshire RE (Railway Vols), 1888–1908; Deputy Assistant-Director, Headquarters Staff, 1906–12. *Address:* Reaseheath Hall, Nantwich, Cheshire. *T:* Nantwich 36; Shallcros-Manor, Whaley Bridge; 2 Portman Square, W. *T:* Paddington 748. *TA:* Jantu, Baker, London. *Clubs:* Carlton, Army and Navy. *Died 13 Oct. 1917.*

COTTRELL, Lieut-Colonel Reginald Foulkes, DSO 1918; late RFA; *b* 1885; *s* of Major W. F. Cottrell, RE; *m* 1920, Margaret (*d* 1921), *d* of late Robert English. *Educ:* privately; Royal Military Academy, Woolwich. Entered Royal Artillery, 1903; resigned, 1909; engaged in business for six years; rejoined Army, 5 Aug. 1914; served European War, 1914–18 (DSO, Bt Lt-Col, Mons Star, Order of the Redeemer, Greek Medal for Military Merit, despatches twice); Assistant-Director, War Office, 1919–21; resigned commission, 1922. Travelled extensively in America, Mexico, India, Europe, etc. *Clubs:* Wellington, New Oxford and Cambridge, Royal Automobile. *Died 9 Nov. 1924.*

COTTRELL, William Henry, CMG 1915; OBE 1919; Captain, RNVR, Eastern Mediterranean Squadron; *b* 17 Aug. 1863; *s* of late Major W. F. Cottrell, RE; *m* 1889, Louise Baglietto, Gibraltar; two *s* three *d. Educ:* SME, Chatham. Started in the Eastern Telegraph Co., 1878; joined the staff afloat, 1881; took part in the bombardment of Alexandria, 1882; appointed Chief Electrician and served in the Mediterranean, Red Sea, India, E and W coasts of Africa, etc, till 1892, when rejoined shore staff on appointment as Superintendent and HM's Consul at Syra, Greece, till 1909, being then appointed Divisional Superintendent at Athens; joined the Rear-Admiral's Staff at Mudros, Feb. 1915; took part in the Gallipoli Campaign with the rank of Commander, RNVR (despatches, CMG); Officer of Communications

and Chief Censor at Mudros; acting Capt., 1918 (despatches OBE); Divisional Manager ET Co. of the Levant, Feb. 1919, and Chairman of British Chamber of Commerce for Greece and the British Club, Athens; retired, 1922. Officer French Legion of Honour and Commander Order George 1st (Greek), 1920. *Publications:* various articles on electrical and kindred subjects. *Recreations:* music, photography, shooting, fishing, most sports. *Address:* c/o Royal Colonial Institute, 18 Northumberland Avenue, WC2. *Club:* Overseas. *Died 18 Nov. 1926.*

COUE, Emile; Professeur de psychologie appliquée; *b* Troyes, France, de parents occupant une situation très modeste; *m* Mlle Lemoine, fille de V. Lemoine de Nancy, qui fut considére comme l'un des plus grands horticulteurs du monde; sans enfants. *Educ:* petit collège de Nogent-sur-Seine; Lycée de Troyes. A été pharmacien à Troyes pendant 30 ans après avoir étudié la pharmacie à Paris où il fut interne des hôpitaux pendant deux ans. *Publications:* n'a jamais publié que quelques articles parus dans les Bulletins de la Société lorraine de Psychologie appliquée dont il est le président, et La Maîtrise de soi-même par l'autosuggestion consciente qui a été traduite en anglais sous le nom "Selfmastery by Conscious Autosuggestion", dans laquelle il a exposé ses théories d'une façon, aussi claire et aussi brève que possible; Ce que j'ai fait (Jugements portés sur mon œuvre). *Recreations:* travaillait autrefois dans son jardin, mais n'a plus le temps de prendre la moindre distraction. *Address:* rue Jeanne d'Arc 186, Nancy, France. *Died 2 July 1926.*

COULCHER, Mary Caroline, CBE 1919 (OBE 1918); *b* 1852; *d* of Rev. George Coulcher, Rector of Wattisfield, Suffolk. *Educ:* Lymington House School, Clapham. Lady of Grace of the Order of St John of Jerusalem; Coronation medal, 1911; Long Service medal with two bars, SJAB; Vice-President for Ipswich of British Red Cross Society, Suffolk Branch. Hon. Secretary and Treasurer Ipswich Centre St John Ambulance Association, 1879–1919; late Lady Superintendent Ipswich Nursing Division and late Lady District Superintendent to X district, SJAB; Town Councillor Ipswich, 1910–12. *Recreation:* music. *Address:* Beechholme, Ipswich. *T:* Ipswich 719. *Clubs:* VAD, St Andrew's House. *Died 15 June 1925.*

COULING, Samuel; *b* 1859; for 25 years a Missionary in Shantung, China. *Publication:* Encyclopædia Sinica; awarded the Prix Stanislas Julien, by the Académie des Inscriptions et Belles Lettres, 1918. Editor and Proprietor of New China Review. *Address:* New China Review, Shanghai, China. *Died 15 June 1922.*

COULL, Hon. William; Registrar-General, Escheator-General, District Magistrate and Coroner (Roseau), and Member of Executive and Legislative Councils, Dominica, Colony of Leeward Islands; *b* 1857; *o* surv. *s* of late Hon. William A. Coull, President of General Legislative Council of Leeward Islands, of Coral Hall, Antigua, and Joyce, 2nd *d* of late Dr Musgrave of Antigua, and *sister* of late Sir Anthony Musgrave, GCMG, Governor of Queensland, Australia; unmarried. *Educ:* The Antigua Grammar School; private tuition. Enrolled law student, Leeward Is, 1875; Clerk Colonial Secretary's Office, Leeward Is, 1878; acted on several occasions as Chief Clerk and Clerk of the Antigua and Federal Executive and Legislative Councils; Dep. Coroner for Dist A, 1880; Acting Magistrate, Dist B, Antigua, 1882; Magistrate and Coroner for Dist E, Roseau, and Registrar-General of births, marriages, and deaths, Dominica, 1882; Member of the Board of Poor Law Guardians; a visiting justice of the gaol, and nominated MLA 1883; Escheator-General, 1885; Member Executive Council, 1895; Official Member Legislative Council, 1895; in charge of out-door poor relief, 1898; Chairman of Quarantine Board under new (Convention) Act, 1906; retired on pension, Dec. 1911. *Address:* Eversleigh House, Roseau, Dominica, BWI. *Died 5 Aug. 1918.*

COULSON, Frederick Raymond; author and journalist; Vexatus and Democritus of the Sunday Chronicle; *b* London, 16 April 1864; *m* 1883, Ada, *d* of Joseph Emery, Berwick; one *s* (and one *s* killed in action). Forsook commercial life for journalism, 1894; before and since contributed articles, short stories, and much verse to magazines and periodicals; wrote many songs and monologues; associated since 1895 with the Sunday Chronicle and allied publications as Member of Literary Staff. *Publications:* A Jester's Jingles, 1899; The Social Scale, 1908; This Funny World, 1911. *Recreations:* reading, travel, gardening. *Address:* 68 Corringham Road, Golders Green, NW4. *Club:* Whitefriars. *Died 4 March 1922.*

COULTER, Robert Millar, CMG 1907; MD; Deputy Postmaster General, Canada, 1897–1924; *b* 9 Sept. 1857; *m* 1887, Emma, *d* of late J. P. Wells. *Educ:* Toronto University; Victoria University. Began practising medicine at Aurora, Ontario. *Address:* 190 Cooper Street, Ottawa, Canada. *Club:* Rideau, Ottawa.

Died Feb. 1927.

COUPER, John, MD; FRCS; Consulting Surgeon, London Hospital, Royal London Ophthalmic Hospital, and Scottish Hospital. *Educ:* Glasgow and Berlin. Was Lecturer in Surgery, London Hospital Medical College. *Address:* 80 Grosvenor Street, W; Ellesborough House, Butlerscross, Bucks. *M:* BH 77.

Died 30 April 1918.

COUPERUS, Louis; Officer of the Order of Orange-Nassau, 1896; novelist; *b* The Hague, 10 June 1863; 4th *s* of John Ricus Couperus and Jonkvrouwe Geertruida Johanna Reynst; *m* 1891, Elizabeth Johanna Wilhelmina Elizabeth, *d* of Ricus Baud. *Educ:* Batavia; The Hague. *Publications* (in England): Eline Vere, 1890; The Footsteps of Fate, 1891; Ecstasy, 1892; Majesty, 1894; Psyche, 1906; Small Souls, 1914; The Later Life, 1915; The Twilight of the Souls, 1917; Dr Adriaan, 1918; Old People and the Things that Pass, 1919; The Tour, 1920; The Law Inevitable, 1921. *Recreation:* travelling. *Address:* c/o A. Teixeira de Mattos, 9 Cheltenham Terrace, SW3.

Died 16 July 1923.

COURROUX, George Augustus, CVO 1903 (MVO 1901); *b* 29 Jan. 1852; *s* of A. F. Courroux, formerly Chief Clerk of the Board of Green Cloth (*d* 1895); *m* 1886, Jane, *d* of late P. T. Renaud, Chief Clerk, Duchy of Lancaster Office. JP 1898, County London, Middlesex, Surrey, Berks; Chief Clerk, Board of Green Cloth, 1888–98; Secretary, 1898; retired, 1 Jan. 1903. *Address:* 17 Chesham Road, Brighton. *Died 5 Jan. 1923.*

COURTENAY, Colonel Arthur Henry, CB 1900; Hon. Lieutenant-Colonel in Army; late Master of the High Court of Justice in Ireland (King's Bench Divison); retired, 1918; *b* 16 Oct. 1852; *s* of late Thomas Lefroy Courtenay, JP, of Grange, Co. Antrim, and 14 Fitzwilliam Square, Dublin, and Jane Caroline, *e d* of late Martin Morris, JP of Spiddal, Co. Galway; *m* 1875, Mary Ellen Mildmay, *d* of David Fullerton, JP of Pennington, Hants; two *d*. *Educ:* privately; Trinity College, Dublin. Called to Irish Bar; Master of the Common Pleas in Ireland, 1883; Lieutenant 2nd Royal Lanark Militia, 1871; Lieut-Colonel and Hon. Colonel 4th Batt. the Cameronians (Scottish Rifles), 1891; Col Commandant 3rd and 4th Batts Scottish Rifles, 1895; served with 4th Batt. Scottish Rifles in South African Campaign, 1900–1 (CB); Commandant of Boshof, Orange River Colony, 1900–1 (despatches, medal and three clasps); on Headquarters Staff, Northern Command, York, 1915–17; attached to Ministry of National Service, 1917–18; Assistant Competent Military Authority London District, 1919–22; DL Lanarkshire; JP, DL Co. Galway; High Sheriff, 1887 and 1909. *Recreations:* shooting, hunting. *Address:* Heathbourne, Lansdown Road, Wimbledon, SW20. *T:* Wimbledon 1186. *Clubs:* Junior Carlton; United Service, Dublin; County, Galway; Royal St George Yacht, Kingstown.

Died 19 May 1927.

COURTENAY, Brig.-Gen. Edward Reginald, CB 1905; CMG 1917; Deputy-Adjutant-General, 2nd Army Central Force; on the General Staff; *b* 27 June 1853; *e s* of Major George Henry Courtenay of Southtown House, Kenton, Devon, and *g s* of Rt Hon. Thomas Peregrine Courtenay, *brother* of 10th Earl of Devon; *m* 1891, Mary Emily, (May), *d* of Major-Gen. F. Hammersley of Ash Grange, Surrey; one *d*. *Educ:* Charterhouse. Lieut 20th Hussars, 1873; Adjt 20th Hussars, 1881–86; Capt. 20th Hussars, 1881; Major 11th Hussars, 1889; Lieut-Col commanding 11th Hussars, 1896–1900; Colonel, 1900; commanded 10th Regimental District, 1900; Assistant Adjutant-General and Chief Staff Officer, NW district, 1900–5; Colonel General Staff Welsh and Midland command, 1905; Inspector of Yeomanry and in Charge of Hussar Records, 1907–10; passed Staff College; served in Zulu War, 1878–79 (despatches, medal and clasp); Nile Expedition with Camel Corps, 1884 (medal and clasps and Khedive's star); Egyptian Frontier Expedition, 1885 (despatches); Tirah campaign, NW Frontier of India, 1897 (medal and clasp); European War, 1914–17 (despatches, CMG). *Address:* 7 Eaton Terrace, SW. *Club:* Cavalry.

Died 29 March 1919.

COURTENAY, Henry, ISO 1903; JP, Co. Dublin; late Assistant Secretary, Irish Local Government Board; a member of several religious and benevolent societies in the City of Dublin; *b* 1843; *m* 1877, Mary, *d* of William J. Stokes; *m* 1916, Victorine Charlotte (Ena), *e d* of Rt Hon. Sir Robert Matheson. *Address:* Rosslyn, Monkstown, Co. Dublin. *Died July 1921.*

COURTHOPE, William John, CB 1895; MA; FBA 1906; FRSL 1907; Civil Service Commissioner, 1887; First Civil Service Commissioner, 1892; retired, 1907; Hon. Fellow New College, Oxford, 1896; Hon. DLitt Durham, 1895; Hon. LLD Edinburgh, 1898; *b* 17 July 1842; *e s* of Rev. William Courthope, Rector of S Malling, Sussex; *m* 1870, Mary, *e d* of John Scott, HM Inspector-General of Hospitals, Bombay; four *s* two *d*. *Educ:* Harrow; New Coll., Oxford. 1st Class Classical Moderations, 1863; 1st class Lit.Hum., 1865; Newdigate Prize Poem, 1864; Chancellor's Prize for English Essay, 1868; Professor of Poetry, University of Oxford, 1895–1901. *Publications:* Ludibria Lunae, 1869; The Paradise of Birds, 1870; Life of Addison (Men of Letters Series), 1882; History of English Poetry vol. i 1895, vol. ii 1897, vols iii and iv 1903, vol v 1905, vol vi 1909; Life in Poetry, Law in Taste, 1901, etc; editor of Pope's Works, and author of his Life. *Address:* The Lodge, Wadhurst, Sussex. *Club:* Athenæum. *Died 10 April 1917.*

COURTNEY OF PENWITH, 1st Baron, *cr* 1906; **Rt. Hon. Leonard Henry Courtney,** PC 1889; MA; *b* Penzance, 6 July 1832; *e s* of John Sampson Courtney, Alverton House, Penzance, and Sarah, *d* of John Mortimer; *m* 1883, Catherine, *d* of Richard Potter of Lancashire and Gloucestershire. *Educ:* St John's Coll., Cambridge, (2nd Wrangler, 1855); equal as Smith's Prizeman, 1855. Barrister Lincoln's Inn, 1858; Bencher, 1889; Prof. of Political Economy, Univ. Coll. London, 1872–75; MP (L) Liskeard, 1876–85; MP (U) for Bodmin Division Cornwall, 1885–1900; Under-Sec. of State for Home Dept, 1880–81; Colonial Office, 1881–82; appointed Financial Sec. to the Treasury; resigned this office in 1884; Chairman of Committees and Deputy Speaker, 1886–92; since this date out of office. Hon. Fellow of St John's Coll., Camb.; Hon. LLD Camb., 1898. *Publications:* The Working Constitution of the United Kingdom and its Outgrowths, 1901; a large contributor to the Times and Nineteenth Century. *Heir:* none. *Recreations:* took considerable interest in literature and art. *Address:* 15 Cheyne Walk, Chelsea, SW. *Clubs:* Athenæum, Reform. *Died 11 May 1918 (ext).*

COURTNEY, Colonel Edward Arthur Waldegrave, CMG 1915; CBE 1918; late RASC; *b* 10 Oct. 1868; *e s* of late Maj.-Gen. Edward H. Courtney CVO, and Mary Dorothy Saunder, *g n* of 7th Earl Waldegrave; *m* 1894, Hilda Maria, *y d* of T. E. Chapman, Silksworth Hall, Co. Durham; three *s* one *d*. Entered army (Lancashire Fusiliers) 1889; RASC 1893; Captain, 1896; Major, 1903; Lt-Col 1912; served South African War, 1899–1901 (Queen's medal, 6 clasps); European War, 1914–18 (despatches, CMG, CBE; Croix d'officier Légion d'Honneur, Croix d'officier l'ordre de Léopold, Croix de Guerre); Staff Captain, Cork District, 1902–3; Deputy Assistant Director of Supplies and Transport, Eastern Command, Sept. 1906–Sept. 1910; Assistant Director of Supplies, 5 Aug. 1914–31 Dec. 1914; Assistant-Director of Requisition Services, 1 Jan. 1915–6 June 1915; Deputy Director of Requisition Services, 1915–16; Director of Requisition Services, 1916–18; Liaison Officer with Army Headquarters, June 1915–May 1918; Assistant Director of Supplies and Transport, Northern Command, 1918–19; Assistant Director of Supplies and Transport, Southern Command, 1919–22; retired pay, 1922. *Club:* United Service. *Died 18 June 1926.*

COURTNEY, Rt. Rev. Frederick, DD; Rector of St James's Church, New York, 1904–15; Rector-emeritus since 1915; *b* Plymouth, 1837; *s* of Rev. S. Courtney, Vicar of Charles, Plymouth; *m* 1865, Caroline (*d* 1909), *d* of Philip Nairn, Waren House, Northumberland; four *s* one *d*. *Educ:* King's College, London. Ordained, 1864; Curate of Hadlow, Kent, 1864–65; Incumbent of Charles's Chapel, Plymouth, 1865–70; St Jude's, Glasgow, 1870–76; Assistant St Thomas's, New York, 1876–80; Rector of St James's, Chicago, 1880–82; of St Paul's, Boston, 1882–88; Bishop of Nova Scotia, 1888–1904. *Address:* St James's Church, 71st Street, and Madison Avenue, New York. *T:* 2185–79th. *Club:* Overseas. *Died Dec. 1918.*

COURTNEY, John Mortimer, CMG 1897; ISO 1903; Knight of Grace, St John of Jerusalem; Deputy Minister of Finance and Receiver-General, and Secretary of the Treasury Board of Canada, 1878–1906; *b* Penzance, Cornwall, 22 July 1838; 2nd *s* of John Sampson Courtney of Alverton House, Penzance, and Sarah, *m* of John Mortimer; *m* 1870, Mary Elizabeth Sophia, 2nd *d* of late Fennings Taylor, Clerk Assistant of the Senate of Canada; one *s*. *Educ:* Penzance. Several years banking; Chief Clerk of the Treasury, Canada, 1869; served on several Commissions; Hon. Treasurer in Canada for the Indian Famine Fund; also of Canadian Patriotic Fund and Association for Prevention of Tuberculosis; President of the Victorian Order of Nurses, Canada. *Recreation:* reading. *Address:* 638 Rideau Street, Ottawa. *Clubs:* Rideau, Royal Ottawa Golf, Ottawa.

Died 8 Oct. 1920.

COURTNEY, Col Richard Edmond, CB 1915; Acting Commandant 5th Military District (WA); *b* 1870; *s* of Capt. T. Wilson Courtney; unmarried. *Educ:* Melbourne University. Barrister and Solicitor, Victoria, 1897. Served European War (Dardanelles), 1914–15 (despatches, CB). *Club:* Naval and Military, Melbourne.
Died 22 Oct. 1919.

COURTNEY, William Leonard, MA, LLD St Andrews; Fellow, New College, Oxford, 1876; editor of the Fortnightly Review, 1894; formerly on editorial staff of the Daily Telegraph; retired; director of Chapman & Hall, Ltd; *b* Poona, 5 Jan. 1850; *y s* of William Courtney, late of ICS, and Anne Edwardes Scott; *m* 1st, 1874, Cordelia Blanche (*d* 1907), *d* of Lionel Place, Commander RN; four *s* three *d*; 2nd, 1911, Janet Elizabeth Hogarth, OBE, writer. *Educ:* Somersetshire College, Bath; Univ. Coll., Oxford (Scholar, 1868). 1st class First Public Examination, 1870; 1st class Greats, 1872; Fellow Merton College, 1872; Headmaster Somersetshire College, Bath, 1873; many years Treasurer OUBC London 1890; editor of Murray's Magazine, 1891. *Publications:* The Metaphysics of John Stuart Mill, 1879; Studies on Philosophy, 1882; Constructive Ethics, 1886; Studies New and Old, 1888; Life of John Stuart Mill, 1889; Kit Marlowe (produced at St James's Theatre), 1893; The Idea of Tragedy, 1900; Undine, 1902; The Development of Maeterlinck, 1904; The Feminine Note in Fiction, 1904; The Literary Man's Bible, 1907; Rosemary's Letter Book, 1909; In Search of Egeria, 1911; The Soul of a Suffragette, 1913; The Literary Man's New Testament, 1915; Old Saws and Modern Instances, 1918; The Passing Hour, 1925; The Bedside Bible, 1926. *Address:* 2 Luxborough House, Northumberland Street, W1. *T:* Mayfair 4009. *Clubs:* Garrick, Beefsteak, Authors'.
Died 1 Nov. 1928.

COUSINS, John Ratcliffe; Metropolitan Police Magistrate sitting at Greenwich and Woolwich, 1922; at West London Police Court since 1925; *b* 22 Aug. 1863; *s* of Edward Ratcliffe Cousins, FRCS; *m* 1887, Eleanor Fanny, *d* of Rev. J. E. Law, Rector of Little Shelford, Cambridge; one *s* two *d*. *Educ:* University College, London; St John's College, Cambridge. Honours, Natural Science Tripos, 1884, and LLB. Called to Bar, Inner Temple, 1887; Western Circuit; Member for Dulwich, London County Council, 1898–1903; Organiser of the Tariff Reform League from its formation until 1906; Stipendiary Police Magistrate of the Borough of West Ham, 1917–22; Ex-Chairman of the Estates Governors of Dulwich College. *Recreations:* golf, bicycling, etc. *Address:* 3 College Gardens, Dulwich, SE. *Club:* Devonshire.
Died 12 March 1928.

COUSINS, William Henry, CB 1887; retired civil servant and country gentleman; *b* Chelsea, 30 Dec. 1833; *e s* of Captain Cousins; unmarried. *Educ:* private tutor; King's Coll., London. Served in Exhibition of 1851 under late Lord Playfair; appointed to the Inland Revenue, 1853; and became Controller of Stamps and Registrar of Joint Stock Companies, 1871–83; and then Secretary of Inland Revenue to 1896; when retired on pension. Decorated for Inland Revenue and Stamp Reforms. *Publications:* editor of the Law List, 1870–82. *Recreation:* collecting old china and curios. *Address:* Vaughan Lodge, Long Ditton, Surrey. *Club:* Constitutional.
Died 7 Sept. 1917.

COUZENS, Sir George Edwin, Kt 1905; JP; *b* 29 Sept. 1851; *s* of George Couzens, Portsmouth; *m* 1885, Mary Ellen (*d* 1908), *d* of James Haming, RN; one *s* one *d*. Mayor of Portsmouth, 1897, 1904–5, 1905–6. Officer Legion of Honour; Order of Holy Redeemer of Greece, member of Board of Guardians; Vice-President, Royal Agricultural Society. *Address:* Glenthorne, Kingston Crescent, Portsmouth.
Died 17 Aug. 1925.

COVENTRY, Henry Arthur; *b* Melton Mowbray, 7 Dec. 1852; *y s* of late Hon. Henry Coventry. Formerly starter to the Jockey Club; a well-known amateur rider; won National Hunt Steeplechase, 1879. *Club:* Turf.
Died 22 Aug. 1925.

COVENTRY, Rev. Henry William, MA; Rural Dean of Bredon; Rector of Severn-Stoke since 1869; JP Worcestershire. *Educ:* Winchester; Pembroke College, Oxford. Rector of Woolston, 1864–69; Rector of Hill-Croome, 1899–1905. *Address:* Severn-Stoke Rectory, Worcester.
Died 10 April 1920.

COWAN, Rev. David Galloway; Prebendary of St Paul's Cathedral, 1917. *Educ:* King's College School; St Edmund Hall, Oxford. Curate of Holy Trinity, Dalston, 1882–89; St John, Isle of Dogs, 1889–92; Vicar, 1892–1902; Vicar of St John Evangelist, Holborn, 1902. *Address:* St John's Clergy House, Red Lion Square, WC1.
Died 15 Sept. 1921.

COWAN, Colonel Henry Vivian; CB 1908; CVO 1904; ADC to the King 1901–11; *b* 10 Nov. 1854; *s* of late Richard Cowan, JP for Midlothian, of St Kilda, Sidmouth; *m* 1894, Mabel Talbot, *d* of late Sir James Laing, Thornhill, Sunderland, and Etal Manor, Cornhill-on-Tweed; three *d*. *Educ:* Winchester College; RMA, Woolwich. Joined Royal Artillery, 1873; served Afghan War, 1878–80 (despatches, medal and 3 clasps); Egypt, 1882 (severely wounded, despatches, Brevet Major, medal and clasp, 5th Class Mejidie, Khedive's star); S Africa, 1899–1900 (despatches twice, Queen's medal and 6 clasps, ADC to King, Brevet Colonel); recently Commandant RMA, Woolwich; AAG Irish Command, 1914–17. *Address:* Ford House, Bideford, N Devon. *Clubs:* United Service, United Sports.
Died 25 Jan. 1918.

COWAN, John, KC 1898; of Cowan, Towers & Cowan, Barristers and Solicitors; President Industrial Mortgage and Savings Co.; Director Canada Trust Co.; *b* on board vessel on Atlantic Ocean, 8 July 1849; *s* of John Cowan and Catherine Sudin; *m* 1881, Eliza A., *d* of John M'Intyre; four *s* four *d*. *Educ:* common schools; Osgoode Hall. Read law with John Idington, later Mr Justice Idington; called to Ontario Bar, 1879; practised Watford, 1879–83; came to Sarnia and practised, in partnership with late Mr Justice Lister, 1883–98; formed present partnership, 1898; City Solicitor, also Solicitor, County Lambton, townships of Moore, Dawn, Brooks, Warwick and Bosanquet, and villages of Watford and Wyoming; Bencher, Law Society of Upper Canada; Liberal; Presbyterian. *Recreations:* horseback riding, gardening. *Address:* Sarnia, Ontario. *Club:* Ontario, Toronto.
Died June 1926.

COWAN, Hon. John; Member of Executive Council and Minister of Finance and Customs, Newfoundland, 1900–6; *b* St John's, Newfoundland, 12 Nov. 1847; parents from Moffat, Dumfriesshire, Scotland; *m* 1874, Eliza Julia Earle, whose parents were from Devonshire. *Educ:* General Protestant Academy, St John's, Newfoundland. At the age of 14 left school; served his apprenticeship to the dry goods business; from that gravitated to office work, for which he was more suited; held the position of book-keeper in two of the principal business houses in St John's for some 17 years, and in 1890 was appointed assistant manager for J & W. Stewart, a large supplying firm; after the bank crash of 1894, went into the commission business on his own account and built up a considerable business; was elected for the District of Bonavesta Bay, 1897. *Recreation:* enthusiastic curler. *Address:* Harbor View, 37 Queen's Road, St John's, Newfoundland. *Club:* Masonic.
Died March 1927.

COWAN, Thomas William, DSc, PhD; FLS, FGS, FRMS, FRHS; Chairman of Council British Bee-keepers' Association since 1874; President since 1922, Chairman Board of Examiners; *b* 1840. *Educ:* private schools; School of Mines. President Somerset Bee-keepers' Association; hon. member Victoria Natural History Society; hon. member of several Bee Associations in Europe, Canada, and United States; Chairman of Committee on the Bee-keeping Industry and Foul Brood in the United Kingdom, 1895; Chairman Joint Committee of BBKA and County Councils to promote legislation against Bee-pest, 1895; lecturer at University of California Farmers' Institutes on fruit-growing and relation of bees to horticulture; steward and judge at shows of the Royal Agricultural Society; also judge at shows of Bath and West of England, Royal Counties, Lancashire, Lincolnshire, and other agricultural societies; member of international juries at shows in France, Germany, and Switzerland. Travelled and studied bees, and lectured in many countries of Europe, in Africa, Canada, and the United States of America; editor of the British Bee Journal (weekly) and Bee-keepers' Record (monthly). *Publications:* The Honey Bee, its Natural History, Anatomy, and Physiology (2nd edition), 1904, translated into French, German, Norwegian, Bulgarian, and Russian; British Bee-keepers' Guide Book, 25th edition, 100th thousand, 1924, translated into French (2 editions), German, Danish, Swedish, Russian (4 editions), Spanish (2 editions), and Dutch; Wax Craft: all about beeswax, its history, production, adulteration and commercial value, 1908, translated into French and Russian (2 editions); Foul Brood and its Treatment; British Bee-keepers' Note Book (3rd edition); Bees and their Management; Wintering Bees (3 editions); How to make an Extractor and Bellows Smoker; Beneficial Results from the Fertilisation of Fruit Blossoms by Bees, 1909, translated into French and Dutch; also author of numerous articles, pamphlets, and lectures on bees in connection with horticulture and agriculture. *Recreations:* natural history, horticulture, wood carving, travelling. *Address:* Sutherland House, Clevedon, Somerset; 23 Bedford Street, Strand, WC. *TA:* Clevedon.
Died 23 May 1926.

COWANS, General Sir John Steven, GCB 1919 (KCB 1913; CB 1911); GCMG 1918; MVO 1902; Knight of Grace of the Order of St John of Jerusalem, 1918; FZS; *b* 11 March 1862; *s* of late John Cowans of Carlisle and Hartlands, Cranford, Middlesex; *m* 1884, Eva May, *d* of Rev. J. E. Coulson, Vicar of Long Preston, Yorkshire. Joined Rifle Brigade (Prince Consort's Own), 1881; Captain, 1890; *psc* 1891; Major, 1898; Lieutenant-Colonel, 1900; Colonel, 1903; Brig.-Gen. 1908; Lt-Gen. 1915; General, 1919; Staff-Captain, Headquarters of Army, 1893-94; Brigade Major, Aldershot, 1894-97; DAQMG, Headquarters of Army, 1898-1903; AQMG, 2nd Division, Aldershot, 1903-6; Director-General Military Education, Indian Army, 1906; Director of Staff Duties and Training, Army Headquarters, India, 1907-8; commanded Presidency Brigade, Calcutta, 1908-10; Director-General of the Territorial Forces, 1910-12; Quartermaster-General of the Forces, War Office, 1912-19; member of HM's Army Council, European War, 1914-19. Grand Officer of the Legion of Honour, Crown of Belgium, Crown of Italy, Sacred Treasure of Japan, Holy Redeemer, Greece, and Chia Ho (Ta Shou) of China. *Address:* 72 Curzon Street, W1. *T:* Mayfair 3967. *Clubs:* Beefsteak, Naval and Military; United Service, Simla; Turf, United Service, Calcutta.   *Died 16 April 1921.*

COWDRAY, 1st Viscount, *cr* 1916; **Weetman Dickinson Pearson,** Bt 1894; Baron 1910; PC 1917; GCVO 1925; DL Aberdeenshire; Rector, University of Aberdeen, 1918-21; President of the Air Board, 1917; Head of the firm of S. Pearson & Son, Ltd; *b* 15 July 1856; *e s* of late George Pearson, Brickendonbury, Hertford, and Sarah, *d* of Weetman Dickinson, High Hoyland, Yorkshire; *m* 1881, Annie, *d* of late Sir John Cass, Bradford, Yorks; two *s* one *d* (and one *s* decd). *Educ:* privately at Harrogate. Contested (L) Colchester, 1892; MP (L) Colchester, 1895-1910; High Steward of Colchester. *Heir: s* Hon. Weetman Harold Miller Pearson, *b* 18 April 1882. *Address:* 16 Carlton House Terrace, SW1; Paddockhurst, Worth, Sussex; Dunecht House, Aberdeenshire. *Clubs:* Reform, Marlborough.

Died 1 May 1927.

COWELL, George, FRCS; Vice-President and Consulting Surgeon to the Westminster and Royal Westminster Ophthalmic Hospitals; Consulting Surgeon to the Victoria and East London Hospitals for Children; *b* Ipswich, 1 June 1836; *e s* of late George Kersey Cowell, surgeon of that town, and Martha, *d* of George Notcutt Conder; *m* 1892, Mary Margaret Elizabeth (*d* 1925), *widow* of W. Hamilton Roe, MB Oxon, and *d* of late John Laurie, MP for Barnstaple. *Educ:* Ipswich, Birmingham, London, and Paris. Surgeon to the Victoria Hospital for Children, 1866-85; Surgeon to Westminster and Royal Westminster Ophthalmic Hospitals, 1869-96; Lecturer on Surgery, 1873-93; took an active part in bringing about the complete rebuilding of the Medical School and the Outpatient Department and Chapel of the Westminster Hospital; filled various offices in the Medical Societies. *Publications:* Lectures on Cataract, and articles and lectures in the medical journals; The Life and Letters of Prof. Cowell. *Recreations:* fishing, golf. *Club:* Athenæum.

Died 18 Nov. 1927.

COWELL, Rev. Maurice Byles, MA; Canon of Norwich since 1911; Vicar of Ash-Bocking since 1862. *Educ:* Wadham College, Oxford. Ordained, 1858; RD Claydon, 1895; Curate of Coseley, Staffs, 1858-60. *Address:* Ash-Bocking Vicarage, Ipswich.

Died 8 Jan. 1919.

COWEN, Richard John; Consulting Surgeon; *b* 1871; *s* of John Cowen, MD; *m* Margaret Isabella, *d* of Captain George Stavers. *Educ:* Dublin University. Diplomate RCSL and RCPL; Gold Medallist in Surgery; Gold Medallist, Académie Parisienne; late Senior Surgeon, Kensington and Fulham General Hospital; late Captain, 4th Middx; served in Egyptian War (wounded, medal and star); working in Cancer Research; Captain Westminster Division National Reserve; rejoined Army, 1914, as Captain, Rifle Brigade; service in Dardanelles and Salonika. *Publications:* What is Life? Electricity in Gynæcology; X-Rays in the Treatment of Cancer and other Diseases; The Social Grindstone; Half-an-hour in a Doctor's Study; The Ideal Trajectory for Conical Bullets; A New Treatment for Leucocythæmia; numerous articles in lay and professional journals. *Recreations:* golf, tennis, shooting. *Address:* 4 Chandos Street, W1. *T:* Langham 2665. *Club:* Devonshire.   *Died 16 Feb. 1928.*

COWIE, William Patrick, CIE 1920; Indian Civil Service; *b* Dunedin, New Zealand, 31 Jan. 1884; *s* of George Cowie and Frances Peter; *m* 1920, Margaret Burne, of Loynton Hall, Newport, Salop; one *d*. *Educ:* Malvern Coll.; Corpus Christi Coll., Oxford. BA 1907. Passed into ICS 1908; Bombay Political Department, 1912-17; 28th Light Cavalry, 1917-18; Private Sec. to the Governor of Bombay, 1918-20;

Collector, Belgaum District. *Recreations:* shooting, all games. *Address:* c/o Grindlay & Co., 54 Parliament Street, SW1. *Club:* East India United Service.   *Died 1 Aug. 1924.*

COWLEY, 3rd Earl, *cr* 1857; **Henry Arthur Mornington Wellesley,** JP; Baron Cowley (UK), 1828; Viscount Dangan, 1857; served with Imperial Yeomanry in South Africa; late Captain 3rd Battalion Wiltshire Regiment; *b* 14 Jan. 1866; *s* of 2nd Earl and Emily Gwendolen, *d* of Col Thomas Peers-Williams, MP; S father, 1895; *m* 1st, 1889, Lady Violet Nevill (by whom he was divorced, 1897; she *d* 1910), *d* of 1st Marquis of Abergavenny; one *s*; 2nd, 1905, Millicent Florence Eleanor (by whom he was divorced, 1913), *d* of 1st Baron Nunburnholme; [she married 1st, Sir Charles Hartopp, 5th Bt, by whom she was divorced; and 3rd, 1914, Major G. William Duberly, Grenadier Guards, Gaynes Hall, St Neots]; one *s*; 3rd, 1914, Clare Florence Mary, (Mrs Buxton), *o c* of Sir Francis Stapleton, 8th Bt; one *d*. *Educ:* Eton. Owned about 4000 acres. *Heir: s* Viscount Dangan, *b* 25 Dec. 1890. *Address:* Draycott House, Chippenham, Wilts. *Clubs:* Carlton, Marlborough, Turf, White's.

Died 15 Jan. 1919.

COWLEY, Hon. Sir Alfred Sandlings Cowley, Kt 1904; Chairman, Bank of North Queensland; Member of the Australian Mutual Provident Society; Speaker of Legislative Assembly, Queensland, 1893-99 and 1903-7; *b* Fairford, Glos, 24 April 1848; *s* of Isaac Cowley, late of Durban; *m* 1880, Marie, *d* of late W. Campbell. Went to Natal; went to NSW, 1871; MLA Herbert, 1888-1907; Member Royal Commissions on Sugar Industry, 1888-89; and on Laws relating to Intoxicating Liquors, 1900-1; Minister Lands and Agriculture 1890-93. *Address:* Silky Oaks, Toowong, Queensland.

Died 1 Dec. 1926.

COWLEY-BROWN, Rev. George James, MA; Canon of Edinburgh Cathedral (retired); Chancellor, 1907-11; Rector of St John the Evangelist, Edinburgh, 1883-1909; *b* Juanpur, India, 1832; *s* of G. F. Brown of the Indian Civil Service and *g s* of Rev. David Brown, scholar of Magdalene Coll., Cambridge, Provost of the College of Fort William; *m* 1868, Isabel, *d* of Charles Tottenham of Ballycurry, many years MP for New Ross; adopted in 1874 by legal deed the name of his great-grandmother, Mrs Cowley, authoress of The Belle's Stratagem, etc. *Educ:* Christ Church, Oxford. Ordained, 1855, by Bishop Wilberforce of Oxford; Rector of Shipton-on-Cherwell, 1867-74; Buckhorn Weston, 1874-77; St Edmund, Salisbury, 1877-83. *Publications:* Daily Lessons on the Life of Our Lord on Earth, 1880; Prayers for a Household from Old Divines, 3rd edn 1908; Some Reasons for believing Christianity to be True, 1897; Verselets and Versions; articles in Blackwood's Magazine, the National Review, and other periodicals. *Address:* 6 Learmonth Grove, Edinburgh. *T:* Central 7150.

Died 17 Dec. 1924.

COWPER, Cecil, JP Surrey; Editor of The Academy; *b* 24 Oct. 1856; *s* of Major Francis Baynton Cowper, 86th Regiment; *m* 1st, Kate, *d* of R. Nevill, 61st Regiment; 2nd, May, *d* of Donald H. Waddell. Barrister, Inner Temple, 1881. *Address:* Cammeray, Burghley Road, Wimbledon Common, SW.

Died 27 April 1916.

COWPER, Sydney, CMG 1901; *b* Kensington, 1854; *s* of late Charles Cowper, CE; *m* 1883, Mary Louisa, *d* of late Richard Cockerton, FRCS. *Educ:* King's College School. Office of Commissioners for Exhibition of 1851, 1871; Technical Assistant, South Kensington Museum, 1875; Cape Civil Service, 1879; in charge of Cape Section, Colonial and Indian Exhibition, 1886; Secretary to Prime Minister, Cape Colony, 1887-91; Principal Clerk, Department of Agriculture, 1892; permanent head of Prime Minister's Department, Cape Town, 1896; retired 1904; OC 4th Batt. Cape Peninsula Regt 1902; Major, and BC Cape Field Artillery, 1903; Trustee of Art Gallery; Pres., Western Province Agricultural Society, 1915-17; MPC and JP; Fellow Royal Colonial Institute; Mayor of Wynberg, 1912-14 and 1918-21; Deputy-Mayor, 1915-17. *Address:* Wynberg, near Cape Town. *Club:* Civil Service, Cape Town.

Died 5 Sept. 1922.

COX, Arthur Frederick, CSI 1901; Indian Civil Service; retired; *b* Kurnool, Madras Presidency, 14 March 1849; 4th *s* of late Major E. T. Cox, MNI, of Ham Common, Surrey; *m* 1873, Flora (*d* 1923), *d* of late Alexander Ranken of Hampstead; two *s* three *d*. *Educ:* Great Ealing School; King's College School and King's College, London. Appointed to the Madras Presidency, 1871; served there in the Revenue and Magisterial Department until 1882, when he joined the Finance Department of the Government of India; returned to

Madras as District and Session Judge, 1887–89; reappointed to the Financial Department as Accountant-General, Bombay; transferred to Calcutta, 1894, to officiate as Comptroller and Auditor-General; confirmed as such in 1898. Kaiser-i-Hind Gold Medal for public service in India, 1900; retired, 1906. *Publication:* The District Manual of North Arcot, Madras Presidency, 1880. *Address:* Cumballa, St John's Road, Meads, Eastbourne. *T:* Eastbourne 1193.

Died 8 Feb. 1925.

COX, A. W.; *b* 1857; *s* of A. R. Cox of Hafod Elwy, North Wales; no occupation; mostly travelling; collector of art, etc; one of original syndicate Broken Hill Mine; won first race, 1888; won One Thousand Guineas with Galeottia, 1895; St Leger with Bayardo, 1909; Derby with Lemberg, 1910; Gold Cup (Ascot), Bayardo, 1910; Chester Cup and Ascot Gold Cup with Aleppo, 1914; Triple Crown Honey, Gay Crusader, 1917; The Oaks with My Dear, 1918. *Address:* 30 St James's Place, SW1. *T:* Regent 1397; The Old Barn, Harrow Weald, Middlesex. *Clubs:* Carlton, Boodle's, Pratt's.

Died 4 May 1919.

COX, Colonel Edgar William, DSO 1915; RE; GSO 1st Grade; *b* May 1882. Entered army, 1900; Captain, 1910; employed on Sierra Leone and Siberia Boundary Commission, 1902–3; Anglo-Portuguese Boundary Commission, Africa, 1904–6; survey duty East Africa Protectorate, 1906–9; General Staff Officer, War Office, 1912–14; served European War, 1914–18 (DSO, despatches, Bt Major and Bt Lieut-Col and Col); Chevalier, Legion of Honour, 1915.

Died 26 Aug. 1918.

COX, Lt-Col Edward Henry, DSO 1902; late Royal Fusiliers; *b* 21 May 1863; *s* of late Arthur Zachariah Cox of Harwood Hall, Essex. Entered army, 1884; Capt., 1892; Maj., 1900; served South Africa, 1899–1902 (despatches, 1900; Queen's medal with 5 clasps, King's medal with 2 clasps). *Died 23 July 1925.*

COX, Francis Albert; Founder and Secretary of The National Equine Defence League; *b* 24 June 1862; 4th and *y* *s* of late George James and Caroline Wintle Cox; *m* 1886, Augusta Elizabeth, *e* *d* of late J. Wildsmith; one *s* two *d*. For 29 years held a post in the Civil Engineers Department of the Great Northern Railway, for the last 12 as Assistant to the Chief Engineer; a life-long worker on behalf of animals, he was impelled to start a public agitation respecting the treatment and conditions of pit ponies, 1908, which work eventually led to his founding the above-mentioned League; this, and his representations to the Government, led to the matter being considered by a Royal Commission, with the result that stringent legislation respecting animals was included in the Mines Act, 1911; eventually resigned his position in order to devote himself entirely to the extended work of the League; engaged in endeavouring to secure just—not kind or merciful—treatment of horses generally, to obtain the total abolition of animal labour in mines, and the use of the Bearing and Hame Reins; promoted in Parliament, 1913–14, a Bill to Prohibit the Docking of Horses; as Assistant Hon. Sec. of the Government Commission for obtaining employment for Belgian refugees (1915), he organised all the work of the Commission in the Metropolitan area. *Publications:* The Tragedy of the Pit Pony; The Pit Pony; Three and eightpence a day; The Unnecessary Whip, A Dog's Life, and other pamphlets; What do you know about a horse; devoted most of his literary efforts to press letters. *Recreations:* reading, particularly Napoleonic literature as a guide to his efforts; "Impossible! a word found only in the dictionary of fools"; loved listening to music; any form of manual labour productive of material results; never played a game. *Address:* Beaconsfield Road, New Southgate, N11. *T:* Finchley 1086. *Club:* National Liberal. *Died 25 May 1920.*

COX, Gen. Sir H. Vaughan, GCB 1921 (KCB 1918; CB 1912); KCMG 1915; CSI 1911; *b* Watford, Herts, 12 July 1860; *e* *s* of late Rev. F. Cox, Rector of Upper Chelsea; *m* 1894, Violet O'Bryen Horsford; one *s* one *d*. *Educ:* Charterhouse; Sandhurst. Second Lieut KOSB 1880; joined Indian Army, 1883; Adjutant SIRVC 1891; DAAGM 1892; DAAGM and Inspecting-Officer, Imperial S Troops, 1894–1902; Officer Commanding 69th Punjabis, 1902–7; AQMG Mobilization Headquarters, 1907; DQMG Headquarters, 1908–11; Military Member, Durbar Committee, 1911; GOC 4th Infantry Brigade, R Pindi, 1912–14; commanded 2nd (Nowshera) Infantry Brigade, Indian Army, 1914; served Afghan War, 1879–80; Khyber Line Force (medal); Burmese War, 1885–89; taking of Minhla Fort, and Mandalay and subsequent operations (despatches, medal, and two clasps); North-West Frontier, 1897; Mohmund Expedition (despatches, medal, and clasp); Tirah, 1907–8 (clasp), Buner (clasp); China, 1901–2 (medal and clasp); European War, 1914–15, command of Gurkha Brigade, in Arabia, Egypt, and Gallipoli (despatches twice,

KCMG, wounded, 2nd class order of White Eagle, Serbia); commanded 4th Australian Division, Egypt and France, 1916–17 (despatches); Secretary Military Department, India Office, 1917–21 (KCB and GCB); member Esher Committee, 1919–20; retired Indian Army, 1921. *Address:* Woodhayes, Camberley, Surrey. *Club:* United Service.

Died 8 Oct. 1923.

COX, Irwin Edward Bainbridge, JP, DL; barrister-at-law; Chairman Petty Sessional Division of Gore, Middlesex, 1894; High Sheriff, Middlesex, 1898–99; *b* Taunton, Somerset, 9 July 1838; *e* *s* of late Mr Serjeant E. W. Cox, Moat Mount, Mill Hill, Middlesex, and Sophia, 2nd *d* of the late W. Harris, MD, RHA; *m* 1865, Katharine (*d* 1898), *d* of late Rev. Bartholomew Nicols, Vicar of Mill Hill, Middlesex. *Educ:* Magdalene Coll., Cambridge (BA). Barrister 1864; elected to Middlesex CC 1889, alderman 1901. MP (C) Harrow Division of Middlesex, 1899–1906; president Harrow Central Conservative Association; Lord of the Manor of Taunton. Owned about 2,000 acres. *Publications:* Anglers' Diary; Hints on Fishing and Shooting; Country House. *Recreations:* fishing, shooting. *Address:* Moat Mount, Mill Hill, Middlesex. *Clubs:* Carlton, 1900, New Oxford and Cambridge.

Died 27 Aug. 1922.

COX, John Charles, LLD; FSA; late Rector of Barton le Street and Holdenby; admitted into the Roman Catholic Church, 1917; *b* 1843; 2nd *s* of Rev. Edward Cox, Rector of Luccombe; *m* 1867, Marian, *d* of E. W. Smith, of Tickton Hall, East Riding, Yorks; seven *s* three *d*. *Educ:* Repton; Som. College, Bath; Queen's College, Oxford. JP, Derbyshire; Member of Royal Archæological Institute and British Archæological Association; Council Member of Canterbury and York Society and British Numismatic Society; Hon. Mem. Derbyshire and East Riding Archæological Societies; formerly Editor of Reliquary, Antiquary, and Derbyshire Archæological Journal; Editor of series of Antiquary's Books; on Advisory Council of Victoria Counties Histories Scheme, and writer therein; contributor to Times, Athenæum, Academy, Country Life, Builder, Guardian, Church Times. *Publications:* Churches of Derbyshire (4 vols), 1876–79; Chronicles of All Saints, Derby, 1881; How to Write History of a Parish, 5th edn, 1910; Lichfield Capitular Monuments, 1886; Three Centuries of Derbyshire Annals (2 vols), 1888; The Sober, Righteous, and Godly Life, 1890; The Gardens of Scripture, 1893; Northampton Borough Records, 1897; Church of St Sepulchre's, Northampton, 1898; Quarter Session Records of Derbyshire, 1899; Strutt's Sports and Pastimes, edited and enlarged, 1901; Little Guide to Derbyshire, 1902; English Monasteries, 1904; Little Guide to Hants, 1904; Royal Forests of England, 1905; History of Canterbury, 1905; Memorials of Old Derbyshire, English Church Furniture (joint), 1907; The Cathedral Church and See of Essex, 1908; Little Guide to Essex, 1909; Parish Registers of England, 1909; Little Guide to Surrey, 1910; Rambles in Surrey, 1910; Churches of Norfolk (2 vols), 1910; Churches of Isle of Wight, 1911; Sanctuaries, 1911; Churches of Cornwall; Churches of Notts, 1912; Memorials of Old Surrey, 1912; Rambles in Kent, 1913; Churchwardens' Accounts, 1913; Churches of Cumberland and Westmorland, 1913; Little Guide to Cambs, 1914; Little Guide to Warwickshire, 1914; The English Parish Church, 1914; Little Guide to Gloucestershire, 1914; Little Guide to Kent, 1915; Pulpits, Lecterns, and Organs, 1915; Bench Ends of English Churches, 1916; contributor to The Tablet and Universe. *Recreation:* archæological research. *Address:* St Albans, Sydenham, SE.

Died 23 Feb. 1919.

COX, John Hugh, CIE 1912; CBE 1919; Excise Commissioner, Central India, since 1906; *b* 1870; *s* of Surg.-Gen. Charles Lindsay Cox, HEICS; *m* 1895, Augusta Edith, *d* of E. C. R. Warner, Barrister-at-law. *Educ:* Clifton College; Balliol College, Oxford. Entered ICS 1888; Joint-Magistrate, 1896; Asst Commissioner, 1899; Deputy Commissioner, 1903; Joint Secretary, Board of Revenue, 1904. *Address:* Indore, Central India.

Died 30 Dec. 1922.

COX, Rt. Hon. Michael Francis, PC; MD; FRCPI, MRIA; Physician St Vincent's Hospital, Dublin; Consulting Physician Children's Hospital, Temple Street; Linden Convalescent Home; and Our Lady's Hospice; Member of Senate and Chairman of Convocation, National University of Ireland; *b* Sept. 1852; *s* of Hugh Cox and Anne, *d* of Richard Kelly, Co. Roscommon; *m* 1886, Elizabeth, *d* of William Nolan, Co. Kildare; one *s*. *Educ:* St Mel's College, Longford; Catholic University of Ireland; London University. When qualified engaged in medical teaching, afterwards in private practice, and as physician and clinical teacher to Hospital; interested in science, in literature, and in public affairs, especially educational. *Publications:* The Country and Kindred of Oliver Goldsmith; Notes on the History of the Irish Horse. *Recreation:* golf. *Address:* 26 Merrion Square, Dublin. *T:* Dublin

1421. *Clubs:* Royal Golf, Dollymount; Leopardstown, Dublin.
Died 20 Feb. 1926.

COX, Palmer; author and artist; *b* Granby, Province of Quebec, Canada, 28 April 1840; 5th *s* of Michael Cox, farmer, and pensioner of the English army; unmarried. *Educ:* Granby Academy. Went to California, 1863; followed railroading, contracting, etc; wrote for newspapers; came to New York, 1875; took up writing and illustrating for children's magazines, and also humorous books. *Publications:* Squibs of Everyday Life, 1874; Hans Von Pelter's trip to Gotham, 1878; How Columbus found America, 1878; That Stanley, 1878; The Brownies, their Book, 1887; Queer People with Wings and Stings, 1888; Comic Yarns (revision of Squibs), 1888; Another Brownies' Book, 1890; Brownies at Home, 1893; Brownies around the World, 1894; Palmer Cox's Brownies, a spectacular play in three acts, 1894; The Brownies in Fairyland, a musical cantata, 1894; Brownies through the Union, 1895; Brownies Abroad, 1899; Brownies in the Philippines, 1904; Palmer Cox's Brownie Primer, 1906. *Recreations:* rifle target shooting, fishing, cycling. *Address:* Granby, Province of Quebec, Canada.
Died 24 July 1924.

COX, Sir Reginald Henry, 1st Bt, *cr* 1921; DL, JP, Berks; *b* 1865; 2nd surv. *s* of late Frederick Cox, DL, JP, of Hillingdon House, and Harefield Place, Uxbridge; *m* 1890, Sybil, *y d* of late T. M. Weguelin, MP. *Educ:* Eton. Senior partner of Cox & Co., Bankers and Army Agents, 16 Charing Cross, SW1. *Address:* 4 Cavendish Square, W1. *T:* Mayfair 6173; Manor Cottage, Old Windsor. *Clubs:* St James', Boodle's. *Died 27 March 1922 (ext).*

COX, Prof. S. Herbert; Emeritus Professor of Mining, Royal School of Mines, South Kensington, SW. *Address:* Vicars Hill Lodge, Boldre, near Lymington, Hants. *Died 11 April 1920.*

COX, Hon. Sir (William Henry) Lionel, Kt 1896; *b* 1864; 2nd *s* of George Cox, MD, of Mauritius; *m* 1st, Lucy (*d* 1900), *d* of S. Pelte; 2nd, 1903, Elizabeth Cushing, *d* of late Lewis Pughe of Scranton, Pennsylvania. *Educ:* Mauritius. Barrister, Middle Temple, 1866; Substitute-Procureur and Advocate-General Mauritius, 1880; Puisne Judge of the Supreme Court, 1881–87; Advocate-Gambling, 1889–93; Chief Justice Straits Settlements, 1893–1906. *Address:* 13 Midvale Road, Jersey. *Clubs:* Athenæum, Sports. *Died 1 Nov. 1921.*

COX-EDWARDS, Rev. John Cox; Chaplain to the King; widower; three *d. Educ:* Emmanuel Coll., Cambridge. Ordained, 1863; Chaplain and Naval Instructor, RN 1871; retired 1899; present at bombardment of Alexandria (medal with clasp, and Khedive's medal); Chaplain of the Fleet and Inspector of Naval Schools, 1888–99; Rector of Ecton, Northants, 1900–8. *Address:* 11 St David's Road, Southsea, Hants. *Died 25 March 1926.*

COXE, Rev. Seymour Richard, MA; Hon. Canon of Newcastle; *b* 23 Jan. 1842; *s* of Ven. Richard C. Coxe, MA, Archdeacon of Lindisfarne; *m* 1872, Fanny, *e d* of Philip S. Coxe; one *s* one *d. Educ:* Durham School; Brasenose College, Oxford; 2nd class mods, BA, MA. Deacon 1866; Priest, 1867; Vicar of Brompton, Yorks, 1873–81; Rector of Baconsthorpe, Norfolk, 1881–85; Vicar of Stamfordham, Northumberland, 1885–95; Rural Dean of Corbridge; Exam. Chaplain to Bishop (Wilberforce) of Newcastle; Proctor in Convocation for Northumberland; Rector of Stoke Bruerne, 1895–1912. *Publication:* The Psalms of Penitence, 1916. *Recreation:* formerly rowing (Captain BNC boat, head of river); Treasurer OUBC. *Address:* The Precincts, Canterbury.
Died 2 Aug. 1922.

COZENS-HARDY, 1st Baron, *cr* 1914, of Letheringsett; **Rt. Hon. Herbert Hardy Cozens-Hardy,** Kt 1899; PC 1901; Chairman of Historical Manuscripts Commission since 1909; Master of the Rolls, 1907–18; *b* Letheringsett, Norfolk, 22 Nov. 1838; 2nd *s* of late William Hardy Cozens-Hardy; *m* 1866, Maria (*d* 1886), *d* of Thomas Hepburn; two *s* two *d. Educ:* Amersham School; Univ. College, London (Fellow). Barrister 1862; QC 1882; a Bencher of Lincoln's Inn. MP (L) N Norfolk, 1885–99; Chairman, General Council of the Bar, to 1899; Judge of the Chancery Division of the High Court of Justice, 1899–1901; Lord Justice of Appeal 1901–7. *Heir: s* Hon. William Hepburn Cozens-Hardy, *b* 25 March 1868. *Address:* 50 Ladbroke Grove, W11. *T:* Park 596; Letheringsett Hall, Holt, Norfolk. *Club:* Athenæum.
Died 18 June 1920.

COZENS-HARDY, 2nd Baron, *cr* 1914, of Letheringsett; **William Hepburn Cozens-Hardy,** KC 1912; JP Norfolk; MP (L) Norfolk,

1918–20; *b* 25 March 1868; *e s* of 1st Baron and Maria, *d* of Thomas Hepburn; *S* father, 1920; *m* 1895, Constance Gertrude Lilian, *e d* of Colonel Sir William Everett, KCMG; one *d. Educ:* New College, Oxford. Called to Bar, Lincoln's Inn, 1893; Commander RNVR, 1914–18; Bencher of Lincoln's Inn, 1916. *Heir: b* Hon. Edward Herbert Cozens-Hardy, *b* 28 June 1873. *Address:* Gunthorpe Hall, Norfolk; 1 Halkin Place, Belgrave Square, SW1; 7 New Square, WC2. *Clubs:* Travellers', Athenæum.
Died 25 May 1924.

CRADDOCK, Charles Robert; *see* Murfree, Mary Noailles.

CRADOCK, Major Sheldon William Keith, DSO 1900; *b* 1 Oct. 1858; *e s* of Christopher Cradock of Hartforth, Yorks, and Georgiana, 3rd *d* of Major Duff. Formerly Captain 5th Dragoon Guards; served Egyptian Campaign, 1882 (medal with clasp, Khedive's star); with Imperial Yeomanry, South Africa (despatches, Queen's medal, 5 clasps, DSO); European War, 1914–16, with 2nd King Edward's Horse (despatches). *Address:* Hartforth, Richmond, Yorks. *TA:* Gilling, West. *Clubs:* Cavalry, Boodle's.
Died 5 July 1922.

CRAFTS, Wilbur Fisk; minister, author, editor, lecturer, traveller, reformer; *b* Fryburg, Maine, 12 Jan. 1850; *s* of Rev. Frederick A. Crafts, a Methodist preacher, of Puritan stock; *m* 1874, Sara J. Timanus, Sunday School writer and speaker. *Educ:* graduated at Wesleyan University, Middletown, Conn; BA 1869; AM 1871; also from Boston University School of Theology, 1871, BD (PhD, Marietta College, 1896). Methodist minister, 1867–79; Congregationalist, 1880–83; Presbyterian since; was pastor of prominent churches in Stoneham, Haverhill, New Bedford, all Mass, Dover, NH, Chicago, Brooklyn, and New York. Since 1871 active in Sunday school work, and participated in scores of Sunday School assemblies, known as Chautauquas, and in countless conventions; founded the American Sabbath Union, later National Lord's Day Alliance, 1889; lectured in all parts of the United States as its Field Secretary, 1889–90; founded The International Reform Bureau, 1895; Superintendent of same down to date; author of 18 laws of Congress, on temperance, gambling, prize fights, impurity, and Sunday; chief editor Christian Statesman, 1901–3; 20th Century Quarterly since 1896; travelled extensively; Chairman of US Government delegates to 12th International Congress on Alcoholism, London, 1909. Member of National Prohibition Amendment Commission, 1915. *Publications:* Through the Eye of the Heart, 1873; Wagons for Eye Gate, Trophies of Song, 1874; Childhood, the Text-Book of the Age, 1875; The Ideal Sunday School, 1876; Fireside Talks on Genesis, Fireside Victories, 1877; the Bible and the Sunday School, The Two Chains, 1878; The Coming Man is the Present Child, Illustrations of the International Sunday School Lessons, Symbols and System in Bible Reading, Normal Outlines, 1879; Rescue of Childsoul, 1880; Normal Half-hours, Plain Uses of the Blackboard, 1881; Talks to Boys and Girls about Jesus, Teacher's Edition of the Revised Testament, Successful Men of To-day, 1883; Must the Old Testament Go? Talks and Stories of Heroes and Holidays, The Sabbath for Man, Rhetoric made Racy, 1884; The Temperance Century, 1885; Reading the Bible with Relish, 1887; The Civil Sabbath, 1890; Practical Christian Sociology, 1895; Social Progress, 1896; Before the Lost Arts, Intoxicating Drinks and Drugs in All Times and Lands, 1900; The March of Christ down the Centuries, 1902; A Primer of Internationalism (editions in Japanese and Arabic); World Book of Temperance, 1908; National Perils and Hopes, 1910; Quarter Century of Moral Legislation, 1911; Bible in Schools Plans of Many Lands, 1914; Illustrated Bible Readings, 1915; Why Dry? Briefs for Prohibition, 1919; Made in Mayflower Land, 1920; Short History of Prohibition, 1921. *Address:* 206 Pennsylvania Avenue, SE Washington, DC. *TA:* Inrefbu.
Died 27 Dec. 1922.

CRAGGS, Sir John (George), Kt 1903; MVO 1902; FCA; *b* 1856; *s* of late James Craggs; *m* 1884, Helen Lewins (*d* 1916), *d* of Andrew Millar; one *s* six *d.* A Chartered Accountant, admitted 1880; Member of the Council of the Institute of Chartered Accountants; Hon. Sec. of King Edward's Hospital Fund, 1897–1906; a member of its Council; received Jubilee Medal, 1897. *Publications:* Rate-supported *v* Voluntary Hospitals; and a technical work on the Agreement of Trial Balances. *Recreation:* golf. *Address:* Redland, Chesham Bois, Bucks. *Clubs:* City Carlton, Ranelagh, Royal Automobile. *Died 2 May 1928.*

CRAIG, Sir Archibald, Kt 1924; MA, LLB, LLD; JP; solicitor, Glasgow; *s* of Andrew Craig, calico printer, Barrhead. *Educ:* High School and University of Glasgow. Clerk of the General Council of the University of Glasgow; Secretary, Glasgow Centre of Franco-Scottish Society; Corresponding Member, Institut d'Etudes Françaises de Touraine; Officier d'Académie; Officier de l'Instruction Publique; Médaille de la Reconnaissance Française; Chevalier de la Légion d'Honneur; Freeman of London; Member of Court of Worshipful Company of Plumbers; Member of Merchants' House, Glasgow; Chairman, Glasgow Unionist Association; Convener (1923) Western Divisional Council Scottish Unionist Association; Member of Council, Faculty of Procurators, Glasgow; Member of Glasgow Council Scottish Ecclesiological Society. *Publications:* Two volumes as to Elder Park, Govan. *Recreation:* foreign travel. *Address:* 174 West George Street, Glasgow. *TA:* Instrument, Glasgow. *T:* Douglas 480. *Clubs:* Glasgow Conservative, Cercle Français, Glasgow.

Died 24 Dec. 1927.

CRAIG, Frank; artist; painter; Member of the National Portrait Society; Hors Concours Société des Artistes Français (Paris Salon); *b* 27 Feb. 1874; 5th *s* of late Hugh Brown Craig and Helen Beet Lloyd Smith; *m* 1898, Katharine, *d* of late R. J. Moser; two *s*. *Educ:* Merchant Taylors' School. Studied on Cook's life class, Fitzroy Street, the Lambeth School of Art, and Royal Academy Schools. Illustrations in the Graphic, Pall Mall, and Nash's Magazine in England, and in Scribner's Magazine, Harper's Magazine, Cosmopolitan, and Hearst's Magazine in America. Following pictures in permanent public collections: Communion on the Velt, Boer War, 1900, in Durban Corporation Gallery; Henley, in National Art Gallery, Sydney; The Heretic, in the National Gallery of British Art (Tate Gallery), London; The Maid, purchased by the French Government for the National Collection, Paris; Goblin Market, purchased by New Zealand Academy of Fine Arts for the proposed National Gallery; and paintings in Government Buildings, Ottawa, and City Hall, Cardiff. Medal of 3rd class, Paris Salon, 1908; medal of 2nd class, Paris Salon, 1910; medal of 2nd class, Barcelona International Exhibition, 1911; medal of 2nd class and award £200, Carnegie Institute, Pittsburg, 1911. *Address:* Shottermill, Surrey. *Club:* Arts.   *Died July 1918.*

CRAIG, Colonel John Francis, CMG 1918; JP Dorset; *b* 1856; *s* of R. M. Craig of Garrane, Co. Tipperary, and *g s* of John Craig of Preston Home, Midlothian, and of Thomas de Quincey; *m* Florence Mary, *d* of James Lyall of Arrat, Forfarshire; two *d*. *Educ:* Shrewsbury; RMA Woolwich. Joined Royal Artillery, 1876; ADC and Private Secretary to Governor of Mauritius, 1879–81; served in S Africa during Boer War, 1881, and in Egypt, 1882 (medal with clasp for Tel-el-Kebir and Khedive's star); served in Chestnut Troop, RHA 1883–85; Adjutant, Clare Artillery Militia, 1887–92; commanded Auxiliary Artillery, Western District, 1902–7; promoted Colonel, 1905, and retired, 1910; volunteered for service, 1914; trained 109th Brigade, RFA, and commanded it at Battle of Loos; took command of DAC of 12th Division, 1916, and served with it until March, 1919 (CMG, despatches 3 times, 1914–15 Star, Victory and Allies medal). *Recreations:* hunting, fishing, bridge. *Address:* Rosehill, Weymouth. *Club:* Royal Dorset Yacht, Weymouth.

Died 8 April 1927.

CRAIG, His Hon. Sir (John) Walker, Kt 1920; KC; Recorder of Belfast and County Court Judge of Antrim, 1911–19; *b* Strabane, Co. Tyrone, 1847; *y s* of late Thomas Craig, of Ardcoen, Strabane; *m* Elsie Oakman, *y d* of late George A. Hume, MD, Crumlin, Co. Antrim. *Educ:* Raphoe Royal School; Queen's Coll., Belfast. 1st classical Scholar, Peel Prizeman, and Senior Scholar in Classics, Queen's Coll., Belfast; gold medallist, Queen's University in Ireland. Called to Irish Bar, 1871; Crown Prosecutor, Co. Louth, 1883–97; Senior Crown Prosecutor, Co. Monaghan, 1892–97; Inner Bar (QC), 1889; Senior Counsel for Belfast Corporation and for Belfast Water Commissioners, 1892–97; contested South Down (LU), 1892; County Court Judge for the counties of Monaghan and Fermanagh, 1897–1911; for many years a Commissioner of Education in Ireland and of Intermediate Education. *Recreation:* motoring. *Address:* 54 The Drive, Hove, Sussex. *Club:* Hove, Hove.

Died 21 July 1926.

CRAIG, Lt-Comdr Norman (Carlyle), KC 1909; RNVR; MP (U) Isle of Thanet Division, Kent, since 1910; *b* 15 Nov. 1868; *s* of William Simpson Craig, MD, and Frances Margaret Morrison; *m* 1918, Dorothy, *d* of E. Storrock Eccles, JP, Hoylake, and *widow* of Lieut Arthur W. Stone, RNVR. *Educ:* Bedford; Peterhouse, Cambridge; Classical Scholar; MA Classical Tripos, 1890. *Recreations:* yachting, motoring, all outdoor sports. *Address:* 10 King's Bench Walk, EC4. *TA:* 50 Temple; *T:* Central 2143; 1 Harley Street, W1. *T:* Mayfair 3958; Fairfield House, St Peter's, Thanet. *T:* Broadstairs 16. *Clubs:* Carlton, St Stephen's, Ranelagh, Prince's, Royal Thames Yacht; Royal Temple Yacht.   *Died 14 Oct. 1919.*

CRAIG-BROWN, Thomas, of Craigend, Midlothian; JP; FSAS; retired manufacturer; *b* 30 July 1844. Accompanied British Commission for negotiating Treaty of Commerce with France, to Paris, 1880; President South of Scotland Chamber of Commerce, 1882; Member Executive Council, Associated Chambers of Commerce of UK, 1883–86, 1896 and 1907; Vice-President, 1904; Member Advisory Committee, Intelligence Branch, Board of Trade, 1900–17; Provost of Selkirk, 1889–94; Member Royal Commission on Exhibitions, 1909, and on International Exhibitions, 1910; Member of Textiles Committee on Trade after War, 1916; Sub-Commissioner, National Serv. Dept 1917; when provincial prisons closed, purchased from Crown the old prison of Selkirk (originally erected at instance of Sheriff Sir Walter Scott), fitted it as public library, and presented it to town. *Publications:* History of Selkirkshire, 2 vols 4to, 1886; Effect of Foreign Tariffs on British Commerce (pamphlet), 1886; Letters of Mrs Cockburn, 1900. *Recreations:* antiquarian research, travel, curling. *Address:* Woodburn, Selkirk. *TA:* Selkirk. *T:* Selkirk 60. *Club:* Royal Societies.   *Died 7 April 1922.*

CRAIGHEAD, Edwin Boone, MA, LLD, DCL; *b* Ham's Prairie, Missouri, 1861; *m* 1889, Kate Johnson; two *s* one *d*. *Educ:* Westminster College, Central College, Mo.; Vanderbilt University; Leipzig; Sorbonne. Professor of Greek, Wofford College, SC, 1890–93; President Clemson College (South Carolina A and M College), Clemson, SC, 1893–97; Central College, Fayette, Mo, 1897–1901; Missouri State Normal School, Warrensburg, 1901–4; Tulane University, New Orleans, 1904–12; President University of Montana, 1912–15; Commissioner of Education, North Dakota, 1915–17; Editor and Owner Billings Star, Weekly and Daily New North-West, Missoula, Mont.; member of American Board, The Hibbert Journal; member Board of Trustees Carnegie Foundation for the Advancement of Teaching; Fellow American Scientific Association; Commissioner of Education for schools of higher education in North Dakota. *Publications:* Skepticism as an Element of Progress; John C. Calhoun; Medical Education in the South; Functions and Limitations of Governing Boards; Inaugural Address at Tulane University and others. *Address:* Missoula, Montana.

Died 1920.

CRAIGIE, Rev. Charles Edward; 2nd *s* of late Admiral Robert Craigie; *m* 1888, Margaret Jane, *d* of late John Dent Goodman; three *s* three *d*. *Educ:* Winchester College; Keble College, Oxford; Wells Theological College. Curate of Woolston, Southampton, 1881; St George's Edgbaston, 1883; Vicar of Kington, 1888–1913; Rural Dean, 1892–1913; Prebendary of Norton in Hereford Cathedral, 1904–22; Rector of Weston-under-Penyard, Ross, Herefordshire, 1913–20; Royal Humane Society Testimonial, 1874. *Address:* Kington, Herefordshire. *Club:* County, Hereford.

Died 30 Aug. 1922.

CRAIGIE, John, KC 1905; Sheriff-Substitute at Glasgow, 1910; *b* 1857. *Educ:* Blairgowrie; Perth Academy; Edinburgh University (MA, LLB). Called to Scottish Bar, 1884. *Publications:* Heritable Rights (3rd edn); Moveable Rights (2nd edn); Elements of Conveyancing; and Conveyancing Statutes. *Recreations:* golf, riding. *Address:* 3 Montague Terrace, Kelvinside, Glasgow.

Died 19 Oct. 1919.

CRAIK, Rt. Hon. Sir Henry, 1st Bt; *cr* 1926; KCB 1897 (CB 1887); PC 1918; MA (Oxon), LLD (Glasgow and St Andrews); MP (C) Glasgow and Aberdeen Universities, since 1906; and one of the Members for the Scottish Universities since 1918; Principal, Queen's College, Harley Street, 1911–14; *b* Glasgow, 18 Oct. 1846; *s* of Rev. James Craik, DD [Moderator of General Assembly, Church of Scotland]; *m* 1873, Fanny Esther (*d* 1923), *d* of late Charles Duffield, Manchester; two *s*. *Educ:* High School, Glasgow; Glasgow University; Balliol Coll., Oxford. Honours in Classics and History, 1869. Examiner in Education Department in 1870; Senior Examiner, 1878; Sec. Scotch Education Department, Whitehall, 1885–1904. *Publications:* Life of Swift, 1882; The State and Education, 1883; Selection from Swift, 1893; English Prose Selections, 1892–96; A Century of Scottish History, 1901; Impressions of India, 1908; Life of Edward, First Earl of Clarendon, 1911. *Heir:* s George Lillie Craik, *b* 1874. *Address:* 5A Dean's Yard, SW1. *T:* Victoria 0256. *Club:* Athenæum.   *Died 16 March 1927.*

CRAMP, Sir William Dawkins, Kt 1908; ISO 1903; *b* Leamington, 29 Dec. 1840; *s* of late James Cramp of Leamington; unmarried. *Educ:* privately. Assistant Master Guilsborough Grammar School, 1860; Clerk in Examiner's Office, HM Customs, London, 1861; HM Inspector of Factories, 1868, in charge successively of North Ireland, Mid-Lancashire, North Staffordshire, and South Midland Districts to 1891; HM Superintending Inspector of Factories, Birmingham, 1891–99; London, 1899–1902; Deputy Chief Inspector, 1902–7. *Address:* Kirkland, Hersham, Walton-on-Thames.

Died 21 Sept. 1927.

CRANE, Robert Newton, KC 1921; MA; *b* 1848; *o s* of late Rev. John Newton Crane, New Jersey, US; *m* 1873, *o d* of late Gerard B. Allen, St Louis, US; three *s* one *d. Educ:* Wesleyan University, Middleton, Connecticut. Founder, with Richard Watson Gilder, Newark (NJ) Morning Register, 1869; Editor St Louis Globe-Democrat, 1873; Consul at Manchester, 1874–80; Member US Supreme Court Bar, 1881; Chancellor Diocese of Missouri, 1882; Barrister Middle Temple, 1894; Bencher, 1919. Chairman American Society in London, 1898; Representative of US Government in South African Deportation Claims Commission, 1901; Agent US Government in Samoan Arbitration Award, 1903–4; US Government Despatch Agent since 1904; Member Ex. Com. Society of Comparative Legislation, 1908; Grand Deacon of Freemasons; Chairman London Branch American Navy League. Doctor Civil Law, Wesleyan University, 1921. *Publications:* contributor to legal and other periodical literatures. *Address:* Sheldon Cottage, Sheldon Avenue, N6. *T:* Mountview 3677; 4 Temple Gardens, EC4. *T:* Central 1083. *Clubs:* Arts, Albemarle, American, Whitefriars.

Died 6 May 1927.

CRANSTON, Brig.-Gen. Sir Robert, KCVO 1905; Kt 1903; CB 1909; CBE 1918; VD, TD; JP, DL; LLD; Officer, Legion of Honour, France, 1904; Knight Commander of St Olaf, Norway, 1906; Col commanded Lothian Brigade; Member of Advisory Committee, War Office; *b* Edinburgh, 2 June 1843; *m* 1868, Elizabeth, *d* of James S. Gilbert, of Edinburgh; two *s* two *d. Educ:* Edinburgh; Tillicoultry; Wilmslow; Paris. Entered The Queen's, 1870; subsequently Lt-Col 2nd Batt.; Fellow of Educational Institute of Scotland and of Royal Scottish Society of Arts; Treasurer of City of Edinburgh, 1899–1903; Lord Provost, 1903–6; contested (C) Leith, 1910. *Address:* Corehouse, 19 Merchiston Avenue, Edinburgh. *T:* Central 823. *Clubs:* Junior Constitutional; Conservative, Edinburgh.

Died 22 Oct. 1923.

CRAUFURD, Rev. Alexander Henry, MA; *b* 1843; *s* of late Rev. C. H. Craufurd, and *g s* of General Robert Craufurd, who commanded the Light Division under Wellington. *Educ:* Oriel Coll., Oxford (Exhibitioner). Life spent chiefly in reading; held few charges, on account of weak health and Broad Church views; preached every autumn in St Peter's, Vere Street, London, 1879–86; spent much time in voluntarily helping to minister to soldiers. *Publications:* General Craufurd and his Light Division; The Unknown God; Enigmas of the Spiritual Life; Christian Instincts and Modern Doubt; Recollections of James Martineau, 1903; The Religion of H. G. Wells and other Essays, 1909; Religion and Ethics of Tolstoy, 1912. *Recreation:* walking. *Club:* Union.

Died 22 Sept. 1917.

CRAVEN, 4th Earl of, *cr* 1901; **William George Robert Craven,** DL; Viscount Uffington, 1801; Baron Craven, 1665; Captain Royal Berks Yeomanry; late ADC to Lord Zetland, Lord Lieutenant of Ireland; HM Lieutenant Co. Warwick; *b* 16 Dec. 1868; *s* of 3rd Earl and Hon. Evelyn Laura Barrington, *d* of 7th Viscount Barrington; *S* father, 1883; *m* 1893, Cornelia, *d* of late Bradley Martin; one *s. Educ:* Eton. Owned 40,000 acres. Coombe Pictures; Elizabeth Queen of Bohemia's collection, left by her to Lord Craven at her death, whom she had previously married. *Heir: s* Viscount Uffington, *b* 31 July 1897. *Address:* Coombe Abbey, Coventry; Ashdown Park, Hampstead Marshall, Newbury, Berks. *Clubs:* Turf, Bachelors', White's; Royal Yacht Squadron, Cowes.

Died 9 July 1921.

CRAVEN, Arthur Scott, (Capt. Arthur Keedwell Harvey James); author and actor; *b* 17 May 1875; *s* of late Stephen Harvey James, Secretary for Law to the Government of India, and Secretary to the Viceroy of India's Council; *m* Lucie, *d* of Colonel Milner, late Royal Irish Regiment; one *s* one *d. Educ:* Cheltenham Junior School; Eton. Formerly special correspondent in India; represented various newspapers in Simla and Calcutta as special correspondent with the Government of India, 1894–97; entered dramatic profession, and assumed the name of Scott Craven; played large number of parts at most of the London Theatres; a frequent contributor to current English and American magazines, and author of several plays. Received commission in the Buffs, 1914; Captain commanding Company, 1915; formerly in the Artists' Rifles, also saw service in India; served European War, Officiating Assistant Provost-Marshal, 15th Div. BEF; Assistant Provost-Marshal, 9th (Scottish) Division BEF, France, Nov.

1915. *Publications:* Poems in Divers Keys; Alarums and Excursions; The Last of the English, a play; The Fool's Tragedy; The Phœnix, etc. *Recreations:* cycling, cricket. *Address:* Hereward House, Westward Ho!, Devonshire. *Clubs:* Garrick, Savage.

Died 14 April 1917.

CRAVEN, Ven. James Brown; Archdeacon of Orkney since 1913; Rector of St Olaf, Kirkwall, 1875–1914; *b* 1850; *s* of Rev. J. E. Craven; unmarried. Hon. DD Aberdeen; ordained 1875; Curate of St Andrew, Aberdeen, 1875. *Publications:* History of Church in Orkney, 1883, 2nd edition, 1912; Journals of Bishop R. Forbes and History of Church in Ross, 1886; The Holy Eucharist (four Sermons), 1889; History of the Church in Moray, 1889; History of the Church in Orkney (1662–88), 1893; (1558–62), 1896; Scots Worthies (1560–1662), 1894; Prayers, etc from Old Scottish Sources, 1894; Scotch Communion Office with Historical Note, 1897; Descriptive Catalogue of Bibliothek of Kirkwall (1683), 1897; Kirkwall Masonic Scroll, 1897; History of the Church in Orkney prior to 1558, 1901; Blazon of Episcopacy in Orkney, 1901; Dr Robert Fludd, the English Rosicrucian, 1902; Ancient Earls of Caithness, 1904; Records of Dioceses of Argyll and The Isles, 1907; History of Church in Caithness, 1908; Count Michael Maier, 1910; Family of Cravie or Craven in Scotland, 1910; Church in South Ronaldshay and Burray, 1911; Sir John Arnot and Arnots in South Ronaldshay, 1913; David, Lord Balcarres, 1913; Esoteric Studies of Archbishop Leighton, 1918. *Address:* Kirkwall, Orkney.

Died 17 April 1924.

CRAVEN, Hon. Osbert William, JP; late Lieutenant Colonel and Hon. Colonel Berkshire Yeomanry; *b* 6 Feb. 1848; 3rd *s* of 2nd Earl of Craven. CC Berks. *Address:* Ashdown Park, Shrivenham. *M:* BL 817. *Clubs:* Turf, Royal Automobile.

Died 5 March 1923.

CRAVEN, Lt-Col Waldemar Sigismund Dacre, DSO 1917; late RFA; *b* 8 Aug. 1880; *s* of late Rev. Dacre Craven and Florence Lees; *m* 1913, Margaret Celia, *d* of late Sir Frederick Mirrielees, KCMG, *g d* of Sir Donald Currie, KCMG; one *s* two *d. Educ:* Haileybury; RMA, Woolwich. 2nd Lieut RFA 1898; served South Africa, 1899–1902 (despatches twice); India, 1907–10; France in BEF Aug. 1914, Nov. 1914, and 1915–17 (severely wounded at battle Ypres, Nov. 1914, despatches four times, DSO); retired pay, 1920; Captain of Blackheath Rugby Football Club, 1911–13, and of Kent RFC 1912 and 1913; Member for Kent on Rugby Union Committee; heavy-weight champion, Army and Navy, 1905 and 1906, and of Western India, 1907. *Recreations:* football, fishing, shooting, big-game shooting, boxing. *Address:* Middleham, Ringmer, Sussex. *M:* P9006, T3123. *Club:* Army and Navy.

Died 11 Dec. 1928.

CRAWFORD, Donald, KC 1903; late Sheriff of Aberdeen, Kincardine, and Banff; DL Aberdeen and Banff; *b* 1837; *s* of Alexander Crawford of Aros, Argyllshire, and Sibella, *d* of Donald Maclean of Kinlochscridan, Writer to the Signet; *m* 1914, Hon. Lilian Mary Susan Moncreiff, 2nd *d* of 3rd Baron Moncreiff. *Educ:* Edinburgh Academy; University of Glasgow; Balliol Coll., Oxford; Heidelberg University. Fellow of Lincoln Coll., Oxford, 1861–81; Advocate at Scottish Bar 1862; Legal Secretary to Lord Advocate, 1880–85; Parliamentary Boundary Commissioner, 1885; MP (L) Lanarkshire NE Division, 1885–95; Member of Scottish University Commission, 1889–97; Sheriff, 1895; Deputy Chairman of Fishery Board for Scotland, 1897 Hon. LLD Aberdeen, 1909. *Address:* 35 Chester Street, Edinburgh. *Clubs:* Brooks's, Oxford and Cambridge; New, Edinburgh.

Died 1 Jan. 1919.

CRAWFORD, Very Rev. John; Canon of Clonfert, 1898; Provost of Kilmacduagh and Canon of Kilconnell; was Member of General Synod, Dublin; Hon. Secretary for many years to Diocesan Board of Education; Member of Senate, Trinity College, Dublin; *m* Mary S., *d* of Rev. Thomas Moore, MA, authoress of Rolf the Imprudent, etc. *Educ:* Portora Royal School, Enniskillen; Trinity College, Dublin (MA, DD). Ordained 1856; Curate of Clontarf, 1856–61 and 1864–70; Kildrought, 1861–64; Curate of Duncavey, 1870–72; Finnes, 1872–77; Woodford, 1877–78; Lickmolassy, 1878–93. *Recreations:* books, nature. *Address:* Clonmoylan Abbey, Portumna, Co. Galway.

Died 8 July 1924.

CRAWFORD, Capt. Lawrence Hugh, CB 1895; RD; RNR; Elder Brother of Trinity House since 1904; *b* Jan. 1857; *e s* of late Lieut William Crawford, RN, formerly Police Magistrate, Williamstown Victoria (*s* of Gen. Robert Crawford, RA), and Marianne Winthrop, *d* of late Admiral Sir Lawrence Halsted, GCB; unmarried. Commander (retired) Royal Naval Reserve. Decorated on recommendation of 1st Lord of the Admiralty. *Recreations:* shooting, golf. *Address:* Holmwood, Claygate, Surrey. *Club:* Junior Constitutional. *Died 19 Oct. 1918.*

CRAWFORD, Col Raymund, CB 1918; retired pay; *b* Paris, 1858; *o s* of Mervyn Archdale Nott Crawford, late of Millwood, Co. Fermanagh, and Emily, *e d* of late Hans Busk; *m* 1st, Evelyn Violet Kempe, *g d* of Robert Bristow, Broxmore Park, Romsey; one *s*; 2nd, Cecilia Grant, *e d* of Wm Grant Henry of Edinburgh and Riga. *Educ:* Stonyhurst. Joined the Royal Irish Regt 1880; transferred permanently to Ordnance Dept 1890; retired as Colonel, 1918. *Club:* Naval and Military. *Died 3 July 1927.*

CRAWFORD, Sir Richard Frederick, GCMG 1919 (KCMG 1911); KBE 1917; Minister Plenipotentiary in HM's Diplomatic Service; a Commissioner of Customs, 1904–11; Adviser to Turkish Minister of Finance since 1911; *b* 18 June 1863; *m* 1894, Augusta, *o d* of late Lieut-Col A. A. D. Lestrange. *Club:* National. *Died 6 Aug. 1919.*

CRAWFORD, Susan Fletcher, ARE; artist; *b* Glasgow; *d* of James R. Crawford, manufacturer in Glasgow. *Educ:* private school; under W. Francis H. Newbery, Glasgow School of Art. Spent most of her life since leaving school at art work in the School of Art and in her own studio; exhibited in most of the principal towns in Europe, Paris, Old and New Salons, the Royal Academy, Royal Scottish Academy, Glasgow Royal Institute of the Fine Arts, Liverpool, Manchester, Leeds, Dundee, and other places, and in Munich, Prague, Vienna and Toronto. *Recreations:* walking, boating, rowing, motoring. *Address:* 10 Lansdowne Crescent, Glasgow, W; Mountgreenan, Tyndrum, Perthshire; (studio) 58 Renfield Street, Glasgow. *T:* 1127 Charing, Glasgow. *Clubs:* Society of Lady Artists; Glasgow Literary, Glasgow. *Died 23 April 1919.*

CRAWFORD, Sir William, Kt 1906; JP, City of Belfast; Chairman of the York Street Flax Spinning Company, Ltd; *b* 1840; *y s* of the late Rev. Alexander Crawford, Presbyterian Minister, Randalstown; *m* 1866, Annie Coulson, *d* of late Rev. James Glasgow, DD, Missionary to India, Fellow of the University of Bombay; four *s* one *d.* Served his apprenticeship with the York Street Flax Spinning Co.; went to Paris, 1862; there for 25 years, represented first the old Company and afterwards the Limited Company; twice President of the Paris British Chamber of Commerce; resident in Belfast since 1888; an ex-President of the Belfast Chamber of Commerce and of the Linen Merchants' Association; took an active interest in the Irish Presbyterian Church and in local charities. *Address:* Mount Randal, Belfast. *T:* Malone 119. *M:* OI 2232. *Clubs:* Ulster, Ulster Reform, Belfast. *Died 12 May 1922.*

CRAWLEY, Alfred Ernest; an authority on social anthropology, and skating, golf, lawn tennis, etc; *b* 1869; *s* of Rev. S. Crawley, Rector of Oddington, near Oxford. *Educ:* Sedbergh; Emmanuel College, Cambridge. Scholar; Classical Tripos, 1st Class (2nd div.). Part ii, 1st class; Sudbury Hardyman Prize; MA. *Publications:* Omar Khayyam in Greek Elegiacs, 1902; The Mystic Rose, a Study of Primitive Marriage, 1902; The Tree of Life, a Study of Religion, 1905; The Idea of the Soul, 1909; The Book of the Ball, 1913; Lawn Tennis, 1919; Lawn Tennis Do's and Dont's, 1922. *Recreations:* lawn tennis, figure-skating, fives, revolver-shooting. *Address:* 78 Redcliffe Square, SW10. *Died 21 Oct. 1924.*

CRAWLEY, William John Chetwode, LLD, DCL; FRGS, FGS, FRHistS, FRSSA; Member of Council of University of Dublin; *b* 15 Nov. 1844; *s* of William Crawley, of Mansfieldtown, Beds, and Margaret Brown Crawley, of Friars' Croft, Irvine, NB; *m* Ellen M., *d* of John M'Carthy, formerly of Desert Serges, Co. Cork; four *s.* *Educ:* Trinity College, Dublin. For many years Director of the Dublin Military Classes; Member of the Academic Body elected to assist the Board of Trinity College in the government of the University of Dublin; sometime Chairman of Dublin Council of Teachers' Guild of Great Britain and Ireland, Council of Classical Association, of Dublin Sanitary Association, and of various local societies; Freemason, for many years Grand Officer of the Freemasons of Ireland. *Publications:* The Handbook of Competitive Examinations (ten editions); Manual of Historical Geography; Caementaria Hibernica, Fasiculus I, 1895, II, 1896, III, 1900; and of numerous Archæological papers, and articles on the History of Freemasonry and kindred subjects; editor and joint author of The Latin Handbook and The French Handbook in the Open Competition Series. *Recreations:* formerly athlete and cricketer. *Address:* Mertonpark, Sandford, Dublin. *Clubs:* New Oxford and Cambridge; University, Dublin; Royal Irish Yacht, Kingstown. *Died 13 March 1916.*

CREAGH, Charles Vandeleur, CMG 1892; Barrister at Law (Middle Temple); *b* 1842; *e surv. s* of late Capt. James Creagh, RN, Cahirbane, Clare, and Grace Emily, *d* of the O'Moore of Cloghan Castle, King's Co.; *m* 1882, Blanche Frances, *e d* of late Captain F. A. Edwardes, 30th Regiment, of Rhydygors, Carmarthenshire; two *s* one *d. Educ:* Royal Naval School, New Cross; Eastman's, Southsea. In 1866, when Assistant District Superintendent Punjab Police, was selected to raise and organise the Sikh Police for the Hong Kong Government; served for sixteen years in the latter colony in magisterial, police, and other appointments; received the thanks of Government for services during the typhoon of 1874; Chief Assistant to Sir Hugh Low, British Resident, Perak, and appointed Judge and Member of Council of that State, 1889; Governor and Chief Judicial Officer, North Borneo, 1888; Governor and Commander-in-Chief of Labuan, 1891–95. Decorated for distinguished services. *Address:* 32 Charlton Road, Blackheath, SE. *Died 18 Sept. 1917.*

CREAGH, General Sir O'Moore, VC 1879; GCB 1909 (KCB 1903; CB 1902); GCSI 1911; Rising Sun of Japan, 2nd class, 1903; *b* Cahirbane, Co. Clare, 2 April 1848; 7th *s* of Captain Creagh, RN, of Cahirbane, Co. Clare; *m* 1st, 1874, Mary Letitia Longfield (*d* 1876), *d* of John Brereton; 2nd, 1890, Elizabeth, *d* of late E. Reade; one *s* one *d. Educ:* private school; Royal Military College, Sandhurst. Ensign, 95th Foot, 1866; Indian Army, 1870; Commanded Merwara Batt. 1882; Commanded 2nd Baluchis, Colonel 129th Duke of Connaught's Own Baluchis, 1912; Asst Quartermaster-General Bombay Command, 1895; Political Resident and General Officer Commanding Aden, 1898–1900; served Afghan War, 1879–80 (despatches, medal, Brevet Major, VC); Zhob Valley Expedition, 1890 (despatches); China Expedition, 1900 (despatches); commanding 1st Class District India, 1903–6; Secretary of Military Department of India Office, 1907–9; Commander-in-Chief, India, 1909–14; retired from the army, May 1914. *Address:* 65 Albert Hall Mansions, Kensington Gore, SW7. *Club:* United Service. *Died 9 Aug. 1923.*

CREAK, Capt. Ettrick William, CB 1901; FRS; RN; *b* 28 May 1835; *s* of late Commander W. Creak, RN; *m* 1867, Grace Mary, *d* of W. B. Brodie; three *s* one *d.* Late Superintendent of Compasses, Hydrographic Department, Admiralty. *Address:* 9 Hervey Road, Blackheath, SE. *Died 3 April 1920.*

CREAN, Major Thomas Joseph, VC 1901; DSO 1915; LRCPI, LRCSI; retired Captain RAMC and 1st Imperial Light Horse; Hon. FRCS; LM Rotunda Hospital, Dublin; late Assistant Master Lying-in-Hospital, Dublin; Arnott Memorial Gold Medal, 1902; Royal Humane Society Testimonial for saving life at sea, 1891; Member of Council Irish Graduate Society, 1908; *b* Dublin, 1873; 2nd *s* of late Michael Theobald Crean, barrister; *m* 1905, Victoria, *o d* of Señor Don Tomás Heredia, Malaga; one *s* one *d. Educ:* Clongowes. Served S Africa and West Africa (wounded Elandslaagte twice dangerously, Tygerskloof); European War, with 1st Cavalry Brigade, 1914–15 (despatches, DSO); officer commanding 44th Field Ambulance, BEF France, 1916; Medical Officer in charge, Hosp., Roy. Enclosure, Ascot; Clin. Asst Samaritan Hosp. for Women, Lond.; Member of the Irish Twenty Club. Decorated for Tygerskloof, South Africa. *Recreations:* Irish International Rugby XV, 1894–96; English team in South Africa, 1896. *Address:* 13 Queen Street, Mayfair, W1. *TA:* Masinto Lond. *T:* 9382 Gerrard. *M:* LM 9850. *Clubs:* Army and Navy, Bucks. *Died 25 March 1923.*

CREASY, Leonard, ISO 1905; MInstCE; *b* 3 Dec. 1854; 3rd *s* of late Sir Edward Creasy, Chief Justice of Ceylon; *m* 1890, Ellen Maud, *d* of late Sir George Elvey, MusD Windsor. *Educ:* University College School, London. Served in Public Works Department, Ceylon, 1874–1905. *Address:* Hurstleigh, Windsor Forest. *Died 9 May 1922.*

CREIGHTON, Charles, MD; *b* Peterhead, 22 Nov. 1847. *Educ:* The Gymnasium, Old Aberdeen; Aberdeen University (MA, 1867). Studied medicine at Aberdeen, Edinburgh, Vienna, and Berlin; occupied with research on cancer for Med. Dep. LGB four years; thereafter Demonstrator of Anatomy at Cambridge for five years (MA King's Coll.); formerly resided in London, occupied with original work in pathology, epidemiology, and microscopic anatomy. *Publications:* Physiology and Pathology of the Breast; Researches on Cancers, etc, of the Breast; Bovine Tuberculosis in Man; Natural History of Cowpox; Jenner and Vaccination; History of Epidemics in Britain; Microscopic Researches on Glycogen, 2 parts; Some Conclusions on Cancer; Shakespeare's Story of his Life; Allegories of Othello and King Lear; Monographs on the second sense in Macbeth, Antony and Cleopatra, Cymbeline, and The Winter's Tale;

Plague in India—conclusions from a visit in 1904-5. *Address:* The Yews, Upper Boddington, Byfield, Northants.

Died 18 July 1927.

CREMIEU-JAVAL, Paul; Consul-General of Monaco for the United Kingdom; Member of the Order of Mercy; Knight of the Order of the Crown of Italy; Grand Officer Order of St Sava, Servia; Commander of the Order of Danilo I of Montenegro; Knight Commander Order of the Redemption, Liberia; Gold Medal of Merit with Ribbon of St Anne, Russia; Officer of the Order of St Charles, Monaco; JP, ACA; *b* 1857; *m* 1893, *d* of Col Bradshaw, JP, of Carrick-on-Shannon. Chairman of Executive of Exhibitions at Earl's Court, 1894-1909. *Recreation:* hunting. *Address:* 39 Ennismore Gardens, SW7. *T:* Western 4095. *Club:* Royal Automobile.

Died 11 April 1927.

CRESSWELL, Colonel George Francis Addison, CVO 1906 (MVO 1901); VD; commanding 5th Battalion Norfolk Regiment, 1904-14; *b* 1852; *m* 1882, Harriet Eva, *d* of Rev. W. H. Gurney, Rector of N Runckton, Norfolk. *Address:* King Street, King's Lynn; Garden House, Hunstanton. *Club:* Royal Thames Yacht.

Died 5 July 1926.

CRESSWELL, Herbert Osborn, FRIBA 1895; architect; *b* Twickenham, 13 June 1860; *s* of late Charles Neve Cresswell, Barrister at Law, of 1 Hare Court, Temple and Ashtead, Surrey; *m* 1911, Mollie, *d* of late Richard Adams, County Court Judge of Limerick. *Educ:* Ewell; private tuition. Articled to Trench and Murray, Surveyors, 1876; in office of Sir Aston Webb, RA, 1879-84; studied in the schools of the RA and the Architectural Association, and travelled abroad; was for a short time in the design branch of the War Office, and started in independent practice in 1885; ARIBA, 1886; served on the Council of the Institute; President of the Architectural Association, 1892-93; during the period of the War was appointed expert adviser to the War Office on questions of Dilapidations and Damage to Buildings in Military Occupation, and made a Captain on the Staff. *Recreations:* water-colour drawing, sketching, photography, mountain climbing, golf, tennis, and other games. *Address:* 12 Charles Street, Knightsbridge, SW. *T:* Western 6644. *Clubs:* Constitutional, Arts.

Died 11 June 1919.

CRESWELL, John Edwards, CBE 1920; MB, BChir (Cantab); retired; *b* 12 March 1864; *s* of late Edmund Creswell of Gibraltar; *m* Catherine Burleigh, *d* of Mathew Towgood, Ceylon. *Educ:* Bruce Castle School; Cavendish College, Cambridge; University College Hospital, London. Served in Egyptian Public Health as PMO at Suez, 1892-1920. *Address:* Charmouth House, Charmouth, Dorset.

Died 25 Oct. 1928.

CRESWICK, Colonel Sir Nathaniel, KCB 1909 (CB 1896); VD; JP for Derbyshire; solicitor; *b* Sheffield, 31 July 1831; *e s* of Nathaniel Creswick, late of Easthill, Sheffield; *m* 1866, Sarah Ann, *o d* of John Walker of York; one *s* one *d*. *Educ:* Sheffield Collegiate School. Received HM Humane Society's Medal, 1861; commanded 4th West York Vol. Artillery (Western Division RA), 1861-97. *Address:* Norton, near Sheffield. *T:* 3028 Sheffield; 127 Beauchief.

Died 20 Oct. 1917.

CREWDSON, Rev. George; Hon. Canon Carlisle; late Rural Dean; *b* Kendal, 18 Aug. 1840; *s* of G. B. Crewdson; *m* 1870, M. S. H. Sweet-Escott (*d* 1910); two *s* two *d*. *Educ:* Windermere College; Trinity College, Cambridge. Curate of All Saints', Mile End, New Town, London, 1864-67; St Andrew's, Clifton, Bristol, 1867-68; St Ann's, Nottingham, 1869-71; Rector of Scaleby, Carlisle, 1871-74; Vicar of St George's, Kendal, 1875-98; Vicar of St Mary's, Windermere, 1893-1911. *Address:* Whitstead, Barton Road, Cambridge. *T:* Cambridge 474.

Died 18 Feb. 1920.

CREWDSON, Wilson, JP; MA; FSA; Chevalier Order of Rising Sun, Japan; Vice-President and Member of Council, Japan Society; Hon. Treasurer Royal Asiatic Society; Hon. Secretary the New East; *b* 13 April 1856; *e s* of Wilson Crewdson, manufacturer, Manchester, and Ellen Waterhouse; *m* Mary Frances Adelaide, *d* of William Bevan of London. *Educ:* Grove House, Tottenham; King's College, Cambridge (Exhibitioner). Joint Hon. Secretary Japan Society, 1904-7; Chairman, 1907-11; SGD English Freemasons, 1914. *Publications:* Japan, Our Ally, 1915; various articles in Nineteenth Century and other Reviews. *Address:* Southside, St Leonards-on-Sea. *TA:* Crewdson Hastings; Queen Anne's Mansions, SW. *T:* 491. *Clubs:* Savage, Oriental, Burlington Fine Arts.

Died May 1918.

CREWE, Sir Vauncey Harpur, 10th Bt, *cr* 1626; JP, DL; *b* 14 Oct. 1846; *s* of Sir John Harpur Crewe, 9th Bt and Georgiana Jane Henrietta Eliza, *d* of Vice-Adm. W. S. Lovell; *S* father, 1886; *m* 1876, Hon. Isabel Adderley, *y d* of 1st Lord Norton; four *d* (and one *s* decd). High Sheriff Derbyshire, 1900. Owned about 28,000 acres. *Heir:* none. *Address:* Calke Abbey, Derby; Warslow Hall, Ashbourne. *Club:* Carlton.

Died 13 Dec. 1924 (ext).

CRICHTON, Lt-Col Hon. Charles (Frederick), JP, DL; *b* 5 Nov. 1841; 2nd *s* of 3rd Earl of Erne; *m* 1873, Madeline Taylour, *e d* of 3rd Marquis of Headfort; one *s* one *d*. *Educ:* St Columba's College, Ireland; Exeter College, Oxford. BA, 1861. Joined 1st Batt. Grenadier Guards, 1861; served in Canada, 1861 and 1864; left the Grenadiers as Captain and Lieut-Colonel in 1876. *Recreations:* hunting, yachting. *Address:* Mullaboden, Ballymore-Eustace, Ireland. *M:* 4799. *Clubs:* Bachelors'; Kildare Street, Dublin; St George's Yacht, Kingstown.

Died 20 Aug. 1918.

CRICHTON, Col Hon. Sir Henry (George Louis), KCB 1911; ADC; DL, JP, Hants; Alderman Hants County Council; Director London and South-Western Railway; Chairman Territorial Association of Hampshire; County Commissioner Boy Scout Association; *b* 7 April 1844; 3rd *s* of 3rd Earl of Erne; *m* 1st, 1869, Letitia Grace (*d* 1888), *d* of Maj. A. W. Cole Hamilton; three *s* one *d* (and two *s* one *d* decd); 2nd, 1890, Lady Jane Emma Baring, CI, CBE 1920, *o d* of 1st Earl of Northbrook. *Educ:* Radley Coll.; Christ Church, Oxford. Served in 10th Royal Hussars, 1863-74; 21st Hussars, 1874-84; Lieut-Col commanding Hampshire Yeomanry Carabiniers, 1884-95; commanding Hampshire Brigade, 1895-1910; ADC to the King; Hon. Col 5th Territorial Batt. Hampshire Regt; Hon. Colonel Hampshire Carabiniers Yeomanry; Commandant Hampshire Volunteer Regiment. *Address:* Netley Castle, Netley Abbey, Hants. *Clubs:* Army and Navy, Cavalry; Royal Yacht Squadron, Cowes; Royal Southern Yacht.

Died 10 May 1922.

CRILLY, Daniel; journalist, reviewer; *b* 14 Dec. 1857; *s* of late Daniel Crilly, Rostrevor, Co. Down; *m* 1887, Mary Ellen Colclough, Dublin. *Educ:* Catholic Institute, Hope Street, Liverpool; Sedgley Park College, Staffordshire. Served his full apprenticeship to a cotton broker in Liverpool; became a journalist; edited the United Irishman, Liverpool, 1876; joined the editorial staff of The Nation, Dublin, 1880; after extension of franchise was selected as National candidate for North Mayo, 1885; stood his trial before a jury in Dublin, 1887, for alleged connection with Plan of Campaign; jury disagreeing, prosecution was abandoned; was Hon. Sec. Home Rule Confederation 1875-77 and Irish National League of Great Britain; MP (AP, HR) North Mayo, 1885-1900. *Publications:* In the Bye-ways with Young Ireland, 1888; The "Felon" Literature of Ireland, 1889; the Celt at Westminster, 1892; Pencillings on Parnassus, 1899; In the Footsteps of John Mitchel, 1900-1. *Recreations:* cricket, cycling.

Died Dec. 1923.

CRIPPS, W. Harrison, FRCS; late Senior Surgeon to St Bartholomew's Hospital; Council Royal College of Surgeons; Chairman Metropolitan Electric Supply Company; *s* of H. W. Cripps, QC; *m* 1st, Blanche, *d* of Richard Potter of Standish House, Gloucestershire; four *s* one *d*; 2nd, Giulia, *d* of Sig. M. N. Ravogli of Rome. *Publications:* Ovariotomy and Abdominal Surgery; Cancer of Rectum. *Recreations:* shooting, fishing. *Address:* Glendaruel, Argyllshire; 19 Bentinck Street, W1. *T:* Mayfair 3514. *Club:* Conservative.

Died 8 Nov. 1923.

CRISP, Sir Frank, 1st Bt, *cr* 1913; Kt 1907; senior partner in firm of Ashurst, Morris, Crisp & Co., solicitors, Throgmorton Avenue, London; *b* 25 Oct. 1843; *o c* of John Shalders Crisp and Harriet, *d* of John Childs of Bungay, Suffolk, opponent of Church Rates and Queen's Printers' Bible Monopoly; *m* 1867, Catherine, *o d* of George D. Howes; four *s* two *d*. *Educ:* privately and University College School; LLB and BA of University of London; admitted Solicitor (Honours), 1869. JP Oxon. Hon. Secretary, Royal Microscopical Society, 1878-89, VP and Treasurer Linnean Society of London, Burlington House, 1881-1906; Member of Board of Trade Committee for Amendment of Companies Act. *Recreations:* Company Law, horticulture, microscopy. *Heir:* *s* Frank Morris, *b* 13 March 1872. *Address:* 17 Throgmorton Avenue, EC; 5 Lansdowne Road, Holland Park Avenue, W; Friar Park, Henley-on-Thames. *Clubs:* Reform, National Liberal.

Died 29 April 1919.

CRISP, Frederick Arthur, JP; *b* Walworth, Surrey, 27 June 1851; *s* of late Frederick Augustus Crisp, of The Hall, Playford, Suffolk and Sarah, *d* of John Steedman, of Walworth; *m* 1880, Gertrude, of John South, of Stutton, Suffolk; six *d*. Lord of the Manor of

Godalming; Patron and Lay Rector of Capel, Surrey. *Publications:* Visitation of England and Wales; Visitation of Ireland; Fragmenta Genealogica; and other genealogical works. *Address:* The Manor House, Godalming, Surrey. *T:* 7 Godalming. *TA:* Crisp, Godalming; Little Wenham Hall, Suffolk. *Clubs:* Royal Societies, Burlington Fine Arts, Royal Automobile.   *Died 25 April 1922.*

CRITCHELL, James Troubridge, JP; late London correspondent of Pastoralists' Review, Sydney Morning Herald, North Queensland Register, and Queensland Sugar Journal; *b* 22 April 1850; *s* of John Critchell of Yeovil. *Educ:* Wootton-under-Edge Grammar School. *Publications:* History of the Frozen Meat Trade, 1912; Polynesian Labour in Queensland, 1892; Preliminary Inquiry into the Markets of the European Continent, 1895; Guide to Queensland; contributor to the Encyclopædia Britannica. *Address:* 22 Basinghall Street, EC; Queensland Cottage, Billericay, Essex. *Club:* Australasian.
Died 8 Nov. 1917.

CRITCHETT, Sir George Anderson, 1st Bt, *cr* 1908; KCVO 1919 (CVO 1905); Kt 1901; MA; FRCSE; Surgeon Oculist to the King, since 1901; Knight of Grace Order of St John; Consulting Ophthalmic Surgeon to St Mary's Hospital, London; 1st President Council of British Ophthalmologists; *b* 18 Dec. 1845; *e s* of late George Critchett, FRCS; *m* 1883, Agnes, *d* of late C. J. Dunphie; one *s* two *d*. *Educ:* Harrow; Caius College, Cambridge. Ex-President of Ophthalmological Society of United Kingdom; President Ophthalmic Section International Medical Congress, 1913; Master of the Oxford Ophthalmological Congress. *Publications:* Eclecticism in Operations for Cataract, 1883; Nature's Speculum in Cataract Extraction, 1886; Conical Cornea, its Surgical Evolution, 1895. *Recreations:* cricket, lawn-tennis. *Heir:* *s* George Montague Critchett [*b* 7 June 1884; *m* 1914, Innes, 3rd *d* of Colonel Wiehe, Littlebourne Lodge, Sandgate. Late Lieut 3rd Batt. Oxfordshire and Bucks LI; Captain 9th London Regiment]. *Address:* 21 Harley Street, W1. *T:* Langham 1065. *Clubs:* Athenæum, Ranelagh, Garrick.
Died 9 Feb. 1925.

CROCKER, George, CB 1902; JP Plymouth; *b* 27 May 1846; *s* of J. W. Crocker; *m* 1st, 1870, Sarah (decd), *d* of J. A. Dodd; 2nd, 1894, Alice, *d* of W. J. Barratt; one *d*. *Educ:* privately; Devonport Dockyard; obtained Queen's Scholarship, 1864. Employed at Admiralty and Portsmouth Dockyard till 1884; Naval Constructor, Bombay and Calcutta, 1884–87; Chatham, 1887–89; Inspector of Admiralty Overseers, 1890–92; Chief Constructor, Devonport, 1892–95; Chatham, 1895–97; Civil Technical Assistant to Adm. Supt at Devonport, 1897–1905; Manager at Devonport, 1906; retired, 1906. *Address:* Coningsby, Mannamead, Plymouth. *TA:* Coningsby, Plymouth.   *Died 21 Feb. 1923.*

CROCKET, Henry Edgar, RWS. *Educ:* Royal College of Art; Julian's, Paris. *Recreation:* concerted music. *Address:* Salterns, Bradford Road, Lewes, Sussex.   *Died 13 March 1926.*

CROFT, Sir Alfred Woodley, KCIE 1887 (CIE 1884); JP Devon; *b* 1841; *s* of C. W. Croft, Plymouth. *Educ:* Mannamead School, Plymouth; Exeter College, Oxford; BA 1863, MA 1870. Sometime Lecturer, Exeter Coll., Oxford; entered Bengal Educational Department, 1866; Director Public Instruction, Bengal, 1877–97; retired 1897; MLC Bengal, 1887–92; President, Asiatic Society of Bengal, 1892–93; Trustee, Indian Museum, 1894–96; Vice-Chancellor, Calcutta University, 1894–96; Hon. LLD 1897. *Address:* Rumleigh, Bere Alston, S Devon. *T:* Bere Alston 13. *TA:* Bere Alston.
Died 29 Oct. 1925.

CROFT, Henry Herbert Stephen; barrister-at-law; Recorder of Tenterden since 1891; *b* Ipswich, 22 Feb. 1842; *e s* of Rev. Stephen Croft, Rector of St Mary, Stoke, Ipswich, Rural Dean; *m* 1876, Emma (*d* 1914), *d* of Mr Kearse, New Brighton; one *s* one *d*. *Educ:* Eton; Trinity Coll., Cambridge. Junior optime, third class Classical Tripos; MA. Appointed Registrar of Courts for trial of Municipal Election Petitions, 1875, 1883–91. *Publications:* editor of Sir Thomas Elyot's Boke named the Governour; joint-editor of Archbold's Quarter Sessions Practice, 4th edn; joint-editor of the Election Manual, 1874. *Address:* 11 King's Bench Walk, EC; 27 Holland Villas Road, W14. *T:* Park 3319.   *Died 8 June 1923.*

CROFTON, Sir Malby, 3rd Bt, *cr* 1838; JP, DL; *b* 20 Aug. 1857; *e s* of Henry Bliss Crofton; *S* grandfather, 1872; *m* 1880, Louisa, *d* of R. J. Verschoyle, Tanrego, Co. Sligo; one *s* two *d* (and one *s* decd). *Educ:* Univ. Coll., Oxford. *Heir:* *s* Major Malby Richard Henry Crofton, *b* 18 Sept. 1881. *Address:* Longford House, Ballisodare, Co. Sligo. *TA:* Beltra.   *Died 17 Sept. 1926.*

CROFTON, Col Morgan, CB 1899; DSO 1886; *b* 2 Jan. 1830; *s* of late Rev. Morgan Crofton; *m* 1894, Ruperta, *d* of late Col Charles Edward Gostling Murray and *widow* of W. H. Willats of Denton Court, Kent. *Educ:* Cheltenham College. Joined army, 1868; served on staff in South Africa, Zulu war, 1879–80; ADC to Gen. commanding Scotland, 1881–85; served Nile Expedition, 1884–86; Chief Staff Officer South Africa, 1894–99. *Address:* 5 Brunswick Terrace, Brighton. *Clubs:* Pratt's, Army and Navy.
Died 9 Jan. 1916.

CROFTS, Major Richard, DSO 1900; RAMC; late Senior Medical Officer, Sierra Leone; retired; *b* 11 Aug. 1859. Served against the Jebus, Lagos, 1892 (despatches, medal with clasp).
Died 16 Jan. 1916.

CROISET, Alfred; Dean of the Faculty of Letters, Paris; Member of the Academy of Inscriptions and Belles-Lettres; Hon DLitt, Oxford, 1903; Corresponding Fellow of the British Academy; *b* 1845. *Publications:* La Poésie de Pindare; Histoire de la Littérature grecque, 5 vols (with Maurice Croiset); Les Democraties antiques. *Address:* 13 rue Cassette, Paris.   *Died 7 June 1923.*

CROKER, Mrs Bithia Mary; novelist; *o d* of late Rev. William Sheppard, Rector of Kilgefin, Co. Roscommon; *m* Lieut-Col John Croker, late Royal Scots and Royal Munster Fusiliers; one *d*. *Educ:* Rockferry, Cheshire; Tours. Spent 14 years in the East (India and Burmah). *Publications:* Proper Pride, 1882; Pretty Miss Neville, 1883; Someone Else, 1884; A Bird of Passage, 1886; Diana Barrington, 1888; Interference, 1891; A Family Likeness, 1892; Mr Jervis, 1894; The Real Lady Hilda, 1895; Beyond the Pale, 1897; Peggy of the Bartons, 1898; Terence (dramatised in the USA); Infatuation, 1899; The Happy Valley; Angel, 1901; The Cat's Paw; Her Own People; The Spanish Necklace, 1907; Katherine the Arrogant, 1910; In Old Madras, 1913; Lismoyle, 1914; Given in Marriage, 1916; The Road to Mandalay, 1917; Odds and Ends, 1919. *Recreations:* reading, travelling, theatre. *Address:* 5 Radnor Cliff, Folkestone. *Clubs:* Writers', Sesame.   *Died 20 Oct. 1920.*

CROKER, Richard; Leader of Tammany Hall, 1884–1903; *b* Clonakilty, Co. Cork, 23 Nov. 1841; *m* 1st, 1873, Elizabeth, *d* of Samuel Fraser, New York; one *s* one *d*; 2nd, 1914, Bula Benton Edmondson, New York. Alderman, New York, 1868–70; Coroner, 1873; served term, 1876; re-elected, served 1879; Fire Commissioner, 1883; City Chamberlain, 1889–90; Freeman of Dublin, 1908. *Recreation:* horse-racing; won the Derby, Irish Derby, Curragh, and Baldoyle Derby with Orby, 1907; also won the English Guineas with Rhodora, Orby's half-sister, 1908. *Address:* Glencairn, Co. Dublin; The Wigwam, Palm Beach, USA. *Club:* Democratic, New York.   *Died 29 April 1922.*

CROLE, Charles Stewart, CIE 1898; late ICS; retired, 1898; *m* 1st, Katharine (*d* 1913); 2nd, 1913, Mary, *e d* of late Walter de Voil. *Educ:* High School and Univ., Edinburgh. Entered service, 1862; District and Sessions Judge, Kistna, 1881; Collector and Magistrate, 1882; Member of Board of Revenue, 1890; Legislative Board, 1893; contested Enfield (L), 1900. *Publication:* Chiuglepat District Manual. *Address:* 28 Queen's Mansions, Victoria Street, SW.
Died 4 May 1916.

CROLE, Gerard Lake, KC; Advocate, Sheriff of Lothian and Peebles since 1918; *b* 22 Nov. 1855; *y s* of late David Crole, Solicitor of Inland Revenue for Scotland, 1893; *m* Elizabeth Ann, *widow* of late Patrick Turnbull, CA, Edinburgh, and 2nd *d* of late George Carrick Coats, Aberdeen; one *s*. *Educ:* The Royal High School and University, Edinburgh. MA 1876; LLB 1880. Called to Scottish Bar, 1881; KC 1904; LLD 1919; Principal Clerk of Justiciary, 1892–1918. Elder, United Free Church. *Recreations:* golf, fishing. *Address:* 1 Royal Circus, Edinburgh. *T:* Central Edinburgh 21572. *Club:* Northern, Edinburgh.
Died 26 Oct. 1927.

CROLY, Very Rev. Daniel George Hayes; Dean of Killala, 1911–15; Incumbent of St Patrick's, 1904–15. *Educ:* Trinity College, Dublin (MA). Ordained 1870; Curate of Kilcommon, 1870–71; Pulathomas, 1871–77; Perpetual Curate of Kilaraught, 1877–78; Vicar of St Anne, Easky, 1878–1904; Examining Chaplain to Bishop of Tuam. *Address:* Hill House, Killala, Ballina.

Died 14 Oct. 1916.

CROMER, 1st Earl of, *cr* 1901; **Evelyn Baring,** GCB 1895 (KCB 1887; CB 1885); OM; GCMG 1888; KCSI 1883; CIE 1876; FRS; PC; Hon. FBA; Baron Cromer, 1892; Viscount Cromer, 1899; Viscount Errington, 1901; Minister Plenipotentiary in the Diplomatic Service;

b Cromer Hall, Norfolk, 26 Feb. 1841; *s* of Henry Baring, MP, and Cecilia Anne, *d* of Vice-Admiral William Windham, Felbrigg Hall, Norfolk; *m* 1st, 1876, Ethel Stanley (*d* 1898), *d* of Sir Rowland Stanley Errington, 11th Bt; two *s*; 2nd, 1901, Lady Katherine Georgiana Louisa Thynne, 2nd *d* of 4th Marquess of Bath; one *s*. *Educ:* Ordnance School, Carshalton; RMA, Woolwich. Hon. DCL Oxford; Hon. LLD Cambridge. Entered Royal Artillery, 1858; Capt. 1870; Major, 1876; ADC to Sir Henry Storks in Ionian Islands, 1861, and Secretary, 1865, during inquiry into outbreak in Jamaica; Private Secretary to Earl of Northbrook, Viceroy of India, 1872–76; Commissioner Egyptian Public Debt, 1877–79; Controller-General in Egypt, 1879; Financial Member of Council of Governor-Gen. of India, 1880; Financial Assistant at Conference in London on Egyptian Finance, 1884; Agent and Consul-Gen. in Egypt, 1883–1907. Protestant. Albert Medal, Society of Arts. *Publications:* Staff College Essays; Paraphrases and translations from the Greek; The War Game; and other military works; Modern Egypt, 2 vols, 1908; Ancient and Modern Imperialism, 1910; Political and Literary Essays, 1908–13; 3rd Series, 1916; Abbas II, 1915. *Recreations:* shooting, fishing. *Heir:* *s* Viscount Errington, *b* 29 Nov. 1877. *Address:* 36 Wimpole Street, W. *T:* Mayfair 473. *Club:* Turf.

Died 29 Jan. 1917.

CROMIE, Commander Francis Newton Allen, DSO 1916; Kt of St George; Chevalier Légion d'Honneur; commanding E19 and English flotilla in the Baltic since 1916; *b* Duncannon Fort, Ireland, 30 Jan. 1882; *s* of late Capt. F. C. Cromie, Hants Regt, Consul-General, Dakar, and Mrs Lennard, *d* of T. I. Webb Bowen, late Chief of Police, Pembrokeshire. *Educ:* Haverfordwest Grammar School; Britannia. Joined Repulse 1898; midshipman, 1898; with Barfleure brigade in Seymour's Expedition, 1900 (China medal, Pekin clasp, despatches); Sub.-Lt 1901; Lt 1903; entered submarine service, 1903; Humane Society's medal (bronze) trying to save a man overboard from A3, 1906; commanded HMS Onyx and III flotilla submarines, 1911–12; Rosario and China flotilla submarines, 1913–14; commissioned E19, August 1915; forced passage into Baltic, 10 Sept. 1915 (4th class St Vladimir with swords); entirely suspended German traffic in Baltic for one week, Oct. 1915 (St Anne, 2nd class); sank German cruiser Undine, 7 Nov. 1915 (St George's Cross, prom. Commander, DSO). *Recreations:* out-door sports, sailing. *Address:* Cromore, Dovercourt, Essex.

Died 31 Aug. 1918.

CROMIE, Rev. William Patrick, MA; Rector of Stoke Newington since 1918; Prebendary of St Paul's, since 1917; Rural Dean of Hackney and Stoke Newington, 1919; Proctor in Convocation for Diocese of London, 1921; *m* 1893, Harriette, 2nd *d* of late John Jones, The Hollies, Oswestry, Shropshire; one *s* two *d*. *Educ:* Corpus Christi College, Cambridge. Deacon, 1891; Priest, 1892; Curate of St Philip, Kingston-on-Hull, 1891–94; St Stephen, Kingston-on-Hull, 1894–96; Curate-in-charge of the Abbey Church (St Andrew the Less), Camb., 1896–1900; Vicar of Harlesden (All Souls) with St Luke's and St Mark's, 1900–18; Surrogate to Master of Faculties, 1902; Chaplain to Willesden Union, 1907–18; Assessor under Clergy Discipline Act, 1912; Chaplain to the Forces, 1914–18; Rural Dean of Willesden, 1914–18. *Recreation:* fishing. *Address:* The Rectory, Stoke Newington, N16.

Died 3 Aug. 1927.

CROMPTON, James Shaw, RI; ARBC; *b* Bootle, near Liverpool, 7 March 1853; *s* of Robert Crompton, author and editor; *m* 1886; two *d*. *Educ:* under John Finnie, Liverpool; Liverpool Academy; Heatherley's School of Art. Member of the Selborne Society (Vice-President and Council); Langham Sketching Club (past-Chairman); Royal Drawing Society; Hampstead Art Society (Council); exhibited at New Gallery, RA, RI, and the Provinces; Picture purchased by the Council for Permanent Collection, Liverpool; did much book illustration. *Recreations:* walking, gardening. *Address:* 1 England's Lane, Haverstock Hill, NW. *Club:* Langham Sketching.

Died 22 July 1916.

CROMPTON, John Gilbert Frederic, JP; *b* 1869; *o s* of late John Gilbert Crompton and 2nd wife Caroline Georgiana, *o d* of late Frederick Chaplin of Tathwell Hall, Lincolnshire. High Sheriff Derbyshire, 1917. *Address:* Flower Lilies, Windley, Derby. *Club:* Boodle's.

Died 31 March 1919.

CRONSHAW, Rev. Christopher; Hon. Canon of Manchester. *Address:* 63 Cambridge Road, Southport, Lancs.

Died 3 Jan. 1921.

CRONSHAW, Rev. George Bernard, MA; Principal of St Edmund Hall, Oxford, since 1928; late Fellow and Bursar, Queen's College,

Oxford; *m* 1926, Dorothy, *d* of Bernard Wardle, of Scarthwaite, nea Lancaster. *Address:* St Edmund Hall, Oxford.

Died 20 Dec. 1928

CROOK, Charles Williamson, BA, BSc (Lond.); MP (U) East Ham (North), 1922–23, and since 1924; Member of Senate, London University; *b* 4 March 1862; *o surv. s* of William Crook and Mary Williamson, Preston, Lancs; *m* 1900, Grace, *e d* of Benjamin and Grace Swinfen, Hackney; one *s* one *d*. *Educ:* St James's National School, Barrow-in-Furness; Alston College, near Preston; St John's College, Battersea. Headmaster Central County Secondary Sch., Wood Green. Member of the Executive NUT fourteen years; Member of the E and O Council, NUT, fifteen years; Member of Board of Teachers Provident Society; Treasurer of the War Aid Fund, NUT; President of the NUT, 1916–17; former Member of the Burnham Committee; on Salaries in Primary, Secondary, and Technical Schools; Hon. Secretary Conservative Teachers' Advisory Committee, and of the National Savings Committee. *Recreation:* walking. *Address:* 15 Manor Road, Sidcup. *TA:* Curriculum, Kincross, London. *T:* Museum 1570 and 1571. *Club:* Constitutional.

Died 29 March 1926.

CROOKE, William, CIE 1919; Hon. DSc Oxon 1919; Hon. LittD Dublin 1920; retired Indian Civil Service; *b* 6 Aug. 1848; *m* 1884, Alice, *y d* of Lieut-Col George Carr, 2nd Madras Native Infantry; two *s*. *Educ:* Trinity College, Dublin. Entered Indian Civil Service, 1871; served as Assistant Magistrate and Collector, and District Magistrate and Collector in the United Provinces of Agra and Oudh; Manager of the Awa Estate, Court of Wards. President Anthropological Section British Association, 1910; President Folklore Society, 1911–12. *Publications:* The Tribes and Castes of the North-Western Provinces, 1896; Popular Religion and Folklore of Northern India, 1896; Anglo-Indian Glossary, 1903; Things Indian, 1906; edited Fryer's New Account of East India and Persia, Hakluyt Society, 1909; Observations on the Mussalmans of India, 1916; Annals of Rajasthan, 1920; Islam in India, 1922; numerous articles in Hastings' Encyclopædia of Religion and Ethics, 1908–18, and numerous papers in Journal Royal Anthropological Institute, Folklore Society Journal, etc. *Address:* Langton House, Charlton Kings, Cheltenham. *Club:* New, Cheltenham.

Died 25 Oct. 1923.

CROOKES, Prof. Sir William, OM 1910; Kt 1897; FRS 1863; Hon. LLD Birmingham; Hon. DSc (Oxon, Cambridge, Ireland, Cape of Good Hope, Sheffield, Durham); proprietor and editor of Chemical News; President, Royal Society, 1913–15 (Foreign Secretary, 1908–12); *b* 17 June 1832; *s* of late Joseph Crookes; *m* 1856, Ellen (*d* 1916), *d* of W. Humphrey of Darlington; four *s* one *d*. *Educ:* Royal Coll. of Chemistry. Professor of Chemistry, Training Coll., Chester, 1855. Discoverer of—the Selenocyanides; Thallium, a new element, 1861; Repulsion resulting from Radiation, 1873; the Radiometer, 1875; Illumination of Lines of Molecular Pressure, 1878; Radiant Matter, 1879, an ultra-gaseous, fourth state, of matter; Radiant Matter Spectroscopy, 1881; New Elements in Gadolinite, etc, 1886; Genesis of Elements, 1887; Some Possibilities of Electricity, Wireless Telegraphy, 1892; Fixation of Atmospheric Nitrogen, 1898; the Spinthariscope, 1903; Eye-Preserving Glass for Spectacles, 1913. Past President, Chemical Society, Brit. Assoc., Inst. Elect. Eng., Soc. Chem. Industry; Hon. Member, Roy. Phil. Soc. Glasgow, Roy. Soc. NSW, Pharm. Soc., Chem. Metall. and Mining Soc. of South Africa, Amer. Chem. Soc., Amer. Philos. Soc., Roy. Soc. Sci. Upsala, Deutsch. Chem. Gesell. Berlin, Psychol. Soc. Paris, Antonio Alzate Sci. Soc. Mexico, Sci. Soc. Bucharest, Reg. Accad. Zelanti; Foreign Mem. Accad. Lincei, Rome; Corresp. Inst. de France (Acad. Sci.), Corresp. Mem. Bataafsch Genoots., Rotterdam, Soc. d'Encouragement pour l'Indust. Paris; For. Assoc. National Acad. Sciences, Washington; Foreign Mem., Royal Swedish Academy of Sciences. International Exhibition, 1862, medal; Académie des Sciences, 1880, gold medal and prize of 3000 frs; Electrical Exhibitions, Paris, 1881, medal; Society of Arts, 1885, Ferguson Gold Medal; Exposition Universelle, Paris, 1889, medal; Society of Arts, 1899, Albert Gold Medal; Franklin Institute, Philadelphia, 1912, Elliott Cresson Gold Medal; Soc. Chem. Industry, 1912, gold medal. Royal medallist, Davy medallist, Copley medallist, and three times Bakerian Lecturer of the Royal Society. *Publications:* Select Methods in Chemical Analysis, 4th edition, 1905; Manufacture of Beetroot-Sugar in England, 1870; Handbook of Dyeing and Calico-Printing, 1874; Dyeing and Tissue Printing, 1882; Kerl's Treatise on Metallurgy, 1868, with Ernst Rohrig; Wagner's Chemical Technology; Auerbach's Anthracen and its Derivatives, 2nd edition, 1890; Ville's Artificial Manures, 3rd edition, 1909; A Solution of the Sewage Question; The Profitable Disposal of Sewage; The Wheat Problem, 1899, 3rd edn 1917; Diamonds, 1909. *Address:* 7 Kensington

Park Gardens, W. *TA:* Crookes, Nottarch, London. *T:* 1601 Park. *Clubs:* Athenæum, Royal Societies, Carlyle.

Died 4 April 1919.

CROOKS, Rt. Hon. William, PC 1916; MP (Lab) Woolwich, 1903–Jan. 1910, and Dec. 1910–Dec. 1918, Woolwich E, 1918–Feb. 1921; *b* 6 April 1852; *m* 1st, 1871, Matilda South (*d* 1892); 2nd, 1893, Elizabeth Coulter; two *s* four *d*. Apprenticed to a cooper, 1866. Member of LCC for Poplar, 1892–1910; Mayor of Poplar, 1901; Chairman Poplar Board of Guardians, 1898–1906. *Address:* 81 Gough Street, Poplar, E.

Died 5 June 1921.

CROOM, Sir (John) Halliday, Kt 1902; LLD, MD; FRCS, FRCP, FRSE; Hon. MD, Dublin; Emeritus Professor of Midwifery, Edinburgh University; late President Royal College of Surgeons, Edinburgh, and British Gynaecological Society; three times President of Edinburgh Obstetrical Society; Hon. Fellow American Society of Gynaecologists, and Société Gynecologie, Belgium; *b* Sanquhar, Dumfries, 15 Jan. 1847; *s* of Rev. D. M. Croom of Lauriston Place UP Church, Edinburgh; *m* 1875, Anna Isabella, *d* of Daniel Walker, HM Inspector of Factories for Scotland; one *s* three *d*. *Educ:* Royal High School, Edinburgh; University of Edinburgh; afterwards studied in London and Paris. Was for several years assistant to Professor of Gynaecology and Obstetrics in the University of Edinburgh; formerly Lecturer on Obstetrics and Gynaecology in the Edinburgh School of Medicine, Minto House; Chairman Central Midwives Board for Scotland; Phys. Roy. Maternity Hosp. Edin.; Consulting Gynaecologist Royal Infirmary; was on the active staff for twenty years; was for fifteen years prior to 1901 in charge of Gynaecological wards at the Royal Infirmary, Edinburgh. *Publications:* Minor Gynaecological Operations and Appliances, 2nd edition, 1883; The Bladder during Parturition, 1883; Collection of Clinical Papers, 1901; numerous contributions to scientific and medical journals. *Address:* 8 Morningside Place, Edinburgh. *T:* Edinburgh 2284.

Died 27 Sept. 1923.

CROPPER, Charles James, JP, DL; Chairman of James Cropper and Co., Ltd; late Director of London and North-Western Railway, and of Cockermouth, Keswick, and Penrith Railway; *b* 1852; *s* of James Cropper, late MP for Kendal; *m* 1876, Hon. Edith Emily Holland (*d* 1923), *e d* of 1st Viscount Knutsford; one *s* four *d*. *Educ:* Rugby; Trinity Coll., Cambridge. High Sheriff, 1905. *Address:* Ellergreen, Kendal. *TA:* Burneside. *T:* Kendal 385 D. *Club:* Brook's's.

Died 6 Oct. 1924.

CROSBIE, Lieut-Gen. Adolphus Brett; Royal Marines; *e* surv. *s* of late Capt. W. A. Crosbie of the Rifle Brigade; *m* 1884, Anne Geraldine, *o d* of late Capt. Thomas Lloyd of Prospect, Co. Limerick, and Huntington Ct, Herefordshire. Entered Army, 1864; Maj.-Gen. 1900; Lieut-Gen. 1903; served China, 1867–69 (despatches); Ashanti in command of Royal Marines (despatches, medal with clasp); commanded Royal Marines, Congo, 1875 (despatches); commanded Royal Marines, Niger, 1876 (despatches), brevet of Major; ADC to Queen Victoria, 1895–1900. *Address:* Harestock House, Winchester. *Club:* Army and Navy.

Died 15 Dec. 1916.

CROSBIE, Henry, CB 1911; late Colonel Commanding 3rd Battalion the Manchester Regiment; *b* 8 Aug. 1852; 4th *s* of Captain W. A. Crosbie, late Rifle Brigade; *m* 1880, Flora (marr. diss. 1910), *d* of late William Leban Holman; two *d*. *Educ:* Royal Military College, Sandhurst. Joined 81st Regiment as Sub-Lieutenant, 1872; Lieutenant, 1874; Captain, 1882; Major 1st Sherwood Foresters, 1894; Reserve of Officers, 1896; Lt-Colonel 5th Manchesters, 1900; granted hon. rank of Colonel, 1901; served E Indies, 1874–83; Afghan War, 1878–79 (medal with clasp); S Africa, 1901–2 (medal with 4 clasps); commanded 5th Bn Manchester Regt (later 3rd Battalion) during the war in S. Africa (despatches); Coronation medal for King George V, 1911. *Recreations:* travelling, boating. *Club:* Naval and Military.

Died 19 Dec. 1928.

CROSBY, Sir Thomas Boor, Kt 1907; FRCS; Lord Mayor of London, 1911–12; Sheriff, 1906–7; *b* 1830. MD, LLD, Dublin and St Andrews. Member and late President Hunterian Society. Medical Officer to the Scottish Amicable, Scottish Provident, and Yorkshire Life Offices; formerly Demonstrator of Anatomy and House Surgeon, St Thomas's Hospital. Legion of Honour (Officier), France; Crown, Germany; St Olaf, Norway; Danebrog, Denmark; Rising Sun, Japan. *Address:* 19 Gordon Square, WC; 136 Fenchurch Street, EC. *Club:* Constitutional.

Died 7 April 1916.

CROSLAND, T. W. H.; *b* 21 July 1868; *s* of William Crosland of Leeds; *m* Annie, *d* of Edward Thomas Moore, Solicitor, Oxford. *Educ:*

privately. Contributed to the Leeds Mercury supplement, Yorkshire Weekly Post, Black and White, Outlook, Academy, Saturday Review, The Gentlewoman, Public Opinion, Evening Standard, etc; Assistant Editor of the Outlook, 1899–1902; Editor of The English Review, 1905; Assistant Editor of the Academy, 1908–11. *Publications:* Literary Parables; Other People's Wings; The Finer Spirit (verse); English Songs and Ballads; The Unspeakable Scot, 1902; Lovely Woman, 1903; The Lord of Creation, 1904; The Enemy, 1904; The Wild Irishman, 1905; The Suburbans, 1905; Red Rose (verse), 1905; The Country Life, 1906; The Beautiful Teetotaller, 1907; Sonnets, 1912; Taffy was a Welshman, 1912; The First Stone, 1912; The Chant of Affection, 1915; The Showmen, 1915; The Soul of a Crown Prince, 1915; War Poems by X, 1911; Collected Poems, 1911; The English Sonnet, 1916; Pop Goes the Weasel, 1924; The Laureate's Job (verse) 1924. *Address:* Mitcham House, Mitcham Street, Marylebone, NW. *T:* Paddington 1354.

Died 23 Dec. 1924.

CROSS, Hon. Alexander George, BA, BCL; Puisne Judge, Quebec, since 1907; Professor of Commercial Law, McGill University; *b* 1858; *m* 1907, Laura M., *d* of late J. J. Buchanan, Dundee, PQ. *Educ:* McGill University. Advocate, 1881; KC 1899; Mayor of Westmount, 1903–4. *Address:* 369 Metcalf Avenue, Westmount, Montreal.

Died 19 Aug. 1919.

CROSS, Hon. Charles Wilson; late Attorney-General of Alberta; *b* Madoc, Ontario, Canada; *s* of Thomas and Marie Cross; *m*; one *s* two *d*. *Educ:* Upper Canada College; Toronto University, and Osgoode Hall, Toronto. Barrister at Edmonton, Alberta. *Address:* Edmonton, Alberta. *Club:* Edmonton.

Died 2 June 1928.

CROSS, Hon. John Edward, JP Cheshire; Land Agent; Member of Council of the Royal Agricultural Society, England, and of Council of the Land Agents Society; Director of the Manchester Branch of the Atlas Assurance Co.; Member of District Council and Board of Guardians; *b* 6 Sept. 1858; *e surv. s* of 1st Viscount Cross; *m* 1st, 1889, Katherine Ellen (*d* 1891), *d* of late Rev. F. Haden Cope; one *d*; 2nd, 1895, Sophy Katherine Mary, *d* of late H. R. Sandbach, DL, JP of Hafodunos, Denbighshire; two *d*. *Educ:* Wellington; Pembroke College, Cambridge. Served in the 1st Royal Lancashire Militia and the Princess Charlotte of Wales Royal Berks Volunteers; acted as private secretary to late Lord Wantage; member of the Cheshire County Council, 1904–7. *Address:* The West Hall, High Legh, Knutsford. TA: Highlegh. *T:* 74 Lymm, Warrington District. *M:* M 3746. *Clubs:* Carlton, Wellington; Union, Manchester.

Died 26 June 1921.

CROSSE, Lieut-Col Charles Robert, CMG 1917; MVO 1909; late Royal West Kent Regiment; Secretary, National Rifle Association since 1899; *b* India, 19 Nov. 1851; 2nd *s* of late Robert Crosse, 73rd BNI; *m* 1874, Catherine, *o d* of late Major-General Whitworth Porter, RE. *Educ:* Paris, private tutor; RM College, Sandhurst. Served 20 years in the army, retiring with the rank of Lieut-Col 1892; was Secretary of the United Service College, Westward Ho; also Brigade-Major of the Hampshire Vol. Infantry Brigade. *Address:* The Secretary's Lodge, Bisley Camp, Surrey. *Club:* Junior United Service.

Died 15 Feb. 1921.

CROSSING, William; author; *b* Plymouth, 14 Nov. 1847; *s* of Joseph Crossing; *m* 1872, Emma (*d* 1921), *d* of Richard Witheridge, Ivybridge; no *c*. *Educ:* South Devon Collegiate School; Mannamead School. The Dartmoor country among earliest recollections; went to sea on leaving school; afterwards settled down on the edge of Dartmoor; Free Churchman; gave much attention to antiquarian investigations; for eight years contributed West-country People and Places to the Western Weekly News; great lover of animals. *Publications:* The Ancient Stone Crosses of Dartmoor; Amid Devonia's Alps; Tales of the Pixies; A Hundred Years on Dartmoor; From a Dartmoor Cot; Gems in a Granite Setting; Guide to Dartmoor; Folk Rhymes of Devon; Echoes of an Ancient Forest; Oranmere and other Poems, 1927, etc. *Recreation:* reading. *Address:* Cross Park House, Hartley, Plymouth.

Died Sept. 1928.

CROSSLEY, Arthur William, CMG 1917; CBE 1919; DSc (Vict.), PhD (Würzburg), Hon. LLD (St Andrews); FRS, FIC; Past-President Chemical Society; FIC; Lieutenant-Colonel, late RE; Officier de la Légion d'Honneur; Director British Cotton Industry Research Association; *b* 25 Feb. 1869; *s* of late Richard Crossley, of Accrington, Lancashire; *m* 1901, Muriel, *d* of Ralph Lamb, of Liverpool; one *s* one *d*. *Educ:* Mill Hill School; Victoria University of Manchester; Würzburg and Berlin Universities; Longstaff Medallist of the Chemical Soc., 1918. Late Berkeley Fellow of the Owens College;

late Lecturer on Chemistry at St Thomas'Hospital; late Professor of Chemistry to the Pharmaceutical Society of Great Britain; late University Professor of Chemistry in University of London, King's College. *Publications:* contributions to the Journals of the Chemical Societies of London and Berlin. *Recreations:* fishing, billiards. *Address:* Shirley Institute, Didsbury, Manchester; Thorngrove, Alderley Edge, Cheshire. *Club:* Devonshire.

Died 5 March 1927.

CROSSLEY, Rt. Rev. Owen Thomas Lloyd, DD; Assistant Bishop to Bishop of Llandaff, 1914–20; Chief Missioner and Superintendent of Special Service Work, Diocese of Llandaff, 1914–21; *b* 30 April 1860; *m* 1896, Grace Mary, *e d* of Robert Joy, JP. *Educ:* Trinity College, Dublin (MA). Ordained 1884; Curate of Sea Patrick, Co. Down, 1884–88; St John, Birkenhead, 1888–92; Vicar of Egremont, 1892–1900; Almondbury, 1901–5; Select Preacher, University of Dublin; Lecturer St Aidan's, Birkenhead, 1900; at Lichfield Theological College, 1903–4; Fellow Australian College of Theology; Lecturer St John's College, Melbourne; Chairman of Governors, Geelong Grammar School; Archdeacon of Geelong, 1905–11; Incumbent of All Saints, St Kilda, 1905–11; Bishop of Auckland, NZ, 1911–13; Chaplain to the Archbishop of Melbourne; Rector of St Andrew's Major, Dinas Powis, Cardiff, 1914–17. *Address:* Wheelers, Bramshott, Liphook, Hants.

Died 3 March 1926.

CROSSLEY, Thomas Hastings Henry, MA Dublin, Hon LittD Queen's University, MA, and late Fellow Royal University of Ireland; *b* 1 Aug. 1846; 3rd *s* of Major Francis Crossley, HEICS, of Glenburn, Co. Antrim, and Elizabeth Helen, 2nd *d* of late William Irwin, JP, Mount Irwin, Tynan, Co. Armagh; *m* Emily Agnes, *y d* of Col F. C. Irwin, Commandant of the Troops and sometime Governor, Western Australia; one *s. Educ:* Bonn; Royal School, Dungannon; Trinity College, Dublin. Honours in Classics, 1st gold medal, Philosophy, 2nd gold medal, Senior Moderatorship, both in 1868; Royal Exhibitioner, University Scholarship in first year, Vice-Chancellor's Prize for Greek Verse; Berkeley gold medal, 1866 for Greek, MA stip. condonato, honoris causa. Senior Classical Master Trinity College, Glenalmond, 1873; deputy Professor of Latin, Queen's College, Belfast, 1875–76; Chair of Classics and Ancient History University College, Bristol, 1876–79; Professor of Greek, Queen's College, Belfast, 1879–90; Classical Examiner to Queen's University and Royal University for twelve years; Examiner to Civil Service Commission; lectured on Ancient History and Literature at Bristol, Belfast, Bridgewater, Eastbourne, Bordighera; studied music with H. Stiehl & Berthold Tours. *Publications:* numerous contributions to Kottabos and Dublin Translations into Greek and Latin Verse; articles in Hermathena on Theocritus, and the Corresp. of Fronto and M. Aurelius; The Fourth Book of M. Aurelius with revised text, trans. and Appendices, 1882; Golden Thoughts of Epictetus, with the Hymn of Cleanthes, Golden Treasury, 1902; contributor to Thackeray and Stone's Anthology of Latin Verse; Style and Composition (National Home Reading Union pamphlet). *Recreations:* sketching, music, photography, gardening. *Address:* Casa del Vallone, Bordighera, Italy. *TA:* Crossley, Bordighera.

Died 23 March 1926.

CROSTHWAITE, Rt. Rev. Robert Jarratt, DD; *b* Wellington, Somerset, 13 Oct. 1837; 3rd *s* of Rev. Canon Benjamin Crosthwaite; *m* 1st, 1867, Eleanor F. (*d* 1885), *d* of Rev. Philip Simpson; 2nd, 1887, Anne Elizabeth (*d* 1921), *d* of Rev. William Moore Crosthwaite, Prebendary of Cork Cathedral; three *s* three *d. Educ:* Leeds Grammar School; Trinity College, Cambridge (Fellow, 1862–67); 8th Wrangler, 1860. Curate, North Cave, Yorkshire, 1862–66; Private Secretary and Domestic Chaplain to Archbishop of York (Thomson), 1866–69; Vicar of Waghem, 1869–73; Vicar of Brayton, 1873–83; Vicar of St Lawrence with St Nicholas, York, 1883–85; Rector of Bolton Percy, 1885–1923; Prebendary of Grindal in Cathedral of York, 1884; Archdeacon of York, 1884–1923; Bishop of Beverley, 1889–1923. *Publication:* The Gospels of the New Testament, their Genuineness and Authenticity, 1887. *Address:* Oliver House, Bolton Percy, Yorkshire. *TA:* Bolton Percy.

Died 9 Sept. 1925.

CROSTHWAITE, Sir Robert Joseph, KCSI 1897 (CSI 1890); *b* 17 Jan. 1841; 3rd *s* of Rev. John Clarke Crosthwaite, Rector of St Mary at Hill, London; *m* 1st, 1868, Charlotte Frances, *d* of W. W. T. Baldwin, Stede Hill, Kent; 2nd, 1877, Mary, *d* of S. Harvey James, St Just, Cornwall; five *s* one *d. Educ:* Merchant Taylors' School; Brasenose College, Oxford (BA). Entered Indian Civil Service, 1863; was Judicial Commissioner of Burmah and of Central Provinces; late Additional Member of Legislative Council, India; Agent to the Gov.-

Gen. for Central India; and Agent to the Gov.-Gen. in Rajputana. Barrister, Middle Temple, 1868. *Address:* Lakenham, Northam, N Devon. *TA:* Northam.

Died 2 July 1917.

CROTHERS, Hon. Thomas Wilson, BA; KC; Minister of Labour, Canada, 1911–19; *b* Northport, 1 Jan. 1850; *m* Mary E. Burns. *Educ:* Victoria College. Headmaster High School, Wardsville, Ont.; contested (C) West Elgin, Canada, 1879; elected, 1908, 1911, and 1917; practised law at St Thomas, 1880–1911. *Address:* Ottawa, Ontario.

Died 11 Dec. 1921.

CROWE, Sir Eyre, GCB 1923 (KCB 1917; CB 1907); GCMG 1920 (KCMG 1911); Permanent Under-Secretary of State for Foreign Affairs since 1920; *b* 30 July 1864; 3rd *s* of late Sir Joseph Archer Crowe, KCMG, CB and Asta, *e d* of G. von Barby; *m* 1903, Clema von Bonin, *e d* of late Professor Gerhardt. Clerk in Foreign Office, 1885; Senior Clerk, 1906; Counsellor of Embassy, 1907; Assistant Under-Secretary of State, 1912; Minister Plenipotentiary, 1919. *Address:* 74 Elm Park Road, Chelsea, SW. *Club:* Travellers'.

Died 28 April 1925.

CROWE, Maj.-Gen. Thomas Carlisle, late RHA; *b* 1830; *e s* of Captain John Crowe, 93rd Sutherland Highlanders; *m* 1859, Ellen, Ellen, *d* of Rev. W. B. Clarke, FRS; one *s.* Entered army, 1847; Lt-Col 1872; Bt-Col 1877; served Persia, 1857 (medal with clasp); Indian Mutiny, 1857–58 (medal with clasp); Canada, 1866; retired, 1878. *Address:* 71 Bouverie Road West, Folkestone. *Club:* United Service.

Died 18 Jan. 1917.

CROWE, William Henry; *b* 1844; *s* of late Edward F. Crowe of Ravenscourt Park, Hammersmith; *m* Violet Mary, 5th *d* of late Col Charles Caldwell Grantham, of 9th and 89th Regts; one *d. Educ:* Godolphin School, Hammersmith; King's Coll., London. Barrister-at-law, Lincoln's Inn; Fellow of the Bombay University. Entered the Indian Civil Service, 1867; Judge and Sessions Judge of Poona and agent for the Sardars in the Deccan, 1881; member of the Legislative Council, Bombay, 1893; Judicial Commissioner and Judge of the Sadar Court in Sind, 1894; additional member of the Legislative Council, Bombay, 1896; Judge of HM's High Court of Judicature, Bombay, 1899–1904. *Address:* 99 Sloane Street, SW1. *T:* 2663 Victoria; Tythe Barn, Cookham Dene, Berks. *Clubs:* East India United Service, Ranelagh, Royal Automobile; Byculla, Royal Bombay Yacht, Bombay.

Died 4 July 1925.

CROWEST, Frederick J.; General Manager and Editor of The Walter Scott Publishing Company, Limited, 1901–17; *b* London (City), 30 Nov. 1860. *Educ:* London and in Italy. Served early life with Messrs Cassell, Petter and Galpin; joined their Editorial staff in 1886; assistant-editor and editor of Work, 1889–93; general editor and reader, 1893–1900; projector and editor of The Year's Music; editor and originator of The Master Musicians Series; projector and editor of The Music-Story Series; London correspondent of Church's Musical Visitor; winner of the Thomas Hughes Prize Essay, The Newspaper Press; contributor to Blackwood, National Review, Westminster and Anglo-Saxon Reviews, and general press; for many years engaged in East London educational and polytechnic work; President Newcastle and Gateshead Master Printers' Association, 1907; re-elected, 1908; President Jarrow Division Tariff Reform League. *Publications:* The Great Tone-Poets, 1874; a Book of Musical Anecdote, 2 vols, 1877; Phases of Musical England, 1881; Advice to Singers, 1878; Musical History and Biography, 1883; Cherubini (Great Musicians Series), 1890; Musical Groundwork, 1890; Dictionary of British Musicians, 1895; The Story of British Music, 1895; Verdi: Man and Musician, 1897; Beethoven (Master Musicians Series), 1899; The Story of Music, 1902; Musicians' Wit, Humour, and Anecdote, 1902. *Address:* Hill House, Fladbury, Worcestershire.

Died 14 June 1927.

CROWFOOT, Rev. John Henchman; Prebendary of Milton Manor, Lincoln Cathedral, 1913; *b* 16 Oct. 1841; 2nd *s* of W. E. Crowfoot, MD, of Beccles, Suffolk; *m* 1872, Mary Elizabeth, *e d* of Robert Bayly, Barrister of Inner Temple; one *s* two *d. Educ:* Rugby School, 1854–60; Trinity Coll., Oxford, 1860–64 (scholar). 1st class Mods; 1st class Lit.Hum.; BA 1864; MA 1867; Fellowship at Jesus Coll., 1866–72. Ordained Deacon, 1866; Priest, 1867; Oxford SPG Missionary at Delhi, 1867–71; Rector of Wigginton, Oxon, 1872–75; Vice-Chancellor of Lincoln Cathedral, 1874–98; Prebendary of Buckden in Lincoln Cathedral, 1874–98; Commissary of Bishop of Likoma, 1896; Chancellor of Lincoln Cathedral, 1898–1913. *Address:* Ravenscourt, West Worthing.

Died 29 March 1926.

CROWLY, Joseph Patrick, CB 1911; Commissioner of Inland Revenue since 1908; *b* 1 Nov. 1859; *s* of John Crowly of Bandon, Co. Cork; *m* 1893, Margaret Caecilia, *d* of A. J. Fox of Hunmanby, Yorkshire; one *d. Educ:* St Stanislaus' College (SJ), Tullamore. Appointed a Class I clerk in the Admiralty, 1881; transferred to Treasury, 1884; private secretary to Sir Reginald (later Lord) Welby, 1891–94; to Sir Francis Mowatt, 1894–97. *Recreations:* travel and anything else that may turn up. *Address:* 17 Leinster Gardens, W.
Died 18 July 1917.

CROZIER, Most Rev. John Baptist, DD; Archbishop of Armagh and Primate of all Ireland (Church of Ireland) since 1911; *b* 8 April 1853; *e s* of Rev. Baptist Barton Crozier, BA, Rockview, Ballyhaise, Co. Cavan, and Kate, *o d* of John Bolland, Yorkshire; *m* 1877, Alice, *d* of Rev. John W. Hackett, MA, and Jane Monck Mason, *g d* of Sir Robert Langrishe, 2nd Bt, Co. Kilkenny; two *s* one *d. Educ:* Trinity Coll., Dublin. Honours and Prizes in Classics, Logics, Ethics, Hebrew, and Irish; Moderator and Medallist in Logics and Ethics; Downes Divinity Prize (first); 1st class Divinity Testimonium; BA 1872; MA 1875; BD and DD 1888; Member of the University Senate. Fellow RS Antiquaries (Ireland), MRIA; President Univ. Philosophical Society, 1874; Auditor Coll. Theological Society, 1875. Ordained 1876; Vicar of Holywood, Co. Down, 1880–97; Chaplain Bishop of Down, 1885–97; to Archbishop of Armagh, 1886; Canon of Down Cathedral, 1887; Chaplain to Lord-Lieutenant of Ireland 1893–97; Canon of St Patrick's National Cathedral, 1896; Hon. Sec. General Synod of the Church of Ireland, 1896; Bishop of Ossory, Ferns, and Leighlin, 1897–1907; of Down, Connor and Dromore, 1907–11. *Recreations:* one of the earliest members of the Wanderers Football Club (Rugby), Dublin; Vice-President of the Holywood Cricket Club and Rugby Football Club; a keen horseman. *Address:* The Palace, Armagh. *Clubs:* Royal Societies; University, Dublin; Ulster, Belfast.
Died 12 April 1920.

CROZIER, John Beattie, LLD; philosopher, historian, and political economist; *b* Canada, 1849; *m* 1877, Katharine Augusta (*d* 1918), *niece* of late Colonel William Anderson, Mount Aboo; two *d. Educ:* Galt Grammar School and Toronto Univ. Univ. medallist and Starr medallist in Medicine, 1872; LLD (honoris causa) Univ. of Toronto, 1899. *Publications:* The Religion of the Future, 1880; Civilisation and Progress, 1885 (translated into Japanese, 1903); Lord Randolph Churchill: a Study of English Democracy, 1887; History of Intellectual Development, vol. i 1897; vol. iii 1901; My Inner Life, being a Chapter in Personal Evolution and Autobiography, 1898; The Wheel of Wealth, 1906; First Principles of Investment, 1910; Sociology applied to Practical Politics, 1911; Last Words on Great Issues, 1917; articles in Fortnightly Review. *Recreations:* formerly boxing, skating, and step-dancing; subseq. (with failing eyesight) music, conversation, and being read to. *Address:* 9 Elgin Avenue, W. *Died 8 Jan. 1921.*

CRUDDAS, Lt-Col Hugh Wilson, DSO 1915; 41st Dogras; *b* 2 Feb. 1868; *s* of John Cruddas of Newcastle-on-Tyne and Bombay; *m* 1909, Alice, *d* of late J. Medhurst; no *c. Educ:* Newton Abbot. Entered army, 1889; Captain Indian army, 1900; Major, 1907; served China, 1900 (medal); European War, 1914–15 (DSO).
Died 20 Jan. 1916.

CRUICKSHANK, Alexander Walmsley, CSI 1898; late Indian Civil Service; *b* 24 July 1851; *y s* of late Major John James Farquharson Cruickshank, HEICS, Bombay Engineers; *m* 1881, Fanny Nina, *d* of late Claremont Daniell; two *s* two *d. Educ:* Wimbledon School. Passed 4th into Woolwich, but entered ICS 1872; Barrister, Middle Temple, 1883; became Junior Secretary to Board of Revenue, NW Provinces, 1878; Under-Sec. to Government, 1886; Settlement Officer, 1886; Deputy Commissioner, 1890; Magistrate and Collector, 1891; Commissioner of the Allahabad Division, 1897; and Commissioner of Rohilkhand Division, 1897; placed on special duty from 9 to 25 Nov. 1897; and reverted to appointment of Comr Rohilkhand Division on 26 Feb. 1898 on return from privilege leave; commanded Rohilkhand Vol. Rifle Corps, 1898–1903, with the rank of Major. Decorated for services in the Indian Famine, 1897, when Comr Allahabad Division; additional member Governor-General's Council, 1903; reappointed member of Council of Lieut-Governor, United Provinces, 1903; Commissioner of Rohilkhand Division, NWP, India, 1898–1905; member Board of Revenue, United Provinces, 1905–8. *Publications:* Settlement Report of Gorakpur District, UP. *Recreations:* shooting, riding, ordinary field sports and games. *Address:* c/o Grindlay & Co., 54 Parliament Street, SW1.
Died 14 April 1925.

CRUICKSHANK, Rev. Alfred Hamilton, MA Oxon, Hon. DLitt Durham; Canon of Durham; Professor of Greek and Classical Literature in the University of Durham; *b* 18 March 1862; *s* of George Cruickshank and Eliza Septima, *d* of Sir Thomas Howell; *m* 1898, Ethel Mary, *d* of Rev. H. J. Wickham; no *c. Educ:* Winchester; New College, Oxford; 1st Class Classical Moderations, 1883; Hertford University Scholar, 1883; 1st Class Final Classical School, 1885. Fellow of New College, and Tutor, 1885; ordained, 1891; Composition Master at Harrow, 1891–93; Assistant Master at Winchester, 1894–1910; Chaplain, 1896. *Publications:* Raochae of Euripides; Fair Copies; Philip Massinger, 1920. *Address:* The College, Durham.
Died 13 May 1927.

CRUM, Sir Walter Erskine, Kt 1920; OBE 1918; partner in Graham & Co., Glasgow; *b* 2 Sept. 1874; *s* of late Ewing Crum and Sara Margaret Tinne; *m* Violet Mary, *d* of late C. H. B. Forbes; two *s* two *d. Educ:* Eton; New College, Oxford. Captain of Boats, Eton, 1892–93; President OUBC 1895–97. President Bengal Chamber of Commerce, 1919–20; Member Imperial Legislative Council, India, 1919–20. *Address:* c/o William Graham & Co., Sackville Street, Manchester. *Died 10 Oct. 1923.*

CRUMLY, Patrick, JP; MP (N) South Fermanagh, 1911–18; was Vice-Chairman, Enniskillen Board of Guardians. *Address:* Town Hall Street, Enniskillen.

CRUMP, Rev. John Herbert, MA; *b* 1849; 2nd *s* of late Rev. Wm Crump, Vicar of Rowley Regis, Staffs; married. *Educ:* St Edmund's School, Canterbury; Jesus Coll., Cambridge. Curate of St Matthew's, Smethwick, 1879–80; St Stephen's, 1881–84; Vicar of Holy Trinity, Smethwick, 1884–92; Rector of Stoke-on-Trent, 1892–97; Vicar of Longdon, 1898–1905; Archdeacon of Stoke-on-Trent, 1905–8; Prebendary of Lichfield, 1901–12. *Address:* Greycourt, Old Colwyn, N. Wales. *T:* Old Colwyn 15. *TA:* Old Colwyn.
Died 12 June 1924.

CRUMP, Sir William John, Kt 1902; ex-High Sheriff, DL, and JP Middlesex; solicitor; past Chairman, National Unionist Association; *b* 1850; *e s* of late Wm Alex. Crump; *m* 1872, Anna Maria (*d* 1921), *d* of late Charles Buttery, 173 Piccadilly, W; three *s* four *d. Educ:* privately. Had a large maritime, mercantile, and company practice in the City of London; was a Member of second Hornsey School Board, and of Hornsey Urban District Council; Past-Master Worshipful Company of Upholders; Past-Master of the City of London Solicitors' Company; past Chairman Metropolitan Division of the National Unionist Association; Chairman of North Islington Unionist Association, 1884–1919, subseq. President; a Member of Council and Executive Committee of City of London Conservative Association; Chairman of the Hendon Division of Middlesex Central Conservative and Unionist Association; a Member of the Middlesex Licensing Committee and a Member of the Territorial Force Association for the County of Middlesex; Member of the Council of the Imperial Society of Knights Bachelor; took an active part in obtaining open spaces for the people in Hornsey; one of the promoters and an original Director of the Crouch End Playing Fields; a Member of the Committee for the acquisition of the Queen's Wood, Highgate, and the Alexandra Palace; first Mayor of Islington, 1900; re-elected, 1901; Vice-Chairman, 1900–2, of the Metropolitan Mayors and ex-Mayors Association; received Coronation Medals from King Edward and King George; Freemasonry; PM of several lodges; PAGDC (Eng.), and PPGW (Essex). *Recreations:* golf, motoring. *Address:* 17 Leadenhall Street, EC. *TA:* Legal, London; Glenthorne, Harrow Weald, Middlesex. *T:* Avenue 1149; Crump, Bushey Heath. *T:* Bushey Heath 291. *Clubs:* Junior Carlton, Royal Automobile, City Carlton, Canada. *Died 8 Jan. 1923.*

CRUTCHLEY, Maj.-Gen. Sir Charles, KCB 1917; KCVO 1913 (MVO 1902); Lieutenant-Governor and Secretary, Royal Hospital, Chelsea, 1909–18; *b* 10 Dec. 1856; 2nd *s* of late Gen. Charles Crutchley; *m* 1887, Sybil Mary, *o d* of Hon. Henry and Lady Katharine Coke of Longford, Derbyshire; one *s. Educ:* Harrow; Sandhurst. Entered army, 1874; Capt. Scots Guards, 1887; Major, 1895; Lt-Col 1897; Col 1900; Staff Captain for Recruiting, 1886–89; DAAG for recruiting, Headquarters of Army, 1889–1900; AAG, recruiting, Headquarters of Army, 1900–8; Director of Recruiting, 1908–9; served Egypt, 1882 (medal with clasp, bronze star, 5th class Medjidie, Bt Major); Soudan, 1884–85 (severely wounded, two clasps). *Address:* 3 Durham Place, Chelsea, SW3. *T:* Kensington 3828.
Died 1 Dec. 1920.

CRUTCHLEY, Commander William Caius, RD; FRGS; RNR; Younger Brother, Trinity House; late Secretary to the Navy League; *b* 1848; *s* of William Crutchley, architect, Wolverhampton; *m* 1st, 1876, Elizabeth, *d* of John Symon, Southampton; 2nd, 1882, Edith, *o d* of Felton Matthew, Cape Town; two *s* one *d. Educ:* private school, Margate. Thirty-one years' sea service, of which seventeen were spent in command of first-class mail steamers; served in HM ships; retired from the sea, 1894; gave considerable attention to matters of maritime interest. *Publications:* My Life at Sea, 1912; contributed (by papers at the RUSI and otherwise) towards the solution of the problem "How to protect the Mercantile Marine in war time"; journalist; made contributions to Meterorology and Nautical Science generally. *Address:* 23 Argyll Mansions, Addison Bridge, W. *Club:* Yorick.

Died 22 Nov. 1923.

CULLEN, Commander Percy, CMG 1902; RNR; late Commanding Naval Forces in British Central Africa; *b* 10 March 1861; *s* of late W. H. Cullen; *m* 1895, Ethel Mary, *d* of F. J. Collart. Served Lake Nyasa, 1895; Mepesu Expedition, 1898 (despatches, medal and clasp).

Died 15 Nov. 1918.

CULLUM, George Gery Milner-Gibson, FSA, FZS; JP, DL; *b* 1857; 5th and *o* surv. *s* of late Rt Hon. T. Milner-Gibson, MP, of Theberton House, Suffolk, and Arethusa Susanna, *o d* of Rev. Sir Thomas Gery Cullum, 8th Bt (*ext*), of Hardwick. *Educ:* Trinity Coll., Cambridge (MA). Inherited Hardwick in 1875, on death of grandmother, Lady Cullum, whose name he assumed. High Sheriff, Suffolk, 1888; admitted to the freedom of Bury St Edmunds, 1911; Hon. Curator of Moyses Hall Museum, 1912; Mayor of Bury St Edmunds, 1913–14. Fellow of the Society of Genealogists, 1916; patron of one living. *Publications:* Pedigree of Middleton or Myddleton of Chirk Castle, 1897; Pedigree of Ray of Denston in Suffolk, 1903; Pedigree of Wittewronge of Ghent in Flanders, and other Families from them descended, 1905; Inscriptions in the Old British Cemetery at Leghorn, 1907; Pedigree of the Family of Corsellis of Essex, 1914; Mary Beale: Suffolk Artist, 1919; contributions to genealogical and archæological publications. *Address:* Hardwick House, Bury St Edmunds; 4 Sterling Street, Montpelier Square, SW. *Clubs:* Athenæum, St James's, Bachelors'.

Died 21 Nov. 1921.

CUMBERBATCH, Henry Alfred, CMG 1896; HM Consul-General for the Vilayet of Beirut, Syria, and for the Lebanon, 1908–14; was also British Post Office Agent; employed at the Foreign Office since Nov. 1914; *b* Berdiansk (Russia), 27 June 1858; *s* of late R. W. Cumberbatch of HM's Consular Service; *m* 1891, Hélène Gertrude, *d* of late T. B. Rees of Smyrna; three *s* two *d. Educ:* Christ College, Finchley. Student Dragoman, Constantinople, 1876; employed at Belgrade, 1876–78; appointed HM's Vice-Con. Bucharest, 1879; HM's Vice-Con. Soulina (Roumania), 1881; Con. Adrianople, 1888; Acting Consul-General, Philippopolis (Bulgaria), 1888 and 1890; Acting Consul-General, Salonica, 1891; Acting Con.-Gen., Smyrna 1892; transferred to Angora, 1893; was at Erzeroum (Kurdistan) during the massacres of Armenians at that place, 1895; Consul for Kurdistan, 1895–96; Consul at Smyrna, 1896–1900; was also British Post Office Agent; Consul-General, 1900–8. Decorated for services rendered in Asia Minor, etc. *Recreation:* golf. *Address:* Foreign Office, SW. *Club:* St James's.

Died 3 Dec. 1918.

CUMBERLAND, Maj.-Gen. Charles Edward, CB 1881; JP Kent; *b* 27 Jan. 1830; *s* of late Rt Hon. T. Milner-Gibson... [*See correction below*] *s* of late R. E. Cumberland; *m* 1st, 1883, Elizabeth Anne (*d* 1891), *d* of late Rev. W. Moss King; 2nd, 1907, Adelaide, *d* of late Philip H. Crampton, of Fassaro, Co Wicklow. *Educ:* RM Academy, Woolwich. Entered Royal Engineers, 1847; Brevet Maj. 1860; Col 1877; retired Maj.-Gen. 1887; served in Crimean Campaign, 1855–56 (medal and Turkish medal); Indian Mutiny, 1857–59 (medal and clasp). *Recreations:* cricket, chess. *Address:* Manor House, Maidstone.

Died July 1920.

CUMBERLAND, Major Charles Sperling; retired; *b* Dec. 1847; *s* of Major G. B. Cumberland, late 42nd Highlanders. *Educ:* Repton School. Joined 39th Regiment, 1867; and served with that regiment until 1882, when he exchanged into the 30th E Lancashire; served Afghanistan, 1878–79; retired 1887; since then travelled for the purpose of big game hunting and exploration in Asia, Africa, Canada, and New Zealand. *Publications:* Sport in the Pamir Steppes; also wrote for Country Life Library of Sport, The Big Game of Asia, and also for Great and Small Game of India. *Recreations:* fishing, shooting, golf. *Address:* County Club, Dorchester. *Club:* Naval and Military.

Died 6 Dec. 1922.

CUMBERLAND, Gerald; dramatic and musical critic, and dramatic author; *b* Manchester, 7 May 1879; *m* Esther Innes Luffman. *Educ:* Victoria University, Manchester. Musical and Dramatic Critic of the Manchester Courier, 1908–13; Critic of the Daily Citizen, 1913. *Publications:* Imaginary Interviews with Great Composers; Set Down

in Malice, 1918; play, The Chivalry of Dreams, 1911; The Poisoner, 1921; Striving Fire, 1924. *Recreation:* swimming. *Club:* Press.

Died 2 June 1926.

CUMMING, Capt. Sir Mansfield, KCMG 1919; CB 1914; RN, retired; *b* 1 April 1859; *m* 1st, 1885, Dora, *d* of T. Cloete of Constantia, SA; 2nd, 1889, Leslie Valiant, *d* of Capt. V. Cumming of Logie, Morayshire. ADC during expedition against Malays, Straits of Malacca, 1875–76 (medal and clasp); served Egypt, 1883 (medal and Khedive's Star); Officer Legion of Honour, St Stanislaus, St Leopold, and St Vladimir; Crown of Italy, 1914 Star, General Service Medal, Victory Medal. *Address:* 1 Melbury Road, W14; Bursledon, Hants. *Clubs:* Naval and Military, Royal Automobile, Garrick; Royal Motor Yacht; Royal Yacht Squadron.

Died 14 June 1923.

CUMMINS, Henry Ashley Travers, CBE 1919; Hon. Paymaster Rear-Admiral, (retired), RN; Director of Petersen & Co., London American Maritime SS Co., and Thompson Steamship Co.; *b* Cork, 25 Jan. 1847; *m* 1876, Frances Wathan Hill (*d* 1923), *d* of late Commander Hugh Price, Royal Navy; one *d. Educ:* Chester College; Eastman's Royal Naval Establishment, Southsea. Entered Royal Navy, 1864; joined Fisgard; Assistant Paymaster, 1868; Octavia, Commodore's ship, East Indies, 1865–69; served in the Abyssinian Expedition (medal); Minotaur, Flagship Channel Fleet; took passage in Megaera for Clio in Australia, 1871; was wrecked on St Paul's Island during the voyage; was on Australian Station, 1872–75; lent to Pearl for duty as Asst Secretary to the Commissioners for the annexation of Fiji; served in Warrior, Channel Fleet, 1875–78, and Flora, Cape of Good Hope Station, 1878–81; during the Boer War of 1881 was Accountant Officer of Flora and Secretary at the Cape Yard; received the special thanks of the Commodore in command of the Station and of the Flag Officer in command of the Detached Squadron; retired list, 1882; Cashier, Royal Naval Hospital, Great Yarmouth, 1882; came to the aid of the Medical Officer in charge, when attacked by a lunatic; received thanks of the Admiralty; Paymaster of Contingencies, Admiralty, 1890–1915; 51 years continuous Naval Service; Coronation Medal, 1911; General Service Medal, 1918; Paymaster-in-Chief, 1914. *Recreation:* golf. *Address:* 86 Oakwood Court, W14. *T:* Park 3890. *Club:* Constitutional.

Died 10 Dec. 1926.

CUMMINS, (William Edward) Ashley, MD; Professor of Practice of Medicine, University College, Cork; Examiner in Medicine, National University, Ireland; Senior Surgeon, Victoria Hospital, Cork; Senior Medical Officer, Cork District Hospital; Consulting Physician, Lying-in Hospital, Cork; also of Cork Eye, Ear, and Throat Hospital; Consulting Physician, Southern Command; *m;* four *s. Educ:* University College, Cork. *Address:* 17 St Patrick's Place, Cork. *T:* 6; Woodville, Glanmire, Co Cork. *TA:* Ashley Cummins, Cork. *T:* 10 Glanmire.

Died 18 Oct. 1923.

CUNARD, Sir Bache Edward, 3rd Bt, *cr* 1859; JP; *b* 15 May 1851; *s* of Sir Edward Cunard, 2nd Bt and Mary, *d* of Bache M'Evers of New York; *S* father, 1869; *m* 1895, Maud Alice, *d* of late E. F. Burke, New York; one *d* (she *m* Sidney Fairbairn, Grenadier Guards). *Educ:* Rugby; Trinity College, Cambridge. *Heir: b* Gordon Cunard [*b* 22 May 1857; *m* 1889, Edith Mary, *d* of late Col John Stanley Howard of Ballina Park, Co Wicklow; three *s. Address:* Shantock Hall, Bovingdon, Herts. *Club:* Arthur's]. *Address:* The Haycock, Wansford, Peterborough. *Club:* Turf.

Died 3 Nov. 1925.

CUNARD, Ernest Haliburton; *b* 1862; 2nd *s* of late William Cunard of Orleans House, Twickenham; *m* 1903, Florence, *d* of late James M'Pheeters, Baltimore, USA, and *widow* of Edward Padelford. *Educ:* Eton. Was a Director of the Cunard Steam Ship Co. (of which Sir Samuel Cunard, 1st Bt, was the original founder); Great Western Railway Co.; Peninsular and Oriental Steam Navigation Co.; The London County and Westminster Bank; The Royal Exchange Assurance Corporation; British India Steam Co.

Died 6 Nov. 1926.

CUNEO, Cyrus Cincinatto, ROI; *b* San Francisco, California; Italian parentage. *Educ:* San Francisco. Studied art in Paris under Girado, Prenet, and Whistler. *Address:* 215 Uxbridge Road, W. *T:* 1558 Hammersmith. *Club:* Langham Sketching.

Died 23 July 1916.

CUNINGHAM, Maj.-Gen. Charles Alexander; Indian Army, and Colonel 127th (Queen Mary's Own) Beluch Light Infantry; *b* 29 Jan. 1842; 2nd *s* of late Alexander Cuningham, Sec. to Northern Lighthouse Board, and Caroline, *d* of General A. D. Faunce, CB;

m 1st, Annie, *e d* of J. M. Balfour, of Pilrig; 2nd, Innes, 3rd *d* of Sir R. Playre, GCB; one *s* two *d*. *Educ:* Edinburgh Academy and privately. Entered Army, 1858; Maj.-Gen. 1899; served Afghan War, 1880 (medal); held various Staff appointments, including Secretary to Govt of Bombay Military Department, and GOC and Political Resident, Aden. *Recreations:* golf, etc. *Address:* 16 Lypiatt Terrace, Cheltenham. *Club:* New, Cheltenham.   *Died 24 Feb. 1925.*

CUNINGHAM, Granville Carlyle, MInstCE, MCanSocCE; Consulting Engineer; *b* Edinburgh, 27 April 1847; 5th *s* of late Alexander Cuningham, WS, Sec. to Comrs of Northern Lighthouses, and Caroline, *d* of Gen. Alured D. Faunce, CB; *m* 1873, Frances Bethune, 3rd *d* of late Robert Pilkington Crooks, Barrister, Toronto, Canada; one *s*. *Educ:* Edinburgh Academy and University. Honduras, Central America, surveying for railway, 1870–71; Ontario, various railway works, 1871–74; preliminary surveys for Canadian Pacific Railway, 1874–75; Engineer-in-charge of Prince Edward Island Railway and of Harbours in the Island, 1875–79; Canada Southern Railway, 1879–81; Chief Engineer, 1881–83; General Asst to Manager of Construction of Rocky Mountain Div. Canadian Pacific Railway, 1884–86; Railway Contractor, Lower Canada, 1886–89; Assistant City Engineer and City Engineer of Toronto, 1889–92; General Manager and Chief Engineer, Montreal (Electric) Street Railway, 1892–97; Managing Director, City of Birmingham Tramways, 1897–99; General Manager, Central London (Tube) Railway, 1899–1911. *Publications:* Imperial Federation, 1895; Bacon's Secret Disclosed, 1911; Wake up, England!, 1919. *Address:* Bedwyn Cottage, Farnham Common, Bucks. *Club:* Constitutional.
                              Died 18 Dec. 1927.

CUNINGHAME, Col John Anstruther Smith, DL; late 2nd Life Guards; *b* 15 Nov. 1852; *m* 1887, Violet Mary (*d* 1917), *e d* of Sir Alfred Slade, 3rd Bt; one *s*. *Address:* Caprington Castle, Kilmarnock, Ayrshire. *Club:* Marlborough.
                              Died 17 Dec. 1921.

CUNINGHAME, John Charles, DL, JP, Renfrew and Inverness, etc; *b* 29 May 1851; *s* of Alexander Cuninghame of Craigends; *m* 1901, his cousin, Alison, *d* of late Alexander L. Pearson, and *g d* of Commander Hugh Pearson, RN; no *c*. *Educ:* Harrow; Cambridge. *Recreations:* shooting, billiards, racing. *Address:* Craigends, Johnstone, NB; Dunragit, Wigtownshire; 25 Hill Street, Mayfair, W. *T:* 3316 Mayfair. *Clubs:* Carlton, Turf; New, Edinburgh.
                              Died 30 Jan. 1917.

CUNLIFFE, 1st Baron, *cr* 1914, of Headley; **Walter Cunliffe,** GBE 1917; Lieutenant City of London; Director of the Bank of England, 1895; Deputy Governor, 1911; Governor since 1913; Director North Eastern Railway Co.; Member of Cunliffe Brothers, White Lion Court, Cornhill, EC; *b* 4 Dec. 1855; *s* of Roger Cunliffe and Anne Edge; *m* 1st, 1890, Mary Agnes (*d* 1893), *d* of Robert Henderson of Randalls Park, Leatherhead; 2nd, 1896, Edith, *d* of Col R. T. Boothby, St Andrews, Fife; two *s* three *d* (and one *s* decd). *Educ:* Harrow; Trinity Coll. Cambridge (MA). Patron of the living of Headley, Surrey. 1st Class, Order of St Anne (Russia), 1915; Grand Cross, Order of the Crown of Italy, 1916. *Heir: s* Hon. Rolf Cunliffe, *b* 13 May 1899. *Address:* Headley Court, Epsom. *TA:* Cunliffe, London. *Club:* New University.   *Died 6 Jan. 1920.*

CUNLIFFE, Sir Foster Hugh Egerton, 6th Bt, *cr* 1759; *b* 17 Aug. 1875; *s* of Sir Robert Alfred Cunliffe, 5th Bt and Eleanor (*d* 1898), *o d* of Major Egerton Leigh, West Hall, Cheshire; *S* father, 1905. *Educ:* Eton; New College, Oxford (MA). Fellow of All Souls. *Heir: b* Robert Nevill Henry, *b* 8 Feb. 1884. *Address:* Acton Park, Wrexham.
                              Died 19 July 1916.

CUNLIFFE, Sir (Robert) Ellis, Kt 1910; *b* 30 Jan. 1858; 2nd *s* of Robert Cunliffe (*d* 1903) and Laetitia (*d* 1899), 3rd *d* of late Ven. John Williams, Archdeacon of Cardigan; *m* 1885, Clementina, 3rd *d* of late Richard Cockerton; two *s* three *d*. Formerly member of Cunliffes and Davenport, Chancery Lane. *Educ:* Bradfield; Corpus Christi Coll., Oxford (MA). Admitted to Roll of Solicitors, 1884; Solicitor to Board of Trade, 1900–20; Member of the Council of Bradfield College, 1914; Chairman of London Society for Teaching and Training of the Blind, Swiss Cottage, NW; Chairman of the Kensington, Fulham, and Chelsea General Hospital. *Address:* 34 The Grove, The Boltons, SW10. *T:* Kensington 5617. *M:* XE 3999.
                              Died 18 Aug. 1927.

CUNNINGHAM, Alfred, MJI; Member Imperial Japanese Order of Rising Sun; *b* Paddington, London, 31 Dec. 1870; 2nd *s* of F. Cunningham, London, journalist; *m* 1893, Cecilia Helen, 3rd *d* of

John Colledge, of Singapore; one *s*. *Educ:* privately. General London and provincial experience; filled editorial appointments, Singapore, Shanghai, Hong Kong, and Cairo; served in Chino-Japanese War (for Central News) as special correspondent; special correspondent for the New York Journal with Spanish forces in Philippines, Spanish-American War; special correspondent at Chinese Rebellion at Tset Tze Lin, and in 1905 for Daily Mail and New York Sun at Camrang Bay with the Baltic Fleet, Russo-Japanese war; special correspondent for South China for the New York Sun; Special Correspondent, Berlin, 1912; Gold Medallist of Hanoi Exposition, Tonkin, of 1902; founded and edited the South China Morning Post, 1903; founded and edited the Review of the Far East. *Publications:* Special articles on Siberia, 1899; History of the Szechuen Riots; The French in Tonkin and South China; The Chinese Soldier and other Sketches; Scrutator's Letters on the Insanitary Condition of Hong Kong; To-Day in Egypt, 1912; acted as Mediator in the Coal Claim Dispute between Viceroy of Canton and the Bank of China, 1906 (thanked by Governor of Hong Kong in despatches); delegate Overseas Press Conference, London, 1901. *Recreations:* tennis, sketching, music, travel. *Address:* Altwood Bailey, Maidenhead, Berks. *Club:* Authors'.
                              Died 14 May 1918.

CUNNINGHAM, Sir Henry (Stewart), KCIE 1889; *b* 1832; *s* of late Rev. J. W. Cunningham, Vicar of Harrow, and Mary, *d* of late Sir H. Calvert; *m* 1877, Hon. Harriett Emily (*d* 1918), *d* of 1st Lord Lawrence; one *d*. *Educ:* Harrow; Trinity College, Oxford. Barrister 1859; Advocate-General, Madras, 1873; Judge of High Court, Bengal, 1877–87. *Address:* 83 Eaton Place, SW1. *T:* 2205 Kensington. *Club:* Athenæum.   *Died 3 Sept. 1920.*

CUNNINGHAM, Rt. Rev. John F., DD; Bishop of Concordia since 1898; *b* Mountcoul, Ireland, 1842. *Educ:* Listowrie, Co. Kerry, Parish of Irremore, Ireland; Atchison, Kans, Milwaukee, Wis. Missionary at Fort Scott, Kans, and south-east part of the State, and five Counties in State of Missouri; Pastor, Laurence, Kans; three years collecting in the country for the Leavenworth Cathedral, and Kansas sufferers; Pastor of Topeka; Vicar-General of the Diocese of Leavenworth, 1881; Rector of the Leavenworth Cathedral; Administrator of the Diocese in absence of the Ordinary Precognised Bishop of Concordia, 1882. *Address:* Concordia, Kansas, USA.
                              Died 23 June 1919.

CUNNINGHAM, Ven. William, DD Cantab; DSc and Hon. LLD Edin.; FBA; Fellow Trinity College, Cambridge, 1891; Archdeacon of Ely, 1907; Hon. Fellow Caius College; *b* Edinburgh, 29 Dec. 1849; 3rd *s* of James Cunningham, WS, and Elizabeth Boyle, *d* of Alexander Dunlop of Keppoch; *m* 1876, Adèle Rebecca, *d* of A. A. Dunlop, Dublin; one *d*. *Educ:* Edin. Acad. and Univ. Jun. Greek Med., 1866; Caius Coll. and Trinity Coll. (scholar) Cambridge; 1st class Moral Science Tripos, 1873; Hulsean, Maitland, and Kaye Prizes, Cambridge. University Extension Lecturer, 1874–78; University Lecturer on History, 1884–91; Deputy to Knightbridge Professor, 1880; Professor of Economics, King's Coll. London, 1891–97; Lecturer on Economic History, Harvard University, USA, 1899; ordained by Bishop of Ely, 1873; Curate at Horningsea and St Saviour's, Everton; Chaplain of Trinity Coll., Cambridge, 1880–91; Hulsean Lecturer, 1885; Vicar of Great St Mary's, Cambridge, 1887–1908; also of St Michael's, Cambridge, 1907–8; Examining Chaplain to the Bishop of Peterborough, 1911. *Publications:* Growth of English Industry and Commerce, 2 vols 4th edition; Outlines of English Industrial History (part); Western Civilisation; Modern Civilisation; Use and Abuse of Money; Alien Immigrants; also S. Austin, Path towards Knowledge; Gospel of Work; Rise and Decline of Free Trade; Cure of Souls; Christianity and Social Questions; Case against Free Trade; Efficiency in the Church of England; Christianity and Economic Science; Christianity and Politics; English Influence on the United States; Progress of Capitalism; Increase of True Religion. *Address:* Trinity College, Cambridge. *Clubs:* Oxford and Cambridge, Albemarle.   *Died 10 June 1919.*

CUNNINGHAME GRAHAM, Commander Charles Elphinstone Fleeming, MVO 1906; Commander on the Emergency List, RN; Groom-in-Waiting to HM the King; *b* 1 Jan. 1854; 2nd *s* of William Cunninghame Graham Bontine, of Ardoch and Gartmore, and Hon. Anne Elizabeth, 4th *d* of Admiral the Hon. Charles Elphinstone Fleeming of Cumbernauld, and *sister* of 14th Baron Elphinstone; *m* 1882, Mildred Emily Barbara, *d* of Rev. C. W. Bagot; one *s* one *d*. *Educ:* Harrow; HMS Britannia. Served in Royal Navy, 1867–86, when he resigned his commission and took service in Royal National Lifeboat Institution, in which he served for 23 years; during his time of service he assisted on various occasions in saving life, and wrote many technical articles on lifeboat matters; invited by Admiralty to join Emergency

List, and commission restored to him, 1901; commander, 1903. Humane Society's silver medal for saving life; Knight Commander of Royal Danish Order of the Dannebrog; 2nd class of Red Eagle of Prussia; Commander of Polar Star of Sweden, and St Stanislas of Russia; 2nd class of White Eagle of Serbia. *Address:* 60 Warwick Square, SW. *Clubs:* Marlborough, Naval and Military; Royal Yacht Squadron (Naval Hon. Member), Cowes.

Died 8 June 1917.

CUNYNGHAM, Sir William Stewart-Dick-, 10th Bt, *cr* 1669, of Prestonfield and Lamburghtoun; CBE 1919; a Gentleman-at-Arms, 1920; Brigade-Major, Lowland Mounted Brigade, Ayr, NB; Major Scottish Horse Imperial Yeomanry; late Capt. 1st Battalion Black Watch (Royal Highlanders); *b* 20 Feb. 1871; *s* of Sir Robert Dick-Cunyngham, 9th Bt and Sarah Mary, *o d* of W. Hetherington; *S* father, 1897; *m* 1903, Evelyn Eleanora, *e d* of Arthur Fraser. *Educ:* Harrow; Sandhurst. ADC to Gen. Sir E. F. Chapman, KCB, Scottish Dist, 1898–1900; Assistant Private Secretary to Gen. Hon. Sir Neville Lyttleton, 1905–7; served South Africa (despatches); European War, commanded 10th Black Watch in France and the Balkans (despatches, CBE); served with Italian Expeditionary Force as Commandant GHQ Reinforcement Camp. *Heir: n* Colin Keith Dick-Cunyngham, *b* 3 March 1908. *Address:* Prestonfield, Edinburgh. *Clubs:* Army and Navy; New, Edinburgh.   *Died 25 March 1922.*

CURE, Sir Edward Capel, Kt 1919; Commercial Counsellor of Embassy, for Italy, 1918–22; *b* 1866; *e s* of late Rev. Edward Capel Cure, Canon of Windsor and Chaplain in Ordinary to Queen Victoria, and Gertrude, 2nd *d* of Sir John Thomas Selwin, 6th Bt, and *sister* of 7th Bt and 1st Baron Rookwood; *m* 1889, Muriel, *e d* of Sir Percy Oxenden, 10th Bt; one *d*. *Educ:* Winchester; New College, Oxford (in honours history). Italian Correspondent for the Engineer, 1906–14; Temporary Italian Correspondent of the Times, 1914; Assistant Commercial Attaché HBM Embassy, Rome, 1914, was on the Anglo-Italian Financial Conference, Nice, 1915, on the British Delegation at the Economic Conference of the Allies, Paris, 1916; and was British Representative on the Servian Revictualling Commission, 1916; accompanied Mr Runciman's Special Mission to Pallanza, Aug. 1916, and the Italian Ministers of the Treasury and the Interior on their Missions to London, 1916–19. Grand Officer of the Order of St Maurice and Lazarus; Commendatore of the Crown of Italy; Serbian Order of the White Eagle. *Publications:* Italian author Risveglio, Sul Meriggio, etc, and articles in Reviews (British and Italian). *Recreation:* driving. *Address:* Villa Della Quercia, Pallanza, Lago Maggiore, Italy. *Club:* Travellers'.

Died 30 Dec. 1923.

CURRAN, His Honour Judge John Adye; *b* 1837; *s* of late John Adye Curran, Barrister, Dublin. *Educ:* Trinity College, Dublin; BA. Called to Irish Bar, 1860; KC 1882; JP Co. Dublin; Divisional Magistrate for Dublin, 1881–83; Chairman of Quarter Sessions and County Court Judge for King's, Longford, Meath and Westmeath Cos, 1883–86, and 1891–1914; Co. Kerry, 1886–91. *Publications:* Recollections of an Irish KC; Reminiscences, 1916. *Address:* 58 Palmerston Road, Dublin.

Died 16 March 1919.

CURRE, John Mathew; MFH Radnors and West Herefords, 1910–19; *b* 1859; *s* of late Edward Mathew Curre, of Itton Court, Chepstow; *m* 1901, Mary, *widow* of Richard Palmer Jenkins, Beachley, Chepstow. *Address:* Titley, Hereford.   *Died 24 Oct. 1919.*

CURRIE, Very Rev. Edward Reid, DD; VD; Dean of the Peculiar of Battle, and Vicar since 1882; Rural Dean of Hastings, 1905–13; *b* Calcutta, 16 Feb. 1844; *s* of late Edward Currie, BCS; *m* 1st, Geraldine Dowdeswell, *o c* of late Richard Tyrrell; one *s*; 2nd, 1889, Hon. Frances Emma (*d* 1920), *o d* of late Rev. W. F. Hotham, Rector of Buckland, Surrey. *Educ:* Cheltenham; Wadham College, Oxford. Curate of Christ Church, Eastbourne, 1868; Senior Curate of Battle, 1869–74; Vicar of St Bartholomew, Chichester, 1874–82; Acting Chaplain to the Forces, Chichester, 1878–82; Acting Chaplain 1st Cinque Ports RV, 1884–1908; Chaplain, 1st Class, Territorial Force, 1908–9. *Address:* Deanery, Battle, Sussex. *Clubs:* Junior Constitutional, Junior Army and Navy.   *Died 4 Feb. 1921.*

CURRIE, Maj.-Gen. Fendall; Bengal Cavalry; *b* 24 Nov. 1841; 6th *s* of Sir Frederick Currie, 1st Bt and Katherine Maria, *d* of George Powney Thompson, BCS; *m* 1st, 1866, Susan (*d* 1868), *y d* of Rev. J. R. Pears, Woodcote House, Windlesham; one *s* one *d*; 2nd, 1869, Julia (*d* 1920), *d* of F. P. Buller; one *s* four *d* (and two *s* decd). Entered army, 1858; Maj.-Gen 1898; Commissioner in Oudh, UP, India, 1888–96.   *Died 4 Dec. 1920.*

CURRIE, Lieut-Col Ivor Bertram Fendall, DSO 1919; late RGA; *b* 2 Aug. 1872; *e s* of Maj.-Gen. Fendall Currie, and 2nd wife, Julia, *d* of F. P. Buller; *m* 1906, May Constance, *d* of late Field Marshal Sir George White, VC, GCB, OM; two *d*. *Educ:* Clifton College; Royal Military Academy, Woolwich. Served European War 1914–19 (despatches, DSO); retired pay, 1921. *Address: c/o* Lloyd's Bank, Ltd, Charing Cross, SW1. *Club:* Army and Navy.

Died 1 April 1924.

CURRIE, Col (Temp. Brig.-Gen.) Ryves Alexander Mark, CMG 1919; DSO 1917; *b* 18 June 1875; *s* of late Lt-Col F. A. Currie, Norfolk Regt; *m* 1908, Ida M., *d* of J. H. Hatchell, MD; no *c*. *Educ:* Wellington College. Joined 1st Batt. Somerset Light Infantry, 1896; Adjutant, 1904; passed Staff College, 1911; Brigade-Major, 13th Infantry Brigade, 1912; served NW Frontier, India, 1897; European War, 1914–18 (despatches, Bt Maj., Bt Lieut-Col, Bt Col, DSO, CMG, Légion d'Honneur). *Address:* Merton, Camberley. *Clubs:* United Service, MCC, I Zingari.

Died 30 March 1920.

CURTEIS, Brig.-Gen. Francis Algernon, CB 1911; CMG 1917; retired, 1912; *b* June 1856; *s* of Capt. H. J. Curteis, late 37th Regt; *m* 1894, Jeannie Hilda Macdonald, *d* of late Philip Myburgh, QC; one *d*. *Educ:* Malvern College. Entered Royal Artillery, 1876; served Soudan, 1885–86; *S* Africa, 1900–2; Brig.-Gen. commanding Western Coast Defences, 1908–12. *Address:* 4 The Croft, Tenby.

Died 1 May 1928.

CURTEIS, Maj.-Gen. Reginald Lawrence Herbert, JP; *b* 3 Jan. 1842. Entered army, 1860; Maj.-Gen. 1900; retired, 1903. *Address:* Glan-yr-afon, Crickhowell.

Died 17 Dec. 1919.

CURTIS, Colonel Edward George, CMG 1916; *b* 1868; 3rd *s* of late Maj.-Gen. Reginald Curtis, RA; *m* 1903, Ethel, *d* of late Walter Coote, FRGS; one *s*. *Educ:* Westminster School; Cheltenham College; RMC Sandhurst. Bedfordshire Regiment, 1888–1909; served with the Chitral Relief Force, 1895 (medal with clasp); commanded 4th Northamptonshire Regt, and served with it in Gallipoli (despatches); and in Egypt, BEF, 1916–19 (despatches); an Organising Secretary of the National Service League, 1909–14. *Recreation:* football; Hon. Secretary, Army Football Association, 1900–1907; several years a member of the Consultative Committee, FA.

Died March 1923.

CURTIS, Maj.-Gen. Sir Reginald Salmond, KCMG 1917 (CMG 1908); CB 1915; DSO 1900; *b* 21 Nov. 1863; *e s* of Maj.-Gen. Reginald Curtis, RA; *m* 1894, Hon. Hilda Margaret, *y d* of 9th Viscount Barrington; three *d*. *Educ:* Cheltenham Coll.; RMA Woolwich. Commissioned in Royal Engineers, 1883; served Egyptian Army, 1890–93; in campaign, Eastern Soudan, 1891, including capture of Tokar (bronze star with clasp, 4th class Medjidie); served in Ashanti expedition, 1895–96, as director of telegraphs (star, brevet of Maj., despatches); special service under Admiralty, Falkland Islands, 1899; served South African war, 1899–1902, as ADC to Engineer-in-Chief, also as Assistant Director of Telegraphs, and with South African Constabulary (DSO, Queen's medal with five clasps, King's medal with two clasps, Brevet Lieut-Colonel, despatches); Chief Staff Officer, SA Constabulary, 1903–5; Inspector General, SA Constabulary, 1905–8; Member of the Intercolonial Council of the Transvaal and Orange River Colony, 1904–8; Commandant Army Signal School, 1912–13; Assistant Adjutant-General, War Office, 1913–17; commanded Cromarty Defences, 1917; in charge of Administration Aldershot Command, 1917–19; retired, 1920; Major-General and KCMG for valuable services rendered in connection with the European War, 1914–17. *Address:* The Croft, West Farleigh, Maidstone. *Club:* Army and Navy.

Died 11 Jan. 1922.

CURTIS, Sir William Michael, 4th Bt, *cr* 1802; *b* Knole, 11 Nov. 1859; *s* of William Edmund Curtis and Ariana Emily, *d* of Col W. C. Master; *S* grandfather, 1870; *m* 1st, 1887, Mabel (*d* 1888), 4th *d* of Sir Somerville A. Gurney, KCVO, of North Runcton Hall, King's Lynn; one *d*; 2nd, 1895, Georgina, *d* of Col J. S. Howard, and *widow* of Capt. Arthur B. Mesham; three *d*. *Recreation:* Master of Ludlow Fox-hounds, 1886–1907. *Heir: c* Edgar Francis Egerton Curtis [*b* 18 Dec. 1875; *m* 1903, Madeline, 3rd *d* of late C. W. Alexander, ICS]. *Address:* Caynham Court, Ludlow, Salop.

Died 19 Dec. 1916.

CURWEN, Eldred Vincent Morris, JP; *b* 1842; 3rd *s* of late Edward Stanley Curwen, of Workington, and Frances Margaret, *d* of late

Edward Jesse; *m* 1st, 1865, Hebe Emily (*d* 1889), *o d* of Sir Chaloner Ogle, 3rd Bt, of Withdeane Court; 2nd, 1913, Evelyn, *y d* of General Sir Edmund Ogle, 6th Bt, of San Remo, Italy. *Clubs:* Arthur's, Conservative; Royal Yacht Squadron, Cowes.

Died 16 Feb. 1927.

CURWEN, John Spencer; editor of the Musical Herald since 1866; *b* Plaistow, Essex, 30 Sept. 1847; *e s* of John Curwen, originator of the Tonic Sol-Fa System; *m* 1877, Annie Jessy, *d* of J. C. Gregg of Dublin; one *s* two *d*. *Educ:* City of London School; Royal Acad. of Music under G. A. Macfarren, Sullivan, and Prout. ARAM 1879; FRAM 1885; Associate Philharmonic Society, 1882; Welsh Bard (ap Derwent Pencerdd), 1896; FZS. Director, J. Curwen & Sons, 24 Berners Street, London. President Tonic Sol-Fa College on death of his father, 1880; travelled much in Europe and America investigating the organisation of music in schools and among the masses of the people; President Tonic Sol-Fa Association. *Publications:* Studies in Worship Music, 1880, 2nd series 1885; Memorials of John Curwen, 1882; The Boy's Voice; School Music Abroad, 1901; Music at the Queen's Accession. *Recreations:* pedestrianism, tennis, dogs, social questions. *Address:* 6 Portland Court, Great Portland Street, W. *T:* 2191 Mayfair. *Died 6 Aug. 1916.*

CURWOOD, James Oliver; author; *b* Owosso, Michigan, USA, 12 June 1879; *s* of James Moran Curwood and Abigail Griffin; descendant on father's side of Captain Marryat, the novelist; *m. Educ:* University of Michigan. In newspaper work seven years; assistant editor and editor, News-Tribune, Detroit; resigned to take up literary work exclusively, 1907; former member Troop B, Michigan State Cavalry; Republican; one of the foremost North American naturalists; spent several months each year in Canadian wilderness, travelling as far north as Arctic coast; the only American ever employed by the Canadian Government as an exploratory and descriptive writer; had one of the largest collections of great game photographs (taken by himself) in America. *Publications:* God's Country—the Trail to Happiness; Baree, Son of Kazan; The Courage of Captain Plum; The Courage of Marge O'Doone; The Danger Trail; Flower of the North; God's Country— and the Woman; The Gold Hunters; The Golden Snare; The Great Lakes; The Grizzly King; The Honor of the the Big Snows; The Hunted Woman; Isobel; Kazan; Nomads of the North; Philip Steele; The Wolf Hunters; The River's End; The Valley of Silent Men; The Flaming Forest; The Country Beyond; Swift Lightning; The Last Frontier; The Alaskan; A Gentleman of Courage; The Ancient Highway; The Black Hunter; The Glory of Living, an autobiography; The Plains of Abraham. *Address:* Owosso, Michigan, USA.

Died 13 Aug. 1927.

CURZON OF KEDLESTON, 1st Marquess, *cr* 1921; **George Nathaniel Curzon,** KG 1916; GCSI 1899; GCIE 1899; PC 1895; JP, DL; DCL, LLD, MA; FRS; FBA 1908; Baron Scarsdale, 1761; Baron (Ireland), 1898; Viscount Scarsdale, 1911; Baron Ravensdale, 1911; Earl Curzon of Kedleston, 1911; Earl of Kedleston, 1921; Irish Representative Peer since 1908; Secretary of State for Foreign Affairs, 1919–24; Leader of the House of Lords, 1916–24; Member of Imperial War Cabinet, 1916; Trustee of the British Museum, 1920; *b* Kedleston, 11 Jan. 1859; *e s* of 4th Baron Scarsdale, and Blanche, *d* of Joseph Pocklington Senhouse, Netherhall; *m* 1st, 1895, Mary Victoria, CI (*d* 1906), *d* of L. Z. Leiter, Washington, USA; three *d*; 2nd, 1917, Grace Elvina, GBE, *d* of late J. Monroe Hinds, USA, Minister, Brazil, and *widow* of Alfred Duggan, Buenos Ayres. *Educ:* Eton; Balliol Coll., Oxford. President of the Union, 1880; Assistant Private Secretary to Marquis of Salisbury, 1885; contested (C) S Derbyshire, 1885; MP (C) Southport Division SW Lancashire, 1886–98; Under-Secretary of State for India, 1891–92; Under-Secretary of State for Foreign Affairs, 1895–98; Viceroy and Gov.-Gen. of India, 1899–1905; Lord Privy Seal, 1915–16; President of the Air Board, 1916; Lord President of the Council, 1916–19. Travelled extensively in Central Asia, Persia, Afghanistan, the Pamirs, Siam, Indo-China, and Korea; received the Gold Medal of Royal Geographical Society, 1895. Lothian Essay Prize, Oxford, 1883; Arnold Essay Prize, 1884; Fellow All Souls' Coll. Oxford, 1883; Hon. DCL (Oxford), 1904; Hon. LLD (Cambridge), 1907; Hon. LLD (Manchester), 1908; Hon. LLD (Glasgow), 1911; Hon. DCL (Durham), 1913; Romanes Lecturer, Oxford, 1907; Chancellor of Oxford University, 1907; Lord Rector, Glasgow University, 1908; Hon. Fellow, Balliol College, 1907; Rede Lecturer, Cambridge, 1913. Lord Warden of the Cinque Ports, 1904–5; President of the Royal Geographical Society, 1911–14; Trustee of the National Gallery, 1911. *Publications:* Russia in Central Asia, 1889; Persia and the Persian Question, 1892; Problems of the Far East, 1894; Lord Curzon in India, 1906; Principles and Methods of University Reform, 1909; Modern Parliamentary Eloquence, 1913; War Poems and Other Translations,

1915; Subjects of the Day, 1915; Tales of Travel, 1923. *Heir:* (to *Viscounty*) *n* Richard Nathaniel Curzon, *b* 3 July 1898; (to *Barony*) *e d* Lady Mary Irene Curzon, *b* 20 Jan. 1896; (to *Marquisate*) none. *Address:* 1 Carlton House Terrace, SW1. *T:* Regent 1628; Hackwood, Basingstoke; Kedleston, Derby; Montacute House, Somerset. *Clubs:* Carlton, Athenæum, Bachelors'.

Died 20 March 1925.

CURZON, Hon. Alfred Nathaniel; *b* 12 March 1860; 2nd *s* of 4th Baron Scarsdale; *m* 1891, Henrietta Mary, *d* of Hon. Spencer Dudley Montagu; one *s* two *d*. *Address:* Weston Underwood, near Derby. *Club:* Wellington. *Died 20 Sept. 1920.*

CURZON, Frank; Theatrical Manager and Racehorse Owner; Lessee and Manager, The Playhouse and Wyndham's Theatre; *b* Wavertree, Liverpool, 17 Sept. 1868; *s* of W. Clark Deeley, Curzon Park, Chester, and Elizabeth, *d* of J. Mallaby of Loxley Hall, Staffordshire; *m* Isabel Jay. *Educ:* privately. Joined the theatrical profession and played with several provincial companies, afterwards touring cos on his own account; took the Avenue Theatre (later the Playhouse) in 1899, and there in conjunction with Mr Charles Hawtrey produced A Message from Mars; following this took the Strand and Globe (both now demolished), and at one time had no less than nine West-End Theatres under his management; produced A Chinese Honeymoon; Miss Hook of Holland; An Englishman's Home, and numerous other plays. *Recreations:* racing, hunting, golfing, fishing. *Address:* 37 Bury Street, St James's, SW1. *T:* Gerrard 2229; Primrose House, Newmarket. *Clubs:* Buck's; Union, Brighton. *Died 2 July 1927.*

CUSACK-SMITH, Sir William, 4th Bt, *cr* 1799; 4th Royal Wurtemberg Lancers (retired); *b* 1822; *s* of Sir Michael Cusack-Smith, 3rd Bt and Elizabeth, *d* of Charles Patrick Moore; S father, 1859. *Heir: cousin* Sir Berry Cusack-Smith, KCMG, *b* 16 Feb. 1859. *Address:* Hope Villa, Southsea. *Died 15 April 1919.*

CUSHNY, Arthur Robertson, MA, MD, LLD; FRS 1907; Professor of Materia Medica and Pharmacology, University of Edinburgh, since 1918; *b* 1866; 4th *s* of late Rev. John Cushny, Speymouth, Morayshire; *m* 1896, Sarah, *d* of Ralph Firbank; one *d*. *Educ:* University of Aberdeen; Berne; Strassburg. Entered University of Aberdeen, 1882; graduated in Arts and Medicine, 1889; Thompson Fellow, 1889; Assistant to Professor of Pharmacology Strassburg, 1892–93; Professor of Pharmacology in the University of Michigan, Ann Arbor, USA, 1893–1905; Professor of Pharmacology and Materia Medica in University of London, University College, 1905–18; member Royal Commission on Whisky and other Potable Spirits, 1908. *Publications:* Textbook of Pharmacology and Therapeutics, 8th edn 1924; The Secretion of the Urine, 1917; The Action and Uses in Medicine of Digitalis and its Allies, 1924. *Recreations:* walking, golf. *Address:* University, Edinburgh. *Club:* Athenæum.

Died 25 Feb. 1926.

CUST, Very Rev. Arthur Perceval Purey-, DD; FSA; JP for Bucks; Dean of York since 1880; *b* 1828; *s* of late Hon. William Cust and Sophia, *d* of Thos Newnham, Southborough; *m* 1854, Lady Emma Bess Bligh, *d* of 5th Earl of Darnley. *Educ:* Proprietary School, Lee, Kent; Brasenose Coll., Oxford. Fellow of All Souls' Coll. 1850–54; MA 1854; DD 1880. Curate of Northchurch, Herts, 1851–53; Rector of Cheddington, Bucks, and Rural Dean, 1853–62; Vicar of St Mary's, Reading, and Rural Dean, 1862–75; Hon. Canon of Christ Church, Oxford; Vicar of Aylesbury, 1875–76; Archdeacon of Buckingham, 1875–80; Chaplain to the Archbishop of Canterbury, 1868. *Publications:* sermons, lectures, papers at Church Congresses; Archidiaconal Charges; magazine articles; The Heraldry of York Minster, 4to, 1st series, 1890, 2nd series, 1896; Picturesque Old York, 1896; York Minster, 1897. *Recreations:* archæology, history, music, etc. *Address:* Deanery, York. *Clubs:* United University; Yorkshire, York. *Died 23 Dec. 1916.*

CUST, Henry John Cockayne, DL, JP; *b* 10 Oct. 1861; *s* of Major Henry Francis Cockayne Cust, Cockayne Hatley, and Sarah Jane, *d* of late Isaac Cookson, and *widow* of Major Sidney R. Streatfeild; *heir* to Barony of Brownlow; *m* 1893, Emmeline Mary Elizabeth, *o d* of Sir William Welby-Gregory, 4th Bt. *Educ:* Eton; Trinity College, Cambridge (Scholar). MP (C) Stamford, 1890–95; MP (C) Bermondsey, 1900–6; editor of the Pall Mall Gazette, 1902–6; member of the French Bar. *Address:* Chancellor's House, 17 Hyde Park Gate, SW; Belton House, Grantham. *Clubs:* Carlton, Travellers', Beefsteak. *Died 2 March 1917.*

CUSTANCE, Colonel Frederic Hambleton, CB 1900; Hon. Colonel 3rd Battalion Norfolk Regiment; *b* 2 Dec. 1844; *e s* of late

Colonel Sir Hambleton Francis Custance, KCB; *m* 1871, Eleanor (*d* 1908), *d* of late Capt. Hylton Jolliffe, *e s* of 1st Lord Hylton; two *d*. Served South Africa 1900–1 (despatches, Queen's medal 3 clasps, CB); Lieut-Col late Grenadier Guards. *Address:* Weston Hall, Norwich. *TA:* Great Witchingham. *M:* AH 46. *Club:* Carlton.

Died 29 Sept. 1925.

CUTLER, Edward, JP; KC 1884; *b* 4 May 1831; *s* of Edward Cutler, Surgeon to St George's Hospital, and Marianne, *d* of Sir Thomas Plumer, Master of the Rolls; *m* Ellen Mona, *d* of late Major Larkins (murdered at Cawnpore); one *s* two *d*. *Educ:* Eton; Paris; Dresden; Balliol Coll., Oxford; graduated with Classical Honours. Barrister 1857. Grand Organist, English Freemasons, 1892, 1893. Imperial Commission for Copyright, 1909; employed in revising International Copyright Bill, 1910. *Publications:* The Teacher's Legal Guide (co-author with H. Lynn); A Treatise on Musical and Dramatic Copyright (co-author with Eustace Smith and Fred. E. Weatherly); A Manual of Musical Copyright Law, 1906; pamphlets in the French language on Les grades Universitaires, and on other subjects; Golden Years, a song published about 1890, and numerous other songs and pieces for full orchestra, organ, and pianoforte. *Recreations:* London Skating Club; gave frequent organ recitals in public. *Address:* 32 Eaton Place, SW. *Clubs:* Junior Carlton, Skating.

Died 22 Dec. 1916.

CUTLER, John, KC; MA; Emeritus Professor of Law, King's College, University of London; formerly Editor, Reports of Patent Design and Trade Mark Cases, published by HM Patent Office; *b* Dorchester, 9 Jan. 1839; *m* 1884, Edith Ruth, *d* of late Thomas Hayes. *Educ:* King's Coll. London; Exeter Coll., Oxford; Edinburgh University. Barrister 1863; QC 1897; Bencher, Lincoln's Inn. *Publications:* Treatise on Law of Naturalisation, 1871; Treatise on Passing Off, 1904; A Brace of Humbugs, Her Début at Court, Dora's Dream, and other dramatic works. *Recreations:* music and the drama. *Address:* 7 Addison Court Gardens, Blythe Road, W14. *T:* Hammersmith 1669; 4 New Square, Lincoln's Inn, WC2.

Died 19 March 1924.

CUYLER, Sir Charles, 4th Bt, *cr* 1814; OBE 1918; reserve of officers since 9 March 1919; Lieut-Colonel commanding Depot Oxford and Bucks Light Infantry and 43rd Recruiting Area, 6 Aug. 1914–9 March 1919; *b* Oakleaze, Gloucestershire, 15 Aug. 1867; *s* of Sir Charles Henry Johnes Cuyler, 3rd Bt and Emma Emilia, *d* of Ansten Cox; *S* father, 1885; *m* 1897, Maud Geraldine, *d* of late Arthur Henry Jenney. *Educ:* Clifton College; RMC Sandhurst. *Recreations:* cricket, golf, shooting, fishing, etc. *Heir: b* George Hallifax Cuyler [*b* 23 April 1876; *m* 1913, Amy, *d* of late Frederick Gordon, of the Briery, Sunderland, and *widow* of Gordon M'Kenzie]. *Address:* Kingswood, Medmenham, Bucks. *TA:* Medmenham.

Died 1 Oct. 1919.

CZAPLICKA, Marie Antoinette, FRAI; FRGS; author, lecturer and traveller; *b* near Warsaw, Poland; *d* of Felix Lubicz de Czaplicki and Sophie de Zawisza. *Educ:* in Poland and Russia. Came to England with Mianowski Research Scholarship (Warsaw), 1910; studied in London and Oxford (Somerville College); took Diploma in Anthropology in Oxford, 1912; Anthropological Expedition to the Yenisei Valley in Siberia, under the auspices of the Oxford University Committee for Anthropology and as Mary Ewart Travelling Scholar, Somerville College, 1914–15; hon. member of Lady Margaret Hall, Oxford, since 1916; Mary Ewart Lecturer in Ethnology to the Oxford School of Anthropology, 1916–19; Murchison Grant, RGS, 1920. *Publications:* Aboriginal Siberia, 1914; My Siberian Year, 1916; The Turks of Central Asia, 1918; essays on East European and North-Central Asiatic subjects in the Hasting's Encyclopædia of Religion and Ethics; various pamphlets and articles on anthropology in English, Polish and Russian. *Recreations:* walking, fencing. *Address:* Lady Margaret Hall, Oxford. *Club:* Lyceum.

Died 27 May 1921.

D

D'AETH, John, MInstCE; ISO 1910; *b* 10 Aug. 1853; *e* surv. *s* of James Death, Waltham Abbey, Waltham Abbey, Essex, and Cheshunt, Herts; *m* 1885, Anna Marie, *d* of Thomas Oughton, Solicitor and

Advocate, and Clerk to the Legislative Council of Jamaica; one *s*. *Educ:* High School, Bishop's Stortford; King's College, London. Selected from King's College, London, and appointed Assistant Draughtsman, PWD, Jamaica, 1873, subsequently Chief Draughtsman, District Engineer, NW District, 1883; Kingston District, 1886; Eastern District, 1889; Southern District, 1892; Eastern District, 1894; in charge of construction of mountain roads. Selected by Sec. of State and seconded 1901 to take charge of alteration and construction of Imperial Road, Dominica, in consequence of wasteful expenditure thereon; invalided home, 1901; acted as Director Public Works, 1902, 1903, 1905, 1907, 1908–9, 1912–13; mentioned in despatches in connection with service rendered on the Relief Works after the severe hurricane of Aug. 1903; Assistant Director Public Works, Jamaica, 1902–14. *Publication:* paper to Institution of Civil Engineers on the Engineering Enterprises of the Victorian Age. *Recreations:* none. *Address:* c/o Lloyds Bank, Torquay.

Died 21 Nov. 1922.

DA FANO, Corrado Donato, MD; FLS; FRMS; Reader in Histology, King's College, University of London, since 1922; *b* Urbino, Italy, 1 June 1879; 3rd *s* of Comm. Alessandro and late Adele Maroni; *m* 1915, Dorothea Landau. *Educ:* Milan. Pupil in Golgi's Institute of Histology and General Pathology, University of Pavia, 1902–5; degree of MD, University of Pavia, 1905; awarded the Fossati Prize by the Istituto Lombardo di Scienze e Lettere, 1906; Resident Physician of the Cernusco Department, Hospital of Milan, 1908; awarded the Sangalli Travelling Scholarship by the Hospital of Milan, 1908; Honorary Assistant in Ziehen's Neurological Klinik, University of Berlin, 1908; Honorary Assistant at the Imperial Cancer Research Fund, London, 1909; 1st Assistant and Presektor of the Pathological Institute, University of Groningen, 1910; degree of LD (Libero Docente) in Morbid Anatomy at the University of Pavia, 1912; Vice-Director of the Pathological Institute of Milan, 1912–15; Captain, Italian RAMC, in command of a Field Ambulance at the Italian Front, 1915–18 (bronze medal, Benemeriti della Salute Pubblica); Lecturer on Histology, University of London, 1918; Member of the Real Sociedad Española de Historia Natural; Member of the Council of the Royal Microscopical Society; Correspondent Member of the Società Medica–Chirurgica di Bologna; Co-editor of Physiological Abstracts. *Publications:* over sixty papers on histological, histopathological and histophysiological subjects published in various scientific periodicals. *Address:* Hypatia Lodge, Sheffield Terrace, W8.

Died 14 March 1927.

DAGA, Sir Dewan Bahadur Kasturchand, Rai Bahadur, KCIE 1911 (CIE 1909); banker, land-owner, mill-owner, etc; *b* 17 Nov. 1855; *s* of Abirchand Daga Rai Bahadur; *m* five times; four *s* five *d*. *Educ:* home. Title of Rai Bahadur from the Bikaner State, 1880; title of Rai Bahadur from the British Government, 1887; title of Dewan Bahadur, 1903; Kaiser-i-Hind Silver Medal, 1898; Coronation Delhi Durbar Medal, 1903; Coronation Delhi Durbar Medal, 1911; Hon. Magistrate with 2nd class powers in Kamptee, CP, 1885; 1st class powers, 1887; Chairman Nagpur Electric Light and Power Co., Ltd; Member of Cantonment Committee, Kamptee; Life Member of the Central Committee of the Imperial Institute in India and a Life Councillor of the Dufferin Fund; exempt from the Arms Act and from personal attendance in Civil Courts, also from payment of Custom duty in the Bikaner State; helped in famine works; constructed a number of tanks, wells, market and pavilion, and did good many other philanthropic works of general utility and public convenience, costing nearly 2 lacs in the British Territory and 1½ lacs in the Bikaner State. *Address:* Bikaner, Rajputana.

Died Jan. 1917.

DAGLISH, Hon. Henry; *b* 18 Nov. 1866; *m* 1894, Edith, *d* of late Charles Bishop, Smythesdale, Victoria. *Educ:* South Geelong School; Melbourne University. MLA Subiaco, 1901; Premier, Western Australia, 1904–5. *Address:* Subiaco, Western Australia.

Died 16 Aug. 1920.

DAGONET; *see* Sims, George Robert.

DALBIAC, Philip Hugh, CB 1911; a Director George Allen and Unwin, publishers, since 1914; *b* 1855; 3rd *s* of Henry Eardley Aylmer Dalbiac, Durrington, and Mary, *d* of Sir Henry E. A. Mainwaring, 1st Bt; *m* 1888, Lilian, 4th *d* of Sir Charles Seely, 1st Bt; one *s* four *d*. *Educ:* Winchester. Joined 70th Regt 1875; exchanged to 45th Foot, 1875; retired as Major, 1890; MP (C) North Camberwell, 1895–1900; Col Commanding 18th Middlesex RV, 1896–1908; raised and commanded Transport and Supply Column, 2nd London Div. Territorial Forces, 1908–12; raised and commanded 60th Div. Train, 1914–17; served in France and Solonika, 1916–17 (despatches).

Publications: Dictionary of Quotations (English), 1896; French and Italian, 1900; History of the 45th Regiment, 1902; History of the Chancellorsville and Gettysburg Campaign. *Recreations:* taken leading part in cricket, as player and organiser; was good runner and athlete generally. *Address:* Heathfield, Freshwater, Isle of Wight.

Died 28 April 1927.

DALBY, Sir William Bartlett, Kt 1886; Consulting Aural Surgeon, St George's Hospital; *b* Ashby-de-la-Zouche, 10 Dec. 1840; *s* of late Charles Allsopp Dalby and Sarah, *d* of William Bartlett, Lymington; *m* 1873, Hyacinthe, *d* of late Maj. Edward Wellesley, 73rd Regiment; one *s* three *d*. *Educ:* Sidney Sussex Coll., Cambridge. President Medical Society, 1894–95; President of the Otological Society of the United Kingdom. *Publications:* Lectures on Diseases and Injuries of Ear; article on same subject in Holmes's System of Surgery, Quain's Dictionary of Medicine. *Recreation:* shooting. *Address:* 14 Montagu Place, Portman Square, W. *Clubs:* Athenæum, Garrick, Carlton.

Died 29 Dec. 1918.

DALDY, Frederick Francis; Barrister-at-law; Master of the Supreme Court, 1916–26; *b* 18 Aug. 1857; *s* of late Frederic Richard Daldy; *m* Elizabeth Violet Frances, *d* of late Judge Melville; two *d*. *Educ:* Charterhouse; Pembroke Coll., Cambridge (MA). Called to the Bar, Inner Temple, 1881; joined the South-Eastern Circuit; devilled for Sir Richard E. Webster (Lord Alverstone), 1884–90; Junior Counsel to HM Customs and Excise, 1900; for many years in practice at the Common Law Bar; was Assistant Executive Officer to the National Rifle Association at Wimbledon and Bisley. *Address:* 12 Pembroke Road, Kensington, W.

Died 11 July 1928.

DALE, Admiral Alfred Taylor; retired; *b* 26 Sept. 1840; *s* of Clement Dale. Entered Navy, 1854; Captain, 1876; Rear-Adm. 1891; Vice-Adm. 1897; Admiral, 1903; served China, 1858. *Address:* 28 Sloane Court, SW.

Died 14 Nov. 1925.

DALE, Sir Alfred (William Winterslow), Kt 1911; MA (Cantab); LLD (Aberdeen, Bristol); *b* 2 Dec. 1855; *s* of R. W. Dale, LLD, Birmingham; *m* 1882, May, 2nd *d* of William Jeeves; three *d*. *Educ:* King Edward's School, Birmingham; Trinity College and Trinity Hall, Cambridge. Chancellor's medal for English poem, 1876 and 1878; Members' Prize, 1880; Hulsean Prize, 1881; Seatonian Prize, 1885, 1920. 8th Classic, 1879; Fellow of Trinity Hall, 1881; Lecturer, Bursar, and Tutor of the College, 1879–99; Examiner in the Classical Tripos, 1883–84; Member of the Council of the Senate, and Secretary of the General Board of Studies; a university representative in the Municipal Council, Cambridge. Principal of University College, Liverpool, 1899; Vice-Chancellor, University of Liverpool, 1903–19; Chairman of the Board of Studies of Victoria University, 1902–4; of Northern Universities Joint Matriculation Board, 1905–16; of Council and Board of Education, Mansfield College, Oxford; Member of the Examinations Council for Secondary Schools, 1918–9; Chairman, 1921. *Publications:* The Synod of Elvira, 1882; The Origenistic Controversies, in Smith's Dictionary of Christian Biography, 1887; Life of R. W. Dale, 1898; completed and edited History of English Congregationalism, 1907; edited Warren's Book: documents and collections relating to the foundation and history of Trinity Hall, Cambridge, 1911. *Address:* Red Lodge, Cold Ash, Newbury. *Club:* Athenæum.

Died 13 Aug. 1921.

DALE, Frank Harry, CB 1913; Chief Inspector for Elementary Schools, Board of Education, since 1911; *b* 1871; *s* of H. J. Dale, manufacturing electrician; *m* Lucy, *d* of C. H. Hanson and *sister* of P. Hanson. *Educ:* St Paul's School, London; Balliol College, Oxford. Fellow of Merton College, Oxford, 1895; Junior Examiner in Board of Education, 1897; HM Inspector of Schools, 1900. *Address:* 33 Clarendon Road, Holland Park, W; Board of Education, Whitehall, SW. *Club:* Royal Societies.

Died 3 Nov. 1918.

DALE, Henry Sheppard, ARE 1909; water-colour painter; *b* 13 Nov. 1852; *s* of B. H. Dale, Bank Manager, Sheffield; *m* 1887, Emily, *d* of S. K. Pollard, Taunton; no *c*. *Educ:* Sheffield Grammar School. After short time at Cary's Art School, entered the Slade on its opening, 1871; studied in Italy, 1874–77; engraved aquatint plates for the coloured numbers of the Graphic, 1879–81; architectural illustrations for several books. *Publications:* portfolios of Etchings of Venice, 1881; Glastonbury, 1885; Wells, 1886; Salisbury, 1887; Exeter, 1888; numerous etchings. *Address:* Green Cliff Studio, Rye.

Died 24 Nov. 1921.

DALE, John Gilbert, FRGS, FZS; *b* Hanley, Staffs, 1869; *s* of James Dale and Sarah Gilbert; *m* Jessie May, *d* of Bernard Collett; two *s*

two *d*. *Educ:* Hanley, Staffs; Congleton, Cheshire. Contested Kennington for LCC, 1910 and 1913; Parliamentary Candidate North St Pancras, 1918 and 1922 in Labour interest; Labour Parliamentary Candidate for Walthamstow East, 1923; First Chairman and one of Founders of National Union of Police and Prison Officers; First President of Prison Officers Federation; Member Society Psychical Research; Member of Council of Industrial Christian Fellowship, also of Council of Union of Democratic Control; Wesleyan Lay Preacher for over thirty years; Member of Fabian Society, Independent Labour Party, etc. *Publications:* Epilepsy: its Causes, Symptoms and Treatment; various articles medical, religious, political. *Recreations:* reading, motoring, foreign travel. *Address:* 68 Holland Park, W11. *T:* Park 3027. *M:* XL 4510. *Club:* Royal Societies.

Died 6 March 1926.

DALE, Rev. Thomas F., MA, Queen's College, Oxford; Senior Chaplain, retired, Bengal Ecclesiastical Establishment. Wrote in The Field as Stoneclink; contributor on sport and travel to various journals in England, America, and India; Steward (resigned 1920 after 18 years' service), appointed Hon. Member of the Council of the National Pony Society; appointed (1912) by President of Board of Agriculture and Fisheries Member of Departmental Committee on Mountain and Moorland Ponies; acted as Official Judge for distribution Ministry of Agriculture Premiums to Mountain and Moorland Stallions in New Forest; Joint-Sec. to Burley and District Society for Improvement of Ponies, Cattle, and Pigs since 1914; Chairman of Mountain and Moorland Pony Committee, 1918. *Publications:* The Game of Polo, 1897; Two Fortunes and Old Patch (with Slaughter), 1898; History of the Belvoir Hunt, 1899; Riding, Driving, and Kindred Sports, 1899; edited Polo in Badminton Series; The 8th Duke of Beaufort and the Badminton Hunt; The Riding and Polo Pony; Fox Hunting in The Shires, 1902; Polo Past and Present, 1905; The Fox (Fur, Fin, and Feather Series), 1906; The Stable Handbook, 1906; Arab and Colonial Horses in Sir H. De Trafford's Horses of the British Empire; editor and part author Polo at Home and Abroad. *Recreations:* hunting, natural history, reading. *Address:* Brush End, Burley, Hants. *Clubs:* Ranelagh, United University.

Died 15 Oct. 1923.

DALE, Rev. William; Secretary of Foreign Missions Committee, 1898–1915, and first Editor and then Joint-Editor of Messenger of Presbyterian Church of England, 1893–1915; *b* Glasgow, 9 Oct. 1841; *m* 1881, Mary Blackhall, Edinburgh; two *s* three *d*. *Educ:* Free Normal School, Glasgow; Glasgow Univ; Free Church Coll., Glasgow. 2nd prize, Senior Logic Class; 1st prize, Sen. Mathematics; twenty guineas for essay on Intellectual Advantages of Sabbath Observance; silver medal for essay on Hobbes; scholarships, etc, in Free Church College. Minister of Free Church, Gordon, Berwickshire, 1868–71; minister of Presbyterian Church, Singapore, 1871–75; minister of New Barnet Presbyterian Church, 1877–1904. *Publications:* Sermons (occasional); The Story of our Missions in the Far East; Presbyterian Missions and the Bible Society; The Opened Door; Foreign Mission Reports. *Address:* New Barnet, Herts.

Died 15 Feb. 1924.

DALGETY, Major Frederick John, DL, JP, county of Southampton; *b* 19 Nov. 1866; *s* of late F. G. Dalgety of Lockerley Hall, Hants; *m* 1897, Hon. Pauline Caroline M'Clintock Bunbury, *d* of 2nd Baron Rathdonnell; three *s* one *d*. *Educ:* Eton. Late Capt. 15th Hussars; served commencement of South African War as Adjutant Imperial Yeomanry; served in 14th Reserve Cavalry Regt and 3rd Reserve Hussars, 1914–19. *Address:* Lockerley Hall, Romsey, Hants. *T:* Lockerley 3. *TA:* Lockerley. *Clubs:* Naval and Military, Wellington.

Died 23 May 1926.

DALGLIESH, Richard, CB 1918; JP, DL; Chairman, Leicester's Territorial Forces Association; Deputy Chairman, Quarter Sessions; Chairman Leicestershire County Council; *b* 1844; *s* of D. Dalgliesh, Carsethorne, Dumfries; *m* 1867, Mary, *d* of late John Pearson, High Sheriff, 1907. *Address:* Asfordby Place, Melton Mowbray.

Died 16 Oct. 1922.

DALHOUSIE, 14th Earl of, *cr* 1633; **Arthur George Maule Ramsay,** DL; Baron Ramsay, 1619; Lord Ramsay, 1633; Baron Ramsay (UK), 1875; Lieutenant Reserve of Officers; *b* 4 Sept. 1878; *s* of 13th Earl and Ida, *d* of 6th Earl of Tankerville; *S* father, 1887; *m* 1903, Lady Mary Adelaide Heathcote Drummond Willoughby, *d* of 1st Earl of Ancaster; two *s* two *d*. Late Forfar and Kincardine Artillery Militia; late Capt. Scots Guards; served S Africa, 1901–2; European War. Owner of about 138,000 acres. *Heir:* *s* Lord Ramsay, *b* 25 July 1904. *Address:* Brechin Castle, also Panmure House, Carnoustie, Forfarshire; Dalhousie Castle, Bonnyrigg, Midlothian; 82 Eaton Square, SW1.

Died 23 Dec. 1928.

DALLAS, Hon. Francis Henry; late Member of Council of Rajah of Sarawak, and Treasurer of independent State of Sarawak; *b* Heworth, near York, 1865; *y s* of William Sweetland Dallas, FLS, CMZS, writer on Zoological subjects, and Frances Esther, *y d* of Liscombe Price, Solicitor, London and Abergavenny; *m* 1889, Ethel Jane, *y d* of Charles Santley, and Gertrude, *e d* of John Mitchell Kemble. Formerly editor of Sarawak Gazette. *Address:* The Borneo Co. Ltd, 73 Fenchurch Street, EC3. *Club:* Sports.
Died 10 March 1920.

DALLAS, Sir George Edward, 3rd Bt, *cr* 1798; late Chief Clerk of the Foreign Office; *b* London, 9 Oct. 1842; *e s* of Sir Robert Charles Dallas, 2nd Bt and Frances, *d* of 1st Baron Ellenborough; *m* 1884, Felicia, *d* of Rev. Canon Welby, Barrowby, Grantham; *S* father, 1874. *Educ:* Eton; Heidelberg; Dresden; Paris. Appointed Clerk in Foreign Office, 1863. *Heir:* none. *Address:* 36 Eaton Square, SW. *Clubs:* Travellers', Wellington.
Died 27 Nov. 1918 (ext).

DALMAHOY, Maj.-Gen. Patrick Carfrae; Bengal Infantry; *b* 7 Sept. 1840; *m* 1868, Emily (*d* 1925), *d* of Edward Wylly; one *s*. Entered Army, 1856; Major-General, 1890; unemployed supernumerary list, 1890; served Indian Mutiny (siege of Delhi), 1857–59 (medal with clasp), and Campaign in Bundelkund, 1858–60. *Address:* 13 Buckingham Terrace, Edinburgh. *Clubs:* New, Edinburgh; Royal and Ancient, St Andrews.
Died 24 Dec. 1926.

DALMAHOY, Patrick Carfrae, DSO 1902; Magistrate; *b* 31 Oct. 1872; *s* of late Maj.-Gen. Patrick Carfrae Dalmahoy; *m* Mabel Houstoun, *d* of late W. H. Rogers of Johannesburg; one *s* four *d*. *Educ:* Haileybury; Edinburgh University. Writer to the Signet, Edinburgh, 1896; served with CIV (MI) in South Africa; gazetted to 1st Batt. The Royal Scots, 1900, and served with them till the end of the war (twice wounded, despatches, DSO); resigned commission, 1903. *Recreation:* golf. *Address:* Magistrate, Benoni, Transvaal, SA; 13 Buckingham Terrace, Edinburgh. *Clubs:* University, Edinburgh; Royal and Ancient, St Andrews; Rand, Johannesburg.
Died 11 Nov. 1928.

DALRYMPLE, Rt. Hon. Sir Charles, 1st Bt, *cr* 1887; PC 1905; DL; MA, LLD (hon); *b* Kilkerran, Ayrshire, 15 Oct. 1839; 2nd *s* of Sir Charles Dalrymple Fergusson, 5th Bt, and Helen, *d* of Rt Hon. David Boyle, Lord Justice-Gen. of Scotland; assumed name of Dalrymple on death of father, 1849; *m* 1874, Alice Mary (*d* 1884), 2nd *d* of Sir Edward Hunter-Blair, 4th Bt; one *s* two *d*. *Educ:* Harrow; Trinity Coll., Cambridge. Barrister 1865; MP (C) Bute, 1868–85; opposed Mr Gladstone in Midlothian, 1885; MP (C) Ipswich, 1886–1906. Member Cathedral Establishments Commission, 1879–85; Reformatories and Industrial Schools Commission, 1882–83; Vaccination Commission, 1890–96; Scottish Univs Commission, 1889–96; Grand Master Mason of Scotland, 1893–96. *Heir: s* David Charles Herbert Dalrymple, late Lieut RN [*b* 29 March 1879; *m* 1906, Margaret Anna, *d* of Sir Mark Mactaggart Stewart, 1st Bt; one *d*]. *Address:* Newhailes, Musselburgh, NB. *TA:* Fisherrow. *Clubs:* Athenæum; New, Edinburgh; Western, Glasgow, etc.
Died 20 June 1916.

DALRYMPLE, Hon. David Hay; Member of Senate, Queensland University, since 1910; *b* Newbury, Dec. 1840. *Educ:* Independent College, Taunton; Bristol Medical School. Went Australia, 1862; MLA, Mackay, 1888–1904; Secretary for Public Instruction, 1895–99, and 1902–3; Public Works, 1896–98; Public Lands, 1899; member of Executive Council, 1899–1901; Sec. for Agriculture, 1901–3. *Address:* Dairy, Crescent Road, Hamilton, Brisbane.
Died 31 Aug. 1912.

DALRYMPLE, Sir Walter Hamilton-, 8th Bt, *cr* 1697; JP, DL; *b* 6 Jan. 1854; *s* of Sir John Warrender Dalrymple, 7th Bt and Sophia, *d* of James Pattle; *S* father, 1888; *m* 1882, Alice, *d* of Maj.-Gen. Hon. Sir Henry Hugh Clifford, VC, KCMG; one *s* three *d* (and one *s* decd). Owner of about 3100 acres. *Heir: s* Hew Clifford Hamilton-Dalrymple [*b* 11 Aug. 1888; *m* 1919, Dorothea Dyce Nicol, *y d* of late Augustus Thorne]. *Seat:* Luchie, North Berwick. *Address:* Villa della Pergola, Alassio, Italy. *Club:* New, Edinburgh.
Died 29 Nov. 1920.

DALTON, Sir Cornelius Neale, KCMG 1908; CB 1894; Hon. DCL, Oxford; *b* 9 March 1842; 3rd *s* of late Rev. John Neale Dalton, MA, Rector of Milton Keynes, Bucks; *m* 1873, Margaret, *d* of late Frederick Gaskell, Chelsea. *Educ:* Blackheath Proprietary School; Trinity Coll., Cambridge. Scholar, 2nd class Classics. Barrister, Inner Temple, 1871; entered Civil Service, 1873; became Asst-Sec. to the Local Govt Board, 1882; was a member of the Royal Commissions on Tithe Redemption (1891–92), Agriculture (1893–97), and Local Taxation (1896–1901); British Delegate to the International Conference at Brussels for protection of industrial property, 1897 and 1900; Comptroller-General of Patents, Designs, and Trade Marks, 1897–1909; Chairman of the East London College Council. *Publications:* The Real Captain Kidd, 1911; The Life of Thomas Pitt, 1915. *Address:* 57 Belsize Avenue, NW3. *T:* Hampstead 3055.
Died 19 Oct. 1920.

DALTON, Frederick Thomas, MA; *b* 29 Oct. 1855; *s* of late Rev. Charles Browne Dalton, Vicar of Highgate, and Mary Frances, *d* of Charles James Blomfield, Bishop of London; *m* 1st, 1895, Mary Edna (*d* 1922), *d* of late Rev. H. G. Evans, headmaster of King Edward VI's School, Stratford-on-Avon; 2nd, 1924, Mary Davenport, *d* of late Rev. C. H. Rice, Rector of Cheam. *Educ:* Highgate School; Corpus Christi College, Oxford (Scholar); 1st class Classical Mods 1876; 2nd class Lit. Hum. 1878; Ellerton Prize, 1879; Chancellor's English Essay, 1880. Assistant Master Radley College, 1879–86; kept terms as student at Lincoln's Inn, and subsequently qualified for admission as a solicitor; joined the staff of The Times, 1893; retired, 1923; assistant editor of Literature, 1897; editor of Literature, 1900–1. *Recreation:* drawing and sketching from Nature. *Address:* Sunningwell, Sandfield Road, Headington. *Club:* Athenæum.
Died 11 Nov. 1927.

DALTON, Rev. Herbert Andrew, DD; *b* Lambeth Rectory, 18 May 1852; *s* of late Rev. Charles Browne Dalton, Vicar of Highgate, Prebendary of St Paul's, and Mary Frances, *d* of Charles James Blomfield, Bishop of London; *m* 1879, Mabel Selina, *d* of Capt. Charles Simeon; four *d*. *Educ:* Highgate School; Corpus Christi Coll., Oxford. Scholar CCC Oxford, 1871; 1st class Classical Mods 1873; 1st class Final School of Lit. Hum. 1875. Senior Student, Christ Church, Oxford, 1875–78; Headmaster St Edward's School, Oxford, 1877–84; Assistant Master Winchester College, 1884–90; Member Essex Education Committee representing Oxford University, 1903–6; Headmaster Harrison Coll., Barbados, 1906–22; Canon of Barbados Cathedral, 1918–22. *Publications:* editor Select Epodes and Ars Poetica of Horace, 1884; Helps to Self-Examination for Boys in Public Schools, 1892; essay on Education in Church Problems, 1900. *Recreation:* croquet. *Address:* 37 Milner Road, Merton, SW19. *Club:* Oxford and Cambridge.
Died 18 May 1928.

DALTON, Norman, MD, FRCP; Fellow King's College, London; Senior Physician to King's College Hospital; late Professor of Pathological Anatomy in King's College, London; Lecturer on Medicine, King's College Medical School; late Examiner in Medicine, University of London; Physician to the National Provident Institution; Medical Officer to the London branch of the Scottish Union and National Insurance Company; Lt-Col RAMC (T); *s* of E.T.E. Dalton, of Demerara, British Guiana. *Educ:* Queen's Coll., British Guiana; Christ's College, Finchley; King's Coll., London. *Publications:* A Method of ascertaining the Position and Size of the Stomach by means of the X-rays and a tube filled with Subnitrate of Bismuth; Influenza in relation to the Digestive Organs; Transactions Clinical Society, 1905. *Address:* 35 Nottingham Place, W1. *T* Mayfair 3976.
Died 9 March 1923.

D'ALVIELLA, Count Goblet, LLD, PhilosD; Belgian Minister of State; Member and late Vice-President, Belgian Senate; Member of the Belgian Cabinet during the War; Professor, University of Brussels; Grand Officer Ordre de Léopold; Grand-Cordon Order of Medjidie; Order of the Crown of Italy; Grand Cross of the Belgian Order of the Crown; Grand Cordon of the French Legion of Honour; war medal of King Albert; *b* Brussels, 10 August 1846; *m* 1879, Margaret Alice Packard, Albany, New York; one *s* one *d*. *Educ:* Brussels and Paris. Member of the Belgian Bar since 1870; Member and late President Royal Academy of Belgium; Member of the Royal Asiatic Society of Great Britain; hon. member of the Oxford Soc. of Historical Theology; Hon. LLD Univ. of Glasgow and of Aberdeen; former MP for Brussels. Late Bampton Lectures Univ.; Hibbert Lecturer at Oxford, 1891; late Envoy-Extraordinary to Constantinople and to Rome; long time director of the Revue de Belgique. *Publications:* Sahara and Lapland, 1874; Inde et Himalaya, 1877, 2nd edn 1880; Contemporary Evolution of Religious Thought in England, America, and India, 1885; Hibbert Lectures, 1892; The Migration of Symbols, 1894; Ce que l'Inde doit à la Grèce, 1897; Eleusinia: de quelques problèmes relatifs aux Mystères d'Eleusis, 1903; A travers le Far West, souvenirs des Etats-Unis 1906; L'Université de Bruxelles pendant son troisième quart de siècle, 1909; Croyances, Rites, Institutions (3 vols), 1911; The True and the False Pacifism, 1917; publications in French. *Address:* 10 rue Faider, Brussels.   *Died 8 Sept. 1925.*

DALY, Ven. Henry Varian, MA; Rector of Gort since 1874; Archdeacon of Clonfert since 1881; Archdeacon of Kilmacduagh since 1891; Member of General Synod since 1882; Member of Committee of Patronage since 1882; Secretary of Diocesan Council since 1869; Member of Representative Church Body, 1915; *b* 20 July 1838; *e s* of late Joseph Daly of The Altar, Co Cork; *m* 1st, 1865, Anne Mary, *e d* of late Robert James Burkitt, AM, MB, of Waterford; three *s* two *d*; 2nd, 1879, Elizabeth Alice, *d* of Rev. W. St George, late Rector of Bryansford, Co Down; two *s* three *d*. *Educ*: Diocesan College, Rosscarbery, Co Cork; Trinity College, Dublin (MA). Ordained 1861; Curate of St Patrick's, Waterford, 1861–65; Bailinasloe, 1866–72; Killinane, 1872–74; Canon of Clonfert, 1872–81. *Recreations*: chess, reading. *Address*: Deanery, Gort, Co Galway. *TA*: Gort.   *Died 3 June 1925.*

DALY, John Archer Blake-, JP, DL; *b* 1835; *s* of late Andrew William Blake, of Furbough, Co. Galway, and Maria Julia, *d* of Malachy Daly of Raford; assumed name of Daly under the will of his maternal grandfather; *m* 1864, Lady Anne Elizabeth Charlotte Nugent (*d* 1907), *d* of 9th Earl of Westmeath. High Sheriff, Galway, 1866; late Lieut-Col and Hon. Col 4th Batt. Connaught Rangers. *Address*: Raford, Kiltulla, near Athenry; Furbough, Galway.
                                              Died 13 June 1917.

DALY, Hon. Sir Malachy Bowes, KCMG 1900; Lieutenant-Governor of the Province of Nova Scotia, Canada, 1890–1900; *b* Quebec, 6 Feb. 1836; *s* of late Sir Dominick Daly of County Galway, Ireland, and Caroline Maria, *d* of Colonel Ralph Gore of Banowmount, Co Kilkenny, Ireland; *m* 1859, Joanna, 2nd *d* of late Sir Edward Kenmy; one *d*. *Educ*: St Mary's College, Oscott (RC), near Birmingham, England. Barrister-at-law; Private Secretary to Sir D. Daly, Lieut-Gov. of Prince Edward Island, and to Sir R. G. Macdonnell and Sir W. Fenwick Williams, while Governors of Nova Scotia; MP (Canada), Halifax, NS, 1878–86; Deputy Speaker, House of Commons, Canada, 1882–86. *Recreations*: cricket, salmon fishing. *Address*: Halifax, Nova Scotia. *Club*: Halifax.
                                              Died 26 April 1920.

DALY, Col Thomas, CMG 1917; LRCPI, LM, LRCSI; RAMC. Served NW Frontier, India, 1897–98 (medal with clasp); S Africa, 1899–1902 (Queen's and King's medals, 5 clasps); European War, 1914–17 (CMG). *Address*: c/o Holt & Co., 3 Whitehall Place, SW.
                                              Died 15 April 1917.

DALYELL, Lt-Gen. John Thomas; Colonel Royal Scots Fusiliers; *b* 22 July 1827; *m* Constance Louisa (*d* 1913), *d* of Rt Rev. Thomas Parry, Bishop of Barbados. Entered army, 1847; Major-General, 1883; retired, 1886; served Crimea, 1854–55 (medal with four clasps, Turkish medal, 5th class Medjidie, brevet Major). *Address*: 10 Merchiston Crescent, Edinburgh.
                                              Died July 1919.

DALZELL, Reginald Alexander, CB 1924; CBE 1920; Director of Telegraphs and Telephones, 1922–27; retired; *b* Poona, Bombay, 1865; *s* of late N. A. Dalzell, MA, Conservator of Woods and Forests; *m* 1895, Katherine Ann, *d* of late James Livingston, Edinburgh; one *d*. *Educ*: Dulwich College. Entered Telephone service, 1881; Provincial Superintendent for the West of England under the National Telephone, 1906–12; Chief Inspector, Telegraph and Telephone Traffic, General Post Office, 1916–22. *Recreation*: golf. *Address*: 1 Cleveland Road, Ealing, W13. *T*: Ealing 1512.
                                              Died 27 Nov. 1928.

DALZIEL OF WOOLER, 1st Baron, *cr* 1927; **Davison Dalziel,** Bt, *cr* 1919; MP (C) Brixton Division, Lambeth, 1910–23, 1924–27; Chairman Pullman Car Company, 1915; President Board of Directors and Managing Committee International Sleeping Car Co., 1919; first introduced motor cabs into London; *b* 17 Oct. 1854; *y s* of Davison Dalziel and Helen, *d* of Henry Gaulter; *m* 1876, Harriet, *d* of J. Godfrey Dunning; one *d* decd. Officer Legion of Honour; Commander Crown of Italy. *Recreation*: yachting. *Heir*: none.
                                              Died 18 April 1928 (ext).

DALZIEL, Sir Kennedy, Kt 1917; JP; MB, CM; FRFPS Glas.; Lieutenant-Colonel late RAMC(T); Surgeon to Western Infirmary and Consultant Surgeon to Glasgow and SW Railway; *b* Merkland, Penpont, Dumfriesshire, 25 Oct. 1861; *m* Margaret, *d* of John Waddell of Inch, Bathgate; two *s* three *d*. *Educ*: Dumfries Private School; Edinburgh University; Berlin; Vienna. House Surgeon to Glasgow Royal Infirmary; joined Staff of Western Infirmary in 1899, and Royal Hospital for Sick Children, 1891; Senior Surgeon of latter institution, and retired 1914; Casualty Surgeon in Central Division of Glasgow,

1885–94; late Professor of Medical Jurisprudence and Public Health, and also of Surgery in Anderson's College; Lecturer on Anatomy in Western Medical School; late Examiner in Final Examination, Glasgow University, and Royal Faculty of Physicians and Surgeons. *Publications*: numerous contributions to medical literature. *Recreations*: shooting, fishing, golf. *Address*: 196 Bath Street, Glasgow; Nether Kinnedder, Oakley, Fife. *Clubs*: Art, Automobile, Glasgow.
                                              Died 10 Feb. 1924.

DAMANT, Lt-Col Frederick Hugh, CB 1902; DSO 1901; Resident Magistrate for District of Lydenburg, Transvaal; *b* District of King Williamstown, S Africa, 1864; *y s* of Hugh Atherstone Damant. Served S Africa, 1899–1902; commanded Rimington's Scouts; promoted Lieut-Col; in a desperate struggle with 800 Boers he received five bullet wounds, but succeeded in saving the guns entrusted to his charge (DSO); later he took part in operations in Western Transvaal until the cessation of hostilities. *Address*: Lydenburg, Transvaal.
                                              Died 13 Oct. 1926.

DANBY, Frank, (Mrs Julia Frankau); *b* 30 July 1864; father an artist; *m* 1883, Arthur Frankau (*d* 1904), merchant; three *s* one *d*. *Educ*: at home by Mme Paul Lafargue, *e d* of Karl Marx. Began work with dilettante journalism; wrote for Saturday Review, etc. *Publications*: Dr Phillips, a Maida Vale Idyll, 1887; A Babe in Bohemia, 1889; abandoned novel writing for a few years in favour of studying engraving; after 10 years wrote Eighteenth Century Colour Prints, 1900; Life of John Raphæl Smith, 1902; The Lives of James and William Ward, 1904; relapsed into novel writing and published Pigs in Clover, 1902; Baccarat, 1904; The Sphinx's Lawyer, 1906; A Coquette in Crape, 1907; The Heart of a Child, 1908; An Incomplete Etonian, 1909; Let the Roof Fall In, 1910; The Story of Emma, Lady Hamilton, 1910; Joseph in Jeopardy, 1912; Concert Pitch, 1913; Full Swing, 1914; Nelson's Legacy, 1915; The Story behind the Verdict, 1915. *Recreations*: needlework, bridge. *Address*: 64 Grosvenor Street, W.   *Died 17 March 1916.*

DANE, Hal; *see* Macfall, Haldane.

DANE, Lt-Col James Auchinleck, DSO 1917; DL; 84th East Anglian Field Brigade, RFA; *b* 18 May 1883; *s* of late Judge Richard Martin Dane, KC; *m* 1909, Elgiva Mary Kathorn Wentworth Fitz-william; two *s* one *d*. *Educ*: Portora Royal School, Enniskillen; Trinity College, Dublin; RM Academy. Joined RA, 1902; Special Reserve, 1910; served with BEF France, Aug. 1914–May 1918 (wounded, April 1918; despatches thrice; DSO). *Recreation*: hunting. *Address*: Harpley Lodge, King's Lynn, Norfolk. *T*: Great Massingham 10. *TA*: Dane, Houghton-Norfolk. *Club*: Royal Automobile.
                                              Died 20 Jan. 1927.

DANGAR, Rev. James George, VD; DD; Rector of Washfield, Tiverton; Hon. Chaplain in the Territorial Force; Officier d'Académie (France); late Principal of the Exeter Diocesan Training College, 1869–1906; Prebendary of Exeter Cathedral; *b* London, 20 Nov. 1841; *s* of late James Dangar; *m* Elizabeth, *d* of Daniel Shilson of Launceston, Cornwall; one *s* one *d*. *Educ*: St John's Coll., Oxford (School Exhibitioner and Lord Camden's Mathematical Medallist); Latin Prose Prizeman; Double Honorary 4th, 1864. Ordained to Curacy of Stoke Climsland, Cornwall, 1864; Vicar of Boyton, Cornwall, 1866–69; formerly Bodleian Lecturer in Exeter, and University Examiner for the Oxford Local Examination; Vice-President Exeter Diocesan Board of Education. *Publications*: Hon. Editor of the Exeter Diocesan Calendar; Notes on the Metric System, 1871; Text-book on Mental Arithmetic, 1873. *Address*: Washfield Rectory, Tiverton.   *Died 31 July 1917.*

DANIEL, Rev. Charles Henry Olive, DD; Provost of Worcester College, Oxford; late Fellow, Bursar, and Chaplain; formerly Tutor; Fellow of King's College, London; Alderman; *e s* of Rev. Alfred Daniel and Eliza Anne, *d* of Clement Wilson Cruttwell; *m* Emily, 3rd *d* of Edmund Crabb Olive. *Educ*: King's College, London; Worcester College, Oxford. 2nd class Mod.; 1st class Lit. Hum. 1858 Classical Moderator, 1864–65; Classical Examiner, 1876–77; Proctor, 1873. Classical Lecturer and Censor of King's College, 1859–68. *Publication*: History of Worcester College. *Recreation*: private press. *Address*: Worcester College, Oxford.
                                              Died 6 Sept. 1919.

DANIEL, Rev. Wilson Eustace; Prebendary and Sub-Dean of Wells Cathedral; *b* 1841; 3rd *s* of Rev. Alfred Daniel, Frome; *m* 1st, O. Gertrude Godfrey of Stow Bedon; 2nd, Mary Nevins Martin, Summit, New Jersey; two *s* three *d*. *Educ*: King's College, London; Worcester College, Oxford. 2nd class Lit. Hum. 1864; Denyer and

Johnson Scholar, 1866. Grinfield Lecturer on Septuagint, 1889–1903; Chaplain of Worcester College, 1865; Curate, St Mark's, Whitechapel, 1866; All Saints', Oxford, 1868; Vicar, Holy Trinity, Frome, 1875; East Pennard, 1890; Horsington, Somerset, 1897–1922; Rural Dean, Shepton Mallet, 1890–97; Merston, 1911–16. *Publication:* Parish Register of Horsington. *Address:* Ansford Lodge, Castle Cary, Somerset.   *Died 15 Feb. 1924.*

DANIELL, Major Francis Edward Lloyd, DSO 1915; Seaforth Highlanders; *b* 19 Dec. 1874. Entered army, 1895; Captain, 1901; Adjutant, 1902–6; Major, 1913; Brigade-Major, India, 1909–11; General Staff Officer, 2nd grade, India, 1911–13; served Nile Expedition, 1898 (despatches); S African War, 1899–1901 (Queen's medal, 4 clasps); NW Frontier, India, 1908 (medal with clasp); European War, 1914–15 (DSO).   *Died 4 March 1916.*

DANIELS, Charles Wilberforce, MB Cambridge; FRCP; *s* of late Rev. T. Daniels, Manchester. *Educ:* Manchester Grammar School; Trinity College, Cambridge; London Hospital. Formerly Medical Services, Fiji, British Guiana; Member of Royal Society Malaria Commission, India and Central Africa; Director Institute Medical Research, Kuala Lumpur, Federated Malay States; Director London School of Tropical Medicine; Consulting Physician to Albert Dock Hospital, E; Lecturer on Tropical Diseases, London School of Tropical Medicine, London Hospital, London School of Medicine for Women, St George's Hospital; retired. *Publications:* Laboratory Studies in Tropical Medicine; Tropical Medicine and Hygiene; various reports. *Recreations:* golf, fishing. *Address:* 283 Wanstead Park Road, Ilford.   *Died 6 Aug. 1927.*

DANKS, Sir Aaron Turner, Kt 1925; Managing Director John Danks & Son Pty Ltd; *b* South Melbourne, 1861; *s* of late John Danks, Melbourne; *m* 1887, *d* of F. G. Miles, late Town Clerk of South Melbourne. *Educ:* Wesley College; Horton College, Tasmania. President Melbourne Hospital since 1918; a Past President of the Melbourne Metropolitan Hospital Association, and Chairman of the Walter and Eliza Hall Research Institute. *Address:* Hazeldene, Balwyn Road, Canterbury, Victoria, Australia.

Died 4 June 1928.

DANKS, Ven. William, MA; Canon of Canterbury, 1907; Archdeacon of Richmond, 1894; *b* Nottingham, 3 Sept. 1845; *y s* of Thomas Danks, Sherwood Rise, and Mary Anne Wheatcroft, Wingfield Park, Derbyshire; *m* 1869, Helena, *y d* of Thomas Manlove, The Park, Nottingham; one *s* two *d. Educ:* Queen's Coll., Oxford. Ordained to New Basford Curacy, Nottingham, 1868; Vicar, St Margaret's, Ilkley, 1884; Rural Dean of South Crave, 1886; Select Preacher at Cambridge, 1888; Rector of Richmond, Yorkshire, and Rural Dean of Richmond West, 1890; Hon. Canon of Ripon, 1891; Canon, 1896–1907; Select Preacher at Oxford, 1909. *Publications:* The Church on the Moor, Sermons, 1886; Canterbury Described, 1910; Memorials of the Cathedral and Priory of Christ in Canterbury, 1912. *Address:* Canterbury.   *Died 4 April 1916.*

DANSON, Sir Francis Chatillon, Kt 1920; JP; FSA, FSS; senior partner of F. C. Danson and Co., of Liverpool and London, average adjusters; Representative of the Board of Trade on the Liverpool and London War Risks Insurance Association, Ltd, since the outbreak of the War; Member of Admiralty Transport Arbitration Board since 1914; Member of the Mersey Docks and Harbour Board; Chairman of Liverpool Institute Schools; Governor of Sedbergh School, 1909–14; Chairman of Liverpool School of Tropical Medicine, and Chairman of Liverpool Shipwreck and Humane Society; Member of Council of Liverpool Chamber of Commerce and Institute of Archaeology; Member of the International Law Assoc.; Member of the Tidal Institute; *b* Barnston, Cheshire, 1855; *s* of John Towne Danson, barrister-at-law; *m* 1888, Edith, *o d* of William Norman Rudolf, of Liverpool, ship-owner; one *s* one *d. Educ:* Liverpool College; Paris. Pres. of the Liverpool Chamber of Commerce, 1896–99; Chairman of the Conservative Party in Birkenhead, 1899–1904; Chairman of the Association of Average Adjusters of Great Britain, 1899; High Sheriff of Westmorland, 1914–15; President Liverpool Philomatic Society, 1913–14; member of Council of University of Liverpool, 1903–18. *Recreations:* motoring, collecting books and antiquities. *Address:* Rosewarne, Bidston Road, Birkenhead. *T:* Birkenhead 616; Dry Close, Grasmere, Westmoreland. *M:* CM 4868, FY 1030. *Clubs:* Burlington Fine Arts, British Empire; University, Conservative, Exchange, Liverpool.

Died 3 July 1926.

DARBISHIRE, Charles William; MP (L) Westbury Division of Wiltshire since 1922; *b* London, 17 June 1875; *s* of Col C. H.

Darbishire, JP, DL, of Plas Mawr, Penmaenmawr, and Mary Lilian, *d* of late William Eckersley; *m* 1905, Frances Middleton, *d* of late Sheriff Davidson, Fort-William. *Educ:* Giggleswick. East India Merchant; one of the Managing Directors of Paterson, Simons & Co., Ltd, of London, Straits Settlements, and Federated Malay States; Member Municipal Commission of Singapore, 1908–10; Unofficial Member of Legislative Council of the Straits Settlements, 1910–19; Member Singapore Harbour Board, 1910–19; Chairman Singapore Chamber of Commerce, 1914–19; Artists' Rifles, 1897–99; Lieut Royal Welch Fusiliers (TF), 1905–8; OC (Temp. Major) Singapore Volunteer Rifles, 1914–19; Singapore Mutiny operations, Feb.–March, 1915; President, Association of British Malay, 1921–22. *Publication:* article on Commerce and Currency in One Hundred Years of Singapore, 1919. *Recreations:* lawn tennis, golf, shooting. *Address:* Elms Cross, Bradford-on-Avon; Queen Anne's Mansions, SW1. *Clubs:* Reform, National Liberal, City of London, Queen's; West Wilts Golf.   *Died 5 June 1925.*

DARBOUX, Jean Gaston; Secrétaire perpétuel de l'Académie des Sciences, Paris; Membre du Bureau des Longitudes; Professeur de Géométrie supérieure à l'Université; *b* Nîmes, 13 Aug. 1842; *m*; one *s* one *d. Educ:* Lycée de Nîmes; l'Ecole Normale Supérieure de Paris. Maître de Conférences à l'Ecole Normale Supérieure; professeur à la Sorbonne; membre de l'Académie des Sciences, 1884; membre étranger des Sociétiés Royales de Londres, Edimbourg et Dublin, de la Royal Institution; correspondant des Académies de Berlin, Petrograd, Rome, Washington, Vienne, etc. *Publications:* nombreux mémoires d'analyse mathématique; 6 à 7 volumes sur la Géométrie infinitésimale. *Address:* 3 rue Mazarine, Palais de l'Institut, Paris.

Died Feb. 1917.

DARBY, Very Rev. John Lionel, DD; Dean of Chester since 1886; *b* Ireland, 20 Nov. 1831; *y s* of Rev. Christopher Darby; *m* 1871, Cecilia C., *d* of Rev. Canon and Lady Ellinor Hopwood; three *s* two *d. Educ:* St Columba's Coll.; Trinity Coll. Dublin. Assistant Curate, Winwick, Lancashire, 1856; Assistant Curate, Mells, Somerset, 1858; Incumbent of Newburgh, Lancashire, 1859–68; Assistant Curate, Kells, Ireland, 1868–70; Assistant Curate, Southam, 1870; Diocesan Inspector for Diocese of Chester, 1871–75; Archbishop's Inspector of Training Colleges, 1875–95; Rector of St Bridget's, Chester, 1875–86; Archdeacon of Chester, 1877–86; Hon. Canon, 1873–85; Canon Residentiary, 1885–86. *Recreations:* microscope, telescope. *Address:* The Deanery, Chester.

Died 5 Nov. 1919.

DARBY, William Evans, BD, STD, LLD, DD; Vice-President Peace Society (Secretary, 1888–1915); *b* Laugharne, Carmarthenshire, 1844; *e s* of Evan Darby, Saundersfoot; *m* 1868, Sarah, *y d* of Joseph Marshall, Hertford; three *s* five *d. Educ:* Tenby; New College, Hampstead; London University. Ordained as Congregational Minister, 1869; Secretary, Preacher, Lecturer, Writer; Vice-President of the International Law Association; Manager of the London Institution; Member of the International Peace Bureau, Berne; of the Grotius Society, etc; Joint Secretary of the Universal Peace Congresses at London, 1890; Chicago, 1893; Glasgow and London, 1908. *Publications:* fiction: Out of the Depths; Walter Vaughan; Worth the Winning, etc; Sermon Notes on Peace Topics; International Tribunals, Modern Pacific Settlements; Proved Practicability of International Arbitration; numerous papers and publications on International Law, Arbitration, and the Peace Question generally; The Christ Method of Peace-making; History of Hague Peace Conferences, etc. *Address:* Jesmond, Norfolk Road, Seven Kings, Essex. *Club:* National Liberal.   *Died Nov. 1922.*

D'ARCY, William Knox; *b* 11 Oct. 1849; *s* of William Francis of Newton Abbott, Devon, and Elizabeth Baker, *d* of late Rev. Robert Bradford of Wolborough, Devon; *m* 1st, 1872, Elena (*d* 1897), *d* of S. B. Birkbeck of Glenmore, Queensland; 2nd, Nina, *d* of A. L. Boucicault of Queensland. *Educ:* Westminster School. In Queensland, Australia, where he followed legal, pastoral, and mining pursuits, 1866–89; returned to England, 1889. *Recreations:* shooting, golf. *Address:* 42 Grosvenor Square, W; Stanmore Hall, Middlesex; Bylaugh Park, East Dereham, Norfolk. *Clubs:* Carlton, Garrick, Wellington.

Died 1 May 1917.

DARE, Adm. Sir Charles Holcombe, KCMG 1919; CB 1917; MVO 1904; *b* 9 Nov. 1854. Entered Navy, 1868; Commander, 1894; Captain, 1900; retired, 1915; Adm. retired, 1918. *Address:* Hill House, Erwarton, Ipswich.   *Died 6 Aug. 1924.*

DARELL, Sir Lionel Edward, 5th Bt, *cr* 1795, of Richmond Hill, Surrey; JP, DL, CC; late Captain Royal Gloucestershire YC;

President, Gloucester Conservative Club and Gloucester Club; High Sheriff, 1887–88; b 6 Sept. 1845; s of Sir William Lionel Darell, 4th Bt and Harriet Mary, o d of Sir Edward Tierney, Bt; S father, 1883; m 1870, Helen Frances, o c of late Edward Marsland, Henbury Park, Cheshire; three s five d. Educ: Christ Church, Oxford. Late President Conservative Club. Recreations: hunting, shooting, etc. Heir: s Lionel Edward Hamilton Marmaduke, Capt. 1st Life Guards [b 2 April 1876; m 1903, Eleanor, d of Capt. J. H. Edwards-Heathcote of Apedale, Staffs; two d (and one s decd). Educ: Eton; Christ Church, Oxford]. Address: 39 Upper Grosvenor Street, W; Fretherne Court, Gloucestershire. T: 2 Saul. M: AD 155. Clubs: Carlton, Junior Carlton, Orleans.   Died 17 Feb. 1919.

DARLEY, Cecil West, ISO 1904; MInstCE; late Inspecting and Consulting Engineer to New South Wales Government; b 20 Oct. 1842; 4th s of late Henry Darley, Wingfield, Co. Wicklow; m 1st, 1877, Rosanne (d 1878), d of late E. C. Close, Morpeth, NSW; 1885, Leila, d of late Hon. Alex. Campbell, MLC, Rosemount, Sydney; two s one d. Educ: King William's Coll., Isle of Man; privately. Resident Engineer, Harbour Works, Newcastle, NSW, 1867; Principal Asst Engineer, Harbour and River Dept, 1881; Engineer-in-Chief for Harbours and Rivers, 1889; Engineer-in-Chief for Public Works, NSW, 1896; President of the Metropolitan WS and S Board, 1892. Address: Longheath, Bookham, Surrey. T: 27 Bookham. Clubs: Overseas; Australian (Hon. Life Member), Sydney.
        Died 18 Oct. 1928.

DARLING, Frank, LLD (Hon.) University of Toronto, 1916; Dalhousie University, 1922; FRIBA; Senior Member of the firm of Darling and Pearson, Architects, 2 Leader Lane, Toronto; b Canada, 17 Feb. 1850; e s of late Rev. W. S. Darling, Rector of Holy Trinity, Toronto; unmarried. Educ: Upper Canada College; Trinity College School; worked under Street and Sir Arthur Blomfield. Began practice in Toronto, 1875; Member Royal Canadian Academy; Royal Gold Medal for architecture, RIBA, 1915. Address: 11 Walmer Road, Toronto. Clubs: York, Toronto, Golf and Hunt, Toronto; Mont Royal, Montreal; Manitoba, Winnipeg; City, New York; Country, Ottawa.   Died June 1923.

DARLINGTON, Edwin, CIE 1897; b 1839; s of James Darlington of St Austell; m 1881, Mary (d 1924), d of David Ring of Templemore. Asst and Junior Sec. to Chief Commissioner, Burma, 1868–72 and 1875–77; Collector of Customs, Akyab, 1872–75; Collector of Customs, Rangoon, 1877–80; Chief Collector of Customs, Burma, 1880–96; Vice-Chairman of Rangoon Port Commissioners, 1881–96. Address: 153 St James's Court, Buckingham Gate, SW. Club: East India United Service.   Died 5 March 1928.

DARLOW, Rev. Thomas Herbert; b Ramsey, Hunts, 26 April 1858; e s of late Thomas Darlow; m 1889, Ellen Frances, e d of late John Stephen Arthur, Liverpool; two s one d. Educ: Clare College, Cambridge (Minor and Foundation Scholar; MA); Lancs Coll., Manchester; Leipzig Univ. Mathematical Master, Royal Institution School, Liverpool, 1881; Minister of Crosby Congregational Church, Liverpool, 1885; Warden of Browning Hall, Walworth, 1891; Minister of New College Chapel, Hampstead, 1892; Literary Superintendent of the British and Foreign Bible Society, 1898–1923. Publications: Christmas Poems; The Print of the Nails; The Upward Calling; Via Sacra; Holy Ground; God's Image in Ebony; At Home in the Bible; Historical Catalogue of Printed Editions of Holy Scripture (with H. F. Moule); Letters of George Borrow to the Bible Society; William Robertson Nicoll: Life and Letters; The Love of God. Recreations: gardening, reading, smoking. Address: Beauleigh, Northwood, Middlesex. TA: Northwood. T: Northwood 160. Club: Authors'.   Died 23 Oct. 1927.

DARNLEY, 8th Earl of, cr 1725; **Ivo Francis Walter Bligh,** DL; Baron Clifton, 1721; Viscount Darnley, 1723; Earl of Darnley, 1725; late Hon. Colonel 4th Battalion Volunteer Royal West Kent Regiment; Irish Representative Peer; County Alderman for Kent; b 13 March 1859; s of 6th Earl and Harriet, d of 3rd Earl of Chichester; S brother, 1900; m 1884, Florence Rose, DBE, d of late John Stephen Morphy of Beechworth, Victoria; two s one d. Educ: Eton; Trinity Coll., Cambridge. Recreations: golf, shooting; Eton XI 1876–77, Cambridge XI 1878–81, Captain 1881; Captain English XI in Australia 1882–83; represented Cambridge v Oxford tennis and racquets. Heir: s Lord Clifton of Rathmore, b 11 Oct. 1886. Address: Puckle Hill, Cobham, Kent. T: Cobham, Kent 14. Club: Carlton.
        Died 10 April 1927.

DARROCH, Alexander; Professor of Education, Edinburgh University, since 1903; b Greenock, 20 Jan. 1862; m 1905, Mabel

(d 1922), d of George Hood, Redcar; one d. Educ: EC Training College, Glasgow; Edinburgh University; MA with First Class Honours in Philosophy; Rhind Phil. Scholarship, 1896. Heriot Research Fellow, 1899; Assistant Lecturer in Educ., University College of N Wales, Bangor, 1900–1; Lecturer in Psychology and Educ. in EC Training College, Edinburgh, 1901–3; also assistant to Professor of Education in Edin. Univ. 1901–3; Chairman of the Edinburgh Committee for the training of Teachers, since 1909; appointed First Chairman of the National Committee for the Training of Teachers in Scotland; Chairman of Edinburgh Education Authority, 1920. Publications: Herbart and the Herbartian Theory of Education, 1903; The Reform of the Scottish Universities Arts Curriculum, 1904; The Children, 1906; The Place of Psychology in the Training of the Teacher, 1911; A History of Educational Thought (cf Teachers' Encyclopædia, vol. VII), 1912; Education and the New Utilitarianism, 1914; articles in Hibbert Journal and in journals devoted to education. Address: 12 Abbotsford Park, Edinburgh. T: 6663 Edinburgh. Club: Northern, Edinburgh.
        Died Sept. 1924.

DARTREY, 2nd Earl of, cr 1866; **Vesey Dawson;** Baron Cremorne, 1797; Baron Dartrey, 1847; b 22 April 1842; s of 1st Earl and Augusta, d of Edward Stanley; S father, 1897; m 1882, Julia, d of Sir George Orby Wombwell, 4th Bt; two d (and one s decd). Formerly Capt. and Lt-Col Coldstream Guards; retired from army, 1876; MP (L) Monaghan, 1865–68; High Sheriff, 1878. Owner of about 25,000 acres. Heir: b Hon. Edward Stanley Dawson, b 16 Aug. 1843. Address: 3 Eaton Place, SW1. T: Victoria 536; Dartrey, Co Monaghan. Clubs: Travellers'; Kildare Street, Dublin.

        Died 14 June 1920.

DARWIN, Col Charles Waring, CB 1911; DL, JP; late Lieutenant Colonel and Hon. Colonel 3rd Battalion Durham Light Infantry; b 28 Aug. 1855; 2nd surv. s of late Francis Darwin, of Creskeld Arthington, Yorks; m 1894, Mary Dorothea, o c of late Rt Hon. John Lloyd Wharton; three s. Educ: Winchester. Entered Army, 1873; Lt-Col 1894; retired, 1895; served S Africa 1902 (medal 3 clasps). Chairman Durham County Territorial Association, 1908–18. Address: Elston Hall, Newark. Club: Arthur's.

        Died 1 Aug. 1928.

DARWIN, Sir Francis, Kt 1913; DSc, MB; FRS 1882; Hon. Fellow, Christ's College, Cambridge; President, British Association, 1908; b Down, Kent, 16 Aug. 1848; 3rd s of Charles Robert Darwin and Emma Wedgwood, g d of Josiah Wedgwood; m 1st, 1874, Amy Ruck (d 1876); one s; 2nd, 1883, Ellen (d 1903), d of John Crofts; one d; 3rd, 1913, Florence (d 1920), Brookthorpe, Gloucester, widow of Prof. F. W. Maitland. Educ: Trinity College, Cambridge; St George's Hospital, London. Did not practise medicine, but became assistant to his father at Down; after the latter's death settled at Cambridge. Publications: Life and Letters of Charles Darwin, 1887; Charles Darwin, 1892; various papers on physiological botany from 1876 onwards; Practical Physiology of Plants (with late E. H. Acton) 1894; Elements of Botany, 1895; More Letters of Charles Darwin (with A. C. Seward), 1903; Foundations of the Origin of Species, 1909; Rustic Sounds, 1917; Springtime, 1920. Address: 10 Madingley Road, Cambridge. Club: Athenæum.   Died 19 Sept. 1925.

DARWIN, Sir Horace, KBE 1918; MA; FRS 1903; MIMechE, AMInstCE; Chairman of the Cambridge Instrument Company, Ltd; b 13 May 1851; 5th s of Charles Robert Darwin, author of the Origin of Species, etc, of Down, Kent; m 1880, Hon. Emma Cecilia Farrer, d of 1st Lord Farrer; two d (and one s decd). Educ: Trinity Coll., Cambridge. Mayor of Cambridge, 1896–97. Address: The Orchard, Cambridge. TA: Horace Darwin, Cambridge. T: Cambridge 17.
        Died 22 Sept. 1928.

DAS, Hon. Satish Ranjan; Barrister-at-law; Member, Governor-General's Executive Council since 1925; b 29 Feb. 1872; 2nd s of Durga Mohun Das; m 1905, Bonolata, d of Behari Lal Gupta, CSI, ICS; two s. Educ: Univ. Coll. School, London; Grammar School, Manchester. Called to Bar, Middle Temple, 1894; Advocate, Calcutta High Court, 1894; Standing Counsel, Govt of India, 1917; Advocate-General, Bengal, 1922. Publications: A Letter to my Son; A New Policy for India, etc. Recreation: tennis. Address: Simla, India.
        Died 26 Oct. 1928.

DASHWOOD, Arthur George Frederick; b 1860; 2nd s of late Capt. G. A. C. Dashwood, 71st Highlanders, and Hon. Harriet Anne, e d of 1st Lord Bateman; m 1st, 1882, Caroline Isabella (d 1920), y d of late Capt. A. O. Lord, 72nd Highlanders; one d; 2nd, 1921, Alice, twin d of Hon. Mrs Kane and late Lt-Col Henry Green-Wilkinson,

Scots Guards. *Address:* Thurlow House, Folkestone. *Clubs:* Arthur's; Royal Yacht Squadron, Cowes.

Died Feb. 1922.

DASHWOOD, Charles James; KC 1906; Crown Solicitor, South Australia, since 1905; *b* 17 July 1843; unmarried. *Educ:* St Peter's Coll., Adelaide; University of Ghent. MHA Noarlungs, 1887–92; Government Resident and Judge in Northern Territory, 1892–1905. *Address:* Adelaide. *Died 9 July 1919.*

DAUNT, Lt-Col Richard Algernon Craigie, DSO 1900; late 1st Battalion Royal Irish Rifles; *b* 1 Oct. 1872; *s* of late Lt-Col Richard Daunt, County Cork; *m* 1903, Feroze, *d* of late Capt. H. J. Cooper; one *s* one *d*. *Educ:* Haileybury College. Joined, 1894; served with 2nd Royal Irish Rifles, Malta, India, Ireland, and South Africa; appointed Divisional Signalling Officer 3rd Division SAF Force, 1900 (despatches, Queen's medal 3 clasps, King's medal 2 clasps, DSO); served European War, 1914–16; commanded 1st Batt. Royal Irish Rifles, 1915–19 ; retired, Aug. 1919. Fellow Royal Astronomical Society. *Address:* Lauston, Pentire, Newquay, Cornwall.

Died 4 July 1928.

DAUNT, Ven. William; Archdeacon of Cloyne since 1909; *b* 23 Dec. 1841; *s* of late Achilles Daunt, JP, Tracton Abbey, Co. Cork; *m* 1877, Rosamond Anne, *y d* of late Sir Gilbert King, 3rd Bt, Charlestown, Co. Leitrim. *Educ:* Trinity Coll., Dublin (MA). Ordained 1865; Curate of Kincurran, 1865–67; Kinsale, 1867; St Mathias, Dublin, 1868–70; Incumbent of St Barnabas, 1870–72; Rector of Kinsale, 1872–81; Clonmel, 1881–1918. *Address:* Ardcæin, St Ann's Hill, Co. Cork. *Died Sept. 1919.*

DAVAR, Hon. Justice Sir Dinsha Dhurjibhai, Kt 1911; one of the Judges of His Majesty's High Court of Judicature, Bombay; *b* Bombay, 6 Nov. 1856; *s* of Dhurjibhai Dinsha Davar, Parsi-Zoroastrian; one *s* two *d*. *Educ:* Proprietary School; Elphinstone College. Joined Middle Temple, 1877; called to Bar, 1880; practised at Bombay; was Law Professor and later Principal of the Government Law School; raised to the Bench 1906. *Recreation:* spent most of his annual summer vacations in London. *Address:* Goolshun, Pedder Road, Bombay. *Clubs:* Orient, Elphinstone, Bombay.

Died 29 July 1916.

DAVERIN, John; *b* Limerick, 1851; *m* 1895, Clotilde Maud Mary, *d* of John E. D'Alton, JP of Ballygriffin, Co. Tipperary. *Educ:* Grey Institute, Port Elizabeth. Went to S Africa, 1859; founded John Daverin & Co., 1876. *Address:* Knockfierna, Park Drive, Port Elizabeth, S Africa. *Died 27 Oct. 1922.*

DAVEY, Henry, MICE; *b* 1843; *s* of Jonathan and Mary Davey, Lewtrenchard, Devon; *m* Elizabeth Barbenson, *d* of Pierre Barbenson Le Ber, JP, of Alderney, Channel Islands; one *s*. *Educ:* Tavistock. Inventor of the Differential pumping engine, and of various improvements in hydraulic machinery; founder of the firm of Hathorn, Davey & Co., Hydraulic Engineers, Leeds, established in 1871; Consulting Engineer in London, 1887; retired. *Publications:* Textbook, The Principles and Construction of Pumping Machinery; papers in Transactions of Institution of Civil Engineers (Watt medal and Telford premium); papers in Transactions of Inst. of Mechanical and other Engineering Societies; The British Association, etc; author of various papers on scientific subjects. *Recreations:* sketching in water-colour, etc. *Address:* Bedford Hotel, Tavistock.

Died 11 April 1928.

DAVEY, Very Rev. William Harrison, MA; Dean of Llandaff, 1897–1913; *b* Thorpe, Norwich, 28 July 1825; *e s* of William Davey. *Educ:* Charterhouse; Lincoln Coll. Oxford (Scholar). 2nd class Lit. Hum; 2nd class Mathematics, 1847. Denyer Theological Prize, Oxford, 1851. Master at Marlborough, 1848–49; Vice-Principal of Chichester Theological Coll. 1852–59; Cuddeson Coll. 1859–64; St David's Coll. Lampeter, 1872–96; 3rd Cursal Prebendary, St David's, 1876–95; Examining Chaplain to Bishop of Llandaff, 1895; Canon and Chancellor of St David's, 1895–97. *Publications:* Articuli Ecclesiae Anglicanae, 1861; The Books of Deuteronomy and Joshua in the Commentary on the Old Testament, 1876, etc, SPCK. *Address:* The Green, Llandaff. *Died 26 March 1917.*

DAVID, Hon. Laurent Olivier; Senator, 1903; City Clerk, Montreal, since 1892; *b* 24 March 1840; *m* 1st, Albina Chenet; one *s* nine *d*; 2nd, Ludivine Garceau. *Educ:* Ste Thérèse College. Admitted to Bar, 1864; practised in partnership with Hon. I. A. Mousseau up to 1873; left profession then to be a journalist; one of the founders of L'Opinion Publique; established Le Bien Public with M. Beausoleil, 1874;

returned to his profession and founded La Tribune; elected i Montreal for local House, 1886. *Publications:* Portraits et Biographie. Les Patriotes de 1837–38; Les Deux Papineau; Le Clergé Canadier Mes Contemporains; L'Union des deux Canadas; Histoire du Canac depuis la Confédération; Souvenirs et Esquisses biographiques Biographies de Mgr Bourget et de Mgr Tachet; drama entitled L Drapeau de Carillon; Laurier et son temps, Mélanges historiques e littéraires, Gerbes Canadiennes. *Address:* Outremont, Canada.

Died 24 Aug. 192€

DAVID, Sir Sassoon Jacob, 1st Bt, *cr* 1911; KCSI 1922; Kt 1905 JP; Member of Viceroy's Council, 1909; head and founder of th firm of Sassoon J. David & Co., Ltd; communal worker; *b* Bombay 11 Dec. 1849; *s* of Jacob David, prominent member of the Jewis community and one of the first to come to Bombay; *m* 1876, Hanna (*d* 1921), *d* of Elias David Sassoon, *n* of late Sir Albert Sassoon, 1s Bt; one *s* one *d* (and two *s* one *d* decd). *Educ:* Bombay. Joined firr of E. D. Sassoon and Co., doing business with China; spent som years in China and was partner in the firm for several years in Chin and Bombay. In 1885 he started his own firm and became agent c the David and Standard Mills and the leading cotton yarn merchan of Bombay; Chairman of the Millowners' Association, 1904–5; Sheri of Bombay, 1905; was for several years a Government nominee on the Bombay Municipal Corporation and the Standing Committee Pres. of the Bombay Municipal Corporation, 1921–22; Director c several public companies and on the committee of several charitabl associations; firms in China, headquarters Bombay. *Heir: s* Perciva Victor [*b* 21 July 1892; *m* 1913, *c* Vere Mozelle, *d* of Aubrey David one *d*. *Educ:* Elphinstone College; Bombay University, BA. Membe of Inner Temple. *Club:* Royal Automobile]. *Address:* Bombay. *TA* (firm) Psalmist; (private) Sanhedrim. *Clubs:* Orient, Willingdon Sports Bombay. *Died 27 Sept. 1926*

DAVID, Bt-Col Thomas Jenkins, DSO 1918; OBE 1924; TD 1919 *b* Margam, South Wales, 1881; *s* of late Lt-Col D. R. David, JP; *n* 1912, Nita, *d* of late Pendrill Charles, Neath, S Wales; one *s* one *d* *Educ:* Malvern; Christ College, Brecon. Solicitor and Notary Publi (Honours), 1904; commissioned 1900; commanding 81st Welsl Brigade RFA; served European War, 1914–18 (despatches, DSO` Brevet Colonel 1924. *Recreations:* golf, riding. *Address:* Prysowen, Pyle Glam. *Clubs:* Junior Army and Navy; Royal Porthcawl Golf.

Died 6 Nov. 1926

DAVIDS, (Thomas William) Rhys, LLD, PhD, DSc; FBA 1901 Professor of Comparative Religion, Manchester, 1904–15; Professo of Pali and Buddhist Literature, University College, Londor 1882–1912; President of the Pali Text Society and India Society; lat President Manchester Oriental Society; Secretary and Librarian o the Royal Asiatic Society, 1885–1904; took part in founding the Britisl Academy, 1901; founded Pali Text Society, 1882; Orienta Translations Fund, 1895; and Indian Text Series, 1900; *b* Colchester 12 May 1843; *s* of Rev. Thomas William Davids; *m* 1894, Caroline Augusta, DLitt, author, *d* of Rev. John Foley, BD, Fellow of Wadhan Coll. Oxford, late Vicar, Wadhurst, Sussex; two *d* (and one *s* decd) *Educ:* Brighton School; Breslau University. Entered Ceylon Civ. Service, 1866; Barrister, Middle Temple, 1877; delivered Hibber Lectures, 1881. *Publications:* Buddhism, 1878 (23rd edn 1914) Buddhist Birth Stories, vol. i 1880; Ancient Coins and Measures c Ceylon, 1877; Buddhist Sutas from the Pali, 1881; Questions of King Milinda, 1890–94; Hibbert Lectures, 1881; American Lectures, 1896 joint-author of Vinaya Texts, 1881–85; Dīgha Nikāya, 1890 and 1902 Sumangala Vilāsinī, 1886; Sacred Books of the Buddhists; Dialogue of the Buddha, 1899, 1910, 1921; Pali-English Dictionary, 1921, etc Buddhist India, 1903 (2nd edn 1905); Early Buddhism, 1908 *Recreation:* Chipstead Golf Club. *Address:* Chipstead, Surrey. *TA:* Rhy Davids, Chipstead, Surrey. *Died 27 Dec. 1922*

DAVIDSON, Col Sir Arthur, GCVO 1921 (KCVO 1906); KCF 1910 (CB 1902); Extra Equerry to the King and Equerry to Queer Alexandra; *b* 12 Nov. 1856; *s* of W. Davidson, Welwyn, Herts, and Louisa, *d* of J. Barnard Hankey, Fetcham Park, Surrey. *Educ:* private tutor; Petersham. Joined 60th Rifles, 1876; served with 2nd Batt. ir Afghan War, 1878–80; occupation of Candahar and Kelati-Ghilzie engagements of Ahmed Khel (mentioned in despatches), and Urzoc near Ghuznee; ADC to Sir Donald Stewart at Cabul; accompaniec Sir F. Roberts's Cabul-Candahar March as ADC to Sir John Ross battle of Candahar (mentioned in despatches, brevet of Major, meda with 2 clasps, bronze decoration); served in Marri Expedition unde: Gen. MacGregor; in Boer War of 1881 with Natal Field Force; ir Egyptian War, 1882; was present battle of Tel-el-Kebir (medal with clasp, 5th class Medjidie, Khedive's star); served in Bechuanalanc Expedition of 1884–85 under Sir Charles Warren (mentioned ir despatches); ADC to HRH the Duke of Cambridge, KG, 1890–95; Groom-in-Waiting to Queen Victoria, 1895–96, and Equerry-in-Waiting, 1896–1901; Equerry and Assistant Keeper of the Privy Purse, and Assistant Private Secretary to King Edward, 1901–10. Received the Orders of the Dannebrög, the Rising Sun, the Sacred Treasure, and the Redeemer. *Recreations:* shooting, riding. *Address:* Red House, Warnham, Sussex. *TA:* Warnham. *Clubs:* United Service, Naval and Military.   *Died 16 Oct. 1922.*

DAVIDSON, Sir Charles, Kt 1919; a Member of the London Stock Exchange; *b* 1 Jan. 1878; *s* of late John Henry Davidson, Glasgow; *m* 1919, Agnes Clare, *d* of late Frederick James Chard. Chairman Statistical Committee, Department of Surveyor-General of Supply, War Office, 1917–18; Deputy Chairman of Establishment, Ministry of Munitions, 1918–21. *Address:* 22 Suffolk Street, SW1. *T:* Regent 4705. *M:* R 4592. *Clubs:* Constitutional, Gresham, Royal Automobile, Ranelagh.   *Died 27 Feb. 1927.*

DAVIDSON, Duncan, of Tulloch, JP, DL Ross and Cromarty; Chief of Clan Dhai; Landed Proprietor; *b* 3 Oct. 1865; *s* of late Duncan H. C. R. Davidson of Tulloch (*d* 1889); *m* Gwendoline, *e d* of William Dalziel Mackenzie of Fawley Court, Bucks. *Educ:* The College, Inverness; Stubbington House, Fareham; private tutors. Was brought up for a Commercial career, and after being in the City for 14 years left it on his health breaking down; lived on his property; took a great interest in County business, and among other things was Hon. Sheriff-Substitute, County Convr of the Boy Scouts, member of the County Com. of Secondary Education, Chairman of the Dingwall Academy, etc; a very keen sportsman and horticulturalist; Tulloch is an old Barony held direct from the Crown, and is one of the few families in which the head member has the real right of signing "of" Tulloch. *Recreations:* farming, gardening, shooting, fishing, and all games, such as cricket, croquet, billiards. *Address:* Tulloch Castle, Dingwall, NB. *T:* Inverness District, 8. *TA:* Tulloch, Dingwall. *M:* JS 369. *Clubs:* Caledonian; Highland, Inverness.   *Died 11 Nov. 1917.*

DAVIDSON, George, CBE 1927; Divisional General Manager, North Eastern Area, London and North-Eastern Railway Company, York; formerly General Manager Great North of Scotland Railway and Solicitor (Scotland) for London and North-Eastern Railway Company; Lt-Col Engineer and Railway Staff Corps RE (TA). *Address:* Clifton Lodge, York. *T:* York 2027.

Died 18 Aug. 1928.

DAVIDSON, Major George Harry, DSO 1900; The Royal Scots; *b* 16 Sept. 1866; *s* of late Archibald Davidson; *m* 1891, Ethel Maud, *d* of J. A. Fairbairn of Ledgerwood, Claremont, Cape of Good Hope; two *d*. Entered Army, 1887; Adjutant 1st Batt. 1894–98; Captain, 1896; Major, 1904; Adjutant 3rd Batt. 1898–1903; served in operations in Zululand with Mounted Infantry, 1888–91; South African War, 1900–2 (despatches, medal with three clasps, King's medal with two clasps, Coronation medal); Reserve of Officers. *Club:* New, Edinburgh.   *Died 17 April 1927.*

DAVIDSON, Sir James Mackenzie, Kt 1912; MB, CM University of Aberdeen; FPhysS, MRI, MRPS; Consulting Surgeon to Röntgen Ray Department, Charing Cross Hospital, Consulting Surgeon in charge of X-ray Department of Royal London Ophthalmic Hospital (Moorfields), Consulting Radiologist to the Military Hospitals of the London district; Past President Röntgen Society; President Radiology Section 17th International Medical Congress, 1913; *b* 6 Dec. 1856; *s* of John Davidson, Estancia, Santo Domingo, Buenos Ayres; *m* 1886, Georgiana, *d* of William Henderson, Aberdeen. *Educ:* Scotch School, Buenos Ayres; tutors in London; studied medicine in Edinburgh, Aberdeen, and London. After graduation at Aberdeen in 1882, became assistant to Professor of Surgery; subsequently Lecturer on Ophthalmology to the University of Aberdeen, and Ophthalmic Surgeon to the Royal Infirmary, Royal Sick Children's Hospital; Physician to Blind Asylum, etc; came to London, 1897, and then devoted attention to X-ray work; invented a precise method of localisation by means of X-rays for foreign bodies in eye and orbit, and for bullets, etc; also a mercury rotary break for coils. *Publications:* The Electric Light applied to the Ophthalmoscope, Lancet, 1886; Röntgen Rays and Localisation, British Medical Journal, 1898; Stereoscopic Skiagraphy, British Medical Journal, 1898; Localisation of Foreign Bodies in Eyeball and Orbit, Trans IX International Ophth. Congress, Utrecht; and various articles in the Trans of the Ophthalmological Society of the United Kingdom; Notes of cases treated by Radium Bromide Rays, British Medical Journal, 1904. *Recreations:* photography, golf, motoring. *Address:* 26 Park Crescent, Portland Place, W. *T:* Mayfair 1137. *M:* A 8699 and LC 1794. *Clubs:* Royal Automobile, Empire, Argentine, Savage.   *Died 31 March 1919.*

DAVIDSON, Colonel John, CB 1902; unemployed supernumerary list, Indian Army; *b* 28 Aug. 1845; *y s* of late Alexander Davidson, MD, Deputy Inspector-General, BMS; *m* 1877, Anna, *e d* of Thomas Elliott, of Dolhaidd, Caermarthenshire. *Educ:* Winchester College. 21st RNB Fusiliers, 1863; 3rd Punjab Cavalry, 1866; Assistant-Adjutant-General, Punjab Frontier Force, 1875; served Jowaki Afridi Expedition, 1877–78; DAQMG Afghan Campaign, 1878–79; Waziri Expedition, 1880, as AQMG; Military Secretary, Punjab Government, 1885–86; Colonel on Staff, Chitral, 1896–98. *Publication:* Notes on Bashgali Kafir Language, 1902. *Address:* 3 Talbot Houses, Blackheath, SE.   *Died 9 Sept. 1917.*

DAVIDSON, Major Leslie Evan Outram, DSO 1915; late RFA; *b* 23 Sept. 1882; *s* of late Duncan Davidson of Inchmarlo; *m* 1914, Matilda Rome, *d* of Lionel Maitland-Kirwan, RN, of Gelston, Castle Douglas; two *d*. *Educ:* Marlborough. Entered army, 1902; Captain, 1914; Major, 1916; served European War, 1914–15 (despatches twice, DSO).   *Died 26 Feb. 1925.*

DAVIDSON, Lt-Col Peers, KC; *b* Montreal, 7 Nov. 1870; *s* of Hon. Sir Charles Peers Davidson; *m* 1897, Louise, *d* of late Rt Hon. Sir William Vallance Whiteway, KCMG, KC, PC, formerly Prime Minister, Newfoundland; two *s* one *d*. *Educ:* McGill University, Montreal (BCL, MA). Barrister; Lt-Col, late OC 73rd Batt. Royal Highlanders of Canada, Canadian Overseas Forces. *Address:* Transportation Building, Montreal. *TA:* Sreep, Montreal. *Clubs:* Junior Army and Navy; Mount Royal, St James, Forest and Stream, Royal St Lawrence Yacht, Montreal; University, New York.

Died 19 July 1920.

DAVIDSON, Sir Samuel C., KBE 1921; Inventor of wind fans for HM ships. *Address:* Sea Court, Princetown Road, Bangor, Co. Down.
                                    Died 18 Aug. 1921.

DAVIDSON, Thomas; editor with W. and R. Chambers, Edinburgh, for 17 years; Presbyterian Chaplain at Vienna, Brussels, Karlsbad from 1898 to the outbreak of the war; Minister at Afton, New Cumnock, since Dec. 1914; *b* Leswalt, near Stranraer, 27 April 1856; 2nd *s* of John Davidson and Anna Pringle; unmarried. *Educ:* Edinburgh Univ. and New College, Edinburgh. Assistant-editor of Globe Encyclopædia, 1876–79, and of Chambers's Encyclopædia, 1888–92. *Publications:* annotated editions, in Chambers's series of English Classics, of parts of Chaucer, Milton, Macaulay, Byron, Scott, Wordsworth, etc; Chambers's English Dictionary, 1898; Chambers's Twentieth Century Dictionary, 1901; contributions to Scots' Observer, Gypsy Love Journal, Dr Hastings' Encyclopædia of Religion and Ethics, etc; preparing an elaborate study of the history of Jeanne d'Arc; a book on Austrian folk-tales; and a novel of cosmopolitan life. *Recreations:* walking, hill climbing; telling stories to children; the study of folk-lore, especially folk-tales, and the problem of their diffusion. *Address:* Afton Manse, New Cumnock, Ayrshire. *Clubs:* Scottish Arts, Edinburgh; Anglo-American, Vienna.

Died 16 June 1923.

DAVIDSON, Sir Walter Edward, KCMG 1914 (CMG 1902); Governor of New South Wales since 1918; *b* 20 April 1859; *s* of late James Davidson of Killyleagh, Co. Down; *m* 1st, 1882, *d* of John Baber, MD, of 34 Thurloe Square, SW; one *s*; 2nd, 1907, Margaret Agnes, DBE, Lady of Grace of St John of Jerusalem, *y d* of late Gen. Hon. Sir Percy Feilding, KCB; two *d*. *Educ:* Christ's College, Cambridge (scholar). Entered the Ceylon Civil Service, 1880; Secretary to Ceylon Commission, Colonial and Indian Exhibition, 1886; Chairman of Municipal Council and Mayor of Colombo, April 1898; Ceylon Commissioner at Paris Exhibition, 1900; Officier d'Instruction Publique; Colonial Sec., Administration, Transvaal, 1902–4; Governor of Seychelles Islands, 1904–12; Newfoundland, 1913–17. Knight of Grace of St John of Jerusalem. *Publications:* two books on Ceylon and its resources; in 1886 for the Colonial and Indian Exhibition, and in 1900 for the Paris Exhibition; in 1909 a volume of Archives of Seychelles prior to 1810. *Address:* Government House, Sydney, New South Wales. *Club:* Savile.

Died Sept. 1923.

DAVIDSON, Sir (William) Edward, KCMG 1907; CB 1897; KC; MA; Legal Adviser to Foreign Office, 1886–1918; held a Commission as Acting Counsellor of Embassy in HM's Diplomatic Service; *b* 17 April 1853; *s* of late William Davidson, Mount House, Braintree, Essex; unmarried. *Educ:* Balliol College, Oxford. Barrister, Inner Temple, 1879; Bencher, 1901; assisted Law Officers of Crown in their official work, 1881–86; one of the Counsel to Board of Trade in Bankruptcy matters, 1884; and in Shipping matters, 1885; Private Secretary and Secretary of Commissions of the Peace to Lord

Chancellor, 1886; QC 1892. *Recreations:* mountaineering and other outdoor sports; tennis, etc; Hon. Sec. Alpine Club, 1880–85; President, 1911–14; President of the Association of Clan Dhai (Davidson), 1909 and 1910; Member of the Society of Dilettanti. *Address:* 12 Lower Sloane Street, SW1. *T:* Victoria 581; 4 Temple Gardens, Temple, EC4. *Clubs:* Athenæum, Brooks's, Oxford and Cambridge.   *Died 12 July 1923.*

DAVIE, Major Arthur Francis Ferguson-, CIE 1906; DSO 1898; *b* 11 July 1867; 3rd *s* of Sir William Augustus Ferguson-Davie, 3rd Bt and Frances Harriet, *d* of Sir William Miles, 1st Bt; *m* 1906, Eleanor Blanche Daphne, *e d* of Charles Topham Naylor of Dean House, Kelmeston, Hants; two *s*. *Educ:* Marlborough. Entered army, 1888; Captain, 1899; served Waziristan Delimitation Escort, present at action at Wana, 1894; Waziristan Expedition, 1894–95 (medal with clasp); Chitral Relief Expedition, 1895 (medal and clasp); Tirah Campaign, 1897–98 (despatches, DSO, two clasps); Mahsud Waziri Expedition, 1901–2 (despatches, clasp); Operations against Darwesh Khel Waziris, 1902; Bazar Valley Field Force, 1908 (medal and clasp); Major, 1906. *Address:* Nowshera, NWFP, India. *Club:* Naval and Military.   *Died 11 April 1916.*

DAVIES, Hon. Charles Ellis, MLC; JP; managing proprietor of The Mercury Hobart, since 1885; *b* New South Wales, 13 May 1848; *m* 1st, 1870, Sophia M. Wilson, Belfast (*d* 1906); 2nd, 1909, Nellie Grace Collins, of Evandale, Tasmania; one *s* one *d*. *Educ:* High School, Hobart (obtained Associate of Arts Degree, Tasmania, 1865). Joined the Victorian Railways, Melbourne, 1866; joined father, proprietor of The Mercury, 1870; president and founder of the Southern Tasmanian Agricultural and Pastoral Society, 1874; Member Legislative Council, Cambridge, since 1897; Grand Master of the Tasmanian Masonic Grand Lodge, 1896–1914; Pro-Grand-Master, 1914–16; Re-elected GM, 1917; District GM of M Masons GLE; Representative of Tasmanian Press at the Imperial Press Conference in London, 1909. *Publications:* Our Trip to Europe; Impressions on a Trip to Japan. *Recreations:* steward, Tasmania Racing Club; specially interested in all outdoor sports, and president and vice-president of several racing, cricket, and football clubs; one of the principal horse-owners—*nom de course,* S. M. Wilson. *Address:* Lyndhurst, Hobart, Tasmania.   *Died 1921.*

DAVIES, Charles Llewelyn, CBE 1918; MA; Assistant Paymaster-General, 1910–24; *b* London, 29 June 1860; *e s* of late Rev. John Llewelyn Davies and Mary (*d* 1895), *d* of late Mr Justice Crompton. *Educ:* Marlborough College; Trinity College, Cambridge (Scholar); Fellow, 1883; First Class in Classical Tripos, 1882; and Bell University Scholar. Clerk in Local Government Board, 1884; transferred to Treasury, 1888. *Address:* 10 Lupus Street, Pimlico, SW.
Died 30 Nov. 1927.

DAVIES, Rt. Rev. Daniel, DD; Bishop of Bangor since 1925; Canon Residentiary of St Asaph, 1910–25; Vicar of Bedelwyddan, near Rhyl, 1923–25; *b* 7 Nov. 1863; *s* of Evan Davies, Llanddewi, Cardigan; *m* Frances Hester Mary, *o d* of Major R. C. Dobbs Ellis, late 1st Batt. 22nd Regiment and Royal Inniskilling Fusiliers; four *s* two *d*. *Educ:* Ystrad Meurig School; St John's College, Cambridge; 2nd Class Theol. Tripos, Part I, 1886, and BA; 2nd Class Theol. Tripos, Part II, 1887. Curate of Conway, 1887; Bangor, 1889; Vicar Choral of St Asaph Cathedral, 1890; Vicar of Brymbo, 1893; Rector of Denbigh, 1897; Rural Dean of Denbigh, 1904; Proctor in Convocation for St Asaph Diocese, 1906; Vicar and Rural Dean of Wrexham, 1907; Chairman of the Executive Committee of the National Eisteddfod of Wales, 1912. *Address:* Bishopscourt, Bangor. *M:* DM 3634.
Died 23 Aug. 1928.

DAVIES, Edward, RI. *Address:* 131 Narborough Road, Leicester.
Died Aug. 1920.

DAVIES, Colonel Edward Campbell, ISO 1910; VD; Public Works Department, Ceylon; retired Aug. 1911 after 33 years' service. *Address:* 129 King's Road, Brighton.   *Died 5 May 1919.*

DAVIES, Rev. Canon Evan Thomas, Canon Residentiary, Bangor Cathedral, since 1906; *m* Anne Catherine (*d* 1923). *Educ:* Lampeter, BA. Curate of Llanwonno, 1870–71; Ferndale, 1871–72; Bettws, 1872–75; Perpetual Curate of St David's, Liverpool, 1875–82; Vicar of Aberdovey, 1882–90; Canon and Preb. of Llanfair, 1897–1906; Vicar of Denio, 1890–1906; Rural Dean, Lleyn, 1897–1906; Rector of Llanfihangel-ysceifiog, 1906–13. *Publications:* Cydymaith y Cymro, 1884; Pregethan ac Anerchiadan, 1894. *Address:* Hafodunos, Bangor.
Died 1927.

DAVIES, Frederick William Samuel, MRCS, LRCP; Senior Anæsthetist to King Edward VII Hospital, Cardiff; MO Llwynarthan Auxiliary Hospital; Acting MO HM Priory, Cardiff; Hon. Medical Attendant Queen's Nurses in Cardiff; Medical Officer St Margaret's House of Mercy and Children's Home; Physician French Consulate, Cardiff; late Clinical Assistant Evelina Hospital for Sick Children; Medical Officer and Anæsthetist Glamorgan and Monmouth Hospital for French wounded, Berckplage. *Educ:* Guy's Hospital.
Died 1919.

DAVIES, Rev. Gerald Stanley, MA; The Master of Charterhouse, since 1908; *b* Banff Castle, 1845; *s* of Admiral George Davies and Julia Hume; *m* 1874, Constance Mary Hilliard (*d* 1922); five *d*. *Educ:* Charterhouse; nominated to Foundation by Edward VII, then Prince of Wales; Christ's College, Cambridge (Scholar). Curate of Shefford and Campton, Beds; Assistant Master, Charterhouse, Godalming, 1873, 1905. *Publications:* St Paul in Greece; Gaudentius; Julian's Dream; Franz Hals; Holbein; Ghirlandaio; Michelangelo; Renaissance Tombs of Rome; History of Charterhouse. *Address:* The Master's Lodge, Charterhouse, EC.   *Died 12 Feb. 1927.*

DAVIES, Lt-Col Henry, CMG 1917; late Army Service Corps; *b* London, 13 July 1867; *s* of late Henry Davies and Ellen Shuttleworth; *m* 1895, Clara Maud, *e d* of late Henry Moore; one *s* one *d*. *Educ:* Cheltenham College; Sandhurst. Joined 1st S Lancs Regt 1887; transferred to ASC 1891; Captain, 1894; Major, 1902; Lt-Col 1914; served S African War, 1899–1902 (Queen's medal, 6 clasps, King's medal, 2 clasps); European War, 1914–18 (despatches thrice, CMG); commanded 6 Divisional Train and Guards Trains; retired pay, 1919. *Recreations:* riding, cycling.   *Died 4 Nov. 1923.*

DAVIES, Hubert Henry; dramatist; *b* Woodley, Cheshire. *Educ:* private schools. Went to San Francisco, 1893, where he became a journalist and produced several vaudeville sketches; returned to England, 1901. *Publications:* Plays—Mrs Gorringe's Necklace; Cousin Kate, 1903; Cynthia, 1904; Captain Drew on Leave, 1905; The Mollusc, 1907; Lady Epping's Lawsuit, 1908; Bevis, 1909; A Single Man, 1910; Doormats, 1912; Outcast, 1914. *Address:* Park Lodge, Park Place, Knightsbridge, SW. *Clubs:* Garrick, Beefsteak.
Died Aug. 1917.

DAVIES, Sir John Cecil, Kt 1922; CBE 1920; JP; Legion of Honour; Vice-Chairman of Baldwins, Ltd; a director of many companies; *b* 23 Sept. 1864; *s* of Thomas Davies, Swansea; *m* 1893, Emma Jane, *d* of late J. Edmunds of Coed-y-Paen, Monmouthshire; four *s* one *d*. Chairman of the South Wales Siemens Steel Association; Chairman of the Welsh Plate and Sheet Manufacturers Association; Member the Executive Com. of the Nat. Federation of Iron and Steel Manufacturers; a Member of the Council of the University College of Swansea; served for many years on the Llanelly Board of Guardians, the Swansea Rural District Council, and the Gowerton Council; one of the founders of the Swansea National Shell Factory, and acted throughout as Chairman of the Board of Management; Member of the Executive Committee appointed by the Ministry of Munitions to control shell factories; represented the Ministry in the allocation of steel supplies in South Wales; was a member of the South Wales and Monmouthshire Railway Transport Joint Committee. *Address:* Stelvio, Newport, Mon. *T:* Newport 2251. *Clubs:* Conservative, Royal Autombile, British Empire.
Died 29 Aug. 1927.

DAVIES, John Humphreys; *s* of late R. J. Davies of Cwrt Mawr, Llangeitho, Cardiganshire; unmarried. *Educ:* University College School; Lincoln College, Oxford (MA). Barrister-at-law (Lincoln's Inn); Principal of the University College of Wales, Aberystwyth; Vice-Chancellor of the University of Wales, 1923–25; late Fellow of Jesus College, Oxford; Member of the Council of the University of Wales; Ex-Chairman of the Cardiganshire County Council; High Sheriff of Cardiganshire, 1912. *Publications:* Letters of Lewis Morris and his Brothers; Bibliography of Welsh 18th Century Ballads; The Works of Morgan Llwyd. *Address:* Cwrt Mawr, Llangeithe, Cardiganshire; Cwm, Aberystwyth.   *Died 10 Aug. 1926.*

DAVIES, Rev. John Llewelyn, MA; Hon. DD (Durham); Hon. LittD (Victoria); Hon. Chaplain to the King; Vicar of Kirkby Lonsdale, 1889–1908; *b* Chichester, 26 Feb. 1826; *s* of Rev. J. Davies, DD; *m* 1859, Mary (*d* 1895), *d* of late Mr Justice Crompton; four *s* one *d*. *Educ:* Repton; Trinity Coll., Cambridge (Bell Scholar, 1845; 1st class in Classics, 1848). Fellow Trinity Coll., Cambridge, 1851–59; Curate of St Ann's, Limehouse, 1851–52; Vicar of St Mark's, Whitechapel, 1852–56; Rector of Christ Church, St Marylebone, 1856–89. *Publications:* Translation of the Republic of Plato (jointly with D. J. Vaughan); Commentary on the Ephesians, Colossians, and Philemon; Social Questions; Order and Growth; Spiritual Apprehension. *Recreation:* original member of the Alpine Club; made first ascents of the Dom and the Täschhorn. *Address:* 11 Hampstead Square, NW.   *Died 18 May 1916.*

DAVIES, Hon. Sir John Mark, KCMG 1918; President Legislative Council, Victoria, since 1910. Solicitor, 1863; MLC, South Yarra, 1889; Melbourne, 1899; Minister for Justice, 1890-2; Solicitor-General, 1899-1900 and 1902-3; Minister of Public Instruction, 1903; Attorney-General and Solicitor-General, Victoria, 1903. *Address:* Valentines, Burke Road, Malvern, Australia.
Died 14 Sept. 1919.

DAVIES, Rt. Hon. Sir Louis Henry, KCMG 1897; PC Can. 1896; PC 1919; KC; Chief Justice of the Supreme Court of Canada (Appeal) since 1918; Deputy Governor-General of Canada since 1918; *b* Prince Edward Island, Canada, 4 May 1845; *s* of Hon. Benjamin Davies; *m* 1872, Susan, *d* of Rev. Dr Wiggins; one *s* three *d*. *Educ:* Prince of Wales Coll.; LLD McGill University, 1922; Barrister, Prince Edward Island, 1867; Solicitor-General, 1869 and 1871-72; Leader of the Opposition, 1873-76; Premier and Attorney-General, Prince Edward Island, 1876-79; QC 1880; elected to Dominion House of Commons, 1882, and re-elected continuously until his appointment to Appeal Court; Counsel for Great Britain before the International Fisheries Arbitration at Halifax in 1877 between Great Britain and United States of America; Joint Delegate to Washington with Sir Wilfrid Laurier, 1897, on Behring Sea seal question; one of Joint High Commissioners on part of Great Britain in 1898 for settlement of all differences with USA in respect of Canada; Minister of Marine and Fisheries, Canada, 1896-1901. KGStJ 1913. *Address:* Ottawa, Canada. *TA:* Ottawa. *T:* 533. *Club:* Rideau, Ottawa: City, Charlottetown.   *Died 1 May 1924.*

DAVIES, Bt-Col Owen Stanley, DSO 1918; *y s* of Sir William Howell Davies; *m* 1923, Ruth Winsome, *o d* of Stanley Gange of Sneyd Park, Bristol. Served European War, 1914-18 (despatches, DSO).   *Died 19 Dec. 1926.*

DAVIES, Rev. Philip Latimer; Vicar of Dalton Parbold, near Wigan, since 1921; Hon. Canon in Liverpool Cathedral; Hon. Secretary, Liverpool Council of Education; *b* Swansea, 1864; unmarried. *Educ:* Swansea Grammar School; Royal University of Ireland; BA. Mathematical Master, Liverpool College, until 1907; Vicar of St James', Toxteth, Liverpool, 1907-12; Vicar of St Thomas', Wavertree, Liverpool, 1912-21. *Address:* Dalton Parbold Vicarage, near Wigan. *T:* Parbold 41. *Clubs:* Athenæum; University, Liverpool.   *Died 18 Sept. 1928.*

DAVIES, Col Richard Hutton, CB 1900; NZ Staff Corps; Brigade Commander 6th Infantry Brigade since 1910; NZ Mounted Rifles; served South Africa, 1900 (despatches, CB); European War, 1914-15 (despatches).   *Died 9 May 1918.*

DAVIES, Robert Gwyneddon; *b* 1870; *s* of John Davies, Gwyneddon; *m* Grace, *d* of Lewis Roberts, Liverpool. *Educ:* University College, Bangor. Solicitor (retired, 1918); Mayor of Carnarvon, 1908; High Sheriff of Carnarvonshire, 1924; Chairman of County Council, 1927; member of Council of University College of North Wales and of Court of University of Wales. *Publication:* Visions of the Sleeping Bard (translated from Welsh). *Address:* Llanwnda, Carnarvon. *T:* Llanwnda 3.   *Died 17 April 1928.*

DAVIES, (Sarah) Emily, Hon. LLD Glasgow; Hon. Secretary, 1867-1904, Mistress, 1873-75, Girton College, Cambridge; *b* Southampton, 22 April 1830; *d* of Rev. J. Davies, DD, Rector of Gateshead. *Educ:* home. Hon. Secretary to Committee for obtaining admission of women to University Examinations, 1862-69; Hon. Sec. of Committee of Proposed New College for Women, 1867; Member School Board of London, 1870-73; Life-Governor of Univ. College, London; late Governor of Grammar School, Hitchin. *Publications:* The Higher Education of Women, 1866; Thoughts on some Questions relating to Women, 1860-1908, 1910. *Address:* 17 Glenmore Road, Belsize Park, NW.   *Died 13 July 1921.*

DAVIES, Rev. Sidney Edmund; Rector of Wyke Regis since 1899; Canon of Sarum since 1896; Surrogate. *Educ:* Worcester College, Oxford, MA. Ordained 1873; Curate of St Martin, Sarum, 1873-79; Vicar of Shipton, Bellinger, Hants, 1879-85; Vicar of Board Windsor, 1885-91; Gillingham, 1891-99; Rural Dean of Shaftesbury, 1891-99. *Address:* Wyke Regis Rectory, Weymouth.
Died 10 July 1918.

DAVIES, T. Witton, BA (Lond); PhD (Leipzig); DTh (Geneva); DD (Durham); MRAS; FRAI; Emeritus Professor of Semitic Languages, University College of North Wales, Bangor; *b* Nantyglo, Monmouthshire, 1851; *s* of late Edmund Davies, Witton Park, Durham; *m* 1st, 1880, Mary Anne (*d* 1910), *o d* of late Henry Moore of Ainger Road, London, and of Great Yarmouth; one *d*; 2nd, 1911, Hilda Mabel, *y d* of late Frederic Everett, Homewood, Swaffham, Norfolk; one *s* one *d*. *Educ:* Witton Park; Baptist Colleges, Pontypool and Regent's Park; Univ. Coll., London; 1st Prize in Logic and Philosophy at University College; also 1st class prize Hebrew, etc, Examination, University of London; Universities of Berlin, Leipzig, and Strasburg. Pastor of High Street Baptist Church, Merthyr-Tydfil, 1878-80; Professor of Classics, Hebrew, and Mathematics, Baptist College, Haverfordwest, 1880-91; Principal Midland Baptist College, Nottingham, 1892-99; Lecturer in Arabic and Syriac, University College, Nottingham, 1897-99; Professor of Hebrew and Old Testament Literature, Baptist College, Bangor, 1899-1906. *Publications:* Oriental Studies in Great Britain, 1892; Magic, Divination and Demonology among the Hebrews and their Neighbours, 1898; The Scriptures of the Old Testament, 1900; Heinrich Ewald, Orientalist and Theologian, 1905; Century Bible, Psalms, vol. ii 1906; and also Ezra, Nehemiah, and Esther, 1909 (Introduction and Commentary); The Survival of the Evangelical Faith, a Lesson and a Warning (Essays for the Times), 1907; (joint) Welsh Political and Educational Leaders, 1907, and Wales To-day and To-morrow, 1907; Out-standing Literary and Human Factors in my Life, 1911 (reprint); Bel and the Dragon, Introduction and Commentary in the Oxford Apocrypha, 1913; contributor to Review of Theology and Philosophy, Biblical World; Expositor, Journal of the Apocrypha, etc. *Recreations:* walking, foreign travel, music, book-hunting. *Address:* Bryn Haul, Victoria Drive, Bangor, North Wales. *Club:* University.
Died 12 May 1923.

DAVIES-EVANS, Herbert; Lord-Lieutenant of Cardiganshire, resigned; *b* 19 Feb. 1842; *o s* of Capt. Delmé Seymour Davies, Scots Guards, Penlan, Carmarthenshire, and Mary Anne, *o d* of Capt. Watkin Evans, RN, Highmead and Dolgadfan, Montgomeryshire; *m* 1869, Mary Eleanor Geraldine (*d* 1926), *e d* of David Jones, MP, Pantglas, Carmarthenshire; three *s* one *d*. Joined RN 1856; and 10th Hussars, 1860. *Address:* Highmead, Llanybyther, S Wales, RSO. *TA:* Llanybyther. *M:* EJ 5.   *Died 4 June 1928.*

DAVIS, Colonel Charles Herbert, CBE 1919; DSO 1917; VD; merchant; *b* Kilmore, Victoria, 4 June 1872; *s* of William Davis, Manager of the Colonial Bank of Australasia, and Ellen May Davis; *m* 1907, Emily Beatrice Deloitte; two *s* one *d*. *Educ:* St Andrew's College, Bendigo; University of Melbourne. A barrister and solicitor at Bendigo, 1895; continued in practice there till the outbreak of war; joined the Militia Forces of Victoria as a Lieut Dec. 1897, and was at the time of the outbreak of war a Lieut-Col in the Commonwealth Forces; appointed Censor, Melbourne, Aug. 1914, and continued in that office till gazetted to a command in the AIF 1916; organised and commanded the 38th Batt. AIF which left Australia June 1916; served with his batt. in France till 1 June 1918, when appointed Commandant to Australian Base Depots at Le Havre, which appointment he retained till demobilisation (despatches, CBE, DSO). *Address:* 81 Clarence Street, Sydney, NSW.
Died Dec. 1922.

DAVIS, Very Rev. Evans; Rector of St James', London, Ont, since 1874; Dean of Huron Cathedral since 1904; *b* 20 May 1848; *m* 1882, Louisa Victoria Greenwood, St Catharine's, Ontario. *Educ:* Western University; DD. Ordained, 1871; Incumbent, Bayfield, 1871-74; Canon of Huron, 1888; Archdeacon of Huron, 1894; member of the General Synod and of the General Board of Missions of the Canadian Church. *Address:* The Deanery, London, Ontario.
Died March 1918.

DAVIS, F. W.; RI; *b* Handsworth, Birmingham. *Educ:* Birmingham Municipal School of Art; Antwerp Academy; L'Ecole des Beaux-Arts (Anatomy Course), Paris. *Works:* Yule-Tide Festival exhibited at National Eisteddfod of Wales Exhibition, Swansea (gold medal); Sword and Pen, Paris Exhibition, 1900; A Forgotten Craft, St Louis Exhibition, 1904; The Love Philtre, New Zealand Exhibition, 1906; Six Large Frescoes for Wootton-Wawen Hall; two large decorative panels for presentation to the Shakespeare Memorial Museum, Stratford-on-Avon; Triptych for St Andrew's Church, Handsworth, 1909, etc; a panel for Reredos, St Patrick's, Earlswood Lakes, 1911; four panels for Triptych, St Stephen's Church, Birmingham, 1912. *Publications:* The Butterfly; A Price on his Head; His Latest Acquisition. *Address:* Oakley Villa, Corbett Avenue, Droitwich.
Died Dec. 1919.

DAVIS, Lt-Col Gronow John, DSO 1916; Military Secretary to the Chief Commissioner NWFP, India; *b* 9 Nov. 1869; *s* of late Major-General Gronow Davis, VC; *m* Evelyn Mary, *d* of W. C. Beloe, JP; three *s* one *d. Educ:* Clifton College; Sandhurst. Joined Scottish Rifles, 1890; Indian Army (22nd Punjabis), 1892; served NW Frontier, India, 1897–98, including Relief of Malakhand (medal, 2 clasps); Tirah, 1897–98 (clasp); NW Frontier, 1898–99; East Africa, 1902–4 (medal, 2 clasps); European War, 1914–16 (despatches twice, DSO). *Address:* Harley Cottage, Clifton Down, Bristol. *Club:* Junior Army and Navy.
Died 20 June 1919.

DAVIS, Henry William Carless, CBE 1918; FBA 1925; Director, Dictionary National Biography, since 1902; Regius Professor of Modern History, Oxford, since 1925; *b* 13 Jan. 1874; *s* of H. F. A. Davis, of Ebley, Stroud; *m* 1912, Rosa Jennie, *o d* of Walter G. Lindup; three *s. Educ:* Weymouth College; Balliol College, Oxford (Scholar, 1891–95). Fellow of All Souls, Oxford, 1895–1902; Fellow of Balliol, 1902–21; War Trade Intelligence Department, 1915; Ford's Lecturer, Oxford, 1924; War Trade Advisory Committee, 1916; Professor of Modern History, University of Manchester, 1921–25. *Publications:* History of Balliol College, 1899; Charlemagne, 1900; England under the Normans and Angevins, 1905; Mediæval Europe, 1911; Regesta Regum Anglo-Norman-uorum, vol. i, 1913; new edn of Stubbs' Select Charters, 1913; Political Thought of Treitschke, 1914; England, 1815–1846, in Story of British Nation, 1923; (joint) Why We are at War, 1914; editor of Oxford Pamphlets, 1914–15; contributions to the English Historical Review, The Quarterly Review, Cambridge Modern History, Helmolt's History of the World (English edition); Encyclopædia Britannica (1910 and 1922); Mowbray's Dictionary of Church History, 1912; History of Peace Conference (ed. Temperley, 1920); etc. *Address:* The Old Vicarage, Summertown, Oxford. *Club:* National.
Died 28 June 1928.

DAVIS, John Samuel Champion, CBE 1918; VD; DL, JP; MA; *b* 21 Feb. 1859; 2nd *s* of Rev. S. Davis, Vicar of Burrington, North Devon; *m* 1880, Minna Sophia, *d* of William Butt of Axmouth; one *d. Educ:* Rossall; Balliol College, Oxford. Entered Indian Civil Service, United Provinces, 1880; Junior Secretary and Joint Secretary, Board of Revenue, 1886–91; Settlement Officer, 1893–97; Deputy Commissioner, 1900–2; Commissioner, 1903–6; special duty with Viceroy, 1903; retired, 1906; held commission in various Indian Volunteer Corps from 1883; Captain United Provinces Light Horse, 1890–1907; retired with rank of Major, 1907; County Director, British Red Cross Society, Devonshire Branch; member of Council of British Red Cross Society; Member of Devon County Council, and Devon Territorial Army Association; Treasurer University College of the South-West, Exeter. *Publications:* Settlement Reports of the Hardoi District, Oudh, 1894–97; Handbook of the Devonshire Voluntary Aid Organisation, 1910; 4th edition, 1912. *Address:* Kingford, Burrington, Umberleigh, N Devon. *Clubs:* National; Devon and Exeter, Exeter.
Died 12 Feb. 1926.

DAVIS, Sir Mortimer (Barnett), Kt 1917; Director of several Industrial Corporations; *b* Montreal, 1866; *m* 1st, 1898, Henriette Marie Meyer; 2nd, 1924, Countess Morini. *Educ:* High School, Montreal. *Address:* Villa Glaieuls, Gulfe Juan, France.
Died 22 March 1928.

DAVIS, Richard Harding, FRGS; American novelist and playwright; Times war correspondent in Greek-Turkish war, Spanish-American war, and for the New York Herald in South African war, also in Russian-Japanese war, Spanish Cuban revolution, Matos revolution in Venezuela, American occupation of Vera Cruz, and representing Daily Chronicle with the allied armies in Belgium and France; *b* 1864; *s* of Rebecca Harding Davis, American novelist, and L. Clarke Davis, editor of the Philadelphia Public Ledger; *m* 1899, Cecil Clark, Chicago; *m* 1912, Bessie McCoy; one *d. Educ:* Lenhigh and Johns Hopkins Universities. *Publications:* Soldiers of Fortune; Gallegher and Other Stories; The Princess Aline; Cuba in War time; Three Gringoes in Venezuela and Central America; The Cuban and Porto Rican Campaigns, 1898; With Both Armies in South Africa, 1900; In the Fog, 1901; Ranson's Folly; Captain Macklin, 1902; Farces, Real Soldiers of Fortune, 1906; The Congo and Coasts of Africa, 1907; The Scarlet Car, 1908; Vera, the Medium, 1908; The White Mice, 1909; Once Upon a Time, 1910; Man who could not lose, 1911; The Red Cross Girl, 1912; The Lost Road, 1913; With the Allies, 1915; Somewhere in France, 1915. *Plays:* The Taming of Helen, 1902; Ranson's Folly, 1903; The Dictator, 1904; The Galloper, 1905; A Yankee Tourist, 1906; Vera, the Medium, 1908; Blackmail, 1912; Who's Who?, 1913. *Address:* The Cross-roads, Mount Kisco, New York, USA. *Club:* The Brook, New York.
Died 11 April 1916.

DAVIS, R. Bramwell, KC; *b* London, 1849; *s* of late Richard Powell Davis of Bedwellty House, Tredegar, Mon.; *m* 1st, Margaret Adelaide Salmond; 2nd, Elaine Beatrice Vaughan; two *s* one *d. Educ:* privately; Trinity Hall, Cambridge. Called to Bar, 1873; QC 1896; practised in the Chancery Courts at first before Mr Justice Kekewich, subsequently before Mr Justice Farwell, Mr Justice Neville, and Mr Justice P. O. Lawrence. *Recreations:* golf, etc. *Address:* 15 Old Square, Lincoln's Inn, WC. *T:* Holborn 4899. *Club:* New University.
Died 25 Aug. 1923.

DAVIS, Major William Hathaway, DSO 1918; MC; MA; Headmaster of the William Ellis School, NW5, since 1919; *b* 1881; *s* of A. J. Davis, Brandesburton, Hull; *m* Isabelle Kathleen Watkins, *d* of T. Watkins Baker; one *s. Educ:* Hymer's College, Hull; The Yorkshire College, Victoria University. BA 1903; MA 1906; Victoria University, Salt Scholar; Gladstone Prizeman; Editor of Gryphon; Chairman of Union. Assistant Master at Leeds Central High School, 1904–6; Second Master of Normanton Grammar School, 1906–14. Served European War, 1914–19; commissioned to KOYLI 1914; transferred to Machine Gun Corps, 1916; service in France as OC Machine Gun Company with rank of Major, 1916–17 (MC, despatches, DSO). *Address:* 141 Woodstock Avenue, NW11. *T:* Speedwell 4618.
Died 7 Dec. 1928.

DAVISON, John Emanuel; MP (Lab) Smethwick, 1918–26; a Labour Whip, 1924–25; *b* Smethwick, 28 Nov. 1870; *s* of John Davison, Sheffield. *Educ:* Sheffield Elementary School. An Official of the Iron-founders' Society; Vice-Chamberlain of the King's Household, 1924. *Address:* 32 Cottingham Street, Attercliffe, Sheffield.
Died 2 March 1927.

DAVY, Sir Henry, KBE 1919; CB 1917; MD (London University); FRCP (London); Honorary DSc, Sheffield; Consulting Physician Royal Devon and Exeter Hospital; Colonel AMS; Consulting Physician Southern Command; *b* 18 Jan. 1855; *y s* of Henry Davy, Solicitor, Ottery St Mary, Devon; *m* 1st, 1885, Beatrice Mary (*d* 1905), *d* of J. T. Tucker, Solicitor, Chard, Somerset; one *d*; 2nd, 1920, A. I. Mary, *d* of late Samuel Octavius Gray and *widow* of Dr John Mortimer. *Educ:* Honiton Grammar School; Guy's Hospital; MD University of London. Took 1st prize for 1st year's students and Gurney Hoare prize for Clinical Medicine at Guy's Hospital; President of the British Medical Association at their Meeting at Exeter, 1907; Vice-President of Association. *Publications:* papers in Pathological Transactions, Guy's Hospital Reports, Lancet, and British Medical Journal. *Address:* Southernhay House, Exeter. *T:* Exeter 209. *M:* T 1806. *Club:* Devon and Exeter, Exeter.
Died 10 May 1922.

DAVY, Richard, FRCS, FRSE; land-owner; *b* 1838; 2nd surv. *s* of John Croote Davy, of Chulmleigh, Devon, and Elisabeth, *d* of late John Sweet, of Burstone Manor; *m* Edith, *d* of George Cutcliffe, of Coombe House, Witheridge, Devon; three *d. Educ:* Univ. of Edinburgh (MB 1862). Practised for 30 years as a consulting surgeon in London; one of the consulting surgeons to the Westminster Hospital. *Publication:* Surgical Lectures, 1880. *Recreations:* superintendence of farm and land improvements. *Address:* Burstone Manor, Bow, North Devon.
Died 25 Sept. 1920.

DAWBARN, Charles; *b* 22 Nov. 1871; *s* of Robert Dawbarn, Solicitor, March, Cambs; *m* 1914, Nora Payne, Durban, S Africa. *Educ:* Edinburgh University. Edited Midland Daily Telegraph; joined Pall Mall Gazette under Sir Douglas Straight; Paris Correspondent, 1900; acted as its special correspondent in Russia 1905, and in America and Canada, 1908; became Observer Correspondent in Paris; joined Paris Staff of The Times, 1914; was in charge of Paris Bureau at battle of Marne; sent special correspondence from Paris and neutral centres to Times, 1915–16; Diplomatic Correspondent, Daily Chronicle, 1917; represented that journal at Peace Conference; likewise in long tour in South and Central Africa, 1920–21; toured Italy for British and American Journals, 1922. *Publications:* France and the French; Makers of New France; France at Bay; Joffre and his Army; My South African Year, 1921; innumerable articles, mostly on French subjects in Nineteenth Century, Fortnightly Contemporary, Atlantic Monthly, Saturday Review, etc. *Address:* Mitchell's Bureau, 23 Fleet Street, EC.
Died 16 Sept. 1925.

DAWES, James Arthur; MP (L) Southwark, SE (formerly Walworth), since 1910; *b* 16 June 1866; *s* of Richard Dawes, of Castle Hill, Ealing; *m* 1920, Violet Maud Garner, *yr d* of Mr and Mrs Pridmore, Penge. *Educ:* Harrow; University College, Oxford (MA, BCL). Admitted a Solicitor, 1891; chairman, Vestry of Newington, 1897–1900; first

Mayor of Southwark, 1900–1; re-elected, 1913–14, 1914–15; member of Metropolitan Water Board, 1904; member of London County Council, 1906; re-elected, 1907, 1910, and 1913; Chairman of the London Insurance Committee, 1912–14; JP, Co. of London; Sub-Lieut RNR 1914; Lieut-Commander, RNVR 1915; Commander (acting), 1918. *Recreation:* yachting. *Address:* 71 Kennington Park Road, SE11; Ravensbury, Dartmouth, S Devon. *T:* Hop 1175. *Club:* Oxford and Cambridge.

Died 14 Nov 1921.

DAWES, William Charles, JP; MFH Tickham; *b* 20 Sept. 1865; *e s* of Sir Edwyn Sandys Dawes, KCMG, of Mount Ephraim, Faversham, Kent, and Lucy Emily, *e d* of late William Bagnall, of Hamstead Hall, Staffordshire; *m* 1893, Jane Margaret, *d* of late James Simpson, JP, of Inverboyndie, Banffshire; two *s* one *d*. *Educ:* Winchester. Director Commercial Union Assurance Co., Ltd. *Address:* Queen Anne's Mansions, SW; Mount Ephraim, near Faversham; Swordanes, Banff. *Clubs:* Gresham, Royal Thames Yacht.

Died 20 July 1920.

DAWKINS, Maj.-Gen. Sir Charles Tyrwhitt, KCMG 1918 (CMG 1897); CB 1915; AQMG Eastern Command 1910–14; *b* 22 Nov. 1858; *s* of late Rev. James Annesley Dawkins; *m* 1887, Hon. Neridah Leeta Robinson, *d* of 1st Baron Rosmead; one *s*. Entered King's (Shrops) Light Infantry, 1878; Capt. 1886; Col 1907; served Afghan War, 1879–80 (medal); S Africa, 1899–1901 (severely wounded, despatches, 1900, 1902; Queen's medal, 4 clasps; King's medal, 2 clasps; brevet of Lt-Colonel); European War, 1914–18 as DQMG at GHQ (despatches 5 times, CB, KCMG). *Address:* 21 Emperor's Gate, SW.

Died 4 Oct. 1919.

DAWNAY, Sir Archibald Davis, Kt 1918; JP; CE; for ten years Mayor of Wandsworth. *Address:* Sheviocke, Cedars Road, Clapham, SW4. *TA:* Yanwad, Clapcom, London. *T:* Battersea 796, 125. *Clubs:* St Stephen's, Junior Constitutional, British Empire.

Died 23 April 1919.

DAWNAY, Hon. Eustace (Henry), JP, DL; *b* 15 April 1850; 5th *s* of 7th Viscount Downe and Mary Isabel, *d* of Hon. and Rt Rev. Richard Bagot; *m* 1883, Lady Evelyn de Vere Capel, *g d* of 6th Earl of Essex; one *s* two *d*. Late Lieutenant Coldstream Guards; served Egypt, 1882 (medal and star). *Address:* 9 Sussex Square, W2. *T:* Paddington 1858. *Clubs:* Guards, Arthur's, Bath.

Died 15 Dec. 1928.

DAWSON, Hon. Edward Stanley; *b* 16 Aug. 1843; *s* of 1st Earl Dartrey and Augusta, *d* of Edward Stanley; *heir-pres.* of 2nd Earl of Dartrey; *m* 1898, Lady Elizabeth Meade, *e d* of 4th Earl of Clanwilliam; one *d*. Retired Captain, RN; High Sheriff Co. Monaghan, 1899. *Address:* 30 Cadogan Square, SW1. *T:* 1654 Victoria. Cannon Hill, Maidenhead. *T:* 62 Maidenhead. *Clubs:* Turf, Travellers', Bachelors'.

Died 24 Oct. 1919.

DAWSON, Rev. Edwin Collas; Canon of St Mary's Cathedral and Synod Clerk of the Diocese of Edinburgh since 1906; *e s* of Rev. John Dawson, MA, late Vicar of Holy Trinity, Weston-super-Mare, and Mary Le Mesurier, *d* of Capt. Peter Collas, RN, of Hauteville, Guernsey; *m* 1875, Lucy, *d* of Lt-Col Robert Wyllie, JP, Mil. Secretary to Govt of India, of Ellerslie, N Devon, and Catherine, *d* of Humphrey Herbert-Jones, JP, DL, MFH, of Llynon Hall, Anglesea, and Tynewdd, Carnavons; one *s* one *d*. *Educ:* Marlborough; Tonbridge; St Mary Hall, Oxford. BA 1872; MA 1876. Deacon, 1873; Priest, 1874; Curate of Hale, 1873; Sandgate, 1875; Incumbent of St Thomas's, Edinburgh, 1878–90; Rector of St Peter's, Edinburgh, 1890–1921; Clerical Secretary FM Board Edinburgh Diocese, 1905; Convener of Publication Committee of FM Board of Scottish Church, and Editor of the FM Chronicle of the Scottish Episcopal Church (now discontinued); Member of every Provincial Synod of the Scottish Church since 1890. *Publications:* The Life and Work of James Hannington, first Bishop of E Equatorial Africa, 1886; Lion-hearted; The Last Journals of Bishop Hannington; Our Work Overseas; In and Out of Chanda; Success to You! Talks with Boys; Comrades; In the Days of the Dragons; The Life of Dr Stern; Heroines of Missionary Endeavour, 1908; The Book of Honour, 1910; articles in various magazines, etc. *Recreations:* fishing, chess. *Address:* University Hall, 9 Ramsay Garden, Edinburgh.

Died March 1925.

DAWSON, Lt-Col (Brig.-Gen.) Frederick Stewart, CMG 1916; DSO 1918; ADC to HM 1917; 1st South African Infantry; *m*; one *s*. Served European War, 1914–18 (despatches, CMG, DSO). *Address:* Intwood, Farnham Royal, Slough.   *Died 26 Oct. 1920.*

DAWSON, Col Harry Leonard, CVO 1902; CB 1900; ISC; late Colonel on Staff Commanding Madras Brigade; *b* 5 Dec. 1854; *s* of late Major-Gen. John Dawson, ISC; *m* 1904, Ada Marion, *e d* of late H. Binny Webster, BCS. *Educ:* Cheltenham College. Entered army, 1873; Lieut-Col 1899; served Soudan, 1885; present at actions of Hasheen and Tamai (medal with clasp, Khedive's Star); Chitral Relief Force, 1895 (medal with clasp); Tirah, 1897–98 (two clasps); South Africa, 1899–1900 (despatches, CB, medal with six clasps); commanded Indian Coronation Contingent, 1902 (CVO, Coronation medal). *Address:* Rosemead, Horley, Surrey.

Died 27 June 1920.

DAWSON, M. Damer, OBE 1918; Chief Officer of the Women Police Service; *b* Sussex, 1875; *d* of Richard Dawson, formerly RA. *Educ:* privately. Studied music under Benno Schönberger and Herbert Sharpe; gold medal and diploma London Academy of Music; worked for the protection of animals in England and on the Continent, 1903–14; Organising Secretary of Congress of International Animal Protection Societies held in London, 1906; silver medal given by King of Denmark for animal protection work; silver medal of Finnish Society for Protection of Animals; founded the Women Police Service, Feb. 1915; was Co-Founder of the Women Police Volunteers, Sept. 1914; Agent to the Minister of Munitions for the training, supplying, and controlling of a force of police-women in HM Munition Factories, 1915. *Recreations:* riding, Alpine climbing, motor cycling. *Address:* Danehill Lodge, Lympne, Kent. *Club:* International Suffrage.

Died 18 May 1920.

DAWSON, Sidney Stanley, OBE 1920; JP; MCom, FCA; Professor of Accounting, Birmingham University, 1907–10; Mayor of the County Borough of Wallasey, 1915–16; head of firm of Dawson, Graves & Co., chartered accountants, Liverpool; *b* 1868. *Educ:* Blue Coat Hospital, Liverpool. *Publications:* The Accountants' Compendium, and other professional works. *Address:* 51 North John Street, Liverpool; Windermere House, Liverpool. *TA:* Problem, Liverpool. *T:* Bank 4163, Royal 546, Liverpool.

Died 19 May 1926.

DAWSON, Rev. William James; Emeritus Pastor of the Old First Presbyterian Church, Newark, NJ; *b* Towcester, Northamptonshire, 21 Nov. 1854; *e s* of Rev. W. J. Dawson, Wesleyan minister; *m* 1879, Jane, *d* of late William Powell, merchant, Lowestoft; three *s* three *d*. *Educ:* Kingswood School, Bath; Didsbury College, Manchester. Entered Wesleyan Ministry, 1875, holding various appointments at Wesley's Chapel, City Road, London, Glasgow, and Southport, until 1892, when he resigned his position as a Wesleyan minister; Minister of Highbury Quadrant Congregational Church, London, N, to 1906. During these years lectured widely on literature and historical subjects. Visited America, 1891, as a delegate of the Methodist Œcumenical Council, held at Washington, and lectured in various cities. *Publications:* A Vision of Souls (poems), 1884; Quest and Vision, Essays on Life and Literature, 1886 (republished with additions, 1892); The Threshold of Manhood, 1889; The Makers of Modern Poetry, 1890; The Redemption of Edward Strahan, A Social Story, 1891; Poems and Lyrics, 1893; London Idylls, 1895; The Comrade-Christ (Sermons), 1894; The Story of Hannah, 1896; The House of Dreams, 1897; Through Lattice Windows, 1897; Table Talk with Young Men, 1898; Judith Boldero, a Tragic Romance, 1898; Makers of Modern Prose, 1899; Savonarola, a Drama, 1900; The Man Christ Jesus, 1901; The Quest of the Simple Life, 1903; The Evangelistic Note, 1905; The Book of Courage, 1911; The American Hymnal, 1913; America, and other Poems 1914; Robert Shenstone: a Novel, 1917; The Autobiography of a Mind, 1925. *Address:* 583 Mount Prospect Avenue, Newark, NJ, USA.

Died 23 Aug. 1928.

DAWSON, Major (temp. Lt-Col) William Robert Aufrère, DSO 1916 and Bar, 1917; commanding 6th Battalion Royal West Kent Regiment; *b* 23 June 1891; *s* of William Dawson, MA, Oxon and Lincoln's Inn. *Educ:* Bradfield; Oriel College, Oxford. Joined the RFA (SR), 1911; regular commission in 1st Batt. Queen's Own (Royal West Kent Regiment), 1914; served with 6th Batt. RWKR till March 1916 (twice wounded that month in the Hohenzollern Redoubt, DSO, severely wounded at Monchy le Preux, May 1917, bar to DSO, Bt-Major); wounded near Cambrai, 30 Nov. 1917; wounded near Albert, 29 March 1918 (2nd Bar to DSO). *Recreations:* fishing, motoring, riding. *Address:* Cold Ash, near Newbury, Berks. *T:* Thatcham 7. *Club:* Army and Navy.

Died 3 Dec. 1918.

DAWSON-SCOTT, Gen. Robert Nicholl, JP; RE; Colonel Commandant RE since 1905; *b* 4 Feb. 1836; *e s* of Colonel Dawson, RE, CB, of Lee Grove, Blackheath; assumed name Scott, 1872; *m*

1870, Grace M., *d* of J. W. Nicholl Carne of S Donat's Castle, Glamorganshire. Entered army, 1854; General, 1897; retired, 1898; Commandant, School of Military Engineering, Chatham, 1888–93. *Address:* Brent House, Penrith.

Died 31 March 1922.

DAY, Rev. Charles Victor Parkerson, CBE 1919; TD; MA; Vicar of Glastonbury, Somerset, since 1912; Commissary to the Bishop of North Queensland; *b* East Hall, Feltwell, Norfolk, 1864; 4th *s* of Rev. T. H. C. Day, Limpenhoe Rectory, Norfolk; *m* Helen Constance, 4th *d* of Mark Lambert of Whitley Hall, Northumberland. *Educ:* Oundle; Durham; Cuddesdon College, Oxon. Priest and Deacon, 1888; served as Curate to St George's, Cullercoats, St Paul's, Beckenham; Chaplain (domestic) to the Bishop of Brisbane and Rector of Christ Church, Milton, 1899; Chaplain to the RAA and QDF Australia; to the Imperial troops in South Africa War (Queen's Medal and King's Medal with 5 clasps); Sub-dean and Canon of Townsville Cathedral, Archdeacon of Mackay, 1903. Returned to England, 1906; Rector of Limpenhoe with Southwood, Norfolk, and Principal of Abbey School, Beckenham, 1907; Rector of Wookey, Somerset, 1910; Chaplain to Somerset RHA, 1914; to SWMB, Dardanelles, 1915; Egypt, 1916; Senior Chaplain, Baghdad, and 3rd Corps HQ, Mesopotamia, 1917 (despatches); returned to England, 1919. *Address:* The Abbey House, Glastonbury.

Died 19 Aug. 1922.

DAY, James Roscoe, STD, DCL, LLD, LHD; Chancellor, Syracuse University; *b* Whitneyville, Maine, USA; *s* of Thomas Day and Mary Plummer Hillman; *m* Anna E. Richards; one *d. Educ:* Maine Wesleyan Seminary and Bowdoin College. Clergyman of Methodist Episcopal Church; pastorates in Portland, Boston and New York City; Chancellor of Syracuse University since 1893; elected Bishop of Methodist Episcopal Church, 1904, but resigned to continue in present position. *Publications:* The Raid on Prosperity; My Neighbour; The Working-Man; magazine articles, sermons, etc. *Address:* Syracuse University, Syracuse, New York. *T:* 973.

Died 13 March 1923.

DAY, Rt. Rev. Maurice, DD; Bishop of Clogher, since 1908; *b* Valentia Island, Co. Kerry, 2 Sept. 1843; *s* of Very Rev. John Godfrey Day, Dean of Ardfert; *m* 1873, Charlotte Frances Mary Forbes Ottley; three *s* one *d. Educ:* Queen's College, Cork (Scholar); Trinity College, Dublin. First Honourman in Mathematics, Trinity; Junior Moderator and Medallist and BA, 1865. Deacon, 1866; Priest, 1867; Curate of St Luke's, Cork, till 1870; Curate of St Matthias's, Dublin, till 1873; Vicar of Greystones, Co. Wicklow, till 1876; Rector of Killiney, Co. Dublin, till 1894; Incumbent of St Matthias's, Dublin, till 1905; Dean of Ossory; Dean of St Canice's Cathedral and Rector of St Mary's, Kilkenny, 1905–8; Commissioner of National Board of Education in Ireland since 1911. *Address:* Bishopscourt, Clones, Ireland. *TA:* Bishopscourt, Clones. *Club:* University, Dublin.

Died 27 May 1923.

DAY, Very Rev. Maurice William; Dean of Waterford and Rector of Holy Trinity with St Olaf, Waterford, since 1913; *b* 23 April 1858; *s* of Rev. M. F. Day, sometime Bishop of Cashel; *m* 1887, Catherine L. F. Garfit; three *s* one *d. Educ:* Repton School; Trinity College, Dublin. Ordained 1882; Curate of Queenstown, 1882–86; of Holy Trinity, Waterford, 1886–93; Rector of St John, Newport, Co. Tipperary, 1893–1904; Rector of Kilbrogan, Co. Cork, 1904–8; Dean of Cashel, 1908–13. *Address:* The Deanery, Waterford.

Died 29 Aug. 1916.

DAY, W. Cave, RBA 1903; *b* Dewsbury, 1862; *s* of Parker Day of Dewsbury; *m* Kathleen G. Maclellan, 2nd *d* of late G. W. Smales of Whitby; one *s* one *d. Educ:* privately. Always desired art as a career, and studied in leisure time from seventeen years of age; followed landscape under various masters; in 1890 devoted himself entirely to art, and exhibited same year at Royal Academy Gossips in St Ives; since then frequent exhibitor at Royal Academy, Royal Society of British Artists, Liverpool Walker Art Gallery, Manchester City Art Gallery, etc; studied in Paris under Benjamin Constant, Jules Lefebvre for painting, and M. Chapu for modelling, and was two years at the Herkomer School, Bushey; painter of Her Own Plot, One O'Clock, Passing, A Lady in White, etc; worked principally at portraits and figure subjects in oils, and fond of water-colour for landscape work. *Recreation:* violin. *Address:* Hilbree, Godrevy Terrace, St Ives, Cornwall.

Died April 1924.

DAYRELL, Elphinstone, FRGS, FRAI; District Officer, Southern Nigeria; *b* 16 Dec. 1869; *s* of late Edmund Marmaduke Dayrell, Captain, RN, and Bella Elphinstone Holloway. *Educ:* Cheltenham College; Germany. Solicitor; served in South African War, 1900–1, with 1st Bucks Yeomanry (Queen's medal and four clasps and commission as temporary 2nd Lieut in Army); Transport Officer and Political on Ebegga Expedition, 1903; Political Officer, Cross River Expedition, 1904; Political Officer, Anglo-Germany Boundary Commission, 1908–9 (African General Service medal and three clasps). *Publications:* Folk Stories from S Nigeria; Ikom Folk Stories. *Recreations:* shooting, fishing, golf. *Clubs:* Junior Army and Navy; Golfers'; Royal Ashdown Forest Golf.

Died 1917.

DEACON, Col William Thomas, CB 1900; retired; late of 13th Australian Light Horse Regiment (Queensland Mounted Infantry); *b* Ipswich, Queensland, 10 July 1850; *s* of W. T. Deacon and Louisa Shenton; *m* 1st, 1874, Elvina Buglar; one *s* two *d*; 2nd, 1884, Isabella M'Nevin; one *d. Educ:* private schools; Collegiate School, Ipswich. Served South Africa, 2nd in Command 4th Queensland Imperial Bushmen Contingent subsequently in command (despatches twice, CB, Queen's medal, four clasps). *Address:* Bellemount, Ipswich, Queensland. *Club:* United Service, Brisbane.

Died 4 May 1916.

DEADMAN, Henry Edward, CB 1904; FRSNA; MINA; *b* London, 7 March 1843; *s* of late John Deadman, of Brockley, SE; *m* 1870, Susannah (*d* 1890), *d* of late Captain Robert Dufill, of Rochester, Kent; one *s* one *d. Educ:* private schools; Royal Dockyard Technical Schools; Royal School of Naval Architecture, S Kensington. After completing professional education as above and obtaining diploma of Fellow of the Royal School of Naval Architecture (FRSNA), employed by Admiralty as follows: Assistant and principal overseer of war-ships building in private yards, also foreman of the yard, HM Dockyard, Devonport, 1867–80; constructor in charge of shipbuilding and engineering departments of the Indian Government Dockyard, Bombay, 1880–83; in this capacity was very highly commended in Government of India despatches for work in connection with the transport of the Indian contingent of the Egypt Expeditionary Force of 1882; constructor, HM Dockyard, Chatham, 1883–86; chief constructor, HM Dockyard, Portsmouth, 1886–92; Admiralty, 1892–1902; Assistant Director of Naval Construction, Admiralty, 1902–6; served as Member of several Admiralty Departmental Committees, and selected to give evidence before other Departmental and House of Commons Committees on subjects connected with naval architecture and dockyard management; several times received the thanks of the Board of Admiralty for services rendered; sometime Director of Cammell, Laird & Co., Ltd; the Fairfield Shipbuilding and Engineering Co., Ltd; and Holzapfels Ltd. *Address:* 10 Bolingbroke Grove, SW.

Died 20 March 1925.

DEAKIN, Hon. Alfred; MP; Barrister-at-Law; late member for Ballarat in the House of Representatives; formerly several times member of Federal Council of Australia, and of the Parliament of Victoria continuously for twenty years; Chairman of Committee of Public Accounts, Victoria; Chairman of Executive of Victorian Federation League; member of the three National Australian Federal Conventions; *b* Melbourne, 8 Aug. 1856; *s* of William Deakin, accountant, Melbourne (*d* 1892); *m* Pattie, *e d* of H. J. Browne, JP, Melbourne; three *d. Educ:* Church of England Grammar School, Melbourne; Melbourne University. Elected West Bourke 1879; Essendon and Flemington, 1889; Minister of Public Works and Water Supply, 1883–86; Solicitor-Gen., 1885; Pres. Royal Commn on Water-Supply, 1884; Chief Sec., 1886–90; senior representative Imperial Conference in London, 1887; member of Federal Council, 1889–95–97–99; member of Federation Conference, Melbourne, 1890; of National Australian Convention, 1891; of National Australian Federal Convention, 1897–98; Australian delegate from Victoria to London to secure passing of the Commonwealth Bill, 1900; first Attorney-General of the Commonwealth of Australia, 1901–3; Prime Minister Commonwealth of Australia, 1903–4, 1905–8, 1909–10; Leader Federal Opposition, 1910–13; represented Australia Imperial Conference, 1907. Bencher of Gray's Inn; received freedom of London, Edinburgh and Manchester; President of the Australian Commonwealth Commission to the San Francisco Exposition, 1915 LLD of the Berkeley University of California. *Publications:* Irrigation in Western America, 1885; Irrigation in Egypt and Italy, 1887 Irrigated India, 1892; Irrigation in Australia, 1893; Temple and Tomb 1894. *Recreations:* reading, a book-lover. *Address:* Llanarth, South Yarra, Melbourne.

Died 6 Oct. 1919

DEAN, Bashford, AM, PhD; Curator of Armour, Metropolitan Museum of Art; Hon. Curator Fishes and Reptiles, American Museum of Natural History; Professor of Vertebrate Zoology, Columbia

University; Professor of Fine Arts, New York University; *b* 1867, Puritan-Huguenot stock; *m* Mary Alice Dyckman. *Educ:* Columbia University; Munich; Col. City, NY. Held appointments US Fishes Commission; organiser of Cold Spring Harbour Biological Laboratory; Advisory Committee NY Aquarium; Major, Ordnance, USA, 1917–18. Chevalier Légion d'Honneur, member, fellow and correspondent of a number of European scientific societies. *Publications:* over two hundred brochures, memoirs, books, dealing with Fishes (anatomy, embryology, fossil), evolution (orthegenesis), and a hundred dealing with Armour ancient and modern. *Address:* Riverdale on Hudson, NY. *Club:* Century, NY.

Died 6 Dec. 1928.

DEANE, Rev. Canon Arthur Mackreth, MA; FRAS; Canon Residentiary, 1897–1923, and Prebendary of Middleton since 1883, in Chichester Cathedral; Vicar of Ferring, 1888–1918; Rural Dean of Storrington (Worthing division), 1904–6; Proctor in Convocation, 1906; *b* 1837; *s* of late Richard T. Deane, of Knutsford, Cheshire; *m* 1883, Mary Jane, *d* of C. Lennox Teesdale, JP, of Whyke House, Chichester; two *s* five *d*. *Educ:* Sedbergh School; Emmanuel College, Cambridge. Foundation scholar, 8th senior optime, 1859; ordained, 1860, and served curacies in Dioceses of Canterbury, Lichfield, and Manchester; Rector of East Marden, near Chichester, 1871–88; formerly secretary of the Diocesan Conference, the Diocesan Association, and Bishop of Chichester's Fund, and was secretary of the Brighton Church Congress, 1901; represented the Diocese on Central Council of Diocesan Conferences, and the Committees of SPG and National Society; gave evidence before the Royal Commissions on Education and Redemption of Tithe Rent Charge; served on Joint-Committee of Upper and Lower Houses of Convocation on Letters of Business, and on Committee of Lower House on Prayer Book Revision. *Publications:* was editor of the Chichester Diocesan Kalendar, and Gazette. *Recreation:* known as a composer of chess problems. *Address:* Apuldram, Chichester. *T:* Chichester 286. *M:* BP 8044.

Died 4 July 1926.

DEANE, Augustus Henry, CIE 1918; VD; *b* Geneva, 5 Nov. 1851; 3rd *s* of Rev. Barry O'Meara Dean, MA, Trinity College, Dublin; *m* 1876, Eugenie Amelia Frederica, *d* of John Frederic Galiffe, late HEICS, and *g d* of Lt-Col J. P. Galiffe, CB; one *s* four *d*. *Educ:* Geneva. Officer Volunteer Forces of India, 1885–1912; attended Coronation King Edward VII, 1902 (medal); Hon. ADC to Viceroy of India, 1905–10; commanded Volunteer dismounted troops at King George V Delhi Durbar (medal); Consul for Belgium in Madras, 1904–13; Consul Pondicherry and Karikal, 1913–20; Member of La Société Académique d'Histoire Internationale, Paris, and of L'Académie latine des Sciences, Arts et Belles Lettres, Paris. *Recreations:* riding, shooting, tennis. *Address:* c/o Mercantile Bank of India, Madras, India. *Clubs:* Madras, Madras; United Service, Bangalore.

Died 25 March 1928.

DEANE, Sir Henry Bargrave; Rt. Hon. Mr Justice Deane, Kt 1905; PC 1917; KC; Judge of Probate and Admiralty Division, High Court of Justice, 1905–17; *o surv. s* of late Sir James Parker Deane; *b* 28 April 1846; *m* 1875, Edith Mary, *e d* of late J. Lindsay Scott, Mollance, Kirkcudbrightshire; one *s*. *Educ:* Winchester; Balliol College, Oxford. International Law Essay Prize, 1870; Barrister, Inner Temple, 1870; South Eastern Circuit; Secretary of Royal Commission on Wellington College, 1879–80; Recorder of Margate, 1885–1905; Bencher of Inner Temple, 1895; Treasurer, 1917; QC 1896. *Publication:* A Treatise on the Law of Blockade. *Address:* 2 King's Bench Walk, Temple, EC; 52 Eaton Place, SW.

Died 21 April 1919.

DEANE, Hermann Frederick Williams, MA; FSA; Librarian and Chapter Clerk to the Dean and Canons of St George's Chapel, Windsor Castle; publisher and editor; Chairman, H. F. W. Deane & Sons, The Year Book Press; *b* Cork, 1858; *y s* of late Sir Thomas Deane, PRHA, of Dundanion Castle, Co. Cork, and Harriet, *d* of Major Williams; *m* Frances Gertrude Emily, *d* of late Rev. W. H. Cartwright; two *s* one *d*. *Educ:* Repton; Trinity College, Cambridge; BA 1881. *Publications:* Editor, Public Schools Year Book, Schoolmasters' Year Book, etc. *Recreations:* fishing, golf, philately. *Address:* Gower Lodge, Windsor. *T:* Windsor 135.

Died 21 Dec. 1921.

e BLAQUIERE, 6th Baron, *cr* 1800; **William de Blaquiere,** JP; Bt 1784; Great Alnager of Ireland; *b* 5 Sept. 1856; *s* of Charles de Blaquiere and Agnes, *widow* of W. Lawson; *S* cousin, 1889; *m* 1888, Marie Lucienne Henriette Adine, OBE, *d* of M. George Desbarats, Montreal; one *d* (and two *s* decd). *Heir:* none. *Address:* 3 The Circus, Bath. *Club:* White's.

Died 28 July 1920 (ext).

de BURGH, Colonel Ulick George Campbell, CB 1902; Knight of Grace of the Order of St John; *b* 19 July 1855; 2nd *s* of Thomas de Burgh (*d* 1872) of Oldtown; *m* 1883, Blanche (*d* 1915), *o c* of Charles Augustus Francis, *s* of Lord William Paget; one *s*. *Educ:* Trinity Coll., Dublin (BA). Entered 7th Dragoon Guards, 1876; Capt. 1881; Maj. 1890; Lt-Col 1897; Col 1900; served as Adjutant 7th Dragoon Guards, Egypt, 1882 (medal with clasp, bronze star); commanded 3rd Dragoon Guards, 1897; special service, 1900; Assistant Director, War Office, 1902; Staff, Gibraltar, 1906; retired 1908; recalled to Army Service, 1914. *Club:* Army and Navy.

Died 17 Nov. 1922.

DEBUSSY, Claude Achille; Chevalier Legion of Honour; composer; *b* St Germain-en-Laye, 22 Aug. 1862. *Educ:* Paris Conservatoire. Gained Grand Prix de Rome, 1884. *Works:* Pelléas et Mélisande; Ariettes oubliées; cinq Poèmes de Baudelaire; Fêtes Galantes; Trois Chansons de France; Trois Chansons de Charles d'Orléans; Quatuor à cordes; Petites Suites; La Damoiselle élue; Prélude à L'après-midi d'un faune; Trois nocturnes; La Mer; Images; Printemps; Ronde de Printemps; Gigue; Iberia; Le Martyre de Saint Sébastien; Ballades de Villon; Jeux; La Boîte à joujoux; Douze Etudes—En Blanc et noir; Children's Corner; 3 Poèmes de S. Mallarmé; Sonate pour Piano et Violoncelle; Sonate pour Harpe, Flute, et Alto; etc. *Address:* 24 Square du Bois de Boulogne, Paris.

Died 26 March 1918.

DECARIE, Hon. Jeremie L.; Chief Justice of the Court of Sessions of the Peace, Montreal, since 1919; *b* Aug. 1870; *m* 1st, 1898, Rose Alba (*d* 1902), *d* of A. C. Decary; 2nd, 1907, Juliette, *e d* of Hon. H. B. Rainville. *Educ:* Montreal College; St Mary's College; Laval University, later Université de Montréal. Advocate, 1896; KC 1906; MP (P) Hochelaga, since 1904; Maisonneuve since 1912; Minister of Agriculture, 1909; Provincial Secretary, Quebec, 1909; Life Governor of Notre Dame Hospital, Montreal; Hon. Lieutenant-Colonel, 85th Regiment, Montreal. *Address:* 857 Dorchester Street, West, Montreal. *Clubs:* Canadien, St Denis, Montreal Jockey, Montreal Hunt, Royal Montreal Golf, Montreal; Laval sur le Lac Golfe.

Died 5 Nov. 1927.

DE CELLES, Alfred Duclos, CMG 1907; FRSC; LLD; Chevalier de la Légion d'Honneur; General Librarian of Parliament, 1880 (then superannuated); *b* 15 Aug. 1844; father, French Canadian; mother, American; *m* Eugenie Dorion. *Educ:* Laval University, Quebec. Lawyer; Editor of Le Journal de Quebec; La Minerve, Montreal; L'Opinion Publique, Montreal. *Publications:* La Crise du régime parlementaire; la conquête de la liberté en France et au Canada; Les Etats Unis; Papineau (Political History of Canada); Papineau and Cartier (in English); La Fontaine, Cartier (in French); The Province of Quebec from 1867 to date; The Habitant in Canada; The Constitutions of Canada. *Address:* 49 Wilton Crescent, Ottawa, Canada.

Died Oct. 1925.

de COLYAR, Henry Anselm, KC 1905; *o surv. s* of late Augustine de Colyar, FRSE (direct descendant of Robert Collier, who came to England from France, temp. Henry VI; *m o d* and *heiress* of Sir John de Doddington and settled at Darlaston, Staffs), and Anne, *d* of Alexander Park; unmarried. *Educ:* The Oratory School, Edgbaston. Barrister, Middle Temple, 1871; Bencher of the Middle Temple, 1914; Gold Staff Officer at Coronation of King Edward VII (silver coronation medal), and at the Coronation of King George V (silver Coronation medal); member of English deputation from Catholic Union to Pope Leo XIII, 1903; a National Service Representative on Military Service Committees, 1918; member of the Court of Assistants of the Poulters' Livery Company, of which Company he was Renter Warden, Upper Warden, and Master. *Publications:* The Law of Guarantees and of Principal and Surety, 3rd edition; County Court-Cases; contributor to Encyclopædia Britannica, The Laws of England, Encyclopædia of the Laws of England, Encyclopædia of Forms, Encyclopædia of Accounting, Journal of Comparative Legislation, Great Jurists of the World, The Life of Colbert, etc. *Recreations:* travelling, golf. *Address:* 24 Palace Gardens Terrace, W; 1 Elm Court, Temple, EC. *Club:* Athenæum.

Died 31 Jan. 1925.

DECOPPET, Camille; *b* Canton of Vaud, 1862. Member of the Swiss Federal Council, 1912; later head of the War Department; President of the Federal Council of Switzerland for 1916; Directeur du Bureau International de l'union postale universelle, 1920; Radical Democrat. *Address:* Berne.

Died 14 Jan. 1925.

DE CUREL, Viscomte François; dramatic author; Member of the French Academy, 1918; Officer Legion of Honour; *b* Metz, 10 June

1854. *Educ:* Ecole Centrale. *Publications:* l'Amour brodé; l'Envers d'une Sainte; la Figurante; les Fossiles; l'Invitée; le Repas du Lion; la Nouvelle idole; la Fille sauvage; le Coup d'aile; la Danse devant le miroir; l'Ame en folie, Terre inhumaine, édit. Crès. *Address:* 5 rue de Solférino, Paris. *T:* Elysèe 6728; Château de Ketzing, Gondrexange, Lorraine.   *Died 26 April 1928.*

DEED, Rev. Canon John George, MA, DD; Vicar of Nuneaton (patron, the Crown), since 1893, and Canon of Coventry, since 1908; *b* 18 Sept. 1842; *s* of John Simpkin Deed and Elizabeth, *d* of John Cornell; *m* 1868, Elizabeth (*d* 1922), *d* of William Snowdon Gard; five *s* three *d. Educ:* University College School; New College, London; Trinity College, Dublin. Deacon, 1867; Priest, 1868; Curate of Paddock, Huddersfield, 1867–69; Hemel Hempsted, 1869–72; Clapham, 1872–73; Blakedown, in the Parish of Hagley, 1873–75; Organising Secretary National Society, 1875–83, also Hon. Secretary Church School Managers and Teachers Association; Secretary of ACS, 1883–93; also Hon. Secretary Ordination Candidates Exhibition Fund; Parochial Missions to the Jews Fund; Incumbents Sustentation Fund; Rural Dean of Atherstone, 1914; Chairman of the Governors of the King Edward VIth Grammar School, Nuneaton, since 1893; Chairman of the Nuneaton Higher Education Committee; Commissary of the Lord Archbishop of Perth, WA; Vice-President of the Additional Curates' Society. *Publications:* Sermons; Continuity of the Church of England, etc. *Recreations:* reading, change of work. *Address:* Nuneaton Vicarage, Warwickshire. *TA:* Deed, Nuneaton. *T:* Nuneaton 52. *Club:* Royal Societies.
                                                        Died 18 Jan. 1923.

DEEDES, Rev. Arthur Gordon; Vicar of St John the Divine, Kennington, 1911; Hon. Canon of Southwark Cathedral, 1911; *b* 4 Feb. 1861; *s* of Rev. Canon Gordon F. Deedes, Vicar of Heydour, Grantham. *Educ:* Haileybury College; Oriel College, Oxford; Cuddesdon Theological College. Ordained, 1884; Assistant Curate of St John the Divine, Kennington, 1884–1911; Warden of the Community of Reparation, Southwark, 1892; Commissary to Bishop Trollope of Corea, 1911. *Address:* 125 Vassall Road, SW. *T:* Brixton 1491. *Club:* New Oxford and Cambridge.
                                                        Died 29 Nov. 1916.

DEEDES, Ven. Brook; Rector of St Vedast, Foster Lane, 1913–21; Archdeacon of Hampstead, 1912–20; *b* 1847; *y s* of William Deedes of Sandling Park, Kent, MP for East Kent; *m* 1889, Mary Caroline, *d* of Hon. Mr. Justice Brodhurst. *Educ:* Harrow; Christ Church, Oxford. Ordained, 1871; Curate of St Mary, Charterhouse, 1871–75; Vicar of St Crispin, Bermondsey, 1875–76; Domestic Chaplain to Bishop of Calcutta, 1877–85; Chaplain at Allahabad, 1885–95; Archdeacon of Lucknow, 1892–97; Naini Tal, 1895–96; Moradabad, 1896–97; Fellow of Allahabad University; Vicar of Hawkhurst, 1897–1900; Vicar of Hampstead, 1900–13. *Address:* 8 Victoria Park, Dover.   *Died 28 Oct. 1922.*

DEEDES, Rev. Cecil, MA; FRHistS; Prebendary of Exceit in Chichester Cathedral, 1903; *b* 1843; *s* of late Rev. Lewis Deedes, MA, Rector of Bramfield, Herts; unmarried. *Educ:* Winchester; Brasenose College, Oxford; 2nd class Law and History School, 1866. Curate of St Philip and St James, Oxford, 1867–72; Chaplain of Christ Church, Oxford, 1868–72; Vicar of St Mary Magdalen, Oxford, 1872–76; Organising Sec. of Central African Mission, 1876–77; Canon of Maritzburg, Natal, 1877–80; Curate of Horspath, Oxford, 1881–82; Rector of Wickham St Paul's, Halstead, Essex, 1882–89; Curate of Brighton, in charge of St Stephen's Chapel-of-ease, 1889–1902; Prebendary of Hova Ecclesia, Chichester, 1902–3; Rector of Saints Martin and Olave, Chichester, 1910–20. *Publications:* articles in Smith's Dictionary of Christian Biography, 1877; Wase's Electra in Stuart Series, 1903; Editor Bishop Praty's Register, 1905; Bishop Rede's Register, 2 vols 1908 and 1910, both for Sussex Record Society; Consecration form of St Bartholomew's Hospital, Chichester, 1909; Church Bells of Essex (jointly with H. B. Walters) 1909; The Muniments of the Bishopric of Winchester, 1912; The Register of John de Pontissara, Bishop of Winchester (part i), for Canterbury and York Society, 1918; (part ii), 1914; (part iv with Introduction), 1916; contributions to Essex Review, 1917–18; Editor of Chichester Diocesan Gazette, 1905–14. *Address:* Frensham, Farnham, Surrey. *Club:* Authors'.   *Died 30 Dec. 1920.*

DEERHURST, Viscount; George William Coventry; JP, DL, Worcester; *b* 15 Nov. 1865; *e s* of 9th Earl of Coventry and Blanche, *d* of 2nd Earl of Craven; *m* Virginia, step-*d* of late Charles W. Bonynge; two *s* two *d. Educ:* Eton; Trinity Coll., Cambridge. Late Lieut-Colonel comdg 2nd Vol. Batt. Worcestershire Regt, 1894; served in European War, 1915–17 (despatches). *Heir: s* Hon. George William

Reginald Victor Coventry [*b* 10 Sept. 1900; *m* 1921, Nesta Donne, *e d* of 1st Baron Kylant]. *Address:* Pirton Court, Worcester. *Club:* Carlton.   *Died 8 Aug. 1927.*

DEERING, William Henry, ISO 1906; FIC; late Chemist, War Department; *b* 1848; *s* of late William Deering. *Address:* Glanmire, Bronshill Road, Torquay, Devon.
                                                        Died 5 Sept. 1925.

DE FREYCINET, C. L.; Sénateur; Ministre of State since 1915; Membre de l'Académie des Sciences et de l'Académie Française. *Educ:* l'Ecole Polytechnique et l'Ecole des Mines. Ingénieur des Mines, puis Inspecteur Général des Mines; Délégué au Ministère de la Guerre, 1870–71; Ministre de Travaux Publics, 1877–79; Ministre des Affaires Etrangères et Président du Conseil des Ministres, 1880, 1882, 1885 et 1886; Président du Conseil et Ministre de la Guerre, 1888–93; Ministre de la Guerre, 1898–99. *Publications:* Traité de Mécanique Rationnelle; Analyse Infinitésimale; Rapport sur l'Assainissement en Europe; La Guerre en Province, 1870–71; Essai sur la Philosophie des Sciences; Sur les planètes télescopiques; Principes de la Mécanique Rationnelle; De l'Expérience en Géométrie; La Question d'Egypte; Souvenirs, etc. *Address:* rue de la Faisanderie 123, XVIᵉ Paris.
                                                        Died 15 May 1923.

DEGAS, Hilaire Germain Edgard, artist; *b* Paris, 19 July 1834. *Educ:* Ecole des Beaux-Arts. *Works:* War in the Middle Ages, Salon, 1865; Steeplechase, 1866; Family Portraits, 1867; Ballet of La Source, 1868; Portraits of Criminals, 1880; Races, 1884; Interior of a Cotton-Broker's Office at New Orleans and The Rehearsal, 1900. *Address:* Rue Victor Massy 37, IXᵉ Paris.   *Died 26 Sept. 1917.*

de GEX, Colonel (temp. Brig.-Gen.) Francis John, CB 1914; CMG 1915; *b* 5 July 1861; Deputy Inspector General of Communications, since 1915; *s* of late George F. de Gex, MA; *m* 1905, Edith Hope, *d* of C. J. Miller, Oughtrington House, Lymm, Cheshire; one *s* one *d. Educ:* Reading; Sandhurst. Lieut West Riding Regiment, 1882; Capt., 1888; Major, 1900; Bt-Lt-Col, 1900; Bt-Col, 1907; Col, 1913; DAAG South Africa, 1901–3; DAQMG, Third Division, 1st Army Corps, DAA and QMG, 3rd Division, Aldershot Army Corps, DAA and QMG, Aldershot Command, 1903–7; AAG Irish Command, 1914; Expeditionary Force, Nov. 1914. Served S Africa, 1899–1902 (despatches, Queen's Medal 3 clasps, King's medal 2 clasps, Bt Lt-Col); European War, 1914–15 (despatches, CMG). *Address:* Highfield House, Rathgar, Dublin. *Clubs:* Army and Navy; Royal Western Yacht.   *Died April 1917.*

de HORSEY, Admiral Sir Algernon (Frederick Rous), KCB 1903; Deputy-Governor (Joint) Isle of Wight, since 1913; *b* 25 July 1827; *s* of late Spencer de Horsey, MP, of Great Glemham, Suffolk and Louisa Maria Judith, *d* of 1st Earl of Stradbroke; *m* 1861, Caroline, *d* of Admiral Drew; one *s* two *d.* Served on coast of Syria, 1840; senior naval officer during Jamaica insurrection, 1865, and Fenian raids on Lakes of Canada, 1866; ADC to Queen Victoria, 1871–75; Commodore in W Indies, 1872–75; Commander-in-Chief, Pacific, 1876–79; in the flagship Shah engaged Peruvian rebel iron-clad Huascar, forcing her to surrender to Peruvian authorities; the Admiral's action being questioned in Parliament, Sir J. Holker, Attorney-General, said "Huascar having committed acts which made her an enemy of Great Britain, de Horsey was justified in what he did"; commanded Channel Squadron, 1884–85; retired list, 1892. JP Hants; Chairman Isle of Wight Bench to 1918. *Publications:* Draysonia; African Pilot; Rule of the Road at Sea; Letters to the Press. *Recreations:* county administration, yachting, astromomy, mechanic's work. *Address:* Melcombe House, Cowes. *Club:* United Service.
                                                        Died 22 Oct. 1922.

DEIGHTON, Frederick, MA, MB Cantab; Consulting Surgeon to Addenbrooke's Hospital; *b* 20 April 1854; *s* of late John Deighton, Surgeon, Cambridge; *m* Louisa Ellen, *d* of late Francis Fisher, Crown Solicitor, Sydney, NSW; two *s* three *d. Educ:* St Peter's College Cambridge; St George's Hospital. Ex-President of the Cambridge Medical Society; Ex-President of the Cambs and Hunts branch o the British Medical Association; Lt-Colonel RAMC(T). *Publications* with the late Prof. Balfour, A renewed Study of the Germinal Layer of the Chick, Quarterly Journal of Microscopic Science; various paper in the Transactions of the Cambridge Medical Society. *Recreations* travel, golf, chess. *Address:* St Bernard's, Hills Road, Cambridge. *T* Cambridge 80. *M:* ER 825. *Club:* Royal Automobile.
                                                        Died 29 Sept. 1924

de KANTZOW, Commander Arthur Henry, DSO 1918; RN (retired); *s* of late Capt. Walter Sidney de Kantzow, RN; *m*; three *d.* Southern Nigerian Civil Service, 1906–13. *Address:* 3 Addison Court Gardens, Kensington, W14. *T:* Riverside 1453.

Died 6 March 1928.

de la BERE, Captain Richard Norman, DSO 1902; late Captain and Hon. Major 3rd Battalion King's Own Royal Lancaster Regiment; *b* 1869; *s* of late Major Charles Reed de la Bere, RMLI. *Educ:* Wellington. Served S Africa, 1900–2 (despatches twice, Queen's medal, 2 clasps, King's medal, 2 clasps). *Club:* Junior United Service.

Died 20 Sept. 1922.

DELAFAYE, Hon. Sir Louis Victor, KC; Chief Judge of the Supreme Court of the Colony of Mauritius since Dec. 1898; *b* 10 March 1842; *m* 1865, Marie Lucia, *o d* of late Theodore Cloarec, DMP. Called to Bar, Middle Temple, 1863; Municipal Councillor, St Louis, 1870; Member Prison Board, 1884; Member Civil Service Commission, 1884–95; Acting Puisne Judge, 1884–85, and 1890–92; QC 1892; Puisne Judge 1894; Acting Chief-Justice, 1898. *Address:* Port Louis, Mauritius. *Died 1920.*

DELAGE, Yves; Professeur de Zoologie à la Faculté des Sciences de Paris; Directeur de la Station Biologique de Rescoff, 1901; *b* Avignon, 13 May 1854; *m;* one *s* one *d. Educ:* divers collèges et lycées de province. Aspirant répétiteur au Lycée de La Rochelle, 1874; Préparateur de Zoologie (Hautes Etudes), 1878; Chargé de Conférences de Zoologie à la Sorbonne, 1880; Préparateur à la Faculté des Sciences de Paris, 1881; Maître de Conférences, 1882; Chargé de Cours à la Faculté des Sciences de Caen et Directeur de la Station Zoologique de Luc-sur-Mer, 1883; Professeur titulaire du même cours et Directeur titulaire de la station, 1884; Chargé du Cours de Zoologie, Anatomie, et Physiologie comparées à la Faculté des Sciences de Paris, 1885; Professeur titulaire du même cours, 1886; Directeur-adjoint du Laboratoire de Recherches de Zoologie expérimentale, 1889; Membre de l'Institut (Académie des Sciences), 1901; Darwin Medal of Royal Society, 1916. *Publications:* L'Appareil circulatoire des crustacés édriophthalmes (thèse), 1881; Evolution de la sacculine, 1884; Fonction des canaux demicirculaires et otocystes des invertébrés, 1887; Embryogénie des éponges, 1892; L'Hérédité et les grands problèmes de la biologie générale, 1895; L'Année biologique (23 vols, 1897–1918); Traité de zoologie concrète (6 vols parus 1896–1903); Nombreux Travaux sur la parthénogenèse expérimentale, 1900–8; Les théories de l'évolution, 1 vol., Bibl. scient. Internat., 1909; La Parthénogénèse naturelle et expérimentale, 1 vol. *ibid.* 1913; Divers travaux d'Océanographie publiés dans les Annales et le Bulletin de Monaco. *Address:* 14 rue du Docteur Berger, Sceaux (Seine), France. *T:* 16. *Died 3 Oct. 1920.*

de LANGE, Daniel; 'cellist, pianist, conductor, critic; Director, Amsterdam Conservatorium since 1895; *b* 11 July 1841; *m* 1st A. M. H. van Oordt (*d* 1910); 2nd, A. M. Gouda; two *s* three *d. Educ:* Rotterdam and Brussels. Virtuose-Violoncellist first at Vienna, afterwards Hungary, Galicia, Roumania, then a short time in Holland (Rotterdam); Paris, 1865–70; established himself in Amsterdam, 1870; was conductor of several choirs and teacher at the music school of the Maatsch. t. Bev. d. Toonkunst; General Secretary of the Society for Music, 1879; erected the Conservatory for Music, 1885; he made a journey with the Amsterdam à Cappella Choir to Vienna, Berlin, Leipzig, Dresden, Koningsberg, Brussels, Paris, London, etc, 1892–93. *Publications:* Symphonie; pieces for fortepiano; Songs; Cantata for Choir and Orchestra; Dramatic Scenes; a Theory of Music, etc. *Address:* Point Loma, California, USA.

Died 30 Jan. 1918.

DELANY, Mgr Patrick, DD; RC Archbishop of Hobart since 1908; *b* near Ballinamore, Co. Galway, Ireland, 1 Feb. 1853. *Educ:* St Ignatius' College, Galway, by the Jesuits; read philosophy and theology at All Hallows' College, Dublin; and higher philosophy and theology at the Catholic Instutute or University, Paris. Graduated there BD in 1879; his teachers included Duchesne, Martin, Bayonne, and Joven. Took the Chair of Civil History at All Hallows' College immediately after his elevation to the priesthood, 1879; proceeded to Australia on a commission from the College, 1885; elected to accept the position of Chancellor offered by the Bishop of Ballarat, 1887; Bishop of Laranda and acting coadjutor to Archbishop of Hobart, with right of succession to See of Hobart, 1893–1908. *Publications:* much on religious and economico-social questions in various publications, the Austral Light, the Ecclesiastical Record, etc, chiefly organs of the Roman Catholic Church in Australia. *Address:* Archbishop's House, Hobart. *Died 7 May 1926.*

DELANY, Rev. William, SJ; LLD; *b* 1835. *Educ:* Carlow College; Maynooth College; Gregorian University, Rome. Entered the Society

of Jesus at St Acheul, near Amiens, 1856; taught classics and mathematics in Clongowes and Tullabeg Colleges, 1858–65; studied in Rome, 1865–68; Priest 1866; Chaplain to Irish Zouaves in Rome, 1867; returned to Tullabeg College, 1868; Prefect of Studies, Tullabeg, 1868–70; Rector, 1870–80; travelled to Canada and the United States, 1881; Rector St Ignatius' College, Dublin, 1882–83; President, Catholic University College, Dublin, 1883–88; Missionary Work in Jesuit Church, Dublin, 1888–97; again President of University College, Dublin, 1897–1909; Provincial in Ireland, 1909–12; Senator of the Royal University, 1885–1909; Senator of the National University, 1909–19; and Member of the Governing Body of the Dublin University College, 1908; gave evidence before the Royal Commissions on University Education in Ireland. *Publications:* Lectures on Christian Reunion, 1897; pamphlets and letters on Irish University Education. *Recreation:* reading. *Address:* 35 Lower Leeson Street, Dublin. *T:* Dublin 532.

Died 1924.

DELANY, William P.; MP (N) Ossory Division, Queen's Co. since 1900; farmer; *b* 1855; *s* of Denis Delany, Roskeen; unmarried. Landholder in King's and Queen's Counties. *Address:* Tullamore, Ireland; House of Commons, SW. *TA:* Commons, London. *T:* 800–801 Victoria; 172, 293, 757 Western.

Died 7 March 1916.

de la RUE, Stuart Andros; *b* 29 May 1883; 3rd *s* of Sir Andros de la Rue, 1st Bt and Emily Maria, *d* of late William Speed, QC; *m* 1912, Margaret Griselda, *o d* of Alexander Wedderburn, KC; four *s* one *d. Educ:* Eton; Magdalen College, Oxford. JP Hertfordshire. *Address:* The Hoo, Willingdon, Sussex. *TA:* Willingdon, Sussex. *T:* Hampden Park 28. *Clubs:* Junior Carlton, Bath, Royal Automobile.

Died 26 Oct. 1927.

de la RUE, Warren William, JP; *b* 27 Feb. 1847; *e s* of Warren de la Rue, DCL, FRS; *m* 1916, Lilla Livingstone, *d* of late W. Forster Smithe, and *widow* of Sir Henry Thobie Prinsep, KCIE. *Educ:* private tutors. Entered the family business of Thos de la Rue & Co at the age of 22; very soon assumed the entire management and developed it fourfold; retired at the age of 42 and then took to racing and shooting; held over 10,000 acres of shooting at Chippenham near Newmarket, and kept a large stud of racehorses; his horse Thayles established a record by winning the Ascot Gold Cup, the Alexandra Plate, and the Goodwood Cup, all in 1889. *Address:* 3 Holland Park, W11. *T:* Park 2049; Thayles, Tenby, S Wales. *Club:* White's.

Died 15 April 1921.

DELAVOYE, Col Alexander Marin, CB 1902; *b* 12 May 1845; *m;* one *s.* Entered Army, 1864; Captain, 1878; Major, 1882; Lieut-Col 1888; Col 1891; Assistant Military Secretary for Education, 1898–1903; retired, 1903. *Died 26 April 1917.*

DELCASSE, Théophile; *b* Pamiers, Ariège, 1 March 1852; *m* Mlle Wallet. Joined staff of journal La République Française, and wrote articles on foreign politics; Conseiller-Général, Ariège, 1888; elected Deputy of Foix, 1889; Under Sec. for Colonies, 1893; Colonial Minister, 1894–95; Foreign Minister, 1898–1905; acted as mediator between United States and Spain, 1899; Minister of Marine, 1905–13; French Ambassador to St Petersburg, 1913–14; Minister of Foreign Affairs, 1914–15. Legion of Honour, 1887; Order of St Andrew, Russia, 1914. *Address:* Boul de Clichy 11, IXᵉ Paris; Les Cascatelles, Ax-les-Thermes, Ariège, France.

Died 21 Feb. 1923.

DE LEMOS, Charles Herman, ISO 1915; *b* 1855; *m* 1885, Guillermina Clemencia, *d* of John Dalton, Consul, USA; one *d. Educ:* private tutor; Continent. British Vice-Consul at Ciudad, Bolivar, 1887–99; HM Consul for the States of Bolivar, Apure, etc (Venezuela), 1899; retired, 1915. *Address:* 11 St John's Road, Harrow. *T:* Harrow 0574. *Club:* Union.

Died 27 Nov. 1928.

DELEPINE, Sheridan, MB, CM, MSc; Professor of Public Health and Bacteriology, (formerly Professor of Pathology), University of Manchester, since 1891; Director of Public Health Laboratories, University of Manchester, since 1901; Hon. Fellow, Incorporated Society Medical Officers of Health; *b* 1 Jan. 1855; *s* of Antoine Delépine of Paris and Henriette Mennet, Canton de Vaud, Switzerland; *m* Florence, *d* of Frederick Rose of London; one *d. Educ:* Collège Charlemagne, Paris; Académie de Lausanne; Université de Genève; Edinburgh University. 1st Class Honours MB CM Examinations; Lecturer in Physiology and Lecturer in Pathology, St George's Hospital Medical School, London, etc; BSc with distinction,

Lausanne, 1872; medical studies, 1877–82; Demonstrator of Anatomy and Pathology, 1881 and 1882. *Publications:* contributions to Anatomy and Physiology, Journal of Physiology, Proceedings of the Royal Society, Transactions of the Pathological Society of London, Practitioner, British Medical Journal, Lancet, Medical Chronicle, Journal of Comparative Pathology and Therapeutics, Journal of State Medicine, Public Health, Journal of Hygiene, Encyclopaedia Medica, Quain's Dictionary, etc, between the years 1883 and 1921. *Address:* 41 Palatine Road, Withington, Manchester. *T:* Didsbury 229; Public Health Laboratory, York Place, Manchester. *TA:* Laboratory, Manchester; *T:* Rusholme 8. *Club:* Authors'.

Died 13 Nov. 1921.

DE L'ISLE and DUDLEY, 3rd Baron, *cr* 1835; **Philip Sidney,** JP; Bt 1818; Major (late), Rifle Brigade; Hereditary Visitor of Sidney Sussex College, Cambridge; *b* 14 May 1853; *s* of 2nd Baron and Mary, *d* of Sir William Foulis, 8th Bt; *S* father, 1898; *m* 1902, Hon. Elizabeth Maria Astell, *d* of 4th Viscount Gort, and *widow* of late W. H. Astell, of Woodbury Hall, Sandy. *Educ:* Eton; Trinity Coll., Cambridge. Owner of about 10,000 acres. *Heir: b* Colonel Hon. Algernon Sidney, RFA, *b* 11 June 1854. *Address:* Penshurst Place, Kent; Ingleby Manor, Great Ayton, Yorkshire. *Club:* Carlton.

Died 24 Dec. 1922.

de LISLE, Edwin Joseph Lisle March Phillipps, DL; FSA; *b* Gracedieu Manor, 13 June 1852; 7th *s* and 13th *c* of Ambrose Lisle March Phillipps de Lisle of Garendon Park and Gracedieu Manor, Leicestershire, and Laura Mary Clifford, *g d* of 4th Lord Clifford of Chudleigh; *m* 1889, Agnes Henriette Ida, *e d* of Adrian Elias Hope and Lady Ida Duff, *sister* of 1st Duke of Fife; four *s* three *d*. *Educ:* Oscott College; Universities of Münster, in Westphalia, and Innsbruck, in Tyrol. Private Secretary to Sir Frederick Weld, GCMG, Governor of the Straits Settlements, 1881–82, and to Lord John Manners, late Duke of Rutland, when Postmaster-General, 1885–86; MP (C) Mid-Leicestershire, 1886–92. *Publications:* The Majesty of London; Centenary Studies on Luther and Wyclif; The Parliamentary Oath; The Royal Declaration Amended; The Evolutionary Hypothesis; joint author with Edmund Sheridan Purcell of Life and Letters of Ambrose Phillipps de Lisle. *Club:* Carlton.

Died 5 May 1920.

DELMEGE, Alfred Gideon, MVO 1898; MD, LRCSI; Hon. Surgeon to the King; Deputy Inspector-General of Hospitals and Fleets (extra); *b* 1846; *s* of Julius Delmege of Rathkeale, Co. Limerick; *m* 1884, Mary Elizabeth, *d* of late Rt Hon. James Anthony Lawson; two *s*. Entered Royal Navy 1869; served with Royal Marines during Ashantee War, 1873 (received thanks of the Admiralty); on board HMS Bacchante during cruise round world of TRH Prince Albert Victor and Prince George of Wales, 1879–82; in Royal Yacht Osborne, 1887–99; Hon. Physician to Prince of Wales, 1899; Hon. Surgeon to King Edward VII. *Address:* 33 Westcombe Park Road, Blackheath, SE.

Died 2 Feb. 1923.

de MAULEY, 3rd Baron, *cr* 1838 (UK); **William Ashley Webb Ponsonby,** JP; *b* 2 March 1843; *s* of 2nd Baron and Mary, *d* of 4th Earl of Bessborough; *S* father, 1896. Formerly Lieut Rifle Brigade and ADC to Gov.–Gen. of Canada. Owner of about 4000 acres. *Heir: b* Hon. Maurice John George Ponsonby, *b* 7 Aug. 1846. *Address:* Langford House, Lechlade, Oxfordshire.

Died 13 April 1918.

de MOLEYNS, Maj.-Gen. Townsend Aremberg; retired list, 1886; late the Royal Artillery; *b* Dublin, 20 June 1838; *o surv. s* of late Thomas de Moleyns, QC; *m* 1866, Selina Harriet, *o d* of Henry Sneyd French; one *s* one *d*. *Educ:* Royal Military Academy, Woolwich. Served at siege and fall of Sebastopol, and Fenian Raid, Canada. *Address:* 5 Brechin Place, South Kensington, SW7. *T:* 2860 Kensington. *Club:* Army and Navy.

Died 13 Nov. 1926.

de MONTMORENCY, Ven. Waller, JP Kilkenny; Archdeacon of Ossory since 1911; *b* 1841; *m* 1872, Mary, 3rd *d* of late Bishop O'Brien of Ossory, Ferns, and Leighlin; two *s*. *Educ:* Trinity College, Cambridge (MA). Ordained, 1865; Treasurer of Kilkenny Cathedral, 1883–91; Chancellor, 1891–1911. *Address:* Castle Morris, Knocktopher, Co. Kilkenny.   *Died 25 Oct. 1924.*

DE MORGAN, William Frend; author; *b* 69 Gower Street, 16 Nov. 1839; *s* of Augustus De Morgan, at the time Professor of Mathematics in University College, London, and Sophia Elizabeth, *d* of William Frend, expelled from Cambridge University for heretical opinions; *m* 1888, Evelyn Pickering, *d* of Perceval Andree Pickering, QC. *Educ:*

University College School, and College, Gower Street. Was student at Royal Academy, 1859, having adopted Art as a profession; in the years following 1864 was chiefly engaged in stained glass-work; in 1870 turned his attention to ceramic work, when his experiments in lustre, at that time not much known in England, attracted some attention among artists; in 1905 he commenced as a writer of fiction. *Publications:* Joseph Vance: an Ill-written Autobiography, 1906; Alice-for-Short: a Dichronism, 1907; Somehow Good, 1908; It Never Can Happen Again, 1909; An Affair of Dishonour, 1910; A likely Story, 1912; When Ghost Meets Ghost, 1914. *Address:* 127 Church Street, Chelsea, SW.   *Died 13 Jan. 1917.*

de MORLEY, 21st Baron in elder line by Writ, Eng., *cr* 1299; **James Thorne Parker Roe de Morley;** title brought in by marriages; Barony of Marshal, *cr* 1309; also the ancient Baronies of Hingham and Rie; claimed at Court of Claims for their Majesties Coronation, 1902, the office of Hereditary Royal Standard Bearer of England and the Marshalship of Ireland—having proved pedigree of blood descent in 1897–98 to the satisfaction of her late Majesty's Attorney-General, by royal command; *b* St Martin's-in-the-Fields, Middlesex, 17 Feb. 1844; *e s* of Freeman Roe, Hydraulic Engineer, late of Bridgefield Hall, Manor of Duntsford, Wandsworth, and Susan, *d* of Timothy Thorne, late of Westminster; *m* Emily Martha, *d* of Wm Passmore, late of Truro, Cornwall. *Educ:* College House, Southgate. Commenced business life with Jackson and Graham of Oxford Street; managed Duntshill Flock Mills for his father; was the leaseholder and proprietor of Ravensbury Wool Mills, Surrey, 1868; became an inventive engineer; took diploma of honourable mention, London International Universal Exhibition, London, 1884, and medals and diploma of special merit 1885 and 1886; travelled in South America, 1899. Staff Captain, Volunteer Civil Force, and Chairman of the Ways and Means Committee, Rusking House, Westminster, 1914–15; engaged making War munitions, Vickers, Ltd, June 1915; Inspector in their Maxim gun department, Jan. 1916; machinery distribution staff, 1917. *Publications:* words to Jubilee Anthem; book of poems on Doré pictures; Bobs' Call, recruiting poem set to music. *Recreations:* various; sketching and painting; founder of the Spencer Cricket Club, Surrey, and an early member of the West London Rowing Club. *Address:* Falcon Lodge, Oppidans Road, Primrose Hill, NW.

Died June 1918.

DEMPSEY, Sir Alexander, Kt 1911; MD; FRCSI; FRSM; Consulting Physician Mater Infirmorium Hospital; Clinical Lecturer in Gynæcology, Queen's University, Belfast; Member of Senate, National University; Member governing body, University College, Dublin; External Examiner, National University; *b* Coldugh, Ballymoney, 15 Feb. 1852; *s* of Bernard Dempsey; *m* 1876 (wife *d* 1905); three *s* four *d*. *Educ:* St Malachy's College, Belfast; Catholic University Medical School, Dublin; Queen's College, Galway. *Publications:* papers in medical journals. *Recreations:* golf, motoring. *Address:* 36 Clifton Street, Belfast; Coldugh, Fortwilliam Park, Belfast. *T:* 214; 2270.   *Died 18 July 1920.*

DENDY, Prof. Arthur, DSc; FRS, FLS, FZS; Hon. Member New Zealand Institute; Corresponding Member Royal Societies of Victoria and Tasmania; Professor of Zoology, King's College, University of London, since 1905; *b* 1865; *s* of Rev. John Dendy, BA; *m* Ada Margaret, *d* of late Louis Courtauld, Barrister; one *s* two *d*. *Educ:* Manchester Grammar School; Owens College, Manchester. Asst in the Zoological Department, British Museum (Natural History), 1887; Demonstrator and Assistant Lecturer in Biology in the University of Melbourne, 1888–94; Professor of Biology in the Canterbury College, University of New Zealand, 1894–1903; Professor of Zoology in the South African College, Cape Town, 1903–5. *Publications:* Outlines of Evolutionary Biology, 1912 (3rd edn 1923); The Biological Foundations of Society, 1924; numerous memoirs on systematic zoology, comparative anatomy, etc. *Address:* King's College, Strand, WC; 118 Corringham Road, NW11. *T:* Speedwell 1283. *Club:* Savile.

Died 24 March 1925.

de NEUFLIZE, Baron Jean; Officer, Legion of Honour; Head of Neuflize and Co.; Regent of the Bank of France; Président de la Compagnie d'Assurances Générales; Vice-Président de la Compagnie des Chemins de Fer, PLM; Président de la Régie de Tabac Ottoman, etc; *b* Paris, 21 Aug. 1850; *m* Miss Dolfus-Davillier (*d* 1926). *Educ:* Lycées St Louis et Buonaparte. *Address:* 7 rue Alfred de Vigny, Paris. *T:* 508–33; Château de Tilles, par Caye, Oise. *Clubs:* Rue Royale, l'Union Artistique, Bois de Boulogne, l'Ile de Pateaux, Paris.

Died 20 Sept. 1928.

DENHAM, Harold Arthur, DSO 1919; MA; Headmaster of the Harvey Grammar School, Folkestone, since 1920; *b* 20 March 1878;

s of Arthur Denham, of Harrogate, formerly of Ilford, Essex; *m* Phyllis Janet, *d* of John Tyrrell, Heston Moor, Stockport; two *d*. *Educ*: St John's College, Cambridge (Foundation Scholar and Prizeman); 1st Class Nat. Sci. Trip. 1901. Senior Science Master, High School, South Shields, 1903–5; Senior Physics Master, Hymers College, Hull, 1905–20; commissioned in 2nd East Riding of Yorkshire Volunteer RGA 1907, and in the East Riding RGA (TF) 1908; Captain, 1912; Major, 1916; served in France as Major commanding various Siege Batteries, 1916–17 and 1918 (DSO, despatches). *Recreations*: geology, photography. *Address*: The Harvey Grammar School, Folkestone.
Died July 1921.

DENHAM, Sir James, Kt 1921; *e* surv. *s* of J. Denham-Smith (*g s* of John Denham of Danescourt), of Bellevue and Vesey Place, Ireland, and York Terrace, London; *m* Grace, *d* of Colonel Hector Stewart Vandeleur of Kilrush and Cahircan and Cadogan Square, London, Lord Lieutenant of County Clare, and Charlotte, *d* of William Orme Foster, MP, of Apley Park, Shropshire, Stourton Castle, Worcestershire, Spratton Grange, Northampton, and Belgrave Square, London. *Educ*: Christ Church, Oxford (BA, MA). Raised considerable sums for charities by his rendering of sections from the English Classics, and addressed large audiences throughout the country on the Social and Political problems of the day. *Publications*: My Ladye and Others; Beauty at a Dinner-party; the Loves of Vandyck; the Log o' the Norseman; Serbelloni; The Roadways of London and sixty miles round; The Cradle of the Hapsburgs; the Byeways of Byron; The Prayer of a Peasant (Oberammergau Passion Play); Queen Mary o' Scots; The Love of Annie Lee; Wake up, England; The Gates of Dream; Songs from Beyond the Night; The Divine Desert; The Holy Shrine; Memoirs of the Memorable—(autobiography); Ode to December; The Passing of Christ; Sowing the Sunrise, etc. *Recreations*: hunting, fishing, cycling (cycled 60,000 miles in twelve different countries), photography; bred and exhibited black spaniels, Clumbers and St Bernards, for which he was a Crystal Palace prize winner. *Club*: White's. *Died 3 Oct. 1927.*

DENIKER, Joseph, DSc (Paris); Librarian of the Musée d'Histoire Naturelle, Paris; anthropologist and ethnographer; *b* Astrakhan, Russia, of French parents, 6 March 1852; *m*; three *s* one *d*. *Educ*: Technological Institute, Petrograd; Faculté des Sciences, Paris. Travelled in Caucasus and Persia, in Italy, Germany, Austria, etc, specially for ethnological research; President or Secretary of many International Congresses; late President of Société d'Anthropologie de Paris; Hon. Fellow of Royal Anthropological Institute of Great Britain, late President of Association des Bibliothécaires français; LLD (Hon.) Aberdeen; Delegate (for France) to International Catalogue of Scientific Literature; Vice-President of Société pour la Propagation des Langues étrangères en France; member of the Comité des travaux historiques et scientifiques; Chevalier de la Légion d'Honneur; Laureat of the Institut de France. *Publications*: Anatomie et Embryologie des Singes anthropoides, 1886; Anthropologie et Ethnographie de la Mission du Cap Horn, 1892 (with Dr Hyades); Les Races de l'Europe, 1896–1908; Bibliographie des Sociétés savantes de la France, 1889–95; The Races of Man, London, 1900; Les six Races de l'Europe (Huxley Memorial Lecture), 1904; Les Races et les Peuples de la Terre (2nd edn), 1916. *Recreation*: fond of collecting ethnographical photographs. *Address*: 36 rue Geoffroy Saint-Hilaire, Paris.
Died 18 March 1918.

DENISON, Col George Taylor; Hon. Colonel Governor-General's Bodyguard; *b* Toronto, 31 Aug. 1839; *s* of late Col George T. Denison; *m* 1st, 1863, Caroline (*d* 1885), *d* of late Oliver Macklem; 2nd, 1887, Helen, *d* of late James Mair, of Perth, Ontario; three *s* four *d*. *Educ*: Upper Canada Coll., Toronto; University of Toronto. LLB; ex-President of the Royal Soc. of Canada, 1903. Served 44 years in the Canadian Militia; commanded the Governor-General's Bodyguard in the Fenian Raid on Fort Erie, 1866 (medal and clasp); and in the North-West Rebellion, 1885 (medal); President of the Imperial Federation League in Canada, 1893–95; President of the British Empire League in Canada since 1896; Vice-President, Royal Colonial Institute, 1911. *Publications*: Manual of Outpost Duties, 1866; The Fenian Raid on Fort Erie, 1866; Modern Cavalry, 1868; History of Cavalry, 1877; Soldiering in Canada, 1900; The Struggle for Imperial Unity, 1909; Recollections of a Police Magistrate, 1920; also magazine articles in the Nineteenth Century, Westminster Review, and Canadian magazines. *Address*: Heydon Villa, Toronto, Canada, *Club*: National, Toronto. *Died 6 June 1925.*

DENISON, William Evelyn, JP and DL for Notts; *b* 25 Feb. 1843; *s* of late Sir W. T. Denison, KCB; *m* 1877, the Lady Elinor Amherst, *d* of 2nd Earl Amherst. *Educ*: Eton; Woolwich. Served in Royal Artillery; retired as Captain in 1878. MP (C) Nottingham, 1874–80.

Recreations: President MCC, 1892, and of Cricketers' Fund Friendly Society. *Address*: Ossington Hall, Newark. *Clubs*: Carlton, Junior United Service. *Died 24 Sept. 1916.*

DENNE, Major William Henry, DSO 1915; 2nd Battalion, The Bedfordshire Regiment; *b* 15 July 1876. Entered army, 1897; Adjutant, 1905–9; Captain, 1906; Major, 1914; Staff Captain number 9 District, Eastern Command, 1909–14; served South Africa, 1899–1902 (despatches; Queen's medal, 3 clasps; King's medal, 2 clasps); European War, 1914–15 (despatches, wounded, DSO for Neuve Chapelle). *Address*: Ingrave Cottage, Brentwood, Essex.
Died 21 Feb. 1917.

DENNEHY, William Francis; Editor, Irish Catholic since 1888, and sole proprietor since 1912; late Editor of Irish Daily Independent and Nation, Dublin; Editor of The Nation from 1896 until the period of its amalgamation with the Independent in 1900; *b* Kingstown, Co. Dublin; *e s* of late Alderman Cornelius Dennehy, JP, of Dublin, and Newtown Cashel, Co. Longford. Secretary to Lord Mayor of Dublin, 1886–87; originated the Irish Institute of Commerce and Industries, 1903; in the same year launched the project of an Irish International Exhibition, to be held in Dublin in 1906, under the patronage of the King; devoted much attention to the study of Irish economic and commercial problems; hon. sec. Irish Institute of Commerce, and also of the Irish International Exhibition of 1907; acted as an hon. sec. of the Citizens' Committees for the reception of King Edward VII and of King George V on their first visits to Dublin after their accession to the Throne; publicly thanked by HE Cardinal Logue, 1915, on behalf of the Bishops of Ireland for his services in securing appointment of sufficiency of catholic chaplains in Army and Navy; a Governor, Royal Hospital for Incurables. *Publications*: The Story of the Union told by its Plotters; many contributions to English and American reviews and journals. *Address*: 23 Leeson Park, Dublin.
Died 2 March 1918.

DENNETT, Richard Edward, FRAI, FZS; *b* Valparaiso, 1857; *s* of Rev. R. Dennett, DCL. *Educ*: Marlborough, 1869–74. Served Thomas Wilson, Sons, and Co., 1876–79; left for Africa in the employ of Hatton and Cookson, 1879; drew attention to irregularities in Congo Free State, 1886; edited manuscript newspaper called Congo Mirror, and accused Congo officials of murders and atrocities; with help he carried on the agitation until the Congo Reform Association was formed; in a series of letters to the African Mail entitled The Lower Congo he pointed out the injustice of the French rule and the concessionaire system in Congo Français; joined the Nigerian Forest Service, 1902; retired on pension, 1918. *Publications*: Seven Years among the Fjort (Fiote); Notes on the Folk-lore of the Fjort (with Preface by the late Mary Kingsley); At the Back of the Black Man's Mind; Nigerian Studies; West African Categories; British and German Trade in Nigeria; My Yoruba Alphabet; The African Table of Periodic Law. *Recreations*: study of the natives, golf. *Address*: c/o H. S. King and Co., 9 Pall Mall, SW1. *Club*: Royal Societies.
Died 28 May 1921.

DENNEY, Rev. James, DD; Principal and since 1897 Professor of New Testament Language, Literature, and Theology, United Free Church College, Glasgow; *b* Paisley, 5 Feb. 1856. *Educ*: Highlanders' Academy, Greenock; Glasgow Univ. and Free Church Coll. MA, BD, and DD (Glasgow); DD (Chicago Theological Seminary); DD (Princeton University and Aberdeen). Minister of East Free Church, Broughty Ferry, 1886–97. *Publications*: The Epistles to the Thessalonians, 1892, and the Second Epistle to the Corinthians, 1894 (Expositor's Bible); Studies in Theology, 1895; The Epistle to the Romans (Expositor's Greek Testament),1900; The Death of Christ, 1902; The Atonement and the Modern Mind, 1903; Jesus and the Gospel, 1908; The Way Everlasting, 1911. *Address*: 15 Lilybank Gardens, Glasgow. *Died 12 June 1917.*

DENNIS, Ven. Thomas John; Archdeacon of Onitsha, S Nigeria, since 1905; Commissary and Examining Chaplain to the Rt Rev. the Bishop in W Equatorial Africa; CMS Missionary in W Africa since 1893; *b* 1869; *m* 1897; three *s* two *d*. *Educ*: CM College, Islington; Durham Univ. (MA). Ordained, 1893; CMS Missionary, Sierra Leone, 1893–94; Onitsha, R Niger, W Africa, 1894–1906; Ebu, Owerri District, S Nigeria, 1906; 1906–13 mainly occupied in making a new translation of the Bible into the Ibo language for the British and Foreign Bible Society. *Address*: CMS, Ebu, Owerri, Southern Nigeria. *Died July 1917.*

DENNIS, Senator William; President of the Halifax Herald; *b* Cornwall, 4 March 1856; *m* 1877, Agnes Miller; two *s* five *d*. Went to Canada 1873; reporter, Halifax Herald, 1875; called to Senate,

1912. *Address:* Cobourg Road, Halifax, Nova Scotia. *Clubs:* Halifax, RNS Yacht, Golf, Halifax; Rideau, Ottawa.

Died 11 July 1920.

DENNISS, Charles Sherwood; Lieutenant-Colonel Engineer and Railway Staff Corps; General Manager, Cardiff Railway, Bute Docks, Cardiff, 1910–17; *b* 1860; *s* of late Henry Denniss, Goods Manager, North Eastern Railway Co., Hull; *m* 1st, 1891, Ethel, *d* of Henry Burnet; one *d;* 2nd, 1899, Edith, *d* of late Rev. Henry J. Pope, DD. *Educ:* Hull and East Riding College, Hull. General Manager, Cambrian Railways, 1895; previously District Superintendent, North Eastern Railway, Darlington; Assistant Docks and District Goods Manager, North Eastern Railway, Hull; formerly in the service of Great Western Railway at Shrewsbury and Reading; Member of the Advisory Trade Committee for South Wales under the Labour Exchange Act, 1909; Member of the Glamorgan County Territorial Association; Member of the Order of St John of Jerusalem (St John Ambulance Assoc.). *Recreations:* golf, cycling. *Address:* South Cliff, Penarth, Glam. *TA:* Denniss, Cardiff. *T:* Penarth 411.

Died 8 Dec. 1917.

DENNISTON, Hon. Sir John Edward, Kt 1917; *b* Scotland, 20 June 1845; *m* 1877, Helen, *d* of late Hon. John Bathgate, New Zealand. *Educ:* Greenock Academy; Blair Lodge; Glasgow University. Went to New Zealand, 1862; called to bar, 1874; Puisne Judge, Supreme Court, New Zealand, 1889–1917. *Address:* Canterbury, New Zealand. *Died 22 July 1919.*

DENNY, Captain Sir Cecil Edward, 6th Bt *cr* 1782, of Tralee Castle, Co. Kerry; Archivist to the Government of Alberta; *b* 14 Dec. 1850; 2nd *s* of late Rev. Robert Day Denny, Vicar of Shedfield, Hants (2nd *s* of Sir Edward Denny, 3rd Bt) and 2nd wife, Frances (who *m* 2nd, Very Rev. A. H. Boyd, Dean of Exeter), *d* of Thomas Waller of Ospringe, Kent; *S* half-brother, 1921; unmarried. *Educ:* Cheltenham Coll.; France and Germany. Sub-Inspector and Superintendent of the Royal North-West Mounted Police of Canada at its original formation in 1874, afterwards Captain and Inspector; was subsequently an official of the Indian Department (in charge of the Western Plain Indians during the Riel Rebellion, 1885), and a Police Magistrate. *Publication:* The Riders of the Plains. *Heir: c* Rev. Henry Lyttelton Lyster Denny, *b* 10 Sept. 1878. *Address:* The Library, Parliament Buildings, Edmonton, Alberta, Canada.

Died 24 July 1928.

DENNY, John M'Ausland, CB 1917; DL, JP; Chairman of William Denny and Brothers Ltd, shipbuilders and engineers, Dumbarton; Director of Caledonian Railway Co.; Hon. Colonel 9th (Dumbartonshire) Argyll and Sutherland Highlanders; *b* 1858; *s* of Peter Denny, Dumbarton; *m* 1885, Janet, *d* of J. Tulloch; four *d. Educ:* Dumbarton; Lausanne. MP (C) Kilmarnock District, 1895–1906. *Address:* Helenslee, Dumbarton. *TA:* Denny, Dumbarton; Rowlocks, London. *T:* Dumbarton 201; (London) Avenue 538. *M:* SN 302. *Clubs:* Oriental; Conservative, Glasgow.

Died 9 Dec. 1922.

DENNY, Sir Robert Arthur, 5th Bt, *cr* 1782; late Lieutenant 22nd Foot; *b* 23 July 1838; *e s* of Rev. Robert Day Denny, 2nd *s* of Sir Edward Denny, 3rd Bt, and Sarah, *d* of G. Grant of Soberton, Hants; *S* uncle, 1889; *m* 1872, Jane, *d* of T. Kirton, Exeter. *Educ:* Harrow. *Heir: half-b* Cecil Edward Denny, *b* 14 Dec. 1850. *Club:* Naval and Military. *Died 24 Nov. 1921.*

DENNYS, Colonel George William Patrick, CIE 1915; MRCS (Eng.), LRCP (Lond.); IMS; Inspector-General of Civil Hospitals, Central Provinces, India, 1911; retired from service, 1917; *b* 28 April 1857; *s* of General J. B. Dennys, Bengal Staff Corps; *m* 1885, Alice Isobel, *d* of Colonel Gordon Young, Bengal Staff Corps; one *s* three *d. Educ:* Bedford Grammar School; St Bartholomew's Hospital and School, London. Joined IMS 1879; entered civil employment, 1882; held appointments as Civil Surgeon successively at Karual, Amritsar, Kangra, Sialkot, Jullundur, Rawal Pindi, Amballa, Delhi, and Peshawar; Administrative Medical Officer, NWFP, 1908; Colonel, 1910; Principal Medical Officer Aden Brigade, 1910; Derajat and Bannu Brigades, 1910; served Afghanistan, 1880 (medal); Delhi Durbar medal, 1911. *Publications:* articles in Lancet and other medical papers in Litholapaxy, with special reference to the operation on male children; Indian Snakes, how they are caught and handled, Cornhill Magazine. *Recreations:* lawn tennis, golf, billiards, modelling in clay. *Address:* South Lea, Milford-on-Sea, Hants.

Died 30 July 1924.

DENNYS, Lt-Col Sir Hector Travers, KBE 1919; CIE 1915; Indian army; *b* 9 March 1864; *s* of General Julius Bentall Dennys, late BSC; *m* 1888, Lucy Maud Massy, *d* of General George Wheeler, late ISC; one *s. Educ:* Cheltenham; Sandhurst. Entered army, Manchester Regt 1885; Captain Indian army, 1896; Major, 1903, Lt-Col, 1911; served in Queen's Own Corps of Guides and 28th Punjabis; joined Punjab Police, 1888; Superintendent of Police, 1891; Deputy Inspector-General Police, 1906; Inspector-General of Police, 1914; retired 1919. *Recreations:* most games. *M:* P 47. *Club:* East India United Service. *Died 2 April 1922.*

DENT, Sir Alfred, KCMG 1888; JP Sussex; High Sheriff, 1908–9; merchant; *b* 1844; 3rd *s* of Thomas Dent; *m* 1896 Margaret, *d* of Charles Aird; one *s. Educ:* Eton. Engaged in business in China, Ceylon etc, since 1864; obtained the Royal charter for British North Borneo Co., 1881; a member of the Indian Silver Currency (1898) Commission. *Recreations:* hunting, shooting, rowing, tennis, etc. *Club.* Oriental, City of London. *Died 23 Nov. 1927.*

DENT, Lt-Col Henry Francis, JP, N and E R Yorks; Master of the Bedale Hounds, 1878–84, and 1896–98; *b* Ribston Hall, Yorkshire 1839; *m* 1870, Isabella (*d* 1908), *o c* of Rev. J. Tomkyns, Greenforth Rectory. *Educ:* Eton; Trinity College, Cambridge. Entered Army, 1859, 17th Foot; exchanged into 3rd Hussars; Major in 7th Dragoon Guards; employed on Remount Department in Canada during Boer War, 1900–2, and given rank of Lt-Col. *Address:* Menethorpe, near Malton. *Club:* Yorkshire, York.

Died 23 Nov. 1916.

DENT, Maj. Joseph Leslie, DSO 1914; South Staffordshire Regiment; *b* 10 April 1889; *y s* of late J. H. and Mrs Dent, Merivale, Edgbaston; *m* 1915, Isabel Doris, *e d* of Arthur T. Keen, Harborne Park, Harborne. Entered army, 1909; Captain, 1915; served European War 1914–15 (despatches, DSO).

Died 11 April 1917.

DENT, Joseph Mallaby; *b* Darlington, 30 Aug. 1849; *s* of George Dent (musician) and Isabella, *d* of Hugh Railton, of Staindrop, Co Durham; *m* 1st, 1870, Hannah (*d* 1887), *d* of George Wiggins London; four *s* two *d;* 2nd, 1890, Alexandra Campbell, *d* of Thomas Main, London; four *d* (and two *s* decd). *Educ:* Elementary Schools. Left Darlington for London at the age of 17 to finish apprenticeship in book-binding and printing; began business as a book-binder, 1872 commenced publishing in 1888, and had great delight in the production of the Temple Shakespeare, Temple Classics, Everyman's Library, the Collection Gallia, the King's Treasuries, complete edition of the Works of W. H. Hudson and Joseph Conrad, etc. *Recreations:* photography, archæology, travel; Member of British Archæological Society. *Address:* Crohamleigh, Harewood Road, South Croydon. *T:* Croydon 2588. *Died 9 May 1926.*

DENTON, Sir George Chardin, KCMG 1900 (CMG 1891); FRGS FZS; Governor of Gambia, 1900–11; *b* 22 June 1851; *y* and *o* surv *s* of Rev. R. A. Denton, Rector of Stower Provost, Dorset, and Mary *d* of George Wroughton, Adwick Hall, Doncaster; *m* 1879, Jean Margaret Alan (*d* 1900), *e d* of Alan Stevenson, FRS, Edinburgh; one *d. Educ:* Rugby; private tutors. Entered 57th Regiment, 1869; Lieut 1871; Capt. 1878; joined Colonial Service as Chief of Police, St Vincent, 1880; Colonial Sec. Lagos, 1888; administered the Govt of St Vincent, 1885–88; of Lagos, 1889–91; 1893–1900. Decorated for service in West Africa; retired 1911. *Recreations:* hunting, shooting, fishing. *Address:* Fairlight, Chigwell Row, Essex. *TA:* Chigwell Row *T:* Chigwell 73. *Clubs:* Windham, Naval and Military.

Died 9 Jan. 1928.

DENYS-BURTON, Sir Francis (Charles Edward), 3rd Bt, *cr* 1813 JP N Riding of Yorkshire and Carlow; *b* 15 March 1849; 2nd *s* of Sir George William Denys, 2nd Bt and Catherine Eliza, *e d* of M H. Perceval, MLC, of Spenser Wood, Quebec; *S* father, 1881 assumed by royal licence surname and arms of Burton under will of late Sir Charles William Cuffe Burton, 5th Bt; *m* 1890, Grace Ellen, *d* of late Col Adolphus W. D. Burton, CB, and *heiress* of Sir Charles William Cuffe Burton, 5th Bt; one *s* four *d* (and one *d* decd). *Educ.* Harrow; Paris. Entered Diplomatic Service, 1871; became 3rd Sec 1873; 2nd Sec., 1878; 1st Sec. of Legation, 1887; served at Athens, Brussels, Washington, Copenhagen, Mexico, Berlin, and Rome; Chargé d'Affaires at Brussels, Mexico, and Copenhagen; retired 1896. High Sheriff, Co. Carlow, 1906. *Heir: s* Charles Peter Denys, *b* 27 May 1899. *Address:* Draycott Hall, Richmond, Yorkshire; Pollacton, Carlow, Ireland. *TA:* Reeth. *Club:* Arthur's.

Died 19 Nov. 1922.

ENZA, Luigi; Chevalier de l'ordre de la Couronne d'Italie; Chevalier de l'ordre de Charles III d'Espagne; a Director of the London Academy of Music; Professor of Singing at the Royal Academy of Music; *b* Castellamare di Stabia, Italy, 24 Feb. 1846; 2nd *s* of Giuseppe Denza, Palermo (*d* 1864); *m* 1890, Mlle Dufour; one *s*. *Educ:* Naples Conservatoire of Music (Diploma); under the celebrated composer Saverio Mercadante, Paolo Serrao, and Carlo Costa (brother of Sir Michael Costa). Scholarship at Naples Conservatoire, 1862; Under-Professor, 1866; opera, Wallenstein, produced Theatre del Fondo, Naples, 1876; travelled through Italy, Russia, France, and England, giving recitals of his songs and singing lessons; first visit to England, 1879; settled in London since 1883. *Publications:* over six hundred songs, the most popular: Funiculì Funiculà; Si tu m'aimais; Come to me; Call me back; Fettered; A May Morning; 'Tis June. *Recreations:* walking, shooting, fishing. *Address:* 9 Clifton Hill, NW.

Died 26 Jan. 1922.

PARAVICINI, Percy John, CVO 1921 (MVO 1908); JP, Bucks; *b* 15 July 1862; 3rd *s* of Baron Prior de Paravicini; *m* 1891, Lady Marcia (Charlotte Sophia) Cholmondeley, 3rd *sister* of 4th Marquis of Cholmondeley. *Educ:* Eton; Trinity College, Cambridge. *Address:* Hillfield, Pangbourne. *T:* Pangbourne 47.

Died 11 Oct. 1921.

EPEW, Chauncey Mitchell, LLD; Chairman Board of Directors New York Central Rail Road Company, and Director in many other railroad companies; *b* Peekskill, New York, 23 April 1834; *s* of Isaac Depew and Martha Mitchell, *g d* of Rev. Josiah Sherman, *brother* of Roger Sherman, one of the signers of the Declaration of Independence; *m* 1st, 1871, Elise Hegeman (*d* 1893); 2nd, 1902, May Palmer; one *s*. *Educ:* Yale. Barrister, 1858; member Legislature, State of New York, 1861, 1862; Secretary of State of New York, 1863; Attorney for New York and Harlem Railroad Company, 1866; US Minister in Japan, 1866, and resigned; General Counsel for Vanderbilt System, 1875; Regent of the University of the State of New York, 1874–1904; Member of Corporation of Yale University, 1893–1905; Boundary Commissioner, 1875; declined United States Senator, 1885; candidate for Presidency, 1888; declined appointment of Secretary of State, 1892; United States Senator, State of New York, 1899, 1905–11; delegate at large to National Republican Conventions to nominate President of 1888, 1892, 1896, 1900, 1904, 1908; delegate, 1912, 1916, 1920, 1924; chosen as orator at unveiling of Statue of Liberty in New York Harbour; at Centennial of inauguration of George Washington as first President; at opening of World's Fair at Chicago; at Centennial Celebration of organisation of Legislature of State of New York, and on other occasions; Hereditary Member Society of the Cincinnati; Officer of the Legion of Honour. *Publications:* Orations and Addresses, eight volumes, 1911; Speeches and Addresses at 80, one volume; Addresses and Literary Contributions at 82, one volume, 1916; also one volume at 86, 1920; My Memories of Eighty Years, 1922; Miscellaneous Speeches at 92, one volume, 1925. *Address:* 27 W 54th Street, New York.

Died 5 April 1928.

E RAMSEY, 2nd Baron, *cr* 1887; **William Henry Fellowes,** JP, DL for Hunts; Custos Rotulorum, Isle of Ely; *b* 16 May 1848; *s* of 1st Baron and Mary, *d* of 4th Lord Sondes; *S* father, 1887; *m* 1877, Lady Rosamond Jane Frances Spencer-Churchill (*d* 1920), *d* of 7th Duke of Marlborough, KG; one *s* four *d* (and one *s* decd). *Educ:* Eton. Conservative. 1st Life Guards, 1867–77; Huntingdonshire Light Horse till regiment disbanded; Hon. Col Hunts Volunteers, 1901; Lord-in-Waiting to Queen Victoria; MP (C) Huntingdonshire, 1880–85; N Hunts, 1885–87. *Heir: g s* Ailwyn Edward Fellowes, *b* 16 March 1910. *Address:* Ramsey Abbey, Huntingdonshire; Haveringland Hall, Norwich; 3 Belgrave Square, SW1. *T:* Vic. 19.

Died 8 May 1925.

ERHAM, Hon. Frederick Thomas; *b* England, 8 Jan. 1844; *m* 1st, 1864, Ada M. Anderson; 2nd, 1878, Frances D. Swallow. Went to Victoria, 1856; MLA Sandridge, 1883–92; Postmaster-General, 1886–90. *Address:* Harptree, Sir William Street, Kew, Australia.

Died 12 March 1922.

ROBECK, Admiral of the Fleet Sir John Michael, 1st Bt *cr* 1919; GCB 1921 (KCB 1916); GCMG 1919; GCVO 1924; Commander-in-Chief Atlantic Fleet, 1922–24; Mediterranean, 1919–22; late High Commissioner, Constantinople; *b* 10 June 1862; 2nd *s* of 4th Baron de Robeck of Gowran Grange, Nass, Ireland; *m* 1922, Hilda, *widow* of Col Sir Simon Macdonald Lockhart, 5th Bt. *Educ:* HMS Britannia. Entered RN as Cadet, 1875; Lieut, 1885; Comdr, 1897; Captain, 1902; Rear-Admiral, 1911; Vice-Admiral, 1917; Admiral of the Fleet, 1925; late Inspector of Boys' Training Establishments; Admiral of

Patrols, 1912–14; Commanded Naval Force in Dardanelles during the time the Expeditionary Force was landed, 1915 (despatches). Legion of Honour; 1st Class Sacred Treasure, Japan; Grand Cross Order Crown of Italy. *Recreations:* hunting, shooting. *Heir:* none. *Address:* 5 Southwick Crescent, W2. *T:* Paddington 1754. *Club:* Army and Navy.

Died 20 Jan. 1928 (ext).

DERRY, Ven. Percy A.; Archdeacon of Auckland since 1914; Residentiary Canon of Durham Cathedral since 1922; *b* 5 Oct. 1859; 4th *s* of late Wm Derry, of Houndiscombe, Plymouth; *m* 1889, Blanche Mary, *d* of Robert R. Broad, Falmouth; three *d*. *Educ:* Harrow; Trinity College, Oxford. Studied for holy orders under Bishop Lightfoot at Auckland Castle; deacon, 1882; priest, 1883; first curacy at Holy Trinity, Stockton-on-Tees; curacy later at Sunderland; Vicar of Rawtenstall, Lancs, 1894–98; Vicar of Norbiton, 1898–1904; Rector of Gateshead, 1904–14; of Sedgefield, 1914–22; Rural Dean of Gateshead; Hon. Canon of Durham Cathedral. *Recreations:* walking, golf, reading. *Address:* The College, Durham. *Club:* County, Durham.

Died 13 Oct. 1928.

DERWENT, 1st Baron, *cr* 1881; **Harcourt Vanden Bempde Johnstone,** JP, DL; Bt 1795; Lieutenant, 2nd Life Guards (retired); *b* 3 Jan. 1829; *s* of Sir John Vanden-Bempde-Johnstone, 2nd Bt, and Louisa, 2nd *d* of Edward Harcourt, Archbishop of York; *S* father, as 3rd Bt, 1869; *m* 1850, Charlotte (*d* 1903), *sister* of 1st Lord Hillingdon; five *s* one *d* (and one *s* two *d* decd). *Educ:* Eton. MP (C) Scarborough, 1869–80. Owner of about 12,800 acres. *Heir: s* Hon. Francis Johnstone, *b* 26 May 1851. *Address:* Hackness Hall, Scarborough. *Club:* Brooks's.

Died 1 March 1916.

de SALES LA TERRIERE, Colonel Fenwick Bulmer, JP Hants and Oxon; the King's Body Guard of the Yeomen of the Guard; *b* 1856; *o s* of late Fenwick de Sales La Terrière, of Alstone, Gloucestershire, and Mary Gurney; *m* 1888, Agneta, *d* of late Charles Hambro, of Milton Abbey, Dorset; one *s*. *Educ:* Eton; Magdalen College, Oxford. Late 18th Hussars, retired 1888; served first Egyptian War (medal and clasp and Khedive's star); Nile Expedition (medal and clasp); Order of the Medjidie. *Publication:* Days that are gone. *Recreations:* shooting, fishing, racing. *Address:* Friary Court, St James's Palace, SW; Solent Cottage, Fawley, Hants. *Clubs:* Bath, Boodle's, Pratt's, Naval and Military.

Died 21 June 1925.

de SARAM, John Henricus, CMG 1901; *b* 1 Sept. 1844; *s* of Frederick John de Saram of Colombo; *m* 1867, Amelia Caroline (*d* 1891), 2nd *d* of Sir Richard F. Morgan, Kt, Queen's Advocate of Ceylon; three *s* one *d*. *Educ:* Colombo Academy (later the Royal College); St Thomas's College, Colombo; King's College School, London. A member of Ceylon Civil Service; became District Judge of Badulla, 1867; District Judge of Kurunegala, 1875; of Kalutara, 1883; Fiscal and Registrar-General, Colombo, 1886; District Judge of Jaffna, 1891; of Galle, 1891; of Kandy, Ceylon, 1893; Acting Treasurer of the Colony, 1902; retired on pension, 1906; acted as Commissioner of Assize in Colombo, 1908. *Address:* Hillside, Kandy, Ceylon.

Died 19 Dec. 1920.

DESBOROUGH, Maj.-Gen. John, CB 1873; retired Colonel, Royal Artillery; *b* 24 Jan. 1824; 2nd *s* of late Henry Desborough of Pilton, N Devon; *m* 1857, Eliza Mary (*d* 1891), *y d* of late Gen. Sir Peregrine Maitland, GCB, and Lady Sarah Maitland; three *s* four *d*. Employed as asst Royal Engineer in Canada during disputed boundary question, 1845–46; commanded the RA attached to 1st Div. of Expeditionary Force, China, 1860–61 (medal and clasps); brevet of Lieut-Col and CB; served in Canada, the Mediterranean, East and West Indies, and China; Governor, Oxford Military Coll., 1876–83. Decorated for China war, 1860–61. *Recreations:* fishing, inlaid wood-work. *Address:* Cross House, Northam, RSO, N Devon. *Club:* National.

Died 14 Jan. 1918.

DESCHANEL, Paul Eugène Louis; Membre de l'Académie Française et de l'Académie des Sciences morales et politiques; *b* 1856; *m* Germaine, *d* de René Brice, député. *Educ:* Collège St-Barbe; Lycée Condorcet. Licencié ès lettres et en droit; Sous-préfet de Dreux, 1878; Secrétaire général de Seine-et-Marne, Sous-préfet de Brest, 1879; de Meaux, 1881; député d'Eure-et-Loir, 1885; Vice-Président de la Chambre des Députés, 1896; Président, 1898–1902; Président de la Commission des Affaires Extérieures et Coloniales, 1905–12; Rapporteur du Budget des Affaires étrangères, 1906–12; Président de la Chambre des Députés, 1912; President of the French Republic, 1920. *Publications:* La Question du Tonkin, 1883; La Politique française en Océanie, 1884; Les Intérêts français dans l'océan Pacifique, 1885; Orateurs et Hommes d'Etat, 1888; Figures de femmes, 1889;

Figures littéraires, 1890; Questions actuelles, 1891; La Décentralisation, 1895; La Question sociale, 1898; La République nouvelle, 1898; Quatre ans de présidence, 1902; L'Idée de Patrie, 1905; Politique intérieure et étrangère, 1906; A l'Institut, 1907; L'organisation de la Démocratie, 1910; Hors des frontières, 1910; Paroles françaises, 1911; Segrais, Madame de Sévigné, 1911; Lamartine, 1913; Gambetta, 1920. *Address:* Palais Bourbon, Paris.
Died 28 April 1922.

DESHON, Edward, CMG 1902; *b* Belgaum, Bombay Presidency, 3 Jan. 1836; *s* of Lieut-Col C. J. Deshon, 17th Regiment; *m* 1863, Emily, *d* of late J. Sawyer. *Educ:* Bath Grammar School. Served in Crimea with 68th Light Infantry, 1854–55 (medal and clasp for Sebastopol, and Turkish medal); passed competitive examination for Staff College, 1861, but retired from service in October of that year; came to Queensland; managed the Cabulture Cotton Company; joined Public Service of Queensland, having amongst other positions filled that of Under-Secretary Public Lands, member of Land Boards, and Auditor-General for twelve years; retired from Public Service of Queensland, 1901; Trustee Agricultural Bank. *Address:* Kemendine, Coorparoo, Queensland. *Club:* Queensland.
Died 4 Sept. 1924.

DESHON, H. F., FRGS; *b* West Ashton, Wilts, 24 April 1858; *s* of Rev. H. C. Deshon, MD, late Vicar of East Teignmouth, Devon; *m* 1889, Nora, *y d* of late George Bird, Madras Civil Service. *Educ:* Sidney College, Bath. Entered the Sarawak Service, 1876, as cadet; appointed Asst Resident in charge of Batang Lupar District, 1881; promoted to Resident of the same district, 1883, which post he held till 1891, when he was promoted to Divisional Resident of the 4th Division; Feb. 1894–Aug. 1896, Acting Resident of the 1st Division; Personal Aide-de-Camp to His Highness the Rajah, GCMG, in which capacity he accompanied His Highness to England in 1883 and in August 1901; in June 1902 commanded a large punitive force sent to punish some turbulent head-hunters in the interior of Batang Lupar; Resident 1st Division March 1903; administered Government during absence of HH the Rajah, 1903–4; retired, 1904; Member Sarawak Station Advisory Council, 1913. *Address:* Southfield, Combe Down, Bath. *Clubs:* Sports, Royal Automobile; Bath and County, Bath.
Died 30 June 1924.

DESIKA-CHARRY, Sir Vembakkam C., Kt 1906; BA; BL,FMU; Judge of the Court of Small Causes, Madras, 1908–18; *b* 29 Dec. 1861; *s* of late V. Rajagopala Charlu. *Educ:* Presidency College, Madras. Member Corporation of Madras, 1896–1908; Lecturer in Law College, 1896–1900; additional Member Madras Legislative Council, 1904–8; High Court Vakil, Madras, 1887–1908; Fellow Madras Univ. since 1903; elected Life Trustee of the Victoria Memorial Fund and Member of the Council of the Victoria Technical Institute, Madras; Hon. Treasurer Madras Agri-Horticultural Society; sometime Vice-President Madras Collegiate Athletic Association, and Vice-President National Indian Association, Madras. *Address:* Padma Vilas, Luz, Mylapore, Madras. *T:* 390. *Clubs:* Cosmopolitan, Madras.

DE SMIDT, Henry, CMG 1901; JP; FSS; late Permanent Head of the Treasury, Accountant-General, Receiver-General, and Paymaster-General of the Colony of the Cape of Good Hope; *b* 6 October 1845; *m* 1878, Jessie, *d* of late Dr. J. Z. Herman, Cape Town. *Educ:* South African College. BA Cape University; certificate in Trigonometrical Surveying; elected a Fellow of the Royal Statistical Society, 1892. Entered Cape Civil Service, Colonial Office, 1865; served continuously in that office until 1898; promoted Under Colonial Secretary, 1891; also held the offices of Permanent Head of Convict Stations and Prisons Department, Inspector of Immigrant Coolie Ships and Controller of Printing; was specially charged with duties of Director of Census of 1891 (congratulations of the Government); Member of Civil Service Commission, 1913. *Publications:* Result of a Census of the Cape on the 5th April 1891; also various reports on convicts, prisons, etc. *Address:* The Cottage, Gordon Road, Kenilworth, Cape Town Suburb.
Died 13 Feb. 1919.

DE SOLA, Rev. Meldola; Rabbi of the Spanish and Portuguese Synagogue, Montreal; 1st Vice-President of the Union of Orthodox Jewish Congregations of the US and Canada; *b* 22 May 1853; *s* of Rev. Prof. Abraham de Sola, LLD, Prof. of Hebrew and Oriental Literature at M'Gill University, Montreal, and Esther Joseph; *m* 1887, Katherine, *d* of Rev. Isaac Samuel, late Senior Minister of the Bayswater Synagogue; one *s* one *d*. Received his theological education under direction of his father; entered ministry, 1882; one of three rabbis who formulated Declaration of Principles at first orthodox Jewish convention, New York, 1898; 1st Vice-President of the Union

of Orthodox Synagogues of the United States and Canada; preac' in England and the United States. *Publications:* numerous pamph and contributions to the press on Orthodox and Reform Juda' *Recreation:* music. *Address:* 35 MacGregor Street, Montreal.
Died 29 April 19

DE SOVERAL, Marquess, GCMG (Hon.) 1897; GCVO (H' 1903; Councillor of State; Portuguese Envoy Extraordinary Minister Plenipotentiary to the Court of St James's, 1897–19 Formerly Attaché and Secretary of Legation at Vienna, Berlin, Madrid; Ambassador Extraordinary to the late Peace Conferenc The Hague; Ambassador Extraordinary to the King's Coronati First Secretary, London, 1885; Minister, 1891; Secretary of State Foreign Affairs, Portugal, 1895–97. *Address:* 6 Granville Place, \ *T:* Mayfair 5337.
Died 5 Oct. 19

D'ESTOURNELLES DE CONSTANT, Baron (Paul He Benjamin); Member of the French Senate; *b* La Flèche, Sarthe Nov. 1852; *m* Miss Sedgwick-Berend; two *s* three *d*. *Educ:* Frar Diplomat eight years French Embassy, London. Member of Fre Parliament; Member of the two Hague Conferences; Member of Hague Court. *Publications:* many on politics, economic scier arbitration, limitation of armaments, organisation of peace; Pygmal' La Vie de Province en Grèce; La politique Française en Tur (couronné par l'académie Française); Les Etats Unis d'Amério Address: 34ter rue Molitor, Paris, 16ème; Château de Créar Clemont - Créans (Sarthe). *T:* Auteuil 05. 77.
Died May 19

DEUCHAR, William, MVO 1918; JP (Aberdeen); Passer Superintendent, Great North of Scotland Railway, 1900–18; retii 1918; *b* 1849; *m* 1881, Charlotte, *d* of late Charles William Sha' Line Engraver, Burnham, Bucks; two *s* one *d*. *Educ:* Auchter' Aberdeen. Local Chairman, St Andrew's Ambulance Associat' Member of Aberdeen Education Authority; Governor of the Nc of Scotland College of Agriculture. *Recreations:* gardening, mechar *Address:* 189 Great Western Road, Aberdeen.
Died 23 May 19

DE VEBER, Hon. Leverett George; Senator since 1906; *b* 10 F 1849; *m* 1885, Rachel Frances Ryan; one *s*. *Educ:* King's Colle Windsor; St Bartholomew's Hospital. MP 1898–1906. Add Lethbridge, Alta, Canada.
Died 9 July 19

DEVENISH, Very Rev. Robert Jones Sylvester; Dean of Cas' since 1913. *Educ:* Trinity College, Dublin (MA). Ordained, 18 Curate of St Patrick, Waterford, 1874–81; Prebendary in Waterf Cathedral, 1883–86; Archdeacon of Waterford, 1886–1913; V of Cahir, 1881–1913. *Address:* The Deanery, Cashel.
Died 16 Sept. 19

DEVITT, Sir Thomas Lane, 1st Bt, *cr* 1916; Senior Partner in firm of Devitt & Moore; late Chairman of Lloyd's Register Shipping; late President, Equitable Life Assurance Society; *b* 28 M' 1839; *e s* of Thomas Henry Devitt; *m* 1863, Fanny Theodora (*d* 19 *d* of late Ebenezer Pye-Smith; three *s* three *d* (and one *s* two *d* de' *Educ:* Madras House Grammar School, Hackney. Twice Maste' the Skinners' Company; President of the UK Chamber of Shipp' 1890; Chairman of the General Shipowner's Society, 1893, and one year of the London Missionary Society; President, Institute Marine Engineers, 1913–14. *Recreations:* travelling, a lover of art. F *g s* Thomas Gordon Devitt, *b* 27 Dec. 1902. *Address:* 6 Buckingh Gate, SW1. *T:* Victoria 1749. *Clubs:* City of London, Burlington F Arts, Arts, Oriental.
Died 8 Dec. 19

DEVLIN, Emmanuel, KC 1906; MP (L) since 1905; *b* 1872; *m* 19 Cecile, *d* of late Hon. L. B. Masson, Lieut-Governor of Quebec. E St Mary's College, Montreal; Mount St Mary's; BA Laval Univers MA Canisins College, Buffalo; BCL M'Gill University. *Address:* Besserer Street, Ottawa; Aylmer, P.Q, Canada.
Died 30 Aug. 19

DEVON, 14th Earl of, *cr* 1553; **Charles Pepys Courtenay;** Bt 16' *b* 14 July 1870; *e s* of Lord Courtenay (*d* 1898), *e s* of 13th Ear' Devon and Lady Evelyn Pepys, *d* of 1st Earl of Cottenham' grandfather, 1904. Major, 3rd Batt. The Prince Albert's (Somersetsl Light Infantry); Temp. Major, 1914–15. Inspector Board Agriculture, 1895–1904. Owner of about 10,000 acres. *Heir: b* P' Hon. Henry Hugh Courtenay, *b* 1 Aug. 1872. *Address:* Powderh' Castle, Exeter; Walreddon Manor, Tavistock; Ford House, New Abbot. *Clubs:* Carlton, Boodle's, Isthmian.
Died 4 Feb. 19

DEWAR, Lord; Arthur Dewar; KC Scotland; Senator of College of Justice, Scotland, since 1910; *b* Perth, 1860; 4th *s* of John Dewar, distiller; *m* 1892, Lettie Dalrymple, *d* of late Robert Bell of Clifton Hall, Midlothian; one *d. Educ:* Edinburgh University; MA. In practice at Scottish Bar since 1885; MP (L) South Edinburgh, 1899–1900 and 1906–10; Solicitor-General, Scotland, 1909–10. *Address:* 8 Drumsheugh Gardens, Edinburgh. *Clubs:* Reform; University, Edinburgh. *Died 14 June 1917.*

DEWAR, Sir James, Kt 1904; MA; FRS 1877; FRSE, FIC, FCS; Hon. LLD Glasgow, St Andrews, Edinburgh, Aberdeen; DSc Victoria, Oxford, and Dublin; Professorial Fellow of St Peter's College, Cambridge; Jacksonian Professor of Experimental Philosophy, University of Cambridge; Fullerian Professor of Chemistry, Royal Institution, London; Director of the Davy-Faraday Research Laboratory; co-inventor with Sir Frederick Abel of cordite, the smokeless powder used by HM Government; introduced into Science and Industry the Silvered Vacuum Vessels known as Dewar Flasks, or popularly as Thermos Flasks, for keeping cold or hot liquids or solids for long periods of time; *b* Kincardine-on-Forth, 20 Sept. 1842; *m* 1871, Helen Rose, *d* of William Banks, Edinburgh. *Educ:* Dollar Academy; Edinburgh Univ. Assistant to Lord Playfair when Professor of Chemistry, Edinburgh University; late member of the Government Explosives Committee; late President of the Chemical Society and the Society of Chemical Industry; President of the British Association, 1902; Hon. PhD (Christiania, Freiburg); Corr. Member of the French Academy of Sciences; Hon. Member of Institution of Civil Engineers and of many Foreign Societies; Foreign Member, Nat. Acad. Sci. USA; R. Acad. dei Lincei, Rome; Deutsch. Chem. Ges. Berlin; Acad. Roy. Sci., Belg.; received Gold Medals from the following Scientific Societies: England—Rumford, Davy, Copley (Royal Society); Albert (Royal Society of Arts); (Society of Chemical Industry). America—First Hodgkins (Smithsonian Institution, Washington); Franklin (Franklin Institute, Philadelphia). France-First English Award Lavoisier (French Academy of Science). Italy—First Award Matteuci (Società Italiana delle Scienze); also recipient of the Gunning Victoria Jubilee Prize of the Royal Society of Edinburgh, 1893; delivered the Bakerian Lecture of 1901 to the Royal Society on the Nadir of Temperature and Allied Problems; investigations include the following: Hydrogenium, Pyridine, and Chinoline Bases; Physiological Action of Light; Problems of Spectroscopy; Liquefaction of Gases; the scientific use of Liquid Oxygen, Air, Fluorine, Hydrogen—by evaporating liquid hydrogen under diminished pressure, a temperature of 13° absolute or 470° F of frost was attained; at this temperature hydrogen became a frozen foam-like mass, air a rigid inert solid; only helium of known gases remained uncondensed; pure metals cooled to this temperature became almost perfect conductors of electricity. By the use of charcoal as an absorbing agent for gases at low temperature the highest vacuum can be rapidly obtained, and gases like hydrogen, helium, and neon separated from air. Problems of capillarity; soap films of the greatest tenuity like the black of Newton's rings, which is about a hundred-thousandth of a millimetre thick, were shown to be exceedingly stable and long-lived, when made in a cryophorus vacuum; soap bubbles when blown in perfectly pure air can be preserved for a period of two months or more, and can reach a thinness when the bubbles are uniformly black, having lost all colour; photographs taken in natural colours of bubbles, 42 cm. diameter (17 inches), in various stages of development, were exhibited at the Royal Society, 22 June 1916. A gold loving cup was presented to Sir James and Lady Dewar on their golden wedding by the Members of the Royal Institution, 17 June 1921. *Publications:* Collected Papers on Spectroscopy (with G. D. Liveing), 1915; numerous papers contributed to the Proceedings of the Royal Societies of London and Edinburgh, the Royal Institution, the British Association, the Chemical Society, etc. *Address:* 21 Albemarle Street, W1. *TA:* Royal Institution, London. *T:* Regent 669; 1 Scroope Terrace, Cambridge. *Clubs:* Athenæum, Garrick. *Died 27 March 1923.*

E WEND-FENTON, West Fenton; Sole Proprietor and Controlling Editor of The World; *b* Oldbury, in Shropshire, 23 Oct. 1881; *e s* of William Fenton de Wend-Fenton, of Underbank Hall, Yorkshire (*d* 1899). *Educ:* Shrewsbury; Christ Church, Oxford (Classical scholar). Represented Oxford *versus* Cambridge in the Inter-University Steeplechase, 1900; whip to the Oxford University Drag Hounds, 1900–1; member of the Bullingdon Club; hunted four days a week at Oxford and kept a string of racehorses, which he rode himself in public; took honours in the final school of history. Owner of Vedas, winner of the Two Thousand Guineas in 1905 and many other races; rode Mark Time in the first hurdle race he won, and rode many other winners; Founder and Editor of the Looking Glass, later incorporated with the Sporting Times; late Editor and Managing Director of the Sporting Times. *Publications:* The Primrose Path; Realities. *Recreations:* hunting, racing, theatre-going. *Address:* 15 Park Square, NW. *TA:* Fentonlike, London. *T:* Gerrard 3807. *Died 6 April 1920.*

DE WET, Gen. Hon. Christian Rudolf; Minister of Agriculture, Orange River Colony, 1907–15; late MLA Vredefort; *b* Smithfield District, 7 Oct. 1854: *s* of Jacobus De Wet of De Wetsdorp; *m* 1873, Cornelia Margaretta Kruger, Bloemfontein; ten *c. Educ:* privately. Field Cornet Heidelburg District, 1881; served Boer War, 1881; Representative Lydenburg in Transvaal Volksraad, 1885; member OFS Volksraad, 1885–97; General and Commander-in-Chief of the Free State Forces during S African War; rebelled during European War, 1914; was defeated and taken prisoner; condemned to six years' imprisonment and a fine of £2000. *Publication:* Three Years' War. *Address:* Bloemfontein, ORC. *Club:* Bloemfontein. *Died 3 Feb. 1922.*

DEWEY, George; Admiral of the United States Navy; *b* Montpelier, Vt, 26 Dec. 1837; *m* 1st, 1867, Susan B. Goodwin (*d* 1872), *d* of Governor Ichabod Goodwin, of New Hampshire; one *s*; 2nd, 1899, widow of General Hazen. *Educ:* Naval Academy, 1854–58. Entered United States Navy, 1858; Commander, 1872; Captain, 1884; Commodore, 1896; Admiral of the Navy, 1899; served in Mississippi River in Farragut's squadron, 1861–63; in command of Asiatic squadron, 1898, when he destroyed Spanish fleet in Manila Bay on May 1. *Publication:* Autobiography, 1913. *Address:* Navy Department, Washington. *Died 16 Jan. 1917.*

DEWEY, Sir Thomas Charles, 1st Bt, *cr* 1917; JP; President Prudential Assurance Co.; Hon. Colonel 4th London (Howitzer) Brigade, RFA, Territorial Force; *b* 31 Aug. 1840; *s* of Charles Dewey of Cheshunt, Herts; *m* 1866, Clara (*d* 1913), *d* of Thomas Daws of Pyrford Place, Surrey; one *s* four *d* (and one *s* one *d* decd). *Educ:* Broxbourne, Herts. General Manager Prudential Assurance Company for thirty years, subsequently Chairman of the Company; Charter Mayor at the Incorporation of Bromley, 1903; Member of the Executive and Trust Fund Committee of King's College for Women, University of London; Deputy Chairman Royal National Pension Fund for Nurses; Member of War Office Expenditure Committee, 1916. *Heir: s* Rev. Stanley Daws Dewey, MA, Rector of Moretonhampstead [*b* 12 Aug 1867; *m* 1891, Emily Rose, *d* of late Rev. H. L. Pryce. *Educ:* Dulwich College; Pembroke College, Cambridge]. *Address:* South Hill Wood, Bromley, Kent. *T:* Bromley 455; Peak House, Sidmouth, Devon. *T:* Sidmouth 036. *M:* LM 3191. *Club:* Constitutional. *Died 13 July 1926.*

DE YOUNG, Michel Harry; proprietor and editor San Francisco Chronicle since 1865; *b* St Louis, 1849; mother's maiden name Morange, *d* nobleman of France; *m* 1880; one *s* four *d. Educ:* San Francisco. Delegate Republican National Conventions, 1888, 1892, 1908; twice member Republican National Committee, and vice-chairman one term; commissioner from California to Paris Exposition, 1889; Vice-President Columbian International Exposition, and originator of its classification plan, 1893; President International League of Press Clubs, 1893; organiser and director-general of California Mid-winter International Exposition, 1894; organiser Mid-winter Fair Memorial Museum, 1894; commissioner-general for California at Omaha Transmississippi Exposition, 1898; President United States Commission at the Paris Exposition, 1900; member French Legion of Honour; director Associated Press since 1882; Vice-President of the Panama Pacific International Exposition. *Recreations:* bicycling, golf, tennis. *Address:* 1919 California Street, San Francisco. *TA:* Chronicle, San Francisco. *T:* Chronicle Exchange 432, 25, and 7119; Tuckerway, Burlingame, Cal. *Clubs:* Lotus, Manhattan, Press, New York; Union League, Commonwealth, Merchants', Olympic, Golf, San Francisco. *Died 15 Feb. 1925.*

DHAR, Lt-Col HH Maharaja Sir Udaji Rao Puar Major, Bahadur, KCSI 1911; KCVO 1922; KBE 1918; Maharajah, 1918; *b* 1886; *m* eldest Princess of Sawantwadi State (Kaiser-i-Hind gold medal); five *c. Educ:* Daly College, Indore. Salute, 15 guns. Area of Dhar State, 1783 square miles. Population, 230,333. Had 8 motor cars. Principal organiser and contributor towards fleet of six motor ambulances in European War, 1915; also a second Ambulance Corps; and other war contributions. *Publications:* Driving in India; With Horses in India; With Rifles and Guns in Dhar State; Training of Vicious Horses. *Recreations:* shooting, polo, cricket. *Address:* Dhar, Central India. *Died 30 July 1926.*

DHARAMPUR, HH Maharana Shri Mohandevji Narandevji, Maharana of; a Sisodia Rajput; *b* 1863; one *s*. His State was 704 square miles in extent, and had a population of 114,995. Salute, 9 guns. Gross revenue, 9½ lacs of rupees. *Address:* Dharampur, Western India. *Died April 1921.*

DIAZ, Maresciallo d'Italia Armando, Duca della Vittoria; Collar of the SS Annunziata; Senator of the Kingdom; Vice-Presidente de Comitato deliberativo della Commissione Suprema di Difesa; *b* Naples, 5 Dec. 1861; *s* of Ludovico Diaz and Baroness Irene Cecconi; *m* 1896, Sara de Rosa; one *s* two *d*. *Educ:* Military Academy, Turin. Served Libyan War, 1912; European War; Commander-in-Chief of the Italian Armies, 1917. *Address:* Via G. Battista Vico 11, Rome. *T:* 20870. *M:* 55-14323. *Died 29 Feb. 1928.*

DIBBS, Sir Thomas Allwright, Kt 1917; General Manager of Commercial Banking Co. of Sydney, Ltd, since 1867; *b* Sydney, 31 Oct. 1832; *s* of Captain John Dibbs, St Andrews;*m* 1857, Tryphena Gaden; one *s* seven *d*. *Educ:* Australia College, Sydney. Joined the Banking Co. 1847. *Address:* Graythwaite, Point Piper, Edgecliff, Sydney. *Died 18 March 1923.*

DIBDIN, William Joseph, FIC, FCS, FRSanI, FMS; Analytical and Consulting Chemist; *b* London, 1850; *y s* of Thomas Colman Dibdin; *m* 1878, Marian, 2nd *d* of Augustine Aglio; three *s* five *d*. *Educ:* privately. Formerly Chief of Chemical and Gas Department, Metropolitan Board of Works and London County Council, 1882-97. Past President of Institute of Sanitary Engineers and of Association of Managers of Sewage Disposal Works; Past Vice-President of Society of Public Analysts; Inventions, etc; utilisation of micro-organisms for purification of sewage in contact and slate beds; Board of Trade standard pentane argand; radial photometer; Dibdin's hand photometer. In private practice since 1897. *Publications:* Practical Photometry; Purification of Sewage and Water; Lime, Mortar, and Cement; Public Lighting; editor and part author vol. iv Churchill's Chemical Technology; Composition and Strength of Mortars (research for and published by Royal Institute of British Architects); Papers (48), including Purification of Thames (1897 Journal Inst. CE), London Water Supply (Journal Soc. Chem. Ind. 1897), Recent Improvements in Biological Treatment of Sewage (*ibid*. 1906.) *Recreations:* golf, photography. *Address:* 31 Idmiston Road, West Norwood, SE27. *T:* Streatham 140.

Died 9 June 1925.

DICCONSON, Hon. Robert Joseph Gerard-; Master of Mr Gerard's Staghounds; *b* 8 Aug. 1857; *y s* of 1st Lord Gerard and Harriet, *d* of Edward Clifton; assumed surname of Dicconson by Royal Licence, 1896; *m* 1888, Eleanor, 2nd *d* of Mrs. Bankes, of Winstanley Hall, Lancashire; one *s* two *d*. Formerly Capt. 3rd Batt. KO Lancaster Regiment. *Address:* Wrightington Hall, near Wigan; 11 Chesterfield Street, W. *Clubs:* Boodle's, Marlborough, Turf.

Died 16 Sept. 1918.

DICEY, Albert Venn, KC; MA, Hon. DCL, Oxford, LLD (Hon.) Cambridge, Glasgow, and Edinburgh; Fellow of All Souls College, Oxford; *b* 4 Feb. 1835; *s* of Thomas Edward Dicey and Anne Mary, *d* of James Stephen; *m*1872, Elinor Mary, *d* of John Bonham Carter, MP. *Educ:* Balliol College, Oxford, late Official Fellow; then Hon. Fellow of Trinity Coll., Oxford. Barrister, Inner Temple, 1863; Vinerian Professor of English Law, 1882-1909. *Publications:* The Privy Council (Arnold Essay), 1860; Treatise on Rules for Selection of Parties, 1870; The Law of Domicil, 1879; Law of the Constitution, 1885; England's Case against Home Rule, 1886; Treatise on the Conflict of Laws, 1896; Lectures on the Relation between Law and Public Opinion in England during the 19th Century, 1905; (with Prof. Rait) Thoughts on the Union between England and Scotland, 1920. *Address:* All Souls College, Oxford; The Orchard, Oxford. *Club:* Athenæum. *Died 7 April 1922.*

DICK, Brig.-Gen. Archibald Campbell Douglas, CB 1900; CMG 1917; late 4th Battalion Argyll and Sutherland Highlanders; *b* 1847; *s* of late William Douglas Dick and Jane Hay, *d* of Sir Francis Walker Drummond, 2nd Bt of Hawthornden; *m* 1883, Isabelle, *d* of late John Parrott of San Francisco; six *d*. *Educ:* Stonyhurst. Served South Africa, 1900-1 (despatches, Queen's medal 3 clasps, CB). *Address:* Pitkerro, by Dundee. *T:* Broughty Ferry 151. *M:* SR 131. *Clubs:* Wellington; New, Edinburgh. *Died 5 Sept. 1927.*

DICK, Sir James (Nicholas), KCB 1895 (CB 1887); Hon. Surgeon to the King, 1901; *b* 1832; *m* 1868, Elizabeth, *d* of Robert Beveridge. Served in Crimean and Abyssinian Wars; Director-Gen. of Medical Department of the Navy, 1888-98. *Address:* 37 Upper Park Fields, Putney, SW; Sea Wood, Bembridge, Isle of Wight. *Club:* United Service. *Died 12 July 1920.*

DICK, Captain Quintin, DL, Co. Wicklow; *b* 1847; 2nd *s* of l Rev. Quintin Dick Hume [assumed by Royal Licence surname Dick, 1892]; *m* 1908, Lorna Katherine, *o d* of Major Penn Curzo Late Captain Derbyshire Yeomanry and Royal Antrim Rifles; Hi Sheriff, Co. Wicklow, 1898. *Recreations:* shooting, fishing, drivi stalking. *Address:* 12 Grosvenor Crescent, SW1. *T:* Vic. 60: Carantrila, Co. Galway. *Clubs:* Carlton, Bachelors', Arthur's; Kild: Street, Dublin. *Died 9 Dec. 19:*

DICKIE, William; Editor, Dumfries and Galloway Standard; *b* 18! 2nd *s* of late George Dickie, Dumfries; *m* 1884, Jane, *d* of R. Paterson, Dumfries (*d* 1917); one *s* three *d*. *Educ:* Moniai Newcastle-upon-Tyne. Ex-Chairman Parish Council; Chairman Books Committee of Public Library; Vice-President, Dumfries a Galloway Natural History and Antiquarian Society; Member Carlyle's House (Chelsea and Ecclefechan) Trust; ex-Preside Dumfries Burns Club; President, YMCA Social Centre; Trustee Foresters' Friendly Society. *Publications:* Dumfries and Round Abo sundry political and archæological pamphlets; papers in Transactic of Dumfries and Galloway Antiquarian Society, relating chiefly Scottish burghal life, and in various reviews. *Recreations:* rural ramb and unscientific observations in natural history. *Address:* Merlewoc Dumfries. *T:* Dumfries 268.

Died 12 Aug. 19!

DICKINS, Rev. Henry Compton, MA; Vicar of St Johr Winchester, since 1871; Fellow of New College, Oxford; *b* 2 O 1838; *s* of William Dickins of Cherrington, Warwickshire; unmarri: *Educ:* Winchester; New College, Oxford. A Master of Winches College, 1861-68. *Publications:* The Moral Lessons of the Fren Revolution in 8 Lectures. *Recreations:* reading, riding, driving. *Addr* St John's Vicarage, Winchester.

Died 4 June 19:

DICKINS, Col Spencer William Scrase-, CB 1916; Brig.-Gene *b* 27 Sept. 1862; 2nd *s* of late C. Spencer Scrase-Dickins, Coolhu: Sussex. Served Egypt, 1882 (medal with clasp, bronze star); N Frontier, India, 1897-8 (medal with clasp); European War, 1914– (despatches, CB). *Died 23 Oct. 19!*

DICKINS, Rev. Thomas Bourne, Doctor of Laws; *b* 7 Jan. 18: *s* of Richard T. Dickins, surgeon of King's Norton, Worcestershi and Amelia, *d* of Thomas Bourne of Highgate; *m* 1853, *o d* of Isa Trow of Balsall Heath, Birmingham; two *s* one *d*. *Educ:* Shrewsbu School; Jesus College, Cambridge. Ordained, 1855; Curate Thurstaston, Cheshire, 1855; St Nicholas, Warwick, 1857; Vicar All Saints, Emscot, Warwick, 1861-1914; Rural Dean of Warwi: 1890-1911; Canon of St Michael's Collegiate Church, Covent 1908. *Address:* Royston, Kenilworth Road, Leamington Spa.

Died 30 Jan. 19!

DICKINS, Ven. William Arthur; Vicar of Over-Stowey, Bridgwat since 1918.*Educ:* Lincoln College, Oxford; Lichfield College. Deac: 1886; Priest, 1888; Curate of Penn, Staff., 1886-91; Chapla Bombay Ecclesiastical Establishment, 1891; Ahmedabad, 18! Nasirabad, 1891-94; Aden, 1894; Kirkee, 1895; Nasirabad, 18! Malabar Hill, 1896; Domestic Chaplain to the Bishop, 1897 and 19(Chaplain of Kirkee, 1897; Senior Chaplain, 1901; Ahmednag 1903-05; Acting Archdeacon, 1905; Bombay Cathedral, 1906; Hc Chaplain to the Bombay Rifle Vols. 1906; Archdeacon of Bomb: 1907, and Commissary. *Address:* The Vicarage, Over-Stowey, ne Bridgwater. *Club:* Westminster.

Died 21 June 19:

DICKINSON, Frederic William; Director and Chief Editor Reuter's Ltd, since 1902; *b* Lee, Kent, 1856; *s* of Henry Dickinsc *m;* two *s* two *d*. *Educ:* Tonbridge School. For 43 years on Editor Staff at Reuter's. *Address:* Sherwell, Blackheath, SE10. *T:* Greenwi 1036. *M:* LK 4544. *Clubs:* Savage; Point House, Blackheath.

Died 2 Sept. 19:

DICKINSON, Lieut-Col William, CSI 1869; retired; *b* 1831; *m* Lau (*d* 1905). Entered army, 1848; Lieut-Col 1876; served Punja (*d* 1905). 1848-49 (medal with two clasps); Sind Irregular Horse, 1857 (me: with clasp); Rajpootana, 1859 (thanked by Gov.-Gen.); Abyssin 1867-68 (medal). *Address:* The Old Bear House, Bisley, Glos.

Died 9 June 19!

DICKINSON, Col William Vicris, CMG 1916; retired; AAG; *b* April 1856; *s* of Douglas J. Dickinson, Glanhonddar, Brecon; *m* 18! Mary Joyce, *d* of Jonathan Ambrose. Served European War, 1914– (despatches twice, CMG). *Died 28 Oct. 19!*

DICKSEE, Sir Francis Bernard, (Sir Frank), KCVO 1917; Kt 1925; DCL Oxford, 1926; RA 1891 (ARA 1881); President of the Royal Academy since 1924; *b* London, 27 Nov. 1853; *e s* of late Thos F. Dicksee. *Educ:* Rev. G. Henslow's School, London. First exhibited at Academy, 1876; since then has painted Harmony, Evangeline, The House Builders, The Symbol, The Love Story, Too Late, Romeo and Juliet, Chivalry, Memories, The Passing of Arthur, The Redemption of Tannhäuser, Mountain of the Winds, The Crisis, Startled, Funeral of a Viking, The Magic Crystal, A Reverie, Paolo and Francesca, The Mirror, The Confession, Dawn, An Offering, The Two Crowns, Yseult, La Belle Dame sans Merci, A Duet, The Ideal, The Shadowed Face, The End of the Quest, The Light Incarnate, The Moon Maiden, This for Remembrance, Daughters of Eve, and Portraits of Lady Aird, The Duchess of Buckingham, The Duchess of Westminster, The Marchioness Camden, The Hon. Mrs Ernest Guinness, Mrs Frank Shuttleworth, etc. *Address:* Greville House, Greville Place, NW6. *T:* Maida Vale 2642. *Clubs:* Athenæum, Arts.   *Died 17 Oct. 1918.*

DICKSON, Right Hon. Lord; Charles Scott Dickson, PC; KC; JP, DL; MA, LLD Glasgow and Aberdeen; Lord Justice Clerk, Scotland, since 1915; *b* Glasgow, 13 Sept. 1850; 2nd *s* of J. R. Dickson, MD; *m* 1883, Hester Bagot, *d* of W. Banks, Edinburgh; two *s. Educ:* Glasgow and Edin. Univs. Practised as law-agent in Glasgow, 1875–76; Advocate, 1877; Advocate Depute, 1892, 1895; Solicitor-General, 1896–1903; Lord-Advocate, 1903–6; Dean of the Faculty of Advocates, 1908–15. MP (C) Bridgeton Division, Glasgow, 1900–6; MP (U) Central Division, Glasgow, 1909–15. *Address:* 22 Moray Place, Edinburgh. *T:* Central, Edinburgh 5454. *M:* S 1799. *Clubs:* Carlton; New, Edinburgh; Western, Glasgow.
                                                              Died 5 Aug. 1922.

DICKSON, Rev. Canon Daniel Eccles Lucas; Vicar of Killeedy, 1872–1916; Canon of Limerick since 1905. *Educ:* Trinity College, Dublin. Ordained 1862; Curate of Aghalurcher, 1862–67; Incumbent of Garvary, 1867–72. *Address:* Hollybank, Lisnaskea, Co. Fermanagh.
                                                              Died 21 Oct. 1924.

DICKSON, Lt-Col George Arthur Hamilton, MVO 1910; Major 5th Worcestershire Regiment, Special Reserve; seconded to Egyptian Army, 1915; *b* 1863; *s* of late Rev. G. Dickson, MA, Vicar of St James the Less, Westminster; *m* Nanne, *d* of Consul Wiborg of Norway. Formerly in the Derby Regt; served through the South African War wth BMI (2 medals, 8 clasps); and was OC Regiment the SA Defence Forces; served on Staff in Egypt and France, 1916. *Club:* Junior Carlton.   *Died 16 Feb. 1918.*

DICKSON, Henry Newton, CBE 1918; Assistant Editor of the Encyclopædia Britannica; *b* Edinburgh, 24 June 1866; *m* 1891, Margaret, *d* of Richard Stephenson; one *s* one *d. Educ:* Edinburgh University; MA, DSc Oxon. Professor of Geography at University College, Reading, 1906–20; President Royal Meteorological Society, 1911–12; President Section E, British Association, 1913; Head of Geographical Section Intelligence Department, Admiralty, 1915–19; FRSE. *Publications:* Elementary Meteorology, 1893; Climate and Weather, 1912; Maps and Map Reading, 1912; papers and articles on Meteorology and Oceanography in Philosophical Transactions, Proceedings of the Royal Society of Edinburgh, Encyclopædia Britannica, Geographical Journal, Journal of the Royal Meteorological Society, Reports of Fishery Board for Scotland, etc. *Club:* Royal Societies.   *Died 2 April 1922.*

DICKSON, Maj.-Gen. John Baillie Ballantyne, CB 1893; CMG 1901; retired; *b* London, 24 Oct. 1842; *s* of late S. Dickson, MD, and Eliza, *d* of late D. Johnstone, Overton, NB; *m* 1st, 1871, Marion (*d* 1876), *d* of late C. F. Huth; 2nd, 1889, Kathleen, *d* of late W. J. Brown, Buckland Filleigh, N Devon. Cornet Bengal Cavalry, 1860; Adjt Lahore Light Horse; Adjt 18th Bengal Lancers; exchanged to Royal Dragoons; special service Zulu War, 1879 (despatches, Zulu medal and clasp); Nile Expedition, 1884–85; DAAG and DAQMG (severely wounded Abu Klea, despatches, medal with two clasps, bronze star); promoted Lieut-Col 5th Dragoon Guards; commanded Regt till 1893; commanded 49th Regimental District, 1895–97; Jubilee medal; commanded 4th Cavalry Brigade, 1897–99; commanded troops Straits Settlements, 1899–1900; commanded 4th Cavalry Brig. S Africa, 1900 (despatches, medal with five clasps); Lord of the Manor of Keevil; JP. *Address:* Keevil Manor, Trowbridge, Wilts. *Clubs:* United Service, Junior United Service, Cavalry.
                                                              Died 15 Aug. 1925.

DIGAN, Lt-Col Augustine J., DSO 1899; late 3rd Battalion (Reserve) Connaught Rangers; *b* 1878; *m* 1914, Helen, *d* of Angus Macregor.

Entered Mid-Ulster Artillery, 1897; served Nigeria, 1898 (despatches, medal with clasp, DSO); European War (wounded, despatches); resigned commission, 1922.   *Died 4 June 1926.*

DIGBY, 10th Baron (Ire.), *cr* 1620; **Edward Henry Trafalgar Digby,** Baron (GB) 1765; JP; Colonel Coldstream Guards; retired 1889; Hon. Colonel Dorset Garrison Artillery, TF; *b* 21 Oct. 1846; *s* of 9th Baron and Theresa, *d* of 3rd Earl of Ilchester; S father, 1889; *m* 1893, Emily, *d* of Hon. Albert Hood, 1893; three *s* three *d.* Lt and Capt. Coldstream Guards, 1868; Instructor of Musketry, 1869–72; Adjt 1874–76; Regimental Adjt 1881; served in Suakim Expedition, 1885. MP (C) Dorset, 1876–85. *Heir: s* Capt. Hon. Edward Kenelm Digby, *b* 1 Aug. 1894. *Address:* 16 Grosvenor Place, SW1. *T:* Victoria 3145; Minterne House, Cerne Abbas, Dorsetshire; Geashill Castle, Tullamore. *Clubs:* Carlton, Travellers'.   *Died 11 May 1920.*

DIGBY, Sir Kenelm Edward, GCB 1906 (KCB 1898); KC 1904; MA; *b* 9 Sept. 1836; *n* of 9th Baron Digby; *m* 1870, Caroline, *d* of 1st Baron Belper; two *s* two *d.* Barrister, Lincoln's Inn, 1865; Bencher, 1891; Vinerian Law Reader at Oxford, 1868–74; County Court Judge, 1892–94; Permanent Under-Secretary of State at Home Office, 1895–1903. *Address:* King's Ford, Colchester. *Club:* Athenæum.
                                                              Died 21 April 1916.

DIGBY, Samuel, CIE 1907; *b* 15 Oct. 1853; *s* of late William Digby of New Walsoken, Norfolk. For many years connected with the English Press in India; formerly Asst Editor of the Times of India; secretary of Indian Section of Royal Society of Arts since 1890, and of Dominions and Colonies Section since 1898; member of Organising Committee and Hon. Secretary for India of Seventh International Congress of Hygiene and Demography (London, 1891), and Hon. Secretary for India of Eighth Congress (Budapest, 1894); assisted in movement which led to appointment of a Select Committee of House of Commons to consider the grievances of Uncovenanted Services of India (1890). *Recreation:* country walks. *Address:* 1 Whitehall Court, SW1; Royal Society of Arts, John Street, Adelphi, WC2.   *Died 22 Sept. 1925.*

DIGGLE, Rt. Rev. John William, DD; Bishop of Carlisle since 1905; *b* Strawberry Hill, Pendleton, 2 March 1847; *e s* of W. Diggle, 19 Cornwall Terrace, Regent's Park, NW; *m* 1st, 1874, Cicely Jane, *y d* of John Butterfield, Broughton, Manchester; 2nd, 1884, Edith Moss, *y d* of Gilbert Winter Moss, The Beach, Aigburth, Liverpool; four *s* one *d. Educ:* Manchester Grammar School; Merton Coll. Oxford. Math. Postmaster, Merton Coll. 1866; 1st class Law and History, 1870. Lectr Merton and CCC Colleges, Oxford, 1871; BA, MA in same Class List of Final Honours School with Rt Hon. A. D. Acland, MP, and late Lord Randolph Churchill, MP. Ordained, 1871; Curate Whalley Range, 1871; All Saints', Liverpool, 1872; St John's, Walton, 1874; Vicar of Mossley Hill, 1875–97, Surrogate; Rural Dean of Childwall, 1882; Hon. Canon of Liverpool, 1887; President of Liverpool Council of Education, 1891; Select Preacher, University of Oxford, 1899; Canon of Carlisle and Archdeacon of Westmorland, 1896–1902; Examining Chaplain to Bishop of Carlisle, 1896–1902; Archdeacon of Birmingham, 1903–4; Rector, Birmingham, 1902–5, and Rural Dean, 1903–4; late Examining Chaplain to Bishop of Worcester. *Publications:* Godliness and Manliness; True Religion; Bishop Fraser's University and Parochial Sermons; Bishop Fraser's Lancashire Life; Rainbows; Religious Doubt; Short Studies in Holiness; Quiet Hours with the Ordinal; Home Life; The Ministry of the Word and Sacraments; The Foundations of Duty; Death and the After-Life. *Recreation:* fishing. *Address:* Rose Castle, Carlisle. *Club:* Athenæum.   *Died 24 March 1920.*

DIGGLE, Joseph Robert, JP; MA; *b* 12 May 1849; *y s* of William Diggle, Park House, Astley; *m* 1878, Janie Wigley, *d* of J. W. Macrae, Aigburth, Liverpool; two *s* two *d. Educ:* Manchester Grammar School; Wadham College, Oxford. 1st class Modern History. Curate, St Mary's, Bryanston Square, W, 1876–79; resigned to devote himself to public work; was nominated at General Election (1885) for West Marylebone to test eligibility of clergy to be nominated; received 101 votes; removed, under the Clerical Disabilities Act, his ineligibility to sit in Parliament in 1889; contested Camberwell (U) 1900. Member London School Board (Marylebone Div.), 1879–97; Chairman London School Board, 1885–94; member of Kent County Council, 1898; Chairman of Elementary Schools Education Committee, Kent, 1903; Mayor of Tenterden, 1896–99; Chairman of the Council of the Royal Botanic Society, 1907; Chairman of the Council of the Ragged School Union and Shaftesbury Society, 1906–8; Hon. Fellow of British Institute of Public Health; Corresponding Member of Société Royale de Médecine Publique de Belgique, 1891; President of Sect. V International Congress of Hygiene and Demography,

London, 1892 and of Sect. VI at Buda Pesth 1894. *Publications:* Pleas for Better Administration upon the London School Board, 1881 and 1885. *Recreations:* tennis, out-door games. *Address:* St Michael's Grange, Tenterden, Kent; 24 Merton Street, Oxford.
Died 16 June 1917.

DILKE, Sir Charles Wentworth, 3rd Bt, *cr* 1862; *b* 19 Sept. 1874; *e s* of Sir Charles Wentworth Dilke, 2nd Bt and Katherine, *o d* of late Capt. Arthur Gore Sheil, *S* father, 1911; *m* 1915, Florence Pearl, *d* of Henry Montague Faithfull, NSW. *Educ:* Rugby; Trinity Hall, Cambridge. *Recreations:* travel, riding, rowing, swimming, golf. *Heir:* *c* Fisher Wentworth Dilke, *b* 5 Jan. 1877.
Died 7 Dec. 1918.

DILL, Sir Samuel, Kt 1909; MA, Hon. LittD Dublin; Hon. LLD Dublin; Hon. LLD Edinburgh and St Andrews; Hon. Fellow, Corpus Christi College, Oxford; Professor of Greek, Queen's College, Belfast, since 1890; *b* 26 March 1844; *e s* of Rev. S. M. Dill, DD; *m* 1884, Fanny Elizabeth, *d* of Richard Cadwallader Morgan; three *d*. *Educ:* Royal Academical Institution, Belfast; Queen's College, Belfast; Lincoln College, Oxford. First-class Moderations, 1867; first class final Classical Schools, 1869. Lecturer, Lincoln College, 1869; Fellow, Dean, and Tutor, Corpus Christi College, 1869–77; High Master of Manchester Grammar School, 1877–88; Governor of Owens Coll. Manchester, and of Victoria Univ., 1880–89; Chairman of Intermediate Board, Ireland; Member of Belfast University Commission, and Pro-Chancellor of Queen's University; Chairman of Vice-Regal Committee on Primary Education, Ireland, 1913. *Publications:* Roman Society in the last Century of the Western Empire, 3rd edn; Roman Society from Nero to Marcus Aurelius, 2nd edn. *Address:* Montpelier, Malone Road, Belfast. *Clubs:* Athenæum; Ulster, Belfast.
Died 26 May 1924.

DILL, Very Rev. S. Marcus, MA, DD; Minister of Alloway Parish, Ayrshire; resigned, 1918; Ex-Moderator of Church of Scotland; *b* Belfast, 1843; *s* of late Professor Robert Foster Dill, MD, Belfast; *m* 1878, Agnes Graham, *d* of late John James Rowe of Dinglefield, Liverpool; two *s* four *d*. *Educ:* Royal Belfast Institution; Queen's College, Belfast (scholar); Assembly's Theological College, Belfast; Theological College, Geneva; graduated MA Queen's University, Ireland (first-class Honours and a gold medal). Early Ministry spent in the Parishes of Lower Cumber, Co. Londonderry, and Ballymena, Co. Antrim; a prominent member of Church Courts, taking an active interest in many Church enterprises, and specially in augmentation of Small Livings. *Publications:* sermons; contributed occasionally to Theological and Literary magazines. *Address:* 23 Greenhill Gardens, Edinburgh. *T:* Edinburgh 6351. *Club:* Scottish Conservative, Edinburgh.
Died 23 Jan. 1924.

DILLON, Captain Constantine Theobald Francis, DSO 1902; late 4th Battalion Worcestershire Regiment; *b* 9 Sept. 1873; *e s* of Lt-Col H. B. C. Dillon, of Redhurst, Cranleigh. Entered army, 1899; Captain, 1902; served South Africa, 1899–1900 (dangerously wounded, despatches, Queen's medal, three clasps, DSO).
Died 27 April 1920.

DILLON, Major Henry Mountford, DSO 1915; Oxford and Bucks Light Infantry; *b* 20 Jan. 1881; *s* of late H. B. C. Dillon. Entered army, 1900; Captain, 1910; Major, 1915; employed in West Africa Frontier Force, 1905–13; served South Africa, 1900 (medal); West Africa, 1906 (medal with clasp); European War, 1914–16 (despatches twice, DSO).
Died 13 Jan. 1918.

DILLON, John; MP (N) Co. Mayo East, 1885–1918; *b* 4 Sept. 1851; *s* of late John Blake Dillon; *m* 1895, Elizabeth (*d* 1907), *d* of late Rt Hon. Sir James Charles Mathew; five *s* one *d*. *Educ:* Catholic Univ., Dublin. Member of Royal Coll. of Surgeons, Ireland. MP (N) Co. Tipperary, 1880–83; Chairman of Irish Nationalist Party, 1918. *Address:* 2 North Great George Street, Dublin.
Died 4 Aug. 1927.

DILLON, Sir John Fox, 7th Bt, *cr* 1801; JP, DL; Baron of the Holy Roman Empire, 1782; *b* 1843; *s* of Sir John Dillon, 6th Bt and Fanny, *d* of Thomas Fox; *S* father, 1875; *m* 1879, Marion Louise, *d* of late Robert Stewart Dykes; one *d*. *Educ:* Magdalene College, Cambridge. Late Major 5th Batt. Prince of Wales' Leinster Regt. Owner of about 3,300 acres. *Heir: kinsman* Robert William Charlier, Dillon, *b* 17 Jan. 1914. *Address:* Lismullen, Navan. *TA:* Tara; Longworth Hall, Hereford. *Club:* Kildare Street, Dublin.
Died 1 Nov. 1925.

DILWORTH, W. J.; Secretary to Board of National Education, Ireland, since 1903; *b* 1863; *m* 1895, Mary Tempe Kildahl; two *s* three

d. Educ: Santry School, Dublin; Trinity College, Dublin. Graduate with First Class Honours in Mathematics in Dublin University, 188 MA 1890; Professor in the Training College of the Commissione of National Education, 1894; Principal of the College, 190 *Publication:* New Sequel to Euclid. *Recreations:* lawn tennis, gol *Address:* Tyrone House, Dublin. *Club:* University, Dublin.
Died 10 Dec. 192

DIMMER, Lt-Col John Henry Stephen, VC 1914; Brig.-Major 92r Infantry Brigade; Lieut KRRC; *b* 1 June 1884. Was with West Afri Regiment; promoted 2nd Lieut KRRC 1908; served European W (VC); served his machine gun at Klein Zillebecke until he w wounded five times and the gun destroyed; was for four years in th office of a firm of civil engineers in Westminster.
Died 21 March 191

DIMSDALE, 7th Baron of the Russian Empire; **Charles Rober Southwell Dimsdale,** DL, JP; *b* 4 June 1856; *s* of 6th Baron ar Cecilia Jane, *d* of Rev. Richard Marcus Southwell; *S* father, 189 *m* 1st, 1882, Alice (*d* 1886), *d* of Charles J. Monk, MP for Glouceste one *s* (and one *s* decd); 2nd, 1891, Mabel Sophia, *d* of Sir Brydg Henniker, 4th Bt and *widow* of Col E. G. G. Hastings, CB; two Educ: Eton; Trinity Coll., Camb. Called to the Bar of the Inn Temple. *Heir: g s* Thomas Dimsdale, *b* 1911 [*s* of Edward Charle Dimsdale (*d* 1915), Capt. Rifle Brigade, and Katharine, *d* of Edwar Barclay]. *Address:* Meesden Manor, Buntingford, Herts. *Club:* Carlto
Died 6 Dec. 192

DIMSDALE, Sir John Holdsworth, 2nd Bt, *cr* 1902; *b* 10 Feb. 187 *s* of Rt Hon. Sir Joseph Cockfield Dimsdale, 1st Bt and Beatrice, of Robert Hunt Holdsworth; *m* 1st, 1901, Edith Kate (*d* 1911), *d* late John Connacher; three *s* (and one *d* decd); 2nd, 1912, Elizabe Grace, *d* of late William John Harling. *Educ:* Eton. *Heir: s* Joh Holdsworth Dimsdale, *b* 31 Dec. 1901. *Club:* Carlton.
Died 10 April 192

DINAJPUR, Maharaja Sir Girijanath Ray, Bahadur of, KCIE 1860; *s* by adoption to Maharaja Taraknath Ray and Mahara Shyammohini of Dinajpur; *m* 1876. *Educ:* Queen's College, Benare Member, Eastern Bengal and Assam Legislative Council, 1906–11 Hon. magistrate, Dinajpur; Vice-President British Indian Associatior Calcutta; former President East Bengal Landholders Associatior Chairman Dinajpur Municipality; former Vice-Chairman Dinajpu District Board; President Dinajpur Landholders' Association; Membe East India Association, London; Asiatic Society, Bengal; Calcut Literary Society; Bangiya Sabitya Parisat. *Recreations:* sports, music *Heir:* Maharaja Kumar Jagadishnath Ray, *m* 1916. *Address:* Dinajpu Rajbati, Dinajpur, Bengal, India; 48 Wellesley Street, Calcutta. *Club* India, Calcutta, Indian Sangita Samaj.
Died 22 Dec. 191

DINES, William Henry, BA Cambridge; FRS 1905; FRMetS, FInstl Hon. FRAeS; *b* 5 Aug. 1855; *s* of George Dines of Hersham, Walton on-Thames, and Grosvenor Road; *m* 1882, Catharine Emma, *d* Rev. Frederic Tugwell; two *s*. *Educ:* Woodcote House School Windlesham; experimental meteorologist; developed pressure-tub anemometer. *Publications:* papers in Proceedings of RS and Quarterl Journal of the Royal Meteorological Society, Journals of Sanitar Institute and Royal Aeronautical Society, and in publications of th Meteorological Office and elsewhere. *Address:* Benson, Wallingford Berks.
Died 24 Dec. 192

DIONNE, Narcisse-Eutrope, LLD, MD; FRSC; Officier d l'Instruction Publique de France; Professeur d'archéologie l'Université Laval, Québec; Librarian of the Legislature of th Province of Quebec, 1892–1913; *b* 18 May 1848; *m* 1st, 1873, Laur Bouchard; 2nd, 1896, Emma Bidégaré; four *s* one *d*. *Educ:* St Ann College; Laval University. Practised medicine at Quebec, 1873–80 Chief Editor of Le Courrier du Canada, 1880–84; Chief Inspecto of federal licences, 1884–86; Chief Editor of Le Journal de Québec 1886; Permanent Secretary of the Quebec Conservative Club 1886–92. *Publications:* (in French): Life of Jacques Cartier, discovere of Canada; La Nouvelle France 1540–1603; Life of Samue Champlain, founder of Quebec; Life of C. F. Painchand, founde of St Ann's College; Serviteurs et servantes de Dieu au Canada; Le Ecclésiastiques et les royalistes français réfugiés au Canada a l'époqu de la Révolution; Inventaire chronologique des livres, brochures journaux et revues publiés en langue française dans la Province d Québec depuis l'établissement de l'imprimerie jusqu'à nos jour (1764–1905); Québec et Nouvelle France; Bibliographie, inventair chronologique des ouvrages publiés à l'étranger en diverses langues depuis la découverte du Canada jusqu'a nos jours (1534-1906); Inventaire chronologique des livres, brochures, journaux et revues publiés en langue anglaise, 1764-1908; Inventaire chronologique des cartes, etc, 1508-1908; Supplément à l'Inventaire chronologique, 1904-12; Life of Champlain (in English); Le Parler populaire des Canadiens français, ou Lexique des Canadianismes, etc, et Galerie historique; Pierre Bédard et ses fils; Les Trois Comédies du Statu Quo; Historique de la paroisse de Ste Anne de la Pocatière; L'Œuvre de Mgr de Forbin-Janson, évêque de Nancy, en Canada; Chouart et Radisson, ou Odyssée de deux Canadiens-français au XVIIe siècle; L'Abbé Gabriel Richard, Sulpicien, second fondateur de la ville de Détroit, Michigan; Les Abbés J. Demers et Thos Maguire—Dispute grammaticale; La Petite Hermine de Jacques Cartier, Etude archéologique; Origine et étymologie des noms de famille canadiens-français, de 1608 à 1908; and fifteen other smaller publications. *Address:* Quebec, Canada. *T:* 1828.   *Died March 1917.*

DIÓSY, Arthur, FRGS; writer and lecturer; Knight Commander of Rising Sun of Japan and of Medjidieh; Knight of Christ of Portugal; Officier de l'Instruction Publique, France; *b* London, 6 June 1856; *s* of Hungarian patriot, Martin Diósy; *m* 1882, Florence, *d* of late George W. Hill of Denton Hall, Lancs; one *d*. *Educ:* in England and Germany. Advocated, for many years, the Anglo-Japanese Alliance; founded, 1891, the Japan Society; chairman, 1901-4, then Vice-President; hon. member Paris Ethnographical Society and Société Franco-Japonaise; member of the Council China Society; Interpreter of the Sette di Odd Volumes (President, 1903-4); member Navy League; Siver Medallist Ligue Maritime Française, 1920; served in Royal Naval Artillery Volunteers, 1875-82; Lecturer for Prince of Wales's National Relief Fund, 1914-15; delivered many Recruiting Lectures, 1914-16; served as Staff-Lecturer, YMCA, with British Expeditionary Forces in Mediterranean War Area, Jan.–June 1917; visited Italian Front, Sept. 1917; attached to First Army, BEF, France, 1918; GHQ Lecturer, British Army of Occupation, Belgium and Germany, Feb. and March 1919, and British Army of the Rhine, May 1919. *Publications:* The New Far East, 1898, 8th edn 1904; History of New Japan in Harmsworth's History of the World, 1907; edited Vols. i and ii of Transactions and Proceedings of the Japan Society. *Recreations:* foreign travel; Europe, Asia, Africa, America; visited ruined Maya cities of Yucatán, 1910. *T:* Gerrard 2927. *Clubs:* Savage, Royal Automobile, London Sketch.
                                                        Died 2 Jan. 1923.

DISNEY, Henry William, Barrister-at-Law; Metropolitan Police Magistrate since 1918; Thames Court since 1922; formerly Revising Barrister on Midland Circuit, Lecturer, London School of Economics, and Legal Correspondent of the Department of Labour Statistics, Ministry of Labour; Member of General Council of the Bar; *b* 1858; *e s* of the late Rev. W. H. Disney, Rector of Winwick, Rugby; *m* 1892, Isabel Wemyss, *d* of late Rev. P. B. Power; two *s* one *d*. *Educ:* Christ's College, Finchley; Hertford College, Oxford (Mathematical Scholar). 2nd Math. Mods, 3rd Math. Greats, BA, 1880; rowed in Oxford University Eight, 1879. Called to Bar, Lincoln's Inn, 1884, and joined Midland Circuit; Recorder of Great Grimsby, 1914-18. *Publications:* The Law of Carriage by Railway, 6th edn, 1923; The Elements of Commercial Law, 3rd edn, 1922; Railways and Canals and other matter in Lord Halsbury's Laws of England. *Address:* 8 West Hill Road, SW18. *T:* Putney 403. *Club:* New University.
                                                        Died 16 Jan. 1925.

DISTANT, William Lucas; *b* 12 Nov. 1845; *o surv.* s of late Capt. Alex. Distant; *m* 1874, Edith Blanche de Rubien (*d* 1914); three *s* three *d*. *Educ:* privately. Director and Hon. Sec. Anthropological Institute, 1878-81; Sec. Entomological Society, 1878-80; Vice-President, 1881 and 1900; Editor of the Zoologist, 1897-1915; travelled and made natural history collections in the Malay Peninsula and in the Transvaal. *Publications:* Rhopalocera Malayana; Monograph of the Oriental Cicadidæ; A Naturalist in the Transvaal; Rhynchota, vol. i in Godman and Salvin's Biologia Centrali Americana; Faun. Brit. India, Rhynchota, vols. i-vii; Insecta Transvaaliensia (in parts); numerous scattered publications on Lepidoptera, Rhynchota, and Coleoptera, and a few on anthropological subjects. *Recreation:* angling. *Address:* Glenside, Birchanger Road, South Norwood, Surrey.
                                                        Died 4 Feb. 1922.

DISTURNAL, William Josiah, KC 1913; *e s* of Thomas Disturnal, late of Walsall and Wednesbury; *m* Charlotte Elizabeth, 2nd *d* of Thomas Southern, late of Walsall and Wednesbury; one *d*. *Educ:* The Leys School; Trinity Hall, Cambridge (Scholar and Prizeman). Law Tripos (Cambridge), 1884; MA and LLB. Called to Bar, Inner Temple, 1885; Bencher, 1921; Oxford Circuit; 1st Recorder of Dudley, 1908. *Address:* 48 Cheyne Walk, Chelsea, SW3. *T:*

Kensington 2360; 2 Temple Gardens, Temple, EC4. *TA:* 71 Temple, EC. *T:* 2470 Central. *Club:* United University.
                                                        Died 2 March 1923.

DIXEY, Sir Harry Edward, Kt 1925; DL, JP Worcestershire; Sheriff, 1921; MD Aberdeen; *b* 26 Aug. 1853; *s* of Charles Anderson Dixey, Highgate; *m* Ellen Mary, *d* of J. Dyson Perrins, Malvern. Alderman Worcestershire County Council; Chairman Worcester City and County Nursing Association; Chairman King Edward VII Memorial Sanatorium, Worcestershire; Chairman St John Brine Bath Hospital, Droitwich. *Address:* Woodgate, Malvern. *T:* Malvern 108. *Club:* Junior Carlton.   *Died 6 Jan. 1927.*

DIXIE, Sir Alexander Beaumont Churchill, 11th Bt, *cr* 1660; *b* 22 Dec. 1851; *o s* of Sir Alexander Beaumont Churchill Dixie, 10th Bt and Maria, *d* of Rev. Charles Walters, Rector of Bramdean, Hants; S father, 1872; *m* 1st, 1875, Lady Florence Caroline Douglas (*d* 1905), *y d* of 7th Marquess of Queensberry and Caroline, *d* of Gen. Sir William Robert Clayton, 5th Bt; two *s*; 2nd, 1906, Alice, *widow* of Edward John Ewart. *Heir:* s George Douglas Dixie [*b* 18 Jan. 1876; *m* 1902, Margaret, *d* of Sir Alexander Jardine, 8th Bt; one *s* two *d*; was a midshipman RN, and late Lieut. 3rd Batt. KOSB].
                                                        Died 21 Aug. 1924.

DIXON, Sir Alfred Herbert, 1st Bt, *cr* 1918; *b* 1857. Chairman of the Cotton Control Board; Fine Cotton Spinners' and Doublers' Association, Ltd; Great Leven Spinning Co. Ltd; Manchester Royal Exchange Ltd. *Address:* Temple Chambers, St James's Square, Manchester.   *Died 10 Dec. 1920 (ext).*

DIXON, Amzi Clarence, BA, DD; Pastor, University Baptist Church, Baltimore; *b* North Carolina, USA, 6 July 1854; *s* of Thomas Dixon and Amanda M'Afee; *m* Mary Faison; one *s* three *d*. *Educ:* Wake Forest College, NC, USA; Southern Baptist Theological Seminary. Began to preach at 19 years of age; ordained at Bear Marsh Church, Duplin Co., NC, USA; Pastor three years of Baptist Church at Chapel Hill, NC; three and a half years of Baptist Church in Asheville, NC; eight years Pastor of Emmanuel Baptist Church in Baltimore, Md; ten years Pastor of Hanson Place Baptist Church, Brooklyn, NY; five and a half years Pastor of Ruggles Street Baptist Church, Boston, Mass; five and a half years Pastor of Moody Church, Chicago, Ill; eight years Pastor of Metropolitan Tabernacle, London; held many evangelistic missions in many places. *Publications:* Heaven on Earth; Evangelism Old and New; Young Convert's Problems; Lights and Shadows; Present-Day Life and Religion; Milk and Meat; The Christian Science Delusion; Back to the Bible; The Bright Side of Life; The Bright Side of Death; Through Night to Morning; The Glories of the Cross; Christian Character; Speaking with Tongues; The Prophet Jonah; The Touches of God; Reconstruction; Why I am a Christian; Victory; Why I am an Evangelical Christian and not a Modernist; many single sermons. *Address:* University Baptist Church, Baltimore, Md, USA.
                                                        Died 15 June 1925.

DIXON, Charles; naturalist, author, journalist, and lecturer; *b* London, 20 July 1858; *e s* of late Charles Thomas Dixon, landscape painter and engraver; *m* 1886, Mary, *o c* of John Knight, Torquay. *Educ:* various public schools. Boyhood passed near Sheffield; London, 1880-91; Devonshire, 1891-1900; devoted his whole life to the study of Natural History; in pursuing this study he visited most parts of the British Islands from the English Channel to St Kilda, where he discovered the wren peculiar to that locality; also travelled in North Africa, where a new species and many rarities were obtained by him; for five years he was associated with the late Henry Seebohm, writing in collaboration with him a work on British Birds; of late years he made the migration of birds and the geographical distribution of species his special study, promulgating several new theories, and suggesting an entirely new law, bearing upon these questions. *Publications:* Rural Bird Life, 1880; Evolution without Natural Selection, 1885; Our Rarer Birds, 1888; Stray Feathers from Many Birds, 1890; Annals of Bird Life, 1890; Idle Hours with Nature, 1891; The Birds of our Rambles, 1891; The Migration of Birds, 1892 (Russian edn 1895; amended English edition, 1897); Jottings about Birds, 1893; The Game Birds and Wild Fowl of the British Islands, 1893; The Nests and Eggs of British Birds, 1893 (illustrated edn 1894); The Nests and Eggs of Non-indigenous British Birds, 1894; The Migration of British Birds, 1895; British Sea Birds, 1896; Curiosities of Bird Life, 1897; Our Favourite Song Birds, 1897; Lost and Vanishing Birds, 1898; Bird-Life in a Southern County, 1899; new and enlarged edition of The Game Birds and Wild Fowl of the British Islands, with 40 coloured plates, 1899; Among the Birds in Northern Shires, 1900; The Story of the Birds, 1900; Birds' Nests; An Introduction to the science of Caliology, 1902; Open Air Studies in Bird Life; Sketches of British Birds in their Homes, 1903; new and popular edition of The Migration of British Birds, 1904; The Bird-Life of London, 1909, etc. *Address:* 50 Crown Hill Road, NW10. *T:* Willesden 848. *Died 17 June 1926.*

DIXON, Charles Harvey; MP (U) Rutland and Stamford Division since 1922; *b* 1862; *s* of Henry Dixon; *m* 1896, *d* of late J. P. Robinson, Esher; one *s* three *d*. MP (C) Boston, 1910–18. *Address:* Gunthorpe, Oakham, Rutland. *Club:* Carlton.

Died 22 Sept. 1923.

DIXON, Maj.-Gen. Edward George; Madras Infantry; *b* 15 Dec. 1837. Entered army, 1857; Maj.-Gen. 1891; retired, 1893.

Died 27 Feb. 1918.

DIXON, Lt-Col Frederick Alfred, CMG 1919; DSO 1917; late RFA; *b* Manchester, 27 March 1880; *s* of late John P. Dixon, JP, The Mount, Marton, Lancs; *m* 1908, Ethel Howard Coulston; one *s* three *d*. *Educ:* Rossall. Commissioned Lancs Vol. Artillery, 1899; Tipperary Militia Artillery, 1900; RH and RFA 1901; served 8 years in India in both RH and RFA; Lt-Col 1915, to command 150th Brigade, RFA, which was raised by him; served European War (CMG, DSO). *Recreations:* big and small game shooting, polo. *Address:* Bramley Meade, Whalley, Lancs. *T:* Whalley 2. *M:* LE 7001. *Club:* Junior Army and Navy.

Died 18 Jan. 1925.

DIXON, Colonel Sir George, 1st Bt, *cr* 1919; late Chairman Cheshire County Council, etc; *b* 23 May 1842; *s* of John Dixon, of Astle Hall; *m* 1885, Emily Katherine, 2nd *d* of George Beacham Cole, of Twickenham; one *s* one *d*. *Educ:* Eton. Joined the King's Own Borderers (the 25th Foot), 1860; took part in the campaign against the Fenians in Canada, 1866 (Canadian medal); in 1873 left the Borderers and entered the 5th Battalion Cheshire Rifle Vols as Major; retired, after serving thirteen years, with the rank of Lt-Col; Colonel Commandant Cheshire Volunteer Training Corps; Vice-Lieutenant for County of Cheshire; JP Cheshire; High Sheriff, 1881; a DL and Chairman of the Cheshire County Council, 1893–1922; was a Councillor since 1889, when County Councils were formed. *Recreations:* travelling, shooting, fishing. *Heir: s* John Dixon [*b* 13 June 1886; *m* 1910, Gwendolen Anna, *d* of Sir Joseph L. E. Spearman, 2nd Bt; two *s* one *d*]. *Address:* Astle Hall, Chelford, Cheshire. *TA:* Chelford. *M:* M4686. *Club:* Arthur's.

Died 1 April 1924.

DIXON, Capt. Kennet, CBE 1919; RN, retired list; *m* Evelyn, *d* of late General Cadwallader Adams. Served European War (CBE). *Address:* Coggeshall, Essex.

Died 13 April 1927.

DIXON, William Gray, MA Glasgow and Melbourne; DD Edinburgh; Minister Emeritus of the Presbyterian Church of New Zealand; *b* Paisley, Scotland, 21 May 1854; *e s* of Rev. James Main Dixon, Minister of Free Martyrs' Church, and Jane Gray Dixon, Ayr; *m* 1900, Elizabeth Aitken, 4th *d* of John Glen of Crosshill, Glasgow. *Educ:* Ayr Academy (Dux); Glasgow University, MA; New College, Edinburgh. Professor of English in the Imperial College of Engineering, Tokyo, Japan, 1876–80; Recording Secretary and Life Member of the Asiatic Society of Japan; Assistant Minister of Scots Church, Melbourne, 1886; Minister of Fitzroy, Melbourne, 1887–89; of St John's, Warrnambool, Victoria, 1889–1900; of St David's, Auckland, NZ, 1900–10; of Roslyn Presbyterian Church, Dunedin, NZ, 1910–21; Examiner in Theology, Ormond College, Melbourne, and Knox College, Dunedin; Theological Tutor; Moderator of the Presbyterian Church of New Zealand, 1919; retired, 1921; Official Delegate of the Presbyterian Church of New Zealand to the World Conference on Faith and Order, Lausanne, Aug. 1927, and to the Alliance of the Reformed Churches holding the Presbyterian System, Budapest, Sept. 1927. *Publications:* The Land of the Morning, 1882; The Romance of the Catholic Presbyterian Church, 1918; revised and enlarged edition, 1928; numerous magazine articles, chiefly descriptive and theological; Acting Editor of various magazines. *Recreations:* mountaineering, bowling, golf. *Address:* Glenfruin, St Leonards, Dunedin, New Zealand. *T:* 18-760.

Died 4 Sept. 1928.

DIXON-WRIGHT, Rev. Henry Dixon, MVO 1912; Chaplain RN College, Dartmouth;*b* 25 April 1870; *m* 1904, Annie Louisa, *d* of late Major J. Paton Lawrie, 2nd Queen's Regt; two *s*. *Educ:* Highgate School; Corpus Christi College, Cambridge; 3rd class Classical Tripos, 1892. Ordained, 1893; Curate of St Stephen, S Lambeth, 1893–94; St James', Paddington, 1894–97; Stoke-Next-Guildford, 1897–98; Chaplain RN, 1899; served in HMS Resolution, 1899–1900;

Ramillies, 1900–3; Bedford, 1903–6; RN Hospital, Malta, 1906–7; RN College, Dartmouth, 1907; HMS Medina, 1911–12. *Address:* Royal Naval College, Dartmouth.

Died 31 May 1916.

DIXSON, Sir Hugh, Kt 1921; retired; Director and Chairman (local) of Alliance Assurance Co., Ltd, London, Royal Prince Alfred Hospital, Dixson Trust, Ltd; *b* 29 Jan. 1841; *s* of Hugh Dixson and Helen Craig, both Edinburgh; *m* 1866, Emma Elizabeth Shaw (*d* 1922); two *s* four *d*. *Educ:* Cape's Academy, Darlinghurst, Sydney. Tobacco manufacturer; Director and Chairman City Bank, Sydney; Contributor Religious, Imperial and Charitable Institutions; Ex-President Baptist Union, NSW. *Recreation:* gardening. *Address:* Abergeldie, Summer Hill, Sydney, NSW. *TA:* Aberdix, Sydney. *T:* V 1013. *M:* 62. *Club:* British Empire.

Died 11 May 1926.

DOBB, His Honour Harry; Judge of County Court, Circuit No 20, 1921–25; of Birmingham County Court, 1925–27; of Lambeth since 1927; Magistrate for County of Leicester and City of Leicester and for City of Birmingham; *b* 15 Aug. 1867; *e s* of Henry and Emily Dobb of Armmore, Frognal, NW, and Kiligarth, Felixstowe, Suffolk; *m* 1st, Florence (*d* 1907), *d* of W. J. Willats of Lansdowne Crescent, Kensington; 2nd, Kathleen Mildred, *e d* of late Henry Caldwell Lipsett, of Ballyshannon, Co. Donegal, and Wickford, Essex; two *s*. *Educ:* Dawlish; Merchant Taylors' School; Pembroke College, Cambridge. BA 1888. Called to Bar, Lincoln's Inn, 1891. *Address:* 5 Essex Court, Temple, EC; The Shrubbery, Stoneygate, Leicester. *Club:* United University.

Died 23 March 1928.

DOBBIE, Sir James (Johnston), Kt 1915; LLD Glasgow, MA, DSc; FRS 1904; *b* 4 Aug. 1852; 2nd *s* of Alexander Dobbie, Glasgow; *m* 1887, Violet, *d* of Thomas Chilton, JP, of Liverpool and Gresford; one *s* two *d*. *Educ:* High School, Glasgow; Universities of Glasgow (George A. Clark Scholar in Natural Science), Edinburgh, and Leipzig. Assistant to the Professor of Chemistry, University of Glasgow, 1881–84; Professor of Chemistry, Univ. Coll. of North Wales, Bangor, 1884–1903; Director Royal Scottish Museum, Edinburgh, 1903–9; Principal of the Government Laboratories, London, 1909–20; President of the Institute of Chemistry, 1915–18; President of the Chemical Society, 1919–21; Member of the Royal Commission on Awards to Inventors; Member of the University Grants Committee. *Publications:* numerous papers on the chemical constitution of alkaloids, and the relation between chemical constitution and absorption spectra of organic compounds. *Address:* The Cottage, Fairlie, Ayrshire. *Club:* Athenæum. *Died June 1924.*

DOBBIE, Brig.-Gen. William Hugh, CB 1912; late Mandalay Brigade, Burma; *b* 9 May 1859; *s* of Lt-Col Robert Shedden Dobbie. Entered army, 1879; Captain, ISC 1890; Major, Indian army, 1899; Lt-Col, 1904; Bt-Col, 1907; AQMG India; served Burmese Expedition, 1885–87 (despatches thrice, medal with clasp); Manipur, 1891 (clasp); S African War, 1899–1900; retired 1920.

Died 25 Nov. 1922.

DOBBIN, Lt-Col William James Knowles, CBE 1919; Indian Army, retired, 1905; *b* 1 June 1856; *s* of Rev. W. P. H. Dobbin and Fanny, *d* of Sheridan Knowles, the dramatist; *m* 1st, 1886, Ethel (*d* 1906), *d* of Major R. Callwell Smith, RA; two *d*; 2nd, 1910, Edith, *d* of Major Octavius Lowry, 96 Regt and Galway Militia. *Educ:* Rathmines School; Trinity College, Dublin. Joined Militia, 1874; Army, 1877; Bengal Staff Corps, 1880; served in six Indian Expeditions, and at the Relief of the Peking Legations, 1900; European War, 1915–19, at Mudros, in Egypt, and the Egyptian Expeditionary Force; commanded 19 Battn, the Rifle Brigade, 1917–19 (despatches twice, CBE, Order of the Nile). *Recreations:* golf, tennis, croquet. *Address:* Charleville, Rostrevor, Co. Down.

Died 27 June 1926.

DOBSON, Henry Austin, LLD; *b* Plymouth, 18 Jan. 1840; *e s* of George Clarisse Dobson, CE; *m* 1868, Frances Mary, *d* of Nathaniel Beardmore, CE, of Broxbourne, Herts; five *s* five *d*. *Educ:* Beaumaris Grammar School; private school, Coventry; Gymnase, Strasbourg. Entered Board of Trade, 1856; First-class Clerk, 1874–84; Principal, 1884–1901; retired, 1901. Hon. LLD, Edinburgh, 1902; Committee of London Library; Council of Society of Authors; Council of Royal Literary Fund. *Publications: poems:* Vignettes in Rhyme, 1873; Proverbs in Porcelain, 1877; Old-World Idylls, 1883; At the Sign of the Lyre, 1885; Collected Poems, 1 vol, 1897, ninth edn 1913; *prose:* Thomas Bewick and his Pupils, 1884; Lives of Fielding, 1883, Steele, 1886, Goldsmith, 1888, Horace Walpole, 1890–1910, William Hogarth, 1891, 1897, 1907, Richardson, 1902, Fanny Burney, 1903; Four

Frenchwomen, 1890; Eighteenth Century Vignettes, three series, 1892, 1894, 1896; A Paladin of Philanthropy, 1899; Side-Walk Studies, 1902; De Libris, 1908; Old Kensington Palace, 1910; At Prior Park, 1912; Rosalba's Journal, 1915; Bookman's Budget, 1917; Later Essays (1917-20), 1921; contributions to the Encyclopædia Britannica, Chambers's Encyclopædia, Chambers's Cyclopædia of English Literature and Dictionary of National Biography; also—besides editing Mme D'Arblay's Diary, 1904-5, and Evelyn's Diary, 1906—edited several books for Clarendon Press, World's Classics, etc, and wrote for many of the more important magazines and reviews. *Address:* 75 Eaton Rise, Ealing, W. *Club:* Athenæum.

Died 2 Sept. 1921.

DOBSON, Henry John, RCA 1920 (ARCA, 1907); RSW 1890; native of Innerleithen, Peeblesshire; *b* 1858; *e s* of Thomas and Rebecca Dobson; *m* 1890, Jeanie Charlotte Hannah Cowan; three *s* one *d*. *Educ:* Innerleithen; Edinburgh. Painter of Scottish character and interiors; studied at School of Design, and Royal Scottish Academy, Edinburgh; Exhibitor at Royal Academy, London, and leading provincial exhibitions; winner of £100 Prize, London, with RA picture The New Toy, open competition best oil picture, 1897; his picture A Scottish Sacrament purchased by Bradford Corporation, 1893; other best-known pictures are The Little Minister, Burns's Grace, The Last Request, The Hand that Rocks the Cradle, The New Arrival, Auld Lang Syne, Burns and Highland Mary, Her Dochter's Bairn, etc; invited to visit America and Canada, 1911, to read paper on Scottish Art at Convention held at Red Oak, Iowa, and presented with Gold Medal in recognition of his work; Newcastle Corporation in 1913 purchased his picture The Sabbath Hat. *Publications:* Scottish Life and Character; Scottish Art. *Recreations:* golf, walking. *Address:* 5 Merchiston Place, Edinburgh.

Died July 1928.

DOCKRELL, Benjamin Morgan; Senior Physician, St John's Hospital for Diseases of Skin, London; Chesterfield Lecturer on Dermatology; *b* 2 Feb. 1860; *s* of late Thomas Dockrell, JP, Monkstown, Co. Dublin, and Anne Morgan Brooks; *m* 1882, Emily, *o d* of late Alexander Oldfield of Cahir, Tipperary; one *s* two *d*. *Educ:* Cheltenham College; University of Dublin; Royal College of Surgeons; Steevens and Adelaide Hospitals; MA, MD (2nd place at MB) BCh; MOSc (1st place) University of Dublin. In practice as a specialist in skin diseases since 1888; President of the London Dermatological Society, 1912; President of the West Kent Medico-Chirugical Society, 1898; Vice-President (for life) of the Balnæological Section of the Royal Society of Medicine; President of the United Hospitals London Swimming Association, 1903-12; for twenty-five years Physician to St John's Hospital; Chesterfield Lecturer on Dermatology since 1895, and Medallist in Dermatology; Fellow of the Medical Society of London, Royal Society of Medicine, and of London Dermatological Society; formerly Physician to the out-patient department Millar Hospital and Royal Kent Dispensary; Dermatologist to the National Society for the Prevention of Cruelty to Children; Pathologist and Director of Laboratory the Hospital for Diseases of Skin, Leicester Square; Lecturer and Demonstrator in the London School of Dermatology. *Publications:* Hydronaphthol as a Specific in the Treatment of Ringworm, 1889; The Skin and how to Keep it Healthy, 1893; Research into the alleged Parasitic Nature of Eczema (Proc. Internat. Congress of Dermatol. Paris, 1900); Lichen from a Histological Point of View, 1901; Atlas of Dermatology, Clinical and Microscopical, 1904; many papers on Syphilis and Diseases of Skin. *Recreations:* research work, golf, swimming, tennis, croquet. *Address:* 9 Cavendish Square, W. *T:* 893 Paddington.

Died 15 March 1920.

DODD, Henry Work, FRCS, LRCP, LSA; Ophthalmic Surgeon; *b* Victoria, Vancouver Island, BC; *s* of late Charles Dodd, HBC; *m* Agnes, *y d* of James Legasick Shuter; two *s* one *d*. *Educ:* Norwich School under Rev. Augustus Jessop, DD; St Bartholomew's Hospital; Ophthalmic Surgeon to, and Clinical Lecturer on Ophthalmic Medicine and Surgery at the Royal Free Hospital; Surgeon to the Royal Westminster Ophthalmic Hospital; Ophthalmic Surgeon to the Hospital for Nervous Diseases, Welbeck Street, W, etc; Major (retired) RAMC Vols. *Publications:* contributed various papers on ophthalmic subjects. *Address:* 136 Harley Street, W1. *T:* 7468 Paddington. *Clubs:* Reform, Savage.

Died 28 June 1921.

DODDS, Rev. Canon Matthew Archbold; Vicar of Chilvers Coton, Nuneaton (the Shepperton of George Eliot's Scenes), since 1914; *b* Galway, 5 June 1864; *e s* of late Jackson and Maria Dodds, Stroud Green, N; *m* Bertha (*d* 1909), *e d* of late Robert Blackman; three *s* two *d*. *Educ:* The Magnus School, Newark; The London College

of Divinity. Deacon, 1887; Priest, 1888; Curate of St Andrew and St Philip, N Kensington, 1887-90; St Chad's, Derby, 1890-92; Missionary West Africa, 1892-93; Curate of Boulton, Derby, 1893-96; Chaplain, Newstead Colliery, 1897-1902; Vicar of St Philip's, Nottingham, and Chaplain of Plumtre Hospital, 1902-14; Canon of Coventry, 1922; Rural Dean of Atherstone, 1923. *Publications:* sundry papers on missionary and temperance matters. *Address:* Chilvers Coton Vicarage, Nuneaton. *M:* NX 9984.

Died 9 Jan. 1928.

DODGE, Grenville Mellen; Major-General USV; President Society Army of the Tennessee, 1892; Vice-President Abilene and Southern Railway; *b* Danvers, Mass, 12 April 1831; *s* of Sylvanus Dodge, and Julia T. Phillips. *Educ:* Norwich University, Vt; CE, AM and LLD. Civil Engineer; Maj-Gen. war rebellion; Commander Regt Brigade, Div. Corps and Army and Department; Chief Engr, United Pacific Rlwy and built that and numerous other railways in the US; member 89th Congress; Comm. MOLL; President of Commission to investigate conduct of the War Dept in war with Spain, 1898; Hon. Member American Society Civil Engineers. *Address:* Baldwin Block, Council Bluffs, Iowa, USA. *Clubs:* Union League, Army and Navy, Republican, New York.

Died 3 Jan. 1916.

DOLGOROUKI, Princess Alexis (Frances); widow of late Prince Alexis Dolgorouki (*d* 1915); *o c* and *heir* of Fleetwood Pellew Wilson of Wappenham Manor, Northants, DL, JP. *Address:* 46 Upper Grosvenor Street, W. *T:* Mayfair 1260; Nashdom, Taplow, Bucks; Wappenham Manor, Northants; Braemar Castle, NB.

Died 23 Aug. 1919.

DOLMAN, Frederick, FJI; Editor of the Art Trade Journal; contributor to the Strand, Pearson's and other magazines; *b* London, 1867; *m*; one *s*. Entered journalism at age of 18—London Echo, Scarborough Evening News, National Press Agency, etc; travelled round the world, 1897; LCC (Brixton) 1901-07; Member of the London War Pensions Committee. *Publication:* Municipalities at Work, 1895. *Recreations:* chess, playgoing, motoring, rambles. *Address:* 9 King's Bench Walk, Temple, EC4. *T:* City 334; 13 Buckingham Street, Strand, WC2. *T:* Regent 3473; The Dell Cottage, Englefield Green, Surrey. *T:* Egham 214. *M:* XC 4961. *Club:* National Liberal.

DOMINGUEZ, Don Vicente J.; Envoy Extraordinary and Minister Plenipotentiary of the Argentine Republic to Great Britain since 1911; *b* Buenos Aires; *s* of Don Luis L. Dominguez and *brother* of Don Florencio L. Dominguez, former Argentine Ministers in London; *m* Helen, *d* of Daniel T. Murphy, New York; one *s*. *Educ:* Buenos Aires. Private Secretary to the Argentine Minister in Peru, 1876; in Brazil, 1878; in the United States, 1882; in England, 1886; First Secretary of Legation in Madrid, 1891; in Washington, 1895; in Paris, 1896; in London, 1899; represented the Argentine Government at the celebrations of the 400th anniversary of the Discovery of America at Huelva and Seville, Spain, 1892; Special Envoy from the Argentine President at the Coronation of King George V, 1911. *Address:* 7 Tilney Street, Park Lane, W; 2 Palace Gate, W. *Clubs:* Argentine, Marlborough, Royal Automobile, St James's.

Died 28 June 1916.

DOMVILE, Sir Compton Edward, GCB 1904 (KCB 1898); GCVO 1903; *b* Worcestershire, 10 Oct. 1842; 2nd *s* of late Henry Barry Domvile; *m* 1876, Isabella, *d* of Capt. Edmund Peel, late 85th Regt; two *s* three *d*. *Educ:* Royal Academy, Gosport. Entered Navy, 1856; appointed to Royal yacht, 1862; Lieut 1862; promoted Commander for service against pirates, 1868; Captain, 1876; Captain of the "Dido", 1879-83; W Africa and Cape during the Boer War; Acting Commodore, Jamaica, 1882; Captain of "Téméraire", 1884-1886; Captain HMS "Excellent"—Gunnery School, Portsmouth, 1886-90; Ordnance Committee, 1891-94; second in command Mediterranean, 1894-96; Adm. 1902; Adm. Supt of Naval Reserves, 1897-1902; Commander-in-Chief Mediterranean Station, 1902-5. *Address:* 7 San Remo, Hove, Sussex.

Died 19 Nov. 1924.

DOMVILLE, Lieut-Colonel Hon. James, FRGS, MIME, FRCI, MInstCE; Senator since 1903; Chairman Select Standing Committee of Senate on Mineral Resources of Canada; Hon. Colonel 8th Princess Louise's New Brunswick Hussars; *b* 29 Nov. 1842; *s* of late Lieut-Gen. J. W. Domville and Frances, *d* of late Hon. W. Usher; *m* 1867, Isabella, *d* of W. H. Scovile. *Educ:* Woolwich. Travelled a great deal; built and sailed the first British steamer on the Yukon; organised the 8th Hussars and commanded it for twenty years (decorations, Long Service, Fenian Medal, Queen's Diamond Jubilee Medal); regiment volunteered for the Soudan, 1884-96; and for South Africa (received the thanks of the Home Authorities); sat as an Alderman, City of St

John, NB, and Chairman Finance Committee; MP 1873; was for four years Chairman of the Select Standing Committee of the House of Commons on Banking and Commerce; founded the St John Free Library; SGIG 33°. *Address:* Rothesay, New Brunswick, Canada. *Clubs:* Rideau, Ottawa; Union, St John; Liberal, Montreal; Moncton, Moncton.   *Died 30 July 1921.*

DOMVILLE, Sir James Henry, 5th Bt, *cr* 1814; Lieutenant RN; commanding destroyer P19; *b* 10 Dec. 1889; *s* of Sir William Cecil Henry Domville, 4th Bt and Moselle, *d* of Henry Metcalfe Ames, Linden, Northumberland; *S* father, 1904; *m* 1912, Kathleen, *d* of Basil Arthur Charlesworth of Gunton Hall, Lowestoft; two *d*. Served European War, 1914–15. *Heir: b* Cecil Lionel Domville, *b* 14 Sept. 1892. *Club:* United Service.   *Died 13 Sept. 1919.*

DON, Sir William, KBE 1918; Deputy-Lieutenant of the County of the City of Dundee; ex-Lord Provost of Dundee; a partner of the firm of Don & Duncan, Ltd, Jute Spinners and Manufacturers; *b* 1861; *s* of late James Don, Dundee; *m* 1894, Martha Nicoll, *d* of J. H. Lindsay; two *s* three *d*. *Educ:* Dundee High School. Seventeen years a member of the Town Council of Dundee. *Recreation:* bowling. *Address:* Ardarroch, Dundee. *T:* Dundee 2709. *Club:* Eastern, Dundee.   *Died 20 Oct. 1926.*

DON, Surg.-Gen. William Gerard, MD; Deputy Surgeon-General, Army Medical Service; retired on the Non-Effective List Army Medical Service, 1885; *b* Stracathro, Forfarshire, 10 Jan. 1836; *y s* of Alexander Don, Ballownie; *m* 1st, 1866, Louisa Jane Elliott; three *s* two *d*; 2nd, 1889, Jean Ann Fairweather; two *s* two *d*. *Educ:* locally; Aberdeen, Edinburgh. Doctor of Medicine, Edinburgh University, 1857. Served medical volunteer in Flagship Duke of Wellington, Baltic Fleet, 1855, and at bombardment of Sweaborg, August (medal); entered army, 1858; served in Mutiny, Central India, in actions with Tantia Topee at Rajpore, and Beilkaira, Nov. 1858 (despatches, medal); served in 28th Regt Royal Engineers, and Royal Artillery, on Staff, and in Medical Branch, War Office; employed in fitting out hospital ships for Egyptian Expedition, 1882; and rewriting and editing the Army Medical Regulations of 1885; as Senior Medical Officer, London Recruiting Staff, for seventeen years; President of the Caledonian Society of London; Life Governor, Royal Scottish Corporation, and connected with Scottish Societies in London. *Publications:* privately, Recollections of the Baltic Fleet of 1855; several Family Genealogies; publicly, Archæological Notes on Early Scotland, 1899; numerous contributions to current medical and other literature. *Recreations:* literature, gardening, fishing, shooting. *Address:* 52 Canfield Gardens, W Hampstead, NW6.   *Died 27 July 1920.*

DONALDSON, Sir George, Kt 1904; *b* 25 May 1845; *s* of late A. Donaldson, of Edinburgh; *m* 1872, Alice (*d* 1907), *d* of John Stronach, Edinburgh; three *s* four *d*. Created and equipped the series of Historic Music Rooms at the Inventions Exhibition of 1885; Vice-President International Jury, Paris Exhibitions, 1889 and 1900; Chevalier Legion of Honour; Member of Royal Commission, St Louis Exhibition, 1904; presented the Donaldson Museum to Royal College of Music, 1894, and a collection of furniture to the Victoria and Albert Museum, 1900; a Director of the Royal Academy of Music and a Member of the Royal Institution; it was solely on his initiative that the fine new buildings of the Royal Academy of Music in the Marylebone Road came into existence. *Address:* 1 Grand Avenue, Hove.
                                                      Died 19 March 1925.

DONALDSON, Sir Hay Frederick, KCB 1911 (CB 1909); Technical Adviser to Minister of Munitions since 1915; *b* 7 July 1856; 2nd *s* of late Sir Stuart Alexander Donaldson, first Premier of New South Wales, and Amelia, *d* of the late Frederick Cowper of Carleton Hall, Penrith, and Unthank, Cumberland; *m* Selina, *y d* of late Col F. M. Beresford, sometime MP for Southwark; one *s* two *d*. *Educ:* Eton; Trinity College, Cambridge; Edinburgh; Zürich; L and NWR Works, Crewe; Past President, Institution of Mechanical Engineers; Member of Council of Institution of Civil Engineers; Member of Iron and Steel Institute, etc; on the Board and Executive Committee of the National Physical Laboratory; Chairman of Sectional Committee on Screw Threads and Limit Gauges of the Engineering Standards Committee; Civil and Mechanical Engineer; employed at Goa, India, 1884–87; Railway and Harbour construction on the Manchester Ship Canal, 1887–89; Chief Engineer, London India Docks Joint Committee, 1892–97; Deputy Director General of Ordnance Factories, 1898–99; Chief Mechanical Engineer of Ordnance Factories, 1899–1903; Chief Superintendent since 1903. *Recreations:* shooting, fishing. *Address:* Wood Lodge, Shooters' Hill, Kent. *Clubs:* Athenæum, St Stephen's, Ranelagh.
                                                      Died 5 June 1916.

DONALDSON, William, CB 1900; *b* 13 March 1838; *s* of George Donaldson, merchant, Edinburgh; *m* 1870, Mary, *d* of the late P. Ross of Leitfie, Meigle, NB. *Educ:* High School; University, Edin. Was in the public service for 43 years; began official career in the office of the Law Agent of the late General Board of Directors of Prisons for Scotland; in 1868 acted as Deputy Governor of Perth General Prison, but a year later returned to Edinburgh to assist the late Dr J. H. Burton in organising the Department of Judicial Statistics and arranging for an Annual Blue-Book on the subject; Secretary of the Prison Commission and Superintendent of the Scottish Department of Judicial Statistics, 1877–1900; gave much assistance in carrying out the provisions of the Prisons Act of 1877; and among other services acted as a member of and Secretary to a Departmental Commission, appointed by Lord Balfour in 1896, to consider in what way the Judicial Statistics could be made of more value to Statisticians and Criminologists; edited the Revised Statistics for the years 1897 and 1898. *Address:* 4 Ravelston Park, Edinburgh.
                                                      Died 22 July 1924.

DONCASTER, Leonard, MA, ScD; FRS 1915; Professor of Zoology, University of Liverpool; Fellow of King's College, Cambridge, 1910; *b* Sheffield, 31 Dec. 1877; *s* of Samuel Doncaster, Sheffield; *m* 1908, Dora, 2nd *d* of Walter Priestman, Birmingham; one *s* two *d*. *Educ:* Leighton Park School, Reading; King's College, Cambridge (Scholar). 1st class Natural Sciences Tripos Part I 1898, Part II (distinction in Zoology) 1900; Walsingham Medallist, 1902. Mackinnon Student of Royal Society, 1904–6; Lecturer on Zoology, Birmingham University, 1906–10; Special Lecturer on Variation and Heredity, 1909; Trail Medal of Linnæan Society, 1915. *Publications:* papers on zoological subjects in Quarterly Journal Microscopical Science, Transactions and Proceedings Royal Society, etc; Heredity in the Light of Recent Research, 1910; The Determination of Sex, 1914. *Address:* University, Liverpool.   *Died 28 May 1920.*

DONELAN, Capt. Anthony John Charles; MP (N) Co. Cork, E, 1892, unseated on petition, 1911; MP (N) Wicklow unopposed, 1911–18; *b* 1846; *s* of late Col Anthony Donelan, 48th Regt. *Educ:* Sandhurst. Was in army. *Address:* Ballymona, Midleton, Co. Cork.
                                                      Died Sept. 1924.

DONELAN, James, MB, MCh; FRSM; Chevalier of the Crown of Italy, 1909, Officer 1918; Surgeon, Throat Department, Italian Hospital, London, and to Royal Society of Musicians of Great Britain and Ireland; Lecturer, Diseases of Nose and Throat, Medical Graduates College, London; President, Section of Laryngology, Royal Society of Medicine, 1918–19; Permanent Organiser of Surgical Staff, Hôpital Régional, Villeneuve-sur-Lot, 1914–18; *e s* of late John Donnellan of Mount Kennett House, Limerick (adopted present form of spelling name 1886); *m* 1889, Sophia Annie, 2nd *d* of late Maj.-Gen. James M'Killop Taylor; one *s* one *d*. *Educ:* privately; Trinity Coll. Dublin. Honours in Surgery and Medicine Royal University of Ireland, 1886; Member of the Royal Italian Military Medical Commission for recruiting, 1915–18; Surgeon in temporary charge of the Ambulance Hospital at Crépy-en-Valois (Oise) during the first battle of the Aisne, Sept. 1914; appointed Medical Referee to the London Committee of the Croix Rouge Française; organised short service system by which over 300 British and Colonial surgeons gave voluntary service to the French wounded, 1914–16; Hon. Laryngologist to Royal Society of Musicians, established and developed the Throat Dept of the Italian Hospital; formerly Hon. Secretary and Member of Council of the Laryngological Society of London now merged in the Royal Society of Medicine. *Publications:* many communications to societies and medical journals on his specialty, as well as on subjects of wider interest. *Address:* 6 Manchester Square, W1. *T:* Pad. 269; Bruntsfield, Harrow-on-the-Hill. *T:* Harrow 24.
                                                      Died 25 Aug. 1922.

DONINGTON, 3rd Baron, *cr* 1880; **Gilbert Theophilus Clifton-Hastings-Campbell;** *b* 29 May 1859; 3rd *s* of Countess of Loudoun (10th in line) and 1st Lord Donington; *S* brother, 1920; *m* 1894, Maud Kemble, *o c* of Sir Charles Edward Hamilton, 1st Bt; two *d* (and two *d* decd). *Address:* 47 Eaton Square, SW1. *T:* Victoria 5781; Glenlee Park, New Galloway, Kirkcudbrightshire. *Clubs:* Bachelors', Carlton, Ranelagh.   *Died 31 May 1927 (ext).*

DONKIN, Sir (Horatio) Bryan, Kt 1911; MD Oxon; FRCP London; Member of Prisons Board, and a Director of Convict Prisons; Consulting Physician to Westminster Hospital, and East London Hospital for Children, King George Hospital, 1915; Hon. Member of the Royal Medico-Psychological Association; Member of Advisory Committee to Home Secretary at HM Preventive Detention Prison at Camp Hill, IoW; Member of Society for the Prevention of Venereal

Disease; *b* Blackheath, Kent, 1 Feb. 1845; *e s* of late Bryan Donkin, CE; *m* 1st, 1888, Auguste Margaretha Elisabeth (*d* 1919), *d* of late Count di Langhi of Cracow; 2nd, 1923, Marie Louise, *widow* of Isaac Bates, Belfast, and *d* of late William Reston, Wilmington, North Carolina, USA. *Educ:* Blackheath Proprietary School; Queen's College, Oxford; Open Scholar; 1st class in Greats (classical). Formerly Physician and Lecturer on Medicine at Westminster Hospital; Physician to East London Hospital for Children; Lecturer on Medicine at London School of Medicine for Women; Examiner in Medicine for Royal College of Physicians on Examining Board for England; HM Commissioner of Prisons; Medical Adviser to the Prison Commission; Member of Visiting Committees at the Borstal institutions; Harveian Orator, Royal Coll. Physicians, on the Inheritance of Mental Characters, 1910; member of Royal Commission on Control of the Feeble-minded, 1904–8, and of several Departmental Committees appointed by Home Office, etc. *Publications:* Diseases of Childhood; Lectures at the Maudsley Hospital on Mental Defect and Criminal Conduct, Lancet, Nov. 1920; many articles in medical journals, and in Reviews, some relating to mental pathology, crime, psychical researchers, medium-craft, the medical prevention of venereal diseases, the fallacies of psycho-analysis, etc. *Address:* 28 Hyde Park Street, W2. *T:* Padd. 5705. *Clubs:* Savile, Athenæum.   *Died 26 July 1927.*

DONKIN, Richard Sims, JP, DL; director of Suez Canal Co.; *b* 1836; *s* of late James Donkin, Tynemouth; *m* 1864, Hannah, *d* of John Dryden. MP (C) Tynemouth, 1885–1900. *Clubs:* Carlton, Junior Carlton; Travellers', Paris.   *Died 5 Feb. 1919.*

DONNELLY, Rt. Rev. Nicholas; RC Bishop of Dublin (auxiliary) since 1883; Bishop of Canea and Vicar-General of Dublin; Parish Priest of St Mary's, Haddington Road, Dublin, since 1904; *b* 23 Nov. 1837; *e s* of John Donnelly of Dublin, merchant. *Educ:* St Vincent's Coll., Castleknock; Irish Coll. Rome. Appointed Curate, 1861, to St Nicholas, Francis St, transferred to Pro Cathedral, Marlborough St, 1864; appointed Administrator St Andrews, 1879; Parish Priest, Rathgar, 1882; Parish Priest of Bray, 1894. *Publications:* English translation of Haberl's Magister Choralis; magazine and newspaper articles. *Recreations:* music, travel. *Address:* St Mary's, Haddington Road, Dublin. *Club:* Royal Societies.

Died 28 March 1920.

DONOHOE, Martin Henry, FJI; journalist and war correspondent; Paris correspondent, London Daily Chronicle; *b* Galway, Ireland, 10 Nov. 1869; *m* 1900, Madge Tilley of Sydney. *Educ:* National and Marist Brothers' Schools; Sorbonne et Ecole des langues Orientales. Began journalistic career, Courrier Australien, Sydney, 1892; subsequently staffs Evening News and Town and Country Journal, Sydney; traced De Rougemont; became war correspondent, London Daily Chronicle, 1899; in the Boer war; with Methuen from the Orange River to Magersfontein; acted as assistant galloper to Hector M'Donald in the fight at Koodoesberg Drift; accompanied Lord Roberts on march from Enslin; present at Paardeberg; subsequently captured; released on fall of Pretoria; in Russo-Japanese war; attached first Japanese army; with Kuroki through Korea and Manchuria; battles of the Yalu, Motien Pass, Towan, Liao-yang, and the Shaho; travelled in America, Australia, China, Japan, Korea, and South Sea Islands; in Turkish Revolution, 1909; witnessed taking Constantinople, Young Turks; first journalist to interview new Sultan; in Portuguese Revolution, 1910; escaped Lisbon with first detailed account fighting, 1911; Italian-Turkish War, with General Caneva in Tripoli; Balkan War (Abdullah Pasha's retreat, Rodosta, Chatalja, etc), 1912–13; in European War was Officer British Intelligence Corps, served Greece, Roumania, Russia; Special Service Officer North Persian Expedition, 1918–19. *Publications:* various. *Recreations:* rowing, cycling, swimming, golf. *Address:* 24 Boulevard des Capucines, Paris.

Died 19 Jan. 1927.

DONOVAN, John Thomas; MP (N) West Wicklow, 1914–18; Barrister; Hon. Secretary, National Volunteers, Ireland; *b* Belfast, 1878; *m* 1915, Alda, *d* of W. J. Ralph, Auckland, New Zealand; one *s.* Visited Australia and New Zealand as Envoy of Irish Party, 1906–7, 1912–13. *Address:* Dunloe, Terenure Road, Dublin.

Died 17 Jan. 1922.

DOOLETTE, Sir George Philip, Kt 1916; JP; *b* Dublin, 24 Jan. 1840; *m* 1st, Mary (*d* 1889), *e d* of George M'Ewin of Glen Ewin, South Australia; 2nd, 1895, Lillie (*d* 1916), *d* of late Dr R. W. Dale, Birmingham; one *s* one *d. Educ:* private tutor. One of the principal pioneers of the Western Australian Goldfields; Director Great Boulder Proprietary, etc; Fellow Royal Geographical Society, Royal Colonial Institute, etc. *Address:* Merlebank, Caterham Valley, Surrey. *TA:*

Doolettian, London. *T:* Caterham 29. *M:* 6641. *Clubs:* City Liberal, Australian, Royal Automobile, British Empire.

Died 19 Jan. 1924.

DOONER, Lt-Col William Dundas, CMG 1918; OBE 1919; BA; pac; late Royal Army Ordnance Corps and formerly Royal Irish Fusiliers; *b* 20 March 1876; *s* of late Col William Toke Dooner of Barton, Rathfarnham, Co. Dublin; *m* 1914, Marion Emily, *e d* of late Walter Wilson, Belvoir Park, Belfast. *Educ:* private tutor; Bradfield College. Entered Army from Militia as 2nd Lieut Royal Irish Fusiliers, 1895; Capt. 1902; Major 1913; Brev. Lt-Col 1915; served South African War, 1899–1900 (severely wounded); transferred to Army Ordnance Department, 1912; retired, 1922. *Address:* Greenan, Dunmurry, Co. Antrim.   *Died 28 Aug. 1927.*

DOONER, Colonel William Toke, CBE 1922; JP, Co. Kent and Rochester; 2nd *s* of John Dooner of Barton Lodge, Rathfarnham, Dublin, and Sarah Georgina, *e d* of Major Lawrence Dundas (*d* 1867), formerly of the 5th Fus; *m* 1875, Augusta, 5th *d* of W. P. Metchim of Petersham Lodge, Surrey; one *s* one *d* (and two *s* killed in War). *Educ:* Aldenham School, Elstree; Trinity College, Dublin; Staff College, Camberley. Entered Army, 1863 (8th King's Liverpool Regt); transferred to Royal Inniskilling Fus as Capt. 1875; Brig. Maj. Gibraltar, Aldershot, and Curragh, 1877–83; DAAG Dublin, 1883–88; Commanded 1st Batt. Royal Inniskilling Fusiliers, 1888–93; 87th Regimental District, 1894–99; Assistant Adjutant-General, 1899–1902; served Ashantee Expedition, 1873–74 (medal with clasp, despatches); retired from Army, 1902; Mayor of Rochester, 1905–6. *Publications:* To Coomassie and Back, 1874; Map of Gibraltar and the Country near, 1878; The Infantry of our Army and Mr Arnold Forster's Proposals, 1903; lectured on military subjects at Royal United Service Institution. *Recreations:* cricket and all games; school eleven. *Address:* Ditton Place, near Maidstone, Kent. *Club:* United Service.

Died 9 Nov. 1926.

DOPPING-HEPENSTAL, Major Lambert John, OBE 1920; DL, JP Co. Longford; *b* 1859; *s* of late Col R. A. Dopping-Hepenstal, DL, of Derrycassan, and Diana, *d* and *heiress* of late Rev. L. W. Hepenstal of Altadore Castle, Delgany; *m* 1920, Amy Maude, *d* of late Maj. C. R. W. Tottenham, DL, of Woodstock, Co. Wicklow, and Plas Berwyn, Llangollen; one *s* one *d. Educ:* Harrow. Commissioned RE, 1879; retired list as Major, 1907; served European War. High Sheriff Co. Wicklow, 1909, and Longford, 1910; inventor of the direct engine-room telegraph for steamers, modified railway points, etc. *Address:* Derrycassan, Granard, Co. Longford; 73 Harcourt Street, Dublin; 1 Albany Road, Bedford. *T:* Bedford 2352. *M:* TM 657. *Club:* Kildare Street, Dublin.

Died 5 Dec. 1928.

DORAN, Alban Henry Griffiths, FRCS, FRSM; President of the Obstetrical Society of London, 1899–1900; Consulting Surgeon, Samaritan Free Hospital; *b* London, 1849; *s* of Dr Doran, FSA, author of Annals of the Stage, Lives of the Queens of the House of Hanover, etc. *Educ:* Nassau School, Barnes, Surrey; St Bartholomew's Hospital. Hon. Fellow of Obstetrical and Gynæcological Societies of Bordeaux, and of Buenos Aires, and American Gynæcological Society. For 8 years was attached to the museum of the Royal College of Surgeons under Sir William Flower; compiler (with Sir James Paget and Sir James Goodhart) of the second edition of the Catalogues of the Pathological Series in that museum; was on the surgical staff of the Samaritan Free Hospital, 1877–1909; practising the operative surgery of the abdomen; lastly, prepared a descriptive Catalogue of Surgical Instruments, Mus. RCS Eng. 1912–25. *Publications:* The Morphology of the Mammalian Ossicula Auditûs, Trans Linn. Soc. 1878; Tumours of the Ovary, 1884; Handbook of Gynæcological Operations, 1887; Shakespeare and the Medical Society (annual oration, Medical Society, 1899); Chapter XIV Medicine in Shakespeare's England, 1916; Burton (Dr Slop), his Forceps and his Foes, Journal of Obstet. etc of British Empire, vol. 23. *Recreations:* literary pursuits, especially Shakespeare, English and French history. *Address:* 3 Lisgar Terrace, Kensington, W14.   *Died 23 Aug. 1927.*

DORAN, Edward Anthony, CIE 1907; *m.* Joined service, 1880; Postmaster-General, Madras, 1904; Bengal, 1904; Bombay, 1906.

Died 11 May 1922.

DORAN, Sir Henry Francis, Kt 1915; JP Cos. Mayo and Roscommon; *b* 15 April 1856; *s* of late Henry Doran of Ardagh, Killarney, Co. Kerry; *m* 1885, Margaret Caroline, *d* of late Thomas Cox of Bunreagh, Croghan, Co. Roscommon; three *s. Educ:* St Brendan's Seminary, Killarney; The Albert Agricultural College, Glasnevin, Dublin. Assistant to Superintendent of Agricultural

Education in Ireland, 1875–77; Estate Surveyor and Valuer for various estates in counties of Roscommon, Mayo and Sligo, 1879–90; Assistant Land Commissioner, 1890–91; Inspector Congested Districts Board for Ireland, 1892; Chief Land Inspector, 1903; Permanent Member of the Congested Districts Board for Ireland, 1910. *Address:* Redcroft, Seaford, Sussex. *Died 23 June 1928.*

DORCHESTER, Baroness (5th in line), *cr* 1899; **Henrietta Anne Leir-Carleton;** *b* 1846; *d* and *co-heiress* of 3rd and *cousin* of 4th and last Baron Dorchester (*d* 1897, when title, *cr* 1786, became extinct, but was revived in her favour, 1899); *m* 1st, 1864, Capt. Francis Paynton Pigott, 16th Lancers, of Banbury, Oxon (who assumed the additional name of Carleton) (*d* 1883); one *s* one *d* (and one *s* decd); 2nd, 1887, Maj.-Gen. Richard Langford Leir, of Ditcheat, Somerset (who assumed additional name of Carleton). *Heir: s* Hon. Dudley Massey Carleton, *b* 28 Feb. 1876. *Address:* Greywell Hill, Winchfield; Ditcheat Priory, Evercreech, Somerset. *TA:* Greywell.
Died 2 March 1925.

DOREZ, Léon Louis Marie; Librarian in the Department of Manuscripts of the Bibiliothèque nationale, Paris, since 1905; *b* Villemaur, Aube, France, 17 July 1864; *m* 1887, Berthe Marie Louise Dorez; one *d*. *Educ:* Ecole des Hautes Etudes; Sorbonne; Ecole des Chartes. Member of the French School at Rome, Palazzo Farnese, 1890–93; entered the National Library, Paris, as an assistant, 1893. Hon. LLD St Andrews, 1911; Editor of the Revue des Biblothèques (26 vols), and of the Bibliothèque littéraire de la Renaissance (17 vols). *Publications:* more than one hundred papers in different French and Italian reviews on the artistic, literary, and political history of the Renaissance in France and Italy; Cronique d'Antonio Morosini, 4 vols; Itinéraire de Jérôme Maurand d'Antibes à Constantinople; La Canzone delle Virtù e delle Scienze di Bartolomeo di Bartoli; Les manuscrits à peintures de Lord Leicester à Holkham Hall, Norfolk; Pétrarque, Vie de César; Le Psautier de Paul III; Pontifical peint pour le cardinal Giuliano Della Rovere par Francesco dai Libri de Vérone; Notice sur un recueil de poésies latines et un portrait de l'humaniste véronais Leonardo Montagna; Tables des Monuments et Mémoires de la Fondation Piot; Catalogue de la Collection Alexandre Bixio; Nouvelles recherches sur Michel-Ange et son entourage; Léonard de Vinci au Service de Louis XII et de François I; Léonard de Vinci et Jean Perréal, etc. *Address:* 10 rue Littré, Paris 6ᵉ; Villemaur-sur-Vanne, Aube. *Died 25 Jan. 1922.*

DORIS, William; *b* 13 April 1860; *s* of Robert and Margaret Doris, Westport; *m* 1910, Sara,*d* of Luke Cannon, Westport. *Educ:* Christian Brothers' Schools, Westport. JP, Westport; late Chm., Westport Urban Council, and Vice-Chairman, Castlebar District Asylum; Harbour Commissioner for Westport; Vice-Chairman, Mayo County Council, 1900–08; Acting Secretary of Irish Land League when no rent manifesto issued, 1881; arrested as suspect in Land League Office, Dublin, on suppression of the League, 1881, and imprisoned in Dundalk Jail for six months; first Secretary of United Irish League; MP (N) Mayo West, 1910–18. *Address:* 37 North Side, Clapham Common, SW; Westport, Co. Mayo. *TA:* W. Doris, Westport.
Died 13 Sept. 1926.

DORLING, Colonel Lionel, CB 1916; CMG 1919; DSO 1902; late Army Pay Department; *b* 7 Aug. 1860; *s* of Henry Dorling of Epsom; *m* 1888, Constance, *y d* of W. H. Price of Karachi. Formerly Captain Yorks Light Infantry; entered army, 1879; served South Africa, 1890–1902 (despatches, Queen's medal, five clasps; King's medal, two clasps; DSO); European War (Dardanelles), 1915 (despatches); Egypt, 1916. *Club:* Naval and Military.
Died 11 July 1925.

DORMER, 13th Baron, *cr* 1615; **Roland John Dormer,** Bt 1615; JP and DL; late Sub-director Egyptian Finance Ministry; Commander of Imperial Order of the Medjidie; *b* St Leonards-on-Sea, 24 Nov. 1862; *e s* of late Lieut-Gen. Hon. Sir James Dormer, KCB; *S* uncle, 1900; *m* 1897, Marie Hanem,*d* of late F. Eywaz of Cairo; one *d* decd. *Educ:* Oscott College. Owner of about 5000 acres. *Heir: b* Hon. Capt. Charles Joseph Thaddeus Dormer, *b* 24 Feb. 1864. *Recreations:* shooting, gardening. *Address:* Maderno, Italy.
Died 9 Feb. 1920.

DORMER, 14th Baron, *cr* 1615; **Charles Joseph Thaddeus Dormer,** Bt 1615; CBE 1919; Captain RN; Gentleman Usher to HM, 1919; *b* 24 Feb. 1864; *s* of Lt-Gen. Hon. Sir James Dormer, KCB; *S* brother, 1920; *m* 1903, May, *y d* of late Col Sir Spencer Clifford, 3rd Bt; two *s* three *d*. *Educ:* Oscott College. Joined Britannia as naval cadet, 1877; sub-Lieut 1883; Lieut 1887; Commander, 1899; retired, 1908; Capt. retired list, 1914; served as Flag-Lieut to Admiral Lord Walter Kerr

in Mediterranean, 1890–92; to Vice-Admiral Sir H. Fairfax in Channel Squadron, 1893–95; Naval Attaché, Tokio, 1906–8. *Heir: s* Hon. Charles Walter James Dormer, *b* 20 Dec. 1903. *Address:* Grove Park, Warwick. *Club:* Naval and Military.
Died 4 May 1922.

DORNHORST, Frederick, KC; *b* Ceylon, 26 April 1849; *s* of Frederick Dornhorst, Notary Public, Trincomalee; *m* Lydia, *d* of E. G. Sisouw, Proctor, Supreme Court; four *s* one *d*. *Educ:* Colombo Academy (later Royal College). Master, Royal College, 1868–73; called to Ceylon Bar, 1874; English Bar, 1901; Member Ceylon Council of Legal Education. *Address:* Calverley House, Colombo, Ceylon. *Club:* Orient, Colombo.
Died 24 April 1927.

DORRIEN-SMITH, Thomas Algernon, JP, DL; *b* Berkhamsted, 7 Feb. 1846; *e s* of late Col Smith-Dorrien, and Mary Ann, *heiress* of Thomas Dorrien, Haresfoot, Gt Berkhamsted; *m* 1875, Edith Anna Maria (*d* 1892), *d* of Christopher Tower and Lady Sophia Tower; two *s* five *d*. *Educ:* Harrow. Served in 10th Hussars, 1864–74; retired as Lieut; afterwards Herts Yeomanry. *Address:* Tresco Abbey, Isles of Scilly; Ashlyns Hall, Herts. *Clubs:* Carlton, Cavalry.
Died 6 Aug. 1918.

DORRITY, Rev. David, BD; Rector of St Ann's, Manchester, since 1895; Hon. Canon of Manchester since 1917; *s* of James and Susan Dorrity, Liverpool; *m* 1891, Mabel Rosa, *y d* of Henry Raine Marriott, Whalley Range, Manchester; one *d*. *Educ:* Liverpool; Dublin University. Ordained, 1883; Curate of Waterhead, Oldham, of Whalley Range, and Chaplain to the Blind at Old Trafford successively. *Recreations:* golf, trout-fishing, chess. *Address:* 62 Platt Lane, Manchester. *T:* Rusholme 205.
Died 1 June 1926.

DOTTIN, Henri Georges; professeur à l'Université de Rennes; conseiller municipal de Rennes; *b* Liancourt (Oise), 29 Oct. 1863; fils de Charles Henri Dottin, homme de lettres; *m* Marie Delaunay, fille du professeur à l'Université de Rennes; two *s*. *Educ:* lycée de Laval. Etudiant à la Faculté des lettres de Rennes, 1883–84; étudiant à la Sorbonne, élévé à l'Ecole des Hautes Etudes, 1884–91; agrégé de grammaire, 1890; docteur ès lettres, 1897; Maître de conférences à la Faculté des lettres de Dijon, 1891–92; Maître de conférences de grammaire et philologie, 1892–1903, puis Professeur de grec à la Faculté des lettres de Rennes, 1903; doyen de la Faculté des Lettres, 1910; correspondant de l'Institut de France, 1919. *Publications:* Les Formations verbales en-r en sanskrit, en italique et en celtique, 1896; De eis in Iliade inclusis hominum nominibus quao non unice propria nomina sunt, 1896; Glossaire des parlers du Bas-Maine, 1899; Contes irlandais traduits du gaélique, 1901; Contes et légendes d'Irlande traduits du gaélique, 1901; Glossaire du parler du Pléchâtel (Ille et Vilaine), 1901; Manuel pour servir à l'etude de l'antiquité, 1906, 2nd edn 1915; Louis Eunius ou le Purgatoire de Saint Patrice, mystère breton, 1911; Manuel d'irlandais moyen, 1913; Les Anciens Peuples de l'Europe, 1916; La langue gauloise, 1920; Les Littératures celtiques, 1924; L'épopée irlandaise, 1925. *Address:* 39 boulevard Sévigné, Rennes. *Died 11 Jan. 1928.*

DOUDNEY, Sarah; novelist; *b* Portsmouth, 15 Jan. 1843; *y c* of G. E. Doudney. *Educ:* by Mrs Kendall, Southsea. Began to write very young, contributing to many magazines. *Publications:* A Woman's Glory, 1885; The Missing Rubies, 1886; When We Two Parted, 1887; Strangers Yet, Stepping Stones, etc, between 1886 and 1896; also several novels for girls: Where the Dew falls in London, 1890; Through Pain to Peace, 1892; A Romance of Lincoln's Inn, 1894; Katherine's Keys, 1895; Pilgrims of the Night, 1896; A Cluster of Roses, etc; Lady Dye's Reparation, 1899; Silent Strings, 1900; One of the Few, 1904; Shadow and Shine, 1906. *Recreations:* walking, antiquarianism. *Died 15 Dec. 1926.*

DOUGALL, Lily; theological writer and novelist;*b* Montreal, 16 April 1858; *y d* of John Dougall and Elizabeth Redpath. *Educ:* privately; Edinburgh University Classes for Women. LLA St Andrews. *Publications:* Beggars All, 1891; What Necessity Knows, 1893; The Mermaid, 1895; Zeitgeist, 1895; Question of Faith, 1895; The Madonna of a Day, 1896; A Dozen Ways of Love, 1897; The Morman Prophet, 1898; The Earthly Purgatory, 1904; The Spanish Dowry, 1906; Paths of the Righteous, 1908; (anonymously) Pro Christo et Ecclesia, 1900; Christus Futurus, 1907; Absente Reo, 1910; Voluntas Dei, 1912; The Practice of Christianity, 1914; The Christian Doctrine of Health, 1916; part author of Concerning Prayer, 1916, Immortality, 1917, The Spirit, 1919, God and the Struggle for Existence, 1919, Arcades Ambo (poems), 1919, The Lord of Thought, 1922. *Address:*

Cutts End, Cumnor, near Oxford. *TA:* Cumnor. *Club:* University Women's. *Died 9 Oct. 1923.*

DOUGHTY, Charles Montagu, MA; Honorary Fellow of Gonville and Caius College, Cambridge; Hon. DLitt Oxford; Hon. LittD Cambridge; *b* 1843; *y s* of late Rev. Charles Montagu Doughty, of Theberton Hall, Suffolk, and Frederica, *d* of late Hon. and Rev. Frederick Hotham, Prebendary of Rochester and Rector of Dennington, Suffolk; *m* 1886, Caroline Amelia, *d* of late General Sir Montagu McMurdo, GCB; two *d. Educ:* Naval School at Portsmouth; Caius College, Cambridge. Began to travel, 1870; joined pilgrimage caravan, 1876, and travelled to Medain Salih, Hail, Kheybar, Kasim and Jiddah, 1878. Royal Founder's medal, Royal Geographical Society, 1912; Hon. Member British Academy. *Publications:* Travels in Arabia Deserta, 2 vols, 1888; Documents Epigraphiques (pub. 1884 par la Commission du Corpus Inscr. Semiticarum); The Dawn in Britain, 6 vols, 1906; Adam Cast Forth, 1908; The Cliffs, 1909; The Clouds, 1912; Mansoul, or the Riddle of the World, 1920. *Address:* Sissinghurst, Kent. *Died 21 Jan. 1926.*

DOUGHTY, Rear-Adm. Henry Montagu, CB 1918; CMG 1919; RN; Rear-Adm. 1st Battle Squadron, Atlantic Fleet; *b* 1870; *s* of H. M. Doughty, Theberton Hall, Suffolk; *m* 1907, Gwendoline, *d* of Lieut-Col C. E. G. Burr. Went as Lieut of HM Theseus to observe eclipse of sun at Santa Pola, 17 May 1900; Captain of Gunnery School, Devonport, 1914; served European War in command HMS Royal Sovereign 1st Battle Squadron (CMG). *Address:* Spencer Place, Bishops Waltham, Hants. *Club:* Naval and Military. *Died 1 May 1921.*

DOUGLAS, Arthur, MD, LSA (graduated University of Ghent, Belgium); physician; *b* 1850; *s* of Dr George Douglas (Friarshaw); *m;* three *s. Educ:* private tuition; Queen's College (Divinity and Medicine). Visited Straits Settlements and China (studying for Navy); also India, Ceylon, Madeira, Canada, Norway, Germany; employed by Colonial Government for some years, also by War Office at the Royal Arsenal, Woolwich, and Royal Small Arms Factory, Enfield Lock; served through Boer War, Staff Surgeon attached RAMC; in charge of several large depots and the insane (two medals, 5 clasps). *Publications:* various articles on Psychology and Hypnotism as a curative agent in certain mental conditions; articles published in the Press on kindred subjects; an exhaustive dissertation on Tabes Dorsalis, embracing Treatment by Suspension, with sketches; an article on Phthisis, copied into French and German medical Press; notes on interesting cases in South Africa; various minor articles. *Recreations:* heavy athletics, walking, riding, cycling. *Address:* 57 Devonshire Street, Portland Place, W1. *TA:* Medicato, London. *T:* Paddington 1488. *Club:* Junior Army and Navy. *Died 22 Dec. 1920.*

DOUGLAS, Arthur Henry Johnstone-, DL, JP; *b* 1846; *e s* of late Robert Johnstone-Douglas of Lockerbie, and Lady Jane Mary Margaret Douglas, 5th *d* of 5th Marquis of Queensberry; *m* 1869, Jane Maitland, *d* of the late Stair Hathorn Stewart of Physgill. Late Lieut Dumfries Militia; was in 42nd Highlanders. *Address:* 9 Doune Terrace, Edinburgh. *Died 26 March 1923.*

DOUGLAS, Cecil George; Chief Clerk, Mansion House Justice Room, London, since 1887; *b* 1 April 1854; *s* of late George Douglas, a Superintendent of the General Register Office, Somerset House; *m* 1885, Sophia Pitt, *d* of late Surgeon-Major Nicolson; two *d. Educ:* University College School, London. Served two years in General Register Office; three years in Board of Trade; five years Bow Street Police Court; two and a half years as Assistant Clerk Mansion House Justice Room; four and a half years as Chief Clerk Guildhall Justice Room. *Address:* Wathla, Surbiton Hill Park. *Died 8 Jan. 1919.*

DOUGLAS, Charles Mackinnon, CB 1918; JP, DL; Officier de l'ordre de la Couronne, Belgium, 1920; *b* Edinburgh, 2 Oct. 1865; *s* of A. Halliday Douglas, MD, and Jessie, *d* of Robert Tod, Clerwood, Corstorphine. MD; *m* 1895, Anne Isabel, *d* of Robert Tod, Clerwood, Corstorphine. *Educ:* Edinburgh Academy; Universities of Edinburgh and Freiburg; MA, DSc; first-class Honours in Philosophy, Univ. of Edinburgh; Vans Dunlop Scholar; Hamilton Fellow; Ferguson Scholar, Scottish Universities; seven years Lecturer in Moral Philosophy, University of Edinburgh. MP (L) NW Division of Lanarkshire, 1899–1906; contested (LU) South Lanarkshire Division, 1910; Chairman, Lanarkshire Territorial Force Association; six years Chairman of Directors of the Highland and Agricultural Society of Scotland; President of the Scottish Agricultural Organisation Society; Ex-Chairman of the Scottish Council of Agriculture; Ex-President of the Scottish Chamber of Agriculture. Owner of about 400 acres. *Publications:* John Stuart Mill, a study of his Philosophy, 1895; Ethics of John Stuart Mill, 1898; minor philosophical writings. *Address:* Auchlochan, Lesmahagow. *T:* Lesmahagow 2. *Clubs:* Brooks's; New, Edinburgh; Western, Glasgow. *Died 3 Feb. 1924.*

DOUGLAS, David, FRSE; publisher in Edinburgh; *b* Stranraer, Wigtownshire, 1823. Business training received in the house of Blackwood, first in Edinburgh and then in London, 1839–47. Bookseller in Edinburgh, 1847; first publication, 1854; editor of North British Review, 1863–69; also Scott's Journal and Familiar Letters, etc, 1890–92; Fellow of the Royal Society of Edinburgh since 1866, and of the Antiquaries since 1861; Treasurer to that body, 1871–83. *Address:* 9 Castle Street, Edinburgh. *Died 5 April 1916.*

DOUGLAS, Brig.-Gen. Douglas Campbell, CB 1917; *b* 19 Aug. 1864; *s* of A. H. Campbell, JP, DL, and Agnes, *d* of J. C. Douglas of Mains, Dumbartonshire; assumed the surname of Douglas in lieu of Campbell on succeeding to Mains, 1925; *m* 1899, Hon. Violet Averil Margaret Vivian, *e d* of 1st Baron Swansea; one *s* two *d. Educ:* Eton, RMC, Sandhurst. Served Hazara Expedition, 1888; Chitral Relief Force, 1895; European War, in France, 1915–17 (despatches, CB); Lieut-Col commanding 2nd Batt. Seaforth Highlanders, 1909–13; Colonel 1913; Brigade Commander, 1914–19; retired pay, 1919. *Address:* Mains, Milngavie, Scotland. *T:* Milngavie 29. *Clubs:* Naval and Military; New, Edinburgh. *Died 17 June 1927.*

DOUGLAS, Rev. Evelyn Keith, MA; Rector of Cheveley, Cambs, since 1895; Hon. Canon of Ely, 1913; Rural Dean of Cheveley; *b* 27 July 1859; *s* of Stewart Douglas and Catherine, *d* of Robert Wright Wood; unmarried. *Educ:* Eton; New College, Oxford. Curate of Newcastle Cathedral, 1884–85; Weybridge, 1885–89; East London Missionary in charge of Eton Mission, Hackney Wick, 1889–90; Curate of Alverstoke, 1891–95; Rural Dean of Thurlow, 1903–14; Fordham, 1914–17; Secretary of Ely Diocesan Sunday School Council, 1907–14; Ely Diocesan Fund, 1912–13; Member of Diocesan Board of Finance, 1913–16; Secretary of Ely Diocesan Conference, 1915. *Recreations:* cricket (Eton XI, 1878); golf. *Address:* Cheveley Rectory, Newmarket. *T:* Cheveley, Newmarket. *Club:* New Oxford and Cambridge. *Died 6 Dec. 1920.*

DOUGLAS, James, LLD, BA; Member and Vice-President, American Institute of Mining Engineers, New York; *b* Quebec, Canada, 1837; *s* of James Douglas, MD, and Elizabeth Ferguson; *m* 1860, Naomi Douglas; two *s* two *d. Educ:* Queen's Univ., Kingston, Canada; Edin. Univ. Mem. of the Iron and Steel Inst. of Great Britain; the North of England Society of ME; the American Geographical Society, NY; the Philosophical Society, Phil.; the Society of Arts, London; Member and Gold Medallist of the Institution of Mining and Metallurgy, London; formerly Professor of Chemistry, Morrin College, Quebec; President of Phelps, Dodge & Co., the Copper Queen Mining Company, Detroit Copper Company and others in Arizona, and of the Moctezuma Copper Company, Mexico; President of the El Paso and SWRR, and the Nacozari RR Companies; twice President of the American Institute of Mining Engineers; President of the Can. Society of New York; representative of the US at the Mining Congress in Paris, 1900. *Publications:* Old France in the New World; New England and New France; Biography of Dr T. Sterry Hunt, FRS; Canadian Independence; Imperial Federation and Annexation; Untechnical Addresses on Technical Subjects; a Cantor Lecturer, Society of Arts, and writer on various subjects in American and English journals. *Recreation:* fishing. *Address:* 99 John Street, New York; Spuyten Duyvil, New York. *Clubs:* Century Association, Engineers, City, Adirondack League; Montmorency, Quebec. *Died 26 June 1918.*

DOUGLAS, Hon. James Moffat; Senator since 1906; *b* Scotland, 26 May 1839; *m* 1861, Jane, *d* of George Smith, Darlington, Ontario. *Educ:* Toronto University; Knox College, Toronto; Princeton Seminary. Ordained Presbyterian Church, 1865; Chaplain to troops at Mhow, 1876–82; MP E Assiniboia, 1896–1904. *Address:* Tantallon, Sask, Canada. *Died 19 Aug. 1921.*

DOUGLAS, Lt-Col Robert Jeffray, CMG 1915; 5th Battalion the Cameronians (Scottish Rifles) (Territorial Force); *b* 4 Oct. 1869; unmarried. *Educ:* Bellahouston Academy; Blairlodge School, Polmont. Served S African War, 1901–2; European War, 1914–15 (CMG). *Address:* Ashlea, Bellahouston, Glasgow. *Clubs:* Conservative, New, Glasgow. *Died 3 July 1916.*

DOUGLAS, Major (Bt Lt-Col) Robert Vaughan, CBE 1919; RGA; *b* 29 June 1881; *s* of late C. P. Douglas, solicitor, Chester; *m* 1917, Gladys Mary, *o d* of Col J. Lewes, JP, late RA, of Llanllyr, Cardiganshire. *Educ:* Cheltenham College; RMA Woolwich. Served European War, 1914–19 (CBE). *Address:* c/o Cox and Co., 16 Charing Cross, SW1. *Club:* Army and Navy.

Died 30 Sept. 1922.

DOUGLAS, Maj.-Gen. Sir William, KCMG 1915; CB 1908; DSO 1900; Royal Scots; Brig.-Gen. commanding 14th Infantry Brigade, 1909–13; commanding a Division since 1913; *b* Cranborne Lodge, Dorset, 13 August 1858; *s* of William Douglas, late East India Civil Service; *m* 1885, Ellen Lytcott, *d* of S. Taylor, Crown Solicitor, Barbados. *Educ:* Bath. Joined 1st Batt. The Royal Scots, 1878; served as Adjutant, 1st Batt. 1880–87; Captain, 1885; Adjutant, 3rd Royal Scots, 1888–93; Adjutant, 1st Royal Scots, 1893–94; Major, 1895; Staff College, 1896–97; Lieut-Col 1900; served with Bechuanaland expedition, 1884–85; South Africa, 1900–2 (despatches, Queen's medal, three clasps; King's medal, two clasps; DSO); Dardanelles, 1914–15 (KCMG) appointed to command a mobile column; Brevet-Colonel, 1904; Colonel, General Staff, 6th Division, 1906. *Club:* Naval and Military.   *Died 2 Nov. 1920.*

DOUGLAS, William Douglas Robinson-, JP, DL; FLS, FRGS; *b* 1851; *o s* of late Rev. George Robinson-Douglas and Jane Eleanor, *o d* of late Boyd Miller, of Colliers Wood, Surrey; *m* 1st, 1879, Frances Mary (*d* 1881), *e d* of late Col William Burnett-Ramsay, of Banchory Lodge, Co. Kincardine; 2nd, 1889, Constance, *d* of Sir Thomas Proctor-Beauchamp, 4th Bt. *Educ:* Christ Church, Oxford. MA. *Address:* Orchardton, Castle Douglas, Kirkcudbrightshire. *TA:* Auchencairn. *M:* SB 18. *Club:* United University.

Died 3 Oct. 1921.

DOUGLAS, Comdr William Ramsay Binny, CIE 1917; RIM; Senior Military Transport Officer, Bombay. *Address:* Senior Transport Officer, Bombay.   *Died 28 June 1919.*

DOUGLAS-SCOTT-MONTAGU, Hon. Robert Henry; *b* 30 July 1867; *s* of 1st Baron Montagu of Beaulieu and Cecily Susan, *d* of 2nd Lord Wharncliffe; *b* and *heir-pres.* to 2nd Baron Montagu of Beaulieu; *m* 1904, Alice, *widow* of Oscar Davies. Formerly Lieut Lothian Regt.

Died 10 Feb. 1916.

DOVER, Rev. Thomas Birkett; Hon. Canon of Southwark; *b* 7 Nov. 1846; *s* of Thomas Dover, late Mayor of Liverpool; *m* 1876, Fenella Smith, *d* of Andrew Low, shipowner; three *s* three *d*. *Educ:* Royal Institution, Liverpool; Exeter College, Oxford; Cuddesdon College. Ordained 1870; Curate at St John the Divine, Kennington, for three years; Chaplain, Stockwell Small-Pox Hospital; Vicar of St Agnes, Kennington Park, 1874–94; Old Malden, 1894–1914; Rector of Shenley, 1917–20; Member London School Board, 1891–94; Domestic Chaplain to the Earl of Home, KT, 1914–15. *Publications:* Some Quiet Lenten Thoughts; The Hidden Word; The Ministry of Mercy. *Address:* 20 Holywell, Oxford. *Clubs:* Oxford and County, Oxford Union, Oxford.   *Died 23 Dec. 1926.*

DOVERDALE, 1st Baron, *cr* 1916; **Edward Partington,** Kt 1912; JP, DL Derbyshire; Director of the Manchester and Liverpool District Bank; Officer's Cross of Order of Francis Joseph of Austria; presented a Convalescent Home to the Borough of Glossop; Freeman of the Borough of Glossop; *b* 1836; *s* of Edward Partington; *m* 1861, Sarah (*d* 1917), *d* of Thomas H. Haworth; one *s* two *d*. Formerly (1874) Captain 23rd Derbyshire (Volunteer) Rifle Corps. Owner of about 5000 acres. *Heir: s* Hon. Oswald Partington, *b* 4 May 1872. *Address:* Easton, Glossop; Westwood Park, Droitwich; 10 Ennismore Gardens, SW.   *Died 5 Jan. 1925.*

DOW, Thomas Millie, RSW; *b* Dysart, Fifeshire; *s* of Thomas Dow, town-clerk and solicitor, and Margaret Millie; *m* Florence Ellen, *d* of William Cox of Snaigow, Perthshire, Scotland. *Educ:* home; Edinburgh. Served law apprenticeship; studied in the Ecole des Beaux-Arts, Paris, under Gérome, and with Carolus Duran. *Address:* Talland, St Ives, Cornwall.   *Died July 1919.*

DOWDING, General Townley Ward; *b* 11 April 1847; *s* of late Rev. Townley W. Dowding, MA, St Peter's, Marlborough, and Elizabeth, *d* of J. Eamonson of Beale, Yorkshire; *m* 1886, Florence Mary, *d* of Hon. Walter Lamb, MLC, Sydney, NSW; one *s*. Entered Royal Marines, 1865; Captain, 1879; Major, 1885; Lieut-Col 1893; Colonel, 1899; Major-Gen. 1902; Lieut-Gen. 1910; retired, 1912. Inspector of Marine Recruiting, 1898–1900; served S Africa, 1877–79 (despatches, medal with clasp, prom. Captain, brevet Major). Jubilee

medal, 1897. *Address:* Singleton, Alverstoke, Hants. *Club:* United Service.   *Died 4 Sept. 1927.*

DOWLING, Rev. Theodore Edward, DD; late Archdeacon in Syria, and Canon of St George's Collegiate Church, Jerusalem; Commissary for Eastern Church intercourse within the Anglican Bishopric in Jerusalem; Chaplain of St Luke's Church, Haifa-under-Mount-Carmel, Palestine; *b* 15 Oct. 1837; *s* of late Rev. John Goulter Dowling, MA, Rector of St Mary de Crypt, Gloucester. *Educ:* St Augustine's College, Canterbury. Twenty-seven years in the Diocese of Fredericton, New Brunswick, Canada; in Turkey since 1890; 3½ years Chaplain of the Crimean Memorial Church, Constantinople, and 22 years in Jerusalem and Haifa, Galilee; visited the United States of America, Mexico, France, Germany, Austria, Hungary, Ceylon, India, Australasia, Denmark, Sweden, Russia, Mount Athos, Damascus, Egypt, The Soudan, Asia Minor, Mount Lebanon, Damascus, Aintab, Petra, Greece. *Publications:* The Orthodox Greek Patriarchate of Jerusalem, 3rd edition; Sketches of Georgian Church History; Gaza: a City of Many Battles; The Armenian Church; The Egyptian Church; The Abyssinian Church; The City of Safed: A Refuge of Judaism; Hellenism in England. *Recreations:* the study of Eastern Churches, numismatics: Jewish, Syrian, and Phœnician coinage. *Address:* 47 Anerley Park, SE.

Died 12 Jan. 1921.

DOWLING, Rt. Rev. Thomas Joseph; RC Bishop of Hamilton since 1889; *b* 23 Feb. 1840; went to Canada, 1951. *Educ:* Hamilton; St Michael's College, Toronto; Grand Seminary, Montreal. Ordained, 1864; Vicar-general, Hamilton, 1881; Bishop of Peterborough, Kingston, Canada, 1887–89. *Address:* King Street West, Hamilton, Toronto, Canada.   *Died 7 Aug. 1924.*

DOWN, Lieut-Commander Sir Charles Edward, KBE 1920 (OBE 1919); RNR; Marine Superintendent, Royal Mail Steam Packet Company, 1917–24; *b* 13 July 1857; *s* of late Rev. Chas J. Down, who was *s* of Rear-Admiral Edward Augustus Down, RN; *m* 1892, Gertrude Louisa, *d* of Dean May of Demerara, British Guiana; one *s* one *d*. *Educ:* Marlborough College; Switzerland. Went to sea, 1876; joined the RMSP Co. as Fifth Officer, 1881; worked up through the various grades, and was promoted to Commander, 1896; commanded the following ships of the said company—Essequibo, Orinoco, Magdalena, Thames, Trent, Aragon, Avon, Arlanza, Desna, Amazon, Descado; was in command of Arlanza when captured by the German armed merchant cruiser Kaiser Wilhelm der Grosse in the early days of the War. *Address:* 15 Whitewell Road, Southsea.

Died 20 Aug. 1927.

DOWN, 8th Viscount, *cr* 1680; **Major-General Hugh Richard Dawnay,** KCVO 1903; CB 1900; CIE 1886; MA; Bt 1642; Baron Dawnay of Danby (UK), 1897; late Steward of Jockey Club; *b* London, 20 July 1844; *s* of 7th Viscount and Mary Isabel, *d* of Bishop of Bath and Wells (Bagot); *S* father, 1857; *m* 1st, 1869, Lady Cecilia Maria Charlotte Molyneux, VA (*d* 1910), *d* of 3rd Earl of Sefton; one *s* three *d* (and one *s* decd); 2nd, 1911, Faith, *d* of Rev. Henry Dening. *Educ:* Eton; Christ Church, Oxford. Cornet and sub-Lieutenant, 2nd Life Guards, 1865; Lieutenant, 1869; Captain, 1873; Major, 1879; Lieut-Col 10th Royal Hussars, 1886; Col 1912; commanded 10th RH, 1887–92; served Zulu War, 1879; ADC to Duke of Connaught, Com. Meerut Div. 1883–85; ADC to Duke of Cambridge, 1892–95; Col Com. Cavalry Brigade at the Curragh, 1897–99; served S Africa, 1899–1900 (despatches twice), and 1901–2; Special Envoy to Shah of Persia, 1903; Brig.-Gen. 1901; retired. Protestant. Conservative. Officer of the Legion of Honour. *Heir: s* Hon. John Dawnay, *b* 23 May 1872. *Address:* Dingley, Market Harborough; Danby Lodge, Grosmont, York. *Clubs:* United Service, Turf.   *Died 21 Jan. 1924.*

DOWNES, Maj.-Gen. Major Francis, CMG 1885; *b* Dedham, Essex, 10 Feb. 1834; *y s* of W. Downes of Dedham; *m* 1858, Helen (*d* 1903), *d* of R. Chamberlin of Catton House, Catton, Norwich; three *s* one *d*. *Educ:* RMA Woolwich. Entered Royal Artillery, 1852; Col 1882; retired as Hon. Maj.-Gen. 1884; Maj.-Gen. South Australia, 1888; Maj.-Gen. Victoria, 1899; served in Crimean Campaign, 1855–56 (medal, clasp, and Turkish medal); Commandant, South Australia, 1877–85; also 1888–93; Secretary for Defence, Victoria, 1885–88; Comm., Victoria, 1899–1902; prepared five contingents for the war in South Africa. Decorated for service in South Australia. *Recreations:* reading, out-of-door amusements. *Address:* Brighton, Melbourne.

Died Oct. 1923.

DOWNES, Sir Joseph, Kt 1900; *b* 1848; *s* of Christopher Downes of Kiltele, Trim, Ireland; *m* 1st, 1884, Teresa, *d* of Dennis Carton;

2nd Johanna, *widow* of Alderman Hennessy, Dublin, and *d* of Thomas Davy, Newtown, Tipperary. Knighthood bestowed in honour of Queen Victoria's visit to Ireland, 1900; High Sheriff of City of Dublin, 1900. *Address:* 40 Eccles Street, Dublin.

Died 22 Sept. 1924.

DOWNES, Rev. Robert Percival, LLD; Wesleyan minister; *b* Ripon, 22 April 1842; *s* of Christopher Downes; *m* 1869, Clara Elizabeth (*d* 1921), *d* of T. W. Trouncer, JP, Shrewsbury; two *s* two *d*. *Educ:* Ripon Grammar School; private tutors. Entered Wesleyan ministry, 1865; started Great Thoughts for the purpose of presenting to the masses something of the best which has been said and written; retired from pastoral work of the ministry for the editorship of the paper, 1885; resigned 1914. *Publications:* John Ruskin; Pillars of Our Faith; Pure Pleasures; Woman: her Charm and Power; The Art of Noble Living; Man's Immortality and Destiny; Seven Supreme Poets; Hours with the Immortals (British Poets); (Foreign Poets); Thoughts on Living Subjects; Cities which Fascinate; Our Fallen Heroes and their Destiny, 1915; Hildebrand, an Historical Play in Blank Verse, 1919, etc. *Recreations:* reading, walking. *Address:* 13 Vallance Road, Hove, Sussex. *Died 20 April 1924.*

DOWNHAM, 1st Baron, *cr* 1919, of Fulham; **William Hayes Fisher,** PC 1911; Chairman, LCC since 1919; a director of the Suez Canal since 1919; *b* Downham, 1853; *e s* of late Frederick Fisher, Rector of Downham, Isle of Ely, and Mary, *d* of late William Hayes; *m* 1895, his *c* Florence Fisher; one *d*. *Educ:* Haileybury; University College, Oxford. Graduated in Classical and Legal Honours Schools, Oxford, 1876 (MA). Barrister, Inner Temple, 1879; Hon. Private Secretary to Sir Michael Hicks-Beach, 1886–87, and Rt Hon. A. J. Balfour, 1887–92; Junior Lord of the Treasury, and a Ministerial Whip, 1895–1902; Financial Secretary to Treasury, 1902–3; Royal Patriotic Commissioner (Chairman), 1904; Alderman LCC 1907–13; MP (C) Fulham, 1885–1906, and 1910; Parliamentary Secretary to Local Government Board, 1915–17, and President, 1917–18; Chancellor of the Duchy of Lancaster, Nov. 1918–Jan. 1919. Knight of the Order of St John of Jerusalem. *Recreations:* President National Skating Association; Leander Rowing Club; Hayling Island and Sandwich Golf Clubs. *Heir:* none. *Address:* 13 Buckingham Palace Gardens, SW1. *T:*Victoria 3365.*Club:* Carlton.

Died 2 July 1920 (ext).

DOWNHAM, Rev. Isaac; Hon. Canon of Manchester. *Address:* Baxendin, Accrington. *Died 10 March 1923.*

DOWNIE, Capt. John, DSO 1916; MB; RAMC TF. Served European War, 1914–16 (despatches, Order of St Anne, DSO). *Address:* Maybush, Bellevue, Wakefield.

Died June 1921.

DOWNIE, Walker, MB, CM; FRFPS Glasgow; Lecturer on Diseases of the Throat and Nose, University of Glasgow; Surgeon, Throat and Nose Department, Western Infirmary; Aurist and Laryngologist to the Royal Hospital for Sick Children, Glasgow; Hon. President Glasgow University Medico-Chirurgical Society; Ex-President, Scottish Otological and Laryngological Society; 2nd surv. *s* of late James Downie of Bertrohill; *m* Elsie, *y d* of late John Maitland, Lauderdale, Liverpool; one *d*. *Educ:* High School and University, Glasgow; London Hospitals. Formerly House Surgeon, Glasgow Western Infirmary; House Physician, Glasgow Royal Infirmary; Assistant Surgeon, Lock Hospital; Clinical Assistant, Central London Throat and Ear Hospital; Vice-President, British Laryngological and Rhinological Association; Lecturer on Diseases of the Throat and Nose, Western Medical School; ex-President, Glasgow Royal Medical-Chirurgical Society; Fellow of the Royal Society of Medicine, London; Fellow of the Royal Philosophical Society, Glasgow; Member of the Medical Consultative Committee, Consumption Sanatoria for Scotland; Examiner for Fellowship, and late Visitor, Royal Faculty of Physicians and Surgeons, Glasgow, etc. *Publications:* History of Med.-Chir. Society of Glasgow, 1908; Clinical Manual for Study of Diseases of the Throat, 2nd edn, 1909; many papers to scientific journals. *Address:* 4 Woodside Crescent, Glasgow. *T:* Charing Cross 520; Cragmohr, Shandon. *Clubs:* Royal Societies; Literary, Glasgow, *M:* G 4218. *Died 21 July 1921.*

DOWNING, Arthur Matthew Weld, MA, DSc (Dubl.); FRS; FRAS; formerly Superintendent of the Nautical Almanac; *b* Ireland, 13 April 1850; *y s* of late Arthur Matthew Downing. *Educ:* Trinity Coll., Dublin. *Publications:* many papers on astronomical subjects; Nautical Almanac, 1896–1912 inclusive. *Address:* 12 Oakcroft Road, Blackheath, SE. *Club:* Royal Societies.

Died 8 Dec. 1917.

DOWNING, Col Cameron Macartney Harwood, CMG 1900; JP County of Suffolk; *b* 8 Dec. 1845; *s* of late Gen. David Downing of The Grange, Plaxtol, Kent; *m* 1877, Adela (*d* 1919), *widow* of Surg. Major Cavendish Johnson, and *d* of Harbut Ward of Carshalton; one *d*. Entered RA 1866; Lt-Col, 1894; retired, 1902; served Abyssinia, 1867–68 (medal); Afghan War, 1878–79 (medal); Chief Instructor, Horse and Field Artillery, School of Gunnery, and Comm. of Okehampton, 1897–99; Colonel on Staff commanding RA Natal Field Force, 1899–1900; Defence of Ladysmith, 1899–1900; commanded the Drakensburg Defence Force, South Africa, with local rank of Maj.-Gen., May–November 1900, when that Force was broken up (despatches twice, medal with 3 clasps); reward for distinguished military service, 1908. *Address:* Thurleston, Whitton, Ipswich, Suffolk. *Club:* United Service.

Died 7 June 1926.

DOWNSHIRE, 6th Marquess of, *cr* 1789; **Arthur Wills John Wellington Blundell Trumbull Hill;** Viscount Hillsborough, Baron Hill, 1717; Earl of Hillsborough, Viscount Kilwarlin, 1751; Baron Harwich (GB), 1756; Earl of Hillsborough and Viscount Fairford, 1772; Hereditary Constable of Hillsborough Fort; Derbyshire Regiment; Captain Berks Yeomanry Cavalry; *b* 2 July 1871; *s* of 5th Marquess and Georgiana, *d* of John Balfour; *S* father, 1874; *m* 1st, 1893, Katherine (from whom he obtained a divorce, 1902), 2nd *d* of Hon. Hugh Hare, Forest House, Bracknell, Berks, and *g d* of 2nd Earl of Listowel; two *s* one *d*; 2nd, 1907, Evelyn Grace May, *d* of E. Benson Foster, Clewer Manor, Windsor. *Educ:* private tutors; Eton. Owner of about 120,000 acres.*Heir: s* Earl of Hillsborough, *b* 7 April 1894. *Address:* 48 Charles Street, Berkeley Square, W; East Hampstead Park, Wokingham, Berks; Hillsborough Castle, also Murlough House, Dundrum, Co. Down. *Clubs:* Carlton, Cavalry, Bachelors'. *Died 29 May 1918.*

DOXFORD, Sir William Theodore, Kt 1900; JP, DL; Director of William Doxford and Sons, Ltd, shipbuilders; *b* 1 Feb. 1841; *s* of late William Doxford, Sunderland; *m* 1863, Margaret (*d* 1916),*d* of R. Williamson; one *s* five *d*. *Educ:* Bramham College. MP (C) Sunderland, 1895–1906. *Address:* Grindon Hall, Sunderland. *Clubs:* Carlton, Constitutional, City of London.

Died 1 Oct. 1916.

DOYEN, Dr E.; claims to have discovered the cancer microbe; *b* 16 Dec. 1859. *Publications:* Traitement de Cancer, 1904; Le Malade et le Meédecin, 1906; Traité de Thérapeutique chirurgicale et de Technique opératoire, 1907; Le Cancer, 1909. *Address:* rue Piccini 6, Paris. *T:* 694-13. *TA:* Clidoyen, Paris.

Died 22 Nov. 1916.

DOYLE, His Honour Charles Francis, KC; Judge of East Circuit Court, Irish Free State, since 1924; County Court Judge and Chairman of Quarter Sessions for the County of Mayo, 1910 till abolition of office, 1924; then Circuit Judge of Eastern Circuit Saorstat Eireann; formerly Professor of Law of Property and Contracts, University College, Dublin; *b* Limerick, 1866; 2nd *s* of late D. Doyle, solicitor; *m* Florence Mary, *y d* of late James Haran, JP, Manager National Bank, Limerick; two *s*. *Educ:* Jesuits' College, Limerick; Trinity College, Dublin; MA (Dublin), Ex-Scholar and Senior Moderator, Berkeley and Vice-Chancellor's Gold Medal. TCD, Ex-Aud. College Historical Society TCD; Society's three medals; MA, and sometime Fellow in Ancient Classics (RUI). Called to Irish Bar, 1888; Inner Bar, 1906; English Bar (Middle Temple), 1902.

Died 30 Sept. 1928.

DOYLE, Major Ignatius Purcell, DSO 1889; Indian Medical Service (retired); *b* 1 June 1863; *s* of Surg.-Maj. William Doyle, IMS. Served Burmah, 1888–89 (twice wounded, despatches, DSO, medal and clasp); Chin-Lushai Expedition, 1889–90 (clasp); Chin Hills, 1891–93 (clasp); Lushai Expedition, 1892 (clasp); Somaliland Field Force, 1903 (medal and clasp). *Died 22 Ooct. 1923.*

DOYLE, Lt-Col John Francis Innes Hay, CMG 1918; DSO 1916; Royal Field Artillery; *s* of late Charles Altamont Doyle, Edinburgh, and *b* of Sir Arthur Conan Doyle; *b* 31 March 1873; *m* 1911, Clara, *d* of Reinhold Schwensen, Copenhagen; two *s*. *Educ:* Richmond, Yorkshire; RMA, Woolwich. Entered RA, 1893; served China, 1900; South Africa, 1902; passed Staff College, 1909; employed on Staff in European War (despatches four times, DSO, CMG, Lt-Col, 1915; Temp. Brig.-Gen. 1917). *Clubs:* Army and Navy, MCC.

Died 19 Feb. 1919.

DOYLE, Very Rev. Thomas; Canon of Westminster since 1918; *b* 1853. *Educ:* Sedgley Park; St Edmund's; Hammersmith Seminary.

Priest, 1880; Chaplain, Manor Park Industrial School; Curate, Saints Mary and Joseph, Poplar, 1880; Rector of Grays and Tilbury, 1887; Our Lady and St Catherine, Bow, 1897; Rector and Parish Priest, Saints Mary and Joseph, Poplar, 1902; Missionary Rector of Saints Mary and Joseph, Poplar, 1903–20; resigned Poplar; Chaplain, Convent Waltham Cross, 1920; retired, 1922. *Address:* 24 Golden Square, W1.   *Died Dec. 1926.*

D'OYLY, Sir Warren Hastings, 10th Bt *cr* 1663; *b* 6 April 1838; *s* of Sir John Hadley D'Oyly, 8th Bt and Mary, *e d* of Hon. John Fendall; *S* half brother, 1900; *m* 1st, 1859, Henrietta Mary (*d* 1904), *d* of Sir Frederick Halliday, KCB; four *s* four *d* (and one *d* decd); 2nd, 1909, Amy, Lady Cotton, *d* of J. G. White, Indian Civil Service. *Educ:* Haileybury. Entered BCS 1858; retired 1891; Inspector-General of Jails, 1876; magistrate and collector, 1st grade; officiating opium agent, Behar, and officiating commissioner, Bhagalpur. *Heir:* s Hastings Hadley D'Oyly, Deputy Commissioner, Andaman Islands, [*b* 26 Jan. 1864; *m* 1st, 1897, Beatrice Alice, *d* of F. B. Clerk, Mysore; two *s* one *d*; 2nd, 1910, Evelyn Maude, *d* of G. Taverner Miller; one *s* two *d*]. *Publications:* Report on the Cultivation of Flax in India; article on the Ganja Tract, published in the Statistical Reporter, Calcutta; illustrated article on The Heart of Queen Anne Boleyn, Jan. 1902 Antiquary. *Recreations:* hunting, pig-sticking in India; cricket, Haileybury and county Dorset Elevens, 1863–69; Calcutta Cricket Club, 1858–68; painting in water-colours.

       Died 16 Feb. 1921.

DOYNE, Charles Mervyn, JP, DL; *b* 27 Sept. 1839; *e s* of late Robert Stephen Doyne, JP, DL, Wells, Co. Wexford and Sarah Emily, *d* of Col Joseph Pratt, of Cabra Castle, Co. Cavan; *m* 1867, Lady Frances Mary Wentworth-Fitzwilliam, *e d* of 6th Earl Fitzwilliam; two *s* three *d. Educ:* Magdalene College, Cambridge, BA 1862, MA 1864. JP and DL Co. Wexford; High Sheriff, 1873; High Sheriff, Co. Carlow, 1875. *Address:* Wells, Gorey, Co. Wexford. *TA:* Kilmuckridge. *Club:* Kildare Street, Dublin.   *Died 24 Aug. 1924.*

DOYNE, Robert Walter, MA Oxon; FRCS; *b* 15 May 1857; 2nd *s* of late Rev. P. W. Doyne; *m* Gertrude Irene Hope, *y d* of late John Hollings; two *s. Educ:* Marlborough; Keble Coll. Oxford. After qualifying, travelled; then entered navy, which he left on marriage; founded Oxford Eye Hospital; Consulting Ophthalmic Surgeon, Radcliffe Infirmary, 1900–15; Reader in Ophthalmology, University of Oxford, 1902–13; late Senior Surgeon Oxford Eye Hosp.; Surgeon Royal Eye Hospital, London; Ophthalmic Surgeon St John's Hospital, Cowley. *Publications:* The More Common Diseases of the Eye; Retinal Extract on the Treatment of Atrophic Retinæ; several papers. *Recreation:* fencing. *Address:* 121 Woodstock Road, Oxford.

       Died 30 Aug. 1916.

DRAGO, Luis Maria, LLD; Member of the Permanent Court of Arbitration at The Hague, and of House of Representatives at Buenos Ayres; *b* Buenos Ayres, 6 May 1859; *s* of Dr Luis M. Drago, Physician, and Estela, *d* of Col Modesto Sanches; *m;* three *s* six *d. Educ:* University of Buenos Ayres. After practising law for some time, became a judge in Buenos Ayres; afterwards elected for Congress; Minister for Foreign Affairs under the Presidency of General Roca; while holding this office he sent to the Argentine Minister in Washington the instructions known as the Drago Doctrine, 1902; one of the Argentine Delegates to the Second Peace Conference; was one of the arbitrators nominated by agreement between Great Britain and the United States for the hearing of the differences regarding fisheries on the North Atlantic coast; Nominated Member of Commission encharged with preparation of Project for Permanent International Court of Justice under the League of Nations; Doctor *honoris causa,* Columbia Univ. *Publications:* La Literatura del Slang; La Idea del Derecho (with D. Matienzo); Colección de Fallos en Materia Civil y Comercial; Los Hombres de Presa (The Men of Prey) translated into Italian with introduction by Professor Lombroso); Cobro Coercitivo de Deudas Publicas; La Republica Argentina y el caso de Venezuela; Les Emprunts d'etat et leur relations avec la politique internationale; El Arbitrage de las Pesquerías del Atlantico Norte. *Address:* Buenos Ayres, Junin 52. *Clubs:* Jockey, Circulo de Armas, Buenos Ayres.

       Died 9 June 1921.

DRAKE, Sir Francis George Augustus Fuller-Eliott-, 2nd Bt, *cr* 1821; *b* 24 Dec. 1837; *o s* of late Capt. Rose Henry Fuller, RN, and Margaret, *d* of late Sir Robert Sheffield, 3rd Bt; *S* uncle, 1870; *m* 1861, Elizabeth, *d* of Sir Robert Andrews Douglas, 2nd Bt, of Glenbervie; one *d.* (The founder of this family was the celebrated Admiral Sir Francis Drake, 1545–96; 1st Bt served under Sir John Moore in Peninsular War, 1808–14.) Joined Royal Horse Guards, 1858; retired (Captain) 1870. Owner of about 7700 acres. Edited Lady Knight's

Letters from France and Italy 1776–95, 1905; *Heir:* none. *Address:* Nutwell Court, Exeter; Buckland Abbey, Plymouth; Sheafhayne House, Devon. *Club:* Carlton.

       Died 25 July 1916 (ext).

DRAKE, Maurice; glass painter and novelist; *b* 31 May 1875; *e s* of Frederick Drake, glass painter, of Exeter; *m* 1897, Alice, *d* of late George Wilson, of Powderham; one *d. Educ:* St James' Grammar School, Teignmouth. *Publications:* novels: The Salving of a Derelict, 1906; Lethbridge of the Moor, 1908; Wrack, 1910; WO$_2$, 1913; The Ocean Sleuth, 1915; The Doom Window, 1923; on glass painting: The Heraldic Glass at Ashton, 1905; The Great East Window of Exeter Cathedral, 1907; A History of English Glass Painting, 1912; Saints and their Emblems, 1915; The Costessey Collection of Stained Glass, 1919. *Address:* 4 The Close, Exeter. *T:* Exeter 876. *Club:* Savage.

       Died 29 April 1923.

DRAKE, Robert James, KC 1914; 3rd *s* of late John Drake, formerly of Dromore; *m* 1897, Edith, *o d* of late W. J. Cooke, formerly of Hereford. *Educ:* privately; Trinity College, Dublin. BA; LLB; King's Inn, Dublin; called to Bar, Middle Temple, 1887; Member Midland Circuit. *Address:* 131 Victoria Street, Westminster, SW1; 1 Essex Court, Temple, EC. *Club:* Royal Automobile. *T:* 1973 Central.

       Died 8 July 1916.

DRAKE, Capt. Thomas Oakley, ISO 1911; *b* 1863; *s* of late T. W. Drake; *m* 1887, Kathleen Maude, *y d* of late Lieut W. Devine; three *s* two *d.* Enlisted, 1878; served in second phase of Afghan Wars of 1878–79–80 (medal), and Mahsud-Waziri Expedition of 1881; retired from the Army with the rank of Commissary (Hon. Captain), 1905; Registrar, Department of Commerce and Industry, Government of India, 1905–16. *Address:* Toongabbie, NSW, Australia.

       Died 28 July 1928.

DRAKE, William James, ISO 1912; Assistant Secretary to the Government of India Public Works Department; *b* 26 Dec. 1872; *s* of Conolly Pakenham Drake, Tyrone Co., Ireland; *m* 1902, *d* of William Maddocks, Bishop Stortford. *Address:* Simla. *Club:* Junior Conservative.   *Died 4 April 1919.*

DRAKE, William Wyckham Tyrwhitt, JP; MFH; Squire of Shardeloes; *b* 27 Sept. 1851; *s* of Thomas T. Drake; *m* Augusta, *d* of late Rev. H. Peel, Thornton, Bucks; one *s* two *d. Educ:* Eton. Studied farming in Hampshire and Shropshire; was given a small farm on the estate by his father until his marriage, when he took a house and some land in Oxfordshire and broke and made hunters; on coming into the property of Shardeloes in 1900 he took the Old Berkeley West hounds for a season; hunted for three years with the Bicester and then took the Old Berkshire hounds for four seasons, 1905–9; Master of them again for two seasons, 1913–14. *Recreations:* hunting, farming. *Address:* Shardeloes, Amersham, Bucks.

       Died 29 July 1919.

DRAPER, Herbert James, RBC; *b* London; *m* Ida, *y d* of W. Walton Williams, JP; one *d. Educ:* Bruce Castle. Studied art RA Schools, and at Paris and Rome; awarded Royal Academy Gold Medal and Travelling Studentship, 1889; spent 1890 in travel; settled in London 1891, painting subject pictures and portraits; has exhibited each year at RA since 1890; Lament for Icarus was bought by the Chantry Trustees for the National Gallery of Brit. Art, 1898; awarded medal at the International Exhibition in Paris, 1900; principal pictures: The Sea Maiden, The Vintage Morn, The Lament for Icarus, The Golden Fleece, Tristram and Yseult, Calypso's Isle, The Foam Sprite, The Dawn Star, Ulysses and the Sirens, etc. Pictures of his have been bought for the permanent collections of the following public galleries: Liverpool, Manchester, Bradford, Preston, Truro, Hull; Durban and Pietermaritzburg, S Africa; The Government of Adelaide, Australia; chief decorative painting, the ceiling of the Livery Hall of the Drapers' Company, City of London; principal portraits, late Duchess of Abercorn, Lord and Lady Inchiquin, Viscountess Ennismore, Hon. Maude Stanley of Alderley, Lord Ninian Crichton-Stuart, Capt. G. A. Boyd-Rochfort, VC, H. Cosmo Bonsor, the children of the Earl of Jersey, etc. *Address:* 15 Abbey Road, NW8. *T:* Hampstead 3949. *Club:* Arts.   *Died 22 Sept. 1920.*

DRAYTON, Edward Rawle, CMG 1902; *b* 2 April 1859; *s* of late Rev. John Drayton; *m* 1882, Edith, *y d* of F. G. Browne, MD, of Barbados; four *s* three *d. Educ:* Harrison College, Barbados. Entered Colonial service, 1878; Chief Clerk to Gov. of Windward Islands, 1882; Provost-Marshal, Grenada, 1885; Registrar, 1886; member, Legislative Council, 1887; Inspector of Prisons, 1888; member, Executive Council, 1888; Chairman, Special Commission Police and

Prisons, St Lucia, 1888; Treasurer of Grenada, 1890; Colonial Secretary of Grenada, 1892–1914; administered Government of Grenada whenever Governor absent between 1890 and 1914; of St Vincent, June 1893, Feb–Sept. 1897, Feb. 1900–April 1901; of Windward Islands, Jan. 1897, Oct. 1907, and Sept. 1913. Delegate to West Indian Quarantine Conferences, 1904 and 1910, and to Canadian Trade Conference, 1908; President, Legislative Council, and Chairman, Harbour Improvement Committee, Grenada, 1912; Administrator, Dominica, 1914; retired on pension, 1915; Chairman, Barbados SPCA, 1916–25. *Publications:* The Grenada Handbook, annually 1896–1914; The Advantages of St George's, Grenada, as a Port of Call for Steamers; West Indian Hurricanes and other Storms. *Address:* Frankfort Villa, Hastings, Barbados.

Died 31 May 1927.

DREAPER, Surgeon Rear-Admiral George Albert, CB 1920; *b* 7 July 1863; *s* of late Richard Henry Dreaper, Finsboro' House, Castlecomer, Co. Kilkenny; *m* 1910, Constance Amy, *d* of late Henry de Blaquiere, JP, of Fiddane, Gort, Co. Galway; no *c. Educ:* Dublin. Surgeon, Royal Navy, 1884; Staff-Surgeon, 1896; served Boer War, 1899; Jubaland Expedition, 1901; Somaliland Expedition, 1904; Fleet-Surgeon, 1904; in charge of the Surgical Wards, Chatham Naval Hospital, 1908–10; Deputy Surgeon-General, 1913; in charge of the Surgical Wards, Plymouth Naval Hospital, 1914–16; in charge of Royal Naval Hospital, Hong-Kong, 1916–19; Surgeon Rear-Admiral, 1919; retired list, 1923. *Recreations:* shooting, fishing, golf, tennis, walking. *Died 28 June 1927.*

DREW, Clifford Luxmoore; Barrister-at-Law; His Majesty's Coroner for the Western Division of London; 2nd *s* of late Charles Drew, HEIC's 3rd Extra Madras Regt; *m* Augusta, *y d* of late William Yeo, Richmond House, N Devon. *Educ:* private tutor and Aberdeen, of which University a graduate. Was in India with his parents during a part of the Indian Mutiny; Past President of the Coroners' Society of England and Wales; formerly held a Captain's commission in the 6th Brigade South Irish Division RA and Argyll and Bute Artillery Militia; subseq. a Captain in the National Reserve; called to bar, 1890; a member of the Middle Temple, Western Circuit, and the Central Criminal Court. *Recreations:* salmon fishing, shooting. *Address:* 15 Pembridge Villas, Kensington. W. *Clubs:* Savage, MCC.

Died 26 May 1919.

DREW, Mary; *b* Nov. 1847; *d* of Rt Hon. William Ewart Gladstone and Catherine, *d* of Sir Stephen Glynne, 8th Bt; *m* 1886, Rev. Harry Drew (*d* 1910), Rector of Hawarden, Canon of St Asaph; one *d. Educ:* home. Was secretary to her father and to her mother until they died, as she lived with them both unmarried and married. *Publications:* The Mothers' Union; Some Hawarden Letters; Catherine Gladstone; Acton, Gladstone and others; Forty Years' Friendship. *Address:* 2 The Boltons, SW10. *T:* Kensington 4530; Hawarden, Chester.

Died 1 Jan. 1927.

DREW, William Wilson; *s* of Rev. William Henry Drew, Professor of Mathematics, King's College, London; *m* 1st, 1894, Mary Louisa, *d* of Rev. S. F. F. Auchmuty; 2nd, 1905, Gertrude Caroline, *d* of George Bowles, 6 Hall Road, NW; one *s* two *d. Educ:* Charterhouse; King's College, Cambridge. Indian Civil Service, 1878; served as Assistant Commissioner in the Punjab until 1882; then transferred to Bombay Presidency; Census Superintendent, 1890–92; member of Anglo-Portuguese Commission, 1892; Commissioner, Southern Division, 1904; Member of the Legislative Council of the Governor-General, 1907–9; Commissioner of Customs, Salt, Opium, and Abkari, Bombay, 1908–11. *Address:* 53 Hamilton Terrace, St John's Wood, NW8. *Club:* East India United Service.

Died 1 Nov. 1923.

DREWRY, Lieut George Leslie, VC 1915; RNR; *b* 3 Nov. 1894. *Educ:* Merchant Taylors' School. Entered Mercantile Marine, 1909; was wrecked on desert island near Cape Horn, 1912; 4th Officer P&OSN Co. Ltd, 1912; joined RNR, 1913; served Dardanelles, 1914–15 (VC); promoted to sub-Lieut and appointed Actg Lieut 2 Sept. 1916. *Address:* 58 Claremont Road, Forest Gate, Essex.

Died 2 Aug. 1918.

DREYER, John Louis Emil, PhD, Hon. MA (Oxon), Hon. DSc (Belfast); *b* Copenhagen, 13 Feb. 1852; 3rd *s* of Lieut-Gen. F. Dreyer; *m* Katherine Hannah (*d* 1923), *d* of John Tuthill, formerly of Kilmore, Co. Limerick; three *s* one *d. Educ:* Copenhagen Univ. Astronomer at Earl of Rosse's Observatory, 1874–78; Asst Astronomer at Dublin Univ. Observatory, 1878–82; Director Armagh Observatory, 1882–1916. Member Royal Danish Academy of Sciences; Knight of the Dannebrog; awarded Gold Medal of Royal Astronomical Society,

1916; President RAS 1923–25. *Publications:* Second Armagh Catalogue of 3300 Stars, 1886; New General Catalogue of Nebulæ and Clusters of Stars 1888; Supplements, 1895 and 1908; Tycho Brahe: a Picture of Scientific Life and Work in the 16th Century, 1890; Planetary Systems from Thales to Kepler, 1906; Copernicus: an International Journal of Astronomy, 1881–84 (jointly with Prof. Copeland); editor of W. Herschel's Scientific Papers, 1912, and of Tycho Brahe's Opera Omnia from 1913. *Recreation:* reading. *Address:* 14 Staverton Road, Oxford.

Died 14 Sept. 1926.

DRISCOLL, Very Rev. James, DD; Canon of Westminster Cathedral; first Headmaster of the Cardinal Vaughan School; *b* London, 20 March 1870. *Educ:* St Edmund's College, Ware; Seminario Romano, Rome. MA of London University; DD of Apollinare University, Rome; Assistant Master for nine years of St Edmund's College, Ware; Headmaster of Westminster Cathedral Choir School, 1903–14; Member of the Catholic Education Council; Hon. Secretary of the Conference of Catholic Colleges. *Address:* Cardinal Vaughan School, Addison Road, W14. *T:* Park 3145.

Died 29 Dec. 1927.

DROMGOOLE, His Honour Charles, KC 1910; MA, LLD; Circuit Judge for the City and County of Dublin; County Court Judge, Kerry, 1913–20, Carlow, Kildare, Wexford, and Wicklow, 1920–24; *b* Newry, Co. Armagh; *o surv. s* of late Charles Dromgoole, Newry; *m* Gertrude, *d* of late John George Fleming, PhD, Head Inspector of National Schools; three *d. Educ:* St Colman's College, Newry; Blackrock College; University College, Blackrock, Dublin. Called to Irish Bar, 1894, and went the North-East Circuit. *Clubs:* St Stephen's Green, Royal Dublin Golf, Dublin.

Died Jan. 1927.

DROUGHT, Rev. Charles Edward, MA; Rector of St John's, Toorak, since 1900; Canon of St Paul's Cathedral, Melbourne; *b* Rectory Aghancon, King's Co., Ireland, 3 Oct. 1847; *s* of Rev. A. T. Drought, of Balliver Estate, King's Co., Ireland; *m* Mary Lillias, *d* of Frederic Race Godfrey; one *s. Educ:* Trinity College, Cambridge. Curate of Hanley Castle and Alvechurch; 3½ years Chaplain of Linares in Spain. *Publications:* Dangers and Duties of the Spiritual Life; The Music of the Cross; Our Church's Standards; My Rectors; My Curates; etc. *Address:* St John's, Toorak, Melbourne.

Died 8 Dec. 1917.

DRUITT, Rt. Rev. Cecil Henry; Bishop of Grafton since 1914; *b* 1874. *Educ:* Corpus Christi College, Cambridge (MA, DD); Ridley Hall, Cambridge. Ordained, 1898; Curate of Christ Church, Torquay, 1898–1900; Theological and Hebrew Lecturer, CM College, Islington, 1900–2; Rector of St Bride, Stretford, 1902–10; Vicar of St Mary, Overchurch, Birkenhead, 1910–11; Lecturer at St Aidan's College, Birkenhead, 1910–11; Coadjutor Bishop of Grafton and Armidale, 1911–14. *Publications:* The Obligation of Prayer; The Missionary Message of St John's Gospel. *Address:* Bishop's Lodge, Grafton, New South Wales. *Died July 1921.*

DRUMMOND, Rev. Arthur Hislop, MA; Hon. Canon of Christ Church, Oxford; Proctor in Convocation, 1907–17; Vicar of All Saints, Boyne Hill, Maidenhead, 1876–1917; *b* 5 April 1843; *s* of Rev. Arthur Drummond, Rector of Charlton, Kent, and Margaretta Maria, *d* of Sir Thomas Maryon Wilson, 7th Bt; *m* 1st, 1868, Armynel Mary, *d* of Rev. C. Baylay; 2nd, Anna Harriet (*d* 1915), *d* of William Dodsworth; one *s. Educ:* Marlborough; Christ Church, Oxford; Cuddesdon Theological Coll. Formerly Curate of Hungerford, Berks, and Long Compton, Warwickshire; presented to Vicarage of Kempley, Glos, by Earl Beauchamp, 1871; was a Guardian of the Poor, and on the Technical Instruction and Education Committees for the borough of Maidenhead. *Address:* 9 Elm Park Gardens, SW10. *T:* Kensington 4361.

Died 19 Feb. 1925.

DRUMMOND, Maj.-Gen. Sir Francis Henry Rutherford, KCIE 1912 (CIE 1897); CB 1908; *b* 9 Sept. 1857; *e surv. s* of late Maj.-Gen. Henry Drummond; *m* 1892, Violet Fraser, *o d* of Col F. J. Home, CSI. *Educ:* Wellington College. Entered army, 1875; Brevet Major, 1887; Major 1895; Lieut-Col 1901; Brevet Col 1904; Substantive Colonel and Brig.-General, 1907; Maj.-Gen. 1909; served Afghan War, 1878–80 (despatches twice, medal with clasp). Served with Afghan Boundary Commission, 1884–86 (Bt-Majority); Afghan Order of Honour; was lately Inspector-General of Imperial Service Troops; an Esquire of the Order of St John of Jerusalem in England. *Address:* Aveland House, Crieff, Perthshire. *TA:* Crieff. *Club:* Cavalry.

Died 27 March 1919.

DRUMMOND, Capt. George Robinson Bridge, MVO 1904; retired, Chief Constable of West Sussex; *b* 1 May 1845; *s* of George Drummond; *m* 1874, Frances, *d* of Thomas Flight. Late 26th Regt Bombay NI. *Address:* 14 The Drive, Hove, Sussex.
Died 27 April 1917.

DRUMMOND, Brig.-Gen. Sir Hugh Henry John, 1st Bt, *cr* 1922; CMG 1918; JP Devonshire; Chairman, The Southern Railway, Co.; Director of National Provincial and Union Bank of England; Deputy Chairman, Alliance Assurance Co.; Member, Royal Bodyguard of Scotland; *b* Clovelly Court, Devonshire, 29 Nov. 1859; 3rd *s* of Sir James Hamlyn Williams Drummond, 3rd Bt of Hawthornden, Midlothian, and Edwinsford, Llandilo; *m* 1889, Gertrude Emily, *e d* of late Hon. Mark G. K. Rolle of Bicton and Stevenston, Devonshire; one *d. Educ:* privately. Joined 1st Devon Militia, 1878; Rifle Brigade, 1879; contested (C) West Carmarthenshire, 1889; in 1895 became a partner in Sanders & Co., Exeter Bank, which was amalgamated in 1894 with Messrs Snow & Co., and Prescott Dimsdale & Co. and later with the Union of London & Smith's Bank; a Director of the London and South Western Railway Co., 1900; Deputy Chairman, 1904; joined Royal North Devon Hussars (Yeomanry) as Captain, afterwards becoming Lieut-Col commanding; on outbreak of war raised second Regiment of Yeomanry, and in Jan. 1915 was given command of the 2nd South Western Mounted Brigade; Hon. Brig.-General, Aug. 1917. *Recreations:* shooting, fishing, golf, yachting. *Heir:* none. *Address:* 98 Eaton Place, SW1. *Clubs:* Carlton, Travellers', Naval and Military; Royal Yacht Squadron, Cowes.
Died 1 Aug. 1924 (ext).

DRUMMOND, Rev. James, MA, LLD; Principal, Manchester College, Oxford, 1885-1906; *b* Dublin, 14 May 1885; *s* of Rev. William Hamilton Drummond, DD; *m* 1861, Frances, *d* of John Classon, Dublin; two *s* six *d. Educ:* Trinity College, Dublin; Manchester New College, London. BA with 1st classical gold medal, Trinity Coll. Dublin, 1855; LLD (TCD), 1882; LittD (Hon. TCD), 1892; MA Oxon 1889; DD (Tufts), 1905. Colleague of Rev. William Gaskell, Cross Street Chapel, Manchester, 1859-69; Professor of Theology in Manchester New Coll. London, 1870; succeeded Dr Martineau as Principal, manchester, 1885; removed with the College to Oxford, 1889; retired, 1906. *Publications:* Spiritual Religion; Sermons on Christian Faith and Life, 1870; The Jewish Messiah: A Critical History of the Messianic Idea among the Jews, 1877; Introduction to the Study of Theology, 1884; Philo-Judæis: or the Jewish-Alexandrian Philosophy in its Development and Completion, 2 vols, 1888; The Epistle of St Paul to the Galatians, 1893; Via, Veritas, Vita (the Hibbert Lectures for 1894, on Christianity in its most simple and intelligible form), 1894; The Pauline Benediction (three sermons), 1897; International Handbooks to the New Testament, edn by Orello Cone, DD, vol. ii, The Epistles of Paul the Apostle to the Thessalonians, etc. 1899; Some Thoughts on Christology (Essex Hall Lecture), 1902; Life and Letters of Dr Martineau (in union with Prof. Upton), 1902; The Character and Authorship of the Fourth Gospel, 1904; Studies in Christian Doctrine, 1908; The Transmission of the Text of the New Testament (a little manual for teachers), 1909; Johannine Thoughts, 1909; Lectures on the Composition and Delivery of Sermons, 1910; Paul: his Life and Teaching, 1911; several articles on theological subjects; College addresses; sermons. *Recreations:* carpentering, cycling. *Address:* 18 Rawlinson Road, Oxford.
Died 13 June 1918.

DRUMMOND, Lister Maurice; Metropolitan Police Magistrate since 1913; *b* 23 Aug. 1856; *o s* of John Drummond, CB, and Hon. Adelaide Lister, *e d* of 2nd Baron Ribblesdale. *Educ:* privately. Called to Bar, Inner Temple, 1879; Revising barrister on South-Eastern Circuit, 1887-1913; Secretary to the Evicted Tenants Commission, Dublin, 1892-93; Commissioner to try the Municipal Election Petition at Grimsby, 1904; and that at Gloucester, 1907; Secretary to Worcester Royal Commission, 1906. A Knight of the Papal Order of St Gregory the Great, 1901. *Recreations:* fencing, swimming, cycling. *Address:* 10 Hampstead Square, SW. *Club:* London Fencing.
Died 27 Feb. 1916.

DRUMMOND, Malcolm, of Megginch and Kilspindie; *b* 2 March 1856; *o s* of John Drummond of Megginch (*d* 1889), late Grenadier Guards and Frances, *d* of late Gen. Sir John Oswald, GCB, of Dunnikier; *m* 1890, Geraldine, *d* of 1st Baron Amherst of Hackney; one *s* three *d. Educ:* Eton. Served in Northumberland Militia, 1873-76; in Grenadier Guards, 1876-90; ADC and private secretary to Governor of Newfoundland, 1881; served with 3rd Battalion Grenadier Guards, Soudan campaign, 1885; Guards' Mounted Infantry (medal and clasp and Khedive's Star); Capt. Grenadier Guards, 1885; retired 1890; Groom of Privy Chamber to Queen Victoria,

1890; groom-in-waiting 1893-1901. JP and DL Perthshire. *Address:* Megginch Castle, Errol, Perthshire. *Club:* Guards.
Died 28 May 1924.

DRUMMOND, His Honour Judge Michael, KC Ireland; County Court Judge, Cos Meath, Westmeath, Longford, and King's County, 1914-24; County Court Judge and Chairman of Quarter Sessions, Cos Cavan and Leitrim, 1904-14; *b* 1850. Irish Bar, 1872; Inner Bar (QC), 1891; Bencher of King's Inns, Dublin, 1899. *Address:* 22 Upper Fitzwilliam Street, Dublin.
Died 1921.

DRURY, Rev. John Frederick William; Vicar of Saddleworth since 1918; Secretary of the Manchester Diocesan Societies, 1891-1918; *b* 18 Oct. 1858; *m* 1900, Charlotte, *d* of Mrs Humphreys of Wyberslegh Hall, Cheshire; two *d. Educ:* Christ Church, Oxford (BA and MA). Curate of St Mary's Cathedral, Glasgow, 1887-89; Morecambe, Lancs, 1889-91; Chaplain to the Hon. Lady Leighton-Warren, Tabley House, Knutsford, 1898-1912; Hon. Canon of Manchester Cathedral, 1911. *Publications:* Manual of Education, 1902; editor of Manchester Diocesan Directory, 1906. *Recreations:* golf, chess, gardening. *Address:* The Vicarage, Saddleworth, Yorks. *T:* Saddleworth 69. *Club:* Old Rectory, Manchester.
Died 1923.

DRURY, Rt. Rev. Thomas Wortley, DD, MA; Master of St Catharine's College, Cambridge, since 1920; *b* 12 Sept. 1847; *m* 1871, Catharine Beatrice (*d* 1914), *d* of Captain Dumergue, Madras Army; two *s* four *d. Educ:* King William's College, Isle of Man; Christ's College, Cambridge (25th Wrangler, 3rd class Classical Tripos and 1st class Theological Honours). Ordained 1871; Curate of Kirk Braddan, 1871-73; Mathematical Master of King William's College, 1873-76; Rector of Holy Trinity, Chesterfield, 1876-82; Principal, Church Missionary College, Islington, 1882-99; select preacher, Cambridge, 1891, 1899, 1905, 1907, etc; Member of the Fulham Conference on Confession and Absolution, 1900-1; and of the Royal Commission on Ecclesiastical Discipline, 1904-6; Principal of Ridley Hall, Cambridge, 1899-1907; Dean of St German's Cathedral, 1908; Bishop of Sodor and Man, 1907-11; Bishop of Ripon, 1911-20; War Office Committee on Chaplains, 1915; Sub-Prelate of the Order of St John of Jerusalem, 1918. *Publications:* Confession and Absolution; How we got our Prayer Book; Two Studies in the Prayer Book; Elevation in the Eucharist, its History and Rationale; A Prison Ministry; The Ministry of Our Lord. *Recreation:* fishing (river and sea). *Address:* The Master's Lodge, St Catharine's College, Cambridge.
Died 12 Feb. 1926.

DRURY, William D., FES, FRHS; Editor of the Bazaar, Exchange and Mart, 1884-1926; *b* Oxford, 1857; *m* 1881; one *s* two *d. Educ:* Nixon's Grammar School, Oxford. Apprenticed to Jas Parker & Son, book and classical printers, passing afterwards to the Oxford University Press (Classical Side); acted as Press Corrector to The Bazaar, Iron, and to Clowes & Sons, Beccles; spent five years on editorial staff of Nicholson's Directory of Gardening. *Publications:* The Collie, Popular Dog Keeping, British Dogs, Popular Toy Dogs, Fruit Culture, Garden Animals, Home Gardening, The Book of Gardening, Hardy Perennials, English and Welsh Terriers, Scotch and Irish Terriers, The Fox Terrier, and The Greyhound; edited numerous books for the Collector, gardening and dogs. *Recreations:* gardening, entomology, curio-collecting. *Address:* Stepaside, 50 St Helen's Park Road, Hastings.
Died 30 March 1928.

DRYSDALE, Hon. Arthur, KC; *b* Nova Scotia, 5 Sept. 1857; *s* of George Drysdale, of Scottish descent; *m* Carrie, *d* of late George P. Mitchell, Halifax. A Judge of the Supreme Court of Nova Scotia, formerly Attorney-General of the Province, and represented Hants County in Provincial Legislature for 16 years. Liberal. *Address:* Halifax, Nova Scotia. *Club:* Halifax.
Died 21 Oct. 1922.

DRYSDALE, Rev. A. H., MA, DD (Edin); ex-Moderator, English Presbyterian Synod; Hon. President of its Historical Society; Governor of Edward VI Royal Grammar School, Morpeth; *b* Bridge of Allan, 1837; *m* 1867; two *s* one *d. Educ:* Stirling High School; Edinburgh Univ.; won the Gray Prize (Essay); Theological training in the United Presbyterian Hall. First charge, Maisondieu, Brechin, 1861; Trinity Church, Rochdale, 1867; St George's, Morpeth, 1883; now Emeritus Publications: Philemon (Epistle to), for English Readers, 1879; Early Hebrew Songs (Bible Bypaths series), 1890; History of the Presbyterians in England, 1889; Ditto, as handbook, 1891; A Moderator's Year, 1904; Christ Invisible Our Gain, 1909; and much current literature. *Recreations:* rambling and ruminating. *Address:* The Stanners, Morpeth.
Died 2 Jan. 1924.

DRYSDALE, Lt-Col William, DSO 1915; Royal Scots; *b* 4 Nov. 1876; *s* of William Drysdale, Kilrie, Kirkcaldy; *m* 1904, Mary Louisa, *d* of Sir John Muir Mackenzie, KCSI; three *s*. Entered army, 1893; Captain, 1902; Brigade-Major 15th Brigade, Irish Command, 1912; served European War, 1914–16 (despatches, prom. Bt Lt-Col, DSO). *Address:* Kilrie, Kirkcaldy, Fife.

Died 29 Sept. 1916.

DUBOIS, Théodore; Directeur honoraire du Conservatoire National de musique et de déclamation; Compositeur de musique; Membre de L'Institut; *b* 1837. *Educ:* Conservatoire de Paris. Entré au Conservatoire, 1854; obtint les prix d'harmonie, d'accompagnement, de fugue, d'orgue, et enfin le grand prix de Rome, 1861; Maître de chapelle de Ste Clotilde, 1863–68, après en avoir été organiste accompagnateur; Maître de chapelle de la Madeleine, 1868–76, puis organiste du grand orgue de cette église jusqu'en 1896, succédant à C. Saint-Saens; Professeur d'harmonie au Conservatoire, 1871; de Composition, 1891; Directeur du Conservatoire, 1896–1905; Inspecteur de l'Enseignement musical, 1884–96; élu Membre de l'Académie des Beaux-Arts, 1894. *Publications:* Sept Paroles du Christ; Le Paradis Perdu; Messes, Motets; La Guzla de l'Emir, opéra comique; Le Pain Bis, opéra comique; La Farandole, ballet de l'opéra; Aben-Hamet, grand opéra; Xavière, Idylle dramatique; Plusieurs Suites d'Orchestre; Concertos de Piano, de Violon; Ouverture de Frithioff et autres ouvertures. Diverses scènes lyriques; L'Enlèvement de Proserpine, Hylas, Le Baptême de Clovis; Notre Dame de la Mer; Prière de France; recueils de pièces de piano, d'orgue, de mélodies sonate pour piano et violon; trios pour piano, violon, and violoncelle; chœurs divers; notes et études d'harmonie; traité de Contrepoint et de Fugue; Petit Manuel d'Harmonie; quintette pour piano, violon, hautbois, alto et violoncelle; sonate pour violoncelle et piano; Fantaisie de Harpe; Quatuor avec piano; 12 Etudes de concert pour le piano, Dixtuor pour double quintette à cordes et à vent; Symphonie française; In Memoriam Mortuorum, pour orchestre; 2ᵉ Symphonie; Exquisses Orchestrales; Fantaisie-Stuck pour violoncelle et orchestre; Fantasietta pour flute, violon, trompette, cor, violoncelle, harpe, timbales et orchestre à cordes; Quatuor à cordes; Poèmes Sylvestres, Virgiliens, Alpestres pour le piano; Sonate pour le piano; traité d'harmonie 2ᵉ quatuor à cordes; nombreuses pièces diverses pour piano, organ, chant, instruments, etc. *Address:* Boulevard Pereire 201, Paris; Rosnay, Marne. *Died 11 June 1924.*

DUBOSE, William Porcher, STD, DCL; Dean since 1894 and Professor Emeritus, Theological Department, University of the South, Sewanee, Tennessee, USA; *b* 11 April 1836; *s* of Theodore Marion and Jane Porcher Dubose, Winnsboro', South Carolina; *m* 1st, 1863, Anne Barnwell Peronneau; 2nd, 1878, Maria Louisa Yorger; one *s* two *d*. *Educ:* Military Academy of South Carolina; University of Virginia. While a student for the ministry of the Church, entered the military service of the Southern Confederacy, 1861; served as an officer through war (several times wounded and once a prisoner); priest in the Protestant Episcopal Church, 1865; served in SC until became Chaplain and Professor, Univ. of South, 1871; STD Columbia Univ., NY, 1874; DCL Univ. of South, 1907; DD General Theological Seminary, NY, 1908; after continuous service in the University of the South for over thirty-six years, resigned active duties in summer of 1908 and elected Dean and Professor Emeritus. *Publications:* Soteriology of the New Testament, 1893; The Ecumenical Councils, 1896; The Gospel in the Gospels, 1906; The Gospel according to St Paul, 1907; High Priesthood and Sacrifice, 1908. *Recreations:* for many years spent winter vacations in Florida, and did there the writing for which duties at Sewanee allowed no leisure. *Address:* Monteagle, Tennessee, USA.

Died 18 Aug. 1918.

DUBOST, Antonin; President of the French Senate since 1906; *b* l'Arbresle, Rhone, 6 April 1844; Member Chamber of Deputies, 1880–97; Minister of Justice, 1893–94; Senator since 1897; President of the Senate, 1906. *Address:* Présidence du Sénat, Paris.

Died 15 April 1921.

DU BOULAY, Ven. Henry Houssemayne, MA; Hon. Canon of Truro, 1882; *b* Lawhitton, 25 Jan. 1840; *s* of late Rev. Francis Du Boulay, Rector of Lawhitton, and Sybella, *d* of Bishop Phillpotts, Exeter; *m* 1870, Emily Henrietta (*d* 1924), *d* of Rev. Richard Stephens, Vicar of Dunsford and Sub-Dean of Exeter; three *d*. *Educ:* Exmouth; Harrow; Exeter Coll., Oxford; Theological Coll., Exeter. Domestic Chaplain and Secretary to the Bishop (Phillpotts) of Exeter, 1864–69; Rural Dean of Kerrier, 1877–80; Proctor in Convocation for the Chapter of Truro, 1887–92; Editor, Truro Diocesan Kalendar, 1877–1902; Vicar of S Sithney, 1869–80; Vicar of Newlyn, 1880–92;

Archdeacon of Bodmin, 1892–1923; Rector of Lawhitton, 1892–1923. *Address:* Chy-an-dour, Falmouth.

Died 6 April 1925.

DU CANE, Colonel Hubert John, CB 1913; MVO 1905; *b* 22 July 1859; 2nd and *o surv. s* of late Major-General Sir Edmund Du Cane, KCB, formerly Chairman of Commissioners of HM Prisons, etc and late Mary Dorothea, *d* of Captain John Mollay, late Rifle Brigade; unmarried. Served Hazara Expedition, 1888 (despatches, medal with clasp); South African War, 1899–1902 (despatches, Bt Lt-Col, Queen's Medal with clasp, King's Medal with two clasps). *TA:* 94 Piccadilly. *Clubs:* Naval and Military, Travellers', Garrick.

Died 15 June 1916.

DUCAT, Ven. William Methven Gordon, MA; Archdeacon of Berkshire since 1903; Hon. Canon, Christ Church, Oxford, 1894. *Educ:* Balliol College, Oxford (Snell Exhibitioner, 2nd Class Mods, 2nd class Lit. Hum.). Ordained, 1873; Curate of All Souls, Langham Place, 1873–76; Chaplain of Cuddesdon College, 1877; Rector of Lamplugh, 1877–80; Principal, Leeds Clergy School, 1880–83; Principal, Cuddesdon College and Vicar of Cuddesdon, 1883–94; Rural Dean, Cuddesdon, 1890–94; Vicar of St Giles's, Reading, 1894–1903; Rural Dean, Reading, 1899–1903. *Publication:* Hints to those who are preparing for Holy Orders, 1909. *Address:* 5 Bath Road, Reading. *Died 17 March 1922.*

DUCHESNE, Mgr Louis Marie Olivier; Hon. DCL Cantab. and Oxon; archæologist; Member of the Institute of France (French Academy and Academy of Inscriptions and Belles Lettres) and of British Academy; Director of the Ecole Française de Rome; *b* St Servan, 13 Sept. 1813. *Address:* passage Stanislas 2, Paris.

Died 21 April 1922.

DUCIE, 3rd Earl of, *cr* 1837; **Henry John Moreton,** GCVO 1906; PC; DL; FRS 1855; Baron Ducie, 1763; Baron Moreton, 1837; Lord-Lieutenant of Gloucestershire, 1857–1911; *b* 25 June 1827; *s* of 2nd Earl and Elizabeth, *d* of 2nd Lord Sherborne; *S* father, 1853; *m* 1849, first cousin, Julia (*d* 1895), *d* of James Haughton Langston, MP, Sarsden, Oxfordshire; one *d* (and one *s* decd). MP for Stroud, 1852–53; Captain of the Yeoman of the Guard, 1859–66; Lord Warden of the Stanneries, 1888–1908. Owner of about 14,000 acres. *Heir: b* Hon. Berkeley Basil Moreton, *b* 18 July 1834. *Address:* Tortworth Court, Falfield, Gloucestershire. *Clubs:* Athenæum, Brooks's, Travellers'; Royal Yacht Squadron, Cowes.

Died 28 Oct. 1921.

DUCIE, 4th Earl of, *cr* 1837; **Berkeley Basil Moreton;** Baron Ducie, 1763; Baron Moreton, 1837; *b* 18 July 1834; 4th *s* of 2nd Earl and Elizabeth, *d* of 2nd Lord Sherborne; *S* brother, 1921; *m* 1862, Emily Eleanor Kent (*d* 1921); two *s* seven *d* (and one *d* decd). *Educ:* Rugby; Magdalen Coll., Oxford; RAC Cirencester. Went to Australia, 1855; MLA Burnet, 1870; Maryborough, 1878; Burnet, 1883; late MLC; PMG, 1885; Colonial Secretary and Minister of Public Instruction, Queensland, 1886–88. Owner of about 14,000 acres. *Heir: s* Lord Moreton, *b* 16 May 1875. *Address:* Tortworth Court, Falfield, Gloucestershire. *Died 7 Aug. 1924.*

DUCKWORTH, Sir Dyce, 1st Bt, *cr* 1909; Kt 1886; Consulting Physician St Bartholomew's Hospital; Consulting Physician Seamen's Hospital, Greenwich; Medical Referee to Treasury, 1904–10; Member of Court, University of Liverpool; *b* Liverpool, 24 Nov. 1840; *y s* of Robinson Duckworth and Elizabeth Forbes, *d* of William Nicol, MD, Stonehaven, NB; *m* 1st, 1870, Annie Alicia (*d* 1886), *widow* of John Smith, of Mickleham Hall, Dorking; one *s* (two *d* decd); 2nd, 1890, Ada, y *d* of G. Arthur Fuller, of the Rookery, Dorking; two *s*. *Educ:* Royal Institution School, Liverpool; Edinburgh University; St Bartholomew's Hospital. MD Edin. 1863 (gold medallist); FRCP Lond. 1870; Hon. MD Cincinnati, 1879; Hon. MD Royal Univ. Ireland, 1887; MD Member Convocation, Queen's University, Belfast; Hon. FRCP Ireland, 1887; Hon. LLD Edin. 1890. Assistant Surgeon, RN, 1864–65; Senior Censor, 1903–4; Representative of RCP in Gen. Med. Council, 1886–91; late President Clinical Soc.; late Hon. Physician to King Edward VII when Prince of Wales. Knight of Justice, Order of St John of Jerusalem. Mem. Corresp. Acad. de Méd., Paris. *Publications:* Views on some Social Subjects, 1915; numerous contributions to medical literature, addresses, etc. *Heir: s* Edward Dyce Duckworth, *b* 10 July 1875. *Address:* 28 Grosvenor Place, SW1. *T:* Gerrard 4745.

Died 20 Jan. 1928.

DUCKWORTH, Rev. William Arthur, JP Somerset; MA; *b* 17 March 1829; *e surv. s* of William Duckworth of Orchardleigh Park,

Frome, and Hester Emily, *d* of Robert Philips of the Park, Manchester; *m* 1859, Hon. Edina, *y d* of John, Lord Campbell, then Lord Chancellor; two *s* four *d*. *Educ:* Eton, 1842–46; Trinity Coll. Camb., 1849–52. Ordained, 1854; Curate of Ashbourne, Derbyshire, 1854–59; Rector of Puttenham, Surrey, 1859–77; Lord of the manors of Frome, Orchardleigh, Lullington, and Buckland Dinham in Somerset; President of the Victoria Hospital, Frome, 1903. *Address:* Orchardleigh Park, Frome. *Clubs:* United University, Athenæum. *M:* LC 6653, Y 1624.   *Died 6 Dec. 1917.*

du CROS, William Harvey; MP (C) Hastings, 1906–8; *b* 19 June 1846; *s* of Edouard Pierre du Cros (the family being of noble Huguenot descent, driven from Montpelier in the Hérault and settled in Dublin, 1702), of the Rectory Moone, Co. Kildare, and Maria, *d* of late John Molloy of Dublin; *m* 1st, 1866, Annie (*d* 1899), *d* of late John Roy of Durrow, Queen's Co.; 2nd, Florence, *d* of William Gibbings of Walson, Bow, N Devon. *Educ:* The King's Hospital, Dublin. JP Sussex. Chevalier of the Légion d'Honneur; Knight of the Order of Isabella la Católica. Founded the pneumatic tyre industry, and now largely interested in the development of the automobile industry. *Recreations:* has been a noted athlete in Irish amateur circles; now an ardent motorist. *Address:* Howbery Park, Wallingford, Berks; Inniscorrig, Dalkey, Co. Dublin; Wildcroft, Putney Heath, SW. *T:* Putney 1753. *Clubs:* Carlton, St Stephen's, Royal Automobile.   *Died 21 Dec. 1918.*

DUDDELL, W., FRS; Consulting Engineer; Past President of the Röntgen Society and of the Institution of Electrical Engineers, and Hon. Treasurer of the Physical Society; *b* London, 1872; unmarried. *Educ:* private school; College Stanislass, Cannes. Served apprenticeship with Davey, Paxman & Company, Colchester, 1890–93; attended courses in engineering and physics, and carried out research work at Central Technical College, London, 1893–1900; obtained a Whitworth Exhibition 1896, and Whitworth Scholarship 1897; in conjunction with Dr E. W. Marchant, read a paper on Experiments on Alternate current Arcs by Aid of Oscillographs before the Institution of Electrical Engineers, 1898; read a paper on Rapid Variations of Current through the Direct Current Arc, 1900; also read papers on Resistance and EMF's of the Electric Arc, before Royal Society, 1901; and on Oscillographs, British Association meeting, 1897; in conjunction with Dr Marchant, contributed to The Electrician an article entitled Experiments on Periodic Variations Occurring in the Exciting Current of an Inductor Alternator, 1901; received a gold medal for oscillographs at Paris Exhibition of 1900; and at St Louis, 1904; was hon. sec. to delegates to International Electrical Congress at St Louis, USA, 1904, and to the International Conference on Electrical Units and Standards, 1908; received the Hughes medal of the Royal Society, 1912. Member of Admiralty Board of Invention and Research, and the Advisory Council for Industrial Research. *Address:* 56 Victoria Street, SW. *T:* Victoria 5753.   *Died 4 Nov. 1917.*

DUDDING, Rear-Adm. Horatio Nelson; retired; *b* 1849; *s* of late Rev. H. N. Dudding, Vicar of St Peter's, St Albans; *m* 1882, Florence Louisa, 3rd *d* of Jas J. Gape, of St Michael's Manor, St Albans, JP; two *s* one *d*. *Educ:* HMS Britannia. With Eastern Soudan Field Force, 1891; 3rd Class Mejidie; Egyptian medal, 1892; Capt. 1893–1902; retired, 1905. *Address:* Ashley Mead, St Albans. *TA:* London Colney.   *Died 1917.*

DUDGEON, Sir Charles John, Kt 1903; *b* 3 Sept. 1855; *s* of late Patrick Dudgeon of Cargen, Dumfries; *m* 1884, Isabelle Annie, *d* of late Maj.-Gen. W. C. O'Shaughnessy; one *d*. *Educ:* Repton; College Hall, St Andrews University. Assistant British Commissioner for Revision of Commercial Treaties with China, 1901–12; President, The China Association, 1911. *Recreations:* fishing, shooting, golf. *Clubs:* Conservative, Thatched House, Bath.   *Died 23 Jan. 1928.*

DUFF, General Sir Beauchamp, GCB 1911 (KCB 1907; CB 1901); GCSI 1916 (KCSI 1910); KCVO 1906; CIE 1897; ADC General to the King, 1914; Commander-in-Chief, India, 1913–16; *b* 17 Feb. 1855; 2nd *s* of late Garden William Duff of Hatton Castle, Aberdeenshire, and Douglas Maria, *d* of late Beauchamp Urquhart of Meldrum; *m* 1877, Grace, *d* of late Oswald Wood; one *s*. *Educ:* Trinity College, Glenalmond; Royal Military Academy, Woolwich. Commissioned as Lieut RA, 1874; Afghan War, 1878–80; transferred to Indian Staff Corps, 1881; Capt., 1886; passed through Staff College, 1888–89; DAAG Indian Army Headquarters, 1891–95; Brigade Major Isazai Expedition, 1892; Major, 1894; DAAG Waziristan Expedition, 1894–95 (despatches twice, brevet of Lieut-Col); Military Secretary to Commander-in-Chief in India, 1895–99; Substantive Col, 1898;

Assistant Military Secretary War Office (for Indian affairs), 1899; South Africa, 1899–1901 (despatches twice, medal with five clasps, CB); DAG Indian Army Headquarters, 1901–2; Brig.-Gen. commanding Allahabad District; Maj.-Gen. 1903; Adjutant-General in India, 1903–6; Sec. Military Department India Office, 1910; Chief of the Staff in India, 1906–9. *Recreations:* shooting, fishing. *Address:* c/o Railway Mail Service, India. *Clubs:* United Service, Caledonian.   *Died 20 Jan. 1918.*

DUFF, Lieut-Col Benjamin Michael, ISO 1903; VD; *b* 1840; *s* of late Captain Benjamin Duff, Edinburgh; *m* 1865, Jane, *d* of late Edward Jones, Port Elizabeth. Entered Civil Service, Cape Colony, 1863; Chief Clerk Postal Department, and Superintendent of Telegraphs, 1886; Secretary, Posts and Telegraphs, 1892; acted General Manager of Telegraphs, and Postmaster-General for various periods from 1883 to 1904; served as lieutenant, Cape Field Artillery, in Transkei campaign, 1880–81, SA (medal and clasp); Lieut-Colonel commanding Cape Town Highlanders, 1895, and Boer War, 1899–1900 (medal and clasp); a MIEE and a JP for the Colony. *Address:* Green Point, near Cape Town, Cape of Good Hope.   *Died 15 Nov. 1926.*

DUFF, Edward Gordon, MA Oxon; Librarian of the John Rylands Library, Manchester, 1893–1900; *b* 16 Feb. 1863; *y s* of late Robert Duff. *Educ:* Cheltenham College; Wadham College, Oxford. Sandars Reader in Bibliography in the Univ. of Cambridge, 1898–99, 1903–4, 1910–11; President of the Edinburgh Bibliographical Society, 1899–1900. *Publications:* Early Printed Books, 1893; Early English Printing, 1896; The Printers, Stationers, and Bookbinders of London, 1899; William Caxton, 1903; A Century of the English Book Trade, 1905; Editor of The Dialogue of Salamon and Marcolphus, 1892; Information for Pilgrims, 1893; writer of many reviews and articles in literary and sporting periodicals. *Recreations:* fishing, swimming, tattooing, book-collecting. *Address:* 293 Woodstock Road, Oxford.   *Died 28 Sept. 1924.*

DUFF, Hon. James Stoddart; Minister of Agriculture, Canada, since 1908; *b* 20 June 1856; *m* Jane Bell, *d* of late John E. Stoddart. MP West Simcoe since 1898. *Address:* Cookstown, Ontario, Canada.   *Died 19 Nov. 1916.*

DUFF, John, ISO 1912; HBM Consul for the West and South coasts of Sweden, 1881–1919; *b* 18 Jan. 1850; 2nd *s* of late Fredrik William Duff, late HBM Consul at Gothenburg; unmarried. *Educ:* Gothenburg. After five years commercial studies, entered the Consular Service as Secretary to HBM Consul at Gothenburg, 1874; Vice-Consul, 1880; Coronation Medal, 1911. *Recreations:* shooting, rowing, sailing. *Address:* 16 Nordhemsgatan, Gothenburg. *TA:* Duff, Gothenburg. *T:* 722.   *Died 13 Feb. 1921.*

DUFF, Thomas Duff Gordon, CBE; JP, Vice-Lieutenant, Banffshire; *b* 1848; *s* of late Major Lachlan G. Duff and Jane Ellen, *d* of late Thomas Butterfield, Chief Justice of Bermuda; *m* 1st, 1875, Pauline (*d* 1880), *d* of late Sir Charles Tennant 1st Bt, of The Glen; 2nd, Mildred, *d* of late E. C. Walker, Chester; three *s* four *d*. *Educ:* Harrow; Trinity College, Oxford. For 20 years member of County Council and other local bodies; during the war Chairman of County Territorial Force Association and Agricultural Executive Committee. *Address:* Drummuir, Keith, Scotland. *Club:* Royal Automobile.   *Died 27 March 1923.*

DUFFERIN and AVA, 2nd Marquess of, *cr* 1888; **Terence John Temple-Blackwood;** Bt 1763; Baron Clandeboye, 1800; Earl of Dufferin, Viscount Clandeboye, 1871; Earl of Ava, 1888; formerly 2nd Secretary, HM Diplomatic Service; *b* 16 March 1866; 2nd *s* of 1st Marquess of Dufferin and Ava, and Hariot, *d* of Archibald Rowan Hamilton; S father, 1902; *m* 1893, Florence, *d* of John H. Davies of New York; three *d*. *Educ:* Harrow. Entered Diplomatic Service 1891; served at Constantinople, Paris, and Stockholm; in Foreign Office since 1896. DL, JP, Co. Down. *Heir: b* Lord Frederick Temple Blackwood, *b* 26 Feb. 1875. *Address:* North House, Putney Hill, SW. *T:* 223 Putney. *Club:* Travellers'.   *Died 6 Feb. 1918.*

DUFFIELD, William Bartleet; *s* of W. W. Duffield, Browning's, Chelmsford. *Educ:* Harrow; abroad; Trinity Hall, Cambridge. Scholar; MA 1890; 1st Class Historical Tripos. Barrister, Inner Temple, 1887; acted as Examiner at various times for Woolwich, Sandhurst, the Diplomatic and Civil Services, etc. Secretary to Royal Commission on Canals and Waterways, 1906–10. *Publications:* contributed to most of the leading reviews (Edinburgh, Nineteenth Century, Fortnightly, Saturday Review, Spectator, etc.) many articles, principally on history, foreign affairs, and current politics; contributor to the Encyclopædia Britannica, 11th edition, and the Dictionary of Nat. Biography. *Recreation:* travel. *Address:* 4 Whitehall Court, SW. *Clubs:* Athenæum, Reform. *Died 5 June 1918.*

DUGAS, Hon. Mr Justice Calixter Aimé; a Judge of the Supreme Court of the Yukon Territory; *b* 1845. *Educ:* St Sulpice College, Montreal. Judge of Sessions, Montreal, 1878–98. *Address:* Dawson City, Yukon Territory, Canada. *Died 24 June 1918.*

DUGAS, Hon. Francois Octave, KC; BCL; *b* St Jacques, Co. Montcalm, 12 April 1857; *s* of Aimé Dugas and Sophie Poirier; *m* 1882, Marie Alix Godin; two *s*. *Educ:* St Mary's Coll., Montreal; McGill University. Town Councillor of Joliette, 1890–1900; Crown Prosecutor for district of Joliette, 1887–92 and 1897–1909; a Puisne Judge of the Superior Court for Province Quebec, 1909; MP, Canada, 1900–9. *Address:* Joliette, Quebec, Canada.
Died 23 June 1918.

DUGDALE, Colonel Frank, CVO 1910 (MVO 1906); TD 1909; DL, JP Warwickshire; Equerry-in-Waiting to the Queen; Extra Equerry to the King; *b* 5 April 1857; 2nd *s* of late James Dugdale, Wroxall Abbey, Warwickshire; *m* 1895, Lady Eva Sarah Louisa Greville (Woman of the Bedchamber to the Queen), *o d* of 4th Earl of Warwick; two *s* one *d*. *Educ:* Harrow; Brasenose College, Oxon. Commanded Warwickshire Yeomanry, 1911–16; Hon. Colonel since 1924. Order of the Redeemer of Greece, and Order of St Anne of Russia. *Address:* Royal Lodge, Windsor Great Park. *T:* Egham 76. *Clubs:* Turf, Marlborough. *Died 26 Nov. 1925.*

DUGDALE, James Broughton, JP, DL; *b* 19 Sept. 1855; *e s* of late James Dugdale, of Wroxall, and Mary Louisa, *d* of John Plummer; *m* 1878, Laura Jane, *e d* of J. T. Arkwright, of Hatton House, Co. Warwick. *Educ:* Harrow; Trinity College, Oxford. Captain and Hon. Major late Warwickshire Yeomanry Cavalry; Alderman Warwickshire County Council; High Sheriff Warwickshire, 1907. *Address:* Wroxall Abbey, Warwick. *T:* Haseley Knob 20. *Clubs:* Carlton, Cavalry. *Died 15 Jan. 1927.*

DUGDALE, John Stratford, KC; Recorder of Birmingham since 1877, and Chancellor since 1905; Chancellor of Diocese of Worcester; Chancellor of Diocese of Coventry; Chairman of Warwickshire Quarter Sessions since 1883; Chairman of Warwickshire County Council from its commencement till 1919; *b* 30 July 1835; 2nd *s* of W. S. Dugdale of Merevale Hall, Warwicks; *m* 1890, Alice, *d* of Gen. Henry Alexander Carlton, CB, RA, of Clare, Co. Tipperary; one *d*. *Educ:* Eton; Merton Coll. Oxford (MA). Barrister Inner Temple, 1862; Recorder of Grantham, 1874; QC 1882; MP (C) Nuneaton, 1886–92. *Address:* Avonside, Barford, Warwick; 1 Paper Buildings, Temple, EC. *Clubs:* Carlton, Oxford and Cambridge.
Died 27 Oct. 1920.

DUGMORE, Rev. Ernest Edward; Canon and Prebendary of Salisbury Cathedral since 1890, and Succentor, 1909; Hon. Chaplain to the Bishop, 1917–21; *b* 1843; 4th *s* of William Dugmore, QC, Bencher of Lincoln's Inn, of Swaffham, Norfolk, and Mary Louisa; *m* 1883, Lady Elizabeth (*d* 1902), *d* of 10th Earl of Kinnoull, and *widow* of Colonel Sir Frederick Arthur, 2nd Bt. *Educ:* Bruce Castle School, Tottenham; Wadham College, Oxford. BA 1867; MA 1869. Ordained deacon, 1867; priest, 1870; assistant-curate, St Peter's, Vauxhall, 1867–71; Vicar of Parkstone, 1872–1910. *Publications:* Sunday Readings on the Collects; From the Mountains of the East, a dramatic poem, 1882; Gospel Idylls and other Sacred Verses, 1884; Some Principles of the Holy Catholic Church, 1898; Hymns of Adoration, 1900; The Church's Prayer Meeting, 1912. *Recreation:* reading. *Address:* 9 The Close, Salisbury.
Died 10 May 1925.

DUGMORE, Lt-Col William Francis Brougham Radclyffe, DSO 1899; 2nd in command 72nd Highlanders (Canada); late Captain North Stafford Regiment; *b* 1 Oct. 1868; *e s* of late Capt. Francis Dugmore, 64th Regt, and Hon. Evelyn Mary, *d* of 2nd Baron Brougham and Vaux; *m* 1910, Phyllis, *d* of J. Wilson Usher. *Educ:* The Oratory, Edgbaston; St Mary's Coll., Oscott. Entered Prince of Wales's (North Staffs) Regt, 1894; served East Africa Arab War, Mzrui Expedition, 1895–96 (medal); Unyoro, 1896–97 (medal); Uganda Mutiny, 1897–98 (medal with 2 clasps, despatches, DSO); South Africa, 1901–2, with Mounted Infantry and Colonial Forces (medal with 5 clasps); Somaliland, 1902–3–4 (medal with clasp), retired 1909; served European War, 1914–15 (despatches). *Recreation:* sport. *Address:* Willhayne, Colyton, Devon. *Club:* East India United Service.
Died 12 June 1917.

DUGUID, Charles; writer on finance and cognate subjects; Founder and Managing Director of General Publicity Agency, Ltd; *b* London, 22 Feb. 1864; *m* 1888, Laura, *e d* of N. Nixon of Brampton, Cumberland; three *s* three *d*. *Educ:* Gordon's Coll. Aberdeen. Asst editor Economist, 1890–92; previously on editorial staff of the Stock Exchange and the Mining Journal; city editor Pall Mall Gazette, 1893–97; Westminster Gazette, 1897–1902; Morning Post, 1902–6; World, 1901–9; Observer, 1906–11; Financial Editor of the Daily Mail, Evening News, and associated newspapers, London, Provincial, and Continental, 1906–20; consulting editor of the financial section of The Times, 1911–20; Director of Associated Newspapers Ltd, 1912–20; organised the Daily Mail Exchange in 1912; signal officer to Hertfordshire Volunteer Regt, 1916–20; presented with sword by City of London National Guard; advisory officer, volunteer signals, Eastern Command, 1918–20; retained rank Hon. Captain. *Publications:* History of the Stock Exchange, 1900; How to Read the Money Article; The Feeding of Finance; The Story of the Stock Exchange, 1901; The Stock Exchange and its Machinery (Lectures), 1902; The Stock Exchange (Books on Business), 1904; Money, Stocks, and Insurance, 1911; The Money Article (Bankers' Institute Lectures), 1914. *Recreation:* golf. *Address:* Park Lodge, New Barnet, Herts. *T:* Barnet 84. *Died 13 Dec. 1923.*

DUHM, Bernhard Laward; Doctor der Theologie; ordentlich Professor der Theologie für die alttestamentliche Wissenschaft an der Universität; Lehrer der hebräischen Sprache am Gymnasium zu Basel; *b* Bingum in Ostfriesland, Provinz Hannover, 10 Oct. 1847; *s* of Johannes Duhm und Friederike Knopf; *m* 1877, Helene Bunjes (*d* 1884); three *s*. *Educ:* Bingum (Dorfschule); Aurich (Gymnasium); Göttingen (Universität, 1867–71). Candidat der Theologie, 1870; Repetent am theolog. Stift zu Göttingen, 1871–72; lic. der Theolog., 1873; Privatdocent für das alte Testament zu Göttingen, 1873–77; ausserordentl. Professor der Theologie zu Göttingen, 1877–89; als ordentlicher Prof. der Theol. nach Basel berufen, 1889. *Publications:* Pauli apostoli de lege judicia dijudicata, 1873; Theologie der Propheten, 1875; Ueber Ziel und Methode der theol. Wissenschaft, 1889–1921; Kosmologie und Religion, 1892; Erklärung des Buches Iesaia, 1892–1902–1913–1922; Erklärung des Buches Hiob, 1897; Das Geheimnis in der Religion, 1896; Die Entstehung des alten Testaments, 1897–1906; Übersetzung des Buches Hiob, 1897; Erklärung der Psalmen, 1899–1922; Übersetzung der Psalmen, 1899; Erklärung des Buches Jeremia, 1901; Übersetzung des Buches Jeremia 1903; Die Gottgeweihten in Israel, 1905; Buch Habakuk, Text, Übersetzung, Erklärung, 1906; Das kommende Reich Gottes, 1909 (englisch durch Prof. A. Duff, 1911); Die zwölt Propheten, 1910 (englisch durch Prof. Duff, 1912); Anmerkungen zu den zwölt Propheten, 1911; Israela Propheten, 1916; 2 Aufl. 1922. *Address:* Basel, Johannrheinweg 101. *Died Sept. 1928.*

DUKE, Sir (Frederick) William, GCIE 1918 (KCIE 1911); KCSI 1915 (CSI 1910); Permanent Under Secretary of State for India since 1919; *b* 8 Dec. 1863; *s* of Rev. William Duke, DD; *m* 1889, Mary Eliza, *d* of James Addison-Scott, of Wooden, Roxburghshire; two *s* one *d*. *Educ:* Arbroath High School; University College, London. Entered ICS 1882; Magistrate and Collector, 1900; Commissioner of Orissa, 1905–8; Chief Secretary to Government of Bengal, 1908; Member Executive Council, Bengal, 1910; last Lieutenant-Governor of Bengal, 1911; Member and Vice-President of the Council of the Presidency of Fort William from its creation, 1912 to 1914; Member of Council of India, 1914–19. *Address:* Peel Street Cottage, Campden Hill Road, W8. *T:* Park 3127. *Clubs:* Athenæum, East India United Service. *Died 11 June 1924.*

DUKE, James Buchanan; late President American Tobacco Co., Continental Tobacco Co., and Consolidated Tobacco Co.; Chairman of Directors British-American Tobacco Co. Ltd; Director American Cigar Co., etc; *b* near Durham, NC, 1857; *m* 2nd, 1907, Nannie Lee Inman, Atlanta, Ga. *Address:* Somerville, New Jersey.
Died 10 Oct. 1925.

DULEEP SINGH, Prince Frederick, MVO 1901; FSA; TF; *b* London, 23 Jan. 1868; 2nd and *o* surv. *s* of late Maharajah Duleep Singh of Lahore, GCSI. *Educ:* Eton; Magdalene College, Cambridge. MA (History Tripos) 1890. Lieut Suffolk Yeomanry, 1893; Captain, 1898; Major, North Norfolk Yeomanry, 1901; resigned, 1909; Gazetted to 2/1 Norfolk Yeomanry, Oct. 1914; served in France, 1917–19. *Publications:* articles in the Proceedings of Norfolk Archæological Society; Suffolk Institution of Archæology; Connoisseur; Burlington Magazine, etc. *Recreations:* archæology, music, gardening, shooting. *Address:* Blo'Norton Hall, Diss, Norfolk. *Clubs:* White's, Carlton.
Died 15 Aug. 1926.

DULEEP SINGH, Prince Victor Albert Jay; *b* London, 10 July 1866; *e s* of late Maharajah Duleep Singh, Lahore, GCSI, and Bamba, *d* of L. Müller, Alexandria, Egypt; *m* 1898, Lady Anne, *y d* of 9th Earl of Coventry. *Educ:* Eton; Trinity and Downing Colleges, Cambridge. Gazetted 1st Royal Dragoons, Feb. 1888; Hon. ADC to Lieut-Gen. Ross, KCB, General commanding at Halifax, Nova Scotia, 1888–90. Captain Royal Dragoons, 1894–8. *Recreations:* shooting, music. *Address:* 40 Avenue du Trocadéro, Paris. *Club:* Carlton.   *Died 7 June 1918.*

DUMARESQ, Rear-Adm. John Saumarez, CB 1916; CVO 1920 (MVO 1908); Commodore 1st Class, commanding the Australian Fleet since 1919; Naval ADC to the King since 1920; *b* 26 Oct. 1873; *s* of late William Alexander Dumaresq, MA, Ferruckabad, Glan Innes, NSW, and Edith Helen, *d* of late Capt. John Neilson Gladstone, RN, MP; *m* 1907, Christian Elizabeth Louisa, *d* of late Rt Hon. Sir Charles Dalrymple, 1st Bt; two *s* two *d*. Entered Navy, 1886; Lieut 1894; Commander, 1904; Captain, 1910; Rear-Adm., 1921; served European War, 1914–18 (CB). *Address:* Monckton Croft, Alverstoke, Hants. *TA:* Alverstoke, Hants. *T:* 55 Alverstoke. *Club:* United Service.   *Died 22 July 1922.*

DUMBLETON, General Charles; Bengal Cavalry; *b* 13 May 1824; *m* 1856, Elizabeth Frances J. (*d* 1910), *e d* of Sir Thomas Reed, KCB. Entered army, 1840; General, 1890; retired list, 1884; served Gwalior Campaign, 1843 (bronze star); Indian Mutiny, 1857 (medal). *Address:* Wyke Lodge, Winchester.

                                    Died 15 March 1916.

DUN, William Gibb, MD; FRFPS Glasgow; ex-President, Royal Faculty of Physicians and Surgeons of Glasgow; ex-President, Glasgow Royal Medico-Chirurgical Society; Hon. Physician, Royal Scottish Society for Prevention of Cruelty to Children; Physician Glasgow City Mission; *s* of Thomas Dun, banker; *m* Margaret Gibb; one *s* three *d*. *Educ:* Glasgow High School and University; Vienna University. Assistant Physician, Western Infirmary; Resident Physician, Royal and Western Infirmaries; Medical Tutor, Glasgow University. *Publications:* Blood Letting in Treatment of Disease, and other papers in Medical Press. *Address:* 15 Royal Crescent, Glasgow C3. *T:* Douglas 4343.   *Died 10 Jan. 1927.*

DUNALLEY, 4th Baron, *cr* 1800; **Henry O'Callaghan Prittie,** DL, JP; Representative Peer for Ireland since 1891; Lieutenant for Co. Tipperary; *b* 21 March 1851; *s* of 3rd Baron and Anne, *o d* of 1st Viscount Lismore; *S* father, 1885; *m* 1876, Mary Frances, MBE, *o d* of Maj.-Gen. Onslow Farmer, RA, Aspley Guise, Bedfordshire; one *s* (and one *s* four *d* decd). *Educ:* Harrow; Trinity Coll. Camb. (BA). Late Lieut Rifle Brigade. *Heir: s* Hon. Henry Cornelius O'Callaghan Prittie, *b* 19 July 1877. *Address:* Kilboy, Nenagh, Co. Tipperary.   *Died 5 Aug. 1927.*

DUNBAR, Rev. Sir Charles Gordon-Cumming, 8th Bt (Scot.), *cr* 1700; *b* 14 Feb. 1844; *s* of Sir Archibald Cumming Dunbar, 6th Bt, and his 2nd wife, Sophia, *d* of George Orred, of Tranmere Hall, Cheshire; *S* half-brother, 1910; *m* 1872, Edith (*d* 1891), *d* of W. C. Wentworth, Pres., Legislative Council, Sydney, NSW; one *d*. *Educ:* Winchester; abroad. Deacon, 1867; Chaplain to Bishop of Colombo, 1867–71; Priest, 1868; Chaplain to HM Forces, Ceylon, 1868–72 (on leave of absence to Europe, 1869–72); appointed Senior Chaplain, 1871; Curate, All Saints', Lambeth, 1869–71; Chaplain to Bishop Claughton, London, 1871–75; DD Jena, 1873; accepted Vicarage, Nether Exe, Exeter, 1875; released from Nether Exe to accept Archdeaconry and First Bishop of Pretoria, 1875; released from that acceptance to take Archdeaconry, Rural Deanery, and Rectorship of St John's and of St Mark's, Grenada, 1875; offered the Episcopate for 2nd time, 1876, but declined; Archdeacon of Grenada, WI, 1875–77; incumbent of St James's, Little Heath, Essex, 1887–90; took charge Parish Church, Walthamstow, 1890–92. *Heir-pres: c* Archibald Edward Dunbar, *b* 17 Feb. 1889. *Recreations:* speaking in public, antiquarian subjects, science, music, art, horticulture, forestry. *Address:* Elmina, Albion Road, East Cliff, Ramsgate. *Club:* Royal Societies.   *Died 8 Jan. 1916.*

DUNBAR, Lieut-Comdr Kenneth James Duff-, DSO 1916; RN; commanding one of HM Submarines; *b* 16 Oct. 1886; *s* of late Garden Duff-Dunbar of Hempriggs, and Jane Louisa Duff-Dunbar; *b* of Sir George Duff-Sutherland Dunbar, 6th Bt of Hempriggs; *m* 1914, Katharine Isabel, *d* of late William Adams Daw. *Educ:* Stubbington House, Fareham. Joined HMS Britannia as naval cadet; Midshipman HMS Good Hope, 1902; Sub-Lieut 1905; Lieut, 1907; joined submarine service, 1907; appointed in command of submarine, Nov. 1909; appointed HMS Princess Royal, 1912; rejoined submarine

service for command, April 1915; served European War, 1914–16 (DSO). *Address:* Ackergill Tower, Wick, Caithness, NB. *Clubs:* United Service; Royal Naval, Portsmouth.

                                    Died Aug. 1916.

DUNBAR, Robert Haig; Editor of Derbyshire Printing Company's papers, 1910–15; *b* Galashiels, NB; 2nd and *e* surv. *s* of late Adam Dunbar, JP, Provost of Huntly, NB; *m* Maria, *y d* of late William Atkinson, retired manufacturer, Sheffield; three *s*. *Educ:* Gala School, Galashiels; privately. Edited Huntly Express (his father's paper) for several years up to 1869, when left north to edit the Sheffield Evening Star (later Yorkshire Telegraph and Star), which he combined with the editorship of the Sheffield Times; joined the staff of Sheffield Daily Telegraph as Chief of Reporting Staff and occasional leader and descriptive writer, 1875; Assistant Editor and Acting Editor; Editor of Sheffield Daily Telegraph, 1902–6; original Member Institute of Journalists (Fellow, 1898), and of Original Society the National Association of Journalists; Member of the Sheffield Chamber of Commerce; Hon. Life Member of the Caledonian Society of Sheffield. *Publications:* several small pamphlets descriptive of enterprises engaged in and travels, the latest of which was Notes in Norway. *Recreations:* golf; cricket (spectator only now); travel, more especially on the moors and hills of Derbyshire. *Address:* Aldersyde, 27 Crescent Road, Sharrow, Sheffield. *Club:* Athenæum, Sheffield.

                                    Died 10 Sept. 1919.

DUNCAN, Alexander Robert, JP; *b* 1844; *s* of John Duncan (*d* 1905), and Catherine, *d* of late Robert F. Gourlay; *m* 1873, Frances Euphemia (*d* 1921), *d* of Sir William Edmonstone, 4th Bt; three *s* two *d*. *Educ:* Cheltenham; Trinity College, Cambridge. Admitted a Member of the Scottish Faculty of Advocates, 1869. *Address:* Parkhill, Arbroath, Forfarshire.   *Died 13 April 1927.*

DUNCAN, Sir David, Kt 1919; JP, County of Glamorgan and City of Cardiff; *b* 1847; *s* of late David Duncan of Penarth, JP; *m* 1891, Elizabeth Beverley, *d* of late Christopher Marshall, Gosport; one *d*. *Address:* Bronyglyn, Penarth, Glamorganshire. *Clubs:* Reform, National Liberal.   *Died 23 Oct. 1923.*

DUNCAN, David, MA, DSc, LLD; *b* 5 Nov. 1839; *s* of David Duncan, Aberdeen; *m* Janet, *d* of Rev. Joseph Morison, Millseat, Aberdeenshire; two *s* one *d*. *Educ:* Grammar School, Aberdeen; Universities of Edinburgh, Aberdeen, and Berlin. Private secretary to Mr Herbert Spencer, 1867–70; entered Madras Educational Service, 1870, as Professor of Logic and Moral Philosophy in the Presidency College; Registrar of the Madras University, 1875–79 and 1881–86; Fellow of the University, 1877; Principal and Professor, Presidency College, 1884; Member of the University Syndicate; Director of Public Instruction and Commissioner for Government Examinations, 1892; Member of the Legislative Council, 1894; Vice-Chancellor of the University, 1899; retired from the service, 1899. One of the trustees of the Herbert Spencer Trust. *Publications:* compiled, under the direction of Mr Herbert Spencer, the four volumes of Descriptive Sociology dealing with uncivilized races; author of The Life and Letters of Herbert Spencer. *Recreations:* tennis, golf, cycling. *Address:* 14 Rubislaw Den North, Aberdeen. *Club:* Athenæum.

                                    Died 18 May 1923.

DUNCAN, Edmondstoune; composer and writer on musical subjects; *b* Sale, Cheshire, 22 April 1866. Professor of Musical Compositions in the Leeds College of Music, 1918. Correspondent of the Musical Standard, Musical Times, Musical Record, Musical Opinion, the Musician (Boston, USA), and the New Music Review (New York, USA). *Chief Compositions:* 50 English Songs in Prose and Verse, 1918–20; Perseus (opera); Tone-poem (op. 108) for Orchestra; Declamatory Songs (op. 115); Editor of 100 Folk-dances of all Countries; Minstrelsy of England, 2 vols; Traditional Nursery Rhymes; Art of Piano-playing. *Literary Works:* Modern Interpreters; Life of Schubert; Story of the Carol; History of Music; History of the Dance; English Lyrical Poems. *Recreations:* swimming, chess, cycling. *Address:* Alexandra Road, Sale, near Manchester.

                                    Died 28 June 1920.

DUNCAN, Sir James, Kt 1922; Managing Director of Steel Bros and Co. Ltd, East India Merchants; Chairman, Royal Insurance Co. Ltd, London Board; Deputy Chairman, British and Foreign Marine Insurance Co. Ltd, London Board. *Address:* Steel Bros & Co. Ltd, 6 Fenchurch Avenue, EC3.   *Died 4 May 1926.*

DUNCAN, Sir (James) Hastings, Kt 1914; MP (R) West Riding, Otley Division of Yorkshire, 1900–18; member William Ackroyd & Co., Otley, worsted spinners; *b* March 1855; *m* 1879, Janette, *d*

of Thomas Hunter, Newall Close; one *s* one *d*. *Educ:* privately. *Address:* Kineholm, Otley, Yorks. *Club:* National Liberal.
Died 31 July 1928.

DUNCAN, John Murray, ISO 1902; Receiver-General of the Land Revenues of the Crown, retired; *b* 19 March 1846; *e* surv. *s* of Robert Duncan of Newton Stewart, Wigtownshire; *m* 1875, Janet, *y d* of Daniel Kemp of Edinburgh. *Educ:* Douglas Academy; Edinburgh University. Entered the Civil Service (Woods and Forests Department), 1874; called to the Bar at Lincoln's Inn, but did not practise. *Address:* Usborne House, Wallington, Surrey.
Died 20 Aug. 1922.

DUNCAN, Leland Lewis, OBE 1918; MVO 1902; FSA; *b* 24 Aug. 1862; *s* of late Leland Crosthwait Duncan of HM Customs, and Caroline Ellen, *d* of late Frederick Lewis of the Paymaster-General's Office. *Educ:* Lewisham Grammar School (Colfe's). Entered War Office, 1882; retired 1922; a member of the Kent Archæological Society. *Publications:* Histories of the Borough of Lewisham, of St Mary's Parish Church, and of Colfe's Grammar School, Lewisham; The Churches of West Kent, their Altars, Images, and Lights; and various contributions to Archæologia Cantiana and St Paul's Ecclesiological Society, Folk Lore Society, etc. *Recreations:* medieval history, ecclesiology, custom. *Address:* Rosslair, Lingards Road, Lewisham.
Died 27 Dec. 1923.

DUNCAN, Norman; author; Adjunct Professor of English Literature, the University of Kansas, 1907-9; *b* Brantford, Ont, 1871. *Educ:* Toronto University; LittD Univ. Pittsburg, 1913. Staff of New York Evening Post, 1896-1901; Professor of Rhetoric, Washington and Jefferson Coll., 1902-6; wrote for McClure's Magazine, Newfoundland and Labrador; for Harper's Magazine, Syria, Palestine, and Arabian Desert; for Harper's Magazine, Australia, Papua, and Dutch East Indies. *Publications:* The Way of the Sea; Dr Luke; The Mother; Dr Grenfell's Parish; The Soul of the Street; The Adventures of Billy Topsail; The Cruise of the Shining Light; Every Man for Himself; The Suitable Child; Billy, Topsail, & Company; Going down from Jerusalem; The Measure of a Man; The Best of a Bad Job; A God in Israel; Australian Byways. *Address:* Fredonia, NY. *Club:* City, New York.
Died 18 Oct. 1916.

DUNCOMBE, Alfred Charles, JP for Staffordshire and Derbyshire; Member of Staffordshire County Council; *b* 5 June 1843; *s* of Very Rev. and Hon. Augustus Duncombe, Dean of York, and Lady Harriet Duncombe; *m* 1876, Lady Florence Montagu, 2nd *d* of 7th Earl of Sandwich. *Educ:* Eton. Late Capt. 1st Life Guards and Hon. Major Staffordshire Yeomanry; High Sheriff for Staffords, 1883. *Address:* Calwich Abbey, Ashbourne. *Clubs:* Guards, Arthur's.
Died 22 Feb. 1925.

DUNCOMBE, Hon. Hubert Ernest Valentine, DSO 1900; Hon. Lieutenant-Colonel in Army, 1900; *b* 14 Feb. 1862; *s* of 1st Earl of Feversham and Mabel Violet, *d* of Rt Hon. Sir James Graham, 2nd Bt. *Educ:* Harrow; RMA Woolwich; Magdalene Coll. Camb. MP (C) Egremont Div. Cumberland, 1895-1900; served South Africa, 1900 (despatches). *Address:* Duncombe Park, Helmsley, York; Clairville, S Norwood. *T:* 540 Croydon.
Died 21 Oct. 1918.

DUNCOMBE, Walter Henry Octavius, JP; *b* 1846; *e s* of late Col Hon. Octavius Duncombe, MP, and Lady Emily Caroline, *e d* of 1st Earl Cawdor. Formerly Captain 1st Life Guards; High Sheriff, Cambridge and Hunts, 1899. *Address:* Waresley Park, Sandy, Beds; Westerdale, Yarm, Yorks. *Clubs:* Carlton; Royal Yacht Squadron, Cowes.
Died 6 Jan. 1917.

DUNCOMBE, Rev. William Duncombe Van der Horst; Prebendary of Hereford since 1916. *Address:* The College, Hereford.
Died 4 Oct. 1925.

DUNDAS OF DUNDAS, Admiral Sir Charles, KCMG 1917; *b* 9 Aug. 1859; *S* father as 28th chief of Dundas, 6 March 1904; *m* 1897, Helen, *d* of E. B. Watson; three *s* three *d*. *Educ:* Clifton Bank, St Andrews. Joined HMS Audacious, China flagship, as Naval Cadet, 1874; Lieutenant, 1883; Commander, 1896; served in Cape Squadron during Boer War, and took part in Delagoa Bay operations (medal, and promoted Captain); served in command of HMS Forte, 1904-5, on the East African Station, and received approval of Admiralty for his prompt action in reference to Russian auxiliary cruisers; presented with order of Brilliant Star by Sultan of Zanzibar; received thanks of French Government for services rendered on East African Station; commanded HMS Ocean, Channel Fleet, 1905-8; Naval Attaché,

Tokio, 1908-10; received 2nd class Order of Rising Sun; ADC to King George V, 1920; Rear-Admiral, 1910; attached to suite of Prince H. Fushimi of Japan at Coronation of King George V; attached to personal staff of Admiral Count Togo during his visit to England, July 1911; Rear-Admiral on the staff at Sheerness, 1911; 2nd in command of 7th Battle Squadron at manœuvres of 1912; Vice-Admiral, 1916; Admiral, 1919; Principal Naval Transport Officer, France, 1915-17; Commandeur Légion d'Honneur, 1917; Commander Order of Redeemer of Greece, 1909. *Publication:* An Admiral's Yarns, 1922. *Address:* Inchgarvie House, South Queensferry, Scotland. *Club:* New, Edinburgh.
Died 1 July 1924.

DUNDAS, Hon. Lord; David Dundas; one of the Senators of the College of Justice in Scotland (under above judicial title), 1905; DL for County of City of Edinburgh; LLD (Edin. Univ. 1909); member University Court of Edinburgh University as assessor to Rt Hon. A. J. Balfour, MP, Chancellor of the University; *b* Edinburgh, 8 June 1854; *y s* of late George Dundas, one of the Senators of the Coll. of Justice in Scotland, and of late Elizabeth, *d* of Colin Mackenzie, Portmore, Peeblesshire; *m* 1885, Helen (*d* 1897), *d* of David B. Wauchope. *Educ:* Edinburgh Academy, 1864-71; Balliol College, Oxford, 1872-76 (BA Oxon); Edinburgh University, 1876-78. Scottish Bar, 1878; was an Advocate Depute, 1890-92; Interim Sheriff of Argyllshire, 1896-98; QC 1897; Solicitor-General for Scotland, 1903-5; contested (C) Linlithgowshire, General Election, 1900. *Address:* 11 Drumsheugh Gardens, Edinburgh. *Clubs:* Wellington; New, Edinburgh.
Died 14 Feb. 1922.

DUNDAS, Colonel Sir Lorenzo George, KCB 1907 (CB 1896); late Commanding 6th Battalion the Royal Fusiliers; *b* 6 April 1837; *e s* of late L. Dundas, JP, Clobemon Hall, Wexford; *m* 1868, Lily, *d* of late R. Adams, 6 Kensington Park Gardens, London; three *s* two *d*. *Educ:* Trinity Coll. Dublin. Joined 62nd Regt, Jan. 1855; served with it in the trenches before Sebastopol and formed one of the stormers at the attack on the Redan, 8 Sept.; retired from Army, 1873, and joined the Militia force; commanded the 17th Brigade on Jubilee day, 1887; and 8th Provisional Batt. Belfast, 1901-7; Hon. Colonel 6th Fusiliers 29 May 1905. Decorated for Crimean War (Crimean medal and clasps, Turkish medal); CB; Jubilee medal. *Recreations:* riding, shooting, boating. *Address:* Gloucester Lodge, East Molesey.
Died 10 Dec. 1917.

DUNDAS, William John, LLD (Edin.); WS; Crown Agent for Scotland, 1895-1905, and 1916-19; *b* 16 March 1849; *s* of late George Dundas, a Senator of the College of Justice. *Educ:* Edinburgh Academy and University. *Address:* 11 Drumsheugh Gardens, Edinburgh. *Club:* New, Edinburgh.
Died 9 July 1921.

DUNFEE, Col Vickers, CBE 1919; VD; JP; *b* 30 April 1861; *m* 1893, Lilla (*d* 1922), *y d* of W. N. Froy; four *s*. *Educ:* King's College School and College. Served in City of London Militia; joined Hamlet's Rifle Brigade, 4th VB Royal Fusiliers; Commanded 2/4th Batt. City of London Regt (Royal Fusiliers) during European War; served Egypt, Gallipoli, Senussi Campaign, Southern Force and France (despatches twice); Commandant City of London Police Reserve. *Recreations:* general. *Address:* 53 St John's Road, Putney, SW15. *Club:* Royal Automobile.
Died 17 Feb. 1927.

DUNHAM, E. K., MD; Emeritus Professor of Pathology, the University and Bellevue Hospital Medical College, New York City; *b* 1 Sept. 1860; *s* of Carroll and Harriet E. Kellogg Dunham; *m* 1903, Mary Dows; one *s* one *d*. *Educ:* Columbia College; School of Mines; Harvard Medical School. *Address:* 35 East 68th Street, New York.
Died 15 April 1923.

DUNKERLEY, Ven. William Herbert Cecil; Rector of Leybourne, Kent, since 1920; *s* of late Rev. William Dunkerley, MA, LLD, and Annie Swann; *m* 1886, Mary Beatrice Taylor; six *c*. *Educ:* Denstone Coll.; Pembroke Coll., Oxford (MA); Cuddesdon (Organ Studentship). Ordained deacon, 1885; priest, 1886; Curate of St Thomas', Toxteth Park, Liverpool, 1885-86; Sigglesthorne, Yorks, 1886-89; Cuddesdon, Oxon, 1889-91; Colonial Chaplain of Malacca, 1891-97; Penang, 1897-1901; Singapore, 1901; JP, Visiting Justice, and Licensing Justice, Malacca, 1892; Acting Headmaster, Govt High School, Malacca, 1893; Assistant Examiner for Government Clerkships, Malacca, 1894-95; passed final Civil Service Malay Examination, 1894; Hon. Chaplain and Captain Penang Volunteer Corps, 1898; Hon. Chaplain and Captain Singapore Volunteer Corps, 1901; Acting Chaplain to the Forces, 1902; Diocesan Surrogate, 1892; Ecclesiastical Registrar, 1902; Archdeacon of Singapore, 1902-5; Vicar of Castle Morton, 1906-9; Vicar of St Mark's, Bush Hill Park, N, and Surrogate, 1909–10; Chaplain of St Paul's, Cannes, 1910–13; Vicar of St John's, Sevenoaks, 1913–20. *Address:* Leybourne Rectory, West Malling.   *Died 21 Aug. 1922.*

DUNLOP, Alexander Johnstone, CIE 1901; *b* 7 April 1848; *s* of late Henry Dunlop of Craigton House, Lanark; *m* 1873, Constance Susan Mary, *d* of late W. R. Myers, of Jamaica. Entered Service, 1869; Director-General of Revenue, His Highness Nizam's Government, 1885; retired 1914. Kaisar-i-Hind Medal. *Address:* Crescent Lodge, Largs, Ayrshire.   *Died 25 Oct. 1921.*

DUNLOP, Col James William, CB 1902; CMG 1916; late RHA; *b* 16 Oct. 1854; *s* of Colin Robert Dunlop (*d* 1896) of Torwood Hill, Row, Dunbartonshire. *Educ:* Cheltenham College; Royal Military Academy, Woolwich. Entered army, 1875, Captain, 1884; Major, 1892; Lt-Col 1900; Colonel, 1904; served Afghan War, 1879–80 (despatches, medal); Burmese Expedition, 1886–87 (medal with clasp); South Africa, 1901–2 (despatches, Queen's medal with five clasps, CB); retired 1908; served European War, 1914–18 (1914 Star, despatches, CMG, British War Medal, Victory Medal). *Recreations:* hunting, shooting. *Address:* Struan, St Boswells, Roxburghshire. *Clubs:* Army and Navy; New, Edinburgh.

      Died 20 Nov. 1923.

DUNLOP, Hon. John, DCL; Puisne Judge of Superior Court of Province of Quebec since 1904, and Admiralty Judge Exchequer Court of Canada since 1906; *b* 1837; 3rd *s* of late Alexander Dunlop of Clober, Stirlingshire, Scotland; *m* 1863, Eleanor, *d* of late David Bellhouse; two *s* three *d*. *Educ:* Edinburgh Academy and University; McGill University, Montreal. Emigrated to Canada, 1857; BCL 1860; DCL 1910; admitted to Bar, Province of Quebec, 1861; KC 1874; Treasurer, Bar of Montreal, 1888–91; Batonnier, Bar of Montreal, 1891–93. *Address:* 299 Peel Street, Montreal, Canada. *TA:* Magdala, Montreal. *T:* Up Town 2028. *Clubs:* Mount Royal, Montreal, Montreal.   *Died 7 Nov. 1916.*

DUNLOP, Sir Nathaniel, Kt 1907; DL; JP; LLD (Glasgow); retired shipowner; formerly Chairman Allan Line Steamship Company and of James and Alexander Allan, Glasgow, the founders and former managing directors of the line; *b* 7 April 1830; *s* of Archibald Dunlop, Campbeltown; *m* 1866, Ellen (decd), *d* of George Smith; one *d*. *Educ:* Grammar School, Campbeltown. *Publications:* various pamphlets on trade and commerce; magazine articles. *Recreation:* country life. *Address:* 21 Bothwell Street, Glasgow; Shieldhill, Biggar, Lanarkshire. *Clubs:* Constitutional; New, Glasgow.

      Died 17 Nov. 1919.

DUNLOP, Col Samuel, CMG 1884; late RA; *b* 8 March 1838; *m* 1864, Martha, *d* of Robert Potts of Belfast. Entered RA 1856; retired 1882; Acting Commissioner of Police, Straits Settlements, 1870; Inspector-General, 1875; served Perak, 1875; retired 1890. *Address:* 74 Cromwell Avenue, Highgate, N.   *Died 28 June 1917.*

DUNLOP, Major William Hugh, DL; Chief Constable of the East Riding of Yorkshire since 1899; *b* 1857; *s* of Colin Robert Dunlop (*d* 1896) of Torwood Hill, Row, Dunbartonshire; *m* 1st, 1882, Clara Helena (*d* 1887), *d* of Hon. H. F. Colthirst, Jamaica; no *c*; 2nd, 1893, Elizabeth Ceorgina, *d* of William Donald of Lisle House, Cheltenham; one *s* one *d*. *Educ:* Cheltenham College; Royal Military College, Sandhurst. Joined the 2nd Royal Lanark Militia, 1877; joined the army as 2nd Lieut, 1879; Captain, 1887; Major, 1898; retired from the Royal Irish Rifles, 1899; served as Adjutant of the 4th Batt. and Depot Royal Irish Rifles, 1893–97; on the Recruiting Staff of the Army, 1897–99; accompanied the Expedition under General Clive Justice to quell a rising of the Ashantis in 1881. *Recreations:* shooting, fishing, golf. *Address:* Beverley, Yorkshire. *TA:* Dunlop, Beverley. *T:* 28 Beverley. *M:* CC89. *Clubs:* Boodle's, Junior Athenæum.

      Died 28 Nov. 1924.

DUNN, Captain Arthur Edward, CBE 1919; RD; ADC, RNR; *b* 1876; *s* of Robert Lowthorpe Dunn; *m* Grace Adeline, *d* of George Glover, Oriental Bay, Wellington, New Zealand. *Educ:* Newark Grammar School; HMS Worcester. Joined RNR as Midshipman, 1893; Commander, King's Birthday Honours, 1914; Captain, 1920; Marine Superintendent The New Zealand Shipping Company Limited, Federal Steam Navigation Company Limited, and the Irish Counties Section of the Union Steamship Company of New Zealand Limited; a Younger Brother of Trinity House, London; Freeman of the City of London. Served European War, 1914 (eleven clasps), Commanding HM ships and latterly Organising Officer of Convoys; despatches for services at evacuation of Serbian troops from Durazzo; Officer of the Order of Redeemer of Greece, rendered services as

Commodore of Convoys and on Staff of British Senior Naval Office, New York; ADC to HM; a selected member of the Royal Naval Reserve Advisory Committee, and a member of the Promotion Board. *Address:* Wakefield, Albion Hill, Loughton. *T:* Loughton 325. *Club:* Junior Athenæum.   *Died 6 Jan. 1927.*

DUNN, James Nicol; London Editor Glasgow News since 1914; Kincardineshire, NB, 12 Oct. 1856; *e s* of Joseph Dunn and Margaret Macleod. *Educ:* Aberdeen. Destined for the law, but wrote for journals and magazines while still a student, and speedily devoted himself to press work; joined staff of the Dundee Advertiser and then that of the Scotsman; when the National Observer was started became managing editor; resigned that position to go on staff of the Pall Mall Gazette; editor of Black and White, 1895–97, and of the Ludgate for the same period; editor of Morning Post, 1897–1905; President of the Institute of Journalists, 1904; Editor of Manchester Courier 1905–10; Star, Johannesburg, 1911–14. *Recreations:* golf, chess. *Address:* Craigallion, Champion Hill, SE. *Clubs:* Press, Yorick, Cecil, Savage.

      Died 30 June 1919.

DUNN, Louis Albert, MS, MB; FRCS; Surgeon, Guy's Hospital; Consulting Surgeon to the East London Children's Hospital; Consulting Surgeon Children's Hospital Plaistow; Member of Court of Examiners, Royal College of Surgeons; Examiner in Surgery at Cambridge University; *b* 1858; *y s* of late J. Roberts Dunn, JP, DL of Stone House, Warbleton, Sussex. *Educ:* Guy's Hospital. *Address:* Dunholme, North Park, Gerrard's Cross, Bucks.

      Died 7 June 1918.

DUNN, Thomas Smith, ISO 1903; late head of Stock and Coupon Department of the Crown Agents for the Colonies; *b* 1836. *Address:* Hazelwood, Brunswick Road, Sutton, Surrey.

      Died 16 Dec. 1916.

DUNN, Sir William (Henry), 1st Bt, *cr* 1917; Kt 1907; Lord Mayor of London, 1916–17; *b* Clitheroe, 8 Oct. 1856; *y s* of late John Quinn Dunn, Clitheroe, and Susannah Scarf; *m* 1885, Ellen, *d* of John Pawley, one *s* one *d*. *Educ:* privately. Late Hon. Col 1st London Div. Transport and Supply Column; Fellow of Surveyors' Institution; Magistrate for the County of London; Alderman of the City of London; 1900–23 (Sheriff, 1906–7); Lieutenant of the City of London, Chairman of the Royal Botanic Society; Trustee and Treasurer Lord Mayor Treloar Cripples Hospital and College; Liveryman of Shipwrights' and other City Companies, being on the Court of several. MP (U) West Southwark, 1910. Orders of the Legion of Honour (France), the Crown (Italy), the Dannebrog (Denmark), St Olaf (Norway), and the Rising Sun (Japan), 4th class; Knight Commander of the Order of St Gregory and Grand Officer of the Order of the Saviour (Greece). *Heir:* *s* John Henry Dunn, *b* 12 Dec. 1890. *Address:* 9 Gloucester Gate, NW1. *T:* Museum 5674. *Clubs:* Carlton, Junior Carlton, Hurlingham.

      Died 12 June 1926.

DUNNE, Rt. Rev. John, DD; First Bishop of Wilcannia since 1887; *b* Rhode, King's Co., Ireland, 21 Sept. 1846. *Educ:* Carlow College, Ireland. Ordained, 1870; Priest in Diocese of Goulburn, 1871–87; stationed in charge of Burrowa and Vicar at Aldbury, 1880–87. *Address:* Bishop's House, Broken Hill, Australia.

      Died 13 Jan. 1917.

DUNNE, General Sir John Hart, KCB 1906; retired; Colonel Duke of Edinburgh's Wilts Regiment; *b* 11 Dec. 1835; *s* of John Dunne of Cartron, Co. Roscommon, and Marianne, *d* of Colonel Hart; *m* 1870, Julia, *d* of W. R. Chapman of Whitby; two *s* one *d*. *Educ:* private schools. Ensign, Wilts Regt, 1852; Lieut, Royal Scots Fusiliers, 1854; Maj.-Gen. 1881; Gen. 1893; served through Crimean campaign, 1854–55, in battles of Alma, Balaclava, Inkerman, and siege of Sevastopol; served throughout the China War of 1860; carried and hoisted the Union Jack at the capture of the Inner North Taku Fort; was with the advance guard at the action of Changiawhan and Poliatchan and capture of Pekin; commanded 2nd Infantry Brigade, Aldershot, 1885–86; Thames District, Chatham, 1887–90; Lieut Tower of London, 1894–97. Grand Cordon, Order of Medjidie, 1907. *Publication:* From Calcutta to Pekin. *Address:* Fortfield, Sidmouth.   *Died 20 April 1924.*

DUNNE, Rt. Rev. John Mary; Bishop of Bathurst since 1901; *b* Ireland, 1843. *Educ:* Mount Melleray Seminary; All Hallows'. Went to Australia, 1871. *Address:* Bathurst, New South Wales.

      Died 22 Aug. 1919.

DUNNING, Albert Elijah, DD Beloit College, 1887; Editor-in-Chief, The Congregationalist, Boston, since 1889; *b* Conn, 5 Jan.

1844; *m* 1870, Harriet W. Westbrook, Kingston, NY. *Educ:* Yale University; Andover Theological Seminary. Pastor Highland Church, Boston, 1870–81; General Secretary for Congregational Churches, 1881–89; Editor-in-chief of The Congregationalist and Christian World, 1889–1911; Lecturer Andover Theological Seminary, 1915–16; Member of Massachusetts Pilgrim Tercentenary Commission, 1915–16. *Publications:* The Sunday School Library, 1883; Bible Studies, 1886; Congregationalists in America, 1894; The Making of the Bible, 1911. *Address:* 43 Druce Road, Brookline, Mass.
Died 14 Nov. 1923.

DUNNING, Sir Edwin Harris, Kt 1904; JP County Devon and Broughton Tiverton; CC Devonshire; *b* 8 April 1858; *s* of Richard Dunning of Exeter; *m* 1881, Hannah Louise (*d* 1914), *d* of Richard Freeman of Hereford; three *s* two *d*. Mayor of Tiverton, 1901. Patron of Rectory of Washfield. *Address:* Jacques Hall, Bradfield, Essex. *Club:* Carlton.
Died 14 Dec. 1923.

DUNNING, William Archibald, PhD, LLD, LittD; Lieber Professor of History and Political Philosophy, Columbia University, New York; *b* Plainfield, New Jersey; *s* of John H. and Catharine D. Dunning; *m* 1888, Charlotte E. Loomis (*d* 1917), Brooklyn, New York. *Educ:* Columbia University. After completing university study with doctor's degree in 1885, began work of instruction in Columbia in history and political science, and rose through various grades to professorship in 1891; entered the editorial board of the Political Science Quarterly in 1889, and was managing editor, 1895–1903; President American Historical Association, 1913; contributed extensively to the Quarterly, American Historical Review, Yale Review, Atlantic Monthly, etc. *Publications:* Essays on the Civil War and Reconstruction, 1898; A History of Political Theories, 3 vols, 1902–20; Reconstruction, Political and Economic, 1907; The British Empire and the United States, 1914. *Address:* Columbia University, New York. *Club:* Century, New York.
Died 25 Aug. 1922.

DUNRAVEN and MOUNT-EARL, 4th Earl of, *cr* 1822; Windham Thomas Wyndam-Quin, KP; CMG 1902; OBE 1914; PC (Ireland) 1899; Baron Adare, 1800; Viscount Mountearl, 1816; Viscount Adare, 1822; Baron Kenry (UK), 1866; Senator Irish Free State; *b* 12 Feb. 1841; *o s* of 3rd Earl and 1st wife, Augusta, *d* of Thomas Goold; *S* father, 1871; *m* 1869, Florence Elizabeth (*d* 1916), *d* of Lord Charles Lennox Kerr; one *d* (and two *d* decd). *Educ:* Christ Church, Oxford. Lieut 4th Oxford Univ. Rifles, 1860–61; late Lieut 1st Life Guards; Hon. Col Glamorgan Artillery Militia; Hon. Col 5th Batt. Royal Munster Fusiliers (disbanded 1922). War Correspondent to Daily Telegraph in Abyssinia, 1867, and in Franco-Prussian War and siege of Paris; ADC to Lord-Lieut of Ireland, 1868; Under-Secretary to Colonies, 1885–86, 1886–87; Chairman of the House of Lords Committee on Sweating, 1888–90; HM's Lieut County Limerick, 1894; Chairman Irish Horse-Breeding Commission, 1896; Chairman Irish Land Conference, 1902–3; President Irish Reform Association; served South Africa, Capt. 18th Batt. Imperial Yeomanry Sharpshooters (Queen's medal with two clasps); Hon. Colonel 5th County of London Armoured Car Company (Sharpshooters). Twice built a yacht for the sailing competitions with the United States; owner of motor yacht Sona; holder, Board of Trade's Extra-master certificate; purchased and fitted out as hospital transport carrier SY Grianaig, 1914 (OBE); Hon. Capt. RNR. Owner of about 39,800 acres. *Publications:* The Great Divide, the Upper Yellowstone, 1874; Irish Question, 1880; Self-Instruction in the Theory and Practice of Navigation, 1900; The Legacy of Past Years, 1911; Canadian Nights, 1914; Past Times and Pastimes, 1922. *Heir: cousin* Windham Henry Wyndham-Quin, *b* 7 Feb. 1857. *Address:* 22 Norfolk Street, Park Lane, W1. *T:* Mayfair 4978; Kenry House, Putney Vale, SW1. *T:* Kingston 465; Danraven Castle, Bridgend, Glamorgan; Adare Manor, Adare, Limerick. *Clubs:* Athenæum, Carlton, Bachelor's, Turf, Jockey, Royal Automobile; Kildare Street, Dublin; Royal Yacht Squadron, Cowes.
Died 14 June 1926.

DUNSMUIR, Hon. James; Lieutenant-Governor, British Columbia, 1906–10; late Premier and President of Executive Council, British Columbia; *b* 8 July 1851; *m* Laura, *d* of W. B. Surles of Fayetteville, North Carolina; one *s* eight *d*. Was owner of Esquimalt and Nanaimo Railway, which was sold to the CPR with a million and a half acres of land; Director of CPR; late owner of the Wellington Colliery Company. *Recreations:* yachting, shooting, fishing, croquet. *Address:* Hatley Park, Victoria, British Columbia. *TA:* Dunsmuir, Victoria, BC. *T:* 531.
Died 6 June 1921.

DUNTZE, Sir George Alexander, 4th Bt, *cr* 1774; *b* 27 Jan. 1839; *s* of late Rev. Samuel Henry Duntze and Frances, *d* of Very Rev. Dr Palmer, Dean of Cashel; *S* cousin, 1884; *m* 1869, Harriet (*d* 1908),

e d of Lloyd Thomas; one *s* two *d*. *Heir: s* George Puxley Duntze [*b* 6 Dec. 1873; *m* 1908, Violet May, *d* of Henry Mark Sanderson; one *s* two *d*]. *Address:* Club Anglais, Dinard, France.
Died 2 May 1922.

DUPUY, Charles Alexander; Sénateur de la Haute-Loire since 1900; Ancien Président de la Chambre de Députés et du Conseil des Ministres; *b* Puy, 5 Nov. 1851. *Educ:* Le Puy (Haute-Loire). Professeur Agrégé de Philosophie, 1879; Inspecteur de l'Académie, 1880; Vice-Recteur de la Corve, 1883; Député de la Haute-Loire, 1889. *Decorations:* plusieurs grands cordons. *Address:* Quai de Bethune 18, IVe Paris.
Died 23 July 1923.

DUPUY, Jean; Sénateur des Hautes-Pyrénées depuis 1891; *b* Saint-Palais (Gironde). Directeur du journal Le Petite Parisien depuis 1888; Président du Comité Général des Associations de la Presse Française depuis 1899; Ministre de l'Agriculture, 1899–1902; Ministre du Commerce et de l'Industrie, 1909–11; Ministre des Travaux Publics, des Postes et des Télégraphes, 1912–13. *Address:* 9 rue Scribe, Paris.
Died 31 Déc. 1919.

DUPUY, Paul; Sénateur des Hautes Pyrénées; Directeur du Petit Parisien depuis 1908; Directeur d'Excelsior depuis 1917; *b* Paris; *m* Miss Browne; two *s* one *d*. Ancien Député des Hautes-Pyrénées. *Address:* 29 rue Octave Feuillet, Paris.
Died 10 July 1927.

DURAND, Colonel Algernon George Arnold, CB 1892; CIE 1897; Gentleman-at-Arms; *b* 31 March 1854; *s* of Maj.-Gen. Sir Henry Marion Durand, RE (*d* 1871); *m* 1895, Elizabeth Marjorie, *d* of late Hon. T. C. Bruce, MP; two *s*. ADC to Lord Ripon, Viceroy of India, 1881–82; British Agent at Gilgit, 1889–93; commanded troops in Hunza Nagar Expedition, 1891; Military Secretary to Viceroy of India, 1894–99. *Publication:* The Making of a Frontier, 1899. *Address:* 47 Egerton Gardens, SW3. *T:* Kensington 6481. *Club:* Travellers'.
Died 7 Oct. 1923.

DURAND, Sir Edward (Law), 1st Bt, *cr* 1892; CB 1887; *b* 5 June 1845; *s* of late Sir Henry Durand, KCSI, RE; *m* 1880, Maude Ellen, *d* of late A. Heber-Percy; three *s* three *d* (and one *s* decd). *Educ:* Bath; Repton; Guildford. Entered 96th Regt 1865; BSC 1868; Assistant Commissioner Afghan Boundary, 1884–86; Resident in Nepaul, 1888–91; retired 1893 (Lieut-Col). *Publications:* Cyrus the Great King, 1906; Rifle, Rod, and Spear in the East. *Heir: s* Edward Percy Marion Durand [*b* 11 July 1884; *m* 1913, Vera Helen, *d* of Sir Robert Lucas Lucas-Tooth, 1st Bt; Lieut Indian Army]. *Address:* 35 Ennismore Gardens, SW7. *T:* Kens. 5013. *Club:* Sports.
Died 1 July 1920.

DURAND, Rt. Hon. Sir (Henry) Mortimer, GCMG 1900; KCSI 1894 (CSI 1881); KCIE 1889; PC 1901; *b* 14 Feb. 1850; *s* of late Major-General Sir Henry Durand, RE, and Anne, *d* of Sir John M'Caskill, KCB; *m* 1875, Ella (*d* 1918), *d* of T. Sandys; one *s* one *d*. *Educ:* Blackheath School; Eton House, Tonbridge. Barrister, Lincoln's Inn, 1872; entered Bengal Civil Service, 1873; Political Secretary to Sir Frederick, afterwards Earl, Roberts during Kabul Campaign, 1879; Foreign Secretary in India, 1884–94; conducted Mission to Ameer of Afghanistan, 1893; Minister at Teheran, 1894–1900; Ambassador and Consul-Gen. at Madrid, 1900–3; Ambassador at Washington, 1903–6. Contested Plymouth (C), 1910. *Publications:* edited Sir Henry Durand's History of the first Afghan War, 1879; Life of Sir Henry Durand, 1883; Helen Treveryan, 1891; Nadir Shah, 1908; A Holiday in S Africa, 1911; Life of Rt Hon. Sir Alfred Comyn Lyall, PC, 1913; Life of Field-Marshal Sir George White, VC, 1915; The 13th Hussars in the Great War, 1921. *Address:* Penmayne House, Rock, Wadebridge, Cornwall. *Clubs:* Athenæum, Ranelagh.
Died 8 June 1924.

DURELL, Henry E. Le Vavasseur dit; Attorney General, Jersey, since 1912; *b* St Helier, Jersey; *m* 1914, Winifred Mary, *d* of late Surg.-Major Lucas G. Hooper, 10th Hussars. *Educ:* Victoria College, Jersey; Caen, Normandy. Called to Bar (Middle Temple), 1868; since practised continuously at Jersey Bar; leader of Local Bar, 1896–99; represented St Helier in the Jersey States Assembly, 1874–96, having been elected on eight consecutive occasions; Mayor of St Helier, 1896–99; Solicitor General, Jersey, 1899–1911. *Address:* The Anchorage, St Luke's, Jersey.
Died July 1921.

DURET, Rt. Rev. Augustin; General Superior of the Society of African Missions since 1914; *b* 1846. Ordained priest, 1870; titular Bishop of Bubastis and Vicar Apostolic of the Nile Delta, Egypt, 1910–14. *Address:* Lyons, Cours Gambetta 150, France.
Died 29 Aug. 1920.

DURHAM, 3rd Earl of, *cr* 1833; **John George Lambton**, GCVO 1912; KG 1909; PC 1912; Baron Durham, 1828; Viscount Lambton, 1833; Lord Lieutenant of Durham, 1884-1928; *b* 19 June 1855; *s* of 2nd Earl and Beatrix, *d* of 1st Duke of Abercorn; *S* father, 1879; *m* 1882, Ethel, 2nd *d* of Henry B. M. Milner, West Retford House, Notts, 2nd *s* of Sir William Milner, 4th Bt. Chancellor University of Durham; Lieut Coldstream Guards, 1877-79. Owner of about 30,500 acres. *Heir:* twin *b* Hon. Frederick Lambton, *b* 19 June 1855. *Address:* 39 Grosvenor Square, W1. *T:* Mayfair 875; Lambton Castle, Fence Houses, Durham; Harraton House, Exning, Newmarket. *Clubs:* Marlborough, Turf.

Died 18 Sept. 1928.

DURHAM, Rev. William Edward, MA; Rector of Trusham, near Chudleigh, Devon, since 1919; Prebendary of Exeter Cathedral, 1912; *b* 15 Aug. 1857; *s* of W. J. Durham; *m* 1880, Priscilla Evelyn, *d* of Rev. T. F. Arthur, Eastdown Rectory, N Devon; one *d*. *Educ:* Cheltenham College; Trinity College, Cambridge. Ordained, 1881; Curate of Tavistock, 1881; Rector of Eastdown, N. Devon, 1882; Vicar of St Matthew's, Burnley, 1888; Rector of Wolborough with Newton-Abbot, 1896; Rural Dean of Morton, 1904. *Publication:* Summer Holidays in the Alps. *Recreation:* mountaineering. *Address:* Trusham Rectory, near Chudleigh, S Devon. *TA:* Lower Ashton. *Club:* Alpine. *Died 16 May 1921.*

DURNFORD, Robert Chichester, DSO 1917; 2nd Lieutenant 1/4th Hampshire Regiment; *b* 19 Oct. 1895; *y s* of Richard Durnford, CB; unmarried. *Educ:* Eton; Scholar elect of King's College, Cambridge, 1913. Newcastle select, 1914; commissioned 4th Hampshire Regt (TF), 1 Oct. 1914; Temp. Lieut, Nov. 1914; went to India with 2/4th Hampshire Regt, Dec. 1914; Quetta, 1915-16; Temp. Captain, Oct. 1915; proceeded to Mesopotamia and joined 1/4th Hampshire Regt Oct. 1916; reverted to Temp. Lieut (wounded, DSO); invalided, March 1917. *Recreations:* cricket, football, etc. *Address:* Hartley Wespall House, Basingstoke, Hants. *Died 21 June 1918.*

DURNFORD, Sir Walter, GBE 1919; VD; JP; LLD; Provost of King's College, Cambridge, since 1918, and Fellow of Eton College; *b* 21 Feb. 1847; *s* of Richard Durnford, Bishop of Chichester, 1870-95. *Educ:* Eton; King's College, Cambridge; 4th in the First Class Classical Tripos, 1869. Scholar and Fellow of King's College, Cambridge, 1865, 1869; Assistant Master, Eton, 1870-99; commanded 2nd Bucks (Eton College) RV; Member of Governing Body of Eton College, 1909; Vice-Provost King's College, 1909-18. *Address:* The Lodge, King's College, Cambridge. *Club:* United University.

Died 7 April 1926.

DURST, Rev. William; Hon. Canon of Winchester since 1885; Proctor in Convocation for the archdeaconries of Winchester and Isle of Wight, 1896-1917; *b* 1838; 2nd *s* of late John Durst of Tunbridge Wells and Walmer; *m* Edith Harriet (*d* 1922), *d* of late Rev. W. Gibson, Rector of Fawley, Hants; three *s* six *d*. *Educ:* King's College School; Emmanuel College, Cambridge (MA). Ordained Deacon, 1861; Priest, 1862, by the Bishop of Worcester; served in curacies at St John's, Ladywood, Birmingham, St John's, Worcester, and Penshurst, Kent; Curate in charge of Crondall, Hants; Vicar of Alton, Hants, 1874; Rural Dean of Alton, 1879; Rector and Rural Dean of Alverstoke, 1881; Canon Residentiary of Winchester, 1887; Rector of St Mary's and Rural Dean of Southampton, 1894-1912. *Address:* St Giles House, Fareham, Hants.

Died 27 Aug. 1922.

DURSTON, Sir Albert John, KCB 1897 (CB 1895); RN; Engineer-in-Chief RN, 1889-1907; *b* Devonport, 25 Oct. 1846; *m* 1869, Agnes Mary (*d* 1887), *d* of C. R. B. Wilkinson; two *s* four *d*. *Educ:* privately; Portsmouth Dockyard and Royal School of Naval Architecture, South Kensington, of which a Fellow. Entered Royal Navy, 1866; Chief Engineer, 1877; Chief Inspector of Machinery, 1893; Chief Engineer, Sheerness and Portsmouth Dockyards, 1881-88; Engineer Vice-Admiral, retired 1906. MInstCE; MInstMechE; Past President Inst. of Marine Engineers; Vice-President Inst. of Naval Architects, Association of Engineers-in-Charge; Royal Naval Benevolent Society; Hon. Mem. Society of Engineers, Inst. of Engineers and Shipbuilders of Scotland and of Junior Engineers, London. *Address:* St Andrews, Westcombe Park Road, Blackheath, SE. *T:* Greenwich 437. *Clubs:* United Service; Royal Blackheath Golf.

Died 18 April 1917.

DUSE, Signora Eleonora; actress; *b* Venice, 1861; father and grandfather actors. Appeared New York, 1893; London, 1893-94 and 1923; appeared before Queen Victoria, Windsor, 1894.

Died 21 April 1924.

DUTHIE, Sir John, KBE 1918; Senior Assistant Director-General o Voluntary Organisations; *b* 15 July 1858; *s* of late William Duthi of Cairnbulg, Aberdeenshire, shipowner, and Martha, *d* of late Jame Biruie of Aberdeen; *m* 1890, Lesley, *d* of late John Fyfe, DL, JF Aberdeen; four *s* two *d*. *Educ:* privately; Aberdeen University Barrister-at-Law, Lincoln's Inn; represented London County Counc on Board of Port of London Authority for seven years; J Aberdeenshire. *Address:* 22 Hyde Park Street, W2; Cairnbulg Castle Aberdeenshire; Kempsons, Whitchurch, Bucks. *Clubs:* Orienta Royal Northern, Aberdeen.

Died 19 June 1922

DU VERNET, Most Rev. Frederick Herbert; Archbishop o Caledonia since 1915; Metropolitan of British Columbia since 1915 President, Anglican Theological College of BC, 1912; *b* 1860; *s* o Rev. Canon Du Vernet and Frances Ellegood; *m* 1885; one *s* on d. *Educ:* Wycliffe College, Toronto. Ordained 1883; Curate St Jame the Apostle, Montreal, 1883-84; Diocesan Missioner, Montrea 1884-85; Professor of Practical Theology, Wycliffe College, 1885-95 Rector of St John, Toronto, 1895-1904; BD, 1893; DD, 1904; Bisho of Caledonia, 1904; Visitor Wycliffe College since 1904. *Addres.* Prince Rupert, British Columbia. *T:* 255.

Died 22 Oct. 1924

DWIGHT, Rev. Timothy, DD, LLD; President of Yale University New Haven, Connecticut, 1886-99; *b* Norwich, Connecticut, 1 Nov. 1828; *s* of James Dwight, *s* of Rev. Timothy Dwight, DD, LLD President of Yale College, 1795-1817, who was *g s* of Jonatha Edwards, the eminent divine, and Susan Breed Dwight, *d* of Joh M'Laren Breed, whose grandfather was Rev. John M'Laren, o Edinburgh, Scotland; *m* 1866, Jane Wakeman Skinner, *d* of Rog Sherman Skinner, *g s* of Hon. Roger Sherman, one of the signers o the Declaration of Independence of the United States, and Mar Lockwood De Forest Skinner, *d* of Lockwood De Forest, of Nev York; one *d*. *Educ:* Yale Coll. BA, 1849; studied Theology in th Divinity School of Yale Coll.; Tutor in the College, 1851-55; studie at the Universities of Bonn and Berlin, 1856-58. Professor of Nev Testament Greek and Exegesis, Yale Divinity School, 1858-86 *Publications:* translated and edited with additional notes the Americal edition of Godet's Commentary on St John's Gospel; edited wit additional notes several volumes of the American edition of Meyer Commentary on the New Testament; volume of sermons entitle Thoughts of and for the Inner Life; Memories of Yale Life and Mer a considerable number of articles on theological and educationa subjects. A member of the American Committee for the Revisio of the English Version of the Scriptures, which was publishe 1881-85. *Address:* New Haven, Connecticut, USA.

Died May 1916

DWYER, Edward, VC 1915; *b* 25 Nov. 1897. Commission i Northumberland Fusiliers, 1915.

Died 4 Sept. 1916

DYCE, Col George Hugh Coles, CB 1896; ISC; late commandin at Mooltan; retired; *b* 19 Feb. 1846; *m* 1876, Marion, *d* of late Matthew Hamilton of Ardmore, Dunoon; two *s*. *Educ:* Cheltenham College Entered army, 1864; Colonel, 1894; Colonel on the Staff a Ferozepore, 1897-98; Multan, 1898; Tochi Valley, 1898-99; Toch Valley and Bannu, 1899-1900; temporary Brigadier-General Allahabad, 1900; temporary Deputy-Adjutant-General with rank o Brigadier-General, Bengal command, Naini Tal, 1900-1; serve Hazara Campaign, 1868 (medal with clasp); Afghan War, 1878-80 (despatches, medal); Mahsood-Wuzeeree Expedition, 1881; Burmese 1886-87 (despatches, clasp); Waziristan Expedition, 1894-95 (clasp) Chitral Relief, 1895 (despatches, CB, medal with clasp). *Addres.* Grindlay & Co., 54 Parliament Street, SW1.

Died 2 Jan. 192

DYER, Henry, MA, DSc, Hon. LLD Glasgow, Kogaku-Hakush (DEng), Japan; JP County and City of Glasgow; CE; Order of Sacre Treasure (2nd Class); Order of Rising Sun, Japan (3rd Class); Emeritu Professor University of Tokyo, Japan; *b* 1848; *s* of John Dyer; *m* 1874 Marie Aquart, *d* of D. Ferguson, Glasgow; three *s* one *d*. *Educ* Anderson's College, and University, Glasgow. Served apprenticeshi as engineer under Alex C. Kirk, LLD; Whitworth Scholar, 1870 attended Glasgow Univ. for five years. Appointed first Principal o the Imperial College of Engineering, Tokyo, Japan, and Professo of Civil and Mechanical Engineering, 1873; in addition, becam director of large engineering works; remained in Japan ten years, an was appointed Hon. Principal of College on retirement, and Hon Member of the Institutions of Civil Engineers, Mechanical Engineers and Naval Architects, Japan. Since return to Britain, has taken an activ part in engineering, education, and social work. A Life Governor of the Glasgow and West of Scotland Technical College, a Governor of the West of Scotland Agricultural College, of the West of Scotland College for Domestic Science, and of the Glasgow School of Art; Chairman School Board of Glasgow, and Convener of the Continuation Classes Committee; Vice-President of the Board of Conciliation and Arbitration of the Manufactured Steel Trade of the West of Scotland, 1894–1916, etc. *Publications:* Dai Nippon; The Britain of the East; Japan in World Politics; The Evolution of Industry; Science Teaching in Schools; Education and National Life; Education and Industrial Training; Education and Citizenship; numerous papers and articles on engineering, educational, literary, and social subjects. *Address:* 8 Highburgh Terrace, Dowanhill, Glasgow. *Club:* Liberal, Glasgow.   *Died 4 Sept. 1918.*

DYER, Captain Sir John Swinnerton, 12th Bt, *cr* 1678; Scots Guards;*b* 27 May 1891; *s* of Sir Thomas Swinnerton Dyer, 11th Bt and Dona Edith, *d* of Sir Charles Roderick M'Grigor, 2nd Bt; *S* father, 1907; *m* 1912, Maude, *d* of W. H. Turner, Western Australia; one *s* one *d* (posthumous). *Educ:* Eton. Entered army 1910; Capt. 1915; served European War, 1914–15 (wounded). *Heir: s* Swinnerton Dyer, *b* 20 Jan. 1914. *Address:* 7 Park Lane, W. *T:* Mayfair 777. *Clubs:* Guards, Boodle's, Pratt's.

Died 31 July 1917.

DYER, Ven. Joseph Perry, MA; late Rector of Datchworth, Stevenage; late Archdeacon of Rangoon; Examining Chaplain and Commissary to the Bishop of Rangoon; Senior Chaplain HM Bengal (Rangoon) Establishment; *b* 19 Oct. 1855; *m* 1909, Mina, *e d* of late Maj.-Gen. C. J. Tyler, RA. *Educ:* Godolphin School; Bishop Hatfield Hall, Durham University. Curate St Jude's, Leeds, 1882; appointed Chaplain on the Bengal Establishment, May 1885; Burma Expeditionary Force (Base), 1886–87; services lent to Punjab Government, 1890; Member of the Governing Council, Royal Army Temperance Association; Chaplain Rangoon Cantonments, 1896; Senior Chaplain Rangoon Cathedral, 1899; Commissary in charge of the Diocese, 1901–2; Lecturer Army Education Scheme. *Recreation:* golf. *Address:* 2 Templeton Place, SW5. *Club:* Overseas.

Died 30 Aug. 1926.

DYER, Brig.-Gen. Reginald Edward Harry, CB 1917; Indian Army, retired; *b* 9 Oct. 1864; *s* of E. Dyer, Simla; *m*; two *s. Educ:* Middleton College, Co. Cork. Commanded 45th Infantry Brigade; retired, 1920. *Publication:* The Raiders of the Sarhad, 1921. *Address:* Ashton Keynes, Swindon, Wilts; St Martin's, Long Ashton, near Bristol.   *Died 23 July 1927.*

DYER, Major Stewart Barton Bythesea, DSO 1903; Hon. Attaché, British Embassy, Madrid, since 1916; *b* 26 Nov. 1875; *s* of Captain Stewart Dyer of Westcroft Park, Surrey; *m* 1906, Mai, *o c* of late Captain S. L. Osborne, RN; one *s.* 2nd Life Guards; entered army, 1899; served with the Kaduma Expedition, 1900 (despatches, medal and clasp); Bornu Expedition, and operations in Warkum Hills and Bussaina country, 1902 (wounded, despatches, medal and clasp); Kano-Sokoto Expedition, 1903 (twice wounded, despatches twice, clasp, DSO); Dakakerri Expedition, in command, 1904 (despatches and clasp); General Staff Officer, 1914; relinquished commission, 1916, on account of ill-health. *Address:* British Embassy, Madrid. *Clubs:* White's, Brooks's, Cavalry, Ranelagh.

Died 26 Jan. 1917.

DYKE, Rev. Edwin Francis, MA; Rector of Mersham, Kent, 1896–1916; Hon. Canon of Canterbury; Rural Dean of North Lympne; *b* 27 Sept. 1842; *s* of Francis Hart Dyke, Queen's Proctor, and Charlotte Lascelles, *d* of Rt Hon. Sir Herbert Jenner Fust; *m* 1870, Katharine Louisa (*d* 1914), 3rd *d* of Sir Frederick Currie, 1st Bt. *Educ:* Eton; Trinity Hall, Cambridge. Deacon, 1866; Priest, 1867; Curate of Crayford, 1866–68; West Wickham, Kent, 1868–76; Vicar of Orpington, Kent, 1877–83; Marchside, 1883–96; Rural Dean of Sutton, 1889–96. *Recreations:* cricket, rowing, tennis, fishing, shooting. *Address:* Normanton, Maidstone.

Died 26 Aug. 1919.

DYKE, Lt-Col John Samuel, OBE 1919; MVO 1908; *b* 14 Aug. 1859; *s* of late Samuel Dyke of Warwick; *m* 1st, 1894, Anna Elizabetha Bergner (*d* 1907); no *c*; 2nd, 1912, Harriet, *widow* of Lt-Col William Wellington Lake. Formerly in Queen's Royal Regt; served Burma Expedition, 1886–88 (medal and two clasps); South African War, 1900–2 (despatches twice, Queen's medal with two clasps, King's medal with two clasps). *Address:* 41 Kingsnorth Gardens, Folkestone. *T:* Folkestone 644.   *Died 5 Feb. 1927.*

DYKES, William Rickatson, MA, L'es-L; Secretary, Royal Horticultural Society; *b* 4 Nov. 1877; 2nd *s* of late Alfred Dykes; *m* 1924, Elsie Katherine Kaye. *Educ:* City of London School; Wadham College, Oxford; Sorbonne, Paris. Assistant Master at Charterhouse, 1903–19. *Publications:* Irises, 1911; The Genus Iris, 1913; Handbook of Garden Irises, 1924; The Lorette System of Pruning, 1925. *Address:* Royal Horticultural Society, Vincent Square, Westminster, SW. *TA:* Hortensia, Sowest, London. *T:* Victoria 5363.

Died 1 Dec. 1926.

DYMOTT, Rev. Sidney Edward; Hon. Canon of Liverpool. *Address:* The Vicarage, Glazebury, near Manchester.

Died 11 April 1924.

DYSON, William, BA, MD, MRCS; JP; *b* Thurgoland, Sheffield, 15 July 1849; *s* of John Dyson, JP; *m* E. J., *d* of Thomas Andrews of Wortley Iron Works. *Educ:* Wesley College, Sheffield; University College, London; London University. Consulting Physician to Sheffield Royal Hospital; Consulting Physician to Sheffield Royal Infirmary; Emeritus Professor of Medicine, University of Sheffield. *Address:* 35 Westbourne Road, Sheffield. *T:* 1817 Central, Sheffield. *Club:* Sheffield.   *Died 9 July 1928.*

E

EADIE, Dennis; actor-manager; *b* Glasgow, 14 Jan. 1875. First appearance in London, 1900; Manager of Royalty Theatre with J. E. Vedrenne, 1911; appeared in Milestones, 1912; My Lady's Dress, 1913; The Man who Stayed at Home, 1915; Billeted, 1917. *Address:* 8 Dorset Square, NW1. *T:* Padd. 3366.

Died 10 June 1928.

EAGLES, Gen. Henry Cecil, RMLI; *b* 25 Feb. 1855; 3rd *s* of late Rev. C. L. Eagles, Longtown, Herefordshire; *m* 1885, Amy, *y d* of T. W. Fox, Hoe House, Plymouth; one *d. Educ:* Marlborough College. Entered Royal Marines, 1873; Capt. 1885; Major 1892; Lt-Col 1899; Col 1902; Maj.-Gen. 1909; Lt-Gen. 1910; Gen. 1912. *Address:* Summerleaze, Yelverton, Devon. *T:* Yelverton 57.   *Died 3 Aug. 1927.*

EALES, Herbert, CSI 1911; MA Hon. Oxon 1916; *b* 20 Aug. 1857; *s* of Charles Eales and Frances Lindstedt Eales of Devon; *m* 1889, Mary, *d* of Joseph Eales, Devon; one *s* four *d. Educ:* Dulwich College; Balliol College, Oxford. Joined Indian Civil Service as Assistant Commissioner, Burma, 1879; Political Officer with Field Force during Burmese War, 1885–88; despatches; received thanks of Viceroy; medal with two clasps; received thanks of Lieut-Gen. Sir Harry Prendergast, commanding forces in Burma, for conduct in a brush with rebels at Magyigon, 16 Feb. 1886; officiated as Secretary to the Chief Commissioner of Burma, 1890; Superintendent of Census, Burma; President of Rangoon Municipality, 1896; Commissioner of Pegu and Member of Legislative Council, 1907; officiated as Financial Commissioner, 1910; Member of Imperial Legislative Council, India, 1912; retired, 1914; joined Catholic Church, 1911. *Publication:* Report on the Census of Burma, 1891. *Recreations:* riding, motoring, billiards. *Address:* Harberton House, Headington Hill, Oxford.   *Died 2 Jan. 1927.*

EAMES, Alfred Edward, ISO 1910; late Controller Central Telegraph Office GPO; *b* 1846; *s* of Edward Eames, Bradford, Wilts; *m* 1869, *e d* of Henry Thorne. *Address:* 54 Alleyn Road, Dulwich, SE.

Died 15 Nov. 1924.

EAMES, James Bromley; Barrister-at-Law; Recorder of Bath since 1914; *b* Bath, 8 Dec. 1872; 3rd *s* of Frederick Eames; *m* 1910, Ellen Lois, *d* of C. H. Price, Worcester; no *c. Educ:* King Edward's School, Bath; Worcester College, Oxford (Exhibitioner; BA 1895; MA, BCL 1898). Professor of Law, Imperial Tientsin University, 1898–1900; served in Boxer Campaign, 1900, with Tientsin Volunteers (medal and clasp, Relief of Legations); Legal Adviser to Tientsin Provisional Government, 1900–1; returned to England, 1901; joined Western Circuit, 1902. *Publications:* The English in China, 1908; joint editor of Odgers on the Law of Libel and Slander, 4th and 5th editions.

Address: 9 Campden Hill Gardens, W; 4 Paper Buildings, Temple, EC. *T:* 924 Park. *Clubs:* Reform, Eighty.

Died 1 July 1916.

EARDLEY-RUSSELL, Lt-Col Edmund Stuart Eardley Wilmot, MVO 1909; RFA; *b* 15 June 1869; *e s* of late Capt. Theodosius Stuart Russell, DL, Chief Constable of West Riding of Yorkshire, and Louisa (of Woodthorpe, Farncombe), *d* of late Rev. Sir Thomas Eardley Wilmot Blomefield, 3rd Bt; assumed by Deed Poll the additional surname of Eardley, 1904; *m* 1903, Aurea Louisa Harriett, *d* of late C. Alfred W. Rycroft of Everlands, Sevenoaks, and late Edith Maud (of Freston Lodge, Sevenoaks), *d* of late Capt. Hugh Berners, RN, of Woolverstone Park, Ipswich; one *s* two *d. Educ:* Charterhouse; RMA, Woolwich. Joined RFA 1888; appointed RHA 1893; Adjutant, RHA, Aldershot, 1896–98; Captain, 1898; qualified as interpreter in German, 1899; and in French, 1900; passed in Russian, 1902; graduated at Staff College, 1900; Instructor at School of Gunnery, H and FA, 1901–4; Staff-Capt. Headquarters of Army, 1904–6; Major, 1904; DAQMG Headquarters of Army, 1906; General Staff, Headquarters of Army, 1907–9; Military Attaché Vienna and Cettinjé, 1909–12; Bucharest, 1909–11, with temporary rank of Lieut-Col; commanded 39th Battery, RFA (4th Division), in Expeditionary Force to France, 1914; Lieut-Colonel, 1914; GSO 1st Grade, War Office, 1914–16; Military Attaché, Stockholm, 1916–17; served on staff in S African War (including actions of Rietfontein and Lombard's Kop and defence of Ladysmith), 1899–1900 (despatches, medal and 2 clasps); China War, 1900–1 (medal); European War, 1914; in attendance upon Prince Albert of Schleswig-Holstein at the Coronation of King Edward VII (Coronation medal), and upon the Archduke Karl Franz Josef at the Coronation of King George V (Coronation medal); Commander, 2nd class, of Dannebrog Order (Denmark), 1905; Commander of the Order of the Crown of Roumania, 1910; Commander of the Austrian Imperial Order of the Iron Crown, 2nd Class, 1912. *Address:* The Park Farm, Berechurch, Colchester. *T:* Colchester 212. *M:* AA6074. *Club:* United Service.

Died 29 March 1918.

EARDLEY-WILMOT, Captain Cecil F.; Commissioner of Prisons since 1909; *b* 4 Aug. 1855; *m* 1888, Alice Maule, *d* of late Edmund Scott, San Francisco. 2nd Lieut the Cheshire Regt, 1877; retired as Captain, 1890; Deputy Governor Wandsworth Prison, 1890; subsequently Governor of Lincoln and Canterbury Prisons, and of Borstal and Parkhurst Convict Prisons; appointed an Inspector of Prisons, 1904; Secretary to Departmental Committee on Education of Prisoners, 1896; Member of Departmental Committee on Vagrancy, 1904–6. *Address:* 35 Tedworth Square, Chelsea, SW. *Club:* Junior United Service. *Died 14 July 1916.*

EARDLEY-WILMOT, His Honour Hugh Eden; *b* 7 Nov. 1850; 6th *s* of Sir John Eardley-Wilmot, 2nd Bt; *m* 1879, Ellen Elizabeth (*d* 1923), *d* of John Williams, S Wales; one *s. Educ:* Charterhouse. Barrister, Lincoln's Inn, 1871. Was Counsel to Mint at Central Criminal Court; Judge of County Courts (Circuit 33), 1891–1920. *Address:* 2 The Avenue, Colchester.

Died 10 March 1926.

EARDLEY-WILMOT, Major-General Revell, CB 1896; *b* 29 Aug. 1842; 2nd *s* of late Sir John Eardley Eardley-Wilmot, 2nd Bt, MP for South Warwickshire, of Berkswell Hall; *m* 1906, Elizabeth, *d* of J. W. Toone Smith, MD. *Educ:* Winchester Coll. (Founder's Kin). Late 14th Bengal Lancers and AAG Meerut Div.; entered Army 1860; Brevet Lt-Col 1881; Maj.-Gen. 1895; Bhotan Expedition, 1864–66 (wounded; despatches, medal with clasp); Jowaki Expedition as ADC (despatches, clasp); Kabul War of 1878–79–80; attack on Ali Musjid Charasiak, capture of Kabul and all operations around Kabul city, 1879 (despatches, medal, three clasps, Bt Lt-Col); in receipt of distinguished service pension. Decorated for military services. *Recreations:* polo, cricket, shooting, fishing, pig-sticking, tent-pegging. *Address:* The Cottage, Lowther Road, Bournemouth.

Died 14 June 1922.

EARLE, Rt. Rev. Alfred, DD; Bishop of Marlborough, 1888–1900; Dean of Exeter, 1900–18; *b* 1827; *s* of Henry Earle, FRCS, Surgeon in Ordinary to Queen Victoria; *m* 1866, Frances Anne (*d* 1911), *e d* of Wm Roope Ilbert of Bowringsleigh, Devon; one *s* two *d. Educ:* Eton; Hertford Coll. Oxford (Lusby Scholar). Ordained, 1858; Curate of St Edmund's, Salisbury; Rector of Monkton-Farleigh, Wilts, 1863–65; Vicar of West Alvington, South Huish, South Milton, Marlborough; joint Vicarage, Devon, 1865–87; Rural Dean; Archdeacon of Totnes, 1872–87; Prebendary of Exeter Cathedral; Examining Chaplain to Bishops Temple and Bickersteth; Canon Residentiary of Exeter Cathedral, 1886–88; Rector of St Michael's,

Cornhill, 1888–95; Rector of St Botolph's, Bishopsgate, and Prebendary of St Paul's Cathedral, 1895–1900; Suffragan Bishop of W and NW London, with the title of Bishop of Marlborough, 1888–1900. *Publications:* charges printed at request of clergy on Church Reform; The Reform of Patronage; Reform of Episcopal Visitations; Our Duty to the Non-conformists; Our Duty to the Masses; Some Pressing Duties of Churchwardens and Clergy, 1874; On Consecutive and Systematic Church Education, Exeter, 1873; Work in West and North-West London, 1897. *Address:* Torquay.

Died 28 Dec. 1918.

EARLE, Arthur, JP, Lancashire; FRGS; *b* 14 Dec. 1838; *y s* of Sir Hardman Earle, 1st Bt; *m* 1867, Ida E. B. (*d* 1903), *e d* of Sir George Buckley-Matthew, KCMG, HM Minister in Brazil; three *s* one *d* (and one *s* decd). *Educ:* Harrow. Merchant; Vice-Chairman of The Liverpool Cathedral Committee; Director, Bank of Liverpool, Liverpool, London, and Glove Insurance Co. Contested Scotland Division, Liverpool, 1885. *Recreations:* visited most of the world, and explored the interior of Brazil with the late Sir Richard Burton; hunting, motoring. *Address:* Childwall Lodge, Wavertree, near Liverpool. *T:* 123 Wavertree; Earles Court, Camberley. *M:* AE 300 and AE 2200. *Clubs:* Windham, Racquet.

Died 5 Feb. 1919.

EARLE, Mrs Charles William, (Maria Theresa Villiers); writer; *b* 8 June 1836; *m* 1864, late Capt. Charles William Earle, Rifle Brigade; two *s. Publications:* Pot-pourri from a Surrey Garden; More Pot-pourri; A Third Pot-pourri, 1903; Letters to Young and Old, 1906; Memoirs and Memories, 1911; Gardening for the Ignorant, 1912; Pot-pourri mixed by Two (with Ethel Case). *Address:* Woodlands, Cobham, Surrey. *Died 27 Feb. 1925.*

EARNSHAW, Albert; Puisne Judge, Supreme Court, Straits Settlements, since 1914; *b* Netherton, Huddersfield, 31 Oct. 1865; *o s* of David Earnshaw; *m* 1898, Sarah Maude, *o d* of William Haley. *Educ:* Huddersfield College; University Coll.; Durham University; Pembroke College, Oxford. MA, Durham; BA, Oxford; Open Classical Scholar and took 1st Class Honours in Classics at both Universities. Fellow of Durham University, 1889–97; called to Bar, 1893; North-Eastern Circuit, 1893–1904; Magistrate, Grenada, 1904–7; British Guiana, 1907–9; Puisne Judge, Gold Coast, 1909–12; British Guiana, 1912–14. *Address:* Supreme Court, Singapore, Straits Settlements. *Died March 1920.*

EAST, Sir George Frederick Lancelot Clayton-, 4th Bt *cr* 1838; 8th Bt *cr* 1732; OBE 1919; Major late RA; *b* 3 Sept. 1872; 2nd *s* of Sir Gilbert Augustus Clayton East, 3rd Bt and Eleanor Theresa, *d* of Maj.-Gen. A. R. Fraser; *S* father, 1925; *m* 1906, Frances Louise Helen, *yr d* of late Lieut-Col James Colquhoun, DL; one *s* two *d.* Served European War, 1914–18 (despatches). *Heir:* *s* Robert Alan Clayton East Clayton, *b* 7 April 1908. *Address:* Hall Place, Maidenhead.

Died 27 April 1926.

EAST, Sir Gilbert Augustus Clayton, 3rd Bt *cr* 1838; 7th Bt *cr* 1732; JP; *b* 25 April 1846; *e s* of Sir Gilbert Clayton East, 2nd Bt and Emma Jane Lucretia, *e d* of Sebastian Smith; *S* father, 1866 and cousin, Sir William Robert Clayton, 6th Bt, 1914; *m* 1867, Eleanor Theresa (*d* 1924), *d* of Maj.-General A. R. Fraser; one *s* one *d* (and one *s* one *d* decd). *Educ:* Eton; Magdalene Coll., Cambridge. Owner of about 1500 acres. *Heir:* *s* George Frederick Lancelot Clayton-East, OBE, *b* 3 Sept. 1872. *Address:* Hall Place, Maidenhead.

Died 26 Sept. 1925.

EAST, Col Lionel William Pellew, CMG 1916; DSO 1895; RA; General Staff Officer 2nd Grade West, since 1909; *b* 27 July 1866; *m* 1897; one *s. Educ:* RMA Woolwich. Entered RA 1885; Captain, 1896; served Hazara and 2nd Miranzai expeditions, 1891 (despatches); NE Frontier, Assam, 1894 (severely wounded, DSO); European War, 1914–18 (CMG, Bt Col). *Address:* Cox & Co., 16 Charing Cross, SW1. *Died 6 Sept. 1918.*

EASTERBROOK, James, MA; *b* Dean Prior, Devonshire, 1851; *m* Edith Montague Hamilton. *Educ:* St Mark's; University College, London. BA Honours in Logic; MA 1878; Master St Mark's College Schools, 1872–75; Mathematical Tutor St Mark's College, 1875–80; Headmaster Owen's School, Islington, 1881–1909; Life Governor University College, London; Vice-President Incorporated Association of Headmasters; Treasurer, 1899–1905; President, 1906; Member LCC Technical Education Board, 1893–98. Chairman Federal Council of Secondary School Associations, 1909–12; Member Consultative Committee, Board of Education, 1910–16. *Club:* Constitutional. *Died 1 Feb. 1923.*

EATON, Sir John Craig, Kt 1915; President of the T. Eaton Co. Ltd, Toronto and Winnipeg; *b* Toronto, 28 April 1876; *s* of late Timothy Eaton and Margaret Wilson Beattie; *m* 1901, Florence M'Crea, Omemee, Ontario; four *s* one *d*. *Educ*: Toronto Public Schools; Upper Canada College. Director of the Dominion Bank; Director of the Canadian Pacific Railway; Hon. Director Canadian National Exhibition; member of Senate, Victoria College; Hon. Governor and member of Board of Trustees, Toronto General Hospital; Member of the Board of Governors of Toronto University. *Recreations*: yachting, automobilism. *Address*: Ardwold, Toronto; Kawandag, Lake Russian, Muskaka. *Clubs*: York, National, Lambton Golf, Caledon Mountain Trout, Royal Canadian Yacht, Toronto; Manitoba, Winnipeg.   *Died 29 March 1922.*

EAYRS, Rev. George, PhD; FRHistS; Minister London, Newington Circuit United Methodist Church; on Executive of Committee for Union of Wesleyan, Primitive, and United Methodist Churches; essayist, at Ecumenical Conference, London; *b* Leicester, 18 Nov. 1864; *s* of Warren and Sarah Burrows Eayrs; *m* Clara Wagg, *d* of Councillor C. Smithurst, Harrogate; two *s* one *d*. *Educ*: Wesleyan School; Manchester and Leeds Universities; Research Student, Durham, PhD. Junior law clerk and cashier; entered ministry, 1887; Circuits in Nottingham, Eccles, Huddersfield, Bradford (Superintendent), Batley, Bristol, Downham, Newcastle; District Chairman, Bristol and S Wales, Lincoln, Norwich and London; Conference Journal Secretary, Hanley, 1912; British Secretary worldwide Methodist Historical Union, founded Toronto Conference, 1911; lectured on Methodist History and Wesley in Canada and United States, 1914, and frequently in England; Member of National Free Church Council Committee for many years, and President Leeds Federation, Bristol Council, etc; Continental Chaplain, Grindelwald, 1902; member of the Aristotelian Society, London; Member League of Nations and Council of Christian Churches. *Publications*: A Son of Issachar—Times of Wesley and Kilham; Alfred to Victoria; Connected Historical Studies; Richard Baxter; Wesley and Kingswood and its Free Churches; co-editor of Free Methodist (1904–7) and United Methodist weekly journals; proposed, edited, and contributed largely to A New History of Methodism in all countries (2 vols); edited Letters of John Wesley; Important and New Letters with Introductions and Biographical Notes; British Methodism as it is, as it was, as it will be; A Methodist Union Handbook and History; Programme and Working Philosophy of Jesus Christ; Wesley, Christian Philosopher and Church Founder. *Recreations*: historical study, great pictures, Wesley relics. *Address*: 74 Sisters Avenue, Clapham Common, North Side, SW11.

     Died 25 Oct. 1926.

EBERTS, Hon. David MacEwen, KC; late Attorney-General, British Columbia; *b* 22 April 1850; 3rd *s* of W. D. MacEwen and Mary Bell; *m* 1884, Mabel Hope, *e d* of William Charles. *Educ*: Chatham Grammar School, Ontario. Called to bar, 1882; QC 1892; in British Columbia Legislature since 1890; Speaker, 1907. *Address*: Victoria, BC. *Clubs*: Union, Victoria; Vancouver, Vancouver.

     Died May 1924.

EBRAHIM, Sir Currimbhoy, 1st Bt, *cr* 1910; Kt 1905; CBE 1918; JP; *b* 21 Oct. 1840; *y s* of late Ebrahim Pabaney, shipowner; family belongs to Cutch; *m* 1st, 1854, Foolbai (*d* 1875), *d* of Asoobhai Gangji; two *s* two *d* (and three *s* three *d* decd); 2nd, 1876, Foolbai, *d* of Vishram Sajan; five *s* eight *d* (and one *d* decd); *m* 1882, Sakinabai, *d* of Jairajbhoy Peerbhoy; one *s*. A leading member of the Khoja community; Past President of the Anjuman-i-Islam; of the Mahomedan Educational Conference in Bombay, and an opium, yarn, cotton, silk, tea, sugar, and cloth merchant of Bombay, Hong-kong, Kobe, Singapore, Shanghai, and Calcutta; owner of the Currimbhoy Mills, the Mahomedbhoy Mills, the Ebrahimbhoy Pabaney Mills, the Fazulbhoy Mills, the Crescent Mills, the Indore Malwa United Mills, and many other factories (ginning and pressing) and the Indian Bleaching, Dying, and Printing Works; established a girls' school, a Madressa at Mandvi; the Currimbhoy Ebrahim Khoja Orphanage in Bombay; dharamsalas at Mandir and Bhuj; gave large donations to Bombay New Museum fund; interested in many charitable institutions. *Heir*: *s* Mahomedbhoy Currimbhoy Ebrahim, *b* Bombay, 11 Sept. 1867. *Address*: Pabaney Villa, Warden Road, Bombay; 13 Esplanade Road, Bombay.

     Died 26 Sept. 1924.

EBRAHIM, Sir Mahomedbhoy Currimbhoy, 2nd Bt, *cr* 1910; Kt 1924; JP; partner in Currimbhoy Ebrahim & Sons; *b* 11 Sept. 1867; *e surv. s* of Sir Currimbhoy Ebrahim, 1st Bt; *m* 1882, Bai Sakinabai, *d* of Jairazbhoy Pirbhoy; one *s* (and one *d* decd). *Educ*: Bombay (privately). Trustee of the Port of Bombay, 1908–23; a member of the Haj Committee since its creation (Gold medal of the Kaiser-i-

Hind); was a member of the Labour Commission; Sheriff of Bombay, 1921–22; a Trustee of the Currimbhoy Ebrahim Khoja Orphanage; a Director of the Alexandra School for Girls; a Treasurer of the Islam Gymkhana. *Heir*: *s* Huseinali Currimbhoy Ebrahim, *b* 13 April 1903. *Address*: Belevedere, Warden Road, Bombay, India. *Clubs*: Willingdon Sports, Orient, Radio, Bombay.

     Died 3 March 1928.

EBURY, 2nd Baron, *cr* 1857; **Robert Wellesley Grosvenor,** DL; Captain 1st Life Guards, retired 1866; *b* 25 Jan. 1834; *s* of 1st Baron and Charlotte, *d* of 1st Lord Cowley; *S* father, 1893; *m* 1867, Hon. Emilie Beaujolais White, *d* of 1st Lord Annaly; two *s* two *d* (and two *s* decd). *Educ*: Harrow; King's Coll. London. Entered 1st Life Guards, 1853; MP (L) Westminster, 1865–74. *Heir*: *s* Hon. Robert Victor Grosvenor, *b* 28 June 1868. *Address*: Moor Park, Rickmansworth, Herts. *Clubs*: Turf, Travellers'.   *Died 13 Nov. 1918.*

EBURY, 3rd Baron, *cr* 1857; **Robert Victor Grosvenor;** *b* 28 June 1868; *s* of 2nd Baron and Hon. Emilie Beaujolais White, *d* of 1st Lord Annaly; *S* father, 1918; *m* 1908, Florence, *d* of Edward Padelford, of Savannah, Georgia, USA. Late Captain 13th Middlesex Rifle Volunteers; served South Africa, 1900–1 (Queen's medal 3 clasps). *Heir*: *b* Capt. Hon. Francis Egerton Grosvenor, *b* 8 Sept. 1883. *Address*: 79 Gloucester Place, W1. *T*: Mayfair 4599; Moor Park, Rickmansworth, Herts.   *Died 5 Nov. 1921.*

ECCLES, Lt-Col Cuthbert John, DSO 1915; retired pay; District Remount Officer; *b* 2 Feb. 1870; *s* of Major-General Eccles. 2nd Lt 16th Lancers, 1894; Captain, 1899; Major, 1909; Lt-Col 1914; served S African War, 1900–2 (Queen's medal, 4 clasps, King's medal, 2 clasps, wounded); European War, 1914–17 (wounded twice, despatches twice, DSO). *Address*: Cowley House, Headington Hill, Oxford. *Club*: Cavalry.   *Died 10 Jan. 1922.*

ECCLES, Rev. Canon John Charles; Vicar Holy Trinity Church, Woodville, 1892–1919; Canon of Waiapu, 1903; *b* 6 March 1845; *m* 1880, Emma Beilby Rabone; four *s* one *d*. *Educ*: St John's College, Auckland. Ordained, 1874; Curate of Waipawa, 1874; Incumbent, 1877; served as Chaplain in the Maori War, 1864 and 1865. *Address*: 4 Alma Street, Newmarket, Auckland, New Zealand.

ECHEGARAY, José; writer; *b* Madrid, March 1832. *Educ*: Grammar School, Murchia; Escuela de Caminos, Madrid. Professor of Mathematics at Engineering College, Madrid, 1888; Member of Academy of Sciences, 1866; Member of Cortes, 1868; Minister of Commerce, of Education and of Finance 1867–74; Minister of Finance, Spain, 1905. Nobel Prize for Literature (jointly with F. Mistral), 1904. *Publications*: La Esposa del Vengador, 1874; El Libro talonario, 1874; La Ultima Noche, 1875; El Gran Galeoto, 1881; Dos Fanatismos, 1887; Mariana, 1892; El hijo de San Juan, 1892; El Loco Dios, 1900; Mancha qua limpia, 1895. *Address*: Madrid.

     Died 15 Sept. 1916.

ECHLIN, Sir Henry Frederick, 8th Bt, *cr* 1721; *b* 14 Aug. 1846; *s* of Sir Ferdinand Fenton Echlin, 6th Bt and Mary, *o d* of William Cavanagh of Grange Beg, Westmeath; *S* brother, 1906; *m* 1890, Mary Dennis (*d* 1913); one *d*. *Heir*: *b* John Fenton [*b* 20 June 1847; *m* 1869, Harriet, *d* of late George Kennedy of Westport, Co. Mayo; three *s* five *d* (and two *s* one *d* decd)]. *Address*: Haddenham, Thame, Oxon.

     Died 8 Nov. 1923.

EDEN, Rev. Frederick Nugent, MA; Hon. Canon of Rochester; *b* 3 Sept. 1857; 5th *s* of late Canon I. P. Eden, Rector of Sedgefield; *m* 1919, Katherine Mary, *e d* of late Bryan Holme Holme, Paull Holme, Holdernesse, Yorks. *Educ*: Reading School; Pembroke College, Cambridge. Assistant Curate of Sedgefield, 1880–85; St James', West Hartlepool, 1885–86; Curate-in-Charge of Norton, Durham, 1886; Vicar of St James', West Hartlepool, 1886–90; Missionary (CMS) on River Niger, W Africa, 1890–91; Vicar of All Saints, Belvedere, Kent, 1892–1904; of St Paul's, Rusthall, 1904–18; Rector of North Cray, 1918–22. *Address*: Verno, Horeham Road, E Sussex.   *Died 11 June 1926.*

EDEN, Hon. George; Partner in Mullens, Marshall & Co., 13 George Street, EC, Stockbrokers; *b* 29 May 1861; 2nd *s* of 4th Lord Auckland; *m* 1888, Amy Violet Powlett, 3rd *d* of late Col Hon. Charles Hay Drummond; two *s* one *d* (and one *s* decd). *Educ*: Eton. *Address*: 6 Cromwell Place, SW7. *T*: Western 522. *Clubs*: Wellington, Royal Automobile.   *Died 14 June 1924.*

EDEN, Brig.-Gen. William Rushbrooke, CMG 1917; DSO 1900; RHA; *b* Bath, 11 Oct. 1873; *s* of Lieut-Col A. D. Eden (late The

Cameronians); *m* 1911, Marjorie, *d* of Major Lyon Campbell, 74th Highlanders; one *s* one *d*. *Educ:* Haileybury College; RMA Woolwich. 2nd Lieut Royal Artillery, 1893; Lieut, 1896; served in South African War, 1900 (despatches, Queen's medal, 6 clasps, DSO), with A Battery RHA; Capt. 1900; Major, 1910; Lt-Col 1915; European War, 1914–17 (CMG); Brig.-Gen. 1916. Officier Légion d'Honneur, 1917. *Address:* 8 Manson Place, Queen's Gate, SW. *Died 11 July 1920.*

EDGAR, George; journalist and writer of fiction; *b* Warrington, 11 June 1877; *e s* of Peter Edgar, Warrington, *m* Jeannie, *y d* of Thomas D. Howard, Dewsbury; one *s* three *d*. *Educ:* privately. Connected with provincial press many years, and later with London journals; edited Modern Business, 1909; Ed. Careers, 1910–11; Associate Editor, Advertisers' Weekly; contributed to many daily and weekly journals, stories, sketches, articles, and essays; wrote on subjects relating to journalism. *Publications:* The Blue Bird's Eye, 1912; Martin Harvey, 1912; Swift Nick of the York Road, 1913; The Red Colonel, 1913; The Pride of the Fancy, 1914; Kent, the Fighting Man, 1916; Honours of War, 1916. *Recreations:* golf, angling. *Address:* 2 Chartham Terrace, Ramsgate. *Clubs:* Savage, Aldwych. *Died April 1918.*

EDGAR, Prof. John, MA Glas.; BA Oxon; Bell Professor of Education, St Andrews University, since 1902; *m y d* of Rev. Thomas Bowman, Catrine; one *s* two *d*. *Educ:* Dumfries Academy; Glasgow University (1st Class Honours, Classics; Snell Exhibition); Balliol College (Honours in Classical Moderations, and Honours in Final School Lit. Hum.). Formerly Master Royal High School, Edinburgh, and Secretary of the Secondary Schoolmasters in Scotland; Examiner in Classics, University of Glasgow, 1897–1901; Examiner in Education, University of Manchester, 1909–11. *Publications:* History of Early Scottish Education; Translation of Homeric Hymns, etc. *Recreations:* golf, angling, photography. *Address:* East Scores, St Andrews, Fifeshire. *Died 5 May 1922.*

EDGE, His Honour James Broughton, JP; Judge of Metropolitan County Courts, 1898–1911; *o s* of Adam Edge, Bolton, and Mary, *d* of Thomas Broughton, Preston; *m* 1859, Alice Ann, *d* of John Whittle, Bolton; two *s*. *Educ:* privately. Admitted solicitor, 1858; Barrister, Middle Temple, 1871; Coroner for Lancashire, 1869–88; Counsel to the Mint for Lancashire, 1872–88; was Judge of Circuit No 58 (Devonshire), 1888–98, and Chairman of Quarter Sessions for Devon; JP for the county of Devon; Hon. Capt. and QM (retired) 5th Batt. Loyal North Lancashire Regt. *Address:* Lynton Lodge, Rickmansworth, Herts. *Died 23 Oct. 1926.*

EDGE, Rt. Hon. Sir John, Kt 1886; PC 1908; KC; *b* 28 July 1841; *o s* of late Benjamin Booker Edge of Clonbrock, Queen's Co.; *m* 1867, Laura, *d* of T. Loughborough; three *d*. *Educ:* Trinity College, Dublin. Irish Barr. 1864; English Barr. Middle Temple, 1866 (elected Bencher, 1898); QC 1886; Chief Justice of High Court of Judicature, North Western Provinces, India, 1886–98; Member of Council of India, 1898–1908; Member of Judicial Committee, Privy Council, 1909. *Address:* 123 Oakwood Court, W14. *T:* Park 0957. *Club:* Junior Carlton. *Died 30 July 1926.*

EDGE, John Henry, MA; KC; Ex-Legal Assistant Land Commissioner, Ireland; *b* 11 June 1841; *o surv. c* of late John Dallas Edge, Barrister-at-Law. *Educ:* Trinity College, Dublin. QC (Ire) 1894. *Publications:* Forms of Leases, 2nd edn 1884; An Irish Utopia, 1906; The Quicksands of Life, 1908. *Address:* 16 Clyde Road, Dublin. *Club:* Dublin University. *Died 22 Sept. 1916.*

EDGEWORTH, Francis Ysidro, MA (Oxon), DCL (Durham); FBA 1903; Emeritus Professor of Political Economy, University of Oxford; Fellow of All Souls College, Oxford; Fellow of King's College, London; sometime President of the Royal Statistical Society; joint editor of the Economic Journal; *b* Edgeworthstown, Ireland, 8 Feb. 1845; *s* of Francis Beaufort Edgeworth; *n* of Maria Edgeworth. *Educ:* at home; Trinity College, Dublin; Balliol College, Oxford. 1st class Lit. Hum. Oxford; Lecturer on Logic, afterwards Tooke Professor of Political Economy at King's College, London, to 1891. *Publications:* Mathematical Psychics, 1881; papers relating to Political Economy, 1925; article on Probability in the Encyclopædia Britannica (11th edition), 1911; articles on Probabilities, Statistics, and Economics in the Philosophical Magazine, Journal of the Statistical Society, Economic Journal, and other periodicals. *Recreations:* boating, golf. *Address:* All Souls College, Oxford. *Clubs:* Athenæum, Savile. *Died 13 Feb. 1926.*

EDGHILL, Rev. John Cox, MA, DD; Chaplain Tower of London, 1887–1902; Fellow of King's College, London; *m*; one *s*. Ordained,

1858; Curate of St Mark, Whitechapel, 1858–60; served at Halifax, NS; Gibraltar; Aldershot, 1881–82; Portsmouth, 1882–85; Chaplain-Gen. to Forces, 1885–1901; Hon. Chaplain to the King; Prebendary of Wells, 1908. *Address:* Soulby, Clarence Park, Weston-super-Mare. *Died 20 Nov. 1917.*

EDIS, Sir Robert William, KBE 1919; CB 1902; VD; DL, JP Norfolk; Colonel, Artists RV; architect since 1862; *b* Huntingdon, 13 June 1839; *m* 1862, Elsie Jane (*d* 1897), *d* of late James Anton of Abingdon Street; five *d*. *Educ:* Huntingdon Grammar School; Brewers' Company School at Aldenham. President of Architectural Association for two years; late Fellow and Member of Council of the Royal Institute of British Architects. Architect of the Constitutional, Junior Constitutional, and Badminton Clubs, London; Conservative Club, Glasgow; Great Central Hotel, London; Ball-room and additions, Sandringham; alterations and additions, York Cottage; mansions at Cheveley Park, Rangemoor, for Lord Burton; School Board additions; Inner Temple Library, etc; largely engaged in building and altering various mansions in England and Scotland; travelled much abroad, and published sketches of old buildings in France, Italy, and Germany; wrote and lectured on domestic art and house sanitation, and published various works on these subjects, including Decoration and Furniture of London Houses, Handbook on Healthy Furniture for the Council of the International Health Exhibition. A keen sportsman and Volunteer; shot big game in North America; joined the Artists Volunteers in 1860, and commanded them for 20 years, after retirement of late Lord Leighton, and was Hon. Col of the Regiment; aide-de-camp to late Earl of Albemarle in the French and German War, in Paris during last days of the Commune, and wrote a paper on Fireproof Materials as the result of his observations during the Paris fires, which was read before the Royal Institute of British Architects. *Address:* The Old Hall, Great Ormesby, Norfolk. *TA:* Ormesby, Norfolk. *T:* Ormesby 11. *Clubs:* Junior Constitutional; The Norfolk, Norwich. *Died 23 June 1917.*

EDMEADES, Lt-Col James Frederick, MVO 1905; JP; *b* 1843; 4th *s* of Rev. William Henry Edmeades, Nurstead Court, Kent; *m* 1883, Mary Erskine, *e d* of late Frederick James Isacke of Wood View, Booterstown, Co. Dublin. *Educ:* Harrow. Major West Kent Imperial Yeomanry, 1901–7. *Address:* Hazells, near Gravesend. *Died 6 Feb. 1917.*

EDMONDES, Ven. Frederic William, MA; Archdeacon of Llandaff, 1897–1913; *b* Llanblethian, near Cowbridge, 1840; 2nd *s* of Thomas Edmondes, MA, Hon. Canon of Llandaff; *m* 1863, Constance Sarah (*d* 1889), 3rd *d* of Rev. Edward Doddridge Knight, of Nottage Court, Glam; one *d*. *Educ:* Cowbridge Grammar School; Jesus College, Oxford. Assistant-master at Trinity Coll. Glenalmond, 1863–64; Curate of Newcastle, 1864–67; Rector of Michaelstone, with St Bride's-super-Ely, 1867–73; Rural Dean, 1876–97; Surrogate; Proctor for Clergy, 1892–1907; Rector of Coity, 1873–1901. *Address:* Nolton Court, Bridgend, Glams. *Died 10 Nov. 1918.*

EDRIDGE, Sir Frederick Thomas, Kt 1897; JP Surrey; DL; *b* 22 Jan. 1843; *s* of Sir Thomas R. Edridge; *m* 1867, Elizabeth Sara, *d* of J. M. Eastty of Wellesley House, Croydon. *Educ:* Marlborough. Five times Mayor of Croydon; High Sheriff of Surrey, 1909; Hon. Col 4th Queen's. *Address:* Bramley Croft, Croydon. *T:* Croydon 1677. *Died 3 Oct. 1921.*

EDSALL, Rt. Rev. Samuel Cook, DD; Bishop of Minnesota (Episcopal Church) since 1901; *b* Dixon, Illinois, USA, 4 March 1860; *s* of James Kirtland Edsall and Caroline Florella More; *m* 1883, Grace Harmon; two *s* one *d*. *Educ:* Racine College, Wisconsin; Western Theological Seminary, Chicago. Early years spent in Dixon, Ill.; from 1870 a good deal of time spent at Springfield, Ill., the State capital, where his father was State senator and attorney-general; studied law under his father in Chicago, and admitted to Bar, 1882; interested in Church work as a layman; candidate for Orders, 1886; Deacon, 1888; founded St Peter's, now largest parish in Chicago, 1887; became Rector thereof on ordination; Missionary Bishop of North Dakota, 1898; resided in Fargo, ND, three years; Bishop Coadjutor of Minnesota, 1901. *Address:* 2642 Portland Avenue, Minneapolis, Minn. *Clubs:* Minikahda, Church. *Died Feb. 1917.*

EDWARDES, General Sir Stanley de Burgh, KCB 1898 (CB 1881); *b* 29 March 1840; *s* of late Capt. George Harris Edwardes, Bengal Army; *m* 1861, Adelaide Jane, *d* of Gen. George Alexander Leckie, ISC; three *s* three *d*. *Educ:* Mount Radford School, Exeter. Entered Bombay Army as Ensign, 1857; Lieut 1858; Capt. 1864; Major, 1869; Lieut-Col 1871; Col 1876; Maj.-Gen. 1885; Lieut-Gen. 1889; Gen. 1896; Col 102nd (KEO) Grenadiers, 1904; served during Indian

Mutiny in pursuit of Tantia Topee, 1858; DAQMG Abyssinian Expedition, 1868 (medal); Chief Director of Transport, Afghan Campaign, 1879-80 (medal and clasp, CB mil.); commanded Quetta District, 1881-84; Northern Division, Bombay Army, 1887-89. *Recreations:* cricket, riding, shooting, carpentering and turning, gardening and bee-keeping. *Address:* Sandhurst, Hawkhurst, Kent. *Clubs:* East India United Service, MCC.

Died 24 Jan. 1918.

EDWARDES, Stephen Meredyth, CVO 1912; CSI 1915; ICS; *b* 1873; *s* of late Rev. Stephen Edwardes, Fellow of Merton College, Oxford; *m* 1895, Celia, *d* of Arthur Darker of Nottingham; two *s* one *d*. *Educ:* Eton; Christ Church, Oxford. Entered Indian Civil Service, 1895; served as Assistant Collector and Magistrate, Under Secretary to Govt, Assistant Collector of Customs, Special Collector, Deputy Secretary to Govt. Compiler and Editor of the Bombay City Gazetteer; Commissioner of Police, 1909-16; Municipal Commissioner for the City of Bombay, 1916-18; Fellow of the Bombay University; Ex-President of the Anthropological Society, Bombay; retired from the service, 1918; represented India at International Conference on Traffic in Women and Children at Geneva, 1921; Joint Editor, Indian Antiquary, 1923. *Publications:* The Rise of Bombay—a Retrospect, 1902; The Ruling Princes of India—a historical and statistical Account of Junagadh and Bhavnagar, 1906; The Gazetteer of Bombay City and Island, 1909; By-ways of Bombay, 1912, and other works on Indian history; Crime in India, 1925; Memoirs of Sir D. Petit and K. R. Cama. *Address:* c/o Grindlays, 54 Parliament Street, SW1. *Clubs:* East India United Service; Orient, Bombay. *Died 1 Jan. 1927.*

EDWARDS, Rev. Canon Allen; Canon Residentiary of Southwark, 1905; *b* 1844; *e s* of Rev. Allen Edwards of Alleyndale, Cambridge Park, Twickenham. *Educ:* Corpus Christi College, Cambridge (MA). Vicar of All Saints and St Augustine's, South Lambeth, 1874; Member of the School Board for London, 1891; Rural Dean of Kennington, 1891; Canon of the Collegiate Church, Southwark, 1897-1905; Proctor in Convocation for the Diocese of Rochester, 1900-5; Proctor in Convocation for the Diocese of Southwark, 1905. *Address:* 248 South Lambeth Road, SW. *Died 7 June 1917.*

EDWARDS, Charles Lewis, CBE; Chief Accountant, London and North-Eastern Railway Co.; *b* 19 March 1865; *o surv. s* of late Charles Edwards, Winchester; *m* Alice, *e d* of late H. Munday, Marlborough; one *s* five *d*. Accountant, North-West Argentine Railway, 1890-95; Buenos Ayres and Rosario Railway, 1895-1902 and re-appointed upon amalgamation with Central Argentine Railway, to 1903; Chief Accountant Great Northern Railway, 1903-22; Fellow of Chartered Institute of Secretaries, Incorporated Society of Accountants and Auditors, Royal Horticultural Society, and of Royal Geographical Society. Liveryman of Company of Turners; Past Grand Deacon of GL of Freemasons of England. *Publications:* various Masonic publications. *Address:* Santa Caterina, Loudwater, Bucks. *T:* Penn 59. *Club:* Constitutional. *Died 11 May 1928.*

EDWARDS, D.; Editor and Managing Director, Nottingham Daily Express and Evening News since 1908; JP County Borough of Nottingham; *b* 11 April 1858; *m* 1888, Annie, *e d* of late G. Lloyd, Carnarvon. Served apprenticeship at Herald Office, Carnarvon; left for Liverpool and engaged on Liverpool Daily Post; returned to Carnarvon; General Manager, North Wales Observer Series, 1884-91; managing editor, Nottingham Daily Express and Nottingham Evening News, 1891-97; assistant-manager Daily News, 1897-1901, editor and manager, 1901-2. *Address:* 10 Ebury Road, Nottingham. *T:* 392 Nottingham. *Died 22 Feb. 1916.*

EDWARDS, Sir Francis, 1st Bt, *cr* 1907; DL, JP; MP (R) Radnorshire, 1892-95, 1900-10, and 1910-18; *b* 28 April 1852; *s* of Edward Edwards and Anne, *d* of John Jones; *m* 1880, Catherine (*d* 1915), *d* of David Davis, Aberdare; one *d* (and one *s* decd). *Educ:* Shrewsbury; Jesus College, Oxford. Sheriff of Radnorshire, 1898. Heir: none. *Address:* The Cottage, Knighton, Radnorshire. *Club:* Reform. *Died 10 May 1927 (ext).*

EDWARDS, G. Spencer; journalist and dramatic critic; *s* of late Henry Francis Edwards, a popular preacher in connection with the Wesleyan body, and *n* of late Rev. William Spencer Edwards, an eminent Congregationalist divine. Joined staff of the Era under the late Frederic Ledger, 1870; became chief of editorial staff, and so remained for more than twenty years; was the original "Carados" of the Referee, and wrote over that signature for thirty-four years; author of numerous short stories, and, with G. H. Snazelle, of Snazelleparilla, a book of foreign travels, adventures, and laughable stories; and contributed to

the once popular periodical Funny Folks under the editorship of late William Sawyer; for six years a regular contributor to the Illustrated Sporting and Dramatic News, and for a considerable time dramatic critic to Lloyds' Newspaper. *Recreation:* an ardent cyclist. *Address:* 147 Clapham Road, SW. *Died 1 Aug. 1916.*

EDWARDS, Lt-Comdr Harington Douty, DSO 1915; RN. Served European War, 1914-15, landing naval guns in Belgium (DSO).

Died 11 March 1916.

EDWARDS, Henry John, CB 1911; CBE 1919 (OBE 1918); TD 1911; MA; Fellow and Lecturer of Peterhouse, Cambridge; *b* Sept. 1869; *e s* of Major Henry Charles Edwards, VD, of Woodbridge, Suffolk, and Sarah Jane, *d* of H. L. Freeman, MRCS, of Saxmundham, Suffolk; *m* 1905, Margaret Ethel, *e d* of Rev. Arthur Ashton, BD, Rector of Uggeshall, Suffolk; one *s*. *Educ:* Woodbridge School; Bath College; Trinity College, Cambridge, Scholar; Browne Medal (Latin Epigram), 1890; BA (1st class, 1st division, Classical Tripos, Part i), 1891; 1st class (Classics and History), Classical Tripos, Part ii, 1892; Jeremie Prize, 1892. Classical Lecturer and Dean of Selwyn College, Cambridge, 1895-99; Fellow and Classical Lecturer of Peterhouse, 1899; Assistant Tutor and Dean, 1900; Tutor, 1907-20; Examiner, Classical Tripos Part i, 1902, 1903, 1907, 1919, 1920, 1921; Part ii, 1906, 1908, 1909, 1912, 1913; CURV, 1891-1908; Lieut-Colonel commanding, 1901-8; "Q" Club gold medal, 1904; Secretary, Board of Military Studies, Cambridge, 1904-20; Colonel Commanding Cambridge University Contingent, Officers' Training Corps, 1908-19; Commandant, Cambridge University School of Instruction, 1914-16; Commanding Officer, Cadet Battalion, 1916-18. *Publications:* Edition of Livy I (Pitt Press); Translation of Caesar's Gallic War (Loeb Classical Library); articles and reviews on classical and military subjects. *Recreations:* music, sketching, rifle-shooting. *Address:* Peterhouse, Cambridge. *Club:* United University.

Died 26 June 1923.

EDWARDS, Captain Hugh, DSO 1915; RN; HMS President; *b* 14 Oct. 1873; *s* of late James George Edwards, JP, Broughton and Fair Oaks, Hants. Served European War, 1914-15 (DSO for services in a patrol cruiser). *Address:* Fair Oaks, Eastleigh.

Died 5 Dec. 1916.

EDWARDS, Lt-Gen. Sir James Bevan, KCB 1912 (CB 1877); KCMG 1891; retired; *b* 5 Nov. 1834; *m* 1st, 1868, Alice (*d* 1899), *d* of late R. Brocklebank; 2nd, 1901, Nina (*d* 1916), *d* of late John Balfour, of Steephurst, Peterfield, and widow of Sir Robert Dalrymple Elphinstone, 3rd Bt; 3rd, 1918, Amy Ann, *d* of late J. N. Harding of Buzzacott, North Devon. *Educ:* Woolwich. Entered Royal Engineers, 1852; Lieut-Gen. 1891; Col Commandant, 1903; served in Crimean War (medal, Turkish medal), Indian Mutiny (despatches thrice, medal with clasp, Brevet-Major, CB); China, 1864 (gold medal); Suakim Expedition, 1885 (despatches, medal with clasp, bronze star); Commandant of School of Military Engineering, 1885-88; commanded the troops in China, 1889-90. MP (C) Hythe, 1895-99. Chairman, Royal Colonial Institute, 1909-15. *Address:* 48 Egerton Crescent, SW3. *T:* Kensington 1444. *Clubs:* United Service, Travellers'. *Died 8 July 1922.*

EDWARDS, Sir John Bryn, 1st Bt, *cr* 1921; MA, LLB; *b* 12 Jan. 1889; *s* of late William Henry Edwards, JP, and late Margaret Hannah Edwards; *m* 1911, Kathleen Ermyntrude, *d* of late John Corfield, JP; one *s* one *d*. *Educ:* Winchester College; Trinity Hall, Cambridge. Member of Swansea Town Council; Director of English Crown Spelter Co. Heir: *s* John Clive Leighton Edwards, *b* 11 Oct. 1916. *Address:* Hendrefoilan, Sketty, Glamorganshire. *T:* Sketty 88. *Clubs:* Swansea and Counties; Bristol Channel Yacht.

Died 22 Aug. 1922.

EDWARDS, Laura Selina, (Lady Edwards); 2nd *d* of J. C. Clark, Bridgefoot House, Iver, Bucks; *m* 1887, as his second wife Sir Henry Coster Lea Edwards, 2nd Bt (*d* 1896); two *s*. *Address:* Ashbrittle, Wellington, Somerset; 17 Wordsworth Road, Worthing. *Clubs:* Caravan, Ladies' Parkside.

Died 24 March 1919.

EDWARDS, Matilda Barbara Betham-; poet, novelist, and writer on French rural life; *b* Suffolk, 4 March 1836; *d* of Edward Edwards and Barbara, *née* Betham; *niece* of Sir William Betham, Ulster King-at-Arms, and Matilda Betham, friend of Charles and Mary Lamb. *Educ:* at home; by herself. Purely literary. Officier de l'Instruction Publique de France, 1891. *Publications:* The White House by the Sea, 1857; Dr Jacob, 1864; Kitty, 1869; John and I; France of To-Day; Poems; The Golden Bee (ballads), 1896; Reminiscences, 1898; A Romance of Dijon; The Lord of the Harvest, 1899; Anglo-French Reminiscences, 1899; A Suffolk Courtship, 1900; Mock Beggars' Hall, 1901; East of Paris, 1902; Barham Brocklebank, MD, 1904; Home Life in France, 1905; Literary Rambles in France, 1907; Poems, 1907; French Men, Women, and Books, 1910; In French Africa, 1913; Hearts of Alsace, 1916. *Recreations:* music, botany, French travel. *Address:* Villa Julia, Hastings. *Died 4 Jan. 1919.*

EDWARDS, Sir Owen Morgan, Kt 1916; HM Chief Inspector of Education for Wales since 1907; Fellow of Lincoln College, Oxford, and Modern History Lecturer, 1889–1907; Hon. Fellow of Lincoln College; *b* 25 Dec. 1858; *s* of late Owen Edwards, Coedypry, Llanuwchllyn; *m* Ellen (*d* 1919), *d* of late Evan Davies, Prys Mawr, Llanuwchllyn. *Educ:* Bala Grammar School; University College of Wales; Balliol College, Oxford. BA, London University; BA and MA, Oxford University; Stanhope Essay; Lothian Prize. MP (L) Merioneth, 1899–1900. *Publications:* Tro yn yr Eidal, Tro yn Llydaw, Er Mwyn Iesu, Cartrefi Cymru, Story of Wales, etc; editor of works of Dafydd ab Gwilym, Goronwy Owen, Ceiriog, Islwyn, etc; editor and proprietor of Cymru till 1907. *Address:* Neuadd Wen, Llanuwchllyn, Bala; Board of Education, Whitehall, SW. *Died 15 May 1920.*

EDWARDS, Rev. Thomas; Rector of Aber, Wales; Hon. Canon Bangor Cathedral. *Address:* The Rectory, Aber, Wales.

EDWARDS, Hon. William Cameron; Member Canadian Senate since 1903; *b* Clarence, Ontario, 7 May 1844; *s* of William Edwards, Portsmouth, England, and Ann Cameron, Fort William, Scotland; *m* 1885, Catherine Margret Wilson, Cumberland, Ontario. *Educ:* Ottawa Collegiate Institute. Entered employ of Cameron and Edwards, lumber manufacturers, 1863; established firm of W. C. Edwards and Co., lumber manufacturers, at Rockland, Ontario, 1868; elected to House of Commons for Co. of Russell, 1887, and again at subsequent elections; largely interested in agriculture and growing of good livestock; President of Russell Agricultural Society for over thirty years; President of W. C. Edwards and Co., Limited, Canada Cement Co., Bathurst Lumber Co., Cascapedia Manufacturing and Trading Co., Ottawa, and Hull Power and Manufacturing Co., and several minor companies; Director of Canadian Bank of Commerce and Toronto General Trusts Corporation. *Recreations:* regular sleep and constant work, also careful diet. *Address:* 80 Sussex Street, Ottawa. *T:* Rideau 340. *M:* Ontario 4199. *Clubs:* Rideau, Country, Golf and Hunt, Ottawa; Mount Royal, St James's, Montreal; Toronto, York, Toronto; Garrison, Quebec. *Died 17 Sept. 1921.*

EDWARDS, Colonel William Egerton, CMG 1918; late RFA; Superintendent of Design, Ordnance Factories, Royal Arsenal, Woolwich, since 1920; *b* 25 June 1875; *s* of late C. F. Edwards, Registrar-General, Mauritius; *m* 1901, Jessie Maud, *d* of late Lt-Col T. G. Thomson, Indian Army; one *s* one *d*. *Educ:* Royal Military Academy, Woolwich. Joined RA 1894; employed with West African Frontier Force, 1899–1901; operations in Ashanti, 1900 (severely wounded, despatches, brev. of Maj., medal); operations in Southern Nigeria, 1901 (dangerously wounded, medal with clasp); Secretary Explosives Committee and Ordnance Research Board, 1904–7; Staff Capt. HQ of Army, 1905–7; Deputy Assistant Director HQ of Army, 1907–9; Inspector Inspection Staff, 1910–14 and 1914–16; Assistant Deputy Director-General, Ministry of Munitions, 1916; Director of Inspection of Munitions, Canada, 1916–19; (temp. Col Oct 1916; temp. Brig.-Gen. Oct. 1918; Col 1920). *Publications:* article, Armour Plates, Encyclopædia Britannica, 11th Edition; sundry papers, RA Journal. *Club:* Junior United Service. *Died 25 July 1921.*

EDWARDS, Hon. Maj.-Gen. Sir William Rice, KCB 1923 (CB 1914); KCIE 1921; CMG 1900; MD; FRCSE, MRCS; King's Hon. Physician, 1917; *b* 17 May 1862; *s* of Rev. Canon Howell Powell Edwards, Monmouthshire, and Elizabeth Evans, Lovesgrove, Cardiganshire; *m* 1st, 1896, Anne Vaughan (*d* 1911), *y d* of late W. H. Darby of Leap Castle, King's County; 2nd, 1919, Nellie, *d* of late Lt-Col R. Dewar and Mrs R. Dewar, 31 Beaufort Gardens, SW, *widow* of Lieut-Colonel R. Bird, CIE, MVO. *Educ:* Magdalen College School, Oxford; Clifton College; London Hospital. Was House-Surg. and House-Physician London Hospital; entered the Indian Medical Service, 1886; served on Lord Roberts' staff, 1890, services lent to War Office, 1900; joined Lord Roberts in S Africa as Surgeon to Headquarters staff (despatches, Queen's medal, 5 clasps, CMG); Superintending Surgeon Kashmir State Hospitals, 1901; Chief Medical Officer of North-West Frontier Provinces, India, 1910; Assistant Director Medical Services Derajat and Bannu Brigades, 1914–15

(British war medal); Surgeon-General, Bengal, 1915; Director-General Indian Medical Service, 1918–22; Member Legislative Assembly Bengal, 1915–18; Govt of India, 1918–20; Council of State for India, 1920–22. *Recreations:* shooting, golf, etc. *Clubs:* Naval and Military, Royal Automobile; United Service, Simla. *Died 13 Oct. 1923.*

EDWARDS, Hon. Sir (Worley) Bassett, Kt 1919; Puisne Judge, Supreme Court, New Zealand, 1896–1920; *b* London, 5 Sept. 1850; *s* of Charles S. Wilson Edwards; *m* 1886, Mary A. Cutten. Went to New Zealand, 1855. *Address:* Auckland, New Zealand. *Died 2 June 1927.*

EFFINGHAM, 4th Earl of, *cr* 1837; **Henry Alexander Gordon Howard,** DL for West Riding of Yorkshire; Baron Howard of Effingham, 1554; *b* 15 Aug. 1866; *s* of 3rd Earl, and Victoria Francisca, *d* of Monsieur Alexandre Boyer of Paris; S father, 1898; unmarried. *Educ:* privately. Patron of 6 livings. Decorated: gold star for services to athletics and cycling in North Oxon, since 1892. Owner of 3013 acres in Yorkshire, 2776 in Oxfordshire, and 910 in Northamptonshire. *Heir-pres.:* *c* Gordon Frederick Henry Charles Howard [*b* 18 May 1873; *m* 1904, Rosamond Margaret, who obtained a divorce, 1914, *d* of late E. H. Hudson; two *s*]. *Recreation:* motoring. *Address:* Tusmore Park, Bicester, Oxon; Thundercliffe Grange, Rotherham, Yorkshire. *TA:* Tusmore Hethe-Oxon. *Died 6 May 1927.*

EGAN, Sir Henry Kelly, Kt 1914; Managing Director Hawkesbury Lumber Company, Bank of Ottawa, Ottawa Stock Exchange, etc; *b* Aylmer, PQ, 15 Jan. 1848; *y s* of late John Egan, MP Canada, Lisswane, Co. Galway, and Anne Margaret, *d* of late Captain Gibson, RN; *m* 1878, Harriet Augusta, *y d* of late W. A. Himsworth. *Educ:* Montreal High School. Conservative. Anglican. *Address:* 30 Cartier Street, Ottawa. *Clubs:* Jockey, Mount Royal, Montreal; Rideau, Golf, Country, Hunt, Ottawa. *Died 19 Oct. 1925.*

EGAN, Hon. Maurice Francis; American Minister to Denmark, 1907–18; *b* Philadelphia, 1852; *m* 1880, Katharine Mullin (*d* 1921), Philadelphia; one *s* two *d*. *Educ:* La Salle College; AB, Georgetown University; LLD (Columbia University, NY), JUD (Ottawa University, Canada), PhD (Villanova College, Pa). Professor of English Literature, University of Notre Dame, India, 1888; Catholic University, Washington, 1895; Member of the American Academy of Arts; President of the Dante League of New York; President of the International Institute of Arts and Letters; Commander of the Danish Order of the Dannebrog; Officer of the Order of King Leopold of Belgium. Holder of the Laslare Medal for poetry. *Publications:* Songs and Sonnets; John Longworthy; Preludes; The Life Around Us; Lectures on English Literature; Studies in Literature; The Wiles of Sexton Maginnis; The Ghost in Hamlet and other Essays in Comparative Literature; Everybody's St Francis. *Address:* 2308 19th Street, Washington, DC. *Clubs:* Century, Players', New York. *Died Jan. 1924.*

EGERTON OF TATTON, 3rd Baron, *cr* 1859; **Alan de Tatton Egerton,** JP; Vice-Lieutenant, Co. Cheshire; *b* 19 March 1845; *s* of 1st Baron Egerton of Tatton and Lady Charlotte Loftus, *d* of 2nd Marquess of Ely; *S* brother, 1st Earl Egerton, 1909; *m* 1867, Anna Louisa, *d* of S. Watson Taylor of Erlstoke Park, Wilts; one *s* (and two *s* decd). *Educ:* Eton. Indentured as an Engineer for three years; Valuing Engineer under the Royal Commission for Railways and Canals, Ireland, 1867; member of St George's Vestry from 1870; and for ten years representative on the Metropolitan Board of Works; held five masonic chairs in Cheshire; Past Deputy Grand Mark Master; first President of the Cold Storage Association; late Captain 5th Batt. Prince Consort's Own Rifle Brigade. MP (C) Mid-Cheshire, 1883–85; Knutsford Division, Cheshire, 1885–1906. *Heir:* *s* Hon. Maurice Egerton, Major Cheshire Yeomanry, *b* 4 Aug. 1874. *Address:* Tatton Park, Knutsford; 9 Seamore Place, W11. *T:* Mayfair 4864. *Clubs:* Carlton, Bath, Bachelors'. *Died 9 Sept. 1920.*

EGERTON, Field-Marshal Sir Charles (Comyn), GCB 1904 (KCB 1903; CB 1895); DSO 1891; Colonel 23rd Cavalry Frontier Force, India; ADC to Queen Victoria and King Edward VII; *b* 10 Nov. 1848; *m* 1877, Anna Wellwood (*d* 1890), *d* of late J. L. Hill, WS, Edinburgh; one *s*. *Educ:* Rossall; Sandhurst. Entered army, 1867; Col 1895; served Afghan War, 1879–80, including battle of Candahar (despatches, medal with clasp, bronze decoration); Murree Expedition, 1880; Black Mountain Expedition, 1888 (despatches, medal); 1st and 2nd Miranzai Expeditions (severely wounded, despatches, Bt Lt-Col, DSO, clasp); Waziristan Field Force, 1894–95 (despatches, CB, clasp); Dongola Expedition, commanded Indian contingent (despatches, British and

Khedive's medals); commanded 1st Brigade, Tochi Force, 1897–98 (despatches, medal with clasp); Waziristan, 1901–2, in command (thanks of Government, clasp); commanded Expedition against Darwesh Khel Waziris, 1902–3; commanded Somaliland Field Force, 1903–4; action of Jidballi (medal, two clasps); commanding troops, Madras, 1904–7; General, 1906; retired, 1907; Field-Marshal, 1917; Member of the Council of India, 1907–17. *Address:* The Staithe, Christchurch, Hants. *Club:* United Service.

Died 20 Feb. 1921.

EGERTON, Rt. Hon. Sir Edwin Henry, GCMG 1902; KCB 1897 (CB 1886); PC 1904; *b* 8 Nov. 1841; *m* 1895, Olga, *widow* of M. Michel Katkoff, and *d* of Prince Nicholas Lobanow Rostowski; one *s.* Entered Diplomatic Service, 1859; Secretary of Legation, Buenos Ayres, 1879; Athens, 1881; Consul-General, Egypt, 1884; Secretary of Embassy, Constantinople, 1885; Paris, 1885; Envoy Extraordinary and Minister Plenipotentiary to the King of the Hellenes, 1892–1904; HM's Ambassador to the Court of Italy, 1904–8. *Club:* Travellers'.

Died 8 July 1916.

EGERTON, Hugh Edward; Beit Professor of Colonial History, Oxford, 1905–20; Fellow of All Souls College, Oxford; *b* 19 April 1855; 2nd *s* of late Edward Christopher Egerton, MP; *m* 1886, Margaret Alice, *d* of Alexander Trotter of Dreghorn, Midlothian; two *s* two *d. Educ:* Rugby; Corpus Christi College, Oxford; 1st class in Literæ Humaniores. Assistant Private Secretary to late Hon. Edward Stanhope, MP, 1885; Member of Managing Committee of Emigrants Information Office since its foundation in 1886 till 1906; Member of L'Institut Colonial International, 1923. *Publications:* A Short History of British Colonial Policy, 1897, 6th edn, 1920; Sir Stamford Raffles, 1900; Origin and Growth of the English Colonies, 1902, 3rd edn, 1920; Canada under British Rule, in Sir Charles Lucas's series on the History and Geography of the British Colonies, 1908, 3rd edn., 1922; Canadian Constitutional Development, 1907 (with Prof. W. L. Grant); Federations and Unions within the British Empire, 2nd edn 1924; British Foreign Policy in Europe, 1917; British Colonial Policy in the 20th Century, 1922; Causes and Character of the American Revolution, 1923; edited Sir William Molesworth's Speeches, 1903, and The Royal Commission on Loyalists' Claims 1783–85, 1915, for Roxburghe Club; contributed to Palgrave's Dictionary of Political Economy; Poole's Historical Atlas of Modern Europe; Cambridge Modern History, vols iv and ix; The Oxford Survey of the British Empire; The (American) Cyclopædia of Government; Supplement to Encyclopædia Britannica; Supplement to Dictionary of National Biography; English Historical Review, and other publications. *Address:* 14 St Giles, Oxford. *Club:* Athenæum.

Died 21 May 1927.

EGERTON, Lady Mabelle, CBE 1918; Lady of Justice of St John of Jerusalem; mentioned in despatches, 1917; *b* 1865; *d* of 1st Earl Brassey, GCB; *m* 1888, Charles A. Egerton of Mountfield Court; four *s* three *d. Address:* 32 Ashley Gardens, SW1. *T:* Victoria 4470.

Died 18 Feb. 1927.

EGGELING, Professor H. Julius, PhD; Professor of Sanskrit and Comparative Philology, Edinburgh University, 1875–1914; *b* Germany, 12 July 1842; *s* of late H. S. Eggeling, country gentleman; *m* 1871, Marie, *d* of W. Homann. *Educ:* Bernburg Gymnasium; Breslau and Berlin Universities. Came to England 1867 to work at Sanskrit MSS in India Office and Royal Asiatic Society's Libraries; Assistant to Professor F. Max Müller, Oxford, 1867–69; Secretary and Librarian of Royal Asiatic Society, 1869–75; Professor of Sanskrit at University College, London, 1872–75. *Publications:* edition of Kātantra Grammar with Commentary (Calcutta), 1874–78; edition of Vardhamāna's Ganaratnamahodadhi, 1879–80; Translation of Satapatha Brāhmana, vols i–v in Sacred Books of the East; Catalogue of Sanskrit Manuscripts in Library of India Office, 1887–99; articles on Brahmanism, Hinduism, and Sanskrit Language and Literature, in Encyclopædia Britannica, 1876–86; and on Veda, and Sanskrit, in Chambers's Encyclopædia; (with E. B. Cowell) Catalogue of Buddhist Sanskrit Manuscripts in the possession of the Royal Asiatic Society, 1875. *Recreation:* gardening. *Address:* Brunstane House, near Joppa, Edinburgh. *Died 3 March 1918.*

:GLINGTON, Rev. Canon Arthur, MA; Vicar of St Anne's, Wandsworth, since 1920; Rural Dean of Wandsworth, since 1924; *b* 13 Feb. 1871; *s* of William Eglington of Southbro, Surbiton; unmarried. *Educ:* Sherborne; Lincoln College, Oxford; Salisbury Theological College. Curate Woolwich Parish Church, 1894–1901; Vicar of St John's, East Dulwich, 1901–9; St Paul's, Lorrimore Square, 1909–20; Chaplain Springfield Mental Hospital, 1920; Hon. Canon of Southwark, 1923; Chaplain Wandsworth Intermediate Schools,

1920; Proctor in Convocation, Diocese of Southwark, 1924. *Address:* St Anne's Vicarage, Wandsworth. *TA:* St Anne's, SW18. *T:* Latchmere 4673. *Club:* New University.

Died 31 Aug. 1925.

EGLINTON and WINTON, 15th Earl of, *cr* 1507; **George Arnulph Montgomerie,** DL; Lord Montgomerie, Baron Seton and Tranent, 1448; Earl of Winton, 1600; Baron Kilwinning, 1615; Baron Ardrossan (UK), 1806; Earl of Winton (UK), 1859; Hereditary Sheriff of Renfrewshire; Lieutenant Grenadier Guards (retired); President Territorial Association; Lord-Lieutenant Co. Ayr, 1897; MFH (Eglinton); *b* 23 Feb. 1848; *s* of 13th Earl and his 1st wife, Theresa (*d* 1853), *d* of C. Newcomen; *S* brother, 1892; *m* 1873, Janet, *d* of B. A. Cunninghame; two *s* two *d* (and one *s* decd). *Educ:* Eton. Owner of about 30,200 acres. *Heir: s* Lord Montgomerie, *b* 23 June 1880. *Address:* Eglinton Castle, also Redburn, Irvine, NB; Skelmorlie Castle, Largs, NB. *T:* Irvine 38. *M:* SD 206, SD 263. *Club:* Carlton.

Died 10 Aug. 1919.

EIFFEL, Alexandre Gustave; engineer; *b* Dijon, 15 Dec. 1832; *m* Marguerite Gaudelet (decd); four *c. Educ:* Colleges of Dijon and Sainte-Barbe; Central School of Arts and Manufacture; late President of Civil Engineers of France Society; Honorary Member of the Mechanical Engineers' Institution of London. Built Eiffel Tower, Paris, 1889; bridge over the Douro, Portugal; Viaduct of Garabit, Cantal; Aerodynamic Laboratory at Auteuil. Officer Legion of Honour; Knight of Iron Crown of Austria; Commander of the Order of Conception, Portugal; of Isabella of Spain; of Crown of Italy; of St Anne of Russia. *Address:* 1 rue Rabelais, Paris; Château des Bruyères, Sèvres, France. *Died Dec. 1923.*

EINTHOVEN, Willem, Medic. and Philosoph. Dr Utrecht, LLD, Aberdeen; Professor of Physiology at the University of Leyden since 1886; *b* Samarang, Java, 21 May 1860; *m* 1886; four *c. Educ:* Utrecht. Student at the University of Utrecht, Scholar of Donders, Koster and Snellen, Assistant of Donders and Snellen, 1879; promotion to medic. doctor, 1885; MD Edin. 1923; Nobel Prize for Physiology or Medicine, 1924. *Publications:* several papers in scientific journals; also a chapter in Heyman's Handbuch der Laryngologie and Rhinologie, and one in Bethe's Handbook der normalen und pathologischen Physiologie; editor of Onderzoekingen Physiol. Laborat., Leyden. *Address:* Leyden, Holland. *Died 29 Sept. 1927.*

ELDER, John Munro, CMG 1918; BA, MD; Colonel AMS (RO); Assistant Professor of Surgery, McGill University since 1905; Surgeon, Montreal General Hospital since 1905; *b* Huntingdon, PQ, Canada, 29 Oct. 1860; *e s* of George Elder and Catherine Munro; *m* 1886, Grace Whitehead Hendrie; two *s. Educ:* McGill University, Montreal, 1st Rank Honours and Prince of Wales Gold Medal; 1st Rank Honours and Sutherland Gold Medal. Surgeon-Major, Com. Heavy Artillery in North-West Rebellion, Canada, 1885 (medal and clasp); Colonial Officers' Long Service Decoration, 1906; Demonstrator of Anatomy, 1890; Lecturer in Surgery, McGill University, 1900; Examiner in Surgery, Dominion Medical Council, Canada, 1912; Lieut-Col, i/c Surgery, No 3 Casualty Clearing Hospital, BEF, France, 1915; OC of same Hospital (despatches four times, CMG) 1917; Consulting Surgeon, British Armies in France (stationed at Rouen), 1918. *Publications:* numerous articles in medical journals; Surgery of Neck in Buck's System Surgery. *Recreation:* golf. *Address:* 781 Sherbrooke Street, Montreal, Canada. *TA:* Eldersurg, Montreal. *T:* Uptown 9654. *Clubs:* Mount Royal, Hunt, University, Montreal.

Died 5 Feb. 1922.

ELDON, 3rd Earl of, *cr* 1821; **John Scott,** DL, JP; Baron Eldon, 1799; Viscount Encombe, 1821; *b* London, 8 Nov. 1845; *s* of 2nd Earl and Hon. Louisa Duncombe, *d* of 1st Lord Feversham; *S* father, 1854; *m* 1869, Henrietta, *d* of Captain Henry Martin Turnor; four *s* two *d* (and one *s* decd). *Educ:* Eton; Christ Church, Oxford. Owner of about 25,800 acres. *Heir: g-s* Viscount Encombe, *b* 29 March 1899. *Address:* Encombe, Corfe Castle, Dorset; 43 Portman Square, W1. *Club:* Carlton. *Died 10 Aug. 1926.*

ELGEE, Captain Cyril Hammond, FRGS; British Resident at Ibadan since 1903; *b* 1871; *e s* of late Rev. W. F. Elgee, Otterbourne, Hants; unmarried. *Educ:* Lancing; France; Sandhurst. First Commission, 16th Foot, 1892; Captain, 1899; served Chitral, 1895 (medal with clasp); Ashanti Campaign, Relief of Kumasi, 1900 (medal); ADC and Private Sec. to Sir William Macgregor, Governor of Lagos, 1900–2; resigned commission, 1904; Member of Court of Enquiry into importation of Liquor into W Africa, 1909; travelled in India, Europe, America, Newfoundland, Labrador, Canada, Africa, Denmark, Sweden, Bohemia, Germany, and Austria. *Publication:* Memorandum on Negro

Education, for which received thanks of Sec. of State, 1906. *Clubs:* United Service, Baldwin, Royal Automobile, Queen's.

Died 17 Aug. 1917.

ELGIN and KINCARDINE, 9th Earl of, *cr* 1633; **Victor Alexander Bruce,** KG 1899; GCSI 1894; GCIE 1894; PC; LLD, DCL; Baron Bruce, 1603; Earl of Kincardine and Baron Bruce of Torry, 1647; Baron Elgin (UK), 1849; *b* Monklands, near Montreal, 16 May 1849; *s* of 8th Earl and his 2nd wife, Lady Mary Louisa (*d* 1898), 4th *d* of 1st Earl of Durham; *S* father, 1863; *m* 1st, 1876, Constance (*d* 1909), 2nd *d* of 9th Earl of Southesk, KT; six *s* four *d* (and one *d* decd); 2nd, 1913, Gertrude, *d* of Commander W. Sherbrooke, RN, and *widow* of Capt. F. Oglivy, RN; one *s* (posthumous). *Educ:* Eton; Balliol Coll. Oxford (MA). Lord Lieut of Fifeshire since 1886; Treasurer of Household and First Commissioner of Works, 1886; Viceroy of India, 1894–99; Secretary of State for the Colonies, 1905–8; Chancellor of Aberdeen University, 1914. *Heir: s* Lord Bruce, *b* 8 June 1881. *Address:* Broomhall, Dunfermline, Fifeshire. *Clubs:* Brooks's, Travellers'. *Died 18 Jan. 1917.*

ELHORST, Hendrik Jan; Professor of Hebraic and Aramaic Language, Antiquities, and Literature, University of Amsterdam, since 1906; *b* Wisch (Guelderland), 21 Oct. 1861; *s* of W. F. G. L. Elhorst and J. van der Ploeg; *m* Hermine Maes; two *d*. *Educ:* University of Amsterdam. Minister of the Mennonites at Irusum (Friesland), 1887; Arnhem, 1888; The Hague, 1898; Harlem, 1900; Member of Teyler's Theological Socety, 1901; Theol. Dr University of Amsterdam, 1891; DD University of St Andrews, 1911; Kt Dutch Lion. *Publications:* De profetie van Micha (a critical introduction to the book of Micah with translation and commentary), 1891; De profetie van Amos (a critical introduction to the book of Amos with translation and commentary), 1899; Israel in het licht der jongste onderzoekingen (Israel in the light of the latest investigations), 1906; the rites of mourning among the Israelites (Festschrift zum 70 Geburtstage Wellhausens); several articles in Dutch and foreign periodicals, *eg* on the ephod; Deut. 21: 1-9 (Zeitschrift für die alttestamentliche Wissenschaft); the books of the Maccabees; the Messiah of the Samaritans; the Hexateuch (Teyler's Theologisch Tydschrift); The Elephantine-papyri; the book of the Wisdom of Solomon (Nieuw Theologisch Tydschrift), etc; editor of Nieuw Theologisch Tydschrift (formerly Teyler's Theologisch Tydschrift). *Address:* P. C. Hooftstraat 170, Amsterdam.

ELIBANK, 1st Viscount, *cr* 1911; **Montolieu Fox Oliphant Murray,** DL, JP; Bt 1628; Baron 1643; Lord-Lieutenant of Peeblesshire, 1896–1908; Commander RN, retired 1870; *b* Edinburgh, 27 April 1840; *e s* of 9th Baron and Emily, *o d* of Archibald Montgomery, *niece* of Sir James Montgomery, 2nd Bt; *S* father as 10th Lord Elibank, 1871; *m* 1868, Blanche, *e d* of Edward John Scott, Portland Lodge, Southsea, Hants; two *s* five *d* (and two *s* decd). *Educ:* privately. Entered Navy, 1854; served in China War, HMS "Cambrian" (medal and Taku clasp), 1860; served in HMS "Wolverine", Jamaica Rebellion, 1865. Conservative. *Heir: s* Master of Elibank, *b* 7 Aug. 1877. *Address:* Darn Hall, Eddleston, Peeblesshire; Elibank, Selkirkshire. *Club:* New, Edinburgh. *Died 20 Feb. 1927.*

ELIOT, Charles William, LLD; *b* Boston, Mass, 20 March 1834; *s* of Samuel Atkins Eliot and Mary Lyman; *m* 1st, 1858, Ellen Derby Peabody (*d* 1869); 2nd, 1877, Grace Mellen Hopkinson; one *s*. *Educ:* Boston Public Latin School; Harvard. Studied Chemistry and investigated Educational Methods in Europe, 1863–65. Tutor in Mathematics, Harvard, 1854–58; Assistant Professor of Mathematics and Chemistry, 1858–61; Chemistry, 1861–63; Prof. of Chemistry in Mass. Inst. of Technology, 1865–69; President of the National Education Association, 1902–3; President Emeritus, 1909. *Publications:* (with F. H. Storer) Manual of Inorganic Chemistry, 1866, and Manual of Qualitative Chemical Analysis, 1869; American Contributions to Civilisation, and other Essays and Addresses, 1897; Educational Reform, 1898; Charles Eliot, Landscape Architect (biography), 1902; More Money for the Public Schools, 1903; Four American Leaders, 1906; The Durable Satisfactions of Life, 1910; The Road toward Peace, 1915; numerous addresses on Education; Annual Reports as President of Harvard, 1869–1909. *Address:* Cambridge, Mass. *Died 22 Aug. 1926.*

ELIOT, Laurence Stirling, CMG 1914; ISO 1903; JP; Under-Treasurer of State of Western Australia since 1891; *b* 20 Nov. 1845; *e s* of late George Eliot, Government Resident, Geraldton, WA; *m* 1871, Eliza Ernestine von Bibra, *d* of late Francis von Bibra of Tasmania; three *s* one *d*. *Educ:* Bishop's College, Perth, WA. Clerk to Magistrates, WA; Landing and Tide Waiter at Bunbury, 1863; also Postmaster and Assistant District Registrar; Clerk in Colonial Secretary's Office, 1872; Secretary to Central Board of Education and Assistant Clerk in Legislative Council, 1873; Registrar General, Registrar of Deeds, and Registrar of Brands, 1876; Acting Chief Clerk Colonial Secretary's Department, 1878–80; First Clerk and Registrar Colonial Secretary's Department, 1880; Chief Clerk and Accountant Treasury, 1881; appointed to take the Census, and to superintend its compilation, 1881; Acting Assistant, Colonial Secretary, 1889; Paymaster of Imperial Pensions, Jan. 1891; Commonwealth Officer July 1902; retired 1914. *Address:* Belmont, near Perth, W Australia

Died 22 Feb. 1922

ELIOT, Very Rev. Philip Frank, KCVO 1909; DD; Dean of Windsor; Domestic Chaplain to His Majesty; Registrar of the Most Noble Order of the Garter since 1891; *b* Weymouth, Dorset, 21 Dec 1835; 3rd *s* of William Eliot, JP, DL, and Lydia, *d* of John Ffoliott MP for Sligo; *m* 1st, 1859, Mary Anna Marriott, *d* of Rev. Frank Smith Rector of Rushton, Dorset; 2nd, 1883, Mary Emma Pitt (*d* 1900) *d* of 4th Lord Rivers; four *s* four *d*. *Educ:* Bath Grammar School Trinity College, Oxford (Exhibitioner). 2nd class Mods, 1855; 2nc class Lit. Hum. 1857. Curate of St Michael's, Winchester, 1858–60 Chaplain at Cally, Gatehouse, NB, 1861–64; Curate of Walcot, Bath 1864–67; Vicar of Holy Trinity, Bournemouth, 1867–90; Hon Canon, Winchester Cathedral, 1881; Canon of Windsor, 1886 Domestic Chaplain to Queen Victoria, 1891–1901; to King Edward VII, 1901–10; Prolocutor of the Lower House of the Convocation of Canterbury, 1904–13. *Address:* Deanery, Windsor Castle. *TA* Windsor. *Club:* Constitutional.

Died 1 Nov. 1917

ELIOT, Sir Whately, Kt 1907; MInstCE; *b* 22 Nov. 1841; *s* of late William Eliot of Weymouth; *m* 1878, Jessy Dingwall Fordyce, *d* o Patrick Jamieson, of Peterhead; one *s* one *d*. *Educ:* Windlesham School; Queenwood Coll. Pupil of Sir J. Coode, CE, at Portland Breakwater; engaged on dock and harbour works at Sunderland Tynemouth, and Isle of Man; conducted survey for harbour works in New Zealand; designed and carried out works for Peterhead Harbour Board and Scarborough Corporation; resident engineer o harbour works for Cape Government, and of Eastham Section Manchester Ship Canal; Admiralty Superintending Civil Engineer in charge of Keyham Dockyard Extension, 1894–1906. *Address:* 1 Inglewood Road, West Hampstead, NW.

Died 12 March 1927

ELIOTT OF STOBS, Sir Arthur Boswell, 9th Bt, *cr* 1666; Chie of ancient family of Eliott; *b* 13 July 1856; *s* and *o c* of Alexande Boswell Eliott, 2nd *s* of Sir William Francis Eliott of Stobs, 7th B and Katherine, *d* of William Craigie; *S* uncle, 1910; *m* 1884, Lilla *d* of John Burbank; one *s* two *d*. *Heir: s* Gilbert Alexander Boswell Eliott of Stobs [*b* 5 May 1885; *m* 1912, Flournoy Adams, *o d* of late Alexander Hopkins, Atlanta, USA; two *s* two *d*]. *Address:* 2! Montague Street, Portman Square, W1. *T:* Paddington 3026.

Died 15 Jan. 1926

ELIOTT, Lt-Col Francis Hardinge, CSI 1915; Indian Army; *b* 1 April 1862; *s* of late Edward Frederick Eliott, ICS; *m* 1900, Mary Agnes Wardrop. *Educ:* Harrow. Entered army, 1881; joined Indian Army, 1885; Burma Commission, 1888; Lt-Col 1907; served Burma 1888–9 (medal, 2 clasps); Commissioner Irrawaddy Division, Burma 1911; retired, 1917. *Club:* Naval and Military.

Died 26 Dec. 1928

ELKAN, John, MVO 1920; Governing Director of John Elkan, Ltd Goldsmiths and Jewellers; *b* 11 Dec 1849; *s* of late Isaac Elkan; *m* 1871 Harriet, *d* of Henry Samuel; three *s* two *d*. *Educ:* privately. Membe of the Corporation of London since 1907; Past Master of the Turners Company. *Recreation:* amateur artist. *Address:* 40 Hanover Gate Mansions, Regent's Park, NW1. *T:* Paddington 5726.

Died 24 July 1927

ELKINGTON, John Simeon, MA, LLB; late Professor of History and Political Economy, University of Melbourne; *b* England, 22 Nov 1841; *m* 1867, Helen Mary Guilfoyle. *Educ:* Grammar School University, Melbourne. *Address:* c/o The University, Melbourne

ELLERTON, Rev. Arthur John Bicknell, MA; Hon. Canon of Southwell; Rector of North Wingfield, Derbyshire, since 1918 Proctor in Convocation, 1920–22; Warden of Community of S Lawrence, Belper; *b* 25 Dec. 1865; 3rd *s* of late Rev. Canon Johr Ellerton; *m* 1896, Evelyn Constance (*d* 1925), 2nd *d* of late Col W M. Barnard, 96th Regiment and Grenadier Guards, and *g d* of late Sir Henry Barnard, KCB; five *d*. *Educ:* Merchant Taylors' School St John's College, Oxford. Curate of Halifax Parish Church, 1890–93

Elland, Yorks, 1893–95; Senior Curate of Nantwich, Cheshire, 1895–96; London Diocesan Home Missionary for Merchant Taylors' School Mission, 1896–1902; Vicar of Chaddesden, Derbyshire, 1902–6; Southwell Diocesan Missioner, 1906–14; Rector of Nuthall, Notts, 1914–18. *Address:* North Wingfield Rectory, Chesterfield. *T:* Clay Cross 64. *M:* NU7782.   *Died 21 March 1928.*

LLICOTT, Rosalind, ARAM 1896; composer and pianist; *b* Cambridge, 1857; *d* of Rt Rev. Charles John Ellicott, late Bishop of Gloucester and Constantia Annie, *d* of Adm. Alexander Becher. *Educ:* Royal Academy of Music, under Frederick Westlake and Thomas Wingham. *Works:* overture (Gloucester Festival), 1886; part-song, Bring the Bright Garlands; choral ballad, Henry of Navarre, 1894; fantasie for piano and orchestra. *Address:* Tresco, Birchington-on-Sea.   *Died 5 April 1924.*

LLIOT, Hon. Arthur Ralph Douglas; *b* 17 Dec. 1846; 2nd *s* of 3rd Earl of Minto and Emma Eleanor Elizabeth, *d* of Gen. Sir Thomas Hislop, 1st Bt, and *heir-pres.* of 5th Earl of Minto; *m* 1888, Madeleine (*d* 1906), *d* of late Sir Charles Lister Ryan, KCB; one *s* (and one *s* decd). *Educ:* Edinburgh Univ.; Trinity Coll. Cambridge (MA); Hon. DCL Durham, 1903. Barrister, 1880, practised on Northern Circuit. MP (L) Roxburghshire, 1880–86; (LU) 1886–92, when he was defeated by Hon. Mark Napier; stood for city of Durham 1895, when he was defeated by one vote; MP (LU) City of Durham, 1898–1906; Financial Secretary to Treasury, 1903; Editor of the Edinburgh Review, 1895–1912. *Publications:* Criminal Procedure in England and Scotland, 1878; The State and the Church, 1881, 2nd edn 1899; Life of the First Viscount Goschen, 1911; Traditions of British Statesmanship, 1919. *Address:* Dimbola, Freshwater Bay, Isle of Wight. *Clubs:* Brooks's, Athenæum; New, Edinburgh.
                Died 12 Feb. 1923.

LLIOT, Major Sir Edmund Halbert, Kt 1911; MVO 1907; Ensign of the King's Bodyguard of Yeomen of Guard since 1908; *b* 7 Nov. 1854 posthumously; *s* of late Lieut-Col Edmund James Elliot, 79th Highlanders, and Matilda, *d* of Charles Craigie-Halkett-Inglis of Cramond; *m* 1898, Isabella, *d* of late James C. H. Colquhoun, and *widow* of 3rd Earl of Limerick, KP. *Educ:* Cheltenham; RM Academy, Woolwich. Lieut. Royal Artillery, 1874; South Africa, 1879; Zulu War; Battle of Ulundi (medal and clasp, despatches); Capt. Royal Artillery, 1883; Adjutant 3rd Middlesex Artillery Volunteers, 1885–91; Major Royal Artillery, 1891; retired, 1892; appointed one of the Exons of HM's Royal Body-Guard of the Yeomen of the Guard, 1892; Clerk of the Cheque and Adjutant, 1901. *Recreations:* golf, hunting, shooting, etc. *Address:* 40 Queen's Gate Gardens, SW7; Friary Court, St James's Palace, SW. *T:* Kens. 6176. *Clubs:* Carlton, Naval and Military.   *Died 20 Sept. 1926.*

LLIOT, Rev. Frederick Roberts, MVO 1906; *b* 15 June 1840. *Educ:* Exeter Coll., Oxford; MA. Ordained, 1864; Curate of Tormohen, 1865–69; perpetual curate of the Lodge, Salop, 1870–75; Chaplain at Kadikeni, Asia Minor, 1875–77; Curate of St John the Evangelist, Kingston-on-Thames, 1881–89; Chaplain to HM Legation Athens, 1891–98; was tutor to Prince Christopher of Greece. *Address:* Tregie, Paignton, Devon.   *Died 25 Dec. 1918.*

LLIOT, Rev. Canon George Edward; retired, on Colonial pension; *b* Tobago, BWI, 29 Jan 1851; *s* of John L. Elliot, MD (Glasgow), and Rosa Eliza Thomas; *m* 1876, Flora Jane Hutson; three *s* five *d*. *Educ:* England; Codrington College, Barbados. Ordained, 1874; Curate of St John, Antigua, 1874–77; Rector of St George, Dominica, 1877–79; Curate of St Luke, Barbados, 1879–85; Vicar of St Martin, 1885–96; Holy Trinity, 1896–97; Rector of St Andrew, 1897–98; of St Peter, 1898, Rural Dean of St Peter, 1905; Canon (St Basil), 1906–9; Assistant Priest at St Lawrence, 1913. *Recreations:* walking, reading. *Address:* 9th Avenue, Belle Ville, Barbados, BWI.
                Died 7 Jan. 1916.

LLIOT, Maj.-Gen. Henry Riversdale; *b* 11 Dec. 1836; *s* of William Elliot, Madras Civil Service; *m* 1866, Carmina Macintire; three *s* one *d*. *Educ:* Cheltenham College; Military Academy, Edinburgh. Joined Madras 42nd Infantry, 1855; served with Madras Sappers and Miners, Abyssinian Campaign, present at assault and capture of Magdala, 1867–68; Brigade-Major; Assistant Quartermaster-Gen. Madras Presidency and Burmah; commanded 11th MNI; returned to England on Colonel's allowances, 1886. *Address:* 1 Fauconberg Villas, Cheltenham. *Club:* New, Cheltenham.
                Died 11 Dec. 1921.

LLIOTT, His Honour Judge Adshead, MA; JP Sheffield and West Riding of Yorkshire; Judge of County Courts on Circuit 13 since

1919; *b* 1869; 5th *s* of late John Matthews Elliott, Manchester; *m* 1904, Florence *o d* of late Joseph Fulton, Paisley. *Educ:* Manchester Grammar School; Oriel College, Oxford. Called to Bar, Inner Temple, 1894; joined Northern Circuit and practised in Manchester; President of Pensions Appeal Tribunal, 1918–19. *Publications:* Treatise on Workmen's Compensation Acts (seven editions). *Address:* Dunluce, Ranmoor, Sheffield. *Club:* The Club, Sheffield.
                Died 7 Sept. 1922.

ELLIOTT, Maj.-Gen. Edward Draper; Colonel-Commandant, Royal Artillery (late Bengal), since 1900; *b* 30 Sept 1838; *o* surv *s* of late Maj.-Gen. W. E. A. Elliott, HEICS; *m* 1899, Maria, 2nd *d* of late Charles Jecks Dixon, Blackheath. *Educ:* Rugby; Addiscombe College. Entered army, 1857; served at the end of Indian Mutiny; Col on Staff Commanding RA Thames District, 1890–95; Maj.-Gen. 1895; retired, 1900. *Clubs:* Naval and Military, MCC, Sandown Park.
                Died 30 Sept. 1918.

ELLIOTT, George; KC 1909; *b* Luton, Bedfordshire, 24 Oct. 1860; *e s* of George Elliott, Buxton Lodge, Luton; *m* 1889, Charlotte, *y d* of Frederick Farr, Surgeon; two *s* three *d*. *Educ:* Mill Hill School. Member of Inner and Middle Temple; called to Bar, 1882; Surrey Sessions and South-Eastern Circuit; pupil of Sir Edward Clarke; engaged in following cases: Edmund Lawrence Levy perjury case, the Great Pearl Case, the Walnut Case, Diamond Jubilee Syndicate Frauds, the Lupton Companies Fraud, and the trials of Chapman the poisoner; Dougal, the Moat Farm murderer; Devereux, the trunk case; Rayner, the murderer of Mr Whiteley; the Stoddart Coupon Case, D. S. Windell Fraud, Lody the German Spy, etc; contested (U) South Bedfordshire, 1900 and 1910. *Publications:* The Law of Newspaper Libel, 1883; assisted the late Walter Shirley in the preparation of his work on Leading Cases in the Common Law; Fifth Edition—Illustrations in Advocacy by Harris. *Recreations:* golf, swimming. *Address:* 1 Garden Court, Temple, EC. *T:* Holborn 660; 29 Clarges Street, Mayfair, W. *T:* Mayfair 6987. *Clubs:* Garrick, United.   *Died 27 Oct. 1916.*

ELLIOTT, Sir George (Samuel), Kt 1917; MP (CU) West Islington, 1918–22; Refreshment Contractor; *b* Islington, 1847; *m* Elizabeth Frances, *d* of Robert Hellier, Upottery, Devonshire; three *s* three *d*. *Educ:* privately; City of London School. Entered municipal life as a member of the Islington Vestry, 1875; for 38 years a member of the Islington Board of Guardians, of which body he was Chairman for 20 years and Vice-Chairman for 9 years; Church-warden twice; Mayor of Islington, 1902–3, 1906–9, 1910–18; Vice-Chairman of the Metropolitan Water Board; member of the Metropolitan Asylums Board; original member of the London County Council, served 18 years; took an active interest in the acquisition of open spaces; raised the memorial to Islingtonians who fell in the Boer War; raiser of the 21st (S) Battalion Middlesex Regiment (Islington); Chairman of the Islington Local Tribunal. Greatly interested in Free Masonry; PM of 11 lodges; PAGDC (England) and PPGSdB Hertford; PPGDC Middlesex. *Address:* 14 Upper Street, Islington, N1; The Chalkpit, Maidenhead, Berks.   *Died 4 May 1925.*

ELLIOTT, Sir Thomas Henry, 1st Bt *cr* 1917; KCB 1902 (CB 1897); British Delegate to the International Institute of Agriculture and Counsellor of Embassy, Rome; *b* London, 7 Sept. 1854; *o s* of late Thomas Henry Elliott of Rue Ruhmkorff, Paris; *m* 1880, Ellen, *d* of late James Rowe; one *s* one *d*. *Educ:* privately. Entered Inland Revenue Department by open competition, 1872; a Principal Clerk, 1887; Private Secretary to Rt Hon. C. T. Ritchie, President of Local Government Board, 1889–92; Sec. to Board of Agriculture and Fisheries, 1892–1913; Deputy-Master and Comptroller of the Mint, 1913–17; Member of the Royal Commission on Local Taxation, 1896–1902; Hon. Member Royal Agricultural Society of England, 1903, and Highland and Agricultural Society, Scotland, 1905; Vice-President of the Land Agents' Society, 1906; Hon. Member Surveyors' Institution, 1906, and of the Society of Agriculturists of Spain, 1911; Hon. Associate Royal College of Veterinary Surgeons, 1914; a Delegate to the International Agricultural Conference, Rome, 1905; a Public Works Loans Commissioner, 1914–19; a Boundary Commissioner, and a Commissioner for the Experimental Application of Proportional Representation, 1917–18; Chairman of the Air Raid Compensation Board, 1917–19. Commander of the French Order du Mérite Agricole and of the Orders of the Crown of Belgium and S Maurizio and S Lazaro, Italy; Officier de l'Instruction Publique, France. *Heir: s* Ivo D'Oyly Elliott, *b* 7 March 1882. *Address:* 12 Queen Anne's Gate, SW; 173 Woodstock Road, Oxford; Institut International d'Agriculture, Rome. *Club:* National.
                Died 4 June 1926.

ELLIS, Arthur; *b* Holloway, 1 Sept. 1856; *s* of late Edward and Catherine Ellis of 33 Lansdowne Crescent, Notting Hill, W; *m* Lydia C. L., *d* of late Basil John Charles Pringle. *Educ:* The King's School, Peterborough. Began life in the City, but after some years left it to follow painting; entered the Royal Academy Schools, 1882; Paris, 1886; exhibitor in chief London and provincial exhibitions; member of the Royal Drawing Society, and on the Board of Examiners. *Address:* 4 Queen's Park Gardens, Seaford. *Club:* Chelsea Arts.
Died 4 April 1918.

ELLIS, Lieut-Comdr Bernard Henry, DSO 1916; RNVR; Commanding Hawke Battalion, RN Division, BEF; *b* Hampstead, 26 May 1885; *s* of Henry Ellis of Potters Bar and Lyme Regis, and Margaret Morley; *m* 1915, Marjorie, *d* of Lieut-Col J. L. Blumfeld, 9th Middlesex Regt TF. *Educ:* University College School, London. Articled to Lieut-Col C. F. T. Blyth; admitted Solicitor, 1908; partner in the firm of Peters & Ellis, Guildhall Chambers, Basinghall Street, EC. Served in ranks of RNVR, London, 27 Jan. 1904, till outbreak of war; was mobilised then having rank of CPO; served with RN Divn Benbow Battalion at Antwerp, Oct. 1914 (despatches, DSM); landed in Gallipoli with Benbow Battalion end of May 1915, and served there and at Suvla till the evacuation; commissioned as Temp. Sub-Lieut RNVR Oct. 1915; promoted Temp. Lieut and Adjt Nov. 1915; Temp. Lieut-Comdr Oct. 1916, served at Stavros Feb.–April 1916; in France May 1916 to present time, with Anson Battalion from June 1915–April 1917 (4 months in command), Hood Batt. 21 to 30 April 1917, Hawke Batt. since, in command (DSO after action near Beaumont Hamel, RNVR long service medal Jan. 1916). *Address:* 2A Guildhall Chambers, Basinghall Street, EC. *Club:* Swiss Alpine.
Died 21 April 1918.

ELLIS, Col Charles Conyngham, CB 1908; CBE 1919; *b* 2 March 1852. Lieut RE, 1872; Captain, 1884; Major, 1891; Lieut-Col, 1899; Col, 1903; served Chitral, 1899 (medal with clasp); retired, 1909. *Club:* Army and Navy. *Died 7 Dec. 1921.*

ELLIS, Sir Evelyn (Campbell), Kt 1914; *b* London, 8 Dec. 1865; *s* of late Robert Ellis, MRCS; *m* 1st, 1900, Margaret (*d* 1918), *d* of George E. Craig, Manchester; one *d*; 2nd, 1920, Kathleen Rose (head sister of St Bartholomew's Hospital for 14 years), *widow* of W. H. P. Jenkins, DL, JP, Frenchay Park, Bristol, and *d* of late Henry John Abernethy. *Educ:* privately. Solicitor, England, 1891; Advocate and Solicitor of the Straits Settlements, 1896; Acting Attorney-General, Straits Settlements, 1912–13; Member Statute Law Revision Commission Straits Settlements, 1912–16; Unofficial Member, Legislative Council, Straits Settlements, 1908–16. *Recreations:* golf, billiards, motoring. *Address:* Farncombe Hall, Godalming. *Clubs:* Carlton, Sports. *Died 1 Sept. 1920.*

ELLIS, Sir Joseph Baxter, Kt 1906; JP; Principal of the firm of Hindhaugh's, millers and merchants; *b* Bramley, near Leeds, 1842; *s* of Mark Ellis; *nephew* of the preacher and controversialist, Joseph Barker; *m* 1st, 1867, Frances (*d* 1886), *d* of William Laidler, Newcastle; four *s* one *d*; 2nd, 1892, Mary Sharp, *d* of late John Taylor, North Shields; two *s* two *d*. *Educ:* East Keswick, near Leeds. Came to Newcastle, 1865; entered the business founded over a century ago by his uncle, J. Hindhaugh. Sheriff of Newcastle, 1887–88; Mayor, 1890–91 and 1904–5; created first Lord Mayor by King Edward VII, July 1906; an Alderman of, and served thirty-seven years on, the Newcastle Council; was the pioneer of wood paving in Newcastle; Chairman of the Tramways Committee; Chairman of the Parks Committee, and a River Tyne Commissioner; Vice-Chairman of Trade and Commerce Committee; entertained Mr Gladstone when the historic Newcastle Programme was launched. *Address:* North Ashfield, Newcastle. *Died 28 Dec. 1918.*

ELLIS, Robert Powley, MVO 1907; late Superintendent of the Line, Great Eastern Railway; *b* 20 July, 1845; *s* of John Erskine Ellis of Bentley, Suffolk; *m* Emily Ann, *d* of William Rose of Bentley, Suffolk; three *s* one *d*. *Educ:* Ipswich. Officer of the Great Eastern Railway for 43 years, 17 of which he was District Goods Manager at Norwich and London, and the last 14 years of his connection with the Company was first Assistant Superintendent and then Superintendent of the Line. In recognition of the large number of Royal journeys so satisfactorily arranged and accompanied, his late Majesty King Edward VII conferred upon him the Royal Victorian Order. *Address:* Rosecroft, Woodford Road, South Woodford, Essex. *T:* Wanstead 125.
Died 16 June 1918.

ELLIS, Tristram, ARE; AKC; artist; *b* Great Malvern, 1844; *s* of Alexander J. Ellis, FRS, LitD, etc; *m*; one *s* two *d*. *Educ:* Queenwood College; King's College, London. Took all scholarships in Applied Science Department; articled to Partner of Sir John Fowler, MIC[…] etc, 1864; worked on District and Metropolitan Railways till 186[…] became AICE; carried out several minor engineering works; entere[…] M Bonnât's Studio in Paris, 1874; travelled through Cyprus direct[…] after its occupation, 1878; travelled in Syria, Asia Minor, ar[…] Mesopotamia and Great Syrian Desert, 1879–80; Egypt 1881–8[…] Portugal, 1883, 1884; Greece and Constantinople, 1885, 188[…] Spitzbergen, 1894. *Publications:* On a Raft and Through the Dese[…] illustrated with 38 etchings on copper by the author, 1881; Sketchir[…] from Nature. *Address:* 15 Gerard Road, Barnes, SW.
Died 25 July 192[…]

ELLIS, T. Mullett; poet and novelist; founder and editor of Th[…] Thrush, a periodical for original poetry; *b* 29 Dec. 1850; 2nd *s* [...] Rev. R. S. Ellis; *m* Gwendoline, *d* of Wm Hayhurst of Billingto[…] one *s* one *d*. Educated as architect. First prize in Architectur[…] Nottingham; ARIBA. After 15 years' practice as architect engage[…] in literature; founded the War Emergency Committee, 1899; assiste[…] to found The Evening News, the first halfpenny Conservativ[…] newspaper in England; one of the earliest members of the Primro[…] League; travelled in Malta, Sicily, Italy, Austria, Hungary, Swede[…] Morocco and Algeria. *Publications:* The Earl's Nose, a book of humo[…] in verse, with illustrations by the author; Bone et Fidelis (a poem[…] Elegy on the Death of Lord Beaconsfield, 1884; Reveries of Wor[…] History, 1893; Seven Sonnets (illustrated); novels: The Beauty [...] Boscastle, 1894; Zalma, 1895; Tales of the Klondyke; God is Lov[…] 1898; The Three Cats'-Eye Rings; Kitty, a story of the Transvaal Wa[…] What can a Woman do for the Empire?, 1915; also several poem[…] and short stories in Illustrated London News, Sketch, To-day, et[…] *Recreations:* caricaturing, boating, gardening. *Address:* Creek Hous[…] Shepperton-on-Thames. *TA:* Shepperton. *Club:* Savage.
Died 20 Aug. 191[…]

ELLIS, William, FRS; FRAS; MIEE; late Superintendent of th[…] Magnetical and Meteorological Department, Royal Observator[…] Greenwich; *b* Greenwich, 20 Feb. 1828; *m* 1st, 1869, Sarah Elizabe[…] (*d* 1906), *e d* of late Edward Campion; 2nd, 1908, Margaret Ann[…] *e d* of late Francis Ellis of Settle. Joined the Royal Observatory[…] attached to the Astronomical Department until 1874, having durin[…] the preceding 18 years had charge of the chronometric and electri[…] branch; was transferred to and had charge of the Magnetical ar[…] Meteorological Department, 1875–93; March 1852–May 1853 ha[…] charge of the University Observatory, Durham. *Recreation:* musi[…] *Address:* 78 Coleraine Road, Blackheath, SE.
Died 13 Dec. 191[…]

ELLIS, Rev. Hon. William Charles; Rector of Bothal, Morpeth[…] 22 July 1835; 2nd *s* of 6th Lord Howard de Walden and Lucy, *d* [...] 4th Duke of Portland; *m* 1873, Henrietta Elizabeth (*d* 1915), *d* [...] Henry Metcalf Ames of Linden; four *s* two *d* (and one *s* decd). Edu[…] Oxford University (MA). *Address:* Bothalhaugh, Morpeth. Clu[…] Athenæum.
Died 20 June 192[…]

ELLIS, William Hodgson, MA, MB, LLD Toronto; LLD McGi[…] FRSCan; Dean of Faculty of Applied Science, Toronto Universit[…] *b* 1845; *s* of John Eimeo Ellis, MRCS, Bakewell, Derbyshire, an[…] Eliza Hodgson; *m* Ellen Maude Mickle; two *s* one *d*. *Educ:* Toront[…] University. *Address:* 86 Woodlawn Avenue East, Toronto, Canad[…] *Club:* York, Toronto.
Died 23 Aug. 192[…]

ELLISON, William Augustine, MVO 1901; VD; Surgeon to HM[…] Household at Windsor Castle; Consulting Physician, King Edwar[…] VII Hospital, Windsor; Lt-Colonel and Hon. Colonel; retired 1[…] Volunteer Battalion, 4th Royal Berks Regiment; Major and Hon. L[…] Colonel TF Reserve; Lt-Colonel Commanding 4th (Reserve[…] Battalion Royal Berks Regiment, 1915–16 (mentioned for wa[…] services); *b* 28 Aug. 1855; *s* of James Ellison, MD; *m* 1894, Catharin[…] May Murray, *g d* of late Rev. H. Headley, of Ashley, Arnewoo[…] Hants; one *s*. *Educ:* Eton; University Coll. Oxford; BA (Honour[…] 1878, MA 1881, MB 1884, MD 1895. Surgeon to Queen Victoria[…] Household at Windsor Castle, 1888; to King Edward VII[…] Household, 1901; Acting Resident Physician to Queen Victoria [...] Balmoral, 1894, 1895, 1897, 1898. *Publications:* contributions t[…] Lancet. *Recreations:* yachting, gardening, boating, music; Eton Eigh[…] 1873–74; "Wall" Football Eleven, 1873; rowed in Head of the Riv[…] Crew, Oxford, 1875, 1877, 1878; in Winning Trial Eight, 1875, 187[…] 1877; Gymnastic Medalist, 1877; rowed in University Boat Rac[…] 1878; won OUBC pairs, 1878; also Visitors' Cup, 1876; Silve[…] Goblets, 1878; and Grand Challenge Cup (stroke of Leander Eigh[…] at Henley Regatta, 1880. *Address:* Eton, Bucks. *T:* Windsor 262. M[…] BL 3477. *Clubs:* New University; Leander, Royal Harwich Yach[…] Royal Cruising.
Died 1 Nov. 1917[…]

LLISTON, Col George Sampson, CB 1911; VD; MRCS; *b* 1844; *s* of late Dr William Elliston of Ipswich. Administrative Medical Officer, East Anglian Division, 1908–12; retired. Knight of Grace, Order of St John of Jerusalem; Commissioner in charge of Eastern District, St John Ambulance Brigade; Member of Suffolk Territorial Association. *Address:* St Edmund's, Felixstowe.
Died 20 Nov. 1921.

LLISTON, Guy; Secretary British Medical Association since 1902; Assistant Secretary 1898; *b* Ipswich, 1872; 3rd *s* of late W. A. Elliston, MD; *m* Clare, *y d* of late Benjamin Warner, Wanstead, Essex, and Newgate Street, EC; four *d. Educ:* Ipswich School. Commenced business career Liverpool, 1888; interested in initiating direct steamship service, Manchester and Paris; joined Weekly Sun, 1897; Manager, Naval and Military Magazine and Public Health Magazine, 1898; joined 1st Lancashire Artillery Volunteers, 1891; retired senior captain, 1897. *Recreations:* golf, tennis, gardening. *Address:* 429 Strand, WC; Belstead, Northwood. *T:* Gerrard 2630. *Clubs:* Savage, Arts; Felixstowe and Northwood Golf.
Died 13 April 1918.

LMHIRST, Capt. Edward Pennell; late 9th Norfolk Regiment; *b* 7 Jan. 1845; *o s* of late Rev. Edward Elmhurst, Shawell Rectory, Leicestershire; *m* 1873, Laura M., *d* of late Stephen P. Kennard. *Educ:* Rugby; Sandhurst. Served in China and Japan with 9th Foot, 1864–68; Musketry Instructor to same, 1871–74; ADC to General C. Elmhirst at Malta and Bangalore, 1874–78; Adj. of Artists' Volunteer Corps, 1878–82; Master and Huntsman Neilgherry Hounds, 1875–77; Woodland-Pytchley Hounds, 1880–81; served in South Africa, 1899–1900 (medal with two clasps). *Publications:* Our Life in Japan, 1869; The Hunting Counties of Great Britain, 1882; The Cream of Leicestershire, 1888; The Best Season on Record, 1884; Foxhound, Forest and Prairie, 1892; The Best of the Fun, 1903. *Recreations:* hunting correspondent of the Field as "Brooksby" since 1870; did much big game shooting in Malay Peninsula, India and the Rocky Mountains of America. *Address:* Blisworth House, Blisworth, Northamptonshire. *Club:* Naval and Military.
Died 2 Dec. 1916.

LPHINSTONE, Sir Howard Warburton, 3rd Bt; *cr* 1816; MA; *b* London, 26 July 1830; *o s* of Sir Howard Elphinstone, 2nd Bt and Elizabeth, *d* of E. J. Curteis, MP; *S* father, 1893; *m* 1860, Constance, *d* of John Alexander Hankey, Balcombe Place, Sussex; three *s* five *d* (and three *s* decd). *Educ:* Eton; Trinity College, Cambridge (Scholar); 17th Wrangler, 1854. Librarian, Trinity Coll. Cambridge; Barrister, Lincoln's Inn, 1862; Lecturer to Incorporated Law Society, 1869–71; Professor of Real Property Law to the Inns of Court, 1889–92; Reader on the Law of Real Property, Inns of Court, 1892–96; Conveyancing Counsel to the Court, 1895–1914. *Publications:* Introduction to Conveyancing, 1871; Patterns for Turning, 1872; joint-author of Key and Elphinstone's Precedents of Conveyancing, 1878; On the Interpretation of Deeds, 1886; On Searches, 1887; joint editor of Goodeve's Real Property, 1897, and Goodeve's Personal Property, 1892. *Recreation:* photography. *Heir: g s* Howard Graham Elphinstone, *b* 28 Dec. 1898. *Address:* Struan, Wimbledon Park. *TA:* Struan, Southfields. *T:* 446 PO Wimbledon. *Club:* Athenæum.
Died 3 Jan. 1917.

LSTOB, Rev. John George; Hon. Canon of Chester, 1911; *m.* Rural Dean of Macclesfield, 1904–12. *Address:* Fanshawe, Chelford, Cheshire.
Died 6 Oct. 1926.

LSTOB, Lt-Col Wilfrith, VC 1919; DSO; MC; 16th Manchester Regiment; *s* of Rev. J. G. Elstob. Served European War. *Address:* Fanshawe, Chelford, Cheshire.
Died 21 March 1918.

LTON, Sir Edmund Harry, 8th Bt, *cr* 1717; JP; *b* 3 May 1846; *s* of Edmund William Elton and Lucy Maria, *d* of Rev. John Morgan Rice; *S* uncle, 1883; *m* 1868, Agnes, *d* of Sir Arthur Hallam Elton, 7th Bt; two *s* three *d. Educ:* Bradfield; Jesus Coll., Cambridge. Hon. Col 1st Gloster Artillery Vol.; County Councillor Somerset; High Sheriff, 1894–95; originator and designer of Elton Ware Pottery; received ten gold and two silver medals in International and other Exhibitions. Owner of about 4200 acres. *Heir: s* Ambrose Elton [*b* 23 May 1869; *m* 1901, Dorothy, *o d* of Arthur Wiggin of Oddington Estate, Ceylon; two *s. Educ:* Lancing Coll.; Jesus College, Cambridge; BA. Barrister, 1896]. *Address:* Clevedon Court, Somerset.
Died 17 July 1920.

LTON, Col Frederick Coulthurst, CB 1882; RA; retired; *b* 15 July 1836; *m* 1866, Olivia, *d* of late Major Power. Entered army, 1854;

Col 1885; served Crimea, 1855 (medal with clasp, Knight of Legion of Honour, Turkish medal); Egyptian War, 1882 (despatches, CB, medal with clasp, 3rd class Medjidie, Khedive's star). *Club:* Army and Navy.
Died 12 Jan. 1920.

ELWELL, Colonel Francis Edwin; Commissioned Speaker for League of Nations; sculptor and writer on art; *b* Concord, Mass, 15 June 1858; Scotch-English; *s* of John W. Elwell and Clara Farrar-Elwell; *m* 1st; two *s*; 2nd, Annie Marion Benjamin-Elwell, British subject before her marriage; one *s. Educ:* Concord, Mass; Paris. Highest award at Columbia Exposition for Statue of Dickens and Little Nell; five medals, one from the King of Belgium; Hon. Member of the Dickens Fellowship of London; Hon. Member Cincinnati Art Club; Hon. Colonel 7th Rhode Island Infantry; Delegate for the State of New Jersey for the Atlantic Congress for the League of Nations; for some years Curator of Ancient and Modern Statuary, Metropolitan Museum of Art, New York City; worked in two Aeroplane Plants, one Ammunition Plant, and unofficial worker in Navy Intelligence Bureau, USN, European War; lectured at Harvard and other Universities; newspaper and editorial work; first to write about the Reuniting of the Anglo-Saxon Race before the war. *Works:* thirty or forty statues and works in Sculpture—three in Europe. *Recreations:* prayer, work, play, sleep. *Address:* Darien, Fairfield County, Connecticut. *T:* Stamford 2723. *Clubs:* Cincinnati Art, Sons of the American Revolution, New York.
Died 23 Jan. 1922.

ELWES, Gervase Henry Cary-, JP, DL, Lincs; JP Northants; Knight of Malta, 1917; professional musician; *b* Billing, Northants, 15 Nov. 1866; *o s* of Valentine D. H. Cary-Elwes, of Billing, Northants, and Roxby and Brigg, Lincs, and Alice, *d* of Hon. and Rev. Henry Ward, *b* of 3rd Viscount Bangor; *m* 1889, Lady Winefride Feilding, 3rd *d* of 8th Earl of Denbigh; six *s* two *d. Educ:* Oratory School, Birmingham; Woburn School; Christ Church, Oxford; Munich; Paris. Served in HM Diplomatic Service, 1891–95. Entered musical profession, tenor, 1903. High Sheriff, Northamptonshire, 1917. *Recreations:* shooting, games. *Address:* Billing Hall, Northampton; Roxby, Lincolnshire. *T:* Cogenhoe 6. *Clubs:* Carlton, Savile; Oxford and Cambridge Musical.
Died 12 Jan. 1921.

ELWES, Henry John, FRS 1897; landowner; *b* 16 May 1846; *o s* of late John Henry Elwes, of Colesborne, and Mary, *d* of late Sir Robert Bromley, 3rd Bt, of Stoke, Notts; *m* 1871, Margaret, *d* of late W. C. Lowndes, of Brightwell Park, Oxon; one *s* (one *d* decd). *Educ:* Eton, and abroad. Served five years in Scots Guards; travelled in Turkey, Asia Minor, Tibet and in India four times, in N America and Mexico three times; in Chile; in Russia and Siberia three times; in Formosa, China and Japan twice; in Nepal and Sikkim; was Vice-President of Royal Horticultural Society, Victoria Medalist of the same; Past President of Royal English Arboricultural Society and of the Royal Entomological Society of London; scientific member of Indian Embassy to Tibet, 1886; represented Great Britain officially at Botanical and Horticultural Congresses at Petrograd and Amsterdam. *Publications:* A Monograph of the Genus Lillium, 1880; The Trees of Great Britain and Ireland, 7 vols, 1906–13; many papers in the Transactions and Proceedings of the Zoological, Linnean, Entomological, Horticultural, and Royal Agricultural Societies, 1869–99. *Recreations:* big game shooting, horticulture, hunting. *Address:* Colesborne Park, near Cheltenham. *Club:* Athenæum.
Died 26 Nov. 1922.

ELWOOD, Hon. Edward Lindsey; a Judge of Appeal for Saskatchewan since 1918; *b* Goderich, Ont, 13 Feb. 1868; *s* of John Yeats and Marion W. Elwood; *m* 1895, Cara A. Slack, Goderich, Ont; four *s* one *d. Educ:* Goderich Collegiate Institute; Osgood Hall, Toronto. Practised Law at South Bend, Washington State, 1890–92; Oxbow, Sask., 1892–97; Moosomin, Sask., 1897–1912; Regina, Sask., 1912–13; public appointment one of the Benchers of Law Society of Saskatchewan, and had been a Bencher of the Law Society of North West Territories; Mayor of Moosomin, 1909 and 1910; Chancellor of the Diocese of Qu'Appelle until 1915; Judge of the Supreme Court of Saskatchewan, 1913–18. *Recreation:* golf. *Address:* 2249 Rae St, Regina, Canada. *T:* 2717. *M:* 21. *Clubs:* Assiniboia, Wascana Country, Regina.

ELY, 5th Marquess of, *cr* 1800; **John Henry Loftus;** Bt 1780; Baron Loftus, 1785; Viscount Loftus, 1789; Earl of Ely, 1794; Baron Loftus (UK), 1801; *b* 6 March 1851; *s* of Rev. Lord Adam Loftus, 3rd *s* of 2nd Marquess and Margaret, *d* of Robert Finnin, Dublin; *S* cousin, 1889; *m* 1895, Margaret, *d* of Frederick A. Clark, Lynton Court, Sussex, and Gracefield Park, Bucks. Owner of about 49,000 acres. *Heir: b* Lord George Herbert Loftus, *b* 19 April 1854. *Address:* Ely

Lodge, Enniskillen; Loftus Hall, Wexford; Rathfarnam Lodge, Brighton; Long Loftus, Yorkshire. *Clubs:* Royal Automobile; Royal St George's, Kingstown; Kildare Street, Dublin.

Died 18 Dec. 1925.

EMANUEL, Samuel Henry, KC 1919; LLD; Barrister; Recorder of the City of Winchester since 1915; Master of the Bench of the Inner Temple; *s* of late Henry Herschel and Julia Emanuel of Southampton; *m* Ethel Gertrude, *d* of late A. L. Lazarus of the Metal Exchange, London; two *s* one *d*. *Educ:* University College School, London; Trinity Hall, Cambridge. Called to Bar Inner Temple, 1886; Member of the Western Circuit. *Address:* 1 Temple Gardens, Temple, EC4; 48 Holland Park, W11. *TA:* 70 Temple. *T:* Central 4257. *Clubs:* Athenæum; Hants County; Royal Southampton Yacht; Dorset County.   *Died 15 May 1925.*

EMARD, Most Rev. Mgr Joseph Médard; RC Archbishop of Ottawa since 1922; *b* 1853. Priest, 1876; Bishop of Valleyfield, 1892–1922. *Address:* Archbishop's Palace, Ottawa.

Died 23 March 1927.

EMERSON, Hon. Charles H., KC; MHA Newfoundland, since 1900; Member of Executive Council without Portfolio since 1899; *b* 1864. *Address:* St John's, Newfoundland.

Died 18 Feb. 1919.

EMERSON, Ven. Edward Robert, DD; Archdeacon of Cork; Rector of Ballymodan since 1890; *b* 1838; *s* of Rev. George Emerson; *m* Annie, *d* of William Roberts, Abbeyville Park, Dublin. *Educ:* Bandon Grammar School; Trinity College, Dublin. Ordained, 1861; Curate of Fanlobus, 1861–65; Rector of St Edmund's, Cork, 1865–90; Canon of Cork, 1884; Chaplain to the Lord Lieutenant of Ireland; Chaplain to Earl of Bandon; formerly Select Preacher to University of Dublin; Diocesan Nominator, Governor Diocesan Education Board; Clerical Member of Diocesan Court. *Address:* Ballymodan, Bandon, Co. Cork.

Died 30 Nov. 1926.

EMERSON, Hon. George Henry; Judge Supreme Court of Newfoundland, since 1896; *b* 1853; *m* Katherine, *o d* of Edward and Jane Maher. *Educ:* Grammar School, Harbor Grace. Barrister, 1876; Bencher, 1888; QC 1890; elected Member of Colonial Legislature (Placentia District), 1885; re-elected, 1889 and 1893; appointed Official Delegate to England on Fisheries Question, 1890, and again on same subject, 1891; Official Delegate to Ottawa to discuss with Dominion Government terms of Union between Canada and Newfoundland, 1895; Commissioner for Consolidation and Revision of Statute Law of Colony, 1888–96; Speaker of Newfoundland Assembly (being twice unanimously elected by House), 1890–94; MEC and MLC, 1895–96; Delegate London Conference, Imperial Court of Appeal, 1901. *Address:* Calvert House, St John's, Newfoundland; Virginia Water, St John's, Newfoundland.

Died 5 March 1916.

EMERSON, Maj. Norman Zeal, DSO 1900; *b* 4 Oct. 1872; *m* 1919. Entered army, 1895; Capt. 1900; Maj. 1914: served North-West Frontier, India, 1897 (medal with two clasps); S Africa, 1899–1902 (despatches, Queen's medal 3 clasps, King's medal 2 clasps); retired, 1911; rejoined for active service, 1914; served in France and Salonica (British War Medal, Victory Medal, 1914–15 Star). *Address:* Crown Point, Ealing, W.   *Died 28 April 1928.*

EMERSON, Sir William, Kt 1902; President, RIBA 1899–1900, 1900–1, 1901–2; *b* 1843; *s* of William Emerson of Whetstone, Middlesex; *m* 1872, Jenny, *d* of Coutts Stone of Prince's Square, Bayswater. *Educ:* King's Coll. Pupil of William Burges, ARA; went to India when 21 years of age; erected there the Bombay markets, several churches, and other buildings; on returning home designed for the Govt of India the Allahabad University, carried out by the Royal Engineers; also designed the Cathedral for the Lucknow Diocese and the Bhounuggur Hospital; was architect of St Mary's Church, Brighton; the Clarence Memorial Wing, St Mary's Hospital; his design was placed first in the competition for Liverpool Cathedral, and Hamilton House, Victoria Embankment, and the New Royal Caledonian Asylum are his work; besides these he was carrying out the Victoria Memorial for India in Calcutta, and designed a large palace for the late Maharajah of Bhounuggur. *Publications:* several papers read before the Royal Institute of British Architects. *Recreations:* golf, billiards. *Address:* Carlton Chambers, 4 Regent Street, SW. *Clubs:* Arts, St Stephen's.   *Died 26 Dec. 1924.*

EMERY, Henry Crosby; *b* 21 Dec. 1872; *s* of Justice L. A. Emery of the Supreme Court of Maine; *m* 1917, Susanne Carey Allinson.

Educ: Bowdoin Coll.; Harvard and Columbia Univs. Taught political economy at Bowdoin College, 1894–1900; Professor of Political Economy, Yale University, 1900–16; Chairman US Tariff Board, 1909–12; Foreign representative of Guaranty Trust Company; while in Petrograd commissioned as Major in US Army to work with American Military Mission in connection with the Mickleson Commission; captured by the Germans, 1918; with Guaranty Trust Company of New York in home office from the Armistice until the spring of 1920, when he became manager of the Asia Banking Corporation, Peking. *Publication:* Speculation on the Stock and Produce Exchanges of the United States, 1896. *Address:* Asia Banking Corporation, Peking, China.

Died 6 Feb. 1924.

EMERY, Walter d'Este, MD, BSc (Lond.); MRCS, MRCP; Captain RAMC (TF); formerly Director of Laboratories and Lecturer on Pathology and Bacteriology to King's College Hospital; late Pathologist Children's Hospital, Paddington Green; late Hunterian Professor Royal College Surgeons; Scholar and Gold Medalist, University, London. *Publications:* Immunity and Specific Therapy; Clinical Bacteriology and Haematology (6 editions); Tumours, Their Nature and Causation; articles in Quarterly Review, Practitioner, etc. *Address:* Old Manor House, Shirehampton, Bristol. *Club:* Savage.

Died 19 June 1923.

EMERY, Winifred, (Isabel Winifred Maud Emery Maude); actress; *b* Manchester; *o d* of Samuel Anderson Emery, actor; granddaughter of John Emery, actor; *m* 1888, Cyril Francis Maude, Chapel Royal, Savoy; one *s* two *d*. *Educ:* London, private school. Made first appearance on the stage at Liverpool at the age of eight years; as a child-actress, Princess Theatre, London, 1875; first appearance in London, 1879, Imperial Theatre, Westminster; at Court Theatre under Wilson Barrett; went to the Lyceum under Henry Irving, 1881; twice to America and Canada with his company, and played at all the principal theatres in London; played at the Haymarket Theatre, 1896–1905. *Recreations:* gardening, reading. *Address:* The Corner, Little Common, Sussex. *T:* Cooden 56. *Club:* Bath.

Died 15 July 1924.

EMMET, Rev. Cyril William, MA, BD; Chaplain and Fellow University College, Oxford; Theological Lecturer, Hertford College; Vice-Principal of Ripon Hall, Oxford; *b* 24 March 1875; *s* of Rev. W. E. Emmet; *m* Gertrude Julia, *d* of James Weir; one *s* two *d*. *Educ:* St Paul's School; Corpus Christi College, Oxford. Classical Scholar, 1894; 1st Class Mods, 1896; 2nd Class Lit. Hum., 1898. Ordained 1898 to Curacy of St Mary's, Plaistow; Curate of St James', Norlands, 1901–6; Vicar of West Hendred, Berks, 1906–20; Select Preacher, Oxford, 1918–20, and Cambridge, 1920; Examining Chaplain to Bishop of Oxford, 1919. *Publications:* The Eschatological Question in the Gospels, 1911; Galatians (Readers' Commentary), 1912; The Third and Fourth Books of Maccabees, 1918; Conscience, Creeds and Critics, 1918; contributor to Oxford Corpus of Apocrypha, Hastings' Dictionaries, Faith and the War, Immortality, The Spirit; articles in Nineteenth Century and theological periodicals. *Recreations:* lawn tennis, golf. *Address:* University College, Oxford; 14 Lathbury Road, Oxford.   *Died 22 July 1923.*

EMMOTT, 1st Baron, of Oldham, *cr* 1911; **Alfred Emmott,** GCMG 1914; GBE 1917; PC; *b* 1858; *e* surv. *s* of late Thomas Emmott of Brookfield, Oldham, and Anchorsholme, Poulton-le-Fylde; *m* 1887, Mary Gertrude, *d* of late John William Lees; two *d*. *Educ:* Grove House, Tottenham. BA, London. Mayor of Oldham, 1891–92. MP (L) Oldham, 1899–1911; Chairman of Ways and Means, 1906–11; Under-Secretary of State for the Colonies, 1911–14; First Commissioner of Works, 1914–15; Director of the War Trade Department, 1915–19. *Recreations:* shooting, etc. *Heir:* none. *Address:* 30 Ennismore Gardens, SW7. *T:* Kensington 1542. *Clubs:* Brooks's, Reform, Ranelagh.   *Died 13 Dec. 1926 (ext).*

EMMOTT, George Henry, MA, LLM; Queen Victoria Professor of Law, University of Liverpool, since 1896, and Dean of the Faculty of Law, since 1903; Barrister, Inner Temple; *b* 28 Sept. 1855; *e s* of late Thomas Emmott, JP, of Brookfield, Oldham and Anchorsholme, Poulton-le-Fylde; *m* 1881, Elizabeth, 4th *d* of late Joseph Bevan Braithwaite, Barrister-at-Law; three *d*. *Educ:* Owens Coll., Manchester; Trinity Hall, Cambridge (Foundation Scholar and twice Law Prizeman); 1st Class Law Tripos, 1878. Barrister-at-Law, 1879; Lecturer in Roman and English Law at the Owens Coll., Manchester, 1880–85; Associate Professor of Logic and Ethics and lecturer in Roman Law at The John Hopkins University, Baltimore, 1885–92; Hon. Sec. to the Board of University Studies, 1887–96; Prof. of Roman Law and Comparative Jurisprudence, 1892–96; lecturer on

Civil Law, Columbia University, Washington, DC, 1892–96; Secretary, Departmental Board of Law, Victoria University, 1901–3; representative of Faculty of Law on Council of University of Liverpool, 1903–5, and 1907–13. *Address:* The University, Liverpool; 10 Cook Street, Liverpool; 64 Park Road West, Birkenhead. *T:* 4866 Bank. *Died 8 March 1916.*

EMRYS-ROBERTS, Edward, MD; Professor of Pathology and Bacteriology, Welsh National School of Medicine; Hon. Pathologist and Bacteriologist to King Edward VII's Hospital, Cardiff; *b* 14 May 1878; *e s* of E. S. Roberts, Brookdale, Dawlish, Devon, and Mary, *y d* of Emrys Evans, Cotton Hall, Denbigh; *m* 1910, Rosamond, *y d* of J. Wynne Paynter, Bryntirion, Amlwch, Anglesey; three *s* two *d*. *Educ:* Liverpool College, Upper School and University of Liverpool. While a student of Medicine served with the Welsh Hospital, South African Field Force, 1900 (medal and 3 clasps); held a Research Fellowship in Pathology at the University of Liverpool, 1903–6, and was subsequently appointed Sub-Curator of the Pathological Museum; Demonstrator of Pathology, University of Bristol, and Pathologist to the Bristol General Hospital, 1908–10; OC Welsh Mobile Bact. Lab., BEF, France, 1915–18; Local Secretary of the Cambrian Archæological Association, and Local Correspondent of the Ancient Monuments Board for Wales. *Publications:* papers in medical and scientific journals. *Recreations:* ethnology, archæology, music, fishing. *Address:* Romarys, Penarth, Glamorgan. *Died 15 Jan. 1924.*

ENGELBACH, Alfred H. H., ISO 1902; *b* 1850. Clerk in the Accounts Branch, Office of Secretary of State for Colonies, 1868; First Class Assistant Clerk, 1879; Book-keeper and Senior Assistant to Financial Clerk, 1884; Accountant in Colonial Office, 1896; retired, 1915. *Address:* 36 Stockwell Park Road, SW. *Died 22 April 1928.*

ENGLEHEART, Sir John Gardner Dillman, KCB 1897 (CB 1884); Kt 1892; MA Oxon; *b* 2 Feb. 1823; *s* of J. C. D. Engleheart, Tunbridge Wells; *m* 1859, Emily (*d* 1911), *d* of Maj. J. A. Willows, ICS. *Educ:* Rugby; Christ Church, Oxford. Barrister, Lincoln's Inn, 1849; Private Sec. to Duke of Newcastle, Sec. of State for Colonies, and accompanied him in suite of Prince of Wales on visit to Canada and US, 1859–64; Comptroller of the Household of the Prince and Princess Christian, 1866–69; Clerk of the Council, Duchy of Lancaster, 1872–99; Member of the Duchy Council, 1901–12. *Address:* 28 Curzon Street, Mayfair, W1. *Club:* Athenæum. *Died 10 April 1923.*

ENNIS, John Matthew, MusDoc; Professor of Music in the University of Adelaide since 1901. *Address:* The University, Adelaide.

ENNISKILLEN, 4th Earl of, *cr* 1789; **Lowry Egerton Cole,** KP 1902; DL, JP, MFH (North Cheshire); Baron Mountflorence, 1760; Viscount Enniskillen, 1776; Baron Grinstead (UK), 1815; *b* London, 21 Dec. 1845; 2nd *s* of 3rd Earl and Jane, *o d* of J. A. Cassamajor; *S* father, 1886; *m* 1869, Charlotte, *d* of Douglas Baird, Closeburn, Dumfriesshire; three *s* two *d* (and one *s* three *d* decd). *Educ:* Eton. Formerly in Rifle Brigade; Hon. Col 3rd Batt. Royal Inniskilling Fusiliers, since 1887; MP (C) Enniskillen, 1880–85. Owner of about 30,300 acres. *Heir: s* Viscount Cole, *b* 10 Sept. 1876. *Address:* Florence Court, Enniskillen, Co. Fermanagh. *Clubs:* Turf, Orleans; Kildare Street, Dublin. *Died 28 April 1924.*

EPPSTEIN, Rev. William Charles; Rector of Lambourne, Essex, since 1916; *b* Bagdad, 8 Feb. 1864; *s* of Rev. J. M. Eppstein, missionary and British chaplain; *m d* of Rev. A. C. H. Bolton, Rector of Shimpling, Suffolk; one *s* two *d*. *Educ:* Corpus Christi College, Cambridge. MA Cambridge and DD Oxford (incorporated St John's College); Mathematical Honours, FRAS; College First Boat, Cricket XI, Football XV. Curate, St Mary's, Spital Square, 1887; Curate of Stowmarket, 1889; Assistant Master, St Lawrence's College, Ramsgate, 1892–94; Bradfield College, Berks, 1894; Headmaster of Reading School, 1894–1914; Select Preacher at Cambridge, 1922. *Publication:* Editor of Gray's Poems. *Recreation:* reading. *Address:* Lambourne Rectory, Romford. *TA:* Abridge. *T:* Loughton 345. *Died 30 Aug. 1928.*

ERNST, Harold Clarence, AM, MD; Professor of Bacteriology in Harvard University; Visiting Bacteriologist to Children's Hospital, and Chairman of the Visiting Staff; late Major, MRC, USA; in command of Laboratory of North Eastern Department; Ex-President of Boston Society of Medical Sciences; Secretary and Ex-President of American Association of Pathologists and Bacteriologists; Editor of the Journal of Medical Research, etc; *b* Cincinnati, Ohio; *s* of

Andrew H. and Sarah (Otis) Ernst; *m* Ellen Lunt Frothingham of Boston. *Educ:* private schools; Harvard University (Academic and Medical Departments); Paris and Berlin. Professor and Teacher in Harvard University; student and editor. *Publications:* many articles in medical journals; special monographs on Infectiousness of Milk, Infection and Immunity, Phagocytosis, Tuberculine; Ultra-Violet Photomicrography. *Recreations:* all outdoor sports; of late years the saddle, sailing, golf. *Address:* The Medical School of Harvard University; in summer—The Cedar-Bushes, Manomet, Plymouth Co., Mass. *T:* Jamaica 108. *Clubs:* St Botolph, Country; Harvard, Boston; Old Colony, Plymouth. *Died 7 Sept. 1922.*

ERNST, Oswald Herbert; Maj.-Gen. US Army, retired; *b* near Cincinnati, 27 June 1842; *s* of Andrew H. and Sarah Otis Ernst; *m* 1866, Elizabeth Amory Lee; two *d*. *Educ:* Harvard College; US Military Academy at West Point. Commissioned First Lieut, Corps of Engineers, 1864; served as Asst Chief Engineer, Army of the Tennessee, to close of Atlanta campaign; as astronomer with the Commission sent by US Government to Spain to observe solar eclipse of Dec. 1870; as instructor of practical military engineering and military signalling and telegraphy at US Military Academy, 1871–78; in charge of improvement of Mississippi river and other western rivers, 1878–86; also of harbour at Galveston, and other harbours on Texas coast, 1886–89; aide-de-camp to President Harrison, 1889–93; superintendent, US Military Academy, 1893–98; in command of 1st Brigade, 1st Div., 1st Corps in the war with Spain; Inspector-General of Cuba, 1898–99; member of Commission to investigate the Isthmus connecting North and South America, with a view to the construction of an inter-oceanic canal, 1899–1903; Division Engineer N West Division; 1901–5; President Mississippi River Commission, 1903–6; Member of the Isthmian Canal Commission, 1905–6; member of International Commission to investigate the condition of the waters adjacent to the boundary lines between the US and Canada, 1905–14; member of numerous Boards of Engineers, 1880–1906. *Publication:* Manual of Practical Military Engineering, 1873. *Recreations:* golf, bridge. *Address:* 1524 18th Street, Washington, DC. *Clubs:* Metropolitan, Chevy Chase, Washington. *Died 21 March 1926.*

ERRINGTON, Sir George, 1st Bt, *cr* 1885 (for services rendered at Rome); JP for Cos Longford, Tipperary and Wexford; *b* 1839; *o s* of late Michael Errington, Clintz, Yorks, and Rosanna, *d* of late Ambrose More O'Ferrall, Balyna, Co. Kildare; *m* 1892, Frances, *d* of H. R. de Ricci, and *widow* of Capt. Shuldham, Moy, Co. Longford. *Educ:* Ushaw Coll. Durham; Roman Catholic University, Ireland. MP (HR) Co. Longford, 1874–85; High Sheriff, Tipperary, 1888; Wexford, 1901. *Heir:* none. *Address:* Ramsfort, Co. Wexford. *Clubs:* Reform, Brooks's, Bachelors'; Rathcline, Hampton Court. *Died 19 March 1920 (ext).*

ERROLL, 20th Earl of, *cr* 1458; **Charles Gore Hay,** KT 1901; CB 1901; JP, DL; LLD, Aberdeen; 24th Hereditary Lord High Constable of Scotland, created 1315; Baron Hay, 1543; Baron Kilmarnock, with seat in House of Lords, 1831; *b* Kingston, Canada West, 7 Feb. 1852; *s* of 19th Earl and Eliza, *d* of Gen. Hon. Sir Charles Gore, GCB, *g d* of 2nd Earl of Arran; *S* father, 1891; *m* 1875, Mary, *d* of Edmund and Lady Harriett l'Estrange; three *s*. *Educ:* Harrow. Cornet Royal Horse Guards, 1869; Lieut-Col commanding, 1891–95; Colonel, 1895; late Brig.-Gen. on staff commanding Yeomanry Brigade, S Africa; retired, 1907; AAG Cavalry Division, SA Field Force; late Col comm. Royal Horse Guards; late ADC to Field-Marshal Lord Wolseley, Commander-in-Chief; Assistant Adjutant-General for Cavalry; Hon. Colonel 3rd Batt. Gordon Highlanders, 1892; Hon. Major-General, 1917; late Lord-in-Waiting to King Edward VII; Commanded 65th (Lowland) Division, April 1915–Feb. 1916; County Commandant for Cumberland, and member of Central Vol. Association; served on staff in France, July 15 1917–Sept. 6 1918. *Heir: s* Lord Kilmarnock, *b* 17 Oct. 1876. *Address:* 34 Sussex Gardens, W2. *T:* Paddington 3998. *Clubs:* Marlborough, Pratt's. *Died 8 July 1927.*

ERROLL, 21st Earl of, *cr* 1453; **Victor Alexander Sereld Hay,** KCMG 1924 (CMG 1919); 25th Hereditary Lord High Constable of Scotland, *cr* 1315; Baron Hay, 1543; Baron Kilmarnock, with seat in House of Lords, 1831; British High Commissioner, Inter-Allied Rhineland High Commission, since 1921; *b* 17 Oct. 1876; *o s* of 20th Earl and Mary, *d* of Edmund and Lady Harriett l'Estrange; *S* father, 1927; *m* 1900, Mary Lucy Victoria, *o d* of Sir Allan Mackenzie, 2nd Bt, of Glen Muick, Aberdeenshire; two *s* one *d*. Attaché, 1900; 3rd Secretary, 1902; 2nd Secretary, 1906; 1st Secretary, 1913; Counsellor,

1919; 1st Secretary, Copenhagen, 1918-19; Chargé d'Affaires, Berlin, on resumption of diplomatic relations with Germany, 1920, till arrival of Ambassador; subsequently Counsellor till Nov. 1921. *Publication:* Ferelith, 1903. *Plays:* The Dream Kiss, produced Wimbledon Theatre, 1924; The Anonymous Letter, produced Q Theatre, 1927. *Heir: s* Lord Kilmarnock, *b* 11 May 1901. *Address:* Inter-Allied Rhineland High Commission, Coblenz, Germany. *Club:* St James's.
Died 20 Feb. 1928.

ERSKINE, David Charles, DL, JP; *b* 1866; *s* of James Erskine of Linlathen. *Educ:* Harrow; France and Germany. Secretary to Governor-General of Canada, 1897-98; MP (L) for West Perthshire, 1906-10; Parliamentary Secretary to Secretary for Scotland, 1906-10; Chairman of the Board of the Trustees for the National Galleries of Scotland since 1908. *Address:* Linlathen, Broughty Ferry, Forfarshire; 33 Brompton Square, SW3. *Clubs:* Brooks's, Burlington Fine Arts; New, Edinburgh.
Died 26 May 1922.

ERSKINE, Sir Henry (David), KCVO 1911 (CVO 1901); JP, DL; Serjeant-at-Arms in House of Commons, 1885-1915; Gentleman Usher to the Robes, 1901-19; *b* 5 Jan. 1838; *s* of James Erskine, Cardross, and Mary, *d* of Major-General Fagan; *m* 1861, Lady Horatia Seymour, *d* of 5th Marquess of Hertford; six *s* one *d. Educ:* Harrow. Served in 30th Regiment and the Scots Fusilier Guards from 1854-61; in Crimea, 1856; became Lieut and Capt. 1859; Groom of the Robes to HM, 1870-1901. *Address:* Cardross, Port of Menteith, Perthshire, NB; 26 Burton Court, SW3.
Died 7 Sept. 1921.

ERSKINE, Colonel Thomas Harry, VD; JP, DL; served on Staff in France, 1917-18; Master of Fife Foxhounds, since 1907; *b* 12 May 1860; 2nd *s* of Sir Thomas Erskine, 2nd Bt of Cambo, Fife; *m* 1913, Kathleen, *d* of Colonel James Crosbie of Ballyheigue Castle, Co. Kerry. *Educ:* Eton. Served in Fife Light Horse, and Fife and Forfar Yeomanry from 1881; commanded the latter, 1905-11; rejoined 1914 on outbreak of war; Hon. Colonel of Fife and Forfar Yeomanry. *Recreations:* hunting, shooting. *Address:* Grangemuir, Pittenweem, Fife. *T:* Pittenweem 13. *M:* SP 401; SP 593. *Clubs:* Boodle's, Wellington; New, Edinburgh.
Died 6 May 1924.

ESCOTT, Thomas Hay Sweet, MA; *o s* of Rev. Hay Sweet-Escott; *m* 1st, 1865, Kate (*d* 1899), 2nd *d* of Colonel Charles Liardet, of the English branch of an old Austrian family ennobled under Maria Theresa for State service; 2nd, Edith, *widow* of Chas Rawnsley Hilton; one *s* one *d. Educ:* Somersetshire College (now by amalgamation with Sidney Coll. become Bath Coll.); Queen's Coll., Oxford. Lecturer in Logic, King's Coll. Strand; Dep. Prof. in Classical Literature, 1866-73; leading-article writer for the Standard since 1866; succeeded Mr John Morley as editor of the Fortnightly Review; since 1865 actively connected with London daily and weekly journalism. *Publications:* England: Its People, Polity, and Pursuits, 1879; editor of Juvenal and Persius, 1867; Politics and Letters, 1886; Lord Randolph Churchill: a Monograph, 1895; Platform, Press, Politics, and Play, 1895; Social Transformations of the Victorian Age, 1897, being a sequel to England, etc; Personal Forces of the Period, 1898; A Trip to Paradoxia, 1899; Gentlemen of the House of Commons, 1902; Sovereigns of the Nineteenth Century, 1902; King Edward VII and his Court, 1903; Society in the Country House, 1906; The Story of British Diplomacy: its Makers and Movements, 1908; Edward Bulwer: First Baron Lytton of Knebworth, 1910; Masters of English Journalism, 1911; Anthony Trollope, His Work and Originals, 1913; Club Makers and Club Members, 1914; Great Victorians, 1916; City Characters in Several Reigns, 1922; National and International Links, 1922. *Address:* 33 Sackville Road, Hove, Brighton.
Died 14 June 1924.

ESCREET, Ven. Charles Ernest; Archdeacon of Lewisham since 1906; Canon of Southwark since 1900; *b* 20 Feb. 1852; *m* 1882, Adelaide, *d* of Charles J. F. Stuart of Harrow Weald. *Educ:* Tonbridge School; Wadham College, Oxford (Smythe Exhibitioner). Ordained Asst Curate, Barham, near Canterbury, 1875; Battersea Parish Church under Canon Erskine Clarke, 1878; Vicar of St Andrew's, Stockwell, 1882-92; Rector of Woolwich, 1892-1909; Vicar of the Church of the Ascension, Blackheath, 1909-17. *Recreations:* cricket, climbing. *Address:* 96 Grove Lane, Camberwell, SE5.
Died March 1919.

ESLER, Erminda Rentoul; novelist; *b* Ireland; *d* of Rev. Alexander Rentoul, MD, DD, Manor Cunningham, Co. Donegal; *m* 1883, Robert Esler, MD, London and Marlow House, Ballymena, Ireland; two *s. Educ:* privately and at schools in Nimes and Berlin. Awarded First Honour Certificate by Royal University, Ireland, 1879.

Publications: Almost a Pauper, 1888; The Way of Transgressors, 1890; The Way they Loved at Grimpat, 1894; A Maid of The Manse, 1895; 'Mid Green Pastures, 1895; The Wardlaws, 1896; Youth at the Prow, 1898; The Awakening of Helena Thorpe, 1901; The Trackless Way, 1904. *Recreations:* walking, reading, conversation with people of individual mind. *Address:* Petherton, Bexley, Kent. *Club:* Lyceum.
Died 1924.

ESMOND, Henry Vernon; actor and dramatic author; *b* Hampton Court, 30 Nov. 1869; 4th *s* of Richard George Jack, MD; *m* 1891, Eva Moore; one *s* one *d. Educ:* by private tutors. Went on stage 1885. *Plays:* produced Rest, Bogey and The Divided Way, One Summer's Day, 1897; Grierson's Way, 1899; The Wilderness, 1901; When we were Twenty-one, 1901; The Sentimentalist; My Lady Virtue, 1902; Billy's Little Love Affair, 1903; The O'Grindles, 1907; Under the Greenwood Tree, 1907; A Young Man's Fancy, 1912; Eliza Comes to Stay, 1913; The Dangerous Age, 1914; A Kiss or Two, 1917; The Law Divine, 1918; Birds of a Feather, 1920. *Recreations:* tennis, golf, cycling. *Address:* 21 Whiteheads Grove, Chelsea, SW3. *T:* Kensington 146. *M:* A 1294. *Club:* Green Room.
Died 17 April 1922.

ESPINAS, Professor Alfred, Doyen honoraire, Docteur ès Lettres, LLD Victoria University; membre de l'Académie des Sciences Morales et Politiques; né le 23 mai 1844, à St Florentin, Yonne. *Educ:* Lycées de Sens et de Paris; Ecole Normale supérieure, 1864-67. Professeur de Philosophie aux Lycées de Bastia (Corse), de Chaumont, du Hâvre, de Dijon; Professeur de Philosophie aux Universités de Douai, Lille, et Bordeaux; Doyen de la Faculté des Lettres de Bordeaux, 1887-90; Professeur d'Histoire de l'Economie sociale (fondation de Chambrun) à la Faculté des Lettres de l'Université de Paris, 1894-1912. *Publications:* Psychologie de Spencer, traduction en collaboration avec T. Ribot, 1874; Des Sociétés animales, 1877 et 1878; La Philosophie expérimentale en Italie, 1880; République de Platon, livres VIII et VI, édition classique, 1886, avec une introduction sur la polit. Platonicienne; Histoire des Doctrines économiques, 1893; Les Origines de la Technologie, 1897; La Philosophie sociale de XVIIIe Siècle et la Révolution (étude sur la Babouvisme), 1898; dans la Revue Philosophique: Collaboration active dès la fondation; chargé pendant 4 ans de la recension des ouvrages Italiens; Le Sens de la Couleur, son origine et son développement: étude critique du livre de Grant Allen sur le même sujet, 1880; La Philosophie en Ecosse depuis le commencement du XVIIIe Siècle, 1881; Les Etudes sociologiques en France, 1882; Etre ou ne pas être, ou du postulat de la Sociologie, 1901; dans les Annales de la Faculté des Lettres de Bordeaux: Essai sur l'Esthétique de Pascal, 1881; Le Sens de l'Espace et les Canaux semi-circulaires, 1882; dans la Revue Internationale de l'Enseignement: L'"Extension" des Universités en Angleterre et aux Etats-Unis, 1892; Le "Système" de Jean-Jacques Rousseau, 1895. *Address:* 84 rue de Ranelagh, Paris.
Died Feb. 1922.

ESSEX, 7th Earl of, *cr* 1661; **George Devereux de Vere Capell,** JP; Baron Capel, 1641; Viscount Malden, 1661; *b* 24 Oct. 1857; *s* of Viscount Malden, *s* of 6th Earl and Emma, *d* of Sir Henry Meux, 1st Bt; *S* grandfather, 1892; *m* 1st, 1882, Ellen Harriet Maria (*d* 1885), *d* of W. H. Harford of Oldown House, Almondsbury; one *s;* 2nd, 1893, Adela, *d* of Beach Grant, New York; two *d.* Entered Grenadier Guards, 1877; retired 1882; served with Imperial Yeomanry in South Africa, 1900; Col Herts Imperial Yeomanry, 1901. Owner of about 15,000 acres. *Heir: s* Viscount Malden, *b* 21 Feb. 1884. *Address:* Bowdon House, Davies Street, W; Cassiobury Park, Watford. *Clubs:* Carlton, Turf.
Died 24 Sept. 1916.

ESSLEMONT, George Birnie, JP; *b* 1860; *e s* of late Peter Esslemont, DL, merchant, Aberdeen; *m* 1890, Clemantina, *d* of late Ranald Macdonald; two *s* four *d. Educ:* privately; Aberdeen Grammar School. Entered business, 1876; served on numerous local Boards, and was Senior Magistrate of the city, 1905-6; Chairman Parliamentary Committee of National Sea Fisheries Protection Association since 1910; MP (L) South Aberdeen 1907-17. *Address:* King's Acre, Aberdeen. *TA:* Esslemont, Aberdeen. *T:* 1699. *Clubs:* Reform, National Liberal; Scottish Liberal, Edinburgh.
Died 2 Oct. 1917.

ESSON, William, MA; FRS; Savilian Professor of Geometry, 1897; Deputy Savilian Professor of Geometry, Oxford, 1894-97; Fellow of New College; Fellow of Merton, 1860-97; Bursar of Merton; Curator of University Chest; *b* 1838. *Educ:* Inverness Royal Academy; Cheltenham Grammar School; St John's Coll. Oxford (Junior and Senior Mathematical Scholar, MA). *Publications:* The Laws of Connexion between the Conditions of Chemical Change and its

Amount, Transactions Royal Society, 1864, 1866, 1895; Notes on Synthetic Geometry, Proceedings of the London Mathematical Society, 1897; Variation with temperature of rate of chemical change, Transactions Royal Society, 1912; The Characters of Plane Curves, a law of connexion between two phenomena which influence each other, International Congress of Mathematicians, 1912. *Address:* Merton College, Oxford. *Died 25 Aug. 1916.*

ESTALL, Thomas, JP; late Senior General Manager, National Provincial Bank of England Ltd; Past Master of the Worshipful Company Turners; *b* 1848. *Address:* 51 Evelyn Gardens, SW7. *T:* Kens. 1380. *Clubs:* Junior Athenæum, County of London Magistrates. *Died 30 July 1920.*

ESTELL, Hon. John; *b* Minmi, NSW, 14 Oct. 1861; *s* of Robert Estell; *m* 1885, Alicia Jane Kirk; two *s*. *Educ:* Public Schools, Rydal and Bathurst. Worked as a coal miner; Minister for Labour and Industry, New South Wales, 1914–16; Minister for Works and Secretary for Railways, New South Wales, 1920–22. *Address:* Wallsend, NSW. *Died 18 Oct. 1928.*

ETCHELLS, Ernest Fiander, Hon. ARIBA, MIStructE, AMICE, AMIMechE, MMathAssoc., FInstP; FPhysS; Fellow of King's College Engineering Society; Structural Engineer in the department of the Superintending Architect of Metropolitan Buildings; *b* 1876; *o s* of Ernest Fiander Etchells, Romiley; *m* 1901, Mary, *y d* of late George Breakwell, Cleobury Mortimer. *Educ:* Old Andersonian College, Glasgow; Royal Technical College, Glasgow; University of London, King's College; University of London, University College. Pupil of Francis Lawrence Lane, Civil Engineer; afterwards Chief Assistant in the office of John Strain, Chartered Civil Engineer; engaged on the design of Rolling Stock for the Pretoria and Pietermaritzburg Railway, Aerial Ropeways for Bolivia, Nitrate Plants for Taltal Chili; was in charge of the structural steelwork for the re-constructions of Lanarkshire Steelworks; was engaged on the Clyde Valley Electric Power Scheme, and the City of Mexico Electricity Supply Scheme; engaged on structural work in all materials, including structural steelwork and reinforced concrete; from 1902 was engaged principally on the duties of an engineer and surveyor under the London Buildings Acts. President of the Concrete Institute, 1920–21, 1921–22; President of the Institution of Structural Engineers, 1922–23; President of the Société des Ingénieurs Civils de France (Section Britannique), 1926–27; President of the Association of Architects, Surveyors and Technical Assistants, 1925–26; Hon. President of the Association of Floor Constructors, 1926; Advisory Member of the Board of Architectural Education, 1922; Superintending Examiner of the Institution of Structural Engineers, 1923; Member of the Grand Committee for the International Congress on Architectural Education, 1924; Membre de la Société des Ingénieurs Civils de France; Hon. Member British Engineering Standards Association; Hon. Member Junior Institution of Engineers; Member of Council of the London Society. *Publications:* Standard Mathematical Notation; Chapters on Steelwork in Rivingtons Notes on Building Construction; Foreword on Standard Mathematical Notation for Engineering Formulae in Twelvetrees' Treatise on Reinforced Concrete, and Foreword on Standard Notation in Harrington-Hudson's Handbook on Reinforced Concrete; Foreword on Standard Notation in Travers Morgan's Tables for Reinforced Concrete; Evolution of Engineering Institutions; also papers on structural engineering in various transactions and journals; also editor of technical transactions. *Address:* Architects' Department, County Hall, Westminster Bridge, SE1. *Died 5 Jan. 1927.*

ETHE, C. Hermann, PhD, Hon. MA Oxford; *b* Stralsund, 13 Feb. 1844; *g s* of Karl Lappe. *Educ:* Stralsund Gymnasium; Greifswald and Leipsic Univs. Lecturer in Oriental Languages in the Univ. of Munich, 1867–71; called to Oxford beginning of 1872, to continue and complete Catalogue of Persian, Turkish, Hindûstâni, and Pushtû MSS in Bodleian Library, and compile supplementary Cat. of Arabic MSS; entrusted same year by Secretary for India with Cat. of Persian MSS in India Office Library; public examiner for Honours School of Oriental Studies, Oxford, 1887–89, and since 1893; Professor of German and Oriental Languages, Univ. Coll. Aberystwyth, 1875–1915. *Publications:* Catalogue of Persian, Turkish, Hindûstâni, and Pushtû MSS in the Bodleian Library, vol. i, 1889; Catalogue of the Persian MSS in the Library of the India Office, vol. i, 1903; Yûsuf and Zalîkhâ, by Firdausi of Tûs, critical edition, fasciculus primus (Anecdota Oxoniensia, Aryan Series, part vi), Oxford, 1908; numerous publications in Germany; a series of articles on Persian literature in the Encyclopædia Britannica. *Address:* 29 Royal York Crescent, Clifton, Bristol. *Died 7 June 1917.*

ETHERINGTON-SMITH, John Henry, FSA; *b* 1841; *o s* of Henry Etherington Smith of Norris Hill, Ashby de la Zouch; *m* 1873, Margaret, *d* of General Sir James Pears, KCB; one *s* three *d*. *Educ:* Repton; University College, Oxford (1st Class Moderations; 2nd Lit. Hum.; BA 1863; MA 1867). Called at the Inner Temple, 1866; Midland Circuit, 1867; Revising Barrister, 1877; Recorder of Newark, 1884–99; Derby, 1899–1918; a Governor of Repton School; Leicestershire Yeomanry, 1863–88, when retired as Major; one of the Wordsworth (Dove Cottage) Trustees; Member Royal United Service Institution and Royal Archæological Institute; Bencher of the Inner Temple, 1900. *Recreations:* travel, rowing, sketching, archæology. *Address:* East Ella, Putney, SW15; *T:* Putney 801; Butharlyp How, Grasmere. *Clubs:* New University, Leander, Skating. *Died 15 April 1923.*

ETTLES, William James M'Culloch, MD, MS; FRCSE; Ophthalmic Surgeon; *b* Brighton, 16 Feb. 1869; *m* Helen Edith, *d* of John Sell Cotman, MRCP; two *s*. *Educ:* Aberdeen, Edinburgh, and Paris Universities. Highest Academical Honours; MD degree, 1896. Late President Optical Society of London; Treasurer (late President) Hunterian Society; Consulting Oculist to the Eastern Public Dispensary and London Spectacle Mission; Foreign Member of the Spanish Red Cross; Knight Hospitaller of the Order of St John the Baptist of Spain; Honorary Fellow and Medallist (1st Class) Italian Physical Academy; Member of the Court of Assistants of the Worshipful Company of Gold and Silver Wyre Drawers; Liveryman of the Worshipful Company of Spectaclemakers; Vice-President and Hon. Medical Officer, London Morayshire Club; late Pathologist, Royal Eye Hospital; Consulting Oculist, Shipping Federation Recuperative Hostels for Sailors and Soldiers, etc. Lecturer on Physiology of Vision, Northampton Institute and Society of Illuminating Engineers; Vice-President of the Institute of Ophthalmic Opticians; silver medal (Paris, 1900); gold medal (London, 1903) for ambulance work; Special Lecturer, London College of Ambulance. *Publications:* Hunterian Oration, 1907; numerous articles on diseases of eye in various medical journals. *Recreations:* cruising (Rear-Commodore, Chichester Harbour Yacht Club), wild-fowling (National Wild-fowling Association), astronomy, violoncello. *Address:* 114A Harley Street, W. *T:* 3245 Mayfair; The Ingle Nook, West Wittering, Sussex. *M:* BP 2713. *Club:* Junior Constitutional. *Died 9 July 1918.*

EUCKEN, Rudolf; *b* Aurich, Ostfriesland, 5 Jan. 1846. *Educ:* Göttingen (DrPhil.); Berlin. War einige Jahre Lehrer an gelehrten Schulen, wurde 1871 Professor der Philosophie in Basel und wirkt seit 1874 als solcher in Jena, seit 1920 im Ruhestand; seine Schriften waren zuerst mehr der Geschichte der Philosophie zugewandt, später überwiegend der systematischen Philosophie; er sucht einen neuen Idealismus zu begründen, der bei voller Anerkennung der Tatsachen und Aufgaben der Gegenwart die Überlegenheit des Geisteslebens behauptet und im besonderen den Konflikt zwischen Religion und moderner Kultur überwinden möchte; 1903 wurde er von der Universität Giessen, und 1910 von der Universität Glasgow zum DD ernannt; seit 1908 ist er auswärtiges Mitglied der Königl. Schwedischen Akademie der Wissenschaften, seit 1911 der Finnländischen Societät der Wissenschaften; 1913 wurde er Dr of Letters (Columbia University), Dr of Humane Letters (Syracuse University), LLD (New York University); 1914 auswärtiges Mitglied der Accademia dei Lincei (Rom); Senator der Deutschen Academie (München); Nobel Prize for Literature, 1908. *Publications:* Grundbegriffe der Gegenwart, 1878; (später Geistige Strömungen), 6th edn, 1920; Die Einheit des Geisteslebens, 1888, 2nd edn, 1925; Die Lebensanschauungen der grossen Denker, 1890, 18th edn, 1922; Der Kampf um einen geistigen Lebensinhalt, 5th edn, 1925; Der Wahrheitsgehalt der Religion, 1901, 4th edn, 1920; Grundlinien einer neuen Lebensan-schauung, 1907, 2nd edn, 1913; Hauptprobleme der Religionsphilosophie der Gegenwart, 1907, 4th and 5th edns, 1912; Der Sinn und Wert des Lebens, 1908, 9th edn, 1923; Einführung in die Hauptfragen der Philosophie, 1908, 4th edn, 1925; Können wir noch Christen sein?, 1912; Erkennen und Leben, 1911, 2nd edn, 1923; Zur Sammlung der Geister, 1913; Present-day Ethics, 1913; Mensch und Welt, 1918, 3rd edn, 1923; der Sozialismus und seine Lebensgestaltung, 1920, 2nd edn, 1926; Lebenserinnerungen, 1920, 2nd edn, 1922; das Lebensproblem in China und in Europa, 1921; Der Kampf um die Religion in der Gegenwart, 1923, 4 edn; Ethik als Grundlage des Staatsbürglichen Lebens, 1924. *Address:* Jena, Botzstr. 5. *Died 14 Sept. 1926.*

EUGENIE, Empress, (Marie Eugénie de Guzman y de Porto-Carrero, Condesa de Teba, Marquesa de Moya); *b* Granada, 5 May 1826; *d* of Cyprien, conde Montijo, duque de Penerauda, and Marie Manuela Kirkpatrick of Closeburn, Scotland; *m* at Paris, 29

January 1853, Napoleon III, Emperor of the French; one *s* decd. *Address:* Farnborough Hill, Farnborough, Hants.

Died 11 July 1920.

EUSTACE, Maj.-Gen. Sir Francis John William, KCB 1913 (CB 1900); *b* 17 Sept. 1849; *s* of late A. T. Eustace-Malpas of Rochestown, Co. Dublin; *m* 1882, Marina, 2nd *d* of late Field Marshal Sir Donald Stewart, 1st Bt, GCB; one *s. Educ:* Somersetshire College, Bath; RM Academy, Woolwich. Joined RA 1870; Captain 1880; Major 1885; Lieut-Col 1896; Col 1900; Maj.-Gen. 1904; was present in the autumn of 1877 at the Schipka Pass and passage of the Balkans during the Russo-Turkish war, and received the Turkish war medal from the Sultan of Turkey for Red Cross services; served throughout the Afghan war, 1878–80 (medal); Boer war, as AAG for RHA on the staff of Lieut-Gen. Sir J. P. French, KCB, Nov. 1899–Nov. 1900 (medal with six clasps, despatches several times, CB); was ADC to Sir D. M. Stewart, Commander-in-Chief in India, 1882–83; commanded RHA Aldershot, 1896–99; Commandant, School of Gunnery for Royal Horse and Field Artillery, 1901–4; Major General on Staff commanding RA, Aldershot, 1904–7; retired; Colonel Commandant Royal Artillery, 1919. *Address:* Doric House, Bath. *T:* Bath 854.   *Died 7 Dec. 1925.*

EUSTACE, Lieut-Col Henry Montague, DSO 1900; JP Co. Wexford; late Middlesex Regiment; *b* 28 Nov. 1863; *e* surv. *s* of late Rev. R. H. Eustace of Sampford Grange, Essex; *m* 1903, Monica Alice, *d* of Col John Thomas Eustace, Bronwylfa, S Africa; two *s* one *d. Educ:* Harrow. Entered army, 1885; Captain, 1893; Major, 1902; served South Africa, 1899–1903 (despatches, Queen's medal six clasps, King's medal two clasps; DSO); European War, 1915; commanded 6th Batt. York and Lancaster Regt in Dardanelles (very severely wounded, despatches). *Address:* Vellore, St Marychurch, Torquay. *Club:* Torquay Yacht.   *Died 27 Feb. 1926.*

EVAN-JONES, Rev. Canon Richard, MA; Vicar of Llanllwchaiarn, since 1884; Rural Dean of Cedewain, 1901; Precentor and Prebendary of Vaenol in St Asaph Cathedral, 1916; *b* Lynesack Vicarage, Durham, Nov. 1849; *e s* of late Reverend J. Evan-Jones; *m* Hannah Rose, 2nd *d* of late Edward Evans, Bronwylfa, Wrexham; one *s. Educ:* Ruthin School; Merton Coll. Oxford. Deacon, 1873; Priest, 1874; Curate of Pont Bleiddyn, near Mold, 1873–76; Llanrhaiadr, near Denbigh, 1876–77; Gresford, near Wrexham, 1877–84; Member of the Governing Body of the Church in Wales. *Publication:* A Few Plain Words to Working Men on Holy Communion, 1887. *Recreation:* walking. *Address:* Llanllwchaiarn Vicarage, Newtown, North Wales.

Died 30 Sept. 1925.

EVAN-THOMAS, Admiral Sir Hugh, GCB 1924 (KCB 1916; CB 1916); KCMG 1919; MVO 1906; LLD; *b* 27 Oct. 1862; *s* of late Charles Evan-Thomas of Gnoll, Glamorganshire; *m* 1894, Hilda, *d* of late Thomas Barnard. Entered Navy, 1875; Commander 1896; Captain 1902; Rear-Admiral 1912; Rear-Adm. First Battle Squadron, 1913–14; commanded Fifth Battle Squadron, battle of Jutland Bank, 1916 (despatches, CB and KCB); Vice-Adm. 1917; Admiral, 1920; Commander-in-Chief the Nore, 1921–24; retired list, 1924. Commander Legion of Honour; Croix de Guerre with palms, Rising Sun, Japan, Order Crown of Italy, St Annes, Russia. *Address:* Charlton House, Shaftesbury. *Club:* Travellers'.

Died 30 Aug. 1928.

EVANS, Rev. Arthur Robertson, MA; Hon. Canon of Ely, 1881. *Educ:* Oriel College, Oxford; Cuddesdon College. Curate of Clifton-Hampden, 1865–67; Kempsford, 1867–68; Leeds, 1868–73; Rector of Newton-in-the-Isle, 1885–1907; Domestic Chaplain to Bishop Woodford (Ely), 1874–85; Chaplain to Bishop Compton (Ely), 1886–1905. *Address:* St Mary Street, Ely.

Died 20 Dec. 1923.

EVANS, Bernard Walter, RI 1887; RBA 1880; landscape painter; *b* Birmingham, 26 Dec. 1843; 2nd *s* of late Walter Evans, who was associated with Pugin in the revival of mediæval architecture; a cousin of George Eliot; *m* 1870, Marian (*d* 1902), *d* of late Samuel Hollyer. Studied painting from 7 years of age under Samuel Lines of Birmingham; studied under late Edward Watson, 1865; came to London at the age of 21; exhibited regularly at Royal Academy from 1870 until his election to Royal Institute of Painters in Water Colours; selected to represent English art in the Paris Exhibition; also St Louis, 1903–4; originated City of London Society of Artists; has pictures in the permanent collection at South Kensington, the Sydney Art Gallery, and the Melbourne Art Gallery; also in Cartwright Hall, Bradford. *Recreation:* smoking. *Club:* Savage.

Died 26 Feb. 1922.

EVANS, Captain Bertram Sutton, MVO 1910; RN; *b* 1872; *s* of Rev. H. J. Evans; *m* 1902. Entered Navy, 1886; Commander 1905; Captain 1913; commanded armed cruiser Macedonia in action of Falkland Islands, 1914 (despatches). *Address:* Little Orchard, St Helen's, Isle of Wight.   *Died 2 March 1919.*

EVANS, Charles Barnard, CMG 1914; Commissioner for Railways, Queensland. *Address:* Dept of Railways, Brisbane.

Died 31 Dec. 1920.

EVANS, Sir David William, Kt 1925; Director and Legal Adviser to the King Edward VII Welsh National Memorial Association since 1913; *b* 4 Nov. 1866; *s* of late Rees Jones, JP, Porthkerry, Glam; two *s* two *d. Educ:* Llandovery School; Jesus College, Oxford. Solicitor; interested in all things pertaining to Wales, particularly matters of health, education, and music; member of the Council of the Cardiff Royal Infirmary, the Prince of Wales' Hospital, the Nursing Association, the National Eisteddfod Association, the National Council of Music, the Ministry of Health Consultative Council (Wales). *Publications:* Reports of the Memorial Association. *Recreations:* golf, formerly Rugby football; Oxford, 1886–87–88; Welsh International, 1889–90–91. *Address:* 199 Newport Road, Cardiff. *TA:* Memorial, Cardiff. *T:* Cardiff 4728 and 32. *Club:* Cardiff and County, Cardiff.

Died 17 March 1926.

EVANS, Sir Edward, Kt 1906; JP; *b* 26 June 1846; 3rd *s* of late Edward Evans, DL, JP, of Bronwylfa, Denbighshire; *m* 1869, Martha, *d* of W. Nevett of Marton, Salop; two *s* three *d. Educ:* Wallace Hall, Dumfriesshire; privately. Chm., Nat. Liberal Fedn, 1894. *Recreation:* golf. *Address:* Spital Old Hall, Bromborough, Cheshire. *T:* 20 Bromborough. *Clubs:* Reform, National Liberal; Liverpool Reform; Glasgow Liberal.   *Died 10 Oct. 1917.*

EVANS, Col Edward Stokes, CB 1900; commanded Royal Munster Fusiliers; retired; *b* 31 July 1855; *s* of late W. Evans, MD; unmarried. The Royal Munster Fusiliers; served South Africa, 1899–1900 (despatches, Queen's medal with clasp, CB). *Address:* Brancaston, King's Lynn.   *Died 27 Aug. 1926.*

EVANS, Sir Edwin, Kt 1927; JP; Fellow of the Auctioneers and Estate Agents Institute; *s* of late John Evans, London; *m* 1880, Elizabeth, *d* of late John Perry, South Street, Manchester Square; three *s. Educ:* various schools. Travelled in South Africa, 1874–76; articled to a local surveyor, 1877; started in business and founded the present firm of Edwin Evans & Sons of Lavender Hill, Clapham Junction, Auctioneers, Surveyors and Land Agents, 1880; member of the London County Council for twelve years, first Wandsworth, later South Battersea; for some time Vice-Chairman of the Housing of the Working Classes Committee; a Director of Arding & Hobbs (Ltd), Clapham Junction; Chairman of the Housing and Land Development Corporation; Director of several building societies. *Recreations:* motoring, work. *Address:* 9 Ashley Gardens, Westminster, SW1. *T:* Victoria 3884. *Club:* Constitutional.

Died 4 April 1928.

EVANS, Evan William, JP Merionethshire; *b* 7 Dec 1860; *s* of David and Jane Evans, Cae Einion, Dolgelley; *m* 1888, *o* of Joseph Roberts, Dolgelley; two *s. Educ:* Dolgelley Grammar School. Editor of the Goleuad, 1879–1914; of the Cymro (Welshman) since 1914; publisher of the Lladmerydd, Gymraes, &c. *Publications:* Travels in the East; With Dr Parker in Switzerland; Egypt; numerous articles on travels through Egypt, Palestine, and Germany. *Recreation:* motoring. *Address:* Frondirion, Dolgelley. *T:* Dolgelley 23; Isfryn, Fairbourne. *T:* Fairbourne 2. *TA:* Cymro, Dolgelley; Cymro, Fairbourne. *M:* HF 103.   *Died 28 Oct. 1925.*

EVANS, Rev. Frederic Rawlins, MA; Rector of Bedworth since 1876; Hon. Canon of Worcester since 1905; *b* 1 June 1842; *s* of Isaac P. Evans, of Griff, Nuneaton, who was brother of George Eliot; *m* 1888, Charlotte, *d* of John Rotherham, Coventry; one *d. Educ:* Rugby; Exeter College, Oxford. Curate, Hagley, Worcestershire, 1866–68; St George's, Kidderminster, 1868–72; Vicar, St George's, Kidderminster, 1872–76; Rural Dean of Monks Kirby, 1886–1924. *Publications:* single sermons. *Recreations:* Oxford University Eleven, 1863–4–5; Gents *v* Players, 1865. *Address:* Bedworth Rectory, Nuneaton. *TA:* Rector, Bedworth. *T:* Bedworth, S Midland 7. *M:* DU 5335.   *Died 4 March 1927.*

EVANS, Rev. Henry, DD; MRIA; Commissioner of National Education in Ireland, 1890–1921, retired; Member of the Board of Technical Instruction. Was Examiner for Board of Intermediate

Education for many years; was Departmental Commissioner of Income Tax for National Board; represented the Commissioners of National Education at International Congresses connected with Education; was Representative of Board of National Education at the British Association, Dublin, 1908, and was Vice-President of Education Section; was a Member of the Royal Commission on Manual and Practical Instruction, 1897; Member of Advisory Committee of Standard Dictionary. *Publications:* articles in quarterly reviews, magazines, weeklies, etc; editions of books for primary and secondary schools. Wrote the articles on The English Versions of the Bible; on Archaic, Obsolete, and Obscure Words in English Bible; and on Biblical Antiquities, Customs, etc, in Aids to Biblical Study for Students. *Address:* St Helens, Blackrock, Co. Dublin. *T:* Blackrock, Dublin, 242. *Died 2 Sept. 1924.*

EVANS, General Sir Horace Moule, KCB 1911 (CB 1894); Hon. Colonel 2nd Battalion 8th Ghurkha Rifles, Indian Army; *b* 8 Dec. 1841; *m* 1866, Elizabeth Anne, *d* of late Surg.-Gen. J. T. Tresidder, IMS; *five s three d*. Served in Dufla expedition, 1874–75 (despatches); Naga expedition, 1879–80 (despatches, medal with clasp, brevet Lt-Col); Manipore operations, 1891 (despatches, clasp). *Address:* Edgecombe, Steyning, Sussex.

Died 28 July 1923.

EVANS, Maj.-Gen. Leopold Exxel; Bengal Infantry; *b* 13 March 1837; *m* Mary, *d* of F. C. Armstrong, Penged Hill, Carmarthenshire. Entered army, 1856; Maj.-Gen. 1891; retired, 1893; served Indian Mutiny, 1857–59 (medal). *Died 8 Oct. 1916.*

EVANS, Maurice Smethurst, CMG 1902; JP; *b* 30 July 1854; *s* of Edward Huddlestone Evans, Manchester; *m* 1886, Elizabeth Fairweather Murray, Edinburgh. Went to Natal, 1875; Member Legislative Assembly, 1897. *Publications:* Black and White in South-East Africa; The Native Problem in Natal; Problem of Production in Natal; Studies in the Southern States from a South African Point of View. *Address:* Hillcrest, Ridge Road, Durban, Natal. *Club:* Durban. *Died 8 April 1920.*

EVANS, Richardson; *b* Cork, 5 April 1846; *s* of late William Evans; *m* 1879, Amy Laura, *d* of late John Frederick Feeney, Edgbaston, Birmingham; *one s five d*. *Educ:* Queen's Coll. Cork; Wadham College, Oxford. MA Royal University of Ireland; Barrister, Middle Temple; Member of Civil Service of India (NWP), 1867–76; leader-writer Pall Mall Gazette and St James's Gazette during the editorship of Mr Frederick Greenwood; leader-writer Standard, 1881–1906; interested in preserving scenery from disfigurement; for many years a Conservator of Wimbledon Common; Chairman of Committee of the Scapa Society; Founder of the John Evelyn Club for Wimbledon; Hon. Sec. of Wimbledon and Putney Commons Extension Fund, 1905–21, and of the Memorial Garden Fund; Hon. Secretary and Treasurer of Wimbledon and Merton Belgian Refugees' Fund, Sept. 1914–18; Hon. Burgess of the Borough of Wimbledon; First Hon. Freeman of the Borough of Wimbledon. *Publications:* The Age of Disfigurement, 1893; (with Mrs Richmond Ritchie) Lord Amherst (Rulers of India Series), 1894; A Beautiful World, Nos i–xi, 1893–1909; Ireland in the Realm: Ulster in Ireland, 1917; Conditions of Social Well-being considered in the Light of the War, 1918; An Account of the Scapa Society, 1925. *Address:* Holly House, Dorking. *Club:* Savile. *Died 10 May 1928.*

EVANS, Rt. Hon. Sir Samuel Thomas, GCB 1916; Kt 1908; PC 1910; KC; President Probate, Divorce and Admiralty Courts since 1910; President of the British Prize Court since the outbreak of the War; *b* 4 May 1859; *s* of John Evans, Skewen, Neath; *m* 1st, 1887, Rachel (*d* 1889), *d* of William Thomas of Skewen; 2nd, 1905, Blanche, *y d* of late Charles Rule, Cincinnati, USA; *one s one d*. *Educ:* University Coll., Aberystwyth; Univ. of London. JP Glamorganshire, Pembrokeshire, and Breconshire; Hon. Freeman of County Borough of Swansea, and of Borough of Neath; Hon. Fellow of Jesus Coll., Oxford; Hon. LLD Univ. of Wales. Barrister, Middle Temple; the last QC appointed, 1901; Bencher and Trustee of the Middle Temple, 1908; Recorder of Swansea, 1906–8; Solicitor-General, 1908–10; MP (L) Glamorganshire (Mid Div.) 1890–1910. *Address:* 11 Lancaster Gate, W; 9 Sussex Square, Brighton. *Clubs:* Athenæum, United Service, Reform, Garrick. *Died 13 Sept. 1918.*

EVANS, Very Rev. Thomas Frye Lewis, MA, DD, DCL; Dean of Montreal since 1902; Rector of St Stephen's Church since 1874; *b* St John's Rectory, Simcoe, Ontario, 17 Dec. 1845; *s* of Rev. Francis Evans, DCL, Rector of Woodhouse, and Maria Sophia Lewis; *m* 1st, 1874, Maria Stuart (*d* 1903), *e d* of Strachan Bethune, KC, Chancellor of the Diocese of Montreal; 2nd 1908, Emily Elizabeth, *d* of late Robert H. Bethune of Toronto. *Educ:* Upper Canada College, and Trinity University, Toronto. 4th Foundation Scholarship, 1863; BA 1866; MA 1871; Hon. DCL 1894; DD 1902; DD jure dignitatis, Bishop's College, Lennoxville, 1902. Deacon, 1869; Priest, 1870 (Huron); Missionary at Norwich, Ontario, 1869–71; Assistant, Christ Church Cathedral, 1871–74; Hon. Canon, Christ Church Cathedral, 1874; Archdeacon of Iberville, 1882; Archdeacon of Montreal, 1886. *Address:* 1 Weredale Park, Westmount, Province of Quebec.

Died Oct. 1920.

EVANS, Rev. Thomas Jones, MA; Vicar of St John Baptist, Knutsford, since 1916; Rural Dean of Bowdon, 1917; *b* April 1856; *s* of late Rev. David Evans, Rector of Llansantffraid, GD, Merionethshire; *two s one d*. *Educ:* Ruthin School; Jesus College, Oxford (Scholar). Powis Scholar; 2nd Class Honours in Classical Moderations; 3rd Class Lit. Hum. Deacon, 1880; Priest, 1881; Assistant Master King's School, Chester, 1880–84; Curate of Eccleston, Chester, 1882–87; Vicar of Hargrave, Chester, 1887–96; Tarvin, 1896–1904; Rock Ferry, 1904–16; Co-opted Member of Cheshire County Education Committee, 1903; Hon. Canon of Chester, 1914; Member of Sub-Committee for Higher, Elementary, and Agricultural Education; Member of Bucklow Union Board of Guardians, etc. *Recreations:* bee-keeping; lecturer on Apiculture to County Education Committee, etc; Chairman of Cheshire Beekeepers' Association. *Address:* The Vicarage, Knutsford, Cheshire.

Died 25 Oct. 1921.

EVANS, Maj.-Gen. Thomas Julian Penrhys, CB 1903; RMLI; retired; *b* 21 Dec. 1854; *s* of late Col H. W. Evans; *m* 1891, Florence Albina, *o d* of Col H. G. Rogers; *one d*. *Educ:* Tonbridge School. Entered army, 1873; Captain, 1884; Major, 1891; Lieut-Col 1898; Colonel, 1902. Served South Africa (Queen's medal and clasp, despatches); European War, Dec. 1914–19 (despatches). *Club:* Junior United Service. *Died 20 May 1921.*

EVANS, Walter Jenkin, JP; MA; Principal, Presbyterian College, Carmarthen, since 1888; *b* 1 April 1856; *e s* of Rev. Titus Evans, Carmarthen, and Rachel, *d* of Rev. John Jeremy of Lampeter, Cardigan; *m* 1888, Annie Wright, *o c* of S. S. Curtis of Upper Clapton and Leadenhall St, EC; *one s two d*. *Educ:* Grammar School and Presbyterian College, Carmarthen; Jesus College, Oxford (Scholar); MA 1880; 2nd class Honours in Classical Moderations, 1875. Assistant-master in Stirlingshire, 1877–78; Brighton, 1879–88; London, 1883–84; Classical Professor at Presbyterian College, Carmarthen, since 1884; Chairman of Carmarthen School Board, 1892–98; President of Carmarthen Literary and Scientific Institute, 1893–96; Chairman of Carmarthen County Governing Body, 1897–1900; President of Carmarthen Liberal Association, 1896–1904; Governor of Bristol, Cardiff and Aberystwyth University Colleges, and in the last (until 1922) Member of Council; Member of Court of University of Wales and formerly of Executive Committee; President of the Theological Board, University of Wales, 1915–19; Dean of Divinity in the University of Wales, 1910–13. *Publications:* Allitteratio Latina, 1921; articles and addresses, chiefly on educational subjects. *Address:* Green Hill, Carmarthen. *TA:* Principal Evans, Carmarthen.

Died 10 Feb. 1927.

EVANS, His Honour Judge William, BA Oxon; Judge of County Courts, Mid Wales, since 1897; *b* Merthyr Tydfil, 27 Dec. 1847; 3rd *s* of the late James Evans and Mary his wife; *m* 1897, Frances Louisa, *o d* of late George Cheatle, 117 Harley Street, W. *Educ:* Jesus College, Oxford. Honours in Classics and Law, Oxford. Inner Temple, 1870; and the South Wales and Chester Circuit, 1874; Assistant Revising Barrister, 1890; went on Commissions to France and Spain, 1879; Australia, 1893; and Griqualand, S Africa, 1894; Deputy County Court Judge, 1895. *Publications:* The Law of Principal and Agent; The Remuneration of Commission Agents; A Fair Reward; Cæsar Borgia and other Poems; Ballads of Wales. *Recreation:* gardening. *Address:* 2 Cambridge Terrace, Hyde Park, W; Ilmington Manor, near Shipston-on-Stour. *Club:* Reform.

Died 15 Feb. 1918.

EVANS, William, CB 1908; *b* 1841; 2nd *s* of Daniel Evans, schoolmaster at Dolgelly and Holyhead; *m* 1st, 1872, Margaret Jane (*d* 1878), *o sister* of J. Kerfoot Evans, JP, Greenfield, Flintshire; 2nd 1881, Caroline, *e d* of Charles Hughes, JP, of Wrexham; *two s one d*. Bank Manager at Holywell and Chester, 1870–84; Official Receiver in Bankruptcy for Chester and North Wales District, 1884–89; First Inspector of Official Receivers for England and Wales, Board of Trade, 1889–1905; Inspector-General, 1906–7. *Address:* 14 Meadway, Golders Green, NW4. *T:* Finchley 1862. *Club:* National Liberal.

Died 7 Dec. 1919.

EVATT, Maj.-Gen. Sir George (Joseph Hamilton), KCB 1919 (CB 1903); MD; RAMC; retired; Member Council British Medical Association, 1904; *b* 11 Nov. 1843; *s* of Capt. George Evatt, 70th Foot; *m* 1877, Sophie Mary Frances, *d* of William Walter Raleigh Kerr, Treasurer of Mauritius, and *g d* of Lord Robert Kerr; one *d*. *Educ*: Royal Coll. of Surgeons, and Trinity Coll. Dublin. Entered Army Medical Service, 1865; joined 25th (KOSB) Regt 1866; Surg.-Maj. 1877; Lt-Col RAMC 1885; Col 1896; Surg.-Gen. 1899; served Perak Expedition with Sir H. Ross's Bengal Column, 1876 (medal and clasp); Afghan War, 1878–80; capture of Ali Musjid (despatches); action in Bazaar Valley, with Gen. Tytler's Column (despatches); advance on Gundamak, and return in "Death March", 1879 (specially thanked in General Orders by Viceroy of India in Council and Commander-in-Chief in India for services); commanded Field Hospital in second campaign, including advance to relief of Cabul under General Sir Charles Gough, 1879; action on the Ghuzni Road; return to India, 1880 (medal and two clasps); Suakin Expedition, 1885, including actions at Handoub, Tamai and removal of wounded from MacNeill's Zareba (despatches, medal and clasp, Khedive's Star); Zhob Valley Expedition, 1890; commanded a Field Hospital (despatches); Medical Officer, Royal Military Academy, Woolwich, 1880–96; Senior Medical Officer, Quetta Garrison, Baluchistan, 1887–91; Sanitary Officer, Woolwich Garrison, 1892–94; Sec. Royal Victoria Hospital, Netley, 1894–96; PMO China, 1896–99; PMO Western District, 1899–1902; Surg.-Gen. 2nd Army Corps, Salisbury, 1902–8; raised with Sir James Cantlie RAMC Volunteers, 1883; founded 1884, Medical Officers of Schools Assoc. London; and 1886, drew up scheme for Army Nursing Service Reserve; Member Committee International Health Exhibition, 1884: Vice-President, British Medical Temperance Association; Member of Council Royal Army Temperance Association, 1903; President Poor Law Medical Officers' Association; President Travelling Medical Board, Western Command, 1915–16; contested (L) Woolwich, 1886, Fareham Division, Hampshire, 1906, and Brighton, 1910); Hon. Col Home Counties Division, RAMC, Territorial Force, 1908; received Distinguished Service Reward, 1910. *Publications*: Travels in the Euphrates Valley and Mesopotamia, 1873; and many publications on military and medical subjects. *Address*: 33 Earl's Court Square, SW5; Wayside, Camberley, Surrey. *Club*: Junior United Service.

Died 5 Nov. 1921.

EVE, Sir Frederic Samuel, Kt 1911; FRCS; Consulting Surgeon to London Hospital and to Evelina Hospital; Member of Council and Vice-President, 1913, Royal College of Surgeons; Lt-Col RAMC (Temp); Consulting Surgeon to the Eastern Command; *s* of late Wm Eve, N Ockendon, Essex; *m* 1889, Ella, *d* of Hon. H. E. Cox, Claremont, Jamaica; one *s* one *d*. *Educ*: St Bartholomew's Hospital; Leipsic. Pathological Curator at Royal College of Surgeons, England, 1881–90; Erasmus Wilson Lecturer (on Pathology of Tumours), RCS, 1882–84; late member of Court of Examiners, Royal College of Surgeons. *Publications*: Monographs on Surgery of Abdomen and Pathological Anatomy. *Address*: 61 Harley Street, W. *TA*: Event, Westdo, London. *T*: Paddington 183. *Club*: Arts.

Died 15 Dec. 1916.

EVELYN, John Harcourt Chichester, JP; *b* 11 August 1876; *o s* of late W. J. Evelyn and Frances Harriet, *e d* of Rev. G. V. Chichester; *m* 1902, Frances Edith, *d* of late Gen. and Hon. Mrs Ives of Moynes Park; two *s* one *d*. *Educ*: Eton; Christ Church, Oxford. *Address*: Wotton House, Dorking. *Clubs*: Arthur's, Carlton.

Died 2 Jan. 1922.

EVEN, Col George Eusebe, CB 1909; late 127th Queen Mary's Own Baluch LI; *b* 12 Aug. 1855; *s* of late Count Rene Even de la Tremblais, Cholet, Brittany; *m* 1885, Susan Ellen, *d* of late Colonel Southey, Madras SC; two *d*. *Educ*: Cheltenham College. Entered army, 1874; Capt. ISC 1886; Major 1895; Lt Col, Indian Army, 1901; Bt-Col 1904; Adjutant, GIP Railway Volunteers, 1883–87; served Afghan War, 1879–80 (medal); Chin-Lushai Expedition, 1889–90 (medal with clasp); operations in Mekran, 1898 (despatches); Indian Army, retired; served European War (England, Egypt, France), 1914–19. *Address*: c/o Thos Cook & Son, Ludgate Circus, EC. *Club*: Junior Army and Navy.

Died 29 June 1924.

EVERARD, Captain Andrew Robert Guy, JP; late 54th Regiment; *b* 1830; *s* of late R. G. Evered, High Sheriff and DL for Somerset; assumed original spelling of his surname, 1904; *m* 1865, Louisa Emily, *d* of Rev. H. Townend; one *s* four *d*. *Educ*: Eton. Lord of the manors of Otterhampton, Exton, and patron of the living of Otterhampton, Somerset. *Address*: Hill House, near Bridgwater; Stone Lodge, Exton, Dulverton.

Died June 1925.

EVERETT, Colonel Edward, CB 1907; DSO 1886; late Cameron Highlanders; *b* 4 June 1837. *Educ*: Marlborough. Entered army, 1855; Colonel, 1899; served Indian Mutiny, 1858–59 (despatches, medal with clasp); Nile Expedition, 1884–85 (despatches, Brevet Lieut-Col, medal with clasp, Khedive's star); Soudan, 1885–86 (despatches, 3rd class Madjidie, DSO).

Died 2 April 1920.

EVERETT, Robert Lacey, JP Suffolk; retired yeoman farmer; *b* 1833; *s* of Joseph David and Elizabeth Everett of Rushmere, Ipswich; *m* 1863, Elizabeth, *d* of O. Nussey, JP of Leeds; four *s* four *d*. *Educ*: private school, Ipswich. Hon. Sec. Ipswich Farmers' Club and E Suffolk Chamber of Agriculture; member of Ipswich School Board from commencement, and Town Council nine years; Alderman E Suffolk County Council from commencement; former candidate for E Suffolk, 1880; MP (L) Woodbridge Division, E Suffolk, 1885–86, 1892–95, 1906–1910; then retired. *Publications*: prize essay on Repeal of the Malt Tax; special report on Cause of Agricultural Depression, written for Royal Commission which sat 1895–97; prize essay on the Silver Question for Bimetallic League. *Address*: Rushmere, Ipswich.

Died 21 Oct. 1916.

EVERINGHAM, Ven. William, BD; Archdeacon of Suffolk since 1917; Diocesan Missioner; late Hon. Canon of Bristol Cathedral; Examining Chaplain to the Bishop; *b* 1856; *m* 1896, Clara Isabella, *sister* of Sir Edward Robert Pearce Edgcumbe. *Educ*: Lincoln Theological College (1st class Camb. Prelim. Theo. Exam). Ordained Deacon, 1879; Priest, 1880; Curate of Beeston and Diss, Norfolk; Chaplain to the Forces at Singapore, 1881; Acting Col Chaplain of Hong Kong, 1884; Col Chaplain of Malacca for five years; Missioner of the Society of St Andrew, Salisbury, 1890–96; commissioned by Archbishop Benson to visit the Armenian Church in Asia Minor, 1892; Special Missioner for Diocese of Salisbury, 1897–1900; Vice-President CETS. *Publications*: pamphlet on Parochial Missions; series of five mission tracts. *Recreations*: travel, sketching, gardening. *Address*: Waveney House, Henley Road, Ipswich.

Died 14 Sept. 1919.

EVERSHED, Arthur, Hon. RE; MRCP London; MRCS and LSA; Physician (retired); *b* Billingshurst, Sussex, 1836; 4th *s* of Peter Evershed, a country doctor; *m* 1864, Mary Hester Field (a direct lineal descendant of Oliver Cromwell); four *s* three *d*. *Educ*: private school; Alfred Clint's Studio and Leigh's School of Art; Guy's Hospital. Studied Art, 1852–59; exhibited at RA 1857; subsequently exhibited several works in oil, water colour and etching; commenced the regular study of medicine, 1859; qualified, 1863; for ten years was in general practice at Ampthill, Beds; subsequently qualified as a physician, and spent twenty years at Hampstead; Senior Physician, Mount Vernon Hospital; Physician to the Artists' Fund; Consulting Medical Adviser to North London Railway; his health failing, retired from practice, 1894, and lived in the country; subsequently spent two years in Italy, where he did several etchings. *Publications*: An Etcher's Rambles—The Thames, 1879–81; contributions on Medicine, Art, and various subjects to daily and other periodicals. *Recreations*: the observation of Nature, and study of Shakespeare. *Address*: Eversfield, Fishbourne, Chichester.

Died 17 Nov. 1919.

EVERSLEY, 1st Baron, *cr* 1906; **George John Shaw-Lefevre,** PC; LCC; *b* 12 June 1831; *o s* of Sir George Shaw-Lefevre, KCB, and Rachel Enid, *d* of Ichabod Wright, Mopperley Hall, Nottingham; *m* 1874, Constance Moreton, *d* of 3rd Earl of Ducie. *Educ*: Eton; Trinity College, Cambridge (MA). Barrister, 1855; contested (L) Winchester, 1859; member of Sea Fisheries Commission, 1862; MP (L) Reading, 1863–85, when defeated by Charles T. Murdoch; Civil Lord of the Admiralty, 1856; Commissioner to negotiate a Convention on Fisheries with French Government, 1858; carried vote in House of Commons for arbitration of the Alabama claims, 1868; Secretary Board of Trade under Mr Bright, 1869–71; carried the General Tramways Act; Under-Secretary, Home Office, 1871; Secretary to Admiralty, 1871–74; First Commissioner of Works, 1881–83; Bencher of Inner Temple, 1882; Postmaster-General, 1883–84; carried Act establishing 6d telegrams; MP (L) Central Bradford, 1885–95; Chairman of Royal Commission on Loss of Life at Sea, 1885; was again First Commissioner of Works and a member of Mr Gladstone's Cabinet in 1892–93; President of Local Government Board, 1894–95; carried Equalisation of Rates of London Act; founded (1866) the Commons Preservation Soc., of which Chairman with short intervals till present time; Chairman Royal Commission on Agricultural Depression, 1893–96 (resigned); elected Member of LCC Feb. 1897, as Progressive for the Haggerston Div. in place of Mr E. R. Turton (resigned); Chairman important Committees in House of Commons—Married Woman's Property Act 1868, the Bright Clauses of Irish Land Act 1877–78, the London

Parochial Charities Act 1879, the Agricultural Holdings Act 1879, Railway Charges 1891–92; President Statistical Society, 1878–79. *Heir:* none. *Publications:* English and Irish Land Questions; Incidents of Coercion; Peel and O'Connell; Agrarian Tenures; English Commons and Forests; Gladstone and Ireland, 1912; The Partitions of Poland, 1915; The Turkish Empire, its Growth and Decay, 1917. *Recreations:* cycling, fishing. *Address:* Abbotsworthy House, Kingsworthy, Winchester. *Clubs:* Athenæum, Reform, National Liberal.

Died 19 April 1928 (ext).

EVERSLEY, William Pinder; Barrister-at-law; Recorder of Sudbury, Suffolk, since 1897; *b* Barbados, West Indies, 23 April 1850; *e s* of William Eversley of Barbados. *Educ:* Somersetshire College, Bath; Queen's College, Oxford. MA; BCL. Called to Bar, 1877; joined South-Eastern Circuit same year; appointed Revising Barrister for South-Eastern Circuit, 1898. *Publications:* The Law of the Domestic Relations, 1885 and 1896; Midnight Tales, 1892. *Recreations:* walking, cricket. *Address:* 13 Upper King Street, Norwich. *Clubs:* Oxford and Cambridge, West Indian; Norfolk County, Norwich.

Died 23 Jan. 1918.

EWART, Admiral Arthur Wartensleben; *b* 23 Dec. 1862; 2nd *s* of late General Sir John Ewart, GCB; *m* Violet Louisa, 3rd *d* of late Colonel B. B. Haworth-Booth of Hullbank and Rolston Halls, Yorkshire; no *c. Educ:* HMS Britannia. Entered Navy, 1875; Commander, 1895; Captain, 1901; Rear-Admiral, 1911; retired through ill-health, 1911; Naval Attaché Maritime Courts, in Germany and Scandinavia, 1900–3. Knight Commander of the Dannebrog; Spanish Naval Order of Merit; French Legion of Honour. *Recreation:* naval history. *Address:* Laneside, Dumfries, Scotland. *M:* SW 164.

Died 18 Nov. 1922.

EWART, David, ISO 1903; Chief Architect, Department of Public Works, Canada; *b* 1841. Entered Civil Service, Canada, 1871; Dominion Consulting Architect, 1914. *Address:* Public Works Department, Ottawa. *Died June 1921.*

EWART, Maj.-Gen. Sir Henry (Peter), 1st Bt, *cr* 1910; GCVO 1902 (KCVO 1897); KCB 1885 (CB 1882); Colonel 7th Dragoon Guards since 1900; Crown Equerry, 1894–1910; *b* 20 Aug. 1838; *s* of late Rev. Peter Ewart, Kirklington, Yorkshire; *m* 1888, Lady Evelyn Clementina Heathcote-Drummond Willoughby (*d* 1924), *d* of 1st Earl of Ancaster; one *s* decd. *Educ:* Eton; Oxford. Joined 2nd Life Guards, 1858; commanded the regiment, 1878; commanded Household Cavalry in Egypt, 1882 (despatches, CB); commanded Cavalry Brigade in Soudan Campaign, 1885 (KCB); Equerry to Queen Victoria, 1884–94. *Heir:* none. *Address:* The White House, Hythe, Southampton. *Clubs:* Carlton, Marlborough. *Died 16 April 1928 (ext).*

EWART, Maj.-Gen. Sir Richard (Henry), KCMG 1918; CB 1915; CIE 1912; DSO 1895; ADC to the King, 1911–16; *b* 26 Dec. 1864; *s* of late Col C. H. Ewart, ISC; *m* 1st, 1889, Charlotte Frewen Laurie; two *d;* 2nd, 1899, Marion Annie (*d* 1920), *d* of Lt-Gen. Norris Baker, Redholme, Folkestone and *widow* of J. R. Thomas; one *d;* 3rd, Ethel Mary, *e d* of the late Sir John Boraston, Beckenham, Kent. Entered army, 1883; Captain, 1894; Major, 1901; Lieut Col 1906; Bt-Col 1910; served with the Hampshire Regiment, 1883–86, then joined 31st Punjabis, Indian Army, afterwards transferring to the Supply and Transport Corps; AQMG, Army Headquarters, Simla, 1905; Director of Military Farming Operations in India, 1906–12; Hazara Expedition, 1891 (medal with clasp); Isazai Expedition, 1892; Waziristan Field Force, 1894–95 (despatches, DSO, clasp); France as Dep. Dir Supply and Transport, Indian Corps, 1914–15 (despatches, CB, 1914 Star); DAQMG, East African Expeditionary Force, 1915–18 (despatches 4 times, prom. Maj.-Gen. for distinguished services in the field, KCMG, General Service and Victory Medals); worked for Central Prisoner of War Committee, first in London and then as Director of Red Cross Depot in Berne, Switzerland; proceeded to Berlin on signature of Armistice as Red Cross Commissioner to repatriate British prisoners of war; Chief of the British Military Mission, Berlin, and President, Inter-Allied Commission for Repatriation of Russian Prisoners of War, Jan.–May 1919; Colonel Commandant Indian Army Service Corps, 1925. American Distinguished Service Medal, Commander of the Orders of the Legion of Honour (France), Saint Maurice and Saint Lazarus (Italy) and Leopold (Belgium); Order of Saint Stanislaus, 2nd Class with Swords (Russia), White Eagle, 2nd Class, with Swords (Serbia). *Address:* Glinton, Farnborough, Kent. *T:* Farnborough (Kent) 202. *Club:* Junior United Service.

Died 27 May 1928.

EWART, Sir William Quartus, 2nd Bt, *cr* 1887; MA, TCD; JP Co. Down; DL Belfast; High Sheriff, Co. Antrim, 1897; Chairman of William Ewart and Son, Ltd, linen manufacturers, Belfast; *b* 14 June 1844; *e s* of Sir William Ewart, 1st Bt, MP (C) N Belfast; *S* father, 1889; *m* 1876, Mary, *d* of Robert Heard of Pallastown, Kinsale; two *s* three *d* (and one *s* decd). *Educ:* Trinity College, Dublin. A Knight of Grace of the Order of St John of Jerusalem. *Heir: s* Robert Heard Ewart, *b* 5 Nov. 1879. *Address:* Glenmachan, Strandtown, Belfast. *Club:* Ulster, Belfast. *Died 17 Oct. 1919.*

EWING, Rev. James Carruthers Rhea, Hon. KCIE 1923 (Hon. CIE 1915); MA, DD, LLD, LittD; Secretary India Council Presbyterian Church (USA) in India; Principal Forman Christian College, Lahore, 1888–1918; Vice-Chancellor Panjab University, 1910–17; *b* Pennsylvania, USA, 23 June 1854; *m* 1879; two *s* three *d. Educ:* Washington and Jefferson, USA. Went to India, 1879; work, that of an Educational Missionary. Kaiser-i-Hind Gold Medal, 1906. *Publications:* numerous magazine articles, addresses, A Prince of the Church in India, etc. *Address:* Lahore, India.

Died 20 Aug. 1925.

EWING, Hon. Norman Kirkwood, KC 1914; *b* 1870; *s* of Rev. T. C. Ewing, Wolligong, New South Wales; *m* 1897, Maude Louisa, *d* of late Hon. Sir Edward Albert Stone, KCMG, Chief Justice and Lt-Gov. of Western Australia. Admitted a solicitor, NSW, 1895; Barrister and Solicitor, Western Australia, 1897; of High Court, Australia, 1903; Supreme Court, Tasmania, 1907; MLA for W Australia, 1898–1901; Federal Senator for W Australia, 1901–3; member of House of Assembly, Tasmania, 1909–15; Leader of the Opposition, 1914–15; a Puisne Judge of the Supreme Court, Tasmania, 1915; Acting Administrator of Tasmania, 1923–24. *Address:* Hobart, Tasmania. *Died 11 July 1928.*

EWING, Hon. Sir Thomas Thomson, KCMG 1908; MP Richmond, NSW, since 1901; Acting Postmaster-General, 1906; Minister for Home Affairs, 1906–7; *b* Pitt Town, Hawkesbury River, NSW, 9 Oct. 1856; *s* of Rev. Thomas Campbell Ewing, RD; *m* 1879, Margaret Russell, *d* of Francis Peter MacCabe. Member of Legislative Assembly of NSW for Richmond, 1885–94; Lismore, 1894–1901; Minister for Defence, Commonwealth of Australia, 1907–8; Vice-President of the Executive Council, 1905–6; Chairman of Parliamentary Public Works Committee of NSW; Chairman of Royal Commission with reference to extension of Railway System of NSW into the city of Sydney; was Staff Surveyor for State of NSW. *Publications:* (with T. A. Coghlan) Progress of Australia during the 19th Century; various publications on Australasian subjects. *Address:* Musgrave Street, Mosman, Sydney, NSW.

Died 15 Sept. 1920.

EXHAM, Col Simeon Hardy, CB 1911; CBE 1919; *b* 5 July 1850; *s* of late Thomas Exham, Monkstown, and Frances, *d* of Simeon Hardy; *m* 1873, Emily, *d* of late Rev. Godfrey Clarke Smith of St Olans, Coachford, Cork. Entered Royal Engineers, 1871; Lt-Col 1896; retired 1901; rejoined 1914; served Afghan War, 1878–79 (medal with clasp); Superintending Engineer, Portsmouth and Rosyth Dockyards, 1895–1911; retired 1911. *Address:* Walton House, Walton, Suffolk. *Died 26 Nov. 1926.*

EXMOUTH, 5th Viscount, *cr* 1816; **Edward Addington Hargreaves Pellew;** Bt 1796; Baron 1814; *b* 12 Nov. 1890; *s* of 4th Viscount and Edith, 3rd *d* of Thomas Hargreaves, Arborfield Hall, Reading, Berks; *S* father, 1899. *Educ:* Eton; Trinity College, Cambridge. *Heir: c* Henry Edward Pellew, *b* 26 April 1828. *Address:* Canonteign House, Lower-Ashton, near Exeter.

Died 16 Aug. 1922.

EXMOUTH, 6th Viscount, *cr* 1816; **Henry Edward Pellew;** Bt 1796; Baron 1814; *b* 26 April 1828; *o s* of Very Rev. the Hon. George Pellew, 3rd *s* of 1st Viscount and Hon. Frances Addington, 2nd *d* of 1st Viscount Sidmouth; *S* cousin, 1922; *m* 1st, 1858, Eliza (*d* 1869), *d* of Hon. Judge William Jay, of New York; one *s* (and one *s* one *d* decd); 2nd, 1873, Augusta, *y d* of Hon. Judge William Jay; one *d. Educ:* Trinity College, Cambridge. MA. *Heir: s* Hon. Charles Ernest Pellew, *b* 11 March 1863. *Address:* Washington, DC, USA.

Died 4 Feb. 1923.

EYLES, Sir George Lancelot, KCMG 1914 (CMG 1902); Lieutenant-Colonel Engineers and Railway Staff Corps; Consulting Engineer for railways to the Crown Agents for the Colonies for Government railways in Ceylon, the Federated Malay States, Straits Settlements, Trinidad, Nyasaland, etc, and for other railways abroad; *b* 15 Feb. 1849; *s* of late George Eyles. *Address:* 12 Dean's Yard, Westminster, SW. *Clubs:* Junior Carlton, St Stephen's, Garrick.

Died 12 March 1919.

EYRE, Ven. Christopher Benson; Archdeacon of Yaoland and Priest-in-charge of Mtonya, Portuguese Nyasaland; Canon of St John the Divine, Likoma Cathedral, 1922; *b* 1849; 2nd *s* of Rev. G. H. Eyre, sometime Fellow of Pembroke College, Cambridge. No education to speak of. Ordained 1894; Curate of Lwynypia, 1894; Missionary, Universities' Mission to Central Africa, 1896. *Address:* Universities' Mission, Mponda's, Fort Johnston, Nyasaland.
Died 28 June 1928.

EYRE, Colonel Edmund Henry, CB 1894; ISC; *b* 26 Nov. 1838; *m* 1862, Louisa, *d* of late Maj.-Gen. C. Pooley, IA. Entered army, 1858; Colonel, 1887; served Zhob Valley Expedition, 1884; Burmah, 1885–86 (despatches, brevet of Col, medal with clasp); QMG Madras, 1890–95. *Address:* Redfield, Newbury, Berks.
Died 4 Dec. 1919.

EYRE, Rev. Edward Vincent, MA; *b* 29 March 1851; *s* of Rev. Edward Eyre, Rector of Larling, Norfolk. *Educ:* Harrow; Corpus Christi College, Oxford. Deacon, 1876; Priest, 1877; Curate at St Philip's, Clerkenwell, 1876–82; appointed Minister of new parish, 1882; first Vicar of the Church of the Holy Redeemer, Clerkenwell, 1888–1904; resigned, 1904; Vicar of Chollerton, Northumberland, 1905–21; Rural Dean of Bellingham, 1917–21; Hon. Canon of Newcastle Cathedral, 1919–21. *Address:* 10 West Cliff Gardens, Folkestone.
Died 4 Feb. 1925.

EYRE, John, RI; ARCA; *b* Staffordshire; one *s* two *d*. *Educ:* Staffordshire. Studied art in the South Kensington schools; in early days designed for pottery, and became a painter in water-colours and enamels; exhibits in the Royal Academy, Royal Institute, French Salon, etc; also book illustrator. *Publications:* illustrations to the English Poets, etc. *Recreations:* fishing, walking. *Address:* Laurel Cottage, The Common, Cranleigh, Surrey.
Died 13 Sept. 1927.

EYSTON, John Joseph, JP; *b* 1867; 2nd *s* of Charles John Eyston (*d* 1883) and Agnes Mary, 5th *d* of late Michael Henry Blount of Mapledurham, Oxfordshire; *m* 1890, Elizabeth, *o d* of late George Dunn of Bath House, Newcastle upon Tyne; one *s* three *d*. High Sheriff of Berkshire, 1915. *Address:* Hendred House, near Steventon, Berkshire. *Club:* Junior Carlton.   *Died 7 June 1916.*

F

FABER, 1st Baron, *cr* 1905, of Butterwick; **Edmund Beckett Faber,** JP and DL for WR of Yorks; senior partner in Beckett's Bank, Leeds and York; director, Yorkshire Post; director, L&NW Railway and Sun Insurance Company, and London County Westminster and Parr's Bank; *b* 9 Feb. 1847; *e s* of Charles Wilson Faber of Northaw, Herts, JP and DL for Herts, and Mary Beckett Faber, *d* of Sir Edmund Beckett, 4th Bt, and *sister* of 1st Baron Grimthorpe. *Educ:* Eton; Trinity College, Cambridge. Contested (C) Pudsey Div., Yorkshire, 1900; MP (C) Andover Div., Hants, 1901–5. *Heir:* none. *Recreation:* shooting. *Address:* Belvedere, Harrogate; 19 Park Street, W1. *T:* Mayfair 3377. *Clubs:* Carlton, Junior Carlton, Yorkshire.
Died 17 Sept. 1920 (ext).

FABER, Lt-Col Walter (Vavasour), DL Hants; partner in Strong's Brewery, Romsey; *b* 11 Feb. 1857; 5th *s* of Charles Wilson Faber of Northaw, Herts, DL for Herts, and Mary Beckett Faber, *e d* of Sir Edmund Beckett, 4th Bt, and *sister* of 1st Baron Grimthorpe; *m* 1915, Mrs Arthur Byass of Bosworth House, Husband's Bosworth, *d* of S. Laing. *Educ:* Cheam; Malvern; Royal Military Academy. Entered Royal Artillery, 1877; Royal Horse Artillery, 1884; Captain 1885; Major 1914; Lt-Col 1915; ADC to Sir Albert Williams, 1888–90; retired, 1890; volunteered during S African War, 1900; entered Wilts Yeomanry, 1901; retired, 1903. MP (C) Andover Division of Hants, 1906–18. *Recreations:* hunting, shooting. *Address:* Welford Grange, near Rugby. *T:* Welford 8. *Club:* Naval and Military.
Died 2 April 1928.

FAGAN, Charles Edward, CBE 1920; ISO; FRGS; Secretary, British Museum (Natural History), since 1919; *b* 25 Dec 1855; *y s* of late George Fagan, Minister Resident, Caracas; *m*; one *s*. *Educ:* private.

Entered the British Museum, 1873; 1st Class Assistant, 1887; Assistant Secretary, 1889–1919; Hon. Treasurer International Ornithological Congress, 1905; British Scientific Expedition to Mt Ruwenzori, 1905–6; British Ornithologists Union's Expedition to Dutch New Guinea, 1910–12; Society for the Promotion of Nature Reserves; Selous National Memorial; Goodman Exploration Fund; Organised British Section International Sports Exhibition, Vienna, 1910; Member Colonial Office Committee for Ghent International Exhibition, 1913; Member of Colonial Office Conference on the Protection of Plumage Birds; British Representative on the International Committee for the Protection of Nature, 1913; President of the Vesey Club, Sutton Coldfield, 1912–13; Council Royal Geographical Society; Member of the Executive Committee of the National Trust; Corresponding Member Lisbon Geographical Society; Knight Order of the Crown Belgium; Order of St Sava, Serbia. *Recreations:* football (Rugby), now as a spectator; country walks. *Address:* 53 FitzGeorge Avenue, West Kensington, W14. *T:* Hammersmith 125; Natural History Museum, Cromwell Road, SW. *Clubs:* Savile, Arts, Savage.   *Died 30 Jan. 1921.*

FAGAN, Maj.-Gen. James Lawtie; Indian Army; *b* 4 Feb. 1843. Entered army, 1859; Maj. Gen. 1899; retired list, 1902; served Afghan War, 1879–80 (despatches, medal). *Address:* 32 Porchester Terrace, W2. *T:* Paddington 8579. *Clubs:* East India United Service, MCC.
Died 12 March 1919.

FAGUET, Emile; Professeur de Littérature Française à la Faculté des Lettres de Paris; *b* 17 Dec. 1847 à La Roche sur Yon (Vendée); *s* de Victor Faguet, Professeur et Homme de Lettres; unmarried. *Educ:* Lycée de Poitiers; Lycée Charlemagne, Paris. Elève de l'Ecole normale en 1867; Professeur dans différents lycées de province, 1869–83; Professeur dans differents lycées de Paris, 1883–90; Professeur à la Faculté des Lettres de Paris, 1890; élu de l'Académie Française en 1900. *Publications:* XVIme Siècle, XVIIme Siècle, XVIIIme Siècle, XIXme Siècle Etudes littéraires (4 vols); Les Moralistes du XIXme siècle (3 vols); Le Libéralisme (1 vol.); Le Socialisme (1 vol.); L'Anticléricalisme (1 vol.); En lisant Nietzsche (1 vol.); Pour qu'on lise Platon (1 vol.); etc. *Address:* Paris, 59 Rue Monge; Poitiers, 39 Rue Carnot.
Died 7 June 1916.

FAHEY, Rt. Rev. Mgr. Jerome, DD; Vicar General of Galway and Kilmacduagh; *b* 1843. *Educ:* Maynooth. *Address:* Gort, Co. Galway.
Died 12 March 1920.

FAIRBANKS, Charles Warren, LLD; Vice-President of the United States, 1905–9; *b* Unionville Center, Ohio, 11 May 1852; *s* of Loriston Monroe and Mary Adelaide Smith Fairbanks; *m* 1874, Cornelia Cole (*d* 1913); four *s* one *d*. *Educ:* Ohio Wesleyan University, Delaware, Ohio. Admitted to bar by Supreme Court of Ohio, 1874; removed to Indianapolis, 1874; elected a trustee of Ohio Wesleyan University, 1885; chairman of Indiana Republican State Conventions, 1892, 1898 and 1914; elected to United States Senate, 1897; re-elected, 1903; resigned, 1905; appointed a member of United States and British Joint High Commission which met in Quebec in 1898 for the adjustment of Canadian questions, and was chairman of United States High Commissioners; was a delegate at large to Republican National Convention at St Louis in 1896, and was temporary chairman of the convention; was a delegate at large to Republican National Convention at Philadelphia in 1900, and as chairman of the committee on resolutions reported the platform; delegate at large to Republican National Conventions at Chicago, 1904 and 1912; chairman Indiana delegation; Vice-President, USA, 1905; representative of USA, Tercentenary Celebration Quebec, 1908; travelled round the world, 1909–10; Republican; Regent Smithsonian Institution, Washington, DC; unanimously nominated for Vice-President, USA, by Republican National Convention at Chicago, June 1916. *Address:* Indianapolis, Ind., USA.   *Died 15 June 1918.*

FAIRBROTHER, William Henry, MA; Lecturer in Philosophy, Lincoln College, Oxford, since 1889; Tutor to the Non-Collegiate Students since 1900; Major (retired) The Royal Warwickshire Regiment; *b* Pendleton, near Manchester, 9 Dec. 1859; *m* 1887, Jeanie Prentice Dunlop, of Southport. *Educ:* Owens College, Manchester (prizeman); Keble College, Oxford. 2nd class Classical Moderations, 1882; 1st class in Literis Humanioribus, 1885; BA 1885; MA 1888. Lecturer at Keble College, 1886–89. *Publications:* several articles and reviews in Mind, in the International Journal of Ethics, and in the Transactions of the Aristotelian Society, London; Philosophy of Thomas Hill Green. *Recreations:* rowing, golf; late Captain in the Oxford University Volunteers. *Address:* Lincoln College, Oxford; Freshwater, IoW. *Clubs:* United Service Institution; Union Society, Oxford.   *Died 20 July 1927.*

FAIRBROTHER, Col William Tomes, CB 1909; FRGS; Indian Army; *b* 19 July 1856; *e s* of late George Berford Fairbrother, Clonsilla, Co. Dublin; *m* 1901, Marie B. L., *e d* of late Rev. Walter Lamb. Entered army, 11th Foot, 1875; Captain, ISC, 1886; Major, 1895; Lt-Col, Indian Army, 1901; Brevet-Col 1904; served Afghan War, 1878–80 (despatches, medal); Sikkim Expedition, 1888 (medal with clasp); NW Frontier, Assam 1894; Chitral, 1895 (medal with clasp); Waziristan, 1901–2 (clasp); was Commandant 13th Rajputs, 1898–1905. *Recreations:* big game shooting, fishing, sketching. *Address:* Bareilly, India; Srinagar, Kashmir. *M:* IF 167.

Died 16 June 1924.

FAIRFAX, Sir James Oswald, KBE 1926 (CBE 1918); a Director of The Sydney Morning Herald and Sydney Mail; *b* Sydney, 1863; *s* of Sir James Reading Fairfax and Lucy Armstrong; *m* Mabel, *d* of Captain Hixson, RN; one *s*. *Educ:* Sydney Grammar School; Balliol Coll. Oxford. Called to Bar, Inner Temple, 1886; Chairman of Australian Section of the Empire Press Union; Chairman of the NSW Division of the Australian Red Cross Society, 1915–21; MA Oxford and Sydney. *Recreations:* yachting, golf. *Address:* Herald Office, Sydney. *Clubs:* Oriental; Union, Sydney.

Died July 1928.

FAIRFAX, Sir James Reading, Kt 1898; senior proprietor of the Sydney Morning Herald and the Sydney Mail; *b* Leamington, 17 Oct. 1834; 2nd *s* of late Hon. John Fairfax, Member of the Legislative Council of New South Wales, and Sarah, *d* of James Reading, Warwick; *m* 1857, Lucy, *d* of John Armstrong, Sydney; five *s* one *d*. *Educ:* private schools (Rev. Dr Woolls and Rev. Henry Cary, MA), Paramatta and Sydney, NSW. Engaged in newspaper work early in life and has continued so up to present time; Trustee, Royal Naval House; Director Royal Prince Alfred Hospital; Trustee, Queen Victoria Homes for Consumptives; President, Nat. Art Gallery of New South Wales; Trustee, National Shipwreck Relief and Humane Society of NSW, Australia; held commission as captain in the Sydney Brigade, Volunteer Rifles; Hon. Treasurer Sydney Boys' Brigade. *Recreations:* yachting; President Royal Sydney Golf Club. *Address:* Ginahgulla, Belle Vue Hill, near Sydney; Woodside, Moss Vale, NSW. *Cable A:* Heralding, Sydney. *T:* Edgecliffe 9, Sydney. *M:* 445; 1806. *Clubs:* Oriental; Union, Sydney; Melbourne, Melbourne.

Died 29 March 1919.

FAIRHOLME, Brig.-Gen. William Ernest, CB 1919; CMG 1890; MVO 1903; late RA; *b* Leamington, 5 Feb. 1860; *s* of late George K. E. Fairholme of Old Melrose, Co. Roxburgh and Baroness Poellnitz-Frankenberg of Bavaria; unmarried. *Educ:* Harrow; RMA Woolwich; FRGS. Joined Royal Artillery, 1879; Staff-Captain, Intelligence Department, War Office, 1893–94; DAAG same department, 1894–98; British Delegate on International Commission for rectification of Turco-Greek Frontier, 1898; Assistant British Military Commissioner in Crete, 1898–99; British Civil Commissioner in Crete, 18th June 1899–24 July 1899; served South Africa, 1899–1900, as AAG; Military Secretary, Gibraltar, 1900–2; Military Attaché, Vienna, Bucharest, Belgrade, and Cettinje, 1902–4; British Staff Officer for the reorganisation of the gendarmerie in Macedonia, 1904–6; Military Attaché, Paris, Madrid and Lisbon, 1909–12; Brig.-General Commanding Artillery 3rd Division, 1912–13; British Delegate for delimitation of Turco-Bulgarian frontier, 1913; Military Attaché, Brussels, The Hague, Copenhagen and Christiania, 1914–15; specially employed at Dunkerque under GHQ in France, 1915; GSO1 (Chief Liaison Officer), British Salonika Force, 1915–16; Military Attaché, Athens, 1916–19. Officer of Legion of Honour; Commander Order of Leopold; Grand Commander Order of the Redeemer; Greek War Cross, 2nd Class; 1915 Star; S African War medal with 2 clasps. *Clubs:* Army and Navy, St James's.

Died 7 Aug. 1920.

FAIRLIE, James Ogilvy Reginald, JP Co. Fife; *b* 28 Dec 1848; 3rd *s* of late James Ogilvy Fairlie, JP, DL, 2nd Life Guards of Coodham, Ayrshire and Elizabeth Constance, *o surv. d* of William Houison Craufurd of Craufurdland, Ayrshire and Braehead, Midlothian; *m* 1880, Jane Mary, 3rd *d* of John Buchanan of Dowanhill; three *s* one *d*. *Educ:* Glenalmond; Christ Church, Oxford; BA 1873. Resided for some time in Rome; for twenty-five years a Privy Chamberlain to HH Leo XIII; appointment confirmed by HH Pius X, 1904, and by HH Benedict XV, 1915; for some years a member of the Catholic Education Council; Captain of the Royal and Ancient Golf Club of St Andrews, 1893; Preses of the Fife Hunt, 1907; Chairman of the Pontifical Court Club, 1910; served for many years on the Rules of Golf Committee. *Recreations:* golf, painting, heraldry. *Address:* Myres Castle, Auchtermuchty, Fife. *Club:* New, Edinburgh.

Died 20 Sept. 1916.

FAIRTLOUGH, Major Edward Charles D'Heillemer, CMG 1900; DSO 1897; late Royal Dublin Fusiliers; *b* 1869; *m* 1901, Gertrude, *d* of Thomas Murray of Milmount House, Westmeath; two *d*. Sierra Leone Frontier Force, 1894; Commanded Expedition against Bandi Tribes, 1896; against Gizehs 1897; appointed District Commissioner, Ronietta, Sierra Leone, 1898; in military charge of operations in Ronietta and Pangoma during Sierra Leone Rebellion, 1898–99; commanded Expedition for relief of Pangoma Fort, June and July 1898, successful after 29 days bush-fighting; Official Member Legislative Council, Sierra Leone.

Died 24 April 1925.

FAIRWEATHER, Lt-Col James McIntyre, DSO 1902; Commanding Rand Light Infantry, Johannesburg; *b* Dundee, 13 Oct. 1876. Served South Africa, 1899–1902 (despatches, Queen's medal, 4 clasps, King's medal, 2 clasps, DSO). *Club:* Athenæum, Johannesburg.

Died 18 Feb. 1917.

FAIYAZ ALI KHAN, Nawab, Sir Mumtazud-Dowlah, Mahomed, of Pahasu, KCVO 1911; KCIE 1907; CSI 1903; CBE 1919; family traces origin to Rama, King of Ayodhya; hereditary head of Lalkhani clan of Rajputs; Prime Minister at Jaipur; *b* 4 Nov. 1851; *s* of late Nawab Sir Faiz Ali Khan Bahadur; married; one *s* one *d*. Served for fourteen consecutive terms on Provincial Legislative Council of United Provinces, and for two years on Viceregal Imperial Council. Represented United Provinces, as guest of nation, at King Edward's Coronation 1902, and at Delhi Durbar 1902; Hon. Magistrate and Munsif of Pahasu; President of Board of Trustees, MAO College, Aligarh; trustee, Government College, Agra, Lady Dufferin Fund, etc. *Address:* Nawab's House, Jaipur, Rajputana; Pahasu, Bulundshahr, UP, India.

Died 26 March 1922.

FALCONBRIDGE, Hon. Sir Glenholme, Kt 1908; MA; Chief Justice of the King's Bench, Ontario, since 1900; a Judge of the Supreme Court of Judicature for Ontario and senior puisne Judge of the King's Bench Division of the High Court of Justice since 1887; President of High Court Division of Supreme Court since 1916; *b* 12 May 1846; *e s* of late John Kennedy Falconbridge, JP, of Richmond Hill, Co. York, Ontario; *m* 1873, Mary Phoebe, *y d* of late Hon. Mr Justice Sullivan; one *s* four *d*. *Educ:* Model Grammar School for Upper Canada; University of Toronto. Scholarship at matriculation, 1862; prizes and scholarships in every year of course; gold medal at grad. 1866; BA 1866; MA 1870. Lecturer in Univ. Coll., Toronto, 1867–68; called to Bar, 1871; bencher of Law Society, UC, 1883; QC 1885; wrote the Introduction to the Canadian Edition de Luxe of Burke's works, 1901; member of several important Royal Commissions, 1897–1902; a Vice-President of the Imperial Maritime League; an Honorary Colonel in the Canadian Militia; President of the Ontario Branch of the Secours National de France; Member of Board of Governors of Upper Canada College. *Recreations:* angling; President of the Ontario Forest, Fish and Game Protective Association; President of Toronto Club. *Address:* Osgoode Hall, Toronto, Ontario, Canada. *Clubs:* Toronto, Royal Canadian Yacht, Toronto.

Died 8 Feb. 1920.

FALCONER, John B., KC; LLD Dublin University. QC (Ire.) 1899. *Address:* 27 Fitzwilliam Square, Dublin.

Died 31 Aug. 1924.

FALCONIO, His Eminence Cardinal Diomed; *b* Pescocostanzo, Monte Casino, Italy, 20 Sep. 1842. Entered Franciscan Order, 1860; sent as Missionary to USA, 1865; Priest, 1866; Professor of Philosophy and Vice-Pres. of St Bonaventure's College, Alleghany, 1866; President, 1868; Secretary and Chancellor to RC Bishop of Newfoundland, 1871–82; Provincial of the Franciscans in the Abrizzi, 1884; Procurator-General of the Franciscan Order, 1889; Bishop of Lacedonia, 1892; Apostolic Delegate to Canada, 1899; to the United States, 1902; Cardinal, 1911; Cardinal Bishop of Velletri, 1914; Prefect of the Sacred Congregation of Religious, 1916. *Address:* 17 Piazza Cavour, Rome.

Died 7 Feb. 1917.

FALKINER, Sir Leslie Edmond Percy Riggs, 7th Bt *cr* 1777, of Annmount, Cork; *b* 2 Oct. 1866; *s* of Sir Samuel Falkiner, 6th Bt, and Blanche, *d* of Sir William Berkeley Call, 3rd Bt; *S* father, 1893; *m* 1st, 1894, Elaine (*d* 1900), *d* of W. M. Farmer of Maynardville, Cape of Good Hope; 2nd, 1902, Kathleen, *e d* of Hon. Henry Robert Orde-Powlett, 2nd *s* of 3rd Baron Bolton; three *s* one *d*. *Educ:* in France; Marlborough; HMS Worcester. Owner of about 6000 acres. *Recreations:* shooting, hunting, fishing. *Heir:* *s* Terence Edmond Patrick, *b* 17 March 1903. *Address:* Burghley Park, Stamford, Lincs. *Clubs:* Junior Carlton; County Cork.

Died 17 Jan. 1917.

FALKLAND, 12th Viscount and 12th Lord Cary, *cr* 1620; **Byron Plantagenet Cary;** Representative Peer for Scotland; late commanding 4th Battalion Yorkshire Regiment; *b* 3 April 1845; *s* of Capt. Hon. Byron Charles Ferdinand Plantagenet Cary, RN, and Selina, *d* of Rev. Francis Fox, of Foxhall, Co. Longford; *S* uncle, 1886; *m* 1879, Mary (*d* 1920), *d* of Robert Reade, New York; two *s* three *d* (and one *s* decd). *Educ:* privately; Cheltenham; Sandhurst. Entered 49th Regt 1863; served in 49th Regt and 35th Regt, 1863–83; retired on a pension with honorary rank of Lieut-Col. A small property in the City worth about £25,000; has no gallery, but owns a few good pictures by Vansommer, Cornelius Jansen, Sir Joshua Reynolds, Sir Peter Lely, Sir Godfrey Kneller, John Riley, and Romney. Church of England. Moderate Conservative. *Recreations:* boating, fishing, shooting; has no hobbies. *Heir: s* Master of Falkland, *b* 23 Sept. 1880. *Address:* 26 Upper Grosvenor Street, W1. *T:* Mayfair 416. *Clubs:* Carlton; Royal Yacht Squadron, Cowes.

Died 10 Jan. 1922.

FALKNER, Rev. Thomas Felton, DSO 1900; MA; *b* 17 July 1847; *s* of Thomas Falkner of Bath; *m* 1877, Maria Louisa, *d* of Rev. James Bacon, BD; two *s* two *d*. *Educ:* Christ's College, Cambridge. BA 1870; MA 1875. Sub-Warden St Thomas's College, Colombo, 1872–79; Domestic Chaplain to Bishop of Colombo, 1873; Acting Colonial Chaplain and Chaplain to Forces at Colombo, 1874–75; Priest-in-charge of Woolland, Dorset, 1879–81; Chaplain to the Forces, 1881; served at Aldershot, Bermuda, Guards Depot, Chatham, Aldershot, Portsmouth, with the S African Field Force, 1899–1900 (despatches, DSO, promoted 1st class), and as Senior Chaplain 1st Army Corps, Aldershot, 1901–3; retired list, 1904; Rector of Burnham Westgate, with Burnham Norton, King's Lynn, 1903–23. *Address:* Oakley Lodge, Claverton Down, Bath.

Died Aug. 1924.

FALMOUTH, 7th Viscount, *cr* 1720; **Evelyn Edward Thomas Boscawen,** KCVO 1905 (MVO 1897); CB 1885; DL, JP; Baron Le Despencer, 1264; Baron Boscawen-Rose, 1720; late Colonel commanding Coldstream Guards and a regimental district; Osmanieh (4th class) and Khedive orders 1882; member Jockey Club since 1898; *b* 24 July 1847; *s* of 6th Viscount and 23rd Baroness Le Despencer; *S* father, 1889, and mother, 1891; *m* 1886, Kathleen, *d* of 2nd Lord Penrhyn; two *s* one *d* (and two *s* decd). *Educ:* Eton. Ensign and Lieut Coldstream Guards, 1866; served Egypt, present at Tel-el-Kebir, 1882; Nile Expedition (despatches); present at Abu Klea and Abu Kru, and commanded at Metemmeh, 1884–85; Assistant Military Sec. to Commander-in-Chief, Ireland; retired, 1902. *Heir: s* Hon. Evelyn Hugh John Boscawen, *b* 5 Aug. 1887. *Address:* Tregothnan, Truro; Mereworth Castle, Maidstone; 2 St James's Square, SW. *T:* Regent 566. *Clubs:* Guards, Bachelors', Travellers'.

Died 1 Oct. 1918.

FANCOURT, Colonel St John Fancourt Michell, CB 1904; JP Suffolk; *b* 30 Sept. 1847; *m* 1897, Ethel Malins, *y d* of Sir Henry Wiggin, 1st Bt. Cornet 5th Lancers, 1869; Major 1st Duke of York's Lancers, 1889; Brevet Lt-Col 1891; Brevet Col 1895; General Officer commanding, Assam, etc, 1898–1901. *Address:* Danecroft, Stowmarket, Suffolk. *Club:* United Service.

Died 11 June 1917.

FANCOURT, Ven. Thomas; Archdeacon of Wellington since 1888; Diocesan Secretary, Bishop's Commissary and Examining Chaplain; *b* 22 Jan. 1840; *s* of Rev. W. J. Fancourt; *m* 1865, Elizabeth Emma, *d* of W. Robinson, Knotstrop, Leeds; one *s* three *d*. *Educ:* Lancing; St Augustine's College, Canterbury. Ordained, 1865; Perpetual Curate of Porirua and Karori, 1865–70; Incumbent of Lower Hutt, 1870–84; Perpetual Curate of Johnsonville, 1886–96; Editor Church Chronicle, Wellington Diocese, 1884–1903. *Address:* Diocesan Office, Mulgrave Street, Wellington, NZ.

Died 1 Feb 1919.

FANE, Capt. Octavius Edward, DSO 1917; MC; RGA; *b* 15 Oct. 1886; 8th *s* of Capt. Henry George Fane and Blanche Louisa, *o d* of Col Hon. R. C. H. Spencer. Served European War (MC, despatches, DSO). *Address:* Bicester House, Bicester. *Club:* United Service.

Died 17 Sept. 1918.

FANE, Maj.-Gen. Sir Vere (Bonamy), KCB 1921; (CB 1914); KCIE 1918 (CIE 1915); FRGS; Indian Army; commanding Burma Independent District; Col of the Manchester Regiment; *b* 16 June 1863; *o s* of Capt. H. J. Fane, late 54th Regt; *m* 1892, Kathleen Emily, 2nd *d* of late James Barratt of Hanslop, Bucks; no *c*. *Educ:* privately; Woolwich. Entered army from Militia, 1884; joined Manchester Regiment and served with that regiment till 1888; then joined 1st

Punjab Cavalry, serving with it till 1908; promoted as 2nd in command of 20th Brownlow's Punjabis; appointed to command 21st Punjabis, 1909; served as orderly officer to Gen. Penn Symons, Waziristan, 1894–95 (medal and clasp); Tochi Field Force, 1897–98; DAAG 1st Brigade (medal and clasp); China, 1900; DAQMG Cavalry Brigade (despatches, medal); China, 1901–2, Chief of Police (despatches, brevet Lt-Colonel); NWF India, 1908; Mohmand, actions of Matta and Kargha (despatches, medal and clasp); commanded at action near Dirdoni, Tochi, 26 March 1915 (despatches, CIE). European War, 1914–18 (despatches six times; promoted Major-General for distinguished service in the field; KCIE, Croix de Guerre (2nd Class), Order of Nile). *Recreations:* golf, tennis. *Clubs:* East India United Service, Junior Army and Navy.

Died 23 May 1924.

FANING, Joseph Eaton, MusDoc Cantab 1900; FRAM; Member of Associated Board of RAM and RCM, 1901–23; of the Royal Philharmonic Society; Council of the Royal College of Music; Board of Studies in Music, University of London; Director of the British Columbia Land and Investment Agency Ltd; Director of the Western Canadian Ranching Co. Ltd; Director of the London and Canadian Investment Co. Ltd; *b* Helston, Cornwall, 20 May 1850; *s* of Roger and Caroline Faning of Helston; *m* 1882, Caroline Pare, 3rd *d* of Thomas Dixon and Emma Amelia Galpin of Bristol House, Roehampton; one *s* three *d*. *Educ:* privately. Played violin at a very early age and studied privately until he entered the Royal Academy of Music, 1870, when he studied pianoforte, harmony and composition, organ, singing and violoncello, and obtained many prizes; Professor of Pianoforte at RAM, 1878; Guildhall School of Music, 1881; Professor and Conductor of the Choral Class at the National Training School of Music; Conductor of several Choral Societies including the Eaton Faning's Select Choir at the Boosey Ballad Concerts, St James' Hall and Queen's Hall; Professor Pianoforte, Harmony and Conductor of the Choral Class at the Royal College of Music, 1883; Director of the Music at Harrow School, 1885–1901; Examiner for Musical Degrees, Cambridge University, 1904–9, and 1919; MusBac, 1894. PGO Grand Lodge of Freemasons; travelled in France, Spain, Portugal, Belgium, Holland, Italy, Switzerland, Germany, Austria, Norway, Denmark, South Africa, China, and Japan. *Publications:* Festival Magnificat and Nunc Dimittis; Te Deum; Benedictus and Jubilate; Anthems; Cantata, Buttercups and Daisies; Operetta, Mock Turtles; various pieces for Pianoforte, Part-songs, Choruses, Odes, Songs; Harrow School Songs. *Recreation:* trout-fishing. *Address:* 19 Preston Park Avenue, Brighton. *Club:* Arts.

Died 28 Oct 1927.

FANNING, Sir Roland Francis Nichol, Kt 1886; JP; *b* 1829; *m* Mary (*d* 1901), *d* of late Thomas Stanton. Late Deputy-Inspector Gen. Royal Irish Constabulary. *Address:* Rosslyn, Bray, Co. Wicklow. *Clubs:* Hibernian, United Service, Dublin; Royal St George Yacht.

Died 20 Feb. 1919.

FANSHAWE, Rev. Gerald Charles; Rector of St Maurice and St Lawrence, Winchester, since 1922; Hon. Canon of Winchester, 1922; *b* 16 Nov. 1870; *s* of late General Charles Fanshawe, RE; *m* 1904, Morforwyn, *d* of late Col Lloyd-Verney; one *s* one *d*. *Educ:* Westminster School; Trinity College, Cambridge; MA. Deacon, 1893; Priest, 1894; Curate of St Thomas, Portman Square, 1893–1900; Domestic Chaplain to Bishop (Ryle) of Exeter, 1900 and Bishop (Ryle) of Winchester on his translation; Hon. Chaplain to Bishop of Winchester, 1904–11; Vicar and Rural Dean of Godalming, 1904. *Address:* St Maurice Rectory, Winchester. *T:* Winchester 555.

Died 15 April 1924.

FANSHAWE, Herbert Charles, CSI 1900; *b* 28 March 1852; *s* of Rev. John Faithfull Fanshawe; *m* 1906, Harriot Wollaston, *widow of* William Ramsay, Bombay Civil Service. *Educ:* Tonbridge; Repton. Entered ICS, 1873; Settlement officer, Rohtak; Under, Junior, Revenue, and Chief Secretary, Punjab Govt; Commissioner (Delhi), Punjab; Member Legislative Council, Punjab, 1898–1901; Additional Member of Legislative Council, Governor-General of India, 1900; retired 1901. FRAS, FRGS, FRHS. *Publications:* Rohtak Settlement Report; Delhi, Past and Present, 1902; Murray's Handbook of India, 1904, 1909, and 1911; Memoirs of Lady Fanshawe, 1907. *Address:* 72 Philbeach Gardens, Earl's Court, SW5. *T:* Western 3121. *Club:* East India United Service.

Died 26 March 1923.

FARDELL, Sir (Thomas) George, Kt 1897; JP; late Chairman Quarter Sessions, Isle of Ely; MP (C) S Paddington, 1895–1910; *b* 26 Oct. 1833; *y s* of late Rev. Henry Fardell, Canon of Ely and Vicar of Wisbech, and Eliza, *e d* of late Rt Rev. B. E. Sparke, Bishop of

Ely; *m* 1862, Letitia Anne (*d* 1905), *o d* of late Henry Swann Oldfield, BCS; two *s* two *d*. *Educ*: Eton; Christ Church, Oxford. BA 1856. Barrister, Lincoln's Inn, 1862, Norfolk Circuit; appointed Registrar in Bankruptcy, Manchester, 1868; engaged in Municipal work since 1877; represented Paddington in Metropolitan Board of Works from 1884, and instrumental in obtaining Royal Commission thereon in 1888, and subsequently in passing into law the Public Bodies Corrupt Practices Act, 1889; and LCC, S Paddington, 1889–98; was twice put forward for the post of Deputy-Chairman of the LCC, and has six years Chairman of the Licensing Committee; travelled in America and Canada; Chairman, 1896–1912, Metropolitan Division National Union Conservative Associations. *Recreation*: shooting. *Address*: 2 South Eaton Place, SW. *T*: Victoria 3080. *Club*: Conservative.
Died 12 March 1917.

FARIDOONJI JAMSHEDJI, Nawab Sir Faridoon Jung, Faridoon Daula Faridoon Mulk Bahadur, KCIE 1915 (CIE 1903); CSI 1911; CBE 1918; Extraordinary Member the Nizam's Executive Council; *b* Sept. 1849; widower; one *s*. Decorated for good services rendered to the Hyderabad State. *Recreation*: used to be big game shooting. *Address*: Saifabad, Hyderabad, Deccan.
Died 26 Nov. 1928.

FARLEY, His Eminence Cardinal John; 4th Archbishop of New York since 1902; *b* Newton Hamilton, Co. Armagh, Ireland, 20 April 1842; *s* of Philip Farley and Catherine Murphy. *Educ*: St Macartan's College, Monaghan; St John's College, Fordham, NY City; St Joseph's Seminary, Troy, NY; North American College, Rome, Italy. Priest, 1870; returned to US 1870; Assistant Pastor, St Peter's Church, New Brighton, Staten Island, 1870–72; Secretary to Archbishop M'Closkey, 1872–84; Private Chamberlain to Pope Leo XIII, with title of Monsignore, 1884; Vicar-General, Archdiocese of New York, 1891; Domestic Prelate to Pope Leo XIII, 1892; Protonotary Apostolic, 1895; Auxiliary Bishop of New York, with titular See of Zeugma, 1895; Administrator of New York, 1902; made Assistant to the Pontifical Throne, 1904; created Cardinal Priest Consistory, 1911. *Publications*: Life of Cardinal M'Closkey, 1900; Neither Generous nor Just (reply to Bishop Potter), Catholic World, 1889; Why Church Property should not be taxed, Forum, 1893; St Patrick's Cathedral, New York, 1908. *Recreation*: walking. *Address*: 452 Madison Avenue, New York City, USA.
Died 17 Sept. 1918.

FARMER, Sir Francis Mark, Kt 1916; LDS, RCS, FRSM; Dental Surgeon and Lecturer on Dental Surgery and Pathology at London Hospital Medical College. Recipient of Presentation from Secretary of State for War, 1902; Member British Dental Assoc. and British Society for Study of Orthodontics. *Publications*: Restoration of Chin after Gunshot Wound, and various articles. *Address*: 53 Wimpole Street, W1. *T*: Padd. 184.
Died 24 Dec. 1922.

FARMER, Colonel George Devey, CBE 1919; Canadian AMC; *b* 6 July 1866; *m* 1895, Eleanour Shelton, *d* of Richard Devey and Margaret Farmer, of Ancaster, Canada; two *s* two *d*. *Educ*: private school; Hamilton College Institute, and Trinity College University, Toronto. Mobilised 5th Canadian Field Ambulance, Nov. 1914; commanded it on the Kemmel, Ypres and Somme fronts till Nov. 1916; commanded No 2 Stationary Hospital at Boulogne, till Dec. 1917; since then in command of No 5 General Hospital, Canadian, Liverpool (despatches). *Address*: Ancaster, Ontario, Canada. *T*: Ancaster 152.
Died 7 May 1928.

FARNALL, Edmund Waterton, CB 1912; Assistant Secretary to GPO since 1906; *b* 1855; *m* 1894, Helen Frances, *d* of late Leonard Bidwell, Blackheath. British Delegate to the International Conferences at Paris on White Slave Traffic Convention and Suppression of Obscene Publications, 1910; British Plenipotentiary to International Wireless Telegraph Conference, London, 1912. *Address*: 2 Morden Road, Blackheath, SE. *T*: Lee Green 501. *Club*: British Empire.
Died 14 April 1918.

FARQUHAR, 1st Earl, *cr* 1922, of St Marylebone; **Horace Brand Farquhar;** Viscount 1917; Baron 1898; Bt 1892; GCB 1922; GCVO 1902 (KCVO 1901); PC; JP, DL; Lord Steward, 1915–22; late Master of the Household of King Edward VII; *heir-pres.* to Sir Robert Townsend-Farquhar, 6th Bt; *b* 19 May 1844; 5th *s* of Sir Walter Minto Townsend-Farquhar, 2nd Bt and Erica, *d* of 7th Lord Reay; *m* 1895, Emily (*d* 1922), *d* of Col Henry Packe, Grenadier Guards, Hurleston, Northamptonshire, and Twyford Hall, Norfolk, and *widow* of Sir Edward H. Scott, 5th Bt. MP (LU) Marylebone, W, 1895–98; LCC Marylebone West, 1889–1901. Grand Officer Legion of Honour. *Heir*: none. *Address*: 7 Grosvenor Square, W1. *T*: Mayfair 5476; Castle Rising, Norfolk. *Clubs*: Marlborough, Turf.
Died 30 Aug. 1923 (ext).

FARQUHAR, Alfred; *b* 25 April 1852; *e s* of late Harvic Morton Farquhar and Hon. Louisa Harriet Ridley Colborne, *d* and *co-heir* of Lord Colborne. *Address*: 11 Belgrave Square, SW1. *T*: Victoria 3465. *Clubs*: Carlton, St James's, Arthur's, Bachelors', White's.
Died 28 Dec. 1928.

FARQUHAR, Very Rev. George Taylor Shillito, DD St Andrews, 1922; Dean of St Andrews, Dunkeld and Dunblane, since 1910; Canon of St Ninian's Cathedral, 1885–1926. *Educ*: Keble College, Oxford (MA 1882); DD (Hon.) St Andrews 1922. Ordained 1881; Precentor of Cathedral, 1885–1926; Diocesan Inspector of Schools, 1895–1900; Synod Clerk, 1900–10. *Publications*: The Episcopal History of Perth, 1894; Our Ancient Scottish Cathedrals, 1897; The Church's Year, 1904; Musicians, 1908; The History of the Lay Claims under the Scottish Bishops, 1911; Three Bishops of Dunkeld, 1915; A Scottish Twelvemonth and Other Poems, 1923. *Address*: Castlegate, St Andrews, Scotland.
Died 30 July 1927.

FARQUHAR, Gilbert; *b* 1 Feb. 1850; *y s* of Sir Minto Farquhar, 2nd Bt, *b* of Sir Robert Farquhar, 6th Bt and Viscount Farquhar, PC. *Educ*: Eton. An actor, 1883–1906. *Publications*: stories and articles. *Clubs*: Bachelors', Beefsteak, Garrick.
Died 1 April 1920.

FARQUHAR, Sir Henry Thomas, 4th Bt, *cr* 1796, of Gilmilnscroft, DL; *b* 13 Sept. 1838; *s* of Sir Walter Rockcliffe Farquhar, 3rd Bt and Lady Mary, *d* of 6th Duke of Beaufort; *m* 1862, Hon. Alice Brand, *d* of 1st Viscount Hampden; one *d* (and two *s* one *d* decd). *Educ*: Harrow. *Recreations*: hunting, shooting, fencing. *Heir*: *n* Walter Randolph Fitzroy [*b* 31 May 1878; *m* 1903, Violet, *d* of Col C. S. Corkran, late Grenadier Guards; three *s* one *d*. *Address*: 3 Eaton Square, SW]. *Address*: 22 Bryanston Square, W; Gilmilnscroft, Mauchline, NB. *Clubs*: Carlton, Travellers', Turf.
Died 15 Jan. 1916.

FARQUHAR, Sir Robert Townsend-, 6th Bt, *cr* 1821; artist; *b* Goldings, 26 Sept. 1841; 4th *s* of Sir Walter Minto Townsend-Farquhar, 2nd Bt, MP, and Erica, *d* of 7th Lord Reay; S brother, 1877; unmarried. *Educ*: RMA Woolwich. Seven years Royal Artillery, retiring 1866; afterwards on Stock Exchange and Lloyd's; active supporter of the Conservative party in Westmoreland; 20 years member of the committee which organised The Grasmere and Lake District Athletic Sports. *Publications*: 2 vols verse, 1870, 1892; pamphlet on Thirlmere Water Scheme, 1878; musical compositions—three songs (words and music); march commemorating Queen's jubilee. Exhibitor at RSA, Dudley Gallery, Liverpool Autumn Exhibition, etc. *Recreations*: angling, shooting. *Address*: 5 Oriental Place, Brighton. *Clubs*: Junior United Service (hon.); New, Brighton.
Died 30 June 1924 (ext).

FARQUHAR, Sir Walter Randolph Fitzroy, 5th Bt, *cr* 1796; *b* 31 May 1878; *s* of Walter Randolph Farquhar, 2nd *s* of Sir Walter Rockcliffe Farquhar, 3rd Bt, and Hon. Kathleen Mary, *d* of 1st Lord Deramore; *S* uncle, 1916; *m* 1903, Violet, *d* of Col Charles Seymour Corkran, late Grenadier Guards; three *s* one *d*. *Heir*: *s* Peter Walter Farquhar, *b* 8 Oct. 1904. *Address*: 3 Eaton Square, SW. *Clubs*: Turf, Arthur's.
Died 15 Oct. 1918.

FARQUHARSON, Rt. Hon. Robert, PC 1906; JP, DL; MD, LLD; *b* Edinburgh, 1836; 2nd *s* of Francis Farquharson, Finzean. *Educ*: Edinburgh Academy and University; Medical Schools of Paris, Berlin, and Vienna. Assistant Surgeon in Coldstream Guards, 1859–68; Medical Officer to Rugby School, and Assistant Physician to St Mary's Hospital; Lecturer on Materia Medica; MP (L) West Aberdeenshire, 1880–1906. Owner of about 16,900 acres. *Publications*: Guide to Therapeutics, 5th edn; School Hygiene; The House of Commons from Within, 1912; In and Out of Parliament. *Recreation*: shooting. *Address*: Finzean, Aboyne, NB; Migvie Lodge, Porchester Gardens, W. *Clubs*: Reform, Junior United Service; Royal Northern, Aberdeen; Scottish Liberal, Edinburgh.
Died 8 June 1918.

FARR, William Edward, CBE 1920; JP; Solicitor, member of Booth, Wade, Farr Lomas-Walker and Foster; Alderman of Leeds City Council; Vice-Chairman Leeds Education Committee; Chairman, Leeds High Education Committee; *b* Weston, Herts, 1872; *e s* of Albert Hart and Louisa Farr; *m* Hilda Lomas-Walker, Harrogate; one *s*. *Educ*: privately. Past Pres. Leeds Incorporated Law Society; Chairman, Leeds Military Advisory Committee, 1916–18; Chairman, Leeds Employment Committee, 1918–20; member of Executive of National Liberal Federation, 1907–19; Hon. Secretary, Leeds Liberal Federation, 1902–22. Hon. Sec. Leeds Luncheon Club; member of Council of Leeds University. *Address*: 1 Central Bank Chambers,

Leeds. *T:* 20787, Leeds; South Gables, Langcliffe Avenue, Harrogate. *TA:* Wafer, Leeds. *Clubs:* Leeds, Leeds Liberal, Leeds.

Died 2 Oct. 1923.

FARRAN, Major George Lambert, DSO 1917; OBE; MC; 2nd Lancers, Indian Army; *s* of late Sir Charles F. Farran and Lady Farran of Brackendale House, Camberley; *m* 1909, Myrtle Keatinge; one *d* one *d*. *Educ:* Rugby; Cheltenham; Sandhurst. Entered Army, 1900; served Waziristan operations, 1901–02 (medal and clasp); European War, France, 1914–15; Egypt, 1915; Mesopotamia, 1915–16; S Persia, 1916–19 (despatches, DSO, OBE, MC); Afghan War, 1919 (medal and clasp); graduated Staff College, Quetta, 1920. *Recreation:* polo. *Address:* 2nd Lancers, Poona, India.

Died 21 Dec. 1925.

FARRAR, Rt. Rev. Walter, DD; Vicar of Bognor since 1915; Assistant Bishop, West Indies, 1912–13; *b* British Guiana, 1865; *s* of late Very Rev. F. W. Farrar, DD, Dean of Canterbury; *m* Alice, *e d* of W. F. Bridges, JP, Administrator-General of British Guiana. *Educ:* Queen's College, Guiana; Keble College, Oxford. Has held, besides various posts of importance in Guiana, the Rectory of Hawkchurch, Dorset; has been Acting Warden of the Jamaica Church Theological College, and Commissary in England of the Bishop of Guiana; was in Jamaica when the call to Antigua came; Bishop of Antigua, 1905–10; resigned, 1910; late Assistant Bishop of Queensland; Asst Bishop in the Diocese of York, and Commissary to the Archbishop of York, 1910; Assistant Bishop of Quebec, and later Archdeacon of St Francis, Canada; on return to England acted for a term as Principal of Bishop's College, Cheshunt; was then asked to go to Honduras on a special mission; Bishop of British Honduras, 1913–15. *Publications:* besides many reviews, etc, a work on the Cultus of the Sacred Heart, co-author of Notes on the History of the Church in Guiana. *Address:* The Vicarage, Bognor, Sussex. *Died 6 Dec. 1916.*

FARRELL, James Patrick; MP (N) North Longford, 1900–18; *b* Longford, 13 May 1865; *s* of Patrick Farrell and Anne, *e d* of late John Lynam, Strokestown, Co. Roscommon; *m* 1888, Bride, *d* of late M. Fitzgerald, Co. Longford; five *s* two *d*. *Educ:* St Mels Coll. Longford. Became a journalist early, Roscommon Herald; always actively engaged in politics in Land League and National League periods; imprisoned two months 1889 for a speech; contested Kilkenny City, 1895; MP (AP) West Cavan, 1895–1900. *Publications:* Fireside Talks about Co. Longford; Historical Notes and Stories of Co. Longford; a large Illustrated History of Co. Longford. *Address:* Market Square, Longford; 10 Gloucester Street, SW.

Died 11 Dec. 1921.

FARRER, Reginald, JP; FRHS; Clerk in the Foreign Office; *b* 17 Feb. 1880; *e s* of James Farrer of Ingleborough, Yorkshire, and Elizabeth Reynell-Pack. *Educ:* privately; Balliol College, Oxford. Second in Mods, third in Greats, 1902. Travelled in Japan, China, Korea, Canada, 1903; yearly journeys of botanical exploration in the Eastern and Western Alps of Europe ever since; Ceylon, 1907; Athens and Constantinople, 1912. Contested (L) Ashford Division, 1911; Yorkshire County Council; Feb. 1914–April 1916 was across Northern China and over the Tibetan Border; was rejected for military purposes on returning, and has since been employed at the Foreign Office. Gill Memorial, RGS, 1920. *Publications: novels:* The House of Shadows; The Sundered Streams; The Ways of Rebellion; The Anne-Queen's Chronicle; Through the Ivory Gate (censored); *horticulture and travel:* My Rock-Garden; Alpines and Bog-Plants; In a Yorkshire Garden; Among the Hills; King Laurin's Garden (the Dolomites); The Garden of Asia; In Old Ceylon; On the Eaves of the World, 1917; *drama:* The Dowager of Jerusalem; Vasanta the Beautiful; Jane Austen's Memorial Article, Quarterly Review, July 1917; The Void of War; The English Rock-Garden. *Recreations:* gardening, being on mountains, talking (without music), indulging in drama. *Address:* Ingleborough, Yorkshire, *via* Lancaster; 50 Ennismore Gardens, SW7. *T:* Ken. 2926. *Clubs:* Travellers', Athenæum, Alpine. *Died 16 Oct. 1920.*

FARRINGTON, Col Malcolm Charles, CB 1887; *b* 4 June 1835. Entered army 1853; Col 1884; retired 1890; served Burmah 1886–89 (thanks of Govt of India, despatches, CB, medal with two clasps).

Died 7 July 1925.

FASKEN, Maj.-Gen. Charles Grant Mansell, CB 1904; *b* 24 May 1855; *s* of late General Edward Thomas Fasken; *m* 1885, Eveline, *d* of late Rev. William Pratt, Rector of Harpley, Norfolk; one *s* two *d*. *Educ:* Marlborough; Royal Military College, Sandhurst. Entered army, Bedfordshire Regt, 1874; BSC (later Indian Army) 1878; Brevet-Col 1904; served Afghan War, 1878–80; present at battle of

Ahmad Khel and action of Arzu, march from Kabul to the relief of Kandahar and battle of Kandahar (medal with 2 clasps and bronze star); Aitchakzai Expedition and operations against the Marri tribe, 1880; served as a Brigade Major in Black Mountain Expedition of 1888 (despatches, medal with clasp); received commendations of Government of India and of Commander-in-Chief for the surprise of village of Maizar, Tochi Valley, NW Frontier, India, 1900; operations in Somaliland, 1903–4; was Brigadier-General commanding 2nd Brigade, action at Jidballi (despatches twice, CB, medal and 2 clasps); Maj.-Gen. 1907; commanded The Southern, Bannu, and Ferozepore Brigades, India, 1906–11; Colonel 52nd Sikhs FF, 1909; retired, 1914; Divisional Commander, European War, Sept. 1914–June 1916 (1914–15 Star, two medals); served in the BEF until invalided. *Address:* c/o Westminster Bank, Wokingham, Berks.

Died 15 April 1928.

FATEH ALI KHAN, Hon. Sir Hajee, Nawab Kizilbash, KCIE 1921 (CIE 1903); *b* 1862; *S* to headship of Kizilbashes, 1896. Placed himself and his great clan at disposal of Government for Chitral campaign, and induced many of tribes across the border to adopt an attitude of pacific non-intervention. For this service received 3000 acres of land in Chenab Canal Colony for settlement of his followers; has served on Punjab Legislative Council; representative of Punjab at Famine Conference, 1897; Life President of Anjumani-Islamia, Lahore, and Imamia Association of Punjab; a Counsellor of the Aitchison Chiefs' College, Lahore; Fellow of the Punjab University; Trustee of the Aligarh College; represented the province as guest of Great Britain at King Edward's Coronation. *Heir: s* Nisor Ali Khan, *b* 1901. *Address:* Aitchison Chiefs' Coll., Lahore, India.

Died 28 Oct. 1923.

FAUCONBERG and CONYERS, Baroness (13th in line) *cr* 1295 and 1509; **Marcia Amelia Mary Pelham, (Countess of Yarborough),** OBE 1920; *b* 18 Oct. 1863; *d* of 12th Baron Conyers and Mary, *d* of Reginald Curteis; *S* father, 1892, as 13th Baroness Conyers; Barony of Fauconberg called out of abeyance, 1903; *m* 1886, 4th Earl of Yarborough; two *s* (and two *s* decd). Lady of Justice of the Order of St John of Jerusalem. Owner of landed estates in North and West Riding of Yorkshire; possessed a collection of miniatures and pictures by Drouet, Kneller, and Sir Thomas Lawrence. *Heir: s* Lord Worsley, *b* 17 Dec. 1888. *Address:* Brocklesby Park, Lincolnshire. *Died 17 Nov. 1926.*

FAUDEL-PHILLIPS, Sir Benjamin Samuel, 2nd Bt, *cr* 1897; *b* 21 July 1871; *s* of Sir George Faudel Faudel-Phillips, 1st Bt and Helen (*d* 1916), *d* of late J. M. Levy, *sister* of 1st Lord Burnham; *S* father, 1922. *Heir: b* Lionel Lawson Faudel, *b* 11 April 1877. *Address:* Balls Park, Hertford. *T:* Hertford 9. *Club:* Reform.

Died 11 Jan. 1927.

FAUDEL-PHILLIPS, Sir George Faudel, 1st Bt, *cr* 1897; GCIE 1897; JP, DL; *b* 29 July 1840; 2nd *s* of Sir Benjamin S. Phillips, Alderman, Lord Mayor of London, 1865–66, and Rachel, *d* of S. H. Faudel; *m* 1867, Helen, (*d* 1916), *d* of late J. M. Levy, *sister* of 1st Lord Burnham; two *s* three *d*. *Educ:* Univ. Coll. School; Berlin; Paris. Sheriff, London and Middlesex, 1884–85; Alderman of Ward of Farringdon Within, 1888–1912; Governor of the Honourable the Irish Society, 1894; High Sheriff, Co. of London, 1895; Lord Mayor of London, 1896–97; an Almoner of Christ's Hospital; Governor of St Bartholomew's; Past Master Spactacle-Makers' Company; High Sheriff Hertford, 1900 and 1901. Commander of the Siamese Order of the White Elephant; 2nd class Osmanieh Order; 2nd class Persian Order of Lion and Sun; Commander of the Order of Leopold; Grand Cross of Servian Order of Takova. *Recreations:* shooting, golfing, riding, driving; a true bibliophile, possessor of a valuable and well-selected library. *Heir: s* Benjamin Samuel Faudel-Phillips, *b* 21 July 1871. *Address:* Balls Park, Hertford. *T:* Hertford 9. *Club:* Reform.

Died 28 Dec. 1922.

FAUNTHORPE, Rev. John Pincher, MA; FRGS; *b* Scotter, 7 Aug. 1839; *m* 1st, C. E. Blackmore, *d* of late Rev. John Blackmore, MA; 2nd, L. J. (*d* 1917), *d* of late James Russell, QC; three *s*. *Educ:* St John's College, Battersea. MA (Lond.); 1st BA; 1st in English Honours; 1st, Holy Scripture Exam. Lond. Univ. Pupil teacher, St George's School, Ramsgate, 1853–57; student, Battersea College, 1858–59; 2nd on QS list for England at entrance; master in Chester Training College, 1860; St John's College, Battersea, Geography Lecturer, 1861–62; Secretary and Lecturer, 1863–66; Vice-Principal (ordained by Bishop of Winchester), 1867–74; Principal, Whitelands College, Chelsea, SW, 1874–1907. *Publications:* Standard Reading-books; Household Science; Map-drawing Atlases; Colonial Geography, British; Complete Index to Ruskin's Fors Clavigera; formerly President of London Ruskin

Society. *Recreation:* driving. *Address:* Elmfield, Bromley Common, Kent. *Died 14 May 1924.*

FAURÉ, Gabriel; General Inspector of the Fine Arts in France; *b* Pamiers, 13 May 1845. Studied at School of Sacred Music directed by Niedermeyer under Dietsch and Saint-Saëns. Maître de Chapelle, Church of the Madeleine, 1877; organist, 1896; Directeur du Conservatoire national de Musique et de Declamation, 1905–20. *Works:* The Birth of Venus, etc. *Address:* Conservatoire Nationale, Paris. *Died 4 Nov. 1924.*

FAVELL, Richard, ChM, MRCS; Professor of Midwifery, University of Sheffield; Surgeon, Jessop Hospital for Women. *Educ:* St Bartholomew's Hospital, Sheffield. *Address:* Brunswick House, Glossop Road, Sheffield. *T:* 2128.
Died Nov. 1918.

FAWCETT, Henry Heath, CB 1918; *b* 7 Dec. 1863; *s* of Peter Fawcett; *m* 1892, Colina, *d* of late John Sharp; one *s* three *d*. *Educ:* Dulwich College; University College, London. Clerk Higher Division War Office, 1886; Private Secretary to Sir Arthur Haliburton and to Sir Ralph Knox, Permanent Under-Secretaries of State for War, 1896–98; Principal Clerk, 1899; Auditor 1st Army Corps 1902–4; Financial Adviser and Auditor, S Africa, 1904; Chief Accountant, Aldershot, 1905–9; Assistant Secretary, War Office, 1916–17; Director of Army Contracts, 1917–19; Director of Finance, War Office, 1919–24; graded as Principal Assistant-Secretary with rank of Assistant Under-Secretary of State; retired on pension, 1924. Officer Legion of Honour. *Recreations:* bicycling, sculling. *Address:* Oaken Cottage, Berkhamsted.
Died 23 Dec. 1925.

FAWCETT, Lt-Col P. H., DSO; retired; Royal Artillery; *b* Torquay, 1867; *s* of E. B. Fawcett, Torquay, and *g s* of Henry Fawcett, of Broadfields, York, and Myra, *d* of Col A. M. McDougall, Bengal Army; *m* Nina, *d* of G. W. Paterson, Ceylon Civil Serivce; two *s* one *d*. *Educ:* Newton College, S Devon; Westminster (Exhibitioner); RMA, Woolwich. Joined RA, 1886; served Ceylon, England, Malta, Hong Kong, Ireland, in RGA and Staff; received RGS Diploma, 1900, for surveying; mission interior Morocco, 1901; lent to Bolivian Government as Boundary Commissioner, 1906–10; retired from Army, 1910, continuing exploration in S America, returning for that, close 1914; commanded Brigade RFA Heavy Artillery; and was CBSO in France till 1919 (DSO, despatches four times); returned S America, 1919–22, for exploration; received Founder's Medal, RGS, 1917. *Publications:* geographical, travel, and journalistic articles in newspapers and magazines. *Recreations:* all sports, exploration, surveying and prospecting, artist (exhibitor Royal Academy in black and white), archaeology, philosophy, yacht designing and building, and navigating, motoring. *Address:* c/o Royal Bank of Canada, Rio de Janeiro, Brazil, S America. *M:* FJ 1867. *Died 1925.*

FAWKE, Sir Ernest (John), Kt 1922; Director of the Central and Western Corporation; *m* Wemyss Gertrude; one *s*.
Died 26 Oct. 1928.

FAWKES, Admiral Sir Wilmot Hawksworth, GCB 1911 (KCB 1907); KCVO 1903 (CVO 1902); LLD Cambridge University, 1913; *b* 22 Dec. 1846; 2nd *s* of Major Richard Fawkes and Fanny, *d* of A. Paris; *m* 1875, Juliana (*d* 1916), *e d* of J. W. G. Spicer, Spye Park, Wilts. *Educ:* St John's College, Cambridge. Entered Royal Navy, 1860; Lieut Nov. 1867; Com. March 1880; Capt. July 1886; Com. Royal Yacht Osborne, 1884–86; HMS Raleigh, 1888–90; Mercury, 1893–96; Terrible; 1896; Canopus, 1899–1900; Naval Adviser to Inspector-General of Fortifications, 1891–92; ADC to Queen Victoria, 1899–1901; Private Secretary to First Lord of the Admiralty, 1897–99, and 1900–2; Rear-Adm. commanding Cruiser Squadron, 1902–4; Commander-in-Chief, Australian station, 1905–8; Plymouth, 1908–11; retired, 1911. *Recreations:* field sports. *Address:* Steel Cross House, Steel Cross, Tunbridge Wells. *TA:* Crowborough. *Clubs:* United Service, Arthur's. *Died 29 May 1926.*

FAYOLLE, Emile; Marshal of France, 1921; *b* Le Puy, Haute Loire, 1852. *Educ:* Polytechnic School. Sub-Lieut Ecole d'Application de l'Artillerie et de Genie, 1875; Professor of Applied Artillery Tactics at the Superior School of War; Lieut-Colonel 1903; General, 1910; commanded the Artillery Brigade of Vincennes; Commander 70th Division of Infantry, 14 Aug. 1914; Commander of the Legion of Honour, Oct. 1914; Commander 33rd Army Corps, June 1915; 6th Army, Feb. 1916; GAC May 1917; Commandant Supérieur des forces françaises en Italie, Nov. 1917; Commander GAR Feb 1918; Grand Officer of the Legion of Honour, Oct. 1916; Croix de Guerre, Oct.

1916; Grand Croix of the Legion of Honour, July 1918; Médaille Militaire, 1919. *Address:* 18 Avenue de la Bourdonnais, Paris.
Died 27 Aug. 1928.

FEARNSIDES, Edwin Greaves, MA, MD, BChir (Cantab.), BSc (London); FRCP (London); Assistant Physician to the Hospital for Nervous Diseases, Maida Vale, W; Beit Memorial Research Fellow; *b* Horbury, Yorks, 17 June 1883; *y s* of late Joshua and Maria Fearnsides; unmarried. *Educ:* Wheelwright Grammar School, Dewsbury; Trinity Hall, Cambridge; London Hospital; Universities of Berlin and Munich; West Riding County Major Scholarship, 1900; Scholar of Trinity Hall, 1902–6; Class I Natural Science Tripos, Part I, 1904; Part II (Physiology), 1906; 1st Class Honours, London, BSc, 1905; Price University Scholar, London Hospital, 1906. After qualification held all the Resident appointments at the London Hospital; Medical Registrar, London Hospital, 1910–14. *Publications:* various papers dealing with nervous and general diseases in medical journals. *Recreation:* travel. *Address:* 46 Queen Anne Street, Cavendish Square, W. *T:* Mayfair 2562; Highfield, Golders Green Road, NW4. *Club:*United University. *Died 26 June 1919.*

FEARON, Daniel Robert, CB 1894; MA; Barrister; *b* Assington, 1 Dec. 1835; *m* 1861, Margaret (*d* 1909), *d* of Prof. Bonamy Price (Political Economy, Oxford). *Educ:* Marlborough; Balliol Coll. Oxford. 1st Class Lit. Hum. Oxford. HM Inspector of Schools, 1860; Assistant-Comr Schools Inquiry Commission, 1865; Assistant Commissioner Endowed Schools Commission, 1870; Assistant Charity Commissioner, 1874; Secretary Charity Commissioners, 1886–1900; Charity Commissioner, 1900–3; retired June 1903. *Address:* Messrs Bury, 47 Lincoln's Inn Fields, WC. *Club:* Athenæum. *Died 20 Oct. 1919.*

FEARON, Rev. William Andrewes, DD; *b* Assington Vicarage, 4 Feb. 1841; 3rd *s* of Rev. Daniel Rose Fearon and Frances Andrewes; *m* Mary, *e d* of late Archdeacon Freeman, Exeter. *Educ:* Winchester; New Coll. Oxford (Hon. Fellow, 1901). Double 1st (Classics and Mathematics) in Moderations and again in the Final Schools. Fellow and Tutor of New College, 1864–67; had a tutor's house at Winchester and the mastership of the Junior VI, 1867–82; Headmaster of Durham School and Examining Chaplain to Bishop of Newcastle, 1882–84; Hon. Canon of Winchester Cathedral, 1889; Headmaster of Winchester College, 1884–1901; Member of Teachers' Registration Council, 1903–4; Examining Chaplain to Bishop of Winchester, 1903–15; Archdeacon of Winchester, 1903–20; Canon of Winchester, 1906–20. *Address:* 12 Cresswell Gardens, SW5. *Club:* Athenæum. *Died 29 April 1924.*

FEETHAM, Brig.-Gen. Edward, CB 1915; CMG 1917; *b* 4 June 1863; *m* 1904, Isabel Beatrix, *d* of Col Ewen Grant; one *d*. Lieut Royal Berks Regt, 1883; Captain, 1892; Adjutant, 1895–6; Major, 1903; Lt-Col 1911; Adjutant, Volunteers, 1896–1901; served Sudan, 1885–86 (medal, 2 clasps; bronze star); South Africa, 1901–2 (despatches, Bt-Major, Queen's medal 5 clasps); European War, 1914–17 (CB, CMG). *Address:* Farmwood, Ascot. *Club:* United Service. *Died 30 March 1918.*

FEILDEN, Maj.-Gen. Sir Henry Broome, KCB 1923 (CB 1893); CMG 1903; *b* 31 July 1834; *s* of Rev. Robert M. Feilden. Entered army, 1852; Maj.-Gen. 1890; served Crimea, 1854–55 (severely wounded, despatches, medal with three clasps, Turkish medal); retired, 1893. *Address:* Wear Giffard, Warwick.
Died 1 Dec. 1926.

FEILDEN, Col Henry Wemyss, CB 1900; retired; *b* 6 Oct. 1838; 2nd *s* of Sir William Henry Feilden, 2nd Bt; *m* 1864, Julia (*d* 1920), *d* of David MacCord of S Carolina. *Educ:* Cheltenham College. Served Indian Mutiny, 1857–58 (medal with clasp); China, 1860 (medal with clasp). Served in army of Confederate States with rank of AAG, 1862–65; surrendering after last battle of war between the States, with the remnant of army of Tennessee, under Gen. J. E. Johnstone, to Gen. Sherman; Naturalist to the British Polar Expedition, 1875–76 (medal); Boer War, 1881; South Africa, Boer War, 1900–1 (medal with three clasps); FGS, FRGS, CMZS. Visited Grinnell Land, Ellesmere Land, Greenland, Spitzbergen, Novaya Zemlya, Waigats, Lapland, and Northern Russia for scientific research. *Publications:* papers in geological, biological, and botanical research. *Address:* Rampyndene, Burwash, Sussex. *Club:* Junior United Service.
Died 18 June 1921.

FELBERMAN, Louis, FRHistS; late Chairman Francis Joseph Institute; Founder and acting President Hungarian Society for Encouragement of Home Industries; Fellow of the Hungarian

Geographical Society; Hungarian Ethnographical Society, and several learned Societies; Knight of the Imperial Order Francis Joseph; Officer of the Royal Orders St Sava and Takova; *b* Hungary, 1861; *s* of a landed proprietor; *m* 1901, Isabelle Maud (*d* 1918), *d* of late Capt. Ross Caldwell, 7th Dragoons, and *widow* of Col H. Webber. Came to England 1881, and devoted several years to study of English language and literature. *Publications:* Hungary and its People; The Puszta; Gypsy Czinká's Prophecy; The Land of the Khedive; The Pyrenees, Auvergne, South Coast of Brittany, Touraine; The Land of the Magyars; Hungary and the Hungarians; Francis Joseph I, The Hungarian Origin of Margaret of Scotland; The House of Teck; edited the Souvenir Album of the Hungarian Millennial Festival; translated Maurice Jokai's In Love with the Czarina; The Blind Poet, Love's Puppets, and numerous other stories. *Recreation:* fond of travelling in order to study the customs and manners of the different nationalities. *Address:* The Boltons, 55 Naphegy Utca (Sun Hill), Budapest. *Clubs:* Authors', Royal Automobile, Albemarle; Radnor, Folkestone.

Died 1 Nov. 1927.

FELL, Thomas Edward, CMG 1918; Colonial Secretary, Fiji, since 1919; *b* 1873; *s* of John Fell, JP, DL, Flan How, Ulverston. *Educ:* Lancaster Royal Grammar School; Owens College, Manchester; Pembroke College, Cambridge, BA 1897. Chief Clerk, Colonial Secretary's Office, Gold Coast, 1897; Inspector of Preventive Services, Gold Coast, 1899; Travelling Commissioner, Gold Coast, 1901; Acting Secretary for Native Affairs, Gold Coast, 1902; District Commissioner, Ashanti, 1905; Provincial Commissioner, 1907; Colonial Secretary, Barbados, 1916; Acting Governor, Barbados, 1918; Acting Governor, Fiji, and Acting High Commissioner, Western Pacific, 1920 and 1921. *Recreations:* games and sport of all kinds. *Address:* Suva, Fiji. *Club:* Sports.

Died 21 May 1926.

FELLING, Sir Christian Ludolph Neethling, Kt 1928; CMG 1922; MInstT; General Manager Kenya and Uganda Railway since 1923; *b* Cape Town, 1880; *m; one s one d. Educ:* Public School, Stellenbosch. Studied law at South African College, Cape Town. Joined Cape Govt Railways, 1895; Chief Asst General Manager, S African Railways, 1918. *Address:* Nairobi, Kenya Colony.

Died 19 Aug. 1928.

FELLOWES, Rear-Admiral Sir Thomas Hounsom Butler, KCB 1911 (CB 1868); JP, DL, Herts; *b* 19 Oct. 1827; *s* of late Sir James Fellowes, MD, of Adbury House, Hants; *m* 1st, 1857, Constance Fanny (*d* 1888), *d* of C. S. Hanson of Constantinople; 2nd, 1890, Margaret, *d* of Rev. W. Jowitt; two *s.* Entered navy, 1845; Senior Lieutenant of Mersey frigate at landing of allied forces at Vera Cruz, 1861; Rear-Admiral, 1886; served Crimea, 1854–56 (Baltic medal); Black Sea (Crimean and Turkish medals, Sebastopol clasp); commanded Naval Brigade, Abyssinian War, 1868 (despatches, promoted, CB, medal); National Lifeboat Institution Medal. *Address:* Woodfield, Stevenage, Herts. *TA:* Stevenage.

Died 26 March 1923.

FELLOWS, Col (Robert) Bruce, CB 1895; JP; *b* 5 Aug. 1830; *s* of late Thomas Fellows, Moneyhill, and Mary, *d* of late Thomas Howard, Batchworth Heath; *m* 1867, Emily Ann (*d* 1917), *d* of John Fellows, Eynsford, Kent; one *s. Educ:* Eton; Christ's Coll. Cambridge. Thirty-seven years in Hertfordshire Militia; commanded it nearly fifteen years; Hon. Col 4th Bedfordshire and Hertfordshire Regiment (Special Reserve), 1908; entered Privy Council Office, 1858; became Deputy Clerk of the Council and Chief Clerk, 1894; retired 1895. *Publication:* Historical Records of the Hertfordshire Militia. *Recreation:* shooting. *Address:* Stanborough Cottage, Hatfield, Herts. *TA:* Hatfield.

Died 6 Jan. 1922.

FELLS, John Manger, CBE 1920; *b* 1858; *s* of late William Fells, Deal; *m* 1897, Henrietta Emily (*d* 1918), *d* of William Julian; three *s* one *d. Educ:* Deal College; privately. Started commercial career in the Accountant's office of a Railway Co.; Accountant and Assistant Secretary of the Anglo-American Brush Electric Light Corporation (later the Brush Electrical Engineering Co Ltd); Superintending Accountant, Salt Union Ltd, 1889, and General Manager, 1895; commenced practice as an Accountant, 1899; Fellow, Member of Council, and Examiner of the Society of Incorporated Accountants and Auditors, Fellow of the Institute of Cost and Works Accountants, an original Fellow, Royal Economic Society; Private Secretary to the Surveyor General of Supply, War Office, 1917; member of several War Office Committees, including Cost Accounting Committee, 1917–19; Hon. Life Member British Red Cross for work in connection with Red Cross. *Publications:* Factory Accounts, their Principles and Practice, 7th edition; various lectures and addresses

on industrial economics, and scientific accountancy. *Recreatio* walking. *Address:* 128 Goldhurst Terrace, NW6; 7 Union Cou EC2. *T:* Central 4506. *Club:* National Liberal.

Died 7 Dec. 192

FENN, Colonel Ernest Harrold, CIE 1894; Royal Army Medic Corps; retired 1907; *b* 16 Feb. 1850; *s* of T. H. Fenn, Naylan Colchester; *m* 1886, Bertha, *d* of Robert Jobson. *Educ:* Sherborn School. Entered Army Medical Staff, Sept. 1875; served in Afgha War, 1879–80; present at affair at Zaidabad; accompanied force und Lord Roberts to relief of Kandahar; present at Battle of Kandah (despatches, medal and clasp, bronze star); joined Grenadier Guard 1881; Soudan Campaign, 1885; Battle of Hasheen and destructio of Temai (medal with clasp and Khedive's star); accompanied S Mortimer Durand on his mission to Cabul, 1893 (thanked t Government of India); served on Lord Lansdowne's Staff in Indi 1888–94; served on Lord Curzon's Staff in India, 1898–1903 (Durb medal). Decorated for services on Durand Mission. *Recreatio* shooting. *Club:* Naval and Military.

Died 24 Nov. 191

FENN, Frederick; dramatist; *b* Bishop's Stortford, 6 Nov. 1868; *e* of late George Manville Fenn, novelist. *Educ:* privately. Was Assistar Editor of The Graphic and Dramatic Critic Daily Graphic. *Publication* Plays: Judged by Appearances (one act); A Married Women (fou acts); The Convict on the Hearth (one act); Amasis (comic opera Dame Nature (four acts), adapted from the French of Henry Batailk (with Richard Pryce) Saturday to Monday (three acts); 'Op 'o m Thumb (one act); etc. *Recreation:* none. *Address:* 12 Gloucester Roac NW. *Clubs:* Savile, Green Room.

Died 2 Jan. 1924

FENN, John Cyril Douglas, CMG 1924; Colonial Secretary of Britis Guiana, 1925–26; *b* 25 Nov. 1879; *y s* of late Colonel E. G. Fenr Shanklin; *m* 1914, Evelyn Blanche, *y d* of late James Lawforc Springvale House, Springvale. *Educ:* Marlborough. Entered Civ Service, Gold Coast, 1903; retired, 1908; reappointed Cyprus, 191C Chief Secretary to Government of Cyprus, 1920–25; administere the Government of Cyprus on several occasions. *Address:* Gastel Zahar, St Jean-de-Luz, France. *Club:* Badminton.

Died 27 Jan. 1927

FENNELLY, Most Rev. Thomas; *b* 28 Jan. 1845. *Educ:* Thurle College; St Vincent's, Castleknock; Maynooth. Ordained 1870; paris priest Moycarkey, 1889; RC Bishop Coadjutor to Archbishop Croke 1901–2; Archbishop of Cashel, 1902–13; retired 1913. *Address* Moycarkey, Co. Tipperary.

Died 24 Dec. 1927

FENTON, Sir Myles, Kt 1889; JP; Consulting Director, South-Easteri and Chatham Railway, since 1896; Lt-Col Engineer and Railwa Volunteer Staff Corps; Chevalier of Legion of Honour of France Officer of Order of Leopold of Belgium; *b* Kendal, 5 Sept. 1830 *s* of Myles Fenton, Kendal; *m* 1883, Charlotte Jane, *d* of George Oakes *Educ:* Kendal. Commenced on Kendal and Windermere Railway 1845; after holding situations on East Lancashire, Great Eastern (ther Eastern Counties), London and S Western, Manchester, Sheffield and Lincolnshire (later Great Central) Railways, and Rochdale Canal became Secretary of East Lancashire Railway, 1856; afterwards Assistant Manager of Lancashire and Yorkshire; General Manager Metropolitan Railway, 1863; South Eastern Railway, 1880. *Address* Redstone Hall, Redhill, Surrey.

Died 14 March 1918

FENTON, Rt. Rev. Patrick; Auxiliary RC Bishop to Cardina Bourne, and Bishop of Amycla since 1904; *b* London, 1837; *s* o Bartholomew Fenton, Cork. *Educ:* St Edmund's, Old Hall, Ware (President, 1882–87). Ordained, 1866; served successively at Ogle Street, at the Bavarian Chapel, and under Mgr Gilbert at St Mary's Moorfields; Conventual Chaplain of the Order of the Knights of St John of Jerusalem since 1878; Domestic Prelate to Leo XIII, 1885–87; Rector of St Thomas, Fulham, 1887; Canon of Westminster, 1895; Titular Bishop of Amycla, and Vicar-General of Westminster; Provost of the Metropolitan Chapter; The First Administrator of the Westminster Cathedral, 1899. *Address:* 30 Morpeth Mansions, Westminster, SW1. *Died Aug. 1918.*

FENTON, (Thomas) Charles, ISO 1912; late of the Parliamentary Branch, India Office. Called to Bar, Middle Temple, 1893. *Recreations:* horticulture, antiquities. *Address:* Cranford, Vineyard Hill, Wimbledon Park, SW. *Died 7 April 1927.*

FENTON, William Hugh, MD, MA; MRCS, LRCP; Senior Surgeon, Chelsea Hospital for Women; Surgeon to Society of Women Journalists; *b* Shardlow, Derbyshire, 1854; *e s* of Michael Thomas Fenton Jones, MD; *m* 1887, Alice Anne, *e d* of William Foster, Hornby Castle, Lancaster, JP, DL; no *c. Educ:* Derby School; Merton College, Oxford (Postmaster in Natural Science); Honours in Natural Science, BA, 1876; MA, 1886. Lecturer on Midwifery and Diseases of Women, Zenana Medical Mission; Vice-President and Hon. Secretary, British Gynæcological Society; Gold Medallist in Surgery and Duckworth Nelson Prizeman, London Hospital; Surgeon to Throat Hospital, Golden Square; Surgeon to London Throat Hospital. *Publications:* contributions to medical journals; also Nineteenth Century. *Recreations:* salmon fishing, shooting, motoring. *Address:* Litley Court, Hereford. *M:* LE 3663. *Club:* Royal Automobile. *Died 5 Oct. 1928.*

FENWICK, Rt. Hon. Charles, PC 1911; MP (GL) Northumberland, Wansbeck, since 1885; *b* Cramlington, Northumberland, 5 May 1850; *s* of late John Fenwick, Bebside, Northumberland; *m* 1869, Jane, *d* of H. Gardner. A working miner, 1860–85; Delegate to Trades Union Congress, 1883; Secretary to Parliamentary Committee on Trades Unions, 1890; Member of Parliamentary Coal-Dust Commission, 1891; served on Royal Commission on Secondary Education, 1894. *Address:* 14 Tankerville Terrace, Newcastle upon Tyne; 95 Vauxhall Bridge Road, SW. *Died 20 April 1918.*

FENWICK, Hon. Sir (George) Townsend, KCMG 1912 (CMG 1904); late senior unofficial member Legislative Council Trinidad and Tobago; *b* 25 Jan. 1846; *s* of John Fenwick of Preston House, Northumberland; *m* 1873, Lucy Frances (*d* 1916), *d* of J. T. Bowen of Trinidad; one *d. Educ:* Stockton; St Mary's College, Windermere. *Address:* Port of Spain, Trinidad, West Indies. *Clubs:* Wellington, West Indian; Union, Savannah, Trinidad.

Died 25 March 1927.

FERGUSON, Lt-Col George Arthur, JP, DL; *b* 17 March 1835; *s* of Rear-Adm. George Ferguson and Hon. Elizabeth Jane Rowley, *d* of 1st Baron Langford; *m* 1861, Hon. Nina Maria Hood (*d* 1923), *e d* of 1st Viscount Bridport; three *s* two *d.* Formerly Grenadier Guards; served Crimea, including Fall of Sebastopol, 1855 (medal and clasp and Turkish medal). *Address:* Pitfour, Mintlaw, Aberdeenshire. *Died 15 Dec. 1924.*

FERGUSON, James, of Kinmundy; DL and JP Aberdeenshire; KC 1902; Sheriff of Forfarshire since 1905; *b* 28 July 1857; *e* and *o* surv. *s* of William Ferguson of Kinmundy, Aberdeenshire; *m* 1885, Georgina Anne, *e d* of Capt. John de Courcy Agnew, RN; one *s. Educ:* Birkenhead School; Craigmount School; Edin. Univ. MA. Called to Scots Bar, 1879; appointed Assistant Advocate-Depute, 1888; Advocate-Depute, 1892; reappointed, 1895; Senior Advocate-Depute, 1896–98; was Honorary Secretary, National Union of Conservative Associations for Scotland, Central Office, 1882–92; Lieut-Col and Hon. Col (VD) 1st Batt. 9th VB (Highlanders) Royal Scots, 1900–4; Lieut-Col 2nd Battalion, 1914–15 and 3rd Battalion since 1915; Sheriff of Argyllshire, 1898–1905; of Inverness, Elgin, and Nairn, Jan.–March 1905. *Publications: legal:* Railway Rights and Duties, 1889; Five Years' Railway Cases, 1894; The Law of Railways in Scotland, by F. Deas, revised and extended, 1897; Scottish Railway Statutes, 1898; The Law of Roads, Streets, and Rights of Way in Scotland, 1904; The Law of Water in Scotland, 1907; Railway Cases and Statutes, 1897–1912, 1913; *general:* Robert Ferguson the Plotter, 1887; Two Scottish Soldiers, 1888; Records of 3rd (the Buchan) Vol. Batt. the Gordon Highlanders, 1894; Records of Clan and Name of Ferguson, etc. (with Rev. J. Menzies Fergusson), 1895 and 1899; papers illustrating the History of the Scots Brigade in the service of the United Netherlands (Scottish History Society), 1899–1901; Records of 9th Vol. Batt. (Highlanders) the Royal Scots, 1909. *Address:* 10 Wemyss Place, Edinburgh; Kinmundy, Mintlaw, NB. *Clubs:* Carlton; New, Edinburgh; Royal Northern, Aberdeen.

Died 25 April 1917.

FERGUSON, John, MA, MD (Toronto); LRCP (Edin.), LFPS (Glas.); Senior Physician, Toronto Western Hospital; Associate Professor of Medicine, University of Toronto; Editor, The Canada Lancet; President, Ontario Publishing Company; Medical Referee, Excelsior Life Assurance Company; Medical Referee, Dominion of Canada Accident Company; sometime Secretary, Ontario Hospital Association; Grand Medical Examiner of the Sons of Scotland Benevolent Association; *b* Glasgow, Scotland, 1854; *s* of Adam Ferguson and Elizabeth Donaldson, both of Glasgow; *m* 1882, Helen Baird of Toronto. *Educ:* Walton Village Public School; Clinton Collegiate Institute; University of Toronto; Edinburgh and London.

Came to Ontario when very young; was Demonstrator of Anatomy in Medical Department, Toronto University, for eleven years; lectured on nervous diseases, and was for some years Examiner in Anatomy; took an active part in the organisation of the Excelsior Life Insurance Company, of the Ontario Publishing Company, of the Toronto Western Hospital, and of the Ontario Hospital Association; sometime Chairman of the Toronto High School Board; in medical practice for 35 years. *Publications:* The Canada Lancet; numerous articles and addresses, as—Diet in Epilepsy, Nerve Path of Taste, Nerve Degeneration in Lead, Arsenic and Alcoholism, Observations on Hemiplegia, The Knee Jerk, Selection of Insurance Risks, The Phrenic Nerve, Reply to Dr Osler, Capital Punishment, Addresses to Students; Text-Book of Pathology; The Physiology and Pathology of the Internal Secretory Glands; The Relation of Sickness and Accidents in Insurance Work; The Medical Aspects of Septic Peritonitis; Sir William Tennant Gairdner, the Ideal Physician, etc. *Recreations:* boating, curling, violin-playing, natural history. *Address:* 264 College Street, Toronto. *Died 3 Nov. 1916.*

FERGUSON, John Macrae, ISO 1911; Collector of Customs and Excise, Edinburgh, since 1907; *b* 11 Nov. 1849; 3rd *s* of Alexander Ferguson, farmer and land steward, Burnside of Newhall, parish of Resolis, Ross-shire, and Flora Mackenzie; *m* 1882, Eliza Jane, *o d* of Henry Kellas, farmer, Strathdon, Aberdeenshire; four *s* two *d. Educ:* Free Church School, Resolis. Entered the Excise Service 1870; passed through all grades in Department; appointed Collector, 1899; promoted to Manchester, 1st Class, 1906. *Address:* Woodfield, Banchory. *Died 15 Dec. 1919.*

FERGUSON, Hon. William Nassau; Justice of Appeal in Supreme Court, Ontario, since 1916; *b* Cookstown, 31 Dec. 1869; 3rd *s* of Isaac Ferguson of Cookstown, Ontario, who came to Canada from Killoughter, County Cavan, Ireland, and Emily J., *d* of late Lieut-Col Ogle R. Gowan, MP for Leeds and Grenville, Ont; unmarried. *Educ:* Upper Canada College and Osgoode Hall, Toronto. Called to the Bar, 1894; Bencher, Law Society, Upper Canada, 1916; KC 1908; member of Board of Governors, Wycliffe College, Toronto, and of Board of Governors of Hospital for Sick Children, Toronto; Anglican; Conservative. *Recreations:* has been identified with outdoor sports. *Address:* 244 St George Street, Toronto. *TA:* Rallim, Toronto. *T:* Hillcrest 1724 and Adelaide 4101. *Clubs:* British Empire; Albany, York, National, Royal Canadian Yacht, Ontario Jockey, Toronto Hunt, Toronto Golf, Toronto.

Died 9 Nov. 1928.

FERGUSSON, Sir James Ranken, 2nd Bt, *cr* 1866; JP, Vice-Lieutenant, Co. Peebles; *b* 10 Aug. 1835; *e s* of Sir William Fergusson, 1st Bt, and Helen Hamilton, *d* of William Ranken of Spitalhaugh; *S* father, 1877; *m* 1st, 1862, Mary Ann (*d* 1868), *d* of late Thomas Colyer of Wombwell Hall, Northfleet; one *s* (and one *s* decd); 2nd, 1877, Louisa (*d* 1878), *d* of late William Forbes; one *s;* 3rd, 1886, Alice, *d* of late J. P. Simpson; one *s* two *d* (and one *s* decd). *Educ:* King's Coll. London; Christ Church, Oxford. Barrister, Lincoln's Inn, 1858; FSA Scot; Member of Royal Archers, King's Bodyguard for Scotland; County Councillor, Peeblesshire, etc. *Publication:* Poems and Ballads, 1876. *Recreations:* books, fishing, shooting, country life and occupations. *Heir: s* Thomas Colyer Colyer-Fergusson, *b* 11 July 1865. *Address:* Spitalhaugh, West Linton, NB. *Clubs:* Constitutional; New, Edinburgh. *Died 28 Oct. 1924.*

FERGUSSON, Lt-Col Vivian Moffatt, DSO 1916; RA; *b* 31 Aug. 1878; 3rd *s* of late James Fergusson, FRCSE, and Mrs Fergusson, Lincoln House, Richmond, Surrey; *m* 1918, Dulce Alice Mollie D'Ewes, *e d* of Percy U. Allen, ICS. Served European War, 1914–18 (despatches, DSO, Bt Lieut-Col). *Club:* Naval and Military.

Died 16 Nov. 1926.

FERMOY, 2nd Baron, *cr* 1856; **Edmund Fitz-Edmund Burke Roche,** DL; *b* 23 May 1850; *s* of 1st Baron and Eliza (*d* 1897), *e d* of J. B. Boothby, Twyford Abbey, Middlesex; *S* father, 1874; *m* 1877, Hon. Cecilia O'Grady (*d* 1919), *d* of 3rd Viscount Guillamore; one *d.* Owner of about 21,400 acres. *Heir: b* Hon. James Boothby Burke Roche, *b* 28 July 1852. *Address:* Rockbarton, Bruff, County Limerick.

Died 1 Sept. 1920.

FERMOY, 3rd Baron, *cr* 1856; **James Boothby Burke Roche,** BA; *b* 28 July 1852; 2nd *s* of 1st Baron Fermoy; *S* brother, 1920; *m* 1880, Frances, *d* of F. Work, New York; twin *s* one *d* (and one *d* decd). *Educ:* Trinity Coll. Cambridge (MA). MP (N) for East Kerry, 1896–1900. *Heir: s* Hon. Edmund Maurice Roche, *b* 15 May 1885. *Address:* 60 St James's Street, SW. *Clubs:* Brooks's, Hurlingham.

Died 30 Oct. 1920.

FERNOW, Prof. Bernhard Eduard, LLD; Dean, Faculty of Forestry, University of Toronto, 1907–19 (Professor Emeritus); *b* Inowradaw, Prussia, 7 Jan. 1851; *m* 1879, Olivia Reynolds of Brooklyn, NY; four *s. Educ:* Forest Academy, Münden; University, Königsberg. Six years Prussian Forest Dept; ten years variously occupied; Chief, Division of Forestry, US Dept of Agriculture, 1886–98; Director Forest School, Cornell University, Ithaca, NY, 1898–1903; private, 1903–6; Professor of Forestry, State College, Pennsylvania, 1907. *Publications:* Economics of Forestry; The Care of Trees; Short History of Forestry. *Address:* University, Toronto.

FERRERO, Baron Augusto; Assistant Editor of La Tribuna, Rome; *b* Turin; *s* of Col F. Ferrero; *m* Gina, *e d* of Senator Roux. *Educ:* Turin University. Journalist, formerly at the Stampa of Turin. *Publications:* Nostalgie d'Amore (verses); From Florence to Rome, a Political Diary of 1870–71; The Cartoons of Teja, a series of humoristic cartoons on recent Italian history; The Marriage Law. *Recreations:* any kind of sport, from horse-riding and fencing to bicycling. *Address:* Office of La Tribuna, Rome.

FERRIER, Sir David, Kt 1911; MA, MD, LLD, DSc; FRCP, FRS; Emeritus Professor of Neuropathology, King's College, London; Consulting Physician to King's College Hospital, and to the National Hospital for Paralysed and Epileptic; *b* 13 Jan. 1843; *m* 1874, Constance, *d* of late Albert C. Waterlow; one *s* one *d. Educ:* Aberdeen, Edinburgh, Heidelberg. Graduated MA (Aberdeen), 1863 (1st class Hons); MD (Edinburgh), 1870. *Publications:* Functions of the Brain, 1876; Cerebral Localisation, 1878, 1890, etc. *Recreations:* various. *Address:* 27 York House, Kensington, W8. *T:* Park 4033. *Club:* Athenæum.   *Died 19 March 1928.*

FESSENDEN, Clementina; Founder of Empire Day; contributor to the Press on current topics; *b* Quebec; *d* of Marion Ridley and Edward Trenholme, Quebec; *m* E. J. Fessenden, BA, late Rector of Ancaster; three *s. Educ:* Quebec. Early identified with national work, a member of the National Council of Women; a representative member of the League of Empire; Convener Flag Committee, Ontario Historical Society; Corresponding Secretary, Wentworth Historical Society; President, Shaftesbury Ragged School Dinner Fund of Hamilton, Ontario. An ardent Imperialist; member of English Church; Conservative; originated the idea of Empire Day, 1897; edited the Niagara Letter Leaflet; author of brochure Our Union Jack; a member of the Anti-Suffrage League, England; hon. member, Canadian Women's Historical Society; hon. Regent, St Hilda's Chapter, Daughters of the Empire; hon. Life Member National Chapter of Canada, Imperial Order Daughters of the Empire, 1913. *Address:* Hamilton, Ontario, Canada.

Died 14 Sept. 1918.

FESTING, Gabrielle; writer; *b* The Residences, South Kensington Museum, *d* of Maj.-Gen. E. Robert Festing, RE, CB, FRS, and Frances Mary Legrew. *Publications:* John Hookham Frere and His Friends; Unstoried in History; On the Distaff Side; From the Land of Princes; When Kings Rode to Delhi; Strangers within the Gates; Honor Among Thieves; The Gift of a Son. *Recreations:* music (Member of Bach Choir), cooking, embroidery. *Address:* 56 Queen's Gate Terrace, SW.   *Died 17 April 1924.*

FESTING, Major Harold England, DSO 1916; *b* 18 Feb 1886; *s* of late Major-Gen. Sir Francis W. Festing, KCMG, CB, Royal Marine Artillery, and Selina Eleanor Mary, *d* of L. W. Carbonell, who *m* 2nd, Col R. C. Drysdale, RA (*d* 1904). *Educ:* Cheltenham College; Sandhurst. Was page of honour to Queen Victoria and King Edward VII, 1897–1902; joined 1st Border Regt, 1905; Captain, 1914; Major, 1922; awarded Royal Humane Society's medal in India, 1914; served European War (Gallipoli), 1915 (wounded, despatches, DSO); France, 1918 (despatches, bar to DSO, French Croix de Guerre). *Recreations:* fishing, shooting. *Club:* Junior United Service.

Died 14 Oct. 1923.

FETHERSTON, Rev. Sir George Ralph, 6th Bt, *cr* 1776; JP Co. Longford; Fellow and Vice President, the Incorporated Guild of Church Musicians, London; Fellow and Vice President, the Victoria College of Music, London; *b* Dublin, 8 April 1852; *o s* of Sir Thomas John Fetherston, 5th Bt, and Sarah, *y d* of Harry Alcock, Wilton Castle, Wexford; *S* father, 1869. *Educ:* Brighton Coll.; Theological Coll. Salisbury. Ordained Salisbury Cathedral, 1880; Priest, 1883; Vicar of Pydeltrenthide, 1887–93; High Sheriff, Co. Longford, 1897; Jubilee medal, 1897; Hon. Assistant Chaplain, the Queen Alexandra Military Hospital, Millbank, SW, 1916; Licensed Curate of St Martin's Parish Church, Worcester; visited North America, Europe, Africa, Malta, Portugal, South America (Brazil), St Vincent, Canada, Canary

Islands, Egypt, Madeira, Corsica. Owner of island Innisclerau n, in Lough Ree. Composer of 150 hymn tunes, also various chants, songs and other music. *Publications:* The Mystery in Maple Street; Loyalty in Sorrow; Interrupted Harmony; Through Corsica with a Pencil. 1914; A Legend of Corpus Christi, 1915; An Incident in the Siege of Antwerp (a poem); A Garden Eastward, and other Sermons; A Marriage Address, 1919; The Rose of England, 1919; The Malvern Hills (a poem), 1921. *Recreations:* music, photography, cycling, fishing, ornithologist, entomologist, philatelist, collector of ancient china. *Heir:* none. *Address:* Cleeve Court, Kempsey, Worcester; Ardagh House, Edgeworthstown, Co. Longford. *M:* NP 268. *Clubs:* Authors', Royal Automobile.   *Died 11 Feb. 1923 (ext).*

FETHERSTONHAUGH, Godfrey, KC 1898; MP (U) Fermanagh N 1906–16 (resigned Oct. 1916); *b* 1858; *s* of Stephen R. Fetherstonhaugh of Milltown, Co. Westmeath, and Rokeby, Co. Dublin. *Educ:* Chard Grammar School; Trinity Coll. Dublin (Scholar in Classics, 1878; First Senior Moderator in Classics, 1880; MA 1883). Called to Irish Bar, 1883; called to English Bar, 1895; Bencher of King's Inn, 1900; JP Fermanagh. *Recreations:* fishing, shooting. *Address:* Glenmore, Crossmolina, Co. Mayo. *Clubs:* Junior Constitutional; University, Dublin.   *Died Sept. 1928.*

FETHERSTONHAUGH-WHITNEY, Henry Ernest William, JP, DL; *b* 21 Nov. 1847; *o* surv. *s* of Rev. Sir Thomas Francis Fetherston, 4th Bt, and 2nd wife Anne, *d* of late Edmund L'Estrange; assumed name of Fetherstonhaugh-Whitney by Royal licence, 1881; *m* 1st, 1876, Jeannie (*d* 1880), *y d* of late Edward Atkinson; 2nd, 1885, Alice Marion Caroline, *e d* of late Col Robert Caulfeild of Camolin House, Co. Wexford. *Educ:* Trinity College, Dublin. High Sheriff, Westmeath, 1887; Capt. and Hon. Major late 7th Batt. King's Royal Rifle Corps; formerly Lieut 60th Rifles. *Address:* Furry Park, Raheny, Co. Dublin; Neupass, Rathowen, Co. Westmeath. *Club:* Junior United Service.   *Died 3 Sept. 1921.*

FEVERSHAM, 2nd Earl of, *cr* 1868; **Charles William Reginald Duncombe;** Baron Feversham (UK), 1862; Viscount Helmsley, 1868; Major, Yorkshire Hussars, Imperial Yeomanry; MFH Sinnington Hounds since 1904; *b* 8 May 1879; *e s* of William Reginald, Viscount Helmsley, MP (*d* 1881), and Muriel, Viscountess Helmsley; *S* grandfather, 1st Earl, 1915; *m* 1904, Lady Marjorie Greville, *e d* of 5th Earl of Warwick; two *s* one *d. Educ:* Christ Church, Oxford. MP (U) Thirsk and Malton Div., NR, Yorks, 1906–15; Assistant Private Secretary to 1st Lord of Admiralty (Lord Selborne), 1902–5. *Heir: s* Viscount Helmsley; *b* 2 Nov. 1906. *Address:* Duncombe Park, Helmsley, Yorkshire. *Clubs:* Carlton, Turf, Bachelors', Pratt's, Ranelagh; Yorkshire, Yorks.

Died 15 Sept. 1916.

FFINCH, Rev. Matthew Mortimer; Chaplain of Huggens College, Northfleet, Kent, since 1870; Hon. Canon of Rochester, 1908; Rural Dean of Gravesend, 1909; *b* Greenwich, Dec. 1838; 2nd *s* of John Drake Ffinch of Greenwich; *m* 1863, Lydia Jane (*d* 1915), *d* of late John Jones Dyer of the Admiralty, Whitehall; four *s* one *d. Educ:* Christ's Hospital; Oriel College, Oxford. Assistant Curate, Holy Trinity and St Peter's, Shaftesbury, 1862; Donhead St Mary, Wilts, 1863–70. *Address:* The College, Northfleet.

Died 8 Feb. 1920.

FFRANGCON-DAVIES, David, MA Oxon; Hon. RAM London; Vocal Artist, and late Professor at the Royal Academy of Music, London; *b* Carnarvonshire, 11 Dec. 1850; *s* of David and Gwen Ffrangcon-Davies; *m* Annie Frances, *d* of late Thomas Rayner, JP, of Manchester; two *d. Educ:* private tutors; Friars School; Jesus College, Oxford (Classical Exhibitioner). Educated for and entered the Church; owing to theological difficulties resigned position and became vocal student; has sung in opera at Covent Garden and Drury Lane, and continues to sing in oratorios at all the principal festivals of the world; has toured 12 seasons in America; resided 3 years in Berlin, taking his position in the German art world; his public work is now confined to festivals and great choral societies. *Publication:* The Singing of the Future. *Recreations:* theology, philosophy.

Died 13 April 1918.

FIASCHI, Col Thomas Henry, DSO 1901; NSW AMC; Surgeon practising in Sydney; Hon. Consulting Surgeon Sydney Hospital; *b* Florence, 3 May 1858; *s* of late Prof. L. Fiaschi of Florence, and Clarissa Fisher; *m* 1st, 1886, Katherine Anna, *d* of James W. Reynolds; 2nd, Amy Curtis, *d* of Capt. W. E. Curtis of Bundaberg, Queensland. *Educ:* Pisa and Florence Universities. MD, ChD, Pisa and Florence. Came to Australia, 1875; practised at first in Windsor, NSW; settled in Sydney, 1883; joined the NSW Army Medical Corps, 1891; was attached as Medical Officer to New South Wales Lancers; obtained leave of absence for six months and joined the Italian army in Abyssinia, 1896, marching with it as far as Kassala; received cross of Cavaliere dei SS Maurizio e Lazzaro from late King Humbert for special merits during Italo-Abyssinian campaign; in Oct. 1899 volunteered for active service in South Africa, where he remained till 1900 in command of the New South Wales No 1 Field Hospital; specially mentioned by Lord Roberts for services rendered at Paardeberg; SMO to Gen. Hutton's Brigade; Col AMC 1911; served with the AIF at Lemnos, OC 3rd Australian General Hospital; invalided to England; went to Italy and served as Surgeon with Italian Red Cross, 73 Ospedale di Guerre, at Schio. *Publication:* Da Cheren a Cassala, 1896. *Address:* 149 Macquarie Street, Sydney. *Club:* Australian.   *Died 16 April 1927.*

FIELD, Major Kenneth Douglas, DSO 1917; RGA; on service in France; *b* 12 Aug. 1880; *s* of late Joshua Field, JP, DL; *m* 1913, Elizabeth Mary, *d* of J. H. Noble, MA, of Selby House, Ham Common; two *d*. *Educ:* Woolwich. Served in Indian Mountain Artillery, and as Instructor in gunnery; active service in Waziristan, 1901; operations against Darwesh Khels, and Tibet (Indian GS medal, medal for Tibet); European War (DSO). *Recreations:* reading, travel. *Address:* Selby House, Ham Common, Surrey.

FIELDHOUSE, William John, CBE 1918; JP; FSA; *b* 1858; *m* 1882, Lucy, *d* of Abraham Wood. *Educ:* Newport Grammar School. Head of George H. Hughes Ltd, St Stephen's Wheel Works, Birmingham. *Address:* Austy Manor, Wootton Wawen, Warwickshire. *Club:* Royal Thames Yacht.   *Died 28 Oct. 1928.*

FIELDING-HALL, Harold; retired; *b* Rathowen, Ireland, 1859; *o s* of H. B. Hall, DCL, last representative of the Halls of Birtley and Consett, Co. Durham, from 1407; *m* 1905, Margaret Evelyn, *d* of J. M. Smith, Ceylon, and Cornwall Gardens; one *s* one *d*. *Educ:* Leamington College. Went round world in sailing ship, 1878; coffee planting in Wynaad, 1879–85; in Upper Burma before the war; entered Government Service, 1886; Political Officer, 1887–91 (medal and two clasps); visited China and Japan, 1891; Famine Officer, 1896–97; District Magistrate, 1901; organised Rural Banks, 1904–6; retired, 1906. *Publications:* The Soul of a People; The Hearts of Men; The World Soul; The Inward Light; Famine Manual; A People at School; The Passing of Empire; Margaret's Book; Love's Legend, 1914; For England, 1916, etc. *Recreations:* shooting, sailing, golf. *Address:* 4 Essex Court, Temple, EC. *Club:* Savage.
                                    Died 5 May 1917.

FIENNES, Gerard Yorke Twisleton-Wykeham, CBE 1920; Chevalier of the Order of Leopold I of Belgium, 1918; *b* 18 July 1864; *e s* of late Rev. Hon. Wingfield T. W. Fiennes, 4th *s* of 16th Baron Saye and Sele, and Alice, *d* of Very Rev. Hon. Grantham Yorke, Dean of Worcester; *m* 1905, Gwendolen, *o c* of late Francis Gisborne of Holme Hall, Bakewell; five *s*. *Educ:* Winchester; New College, Oxon, 3rd class Mod. Hist., BA 1888. Tutor to sons of Rajah of Sarawak, 1887; visited Sarawak with them; Assistant Editor New Review, 1891–3; member London School Board, 1893–6 (Hackney); Secretary, Unionist Association, N Bucks Division, 1896–1900; Asst Editor, St James's Gazette, 1901–3; Editor, 1903; Editor Birmingham Gazette and Express, 1904–5; Asst Editor Standard, 1905–7; Asst Editor Pall Mall Gazette, 1912–15; again of Standard, 1915–16; writer on naval matters for Observer, Daily Graphic, etc; General Editor National War Aims Committee, Oct. 1917–Dec. 1918; Church of England; no Party. *Publications:* The Ocean Empire, 1911; Navy at War, 1916; Sea Power and Freedom (a course of Lectures to LCC Teachers), 1917; and with L. G. Pilkington, Getting our Living, an easy Handbook of Economics for Schools, 1924; articles in Nineteenth Century, Fortnightly, New Review, Navy League Annual, etc. *Recreations:* cricket, lawn tennis, rowing till too old. *Address:* Wellwick, Wendover. *T:* Wendover 68. *Club:* Savile.
                                    Died 13 Jan. 1926.

FIFE, Colonel Sir Aubone, Kt 1902; CVO 1909; standard-bearer of HM's Bodyguard of Gentlemen-at-Arms; *b* 1 Feb. 1846; 3rd *s* of late W. H. Fife and *g s* of late Sir John Fife of Ghortanloisk, Argyll. *Educ:* Cheltenham College. Entered army, 1866; served Canadian Frontier, 1866; Afghan War, 1879–80 (medal); Burmese Expedition, 1886–87 (medal with clasp); formerly Adjutant and Clerk of the Cheque HM's Bodyguard. *Address:* St James's Palace, and 42 Jermyn Street, SW; Lee Hall, Wark, Northumberland.
                                    Died 5 Feb. 1920.

FIGG, Captain Donald Whitly, DSO 1915; 24th (County of London) Battalion, the London Regiment (the Queen's), Territorial Forces;

b 17 March 1886. Served European War, 1914–15 (DSO). *Address:* Garlands, Redhill, Surrey.   *Died 5 March 1917.*

FIGGIS, Rev. J. B., MA; Chairman of the Countess of Huntingdon's Trustees; *b* Dublin; *m* 1862, Harriet Webb Chaffey (*d* 1914); two *s*. *Educ:* Taunton School; Trinity College, Dublin (MA); New College, London (Scholar). Ordained, 1861; Pastor, North Street Church, Brighton, 1861–97; Emmanuel Church, Hove, 1897–1912. *Publications:* Keswick from Within; Agnosticism; Christ and Full Salvation; The Christ Life; Visions, etc. *Address:* 38 Compton Avenue, Brighton.   *Died 4 Sept. 1916.*

FIGGIS, Rev. John Neville, DD, LittD; Member of Community of Resurrection since 1909; Hon. Fellow, St Catharine's College, Cambridge; *b* Brighton, 2 Oct. 1866; *s* of late Rev. John Benjamin Figgis, MA. *Educ:* Brighton College; St Catharine's College, Cambridge (Scholar); Wells Theological College. Senior Optime, 1888, and BA; 1st class Hist. Tripos, 1889; Lightfoot Scholarship, 1890; 2nd Whewell Scholarship, 1891; Prince Consort Prize, 1892, MA. Curate of Kettering, 1894–95; Great St Mary's, Cambridge, 1895–98; Lecturer in St Catharine's College, 1895–1901; Chaplain Pembroke College, 1898–1900; Birkbeck Lecturer in Trinity College, 1900; Rector of Marnhull, Dorset, 1901–7; Examiner to Univ. of Cambridge in Historical Tripos, Lightfoot, etc; Hulsean Lecturer, 1908–9; Noble Lecturer, Harvard, 1911; Bishop Paddock Lecturer, General Theological Seminary, New York, 1913; Bross Lecturer, Lake Forest, Illinois, 1915. *Publications:* Divine Right of Kings, 1896; Illustrations of English History 1660–1715, 1902; Christianity and History, 1904; From Gerson to Grotius, 1907; The Gospel and Human Needs, 1909; Religion and English Society, 1910; Civilisation at the Cross Roads, 1912; Antichrist, 1913; Churches in the Modern State, 1913; The Fellowship of the Mystery, 1914; Some Defects in English Religion, 1916; The Will to Freedom (lectures on Nietzsche), 1917; contributor to Cambridge Modern History; editor with R. V. Laurence of Lord Acton's Lectures and Essays. *Address:* House of Resurrection, Mirfield.   *Died 13 April 1919.*

FILDES, Sir (Samuel) Luke, KCVO 1918; Kt 1906; RA 1887 (ARA 1879); *b* England, 18 Oct. 1843; *m* 1874, Fanny, *d* of William Woods, Warrington; four *s* two *d*. *Educ:* private school. Studied South Kensington Art Schools and Royal Academy, London; illustrator of books and magazines for several years; afterwards painted English and Venetian subjects; latterly portraits. *Paintings:* first picture, Fair Quiet, and Sweet Rest, exhibited RA 1872; The Casual Ward, 1874; The Widower, 1876; The Return of the Penitent, 1879; The Village Wedding; Venetian Life; The Al Fresco Toilette; The Doctor, 1892; The State Portrait of the King, 1902; The State Portrait of the Queen, 1905; The State Portrait of the King, 1912. *Address:* 11 Melbury Road, Kensington, W14. *T:* Park 4552. *Club:* Athenæum.
                                    Died 27 Feb. 1927.

FILGATE, William de Salis, JP, DL; High Sheriff, Co. Louth, 1879; *b* 2 Dec. 1834; *m* 1870, Georgiana Harriet, *e d* of late William John French of Ardsallagh, Co. Meath; two *d*. *Educ:* Rugby; Cheltenham College. Louth Rifle Militia, 1855–58; permanent duty, retired as Captain; Master of Louth Hounds since 1860. *Address:* Lissrenny, Ardee, Co. Louth. *Club:* Sackville Street, Dublin.
                                    Died 14 June 1916.

FILMER, Sir Robert Marcus, 10th Bt, *cr* 1674; *b* 25 Feb. 1878; *s* of Sir Edmund Filmer, 9th Bt and Mary Georgiana Carolina, *e d* of Lord Arthur Marcus Hill, 4th *s* of 2nd Marquess of Downshire, who succeeded his brother as 3rd Baron Sandys, 1880; *S* father, 1886. Served in Grenadier Guards, 1897–1904; Soudan campaign, 1898; South African War, 1899–1902; Lt Reserve of Officers, 1904; contested (U) NW Durham, 1906, Lincoln, Jan. and Dec. 1910; Lieut Royal East Kent Mounted Rifles, 1907; Major, 1912; rejoined the Grenadier Guards from the Royal East Kent Yeomanry, Feb. 1915, for the duration of the War. Owner of about 10,000 acres. *Heir:* none. *Address:* Little Charlton Manor, East Sutton, Maidstone, Kent. *Clubs:* Guards, Turf, Carlton, Beefsteak.
                                    Died 27 Jan. 1916 (ext).

FILOSE, Lt-Col Sir Michael, KCIE 1911 (CIE 1908); Chief Secretary Huzur Durbar, Gwalior, since 1894; *b* 18 April 1836; *s* of Major Julien Filrose, Gwalior; *m* 1853, Annie Donnery; two *s* five *d*. *Educ:* London University College. Accompanied Jiageerao Maharaja Scindia on his retreat to Agra during the mutiny of 1857; Major and Director of Public Instruction, Educational Department, 1863; designed and built Jai Vilas Palace, Gwalior, 1872–74; constructed Jal Mahal Moti Mahal, Law Courts, Central Jail, etc; carried out first revenue survey of the Malwa Praut, 1879–81; Governor of the Province of Malway, 1882;

Lt-Col 1891. Knight of the Order of St Sylvester, 1874. *Address:* Gwalior, India. *Clubs:* Aligha, Elgin, Gwalior.

Died 5 Feb. 1925.

FINCK, Henry T., AB; on editorial staff, New York Evening Post and Nation, 1881–1924 (specialty, musical criticism); *b* Bethel, Shelby Co., Missouri, 22 Sept. 1854; *s* of Henry C. Finck and Beatrice; *m* 1890, Abbie H. Cushman. *Educ:* Harvard (1872–76); Heidelberg, Berlin (1878–81) (specialties, psychology, sociology). Harris Fellowship (1878–81) of Harvard; highest honours in philosophy. Professor of Musical History at National Conservatory. *Publications:* Anton Seidl, a Memorial; Wagner and his Works; Chopin and other Musical Essays; Songs and Song-Writers; Paderewski and his Art; Grieg and his Music; Development of Musical Instruments; Success in Music; Massenet and his Operas; Romantic Love and Personal Beauty; Primitive Love and Love Stories; Pacific Coast Scenic Tour; Spain and Morocco; Lotos Time in Japan; Food and Flavour; Richard Strauss; Gardening with Brains; Girth Control; Musical Progress; Musical Laughs; My Adventures in the Golden Age of Music, 1926; magazine articles on woman question, psychology, gastronomy, etc; Editor of Fifty Master-Songs, Thirty Sterling Songs for High Schools, Fifty Grieg Songs and Fifty Schubert Songs. *Recreations:* travel, walking, gardening. *Address:* Bethel, Maine, USA.

Died 1 Oct. 1926.

FINDLAY, Alexander, MA, DSc (Aberdeen), PhD (Leipzig); FIC; Professor of Chemistry, University of Aberdeen, since 1919; *b* 24 Sept. 1874; *y s* of William Findlay and Catherine Fyfe; *m* 1914, Alice Mary, *y d* of late Herbert de Rougemont of Lloyd's; two *s*. *Educ:* Grammar School, Aberdeen; Universities of Aberdeen and Leipzig. Interim Lecturer on Organic Chemistry, University of St Andrews, 1900; Lecturer on Chemistry and Special Lecturer on Physical Chemistry, University of Birmingham, 1902–11; Professor of Chemistry, University College of Wales, Aberystwyth, 1911–19. Member of Council, Institute of Chemistry, 1915–18; Member of Council, Chemical Society; Thomson Lecturer, United Free Church College, Aberdeen, 1915–16; Editor of Monographs on Inorganic and Physical Chemistry. *Publications:* The Phase Rule and its Applications; Physical Chemistry and its Application in Medical and Biological Science; Practical Physical Chemistry; Osmotic Pressure; Chemistry in the Service of Man; The Treasures of Coal Tar; Translation of Ostwald's Principles of Inorganic Chemistry; a number of memoirs contributed to various scientific journals. *Recreation:* golf. *Address:* Marischal College and Broomhill Park, Aberdeen. *T:* 2793.

Died 2 Feb. 1921.

FINDLAY, Rev. George Gillanders, BA, DD; Tutor in New Testament Exegesis and Classics at the Headingley Branch of the Wesleyan Theological Institution, 1881–1917, now retired; *b* 3 Jan. 1849; *s* of late Rev. James Findlay, Wesleyan minister; *m* 1875; three *s* four *d*. *Educ:* Woodhouse Grove School and Wesley College, Sheffield; Richmond Theological College. BA Lond. 1867, University Scholar in Classics; DD (Hon.) St Andrews, 1901. Assistant Tutor at Headingley College, 1870–74; Classical Tutor at Richmond, 1874–81; Fernley Lecturer, on Christian Doctrine and Morals, 1894. *Publications:* several commentaries on St Paul's Epistles in the Expositor's Bible, Expositor's Greek Testament, Cambridge Greek Testament and Bible for Schools and Colleges; Epistles of Paul, and Books of the Prophets, in Handbooks for Bible Students; vol. of Sermons on The Things Above; Fellowship in the Life Eternal, an Exposition of the Epistles of St John; Life of Wm F. Moulton; Wesley's World Parish, etc. *Address:* Headingley College, Leeds.

Died 2 Nov. 1919.

FINDLAY, James Thomas; FRHistS; FSAScot.; author; *b* Peterhead, Aberdeenshire, 22 July 1875; *e s* of late William Findlay, and Isabella, *d* of James Scott, Peterhead; *m* 1922, Mary Katherine, *o d* of late Alexander Keith of Pitmedden, Aberdeenshire. *Educ:* Peterhead Academy; Gordon's College, Aberdeen; Edinburgh University; abroad. Editor, Peterhead Sentinel; assistant-editor and leader-writer of Shields Daily Gazette, 1898–1900; acting editor, Ripon Observer, 1903–5; chief sub editor, The Shipping World, 1905–19; editor, 1920–27. *Publications:* Socialism in France, a study of contemporary French Socialism; The Secession in the North, and The Ingenious and Learned William Meston, AM—two historical studies of the North-East of Scotland; three novels—A Deal with the King, Silent Places, The Chosen. *Recreation:* skating, when there's ice. *Address:* Cairnbrogie, Old Meldrum, Aberdeenshire. *T:* Udny Green 24. *Club:* Savage.

Died 31 Oct. 1927.

FINDLAY, Surg.-Maj. John, CIE 1889; MB, CM; *b* 29 July 1851. *Educ:* Edinburgh University. Joined Army Medical Staff, 1875; served

in Afghan War; Burmah Campaign; on personal staff of Governor of Bombay, 1881–85; and of Viceroy of India (Marquess of Dufferin), 1885–89; retired 1890. *Recreations:* shooting, golf. *Club:* Junior United Service.

Died 14 Jan. 1920.

FINLAY, David White, BA, MD (Glasg.), LLD (Yale and Aberdeen); DPH (Camb.); FRCP, FRSE; Hon. Physician-in-Ordinary to King in Scotland; Emeritus Professor of Practice of Medicine, Aberdeen University; Consulting, late Senior Physician to Aberdeen Royal Infirmary; Member of the General Medical Council, 1901–11; *b* Glasgow; *m* Catherine Mary, *e d* of late Stephen Thompson, shipowner, London; two *s* four *d*. *Educ:* High School and University, Glasgow; Vienna. Was physician and lecturer at Middlesex Hospital; London; also physician to Royal Hospital for Diseases of the Chest and to Royal Scottish Hospital, and consulting physician to the Caledonian Asylum, London; formerly Inspector of Examinations in Medicine to General Medical Council; recently Hon. Lt-Col RAMC; Commandant, Scottish National Red Cross Hospital, Glasgow. *Publications:* on medical subjects in the medical papers, and in the Transactions of various Medical Societies in London; also Reminiscenses of Yacht-Racing and some Racing Yachts, 1910. *Recreations:* yachting (was a member of the first council of Yacht-Racing Association), photography. *Address:* Balgownie, Helensburgh, Dunbartonshire. *T:* 164. *Clubs:* Royal Clyde Yacht, Conservative, Glasgow.

Died 4 Nov. 1923.

FINLAY, Ian Archibald; late Major North Irish Horse and Lieutenant Royal Scots Greys; *b* 1878; *s* of late Major John Finlay of Castle Toward, Argyll, and Mary Marcella, 2nd *d* of late Thomas Taylor, BCS; *m* 1904, Elizabeth Muriel, *o d* of 1st Baron Glenarthur; two *s* one *d*. *Educ:* Eton. Served South African War, 1899–1901 (despatches twice; severely wounded; Queen's medal with 7 clasps); European War, 1914–19 (wounded). *Address:* Temple Hall, Coldingham, Berwickshire. *TA:* Coldingham. *Club:* Cavalry.

Died 9 Nov. 1925.

FINLAY, Very Rev. John, MA; Dean of Leighlin, 1895–1912; Rector of Carlow, 1890–1912; Rural Dean of Carlow, 1899–1912; *b* 27 June 1842; 6th *s* of John Finlay, JP, Brackley House, Bawnboy, Co. Cavan; *m* Isabella Anne, *d* of Very Rev. W. Smyth-King, Dean of Leighlin; no *c*. *Educ:* Trinity College, Dublin. Ordained, 1867; Curate of Clonenagh, 1867–73; Rector of Lorum, 1873–90; Prebendary of Ullard in Leighlin Cathedral, 1876–95; Chaplain Lord-Lieutenant, 1902; Dio. Nominator, 1890–1912; Member of Church Representative Body. *Address:* Brackley House, Bawnboy, Co. Cavan.

Died 11 June 1921.

FINLAYSON, Lt-Col Walter Taylor, DSO 1917; LRCP (London); MRCS (England); *b* Broughty Ferry, Scotland, 14 July 1877; *s* of David Finlayson and Katheen Nina Macarthur; *m* 1905, Elizabeth Mary Dorothea, 6th *d* of late Benjamin Neville, Winchester; two *d*. *Educ:* Haileybury College; Melbourne University; St Mary's Hospital, London. Qualified in medicine and surgery, 1903; entered the Indian Medical Service, 1904; Captain, 1907; Major, 1915; Lt-Col 1923; served European War, 1914–18 (despatches, DSO). *Publications:* Some Effects of Hornet Stings, Indian Medical Gazette; Notes and Observations on the Borstal System as carried out at Borstal, England. *Recreations:* cricket, golf, lawn tennis. *Address:* c/o Lloyds Bank Ltd, Bombay, India. *Club:* East India United Service.

Died 10 June 1928.

FINN, Alexander, FRGS; *b* 5 Nov. 1847; *s* of James Finn, Consul for Palestine; *m* 1887, Mary Margaret, *d* of late Jos. Sanders; two *s*. *Educ:* Royal Institution School, Liverpool; Royal School, Dungannon; King's Coll. London. Was some time in Home Civil Service; Clerk to HM Legation, Tehran, 1873; Vice-Consul, 1880; Consul, Resht, 1883; special service on Perso-Afghan Frontier, 1884–5; Consul, Malaga, 1887–1904; in charge of United States interests during Spanish-American War; received thanks of German Government for assistance rendered at shipwreck of their training corvette the Gneisenau, Dec. 1901; Consul, Chicago, 1904–7; Consul-General, 1907–9; Consul-General, Chile, 1909, and in charge of Turkish Consular affairs at Valparaiso; retired, 1912. *Recreations:* anything and everything out of doors. *Address:* 2 Park Road, Richmond, Surrey. *Club:* Royal Societies.

Died 15 Feb. 1919.

FINN, Brig.-Gen. Harry, CB 1907; DCM; FRCO; Secretary, The Walter and Eliza Hall Trust, Sydney, 1912; half-pay, 1907; retired, 1907; *b* 6 Dec. 1852; *y s* of late Samuel Finn of Tenterden, Kent; *m* 1886, Kate, *e d* of late William Scott, 9 Leeson Park, Dublin; one *s* two *d*. *Educ:* British School, Tenterden. Enlisted 9th Lancers, 1871; 2nd Lt 21st Hussars, 1881; Capt. 1887; Major, 21st Hussars, 1894;

Lieut-Col 21st Lancers, 1900; Brevet Col 1904; Col 1907; Brig.-Gen. 1912; DAAG, Madras, 1893–95; AAG, Madras, 1895–98; Commandant, Military Forces, Queensland, 1900–1; New South Wales, 1902–4; Inspector-General (local Major-General) of Forces, Australia, 1905–6; served Afghan War, 1878–80 (despatches, medal for distinguished conduct in the field, medal with clasp); Nile, 1898 (despatches, Brevet Lieut-Col, two medals and clasps). *Address:* Ashmore, Point Piper, Sydney, New South Wales, Australia. *Clubs:* Junior Constitutional; Union, Sydney.

Died 24 June 1924.

FINNEY, Sir Stephen, Kt 1913; CIE 1904; Member of the Indian Railway Board; *b* 8 Sept. 1852; *s* of J. D. Finney of Old Charlton, Kent; *m* 1888, Constance, *d* of Colonel Pilcher, IMS; one *s* one *d*. *Educ:* Clifton; Cooper's Hill. Entered Indian Public Works Dept, 1874; served four years as assistant and district engineer; joined the administrative branch of the railway dept; Manager, Eastern Bengal State Railway, 1891–99; North-Western Railway, India, 1899–1907. *Publications:* a series of lectures on Railway Construction and Working in Bengal, and papers on subjects connected with railway economics. *Recreations:* plays tennis, was formerly fond of games of all kinds, played for England against Scotland, Rugby, in 1872 and 1873. *Address:* 28 Evelyn Gardens, SW7. *T:* 6220 Kensington. *Club:* Oriental.

Died 1 March 1924.

FINNIS, Admiral Frank, CVO 1907; retired; *b* 8 Nov. 1851; *s* of late Steriker Finnis, Dover; *m* 1906, Anna, *d* of late Prof. John MacRobin, Aberdeen, and *widow* of Herbert Lake. Entered Navy, 1864; Lieut, 1874; Commander, 1886; Capt, 1893; Rear Admiral, 1905; late commanding Chatham Division, Home Fleet. *Address:* Lightlands, Frant, Sussex. *Club:* United Service.

Died 17 Nov. 1918.

FINNY, John Magee, BA, MD Dublin; Fellow and Past President Royal College Physicians, Ireland; Consulting Physician to Sir Patrick Duns' Hospital, Mercer's Hospital, Masonic Female Orphan School, Bloomfield Asylum, and Royal Hospital for Incurables, Dublin; Member of Senate, Trinity College, Dublin, and of Board of Superintendence of Dublin Hospitals; Visitor in Lunacy; *b* 9 Feb. 1841; 3rd *s* of Rev. T. H. C. Finny, Rector of Clondulane, Co. Cork, and Frances, *d* of William Magee, Archbishop of Dublin; *m* 1873, Agnes Anne, *y d* of William Watson, Dublin; four *s* three *d*. *Educ:* private school; Trinity Coll. Dublin (Med. scholar and senior exhibitioner, 1864). President Royal College Physicians, Ireland, 1890–92; ex-President of Royal Academy of Medicine in Ireland and of Leinster Branch, BMA; ex-King's Professor of Practice of Medicine, Trinity Coll. Dublin; ex-Physician to Sir Patrick Duns' Hospital; late Examiner in Medicine, RAMC. *Publications:* on various medical subjects, and contributions to British Medical Journal and other journals. *Address:* Erith Lodge, Sandymount, Dublin. *T:* Ballsbridge 460. *Club:* University, Dublin.

Died 7 Dec. 1922.

ꞋINOT, Jean; Directeur de La Revue; officier de la Légion d'Honneur; membre de l'Académie des Sciences de Lisbonne; membre de l'Académie de Rio-de-Janeiro; membre de l'Institut de Coimbra, Président de l'Alarme; Vice-Président des Amitiés francoétrangères, etc; Commandeur de Maurice et Lazare et de la Couronne d'Italie; Commandeur du Soleil Levant, etc; *b* 1856; *m*; one *s*. *Publications:* Race Prejudice; Philosophy of Longevity; Problems of the Sexes; Science of Happiness; (ouvrages non traduits en anglais): Progrès et Bonheur (2 vols); Civilisés contre Allemands; Anglais et Française. Tous ces ouvrages sont traduites dans beaucoup de langues: espagnole, allemande, italienne, russe, grecque, polonaise, etc, et plusieurs d'entre eux ont été couronnés par l'Académie française, l'Académie des Sciences Morales, etc. *Address:* La Revue, Paris.

Died 25 April 1922.

ꞋRBANK, (Arthur Annesley) Ronald; writer; *b* 1886; 2nd and *o* surv. *s* of late Major Sir Thomas Firbank, MP, St Julian's, Monmouthshire, and Jane Harriette, 4th *d* of late Rev. James Perkins Garrett, of Kilgarron, Co. Carlow. *Educ:* abroad; Trinity Hall, Cambridge. *Publications:* Odette, 1905; Vainglory, 1915; Inclinations, 1916; Caprice, 1917; Valmouth, 1919; The Princess Zoubaroff (play), 1920; Santal, 1921; The Flower Beneath the Foot, 1922; Sorrow in Sunlight, 1924; Concerning the Eccentricities of Cardinal Pirelli, 1925; *posthumous publications:* The Artificial Princess, 1934; The New Rhythum and other Pieces, 1962. *Recreations:* travelling, literature, art. *Club:* Junior Carlton.

Died 21 May 1926.

ꞋSET, Hon. Jean Baptiste Romuald, MD; *b* St Cuthbert, PQ, 7 Feb. 1843; *s* of Henri Fiset of St Cuthbert; *m* 1st, 1869, Aimée, *d*

of late Honoré Plamondon of Quebec; 2nd, Emelina Loranger, *widow* of Captain H. Pouliot; five *s* three *d*. *Educ:* Montreal College, classical course; Laval University, Quebec, as MD, 1868. A Governor of the College of Physicians and Surgeons of Quebec; has been Councillor and subsequently Mayor of Rimouski, Quebec, 1871; took his certificates of Captain, Military School, Quebec, 1865; served Fenian raids, 1865–66 and 1870; Surgeon of 89th Battalion Rimouski, 1871; Surgeon-Major, 1895; retired, 1899, with rank of Lieut-Col; Member for Rimouski, Quebec, House of Commons, 1872–82, 1887–91, and 1896; Senator, 1897; Liberal. *Recreations:* hunting, fishing. *Address:* Rimouski, Province of Quebec, Canada. *Club:* President of Fishing and Game Club, Rimouski, Quebec.

Died 6 Jan. 1917.

FISH, Ven. Lancelot John, MA; Archdeacon of Bath, since 1909; *b* 1861; *s* of late Rev. J. D. Fish; *m* 1891, Mary, *d* of Rev. H. Girdlestone; no *c*. *Educ:* Harrow; Trinity College, Cambridge. Chaplain at Christ Church, Cannes, 1900–3; Vicar of Bathampton, Bath, 1894–1907; Diocesan Inspector of Schools, 1899–1902; Hon. Sec. Bath and Wells Diocesan Societies, 1902–7; Proctor in Convocation, 1906; Prebendary of Wells Cathedral, 1906; Chaplain at St Andrew's Church, Biarritz, France, 1907–9; Vicar of St Stephen Lansdown, Bath, 1909–23. *Address:* 12 Lansdown Place East, Bath. *Clubs:* New University, MCC; Bath and County, Bath.

Died 29 Sept. 1924.

FISH, Stuyvesant; *b* New York, 24 June 1851; *s* of late Hon. Hamilton Fish, Secretary of State in Grant's Administration; *m* Marian G. Anthon. *Educ:* Columbia College. Clerk in New York office, Illinois Central RR, 1871; Secretary to President, 1872–74; Director since 1877; Clerk with Morton, Bliss and Co., New York and Morton, Rose and Co., London; Mem., New York Stock Exchange; Treas. and Agent for purchasing co. New Orleans, Jackson and Great Northern RR; Secretary, 1877–82, Chicago, St Louis and New Orleans RR; Vice-President, 1883–84; 2nd Vice-President, 1884–87; President, Illinois Central RR, 1887–1906; member, Monetary Commission created by Indianapolis Monetary Conference, 1897; Pres. American Railway Association, 1904–6; Chairman, 7th Session International Railway Congress, 1906; Trustee of New York Life Insurance and Trust Co.; for many years Vice-President and Director, National Park Bank, New York, and Director of other fiscal and fiduciary institutions; Trustee of Mutual Life Insurance Company of New York from 1883 until his resignation in 1906, owing to disapproval of "ring" methods then brought to light among certain of his co-trustees and disclosed at that time in the press; Member, St Nicholas Society. *Address:* 52 Wall Street and 25 E 78th Street, New York. *Clubs:* Union, Metropolitan, Down Town, St Anthony's, New York.

Died 10 April 1923.

FISHER, 1st Baron, *cr* 1909, of Kilverstone; **Admiral of the Fleet John Arbuthnot Fisher,** GCB 1902 (KCB 1894; CB 1882); OM 1905; GCVO 1908; Chairman of Inventions Board since 1915; Grand Cordon of Legion of Honour, 1906; Member, Committee Imperial Defence; *b* 25 Jan. 1841; *s* of Capt. William Fisher, 78th Highlanders, and Sophia, *d* of A. Lambe of New Bond Street, and *g d* of Alderman Boydell; *m* 1866, Frances (*d* 1918), *d* of Rev. T. Delves Broughton; one *s* three *d*. Entered Navy, 1854; Lieut, 1860; took part in capture of Canton and Peiho forts; obtained Beaufort Testimonial; Rear-Adm. 1890; served Crimean War, 1855; China War, 1859–60; Egyptian War, 1882; in command of the "Inflexible", Bombardment of Alexandria, 1882; Director Naval Ordnance, 1886–91; Admiral Superintendent at Portsmouth Dockyard, 1891; Controller of the Navy; Lord of the Admiralty, 1892–97; Commander-in-Chief on the North American and West Indies Station, 1897–99; Delegate to Peace Conference at The Hague, 1899; Commander-in-Chief, Mediterranean Station, 1899–1902; 2nd Sea Lord of Admiralty, 1902–3; Commander-in-Chief, Portsmouth, 1903–4; First Sea Lord of Admiralty, 1904–10 and 1914–15; Chairman Royal Commission on Oil Fuel, 1912. *Heir: s* Hon. Cecil Vavasseur Fisher, *b* 18 July 1868. *Club:* Athenæum.

Died 10 July 1920.

FISHER, Rt. Hon. Andrew; PC 1911; *b* Crosshouse, Kilmarnock, 29 Aug. 1862; *s* of Robert Fisher; *m*; five *s* one *d*. *Educ:* Crosshouse. Went to Queensland, 1885; entered Queensland Parliament, 1893; Minister of Railways in Dawson Ministry; represented Wide Bay in the Commonwealth Parliament for first fifteen years of the Parliament; Minister for Trade and Customs, Commonwealth of Australia, 1904; Leader of Federal Parliamentary Labour Party, 1907–15; Prime Minister, Australia, 1908–9; Leader of Federal Opposition, 1909–10; Prime Minister, 1910–13, and 1914–15; represented Australia at opening of Union Parliament, S Africa, 1910; at Imperial Conference, 1911, and at Coronation of King George V; High Commissioner of

Australia in England, 1916-21. *Address:* 57 South Hill Park, NW3.
Died 22 Oct. 1928.

FISHER, Rev. Cecil Edward; Prebendary of Lincoln since 1877; *b*
12 Aug. 1838; *y s* of Rev. William Fisher, Rector of Poulshot, Devizes,
Canon of Salisbury; *m* 1862, Agnes, *y d* of John Mirehouse of
Brownslade, Pembroke, Common Serjeant of London; two *s* six *d.*
Educ: Westminster School; Christ Church, Oxford (Student). Curate
of Bremhill, Wilts, 1864; Rector of Stoke Rochford, Lincs, 1865-78;
Vicar of Grantham, 1878-83; Rector of Hagworthingham, Lincs,
1883-90; Rural Dean of Hill, 1885-86; Vicar of St Peter's,
Bournemouth, 1890-1904. *Address:* Ankerwyke, Shirley Warren,
Southampton. *TA:* Canon Fisher, Shirley, Southampton.
Died 13 Jan. 1925.

FISHER, Frederic Henry; Editor of the Literary World, 1883-1915;
b London, 13 April 1849; *e s* of late Rev. F. W. Fisher; *m* 1872, Clara
(*d* 1914), 2nd *d* of late James Clarke, Beechhanger, Caterham; one
s one *d. Educ:* Boston Grammar School; BA London University.
Entered Indian Civil Service by open competition, 1868; Officiating
Civil and Sessions Judge, Saharanpur, North-Western Provinces,
1881; editor of North-Western Provinces Gazetteer, 1881-83; retired
1885. Barrister, Middle Temple, 1885. *Publications:* Cyprus our New
Colony and What we Know about it, 1878; Afghanistan and the
Central Asian Question, 1878. *Recreation:* chess. *Address:* Westover,
Cobham Road, Westcliff-on-Sea, Essex. *Club:* Alexandra Yacht,
Southend-on-Sea. *Died 30 Dec. 1926.*

FISHER, Rt. Rev. George Carnac, DD; *b* 1844; *s* of William Fisher,
HM Madras Civil Service, and Frances Ruggles-Brise, *d* of Rev. C.
J. Fisher, Ovington Rectory, Essex; *m* 1876, Mary Penelope
Gwendoline, *o d* of late T. C. Thompson, at one time MP for
Durham, of Sherburn Hall, Durham, and Ashdown Park, Sussex; four
s four *d. Educ:* Harrow; Brasenose Coll. Oxford (MA). Vicar of Forest
Row, Sussex, 1874-79; St George, Barrow-in-Furness, 1879-81; St
Mary, Beverley, 1882-89; Croydon, 1889-94; Bishop of
Southampton (Suffragan to Bishop of Winchester), 1896-98; Bishop
of Ipswich (Suffragan to Bishop of Norwich), 1899-1905; resigned,
1905. *Address:* Burgh House, Fleggburgh, Norfolk.
Died 9 April 1921.

FISHER, Inspector-Gen. James W., MD; RN. *Address:* Failthe,
Dover Road, Walmer, Kent.
Died 3 Feb. 1919.

FISHER, Maj.-Gen. John Frederick Lane; Indian Army; *b* 10 Dec.
1832. Entered army, 1848; Maj.-Gen., 1890; unemployed list, 1890;
served Indian Mutiny, 1857-59 (slightly wounded, medal with clasp).
Died 20 June 1917.

FISHER, Mark, RA 1919 (ARA 1911); *b* Boston, USA, of English and
Irish parents. *Educ:* Boston Pub. School. When quite a child showed
a marked talent for drawing, his taste and talent developing rapidly
in this direction; the opportunities for studying Art at that time being
much fewer than now, his earliest instruction was gained at Lowell
Institute; his first efforts were portraits and figures, but his love of
outdoor subjects and life induced him to take up landscape and animal
painting; at the age of twenty he went to Paris, and was for a short
time in Gleyre's studio; on his return to Boston he met with scant
encouragement, so came to England, married and settled here;
represented in the following permanent exhibitions—Dublin,
Manchester, Birmingham, Leeds, Bradford, Oldham, Huddersfield,
Dudley, Rochdale, Adelaide, Perth (Australia), Johannesberg;
Medals—Paris, Chicago, St Louis. *Address:* Hatfield Heath, Harlow,
Essex. *Died 30 April 1923.*

FISHER, Hon. Sydney Arthur, BA, DCL (Hon.) McGill; Minister
of Agriculture, Canada, 1896-1911; *b* Montreal, Canada, 12 June
1850; *s* of Dr Arthur Fisher, FRCS, Edinburgh, and Susan Corse,
both of Montreal; unmarried. *Educ:* High School and McGill Coll.,
Montreal; Trinity College, Cambridge (BA). Farmer by profession,
at Knowlton, in Eastern Townships, PQ; entered Parliament of
Canada as MP for County Brome, 1882; re-elected 1887, 1896, 1900,
1904 and 1908; defeated, 1891 and 1911; First Vice-President
International Institute of Agriculture, convened at Rome, 1908.
Church of England; Liberal. *Recreations:* riding, cricket. *Address:* Alva
House, Knowlton, PQ, Canada; 4 Range Road, Ottawa. *Clubs:*
University, Reform, Montreal; Rideau, Golf, University, Ottawa.
Died April 1921.

FISHER, Commander Sir Thomas, KBE 1920; RN; General
Manager, Canadian Pacific Steamships Ltd; *b* Birmingham, 1883; *s*

of Thomas Fisher, and Margaret, *d* of Sir Alfred Hickman, 1st Bt
Wolverhampton; *m* 1912, Aimée, *d* of Walter Loveridge of Codsall
one *s* one *d.* Entered RN, 1897; served in China (medal)
Mediterranean, and Home Fleets; specialised in Gunnery; qualified
as War Staff Officer; Flag Commander in Reserve Fleet, 1914
Admiralty Trade Division, 1915-17 (CBE); represented Ministry o
Shipping in Washington, USA, 1918-19; retired 1920. *Address:* E
Waterloo Place, SW. *T:* Regent 2925; 103 Sloane Street, SW. *T*
Victoria 6972. *Clubs:* United Service, St James's.
Died 22 Feb. 1925

FISHER, Adm. William Blake, CB 1900; RN; *b* 19 Feb. 1853; *.*
of late Capt. W. E. Fisher, RN; *m* 1887, Edith Lilian, *d* of Francis
A'Beckett Chambers of NSW; one *s.* Entered Navy, 1866; Captain
1896; Commodore, 1905; commanded punitive expedition, New
Hebrides, 1885; Senior Officer commanding Delagoa Bay Blockading
Squadron (medal and Natal clasp); commandant of Base Jubaland
Expedition, 1901; GS East African Medal, Jubaland clasp
Commodore RN Barracks, 1905-7; Rear-Admiral, 1906; Rear-
Admiral, Second in Command of Atlantic Fleet, 1908; Vice-Admiral
1911; retired, 1914; commanded HM Yacht Medusa, 1915; also
served as Admiralty representative for Munition Supply; Roya
Humane Society's medal and clasp for saving life on two occasions
Club: United Service. *Died 8 May 1926*

FISHER, William James, JP London, 1906; Chairman, Holborr
Bench of Justices; Member, County Licensing Committee, since
1910; Visiting Justice, Wormwood Scrubs Prison, since 1915; *e* surv
s of late Walter Fisher; *m* 1st, Emma, *d* of late J. J. Florac; one *s* twe
d; 2nd, 1897, Adrienne Dairolles. Joined the staff of the Daily
Chronicle as foreign editor in 1883; assistant editor, 1894; editor-in-
chief, 1899-1904; contested (L) Canterbury, general elections 190!
and Dec. 1910; Director, Edmond Coignet Ltd, and other publi
companies. *Recreations:* fishing, swimming, golfing. *Address:* 3.
Cathcart Road, SW10. *T:* Kensington 5567. *Clubs:* Reform; Mid
Surrey Golf. *Died 28 Feb. 1924*

FISON, Alfred Henry, DSc London; Secretary to the Gilchris
Educational Trust since 1912; Lecturer on Physics at Guy's Hospita
since 1906, and the London Hospital since 1910; *b* Hendon, 1857
s of Rev. Thomas Fison, Congregational Minister; *m* 1888, Alice
Maud, *d* of Alexander W. Williamson, FRS, Professor of Chemistry
at University College, London; one *s* two *d. Educ:* Mr. Munro'
School, Elstree; Royal School of Mines. Mathematical Master at three
private schools, 1879-84; Demonstrator of Physics at University
College London, 1884-92; Lecturer to the Oxford University
Extension Delegacy, 1892-1912. *Publications:* Recent Advances in
Astronomy, 1898; article on the Evolution of Double Stars in Lecture
on the Methods of Science, 1905; A Text Book of Practical Physics
1911; re-written, 1922. *Address:* 147 Dartmouth Road, Cricklewood
NW2. *T:* 1551 Willesden. *Club:* Sandy Lodge Golf.
Died 4 Feb. 1923

FISON, Sir Frederick William, 1st Bt *cr* 1905; JP, DL; *b* 4 Dec. 1847
o s of late William Fison, Greenholme, Burley-in-Wharfedale
Yorkshire; *m* 1872, Isabella, *d* of late Joseph Crossley, Broomfield
Halifax; two *s* two *d* (and one *s* decd). *Educ:* Rugby; Christ Church
Oxford; 1st Class Natural Science. Contested (C) Otley Division 1885
Buckrose Division 1892; MP (C) for Doncaster Div., Yorkshire
1895-1906. *Heir: s* Capt. Francis Geoffrey Fison, MC, late KRRC
[*b* 12 March 1873. *Educ:* Harrow; Christ Church, Oxford (BA)]
Address: Boarzell, Hurst Green, Sussex. *T:* Hurst Green 7. *Clubs*
Carlton, United University.
Died 20 Dec. 1927

FITCHETT, Rev. William Henry, LLD Toronto University; edito
of Life, a monthly magazine; of a weekly paper, The Southern Cross
principal of the Methodist Ladies' College, Hawthorn, Melbourne
b Lincoln; married. *Educ:* Melbourne University (BA). Wesleyan
minister (ex-Pres. of the Wesleyan Conference of Victoria an
Tasmania); President of the General Conference of the Methodi
Church of Australasia; also educationist and journalist, having edite
the Melbourne Daily Telegraph at one time. *Publications:* Deeds tha
won the Empire, 1897; Fights for the Flag, 1898; The Tale of the
Great Mutiny; How England saved Europe, 1899; Wellington's Men
1901; Nelson and his Captains, 1902; The Commander of th
Hirondelle, 1904; The Unrealised Logic of Religion, 1905; Life c
Wesley, 1905; Ithuriel's Spear, 1906; The Pawn in the Game, 1907
The Beliefs of Unbelief, 1907; The Great Duke, 1911; The New
World of the South, 1913; The Romance of Australian History, 1913
Recreations: golf, takes considerable interest in cricket. *Address*
Hawthorne, Melbourne. *Died May 1928*

FITTON, Col Hugh Gregory, CB 1911; DSO 1896; ADC to the King, 1907; Royal West Kent Regiment; *b* 15 Nov. 1863; *m* 1910, May, 6th *d* of late Sir Alfred Hickman, 1st Bt. Entered Royal Berks, 1884; Brevet-Major, 1898; served Eastern Soudan, 1885 (medal with clasp, Khedive's star); Egyptian Frontier Field Force, 1885–86; Dongola Expeditionary Force, 1896 (despatches, DSO, Khedive's medal, two clasps); DAAG 7th Division South Africa, 1900–4 (despatches twice, Bt Lt-Col, Queen's medal, 8 clasps); PSC; Colonel, 1907. *Address:* 42 Albert Court, SW.

Died 20 Jan. 1916.

FitzCLARENCE, Hon. Harold Edward, MC; Governor HM Prison Manchester since 1919; *b* 15 Nov. 1870; *s* of 2nd Earl of Munster and Wilhelmina, *d* of Hon. John Kennedy-Erskine; *b* and *heir-pres.* to 4th Earl of Munster; *m* 1902, Frances Isabel, *d* of late Lieut-Col William Keppel, of Lexham Hall, Norfolk; one *s* one *d*. Late Lieut 3rd Batt. Yorkshire Light Infantry; served South Africa with Imperial Yeomanry, 1900–1; Governor of Worcester Gaol, 1909; on active service BEF, 1915; Assistant Provost Marshal 31st and 47th Divisions (despatches, MC). *Died 28 Aug. 1926.*

FitzGEORGE, Rear-Admiral Sir Adolphus (Augustus Frederick), KCVO 1904 (CVO 1901); Deputy Ranger of Richmond Park; *b* 1846; *s* of late Duke of Cambridge; *m* 1st, 1875, Sophia Jane (*d* 1920), *d* of Thomas Holden, of Winestead Hall, Hull; one *d*; 2nd, 1920, Margarita Beatrice, *d* of late John Watson of Waresley Hall, Worcestershire. *Address:* 20 Eccleston Square, SW1. *Clubs:* Carlton, Naval and Military, Marlborough.

Died 17 Dec. 1922.

FITZGERALD, Admiral Charles Cooper Penrose; Admiral, 1905; *b* Corkbeg, Co. Cork, 30 April 1841; 2nd *s* of Robert Fitzgerald and Frances, *d* of Rev. Robert Austin; *m* 1882, Henrietta, *d* of late Rev. F. Hewson; two *s* two *d*. *Educ:* at sea. Joined the "Victory", 1854; Midshipman of "Colossus" in the Baltic; "Retribution", round the world; Lieut of "Ariadne", First Lieut "Cordelia", "Hercules"; Commander, "Agincourt", "Asia", "Rapid"; Capt. "Inconstant", RN College, "Bellerophon", "Inflexible", "Collingwood"; Superintendent, Pembroke Dockyard; second in command of the China Station, 1898–99. *Publications:* a book on Boat Sailing, 1883; Life of Sir George Tryon, 1897; Memories of the Sea 1913; From Sail to Steam, 1916. *Address:* 2 Trinity Road, Folkestone.

Died 11 Aug. 1921.

FitzGERALD, Charles Edward, MD, MCh; Ex-President Royal College of Physicians of Ireland; Hon. Surgeon-Oculist-in-Ordinary to the King in Ireland; Professor of Ophthalmic Surgery, Royal College of Surgeons, Ireland; Consulting Ophthalmic Surgeon, Richmond Hospital; *b* 9 Feb. 1843; *s* of F. A. FitzGerald, late Baron of Exchequer, Ireland; *m* 1st, Isabel, *d* of late Peter Roe Clarke; four *s*; 2nd, Edythe, *d* of late John Overend. *Educ:* Trinity Coll. Dublin. *Address:* 27 Upper Merrion Street, Dublin.

Died 27 May 1916.

FitzGERALD, Hon. David, KC; **His Honour Judge FitzGerald;** County Court Judge, Cos Waterford, Kilkenny, and Queen's, since 1892; *b* 14 Jan. 1847; *s* of late Rt Hon. Lord FitzGerald (Lord of Appeal); *m* 1894, Isabel, *d* of Luke J. M'Donnell. *Educ:* Downing College, Cambridge, BA. Called to Bar, Lincoln's Inn, 1871; King's Inns, Dublin, 1872; QC 1889. *Address:* 18 Clyde Road, Dublin. *Clubs:* Reform; University, Kildare Street, Dublin.

Died 5 March 1920.

FitzGERALD, Capt. Lord Desmond; Captain, Irish Guards; *b* 21 Sept. 1888; *s* of late 5th Duke of Leinster and Lady Hermione Duncombe, *d* of 1st Earl of Feversham; *b* and *heir-pres.* to 6th Duke of Leinster. *Educ:* Eton. Served European War, 1914 (despatches, wounded). *Died 5 March 1916.*

FITZGERALD, Sir Edward, 1st Bt *cr* 1903; JP; *b* 24 Nov. 1846; *m* 1872, Anne, *d* of John O'Donoghue, Cork; four *s* four *d* (and one *s* one *d* decd). Contested (N) Cork City, 1910. Lord Mayor of Cork, 1901–3. Decorated on King's visit to Ireland. Order of Sacred Treasure of Japan. *Heir: s* John Joseph Fitzgerald, *b* 20 Feb. 1876. *Address:* Geraldine Place, Finn Barr, Co. Cork.

Died 22 June 1927.

FitzGERALD, Lt-Col Lord Frederick; *b* 18 Jan. 1857; 3rd *s* of 4th Duke of Leinster and Lady Caroline, *d* of 2nd Duke of Sutherland. *Educ:* Eton. Late Major King's Royal Rifle Corps; served Afghan Campaign (medal with 2 clasps and bronze star), 1878–80; South African Campaign, 1881; Egyptian Campaigns, 1882; Nile Expedition (medal with two clasps and bronze star), 1884–85. JP, Co. Kildare. *Address:* Carton, Maynooth. *Clubs:* Junior United Service; Kildare Street, Dublin. *Died 8 March 1924.*

FitzGERALD, Hon. George Parker, MEC, Tasmania; Head of firm of G. P. FitzGerald & Co., Merchants, Hobart, Tasmania; *b* Hobart, 13 Feb. 1843; twice married; four *s* two *d*. *Educ:* Hutchins School, Hobart. Was Minister of the Crown, Tasmania, 1888–91; President of Tasmanian Section at Melbourne International Exhibition; also Chairman of the Board of Technical Education, and succeeded in getting a vote through Parliament for the construction of Technical College at Hobart; appointed chief liquidator of the Bank of van Diemen's Land, which closed, 1901. *Recreations:* fishing, yachting, rowing. *Address:* Hobart, Tasmania.

Died 1917.

FitzGERALD, Hon. Gerald, KC; *b* 12 Aug. 1849; 3rd *s* of late Rt Hon. Lord FitzGerald (Lord of Appeal). *Educ:* Oscott; Trinity Coll. Dublin. Called to Irish Bar, 1871; County Court Judge, 1886–90; QC 1892; Land Commissioner in Ireland, 1890; Judicial Commissioner, 1903. *Address:* 6 Fitzwilliam Square, Dublin. *Clubs:* Brooks's, Wellington; Kildare Street, University, Dublin; Royal St George Yacht, Kingstown.

Died 30 Oct. 1925.

FitzGERALD, Gerald A. R., KC 1909; Barrister; *b* 1844; *e s* of late Rev. A. O. FitzGerald, Archdeacon of Wells; *m* 1875, Alice Caroline Frances (*d* 1917), *e d* of late H. D. Skrine of Warleigh and Claverton Manors, Co. Somerset; two *s*. *Educ:* Sherborne; Corpus Christi Coll., Oxford; late Fellow of St John's Oxford. Called to Bar, 1871; employed in office of the Parliamentary Counsel for 3 or 4 years; then practised as draftsman of private Bills, etc, and before Parliamentary Committees; Light Railway Commissioner (unpaid), 1896–1900. JP Wilts 1904. *Publications:* Editor of two editions of Thring's Companies Acts; Manual of Ballot Act, 1872; The Public Health Act, 1875. *Address:* 9 Parktown, Oxford.

Died 1 Aug. 1925.

FitzGERALD, Brig.-Gen. Herbert Swayne, CB 1900; retired; *b* 12 March 1856; 2nd *s* of Major C. M. Fitz-Gerald, Bengal Staff Corps; *m* 1884, Charlotte, *d* of J. Baumgartner. Entered 68th Durham Light Infantry, 1875; attached 15th Sikhs, Afghan War, 1880, including Candahar (medal with clasp, bronze decoration); Marri Expedition, 1881; DAAG for Intelligence, Soudan Frontier Field Force, 1885–86 (medal, Khedive's Star); operations on Niger, 1897–98 (despatches, Brevet Lieut-Col, medal with clasp); commanded 1st Bn Durham LI; South Africa, 1899–1902, including Colenso, Tugela, Vaal Krantz (severely wounded, despatches twice, CB); commanded 64th Brigade, 1914–15; 226th, 1915–16. *Club:* Army and Navy.

Died 2 July 1924.

FITZGERALD, Hon. John Donohoe, KC; *b* Dublin, 20 Jan. 1848; 2nd *s* of late Rt Hon. Lord FitzGerald and Rose, *d* of late John Donohoe; *m* 1881, Emma Ysolda, 2nd *d* of Sir Thomas Barrett Lennard, 2nd Bt; one *s* four *d* (and two *s* decd). *Educ:* Christ's Coll. Camb. LLB Cambridge, 1st class Law Tripos, 1870; LLM 1873. Barrister, Inner Temple, 1872; QC 1896. *Address:* 33 Harrington Gardens, South Kensington; 38 Parliament Street, SW. *Clubs:* Athenæum, Brooks's, Reform. *Died 11 May 1918.*

FitzGERALD, Sir Maurice, 2nd Bt, *cr* 1880; 20th Knight of Kerry; CVO 1905; DL, JP for Cambridgeshire, Suffolk and Cos Kerry and Carlow; formerly Equerry of Duke of Connaught; Captain Rifle Brigade, 1875; retired, 1881; [the title Knight of Kerry has been considered prescriptive from early times; the founder of this family, John Fitz Thomas FitzGerald, Lord of Decies and Desmond, created three of his sons by his second marriage hereditary Knights—The White Knight, the Knight of Glin, and the Knight of Kerry]; *b* 5 Feb 1844; *s* of Sir Peter George FitzGerald, 1st Bt and Julia, *d* of Peter Bodkin Hussey; *S* father, 1880; *m* 1882, Amelia, *d* of late H. L. Bischoffsheim; two *s* one *d* (and one *s* decd). *Educ:* Harrow. Served in Ashanti War, 1873–74. Owner of about 10,000 acres. *Recreations:* owner of yacht "Satanita", owner of race horses. *Heir: s* John Peter Gerald Maurice FitzGerald, Captain RHG, *b* 14 May 1884. *Address:* Buckland, Berkshire; The Severals, Newmarket; Valencia Island, Co. Kerry. *Clubs:* Travellers', Brooks's; Royal Yacht Squadron, Cowes. *Died 22 Oct. 1916.*

FitzGERALD, Maurice F., DSc; Professor of Civil Engineering, Queen's College, Belfast, 1884–1910; Professor Emeritus since 1910. *Educ:* Trinity Coll., Dublin; Eastons and Anderson, Erith. *Address:* Queen's University, Belfast. *Died 5 May 1927.*

FITZGERALD, Michael, CMG 1897; *b* Dysert, Co. Clare, 1851; 2nd *s* of George Fitzgerald, Roughan, Co. Clare; *m* 1887, Florence, *d* of Deputy-Inspector-Gen. Daniel Finucane, RN. *Educ:* Ennis Coll.; Royal Coll. of Surgeons, Ireland. LRCSI 1871; LM, LRCPI 1872. Surgeon in charge of HMS "Magpie", 1874 (officers and men thanked by Admiralty for services in disturbances at Masnaah, Persian Gulf); received thanks of Admiralty for services at Malta Hospital during operations in Egypt, 1882; of Secretary of State for War; of Dutch Government; of United States Government for services to Admiral, then Capt. Dewey; PMO of hospital ship "Malacca", and of forces landed with Admiral Rawson in punitive naval expedition against King of Benin, 1897 (mentioned in despatches; decorated for this latter service); RN Dep. Insp.-Gen. of Hospitals and Fleets, 1901–5; retired, 1905, with rank of Insp.-Gen. of Hospitals and Fleets. *Recreations:* cricket, fishing, shooting, boxing, cycling. *Club:* Royal Naval, Portsmouth. *Died 13 March 1918.*

FITZGERALD, Lieut-Col Oswald Arthur Gerald, CMG 1915; 18th KGO Lancers; Personal Military Secretary to Secretary of State for War since Aug. 1914; *b* 8 July 1875; *s* of late Col Sir Charles Fitzgerald. *Educ:* Wellington. Received first commission Indian Staff Corps, 1895; gazetted to 18th KGO Lancers, 1897; served NW Frontier of India, 1897–98 (medal with 2 clasps); ADC to Commander-in-Chief in India, 1904–6; Assistant Military Secretary to Lord Kitchener, Commander-in-Chief in India, 1907–8; Staff Officer to Lord Kitchener on his mission to Japan, Australia, and New Zealand, 1909; Staff College, 1909–10; Military Secretary to Lord Kitchener, commanding troops at Coronation, 1911; General Staff Officer Egypt, 1911–12; Military Attaché Egypt, 1912–14. *Club:* Cavalry. *Died 5 June 1916.*

FitzGERALD, Percy Seymour Vesey, CSI 1906. Assistant Political Agent, Kathiawar, 1874; Mahi Kantha, 1875; Kathiawar, 1877; Baroda, 1878; Kathiawar, 1879; Administrator, Gondal State, 1881; Administrator, Sangli State, 1883; Assistant Political Agent, Kolhapur, 1884; Kathiawar, 1885; Aden, 1889; Political Agent, Sawantwadi, 1893; Mahi Kantha, 1894; Cutch, 1895; Palanpur, 1898; Mahi Kantha, 1901; Agent to Governor in Kathiawar, 1906–8; retired 1908. *Club:* Carlton. *Died 17 Nov. 1924.*

FitzGERALD, Mrs Robert, (Marion), CBE 1920; *b* 1860; *d* of late Mahony Harte, BL, of Batterfield House, Co. Kerry; *m* 1878, Robert FitzGerald, JP, DL, 2nd *s* of Sir Peter FitzGerald, 1st Bt, Knight of Kerry; two *s*. President, Soldiers' and Sailors' Families Association for Co. Kerry; Chairman, War Pensions Committee for Co. Kerry; District Head, Soldiers' and Sailors' Help Society for Tralee; President, Tralee Women's National Health Association; Hon. Secretary, Tralee Red Cross Association; Commandant, Kerry 4 VAD during European War. *Address:* 40 Onslow Square, SW3. *T:* Kens. 2108. *Died 11 Feb. 1928.*

FITZGERALD, Sir Robert Uniacke-Penrose-, 1st Bt, *cr* 1896; DL, JP; *b* Cork-Beg Island, Co. Cork, 10 July 1839; *e s* of Robert Penrose-Fitzgerald and Frances, *d* of Rev. Robert Austen; *m* 1867, Jane, *d* of General Sir William Codrington, GCB. *Educ:* Westminster; Trinity Hall, Cambridge. Travelled in India and Thibet, 1863–67; Hon. Col of North Cork Rifles. Contested (C) Youghal, 1874; MP (C) Cambridge, 1885–1906; working member of Committee of Royal National Lifeboat Society; President of the Council of the Yacht-racing Association; director Property Defence Association and Cork Defence Union against Land League. Owner of about 6000 acres in Co. Cork, of which 1000 are farmed by himself. *Recreations:* sailing, shooting, farming, gardening. *Heir:* none. *Address:* Cork-Beg Island, Co. Cork; 35 Grosvenor Road, Westminster, SW. *Clubs:* Carlton; Kildare Street, Dublin; Royal Cork Yacht. *Died 10 July 1919 (ext).*

FitzGERALD, Hon. Rowan Robert, (Hon.) DCL; Vice-Chancellor, and Judge Supreme Court of the Province, Charlotte-town, since 1894; *b* 1847. *Educ:* Prince of Wales' College, Prince Edward Isle. Barrister, 1869; Stipendiary Magistrate, 1875; KC 1880; Recorder to 1894. *Address:* Charlotte-town, PEI.

Fitz-GERALD, Shafto Justin Adair; novelist and dramatist; *b* 9 Nov. 1859; 2nd *s* of late Captain Thomas Justin Fitz-Gerald; *m* 1899, Blanche Adeline Cawse. *Educ:* privately. *Publications:* Sketches from Bohemia, 1890; The Wonders of the Secret Cavern, 1892; Ballads of a Bohemian, 1893; A Book of Words, 1895; The Zankiwank and the Bletherwitch, 1896; The Mighty Toltec, 1897; A Tragedy of Grub Street, 1897; Stories of Famous Songs, 1897; Fame the Fiddler, 1898; That Fascinating Widow, 1898; The Grand Panjandrum, 1898; The Black Tulip, 1899; Rip Van Winkle, 1900; How to Make Up, 1901;

Drink (from L'Assommoir), 1902; The Love Thirst of Elaine, 1903; Prince Conan, 1907; Dickens and the Drama, 1910; Nine One-Act Plays (three volumes), 1914; The Idol of Paris (from the French of Sarah Bernhardt), 1921; The Story of the Savoy Opera, 1924. *Plays:* The Barringtons, 1884; A Lucky Girl, 1889; The Parson, 1891; Two Hearts, 1894; The Bric-a-Brac Will, 1895; A Jealous Mistake, 1899; The Parting, 1899; Waiting for the Train, 1899; Rip Van Winkle, 1899; Cinq Mars, 1900; That Sister of Mine, 1900; The Forgotten Favorite, 1902; Son of a Duke, 1903; Her Answer, 1907; The Lilac Domino (part author), 1918; and several pantomines and children's plays; for over thirty years one of the chief writers on The Era, and contributor, at one time or another, to nearly every London daily newspaper. *Recreations:* carpentry, music. *Address:* 8 Lancaster Road, Bowes Park, N11. *Club:* Actors'. *Died 23 Oct. 1925.*

FitzGERALD, Lord Walter, JP Co. Kildare; *b* 22 Jan. 1858; 4th *s* of 4th Duke of Leinster; unmarried. *Educ:* Cheam, Surrey; Eton; Sandhurst. Gazetted to 4th Battalion 60th Rifles, 1879; served in India; retired as a Captain, 1888; served with the Carlow Militia, 1888–98. *Publications:* papers on archæological subjects in the Journal of the Royal Society of Antiquaries of Ireland, and in the Journal of the County Kildare Archæological Society. *Recreations:* shooting, archæologising. *Address:* Kilkea Castle, Maganey, Co. Kildare, Ireland. *Died 31 July 1923.*

FitzGIBBON, John; MP (N) South Mayo, 1910–18; *b* 1 June 1849; *m* 1873, Mary A. O'Carroll. *Educ:* St Kyran's College, Kilkenny. Chairman Roscommon County Council; a trustee of the Irish Parliamentary Fund; on Congested Districts Board, Ireland (unpaid). *Address:* Castlerea, Co. Roscommon. *Died 8 Sept. 1919.*

FITZHARDINGE, 3rd Baron (UK), *cr* 1861; **Charles Paget Fitzhardinge Berkeley,** DL; MFH (Fitzhardinge); *b* 19 April 1830; *s* of 1st Baron and Charlotte, *d* of 4th Duke of Richmond; *S* brother, 1896; *m* 1856, Louisa Elizabeth (*d* 1902), *o d* of Henry Lindow Lindow. MP (L) Gloucester, 1862–65. *Heir:* none. *Address:* Berkeley Castle, Berkeley, Gloucestershire; Cranford House, Hounslow. *Club:* Travellers'. *Died 3 Dec. 1916.*

FITZHERBERT, Basil Thomas, JP, DL; *e surv. s* of late Francis Fitzherbert and Maria Teresa, *d* of late John Vincent Gandolfi, of East Sheen, Surrey; *b* 1836; *m* 1st, 1858, Emily Charlotte (*d* 1881), *e d* of late Hon. Edward Stafford-Jerningham; 2nd, 1887, Emma Eliza (*d* 1912), 2nd, *d* of late Frederick Sewallis Gerard, and *widow* of 9th Lord Stafford. *Educ:* Oscott. *Address:* Ensleigh, Grayshott, Haslemere. *Died 13 April 1919.*

FITZHERBERT-BROCKHOLES, William Joseph, CBE 1918; JP, DL, and County Alderman, Lancaster; MBOU; Lord of the Manors of Claughton and Heaton; *b* 1851; 2nd surv. *s* of Francis Fitzherbert of Swynnerton, and Maria Teresa, *d* of late John Vincent Gandolfi of East Sheen, Surrey; *m* 1st, 1876, Mary Ida (*d* 1883), 2nd *d* of late Robert Berkeley of Spetchley, Co. Worcester; two *d;* 2nd, 1885, Blanche (*d* 1918), 2nd *d* of late Maj.-Gen. Hon. Sir Henry Hugh Clifford, VC, KCMG; three *s* two *d*. *Educ:* St Mary's College, Oscott. Farmed in Staffordshire, 1870–75; on the Council of the Royal Agricultural Society; an active Member of the Central Chamber of Agriculture and other agricultural bodies; Member of the Lancs CC since its inception. *Recreations:* shooting, ornithology, formerly hunting. *Address:* Claughton Hall, Garstang, Lancs. *TA:* Claughton, Bilsborough. *T:* Preston, Brock 5. *Clubs:* Junior Carlton, Wellington. *Died 21 Jan. 1924.*

FITZMAURICE, Sir Maurice, Kt 1912; CMG 1902; FRS 1919; Consulting Engineer; member of firm of Coode, Fitzmaurice, Wilson & Mitchell, Consulting Engineers for Harbours to the Crown Agents for the Colonies; Consulting Engineers for Harbours and Docks at Singapore, Colombo, Hong-Kong, Lagos, and other ports; Chief Engineers of the National Harbours at Dover and Peterhead; Consulting Engineers to the Sudan Government for Blue Nile Irrigation Works; Chief Engineer to the London County Council, 1901–12; *b* 11 May 1861; *m* 1911, Ida, *d* of late Colonel Edward Dickinson, RE, of West Lavington Hill, Midhurst, Sussex; two *d*. *Educ:* Trinity College, Dublin. MA, MAI (Dublin); Hon. LLD (Birmingham). Apprenticed to late Sir Benjamin Baker, KCB. MInstCE (President, 1916–17); MnstMechE; Chairman Engineering Joint Council, 1923–24; Hon. Member American Society of Civil Engineers; Hon. Fellow Society of Engineers; Hon. Member Royal Engineers Institution; Member Engineering Institute of Canada. Member of Advisory Council on Scientific and Industrial Research;

Member of International Technical Commission Suez Canal; Chairman of Admiralty Advisory Committee on Naval Works, 1912–18; Chairman Canal Control Committee (Board of Trade), 1917–19; Chairman of Committee dealing with Civilian Labour London Defences (War Office), 1914–19; Member of War Office Committee on Hutted Camps, 1915–18; Chairman Nile Projects Committee (Foreign Office), 1918–19; Chairman of Committee on Aerodrome Accounts, etc. (Treasury), 1919; Member of Royal Commission on Fire Prevention; Member of Advisory Council Science Museum, 1915–21; Commandant Engineer and Railway Staff Corps; Engineer of the Rotherhithe Tunnel; New Vauxhall Bridge; visited Australia in 1913 at request of Commonwealth Government to advise on Naval Harbours and Works; visited British Front in Flanders in 1915 at request of War Office to advise on questions of drainage, and in 1918; also engaged on the Forth Bridge; Railways and Docks in Canada; the Blackwall Tunnell; Nile Reservoir Dam, Assouan, Egypt. Order of Mejidieh, 2nd Class, 1901; Telford and Watt gold medals of Institution of Civil Engineers. *Publications:* Plate Girder Railway Bridges; The Thames and Lea; London County Bridges; Main Drainage of London; and many papers. *Recreations:* shooting, fishing. *Address:* 9 Victoria Street, Westminster, SW. *T:* Victoria 47; 54 Onslow Square, SW7. *T:* Kensington 6241; West Bay, Bridport, Dorset. *Club:* Reform.

Died 17 Nov. 1924.

FITZ MAURICE, Vice-Admiral Sir Maurice Swynfen, KCVO 1925; CB 1921; CMG 1916; Commander-in-Chief, Africa Station, since 1924; *b* 12 Aug. 1870; *e s* of late J. G. Fitz Maurice, Barrister; *m* 1896, Mabel Gertrude, *y d* of late S. W. Gray; one *s*. Served Vitu, East Africa, 1898 (wounded, despatches, medal, clasp); River Gambia, 1894 (despatches, clasp); Boer War, 1899–1901 (medal 2 clasps); European War, 1914–18 (CMG); Assistant Director of Naval Intelligence, 1910; of Intelligence Division, Admiralty War Staff, 1912–14; Senior Officer on the Yangtse, 1914; Captain of Triumph, 1914, until torpedoed and sunk May 1915; Principal Naval Transport Officer, Dardanelles and Salonika, 1915–16; Chief of Staff Eastern Mediterranean, 1916–17; Capt. of Dreadnought, 1918; SNO Coast of Palestine, 1918; Commodore Commanding British Aegean Squadron, 1919; Director of Naval Intelligence Admiralty, 1921–24; Vice Admiral, 1926. Sacred Treasure of Japan (2nd cl.), 1917; Legion of Honour (officer), Royal Order of Redeemer, Greece; Croix de Guerre, Greece. *Clubs:* White's, United Service, Royal Automobile; Royal Norfolk and Suffolk Yacht.

Died 23 Jan. 1927.

FITZPATRICK, Rt. Rev. Mgr. Bartholomew; Vicar-General, Dublin, and Dean of the Chapter; Priest of St Kevin's, Dublin; *b* Dublin, 1847. *Educ:* Carlow; Clonliffe; Irish College, Rome. Priest, 1870; Privy Chamberlain to the Pope, 1873; Domestic Prelate since 1905. *Address:* St Kevin's, Heytesbury Street, Dublin.

Died 16 Feb. 1925.

FITZPATRICK, Sir Dennis, GCSI 1911 (KCSI 1890; CSI 1887); late Lieutenant-Governor of Punjab; and afterwards Member of Council of India, 1897; *b* 1837; *s* of late Thomas Fitzpatrick, MD, Dublin; *m* 1862, Mary, *d* of Col H. Buller; two *s* two *d*. *Educ:* Trinity College, Dublin. Barrister, Inner Temple, 1872; was Resident at Hyderabad, and Secretary to the Government of India, Judge of the Chief Court of the Punjab, and Chief Commissioner of Assam and of the Central Provinces; Member of Public Service Commission; Acting Resident at Court of Maharajah of Mysore, 1877. *Address:* 2 Queen's Gate Gardens, SW. *Club:* Athenæum.

Died 20 May 1920.

FitzROY, Lord Frederick (John); Magistrate for Sussex and Northamptonshire; *b* 4 April 1823; 3rd *s* of 5th Duke of Grafton and Mary, *d* of Adm. Hon. Sir George Berkeley, GCB; *m* 1853, Catherine Sarah Wilhelmina (*d* 1914), *d* of late Rev. William Wescomb, Rector of Langford; two *d* (and one *s* two *d* decd). *Educ:* at sea. Entered the Navy, 1836; served in Syria, 1840; Grenadier Guards, 1843; served in Crimea, 1855; Canada, 1861–62; retired Lieut-Col, 1862; MP (L) Thetford, 1863–65. *Recreations:* shooting, farming. *Address:* 23 Grosvenor Street, W; Forest Farm, Balcomb, Hayward's Heath. *Clubs:* Travellers', Wellington.

Died 13 Feb. 1919.

FITZWILLIAM, Captain Hon. Sir (William) Charles Wentworth, GCVO 1921 (KCVO 1911; CVO 1910); DL; Crown Equerry to King George, 1910–24; *b* 31 March 1848; *s* of 6th Earl Fitzwilliam and Lady Frances Harriet, *e d* of 19th Earl of Morton; *m* 1882, Constance Anne, *d* of late Henry Brocklehurst; one *s*. Late Captain Royal Horse Guards; ADC to Marquess of Ripon, Governor-General of India, 1880–82; Extra Equerry and Master of the Stables

to the King (when Prince of Wales), 1901–10; High Sheriff of Rutland, 1898. *Address:* Barnsdale, Oakham. *Clubs:* Brooks's, Bachelors', Turf.   *Died 17 April 1925.*

FITZWILLIAM, Hon. William Henry Wentworth-; DL Co. Wicklow; *b* 26 Dec. 1840; 2nd *s* of 6th Earl Fitzwilliam; *m* 1877, Lady Mary Grace Louisa Butler, *d* of 2nd Marquess of Ormonde; three *d*. *Educ:* Eton; Trinity Coll. Cambridge. MP (L) Co. Wicklow, 1868–74; WR Yorks, South Division, 1880–85; WR Yorks, Doncaster Division (LU), 1888–92. Member of Jockey Club since 1875. Hon. Lt-Col and Commandant 2nd Battalion North Riding of Yorkshire Volunteer Regt; Hon. Major 1st West Yorks Yeomanry, 1881. *Address:* Wigganthorpe, York. *TA:* Wigganthorpe, Terrington, Yorks. *Clubs:* Turf, Brooks's, Yorkshire.

Died 10 July 1920.

FITZWYGRAM, Sir Frederick Loftus Francis, 5th Bt, *cr* 1805; *b* 11 Aug. 1884; *o s* of Sir Frederick Wellington John Fitzwygram, 4th Bt and Angela, *d* of Thomas Nugent Vaughan and Viscountess Forbes; *S* father, 1904. *Educ:* Eton; Magdalen College, Oxford (MA). Captain Scots Guards; served European War, 1914–15 (despatches, wounded twice). Owner of 2000 acres in Hants. *Heir-pres.: c* Edgar Thomas Ainger Wigram, BA [*b* 23 Nov. 1864. *Educ:* Trinity Hall, Cambridge. *Address:* Watling House, St Albans]. *Address:* Leigh Park, Havant, Hants. *Clubs:* Guards, Carlton.

Died 5 May 1920.

FLAMMARION, Camille; astronomer; *b* Montigny-le-Roi (Haute Marne), 26 Feb. 1842; *m* 1st, 1874; 2nd, 1919, Gabrielle Renaudot. *Educ:* Langres, 1853–56; Paris Observatory under Le Verrier, 1858–62; Sorbonne, under Delaunay, 1862; Bureau des Longitudes, 1862–66. Founded monthly review l'Astronomie, 1882; founded Observatory of Juvisy, 1883; founded Astronomical Society of France, 1887. *Publications:* (translated into English) Marvels of the Heavens, 1870; The Atmosphere, 1873; Urania, 1891; Omega, the Last Days of the World, 1893; Popular Astronomy, 1894; Lumen, 1897; The Unknown, 1900; Astronomy for Amateurs, 1904; Mysterious Psychic Forces, 1907; Death and its Mystery, in three parts, 1920, 1921, 1922; Dreams of an Astronomer, 1923. *Address:* The Observatory, Juvisy, Seine-et-Oise, France.   *Died 4 June 1925.*

FLANAGAN, Rev. J.; minister of the Primitive Methodist Church; *b* Mansfield, 18 Dec. 1851; *s* of William Patrick Flanagan, Co. Waterford, Ireland, and Elizabeth Robinson, Edwinstowe, Notts; *m* 1872, Mary Jane Richardson of Newark-on-Trent; four *s* four *d*. *Educ:* became a Christian after marriage; commenced education while toiling as a miner. Called by Providence to be a mission preacher; toiled at this for about 15 years; then pastor of the United Gospel Mission, Albert Hall, Nottingham, 4 years; received into full ministry of Primitive Methodist Church, 1890; sent to London; built up a mission church in the Boro', SE; erected St George's Hall and Schools, Old Kent Road; earned and raised £20,000 in 13 years for the poor of slums; now minister without charge. *Publications:* Romance of Evangelism; Man's Quest in Sermon and Song; Scenes from my Life, both Grave and Gay; Thy Brother's Blood. *Recreations:* preaching, travelling and lecturing. *Address:* 20 Patrick Road, West Bridgford, Nottingham.   *Died 30 March 1918.*

FLATHER, James Henry, MA; late Secretary for Examinations to the Local Examinations and Lecturers Syndicate of the University of Cambridge; *b* Sheffield, 11 Aug. 1853; *y s* of late Rev. John Flather; *m* Jane, *y d* of late Charles Thomas Shaw of Birmingham. *Educ:* Collegiate School, Sheffield; Emmanuel College, Cambridge. First Class in Classical Tripos, 1876; Lightfoot University Scholar, 1877; Assistant Master at Lancaster Grammar School, 1877; Tutor (1878) and Master (1888–91) of Cavendish College; Asst Secretary to Local Examinations and Lectures Syndicate, 1892. *Publications:* contributions to Smith's Dictionary of Greek and Roman Antiquities (3rd edn); editions of works by Scott, etc. *Address:* Lawden Cottage, Newton Road, Cambridge. *T:* Cambridge 838.

Died 3 Nov. 1928.

FLEET, Vice-Adm. Henry Louis, CBE 1918; *b* 1 May 1850; 3rd *s* of J. G. Fleet, late of Roystons, Chiswick, and Esther Faithfull, *d* of Rev. F. F. Faithfull; *m* Alice Mary, *d* of W. F. Elliot of Wilton, Somerset. *Educ:* St Paul's School; St Mary's Hall, Southsea. Entered Royal Navy, 1864; Captain, 1895; commanded Indian Naval Defence, Bombay, 1897–1900; JP, Bombay; Flag Capt. at Queenstown, 1900–3; Capt. Western District, 1903; Rear-Admiral (retired), 1905; possesses the Canadian Medal, Egyptian Medal, Khedive's Star, and Coronation Medal; awarded Humane Society's Certificate, 1884; Nautical Assessor to House of Lords, 1910; County Director Auxiliary

Hospitals of VAD, Berkshire. *Publications:* An Admiral's Yarns; My Life and a Few Yarns, 1922. *Address:* The Camber, Coley Avenue, Reading. *Club:* United Service.

Died 17 Sept. 1923.

FLEET, John Faithfull, CIE 1884; *b* 1847; *s* of John George Fleet. *Educ:* Merchant Taylors' School. Was in Indian Civil Service, 1867–97; Commissioner of Central and Southern Divisions of Bombay, 1891–97. *Publications:* Inscriptions of the Early Gupta Kings, vol. iii of the Corpus Inscriptionum Indicarum, 1888; numerous other writings on the ancient history and antiquities of India, in the Indian Antiquary, the Epigraphia Indica, the Journal of the Royal Asiatic Society, and elsewhere; Triennial Gold Medal, Royal Asiatic Society. *Address:* 8 Leopold Road, Ealing Common, W. *Club:* East India United Service.

Died 21 Feb. 1917.

FLEMING, Sir Andrew Fleming Hudleston le, 8th Bt, *cr* 1705; *b* Easedale, near Canterbury, New Zealand, 1855; *s* of Sir Michael Le Fleming, 7th Bt and Mary, *d* of Capt. Boddie, Russian Navy; *S* father, 1883; *m* 1895, Jeannette, *d* of late Roderick Frazer, Otago. *Educ:* Christ Coll., Canterbury. *Heir: c* William Hudleston Le Fleming, *b* 26 May 1861. *Address:* Woodgrove, Canterbury, NZ.

Died 20 Oct. 1925.

FLEMING, Major Charles Christie, DSO 1898; late Royal Army Medical Corps; Assistant Director of Medical Services, Highland Division, with rank of Colonel, since 1915; late Secretary (Scottish Branch) British Red Cross Society, Headquarters, Glasgow; *b* 6 Nov. 1864; 2nd *s* of late Dep.-Surg.-Gen. A. Fleming and Catherine, *d* of Capt. Joseph Henry Garner. *Educ:* Edinburgh University (MB, CM). Entered Army Med. Service, 1892, and became Surg.-Capt. (later Capt. Royal Army Med. Corps), 1895; Major, 1904; served as Senior Med. Officer at Suakim (1896–97), at Kassala (1897–98), and at actions at Gedaref, 1898 (despatches, medal with clasp, Soudan medal (Queen's), DSO); South Africa as MO in charge No 2 Ambulance Train, 1899–1902 (medal with five clasps; King's medal, 2 clasps). *Recreations:* fishing, shooting. *Address:* 8 Napier Road, Edinburgh. *Clubs:* Junior Constitutional; Caledonian United Service, Edinburgh; Western, Glasgow.

Died 24 Dec. 1917.

FLEMING, Rev. David; Hon. Canon of Durham. *Address:* Coxhoe Vicarage, County Durham.

Died 15 Dec. 1920.

FLEMING, Sir Francis, KCMG 1892 (CMG 1887); JP; *b* 1842; *s* of late James Fleming, QC,and Julia, *d* of late Maj. John Canning; *m* 1892, Constance Mary, *d* of M. D. Kavanagh, barrister, and Hon. Mrs Kavanagh. *Educ:* Downside College. Barrister, Middle Temple, 1866; Crown Solicitor, Mauritius, 1869; District Magistrate, 1872; District Judge, Jamaica, 1876; Attorney-General, Barbados, 1878; acted as private sec. to Sir G. C. Straban, KCMG; Gov. of Cape Colony, 1880; Puisne Judge, British Guiana, 1882; Queen's Advocate, Ceylon, 1883; Col Sec. Mauritius, 1886; Col Sec. Hong-Kong, 1889; Actg Gov. Mauritius, 1886–87; of Hong-Kong, 1890; Gov. Sierra Leone, 1892; Consul for Liberia, 1892; Governor of Leeward Islands, 1895–1901; late Poor Law Guardian for Parish of St Mary Abbots, Kensington. *Address:* 9 Sydney Place, SW7. *T:* Kens. 568.

Died 4 Dec. 1922.

FLEMING, Frederick, QC Ireland 1896. *Address:* 69 Merrion Square, Dublin.

FLEMING, Rev. Herbert James, CMG 1916; MA; Chaplain to the Forces, 1st class; *b* 1 Jan. 1873. *Educ:* Pembroke College, Oxford (Scholar). Ordained 1897; Curate of St Mary, South Shields, 1897–99; South Petherton, 1899–1902; Chaplain to Forces, Aldershot, 1902–4; Ballincollig, 1904–6; Woolwich, 1906–7; Crete, 1907–9; Gibraltar, 1909–11; RMA, Woolwich, 1911–14; served European War, 1914–18 (despatches twice, CMG); RMA, Woolwich, 1918–22; Shorncliffe, 1922–23; Royal Hospital, Chelsea, 1923. *Address:* Royal Hospital, Chelsea, SW.

Died 17 Nov. 1926.

FLEMING, James, ISO 1908; late Collector of Customs, London and Chief Registrar of Shipping; retired, 1906; *b* Aghadowey, Co. Londonderry, 1841; 5th *s* of late Edward Fleming of Coleraine; *m* 1868, Jane, *d* of late William Hastings of Portstewart; two *s* four *d*. Clerk in Customs, London, 1858; Surveyor, 1882; Inspector, 1894; Surveyor-General, 1900; witness before Playfair, Ridley, Port of London, and Civil Service Superannuation Royal Commissions; Chairman of Inter-departmental Committee on Tobacco Drawback, 1904; Member of Committee of Civil Service Supply Association,

Ltd. *Address:* Hastings Villa, Rudall Crescent, Hampstead Heath, NW.

Died 22 Dec. 1922.

FLEMING, James Alexander, KC 1903; Sheriff of Fife and Kinross since 1913; Vice-Dean of the Faculty of Advocates, 1905–21; *b* 1855; *e surv. s* of late James Simpson Fleming, Cashier and General Manager of the Royal Bank of Scotland, and Elizabeth, *d* of Thomas Reid of Hayston, Stirlingshire; *m* 1893, Helen Mary, *d* of William Hudson Swire, merchant, London. *Educ:* Glasgow Academy; Uppingham; Edinburgh University. Apprenticed to mercantile firms of James Finlay & Co., Glasgow and London; Steel, Macfarlane & Co., Port Elizabeth, Cape Colony; served with James Finlay & Co., Liverpool; Heugh Balfour & Co., and Robert Barclay & Co., Manchester, and Royal Bank of Scotland; passed as advocate, 1883; Scottish Counsel to Statute Law Committee, 1890–98 and 1900; Counsel to Post Office in Scotland, 1891–1900; Sheriff-Court Depute, 1892, and again in 1895; Extra Advocate Depute, 1896; Advocate Depute, 1898; Sheriff of Dumfries and Galloway, 1900–13. *Address:* 33 Melville Street, Edinburgh. *T:* Central 2373, Edinburgh. *Clubs:* Junior Carlton; New, University, Edinburgh; Western, Glasgow.

Died 12 April 1926.

FLEMING, Sir John, Kt 1908; JP, DL; LLD; *b* 1847; *s* of John Fleming, Dundee; *m* 1870, Elizabeth, *d* of John Dow, Dundee; three *s* four *d*. *Educ:* Brown Street and High Schools, Dundee. Timber Merchant, Aberdeen; has been Member of Aberdeen Town Council, Harbour Board, and Chamber of Commerce; Vice-Chairman Aberdeen Territorial Force; Lord Provost of Aberdeen, 1898–1902. *Address:* Dulmumzie, Murtle, near Aberdeen.

Died 25 Feb. 1925.

FLEMING, His Honour Patrick D., KC; MA; County Court Judge for King's Co., Longford, Meath, and Westmeath, 1918–24; *b* Sunville, Kilmallock, Co. Limerick. *Educ:* Trinity College, Dublin (MA Senior Moderator and Gold Medallist); Middle Temple (Scholar). Called to Irish Bar, 1881; Inner Bar, 1904. *Address:* 15 Herbert Street, Dublin. *Club:* Stephen's Green, Dublin.

Died April 1928.

FLEMING, Lt-Col Samuel; Metropolitan Police Magistrate, Greenwich and Woolwich, 1921–24; Lambeth, since 1924; *b* 1865; *s* of late Frederick Green Fleming; *m* 1892, Elizabeth Knox, *d* of Col. William Clare Ball, CB. Barrister, Gray's Inn and Middle Temple, 1897; legal adviser and Judge Advocate Aldershot Command, and subsequently legal adviser at War Office during European War, 1914–19; Deputy Assistant Director-General, 1917; Recorder of Doncaster, 1920–21; Member of Bar Council; JP Surrey, 1921. *Address:* 315 St James's Court, Buckingham Gate, W1. *Clubs:* Conservative, Royal Automobile.

Died 20 Dec. 1925.

FLEMING, Valentine; MP (C) South Oxfordshire (Henley Division) since 1910; Barrister-at-Law; Major Oxfordshire Yeomanry; *b* Newport, Fife, NB, 17 Feb. 1882; *e s* of Robert Fleming, of Joyce Grove, Nettlebed, and 8 Crosby Square, EC; *m* 1906, Evelyn B. St C. Rose, *d* of George A. St C. Rose, The Red House, Sonning; four *s*. *Educ:* Eton; Magdalen Coll., Oxford; BA (Honours in History), 1905. Rowed in Eton Eight, 1900; Magdalen College Eight three years; won Ladies' Plate at Henley, 1904, and Final of Visitors Cup; rowed University Trial Eights. Called to Bar, Inner Temple, 1907; partner in Robert Fleming and Co., 8 Crosby Square, EC; travelled in Europe and America; served European War (despatches). *Recreations:* deerstalking, salmon fishing, fox-hunting, hunts a pack of Basset hounds. *Address:* Arnisdale, Lock Hourn, Inverness-shire; Pitt House, Hampstead Heath, NW. *Clubs:* Carlton, Travellers', White's, Bath.

Died 20 May 1917.

FLEMMING, Hon. James Kidd, LLD; MP for Carleton, Victoria, New Brunswick, since 1925; *b* 27 April 1868, of Irish parentage; *m* 1890, Helena S. Fleming; three *s* two *d*. *Educ:* common schools and Provincial Normal School. Since 1890 engaged in commercial pursuits; contested the provincial election for native county in 1895, and again in 1899; in a by-election, Jan. 1900, was successful, and was re-elected 1903, 1908 and 1912; Provincial Secretary and Receiver-General in the Hazen Administration, 1908–11; Premier of New Brunswick, 1911–16; President and Manager, Flemming and Gibson Ltd, and engaged in lumbering business. *Address:* Box 297, House of Commons, Ottawa, Ontario; Juniper, New Brunswick. *T:* 10–3.

Died 10 Feb. 1927.

FLEMWELL, George Jackson; artist and author; *b* The Chesnuts, Mitcham, Surrey, 29 May 1865; *e s* of John Flemwell and Anne

Catherine Lancefield; *m* 1912, Grace, *y d* of John Priddle, of Muswell Hill. *Educ:* Thanet College, Margate; private tutor. Studied four years with W. P. Frith, RA; afterwards, on the advice and introduction of Sir Alma Tadema, RA, going to Antwerp and studying with Prof. Rosier; then to Nuremberg and Munich; exhibited figure subjects at the Royal Academy for four or five years, but abandoned this branch of work; settled in Switzerland and devoted himself to painting and studying the Alps and Alpine wild life. *Publications:* Alpine Flowers and Gardens; The Flower Fields of Alpine Switzerland; Sur l'Alpe Fleurie; Beautiful Switzerland; Lucerne; Locarno; Lugano; Lausanne; Villars and Champery; Chamonix; Zermatt; Known and Little-Known; Mooning in Paradise; the plates for H. Stuart Thomson's Sub-Alpine Plants; essays and illustrations in various English, Continental and American publications. *Recreations:* nature-study, gardening. *Address:* c/o Swiss Office of Tourism, Löwenstrasse, Zürich, Switzerland. *Clubs:* Alpin Suisse; Alpin Français.

Died 5 March 1928.

FLERS, Marquis de, (Robert de Flers); Membre de l'Académie Française 1920; Directeur littéraire du Figaro; *b* Pont l'Evêque, 25 Nov. 1872; petit-fils d'Eugène de Rozière, membre de l'Institut; arrière-petit-fils de Charles Giraud, membre de l'Institut et ministre de l'Instruction Publique; *m* 1901, G., *d* of Victorien Sardon, de l'Académie Française; one *s*. *Educ:* Lycée Condorcet, Paris. Licencié en Droit et ès Lettres, Lauréat de l'Académie Française en 1894; homme de lettres, journaliste et auteur dramatique; plusieurs fois président de la Société des Auteurs et Compositeurs Dramatiques; Officier de la Légion d'Honneur 1913. *Publications:* articles parus dans la Liberté, le Gaulois et dans le Figaro; Vers l'Orient; La Courtisane Taïa et son singe vert; Illsée, princesse de Tripoli; Entre cœur et chair; Sur les chemins de la Guerre; La Petite Table Théâtre; Le Cœur a ses raisons; La Chance du mari; Les Sentiers de la vertu; La Montansier; L'Ange du foyer; Miquette et sa mère; L'Amour veille; Les Travaux d'Hercule; Le Sire de Vergy; Paris ou le Bon Juge; Monsieur de la Palisse; Papa; Le Roi; L'Habit vert; L'Ane de Buridan; Le Bois sacré; Monsieur Brotonneau; Primerose; Venise; Le Retour; Fortunio; Béatrice; (Collaborateurs; pour la plupart de ses pièces; G. A. de Caillavet; pour le Retour, F. de Croisset. Musiciens collaborateurs A. Messager; Claude Terrasse). *Address:* 70 boulevard de Courcelles, Paris 17. *T:* Wagram 01-09. *Died 30 July 1927.*

FLETCHER, Hon. Edward Ernest; Judge of the Supreme Court, Calcutta; *m* Millicent Valentine (*d* 1917); *e d* of Horace Waddington, late HMI of Schools. *Address:* Supreme Court, Calcutta.

FLETCHER, Lt-Col Sir Henry Arthur, Kt 1919; CVO 1909; Lieutenant HM Bodyguard of the Honourable Corps of Gentlemen-at-Arms since 1922; *b* 20 April 1843; *s* of the late Charles William Fletcher, Board of Control, India Office; *m* 1881, Constance (*d* 1921), *d* of E. Headland, 93 Portland Place, W; no *c*. *Educ:* private schools. Served in Bengal Cavalry, 1860–89; North-West Frontier of India, 1863–64; affair of Shabkadar, etc (medal and clasp); Egyptian Campaign, 1882 (medal and bronze star); appointed to the Honourable Corps of Gentlemen-at-Arms, 1892; Clerk of the Cheque and Adjutant, 1900–20; Standard Bearer, 1920–22. *Address:* 17 Victoria Square, SW1; St James's Palace, SW. *Clubs:* United Service, Garrick. *Died 24 Dec. 1925.*

FLETCHER, Herbert Phillips, FRIBA, FSI, AMICE; architect; *b* 27 Feb. 1872; *s* of late Professor Banister Fletcher, MP, JP, etc; *m* Lydia, *o d* of late T. T. Lindrea, JP, Westbury, Glos. *Educ:* King's College, London (Gold Medal in the Architectural and Engineering Course.) Travelled round the world; obtained the highest examination diplomas at the Institute of British Architects, Surveyors' Institute, and the Institution of Civil Engineers. Called to Bar at Middle Temple; Architect to the Worshipful Company of Carpenters, and Technical Adviser to six of the associated City Companies; Director of their Trades Training Schools; lately Lecturer on staff of King's College, and acting District Surveyor for Newington; Godwin Bursar, RIBA, 1904; partner in firm of Banister Fletcher and Sons, whose works include King's Coll. School, and numerous banks, schools, churches, city buildings, and country houses; alterations and additions King's College, London, Carpenters' Hall, London Wall, etc; was lent to the French Navy as senior military observer for reconnaissance work in seaplanes from Aden to Gallipoli, March 1915—Feb. 1916; awarded Croix de Guerre three times, twice by the French navy and once by the army; afterwards attached to the RNAS in same capacity when they took over this patrol, and was OC of Military Observers' School at Port Said; seconded to the Royal Flying Corps, 1916. *Publications:* The English Home, Architectural Hygiene, Carpentry and Joinery, Arbitrations, Quantities, London Building Acts, Valuations and Compensations, Light and Air, Dilapidations, and other text-books. *Recreations:* hunting; late deputy master and joint-huntsman

of the North Bucks Harriers, shooting, sailing, golf; Major Middlesex Hussars. *Address:* 29 New Bridge Street, EC. *TA:* Banister, London. *T:* 741 Holborn; Park House, Marden, Kent; Cuthbert Villa, Westgate-on-Sea. *Clubs:* Cavalry, Pegasus; various golf.

Died Aug. 1917.

FLETCHER, James Douglas, JP, DL; *b* 1857; *e surv. s* of late James Fletcher, and Frederica Mary, *d* of John Stephen and *widow* of Alexander Hay, 58th Regt; *m* 1909, Lilian, *y d* of late Col Stephen, CB. *Educ:* Eton; Balliol College, Oxford. *Address:* Rosehaugh, Avoch, Ross-shire; 26 Curzon Street, W1. *T:* Mayfair 1925. *Clubs:* Arthur's, Carlton.

Died 30 Aug. 1927.

FLETCHER, Rev. John Charles Ballett; Canon of Chichester. *Address:* North Mundham Vicarage, Chichester.

Died 6 May 1926.

FLETCHER, Sir John Samuel, 1st Bt, *cr* 1919; JP; *b* 3 Nov. 1841; 2nd *s* of Samuel Fletcher, Manchester; *m* 1895, Sara, *d* of late Jonathan Clark of Winchendon, Bucks. *Educ:* Harrow; Christ Church, Oxford. Chairman, Hampstead Board of Guardians, 1880–98; Member LCC, 1889–1904; Deputy Chairman, 1900. Barrister, Lincoln's Inn, 1868; MP (U) Hampstead, 1905–18. *Heir:* none. *Address:* Bryony Hill, Hambledon, Surrey. *Clubs:* Albemarle, St Stephen's.

Died 20 May 1924 (ext).

FLETCHER, Sir Lazarus, Kt 1916; MA (Oxon), Hon. LLD (St Andrews), Hon. PhD and AM (Berlin); FRS; Hon. Fellow of University College, Oxford, 1910; *b* Salford, 3 March 1854; *e s* of Stewart Fletcher, Manchester; *m* 1st, Agnes Ward (*d* 1915), *d* of Rev. Thomas Holme, Vicar of Moorside, Oldham; one *d*; 2nd, 1916, Edith, *sister* of the above. *Educ:* Manchester Grammar School; Balliol Coll. Oxford (Brakenbury Science Scholar); 1st class Math. Mods; 1st class Final Mathematical School; 1st class Nature Science School. National Gold Medal (Mechanics) and Bronze Medal (Mathematics) awarded by Science and Art Department, 1872; highly distinguished for the University Junior Mathematical Scholarship, Oxford, 1874. Demonstrator in the Clarendon Laboratory, Oxford, 1875–77; Fellow Univ. Coll. Oxford, 1877–80; Millard Lecturer in Physics, Trinity Coll. Oxford, 1877–78; University Senior Mathematical Scholarship, Oxford, 1876; Keeper of Minerals in British Museum (Natural History), 1880–1909; Director of the Natural History Depts of the British Museum, 1909–19; Public Examiner (Natural Science) Oxford, 1880; Examiner for Natural Sciences Tripos, Camb. 1882–83, 1889–91, 1896–97; Vice-Pres. Royal Soc., 1910–12; Vice-Pres. Geological Society, 1890–92, and Vice-Pres. of Physical Society, 1895–97; Council of Royal Society, 1895–97 and 1910–12; Pres., Mineralogical Society, 1885–88; General Secretary, 1888–1909; Pres. of the Geological Section of the British Association at Oxford, 1894; Wollaston Medallist, Geological Society, 1912; Member of the Boards of Electors to the Professorships of Mineralogy at Oxford and Cambridge; Corresponding Member of the Royal Society of Göttingen, the Academy of Sciences, Munich, and the New York Academy of Sciences. Honorary Member of the Sociedad Cientifica Antonio Alzate, Mexico; Association Scientifique et d'Enseignement Médical complémentaire; Selborne Society; Hertfordshire Natural History Society and Field Club; Ealing Scientific and Microscopical Society; Museums Association. *Publications:* Introduction to the Study of Meteorites, 1881; Introduction to the Study of Minerals, 1884; The Optical Indicatrix, 1892; Introduction to the Study of Rocks, 1895; papers on crystallographical, physical, and mineralogical subjects and on meteorites; article on Meteorites in the Encyclopædia Britannica and on Precious Stones of the Bible in the International Standard Bible Encyclopædia. *Recreation:* gardening. *Address:* The White House, Ravenstonedale, Westmorland. *Clubs:* Athenæum, Savile.

Died 6 Jan. 1921.

FLETCHER, Rev. Philip; *b* Ashley Park, Walton-on-Thames, 30 Oct. 1848; 5th *s* of Sir Henry Fletcher, 3rd Bt. *Educ:* Exeter College, Oxford (MA). For six years curate at St Bartholomew's Church, Brighton; received into the Catholic Church, 1878; Priest, 1882; Founder of the Guild of Our Lady of Ransom for the Spread of the Catholic Religion and the organisation of Public Processions and Pilgrimages; these have been carried on for 30 years; has contributed weekly articles to the Catholic Press since 1886. Chevalier d' l'Ordre de la Couronne (Belgium), 1919; Knight Commander of the Order of the Holy Sepulchre, 1920. *Address:* 29 Portugal Street, Kingsway, WC.

Died 13 Jan. 1928.

FLETCHER, Rev. Robert, MA; Prebendary of Hereford since 1902. *Address:* Armidale, Roumania Crescent, Llandudno.

Died 15 April 1921.

FLETCHER, Ven. Robert Crompton; Archdeacon of Blackburn since 1901; Rector of Chorley, Lancashire, 1907; Alderman of Lancashire County Council since 1889; Surrogate of diocese of Manchester since 1888; *b* Fremantle, W Australia, 9 Dec 1850; *e s* of late Rev. Matthew Fox Fletcher, Rector of Tarleton, and Louisa Jane Crompton, *d* of Andrew Todd of Lower Darley Hall; *m* 1st, 1878, Nina Helen (*d* 1904), *e d* of Henry Rawcliffe, JP, of Gillibrand Hall, Lancs; three *s* five *d*; 2nd, 1909, Jessie, *d* of late James Knowles, and *widow* of Rev. J. Tyas. *Educ:* Rossall; Sidney Sussex College, Cambridge (MA). Asst Master, King William's College, Isle of Man, 1872-73; ordained, 1874; Curate of Tarleton, 1874-75; Rector and Vicar of Tarleton, 1875-1907. *Address:* The Rectory, Chorley, Lancashire. *TA:* Archdeacon, Chorley, Lancashire. *T:* 140 Chorley. *Club:* Royal Societies. *Died 27 Feb. 1917.*

FLETCHER, Major William Alfred Littledale, DSO 1900; Lieutenant-Colonel, 2/6 Rifle Battalion King's Liverpool Regiment; *b* Childwall, 25 Aug. 1869; *s* of Alfred Fletcher, JP, DL. *Educ:* Eton; Christ Church, Oxford. Served South Africa, Lieut, 2nd Batt. Imperial Yeomanry, 1900 (DSO); European War, 1914-18 (Bt Major), then commanding in France (despatches thrice, Legion of Honour). *Recreations:* rowing (Eton Eight, 1890; Oxford Eight, 1890-93), big game shooting, travelling. *Address:* Allerton, Liverpool. *Clubs:* Bath, Sports, Leander. *Died 14 Feb. 1919.*

FLETCHER, Ven. William Henry, MA; Archdeacon of Wrexham, 1910-25; *s* of late Rev. Henry Fletcher and Mrs Fletcher of Ulceby Grange, Lincs; *m* Agnes (*d* 1922), *d* of George Crawfurd, Thornwood, Lanarkshire; one *s*. *Educ:* Shrewsbury School; Careswell Scholar of Christ Church, Oxford; 2nd Class Moderations, 1874; BA 1876. Curate of Holy Trinity, Shrewsbury, 1876-78; Vicar of Criftins by Ellesmere, 1878-82; Vicar of Holy Trinity, Shrewsbury, 1882-88; Vicar of Oswestry, 1888-91; cursal canon of St Asaph Cathedral, 1891-97; Vicar of Wrexham, 1891-1907; Rural Dean of Wrexham, 1891-1907; Rector of Marchwiel, Denbighshire, 1907; Canon Residentiary, 1897-1910; Proctor in Convocation for Cathedral Chapter, 1897-1910. *Address:* Marchwiel Rectory, Wrexham. *Died 2 April 1926.*

FLINN, D. Edgar, VD; FRCS, DPH, MRCP; Medical Member General Prisons Board, Ireland; HM Chief Inspector, Reformatory and Industrial Schools, Ireland, 1910-17; *b* 1850; *s* of late David Edgar Flinn, Buenos Ayres. *Educ:* Clongowes; Royal College Surgeons, Ireland; Univ., Dublin. Served for 25 years in the Volunteer and Territorial Forces, and Army Medical Reserve, retiring with rank of Colonel, 1904. Fellow of the Royal Sanitary Institute, London; Medical Inspector, Local Government Board, Ireland, 1896-1910; Member of Belfast Vice-Regal Commission, 1907-8; Member of Committee of Inquiry as to the causes of Typhoid Fever in Dublin, 1893; President State Medicine Section, Royal Academy Med., Ireland, 1894 and 1895; Editor Health Record, 1890-94; Fellow and Member of Council, Royal College Surgeons, Ireland, 1906-11 and 1916-21; formerly MOH, East Staffordshire, combined Urban and Rural Districts; Examiner in Hygiene and Public Health, Royal Colleges Physicians and Surgeons, Ireland. *Publications:* Ireland, its Health Resorts and Watering Places; Refuse Disposal; Public Cleansing of Towns; Rural Water Supplies; Our Dress and Our Food; The Administration of the Public Health Acts in Ireland, the Public Health of Dublin, and many Government Reports. *Recreations:* golf, travel, reading. *Club:* Stephen's Green, Dublin. *Died 18 Aug. 1926.*

FLINT, Joseph, CMG 1900; formerly Agent-General Niger Co. Ltd; *b* 7 Sept. 1855. Twenty-four years in Nigeria; transferred the administration of Royal Niger Co. Ltd to the Govt of Northern Nigeria to Sir Frederick Lugard, KCMG, CB, and S Nigeria to Sir Ralph Moor, KCMG, Jan. 1900; Agent-Gen. for the Royal Niger Co. Ltd. in conjunction with W. Wallace, CMG, from 1886 to time of transfer to Government, Jan. 1900. *Address:* Rosemount, Sanderstead. *Died 26 Aug. 1925.*

FLINT, Thomas Barnard, MA, LLB, DCL; Clerk of the House of Commons of Canada since 1902; *b* Yarmouth, Nova Scotia, Canada, 28 April 1847; *s* of late John Flint, Shipowner, and Anne Barnard Flint of Yarmouth, NS; *m* 1874, Mary Ella, *d* of Yarmouth, *d* of late Thos B. Dane. *Educ:* Mt Allison University, Sackville, New Brunswick, Canada; Harvard University, Cambridge, Mass, USA. Admitted to the Supreme Court Bar of Nova Scotia, 1871; Commissioner of the Supreme and County Courts and in Admiralty, 1873; High Sheriff of the County of Yarmouth, Nova Scotia, 1884-87; Assistant Clerk of the Provincial Assembly, 1887-91; Member (L) for the County of Yarmouth, House of Commons of Canada, 1891; re-elected, 1896 and 1900; Chief Government Whip

for Maritime Provinces, 1896-1900; Chairman of the Committe on Standing Orders of the House, 1898-1902; Grand Master of th Grand Lodge of Nova Scotia, AF and AM, 1897, 1898 and 189 *Publications:* editor 3rd and 4th editions Bourinot's Parliamentar Practice and Procedure. *Recreations:* travel, research. *Address:* Hous of Commons, Ottawa, Canada. *Club:* Canadian, Ottawa. *Died 7 March 191*

FLOOD, Chevalier William Henry Grattan, Hon. MusD, NUI KSG; Organist of Enniscorthy Cathedral since 1895; *b* Lismore, Cc Waterford, 1 Nov. 1859; *e s* of William Flood and Catherine, *d* c Andrew Fitzsimon; *m* 1898, Margaret, *e d* of Patrick Delane Enniscorthy; two *s* four *d*. *Educ:* Mount Melleray, Catholic Universit All Hallows College, and Carlow College. Successively Organist c Belfast pro-Cathedral; Professor at Tullabeg and Clongowes Woo Colleges; Organist of Thurles Cathedral; Professor at St Wilfrid's Cotton Hall (Staffs), and St Kieran's College, Kilkenny. Decorate by Pope Leo XIII and by Pius X and XI; received the Cross Pr Ecclesia et Pontifice, 1917; Vice-President of the Irish Folk Son Society; Council Member of the Catholic Record Society of Irelan Foundation Member of the National Academy of Ireland. *Publication* History of Enniscorthy; History of Irish Music, 4th edn. 1927; Stor of the Harp; Story of the Bagpipe; Memoir of W. Vincent Wallac History of the Diocese of Ferns, 1916; Introductory Sketch of Iris Musical History, 1921; Memoir of John Field, Inventor of th Nocturne, 1921; Early Tudor Composers, 1925; Late Tudo Composers, 1929; two Masses, numerous Motets and Services, song part music, hymns, etc; Editor of Moore's Irish Melodies, the Spir of the Nation, and Selected Airs of O'Carolan; musical editor of th standard Catholic Hymnal for Ireland; contributions to the Dictionar of National Biography, Grove's Dictionary of Music and Musician 3rd edn 1927-28, Catholic Encyclopædia, home and foreig periodicals, etc. *Recreation:* tracing the sources of old songs and tunes *Address:* Rosemount, Enniscorthy, Co. Wexford. *Died 6 Aug. 192*

FLORENCE, Lt-Col Henry Louis, VD; FGS; Past Vice-Presiden RIBA; architect; *b* 9 June 1843; *e s* of late John Henry Florenc Streatham, Surrey. *Educ:* privately. Articled, 1860; subsequentl studied in Atelier Questel, Paris; Soane medallist, RIBA, 1869 travelling student and gold medallist, RA 1870. Travelled in Italy 1870; commenced practice as an architect, 1871; for 21 years Volunteer officer, retiring with rank of Lt Col in 1892, and receivin the Volunteer decoration. *Professional works:* Holborn Viaduct Hote and Station; Holborn Town Hall; mansion for Edward Lloyd, Delaha St; Hotel Victoria; Paddington Branch of the London Joint-Stoc Bank; new library, pension-room and class-rooms, Gray's Inn restoration of Gray's Inn Hall; offices for Edward Lloyd, Ltd, Salisbur Square, EC; Coombe House and Coombe Farm, near Croydon Coburg Hotel; Carlton Hotel; Buildings for Woolland Bros, Lownde Terrace; new station, St James's Park, for Met. Dist Railway; Empir Hotel, Lowestoft; extension of First Avenue Hotel; Queen Victori Memorial, Kensington; the Institute of Journalists; new Library Museum, and exit staircase, Freemasons' Hall; alterations and addition to the United Service Club. *Recreations:* travel, music. *Address:* S Princes Gate, Hyde Park, SW; 16 Royal Crescent, Bath. *Club:* Arts *Died 20 Feb. 1916*

FLOWER, Benjamin Orange; author; editor Twentieth Century Magazine since 1910; *b* Albion Ill., 19 Oct. 1858; *s* of Rev. Alfred and Elizabeth Orange Flower; *m* 1885, Hattie Cloud, Evansville, Ind *Educ:* public schools of Evansville, Ind; Kentucky University Lexington, Ky. Editor, The American Sentinel Albion, Ill., until 1880 went to Philadelphia, and later to Boston; established The American Spectator, which subsequently was merged into The Arena, which he founded; remained at its head until the end of 1896, then was for a short time in 1897-98 one of the editors of The New Time, a Chicago magazine; subsequently became editor of The Coming Age; which position he held until that magazine was merged into The Arena; editor till it ceased publication in 1910; extensive contributor to leading magazines and periodicals. *Publications:* Lessons Learned from Other Lives, 1891; Civilisation's Inferno, 1893; The New-Time, Essays on Social Problems, 1894; Gerald Massey, Poet, Prophet, and Mystic, 1895; Whittier, Prophet, Seer, and Man, 1895; The Century of Sir Thomas More, 1896; Persons, Places, and Ideas, 1896; How England averted a Revolution of Force, 1901; Progressive Men, Women, and Movements of the Past Twenty-Five Years. *Address:* 145 Aspinwall Avenue, Brookline, Mass; 5 Park Square, Boston. *Died 1918.*

FLOWER, Sir Ernest (Francis Swan), Kt 1903; *b* 24 Aug. 1865; *o* surv *s* of John Flower. Member of the Grand Council of Primrose

League; Fellow of the Royal Colonial Institute; member London School Board, 1897; Member of the Committees of the Metropolitan and Royal Orthopaedic Hospitals; one of the founders and hon. secs. of the People's Palace and East London Horticultural Society; has been much engaged in philanthropic work in East London; Hon. Treasurer of Queen Mary's Royal Naval Hospital, Southend-on-Sea; Chairman of the Blue Cross Fund; Hon. Treasurer of Red Cross and St John Hostel for Nurses; a Governor of St Bartholomew's Hospital. Contested (C) Bradford, 1892; MP (C) Bradford (W Div.), 1895–1906; contested same Division, 1910; a JP Co. of London; one of HM's Lieutenants for the City; a Knight of Grace of the Order of St John of Jerusalem; decorated by the French Government for services in the Great War; Member of the Council of the Imperial Society of Knights Bachelor. *Address:* 6 Upper Phillimore Gardens, Kensington, W. *T:* Western 2464. *Clubs:* Carlton, Junior Carlton, Bath, Cecil, 1900, Savage.

Died 30 April 1926.

FLOWER, Major Horace John, DSO 1916; MC; 60th Rifles; *b* The Hyde, Luton, Herts, 6 April 1883; *s* of late Arthur and Isabel Flower; *m* 1912, Richenda Louisa, *d* of H.G. Barclay, MVO, of Colney Hall, Norwich; two *d. Educ:* Winchester; Sandhurst. Joined 60th Rifles in S Africa, 1902; served SA, Cork, Bermuda, Malta, India; Adjt, Queen's Westminsters TF, 1913; served European War in France Oct. 1914–Sept. 1915 (wounded battle of Loos and invalided out of the service, DSO, MC). *Recreations:* hunting, polo, etc. *Address:* Camp House, Gerrard's Cross, Bucks. *Club:* Army and Navy.

Died 31 Jan. 1919.

FLOWER, Major Victor Augustine, DSO 1917; Temp. Lieut-Col Commanding 1/22nd Battalion London Regiment (the Queen's); *b* London, 1875; *y s* of late Sir William Henry Flower, KCB, FRS, and Georgiana Rosetta, *d* of Admiral W. H. Smyth, FRS; *m* 1914, Winifride, *d* of Sir T. Digby Pigott, CB, JP; one *s. Educ:* Winchester. Licentiate, RIBA; practised in the Straits Settlements, 1900–12; formerly Captain, West London Rifles, 1898, and Captain and OC Singapore RE (V), 1905; Captain 13th Kensington Battalion, London Regiment, 1914; Brevet Major, 1916; Major, 1916; Temp. Lieut-Col 1917; served European War (DSO, despatches twice). *Recreations:* rifle-shooting, walking. *Address:* 42 Earl's Court Square, SW5.

Died 15 Aug. 1917.

LOWERDEW, Herbert; novelist; *b* York, 14 June 1866. *Educ:* Nottingham High School. *Publications:* In an Ancient Mirror, 1897; A Celibate's Wife, 1898; The Realist, 1899; Retaliation, 1901; The Woman's View, 1903; The Third Kiss, 1905; Maynard's Wives, 1907; The Ways of Men, 1909; The Second Elopement, 1910; The Third Wife, 1910; The Villa Mystery, 1912; Mrs Gray's Past, 1913; Love and a Title, 1914; The Seventh Postcard, 1914. *Recreation:* invention of mechanical toys. *Address:* 7 Clarendon Gardens, Ramsgate.

Died 29 May 1917.

LOWERS, Hon. Frederick, MLC; President of Legislative Council, New South Wales since 1915; *b* Sandon, March 1864; *s* of William Flowers, Leamington, Warwickshire; *m* Annie, *d* of J. C. Foster, Manchester; one *s* two *d. Educ:* Church of England Grammar School, Wolstanton. MLC 1900; Vice-President of the Executive Council and Representative of the Government in Legislative Council, 1910–15; Secretary for Lands, 1911; Acting Chief Secretary, 1910–11; Minister for Public Instruction, 1911–12; Minister for Public Health, 1913–15. *Address:* Parliament House, Sydney, New South Wales.

Died 14 Dec. 1928.

LUDYER, Sir Arthur John, 5th Bt, *cr* 1759; JP; *b* 12 Oct. 1844; 2nd *s* of Sir John Henry Fludyer, 4th Bt and Augusta, *d* of Sir Richard Borough, 1st Bt; *S* father, 1896; *m* 1876, Augusta, 3rd *d* of Sir Edward Borough, 2nd and last Bt. Late Lieut-Col, 3rd Northants Regiment. Owner of about 4900 acres. *Heir:* none. *Address:* Ayston Hall, Uppingham. *Clubs:* Windham, Carlton.

Died 27 Jan. 1922 (ext).

UDYER, Colonel Henry, CVO 1901; Gentleman Usher in Ordinary to His Majesty; *b* 22 May 1847; 2nd *s* of Rev. Sir John Henry Fludyer, 4th Bt, and Augusta, *d* of Sir Richard Borough, 1st Bt; *m* 1891, Mary Stuart, *d* of A. R. Hordern. Joined Scots Fusilier Guards as Ensign; Lieutenant, 1866; Captain, 1869; Lieut-Colonel Scots Guards, 1877; Regtl Major, 1884; Colonel, 1887; Lieut-Col commanding 2nd Battalion 1892; retired on half-pay, 1896; served in the Egyptian Campaign, 1882; in Suakim Expedition, 1885 (Egyptian medal with clasps for Tel-el-Kebir and Suakim, 1885; Khedive's bronze star and Jubilee medal, 1897); King Edward's and King George's Coronation medals; commanding Scots Guards and Regimental District, 1898–1903; retired; reappointed Command of

Scots Guards, Aug. 1914. *Recreations:* racing, hunting, shooting. *Address:* 62 Warwick Square, SW1. *T:* Victoria 1916. *Clubs:* Turf; Jockey Club Rooms, Newmarket.

Died 8 April 1920.

FLYNN, Hon. Edmund James, KC; LLD; Judge of the Court of Appeals (Court of King's Bench) since 1920; Professor of Law, Laval University, since 1874; heretofore Dean of Law Faculty; *b* Percé, Co. Gaspé, PQ, 16 Nov. 1847; *s* of late James Flynn, trader, and late Elizabeth Taudevin (father of Irish descent, mother of Guernsey descent); *m* 1st, 1875, Augustine, *d* of Augustin Côte, JP, printer and Editor of Journal de Quebec; four *c*; 2nd, 1912, Cecile Pouliot, *widow* of Eugene Globenski, of Montreal. *Educ:* Quebec Seminary; Laval University. Admitted to Bar, 1873; QC 1887; Member for Gaspé in Quebec Legislative Assembly, 1878–1900; Nicolet, 1900–4; contested the County of Quebec, 1891, and Dorchester, 1908, for House of Commons; Commissioner of Crown Lands, 1879–82; Minister of Railways and Solicitor-General, 1884–87; Minister of Crown Lands, 1891–96; Prime Minister, 1896–97; Leader of Quebec Opposition, 1897–1905; a Liberal-Conservative; has been batonnier of Quebec Bar; has practised his profession with his son Francis as Flynn and Flynn. *Address:* 9 Hamel Street, Quebec City. *T:* 848.

Died June 1927.

FLYNN, James Christopher; MP (N) Cork Co. N, 1885–1910; *b* London, 1852; 2nd *s* of late Daniel Flynn, Whitechurch, Co. Cork, and Sarah Nicholls, Northampton; *m* 1st, Maggie (*d* 1894), *d* of P. Malone, Rathmines, Dublin; 2nd, 1897, Rebecca, *widow* of J. F. Rice, Co. Kerry. *Educ:* Christian Brothers' College; Keogh's Classical Schools, Cork. Secretary Evicted Tenants' Association, 1882, 1886–91; imprisoned under Coercion Act, 1888. *Recreations:* cricket, rowing, cycling. *Address:* 4 York Terrace, Cork.

Died 15 Nov. 1922.

FOGG, Ven. Peter Parry, MA Oxon; Archdeacon of George, Cape of Good Hope, since 1871; *b* Coppa, Mold, Flintshire, 1832; 3rd *s* of J. Barratt Fogg. *Educ:* Germany; Christ College, Tasmania; Jesus College, Oxford. Third Class Lit. Hum.; secretary, treasurer and president of Oxford Union Society. Ordained, 1860; curate of St Mary the Less, Lambeth, St Michael's Highgate, All Saints', N Hill St, and Streatham; member of the first council of the university of the Cape of Good Hope, 1873; vicar-general of St Helena, 1899. *Address:* George, Cape of Good Hope.

Died 22 March 1920.

FOLEY, 6th Baron, *cr* 1776; **Fitzalan Charles John Foley,** JP County of London and JP and DL County of Surrey; *b* 27 Sept. 1852; *s* of 4th Baron, and Lady Mary Charlotte Howard, *e d* of 13th Duke of Norfolk; *S* brother, 1905. Late Major, Sherwood Foresters. *Heir: c* Gerald Henry Foley, *b* 15 April 1898. *Address:* Ruxley Lodge, Claygate, Surrey.

Died 14 Feb. 1918.

FOLEY, 7th Baron, *cr* 1776; **Gerald Henry Foley;** late Flight-Lieutenant RAF; *b* 15 April 1898; *s* of late Henry St George Foley and Lady Mary Adelaide Agar, *y d* of 3rd Earl of Normanton; *S* cousin, 1918; *m* 1922, Mrs Min Barrie, widow, and *d* of H. Greenstone, South Africa; one *s. Heir: s* Hon. Adrian Gerald Foley, *b* 9 Aug. 1923. *Address:* Westbrook, Meads, Eastbourne. *T:* Eastbourne 1969. *Clubs:* Royal Aero, Bachelors', Royal Automobile.

Died 3 April 1927.

FOLEY, Rt. Rev. Patrick, DD; RC Bishop of Kildare and Leighlin; consecrated April 1896; *b* Mensal Lodge, Leighlinbridge, Carlow, 8 March 1858; 4th *s* of Patrick Foley and Mary Delaney. *Educ:* Carlow College. Solus Theological Prizeman, 1881; Solus Sacred Scripture Prizeman, 1881; BA Lond. Ordained Priest, 1881; Professor of Mental and Moral Philosophy and Sacred Scripture, Carlow College, 1885–92; President of same institution, 1892–96; Commissioner of National Education, 1905; Member of Governing Body, University College, Dublin, 1908. *Address:* Braganza House, Carlow.

Died 24 July 1926.

FOLEY, Paul Henry, JP, DL; *b* 1857; *o s* of late Henry John Wentworth Hodgetts-Foley of Prestwood and Hon. Jane Frances Anne (*d* 1860), 2nd *d* of 1st Lord Vivian; *m* 1904, Dora, *o c* of Hamilton W. Langley. *Educ:* Eton; Christ Church, Oxford. MA. Called to Bar, Inner Temple, 1881; Lord of several manors in Herefordshire and Staffordshire; patron of 3 livings. *Address:* Stoke Edith, Hereford. *Club:* Travellers'.

Died 21 Jan. 1928.

FOLJAMBE, Rt. Hon. Francis John Savile, PC 1895; MA; High Steward of Burgh of E Retford; *b* Osberton, 9 April 1830; *e s* of late

George Savile Foljambe; *m* 1856, Lady Gertrude Emily Acheson, *e d* of 3rd Earl of Gosford; two *s*. *Educ:* Eton; Christ Church, Oxford. MP (L) E Retford and Hundred of Bassetlaw, 1857–85, continuously. Owner of about 14,500 acres. *Recreations:* field sports. *Address:* Osberton, Worksop. *TA:* Worksop. *Club:* Brooks's.
Died 5 Feb. 1917.

FOLJAMBE, George Savile, CB 1917; VD; DL and JP for Notts; Lieutenant-Colonel Territorial Force; late commanding 8th Sherwood Foresters; *b* 30 Oct. 1856; *e s* of late Rt Hon. Francis John Savile Foljambe and Lady Gertrude Emily, *e d* of 3rd Earl of Gosford; *m* Dora M., *e d* of late Rev. E. Warre, Provost of Eton; two *s* three *d*. *Educ:* Eton; Christ Church, Oxford. Joined the 8th Sherwood Foresters (then the first Administrative Battalion, Notts Volunteers), 1875; served in the regiment till 1913; Lt-Colonel Commanding, 1908; employed at Depot and in command of 3rd line, Aug. 1914–Dec. 1915; then served with Red Cross in France till Feb. 1917; employed on Staff of Northern Command as president of an Area Quartering Committee, 1917–19. *Recreations:* hunting, fishing, and in early days cricket, football and tennis. *Address:* Osberton, Worksop, Notts. *TA:* Ranby, Retford. *T:* Worksop 89. *Club:* Brooks's.
Died 13 Sept. 1920.

FOLLETT, Sir Charles John, Kt 1902; CB 1891; *b* 1838; *s* of John Follett of Countess Wear, Devon; *m* 1st, 1863, Eliza (*d* 1895), *e d* of William Nation of Rockbeare House, Devon; 2nd, 1897, Blanche, *e d* of Lieut-Col Henry Green-Wilkinson and the Hon. Mrs Green-Wilkinson; one *s* three *d*. Late Fellow St John's Coll., Oxford; BCL, MA; Solicitor of His Majesty's Customs to 1903. Decorated for official work. *Address:* Culm Davy, Hemyock, Devon.
Died 11 Sept. 1921.

FOLLETT, Lt-Col Gilbert Burrell Spencer, MVO 1907; DSO 1917; Coldstream Guards; *b* 31 July 1878; *m* 1904, Lady Mildred Murray, 3rd *d* of 7th Earl of Dunmore; one *s* one *d*. *Educ:* Eton; Sandhurst. Entered army, 1899; Captain, 1908; Major, 1915; served S Africa, 1899–1900 (wounded, Queen's medal, two clasps); European War, 1914–18 (wounded thrice, despatches thrice, DSO, Bt Lt-Col). *Clubs:* Guards, Bachelors'. *Died 27 Sept. 1918.*

FOLLETT, Colonel Robert William Webb; *b* 1844; *e s* of late Sir William Webb Follett, MP, of Culm Davy, Devon, and Jane Mary, *e d* of late Sir Ambrose Hardinge Giffard, Chief-Justice of Ceylon; *m* 1869, Lady Julia Alice Kennedy, *d* of 2nd Marquis of Ailsa. *Educ:* Eton; Christ Church, Oxford; 1st Class Law and Modern History. Late Colonel Coldstream Guards; served Egyptian Campaign, 1882; Suakim, 1885. *Address:* Woodside, Old Windsor. *Clubs:* Guards, Travellers', Turf. *Died April 1921.*

FOOTE, John Alderson, KC; Recorder of Exeter since 1899; *b* Plymouth, 15 Dec. 1848; *e s* of Capt. John Foote, RN; *m* 1877, Jessie, *d* of J. A. Eaton, CE, of The Priory, Shrewsbury; one *d*. *Educ:* Charterhouse; St John's College, Cambridge (Minor Scholarship, 1868; Scholar, 1870); 1st class Classical Tripos, 1872; Chancellor's Legal Medallist, 1873; Sen. Whewell Scholar of International Law, 1873; Senior Studentship (Inns of Court Examination), 1874; Barrister, 1875; joined Western Circuit; Revising Barrister, 1892; Counsel to the Post-Office (Western Circuit), 1893; QC 1897; Bencher Lincoln's Inn, 1905; a Commissioner of Assize, NE Circuit, 1913; Counsel to Cambridge University, 1915. *Publications:* Treatise on Private International Jurisprudence, 1878, 2nd edn 1892. *Address:* 8 Albert Hall Mansions, Kensington Gore, SW7; *T:* Kensington 3077; 2 Dr Johnson's Buildings, Temple, EC4. *T:* City 7081; Beacon Beech, Dormansland, East Grinstead. *TA:* 3 Temple, London.
Died 26 April 1922.

FORBES, 21st Lord, *cr* 1442 or before; **Atholl Monson;** JP, DL; landed proprietor; *b* Castle Forbes, Aberdeenshire, 15 Feb. 1841; *s* of 19th Baron and 1st wife, Horatia, *d* of Sir John Gregory Shaw, 5th Bt; *S* brother, 1914; *m* 1876, Margaret Alice, *d* of Sir William Hanmer Dick-Cunyingham of Prestonfield, Midlothian, 8th Bt; one *s* one *d* (and one *s* decd). *Educ:* Magdalen College School, Oxford; private tutor. *Heir: s* Master of Forbes, *b* 14 Sept. 1882. *Address:* Castle Forbes, Littlewood Park, Aberdeenshire; Brux Lodge, Co. Aberdeen. *Club:* Wellington. *Died 31 Jan. 1916.*

FORBES, Arthur, CSI 1895; late ICS; *b* 1843; *s* of late Rev. E. Forbes, DD, formerly chaplain in Paris; *m* 1879, May Grace, *d* of late Andrew Cassels, a member of the Indian Council; one *s*. *Educ:* Sedbergh; St John's College, Cambridge. Exhibitioner; BA 1867. Entered ICS 1867; served as Asst and Joint Magistrate in different districts and through Behar famine, 1874; Deputy-Commissioner, Assam, 1875;

Magistrate-Collector, Dacca, 1879; Junior Secretary, Board Revenue, Lower Provinces, 1880–84; member and secretary Opium Commission, 1883 (thanked by Government of India a Secretary of State); subsequently Magistrate-Collector of Sarun, Pergunnahs, Shahabad, and Mozafferpur; acted as Commissioner Excise, Bengal, 1890, and as Commissioner of Dacca, 18⁹ Commissioner of Patna Division, 1892–96; of Chutia-Nagp Bengal, 1896–1902; retired, 1902. *Recreations:* yachting, Ca Lymington Cadet Corps 7th Batt. Hants Regt. *Address:* Yaldhu Lymington, Hants. *Died 5 April 19.*

FORBES of Pitsligo, Sir Charles Hay Hepburn Stuart-, 10th *cr* 1626; *b* 3 June 1871; *s* of Sir William Stuart Forbes, 9th Bt, a Marion, *d* of J. Watts; *S* father, 1906; *m* 1896, Ellen, *d* of Capt. Huntley of Picton, Marlborough, NZ; five *s* six *d*. *Heir: s* Hugh Stua Forbes, *b* 9 Nov. 1896. *Address:* Picton, Marlborough, New Zeala *Died Aug. 19.*

FORBES, Sir Charles (Stewart), 5th Bt, *cr* 1823; JP, DL; *b* 19 J 1867; *o s* of Sir Charles John Forbes, 4th Bt and Helen (*d* 1913), 2 *d* of Sir Thomas Moncreiffe of Moncreiffe, 7th Bt; *S* father, 18⁸ *m* 1888, Emma Theodora, *d* of Robert Maxwell; one *s* four *d* (a one *s* three *d* decd). Owner of about 9000 acres in Aberdeenshi *Heir: s* John Stewart Forbes, *b* 8 Jan. 1901. *Address:* 25 Holland Pa W; Castle Newe, Strathdon, Aberdeen.
Died 12 Dec. 19.

FORBES, Daniel, ISO; *b* 1 May 1853; *e s* of Alexander Forb Edinburgh; *m* Frances Gray, *d* of George Leitch, Norham-on-Twee two *d*. *Educ:* Western Institution and Hamilton Place Academ Edinburgh. Junior clerk, Department of General Board of Luna for Scotland, 1875; chief clerk, 1905; retired, 1918. *Recreations:* cycli golf. *Address:* 19 Cluny Terrace, Edinburgh. *T:* Central 7425. *Cl* Scottish Conservative, Edinburgh.

FORBES, Lady Helen (Emily); author; *b* London, 13 Dec. 18 2nd but *o* surv. *d* of 3rd Earl of Craven and Evelyn, *d* of 7th Visco Barrington; *m* 1901, Ian Forbes; two *s* four *d*. *Educ:* Ashdown Pa Began writing in 1885. Tory. Roman Catholic. *Publications:* No of a Music Lover, 1897; Katharine Cromer, 1897; His Eminen 1898 (book form, 1904); The Outcast Emperor, 1900; T Provincials, 1905; Its a Way they have in the Army, 1905; La Marion and the Plutocrat, 1906; The Bounty of the Gods, 1910; T Polar Star, 1911; The Saga of the Seventh Division, 1920. *Recreatio* hunting, riding, music, very fond of languages, literature, histo heraldry. *Address:* Hill House, Purton, Wilts. *M:* MS358. *Club:* Lad Athenæum. *Died 13 Oct. 19.*

FORBES, James, MVO 1904; late HM's Commissioner at Balmo *b* 1862; *s* of late Alex. Forbes, Edinburgh; *m* 1887, Barbara, *d* of J Jackson, Shawhill, Dumfriesshire. Agent to Duke of Atholl, 19(*Address:* Eallabus, Bridgend, Islay, Argyllshire.
Died 25 March 19.

FORBES, John Colin, RCA; Canadian artist; *b* Toronto, 3 Jan 18 *s* of late Duncan Forbes, Doune, Perth; *m* 1888, Laura Gertrude of George M. Holbrooke, Ottawa. *Educ:* UC College, Toronto; R and South Kensington Museum. *Principal Works:* Mr Gladstone; H. Campbell-Bannerman; King Edward VII; Queen Alexan (Canadian House of Parliament); Earl of Dufferin; Sir J. Macdona etc. *Address:* Sherwood Studio Buildings, 57th and 6th Avenue, N York. *Club:* Salmagundi. *Died Oct. 19.*

FORBES, Hon. Mrs Walter, (Eveline Louisa Michell Farwe *b* The Lowlands, Tettenhall, 1866; *d* of late Frederick Cooper Farw and Louisa Whitbread, *o c* of late Admiral Sir Frederick Michell, KC *m* 1888, Hon. Walter Robert Drummond Forbes, Capt. Gord Highlanders, *s* of 18th Baron Forbes; one *s*. *Educ:* at home. *Publicatio* Fingers and Fortune, 1886; Her Last Run, 1888; Blight, 1897; Gentleman, 1900; Dumb, 1901; Unofficial, 1902; Leroux, 1908; Va Royal, 1908; Nameless, 1910; His Alien Enemy, 1918. *Recreatio* riding, theatre, reading. *Address:* 47 Onslow Gardens, SW7. Kensington 279. *Died 18 April 19.*

FORBES, Brig.-Gen. Willoughby Edward Gordon, CB 189⁸ 11 Sept. 1851; 3rd *s* of late Gordon Forbes and Charlotte, *d* of Ma Edward Lake; *m* 1882, Edith, *d* of late Francis Forbes, ICS; three *Educ:* private school. Joined 6th (Royal Warwickshire) Regt, 18⁷ served Afghan Campaign, 1879–80; Orderly Officer to Brig.-Ge Palliser; present at engagements of Ahmed Khel, Urzoo, and Deh Shana (despatches, medal with clasp); Com. 1st Batt. Royal Warwic shire in Egyptian Soudan Campaign, 1898; present at engageme of Atbara and Omdurman (despatches, medal with clasp, CB); AAG IX Secunderabad Division, 1902–7; retired, 1907; com. 2/1 Lothian Inf. Brigade (T), Jan.–Nov. 1915, and "B" Group Lowland Division, Feb.–July 1916; Gazetted Hon. Brig.-Gen. Aug. 1917. *Address:* Shorebank, Bognor, Sussex. *Died 13 Dec. 1926.*

)RD, Charles, ISO 1904; FLS; *b* 1844; *m* 1871. Superintendent Botanical and Afforestation Department in the Colony of Hong Kong, 1871–1902. *Address:* Lindeth, Stanmore.
Died 14 July 1927.

)RD, Ernest A. C., FRAM; Conductor Royal Amateur Orchestral Society, 1897–1908; Professor of Singing at Guildhall School of Music; *b* 17 Feb 1858, of Celtic descent; *s* of a Local Government official; *m* 1896, Alice, 2nd *d* of James Philp of East Finchley and Partridge Green, Sussex. *Educ:* RAM and afterwards in Paris; pupil of Sir Arthur Sullivan; was the first holder of the Sir John Goss Scholarship. Visited America, 1887, where his motet Domine Deus, which, with English words has become a standard work of modern Church music, was the principal work performed at the 250th anniversary of Harvard University; in 1889 was selected by Sir Arthur Sullivan to conduct Ivanhoe at the Royal English Opera House; he was subsequently engaged to write the ballets for the Empire. *Publications:* Short History of Music in England; Cantata, The Eve of the Festa; much sacred music and many songs; orchestral works; Scène Bacchanale, produced by Robert Newman at the Queen's Hall, 1897. *Recreation:* golf. *Address:* 45 Prince of Wales Mansions, Prince of Wales Road, SW.
Died 2 June 1919.

)RD, Rev. Gabriel Estwick, BA; Vicar of Bilston since 1909; Hon. Canon, Birmingham, 1905–9. *Educ:* University of London. Curate of Stepney, 1881–85; Vicar of Holy Trinity, Bristol, 1885–98; Rector All Saints, Birmingham, 1898–1901; Rector of St George's Birmingham, 1901–9. *Publications:* Gambling: an Analysis; The New Testament Doctrine of the Holy Communion. *Address:* The Vicarage, Bilston, Staffs.

)RD, John; *s* of late Rt Hon. Sir F. Clare Ford, GCB, GCMG, HM's Ambassador at Madrid, Constantinople and Rome, and Anna, *d* of the Marquis Garofalo; *m* Mary Augusta, *d* of George Cavendish-Bentinck. *Educ:* Eton. Entered Diplomatic Service, 1892; Attaché, Athens and Washington; 3rd Secretary, 1894, Copenhagen, Rome and Brussels; 2nd Secretary, 1898, Teheran, Munich and Paris; 1st Secretary, 1906, Copenhagen and Rome; a trustee of National Portrait Gallery. *Club:* St James's. *Died 11 Oct. 1917.*

)RD, Surgeon-General Sir Richard (William), KCMG 1917; CB 1916; DSO 1900; late RAMC; *b* 26 Sept. 1857; *m* 1884, Mary Augusta, *d* of late Rear-Admiral Wainwright, RN. Deputy Surgeon, Royal Hospital, Chelsea, 1901–6; served European War 1914–17 (CB, KCMG). *Club:* Army and Navy. *Died 31 March 1925.*

)RD, Sir Theodore Thomas, Kt 1888; *b* 1829; *m* 1859, Ellen, *d* of George Watson; four *s* two *d*. Barrister, Middle Temple, 1866. Judge in Straits Settlements, 1874; Chief Justice, 1886–89. *Address:* Devon House, Harold Road, Upper Norwood, SE.
Died 23 May 1920.

)RDE, Col Lionel, CMG 1917; retired pay, late RA; *b* 18 April 1860; 3rd *s* of late Henry Charles Forde, MICE, St Brendan's, Wimbledon; *m* 1895, Gertrude Emily Meredith, *d* of late Frederick Pollen, ICS (Bengal); one *s* two *d*. *Educ:* Cheltenham College; RMA Woolwich. Entered Army, 1879; Lt-Col 1905; retired 1910; served Burma, 1885–87 (medal with clasp); Chin-Lushai, 1889–90 (clasp); NW Frontier, India, 1897–98 (medal with clasp); European War (France and Flanders), 1915–19 (CMG, 1914–15 Star, British War Medal, Victory Medal, Oak Leaf). Church of England. *Publication:* Lord Clive's Righthand Man, 1910. *Recreations:* genealogical research, gardening, lawn tennis. *Address:* St Mary's, Battle.
Died 25 Oct. 1926.

)RDHAM, Edward Snow, JP, DL, Herts, Cambs and Beds; JP Kent, Surrey, London, Middlesex and Essex; Metropolitan Police Magistrate, North London, 1898–1910; West London, 1910; retired, 1917; Chairman, Quarter Sessions for Cambridgeshire, 1901–12; *b* Ashwell, Herts, 15 Jan. 1858; *e s* of late Edward King Fordham, JP, DL, Ashwell Bury; *m* 1880, Annie, *d* of late T. Carr-Jackson, FRCS; three *s* two *d*. *Educ:* Caius Coll., Camb. BA 1880; MA, LLM 1883. Barrister, Inner Temple, 1883; pupil of Mr Justice Channell; practised on Midland Circuit. Owner of about 450 acres. *Address:* Elbrook House, Ashwell, Herts. *M:* AR 2345. *Club:* Brooks's.
Died 28 Jan. 1919.

FOREMAN, Sir Henry, Kt 1921; OBE 1918; MP (U) North Hammersmith 1918–23; *b* 1852; *m* 1st, 1873, *d* of W. Howe of Bayswater, W; 2nd, 1901, *d* of A. J. Randall. Mayor of Hammersmith, 1913–20; Alderman since 1919; Hon. Col and Founder 20th London Cadet Corps; Chm. and Hon. Comdt Hammersmith Div. Red Cross Society; presented to War Office Ravenscourt Park Hospital for Officers; raised 140th Heavy Battery RGA, and 40th Division Ammunition Column during European War (OBE). *Address:* 17 Kensington Court, Kensington, W8. *T:* Western 1244. *Clubs:* Carlton, Constitutional, Royal Automobile.
Died 11 April 1924.

FORESTER, 5th Baron (UK), *cr* 1821; **Cecil Theodore Weld-Forester,** JP, DL; *b* 3 Aug. 1842; *s* of 4th Baron and Sophia Elizabeth, *d* of Richard Norman; *S* father, 1894; *m* 1866, Emma, *d* of Sir Willoughby Wolstan Dixie, 8th Bt; five *s* (incl. twins) one *d* (and two *s* one *d* decd). *Educ:* Harrow; Trinity Coll. Camb. MP (C) Wenlock, 1874–85. Owner of about 15,700 acres. *Heir: s* Capt. Hon. George Cecil Beaumont Weld-Forester, *b* 9 Sept. 1867. *Address:* Rose Bank, Birchington; Willey Park, Broseley, Shropshire. *Clubs:* Carlton, Turf; Royal Yacht Squadron, Cowes.
Died 20 Nov. 1917.

FORGET, Sir (Joseph David) Rodolphe, Kt 1912; President Quebec and Saguenay Railway and Quebec Railway Light, Heat and Power Company; Vice-President Montreal Light, Heat and Power Co., Ltd; *b* Terrebonne, Quebec, 10 Dec. 1861; *s* of David and Angèle Limoges Forget; *m* 1st, 1885, Marie Alexandra, *d* of late Hon. Louis Tourville, MLA; 2nd, 1894, Marie Louise Blanche, *d* of late Robert Macdonald; three *s* two *d*. *Educ:* Masson College, Terrebonne. Partner L. J. Forget & Co., 1887–97; founded Rodolphe Forget, Montreal, 1907; MP, Charlevoix and Montmorency, since 1911; Hon. Col, 1914. *Address:* 71 Ontario Avenue, Montreal; Gil Mont, St Irenee les Bains, Quebec. *Clubs:* St James, Mount Royal, Canadien, Montreal, Canada, Montreal Hunt, Montreal; Rideau, Ottawa; Garrison, Quebec.
Died 19 Feb. 1919.

FORMAN, E. Baxter, JP Co. of London; MD, MRCP, MRCS; Member of London County Council, 1891–1910. *Educ:* privately; Guy's Hospital (scholarship in Medicine). Represented North Hackney on the LCC ten years; Alderman six years; South Kensington, three years; belongs to Municipal Reform party; has filled many offices on Council; Deputy Chairman of Council; Vice-Chairman of Education Committee; Chairman third time of Public Health Committee and of Midwives Committee; many years Chairman of Hackney Institute. *Publications:* papers on medical and municipal subjects. *Address:* Newmount, Chalfont St Giles, Bucks. *TA:* Chalfont St Giles. *T:* 25 Chalfont St Giles.
Died 25 Nov. 1925.

FORMAN, Harry Buxton, CB 1897; late Second Secretary General Post Office, and Controller of Packet Services; *b* London, 1842; *m* 1869, Laura, *d* of W. C. Selle; two *s* one *d*. *Educ:* Teignmouth. Entered Civil Service, 1860; retired 1907. *Publications:* Our Living Poets, 1871; The Works of Shelley (ed), 1876–80; Letters of John Keats to Fanny Brawne, 1878; Poetical Works and other writings of John Keats, 1883; The Shelley Library, 1886; Elizabeth Barrett Browning and her Scarcer Books, 1896; The Books of William Morris, 1897; Letters of Edward John Trelawny, 1910; Note Books of Shelley deciphered, with a Commentary, 1911; Elopement of Shelley and Mary as narrated by Godwin, 1911; Medwin's Life of Shelley, enlarged and fully commented, 1913. *Address:* 46 Marlborough Hill, NW.
Died 15 June 1917.

FORNERET, Ven. George Augustus, MA; DD, Queen's Kingston; Rector All Saints' Church, Hamilton, Ontario; Archdeacon of Hamilton; Chaplain and Hon. Lt-Col, 13th Royal Regiment; *s* of Lt-Col C. Alexr Forneret, JP, of Berthier-en-haut, Quebec; *g s* of Maj. Forneret, 60th Regt Imperial Army; *m* Adelaide Robbins; one *s* one *d*. *Educ:* Berthier Grammar School; Bishop's College School; M'Gill University; Montreal Diocesan Theological College. Curate Christ Church Cathedral, Montreal, 1875; SPG Missionary Diocese Saskatchewan, 1877–79; Rector Dunham, PQ, 1879–81; Curate St Thomas Church, St Catharine's, Ont., 1881–82; Curate-in-Charge St James', Dundas, Ont., 1882–85; Rector All Saints', Hamilton, 1886; has served as Rural Dean of Hamilton. *Publication:* How Shall I Give? *Recreation:* militia. *Address:* 13 Queen Street, South Hamilton, Ontario, Canada. *T:* 153. *Club:* Military Institute, Toronto.
Died 1927.

FORRER, Ludwig; *b* Winterthur, 9 Feb. 1845. Member of Swiss Federal Council, 1877–1900; Minister of Commerce and Agriculture,

1902; President of the Swiss Confederation, 1906 and 1912. *Address:* Elfenauweg 88, Berne.   *Died 29 Sept. 1921.*

FORREST, 1st Baron, *cr* 1918; **John Forrest,** GCMG 1901 (KCMG 1918; CMG 1882); PC 1897; LLD Camb. 1897; Adelaide, 1902; Perth, 1916; FLS, FRGS, FGS; Treasurer, Australia, 1917-18; Hon. Fellow of the Geographical Societies of Rome, Vienna, and St Petersburg; Knight of Order of Crown of Italy, 1875; *b* W Australia, 22 Aug. 1847; 3rd *s* of William Forrest, Leschenault, near Bunbury; *m* 1876, Margaret Elvire, *e d* of Edward Hamersley, JP, Pyrton, near Guildford, W Australia, and *niece* of Hugh Hamersley, JP, DL of Pyrton Manor, Oxon. *Educ:* Bishop's School, Perth. Entered Survey Department, 1865; commanded exploring expedition into interior in search of Dr Leichhardt, 1869; exploring expedition Perth to Adelaide, via the head of Great Australian Bight, 1870; exploring expedition from Champion Bay to overland telegraph line between Adelaide and Port Darwin, nearly 2000 miles, through centre of Australia, without aid of camels, with horses only, 1874; received thanks of Governor and Legislative Council, Gold Medal RGS London 1876; presented by Government with grant of 5000 acres; Deputy Surv.-Gen. W Australia 1876; conducted trigonometrical surveys of Murchison District, Nickol Bay District, and Gascoyne and Lyons District, W Australia, 1876-78-82; Acting Comr of Crown Lands and Surv.-Gen., 1878-79; Acting Controller of Imperial Expenditure, 1880-81; Commissioner of Crown Lands and Surveyor-Gen. W Australia, with seat in Executive and Legislative Councils, 1883-1900; in 1883 proceeded to Kimberley district, NW Australia, on behalf of Government, to report on its character and capabilities; proceeded to Cambridge Gulf, and selected site of town of Wyndham, 1886; introduced and passed the Land Act, 1887; First Premier and Treasurer of W Australia under responsible government, 1890-1901; represented Western Australia at the Colonial-Imperial Conferences in London, 1887-97, at National Australian Convention, 1891, and at Federal Conventions, 1897-8; President Australian Federal Council, 1897. Introduced system of giving free grant of 160 acres of land to persons willing to reside upon it and make specified improvements, and established the Agricultural Land Bank. During his administration was responsible for the construction of the great harbour at Freemantle and the project of conveying, by pumping through steel pipes, 6,000,000 gallons of water daily to the Coolgardie Goldfields, a distance of 350 miles. Has been a member of the Federal Parliament since 1901. Postmaster-General, 1901; Minister of Defence, 1901-3; Minister of Home Affairs, 1903-4; Treasurer of the Commonwealth, 1905-7, 1909-10, and 1913-14; acting Prime Minister of the Commonwealth, March-June 1907; strongest and most persistent advocate of the East to West Trans-Australian Railway, 1060 miles, now nearly completed; represented Western Australia at Queen Victoria's two Jubilees, 1887 and 1897; attended as a Privy Councillor the coronation of King Edward VII, 1902 and of King George V, 1911. *Publications:* Explorations in Australia, 1875; Notes on Western Australia, 1884-87. *Heir:* none. *Address:* The Bungalow, Perth, Western Australia. *Clubs:* Athenæum; Weld, Perth; Melbourne, Melbourne.   *Died 3 Sept. 1918 (ext).*

FORREST, Rev. David William, MA, DD (Glasgow); Professor of Systematic Theology and Apologetics, United Free Church College, Glasgow, since 1914; *s* of Rev. David Forrest, St Rollox United Presbyterian Church, Glasgow. *Educ:* High School, Glasgow; Universities of Glasgow and Leipzig; United Presbyterian College, Edinburgh. Minister of Saffronhall Church, Hamilton, 1882-87; United Presbyterian Church, Moffat, 1887-94; Wellington Church, Glasgow, 1894-99; United Free Church, Skelmorlie, Wemyss Bay, 1899-1903; North Morningside Church, Edinburgh, 1903-14; Kerr Lecturer at Edinburgh, 1897; was offered, but declined, Professorship of Apologetics in Knox College, Toronto, and also Principalship of United College, Bradford; Special Lecturer at Yale University, USA, 1901. *Publications:* The Christ of History and of Experience (Kerr Lectures), 1897 (seventh edition, 1914); The Authority of Christ, 1906 (fourth edition, 1914); joint-editor of Letters of Dr John Brown, 1907; various articles in magazines. *Recreations:* cycling, golf. *Address:* 15 Bute Gardens, Glasgow. *Clubs:* Liberal, Glasgow; Scottish Liberal, Edinburgh.   *Died 3 March 1918.*

FORREST, Sir George William, Kt 1913; CIE 1899; FRGS; FRHS; *b* Nusseerabad, 8 Jan. 1846; 2nd *s* of Captain George Forrest, VC; *m* Emma G., *d* of late Thomas Viner, Broadfield, Crawley, Sussex; one *s* one *d. Educ:* private tutor; St John's College, Camb. (BA). Fellow of Bombay University; read for Bar, 1870-72; member of Inner Temple; contributed to the Saturday Review and other London journals; appointed by Secretary of State for India to Bombay Educational Department, 1872; acted as Census Commissioner, Bombay, 1882; employed on special duty in connection with Bombay

Records, 1884-88; Professor of English History, Elphinstone C 1887; Director of Records, Bombay, 1888; Director of Rec Government of India, 1891-1900; Assistant Secretary to Government of India, 1898; Secretary to the Government of Patents Branch, 1894-1900; retired, 1900. *Publications:* Selections the State Papers preserved in the Bombay Secretariat (Home Se (Mahratta Series); Selections from the State Papers preserved in Foreign Office Government of India, relating to Warren Hast The Administration of Warren Hastings; Selections from the Papers preserved in the Military Department of the Govt of relating to the Mutiny, vol i, Delhi; vol ii, Lucknow; Administration of the Marquis of Lansdowne; Sepoy Generals; C of India; History of the Indian Mutiny, vols i, ii and iii; Life o Nevile Chamberlain, 1909; Life of Lord Roberts, KG, VC, 1 Life of Lord Clive, 1918. *Address:* Iffley Turn, Oxford. *Clubs:* Sa Burlington Fine Arts.   *Died 28 Jan. 1*

FORREST, Lt-Col William, DSO 1900; DL; late 3rd Battalion W Regiment; *b* 30 Sept. 1868; *s* of late Col Peter Forrest; *m* 1898, Marie Spencer Lewis, *d* of 1st Baron Merthyr; one *s.* Served S Africa, 1900-2 (despatches, Queen's medal with clasp, King's m 2 clasps, DSO). *Address:* Greenwood, St Fagans, Co. Glamorgan L9149. *Club:* Junior United Service.
                                                      Died 1 Nov. 1

FORREST, Sir (William) Charles, 5th Bt of Comiston, Midlot *cr* 1838; *b* Kinross, 5 Jan. 1857; 2nd *s* of late Sir William Forrest Bt; *S* brother, 1899; *m* 1892, Edith I., *e d* of late A. J. T. Me Incumbent, St Columba's, Crieff; one *s* decd. *Educ:* Glas Academy; Merchiston Castle School, Edinburgh. Formerly mar of Imperial Bank of Canada, Fergus, Ontario. *Heir:* none. *Recrea* golf, boating. *Club:* Caledonian United Service, Edinburgh.
                                                      Died 25 Sept. 1928 (

FORREST, Sir William (Croft), Kt 1919; JP West Riding; M of Pudsey, 1913-19; Chairman of Local Food Control Commi Chairman War Pensions Association. *Address:* Aldingham, Round Leeds. *T:* Roundhay 625.   *Died 12 April 1*

FORSTER, Lt-Gen. Bowes Lennox, RA; Colonel Comman RA, since 1904; *b* 9 Oct. 1837; *m* 1868, Jessie Kate, 3rd *d* of Sir Wi Mackenzie, KCB. Entered army, 1855; Lt-Gen 1895; retired, 1 served New Zealand War, 1860-61 (despatches, medal, brevet M Commanded RA, Gibraltar, 1888-92; Thames District, 1892 *Address:* Hillsides, Parklands, Surbiton.
                                                      Died 7 Oct. 1

FORSTER, Lt-Col George Norman Bowes, DSO 1 Commanding 1st Battalion, The Royal Warwickshire Regime 26 Oct. 1872; 3rd *s* of Lieut-General Bowes Lennox For Commandant Royal Artillery; *m* 1902, Margaret (Daisy) Ethel, Brig.-General R. A. Gilchrist, Indian Cavalry; no *c. Educ:* Ur Services College, Westward Ho; RM College, Sandhurst. Sec Lieut Royal Warwickshire Regiment, 1893; Lieut, 1898; Cap 1900; Major, 1911; Lieut-Col 1916; served Nile Expedition, (Queen's medal, 1898; Khedive's medal with clasps, Atbara Khartoum); S African War, 1899-1902 (despatches, Queen's m with 5 clasps); European War (despatches thrice, DSO, wour twice); Adjutant of 1st Batt., 1902-4. *Address:* c/o Cox & Co. Charing Cross, SW. *Club:* Army and Navy.
                                                      Died 4 April 1

FORSTER, Robert Henry, MA, LLB; author, archæologist; barr at-law (not in practice); *b* Backworth, near Newcastle upon T 10 March 1867; 3rd surv. *s* of late George Baker Forster, mi engineer, of Newcastle upon Tyne, and Hannah Elizabeth, *d* of Rev. Isaac Todd, formerly Vicar of Shincliffe, near Durham; *m* 1 Margaret Hope, *e d* of A. G. Payne, Dartmouth. *Educ:* Aysg School, Harrow; St John's College, Cambridge. Entrance Scholar Harrow, 1881; Leaf Scholarship, 1885; Minor Scholarship, St Jo 1884; Foundation Scholarship, 1887; M'Mahon Law Student, 1 1st Class (3rd Div.) Classical Tripos, 1888; 1st Class (Senior) Tripos, 1889. Called to the Bar; 1892; was many years captain o Thames Rowing Club, Putney, and a member of the Committe the Amateur Rowing Association. *Publications:* The Hand of Spoiler, 1898; The Amateur Antiquary, 1899; Down by the R 1900; A Tynedale Comedy, 1902; The Last Foray, 1903; In S and Leather, 1904; Strained Allegiance, 1905; The Arrow of North, 1906; The Mistress of Aydon, 1907; A Jacobite Admiral, 1 Harry of Athol, 1909; Midsummer Morn, 1911; The Little Mai 1912; Idylls of the North (verse), 1903; In Old Northumbria (ve 1905; War Poems of a Northumbrian, 1st series, 1914, 2nd se

1915; The Double Realm, 1920. *Recreation:* walking. *Address:* Rest Dod, Coombeinteignhead, S Devon.

Died 6 June 1923.

ORSYTH, Lt-Col James Archibald Charteris, CMG 1919; DSO 1916; RFA; *b* 15 June 1877; *o s* of late Archibald Forsyth of Culeaze, Wareham, Dorset; *m* 1917, Ethel Winifred, twin *d* of late Janvrin Robin of Steephill, Jersey, Channel Isles; one *d*. *Educ:* Haileybury College; Royal Military Academy, Woolwich. Commissioned Second Lieut, 1897; Lt, 1900; Captain, 1904; Major, 1914; Lieut-Col, 1916; served South Africa, 1899–1900 (Queen's medal 3 clasps); China, 1900 (medal) European War, 1914–18 (despatches four times, CMG, DSO, Bt Lt-Col, 1917). *Recreations:* hunting, pig-sticking, polo, fishing. *Address:* Culeaze, Wareham, Dorset. *Clubs:* Army and Navy, Bath.

Died 21 Nov. 1922.

ORSYTH, Maj.-Gen. John Keatly, CMG 1917; *b* 1867; *s* of late William Forsyth; *m* 1897, Kate, *d* of John M'Master, MLC, Brisbane. *Educ:* Fortitude Valley State School, Normal School, Brisbane. Served European War, 1914–16 (despatches, CMG); QMG Australian Forces, 1919–22; sometime member Australian Military Board; retired 1922. *Address:* 6 Hepburn Street, Auburn, Melbourne, Australia.

Died 12 Nov. 1928.

ORSYTH, Rev. Dr Peter Taylor, MA, DD; Principal of Hackney Theological College, Hampstead, since 1901; Chairman of Congregational Union of England and Wales, 1905; *b* Aberdeen, 1848; twice married; one *d*. *Educ:* Grammar School and University Aberdeen (1st class honours Classics); some time Assistant to Professor of Humanity, Aberdeen; Göttingen under Ritschl; New College, Hampstead; also under Dr Fairbairn. Has held ministries at Shipley, Hackney, Manchester, Leicester, Cambridge; Congregational. *Publications:* Children's Sermons; Religion in Recent Art; The Charter of the Church; The Holy Father and the Living Christ; On Christian Perfection; Rome, Reform and Reaction; The Taste of Death and the Life of Grace; Positive Preaching and Modern Mind (Yale Lectures, 1907); Missions in State and Church; The Cruciality of the Cross; The Person and Place of Christ (Congregational Lecture, 1909); The Work of Christ; Christ on Parnassus (Lectures on Art, Ethic, and Theology), 1911; Faith, Freedom, and the Future, 1912; The Religion and Ethic of Marriage, 1912; The Principle of Authority, 1913; Theology in Church and State, 1915; The Christian Ethic of War, 1916; The Justification of God, 1916; The Soul of Prayer, 1916; The Church and Sacraments, 1917; This Life and the Next, 1918; articles in the Contemporary Review, London Quarterly, Hibbert Journal etc. *Recreations:* novels, friends, travel. *Address:* Hackney College, Hampstead. *T:* PO Hampstead 3719.

Died 11 Nov. 1921.

ORT, Sir Hugh, Kt 1911; *b* 14 May 1862; 4th *s* of Richard Fort, MP Clitheroe, and Margaret Ellen, *d* of Major-General Smith, HEICS; unmarried. *Educ:* Winchester; New College, Oxford. Barrister, Inner Temple, 1887; Advocate and Solicitor of the Straits Settlements, 1893; Acting Unofficial Member of the Legislative Council of the Straits Settlements, 1903; Unofficial Member of the Legislative Council of the Straits Settlements, 1905–8, and 1909–11. *Recreations:* racing, lawn-tennis. *Address:* 11 Portland Place, W. *Clubs:* United University, Sports.

Died 28 May 1919.

ORT, Richard; Master of the Meynell Hounds, 1898–1903 and since 1915; *b* 29 July 1856; *s* of Richard Fort, MP for Clitheroe, and Margaret Ellen, *d* of Maj.-Gen. Smith, HEICS; *m* 1882, Anna Alice, *d* of Henry Blundell Leigh. *Educ:* Eton; Brasenose College, Oxford. Served in the 11th PAO Hussars, 1878–81; MP (L) Clitheroe 1880–85. *Recreations:* hunting, reading. *Address:* King's Standing, Burton-on-Trent. *T:* 3 National, Burton-on-Trent. *Clubs:* Arthur's, Brooks's, Boodle's, and Naval and Military.

Died 31 Jan. 1918.

ORTESCUE, Rev. Adrian, DD, DPh; *b* 1874; *s* of Rev. Edward Bowles Knottesford Fortescue, sometime Provost of St Ninian's, Perth, and Gertrude M., *d* of Rev. Sanderson Robbins, MA. *Educ:* Scots College, Rome; Innsbruck University. Priest 1898; first resident priest at the Garden City, Letchworth, 1907. *Publications:* The Orthodox Eastern Church; The Greek Fathers; The Liturgy of St John Chrysostom; The Mass, a Study of the Roman Liturgy; The Lesser Eastern Churches; The Ceremonies of the Roman Rite Described, 1918, etc. *Address:* St Hugh, Letchworth, Herts.

Died 11 Feb. 1923.

ORTESCUE, Laurence Knottesford-, CMG 1916; ISO 1905; *b* 17 Aug. 1845; 3rd *s* of late Very Rev. E. B. Knottesford-Fortescue

of Alveston Manor, Warwickshire; *m* 1877, Emily Alison, *d* of late A. J. Russell, Ottawa. *Educ:* Trinity College, Glenalmond. Joined Royal Marine Light Infantry, 1862; retired on half pay, 1871; entered Royal North West Mounted Police Force of Canada on its organisation, 1873; Assistant Comptroller, 1908–13; Comptroller, 1913–16. *Address:* 11 Polstead Road, Oxford.

Died 26 Jan. 1924.

FORTESCUE-BRICKDALE, John Matthew, MA, MD, Oxon; MRCP Lond.; Captain RAMC (TF); Physician to Clifton College; Physician, Bristol Royal Infirmary; Clinical Lecturer, University of Bristol; 2nd *s* of late M. I. Fortescue-Brickdale, barrister of Lincoln's Inn; *m* Edith Augusta, 3rd *d* of late George White; two *s*. *Educ:* Dulwich College; Christ Church, Oxford; Guy's Hospital. House Physician, Guy's Hospital, 1898–99; Registrar, Assistant-Physician and Physician, Royal Hospital for Sick Children, Bristol, 1903–7; Lecturer on Pharmacology, University of Oxford, 1909–10. *Publications:* Chemical Basis of Pharmacology (jointly); Practical Guide to the Newer Remedies; numerous papers in medical journals. *Address:* 52 Pembroke Road, Clifton, Bristol. *T:* Bristol 1797.

Died 2 June 1921.

FORTH, Francis Charles, FRCScI; Principal, Municipal Technical Institute, Belfast, and Director of Technical Instruction, Belfast; *m;* two *s* three *d*. *Educ:* Royal College of Science, Dublin. Now serving as a Captain in the 18th Batt. Royal Irish Rifles, 1915. *Publications:* various, on educational subjects. *Address:* Ravenswood, Belfast. *T:* 1228 Belfast. *Club:* Ulster Reform. Belfast.

Died 28 Feb. 1919.

FORTIN, Ven. Octave, BA, DD; *b* 5 Jan. 1842; *s* of William and Sophia Fortin of Iberville, Province of Quebec; *m* 1874, Margaretta Elizabeth, *e d* of Edward Stayner Freer of Montreal; two *s* two *d*. *Educ:* St John's, PQ; Bishop's Coll., Lennoxville; and M'Gill Univ., Montreal. Ordained deacon, 1865; priest 1866; his first charge was among the Abenakis Indians of St Francis, where he built a substantial church and parsonage; after spending a year in England in deputation work for the CCCS, he became assistant minister at Trinity Church, Montreal, where he remained till 1875; Rector of Holy Trinity, Winnipeg, Man., 1875–1917, and Archdeacon of Winnipeg, 1888–1920; was one of the professors of St John's College, an examiner in the University of Manitoba, and a member of the Diocesan Provincial and General Synods.

Died Oct. 1927.

FORWOOD, Sir William Bower, KBE 1918; Kt 1883; DL; Hon. Freeman of Liverpool; High Sheriff of Lancashire, 1909; *b* Liverpool, 21 Jan. 1840; 2nd *s* of late Thomas B. Forwood, Thornton Manor, Cheshire; *m* 1st, 1862, *d* of William Miles Moss, Liverpool (*d* 1896); 2nd 1898, Elizabeth, *d* of late General le Fleming, JP, DL, Rydal Hall, Westmorland. *Educ:* Liverpool College. Formerly Merchant and Shipowner, Liverpool; President Liverpool Chamber of Commerce, 1871–77; Pres. Joint Committee on Railway Rates, which led to formation of Railway Commission; one of the founders and the first Chairman, Liverpool Overhead Railway, the first full-gauge Electrical Railway ever built; Member of the City Council 58 years; Mayor of Liverpool, 1880–81; Lord Mayor 1903; a Founder of the Liverpool Cathedral and raised the funds for its construction, Chairman 1900–13; Chairman Quarter Sessions, Lancashire, 1890–1910; Chairman Lancashire Magistrates (Kirkdale Division); Chairman Liverpool Public Libraries, Museum and Art Committee, 1890–1909; President Seaman's Orphanage; Director Cunard Steamship Co.; Bank of Liverpool. *Publications:* sundry pamphlets and papers on economical questions and on literary subjects. *Recreation:* yachting, one of the founders of the Yacht Racing Association, and for many years member of council, built and sailed many well-known racing yachts. *Address:* Bromborough Hall, Cheshire. *T:* Bromborough 39. *M:* M 491.

Died 23 March 1928.

FOSBERY, Hon. Edmund Walcott, CMG 1902; Member of the Legislative Council of New South Wales; *b* Wootten, 6 Feb. 1834; *s* of late Capt. Godfrey Fosbery, RN. *Educ:* Royal Naval School. Went to Australia, 1852; Inspector-General, Police Department, NSW, 1874–1904. *Address:* Eaton, Bayswater Road, Sydney. *Club:* Union.

Died 1 July 1919.

FOSTER, Ernest; *b* Purwell, Herts; *y s* of William Foster; *m* 1892, Annie, *d* of James Relley. *Educ:* privately. Editor of Little Folks Magazine, 1880–94; Cassell's Saturday Journal, 1887–1907; Chums, 1894–1907; Family Reader, 1910. *Publications:* An Editor's Chair; Heroes of the Indian Empire; Men of Note: their Boyhood and School Days; Abraham Lincoln; miscellaneous journalistic and other contributions. *Recreations:* cycling, walking, outdoor pursuits. *Address:* 35 Surrey Street, Strand, WC2. *Club:* Constitutional.

Died 11 Jan. 1919.

FOSTER, Very Rev. Ernest, MA; Dean of Perth, WA, since 1918; *b* North Curry, Somerset, 22 April 1867; *s* of Charles Millett Foster, solicitor, and Helen Jane Drury; *m* 1922, Cassie, *o c* of late George Hickman Johns, ICS. *Educ:* King's School, Taunton; New College, Oxford; Wells Theological College; Auckland Castle. 2 Cl. Mod., 1888; 2 Cl. Lit. Hum., 1890; BA 1891; MA 1893. Deacon 1892; Priest 1893; Curate, St Jude's, South Shields, 1892–96; St Hilda, South Shields, 1896–99; Vicar of St Aidan's, Gateshead, 1899–1907; DL Dio. Winchester, 1907; Minor Canon, St George's Cathedral, Perth, WA 1908–13; Rector of Guildford, WA, 1913–18; Chaplain, CMF 4th Class, 1914; Examining Chaplain to the Archbishop of Perth, 1922. *Address:* Deanery, Perth, Western Australia.

Died 13 Sept. 1925.

FOSTER, George Carey, JP; BA, LLD, DSc; FCS, FRS; *b* 1835; *s* of late George Foster, Sabden, Lancashire; *m* 1868, Mary Anne F., *e d* of late Andrew Muir, Rosebank Greenock; four *s* four *d.* *Educ:* University College, London; Universities of Ghent, Paris, Heidelberg. Professor of Physics, Univ. Coll. London 1865–98; Principal of Univ. Coll. London, 1900–4. Pres., Physical Soc., London, 1876–78; Society Telegraphic Engineers (subseq. Institution of Electrical Engineers), 1881; General Treasurer Brit. Association for Advancement of Science, 1898–1904. *Address:* Ladywalk, Rickmansworth. *Clubs:* Athenæum, National Liberal.

Died 9 Feb. 1919.

FOSTER, Rev. Herbert Charles, TD; *s* of Pebendary Henry Foster, late Rector and Vicar of Selsey, Chichester, and Augusta Georgiana, *d* of General Knollys; *m* 1889, Edith Susan, *d* of Prebendary Sutton, late Rector of Rype, and Henrietta, *d* of Thomas Woodward, of Winkenhurst and Highlands, Sussex. *Educ:* Chigwell Grammar School; St Edmund Hall, Oxford; Gloucester College. Curate of All Saints, Gloucester, 1875–84; Vicar, 1884–1910; Vicar of Groombridge, Sussex, 1910–17; Hon. Canon, Gloucester Cathedral, 1901; Rural Dean, Gloucester, 1904–10. *Recreations:* gardening, bowls. *Address:* 22 West Hill, St Leonards-on-Sea.

Died 13 Nov. 1926.

FOSTER, Rev. Canon Herbert Henry; *b* 1864. *Educ:* Sherborne School; St Edmund's College, Salisbury; Pembroke College, Oxford, MA; Wells College. Ordained 1887; Curate of Rowbarton, 1887–88; St John's Pro-Cathedral, Umtata, 1888–91; Vice-Principal Burgh Missionary College, 1891–94; Curate of Claremont, Cape Town, 1894–95; Priest in charge, Salisbury, Mashonaland, and Chaplain to the Bishop, 1895–1901; Incumbent of Estcourt, 1901–6; Vicar and Sub-Dean of St Saviour, Pietermaritzburg, 1906–8; Archdeacon of Matabeleland, 1908–13; Rector of Bulawayo, 1910–13; Principal St Paul's Miss. College, Burgh, Lincs, 1912–20; Prebend of Welton Beckhall in Lincoln Cathedral, 1916; Vicar of Orby, Lincs, 1918–20; on special service, NZ, 1920–23; Commissary Bishop of Auckland, 1923. *Address:* Shiba, Tokyo, Japan.

Died June 1927.

FOSTER, Rev. James, DCL; Prebendary of Lincoln. *Address:* Tathwell Vicarage, Louth, Lincs. *Died 17 Dec. 1926.*

FOSTER, John Watson; International Lawyer; *b* Indiana, USA, 2 March 1836; *m* 1859, Mary Parke M'Ferson. *Educ:* University of Indiana; Harvard. Doctor of Laws, Yale, Princeton, Indiana and Pennsylvania Universities. Served in Union Army during Civil War, 1861–64; Minister to Mexico, Russia and Spain, 1873–86; Agent of United States before Bering Sea Tribunal of Arbitration, Paris; Secretary of State of the United States, 1892–93; Counsel of Emperor of China in peace negotiations with Japan, 1895; Special Ambassador to Russia, 1897; Member, Anglo-American Commission on Canadian questions, 1898–99; Agent of United States before the Alaskan Boundary Tribunal, 1903; Delegate of Chinese Government to second Hague Conference, 1907. *Publications:* A Century of American Diplomacy; American Diplomacy in the Orient; The Practice of Diplomacy; Arbitration and the Hague Court; Diplomatic Memoirs; and various diplomatic papers and addresses. *Recreations:* golf, fishing. *Address:* Washington, DC, USA. *Club:* Cosmos, Washington.

Died Nov 1917.

FOSTER, Joshua James, FSA; *b* Dorchester; *o s* of James Foster; *m* 1883, Bertha Woodman, 5th *d* of George Carter, Stone Hall, Wallingford; one *s* one *d.* Hon. Sec. Folk-Lore Society, 1885–92; Hon. Sec. Folk-Lore Congress, 1891; Member British Committee

International Exhibition of Miniatures, Brussels, 1912. *Publications:* British Miniature Painters and their Works, 1898; The Stuarts in 16th, 17th and 18th Century Art, 2 vols, 1902; Miniature Painters, British and Foreign, 2 vols, 1903; Concerning the True Portraiture of Mary Stuart, 1904; Life of George Morland, 1904; French Art from Watteau to Prudhon, 3 vols, 1905; Chats on Old Miniatures, 1908; Samuel Cooper and English Miniature Painters of the XVII Century, 1915; Wessex Worthies, 1920; numerous reviews and articles, chiefly on Art subjects. *Address:* Aldwick, Holland Road, Sutton, Surrey. *T.* Sutton 957. *Died 24 March 1923.*

FOSTER, Sir Norris Tildasley, Kt 1920; CBE 1920; *b* Bromsgrove, 15 Dec. 1855; *s* of late Frederick F. Foster; *m* 1st, 1875, Alice Maud, *e d* of late Rev. H. Dewhurst; 2nd 1905, Eliza, *e d* of late Elijah Barnett. *Educ:* King Edward's School, Birmingham; Oxford University, MA. Called to Bar, Inner Temple, 1891; joined the Midland Circuit; on the passing of the Military Service Act, 1916, was elected member of Warwickshire County Appeal Tribunal and continued an active member until its close; Chairman (for Ministry of Labour) at Court of Referees, 1919–20; Vice-President of University Graduates Club; Member of General Purposes, Finance and Administration Committee of War Pensions and Citizens Committee, 1914–19; Chairman of Committee of Appeals against decisions from any of the 29 districts of the city; founder and chairman and organiser of Birmingham Streets' Collection Committee, 1915–18; Hon. Treasurer of War Pensions Committee, 1920; for 15 years Chairman of East Birmingham Conservative Association; on formation of Birmingham Unionist Association elected Hon. Secretary; Vice-President of Erdington Parliamentary Division; Hon. Secretary of Midland Unionist Association for 7 years. *Address:* Southfield, Priory Road, Edgbaston, Birmingham. *T:* South 850.

Died 5 Dec. 1925.

FOSTER, Robert John, JP; DL; *b* 1850; 2nd *s* of late William Foster, JP, DL, of Hornby Castle, County Lancaster, and of Harrowins, Queensbury, Yorks, and first wife, Emma Eliza, *d* of Swithen Anderton of Ashfield, Yorks; *m* 1st, 1884, Hon. Evelyn Augusta Bateman-Hanbury (*d* 1907), 2nd *d* of 2nd Lord Bateman; three *s* one *d*; 2nd, Susan R. H., *d* of late Rev. Frederick Fawkes, Farnley Hall, Yorkshire. High Sheriff, County York, 1898. *Address:* Stockeld Park, Wetherby, Yorkshire. *T:* Wetherby 3. *Clubs:* Arthur's; Yorkshire, York. *Died 25 July 1925.*

FOSTER, Sir Tom Scott, Kt 1911; JP; LDS; *b* 1845; *s* of William Foster; *m* Elise, *d* of D. Godden; one *s* three *d.* *Educ:* Portsmouth Grammar School. Entered public life, 1876; Mayor of Portsmouth, 1891, 1898, 1911, 1912; Alderman 1892; Hon. Freeman of Portsmouth; Past Chairman Board of Guardians and Chairman of Governing Body of Grammar School; President of Portsmouth Hospital; entertained Sanitary Congress, British Medical Association, British Association; presented Freedom to Earl Roberts during office as Mayor; Deputy Chairman of Directors of Portsmouth Water Co.; Director Gas Co. etc; Chairman of Finance Committee of Portsmouth Corporation for 18 years; governor and trustee of several charities; King's Coronation Medal and Volunteer Veterans' Badge; Member Imperial Society Knights. *Recreation:* motoring. *Address:* Braemar, St Helen's Parade, Southsea. *T:* Post Office 4715. *M:* BK 1; BK 58. *Club:* Hants Automobile. *Died 18 Sept. 1918.*

FOSTER, Sir William Edward, Kt 1918; FSA; *b* Manor House, Moulton, Lincolnshire, 1846; *o s* of late Thomas Foster and Susanna Mary Hunnings; *m* 1879, Alexandrina Macpherson, *y d* and co-heiress of late Hugh Matheson and Christina Macpherson; two *s. Educ:* The Grammar School, Moulton. Admitted a solicitor, 1869; late head of firm of Foster and Wells, Solicitors, Aldershot; Coroner for the Aldershot District; held a number of public appointments; largely interested in Church work in the Aldershot District—in the Church of England Soldiers' Institute, of which he was Hon. Solicitor, also in hospital work; a trustee and a vice-president of the Aldershot Hospital and Hon. Solicitor; takes great interest in Freemasonry; a member of several Antiquarian Societies; and of the Spalding Gents' Society; for eight years a member of the Council of the Law Society; a founder and past-president of the Hampshire Law Society. *Publications:* has written and published a number of works, antiquarian and genealogical, relating to South Lincolnshire and its families. *Address:* Lindum House, Aldershot. *T:* 345.

Died 7 July 1921.

FOSTER, William Henry, JP, DL, Shropshire; High Sheriff, 1903; JP Northamptonshire; *b* 9 April 1846; *s* of late W. O. Foster, Apley Park, Bridgnorth; *m* 1874, Henrietta Grace, *d* of late H. Pakenham Mahon, Strokestown House, Roscommon; one *s* three *d.* *Educ:* Eton;

Christ Church, Oxford. MP (L) Bridgnorth, 1870–85. *Address:* Apley Park, Bridgnorth, Shropshire; Spratton Grange, Northampton. *Clubs:* Carlton, Wellington.   *Died 9 March 1924.*

FOSTER, Bt-Col (temp. Col Comdt) William James, CB 1919; CMG 1918; DSO 1916; commanding 2nd Cavalry Brigade since 1927; late Brigade-Major, Staff Australian Imperial Force; *b* 8 Dec 1881. Served European War, including Egypt, 1914–18 (despatches, CB, CMG, DSO); Director of Military Operations and Intelligence, Australian Staff. *Address:* Tidworth, Wilts.
                    Died 15 Nov. 1927.

FOTHERGILL, William Edward, MA, BSc, MD (Edin); Hon. Consulting Gynæcological Surgeon, Manchester Royal Infirmary, and Hon. Surgeon, St Mary's Hospital; Professor of Clinical Obstetrics and Gynæcology, University of Manchester; *b* 1865; *s* of late Samuel Fothergill of Darlington; *m* 1895, Edith A., *d* of late J. Dillon Woon of Chelsea. *Educ:* Edinburgh; Paris; Jena. Neil Arnott Prize, 1886; Essay Prize Edin. Univ. Club of London, 1888; MB, CM, 1st class honours and Buchanan Scholarship, 1893; Gold Medal for MD thesis, and Milner-Fothergill Gold Medal, 1897; late Resident, Royal Maternity and Royal Infirmary, Edin.; Consulting Practice in Manchester since 1895; former honorary appointments, Northern and Southern Hospitals for Women, and Maternity; some years Director Clinical Laboratory, Royal Infirmary, Manchester. *Publications:* Manual of Midwifery, 1896, 5th edn 1922; Golden Rules of Obstetrics, 1898 (6 editions); Handbook for Midwives, 1907, 5th edn 1925; Manual of Diseases of Women, 2nd edn 1922; over 60 articles in various medical journals and transactions; Green's Encyclopædia Medics, Churchill's System of Treatment, and Eden & Lockyer's System of Gynæcology. *Address:* 337 Oxford Road, Manchester. *T:* Ardwick 2950; 21 Rathen Road, Withington, Manchester. *T:* Didsbury 767.
                    Died 4 Nov. 1926.

FOTTRELL, Sir George, KCB 1919; Clerk of the Crown and Peace, County and City of Dublin; *b* 6 Feb. 1849; *s* of late George Drevar Fottrell, Solicitor; *m* 1872, Mary, *d* of William Watson, Dublin; one *s* five *d*. *Educ:* Belvedere College, Dublin; Catholic University of Ireland. *Address:* 8 North Great George's Street, Dublin; Dunmara, Ballybrack, Co. Dublin. *T:* Dublin 2363, Killiney-Dublin 23. *Clubs:* Reform; Stephen's Green, Dublin; Royal Irish Yacht, Kingstown.
                    Died 1 Feb. 1925.

FOULIS, Sir William Liston-, 10th Bt, *cr* 1634; *b* 27 Oct. 1869; *e s* of Sir James Liston-Foulis, 9th Bt and Sara Helen, *e d* of Sir Charles M. Ochterlony, 2nd Bt; *S* father, 1895. Owner of about 2900 acres in Midlothian. *Heir: b* Charles James Liston Foulis [*b* 4 Jan 1873; *m* 1903, Maria, *d* of Richard Moore; one *s*]. *Address:* 14 Murrayfield Avenue, Edinburgh; Millburn Tower and Woodhall, Midlothian. *Club:* Caledonian United Service, Edinburgh.
                    Died 16 April 1918.

FOWKE, Frank Rede; late Assistant Secretary, Board of Education; *b* 17 March 1847; 2nd *s* of Captain Francis Fowke, RE, and Louisa Charlotte, *e d* of Rev. Robert Rede Rede; *m* 1870, Isabella Langdale, 4th *d* of Sir Henry Cole, KCB; three *d*. *Educ:* Eton, and by tutor. On the staff of L'Exposition Universelle de 1867 à Paris; after serving temporarily in the Department of Science and Art (subsequently merged in the Board of Education), joined its permanent staff, 1868; Hon. Secretary of the Committee on Solar Physics throughout its duration, 1879–1913. *Publications:* The Bayeux Tapestry reproduced in Autotype Plates, with Historic Notes, published under the sanction of the Science and Art Department of the Committee of Council on Education, by the Arundel Society, 1875; partially reprinted in Ex Libris Series and in Bohn's Library. *Recreations:* painting, books. *Club:* Chelsea Arts.   *Died 2 Jan. 1927.*

FOWLE, Col John, CB 1911; CMG 1918; Inspector of Remounts Irish Command; *b* 26 May 1862; *m* 1908. Entered Army, 1881; Captain 1887; Major, 1898; Lieut-Colonel, 1902; Colonel 1907; ADC to Governor Madras and Bombay, 1889–1903; Commander SE Mounted Brigade 1908–10. Served Soudan, 1884–5 (medal with clasp, bronze star); Nile Expedition, 1898 (despatches, 4th class Osmanieh, Egyptian medal with clasp, medal); South Africa, 1900–1 (Queen's medal, 2 clasps). *Clubs:* Naval and Military, Cavalry.
                    Died 25 Sept. 1923.

FOWLER, James Stewart, MD, FRCPE; Physician, Royal Edinburgh Hospital for Sick Children and Chalmers' Hospital; University Clinical Lecturer on Diseases of Children; Editor Edinburgh Medical Journal; *b* 22 Oct. 1870; *s* of James Stewart Fowler, MD, Demerara; *m* 1902,

Edith (*d* 1924), *d* of Philip Sharkey Hudson, CE, Hyderabad; one *d*. *Educ:* Edinburgh Academy; Universities of Edinburgh and Vienna. *Publications:* contributions on medical subjects in Journals and Treatises. *Recreations:* fishing, photography. *Address:* 55 Northumberland Street, Edinburgh. *T:* Central 1361. *Club:* University, Edinburgh.
                    Died 24 Aug. 1925.

FOWLER, Rev. Joseph Thomas, MA, Hon. DCL Dunelm; FSA, MRCS, LSA; Vice-Principal of Bishop Hatfield's Hall, Durham, 1870–1917; University Hebrew Lecturer, 1872–1917; Librarian, 1874–1901; Maltby Librarian, 1881–1911; Keeper of Bishop Cosin's Library, 1889–1911; Hon. Canon of Durham, 1897; *b* Winterton, Co. Lincoln, 9 June 1833; *e s* of Joseph, *e s* of William Fowler, the Antiquary and Engraver of Winterton, and Elizabeth, *e d* of Thomas Fowler, Owmby, near Spital, Co. Lincoln; unmarried. *Educ:* at home (by his father); West Riding Proprietary School, Wakefield; St Thomas' Hosp. London; Bishop Hatfield's Hall, Durham. Hospital appointments at St Thomas'; House Surgeon St Thomas', 1856–57; Bradford Infirmary, 1857–58; Hebrew Prizes; Theological, Entrance and Barry Scholarships at Durham; Curate of Houghton-le-Spring, Co. Durham, 1861–63, Chaplain and Precentor at St John's College, Hurstpierpoint, 1864–69; Curate of North Kelsey, 1870; a Local Sec. for Durham of Society of Antiquaries, *c* 1873–1917; a Vice-President of Surtees Society. *Publications:* editor of Ripon Chapter Acts; Newminster Cartulary; Memorials of Ripon, 4 vols; Metrical Life of St Cuthbert (Surtees Society); The Coucher Book of Selby, 2 vols (Yorkshire Record Society); Cistercian Statutes (Yorkshire Archaeol. Society); Adamnani Vita S Columbæ (two edns), and Translation; Durham Account-Rolls, 3 vols; Memorials of Fountains Abbey, vol. 3, and Rites of Durham (Surtees Society); Durham Cathedral; Life and Letters of Dr Dykes; St Cuthbert, a sermon preached in York Minster; History of the University of Durham, 1904 (College Histories); Correspondence of W. Fowler, 1907 (privately printed); many articles in various periodicals, 1862–1920. *Recreations:* formerly part-singing, bell-ringing, cycling, photography. *Address:* Winterton, Scunthorpe. *TA:* Winterton, Lincs.
                    Died 22 March 1924.

FOWLER, Robert, RI; artist; *b* Anstruther, Fifeshire; married. *Educ:* Liverpool Coll. First exhibition at Royal Academy, 1876; has exhibited at Grosvenor, Grafton, and New Galleries, London, and Champ de Mars, Paris; also in Munich, Berlin, Brussels, Venice, Vienna, and other cities of the Continent. *Principal Pictures:* Coming of Apollo, RA, 1896; Some Enchantment Old, RA, 1897; Conway Castle, RA 1903; After Music, New Gallery, 1896; The Enchanted Glade, Grafton 1895; Shy Nymph, now in Magdeburg Museum; Eve, Ariel, and Sleeping Nymphs discovered by a Shepherd, belonging to Corporation of Liverpool; Light and Shadow in the Gipsy Camp, RA, 1908; Light and Laughter in Kentish Hopfields, RA, 1909 etc.
                    Died 28 Oct. 1926.

FOWLER, William Warde, MA; Hon. DLitt Manchester; Hon. LLD Edinburgh; *b* Somerset, 1847; 2nd *s* of J. Coke Fowler, Stipendiary Magistrate of Swansea; unmarried. *Educ:* Marlborough; Lincoln College, Oxford (Scholar, 1866); Fellow, 1872; Sub-Rector, 1881–1904; Gifford Lecturer Edinburgh Univ. 1909. *Publications:* A Year with the Birds, 1886; Tales of the Birds, 1888; Life of Julius Cæsar, 1892; The City-State of the Greeks and Romans, 1893; Summer Studies of Birds and Books, 1895; The Roman Festivals of the Republican Period, 1899; More Tales of the Birds, 1902; An Oxford Correspondence of 1903, 1904; Social Life at Rome in the Age of Cicero, 1909; The Religious Experience of the Roman People, 1911; Kingham Old and New, 1913; Roman Ideas of Deity, 1914; Virgil's Gathering of the Clans, 1916; Essays in Brief for War-Time 1916; Æneas at the Site of Rome, 1917; The Death of Turnus, 1919; Roman Essays and Interpretations; articles of Zoologist, Classical Review, etc. *Recreations:* observation of bird-life, especially in England and Switzerland; trout-fishing. *Address:* Lincoln College, Oxford; Kingham, Oxford.   *Died 14 June 1921.*

FOWLER, Rev. William Weekes, DSc, MA; Vicar of Earley, Reading, since 1904; Prebendary and Canon of Lincoln Cathedral, 1887; *b* Jan. 1849; *s* of Rev. Hugh Fowler, Barnwood Vicarage, Gloucester; *m* 1875, Anne Frances, *d* of B. Bonnor, JP, Gloucester; two *s* two *d*. *Educ:* Rugby; Jesus College, Oxford. Assistant and House Master at Repton, 1873–80; Head Master of Lincoln School, 1880–1901; President of the Incorporated Association of Head Masters, 1897; Rector of Rotherfield Peppard, Oxon, 1901–4. President of the Entomological Society of London, 1901–2; Vice-President of the Linnean Society, 1906–7; Member of the Scientific Committee, Royal Horticultural Society. *Publications:* The Coleoptera of the British Islands (5 vols); The Membracidæ and other groups of Honoptera of Central America (Biologia Centrali Americana); Notes on new species of Ianguriidæ, etc; Fauna of British India (India Office); Coleoptera, General Introduction: Cicindelidæ and Paussidæ. *Recreations:* gardening, natural history. *Address:* Earley Vicarage, Reading. *TA:* Earley. *Died 3 June 1923.*

FOWLER-BUTLER, Maj.-Gen. Robert Henry; retired list; *b* 11 May 1838; *s* of Richard Fowler-Butler, late Rifle Brigade; *m* Agnes, *d* of Rev. J. de Courcy O'Grady, Knockany, Co. Limerick; one *s*. *Educ:* Cheltenham. Served in Royal Fusiliers, 1858–87; commanded 1st battalion; Colonel of Chichester district 1888–93; commanded troops, West Indies, 1895–1900; Major–General 1898; served Kandahar campaign, 1881. *Address:* The Hall, Barton-under-Needwood, Staffs. *TA:* Barton-under-Needwood. *Club:* Naval and Military. *Died 17 Nov. 1919.*

FOX, Lt-Col Arthur Claude, DSO 1915; RAMC; *b* 23 April 1868. Captain, 1897; Major, 1905; Lt-Col, 1915; served European War, 1914–16 (despatches, DSO).
Died 15 April 1917.

FOX, Sir (Charles) Douglas, Kt 1886; JP London, Kent, and Surrey; Past President, Institution of Civil Engineers; civil and mechanical engineer; *b* 14 May 1840; *s* of late Sir Charles Fox; *m* 1863, Mary (*d* 1920), *d* of Francis Wright of Osmaston Manor, Derby; one *s* four *d*. *Educ:* Cholmondeley School; King's College, London. Fellow of King's College, London. Has practised in London since 1861. *Publications:* several professional papers. *Address:* 27 Campden House Road, Kensington, W8. *Died 13 Nov. 1921.*

FOX, Sir Charles Edmund, KCSI 1917; Kt 1907; *b* 18 Feb. 1854; *s* of late John Fox of St John's, Newfoundland; *m* 1877, Ethel Mary, *e d* of Sir Charles Parry Hobhouse, 3rd Bt. *Educ:* Prior Park College, Bath. Called to Bar, 1877; Government Advocate, Burma, 1884–1900; Judge of Chief Court, Lower Burma, 1900; Chief Judge, 1906–17. *Address:* Bigswear House, St Briavels, Glos. *Club:* East India United Service. *Died 9 Oct. 1918.*

FOX, Major Charles Vincent, DSO 1914; late 2nd Battalion Scots Guards; *b* 31 Dec. 1877; *e s* of late Capt. H. C. Fox, King's Dragoon Guards, of Glen-a-gearagh Hall, Co. Dublin. *Educ:* Clongowes; Oxford University. Gazetted into Scots Guards, 1900; Captain, 1906; Major, 1915; Second in Command and Commanding Battalion, 1919; Lieut-Col 1921, on appointment as Deputy Inspector-General. Employed with South Nigeria Regiment, West African Field Force, 1901–7; served West Africa, 1901–2; Aro Expedition (despatches, medal and clasp, wounded); again in 1902; operations in N Hibio District (despatches, clasp); again in 1904–5; Onitsha Hinterland Expedition (despatches); again in 1905–6; Bende-Onitsha Hinterland Expedition (despatches, clasp); attached Egyptian Army, 1908–12; Political Inspector, Mongalla Province, Sudan, 1911–13; Annak and Bier Patrol Expeditions (despatches, medal and 2 clasps); conducted elephant poacher hunt, 1911, and taken prisoner by the Belgians (despatches, Order of the Mejidieh); special war correspondent in Turco-Balkan War (Turkish Army), 1912; European War, 1914 (despatches twice, DSO for conspicuous gallantry at Kruiseik, in which action he captured five officers and 200 prisoners, thrice wounded, 1914 Star); taken prisoner Kruiseik, 26 Oct. 1914; escaped from Crefeld; escaped from Berlin express; recaptured; escaped from Schwarmstedt, 1917 (received in special audience by the King, despatches); President of the Escapers, 1918; Deputy Inspector-General Iraq Levies, 1921–22; retired pay, 1923. *Publications:* (serial) various, on war and sport. *Recreations:* Record-holder Oxford University and Wingfield Sculls (Championship Great Britain); won Diamond Sculls, 1901; also Championships of France and Ireland; runner-up Army Middle Weight Championship, 1900; yachtsman, oar, big game, Rugby, polo, hunting, cricket, golf. *Address:* Brookfield, Milltown, Co. Dublin. *Clubs:* Guards, Army and Navy, Royal Automobile. *Died 8 Nov. 1928.*

FOX, Sir Francis, Kt, 1912; JP; MInstCE; Hon. ARIBA; *s* of late Sir Charles Fox; *b* 1844; *m* 1st, 1869, Selina, *d* of Francis Wright of Osmaston Manor, Derby; two *s* three *d*; 2nd, 1901, Agnes, *d* of H. King Horne, of Guerres, Normandy. Appointed by the Federal Government of Switzerland, on the nomination of the British Government, as Member of Committee of Three Experts on Tunnelling, for the construction of the Simplon Tunnel. *Publications:* River, Road, and Rail; Sixty-three years of Engineering Science and Social Work; The Mersey Tunnel; The Simplon Tunnel; The Cape and Cairo Railway; The Saving of Winchester Cathedral, etc. *Address:* Alyn Bank, 12 The Downs, Wimbledon, SW20. *T:* 35 PO Wimbledon. *Died 7 Jan. 1927.*

FOX, Sir Gilbert Wheaton, 1st Bt, *cr* 1924; JP; *b* 1 July 1863; *y s* of John Palk Fox, shipowner, Liverpool; *m* 1902, May, *e d* of Edward William Jones, Hoylake, Cheshire; one *s* one *d*. *Educ:* privately. Sole partner Edward Grey and Co., sugar merchants, of Liverpool and Mincing Lane, London; went to America and Cuba on behalf of the Sugar Commission, 1919–20; Director Colonial Bank and Guardian Insurance Co.; Chairman Reliance Marine Co.; one of the Auditor Commissioners of the Mersey Docks Harbour Board; member of the Executive Committee of the Empire Exhibition at Wembley; Government Respresentative on the Wallasey Board of Commissioners; Director at Lever Bros, 1916–20. *Heir:* *s* Gifford Wheaton Grey Fox, *b* 2 Feb. 1903. *Address:* 37 Aigburth Drive, Liverpool; Pinfold, West Kirby, Cheshire. *Clubs:* Portland; Down Town, New York; Travellers', Paris; Racquet, Liverpool.
Died 21 Feb. 1925.

FOX, H. B. Earle; Secretary of the British Numismatic Society and Editor of the British Numismatic Journal since 1918. *Address:* 43 Bedford Square, WC. *Died 21 March 1920.*

FOX, Rev. Henry Elliott, MA; Prebendary of Holborn in St Paul's Cathedral; *b* Masulipatam, S India, 21 Oct. 1841; *e s* of late Henry Watson Fox (*d* 1848) and Elizabeth James (*d* 1845); *m* 1st, 1866, Emily Stebbing Sandle, (*d* 1867); 2nd, 1871, Frances Alice Highton (*d* 1904); 3rd, 1906, Effie, *d* of Rev. H. James; one *s* five *d*. *Educ:* Harrow; Trinity College, Cambridge. Entered Lincoln's Inn, 1864; ordained to the Curacy of St Ebbe's, Oxford 1869; Vicar of Christ Church, Westminster, 1873; Vicar of St Nicholas', Durham, 1882; Hon. Clerical Secretary Church Missionary Society, 1895–1910. *Publications:* Our Lord and His Bible; Christian Inscriptions in Ancient Rome; occasional sermons, pamphlets, papers. *Address:* The Croft, Putney Hill, SW15. *T:* 484 Putney Post Office. *Club:* National.
Died 12 May 1926.

FOX, Henry Wilson-; MP (U) North Warwicks, since 1917; *b* London, 18 Aug. 1863; 2nd *s* of late Dr Wilson Fox, FRS; *m* 1898, Hon. Eleanor Birch Sclater-Booth, CBE, 5th *d* of 1st Baron Basing; one *s*. *Educ:* Charterhouse; Marlborough; University College, London; Trinity College, Cambridge (BA, Scholar). Barrister-at-Law, Lincoln's Inn (Exhibitioner), 1888; Johannesburg, 1889; editor South African Mining Journal, 1892; Public Prosecutor of Rhodesia, 1894; served Matabeleland rebellion, 1896; Director of Transport and Commissariat, Mashonaland, 1897 (despatches, medal with clasp); Manager of the British South Africa Company, 1898; Director, 1913. Vice-President of the Royal Geographical Society; Member Conjoint Board Scientific Societies; Fellow of the Royal Statistical Society; Fellow, Royal Colonial Institute; Member of Committee of the All England Lawn Tennis and Croquet Club. *Publications:* articles in Nineteenth Century, etc. *Recreations:* lawn tennis, golf, fishing. *Address:* 20 Lowndes Square, SW1. *T:* Victoria 462. *Clubs:* Carlton, St Stephen's, Wellington, Prince's.
Died 22 Nov. 1921.

FOX, John (Junior); *b* Bourbon, County Kentucky, 1863. *Educ:* Kentucky (Transylvania University); Harvard; Columbia Law School. Acted as Correspondent of Harper's Weekly in Spanish-American War; and for Scribner's Magazine in Russo-Japanese War. *Publications:* A Mountain Europa; A Cumberland Vendetta; Hell for Sartain; The Kentuckians; Crittenden; Bluegrass and Rhododendron; The Trail of the Lonesome Pine; The Heart of the Hills; Following the Sun-Flag; Christmas Eve on Lonesome; The Little Shepherd of Kingdom Come. *Address:* Bigstone Gap, Virginia.
Died 8 July 1919.

FOX, His Honour Judge John Scott, KC; Judge Leeds Circuit since 1916; *b* Selby, Yorkshire, 17 January 1852; *s* of Rev. William Fox; *m* 1901, Agnes Maria Theresa Hammer; two *s* one *d*. *Educ:* Bedford Grammar School; University College, Oxford. Double First in Moderations, 1872; 1st class Classical Greats, 1874; BA 1875; MA and BCL 1877. Barrister, 1877; joined the North-Eastern Circuit, 1881; Examiner to the Court, 1884–94; revising barrister on the North-Eastern Circuit, 1885–96; Queen's Counsel, 1898; Solicitor-General, Co. Palatine, Durham, 1901; Bencher Middle Temple, 1905; Chancellor County Palatine of Durham, 1905–15; Recorder of Sheffield, 1903–15; CC Judge Circuit 7 (Birkenhead, etc), 1915–16. *Recreations:* travel, golf. *Address:* Fountain Court, Temple, EC. *T:* Central 1727; 13 Cornwall Gardens, SW. *T:* Western 1559. *TA:* Scott Fox, 86 Temple, EC. *Club:* United University.
Died 3 March 1918.

FOX, Colonel Sir Malcolm, Kt 1910; *b* Derby, 4 March 1843; *s* of Douglas Fox, Derby, and Marian, *d* of J. Strutt, Green Hall, Belper;

m 1st, 1881, Mary Rose, *d* of Captain William Newall, Gordon Highlanders; one *d*; 2nd, 1884, Marion Jane, *d* of John Remington Mills of Tolmers, Hertford; one *d*. Served in 100th Royal Canadians and 42nd Royal Highlanders; served Egyptian Campaign (severely wounded, medal and clasp, Khedive's star); Assistant Inspector of Army Gymnasia, 1883-87; Inspector, 1889-96; Assistant Adjutant General NE District, 1897-1900; Inspector of Physical Training to Board of Education, 1901-10; was member of Inter-Departmental Committee which drew up a course of physical training for elementary schools and training colleges. Commander of the Royal Order of the Sword, Sweden. *Address:* 118 Eaton Square, SW. *Club:* Naval and Military. *Died 10 March 1918.*

FOX, Sir Robert Eyes, Kt 1913; Town Clerk of Leeds since 1904; *b* 22 Oct. 1861; *s* of Rev. George Fox; *m* 1890, Laura Stuart, *d* of late Edward Pearson; one *s* one *d*. Solicitor 1883; Deputy Town Clerk, Birkenhead, 1886-88; Town Clerk of Burnley, 1888-92; of Blackburn, 1892-1904. *Address:* Moorlands, Moortown, Leeds. *T:* Chapeltown, Leeds, 158. *Clubs:* National; Leeds. *Died 2 Oct. 1924.*

FOX, Thomas Colcott, BA (Cantab), MB (Lond.); FRCP; Consulting Physician for Diseases of the Skin to the Westminster Hospital; Consulting Medical Referee to the Mutual Life Insurance Company of New York; *b* 1849; 8th *s* of Dr L. O. Fox, of Broughton, Hants; *m* 1890, Ida Mary *y d* of J. S. Hay-Newton of Newton Hall, Gifford, NB. *Educ:* Queenwood Coll.; Univ. Coll. School and Coll., London; Peterhouse, Cambridge (Natural Science Scholar). Formerly Medical Superintendent of Fulham Smallpox Hospital, Physician to Victoria Hospital for Children and for Skin Diseases to the Paddington Green Children's Hospital. *Publications:* numerous medical contributions, chiefly on Diseases of the Skin. *Recreations:* various games and sports; formerly played cricket for Hampshire and Incogniti. *Address:* 10 Walpole Street, Chelsea, SW. *T:* 798 Victoria. *Died 11 April 1916.*

FOXCROFT, Frederick Walter, MD, CM Edin. Aural Surgeon and Laryngologist to the General Hospital, Birmingham; Clinical Lecturer on Otology and Laryngology to the University of Birmingham; *b* Broughton, Manchester, 16 Jan. 1858; *y s* of late Joseph Foxcroft, Manchester, and Margarette Anne, *o d* of late Thomas Slatter, Hope House, Pendleton; *m* 1904, Mary Lydia, *d* of late Thomas Cockbain, Liverpool. *Educ:* private school; Universities of Edinburgh, Berlin and Vienna. Late Clinical Assistant at the Saughton Hall Lunatic Asylum, Edinburgh; House Surgeon and Resident Medical Officer, General Hospital, Birmingham; Assistant Surgeon to the Birmingham and Midland Ear and Throat Hospital for five years. *Recreations:* cricket, yacht and boat sailing, golf. *Address:* 47 Newhall Street, Birmingham. *T:* 33 Central. *Clubs:* Royal Societies; Union, Birmingham. *Died 1916.*

FOX-DAVIES, Arthur Charles; *b* Bristol, 28 Feb 1871; 2nd *s* of late T. Edmond Fox-Davies of Coalbrookdale, Shropshire, and Maria J., *e d* and co-heiress of John Fox, JP, of Coalbrookdale; *m* 1901, Mary E. B., *e d* of Capt. Septimus Wilkinson Crookes of The Wyke, Shifnal; one *s* one *d*. *Educ:* Ackworth, Yorks. Barrister-at-Law, Lincoln's Inn (Surrey and South London Sess., CCC, and SE Circuit); late Editor of Dod's Peerage and Burke's Landed Gentry; Editor of Armorial Families; contested (C) Merthyr Tydfil, 1910, 1923 and 1924; formerly Member of Holborn Borough Council; Gold Staff Officer at Coronation of King George V; member of Anti-Aircraft Corps, 1914-16; Naval Law Branch at Admiralty, 1916-20. *Publications:* The Book of Public Arms; The Art of Heraldry; The Law of Names and Changes of Name; Heraldic Badges; Heraldry Explained; The Complete Guide to Heraldry; Their Majesties' Court; The Dangerville Inheritance; The Average Man; The Mauleverer Murders; The Finances of Sir John Kynnersley; The Sex Triumphant; The Troubles of Colonel Marwood; The Duplicate Death; The Testament of John Hastings; The Ultimate Conclusion; The Book of Public Speaking; and various other works, including printed "cases" for numerous claims of peerage. *Address:* 23 Old Buildings, Lincoln's Inn, WC2. *T:* Holborn 1912; 65 Warwick Gardens, Kensington, W14. *T:* Western 6084; Coalbrookdale, RSO, Shropshire. *Died 19 May 1928.*

FOX-PITT, Douglas; 5th *s* of late General Pitt Rivers, FRS. Member of The London Group; edited and illustrated Count Sternberg's book, The Barbarians of Morocco, 1908; has a water-colour drawing of British Museum Library in Print Room of British Museum presented by late Lord Avebury; a water-colour drawing, Under the Pier, bought by the Brighton Corporation, 1912; water-colour drawing of Ceylon at the Imperial Institute; water-colour drawing at the Fitzwilliam Museum, Cambridge; oil painting, The Indian Hospital at the Dome, Brighton, purchased for the Imperial War Museum. *Recreations:* travelling, reading. *Address:* The Cottage, Thorpe, Chertsey, Surrey. *Died 19 Sept. 1922.*

FOXTON, Col Hon. Justin Fox Greenlaw, CMG 1903; VD; ADC to Governor-General of Australia; *b* 24 Sept. 1849; *e s* of late John Greenlaw Foxton, HEICS (naval); *m* 1874, Emily Mary, 3rd *d* of late Hon. John Panton, MLC Queensland; two *s* two *d*. *Educ:* Melbourne Grammar School and privately. A Solicitor of Supreme Court of Queensland; received commission as Lieut and afterwards as Captain, in old volunteer force, Queensland, 1879; Captain in Militia (Artillery), 1885; late Brigadier in command of Queensland Field Force (Commonwealth Military Forces); retired, 1912. Elected member for district of Carnarvon in Queensland Parliament, 1883; five times re-elected for same constituency, which he represented for 21 years; Minister for Lands in Nelson and Byrnes ministry; Home Secretary in Dickson ministry; Home Secretary and afterwards Minister for Lands in Philp ministry; was a member of Federal Council of Australasia until its abolition on the establishment of the Commonwealth; was member of late Defence Committee for Queensland; member for Brisbane in Commonwealth Parliament, 1906-10; Minister without portfolio, Deakin Ministry, and as such represented Australia at Imperial Conference on Naval and Military defence of Empire, 1909. President Charity Organisation Society, Brisbane; holds medal of Royal Humane Society, having received the Society's award on two occasions for saving life. *Recreations:* cricket (Pres. Queensland Assoc.), yachting, shooting, tennis, golf. *Address:* Bulimba House, Bulimba, near Brisbane, Queensland. *TA:* Circe, Brisbane. *T:* 79 and 3127 Brisbane. *Clubs:* Queensland, Johnsonian, United Service Institution of Queensland, Brisbane; Naval and Military, Melbourne. *Died 23 June 1916.*

FOY, Hon. James Joseph, KC; LLD; Attorney-General of Ontario; *b* Toronto, Canada, 22 Feb. 1847; *s* of Patrick Foy; *m* 1879, Marie Cuvillier (*d* 1903) of Montreal. *Educ:* St Michael's College, Toronto; Ushaw College, Durham, England. Barrister-at-Law, Osgoode Hall, 1871; Bencher of Law Society of Ontario; QC 1883; LLD Toronto University; elected Ontario Legislature, 1898, 1902, 1905, 1908 and 1911. *Address:* 90 Isabella Street, Toronto. *Clubs:* Albany, Toronto, Royal Canadian Yacht, York, Granite, Toronto. *Died 12 June 1916.*

FRAMPTON, E. Reginald, ROI, 1904; painter; Staff of LCC Higher Education Art Section; *s* of Caroline and Edward Frampton, artist; *m* Lola, *d* of Francis Mallard Clark, late of the Admiralty, London. *Educ:* Brighton; Westminster School; France and Italy. RBA, 1894, resigned; Tempera Society, 1907; Art-Workers' Guild, 1910; Exhibitor: International Art Exhibitions at Rome, Ireland, Canada, Brussels, Ghent, etc; Salon, RA, New Gallery, Franco-British, Japan, Pittsburg 1922; Liverpool, Glasgow, Birmingham, Manchester and other Provincial Galleries. Principal pictures painted: Annunciation; St Cecilia; Navigation; St Brandan (Mention Honourable Paris Salon); The Kiss of Spring (Silver Medal, Paris Salon 1920); Holy Grail; Jeanne d'Arc; Love and the West Wind; A Madonna of Brittany, bought by Corporation of Bradford; Our Lady of Snows, bought by Corporation of Liverpool; The Sleep of Summer; One Man Show, London, 1914; executed Mural Paintings in All Saints, Hastings; Rushall Church, Mellish Memorial, St Peter's, Birstall; Batty Memorial, Southampton; Seaforth Church, Waddington Hall, Yorks; Liverpool High School, Smithwick Memorial; Ranmore Church, Lord Ashcombe Memorial. *Publications:* Reproduction and Account of Work, Art Journal, 1907, Studio, 1906 and 1914; Colour-print of the Island of Brechou, Sark, 1923; Illustrations for Poems of William Morris. *Recreations:* chess, sailing etc. *Address:* 1 Brook Green Studios, Brook Green, W14. *Died 4 Nov. 1923.*

FRAMPTON, Sir George James, Kt 1908; RA 1902 (ARA 1894); LLD, 1894; FSA 1904; sculptor; an Honorary Life Member of the Oxford Union Society, 1904; Hon. Associate, Royal Institute of British Architects; Member Royal Academy of Fine Arts, Milan; past Master of the Art Workers' Guild; President Royal Society British Sculptors, 1911-12; *b* 16 June 1860; *m* 1893, Christabel Cockerell; one *s*. Studied under W. S. Frith; entered Royal Acad. schools, 1881; Gold Medal and Travelling Studentship, 1887; since then gold and silver medals, and other honours in France, Germany, Belgium, Spain and America, including Médaille d'Honneur at the Paris Exposition, 1900; Mem. of l'Academie Royale de Belgique, 1926; Member of Corps Académique, Antwerp; Commandeur de l'ordre de Leopold II; Commandeur de l'ordre de la Couronne; Liveryman of the Merchant Taylors' Company and Founders' Company; Master of the Merchant Taylors' Company, 1918-19. Executed many memorials and statues, including that of HM Queen Victoria for Calcutta, Southport, St Helens, Newcastle upon Tyne, Winnipeg and Leeds; designed the terra-cotta decoration on the Constitutional Club; the sculpture on the Glasgow Art Galleries; the whole of the sculpture on the exterior of Lloyd's Register, City; the entrance to Electra House, Moorgate Street, City; spandrels at entrance of the Victoria and Albert Museum; Peter Pan, Kensington Gardens; figures on the spire of St Mary's, Oxford; saints on the shrine of William of Wykeham, Winchester Cathedral; lions at the entrance to the new extension to the British Museum; statues of Queen Mary for Victoria Memorial Hall, Calcutta and Government House, Delhi; portrait-busts of King George V and Queen Mary for the Guildhall; the Edith Cavell Memorial, London; designed and executed works in ivory, silver, enamels, etc; the CIV medal; many other medals, including Coronation medal. *Address:* 90 Carlton Hill, St John's Wood, NW. *Clubs:* Athenæum, Garrick. *Died 21 May 1928.*

FRANCE, Anatole, (Jacques Anatole François Thibault); French author; Officer Legion of Honour; Member of French Academy; *b* Paris, 16 April 1844; *m* 1920, Emma Leprévotte. *Educ:* Collège Stanislaus. Nobel Prize for Literature, 1921. *Publications:* Alfred de Vigny, 1868; Les Poèmes dorés, 1873; Les Noces corinthiennes, 1876; Jocaste et le Chat maigre, 1879; Le Crime de Sylvestre Bonnard, 1881; Les Désirs de Jean Servien, 1882; Le Livre de mon ami, 1885; Nos enfants, 1886; Balthazar, 1889; Thaïs, 1890; La Vie littéraire, 1890; L'Etui de Nacre, 1892; L'Elvire de Lamartine, 1893; Les Opinions de Monsieur Jérôme Cogniard, 1893; La Rôtisserie de la Reine Pédauque, 1893; Le Lys Rouge, 1894; Le Puits de Sainte-Claire, 1895; Le Jardin d'Epicure, 1895; Poesies, 1896; Le Mannequin d'osier, 1897; L'Orme du Mail, 1897; L'Anneau d'améthyste, 1899; Clio, 1899; M. Bergeret à Paris, 1901; Le Procurateur de Judée, 1902; Mme de Luzy, 1902; Mémoires d'un volontaire, 1902; Histoire comique, 1903; L'Eglise et la République, 1905; Sur la pierre blanche, 1905; Le Jongleur de Notre-Dame, 1906; Sainte Euphrosyne, 1906; Histoire de Jeanne d'Arc, 1908; Les Sept Femmes de la Barbe Bleue, 1909; La Révolte des Anges, 1914; La Vie en'fleur, 1922. *Address:* Villa Said V, XVIᵉ, Paris. *Died 13 Oct. 1924.*

FRANCILLON, Robert Edward, LLM; novelist, journalist; *b* Gloucester, 25 March 1841; *e s* of James Francillon, County Court Judge; *m* 1872, Rosamond, *d* of John Barnett, the musical composer. *Educ:* Cheltenham College; Trinity Hall, Camb. Barrister, Gray's Inn, 1864; on staff Globe newspaper, 1872–94. *Publications:* Earl's Dene; Pearl and Emerald; Olympia; Strange Waters; Zelda's Fortune; A Real Queen; Queen Cophetua; A Dog and his Shadow; King or Knave; Jack Doyle's Daughter; Ropes of Sand; Gods and Heroes; Nine Christmas Numbers of the Gentleman's Magazine; Mid-Victorian Memories, 1913. *Address:* St Paul's House, Warwick Square, EC. *Died 11 May 1919.*

FRANCIS, Augustus Lawrence, MA; *b* Hurley-on-Thames, Berkshire, 16 Jan. 1848; *s* of late Henry Ralph Francis, formerly Fellow of St John's College, Cambridge, and Judge, NSW, and Beata, *d* of John Lloyd-Jones of Plasmadoc, N Wales; *m* 1874, Emily Constance, *d* of Major-General Robert Unwin; two *s* two *d*. *Educ:* Christ's Hospital; Jesus College, Cambridge, sometime Fellow; First Class Classical Tripos, 1870. Assistant Master at Dulwich College, 1872; Headmaster, Blundell's School, Tiverton, 1874–1917. *Publications:* (Joint) An Advanced Latin Syntax and an English Verse translation of Martial's Epigrams. *Recreations:* golf, shooting, fishing. *Address:* Blundell House, Tiverton. *T:* Tiverton 1Y4.
Died 18 Oct. 1925.

FRANCIS, Charles King, JP Home Counties; Metropolitan Police Magistrate, at Westminster, since 1896; *b* 3 Feb. 1851; 2nd *s* of late Fred. Francis, East Molesey Court, Surrey; *m* 1881, Edith Rose Alma, *e d* of late Francis Frederick Lovell, Hinchelsea, Brockenhurst, Hants, and late Lady Rose Lovell, *sister* of 8th and *d* of 7th Duke of Beaufort; one *s*. *Educ:* Rugby; Brasenose Coll. Oxford (BA). Barrister, 1876; practised in London and SE Circuit. *Recreation:* cricket—Rugby Eleven, 1867–69; captain in 1869; Oxford Eleven, 1870–73; played for Gentlemen *v* Players, 1870–75, and for Middlesex. *Address:* 7 Granville Place, Portman Square, W1. *T:* Mayfair 1305; East Molesey Court, Surrey. *Clubs:* Boodle's, Pratt's.
Died 28 Oct. 1925.

FRANCIS, Very Rev. Henry, MA; Dean of the Peculiar of Battle and Vicar since 1920; late Rector of Garboldisham, Thetford. *Address:* Deanery, Battle, Sussex. *Died 27 Jan. 1924.*

FRANCIS, John Collins; *b* 11 Sept 1838; *e s* of late John Francis, who from 1831 until his death, 1882, was publisher of The Athenæum,

and from 1872 also author of Notes and Queries; took leading part in agitation for repeal of fiscal restrictions on the press; *m* 1868, Louise Anne Martel. *Educ:* owing to ill-health mostly private, but for three years went to City of London School. Joined The Athenæum Staff, 1881, and on his father's death took entire management. In 1911 he became proprietor of The Athenæum and Notes and Queries with his nephew, John Edward Francis, who five years previously had joined him in the management. In the same year he became editor of Notes and Queries. Retired from both papers in favour of his nephew, in order to devote himself to continuing the history of The Athenæum till MacColl's death, with memoir of him. *Publications:* John Francis and The Athenæum, being the history of the paper to 1882, 1888; Notes by the Way, containing Memoirs of Joseph Knight and the Rev. Joseph Woodfall Ebsworth, 1909. *Address:* Florence House, Christchurch Road, Streatham Hill, SW.
Died 27 Dec. 1916.

FRANKAU, Mrs Julia; *see* Danby, Frank.

FRANKFORT DE MONTMORENCY, 4th Viscount (Ireland) *cr* 1816; **Willoughby John Horace de Montmorency;** Baron Frankfort, 1800; *b* 3 May 1868; *s* of 3rd Viscount Frankfort de Montmorency and Rachel Mary, *d* of Field-Marshal Sir John Michel; *S* father, 1902; *m* 1916, Mabel Augusta Pearson, *y d* of late C. L. Throckmorton and Mrs Wrench, of Woollahra, Sydney, NSW. *Educ:* Marlborough. Capt. 1st Batt. Duke of Cornwall's LI; with Egyptian army. Entered army, 1888; Capt., 1897; commanded Wuntho Expedition, 1891 (medal with clasp); North-West Frontier India, 1897–98 (medal with two clasps). Owner in Co. Kilkenny 5500 acres, Co. Carlow 1631 acres, and in Co. Cavan 1045 acres; houses in Dublin and environs. *Heir:* none. *Address:* 56 Warwick Square, SW.
Died 5 July 1917 (ext).

FRANKLEN, Sir Thomas Mansel, Kt 1921; Clerk of the Peace for Glamorgan since 1878; *b* 1840; *s* of Richard Franklin of Clemenstone, Glamorgan; *m* 1872, Florence, *o d* of late Thomas Allen of Freestone, Co. Pembroke. *Address:* St Hilary, Cowbridge, Glamorgan. *T:* Cowbridge 40. *Died 29 Sept. 1928.*

FRANKLIN, Surgeon-General Sir Benjamin, KCIE 1903 (CIE 1896); IMS, retired; Hon. Physician to the King; late Director-General Indian Medical Service and Sanitary Commissioner with the Government of India; Knight of Grace of the Order of St John of Jerusalem, 1905; Member of Council of British Red Cross Society; *b* 1 May 1844; *m* 1871, Harriette, *d* of John Ferra Watson, of Heigham Hall, Norwich; one *s* two *d*. *Educ:* Univ. Coll. London; Paris. Entered IMS, 1869; Civil Surgeon, Lucknow, 1878–80; Civil Surgeon, Simla, 1881–86; Surgeon to HE the Viceroy of India (Earl of Elgin), 1894–99; officiated as Inspector-General of Hospitals, Bengal, 1897; Inspector-General of Hospitals, NW Province and Oudh, 1899; Inspector-Gen. of Hospitals, Punjab, 1900–1; Hon. Physician to Queen Victoria and to King Edward VII; a British Delegate to the International Sanitary Conferences at Rome, 1907, and Paris, 1911–12. *Address:* Westhay, East Sheen, Surrey. *Club:* United Service.
Died 17 Feb. 1917.

FRANKLIN, Sir George, Kt 1916; JP; LittD; FCA; Pro-Chancellor, University of Sheffield; late Chairman and Managing Director, National Telephone Co. Ltd; *b* 19 July 1853; *s* of late Alexander Franklin; *m* 1876, Ann, *d* of George Hawksley, Sheffield. Lord Mayor of Sheffield, 1897–98; Alderman and Councillor, 1881–1909; Senior Partner of Franklin, Wild & Co., London, and Franklin Greening & Co. Sheffield; engaged in important negotiations for sale and purchase of Electric Light and Telephone undertakings; carried through negotiations for transfer of telephones to Post Office, 1911; Member of Departmental Committees on University of London and Employment of Disabled Soldiers and Sailors and Admiralty Expenditure. *Address:* Tapton Holt, Sheffield; 10 Cavendish Square, W. *T:* 218; Gerrard 300. *Clubs:* Carlton, Bath, Royal Automobile, Constitutional. *Died 23 Sept. 1916.*

FRANKLIN, George Cooper, MBE 1918; JP; LLD (Hon.) Toronto; FRCS; Consulting Surgeon, Royal Infirmary, Leicester; President, British Medical Association, 1905–6; *b* Leicester, 16 April 1846; *m* Lucy Hannah Denne; three *s* two *d*. *Educ:* Leatherhead, Surrey; St Thomas' Hospital. Surgeon Leicester Provident Dispensary, 1875–80; Hon. Surgeon, Leicester Infirmary, 1886–1906; late Surgeon, Midland and London & North-Western Railway Companies; Vice-President, BMA. *Publications:* reports and contributions to medical journals. *Address:* 18 High Street, Fareham.
Died 2 June 1919.

FRANKS, Lieut-Colonel George Despard, DSO 1917; Commanding 19th Royal Hussars; 2nd *s* of Matthew Henry Franks, DL, of Garrettstown, Kinsale, and of Westfield, Mountrath, Ireland; *m* 1908, May Geraldine, *e d* of late Lt-General Sir Gerald de Courcy Morton, KCIE, CB, CVO; one *s*. *Educ:* Repton School; RMC Sandhurst. Joined 19th Hussars, 1894; served in India, 1894–99; ADC to Governor of Madras, 1898–99; served South Africa with 19th Hussars, 1899–1900 (despatches); ADC to General Officer Commanding Dublin and Curragh, 1902–6; Capt. 1904; Major 1908; Lt-Col 1915; served European War in France, 1914–17 (despatches twice, DSO). *Address:* 3 Halkin Place, SW. *Clubs:* Cavalry, White's.

Died 8 Oct. 1918.

FRANKS, Sir Kendal, Kt 1904; CB 1900; MD; FRCSI; *b* 8 Feb. 1851; *s* of late R. F. Franks of Kilkenny and *g s* of Rt Hon. Charles Kendal Bushe, Lord Chief-Justice of Ireland; *m* 1st, 1879, Charlotte Selira (*d* 1883), *e d* of R. J. and Hon. Mrs Greene; 2nd, 1885, Gertrude (*d* 1896), *d* of Lieut-Col T. B. Butt, 79th Highlanders; three *s* one *d*. *Educ:* Trinity College, Dublin; Leipzig. Served S Africa; Consulting Surgeon to HM Forces (despatches thrice, CB); Hon Consulting Surgeon, Johannesburg Hospital; Lt-Col SA Defence Force (Reserve); President SA Committee, British Medical Association; formerly Surgeon, Adelaide Hospital, Dublin; Vice-President, Royal College of Surgeons; Examiner in Surgery, Univ. Dublin; Surgeon-in-Ordinary to Lord-Lieutenants. *Address:* Kilmurry, Hospital Hill, Johannesburg. *Clubs:* Junior Constitutional; Kildare Street, Dublin; Royal St George Yacht, Kingstown, Rand, Johannesburg.

Died May 1920.

FRANKS, Captain Norman, CIE 1896; late The Buffs Regiment; *b* 1843; *e s* of late Robert Fergusson Franks, of Jerpoint, Co. Kilkenny; *m* 1875, Frances Mary, *d* of late Charles Yorke Lucas-Calcraft, JP, DL, of Ancaster Hall, Lincolnshire. *Educ:* Marlborough. Entered the army, 1862; became captain, 1871; retired 1874. *Address:* 65 Onslow Square, SW7. *T:* Western 2930. *Club:* Army and Navy.

Died 5 Feb. 1923.

FRANKS, William Temple, CB 1914; BCL; Comptroller-General of Patents, Designs and Trade Marks; *b* 1863; 2nd *s* of late J. F. Franks of Shanghai and Streatham, Surrey, and Catherine Smithwayte Temple. *Educ:* Dulwich; Wadham College, Oxford. Classical Scholar, 1883; Hody Greek Prizeman, 1885; 1st Class Honours Literae Humaniores, 1885; BA 1887; BCL degree, 1889; Stowell Law Fellow, University College, Oxford, 1888; 1st Class Studentship (Inns of Court), Roman Law, Jurisprudence and International Law, 1888. Barrister, Inner Temple, 1890; practised at Bar, South Eastern Circuit and Surrey Sessions, 1890–1902; Assistant Librarian House of Commons, 1902–5; Secretary Railway Companies Association, 1905–9; Member of Board of Trade Railway Conference, 1908; Departmental Committee on Railway Amalgamations, 1909; Colonial Conference Copyright, 1910; British Delegate Industrial Property Conference, Washington, 1911; Delegate Peace Conference (Economics Section), 1919; Departmental Committee Merchandise Marks, 1919–20; Royal Commission Awards to Inventors, 1919–20; Lecturer on Railway Law and History, London School of Economics, 1907–8. Lieutenant Inns of Court Mounted Infantry, 1902; Sub-Lieut RNVR, 1915–16. *Recreations:* fishing, shooting, riding. *Address:* 46 Westminster Mansions, SW; HM Patent Office, Southampton Buildings, WC. *Clubs:* Carlton, Bath, St Stephen's.

Died 4 July 1926.

FRANQUEVILLE, Amable Charles Franquet, Comte de; Member and late President of the Institut de France; LLD Cambridge, Dublin, Edinburgh, Glasgow, St Andrews, etc; *b* Paris, 1840; *m* 1903, Sophia Matilda (*d* 1915), 3rd *d* of 1st Earl of Selborne. Member of the Council of State, 1860–79; Officer of Legion of Honour, 1873. *Publications:* Les Institutions politiques, judiciares et administratives de l'Angleterre, 1863; Du régime des travaux publics en Angleterre, 4 vols, 1875; Le Gouvernement et le Parlement britanniques, 8 vols, 1887; Le système judiciaire de l'Angleterre, 2 vols, 1893; Le premier Siècle de l'Institut de France, 2 vols, 1895, etc. *Address:* Château de la Muette, Paris XVIᵉ; de Bourbilly, par Semur, Côte-d'Or.

Died Dec. 1919.

FRASER, Sir Andrew Henderson Leith, KCSI 1903 (CSI 1897); JP, Forfarshire; MA, LLD, DLitt; *b* 14 Nov. 1848; *e s* of Rev. A. G. Fraser, DD, and Joanna, *d* of Rev. J. Shaw; *m* 1st, Agnes (*d* 1877), *d* of R. Archibald, Devonvale, Tillicoultry; 2nd, 1883, Henrietta, *d* of Col H. I. Lugard, ISC; four *s* one *d*. *Educ:* Edinburgh Academy, Institution, and University (MA). Barrister-at-Law, Middle Temple, 1874; Indian Civil Service, 1871; Commissioner of Division, 1888; Member of Hemp Drugs Commission, 1893–94; Officiating Secretary

to Government of India, Home Department, 1898–99; Chief Commissioner Central Provinces, 1899; President Police Commission, 1902; Lt-Gov. of Bengal, 1903–8; Moderator Indian Presbyterian Church, 1907. Decorated for services in India. *Publication:* Among Indian Rajahs and Ryots. *Recreation:* golf. *Address:* Auchenleish, Glenisla, Alyth, NB. *Club:* University Edinburgh.

Died 26 Feb. 1919.

FRASER, Major Arthur Ion, DSO 1917; 9th Hodson's Horse, Indian Army; *b* 28 Dec. 1879; *e s* of Arthur Matheson Fraser, Barrister-at-law, and Mary Gordon; unmarried. *Educ:* Haileybury College; Sandhurst. Gazetted to Indian Army, 1900; Captain 1909; Major 1915; served European War in France, 1914–17 (despatches, DSO). *Club:* United Service.

Died 30 Nov. 1917.

FRASER, Mrs Augusta Zelia, (Alice Spinner); writer; *e d* of W. F. Webb; *m* 1889, Affleck Fraser, of Reelig, Inverness-shire, NB; one *s* two *d*. *Educ:* home. Spent some years abroad before her marriage; in 1892 accompanied her husband to Jamaica, where he held a Government appointment and on her return wrote the W Indian stories which first appeared in 1894. They were first written at a friend's suggestion, and without any idea that the public would care for them. *Publications:* A Study in Colour, 1891; Lucilla, 1895; A Reluctant Evangelist, 1896; Livingstone and Newstead, 1913; and occasional magazine stories. *Address:* Newstead Abbey, Nottingham.

Died Dec. 1925.

FRASER, Sir Charles Frederick, Kt 1915; LLD; Superintendent of the School for the Blind, Halifax, Nova Scotia, 1873–1923; *b* Windsor, NS, 4 Jan. 1850; *s* of late Dr B. D. Fraser; *m* 1st, 1891, Ella J. (*d* 1909), *d* of late James Hunter; 2nd, 1910, Janie C. R., *d* of William Stevens; one *s*. *Educ:* Windsor; Perkins School for the Blind. Lost sight at six years of age. Publicly thanked by House of Assembly in Nova Scotia for his forty years' service; President or Director of a number of public companies. *Address:* Beaufort, Halifax, Nova Scotia.

Died July 1925.

FRASER, Sir Edward Cleather, Kt 1923; CMG 1912; Member of Legislative Council of Government, Mauritius, 1902–23; *b* 1853; *e s* of late James Fraser of Newfield, Blackheath; *m* 1st, 1882, Mary (*d* 1901), *d* of late Thomas Howie; two *d*; 2nd 1903, Aimée, *d* of late John Ferguson. *Educ:* Blackheath Proprietary School; Merton College, Oxford. *Recreations:* shooting, golf. *Address:* Port Louis, Mauritius. *Clubs:* Junior Carlton; Norfolk County, Norwich.

Died 15 Oct. 1927.

FRASER, Sir Edward Henry, Kt 1908; JP; DCL; solicitor; admitted 1872; *b* 15 Feb. 1851; *m* 1877, Jane, *d* of Charles Keightley of Nottingham; one *s* three *d*. *Educ:* Sherwood House School, Nottingham. Sheriff for City of Nottingham, 1884; Mayor, 1896–97, 1897–98, 1898–99, 1910–11. Hon. DCL Cantuar, 1897; Director of Great Central Railway and other Companies. Contested (L) East Nottingham, 1900; (L) Kidderminster, 1910. *Address:* Wellington House, Nottingham. *Clubs:* National Liberal; Notts County, Nottingham.

Died 10 Nov. 1921.

FRASER, Sir Everard Duncan Home, KCMG 1912 (CMG 1901); HM Consul-General, Shanghai, since 1911; *b* 27 Feb. 1859; *s* of Lt-Col R. W. Fraser, BNI; *m* 1899, Constance, *d* of A. W. Walkinshaw, of Foochow. *Educ:* Aberdeen. Vice-Consul, Canton, 1895–97; Vice-Consul, Pagoda Island, 1897; acting Consul, Foochow, 1897–99; Consul, Chinkiang, 1899, but acted as Consul, Hankow, till 1901, when made Consul-General there; Consul-General, Hankow, 1901–11; Coronation Medal, 1911. *Address:* Shanghai, China.

Died 20 March 1922.

FRASER, Galloway; former editor of Tit-Bits. *Educ:* St Andrew's School, Dundee; Glasgow and Edinburgh Universities. Edited in Edinburgh The Scottish Liberal; came to London as Parliamentary representative of Dundee Courier in Press Gallery and Lobby of House of Commons; wrote largely for Scottish press; invited by late Sir George Newnes to join his staff, July 1890; retired 1921. JP Middlesex. *Address:* St Nicholas, Strawberry Hill.

Died 26 Sept. 1925.

FRASER, Gilbert; *b* Inverness, 5 Sept. 1848; *y s* of Gilbert Fraser, shipbuilder; *m* Josephine, *d* of Henry A. Kellogg of Ohio; one *d*. *Educ:* public schools and privately. Trained for the Bar; second Vice-Consul at New York, 1874; first Vice-Consul, 1880; Consul, 1891; Consul-General, Baltimore, 1913; on numerous occasions acted Consul-General at New York; retired, 1919. *Recreations:* horseback riding, cricket, tennis, golf, cycling. *T:* St Paul 6096. *Clubs:* Century, New

York; Maryland; Elkridge Fox Hunting; Baltimore Country; Baltimore Yacht, Baltimore.

FRASER, Hon. Sir Hugh, Kt 1917; JP County of Ross and Cromarty; MA, LLD; **Hon. Mr Justice Fraser;** Judge of the King's Bench Division of the High Court of Justice since 1924; Honorary Fellow of Trinity Hall, Cambridge; Arbitrator, Building Trade Dispute, 1923; Member, Irish Deportees Compensation Tribunal, 1923-24; Member, Committee for dealing with claims of Police Strikers, 1924; *e s* of late Thomas Fraser (*y s* of John Fraser of Gortuleg and Farraline, Inverness-shire); *m* 1888, Ethel Mary, *e d* of late Rev. James Milne Hamilton, MA, Vicar of Ridgmount, Bedfordshire; one *s* three *d*. *Educ:* Charterhouse; Trinity Hall, Cambridge (Exhibitioner, Scholar, Law Student, Cressingham prizeman); Inns of Court Studentship, 1884; Proxime Accessit Chancellor's medal for Legal Studies, Cambridge, 1885; Inner Temple Scholarship, 1886. Called to Bar, 1886; Bencher, Inner Temple, 1918. Lecturer on Equity to Incorporated Law Society, 1888-91; Reader and Examiner in Common Law at the Inns of Court, 1897-1924; sometime Examiner for Honours in Law at the Universities of Oxford, Cambridge and London. *Publications:* Law of Torts, 11th edn; Law of Libel and Slander, 6th edn; Law of Parliamentary Elections and Election Petitions, 3rd edn; Representation of People Act, 1918, 2nd edn; Amid the High Hills, 1923. *Recreations:* shooting, fly-fishing. *Address:* 43 Linden Gardens, W2. *T:* Park 3566; Stromeferry, Ross-shire. *Club:* Athenæum.   *Died 8 July 1927.*

FRASER, Mrs Hugh, (Mary); novelist and writer of travels; *b* Rome, 1815; *d* of Thomas Crawford, sculptor, and Louisa Cutler Ward; *sister* of late Marion Crawford, novelist; *m* Hugh Fraser (*d* 1894), late HM Minister to Japan. *Educ:* Bonchurch, by Miss E. M. Sewell, and in Rome. Accompanied her husband to China, South America and Japan, as well as to various Courts of Europe; travelled much in the United States; became a Catholic in 1884. *Publications:* The Brown Ambassador, 1895; Palladia, 1896; A Chapter of Accidents, 1897; The Looms of Time, 1898; A Diplomatist's Wife in Japan, 1899; The Customs of the Country, or, Tales of New Japan, 1899; The Splendid Porsenna, 1899; A Little Grey Sheep; Marna's Mutiny, 1901; The Stolen Emperor: a Tale of Old Japan, 1903; The Slaking of the Sword, 1904; A Diplomatist's Wife in many Lands, 1911; Further Reminiscences of a Diplomat's Wife, 1912; Captain Corbeau's Adventure, 1913; Italian Yesterdays, 1914; Seven Years on the Pacific Slope, 1915; Storied Italy, 1916. *Recreations:* reading old books, seeing old friends, drama of the day.

Died 7 June 1922.

FRASER, Captain Ian Mackenzie, DSO 1893; RN; *b* Dundee, 15 Nov. 1854; *e s* of late Captain Ian Fraser, 93rd Sutherland Highlanders, of Whitehill, county of Fife, and Charlotte, *d* of late John Mackenzie of Ness House, Inverness; *m* 1887, Effie, *e d* of late William P. Edwards, JP, 17 Belgrave Crescent, Edinburgh, and Broadwell, Perth. Joined Royal Navy, 1868; Lieutenant, 1879; Commander, 1893; Captain (retired), 1904; in command of HMS Sparrow and second in command of Naval Brigade at night attack on Fodey Kabba at Marigé, Gambia, 1891 (highly mentioned in despatches, received the thanks of Governor of Gambia, specially commended by him to Secretary of State for Colonies); in command of Sparrow with Gambia Expedition, 1892, resulting in capture of Tambi and Toniataba (medal with clasp, DSO). *Address:* 7 Albert Park, Liverpool. *Club:* Naval and Military.   *Died 2 Dec. 1922.*

FRASER, John, ISO 1908; Auditor-General of Canada since 1905; *b* 13 Dec. 1852; *s* of James Fraser and Isabella M'Donald; *m* 1876, Mary Atchison; six *s* three *d*. *Educ:* Loch Garry, Ont., Canada. Entered Civil Service of Canada as clerk in the Department of Finance, 1875; chief clerk, 1898. *Recreations:* motor boating, lawn bowling, curling. *Address:* Ottawa, Ont. *T:* 1101. *Club:* Civil Service.

FRASER, John, MB, CM, Edin.; Lunacy Commissioner for Scotland, 1895, retired, 1910. *Educ:* Edinburgh Univ. (1st class honours); 1870; MB, CM, 1882 (Edin.). FRCP (Edin.), 1896; FRSE, and Fellow of Royal Botanical Society, Edin. *Recreations:* golf, shooting. *Address:* 54 Great King Street, Edinburgh. *T:* 2299. *Club:* University, Edinburgh.
Died 18 Jan. 1925.

FRASER, Sir John George, Kt 1905; LLD Aberdeen; MLC; *b* Beaufort West, SA, 17 Dec. 1840; *s* of Rev. Colin Mackenzie Fraser, minister of Dutch Reformed Church; *m* 1866, Dorothea, 2nd *d* of A. A. Ortlepp, Colesberg; three *s* six *d*. *Educ:* Free Church Inst., Inverness; Marischal and King's Colleges, Aberdeen. Returned to South Africa, 1861; fought in Basuto War, was Secretary to Sir John Brand; Registrar of High Court, Secretary to Volksraad, and Master

of Orphan Chamber, Orange Free State; retired from Government service, 1877; represented Bloemfontein in Volksraad, 1880-99; stood for President, 1896; MLC Orange River Colony, 1902; Member Inter-Colonial Council, ORC and Transvaal, 1904; Member of Parliament and Leader of Opposition in Parliament, ORC; Senator, Union Parliament of South Africa, 1910-20. *Address:* Clach-na-Cuddin Lodge, Bloemfontein.   *Died June 1927.*

FRASER, Lovat; Chief Literary Adviser and Contributor, Sunday Pictorial and Daily Mirror; Editorial Staff of The Times, 1907-22; *b* 18 Nov. 1871. Was Editor of the Times of India for several years; afterwards went on various special missions for The Times (London) to India, China and the Dominions, and round the world; attended Imperial Coronation Durbars at Delhi in 1903 and 1912; travelled extensively in many parts of the world, notably the Persian Gulf, the Balkans, the China Seas, Manchuria, Siberia, Egypt, Japan and most European countries. *Publications:* At Delhi, 1903; India under Curzon and After, 1912, etc. *Recreations:* visiting islands, sea-fishing, small boat sailing. *Address:* Bucklands, Churt, Farnham, Surrey (station Haslemere). *T:* Hindhead 74.

Died 20 April 1926.

FRASER, Brig.-Gen. Lyons David, CB 1918; CMG 1916; RA; *b* 15 April 1868; *s* of late Colonel Lyons Fraser, Indian Army; unmarried. *Educ:* Tonbridge; RMA, Woolwich. Commissioned in RA 1887; Capt. 1896; Major 1906; Lt-Col 1914; Col 1917; temp. Brig.-General, 1916; employed with Intelligence Branch, India, 1898-1903 (MacGregor medallist, 1904); GSO 3rd grade, Military Operations, 1906-9; 2nd grade, 1909-11; served European War, 1914-18 (despatches 6 times, Bt Col, CB, CMG); Commanding Heavy Artillery, Australian Corps (France), 1916-18; Brig.-Gen RA Scottish Command, 1919; retired, 1921. FRGS 1900. *Club:* United Service.
Died 4 Feb. 1926.

FRASER, Senator Hon. Sir Simon, Kt 1918; politician and pastoralist; *b* Nova Scotia, 21 Aug. 1832; *s* of William Fraser, farmer and mill owner; *m* twice; three *s* one *d*. *Educ:* West River Seminary, Picton County. Came to Australia, 1852; some months gold-digging, afterwards contracting for bridges, etc; later with partners built several railways in Victoria, New South Wales, including one in South Australia 200 miles long, first section transcontinental railway; the Deniliquin and Moama Railway Company, being private line and worked as private company, 45 miles long, in New South Wales; with exception of three years spent in travelling throughout the world, been in Parliament in Victoria forty years; Legislative Assembly, Legislative Council of Victoria; Member of the Convention which framed the Commonwealth Constitution, and Member of Federal Senate from its beginning to the present time, retiring in his eighty-first year; largely interested as a pastoralist in New South Wales and Queensland. *Recreations:* in early life, hunting and shooting. *Address:* Toorak, Melbourne. *Club:* Australian, Melbourne.
Died 30 July 1919.

FRASER, Major-Gen. Sir Thomas, KCB 1900 (CB 1891); CMG 1882; psc; *b* 15 Nov. 1840; *s* of G. R. Fraser, barrister-at-law, and Elizabeth Allen, *d* of S. Chichester Smythe; *m* 1865, Matilda, *d* of late James Beckford Wildman, MP, formerly of Chilham Castle, Kent; two *s*. *Educ:* abroad; RM Academy, Woolwich. Entered RE 1862; Brevet Major, 1878; Brevet Lieut-Col 1882; Brevet Colonel 1885; Local Maj.-Gen. 1896; Maj.-Gen. 1898; in France after military operations of 1871; Paris during Communist Revolution and Siege, 1871; on military duty in Turkey, 1876; Military Officer with British Naval C-in-C Besica Bay, 1877; accompanied Turkish C-in-C in Russo-Turkish Bulgarian Campaign, 1877; Transvaal War, 1881, as DAA, and QMG, and as AQMG (despatches); Political and AMS to Sir Evelyn Wood, 1881-82; Egyptian Campaign, 1882, on HQ Staff, as Brigade Major, RE (despatches, bronze star, medal with clasp, Osmanieh); AG and QMG Egyptian Army, 1882-85; Nile Expedition, 1884-85 (despatches, clasp, Medjidie); Member of Royal Commission on Piers and Roads, Ireland, 1886-88 and 1900; Assistant Inspector-Gen. of Fortifications, 1891-94; Col on the Staff CRE S District, 1894-96; Commandant School of Military Engineering, Chatham, 1896-1902; Substantive Maj.-Gen. and GOC Thames District, 1898-1902; Col Commandant RE, 1913. *Publications:* The Military Danger of Home Rule for Ireland, 1912; Recollections with Reflections. *Address:* 83 Onslow Square, SW. *Club:* Athenæum.
Died 5 May 1922.

FRASER, Sir Thomas Richard, Kt 1902; MD Edin., Hon. LLD Aberdeen, Glasgow and Edinburgh; Hon. ScD Camb; Hon. MD Dublin; FRS 1877; FRSE, FRCPE; Hon. Physician to King in Scotland; Professor of Materia Medica, 1877-1918, and of Clinical

Medicine, Edinburgh University, since 1878; Emeritus Professor since 1918; *b* Calcutta, 5 Feb. 1841; *m* 1874, Susanna Margaret, *d* of Rev. R. Duncan; four *s* three *d*. *Educ:* Public Schools in Scotland; University, Edinburgh. Pres. of Royal College of Physicians of Edinburgh, 1900–2; President Medico-Chirurgical Society of Edinburgh, 1901–3; Laureate of the Institute of France; Macdougall-Brisbane and Keith Prizeman of the Royal Society of Edinburgh; Cameron Prizeman in Therapeutics of the University of Edinburgh; Medical Adviser to HM Prison Commission for Scotland; Consulting Physician to the Standard Life Assurance Company; Member of University Court, 1904–13; representative of the University on the General Medical Council since 1905; President of the Indian Plague Commission, 1898–1901; President of the Association of Physicians of Great Britain and Ireland, 1908–9; Asst Physician to Royal Infirmary, 1869–74; Examiner in Materia Medica, 1870–75, and in Public Health, 1876–79, in the Univ. of London; Member Admiralty Committee on Sir George Nares' Arctic Expedition, 1877; Dean of Faculty of Medicine, 1880–1900. *Publications:* many papers in practical medicine, on the action and therapeutic uses of medicinal substances and on Serpent's Venom in Transactions Royal Societies of London and Edinburgh, etc. *Recreations:* fishing, shooting, golf, photography. *Address:* 13 Drumsheugh Gardens, Edinburgh. *T:* Edinburgh 2485; Druimbeg, Acharacle, Argyllshire. *Clubs:* Athenæum, Royal Societies; University, Edinburgh.   *Died 4 Jan. 1920.*

FRASER, Rev. William; Moderator of the Free Church of Scotland, 1912; Minister of the Free Church, Strathpeffer; *b* Parish of Urquhart, 1851; *s* of William Fraser, stone mason, builder; *m* 1881; three *s* one *d*. *Educ:* Beauly Public School; Glasgow University; Free Church Divinity College, Edinburgh. Began life as artisan joiner; after serving apprenticeship and working for a few years, at same time attending clases in Latin and Greek, etc, entered Glasgow University; finished Arts and Divinity, 1884. Ordained at Sleat, Isle of Skye, 1886; translated to Plockton, 1905; Strathpeffer, 1908; at the Church crisis 1900, one of the twenty-five who remained faithful and gained the case in the House of Lords. *Publications:* Sketches of Noted Ministers in the Free Church of Scotland; the Opening and Closing Addresses as Moderator of Assembly. *Recreations:* visiting the sick, preaching. *Address:* Manse, Strathpeffer.   *Died July 1919.*

FRASER, Hon. Sir William, KCVO 1920; Kt 1918; Member of Legislative Council since 1920; Minister of Mines, New Zealand; *b* 1840; *s* of Capt. Hugh Fraser, 5th Madras Light Cavalry of Leadclune, Invernessshire; *m* 1874, Ellen Isabel, *d* of Alfred Edward Chetham Strode of Dunedin, NZ; one *d*. *Educ:* Elizabeth College, Guernsey; Lycée Imperiale de Ste Brieux and Victoria College, Jersey. Arrived in New Zealand, 1858; elected to Otago Provincial Council, 1866; to NZ Parliament, 1893; retired 1919; joined Massey Cabinet, 1912, as Minister of Public Works, and the National Cabinet in same capacity, 1915–20; resigned Portfolio in 1920, but retained position as Member of Cabinet, and was appointed to Legislative Council. *Clubs:* Wellington, Wellington, NZ; Dunedin; Christchurch.   *Died 16 July 1923.*

FRASER, William Henry; Professor of Italian and Spanish, University of Toronto, since 1901; *b* Bond Head, Ontario, Canada, 1853; 5th *s* of late Rev. William Fraser, DD; *m* 1883, Helene Zahn. *Educ:* Bradford Grammar School; University of Toronto. After graduation in 1880, taught as resident master in Upper Canada College for three years; and was French and German master there, 1884–87; lecturer in Italian and Spanish in the University of Toronto, 1887–92; associate-professor, 1892–1901; has taken considerable interest in educational affairs, and has held various offices in connection therewith. *Publications:* joint author with Professor Van der Smissen of German Grammars, 1887, 1909, and with Professor Squair of French Grammars, 1891, 1900, 1913; also published various papers on literary and education subjects. *Address:* York Mills, Ontario.   *Died 1916.*

FRASER-TYTLER, Edward Grant, of Aldourie, JP, DL; Lieutenant-Colonel in Lovat's Scouts, Imperial Yeomanry; *b* 19 July 1856; *e* surv. *s* of C. E. Fraser-Tytler and Harriet Jane, 2nd *d* of late Rev. John Pretyman; *m* 1st, 1881, Edith Adriana (*d* 1910), *d* of late Rt Hon. Sir Charles J. Selwyn, Lord Justice of Appeal; one *s* one *d*; 2nd, 1912, Christian, *d* of late William Scott-Kerr of Chatto and Sunlaws, Roxburghshire, and *widow* of late J. W. Fraser-Tytler of Woodhouselee, Midlothian. *Educ:* Eton. Was Captain in 3rd Battalion Cameron Highlanders for some years; Lieutenant in 1st Invernessshire Highland Volunteer Batt. *Recreations:* deer-stalking, hunting, shooting, pig-sticking and tiger-shooting in India and Ceylon; has travelled in South America, etc. *Address:* Aldourie Castle, Inverness, NB. *TA:* Dores. *Clubs:* Junior Carlton, Bath.   *Died 12 March 1918.*

FRAYLING, Frederick George, ISO; Senior First Class Clerk, Department of Director of Public Prosecutions, Whitehall; *b* 1846; *m* 1873, Ellen *d* of late Thomas Cooper, Oxford; one *s* two *d*. *Educ:* Dulwich College. Entered firm of Maples, Teesdale and Co., City Solicitors, 1864; received an appointment in the old Court of Queen's Bench at Westminster, 1866; while there received temporary appointments from 14 judges and the three associates; appointed one of the 8 clerks in the newly created Office of Director of Public Prosecutions, 1880; transferred to the Treasury Solicitor's Department, 1884; Senior Representative of the Director of Public Prosecutions at the Central Criminal Court, 1885–1911, when retired from Civil Service. *Publications:* Infanticide, Law and Punishment; Reminiscences of Criminal Courts and views and observations thereon. *Recreations:* walking, literary pursuits. *Club:* Croydon Constitutional.

FRAZER, Robert Watson, LLB; CE; Indian Civil Service, retired; late Principal Librarian and Secretary London Institution, and Lecturer in Tamil and Telugu, School of Oriental Studies, London Institution, Finsbury Circus, EC; *b* Dublin, 1854. *Educ:* Royal College of Science; Dublin University. ICS; in charge disturbed tracts during Rumpa rebellion; invalided in consequence of fever there contracted; formerly Lecturer, University Extension, on Indian Architecture. *Publications:* Silent Gods and Sun-Steeped Lands, 1895, 2nd edn 1896; British India, Story of Nations Series, 1897, 2nd edn 1893; A Literary History of India, 1898; Text-Book Indian History (League of the Empire), 1907; Indian Thought, Past and Present, 1915; articles, Encyclopædia of Religion and Ethics, etc. *Address:* The Hollies, Balcombe, Sussex.   *Died 30 Nov. 1921.*

FREAKE, Sir Thomas George, 2nd Bt, *cr* 1882; Mayor of Dartmouth since 1897; *b* 12 Oct. 1848; *s* of Sir Charles James Freake, 1st Bt and Eliza Pudsey, *d* of Charles Wright; *S* father, 1884; *m* 1868, Frederica, *d* of Col. F. T. Maitland, Holywich, Sussex; one *s* two *d* (and one *s* two *d* decd). *Educ:* Magdalene Coll. Camb. *Heir: s* Frederick Charles Maitland Freake [*b* 7 March 1876; *m* 1902, Alison, *d* of late Christopher Ussher of Eastwell, Co. Galway; one *s*. *Address:* Halford Manor, Shipstone, Warwicks]. *Address:* 43 Sloane Street, SW. *T:* Western 3946. *Clubs:* Conservative, Ranelagh, Hurlingham.   *Died 21 Dec. 1920.*

FRÉCHETTE, Achille, KC; ISO 1910; formerly Chief of Translation Department, House of Commons, Canada; *b* Levis, PQ, 13 Oct. 1847; *s* of Louis and Marguerite Martineau Fréchette; *m* Annie Thomas Howells; one *s* one *d*. *Educ:* Lévis College; Quebec Seminary; Royal Military School, Quebec; Art Students' League, New York. Barrister; journalist; for many years a Director, and also Secretary, Art Association, Ottawa; exhibited Royal Canadian Academy of Arts; edited the French papers in Transactions of Royal Society of Canada; for a time Chairman French Section Separate School Board, Ottawa; commissioned by Canadian Government to report upon the organisation of the parliamentary translation services in Belgium and Switzerland. *Publications:* occasional poems and papers; Member Canadian Authors' Association. *Address:* c/o Howells Fréchette, Department of Mines, Sussex Street, Ottawa, Canada.   *Died 15 Nov. 1927.*

FREELING, Sir Clayton Pennington, 8th Bt, *cr* 1828; *b* 26 Nov. 1857; *s* of late Sir Stanford Freeling, KCMG, *b* of Sir Arthur Henry Freeling, 5th Bt and Frederica Selina Owen, *d* of late George James Pennington; *S* uncle, 1916. *Heir: c* Charles Edward Luard Freeling [solicitor; *b* 1858; *m* 1913, Ethel Amy, *d* of late Iltid Nicholl. *Address:* Beenham Lodge, Reading]. *Address:* 57 Hurlingham Court, SW6.   *Died 8 July 1927.*

FREELING, Rev. Sir James Robert, 7th Bt *cr* 1828; *b* 3 June 1825; *s* of John Clayton Freeling, 2nd *s* of Sir Francis Freeling, 1st Bt, and Mary, *d* of Edward Coxe; *S* nephew, 1914; *m* 1851, Annabella Elizabeth (*d* 1903), *e d* of Walpole Eyre; one *d*. *Educ:* Exeter College, Oxford; Durham University. Ordained, 1852; Curate of Farley, Wilts, 1852–55; Shanbrook, 1861–68; Chaplain at Chantilly, 1868–70; Assistant Chaplain, Brussels, 1870–77; Chaplain at Bonn, 1878–82. *Heir: n* Clayton Pennington Freeling, *b* 26 Nov. 1857. *Address:* 414 Avenue Louise, Brussels.   *Died 30 Oct. 1916.*

FREEMAN, Edward Bothamley, ISO 1903; *b* London, 5 Jan. 1838; *y s* of late Luke Freeman, solicitor, and Henrietta Illingworth; *m* 1884, Minna, *d* of Baron Carl Cnobloch; one *d*. *Educ:* Rev. Edward Wickham's, Brookgreen, Hammersmith; private tutor; Rev H. A. Box's, Heavitree, Exeter. Assistant Superintendent of the Dardanelles Depot of the Land Transport Corps, 1855–56; Chancelier in the Consulates of Diarbekir and Serajevo, 1858–76; Vice-Consul, Mostar, 1876; Consul, Serajevo, 1879 (Jubilee medal, 1897); Con.-Gen for

Bosnia and the Herzegovina, 1891–1905. *Address:* Clyde Lodge, Cyprus Road, Exmouth. *Club:* Exmouth.

Died 30 Oct. 1921.

FREER, Charles L.; *b* Feb. 1854; unmarried. *Educ:* public and private schools; Hon. MA University of Michigan, and Rutgers College. Ex-railroad supply manufacturer, traveller, art collector; gave collection of Whistler paintings (including the Peacock Room), etchings, lithographs, and drawings, also Oriental collection of paintings, potteries, bronzes and sculptures, to the National Gallery at Washington, DC; special building at Washington to hold and exhibit the collections now being built. *Publications:* Facsimiles of the Washington Biblical Manuscripts. *Recreation:* travel. *Address:* 33 Ferry Avenue, East, Detroit, Michigan, USA. *TA:* Freer, Detroit.

Died 25 Sept. 1919.

FREEMANTLE, Very Rev. Hon. William Henry, DD; Dean of Ripon, 1895–1915; *b* 12 Dec. 1831; 2nd *s* of 1st Lord Cottesloe and Louisa, *d* of FM Sir George Nugent, 1st Bt; *m* 1st, 1863, Isabella (*d* 1901), *d* of Sir Culling Eardley, 3rd Bt; three *s* two *d* (and four *s* decd); 2nd, 1903, Sophia Frances, *e d* of late Major G. F. Stuart of the 88th and 49th Regts. *Educ:* Cheam; Eton; Balliol College, Oxford. First class Final Classical Schools; Newcastle Medallist, 1849; English Essay Prize. Fellow of All Souls, 1854–64; of Balliol, and Theological tutor, 1883–94; Select Preacher, 1879–80; Bampton Lecturer, 1883. Ordained, 1855; Vicar of Lewknor, Oxon, 1857–66; chaplain to Bishop of London (Tait), 1861, and to Archbishop of Canterbury (Tait), 1868–82; Rector of St Mary's, Bryanston Square, 1866–83; Canon of Canterbury, 1882–95. *Publications:* The Influence of Commerce on Christianity (Oxford Prize Essay), 1854; The Ecclesiastical Judgments of the Privy Council (with Hon. G. C. Brodrick), 1865; Reconciliation to God through Jesus Christ, 1870; Lay Power in Parishes, 1870; The Gospel of the Secular Life (University Sermons), 1882; The World as the Subject of Redemption (Brampton Lectures), 1885; Works of St Jerome and Refinus, translated, 1893; Church Reform (Imperial Parliament Series), (with Earl Grey and others), 1887; Christian Ordinances and Social Progress (published in America), 1900; Natural Christianity (Harper's Library of Living Thought), 1911. *Address:* 25 Barkston Gardens, SW.

Died 24 Dec. 1916.

FRENCH, General Arthur, CB 1892; Royal Marine Artillery; retired; *b* Chester, 20 Aug. 1840; *s* of Major E. F. French, 82nd and 22nd Regts; *m* 1875, Mary Julia Eveleigh, *d* of Capt. Belson, Royal Engineers; one *s*. *Educ:* Fairfield, near Manchester; Brindley's Collegiate School, Leamington. Joined Royal Marine Artillery, 1858; served in HM Ships "Diadem", "Nile", "Valiant", "Revenge", "Zealous", "Lord Warden", "Hercules" and "Minotaur"; served with Egyptian Expedition, 1882 (despatches Brevet Lieut-Col, medal, bronze star, CB, and Jubilee medal); was ADC to Her Majesty, 1888–93. Decorated for Egyptian Expedition, 1882. *Recreations:* fishing, shooting, otter-hunting, field sports generally. *Address:* Eastney Lodge, Wilton, Salisbury.

Died 22 March 1928.

FRENCH, Hon. Charles, JP; *b* 1851; *s* of 3rd Lord de Freyne and Catherine, *d* of Luke Maree; *m* 1880, Constance, 2nd *d* of Lt-Col Charles Raleigh Chichester of Runnamoat, Co. Roscommon; one *s* six *d*. *Educ:* Downside. High Sheriff Co. Roscommon, 1887; MP (HR) Co. Roscommon, 1873–80. *Address:* Headlands, Dalmeny Road, Southbourne-on-Sea.

Died 27 Oct. 1925.

FRENCH, Sir Edward Lee, KCVO 1911; *b* 22 July 1857; 2nd *s* of late Rev. F. French, Rector of Worlingworth, Suffolk; *m* Wilna, *d* of late David Ross, CIE. *Educ:* Marlborough College. Entered Indian Police, 1879; Deputy Inspector-General, Criminal Investigation Department, Punjab, 1905; Inspector-General, NW Frontier Police, 1908; Punjab Police, 1909; in charge of Police arrangements Coronation Durbar, 1911. *Recreations:* cricket, tennis, golf, billiards. *Address:* c/o H. S. King and Co., 9 Pall Mall, SW. *Club:* United Empire.

Died 17 May 1916.

FRENCH, Maj.-Gen. Sir George Arthur, KCMG 1902 (CMG 1877); Colonel Commandant RA since 1912; *b* Roscommon, Ireland, 19 June 1841; *e s* of John French, Mornington Park, Co. Dublin, and Isabella Hamilton, his wife; *m* 1862, Janet Clarke (*d* 1917), *d* of Robert Long Innes, formerly 37th Regiment; two *s* three *d*. *Educ:* RMC Sandhurst and RMA Woolwich. Joined Royal Artillery, 1860; Adjutant RA Kingston, Canada, 1862–66; Inspector of Artillery, Canada, with rank Lt-Col, 1870–73; Commissioner North-West Mounted Police, 1873–76; IWS Devonport, 1878–83; Commandant of Forces, Queensland, with rank Colonel, 1883–91; received thanks

of both Houses of Parliament; commanding RA Dover, 1891–92; Chief Instructor School of Gunnery Shoeburyness, 1892–93; Col-on-Staff and Brigadier-Gen. RA Bombay, 1894–96; Major-General commanding NSW Forces, 1896–1902; retired full pay, Sept. 1902. Decorated for services in Canada, and specially with reference to an expedition from Red River to Rocky Mountains in command North-West Mounted Police in 1874; was promoted Colonel for "distinguished services other than in the field", Nov. 1892. *Recreations:* shooting, fishing, sailing. *Club:* Junior Constitutional.

Died 7 July 1921.

FRENCH, Sir John Russell, KBE 1918; General Manager, Bank of New South Wales; President of Institute of Bankers; *b* 1847; *m d* of late W. L. Hawkins, Christchurch, NZ; two *s* one *d*. *Educ:* Cheltenham College.

Died 30 June 1921.

FRENCH, Percy, BA; CE; humorist, artist and poet; *b* 1854; 2nd *s* of Christopher French, Cloonyquin, Co. Roscommon; *m* 1st, 1890, Ethel Armytage Moore (*d* 1891), of Arnmore, Co. Cavan; 2nd, 1894, Helen May Sheldon, of Burmington, Co. Warwick; three *d*. *Educ:* Windermere College; Trinity College, Dublin. After College tried Civil Engineering for six years; editor of a Dublin humorous journal for two years; composed music and words of about thirty songs; took up Art, and painted some Irish scenes for the King; has united his talents in a combined song, story, and sketching entertainment; gave a series of recitals in London in 1899. *Publications:* The First Lord Liftinant, and other Stories; Phil the Fluter's Ball; The Mountains of Mourne; Abdallah Bulbul Ameer; and Come Back Paddy Reilly; Noah's Ark, a fairy play produced at the Waldorf, 1905. *Recreations:* cycling, lawn tennis, water-colour sketching, writing pathetic poems. *Address:* 27 Clifton Hill, NW8. *T:* Hampstead 155. *Club:* St John's Wood Arts.

Died 24 Jan. 1920.

FREND, Col George, CB 1919; Military Knight of Windsor; *b* 1857; *s* of Col George French, Ardsallagh, Fethard, Co. Tipperary. *Address:* Salisbury Tower, Windsor Castle.

Died 24 Sept. 1923.

FRERE, John Tudor, JP; *b* 12 Jan. 1843; *e s* of George Edward Frere, FRS, and Isabella Tudor; *m* 1st, 1869, Constance, *d* of Forbes Winslow, MD, DCL; two *d*; 2nd, 1893, Agatha Mary Gabrielle (*d* 1913), *d* of Rev. Edmund Thomas Daubeney. *Educ:* Trinity Coll. Oxford (BA 1866). Entered as student at the Inner Temple, 1863; practised as a special pleader, not at the bar, 1867–80. *Address:* Roydon Hall, Diss. *Clubs:* New University, Queen's; Norfolk, Norwich.

Died Feb. 1918.

FREWEN, Colonel Edward, CB 1911; DL, JP; Colonel commanding RE Kent Yeomanry since 1908; *b* 25 July 1850; *m* 1873, Anne Mary, *d* of Capt. H. Byng, RN, Quendon Hall, Essex; two *s*. Sheriff of Rutland, 1876; Major Imp. Yeo. S Africa, 1900–1. *Address:* Brickwall, Northiam, Sussex. *Club:* Carlton.

Died 13 Jan. 1919.

FREWEN, Moreton, JP Cos Galway and Cork; MP (N) North-East Cork, 1910–11; *b* 1853; *s* of late Thomas Frewen, Northiam, Sussex; *m* Clare, *d* of Leonard Jerome of New York; two *s* one *d*. *Educ:* Trinity College, Cambridge (BA). A Vice-President Imperial Federation League and a frequent writer in the Reviews on economic problems, Tariff and the Exchanges. Has travelled extensively. *Publications:* The Economic Crisis, etc; Melton Mowbray and other Memories, 1924. *Address:* Brede Place, Sussex. *TA:* Frewen, London. *Club:* Carlton.

Died 2 Sept. 1924.

FREYER, Sir Peter J., KCB 1917 (CB 1917); Lieut-Col (retired list) IMS; Consulting Surgeon; Surgeon to St Peter's Hospital, Consulting Surgeon Queen Alexandra's Military Hospital, and to the Eastern Command; late Examiner in Surgery at the University of Durham; *e s* of late Samuel Freyer, Selerna, Galway; widower; one *s* one *d*. *Educ:* Erasmus Smith's Coll. Galway; Royal Univ. of Ireland; Steeven's Hospital, Dublin; and Paris. BA, RUI (First Class Honours and Gold Medal), 1872; MA (*hon. causa*), 1886; MD (First Class Honours and Gold Medal), MCh and LM 1874. Obtained first place at the open competition for Indian Medical Service, 1875; after period of military employment, services lent to govt of NW Provinces, India, under which held consecutively the appointments of Civil Surgeon, Moradabad, Bareilly, Allahabad, Mussoorie and Benares; Surgeon to Prince of Wales' Hospital, Benares; was for some time Medical Officer to the Lt-Governor, NW Provinces and Oudh, and subsequently to His Highness the late Nawab of Rampur; Delegate from the Indian Govt to the International Medical and Surgical Congress at Rome, 1894; awarded Arnott Memorial Medal, for original surgical work,

1904; on retirement from the Indian army practised as consulting surgeon, London. *Publications:* The Modern Treatment of Stone in the Bladder; Clinical Lectures on Stricture of the Urethra and Hypertrophy of the Prostate; Total Enucleation of the Prostate for Enlargement of that Organ; lectures and articles on surgical subjects. *Recreations:* big game shooting in India, shooting, golf. *Address:* 27 Harley Street, Cavendish Square, W1. *T:* Paddington 1704. *Clubs:* Junior United Service, Reform.^{NL}

Died 6 Sept. 1921.

FRICK, Henry Clay; *b* W Overton, Pa, 19 Dec. 1849; *m* 1881, Adela de Howard, *d* of late Asa P. Childs. Began business life as a clerk for his grandfather, a flour merchant and distiller; later embarked in coke business; founded the H. C. Frick Coke Co. and was its President until it was absorbed by the US Steel Corporation; was Chairman of the Board of the Carnegie Steel Co. until absorbed by the US Steel Corporation; is now a Director of the US Steel Corporation, Pennsylvania Railroad Co., Chicago and Northwestern Railway Co., Norfolk and Western Railway Co., Atchison, Topeka and Santa Fe Railroad Co., and a member of the Executive and Finance Committees of those Companies; also a Director of the Union Trust Co. and Mellon National Bank of Pittsburgh, Pa. *Address:* Pittsburgh, Pa; 1 East 70th Street, New York; Prides Crossing, Mass.

Died 2 Dec. 1919.

FRICKER, Edward T.; Editor, The Australasian, Melbourne, since 1903; *s* of Henry R. Fricker, architect, of South Hackney, London; *m* 1883, Emily May, *d* of Capt. J. Cousens of Victoria; two *s* two *d*. *Educ:* London; Margate. After short commercial experience in London and Adelaide, joined staff of Otago Daily Times, Dunedin, New Zealand, 1881; joined The Argus, Melbourne, 1889; for several years dramatic critic and leader writer. *Recreations:* cycling, billiards. *Address:* Australasian Office, Melbourne, Victoria, Australia. *Club:* Yorick.

Died 4 April 1917.

FRIEDERICHS, Miss Hulda; *b* Ronsdorf, Rhenish Prussia. *Educ:* Ronsdorf; Cologne; St Andrews. Joined the staff of Pall Mall Gazette 1883 (the first woman journalist engaged on exactly the same terms, with regard to work and pay, as male members of the staff); left PMG when that paper changed politics 1893, and joined Westminster Gazette. *Publications:* Translated Poems (into German and English) from Russian, Swedish, Spanish and French; Mr Gladstone in the Evening of his Days, 1895; co-author of Half-Holidays at the Zoo, 1895; translator of Dr Martin's The Future of Russia, 1906; The Romance of the Salvation Army, 1907; The Life of Sir George Newnes, Bt, 1911; editor, Westminster Budget, 1896–1905. *Recreations:* reading, writing. *Address:* Westminster Gazette, 104 Shoe Lane, EC. *TA:* Lobby, Lud, London. *T:* Central 7600–6.

Died 11 Feb. 1927.

FRISWELL, Sir Charles Hain, Kt 1909; *b* 30 Dec. 1871; *s* of George Friswell; *m* 1915, Edith Kate, *d* of William Frewer; no *c*. *Educ:* privately. Has travelled considerably in India, Africa, Ceylon, Burmah. *Recreations:* shooting, riding, sports generally. *Address:* Woodland, Ewhurst, Surrey.

Died 15 Dec. 1926.

FRITH, W. S., RBS. *Address:* Elgin Studios, Trafalgar Square, Chelsea, SW3.

Died Aug. 1924.

FRIZELL, Rev. Charles William, MA; Registrar, Secretary and Surrogate for the Diocese of Down and Connor and Dromore; Chaplain to the Bishop of Down and Connor; Member of the General Synod of Church of Ireland; *e s* of Charles Frizell, JP, Castle Kevin, Co. Wicklow; unmarried. *Educ:* Harcourt Street School, Dublin; Trinity College, Dublin. President of the University Philosophical Society, TCD, 1872; BA 1873; MA 1897. Curate of Coleraine, 1873–77; Castlerock, Co. Derry, 1877–79; Rector of Dunluce, Co. Antrim, 1879–93; Diocesan Chaplain and Assistant Diocesan Inspector of Religious Education, 1897–99; Minor Canon of Belfast Cathedral, 1899–1904; Examining Chaplain to the Bishops of Down, 1899–1907. *Address:* Knocknamona, Fortwilliam Park, Belfast. *T:* Fortwilliam 120.

Died 13 Jan. 1920.

FRIZELLE, Sir Joseph, Kt 1899; *b* 1841; *m* 1868, Elizabeth, *d* of late J. W. Keene. *Educ:* Royal School, Dungannon; Trinity College, Dublin. Entered Indian Civil Service, 1863; Assistant Magistrate and Collector, NWP, 1864; Punjab Commission, 1864–98; Judge of Chief Court, Punjab, 1889–98; Chief Judge, 1898. *Address:* Jersey.

Died 17 Oct. 1921.

FROST, Edward Purkis, JP, DL Co. Cambs; AFAS; Past-President Royal Aeronautical Society of Great Britain, now Vice-President; Vice-President of Tariff Reform League; Commissioner of Income Tax; Chairman of Linton Bench; Member of various Scientific Associations; Member of the Council of the Aerial League of Great Britain; *b* 1842; *s* of late Edward Frost, JP; unmarried. *Educ:* Blackheath, Brentwood and Bishop's Stortford. Joined Cambs Rifle Volunteers, 1861; served on various County Committees prior to the County Councils; served on County Bench since 1871; Aeronautical since 1863; Agricultural, Horticultural, Scientific, Political Associations. *Publications:* Union of Science and Religion; The Influence of Physiological Discovery on Thought; Safeguards for Peace; National Insurance against War, etc. *Recreations:* shooting, fishing, natural history, science, aviation, art, music. *Address:* West Wratting Hall, Cambridge. *TA:* West Wratting. *M:* CE 1113. *Clubs:* Constitutional, Royal Aero; Cambridge County.

Died 26 Jan. 1922.

FROST, Hon. Sir John, KCMG 1904 (CMG 1879); *b* 1828; *s* of William Frost, farmer, Leicestershire. Emigrated to S Africa, 1849, and farmed for three years in the div. of Graaf Reinet; served with the Somerset Burghers under Commandant Bowker, 1850–51, for which service he received a grant of land in the div. of Queenstown, 1857; served under Sir Walter Currie when the Kaffir Chief Kreile was expelled from the territory now known as the Transkei; elected member for House of Assembly for div. of Queenstown, 1874, and has represented that district continuously for 27 years; when the war of 1877–78 broke out he was appointed Commandant of Queenstown Div. and of all the burghers operating in Gaikaland, and in 1880–81 was appointed Chief Commandant of the Burghers and of several bodies of levies in the Transkei; joined Mr Rhodes' Ministry as Sec. of Native Affairs, 1893; this office was abolished, when he became Minister of Agriculture during the same year; joined Sir Gordon Sprigg, 1900, as minister without portfolio, and represented the Cape Govt in Australia at the inauguration of the Commonwealth and opening of the Federal Parliament by HRH the Duke of York; appointed Minister of Agriculture on reconstruction of Ministry in June, 1902. *Address:* Eastbrooke, Rondesbosch, Cape Town; Thibet Park, Cape Colony.

Died 2 April 1918.

FROST, Lieut-Col John Meadows, DSO 1918; RFA (TF); *b* 1885; *e s* of Sir J. M. Frost; *m* 1910, Olivia, *e d* of Henry Shelmerdine, South Lawn, Southport; three *s* two *d*. *Educ:* Charterhouse; Christ Church, Oxford. Served European War, 1914–1918 (despatches, DSO). *Address:* The Dene, Hoole, Chester.

Died 15 Aug. 1923.

FROUDE, Robert Edmund, CB 1911; LLD; FRS; CE; Superintendent Admiralty Experiment Works, Haslar, Gosport, 1879, retired, 1919; *b* Devonshire, 22 Dec. 1846; 3rd *s* of William Froude, CE, FRS, *n* of Hurrell Froude of the Oxford Tract Movement and James Anthony Froude the historian. *Educ:* Bradfield College, Berkshire; Oratory School, Edgbaston, Birmingham. Served under his father, Admiralty Experiment Works, then at Torquay, 1871–79; afterwards Superintendent of same; late at Haslar (Gosport); retired, 1919. *Publications:* papers on scientific subjects bearing on Naval Architecture. *Recreations:* cycling, boating, photography. *Address:* North Lodge, Alverstoke, Gosport.

Died 19 March 1924.

FROWDE, Henry; Publisher to the University of Oxford, 1883–1913; *b* 8 Feb. 1841; *m* 1874, Mary Blanche Foster; three *d* (and one *s* decd). Manager, London Office, OUP, 1874–1913. *Address:* 25 The Waldrons, Croydon, Surrey. *T:* Croydon 726.

Died 3 March 1927.

FRY, Rt. Hon. Sir Edward, GCB 1907; Kt 1877; PC 1883; BA, DCL, LLD; FRS 1883; FBA, FSA, FLS; Judge of High Court, Chancery Division, 1877–83; Lord Justice of Appeal, 1883–92; *b* Bristol, 4 Nov. 1827; 2nd *s* of Joseph Fry, Bristol, and Mary Anne, *d* of Edward Swaine, Reading; *m* 1859, Mariabella, *d* of John Hodgkin, Lewes; two *s* six *d* (and one *d* decd). *Educ:* Bristol College; University College, London. Fellow University of London; Hon. Fellow of Balliol College, Oxford. Barrister, 1854; QC and Bencher of Lincoln's Inn, 1869; Treasurer Lincoln's Inn, 1892; presided over the Royal Commission on the Irish Land Acts, 1897–98; Conciliator in the S Wales Colliery dispute, 1898; Alderman and Chairman of Quarter Sessions, County of Somerset, 1899–1913; Chairman of the Departmental Committee on the Patent Laws, 1900; a Judge, Permanent Court of Arbitration, The Hague, 1900–12; Arbitrator in the Grimsby Fishery dispute, 1901; was Chairman of the Court of Arbitration under the Metropolis Water Act, 1902; and of University College, London, Transfer Commission, 1906; and was legal assessor to the International Commission on the North Sea

incident, 1904–5; Arbitrator between the US of America and Mexico in the Pious Funds case, 1902, and between France and Germany on the Casa Blanca incident, 1909; was Chairman of the Royal Commission on Trinity College, Dublin, and on the University of Dublin, 1906–7; Arbitrator between the London and NW Rly Company and their employees, 1908; was Ambassador Extraordinary and First British Plenipotentiary to The Hague Peace Conference in 1907. Formerly a Trustee of the Hunterian Museum, College of Surgeons; a member of Historical MSS Commission. *Publications:* Essays on the Accordance of Christianity with Nature of Man, 1857; The Doctrine of Election, an Essay, 1864; A Treatise on the Specific Performance of Contracts, edns 1858, 1881, 1892, 1903 and 1911; British Mosses, 1892 and 1908; James Hack Tuke, 1899; and The Mycetozoa, 1899, 1915; Studies by the Way, 1900; The Liverworts, 1911. *Address:* Failand House, Failand, near Bristol. *TA:* Failand, Abbots-Leigh. *Clubs:* Athenæum; County, Taunton.
Died 18 Oct. 1918.

FRY, Francis James, DL, JP; Lord of the Manor of Cricket St Thomas, Chard; *b* 1835; *e s* of Francis Fry, FSA; *m* 1st, 1861, Elizabeth Greer, *d* of Joseph Rake, Bristol; 2nd, 1885, Elizabeth, *d* of A. Capper Pass, Bristol; four *s* one *d. Educ:* a private school in Bristol. Sheriff, Bristol, 1887; Somersetshire, 1906; spent the greater part of life in Bristol on business and in public matters; was for many years an alderman of the city, and a member of the Council of University College; now a member of the Court of Bristol University. *Recreations:* foreign travel, shooting, art, science. *Address:* Cricket St Thomas, Chard. *TA:* Cricket, Winsham. *T:* 37 Chard. *Club:* Royal Societies.
Died 4 Nov. 1918.

FRY, Sir Henry James Wakely, Kt 1916; CIE 1914; Director General of Stores, India Office, 1912–15; *b* 13 Nov. 1849; 2nd *s* of William Wakely Fry of Taunton, Somerset; *m* 1877, Elizabeth, *y d* of Charles Parsons of Steepleton Preston, Dorset; five *d. Educ:* Church College, Taunton; privately. BA (honours) London University, 1875. Junior Clerk, India Office, 1873; Senior Clerk, 1896; Deputy Director General of Stores, 1909. *Address:* Holly Cottage, Englefield Green, Surrey.
Died 18 Dec. 1920.

FRY, Rt. Hon. Lewis, PC 1901; JP, DL; LLD; Governor of Clifton College; Pro-Chancellor of University of Bristol; President of Clifton High School for Girls; *b* 16 April 1832; *s* of late Joseph Fry, Bristol; *b* of late Rt Hon. Sir Edward Fry; *m* 1859, Elizabeth Pease (*d* 1870), *o d* of late Francis Gibson of Saffron Walden, Essex; one *s* three *d.* Formerly a Solicitor; member of Bristol Town Council, and Chairman of School Board. MP (LU) for Bristol, 1878–85; N Bristol, 1885–92, 1895–1900; Chairman of Parliamentary Committee on Town Holdings, 1886–92; and author of two reports of same. *Address:* Goldney House, Clifton, Bristol. *Club:* Burlington Fine Arts.
Died 10 Sept. 1921.

FRY, Peter George, CMG 1919; DSO 1916; TD; FRIBA; *b* 1875; *s* of Peter Fry; *m* 1901, Minnie, *d* of Llewellin Llewellin; one *s.* Served European War, 1914–18 (despatches, DSO, Brevet Lieut-Col, CMG, White Eagle of Serbia). *Address:* c/o Barclays Bank, Weston-super-Mare.
Died 28 Oct. 1925.

FRYER, Sir Charles (Edward), Kt 1915; ISO 1907; FLS; AA, Oxford; Hon. Member American Fisheries Society; Hon. Member Salmon and Trout Association; *b* 19 July 1850; *e s* of late Charles Biden Fryer of Leamington; *m;* one *s. Educ:* privately. Clerk to Inspectors of Fisheries, Home Office, 1869; Inspectors' Assistant, 1883; Inspector, 1886; transferred to Board of Trade, 1886, and to Board of Agriculture and Fisheries (as Superintending Inspector), 1903; Secretary to, or Member of, various Commissions and Committees of Inquiry into Fisheries of England, Wales and Scotland, 1874–1915; received thanks of Government of New Zealand for services in connection with introduction of trout and efforts to acclimatise salmon in the colony, 1873, 1910–13; awarded silver medal Society of Arts for invention of preserving pilchards as sardines—a new industry in this country—1876; silver medal Royal Cornwall Polytechnic Society, 1875; bronze medal Philadelphia International Exhibition, 1876; first prize for essay on Relations of the State with Fishermen and Fisheries, International Fisheries Exhibition, 1883, and diploma of Royal Commission for services rendered; official English Delegate and Juror, International Fisheries Exhibition, Bergen; Official English Delegate, Internat. Fish. Congress, Dieppe, 1898; member of Committee, Internat. Fish. Congress, Paris, 1900; Vice-Pres. Washington, 1908; Official English Delegate, Rome, 1911; Official English Delegate and Pres. Maritime Section, Internat. Fish. Congress, Ostend, 1913; Member of Organising Committee for ensuing Internat. Fish. Congress, San Sebastian. *Publications:* Handbook on Salmon Fisheries,

1883; A National Fisheries Society, 1883; Relations of the State with Fishermen and Fisheries, 1883; International Regulation of the Fisheries on the High Seas, 1910; The Management of our Salmon Rivers, 1916; annual and other reports on Fisheries, etc, 1886–1915; editor of The Colonies and India, 1874–90; contributor to various journals and other publications. *Clubs:* Royal Automobile, Fly-Fishers'.
Died 19 Nov. 1920.

FRYER, Sir Frederic William Richards, KCSI 1895 (CSI 1890); *b* 1845; *s* of F. W. Fryer of West Moors, Dorset, and Emily Frances, *d* of John Richards, MP; *m* 1870, Frances (*d* 1920), *d* of W. C. L. Bashford, JP, DL; one *s.* Entered Bengal Civil Service, 1864; Barrister, Middle Temple, 1880; Deputy-Commissioner Punjaub, 1877; Commissioner Central Division Upper Burma, 1886; Financial Comr of Burma, 1888; Acting Chief Comr of Burma, 1892–94; Officiating Financial Comr of the Punjaub, and Additional Member of the Viceroy's Council, 1894–95; Chief Comr, Burma, 1895–97; Lieut-Governor, Burma, 1897–1903. *Address:* 23 Elvaston Place, SW7. *T:* 3779 Kensington. *Clubs:* Athenæum, East India United Service.
Died 20 Feb. 1922.

FRYER, Lt-Gen. Sir John, KCB 1903 (CB 1881); Colonel 6th Dragoon Guards (The Carabiniers), 1902; *b* Wimborne Minster, Dorset, 27 June 1838; *e s* of late John Fryer (*d* 1854), and Mary, *d* of late Christopher Hardinge; *m* 1862, Catherine (*d* 1914), *d* of late George Reed, East Brent Manor, Somerset; one *s* two *d. Educ:* Exeter Coll. Oxford. Entered army, 1860, as a cornet 6th Dragoon Guards (The Carabiniers), and passing through every grade, commanded that regiment as Lieut-Col, 1877–82; as a Colonel commanded 17th Leicester regimental District, 1883–88; as a Maj.-Gen. commanded the South Irish (Cork) District 1893–98; war service, command of the Carabiniers throughout campaign, Afghanistan, 1879–80; command of 2nd movable column, Khaibar Field Force, etc, etc, 1879–80; Afghan medal; Victoria Jubilee medal; in receipt of Reward for Distinguished Service. *Recreations:* polo (winner of silver cup); rowing (winner of cups); won presentation sword as best swordsman of officers of The Carabiniers, 1872; steeple-chasing (won his regimental cup twice); on the Councils of the Hunters Improvement Society, Army and Navy Pensioners Employment Society, etc; hunting, shooting, deer-stalking, golf. *Address:* 42 Evelyn Gardens, SW. *Clubs:* Army and Navy, Cavalry, Hurlingham, MCC.
Died 28 Jan. 1917.

FUKUSHIMA, Gen. Baron, Hon. KCB 1902; Governor-General of Kwantung, 1912–17; *b* Matsumoto, Shinano Province, 1853 (Samurai); married; four *s* one *d.* Began life as a drummer-boy; studied in Tokio University; entered Judicial Department, 1874; transferred to General Staff Office, 1875; visited Philadelphia Exhibition, 1876; Lieut in army, 1877; travelled in Mongolia, 1879; Military Attaché, Peking, 1882–84; sent to India, 1886; Military Attaché, Berlin, 1887–92; travelled on horseback, Berlin to Vladivostock, through Russia, Siberia, Mongolia, Manchuria (9000 miles), 1892–93; General Staff Officer, 5th Division, First Army; then Chief of Administrative Bureau of Territory occupied by Japan during war with China; sent to Egypt, Turkey, Persia, Causasia, Arabia, Turkestan, India, Burma, Siam and Annam, 1895–97; in command of Japanese contingent till fall of Tientsin, then attached to General Yamaguchi, then to Field-Marshal Waldersee as General Staff Officer during Boxer troubles, 1900–1; attended King Edward's Coronation; General Staff Officer, Headquarters, Manchurian Army, Russo-Japanese War, 1904–5; Gen. 1914 (retired). *Address:* Tokio, Japan.
Died 18 Feb. 1919.

FULFORD, Francis, JP, Devon; AKC; District Councillor St Thomas's RDC; *b* 15 Sept. 1861; *e s* of Francis Drummond Fulford of Fulford, DL, JP; *m* 1897, Constance, *d* of late Edgar Drummond of Cadland, Hants, DL, JP, and Louisa Theodosia, *d* of 3rd Baron Muncaster; three *s. Educ:* Sherborne; King's College, London. Assistant Engineer on Canadian Pacific Railway, 1883–85; Assistant Secretary to Royal Commission on Civil Establishments, 1886–91; Inspector Board of Agriculture, 1891; private secretary to Rt Hon. Walter Long, 1899; to Rt Hon. R. W. Hanbury, 1900; Superintending Inspector Ministry of Agriculture and Fisheries, 1901–21. *Address:* Great Fulford, Dunsford, Exeter; *TA:* Fulford, Dunsford. *Clubs:* National, MCC.
Died 4 Nov. 1926.

FULFORD, Rev. Frederick John; Rector of Fornham All Saints with Westley, 1904–25; Rural Dean of Thingoe, 1917–24; Hon. Canon of St Edmundsbury and Ipswich; *b* London, 1860; *y s* of William Fulford; *m* 1890, Emily Constance, *d* of W. H. Ellis of Ottermouth, Budleigh Salterton; two *s* one *d. Educ:* King's College School, London; Clare College, Cambridge. Vice-Principal of Gloucester Theological

College, 1888–90; Vicar of Flaxley, Gloucestershire, 1890–1904; Representative of the Senate of Cambridge University on the West Suffolk Education Committee; Chairman of the Governors of the West Suffolk County School and Pupil Teachers' Centre; Chairman of the Diocesan Education Committee and Member of the Diocesan Board of Finance of St Edmundsbury and Ipswich; Chm. of the West Suffolk Local War Pensions Committee. *Recreations:* walking, croquet, poultry-keeping. *Address:* 5 Louisa Terrace, Exmouth.

Died 8 Jan. 1927.

FULLER, George Pargiter, JP; *b* Baynton, Wilts, 8 Jan. 1833; *o* surv. *s* of John Bird Fuller, Neston Park, Wilts, and Sophia, *d* of John Hanning, Dillington Park, Ilminster, Somerset; *m* 1864, Emily, 2nd *d* of Sir Michael Hicks-Beach, 8th Bt; five *s* one *d*. *Educ:* Winchester; Christ Church, Oxford (Ma). MP (L) for West Wilts, 1885–95. *Recreations:* coaching, hunting, cricket. *Address:* Neston Park, Corsham, Wiltshire. *TA:* Fuller, Corsham. *T:* Corsham, 1. *M:* AM 3247. *Clubs:* United University, National Liberal.

Died 2 April 1927.

FULLER, James Franklin, FSA; FRIBA; FRIAI; architect, author; *b* 1835; *m* Helen, *d* of J. P. Gouvion. Principal professional works: churches of Clane, Arthurs-town, Killadease, Rattoo, Kylemore, Syddan, Rathdaire, etc; Lord Ardilaun's mansions at St Ann's, Dublin and Ashford, Co. Galway; Harristoun House, Kildare, Ballyburley House, King's Co.; Mount Falcon, Co. Mayo; Lord Ventry's, Co. Kerry; has been Architect to the Church Representative Body, to the Honourable the Benchers of King's Inns, and to the National Board of Education. *Publications:* John Orlebar; Culmshire Folk; The Young Idea; Doctor Quodlibet; Chronicles of Westerly; Omniana, the Autobiography of an Irish Octogenarian; has been a frequent contributor to genealogical and heraldic periodicals, such as the Miscellanea Genealogica et Heraldica, The Genealogist, and Walford's Antiquarian Magazine. *Recreations:* genealogy, heraldry. *Address:* Glashnacree, Kenmare, Co. Kerry; Lissatier, Eglinton Road, Dublin.

Died 8 Dec. 1924.

FULLERTON, Hugh, JP; *b* 1851; *s* of Samuel and Mary Fullerton, of Manchester; *m* 1891, Ada, *d* of Joseph Copley. *Educ:* public school. Working man, then foreman, then master, now retired; taken active part in various educational, social, and political movements; been Guardian of Poor; was Chairman of School Board Progressive Party, Manchester; was Member of a Trades Council; Executive Treasurer, Discharged Prisoners' Aid Society, Manchester; Member of Executive for seven years of National Liberal Federation; Magistrate, City of Manchester and Cumberland; MP (L) Egremont West, Cumberland, 1906–10. *Address:* Brackenhoe, Sale, Cheshire. *Clubs:* National Liberal; Reform, Manchester.

Died 31 Aug. 1922.

FULLERTON, Admiral Sir John Reginald Thomas, GCVO 1901 (KCVO 1899); CB 1896; Extra-Groom-in-Waiting to the King; *b* 10 Aug. 1840; *m* 1874, Ada, *d* of late Col E. S. Capell, Lady's Close, Watford, Herts; two *s* three *d*. Entered Royal Navy, 1853; Commander, 1872; Capt. 1878; Rear-Admiral, 1893; Lieut of "Bombay" when that vessel took fire and blew up off Monte Video, 1864. Order of St Anne, 1st class; Order of the Prussian Crown, 1st class. *Recreations:* yachting, motoring. *Address:* Hamble, South Hants. *Clubs:* United Service, Royal Automobile.

Died 29 June 1918.

FULTON, Lt-Col Harry Townsend, CMG 1917; DSO 1900; Indian Army; 2nd King Edward's Own Gurkhas; *b* 15 Aug. 1869; 6th *s* of late Lieut-Gen. John Fulton, RA; *m* 1905, Ada Hermina, 2nd *d* of John James Dixon. Entered army, 1892; served NW Frontier of India, 1897–98 (medal and clasp); Tirah, 1897–98 (clasp); S Africa, 1899–1901 (medal, three clasps, despatches, DSO); European War, 1914–17 (despatches twice, CMG, Bt Lt-Col, Croix de Guerre). *Address:* Dehra Dun, India.

Died 29 March 1918.

FULTON, Sir (James) Forrest, Kt 1892; KC; JP, Norfolk; LLB; Recorder of London, 1900–22; one of HM's Lieutenants for the City of London; *b* Ostend, 12 July 1846; *y s* of late Lieut-Col Fulton, KH, and Fanny, *d* of John Sympson Jessopp; *m* 1875, Sophia Browne, *e d* of John B. Nicholson; three *s*. *Educ:* Norwich Grammar School, under his uncle the Rev. Augustus Jessopp, DD; London University, BA 1867; LLB 1873. Barrister, Middle Temple 1872; QC 1892; Bencher 1898; Treasurer 1921–22; Counsel to Treasury at Middlesex Sessions and Central Criminal Court; Senior Counsel to Post Office; Counsel to Mint, Hertfordshire; Common Serjeant, 1892–1900. MP (C) West Ham (North), 1886–92. *Address:* The Cottage, Sheringham, Norfolk. *Club:* Carlton. *Died 25 June 1925.*

FULTON, Robert Burwell, AM, LLD; President Miller Technical School since 1906; *b* Sumter Co., Alabama, 8 April 1849; *s* of William and Elizabeth K. Fulton; *m* 1st, 1871, Annie Rose Garland (*d* 1893); four *s* one *d*; 2nd, 1903, Florence Thompson. *Educ:* private schools; University of Mississippi. AB 1869; AM 1873; LLD University of Nashville, 1893; South Carolina College, 1905; University of Alabama, 1906; University of Mississippi, 1909. Taught in high schools, Alabama, 1869–70; New Orleans, 1870–71; Tutor, University of Mississippi, 1871; Adjunct Professor Physics, 1872; Professor Physics and Astronomy, 1875–1906; Fellow AAAS since 1888; President Department of Higher Education, National Educational Association, 1898; Pres. Southern Educational Association, 1899; Pres. National Association of State Universities, 1896–1902; Chancellor of the University of Mississippi, 1892–1906; member of the Board of Trustees of the Miller Fund of the University of Virginia since 1910. *Publications:* contributions to Ency. Brit., 1878, and revisions 1903; author of various reports and addresses on educational and scientific topics; Virginia and the Cession of the North-west Territory, a historical review, 1910. *Address:* Miller School, Albemarle Co., Va. *TA:* Charlottesville, Va. *T:* Charlottesville 915R. *Club:* Chi Psi. *Died 28 May 1918.*

FULTON, Sir Robert Fulton, Kt 1908; MA, LLD; *b* 1844; *m* 1887, Margaret Edith, *d* of Brigade-Surgeon R. G. Mathew; one *d*. *Educ:* Edinburgh Academy, and University. Entered Bengal Civil Service, 1864; District Judge, 1875–93; Barrister-at-law, Inner Temple, 1884; Acting Puisne Judge, High Court, Calcutta, 1888, 1889, 1890, 1892; Puisne Judge, 1893; additional Member of Legislative Council of Viceroy of India, 1902–3; Acting Chief-Justice of Bengal, 1907, 1908; retired, 1908. *Publications:* Commentary on Bengal Tenancy Act; revised editions of Field's Law of Evidence, Alexander's Law of Torts, O'Kinealy's Code of Civil Procedure. *Address:* 7 Sloane Gardens, SW1. *T:* Victoria 1582. *Clubs:* East India United Service; Bengal, Calcutta. *Died 15 Oct. 1927.*

FUNSTEN, Rt. Rev. James Bowan, BL, DD; Bishop of Idaho since 1907; *b* Clarke, Co. Virginia; *s* of Colonel Oliver Ridgeway Funsten, of 11th Virginia Cavalry, USA, and Mary Bowen of Mirador, Virginia; *m* Ida Vivian Pratt of Camden, Virginia; four *s* one *d*. *Educ:* University High School; Virginia Military Institute; University of Virginia; Virginia Theological Seminary. Till 20 years manager of mother's Plantation (Mirador) in Virginia; practised law in Baltimore; deacon at 23; missionary in charge of Bristol and Marion, Virginia; priest; spent some time in travel abroad, 1884; rector of Christ Church, Richmond, 1884–90; general missionary, Virginia, 1890–92; rector of Trinity Church, Portsmouth, Virginia, 1892–99; first Missionary Bishop of Boisé, 1899; Bishop in charge of Wyoming, 1907–9; Chaplain 2nd Regt Idaho National Guards, USA. Founder and President of St Luke's Hospital, Boisé, Idaho. *Publications:* tracts, occasional magazine articles, sermons, monograms. *Recreation:* travelling. *Address:* Boisé, Idaho, USA.

Died 1918.

FUNSTON, Brig.-Gen Frederick; *b* New Carlisle, Ohio, 9 Nov. 1865; *m* 1898, Eda Blankart. *Educ:* Kansas University. Commissioner Department of Agriculture to explore Alaska and report on its flora, 1893; Captain Major and Lt-Col Cuban Insurgent Army, 1896–97; Col Comdg 20th Kansas Infantry, 1898; went to Philippines (prom. Brig-Gen., medal of honour); organised and commanded an expedition resulting in capture of Aguinaldo; Commandant Army Service School, Fort Leavenworth, 1909. *Publication:* Memories of Two Wars, 1912. *Address:* Iola, Kansas, USA.

Died 9 Feb. 1917.

FURLEY, Sir John, Kt 1899; CH 1918; CB 1902; JP, DL; late Captain East Kent Rifle Volunteers; *b* Ashford, Kent, 19 March 1836; *s* of Robert Furley, JP; *m* 1874, Maria Turner (RRC, Lady of Justice Order of the Hospital of St John of Jerusalem, S Africa war medal), *d* of George Baker of Holmfels, Reigate, JP. *Educ:* Harrow. Commissioner of British National Aid Soc., Franco-German War, 1870–71; Director of Ambulances Volantes of French Army during War of Commune, 1871; Delegate of British Seed Fund Committee for French peasant Farmers (Lord Vernon's Fund), 1871; Director of Ambulances in Spain during Carlist War, 1874; special Commissioner of Mansion-House Fund for relief of sufferers from inundations in valley of Garonne, 1875; Special Commissioner of British National Aid Society to inspect and report on Ambulance arrangements, and to afford necessary assistance to wounded in Montenegro during Russo-Turkish war, 1876; Chief Commissioner Central British Red Cross Committee in S Africa, 1900 (despatches twice); one of original organisers of St John Ambulance Association, 1877; Deputy-Chairman and Director of Ambulance Dept of Order of St John of Jerusalem; member of

International Congress of Red Cross Societies, held at Berlin, 1868; Hon. Sec. of similar Conference held at Vienna, 1873; member of the Conference at Geneva, 1884; Hon. Sec. of the Conference at Carlsruhe, 1887; Vice-President of the Conference at Rome, 1892; Vice-President of Conference at Vienna, 1897; Vice-President of Conference at Petrograd, 1902; one of the delegates for Great Britain at International Conference for revision of the Convention of Geneva, 1906; Vice-Pres. of International Conference, London, 1907; Vice-President of 9th International Conference, Washington, 1912; Hon. Pres. of first International First-Aid and Life-Saving Congress, Frankfort-on-Main, 1908; Knight of Justice and Hon. Bailiff, Order of St John of Jerusalem; Jubilee medal, 1887; Jubilee bar, 1897; Coronation medal, 1902; Order of St John Service medal; South African War medal and 3 bars; Knight Commander Royal Order of Wasa; Knight of the Dannebrog; Grand Star of Honour and Knight Commander of Isabel the Catholic; Knight Commander Montenegro; Officer of Légion d'Honneur; French Commemoration medal (Decree 1910) for Campaign of 1870–71. *Publications:* War and Charity (translation of La Guerre et la Charité, by MM Moynier and Appia), 1870; Struggles and Experiences of a Neutral Volunteer (2 vols), 1871; In Spain Amongst the Carlists (1 vol.), 1876; The Red Cross, its Past and Future (translation of La Croix Rouge, son Passé et son Avenir, by M Gustave Moynier), 1883; In Peace and War, 1905. *Address:* 14 Evelyn Gardens, SW.
Died 27 Sept. 1919.

FURLONG, Robert O'Brien, CB 1901; Solicitor of Inland Revenue for Ireland; and Special Commissioner of Income Tax 1880–1907; *b* 1842; *s* of William Croker Furlong; *m* 1871, Henrietta (*d* 1915), *d* of Henry Courtney; one *s* two *d*. *Educ:* Trinity College, Dublin (MA). Irish Barrister, 1867; Secretary, Royal Sanitary Commission, Dublin, 1879–80; Counsel, Post Office (Ireland), 1879; JP, Hants. *Addresss:* Maesbury, Cavendish Road, Bournemouth. *Clubs:* Constitutional; University, Royal St George Yacht, Dublin; Bournemouth.
Died 5 July 1917.

FURNEAUX, Rev. William Mordaunt, DD; *b* 29 July 1848; *e s* of Rev. W. D. Furneaux, Swilly, Devon; *m* 1877, Caroline Octavia (*d* 1904), *d* of Joseph Mortimer, of Weymouth; three *d*. *Educ:* Marlborough; Corpus Christi Coll., Oxford. 1st class Classical Moderations, 1870; 1st class Lit. Hum. 1872. Assistant Master at Clifton, 1873; at Marlborough, 1874–82; Headmaster of Repton to 1900; late Canon of Southwell; Dean of Winchester, 1903–19. *Publications:* Commentary on the Acts of the Apostles; The Book of Psalms; Introduction to the Lessons of the Lectionary. *Club:* Church Imperial.
Died 10 April 1928.

FURNISS, Harry; caricature artist, author and lecturer; *b* Wexford, 26 March 1854; *s* of James Furniss, English engineer, and Isabella Cornelia, *d* of Eneas Mackenzie, Newcastle upon Tyne; *m* 1877, Marian, *d* of Alfred Rogers; three *s* one *d*. Settled in London at nineteen; many years contributor to Illustrated London News, The Graphic, Black and White, Illustrated Sporting and Dramatic News, and the principal magazines in England and America; Punch; joined Punch staff 1880; Humorous Lecturer; has toured in America, Canada, Australia, etc; illustrated Happy Thoughts, Incompleat Angler, Comic Blackstone, Lewis Carroll's Sylvie and Bruno; founded Lika Joko, New Budget. *Publications:* Romps, Flying Visits; exhibited Artistic Joke in Bond Street, 1887; Royal Academy Antics; Humours of Parliament, America in a Hurry, 1900; illustrated London Letter; Peace with Humour; P and O Sketches, 1898; Confessions of a Caricaturist, 1901; Harry Furniss at Home, 1903; Poverty Bay, a novel, 1905; How to Draw in Pen and Ink, 1905; Friends without Faces, a book for children, 1905. Illustrated all the works of Charles Dickens, 1910; illustrated all the works of W. M. Thackeray (the Furniss Centenary Edition), 1911; Our Lady Cinema, 1914; More about How to draw in Pen and Ink, 1915; humorous lectures throughout England, What you are Thinking About, The Frightfulness of Humour; The Blue Moon, an intermittent publication for concrete objects; The Cranks No (Brewers), Peace in War (Salvation Army War Work Fund), and so on, 1917; Deceit, a reply to Defeat, 1917; My Bohemian Days; The Byways and Queer Ways of Boxing, 1919; Stiggins, 1920; Some Victorian Women (Good, Bad, and Indifferent), 1923; Some Victorian Men, 1924. Has written many photo-plays for the cinematograph, produced and acted in them both in the United States and in England, 1912. *Address:* The Mount, High Wickham, Hastings. *Club:* Garrick.
Died 14 Jan. 1925.

FYFE, Thomas Alexander, CBE 1918; Sheriff-Substitute of Lanarkshire at Glasgow since 1900; *b* Dundee, 1852. *Educ:* Perth; Edinburgh University. Appointed Sheriff-Substitute at Lanark, 1895. *Publications:* The Law and Practice of the Sheriff Court; The

Bankruptcy Code (Scotland); Employers and Workmen under the Munitions of War Acts. *Address:* 1 Kingsborough Gardens, Glasgow, W. *T:* W 606.
Died 13 March 1928.

FYSH, Hon. Sir Philip Oakley, KCMG 1896; Hon. DCL Oxon; *b* 1 March 1835; *s* of John Fysh, Highbury; *m* 1856, Esther (*d* 1912), *e d* of William Willis, manufacturer, Luton, Beds. MLC Hobart, 1866–69; Buckingham, 1870–73, 1884, 1887, 1890; MHA for East Hobart, 1873–78; Treasurer in Mr Kennerly's Ministry, 1873–75, and without portfolio to 1876; Leader of the Opposition, July 1877–Aug. 1877; Premier without office, 1877–78; held portfolio without office in Mr Giblin's first Administration, 1878; Premier and Chief Secretary, March 1887–Aug. 1892; Leader of the Opposition in Legislative Council, 1892–94; member of the Executive Council; a Magistrate for the Territory; President of the Central Board of Health; Chairman of Metropolitan Drainage Board; Major commanding the Tasmanian Volunteer Rifle Regiment, 1880–84; Alderman of Hobart, 1868–69; one of the Delegates from Tasmania to the Federal Conventions held in Sydney, Adelaide, and Melbourne, 1891, 1897, 1898; one of the Representatives of Tasmania in the Federal Council of Australasia; Treasurer in Sir Edward Braddon's Ministry, 1894–99; member for North Hobart, 1894–99; one of the Australian Delegates to London 1900, in connection with the Commonwealth Bill of Australia; Postmaster-General, Commonwealth of Australia, 1903–4; late Minister without Portfolio; Agent-General for Tasmania in London, 1899–1900; retired from public life, 1910. *Address:* Hobart, Tasmania.
Died 21 Dec. 1919.

FYSON, Rt. Rev. Philip Kemball, DD; *b* 1846; *m* 1874, Eleanor Furley of Hull; five *s* four *d*. *Educ:* Christ's Coll., Camb. 1st class Classical Tripos, 1870. Ordained 1871; missionary, CMS Japan, 1874–96; Bishop of Hokkaido, N Japan, 1896–1908. *Address:* Sutton Valence, Maidstone.
Died 30 Jan. 1928.

G

GADOW, Hans Friedrich, PhD, Hon. MA Cantab; FRS 1892; Strickland Curator since 1884 and Reader in Morphology of Vertebrates, Cambridge University; *b* Pomerania, 8 March 1855; *e s* of late M. L. Gadow, Inspector Royal Forests, Prussia; *m* Clara Maud, *e d* of late Sir George Edward Paget, KCB, FRS, Regius Professor of Physic, Cambridge. *Educ:* Frankfurt-on-Oder; Berlin, Jena and Heidelberg Universities. British Museum, Natural History Department, 1880–82. *Publications:* In Northern Spain, 1897; A Classification of Vertebrata, 1898; The Last Link by E. Haeckel, 1898; Through Southern Mexico, 1908; vol. Aves in Bronn's Animal Kingdom; vol. Amphibia and Reptiles, Camb. Nat. Hist.; The Wanderings of Animals; and papers in Royal Society Philosophical Transactions and other scientific periodicals. *Address:* Museum of Zoology, Cambridge; Cleramendi, Great Shelford.
Died 16 May 1928.

GADSBY, W. H., RBA. *Address:* 5 Carleton Road, Tufnell Park, N.
Died 15 Oct. 1924.

GADSDEN, Edward Holroyd, ISO 1914; *b* 21 Aug. 1859; *s* of late Maj.-Gen. Frederick Gadsden, Madras Staff Corps; *m* 1885, Hester Sinclair, *d* of George Hamnett, CDE, Inspector General of Registration, Madras; three *s* two *d*. *Educ:* Monmouth Grammar School. Joined the Madras Police for special service in Rumpa, 1879; Asst Superintendent Police, 1883–86; Services transferred to the Jail Department, 1886; Superintendent Central Jail, Coimbatore, 1893–1914; Inspector General of Prisons, Madras, 1914; retired, 1918. Awarded Delhi Durbar Medal in 1912. *Address:* Commercial Bank of Tasmania, Latrobe, Tas.
Died 17 Feb. 1920.

GAFFNEY, Thomas Burke, ISO 1903; CE; *b* 23 Jan. 1839; *s* of Edward Gaffney, CE, late Sub-Commissioner of Valuation in Ireland, and Bridget Burke of Bekan, Co. Mayo; *m* 1885, Joan, *d* of P. O'Donnell, High Constable of Glenquin, Killeedy, Co. Limerick; six *s* two *d*. *Educ:* Catholic University, Dublin. Served his apprenticeship to his father; began in 1855 and completed his career in the Valuation and Boundary Survey Department (Ireland); during the last twelve years of his service was chief of the technical branch of that service; retired under the 65 rule, 1904. *Address:* 23 Waterloo Road, Dublin.   *Died 1 April 1927.*

GAGE, Hon. Lyman Judson; President of the United States Trust Company of New York City, 1902–6; *b* 28 June 1836; *m* 2nd, 1909, Mrs Francis Ballon. *Educ:* common school; Rome (NY) Academy. LLD Beliot College, Wis.; LLD (Hon.) New York University, 1903. Banker and financier; in 1858 book-keeper and in 1868 cashier, Merchants' Loan and Trust Co., Chicago; cashier, 1st National Bank, Chicago, 1868; Vice-Pres. and General Manager, 1882; President, 1891; Secretary of the Treasury, 1897–1902; was three times Pres. American Bankers' Association; first Pres. and organiser of Chicago Clearing-House Association; first Pres. and organiser of Chicago Civic Federation; devoted to municipal reform; first Pres. of World's Columbian Exposition at Chicago. *Publications:* contributor to popular and technical magazines; pamphlets on money questions. *Address:* San Diego, California.   *Died Jan. 1927.*

GAGE, Sir William James, Kt 1918; publisher; *b* Peel County, Ontario, 1849; *s* of Andrew Gage and Mary Jane Grafton; *m* 1880, Ina, *d* of David Burnside, FEIS; four *d. Educ:* Brampton High School and Toronto Normal School (First-Class Certificate). Taught for several years; entered into partnership with Adam Miller & Co., Publishers, 1874; on death of Mr Miller, 1876, became head of Firm; later changed to W. J. Gage & Co., Ltd; President, Educational Book Co. of Toronto, and Kinleith Paper Mills Ltd, St Catherine's, Ont.; Vice-President, Chartered Trust and Executor Company. Chairman, Executive Committee of Toronto Branch, Victorian Order of Nurses; Founder and President of National Sanatorium Association, controlling Muskoka Cottage Sanatorium and Muskoka Free Hospital for Consumptives near Gravenhurst; Chairman of Toronto Free Hospital for Consumptives; also the Queen Mary Hospital for consumptive children; originated and successfully established in 1912 The King Edward Memorial Fund of One Million Dollars for Consumptives; President of the Toronto Board of Trade in 1910; organised and became First President of Associated Boards of Trade of Ontario, 1911; Delegate to 6th Chamber of Commerce in Australia, 1911; Knight of Grace of St John, 1913; contributed with his wife one hundred thousand dollars for the establishment of widows and children of Canadian soldiers, 1916; Hon. Degree of LLD was conferred by Mount Allison University for educational and philanthropic work, 1917. *Recreation:* golf. *Address:* Wychwood Park, Toronto, Canada. *Clubs:* National, York, Lambton, Toronto.
Died 14 Jan. 1921.

GAIMES, John Austin, DSO 1918; *b* 1886; *s* of Henry Austin Gaimes. *Educ:* Tonbridge School; entered HMS Britannia, 1901; Lieut-Comdr 1916. *Address:* c/o Admiralty, SW1.
Died 20 Jan. 1921.

GAINER, Rev. Canon Harry; Canon of the Cathedral, Georgetown, Guiana, since 1908; *b* 1858; *s* of late E. J. Gainer of Gloucester; unmarried. *Educ:* Grammar School, Gloucester; St Augustine's College, Canterbury. Ordained 1882, curate of the Cathedral, Georgetown, Guiana, 1883; Curate of St Philip's, Georgetown, 1883–85; perpetual Curate of St Mary's on the East Coast Demerara, 1885; Vicar of Enmore, 1892, and Rural Dean of Demarara, British Guiana, 1905; Secretary to the Synod of the Diocese for 14 years; retired on pension, 1914. *Publications:* Editor of the Diocesan Magazine for about 10 years, and as Secretary was responsible for Diocesan Synod Report for many years. *Recreations:* ecclesiastical architecture, church music, croquet. *Address:* Greenfield House, Greenfield, East Coast Demerara.   *Died 2 May 1920.*

GAINSBOROUGH, 3rd Earl of, *cr* 1841; **Charles William Francis Noel,** JP Cos of Gloucester and Worcester; JP, DL Co. of Rutland; Bt 1781; Baron Barham, 1805; Viscount Campden, Baron Noel, 1841; Lieutenant 10th Hussars, retired 1876; *b* 20 Oct. 1850; *s* of Charles George, 2nd Earl, and Lady Ida Adelaide Harriet Augusta Hay, *d* of 18th Earl of Erroll; *S* father, 1881; *m* 1st, 1876, Augusta Mary Catherine (*d* 1877), *e d* of late Robert Berkeley, Spetchley; one *d* decd; 2nd, 1880, Mary, *d* of James Arthur Dease, Turbotston, Co. Westmeath; two *s* two *d* (and one *s* decd). *Educ:* Oscott Roman Catholic Coll. *Heir:* *s* Viscount Campden, *b* 30 June 1884. *Address:* Exton Park, Oakham. *T:* Oakham 53. *Clubs:* Junior United Service, Marylebone Cricket.   *Died 17 April 1926.*

GAINSBOROUGH, 4th Earl of, *cr* 1841; **Arthur Edward Joseph Noel,** OBE 1919; TD 1919; JP Co. Rutland; Bt 1781; Baron Barham, 1805; Viscount Campden, Baron Noel, 1841; Major, the

Gloucestershire Regiment (TAR); *b* 30 June 1884; *e s* of 3rd Earl and Mary, *d* of James Arthur Dease, Turbotston, Co. Westmeath; *S* father, 1926; *m* 1915, Alice Mary, *e d* of Edward Eyre, Gloucester House, Park Lane, W1; one *s* one *d. Educ:* Downside; Exeter College, Oxford. Private Chamberlain of Sword and Cape to the late Pope and to Pope Pius XI; President of the Amateur Gymnastic Association; Vice-President, British Olympic Association; Attaché to the British Legations at Christiania and Stockholm, 1908–12, and to the British Embassy at Washington, USA, 1913–14, when he resigned; accompanied Dr Charles Harriss's Musical Festival throughout the British Empire, 1911. Served European War, France, 1915; DAMS Forces in Great Britain, Horse Guards, 1917–19; mentioned for valuable service during the War; organised, with Dr Harriss, Imperial Concert of 10,000 voices in Hyde Park on Empire Day, 1919. *Recreations:* hunting, shooting, lawn tennis. *Heir:* *s* Viscount Campden, *b* 24 Oct. 1923. *Address:* Exton Park, Oakham, Rutland; 30 Pont Street, SW1. *T:* Ken. 4534. *Clubs:* White's, Turf, Beefsteak, MCC.
Died 27 Aug. 1927.

GAIRDNER, Rev. Canon W. H. Temple, BA; Missionary of the Church Missionary Society, Cairo; *b* Ardrossan, Ayrshire, 31 July 1873; *s* of late Sir William Tennant Gairdner, KCB, MD, LLD, FRS; *m* Margaret Dundas, *d* of late J. O. Mitchell, LLD, Glasgow; three *s* two *d. Educ:* St Ninian's, Moffat; Rossall; Trinity College, Oxford (Exhibitioner). Missionary at Cairo, Egypt, 1899; Canon-Missioner of the Pro-Cathedral, Cairo. *Publications:* Life of D. M. Thornton; The Rebuke of Islam; Edinburgh, 1910; the Mishkāt al Anwār of al-Ghazzāli, an Introduction and Translation; The Phonetics of Arabic; Egyptian Colloquial Arabic; Arabic Syntax; Bible Dramas (Joseph and his Brothers; Passover-night; Saul and Stephen; King Hezekiah, a Tragical Drama). *Recreation:* music. *Address:* CMS, Boulac, Cairo. *TA:* Jardinier, Cairo.   *Died 22 May 1928.*

GAISFORD, Brig.-Gen. Richard Boileau, CB 1911; CMG 1900; *b* 14 Dec. 1854; *s* of late Rev. S. H. Gaisford, Cowthorpe Rectory, Wetherby, Yorkshire, and *g s* of late Joseph Yarker, of Ulverston; *m* Elsy, *d* of late Major-General A. H. Lindsay, CB, RHA; one *s* one *d. Educ:* Haileybury College; St John's College Oxford (BA Hons 1876). RMC Sandhurst, 1877; passed Staff College, 1893. Entered 21st Royal Scots Fusiliers, 1878; Adjutant, 1885–90; Brig.-Maj., Shorncliffe, 1896–99; DAAG South Africa, 1899; Assistant Adj.-General, Headquarters, South Africa, 1900–2; selected to command 3rd Battalion Royal Fusiliers, 1903–7; AQMG Scottish Command, 1908–11; was an Inspector of Infantry with temp. rank of Brig.-Gen., 1914–16; Hon. Brig.-Gen., 1917; served Boer War, 1881; Burmese Expedition, 1886–87 (medal with clasp); Boer War, 1899–1902 (despatches, Queen's medal four clasps, King's medal two clasps, CMG); European War, France, 1917 (British Victory and War Medal). *Address:* Conynger Hurst, Ulverston, Lancashire. *Club:* Naval and Military.   *Died 25 Sept. 1924.*

GAJJUMAL, Rai Sahib, Lala, ISO 1911; *b* 1857; descended from a respectable family of Kapur Khatris of Peshawar; father's name, Lala Jaggan Nath. *Educ:* C Mission School, Peshawar. Passed Matriculation Exam., Calcutta University, 1877; entered Govt Service as Record Keeper Commissioner's Office, 1879; joined the Khyber Agency as HC, 1880, and accompanied the Khyber Column during the 2nd Afghan war, 1879–80, and the Tirah Campaign of 1897–98; was present in the Fort at Landi Kotal when the Afghans attacked the Fort, and throughout the disturbances of 1908 (medals with clasps); title of Rai Sahib, 1910; coronation medal in 1911; retired 1912, on completion of 33 years of active service. *Address:* Peshawar City, India.

GALDOS, Benito Perez; Spanish novelist; Member of Spanish Academy and Deputy in the Cortes; *b* Las Palmas, Canary Islands, 1845. *Educ:* Madrid. Holds Medal of the Royal Society of Literature, Great Britain, 1917, as "most distinguished living representative of Spanish Literature." *Publications:* (novels, 1st, 2nd, 3rd, and 4th series, Episodios nacionales, 1873–1907); La Fontana de Oro, 1871; El Audaz; Doña Perfecta, 1876; Gloria (2 vols); Marianela; La familia de Léon Roch (12 vols); La Sombra; La Desheredada, 1881; El Doctor Centano; El Amigo Manso, 1883; Tormento; La de Bringas; Lo Pronibido; Fortunana y Jacinta (4 vols), 1887; Miau; La Incognita; Realidád; Angel Guerra (3 vols), 1890; Tristana; La Loca de la casa; Torquemada; Nazarin; Halma; Misericordia; El Abuelo, 1898; El Caballero Encantado; Casandra; (Plays) Realidád; La de San Quintin; Los Condenados; Voluntad; La Fiera; Electra, Marincha, Bárbaral; Amor y Ciencia; Pedro Minio; Casandra (drama). *Address:* Madrid, Hilarión Eslava 5, hotel.   *Died 4 Jan. 1920.*

GALER, John Maxcey, ISO 1903; *b* Rochester, Kent, 10 June 1839; *s* of late John Galer; *m* 1866, Louise Jane, *d* of late Henry Hughes

Allen of HM Civil Service; five s two d. *Educ:* private schools, Rochester. Appointed after competition to a Clerkship in HM Stationery Office, 1859; Accountant in HM Stationery Office, 1892–1904. *Recreations:* music, horticulture. *Address:* 110 Croxted Road, West Dulwich.   *Died 16 Nov. 1919.*

GALLAGHER, Sir James Michael, Kt 1917; *b* 1860; *s* of Patrick Gallagher, of Kilty Clogher, Co. Leitrim; *m* Annie, *d* of John O'Brien, Limerick. Lord Mayor of Dublin, 1916. *Address:* 149 Lower Baggott Street, Dublin.   *Died 2 Jan. 1926.*

GALLAGHER, Rt. Rev. John, DD; RC Bishop of Goulburn since 1900; *b* Castlederg, Co. Tyrone, 4 July 1846. *Educ:* St Patrick's College, Maynooth. Ordained, 1869; arrived at Goulburn, 1870; engaged in missionary work for first four years; President St Patrick's College for fourteen years; Permanent Rector of Wagga Wagga, 1887; Coadjutor Bishop, 1895. *Publications:* numerous lectures, sermons, addresses, and ssays, published in newspapers, magazines, and pamphlets. *Recreations:* incessant travelling by train and coach for official duties in his extensive diocese and to other dioceses and cities for special functions occupy nearly all his time. *Address:* Bishop's House, Goulburn, NSW. *T:* 16.

Died 26 Nov. 1923.

GALLAHER, Thomas, JP; Founder and Head of Gallaher, Limited, tobacco manufacturers; Member of Tariff Commission; *b* 1840. *Address:* Belfast. *TA:* Tobacco, Belfast. *T:* 6646 and 6647.

Died May 1927.

GALLETTI DI CADILHAC, Countess, (Hon. Margaret Isabella Collier); author; *b* 1846; *d* of 1st Baron Monkswell; *m* 1873, Count Arturo Galletti di Cadilhac (*d* 1912), Colonel in the Reserve, and Deputy in Italian Parliament; two *s* one *d*. *Publications:* The Camorristi and Other Tales, 1882; Our Home on the Adriatic, 1886; Prince Peerless, 1886; Babel, 1887; Rachel and Maurice, 1892; Annals of an Italian Village, 1896. *Address:* 4 Hillside, S Brent, Devon.

Died 27 June 1928.

GALLIENI, Joseph; général de division; Gouverneur militaire de Paris et Commandant en chef de l'armée de Paris; *b* St Beat, Haute Garonne, le 24 avril 1849; *m* 1882, Mlle Savelli; one *s* one *d*. *Educ:* Prytanée militaire de la Flèche, Saint Cyr. Lieutenant pendant la guerre de 1870–71; Commandements aux colonies: Soudan, Tonkin, Madagascar; Gouverneur général de Madagascar, 1896–1905; Général commandant le XIVe Corps; Gouverneur militaire de Lyon; membre du Conseil supérieur de la Guerre; Grand Croix de la Légion d'honneur; médaille militaire; membre correspondant de l'Academie des Sciences; membre d'honneur de nombreuses Sociétés scientifiques, géographiques; titulaire de la grande médaille d'or de la Société de Géographie et de nombreuses autres médailles de Sociétés scientifiques et de Chambres de Commerce. *Publications:* Voyage au Soudan Français, 1880–81; Deux Campagnes au Soudan Français, 1886–88; Trois Colonnes au Tonkin, 1894–95; Rapport sur Madagascar, 1896–99; Le Guide de l'immigrant, 1898; Rapport sur la pacification, l'organisation et l'administration de Madagascar, 1896–1905; Neuf ans à Madagascar, 1908. *Recreations:* marche à pied, lectures; mémoires et voyages, collection d'objets des colonies. *Address:* La Gabelle, St Raphael, Var, France. *Club:* Cercle militaire.

Died 27 May 1916.

GALLOP, Rev. Edward Jordan, MA; Hon. Canon of St Albans; *b* 1850; *s* of John Gallop, of Rio de Janeiro and New York, afterwards of Streatham, Surrey; *m* 1874, Julia, *d* of E. S. Judkins; three *s* one *d*. *Educ:* North America; Germany; King's College, London; Lincoln College, Oxford. Vicar of St Paul, Hemel Hempstead, 1878–1905; Chaplain, St Margaret's School, Bushey, 1906–17. *Address:* Denford, St Albans. *T:* St Albans 158. *M:* XN 8288. *Clubs:* Royal Societies, Royal Automobile.   *Died 26 April 1928.*

GALLOWAY, 11th Earl of, *cr* 1623; **Randolph Henry Stewart;** Lord Garlies, 1607; Bt 1627; Baron Stewart of Garlies (GB), 1796; *b* Galloway House, 14 Oct. 1836; *s* of 9th Earl and Lady Harriet Blanche Somerset, 7th *d* of 6th Duke of Beaufort; *S* brother, 1901; *m* 1891, Amy Mary Pauline, *d* of late Anthony John Cliffe of Bellevue, Co. Wexford; two *s* (the 2nd *s*, Lieut Hon. Keith Stewart, Black Watch, Royal Highlanders, killed in action at the head of his platoon, at Aubers Ridge, 9 May 1915. Formerly Captain 42nd Royal Highlanders; served Crimea, 1855 (medal with clasp, for Sebastopol, Turkish medal); Indian Mutiny, 1857–59 (medal with clasp, for Lucknow). Owner of about 69,000 acres. *Heir: s* Lord Garlies, *b* 21 Nov. 1892. *Address:* Cumloden, Newton-Stewart, NB; Garlies Lodge, Bargrennan, NB; Glen Trool Lodge, Bargrennan, NB. *TA:* Randolph,

Newton-Stewart, Scotland. *M:* LB 7843. *Clubs:* Army and Navy Bachelors'.   *Died 7 Feb. 1920*

GALLOWAY, Admiral Arthur Archibald Campbell; *b* Delhi, 30 June 1855; *s* of A. Galloway, Magistrate in Indian Civil Service, who was *s* of Major-General Sir A. Galloway, Chairman East India Company; mother was of the Campbells of Melfort; *m* Evelyn Royston, 2nd *d* of Edward Rawson-Walker, late HM Consul Philippine Islands; two *s* one *d*. *Educ:* Carshalton House, Carshalton Burney's Naval Academy. Joined navy, 1869; Lieut 1876 Commander, 1891; Captain, 1898; Rear-Admiral, 1907; Vice-Admiral, 1913; Admiral, retired 1916. ADC to King Edward VII 1906–7; served in Egypt, 1882; saved lives from drowning in 1873 1877, 1882, 1885, 1911 (2); seen much service in revolutions; selected to command Portsmouth Barracks after the mutiny, 1906; has commanded 11 ships, 2 establishments, and 1 squadron. *Recreations* formerly boxing, rowing, football, now cycling, swimming, rowing. *Address:* Barsham House, Bedford. *Club:* Junior United Service.

Died 12 Feb. 1918.

GALLOWAY, Sir James, KBE 1918; CB 1917; MD, LLD 1919; FRCP, FRCS; Colonel AMS; Senior Physician, and Lecturer on Medicine, Charing Cross Hospital; Censor, Royal College of Physicians; Consulting Physician, Metropolitan Asylums Board; Examiner in Medicine, University of London; late Consulting Physician, 1st and 2nd Armies, BEF, and Chief Commissioner for Medical Services, Ministry of National Service; Examiner Conjoint Board, Royal Colleges of Physicians and Surgeons, England; Member Examining Board, Royal Navy, Medical Service; *b* Calcutta, 10 Oct. 1862; *s* of James Galloway, Calcutta, and Jeanne Hermina de Villeneuve; *m* 1898, Jessie Hermina Sawers; two *s* two *d*. *Educ:* Chanonry School, Aberdeen; Aberdeen University. AM 1883; MD 1892 (Highest Honours). Subsequently became a Fellow of the Royal Colleges of Physicians, and of Surgeons in London, and an Examiner in Medicine in the University of Aberdeen. After a period of study and of teaching at the London Hospital, was appointed to the Medical Staff of Charing Cross Hospital (1894), and engaged in the teaching and practice of medicine. After the South African War, appointed to serve on the Advisory Board for Army Medical Services. *Publications:* Morton Lecture on Cancer, Royal College of Surgeons, England; late editor of the British Journal of Dermatology; numerous papers in scientific and medical journals; Story of Saint Mary Roncevall; Eleanor of Castile; Historical Sketches of Old Charing. 1914. *Recreation:* field studies. *Address:* 54 Harley Street, W1. *T:* 1148 Paddington.   *Died 18 Oct. 1922.*

GALLOWAY, Maj.-Gen. John Mawby Clossey, JP Co. Southampton; Colonel; 27th Light Cavalry, Indian Army; *b* 19 April 1840; *s* of Major Thomas Leech Lennox Galloway, 10th Foot, and Isabella Ann Coffin; *m* Emilie, *d* of Aylmer G. W. Harris, Mysore and Nagpore Commissions; three *s* one *d*. *Educ:* Cheltenham Coll. Served Indian Mutiny, 1858–59 (medal with clasp); Burmese War, 1886 (medal with clasp); granted the Distinguished Service Reward, 1894. *Address:* Egmore, East Cliffe, Bournemouth. *Clubs:* Bournemouth, Bournemouth Golf.

Died 25 Oct. 1916.

GALLOWAY, Sir William, Kt 1924; Hon. DSc Wales; FGS; Hon. MIME; *b* 12 Feb. 1840; *s* of late William Galloway, JP, of Paisley; *m* 1st, Christiana Maud Mary, *d* of late W. F. Gordon, of Milrig, Ayrshire; two *s*; 2nd, Mary Gwenap Douglas, *d* of late Captain Wood, RMLI, of Nunlands, Surrey. *Educ:* private school; University of Giessen; Bergakademie, Freiberg; University College, London. Formerly HM Inspector of Mines in the West of Scotland and South Wales Districts; past Professor of Mining in the University College of South Wales and Monmouthshire; Fellow of the Institute of Directors; Past President and Hon. Member S Wales Institute of Engineers; a member of the Panel of Referees appointed under the Coal Mines Act, 1911; one of the Central Examiners appointed by the Board for Mining Examinations; External Examiner in Mining for the University of Birmingham, the Treforest School of Mines, etc; author of the coal-dust theory of great colliery explosions; investigated the causes and mode of occurrence of colliery explosions; suggested the use of stone-dust as a means of preventing great colliery explosions, 1896; again suggested in 1908, after which it was universally adopted; made series of experiments with different kinds of explosives fired into mixture of gas, air, and coaldust for the Royal Commission on Accidents in Mines; determined the relation between height of firedamp cap and proportion of firedamp in the air of mines; invented the guides for sinking pits. Presented with the Shaw gold medal by the Royal Society of Arts, a special gold medal and later an illuminated album by the South Wales Institute of Engineers, the medal of the Institution of Mining Engineers, and his portrait and later a gold watch by the Monmouthshire and South Wales Coalowners' Assoc. in recognition of his researches into the action of Coaldust in Colliery Explosions; described External Capillarity in 1926. *Publications:* twenty-one papers (four in collaboration with R. H. Scott, FRS) on researches as to the causes of colliery explosions, eight of which were read before, and published by the Royal Society; paper on the Flying Fish; nineteen papers, mostly on mining and kindred subjects; course of lectures delivered before, and published by the South Wales Institute of Engineers; four of the subjects in Practical Coal-Mining, etc. *Recreation:* bicycling. *Address:* 17 Park Place, Cardiff. *T:* 8907 Cardiff. *Club:* Athenæum.

Died 2 Nov. 1927.

GALLWEY, Col Edmond Joseph, CB 1900; *b* 7 Feb. 1850; *s* of late H. Gallwey, JP, of Tramore, Co. Waterford; *m* 1871, Augusta, *d* of J. Burtchaell, JP, of Carbally, Co. Clare. Entered 13th Light Infantry, 1870; Capt. 1880; Major, 1886; Lieut-Col commanding 2nd Somerset Lt Infantry, 1898; Col 13th Regt Dist, 1902; Zululand, 1877–79, including Kambula Hill and Ulundi (medal with clasp); S Africa, 1899–1902 (Queen's medal 5 clasps, King's, 2 clasps); Tugela Heights and Relief of Ladysmith (CB, despatches 3 times); commanding 13th Regimental District, 1902–5; Col in charge of Records, Western Counties, 1906; retired, 1907; 11 District, 1915–18 (mentioned). *Recreations:* shooting, stag-hunting, rackets, cricket, golf. *Club:* Junior United Service.

Died 11 May 1927.

GALLWEY, Sir Ralph William Frankland Payne-, 3rd Bt, *cr* 1812; formerly Lieutenant Rifle Brigade; *b* 19 Aug. 1848; *e* s of Sir William Payne-Gallwey, 2nd Bt and Emily Anne, 3rd *d* of Sir Robert Frankland-Russell, 7th Bt; *S* father, 1881; *m* 1877, Edith Alice, *d* of T. M. Usborne, Clifton, Co. Cork; four *d* (and one *s* decd). *Educ:* Eton. *Publications:* The Fowler in Ireland, 1882; The Book of Duck Decoys, 1886; Letters to Young Shooters, 3 vols, 1891–96; The Cross-Bow, 1903; The Mystery of Maria Stella, Lady Newborough, 1907; The History of the George of Charles 1st, 1908; High Pheasants in Theory and in Practice, 1913. *Recreations:* shooting, golf, cricket, fishing, well known as experienced and enthusiastic wild-fowler. *Heir:* *n* Frankland-Payne-Gallwey, *b* 23 Dec. 1889. *Address:* Thirkleby Park, Thirsk. *Clubs:* Carlton; Yorkshire, York.

Died 24 Nov. 1916.

GALLWEY, Capt. William Thomas Frankland Payne-, MVO 1908; Grenadier Guards; *b* 5 March 1881; *o* s of Sir Ralph William Frankland Payne-Gallwey, 3rd Bt. Entered Army, 1900; Capt. 1908; served S Africa, 1901–2 (medal, 2 clasps); Coronation medal. *Address:* Thirkleby Park, Thirsk.

Died 14 Sept. 1914 (Presumed).

GALPIN, Rev. Arthur John, DD Oxford; Hon. Canon of Canterbury Cathedral since 1910; Rector of Saltwood, Hythe, since 1910; Member of Kent Education Committee since 1911; *b* Dorchester, Dorset, 3 March 1861; *s* of John Galpin, JP; *m* 1900, Millicent Jane, *d* of late Rev. F. H. Hichens, Hon. Canon of Canterbury; one *s* one *d*. *Educ:* Sherborne School; Trinity Coll., Oxford (Senior Scholar, 1st Class Classical Mods, 1880, 1st Class Final School of Lit. Hum., 1883). Assistant Private Secretary to Lord Lansdowne, Governor-General of Canada, and Tutor to his sons, 1883–85; Classical Lecturer, Trinity College, Oxford, 1886–87; Assistant Master, Marlborough College, 1887–96; Housemaster, 1893–96; Headmaster, King's School, Canterbury, 1896–1910. *Recreations:* music, motoring, archæology. *Address:* Saltwood Rectory, Hythe, Kent. *M:* KE 7069.

Died 2 Oct. 1926.

GALSWORTHY, Sir Edwin Henry; Kt 1887; JP, DL; late Chairman of Metropolitan Asylums Board, resigned 1901; *b* 24 Dec. 1831; *m* 1st, 1858, Eleanor (*d* 1872), *d* of late Charles Pennington, Manchester; 2nd, 1873, Laura, *d* of late John Oakes, Manchester; five *s* three *d*. *Educ:* City of London School. *Address:* 26 Sussex Place, Regent's Park, NW1. *T:* Paddington 147.

Died 21 Dec. 1920.

GAMBLE, Admiral Edward Harpur, CB 1902; RN; *b* 6 Sept. 1849; *m* 1904, Charlotte Mainwaring, 3rd *d* of W. H. Prance. Served Egypt, 1882 (medal, Khedive's star); Gambia, 1894 (despatches, medal with clasp); Brass River, 1895 (medal). *Address:* Rowe House, Verham Dean, near Hungerford.

Died 18 Nov. 1925.

GAMBLE, Frederick William, DSc 1900; FRS 1907; FZS; Professor of Zoology, University of Birmingham, since 1909; late Assistant-Director of the Zoological Laboratories, and Lecturer in Zoology, University of Manchester; President of Zoology Section, British Association, Toronto, 1924; *b* Manchester, 13 July 1869; *e* surv. *s* of late William Gamble and late Mrs Gamble of Brantfell, Arnside, Westmorland; *m* 1904, Ellen, *d* of Rev. J. M. Bamford, Arnside. *Educ:* Manchester Grammar School; Manchester and Leipzig Universities. 1st Class Hons BSc 1891; Bishop Berkeley Fellowship, 1892; MSc, 1893. Junior Lecturer and Demonstrator in Zoology, 1893; Senior Lecturer and Demonstrator, 1895. *Publications:* Animal Life; The Animal World; editor of 5th, 6th, and 7th editions of Practical Zoology, by Marshall and Hurst; author of many papers in the Transactions and Proceedings of the Royal Society, Quarterly Journal of Microscopical Science, and other scientific journals. *Recreation:* gardening. *Address:* The University, Birmingham.

Died 14 Sept. 1926.

GAMBLE, James Sykes, CIE 1899; FRS, FLS; retired officer of the Indian Forest Service; *b* London, 2 July 1847; *s* of late Harpur Gamble, MD, RN; *m* 1911, Gertrude, *d* of late Rev. A. S. Latter. *Educ:* Royal Naval School, New Cross; Magdalen College, Oxford (MA); Ecole Nationale des Eaux et Forêts, Nancy, France. Entered Indian Forest Department, 1871; last appointment, Conservator of Forests, School Circle, NWP and Oudh, and Director of the Imperial Forest School, Dehra Dun, India; for some time Fellow of the University of Madras; Jury Medal and Diploma, Paris International Exposition, 1900, Barclay Medal, Asiatic Society of Bengal, 1915; Examiner in Forestry, University of Oxford, at various times and Lecturer on Indian Forest Botany. *Publications:* List of Trees, Shrubs, and Climbers of the Darjeeling District, Bengal, 1877, 2nd edn 1895; A Manual of Indian Timbers, 1881, 2nd edn 1902; The Bambuseæ of British India (Ann. R. Bot. Gard., Calcutta, 1895); Materials for a Flora of the Malay Peninsula (with late Sir George King); Flora of the Madras Presidency. *Address:* Highfield, East Liss, Hants. *T:* East Liss 10; 63 Kew Green, Surrey. *Club:* Athenæum.

Died 16 Oct. 1925.

GAMLEY, Henry Snell, RSA 1920 (ARSA 1908); RBS 1926; sculptor; *b* Logie-Pert, Craigo, 1865; *m* 1898, Margaret, *e* d of Alexander Hogg, Carnoustie; one *s* one *d*. *Educ:* James Gillespie's School, Edinburgh; Royal Institution, Edinburgh. National Gold and Silver Medals. *Works:* Ideal works; The Whisper, A Message to the Sea; Inspiration and Achievement, for Usher Hall, Edinburgh; St Andrew, for Grand Lodge of Scotland. Statue of His Majesty King Edward, Holyrood Palace; War Memorial, Cupar, Fife; War Memorial, Montrose; War Memorial, St Giles' Cathedral, Edinburgh. Portraits: J. B. Dunlop, Joseph Laing Waugh, John Geddie, Sir William Marris, Charles Murray, LLD; Medallions: William Murdoch, Alexander Anderson, Surfaceman, Sir Alexander R. Simpson, Lord Salvesen, Clarinda. *Recreation:* music. *Address:* The Studio, 7 Hope Street Lane, Edinburgh.

Died 24 Oct. 1928.

GANGA RAM, Rai Bahadur Sir Lala, Kt 1922; CIE 1903; MVO 1911; MIME, MICE; *b* May 1851; *m*; three *s*. *Educ:* Thomason College. Entered India Public Works Department, 1873; Executive Engineer, 1883; Superintendent Coronation Durbar Works, Delhi, 1903; retired, 1903; Superintending Engineer Patiala State; retired, 1911; Consulting Engineer, Delhi Durbar, 1911; patentee slide rule, bricks for wells. *Publication:* Pocket-Book of Engineering. *Address:* Lahore. *TA:* Ganganivas, Lahore. *M:* P340.

Died 10 July 1927.

GANNON, Hon. James Conley, KC; MLC, New South Wales since 1904; *b* 1860. Called to Bar, NSW, 1887; Attorney-General, 1907. *Address:* 165 Phillip Street, Sydney, NSW.

Died 1 Oct. 1924.

GANT, Hon. Tetley, CMG 1918; MA Oxon; President of the Legislative Council of Tasmania, 1907–26; Chancellor of the University of Tasmania, 1914–24; *b* Bradford, Yorkshire, 19 July 1856; *s* of James Greaves Tetley Gant; *m* Frances Amy, *d* of Lavington Roope, of Hobart; one *d*. *Educ:* Rugby; St John's College, Oxford. Called to Bar, Inner Temple, 1884; elected to the Legislative Council of Tasmania for Buckingham, 1901; Chairman of Committees of the Council, 1904–7. *Club:* Tasmanian, Hobart.

Died 7 Feb. 1928.

GARDE, Engineer Captain Robert Boles, CBE 1919; RN (retired); Marine Engineer Superintendent South-Eastern & Chatham Railway, Dover; *b* 1863; 3rd *s* of Dr H. W. Garde, MB, Timoleague, Co. Cork; *m* 1899, Amy Ethel, *y* d of T. Richards, Mutley, Plymouth; no *c*. *Educ:* Midleton College, Co. Cork. Joined HMS Marlborough as Naval Engineering Student, 1879; spent the whole of life in Navy up to 1919; during European War was Admiralty Engineer Overseer at J. S. White & Co, Cowes, and later at Sunderland and Hartlepool districts (CBE). *Recreations:* all sports, particularly cricket, shooting, boat-sailing. *M:* DL 473.

Died 29 Oct. 1921.

GARDINER, Rev. Frederic Evelyn; Hon. Canon of Truro; Rector of Bishopsbourne, Kent, 1918–23; late Vicar of Holy Trinity, Folkestone. *Address:* 15 Castle Hill Avenue, Folkestone.
Died 30 May 1928.

GARDINER, Frederick William, ISO 1902; Clerk in the Office of the Parliamentary Counsel, 1871–1914; *b* 1849; *s* of late W. Gardiner, of Tetbury. *Address:* 25 Malwood Road, Balham Hill, SW.
Died 24 April 1918.

GARDINER, James; MP (L) Kinross and Western Perthshire, 1918–22, (NL) 1922–1923; *b* near Crieff, 1860; *s* of John Gardiner, Eastmill, and Harriet A. B. D. Allan; *m* 1st, 1887, Elizabeth Maule (*d* 1921), *d* of John Christie, Engineer, Ruthvenvale; 2nd, 1922, Elizabeth, *y d* of late Daniel Christie, Mokameh, Bengal, and Drummondearnoch, Comrie. *Educ:* Morrison's Academy, Crieff; privately. Director of Scottish Chamber of Agriculture; Hon. President of Scottish National Farmers' Union; Member of Ministry of Foods, Potato Advisory Committee; Member of Council National Institute of Agricultural Botany; Expert in Agricultural Plant Breeding and raiser of several of the most popular immune varieties of potatoes now in cultivation. JP Perthshire; keen on social and temperance reform; authority on practical agriculture in all its advanced branches. *Address:* Dargill, Crieff. *T:* Crieff 133. *Clubs:* Scottish National Liberal, Edinburgh; Liberal, Glasgow.
Died 31 Dec. 1924.

GARDINER, Rev. Canon William; Vicar of Southbroom, Wilts, 1897–1918; Canon of Salisbury; Prebendary of Teignton Regis since 1910; Rural Dean of Avebury (Cannings Portion), 1906–19; Acting Chaplain to the Forces at Devizes; *b* 24 March 1848; *s* of Rev. R. Gardiner of Wellesford Manor and Bindon House, Somersetshire, and Augusta Elizabeth, *d* of Robert Jackson of Swallowfield, Wellington, Somerset; *m* 1873, Jessie, *d* of Rev. William T. Redfern, Vicar of St James, Taunton; two *s* three *d*. *Educ:* Taunton College School; private tuition; Exeter College, Oxford; BD Oxon; *ad eundem* MA, TCD, and Member of the Senate. Captain Oxford University Volunteers; Grand Chaplain of English Freemasons, 1899. Vicar of St George's Claines, Worcester, 1873; St Mary's, Marlborough, 1887; Rural Dean of Marlborough, 1891–97; member of Worcester School Board; Hon. Secretary of Royal City and County of Worcester Nursing Institution, of Savernake Hospital, Wilts. *Publications:* Southbroom Catechisings on the Church Catechism; Benefice Record Book for Deanery of Cannings. *Recreation:* fishing. *Address:* St Alban's Priory, Wallingford, Berks.
Died 10 April 1925.

GARDNER, Alice, MA Bristol; Associate of Newnham College, Cambridge, since 1893; Reader in Byzantine History in the University of Bristol since 1919; *b* Hackney, 1854; *y d* of late Thomas Gardner, of the Stock Exchange, and Ann, *d* of Peter Pearse. *Educ:* Laleham, Clapham Park, etc; Newnham College, Cambridge (student, 1876–79); First Class in Historical Tripos. Assistant Mistress in the Girls' High School, Plymouth, 1880–82; Professor of Ancient and Modern History in Bedford College, London, 1883–84; Lecturer in History at Newnham College, Cambridge, 1884–1914; temporary lecturer in the University of Bristol, 1915–19; first Secretary of the University Association of Women Teachers; a Vice-President of the Historical Association; on Council of Royal Historical Society; Member of British Institute of Pilosophical Studies. *Publications:* Synesius of Cyrene, Philosopher and Bishop; Friends of the Olden Time (for children); Rome the Middle of the World (a sequel to above); Julian, Emperor and Philosopher; Studies in John the Scot; The Conflict of Duties, and other Essays; Theodore of Studium, his Life and Times; Letters to a Godchild; Supplementary Chapter to English Translation of Professor Hans von Schubert's Church History; The Lascarids of Nicæa; Within our Limits; Chapter in the Faith and the War; article in History on some Episodes in the History of Mediæval Salonika; History of Sacrament in Relation to Thought and Progress; A Short History of Newnham College; various reviews. *Recreation:* country walking. *Address:* 8 Canynge Road, Clifton, Bristol. *Clubs:* Ladies' University; Ladies', Clifton.
Died 11 Nov. 1927.

GARDNER, Sir Ernest, Kt 1923; JP; MP (C) Wokingham Division of Berks, 1901–18; Windsor Division, 1918–22; *b* 1846; *s* of Joseph Goodwin Gardner, of Havering, Essex; *m* 1st, 1878, Mary (*d* 1903), *d* of William Peto of Cannon Court, Cookham, Berks; 2nd, 1910, Amy Inglis, *y d* of Lt-Gen. J. W. Laurie, CB. *Educ:* Orsett House, Essex. Successor to Berkshire property of his uncle, John Silvester, Spencers, Maidenhead, 1864; JP, Maidenhead, 1887; Mayor, Maidenhead, 1892–93; JP, Berkshire, 1895; County Councillor, 1889;

Alderman, 1898; Liveryman Drapers' Company, 1873, member of Court, 1895, Master of Company, 1901–2; yeoman. *Address:* Spencers, Maidenhead.
Died 7 Aug. 1925.

GARDNER, Ven. George Lawrence Harter, MusB Oxon. *Educ:* Cheltenham College; Corpus Christi, Cambridge (MA). Curate of St Mary's, Nottingham, 1875–84; All Saints, Cheltenham, 1884–1911; Diocesan Chaplain to the Bishop of Birmingham, 1911; Archdeacon of Aston, 1913–20; Archdeacon of Cheltenham, 1920–24; Hon. Canon, Gloucester Cathedral, 1906–11–20; Hon. Canon, Birmingham Cathedral, 1911. *Publications:* Worship and Music; English Catholicism; joint Editor of a Manual of English Church Music. *Address:* The Deanery, Marlow, Bucks. *T:* Marlow 29. *Club:* Church Imperial.
Died 20 Sept. 1925.

GARDNER, Rt. Hon. Sir James Tynte Agg, Kt 1916; PC 1924; MP (U) Cheltenham since 1917; *b* Cheltenham, 25 Nov. 1846; *e s* of late James Agg Gardner of Cheltenham and Emily Hopkyns Northey of Oving House, Bucks; unmarried. *Educ:* Harrow; Trinity College, Camb. Barrister, Inner Temple. Contested (C) Cheltenham, 1868, 1880, and 1906; MP (C) Cheltenham, 1874–80, 1885–95, 1900–6. JP Glos; Lord of the Manor of Cheltenham. *Address:* Queen's Hotel, Cheltenham. *Clubs:* Carlton, St James's, Garrick, Windham.
Died 9 Aug. 1928.

GARDNER, Sir Robert, Kt 1905; member of firm of Craig, Gardner, and Co., Chartered Accountants of Dublin; *b* 14 April 1838; *s* of late John Gardner, of Ballymoney, Co. Antrim; *m* 1895, Norah Kathleen, *d* of Captain P. L. Peacocke of Villaggio, Dalkey. *Educ:* Ballymoney. JP for Dublin. *Address:* Ashley, Clyde Road, Dublin. *Clubs:* Royal Irish Yacht, Stephen's Green, Dublin.
Died 1920.

GARDNER, William, MD, CM; Emeritus Professor of Gynæcology in McGill University, Montreal; Consulting Gynæcologist to the Royal Victoria Hospital; *b* Province of Quebec, 1845; *e s* of William Gardner; *m* Jane, *d* of A. Cantin, of Montreal; no *c*. *Educ:* McGill University, Montreal. Graduated with honours, 1867; general practice for several years, then specialist in Gynæcology; Professor of Medical Jurisprudence, Bishop's Coll., 1870–75; McGill University, 1875–83; Professor of Gynæcology, 1883–1910; Consulting Gynæcologist to the Montreal General Hospital; Past President of the Montreal Medico-Chirurg. Society; Past President and present Member of Council of the Montreal Art Association. *Recreation:* billiards. *Address* 457 Sherbrooke Street West, Montreal. *T:* Up 1263. *Clubs:* Mount Royal, University, Montreal.
Died 20 Sept. 1926.

GARFIT, William, JP, DL; Sheriff of Lincolnshire, 1892; Chairman of Holland Division Lincolnshire Quarter Sessions, 1900–14; banker; Director Lloyds Bank; *b* 9 Nov. 1840; *s* of late William Garfit, Boston; *m* 1868, Mary, *d* of C. Norman; one *d*. *Educ:* Harrow; Trinity College, Camb. Capt, 2nd Lincoln RV, 1874–81. MP (C) Boston, 1895–1906. *Address:* Mortimer House, Egerton Gardens, SW. *Clubs:* Carlton, New University, Wellington. *M:* DO 94.
Died 29 Oct. 1920.

GARFORTH, Rear-Admiral Edmund St John, CB 1887; DL, JP, Sussex; *b* 1836; *s* of late William Garforth, Wiganthorpe, near York, JP, and Louisa, *d* of St John Charlton, Apley Castle, Salop; *m* 1871, Haidie, *d* of late E. Cooper, Failand House, near Bristol; one *s* two *d*. Served in Baltic War, 1854 (medal); Crimean War, 1854–55; present at siege of Sebastopol (medal with clasp, Turkish medal); New Zealand War (medal), 1859–60; in command of expedition against Masnàah Forts (Persian Gulf), 1874 (thanked by Indian Government); in command of Naval Brigade attached to Larut Field Force, 1875–76 (Perak medal); in Egyptian War, 1882 (medal, bronze star, and 3rd class Order of Osmanieh); while in command of Hastings Div. of Coast Guards, 1870, was presented by German Emperor with a silver telescope for assisting in saving lives of German emigrants wrecked off that coast; created CB on occasion of HM Jubilee, 1887. *Address:* 14 Upper Maze Hill, St Leonards-on-Sea. *Clubs:* United Service; Honorary member Royal Yacht Squadron, Cowes.
Died 27 Dec. 1920.

GARFORTH, Sir William Edward, Kt 1914; JP Cheshire, 1876, and WR Yorks, 1892; LLD; *b* 30 Dec. 1845; 2nd *s* of late William Garforth of Dukinfield, Cheshire, JP; *m* 1882, Mary E., *d* of late Rev. Canon Eager, MA, RD, Rector of Ashton-under-Lyne. MInstCE; Past President Mining Association of Great Britain; President InstME; Chairman of Mining Committee, University of Leeds; awarded Fothergill gold medal RSA; First Medal InstME; Peake Gold Medal,

Mid. InstME; Vice-Pres. Jurors Brussels Exhibition, 1910. *Address:* Snydale Hall, near Pontefract. *Club:* Author's.

Died 1 Oct. 1921.

GARLAND, Charles Tuller. *Address:* 26 Grosvenor Street, W1. *T:* Mayfair 5540; Avenue House, Newmarket; Moreton Hall, Moreton Morrell, Warwick. *Died 10 June 1921.*

GARLAND, Hon. John, KC 1910; MLC since 1908; *b* Cowhythe, Banffshire, 17 Sept. 1863; *s* of Robert Garland; *m* 1896, Isabel, *d* of Edward Chisholm, Sydney; one *d*. *Educ:* Fordyce Academy; Aberdeen and Edinburgh Universities. MA (Phil. Honours), Aberdeen, 1882; LLB (Highest Distinction), Edinburgh, 1886; called to Bar, New South Wales, 1888; Member of the Legislative Assembly for Wollahra, 1898–1901; and for Tamworth, 1903–4; Minister for Justice and Solicitor-General, 1909–10; Minister for Justice and Solicitor-General since 1916; Representative of the Government in the Legislative Council; Procurator of the Presbyterian Church of New South Wales since 1894; of Australia since 1901; Councillor of St Andrews College; representative of the Legislative Council on Senate of Sydney University since 1915; President, Sydney University Law Society, 1915; Vice President of the National Association of New South Wales. *Recreation:* golf. *Address:* Cairnton, Belle Vue Hill, Sydney, NSW. *Clubs:* Australian, University, Royal Sydney Golf, Sydney.

Died Feb. 1921.

GARNER, Col Cathcart, CMG 1919; CBE 1919; MB, BCh Trinity College, Dublin, 1885; Kt of Grace, Order of St John of Jerusalem; Officer, Legion of Honour; AMS Retired Pay; late Under Secretary of State (Health), Ministry of Interior, Egypt; *b* 9 Aug. 1861; *e s* of late Wm Hastings Garner of St Grellans, Monkstown, Co. Dublin; *m* 1900, Annette Jane, *y d* of late J. Nadin, MRCS, LRCP, Tipperary; one *s*. *Educ:* St Columba; Trinity College, Dublin. Entered Army Medical Dept, 1886; seconded for Civil Service Egyptian Govt, 1896; President International Quarantine Board, Alexandria, 1898; Deputy Director General Public Health Dept, Cairo, 1907; rejoined Army for war service, 8 Aug. 1914; Gallipoli, Egypt and Palestine (despatches three times); ADMS of Occupied Enemy Territory, Palestine, 1917–19. Commander Order of George I of Greece; for former services in Egypt, 2nd Class Medjidie and 3rd Class Osmanieh; Grand Officer Order of the Nile. *Recreations:* sailing, shooting. *Address:* 19 St Helen's Parade, Southsea. *Clubs:* Windham, Royal Thames Yacht; Royal Albert Yacht, Southsea.

Died 5 Feb. 1928.

GARNETT, Frank Walls, CBE 1918; JP; President, Royal College of Veterinary Surgeons, 1914–19; *b* 1867; *s* of late Wm Garnett, Bowness, Westmorland; *m* 1895, Susannah, *d* of Joseph Goddard, The Priory, Hampstead. *Address:* 10 Red Lion Square, WC1; Dalegarth, Windermere. *Died 22 Aug. 1922.*

GARRATT, Brig.-Gen. Sir Francis Sudlow, KCMG 1918 (CMG 1915); CB 1902; DSO 1900; JP, Devon; *b* 18 June 1859; *e s* of late Rev. Sudlow Garratt, Merifield, Devonport; *m* 1st, 1897, Frances Lucy (*d* 1921), *e d* of Colonel Troyte of Huntsham Court, Devon; three *d*; 2nd, 1925, Florence Kate, *d* of late David L. Gooch of Anerley. *Educ:* Winchester; Sandhurst. Appointed 2nd Lieut 6th Dragoon Guards, 1878; Captain, 1887; Major, 1897; second in command 6th Dragoon Guards, 1900; commanded a column in South Africa with local rank of Lieutenant-Colonel 3rd Dragoon Guards, 1903; Lieutenant-Colonel 6th Dragoon Guards, 1904; commanded Jhansi Brigade, 1905–6; Ambala Cavalry Brigade with temporary rank Brigadier-General, 1907–9; 4th Cavalry Brigade, 1909–11; served Afghanistan, 1879–80 (medal); South Africa, 1899–1902 (despatches, Queen's medal 6 clasps, King's medal 2 clasps, CB, DSO); European War, 1914–18 (despatches five times, CMG, KCMG). *Address:* Ashbury, Devon. *Club:* Naval and Military.

Died 23 June 1928.

GARRATT, Lieut-Col John Arthur Thomas, JP, DL; late Lieutenant-Colonel Grenadier Guards, and Captain, 1st Devon Yeomanry Cavalry; *b* 1842; *o s* of late John Garratt, and Anne, *d* of Richard Heming; *m* 1867, Georgina Henrietta, *d* of John Henry, *s* of Jerome, Count Fane-De Salis, of Dawley Court; two *s* two *d*. *Educ:* Eton; Christ Church, Oxford. *Address:* Bishop's Court, Exeter. *Clubs:* Guards, Travellers'. *Died 10 June 1919.*

GARRETT, R. W., MA, MD, CM; late Professor of Obstetrics, Queen's University, Kingston, Canada; *b* Brock, Ontario, 31 May 1853; father English, mother Irish; *m* 1887, M. L., *d* of A. S. Kirkpatrick, County Crown Attorney; two *s* one *d*. *Educ:* Preliminary Ontario College, Picton; MA Trinity College, Toronto; MD Queen's

University, Kingston, Ontario. Practised profession in Kingston; Professor of Anatomy in the Women's Medical School; Demonstrator of Anatomy Royal College of Physicians and Surgeons; Professor of Anatomy; Senior Surgeon Kingston General Hospital, and Surgeon Major in the 14th Batt. Princess of Wales' Own Rifles. *Publications:* Medical and Surgical Gynæcology; editor, Kingston Medical Quarterly. *Recreations:* boating, fishing, and cycling; also very fond of photography. *Died 1925.*

GARRETT, Samuel; JP Suffolk; late Head of firm of Parker Garrett & Co., Solicitors, St Michael's Rectory, Cornhill, EC; on retirement from business in 1921 elected Hon. Member of Lloyd's and of Institute of London Underwriters and Association of Average Adjusters; *b* 20 Nov. 1850; 3rd *s* of late Newson Garrett of Aldeburgh, Suffolk; *m* 1882, Clara, *d* of late Col Thornbury, Bombay Army; three *s* one *d*. *Educ:* Rugby; Peterhouse, Cambridge. 8th in First Class in Classical Tripos; Le Bas Prize; Fellow of Peterhouse, 1875. Admitted as solicitor, 1876; entered into partnership with late Sir Henry Parker in 1879, and became head of the firm on the latter's death in 1894; Member of the Council of the Law Society, 1907, and served as President of the Society, 1917–18; served on Departmental Committees appointed by Lord Chancellor in 1918 on British and Foreign Legal Procedure, and in 1919 on the Public Trustee's Office. *Publications:* Address to the Law Society in 1910 on Codification; Address to the Law Society as President in 1918 on A Ministry of Justice and its Task; Dissenting Report as Member of the Committee on the Public Trustee's Office in 1919, in which radical changes in the organisation of the office were recommended. *Recreations:* yachting, gardening. *Address:* Gower House, Aldeburgh, Suffolk. *Clubs:* City of London, Royal Thames Yacht.

Died 22 April 1923.

GARRICK, Rev. James Percy; late Rector of Blofield, Norwich; Hon. Canon, Norwich, 1889. *Educ:* Caius College, Cambridge (MA, 9th Wrangler, Senior Fellow, and Tutor). Curate of St Marylebone. *Address:* Merlewood, Old Cotton, Norwich.

Died 27 Feb. 1919.

GARROW, Hon. James Thompson; Justice of the Court of Appeal, Ontario, since 1902; *b* 1843. Called to Bar, 1869; member of Ontario Legislature, 1890–1902. *Address:* Toronto, Ontario, Canada.

Died 31 Aug. 1916.

GARSTIN, John Ribton, DL, JP; FSA (Lond. and Scot.); ex-President Royal Society Antiquaries of Ireland; ex-Vice-President Royal Irish Academy; a Visitor of the National Museum Dublin, and Governor of Armagh Library and Observatory; *b* 27 Dec. 1836; *o c* of William Garstin of Dublin; *m* 1864, Martha (*d* 1910), *o d* of J. A. Durham of Elm Lodge, Hampton, Middlesex; three *d*. *Educ:* Cheltenham College; Dublin Univ., MA, LLB and BD Dublin. Educated for Holy Orders; purchased the family estate in the Co. Louth, 1877; High Sheriff, Co. Louth, 1879. *Recreations:* reading, bibliography, public duties. *Address:* Braganstown, Castlebellingham, Co. Louth.

Died 16 June 1917.

GARSTIN, Sir William Edmund, GCMG 1902 (KCMG 1897; CMG 1894); GBE, 1918; Grand Cordon Medjidie and Grand Cordon Osmanieh; Chevalier of Légion d'honneur; British Government Director Suez Canal Co. since 1907; engaged on Red Cross work in England during the War; *b* India, 29 Jan. 1849; 2nd *s* of late Charles Garstin; *m* 1888, Mary Isabella, *d* of late Charles Augustus North, 56 York Terrace, NW. *Educ:* Cheltenham College; King's College, London. Entered Indian Public Works Dept, 1872; sent to Egypt, 1885, and retired from India 1892; Inspector-General of Irrigation, Egypt, 1892; Under-Secretary of State for Public Works, 1892; Adviser to the Ministry of Public Works in Egypt, 1904–8. *Address:* 17 Welbeck House, Wigmore Street, W. *Clubs:* Turf, Brooks's.

Died 8 Jan. 1925.

GARTH, Sir William, Kt 1914; KC 1919; Barrister, Middle Temple; *b* 26 Aug. 1854; 3rd *s* of late Rt Hon. Sir Richard Garth, PC. *Educ:* Eton; Merton College, Oxford (BA). Advocate, Calcutta High Court, 1885–1913. *Address:* 132 Oakwood Court, W14. *T:* Park 3545. *Clubs:* United University, Oriental.

Died 20 Feb. 1923.

GARTSIDE-TIPPING, Colonel Robert Francis, CB 1900; ISC; JP Co. Chester; *b* 17 Aug. 1852; *s* of G. Gartside-Tipping of Rossferry, Co. Fermanagh, Ireland, and Jane, *d* of R. Fowler, of Rabinston, Co. Meath; *m* 1885, Jane, *d* of J. Sclater of Newick Park, Sussex; one *d*. *Educ:* Oswestry. Entered army, 1872 (51st KOLI); Indian Staff Corps (2nd Bengal Lancers), 1875; 1st Bengal Lancers, 1879; served Afghan

War, 1879–80; Zaimukt Expedition, 1880; Takt-i-Suleman Expedition, and Egypt, 1882; Miranzai Expedition, 1890; Isazai Expedition, 1892; China, 1900. *Address:* 30 Redcliffe Gardens, SW10. *T:* Kensington 6227. *Club:* East India United Service.

Died 16 Dec. 1926.

GARVAN, Sir John Joseph, Kt 1927; *b* Hill End, New South Wales, 17 Jan. 1873; *s* of late James P. Garvan. Managing Director of Mutual Life and Citizens Assurance Co. Ltd; Chairman of Commonwealth Bank, 1924–26. *Address:* Sydney, New South Wales.

Died 18 July 1927.

GARVICE, Charles, FRSL; novelist, dramatist, and journalist; correspondent for several English and American papers; President of Institute of Lecturers; late President Farmers' and Landowners' Association; CC for Northam, Devon; Conservator of Rivers. *Publications: poems:* Eve, 1873; *novels:* Maurice Durant, 1875; Nance, 1900; Her Heart's Desire, 1900; The Outcast of the Family, 1900; A Coronet of Shame, 1900; Just a Girl; In Cupid's Chains; Love Decides; Linked by Fate; Love the Tyrant; A Girl of Spirit; Diana and Destiny; Where Love Leads; The Gold in the Gutter; In Wolf's Clothing; Queen Kate; The Scribbler's Club; Love in a Snare; Two Maids and a Man; The One Girl in the World, 1915; *plays:* The Fisherman's Daughter; A Life's Mistake; part author of A Heritage of Hate and Marigold Comes to Town. *Recreations:* riding, fishing, motoring, amateur farming. *Address:* 4 Maids of Honour Row, Richmond, Surrey; The Thatch Cottage, Hambleden, Henley-on-Thames. *T:* Richmond 899. *Clubs:* Garrick, Authors'.

Died 1 March 1920.

GARVICE, Major Chudleigh, OBE 1919; DSO 1900; Royal Dublin Fusiliers; *b* 12 Jan. 1875; *s* of Charles Garvice, of Bradworthy, N Devon; *m* 1920, Isabel, *d* of Andrew Ormiston. Entered army, 1896; served South Africa, 1899–1902 (despatches, Queen's medal, 3 clasps, King's medal, 2 clasps, DSO); Sudan medal with clasp; holds 4th Class Osmanieh and 3rd Class Order of the Nile. *Address:* Alexandria City Police, Egypt. *Club:* Naval and Military.

Died 23 March 1921.

GARVIN, Thomas, ISO 1909; formerly Inspector-General of Police, New South Wales; *b* Sydney, 7 Aug. 1843; *m* 1865, Harriet, *o d* of late Charles Field, Sydney. Joined NSW Mounted Police, 1862. *Address:* Carbethon, 69 Edgecliffe Road, Woolluhra.

Died 6 Feb. 1922.

GARY, Elbert Henry, LLD, ScD, LLB; Chairman, United States Steel Corporation; *b* father's farm near Chicago; *s* of Erastus Gary and Susan A. Vallette Gary; *m* 1st, Julia E. Graves (*d* 1902); 2nd, 1905, Emma T. Townsend; two *d*. *Educ:* Wheaton Public Schools and Wheaton College; Chicago University; LLB 1867; LLD M'Kendree College, 1906; Lafayette College, 1915; Lincoln Memorial University, 1919; Trinity College 1919; Syracuse University, 1921; Northwestern University, 1922; ScD, University of Pittsburgh, 1915; DCS New York University, 1925. Practised law in Chicago twenty-five years; County Judge eight years; first Mayor, City of Wheaton; prominently connected with organisation Federal Steel Co., 1898; removed from Chicago to New York to become its President; identified with organisation of the United States Steel Corporation 1901, of which became Chairman Board of Directors, Chairman Finance Committee and Chief Executive Officer; President Chicago Bar Association, 1893–4; President American Iron and Steel Institute since its organisation in 1910; Trustee, Northwestern University, Syracuse University; Member US Section International High Commission, 1915–17; Member of Society of Colonial Wars and Sons American Revolution. Grand Cordon of the Order of Leopold II; Second Class Order of the Sacred Treasure; Officer of the Legion of Honour; Grand Cross Knight of the Crown of Italy; Grand Commander, Morocco; Golden Cross of the Commandership of the Royal Battalion of George I of Greece. *Publications:* numerous addresses; Gary genealogy. *Recreation:* farming. *Address:* 856 Fifth Avenue, New York City; 71 Broadway, New York City; Jericho, Long Island, NY. *TA:* 71 Broadway, New York City; Jericho, Long Island, New York. *T:* Syosset 800. *Clubs:* Chicago, Chicago Golf, Union League, Chicago; Metropolitan, Automobile of America, National Golf Links, New York Yacht, Piping Rock, Meadowbrook, Sleeping Hollow Country, New York.

Died 15 Aug. 1927.

GASCOIGNE, John Henry, MVO 1911; Senior Clerk, Scottish Office, 1902–17; *b* 1856; *m* 1883, Florence, *d* of Benjamin Gregory. Scottish official delegate to Diplomatic Conference on International Circulation of Motor Cars, Paris, 1909. Jubilee Medal, 1897; Coronation Medals, 1902 and 1911. *Address:* 14 Beatrice Avenue,

Norbury, SW16. *T:* Streatham 3969. *Club:* North Surrey Golf.

Died 2 Oct. 1928.

GASCOIGNE, Maj.-Gen. Sir William Julius Gascoigne, KCMG 1901 (CMG 1899); late commanding at Hong Kong; *b* 29 May 1844; *m* 1875, Helen, *d* of Martin T. Smith and *widow* of Hon. Arthur F. Egerton. Entered army, 1863; Maj.-Gen. 1895; served Egyptian War, 1882 (medal with clasp, Khedive's star); Soudan, 1885 (clasp). *Address:* Boyton House, Boscombe, Hants. *Clubs:* Travellers', United Service.

Died 9 Sept. 1926.

GASELEE, Gen. Sir Alfred, GCB 1909 (KCB 1898; CB 1891); GCIE 1900; Colonel 54th Sikhs (Frontier Force), Indian Army, since 1904; *b* 3 June 1844; *s* of Rev. John Gaselee; *m* 1895, Alice Margaret, *d* of late G. Gartside-Tipping of Rossferry, Co. Fermanagh. Entered army, 1863; Capt., 1875; Maj., 1881; Col, 1893; Col-on-Saff, Cawnpore, 1896; temporary Brig.-General, 1898. NW Frontier, 1863 (medal with clasp); Abyssinia, 1868; Bizoti expedition, 1869 (despatches; thanked by Governor-General); Jowaki Afridi expedition, 1877–78 (despatches, clasp); Afghan, 1878–80 (despatches); Candahar (Bt of Major, medal with two clasps, bronze decoration); Zhob Valley expedition, 1884 (despatches); Hazara expedition, 1891 (despatches, CB and clasp); Isazai expedition, 1892; Waziristan Field Force, 1894–95 (despatches, clasp); Tirah Expeditionary Force and Khyber Field Force, commanding 2nd Brigade (KCB, despatches, medal, two clasps); officiated QMG in India, 1898; commanded second class district, India, 1898–1901; commanded British Forces in North China, 1900 (medal and clasp, promoted Maj.-Gen.); Lt-Gen. 1903; Gen. 1906; commanded Northern Army, India, 1907–8. *Address:* 54th Sikhs, Kohat, India. *Clubs:* United Service; Guildford.

Died 29 March 1918.

GASKELL, Rt. Hon. Charles George Milnes, PC 1908; DL, JP; LLD, MA, Chairman West Riding County Council, 1893–1910; *b* 23 Jan. 1842; *e s* of J. Milnes Gaskell (*d* 1873) of Thornes House, Yorks, MP, and Mary, 2nd *d* of Rt Hon. Charles Williams-Wynn, MP; *m* 1876, Lady Catherine Henrietta [author of Old Shropshire Life], *d* of 5th Earl of Portsmouth; one *s* one *d*. *Educ:* Eton; Trinity Coll. Camb. Third class classical tripos. Barrister Inner Temple, 1866. MP (L) Morley Division, West Riding, Yorks, 1885–92. *Address:* Thornes House, Wakefield; Wenlock Abbey, Shropshire. *Club:* Travellers'.

Died 9 Jan. 1919.

GASKIN, Arthur J.; Director of the Jewellers' and Silversmiths' School, Vittoria Street, Birmingham; retired, 1925; *b* Birmingham, 1862; *s* of Henry and Harriet Gaskin; *m* 1894, Georgie Evelyne Cave France; two *d*. *Educ:* Wolverhampton Grammar School. Painter and goldsmith; member of London Arts and Crafts, and Royal Birmingham Society of Artists. *Publications:* various illustrated books, including work for the Kelmscott Press. *Recreation:* golf. *Address:* Chippen Campden. *M:* D 9034.

Died 4 June 1928.

GATES, Lewis Edwards; *b* 23 March 1860; *s* of Seth M. Gates, Member of Congress and abolitionist. *Educ:* Harvard; studied in France, Germany, England. Assistant Professor of English, Harvard Univ., till 1901, and of Comparative Literature till 1902. *Publications:* Selections from Jeffrey, 1894; Selections from Newman, 1895; Three Studies in Literature, 1899; Studies and Appreciations, 1900. *Address:* The Wareham, 88 Willett Street, Albany, NY.

Died 1 Oct. 1924.

GATHORNE-HARDY, Hon. Alfred Erskine, JP, DL; a Railway Commissioner since 1905, and Chairman of the Light Railway Commission; barrister; formerly Counsel for Woods and Forests, and Commissioner of Works; *b* London, 27 Feb. 1845; 3rd *s* of 1st Earl of Cranbrook; *m* 1875, Isabella Louisa, *o d* of late John Malcolm of Poltalloch, Argyllshire; one *s* one *d* (and one *s* decd). *Educ:* Eton; Balliol Coll., Oxford. First class Honours in History. Called to Bar, Inner Temple, 1869. MP (C) Canterbury, 1877; re-elected 1880, but unseated on petition; contested Northern Division Yorkshire, West Riding, 1883, on assassination of Lord Frederick Cavendish; and Doncaster Division, Yorkshire, 1885; MP (C) North Sussex, 1886–95; retired, 1895. *Publications:* The Salmon: Fur, Feather, and Fin Series, 1898; Autumns in Argyllshire with Rod and Gun, 1900; Life of Gathorne-Hardy, First Earl of Cranbrook, 1910; My Happy Hunting-Grounds, 1914. *Address:* Donnington Priory, Newbury, Berks. *Clubs:* Carlton, Burlington Fine Arts. *Died 11 Nov. 1918.*

GATHORNE-HARDY, Col Hon. Charles Gathorne; *b* 11 May 1841; 2nd *s* of 1st Earl of Cranbrook; *m* 1872, Lady Cicely Louisa

Nevill, *d* of 1st Marquess of Abergavenny; two *d*. Formerly Lt-Col Grenadier Guards. *Address:* 43 Lennox Gardens, Chelsea, SW. *Clubs:* Turf, Carlton.   *Died 17 Feb. 1919.*

GATLIFF, General Albert Farrar, DL Sussex; *b* 1857; *s* of late Henry Gatliff and *g s* of Rev. John Gatliff, Canon of Manchester Cathedral of Brinkworth Hall, York; *m* Rosamund (*d* 1923), *widow* of Lt-Col C. F. Dashwood, late Gordon Highlanders; no *c*. *Educ:* Alston College; London University; Royal Naval College, Greenwich. Entered Royal Marine Light Infantry, 1876; Capt. 1885; Major 1892; Brevet Lt-Col 1899; Col 1903; Maj.-Gen. 1910; Lt-Gen. 1911; Gen. 1915; served in Mendiland Expedition (West Coast of Africa), 1898 (medal and clasp); commanded Royal Marines on Cape Station (HMS Doris), 1897–99; special service South African War. 1899–1901; Press Censor Capetown; Assistant Adjutant-General, operations in Orange Free State and Cape Colony; present at Paardeberg (medal and three clasps); Senior Officer Royal Marines for fourteen months during the War; appointed to command 37th Battalion of Imperial Yeomanry; Passed Staff College, 1888; Instructor of Fortifications, Royal Military College, 1890–97. Called to Bar, Middle Temple, 1897; passed first in Common Law and gained J. J. Powell prize; Member of Admiralty Volunteer Committee, 1903–7 and compiled regulations for RM Volunteers (received thanks of Admiralty); Times correspondent on various occasions; specially selected to assist in writing official history of South African War. Colonel Commandant Portsmouth Division, RMLI, 1908–10; awarded Good Service Pension, 1909; retired pay, 1922; Member of Council, Royal United Service Institution and British Legion, etc; in attendance on HIH The Hereditary Prince of Turkey representing the Sultan at the Coronation (medal); a pall-bearer at Funeral of Unknown Warrior at Westminster Abbey, 11th Nov. 1920; JP, Cape Colony. *Recreations:* cricket (I Zingari and Free Foresters), golf, shooting. *Address:* 5 Clarendon Mansions, Brighton; Silverstream, Thorpe, Chertsey. *Clubs:* Army and Navy; New, Brighton.   *Died 28 Sept. 1927*

GATT, Hon. Camillo. *Educ:* Malta University. Private Secretary to Sir Richard Wood, HM's Diplomatic Agent and Consul General, Tunis, 1868–71; Superintendent of the Government Printing Office, Malta, 1882; Assistant Secretary to Government, Gozo, 1892; Receiver-General, 1899; Auditor-General, 1902; member of the Executive Council and of the Council of Government, 1903; Pensioned. *Address:* Malta.

GATTIE, Alfred Warwick; Chairman of Gattie Springs Limited; *b* London, 21 June 1856; 2nd *s* of William and Henrietta Warwick Gattie; *m* Carlotta, *d* of Walter Elliot. *Educ:* Brighton Grammar School. Began life as a clerk in the Bank of England; inventor of the Gattie System of Goods Clearing Houses; inventor of Gattie co-ordinating springs for vehicles, aeroplanes, etc. *Publications:* The Transgressor; The Honourable Member; Sir Jackanapes; The Millionairess; and a number of other plays; articles in the Nineteenth Century and Fortnightly Reviews, etc; a number of lectures on Transport Reform by Road, Rail and Water. *Recreations:* reading, music, drama, science, sociology. *Address:* 11 Montague Gardens, Acton, W3. *T:* Chiswick 653.   *Died 21 Sept. 1925.*

GATTY, Sir Stephen Herbert, Kt 1904; KC; *b* 9 Oct. 1849; *s* of late Rev. Alfred Gatty; *m* 1st, 1876, Alice Georgina (*d* 1894), *e d* of late Rev. G. Rawlinson; 2nd, 1905, Katharine, *d* of late Alfred Morrison; two *s* one *d*. *Educ:* Winchester; New Coll. Oxford. Called to Bar, Middle Temple, 1874; NE Circuit; QC 1891; Attorney-Gen. Leeward Isles, 1883; Acting Chief-Justice Antigua, 1884; Attorney-Gen. Trinidad, 1885; Puisne Judge Straits Settlements 1892; Chief-Justice of Gibraltar, 1895–1905. *Address:* Ossemsley Manor, Christchurch, Hants. *TA:* New Milton. *T:* New Milton 13.
                                          Died 29 March 1922.

GAUGHRAN, Rt. Rev. Laurence; RC Bishop of Meath since 1906; *b* 1842. *Educ:* Maynooth. Ordained, 1868; Professor at St Finian's, 1872–77; at Mullingar, 1877–85; Pastor of Kells, 1885; Vicar-General of Meath, 1894; Domestic Prelate to the Pope, 1895. *Address:* The Palace, Mullingar, Ireland.   *Died 14 June 1928.*

GAUL, Rt. Rev. William Thomas, DD; Hon. Canon Cape Town Cathedral since 1913. *Educ:* Trinity Coll. Dublin (MA). Ordained, 1873; Vicar of Bloemfontein, 1875–80; Rector of All Saints, Dutoitspan, 1880–84; of Kimberley, 1884–95; Archdeacon of same, 1887–95; Bishop of Mashonaland, 1895–1907. *Address:* Capetown, S Africa.   *Died 17 May 1928.*

GAULT, James, AKC; late Professor of Commerce and Commercial Law, King's College, London; *b* Jersey, 21 June 1850; *s* of D. Gault

of Ahoghill, Co. Antrim, Ireland; *m* 1887, Ellen Sarah, *y d* of R. Rixon of Woolwich; two *d*. *Educ:* King's Coll., London. Called to the Bar, 1887; appointed by the Council of King's College lecturer in Roman Law; for several years was Dean of the Evening Classes of the College. *Publications:* revised and edited, under the title of Lessons in Commerce, The Law and Customs of British Trade by Prof. Gambaro of Genoa; assisted with J. E. Forster's Registration of Business Names Act; Excess Profits Duty and Corporation Tax. *Recreations:* rowing, music. *Address:* 3 Elm Court, Temple, EC. *T:* Central 1234.
                                          Died 13 Dec. 1927.

GAUNT, Percy Reginald, CBE 1920; Mill Manager and a Director of Reuben Gaunt & Sons, Ltd, Broom Mills, Farsley, near Leeds; *b* Farsley, near Leeds, 6 Nov. 1875; *s* of John Wm Gaunt of Summerfield, Bramley, near Leeds; *m* 1902, Ethel Mary, *d* of late Abimelech Hainsworth of Farsley, near Leeds; two *s* two *d*. *Educ:* Leeds Boys' Modern School; Leeds University. District Commissioner for the Farsley District (West Riding of Yorkshire) Baden-Powell Boy Scouts' Association; Freeman of the City of London; Liveryman of the Worshipful Company of Dyers; President of the Leeds University Textile Association; Member of Council and Research Control Committee, The British Research Assoc. for the Woollen and Worsted Industries, Leeds, etc, Honorary Assistant Director of Wool Textile Production, War Dept, Bradford; Member of the Board of Control of Wool Textile Production, and Chairman of various Sub-Committees in relation thereto; responsible for the following Sections: Costing of Textile Fabrics and Commission Rates for Textile Processes, Costings in Consultation with Directorate of Costings, Dyewares, Dyeing, ie, Piece-dyeing, Wool-dyeing, and Slubbing-dyeing. *Recreations:* golf, gardening. *Address:* Elmwood, Calverley, near Leeds. *T:* Stanningley, Leeds 111. *Clubs:* National Liberal; Union, Bradford; New Leeds and County Liberal, Leeds.
                                          Died 3 Dec. 1926.

GAUSSEN, Perceval David Campbell, KC 1909; *b* 1862; *m* 1908, Letitia Elisabeth, *d* of Rev. J. Wilson, Rector of Tyholland, Co. Monaghan; one *d*. *Educ:* Trinity College, Dublin. Wray Prizeman in Logics and Ethics; Senior Moderator in Moral and Mental Philosophy; BA 1884; ex-President of Dublin University Philosophical Soc. Called to Bar, 1885; Senior Crown Counsel, Co. Cavan; JP for Cos Londonderry, Antrim, and Tyrone. *Address:* Clifton, Monkstown, Co. Dublin. *T:* 308 Dun Laoghaire, Co. Dublin; Shanemullagh House, Castledawson, Co. Londonderry.
                                          Died 19 Oct. 1928.

GAUTHIER, Most Rev. Charles Hugh; RC Archbishop of Ottawa since 1910; *b* Alexandria, Ont, Canada, 1843. *Educ:* Regiopolis College, Kingston; later Professor of Rhetoric there. Priest, Gananoque, Westport, Williamstown, Glen Nevis, and Brockville; Dean, 1886; Vicar-General, 1891; Archbishop of Kingston, 1898–1910. *Address:* Archbishop's Palace, Ottawa, Canada.
                                          Died 19 Jan. 1922.

GAUTIER, C. Lucien; Honorary Professor of Theology; *b* Cologny, near Geneva, Switzerland, 17 Aug. 1850; *s* of late Col E. A. Emile Gautier, Director of the Observatory of Geneva, and P. E. Victorine (*née* Sarasin); *m* 1878, Bertha V. Hentsch of Geneva; three *s* two *d*. *Educ:* Geneva, Collège Lecoultre and State Gymnasium. BLit 1867; BSc 1869; BTheol 1874; studied evangelical theology and Semitic languages at the Universities of Geneva, Leipzig, and Tübingen; PhD Leipzig, 1877. Appointed 1877 to the Professorship of Hebrew and Old Testament Exegesis at the Theological Faculty of the Free Evangelical Church of Canton de Vaud at Lausanne; resigned and was nominated Honorary Professor, 1898; Hon. DD Berne, 1906, and Glasgow, 1908; Hon. Professor University of Geneva, 1909; President of the Synod of the Free Evangelical Church of the Canton de Vaud, 1885, 1886, 1891, 1892, of the Geographical Society of Geneva, 1906–7, of the Christian Evangelical Association of Geneva, 1906–9, of the Société Pastorale Suisse, 1916–17; Chairman of the Association of the International Monument of the Reformation, 1906–17; Central President of the Société Suisse des Vieux-Zofingiens, 1915–19; President of the Board of Delegates of the South African Swiss Mission, 1918–20; Member of the International Committee of the Red Cross since 1919; one of the editors of the Review La Liberté Chrétienne, Lausanne, 1898–1907; travelled in the Holy Land, 1893–94, and 1899. *Publications:* Le Sacerdoce dans l'Ancien Testament, 1874; Ad-Dourra al-Fâkhira, la Perle Précieuse de Ghazâli, Traité d'Eschatalogie musulmane, 1878; La Mission du Prophète Ezéchiel, 1891; Au delà de Jourdain, 1896, 2nd edn; Souvenirs de Terre-Sainte, 1898, 2nd edn; Vocations de Prophêtes, 1922, 2nd edn (German translation, 1903); Autour de la Mer Morte, 1901; Introduction à l'Ancien Testament (2 vols), 1914, 2nd edn;

La Loi dans l'ancienne alliance, 1908; l'Evangéliste de l'Exil, 1911; le Prophète Jérémie, 1916, etc. *Address:* Cologny, Geneva, Switzerland. *TA:* Lucien Gautier, Cologny. *T:* St 6687.

Died Feb. 1924.

GAUTIER, Judith; *d* of Théophile Gautier; Member Goncourt Academy; Chevalier de la Légion d'Honneur. *Romans:* Le Dragon Impérial (Chinois); Iskender (Persan); La Sœur du Soleil (Japonais); Le Vieux de la Montagne (Croisade); Khou 'N Atonon (Egyptien); L'Inde Eblouie (Hindou); etc. *Théâtre:* La Marchande de Sourires (Odéon); L'Avare Chinois (Odéon); Princesse d'Amour (Vaudeville); etc; La Fille du Ciel (en collaboration avec Pierre Loti) (New York). *Traductions:* Parsifal; Le Livre de Jade (Poèmes Chinois). *Poésie:* Poèmes de la Libellule (Japon). *Mémoires:* Collier des jours, 3 volumes. *Address:* 30 rue Washington, Paris; Pre' des Oiseaux, Dinard, Ille-et-Vilaine.

Died Dec. 1917.

GAVEY, Sir John, Kt 1907; CB 1903; MICE; Engineer-in-Chief to the Post Office, 1902-7; Consulting Engineer to Post Office, 1908-13; *b* Aug. 1842; *o s* of J. Gavey, St Helier, Jersey; *m* 1870, Mary de Gruchy; two *s* three *d*. *Educ:* Victoria College, Jersey. Received professional training under Mr, Later Sir, W. H. Preece, in the service of Electric International Co.; on the transfer of the telegraphs to the State appointed Superintendent of the South-Eastern Subdivision, 1870; and of the Great-Western Subdivision, 1872; Superintending Engineer, South Wales District, 1878; Chief Technical Officer, General Post Office, 1892; Assistant Engineer-in-Chief, 1897, and Electrician, 1899; closely associated with all telegraphic and telephonic developments of the Post Office; Past President of the Institution of Electrical Engineers. *Publications:* papers read before Engineering Institutions, contributions to technical press. *Recreation:* boating. *Address:* The Croft, Hampton Wick. *T:* Kingston 1616. *Died 1 Jan. 1923.*

GAVIN, Ethel, MA, Dublin; Head Mistress, Wimbledon Hill School, since 1908; 4th *d* of late John Gavin of Kandy, Ceylon. *Educ:* Maida Vale High School; Girton Coll. Classical Tripos, Cambridge, Class II; Russell Gurney Scholar, Girton College. Assistant Mistress, Maida Vale High School, 1888-93; Head Mistress Shrewsbury High School, 1893-1900; Head Mistress, Notting Hill High School, 1900-8. *Address:* Wimbledon Hill School, SW. *Club:* Ladies' University.

Died 2 March 1918.

GAVIN, Michael; Jesuit Priest; Member of the Staff attached to Farm Street Church, Berkeley Square, London, W, since 1882; *b* Limerick, Jan. 1843; *s* of Capt. Michael Gavin, Limerick, and Eliza Gallwey, Kilkenny. *Educ:* Castleknock, near Dublin; Stonyhurst College. Taught literature at Beaumont College, Old Windsor, 1869-74; Theology at St Beuno's College, St Asaph, 1878-81. *Publications:* The Sacrifice of the Mass; Memoirs of Father P. Gallwey, SJ; the Decay of Faith; the Devotion to the Sacred Heart; the Salvation of God; and other Sermons. *Address:* 114 Mount Street, W.

Died 28 June 1919.

GAWAN TAYLOR, His Honour Judge Henry, BA, LLB (Cantab); JP Lancashire, Cumberland, and Westmorland; County Court Judge, on Circuit No 3, since 1912; *b* 16 Dec. 1855; 2nd *s* of late William Taylor, Cober Hill, Cloughton, Yorkshire, and of Scarborough; *m* 1883, Rachel (*d* 1927), 3rd *d* of late T. J. Candler of Low Hall, West Ayton, Yorks; one *s* three *d*. *Educ:* Trinity Hall, Cambridge (Law Scholar and Prizeman); Lond. Univ.; Honours 1st LLB. Called to Bar, Lincoln's Inn, 1882; Lincoln's Inn Scholarship in International and Constitutional Law; a Revising Barrister on the North-Eastern Circuit, 1895-1911; Chairman of the Joint Commitee of the Durham Coal Trade, 1906-10. *Address:* Croftlands, Heads Nook, Carlisle. *Club:* Cumberland County, Carlisle. *Died 9 Dec. 1928.*

GEAKE, Charles; Secretary Liberal Publication Department, and editor Liberal Magazine, Liberal Monthly, and Liberal Year Book since 1894; member Editorial Staff of Westminster Gazette since 1896; *b* 7 May 1867; *e s* of late Joseph Ford and Ellen Geake of Launceston, Cornwall; *m* 1899, Jessie Margaret, *d* of late Robert and Jessie Hudson of Lapworth, Warwickshire; one *d*. *Educ:* Dunheved College, Launceston; Clare College, Cambridge (Scholar); Eighth Wrangler, 1889; First Class (3rd Div.), Part II, Math. Tripos, 1890. Fellow Clare College, 1891; read in Chambers for Bar, 1892-94; called at Lincoln's Inn, 1894; Cambridge Editor of the Granta, 1890-2; frequent contributor to Punch, 1891-96. *Publications:* John Bull's Adventures in the Fiscal Wonderland (with Sir F. C. Gould); Appreciations and Addresses by Lord Rosebery (editor). *Address:* Percy Lodge, Campden Hill, W8. *T:* Park 3141. *Clubs:* Union, National Liberal, Eighty, Whitefriars, Omar Khayyam. *Died 29 April 1919.*

GEARY, Lieut-Gen. Sir Henry Le Guay, KCB 1900 (CB 1891); Colonel Commandant RA; *b* 29 April 1837; *s* of late Frederick Augustus Geary, Platt House, Putney, Surrey; *m* 1865, Sophia Mary, *d* of George Symes, Bridport, Dorset; one *s* three *d*. *Educ:* RMA Woolwich. Joined RA, 1855; Crimea, 1855-56 (medal, clasp for Sebastopol, Turkish medal, 5th class Medjidie for distinguished conduct in the field); Indian Mutiny Campaign, 1858-59 (medal); Abyssinian Campaign (medal, despatches, Brevet Major); Brig. Major, and AA Gen. RA Ireland, 1873-77; DAAG and AAG Army Headquarters, 1879-84; Asst Director of Artillery, War Office, 1885-90; Maj.-Gen. com. RA South. Dist. 1890-95; Maj.-Gen. com. Belfast Dist. 1895-99; President of Ordnance Committee, 1899-1902; Governor of Bermuda, 1902-4; Jubilee medal, 1897. *Recreations:* nothing special. *Address:* Arreton, Camberley. *T:* 169 Camberley. *Club:* Junior United Service.

Died 31 July 1918.

GEDDES, Brig.-Gen. John Gordon, CB 1915; CMG 1918; RA; *b* 4 Nov. 1863; *s* of Col John Geddes, Cheltenham; *m* 1898, Eling Esther, *y d* of Brig.-Gen. C. H. Spragge, CB. Entered army, 1883; Capt., 1892; Maj., 1900; Lt-Col 1910; Col, 1913; Brig.-Gen. 1915; DAAG, India, 1897-1900; Instructor, School of Gunnery, 1901-4; DAA and QMG, 3rd Div. Southern Command, 1908-10; served Tirah Expedition, 1897-8 (medal with clasp); European War, 1914-18 (wounded, despatches four times, CB, CMG). *Address:* 4 Suffolk Square, Cheltenham.

Died 26 Aug. 1919.

GEDDES, Colonel Robert James, CB 1915; DSO 1900; MB; late AMS; *b* 13 Aug. 1858; *m* 1907, Christina Gowans, *d* of late J. G. Whyte. Entered army, 1884; Maj. 1896; Lt-Col 1904; Col 1913; served Burmah, 1885-88 (medal, 2 clasps); Chin-Lushai, 1889-90 (clasp); Mekran Expedition, 1898; South Africa, 1899-1902 (despatches, Queen's medal four clasps, King's medal two clasps, DSO); European War, 1914-17; DDMS 4th and 2nd Corps, BEF (despatches twice, CB); Inspector Medical Services for Scotland, 1917-19. *Address:* Westcliff, St Andrews, Fife.

Died 27 Sept. 1928.

GEDGE, Rev. Hugh Somerville, MA; Hon. Canon of Peterborough, 1900; *b* 24 Oct. 1844; *s* of Rev. Sydney Gedge, MA, formerly Fellow of St Catharine's College, Cambridge; some time Second Master of King Edward's School, Birmingham, afterwards Vicar of All Saints', Northampton; *m* 1882, Georgiana Caroline, *d* of Lieut-Col Clunes, IA. *Educ:* King Edward's School, Birmingham; Marlborough; St Catharine's College, Cambridge. BA 1866 (2nd class Classical Tripos); MA 1873; Carus Greek Testament Prize, 1867; 2nd class Theological Hons 1867. Ordained Deacon, 1868; Priest, 1869; Curate of St Peter's, Sowerby, Halifax, 1868-71; All Saints', Northampton, 1871-77; Perpetual Curate of St Paul's, Northampton, 1877-82; Vicar of All Saints', Leicester, 1882-91; Rural Dean of Christianity on Leicester, 1908-10; Rector of Aylestone, Leicester, 1891-1912; Proctor in Convocation, 1906-16. *Recreation:* travel. *Publications:* editor of Peterborough Diocesan Calendar, 1902-8-13-20; several Tracts. *Address:* Park House, Stoneygate, Leicester. *TA:* Leicester.

Died 10 April 1923.

GEDGE, Sydney, MA; solicitor; head of Gedge, Fiske, and Gedge; Governor and Almoner Christ's Hospital; Governor Westfield College, Ridley Hall, and Wycliffe Hall; Director Henley's Telegraph Works Co.; *b* 16 Oct. 1829; *e s* of Rev. Sydney Gedge; *m* 1857, Augusta, *d* of R. Herring. *Educ:* King Edward's School, Birmingham; Corpus Christi Coll. Cambridge. 1st class Moral Science Tripos, 1854. Contested (C) South Bedfordshire, 1885; MP (C) Stockport, 1886-92; MP (C) Walsall, 1895-1900; contested Walsall, 1900. Member House of Laymen, Rep. Church Council; Vice-Pres. CMS; Licensed Preacher Dioceses of London and Southwark. *Publications:* articles in the Churchman on Church subjects. *Address:* Mitcham Hall, Surrey. *T:* Mitcham 825; 10 Norfolk Street, Strand, WC. *T:* Central 4220. *Club:* Junior Constitutional. *Died April 1923.*

GEE, William Winson Haldane, BSc (Lond), MScTech (Manchester); Professor of Pure and Applied Physics at the College of Technology, Manchester, 1902; retired under superannuation, 1924; *b* near Bolton, Lancs, 29 June 1857; *s* of William Gee, formerly of Manchester; *m* Caroline, *e d* of M. M. Rooker, of Sale, Cheshire; one *d*. *Educ:* Manchester Grammar School; the Royal College of Science; Owens College. Demonstrator and Assistant Lecturer in Physics at Owens College, Lecturer of the Victoria University, 1881-91; Chief Lecturer in Physics and Electrical Engineering at the Municipal Technical School, Manchester, 1891-1902; largely responsible for the design and equipment of the laboratories, etc, in

Physics, Electrical Engineering, and Electro-Chemistry at the College of Technology; Hon. Curator Manchester Literary and Philosophical Society. *Publications:* papers relating to Physics and Electro-Chemistry, etc; with the late Balfour Stewart, three volumes on Practical Physics; joint translator of Rosenberg's Electrical Engineering. *Address:* Oak Lea, Whalley Avenue, Sale, Cheshire.   *Died 3 March 1928.*

GEER, Ven. George Thomas; *b* 1844; *s* of G. T. and Sarah Geer, London, England; *m* 1870, Davinia Louisa Macdougall. *Educ:* English Public School; Moore College, Liverpool; New South Wales. Licensed as Reader at Timor, by Bishop of Melbourne, Victoria, 1874; ordained Deacon, by Bishop of Ballarat, Victoria, 1877; Priest, 1879. Incumbent of East Charlton, 1878; Dimboola, 1881; Rector of Condobolin, New South Wales, 1883; Coonamble, 1884; Cowra, 1891; Carcoar, 1896; Bourke, 1898; appointed Canon, All Saints Cathedral, Bathurst, 1891; Archdeacon of the Lachlan, 1895; Rector of Bourke, Archdeacon of Bourke, 1901-6; Rector of Gulgong, 1904-13; late Hon. Archdeacon and Rural Dean; licensed for general work, Diocese of Sydney, 1913. *Recreations:* photography; horticulture (prize-taker), ferns, cut flowers, chrysanthemums; portraits, landscape, lantern slides, buildings, etc. *Address:* Magic Street, Mosman, New South Wales.   *Died 2 Feb. 1918.*

GEIKIE, Sir Archibald, OM 1914; KCB 1907; Kt 1891; FRS 1865; FRSE 1861; FGS; Hon. MRIA; Officier de la Légion d'Honneur; President Royal Society, 1908-13; *b* Edinburgh, 28 Dec. 1835; *e s* of late James Stuart Geikie; *m* 1871, Alice Gabrielle (*d* 1916), *y d* of late Eugène Pignatel of Lyons; two *d* and one *s* one *d* decd). *Educ:* High School and University, Edinburgh. Hon. DCL Oxford; DSc Cambridge and Dublin; LLD Edinburgh, Glasgow, Aberdeen, St Andrews, Durham, Birmingham, Sheffield, Liverpool; PhD Upsala, Leipzig, Prague, Strasbourg. Entered Geological Survey, 1855; Director Geo. Survey of Scotland, 1867; first Murchison Prof. of Geology and Mineralogy, University of Edinburgh, 1871-82; Foreign Secretary Royal Society, 1890-94, and Secretary, 1903-8; President Geological Soc., 1891-92, 1906-8; President British Association, 1892; Director-General Geological Survey of United Kingdom, and Director Museum of Practical Geology, 1882-1901. Wollaston medallist and Murchison medallist of Geological Society; twice Macdougal-Brisbane medallist of Royal Society, Edinburgh; Royal medallist, Royal Society; Hayden gold medallist, Philadelphia Academy of Natural Sciences; Livingstone Gold Medallist of Royal Geog. Soc. Scotland; Gold Med. of Inst. of Mining and Metallurgy. Governor of Harrow School, 1892-1922; Trustee of the British Museum; Member of the Royal Commission for the Exhibition of 1851; Member of Council of the British School at Rome; Chairman of Royal Commission on Trinity College, Dublin, 1920. Foreign Associate Institute of France; Member Lincei, Rome; Academies of Berlin, Vienna, Petrograd, Belgium, Stockholm, Turin, Naples, Munich, Christiania, Göttingen, Kais. Leopold Carol., Philadelphia, New York, National Academy of Sciences of United States, etc. *Publications:* The Story of A Boulder, or Gleanings from the Notebook of a Field-Geologist, 1858; Memoir of Edward Forbes (with G. Wilson), 1861; Geological Map of Scotland (with Murchison), 1862; The Scenery of Scotland viewed in connection with its Physical Geology, 1865, 3rd edn 1901; Memoir of James David Forbes, 1869; Life of Sir Roderick I. Murchison, 2 vols, 1875; Geological Sketches at Home and Abroad, 1882; Text-book of Geology, 1882, 4th edn in two vols, 1903; Class-book of Geology, 6th edn 1915; Field-Geology, 5th edn 1900; New Geological Map of Scotland, with descriptive notes, 1892, 2nd edn 1910; Memoir of Sir Andrew Crombie Ramsay, 1895; The Ancient Volcanoes of Britain, 2 vols, 1897; The Founders of Geology, 1897, 2nd edn 1906; Geological Map of England and Wales, with descriptive notes, 1897; Types of Scenery, and their Influence on Literature (Romanes Lecture), 1898; The Geology of Central and Western Fife and Kinross (Mem. Geol Surv.), 1901; The Geology of Eastern Fife (Mem. Geol Surv.), 1902; Scottish Reminiscences, 1904; Landscape in History, 1905; Charles Darwin as Geologist, the Rede Lecture for 1909; The Love of Nature among the Romans, Presidential Address to Classical Association, 1911, expanded into a volume, 1912; The Birds of Shakespeare, 1916; Annals of the Royal Society Club, the Record of a London Dining Club in the Eighteenth and Nineteenth Centuries, 1917; John Michell, MA, FRS, of Queens' College, Cambridge (1724-93), 1918; A Long Life's Work, an Autobiography, 1924; smaller school-books on Physical Geography and Geology, which have been translated into most European languages; many original contributions to science in the journals and transactions of learned societies and in the Memoirs of the Geological Survey, and literary papers in the Quarterly and Edinburgh Reviews, and other periodicals. *Address:* Shepherd's Down, Haslemere, Surrey. *Club:* Athenæum.
          Died 10 Nov. 1924.

GEIL, William Edgar, MA, LittD, LLD; FRGS, FRAS; explorer; *b* near Philadelphia; mother Scotch; *m* L. Constance Emerson, BA, *d* of Hon. E. O. Emerson. Crossed Africa; penetrated as far as Mount Douglas in New Guinea; visited the Dyacks in Borneo; visited the D'Entrecasteaux Archipelago; crossed China from Shanghai to Burma; followed the Great Wall of China from the Yellow Sea to Tibet; visited the Koko Nor; visited Australia, Friendly Islands, Samoa, Fiji, Friday Island, New Zealand, Timour, Japan, Corea, Siberia; visited all the capitals of China; explored the five sacred mountains of China, 1919-20. *Publications:* A Yankee on the Yangtze; A Yankee in Pigmyland; The Isle Called Patmos; The Men on the Mount; The Man of Galilee; Ocean and Isle; The Great Wall of China; Eighteen Capitals of China; Hunting Pigmies. *Recreation:* golf. *Address:* The Barrens, Doylestown, Pa, USA.
          Died 11 April 1925.

GELDART, William Martin, CBE 1917; MA, BCL; Vinerian Professor of English Law, and Fellow of All Souls College, Oxford, since 1909; *b* 7 June 1870; *s* of Rev. Edmund Martin Geldart; *m* 1905, Emily Falk. *Educ:* Whitgift Grammar School, Croydon; St Paul's School; Balliol College, Oxford (Scholar). Fellow of St John's College, Oxford, 1892-99; called to Bar, Lincoln's Inn, 1897; Official Fellow and Lecturer in Law at Trinity College, Oxford, 1901-9; All Souls Reader in English Law in the University, 1906-9; member of the Hebdomadal Council since 1905. *Publications:* Joint-Editor with F. W. Hall of Aristophanes in Oxford series of Classical Texts; Contributor to A Digest of English Civil Law, edited by E. Jenks; Elements of English Law, in Home University Library. *Recreation:* entomology. *Address:* 10 Chadlington Road, Oxford; All Souls College, Oxford. *T:* Oxford 126.
          Died 12 Feb. 1922.

GELL, Philip Lyttleton, JP Oxfordshire and Middlesex; *b* 29 April 1852; *s* of Rev. John Philip Gell and Eleanor, sole issue of Admiral Sir John Franklin, the Arctic explorer; *m* 1889, Hon. Edith Mary, *d* of 8th Viscount Midleton. *Educ:* King's Coll., London (Hon. Fellow); Balliol College, Oxford (Scholar). 1st class Mod. History, 1876; Arnold Prize Essay on Turkish Races in Europe, 1877. Director, Guardian Assurance Co.; Director and late President of British South Africa Company. First Chairman of Council Universities Settlement in East London (Toynbee Hall), 1884-96; Archbishops' Church Finance Committee, Empire Settlement Committee, 1917. *Address:* Hopton Hall, Wirksworth, Derbyshire; Haven Hill, Kingswear, S Devon. *Clubs:* Brooks's, Athenæum; Derbyshire County.
          Died 29 May 1926.

GEMMILL, James Fairlie, FRS; FRSE; FZS; Professor of Natural History, University College, Dundee, since 1919; *s* of late Cuthbert Gemmill, Hillhead, Mauchline, and Jeanie Leiper. *Educ:* Mauchline Public School; Kilmarnock Academy; Glasgow University; Cowan Medallist, Blackstone Medallist, Coulter Prizeman, Bellahouston Medallist; MA (Hons Classics, 1890); MD (Hons 1900), DSc (1910); Leipzig and Naples. First President (then Hon. Vice-President) of the Marine Biological Association of the West of Scotland (later Scottish Marine Biological Association); late Research Fellow in Embryology at Glasgow University, and Lecturer in Zoology at the Glasgow Provincial Training College. *Publications:* various on embryological, zoological, and teratological subjects, including work on Ovogenesis; Origin of Müllerian Duct; Vitality of Ova and Sperm; Aquarium Aeration; Development of Sun Star (Trans Zool Soc. Lond. 1912); Locomotor Function of Lantern of Aristotle (Proc. Roy. Soc. Lond. 1912); The Teratology of Fishes, Glasgow, 1912; Development of Common Crossfish, etc. (Phil. Trans Roy. Soc. Lond. 1914, and Quart. Journ. Micr. Sc. 1915); Development of Sea Anemones (Phil. Trans Roy. Soc. Lond. 1920). *Address:* Hawkhill House, Dundee. *T:* 2412.   *Died 10 Feb. 1926.*

GEMMILL, Lt-Col William, DSO 1915; JP; 8th Battalion Royal Scots (TF); *b* 4 Sept. 1878; *s* of late William Gemmill of Greendykes. Served South Africa, 1899-1901 (Queen's Medal with 4 clasps); European War, 1914-15 (DSO, despatches). *Address:* Greendykes, Gladsmuir, East Lothian, Scotland.   *Died April 1918.*

GENESE, Robert William, MA; Professor of Mathematics, University College of Wales, 1879-1919; *b* Dublin, 8 May 1848; *m* Margaretta, *d* of Capt. Richards, Aberystwyth. Educ: The Institute, Liverpool; St John's College, Cambridge (Local Examinations, Holt Scholar, Liverpool, Minor and Foundation Scholar, St John's, Cambridge, 8th Wrangler, 1871). Vice-principal of the Training College, Carmarthen, and minor appointments; a Vice-President of the Council of the Association for the Improvement of Mathematical Teaching; member of the General Committee of the British Association. *Publications:*

problems in the Educational Times; articles in the Messenger of Mathematics, Quarterly Journal, and Nouvelles Annales des Mathématiques: papers in the Proceedings of the London Mathematical Society, British Association, Association Française, and International Congresses. *Recreations:* wireless, chess. *Address:* 49 Prospect Road, Southborough, Tunbridge Wells.

Died 21 Jan. 1928.

GENT, His Honour John; County Court Judge, Halifax Disctrict, 1906; transferred to Cornwall, 1911; retired, 1919; *b* Northumberland, 19 July 1844; *s* of William and Anne Gent; *m* 1886, Harriet Frankland, *d* of Edward Randall of Loders, Dorset; three *s* two *d. Educ:* Durham School; Trinity College, Oxford. Scholar and Fellow, 1st class Mods and Final Classical Schools; Hertford, Ireland, and Craven scholarships; Arnold History Essay; Eldon Law Scholar. Called to Bar, Lincoln's Inn, 1874. *Address:* 8 Crescent Road, Kingston Hill, Surrey.

Died 14 March 1927.

GENTILI, Most Rev. Dr Charles, OSFC; RC Archbishop of Agra since 1898; *b* Italy, 1842. *Educ:* Italy. Entered the Order of Capuchins; Missionary Apostolic in India, 1870; Bishop of Allahabad, 1897. *Address:* Agra, India.   *Died 6 Jan. 1917.*

GEOFFRION, Victor, KC Canada; BCL; *b* St Simon, Quebec, 23 Oct. 1851; *s* of Felix Geoffrion and Catherine Brodeur; *m* 1884, Francesca, *d* of late Hon. Senator Paquet, of St Cuthbert. *Educ:* St Hyacinthe Seminary; the Guild College, Montreal. Member Canadian House of Commons since 1900; Liberal; head of legal firm, Geoffrion, Geoffrion, and Coussin, Montreal. *Address:* House of Commons, Ottawa.   *Died 31 May 1923.*

GEORGE, Sir Ernest, Kt 1911; RA 1917 (ARA 1910); architect; *b* London, 13 June 1839; *s* of late John George of Streatham; *m* 1865, Mary Allan, *d* of late Robert Burn of Epsom; three *s* two *d. Educ:* Brighton; Reading. RA gold medal for Architecture, 1859; Queen's gold medal of the Royal Institute British Architects, 1896. President RIBA 1908-9. Articled to Samuel Hewitt; entered Royal Academy as student; began practice with Thomas Vaughan; at Vaughan's death was joined by Harold Peto, and on Peto's retirement by A. B. Yeates. *Professional work:* Stoodleigh Court, Devon; Rousdon, Devon; Motcombe, Dorset; Batsford, Gloucester; Edgeworth Manor, Gloucester; Monk Fryston, Yorks; Poles, Herts; North Mymms, Herts; Buchan Hill, Sussex; Dunley Hill, Surrey; Welbeck Abbey; Eynsham Hall, Oxon; Sedgwick Park, Sussex; Ruckley Grange, Salop; Foxcombe, Oxon; Putteridge Bury, Herts; Busbridge Park, Surrey; Crathorne Hall, Yorks; Shiplace Court; Harrington Gardens; Mount Street; 17 Grafton Street; Collingham Gardens, S Kensington; houses in Cadogan Square and Berkeley Square; Royal Exchange Buildings, EC; The Golders Green Crematorium; The Shirpur Palace, India; Royal Academy of Music; Ossington, Newark; Church of St Andrew, Streatham; St Pancras, Rousdon, Devon; the Churches of Samaden and Tarasp in the Engadine; villa at Antibes, France; Restorations, Berkeley Castle. *Publications:* as an etcher—Etchings on the Mosel; Etchings on the Loire; in Belgium; in Venice, and Old London. *Address:* 71 Palace Court, W2. *T:* Park 696. *Club:* Arts.

Died 8 Dec. 1922.

GEORGE, W. L.; author; *b* of British parents, Paris, 20 March 1882; *m* 1st, 1908, Helen (*d* 1914), *d* of Richard Porter; 2nd, 1916, Helen Agnes (*d* 1920), *y d* of late Col Travers Madden, BSC; two *s*; 3rd, 1921, Kathleen, *o d* of Herbert Geipel, JP, the Old Hall, Coxwold, York. *Educ:* Paris (school and university); Germany. Contributed to most London publications; special correspondent of various papers in France, Belgium and Spain; served in the French army; during the War, Section Officer in the Ministry of Munitions. *Publications:* various political and economic works; *novels:* A Bed of Roses, 1911; The City of Light, 1912; Israel Kalisch, 1913; The Making of an Englishman, 1914; The Second Blooming, 1914; The Strangers' Wedding, 1916; Blind Alley, 1919; Caliban, 1920; The Confession of Ursula Trent, 1921; The Stiff Lip, 1922; One of the Guilty, 1923; The Triumph of Gallio, 1924; Gifts of Sheba, 1926; *miscellaneous:* Woman and To-Morrow, 1913; Dramatic Actualities, 1914; Anatole France, 1915; Olga Nazimov, stories, 1915; The Intelligence of Woman, 1917; A Novelist on Novels, 1918; Eddies of the Day, 1919; Hail, Columbia! 1921; A London Mosaic, 1921; How to Invest your Money, 1924; The Story of Woman, 1925. *Recreation:* travel. *Address:* 2 Hyde Park Terrace, W2. *T:* Paddington 137. *Club:* Savile.

Died 30 Jan. 1926.

GEPP, Rev. Nicolas Parker, MA; Hon. Canon of Ely, 1915; Hon. Canon, Norwich, 1899; *s* of Thomas Morgan Gepp, Maynetrees, Chelmsford; *m* Alice P. Melvill (*d* 1915), *y d* of Philip Melvill, BSC,

e s of Sir James Cosmo Melvill, KCB; one *s* two *d. Educ:* New College, Oxford. Curate of St George's Bloomsbury, 1866-69; Aspley-Guise, 1870; Great and Little Henny, 1870; Vicar of Sandon, Herts, 1871-77; Rector of St James's, Colchester, 1877-86; Vicar and Rector of Great and Little Witchingham, 1886-1910; Rector of Northwold, 1910-19. *Address:* Oakdene, 201 Richmond Road, Kingston-on-Thames.

Died 6 June 1921.

GERALD, William John, ISO 1909; *b* Prescott, Ont, 27 July 1850; *m* 1869, Elizabeth Hainsworth, *d* of William Billyard, CE, of Windsor, Ont; two *d. Educ:* St Joseph's College, St Laurent, Montreal. Entered Inland Revenue Department, 1867; Collector at Brantford and London; Chief Inspector and Assistant Commissioner; late Deputy Minister of Inland Revenue; retired, 1912; later Parliamentary and Departmental Agent. *Recreation:* angling. *Clubs:* Canadian, Rotary, Ottawa.   *Died 19 Nov. 1923.*

GERRANS, Henry Tresawna, MA; Fellow, Vice-Provost, and Lecturer, sometime Bursar and Tutor, Worcester College, Oxford; Secretary to Delegates of Local Examinations since 1887; *b* Plymouth, 23 Aug. 1858; *e s* of Sampson Tresawna Gerrans and Jane, *d* of Robert Dunn; *m* 1889, Anna Elizabeth, 2nd *d* of late Rev. N. F. English. *Educ:* Cheltenham and Bristol Grammar Schools; Christ Church, Oxford. Junior and Senior Mathematical Scholar; 1st class in Mathematics, Mods and Greats; 2nd class in Natural Science, Junior Student, Christ Church, 1877. Fellow, Worcester College, Oxford, 1882; Pro-proctor, 1889; Asst-Commissioner to Mr Bryce's Royal Commission, 1894; Proctor, 1895; Member of Hebdomadal Council; Curator of the Chest; Member of the Board of Finance; Curator of Taylor Institution; Delegate of the Oxford University Press, Museum, Local Examinations, and for Training of Teachers; FRAS, FCS, FSA; member of the London Mathematical Society, the Mathematical Association, the Physical Society, the American Mathematical Society, the Société mathématique de France, and the Circolo matematico di Palermo; Member of the Teachers' Registration Council and of the Secondary School Examinations Council. *Address:* 20 St John Street, Oxford. *Clubs:* Savile, Royal Societies.

Died 20 June 1921.

GERRY, Hon. Elbridge Thomas; President, New York Society for Prevention of Cruelty to Children, 1876-1901; Counsellor at Law; *b* New York, 25 Dec. 1837; *s* of Thomas R. Gerry (formerly US Navy) and Hannah G., *y d* of Peter P. Goelet; *g s* of Elbridge Gerry, Vice-President, USA, and a signer of the Declaration of Independence; *m* 1867, Louisa M. (*d* 1920), *o d* of Robert J. Livingston and Louisa M. Storm. *Educ:* Columbia College, NY. AB 1857; AM 1858; Nashotah, LLD, 1910. Admitted to Bar, 1860; Member NY State Constitutional Convention, 1867; Vice-President, American Society for Prevention of Cruelty to Animals until 1899; Governor of NY Hospital, 1878-1912; Commodore NY Yacht Club, 1886-93; Chairman, NY State Commission on Capital Punishment (which substituted electricity for hanging), 1886-88; Chairman, Executive Committee, Centennial Inauguration of George Washington, 1889; President, Annual Conventions, NY Societies for Prevention of Cruelty, 1889-1903; Trustee, General Theological Seminary, PE Church, 1877-1913; Trustee, American Museum of Natural History, 1895-1902; Director of Fifth Avenue Trust Co., 1897-1907; Director of Newport Trust Co., 1901-13; Director of Industrial Trust Co. of Providence, 1902-10. *Publications:* Manual of Prevention of Cruelty to Children, several editions; the following articles in North American Review, "Cruelty to Children", July 1883; "Capital Punishment by Electricity", Sept. 1889; "Children of the Stage", July 1890. *Recreations:* yachting; private law library of 30,000 volumes. *Address:* Newport, Rhode Island, USA; 258 Broadway, New York; Private Park, Lake Delaware, New York. *Clubs:* Newport Reading Room; Hope, Providence; Metropolitan, Knickerbocker, New York Yacht, NY; Metropolitan, Washington, DC.

Died 18 Feb. 1927.

GERVIS, Henry, JP Middlesex; MD (Lond); FRCP, FRSM, FSA; Consulting Obstetric Physician to St Thomas' Hospital; Consulting Physician to the Grosvenor Hospital and the Royal Maternity Charity; Fellow (late President) of the Obstetrical Society and of the Hunterian Society; Member, Huguenot Society of London, British Numismatic Society, London and Middlesex Archæological Society, Somersetshire Archæological Society, and Devonshire Association; *b* 1837; *e s* of late F. S. Gervis, Tiverton; *m* Phœbe Louisa Pollard (*d* 1918); one *s* one *d. Educ:* St Thomas' Hospital. Successively Assistant Obstetric Physician, Lecturer on Forensic Medicine, and Obstetric Physician and Lecturer on Obstetric Medicine at St Thomas'; Examiner in Obstetric Medicine at the Universities of Cambridge and London, and at the Royal College of Physicians. *Publications:* contributions to the Transactions of various medical and other societies, and of articles in Quain's Dictionary of Medicine, and Prof. Allbutt's System of Medicine. *Address:* 15 Royal Crescent, Bath. *Club:* Bath and County, Bath.   *Died 25 Sept. 1924.*

GETHIN, Sir Richard Charles Percy, 7th Bt, *cr* 1665; late Major 4th Battalion Suffolk Regiment; *b* 20 Nov. 1847; *s* of Sir Richard Gethin, 6th Bt; *S* father, 1885; *m* 1876, Catherine, *d* of F. E. B. Scott, Ingham Lodge, Cheshire; three *s*. Barrister, Inner Temple, 1879. Served South Africa, 1900-2 (Queen's medal, one clasp, King's medal, two clasps); JP, Hampshire. *Heir: s* Col Richard Walter St Lawrence Gethin, *b* 16 Feb. 1878. *Address:*The Grove, Hythe, Hants. *Club:* Junior United Service.   *Died 17 June 1921.*

GHOSE, Sir Chunder Madhub, Kt 1906; Senior Puisne Judge, High Court, Calcutta, 1885-1906; President (Hon.) of the Board of Examiners of Candidates for Professional Pleadership and Mukhlearship, 1898-1906; *b* 26 Feb. 1838; *s* of late Rai Doorga Persad Ghose Bahadoor; *m* Srumutty Hemunt Coomary Ghose; three *s* two *d. Educ:* Hindu College; Presidency College, Calcutta University (Fellow). Began his professional career as a Pleader at Burdwan in 1860, where he held the position of Government Pleader for sixteen months; was enrolled as Vakel, Sudder Court (subseq. High Court), at Calcutta in 1861; Member of the Bengal Legislative Council, 1884; President of the Faculty of Law, Calcutta University, for three years; officiating Chief-Justice at Bengal, 1906; took an active part (President, 1905) in the establishment of the Bengal *Kyasht Shobha* (for the amalgamation of the different subsections of the *Kyashts* of Bengal, for the improvement of their social condition and status, and for the curtailment of their extravagant marriage expenses); President Indian Social Conference, Dec. 1906; retired from office as Judge, 1907. *Address:* Bhowanipore, Calcutta.

Died 2 March 1918.

GHOSE, Sir Rashbehary, Kt 1915; CSI 1909; CIE; MA, DL; Member Vice-regal Council; *b* 23 Dec. 1845; *s* of Jagabandho Ghose of Torekona, Burdwan, India; *m* 1st, 1867, Priambada Dassi (*d* 1879); 2nd, 1880, Matibala Dassi (*d* 1882); no *c. Educ:* Presidency College, Calcutta. MA 1st Class Honours, 1866; DL 1884. Tagore Law Professor, Calcutta University, 1876; Fellow, 1879; member of Bengal Legislative Council, 1888-91; Council of Viceroy of India, 1891-94; re-nominated, 1906. *Publication:* Law of Mortgage. *Address:* Sans Souci, Alipore, India. *Clubs:* Landholders, Calcutta, Calcutta.

Died March 1921.

GIBB, Sir George Stegmann, Kt 1904; LLB (London); Chairman Oriental Telephone Co. Ltd; *b* Aberdeen, 30 April 1850; *y s* of late Alexander Gibb, CE, Willowbank, Aberdeen, and Margaret, *d* of John Smith, architect, of Aberdeen; *m* 1881, Dorothea Garrett Smith; four *s* one *d. Educ:* Aberdeen Grammar School and University. Entered solicitor's office as articled clerk, 1872; Assistant in Great Western Railway Solicitor's Office, 1877; practised as Solicitor in Fenchurch Avenue, 1880-82; Solicitor to the North-Eastern Railway at York, 1882; acted as Arbitrator for the Company in Wages Arbitration before Lord James of Hereford, 1897; Member of Committee on War Office Reorganisation, 1901; Member of Royal Commission on London Traffic, 1903; General Manager, North Eastern Railway, 1891-1906; Director, 1906-10; Chairman Metropolitan District Railway Co. and of Tube Railways controlled by Underground Electric Railways Co. of London Ltd, of which company was Managing Director, 1906-10; Chairman of the Road Board, 1910-19; Member (Chairman, 1918) of Government Arbitration Board (Committee on Production), 1915-18. *Address:* South Corner, Alan Road, Wimbledon, SW19. *T:* Wimbledon 568. *Club:* Reform.

Died 17 Dec. 1925.

GIBB, James A. T., ISO 1902; *b* 18 April 1842; *m* 1868, Margaret Bridget (*d* 1912), *e d* of William Scott, Lanark. Late Accountant and Registrar of Bonds, Post Office, Edinburgh. *Address:* 7 Dalkeith Street, Joppa, Midlothian.   *Died 5 April 1922.*

GIBBES, Cuthbert Chapman, MD, MCh (Aberdeen); DPH (Camb), MRCP (London); FLS, FCS; Consulting Physician to the National Hospital for Diseases of the Heart; *b* 5 Sept. 1850; *s* of Rector of Bradstone, Devon, and Margareta Murray. *Educ:* Aberdeen University; Westminster Hospital. Graduated MB, MCh, Aberdeen, 1872, and shortly after was appointed RMO to the Public Hospital, Kingston, Jamaica; after returning to England held the following appointments: RMO, Tiverton Infirmary; House Surgeon and Physician, South Devon and East Cornwall Hospital, Plymouth; Surgeon, Surbiton Cottage Hospital; Medical Officer, Kingston Rural Sanitary District; Medical Superintendent, Tolworth Isolation

Hospital; Physician, Western General Dispensary; Pathologist, National Hospital for Diseases of the Heart. *Publications:* The Effect of Pregnancy on Chronic Heart Disease; Sleeplessness in Heart Disease and its Treatment; many other papers in the medical journals of Great Britain and America. *Recreations:* entomology, botany. *Address:* 89 Harley Street, Cavendish Square, W1.

Died 25 Aug. 1927.

GIBBON, Perceval; novelist and short story writer; *b* Trelech, Carmarthenshire, 4 Nov. 1879; *e s* of Rev. J. Morgan Gibbon; *m*; two *d. Educ:* Moravian School, Königsfeld, Baden. Formerly in merchant service in British, French, and American ships; as journalist and war-correspondent, travelled in South, Central, and East Africa, America, and Europe; Major, Royal Marines, 1918-19. *Publications: verse:* African Items; *novels:* Souls in Bondage, Salvator, Margaret Harding; *volumes of stories:* The Vrouw Grobelaar's Leading Cases, Adventures of Miss Gregory, The Second-class Passenger, Those Who Smiled; many contributions to all English and American magazines. *Recreations:* golf, motoring, shooting. *Address:* c/o J. B. Pinker, Talbot House, Arundel Street, Strand, WC. *TA:* Gibbon, Bookishly, London.   *Died 30 May 1926.*

GIBBON, Thomas Mitchell, CIE 1878; formerly Member of Council of India. *Address:* The Hern, Beddington Lane, Croydon. *T:* Croydon 657.   *Died May 1921.*

GIBBON, Sir William Duff, Kt 1912; *b* 22 July 1837; *s* of Rev. Charles Gibbon, DD, Church of Scotland, Lonmay Parish, Aberdeenshire; *m* Katherine (*d* 1916), *d* of Andrew Murray of Allathan, Aberdeen; three *s* three *d. Educ:* Banff Academy; Grammar School and University, Aberdeen. Went to Ceylon when eighteen years of age; Chairman, Ceylon Planters' Assoc. 1878; member Kandy Municipal Council; JP, Ceylon; acting Planting Member Legislative Council, Ceylon; Fellow of Royal Colonial Institute. *Address:* Hathaway Cottage, Surrey Road, Bournemouth, W. *T:* Bournemouth Area 1636.   *Died 18 March 1919.*

GIBBONS, Major Edward Stephen, DSO 1914; 1st Battalion Middlesex Regiment; *b* 18 June 1883; *s* of Sir William Gibbons, KCB; *m* 1914, Annie MacGregor, *e d* of late John Lyle, Finnart House, Weybridge; one *s* one *d*. Entered army, 1902; Captain, 1912; served NW Frontier of India (Mohmand), 1908 (medal and clasp); European War, 1914-18 (despatches, DSO). *Address:* Finnart House, Weybridge.   *Died 19 Sept. 1918.*

GIBBONS, Sir George Christie, Kt 1911; KC Can.; President London and Western Trusts Co.; President City Gas Co.; Life Bencher Law Society; *b* 2 July 1848; *m* 1876, Elizabeth, *d* of Hugh Craig, Montreal. *Address:* London, Canada. *Clubs:* London, Toronto, York, Toronto; Rideau, Ottawa; St James's, Montreal.

Died 8 Aug. 1918.

GIBBONS, His Eminence Cardinal James; *b* Baltimore, 23 July 1834. *Educ:* St Charles' Coll. Maryland; St Mary's Seminary, Baltimore. Ordained Priest, 1861; Vicar Apostolic, North Carolina, 1868; Bishop of Richmond, 1872; Archbishop of Baltimore, 1877; Cardinal, 1886. *Publications:* The Faith of Our Fathers; Our Christian Heritage; The Ambassador of Christ. *Address:* 408 N Charles Street, Baltimore.   *Died March 1921.*

GIBBONS, John Lloyd, JP Co. Stafford; County Councillor N Bilston, 1891-98; *b* 1837; *e surv. s* of late Henry Gibbons, agricultural chemist, Wolverhampton. MP (U) S Wolverhampton, 1898-1900. *Address:* Ellowes Hall, Sedgley, Staffs. *TA:* Sedgley, Dudley. *T:* 43 Sedgley.   *Died 27 April 1919.*

GIBBS, Sir Charles Henry, Kt 1918; Mayor of Lambeth, 1907-8 and 1914-18; Leader of the Unionist Party in Lambeth since 1900; *b* 1854. *Address:* 3 St Saviour's Road, SW2. *T:* Brixton 1976. *Clubs:* Constitutional, City Carlton.

Died 12 May 1924.

GIBNEY, Rt. Rev. Matthew, DD; RC Bishop of Perth, 1887-1910; *b* 1838. Priest, 1863; arrived in Western Australia, 1863; attended to Ned Kelly of the Ned Kelly gang after his capture, when he was supposed to be dying, and in the afternoon, whilst the other members of the gang were making their final stand in the burning hotel at Glenrowan, Victoria, in 1880, entered the burning building to endeavour to rescue them, but found Dan Kelly and his comrade, Steve Hart, lying side by side, both dead, with no signs of wounds on either. *Address:* Lourdes, Vincent Street, North Perth, Western Australia.   *Died 22 June 1925.*

GIBSON, Rt. Rev. Alan George Sumner, DD; General Licentiate, Diocese of St John's, 1911; *b* 1856; *y s* of Rev. William Gibson, Rector of Fawley, and Louisanna, *d* of Rt Rev. Charles Richard Sumner, Bishop of Winchester; unmarried. *Educ:* private school (Kineton), 1866–67; Haileybury Coll. 1867–75; Oxford, 1875–79. Scholar of Haileybury College, 1869; Exhibitioner of Haileybury College, 1875; Scholar of Corpus Christi College, Oxford, 1875; 1st class Class. Mods 1876; 1st class Lit. Hum. 1879; Prox. Acc. Junior Univ. GT Prize, 1880; Senior Univ. GT Prize, 1881; MA 1882. Deacon, 1879; Priest, 1881; Vice-Principal Burgh Missionary Coll. 1879–80; Curate of Croft, Lincolnshire, 1879–82; Incumbent of Pro-Cathedral, Umtata, 1882–84; Missionary at Ncolosi, 1884–93; Canon of Umtata, 1885–94; Archdeacon of Kokstad, 1886–91; Dioc. Sec. 1882–4, 1893–4; Rector of Claremont, Cape Colony, 1894–97; Coadjutor-Bishop of Cape Town, 1894–1906; Canon of St George's, Cape Town, 1895–1906. *Publications:* Intloko Zentshumayelo (Kaffir Sermon Sketches), 1890; Eight Years in Kaffraria, 1891; Some Thoughts on Missionary Work and Life, 1894; Sermon Sketches for a Year, 1898; Between Cape Town and Loanda, 1905; joint-author of Translations from the Organon of Aristotle, 1877; edited Reminiscences of the Pondomisi War of 1880, 2nd edn, 1900; Sketches of Church Work and Life in the Diocese of Cape Town, 1900; joint editor Hand-boek voor Communicanten. *Recreations:* football XX Haileybury, 1873, 1874; paperchases, fives, cricket, football, music, literature, swimming, at school; walking, riding, music, literature, swimming, in manhood. *Address:* Matatiele, Griqualand East, S Africa.   *Died 20 Oct. 1922.*

GIBSON, Rt. Rev. Edgar Charles Sumner, DD; *b* Fawley, Southampton, 23 Jan. 1848; 4th *s* of late Rev. William Gibson, Rector of Fawley; *m* 1875, Mary Grace, *e d* of Rev. R. S. Philpott, MA, Vicar of Chewton Mendip; three *s*. *Educ:* Charterhouse; Trinity Coll. Oxford (Hon. Fellow, 1921). Priest, 1872; Chaplain of Wells Theological College, 1871–74; Vice-Principal, 1875; Principal of Leeds Clergy School, 1876–80; Principal of Wells Theological College, 1880–95; Lecturer on Pastoral Theology, Cambridge 1893; Exam. Chap. to Bishop of Bath and Wells, 1894–1904; Hon. Chaplain to Queen Victoria, 1901; Vicar of Leeds and Rural Dean, 1895–1905; Bishop of Gloucester, 1905–22; Warburton Lecturer, 1903–7; Member Royal Commission on Ecclesiastical Discipline, 1904; a Governor of the Charterhouse; late Preb. of Wells; Chaplain-in-Ordinary to King Edward VII. *Publications:* Northumbrian Saints, 1884; Commentary on St James in Pulpit Commentary, 1886; translation of the Works of Cassian, in Nicene and Post-Nicene Library, 1894; Self-dicipline, 1894; Commentary on the XXXIX Articles, 2 vols 1896–97, 2nd edn (1 vol.) 1898, 9th edn 1915; Commentary on the Book of Job, 1898, 2nd edn 1905; John Howard, 1901; Messages from the Old Testament, 1904, 3rd edn 1906; The Old Testament in the New, 1907; The Three Creeds, 1908, 2nd edn 1909; The Revelation of St John the Divine (Churchman's Bible), 1910; The Declaration of Assent, 1918; Editor George Herbert's Temple, 1899, 2nd edn 1906. *Address:* St Giles' House, Fareham, Hants.   *Died 8 March 1924.*

GIBSON, Hon. Edward Graves Mayne, JP; Barrister; *b* 28 July 1873; *s* of 1st Baron Ashbourne and Frances Maria Adelaide, *d* of Henry Cope Colles; *b* and *heir-pres.* to 2nd Baron Ashbourne; *m* 1st, 1900, Mary Philips (*d* 1919), *d* of late H. R. Greg, Lode Hill, Cheshire; three *s* three *d*; 2nd, 1922, Deloraine Amy Norah, *d* of C. W. E. Henslowe of Pinewood, Grayshott, Hants. *Educ:* Wellington; Trinity College, Cambridge. Barrister-at-law. *Address:* Highlands, Haslemere, Surrey. *T:* Haslemere 108. *Club:* Carlton.

Died 26 April 1928.

GIBSON, Hope, CBE 1919; Argentine landowner and stockbreeder; Senior partner in the house of Gibson Brothers, produce brokers and export merchants, Buenos Aires; *b* 23 May 1859; *s* of late Thomas Gibson, of the estancia Los Yngleses, and 1 Eglinton Crescent, Edinburgh; *m* Agnes Russell, MBE, *d* of late John Waddell, JP, of The Inch, Bathgate, and 4 Belford Park, Edinburgh; two *d*. *Educ:* England. Civil engineer, engaged on the construction of public works at home and abroad; joined the house of Gibson Brothers, 1889; held office as first Chairman of the British Chamber of Commerce in the Argentine Republic for five years; President of a Committee composed of Chairmen and Representatives of six Allied Chambers of Commerce in Buenos Aires during the war. *Recreations:* shooting, fishing. *Address:* estancia Los Ynglesitos, Province of Buenos Aires; 1833 Rodriguez Pena, City of Buenos Aires. *Club:* Jockey, Buenos Aires.   *Died 10 Oct. 1928.*

GIBSON, Rev. John Campbell, MA (Glasgow), DD (Glasgow); Missionary of the Presbyterian Church of England, Swatow, South

China; *b* Kingston, Glasgow; *s* of Rev. James Gibson, MA, DD, Prof. of Divinity and Church History in Free Church College, Glasgow; *m* 1883, Agnes Gillespie Barclay (*d* 1915); one *s* one *d*. *Educ:* Academy and University of Glasgow; United Free Church Theological College. First holder, along with T. Barclay, Tai-nan, of the Thompson (Lord Kelvin) Experimental Scholarship, University of Glasgow, 1869–72. Ordained Missionary of Presbyterian Church of England to China, 1874; arrived Swatow, 1874; Lecturer on Evangelistic Theology in United Free Church Colleges of Edinburgh, Glasgow, and Aberdeen, 1898–99; British Chairman of Protestant Missionary Centenary Conference, Shanghai, 1907; Moderator of Synod of the Presbyterian Church of England, 1909; Hon. Moderator of General Assembly of Presbyterian Church of China, 1918. *Publications:* The Number of Readers in China, 1887; Learning to Read in South China, 1888; A Swatow Index to the Syllabic Dictionary of Chinese, 1886; Mission Problems and Mission Methods in South China; various papers and articles chiefly relating to Missions in China; in collaboration with others: Translations of Books of the Old Testament, and the whole of the New Testament in Swatow Vernacular in Roman Letter; the whole New Testament in Simple Classical Chinese (in Chinese character); in collaboration with T. Barclay (afterwards of Tai-nan): Paper on Measurements of Specific Inductive Capacity of Dielectrics in Transactions of Royal Society, London. *Address:* Swatow, China; Kirnan, Bearsden, Scotland.

Died 25 Nov. 1919

GIBSON, Rev. John George, LLD (Washington Coll.), 1904; DD 1923; Tusculum Coll., DD 1924; FSA (Scot); FEIS; Rector of Ebchester, Durham, since 1895; District Head, Incorporated Soldiers and Sailors Help Society; *b* North Shields, 14 February 1859; *o s* of late Captain Ralph Coxon-Gibson, RN, and Margaret, 3rd *d* of late John Rossiter, of Topsham and Murton; *m* 1902, Harriette, *y d* of late Nathan Meanock (Mannock) of Thorn Mount Royton, Co. Lancaster. *Educ:* Albion Street, Academy, North Shields; private tutors; University Coll., Durham; Heidelberg and USA; First Class Prelim Theol. 1886. Formerly HMIS; Deacon, 1887; Priest, 1888; Curate of St Mary, Preston, 1887–89, Royton, near Oldham, 1889–91; East Rainton, Co. Durham, 1891–93; Vicar of Irchester, Wellingborough, 1893–4; Hartford, near Huntingdon, 1894–95. FRGS, FRSL; Member British Institute of Philosophical Studies; Freeman and Liveryman, City of London. *Publications:* Series on Primary School Books, 1881–86; Primary School Arithmetic, 15th edn 1889; Stepping Stones to Life, 3rd edn 1893; Divine Song in its Human Echo, or Song and Service, 2nd edn, 1899; History and Folk-lore of Ebchester and District, 1900; The Registers of the Parish of Ebchester, County and Diocese of Durham, 1901; Watching for the Daybreak, 1902; Along the Shadowed Way, 1903; From Blanchland to the Tyne, or in Derwent Dale, 1905, 2nd edn 1924; Orations of Freemasonry; The King in the East; A Casket of Masonic Verse, 1906; Freemasonry in its Relation to the Social Questions of Modern Times and other Essays, 1906; Illustrated Guide to Whitley Bay, Tynemouth, Cullercoats, Monkseaton, and District, 15th edn 1924; Dermatographs and Criminal Investigation; Through Fast and Festival in Metre, 1907; Cleveland Watering-Places, 1909; Heroic Northumbria, 1909; The Masonic Problem, 1911; Masonry and Society, 1914, 7th edn 1924; Masonic Problem, 2nd Series, 1915; War-time Sermons from an Old Norman Church, 1916; Fair Marjorie's Trust; The Metaphysic of Ethics, 1917; The Problem of Origin, 1919; Builders of Man, 1924; The Romance of Ebchester and its Parish Church, 1926. *Recreations:* reading and writing for the Press; mission work and lecturing; historical research and antiquities; freemasonry, cycling, golfing, photography, walking. *Address:* The Rectory, Ebchester, Co. Durham. *TA:* Rector, Ebchester. *T:* Ebchester 5; Saint Ebba's, 1 Greenfield Place, Newcastle upon Tyne. *T:* Newcastle upon Tyne 120; St George's, Ormonde Avenue, Blackpool, Lancs. *Clubs:* Authors', Canadian; Arts, Manchester.

Died 2 March 1927.

GIBSON, Rt. Hon. John George, PC 1887; Judge, Queen's Bench Division, High Court of Justice, Ireland, 1888–1921; *b* Dublin, 13 Feb. 1846; *y s* of late William Gibson, Rockforest, Tipperary, and Louisa, *d* of Joseph Grant; *m* 1871, Anna, *d* of Rev. John Hare. *Educ:* Portora Royal School, Enniskillen; Trinity Coll. Dublin; scholar, double first gold medallist; Vice-Chancellor's prizeman, Trinity Coll. Dublin. Barrister, 1870; QC 1880; Serjeant, 1885; Solicitor-General, 1885, 1886–87; Attorney-General, 1887–88. MP (C) Walton Division of Liverpool, 1885–88. *Address:* 38 Fitzwilliam Place, Dublin. *Clubs:* Athenæum; University, Dublin.

Died 28 June 1923.

GIBSON, Rev. John Monro, MA, DD, LLD; Minister St John's Wood Presbyterian Church, London, since 1880; *b* Whithorn,

Scotland, 24 April 1838; *s* of Rev. James Gibson, UP Minister; *m* 1864, Lucy (*d* 1909), *d* of Rev. Henry Wilkes, DD, Principal of Theological College of British N America (Congregational); two *s* one *d*. *Educ:* Brechin High School; University Coll. and Knox College (Theological), Toronto. Double 1st class Honours, 1862–63. Minister, Erskine Church, Montreal, as colleague to Dr William Taylor, 1864–74; Lecturer in Greek and Hebrew Exegesis in Montreal Theological Coll., 1868–74; Minister Second Presbyterian Church, Chicago, 1874–80; Moderator Presbyterian Church of England, 1891 and 1915; President Nat. Council of Free Churches, 1897. *Publications:* Ages before Moses, 1879; The Foundations (Lectures on Sources of Christianity), 1880; The Mosaic Era, 1881; Rock versus Sand, 1883; Pomegranates from an English Garden, 1885; Christianity according to Christ, 1888; Gospel of Matthew (in Expositor's Bible), 1890; From the Outpouring of the Spirit to the Death of St Paul (in the People's Bible History), 1895; Unity and Symmetry of the Bible, 1896; From Fact to Faith, 1898; A Strong City, and other Sermons, 1899; The Glory of Life, 1900; Apocalyptic Sketches, 1901; Protestant Principles, 1901; Devotional Study of Holy Scripture, 1904; The Inspiration and Authority of Holy Scripture, 1908. *Recreations:* music, travel, in old days cricket and chess. *Address:* Linnell Close, Hampstead Garden Suburb, NW. *T:* Finchley 1461. *Died 13 Oct. 1921.*

GIBSON, Margaret Dunlop, Hon. DD Heidelberg; LLD St Andrews; Hon. LittD Dublin; *yr* twin *d* of John Smith, solicitor, Irvine, Ayrshire, one of the original Ferguson's trustees, and Margaret Dunlop; *m* 1883, Rev. James Young Gibson (*d* 1886), translator of Cervantes' poetry. *Educ:* chiefly by private tuition, in classics and Oriental and modern languages by university men. Gold Medallist, Royal Asiatic Society, 1915. Visited Sinai six times. In 1892 assisted her sister, Mrs Agnes Smith Lewis, to photograph the famous Syriac palimpsest of the Gospels; in 1896 they brought to England the first leaf of the Hebrew Ecclesiasticus; they also gave the site for Westminster Theological College, Cambridge, and laid its memorial stone 25 May 1897. *Publications:* How the Codex was found; Studia Sinaitica: Arabic versions of some of St Paul's epistles, the Acts, and Catholic epistles; Catalogue of Arabic MSS; Apocrypha Sinaitica; Apocrypha Arabica; Horæ Semiticæ, No 1; Didascalia Apostolorum, in Syriac and English; The Gospel Commentaries of Ishodad, in Syriac and English; Commentaries on Acts, 1913; on St Paul's Epistles, 1916; co-editress of Palestinian Syriac Lectionary of the Gospels, of Pal.-Syr. Fragments, and of 41 facsimiles of dated Christian Arabic MSS. *Recreation:* travel. *Address:* Castlebrae, Chesterton Road, Cambridge. *M:* CE 2078. *Died 11 Jan. 1920.*

GIBSON, Rt. Rev. Robert Atkinson, DD; Bishop of Virginia since 1897; *b* Petersburg, Virginia, 9 July 1846; *s* of Rev. Churchill Jones Gibson, DD, and Lucy FitzHugh Atkinson; *m* 1872, Susan Baldwin Stuart; two *s* three *d*. *Educ:* Hampden, Sidney College, Virginia; Virginia Theological Seminary. Private in the Rockbridge Battery of Virginia Artillery, CSA, 1864; Assistant Minister St James' Church, Richmond, Virginia, 1872–78; Rector Trinity Church, Ponkersburg, West Virginia, 1878–88; Rector Christ Church, Cincinnati, Ohio, 1888–97. *Address:* 906 Park Avenue, Richmond, Virginia. *Died 17 Feb. 1919.*

GIBSON, Thomas, CMG 1919; DSO 1918; Médaille d'Honneur avec Glaives en Vermeil, 1921; barrister-at-law; *b* 14 June 1875; *s* of Joseph Gibson and Janet Buchanan; *m* 1903, Clara Annie, *d* of F. Sharon; two *s* three *d*. *Educ:* Ingersoll Collegiate Institute; Toronto University; Osgoode Hall. Read law with Maclaren, Macdonald, Shepley, and Middleton, Toronto, 1897–1900; called to Ontario Bar, 1900; practised law Ingersoll, 1900–3; partner, Rowell, Reid, Wilkie, Wood, and Gibson, Toronto, 1903–9; General Counsel for Lake Superior Corporation and Subsidiary Companies since 1909; Head of firm, Gibson & Gibson, Barristers, Toronto; Vice-President and General Counsel, Spanish River Pulp and Paper Mills, Ltd; President and General Counsel Fort William Paper Co. Ltd. Assisted in recruiting and went overseas as second-in-command 168th Batt. Oxford's Own, CEF; upon this Battalion being broken up in England, was appointed Senior Major, 4th Pioneer Batt.; after service in field, later appointed assistant Deputy Minister Overseas Militia Forces, Canada, London. Conservative, Methodist. *Recreations:* golf, gardening. *Address:* 707 Bank of Hamilton Building, Toronto; 88 Roxborough Drive, Toronto, Ont. *TA:* Songib. *T:* M 5780. *M:* 47,402. *Clubs:* Toronto, Albany, University, Toronto; Rideau, Ottawa; Lawyers, New York. *Died Feb. 1925.*

GIBSON, Very Rev. Thomas B., AM; Dean of Ferns 1908–26; Rector of Kilbride and Ferns, 1896–1925; Canon of Kilrane and Taghmon, 1896–1908; Rural Dean of Gorey, 1901–25; member of Diocesan Council, etc; *b* 17 March 1847; *s* of Joseph and Mary Gibson

of Stackallan, Co. Meath; *m* 1st, 1878, Caroline O. Leney; 2nd, 1887, Annie M. Lowry; one *s* four *d*. *Educ:* Trinity College, Dublin. Ordained for Curacy of Dunmanway (Fanlobbus), Co. Cork, 1876; Headmaster of King's Hospital, Dublin, 1878–96; Member of General Synod and Diocesan Nominator. *Publications:* Essays and Reviews in Hibernia and Dublin University Review, etc; Ferns Cathedral Restorations; Jottings from a Parish Registrar; Sermons, etc. *Recreations:* founded Hockey Union in Ireland and held Presidency for 25 years, Fellow of Antiquarian Society, etc. *Address:* 60 Grosvenor Square, Dublin. *Died 19 Jan. 1927.*

GIBSON-CARMICHAEL, John Murray; Lieutenant, Royal Defence Corps; *b* 27 Dec. 1860; *s* of Rev. Sir William Henry Gibson-Carmichael, 10th Bt and Eleanora Anne, *d* of David Anderson; *b* of 1st Baron Carmichael, and *heir pres.* to his baronetcy; *m* 1892, Amy Katherine (*d* 1899), *d* of Frederick Archdale of Baldock, Herts; two *d* (and one *s* decd). *Died 6 May 1923.*

GIBSON-CRAIG-CARMICHAEL, Captain Sir Henry Thomas, 5th Bt *cr* 1831; 12th Bt *cr* 1702; late 4th Battalion (Extra Reserve) Highland Light Infantry; *b* 5 Jan. 1885; *s* of Sir James Henry Gibson-Craig, 3rd Bt and Julia, *o d* of Archibald Buchanan, Curriehill, Midlothian; *S* brother, as 5th Bt, 1914, and kinsman, 1st Baron Carmichael, as 12th Bt, 1926; assumed additional surname Carmichael, 1926. *Heir: c* Eardley Charles William Gibson-Craig, *b* 22 Nov. 1887. *Address:* Riccarton, Currie, Midlothian. *Died 5 Sept. 1926.*

GIDDENS, George; comedian; *b* Bedfont, 17 June 1855; his forebears were farmers in Berks and Wilts. *Educ:* National Schools. Commenced career at Theatre Royal, Edinburgh, and went to America; remained there till 1878, and joined Criterion Theatre; remained there till 1894; thereafter played at Drury Lane in Derby Winner; Cheer, Boys Cheer; The Passport; and A Night Out, Never Again, On and Off, and Elixir of Youth, at Vaudeville; Dandy Dick, and Cyrano de Bergerac, as Wyndham's Theatre; Noble Lord, at Criterion; Women are so Serious, at Court; Are you a Mason?; Sam Gerridge in Caste. *Recreations:* fly-fishing, landscape-painting, gardening. *Clubs:* Garrick, Green-Room, Crichton, Kinsmen. *Died 11 Nov. 1920.*

GIDHOUR, Maharajah Sir Ravneswar Prasad Singh, Bahadur of, KCIE 1895; the premier nobleman in the Province of Bihar and Orissa; *b* 1860; *m* 1886; one *s*. Member of Bengal Legislative Council, 1893–95 (thanked for services); again elected, 1895–97; 3rd time, 1901–3; 4th time, 1903; has been member of Local Board and District Board; Hon. Magistrate; Life Vice-President BL Association; title of Maharajah Bahadur made hereditary, 1877; Hon. Member of the Legislative Council of the new Province of Behar, 1913–22. *Heir:* Gidhour, Maharaj Kumar Chandra Moulesshur Prasad Sing [*b* 1890; *m* 1913. Formally installed on the Gudee on the 17th May 1915 for investiture with powers of management over a major portion of the Raj. Member, District Board; Member Legislative Council, Patna; Honorary Magistrate]. *Address:* Gidhour, Monghyr, Behar, India. *Died 21 Nov. 1923.*

GIFFARD, Admiral George Augustus, CMG 1902; JP; *b* Feb. 1849; *e s* of late Capt. H. W. Giffard, RN, and Ella Emilia Stephenson; *m* 1884, Eleanor, *y d* of Col and Mrs Bruce Brine; one *d*. *Educ:* sea. Entered Navy, 1862; served on the Canadian Lakes, 1866; Fenian raid (medal), Victoria and Albert, 1870; in HMS Alert, Arctic Expedition, 1875–76 (medal); operations in Egypt, 1882 (medal and bronze star); Commodore and senior officer, Newfoundland fisheries, 1899–1901 (CMG); Admiral-Superintendent of HM Dockyards at Chatham, 1907–9; retired, 1913. *Address:* Highfield, Bishops Waltham, Hants. *TA:* Bishops Waltham. *T:* 19 Bishops Waltham. *Club:* Royal Naval, Portsmouth. *Died 23 Sept. 1925.*

GIFFARD, Major-General Sir Gerald Godfray, KCIE 1923; CSI 1913; MRCP, MRCS; *b* 19 Jan. 1867; *m* 1898, Alice Melicent, *e d* of James Grose, CIE, ICS; two *s* two *d*. *Educ:* St Bartholomew's Hospital. Lieutenant IMS 1890; Captain, 1893; Major, 1902; Lt-Col 1910; Major-General, 1918; Resident Surgeon, General Hospital, Madras, 1897; District Medical and Sanitary Officer, Chingleput, 1899; Professor, Materia Medica, Madras College, 1901; Professor, Surgery, 1903; Professor of Midwifery and Superintendent Government Maternity Hospital, 1906; Commandant Hospital Ship, Madras, 1914–15; ADMS 6th Poona Div., 1915; Surgeon-General with the Govt of Madras, 1919–23; retired, 1924. *Address:* c/o Grindlay & Co., 54 Parliament Street, SW1. *Died 5 Jan. 1926.*

GIFFARD, Sir Henry Alexander, Kt 1903; KC; Bencher of Lincoln's Inn since 1885; *b* 1838; *e s* of Col Henry Giffard, RGA, and Elizabeth, *d* of James Agnew; *m* 1866, Helen Agnes (*d* 1913), *o d* of Stephen Alers Hankey; two *s. Educ:* Elizabeth College, Guernsey; Corpus Christi College, Oxford (MA). Exhibitioner, 1857; Junior Mathematical Scholar, 1858; 1st class Mods (classics and mathematics), 1859; Taylorian scholar, 1860; 1st class Lit. Hum. and 1st class Math. 1861; Eldon scholar, 1861; Senior student of Christ Church, 1863. Called to the Bar, Lincoln's Inn, 1865; QC 1882; Assistant Commissioner on Schools Inquiry Commission, 1865–66; contested East Cambs 1892; Reader in Equity to Inns of Court, 1888–91; Bailiff of Guernsey, 1902–8. *Recreations:* golf, shooting. *Address:* Braye du Valle, Guernsey. *Clubs:* New University, Cecil.
Died 1 July 1927.

GIFFARD, Walter Thomas Courtenay, DL, JP Co. Stafford; *b* 11 Jan. 1839; *s* of Walter Peter Giffard of Chillington, Co. Stafford, and Henrietta Dorothy, 2nd *d* of late Sir John Fenton Boughey, 2nd Bt of Aqualate, Co. Stafford; *m* 1879, Mary Constance, *e d* of Richard Holt Briscoe, Somerford, Co. Stafford; two *s* two *d. Educ:* Leamington Coll. *Address:* Chillington, Wolverhampton. *TA:* Codsall. *Club:* Conservative, Wolverhampton.
Died 31 Oct. 1926.

GIFFARD, Colonel William Carter, DSO 1900; Welsh Regiment; retired; *b* 25 June 1859; *s* of late Major E. C. Giffard; *m* 1906, Cecile Margaret Stewart, *d* of Mrs Schwabe. Served Suakin, 1888 (despatches, medal with clasp, 4th Medjidie, Khedive's Star); Gold Coast, 1897–98 (despatches, brevet Lt-Col, medal with clasp); South Africa, 1899–1902 (wounded, despatches, Queen's medal, 5 clasps, King's medal, 2 clasps, DSO); European War (despatches, Bt-Col). *Address:* Skiddaw View, Keswick.
Died 25 April 1921.

GIFFORD, Charles Edwin, CB 1894; retired Paymaster-in-Chief, Royal Navy; *b* Milton Abbott, Devon, 8 April 1843; *s* of George Mitchell Gifford; *m* 1880, Effie (*d* 1902), *d* of Mark A. Neef, Chicago, USA; one *s* two *d. Educ:* King Edward's School, Launceston. Entered RN 1861; served as Secretary to Naval Commanders-in-Chief of Channel Squadron, Cape of Good Hope, Portsmouth, The Nore, Mediterranean; Secretary at Portsmouth during Jubilee Naval Review, 1887; Naval Review, 1897; employed at Admiralty on manning and recruiting duties, 1897–1908. *Publication:* (joint) Manual of Naval Law and Court-Martial Procedure. *Address:* Chesterton House, West Ewell, Surrey. *T:* Epsom 476.
Died 18 Feb. 1922.

GILBERT, Albert, ROI; Art Master, Leys School, Cambridge; Governing Member of the Artists Society and Langham Sketching Club; *b* London. *Educ:* Southport. Exhibitor at Royal Academy and other London exhibitions; also the Provincial Galleries; illustrator. *Address:* 39 Fairfax Road, Bedford Park, W4. *T:* Chiswick 2143. *Club:* Chelsea Arts.
Died 15 June 1927.

GILBERT, Rev. Charles Robert; Rector of Seagrave, Leicestershire, since 1906; *b* Oxford, 12 July 1851; *s* of late Charles Gilbert, CE; *m* 1877, Edith Mary Walton, 2nd *d* of Rev. J. Dawson, Vicar of Holy Trinity, Weston-super-Mare; three *d. Educ:* Rugby; Christ's Coll. Cambridge (Open Scholar), 19th wrangler, and 2nd class Moral Sciences Tripos; BA 1874; MA 1877. Private coaching at Cambridge after degree till 1875; Mathematical Master, Derby School, 1875–78; Deacon, 1876; Priest, 1877; Head Master of Weymouth Coll., 1879–85; Master of Modern Side and Senior Mathematical Master, St Peter's School, York, 1885–90; Head Master of King Henry VIII School, Coventry, 1890–1905; Select Preacher at Cambridge, 1891; Domestic Chaplain to Lord Leigh at Stoneleigh Abbey, 1891–1905; Chaplain of Ragdale, Leics., 1910–15; Editor of Shakespeare's King Henry V, 1911; As You Like It, 1912. *Publication:* Notes on St Matthew's Gospel, 1914. *Recreations:* cycling, bowls, reading, singing. *Address:* Seagrave Rectory, near Loughborough. *TA:* Gilbert, Seagrave, Sileby.
Died 29 Dec. 1919.

GILBERT, Rosa, (Lady Gilbert), (Rosa Mulholland); authoress; *b* Belfast, 1841; 2nd *d* of Joseph Stevenson Mulholland, MD, Belfast; *m* 1891, Sir John Thomas Gilbert, LLD (*d* 1898). *Educ:* home. *Publications:* (as Ruth Murray) Dunmara, 1864; Hester's History; The Wild Birds of Killeevy; Marcella Grace, 1886; A Fair Emigrant, 1889; The Late Miss Hollingford; Banshee Castle; Giannetta; Vagrant Verses; Hetty Gray, 1899; Four Little Mischiefs; Puck and Blossom; The Walking Trees; Nanno; Onora, 1900; Cynthia's Bonnet Shop, 1900; Terry; The Squire's Granddaughters; The Tragedy of Chris; A Girl's Ideal; The Life of Sir John T. Gilbert; Our Sister Maisie; The Return of Mary O'Murrough; Spirit and Dust (poems); Cousin Sara; The

O'Shaughnessy Girls; Father Tim; Fair Noreen; Twin Sisters; Old School Friends; The Daughter in Possession; Narcissa's Ring, 1915; etc. *Recreations:* gardening, reading, seeing friends. *Address:* Villa Nova, Blackrock, Co. Dublin.
Died April 1921.

GILBERT, Rev. Thomas Morrell; Vicar of Heversham, 1866–1921; Hon. Canon of Carlisle since 1877; *m* Esther Anne Harrison (*d* 1917). *Educ:* Trinity College, Cambridge (Fellow). Ordained 1861; Curate of Hurstpierpoint, 1861–63; St Bartholomew's, Chichester, 1863–64; Incumbent, 1864–66; Vice-Principal Chichester College, 1863–66; RD Kirkby Lonsdale, 1888–1912. *Address:* 21 Warwick Square, SW1.
Died 16 Dec. 1928.

GILBERT-CARTER, Sir Gilbert Thomas, KCMG 1893 (CMG 1890); FZS, FSA, FES, FRCI, FRGS; *b* 14 Jan. 1848; *o s* of Commander Thomas Gilbert Carter, RN; *m* 1st, 1874, Susan Laura (*d* 1895), 4th *d* of Lieut-Col Edward Hocker, CB; 2nd, 1903, Gertrude Codman, *o c* of late Francis Parker of Boston, USA; three *s* two *d. Educ:* Royal Naval School, Greenwich; private tutors. Royal Navy, 1864–75; Private Sec. to Governor Leeward Islands, 1875–79; Treasurer and Collector of Customs, Gold Coast, 1879–82; transferred to Gambia in same capacity, 1882–88; Administrator, 1888–91; Governor and Commander-in-Chief, Lagos, 1891–96; Bahama Islands, 1897–1904; Barbados, 1904–10; transferred temporarily to Trinidad, 1907; retired, 1910; by deed-poll name changed to Gilbert-Carter, 1919. *Recreations:* lawn tennis, archery, natural history pursuits, gardening. *Address:* 43 Charing Cross, SW; Ilaro Court, Barbados, West Indies.
Died 18 Jan. 1927.

GILBERTSON, Rev. Lewis, MA; FSA; Rector of St Martin's, Ludgate, with St Gregory by St Paul, and St Mary Magdalen, Old Fish Street; Hon. Minor Canon of St Paul's since 1913; *b* 1857; *m* 1912, Edith, *d* of Sir Brydges Henniker, 4th Bt. *Educ:* Magdalen School; Queen's College, Oxford (honours, Natural Science, 1876). Curate of Fulham, 1880; Minor Canon, St Paul's Cathedral, 1882; Succentor, 1893–1903; Librarian, 1897–1903. *Address:* 32 Dorset Square, NW1. *T:* Paddington 0662. *Clubs:* Athenæum, Burlington Fine Arts.
Died 12 June 1928.

GILBEY, Lt-Col Alfred, VD; JP; Director of Barclays Bank and W. & A. Gilbey; *b* Jan. 1859; *s* of late Alfred Gilbey, one of the founders of W. and A. Gilbey; *m* 1885, Beatrice Elizabeth (*d* 1926), *d* of W. J. Holland of Cadogan Gardens; five *s*. Contested (L) South Bucks, 1886; member of Tariff Reform Commission; commanded Buckinghamshire Vol., 1900–6; Master of the Old Berkeley Hunt West Hounds, 1895–1902; High Sheriff, Bucks, 1906; raised and commanded a Bucks Territorial Battalion, in 1915–16. *Address:* 78 Upper Berkeley St, W1. *T:* Mayfair 7114. *Clubs:* Carlton, Marlborough.
Died 24 Oct. 1927.

GILCHRIST, Douglas Alston, BScA (Edin.), Hon. MSc, Durham; FRSE, FHAS; Professor of Agriculture, Armstrong College (University of Durham), Newcastle upon Tyne; Director of Northumberland Agricultural Experiment Station at Cockle Park; *s* of late Wm Gilchrist, Bothwell, Scotland; *m* Jessie Kathleen, *d* of late J. F. Ferguson, Reading. *Educ:* Hamilton Academy; Technical College, Glasgow; Edinburgh University. Director of the Agricultural Department, University Coll., Reading, 1894–1902; head of Agricultural Department of University College of North Wales, Bangor, 1889–94. *Address:* The Quarries West, Clifton Road, Newcastle upon Tyne.
Died 4 April 1927.

GILCHRIST, John Dow Fisher, MA, DSc, PhD; FLS, CMZS; Professor of Zoology, University of Cape Town, since 1918; *b* 1866; 2nd *s* of late Andrew Gilchrist, Anstruther, Scotland; *m* Elfreda Ruth, *d* of late S. H. Raubenheimer, Heimers River, George; one *s* one *d. Educ:* Madras College, St Andrews; Universities of St Andrews, Edinburgh, Munich, and Zürich. Assistant in Zoological Department, University of Edinburgh, 1893; Marine Biologist to the Government of the Cape of Good Hope, 1895; carried out Marine Biological and Fisheries Survey of Cape Coasts, 1896–1904; discovered trawling ground on Agulhas Bank, 1898; carried out Marine Biological and Fisheries Survey for Natal Government, 1902; President of the S African Philosophical Society, Cape Town, 1903–4; Hon. Member Soc. Centrale d'Aquiculture; Joint Hon. Secretary S African Association for the Advancement of Science, 1902–5; Professor of Zoology, South African College, Cape Town, 1905–17; Chairman of Fishery Board of Cape Province, 1908; Marine Biological and Fisheries Adviser for Cape Province, 1912; President of the Royal Society of South Africa, 1918; Hon. Director S Africa Fishing and Marine Biological Survey, 1920; President S Africa Association for Advancement of Science, 1922. *Publications:* Annual Reports of

Marine Biologist to Cape Government, 1895–1904; editor and part author of Marine Investigations in S Africa (5 vols), 1902–8; Joint Editor Science in S Africa, 1905; South African Zoology, 1911; Marine Biological Reports to Cape Province from 1913; Reports on the Fisheries and Marine Biological Survey of S Africa, since 1920; papers, chiefly on Fishes, Mollusca, Crustacea, Hemichordata, Temperatures and Currents of S African Seas, etc, in various scientific publications. *Address:* University of Cape Town.

Died Oct. 1926.

GILCHRIST, Robert Murray; novelist; *b* Sheffield, 6 Jan. 1868; 2nd *s* of Robert Murray Gilchrist and Isabella, *d* of Peter Murray; unmarried. *Educ:* Sheffield Royal Grammar School; privately. Began to write at an early age; spent many summers in Derbyshire; and afterwards lived for several years in a remote part of the High Peak, studying the country folk; contributed to the National Observer in W. E. Henley's day. *Publications:* Passion the Plaything, 1890; Frangipanni, 1893; The Stone Dragon and other Tragical Romances, 1894; Hercules and the Marionettes, 1894; A Peakland Faggot, 1897; Willowbrake, 1898; The Rue Bargain, 1898; Nicholas and Mary, 1899; The Courtesy Dame, 1900; The Labyrinth, 1902; Natives of Milton, 1902; Beggar's Manor, 1903; Lords and Ladies, 1903; The Wonderful Adventures, 1905; The Gentle Thespians, 1908; Good-bye to Market, 1908; The Abbey Mystery, 1908; The Two Goodwins, 1909; Pretty Fanny's Way, 1909; The Peak District, 1911; Willowford Woods, 1911; The Firstborn, 1911; The Secret Tontine, 1912; Damosel Croft, 1912; The Dukeries, 1913; Roadknight, 1913; Weird Wedlock, 1913; The Chase, 1913; Ripon and Harrogate, 1914; Scarborough, 1914; Under Cover of Night, 1914; Honeysuckle Rogue, 1916. *Recreations:* long moorland walks, motoring, music. *Address:* Cartledge Hall, Holmesfield, Sheffield.

Died 4 April 1917.

GILDEA, Col Sir James, GBE 1920; KCVO 1908 (CVO 1901); Kt 1902; CB 1898; FSA, FRGS; Knight of Justice Order of St John of Jerusalem; Jubilee (Queen Victoria) and Coronation medals, King Edward VII and King George V; King Edward and Queen Alexandra Personal Gold Medal; Colonel commanding 6th Royal Warwickshire Regiment, 1890–98; Hon. Colonel 4th Battalion (Special Reserve) Royal Warwickshire Regiment, 1909; *b* Kilmaine, Co. Mayo, 23 June 1838; 3rd *s* of late Very Rev. George Robert Gildea, Provost of Tuam; *m* 1864, Rachel Caroline (*d* 1888) (a Lady of Justice Order of St John of Jerusalem), *d* of Arthur Kett Barclay of Bury Hill, Dorking; one *s* two *d*. *Educ:* St Columba's College, Ireland; Pembroke Coll. Cambridge. Served in Franco-German War (Nat. Soc. for Aid to Sick and Wounded in War); mainly instrumental in raising a fund of £12,000 for relief of widows and orphans of those killed during the Zulu War, 1879; raised a similar fund in connection with the Afghan War, 1880; to these funds he acted as Treasurer and Hon. Secretary; Treasurer in England at the same time to the Indian Patriotic and Bombay Military Relief Funds; Organising Secretary of Queen Victoria's Jubilee Institute for Nurses, 1890–95; founded the Soldiers' and Sailors' Families Association, of which he is Chairman, Treasurer, and one of Trustees, 1885; founded also in connection with this the "Officers", "Nursing", and "Clothing" branches, Royal Homes for Officers' Widows and Daughters, Queen Alexandra's Court, Wimbledon, 1899; was instrumental in raising the "Serpent" and "Edgar" Boat Funds, as also the NW Frontier Fund, all of which are administered by the Assoc.; over one million and a quarter was placed in the hands of and administered by the Assoc. during the South African War, 1899–1902; and two million and a half during the European War, 1914–17; is one of the members of the Royal Patriotic Fund Corporation (1903); has taken an active part (being one of its promoters) in the St John Ambulance Association, of which he was treasurer, as well as assistant almoner of the Order of St John of Jerusalem. *Publications:* The Order of St John of Jerusalem in England; The St John Ambulance Association; Naval and Military Funds and Institutions; For King and Country, being a Record of Funds and Philanthropic Work in connection with the South African War, 1899–1902; For Remembrance, being memorials erected in memory of those who lost their lives in the same war; Memorials to His late Majesty King Edward VII; The Gildeas of Port Royal and Clooncormack; Historical Record of the Work of the Soldiers' and Sailors' Families Association from 1885 to 1916; and History of the Royal Homes from 1899 to 1918. *Recreations:* oarsman at Cambridge; cycling. *Address:* 11 Hogarth Road, SW5.

Died 6 Oct. 1920.

GILDEA, Rev. William; Rector of Upwey, 1901–22; Canon of Salisbury since 1893; *b* Dec. 1833; 2nd *s* of Very Rev. George Robert Gildea, Provost of Tuam, and Esther, *o d* of Thomas Green of Green Mount, Enniscorthy; *m* 1862, Sarah Caroline (*d* 1924), *e d* of N. P.

Simes, Strood Park, Horsham; five *s* four *d*. *Educ:* Marlborough; Exeter College, Oxford. BA (4th class Lit. Hum.), 1856; MA 1858. Deacon, 1856; Priest, 1858; Curate of Compton Valence, 1856–61; Vicar of West Lulworth, Dorset, 1862–79; Netherbury, Dorset, 1879–1901; Rural Dean, Beaminster Portion, 1890–1901; Chaplain of Beaminster Union, 1883–1901; Acting Chaplain, Valparaiso, 1897–98. *Publication:* an article in the National Review in answer to the late H. Farquharson, MP, on Tithe. *Recreations:* wood work, shooting, salmon fishing, yachting. *Address:* Innellan, Verne Road, Rodwell, Weymouth. *TA:* Weymouth. *Club:* Royal Dorset Yacht, Weymouth.

Died 11 Dec. 1925.

GILDER, Jeannette Leonard; special literary agent since 1908; *b* Flushing, New York, 3 Oct. 1849; *d* of Rev. William H. Gilder. Left school at fourteen to accept clerical position, father having died during Civil War; journalist since 1872, first on New York Tribune; was musical, dramatic, and literary critic on NY Herald seven years; left Herald to start The Critic, later Putnam's Magazine, with J. B. Gilder, in 1881; literary correspondent of Chicago Tribune since 1888; established The Reader, 1911. *Publications:* Taken by Siege, pub. anonymously, 1886, repub. with name, 1897; The Autobiography of a Tomboy, 1900; The Tomboy at Work, 1904; dramatic versions of Quo Vadis, Folly Corner, Joan of the Sword Hand, and other popular novels; edited Representative Poems of Living Poets, 1888, Pen Portraits of Literary Women, with Helen Gray Cone, 1889, and Authors at Home, with J. B. Gilder, 1888. *Recreation:* loafing in Europe, and among the hill farms of Connecticut. *Address:* 100 East 17th Street, New York. *Club:* Colony.

Died 17 Jan. 1916.

GILDERSLEEVE, Basil Lanneau, PhD, LLD; Hon. DLitt Oxford and Cambridge; Professor of Greek, Johns Hopkins University, Baltimore, 1876–1915; *b* Charleston, SC, 23 October 1831; *e s* of Rev. Benjamin Gildersleeve and Louisa Lanneau; *m* Elizabeth Fisher, *e d* of Raleigh Colston and Gertrude Powell; one *s* one *d*. *Educ:* Princeton (BA 1849, MA 1852); Berlin; Göttingen (PhD 1853); Bonn. Professor of Greek, Univ. of Virginia, 1856–76; of Latin, 1861–66. Corresponding Fellow of British Academy; Member of American Academy of Arts and Letters. *Publications:* Latin Grammar, 1867; 3rd edn, with Lodge, 1894; and other Latin school books; joint-editor of Gildersleeve-Lodge Latin Series; Ed. Persius, 1875; Justin Martyr's Apologies, 1877; Pindar's Olympian and Pythian Odes, 1885; Essays and Studies, 1890; Syntax of Classical Greek, First Part, 1901; Second Part, 1911; Problems in Greek Syntax, 1903; Hellas and Hesperia, 1909; Creed of the Old South, 1915; Associate Editor for Greek Literature, Johnson's Cyclopædia; Founder and Editor of the American Journal of Philology, 1880–1919. *Address:* The Johns Hopkins University, Baltimore, Maryland, USA. *Clubs:* University, Country, Johns Hopkins, Baltimore.

Died Jan. 1924.

GILES, Sub-Lieut Alfred Edward Boscawen, DSO 1915; RN; served European War, Dardanelles, in HMS Inflexible, 1914–15 (despatches, DSO).

Died Oct. 1917.

GILES, Bertram, CMG 1916; Consul-General, Nanking, since 1924; *b* Hankow, 24 Sept. 1874; *s* of Prof. H. A. Giles; *m* 1903, Violet Jessie, 2nd *d* of David Gilmour of Shanghai; one *s*. *Educ:* Belgium (Liège); Austria (Feldkirch); Scotland (Aberdeen). Student Interpreter, China, 1894; 1st Class Asst 1902; Asst in Mixed Court, Shanghai, 1902–4; Vice-Consul at Canton, 1904–5; Hankow, 1910; Acting Consul at Foochow, 1905; Changsha, 1905–7; Tsinan, 1908–10; Consul at Changsha, 1910–13; Nanking, 1914–21; Consul-General, Tsinan, 1922; Senior British Delegate on Joint Commission for Rendition of Wei-hai-wei, 1922–23; Consul-General, Canton, 1923–24. *Recreations:* billiards, croquet, pedestrianism. *Address:* HBM Consulate-General, Nanking, China. *TA:* Britain, Nanking.

Died 26 March 1928.

GILES, Peter Broome, CB 1911; VD, TD; JP; *b* 5 April 1850; *e s* of Peter Broome Giles and Caroline, *d* of late Admiral T. Bennett; *m* 1879, Florence, *e d* of late J. C. Houghton, of the Quinta, Brobury, Hereford, and 20 Devonshire Place, W; one *s* one *d*. *Educ:* St Catherine's Hermitage, Bath; University College. JP Hereford, Bucks and Kent; High Sheriff, Bucks, 1907; Member of County Council; County Director for the City of London Branch of the British Red Cross Society since 1905; Commandant of the Military Convalescent Hospital, Alnwick, 1915; Commandant of Vol. Ambulance School of Instruction; Commandant of the Military Convalescent Hospital, Ashton-in-Makerfield, 1917; Master of Herefordshire Staghounds. *Publications:* a large number of articles upon Ambulance work, the organisation of Royal Army Medical units, sanitation. *Recreations:*

hunting, shooting, fishing. *Address:* 51 Earls Avenue, Folkestone. *T:* 187. *Club:* Junior Army and Navy.

Died 19 Dec. 1928.

GILES, Robert, CIE 1899; MA (Cantab); *b* 27 Sept. 1846; *s* of late Archdeacon Giles, Precentor of Lincoln and Rector of Willoughby, Lincolnshire; *m* 1885, Isabel, *d* of General Thom, IMS. *Educ:* Durham Grammar School; St John's Coll. Cambridge. Joined the Sind Commission; Collector of Karachi, 1895; acted repeatedly as Commissioner in Sind, 1896–1900, and confirmed in than appointment; retired, 1902. JP West Sussex; Member of West Sussex County Tribunal. *Address:* Ash, Stedham, Midhurst, Sussex. *Club:* East India United Service.

Died 17 March 1928.

GILHOOLY, James Peter, JP; MP (N) Co. Cork, W, 1885–1910, and since 1910; *b* 1847; *s* of late P. Gilhooly, Bantry, Cork; *m* 1882, Mary, *d* of J. Collins. Draper, Bantry; member of Poor Law Board; President of Local National League; Chairman of Town Commissioners, Rural District Council, and local branch United Irish League; Representative of Provincial Executive of United Irish League; was imprisoned several times under the Coercion régime. *Address:* Bantry, Co. Cork. *Died 16 Oct. 1916.*

GILKES, Rev. Arthur Herman, MA; Curate of St James's Church, Bermondsey, since 1915; *s* of William Gilkes, chemist, Leominster, Herefordshire; *m* 1892, *d* of B. M. Clarke, Clairville, Sydenham Hill; four *s*. *Educ:* Shrewsbury School; Christ Church, Oxford. 1st class in Mods and in Final Schools Litteris Humanioribus. Assistant Master at Shrewsbury, 1873–85; Head Master of Dulwich College, 1885–1914; ordained 1915. *Publications:* School lectures on Electra and Macbeth; Boys and Masters; The Thing that Hath Been; Kallistratus; The New Revolution; A Dialogue; A Day at Dulwich; Four Sons. *Recreations:* cycling, cricket. *Address:* St James's Church, Jamaica Road, Bermondsey, SE.

Died 13 Sept. 1922.

GILL, Andrew John Mitchell-, JP and Commissioner of Supply for Cos of Aberdeen and Elgin; FSA (Scot); *b* 1 Aug. 1847; *o surv. s* of late David Gill, JP, of Blairythan and Savock, Aberdeenshire, and Margaret, *d* of Gilbert Mitchell of Savock; assumed the additonal surname of Mitchell; *m* 1894, Margaret, 2nd *d* of late Charles S. Lindsell of Holme, JP, DL Bedfordshire; three *d*. *Educ:* Marischal College and Univ. Aberdeen; Royal Agricultural College, Cirencester. Travelled extensively in Australia, S Africa, Morocco, etc. An authority in Genealogy and Heraldry, particularly so far as the north country families are concerned. *Publications:* The Houses of Moir and Byres; many genealogical articles and pamphlets. *Address:* Auchinroath House, Rothes, Savock House, Newburgh, Aberdeenshire. *Club:* Conservative, Edinburgh. *Died 1 March 1921.*

GILL, Sir Charles Frederick, Kt 1921; KC; Recorder of Chichester, 1890–1921; *b* 10 June 1951; *s* of late Charles Gill of Dublin; *m* 1878, Ada, 7th *d* of John Crossley Fielding of Forest Hill, Kent; one *s* one *d*. *Educ:* Royal School, Dungannon. Barrister, Middle Temple, 1874, Bencher 1905, Lent Reader 1919; QC 1899; Junior Counsel to Post Office, 1886–87; Senior Counsel to Post Office, 1887–89; Junior Counsel to Treasury, 1889–92; Senior Counsel to Treasury, 1892–99; Junior Counsel to London Bankers' Association, 1889–98; Senior Counsel to London Bankers' Association, 1901; Senior Counsel to Jockey Club, 1903–22; Hon. Member of the Jockey Club. *Address:* Tappington, Birchington, Thanet. *T:* Birchington 10; 1 Brick Court, Temple, EC4. *Clubs:* Carlton, Garrick, Beefsteak, Turf.

Died 22 Feb. 1923.

GILL, L. Upcott, FJI; part proprietor of the Bazaar, Exchange and Mart newspaper; formerly Governing Director and Chairman L. Upcott Gill and Son, Ltd; past Chairman of the Master Printers' Association; *b* 7 Nov. 1846; 2nd and *e surv. s* of Chas J. Gill and Emma Gill, *sister* of late Serjeant Cox (last of the Serjeants-at-Law); *m* 1874, Gertrude Alice, *e d* of late Dr A. Sumner, St John's Wood; two *s* four *d*. *Educ:* City of London School. Entered Life Assurance Office of which his father was secretary, and subsequently joined staff of The Field and Queen, and when the Exchange and Mart was started, 1868, was appointed manager and editor. Entered for the Bar, Lincoln's Inn, for a time, but subsequently relinquishing law to devote himself to journalism. Edited a large number of technical handbooks. *Recreations:* fly-fishing, gardening. *Address:* The Old Manor House, Feltham, Middlesex. *Died 9 March 1919.*

GILL, Thomas, CMG 1918; ISO 1903; Under Treasurer of South Australia, 1894–1920; *b* 23 Feb. 1849; *m* 1876, Louisa Jane (*d* 1915),

d of John Bristow. Entered Civil Service, 1865; retired 1920; Member of Public Library Board, etc, since 1896; Hon. Treasurer Royal Geographical Soc. of Australasia, SA Branch, since 1885; Government Member Adelaide Tramways Trust since 1896; a Trustee of the State Savings Bank since 1920; a SA Commissioner of Charitable Funds; a Governor of the Wyatt Benevolent Institution, and Member of Board Da Costa Charitable Fund. *Publications:* Bibliography of South Australia; The History of Glen Osmond; Colonel William Light; Coinage and Currency of SA. *Address:* Willalar, Glen Osmond, South Australia. *Died 22 July 1923.*

GILLESPIE, Robert Alexander; Stipendiary Magistrate for the Borough of West Ham; *b* 30 March 1848; *s* of Alexander Gillespie, merchant, of London, and Montreal, Canada, and Eliza Greenshields; *m* 1896, Helen Duncan, *d* of John Inglis of 10 Upper Phillimore Gardens, Kensington. *Educ:* Weybridge School; St John's College, Cambridge. BA 1869. Barrister, Middle Temple, 1871; practised on the Home and South-Eastern Circuits, and at Surrey and South London Sessions. *Address:* 3 Plowden Buildings, Temple, EC. *Club:* United University. *Died 11 April 1917.*

GILLETT, Major William, FRGS, FZS; DL Herefordshire; *b* 1839; *o surv. s* of late Joseph Ashby Gillett, of Banbury, Oxfordshire, banker; unmarried. *Educ:* private tutors. Originated and carried out clearing of Country Bankers' Cheques, 1859–60, for which he was presented with a testimonial by the Country Bankers of England and Wales. Travelled United States, Canada, West Indies, and in Europe, 1860–61; visited Russia, Turkey, Palestine, and North Africa, 1867–68; travelled with American Army Commission through Japan, China, and India, 1875–76; visited South America, Mexico, Sandwich Islands, New Zealand, and Australia, 1877–78; Middlesex Yeomanry Cavalry, 1869–81; Major 1873–81; attached to 1st Life Guards, 1870–72. In conjunction with the late Colonel Farquharson of Invercauld, and the late Mr Augustus Savile of Rufford Abbey, established the Bachelors' Club in 1881, of which club he is President and one of the Trustees. *Publications:* A British Zollverein, 1879; The Revival of British Industries, 1885; Detailed Proposals for a Tariff Bill, 1904; House of Lords Reform, 1911; Reduction of the National Debt and Decrease of Taxation, 1920. *Recreations:* hunting, shooting, yachting. *Address:* 19 Lowndes Square, SW1. *T:* Victoria 3114. *Clubs:* Carlton, Junior Carlton, Bachelors', Royal Thames Yacht.

Died 5 Dec. 1925

GILLIES, Hon. William Neal; lay member of Queensland Board of Trade and Arbitration since 1925; *b* 28 Oct. 1868; *s* of Dugald Gillies, *m* 1897, Margaret, *d* of late Shelton Smith, Queanbeyan, NSW; one *s* one *d*. MLA 1912–25; Chairman of Public Works Commission 1916; Minister of Justice, 1918; Secretary for Agriculture and Stock 1919–25; Premier, Vice-President of the Executive Council, Chief Secretary and Treasurer of Queensland, 1925; resigned premiership 1925. *Address:* St Osyth Street, Toowong, Brisbane, Queensland *Died 9 Feb. 1928*

GILLMAN, Herbert Francis Webb, CSI 1917; ICS; Ordinary Member of Council of Governor of Madras; Collector and Magistrate Madras, since 1907. *Educ:* Dulwich College; Emmanuel College Cambridge. Entered ICS 1886. *Address:* Madras. *Club:* East India United Service. *Died 23 Nov. 1918*

GILLOT, E. Louis; painter, engraver; Official Painter to the French Armies; Member of Committee of the Société Nationale des Beaux Arts; Vice-President of the Société des Peintres-Graveurs de Paris Member of the Committee of Peintres Orientalistes Français; Hon Concours; Knight of Legion of Honour; MVO; *b* Paris, 14 April 1867 *s* of August Nicholas Gillot, architect. *Educ:* Lycée Ste Barbe, Paris Ecole des Beaux Arts. Inventor of the monotype in colours; chiefly known for paintings representing great industrial works. *Works:* Mine of St Etienne; Records of President Loubet's visits to London and Naples, and an impression of the Thames (gold medal at the Barcelona Exhibition); The Naval Review at Spithead, 1911 (ordered by the French Government for presentation to King George); The Coronation of George V in Westminster Abbey; Investiture of the Prince of Wales at Carnarvon; in addition to etchings and engravings he has also done a number of portraits, among which may be mentioned that of Baron Dard. *Recreations:* fishing, shooting, boating *Address:* 15 rue Théophile Gautier, Paris. *T:* 675–47.

GILMAN, Harold John Wilde; Artist-Painter; *b* England, 1878; 2nd *s* of Rev. John Gilman, Rector of Snargate, Romney Marsh, Kent and Emily Purcell Gulliver. *Educ:* Tonbridge School. *Address:* Maple Street, W. *Died 12 Feb. 191*

GILMOUR, Sir John, 1st Bt; *cr* 1897, of Lundin and Montrave, Fife, and of South Walton, Renfrewshire; JP, DL Fifeshire; Convener of Commissioners of Supply for Fife; Hon. Colonel Fife and Forfar Imperial Yeomanry; *b* 24 July 1845; *e s* of Allan Gilmour of Lundin and Montrave and of South Walton; *m* 1873, Henrietta, 2nd *d* of David Gilmour, Quebec, Canada; two *s* two *d* (and three *s* decd). *Educ:* Glasgow and Edinburgh Academies; Edinburgh University. President of Royal Caledonian Curling Club, 1913. *Recreations:* hunting, stalking, shooting. *Heir: s* Major John Gilmour, *b* 27 May 1876. *Address:* Montrave, Leven, Fife. *TA:* Leven. *Clubs:* Carlton, Junior Carlton; New, Conservative, Scottish Unionist, Edinburgh; Conservative, Glasgow.   *Died 20 July 1920.*

GILMOUR, William Ewing, DL; *b* 21 May 1854; 3rd *s* of late Allan Gilmour, of Eaglesham, and Isabella Buchanan Ewing; *m* 1882, Jessie Gertrude (*d* 1923), 3rd *d* of late James Campbell, of Tullichewan; one *s* three *d*. *Educ:* Edinburgh Academy and University. JP, Dunbarton, Sutherland, and Ross. *Address:* Glencassley Castle, Sutherland. *Clubs:* University, Edinburgh; Western, Glasgow.   *Died 31 Jan. 1924.*

GILPIN, Peter Valentine, JP; *b* 1858; *o s* of late Peter Valentine Purcell of Halverstown, Capt. 13th Light Dragoons, and Agnes Maria (she *m* 2nd, 1866, Col Henry St John Le Marchant, RHA), 8th *d* of Sir John Hesketh Lethbridge, 3rd Bt; *m* 1883, Amy Mary Louisa, *e d* of late Capt. Henry Meux-Smith of Hockliffe; seven *s* two *d*. Assumed the name of Gilpin, 1883. *Address:* Clarehaven, Newmarket; Dollanstown, Kilcock, Ireland. *T:* 17 Newmarket. *Clubs:* Cavalry, Orleans.   *Died 9 Nov. 1928.*

GILRAY, Thomas, MA; FRSE; Hon. LLD Edin.; Professor of English Language and Literature since 1889, and Dean of the Faculty of Arts and Science, Otago University; *b* Scotland, 1851; *m*; four *s* one *d*. *Educ:* High School and University, Edinburgh; Berlin and Heidelberg Universities; one of the trustees of Carlyle's House, Cheyne Row; Member of Board of Studies, New Zealand University, and Member of the New Zealand University Senate. *Address:* Ellangowan, Sargood Street, Dunedin, New Zealand.

Died 3 Feb. 1920.

GINGRAS-DALY, Lt-Col Ludger Jules Olivier, DSO 1917; Commanding 2nd/2nd Quebec Regiment, Canada; *b* 11 July 1876; *m* 1899; no *c*. *Educ:* St Patrick's College, Quebec. Served European War in France, 20 May 1915–Sept. 1917 (wounded at Courcelette with 22nd French-Canadians, DSO, despatches). *Recreations:* golf, equitation. *Address:* 122 Arlington Avenue, Westmount, Montreal, Canada.   *Died 20 Feb. 1919.*

GINNELL, Laurence, BL; MP N Westmeath, 1906–18, Westmeath Co., since 1918; Barrister, Middle Temple, 1893 and also of King's Inns, Dublin, 1906; *b* 1854; 3rd *s* of Laurence Ginnell; *m* 1902, Alice, *d* of J. King, JP, Kilbride. *Educ:* self-educated. One of the founders of the Irish Literary Society, London. Sat as a Nationalist from 1906 but expelled from party 1909; associated with Sinn Fein from 1916; TD for Westmeath, then for Longford and Westmeath 1921–23. *Publications:* Brehon Laws, 1894; Doubtful Grant of Ireland, 1899, and presented personally to Pope Leo XIII; Land and Liberty, 1908. *Recreations:* literary.   *Died 17 April 1923.*

GIOLITTI, Giovanni; *b* Mondovi, Piedmont, 27 Oct. 1842. *Educ:* Turin. Deputy for Dronero (Coni), 1882; Minister of the Treasury, Italy, 1889–90; Premier, 1892–93; Interieur, 1901–3; Premier, 1903–5, 1906–9, 1911–14, 1920–21. *Publication:* Memoirs of My Life. *Address:* Rome.   *Died 17 July 1928.*

GIRARD, Robert George, ISO 1912; Uncovenanted Civil Service of India; *b* 11 Aug. 1859, *s* of late Henry Charles Girard, HEICS (Bengal); *m* 1911, Marie, *d* of late Charles Frederick Pitlar, Solicitor, Calcutta. *Educ:* Bedford Grammar School. Military Accounts Dept Govt of India, 1876–84; Revenue Dept (Stamps and Excise) Govt of Bengal, 1884–96; Collector of Income Tax, Calcutta, since 1896; Major, VD, and Officiating Commandant, Calcutta Volunteer Rifles. *Clubs:* Oriental; Bengal, Calcutta.   *Died 17 May 1921.*

GIRAUD, Surg.-Maj.-Gen. Charles Herve. Entered army, 1858; retired, 1896; served Indian Mutiny, 1858 (medal with clasp); China War, 1860 (medal with clasp); Taeping Rebellion, 1863–64; South African War, 1879–81.   *Died 10 May 1918.*

GIRDLESTONE, Rev. Robert Baker, MA; Hon. Canon of Christ Church, Oxford; *b* 1836; *s* of Rev. Charles Girdlestone, formerly Fellow of Balliol; *m* 1st, Maude, *d* of Rev. J. Richey; 2nd, Mary, *d* of J. Wood of Thedden Grange; three *s*. *Educ:* Charterhouse; Christ Church, Oxford. Supt of the Translation Department of the Bible Society, 1866–76; Principal of Wycliffe Hall, Oxford, 1877–89; Minister of St John's, Downshire Hill, NW, 1889–1903. *Publications:* Synonyms of the Old Testament; Students' Deuteronomy; Foundations of the Bible; Grammar of Prophecy; Deuterographs; How to Study the English Bible; Age and Trustworthiness of Old Testament; Doctor Doctorum; Churchman's Guide; Why do I Believe in Jesus Christ; OT Theology; Outlines of Bible Chronology; Commentary on Galatians; Building up of Old Testament; Mission of Christ. *Address:* Saxholme, Wimbledon, SW19. *T:* Wimbledon 550.   *Died 6 April 1923.*

GIRDWOOD, Gilbert P.; Emeritus Professor of Chemistry, McGill University, since 1902; *b* London, 22 Oct. 1832; *s* of G. F. Girdwood, MD, Edinburgh, from Polmont, Scotland, and *d* of Rev. Thos Bazely, Rector of Lavenham, Suffolk; *m* 1862, F. M., *d* of late T. E. Blackwell, CE, Managing Director Grand Trunk Railway; five *s* three *d*. *Educ:* private school, and St George's School of Medicine, London. Passed Coll. of Surgeons, London, 1854; House Surgeon Liverpool Infirmary, 1854; joined 1st Battalion Grenadier Guards, as Assistant Surgeon, 1854; went to Canada with 1st Battalion; at Trent Affair, 1862; stationed in Montreal; left the service on the regiment returning to England; joined the Victoria Rifle Volunteer Militia as surgeon; called out with regiment at Fenian disturbance, 1866 (medal); promoted to Medical Staff Officer of Militia of Canada; MD, CM M'Gill University, 1865; Lecturer in Practical Chemistry in Medical Faculty of M'Gill University, 1869; Professor of Practical Chemistry, 1872–94; Professor of Chemistry, 1879–1902; 12 years Surgeon to Montreal Dispensary, and to Montreal General Hospital; Consulting Surgeon to both institutions; Consultant Physician in X-Rays Department, Victoria Hospital, Montreal; Chief Medical Officer Canadian-Pacific Railway; ex-President Roentgen Society of America; Vice-President Canadian Branch Society of Chemical Industry; Fellow Chemical Society, Chemical Institute of Great Britain, Society of Public Analysts, Society of Chemical Industry, Royal Society of Canada, Natural History Society and Microscopical Society of Montreal. *Publications:* various articles. *Recreations:* worn mile race open to all officers in British Army, Aldershot, 1856; athletic exercise; boating. *Address:* 615 University Street, Montreal, Canada. *Club:* St James's, Montreal.   *Died 2 Oct. 1917.*

GISBORNE, Lt-Col Lionel Guy, CMG 1916; late RFA, TF; *b* 1866; *s* of late Hon. William Gisborne, MLC, New Zealand, and Allestree Hall, Derby; *m*; one *s* one *d*. Served S Africa, 1899–1900 (Queen's medal 3 clasps); European War, 1914–18 (despatches, CMG). *Address:* Lingen Hall, Bucknell, Shropshire; Ros Vean, Mullion, S Cornwall.   *Died 24 Oct. 1928.*

GIUFFRIDA-RUGGERI, Dr Vincenzo; Professor Ord. of Anthropology and Director of Anthropological Institute in the Royal University of Naples since 1907; Professor of Ethnology at Royal Oriental Institute of Naples since 1914; *b* Catania, 1 Feb. 1872; *m* 1914, Lilian C. Strachan of Newcastle upon Tyne; two *s*. Physician at Rome, 1896; later, Libero Docente of Anthropology; Assistant Professor of Anthropology, University of Rome, 1900–5; Professor of Anthropology at University of Pavia, 1906–7; late Vice-President of Società Italiana di Antropologia ed Etnologia, and of Società Romana di Antropologia; Hon. Fellow of the Royal Anthropological Institute of Great Britain and Ireland; Corres. Member Anthropological Societies Paris, Vienna, Moscow, Lyons, Bruxelles, Porto, Liége, Ord. Member of the R. Accad. delle scienze fis. e matem. di Napoli, Member of the Institut suisse d'Anthropologie générale; and the Ecole d'Anthropologie de Paris. *Publications:* Sullà dignità morfologica dei segni degenerativi, Roma, 1897; Homo sàpiens, Einleitung zu einem Kurse der Anthropologie, Wien, 1913; L'Uomo attuale, Una specie collettiva, Roma (Albrighi-Segati), 1913; Antropologià dell' Africa orientale, Firenze, 1915; A Sketch of the Anthropology of Italy, Lond. 1918; Antropologia sistematica dell' Asia, Firenze, 1919. *Address:* Istituto Antropologico, R. Università, Napoli.

GIVENS, Hon. Thomas; President of the Commonwealth Senate, 1913–26; Senator for Queensland since 1903; *b* Co. Tipperary, Ireland, 12 June 1864; *m* 1901, Katie, *d* of J. Allen, Cairns, Queensland. MLA Queensland, 1899–1902. *Address:* Federal Parliament House, Melbourne.   *Died 19 June 1928.*

GJELLERUP, Karl; Danish novelist; *b* 1859. Nobel prize for literature (jointly with Henrik Pontoppidan), 1917. *Publications:* En Idealist, 1878; Antigonos, 1880; Rödtjörn, 1881; Germanernes Laerling, 1882; Minna, 1889; Möllen, 1896; Der Pilger Kamanoto, 1906.

Died 14 Oct. 1919.

GLADSTONE, Helen; b 28 Aug. 1849; y d of late Rt Hon. William Ewart Gladstone. *Educ:* home; Newnham College, Cambridge. Vice-Principal of Newnham College, 1882–96; Warden of Women's University Settlement, 1901–6. *Address:* Sundial, Hawarden, Chester.
Died 19 Aug. 1925.

GLADSTONE, Sir John Robert, 3rd Bt, cr 1846; DL; Captain Coldstream Guards; retired; b 26 April 1852; o s of Sir Thomas Gladstone, 2nd Bt and Louisa, 2nd d of Robert Fellowes of Shotesham Park, Norfolk; S father, 1889. *Educ:* Eton; Christ Church, Oxford. Served Egyptian Expedition, 1882; Suakin, 1885. *Heir:* c John Evelyn Gladstone, b 23 Nov. 1855. *Address:* Fasque, Fettercairn, NB; Glendye Lodge, Banchory, Kincardineshire. *Clubs:* Guards, Travellers', Carlton.
Died 25 June 1926.

GLADSTONE, Robert, JP Co. of Lancashire; late Chairman Mersey Docks and Harbour Board; b 1833; e s of late Thomas Steuart Gladstone of Capenoch, Dumfriesshire, NB; m 1860, Mary Ellen (d 1895), d of Robertson Gladstone of Court Hey, near Liverpool; four s five d. *Educ:* Eton; Edinburgh University. JP for Liverpool for 32 years; Treasurer of University College, Liverpool, for 22 years. LLD University of Liverpool, and Hon. Freeman of Liverpool. *Address:* Woolton Vale, Liverpool. *TA:* Gladstone, Woolton. *T:* Gateacre 59. *Club:* Palatine, Liverpool.
Died 12 July 1919.

GLADSTONE, Rev. Stephen Edward; b 4 April 1844; 2nd s of late Rt Hon. William Ewart Gladstone; m 1885, Annie Crosthwaite, d of late C. B. Wilson, Surgeon, Liverpool; three s two d (and one s decd). *Educ:* Eton; Christ Church, Oxford (2nd Mods; 2nd class Lit. Hum.); MA, 1868. Priest, 1870; Curate of St Michael the Less, Lambeth, 1868–72; Rural Dean of Mold, 1884–92; Rector of Hawarden, 1872–1904; Rector of Barrowby, Lincs, 1904–11. *Address:* Manley Hall, Helsby, Cheshire.
Died 23 April 1920.

GLAIHER, James Whitbread Lee, MA, ScD; FRS 1875; Fellow of Trinity College, Cambridge, since 1871; b Lewisham, Kent, 5 Nov. 1848; e s of late James Glaisher, FRS, and Cecilia Bellerville; unmarried. *Educ:* St Paul's School, London; Trinity Coll. Camb. Campden Exhibitioner, St Paul's School, 1867; Scholar of Trinity Coll. Camb. 1868; graduated (2nd Wrangler), 1871. President of the Cambridge Philosophical Society, 1882–84; of the London Mathematical Society, 1884–86; of the Royal Astronomical Society, 1885–87, 1900–2; of Section A of the British Association, 1890; of the Cambridge Antiquarian Society, 1899–1901; ScD Cambridge, 1887; Dublin, 1892; Victoria University, 1902; Tutor of Trinity, 1883–93; Lecturer, 1871–1901; De Morgan Medal of London Mathematical Society, 1908; Sylvester Medal of Royal Society, 1913. *Publications:* editor of the Messenger of Mathematics since 1871, and of the Quarterly Journal of Pure and Applied Mathematics since 1878; numerous papers on Pure Mathematics. *Recreations:* President Cambridge University Bicycle Club, 1882–85; interested in faience and pottery. *Address:* Trinity College, Cambridge. *Club:* Athenæum.
Died 7 Dec. 1928.

GLAISTER, Rev. William; Hon. Canon of Southwell since 1908; Chancellor of the Cathedral; s of late Rev. W. Glaister, Vicar of Beckley, Sussex. *Educ:* Marlborough; University Coll. Oxford (MA, BCL). Vicar of Grantham, 1883–1905; Rural Dean and Surrogate; Hon. Canon Lincoln Cathedral, 1890–1908. *Publications:* Life of St Wulfram; Life of Karl the Great. *Recreations:* cricket, boating (winner of Grand Challenge, Ladies' Plate, and Stewards' Cup, Henley, 1863). *Address:* The Burgage, Southwell.
Died 7 Feb. 1919.

GLANCEY, Rt. Rev. Mgr Michael Francis; Bishop of Flaviopolis since 1924; Auxiliary of the Archbishop of Birmingham; Provost of Birmingham Metropolitan Chapter; b Wolverhampton, 25 Oct. 1854. *Educ:* Sedgley Park School; Oscott College. Priest, 1877; Professor at Oscott College, 1877–88; Diocesan Inspector of Schools, 1888–97; Diocesan Chancellor, 1897–1918; Pastor at Solihull, 1899–1908; Principal St Charles', Begbroke, 1908–14; Canon of Chapter, 1905; Provost of Chapter, 1922; Protonotary Apostolic, 1916; Vicar-General of Birmingham, 1921–25; Chairman of Education Committee of Old Birmingham School Board, 1899–1902. *Publications:* Characteristics from the Writings of Archbishop Ullathorne; English version of Knecht's Commentary on Scripture; translation of Schanz's Christian Apology, 3 vols, 1890; Editor Birmingham Catholic Directory, 1900–12; Birmingham Provincial Directory, 1912–16; Orbis Catholicus: A Directory of the Catholic World, 1916; The Present Position of the Education Question: A Course of Lectures, 1896; Catholics and the Education Question, 1902. *Address:* Archbishop's

House, 6 Norfolk Road, Edgbaston, Birmingham. *T:* Edgbaston 564. *M:* AC 2877.
Died 16 Oct. 1925.

GLANFIELD, Sir Robert, Kt 1920; Chairman G. Glanfield & Son, Ltd, London; b London, 16 Oct. 1862; 2nd s of George Glanfield, Hale End, Woodford; m 1888, Mabel, e d of late H. H. C. Baker of King William's Town, South Africa; two s two d. *Educ:* Campden Grammar School; Oundle. *Recreation:* golf. *Address:* 34 Eton Avenue, NW3. *T:* Hampstead 5689. *Clubs:* Devonshire, Royal Automobile.
Died 17 Aug. 1924.

GLANUSK, 2nd Baron, cr 1899; **Joseph Henry Russell Bailey,** CB 1911; CBE 1919; DSO 1900; JP Breconshire; Bt 1852; Lord-Lieutenant of Brecknock since 1905; retired; late Major Grenadier Guards; commanded Guards Depot, Caterham, 1901–3; 3rd Battalion, South Wales Borderers, 1905–10; Brecknockshire Battalion, 1911–16; London Command Depot since 1916; b 26 Oct. 1864; e s of 1st Baron Glanusk, and Mary, d of Henry Lucas, MD; S father, 1906; m 1890, Editha Elma, CBE 1920, o d of late Warden Sergison of Cuckfield Park, Sussex; one s one d (and two s decd). *Educ:* Eton; RMC Sandhurst. Joined Grenadier Guards, 1885; was adjutant to CIV, South Africa. *Recreations:* cricket, football (capt. of Eton Football, 1883), shooting, fishing, hunting, etc. *Heir:* s Hon. Wilfred Russell Bailey, b 27 June 1891. *Address:* Pwll-y-faedda, Erwood. *Club:* Guards.
Died 2 Jan. 1928.

GLASSE, John, MA, DD; Minister Emeritus of Old Greyfriars, Edinburgh; b Auchtermuchty, Fifeshire, 27 Jan. 1848; m 1st, 1878, Jane Scott (decd), d of Provost White, Auchtermuchty; one s one d; 2nd, Louisa Plymer, d of Alexander Gibson, Ceylon. *Educ:* Free Church School, Auchtermuchty; St Andrews Univ.; New Coll. Edinburgh. Licensed by Presbytery of Edinburgh, 1876; Asst in Old Greyfriars and ordained Minister, 1877; intimately associated with public movements and public bodies; Vice-President of Sunday Society; ex-President Edinburgh Burns Club; a prominent advocate of Christian Socialism; an enthusiastic Freemason. *Publications:* John Knox, a Criticism; Pauperism in Scotland, Past and Present; Poor Law Amendment; Modern Christian Socialism; The Relation of the Church to Socialism; Robert Owen and his Life-Work; has written and lectured extensively on ethical and social questions. *Recreation:* an occasional game of golf. *Address:* 16 Tantallon Place, Edinburgh; Bayview, Upper Largo, Fifeshire. *Club:* Scottish Liberal, Edinburgh.
Died 8 Feb. 1918.

GLASSINGTON, Charles William, MRCS, LDSEd; Senior Dental Surgeon, Westminster Hospital; Member of the British Dental Association, etc; b 1857; m 1892; widower; no c. *Educ:* St Mark's College, SW; Westminster Hospital; National Dental Hospital. House Surgeon; Administrator of Anæsthetics; Assistant Dental Surgeon; Dental Surgeon and Lecturer; formerly Dental Surgeon at the Duke of York's Royal Military School, Chelsea. *Publications:* Dental Materia Medica and Therapeutics, 2nd edn; Golden Rules of Dental Surgery, 4th edn; contributions to various dental journals. *Recreations:* sea angling, bowls. *Address:* 6 Pelham Crescent, South Kensington, SW7. *T:* 615 Kensington.
Died 7 Feb. 1922.

GLAZEBROOK, Rev. Michael George, DD; Canon of Ely since 1905; b London, 4 Aug. 1853; s of M. G. Glazebrook; m 1880, Ethel, 4th d of Sir Benjamin Collins Brodie, 2nd Bt. *Educ:* Dulwich College; Balliol Coll. Oxford; double 1st in Mods; 1st class Lit. Hum. Asst Master at Harrow, 1878; High Master of Manchester Grammar School, 1888; Hon. Canon of Bristol Cathedral, 1898; Headmaster of Clifton Coll., 1891–1905. *Publications:* editions of the Prometheus and Medea; Lessons from the Old Testament; various educational essays; Sermons; Studies in the Book of Isaiah; The End of the Law: The Layman's Old Testament; The Faith of a Modern Churchman. The Letter and the Spirit; The Apocalypse of St John. *Recreations:* rowing, golf. *Address:* The College, Ely. *Club:* Athenæum.
Died 1 May 1926.

GLAZEBROOK, Philip Kirkland; MP (U) South Manchester since 1912; Major, Cheshire Yeomanry; b 1880; s of John K. Glazebrook; unmarried. *Educ:* Eton; New College, Oxford. Left Oxford, 1903 and travelled a good deal until 1910; contested S Manchester, 1910 but owing to a mistake was not nominated. *Recreations:* travelling, shooting. *Address:* Twemlow Hall, Holmes Chapel, Cheshire. *TA* Glazebrook, Goostrey. *M:* 3515. *Clubs:* Bath, Prince's; Vincent's, Oxford.
Died 11 March 1918.

GLEADOWE-NEWCOMEN, Colonel Arthur Hills, CIE 1907 VD; FRGS, FRSA, FAGS; late Officer Commanding 1st United Provinces Horse, and Hon. ADC, Lords Curzon, Minto, and

Hardinge, Viceroys of India; *b* 9 Nov. 1853; *o s* of Robert Gleadowe-Newcomen of Killester House, Co. Dublin; *m* 1st, 1876, Clara, *d* of Capt. J. Masson, IA; one *s* one *d*; 2nd, 1925, Marye Eveleen, *d* of Rev. Algernon Clementi Smith; no *c*. *Educ:* Ripon and Durham Schools. Travelled over the greater part of the world, and served 40 years in India, seeing much service, and spent many years exploring; served in Egypt, Soudan, and in South Africa during Boer War; in Japan and China during Russo-Japanese War, also in France and Flanders during European War, 1914–15. *Publication:* Report on the Trade and Commerce of SW Persia, of which commission he was in command. *Recreations:* cricket, football, racquets, tennis, polo, pig-sticking, big-game shooting, etc. *Address:* Killester Ranch, Coppice Hill PO, Ardrossan, Alberta, Canada. *Club:* Junior Army and Navy.
Died 30 May 1928.

GLEGG, Edward Maxwell; owner of Backford Hall and Irby Hall, Cheshire; *b* 24 June 1849; *o* surv. *s* of late Col Edward Holt Glegg, Rifle Brigade, and Margaret Maxwell, *o c* of John Maxwell Logan of Fingalton, NB; *m* 1901, Elizabeth, 2nd *d* of late Stuart Hawkins of Hayford Hall, Devon; no *c*. *Educ:* Harrow. Late Lieut 32nd Light Infantry. *Address:* Backford Hall, Chester. *Clubs:* Naval and Military, Wellington.
Died 6 Feb. 1927.

GLEICHEN, Lady Feodora; sculptor; *b* London, 20 Dec. 1861; *d* of late Admiral Prince Victor of Hohenlohe-Langenburg; unmarried. *Educ:* Slade School and University College, London, under Professor Legros. Hon. Member Royal Institute of Painters in Water-colours and Royal Society of Painter Etchers. Worked as sculpture in London and Rome; exhibited at the Royal Academy regularly since 1893, previously at the New Gallery and Grosvenor Gallery; completed life-size group of Queen for Victoria Hospital, Canada, 1895; fountain in Paris, 1901; fountain for Sir Walter Palmer, 1902, placed in Hyde Park; external decoration, Foundling Hospital, Cairo, 1904; Panel for exterior of National Art Gallery; King Edward VII Memorial, Windsor; Florence Nightingale Memorial, Derby; two Busts of Queen Victoria, and several other busts, etc; bronze medal for Sculpture, Paris Exhibition, 1900. *Recreations:* travelling, country pursuits. *Address:* Engine Court, St James's Palace, SW1. *T:* Gerrard 7187.
Died 22 Feb. 1922.

GLENARTHUR, 1st Baron, *cr* 1918, of Carlung, Ayrshire; **Matthew Arthur;** Bt, 1903; *b* 9 March 1852; *e s* of late James Arthur of Carlung, Ayrshire, and Barshaw, Renfrewshire, and Jane, *d* of Thomas Glen, Thornhill, Co. Renfrew; *m* 1879, Janet Stevenson Bennett, OBE, JP Co. Ayr, President Ayrshire Branch British Red Cross Society, *y d* of late Alexander Bennett M'Grigor, LLD, of Cairnoch, Stirlingshire; one *s* one *d*. *Educ:* Glasgow University. JP and DL Co. Ayr and County of City of Glasgow; LLD Glasgow; Member Royal Company of Archers (King's Bodyguard for Scotland); Chairman of Arthur & Company, Ltd, and of Lochgelly Iron & Coal Company, Ltd; President Glasgow Unionist Association; President of Scottish Unionist Association, 1914–18; Chairman of West of Scotland Liberal Unionist Association, 1893–1912; Convener Western Divisional Council Scottish Unionist Association, 1913; Member of Executive Committee National Unionist Association, 1912–18; Chairman of Western Infirmary, Glasgow, 1904–21; Chairman Glasgow and South-Western Railway, 1920–22. *Heir: s* Hon. James Cecil Arthur, *b* 2 June 1883. *Address:* Fullarton, Troon, Ayrshire. *TA:* Fullarton Troon. *T:* Troon 21. *Clubs:* Brooks's, Carlton, Boodle's, Windham; Western, Glasgow; New, Edinburgh.
Died 23 Sept. 1928.

GLEN-COATS, Sir Thomas Glen, 1st Bt, 1894; CB 1911; Chairman, J. & P. Coats, Ltd; Lord-Lieutenant of Renfrewshire, 1908; *b* 19 Feb. 1846; *s* of Thomas Coats, Ferguslie, and Margaret, *d* of Thomas Glen, Thornhill, Renfrewshire; assumed additional surname of Glen, 1894; *m* 1876, Elise Agnes (*d* 1910), *d* of Alexander Walker, Montreal; two *s* one *d*. *Educ:* Queenwood College, Hants. Hon. Colonel (VD), 6th Argyll and Sutherland Highlanders; contested (L) West Renfrewshire, 1900; MP (L) West Renfrewshire, 1906–10. *Recreations:* shooting, yachting. *Heir: s* Thomas Coats Glen Glen-Coats [*b* 5 May 1878. *Educ:* Merton College, Oxford, BA]. *Address:* Ferguslie Park, Paisley. *Clubs:* Reform, National Liberal; Western, Glasgow.
Died 12 July 1922.

GLENCONNER, 1st Baron, *cr* 1911; **Edward Priaulx Tennant;** 2nd Bt, *cr* 1885; Lord High Commissioner to General Assembly of Church of Scotland, 1911–12–13–14; Lord-Lieutenant, Peeblesshire; *b* 31 May 1859; *e* surv. *s* of Sir Charles Tennant, 1st Bt, and Emma, *d* of Richard Winsloe, Mount Nebo, Taunton; *S* father, 1906; *m* 1895, Pamela, [author of The White Wallet, The Sayings of the Children, and other books], *y d* of late Hon. Percy Wyndham; three *s* one *d* (and one

s one *d* decd). *Educ:* Eton; Trinity College, Cambridge; MA 1885. Inner Temple. Travelled extensively in Africa, India, and America; Assistant Private Secretary to Sir George Trevelyan at the Scottish Office, 1892–95; contested (L) Partick Division of Lanarkshire, 1892; united counties of Peebles and Selkirk, 1900; MP (L) Salisbury, 1906–10. Owner of about 7000 acres. *Heir: s* Hon. Christopher Grey Tennant, *b* 14 June 1899. *Address:* Glen, Innerleithen, Peebles; 34 Queen Anne's Gate, SW1; Wilsford Manor, Salisbury. *T:* Victoria 2501. *Club:* Brooks's.
Died 21 Nov. 1920.

GLENDINNING, Rt. Hon. Robert Graham, PC Ireland 1911; JP Belfast; DL of County of City of Belfast, 1914; MP (L) North Antrim, 1906–10; Linen Merchant; *b* 5 April 1844; *s* of William Bell Glendinning of Brakagh, Co. Tyrone; *m* 1st, 1874, Elizabeth Harden (*d* 1882); 2nd, 1886, Mary W. Hastings; four *s* three *d*. *Educ:* privately. *Recreations:* motoring, golf. *Address:* Knock-Dhu, Sans Souci Park, and Murray Street, Belfast. *TA:* Eccles, Belfast. *T:* 474. *Club:* National Liberal.
Died 8 June 1928.

GLENN, Very Rev. Henry Patterson, BA, TCD; Ex-Moderator of General Assembly of Presbyterian Church in Ireland; Ex-Senator, Irish Free State; *b* Indianapolis, USA, 4 Sept. 1858; *s* of Wm Glenn, JP, and Maria Morgan; *m* 1908, Ida Moncreiff, *d* of Rev. John Sturrock, Edinburgh; no *c*. *Educ:* Trinity College, Dublin; Edinburgh University; New College, Edinburgh; and Leipzig University. Licensed 1883; Assistant Free High Church, Inverness, 1883–84; Minister of Tullamore, 1884; Minister of Bray since 1892; Synodical Convener of Sustentation Fund, 1890; Assembly Convener of Sustentation Fund, 1912; Convener of Committee on Bequests, 1898. *Recreation:* golf. *Address:* The Manse, Bray, Co. Wicklow. *T:* Bray 46.
Died 12 Sept. 1923.

GLENNIE, Rev. Herbert John, MA; Canon of Bradford 1921; *b* 22 Jan. 1860; *s* of Rev. John David Glennie, late Vicar of Croxton, Staffs; *m* 1886, Mary Nathalie Katherine, *e d* of Rev. Nathaniel Cooper, Vicar of Oxon, Salop; one *s* one *d*. *Educ:* Marlborough; Keble College, Oxford. Deacon, 1885; Priest, 1886; Curate of St Mary's, Shrewsbury, 1885; Leeds Parish Church (and Acting Chaplain of Gen. Infirmary), 1889; Vicar of Holbeck, 1894; Rector of Goldsborough, 1904; Ripon Diocesan Inspector of Schools, 1905; Vicar of St Margaret's, Ilkley, 1908–22; Chaplain Middleton Sanatorium 1916; Vicar of Hawley Green, Hants, 1922–26. *Publications:* A Battalion in Training; Ripon Diocesan Dialogues. *Recreations:* cricket, football, hockey, rowing, tennis, sketching, motoring. *Address:* Redheath, Wokingham, Berks. *M:* DL 6096.
Died 19 Oct. 1926.

GLENTANAR, 1st Baron, *cr* 1916; **George Coats,** JP, Ayrshire; Director of J. and P. Coats, Limited; *b* 11 Feb. 1849; *s* of late Thomas Coats of Ferguslie; *m* 1880, Margaret Lothian Black; one *s* two *d*. *Educ:* Queenwood College, Hampshire. *Recreations:* hunting, fishing, yacht-racing, shooting. *Heir: s* Hon. Thomas Coats, *b* 4 Dec. 1894. *Address:* Forest of Glen Tanar, Aboyne, NB; Belleisle, Ayr, NB; 11 Hill Street, Berkeley Square, W. *T:* Gerrard 6515. *Clubs:* Carlton; Royal Yacht Squadron, Cowes; Western, Glasgow; Northern, Aberdeen.
Died 25 Nov. 1918.

GLENTWORTH, Viscount; Edmond William Claude Gerard de Vere; RFC; *b* 14 Oct. 1894; *e s* of 4th Earl of Limerick. *Educ:* Eton. Lieut Warwickshire Yeomanry. *Address:* Dromore, Pallaskenry, Limerick.
Died 18 May 1918.

GLOSSOP, Rev. George Henry Pownall; Hon. Canon of St Albans Cathedral, 1907; *b* 1858; *s* of F. H. N. Glossop of Silver Hall, Isleworth, JP, DL, and Ann, *e d* of Henry Pownall, JP, DL; *m* 1886, Frances Mary, JP, *d* of Maj. Gape, JP, of St Michael's Manor, St Albans; one *s* three *d*. *Educ:* Harrow; St John's College, Oxford; Wells Theological College. Curate of Uffculme, Devon, 1882–4; Curate St Albans Cathedral, 1884–1905; has been Chairman St Albans Board of Guardians, School Board; is an Alderman of Herts County Council; Hon. Secretary, St Albans Diocesan Conference and of the St Albans Diocesan Board of Finance; Chairman Herts Mental Hospital, Hill End; Chairman Hertfordshire Education Committee; Member of Executive of Poor Law Unions Associations and of Board of Health Advisory Committee for the Blind. *Address:* Romeland House, St Albans; Whitechapel Manor, South Molton. *T:* 64 St Albans.
Died 8 June 1925.

GLOSTER, Brig.-Gen. Gerald Meade, CMG 1916; retired pay; *b* 8 June 1864; *s* of late Rev. Thomas Gloster, MA, Castleterra Rectory, Co. Cavan; *m* Wilhelmina Ormonde, *o c* of C. Brown, CIE. Lieut Devon Regt 1884; Col 1914; served NW Frontier, India, 1897–98 (medal 2 clasps); S Africa, 1899–1900 (Queen's medal and clasp);

European War, 1914–18 (despatches, CMG, 1914 Star, General Service medal, Allied medal). *Address:* Oak Manor, Cheltenham.
Died 14 April 1928.

GLOVER, Elizabeth Rosetta, (Lady Glover); *d* of late J. W. Butler-Scott, Annegrove Abbey, and Elizabeth Rosetta, *d* of late John Bolton-Massy of Ballywire, Tipperary, and Clareville, Co. Dublin; *m* 1876, Captain Sir John Hawley Glover, GCMG, RN (*d* 1885); one *d*. *Publications:* The Life of Sir John Hawley Glover, GCMG, RN; Lest We Forget Them; Memories of Four Continents; short stories, and a number of magazine articles in various journals. *Address:* 68 Carlisle Mansions, Victoria Street, SW1. *T:* 3642 Victoria.
Died Feb. 1927.

GLOVER, George Wright, DSO 1916; MA, PhD; 2nd Lieutenant 1st Battalion, The Rifle Brigade; *b* Pretoria, S Africa, 1 Oct. 1884; English parents. *Educ:* Leigh Grammar School; Manchester, Berlin, Marburg Universities. Graduated 1911, 1st Class Hons Mod. Langs, Manchester. Gilchrist travelling studentship to Berlin University; English Lektor at Marburg (Hesse), 1912–14; PhD there, 1914; instructor in German at Princeton University, NJ, USA, 1914–15; Commissioned Spec. Res. 6th Batt. Rifle Brigade, Nov. 1915; joined 1st Batt. in France, April 1916 (wounded, DSO, despatches); with 1st Batt. again since Nov. 1916. *Address:* Ivy Cottage, Croft, Lancs.
Died 1 Sept. 1918.

GLOVER, Sir John, Kt, 1900; *b* 6 Sept. 1829; *s* of late Terrot Glover of South Shields; *m* 1854, Louisa (*d* 1915), *d* of Richard Moser of Penge, Surrey; three *s* three *d*. JP Middlesex and London; Ex-Chairman of Liberal Unionist Association of the City of London; and of Lloyd's Registry of British and Foreign Shipping; Ex-Chairman of the Mercantile Steamship Company, Limited; senior partner in the firm of Glover Brothers, ship-brokers, 59 Bishopsgate, EC2. *Address:* Highgate Lodge, Highgate. *T:* Hornsey 148. *Club:* Reform.
Died 24 March 1920.

GLOVER, Dr Richard, DD Edin.; LLD Bristol; *b* South Shields, 1837; *s* of Terrot Glover, JP; *m* Anna, *d* of R. G. Finlay, Glasgow; one *s* two *d*. *Educ:* Edin. Univ.; King's Coll. London; English Presbyterian College. Educated for Presbyterian Ministry, but joined Baptist Ministry, becoming minister in Glasgow, 1861, and in Bristol, 1869; President of the Baptist Union of Great Britain, 1884; for many years member of Baptist Missionary Committee and Chairman of China Committee; visited China in 1890–91; retired from ministry, 1911. *Publications:* Teacher's Commentary on St Mark; Teacher's Commentary on St Matthew; Lectures on Lord's Prayer; Lectures on Beatitudes; Lectures on the Ministry to the Young; The Comforts of God, Lectures on XIV Chap. of St John. *Address:* Bristol. *TA:* Redland, Bristol. *T:* 1336.
Died 26 March 1919.

GLUCKSTEIN, Montague; Chairman, J. Lyons & Co., Ltd; Chairman, Salmon & Gluckstein, Ltd; Chairman, Strand Hotel, Ltd; Director A. I. Jones & Co., Ltd, Westminster Electric Light Corporation, St James Pall Mall Electric Light Corporation and Guardian Eastern Insurance Co.; *b* 13 July 1854; *m* 1884, Matilda Franks; two *s* one *d*. *Educ:* Foundation School, St Mary's, Whitechapel. *Address:* 38 Hyde Park Gate, Kensington, SW7. *T:* Kensington 1186.
Died 7 Oct. 1922.

GLYN, Hon. Alice Coralie; author; *d* of late Admiral Hon. Henry Carr-Glyn, and *sister* of 4th Baron Wolverton; unmarried. Has written and lectured on Industrial Questions, is identified with the movement for better Housing, and is connected with various undertakings for the furtherance of Humanitarian and Progressive Ideals; Founder of a Sunday Institution which was carried on for the benefit of working women. *Publications:* A Woman of To-morrow; The Idyll of the Star-Flower, being a study of the mystic interpretations of Norwegian Sagas. *Address:* Ernstein House, Tunbridge Wells.
Died 28 Sept. 1928.

GLYN, Rt. Rev. Hon. Edward Carr; *b* London, 21 Nov. 1843; 9th *s* of 1st Lord Wolverton and Marion, *d* of Pascoe Grenfell, MP, of Taplow Court; *m* 1882, Lady Mary Emma Campbell, *d* of 8th Duke of Argyll; one *s* two *d*. *Educ:* Harrow; University College, Oxford (MA). Ordained, 1868; curate of Doncaster under Dr Vaughan; domestic chaplain to the Archbishop of York, 1871; Vicar of St Mary, Beverley, 1872–75; Vicar of Doncaster, 1875–78; Vicar of Kensington, 1878–97; hon. chaplain to the Queen, 1881; chaplain-in-ordinary, 1884; proctor for the clergy of London in Canterbury Convocation, 1891; Bishop of Peterborough, 1897–1916. *Publications:* sermons and pamphlets. *Address:* 23 Chester Square, SW1. *T:* Victoria 7867. *Club:* Athenæum.
Died 14 Nov. 1928.

GLYN, Rev. Frederick Ware, JP Co. Durham; MA; Rector of Brancepeth since 1900; Private Chaplain to Viscount Boyne; 4th *s* of late Rev. Canon Glyn, Rector of Fontmell, Dorset; *m* Eleanor, *e d* of late John Bayntun Stanley, Spye Park, Wilts; three *d*. *Educ:* Marlborough; Keble College, Oxford. Spent fifteen months at Auckland Castle with the late Bishop Lightfoot; Curate of St Andrew, Auckland, 1880; Vicar of Lanchester, 1885; Rector of Fontmell Magna and West Orchard, 1893; keenly interested in social matters and an active Magistrate, Guardian, District Councillor, etc. *Publications:* The Bishopric (before the War); editor of the Durham Diocesan Calendar since 1901. *Recreation:* driving. *Address:* Brancepeth Rectory, Durham.
Died 30 Oct. 1918.

GLYN, Sir Gervas Powell, 6th Bt, *cr* 1759; *b* Ewell, 3 Oct. 1862; 3rd *s* of Sir George Lewen Glyn, 4th Bt and Henrietta Amelia, *d* of Richard Carr Glyn; *S* half-brother, 1891; *m* 1898, Dorothy, *d* of late Edmund Charles Hislop of Clapham Park. *Educ:* Winchester Coll.; New Coll. Oxford (MA). Studied medicine at Univ. Coll. London; afterwards visited, besides European countries, Ceylon, India, Straits Settlements, China, Japan, British Columbia, Alaska, United States, New Zealand, Australia, Tasmania, Egypt, Syria, Tunis, and Algiers. *Recreations:* violoncellist; collector of foreign and antique musical instruments; photography. *Heir: b* Arthur Robert Glyn, *b* 5 Aug. 1870. *Address:* Rectory House, Ewell, Surrey; The Close, Burcote, Oxon.
Died 16 July 1921.

GLYN, Lewis Edmund, KC 1901; *b* 1849; 2nd *s* of late William Glyn, one of the Clerks of the House of Commons; *m* 1875, *o d* of late Rev. Richard Dugdale. Barrister, Middle Temple, 1871; Bencher, 1907; South-Eastern Circuit. *Address:* 3 Essex Court, Temple, EC; Broom-Hills, Bexley, Kent; Thistlewood, Cumberland.
Died 27 Feb. 1919.

GLYN, Maurice George Carr, JP; Partner in Glyn, Mills, Currie, and Co., Bankers; *b* 12 March 1872; 2nd *s* of Hon. Pascoe Charles Glyn; *m* 1897, Hon. Maude Grosvenor, *e d* of 2nd Baron Ebury; six *s* two *d*. Sheriff Herts, 1912; late 2nd Lieut Dorsets Yeomanry. *Address:* 21 Bryanston Square, W1; *T:* Padd. 2676; Albury Hall, Hadham, Herts. *Club:* Arthur's.
Died 20 Aug. 1920.

GLYN, Sir Richard George, 3rd Bt, *cr* 1800; JP, DL; Captain Royal Dragoons, retired 1859; *b* London, 22 Nov. 1831; *e s* of Robert Glyn and Frederica, *d* of Henry Harford, Down Place, Berks; *S* uncle, 1863; *m* 1868, Frances, *d* of Maj. H. T. G. Fitzgerald, Maperton House, Somerset; one *s* one *d*. *Educ:* Cheam School; Merton Coll. Oxford. Joined Royal Dragoons, 1852; sailed with them to Varna, 1854, present at battles of Balaclava and Inkerman, returned with Regt, 1856; made an expedition from Natal to the interior of Africa, was one of first Europeans after Dr Livingstone to reach the Victoria Falls of River Zambesi, 1863; Master Blackmoor Vale Hounds, 1865–84. Owner of about 9800 acres. *Heir: s* Richard Fitzgerald Glyn [*b* 13 May 1875; late Lieut Royal Dragoons; *m* 1906, Edith Hilda, *e d* of G. D. Hamilton-Gordon; two *s* one *d*]. *Address:* Gaunt's House, Wimborne; Fontmell-Magna, Shaftesbury. *Club:* Arthur's.
Died 9 Aug. 1918.

GLYN, Hon. Sidney Carr; *b* 11 Oct. 1835; 7th *s* of 1st Baron Wolverton; *m* 1868, Fanny (*d* 1907), *d* of M. Adolphe Marescaux of St Omer, France; one *s* (and one *s* decd). MP (L) Shaftesbury, 1880–85; late Capt. Rifle Brigade. *Address:* 27 Grosvenor Place, SW. *Clubs:* Army and Navy, Brooks's.
Died 26 Feb. 1916.

GLYN-JONES, Sir William Samuel, Kt 1919; JP Middlesex; Chairman of Council of the Proprietary Articles Trade Association, and since 1926 of the Canadian Proprietary Articles Trade Association; pharmacist; Secretary to the Pharmaceutical Society of Great Britain, 1918–26; *b* Worcester, 1869; *m* 1894, Mary, *d* of John Evans of Tower Hill, Llanybyther, Carmarthen; two *s* two *d*. *Educ:* Merthyr Tydfil Grammar School. Called to Bar, Middle Temple, 1904. MP (L) Stepney, 1911–18. *Publication:* The Law of Poisons and Pharmacy. *Address:* 43 Gordon Square, WC1. *T:* Museum 8885. *Club:* National Liberal.
Died 9 Sept. 1927.

GOAD, Col Howard, CSI 1907; *b* 15 Sept. 1857; *s* of late C. W. Goad, formerly 5th Dragoon Guards, and Sophia, *d* of Col T. B. Thoroton Hildyard, MP, of Flintham Hall, Newark; *m* 1908, Ethel May, *y d* of late John Groome Howes of Kingscliffe, Northants. *Educ:* Marlborough. Entered Army, 1875; Capt. ISC, 1886; Major, 1895; Lt-Col Indian Army, 1901; Col 1904; Director Army Remount Dept, 1898–1903; Director-General Army Remount Department, India, 1903–8; served Afghan War, 1879–80 (medal); Commandant

Swaythling Remount Depot, 1915–18. *Address:* Kennedy, Thurlestone, South Devon. *Club:* Naval and Military.

Died 18 Dec. 1923.

GOBEIL, Antoine, ISO 1904; *b* St Jean, Island of Orleans, Quebec, 22 Sept. 1854; *m* Blanche Gingras; two *s* two *d*. *Educ:* Seminary of Quebec; Laval University. Entered Civil Service, 1872; retired, 1908; admitted to Bar, Province of Quebec, 1902; Law Clerk, Dept of Public Works, Ottawa, 1880–85; Secretary, 1885–91; Deputy Minister, 1891–1908; resumed practice of Law in Quebec, 1911. *Address:* 81 St Peter Street, Quebec; Aux Quatre Vents, St Laurent, Island of Orleans, Quebec. *Club:* Rideau, Ottawa.

GODDARD, Arabella, (Mrs J. W. Davison); pianist; *b* St Servan, Brittany, 12 Jan 1836; parents English; *m* 1859, J. W. Davison, music critic of The Times. *Educ:* at 8 years old had lessons from Kalkbrenner in Paris, afterwards under Mrs Anderson, Thalberg, and J. W. Davison in England. Played to Chopin as a child of seven, and was caressed by Georges Sand on that occasion; début at Grand National Concerts at Her Majesty's Theatre, 1850; was the first pianist to play Beethoven's Posthumous Sonatas publicly in England; travelled in Germany and Italy and gave concerts, 1854–55; played at the Gewandhaus Concert, Leipsic, 1855, receiving an enthusiastic reception; at the Philharmonic Concert in England, 1856 (gold medal); later at the Monday Popular Concerts; toured through America, Australia, India, Java and China, 1873–76; took part in Sir Arthur Sullivan's Concerts, Paris Exhibition, 1878 (medal); retired from public life the same year; played many times before the Queen Victoria, the German Emperor and Empress William, and King Edward and Queen Alexandra; was asked to join the professional staff of the Royal College of Music.

Died 6 April 1922.

GODDARD, Arthur; *b* 1853. One of the originators and subsequently editor of Society; joined the editorial staff of the Lady's Pictorial, 1887; editor, 1900–14; has been a dramatic critic since 1884. *Publications:* Players of the Period, 2 vols, 1891; Windsor, the Castle of our Kings, and some Notes on Eton College, 1911. *Recreation:* book and print collecting. *Address:* Redholme, 23 Holmdene Avenue, Herne Hill, SE24. *T:* Brixton 1895. *Died Aug. 1920.*

GODDARD, Rt. Hon. Sir Daniel Ford, Kt 1907; PC 1916; JP; *b* 17 Jan. 1850; *o s* of late Ebenezer Goddard; *m* 1st, 1874, Lucy, *d* of Thomas Harwood, Belstead Hall, Suffolk; 2nd, Elizabeth, *d* of Ebenezer Hitchcock, Bramford; one *d*. *Educ:* privately at Ipswich and Hastings; articled to Messrs E. R. and J. Turner, engineers, Ipswich; Associate member of the Instn of Civil Engineers; studied Chemistry in London and Newcastle; succeeded father as Engineer and Secretary Ipswich Gas Co. 1871; Mayor of Ipswich, 1891; contested (L) Ipswich, 1892; MP (L) Ipswich, 1895–1918; Chairman of Directors, Ipswich Gas Co. since 1887; founded and built Ipswich Social Settlement. *Recreations:* travelling, photography. *Address:* Oak Hill, Ipswich. *TA:* Sir Daniel Goddard, Ipswich. *T:* Ipswich 583. *M:* DX 520. *Clubs:* National Liberal, Reform.

Died 6 May 1922.

GODFRAY, Brig.-Gen. John William, CB 1900; CVO 1905; CBE 1919; ADC to the King, 1911; late The King's Own Scottish Borderers; retired; *b* 20 Oct. 1850; *m* 1880, Annie Julia, *d* of late J. D. Muntz of Baddesley, Clinton, Warwick; one *s*. *Educ:* Cheltenham College. Entered army, 1871; Capt., 1879; served Chitral, 1895 (despatches, medal and clasp, brevet of Lieut-Colonel); Tirah Campaign, 1897–98 (two clasps, NW Frontier and Tirah); commanded 1st KOSB, South Africa, 1900, then Chief Staff Officer VII Division, and afterwards CSO Orange River Colony to end of war (despatches, CB, Queen's and King's South African medals); commanded 25th Regimental District, 1902–5; Brig.-Gen. in charge of Administration, Scottish Command, 1905–7; AAG Jersey Militia, 1908–14; AA and QMG Jersey Defences to 1919. *Address:* 3 Hastings Terrace, Jersey. *Died 10 Jan. 1921.*

GODFREY, Charles, MVO 1910; MA; Professor of Mathematics at RN College, Greenwich; *b* 4 Oct. 1873; *e s* of G. H. Godfrey, Birmingham; *m* 1908, Evelyn Patience, *d* of J. Armine Willis; one *s* three *d*. *Educ:* King Edward's School, Birmingham; Trinity College, Cambridge. 4th Wrangler, 1895; 1st div. 1st class in second part of Mathematical Tripos, 1896; Senior Mathematical Master at Winchester College, 1900–5; Head Master of the Royal Naval College, Osborne, 1905–21. *Address:* 57 Westcombe Park Road, Blackheath, SE3. *T:* Greenwich 1338. *Club:* Savile.

Died 4 April 1924.

GODFREY, Sir William Cecil, 5th Bt, *cr* 1785; *b* 21 July 1857; *s* of Sir John Fermor Godfrey, 4th Bt and Mary, *d* of T. W. Scutt, late of Clapham House, Litlington, Sussex; *S* father, 1900; *m* 1st, 1885, Adela Maud (*d* 1890), *d* of F. F. Hamilton; one *d*; 2nd, 1901, Mary, *e d* of late Richard Leeson-Marshall of Callinafercy, County Kerry. Late Lieut South Wales Borderers; served S Africa, 1879 (medal with clasp). Owner of about 6100 acres. *Heir:* *b* John Ernest Godfrey [*b* 6 Oct. 1864; *m* 1897, Eileen Mary, *e d* of S. Curry, MD, Lismore; one *s* three *d*]. *Address:* Kilcoleman Abbey, Milltown, Co. Kerry.

Died Nov. 1926.

GODLEE, Sir Rickman John, 1st Bt, *cr* 1912; KCVO 1914; BA, MS, LLD, MD Dublin; FRCS; Hon. Surgeon in Ordinary to the King; Fellow and Emeritus Professor of Clinical Surgery, University College, London; late Surgeon at University College Hospital; *b* 15 April 1849; *m* 1891, Juliet Mary, *d* of Frederic Seebohm, LLD, of Hitchin, Herts. *Educ:* University College, London. *Publications:* Lord Lister, 1917; numerous works on professional subjects. *Heir:* none. *Address:* Coombe End Farm, Whitchurch, Oxon. *T:* Pangbourne 96. *Clubs:* Athenæum, Burlington Fine Arts, University of London.

Died 20 April 1925 (ext).

GODLEY, Alfred Denis, OBE 1919; MA; Public Orator, Oxford, since 1910; *b* Ireland, 1856; *e s* of late Rev. James Godley, Carrigallen, Co. Leitrim, and Eliza, *d* of P. La Touche; *m* 1894, Amy, *d* of late C. H. Cay. *Educ:* Harrow; Balliol Coll., Oxford. Craven Scholar, 1880; various University prizes, 1874–79; Classical Moderator, 1887–88, 1895–96, 1906–7; Deputy Public Orator, 1904–6; Assistant Master at Bradfield College, 1879–82; Fellow and Tutor of Magdalen College, Oxford, 1883–1912; Hon. Fellow of Magdalen College since 1912; Hon. LLD Princeton, 1913; Hon. DLitt(Oxon), 1919; Lieut-Col, Oxfordshire Volunteer Corps, 1916–19; Member of the Governing Body of Harrow School; an Alderman in the Oxford City Council. *Publications:* Verses to Order, 1892 and 1903; Aspects of Modern Oxford, 1893; Socrates and Athenian Society, 1895; edition of Tacitus' Histories, 1887 and 1890; translation of the Odes of Horace, 1898; Lyra Frivola, 1899; Nova Anthologia Oxoniensis (edited with Prof. Robinson Ellis), 1899; Fables of Orbilius, 1901 and 1902; Second Strings, 1902; Oxford in the Eighteenth Century, 1908; The Casual Ward, 1912; Translation of Herodotus (Loeb series), 1921–23; Joint editor of the Classical Review, 1910–20; of Horace, Book V, 1920; various magazine articles and introductory essays. *Address:* 27 Norham Road, Oxford. *Club:* Alpine (Vice-Pres. 1924).

Died 27 June 1925.

GODMAN, Frederick Du Cane, DCL; FRS; MRI; Trustee of the British Museum; *b* 1834; *3rd s* of J. Godman, Park Hatch, Surrey; *m* 1st, Edith Mary (*d* 1875), *d* of late J. H. Elwes, Colesborne, Gloucestershire; 2nd, Alice Mary, *d* of late Maj. Percy Chaplin, JP, 60th Rifles. *Publications:* Natural History of the Azores, 1870; Monograph of the Petrels, 1910; Biologia Centrali-Americana, 1916. *Address:* 45 Pont Street, SW; South Lodge, Horsham. *Club:* Athenæum.

Died 19 Feb. 1919.

GODMAN, Major Laurence, DSO 1916; Royal Artillery; *b* 4 Sept. 1880; *3rd s* of Colonel A. F. Godman, CB. *Educ:* Rugby; RMA Woolwich. Joined Royal Artillery, 1899; Captain, 1908; Major, 1914; served European War (despatches twice, DSO). *Address:* Smeaton Manor, Northallerton. *Club:* Army and Navy.

Died 30 Sept. 1917.

GODSELL, Sir William, Kt 1903; *b* 23 Feb. 1838; *e s* of late Thomas Godsell of King's Caple, Herefords; *m* 1st, 1864, Georgina Mary (*d* 1903), *d* of late Rev. James Buckoll; 2nd, 1908, Emily Helen, *d* of late George Grimmette. Entered Government Service, 1860; Auditor of Accounts of Secretary of State for India, 1895–1903. *Address:* 15 Grosvenor Avenue, Carshalton, Surrey.

Died 27 Sept. 1924.

GODWIN, Sir Arthur, Kt 1913; *b* 17 Oct. 1852; *o s* of John Venimore Godwin, JP, Mayor of Bradford (*d* 1898), and Rachel Catherine, *d* of late Rev. James Acworth, LLD; *m* 1887, Mary Elizabeth, *d* of late William Geddes, Liverpool. *Educ:* Edinburgh University. Taken active part in political, municipal, and philanthropic life of city; JP City of Bradford, 1892; entered City Council, 1900; Alderman, 1903; first Lord Mayor of Bradford, 1907; a Freemason and Senior Grand Deacon of England, 1908. *Recreations:* fishing, sketching. *Address:* Colvend, Grassington, near Skipton. *TA:* Godwin, Bradford. *T:* Grassington 21. *M:* DU 3631, WR 1690. *Clubs:* Royal Canoe; Bradford. *Died 29 April 1921.*

GODWIN-AUSTEN, Henry Haversham, JP; FRS 1880; FZS; FRGS, etc; Lieutenant-Colonel, retired 1877; *b* Teignmouth, 6 July 1834; *e s* of Robert A. C. Godwin-Austen, FRS, a distinguished geologist, and Maria, *d* of General Godwin, CB; *m* 1st, 1861, Pauline (*d* 1871), *d* of Major Chichele Plowden; one *s*; 2nd, 1881, Jessie (*d* 1913), *d* of J. H. Robinson. *Educ:* RMC Sandhurst. Gazetted HM's 24th Regt of Foot, 1851; went to India, 1852; served in 2nd Burmese War (medal and clasp, Pegu) and Punjab; appointed Topographical Assistant in Trigonometrical Survey of India, and joined the Kashmir Survey party, 1857; surveyed very large extent of country in Kashmir and Baltistan; in latter country the enormous glaciers at head of Shigar river and Hunza Nagar frontier, which included the Baltoro glacier, which he was the first to discover, coming down in part from the second highest mountain in the Himalayas; surveyed the lofty country of Rupshu and Zaskar in Ladakh, 1862; in July and August of that year he made 13 different ascents of a mean height of 17,900 feet, the highest peak, Mata, being 20,607; took up the Changchingmo and carried the topography to the eastern end of the Pang Kong lake, close up to Rudok in Chinese territory, where he was met and stopped by the Lhassan Governor, 1863; in winter of 1863–64 on special duty with last mission to Bhutan, and mapped the country between Darjeeling and Punakha, the capital; 1864–65 on special duty with the Bhutan Field Force, and was present at the capture of Dalingkote and Chamurchi Forts (clasp for Bhutan); 1866–76 in charge of Survey Operations in the Garo, Khasi, Jaintia, North Cachar and Naga Hills, and Manipur, including in 1874 the expedition against the Dafla tribe at base of the Eastern Himalayas, when a large area of new country was mapped and many distant peaks fixed. President of Section E (Geography) British Association, 1883; President Malacological Society, 1897–99; President Conchological Society of Great Britain and Ireland, 1908–9; awarded by the Royal Geographical Society the Founder's medal (1910) for his exploration work. *Publications:* On the Land and Fresh-water Mollusca of India, 1882–1920; (with late Dr W. T. Blanford, FRS) The Fauna of British India, vol. Mollusca, 1908; 131 papers in the journals of various scientific societies on geology and physical features, ethnology and natural history. *Recreations:* shooting, fishing, drawing. *Address:* Nore, Godalming.
Died 2 Dec. 1923.

GOETHALS, George Washington; army engineer; *b* Brooklyn, 29 June 1858. *Educ:* College, City of New York; United States Military Academy; LLD University of Pennsylvania, 1913; Princeton University, 1915. 2nd Lieut, Engineers, 1880; 1st Lieut, 1882; Capt., 1891; Lieut-Col, Chief Engineer Volunteers, 1898; hon. discharged from Volunteer service, 1898; Major, Engineer Corps, 1900; graduated Army War College, 1905; Lieut-Col, Engineers, 1907; Col, 1909; Major-General, 1915; retired, 1916; Instructor in Civil and Military Engineering, US Military Academy; in charge of Mussel Shoals Canal construction on Tennessee River; Chief of Engineers during Spanish-American War; Member Board of Fortifications (coast and harbour defence); Chief Engineer Panama Canal, 1907–14; 1st Civil Governor Panama Canal Zone, 1914–16; Chairman Board appointed to report on Adamson 8-Hour Law, 1916; State Engineer, New Jersey, 1917; General Manager, Emergency Fleet Corporation, 1917 (resigned); Acting Quarter-Master-General, USA, 1917; Chief Division of Storage and Traffic of General Staff, 1918; Chief of Division of Purchase, Storage and Traffic, 1918; Member War Industries Board; relieved from the active duty at own request, 1919; received thanks of Congress, 4 March 1915, for distinguished service in constructing Panama Canal; DSM 1918, for especially meritorious and conspicuous service in reorganising OM Dept; Commander Legion of Honour, 1919; medals: Nat. Geog. Soc., Civic Forum, and Nat. Inst. Social Sciences. *Address:* 40 Wall Street, New York.
Died 21 Jan. 1928.

GOFF, Sir Herbert William Davis-, 2nd Bt, *cr* 1905; *b* 20 Oct. 1870; *o* surv. *c* of Sir William Goff Davis-Goff, 1st Bt, and Anna, *d* of M. D. Hassard; *S*, father 1917; *m* 1903, Margaret Aimée, *d* of Rt Hon. Sir Charles Stewart Scott; three *s* one *d*. *Educ:* Wellington; Trinity College, Cambridge (BA). Lieut Army Motor Reserve; Capt. in command of ASC Co., attached to No 6 Motor Ambulance Convoy, BEF, France, 1914–16. *Heir: s* Ernest William Davis-Goff, *b* 11 June 1904. *Address:* Maypark, Waterford. *Clubs:* Bath, Royal Automobile; Kildare Street, Dublin.
Died 26 June 1923.

GOFF, Colonel Robert Charles; late of the Coldstream Guards; retired 1878; *m* 1899, Clarissa Catherine, *d* of 8th Baron de Hochepied. Fellow of the Royal Society of Painter Etchers; frequent exhibitor both of water-colours and of etchings in London and abroad; Hon. Member of the Florence and Milan Academies of Arts. *Address:* Wick Studio, Holland Road, Hove, Sussex; Villa dell' Ombrellino, Via della Piazzola, Florence. *Club:* Army and Navy.
Died 1 July 1922.

GOFF, Sir William Goff Davis-, 1st Bt, *cr* 1905; JP, DL; *b* 12 Sept. 1838; *s* of late S. Davis Goff and Susan, *d* of late Arthur Ussher; *m* 1866, Anna, *d* of M. D. Hassard; one *s* (and one *s* decd). *Educ:* Trinity College, Dublin (MA). Formerly Cornet, 2nd Dragoon Guards. *Recreations:* yachting, motoring. *Heir: s* Herbert William Davis-Goff, *b* 20 Oct. 1870. *Address:* Glenville, Waterford. *T:* 5 Waterford Exchange. *M:* WI 20, WI 36. *Clubs:* Constitutional, Royal Automobile; Royal St George Yacht, Royal Mersey; Kildare Street, Dublin.
Died 23 Nov. 1917.

GOLD, Sir Charles, Kt 1906; DL, JP; Director of W. and A. Gilbey; *b* 1837; *s* of Michael Gold, Birmingham; *n* of Sir J. Allport; *m* 1859, Fanny Georgina (*d* 1910), *sister* of Sir Walter Gilbey, 1st Bt; two *s*. MP (GL) Saffron-Walden, Essex, 1895–1900. *Address:* The Limes, Birchanger, Essex. *Clubs:* Orleans, Devonshire.
Died 2 Nov. 1924.

GOLDIE, Rt. Hon. Sir George Dashwood Taubman, KCMG 1887; PC 1898; DCL (Hon.), Oxford; LLD (Hon.), Camb.; FRS 1902; founder of Nigeria; *b* The Nunnery, Isle of Man, 20 May 1846; *y s* of Col J. T. Goldie-Taubman, Scots Guards, and Speaker of the House of Keys; *m* 1870, Matilda (*d* 1898), *d* of John Elliot, Wakefield; one *s* one *d*. *Educ:* Royal Military Academy, Woolwich. Lieut RE; attended Berlin Conference, 1884–85, as expert on Niger questions; Royal Commissions on South African War, 1902–3, and on War Stores, 1905–6; President National Defence Association, 1905–14 and 1915–20. *Clubs:* Naval and Military, Athenæum; Royal Yacht Squadron, Cowes.
Died 20 Aug. 1925.

GOLDNEY, Sir (Gabriel) Prior, 2nd Bt, *cr* 1880; CB 1902; CVO 1903; DL, London; JP, Wilts and Somerset; late Major Royal Wiltshire Yeomanry Cavalry; *b* 4 Aug. 1843; *s* of Sir Gabriel Goldney, 1st Bt and Mary, *o d* of R. H. Alexander, Corsham, Wilts; *S* father, 1900. *Educ:* Harrow; Exeter Coll., Oxford. Called to Bar, Inner Temple, 1867; Recorder of Helston, 1876–79; Poole, 1879–82; Remembrancer of City of London, 1882–1902. *Heir: b* Frederick Hastings Goldney, *b* 26 May 1845. *Address:* Derriads, Chippenham, Wilts; Manor House, Halse, Somerset. *Club:* Junior Carlton.
Died 4 May 1925.

GOLDNEY, Hon. Sir John Tankerville, Kt 1893; JP Wilts; Lay-Rector of Corsham; *b* 15 June 1846; 3rd *s* of Sir Gabriel Goldney, 1st Bt; *m* 1st, 1875, Jane (*d* 1911), *d* of J. Laird, MP; one *d* decd; 2nd, Alice Frances Holbrow, *d* of Major F. C. Goldney, late 8th Gurkha Rifles. *Educ:* Harrow; Trinity Coll., Camb. (BA, LLB). Barrister, Inner Temple 1869; Acting Chief Justice, Leeward Islands, 1881; Judge of Supreme Court of British Guiana, 1883; Judge of Straits Settlements, 1887; Chief Justice of Trinidad, 1892–1900; High Sheriff for Wilts, 1910–11. *Address:* Monks Park, Corsham; Hanover Court, Hanover Square, W. *Clubs:* Junior Carlton, Oxford and Cambridge.
Died 11 April 1920.

GOMEZ, Alice; singer; *b* Calcutta, of Eurasian parentage; *m* T. H. Webb, Professor of Music. Made debut in London 1885. Resided in Calcutta.
Died 1922.

GOMME, Sir (George) Laurence, Kt 1911; JP; FSA; FSS; Fellow of the Anthropological Institute; original founder and some time secretary; formerly President and then Vice-President of the Folklore Society; Hon. Member of the Glasgow Archæological Society; author; Secretary to the Lieutenancy of London; *b* London, 1853; *m* 1875, Alice Bertha Merck, author of Traditional Games of Great Britain, 1896–98; seven *s*. *Educ:* City of London School. Formerly edited the Antiquary, the Archæological Review, and the Folklore Journal; lecturer at the London School of Economics and University Extension; formerly Statistical Officer and Clerk to the London County Council. *Publications:* Index of Municipal Offices, 1879; Primitive Folk-Moots, 1880; Folklore Relics of Early Village Life, 1883; The Gentleman's Magazine Library (ed), 1883–1906; Chap-Books and Folklore Tracts, 1885; The Literature of Local Institutions, 1886; The London County Council, 1888; The Village Community, 1889; Ethnology in Folklore, 1892; Lectures on the Principles of Local Government, 1898; Editor of: the King's Story-Book, 1897; Queen's Story-Book, 1898; Prince's Story-Book, 1899; Princess's Story-Book, 1900; *historical novels:* Lytton's Harold, Macfarlane's Camp of Refuge and Reading Abbey, and Kingsley's Westward Ho!; Governance of London, 1907; Index of Archæological Papers (edited), 1907; Folklore as an Historical Science, 1908; The Making of London, 1911; London, 1914. *Recreation:* change of work. *Address:* 20 Marlborough Place, NW; The Mound, Long Crendon, Bucks. *Clubs:* Royal Societies, Municipal and County.
Died 24 Feb. 1916.

GOMPERS, Samuel; President American Federation of Labour; Editor American Federationist; 1st Vice-President Cigarmakers' International Union; President Pan-American Federation of Labour; *b* London, England, 27 Jan. 1850; *s* of Solomon Gompers and Sarah Rood; *m* 1st, 1867, Sophia Julian (*d* 1920); three *s*; 2nd, 1921, Gertrude Gleaves Neuscheler. *Educ:* from sixth year until little more than ten years of age attended the public schools of London. Cigarmaker by trade; came to USA 1863; helped develop the Cigarmakers' International Union, of which an officer since 1887; one of the founders of the Federation of Trades and Labour Unions organised in 1881, of which he was president 3 years; one of the founders of the American Federation of Labour organised in 1886, of which elected president annually, with the exception of the year 1895; member of New York Factory Investigating Committee, 1912; member of Advisory Committee to the Council of National Defence, 1916–19; President of the International Commission on Labor Legislation of the Paris Peace Conference, 1919; member Advisory Committee to American Delegates in the Conference for the Limitation of Armaments; member President's First Industrial Conference, 1919; member President's Unemployment Conference, 1921; member Sulgrave Institute. *Publications:* Labor in Europe and America; American Labor and the War; Labor and the Common Welfare; Labor and the Employer; Out of Their Own Mouths; and a number of pamphlets on the labour question and the labour movement. *Address:* 318 West 51st Street, New York City; American Federation of Labour Building, Washington, DC. *TA:* Afel. *T:* Main 3871. *Died 13 Dec. 1924.*

GONNER, Prof. Sir Edward Carter Kersey, KBE 1921 (CBE 1918); MA Oxford; Hon. MA Sydney; Hon. LittD, Manchester; Professor of Economic Science in the University of Liverpool; sometime Economic Adviser to the Ministry of Food; Director of Statistics, Ministry of Food; a Chairman in the Committee on Production; *b* 1862; *s* of Peter Kersey and Elizabeth Gonner; *m* 1890, Nannie Ledlie; one *d*. *Educ:* Merchant Taylors' School, London; Lincoln Coll., Oxford. Lecturer for the London Extension Society, 1885; Lecturer at University College, Bristol, 1885; Lecturer at University Coll., Liverpool, 1888; Professor at University College, Liverpool, 1891; Rae Lecturer, University College, Bangor, 1911; President of Section F, Economics and Statistics, of the British Association (Toronto), 1897; President of Section F, British Association (Australia), 1914; Vice-President Economic History Sub-section, International Historical Congress, London, 1913; Member of the Royal Commission on Shipping Conferences, 1906–9; Chairman of the Sub-Committee for Elementary Education, County of Chester; Chairman of the War Savings Committee, County of Chester, 1917–18. *Publications:* edited Ricardo's Principles of Political Economy and Taxation; The Socialist State; The Social Philosophy of Rodbertus; Commercial Geography; Interest and Saving; Common Land and Inclosure; The Economic History of Germany in the Nineteenth Century; contributor to Dict. of Nat. Biography, Dict. of Political Economy, Conrad's Handwörterbuch der Staatswissenschaften, etc. *Address:* Red Gables, Headington, Oxford. *Died 24 Feb. 1922.*

GOOCH, Sir Daniel Fulthorpe, 3rd Bt, *cr* 1866; *b* 25 May 1869; *s* of Sir Henry Daniel Gooch, 2nd Bt and Mary Kelsall, *d* of Joseph Rodney Croskey; *S* father, 1897; *m* 1896, Mary Winifred (*d* 1921), *d* of late Edward William Monro; one *s* two *d* (and one *s* decd). *Heir:* *s* Robert Douglas Gooch, *b* 19 Sept. 1905. *Address:* Tatchbury Mount, Totton, Hampshire. *Club:* Boodle's. *Died 22 Dec. 1926.*

GOODDEN, Rev. Edward Wyndham; Rector of Nether and Over Compton since 1884; Canon and Prebendary of Salisbury since 1904; *b* 17 Feb. 1847; 2nd *s* of late John Goodden of Compton House, Sherborne; *m* 1871, Georgina, *e d* of late Rev. J. Frewen Moor of Bradfield, Berks, and Sion Place, Bath. *Educ:* Harrow; Merton Coll., Oxford. Curate of Limpsfield, Surrey, 1870–72; Nether and Over Compton, 1872–84; Alderman Dorset County Council since 1889; Chairman of Dorset Education Committee since 1903. *Recreations:* fishing, motoring, yachting. *Address:* Nether Compton Rectory, Sherborne, Dorset. *T:* Yeovil 20. *TA:* Nether Compton. *M:* FX 5810. *Clubs:* Royal Societies; Royal Dorset Yacht. *Died 19 May 1924.*

GOODE, Sir Charles Henry, Kt 1912; Chairman of Goode, Durrant & Co., Limited, Adelaide, Perth, Broken Hill, NSW and 27 Milton Street, EC; *b* 26 May 1827; *m* 1st, 1856; 2nd, 1890; no *c*. *Educ:* Docklow Academy, Herefordshire. Left school at 10 years of age; apprenticed to draper, 1839; went to London, 1845; went to Adelaide, 1849; started business in a cart; gradually climbed up; visited London four times, staying 4 years, 12 years, and 2 short visits; right round

the world twice after he was 70. *Publications:* none of consequence; only Letters to Young People from Japan. *Recreations:* looking after the blind, deaf and dumb, consumptives, state children, etc; taking carriage drives occasionally. *Address:* North Adelaide, South Australia. *Died 5 Feb. 1922.*

GOODEVE, Mrs Arthur, (Florence Everilda); composer of many popular songs; *d* of Thomas John Knowlys, JP, of Heysham Tower, Lancashire, and Hollybrook, Hants; *niece* of Sir Peter Fleetwood-Hesketh, Bt, MP, of Rossall; *m* Louis Arthur Goodeve, Advocate, High Court, Calcutta, *s* of late Joseph Goodeve, Master in Equity, Supreme Court, Bengal. Composer of Fiddle and I; Ah, Well a Day!; The Jovial Beggar; Come Again; Litany for the War; Round the Clock, etc. *Address:* 36 Harcourt Terrace, S Kensington, SW; Clayton, Clifton. *Club:* Ladies' Park. *Died 15 Jan. 1916.*

GOODEVE, Hon. Arthur Samuel; Member of Board of Railway Commissioners for Canada since 1912; *b* Guelph, Ontario, 15 Dec. 1860; *s* of Arthur Henry Goodeve and Caroline Higginson; *m* 1884, Ellen Edith Spence; four *s* two *d*. *Educ:* Guelph Collegiate Institute. Druggist; Mayor of Rossland, BC, 1889 and 1900; Provincial Secretary, 1902; MP Kootenay, BC, 1908 and 1911. *Recreations:* tennis, bowling. *Address:* Ottawa, Canada. *T:* Q 8651, Q 3204. *Clubs:* Country, Rideau, Ottawa; Rossland, Rossland. *Died Nov. 1920.*

GOODHART, Comdr Francis Herbert Heveningham, DSO 1916; RN; *b* Sheffield, 10 July 1884; *s* of the Vicar of St Barnabas, Sheffield, later Rector of Lambourne, Essex for 23 years, and of *d* (*d* 1885), of late C. Warner of Birmingham; *m* 1912, Isabella, *y d* of Mrs Turner of Eastbourne and S Africa, and *g d* of late Thomas Turner of Worksop; two *d*. *Educ:* Chigwell Grammar School, Essex; HMS Britannia, Dartmouth. Served as midshipman in Mediterranean, HMS Ramillies, 1900–3; passed exams for Lieutenant, 4 firsts, 1903–4; Lieutenant, 1905; served in Submarine Service since June 1905; also in HM ships Magnificent and Agamemnon, 1910–11; served in HMS Maidstone for command of submarine E8, Aug. 1914 (despatches) for reconnaissance of Heligoland Bight; Commander, 1915 (DSO) for services in command of a submarine; Order of St Vladimir, 4th class; Order of St George, 4th class; Chevalier of Légion d'Honneur. *Recreations:* tennis, golf. *Address:* c/o Admiralty, SW. *Died 30 Jan. 1917.*

GOODHART, Sir James Frederic, 1st Bt, *cr* 1911; MD, CM; Hon. LLD Aberdeen; FRCP; Consulting Physician to Guy's Hospital, the Evelina Hospital for Sick Children, Royal Hospital for Incurables, Putney, Female Orphan Asylum, Beddington, and Spurgeon Orphan Asylum; on Consulting Committee of King Edward VII Sanatorium, Midhurst; late one of the Hon. Staff of King Edward VII Hospital for Officers and Osborne Convalescent Home; *b* London, 24 Oct. 1845; *m* 1879, Emma Sandford (*d* 1915), *d* of William Bennett, JP, of Ashgrove, Herefordshire; two *s*. *Educ:* Aberdeen Univ. Fellow of the Royal Society of Medicine; President Harveian Society, 1898. *Publications:* Common Neuroses; the Diseases of Children, 10th Edition; many medical addresses. *Heir:* *s* Ernest Frederic Goodhart, barrister [*b* 12 Aug. 1880; *m* 1906, Frances Evelyn, *d* of M. F. Armstrong; one *s* one *d*. *Educ:* Merton College, Oxford]. *Address:* 25 Portland Place, W; Holtye Corner, Cowden, Kent. *Club:* Conservative. *Died 28 March 1916.*

GOODIER, Rev. Joseph Hulme; Hon. Canon of Ripon. *Address:* 11 Crescent Parade, Ripon. *Died Feb. 1920.*

GOODLIFFE, Francis Foster, CIE 1924; MLC; Managing Director, Barnett Bros, Ltd, Rangoon; *s* of W. G. Goodliffe, late Accountant-General, India Office; *m* Alice Hilda, *d* of W. D'Arcy Porter, Rangoon; two *d*. *Educ:* University College School, London. Came to Burma, 1887; Member of the Legislative Council, Burma; Trustee of the Rangoon Development Trust; Commissioner of the Port of Rangoon. *Recreation:* stock-breeding. *Address:* Rangoon, Burma. *Died 7 Oct. 1925.*

GOODMAN, Hon. Sir Gerald Aubrey, Kt 1920; JP, KC; Attorney-General of Straits Settlements since 1913; *b* 6 Sept. 1862; *s* of late Flavius Augustus Goodman; *m* 1885, Gertrude Winifred, *y d* of E. J. Cobbett, RBA; three *s*. *Educ:* Lodge School and Harrison College, Barbados; University College, London. First Common Law Scholar, Middle Temple, 1885; called to Bar, Middle Temple, 1885; practised Barbados; acted Judge of Petty Debt Court and of Assistant Court of Appeal, 1889; acted Solicitor General in 1890-91-92; appointed Solicitor General, 1896; acted Attorney General, 1891, 1898, 1900-1-2-3-4; Attorney-General, Barbados 1907-13; Member of the Barbados House of Assembly, 1889–1912; of the Board of Education, 1891–1912; of the Quarantine Board and General Board of Health, 1902–12; Delegate to Canadian Reciprocity Conference at Barbados, 1908. *Address:* Cahore, Goodwood Hill, Singapore.

Died 20 Jan. 1921.

GOODMAN, Hon. Sir William Meigh; Kt 1902; KC; *b* 1847; *m* 1st, 1874, Fanny, 2nd *d* of B. B. Breach of Burwash, Sussex; 2nd, 1892, Katie, *d* of F. J. Smith. *Educ:* University College; University of London (BA Honours). Called to the Bar, Middle Temple, 1870; went SE Circuit; Attorney-General Brit. Honduras, 1883; Chief-Justice, 1886; Attorney-General, Hong-Kong, 1889; Chief-Justice Supreme Court, Hong-Kong, 1902–5; retired, 1905. *Address:* Clavadel, Guildford, Surrey. *Club:* Constitutional.

Died 3 May 1928.

GOODRICH, Rev. Dr A.; *b* 8 March 1840; *s* of William Goodrich, wholesale furniture manufacturer, Curtain Road, London, and Harriet Gale of Bath; *m* 1865, Emma Susan, *e d* of John Barr, wholesale furniture manufacturer; one *s* five *d*. *Educ:* The Hoxton Acad.; Hackney Coll. Ordained to the Congregational Ministry, 1865; Minister of the Braintree Congregational Church, 1865–76; Elgin Place Congregational Church, Glasgow, 1876–90; Congregational Church, Chorlton Road, Manchester, 1890–1912; Chairman of the Congregational Union of Scotland, 1885; Lecturer in the Congregational Theological Hall; received the degree of Doctor of Divinity from Glasgow University, 1889; Chairman of the Congregational Union of England and Wales, 1904. *Publications:* Primer of Congregationalism; Primer of the Christian Life; Sundry Sermons and Addresses. *Recreation:* golf. *Address:* Candor, Whitehall Road, Colwyn Bay. *Died 26 Sept. 1919.*

GOODRICH, Admiral Sir James Edward Clifford, KCVO 1908 (MVO 1903); *b* Maisemoor Court, Gloucester, 23 July 1851; *s of* James Pitt Goodrich, JP, of Energlyn, Glamorganshire, and Mary, *o c* of Richard Miles Wynne of Eyarth House, Denbighshire; *m* 1897, Adeline Rose, *d* of Capt. Frederic John Helbert, Indian Army, and Sarah Magdalene, *d* of Richard Lane. *Educ:* HMS Britannia. Commodore 2nd Class of Pacific Squadron, 1903–5; Admiral Superintendent of the Gibraltar Dockyard, and in charge of all His Majesty's Naval Establishments at Gibraltar to 1909. JP Gloucestershire. *Address:* Stinchcombe Manor, Dursley, Gloucestershire. *Club:* United Service.

Died 21 Dec. 1925.

GOODWIN, Harvey, JP, DL; *b* 3 Feb. 1850; *e s* of late Rt Rev. Harvey Goodwin, DD, Bishop of Carlisle, and Ellen, *e d* of George King of Higher Bebington Hall, Cheshire; *m* 1879, Ruth, 2nd *d* of W. H. Wakefield of Sedgwick, Westmorland; two *s* one *d*. High Sheriff, Westmorland, 1904. *Address:* Orton Hall, Tebay, Westmorland. *Club:* Carlton. *Died 25 Oct. 1917.*

GOODWIN, Nathaniel Carl; actor; *b* Boston, 25 July 1857; *s* of Nathaniel C. and Caroline R. Goodwin; *m* 1st, Eliza Weathersby (*d* 1887), actress; 2nd, 1898, Maxine Elliott, actress; 4th, 1908, Edna Goodrich, actress. *Educ:* public and private schools. Made his debut with Stuart Robson, Howard Athenæum, Boston, in The Law in New York, 1873; played comedy parts until 1879; appeared as Modus in The Hunchback and as a grave-digger in Hamlet, Cincinnati, 1883; at Bijou Theatre, New York, 1885; played in A Gold Mine and The Bookmaker, London, and in The Nominee, 1890; starred as Captain Crosstree in Black-Eyed Susan, Evangeline, Hobbies, The Member from Slocum, In Mizzoura, Nathan Hale, The Skating Rink, Cruets, Confusion, Turned Up, A Gilded Fool, David Garrick, The Rivals, An American Citizen, 1896; Nathan Hale, 1898; The Cowboy and the Lady, 1899; When we were Twenty-One, 1900; played Shylock in The Merchant of Venice, 1901; appeared in The Altar of Friendship, 1902; The Usurper, 1903; played Bottom in A Midsummer Night's Dream, 1904; starred in The Beauty and the Barge, 1905; Wolfville, and The Genius, 1906; What Would a Gentleman Do?; The Master Hand; The Easterner, 1908–9; Nat Goodwin's Book, 1915. *Address:* Ocean Park, California.

Died 31 Jan. 1919.

GOODWIN, Shirley, MA; Headmaster of Emanuel School, Wandsworth Common, SW, since 1914; *b* 1 Feb. 1880; 2nd *s* of Alfred Goodwin, MA, FSA (Scholar, Tutor, and Fellow of Balliol College, Oxford; Professor of Latin and Greek at University College, Gower Street, WC), and Sara, *d* of Samuel Ford Simmons, Coventry. *Educ:* University College School; Balliol College, Oxford. Master at Malvern Link Preparatory School, 1905; Loretto School, Musselburgh, 1905–7; Perse School, Cambridge, 1907–9; Rector of

the High School, Glasgow, 1909–13. *Recreations:* fishing, golf. *Address:* The Headmaster's House, Emanuel School, SW11.

Died 2 June 1927.

GOODYEAR, William Henry; Curator of Fine Arts, Brooklyn Institute of Arts and Sciences since January 1899; *b* New Haven, Conn, 21 April 1846; *s* of late Charles Goodyear. *Educ:* Yale; Heidelberg; Berlin. Visited Cyprus, Syria, Greece, and Italy, 1869–70; Curator Metropolitan Museum of Art, 1881–88; visited Egypt for studies of lotus ornaments, 1891; surveyed many cathedrals in Italy and Northern Europe for studies of architectural refinements; founder American Anthropological Association, 1902; MA; Honorary Member, Royal Academies of Milan and Venice, Architectural Associations of Rome and Edinburgh, Society of Architects, London, Royal Institute of Architects of Ireland; Corresponding member of the American Institute of Architects. *Publications:* Ancient and Modern History, 1883; A History of Art, 1887; The Grammar of the Lotus, 1891; Roman and Mediæval Art, 1893; Renaissance and Modern Art, 1894; Greek Refinements, 1912; contributions to periodical literature. *Address:* 329 Lincoln Place, Brooklyn. *Club:* Elizabethan, New Haven.

Died 19 Feb. 1923.

GOOLD, Sir James Stephen, 4th Bt, *cr* 1801; *b* 13 Oct. 1848; *s* of George Ignatius Goold, late Resident Magistrate, Waterford, and Clara, *d* of Maj.-Gen. James Webber Smith, CB; *S* uncle, 1893; *m* 1873, Bridget Mary (*d* 1898), *d* of Patrick Goold Jordan; three *s* three *d*. Went to Australia, 1863. *Heir: s* George Patrick Goold [*b* 9 July 1878; *m* 1902, Mary, *d* of Nicholas Browne; two *s*]. *Address:* Gladstone, Adelaide, South Australia.

Died 12 Aug. 1926.

GOOLD-ADAMS, Major Sir Hamilton (John), GCMG 1907 (KCMG 1902; CMG 1894); CB 1898; Governor of Queensland since 1914; *b* 27 June 1858; *s* of late R. W. Goold-Adams; *m* 1911, Elsie, *y d* of Charles Riordan, Montreal; one *s* one *d*. Lieut 1878; Captain, 1885; Major Royal Scots, 1st Batt., 1895; served with Bechuanaland Expedition under Sir Charles Warren, 1884–85; commanded the Field Force against the Matabele, 1893; late Resident Commissioner Bechuanaland Protectorate; served South Africa, 1899–1901 (despatches); Lt-Gov. Orange River Colony, 1901–7; Governor, 1907–10; High Commissioner, Cyprus, 1911–14. *Address:* Government House, Brisbane. *Club:* Army and Navy.

Died 12 April 1920.

GOOLD-ADAMS, Ven. John Michael, MA; Archdeacon of Derry since 1914; Rector of Clonleigh, Lifford, Co. Donegal, since 1914; Examining Chaplain to the Bishop of Derry and Raphoe; *b* 7 April 1850; *e s* of Michael Goold Adams of Rhincrew Abbey, Co. Waterford; *m* 1878, Emma, 4th *d* of Robert M'Clintock, DL of Dunmore, Carrigans, Co. Donegal; one *d*. *Educ:* Midleton College, Co. Cork; Trinity College, Dublin; 1st Prizeman Greek Prose Composition, 1869; 1st Classical Honourman, 1870; awarded by decree of the Board a special Exhibition in lieu of Scholarship, 1873. Ordained, 1875; Curate of Taughboyne, 1876–78; Derry Cathedral, 1878–81; Vicar of Clooney, Londonderry, 1881–1914; Canon of Derry Cathedral, 1893–1914. *Address:* The Rectory, Lifford, Co. Donegal. *Clubs:* Primrose; University, Dublin.

Died 19 July 1922.

GORDON, Lt-Col Adrian Charles, DSO 1915; 16th County of London Battery, 6th London Brigade, Royal Field Artillery, Territorial Force; *b* 4 July 1889; *s* of Charles Gordon; *m* 1912; one *s* twin *d*. *Educ:* Bishop Stortford School. Employed in shipping; served European War, 1914–16 (despatches twice, DSO). *Address:* 8 Park Crescent, Finchley, N3; 36 Lime Street, EC3. *T:* Avenue 1315. *TA:* Gordonia, London. *Died 12 Dec. 1917.*

GORDON, Brig.-Gen. Alister Fraser, CMG 1915; DSO 1900; commanding 2nd Battalion Gordon Highlanders; *b* 1 Feb. 1872; 3rd *s* of W. G. Gordon, Drumdevan, Inverness; *m* 1908, Pilar Mary, *d* of late C. E. H. Edmondstoune Cranstoun of Corehouse; one *s* two *d*. *Educ:* the College, Inverness; RMC Sandhurst. Served Chitral, 1895; NW Frontier, India, 1897–98, including storming of Dargai (despatches); with 2nd British Central Africa Regt, Ashanti, 1900 (DSO, despatches); S Africa (Gordon Highlanders), 1901 (Queen's medal, 3 clasps); European War, 1914–16 (despatches thrice, CMG). *Club:* Naval and Military. *Died 29 June 1917.*

GORDON, Rev. Hon. Arthur, MA, DD; Chaplain to the Royal Company of Archers (King's Body Guard for Scotland); formerly Minister of St Andrew's Church, Edinburgh, and Monzievaird, Perthshire; *b* 20 Dec. 1854; 3rd *s* of Rt Hon. Lord Gordon, of

Drumearn, and Agnes Joanna McInnes; *m* 1893, Emily Olga Marion, *d* of late F. S. S. Constant; two *s* one *d*. *Publication:* The Life of Archibald Hamilton Charteris, 1912. *Address:* 16 Hermitage Drive, Edinburgh. *Club:* Scottish Conservative.

Died 11 June 1919.

GORDON of Ellon, Arthur John Lewis, CMG 1876; JP and DL for Aberdeenshire; landed proprietor; *b* 19 March 1847; 2nd *s* of G. T. R. Gordon of Ellon; *m* 1885, Caroline, 2nd *d* of Gen. Hon. Sir Alexander Hamilton Gordon, KCB; one *s*. *Educ:* Radley Coll. Private Sec. to Governor of Trinidad, 1866–70; Acting Colonial Secretary, 1870; Private Secretary to Governor of Mauritius, 1870; to Governor of Fiji, 1875–80; to Governor-General of Canada (Earl of Aberdeen), 1893. Decorated for services connected with the suppression of rebellion of native tribes in Fiji. *Address:* Ellon Castle, Aberdeenshire. *Club:* Caledonian.

Died 13 Aug. 1918.

GORDON, Lt-Gen. Sir Benjamin Lumsden, KCB 1899 (CB 1881); late Royal Horse Artillery; *b* Revack, Inverness-shire, 8 July 1833; *s* of Captain James Gordon of Revack and Ivybank, and Janet, *d* of Major Grant of Auchterblair; *m* 1860, Laura Sophia, *d* of R. R. Caton of Binbrook; one *s* three *d*. *Educ:* Edin. Military Acad.; Addiscombe. Joined Madras Artillery, 1852; served with Horse Artillery in Indian Mutiny, and was present at Relief of Lucknow, battle of Cawnpore, and several minor engagements (medal and clasp); Captain RHA 1863; Major, 1872; Lieut-Col 1875; Colonel, 1880; commanded RA in Sir Frederick Roberts's advance on Kabul; present at Charasiah and Kabul (despatches, medal with two clasps, CB); commanded a brigade in Madras, 1884–86, and was then appointed as Maj.-Gen. to command in Lower Burmah; in 1889 assumed command of the whole of Burmah (despatches twice, three times thanked by Viceroy of India, medal with two clasps); retired, 1891. Decorated for Afghan campaign. *Address:* Moustows Manor, Henfield, Sussex. *TA:* Henfield.

Died 20 Nov. 1916.

GORDON, Very Rev. Daniel Miner, CMG 1915; DD, LLD; Vice-Chancellor and Principal of Queen's University, Kingston, Canada, 1902; retired and was appointed Principal Emeritus, 1917; *b* Pictou, Nova Scotia, 30 Jan. 1845; *s* of William Gordon, merchant; *m* 1869, Eliza S. (*d* 1910), *d* of Rev. John Maclennan; three *s* two *d*. *Educ:* Pictou Academy; Universities of Glasgow (MA, BD) and Berlin. Ordained a Minister of the Church of Scotland by the Presbytery of Ayr, 1866; Pastor of St Andrew's Church, Ottawa, 1867–82; Knox Church, Winnipeg, 1882–87; St Andrew's Church, Halifax, 1888–94; Professor of Theology in Presbyterian College, Halifax, 1894–1902; Moderator of the General Assembly of the Presbyterian Church in Canada, 1896. DD Glasgow University, 1895; LLD St Andrew's University, 1911, and University of Toronto, 1913. *Publication:* Mountain and Prairie, an account of a journey across Northern British Columbia, the Peace River Country, and the Western Canadian Prairies, 1880. *Recreations:* golf, boating, skating. *Address:* 122 University Avenue, Kingston, Ontario, Canada. *TA:* Gordon, Kingston, Ontario. *T:* 623. *Club:* Frontenac, Kingston.

Died Sept. 1925.

GORDON, Major Duncan Forbes, MVO 1906; DL; Chief Constable, Aberdeen; *b* 30 May 1849; *m* 1st, Elizabeth Alexandrina (*d* 1913); 2nd, 1915, Edith, *widow* of Col T. S. Gildea. Entered Army, 1867; Major, 1885; retired, 1889; served Afghan War, 1878–79 (severely wounded, despatches, medal, two clasps, brevet Major). *Address:* 19 Queen's Road, Aberdeen. *Club:* Junior United Service.

GORDON, Francis Frederick, JP; Hon. Presidency Magistrate; Governing Director of the Advocate of India and Illustrated Sunday Advocate, Bombay; *b* 1866. Went to India on literary staff of Bombay Gazette, 1890, since when closely connected with Indian journalism; purchased the Advocate of India, 1894; pressed and obtained the introduction of the anna nickel coin into the Indian currency; took an active part in plague suppression measures; and, through his efforts, succeeded in inducing the Government to abolish the quarantine imposed at Bombay on Mahomedan pilgrims to Mecca, for which he received the thanks of leading Mahomedans of India. *Address:* Advocate of India, Bombay.

Died 27 Feb. 1922.

GORDON, Lt-Col Francis Lewis, DSO 1917; *b* 28 March 1878; *s* of Francis Frederick Gordon, *y s* of Lord Francis Gordon; unmarried. *Educ:* Haileybury. 3rd Gordon Highlanders; joined 2nd Gordon Highlanders; served South Africa (Queen's medal, 3 clasps); retired, 1903; Major, Royal Irish Rifles, Sept. 1914; 2nd in Command, 1915; Commanded, 1915–17; Commanded 2/1 Leicester Yeo., Sept. 1917–Feb. 1919; served European War, 1914–19 (DSO). *Recreations:*

shooting, hunting, fishing, dog-breaking; a partner in the Hollingbourne Retriever Kennel. *Club:* Bachelors'.

Died 30 Jan. 1920.

GORDON, Maj.-Gen. Hon. Sir Frederick, KCB 1917 (CB 1915); DSO 1900; late commanding 1st Battalion Gordon Highlanders; retired pay since 1920; *b* 9 Oct. 1861; 4th *s* of late Lord Gordon, of Drumearn; *m* 1897, Mabel Rose, *d* of late J. D. Robinson, MCS; one *s* one *d* (and one *d* decd). Served Egypt, 1882–85, including Tel-el-Kebir, El Teb, Tamaai (medal with 3 clasps, and bronze star); Soudan, 1889 (clasp); South Africa, 1899–1902 (despatches four times; Brevet Lt-Col; Queen's medal, 6 clasps, King's Medal, 2 clasps; DSO); European War, 1914–17 (despatches 5 times; specially promoted Maj.-Gen.; KCB); Order of White Eagle, 2nd Class, Serbia; Grand Officer Crown of Rumania. *Address:* Lloyds Bank Ltd, 6 Pall Mall, SW1.

Died 18 Oct. 1927.

GORDON, Col George Grant, CIE 1911; *b* 20 March 1863; *s* of late Capt. G. Grant Gordon, Bengal HA, of Milton, Kilravrock, Nairn; *m* 1891, Mary, *d* of late John Fergusson of Kirkcudbright. Late Manager and Proprietor of Tea Estates in Darjeeling District. *Address:* The Elms, 60 Queen's Road, Richmond, Surrey. *T:* Richmond 578.

Died 12 Nov. 1926.

GORDON, Rt. Hon. John, PC 1915; BA, LLD; **Hon. Mr Justice Gordon;** Judge of High Court (King's Bench Division), Ireland, since 1916; *b* 23 Nov. 1849; *s* of Samuel Gordon, Shankhill, Co. Down; *m* 1887, *d* of late Robert Keating Clay, Dublin. Called to Bar, King's Inn, Dublin, 1877; QC 1892. MP (LU) South Londonderry, 1900–16; Attorney-General, Ireland, 1915–16. *Club:* Constitutional.

Died 26 Sept. 1922.

GORDON, Colonel John Charles Frederick, CIE 1897; JP County Waterford; *b* 4 May 1849; *s* of J. Tomline Gordon, JP; *m* 1879, Grace Hay, *d* of late Fleetwood Williams, CSI. Entered army, 1869; Col 1899; served Mahsood Wuzeeree Expedition; Egyptian war, 1882 (despatches, medal with clasp, Khedive's Star); North-West Frontier, India, in command of 6th Bengal Cavalry, with Kurram movable column, and afterwards Tirah Expeditionary force, 1897–98 (despatches, medal with two clasps); S African War, 1901–2 (medal, 2 clasps); commanded Her late Majesty's Guard of Honour, Diamond Jubilee, 1897.

Died 2 Sept. 1923.

GORDON, Hon. Sir John Hannah, Kt 1910; CMG 1908; KC; Judge of the Supreme Court, South Australia, since 1904; *b* Kilmacolm, NB, 26 July 1850; *s* of Rev. James Gordon, Presbyterian Minister of Gawler, South Australia; *m* 1876, Ann Wright, *d* of late William Rogers of Sandergrove. *Educ:* under private tutors. Admitted to South Australian Bar, 1876; entered Parliament, 1888; Minister of Education in Cockburn Government; Minister of Education in Holder Government; Chief Secretary in Kingston Government; Attorney-General in Holder Government; Attorney-General and Minister of Education in Jenkins Government; Delegate to Federal Convention and Member of the Constitutional Committee of the Convention; Attorney-General for South Australia to 1904. *Address:* Clairmont, Glen Osmond, South Australia.

Died Dec. 1923.

GORDON, Maj.-Gen. Lochinvar Alexander Charles, CB 1915; CSI 1916; late Royal Artillery; *b* 26 May 1864; *m* 1895, Maria, *d* of J. T. Withers; one *s* one *d*. Entered army, 1883; retired, 1919; served European War, 1914–18 (CB, CSI, despatches); Order of White Eagle, Serbia, 3rd class. *Address:* Snowhill, Midhurst, Sussex.

Died 7 Aug. 1927.

GORDON, Col Philip Cecil Harcourt, CMG 1918; Assistant Director Medical Services, Calais, British Expeditionary Force; *b* London, 17 Jan. 1864; *s* of Philip Brodie Gordon, solicitor; *m*; one *s* two *d*. *Educ:* Edinburgh. Entered Army Medical Service, 1885; served Burmese War, 1886–87 (medal and two clasps, despatches); South African War, 1901–2 (medal, three clasps); European War since Dec. 1914. *Recreations:* shooting, cycling, motoring. *Address:* Sunny Corner, Queen's Road, Jersey, CI. *Club:* East India United Service.

Died 4 May 1920.

GORDON, Reginald Hugh Lyall; *b* 14 July 1863; *e s* of late Lewis Gordon of Abergeldie Castle, Aberdeen, and Louisa Isabella, 4th *d* of William Lyall; *m* Rose (*d* 1906); one *d*. *Educ:* Blackheath School. *Address:* 15 Belmont Park, Lee, Kent.

Died 17 July 1924.

GORDON, Victor, CMG 1926; High Commissioner for Newfoundland in London since 1924; *b* St John's, Newfoundland,

28 June 1884; *y s* of late James Gordon, merchant; unmarried. *Educ:* St John's; Academical Institution, Coleraine. Received early business training in Bank of Montreal; called to Bar, Middle Temple, 1912. Served in European War, 1914–18; in Gallipoli Campaign, Egypt and France; temporary Captain King's Own Scottish Borderers; severely wounded at Monchy le Preux, April 1917. Secretary, High Commissioner for Newfoundland, 1919; Acting High Commissioner, 1922–24; represented Newfoundland at Imperial Economic Conference 1923 in advisory capacity, and on Imperial Economic Committee, 1925–26; Chairman, London Advisory Committee, Newfoundland Section, British Empire Exhibition. *Publications:* numerous articles on Newfoundland. *Recreation:* golf. *Address:* 58 Victoria Street, SW1. *T:* Victoria 2302. *TA:* Rurality. *Clubs:* National, British Empire. *Died 6 Oct. 1928.*

GORDON, General William, CIE 1878; General, unemployed list; *b* 10 Feb. 1824; *y s* of late Adam Gordon of Cairnfield, DL Banffshire; *m* 1871, Harriet Elizabeth (*d* 1908), *e d* of Andrew Steuart of Auchlunkart, Banffshire; five *s* three *d. Educ:* Addiscombe College; private schools. Ensign, 1841; arrived in India 30 Dec.; joined 49th Bengal NI 1842; Lieut 1845; at siege of Mooltan as Asst Field Engineer, and with Sappers and Pioneers, 1848–49; present at the surrender of Fort Chiniout, 1849; battle of Goojerat, in command of 2nd and 6th Companies Pioneers (medal and 2 clasps); throughout the Mutiny as Brigade-Major and Deputy-Asst QMG, Mooltan (medal); District Inspector of Musketry, 1860–62; Chief Insector of Musketry, Army Headquarters, 1862–63; twice reappointed, 1868, 1873; Brig.-Gen. 1878; commanded districts Rawal Pindi, Gwalior, and Peshawar; Maj.-Gen. 1882; left India, 1883. *Address:* 9 Tavistock Road, Croydon, Surrey. *Died 3 April 1917.*

GORDON-CUMMING, Miss Constance Frederica; *b* Altyre, 26 May 1837; 12th *child* of Sir William Gordon-Cumming, 2nd Bt, Altyre and Gordonstoun, and Eliza, *d* of John Campbell, Islay. *Educ:* home; school at Fulham, London. An invitation to spend a year with a married sister in India, 1867, awoke the taste for travel and led to very extensive wanderings extending over twelve years. *Publications:* Memories, Autobiography; At Home in Fiji and New Zealand; A Lady's Cruise in a French Man-of-War among the South Sea Isles; Fire Fountains of Hawaii; Granite Crags of California; Wanderings in China; In the Hebrides; In the Himalayas; *Via* Cornwall to Egypt; Two Happy Years in Ceylon. *Recreations:* water-colour painting, but especially, later, working for the development of the invention of the Numeral-Type for the use of illiterate Chinese, both blind and seeing, in Mandarin-speaking districts of China. *Address:* College House, Crieff, Scotland. *Died 4 Sept. 1924.*

GORDON-LENNOX, Colonel Lord Algernon (Charles); Colonel on Retired List; *b* 19 Sept. 1847; 2nd *s* of 6th Duke of Richmond and Gordon and Frances, *e d* of Algernon Frederick Greville (Warwick); *m* 1886, Blanche, DBE, *d* of late Col Hon. Charles Maynard and Blanche, Dowager Countess of Rosslyn; one *d. Educ:* Eton, 1859–61. Served in Royal Navy, 1862–65; joined 1st Life Guards, 1867; transferred to Grenadier Guards, 1867; served with 2nd Batt. Grenadier Guards in Egyptian campaign, 1882 (medal and Khedive star); ADC to Duke of Cambridge, 1883–95; served South Africa, 1900, as Asst Military Secretary to Sir Alfred Milner, and latterly on the staff of General French (medal and three clasps); Jubilee medal, 1887. *Recreations:* hunting, shooting, yachting, fishing, golf. *Address:* 20 Queen Street, Mayfair, W1. *T:* Mayfair 5833. *Clubs:* Guards, Turf; Royal Yacht Squadron, Cowes.

Died 3 Oct. 1921.

GORDON-LENNOX, Cosmo Charles; *b* 17 Aug. 1869; *e s* of Lord Alexander Gordon-Lennox and Emily, *d* of Col Charles Towneley of Towneley; *m* 1898, Marie Tempest. *Educ:* Woburn. *Publication:* Letters of Two People in War Time, 1916. *Plays:* The Impertinence of the Creature, etc. *Died 31 July 1921.*

GORDON-LENNOX, Rt. Hon. Lord Walter Charles, PC 1891; *b* London, 29 July 1865; *y s* of 6th Duke of Richmond and Gordon; *m* 1889, Alice, *d* of late Hon. George Henry Ogilvie-Grant of Grant; one *s. Educ:* Eton; Christ Church, Oxford. Private Secretary to Marquis of Salisbury, 1886; MP (C) SW Sussex, 1888–94; Treasurer of HM Household, 1891–92. *Recreations:* shooting, fishing, golf. *Address:* 19 Palace Court, W. *T:* Park 1501. *Clubs:* Carlton, Beefsteak. *Died 21 Oct. 1922.*

GORDON-SMITH, Richard, FRGS; *b* 20 April 1858; *s* of late John Bridson Smith and Elizabeth Anne, *d* of late George Lawrence of Moreton Court, Herefordshire; *g g s* of James Gordon-Smith of the Manor of Poulton-cum-Seacombe, Cheshire; *m* Ethel, *y d* of late

William Newcomb, of Montreal, Canada; three *d. Educ:* Cheltenham College. Entered Royal South Lincoln Militia, 1877; resigned, 1879; rest of life spent big game hunting, travel, and sport. 4th Class Order of Rising Sun, Japan. *Publication:* Ancient Tales and Folklore of Japan, 1908. *Clubs:* Arthur's, Hurlingham; Royal Albert Yacht, Southsea. *Died 8 Nov. 1918.*

GORE, Arthur (William Charles) Wentworth; *b* Lyndhurst, 2 Jan. 1868; 3rd *s* of Augustus Wentworth Gore, late 7th Hussars, and Emily Ann, *d* of Hon. Edward Curzon; *m* 1893, Minnie, *e d* of Francis Rutledge Alexander. Captain of the first international lawn tennis team England *v* America, 1900; International, 1900, 1906, 1907, 1912, 1913; lawn tennis champion of England, 1901, 1908, and 1909 and Doubles, 1909; Scotland, 1892. *Recreations:* lawn tennis, golf. *Address:* 12 Hereford Square, SW7. *T:* Kensington 5847.

Died 1 Dec. 1928.

GORE, Col Charles Clitherow, MVO 1914; one of HM's Hon. Corps Gentlemen-at-Arms, 1887–1921; *b* 1839; *m* 1st, 1875, Maria (*d* 1881), *d* of Rev. Thomas and Lady Louisa Cator; 2nd, 1882, Lavinia (*d* 1912), *d* of Francis Charles Fitzroy. Served Indian Mutiny, 1857–59 (medal and clasp); Boer War, 1881. *Address:* 56 Stanhope Gardens, SW7. *Club:* Junior United Service.

Died 13 Aug. 1926.

GORE, Lt-Col J. C.; Acting Chief Secretary to the Government of Cyprus several times; *b* 16 Jan. 1852; *y s* of late Lieut-Col Henry Ross Gore, CB; *m e d* of late Major M. Doorly, Police Magistrate, Sierra Leone; two *s* four *d.* Auditor-General West African Settlements, 1882–87; appointed to administer the Government of the Gambia, June–Nov., 1894; Colonial Secretary, Sierra Leone, 1894–1901; Receiver-General Cyprus, 1901–9; served Ashanti War (medal), 1873–74; Expedition against Yonnie Tribes, Sierra Leone, 1887–88 (medal and clasp, despatches). *Address:* c/o Westminster Bank, Jersey. *Club:* Victoria, Jersey. *Died 11 Nov. 1926.*

GORE, Col Robert Clements, CMG 1916; Temporary Brigadier-General; 2nd Battalion Argyll and Sutherland Highlanders; *b* 3 Feb. 1867; *s* of Nathaniel Gore; *m* 1899, Rachel Cecilia, 3rd *d* of Llewellyn Saunderson; one *s. Educ:* Haileybury; Sandhurst. Joined 1st Batt. Argyll and Sutherland Highlanders, 1886; served European War, 1914–17 (despatches, CMG, and Bt-Col). *Club:* Army and Navy.

Died 14 April 1918.

GORE-BOOTH, Eva Selina; writer; 2nd *d* of Sir Henry Gore-Booth, 5th Bt of Lissadell, Sligo. *Publications:* Poems; Unseen Kings; The One and the Many; The Three Resurrections and the Triumph of Maeve; The Egyptian Pillar; The Sorrowful Princess; The Agate Lamp; The Perilous Light; The Death of Fionavar; The Sword of Justice; Broken Glory; articles in reviews and leaflets.

Died 30 June 1926.

GORE-BROWNE, Sir Francis, Kt 1921; KC 1902; JP Berks; MA Oxon; Master of the Bench of the Inner Temple, 1911; Chairman Civil Service Arbitration Board, 1918–20; Chairman Rates Advisory Committee, Ministry of Transport, 1919–21; *b* 1860; *s* of Col Sir Thomas Gore-Browne, KCMG, CB; *m* Helenor, *e d* of J. A. Shaw Stewart; two *s* one *d. Educ:* Harrow; New College, Oxford. Called to the Bar, 1883. *Address:* 8 Pont Street, SW. *T:* Kensington 7248; Oakley House, Abingdon; 4 Crown Office Row, Temple, EC4. *T:* Central 758. *Clubs:* Athenæum, Carlton.

Died 2 Sept. 1922.

GORE-BROWNE, Rt. Rev. Wilfred, MA; Bishop of Kimberley and Kuruman since 1912; *s* of late Colonel Sir Thomas Gore-Browne, KCMG. *Educ:* Harrow; Trinity Coll., Camb., MA. Ordained, 1882; Curate of Pallion, 1882–83; St Hilda, South Shields, 1883–87; St John Evangelist, Darlington, 1887–89; Perpetual Curate, St Hilda's, Darlington, 1889–1902; Rector of Pretoria, 1902–9; Dean of Pretoria, 1909–12. *Address:* Bishopsgarth, Kimberley. *T:* 330.

Died 15 March 1928.

GORELL, 2nd Baron, *cr* 1909; **Henry Gorell Barnes,** DSO; MA; *b* 21 Jan. 1882; *e s* of 1st Baron and Mary Humpston, *d* of T. Mitchell of West Arthurlie; *S* father, 1913. *Educ:* Winchester; Trinity College, Oxford; Harvard University. Barrister, 1906; Secretary to the President of the Probate, Divorce, and Admiralty Division of the High Court of Justice, 1906–10; to County Courts Committee, 1908–9; to Royal Commission on Divorce and Matrimonial Causes, 1909–12; Chairman Kensington Division Red Cross Society; Member of TF Association, County of London; Capt. 19th Battery, 7th London Brigade, RFA (TF). *Publication:* The Divorce Commission: The

Reports Summarised (with J. E. G. de Montmorency). *Recreations:* travelling, shooting, riding, fishing, golf. *Heir: b* Hon. Ronald Gorell Barnes, Barrister [*b* 16 April 1884. *Educ:* Balliol College, Oxford. *Address:* 6 John Street, WC. *Club:* Garrick]. *Address:* 14 Kensington Park Gardens, W. *T:* Park 1424. *Clubs:* Garrick, Ranelagh.

Died 16 Jan. 1917.

GORGAS, William Crawford; *b* Mobile, Ala, 3 Oct. 1854; *s* of Josiah Gorgas, Brig.-Gen. and Chief of Ordnance in the Confederate States Army, and Amelia, *d* of Governor Gale of Alabama; *m* 1885, Marie Cook, *d* of William Doughty; one *d. Educ:* University of the South; Bellevue Hospital Medical College, New York. Entered Medical Corps, United States Army; served in Florida, Western Texas, Indian Territory, and the Territory of Dakota; Captain, 1885; Major, 1898; served Santiago, 1898; Chief Sanitary Officer of Havana; Colonel, 1903; Surgeon-General, 1914; Chief Health Officer of the Isthmian Canal Commission, 1904; Member Isthmian Canal Commission, 1907; United States' delegate to first Pan-American Congress at Santiago, 1908; Associate Fellow of Philadelphia College of Physicians and Surgeons; Doctor of Science, University of Pennsylvania, 1903, Harvard University, 1908, Jefferson Medical College and Brown University, 1909, Columbia University, 1913, Oxford, Princetown University, 1914; LLD University of Alabama, 1910, Tulane University, 1911, Johns Hopkins University, 1912; Hon. Fellow of New York Academy of Medicine; Associate Member of Société de Pathologie Exotique, Paris, 1908; President, American Medical Association and American Society of Tropical Medicine; Vice-President, Association of Military Surgeons, 1909; was the recipient of the Mary Kingsley medal from the Liverpool School of Tropical Medicine, 1907. *Address:* War Department, Washington, USA. *Clubs:* Army and Navy, Chevy Chase, Cosmos, Washington.

Died 3 July 1920.

GORGES, Sir (Edmond) Howard (Lacam), KCMG 1919 (CMG 1917); MVO 1911; Chairman, Board of Trade and Industries, Union of South Africa, 1921; *b* King William's Town, Cape of Good Hope, 16 Jan. 1872; *s* of late Col E. H. Gorges, APD; *m* 1901, Dora, *d* of late Rev. D. P. Faure of Cape Town; two *s. Educ:* South African College, Cape Town. Cape Civil Service, 1889–1901; Transvaal Civil Service, 1901–10; Chief Clerk Colonial Secretary's Office, 1901; Under-Secretary, 1903; Secretary to the Prime Minister and Clerk of Executive Council, 1907; Assistant Colonial Secretary, 1907; Chairman, Transvaal Public Service Board, 1908–10; on formation of the Union of South Africa appointed Secretary for the Interior; Chairman, Union Public Service Advisory Committee, 1910–12; Deputy Chief Censor (Cablegrams and Radiograms) for South Africa, and Chief Press and Postal Censor for the Union, 1914–15; seconded on Gen. Botha's personal staff as Chief Civil Secretary to organise the Public Service and establish Civil Government in South-West Africa; Chief Secretary for the Protectorate, July–Oct. 1915; Administrator of the Protectorate, 1915–20; Chairman Board of Control under Union of South Africa Anti-Profiteering Legislation, 1920–22; also a Member of the Transvaal Mining Leases Board. *Clubs:* Pretoria; Civil Service, Cape Town.

Died Nov. 1924.

GORMAN, Ven. William Charles; *b* 25 Sept. 1826; *o s* of Rev. Fortescue Gorman, of Tanaghmore, Co. Antrim, Ireland, and Harriet, *d* of Sir Jonas Greene, Recorder of Dublin; *m* 1856, Harriet Pitcairn, *o d* of Lieut H. A. West and Eliza Deane West; one *s* one *d. Educ:* Trinity College, Dublin (MA). Ordained, 1850; Curate of Kiltegan, 1850–52; Archdeacon's Vicar of Kilkenny Cathedral, 1852–59; Vicar of Kilmocar, 1859–63; Kilsheelan, 1863–69; Rector of Thomastown, 1869–1908; Archdeacon of Ossory, 1883–1911. *Address:* Mall House, Thomastown, Co. Kilkenny.

Died 20 May 1916.

GORMANSTON, 15th Viscount, *cr* 1478; **Jenico Edward Joseph Preston;** Baron Loundres, 1478; Baron Gormanston (UK), 1868; late Lieutenant Reserve of Officers; Lieutenant 15th Company of London Regiment, Railway Transport Officer; *b* 16 July 1879; *s* of 14th Viscount and Georgina, *d* of Peter Connellan, Coolmore, County Kilkenny; *S* father, 1907; *m* 1911, Eileen, *y d* of late Lt-Gen. Sir William Butler, GCB; three *s* one *d. Educ:* Prior Park Coll., Bath. Late Lieut Manchester Regt. Owner of about 11,000 acres. *Heir: s* Hon. Jenico William Richard Preston, *b* 7 Oct. 1914. *Address:* Gormanston Castle, Co. Meath; Whitewood House, Co. Meath. *Clubs:* Carlton; Sackville Street, Dublin.

Died 7 Nov. 1925.

GORST, Mrs Harold, (Nina Cecilia Francesca); novelist and dramatist; *b* 2 Nov. 1869; *d* of E. R. Kennedy, whose father and uncles, all senior classics, were known at Cambridge as the four Kennedys; *m* Harold Gorst; three *s* one *d. Educ:* home. *Publications:* Possessed of Devils, 1897; And Afterwards?, 1901; This our Sister, 1905; The Light, 1906; The Soul of Milly Green, 1907; The Thief on the Cross, 1908; The Leech, 1911; The Night is Far Spent, an Autobiography, 1919; The Misbegotten, 1921; Ede's Trouble; Timfy's Mother; That Fascinating Foreigner; The Cloche; The Curate and the Columbine; Moll o' the Clothes' Line. *Recreation:* talking. *Address:* 92 Abingdon Road, W.

Died 19 Oct. 1926.

GORST, Rt. Hon. Sir John Eldon, Kt 1885; PC 1890; KC; MA, LLD; FRS; *b* Preston, 24 May 1835; 2nd *s* of E. C. Lowndes (formerly Gorst) and Elizabeth, *d* of John D. Nesham, Houghton-le-Spring, Durham; *m* 1st, 1860, Mary (*d* 1914), *d* of Rev. Lorenzo Moore, Christ Church, NZ; two *s* five *d*; 2nd, 1914, Ethel, *d* of late Edward Johnson. *Educ:* Preston Grammar School; St John's College, Camb. Fellow and Hon. Fellow, 1890; 3rd Wrangler, 1857; Barrister Inner Temple, 1865; QC 1875; Civil Commissioner, Waikato, NZ, 1861–63; Solicitor-General, 1885–86; Under Secretary for India, 1886–91; Financial Secretary to Treasury, 1891–92; MP (C) for Cambridge, 1866–68, for Chatham, 1875–92; Deputy Chairman of Committees, House of Commons, 1888–91; Lord Rector, Glasgow University, 1893–94; Vice-President of Committee of Council on Education, 1895–1902; British Plenipotentiary, Labour Conference, Berlin, 1890; MP (C) Cambridge University, 1892–1906; contested (L) Preston, 1910. *Publications:* The Children of the Nation, 1907; New Zealand Revisited, 1908. *Address:* Castle Combe, Wilts; 84 Campden Hill Court, W. *Club:* Royal Societies.

Died 4 April 1916.

GOSCHEN, Hon. George Joachim; Lieutenant 5th Battalion East Kent Regiment; *b* 18 Nov. 1893; *e s* of 2nd Viscount Goschen.

Died 19 Jan. 1916.

GOSCHEN, Rt. Hon. Sir William Edward, 1st Bt, *cr* 1916; GCB 1911; GCMG 1909 (KCMG 1901); GCVO 1904; PC 1905; *b* 18 July 1847; *y s* of late W. H. Goschen, Templeton House, Roehampton; *m* 1874, Harriet Hosta (*d* 1912), *d* of Darius Clarke; two *s. Educ:* Rugby; Oxford. Attaché, 1869; Madrid, 1870; 3rd Sec., 1873; Buenos Aires, same year; Paris, 1875; 2nd Secretary at Rio de Janeiro, 1877; attached to Rt Hon. George J. Goschen's special embassy to Constantinople, 1880; 2nd Secretary, Constantinople, 1881; Secretary of Legation, Pekin, 1885; Copenhagen, 1888; Lisbon, 1890; Secretary of Embassy, Washington, 1893; Petrograd, 1894; Minister Plenipotentiary during absence of ambassador; acted as Chargeé d'Affaires at Copenhagen, Lisbon, Washington, and Minister Plenipotentiary at Petrograd during absence of Ambassador; Envoy Extraordinary and Minister Plenipotentiary at Belgrade, 1898–1900; at Copenhagen, 1900–5; Ambassador, Vienna, 1905–8; Berlin, 1908–14. Grand Crosses of the Danebrog of Denmark, the Leopold Order of Austria, and the Red Eagle of Prussia. *Heir: s* Edward Henry Goschen, *b* 9 March 1876. *Address:* Beacon Lodge, Christchurch, Hants. *TA:* Highcliffe. *T:* Highcliffe 15. *Clubs:* Travellers', St James', Beefsteak.

Died 20 May 1924.

GOSFORD, 4th Earl of, *cr* 1806; **Archibald Brabazon Sparrow Acheson,** KP; Bt of Nova Scotia, 1628; Baron Gosford, 1776; Viscount Gosford, 1785; Baron Worlingham (UK), 1835; Baron Acheson (UK), 1847; Vice-Chamberlain to HM Queen Alexandra since 1901; *b* 19 Aug. 1841; *s* of 3rd Earl and Theodosia, *o d* of 10th Earl of Meath; *S* father, 1864; *m* 1876, Lady Louise Augusta Beatrice Montagu (Lady of the Bedchamber to HM The Queen), 2nd *d* of 7th Duke of Manchester; two *s* three *d. Educ:* Harrow. Kt Grand Cross of the Dannebrog; St Saviour of Greece; The White Eagle of Russia. *Heir: s* Viscount Acheson, *b* 26 May 1877. *Address:* 24 Hyde Park Gardens, W2. *T:* Paddington 4003. *Clubs:* Travellers', White's; Royal Yacht Squadron, Cowes.

Died 11 April 1922.

GOSLING, Col (Temp. Brig.-Gen.) Charles, CMG 1916; King's Royal Rifle Corps; *b* 24 June 1868. Brigade-Commander; served S Africa, 1899–1900, and 1902 (Queen's medal with clasp); European War, 1914–16 (despatches, CMG).

Died 12 April 1917.

GOSSE, Sir Edmund, Kt 1925; CB 1912; LLD; LittD; Librarian, House of Lords, 1904–14; a Trustee of the National Portrait Gallery; *b* London, 21 Sept. 1849; *o s* of late Philip Henry Gosse, FRS, the eminent zoologist and Emily, *d* of William Bowes; *m* 1875, Ellen, *d* of late Dr G. N. Epps; one *s* two *d. Educ:* privately in Devonshire. Member of the Academic Committee; Assistant Librarian British Museum, 1867–75; Translator to Board of Trade, 1875–1904; Clark

Lecturer in English Literature, Trinity Coll., Camb., 1884–90; Chairman of the Board of Scandinavian Studies, University College, London, since 1917; President of the English Association, 1921. Hon. MA Trinity College, Cambridge; Hon. LLD St Andrews, 1899; Hon. LittD Cambridge, 1920; Hon. Dr Strasburg, 1920; Hon. Dr Gothenburg, 1923; Hon. Dr Paris (Sorbonne); Commander Legion of Honour, 1925; Knight of the Royal Norwegian Order of St Olaf, First Class, 1901; Knight of the Royal Swedish Order of the Polar Star, 1908; Knight of the Royal Danish Order of the Dannebrog, 1912. *Publications: verse:* On Viol and Flute, 1873; King Erik, 1876; New Poems, 1879; Firdausi in Exile, 1885; In Russet and Silver, 1894; Hypolympia, 1901; The Autumn Garden, 1908; Collected Poems, 1911; *prose:* Northern Studies, 1879; Life of Gray, 1882; Seventeenth Century Studies, 1883; Life of Congreve, 1888; History of Eighteenth Century Literature, 1889; Life of P. H. Gosse, 1890; Gossip in a Library, 1891; The Secret of Narcisse, 1892; Questions at Issue, 1893; The Jacobean Poets, 1894; Critical Kit-Kats, 1896; History of Modern English Literature, 1897; Life and Letters of Dr John Donne, Dean of St Paul's, 1899; Illustrated Record of English Literature, vols iii and iv, 1903; Life of Jeremy Taylor, 1904; French Profiles, 1905; Coventry Patmore, 1905; Life of Sir Thomas Browne, 1905; Father and Son, 1907 (crowned by the French Academy, 1913); Henrik Ibsen, 1908; Two Visits to Denmark, 1911; Portraits and Studies, 1912; Collected Essays (5 vols), 1913; Inter Arma, 1916; The Life of Algernon Charles Swinburne, 1917; Three French Moralists, 1918; Diversions of a Man of Letters, 1919; Malherbe, 1920; Books on the Table, 1921; Aspects and Impressions, 1922; More Books on the Table, 1923; Silhouettes, 1925; Leaves and Fruit, 1927. *Address:* 17 Hanover Terrace, Regent's Park, NW1. *T:* Paddington 4524. *Clubs:* Marlborough, Savile, National, Grillions.

Died 16 May 1928.

GOSSELIN, Major Sir Nicholas, Kt 1905; DL; *b* 12 Feb. 1839; *s* of late Nicholas Gosselin, Capt. 46th Regiment; *m* 1865, Katherine Rebecca, *e d* of William Haslett, JP, Carrownaffe, Moville, Co. Donegal; two *s* two *d*. Entered Army, 1855; Civil Service, 1882; retired, 1905, after fifty years of public service. *Address:* Westaria, West Malling, Kent; Lackenagh, Burton Port, County Donegal.

Died 4 Feb. 1917.

GOSSELIN-GRIMSHAWE, Hellier Robert Hadsley, JP; *b* 1849; 2nd *s* of late Martin Hadsley Gosselin, JP, of Ware Priory, and Blakesware, Hertfordshire, and Frances, *e d* of late Admiral Sir John Marshall, KCH, CB; *m* 1902, Mary Ambrose Louisa, *e d* of late Samuel Grimshawe of Errwood Hall; assumed additional surname of Grimshawe by deed poll, 1902; Mrs Gosselin-Grimshawe was joint owner, with her sister, the Hon. Mrs Preston, of Errwood Hall. High Sheriff Herts, 1906. *Address:* Bengeo Hall, Hertford.

Died 31 March 1924.

GOSSET, Ven. Charles Hilgrove; Archdeacon of Christchurch, NZ, 1909–18; 4th *s* of Rev. I. H. Gosset, Vicar of Northam, N Devon; *m* Helen L. Morison; four *d*. *Educ:* Clifton; University of St Andrews. Ordained, 1877; Curate of Masterton, 1877–80; Perpetual Curate of Bank's Peninsula, 1880; Rangiora, 1881–83; Vicar of Woodend, 1883–87; Woodend, Ashley, and Loburn, 1887–91; Heathcote, 1891–1902; Merivale, 1902–15; Archdeacon of Akaroa, 1909; late Member of General Synod, also of Standing Committee, Diocese of Christchurch, and Assessor of Bishop's Court. *Publications:* Notes on Charagia Virescens; Transactions of NZ Institute. *Recreations:* played rugby football for University, for Kidderminster, England, and for Masterton, New Zealand; represented University in mile, 1st Scotch Inter-University sports; member of golf clubs. *Address:* Christchurch, NZ. *T:* Christchurch 2209, NZ. *Club:* Union, Westward Ho.

Died 31 March 1923.

GOSTLING, Col Ernest Victor, DSO 1916; MA, BCh(Cantab); MRCS, LRCP; late Army Medical Staff, Territorial Army; *b* 6 April 1872; *m* 1917; Joan Edith, *d* of Rev. C. Wilton, Beverley, Yorks; one *s* one *d*. *Educ:* Cambridge; St Thomas' Hospital. Late House Physician, Royal Infirmary, Derby, and Senior House Surgeon, Addenbrooke's Hospital, Cambridge; served European War, 1914–16 (DSO); Asst Dir of Medical Services, East Anglian Div. TA, 1920. *Address:* Bedingfield House, Needham Market, Suffolk. *T:* Needham 18.

Died 30 Dec. 1922.

GOUDY, Henry, MA, DCL (Oxon); Hon. LLD (Edin.); Fellow of All Souls College, Oxford; *b* Ireland, 16 Sept. 1848; *e s* of late Rev. Alexander P. Goudy, DD, of Strabane, Co. Tyrone; unmarried. *Educ:* private schools; Glasgow, Edinburgh, and Königsberg Universities. Advocate of the Scottish Bar; elected Professor of Civil Law, Edinburgh University, 1889; editor Juridical Review from foundation

till 1893; Regius Professor of Civil Law, Oxford, 1893; resigned, received the hon. title of Emeritus Prof. from the University, 1919; Ex-Pres. of the Soc. of Public Teachers of Law and the Grotius Society; Honorary Bencher of Gray's Inn. *Publications:* joint author of Manual of Local Government in Scotland, 1880; A Treatise on the Law of Bankruptcy in Scotland, 1886, 4th edn 1914; Inaugural Lecture on the Fate of the Roman Law north and south of the Tweed, 1894; edited 2nd edn of Muirhead's Private Law of Rome, 1898; translated, with notes and additions, Von Jhering's Jurisprudenz d. täg. Lebens, 1904; Trichotomy in Roman Law, 1910 (translated into German by Prof. E. Ehrlich, 1913); contributor of various articles to the Encyclopædia Britannica, etc. *Recreations:* golf, angling. *Address:* All Souls College, Oxford; Strathmore, West Malvern. *Club:* Reform.

Died 3 March 1921.

GOUGH, 3rd Viscount, of Goojerat, Punjab, and Limerick, *cr* 1849; **Hugh Gough,** KCVO 1904; MA; Bt 1842; Baron Gough, 1846; Minister Resident at Coburg and Dresden, 1901–7; *b* 27 Aug. 1849; *s* of 2nd Viscount and Jane, *d* of George Arbuthnot, Elderslie, Surrey; *S* father, 1895; *m* 1889, Lady Georgiana Frances Henrietta Pakenham, *e d* of 4th Earl of Longford, GCB; one *s* one *d* (and one *d* decd). *Educ:* Eton; Brasenose Coll., Oxford. Entered Diplomatic Service, 1873; Secretary to Legation at Rio de Janeiro, 1887–88; Stockholm, 1888–94; Secretary of Embassy, Washington, 1894–96; Berlin, 1896–1901. *Heir:* s Hon. Hugh William Gough, *b* 22 Feb. 1892. *Address:* 9 Upper Belgrave Street, SW1. *T:* Victoria 5810; Lough Cutra Castle, Gort, Co. Galway. *Clubs:* Oxford and Cambridge, Travellers'; Kildare Street, Dublin.

Died 14 Oct. 1919.

GOUGH, Rev. Edwin Spencer, MA; Rector of Barningham, Darlington, 1889–1924; Rural Dean, Richmond North, Surrogate; Hon. Canon, Ripon Cathedral; *b* Feb. 1845; *s* of Edwin Twizell Gough; *m* Caroline Lydia Gough (*d* 1902), *d* of Augustus Morand of Philadelphia; two *s* three *d*. *Educ:* Godolphin Grammar School, Hammersmith; Trinity Coll., Dublin; King's College, London. Curate of St Paul's, Leeds, 1868; Chaplain of the Leeds General Infirmary, 1870–77; Vicar of Burley, Leeds, 1877–89. *Address:* c/o Barningham Rectory, Darlington.

Died 12 Feb. 1927.

GOUGH, Frederic Harrison, MA Oxon; *b* 1863; *e s* of Rev. R. L. H. Gough, Vicar of Chilton Moor, Co. Durham; *m* 1904, Emma Briscoe, *d* of John Tompsett, Merefield House, Crewkerne. *Educ:* Durham School; Oriel College, Oxford. Barrister-at-Law, Inner Temple, 1894; Police Magistrate, Freetown, Sierra Leone, 1903; Solicitor-General, 1903; Solicitor-General, Gold Coast Colony, 1908; Puisne Judge, 1908; Senior Puisne Judge, Gold Coast Colony, 1911. *Publication:* prepared revised edition of The Ordinances of the Gold Coast Colony, Ashanti and Northern Territories, 1910.

GOUGH, Maj.-Gen. Hugh Sutlej, CB 1899; CMG 1886; JP, DL, Carnarvonshire; *b* 4 Feb. 1848; *e s* of late General Sir John B. Gough, GCB; *m* 1886, Beatrice Sophia, Lady of Grace of the Order of St John of Jerusalem, *d* of late Richard Hemming, of Bentley Manor; one *s*. *Educ:* Royal Naval School, Gosport; Emmanuel Coll., Cambridge. Served in RN, 1862–65; entered 10th Royal Hussars as Cornet, 1868; Capt. 1875; Major, 1881; Bt Lieut-Col 1884; Colonel, 1888; Maj.-Gen. 1900; ADC to Commander-in-Chief, India, 1876–81; served in Afghan war, 1878–79; Egyptian campaign, 1884 (despatches); Bechuanaland expedition, 1884–85, where he raised and commanded 3rd Mounted Rifles; commanded 18th Hussars, 1889–93; Asst-Adjt for Cavalry at Headquarters, 1893–98; Lt-Governor and Commander of the Troops in Jersey, 1904–10; Col-in-Chief, 20th Hussars; Hon. Colonel Royal Militia of the Island of Jersey; Distinguished Service Reward, 1905. Decorated: Afghan war; Egyptian war; Bechuanaland expedition. *Recreations:* hunting, shooting, etc. *Address:* Caer Rhùn, Tal-y-Cafn, North Wales.

Died 30 March 1920.

GOULD, Sir Alfred Pearce, KCVO 1911; CBE 1919; FRCS; Lieutenant-Colonel Royal Army Medical Corps (Territorial Force); Officer-in-Command, 3rd London General Hospital, Wandsworth; late Vice-Chancellor of University of London; President, Boys' Life Brigade; late President of the Clinical Section of the Royal Society of Medicine; late President of Medical Society of London; Consulting Surgeon and Emeritus Lecturer on Surgery to Middlesex Hospital; late Lecturer on Surgery to Medical School; late President of Röntgen Society; *b* Norwich, 2 Jan. 1852; 2nd *s* of Rev. George Gould; *m* 2nd, 1885, Florence Jane, *y d* of late Rt Hon. Lord Justice Lush; two *s* four *d*. *Educ:* Amersham Hall School; University Coll. London. Entered Medical School of University Coll. London, 1868; graduated

at University of London, 1874; Master in Surgery, London Univ. Was appointed Assistant-Surgeon to Westminster Hospital and Lecturer on Anatomy, 1877; in 1882 was elected at Middlesex Hospital. *Publications:* The Elements of Surgical Diagnosis; joint-editor with Dr Collins Warren of The International Text-Book of Surgery; The Evolution of Surgery; Bradshaw Lecture on Surgery, Royal College of Surgeons of England, 1910; and several papers and contributions to various scientific societies. *Address:* 26 Ferncroft Avenue, Hampstead, NW3. *T:* Hampstead 2829; Ashe, Ashburton, S Devon. *M:* LA 7500. *Clubs:* Athenæum, University of London.
Died 19 April 1922.

GOULD, Edward, ISO 1902; late Deputy Chief Inspector of Factories and Workshops; *b* 1837. *Educ:* Eton; Trinity College, Cambridge (BA). *Clubs:* St James's, Garrick.
Died 23 July 1922.

GOULD, Edward Blencowe, ISO 1903; *b* Stokeinteignhead, Devon, 9 Aug. 1847; *e surv. s* of Rev. John Nutcombe Gould and Katharine, *d* of General James Grant, CB; *m* 1895, Alice Elizabeth, *e d* of George Gordon of Ellerslie, Toorak, Melbourne. *Educ:* private school. Entered Consular Service in Siam, 1868; 1st Vice-Consul in Siamese Shan States, 1883; Consul at Bangkok, 1885; Chargé d'affaires in Siam, 1886 and 1887–89; Consul, Port Said, 1891; Consul-General, Alexandria, 1897; retired, 1909. *Recreations:* shooting, fishing. *Address:* 7 Alfred Place West, SW. *Club:* Conservative.
Died 16 Nov. 1916.

GOULD, Sir Francis Carruthers, Kt 1906; caricaturist; assistant editor Westminster Gazette; *b* Barnstaple, 2 Dec. 1844; 2nd *s* of Richard Davie Gould, architect; *m* 1869, Emily (*d* 1920), *d* of Hugh Ballment, Barnstaple; three *s* two *d*. *Educ:* private schools in Barnstaple. Over twenty years a member of the London Stock Exchange; illustrated the Christmas Number of Truth many years, and constant contributor to Pall Mall Gazette, till it passed to Mr Astor; since then attached Westminster Gazette; lectured for four years on parliamentary subjects in different parts of England and Scotland; retired Major, London Irish Rifles; JP London and Somerset. *Publications:* a large number of Stock Exchange sketches and caricatures for private circulation; Who killed Cock Robin?, 1897; Tales told in the Zoo (with one of his sons), 1900; Froissart's Modern Chronicles, 2 vols; also Westminster cartoons; editor and illustrator of Picture Politics. *Recreations:* sketching in Normandy and Brittany; natural history, especially ornithology. *Address:* Upway, Porlock, Somerset. *Clubs:* National Liberal, Eighty, Johnson, Whitefriars', Omar Khayyam.
Died 1 Jan. 1925.

GOULD, George Jay; President Texas and Pacific Railway since 1893; *b* New York, 6 Feb. 1864; *s* of late Jay Gould and Helen Day Miller; *m* 1st, 1888, Edith M. Kingdon (*d* 1921); three *s* four *d*; 2nd, 1922, Alice Sinclair. *Educ:* privately. Preferred business to college; became clerk in banking house of W. E. Connor and Co., in which his father was partner; on father's retirement he became member of firm; member of NY Stock Exchange, 1886; entered railway service, 1888, as President Little Rock and Fort Smith Railway; Pres. International and Great Northern RR, 1893–1911; Manhattan Railway, 1888–1913; President and Director Weatherford Railway; Chairman of the Board, St Louis Iron Mountain and Southern RR since 1911; Chairman Missouri Pacific Co.; and Director of numerous railway and other companies. *Recreations:* riding, hunting, polo, yachting, photography. *Address:* Georgian Court, Lakewood, New Jersey; 857 Fifth Avenue and 165 Broadway, New York. *Clubs:* Royal Thames Yacht; Lawyers, New York; NY Athletic, NY Yacht, New York; Royal Southampton Yacht.
Died 16 May 1923.

GOULD, Rev. George Pearce, MA, DD; President of Regent's Park College, 1896–1920; *b* 1848; *e s* of late Rev. G. Gould, Norwich; unmarried. *Educ:* Grey Friars' Priory, Norwich; Amersham Hall School; Glasgow University. Hibbert Travelling Fellow, 1874–76, studying at Berlin, Göttingen, Leipzig. Minister of Bournemouth and Boscombe Baptist Church, 1876–80; Cotham Grove Baptist Church, Bristol, 1880–85; Professor of Hebrew and Old Testament Exegesis, Regent's Park College, 1885–96; President of the Baptist Union of Great Britain and Ireland, 1913–14. *Publications:* Memoir of Rev. G. Gould; Editor of Baptist Historical Manuals; sundry articles. *Recreations:* walking, foreign travel. *Address:* 5 Kidderpore Gardens, NW3. *T:* Hampstead 1476.
Died 21 March 1921.

GOULD, Nathaniel; novelist; *b* Manchester, 21 Dec. 1857; *s* of late Nathaniel Gould, Manchester, and Pilsbury Grange, Derbyshire; *m* 1886, Elizabeth Madelin Ruska; three *s* two *d*. *Educ:* Strathmore House, Southport. Journalist of wide experience for 25 years in

England and Australia; travelled in Queensland, Victoria, NSW, S Australia, Tasmania, and elsewhere. *Publications:* The Double Event, 1891; Running It Off, 1892; Jockey Jack, 1892; Harry Dale's Jockey, 1893; Banker and Broker, 1893; Thrown Away, 1894; Stuck Up, 1894; Only a Commoner, 1895; The Miner's Cup, 1896; The Magpie Jacket, 1896; Who Did It?, 1896; On and Off the Turf in Australia; Town and Bush, 1896; The Doctor's Double, 1896; A Lad of Mettle, 1897; Horse or Blacksmith (later Hills and Dales), 1897; A Gentleman Rider, 1898; The Pace that Kills, 1899; Sporting Sketches; The Roar of the Ring, 1900; A Stable Mystery, 1901; A Racing Sinner, 1902; Bred in the Bush, 1903; The Rajah's Racer, 1904; The Second String; Charger and Chaser, 1906; The Chance of a Lifetime; The Little Wonder; The Dapple Grey; A Run of Luck, 1907; The Stolen Racer, 1908; A Reckless Owner, 1909; The Magic of Sport; The Roarer; The Lucky Shoe; A Great Coup, 1910; The King's Favourite; Good at the Game; The Phantom Horse; The Cast-Off; The Trainer's Treasure, 1911; A Northern Crack; The Head Lad; Fast as the Wind; At Starting Price; A Fortune at Stake; A Gamble for Love; The Wizard of the Turf; Lost and Won; The Smasher; The White Arab; Never in Doubt; in all about a hundred and thirty novels; short stories and newspaper articles. *Address:* Newhaven, Bedfont, Middlesex. *Club:* Authors'.
Died 25 July 1919.

GOULDING, Rt. Hon. Sir William Joshua, 1st Bt, *cr* 1904; PC 1917; JP, DL; Chairman, Great Southern and Western Railway of Ireland; Deputy-Chairman, Fishguard and Rosslare Harbours and Railway Company; an Irish Lights Commissioner; Chairman Irish Railway Clearing House; Chairman Property Losses Committee (Ireland), 1916; Director National Bank, Ltd; Chairman W. & H. M. Goulding, Ltd; Irish Convention, 1917–18; a Senator for Southern Ireland; Member of the Church Representative Body of Ireland; a Steward of the Turf Club of Ireland; *b* 7 March 1856; *e s* of W. Goulding, DL, MP, Summerhill House, Co. Cork; *m* 1881, Ada, *d* of Charles Lingard Stokes of Pauntley, Worcs; one *s* four *d*. *Educ:* Cambridge (MA). High Sheriff, Co. Dublin, 1906; Co. Kildare, 1907. *Heir: s* William Lingard Amphlett Goulding, Capt. Royal Irish Fusiliers, ADC [*b* 5 Oct. 1883; *m* 1908, Nesta Violet, *d* of late Hon. Mr Justice Wright, and *g d* of Sir Croker Barrington, 4th Bt; two *s*]. *Recreation:* hunting. *Address:* Luttrellstown, Clonsilla, Co. Dublin; Millicent, Sallins, Co. Kildare. *T:* Naas 14. *Clubs:* Carlton; University, Kildare Street, Dublin; Royal St George Yacht.
Died 12 July 1925.

GOURLAY, Charles, BSc; FRIBA, FSAScot; Professor of Architecture and Building, the Royal Technical College, Glasgow, since 1895; *b* Edinburgh; *s* of Charles Gourlay and Anne Ingram Clark; *m* 1905, Helen Mary Ramsay (*d* 1920), Constantinople; one *d*. *Educ:* Glasgow University. Served apprenticeship as an architect in Glasgow; afterwards began professional practice, and executed several buildings; began teaching architecture and building subjects, 1886; resolved to devote all his time to teaching, 1890; Lecturer, Royal Technical College, Glasgow, 1888. *Publications:* Elementary Building Construction and Drawing for Scottish Students; The Construction of a House; The Italian Orders of Architecture; Rheims Cathedral in The Architect; The Parthenon; Santa Sophia; The Churches of Constantinople; The Churches of Salonica, in the RIBA Journal; etc. *Recreations:* photography (Hon. Pres. of the Royal Technical College Architectural Craftsmen's Society), archæology pertaining to architecture. *Address:* Coniston, Craigdhu Road, Milngavie, Glasgow.
Died 30 June 1926.

GOW, Andrew Carrick, RA 1891 (ARA 1881); artist; Keeper of the Royal Academy since 1911; *b* London, 15 June 1848; *m* Ethel, *d* of Frederick Relfe; one *s* four *d*. Studied at Heatherley's School of Art; elected RI 1868; since 1869 exhibited continuously at Royal Academy. *Principal Pictures:* The Relief of Leyden, 1876; No Surrender, 1878; The Last Days of Edward VI, 1880; Cromwell at Dunbar, 1886 (purchased by Chantrey Fund); The Garrison Marching out with the Honours of War, Lille 1705, 1887; Flight of James II after the Battle of the Boyne, 1888; After Waterloo, 1890; Queen Mary's Farewell to Scotland, 1892; The Queen's Diamond Jubilee at St Paul's (for the Corporation); Nelson Cartoon in the Royal Exchange, etc; Cartoon presented by the Royal Academy to the Houses of Parliament. *Address:* Burlington House, Piccadilly, W. *Club:* Athenæum.
Died 1 Feb. 1920.

GOW, Rev. James, LittD; Headmaster of Westminster School, 1901–19; *b* 1854; *s* of James Gow, member of Royal Soc. of British Artists; *m* Gertrude Sydenham, *d* of the late G. P. and M. A. Everett Green; two *s*. *Educ:* King's College School; Trinity College, Cambridge (MA). 3rd Classic and Chancellor's Classical Medallist, Cambridge, 1875; Fellow of Trinity College, 1876; Fellow of King's

College, London, 1876; Litterarum Doctor (Cambridge), 1885. University Extension Lecturer, Cambridge, 1876–78; Barrister, Lincoln's Inn, 1879; President of Headmasters' Association, 1900–2; Chairman of Headmasters' Conference, 1906–8, 1911–12; Master of the High School, Nottingham, 1885–1901. *Publications:* A Short History of Greek Mathematics, 1884; A Companion to School Classics, 1888; A Method of English, 1893; Odes and Epodes of Horace, 1896; articles in Smith's Dictionary of Antiquities, etc. *Recreation:* walking. *Address:* 40 West End Lane, Hampstead, NW6. *Club:* Athenæum. *Died 16 Feb. 1923.*

GOW, William; Secretary of the British and Foreign Marine Insurance Co. Ltd, Liverpool, since 1908; occasional Lecturer on Marine Insurance at University College, Liverpool; *b* 1853; *e s* of John Gow, JP, banker and worsted spinner, Dalry, Ayrshire; *m* 1884, Katharine Mary, 2nd *d* of late John Thornborrow Manifold, Government Engineer, British Guiana; one *s* one *d*. *Educ:* Glasgow Academy; Glasgow and St Andrews Universities and University College, London (MA Glasgow); afterwards Paris (Conservatoire de Musique, etc), Berlin, Jena, Heidelberg. Secretary of Union Marine Insurance Company, Liverpool, 1883–92; then appointed Liverpool underwriter for the Marine Insurance Company of London; in 1897 went to New York as American manager of the London Assurance Corporation, marine branch; returned to Liverpool to be underwriter of Union Marine Insurance Co. there, 1899. *Publications:* Marine Insurance; British Imperial Customs Union; Sea Insurance according to British Statute. *Address:* Druid's Lodge, Hoylake, Cheshire. *TA:* c/o Elysium, Liverpool. *T:* Liverpool Central 26; Hoylake 426. *Club:* Exchange, Liverpool. *Died 21 Nov. 1919.*

GOWER, Lord Ronald Sutherland–; MP (L) County of Sutherland, 1867–74; *b* 2 Aug. 1845; *y s* of 2nd Duke and 20th Earl of Sutherland and Harriet Howard, *d* of 6th Earl of Carlisle; uncle and great uncle of the Dukes of Argyll, Sutherland, Leinster, and Westminster, etc. *Educ:* home; Eton; Trinity Coll., Cambridge. A Trustee of the National Portrait Gallery, and of the Birthplace and Shakespeare Memorial Building at Stratford-on-Avon; Sculptor of statues of Marie Antoinette on her Way to Execution; The Old Guard at Waterloo; the Shakespeare Monument at Stratford-on-Avon, consisting of colossal statue of the poet, with four life statues at the base of the Memorial, etc. *Publications:* many on the Fine Arts; My Reminiscences; Life of Joan of Arc; Rupert of the Rhine; Stafford House Letters; Bric-a-Brac; Last Days of Marie Antoinette; De Brosses' Letters from Italy; Life of Sir Thomas Lawrence; Life of Sir D. Wilkie; History of the Tower; Old Diaries; Life of Michael Angelo; Life of Thomas Gainsborough; Records and Reminiscences, 1903; Life of George Romney, etc. *Recreations:* literature, art. *Address:* 66 Mount Ephraim, Tunbridge Wells. *Clubs:* Royal Societies, Royal Automobile, Authors'. *Died 9 March 1916.*

GOWING, Lionel Frances; journalist; on staff of Daily Telegraph; *b* Ipswich, 1859; *s* of late Richard Gowing; *m* 1898, Florence, *d* of William Senior; one *s* one *d*. On staff of North China Daily News, and Weekly Herald, Shanghai, 1882–87; and acted for over thirty years as London correspondent; published at Shanghai, Notes of a Visit to Corea; travelled with one companion (the late Mr C. J. Uren) through Siberia in mid-winter in a sledge, from Vladivostock to Moscow. *Publication:* Five Thousand Miles in a Sledge: a Mid-Winter Journey across Siberia, with illustrations by Mr Uren, 1889. *Address:* 11 Thornton Avenue, Streatham Hill, SW2.

Died 2 Dec. 1925.

GOWLAND, Professor William, FRS; ARSM; Chevalier Imperial Order of the Rising Sun; Emeritus Professor of Metallurgy, Royal School of Mines, London; late Member of the Governing Body of the Imperial College of Science and Technology; a Governor of the School of Metalliferous Mining, Camborne; late Examiner in Metallurgy Board of Education and London University; *b* Sunderland, 1842; *e s* of late George Thompson Gowland; *m* 1st, 1890, Joanna (*d* 1909), *y d* of late Murdoch Macaulay, JP, of Linchader, Isle of Lews; one *d*; 2nd, 1910, Maude Margaret, *e d* of late D. J. Connacher. *Educ:* Royal College of Chemistry; Royal School of Mines. 1st and 2nd years Scholarships; Murchison and De la Beche Medallist; Associateship in Mining and Metallurgy; Chemist and Metallurgist Broughton Copper Co., 1870–72; Chemist, Assayer, and Foreign Head of Imperial Japanese Mint, 1872–88; sometime Metallurgical Adviser to the War Dept, Japan; Chief Metallurgist Broughton Copper Company, 1889–91; Past President Institute of Mining and Metallurgy, of Royal Anthropological Institute, and of the Institute of Metals; gold medallist of the Institute of Mining and Metallurgy; Fellow or Member of Society of Antiquaries, Institute of Chemistry, Chemical Society, American Institute of Mining and Metallurgical

Engineers, Society Chemical Industry, Royal Society Arts, and Royal Institution. *Publications:* The Metallurgy of the Non-Ferrous Metals; Imperial Mint Technical Reports; various papers in the Journals of the Institute of Mining and Metallurgy, Chemical Society, Society Chemical Industry, Royal Anthropological Institute, and in Archæologia and Proceedings Society Antiquaries, etc. *Address:* 13 Russell Road, Kensington, W14; Royal School of Mines, S Kensington, SW. *T:* Park 4540.

Died 10 June 1922.

GRAAFF, Senator Hon. Sir Jacobus Arnoldus Combrinck, KCMG 1917; Minister without Portfolio, South Africa, 1913–20; Minister of Public Works, Posts and Telegraphs, 1920–21; *s* of late Petrus Novbertus Graaff and Annie Elizabeth de Villiers; *m* 1889, Susan Elsebie Maria Theunissen. Director of Messrs Graaffs' Trust Limited, Cape Town and Pretoria; keen politician, and was for many years Chairman of the Cape Town Branch of the Afrikander Bond; commenced Parliamentary career in 1903, and at successive elections successfully contested the seat for the North Western Circle in the Legislative Council of the Cape Colony; Chief Whip of South African Party in Legislative Council, which position he continued to fill in the Union Senate; an ardent Protectionist. *Address:* Bordeaux, Sea Point, Cape Province. *Clubs:* National Liberal; City, Royal Automobile of South Africa, Cape Town; Country, Pretoria.

Died 5 April 1927.

GRACE, Ven. Thomas Samuel; Archdeacon of Marlborough since 1890; Canon of Christchurch Cathedral, Nelson, since 1916; Vicar of Church of Nativity, Blenheim, since 1885; *b* at sea, 1850; *s* of Rev. T. S. Grace, CMS Missionary; *m* Rhoda Caroline, 2nd *d* of Capt. Colt; five *s* four *d*. *Educ:* Church of England Grammar School; Bishopdale College, Nelson; University of New Zealand. Ordained, 1873; Domestic Chaplain to Bishop of Nelson: Asst Tutor Bishopdale College; and Perpetual Curate of Suburban North Nelson, 1874–81; CMS Missionary, Putiki, 1881–85; Superintendent of Maori Mission, Diocese of Nelson, NZ, since 1890. *Publications:* Sketches of Church History in Maori; Outline of Scripture History in Maori. *Address:* Blenheim, Marlborough, NZ.

Died 1 April 1918.

GRACEY, Col Thomas, CSI 1897; late India Public Works Department; *b* 21 Jan 1843; *s* of Thomas Gracey, of Ballyhosseth, Co. Down. *Educ:* Enniskillen Royal School. Entered RE 1862; Col 1895; 1st assistant engineer, 1867; executive engineer, 1870; engineer-in-chief, Pindi-Kohat section of Punjab Railway, 1879; North-West Provinces and Oudh, 1882; secretary to Chief Commissioner, Public Works Department, Burma, 1887; superintending engineer, 1888; consulting engineer to Government of India, 1891; chief engineer, 1892; director-general of railways, 1895; secretary to Government of India, railway branch, 1897; retired 1898. *Address:* 22 Kidbrooke Grove, Blackheath, SE. *Died 16 June 1921.*

GRAFTON, 7th Duke of, *cr* 1675; **Augustus Charles Lennox FitzRoy,** KG 1883; CB 1873; DL, JP; Baron Arlington, 1664; Earl of Arlington and Euston, Viscount Thetford and Ipswich, Baron Sudbury, 1672; late Coldstream Guards; General, retired 1881; Hereditary Ranger of Whittlebury Forest, Northamptonshire; Equerry to Queen Victoria, 1849–82; Hon. Equerry, since 1882, to late King Edward VII and to King George V; *b* 22 June 1821; *s* of 5th Duke and Mary, *d* of Adm. the Hon. Sir George Cranfield Berkeley, GCB; *S* brother, 1882; *m* 1847, Anna (*d* 1857), *y d* of late James Balfour, Whittingehame, Haddingtonshire; one *s* (and two *s* one *d* decd). *Educ:* Harrow. Entered 60th Rifles, 1837; Coldstream Guards, 1839; served Crimea (severely wounded at Inkerman). *Heir:* *s* Earl of Euston, *b* 3 March 1850. *Address:* 6 Chesterfield Gardens, W; Euston Hall, Thetford; Wakefield Lodge, Stony-Stratford. *Clubs:* Travellers', United Service. *Died 4 Dec. 1918.*

GRAHAM, Flt-Lt Charles Walter, DSO 1916; Royal Naval Air Station, Eastchurch, Kent; *b* 12 Nov. 1893; *s* of Charles Knott Graham and Helena Reutt; unmarried. *Educ:* two years college in France; Merchant Taylors' School. Joined the Triumph Engineering Co., Coventry, to study motor engineering; after about 1¼ years went to Germany to the Bosch Magneto Factory at Stuttgart; was in Germany at outbreak of war; got out *via* Switzerland; on arriving in England immediately started to study science of Aviation at Hendon, finally buying an aeroplane and teaching himself to fly; joined RNAS 12 April 1915; sent to France May 1915; attacked and destroyed a German seaplane off the Belgian coast (with Flight Sub-Lieut Ince), Dec. 1915 (DSO); seriously injured at Dunkerque, 8 Feb. 1916. *Recreations:* everything, particularly gymnastics and motoring. *Address:* 9 Kitson Road, Barnes, SW. *Died Sept. 1916.*

GRAHAM, Sir Claverhouse Frederick Charles, Kt 1905; JP, Derbyshire; *s* of Sutherland Graham; *m* 3rd, Emily, 2nd *d* of George Moulson, Hove. Past Grand Master, Parliamentary Secretary, and Trustee of the Manchester Unity Friendly Society; Founder and Past President of the National and State Paid Old Age Pension League, 1890; Past Pres. Licensed Victuallers' Society; Past Prov. Senior Grand Warden Prov. of Staffs; formerly CC for Staffs; Founder and Past Pres. of the Pioneer Three Counties Conference. *Publications:* House of Lords, Past, Present, and Future; Friendly and Thrift Progress and Development; Old Age Pensions, a Duty of the State, 1884, 10 edn 1904; State Pensions for all the Thrifty (Address, Church Congress, Norwich, 1905); Labour, Religion, and Science; The Parliamentary Committee Old Age State Pension Bill. *Address:* Helmsley, Lennox Road South, Southsea.   *Died 19 May 1924.*

GRAHAM, Edward John; MP (IN) Tullamore, King's County, since 1914. *Address:* House of Commons, SW.
Died 26 March 1918.

GRAHAM, Capt. (temp. Major) Francis, DSO 1915; MC 1916; 71st Brigade Royal Field Artillery; *b* 29 March 1894. Entered army, 1913; served European War, 1914–17 (despatches, DSO, MC). *Address:* Forston House, near Dorchester, Dorset.
Died 28 March 1918.

GRAHAM, Sir Frederick, KCB 1907 (CB 1899); late Assistant Under Secretary of State, Colonial Office; *b* 1848; *s* of late Frederick Graham of Cherry Bank, Newhaven, NB, and Marjory, *d* of Rev. Alexander Niven, DD, of Dunkeld. *Educ:* Edinburgh. Entered Colonial Office, 1870; Principal Clerk, 1896; retired, 1907. *Address:* Aros, Haslemere, Surrey. *Club:* St Stephen's.   *Died 21 Feb. 1923.*

GRAHAM, Hon. George; *b* Scotland, 1838; *m* 1863, Miss Welch, of Langer, Nottinghamshire. MLA Moira, 1883; Numurkah and Nathalie, 1889; Goulburn Valley, 1894; Minister for Water Supply, 1890–92; Agriculture, 1891–92; Public Works, Water Supply, and Agriculture, 1892–93; Public Works and Agriculture, 1899–1900; Minister of Water Supply and of Agriculture, 1912–13. *Address:* Wungburn, Australia.

GRAHAM, Rev. Chancellor George R.; Vicar of Lea, 1890–1923; Chancellor of Kildare Cathedral, 1909–23; *b* 1850; *s* of Rev. Christopher Graham, rector of Derver, Co. Louth, and Frances Caroline Skelton; *m* 1876, Emily Mary, *d* of Capt. F. Page; two *s* two *d*. *Educ:* Dundalk Grammar School; Dublin University. Curate, Irishtown, Dublin, 1873–75; Carbury, Co. Kildare, 1875–79; Vicar, Carnalway, Co. Kildare, 1879–87; Eyrecourt, Co. Galway, 1887–90; 1st Canon of Kildare, 1905. *Address:* Killylea House, Killylea, Co. Armagh.   *Died 1927.*

GRAHAM, John, ISO 1903; late a Chief Clerk, Board of Agriculture and Fisheries; *b* 1844; *m* 1880, Louise (*d* 1913), *d* of late Rev. George Yenkins, Rector of Manatan, Devon. *Address:* 26 Sandringham Court, Maida Vale, W.   *Died 9 Jan. 1918.*

GRAHAM, Sir John Hatt Noble, 1st Bt, *cr* 1906, of Larbet and Househill, Stirlingshire; *b* 14 Aug. 1837; *s* of John Graham of Lancefield, Glasgow, and Elizabeth Hatt Noble; *m* 1st, 1862, Jane Brown (*d* 1890), *d* of James Graham Adam of Denovan, Stirlingshire; two *s* five *d*; 2nd, 1891, Frances Lucy, *d* of Martin Collingham Clodd, of Bury St Edmunds. *Educ:* Merchiston Castle, Edinburgh; Glasgow University. Partner of William Graham & Co., Glasgow, and all its corresponding firms in England, India, Portugal, since 1855. JP Lanark, Glasgow, and Stirling Counties. *Recreation:* shooting. *Heir: s* John Frederick Noble Graham, *b* 25 July 1864. *M:* MS 181. *Club:* Western, Glasgow.   *Died 25 May 1926.*

GRAHAM, Sir John (James), KCMG 1905 (CMG 1899); Secretary to Law Department, Cape of Good Hope, 1889–1908; *b* Wynberg, 21 Feb. 1847; *e s* of Robert Graham of Fintry; *m* 1873, Annie Julia, *d* of Hon. J. Murison, MLC; four *s* one *d*. *Educ:* St Andrew's College, Grahamstown. Clerk to Civil Commissioner and Resident Magistrate, Albany, 1864; to Registrar Eastern Districts Court, 1865; Assistant Registrar Supreme Court, 1872; Registrar and Master Eastern Districts Court, 1875; Chief Clerk to Attorney-General and Clerk of Peace for Cape Town, 1878; Secretary to Law Department, 1882; High Sheriff and Taxing Officer Supreme Court, 1884; reappointed Secretary to Law Dept with control of convict stations and prisons, 1889; retired, 1908. *Address:* Monorgan, Newlands, Cape Town.
Died 17 Dec. 1928.

GRAHAM, Michael, JP; *b* Glasgow, 22 Jan. 1847; *m* 1887; one *s* one *d*. *Educ:* St Andrew's Parish School, and Andersonian University, Glasgow. Sub-Editor and Leader-Writer, Glasgow Herald, 1872–86; Editor The Evening Times, Glasgow, 1886–1919. *Recreations:* books, walking. *Address:* Hillend, Old Cathcart, Glasgow. *T:* Langside 75.
Died 1925.

GRAHAM, Sir Reginald (Henry), 8th Bt, *cr* 1662, of Norton Conyers, JP, DL; late Captain Rifle Brigade; *b* 22 April 1835; *e s* of Sir Bellingham Reginald Graham, 7th Bt and 2nd *wife*, Harriet, 3rd *d* of late Rev. Robert Cottam; *S* father, 1866; *m* 1876, Annie Mary (*d* 1917), *d* of late Thomas Shiffner, Westergate House, Sussex; two *s* (and one *s* decd). Served with 14th Foot in Crimean campaign at Sebastopol, 1854–56 (medal and clasp); Crimean and Turkish medals; Capt. Rifle Brigade, 1856 (retired 1863). *Publications:* Fox-hunting Recollections, 1907; Poems of the Chase, 1912. *Heir: s* Reginald Guy Graham, *b* 28 May 1878. *Address:* Norton Conyers, near Ripon, Yorkshire. *Clubs:* Carlton, Jockey; Yorkshire, York; Royal Yacht Squadron, Cowes.   *Died 27 Dec. 1920.*

GRAHAM, Sir Robert James Stuart, 10th Bt, *cr* 1629; *b* 2 Dec. 1845; *s* of Sir Edward Graham, 9th Bt and Adelaide Elizabeth, *d* of James Dillon Tully; *S* father, 1864; *m* 1874, Eliza, *d* of Charles Burns, Brooklyn, NY; four *s*. *Heir: s* Montrose Stuart Graham [*b* 20 May 1875; *m* 1903, Helen Ursula, *d* of John Henderson, Lerwick; one *s* one *d*. *Address:* 563 52nd Street, New York]. *Address:* 629 54th Street, Bay Ridge, Brooklyn, New York, USA.
Died 12 May 1917.

GRAHAM, General Sir (Samuel) James, KCB 1902 (CB 1882); Royal Marines; retired; *b* Malta, 30 Jan. 1837; *s* of late Col J. J. Graham, at one time Military Secretary Turkish Contingent; *g s* of late General Graham, Lieut-Governor of Stirling Castle; *m* 1st, 1862, Laura Christiana (*d* 1874), *d* of late A. H. Williams, HEICS; three *s*; 2nd, 1879, V. Rosabel, *d* of late Gen. T. Conyngham Kelly, CB, of Loughbrown, Co. Kildare, Ireland. Served in Baltic campaign, 1854–55 (medal); served in HMS "Agamemnon" when engaged in laying Atlantic Telegraph Cable; HMS "Black Prince" when towing Floating Dock to Bermuda; commanded a Batt. of Marines sent to Port Said to assist Navy in seizing Suez Canal during insurrection under Arabi Pasha; landed at Ismailia (despatches); present at actions of Tel-el-Mahuta, Mahsemah, Kassassin, and battle of Tel-el-Kebir (despatches twice, medal and clasp, CB); selected to receive Egyptian War Medal at hands of HM at Windsor; Queen's Jubilee Medal; 4th class of the Order of the Osmanieh. *Address:* 3 Kensington Court Mansions, Palace Gate, SW. *Club:* United Service.
Died 11 May 1917.

GRAHAM, Peter, RA 1881 (ARA 1877); HRSA 1877 (ARSA 1860); *b* Edinburgh, 1836; *m.* *Educ:* Trustees Acad., Edinburgh. Studied with Robert Scott Lauder and John Ballantyne, 1850–56. First painting to be exhibited at RA, A Spate in the Highlands, 1866; commnd by HM the Queen to paint Bowman's Pass, Balmoral Forest, 1868. *Address:* Westoun, St Andrews, Scotland. *Club:* Athenæum.
Died 19 Oct. 1921.

GRAHAM, P. Anderson; Editor of Country Life. A Northumbrian, who early in life took to journalism and literature; edited or helped to edit several journals before coming to Country Life about 1900; acted as special commissioner to the Standard, Morning Post, and St James's Gazette at various times. *Publications:* Nature in Books; Seven Studies in Biography; The Rural Exodus; The Problem of the Village and the Town; All the Year with Nature; Country Pastimes for Boys; The Victoria Era; The Red Scaur: A Novel of Manners; edited the Country Life Anthology of Verse, 1916; Highways and Byways in Northumbria, 1919; The Collapse of Homo Sapiens, 1923; Iwerne, Before, During and After the War, 1923 (for private circulation only); editor of the Country Life Increased Productivity Series. *Recreations:* chess, billiards, golf. *Address:* 20 Tavistock Street, WC. *TA:* Countrylife, London. *T:* Gerrard 2748. *Club:* Constitutional.   *Died 25 Oct. 1925.*

GRAHAM, Maj.-Gen. Sir Thomas, KCB 1908 (CB 1889); late Royal Bengal Artillery; *b* 26 Jan. 1842; *s* of late Gen. Joseph Graham; *m* 1869, Elizabeth, *d* of Maj.-Gen. Bean, BSC; two *s* (younger killed in action in France, 21 Dec. 1914). Entered army, 1858; Major-General, 1891; retired; served Hazara expedition (medal with clasp); Afghan war, 1878–80 (despatches, Brevet Lieut-Col, medal, bronze decoration); Burmah (despatches, clasp); Sikkim, 1888–89 (CB, clasp); Manipur, 1891 (thanks of Government, despatches, clasp). *Address:* Glencoe, Camberley.   *Died 4 Nov. 1925.*

GRAHAM, Hon. Sir Wallace, Kt 1916; Chief Justice of Nova Scotia since 1915; Governor of Dalhousie College, Halifax, NS; *b* Antigonish, NS, 15 Jan. 1848; *s* of David Graham and Mary Elizabeth Bigelow; *m* Annie Lyons, of Cornwallis, NS; one *s* two *d. Educ:* Acadia Coll. (BA 1867). Called to Bar, 1871; QC 1881; Standing Counsel in NS for Govt of Canada 8 years; appointed on Commission to revise Statutes of Canada, 1883; and to revise Statutes of Nova Scotia, 1898; Judge in Equity of Supreme Court and of Court for Divorce in Nova Scotia, 1889. *Address:* 37 South Park Street, Halifax, NS. *TA:* Halifax. *T:* St Paul 517. *Club:* Halifax.

Died 12 Oct. 1917.

GRAHAM, William Perceval Gore; one of HM's Inspectors at the Home Office since 1914; *b* 1 July 1861; 3rd *s* of late Robert Gore Graham, JP, of Southmead, Westbury, Gloucestershire; *m* 1st, Isabel Mary, *d* of late Sir Thomas Longmore, CB, of Woolstone, Hants; 2nd, Isabel Margaret, *d* of Frederick W. Harris, JP, DL, of Park Grove, Withyham, Sussex; two *s* two *d. Educ:* privately; University College School; Caius College, Cambridge; Scholar and Prælector 1st Class Nat. Sci. Tripos. Entered Royal Army Medical Corps, 1887 (Montefiore Prizeman and Medallist in Military Surgery); joined Egyptian Army, 1890; served Tokar Expedition, 1891 (despatches, star and clasp, Osmanieh); transferred to Public Health Department, 1896; Administrator of the International Municipality of Alexandria, 1902–4; Deputy Director-General Public Health Dept, 1905–7; Director-General Department of Public Health, Egypt, 1907. *Address:* Cheriton House, Alresford, Hants. *Clubs:* Arthur's, Leander, Royal Automobile. *Died 30 Dec. 1918.*

GRAHAME, Thomas George; in charge of British Consulate Canea, Crete, since May 1917; *b* 10 Jan. 1861; *s* of Robert Vetch Grahame. *Educ:* Harrow. Travelled extensively on the Continent and in Far East; resided at Paris for many years; Vice-Consul, Teheran, 1900; Consul, Shiraz, 1903; Consul-General, Ispahan, 1908–16. *Publications:* articles, chiefly on travel and art, to various English and continental periodicals. *Recreations:* travel, riding. *Club:* Royal Societies.

Died 22 Oct. 1922.

GRAINGER, Francis Edward; see Hill, Headon.

GRAMIGNA, Rt. Rev. Fr Petronius, DD; OSFC; RC Bishop of Allahabad since 1904; *b* Castel-Bolognese, Italy, 13 Dec. 1844. Admitted into Capuchin branch of Franciscan Order at age of 19; priest, 1868; Missions in East India, 1871; was Principal of Schools, Chaplain to Cathedral, and in charge of troops, Allahabad; was elected Superior of his Order in the Missions; Vicar-General of the Diocese and Administrator Apostolic, 1896. *Recreation:* walking. *Address:* Allahabad, India. *Died 18 Dec. 1917.*

GRANET, Col Edward John, CB 1911; Military Attaché, Rome, since 1911; *b* 2 Aug. 1858; *m* 1885, Evelyn Pulcherie, *d* of David Ward Chapman. Lieut RA 1878; Captain, 1886; Major, 1896; Lieut-Col 1903; Colonel, 1906; Staff Captain NE District, 1892–95; Brigade Major Southern District, 1896–99; DAAG S Africa, 1901–2; Headquarters of Army, 1902–5; Asst Director Remounts, 1906–10; served European War, 1914–15 (wounded). *Address:* British Embassy, Rome. *Club:* Naval and Military.

Died 22 Oct. 1918.

GRANGER, His Honour Sir Thomas Colpitts, Kt 1921; JP; County Court Judge, Greenwich, Woolwich, and Southwark, since 1911; *b* 30 Aug. 1852; 3rd *s* of late T. Colpitts Granger, QC, MP; *m* 1st, 1886, Lilian (*d* 1910), *d* of James Payn, the novelist; 2nd, 1919, Ellen, *widow* of Godfrey Walker of Northbrook Park, Countess Wear, Devon. Called to Bar, Inner Temple, 1874; County Court Judge, Cornwall, 1891–1911; Joint Chairman of Quarter Sessions, Cornwall, until 1918. *Address:* 25 Lower Belgrave Street, SW1. *T:* Victoria 6275. *Club:* Reform. *Died 13 Jan. 1927.*

GRANNUM, Edward Thomas, CMG 1911; JP; Auditor-General, Barbados, 1894; retired 1918; *b* 1843; *s* of Henry Grannum; *m* 1864, Mary, *d* of William Jordan; three *s. Educ:* Codrington Grammar School, Barbados. Member for Bridgetown, Barbados House of Assembly, 1883–95; Member of Finance Commission, 1885; of Executive Committee, 1885–89 and 1900–4; of General Board of Health, 1885; represented Barbados in negotiations at Washington in connection with McKinley Tariff Act, 1891; Member of Technical Education Committee, 1892; of Emigration Commission, 1893; Director of General Hospital, and Member of House Committee, 1906; Member of Education Commission, 1894 and 1907; Chairman of Conference at Barbados to consider trade relations with Canada, 1908; Member Customs Commission, 1908; administered

government of Barbados for a short time in 1907; MLC 1906; Acting Colonial Secretary and Member of Executive Council. *Club* Bridgetown, Barbados. *Died 6 June 1922*

GRANT, Col Alexander Brown, MVO 1905; VD; DL, JP; *b* 20 Oct 1840; *m;* three *s* two *d. Educ:* Irvine Royal Academy. Joined Volunteer Force, 1859; retired, 1907; gave evidence before many committee at War Office; Commandant Glasgow National Reserve; Militar Member, Glasgow Territorial Force Association; Lord Rector Assessor, Glasgow University; Hon. Colonel 4th Lowland (H) Brigad RFA (T). *Recreations:* fishing, shooting, country life. *Address:* Killocha Castle, Ayrshire; 7 Athole Gardens, Glasgow. *TA:* Grant, Glasgow *T:* Glasgow 2525 Bell, 796 Hillhead. *Clubs:* National Liberal, Junio Army and Navy; Liberal, Art, Glasgow. *M:* LA 8072.

Died 2 April 1921

GRANT, Sir Arthur Henry, 9th Bt, *cr* 1705; JP, DL; late Lieutenan 27th Inniskillings; Captain and Hon. Major Hampshire Yeomanr (Carabiniers), retired; Hon. Colonel 1st Aberdeenshire Roya Engineers (Volunteers); *b* 1849; *s* of Arthur Grant, *g s* of Sir Archibal Grant, 3rd Bt; *S* cousin, 1887; *m* 1878, Mary, *d* of Capt. H. Sholto Douglas, late 42nd Highlanders; two *s. Educ:* Oriel Coll., Oxford MA 1873. Contested (U) W Aberdeenshire 1892, 1895, and 1900 *Heir: s* Arthur Grant, *b* 14 Sept. 1879. *Address:* House of Monymusk Aberdeen, NB; Fairoak Lodge, Bishopstoke, Hants. *Clubs:* Junio Carlton, Carlton, Cavalry. *Died 1 March 1917*

GRANT, Corrie; KC 1906; MP (R) for South-East (Rugby) Division of Warwick, 1900–10; *b* 14 Nov. 1850; *s* of James Brighton Grant Kettleburgh, Suffolk; *m* 1885, Annie Adams. *Educ:* City of London School. Called to Bar, Middle Temple, 1877. Contested (R Woodstock, 1885; W Birmingham, 1892; Rugby Div. 1895; Harrow Div. 1899. *Address:* 26 The Avenue, Bedford Park, Chiswick. *Club* National Liberal. *Died Dec. 1924*

GRANT, Rev. Cyril Fletcher, MA; Hon. Canon, Rochester, 1890 *m* 1909, Alicia, *d* of late Capt. W. P. Salmon, 60th Rifles. *Educ:* Ballio College, Oxford. Curate of St John's, Chatham, 1871–74; St James's Gravesend, 1874–75; St Margaret's, Lee, 1875; Aylesford, 1876–78 Vicar, 1878–95; Rector of Holy Trinity, Guildford, 1895–1907; Rura Dean, Guildford, 1905–7; Chaplain at Rome, 1909–10. *Publication* North African Shores of the Mediterranean. *Address:* 1 Sloane Gardens, SW. *Died 9 Feb. 1916*

GRANT, Lt-Col and Hon. Col Edward James, CB 1900; late Roya Scots; *b* 31 Aug. 1854; *s* of late Col A. G. Grant; *m* 1882, Mary (*d* 1926), *y d* of Rev. H. Addington of Henlow Grange, Beds. *Educ* Cheltenham College. Served Egypt 1882 with Royal Irish Regiment, Battle of Tel-el-Kebir; South Africa, 1899–1902, in command of 3rd Royal Scots (despatches, Queen's medal three clasps, King's medal two clasps, CB). *Address:* 71 Philbeach Gardens, SW5. *Club:* Naval and Military. *Died 2 Sept. 1928.*

GRANT, General Sir Henry Fane, GCVO 1909; KCB 1908 (CB 1885); retired; *b* 4 May 1848; *s* of late Field-Marshal Sir Patrick Grant, GCB, GCMG, and Hon. Lady Grant, *d* of 1st Viscount Gough; *m* 1898, Lily, *widow* of late Colonel Pemberton, RA, and *d* of late E. Sandys, ICS. *Educ:* Eton. Entered army, 1868; Col 1888; served Egyptian army, 1884 (Brevet Lt-Col, 3rd Class Medjidie); Nile Expedition, 1884–85 (despatches, CB, medal with two clasps, Khedive star); Comd 5th Div. 2nd Army Corps, 1903–7; Governor and Commander-in-Chief of Malta, 1907–9; Lieut Tower of London, 1909–13. *Address:* Laggan Lodge, Scaniport, Inverness-shire. *Club:* United Service. *Died 28 July 1919.*

GRANT, Colonel Hugh Gough, CB 1900; late commanding Regimental Districts, Fort-George and Inverness; retired; *s* of late Field-Marshal Sir Patrick Grant, GCB, GCMG; *b* 23 July 1845; *m* 1885, Isabel, *d* of Eneas Mackintosh of Balnespick, Inverness-shire; two *s* one *d. Educ:* Eton; RMC Sandhurst. Served with Seaforth Highlanders, 1863–95; received thanks of Indian Government for special services during Madras Famine, 1877–78; Brigade-Major Kurram Column during Afghan War, 1879–80 (despatches, medal); Brig.-Major 2nd Column during Mahsud Waziri Expedition, 1881 (despatches); served in Black Mountain Expedition, 1891 (medal); was Assistant Adjutant-General Punjab Command, 1895–97.

Died 19 Aug. 1922.

GRANT, Sir James Alexander, KCMG 1887; MD; MRCS, FRCP, FRCSE; *b* Inverness, 11 Aug. 1831; *m* 1856, Maria, *d* of Edward Malloch, MP. *Educ:* Queen's Coll., Kingston, Ont; London; Edinburgh. MP (Canadian) for Co. of Russell, 1865–73; Ottawa,

1892–96; introduced Pacific Railway Bill to construct the present Trans-continental Railroad, 1872; President Tuberculosis Association of Canada, 1901–2; President Royal Society of Canada, 1903; Ex-President Medical Council, Ontario; Hon. Member British Medical Association; awarded gold medal of Palermo, Sicily, for Medical Science; also Legion of Honour of Italy; Hon. President Medico-Chirurgical Society, Ottawa; President International Congress of Hygiene for Canada, 1909; and of Canadian Section 4th International Hygienic Congress, Buffalo, 1913; Hon. Member Canadian Medical Association, 1912; Hon. President Ottawa Valley Graduates, McGill University; discoverer of serum therapy, 1861; Hon. President Medico-Chirurgical Society, Ottawa. *Publications:* essays on medical, surgical, and scientific subjects in the journals of Canada, United States, and England; Organic Heart Disease (Montreal Med. Mal. Dec. 1897). *Recreations:* chiefly in field of geology (large collection Silurian fossils). *Address:* Roxborough Apartments, Ottawa, Canada. *Club:* Rideau, Ottawa.   *Died Feb. 1920.*

GRANT, John Peter, of Rothiemurchus; DL for Cos Inverness and Banff; JP for Co. Inverness; Sheriff-Substitute of Inverness-shire; *b* 1860; *s* of late John Peter Grant, Rothiemurchus; *m* 1st, 1882, Edith Mary, *d* of Lt-Col David Macpherson, Belleville, Inverness-shire; 2nd, 1899, Lady Mary Augusta Pierrepont (*d* 1917), *d* of 3rd Earl Manvers; four *s* one *d*. *Educ:* Marlborough; Trinity Coll., Oxford; University of Edinburgh. MA Oxon (2nd Cl. Hon. History); LLB Edin. Barrister-at-law (Inner Temple), 1883; Advocate (in Scotland), 1883; Sheriff-Substitute of Banffshire, 1890–1900; Major 1st Vol. Batt. Queen's Own Cameron Highlanders (retired, 1898). *Address:* The Doune of Rothiemurchus, near Aviemore, Inverness-shire. *Clubs:* New, Edinburgh; Highland, Inverness.
                                                     Died 18 Feb. 1927.

GRANT, Hon. MacCallum, LLD, DCL; *b* Hants County, Province of Nova Scotia, 17 May; *m* Laura McNeill, *d* of Hon. D. McN. Parker, MD; four *s* one *d*. *Educ:* Newport, Hants Co., NS. Commenced business career 1873; Lieutenant-Governor Province Nova Scotia, 1916–25; Director Bank of Nova Scotia; Vice-President Nova Scotia Loan Society; Chairman Old Ladies' Home; Director Halifax Dispensary, etc. *Recreations:* golf, tennis. *Address:* 114 Young Avenue, Halifax, Nova Scotia, Canada. *Clubs:* Halifax, City, Halifax, NS.
                                                     Died 23 Feb. 1928.

GRANT, Rear-Adm. Noel, CB 1915; Royal Navy; in command of Air Store Depot, White City; *b* 13 Sept. 1868; *s* of John Miller Grant; *m* Mary Annette, *d* of E. Allen; no *c*. *Educ:* Burney's School; HMS Britannia. In command of the Carmania at sinking of German cruiser, Cape Trafalgar, 1914. *Club:* United Service.
                                                     Died 6 March 1920.

GRANT, Major Robert Francis Sidney, DSO 1900; MVO 1911; late Rifle Brigade; *b* 18 Sept. 1877; *s* of late Sir Charles Grant, KCSI, and Ellen, *d* of Rt Hon. Henry Baillie, of Redcastle, NB; *m* 1917, Vera, *d* of Lt-Col Walter Campbell, The Ivy House, Hampton Court. *Educ:* Eton. Entered army, 1898; Captain, 1904; Major, 1914; served South Africa, 1899–1902 (despatches, Queen's medal 6 clasps, King's medal 2 clasps, DSO); European War, 1914–15 (despatches twice, severely wounded, Feb. 1915). *Address:* 29 Sussex Square, Brighton. *Clubs:* Travellers', Army and Navy.
                                                     Died 4 Aug. 1927.

GRANT, William, CMG 1899; 1st Class Assistant, Sub-Commissioner Uganda Protectorate Service, 1893–1904; *b* 22 Sept. 1863; *s* of Alex. Grant and Bella Young of Inverness. *Educ:* Rhumaharime Public School, Kintyre, Argyllshire, Scotland. Left home, 1883; was variously employed until 1890; in IBEA Co.'s service, 1890–93; left Mombasa for Uganda, 1890. *Address:* Pennygowan, Campbeltown, Argyllshire.
                                                     Died 28 Oct. 1919.

GRANT-DUFF, Sir Evelyn, KCMG 1916 (CMG 1911); British Envoy to Swiss Confederation, 1913–16; *b* 9 Oct. 1863; 2nd *s* of late Rt Hon. Sir Mountstuart Grant-Duff, GCSI; *m* 1900, Edith Florence, CBE, a Lady of Grace of the Order of St John of Jerusalem, *e d* of Sir George (Francis) Bonham, 2nd Bt. Entered Foreign Office, 1888; appointed to Rome, 1889; 3rd Secretary, 1890; Tehran, 1892; 2nd Secretary, 1894; St Petersburg, 1895; Stockholm, 1896; Berlin, 1897; Stockholm, 1898; employed Foreign Office, 1899–1903; Secretary of Legation, Tehran, 1903–6; Councillor of Embassy, Madrid, 1906–10; appointed Minister to Venezuela, 1910, bud did not proceed; Consul-General for Hungary, 1911–13. *Address:* 14 Marlborough Buildings, Bath.
                                                     Died 19 Sept. 1926.

GRAVES, Rev. Charles Edward, MA; Fellow of St John's College, Cambridge, 1863–65 and since 1893; *b* London, 11 Nov. 1839; *o* surv. *s* of J. J. Graves, Partner in H. Graves and Co., silk manufacturers, and Mary, *d* of J. Barlow, Ardwick, Manchester; *m* 1865, Ann Hughes, *d* of Rev. Richard Gwatkin, sometime Fellow and Tutor of St John's Coll., Camb., and afterwards Vicar of Barrow-on-Soar; one *s* four *d*. *Educ:* Leamington College; Shrewsbury School; St John's Coll., Cambridge. Porson Prize, 1861; 2nd in 1st class Classical Tripos, 1862; Naden Divinity Student, 1862. Mostly lived in Cambridge; worked as a private tutor for some years; Lecturer at St John's College, 1866–1901; at Sidney Sussex College, 1871–82; at Jesus College, 1877–90; Tutor St John's College, 1895–1905; ordained in 1866; Curate of Chesterton, Cambridge, 1866–68; Chaplain of Magdalene Coll., 1886–94; Select Preacher, Camb., 1875, 1886, and 1892. *Publications:* editor of Thucydides, books iv and v; Plato's Menexenus and Euthyphro; Aristophanes' the Acharnians, Clouds, Wasps, and Peace. *Address:* St Martin's, Cambridge.
                                                     Died 21 Oct. 1920.

GRAVES, Robert Ernest, CBE 1918; HM Chief Inspector of Factories, Home Office, since 1920; Deputy Commissioner for Trade Exemptions, Ministry of National Service, Aug. 1917–Dec. 1918; *b* Waterford, Ireland, 22 Dec. 1866; *s* of James Palmer Graves, JP, Waterford; *m* Marion Burt, Ventnor, Isle of Wight; one *d*. *Educ:* Portora Royal School, Enniskillen. HM Inspector of Factories, 1890; Superintending Inspector, 1908; Deputy Chairman of Reserved Occupations Committee; Director of Substitution in the National Service Department, Feb.–Aug. 1917. *Recreations:* fishing, sailing, gardening. *Address:* Cowley Cottage, Cowley, Uxbridge. *Club:* Royal Automobile.   *Died 21 May 1922.*

GRAVES, Rev. Walter Eccleston; Hon. Canon of Truro. *Address:* St Clement's Vicarage, Truro.
                                                     Died 21 May 1922.

GRAY, Baroness, 19th in line, *cr* 1445; **Eveleen Smith Gray;** *b* Dresden, 3 May 1841; *o d* of Lady Jane and Capt. Lonsdale Pounden; *S* to Barony of Gray, 1895; claim established, 1896; *m* 1863, James Maclaren Smith (*d* 1900), Hazelgreen, Lancs; one *s* three *d* (and one *s* decd). Heir: *s* Master of Gray, *b* 4 June 1864. *Address:* 14 The Boltons, South Kensington; Brownswood, Enniscorthy, Co. Wexford.
                                                     Died 24 Dec. 1918.

GRAY, 20th Lord, *cr* 1445; **James Maclaren Stuart Gray,** *b* 4 June 1864; *S* mother, 1918. *Educ:* Pembroke Coll., Camb. Formerly Captain, 5th Batt. Rifle Brigade. Heir: *sister* Ethel Eveleen Gray, *b* 16 Jan. 1866. *Address:* Cwmeron, Llanwrtyd Wells, RSO, S Wales. *Club:* Junior Athenæum.   *Died 2 May 1919.*

GRAY, Sir Albert, KCB 1919 (CB 1916); KC 1905; Counsel to the Chairman of Committees in the House of Lords, 1896–1922; *b* 10 Oct. 1850; 4th *s* of George Gray of Bowerswell, Perth, NB; *m* 1895, Sophie, *d* of S. Wells Williams, of the US Legation, Peking, and *widow* of the Hon. Thos G. Grosvenor, CB. *Educ:* Rugby. Entered the Ceylon Civil Service, 1871; resigned 1875, and was called to the Bar at the Inner Temple, 1879; Bencher, 1914; Chancellor of the Diocese of Ely, 1894–97; President of the Hakluyt Society, 1908; Mayor of Chelsea, 1924–25. *Address:* Catherine Lodge, Trafalgar Square, Chelsea, SW3. *T:* Kensington 0234. *Clubs:* Athenæum, Brooks's.
                                                     Died 27 Feb. 1928.

GRAY, Andrew, MA, DSc, LLD; FRS; Emeritus Professor of Natural Philosophy, University of Glasgow; Professor of Natural Philosophy, 1899–1923; *b* Scotland, 1847; *e s* of John Gray, Lochgelly, Fifeshire; *m* Annie, *d* of James Gordon; three *s* four *d*. *Educ:* Subscription School, Lochgelly; privately; Glasgow University. Eglinton Fellow in Mathematics, Glasgow University, 1876. Private Secretary and Assistant to Sir William Thomson (Lord Kelvin), 1875–80; Official Assistant to Prof. of Nat. Phil. in Glasgow University, 1880–84; Professor of Physics University Coll. of North Wales, 1884–99. *Publications:* Absolute Measurements in Electricity and Magnetism, 1883; Theory and Practice of Absolute Measurements in Electricity and Magnetism, vol. i 1888, vol. ii (pts 1 and 2), 1893 (new edition, 1921); A Treatise on Bessel Functions (with late Dr G. B. Mathews, FRS), 1895, revised edition (with Dr MacRobert), 1922; Magnetism and Electricity, vol. i 1898; Dynamics and Properties of Matter, 1901; The Scientific Work of Lord Kelvin, 1908; A Treatise on Dynamics (with Prof. J. G. Gray), 1911, revised edition, 1920; A Treatise on Gyrostatics and Rotational Motion, 1919; and various scientific papers. *Address:* The University, Glasgow.
                                                     Died 10 Oct. 1925.

GRAY, George Buchanan, MA, DLitt (Oxon); Hon. DD Aberdeen; MRAS; Tutor since 1891, and since 1900, Professor of Hebrew and Old Testament Exegesis in Mansfield College, Oxford; Speaker's Lecturer in Biblical Studies in the University of Oxford, 1914–19; Grinfield Lectures on the Septuagint, 1919–21; *b* Blandford, Dorset, 13 Jan. 1865; 2nd *s* of Rev. Benjamin Gray, BA, and Emma Jane, *d* of late George Buchanan Kirkman; *m* Frances Lilian, *o d* of Alfred Williams, JP, FRGS, of Salisbury; one *s* one *d. Educ:* private schools; New and University Colls, London; Mansfield Coll., Oxford; Marburg. BA London, 1886; Prizeman, 1887; Oxford, 1st class in School of Semitic Studies, 1891; Pusey and Ellerton Scholar, 1889; Junior Septuagint Prizeman, 1890; Junior Kennicott Scholar, 1891; Sen. Kennicott Scholar, 1893; MA 1895. Entered Ind. ministry, 1893; Examiner in Oriental Languages in Univ. of Oxford, 1896, 1898–1900, and frequently since; Lecturer on the Old Testament to the Friends Summer School, 1897–99; Fellow of the German Oriental Society, 1898. *Publications:* Studies in Hebrew Proper Names, 1890; The Divine Discipline of Israel, 1900; Numbers (Temple Bible), 1902; Numbers, 1903, and Isaiah, i–xxvii, 1911, and (with the late S. R. Driver) Job, 1921 (International Critical Commentary); A Critical Introduction to the Old Testament, 1913; The Forms of Hebrew Poetry, 1915; Names of Places, and several other articles in Encyclopædia Biblica; contributions, chiefly on Semitic Philology and Old Testament Criticism, to the Academy, Expositor, Jewish Quarterly Review, Contemporary, etc. *Recreations:* lawn-tennis, cycling, climbing. *Address:* 33 Norham Road, Oxford.
Died 2 Nov. 1922.

GRAY, Hon. George Wilkie; MLC Queensland; Chairman of Directors, Quinlan, Gray & Co., Ltd, and Castlemain Brewery; *b* Sydney, 1844. Minister without Portfolio, 1889, 1899–1903. *Address:* Eldernel, Brisbane, Queensland.
Died 22 Sept. 1924.

GRAY, James Hunter; KC 1918; MA, BSc; MIEE; called to Bar, Middle Temple, 1895; *b* 3 Sept. 1867; *m* Julie, *d* of late Professor Dittmar, LLD, FRS. Chiefly engaged in Patent Trade Mark and Technical Litigation. *Address:* 17 Chantrey House, SW1. *T:* Victoria 5581; 5 Fig Tree Court, Temple, EC4. *T:* Central 978. *Clubs:* Garrick, Beefsteak, Royal Automobile. *Died 1 June 1925.*

GRAY, Maxwell, (Mary Gleed Tuttiett); novelist; general writer; *b* Newport, Isle of Wight, 1847; *o d* of late F. B. Tuttiett, MRCS, and Eliza, *d* of the late Thomas Gleed. *Publications:* The Silence of Dean Maitland, 1886; Reproach of Annesley, 1888; Westminster Chimes and other Poems, 1889; In the Heart of the Storm, 1891; An Innocent Imposter, 1892; The Last Sentence, 1893; A Costly Freak, 1893; Lays of the Dragon-Slayer, 1894; Sweethearts and Friends, 1897; Ribstone Pippins, 1898; The House of Hidden Treasure, 1898; The Forest Chapel and other poems, 1899; The World's Mercy, 1900; Four-Leaved Clover, 1901; Richard Rosny, 1903; The Great Refusal, 1906; The Suspicions of Ermengarde, 1908; England's Son and other Poems, 1910; Unconfessed, 1911; Something Afar, 1913; The Worldmender, 1916; The Diamond Pendant, 1918; A Bit of Blue Stone, 1923; essays, poems, etc. *Address:* 144A Argyle Road, West Ealing, W. *Died 21 Sept. 1923.*

GRAY, Sir Walter, Kt 1902; JP for the City of Oxford; Alderman of City of Oxford; *b* 1848; *s* of late Thomas Gray of Litlington, Cambs; *m* 1874, Emily Alice, *d* of late James Savage of Box Hall, Herts; one *s* two *d. Educ:* Grammar School, Stevenage, Herts. Prominent in municipal life in Oxford since 1875; Mayor four times. *Address:* Oxford. *Died 17 March 1918.*

GRAY, Rt. Rev. William Crane, DD; Missionary Bishop of the Episcopal Church in Southern Florida since 1892; *b* Lambertville, New Jersey, 6 Sept. 1835; *e s* of Dr Joseph Gray; *m* 1st, 1863; Maggie Trent; one *s*; 2nd, 1877, Fannie Bowers; one *s. Educ:* Kenyon College and Bexley Hall, Gambier, Ohio. Deacon, 1859; Priest, 1860; spent a year and a half in Missionary work in West Tennessee; Rector St James' Church, Bolivar, Tenn, 20 years; charge of the Church of the Advent, Nashville, Tenn, 1881; Delegate to General Convention since 1868; has work going on among red men, black men, brown men, and white men. *Publications:* sermons, addresses, and brief treatises on Church subjects. *Recreations:* very few, and coming only in the line of duty; no vacations as such, but councils, conventions, and especially the Lambeth Conference, much enjoyed. *Address:* Bishopstead, Main Street, Orlando, Fla, USA. *T:* 361.
Died 14 Nov. 1919.

GRAY, Sir William Cresswell, 1st Bt, *cr* 1917; DL, JP; Chairman of William Gray & Co., Ltd; late Sheriff of Durham; *b* 1 May 1867;

o surv. *s* of late Sir William Gray of Greatham, Durham; *m* 1891 Kate, *d* of late C. T. Casebourne, CE; one *s* four *d. Educ:* Leys School Cambridge. *Heir: s* William Gray, Captain Yorkshire Regt [*b* 18 Aug 1895. *Educ:* Loretto School, Edinburgh. Served European war 1915–17 (despatches)]. *Address:* Tunstall Manor, West Hartlepool
Died 1 Nov. 1924

GRAY, Col William Lewis, CMG 1917; MB, CM, Glasgow; BSc Edin.; Army Medical Staff, retired; *b* 1864; 2nd *s* of Alexander Gray MD, Selby; *m* 1897, Janet, *d* of Thomas Orr, Accountant, London no *c. Educ:* Universities of Glasgow and Edinburgh. Examiner in Chemistry, Malta University, 1906; served Anglo-Siamese Boundary Commission, 1889–90; Kaingtung-Chiengmai Mission, 1890–91 Chitral, 1895 (medal with clasp); S Africa, 1899–1901 (despatches Queen's medal 4 clasps); European War, 1914–17 (CMG, despatches) *Address:* North Holt, Hythe, Kent. *Club:* Junior United Service.
Died 3 Nov. 1924.

GRAYFOOT, Col Blenman Buhot, CB 1916; MD; Indian Medical Service. Served European War, 1914–16 (despatches, CB).
Died Oct. 1916.

GREANY, Surg.-Gen. John Philip, MD; Indian Medical Service (retired); *b* 21 July 1851; *m* 1889, Agnes Norah, *d* of late Andrew Wingate, Glasgow; one *s* one *d. Educ:* Queen's College, Cork. Graduated MD, MCh, LM from the Royal University, Ireland, 1874; joined the Indian Medical Service, 1875; Surg.-Gen. with the Government of Bombay, 1905–8. *Address:* 31 Woodville Gardens, Ealing, W5. *Died 7 Oct. 1919*

GREANY, Capt. John Wingate, DSO 1915; *b* 1892; *s* of Surg.-Gen. J. P. Greany, IMS. Served European War in Gallipoli, 1915 (despatches, DSO). *Address:* 31 Woodville Gardens, Ealing, W.
Died April 1916.

GREAVES, Gen. Sir George Richards, GCB 1896 (KCB 1885; CB 1875); KCMG 1881; General, 1896; retired, 1896; *b* 9 Nov. 1831; *s* of late Capt. George Greaves, 60th Rifles, who served in Peninsular War as a Lieut in the 5th Fusiliers and received the war medal with five clasps; *m* 1st, 1859, Ellen (*d* 1880), *d* of Brig.-Gen. Hutchison; 2nd, 1903, Julia Rose, *d* of Rev. E. Morris, Rural Dean, Vicar of Llanelly, and *widow* of Surg.-Major W. Venour, AMS. *Educ:* Sandhurst. Ensign 70th Foot; served in Indian Mutiny, 1857–58; Ensfozie Expedition, 1858; New Zealand War, 1860–66; Ashantee Campaign, 1874; Soudan, 1885; on the staff at the War Office, 1870–78; Chief Secretary and Commissioner, Cyprus, 1878; Adjt-Gen. in India, 1879; commanded Division in India, 1886; Commander-in-Chief, Bombay, 1890; resigned 1893; Colonel East Surrey Regiment, 1898. *Recreations:* shooting, fishing, yachting. *Address:* Netherwood, Saundersfoot, South Wales. *TA:* Saundersfoot.
Died 11 April 1922.

GREEN, Col Bernard Charles, CMG 1915; TD; DL; late Commanding 14th Battalion London Regiment (London Scottish); *b* 1866; *m* 1922, Marguerite Mary, *d* of late Captain Whiteway, RNR, and Mrs Whiteway, 190 Earl's Court Road, SW5. Served with City of London Imperial Volunteers and Gordon Highlanders S African War, 1900–2 (despatches, Queen's medal 4 clasps, King's medal 2 clasps); European War, 1914–16 (despatches, CMG). *Address:* Warren Grange, Crowborough, Sussex.
Died 26 March 1925.

GREEN, Charles Edward, FRSE; publisher; *b* Edinburgh, 1866; *m* 1897, *y d* of late John Dalrymple, Edinburgh. *Educ:* Edinburgh University. Founded Juridical Review, 1887; Scots Law Times, 1891; Green's Encyclopædia, 14 vols 1895; Encyclopædia of English Law, 12 vols 1896; Scots Revised Reports, 45 vols 1897; Encyclopædia Medica, 15 vols 1898; Scots Statutes Revised, 10 vols 1899; English Reports, 180 vols 1900; Encyclopædia of Accounting, 8 vols 1903; Encyclopædia of Agriculture, 4 vols 1907. *Publications:* Lives in a Lowland Parish; History of East Lothian; The Cancer Problem, 4th edn; editor, Juridical Review; editor, Encyclopædia of Agriculture. *Address:* Gracemount House, Midlothian. *TA:* Viridis, Edinburgh. *T:* Edinburgh 766 and 968. *Died 6 Jan. 1920.*

GREEN, David, RI. *Publication:* Marine Painting in Water-colours. *Address:* 117 Finchley Road, NW. *Club:* St John's Wood Arts.
Died 6 March 1918.

GREEN, Sir Edward, 1st Bt, *cr* 1886; DL, JP; head of E. Green and Son, Ltd; MP (C) Wakefield, 1874, 1885–92; contested Pontefract, 1880; Director of Lancashire and Yorkshire Railway; *b* Wakefield,

4 March 1831; *e s* of Edward Green, Wakefield; *m* 1859, Mary (*d* 1902), *d* of W. E. Lycett; two *s*. Owner of about 5,000 acres. *Recreations:* business, hunting, shooting. *Heir: s* Edward Lycett Green, *b* 25 May 1860. *Address:* Treasurer's House, York; Ken Hill, Snettisham, Norfolk. *Clubs:* Carlton, Marlborough.

Died 30 March 1923.

GREEN, Everard, FSA; Somerset Herald since 1911; formerly Rouge Dragon Pursuivant of Arms; *b* 1844; *y s* of Charles Green, Holdich House, Spalding, Lincolnshire, and Mary, *d* and *co-heir* of Henry Everard, Spalding, and Anne, *d* of George Toynbee, Waddington, Lincolnshire. *Publications:* A Plea for the Resurrection of Heraldry; O Sapientia; The Insignia of an Archbishop; The Westminster Tournament Roll of 1510; Arms of the Popes; Lincolnshire Pedigrees, etc. *Address:* College of Arms, EC.

Died 22 June 1926.

GREEN, Sir Frederick, KBE 1918; Kt 1912; *b* Essex, 17 June 1845; *s* of late Frederick Green of Princes Gardens, Kensington, W; *m* 1868, Alice, 2nd *d* of late Sir Daniel Cooper, 1st Bt; four *s* three *d*. *Educ:* Harrow. JP Essex; High Sheriff, 1918; Director, Suez Canal Co., Bank of New South Wales; Member of the Council of King Edward's Hospital Fund. *Address:* Oaklawn, Wimbledon Park, Surrey. *Clubs:* City of London; Travellers', Paris.

Died 18 Feb. 1927.

GREEN, Frederick Ernest; author and farmer; *b* Hongkong, 16 Oct. 1867; *s* of Thomas Green, Hongkong, and Jane Stuart, Aberdeen; *m* 1st, Gertrude Beane (*decd*); one *s*; 2nd, her sister Constance. *Educ:* Southampton. After leaving school was perched on a stool in the City to earn a living; hating the regimentation of commercialism and the boredom of suburbanism, after enduring City life for some years flung up his job to seek a living on the land; but it is as a freelance he chiefly won his way in the republic of letters; aloof from political parties and boldly criticising the agricultural policy or lack of policy of succeeding Governments he contributed much towards creating the new agricultural atmosphere; Member Royal Commission on Agriculture; Surrey District Wages Committee; Surrey CC Small Holdings Committee. *Publications:* The Awakening of England; The Tyranny of the Countryside; The Surrey Hills; A Few Acres and a Cottage; The Small Holding; How I Work my Small Farm; The Settlement of Ex-Service Men; Everyman's Land and Allotment Book; First Advice to Would-be Farmers; History of the Agricultural Labourer, 1870–1920; A New Agricultural Policy; Life of Cobbett. *Recreations:* tramping, tennis. *Address:* Barings Field, Newdigate, Surrey. *TA:* Green, Newdigate. *Died 20 Jan. 1922.*

GREEN, Sir George, Kt 1911; Inspector for Scotland for Prudential Assurance Company; *b* Stockport, 15 Dec. 1843; *s* of Thomas Green and Elizabeth Meadows; *m* Jane, *d* of John and Anne Heywood, Stockport; one *s* six *d*. *Educ:* St Thomas's School, Stockport. With Prudential Assurance Co. since 1870; risen from the ranks to highest position attainable; Methodist lay preacher since 1861; contested Glasgow, 1895; Stockport, 1900; for eighteen years member of Lanarkshire County Council; sometime Vice-Convener and also Convener of that Council; Chairman of the Scottish Liberal Association, 1905–12; Chairman of Executive Scottish Band of Hope Union; JP Lanarkshire; sometime Vice-President, Primitive Methodist Conference. *Address:* Methven, Balshagray Avenue, Partick, Glasgow. *T:* 243 Hillhead, Glasgow. *Clubs:* National Liberal; Liberal, Glasgow. *Died 8 April 1916.*

GREEN, Mrs Hetty Howland Robinson; financier; *b* New Bedford, Mass, 21 Nov. 1835; *d* of late Edward Mott Robinson; *m* 1867, Edward H. Green (*d* 1902), New York. *Address:* Bellows Falls, Vermont, USA. *Died 2 July 1916.*

GREEN, John Alfred, BA (London), MA (Sheffield); Professor of Education, University of Sheffield, since 1906; *b* 15 October 1867; *m* Adeliza Norman, *d* of Alderman J. Johnston, Manchester. *Educ:* Firth College, Sheffield; Borough Road Training College. Junior Tutor at the Borough Road College, 1881–92; Assistant Master in a London Pupil Teachers' School, 1893–94; Lecturer in Education at Bangor, 1894; studied educational systems of Germany, Austria, and Switzerland, 1904–5; Professor of Education, Bangor, 1900–6; Member of Central Welsh Board, 1898–1906; Member of Executive Council, Teachers' Guild; Member of Teachers' Registration Council, 1912–16; Recorder (Section L) British Association; Secretary of Committee (Sect. L), dealing with research into Mental and Physical Factors involved in Education, and Chairman of Committee appointed to enquire into development of Museums as Educational Institutions; Chairman of Executive Committee, Educational

Handwork Association; Secretary of Board of Examinations for Educational Handwork; Member of Sheffield Education Committee. *Publications:* Educational Ideas of Pestalozzi, 1904; (Joint) Primer of Teaching Practice, 1911; Life and Work of Pestalozzi, 1912; (Joint) Introduction to Psychology, 1912; Educational Writings of Pestalozzi, 1912; Editor, Journal Experimental Pedagogy; various articles. *Address:* The University, Sheffield.

Died 12 March 1922.

GREEN, Max Sullivan, JP; Chairman of the Irish Prison Board since 1912; *b* 1864; *s* of late J. S. Green, Air Hill, Co. Cork; *m* 1913, Johanna (author of several plays), *y d* of late John Redmond, MP. *Educ:* Trinity College, Dublin; Royal College of Sciences (Diploma in Civil Engineering); AMICE, 1890. Engaged on harbour and railway construction and public works, 1885–97; Engineer to Prison Service, 1897–1906; Inspector Local Government, 1907; Private Secretary to Viceroy of Ireland, 1907–12. *Address:* General Prisons Board, Dublin Castle; Windsor House, Windsor Road, Dublin.

Died 4 March 1922.

GREEN, Rev. Professor Samuel Walter, MA (London); Professor of New Testament Exegesis and Criticism, Regent's Park College, New College, and Hackney College (University of London); *b* Bradford, 1853; *s* of Rev. S. G. Green, DD, President of Rawdon College, near Leeds, and late Editorial Secretary of the Religious Tract Society, London; *m* 1881, *e d* of Charles Hemming, MD; one *s* two *d*. *Educ:* University College, London. Graduated MA London, 1878; Tutor at Regent's Park College, 1878; Dean of the Faculty of Theology; Representative of the Faculty on the Senate of the University of London. *Publications:* Commentary on St Mark's Gospel (Westminster New Testament); Lessons in New Testament Greek; The Early Witness to the Four Gospels; minor writings. *Address:* 9 Bellasis Avenue, Streatham Hill, SW2.

Died 12 July 1926.

GREEN, Rev. William Spotswood, CB 1907; JP 1917; MA; Government Inspector of Irish Fisheries, 1889–1914; Commissioner of Congested Districts Board for Ireland 1892–1909; *b* 10 Sept. 1847; *o c* of Charles Green, JP, of Youghal, Co. Cork, and Catherine Frances, *d* of Mr Fitzsimons; *m* 1875, *cousin*, Belinda Beatty, *d* of James Butler, JP, of Waterville House, Waterville, Co. Kerry, and *g d* of Roger Green Davis, JP, of Dromdiah, Co. Cork; one *s* five *d*. *Educ:* Trinity Coll., Dublin; BA 1871, MA 1874. Ordained 1872; Incumbent Carrigaline, Co. Cork, 1880–89; first to ascend Mount Cook, New Zealand. *Publications:* The High Alps of New Zealand; The Selkirk Glaciers, etc. *Address:* Westcove House, Cahirdaniel, Co. Kerry.

Died 22 April 1919.

GREENE, Sir (Edward) Walter, 1st Bt, *cr* 1900; JP, DL; Hon. Colonel of 3rd Battalion Suffolk Regiment; late Lieutenant-Colonel (Hon.) Loyal Suffolk Hussars; High Sheriff for Suffolk, 1897; *b* 14 March 1842; *s* of Edward Greene, MP for Stowmarket Division of Suffolk, 25 years MP for Bury St Edmunds; *m* 1864, Emma Elizabeth (*d* 1912), *d* of Rev. C. Royds of Haughton Rectory, Prebendary of Lichfield Cathedral; two *s* three *d* (and two *s* one *d* decd). *Educ:* Rugby. MP (C) for Bury St Edmunds, 1900–6. *Recreations:* hunting (hunted Suffolk Foxhounds, Croome Hounds, and kept harriers and staghoods at own expense; hunted hounds 34 years), shooting, yachting. *Heir: s* Walter Raymond Greene, *b* 4 Aug. 1869. *Address:* Nether Hall, Bury St Edmunds. *Clubs:* Carlton, Cavalry; Royal Yacht Squadron, Cowes.

Died 27 Feb. 1920.

GREENE, Gen. Francis Vinton; Major-General US Volunteers in Spanish-American War. *Publications:* The Russian Army and its Campaigns in Turkey; Army Life in Russia; Life of Major-Gen. Nathanael Greene; The Mississippi Campaigns of the Civil War; The Revolutionary War and the Military Policy of the United States; The Present Military Situation in the United States, 1915; Why Europe is at War, 1915; Our First Year in the Great War, 1918; and numerous magazine articles on military and historical subjects. *Address:* 62 East 77th Street, New York City.

Died 15 May 1921.

GREENE, George Arthur, LittD; FRHistS; author and lecturer; employed on National work under War Office; *b* 1853; *e surv. s* of late Rev. Henry Greene, and *g s* of late Sir Jonas Greene, Recorder of Dublin; *m* 1885, Mary Dorothea Lucy (*d* 1914), *d* of late Rev. Henry Roundell, Vicar of Buckingham; two *s*. *Educ:* Florence; Trinity College, Dublin. First in Modern Literature Tripos, with large gold medal; Vice-Chancellor's Prizeman; member of Academic Senate; President and Gold Medallist, University Philosophical Society. Professor of English Literature at Alexandra College, 1877–80;

afterwards an Examiner to the Board of Intermediate Education; sometime Taylorian Examiner at Oxford; was long Vice-Chairman of the Irish Literary Society. *Publications:* Italian Lyrists of To-day, second edition, 1898; Dantesques, 1903; Songs of the Open Air (verse), 1912; editions of Southey's Life of Nelson, Irving's Life of Columbus; selections from Lamb's Essays of Elia and from Prescott's Peru; editor and part author of the two Books of the Rhymers' Club; contributed to various miscellanies and periodicals; a novel, The Lost Prima Donna (in collaboration with A. C. Hillier) appeared in serial form; translated Giacosa's Tristi Amori, acted in America as The Wife of Scarli; The Wartburg, 1907; and several works on art and history from the German. *Recreations:* reading, walking. *Address:* 2 Tanfield Court, Temple, EC. *Club:* Authors'.

Died 12 May 1921.

GREENE, H. Barrett; Editor and Leader-writer Staffordshire Daily and Weekly Sentinel, Stoke-on-Trent, since 1899; *b* Bridport, 24 Nov. 1861; *e s* of late J. C. Greene, over fifty years on Somerset County Gazette, Taunton; *m;* one *s. Educ:* Huish's, Taunton; private study and experience. Early training in journalism at Taunton, Wigan, and Sunderland; joined Newcastle Chronicle, 1883; Editor of Newcastle Evening Chronicle for some years; sent many verbatim of W. E. Gladstone, J. Morley, R. Churchill, A. Balfour, and J. Chamberlain to The Times; persistently advocated federation of six Potteries towns into one County Borough (Stoke-on-Trent), leading up to Act of Parliament, 1908, which came into operation March 1910; helped to raise £50,000 for North Staffordshire Infirmary by Sentinel Funds; Hon. Vice-President, North Staffordshire Infirmary; JP County Borough of Stoke-on-Trent; Democrat and Imperialist; interested in educational and industrial questions. *Address:* Elmhurst, Wolstanton, Staffs. *Died 30 Oct. 1927.*

GREENFIELD, Brig.-Gen. Richard Menteith, CB 1907; Brigadier-General, General Staff, Ireland; Commander Bombay Brigade, 1905-9; *b* 27 Dec. 1856; *s* of James Greenfield of Brynderwen, Monmouth; *m* 1893, Mary Frances, *d* of Col Bateman, IMS. *Educ:* Winchester. Entered army, 1874; Captain Royal Inniskilling Fusiliers, 1881; Major, 1890; Lieut-Col 1897; Col 1899; AAG India, 1899-1902; DAG Headquarters, India, 1902-5; served Burma, 1892-93 (despatches, medal with clasp, Brevet Lieut-Col); NW Frontier, 1897-98 (medal with two clasps). *Address:* Parkgate, Dublin. *Died 5 April 1916.*

GREENFIELD, William Smith, LLD Edin.; MD London; FRSE; FRCP, FRCPE, MRCS; *b* 9 Jan. 1846. *Educ:* University Coll. London. Emeritus Professor of Pathology and Clinical Medicine, Edinburgh University, 1881-1912; Fellow University College, London. *Address:* Muir House, Juniper Green, Midlothian. *Died 12 Aug. 1919.*

GREENHILL, Sir George, Kt 1908; MA; *b* 29 Nov. 1847. Formerly Professor of Mathematics in the Artillery College, Woolwich. *Publications:* Differential and Integral Calculus with Applications, 1885; Applications of the Elliptic Function, 1892; Hydrostatics, 1894; Notes on Dynamics, 1908; Report 19, Theory of a Stream Line with application to an Aeroplane, 1910, 1916; Dynamics of Mechanical Flight, 1912; Report 146, Gyroscopic Theory, 1914. *Address:* 1 Staple Inn, WC1. *Club:* Athenæum. *Died 10 Feb. 1927.*

GREENHILL-GARDYNE, Lt-Col Charles; *b* 1831; *m* 1858, Hon. Amelia Anne Drummond (*d* 1912), *d* of 9th Viscount Strathallan; two *s* four *d.* Late Coldstream Guards; retired, 1868; JP and DL for Argyll and Forfar. *Address:* Finavon, Forfarshire. *TA:* Tannadice. *Club:* New, Edinburgh. *Died 25 Nov. 1923.*

GREENHOW, William Thomas; *b* Newcastle-on-Tyne, 6 Feb. 1831; 2nd *s* of late Thos Michael Greenhow, MD, FRCS, of Newcastle-on-Tyne, and subsequently of Leeds; *m* 1857, Marion, *e d* of the late Charles Martineau of London; one *d. Educ:* Proprietary School, Edgbaston; University College, London (BA, LLB). Barrister 1854; joined Northern Circuit and Durham Sessions; Recorder of Berwick-on-Tweed, 1870-99; County Court Judge of Leeds and Wakefield, 1880-1916. *Recreations:* cricket, skating, rowing. *Address:* Warling Dean, Esher, Surrey. *T:* Esher 154. *TA:* Kitcat, Esher. *Died 30 April 1921.*

GREENLY, Edward Howorth, JP, DL; *b* 1837; *o s* of Charles Williams Allen (afterwards Greenly) (*d* 1878), and Frances, *d* of late Richard Rosser; *m* 1869, Sarah Caroline (*d* 1892), 2nd *d* of Lt-Gen. Bowes Forster. *Educ:* Harrow; Balliol College, Oxford. MA 1863. Called to Bar, Lincoln's Inn, 1862; High Sheriff, Herefordshire, 1881; Lord

of the Manor of Titley. *Address:* Titley Court, Titley, RSO, Herefordshire. *Club:* New University. *Died 1 March 1926.*

GREENWELL, Sir Walpole Lloyd, 1st Bt, *cr* 1906; JP; *b* 9 June 1847; 2nd *s* of late Walpole Eyre Greenwell and Eliza Theophila, *d* and heiress of John Morris, Hastings; *m* 1873, Kathleen Eugenie, *e d* of John Tizard of Radipole, Weymouth; four *s* seven *d* (and one *s* one *d* decd). High Sheriff, Surrey, 1903; one of HM Lieuts, City of London; Breeder of Pedigree Stock. *Heir: s* Bernard Eyre Greenwell, Major Hants Carabineers, Imp. Yeomanry [*b* 29 May 1874; *m* 1902, Anna Elizabeth, *e d* of Admiral Sir Francis Leopold McClintock, KCB; one *s* five *d. Educ:* Harrow; Trinity Coll., Camb. Served S African War (Queen's medal, 5 clasps). *Address:* Woodcock Lodge, Little Berkhamsted, Herts. *Club:* Junior Carlton]. *Address:* Marden Park, Godstone, Surrey; Greenwell, Wolsingham, Co. Durham; 17 Portman Square, W1. *TA:* Greenwell, Wolsingham. *T:* Mayfair 1050. *Clubs:* Carlton, Bachelors'; Royal Yacht Squadron, Cowes. *Died 24 Oct. 1919.*

GREENWELL, Rev. Dr William, JP; MA, DCL; FRS 1878; FSA; Rector of St Mary in the South Bailey, Durham; *b* Greenwell Ford, Durham, 23 March 1820; *e s* of late William Thomas Greenwell, JP, DL; unmarried. *Educ:* Grammar School and University Coll., Durham. MA; Hon. DCL Durham. Fellow of University Coll., Durham, 1844-54; Vicar of Ovingham and Mickley, Northumberland, 1848-50; Principal of Neville Hall, Newcastle-on-Tyne, 1852-54; Minor Canon of Durham, 1854. *Publications:* British Barrows, 1877; Durham Cathedral, 1881; Electrum Coinage of Cyzicus, 1887; editor of Boldon Buke, 1852; Bishop Hatfield's Survey, 1856; Wills and Inventories from the Durham Registry, vol. ii 1859; Feodarium Prioratus Dunelmensis, 1872 (all Surtees Society); papers in Archæologia, the Journal of the Royal Archæological Institute, the Numismatic Chronicle, Transactions of the Durham and Northumberland Archæological Society, etc. *Recreation:* angling (trout and salmon). *Address:* 27 North Bailey, Durham. *Died 27 Jan. 1918.*

GREENWOOD, Sir (Granville) George, Kt 1916; Barrister-at-law; MP (L) Peterborough, 1906-Dec. 1918; *b* 3 Jan. 1850; 2nd *s* of late John Greenwood, QC, of the Western Circuit, and for many years Solicitor to the Treasury, and late Fanny H. Welch, *d* of William Collyns of Starcross, Devon; *m* 1878, Laurentia Trent, *d* of the late L. T. Cumberbatch, MD; one *s* three *d. Educ:* Trinity College, Cambridge. Foundation Scholar, 1871; first-class in Classical Tripos, 1873; called to Bar, Middle Temple, 1876; joined the Western Circuit; original member of the Eighty Club previously to the election of 1880; contested (L) Central Hull, 1886; Central Hull, 1900. *Publications:* The Shakespeare Problem Restated, 1908; *In re* Shakespeare, 1909; The Vindicators of Shakespeare, 1911; Is there a Shakespeare Problem?, 1916; The Faith of an Agnostic, 1919; Shakespeare's Law, 1920; Ben Jonson and Shakespeare, 1921; The Powers and the Turk, 1923; The Shakespeare Signatures and Sir Thomas More, 1924; The Stratford Bust and the Droeshout Engraving, 1925. *Address:* 33 Linden Gardens, W2. *T:* Park 0237. *Club:* United University. *Died 27 Oct. 1928.*

GREENWOOD, Rev. Sydney; Canon of York since 1903. *Educ:* Magdalene College, Cambridge (Scholar). Priest, 1869; Vicar of Wortley, 1880-97. *Address:* The Croft, Kirkby-Wharfe, Tadcaster. *Died 14 July 1926.*

GREENWOOD, William; MP (U) Stockport, since 1920; Cotton Spinner; *b* 25 Feb. 1875; *s* of Edmund Greenwood; *m* 1900, Elizabeth Marion (*d* 1923), *d* of T. S. Whittaker, Marple, Cheshire. *Address:* House of Commons, SW; 35 Belgrave Road, Oldham. *Died 12 Aug. 1925.*

GREER, Rt. Rev. David Hummell; Bishop of New York since 1908; *b* Wheeling, West Virginia, 20 March 1844; *s* of Jacob R. Greer and Elizabeth Armstrong; *m;* two *s* two *d. Educ:* Washington College, Pennsylvania. In charge of Christ Church, Clarksburg, West Virginia, during Diaconate; Rector, Trinity Church, Covington, Ky, 1868-71; Grace Church, Providence, Rhode Island, 1872-88; St Bartholomew's Church, New York, 1888-1904; Bishop-Coadjutor of New York, 1903. *Publications:* The Historic Christ; Visions; The Preacher and His Place (Yale Lectures); From Things to God. *Address:* Amsterdam Avenue and 110th Street, New York City. *Died 18 May 1919.*

GREER, Sir Francis (Nugent), KCB 1923 (CB 1913); Kt 1920; Third Parliamentary Counsel to the Treasury since 1923; *b* 24 Feb. 1869;

s of Samuel M'Curdy Greer, County Court Judge, one time MP for Co. Londonderry; *m* 1897, Mary Elizabeth, *d* of F. A. Barlow, solicitor; one *s*. *Educ:* High School and Trinity College, Dublin (Scholar, Senior Moderator, Brooke Prizeman); Degree, 1891. Auditor College Historical Society, 1893; Parliamentary Draftsman, Irish Office, 1908–23; called to Bar, Ireland, 1893; England, 1912; KC (Ireland), 1918. *Address:* Arundel House, The Bank, Highgate, N6. *T:* Hornsey 876. *Club:* University, Dublin.

Died 6 Feb. 1925.

REER, Rev. George Samuel; Incumbent of Ballyphilip; *m*. *Address:* Ballyphilip, Portaferry, Co. Down.

Died 24 June 1921.

REER, Joseph, CMG 1900; *b* Armagh, 6 Aug. 1854; *s* of late Robert Greer, Armagh; *m* 1890, Emily, *d* of late W. Wheeler. *Educ:* Dundalk; Santry, near Dublin. Clerk SW Postal District, London, 1873; Chief Officer Sorting Office, SW District, London, 1887; Chief Clerk E District, London, 1889; Chief Clerk SW District, London, 1890; Postmaster N District, London, 1899; Director of Military Postal Services, S Africa, 1900-2; Postmaster, E District, London, 1903–8; Assistant Controller London Postal Service Department, 1908–15. Decorated for service in S Africa on postal work. *Recreations:* walking, bowls. *Address:* 41 Dowsett Avenue, Southend-on-Sea.

Died 16 Jan. 1922.

REER, Thomas Macgregor, JP, DL; retired County Solicitor, Land Agent, etc; Senator Parliament of Northern Ireland since 1921; *b* 1853; *s* of Samuel Macurdy Greer, County Court Judge, one time MP for Co. Londonderry, and Marion, *d* of James McCrone, Crown Agent, Isle of Man; *m* Margaret Baines, *d* of Sir Charles Reed, MP, Chairman London School Board; one *d*. *Educ:* Coleraine Academical Institution; Trinity College, Dublin, MA. Admitted Solicitor, 1875; County Solicitor for Antrim, 1900; Delegate for Co. Antrim on Council of Incorporated Law Society of Ireland; Convener of General Assembly's Northern Committee on Tenures and Trusts. *Recreations:* foreign travel, golf. *Address:* Ballycastle, Co. Antrim. *T:* Ballycastle 31. *M:* YN 888. *Club:* Ulster, Belfast.

Died 19 Feb. 1928.

REGG, Sir Henry, Kt 1920; *b* 1859; *m* 1922, Annie Gladys Samuels. Mayor of Tynemouth, 1913–18; member of Central Organisation for the County. *Address:* Leonie House, Whitley Bay, Northumberland. *Died 6 Aug. 1928.*

REGGE-HOPWOOD, Major Edward Byng George, DSO 1915; 1st Battalion Coldstream Guards; *b* 24 Dec. 1880; *s* and *heir* of Edward Robert Gregge-Hopwood. Entered army, 1902; Captain, 1910; served European War, 1914–15 (despatches, Bt Major, DSO). *Address:* Hopwood Hall, Middleton, Lancs.

Died July 1917.

REGORIE, Maj.-Gen. Charles Frederick, CB 1882; Colonel Royal Irish Regiment since 1897; *b* 25 Nov. 1834; *m* 1859, Henrietta Amy (*d* 1904), *d* of George Lawrence of Moreton, Hereford. Entered army, 1855; Maj.-Gen. 1890; served Indian Mutiny, 1857–58 (medal, two clasps); Egyptian War, 1882 (despatches, CB, medal, clasp, 3rd class Medjidie, Khedive's star).

Died 18 April 1918.

REGOROWSKI, Hon. Reinhold; Judge of the Supreme Court of South Africa since 1913; *b* Somerset East, Cape Colony, 1856; *s* of Rev. R. T. Gregorowski; *m* Mary Brown; five *c*. *Educ:* Gill College, Somerset East; Gray's Inn (studentship). Called to Bar, 1878; Advocate, Cape Supreme Court, 1878; Judge of the High Court, Orange Free State, 1881–92; State Attorney, 1892–4; State Attorney and Chief Justice, South African Republic; MLA Pretoria. *Address:* Pretoria. *Club:* Pretoria. *Died Nov. 1922.*

REGORY, Hon. Alexander Frederick; *b* 20 May 1843; 3rd *s* of 3rd Viscount Hood and Mary Isabella, *d* of late Richard Tibbits; succeeded his cousin, Major F. Hood Gregory, to Styvechall Estates, 1909, and took the name of Gregory by Royal licence, 1911; *m* 1870, Ethel Cecilia (*d* 1923), *d* of Algernon C. Heber Percy of Hodnet, Co. Salop; one *s* two *d* (and two *s* one *d* decd). *Educ:* Eton. Lieut RN and Lieut 15th Hussars; JP E and W Ridings, Yorks, and Warwickshire. *Address:* Styvechall Hall, Coventry, Warwickshire.

Died 20 May 1927.

REGORY, Charles, RWS. *Address:* Maisemore, Marlow-on-Thames. *Died 21 Oct. 1920.*

GREGORY, Rt. Rev. Francis Ambrose, DD; *b*1848; *s* of late Very Rev. Robert Gregory, Dean of St Paul's; *m* 1924, Mildred, *d* of late W. H. Peel, Trenant Park, Cornwall. *Educ:* Corpus Christi College, Oxford, MA. Ordained, 1873; Curate of Cheam, 1873–74; Warden of St Paul's College, and SPG Missionary at Ambatoharanana, Madagascar, and Chaplain to Bishop of Madagascar, 1874–1900; Legion of Honour for services with French troops, 1900; Chancellor of Cathedral of St Laurence, Antananarivo, 1880–1901; Chaplain of St John's, Mentone, 1901–3; Bishop of Mauritius, 1904–19. *Publications:* commentaries and manuals in Malagasy (translations). *Address:* Elmside, Northiam, Sussex.

Died 31 Jan. 1927.

GREGORY, Frederick; *b* near Wakefield, 15 March 1831; widower. *Educ:* Winterton, Lincolnshire, at the private school of the Vicar. Followed his father and grandfather's occupation, dating two centuries back, as corn merchants at Wakefield, and came to London on his own account in 1854. Late Master of Surrey Staghounds. *Recreation:* golfing. *Address:* Woodlands Road, Earlswood, Surrey. *T:* Redhill 96. *Clubs:* Overseas; New, Brighton.

Died Aug. 1919.

GREGORY, George Frederick; Supreme Court Judge, New Brunswick, since 1900, and Judge of the Court of Divorce and Matrimonial Causes since 1901; *b* Fredericton, New Brunswick, 31 Aug. 1839; *s* of John Gregory, originally of Edinburgh, Scotland, clerk assistant Legislative Council of NB, and Mary, *d* of Samuel Grosvenor of Fredericton; *m* 1st, 1860, Marion (*d* 1871), *d* of Francis Beverly of Fredericton, stationer; 2nd, 1879, Isabella, *widow* of C. J. Davis of Fredericton, druggist. *Educ:* Collegiate School and King's College, Fredericton. Admitted to Bar of NB, 1865; elected and served as Mayor of Fredericton, 1869–73, and 1878–81; QC, Bar of Canada, 1891. Presbyterian. *Address:* Fredericton, New Brunswick.

GREGORY, Sir Philip Spencer, Kt 1913; barrister; one of the Conveyancing Counsel to the Supreme Court since 1902; *b* 2 Feb. 1851; *y s* of late John Gregory, Governor of the Bahamas; *m* 1876, Edith Anne, *d* of late Rev. Edward James, Rector of Hindringham, Norfolk; one *s*. *Educ:* Eton; King's College, Cambridge (Scholar). BA 1873, 10th Wrangler and 2nd Class Classical Tripos; Fellow of King's College, 1873–77; MA 1876; called to Bar, Lincoln's Inn, 1875; Bencher, 1907. Additional Member of the General Council of the Bar; Member of the Royal Commission on the Land Transfer Acts, 1908; Member of the Rule Committee under the Land Transfer Acts. *Address:* 9 Lowndes Square, SW; 1 New Square, Lincoln's Inn, EC. *Club:* Athenæum. *Died 28 Oct. 1918.*

GREGORY, Reginald Philip; Fellow since 1904 and Tutor since 1912, St John's College, Cambridge; University Lecturer in Botany since 1907; *b* 7 June 1879; *s* of Arthur Gregory of Trowbridge, Wilts; *m* 1908, Joan Laidlay, *d* of T. G. Bisdee, Hutton Court, Weston-super-Mare; three *d*. *Educ:* St John's College, Cambridge. Walsingham medal, 1904; University Demonstrator in Botany, 1902–7; 2nd Lt the Gloucestershire Regiment. *Publications:* papers on genetics and cytology in various scientific publications. *Recreations:* golf, other games. *Address:* 7 Harvey Road, Cambridge. *T:* Cambridge 959.

Died 24 Nov. 1918.

GREGSON, Ven. Francis Sitwell Knight, MA Oxon; Rector of Steeple Aston, Oxfordshire, since 1918. Ordained, 1888; Curate of Christ Church, Gateshead, 1888–95; Vicar of All Hallows, Leeds, 1895–1903; Vicar of St Thomas's, Durban, 1903–14; Archdeacon of Durban and Canon of St Saviour's Cathedral, Pietermaritzburg, 1908–14; Vicar of All Souls, Leeds, 1914–18. *Address:* Steeple Aston Rectory, Oxford. *Died 26 May 1926.*

GREIG, Capt. Ronald Henry, DSO 1900; Royal Engineers; *b* 4 April 1876; *s* of Lt-Col Banks Robinson Greig, and Florence Louisa Sibbald, 2nd *d* of late Sir J. D. Sibbald Scott, 3rd Bt of Dunninald; *m* 1909, Mary Hope Letitia, *d* of Mr and Mrs Clutterbuck of Hardenhuish Park; one *s* one *d*. Entered army, 1896; served South Africa, 1899–1902 (severely wounded, despatches, Queens' medal, 4 clasps; King's medal, 2 clasps, DSO). *Address:* Woolmer Lodge, E Liss, Hants.

Died 27 Aug. 1916.

GRENFELL, 1st Baron, *cr* 1902 of Kilvey; **Francis Wallace Grenfell,** PC; GCB 1898 (KCB 1886; CB 1885); GCMG 1892; FSA; Hon. LLD, Cambridge and Edinburgh; Field Marshal, 1908; Colonel 1st Life Guards and King's Royal Rifles; *b* 29 April 1841; *s* of Pascoe St Leger Grenfell, JP, and Madelena Du Pré; *m* 1st, 1887, Evelyn (*d* 1899), *d* of General Robert Wood, CB; 2nd, 1903, Hon. Aline (*d* 1911), *o d* of late Lewis A. Majendie of Hedingham Castle, Essex;

two s one d. Entered 60th Rifles, 1859; served in Kaffir War, 1878; Zulu War, 1879; QMG in Transvaal, 1881–82; Egyptian Expedition, 1882; Nile Expedition, 1884; Sirdar Egyptian Army, 1885–92; commanded Forces, Suakim, 1889; at Toski, 1889; Inspector-General of Auxiliary Forces, War Office, 1894–97; Inspector General of Recruiting, 1896; commanded the forces in Egypt, 1897–98; Governor and Commander-in-Chief of Malta, 1899–1903; commanded 4th Army Corps, 1903–4; Commander-in-Chief in Ireland, 1904–8. *Heir: s* Hon. Pascoe Christian Victor Francis Grenfell, *b* 12 Dec. 1905. *Address:* Foresters, Windlesham, Surrey. *Clubs:* Army and Navy, Travellers'.   *Died 27 Jan. 1925.*

GRENFELL, Bernard Pyne, DLitt, MA; Hon. LittD (Dublin); Hon. PhD (Koenigsberg); Hon. DJur (Graz); FBA 1905; late Fellow of Queen's College, Oxford; Drexel Medallist of the University of Pennsylvania, 1903; Socio delle reale Academia dei Lincei, Rome; Corresponding Member of the Munich Academy of Sciences; Professor of Papyrology, Oxford, 1908. Hon. Professor, 1916; *b* Birmingham, 16 Dec. 1869; *e s* of late John Granville Grenfell, Master at Clifton College. *Educ:* Clifton College; Queen's College, Oxford. Craven Fellow in the University of Oxford, 1894–95; Fellow of Queen's College, 1894; engaged in the discovery and editing of Greek Papyri since 1894. *Publications:* The Revenue Laws of Ptolemy Philadelphus, 1896; An Alexandrian Erotic Fragment and other Greek Papyri, 1896; and, in collaboration with A. S. Hunt, New Classical Fragments and other Greek and Latin Papyri; Sayings of Our Lord from an Early Greek Papyrus; New Sayings of Jesus and Fragment of a Lost Gospel; The Geneva Fragment of Menander; The Oxyrhynchus Papyri; The Amherst Papyri; Fayûm Towns and their Papyri; The Tebtunis Papyri; Greek Papyri in the Cairo Museum; Hellenica Oxyrhynchia; The Hibeh Papyri. *Recreation:* travelling. *Address:* Queen's College, Oxford. *Club:* Athenæum.

Died 17 April 1926.

GRENFELL, Lt-Col Cecil Alfred; *b* 13 Feb. 1864; *s* of Pascoe du Pre Grenfell; *m* 1898, Lady Lilian Spencer-Churchill, *sister* of 9th Duke of Marlborough; two *d* (and one *d* decd). *Educ:* Eton. Member of Stock Exchange; served as Capt., South African War; Col of Bucks Yeomanry; Member of Bucks Territorial Association and Political Council City Liberal Club; MP (L) Bodmin, SE Cornwall, 1910; served European War (despatches). *Recreations:* hunting, polo, golf; rode Father O'Flynn in Grand National Steeplechase, 1896. *Address:* 4 Great Cumberland Place, W1. *T:* Paddington 856. *Clubs:* Turf, Garrick.   *Died 11 Aug. 1924.*

GRENFELL, Charles Seymour; banker; *b* Carshalton Park, Surrey, 14 Sept. 1839; *s* of late Riversdale Grenfell of Ray Lodge, Maidenhead; *m* 1862, Elizabeth Graham; one *s* three *d*. Bucks Yeomanry for many years as Captain; for over 30 years a partner in the firm of Pascoe, Grenfell and Sons; sub-Governor of the Royal Exchange Assurance Corporation, and Director of the London and County Bank. *Recreations:* only a bicyclist and golfer; formerly hunting, shooting, fishing. *Address:* Elibank, Taplow, Bucks. *Club:* Arthur's.

Died 11 Jan. 1924.

GRENIER, Gerard, ISO 1905; Registrar of Superior Court, Ceylon; retired, 1906.   *Died Feb. 1917.*

GRENIER, Gustave, ISO; JP; Clerk of the Executive Council, Province of Quebec, since 1886; Deputy Lieutenant-Governor for signing warrants; *b* Montreal, June 1847; *m* 1st, 1879, Kate Winifred Heatley (*d* 1880), of Quebec; 2nd, 1889, Helen, *d* of late Hon. F. G. Marchand, Premier of the Province; one *s* three *d*. *Educ:* Toronto and Quebec. Entered Civil Service of Province, 1867, as a junior clerk in the Executive Council Dept. *Address:* 89 Berthelot Street, Quebec. *TA:* Quebec, Canada. *T:* 1022.

GRENIER, Joseph Richard; late a Judge of the Supreme Court of Ceylon; Barrister-at-law, Gray's Inn; *b* 4 July 1852; *s* of F. C. Grenier and Matilda Aldons; French by descent; *m* Lydia, *d* of John Drieberg; six *s* three *d*. *Educ:* St Thomas' College. Admitted an Advocate of the Supreme Court, 1873; Commissioner of Assize on several occasions; acted twice as HM's Solicitor-General; permanent District Judge of Colombo, 1903; a Puisne Justice of the Supreme Court, 1910; retired on attaining the age limit of 60, 1912; KC 1913; a leader of the Ceylon Bar; President YMCA of Ceylon. *Recreations:* fishing, shooting. *Address:* Meadowsweet, Barnes Place, Colombo.

Died June 1926.

GRENSTED, Rev. Frederic Finnis; Vicar of Melling, near Liverpool, since 1912; Diocesan Inspector of Religious Education for Diocese

of Liverpool since 1895; Hon. Canon of Liverpool, 1908; *b* Maidstone, 14 Dec. 1857; *s* of William and Julia Theresa Grensted *m* 1884, Gertrude Ellen, *y d* of Alexander Plimpton of Spring House Merton, Surrey; one *s* one *d*. *Educ:* Maidstone Grammar Schoo (Lubbock Scholar); University College, Oxford (Gunsley Exhibitioner). First-Class Honours in Natural Science. Ordained 1883; Curate of St Nicholas, Blundellsands, 1883–90; Second Master of Merchant Taylors' School, Great Crosby, 1883–95. *Publications* a few scientific papers, Liverpool Geological Society, etc; article in Hibbert Journal, Timelessness of the Eternal, Jan. 1907; and in the Interpreter, Rev. xii, Oct. 1911; articles in The Prayer Book Dictionary, 1912, on The Calendar, The Punctuation of the Prayer Book, etc. *Address:* Melling Vicarage, Liverpool. *TA:* Melling Maghull.   *Died Feb. 1919.*

GRESLEY, Rear-Adm. Richard Nigel; *b* 3 March 1850; *e s* of late Major F. Gresley; *m* 1892, Ruth Slingsby (*d* 1925), *d* of G. Peirse-Duncombe; one *d*. Retired list, 1902; Rear-Adm. 1905. *Address:* Drakelow, Compton, Winchester. *Club:* Naval and Military.

Died 11 Sept. 1928.

GRESSON, Lt-Col Thomas Tinning, DSO 1900; York and Lancaster Regiment; *b* 29 April 1870; *s* of Major W. H. Gresson. Entered army, 1889; Captain, 1899; Adjutant, Dec. 1896–June 1901; special service South Africa, Nov. 1899–Feb. 1900; rejoined Batt. as Adjutant, Feb. 1900; served with 5th Division MI (despatches twice, Queen's medal, 6 clasps, King's medal, 2 clasps, DSO). *Club:* Army and Navy.   *Died 1921.*

GRESWELL, Rev. William Henry Parr, MA; FRGS; Rector of Dodington, Somerset, 1888–1913; *e s* of Rev. William Parr Greswell, late Fellow of Balliol Coll., Oxford and Rector of Kilve, Somerset; *m* 1895, Blanche Caroline Annie, *y d* of late Coventry Carew of Crowcombe, Somerset. *Educ:* Somersetshire College, Bath; Brasenose College, Oxford. Classical Scholar and Hulme Exhibitioner; 2nd class Moderations (Classical); 3rd class Greats (Classical). Lecturer of Classics and English Literature under the Higher Education Act of the Cape Legislature, 1876–84; Secretary Coleridge Cottage Fund, 1893–1908. *Publications:* Our South African Empire, 1885; Imperial Federation, 1887; A History of the Canadian Dominion, 1890; A Geography of the Canadian Dominion, 1891; A Geography of Africa South of the Zambesi, 1892; The British Colonies and their Industries, 1893; Outlines of British Colonisation, 1893; The Growth and Administration of the British Colonies, 1897; The Land of Quantock, 1903; The Forests and Deerparks of Somerset, 1905; Chapters on Glastonbury Abbey, 1909. *Recreations:* cricket, ornithology. *Address:* Martlet House, Minehead.   *Died 19 Jan. 1923.*

GRETTON, Major Frederic; Director of Bass & Co.; *s* of the late John Gretton; unmarried. *Educ:* home. *Recreations:* hunting, racing, shooting, yachting. *Address:* Egginton Hall, Derby. *Clubs:* Marlborough, Boodle's; Royal Yacht Squadron, Cowes.

Died 19 July 1928.

GREVILLE, Hon. Sir Sidney Robert, KCVO 1912 (CVO 1901); CB 1899; Groom-in-Waiting to King George V, 1910–1911 and since 1920; *b* Warwick Castle, 16 Nov. 1866; 4th *s* of 4th Earl of Warwick and Lady Ann Charteris, *d* of 8th Earl of Wemyss and March. *Educ:* Marlborough. Assistant Private Sec. to Sir John Gorst as Under-Secretary for India, 1887; Private Sec. to Marquess of Salisbury as Prime Minister, 1888–92, 1896–98, 1900–1; Equerry to Prince of Wales, 1898–1901; Groom-in-Waiting to King Edward VII; Private Sec. to HM Queen Alexandra, 1901–10; Paymaster to HM's Household, 1911–15; Comptroller and Treasurer to HRH the Prince of Wales, 1915–20. *Address:* St James's Palace, SW1. *T:* Gerrard 6226. *Clubs:* Carlton, Marlborough, Bachelors'.

Died 12 June 1927.

GREY, 4th Earl, *cr* 1806; **Albert Henry George Grey,** GCB 1911; GCMG 1904; GCVO 1908; PC 1908; JP; LLM; Bt 1746; Baron Grey, 1801; Viscount Howick, 1806; *b* 28 Nov. 1851; *s* of General Hon. Charles Grey and Caroline, *d* of Sir Thomas Harvie Farquhar, 2nd Bt; *S* uncle 1894; *m* 1877, Alice, 3rd *d* of Robert Stayner Holford, MP, Westonbirt, Gloucestershire; one *s* two *d* (and 2 decd). *Educ:* Harrow; Trinity Coll., Camb. (Senior in Law and History Tripos, 1873). MP (L) S Northumberland, 1880–85; Northumberland (Tyneside), 1885–86; Administrator of Rhodesia, 1896–97; Director of British South Africa Company, 1898–1904; Governor-General and Commander-in-Chief of Canada, 1904–11; Lord-Lieutenant of Northumberland, 1899–1904; Chancellor of the Order of St Michael and St George since 1916. Owner of about 17,600 acres. *Publication:* Hubert Hervey, a Memoir, 1899. *Heir: s* Viscount Howick, *b* 15 Dec.

1879. *Address:* 22 South Street, Park Lane, W; Howick House, Lesbury, Northumberland. *Club:* Brooks's.

Died 29 Aug. 1917.

GREY OF FALLODON, Viscountess; (Pamela); *y d* of late Hon. Percy Wyndham; *m* 1st, 1895, 1st Baron Glenconner (*d* 1920); three *s* one *d* (and one *s* one *d* decd); 2nd, 1922, Viscount Grey of Fallodon. Fellow of the Royal Society of Literature. *Publications:* The Earthen Vessel; The Sayings of the Children; Shepherds' Crowns, 1923; Edward Wyndham Tennant, 4th Grenadier Guards, and other books. *Address:* Mulberry House, 37 Smith Square, SW1. *T:* Victoria 0961; Wilsford Manor, Salisbury; Fallodon Hall, Christen Bank, Northumberland. *Died 18 Nov. 1928.*

GREY, Colonel Arthur, CIE 1910; VD; *b* 3 July 1855; *s* of late Col Francis D. Grey, *g s* of late Rt Rev. Hon. Edward Grey, Bishop of Hereford; *m* 1907, Teresa Mary, *d* of Rev. A. Alleyne; four *s* one *d*. *Educ:* Wellington; New College, Oxford. Barrister Inner Temple, 1886; sometime President Punjab Chief Court Bar Association; practised before the Judicial Committee of the Privy Council; raised the Punjab Light Horse, 1893, which he commanded until retirement, 1912; commanded Volunteer Cavalry at Delhi Durbar, 1902, and at HM Coronation, 1911; special appointment War Office, 1915. *Address:* 1 Essex Court, Temple, EC4. *T:* Temple 1304; Richmond 522. *M:* EK90. *Clubs:* St Stephen's, Royal Automobile.

Died 13 Oct. 1924.

GREY, Rev. Harry George, MA; *b* 1 Oct. 1851; 2nd *s* of Adm. Hon. George Grey and Jane Frances, *d* of Gen. Hon. Sir Patrick Stuart. *Educ:* Wadham Coll., Oxford (3rd class Mods, 2nd class Lit. Hum.). Ordained 1874; Curate of St Giles in the Fields, 1874–77; Vicar of Holy Trinity, Oxford, 1877–85; Curate of St James's, Clapham Park, 1885; CMS Missionary, Quetta, Panjab, India, 1887–1900; Principal of Wycliffe Hall, Oxford, 1900–5; Examining Chaplain to Bishop of Liverpool, 1900–5; returned to India, 1905–9; Principal Wycliffe Hall, Oxford, 1910–18; resigned. *Address:* 17 New Inn Hall Street, Oxford. *Died 22 Jan. 1925.*

GREY, Colonel Leopold John Herbert, CSI 1877; *b* 1 July 1840; *s* of late Leopold James Henry Grey; *g s* of late Rt Rev. Hon. Edward Grey, Bishop of Hereford; *m* 1864, Josephine Catherine (*d* 1915), *d* of General H. C. van Cortlandt, CB; two *s* one *d* (and three *d* decd). *Educ:* Cheltenham College. Served through the Mutiny and on the North-West Frontier, 1857–62; Bhutan Campaign, 1865–66, as political officer with Eastern Column; Superintendent Bahawalpur State, 1871–73, 1877–79, 1899–1903; Commissioner Hissar Division, 1882; retired, 1894. *Publications:* A Manual of the Construction and Management of Canals, 1884; The India of the Future, 1907.

Died 1921.

GREY, Major Robin, DSO; 2nd Battalion Grenadier Guards; *b* 28 June 1874; *s* of Sir William Grey, KCSI, late Governor of Bengal and Jamaica; unmarried. *Educ:* Harrow. Was ADC to Sir Trevor Plowden in India; served Mateleland campaign, 1896; Secretary to Lord Beresford, 1898–1900; served South African War; Unionist Candidate for the Bishop Auckland Division, 1911–13; seconded for service with the RFC 1913; flew to France on outbreak of war as 2nd in command 5th Squadron RFC; Chevalier de la Légion d'Honneur at the end of the retreat; later taken prisoner; after the Armistice went to Archangel; became CRAF in North Russia (DSO, despatches twice). *Recreation:* travelled much in America, China, Japan, India, Africa, and Europe. *Clubs:* Guards, Travellers', 1900.

Died 15 May 1922.

GREY-WILSON, Sir William, KCMG 1904 (CMG 1891); KBE 1918; Commander of the Star of Roumania, 1921; *b* Kent, 7 April 1852; *y s* of late Andrew Wilson, Inspector-Gen. of Hosps, HEIC, and Charlotte, *g d* of 1st Earl Grey; *m* 1884, Margaret, *o d* of Robert Glasgow Brown, of Broadstone, Ayrshire; two *s* one *d*. *Educ:* Cheltenham Coll.; France. Private Secretary to Sir William Grey, Governor of Jamaica, 1874; to Sir Frederick Barlee, 1877; Clerk of the Executive and Legislative Councils, British Honduras, 1878; Magistrate in command of scouts on Mexican Frontier, 1879; Special Commissioner to take over territory between Sierra Leone and Liberia, West Africa; Asst Colonial Secretary, Gold Coast, 1884; Colonial Secretary, St Helena, 1886; Governor, 1887–97; Governor, Falkland Isles, 1897–1904; Governor of the Bahamas, 1904–12; Chairman The Central Committee for National Patriotic Organisations; Chairman Institute of Patentees (incorporated) and Past President. *Address:* 188 Cromwell Road, SW5. *Recreations:* riding, mechanics. *Club:* Junior Carlton.

Died 14 Feb. 1926.

GRIBBLE, George James, JP; *b* 1846; *s* of Thomas Gribble; *m* 1881, Norah (*d* 1923), *d* of Rev. F. C. Royds, Rector of Coddington and Hon. Canon of Chester; two *s* three *d*. *Educ:* Harrow. High Sheriff of Bedfordshire, 1897. *Recreation:* yachting. *Address:* 34 Eaton Square, SW1; Kingston Russell House, Dorset. *T:* Victoria 7214. *Clubs:* Junior Carlton, Burlington Fine Arts; Royal Yacht Squadron, Cowes.

Died 16 June 1927.

GRICE, Col Walter Thomas, CIE 1915; VD; FCS; late Colonel Commanding 1st Battalion Calcutta Volunteer Rifles and 5th Battalion Indian Defence Force; Member Legislative Council, Bengal, 1914–16; *b* 11 Sept. 1868; 3rd *s* of late William Grice, Yardley, Birmingham; *m* 1908, Helen, 2nd *d* of Archibald Symington, JP, Allanton, Auldgirth, Dumfriesshire; one *s*. *Educ:* Solihull Grammar School; Mason's College, Birmingham. Hon. ADC to Viceroy of India, 1912–17; to Commander-in-Chief, 1918–19. *Address:* The Coppice, Cookham Dean, Maidenhead. *T:* 1Y3 Marlow. *M:* SM 1806. *Clubs:* Junior Constitutional, Royal Automobile.

Died 28 Feb. 1926.

GRIEP, Louis Monro, RBA; Principal of St Ives School of Landscape and Marine Painting; *b* Melbourne, Australia, 1864; *s* of Dr Charles Grier and Maria Agnes Monro of Craiglochart. *Educ:* Upper Canada College, Toronto; King's College School, London. Was a banker in Canada; returned to England to devote himself to Art; visited many countries and voyaged round the world; exhibited in principal European Galleries; Medal at Paris Salon for The Night Watch, 1891. *Address:* The Foc'sle, St Ives, Cornwall. *Club:* St Ives Arts.

Died 24 Oct. 1920.

GRIERSON, Francis; musician and author of books on philosophy, art, and literature; *b* Birkenhead, Cheshire, 1848. Began musical career in Paris, 1869, under the patronage of Auber, Director of the Conservatoire; gave improvisational piano recitals in all the principal cities and at the Courts of Continental Europe for many years before turning his attention to literature; made long sojourns in France, Russia, Germany, Austria, and Italy; studied political economy and psychology in Berlin and Paris; made exhaustive art studies in the principal galleries of the world; lectured at leading clubs and universities in the United States; contributed critical articles to La Nouvelle Revue and La Nouvelle Revue Internationale, of Paris; the English Review, the Nation, Westminster Review, the New Age, Oxford and Cambridge Review, Atlantic Monthly, Century Magazine, Washington Herald, New York Tribune, Philadelphia Ledger. *Publications:* La Revolte Idéaliste, Paris, 1889; Modern Mysticism, London, 1899; The Celtic Temperament, 1901; The Valley of Shadows, 1909; Parisian Portraits, 1910; La Vie et Les Hommes, Paris, 1911; The Humour of the Underman, London, 1911; The Invincible Alliance, 1913; Illusions and Realities of the World War, 1918; Abraham Lincoln, 1919. *Recreations:* walking, nature studies. *Address:* Los Angeles, California.

Died 29 May 1927.

GRIERSON, James Cullen, JP; *b* 1863; *e s* of late Andrew John Grierson and Alice, *d* of Herbert John Clifford; *m* 1895, Alice Stanley, *d* of late Henry Peake of Westholme, Sleaford; three *s* two *d*. Convener of Shetland; Captain, Shetland Companies, Gordon Highlanders; Member of Committee to enquire into adequacy of medical relief in Highlands and Islands of Scotland, 1912. *Address:* Quendale House, Lerwick, NB. *Died 1919.*

GRIERSON, Sir Philip James Hamilton-, Kt 1910; JP; LLD Edin.; Solicitor for Scotland to the Board of Inland Revenue, 1892, till retirement in 1919; *b* 9 March 1851; *o surv. c* of late John Hamilton, Chartered Accountant, Edinburgh; took the name of Grierson in 1879 on succeeding his uncle, James Grierson of Dalgoner, Dumfriesshire; *m* 1881, Lilias, *d* of late Deputy Surg.-Gen. James Kirkpatrick; one *s* two *d*. *Educ:* Cheltenham College; Oxford University. BA 1876. Called to Scots Bar, 1880; Sheriff-Substitute of Aberdeen, Kincardine, and Banff, 1887; removed to Aberdeen, 1890. *Publications:* contributed frequently to current literature; editor and author of several law books; also The Silent Trade, a contribution to the Early History of Human Intercourse, 1903, and several articles in Hastings' Encyclopedia of Religion and Ethics. *Address:* 7 Palmerston Place, Edinburgh. *Club:* New, Edinburgh. *Died 25 April 1927.*

GRIEVE, Hon. Walter Baine, CBE 1918 (OBE 1918); MLC Newfoundland; Merchant and Shipowner; *b* 1850; *s* of James Johnston Grieve, formerly MP for Greenock; *m* 1880, Helen Marion, *d* of Henry Stone, Ryde, Isle of Wight; one *s*. *Educ:* St Andrew's; Glasgow Univ. Liberal; Church of England. *Recreations:* fishing, golf. *Address:* Musgrave Terrace, St John's, Newfoundland. *TA:* Baine St John's.

T: 43. *M:* M 363, Motor Association. *Clubs:* Devonshire; City, St John's; Greenock, Greenock. *Died 3 Feb. 1921.*

GRIFFIN, Lt-Col Cecil Pender Griffith, DSO 1900; Indian Staff Corps; 1st (DYO) Lancers; *b* 22 Jan. 1864; *s* of late Col Griffin, commanding 45th Regiment; *m* 1893, Annie, *o d* of E. Janes, Plymouth; one *d. Educ:* Wellington College; RMC, Sandhurst. Served Frontier, India, 1898 (medal and 2 clasps); China, 1901 (despatches, DSO); retired, 1912; European War, 1914–16 (wounded). Granted Silver Medal Royal Humane Society, 1893. *Address:* Berridon Hall, Bradworthy, N Devon. *Club:* Cavalry.
Died 2 April 1922.

GRIFFIN, Charles Thomas, ISO 1911; late Assistant Principal Civil Medical Officer and Inspector-General of Hospitals, Island of Ceylon; *m* Katherine Agnes Iago-Lucas (*d* 1913). *Club:* Badminton.
Died 15 Dec. 1923.

GRIFFIN, Lt-Gen. Edward Christian; Colonel Commandant, Royal Artillery; *b* 2 June 1836. Entered army, 1854; Lieut-General, 1895; unemployed list, 1895; served Indian Mutiny, 1857–58 (despatches twice, medal). *Died 6 May 1917.*

GRIFFIN, Martin Joseph, CMG 1907; LLD; Parliamentary Librarian, Ottawa, since 1885; *b* St John's, 7 Aug. 1847; *m* 1872, Harriet, *d* of late D. Starratt, Liverpool, NS. *Educ:* St Mary's College, Halifax. Called to Bar, 1868; Conservative candidate for Legislature, 1874; Editor of The Express, 1868–74; Secretary and Assistant to Counsel for Fisheries, 1873; Secretary to Civil Service Commission, 1880; Editor Toronto Mail, 1878–85; Roman Catholic. *Publications:* many articles to magazines. *Address:* 319 Daly Avenue, Ottawa.
Died March 1921.

GRIFFIS, Rev. William Elliot, AM, DD, LHD; President of the De Witt Historical Society; Dudleian Lecturer at Harvard and on Missions at Yale University; Preacher at Yale, Chicago, Pennsylvania and Cornell University; *b* Philadelphia, 17 Sept. 1843; 2nd *s* of late Capt. John L. Griffis; *m* 1st, Katharine Lyra (*d* 1898), *d* of late Prof. B. I. Stanton, Union College, Schenectady, NY; 2nd, Frances King, *d* of late Don King of Pulaski, NY; two *s* one *d. Educ:* Philadelphia public schools; Rutger's College; Union Theological Seminary. Served in 44th Pennsylvania Volunteer Militia during Gettysburg Campaign, 1863; in service of Japanese Government organising schools according to American methods, 1870–74; the only white man living who at a daimio's capital saw the feudal system in full operation; Order of Rising Sun, 1908; active pastor in Schenectady, Boston, and Ithaca, 1877–1903; eleven times in Europe; made nine preaching tours in Great Britain. *Publications:* The Mikado's Empire, 1876, 12th edn 1912; Japanese Fairy World, 1880; Corea, the Hermit Nation, 1882, 9th edn 1911; Matthew Calbraith Perry, 1887; The Lily Among Thorns, 1889; Sir William Johnson; Japan in History, Folk-lore and Art, new edn 1906; Brave Little Holland and What She Taught Us; The Religions of Japan; Townsend Harris, First American Envoy in Japan; The Romance of Discovery; Motley's Dutch Nation, 2nd edn 1908; Romance of American Colonisation; The Pilgrims in their Three Homes, 2nd edn 1910; America in the East; Romance of Conquest; The American in Holland; Verbeck of Japan, 1900; In the Mikado's Service, 1901; Youth's History of Holland, 1902; A Maker of the New Orient; Sunny Memories of Three Pastorates, 1903; Dux Christus, 1904; Christ the Creator of the New Japan, 1907; The Japanese Nation in Evolution, 2nd edn 1911; The Fire-Fly's Lovers and other Fairy Tales of Old Japan, 1908; The Story of New Netherland, 1909; China's Story, 1911; The Unmannerly Tiger and other Korean Fairy Stories, 1911; Belgium: The Land of Art, 2nd edn revised and enlarged, 1916; A Modern Pioneer in Korea; The Call of Jesus to Joy, 1912; Mighty England; Hepburn of Japan; The House We Live In, 1914; Japan and America: A Chronicle of Friendship, 1914; Millard Fillmore, Constructive Statesman, 1915; The Mikado, Institution and Person, 1915; Bonnie Scotland and What We Owe Her, 1916; Dutch Fairy Tales, 1917; Belgian Fairy Tales, 1919; Swiss Fairy Tales, 1920; Young People's History of the Pilgrims, 1920; Welsh Fairy Tales, 1921; (with H. D. Sawyer) The Pilgrim and Puritan Fathers of New England, 1922; (with H. de H. Scheffer) History of the Free Churchmen in the Dutch Republic, 1581–1701, 1922; Korean Fairy Tales, 1922; Japanese Fairy Tales, 1923; The Story of the Walloons, 1923; Japanese Proverbs, 1924; Jesus: of the International Mind, 1925; Things Borrowed from Japan; Why Americans should visit Holland, 1926; The Stripes and Stars, a History of the American Flag, 1926. *Recreations:* lecturing, pedestrianism, Japanese art, collector of monographs on Japan, Pilgrim history, Dutch prints of American interest. *Address:* Pulaski, NY.
Died Feb. 1928.

GRIFFITH, Arthur; MP (Sinn Fein) East Cavan since 1918; *b* Dublin, 1872; *s* of Arthur Griffith, printer. *Educ:* Christian Brothers School, Dublin. Founder and first editor of Sinn Fein, 1906–15; Editor of Nationality since 1916. *Address:* 6 Harcourt Street, Dublin.
Died 12 Aug. 1922.

GRIFFITH, Rev. David; Prebendary of St David's. *Address:* Clyro Vicarage, Hereford.

GRIFFITH, Rt. Hon. Sir Ellis Jones Ellis-, 1st Bt, *cr* 1918; PC 1914; KC 1910; Under-Secretary of State, Home Department, 1912–15; MP (GL) Anglesey, 1895–1918; (L) Carmarthen Division, 1923–24; *b* 23 May 1860; *s* of T. M. Griffith, Anglesey; *m* 1892, Mary, *d* of Rev. R. Owen, Mold; one *s* (and one *s* one *d* decd). *Educ:* University Coll. of Wales, Aberystwyth; Downing College, Cambridge (Hon. Fellow; late Fellow). President of the Union, 1886. Barrister 1887; contested (L) Toxteth Division Liverpool, 1892; Recorder of Birkenhead, 1907–12. *Heir:* *s* Elis Arundell Ellis-Griffith, *b* 15 Sept. 1896. *Address:* New Court, Middle Temple, EC4; (chambers) 3 (North) King's Bench Walk, Temple, EC4. *T:* Central 2552; Towyn Capel, Trearddur Bay, Anglesey. *Clubs:* Athenæum, National Liberal.
Died 30 Nov. 1926.

GRIFFITH, Lt-Col George Richard, DSO 1896; late Principal Veterinary Officer, Egyptian army; *b* 5 July 1857; *m* 1909, Alice Maud, *e d* of Rev. G. D. Redpath, of Harbledown. Entered Army Veterinary Department 1880; Major 1900; served Egyptian War, 1882 (medal with clasp, Khedive's star); Nile Expedition, 1884–85 (clasp); Suakim, 1888 (clasp); capture of Tokar, 1891 (4th class Osmanieh, clasp, Khedive's star); Dongola, 1896 (despatches, DSO, British medal, Khedive's medal with two clasps); Soudan, 1898 (despatches, 2nd class Medjidie, clasp); Reserve of Officers.
Died 21 March 1920.

GRIFFITH, Rt. Hon. Sir Samuel Walker, GCMG 1895 (KCMG 1886); PC 1901; Hon. FBA; a Member of the Judicial Committee of the Privy Council; Chief Justice of Australia, 1903–19; *b* 21 June 1845; *s* of Rev. Edward Griffith; *m* 1870, Julia, *d* of J. Thomson; one *s* four *d. Educ:* Univ. of Sydney (BA 1863; MA 1870). LLD Universities of Queensland and Wales; Barrister Queensland, 1867, also of NSW and Victoria; QC 1876; Attorney-Gen. of Queensland, 1874–78, 1890–93; Sec. for Public Instruction, 1876–79, 1883–84; Sec. for Public Works, 1878–79; Premier of Queensland, 1883–88, 1890–93; Colonial Treas., 1887–88; President of Federal Council of Australasia, 1888, 1891, 1893; Chief Justice of Queensland, 1893–1903; Lt-Governor of Queensland, 1899–1903. *Publications:* The Queensland Criminal Code; translator of Dante's Divina Commedia. *Address:* Sydney, NSW.
Died 9 Aug. 1920.

GRIFFITHS, Rev. Charles; Vicar, St Paul's Church, Bedminster, Bristol, 1888–1914; *b* London, 19 April 1847; *s* of Thomas Griffiths of Kirkby Wharf, Tadcaster, Yorkshire; *m* Fanny Pote, *d* of Rev. Frederic Williams, BA, Vicar of Saltley, Warwickshire; one *s. Educ:* privately; Gloucester Theol Coll.; Oxford Univ. Ordained, 1877; first curacy, St Peter's, Clifton Wood, Bristol; appointed Missions to Seamen; Chaplain to the Port of Bristol, 1879; Bristol Seamen's Church and Institute built 1881; place found so suitable to the wants of seamen that same kind of erection placed in many ports at home and abroad; restoration and enlargement of Parish Church, 1892; Hon. Canon of Bristol Cathedral, 1900; Proctor in Convocation, 1900–19; member of the Bristol Board of Guardians, 1898–1914; Governor of Bristol General Hospital, 1889; Governor of Queen Victoria Convalescent Home, 1901; selected Speaker Cardiff Church Congress. *Publications:* Numerical Decline of British Seamen; Haddon, a Child's Doctor; A Short Record of the Life of Melville Charles Griffiths, First Vicar of All Saints', Fishponds, Bristol. *Recreation:* chess. *Address:* Hazelwood, Stoke Bishop, Bristol. *T:* 107 Stoke Bishop, Bristol. *Club:* Authors'. *Died 9 May 1924.*

GRIFFITHS, Ven. David Henry, MA; Archdeacon of Monmouth since 1922; *b* 1864; *s* of late Thomas Griffiths, JP, Aberystwyth; *m* 1901, Jennie Isabella Wailes, Cardiff; three *s* two *d. Educ:* The Grammar School, Aberystwyth; Christ College, Brecon; Corpus Christi College, Cambridge. Deacon, 1888; priest, 1889; Vicar of Aberavon, 1901–8; St Woolos, Newport, 1908; Rural Dean of Newport, 1915–22; Grand Chaplain of Grand Lodge of England, 1924. *Address:* St Woolos Vicarage, Newport, Mon.
Died 27 Aug. 1926.

GRIFFITHS, John G., CVO 1917 (MVO 1916); Fellow and late President of Institute of Chartered Accountants; *b* 1845; *s* of George

Griffiths; *m* 1874, Emily Wilhelmina (*d* 1918), *d* of E. W. Dubois. *Educ:* private schools in England and under tutors in France. Appointed to an Ensigncy in the 100th Foot, 1865; shortly afterwards entered the office of Deloitte and Co., Accountants in the City of London, of which firm he was for some years the senior partner, and retired in 1902; was engaged, on behalf of the Electric and International Telegraph Co., when the Govt took over the Electric Telegraph business in Great Britain, and, on behalf of the Khedive, during the inquiry into the financial condition of Egypt in 1875–6 by the Rt Hon. Stephen Cave, MP, and again, in 1876–77, during the investigation by Lord Goschen and Mr Joubert; acted as advising accountant or auditor to most of the Telegraph Cable Companies and of the English Railway Companies in the Argentine Republic, as well as to the Great Western Railway Co., the London Joint Stock Bank, and many other of the larger English business enterprises; an original member of the council of the Institute of Chartered Accountants, of which he was president during the two years from June 1897 to June 1899; a Director of the Western Telegraph Company, and Great Western Railway. *Address:* 4 Hyde Park Gardens, W2. *T:* Paddington 5394. *Clubs:* Arts, Burlington Fine Arts, Ranelagh.

Died 16 Nov. 1922.

GRIFFITHS, Vincent, CB 1897; a Magistrate for Middlesex; *b* 27 Oct. 1831; *y s* of late Thos Griffiths; *m* 1869, Louisa Emily Caroline (decd), *d* of Edmund Bechinoe Ashford of Westbury, Sherborne; two *s* two *d*. Entered Poor Law Commission, 1845; Private Secretary to Parliamentary Sec., Poor Law Board, 1852; Principal of Poor Law Audit Department, 1860; HM Treasury Inspector and Valuer, 1869–99. Decorated for official services. *Address:* Yelverton Lodge, Twickenham.
Died 9 May 1917.

GRIGGS, Hon. John William; *b* New Jersey, 10 July 1849. *Educ:* Lafayette University. Admitted to Bar, 1871; Member General Assembly, NJ, 1876–77; State Senator, 1882–88; President Senate, NJ, 1886; Governor of New Jersey, 1896–98; Attorney-General, 1898–1901. Republican. *Address:* Paterson, New Jersey.
Died 28 Nov. 1927.

GRIGGS, Sir (William) Peter, Kt 1916; JP Essex; MP (U) Ilford since 1918; Alderman for County Council, Essex; *b* 1 Nov. 1854; *s* of late John Griggs; *m* Georgina, *d* of Thomas Hodges of Kensington; no *c. Educ:* private school. Had to make his own way in the world, his father dying when he was seven years old; apprenticed himself to the water, but left it to find a path not quite so rough and on firm ground. Ilford Councillor, since 1899; Chairman, Ilford District Council, 1910; Essex County Councillor, since 1901; Governing Director of W. P. Griggs & Co. Ltd and of the South Essex Recorders, Ltd. *Address:* The Drive, Ilford. *Died 11 Aug. 1920.*

GRIMBLE, Augustus; *b* 1840; *s* of late William Grimble of The Distillery, Albany Street, Regent's Park; *m* 1880, Alice, *e d* of late Edward Mathew Ward, RA. Served in 25th and 41st Regiments. *Publications:* Deerstalking; Shooting and Salmon-fishing; Highland Sport; The Deer Forests of Scotland; Leaves from a Game Book; The Salmon Rivers of Scotland. *Recreations:* all outdoor sports. *Address:* 44 Duke Street, SW1. *Died 1 Feb. 1925.*

GRIMES, Mary Katharine, FRHS; Hon. Secretary of Church Emigration Society since 1901; Member Emigration Committee Church of England Waifs and Strays Society since 1904; Associate Royal Colonial Institute, 1910, and Member of RCI Standing Committee on Emigration; *b* Funchal, Madeira, 26 Sept. 1861; *e d* of John Ralph Grimes and Mary Ann, *o d* of George Lund, MD, etc, of Edinburgh, Scarborough, and Madeira. *Educ:* at home. Voluntary worker, Battersea parish; Hon. Sec. and Librarian, parochial library; Poor-law Infirmary Visitor, and Visitor for Metropolitan Association for Befriending Young Servants, Wandsworth and Battersea, 1885–94; Hon. Secretary, Clapham and East Battersea Committee of Charity Organisation Society, 1894–97; Representative at Council for Brixton Committee Charity Organisation Society, 1898–99; Poor-law Infirmary Visitor, and Visitor for Metropolitan Association for Befriending Young Servants for Lambeth, 1897–1901; Visitor for Ministry of Pensions, 1918; Member National Union of Women's Suffrage Societies, and of Conservative and Unionist Women's Franchise Society; visited Canada, British Columbia, and Vancouver Island, 1905; South Africa, 1914. *Recreations:* music, photography, travelling. *Address:* Church House, Dean's Yard, Westminster, SW; 312a Vauxhall Bridge Road, SW. *TA:* Emigration. *T:* Victoria 1298.
Died 10 Jan. 1921.

GRIMSTON, Rev. Hon. Robert; Vicar of St Michael's, St Albans, since 1915; Hon. Canon of St Albans, 1914; Member of Industrial

Christian Fellowship; *b* 18 April 1860; *s* of 2nd Earl of Verulam and Elizabeth Joanna, *d* of Maj. Richard Weyland; *m* 1896, Gertrude Mary Amelia, *d* of late Rev. Charles Villiers; two *s* two *d. Educ:* Harrow; Trinity Coll., Cambridge, MA. *Address:* Darrowfield, St Albans. *T:* St Albans 232. *Died 8 July 1927.*

GRIMSTON, Brig.-Gen. Sir Rollo Estouteville, KCVO 1911; CIE 1906; Inspector-General Imperial Service Troops, India; *b* 26 Oct. 1861; *s* of Col O. J. A. Grimston of the Lodge, Itchen, Hants. *Educ:* United Services College. Entered army, 1881; Captain, Indian Cavalry, 1892; Major, 1901; Lieutenant-Colonel, 1907; Brig.-Gen., 1911; ADC to Viceroy, 1893–98; ADC to Prince of Wales during tour in India, 1905–6; extra Equerry-in-Waiting to HRH, 1906; extra Equerry-in-Waiting to King George V, 1910; Military Secretary to King George V during tour in India; served NW Frontier, India, 1897–98 (despatches, medal with clasp); Tirah, 1897–98 (despatches, clasp). *Clubs:* Cavalry, Hurlingham.

Died 29 Jan. 1916.

GRIMSTON, Brig.-Gen. Sylvester Bertram, CMG 1916; 18th Lancers, Indian Army; *b* 27 Nov. 1864; *s* of Col Oswald Augustus Grimston and Frances Campbell; *m* 1904, Nina, *d* of late Colonel G. W. Macauley; one *s* one *d. Educ:* US College, Westward Ho! Joined King's Liverpool Regiment, 1884; 2nd Queen's Own BLI (Indian Army), 1886; 18th Lancers, 1887; was on Staff as DAAG China Field Force, 1901–2; DAAG Div. Staff, India, 1904–8; AQMG Divisional Staff, India, 1916; commanded Brigade, India, Dehra Dun, 1917, March–Nov. 1918; Delhi, Dec. 1918–Feb. 1919; retired 1919; served Burma, 1885–1887 (medal and clasp); NW Frontier, India, and Tirah, 1897–98 (medal and 3 clasps); China, 1900 (medal); European War in France 1914–1916 (4th Class Legion of Honour, CMG, despatches, 1914–15 Star, Medal 1914–18, Victory Medal 1914–19). *Address:* The White House, Willingdon, Sussex. *Club:* United Service. *Died 24 March 1928.*

GRIMTHORPE, 2nd Baron, *cr* 1886; **Ernest William Beckett;** Bt 1813; Hon. Colonel Yorkshire Hussars; *b* 25 Nov. 1856; *s* of William Beckett-Denison, MP, Nun Appleton, Yorkshire, *b* of 1st Baron Grimthorpe, and Helen, *d* of 2nd Baron Feversham; *S* uncle 1905; *m* 1883, Lucy Tracy Lee, New York (*d* 1891); one *s* one *d* (and one *d* decd). *Educ:* Eton; Cambridge. MP (C) Whitby Div. Yorkshire, 1885–1905; formerly partner in Beckett and Co., Bankers, Leeds. DAG Imperial Yeomanry, 1900; late Lt-Col Yorkshire Hussars. *Heir:* *s* Hon. Ralph William Ernest Beckett, *b* 4 May 1891. *Recreations:* shooting, golf, travelling, amateur and collector of works of art. *Address:* 27 Welbeck Street, W. *T:* Mayfair 3864. *Clubs:* Brooks's, Turf, Marlborough, St James'.

Died 9 May 1917.

GRISDALE, Rt. Rev. John, DD, DCL; *b* 25 June 1845; *m* 1871, Anne, *d* of J. Chaplin, Hinckley, Leicestershire. *Educ:* Missionary College, Islington. Ordained, St Paul's Cathedral, 1870; Lambeth BD 1876; Professor of Systematic Theology, St John's College, Winnipeg, and Canon of St John's Cathedral, 1878–82; Dean of Rupert's Land and Professor of Pastoral Theology, 1882–96; Bishop of Qu'Appelle, 1896–1911. Hon. DCL Trinity, Toronto, 1893. *Address:* 341 Redwood Avenue, Winnipeg.

GROGAN, Col Sir Edward Ion Beresford, 2nd Bt, *cr* 1859; CMG 1920; DSO 1917; late Rifle Brigade; *b* 29 Nov. 1873; *o s* of Sir Edward Grogan, 1st Bt and Katherine Charlotte, *e d* of Sir B. B. McMahon, 2nd Bt; *S* father, 1891; *m* 1907, Ellinor, *d* of R. Bosworth Smith, and *widow* of Sir H. Langhorne Thompson, KCMG. Served South Africa, 1899–1900 (despatches, Queen's medal 5 clasps); psc; at War Office, 1904–6; served in Imperial Ottoman Gendarmerie, 1906–8; Military Attaché, South America, 1911–14; served European War, 1914–19 (despatches, DSO, Bt Col); retired pay, 1924. *Heir:* none. *Address:* Shropham Hall, Norwich, Norfolk. *Club:* United Service. *Died 11 July 1927 (ext).*

GROOME, Admiral Robert Leonard, CVO 1905; RN; *b* 10 Sept. 1848. Entered navy, 1861; Commander, 1882; Captain, 1890; Rear-Admiral, 1903; Vice-Admiral, 1907; commanded SE Coast of America; Reserve Division Portsmouth, 1905; Rear-Admiral, Channel Fleet, 1905–6; Director of Transports, 1907–11; retired, 1911. *Address:* St James's Court, SW.

Died 22 Nov. 1917.

GROSS, Edward John, MA; Senior Fellow since 1878 and President since 1923 of Caius College, Cambridge; *b* Alderton, Suffolk, 3 Feb. 1844; *s* of Samuel Chilton Gross; *m* 1st, 1877, Maria Isabella Chance of Malvern; 2nd, 1896, Constance Bertha King of Wimbledon; one s five d. Educ: Ipswich School; Caius College, Cambridge (Scholar; 8th Wrangler, 1866). Fellow, 1866; Bursar, 1876–86; Secretary to the Board of Examinations, 1874–1921; Secretary to the Oxford and Cambridge Schools Examination Board, 1875–1915. Publications: Treatise on Algebra, 1874; Treatise on Kinematics and Kinetics, 1876; Chronicle of the Estates of Gonville and Caius College, 1912. Address: Gonville Lodge, Cambridge.

Died 30 Aug. 1923.

GROSSMITH, (Walter) Weedon; artist, actor and author; b 9 June 1854; s of late George Grossmith, lecturer and journalist; m 1895, May Lever, y d of late Dr James Palfrey; one d. Educ: Simpson's School, Hampstead; Slade School; London University; RA Schools. First picture in Academy three-length portrait of his father; exhibited many times at the RA and Grosvenor Gallery. First appearance on stage at old Prince of Wales Theatre, Liverpool, as Specklebury in Time Will Tell, 1885; and in New York same year; first appearance in London as Woodcock in Woodcock's Little Game (Gaiety), 1887; started management at Terry's Theatre, 1894; lessee and manager of Vaudeville Theatre, 1894–96; lessee of Avenue Theatre, 1901; produced The Lady of Ostend at Terry's Theatre, 1900. Principal parts (out of numerous others): appeared in the M'Haggis, The Nobel Lord, and The Duke of Killiecrankie; at the Haymarket Theatre, 1906 and 1907, in The Man from Blankley's and Lady Huntworth's Experiment, and at His Majesty's Theatre in The Vandyk, 1907; Mrs Ponderbury's Past; The Worm; Sir Anthony, 1908; produced under own management at Criterion Theatre Mr Preedy and the Countess, 1909; went to Canada and America, 1910; at the command performance, Drury Lane, 1911, played Frantz in Money; at the Gala performance, His Majesty's, 1911, played Jones in David Garrick; appeared with Miss Marie Tempest in a revival of The Duke of Killiecrankie at the Playouse, June 1914. Publications: The Diary of a Nobody (with George Grossmith), 1894; written articles for Punch and Art Journal. Plays: A Commission; The Night of the Party; The Cure; The Duffer, 1905; The Mystery of Redwood Grange; Billy's Bargain, 1910; From Studio to Stage, 1912. Recreations: shooting, fishing, books, old furniture, antiquities, etc. Address: 1 Bedford Square, WC. Clubs: Beefsteak, Savage, Garrick.

Died 14 June 1919.

GROSVENOR, Capt. Lord Hugh (William); 1st Life Guards; b 6 April 1884; 4th surv. s of 1st Duke of Westminster and Hon. Katherine Caroline Cavendish; m 1906, Lady Mary Florence Mabel Crichton, d of 4th Earl of Erne; two s. Entered Army, 1903; Captain, 1908; served European War, 1914–15 (despatches). Address: 9 Southwick Crescent, W. T: Paddington 1382.

Died 30 Oct. 1914.

GROSVENOR, Hon. Richard Cecil; barrister-at-law; b 27 Jan. 1848; y s of 1st Baron Ebury and Hon. Charlotte Arbuthnot; m 1898, Jessie Amelia, d of late Rev. Charles Clarke Esher. Director-General Life Assurance Company. Address: Morrisburne House, Woking.

Died 29 Oct. 1919.

GROUT, Rev. George W. G., MA; Clerical Secretary since 1901, and Registrar since 1903, Diocese of Ontario; Senior Canon, St George's Cathedral, Kingston; b 12 June 1837; s of Rev. G. R. F. Grout, Rector of Grimsby, and Eliza Walker; m 1863, C. E., d of Rev. F. J. Lundy, DCL, Rector of Grimsby; four s. Educ: Trinity College, Toronto. Diocese of Ontario, North Gower, 1860–63; Loughboro, 1863–65; Stirling, 1865–72; Carleton Place, 1872–81; Elizabethtown, 1881–1901; Rural Dean of Lanark and Renfrew, 1881–88; Leeds, 1888–98. Publications: compilation and publication of the Journal of Synod, 1901–11, etc. Address: St George's Hall, Wellington Street, Kingston, Ontario.

Died 14 Feb. 1917.

GROVE, Agnes, (Lady Grove); b 25 July 1864; d of Maj.-Gen. Augustus Henry Lane Fox Pitt Rivers and Hon. Alice, d of 2nd Baron Stanley of Alderley; m 1882, Sir Walter John Grove, 2nd Bt; two s two d (and one s deced). Educ: home and Oxford. First essay appeared in Oxford High School Magazine when aged 15; has written many articles for magazines, Nineteenth Century, Fortnightly, Cornhill, etc; has travelled since marriage in Europe, America, and Africa; in Morocco crossed the Atlas Mountains and made the acquaintance of the then reigning Sultan Abdul-Aziz; has visited Spain, Italy, France, Germany, Switzerland; was Member of Executive Committee of Women's Liberal Federation, Anti-Vivisection Society, and President of the Forward Suffrage Union; also member of National Union of Women Suffrage Societies, and Pres. of National Anti-Vaccination League, etc; speaks at public meetings; represented Berwick St John, in Wiltshire, on District Council, 1898–1903. Publications: Seventy-

one Days' Camping in Morocco, 1902; The Social Fetich, 1907; The Human Woman, 1908; On Fads, 1910. Recreations: reading, motoring, entertaining friends; chief interest and pleasure her home and children and grandchildren. Address: Sedgehill Manor, Shaftesbury, Wiltshire.

Died 7 Dec. 1926.

GROVE, Maj.-Gen. Sir Coleridge, KCB 1898 (CB 1887); Colonel East Yorks Regiment since 1901; b Wandsworth, 26 Sept. 1839; 2nd s of late Rt Hon. Sir William Robert Grove (d1896), and Emma, d of late John Powles. Educ: private school; Balliol Coll. Oxford (exhibitioner; BA, first class in Mathematics, Moderations and Greats). Joined 15th Regiment, 1863; passed through Staff College, 1879; Private Secretary to three successive war ministers, viz. Mr Campbell-Bannerman, Mr W. H. Smith, and Mr Stanhope; ADC to Lieut-Gen. and Gen. Gov. of Ireland, 1882; DAA and QMG Exped. Force, Egypt, 1882; DAAG, HQ of Army, 1883–84; Spec. Serv. Egypt, 1884–85; Mil. Sec. to GOC-in-Chief, Egypt, 1885; AA and QMG, Gibraltar, 1885–86; Priv. Sec. to Sec. of State for War, 1886–88; AAG, HQ of Army, 1888–94; Mil. Sec. War Office, 1896–1901; Col East Yorks Regt, 1901; war services, Egyptian Expedition, 1882; DAAG, HQ (despatches, medal with clasp, bronze star, Brev. of Lt-Col, 4th class Osmanieh); Soudan Expedition, 1884–85; Nile and Suakin; as AAG for Boat Service, Commandant at Gemai, and AAG and Acting Military Secretary at Headquarters (despatches, 2 clasps, promoted Colonel). Address: 7 Wellington Court, Knightsbridge, SW1. T: Western 4481. Clubs: Oxford and Cambridge, Army and Navy.

Died 17 May 1920.

GROVE, (Thomas Newcomen) Archibald, JP for Bucks and Essex; MP (L) Northants South, 1906–10; b 1855; 2nd s of late Capt. Edward Grove and Elizabeth, d of Colonel Ponsonby Watts; m 1889, Kate Sara, d of Henry James Sibley; one s. Educ: private tutors; Oriel College, Oxford; double Honours. Educated for Barrister; ate dinners and passed all examinations at the Inner Temple; founded New Review and edited it from commencement till 1894; contested (L) Winchester, 1886; MP (L) West Ham (North), 1892–95; travelled extensively on Continent, Asia, and in Africa. Publications: Co-operation or Spoliation; The Big Black Hog; and many political and social articles. Recreations: fishing, shooting, golf. Address: Pollards Park, Chalfont St Giles, Bucks. TA: Chalfont St Giles. T: Amersham Common 18. Clubs: White's, Eighty.

Died 4 June 1920.

GROVE-HILLS, Col Edmond Herbert, CMG 1902; CBE 1919; DSc; FRS 1911; RE; President Royal Astronomical Society, 1913–15; b 1 Aug. 1864; s of late Herbert A. Hills of High Head Castle, Cumberland; m 1892, Juliet, d of late James Spencer-Bell, MP; assumed name Grove-Hills, 1920. Educ: Winchester; Woolwich. Entered army, 1884; Captain, 1893; Major, 1901; Assistant-Instructor, School of Military Engineering, 1898–99; rejoined, Aug. 1914; Col 1914; Brig.-Gen. 1918; DAAG Headquarters, 1899–1905; contested (C) Portsmouth, 1906. Publications: many papers on astronomical and allied subjects. Address: 1 Campden Hill, W8. T: Park 4655. Club: Athenæum.

Died 2 Oct. 1922.

GROZIER, Edwin Atkins; editor and publisher, Boston Post; b San Francisco, 12 Sept. 1859, New England parentage; m 1885, Alice G. Goodell of Salem. Educ: Brown University, Providence, RI; Boston University, PhB. Reporter, 1882; private sec. to Governor of Massachusetts, 1884–85; editorial and business positions on New York World, 1886–91; controlling owner of Boston Post, 1891–1922. Publications: chiefly newspaper and magazine work; Editor, One Hundred Best Novels—Condensed. Address: 168 Brattle Street, Cambridge, USA. Clubs: Algonquin, Boston Athletic, Oakly, Country, Press, Boston Chess, Belfry, Economic, Bostonian Society, Mass. Society of Mayflower Descendants.

Died 9 May 1924.

GRUBBE, Walter John; Stipendiary Magistrate for the Borough of East Ham, 1906–25; 2nd s of late John Eustace Grubbe, Barrister Inner Temple and Parliamentary Agent, and Julia Catharine, d of Rev. George William Hall, DD, Master of Pembroke College, Oxford; m 1912, Dora, d of late Rev. William Jowitt, Rector of Stevenage, Herts, and widow of Charles Arnold Edgell. Educ: Cheltenham College; Pembroke College, Oxford (MA). Barrister Inner Temple, 1874; South-eastern Circuit; Herts and Essex Sessions. Address: 7 Dr Johnson's Buildings, Temple, EC; Southlands, Margaretting, Essex; Southwold, Suffolk. Club: New University.

Died 16 March 1926.

GRUEBER, Herbert Appold, FSA; Keeper of Department of Coins and Medals, British Museum, 1906–12; b 1846; s of Rev. C. S.

Grueber, Hambridge, Somerset; *m* Alice Emily (*d* 1926), *d* of W. H. Hewitt of Lancaster Gate, Hyde Park. *Educ:* private tuition. Barrister Middle Temple, 1872. Assistant, British Museum, 1866; Assistant Keeper, Coins and Medals, 1893–1906; Hon. Sec. and Vice-President of Royal Numismatic Society, 1874–1912; Hon. Treasurer of Egypt Exploration Fund, 1883–1912; Hon. Member of French, Austrian, Italian, and American Numismatic Societies. *Publications:* Joint editor of the Numismatic Chronicle; edited Medallic Illustrations of the History of Great Britain and Ireland, and Thorburn's Guide to the Coins of Great Britain and Ireland; Roman Medallions in the British Museum; Guide to English Medals exhibited in the British Museum; Catalogue of Anglo-Saxon Coins in the British Museum, vol. ii; Handbook of the Coins of Great Britain and Ireland (British Museum); Roman Republican Coins in the British Museum; Illustrated Edition of the Medallic Illustrations of British History; numerous articles on Numismatics. *Address:* Bembridge, Isle of Wight.

Died 21 Nov. 1927.

GRUNING, John Frederick, CIE 1915; ICS; Member of the Board of Revenue since 1921; *b* 1 Oct. 1870; *s* of late Henry Gruning; *m* Mabel, *d* of E. B. Baker, late Deputy-Inspector-General Bengal Police; three *s* two *d*. *Educ:* Eastbourne College; St John's College, Cambridge. Entered ICS, 1892; Magistrate and Collector, 1906; Secretary to Government, Revenue and Gen. Departments, 1911; Magistrate and Collector, Shahabad; Magistrate Collector, Patna; Additional Commissioner, Patna, Bihar and Orissa; Commissioner of the Orissa Division, 1917–21. *Publications:* a Gazetteer; pamphlet on emigration to Assam. *Recreations:* any available game—tennis, polo, racquets. *Address:* Patna, EIR, India. *Clubs:* East India United Service; United Service, Calcutta and Simla.

Died 3 Oct. 1923.

GUARD, Lieut-Col Frederic Henry Wickham, CMG 1919; CBE 1922; DSO 1918; late Royal Scots; Squadron Leader, RAF, since 1922. Served European War, 1914–18 (despatches, DSO). *Address:* c/o Air Ministry, WC. *Died 17 June 1927.*

GUBBINS, Lieut-Col Richard Rolls, DSO 1900; JP Cumberland; King's Shropshire Light Infantry; Reserve of Officers, employed on Staff as AA and QMG, BEF; *b* 14 Dec. 1868; *e s* of late Rev. Richard Shard Gubbins, Rector of Upham, Hants, and Ellen Rolls, *sister* of 1st Baron Llangattock; *m* 1902, Agnes Edith, *e d* of late G. W. Mounsey Heysham of Castletown, Carlisle; two *s*. Entered army, 1890; Captain, 1899; Major, 1908; retired, 1912; served South Africa, 1899–1902 (despatches, Queen's medal, 3 clasps, King's medal, 2 clasps, DSO); European War, 1914–17 (despatches). *Address:* The Old Hall, Rocliffe, Carlisle. *Club:* Army and Navy.

Died 24 Jan. 1918.

GUBBINS, Lieut-General Sir (William) Launcelotte, KCB 1911 (CB 1905); MVO 1902; KHS 1909; JP (Surrey); MB; late Director-General Army Medical Service; *b* 26 July 1849; *s* of late Rev. George G. Gubbins, MA, Prebendary and Chancellor of Limerick, and Dora, *d* of Edward Purdon, JP, Lisnabin, Killucan Westmeath; *m* 1885, Florence Margaret, 2nd *d* of Rev. H. Tripp (formerly Fellow of Worcester College, Oxford) of Huntspill and Winford, Somerset; one *d*. *Educ:* Trinity College, Dublin; Erasmus Smith Scholar. Entered Army Medical Service, 1873; served Afghan War, 1878–79, with 5th Fusiliers, and subseq. on Staff of Lt-General Sir Frederick Maude, VC, was present at numerous engagements in Khyber Pass; again in Afghanistan in 1879–80, as Sanitary Officer on Staff of Lt-General Sir R. Bright, present with Expeditions against Mohmunds and Gilzais (despatches); with Egyptian Expedition, 1882; with Burmah Expedition, 1886, and in S Africa, 1899–1901, as Principal Medical Officer; 6th Division; present at relief of Kimberley; battles of Paardeberg and Driefontein; occupation of Bloemfontein, and subsequently as Principal Medical Officer, Pretoria and Pietersburg Districts (despatches, promoted Colonel); filled also various posts during Great War; was Assistant Director, Army Medical Service, War Office, 1894–99; Principal Medical Officer Home District, 1902–3; since when in a similar post in Western and Eastern Commands and Army Headquarters, India; a Commissioner Royal Hospital, Chelsea. *Recreations:* hunting, golf, cycling. *Address:* Belvedere Drive, Wimbledon. *Club:* United Service.

Died 8 July 1925.

GUEST WILLIAMS, Rev. Samuel Blackwell; Vicar of Pittington since 1895; Rural Dean of Easington, 1905; Hon. Canon of Durham, 1913; *b* 1851; *s* of late Mr Guest Williams, formerly of Manchester; *m* 1884, Catherine, *d* of late William Gray, formerly of York; three *s* one *d*. *Educ:* Shrewsbury School; Exeter College, Oxford. (Scholar) first-class Moderations; Assistant Master at Hereford and Marlborough

College; Second Master at Durham Grammar School, 1877–95; ordained, 1878. *Publications:* reviews and magazine articles. *Recreations:* cycling, golf, photography. *Address:* Prior's Hallgarth, Durham. *TA:* Littletown. *Club:* Constitutional, Durham.

Died 11 Dec. 1920.

GUILLAMORE, 5th Viscount, *cr* 1831; Hardress Standish O'Grady; Baron O'Grady, 1831; Major RA Madras (retired); *b* 20 Oct. 1841; 4th *s* of 2nd Viscount and Gertrude Jane, *d* of Hon. Berkeley Paget; *S* brother, 1877. *Educ:* Addiscombe. *Heir:* *b* Hon. Frederick Standish O'Grady, *b* 20 April 1847. *Address:* Cahir Guillamore, Kilmallock, Co. Limerick. TA: Bruff.

Died 6 Feb. 1918.

GUILLAMORE, 6th Viscount, *cr* 1831; Frederick Standish O'Grady, FZS; Baron O'Grady of Rockbarton, 1831; *b* Cahir Guillamore, Co. Limerick, 20 April 1847; *s* of 2nd Viscount Guillamore, and Gertrude Jane, *d* of Hon. Berkeley Paget; *S* brother, 1918; *m* 1st, 1881, Mary Theresa Burdett (*d* 1910), *d* of late Hon. William James Coventry; 2nd, Gertrude Lily, *y d* of J. Langford of Draycott; one *d*. *Educ:* Charterhouse; St John's College, Oxford. Winner of High Jump, Inter-Varsity Sports, 1868. Formerly Lieut Isle of Wight Artillery; travelled and resided in New Zealand, Hawaii, etc. *Recreation:* fishing and fish culture. *Heir:* *c* Hugh Hamon Massy O'Grady, *b* 5 July 1860. *Address:* Ingleside, Holt, Trowbridge, Wilts. *TA:* Holt, Wilts; Cahir Guillamore, Co. Limerick. *M:* CH 567.

Died 11 Oct. 1927.

GUINEY, Louise Imogen; *b* Boston, Mass; *o c* of Gen. P. R. Guiney and Janet Margaret Doyle. *Educ:* Elmhurst Academy, Providence; and private tutors. *Publications:* Goosequill Papers, 1885; The White Sail and other Poems, 1887; Monsieur Henri, a Footnote to French History, 1892; A Roadside Harp (poems), 1893; A Little English Gallery, 1894; Patrins (essays), 1897; "England and Yesterday", 1898; The Martyrs' Idyl and shorter Poems, 1899; Robert Emmet: his Rebellion and his Romance, 1904; Hurrell Froude: Memoranda and Comments, 1905; Blessed Edmund Campion (in St Nicholas Series), 1908; Happy Ending (collected poems), 1910; edited Selected Poems of James Clarence Mangan, Matthew Arnold, The Matchless Orinda, and Thomas Stanley; Dr T. W. Parsons' translation of Divina Commedia, 1893; Henry Vaughan's Mount of Olives, 1902; has contributed to various magazines since 1885. *Recreations:* walking, canoeing. *Address:* Grangeleigh, Amberley, Glos.

Died 2 Nov. 1920.

GUINNESS, Lieut Eric Cecil, DSO 1918; Adjutant, 2nd Irish Regiment since 1920; *b* 30 Aug. 1894; *s* of Robert Cecil Day Guinness and Madeline Ride Guinness, of Bury House, Baldock, Herts; *m* 1916, Hannah Mary, *d* of late Robert Marlborough Pryor of Western Park, Stevenage, Herts; one *s* one *d*. Served European War, 1914–18 (despatches, DSO). *Club:* Junior Army and Navy.

Died 11 Sept. 1920.

GUINNESS, Col Henry William Newton, CB 1900; late Assistant Adjutant General, 5th Division; *b* 5 Aug. 1854; *s* of late Rev. W. N. Guinness, Collooney, Co. Sligo; *m* 1893, Frances Helen, *d* of late Henry West, QC, Loughlinstown House, Co. Dublin; one *s*. *Educ:* Newton Abbot College. Joined 18th Regt 1873; Captain Royal Irish Regt, 1881; Brevet Major, 1885; Lieut-Col, 1889; served in Afghan War, 1880 (medal); Nile Expedition, 1884–85 (despatches, medal and clasp, Khedive's Star, Brevet Major); S Africa, 1900–1 (despatches, CB, medal and three clasps, King's medal and two clasps).

Died 5 Aug. 1925.

GUISE, Sir William Francis George, 5th Bt, *cr* 1783; JP, DL; Hon. Colonel 3rd Battalion Gloucestershire Regiment; *b* 14 Dec. 1851; 2nd *s* of Sir William Vernon Guise, 4th Bt and Margaret Anna Maria, *e d* of Rev. D. H. Lee-Warner of Tyberton Court, Herefords, and Walsingham Abbey, Norfolk; *S* father, 1887; *m* 1887, Ada Caroline, *d* of late Octavius Edward Coope, MP, Rochetts, Brentwood; one *s* one *d* (and one *s* decd). *Educ:* Elton. Patron of two livings; High Sheriff, 1893. Owner of about 2100 acres. *Heir:* *s* Anselm William Edward Guise, *b* 18 Sept. 1888. *Address:* Elmore Court, Gloucester. *Clubs:* Brooks's, Wellington.

Died 17 Jan. 1920.

GUITRY, Lucien; actor; *b* Paris, 1860; *m* 1882; one *s*. Spent nine years in Russia, Théâtre Michael, Petrograd; Manager of Porte St Martin; Director of Renaissance Theatre. Principal parts: L'Assommoir; La Veine; L'Adversaire; Le Mannequin d'osier; La Griffe; Le Voleur; Sampson; L'Emigré; Chantecler.

Died 1 June 1925.

GULL, Cyril Arthur Edward Ranger; *b* 1876; *e s* of Rev. J. E. Gull, Rector of Rushall. *Educ:* Denstone; Oxford University. Member Literary Staff, Saturday Review, 1897–98; also Bookman, and Academy; Editor, London Life, 1899; then joined Editorial Staff, Daily Mail, afterwards Daily Express; gave up journalism for novel writing. *Publications:* The Hypocrite, 1898; Miss Malevolent, 1899; From the Book Beautiful, 1900; Back to Lilacland, 1901; The Cigarette Smoker, 1901; The Serf, 1902; His Grace's Grace, 1903; Portalone, 1904; The Harvest of Love, 1905; The Soul Stealer, 1906; When Satan Ruled, 1911; under name of Guy Thorne published When It Was Dark (500th thousand); A Lost Cause; First It Was Ordained; Made In His Image; The Charioteer, 1907; I Believe, 1907; The Angel, 1908; The Socialist, 1909; Not in Israel, 1913; The Drunkard, 1912; Love and the Freemason, The Secret Service Submarine, The Cruiser on Wheels, the Secret Seaplane, 1914–15. *Recreations:* shooting, especially wild fowling, French literature, travelling. *Clubs:* Primrose, Cocoa Tree.   *Died 9 Jan. 1923.*

GULL, Sir (William) Cameron, 2nd Bt; *cr* 1872; OBE 1918; JP; Alderman, County Council, Berks; *b* 6 Jan. 1860; *s* of Sir William Withey Gull, 1st Bt and Susan Anne, *d* of Col J. Dacre Lacy; *S* father, 1890; *m* 1st, 1886, Hon. Annie Clayton Lindley (*d* 1908), *d* of Rt Hon. Lord Lindley; one *s* three *d* (and one *s* one *d* decd); 2nd, 1910, Evelyn Louisa (*d* 1914), *d* of late His Hon. Sir Thomas Snagge; one *s* one *d*. *Educ:* Eton; Christ Church, Oxford. 1st Class Law and Vinerian Scholar; Barrister, Lincoln's Inn, 1886. London School Board, 1891–94. Contested (LU) Moray and Nairn, 1892; MP (U) Barnstaple Div. Devon, 1895–1900; High Sheriff of Berks 1908. *Heir:* *s* Richard Cameron Gull, Rifle Brigade [*b* 18 March 1894; *m* 1917, Dora, *d* of late Sir T. Dyer, Bt. *Educ:* Eton; Christ Church, Oxford; Sandhurst. Served European War, 1914–16 (despatches, wounded)]. *Address:* Frilsham House, Yattendon, Berks. *Club:* Athenæum.
                                          Died 15 Dec. 1922.

GULLAND, Rt. Hon. John William, PC 1917; MP (L) Dumfries Burghs, 1906–18; *b* Edinburgh, 1864; *s* of late John Gulland, Magistrate of City of Edinburgh; *m* 1912, Edith Mary, *d* of late Walter Allen of Whitefield. *Educ:* Edinburgh High School and University. Was a corn merchant; director of Edinburgh Chamber of Commerce; lecturer on Practice of Commerce in Heriot-Watt College, 1898–99; member Edinburgh School Board, 1900–6; Edinburgh Town Council, 1904–6; JP, County of City of Edinburgh; on Advisory Committee of United Free Church; Hon. Treas. of Scottish Liberal Association; late Hon. President Young Scots Society; Secretary to Scottish Liberal Committee in House of Commons, 1906–9; Junior Lord of the Treasury and Scottish Whip, 1909–15; Joint Parliamentary Secretary to Treasury, 1915–17. *Publications:* numerous pamphlets, leaflets, and magazine articles. *Recreations:* cycling, golf, angling. *Address:* 23 Sumner Place, SW7. *T:* Kensington 5895. *Clubs:* Reform, National Liberal; Scottish Liberal, Edinburgh; Glasgow Liberal.
                                          Died 26 Jan. 1920.

GUNDRY, Richard Simpson, CB 1904; *b* 1838; *s* of Richard Hickley Gundry of Hillworth Cottage, Devizes. *Educ:* privately; Brussels. Editor of the North China Herald and correspondent of the Times in China, 1865–78; Hon. Sec. to the China Association in London from its formation in 1889 to 1901; President, 1905–8; a frequent contributor to the principal reviews. *Publications:* China and Her Neighbours; China Present and Past, etc. *Address:* Hillworth Cottage, Devizes. *Club:* Conservative.
                                          Died 13 March 1924.

GUNN, Sir John, Kt 1898; *b* 28 Oct. 1837; *s* of Donald Gunn of Achalybster, Caithness; *m* 1st, 1871, Sarah Jane (*d* 1874), *o d* of Thomas Hill of Cardiff; 2nd, 1877, Harriette (*d* 1914), *d* of James Boyle of Ballymacrea, Co. Antrim. President, Cardiff Chamber of Commerce, 1886–87, Chamber of Shipping, 1889. JP Co. Glamorgan and City of Cardiff. *Address:* Ty-to-Maen, St Mellons, near Cardiff; Mountstewart Square, Cardiff. *Clubs:* Reform; County Cardiff.
                                          Died 20 Jan. 1918.

GUNNING, Col Orlando George, CMG 1915; DSO 1917; 3rd Battalion (Reserve) Manchester Regiment; late Indian Army; *b* 31 July 1867; *m* 1902, Margaret Cecilia, *d* of late Clinton Dawkins; one *s* two *d*. Joined Manchester Regt 1888; Captain Indian army, 1899; Major, 1906; Lt-Col 1914; served Miranzai Expedition, 1891 (medal with clasp); Expedition to Dongola, 1896 (Egyptian medal, medal); NW Frontier, India, 1897–98 (severely wounded, despatches twice, medal with clasp); European War, 1914–15 (CMG, Bt Col); Mesopotamia, 1916–17 (despatches, DSO). *Club:* East India United Service.   *Died 15 Nov. 1917.*

GUNSAULUS, Frank Wakeley, DD, LLD; President of Armou[r] Institute of Technology since 1892; Lyman Beecher Lecturer o[n] Preaching at Yale Divinity School, 1911; *b* Chesterville, Ohio, 1 Ja[n] 1856; *s* of Hon. Joseph Gunsaulus, of Spanish extraction, and Mar[y] J. Hawley, of English extraction; *m* 1875, Anna Long of West Virgini[a;] one *s* four *d*. *Educ:* Delaware Wesleyan Coll., Ohio. Began preachin[g] in the ME Church at 19 years; Columbus, Ohio, first importan[t] church; left ME Church for Congregational, 1881; called t[o] Newtonville, Massachusetts; Baltimore, Maryland, and Chicag[o,] Illinois; Divinity Lecturer at Yale University, 1890; Professoria[l] Lecturer at University of Chicago, 1896; Lecturer Chicag[o] Theological Seminary, 1905; DD Beloit College, 1889; LLD Ohi[o] Wesleyan University, 1905; Miami University, Oxford, LLD 1908[.] *Publications:* November at Eastwood; Transfiguration of Chris[t;] Sermons, 1881–86; Monk and Knight, historical romance; Phidia[s] and other Poems, 1891; Loose Leaves of Song, 1893; Songs of Nigh[t] and Day, 1895; Gladstone, the Man and His Times, 1898; Man o[f] Galilee, 1899; *sermons:* Paths to Power, 1905; Paths to the City o[f] God, 1906; *essays:* The Higher Ministries of Recent English Poetry[,] 1907; The Minister and the Spiritual Life, 1911; *lecturing:* Savonarola[;] John Hampden; Oliver Cromwell; Washington; Wendell Phillips[;] Five Points of American Statesmanship. *Address:* Armour Institut[e] of Technology, Chicago, Ill. *Clubs:* Union League, Congregational[,] Mayflower, Colonial Wars, Society, University.
                                          Died 17 March 192[1]

GUNTER, Col Sir Robert Benyon Nevill, 2nd Bt, *cr* 1901; JP; 3r[d] Battalion Yorkshire Regiment; *b* 4 Aug. 1871; *e s* of Sir Robert Gunter[,] 1st Bt, MP, and Jane Marguerite, *d* of Thomas Benyon, of Gledhow Hall, Yorkshire; *S* father, 1905; *m* 1902, Clara Lydia, *widow* of John Pritchard-Barrett; one *s*. Served S African War, 1900–2 (despatches[,] Queen's medal with two clasps, King's medal with two clasps). *Heir:* *s* Ronald Vernon Gunter, *b* 8 March 1904. *Address:* Wetherby Grange[,] Wetherby, Yorkshire. *Clubs:* Carlton, Hurlingham; Yorkshire, York[.]
                                          Died 20 Aug. 1917

GUNTHER, Ven. William James, MA; Canon of St Andrew['s] Cathedral, Sydney; Archdeacon of Camden; Administrator of th[e] Diocese, 1910; *b* Wellington, NSW, 28 May 1839; *s* of Archdeaco[n] Günther; *m* 1868, Mary Jane Willis; three *s* two *d*. *Educ:* The King['s] School, Parramatta; Queen's College, Oxon. Ordained Deacon, 1863[,] Priest, 1864; Curate of Stapenhill, Derbyshire, 1863–65; St Philip's[,] Sydney, 1866–68; Rector of St John's, Parramatta, 1867–1910; Fellow[w] of St Paul's Coll., University of Sydney, 1884; Commissary, 1902–9[;] Vicar-General diocese of Sydney, 1902. *Publications:* Sermons, an[d] Lecture, The Church of England in Australia; various papers. *Address[:]* 259 Walker Street, North Sydney, NSW.

                                          Died 1918[?]

GUPPY, Henry Brougham, MB, CM Edin. 1876; FRS 1918; FRSE[;] FLS; Gold Medallist, Linnæan Society, 1917; *b* Dec. 1854; *s* of T[.] S. Guppy, MD, Falmouth; *m* 1st, 1887, Annie, *d* of J. Jordon; 2nd[,] 1900, Letitia, *d* of A. J. Warde, Yalding, Kent; no *c*. *Educ:* King['s] School, Sherborne; Queen's College, Birmingham; St Bartholomew's[s] Hospital, London; Edinburgh University. Served in the Medica[l] Service of the Royal Navy, 1876–85, being Surgeon of HMS Horne[t] on the China and Japan station, 1877–80, and of HMS Lark, [a] surveying schooner in the Western Pacific, 1881–84; investigate[d] coral-reef formation and plant-dispersal in the Keeling Islands an[d] West Java, 1887–88; botanical and geological exploration in th[e] Hawaiian and Fijian Islands, 1896–1900; investigating the littoral flor[a] of the Pacific side of South America from the Straits of Magellan t[o] Panama, 1903–4; after a short visit to Teneriffe, 1905, spent th[e] winters of 1907–11 in the West Indies in botanical work; made [a] detailed examination of the flora of Mount Pico in the Azores[,] 1913–14. *Publications:* two volumes on the Solomon Islands, 1887[;] one volume on the Homes of Family Names, 1890; two volumes[s] on his observations in the Pacific in Hawaii and Fiji, 1903–6; on[e] volume on Studies in Seeds and Fruits, 1912; and one volume dealing[g] with results obtained in the West Indies and Azores, 1917. *Recreations[:]* walking, boating. *Address:* Red House, Fowey.

                                          Died 23 April 1926

GUPTA, Bihari Lal, CSI 1914; retired Indian Civil Service Pensioner[;] *b* Calcutta, of Hindu parents of high caste, 26 Oct. 1849; *m* 1872[,] widower; three *s* four *d*. *Educ:* Calcutta; London University. Passed[d] ICS open competitive examination, 1869; called to Bar, Middl[e] Temple, 1871; joined the Civil Service in India (Bengal); served in[n] various districts; was Presidency Magistrate and Coroner of Calcutt[a] for 5 years, and then District and Sessions Judge; was Remembrance[r] and Superintendent of Legal Affairs, Bengal, and member Benga[l] Council; raised to the Bench of the Calcutta High Court whenc[e] he retired, 1907; Minister of Law and Justice in the Baroda State, 1909; chief minister, 1912; retired 1914 to travel in Europe with HH the Maharaja Gaekwar; Degrees of Honour in Sanskrit and Persian; Delhi Durbar medals of 1903 and 1912. *Address:* 9 Lower Rawdon Street, Calcutta. *Club:* Calcutta.

Died 20 Nov. 1916.

GUPTA, Sir Krishna Govinda, KCSI 1911 (CSI 1909); Barrister-at-law, Middle Temple, 1873; late ICS; *b* Bhatpara, Dacca, 28 Feb. 1851; *e s* of Kali Narayan Gupta; *m* 1866, Prasannatara (*d* 1908), *d* of Nabin Chandra Das; three *s* five *d*. *Educ:* Mymensing Government School; Dacca Coll.; London University College. Joined Indian Civil Service, 1873 (2nd at the final examination); passed through all the grades in Bengal; Secretary, Board of Revenue, 1887; Commissioner of Excise, 1893; Divisional Commissioner, 1901; Member Board of Revenue, 1904, being the first Indian to hold that appointment; Member Indian Excise Committee, 1905; on special duty in connection with the Fisheries of Bengal, 1906; deputed to Europe and America in 1907 to carry on fishery investigation, as a result of which a new department has been organised to conserve and develop the provincial fisheries; nominated to the Indian Council, 1907, being one of the two Indians who were for the first time raised to that position; retired from India Office on completion of term, March 1915; Member, Lord Esher's Army in India Committee, 1920. *Clubs:* National Liberal; Calcutta. *Died March 1926.*

GURDON, Maj.-Gen. Evelyn Pulteney; Indian Army; *b* 4 June 1833; *e s* of late Rev. Philip Gurdon, MA, JP, of Cranworth, Norfolk, and Henrietta Laura, *e d* of late J. Pulteney of Northerwood House, Lyndhurst, Hants; *m* 1858, Mary, 2nd *d* of late Maj.-Gen. R. T. Sandeman, Indian Army, and *sister* of late Col Sir Robert Sandeman, KCSI; three *s* one *d*. Entered army, 1852; Maj.-General, 1892; Punjab Commission, 1860–90; Commissioner and Divisional Judge and JP Punjab; served Indian Mutiny, 1857 (despatches, medal). *Address:* 12 Norton Road, Hove, Brighton. *Club:* Hove.

Died 5 Feb. 1921.

GURNEY, Sir Eustace, Kt 1911; JP; Lord Mayor of Norwich, 1910–11; *b* 4 Oct. 1876; 2nd *s* of late John Gurney, Sprowston Hall, Norfolk, and Isabel, *d* of Robert Blake Humfrey (she *m* 2nd, 1901, 5th Lord Talbot de Malahide); *m* 1904, Anne Agatha, *d* of late John Lee-Warner; three *s* four *d*. *Educ:* Eton; New College, Oxford. *Address:* Walsingham Abbey, Norfolk. *Clubs:* Athenæum, New University. *Died 3 Dec. 1927.*

GURNEY, John Henry, JP, DL; *b* 31 July 1848; *m* Margaret Jane, *d* of Henry Edmund Gurney; one *s* three *d*. *Educ:* Harrow. Elected member of the Zoological Society, 1868, of the British Ornithologists Union, 1870, and of the Linnæan Society, 1885. *Publications:* works on ornithology. *Address:* Keswick Hall, Norfolk. *Club:* Athenæum. *Died 8 Nov. 1922.*

GURNEY, Sir Somerville Arthur, KCVO 1909; JP, DL; Director of Barclay and Co., Ltd; *b* 21 Oct. 1835; *y s* of late Daniel Gurney and Lady Harriet Jemima, 3rd *d* of 17th Earl of Erroll; *m* 1857, Katharine, *d* of A. Hamond of Westacre, Norfolk; two *s* four *d*. *Address:* North Runcton Hall, Lynn. *Club:* White's.

Died 17 May 1917.

GURNEY, Sir Walter Edwin, Kt 1919; Auditor-General, Union of South Africa, since 1910. *Address:* Cape Town, South Africa.

Died 8 Jan. 1924.

GURNHILL, Rev. James, BA; Canon of Lincoln; Member of the Aristotelian Society. *Educ:* Emmanuel College, Cambridge. *Publication:* Through Creative Evolution to Incarnation and the Goal of Humanity, 1926. *Address:* The Priory, Minster Yard, Lincoln.

Died 5 Feb. 1928.

GUTHRIE, Hon. Lord; Charles John Guthrie, MA; FRSE; FSA (Scot.); Hon. LLD Edin.; Senator of the College of Justice in Scotland since 1907; Sheriff of Ross, Cromarty, and Sutherland, and one of the Commissioners of Northern Lights, 1900–7; *b* Edinburgh, 1849; *s* of late Rev. Thomas Guthrie, DD, Edinburgh, one of the founders of Ragged Schools, and first editor of The Sunday Magazine; *m* 1876, Anne, *d* of Rev. J. C. Burns, DD, Kirkliston; two *s* three *d*. *Educ:* High School and Univ. of Edin. Admitted Advocate at the Scotch Bar 1875; QC 1897; Mem. Edin. School Board, 1879–81; Legal Adviser of Free Church of Scotland, 1881–1900, and of United Free Church, 1900–2; Chairman, House-letting Commission, 1906–7; Member of the Royal Commission on Historical Monuments in Scotland, 1908; Member of the Royal Commission on Divorce, 1910;

Chairman of Early Scottish Text Society, 1910; President of the Boys' Brigade of Great Britain and Ireland, 1910–19; President of Royal Scottish Geographical Society, 1917–19; member of Councils of Antiquarian and Scottish History Societies. *Publications:* joint-author of Memoir of Thomas Guthrie, DD, 1875; John Knox and his House, 1898; editor of The History of the Reformation in Scotland, by John Knox, 1898; Cummy, R. L. Stevenson's nurse, an Appreciation, 1914. *Recreations:* travel, antiquities, music. *Address:* 13 Royal Circus, Edinburgh; Swanston Cottage, Midlothian. *T:* Edinburgh 2049. *Clubs:* Royal Societies; University, Edinburgh.

Died 28 April 1920.

GUTHRIE, David Charles; *b* 25 July 1861; *e s* of late James Alexander Guthrie and Ellinor, 2nd *d* of late Admiral Sir James Stirling (she *m* 2nd, 1879, Forster Fitzgerland Arbuthnot); *m* 1891, Mary, *d* of late Andrew Low, of Savannah, USA; one *s* two *d*. *Educ:* Eton; Christ Church, Oxford. MP (L) Northamptonshire (S Div.), 1892–95. *Address:* Craigie, Dundee; East Haddon Hall, Northampton.

Died 12 Jan. 1918.

GUTHRIE, John Douglas Maude, JP, DL; *b* 1856; *o s* of John Guthrie (*d* 1877) and Harriet (*d* 1879), *e d* of late Barnabas Maude; *m* 1884, Mary Macpherson (Myra), *d* of late Duncan Davidson, of Tulloch, Ross-shire; four *s* one *d*. *Educ:* Harrow. Captain, retired, late 19th Hussars; served Egypt, 1882 (medals, Tel-el-Kebir and Khedive's Star). Lord of the Barony of Guthrie. *Recreations:* hunting, coaching, fishing, shooting. *Address:* Guthrie Castle, Guthrie, Scotland. *Club:* Junior United Service. *Died 27 Jan. 1928.*

GUTHRIE, Leonard George, MA, MD Oxon; FRCP Lond.; Senior Physician Children's Hospital, Paddington Green; Physician Hospital for Epilepsy and Paralysis, Maida Vale, W; Consulting Physician Home of Rest for the Dying, Clapham, and Potters Bar Cottage Hospital; *b* 7 Feb. 1858; 2nd *s* of late Thomas Anstey and Augusta Guthrie, of Kensington; unmarried. *Educ:* King's College School; Magdalen College, Oxford University; St Bartholomew's Hospital, London. *Publications:* various contributions to medical journals and societies. *Recreation:* study of antiquities of all sorts. *Address:* 15 Upper Berkeley Street, Portman Square, W. *T:* 1623 Pad. *Club:* United University. *Died 28 Dec. 1918.*

GUTTERY, Rev. Arthur Thomas, DD; Minister, Princes Avenue Primitive Methodist Church, Liverpool; President National Free Church Council; *b* Birmingham, 15 June 1862; *s* of Rev. Thos Guttery; *m d* of Rev. E. Alford; three *s* three *d*. *Educ:* Elinfield College, York; London University. Entered Ministry, 1883; General Secretary Primitive Methodist Missionary Society, 1908–13; President, Primitive Methodist Conference, 1916; Hartley Lecturer, 1920. *Publications:* constant writer in weekly and daily press both in England and America. *Recreations:* golf, chess. *Address:* Elmfield, Hartington Road, Sefton Park, Liverpool. *T:* Wavertree 420, Liverpool. *Club:* Liverpool Reform. *Died 17 Dec. 1920.*

GUY, John Crawford, MA, LLB; Advocate; Sheriff-Substitute of the Lothians and Peebles at Edinburgh, 1904–21; *b* Shawlands, Renfrewshire, 10 March 1861; *s* of John Guy, solicitor, Glasgow; *m* 1891, Jessie, *d* of John Morrison, Ruadhsgeir, Pollokshields, Glasgow; two *s*. *Educ:* Church of Scotland Training College, and University, Glasgow. Advocate, 1886; appointed Counsel for the Crown in *ultimus hæres* cases, 1895; Sheriff Court Depute, 1899; Extra Advocate Depute, 1899; Advocate Depute, 1901. *Address:* Carsaig House, North Knapdale, Argyllshire.

Died 18 Jan. 1928.

GUY, Lt-Col Robert Francis, CMG 1919; DSO 1916; Duke of Edinburgh's (Wiltshire) Regiment; *b* 1878; *e s* of late R. J. Guy; *m* 1915, Mrs M. A. Dolphin (*née* de Blaquière) of Turoe, Loughrea, Co. Galway. *Educ:* Monkton Combe School, near Bath. Joined the Wiltshire Regt in South Africa, from the 9th KRRC, 1900; served S African War, 1900–2 (Queen's medal with 3 clasps, King's medal with 2 clasps); Railway Staff Officer, 1901–2, at railhead, N Transvaal; Adjutant, 1st Batt. Wiltshire Regt in India, 1905–8; Brigade-Major to York and Durham Infantry Brigade (TF), 1912–16; served European War, 1915–19, as a General Staff Officer (despatches 8 times, DSO, CMG, Bt Lt-Col). *Address:* The Barracks, Devizes, Wilts.

Died 2 Oct. 1927.

GWALIOR, HH Maharajah Scindia of; Hon. Lt-Gen. HH Mukhtar-ul-Mulk, Azim-ul-Iktidar, Raflush Shan, Wala Shikoh, Mohtasham-i-Dauran, Umdat-ul-Umara, Maharajadhiraja, Alijah Hisam-us-Saltanat; **Maharaja Sir Madhav Rao Scindia,** GCSI 1895; GCVO 1902; GBE 1917; Bahadur Srinath, Mansur-i-Zaman,

Fidvi-i-Hazrat-i-Malika-i-Muazzam-i-Rafl-ud-Darja-i-Inglistan, Hon. LLD Cambridge; DCL Oxon; Hon. Lt-Gen. in the Army; Hon. and Extra ADC to the King; Hon. Col 1st Duke of York's Own Lancers, 1906; *b* 20 Oct. 1876; *S* 1886. Made Hon. Col British Army, 1898; Maj.-Gen.; went to China as Orderly Officer to General Gaselee, 1901 (medal); provided the expedition with a hospital ship; organised the hospital ship Loyalty in 1914 and financed it for the duration of the war; his troops fought with distinction in France, East Africa, Egypt, and Mesopotamia; granted salute of 21 guns at 1911 Durbar; salute made hereditary in 1917; Kaiser-i-Hind medal, 1900; London Coronation medals 1902 and 1911; Delhi Coronation medals, 1903 and 1911. *Heir: s* George Jivaji Rao, *b* 26 June 1916 (to whom the King stood sponsor). *Address:* Gwalior, Central India; Shivpuri, Central India. *Club:* Marlborough.

Died 5 June 1925.

GWATKIN, Rev. Henry Melvill, MA; Dixie Professor of Ecclesiastical History, Cambridge University, and Fellow of Emmanuel College since 1891; Gifford Lecturer, Edinburgh University, 1903–5; Hon. DD Edin.; *y s* of Rev. R. Gwatkin, formerly Tutor of St John's College, Cambridge; *m* 1874, Lucy de L., *d* of Rev. Thos Brock, Vicar of St John's Guernsey; one *s* one *d. Educ:* Shrewsbury School; St John's College, Cambridge; 1st Class Honours Math., Classics, Moral Science, Theology; Carus Greek Test Prize, 1865 and 1869; Crosse Scholar, 1869; Tyrwhitt Hebrew Scholar, 1870. Fellow, St John's Coll., Cambridge, 1868–74; Theological Lecturer, 1874–91. *Publications:* Studies of Arianism, 1882; The Arian Controversy, 1889; Selections from Early Christian Writers, 1893; Editor of the Church Past and Present, 1899; The Eye for Spiritual Things (Sermons); The Knowledge of God (Gifford Lectures, 1906); Early Church History, 1909; Joint Editor of Cambridge Medieval History since 1911. *Address:* 8 Scrope Terrace, and Emmanuel College, Cambridge.   *Died 14 Nov. 1916.*

GWATKIN, Maj.-Gen. Sir Willoughby Garnons, KCMG 1920 (CMG 1918); CB 1916; LLD Toronto; Hon. Major-General (retired); Major-General and Hon. Lieutenant-General Canadian Militia; *b* 11 Aug. 1859; 4th *s* of late Frederick Gwatkin of 9 New Square, Lincoln's Inn, and Grove House, Twickenham. *Educ:* Shrewsbury; King's College, Cambridge; Sandhurst. Appointed to Manchester Regiment, 1882, and Colonel of it since 1924. Grand Officer of the Order of St Sava; Commander of the Legion of Honour; Commander of the Crown of Belgium. *Clubs:* United Service, Garrick, Sports.

Died 2 Feb. 1925.

GWILLIM, John Cole, BSc; Professor of Mining, Queen's University, Kingston, since 1902; *b* England; *m* 1900, Jane Birch, Vancouver, BC. *Address:* Queen's University, Kingston, Ontario. *Club:* Frontenac, Kingston.   *Died 1920.*

GWYNN, Rev. John, DD Dublin; DCL Oxon; Regius Professor of Divinity, Dublin University, 1888–1907; *b* Larne, 28 Aug. 1827; *e s* of Rev. Stephen Gwynn; *m* 1862, Lucy (*d* 1907), *e d* of late Wm Smith O'Brien, of Cahirmoyle, Co. Limerick; six *s* two *d. Educ:* Royal School, Enniskillen; Trinity Coll. Dublin. Fellow 1853–64; Warden of St Columba's, 1856–64; Rector of Tullyaughnish, 1863–82; Dean of Raphoe, 1873–82; Rector of Templemore and Dean of Derry, 1882–83; Archbishop King's Lecturer in Divinity (Dublin Univ.), 1883–88. *Publications:* Commentary on Epistle to Philippians, with Introduction (in Speaker's Commentary), 1881; several articles in Smith and Wace's Dictionary of Christian Biography, and in Hermathena; also, The Apocalypse in a Syriac Version hitherto unknown, with critical notes, etc; with Introductory Dissertation on the Syriac Versions of the Apocalypse, 1897; Selections from Ephraim and Aphrahat, translated from the Syriac, with Introduction, 1898; Remnants of the later Syriac Versions of the Old and New Testament, 1909; the Book of Armagh, with Introduction, 1913. *Address:* Trinity College, Dublin; Ashbrook, Clontarf.

Died 2 April 1917.

GWYNNE, Major-General Nadolig Ximenes; Hon. Major-General (retired); *b* Glanbràn, Carmarthenshire, 25 Dec. 1832; *m* Mary Shee Jackson, *d* of Major G. C. Jackson, 16th Lancers. *Educ:* Cheltenham; Llandovery. Received Commission in 41st The Welch Regt 1855; served on the Staff in India and in the Afghan Expeditions of 1878–80; commanded the 85th, 2nd King's Shropshire Light Infantry; half pay, 1887; PSC; raised 5th Batt. Devon Volunteers, 1914. *Address:* Brockendean, Bournemouth.

Died 9 May 1920.

GWYNNE, Rupert Sackville; MP (C) Eastbourne, Southern Division of Sussex, 1910–24; Financial Secretary, War Office, 1923–24; *b* 2

Aug. 1873; *s* of late James Eglinton Anderson Gwynne, of Folkington Manor, Sussex; *m* 1905, Hon. Stella Ridley, *d* of 1st Viscount Ridley; four *d. Educ:* Shrewsbury; Pembroke College, Cambridge (BA 1895). Called to Bar, Inner Temple, 1898. *Address:* Wootton Manor, Polegate, Sussex; 47 Catherine Street, SW1. *T:* Victoria 5335. *Clubs:* Bachelors', Carlton.   *Died 12 Oct. 1924.*

GWYNNE-EVANS, Sir William, 1st Bt, *cr* 1913; Director of the Real Estate Corporation of South Africa; *b* 3 Feb. 1845; *m* 1st, 1886, Mary Anna (*d* 1902), *d* of Evan Williams; one *s* four *d* (and one *d* decd); 2nd, 1909, Blanche Sophia, *d* of Rev. J. C. E. Besant, Vicar of Lydney; one *s* one *d.* Gave to the nation the Arthur Morrison collection of Chinese and Japanese Paintings now at the British Museum. *Heir: s* Evan Gwynne Gwynne-Evans [*b* 4 May 1877; *m* 1908, Ada, *d* of W. S. Andrews, New York; two *s. Address:* Oaklands Park, Newnham, Co. Gloucester]. *Address:* 93 Queen's Gate, SW1. *T:* Western 4096; Penlan Hall, Fordham, Essex. *Clubs:* Queen's; Rand, Johannesburg.   *Died 23 Jan. 1927.*

GWYTHER, Ven. Arthur; Archdeacon of Demerara, 1896–1910; Canon of St George's Cathedral, Georgetown, 1894–1910; Incumbent of St Philip's, Georgetown, 1896–1910. *Educ:* St John's College, Cambridge (MA). Ordained, 1874; Curate of Weybridge, 1874–75; Headmaster, Queen's College Grammar School, Georgetown, 1875–77; Vicar of St Paul's, Wakenaam, 1877–80; missionary, Demerara River, 1880–88; Chaplain, HM Penal Settlement, Mazaruni, 1888–90; Rector of Holy Trinity, Essequibo, 1890–96; Clerical Assessor, 1896–1910; Vicar-General, 1897, 1899, 1902, 1904–10; Administrator of Diocese, 1900; Chaplain Georgetown Gaol (unpaid), 1897–1910 (retired 1910); Licensed Preacher, Diocese Lincoln, 1912–15. *Address:* Rawnsley, Capstone Road, Bournemouth.   *Died 21 Feb. 1921.*

GWYTHER, Frank Edwin, CIE 1914; Secretary to Government, Punjab, since 1912. *Educ:* Thomasson College. Entered Public Works Department, India, 1881; Executive Engineer, 1895; Under Secretary to Government, 1904; Superintending Engineer, 1908. *Address:* Public Works Department, Lahore, Punjab.

Died 6 Sept. 1918.

GYE, Percy; His Honour Judge Gye; County Court Judge for Hampshire since 1896; *b* 25 Nov. 1845; 4th *s* of late Frederick Gye; *m* 1880, Constance, 3rd *d* of James Sant, RA; two *s* one *d. Educ:* privately. Called to Bar, Inner Temple, 1872. *Address:* Piper's Field, Winchester, Hants. *TA:* Gye, Winchester. *Club:* Hampshire County.

Died 13 June 1916.

H

HABBERTON, John; author; *b* 24 Feb. 1842; father, English; mother, American; *m* 1868; two *s* two *d. Educ:* various schools, no college. Printer, soldier, merchant, journalist, author. *Publications:* Helen's Babies; All He Knew; Life of George Washington; Brueton's Bayou; Caleb Wright; Some Boys' Doings; The Tiger and the Insect, and other books; his only play, Deacon Crankett, had a two years' run. *Recreations:* sailing and gardening. *Address:* Montclair, New Jersey, USA.   *Died 25 Feb. 1921.*

HACKER, Arthur, RA 1910 (ARA 1894); RI 1918; figure painter; *b* London, 25 Sept. 1858; 2nd *s* of Edward Hacker, line engraver; *m* 1907, Lilian, 3rd *d* of late Edward Price-Edwards. *Educ:* London, Paris. Student Royal Academy, 1876; studied Atelier Bonnat, Paris, 1880–81; travelled in Morocco, Algeria, Spain, Italy, etc. *Pictures:* Her Daughter's Legacy, 1880; The Mother; Children's Prayer, and other domestic subjects; Pelagia and Philammon, 1887; Via Victis; Christ and the Magdalen; Annunciation; The Cloud; Vale; Studies of London, etc; also many portraits. *Recreations:* river, billiards. *Address:* 178 Cromwell Road, SW. *Club:* Arts.

Died 12 Nov. 1919.

HACKETT, Hon. Sir John Winthrop, KCMG 1918; Kt 1911; JP; MLC; MA; Hon. LLD Dublin 1902; Member Legislative Council, West Australia, 1890, subseq. Senior Member; *b* Ireland, 1848; *s* of late Rev. J. W. Hackett, MA, and Jane, *d* of late H. Monck Mason, LLD, Librarian, King's Inns; *m* 1905, Deborah, *d* of Frederick Slade Drake-Brockman, Perth; one *s* four *d*. *Educ:* Trinity College, Dublin. Editor and Proprietor of the West Australian and Western Mail, Perth; member of Irish, NSW, WA, and Victorian Bars; late member Federal Council of Australasia. Offered Knighthood 1902, but declined; Delegate National Australasian Federal Convention, 1891, and Federal Convention, 1897–98; Past Grand Master Freemasons, West Australian Grand Lodge; President Zoological Gardens, West Australian Museum, Library, and National Gallery, etc; Registrar of diocese of Perth, and Chancellor of Cathedral; Chairman of Royal Commission on the establishment of a State University in WA; First Chancellor of the University, 1912; First Hon. degree in University of LLD; founded first Chair, that of Agriculture, in University. *Address:* St George's Terrace, Perth, Western Australia. *Clubs:* National Liberal; Weld, Perth, WA; South-Western, Bunbury; Albany, Albany, WA. *Died 19 Feb. 1916.*

ACKETT, Col Robert Isaac Dalby, CBE 1919; MA, MD with honours; retired pay; *b* 31 March 1857; *s* of Thomas Hackett, JP, Castletown, King's County; *m* 1895, Evelyn Mary Wynne Jones; one *s* one *d*. *Educ:* Chesterfield School; Queen's University, Ireland. Entered Army Medical Service, 1881; served in Cyprus and Egypt, 1882; Sudan, 1885; in Nova Scotia, 1886–7; South Africa, 1888–94, in Denizulu Rebellion; South African War, 1899–1902; South Africa 1902–6 and 1910–11; in India as Administrative Officer, Sialkote and Abbotabad Brigades, 1911–12; retired, 1912; rejoined for European War. *Address:* Ocala, Eldorado Road, Cheltenham. *Club:* New, Cheltenham. *Died 15 Feb. 1925.*

ACKETT, Very Rev. T. Aylmer P., DD; Dean of Limerick since 1913; Chaplain to Forces; *b* 5 December 1854; *e s* of Thomas Hackett, JP, Castletown, King's Co.; *m* 1st, 1880, Helen, *d* of James Whiteside, MD, Ballyarton, Coleraine; two *s* one *d*; 2nd, Ella T., *d* of Col T. H. Maginniss. *Educ:* Chesterfield College; Trinity College, Dublin. Graduated 1877 as Senior Moderator in Mental and Moral Philosophy, after taking honours in several subjects; BD 1889, DD 1890. Curate of Coleraine, 1877–80; Curate in Charge of Newcastle West, 1880–81; Rector of Kilmallock, 1881–1910; Chancellor, 1904; Archdeacon of Limerick, 1912–13; Rector of St Michael's, Limerick, 1910–13; Canon of St Patrick's, 1907; Member of Board of Patronage, Diocesan Court; Church Representative Body, Diocesan Council; Board of Education and Board of Missions. *Publications:* The Intermediate State; Papal Infallibility and Supremacy; The Parson and Priest. *Recreations:* in college days cricket, fond of athletics. *Address:* The Deanery, Limerick. *Clubs:* Dublin University; Limerick County. *Died 4 Dec. 1928.*

ACKETT, William Henry, FJI; writer on finance and allied subjects; *b* Leicester, 11 June 1853; *s* of late T. Sandys Hackett; *m* Helen Louisa, *d* of late Thomas Whitehead, Liverpool; two *s* two *d*. *Educ:* Grammar School, Manchester. Apprenticed to, and subsequently foreign correspondent in a Manchester shipping firm; began contributing to Manchester Guardian, 1881, and accepted appointment on London staff, 1883; City Editor, Yorkshire Post, 1890–1920; for ten years chief sub-editor of Statist; commercial contributor to Glasgow Herald, 1894–1907; financial correspondent and leader writer for the Scotsman, 1909–19; relinquished all journalistic work in 1920 owing to failing health. *Recreations:* gardening and billiards. *Address:* Sandhills, Wethersfield, near Braintree, Essex. *Died 19 Oct. 1926.*

ADDEN, Sir Charles Frederick, KCB 1908 (CB 1902); Major-General, RA retired; JP, DL; Sheriff for Herts, 1919; Member Herts County Council; *b* Nottingham, 2 June 1854; *o s* of late Charles Stanton Hadden, Ingleside, Sunningdale; *m* 1885, Frances Mabel, 3rd *d* of late Col Clement Strong, Coldstream Guards. *Educ:* Elstree School; Cheltenham College; RMA. Passed out of RMA first for Royal Engineers, but selected Royal Artillery; commissioned Lieut, 1873; assistant to superintendent Royal Laboratory, 1885; Inspector of laboratory stores, 1888; Chief Inspector, Royal Arsenal, Woolwich, 1893; Member of the Ordnance Committee, and Associate Member of the Explosives Committee, 1901; Commandant Ordnance College, 1904; Director of Artillery, Headquarters, 1904–7; Master-General of the Ordnance and Member of the Army Council, 1907–13; President Ordnance Board and Royal Artillery Committee, 1913–15. *Recreations:* shooting, fishing, motoring. *Address:* Rossway, Berkhampstead, Herts. *TA:* Northchurch. *Club:* United Service. *Died 13 Sept. 1924.*

ADDINGTON, 11th Earl of, *cr* 1619; **George Baillie-Hamilton Arden,** KT 1902; JP; Baron Binning, 1613; Representative Peer for Scotland since 1874; Lord-Lieutenant Haddingtonshire since 1876; ADC to the King; Hon. Colonel Lothians and Berwickshire Yeomanry; *b* 26 July 1827; *s* of 10th Earl and Georgina, *d* of Ven. Robert Markham; *S* father, 1870; *m* 1854, Helen (*d* 1889), *d* of Sir John Warrender, 5th Bt, and Frances, *d* of 1st Lord Alvanley; one *s* three *d* (and two *s* one *d* decd). Vice-Lieutenant, Co. Berwick. Owner of about 34,100 acres. *Heir: g s* Hon. George Baillie-Hamilton, *b* 18 Sept. 1894. *Address:* Tyninghame, Prestonkirk, Haddington; Arderne Hall, Tarporley, Cheshire. *Clubs:* Carlton, Hurlingham; New, Edinburgh. *Died 11 June 1917.*

HADDOCK, Edgar Augustus; Principal of the Leeds College of Music; *b* Leeds, 23 Nov. 1859; *y s* of G. Haddock; *m* 1896, Hilda, *d* of Joseph Sykes, Harrogate and Morley; one *s*. *Educ:* private schools in Leeds. Made debut at Crystal Palace, 1883; given many concerts of programmes entirely of British music, recitals devoted to Schumann, Brahms, the complete sonatas for pianoforte and violin of Beethoven in chronological order, historical recitals, etc, 1884; he began his series of musical evenings at Leeds, 1885; played with Joachim one of the unaccompanied duets of Spohr at a Huddersfield Subscription Concert, 1890; founded the Leeds College of Music in 1894, the Leeds Orchestra in 1899; instituted in 1923 the Leeds Competitive Musical Festival. *Publications:* violin music: Practical Violin School; The Student's Series of Violin Solos; Scale Manual; The Complete Soloist for Violinists; orchestral music: Ballade Norvégienne for Violin and Orchestra; Triumphal March; church music: Jesu, my Lord; Lord God Almighty; numbers of fugitive instrumental and vocal pieces; literature: Music in Yorkshire; A Retrospect: Then—and Now; Pages from a Music-Lover's Note-book; The Art of Clear Speech, etc. *Recreations:* chess, collecting curios. *Address:* 37 University Road, Leeds; Kearby, via Wetherby, Yorkshire. *TA:* Haddock, Leeds. *T:* Leeds, Central 24641 and 27924. *M:* NW 2913. *Died 9 Aug. 1926.*

HADEN, Francis Seymour, CMG 1890; *b* 7 March 1850; *e s* of late Sir Francis Seymour Haden; *m* 1885, Ethel, *d* of Lt-Col B. A. Branfill (late 10th Hussars), Upminster Hall, Essex; one *d*. *Educ:* Westminster School; Christchurch, Oxford (BA with honours, 1873). Asst private secretary 1876, and private secretary 1877, to Sir Henry E. G. Bulwer, GCMG, Lt-Gov. of Natal; Chief Clerk, Colonial Secretary's Office, Natal 1880; Asst Colonial Secretary, 1881; Acting Colonial Treasurer, 1885, and Acting Colonial Secretary in same year; Colonial Secretary, 1887, and on several occasions Deputy-Governor of Natal and Zululand; in 1892 was granted a Dormant Commission, under which he twice administered the Governments of Natal and Zululand; a member of the Executive and Legislative Councils of the Colony from 1885; was President of the Natal Trade Commission in 1885; and on various occasions a delegate to the Governments of the Cape Colony and the South African Republic on customs and railway matters; retired in 1893 on the adoption by Natal of responsible government. Decorated 1890, for services in connection with proposed Customs and Railway Union between the Orange Free State, Cape Colony, and Natal. *Recreations:* golf, shooting, fishing—especially the last-named. *Club:* Whites'. *Died 21 March 1918.*

HADLEY, William Sheldon, LLD; Master of Pembroke College, Cambridge, since 1912; Lecturer in Classics and Modern History; Fellow of Pembroke College, 1882; Treasurer, 1887; Assistant Tutor, 1891; President and Tutor, 1902; *b* 1859; *m* 1894, Edith Jane, *d* of late Rev. R. Foster, formerly Chaplain of Royal Hibernian Military School, Phoenix Park, Dublin, and Vicar of Upavon, Wilts; one surv. *s*. *Address:* Master's Lodge, Pembroke College, Cambridge; Shallcross, Heacham, Norfolk. *Club:* Junior Carlton. *Died 25 Dec. 1927.*

HADOW, Col Reginald Campbell, DSO 1896; retired; late Commanding 15th Sikhs, ISC; *b* 6 July 1851; *s* of late Patrick Douglas Hadow, JP (Chairman of P & O Steam Navigation Co.) of the Priory, Sudbury, Middlesex; *m* 1876, Annie Sophia Erskine (*d* 1912), *d* of late Gen. David Pott, CB, of Borthwickshiel, Hawick, NB. *Educ:* Cheltenham. Entered 55th Regt, 1870; BSC, 1876; Capt. (15th Sikhs) BSC (later ISC) 1882; Major, 1890; Lt-Col 1896; Brevet Colonel, 1902; served Afghan War, 1878–80; present at actions of Ahmed Khel and Urzoo; march from Kabul to Khandahar, and battle of Khandahar (medal with 2 clasps, bronze star); Soudan Expedition, 1885; present at actions of Tofrek and Tamai (medal with 2 clasps, bronze star); Miranzai Expedition (medal with clasp), 1891; Chitral relief force, 1895; present at storming of Malakand Pass, and forcing passage of Swat River (despatches, medal with clasp, DSO); Tirah Expedition, 1897; present at actions of Dargai and operations in Khanki Valley (very severely wounded, 3 clasps). *Recreations:* cricket, golf, shooting.

Address: The Ferns, Spencer Road, Eastbourne. *Clubs:* United Service; Sussex, Eastbourne.   *Died 10 Oct. 1919.*

HAGGARD, Lieut-Col Andrew Charles Parker, DSO 1886; author, novelist, historian, poet; *b* Bradenham Hall, Norfolk, 7 Feb. 1854; 5th *s* of late William Meybohm Rider Haggard and Ella, *d* and co-heiress of late Bazett Doveton, EICS; *m* 1906, Ethel Fowler, *widow* of late Edward Fowler. *Educ:* Westminster School. Joined 25th Regt (King's Own Borderers), 1873; served in India, Aden; also on Staff, Egypt, 1882; joined Egyptian Army, 1883; on special service on the Red Sea Littoral (special naval despatches), 1884; present at battle of Tamai (despatches), 1884; investment of Suakin by Osman Digna, in command of 1st Batt. Egypt. Army (4th Class Osmanieh), 1884–85; reconaissance to Hasheen, 1885; operations at Suakin, 1885; Special Recruiting Commission with Brig.-Gen. Yusuf Pasha Schudi to investigate abuses of the conscription, 1885; commanded 1st Batt. Egypt. Army operations on the Nile, including the battle of Ginness, 1885–86; commanded Egyptian troops on the frontier (despatches, medal and star, several clasps, DSO, 3rd class Medjidie), 1886. Co-founder Veterans' Club of British Columbia, 1915. *Publications:* Ada Triscott, written 1881, published 1890; articles on sport and travel, in Blackwood and the Field, constantly from 1884; Polyglot Poems, 1887; Dodo and I, 1889; Leslie's Fate, 1889; A Strange Tale of a Scarabaeus, 1891; Tempest-Torn, 1894; Under Crescent and Star, 1896; Hannibal's Daughter, 1898; Love rules the Camp, 1901; Sporting Yarns, 1903; Sidelights on the Court of France, 1903; A Canadian Girl, 1904; Louis XIV in Court and Camp, 1904; A Bond of Sympathy, published in America under name of Silver Bells, 1905; The Regent of the Roués, 1905; The Real Louis XV, 1906; A Persian Roseleaf, 1906; Louis XVI and Marie Antoinette, 1909; Two Great Rivals, 1910; The Amours of Henri de Navarre and of Marguerite de Valois, 1910; The France of Joan of Arc, 1911; Two Worlds, a Romance, 1911; The Romance of Bayard, 1912; Louis XI and Charles the Bold, 1913; Remarkable Women of France (1431–1749), 1914; Women of the Revolutionary Era, 1914; Thérèse of the Revolution, 1921; Madame de Stäel, Her Trials and Triumphs, 1922. *Recreations:* fishing, shooting, especially in connection with exploration of little-known rivers, forests, and mountain ranges in Canada. *Address:* Camp Haggard, Vancouver Island. *Club:* Fly Fishers'.
Died 13 May 1923.

HAGGARD, Major Edward Arthur, (*pseudonym* Arthur Amyand); author; *b* Bradenham Hall, Norfolk, 5 Nov. 1860; *y s* of late William Meybohm Rider Haggard, Bradenham Hall; *m* 1887, Emily, *d* of late Edmund Calvert of Walton-le-Deale, Lancashire; one *s* one *d. Educ:* Shrewsbury; Pembroke Coll., Camb. (BA); Royal Military Coll. Joined 1st Batt. King's Shropshire Light Infantry, 1884; appointed to Army Service Corps, 1889; retired and joined 3rd Batt. Bedfordshire Regt (Militia), 1892; retired May 1904; served in Suakim Campaign, including march to Tamai, 1885, and throughout British occupation until May 1886 (Egyptian medal with clasp and star); on special service attached to ASC, South Africa, March 1900–May 1901 (medal, four clasps); First Secretary, Union Jack Club, 1902–7; Founder and Chairman Veterans' Club, 1907; Founder of the Veterans' Corps, 1908; Joint-Founder (with Mr J. A. Malcolm) of the Veterans' Association, 1915. *Publications:* Only a Drummer Boy, 1894; With Rank and File, or Sidelights on Soldier Life, 1895; Comrades in Arms, 1895; The Kiss of Isis, 1900; The Social Status of the Soldier in connection with Recruiting, 1906; Malcolm the Patriot, 1907. *Recreations:* hunting, fishing, shooting, travelling. *Address:* 27J Bramham Gardens, S Kensington, SW5. *T:* Kensington 8727. *Clubs:* Army and Navy, Junior Naval and Military.
Died 19 Jan. 1925.

HAGGARD, Sir (Henry) Rider, KBE 1919; Kt 1912; JP for Norfolk and Suffolk; Chairman of Justices Petty Sessional Division of Bungay; barrister-at-law; an Authority on Empire Migration and on Imperial, Agricultural, and Social Conditions; author; *b* Bradenham, Norfolk, 22 June 1856; 6th *s* of William Meybohm Rider Haggard, Bradenham Hall; *m* 1880, Mariana Louisa, *o c* of late Major Margitson, Ditchingham, Norfolk; three *d* (and one *s* decd). Secretary to Sir Henry Bulwer, Governor of Natal, 1875; on the staff of Sir Theophilus Shepstone, special commissioner to the Transvaal, 1877; with late Gen. Brooke, RE, formally hoisted the British flag over the South African Republic at Pretoria, on the Queen's Birthday, 1877; Secretary to Secocoeni Commission; Master High Court of the Transvaal, 1878; Lieutenant and Adjutant Pretoria Horse, 1879. Barrister, Lincoln's Inn, 1884; Chairman of Committee, Society of Authors, 1896–98; journeyed through England investigating condition of agriculture and of the rural population, 1901 and 1902; appointed British Government Special Commissioner to Report on Salvation Army Settlements USA, etc, 1905; Chairman Reclamation and Unemployed Labour Committee of the Royal Commission on Coast Erosion a Afforestation, 1906–11; travelled round the world as Memb Dominions Royal Commission, 1912–17; visited all the Over Dominions as Honorary Representative of the Royal Colonial Institi in connection with the After-War Settlement of Ex-Service Mc 1916; nominated Hon. Life Fellow of Royal Colonial Institute a presented with inscribed address of thanks signed by President a Council of the Institute in recognition of "conspicuous service the British Empire," 1916; elected a Vice-President Royal Color Institute, 1917; Member Empire Settlement Committee, 191 Member East Africa Committee, 1924; Member of Council Imperial Society of Knights; travelled much throughout the wor *Publications:* Cetywayo and his White Neighbours, 1882; Dawn, 188 The Witch's Head, 1885; King Solomon's Mines, 1885; She, 188 Jess, 1887; Allan Quartermain, 1887; Maiwar's Revenge, 1888; ! Meeson's Will, 1888; Colonel Quaritch, VC, 1888; Cleopatra, 188 Allan's Wife, 1889; Beatrice, 1890; Eric Brighteyes, 1891; Nada ￼ Lily, 1892; Montezuma's Daughter, 1894; The People of the M 1894; Joan Haste, 1895; Heart of the World, 1896; Dr Therne, 189 Swallow, a Story of the Great Trek, 1899; A Farmer's Year, 189 Black Heart and White Heart, 1900; Lysbeth, a Tale of the Dutc 1901; A Winter Pilgrimage, 1901; Rural England (2 vols), 1902; Pe Maiden, 1903; Stella Fregelius, 1903; The Brethren, 1904; Gardener's Year, 1905; Ayesha, or The Return of She, 1905; Rep￼ to British Government on Salvation Army Colonies, USA, and Hadleigh, England, with Scheme of National Land Settlement, 19 The Poor and the Land, 1905; The Way of the Spirit, 1906; Ben￼ 1906; Fair Margaret, 1907; The Ghost Kings, 1908; The Yellow Gc 1909; Morning Star, 1910; Queen Sheba's Ring, 1910; Regenerati (Report on Social Work of Salvation Army), 1910; Rural Denma and its Lessons, 1911; The Mahatma and the Hare, 1911; Red E 1911; Marie, 1912; Child of Storm, 1913; The Wanderer's Neckla 1914; The Holy Flower, 1915; The Ivory Child, 1916; Report Royal Colonial Institute, 1916; Finished, 1917; Love Eternal, 191 Moon of Israel, 1918; When the World Shook, 1919; The Ancie Allan, 1920; Smith and the Pharaohs, and other stories, 1920; S and Allan, 1921; The Virgin of the Sun, 1922; Wisdom's Daught 1923; Heu-Heu: or The Monster, 1924; The World's Desire (w￼ Andrew Lang), 1891. *Address:* Ditchingham House, Norfolk. T Haggard, Ditchingham. *Clubs:* Athenæum, National, Cecil.
Died 14 May 192

HAGGARD, Sir William Henry (Doveton), KCMG 1908; (1903; JP; *b* 25 June 1846; *e s* of William Meybohm Rider Hagga Bradenham Hall, Norfolk, and Ella, *d* of Bazett Doveton; *m* 188 Emily Margaret (Nitie) (*d* 1924), *d* of Joseph Hancox; one *s* two *Educ:* Tonbridge School; Winchester; Magdalen College, Oxfo Entered Diplomatic Service, 1869; Secretary of Legation, Rio Janeiro, 1885; Athens, 1887; Minister Resident at Quito, 189 Consul-General at Tunis, 1894; Minister Resident at Carac 1897–1902; Envoy Extraordinary and Minister Plenipotentiary Buenos Aires and Asuncion, 1902–6; Brazil, 1906–14; retired, 191 Diamond Jubilee and Coronation Medals of King Edward VII a King George V; Fellow of the Royal Geographical and Royal Asia Societies. *Publication:* (with Mr Guy Le Strange) The Vazir Lenkuran—a standard book for the study of modern Persia *Recreation:* fond of all sports, specially of hunting. *Address:* Hartl House, Sittingbourne. *Club:* National.
Died 22 Jan. 192

HAGGERSTON of Haggerston, Sir Edward Charlton de Mari 10th Bt, *cr* 1643; JP; *b* Teignmouth, Devonshire, 8 Feb. 1857; *s* Sir John Haggerston, 8th Bt and Sarah, *d* of Henry Knight, Axminst S brother, 1918; *m* 1904, Florence, 3rd *d* of W. H. Perrin; two two *d. Educ:* Ushaw; Prior Park. Passed exams for Solicitor, but ne practised; a Member of Belford Guardians and RDC for 30 yea served on the Northumberland Military Appeal Tribunal (Berwi Panel) during the War. Owner of about 13,000 acres in Northumberland. *Heir: s* Hugh Carnaby de Marie Haggerston, *b* March 1906. *Address:* Ellingham Hall, Chathill, RS￼ Northumberland. *T:* Chathill 4. *Club:* Junior Carlton.
Died 1 April 192

HAGGERSTON of Haggerston, Sir John de Marie, 9th Bt, 1643; *b* Axminster, Devonshire, 27 Nov. 1852; *e s* of Sir Jo Haggerston, 8th Bt and Sarah, *d* of Henry Knight, Axminster; S fath 1858; *m* 1887, Marguerite, *d* of Lewis Eyre. *Educ:* Ushaw. *Recreatio* shooting, hunting. Owner of about 15,000 acres in Northumberlan *Heir: b* Edward Charlton de Marie Haggerston [*b* 8 Feb. 1857; *m* 19 Florence, 3rd *d* of W. H. Perrin; two *s* two *d. Club:* Junior Carlto *Address:* Ellingham Hall, Chathill, RSO.
Died 29 Nov. 19

AGUE, Anderson, RI. *Address:* Vardre, Deganwy, Llandudno.
Died 24 Dec. 1916.

AGUE, Arnold, DSc Columbia, 1901; LLD Aberdeen, 1906; Geologist, US Geological Survey, since 1880; *b* Boston, 3 Dec. 1840; *s* of Rev. Dr William Hague and Mary Bowditch Moriarty; *g s* of James Hague, Yorkshire. *Educ:* Yale; Göttingen; Heidelberg. Geologist, US Geological Exploration of 40th Parallel, 1867–78; Geologist in the service of Chinese Government, 1878–79; Field service in Rocky Mountains and for several years in Yellowstone National Park and adjacent country; Secretary, National Academy of Sciences, since 1901; President Geological Society of America; Member of many scientific societies. *Publications:* Descriptive Geology, vol. ii, US; Geological Exploration of 40th Parallel, 1877; Geology of the Eureka District, 1892; Tertiary Volcanoes of the Absaroka Range, 1898; Geology, Yellowstone National Park, 1899; Geological Atlas of Yellowstone Park, 1904. *Recreations:* mountain climbing, sailing, fishing. *Address:* Washington, USA.
Died 15 May 1918.

AIG, 1st Earl, *cr* 1919; **Douglas Haig,** KT 1917; GCB 1915 (KCB 1913; CB 1900); OM 1919; GCVO 1916 (KCVO 1909); KCIE 1911; Viscount Dawick 1919; Baron Haig and 29th Laird of Bemersyde; ADC General to HM, 1914–17; Colonel of RHG, 17th Lancers, KOSB and London Scottish; Chairman of Council of the United Services Fund since 1921; *b* 19 June 1861; *y s* of John Haig, JP, of Cameronbridge, Fife, and Rachael, 4th *d* and *co-heiress* of Hugh Veitch of Stewartfield, Midlothian; *m* 1905, Hon. Dorothy Vivian, *d* of 3rd Lord Vivian; one *s* three *d*. *Educ:* Clifton; Brasenose College, Oxford (Hon. Fellow, 1915). Joined 7th Hussars, 1885; psc; served Soudan, 1898, including Atbara and Khartoum (despatches, Bt-Major, British medal, Khedive's medal with two clasps); South Africa, 1899; DAAG for Cavalry, Natal; CSO to General French during the Colesberg operations; AAG Cavalry Division, 1900; commanded group of columns, 1901–2 (despatches, ADC to King, Brevet-Colonel, CB, Queen's medal with seven clasps, King's medal); Lt-Col Comdg 17th Lancers, 1901–3; Inspector-Gen. Cavalry, India, 1903–6; Major-General, 1904; Lieut-General, 1910; General, 1914, for distinguished service; Field-Marshal, 1914, for distinguished service; Director of Military Training, 1906–7; Director of Staff Duties at Army Headquarters, 1907–9; Chief of Staff, India, 1909–12; General Officer Commanding, Aldershot, 1912–14; Commanding 1st Army, 1914–15; Commander-in-Chief of the Expeditionary Forces in France and Flanders, 1915–19; Field-Marshal Commander-in-Chief the Forces in Great Britain, 1919–20. Lord Rector, St Andrews Univ., 1916–19; Chancellor of St Andrews Univ., 1922. Served European War, 1914–18 (despatches five times, prom. Gen., Field-Marshal, GCB, GCVO, KT); Grand Cordon Legion of Honour; Médaille Militaire; Grand Cross Order of Leopold; Grand Cross St Maurice and St Lazarus; Obolitch Gold Medal (Montenegro) and 1st Class Order of Danilo, 1917; 4th Class of St George (Russia). *Publication:* Cavalry Studies, 1907. *Heir: s* Viscount Dawick, *b* 15 March 1918. *Address:* Bemersyde, St Boswells, Roxburghshire. *Clubs:* Cavalry, Marlborough, United Service. *Died 29 Jan. 1928.*

AIG, Alexander, MA, MD (Oxon); FRCP; Consulting Physician to Metropolitan Hospital; Consulting Physician Royal Hospital for Children and Women; *b* 1853; *o s* of late George Andrew Haig, formerly of Maulesden, Brechin, Forfarshire; *m* 1878, Gertrude Mary, *d* of late James Haig, Barrister, Lincoln's Inn; one *s* one *d*. *Educ:* Harrow; Exeter College, Oxford. Second Class Honours in the School of Natural Science, Oxford, 1876. Practised as a physician in London from 1882; spare time spent in physiological researches. *Publications:* Uric Acid as a Factor in the Causation of Disease, 1892, 7th edn 1908; Diet and Food, 1898, 6th edn 1906; Uric Acid, an Epitome of the Subject, 2nd edn 1906; Uric Acid in the Clinic, 1910. *Recreations:* cycling, the natural sciences. *Address:* 57 Inverness Terrace, W2.
Died 6 April 1924.

AIG, Lt-Col Arthur Balfour, of Bemersyde, CMG 1880; CVO 1902; JP Co. Berwick; RE; Extra Equerry to the King; Principal Conservative Agent, 1905–6; *b* 10 July 1840; *s* of late Robert Haig and Magdalene Murray; *m* 1874, Hon. Frances Charlotte Harris, *o d* of 3rd Baron Harris; one *s*. *Educ:* Rugby; Royal Academy, Woolwich. Entered RE 1859; Equerry to Duke of Edinburgh, 1864–80; Extra Equerry to King Edward VII, 1902. Companion of Ernestine Order of Saxe-Coburg and Gotha; Companion of Imperial Russian Order of St Vladimir; Jubilee Medal and clasp; Coronation Medal. *Decorated* for services rendered in Colonies when in attendance upon HRH, 1867–71, and in Russia and Coburg. *Recreations:* salmon fishing, shooting. *Address:* 75 Elm Park Gardens, SW10. *T:* Kensington 1841. *Club:* Marlborough.
Died 15 April 1925.

HAIG, Axel Herman, RE; Member of the Royal Swedish Academy, Stockholm; Knight Commander of the Swedish Order of the Vasa, and Knight of the Order of Nordstjernan (Northern Star); *b* Katthamra, island of Gotland, in the Baltic, 1835; *m*; one *s*. *Educ:* Wisby, the town of Gotland. In early life studied naval architecture at the Swedish Naval Dockyard, Cariskrona, and had a diploma as Naval Architect; came to Scotland and worked under Laurence Hill, shipbuilder, at Port-Glasgow; drifted by degrees into other architecture, came to London and worked under Evan Christian, architect to the Ecclesiastical Commissioners; worked for William Burges, ARA, and other architects; did numerous water-colour drawings, lithographs, etc; designs for churches and mural decorations in Sweden, and during the last thirty years mostly devoted himself to etching, finding many subjects abroad and in England; lived and worked at Haslemere, Surrey, and exhibited at the Royal Academy, Fine Art Society, and many other English exhibitions, as well as at various places abroad; Gold Medal at the Paris Salon, 1882; Medal and First Order of Merit at the Adelaide Intern. Exhibition, 1887; Diploma Chicago Exhibition, 1891; Gold Medal, 1st Class, Paris International, 1889; Gold Medal, Munich, 1890; Diploma, Berlin, 1891; Gold Medal, 1st Class, Paris International, 1900, and every year afterwards an exhibitor in London, Paris, and various places abroad. *Publications:* over 400 etchings, among them The Vesper Bell; The Quiet Hour; The Morning of the Festival; Burgos Cathedral, Spain; Chartres Cathedral; San Marco, Venice; Toledo Cathedral, Seville; Notre Dame, Paris; Tarragona; Capella Palatina, Palermo; Reims, etc. *Recreations:* travelling, going over to Sweden every year to visit relatives and friends. *Address:* Grayshurst, Haslemere, Surrey. *Club:* Savage.
Died 23 Aug. 1921.

HAIG, Brig.-Gen. Neil Wolseley, CB 1919; CMG 1917; late Inniskilling Dragoons; *b* 30 Oct. 1868; 2nd *s* of late Henry Haig and Annie, *d* of Edward Meyer, East Sheen; *m* 1913, Gerard Fitz-Gerald, *o c* of late Major-Gen. Fitz-Gerald Creagh, of Co. Clare, Ireland. Served S Africa, 1899–1900 (Queen's medal 3 clasps); European War, 1914–18 (CMG, CB), retired, 1922. *Address:* The Dale House, Hassocks, Sussex. *Clubs:* Boodle's, Cavalry.
Died 18 April 1926.

HAIGH, Rev. Henry, DD; ex-President of the Wesleyan Methodist Conference; Secretary of Wesleyan Methodist Missionary Society; *b* Ossett, Yorks, 26 June 1853; *s* of John Haigh; *m* Miss Shillington, Portadown, Ireland; one *s* three *d*. *Educ:* privately; Richmond College. For 27 years a missionary in the Mysore, South India; founder of a very large missionary printing-press; founder and editor of a Kanarese newspaper and Missionary Magazine; after returning to England, Chairman for nine years of the Wesleyan Synod of the Newcastle upon Tyne District; member of Edinburgh Continuation Committee; travelled extensively in Asia, Australasia, United States, Canada, and West Indies. *Publications:* many theological works and commentaries in the Kanarese language; chief reviser of Kanarese New Testament; Fernley Lecture, Some Leading Ideas of Hinduism. *Recreations:* formerly riding, tennis, cricket, golf. *Address:* 24 Bishopsgate, EC. *TA:* Wesley Led, London. *T:* London Wall 421.
Died 14 July 1917.

HAIN, Sir Edward, Kt 1910; member of Edward Hain and Son, St Ives; Foster, Hain, and Co., Cardiff; Foster, Hain, and Read, London, steamship owners; JP Cornwall and St Ives; *b* 1851; *o s* of late Edward Hain of St Ives; *m* 1882, Catherine, *d* of James Hughes of Whitehaven, Cumberland; one *s* one *d*. MP (LU) West (St Ives) Cornwall, 1900–6; President of the Chamber of Shipping of the United Kingdom, 1910–11; member St Ives Town Council over 20 years, six times Mayor; 12 years member Cornwall County Council; Sheriff of Cornwall, 1912. *Address:* Exchange Chambers, St Mary Axe, EC; Treloyhan, St Ives, Cornwall. *TA:* Trelawny, London. *T:* 13 and 14 St Ives, Cornwall, and 182 London Wall. *Clubs:* Reform, City of London, Royal Automobile, Ranelagh.
Died 20 Sept. 1917.

HAITÉ, George Charles, FLS; RBA, RI, ROI, RBC; decorative artist, designer, painter, and illustrator; writer and lecturer on art; President Institute of Decorative Designers; Examiner to Board of Education in Principles of Ornament; *b* 8 June 1855; *e s* of George Haité, designer. *Educ:* Mitcham College. Absolutely self-taught in art; commenced work before 16, owing to father's sudden death; came to London, 1873; early part of career devoted to design; exhibited at RA since 1883; exhibited oil and water colours at all leading galleries; has worked in black and white illustrations in all leading magazines; designed the covers to the Strand Magazine and the Strand Musical Magazine, etc. Pres. Langham Sketching Club, 1883–87 and 1908; late Pres. London Sketch Club; President Nicholson Institute, 1897;

Past-Pres. Artists' Society; Vice-Pres. South Wales Art Society; Vice-Pres. and Member of Council since 1881, Society Encouragement of Fine Arts; elected Life Member of the National Association of House Painters and Decorators of England and Wales. *Publications:* Haité's Plant Studies, Lectures, etc. *Recreations:* football, cricket, running, boxing, of the past; cycling, golf, shooting, present. *Address:* Ormsby Lodge, The Avenue, Bedford Park, W. *Clubs:* Arts, Sette of Odd Volumes (past president).

Died 31 March 1924.

HAJIBHOY, Sir Mahomedbhoy, Kt 1925; merchant. *Address:* Bombay. *Died 24 Feb. 1926.*

HALAHAN, Very Rev. John; Dean of Ross since 1905; married. *Educ:* Trinity College, Dublin (MA). Ordained, 1846; Curate of Berehaven, 1846–62; Rector, 1862–1918. *Address:* Black Rock Terrace, Bantry, Ireland. *Died 28 Sept. 1920.*

HALDANE, 1st Viscount, *cr* 1911, of Cloan; **Rt. Hon. Richard Burdon Haldane,** KT 1913; OM 1915; PC 1902; LLD; FRS 1906; FBA 1914; Member of Judicial Committee of Privy Council; Rector of Edinburgh University, 1905–8; elected Chancellor, University of Bristol; Chancellor St Andrews University, 1928; *b* 30 July 1856; 4th *s* of late Robert Haldane, WS, Cloanden, and Mary Elizabeth Burdon Sanderson. *Educ:* Edinburgh Academy; Edinburgh and Göttingen Universities. MA 1st Class Honours in Philosophy, Edinburgh University; Gray Scholar and Ferguson Scholar in Philosophy of four Scottish Univs, 1876. Called to the Bar, Lincoln's Inn, 1879; QC 1890. Gifford Lecturer in St Andrews University, 1902–4. MP (L) Haddingtonshire, 1885–1911; Secretary of State for War, 1905–12; Lord High Chancellor of Great Britain, 1912–15 and 1924. Hon. DCL (Oxon). *Publications:* Essays in Philosophical Criticism (with Prof. Seth); Life of Adam Smith; translator (with John Kemp) of Schopenhauer's World as Will and Idea, 3 vols; Education and Empire, 1902; The Pathway to Reality, 1903; The Reign of Relativity, 1921; The Philosophy of Humanism, 1922; Human Experience: a Study of its Structure, 1926. *Heir:* none. *Address:* 28 Queen Anne's Gate, SW1. *T:* Victoria 5193; Cloan, Auchterarder, Perthshire. *Clubs:* Brooks's, Athenæum, National Liberal; New, Edinburgh.

Died 19 Aug. 1928 (ext).

HALE, Col Charles Henry, CMG 1916; DSO 1896; Army Medical Service; *b* Eastbourne, 9 March 1863; 2nd *s* of G. W. Hale, MA, Trinity Coll. Camb.; *m* 1889, Elsie Innes MacGeorge Brown (whom he *div.* 1904); one *d. Educ:* Plymouth Grammar School. Decorated for Matabele Campaign, 1896; served S Africa, 1890–97 (despatches, DSO); S Africa, 1901–3 (Queen's medal with clasp); European War, 1914–16 (despatches, CMG); retired on retired pay owing to heart trouble, 1917. *Recreations:* various. *Address:* c/o Holt and Co., 3 Whitehall Place, SW1. *Died 20 July 1921.*

HALE, Col E. Matthew, VD; ROI; late Lieutenant-Colonel 24th Middlesex Post-Office Rifle Volunteers. Served as special artist to Illustrated London News during Russo-Turkish War, 1877–78. *Address:* Shackleford, Godalming. *Club:* Savile.

Died 24 Jan. 1924.

HALE, Sarah J.; Principal, Edge Hill Training College for Teachers in Elementary Schools, since 1890; *y d* of late John Hale of Burton Latimer, Northants. *Educ:* Wellingborough, Northants. Prepared for the profession of a Teacher in Elementary Schools, at Freeman's Endowed School, Wellingborough, and at Whiteland's College, Chelsea; took charge successively of the Derby Girls' School, Great Windmill St, W; of Park St Girls' School, Wellingborough, and of Holy Trinity School, Leicester; was appointed to the New Training College of St Katharine's, Tottenham, 1878, leaving it for Newnham College, Cambridge, 1885; after the Cambridge course (Moral Science Hons) some few months were spent as Mistress of Method at St Mary's Hall, Cheltenham; one of a select committee appointed to inquire into the conditions of the training of pupil teachers, 1908. *Publications:* The Teaching of Infants; Diagram Sheets for the Teaching of Needlework. *Recreations:* travelling, cycling, walking, etc, reading, drama. *Address:* Edge Hill College, Liverpool. *T:* 791 Royal.

Died 1 April 1920.

HALKETT, George Roland; artist and writer on art; *b* Edinburgh, 11 March 1855; *m* 1891, Lucy Marion, *d* of Joseph Lees, JP, of Minnickfold, Holmwood; two *d. Educ:* privately. Studied art in Paris; became a regular contributor to journalism and the art magazines; art critic, Edinburgh Evening News, 1876; joint-compiler and artist of the New Gleanings from Gladstone and Gladstone Almanack; and author and artist of The Irish Green Book (1887), which had an

enormous circulation during the first Home Rule controversy; join the Pall Mall Gazette, 1892, as political cartoonist and writer on a contributed many drawings and caricatures to Punch; became editor of the Pall Mall Magazine, 1897; editor of the Pall M Magazine, 1900–5; has travelled extensively in the Colonies and the East; his chief recreation in politics and motoring. *Address* Aubrey Road, Campden Hill, W. *T:* Park 1993. *Club:* Garrick

Died Dec. 191

HALL, Alexander Cross, JP in Cambs and Oxon; landowner; l Captain and Hon. Major 3rd Battalion Suffolk Regiment; *b* 16 Se 1869; *s* of late William Henry (Bullock) Hall (who changed his na to Hall in 1872 to succeed his uncle, the late Gen. John Hall, 1st L Guards), and 1st wife, Elizabeth Dennistoun, *d* of William Cross; 1899, Favell Helen, *y d* of late Lt-Col H. C. Jones-Mortimer of P Newydd, Denbigh; two *s* one *d. Educ:* Marlborough; Trinity Colle Cambridge; BA 1893; MA 1899. While at Cambridge hunted t Trinity beagles, 1889–91; on leaving Cambridge studied agricult and land management with late W. T. Scarth at Raby Castle and Downton Agricultural College; travelled and hunted big game Canada and USA in 1896; and in India and Kashmir in 1898; bree of pedigree shorthorns and Southdown sheep. *Recreations:* hunti shooting, fishing, golf. *Address:* The Manor, Great Rollright, Ox *Club:* Brooks's. *Died 2 Oct. 191*

HALL, Alexander William, JP, DL; *b* 1838; *e s* of late Henry H and Hon. Catherine Louisa, 4th *d* of 2nd Lord Bridport; *m* 18 Emma Gertrude, 2nd surv. *d* of late Edward Jowitt of Eltofts, C York. *Educ:* Eton; Exeter College, Oxford. High Sheriff, Oxfordshi 1867; MP (C) Oxford, 1874–80, 1885–92. *Address:* Barton Abb Steeple Aston, Oxfordshire.

Died 29 April 191

HALL, Sir Douglas Bernard, 1st Bt, *cr* 1919; *b* 24 Dec. 1866; of Bernard Hall, JP (*d* 1890), and Margaret, *d* of William Calro DL, JP; *m* 1890, Caroline, *o d* of T. Y. Montgomery, of Larchm Manor, New York State, USA; one *s. Educ:* Charterhouse; Ch Church, Oxford. On outbreak of War, 1914, employed with his ya on patrol work on the Solent and in the Channel, assisting in t transport of the original British Expeditionary Force; later on he w out to the Seine and assisted in conveying wounded officers on t river; started the first Hospital Barge Flotilla of 200 beds, under title of British Water Ambulance Fund, of which he was Preside (special thanks of the Army Council); taken over by the War Off as No 1 Ambulance Flotilla, which he commanded; relinquish command for a post in the High Explosives Department, Minis of Munitions. MP (U) Isle of Wight, 1910–22. JP Sussex, High Sher 1907; 1st Lieut RNR (retired); Capt. RE; Lord of the Manors Barlavington, Burton, and Crouch. *Heir: s* Capt. Doug Montgomery Bernard Hall, *b* 30 Dec. 1891. *Recreations:* shooti golf. *Address:* 10 Cadogan Gardens, SW3. *T:* Victoria 2170; Cas Priory, Berks. *Clubs:* Carlton, White's, Boodle's.

Died 30 June 192

HALL, Edwin Thomas; a Fellow and Past Vice-President of the Ro Institute of British Architects; Fellow and Member of Council Royal Sanitary Institute; Architect to the British Home and Hospi for Incurables, and the City of Westminster Union; *b* Suffolk, 18 *m* 1878, Florence, *e d* of Julian Byrne; three *s* four *d. Educ:* Sou Kensington School of Art; office of late J. Fogerty. Commenc practice, 1876. Past-Chairman Estates Governors of Dulwich Colle a Governor of Dulwich College; Chairman of the Dulwich Pict Gallery; a Vice-President of the London Society; President of Secti of Architecture and Engineering at Sanitary Congress at Bristol, 19 *Professional work:* churches, mission halls, mansions, public buildi hospitals etc, including St Ermin's Hotel, Westminster, Park Hospit Hither Green, SE, Plaistow Hospital, St George's Children's Hon Chelsea; Library, Dulwich College; head offices of the Metropolit Asylums Board, Victoria Embankment; National Press Agen building; Seacroft and Killingbeck Hospitals, City of Lee Camberwell Infirmary and Guardians' Offices; Sanatorium, Friml New Royal Infirmary, Manchester, in conjunction with a Manches colleague; the new wing and Nurses' Home for the Lond Homœopathic Hospital; the Barnato Memorial additions to t Middlesex Hospital; the South Wales Sanatorium and Meadows Hospital, Cheshire, for the King Edward VII Memorial; Liberty Regent Street, London; the King George Hospital for wounded London; the Welsh War Hospital at Netley (in conjunction with Stanley Hall); Sanatoria for London at Godalming and East Grinstea etc; Consulting Architect to King Edward VII Sanatorium, Midhur to the Leeds General Infirmary, and to St Bartholomew's Hospit London; designed several houses in Cadogan Square and Pont Stre and in the country. *Literary work:* Victoria, the Last Progress; Architecture and the other Arts; Art Museums and Picture Galleries; Modern Hospitals; Sanatoria for Consumptives; Flats and Apartment Houses on the Continent, etc. *Recreation:* golf. *Address:* 54 Bedford Square, WC1. *T:* 37 Museum; Hillcote, Dulwich, SE21. *T:* 1388 Brixton. *Clubs:* Arts; Dulwich.

Died 15 April 1923.

HALL, Brig.-Gen. Francis Henry, CB 1900; CVO 1907; retired 1909; *b* 21 March 1852; *s* of Rev. F. H. Hall of Drum-Cullen, Co. Down. Served Afghan War, 1878–80 (despatches, medal); South Africa, 1899–1900 (despatches twice, CB); Brig.-Gen. in charge of Administration, Malta, 1906–7, Scottish Command, 1908–9.

Died 19 Nov. 1919.

HALL, Granville Stanley; President, Clark University; retired 1920; *b* Ashfield, Mass, 1 Feb. 1846; *s* of Granville Bascom Hall and Abigail Beals; married. *Educ:* Williams Coll.; AB 1867; AM 1870; PhD Harvard, 1878; LLD University of Michigan, 1888; Williams Coll., 1889; Johns Hopkins, 1902. Professor of Psychology, Antioch (Ohio) Coll., 1872–76; studied in Berlin, Bonn, Heidelberg and Leipzig; Lecturer on Psychology in Harvard and Williams, 1880–81; Professor of Psychology, Johns Hopkins, 1881–88. *Publications:* Aspects of German Culture; Hints toward a Select and Descriptive Bibliography of Education (with John M. Mansfield); Adolescence (2 vols); Youth: its Education, Regimen, and Hygiene, 1907; Aspects of Child Life and Education, 1907; Educational Problems, 1911; Founders of Modern Psychology, 1912; Jesus, the Christ, in the Light of Psychology (2 vols), 1917; Morale: The Supreme Standard of Life and Conduct, 1920; Recreations of a Psychologist, 1920; Senescence, 1922; Life and Confessions of a Psychologist, 1923; has contributed largely to periodical literature in the fields of experimental psychology, genetic psychology, psychology of religion and education. Founder of the American Journal of Psychology, Editor of The Pedagogical Seminary, and Founder of Journal of Applied Psychology. *Recreations:* walking, farming. *Address:* 156 Woodland Street, Worcester, Mass, USA. *T:* Cedar 4125. *Died 24 April 1924.*

HALL, Sir Henry, Kt 1919; *b* 1860; *s* of late Henry Thomas Hall, of Oxford, and Jemima, *d* of Thomas Gill, of Middlesex. *Educ:* privately. Chairman of Stephen Smith & Co., Ltd, London, Adelaide, and Toronto; Organiser of the Fertiliser Section in the Ministry of Munitions, 1917. *Address:* Gloverswood, Charlwood, Surrey. *T:* Norwood Hill 12. *Clubs:* Constitutional, Royal Automobile.

Died 30 March 1928.

HALL, Ven. Henry Armstrong, CBE 1919; BD; Archdeacon of Richmond; Chaplain to the King; Rector of Methley; Chaplain to the Forces, 1st Class, and Deputy Assistant Chaplain General (Northern Command), 1915–19; *b* Parkhurst, Isle of Wight, 2 June 1853; *s* of George Hall, late 2nd Light Infantry, and Julia, *d* of Col Geo. Gawler, KH; *m* 1878, Catherine Gertrude, *d* of John Ross Hutchinson, HEICS; one *d*. *Educ:* Christ's Hospital; Vevey; King's College, London. Curate of Holy Trinity, Lee, Kent, and successively incumbent of St George's, Douglas, I of M; Holy Trinity, Bristol; Swindon, Wilts; St Mary's, Spring Grove, Isleworth; St John's, Perth, NB; and Methley, Yorks; conducted parochial missions in all parts of the country during his last thirty years. *Recreations:* golf, fishing. *Address:* Methley Rectory, Leeds.

Died 12 May 1921.

HALL, Col Henry Samuel, CB 1902; VD; late Captain 6th Dragoon Guards and late Lieutenant-Colonel and Hon. Colonel 2nd Volunteer Battalion Oxford Light Infantry; 2nd *s* of late Henry Hall of Barton Abbey, Oxon, and Hon. Catherine Louisa Hood, 4th *d* of 2nd Baron Bridport; *m* 1874, Eleanor, *d* of late Gen. Edward Boxer, RA, FRS. Served in Indian Mutiny. *Address:* 25 Longride Road, SW. *Club:* Army and Navy. *Died 24 May 1923.*

HALL, Rev. Herbert, MA, SCL; Rector of Glemsford, Suffolk, since 1887; Hon. Canon, Diocese of St Edmundsbury and Ipswich; *b* 11 July 1845; *s* of late Charles Ranken Hall, Rector of Shirenewton, Mon., and Harriett, *d* of John Baker of Aldwick Court, Somerset and Weston-super-Mare; unmarried. *Educ:* Cheltenham and Marlborough Colleges; BNC, Oxford. Curate of St James's, Bury St Edmunds, 1869–76; Vicar of Linton, Cambridgeshire, and Chaplain of the Union until 1887. *Address:* The Rectory, Glemsford, Suffolk. *TA:* Glemsford. *Died 16 Feb. 1921.*

HALL, John Basil, JP, Bradford; MA, MCh (Camb.); FRCS, FRCSE; Hon. Consulting Surgeon, Bradford Royal Infirmary; *b* 1866; *s* of William Hall of Leeds; *m* Lisbeth, *d* of late Thomas Mackenzie, JP,

of Achnaaird, Scotland; one *d*. *Educ:* King's School, Canterbury; Cambridge University; St Thomas' Hospital; Leeds and Vienna. Qualified in 1890; held several appointments at the Leeds General Infirmary; Hon. Surgeon, Bradford Royal Infirmary, 1900. *Publications:* various papers in medical journals. *Recreations:* fishing, motoring, outdoor sports. *Address:* Eldon Place, and North Park Road, Bradford. *T:* Bradford 1358. *M:* AK 1358. *Club:* Bradford.

Died 12 Jan. 1926.

HALL, John Carey, CMG 1912; ISO 1902; *b* Coleraine, Co. Londonderry, 22 Jan. 1844; *s* of John Hall of Coleraine and Portrush, Co. Antrim; *m* 1876, Agnes, *d* of Charles Wyclif Goodwin, Assistant Judge of British Supreme Court for China and Japan; two *s* four *d*. *Educ:* Coleraine Academical Institution; Queen's Coll. Belfast. Entered Consular Service, Japan, 1868; Acting Vice-Consul at Yedo (Tokio), 1869–70; services lent to Japanese Commission for Prison Reforms, 1871; called to Bar, Middle Temple, 1881; Assistant Japanese Secretary to Legation at Tokio, 1882; Acting Japanese Secretary, 1884–86; Acting Assistant Judge, Supreme Court for China and Japan at Shanghai, 1888–89; HM's Consul-General for Yokohama, 1902–14; acted or officiated as Consul at all the open ports of Japan; one of the founders of the China Society, London; President Asiatic Society of Japan, Tokio, 1913. Coronation medal, 1911. *Publications:* General View of Chinese Civilisation; The Positive Science of Morals, both translated from the French of Pierre Laffitte, etc; Papers on Japanese Feudal Law and other subjects in the Trans of the Japan Asiatic Soc.; occasionally contributor to Positivist Review. *Recreation:* reading. *Club:* Royal Societies.

Died 21 Oct. 1921.

HALL, Col Sir John (Richard), 9th Bt, *cr* 1687; CBE 1919; late Major 3rd (Reserve) Battalion Irish Guards; late Coldstream Guards; *b* 14 Nov. 1865; *s* of late Lt-Gen. Julian Hamilton Hall, 5th *s* of Sir John Hall, 5th Bt, and Augusta Wilhelmina Louisa, *d* of late Col John Fremantle; *S* uncle, 1913; *m* 1903, Sophia, *d* of Henry Duncan and *widow* of Captain S. A. Olliver, DSO. *Publications:* The Bourbon Restoration; England and the Orleans Monarchy; General Pichegru's Treason, 1915; Four Famous Mysteries, 1922; The Bravo Mystery, and other Cases, 1923. *Heir: b* Martin Julian Hall, *b* 23 March 1874. *Address:* 6 Chichester Terrace, Brighton. *T:* Kemp Town 7248. *Clubs:* Turf, Beefsteak, Guards, Carlton.

Died 15 Feb. 1928.

HALL, Joseph, MA, DLitt; *b* Portadown, Ireland, 23 April 1854; *e* surv. *s* of William Hall of Portadown, Ireland; unmarried. *Educ:* Coleraine Institution; Queen's College, Belfast. BA with honours in classics, Queen's University, 1875; Peel Prize for English Essay, 1878; MA 1882. Hon. DLitt Durham University, 1904; representative of secondary schoolmasters on Lancashire Education Committee, 1904–6; Assistant Master, Manchester Grammar School, Manchester, 1887–1913. *Publications:* Poems of Laurence Minot, 1887, third edition, 1914; King Horu, 1901; Selections from Early Middle English, 1920; Selections from Layamon, 1924; collaborated with late Professor Kölbing and others in Middle English and other books, and contributed to Englische Studien and other periodicals. *Recreation:* gardening. *Address:* Woodstock, Oxfordshire.

Died 8 Nov. 1927.

HALL, Brig.-Gen. Lewis Montgomery Murray, CB 1907; retired 1910; *b* 10 Sept. 1855; *s* of Maj.-Gen. Lewis Hall, RA; *m* 1880, Blanche, *d* of Captain Symons, Royal Navy; three *s* one *d*. Entered RMA 1873; Captain ISC 1885; Major 1893; Lieut-Col Indian Army, 1899; Bt-Col 1903; Col 1906; Brig.-Gen. 1907; served Chin-Lushai, 1899–90 (despatches, medal with clasp); NW Frontier, 1897–98 (medal with clasp); commanded a brigade in India, 1906–10; Aviator's Certificate, 1915. *Address:* 12 Kent Gardens, Ealing, W. *Club:* Junior Army and Navy. *Died 14 April 1928.*

HALL, Lt-Col Montagu Heath, DSO 1900; late commanding 3rd Battalion South Lancashire Regiment; *b* 26 Dec. 1856; *s* of late Isaac Hall of Upton Bank, Macclesfield, and Castleton, Derbyshire. *Educ:* Repton; Trinity Hall, Camb. Joined 4th Royal Lancashire Militia, 1876; served South Africa, 1900–1 (despatches twice, medal and 3 clasps). *Address:* The Cottage, Cranleigh, Surrey.

Died 22 June 1928.

HALL, Hon. Robert Newton, BA, LLD; KC; Puisne Judge, Court of King's Bench of Province of Quebec, from 1892; *b* 26 July 1836; *s* of Rev. R. V. Hall, Stanstead, Province of Quebec; *m* 1862, Celina, *d* of A. W. Kendrick, Warden of Compton County, PQ. *Educ:* Burlington University (BA honours, 1857). Admitted to Bar of Lower Canada, 1861; appointed QC by Lord Lorne, 1877; President St

Frances' section of Bar, 1877–81; President of Bar of Province of Quebec, 1878; Crown Prosecutor, 1878–79; Dean of Faculty of Law of Bishop's College, LLD 1880; Government Director first Canadian Pacific Railway Co.; President Massawippi Valley Railway Co., 1880–91; sat in Dominion House of Commons as MP for City of Sherbrooke, 1882–91, during part of which time he was Chairman of Committee on Banking and Insurance. *Address:* Montreal, Canada. *Club:* St James's, Montreal.   *Died 1 July 1917.*

HALL, Sydney Prior, MVO 1901; MA; painter; *b* 18 Oct. 1842; *e s* of late Harry Hall, painter, of Newmarket; *m* 1st, Emma Holland (*d* 1894); 2nd, Mary, *d* of late James Gow. *Educ:* Merchant Taylors'; Pembroke College, Oxford. 1st Class Lit. Hum. (Greats), 1865; MA 1871. Special artist of The Graphic during Franco-German War, 1870–71; member of the suite of King Edward VII on his voyage to India in 1875–76; member of the suite of the Marquess of Lorne and HRH Princess Louise on going out to Canada as Governor-General, 1879; accompanied the Marquess of Lorne on his journey in the North-West Territories, 1881; member of the suite of TRH the Duke and Duchess of York, and special artist of The Graphic on board HMS Ophir, 1901. *Address:* 36 Grove End Road, NW.
Died 15 Dec. 1922.

HALL-DEMPSTER, Col Reginald Hawkins, DSO 1900; *b* 14 March 1854; *e s* of late Capt. Henry Hall, formerly of 1st Madras Light Cavalry; assumed additional name of Dempster under Deed of Entail, 1918; *m* 1894, Edith Gertrude Dickson, *e d* of late Rev. Francis Home Atkinson of Morland Hall, Westmorland; one *d*. *Educ:* Wellington College. Entered 82nd Regt 1873; Capt. 1883; Major, 1893; Lt-Col 1st Bn South Lancashire Regt 1900; Bt-Colonel, 1904; retired, 1904; served Boer War, 1899–1903, and was at Spionkop and Relief of Ladysmith (despatches 4 times, DSO, Queen's Medal 5 clasps, King's Medal 2 clasps); JP Co. Forfar. *Recreations:* shooting, golf. *Address:* Dunnichen, Forfar. *Club:* Naval and Military.
Died 17 May 1922.

HALL-EDWARDS, John Francis, LRCP, LM (Edin), DMRE (Cantab); FRSE, Hon. FRPS; Major, RAMC 1914; Councillor for the City of Birmingham; Vice-Chairman of the Birmingham and Sutton Coldfield War Pensions Committee, and Vice-Chairman of the Birmingham King's Roll Committee; Hon. Life Member of the Roentgen Society, of the Electro-Therapeutic Section of the Royal Medical Society, of the British Institute of Radiology, of the American Roentgen-Ray Society, of the American Electro-Therapeutic Society, and of the Birmingham Natural History and Philosophical Society; late Vice-President of the Roentgen Society; Vice-President of the Midland Institute; Hon. Fellow of the American Electro-Therapeutic Society; *b* 19 Dec. 1858; *e s* of John Edwards, MD, MRCS. *Educ:* King Edward's School and Queen's College, Birmingham. Late Consulting Radiographer to 1st Southern General Hospital; Radiographer to 1st Birmingham War Hospital, Rubery; Military Orthopædic Hospital, Hollymoor; Monyhull Military Hospital; Consulting Radiographer to the Guest Hospital, Dudley; Surgeon Radiographer to the Royal Orthopædic, and Dental Hospitals, Birmingham; Fellow of the Royal Society of Medicine; late Vice-President Birmingham Photographic Society; President Birmingham and Midland Institute Scientific Society; Editor of Archives of Roentgen Ray, and President British Electro-Therapeutic Society; British Correspondent to the American X-Ray Society; served as surgeon X-ray expert to the Imperial Yeomanry Hospitals in South Africa, 1900–1 (medal and four clasps); a pioneer in X-ray investigation, during which lost both hands as the result of burns; awarded Civil List Pension, 1908, in recognition of services rendered to the country by the application of the X-rays to medicine and surgery; mentioned for valuable services rendered during the war, 1916; mentioned for valuable medical services, 1917; lecturer on scientific subjects; awarded the Carnegie Hero Trust Medallion, Jan. 1922. *Publications:* Bullets and their Billets, or Experiences with the X-Rays in South Africa; X-Ray Dermatitis—its Cause, Cure, and Prevention; Carbon-dioxide Snow: its Therapeutic Uses; The Radiography of Metals; The Metal Industry; numerous papers on the application of Electricity, Photography, X-Rays, and Radium to Medicine and Surgery. *Address:* 141 Great Charles Street, Birmingham. *T:* Central 6807; 112 Gough Road, Edgbaston, Birmingham. *T:* Midland 2173. *Clubs:* Conservative, Press, Birmingham.   *Died 15 Aug. 1926.*

HALLAS, Eldred; MP (Lab) Duddeston Division of Birmingham, 1918–22; *b* 1870; *s* of Edward Hallas; *m* 1892, Clara, *d* of Arthur Bottomley. Lecturer at the Ethical Church, 1906; Birmingham City Council, 1911; District President of the National Union of General Workers.   *Died 13 June 1926.*

HALLÉ, Charles E.; late Director of New Gallery; *b* Paris, 1846; *s* of late Sir Charles Hallé; unmarried. Learnt drawing from Baron Marochetti and Victor Mottez. Exhibited four pictures at Royal Academy, 1866; practised portrait-painting for several years; assisted Sir Coutts Lindsay in founding the Grosvenor Gallery, 1876; resigned directorship of Grosvenor, 1887, and built the New Gallery; besides organising and arranging the many exhibitions of the Grosvenor and New Galleries, painted about 100 portraits and many subject pictures, which passed into well-known collections here and abroad; principal works: Madonna and Child with attendant Angels; Sic transit Gloria Mundi; Buondelmonte and the Donati; Paolo and Francesca; The March of the Seasons; The Wishing Well; Fleeting Beauty; An Invocation; The Rock of the Sirens; besides single figures, generally life size half length, of beautiful women and children, in which he made study of expression his principal aim. *Publication:* Notes from a Painter's Life, 1909. *Address:* 5856 Campo Sta Maria Formosa, Venice. *Club:* Burlington Fine Arts.   *Died 31 Jan. 1919.*

HALLIDAY, Lt-Gen. George Thomas; Bengal Cavalry; *b* 1841; *y s* of late Sir Frederick James Halliday, KCB; *m* Minnie, *d* of late General G. W. Bishop, Indian Army. Entered army, 1858; Brigade Major and Deputy Asst Adjutant-General, India, 1874; Commandant 16th Bengal Cavalry, 1889; Colonel on the Staff, 1894; Commanding Oudh District (Officiating), 1895; Colonel, 16th Cavalry, Indian Army; Lt-General, 1900; Hazara expedition, 1888 (medal with clasp). *Address:* 75 Redcliffe Gardens, SW10. *T:* Kensington 294.
Died 15 Sept. 1922.

HALLIDAY, Gen. John Gustavus; unemployed supernumerary list; *b* May 1822; 3rd *s* of Thomas Halliday of Ewell, Surrey; *m* 1845, Lucy (*d* 1888), *d* of W. M. Cotton of Petrograd; one *s* three *d*. *Educ:* Switzerland. Appointed to the Indian Army, Madras Establishment, 1838; appointed by Lord Dalhousie to the Mysore Commission under Sir Mark Cubbon, KCB, in which served for several years, leaving it on promotion; Vice-President, Victoria Institute. *Address:* 5 Church Terrace, Blackheath, SE.   *Died 4 Feb. 1917.*

HALLINAN, Most Rev. Denis; Bishop of Limerick since 1918; *b* Coolcappa, Co. Limerick, 1849. *Educ:* Irish College, Rome. Priest, 1874; Curate, Newcastle West, 1875–86; St Michael's, Limerick, 1886–94; Parish Priest of St Mary's, Limerick, 1894–98; Newcastle West, 1898–1918; Domestic Prelate to the Pope, 1900; Chancellor, Cathedral Chapter, 1912. *Address:* Bishop's House, Corbally, Limerick.   *Died 2 July 1923.*

HALLOWES, Maj.-Gen. Henry Jardine; *b* 13 Nov. 1838; *s* of Admiral John Hallowes; *m* Charlotte Elizabeth Ormonde (*d* 1916), *d* of Hon. J. Hamilton Gray, DCL; one *d*. *Educ:* privately. Served in army from 1855; Adjutant, 15th Foot; Adjutant-General, New Brunswick Militia; Adjt School for Officers of Reserve Forces; ADC to Hon. A. Gordon, Gov. of Trinidad, etc; Inspector of Gymnasia, India; AAG of Division, India; commanded 15th Regimental District; General Officer commanding the troops, Jamaica; commanded a brigade of National Reserve, London Division; Colonel-in-Chief the West India Regt. European War, 1914–19 (medal); war medals, etc— Canada medal and clasp, 1866; Afghan medal and clasp, despatches; Jubilee decoration and Coronation medal; Collar of Commandeur de la Légion d'Honneur; Croix de Guerre avec Palmes. *Publications:* The Drill and Working of the Three Arms; Thirteen Lectures on Tactics with regard to Fortification. *Recreations:* all outdoor games, riding, golf, cycling. *Address:* Inwoodbarn, by Tongham, Surrey. *Club:* Naval and Military.   *Died 28 June 1926.*

HALSBURY, 1st Earl of, *cr* 1898; **Hardinge Stanley Giffard,** Kt 1875; PC 1885; FRS 1887; MA; JP; VPLSL; Baron Halsbury, 1885; Viscount Tiverton, 1898; President Royal Society of Literature; Senior Grand Warden of English Freemasons; High Steward of University of Oxford since 1896; Hon. Fellow, Merton; *b* London, 3 Sept. 1823; *s* of Stanley Lees Giffard, LLD, and Susanna, *d* of late Frank Moran; *m* 1st, 1852, Caroline (*d* 1873), *d* of C. O. Humphreys; 2nd, 1874, Wilhelmina, *d* of late Henry Woodfall; one *s* one *d* (and one *d* decd). *Educ:* Merton Coll., Oxford. BA 1855; Barrister, Inner Temple, 1850; QC 1865; Treasurer of Inner Temple, 1881; Solicitor-General, 1875–80; Lord Chancellor, 1885–86, 1886–92 and 1895–1905. MP (C) Launceston, 1877–85. Oversaw complete The Laws of England, 1905–1916. *Heir: s* Viscount Tiverton, *b* 20 June 1880. *Address:* 4 Ennismore Gardens, SW7. *T:* Kensington 1557; Pendruccombe, Launceston. *Clubs:* Athenæum, Carlton, Junior Carlton, St Stephen's.
Died 11 Dec. 1921.

HALSEY, Rt. Hon. Sir (Thomas) Frederick, 1st Bt, *cr* 1920; PC 1901; JP; Deputy Grand Master, England, 1903–26; Provincial Grand

Master, Herts, 1873–1928; *b* 9 Dec. 1839; *s* of late Thomas Plumer Halsey, MP; *m* 1865, Mary Julia (*d* 1922), *d* of late F. O. Wells; six *s* two *d* (and one *s* one *d* decd). *Educ:* Eton; Christ Church, Oxford (MA); rowed in 'Varsity Boat Race. MP (C) Herts, 1874–85, Herts, Watford Division, 1885–1906. Major, Hon. Lt-Col (retired), Herts Yeo. Cavalry. *Heir: s* Lt-Col Walter Johnston, *b* 1 June 1868. *Address:* Gaddesden, Hemel Hempstead. *Club:* Carlton.

Died 12 Feb. 1927.

IALTON, Herbert Welch, LLD; Vice-President of Court of Appeal, Cairo, since Oct. 1916; British Red Cross Commissioner in Cairo; *b* London, 26 July 1863; *e* surv. *s* of late Walter Fox Halton of the Home Civil Service; unmarried. *Educ:* University College School, London. Studied law in London and Paris; barrister-at-law Middle Temple, 1890; LLD University of Paris, 1898. Formerly an Inspector attached to the Committee of Judicial Control at the Ministry of Justice, Cairo; one of the pioneers of the English section of the School of Law, Cairo (Lecturer, 1900–4); a judge of the Native Court of Appeal, Cairo, 1897, transferred to the Mixed Tribunal, Cairo, 1909; President, 1914–16; Mixed (International) Court of Appeal, Alexandria, March 1916. Decorations: 2nd Class Mejidieh, 3rd Class Osmanieh, Grand Officer of the Order of the Nile. *Publications:* (English) An Elementary Treatise on the Egyptian Civil Codes, 2 vols; (French) Étude sur la Procédure Criminelle en France et en Angleterre. *Recreations:* modest golf and a dilettante pleasure in visiting places of historic interest. *Address:* Court of Appeal, Cairo. *Clubs:* Royal Societies, Royal Automobile; Turf, Cairo.

Died 8 Sept. 1919.

IAMBIDGE, Jay; lecturer and writer on Fine Art; *b* Simcoe, Elgin Co., Ontario, Canada, 13 Jan. 1867. Artist and investigator of design principles. *Publications:* Dynamic Symmetry, The Greek Vase, The Diagonal, The Parthenon and its Plan, The Erechtheum and its Plan, The Nike Temple and its Plan, Greek Bronzes, Classic Surveyors and Classic Designers. *Recreation:* golf. *Address:* Department of Fine Arts, Yale University, New Haven, Conn, USA.

Died 20 Jan. 1924.

IAMBLEDEN, 2nd Viscount, *cr* 1891; **William Frederick Danvers Smith,** JP, DL; partner in W. H. Smith & Son; *b* 12 Aug. 1868; *o s* of Rt Hon. William Henry Smith, PC, MP, and Viscountess Hambleden (1st in line), *d* of Frederick Dawes Danvers, formerly Clerk of Council, Duchy of Lancaster; *S* mother, 1913; *m* 1894, Lady Esther (Caroline Georgiana) Gore, 3rd *d* of 5th Earl of Arran; three *s* two *d*. *Educ:* Eton; New College, Oxford. Late Lt-Col Royal 1st Devon Yeomanry; served European War, Gallipoli and Egypt, 1915–16 (despatches). MP (C) Strand, 1891–1910. *Heir: s* Hon. William Henry Smith, *b* 25 July 1903. *Address:* 3 Grosvenor Place, SW1. *T:* Kensington 2200; Greenlands, Henley-on-Thames; The Manor House, North Bovey, Moretonhampstead. *Clubs:* Carlton, Wellington, Travellers'.

Died 16 June 1928.

IAMBRO, Sir Everard Alexander, KCVO 1908; JP, DL; Director of the Bank of England; *b* 11 April 1842; *s* of Baron Hambro, Milton Abbey, Dorset, and Caroline Gostenhofer; *m* 1st, 1866, Gertrude Mary (*d* 1905), *d* of late Henry Stuart; four *s* one *d*; 2nd, 1911, Ebba, *y d* of C. Beresford Whyte, of Hatley Manor, Co. Leitrim. *Educ:* Trinity Coll., Camb. *Address:* Hayes Place, Kent. *T:* Bromley 135; Milton Abbey, Dorset. *Club:* Travellers'.

Died 26 Feb. 1925.

IAMBURGER, H. J., ScD, MD, LLD (Aberdeen and St Andrews); FRS (Netherlands, Copenhagen, and Turin); Professor of Physiology in the University of Groningen since 1901; *b* 9 March 1859; *m* Frédérique Coben Gosschalk; one *s* one *d*. *Educ:* Alkmaar; University of Utrecht. Assistant to late Professor Donders at the Physiological Laboratory at Utrecht, 1882–88; Professor in the Royal Veterinary School in Utrecht, 1888–1901; introduced the application of physical chemistry in the medical sciences, 1883; and published a work containing the researches of himself and others on this subject: Osmotischer Druck and Ionenlehre in den medicinischen Wissenschaften, 1902–4; on 4th June 1908, date of commemoration of his first 25 years doctorship (chemistry), the merits of his scientific work were celebrated by the publication of an international jubilee book, containing a great number of biochemical contributions of medical and chemical scientists of the old and new world; President ix International Physiological Congress, Groningen, 1913; First Charles E. Dolme Lecturer, Johns Hopkins University, Baltimore, 1922; Herter Lecturer, New York, 1922. *Address:* Praediniussingel 2, Groningen. *T:* 939.

Died 5 Jan. 1924.

HAMEL, Prof. Auguste-Charles, MD; Professor of Histology and Bacteriology, Laval University, since 1895; *b* Quebec, 21 June 1854; *s* of Abraham Hamel and Dame Cécile Roy; *m* 1881, Sussie Vallière; five *s* three *d*. *Educ:* Jesuit College; Laval Univ. *Address:* Laval University, Quebec, Canada.

Died 25 April 1923.

HAMEL, Gustav, MVO 1901; MD; *b* 12 Sept. 1861. *Educ:* Sweden; Switzerland; St Bartholomew's Hospital. *Address:* 1 Stratford Place, W1. *T:* Paddington 5656; Westfield House, Portsmouth Road, Surbiton. *T:* Kingston 1182.

Died 3 May 1922.

HAMILL, Rev. Thomas Macafee, MA, DD; Professor of Systematic Theology, Assembly's College, Belfast, Presbyterian Church in Ireland, since 1895; *b* Ballymoney, Co. Antrim. *Educ:* Coleraine Academical Institution; Queen's College, Belfast; theological course at Assembly's College, Belfast; University, Edinburgh. Ordained, 1879; minister, Presbyterian Church, Omagh, Co. Tyrone, 1879–84; Lurgan, Co. Armagh, 1884–95; Moderator of the General Assembly, 1915. *Address:* College Park, Belfast. *TA:* Professor Hamill, Belfast.

Died 17 Feb. 1919.

HAMILTON, Hon. Brig.-Gen. Alex. Beamish, CB 1915; retired pay; *b* 22 Dec. 1860. Entered army, 1881; Captain KOSB 1889; Adjutant, 1890–1903; Major, 1901; Lt-Col 1908; Col 1911; DAAG Egypt, 1893–98; China and Hongkong, 1891–94; DAQMG S Africa, 1905–8; Embarkation Staff Officer, S Command, 1911–13; Embarkation Commandant from 1914; served Chin-Lushai Expedition, 1899–90 (medal with clasp); Nile Expedition, 1898 (despatches, Bt Major); European War, 1915 (despatches, CB). *Club:* Junior United Service.

Died 30 Dec. 1918.

HAMILTON, Allan M'Lane, MD, LLD; FRSE; one of the Consulting Physicians at the Manhattan State Hospital for the Insane, New York; *s* of Philip Hamilton, *y s* of Alexander Hamilton, the statesman, and author of the Federalist, and Rebecca, *d* of Louis M'Lane, US Senator and Secretary of the Treasury, Minister to England, 1829–30; *m* 1902, May C. Tomlinson; no *c*. *Educ:* preparatory school; Medical Department, Columbia University, New York. Took 1st Faculty and 1st Harren Prizes at graduation; 1st Prize Amer. Med. Assoc. 1879; has since made special study of Nervous and Mental Disease and Legal Medicine; expert witness for government in case of US *v* Guiteau, assassin of President Garfield; also connected with Czgolz, Thaw, and most important cases for past 40 years; ex-President Psychiatrical Society; Honorary Member American Neurological Association, Psychiatrical Society, NY Medical and Surgical Society; Fellow Medical Society of London; has made contributions to Study of Eugenics, and in 1896 further elaborated a suggestion of vocational fitness in young people; introduced Educational System in American Asylums. *Publications:* Prize Thesis on Galvano-Puncture, 1870; A Treatise on Nervous Diseases, 1873; A System of Legal Medicine, 1900; Accidents and Injuries of the Nervous System, 1904; An Intimate Life of Alexander Hamilton, 1911; Recollections of an Alienist, 1916; besides many contributions to special journals and encyclopædias. *Recreations:* writing, reading, fishing, photography, mechanical work. *Address:* 43 East 25 Street, New York; Great Barrington, Mass. *Club:* Beefsteak.

Died 23 Nov. 1919.

HAMILTON, Charles Boughton, CMG 1895; *b* British Guiana, 2 May 1850; *o s* of Rev. William Hamilton, MA; *m* 1880, Elizabeth Hermina (*d* 1897), *d* of P. van Eeden of British Guiana; one *s* two *d*. *Educ:* Queen's Coll., British Guiana; South Devon Collegiate School, Exeter. Entered Colonial Civil Service, 1865; acted Receiver-General and Auditor-General of British Guiana, 1881–86; in which Colony thanked by Council for services; Receiver-General of Trinidad, 1886–92; acted as Colonial Sec. twice; returned to British Guiana, 1892; Receiver-General of British Guiana, 1892; member of Executive Council of Government, 1895; member of Court of Policy of British Guiana, 1898; Govt Director Demerara Railway, 1910–23; Chm. of various important Commissions; Chairman Education Commission, 1902; thanked by Combined Court for special services gratuitously rendered in Public Road Administration, 1905; Secretary of State for colonies recorded high appreciation of his services, 1908. Freeman of city of Exeter, Devon. Esq.OStJ. *Recreations:* fishing, shooting, boating, tropical bush life. *Address:* Orbieston, Purley, Surrey.

Died 13 March 1927.

HAMILTON, Sir Charles Edward, 1st Bt, *cr* 1892; *b* 28 May 1845; *s* of late John Hamilton and Jessie, *d* of Peter Kemble, late Capt. 4th

Regt; *m* 1867, Mary (*d* 1906), *d* of late George M'Corquodale, Gladys, Anglesey; one *d* (and one *d* decd). MP (C) Southwark (Rotherhithe Div.), 1885–92. *Heir:* none. *Address:* 38 Eaton Place, SW1. *T:* Victoria 5181. *Clubs:* Carlton, Constitutional.

Died 15 Nov. 1928 (ext).

HAMILTON, Rev. Charles James, MA; Hon. Canon of Southwell; *b* 1840; *s* of Rev. J. H. Hamilton, Canon of Rochester; *m* 1870, Alice Catherine, *d* of Elliot Macnaghten of HM Indian Council; three *s* two *d*. *Educ:* Harrow; Trinity College, Cambridge; BA (Sen. Opt.), 1863. Deacon, 1864; Priest, 1865; Curate of Southwold, 1864–66; St Michael's, Chester Square, 1866–70; Vicar of Doveridge, Derbyshire, 1870–99; St John's, Derby, 1899–1908; Rural Dean of Derby, 1901–8; Proctor in Convocation for Diocese of Southwell, 1891–1916. *Address:* Walton-on-Trent, near Burton-on-Trent.

Died 15 Nov. 1917.

HAMILTON, Rt. Hon. Lord Claud (John), PC 1917; High Steward, Borough of Great Yarmouth, and of the Borough of Harwich; *b* Middlesex, 20 Feb. 1843; 2nd *s* of 1st Duke of Abercorn and Lady Louisa Russell, 2nd *d* of 6th Duke of Bedford; *m* 1878, Carolina (*d* 1911), *d* of late Edward Chandos Pole, Radbourne Hall, Derby, and Lady Anna Chandos Pole; one *s* one *d*. *Educ:* Harrow. Entered Grenadier Guards, 1862; retired, 1867; Col 5th Battalion Royal Inniskilling Fusiliers, 1867; Hon. Col 1892; Aide-de-Camp to the Queen, 1887. MP (U) Londonderry, 1865–68; Lord of the Treasury, 1868; MP King's Lynn, 1869–80; Liverpool, 1880–88; South Kensington, 1910–18. KJStJ. *Recreations:* cricket, football, racquets, all sports. *Address:* 28 Cambridge Square, W. *T:* Paddington 4919. *Clubs:* Carlton, 1900, Bachelors'.

Died 26 Jan. 1925.

HAMILTON, Edwin, JP; MA; MRIA 1879; barrister; *o s* of late Rev. Hugh Hamilton, Rochfort House, Balbriggan; *m* 1891, Helen, 2nd *d* of late Daniel Delacherois, DL, Manor House, Donaghadee; one *s*. *Educ:* Durham Grammar School (King's Scholar, 1864–68); Trinity Coll., Dublin. Prizeman in classics, honourman in science, Vice-Chancellor's prizeman in English verse, 1872; MA 1877. Edited several Dublin weekly papers, annuals, etc; contributed to many London weeklies, chiefly humorous verse. Called to Irish Bar, 1887; secretary Queen's Jubilee Local Committee, same year; Chairman, Conservative Club, Dublin, 1892–94; received Com. of the Peace, 1896; Chairman, Dublin District, Institute of Journalists, 1900. *Publications:* Ariadne, a Drama (University prize poem); Dublin Doggrels; Mongrel Doggrels; Waggish Tales (prose); The Moderate Man, and other verses; Ballymuckbeg (political satire); Dublin University Tercentenary Prologue, 1892; Gaiety Theatre, Dublin, Silver Jubilee Address, 1896; New Theatre Royal, Dublin, Opening Prologue, 1897; numerous libretti, comediettas, etc, produced in Dublin theatres, and elsewhere. *Address:* The Crossways, Donaghadee, Co. Down.

Died June 1919.

HAMILTON, Sir Frederic Harding Anson, 7th Bt, *cr* 1647; late Major 60th Rifles; *b* 24 Sept. 1836; 2nd *s* of Sir Robert Nortu Collie Hamilton, 6th Bt and Constantia, 3rd *d* of Gen. Sir George Anson, GCB; *S* father, 1887; *m* 1865, Mary (*d* 1918), *d* of H. Willan; two *s* four *d*. *Educ:* Eton. *Heir: s* Robert Caradoc Hamilton, Lieut Norfolk Regt, [*b* 22 March 1877; *m* 1907, Irene, 3rd *d* of Sir C. Mordaunt, 10th Bt; one *s* one *d*]. *Recreations:* shooting, etc. *Address:* Avon Cliffe, Alveston, Stratford-on-Avon.

Died 19 Sept. 1919.

HAMILTON, Lord Frederic (Spencer); *b* 13 Oct. 1856; 6th *s* of 1st Duke of Abercorn, KG. *Educ:* Harrow. Formerly in Diplomatic Service, and successively Secretary in the British Embassies at Berlin and Petrograd and in the Legations at Lisbon and Buenos Ayres; travelled much. MP (C) SW Manchester, 1885–86; North Tyrone (U), 1892–95; Editor Pall Mall Magazine to 1900. *Publications:* The Holiday Adventures of Mr P. J. Davenant, 1915; Some Further Adventures of Mr P. J. Davenant, 1915; The Education of Mr P. J. Davenant, 1916; The Beginnings of Mr P. J. Davenant, 1917; Lady Eleanor, Private Simmons, and others, 1918; The Vanished Pomps of Yesterday, 1919; Here, There, and Everywhere, 1921. *Address:* 13 Great College Street, Westminster, SW1. *T:* Victoria 6180. *Clubs:* Carlton, St James', Beefsteak.

Died 11 Aug. 1928.

HAMILTON, Adm. Sir Frederick Tower, GCB 1917 (KCB 1913); CVO 1908; Commander-in-Chief, Rosyth, since 1916; Grand Officer of the Legion of Honour; *b* 8 March 1856; *m* 1889, Maria, *d* of late Admiral of the Fleet Hon. Sir Henry Keppel; two *s* two *d*. Entered Navy, 1869; Commander, 1892; Captain, 1898; Rear-Adm. 1907; Adm., 1916; served Zulu War, 1879 (despatches, promoted, Zulu medal and clasp); ADC to the King, 1906–7; Inspector of Target Practice, 1907–9; commanding 5th Cruiser Squadron Atlantic Fleet, 1909–11; 2nd and 3rd Fleets, 1911–13; 2nd Sea Lord of the Admiralty, 1914–16. *Address:* Admiral's Office, Rosyth, Scotland; Anmer Hall, Lynn, Norfolk. *Clubs:* United Service, Naval and Military, Marlborough.

Died 4 Oct. 1917.

HAMILTON, G. E.; Hon. MA, Cambridge; late Chairman of Finance Committee, National Union of Teachers, and Treasurer, 1884–1916. *Address:* Hamilton House, Mabledon Place, WC.

HAMILTON, Rt. Hon. Lord George (Francis), GCSI 1903; PC 1878; DCL; LLD Glasgow; Captain of Deal Castle, 1899–1923; Provincial Grand Master, Middlesex, 1892–1924; Chairman of Governors of Harrow School, 1913–24; *b* 17 Dec. 1845; 3rd *s* of 1st Duke of Abercorn; *m* 1871, Lady Maud Lascelles, *y d* of 3rd Earl of Harewood; three *s*. *Educ:* Harrow. MP (C) County of Middlesex, 1868–85; Ealing Division, 1885–1906; Under-Secretary of State for India, 1874–78; Vice-President of Council, 1878–80; First Lord of the Admiralty, 1885–86, 1886–92; Chairman London School Board, 1894–95; Secretary of State for India, 1895–1903; Chairman of Royal Commission upon Poor Law and Unemployment, 1905–9; Chairman Mesopotamia Commission, 1916–17. *Publications:* Parliamentary Reminiscences and Reflections, 1868–85, 1916, and 1886–1906, 1922. *Recreations:* shooting, golf. *Address:* 17 Montagu Street, Portman Square, W1. *T:* Mayfair 700. *Club:* Carlton.

Died 22 Sept. 1927.

HAMILTON, Henry; dramatic author; *b* Nunhead, Surrey; *y s* of late James Hamilton, Captain HEICS; unmarried. *Educ:* Christ's Hospital. Originally an actor. *Plays:* first play produced Prince's Theatre, Manchester; Blank-verse Drama, A Shadow Sceptre; Moths (adaptation of Ouida's novel); Our Regiment, 1884; The Lady of the Locket, musical play, 1884; Harvest, 1886; Lord Anerley (in collaboration), 1889; La Tosca (adaptation), 1889; The Three Musketeers, 1898; Robin Hood (collaboration), 1906. Musical Plays: The Duchess of Dantzic, 1903; (adaptations)—Veronique, 1904; The Little Michus, 1905; Autumn Manœuvres, 1912. Plays (in collaboration) at Drury Lane—The Armada, 1888; the Royal Oak, 1889; The Derby Winner, 1894; Cheer Boys, Cheer! 1895; The White Heather, 1897; The Great Ruby, 1898; The Sins of Society, 1907; The Whip, 1909; The Hope, 1911; Sealed Orders, 1913; The Best of Such, 1916. *Address:* The Haven, Sandgate. *T:* Sandgate 16. *Club:* Isthmian.

Died 3 Sept. 1918.

HAMILTON, Col Henry Blackburne; *b* 1841; *e s* of late Rev. Henry Hamilton, MA, Devonshire Place, London, formerly Rector of Thomastown, Co. Kildare, Ireland, previously Ensign 85th (Duke of York's Own) Light Infantry, and Frances Margaret, *d* of late Ralph Peters, Platbridge House, Lancashire; *m* 1st, 1874, Isabella Lottie (*d* 1881), *d* of J. K. Wedderburn; one *s*; 2nd, 1888, Florence Emily, *e d* of Lieut-Gen. C. B. Ewart, CB, RE. *Educ:* Eton; Christ Church, Oxford. MA 1868. Cornet, 6th Dragoon Guards (Carabiniers), 1864; Lieutenant-Colonel, 1886; commanded 14th Hussars, 1887–91; Brevet-Colonel, 1890; retired, 1896; served Afghan Campaign, 1880 (despatches, medal); awarded Order of Mercy, 1901; Member of the Westminster City Council, 1900–3; President of St George's, Hanover Square District, League of Mercy, 1909–19; KGStJ 1916. *Publications:* Regimental Almanac of 14th (King's) Hussars, 1889–91; Regimental Standing Orders for the 14th (King's) Hussars, 1891; Historical Record of 14th (King's) Hussars from 1715 to 1900. *Recreations:* field sports in early life, then riding, golf, croquet, walking. *Address:* Cumloden, Bournemouth. *T:* Bournemouth 1293. *Clubs:* Carlton, Wellington, Royal Automobile; Bournemouth; Kildare Street, Dublin.

Died 2 April 1920.

HAMILTON, Very Rev. James; Dean of Clonmacnois since 1913. *Educ:* Trinity College, Dublin. Ordained, 1878; Curate of Fivemiletown, 1878–79; Rector of Donoughmore, 1879–82; Curate of St Matthew, Irishtown, 1882–84; Incumbent of Dunboyne, 1884–88; Ardmurcher, 1888–94; Rector of Mayne, 1894–1906; Incumbent of Kilbride, Clara, 1906–13. *Address:* The Deanery, Clara, King's Co., Ireland.

Died 8 May 1925.

HAMILTON, Capt. Keith Randolph, DSO 1900; late DAA&QMG Lowland Division, Territorial Force, Oxfordshire Light Infantry; *b* 28 Feb. 1871; 4th *s* of Lt-Gen. Henry Meade Hamilton, CB; *m* 1895, Ella Marcella, *d* of late Major John Finlay (late 78th Highlanders) of Castle Toward, Argyllshire; one *s*. Entered army, 1892; Captain, 1899; served North-West Frontier India, 1897–98 (medal with two clasps);

South Africa, 1899–1902 (severely wounded, DSO, Queen's medal 5 clasps, King's medal 2 clasps); retired 1913.
Died 7 Dec. 1918.

HAMILTON, Lillias, MD; Warden, Studley Horticultural College for Women, 1908–24. Private practice in Calcutta, 1890–94; Physician in charge of the Dufferin Hospital, Calcutta, 1893–94; Physician to the late Ameer of Afghanistan, 1894–97. *Publications:* A Vizier's Daughter, 1900; A Nurse's Bequest, 1907; The Powers that Walk in Darkness, 1924. *Address:* c/o Studley College, Warwickshire.
Died 6 Jan. 1925.

HAMILTON, Pryce Bowman, JP; *b* 1844; *o s* of late John Hamilton of Hilston Park, and Anne, *e d* of late Pryce Jones of Cyfronydd, Co. Montgomery; *m* 1873, Julia Annie, *o d* of late George H. Reynard-Cookson of Whitehill Park, Co. Durham. *Educ:* Harrow. Late Lieut 13th Hussars. *Address:* Seaford, Ryde; Villa Valetta, Nice. *Clubs:* Army and Navy; Royal Yacht Squadron, Cowes.
Died 8 Dec. 1918.

HAMILTON, Very Rev. Robert Smyly Greer; Dean of Armagh since 1924; *b* Castle Caulfield, Co. Tyrone, 1861; *m* Constance Helen Kinahan. *Educ:* Trinity College, Dublin. Curate of Cavan, 1886–96; Rector of Six-mile Cross, 1886–96, Cookstown, 1896–1905, Dundalk, 1905–24. *Recreations:* tennis, golf. *Address:* The Library, Armagh. *M:* IB 2661.
Died 23 Oct. 1928.

HAMILTON, Rt. Hon. and Rev. Thomas, PC (Ireland) 1921; MA, DD, LLD; President and Vice-Chancellor of the Queen's University of Belfast, 1908–23; *b* Belfast, 28 Aug. 1842; *s* of late Rev. David Hamilton (Moderator of General Assembly, 1854–55) and Eliza, *d* of Henry Weir, Banbridge, Co. Down; *m* 1876, Frances, *d* of Robert Allen, The Farm, Co. Londonderry; one *s* two *d*. *Educ:* Royal Academical Institution, Belfast; Queen's Coll., Belfast; BA, MA, with 1st Class Honours and two gold medals in Natural Science in Queen's Univ. of Ireland, 1863 and 1864; DD (hon.) Belfast and Aberdeen; LLD (hon.) Ireland, 1891. Ordained 1865; Examiner in Botany and Zoology to Intermediate Education Board, Ireland, 1878–80; President of Queen's College, Belfast, 1889; Senator of Royal University of Ireland, 1890. *Publications:* Faithful unto Death, a Memoir of Rev. David Hamilton, 1875; Irish Worthies, 1875; Our Rest Day (A Prize Essay), 1885; History of the Irish Presbyterian Church, 1886; Beyond the Stars, 1888; many articles in Dict. of Nat. Biography, 1886–1912. *Recreations:* autograph collecting, gardening. *Address:* Chlorine Gardens, Belfast. *T:* Belfast 50.
Died 18 May 1925.

HAMILTON, Col Thomas William O'Hara, CMG 1900; BA, MB; late RAMC; *b* 24 May 1860; *e s* of late Col T. Hamilton, Maldon, Surrey; *m* 1891, Hannah, *d* of late C. de Gallye Lamotte, MD, of the Cloisters, Sunderland; one *s*. *Educ:* King's School, Canterbury; Trinity College, Dublin. Entered army, 1883; Major 1895; served South Africa, 1899–1902 (despatches, Queen's medal, 6 clasps, King's medal, 2 clasps, CMG); Reserve of Officers.
Died 22 April 1918.

HAMILTON, William Frederick, KC; Chancery Division; *b* 25 Dec. 1848; *e s* of late Andrew Hamilton of Southampton; *m* 1884, Ada Margaret, *e d* of W. Morris of Caversham House, Brixton Rise; one *s*. *Educ:* London University (LLD). Called to Bar, 1879; Bencher Middle Temple. QC 1900; Member of War Compensation Court. *Publications:* Hamilton's Company Law; Compulsory Arbitration in Industrial Disputes. *Address:* 4 Whitehall Court, SW1. *T:* 3160 Victoria. *Clubs:* Reform, Argentine.
Died 17 Sept. 1922.

HAMLEY, Col Francis Gilbert, CMG 1900; Army Pay Department; *b* 1 Feb. 1851; *s* of General Hamley, CB; *m* 1878, Grace *d* (1916). *Educ:* St John's College, Auckland, New Zealand. Royal Cornwall Rangers (Militia), 1872–73; Control Department, 1873; Army Pay Department, 1878. Decorated for South Africa. *Address:* Cox and Co., Charing Cross, SW.
Died 14 Sept. 1918.

HAMMERSLEY, Maj.-Gen. Frederick, CB 1908; *b* 21 Oct. 1858; *s* of Maj.-Gen. F. Hammersley; *m* 1891, Edith, *d* of George Grant; two *d*. *Educ:* Eton; Sandhurst. Joined army, 1876; posted to 20th Regt, later Lancashire Fusiliers, 1877; raised and commanded 4th Batt. of the regiment; served on the staff at Aldershot, Dublin, and the War Office; served Egypt, 1884–85; Soudan, 1898; South Africa, 1899–1900. *Club:* Naval and Military.
Died 28 March 1924.

HAMMERSTEIN, Oscar; *b* Berlin, 1847. Built Haarlem Opera House, New York, 1889; Columbus Theatre, New York, 1890; Manhattan Theatre, New York, 1892; Victoria Theatre, New York, 1899; Republic Theatre, 1900; opened Manhattan Opera House, New York, 1906; and London Opera House, 1911. *Works:* Koh-i-nor; Santa Maria; War Bubbles; Sweet Marie; Marguerite; Mrs Radley Bradley Bore; etc. *Address:* New York Opera House, Manhattan, USA.
Died 1 Aug. 1919.

HAMMICK, Ven. Ernest Austen, MA; *b* 3 Jan. 1850; 4th surv. *s* of Rev. Sir St Vincent Hammick, 2nd Bt; *m* 1897, Mary Elizabeth Amy, *widow* of William Popham, Bray Hill, Natal. *Educ:* Exeter College, Oxford. Ordained, 1874; Curate of Christ Church, Albany Street, 1874–77; Rector of Forrabury, 1877–85; St John, Westminster, 1885–86; Archdeacon of Zululand, 1886–89; Priest in Charge of Kwamagwaza, Zululand, 1888–89; Incumbent of Blackall, Rockhampton, 1889–92; Pitsworth, Brisbane, 1892–94; Priest in Charge, Bulawayo, 1895–97; Vicar of Ulhmatulzi, 1897–1904; Archdeacon of Durban, 1899–1907; Vicar of St James, Umgeni, 1904–7; Rector of Elford, 1909–17. *Address:* Manor Road, St Marychurch, Torquay.
Died 2 Sept. 1920.

HAMMICK, Vice-Adm. Robert Frederick, JP; *b* 22 Oct. 1843; 2nd *s* of Rev. Sir Vincent Love Hammick, 2nd Bt, and *b* and *heir-pres.* of Sir St Vincent Alexander Hammick, EICS; *S* father, 1888; *m* 1st, 1869, Grace, *d* of William Longman of Ashlins, Herts; two *s* one *d* (and one *s* decd). China medal, 1856; Acting Lieut commanding the Ant at Rangarei, 1863 (promoted); served with Naval Brigade, Pukehinahina, 1864 (medal); good service pension, 1897. *Address:* Beaumont House, Stoke, Devonport.
Died 3 Dec. 1922.

HAMMICK, Sir St Vincent Alexander, 3rd Bt, *cr* 1834; Colonel, retired, 1896; *b* Devonshire, 10 April 1839; *e s* of Rev. Sir St Vincent Hammick, 2nd Bt and Mary, *d* of Robert Alexander, EICS; *S* father, 1888; *m* 1st, 1869, Penelope Sarah Blanche (*d* 1886), 2nd *d* of late C. W. Beauclerk; two *d* (one *s* decd); 2nd, Elinor, 2nd *d* of late Rev. Sir Gilbert Frankland Lewis, 3rd Bt. *Educ:* Harrow; Balliol Coll., Oxford. BA 1861. Joined 43rd Light Infantry 1861; served in New Zealand War, 1863–66 (medal, despatches). *Heir:* n George Frederick Hammick, RNVR [*b* 24 Sept. 1885; *m* 1916, Eileen Laura, *d* of Lt-Col F. Newton-King; one *d*]. *Address:* Treneere, Torquay. *T:* 368.
Died 8 Nov. 1927.

HAMMOND, Col Sir Arthur George, VC 1879; KCB 1903 (CB 1891); DSO 1889; *b* 28 Sept. 1843; *m* 1886, Edith Jane, *d* of Major J. H. Wright, ISC; one *s* two *d*. Entered ISC 1861; Col, 1890; served Jowaki Afridee (despatches, medal with clasp), 1877–78; Afghan War (despatches, VC, medal with two clasps), 1878–80; Hazara Expedition (DSO, clasp), 1888; ADC to the Queen, and Colonelcy, 1890; Hazara Expedition (despatches, CB, clasp), 1891; Isazai Expedition, 1892; Chitral Relief Force (received thanks of Govt of India, despatches, medal with clasp), 1895; Tirah Expedition, 1897–98, commanding a brigade (two clasps, despatches). *Address:* Camberley, Surrey.
Died 20 April 1919.

HAMMOND, Basil Edward; Fellow of Trinity College, Cambridge, since 1867; *b* Sopley, near Ringwood, Hants, 10 Aug. 1842; *s* of late Rev. J. P. Hammond, Vicar of Sopley; *m* 1900, Margaret Dorothea, *d* of late Rev. Francis Salter, Vicar of St Giles, Cambridge. *Educ:* Rugby; Trinity College, Cambridge. BA 1865. Assistant-Master, Haileybury College, 1865–66; Wellington College, 1868–70; Lecturer of Trinity College, 1871–97; Tutor of Trinity, 1881–85; Lecturer on History for Cambridge University, 1884–1912. *Publications:* The Political Institutions of the Ancient Greeks, 1895; Outlines of Comparative Politics, 1903; Bodies Politic and their Governments, 1915. *Recreations:* variable. *Address:* Trinity College, and Wentworth House, Cambridge. *Club:* Savile.
Died 6 Dec. 1916.

HAMOND-GRAEME, Sir Graham Eden William, 4th Bt, *cr* 1783; JP, DL; *b* 20 Aug. 1845; *e s* of Sir Andrew Snape Hamond-Graeme, 3rd Bt and Mary, *d* of Edward Miller; *S* father, 1874; *m* 1876, Evelyn, *d* of R. B. Lawes, Old Park, Dover; one *s*. Late 16th Lancers; served Abyssinian War, 1867–68 (medal). *Heir:* s Egerton Hood Murray Hamond-Graeme, Major Hampshire Carabiniers [*b* 23 May 1877. *Educ:* Cambridge (BA). *Club:* Brooks's]. *Address:* Norton, Yarmouth, Isle of Wight; St James's Court, Buckingham Gate, SW. *Club:* Cavalry.
Died 12 Jan. 1920.

HAMPSON, Sir Robert Alfred, Kt 1904; JP; Chairman of C. Tinling & Co., Ltd., Liverpool, proprietors of The Liverpool Daily Courier, The Liverpool Weekly Courier, and The Liverpool Evening Express;

b 23 Sept. 1852; *s* of William Hampson of Plas Onn, Mold, Co. Flint; *m* 1884, Kate Bolland, *d* of Walter Ashton, Warrington, Co. Lancaster; one *s* three *d*. *Educ:* Liverpool College. Solicitor; Lord Mayor of Liverpool, 1903–4. *Address:* Brown Howe, Ulverston. *Clubs:* Conservative, Athenæum, Liverpool.

Died July 1919.

HAMPSON, William, MA (Oxford), LMSSA (London); late Medical Officer in charge of Electrical and X-ray Departments, Queen's Hospital for Children, and St John's Hospital, Leicester Square; Member of the Council of the Röntgen Society; 2nd *s* of late William Hampson; *m* Amy, *d* of late J. Bolton, Nannerch. *Educ:* Liverpool College; Manchester Grammar School; Trinity College, Oxford (open scholarship). Inventor of the self-intensive method of refrigeration of gases, by which air was first liquefied cheaply, and by which hydrogen and helium were subsequently liquefied; his self-intensive air liquefier is now used in most of the universities of this country and on the Continent, and in the United States, Canada, and Australia; inventor of the first apparatus for making surgical pencils of carbonic acid snow; inventor of the Hampson radiometer for measuring doses of X-rays; discoverer of the method of controlling the beats of the heart by electrically stimulated muscle contractions. *Publications:* Radium Explained; Paradoxes of Nature and Science; Modern Thraldom—a New Social Gospel; numerous contributions to Nature and other scientific journals. *Address:* 8 West Chapel Street, Mayfair, W1. *T:* Mayfair 65; 12 Royal Crescent, W11. *T:* Park 1258.

Died 1 Jan. 1926.

HANBURY, Evan, JP; Master of the Cottesmore Foxhounds; *b* 1854; 2nd *s* of late Robert Culling Hanbury, MP, of Poles, Herts and Caroline, *e d* of Abel Smith, of Woodhall, Herts; *m* 1886, Gwendoline, 2nd *d* of George Henry Finch, MP, of Burley-on-the-Hill, Oakham. *Educ:* Eton; Christ Church, Oxford. High Sheriff, Rutland, 1892. *Address:* Braunston, Oakham. *Clubs:* Boodle's, Turf.

Died 8 Sept. 1918.

HANCOCK, Rev. Frederick, JP Somersetshire; MA; SCL; FSA; Vicar of Dunster, since 1898; Prebendary of Wells since 1899; Proctor in Convocation for diocese of Bath and Wells, 1899–1910; Treasurer of Wells Cathedral, 1914; *b* 30 Aug. 1848; *s* of Philip Hancock of Ford, and Anne Blake, *d* and *heiress* of Robert Hancock of Lydeard St Lawrence; *m* 1874, Baptista J. W., *d* of Rev. John Woodhouse of Huish Champflower, Somerset; four *s* two *d*. *Educ:* Sherborne; Wadham Coll., Oxford. 2nd class in Law and History, 1872; BA and SCL 1872; MA 1885. Deacon, 1873; priest, 1874; Curate of Luccombe, Somerset, 1876–77; domestic chaplain to Rt Hon. Sir Thomas Dyke Acland, 11th Bt, 1877–78; Rector of Meshaw, Devon, 1879–84; Rector of Selworthy, Somerset, 1884–98; Assistant Dio. Inspector of Schools, 1884–90; Rural Dean of Dunster, 1899; CC for Minehead division of Somerset, 1896–1913; Treasurer of the Cathedral Church of St Andrew, Wells, 1913. *Publications:* A History of Selworthy; A History of Minehead; Dunster Church and Priory; Wifela's Combe; A History of the Parish of Wiveliscombe. *Address:* The Priory, Dunster; Combe End, Huish Champflower, Somerset. *Clubs:* Royal Societies; Somerset County, Taunton.

Died 7 Jan. 1920.

HANCOCK, Comdr Reginald L., DSO 1916; RN; *b* 4 June 1880; *m* 1905, Millicent George, 2nd *d* of D. T. Stuart, of Wellington, New Zealand; two *s*. Served European War, 1914–17; surveying operations (DSO). *Address:* 36 Vineyard Hill, Wimbledon Park. *Club:* Junior Army and Navy. *Died 4 Aug. 1919.*

HANCOCK, Rev. William Edward; Hon. Canon of Ripon; Vicar of Knaresborough, 1888–1920; *m* Margaret Patience (*d* 1926), *d* of late Charles Carr, of Seghill House and Cramlington Hall, Northumberland. *Educ:* Trinity Hall, Cambridge. Deacon, 1869; Priest, 1870. *Address:* Chunocke Hotel, Winchester.

Died 25 Feb. 1927.

HANDFIELD-JONES, Montagu, MD (Lond.); FRCP; Obstetric Surgeon to St Mary's Hospital and to the British Lying-in Hospital; lecturer on Midwifery and Diseases of Women to St Mary's Hospital Medical School; examiner in Midwifery and Gynæcology in the University of Cambridge; *b* 12 May 1855; *e s* of Charles Handfield-Jones, FRS; *m* Maud Kathleen Dawson. *Educ:* Rugby; London University. *Publications:* contributions to various medical journals and to works on obstetric medicine and surgery. *Address:* 36 Cavendish Square, W1. *T:* Mayfair 1207. *M:* Y 382.

Died 2 July 1920.

HANDLEY, Lt-Col Arthur, CB 1918; Director of Cammell, Laird & Company; *b* 30 Sept. 1861; *m* Clara Mabel, *e d* of George Wilson, JP, late of Banner Cross, Sheffield; four *d*. *Educ:* Marlborough; RM Academy, Woolwich. Entered Royal Artillery, 1881; Capt. 1889; Major, 1899; retired, 1905; Instructor in Gunnery, 1900–2; Assistant Director of Artillery, War Office, 1902–5, and 1917–19. Officer of the Order of the Crown of Italy, 1919. *Address:* Rusthall Elms, Tunbridge Wells. *Club:* United Service.

Died 22 July 1927.

HANDS, Rev. John Compton, JP; Hon. Canon, St Paul's Cathedral, St Helena, 1895–1910; *b* Daventry, May 1842; *m* 1869, Alice Mary Metcalfe; two *s* two *d*. *Educ:* private schools, Banbury, and other places; St Augustine's College, Canterbury. Ordained, 1868; Curate of St Matthew's Longwood, 1868–75; Vicar of St Matthew's, 1875–1910; Curate of St John's, Jamestown, 1892–1900; Vicar-General of St Helena, 1890–91, 1904–5, 1909; Acting Chaplain to Forces, 1884–1906. *Recreation:* driving. *Address:* Willow Bank, Island of St Helena.

Died Nov. 1928.

HANDS, Rev. Thomas, MA; *b* Shipston-on-Stour, 19 Dec. 1856; father a corn-merchant. *Educ:* All Saints' School, Bloxham; Cowbridge Grammar School; Queen's College, Oxford (Mathematical Scholar). Degree, 1878, 1st Class Math. Mods, 1st Class Math. Greats, 2nd Class Physics. 2nd Master, Carlisle Grammar School, 1880–84; Assistant Master Clifton College, 1885–86. Deacon, 1885; Curate of St Agnes, Bristol; Priest, 1886; Curate, St Margaret's Leicester, 1887–88; Hinckley, 1888–90; Vicar of St Lawrence, Northampton, 1890–1921; Hon. Canon of Peterborough, 1919. *Recreations:* walking, gardening. *Address:* Holy Trinity Vicarage, Shoreditch, E2.

Died Nov. 1926.

HANINGTON, Rev. Canon Edward A. W., BA; Rector of St Bartholomew's Church, and Canon of Christ Church Cathedral, Ottawa; *b* New Brunswick; grandparents English; *m* 1866; one *s* six *d*. *Educ:* University of New Brunswick. Rector of Princetown, New Brunswick; Rural Dean of Woodstock, NB; Chaplain to Government House, Ottawa; Secretary of the Diocese of Ottawa. *Publication:* Short Tracts. *Recreations:* cricket, boating, chess. *Address:* St Bartholomew's Rectory, Ottawa, Canada. *TA:* Hanington, Ottawa. *T:* Rideau 2115.

Died 13 May 1917.

HANLEY, Allan Hastings, CMG 1903; FRCSI; Medical Superintendent Peamdunt Sanatorium since 1913; *b* 19 May 1863; *s* of Lt-Col Dudley Hanley of Ballycomin, Co. Roscommon. Late Deputy Principal Medical Officer, Southern Nigeria. *Address:* Peamdunt, Hazlehatch, Dublin. *Died 1921.*

HANMER, Adm. John Graham Job; *b* 1836; 2nd *s* of Capt. T. J. S. Hanmer, RN, of Holbrook Hall, Suffolk; *m* 1864, Mary Caroline, *d* of Rev. John Cobbold Aldrich; one *s* three *d*. Served China War, 1858; North China Expedition, 1860. *Address:* The Priory, Little Waldingfield, Suffolk. *Died 21 May 1919.*

HANMER, Sir Wyndham Charles Henry, 6th Bt, *cr* 1620, *re-cr* 1774; *b* 17 Sept. 1867; *s* of Sir Edward John Henry Hanmer, 5th Bt and Mary Elizabeth, *d* of Col Richard Tottenham Fosse; *S* father, 1893; *m* 1890, Essex, *d* of W. Selby Lowndes, Whaddon Hall, Bucks; one *s* four *d*. *Educ:* Eton; Christ Church, Oxford. Major in Remount Service, 1917–18. Owned about 9,000 acres. *Heir: s* Griffin Wyndham Edward Hanmer, Lieut, Shropshire Yeomanry, *b* 30 Aug. 1893. *Address:* Bettisfield Park, Flintshire. *Club:* Carlton.

Died 3 June 1922.

HANNA, Hon. William John, KC; Provincial Secretary and Registrar-General, Ontario, 1905–16; Food Controller for Canada, 1917–18; President The Imperial Oil Co., Ltd, and of Imperial Oil, Ltd; *b* Adelaide, Ontario, 13 Oct. 1862; *s* of Geo. Hanna and Jane Murdock; *m* 1st, 1891, Jean G. Neil; 2nd, Maud MacAdams, Sarnia; one *s* two *d*. *Educ:* Public Schools, Brooke, Lambton. Contested West Lambton, 1896, 1900; MPP 1902, 1905. Methodist. *Address:* Toronto, Ontario. *Clubs:* Toronto, York, Toronto.

Died 20 March 1919.

HANNAH, Rev. Joseph Addison, MA; Chaplain, Norwich Training College, 1926; Principal, Diocesan Training College at Norwich, 1895–1924; Hon. Canon of Norwich, 1918; *b* Warrington, 1 Dec. 1867; *e s* of late James Hannah of Whitehaven and Warrington. *Educ:* The Boteler Grammar School, Warrington, 1880–86; Queens' Coll., Cambridge, 1886–90; Classical Scholar; 1st class Classical Tripos, 1889; special mention for Berney University Prize. Assistant master at Warrington Grammar School, 1890–91; chaplain and tutor St John's

College, Battersea, 1892–95; deacon (Rochester diocese) gospeller, 1892; priest, 1893. *Address:* 14 Clarendon Road, Norwich.
Died Oct. 1928.

HANNYNGTON, Col (temp. Brig.-Gen.) John Arthur, CB 1918; CMG 1911; DSO 1916; 129th DCO Baluchis; *b* 26 Feb. 1868; *s* of late John Child Hannyngton, ICS; *m* 1907, Mary Gertrude, *d* of late Surgeon-Major J. R. Lewis, AMD, FRS; one *d. Educ:* United Service College, Westward Ho. Joined 1st Batt. Worcestershire Regt, 1889; transferred to Indian Army, 1892; served British E Africa, 1896, operations against Mazrui rebels (medal); Uganda, 1897–99; operations against Soudanese mutineers and rebel Waganda (medal and clasp); Somaliland, 1908–10; in command of troops (despatches, medal and clasp, CMG); European War, 1914–17 (despatches, DSO, Bt Col). *Club:* United Service.   *Died 21 Aug. 1918.*

HANSARD, Col Arthur Clifton, CMG 1917; retired, late Royal Artillery; *b* 11 June 1855; *s* of Colonel L. H. Hansard, JP; *m* Marion S., *d* of H. Minchin Simons; one *s* one *d. Educ:* Winchester College; RMA Woolwich. Commissioned in Royal Artillery, 1874; held several appointments including DAQMG at Headquarters; Lt-Col RA 1900; Colonel, 1906; retired, 1912; re-employed, Oct 1914; retired on account of health, Nov. 1916 (mentioned for distinguished service in connection with the War, 1917; awarded CMG). *Publications:* handbook and articles on professional subjects. *Recreation:* golf. *Address:* 17A Cadogan Gardens, SW3. *T:* Kensington 2498. *Clubs:* Junior United Service, Hurlingham.
Died 6 Jan. 1927.

HANSON, Sir Charles Augustin, 1st Bt, *cr* 1918; JP, DL; MP (Coal. U), Bodmin Division of Cornwall since 1916; *b* 11 Sept. 1846; *e s* of Joseph Hanson (*d* 1870) and Mary Ann (*d* 1905), *d* of late William Hicks; *m* 1868, Martha Sabina, *d* of late James Appelbe of Trafalgar, Halton, Canada; one *s* one *d. Educ:* Fowey. Alderman, City of London, 1909–21; High Sheriff, Cornwall, 1907; Sheriff of London, 1911–12; Lord Mayor of London, 1917–18. Knight of the Order of Francis Joseph; Knight Commander of the Order of the Saviour (Greece); Commander Legion of Honour (France); Grand Officer of Crown of Italy; Order of the Rising Sun, 3rd Class, Japan. *Heir:* *s* Major Charles Edwin Bourne Hanson, W Riding Regt [*b* 17 May 1874. Served South African War, 1899–1902 (Queen's medal and clasp, King's medal and two clasps). *Club:* United University]. *Address:* Fowey Hall, Cornwall. *Club:* Carlton.
Died 17 Jan. 1922.

HARBEN, William Nathaniel; novelist; *b* Dalton, Ga, 5 July 1858; *e s* of Nathaniel Parks Harben, planter, and Myra, *d* of Hiram Lewis Richardson; *m* Maybelle, *d* of Joseph B. Chandler; one *s* one *d. Educ:* high schools; privately. Travelled extensively; associate editor, The Youth's Companion, Boston, 1891–93; Member of the National Institute of Arts and Letters. *Publications:* White Marie, 1889; Almost Persuaded, 1890; A Mute Confessor, 1892; The Land of the Changing Sun, 1894; From Clue to Climax, 1896; The Caruthers' Affair, 1898; Northern Georgia Sketches, 1900; The Woman Who Trusted, 1901; Westerfelt, 1901; Abner Daniel, 1902; The Substitute, 1903; The Georgians, 1904; Pole Baker, 1905; Ann Boyd, 1906; Mam' Linda, 1907; Gilbert Neal, 1908; The Redemption of Kenneth Galt, 1909; Dixie Hart, 1910; Ann Boyd, a drama produced in Boston, 1911; Jane Dawson, 1911; Paul Rundel, 1912; The Desired Woman, 1913; The New Clarion, 1914; The Inner Law, 1915; Second Choice, 1916; The Triumph, 1917; The Hills of Refuge, 1918. *Recreations:* long walks, character study. *Address:* 854 West 181st Street, New York City; Dalton, Georgia. *T:* St Nicholas 9892. *Club:* Authors', New York City.   *Died 7 Aug. 1919.*

HARBOTTLE, Frank, DSO 1917; *b* Hobart, 1872; *s* of Joseph Harbottle; *m* 1912, Olive, *d* of Major P. W. Grant Pinnock, Brisbane; one *s* one *d. Educ:* Christ College, Hobart. Entered Civil Service; remained two years and left to follow business pursuits as Accountant and Company Secretary; joined Volunteer Artillery, 1889; Hon. Secretary to Tasmanian Rifle Association for some years before War; invented mechanical miniature rifle target, which was approved by British War Office about 1910; also an apparatus explaining gunnery problems and working of automatic sight, which was adopted by Australian military authorities. Took keen interest in trout fishing, and personally introduced English and rainbow trout into several mountain lakes in Tasmania. Served European War, 1914–17; first six months as OC Australian Garrison Artillery, Fort Nelson, Tasmania; eight months as Camp Commandant Tasmanian Reinforcement Camp, and joined 2nd Australian Division Field Artillery, Sept. 1915; was in Egypt, Dec. 1915–March 1916; and in France (DSO); gassed at Paschendaale, Nov. 1917; invalided to

Australia, Jan. 1918; joined Censor's Staff on reaching Australia; held position of Censor for Tasmania to end of War. *Recreations:* trout-fishing, golf, motoring, music. *Address:* Undruba, Queenborough, Tasmania. *Club:* Naval and Military, Hobart.
Died Sept. 1923.

HARBOTTLE, Sir John George, Kt 1918; JP; *b* 17 May 1858; *s* of William Harbottle of Great Ayton; *m* Mary Cowper, *d* of Cowper Cain, Darlington; four *d. Educ:* Preston Grammar School; Stokesley, Cleveland. Entered Municipality of Darlington, 1896; Mayor, 1900 and 1914–17; presented with the freedom of the borough, 1917. Hon. MA Cambridge, 1917. *Recreations:* golf, tennis, climbing. *Address:* Millburn, Darlington. *TA:* Harbottle, Darlington. *T:* 2385. *Club:* National Liberal.   *Died 18 Aug. 1920.*

HARCOURT, 1st Viscount, *cr* 1916; **Lewis Harcourt,** PC 1905; Baron Nuneham 1916; a Trustee of the Wallace Collection, British Museum, London Museum and National Portrait Gallery; Member of Council and Executive of British School at Rome; *b* 31 Jan. 1863; *e* surv. *s* of late Rt Hon. Sir William Harcourt and Thérèse, *d* of Thomas Henry Lister and Lady Theresa Lewis, *sister* of 4th Earl of Clarendon; *m* 1899, Mary Ethel, GBE, *o d* of late Walter H. Burns of New York and North Mymms Park, Hatfield; one *s* three *d. Educ:* Eton. MP (L) Rossendale Division, Lancashire, 1904–17; Secretary of State for the Colonies, 1910–15; First Commissioner of Works, 1905–10, and 1915–17. Hon. FRIBA; Hon. DCL (Oxford). *Heir:* *s* Hon. William Edward Harcourt, *b* 5 Oct. 1908. *Address:* 69 Brook Street, W1. *TA:* Harcourt, Wesdo, London. *T:* Mayfair 5702; Nuneham Park, Oxford. *Clubs:* Reform, National Liberal.
Died 24 Feb. 1922.

HARDCASTLE, Joseph Alfred; Astronomer at the Armagh Observatory since 1917; *b* 27 Aug. 1868; *s* of Henry Hardcastle, *g s* of Sir John Herschel, 1st Bt, and of Joseph Alfred Hardcastle, MP; *m* Theresa S. C., *d* of late Sir E. Clive Bayley, KCSI, CIE; one *s* one *d. Educ:* Harrow; Trinity College, Cambridge. Lecturer to University Extension Delegacy, Oxford, 1901; lecturer to University Extension Syndicate, Cambridge, 1908. *Address:* The Observatory, Armagh. *Club:* Athenæum.   *Died 10 Nov. 1917.*

HARDIE, Charles Martin, JP County of Fife; RSA 1895 (ARSA 1886); painter of portraits, subject pictures, and landscapes; *b* East Linton, Haddingtonshire, 16 March 1858. *Educ:* Free Church School, East Linton. Entered School of Design, Edinburgh, 1875; Royal Scottish Academy's Life School, 1877; Stuart Prize for composition, 1878; Keith Prize for best work by RSA student in Exhibition, 1880. *Principal pictures:* An Unrecorded Coronation, 1889; Burns reading his poems to the Edinburgh literati, 1887; The meeting of Burns and Scott, 1893; The Judgment of Paris, 1897; Stepping Stones and The Ford, 1913. *Recreation:* golf. *Address:* Lynedoch Studio, Edinburgh; Garthhill, North Queensferry, Fife. *Clubs:* Scottish Arts, Scottish Conservative, Edinburgh.   *Died 1 Sept. 1916.*

HARDIE, William Ross, MA Edin. and Oxon; Hon. LLD St Andrews; Professor of Humanity, Edinburgh University, since 1895; *b* Edinburgh, 6 Jan. 1862; *m* 1901, Isabella Watt, 3rd *d* of Rev. W. Stevenson; three *s* one *d. Educ:* Edin. Univ.; Balliol Coll., Oxford; Hertford and Ireland Scholarships, 1882; Gaisford Prizes (Prose and Verse), 1882; Latin Verse, 1883; 1st class in Literæ Humaniores, 1884; Craven Scholarship, 1884; Derby Scholarship, 1885. Fellow and Tutor of Balliol College, 1884–95; Junior Proctor, 1893–94. *Publications:* Lectures on Classical Subjects, 1903; Latin Prose Composition, 1908; Silvulæ Academicæ, Verses and Verse Translations, 1912; *posthumous publication:* Res Metrica, 1920. *Address:* 4 Chalmers Crescent, Edinburgh. *Clubs:* Scottish Arts, Hon. Company of Edinburgh Golfers, Edinburgh.   *Died 3 May 1916.*

HARDING, Rt. Rev. Alfred, DD, LLD; Bishop of Washington since 1909; *b* Lisburn, Ireland, Aug. 15, 1852; *s* of Richard Harding and Mary Ferguson; *m* 1887, Justine Butler Prindle; two *s* one *d. Educ:* Pyper's Academy, Belfast; Public Schools, Dublin; Trinity College (America), and Berkeley Divinity School. Served as Deacon at Trinity Church, Geneva, NY, 1883–87; Assistant, St Paul's Church, Baltimore, Maryland, and Rector, St Paul's Church, Washington, DC, 1887–1908. *Address:* Bishop's House, Cathedral Close, Mount St Alban, Washington, DC. *T:* Cleveland 948. *M:* 13337 DC, 88831 Md. *Clubs:* Alpha Delta Phi, New York City; Cosmos, Washington.
Died 30 April 1923.

HARDING, Rev. John Taylor, MA; Prebendary of St Nicholas in Llandaff Cathedral; Rural Dean of Monmouth, 1884–1919; Proctor in Convocation for Chapter of Llandaff, 1886–1919; *b* 1835; *e s* of

John Harding of Henbury Hill, Gloucestershire; *m* Patty (*d* 1919), *d* of John Etherington Welch Rolls of the Hendre, Monmouthshire; three *s*. *Educ*: Eton; Merton College, Oxford. Deacon, 1859; Priest, 1860; Curate of Cirencester, 1859–61; Curate of Stratton, Gloucestershire, 1861–64; Vicar of Rockfield, 1873–1902. *Address*: Pentwyn, Rockfield, Monmouth. *M*: AX 765 and AX 5796.

Died 30 May 1928.

HARDING, Col (Thomas) Walter, JP West Riding of York, County Borough of Leeds, and County of Cambridge; DL Cambridgeshire and Hunts; High Steward of the Borough of Cambridge; *b* 1843; *s* of T. R. Harding, DL, JP, of Leeds and Doddington, Cambs; *m* 1869, Annie Heycock (*d* 1923), *d* of Ambrose Edmund Butler of Kirkstall, Leeds; one *s*. *Educ*: France and Germany. Commanded for 20 years the 1st West York Artillery Volunteer Brigade at Leeds; President for 2 years of the Leeds Chamber of Commerce; Lord Mayor of Leeds, 1898–99; High Sheriff of the Counties of Cambs and Hunts, 1900; Hon. Freeman of the City of Leeds; contested West Leeds, 1900; Chairman of Harding, Rhodes, and Co., Ltd, Leeds. Hon. LLD Leeds 1909. *Address*: Madingley Hall, Cambridge. *TA*: Harding, Madingley. *T*: 2 Madingley. *Clubs*: Constitutional, Leeds; County, Cambridge.

Died 26 March 1927.

HARDING, Warren Gamaliel; President of the United States of America since 1920; *b* Corsica, Morrow Co., Ohio, 2 Nov. 1865; *s* of George Tyron Harding and Phebe Elizabeth Dickerson; *m* 1891, Florence Kling, of Marion, Ohio. *Educ*: Ohio Central College, Iberia. Engaged in newspaper business at Marion, Ohio, since 1884; President, Harding Publishing Co., publishers of Star (daily); member Ohio Senate, 1900–4; Lieut-Gov. of Ohio, 1904–6; Republican nominee for Governor of Ohio, 1910; member US Senate from Ohio, 1915–21; Baptist. *Address*: The White House, Washington, USA; Marion, Ohio, USA. *Club*: Marion, Marion.

Died 2 Aug. 1923.

HARDINGE, 3rd Viscount, *cr* 1846, of Lahore, and of King's Newton, Derbyshire; **Henry Charles Hardinge,** CB 1911; late Captain Rifle Brigade; late Colonel commanding 7th Battalion Rifle Brigade; ADC on Staff of Lord Roberts; ADC to the King; *b* 1 Aug. 1857; *s* of 2nd Viscount and Lavinia, *d* of 3rd Earl of Lucan; *S* father, 1894; *m* 1891, Mary, *d* of Hon. Ralph Nevill, Birling Manor, Kent, *b* of 1st Marquis of Abergavenny; one *s* two *d* (and one *s* decd). *Educ*: Harrow. Served in Nile Expedition, 1885. *Heir*: *s* Hon. Caryl Nicholas Charles Hardinge, *b* 25 Dec. 1905. *Address*: South Park, Penshurst, Tonbridge. *Clubs*: Carlton, Pratt's.

Died 30 April 1924.

HARDINGE, Sir Edmund Stracey, 4th Bt, *cr* 1801; JP, DL; *b* 27 March 1833; *s* of Rev. Sir Charles Hardinge, 2nd Bt and Emily Bradford, *d* of Kenneth Callander; *S* brother, 1873; *m* 1877, Evelyn, *d* of late Maj.-Gen. Evan Maberly, CB; one *s* two *d* (and one *d* decd). *Educ*: Tonbridge School; University Coll. Oxford. *Heir*: *s* Charles Edmund Hardinge, *b* 15 Nov. 1878. *Address*: 15 Durham Villas, W8. *T*: Western 4509. *Club*: Junior Carlton.

Died 8 April 1924.

HARDWICK, John Jessop, ARWS 1882; *b* Bow-by-Stepney, 22 Sept. 1831; *s* of William Hardwick, Beverley, Yorks; *m* 1862, Caroline, 3rd *d* of John Humphrey of Coptgilders Hall, Chessington, Surrey; one *s* one *d*. *Educ*: Bow, under Rev. John Dawson; studied under Royal Academicians, Redgrave, Herbert, and Danby. Apprenticed to Mr Henry Vizetelly, draughtsman and engraver on wood, 1847; attended School of Art, Somerset House (first prize for water-colour landscape painting from nature, 1851); on staff of The Illustrated London News, 1858; first exhibited Royal Academy, 1860. Friend of late John Ruskin, and assisted him with his classes at the Working Men's College, Great Ormond Street; Trustee and Churchwarden for Parish of Thames Ditton from 1881. *Recreation*: working in his garden. *Address*: The Hollies, Thames Ditton, Surrey.

Died 15 Jan. 1917.

HARDWICK, Lt-Col Philip Edward, DSO 1916; Commanding 10th Royal Hussars; *b* 1875; *s* of late Philip Hardwick, FSA; *m* 1904, Guina, *d* of late W. Hargrave Pawson and the Hon. Mrs Howard; one *s*. *Educ*: Eton. Joined Royal Dragoons, 1897; Captain, 1905; Major, 1914; Lt-Colonel, 10th Hussars, 1916; served with Royal Dragoons in South African War, 1899–1902 (Queen's medal 5 clasps, King's medal 2 clasps); served European War in Belgium, Flanders and France (twice wounded, despatches, DSO, 1914 Star). *Address*: 7 Albert Place, Kensington, W8. *T*: Western 4727. *Clubs*: Army and Navy, Cavalry.

Died 9 June 1919.

HARDWICKE, Herbert Junius, MD; FRCS, MRCP; 3rd *s* of late Junius Hardwicke of Chilton Lodge, Rotherham, MD, FRCS, MRCP, and *g s* of William Hardwicke of Diamond Hall, Bridgnorth, solicitor and Proctor of Bridgnorth Royal Peculiar, and *g g s* of William Hardwicke of Burcott Hall, Salop; *m* Mary Elizabeth, *o c* of late William Allen of Southfield Grange and Wink House, Yorkshire; two *s* two *d*. Late Fellow Lond. Med. Soc., and corresponding Fellow, Med. Soc. Paris, Madrid, and Athens; formerly editor of The Specialist, and Surgeon in Tevükiyeh Service, Upper Egypt; founder and formerly Physician to Sheffield Public Hospital for Ear, Throat, etc. *Publications*: Medical Education and Practice in all Parts of the World; European Health Resorts and Spas; Evolution and Creation; The Popular Faith Unveiled; Rambles Abroad; From Alps to Orient; Egypt for Invalids; Alpine Climates for Consumption; Medical Notes on the Spanish Peninsula and Marocco; Ascent of Mind; Evolution of the Special Senses; Mr Gladstone and Supernaturalism, etc. *Address*: Southfield Mount, St Leonards-on-Sea.

Died 13 Aug. 1921.

HARDY, Dudley, RI, RMS; artist; *b* Sheffield, 15 Jan. 1867; *e s* of T. B. Hardy, marine painter; *m* 1st, 1899, Mrs Burnside, (*née* Mulholland) (*d* 1906); 2nd, 1907, Annie Morrison; one *s* one *d*. *Educ*: Boulogne School; Univ. Coll. School, London. Studied at Düsseldorf, Antwerp, Paris. Member, Society Oil Painters, Society 25 English Painters and Pastel Society. *Publications*: in Illustrated London News, The Sketch, Pictorial World, Lady's Pictorial, Gentlewoman, Pick-me-up, Black and White, Graphic, and foreign papers, Punch, Sphere, etc; book illustrations, and many posters. *Recreation*: cycling. *Clubs*: Savage, Ye Punch Bowle, London Sketch.

Died 11 Aug. 1922.

HARDY, Ernest George, MA, DLitt; Principal of Jesus College, Oxford, since 1921, formerly Vice-Principal and Tutor; *b* Hampstead, 15 Jan. 1852; *e s* of George Hardy, sometime Chief Clerk in the GPO; *m* 1st, 1877, Mary, *d* of late John Mann; 2nd, 1920, Daisy Anne, *widow* of Dr Percy Gardiner, and *d* of late John Spear, surgeon. *Educ*: Highgate School; Scholar of Exeter College, 1871–74; 1st class in Classical Moderations; 1st class in final Classical School. Fellow of Jesus College, 1875; Assistant Master, Felstead School, 1877–79; Headmaster of Grantham School, 1879–87; Fellow and Tutor of Jesus College, 1894; Public Examiner in final Classical School, 1900–1. *Publications*: translator (with J. S. Mann) of Schömann's Greek Antiquities; editor of Plato's Republic, book i; Juvenal's Satires; Pliny's Correspondence with Trajan; Plutarch's Lives of Galba and Otho; author of Christianity and the Roman Government; a History of Jesus College; Studies in Roman History, first series, 1907, second series, 1910; Roman Laws and Charters, translated with introductions, etc, 1912; Monumentum Ancyranum, edited with notes, 1923; Some Problems in Roman History, 1924; Catilinarian Conspiracy, 1924; articles in Classical Review, Journal of Philology, Journal of Roman Studies, etc. *Address*: The Lodgings, Jesus College, Oxford; Jesmond, Chester Road, Bournemouth.

Died 26 Oct. 1925.

HARDY, Rev. E. J., MA; Chaplain to HM Forces; retired; *b* Armagh, Ireland, 7 May 1849; *s* of Rev. James Hardy, Rector of Moylary, Ireland; *m* 1876, Margaret, *d* of Rev. William Noble. *Educ*: Royal School, Portora; Trinity Coll. Dublin. Senior Moderator and Gold Medallist; Elrington, etc, Prizeman. Deacon, 1874; Priest, 1875; army chaplain, 1878–1908; served at Cork, Bermuda, Halifax, Dover, Gosport, Netley, Malta, Plymouth, Dublin, Hong-Kong, Egypt, Lichfield, Winchester, Aldershot. Donnellan Lecturer, Trinity Coll. Dublin, 1898–99. When at Hong-Kong visited Japan and many parts of China; gave some lectures in the large towns of England. *Publications*: How to be Happy though Married, 1884 (translated into many languages); Manners Makyth Man, 1885; Faint yet Pursuing, 1886; Uncle John's Talks with his Nephews, 1886; The Five Talents of Woman, 1888; The Business of Life, 1892; Sunny Days of Youth, 1895; The People's Life of their Queen, 1896; In the Footprints of St Paul, 1896; The Love Affairs of Some Famous Men, 1897, which is dedicated to his "only wife"; Doubt and Faith, 1899; Mr Thomas Atkins, 1900; Concerning Marriage, 1901; Love, Courtship, and Marriage, 1902; Pen Portraits of Our Soldiers, 1902; Love Rules the World, and John Chinaman at Home, 1905; How to be Happy Though Civil, 1909; The Unvarying East, 1912; The British Soldier, His Courage and Humour, 1915. *Recreations*: riding on horse, camel, ass, bicycle, top of a motor bus; talking to simple, hard-working people; looking at flowers and picking fruit in a garden; taking a sun bath; thinking of the queer things of life; swimming. *Address*: c/o Rev. F. Stoney, Tashinny Rectory, Mullingar, Ireland. *Club*: his wife's tea-table.

Died 11 Oct. 1920.

HARDY, Maj.-Gen. Frederick, CB 1907; Colonel York and Lancaster Regiment, 1903; *b* 25 Dec. 1830; *m* 1863, Kate, *y d* of Ven. S. M. Kyle, Archdeacon of Cork. Entered army, 1849; Maj.-Gen. 1885; retired, 1889; served Indian Mutiny, 1857–59 (despatches twice, medal with 2 clasps). *Address:* Ashton, Wyke Hall, Winchester. *Club:* Junior United Service.   *Died 24 Feb. 1916.*

HARDY, George Alexander, JP County of London; Alderman of London County Council; Member LCC, Dulwich Division, 1898–1907; *b* Islington, 29 Dec. 1851; *s* of late Edward Septimus Hardy; *m* 1875, Florence Marianne, *d* of late Francis Deacon Wilson; one *s*. *Educ:* privately. Merchant and manufacturer since 1874; Director London Missionary Society; Chairman of Governors, Cheshunt College; Chairman Managing Committee, National Liberal Club; Member of Tribunal, Camberwell; interested in social and philanthropic work; Captain 2/12 C of London VTC. MP (L) Stowmarket, Suffolk, 1906–10; contested Bath, 1910. *Recreations:* golf, chess, tennis, etc. *Address:* Highlands, Champion Hill, SE. *TA:* Osprey, London. *T:* 430 Brixton. *Clubs:* National Liberal, Reform.   *Died 2 Oct. 1920.*

HARDY, Iza Duffus; *o d* of the late Sir Thomas and Lady Duffus Hardy. *Publications:* A New Othello; Glencairn; Only a Love Story; A Broken Faith; Love, Honour, and Obey; Hearts are Diamonds; The Love that he Passed By; Love in Idleness; Between Two Oceans; Oranges and Alligators; The Lesser Evil; A Woman's Loyalty; MacGilleroy's Millions; Man, Woman, and Fate; A Butterfly, His Silence; The Silent Watchers, etc. *Address:* c/o London County and Westminster Bank, Temple Bar Branch, EC.
                                    Died 30 Aug. 1922.

HARDY, Richard Gillies, CSI 1900; JP and CC, Gloucestershire; Member Board of Revenue, United Provinces, India, 1902–6; *b* London, 12 Feb. 1852; *s* of late Rev. R. Hardy of Anerley; *m* 1887, Charlotte Annie, *e d* of Admiral Sir William Garnham Luard, KCB, of The Lodge, Witham, Essex; three *d*. *Educ:* Victoria College, Jersey. Served in Indian Civil Service from 1871; Magistrate and Collector of Jhansi and Moradabad districts; Commissioner Lucknow Division, 1896–1900; Member of Legislative Council, UP, 1899–1901; Chief Secretary, UP Govt, 1901; Member Viceroy's Legislative Council, 1901–2; Acting Sec. to Government of India, Revenue and Agriculture, 1902. Decorated for general and famine services. *Club:* East India United Service.   *Died 1 June 1923.*

HARDY, Rev. Theodore Bayley, VC 1918; DSO 1917; MC; CF; attached Lincoln Regiment; Priest in Charge, Hutton Roof, since 1913; Chaplain to the Forces since 1916; *b* 1866; widower; one *s* one *d*. *Educ:* City of London School; University of London. Ordained 1898; Curate Bulcott, Notts, 1898–1902; Assistant Master, High School, Nottingham, 1891–1907; Curate New Basford, 1902–7; Headmaster Bentham Grammar School, 1907–13. *Address:* Hutton Roof, Kirkby, Lonsdale.   *Died 18 Oct. 1918.*

HARDY, Thomas, OM 1910; JP Dorset; author; Hon. LLD Aberdeen; LittD Cambridge; DLitt Oxford; LLD St Andrews and Bristol; Hon. Fellow, Magdalene College, Cambridge, and Queen's College, Oxford; *b* Dorsetshire, 2 June 1840; *s* of late Thomas and Jemima Hardy; *m* 1st, 1874, Emma Lavinia (*d* 1912), *d* of J. A. Gifford, and *niece* of Archdeacon Gifford; 2nd, 1914, Florence Emily, JP for Dorchester, *d* of Edward Dugdale, and author of numerous books for children, magazine articles, and reviews. *Educ:* Dorchester; King's College, London. Pupil of John Hicks, ecclesiastical architect, 1856–61; read Latin and Greek with a fellow-pupil, 1857–60; sketched and measured many old country churches later pulled down or altered; removed to London and worked at Gothic architecture under Sir Arthur Blomfield, ARA, 1862–67; prizeman of Royal Institute of British Architects, 1863; the Architectural Assoc., 1863; wrote verses, 1865; gave up verse for prose, 1868–70; but resumed it later. Pres., Society of Authors, 1909. Gold Medal of Royal Society of Literature; Member of the Council of Justice to Animals; against blood-sport, dog-chaining, and the caging of birds. *Publications:* Prose—Desperate Remedies, 1871; Under the Greenwood Tree or The Mellstock Quire, 1872; A Pair of Blue Eyes, 1872–73; Far from the Madding Crowd, 1874; Hand of Ethelberta, 1876; Return of the Native (with map), 1878; The Trumpet-Major, 1879; A Laodicean, 1880–81; Two on a Tower, 1882; The Life and Death of the Mayor of Casterbridge, 1884–85; The Woodlanders, 1886–87; Wessex Tales (collected), 1888; A Group of Noble Dames, 1891; Tess of the d'Urbervilles, 1891; Life's Little Ironies (collected), 1894; Jude the Obscure, 1895; The Pursuit of the Well-Beloved, serially 1892, revised and re-written as The Well-Beloved, 1897; A Changed Man, etc (collected), 1913. Verse—Wessex Poems (written 1865 onwards),

1898; Poems of the Past and the Present, 1901; The Dynasts (epic-drama), Part I, 1903; Part II, 1906; Part III, 1908; Select Poems of William Barnes, with Preface, 1908; Time's Laughing-stocks and other Verses, 1909; Satires of Circumstance (serially), 1911 (with Lyrics and Reveries), 1914; Selected Poems, 1916; Moments of Vision, 1917; Late Lyrics, 1922; Queen of Cornwall (play), 1923; Human Shows, 1925; definitive Wessex edition of works in prose and verse with new prefaces and notes, 1912 onwards; complete Poetical Works, 2 vols, 1919; limited Mellstock Edition of works, 1920. *Address:* Max Gate, Dorchester, Dorset. *Club:* Athenæum.
                                    Died 11 Jan. 1928.

HARDY, William John, Hon. MA Durham, 1909; FSA; legal and genealogical record searcher and translator; *b* London, 29 Sept. 1857; 2nd *s* of Sir William Hardy, Deputy-Keeper of the Public Records, and Miss E. C. S. Lee, West Cholderton Manor, Wilts; *m* 1886, Margaret (*d* 1911), *e d* of Henry Page, London and Oporto; one *s* one *d*. *Educ:* privately. Council, Society of Antiquaries, 1887–89, 1891–93, 1895–97, 1907, 1912–13; Inspector, Historical MSS Commission; editor of Calendar of State Papers, William and Mary (Master of the Rolls Series); Middlesex and Hertfordshire Notes and Queries, 1895–98; Home Counties Magazine, 1899–1904. *Publications:* Handwritings of the Kings and Queens of England, 1893; Book Plates, 1893, 2nd edn 1897; Lighthouses, their History and Romance, 1895; Documents Illustrative of English Church History (jointly with Rev. H. Gee), 1896; The Stamp Collector (jointly with E. D. Bacon), 1898. *Recreations:* archæology, entomology, the collection of book-plates. *Address:* The Firs, St Albans, Herts; 15 Old Square, Lincoln's Inn, WC.
                                    Died 17 July 1919.

HARE, Francis, MD Durham; MRCS; Medical Superintendent, Oaklands, Beckenham; late Medical Superintendent, Norwood Sanatorium; *b* Dublin, 13 Feb. 1858; *s* of Matthias Hare, LLD, and Frances Louisa Everard; *m* 1902, Ethel Maud Bell; one *s*. *Educ:* Fettes College, Edinburgh. Surgeon, P&O; Surgeon-Superintendent Queensland Immigration Service; Resident Medical Officer and acting Medical Superintendent, Brisbane General Hospital; Medical Superintendent, Charters Towers District Hospital, Queensland; Inspector-General of Hospitals for Queensland; Medical Superintendent and Visiting Physician, Diamantina Hospital for Chronic Diseases, Queensland; Consulting Physician, Brisbane General Hospital. *Publications:* The Cold-Bath Treatment of Typhoid Fever; The Food Factor in Disease; On Alcoholism: its clinical aspects and treatment. *Recreations:* various. *Address:* Oaklands, 15 The Avenue, Beckenham, Kent.   *Died 9 Dec. 1928.*

HARE, Henry Thomas; President, Royal Institute of British Architects; *b* Scarborough; *m* 1884, 2nd *d* of late W. H. Ferons, Durham; one *d*. *Educ:* privately at Sheffield and Harrogate. Articled in 1876; studied subsequently at Ecole des Beaux Arts, Paris; ARIBA, 1887; FRIBA, 1898; Vice-President, 1904–8; Hon. Secretary, 1909–13; Ashpitch Prizeman, 1886. Buildings executed: City Buildings, Oxford; County Buildings, Stafford; Westminster College, Cambridge; North Wales University, Bangor, and others. *Address:* 2 Gray's Inn Square, WC1. *T:* Central 2507; Egypt, Farnham Common, Bucks.   *Died 10 Jan. 1921.*

HARE, Sir John, Kt 1907; actor and theatre manager; *b* London, 16 May 1844; *m* 1864, Mary Adela Elizabeth, *d* of John Hare Holmes; one *s* two *d*. *Educ:* Giggleswick Grammar School, Yorkshire. First appearance on the stage, Prince of Wales' Theatre, Liverpool, 28 Sept. 1864; in London, 25 Sept. 1865, where he appeared in the entire series of Robertson Comedies, Sir Peter Teazel in School for Scandal, and other parts; became manager of the Court Theatre, 13 March 1875, when he produced Olivia and other plays; manager of St James' Theatre in partnership with Mr Kendal, 1879; opened and became manager of the Garrick Theatre, 1889–94; amongst other characters played by him during this period were Col Daunt in Queen's Shilling, Lord Kilclare in Quiet Rubber, Duke of St Olpherts in Notorious Mrs Ebbsmith, Goldfinch in Pair of Spectacles, and Lord Quex. *Address:* 47 Westbourne Terrace, W3. *T:* Paddington 6660. *Clubs:* Garrick, Beefsteak.   *Died 28 Dec. 1921.*

HARE, Sir Lancelot, KCSI 1907 (CSI 1906); CIE 1900; Indian Civil Service, Bengal; *b* London, 7 Jan. 1851; *y s* of late Thomas Hare of Hook, Surrey; *m* 1st, 1881, Laura Maud (*d* 1916), *e d* of late General Sir John Nation, KCB; 2nd, Marjorie Edith, *d* of late Capt. Eustace Maudslay. *Educ:* Hurstpierpoint, Sussex; City of London School. Served in Bengal and Assam from 1873; member Board of Revenue, Calcutta, 1903; member of Governor-General's Council, 1905–6; Officiating Lt-Governor, Bengal, 1906; Lieut.-Gov. East Bengal and

Assam, 1906–11. Decorated for service in India. *Address:* 8 Embankment Gardens, Chelsea, SW. *Club:* Albemarle.

Died 7 Oct. 1922.

HARE, Col Richard Charles, CB 1900; retired pay; *b* 8 Aug. 1844; *e s* of late Col Hon. Richard Hare and *g g s* of 1st Earl of Listowel; *m* 1875, Mary, *o d* of late Lieut-Gen. Sir Charles Ashe Windham, KCB; two *s* two *d* (and two *s* one *d* decd). Appointed Ensign in 22nd Foot, 1863; was Adj. for 1st Batt., and commanded the 2nd Batt., 1892–96; commanded 63rd Regimental District, 1898–1900; and the 24th Regimental District, 1900–2; passed the Staff College; served as ADC to Commander-in-Chief of Canada, 1867–70; DAQMG under Lord Wolseley in Cyprus, 1878–79; Brigade-Major, Aldershot, 1879–83; served in Ashanti Expedition, 1873–74 (medal and clasp), as Acting RE Officer; also in Egyptian Campaign, 1882, as Brigade-Major (despatches, and Brevet-Major, Egyptian medal and Khedive's bronze star, 4th class Medjidie). *Address:* Reymerston Hall, Attleborough, Norfolk. *Club:* United Service.

Died 31 Oct. 1917.

HARFORD, Charles Forbes, MA, MD; MRCS, LRCP; Refraction Assistant St Bartholomew's Hospital; Oculist to School Clinics London and Herts CC; Emeritus Lecturer, late Principal of Livingstone College; Instructor in Health and Outfit to Royal Geographical Society; Joint Secretary Fédération Internationale pour la Protection des Races Indigènes contre l'Alcoolisme; *y s* of late Rev. Canon Harford-Battersby, Keswick; *m* Adeline, *d* of William Clapton, FRCS; one *d. Educ:* Repton; Trinity College, Cambridge; St Thomas' Hospital. Medical Missionary of the CMS in West Africa, 1890–92; with others founded Livingstone College and became its first Principal, 1893; Honorary Secretary (later Chairman of Executive) of Native Races and the Liquor Traffic United Committee, 1896–1904; Physician of CMS 1903–11; Secretary Medical Committee CMS, 1911–19; Joint Secretary Society of Tropical Medicine and Hygiene, 1908–17; Temp. Captain, RAMC; Secretary Church of England Temperance Society, 1919; Diocesan Reader in London, St Albans, and Chelmsford Dioceses. *Publications:* Pilkington of Uganda; Do you Pray? Daily; Hints on Outfit for Travellers in the Tropics; Mind as a Force. *Address:* 30 Finsbury Square, EC2. *T:* Clerkenwell 1258; Shirley, Ox Lane, Harpenden. *T:* Harpenden 165.

Died 4 July 1925.

HARFORD, Rev. Edward John; Canon Residentiary of Wells since 1903; Rural Dean of Keynham; *m* 1864, Gertrude Emma, *y d* of Rev. Sir Thomas Pym Bridges, 7th Bt; one *s* four *d. Educ:* Oxford (2nd class Law and History). Ordained, 1857; Curate of Deal, also Curate and Lecturer of Henbury, Bristol, 1860–70; Vicar of Bathford, 1870–92; Rector of Marston-Biggott, 1892–1905; late Rural Dean of Frome. *Address:* The Liberty, Wells, Somerset. *TA:* Nunney, Frome.

Died 27 Aug. 1917.

HARFORD, Rev. George, MA; Vicar of Mossley Hill, Liverpool; Hon. Canon of Liverpool; Joint Editor of The Hexateuch according to the Revised Version and of the Prayer Book Dictionary; *b* 1860; *s* of T. D. Harford-Battersby, late Vicar of St John's, Keswick, and Hon. Canon of Carlisle; *m* 1889, Helen Antoinette, *d* of Col E. C. Impey, CIE; one *s* three *d. Educ:* Harborne Vicarage; Repton School; Balliol College, Oxford (1st Class Math. Mods, 2nd Class Math. Finals, 1st Cl. Theol.); Liverpool (MA by Diss. in Philos. 1915). Held curacy in South Lambeth and benefice of Middle w. East Claydon, Bucks. *Publications:* articles in Hastings' Dictionary of the Bible; the Church Congress Manual; Church Song and Prayer with Tunes. *Address:* Mossley Hill Vicarage, Liverpool. *T:* 3 X Mossley Hill.

Died 21 Feb. 1921.

HARGREAVES, John, MFH; *b* Leighton Park, near Reading, 1 March 1864; *e s* of late John Hargreaves of Broad Oak, Whalley Abbey, and Maiden Erleigh, Berkshire, and Mary Jane, *o d* of Alexander Cobham Cobham of Shinfield Manor, Berks; *m* 1889, Evelyn Kennard, 5th *d* of William Bunce Greenfield; three *d. Educ:* Eton. Entered 15th Hussars, 1887; Master of the Cattistock, 1897–1900; Master of the Blackmore Vale, 1900–5. *Address:* Templecombe House, Templecombe, Somerset. *Club:* Junior Carlton.

Died 21 April 1926.

HARKER, Ven. Archdeacon Ernest Gardner; Archdeacon of Matabeleland and Rector of Bulawayo, 1913–27. *Educ:* Exeter College, Oxford (MA). Ordained 1893; Curate of St Paul, Burton-on-Trent, 1893–96; Holy Cross, Shrewsbury, 1897; Rector of Castle Bromwich, 1897–1911; Diocesan Inspector of Schools, Birmingham, 1897–98; Dean and Archdeacon of Salisbury, Rhodesia, 1911; Vicar-general of Diocese of Southern Rhodesia, 1923–24 and 1926; Chaplain

of Queen Margaret's School, Scarborough, 1927. *Address:* 1 Princess Royal Park, Scarborough, Yorkshire.

Died 25 Dec. 1928.

HARKER, John Allen, OBE 1918; DSc; FRS; Member of the firm of J. T. Crowley and Partners, Consulting Engineers; Director of Research, Ministry of Munitions, 1916–21; formerly Chief Assistant at the National Physical Laboratory, Teddington; *b* Alston, Cumberland, 23 Jan. 1870; *s* of late Rev. John Harker, Congregational minister; *m* Ada, *d* of late Thomas Richardson, CC, JP, of Alston; two *s* three *d. Educ:* Stockport Grammar School; Universities of Manchester and Tübingen. Dalton Chemical Scholarship at Owens College, 1891; Berkeley Fellowship in Physics, 1892; Member of the Councils of the Physical Society of London and of the Faraday Society; Member of the British Association Committee on Gas Engines; Member of the Royal Institution; was the delegate of the British Government at the International Petroleum Congress, Vienna, 1912; Superintendent (*pro tem.*) Eskdalemuir Observatory, 1913; was responsible during the war for the organisation of the work of the Nitrogen Products Committee of the Ministry of Munitions, and was Director of the Research Laboratories set up to study modern nitrogen fixation processes; was on board the Cunard liner Andania torpedoed off the north coast of Ireland Jan. 1918; later visited the United States and Canada on behalf of the Ministry at the request of the American Government; was member during the war of a large number of Government Committees on Scientific Problems, including the Oxygen Committee and the Gas Cylinders Committee of the Dept Sci. and Ind. Research. *Publications:* a number of papers, mostly on thermal and electrical subjects, in Philosophical Transactions and Proceedings Royal Society, Philosophical Magazine, etc. *Address:* 16 Victoria Street, SW1; 6 Cambridge Terrace, Regent's Park, NW1; Clarghyll Hall, Alston, Cumberland. *Club:* National Liberal.

Died 10 Oct. 1923.

HARKER, Joseph Cunningham; painter; *b* Levenshulme, Manchester, 17 Oct. 1855; father was well-known character actor in Manchester; mother before her marriage was Maria O'Connor, an actress, sister of John O'Connor, artist; *m* 1877, Sarah Hall, *d* of scene painter of that name; six *s* three *d.* Came to London, 1870; apprenticed to T. W. Hall, scene painter, and assisted in many notable productions at the Haymarket Theatre under Buckstone's management; then followed seasons in Glasgow and Dublin in 1882–83; in 1885-6-7-8 went for seasons to United States to paint some huge panoramic pictures, then much in vogue; returning to England, was then engaged by Sir Henry Irving for all of his productions until his death, and was associated with all the leading London theatrical managements. *Publication:* Studio and Stage, 1924. *Recreations:* music, sailing. *Clubs:* Savage, London Sketch.

Died 15 April 1927.

HARKNESS, James, MA; FRSC 1909; *b* Derby, 24 Jan. 1864; *s* of late John Harkness, Derby; *m* 1908, Katherine E., *e d* of Rev. W. H. Cam, Paulers-Pury Rectory, Towcester; two *s* one *d. Educ:* Derby School; Trinity Coll., Cambridge (Major Scholar); first in Mathematics in the Honour Examinations for the Intermediate and BA at London University. Successively Associate, Associate Professor, and Professor of Mathematics at Bryn Mawr College, Pennsylvania, USA, 1888–1903; Peter Redpath Prof. of Pure Mathematics, McGill University, Montreal, 1903–13. Formerly Vice-President of the American Mathematical Society, and sub-editor of Transactions of the American Mathematical Society; LLD McGill University, 1921. *Publications:* (with Prof. Frank Morley) two treatises on the Theory of Functions; assisted in the article on Elliptic Functions in the German Encyclopædia of Mathematics; scientific papers in the Transactions of Royal Society of Canada, etc. *Recreation:* lawn tennis. *Address:* Arts Building, McGill University, Montreal; 23 Lorne Avenue, Montreal, Canada.

Died Dec. 1923.

HARLEY, Lt-Col Henry Kellett, DSO 1895; late 7th Hussars; *b* 2 Dec. 1868; *m* 1st, 1899, Hon. Margaret Holland, *d* of 1st Baron Rotherham; one *s* one *d*; 2nd, Thella, *d* of Henri Bluston, of Kovno, Russian Poland; three *s*. Entered army, 1890; served Chitral Expedition, 1895; defence of Chitral Fort (despatches, DSO, medal and clasp); Sudan Expedition, 1897 (medal and clasp); Sudan Expedition, 1898; Battle of Atbara (despatches, severely wounded, clasp, and English-Sudan medal, 4th Class Medjidie); Brevet of Major, 1898; South African Field Force, 1901–2 (medal, 5 clasps); served European War, in France with RFA and RGA, 1916–17 (Croix de Guerre, Bronze Military Medal for valour, despatches); later on the Staff of British Mission, GHQ, Italy. *Address:* Raycroft, Maidenhead. *Clubs:* White's, Cavalry.

Died 9 Jan. 1920.

HARLEY, Vaughan, MD; MRCP; late Professor, University College London; physician; *b* London, 28 Dec. 1863; *s* of late Dr George Harley, FRS, and Emma, *d* of James Muspratt, Seaforth Hall; *m* 1905, Mary, *e d* of Rev. Canon Blagden, of Peverel Court, Aylesbury; two *d*. *Educ:* Edinburgh Univ.; Paris, Leipzig, Vienna, Buda Pest, Turin, etc. MD Edinburgh, Gold Medallist; Bronze Medallist in Pathology; Grocer Research Scholarship. Travelled round the world, 1887–88; studied at foreign universities, 1888–92; from 1892 practising in London as a physician. *Publications:* The Chemical Investigation of Diseases of the Stomach and Intestines; numerous—in Royal Soc. Transactions, English and foreign physiological journals and medical papers. *Recreations:* travelling, farming. *Address:* 25 Harley Street, W1. *T:* Mayfair 2643; Walton Hall, Bletchley, Bucks. *Club:* Junior Carlton.
Died 21 May 1923.

HARMAN, Edward George, CB 1911; *b* 28 Nov. 1862; 2nd *s* of late Rev. Edward Harman. *Educ:* Uppingham (Scholar); King's College, Cambridge. Entered the Home Civil Service, Admiralty, 1886; Home Office, 1886; Treasury, 1889; seconded for service under Lord Kitchener of Khartoum as Financial Secretary to the Soudan Government, 1898–1900; accompanied Sir David Barbour on financial mission to South Africa, 1900–1; a Principal Clerk in HM Treasury, 1907–12; retired, 1912. *Address:* 3 Middle Temple Lane, EC4. *Club:* New University.
Died 20 Dec. 1921.

HARMER, Frederic William, JP; MA (Hon.) Cantab; FGS, FRMetS; *b* Norwich, 24 April 1835; *s* of Thomas and Emily Harmer; *m* Mary, *d* of Adam Lyon; four *s* one *d*. *Educ:* Norwich. Mayor of Norwich, 1887–8; Alderman, 1880–1902; Geological Society, London, Council, 1896–1900; Murchison Medallist, 1902; Palaeontographical Soc., Council, 1878–82; Norfolk and Norwich Nat. Soc., Pres., 1877–79; late Chairman and Man. Director, Norwich Electricity Co., Ltd; Trustee King Edward VI Grammar School, Norwich; Dep. Chairman, 1909–13; Member of Mousehold Heath Conservators; Committee Norfolk and Norwich Horticultural Soc.; Norwich Castle Museum; Norwich Public Library; Income Tax Commissioners, etc; 1864–72 carried out with the late Searles V. Wood, Jr, the first survey of the glacial beds of the East of England, a portion of the map being published in 1872 by the Palaeont. Soc.; travelled some thousands of miles in the investigation of the Pliocene and Pleistocene deposits of the eastern and midland counties, and of those of Belgium and Holland. Mem. Hon. Soc. Belge Géol. 1904; Mem. Géol. Soc., France. *Publications:* Pliocene Mollusca of Great Britain, six parts issued by the Palæontographical Soc., 1914–21, and in progress; many original papers on Geology, Palæontology, and Palæometeorology, by the Geol Soc. of London, Geol Assoc. Lond., Soc. Belge de Géol., Norfolk and Norwich Nat. Soc., Yorks Geol Soc., etc. *Recreations:* horticulture, scientific work. *Address:* Oakland House, Cringleford, near Norwich. *TA:* Harmer, Eaton, Norwich. *T:* Eaton 81.
Died 11 April 1923.

HARMOOD-BANNER, Sir John Sutherland, 1st Bt, *cr* 1924; Kt 1913; JP, DL; MP (C) Everton Division, Liverpool, 1905–24; *b* Liverpool, 8 Sept. 1847; *m* 1st, 1875, Elizabeth, *d* of late Thomas Knowles of Darnhall, Cheshire, MP for Wigan; two *s* one *d* (and two *s* two *d* decd); 2nd, 1908, Ella, *d* of John Ernest Herbert Linford. *Educ:* Radley. Entered father's office, Harmood-Banner and Sons, Accountants, Liverpool, 1865; partner, 1870; Auditor Bank of Liverpool. Pres., ICA, 1904–5, AMC, 1907. High Sheriff, Cheshire, 1902; Lord Mayor of Liverpool, 1913. *Heir:* s Harmood Harmood-Banner, *b* 28 Oct. 1876. *Address:* 63 Lowndes Square, SW. *T:* Victoria 377; Ingmire Hall, Sedbergh, Yorkshire. *Clubs:* Junior Carlton, Carlton.
Died 24 Feb. 1927.

HARNESS, Maj.-Gen. Arthur, CB 1879; retired from Royal Artillery; *b* 2 June 1838; *s* of General Sir Henry Harness, KCB; unmarried. *Educ:* Carshalton; Woolwich. Entered army, 1857; served in Cape and Zulu Wars, 1877–78–79; Brevet of Lieut-Colonel and CB; extra ADC to HRH the Commander-in-Chief, 1887–92; Maj.-Gen., 1894; Colonel Commandant RA, 1906. Decorated for service in the field. *Address:* 19 Montpelier Villas, Brighton. *Club:* Army and Navy.
Died 13 Oct. 1927.

HAROLD, John, MB, BCh, BAO; MRCS, LRCP; *b* Dublin; 2nd *s* of William Harold, Dublin; *m*; three *s* two *d*. *Educ:* Belvedere College, Dublin; University College, London; Charing Cross Hospital, London. Physician to Hospital of St John and St Elizabeth; Senior Assistant Editor of Quain's Dictionary of Medicine; Advisory Editor of The International Clinics; late Medical Registrar, Charing Cross Hospital. *Publications:* many contributions to Quain's Dictionary of Medicine. *Recreation:* country life. *Address:* 65 Harley Street, W. *T:*

1039 Pad.; Milford, Surrey. *T:* Milford 3. *Clubs:* Garrick, Caledonian; West Surrey Golf.
Died 27 May 1916.

HARPER, Lt-Gen. Sir George Montague, KCB 1918 (CB 1915); DSO 1900; GOC Southern Command since 1919; *b* 11 Jan. 1865; *s* of late Charles Harper; *m* 1893, Hon. Ella Constance Jackson, 2nd *d* of 1st Baron Allerton. Entered army, 1884; Captain, 1892; Lt-Col 1907; Col 1911; served South Africa, 1899–1900 (despatches four times, Queen's medal, four clasps, DSO); European War, 1914–18 (despatches, CB, prom. Maj.-Gen., KCB); Commander Legion of Honour. *Club:* Naval and Military.
Died 15 Dec. 1922.

HARPER, Ven. Henry William. *Educ:* Eton; Merton College, Oxford (MA). Ordained 1857; Curate of Waimakariri District, 1857–64; Commissary of Bishop of Christchurch in England, 1864–66; Vicar of Hokitika, 1866–75; Canon of Christ Church Cathedral and Archdeacon of Timaru, 1875–1911. *Address:* 58 Kensington Palace Mansions, De Vere Gardens, W.
Died 20 Jan. 1922.

HARPIGNIES, Henri Joseph; artist; *b* Valenciennes, 1819. *Educ:* Paris, under Achard; two years in Italy. First exhibited in Salon, 1853; accompanied Corot to Italy, 1860. Legion of Honour, 1875; Médaille d'Honneur of the Salon, 1897. *Address:* Rue Coetlogon 9, Paris.
Died 29 Aug. 1916.

HARRIES, Arthur John, MD; FRSM; consulting physician; *b* 1856; father, colliery owner; *m* 1st, 1879; 2nd, 1907; five *s* one *d*. *Educ:* University College, London; Brussels University. Formerly Physician and Lecturer on Clinical Dermatology to St John's Hospital for Diseases of Skin, Leicester Square; later Physician to Electrical Department, Western Skin Hospital; in 1885 first suggested aseptic vaccination in his appendix to his translation of Warlomont's Animal Vaccination; in 1886, lecturing at St John's Hospital, expressed reasons why the bacillus of lupus was different from that of human tuberculosis; showed intimate relation between band alopœcia and hyper-thyroidism in exophthalmic goitre; was a pioneer of electro-therapeutics in England; demonstrated discomfort and fixation points for battery-produced alternating currents at Institution Electrical Engineers in 1890, and for dynamo currents at British Association the same year; also showed how local anæsthesia could be produced by cataphoresis (Lancet, 1890). Past-President Bartholomew Club, City, and Past President City of London Tradesmen's Club. *Publications:* Animal Vaccination (Warlomont), translator and editor, with Appendix, 1885; Lectures on Lupus, 1886; Electrolysis in Stricture, 1891; Manual of Electro Therapeutics, 1890; papers on Cataphoric Medication, 1889 (Med. Press and Circ.); Dangers and Uses of Electricity (Trans Soc. of Arts, 1891), and Therap. Application of Continuous Current (Therap. Soc., later Royal Soc. Med. 1904). *Address:* 30 St James's Square, St James's, SW; 118 Dartmouth Road, Brondesbury, NW. *T:* Gerrard 938.
Died 27 July 1922.

HARRIES, Robert Henry, JP; Master of the Carmarthenshire Foxhounds, 1902–14; *b* 11 Dec. 1859; *o s* of late Essex Harries of Upper Scolton, near Haverfordwest; *m* 1893, Arabella, *d* of late George Blaney Meager of Marine Villa, The Mumbles, Glamorganshire, and The Penrhyn, Goodwick, Pembrokeshire; one *s* one *d*. *Educ:* Cowbridge. Began his hunting career at the age of 8 with the Pembrokeshire, which he followed until he took over the Carmarthenshire; a hunter judge in all the shows in England, Ireland, and Wales; during the summer months acted as Deputy-Master of the Pembrokeshire and Carmarthenshire Otter Hounds. Joined the ASC at the Remount Depot, Shirehampton, and was made Lieutenant, 12 March 1917. *Recreations:* keen on shooting and other sports. *Address:* The Croft, St Clears, Carmarthenshire. *Club:* County, Carmarthen.
Died 25 Dec. 1918.

HARRINGTON, 8th Earl of, *cr* 1742; **Charles Augustus Stanhope;** Baron Harrington, 1729; Viscount Petersham, 1742; CE (retired); ADC to the King; Commandant of the South Derbyshire Battalion Home Guards; Lieutenant-Colonel commanding Cheshire Yeomanry; MFH (Harrington); *b* 9 Jan. 1844; *s* of 7th Earl and Elizabeth Still, *d* of Robert Lucas de Pearsall; *S* father, 1881; *m* 1869, Hon. Eva Elizabeth Carington, *y d* of 2nd Lord Carrington. *Educ:* Queen's Coll. Belfast; Christ Church, Oxford. Owned about 13,000 acres. *Publication:* Polo-Pony Stud Book, vol. i. *Recreations:* MFH, South Notts, polo, yachting, gardening. *Heir:* *b* Hon. Dudley Henry Eden Stanhope [*b* 13 Jan. 1859; *m* 1883, Kathleen, *d* of J. C. Wood, Felcourt, Sussex; one *s* one *d* (and one *s* decd). *Address:* Bartley Close, Totton, Hants]. *Address:* Elvaston Castle, Derby; Gawsworth,

Macclesfield; Harrington House, Charing Cross, SW. *Clubs:* Carlton, White's, Hurlingham, Marlborough; Royal Yacht Squadron, Cowes.
Died 5 Feb. 1917.

HARRINGTON, 9th Earl of, *cr* 1742; **Dudley Henry Eden Stanhope;** Baron Harrington, 1729; Viscount Petersham, 1742; *b* 13 Jan. 1859; 6th *s* of 7th Earl and Elizabeth Still, *d* of Robert Lucas de Pearsall, Wartensee Castle, Switzerland; *S* brother, 1917; *m* 1883, Kathleen, *d* of J. C. Wood, Felcourt, Sussex; one *s* one *d* (and one *s* decd). Owned about 6,000 acres. *Heir: s* Viscount Petersham, *b* 9 Oct. 1887. *Address:* Elvaston Castle, Derby; Gawsworth, Macclesfield.
Died 13 Nov. 1928.

HARRINGTON, Sir John Lane, KCMG 1909; KCVO 1903 (CVO 1901); CB 1902; late Major, Indian Army; Lieutenant-Colonel (Hon.) 1917; *b* 16 Jan. 1865; *s* of late Nicholas Harrington, MRCS; *m* 1907, Amy, *d* of late US Senator Macmillan. *Educ:* Stonyhurst Coll. Entered army, 1884; Vice-Consul at Zaila, 1895–98; Consul, 1898; Minister Plenipotentiary at Court of Emperor Menelek of Ethiopia, 1903; Minister Plenipotentiary and Envoy Extraordinary, 1908–9; Agent, 1898; Agent and Consul-General, 1900. Contested (C) Crewe Division, Cheshire, 1910, and Battersea, 1910, (IU) North Southwark, 1918. Served with BEF France, 1915–16, in command of a Batt. (despatches). *Address:* Midland Bank Ltd, 36 Old Bond Street, W1. *Clubs:* Turf, Carlton, Marlborough, White's, Beefsteak.
Died 8 Sept. 1927.

HARRIS, Hon. Addison C.; late US Minister to Austria; *b* Wayne Co., Ind., 1840. *Educ:* NW University. Member State Senate, 1870–79. Pres. Board Trustees, Purdue University. *Publication:* Indiana (9th edn Ency. Brit.). *Address:* Indianapolis, Ind., USA.
Died 1916.

HARRIS, Rt. Hon. Frederick Leverton, PC 1916; Officer of the Legion of Honour (France); Officer St Maurice and St Lazarus (Italy); Parliamentary Secretary to Ministry of Blockade, 1916–18; *b* 17 Dec. 1864; *s* of late F. W. Harris, JP; *m* 1886, Gertrude, *d* of John G. Richardson of Moyallon and Bessbrook, Ireland; no *c*. *Educ:* Winchester; Gonville and Caius Coll., Cambridge (MA). Member of Tariff Commission, 1904; MP (C) Tynemouth, 1900–6; MP (U) Stepney, 1907–10; MP E Worcestershire, 1914–18; LCC Stepney, 1907–10; Hon. Capt. RNVR. *Publications:* various articles in National Review and other journals; pamphlets on Tariff Reform. *Recreations:* shooting, fishing, painting, travelling. *Address:* 70 Grosvenor Street, W; Small Downs House, Sandwich. *Club:* Carlton.
Died 14 Nov. 1926.

HARRIS, Frederick Rutherfoord, JP; financier and surgeon; MP (U) Dulwich, 1903–6, resigned seat through going abroad; MP (C) Monmouth District, 1900, unseated on petition, 1901; *b* 1 May 1856; *m* 1884, Florence, *d* of W. Ling of Hempstead Hall, Norfolk. *Educ:* Leatherhead Grammar School; Baden; matriculated at Edinburgh University, and graduated at Royal College of Surgeons. Went to South Africa, 1882; became Mr Rhodes's confidential agent; appointed first Secretary to British South Africa Company; elected to Cape Parliament as one of four members for Kimberley, 1894–96; re-elected, 1898; one of Whips for Rhodes' Administration; gave evidence before House of Commons Committee (Jameson Raid) of 1897; was one of chief members of Progressive party in Cape Colony. *Recreations:* coursing, shooting, fishing. *Address:* Llangiby Castle, Usk, Monmouthshire. *Clubs:* Carlton, Union.
Died 1 Sept. 1920.

HARRIS, Frederick William, JP Co. Glamorgan; one of HM Lieutenants, City of London; Member of the Council of the University College of Wales; Past Master of the Drapers' Company; Chairman of Harris and Dixon, Ltd; Director of the Commercial Union Assurance Co. Ltd; Founder of the Deep Navigation Colliery, and of the Town of Treharris in Glamorganshire; *b* 1833; *s* of late Edward Harris and Isabella, *d* of late John Tindall of Knapton Hall, Co. York; *m* Elizabeth Rachel, *d* of late Peter Macleod Wylie, Edinburgh. *Educ:* Private School of Society of Friends. Chairman of the Coal Factors Society, 1887–1905. *Address:* 23 Devonshire Place, W; Park Grove, Withyham, Sussex. *Clubs:* City of London, Oriental.
Died 4 Feb. 1917.

HARRIS, George, DD, LLD; President Emeritus of Amherst College; *b* East Machias, Maine, USA, 1 April 1844; *o s* of George and Mary A. Harris; *m* 1873, Jane A. Viall, Providence, Rhode Island; one *s*. *Educ:* Amherst College; Andover Theological Seminary. Pastor High Street Congregational Church, Auburn, Maine, 1869–72; pastor Central Congregational Church, Providence, Rhode Island, 1872–83;

Professor of Theology in Andover Theological Seminary, 1883–99; President of Amherst College, 1899–1912. *Publications:* Moral Evolution, 1896; Inequality and Progress, 1897; A Century's Change in Religion, 1914. *Address:* 35 West 81st Street, New York City.
Died 1 March 1922.

HARRIS, John Mitchell, JP Co. Wilts; *b* Sept. 1856; *e s* of Thomas Harris, JP, of Caine; *m* 1881, Emma, *d* of James Cox, The Elms, Stow on the Wold; two *s* two *d*. Has given evidence before various Royal and Parliamentary Commissions. *Publications:* writer of various pamphlets, also articles to Live Stock Jl, Farmer and Stock Breeder, and other papers. *Recreations:* fond of any kind of sport, but principally shooting. *Address:* Chilvester Hill, Calne. *TA:* Chilvester, Calne. *T:* Calne 57. *M:* HR 9702. *Club:* Junior Constitutional.
Died 12 Oct. 1927.

HARRIS, Lloyd; MP, 1908–11; *b* Beamsville, Ont, 14 March 1867; *s* of John and Alice Jane Harris; *m* Evelyn F. Blackmore; one *d*. *Educ:* Brantford Public School; Woodstock College; Brantford Collegiate Institute. President Russell Motor Car Co. Ltd, Canada Glue Co. Ltd; Vice-President Willys Overland, Ltd, Canada Cycle and Motor Co. Ltd; Director Steel Co. of Canada, Ltd, Massey-Harris Co. Ltd, Dominion Power and Transmission Co., Trusts and Gaurantee Co.; Ex-Chairman Canadian War Mission, Washington; Ex-Chairman Canadian Mission in London; a Liberal. *Address:* 110 Brant Avenue, Brantford, Ont. *Clubs:* Brantford, Toronto, National, Toronto Hunt, RCYC, York, Toronto; Rideau, Ottawa.
Died Sept. 1925.

HARRIS, Sir Matthew, Kt 1899; late Mayor of Sydney; *b* Magherafelt, Co. Derry, 1840; *s* of John Harris of same place, merchant; *m* 1868, Frances Snowden, *d* of William Owen Lane of Windsor, NSW. *Educ:* Sydney Grammar School and University (BA 1863). Alderman of City of Sydney; member of Legislative Assembly for Denison Division; vice-president of Royal Agricultural Society; JP; director of Sydney Hospital; chairman of Wanset Commission. *Recreations:* cricket, bowls. *Address:* Warrane, Ultimo, NSW.
Died 8 June 1917.

HARRIS, Richard Hancock William Henry, CB 1900; retired, 1906; late commanding Regimental District of West Riding; *b* 17 July 1851. *Educ:* Cheltenham Coll. East Surrey Regt; half-pay; served South Africa, 1899–1900 (dangerously wounded, despatches, Queen's medal, two clasps, CB). *Address:* 26 St Aubyn's, Hove.
Died 11 Feb. 1927.

HARRIS, Robert, CMG 1902; *b* Wales, 18 Sept. 1849; *s* of William Critchlow Harris; taken by parents as a child to Charlottetown, Prince Edward Island, 1856; *m* 1885, Elizabeth, *d* of late L. N. Putnam, Montreal. *Educ:* Prince of Wales's College, Charlottetown. Painted in Charlottetown as a self-taught artist. Studied Slade School, London, and at Paris atelier Bonnat, Italy, Belgium and Holland; after a few years in Toronto settled in Montreal. Director of Art School, Montreal, 1883–87; Pres. of the Royal Canadian Academy, 1893–1906. *Works:* has produced many pictures of Canadian life; best known as a portrait painter, very many prominent Canadians having sat to him; awards for pictures exhibited in the International Exhibitions of Paris and Chicago, and gold medals at the Pan-American at Buffalo and the St Louis International, 1904. *Address:* 11 Durocher Street and Art Association, Montreal. *T:* Uptown 2278.
Died 27 Feb. 1919.

HARRIS, Adm. Sir Robert Hastings, KCB 1900; KCMG 1898; *b* 12 Oct. 1843; *s* of Capt. Robert Harris, RN; *m* 1875, Florence, *d* of late Commander Henn-Gennys, RN; two *s* five *d*. *Educ:* Royal Naval School, New Cross. Inspecting Captain of Training Ships, 1890–93; Commodore commanding Training Squadron, 1893–95; second in command Mediterranean Squadron, 1896–98; Commander-in-Chief Cape of Good Hope and West Coast of Africa Station, 1898–1902; President Royal Naval College, Greenwich, 1903–6; Admiral, 1904. JP Devon. *Address:* The Brake, Yelverton, RSO, S Devon. *Club:* United Service.
Died 25 Aug. 1926.

HARRIS, Sir Walter Henry, Kt 1919; CMG 1895; JP Surrey and Kent; one of HM Lieutenants for City of London; Director Neath and Brecon Railway Company; *b* 6 Dec. 1851; *o s* of Henry Harris (*d* 1889), builder, Clapham, Surrey; *m* Grace, *o d* of late Captain Thomas Hylands of Brighton, Sussex. *Educ:* Clapham Park School. Member of London Stock Exchange from 1884; British Royal Commission, Chicago, 1892–94; British Committee, Antwerp, 1894; British Committee, Amsterdam, 1895; British Committee, Vienna,

1895; British Committee, Tasmania, 1895; Mem. Council Soc. of Arts, 1892–95. Sheriff City of London, 1889–90; Master of the Lorimers' Company, 1896–97; Master of the Innholders' Company, 1902–3; Prime Warden of the Blacksmiths' Company, 1917–18, 1918–19; a Grand Officer of Freemasons, 1890; President City of London General Pension Society from 1902. Decorated for services to the Colonies at Chicago. Officer of the Order of Leopold of Belgium. *Publication*: History of the Royal Windsor Tapestry Works. *Recreation*: golf. *Address*: Rothley House, Macaulay Road, Clapham Common, SW4. *T*: Battersea 572. *Clubs*: Junior Carlton, Orleans; Mid-Surrey Golf. *Died 3 March 1922.*

HARRIS, William; Chairman, Mappin and Webb, Carlton Hotel, Ritz Hotel, and Meux's Brewery Company; President, Ritz-Carlton Hotel, New York; *b* 16 June 1864; *m* 1st, 1883, Elizabeth (*d* 1902), *d* of William Sumner Edge, Manchester; 2nd, Madeleine, *d* of Samuel Kordy, London; one *s* one *d*. *Educ*: Victoria University, Manchester. *Address*: Westfield, Reigate. *T*: Reigate 132.

Died 26 Oct. 1923.

HARRIS-BURLAND, John Burland; *b* 1870; *e s* of late Major-General W. Harris-Burland, 9th and 19th Foot, and *g s* of late J. B. Harris-Burland, JP, of New Court, Newent, Glos; *m* 1906, Florence, *d* of late Albert Marley. *Educ*: Sherborne; Exeter College, Oxford. Theological Scholarship, Durham (won, but not accepted), 1892; Newdigate Prize, 1893; while at Oxford edited Isis for a year, and was secretary of Union Oct. term, 1894; BA 1895. *Publications*: Dacobra, 1903; Dr Silex, 1905; The Black Motor Car, The Financier, The Broken Law, 1906; The Gold Worshippers, Love the Criminal, 1907; Workers in Darkness, 1908; The House of the Soul, The Disc, 1909; The Secret of Enoch Seal, The Torhaven Mystery, 1910; The Shadow of Maireward, 1911; Lord of Irongrey, 1912; The Grey Cat, 1913; Baldragon, The Curse of Cloud, 1914; The White Rook, 1917; The White Yawl; The Builder; The Avalanche; The Temple of Lies; The Watchman; The Lion's Claws; Gabrielle Janthry; The Golden Sword; The Spy; The Greed of Conquest, 1919; The Poison League, 1921; The Red Moon, 1922; The Brown Book, 1923; The Hidden Hour, 1925. *Recreations*: motoring, gardening. *Address*: The Lyon's Close, Pevensey, Sussex. *T*: Pevensey 37; Stanton, near Broadway, Worcs. *M*: PM 5339. *Club*: Savage.

Died 22 July 1926.

HARRISON, Alfred Hayford; *b* 1845; *y s* of George Harrison of Grosvenor Street and Walton-on-Thames; *m* 1871, Frances Annie, *d* of Inspector-General John Robert Taylor, CB; one *s* three *d*. *Educ*: Cheltenham College. Appointed a Junior Clerk in the Parliament Office, House of Lords, 1864; Clerk attending the Table of the House, 1876; Clerk of Printed Papers, 1896; Principal Clerk of Public Bills, 1902; Chief Clerk, House of Lords, 1908–10; Barrister, Inner Temple, 1869. *Recreations*: golf, music. *Club*: Bournemouth.

Died 6 May 1918.

HARRISON, Austin; late Editor of The English Review; *b* 27 March 1873; *s* of late Frederic Harrison; *m* Mary Medora Greening, USA; one *s* two *d*. *Educ*: Harrow; subsequently at various foreign universities. *Publications*: The Pan-Germanic Doctrine; England and Germany; The Kaiser's War; Then and Now; Lifting Mist; Pandora's Hope; Frederic Harrison: Thoughts and Memories; Essays of To-day and Yesterday. *Recreation*: travel. *Address*: Lychgate House, Seaford. *T*: Seaford 97.

Died 13 July 1928.

HARRISON, Constance Cary, (Mrs Burton Harrison); novelist; *b* Virginia; *d* of Archibald Cary, Carisbrooke, Virginia, and Monimia, *d* of 9th Lord Fairfax; *m* Burton Harrison, Louisiana, a barrister of New York (*d* 1904). Youth spent in country house of Virginia; educated at home by governess; was in Richmond with her widowed mother during war as refugees from their home in Fairfax county; after war resided abroad with her mother for a year or two, then married, and subseq. lived in New York; travelled a great deal in Europe, visiting most of its countries, as well as Africa, Syria, Turkey, and Asia Minor. *Publications*: Golden Rod, an Idyll of Mount Desert, 1880; Woman's Handiwork, 1881; Old Fashioned Fairy Book, 1884; Folk and Fairy Tales, 1885; Bar Harbour Days, 1887; The Anglomaniacs, 1887; Flower-de-Hundred, 1891; Crow's Nest and Belhaven Tales, 1892; A Daughter of the South, 1892; Sweet Bells out of Tune, 1893; A Bachelor Maid, 1894; An Errant Wooing, 1895; Externals of Modern New York, 1896; A Merry Maid of Arcady, and other Stories, 1896; A Son of the Old Dominion, 1897; Good Americans, 1897; A Triple Entanglement, 1898; A Princess of the Hills, 1901. Her play, The Unwelcome Mrs Hatch, was brought out by Mrs Minnie Maddern Fiske, at the New Manhattan Theatre, New York, 1901. *Recreations*: country life, travel. *Address*: 43 East Twenty-Ninth Street, New York; Sea Urchins, Bar Harbour, Mount Desert, Maine. *Died Nov. 1920.*

HARRISON, Frederic; President of English Positivist Committee, 1880–1905; *b* London, 18 Oct. 1831; *e s* of late Frederick Harrison, Threadneedle Street, EC, and Sutton Place, Guildford, and Jane, *o d* of Alexander Brice, Belfast; *m* 1870, Ethel (*d* 1916), *o d* of William Harrison, Craven Hill Gardens, W; three *s* one *d* (and one *s* decd). *Educ*: King's Coll. London; Wadham Coll. Oxford (MA, Fellow and Tutor, 1854–56); Hon. Fellow, 1899; Hon. DCL Oxford; Hon. LittD Cambridge; Hon. LLD Aberdeen. Barrister, Lincoln's Inn, 1858; member of Royal Commission of Trades Unions, 1867–69; secretary Royal Commission for Digesting the Law, 1869–70; Prof. of Jurisprudence and International Law to Inns of Court, 1877–89; Alderman, London County Council, 1889–93; Rede's Lecturer, Cambridge, 1900; Washington Lecturer, Chicago, 1901; Herbert Spencer Lecturer, Oxford, 1905; Vice-Pres. Royal Historical Society, and London Library. JP Kent and Somerset. *Publications*: Meaning of History, 1862; Order and Progress, 1875; Social Statics—Comte's Positive Polity, vol. ii, 1875; The Choice of Books, 1886; Oliver Cromwell, 1888; Annals of an Old Manor House, 1893, new edn 1899; (editor and part author) The New Calendar of Great Men, 1892; The Meaning of History, enlarged 1894; Victorian Literature, 1895; Introductions to Comte's Positive Philosophy, to Carlyle's Past and Present, 1896; Carlyle's Essays, 1903; Bacon's Essays, 1905; Trollope's Barsetshire Tales, 1906; to Trollope's Phineas Finn and Phineas Redux, 1911, and to Miss Betham-Edwards' Lord of the Harvest; William the Silent, 1897; The Millenary of King Alfred, 1897; Tennyson, Ruskin, Mill and others, 1899; Byzantine History in the Early Middle Ages, 1900; American Addresses, 1901; Life of Ruskin, 1902; Theophano, 1904; Chatham, 1905; Herbert Spencer Lecture, Oxford, 1905; Nicephorus: A Tragedy of New Rome, 1906; Memories and Thoughts, 1906; Carlyle and the London Library, 1907; The Creed of a Layman, 1907; The Philosophy of Common Sense, 1907; My Alpine Jubilee, 1908; National and Social Problems, 1908; Realities and Ideals, 1908; Autobiographic Memoirs, 1911; Among My Books, 1912; The Positive Evolution of Religion, 1912; The German Peril, 1915; On Society, 1918; Jurisprudence and Conflict of Nations, 1919; Obiter Scripta, 1919; Novissima Verba, 1920. *Address*: 10 Royal Crescent, Bath. *Club*: National Liberal.

Died 14 Jan. 1923.

HARRISON, Frederick, MA; *s* of Frederick Burgoyne Harrison and Ellen Maria Norton. *Educ*: King's College School; Trinity College, Cambridge. Private tutor and lecturer; travelled extensively for some years; went on stage, 1886; several years with Mr Tree; joint manager of Lyceum with Mr Forbes Robertson, 1895–96; sole lessee of the Haymarket Theatre from 1896; joint manager of Haymarket with Mr Cyril Maude, 1896–1905. Esq.OStJ. *Recreations*: gardening, motoring. *Address*: Kemnal, Haslemere, Surrey. *Clubs*: Conservative, Bath, Royal Automobile. *Died 13 June 1926.*

HARRISON, James Jonathan, JP; *b* 1858; *s* of late Jonathan Stables Harrison, JP, DL, of Brandesburton Hall, Yorks, and 70 Harley Street, London, and Eliza Whitehead, *sister* of George Whitehead, JP, DL, of Deighton Grove, York; *m* 1910, Mrs Sumner Clarke, of Peoria, Illinois. *Educ*: Elstree; Harrow; Christ Church, Oxford. Took his first big game shoot 1885, and hardly missed a subsequent year; his collection of trophies—birds and small animals collected in all parts of the globe. Joined the Prince of Wales Yorkshire Hussars, 1884; retired, after 21 years' service, with the rank of Lt-Colonel. *Recreations*: hunting, shooting, cricket. *Address*: Brandesburton Hall, Hull. *TA*: Brandesburton. *Clubs*: Carlton, Bachelors', Oxford and Cambridge, Hurlingham, Ranelagh; Yorkshire, York.

Died 12 March 1923.

HARRISON, Jane Ellen, Hon. LLD Aberdeen; Hon. DLitt Durham; sometime Fellow and Lecturer in Classical Archæology, Newnham College, Cambridge; *b* Yorkshire, 9 Sept. 1850; 3rd *d* of late Charles Harrison, Cottingham, Yorks, and Elizabeth Hawksley, *d* of Thomas Nelson, Limber, Lincolnshire; unmarried. *Educ*: home; Cheltenham; Newnham College, Cambridge. Vice-President Hellenic Society, 1889–96; Corr. Member of K. Arch. Institute, Berlin. *Publications*: Myths of the Odyssey in Art and Literature, 1882; Introductory Studies in Greek Art, 1885; Mythology and Monuments of Ancient Athens (joint-author Mrs A. W. Verrall), 1890; Greek Vase Painting (joint-author Mr D. S. MacColl), 1894; Prolegomena to Study of Greek Religion, 1903; Religion of Ancient Greece: Themis, 1912; Ancient Art and Ritual, in Home University Library, 1913; Alpha and Omega, 1915; Russia and the Russian Verb, 1915; Aspects Aorists and the Classical Tripos, 1919; Epilegomena to Study of Greek Religion, 1921; (with Hope Mirrlees) Life of the Archpriest Avvakum, trans. from the Russian, 1925; Reminiscences of a Student's Life, 1925; (with Hope Mirrlees) The Book of the Bear—translations from the Russian. *Address:* Newnham College, Cambridge. *Club:* University Women's. *Died 15 April 1928.*

HARRISON, John, CBE 1918; DL; LLD Edin.; FRSE; Chairman Public Library, Savings Bank; *b* 17 Aug. 1847; *s* of late Sir George Harrison, MP, Lord Provost of the City of Edinburgh; *m* 1879, Helen Georgina, *d* of George Roberts, Manufacturer, Selkirk; two *s* three *d. Educ:* Royal High School, Edinburgh. Head of the firm of Harrison and Son, clothiers, Edinburgh; retired from business; has given much work in connection with the public life of Edinburgh, especially to the institutions carrying on the education of the city. *Publications:* The Scot in Ulster; Oure Tounis Colledge; The History of the Monastery of Holyrood and of the Palace of Holyrood House. *Recreations:* golf, walking. *Address:* Rockville, Napier Road, Edinburgh. *T:* Central, Edinburgh 6958. *Clubs:* Northern, Edinburgh; Gullane Golf. *Died 10 July 1922.*

HARRISON, Sir John Burchmore, Kt 1921; CMG 1901; Government Analyst and Professor of Chemistry, British Guiana, since 1889; Director of the Department of Science and Agriculture since 1904; Member Executive Council, 1918; *b* Birmingham, 29 May 1856; *e s* of John Harrison; *m* 1881, M. E. Hortense, *d* of late J. P. Carter, Barbados; one *d. Educ:* Edgbaston Proprietary School; Christ's Coll. Camb. (MA). Island Prof. of Chem. and Agricultural Science, Barbados, West Indies, 1879–89; travelled for geological purposes in the West Indian Islands and in the interior of British Guiana; awarded the balance of the Wollaston Donation Fund 1899 by the Geological Society of Lond. Decorated for scientific services in connection with the West Indian Colonies. *Publications:* many reports and papers dealing with agricultural chemistry of tropical products, and with the geology of the West Indian Islands and British Guiana. *Recreations:* microscopy, geology. *Address:* Georgetown, Demerara, British Guiana. *Died 8 Feb. 1926.*

HARRISON, Rev. Robert; President of the Primitive Methodist Connexion, 1904; *b* Carlisle, 6 Dec. 1841; *m* 1st, Maria E. Wright, Hull; 2nd, S. A. Andrew, Hull. Entered ministry, 1864; served at Selby, Market Rasen, Gainsborough, Hornsea, Hull, Grimsby, Driffield, Sunderland; was Governor of Elmfield College, York, and Chairman of the Primitive Methodist Insurance Company and Chapel Aid Association. *Address:* West Gable, Hymers Avenue, Hull. *Died 27 Jan. 1927.*

HARRISON, Robert Francis, KC 1899; *b* 26 Dec. 1858; *o s* of late Mr Justice Harrison and Fanny Letitia Bolden Davison; *m* 1884, Agnes Blanche, *e d* of late John Bagwell; two *s* two *d. Educ:* Temple Grove, East Sheen; Wellington College (Scholar); Trinity College, Dublin (Senior Exhibitioner, Scholar, and Senior Moderator). Scholar in Constitutional and International Law, and also in the Law of Real and Personal Property, Middle Temple, and John Brooke Scholar at King's Inns, Dublin. Called to the Bar, King's Inns, Dublin, 1882; Bencher 1904. *Recreation:* golf. *Address:* 17 Fitzwilliam Square, Dublin. *T:* 62072. *M:* XP 8867. *Club:* Kildare Street, Dublin. *Died 24 Nov. 1927.*

HARRISON, Robert Hichens Camden, JP, DL; 4th *s* of late Frederick Harrison; married. *Educ:* Blackwater. High Sheriff, Oxfordshire, 1900. *Address:* Shiplake Court, near Henley-on-Thames, Oxfordshire. *Club:* Junior Athenæum. *Died 21 Oct. 1924.*

HARRISON, Thomas Fenwick, JP Herts; *b* 9 Jan. 1852; *s* of Thomas Harrison (*d* 1888) of Liverpool and Mary Anne, *d* of Cuthbert Fenwick, Newcastle; *m* 1881, Florence Emily (*d* 1899), *d* of Henry Edwards of Winchester. *Educ:* Rugby. In business at Liverpool until retirement in 1889. *Recreations:* hunting, shooting. *Address:* Kings Walden Bury, Hitchin, Herts. *Club:* Junior Carlton. *Died 29 Dec. 1916.*

HARRISON, Rt. Rev. William Thomas, DD; Assistant Bishop of Ely, 1903–17; *b* 22 Sept. 1837; *y s* of Rev. T. T. Harrison, Rector of Thorpe Morieux; *m* 1870, Elizabeth B. Colvin, *d* of Col John Colvin, CB, Leintwardine House, Ludlow; two *s* three *d. Educ:* Brighton College; Marlborough; Trinity College, Cambridge. Curate at Parish Church, Great Yarmouth, 1861; in charge of St John's Church, Great Yarmouth, 1864; Rector of Thorpe Morieux, 1868; Vicar of Christ Church, Luton, 1875; Hon. Canon of Ely, 1881; Rural Dean of Luton, 1881; Vicar of St James's, Bury St Edmunds, 1883; Rural Dean of Thingoe, 1886; Bishop of Glasgow and Galloway, 1888–1908; Rector of Thorpe Morieux, 1903–12. *Address:* Olivers, Colchester. *Died 11 Dec. 1920.*

HARRISON-SMITH, Sir Francis, KCB 1919 (CB 1911); Chairman of Grand Trunk Pacific Railway 4 per cent Debenture Committee; Paymaster Rear-Admiral (retired), 1920; *b* 1861; *s* of Horace Harrison-Smith, MD, RN, and Georgiana Amelia Way; *m* 1890, Eleanor Catherine, *d* of Alexander Hellard; one *s* one *d. Educ:* RN School, New Cross. Joined RN as Assistant Clerk, 1878; Egyptian Campaign, 1882 (medal and bronze star); Eastern Soudan Campaign, 1883–84 (El Teb and Suakim clasps, Mejidieh, 5th Class, despatches); Admiral Sir William Hewett's Mission to Abyssinia, 1884 (despatches); sent by Lord Salisbury on Mission to Abyssinia, 1885–86 (received thanks of HM Government); specially promoted for services, 1889; Naval Sec. to Commander-in-Chief, Plymouth, 1896–1900; China, 1901–4; Plymouth, 1908–11; Portsmouth, 1911–16; Private Sec. to HE the Governor of New South Wales, 1904–8. *Publications:* Through Abyssinia: an Envoy's Ride to the King of Zion; (part) The Manual of Naval Law; The King's Regulations 100 Years ago; The Curiosities of an Old Navy List; Office Work in the Navy; various magazine articles on African and Naval subjects. *Recreation:* restoration of old clocks and furniture. *Address:* Wilcot Lodge, Marlborough, Wilts. *Died 10 June 1927.*

HARRISSON, Damer, MCh (*hon. causa*); FRCSE; late Hon. Surgeon to the King; Hon. Consulting Surgeon, Liverpool Northern Hospital; late Clinical Lecturer on Surgery, Liverpool University; Colonel, AMS, TF; *b* 1852; *y s* of John Harnett Harrisson of Sandwich; *m* 1880, Constance, 2nd *d* of Rev. John Vaughan Lloyd, MA (Oxon), Rector of Hope. Resident Medical Officer, Liverpool Royal Infirmary, 1877–79; late Surgeon Lancashire Hussars Imp. Yeo.; late Assistant Director Medical Services, West Lancs Division (Territorial decoration). *Publications:* papers on General Surgery; Cerebral Surgery; Surgery of Nerves; The Eugenic Aspect of the Feeble-Minded Child. *Recreations:* golf, riding, fishing, and other kinds of sport. *Address:* 53 Rodney Street, Liverpool. *T:* 2374 Royal. *Clubs:* Athenæum, University, Liverpool. *Died 1 Sept. 1918.*

HART, Charles Henry; lawyer, art expert and writer; Director of Pennsylvania Academy of Fine Arts, Philadelphia; resigned 13 Jan. 1902, at the close of 20 years' service; *b* Philadelphia, Pa, 4 Feb. 1847; *s* of Samuel Hart of Philadelphia, and Julia Leavey of London, England; *m* 1st, 1869, Armine Nixon (*d* 1897), *g g d* of Robert Morris, Signer Declaration of Independence and Financier of American Revolution; 2nd, 1905, Marianne Livingston Phillips; 3rd, 1912, Anita Arabe; one *s. Educ:* private schools; University of Pennsylvania. Studied Law; admitted to Bar, 1868; practised until 1894, when met with severe railroad accident that left him on his back for 14 months; since recovery abandoned the Law, and devoted himself to Literature and Art; recognised as first Art Critic and Expert in Historical Portraiture in America; was Chief Commissioner on Retrospective Art at World's Columbian Exposition, Chicago, 1893; exposed frauds in so-called portraits of celebrities; made the work of Gilbert Stuart, America's master painter, a special study; member of twenty learned societies. *Publications:* Life Portraits of Great Americans; Turner the Dream Painter; Bibliographia Lincolniana; Mary White—Mrs Robert Morris; Browere's Life Masks of Great Americans; Gilbert Stuart's Portraits of Women; Catalogue Raisonnée of the Engraved Portraits of Washington; Abraham Lincoln's Place in History; Hints on Portraits and how to Catalogue them; The Last of the Silhouettists; First Century and a half of American Art; Franklin in Allegory; The Earliest Painter in America; The Original Portraits of Washington; Benjamin West Not a Quaker; Register of Portraits painted by Thomas Sully; Memoirs of the Life and Works of Jean Antoine Houdon, sculptor, of Voltaire, and of Washington; the Wright Portrait of Franklin in Royal Society, London; Descriptive Catalogue of the Collection of Miniatures owned by Lucy Wharton Drexel, 1911; articles on Philadelphia in Ency. Brit. 1885 and 1903; Who was the Mother of Franklin's Son?; editor of Letters from William Franklin to William Strahan; Frauds in Historical Portraiture, or Spurious Portraits of Historical Personages, 1913; Charles Willson Peale's Allegory of William Pitt, 1915; Peter Harrison (1716–1775), First Professional Architect in America, 1916; contributor to Art in America, a number of articles on American Portrait Painters and their Works; also about 150 magazine articles on art and history; selected and edited the illustrations for Elson's History of the United States, 1905; Lodge's Story of the American Revolution; Tarbell's The American Woman, 1910, etc. *Address:* 970 Park Avenue, New York. *T:* Lenox 8513. *Clubs:* Royal Societies; Players', New York. *Died Aug. 1917.*

HART, Col Charles Joseph, CB 1909; CBE 1919; VD; TD; Temporary Lieutenant-Colonel in the Army, 1914–20, as Recruiting Officer, Officer Commanding Troops, Competent Military Authority for Arms and Ammunition, Birmingham, and President Northern

Area Quartering Committee Southern Command; *b* 15 Aug. 1851; *s* of late Chas Hart, The Hall, Harborne, Staffordshire; unmarried. *Educ:* Haileybury College. DL, JP Warwickshire; Member of the Warwickshire Territorial Army Association. Officer of Order of Crown of Belgium. *Publications:* History of the 1st VB The Royal Warwickshire Regt and its Predecessors; The Antiquity of Iron; The Old Ironwork of Warwickshire; Old Church Chests. *Recreations:* archaeology, golf, Leamington Tennis Court Club. *Address:* South Bank, Warwick New Road, Leamington.

Died March 1925.

HART, Henry George, MA; *b* 16 April 1843; *s* of W. Hart, ICS; *m* H. L. Lawrence, *d* of late Sir Henry Lawrence, KCB. *Educ:* Rugby; St John's Coll. Camb. (Scholar, afterwards Fellow); 7th in 1st class Class. Tripos, 1866. Asst Master, Haileybury Coll., 1866–73; Harrow School, 1873–80; Head Master of Sedbergh School, 1880–1900. *Publication:* Sedbergh School Sermons, 1901. *Recreation:* fishing. *Address:* Sedbergh, Hillside, Wimbledon.

Died 12 Jan. 1921.

HART-DAVIES, Thomas, FRGS; *s* of late Ven. Archdeacon Hart-Davies; *b* 1849; *m* 1913, Cora, 3rd *d* of George Boothby, RN, Ashbourne, Derbys, and *widow* of Colonel G. B. Wanhope, Lancs Fusiliers. *Educ:* Marlborough; Pembroke College, Oxford (Exhibitioner). Entered ICS 1869; served in numerous departments in Bombay Presidency, chiefly in Sind, where he was Educational Inspector, Assistant Commissioner, and Manager of Estates; subsequently Judge of Karachi, and Acting Judicial Commissioner; retired, 1897; contested (L) Rotherhithe, 1900; MP (L) North Hackney, 1906–10. Travelled extensively: eight times round the world, in Siberia, Persia, South America, and nearly every other country of the globe; fond of languages. *Publications:* translated works from Russian, and wrote short stories for magazines. *Recreations:* music, conjuring, fishing, golf, travelling. *Clubs:* Reform, East India United Service, Savile. *Died 3 Jan. 1920.*

HARTING, James Edmund, FLS, FZS; formerly Librarian and Assistant Secretary Linnean Society of London, retired, 1902; *b* London, 1841; *s* of James V. Harting, Lincoln's Inn Fields, Harting, Sussex, and Kingsbury, Middlesex, and Alexine, *d* of Col R. H. Fotheringham, RE; *m* 1868, Elizabeth, *d* of James M. Lynch, Whiteleas, Co. Kildare, and Newcastle, Co. Dublin; one *s* one *d*. *Educ:* Downside College; University of London. Admitted to practice as a solicitor, 1866; retired, 1878. Gave evidence before the Select Committee of the House of Commons on Wild Birds Protection, 1873; travelled in France, Holland, Belgium, Italy, Greece, and Thessaly; went to Paris in 1889 for The Field, to report on guns and rifles at the Paris Exhibition; and to Thessaly in 1893 for the Board of Agriculture, to report on the Vole Plague; prepared a catalogue of the Library of the Zoological Department, British Museum, published by order of the Trustees, 1884, and a catalogue of the Library of the Society of Apothecaries, 1913, for which he was awarded the gold medal of the Society; the Acclimatization Society of Paris also awarded him a medal of the 1st class for scientific publications. *Publications:* The Birds of Middlesex, 1866; The Ornithology of Shakespeare, 1871; A Handbook of British Birds, 1872; new and revised edition, with coloured plates, 1901; Our Summer Migrants, 1875; White's Natural History of Selborne, 1875–76; Rambles in Search of Shells, 1876; Ostriches and Ostrich Farming, 1877; British Animals Extinct within Historic Times, 1880; Glimpses of Bird Life, 1880; Rodd's Birds of Cornwall, 1880; Essays on Sport and Natural History, 1883; A Perfecte Booke for Keeping Sparhawkes (1575), 1886; Bert's Treatise on Hawks (1619), 1891; Bibliography of Falconry, 1891; Walton's Angler, Tercentenary Edition, 1893; Hints on the Management of Hawks, 1897; the vol. on the Rabbit in Fur and Feather Series, 1898; The Encyclopædia of Sport (24 articles), 1897–98; Recreations of a Naturalist, 1906; editor of The Zoologist, 1877–96; and of the Natural History and Falconry Columns in The Field, 1871–1925. *Recreations:* shooting, hawking, fishing, lawn-tennis. *Address:* Portmore Lodge, Weybridge, Surrey. *Club:* Royal Societies. *Died 16 Jan. 1928.*

HARTLAND, Edwin Sidney, Hon. LLD St Andrews, Hon. DLitt University of Wales; FSA; Honorary FSA Ireland; Registrar, County Court, Gloucester and District Registrar of the High Court, 1889–1923, and District Probate Registrar, 1918–24; *b* Islington, 23 July 1848; *e s* of Rev. E. J. Hartland, Congregational minister; *m* 1873, Mary Elizabeth, *d* of Rev. M. R. Morgan, Vicar of Llansamlet. Solicitor at Swansea, 1871–90; Chairman of Folk-tale Section of the International Folklore Congress, London, 1891; President of the Folklore Society, 1899; Mayor of Gloucester, 1902; President of the Anthropological Section of the British Association, 1906; President

of Section I (Religions of the Lower Culture), Congress for the History of Religions, Oxford, 1908; 1st Frazer Lecturer, Oxford, 1922; awarded Huxley Medal, 1923. *Publications:* English Fairy and other Folktales, 1890; The Science of Fairy Tales, 1890; The Legend of Perseus (3 vols), 1894, 1895, 1896; Primitive Paternity, 1910; Ritual and Belief, 1914; Primitive Society, 1921; Primitive Law, 1924; edited Walter Map's De Nugis Curialium, 1923; and numerous essays and papers, chiefly on archæological and anthropological subjects. *Address:* 13 Alexandra Road, Gloucester.

Died 19 June 1927.

HARTLEY, C. Gasquoine, (Mrs Arthur D. Lewis); author and journalist; *b* Antananarivo, Madagascar, 1869; 2nd *d* of Rev. Richard Griffiths Hartley, MA, London, and Catherine Gasquoine; *m* 1st, Walter M. Gallichan; 2nd, Arthur D. Lewis; one *s*. *Educ:* private; almost no education until the age of 16. First occupation teaching; Headmistress of Babington House School, Eltham, Kent, 1894–1902; came to London in 1903 and began to write; first book a novel which was not successful; afterwards wrote on Spain and Spanish Art; in later years has been entirely occupied with books on education, social questions, and in particular subjects of feminist interest. *Publications:* Life the Modeller; Stories of Early British Heroes; Stories from the Greek Legends; The Weaver's Shuttle; Pictures in the Tate Gallery; The Story of Santiago de Compostela; The Cathedrals of Southern Spain; History of Spanish Painting; Moorish Cities; Spain Revisited; The Truth about Woman; The Position of Woman in Primitive Society: a study of the matriarchy; Motherhood and the Relationships between the Sexes; Women's Wild Oats; Sex Education and National Health; Divorce, To-Day and Tomorrow; The Mind of the Naughty Child; Mother and Son: a psychological study of character formation in children; Women, Children, Love and Marriage, etc. *Recreations:* country walks, gardening, reading. *Address:* c/o Bate & Co., 35 Bedford Row, WC. *Died 7 June 1928.*

HARTLEY, Edmund Baron, VC 1881; CMG 1900; Col (retired), Medical Staff, Cape Mounted Riflemen; Col Commanding Cape Medical Corps; Principal Medical Officer, Cape Colonial Forces, since 1878; *b* Ivy Bridge, S Devon, 6 May 1847; *e s* of Dr Edmund Hartley; *m* 1886, Ellen, *d* of J. Rose-Innes, CMG, Under Secretary, Native Affairs, Cape Town. *Educ:* private school; St George's Hospital, London. MRCS, England; LRCP, Edinburgh. Clerk in HM Inland Revenue, 1867–69; District Surgeon, Basutoland, 1874–77; joined Colonial Forces, 1877; served in Galeka, Gaika, Morosi (VC), Tembu (medal and clasps), Basuto Campaigns, 1877–80; Bechuanaland, 1897 (wounded); S Africa (medal, clasps, 1877–78–79); S Africa, 1900–2 (despatches, CMG, medals, five clasps). Decorated for rescuing wounded under fire at Morosi's Mountain, 5th June 1879. *Recreation:* travelling. *Club:* Royal Societies.

Died 20 March 1919.

HARTLEY, Rev. Marshall; Wesleyan Minister, retired, 1926; President of Wesleyan Conference, 1903–4; *b* Stamford Hill, 26 Jan. 1846; *m* Millie Ryall (*d* 1914), *d* of late Rev. W. W. Rouch, Wesleyan Minister. *Educ:* Woodhouse Grove School; Richmond College. Entered Wesleyan Ministry, 1868; ordained, 1872; Secretary of the Schools Fund, 1881; Assistant Secretary of the Conference, 1886; elected into the Legal Hundred, 1890; Secretary, Conference, 1895–1902; Secretary, Wesleyan Missionary Society, 1888–1919; Connexional Funds Secretary, 1919–26; visited Mission Stations in India, China, and Ceylon, 1898; South Africa, 1902; India, Ceylon, and Burma, 1915. *Address:* 27 Cedar Road, Sutton, Surrey. *T:* Sutton 498. *Died 21 Dec. 1928.*

HARTLEY, Sir William Pickles, Kt 1908; JP; President, Primitive Methodist Church, 1909; *b* Colne, Lancs, 1846; *s* of John Hartley; *m* Martha, *d* of H. Horsfield; one *s* seven *d*. *Educ:* Colne Grammar School. Manufacturer of grocers' sundries, and jam, marmalade, and table jellies at Colne; removed to Bootle, Liverpool, 1874; to Aintree, 1886; benefactor to Liverpool University, to hospitals and chapels. *Publication:* The Use of Wealth, published by the National Council of the Evangelical Free Churches. *Recreations:* none except driving. *Address:* Sea View, Southport. *T:* Southport 349. *M:* FY 282. *Club:* Reform, Liverpool. *Died 25 Oct. 1922.*

HARTMANN, William, JP; *b* Bremen, 21 March 1844; *s* of Henry and Meta Hartmann. *Educ:* Bremen. Came to England, 1864; established as merchant in London, 1866; founder of Suter Hartmann and Rahtjens Compo. Co. Ltd (The Red Hand Compositions Ltd, of which he was the chairman). *Recreations:* shooting, fishing, foreign travels. *Address:* Milburn, Esher, Surrey. *TA:* Hartmann, Esher, Surrey. *T:* Esher 10. *M:* XH 6259. *Club:* Ranelagh.

Died 11 Dec. 1926.

HARTOG, Marcus, MA (Cantab), DSc (Lond. and RUI); FLS, Hon. FRHS, late Fellow Royal University, Ireland; 2nd *s* of Prof. Alphonse Hartog and Marion, *d* of Joseph Moss; *m* 1874, Blanche, *d* of R. Levy-Brandeis of Paris; one *s* one *d. Educ:* N London Collegiate School; University College, London; Trinity College, Cambridge. 1st Class Nat. Sci. Tripos, 1874; Assistant to Director Royal Botanic Gardens, Ceylon, 1874-77; Demonstrator, and later Lecturer in Natural History, Owens College, Manchester, 1878; Professor of Natural History, Queen's College, Cork, 1882-1909; of Zoology in University College, Cork, 1909-21; Member Scientific Committee RHS. *Publications:* chiefly memoirs in zoology, botany, and general biological science; The Dual Force of the Dividing Cell, Pt I, PRS, 1905; and other researches on the physics of nuclear division; A Study on the Irish Dialect of English (with Miss Mary Hayden, MA); Problems of Life and Reproduction, 1913; The Function of Examinations in Education, Merit Proficiency, 1919. *Recreations:* cycling, walking, music. *Address:* 33 rue d'Alsace-Lorraine, Choisy-le-Roi, France (Seine). *Club:* Maccabæans.
Died 21 Jan. 1923.

HARTRIDGE, Gustavus, FRCS; late Ophthalmic Surgeon to the Royal Flying Corps Hospital; Consulting Surgeon to the Royal Westminster Ophthalmic Hospital; Consulting Ophthalmic Surgeon and Lecturer on Ophthalmology to the Westminster Hospital; Consulting Ophthalmic Surgeon to St Bartholomew's Hospital, Rochester, etc; *s* of James Hartridge, Yalding, Kent; *m* Susan C., *d* of Colonel Murray, 42nd Highlanders (Black Watch). *Educ:* King's College. *Publications:* Refraction of the Eye, 16th edn, and numerous other works on the Eye. *Recreations:* yachting, cycling. *Address:* 12 Wimpole Street, W1. *T:* 831 Paddington. *Clubs:* Bath, Royal Auto.
Died 8 Sept. 1923.

HARTVIGSON, Fritz; Knight of Dannebrog and Dannebrogsmand; pianist to HM Queen Alexandra; *b* Grenaae, Denmark, 1841; unmarried. *Educ:* Copenhagen and Berlin. Studied piano-playing, etc, with Niels W. Gade and Anton Rée in Copenhagen, and with Dr Hans von Bülow in Berlin; appeared in public in Denmark, Berlin, Leipzig, Munich, St Petersburg, Moscow, Helsingfors, Christiania, Edinburgh, and in the Crystal Palace Saturday concerts, the Philharmonic Society, the Richter and Henschel orchestral concerts in London; lived in Russia, 1872-75; in London, 1875-1911; Professor and Examiner Royal College of Music; Hon. RAM. *Recreations:* pistol-shooting, dancing, mountaineering, collected old Japanese colour-prints and old Nankin porcelain. *Address:* 3 Martensens Allé, Copenhagen. *Died March 1919.*

HARTZELL, Dr Joseph Crane; Methodist Episcopal Bishop of Africa, 1896-1916; *b* Moline, Illinois, 1 June 1842; *m* 1869, Miss Jennie Culver, Chicago. *Educ:* High School, Moline, Illinois; Illinois Wesleyan University, Bloomington, Illinois, BA, MA, DD. BD, Garrett Biblical Institute, Chicago, Illinois; LLD US Grant University, Tennessee; and Gedding College, Illinois. Pastor Methodist Episcopal Church, Pekin, Illinois, 1868-69; New Orleans, La, 1870-72; Presiding Elder New Orleans District, and founder and editor South-Western Christian Advocate, 1872-81; Member Public School Board of Education, New Orleans, 1873-76; Assistant Corresponding Secretary, 1882-87; Chief Secretary, 1888-95, of Southern Education Society, Methodist Episcopal Church, Member General Conference Methodist Episcopal Church, 1876, 1880, 1884, 1888, 1892; and of Methodist Œcumenical Conference, Washington, 1878; and London, 1898. *Publications:* Methodism and the Negro; Africa Mission; Address World Exposition, Congress of Religions, Chicago; and many addresses and magazine articles on educational and racial topics in America and Africa; also several sermons. *Recreations:* only such as were incidental to an intensely active and very responsible administration, while secretary of over forty-five institutions of learning of higher grade, or superintending work of missions in Eastern Rhodesia and Portuguese East Africa, on East Coast and in Liberia, on the Congo and in Angola, in the West Coast and in Madeira Islands; during twenty-six years in America and twenty years in Africa travelled over 1,300,000 miles and administered over $6,000,000,00 in educational, industrial, and church work. *Address:* Cincinnati, Ohio.
Died 6 Sept. 1928.

HARVEY, Alexander Gordon Cummins; MP (L) Rochdale, 1906-18; *b* Manchester, 31 Dec. 1858; *s* of Cummins Harvey. Cotton manufacturer and merchant, Manchester and Littleborough. Co. Alderman of Lancs; JP Lancashire. *Address:* Town House, Littleborough. *Club:* Reform. *Died 6 Nov. 1922.*

HARVEY, Sir Charles, 2nd Bt, *cr* 1868, of Crown Point; JP; *b* 25 Feb. 1849; *s* of Sir Robert John Harvey Harvey, 1st Bt; *S* father, 1870;

m 1st, 1870, Jane (*d* 1891), *d* of Benjamin Green, Newcastle; one *s* two *d* (and one *d* decd); 2nd, 1893, Edith, *d* of G. F. Cooke, Holmwood, Norwich; one *s. Educ:* Magdalene Coll., Cambridge. Formerly Hon. Col 4th Batt. Norfolk Regt. *Publication:* History of Norfolk Militia and Militias. *Recreations:* hunting, shooting, yachting. *Heir: s* Charles Robert Lambart Edward Harvey [*b* 16 April 1871; *m* 1891, Jessie (*d* 1913), *d* of late Ebenezer Turnbull, of Smedley, Manchester; one *d. Club:* Bath]. *Address:* Rainthorpe Hall, Norwich. *TA:* Saxlingham, Norfolk. *Clubs:* Royal Thames Yacht, Junior United Service. *Died 30 Jan. 1928.*

HARVEY, Rev. Clement Fox, MA; Hon. Canon of St Carantoc in Truro Cathedral since 1878; *b* 28 Oct. 1847; *s* of late Prebendary Harvey, Rector of Truro; *m* 1st, Emma Mary, *d* of Rev. J. Hardwicke Dyer; 2nd, Helen Cornelia, *d* of J. G. Chilcott; four *s* three *d. Educ:* Winchester; Trinity College, Oxford. Student of Lincoln's Inn, 1869-70. Ordained deacon, 1872; priest, 1873; Assistant Curate of Prittlewell, 1872-75; Rector of Truro, 1875-85; Vicar of Probus, Cornwall, 1885-1910; of Probus-with-Cornelly, 1897-1910; Commissioner under Pluralities Acts Amendment Act for Chapter of Truro Cathedral, 1897-1915; Surrogate for Diocese of Truro from 1878. *Publications:* several sermons. *Address:* Lanprobus, Falmouth.
Died 25 Sept. 1917.

HARVEY, Sir Ernest Maes, KBE 1920; banker; partner of Allen, Harvey & Ross since 1904; *b* Ipswich, 1 Jan. 1872; *s* of Julius Harvey, Engineer, Ipswich; *m* 1898, Blanche, *d* of Edward Pogson, St Kitts, West Indies; two *s. Educ:* Ipswich; Germany. Partner, firm of Clare & Harvey (Bankers), 1894; served as Treasury Representative in Archangel, 1918; as Financial Adviser to the British Representative on the Inter-Allied Rhineland Commission, 1919; Inter-Allied Financial Adviser to the Austrian Section of the Reparations Commission in Vienna, 1920; Hon. Consul-General for Austria. *Publications:* articles on money matters. *Recreations:* golf, bridge. *Address:* 6 Cornwall Terrace, Regent's Park, NW1. *T:* Mayfair 6346; Hill House, Aldeburgh, Suffolk. *T:* Aldeburgh 65. *Clubs:* Union, City of London. *Died 13 Sept. 1926.*

HARVEY, Rev. Francis Clyde; Prebendary of Chichester; Vicar of Hailsham since 1872. *Educ:* Trinity College, Cambridge. Deacon, 1868; Priest, 1869. *Address:* The Vicarage, Hailsham, Sussex.
Died 18 Sept. 1922.

HARVEY, Col George; editor and proprietor of North American Review, 1899-1926; American Ambassador at the Court of St James's, 1921-24; formerly editor Harvey's Weekly; *b* 16 Feb. 1864, of Scotch and English descent, in New England; *m* 1887, Alma Parker. *Educ:* Peacham, Vermont. Entered journalism at age of 20, becoming managing editor of New York World at 27; withdrew because of ill-health; bought North American Review, 1899; was elected president of publishing house of Harper and Brothers, 1900; Editor of Harper's Weekly and its successor, Harvey's Weekly. Served as ADC on staff of Governor Green, and chief of staff of Governor Abbett of New Jersey. Hon. Doctor of Laws, Erskine Coll. of South Carolina, 1905; University of Nevada, 1908; Middlebury College, 1912; and Univ. of Vermont, 1914; Hon. Dr of Letters, Dartmouth College, 1916; Hon. Member Phi Beta Kappa Alpha Chapter, 1914; Bromley Lecturer on Journalism at Yale, 1908; Trustee Stevens Institute of Technology; Hon. Member Cottage Club of Princeton. *Publications:* Women, etc; The Power of Tolerance. *Recreations:* golf, automobiling. *Address:* 9 East 37th Street, New York City. *Clubs:* Savage, Royal Automobile; Stoke Poges, Hanger Hill; Racquet, Metropolitan, Lotos, New York; Metropolitan, Washington; Travellers', Paris. *Died 20 Aug. 1928.*

HARVEY, John Edmund Audley, JP, DL; *b* 1851; *o s* of late John Harvey and Anne Jane, *d* of Henry Tennant, Cadoxton Lodge, Co. Glamorgan; *m* 1873, Rosa Frances (*d* 1880), 6th *d* of Admiral Hon. Keith Stewart, CB. High Sheriff, Beds, 1886; Patron of 1 living; late Capt. 42nd Highlanders. *Address:* Ickwellbury, Biggleswade; Finningley Park, Bawtry. *Died 15 May 1927.*

HARVEY, Lt-Col John Robert, DSO 1902; JP Norfolk; *b* 31 July 1861; *e s* of late Col John Edmund Harvey, 41st Regiment, of Springfield, Taplow, Bucks, and Thorpe, Norfolk, and Octavia Lettice, *d* of Rev. R. Stephens; *m* 1st, 1888, Nora (*d* 1889), 2nd *d* of H. Adams of Canon Hill, Bray, Berks; 2nd, 1890, Florence, *d* of F. W. Parsons of Risley Hall, Derby; one *s* two *d. Educ:* Rugby; Trinity Coll. Camb. Served in 5th Lancers; commanded 25th Battalion Imperial Yeomanry in South Africa, 1900-2 (despatches, Queen's medal, 3 clasps, King's medal, 2 clasps); 4th Norfolk in Gallipoli, 1915. Mayor of Norwich, 1902-3. *Publications:* Records of the Norfolk

Yeomanry Cavalry, 1782 to 1908; Hunting in Norfolk; Shannon and its Lakes. *Recreations:* hunting, polo, shooting, fishing, yachting. *Address:* Holmwood, Thorpe, Norfolk. *T:* Thorpe 44. *Club:* Army and Navy. *Died 2 July 1921.*

HARVEY, William, BA, LLB; advocate; Sheriff-Substitute of Lanarkshire since 1917; of Caithness, Orkney and Shetland at Kirkwall, 1904–12; of Ross and Cromarty, 1912–17; *b* 8 Dec. 1859; *s* of Thomas Harvey, MA, LLD, late Rector of the Edinburgh Academy; *m* 1902, Eveline Cecil la Cour; two *s* two *d. Educ:* Edinburgh Acad.; King's Coll., Camb. (Exhibitioner and Scholar); Edinburgh Univ. First Class Mathematical Tripos, Parts I and II; Div. I, Pt III, 1883. Called to the Scottish Bar, 1886; Editor of the Scottish Law Reporter, 1895–1900; additional Examiner for degrees in Mathematics and Science in Edinburgh University, 1888–94. *Publication:* Lectures on Law of Insurance, delivered to Faculty of Actuaries, Edinburgh, 1895. *Address:* Eddlehurst, Lanark. *T:* Lanark 12. *Clubs:* University, Edinburgh; Western, Glasgow.
Died 1 June 1927.

HARVIE-BROWN, John A., LLD; FRSE, FZS; JP Stirlingshire; Member British Ornithologists' Union; Hon. Life Fellow of the American Ornithologists' Union; landed proprietor; *b* Scotland, 27 Aug. 1844; *o s* of John Harvie-Brown, Quarter and Shirgarton, who took the name Brown by the will of the late Alexander Brown, Quarter, and Elizabeth Spottiswoode, *d* of late Thomas Spottiswoode, Dunipace. *Educ:* Merchiston Castle, near Edinburgh; Edinburgh and Cambridge Universities. Devoted much time to the Vertebrate Fauna of Scotland, Britain, and foreign countries; to a study of Migration of Birds (member of the British Association Committee on the subject); Dispersal and Distribution of Species and kindred subjects; and for the purposes of natural history observations travelled in Norway, Russia, and Transylvania, Faroe Isles and Rockall, and all around Scottish coasts and amongst Scottish Archipelago of islands. Owner of about 2,100 acres. *Publications:* some 250 books and papers and notices of Natural History facts, etc. *Recreations:* travel, shooting, fishing (salmon and trout), collecting objects of natural history in connection with work above mentioned, library ditto. *Address:* Dunipace House, Larbert, Stirlingshire, NB. *Clubs:* University, Edinburgh; County, Stirling. *Died 26 July 1916.*

HARWOOD, Henry William Forsyth; Editor of the Genealogist since 1894; *b* Porchester Terrace, London, 9 March 1856; *e s* of late Henry Harwood Harwood, JP and DL for Middlesex, and Mary Elizabeth, *o c* of John Forsyth, Bengal Civil Service. Called to Bar, Middle Temple, 1880. *Address:* 15 Rugby Mansions, Addison Bridge, Kensington, W. *Died 3 Jan. 1923.*

HASLAM, Sir Alfred Seale, Kt 1891; principal proprietor Haslam Engineering Co., Derby; *b* 27 Oct. 1844; 4th *s* of William Haslam, Derby; *m* 1875, Annie (*d* 1924), *d* of Thomas Tatam, The Elms, Little Eaton, Derbys; one *s* two *d.* Trained as engineer at Midland Railway Works, Derby, later under Lord Armstrong's Co.; started the Haslam Engineering Works, Derby, 1868; first to invent, manufacture, and to fit up Haslam's patent refrigerating plant in Colonies, and to fit up the machinery and cold chambers on board ship and on shore, which established an important business in conveying perishable food from the Colonies to Great Britain. Mayor of Derby, 1890–91, when he received HM Queen Victoria when she paid a State visit to the town; Mayor of Newcastle-under-Lyme, 1901–2–3–4; contested (LU) Derby, 1892; MP (LU) Newcastle-under-Lyme, Staffords, 1900–6; contested Newcastle-under-Lyme, 1906. Donated to the Nation statues of Queen Victoria erected in the City of London, Newcastle-under-Lyme, and Derby. *Recreations:* riding, shooting. *Address:* Breadsall Priory, near Derby. *T:* Duffield 13. *Clubs:* Reform, Devonshire, City of London. *Died 13 Jan. 1927.*

HASLAM, Lewis, JP Co. Lancaster; MP (L) Newport (Monmouth) since Dec. 1918; *b* Bolton, 25 April 1856; *s* of John Haslam, Gilnow House, Bolton, Lancashire, and Jane, *d* of J. Crook, White Bank, Bolton; *m* 1893, Helen Norma, *d* of Henry Dixon of Watlington, Oxon. *Educ:* University College School and University College, London. MP (L) Monmouth Boroughs, 1906–18. *Address:* 8 Wilton Crescent, SW1. *Clubs:* Reform, National Liberal, Bath, Ranelagh. *Died 12 Sept. 1922.*

HASLAM, Rev. Samuel Holker; Hon. Canon of Truro, 1918; Rector of Week St Mary, 1900–19. *Address:* 2 King's Road Villas, Paignton, Devon. *Died 1922.*

HASSARD, Rev. Richard Samuel, MA; Canon Residentiary and Sub-Dean of Truro Cathedral; Rector of Truro; Proctor in Convocation for Chapter of Truro; *b* 1848; *s* of late Rev. Henry Hassard, Rector of Stockton Forest, Yorks; *m* Edith (*d* 1920), *d* of late John Costeker, of Midhurst, Sussex. *Educ:* Queen's College, Oxford; BA 1869. Ordained 1871; incumbent of St Matthew's, Auckland, New Zealand, 1874–79; Vicar of Holy Trinity, Dalston, 1879–93; St James', Norlands, Kensington, 1893–1906; a Vice-President of SPG; and one of the Mission of Help to the Church in South Africa, 1904; Rural Dean of Powder, 1912–15. *Publication:* Confirmation and Holy Communion. *Address:* Rectory, Truro. *Club:* The Church Imperial. *Died 22 Oct. 1921.*

HASTINGS, Adm. Alexander Plantagenet, CB 1882; JP; *b* India, 31 Dec. 1843; 2nd *s* of late Capt. Hon. Edward Plantagenet Robin Hastings and Caroline, *e d* of G. J. Morris, BCS; *m* 1885, Edith Caroline, 2nd *d* of Col Frederic Rodolph Blake, CB; one *s* one *d. Educ:* Elm Grove, Ealing; HMS Britannia. Entered RN 31 Dec. 1858; Vice-Admiral, 1900; served Egyptian War, 1882 (Egyptian medal, Khedive's bronze star, CB); Soudan, 1884; commanded Naval Brigade landed for protection of Suakim, 1884; Governor of Massowah, 1884 (clasp); Captain of Royal Naval College, Greenwich, 1885–89; ADC to the Queen, 1891–93. Decorated for engagement at Chalouf in the Suez Canal during Egyptian Campaign, being Capt. HMS Euryalus at the time. *Address:* Bayford Hall, Bayford, near Hertford. *TA:* Bayford. *Club:* Army and Navy.
Died 7 Dec. 1925.

HASTINGS, Basil Macdonald; author; *b* London, 20 Sept. 1881; 2nd *s* of S. J. E. Hastings, solicitor; *m* Wilhelmina Creusen White; one *s* one *d. Educ:* Stonyhurst. On War Office Staff for eight years; then asst editor of The Bystander for three years; during War, 2nd Lt RAF, and Cpl, KRRC; founder and editor of The Fledgling; subsequently Roosters and Fledglings (the RAF Journal). *Publications:* The Tribe; Letters of Sympathy; Faithful Philanderers; My Permitted Say (Essays); Memoirs of a Child; Essays of To-day and Yesterday; Ladies Half-Way; The Laughers; and the following plays: The New Sin; Love, and What Then?; The Tide; Such Nice People; Advertisement; Bed Rock (with Eden Phillpotts); Played Out (one act); The Angel in the House (with Eden Phillpotts); The Fourth Act (one act); A Best Seller (one act); Q (one act, with Stephen Leacock); Razzle-Dazzle (Drury Lane revue); The Johnson 'Ole (with Capt. B. Bairnsfather); A Certain Liveliness; Victory (from Conrad's novel); Pep; Hanky-Panky John; Any Woman Would; If Winter Comes (with A. S. M. Hutchinson); The Jackdaw of Rheims (vocal ballet); Faithful Philanderers. *Address:* 30 Holland Road, Kensington, W. *T:* Park 2393. *Club:* Savage.

Died 21 Feb.1928.

HASTINGS, Charles Godolphin William, CIE 1897; *b* 29 June 1854; 2nd *s* of late Rev. Hon. Richard Godolphin Hastings, 4th *s* of 11th Earl of Huntingdon; *m* 1882, Margaret Logie, *d* of late Gen. Sir James D. Macpherson, KCB; one *s. Educ:* Haileybury. Entered Punjab Police, 1873; Political Officer, Kurram; served Jowaki Expedition (medal with clasp); Afghan War (medal); Chitral Relief Force (medal with clasp); Tirah Campaign (medal, 3 clasps); Inspector-General Police, NWF Province, 1901; Punjab, 1904; Under-Secretary to Government, 1904–7; retired, 1909.
Died 26 Feb. 1920.

HASTINGS, Graham, KC; *b* London, 7 Oct. 1830; 2nd *s* of late Dr John Hastings; *m* Constance Arabella, *e d* of Rev. E. C. Holt. *Educ:* Paris, Edinburgh, King's Coll. and Worcester Coll. Oxford. Called to Bar, 17 Nov. 1854; QC 1875; Bencher of Lincoln's Inn, 1877; retired 21 Dec. 1897. *Address:* 19 Hyde Park Street, W2. *Club:* Lord's.
Died 5 Dec. 1922.

HASTINGS, Rev. James; editor of The Expository Times, Dictionary of the Bible, Encyclopædia of Religion and Ethics, etc; *b* Huntly, Aberdeenshire; *m* 1884, Ann Wilson Forsyth; one *s* one *d. Educ:* Public School, Huntly; Old Aberdeen Grammar School; Aberdeen University (MA and Hon. DD). Hon. DD Halifax, 1920; Divinity College of Free Church in Aberdeen. Ordained minister at Kinneff in Kincardineshire, 1884; called to Willison Church, Dundee, 1897; St Cyrus Church, 1901; surrendered pastoral charge of St Cyrus, 1911, and removed to Aberdeen; Mem. of the General Council of the Palestine Exploration Society. Dyke-Acland Medallist, 1913. *Publications:* The Expository Times (vols i–xxxii), 1890–1921; Dictionary of the Bible (vols i, ii, iii and iv), 1898–1902, with extra volume, 1904, as editor; Dictionary of Christ and the Gospels, in two vols, 1906–7; a Dictionary of the Bible in a single volume, 1903; Encyclopædia of Religion and Ethics, vols i–xii, 1908–22; Dictionary of the Apostolic Church, vol. i 1915, vol. ii 1918; commenced in 1910 the publication of a series of volumes entitled The Great Texts of the Bible, and in 1913 a similar series entitled The Greater Men and Women of the Bible; also a series on the Great Christian Doctrines, vol. i on Prayer, 1915; vol. ii on Faith, 1919; vol. iii on Peace, 1921; editor of The Scholar as Preacher series. *Recreation:* bowling. *Address:* King's Gate, Aberdeen.

Died 15 Oct. 1922.

HASTINGS, Lt-Col Wilfred Charles Norrington, DSO 1902; late Manchester Regiment; *b* Devonport, 24 Dec. 1873; *s* of Rev. Francis Henry Hastings, retired Captain RN; unmarried. *Educ:* Trinity College School, Stratford-on-Avon. Entered 4th Batt. South Wales Borderers, 1892; seconded for Sierra Leone Frontier Force, 1898; served in Hut Tax War, 1898–99 (wounded, medal and clasp); entered Manchester Regiment, 1899; served South African Campaign, 1900–2 (South African and King's medal, despatches, DSO); with 1st Batt. Northern Nigerian Regt, 1903; Munshi Expedition, 1906; France, 1914; Cameroon, 1915–16; Commanded Sierra Leone Batt. W African Frontier Force, 1915; West African Regiment, 1920; retired pay, 1923. *Recreations:* shooting, fishing, boxing. *Address:* Daylesford Lodge, Stratford-on-Avon. *Club:* Sports.

Died 19 Jan. 1925.

HASWELL, Prof. William A., MA, DSc; FRS 1897; CMZS; Challis Professor of Biology, University of Sydney, 1890–1917, Dean of the Faculty of Science, 1913–17, Emeritus Professor of Biology since 1917; *b* Edinburgh, 5 Aug. 1854; *m* 1894, Josephine Gordon, *d* of W. Gordon Rich, Toi Toi, New Zealand; one *d. Educ:* Edinburgh Institution and University (Baxter scholar). Curator of Queensland Museum, 1880; zoological cruise on coasts of tropical Queensland (as guest on HMS "Alert"), 1881; Demonstrator of Zoology, Comparative Anatomy, and Histology, Sydney University, 1882; Acting Curator of Australian Museum, 1882; President of Section D of Australasian Association for Advancement of Science, 1891; President of Linnean Society of NSW, 1892–93; Clarke Memorial Medal, Royal Society, NSW, 1915; Editor of the Biological Reports of the Australasian Antarctic Expeditions since 1916. *Publications:* A Text Book of Zoology (with T. Jeffrey Parker), 1897; A Manual of Zoology, 1899. *Recreations:* trout-fishing, golf, gardening. *Address:* 33 Wolseley Road, Edgecliff, Sydney. *Club:* Australian, Sydney.

Died 24 Jan. 1925.

HATCH, Sir Ernest Frederic George, 1st Bt, *cr* 1908; KBE 1920; founder and Chairman of Hatch, Mansfield and Company; Director, Fine Art and General Insurance Co.; *b* 12 April 1859; *s* of late John William Hatch and Matilda, *o d* of late Hugh Snell; *m* 1900, Lady Constance Blanche Godolphin Osborne, *y d* of 9th Duke of Leeds; one *d.* Contested (C) Gorton Div. of Lancashire, 1889, 1892; MP (C) Gorton Division, 1895–1906; travelled in United States, Canada, India, South Africa, Japan, and China; special interest in South African affairs and in the Colonies generally throughout the Empire; acted as special Commissioner of various industrial matters for Home Office, and Chairman of many Departmental Committees (Home Office, Board of Trade, and Insurance Commissioners); Chairman of Government Commission for Belgian Refugees; Treasurer and Chairman of University College Hospital. KGStJ. Commander of the Order of the Crown (Belgium). *Publications:* Far Eastern Impressions, 1904; In Support of Free Trade, 1905. *Recreation:* a keen interest in athletics. *Heir:* none. *Address:* 20 Portland Place, W1; Ridge Mount, Sunningdale. *Clubs:* Reform, Ranelagh.

Died 17 Aug. 1927 (ext).

HATCH, Lt-Col George Pelham, CMG 1898; late Commandant of Military Force in British East Africa; *b* 1855; *s* of late Gen. George Cliffe-Hatch; *m* 1895, Helen Sophia, *d* of late Rev. C. H. Raikes. *Educ:* Rugby. Served Afghan War, 1879–80 (medal); Egypt, Tel-el-Kebir, 1882 (medal and clasp, bronze star); in command of Troops and Police of Sultan of Zanzibar, 1891–94 (twice thanked by British Government, received the Brilliant Star of Zanzibar); present at the operations in the Witu District, 1893 (British medal and clasp, and Sultan's medal, with two clasps); raised and commanded the troops in the East Africa Protectorate, 1895–1903; served with the Somaliland Field Force, 1901–2 (medal and clasp). *Address:* 10 Clarence Road, Walmer, Kent.

Died 23 May 1923.

HATFIELD, Henry, ISO 1904; barrister-at-law; *b* 22 May 1854; *e s* of late Abraham Hatfield of Stockport; *m* 1879, Mary Homena, *e d* of late Thomas Stafford of Macclesfield; one *s. Educ:* Owens College; Royal College of Science, Dublin. Entered Patent Office, 1878; Examiner, 1884; Chief Examiner, 1888; authorised by Board of Trade to act for Comptroller-General; retired, 1919. *Recreation:* golf. *Address:* North Bank, New Barnet.

Died 26 Feb. 1926.

HATHERELL, William, RI 1888; RWA; illustrator and painter; on the Staff of the Graphic since 1892; *b* 18 Oct. 1855; *y s* of late Abraham Hatherell, Westbury-on-Trym; *m* 1887, Emily Agnes, *d* of John Newell Logan. *Educ:* private schools. Entered Royal Academy Schools, 1877; made a member of the Society of Oil Painters, 1898; hon. member of the Langham Sketching Club, 1900; member of Royal West of England Academy, 1903; member of the American Society of Illustrators, 1905; first illustrating work done for Cassell's; illustrated many works by Thomas Hardy, William Black, J. M. Barrie, etc, for Graphic, Harper's, Scribner's, etc. *Recreations:* cycling, fishing. *Address:* 15 Cavendish Road, Brondesbury, NW. *Club:* Arts.

Died 7 Dec. 1928.

HATTON, Richard George, MA; Hon. ARCA (Lond.); Professor of Fine Art and Director, King Edward VII School of Art, Armstrong College, Newcastle-upon-Tyne; *b* 1864; *e s* of George Hatton, Birmingham, and Ellen, *d* of Richard Timmins; *m* 1892, Gertrude Helen, 3rd *d* of George Young, London; one *d. Educ:* King Edward's School, Birmingham; Birmingham School of Art. President, National Society of Art Masters, 1911; Member of the Board of Education's Standing Committee of Advice for Education in Art, 1911. *Publications:* Design, 1902; Perspective for Art Students, 1902; Figure Drawing, 1905; Figure Composition, 1905; The Craftsman's Plant-Book, 1910; The Principles of Decoration, 1925. *Address:* 31 Elmfield Road, Gosforth, Newcastle.

Died 19 Feb. 1926.

HAUGHTON, Benjamin; landscape painter; *b* 1865; *o s* of late David Haughton, JP, of Sutton Hall, E Yorks; *m* 1894, Janet, 2nd *d* of late Thomas Mason, JP, of Alkincoats, Lancs; one *d. Educ:* Caius College, Cambridge (BA 1885). *Address:* East Downe House, near Barnstaple.

Died 31 July 1924.

HAUPT, Dr Paul; W. W. Spence Professor of the Semitic Languages and Director of the Oriental Seminary in the Johns Hopkins University, Baltimore; Associate in Historic Archæology in the US National Museum, Washington; *b* Görlitz, Germany, 1858. *Educ:* Görlitz Gymnasium; Universities of Leipzig and Berlin under Friedrich Delitzsch in Assyriology, and Franz Delitzsch in Hebrew; for Rabbinical Hebrew as found in the Talmud he went to the local rabbis; studied Arabic with H. L. Fleischer; and A. Dillmann taught him Ethiopic. Appointed *privat-docent* at the University of Göttingen, 1880; Professor of the Semitic languages in the Johns Hopkins University, 1883, retaining his connection with the University of Göttingen until 1889 as Professor Extraordinarius of Assyriology. *Publications:* editor, with Friedrich Delitzsch, of the Johns Hopkins Contributions to Assyriology and Comparative Semitic Grammar, as well as of the Assyriological Library, and has published a number of important works, including a critical edition of the cuneiform text of the Babylonian Nimrod Epic with the Chaldean account of the Deluge, besides contributing to many philological journals; editor of The Polychrome Bible; bibliography of his publications (more than 500 numbers) given in the Haupt Memorial Volume, 1926. *Address:* 215 Longwood Road, Roland Park, Baltimore, Md.

Died 15 Dec. 1926.

HAUSSONVILLE, Othenin Bernard Gabrielle de Cleron, Comte d'; Chevalier de la Légion d'Honneur; Membre de l'Académie Française; *m* 1865, Pauline (*d* 1922), *d* of 4th Marquis d'Harcourt; four *d.* Député de Seine-et-Marne, 1871–75. *Publications:* Misères et Remèdes; Socialisme et Charité; A travers les Etats Unis; Sainte-Beuve, sa vie et ses œuvres; Le Salon de Mme Necker (with G. Hanotaux); Souvenirs sur Mme de Maintenon; Mémoires et lettres inédites de Mlle d'Aumale; Les Cahiers de Mlle d'Aumale; Mme de Maintenon et St-Cyr; La Duchesse de Bourgogne et l'Alliance Savoyarde. *Address:* 6 rue Fabert, Paris. *T:* 703–53; Château de Coppet, Canton de Vaud, Suisse.

Died 1 Sept. 1924.

HAVERFIELD, Francis John, FBA; FSA; Camden Professor of Ancient History in the University of Oxford since 1907; *b* Shipston-on-Stour, 1860; *o s* of late Rev. W. R. Haverfield and Mary, sister of Rt Rev. John Mackarness, late Bishop of Oxford; *m* 1907, Winifred Breakwell. *Educ:* scholar of Winchester (1873–79); scholar of New College, Oxford (1879–84); MA Oxon. Hon. LLD Aberdeen; Hon. DLitt Leeds; Hon. FSAScot; Schoolmaster, 1884–91; Senior Censor, Student, Tutor, and Librarian of Christ Church, Oxford, 1891–1907; Rhind Lecturer, Edinburgh, 1905–6; Ford Lecturer, Oxford, 1906–7; Creighton Lecturer, London University, 1910; a Governor of Westminster School, 1900–8; member of the Hebdomadal Council, Oxford, 1908–14. Visitor of the Ashmolean Museum, Oxford, from 1901; Fellow of Brasenose College, Oxford; Member of General

Board of Faculties, Oxford; Member of Royal Commission on
Ancient Monuments, England; a Governor of Roysse's School,
Abingdon; first President Society for Promotion of Roman Studies,
1910–16; President of several English local archæological societies.
Publications: The Romanization of Roman Britain, 3rd edn 1915;
Ancient Town-planning, 1913; Military Aspects of Roman Wales;
and other monographs on Roman History, and on Roman Britain;
fifth edition of Conington and Nettleship's Virgil; Guide to the
Portraits in Christ Church Hall; Relief Map of Syracuse (with J. B.
Jordan); editor of H. Nettleship's Lectures and Essays (1895) and H.
Pelham's Essays (1911); occasional contributor to Edinburgh Review,
Quarterly, etc. Address: Winshields, Oxford. T: Oxford 110. Clubs:
Athenæum; County, Carlisle.

Died 1 Sept. 1919.

HAVERSHAM, 1st Baron, cr 1906, of Bracknell; Arthur Divett
Hayter, Bt 1858; PC 1894; MA; JP, DL; b London, 19 Aug. 1835;
o s of Rt Hon. Sir William Hayter, 1st Bt and Ann, d of William
Pulsford, Linslade Manor, Bucks; S father as 2nd Bt, 1878; m 1866,
Henriette, y d of Adrian J. Hope, and niece of late Rt Hon. A. J.
Beresford-Hope, MP. Educ: Eton; Balliol and Brasenose Colls,
Oxford. Open classical Scholarship Brasenose Coll., classical Honours,
Moderations and Final Schools. MP (L) Wells, 1865–68; Bath,
1873–85; Walsall, 1893–95; 1900–5. Served ten years in Grenadier
Guards, of 2nd Batt. of which he acted as Adjutant; was in command
of London Rifle Brigade for nine years; moved resolution against Earl
Russell's Redistribution of Seats Bill in 1866; a Lord of the Treasury,
1880; Financial Secretary at War Office, 1882; remained in office
during the two expeditions to Egypt and Suakim, until defeat of the
Government, 1885; Chairman Public Accounts Committee, 1901–5;
served for 15 years on the Executive Committee of the Royal Patriotic
Fund; Chairman Macedonian Relief Committee; Chairman Berks
Territorial Association. Publications: Essays on Production and its
Increase; articles in reviews. Recreations: cricket (played 3 years in Eton
Eleven at Lord's); formerly winner of running at Eton and Oxford,
and a public match at Lord's of 100 yards. Heir: none. Address: 9
Grosvenor Square, W. T: Mayfair 2195; South Hill Park, Bracknell,
Berks; Tintagel, Camelford, Cornwall; Linslade Manor, Leighton
Buzzard, Bucks. M: 1958. Clubs: Brooks's, Travellers', Devonshire,
National Liberal.   Died 1 May 1917 (ext).

HAWARD, J. Warrington, FRCS, LRCP; Consulting Surgeon to
St George's Hospital, to Cripples Nursery and to Santa Claus Home;
Vice-President of Society for Relief of Widows and Orphans of
Medical Men; Director Guardian Assurance Company; Director and
Member of Medical Board of Royal Sea-bathing Hospital, Margate;
Vice-President of Invalid Children's Aid Association; b 1841; s of
James Haward; m 1876, Amy Cecilia, d of James Nicholls, MD, FRCS.
Formerly President of Royal Medical and Chirurgical Society, and
of Surgical Section Royal Society of Medicine; Vice-President Clinical
Society and Pathological Society; Hunterian Professor, Royal College
of Surgeons; Asst Surgeon to Hospital for Sick Children, Great
Ormond Street; Surgical Registrar, Curator of Museum,
Demonstrator of Anatomy, Lecturer on Practical Surgery and Clinical
Surgery, Assistant Surgeon and Surgeon to St George's Hospital, and
Treasurer of Medical School. Publications: Lecture on Liberty and
Authority in Relation to Medicine; and various surgical works, essays,
lectures, and scientific papers. Address: Manor End, Berkhamsted,
Herts. Club: Athenæum.   Died 20 Aug. 1921.

HAWES, Alexander Travers, JP; solicitor; b 1851; s of late William
Hawes, of Russell Square, WC; m 1st, 1874, Catherine (d 1891), d
of Henry Honey; 2nd, 1897, Ada Lucy, d of Col P. S. Court; two
s two d. Partner in firm Baker, Blaker and Hawes; Treasurer and
Chairman Royal Humane Society; Director Phœnix Assurance
Company. Address: Nizels, Chislehurst, Kent. TA: Chislehurst 46.
Clubs: Conservative, City Carlton.

Died 20 May 1924.

HAWKER, Squadron Commander Lance George, VC 1915; DSO
1915; Royal Engineers and Royal Flying Corps; b 30 Dec. 1890.
Entered RE 1911; Squadron Commander, 1916; served European
War, 1914–15 (DSO for dropping bombs on the German airship shed
at Gontrode from a height of only 200 feet, under circumstances of
the greatest risk; VC for attacking three German aeroplanes, damaging
one and destroying one).   Died Nov. 1916.

HAWKINS, Maj.-Gen. Alexander Caesar, CB 1871; b Kelston Park,
near Bath, 3 Nov. 1823; 8th s of Sir John C. Hawkins, 3rd Bt; m
1895, Janet, d of Lieut-Gen. E. A. Williams, CB. Educ: RMA,
Woolwich. Joined Royal Artillery, 1842; served West Indies as Fort
Adjutant, 1842–47, and as Captain, 1848–50; in the trenches of the

left attack in the Crimea, March 1855–Aug. 1856, and was engaged
in five bombardments of Sebastopol (despatches); served in India as
Lt-Col, 1863–70. Decorated for service in the Crimea; CB, 5th class
Medjidie, Turkish medal, Crimean medal, Sardinian medal. Address:
St Winifred's Lodge, Bath.   Died 17 Dec. 1916.

HAWKSHAW, John Clarke, MA; MICE, FGS, FES; JP (Sussex);
b 17 Aug. 1841; s of late Sir John Hawkshaw; m Cicely (d 1917),
d of F. Wedgwood of Barlaston, Staffordshire; one s four d. Educ:
Westminster (Triplet Scholarship); Trinity College, Cambridge;
Mathematical Tripos Senior Opt. No 9. President of the CUBC, won
Colquhoun Sculls, Capt. of 3rd Trinity Boat (Head of the River),
rowed at Putney, 1863 and 1864. Hon. Col, late Lt-Col commanding
Engineers and RT Staff Corps; President of the Institution of Civil
Engineers, 1902; retired from professional work as Civil Engineer,
1915. Publications: papers on various subjects published in Proceedings
of Institution of Civil Engineers (Telford Medal), Journal of
Geological Society, Journal of Linnean Society, British Association
reports, and Society of Arts (medal). Recreations: alpine climbing
(Member of Alpine Club from 1860), natural history, arboriculture,
etc. Address: Hollycombe, Liphook, Hants. Club: Athenæum.
                                                    Died 12 Feb. 1921.

HAWLEY, Sir Henry Cusack Wingfield, 6th Bt, cr 1795; b 23 Dec.
1876; e s of Sir Henry Michael Hawley, 5th Bt, and Frances Charlotte,
d of John Wingfield-Stratford of Addington Park, near Maidstone;
S father, 1909; m 1913, Marjorie Florence, o d of R. M. Curteis,
Winkenhurst, Hellingley. Educ: Eton; Magdalen Coll., Oxford.
Owner of about 8,500 acres. Heir: n David Henry Hawley, b 13 May
1913. Address: The Manor House, Lytchett Maltravers, Poole, Dorset.
                                                    Died 18 Nov. 1923.

HAWLEY, Maj.-Gen. William Hanbury; b 9 May 1829; 4th s of
late Capt. R. T. Hawley of the King's Dragoon Guards, and a
Waterloo Officer, and o d of late John Hanbury Beaufoy of Upton
Grey, Hants; m 1864, Eliza Jane, 2nd d of late Henry Warner, Barrister,
Trinidad; four s two d. Ensign 14th Foot, 1846, with which regiment
he served 31 years; Maj.-General, 1886; retired, 1890; served Crimea,
1855 (medal with clasp, Turkish medal); commanded troops
Mauritius, 1882–87; Colonel Prince of Wales Own West Yorkshire
Regiment, 1904. Address: Shiplake, Henley-on-Thames.
                                                    Died 20 March 1917.

HAWTAYNE, Lionel Edward; Puisne Judge, Gold Coast, since 1912;
s of late George Hammond Hawtayne, CMG. Barrister, British
Guiana, 1891; Stipendiary Magistrate, 1905. Address: Accra, Gold
Coast.   Died 28 March 1920.

HAWTREY, Sir Charles, Kt 1922; actor-manager; b 21 Dec. 1858;
6th s of late Rev. John Hawtrey, Slough; m 1919, Hon. Mrs Albert
Petre. Educ: Eton; Rugby; Oxford University. Made wonderful
success in The Private Secretary and A Message from Mars. Address:
37 Hertford Street, Mayfair, W1. Club: Orleans.
                                                    Died 30 July 1923.

HAY, Hon. Claude George Drummond; Director of the Fine Art
and General Insurance Co., Ltd; b 24 June 1862; 5th s of 11th Earl
of Kinnoull; unmarried. Educ: Radley College; abroad. Was first
Secretary of Primrose League, and Assistant Secretary, Lloyd's.
Contested (C) Hoxton, 1892 and 1895; MP (C) Hoxton Division
of Shoreditch, 1900–10. Temp. Capt., HM Army, 1915. Recreations:
fond of outdoor sports, pictures, music; travelled a good deal. Clubs:
St James', Turf.   Died 24 Oct. 1920.

HAY, Francis Stuart; Vice-Lieutenant and Convener Berwickshire;
b 22 July 1863; 2nd s of late Major-General A. C. Hay; m 1903, Laura
Elizabeth, e d of late Colonel G. Fordyce-Buchan of Kelloe,
Berwickshire. Educ: Repton. Recreation: shooting. Address: Duns
Castle, Duns, Berwickshire. TA: Hay, Duns. T: Duns 11. Clubs:
Junior United Service; New, Edinburgh.

Died 27 Nov. 1928.

HAY, Col Sir George Jackson, KCB 1911 (CB 1896); Kt 1906; CMG
1902; JP, DL Co. Durham; JP, NR Yorkshire; late Lieutenant-
Colonel commanding 3rd Battalion Prince of Wales's Own (W Yorks)
Regiment; Hon. Colonel Militia, and Hon. Lieutenant-Colonel in
the Army; b 18 Feb. 1840; e s of late John Hay, JP, DL, of Creswell,
Sunderland, Co. Durham, and Hilton Manor, Yorkshire; m 1865,
Minnie, o c of Richard Cail, JP of Beaconsfield, Low Fell, Co.
Durham. Educ: private schools. Publications: The History of the
Constitutional Force, 56BC to 1905, etc. Club: Junior Army and
Navy.   Died 7 Oct. 1921.

HAY, Sir Hector Maclean, 7th Bt, *cr* 1703, of Alderston; *b* 28 March 1821; *s* of Sir James Douglas Hamilton Hay, 6th Bt and Jane, *d* of William Sanderson; *S* father, 1873; *m* 1st, 1852, Anne (*d* 1888), *d* of Dr J. White, 17th Light Dragoons; 2nd, 1889, Julia (*d* 1906), *widow* of William Johnson, Appleby, Lincolnshire; 3rd, 1906, Florence Anne, *widow* of Major A. Dingwall Fordyce of Aberdeen. Formerly Major London Rifle Brigade. *Heir: n* William Henry Hay, *b* 30 May 1867. *Address:* 30 Holland Road, Hove, Sussex.

Died 15 Sept. 1916.

HAY, Col James Adam Gordon Richardson-Drummond-, of Seggieden and Aberargie, Perthshire; JP Co. Perth; a Lieutenant-Colonel in the Reserve of Officers, Coldstream Guards; commanded Coldstream Guards Regiment and Regimental District, Aug. 1914–Feb. 1917; *b* 5 Aug. 1863; *s* of Henry Maurice Drummond (*y s* of Admiral Sir Adam Drummond, KH, of Megginch Castle, Perthshire), who assumed name of Hay on marriage with Charlotte Elizabeth, *d* and *heiress* of Captain James Richardson-Hay (late the Carbineers), of Seggieden and Aberargie, Perthshire; *m* 1903, Evelyn, 2nd *d* of late Sir James T. Stewart-Richardson, 14th Bt of Pitfour Castle, Perthshire; three *s* one *d. Educ:* Twyford School, near Winchester; Winchester; Sandhurst. Joined Coldstream Guards, 1884; Capt. 1895; Major, 1899; Bt Lieut-Colonel, 1900; Bt Colonel, 1906; Substantive Lieut-Colonel to command 2nd Battalion, 1907; retired, 1911. Served with 1st Battalion at Suakim, Alexandria and Cyprus, 1884 (Egyptian Medal and Clasp and Khedive's Star); granted Jubilee Commemoration Medal for services in command of a Rest Camp at the Tower of London, 1897; served with the 1st Battalion at Gibraltar, 1899, and in South Africa, 1899–1902 (Queen's medal and six clasps, King's medal and two clasps; despatches and Bt Lieut-Colonel); Major 2nd in command 3rd Battalion at Cairo, Oct. 1906, March 1907. *Recreations:* shooting, fishing, gardening, entomology, ornithology (MBOU), philately. *Address:* Seggieden, by Perth. *TA:* Glencarse.

Died 27 Dec. 1928.

HAY, James Paterson, MVO 1906; *b* 1863; *m* 1899, Janey, *d* of William Alexander, Alticane, Pinwherry, Ayrshire, NB. Late manager, Irrawaddy Flotilla Co., and late Member, Burma Legislative Council. *Address:* Craigwell, Ayr, NB. *Club:* Oriental.

Died 12 Dec. 1925.

HAY, Brig.-Gen. James Reginald Maitland Dalrymple, CB 1910; DSO 1900; *b* 31 July 1858; Scotch; *e s* of late Col George James Dalrymple Hay, BSC; *m* 1892, Catherine Margaret, *yr d* of late Henry Billinghurst, MD, Stedham Hall, Sussex. Joined 21st Royal Scots Fusiliers, 1879; Captain, 1890; Major, 1895; served Boer War, 1880–81; siege of Potchefstroom (wounded, despatches); with West India Regt West Coast Africa, in operations Hinterland of Lagos, 1897–98 (despatches, Bt Lt-Col, medal, clasp); Hinterland, Sierra Leone, 1898–99 (medal, clasp); Boer War, 1899–1901, Special Service Officer; District Commissioner, Wakkerstroom, 1900–1; Commandant, Paarl District, Cape Colony, 1901 (despatches, Queen's medal and four clasps, DSO); commanded troops St Lucia, BWI 1902; Acting Administrator of the Colony, Feb.–Nov. 1902; commanded 2nd WIR, 1904–7; Brevet of Col 1904; wounded in Jamaica Earthquake, 1907; Brig.-Gen. commanding troops in Jamaica and Inspector of West India Local Forces, 1910–14; European War, commanded Infantry Brigade Colchester and East Coast, Nov. 1914–17 (despatches); retired with rank of Brig.-Gen. 1917; special appointment Commandant Corps Troops 6th Corps BEF, 1917–19. *Address:* c/o Cox's Branch, 6 Pall Mall, SW1.

Died 6 Nov. 1924.

HAY, Sir James Shaw, KCMG 1889 (CMG 1887); *b* 25 Oct. 1839; *s* of late Colonel Thomas Pasley Hay and *cousin* of Sir Hector Hay, 7th Bt, of Alderston; *m* 1st, Jane, *e d* of John Morin, Allington, Dumfries; one *d*; 2nd, Frances Marie (*d* 1893), *d* of Jacques Polatza of Brussels; 3rd, 1894, Isabella, *d* of late G. F. Cockburn and *g d* of Lord Cockburn. Was Lieutenant 89th Foot; served Indian Mutiny; served Yonnie Expedition, 1887–88 (medal and clasp); Administrator of the Gambia, 1886–88; Governor of Sierra Leone and Consul-Gen. for Liberia, 1888–92; Governor of Barbados 1892–1900. *Club:* United Service.

Died 20 June 1924.

HAY, Lord John, GCB 1886; Admiral of the Fleet, 1888; *b* Geneva, 23 Aug. 1827; 4th *s* of 8th Marquis of Tweeddale; *m* 1876, Christina, *y d* of N. G. Lambert, MP, Denham Court, Bucks; two *s* one *d* (and one *d* decd). Entered Navy, 1839; served in China War, 1842; before Sebastopol; Commodore East India Station, 1861–63; MP (L) for Wick, 1857–59; for Ripon, 1866–67 and 1868–71; a Lord of the Admiralty, 1866, 1868–71, 1880–83, 1886; commanded Channel Squadron, 1877–79; took possession of and administered Cyprus,

1878; commanded Mediterranean Station, 1883–86; Com.-in-Chief, Devonport, 1887–88; retired 1897. *Address:* Fulmer Place, Fulmer, Slough.

Died 4 May 1916.

HAY, Sir Lewis John Erroll, 9th Bt, *cr* 1663, of Park; indigo planter; retired; *b* Stirling, NB, 17 Nov. 1866; *e s* of Sir Arthur Graham Hay, 8th Bt and Thomasina Isabella, *d* of John Brett Johnston, of Ballykilbeg, Co. Down; *S* father, 1889; *m* 1895, Lizabel Annie, *o d* of late Lachlan Mackinson Macdonald, Skeabost, Isle of Skye; one *s* eight *d. Educ:* Fettes Coll. Edin. *Recreation:* golf. *Heir: s* Arthur Thomas Erroll Hay, *b* 13 April 1909. *Address:* 6 Ravelston Park, Edinburgh. *T:* Central 4286.

Died 14 May 1923.

HAY, Sir Robert Hay-Drummond-, Kt 1906; CMG 1902; *b* Tangier, 25 July 1846; *o s* of late Rt Hon. Sir John Hay Drummond Hay, GCMG, KCB, HM's Envoy Extraordinary and Minister Plenipotentiary in Morocco; *m* 1st, 1868, Euphemia Katharine (*d* 1918), *e d* of late Thomas Willis-Fleming, formerly of South Stoneham, Hampshire; two *s* one *d*; 2nd, 1920, Grace Marguerite, *e d* of Sidney Thomas Lethbridge, Hampstead. *Educ:* Eton; Trinity College, Camb. Attached to British Legation at Tangier, 1869–75; Consul at Mogador, 1876; transferred to Stockholm, 1879; to Tunis, 1889; Consul-General there, 1891; Consul-General in Syria, to reside at Beirut, with superintendence over Consuls at Damascus and Jerusalem, 1894; retired 1908; received the Jubilee medal, 1897. *Recreations:* field sports. *Club:* Travellers'.

Died 15 Oct. 1926.

HAY, Sir William Henry, 8th Bt, *cr* 1703, of Alderston; *b* 30 May 1867; *s* of William Thomas Hay, *s* of Sir James Douglas Hamilton Hay, 6th Bt, and Isabella, *d* of Robert Charles, Melbourne; *S* uncle, 1916. Heir: *b* Edward Hamilton Hay, *b* 30 May 1870.

Died 3 July 1927.

HAY-DRUMMOND, Col Hon. Charles Rowley, JP; *b* 10 Oct. 1836; *y s* of 10th Earl of Kinnoull and Louisa Burton, 2nd *d* of Adm. Sir Charles Rowley, 1st Bt, GCB; *m* 1858, Arabella Augusta (*d* 1899), *d* of late Col William Henry Meyrick, of Goodrich Court, Herefordshire; three *s* four *d. Educ:* Sandhurst. Assumed additional surname of Drummond, 1900; formerly Capt. and Lt-Col Scots Guards; served Crimea. *Address:* Harewood Lodge, Sunninghill; 8 Eccleston Square, SW. *T:* Victoria 5476.

Died 23 May 1918.

HAYCRAFT, Prof. John Berry, MD, DSc, Gold Medallist; FRSE; Emeritus Professor of Physiology, University College, South Wales; formerly interim Professor of Physiology, Edinburgh University. *Publications:* Darwinism and Race Progress; The Human Body; papers before the Royal Societies of London and Edinburgh; papers in Brain, the Journal of Physiology, Text-book of Physiology (Schafer), in several German and French periodicals. *Address:* 3 Whitehall, Royston, near Cambridge.

Died 30 Dec. 1922.

HAYDEN, Sir Henry Hubert, Kt 1920; CSI 1919; CIE 1911; BA, BAI; FRS 1915; FGS; late Director, Geological Survey of India; *b* 1869; *s* of late James Hayden of Lisardahla, Londonderry. *Educ:* Hilton College, Natal; Trinity College, Dublin. Joined Geological Survey of India, 1895; attached to Tirah Expeditionary Force, 1897–98; Tibet Frontier Commission, 1903–4; services lent to Amir of Afghanistan, 1907–8. Hon. DSc, Calcutta. *Publications:* papers in Records and Memoirs of the Geological Survey of India; in conjunction with Colonel S. G. Burrard, FRS, Sketch of the Geography and Geology of the Himalaya Mountains and Tibet. *Clubs:* Oriental; Bengal, Calcutta.

Died Aug. 1923.

HAYES, Claude, RI, ROI; landscape painter; *b* Dublin, 1852; 2nd *s* of late Edwin Hayes, RHA, and Ellen Brisco. *Educ:* Loughborough. Began life as a sailor at 19 years of age; was in the Abyssinian Expedition; left the calling of the sea and went to America; returned and studied at Heatherley's School of Art; entered the Royal Academy as student at 22 years of age, and was exhibiting on the walls of RA at 24 years of age; elected Royal Institute of Painters in Water Colours at 32 years of age. *Recreations:* bicycling, golf, hockey. *Address:* c/o Messrs Bourlet, 17 Nassau Street, Mortimer Street, W1. *Club:* Arts.

Died 1922.

HAYES, Frederick William, ARCA; FRGS; landscape painter; illustrator, author; *b* 13 July 1848; *e s* of W. W. Hayes, Freshfield, Lancs; *m* 1st, 1876, Margaret, and 2nd, 1886, Elise, *ds* of John Robinson, of Talysarn Hall, late High Sheriff of Carnarvonshire; two *s* two *d. Educ:* Liverpool College and privately. Brought up as architect, but abandoned this for landscape painting, especially of North Wales scenery; one of the founders and for some years hon. secretary of Liverpool Water Colour Society; exhibited at Royal Academy from 1871 onwards; active worker in Fabian Society from 1891, also in the Psychical Research, Land Nationalisation, and Commons and Footpaths Preservation Societies. *Publications:* (novels, with own illustrations) A Kent Squire, 1900; Gwynett of Thornhaugh, 1900; The Shadow of a Throne, 1904; A Prima Donna's Romance, 1905; Captain Kirke Webbe, 1907; (sociological) The Story of the Phalanx, 1894; The United Kingdom, Ltd, 1910; miscellanea; comedy, Medusa, at St James's Theatre, 1882; various songs. *Recreations:* music, Royal Choral Society from 1882, local parliaments, cycling, walking. *Address:* 12 Westcroft Square, W.

Died 7 Sept. 1918.

HAYES, Hugh; a practising solicitor, since 1882; MP (U), West Down, 1922. *Address:* Lurgan, Co. Down.

Died 5 Sept. 1928.

HAYES, John; MP (Sinn Fein) West Cork, Dec. 1918–22; member of Dail Eireann, Cork, 1921–23; late Editor of Skibbereen Southern Star. *Address:* Skibbereen, Co. Cork.

HAYES, Captain William, DSO 1917; The Queen's Regiment; *b* 11 April 1891; *e s* of late Major P. A. Hayes and Edith Mary, Lady Babtie, *d* of late W. H. Barry, of Ballyadam, Co. Cork; unmarried. *Educ:* Beaumont; RMC, Sandhurst. Entered army, 1911; Captain, 1915; Temp. Major, 1916–18; served European War, 1914–18 (despatches, DSO). *Address:* 7 Campden Hill Gardens, W8. *Club:* Junior United Service. *Died 20 Oct. 1918.*

HAYFORD, John Fillmore; Director, College of Engineering, Northwestern University, since 1909; *b* Rouse's Point, New York, 19 May 1868; *s* of Hiram Hayford and Mildred Alevia Fillmore; *m* 1894, Lucy Stone, of Charlotte, New York. *Educ:* Cornell University. Computer US Coast and Geodetic Survey, 1889; Assistant Astronomer to International Boundary Commission, US and Mexico, in charge of one of field parties, 1892–93; with US Coast and Geodetic Survey, 1894–95; Instructor, Civil Engineering, Cornell University, 1895–98; Expert Computer and Geodesist, US Coast and Geodetic Survey, 1898–99, and Inspector of Geodetic Work and Chief of Computing Division, 1900–9. Member Nat. Advisory Cttee for Aeronautics; FAAAS; Member National Acad. Sciences; Am. Philos. Soc., Am. Astron. Soc., Am. Soc. CE, Western Soc. Engrs. *Publications:* Geodetic Astronomy, 1898; numerous monographs in reports of US Coast and Geodetic Survey. *Address:* 574 Ingleside Park, Evanston, Ill, USA. *Died 10 March 1925.*

HAYMAN, Ven. Reginald John Edward; Archdeacon of Geelong since 1916; Organising Secretary Bishop of Melbourne's Fund, 1913; Organising Secretary for Completion of St Paul's Cathedral, Melbourne, 1925 (pro tem.); *b* Axminster, 1861; *s* of Philip Hayman, medical practitioner; *m* 1890, Mercy, *d* of Supt Barclay; four *s* three *d*. *Educ:* Oakhouse School, Axminster; Hamilton College, Victoria; Moore College, NSW (First Class honours). Ordained, 1884; Curate of Dimboola, 1885–86; Casterton, 1887–88; Incumbent of Branxholme, 1888–89; Vicar of Stawell, 1889–98; Incumbent of Hamilton, 1898–1906; Archdeacon of Grampians, 1902–6; Vicar of Maryborough, 1906–13; Canon of Ballarat Cathedral, 1895–1913; Archdeacon of the Loddon, 1906–13; Chairman of Committees in Ballarat Diocesan Synod, 1901–12; took part in securing Federal Provident Fund for Diocesan clergy. *Address:* St Paul's Cathedral, Melbourne, Australia. *Died Nov. 1927.*

HAYNE, Louis Brightwell, MBE 1920; MD Cantab, MA; Hon. Physician, Harrogate Infirmary; *b* 19 July 1869; *s* of late Henry Hayne, The Ferns, Tunbridge Wells; *m* Margaret L., *d* of late Murdoch Shaw Morison; no *c*. *Educ:* Tonbridge School; Gonville and Caius College, Cambridge; St George's Hospital, London (House Surgeon and House Physician). House Physician, Victoria Hospital for Children, Tite Street, Chelsea; private practice in Harrogate from 1901; Hon. Medical Officer in charge of Grove House Hospital, Harrogate, 1914–19. *Recreations:* fishing, shooting, natural history. *Address:* Sheen House, Harrogate. *T:* Harrogate 199.

Died 14 Feb. 1926.

HAYNES, Richard Septimus, KC 1904; practising in the city of Perth; *b* Picton, NSW, 14 Aug. 1857; *s* of late John Haynes, Sydney, Civil Servant; *m* 1st, 1881, Marion Adelaide Goodwin, Sydney; 2nd, 1907, A. D'Arcy, Perth; three *s* four *d*. *Educ:* Sydney Grammar School. Admitted Solicitor, NSW, 1881; Barrister, etc, WA, 1885; City Councillor, 1886–95; Member Legislative Council, 1896–1902;

Mayor North Perth, 1901–4; Consul for Norway, 1906–14; Trustee Public Library and Museum from 1913; Member Barristers' Board from 1889. *Publications:* The Licensing Law of WA, 3 editions; The Trespass Law of WA. *Recreation:* angling. *Address:* Windsor Hall, Queen's Crescent, Mount Lawley, Perth, W Australia. *TA:* Senyah. *T:* A 1042, A 3257. *Died 20 Feb. 1922.*

HAYSOM, Sir George, Kt 1917; Sheriff, City of London, 1917; Chairman, G. Haysom, Ltd, and Miller, Rayner & Haysom, Ltd; *b* London, 6 May 1862; *m* 1881, Lydia, *d* of Samuel Archer; one *s* four *d*. Member of Court of Common Council, Aldgate Ward, from 1903; Liveryman Basket Makers' and Spectacle Makers' Companies. *Recreations:* golf, fishing. *Address:* The Welkin, Lindfield, Sussex. *Club:* Constitutional. *Died 7 Sept. 1924.*

HAYTER, Sir William Goodenough, KBE 1920 (CBE 1917); *b* 28 Jan. 1869; *s* of Henry Goodenough Hayter of Winterbourne, Sidmouth; *m* Alethea, 2nd *d* of Rev. J. H. Slessor; one *s* two *d*. *Educ:* Winchester; New College, Oxford. Barrister, Lincoln's Inn, 1895; Civil Judge in the Sudan, 1904; Asst Legal Adviser in Egypt, 1904; Khedivial Counsellor, 1913; Counsel to the Sultan of Egypt, 1915; Legal Adviser to HBM Residency, Cairo, 1918; and to Egyptian Govt; Chairman, Cotton Control Commission, 1919; acted as Judicial Adviser, and in 1919 as Financial Adviser. Grand Officer of Orders of Medjidieh and Nile. *Recreation:* golf. *Address:* Zamalek, Gezira, Cairo. *Died 5 Aug. 1924.*

HAYTHORNTHWAITE, Rev. John Parker, MA; Vicar of Kings Langley since 1916; *b* 22 May 1862; *s* of late Rev. Richard Haythornthwaite, Vicar of Cleator Moor, Cumberland; *m* 1892, Iszet Mead, LRCP, LRCS, Lucknow Medical Mission; one *s* two *d*. *Educ:* Sedbergh School; St John's College, Cambridge. Curate of St Luke's, Barrow-in-Furness, 1885–88; Organising Secretary for the Church Missionary Society in the South of Ireland, 1888–90; Principal of St John's College, Agra, in North India; Fellow of Allahabad University; Examiner in Logic, History, etc, 1890–1911; Educational Deputation of the Church Missionary Society, 1911–14; Metropolitan Secretary of the Church Missionary Society, 1914–16. *Publications:* History of Parish of Kings Langley, its Ancient Church and Historic Associations, 1924; The Romantic Life and Notable Tomb of Edmund de Langley, 1927; articles in CM Review, East and West, etc. *Recreations:* cricket, tennis, cycling. *Address:* The Vicarage, Kings Langley, Herts. *Club:* Church Imperial. *Died 12 Aug. 1928.*

HAYWARD, William Thornborough, CMG 1918; Hon. LLD (Aber. and Adel.); MRCS, LRCP; Consulting Physician, Adelaide Hospital; Vice-President of British Medical Association; Col (retd); *b* 26 June 1854; *e s* of W. G. Hayward, Reading; *m* Florence Burden, Adelaide; seven *s* two *d*. *Educ:* St John's College, Hurstpierpoint; Liverpool School of Medicine. Hon. Physician Adelaide Hospital, 1885–1914; Hon. Medical Officer Children's Hospital; Lecturer on Clinical Medicine, Materia Medica, Therapeutics, Adelaide University; Member of Council of Adelaide University; Chairman of Australian Federal Committee British Medical Association, 1913–22; OC 1st Australian Auxiliary Hospital, Harefield, 1915–17 (despatches); Physician to 3rd Australian Gen. Hosp., France. *Publications:* various papers to medical journals. *Recreations:* bowls, bridge. *Address:* 20 Alexandra Avenue, Rose Park, South Australia. *Club:* Adelaide. *Died 21 Dec. 1928.*

HAZELL, Walter; *b* 1843; *o c* of Jonathan Hazell; *m* 1886, Anna, *e d* of James Tomlin; three *s* two *d*. *Educ:* privately. Chairman, Hazell Watson and Viney, Ltd, printers; first President of the Federation of Employing Printers of the United Kingdom; actively connected with various social reform and philanthropic movements; Treasurer British Institute of Social Service; Treasurer Land Law Reform Assoc.; President and Joint Founder of Children's Fresh Air Mission; Chairman, Women's Settlement Canning Town; Chairman Emigration Committee of Central Unemployed Body; and in furtherance of emigration has travelled through Australasia and Canada; carried on a farm for unemployables, 1892–1900; President Bloomsbury House Club, and also of Cartwright Gardens Ladies' Club; Chairman, Homes for Little Boys at Farningham and Swanley. MP (L) Leicester, 1894–1900; Mayor of Holborn, 1911–12; JP for Bucks; a Commissioner of Income Tax. *Recreations:* farming, travel. *Address:* 52 Long Acre, WC; 82 Bedford Avenue, WC. *T:* Gerrard 605; Walton Grange, Aylesbury. *T:* Aylesbury 15. *Clubs:* Reform, New City. *Died 12 Feb. 1919.*

HAZELL, Captain William, CB 1911; RD; RNR; *b* 9 Dec. 1857; *e s* of late Joseph Hazell and late Frances Helen Hornsby; *m* E. Hooper of Mount Pleasant, Warfield, Bracknell, Berks; no *c*. *Educ:* Clewer

House, Windsor. Served in ships and vessels employed in, or otherwise associated with, the following wars: Egyptian, 1882; Burma, 1886; China-Japan, 1894-95; Boer, 1900-2; European War, 1914-18; in the ranks successively of the late Royal Naval Artillery Volunteers, the East Indian Railway Volunteers, and the Calcutta Naval Volunteers, 1877-90; the Rangoon Pilot Service, as Mate of the pilot brig Guide, and Probationary Pilot for the Rangoon River, Burma, 1884; equal service in Merchant Service and in Royal Navy; at the Admiralty, in the Office of the Admiral Commanding Coast Guard and Reserves, 1904-5; member of the Military Council of the British League for the Support of Ulster and the Union, 1914; Sub-Lieutenant, 1890; Lieutenant, 1895; Commander (retired), 1910; and Captain (retired), 1918 (in recognition of services rendered during the war). Constitutional Imperialist and Royalist. Church of England; student and practician in divine metaphysics. *Address:* 8 Sheet Street, Windsor, Berks. *Died 26 June 1927.*

HAZLEHURST, Thomas Francis, JP, DL; *o s* of late John Hazlehurst, and Sarah, *d* of late F. Salkeld; *m* 1867, Hon. Blanche, *y d* of 15th Viscount Hereford. Was Capt. 3rd Warwickshire RV; High Sheriff, Northampton, 1900. *Address:* Cold Ashby Hall, Rugby. *Clubs:* Junior Carlton, Orleans.
Died 26 Jan. 1918.

HEAD, Lt-Col Arthur Edward Maxwell, DSO 1917; late Royal Field Artillery; *b* 18 June 1876; 2nd *s* of late H. H. Head, JP; unmarried. *Educ:* Charterhouse; RMA, Woolwich. Joined RA 1896; Lieut 1899; Captain, 1902; Major, 1913; Lt-Col, 1917; served China, 1900 (medal); European War (despatches twice, DSO); retired pay, 1920. *Address:* Ferry Quarter, Strangford, Co. Down, Ireland. *Club:* Army and Navy. *Died 15 Nov. 1921.*

HEAD, Ernest; News Editor and Chief Sub-Editor, Pall Mall Gazette; *b* 16 April 1871; *s* of Rev. A. T. Head, Ford, Devonport. Formerly on staff of the Western Morning News and Managing Editor Cornish Telegraph. *Address:* 85 Harborough Road, Streatham, SW.
Died 16 June 1923.

HEAD, George Herbert, MA; County Court Judge, Circuit No 16 since 1922; holds courts at Beverley, Bridlington, Goole, Great Driffield, Howden, Kingston-upon-Hull, New Malton, Scarborough, Thorne and Whitby, with jurisdiction in Admiralty at Hull and in bankruptcy at Hull and Scarborough; *e s* of late Rev. George Frederick Head, Vicar of Clifton Parish Church and Hon. Canon of Bristol Cathedral, and Mary Henrietta (*d* 1912), *d* of late Captain Charles Nelson Bolton, RN; *m* 1913, Geraldine Maria, *y d* of late Major-General Henry Pipon, CB, His Majesty's Resident Governor of the Tower of London, and Louisa Ann (*d* 1921), *d* of the late Admiral Sir William Edmonstone, 4th Bt, CB of Duntreath, Stirlingshire; two *s. Educ:* Repton School (Entrance Exhibitioner); Pembroke Coll., Cambridge (Classical Scholar). Called to the Bar Inner Temple; joined Western Circuit; JP for E Riding and Ouse and Derwent Division of Yorkshire, Hull and Scarborough. *Recreations:* golf, sailing. *Address:* The Lodge, Acomb, York. *T:* York 2837. *Clubs:* New University; Yorkshire, York. *Died 11 Feb. 1927.*

HEAD, John Joshua, ISO 1902; Collector of Customs (retired); *b* 30 Sept. 1838; *e s* of late John Head of Ipswich; *m* 1868, Charlotte, *d* of late Henry St John Diaper; two *d. Educ:* Queen Elizabeth's School, Ipswich. Entered the Customs Service at Ipswich, 1856; subsequently held the appointment of Collector of Customs at the ports of Cardigan, Deal, Dartmouth, Newhaven, Swansea, Harwich, Leith, Newcastle-on-Tyne, Hull, and Belfast, and for some years was the senior collector in the United Kingdom. *Address:* Highlands, Seaford, Sussex. *Died 5 Nov. 1925.*

HEAD, Sir (Robert Pollock) Somerville, 4th Bt, *cr* 1838; FRGS; 1st Secretary, Diplomatic Service; *b* 7 April 1884; *s* of Sir Robert Garnett Head, 3rd Bt and Florence Julia, *d* of R. Pollock, 8th Madras Cavalry, and *g d* of Sir Frederick Pollock, 1st Bt; *S* father 1907; *m* 1915, Grace Margaret, *d* of late David Robertson; two *s* one *d. Educ:* Wellington Coll. Nominated an Attaché in HM Diplomatic Service, 1905; passed a competitive examination, 1906; appointed to Lisbon, 1907; transferred to Madrid, 1907; 3rd Secretary, 1908; transferred to Peking, 1911; 2nd Secretary, 1914; transferred to Vienna, 1914; to Petrograd, 1914; to Peking, 1917; 1st Secretary, 1919; to Berlin, 1920. *Heir: s* Francis David Somerville Head, *b* 17 Oct. 1916. *Address:* 13 Sussex Square, W2. *T:* Paddington 1143; British Embassy, Berlin. *Died 21 June 1924.*

HEADINGTON, Arthur Hutton; Captain Berkshire Yeomanry; Joint-Master of the Berkshire and Buckinghamshire Farmers

Staghounds since 1907; Member Maidenhead Board of Guardians; *b* Scarletts, Twyford, Berks, 6 Oct. 1878; *s* of Frederick and Fanny Headington; unmarried. *Educ:* St Leonard's; Uppingham. Member of National Rifle Association, Bisley. *Recreations:* hunting, shooting, fishing. *Address:* Highway, Maidenhead. *T:* 231 Maidenhead. *M:* LH 3565. *Died Nov. 1917.*

HEADLAM, Rev. Stewart Duckworth; Member London School Board, 1888-1904; London County Council (P) SW Bethnal Green since 1907. *Educ:* Wadhurst; Eton; Trinity Coll., Camb. Ordained, 1870; Curate of St John's, Drury Lane, 1870-73; St Matthew's, Bethnal Green, 1873-77; St Thomas's, Charterhouse, 1879-81; St Michael's, Shoreditch, 1881-84. *Publications:* Laws of Eternal Life; Lessons from the Cross; Priestcraft and Progress; The Ballet; Theory of Theatrical Dancing; The Place of the Bible in Secular Education; The Meaning of the Mass; The Socialist's Church; Fabianism and Land Values; Some Old Words on the War. *Address:* Wavertree, St Margaret's on Thames. *Died 18 Nov. 1924.*

HEADLAND, John, ISO 1904; late a Principal Clerk in Supreme Court Pay Office; *b* 1840. *Address:* Russell Villa, New Barnet.
Died 22 Jan. 1927.

HEALY, Most Rev. John, DD, LLD; MRIA; Archbishop of Tuam; *b* Ballinafad, Co. Sligo, 14 Nov. 1841; *e s* of Mark Healy. *Educ:* Summer Hill College, Athlone; Maynooth College (First Honours). Classical Professor, 1867-70; Missionary Priest, Professor of Theology, Maynooth College; Præfect of the Dunboyne Establishment, Maynooth College; Senator Royal University of Ireland and of new Dublin University; ex-Member Board of Agriculture for Ireland; Commissioner for publication of the Brehon Laws; Vice-President Royal Society of Antiquaries of Ireland; member Royal Commission on University Education in Ireland, 1901. *Publications:* Ireland's Ancient Schools and Scholars; Centenary History of Maynooth College; Centenary Record of Maynooth College; Life of St Patrick; Irish essays, literary and historical; papers and addresses. *Recreations:* fishing, yachting, where chance offers; otherwise, recreation spent in antiquarian researches throughout Ireland. *Address:* St Jarlath's, Tuam, Ireland. *Died 16 March 1918.*

HEALY, Maurice; MP (IN) Cork City, 1910-18; solicitor; *b* 3 Jan. 1859; *s* of Maurice Healy, Bantry; *y b* of Timothy Michael Healy, MP; *m* 1887, Annie, *d* of late A. M. Sullivan, MP; two *s* one *d. Educ:* Christian Bros, Lismore. MP (N) Cork City, 1885-1900, 1909-10; NE Cork, March-Dec. 1910. *Address:* Ashton Lawn, Cork.
Died 9 Nov. 1923.

HEALY, Thomas Joseph; solicitor; *b* 1854; *s* of Maurice Healy, Bantry, Cork; *m* 1879, Kathleen, *d* of M. F. Shine, Dungarvan. Admitted a solicitor, 1888. MP (N) Co. Wexford, N, 1892-1900. *Address:* Tullow, Co. Carlow. *Died 1925.*

HEAN, Hon. Alexander, CMG 1912; a Member for Franklin, House of Assembly, Tasmania, since 1909; *b* 11 June 1859; *s* of late Captain A. B. Hean, Dundee, Scotland; *m* Amy Mary, *d* of late J. W. Allanby, of Dunalley, Tasmania; four *s* four *d. Educ:* Highlanders' Academy, privately, Greenock. Arrived in Australia from Scotland, 1877; Council of Sorell Municipality, 1886-1906; Warden, 1899-1904; Member for Sorell, House of Assembly, 1903, and 1906; sometime Minister for Mines; Attorney-General, Tasmania, 1923; Minister of Lands and Works, Agriculture and Railways, and Commissioner of Main Roads, 1904; for some time in 1911 held Office of Acting Premier; a Coroner and Magistrate for the Territory, and Member of the Licensing Bench of Sorell. *Recreations:* cricket; engaged in pastoral pursuits. *Address:* Parliament House, Hobart. *Club:* Athenæum, Hobart. *Died 11 Jan. 1927.*

HEARD, Rev. William Augustus, MA; Hon. LLD Edinburgh; FRSL; Headmaster of Fettes College, Edinburgh, 1890-1919; *b* 9 Aug. 1847; *s* of James Heard, Spey Lodge, Withington, Manchester; *m* Elizabeth, *d* of Henry Burt, Southport; three *s* three *d. Educ:* Manchester Grammar School; Trinity College, Oxford (Scholar). House-master at Fettes College, subsequently House-master at Westminster School; on committee of St George's Training College, Edinburgh, St Leonard's College, St Andrews; President Classical Association (Scotland). *Address:* Fettes College, Edinburgh. *T:* 19 Central, Edinburgh. *Club:* New University.
Died 12 March 1921.

HEATH, Col Edward, CMG 1918; late Army Ordnance Department; *b* 5 July 1854; *m*; one *s.* First Commission in the Control Dept, 1873; Col 1901; retired, 1904; served Bechuanaland, 1884-85; re-employed as Chief Ordnance Officer, Tidworth, Salisbury Plain, 1915-19. *Address:* Parkstone. *Died 4 June 1927.*

HEATH, Col Harry Heptinstall Rose, CB 1905; *b* 24 June 1850. Entered 10th Hussars, 1872; Captain Indian Staff Corps, 1884; Major, 1892; Lt-Col, 1898; Col, 1900; served Jowaki Expedition, 1877-78 (despatches, medal with clasp); Afghanistan, 1878-79 (despatches, medal with clasp); Hazara Expedition, 1891 (clasp); Chitral, 1895 (despatches, Bt Lt-Col); employed with Afghan Boundary Commission, 1884-86; retired, 1910. *Address:* Dunley, Bovey Tracy, S Devon. *Died 17 Dec. 1922.*

HEATHCOTE, Justinian Heathcote Edwards-, JP, DL; *b* 1843; *e s* of Rev. Edward James Justinian Edwards, Vicar of Trentham, Co. Stafford, and Elizabeth Anne, *d* of late Richard Edensor Heathcote, of Apedale and Longton Halls; *m* 1870, Eleanor (*d* 1927), *d* of Spencer Stone, of Callingwood, Co. Stafford; one *s* one *d. Educ:* Winchester. Capt. 63rd Foot and Staffordshire, 1886-92. *Address:* Betton Hall, Market Drayton, Shropshire; Longton Hall, Stoke-on-Trent. *Clubs:* Carlton, Windham. *Died 21 Jan. 1928.*

HEATHCOTE, Rev. Sir William Arthur, 7th Bt, *cr* 1733; SJ; *b* 22 July 1853; *e s* of Sir William Perceval Heathcote, 6th Bt and Letitia Maria, *d* of David Daly; *S* father 1903. *Educ:* Beaumont College. In remainder to the earldom of Macclesfield. *Heir:* brother Lt-Col Gilbert Redvers Heathcote, JP Hants, late 1st Bn Cameronians [*b* 25 Dec. 1854; *m* 1st, 1891, Pauline (*d* 1897), *d* of Sir Alfred Trevelyan, 7th Bt; 2nd, 1901, Mabel, *y d* of late H. D. Silvertop, of Minster Acres, Northumberland. *Address:* Bighton Wood, Alresford, Hants. *TA:* Bighton. *T:* Alresford 42; 27 Green Street, Park Lane, W1. *T:* Mayfair 3951. *Club:* Army and Navy]. *Address:* Stonyhurst College, Blackburn. *Died 9 Sept. 1924.*

HEATON-ARMSTRONG, William Charles; MP (L) Sudbury Division, Suffolk, 1906-10; Fellow of the Royal Astronomical, Zoological, Botanical, Statistical, and other learned Societies; Lord of the Manor of Roscrea; merchant and banker; *b* 1 Sept. 1853; *s* of John Heaton-Armstrong; succeeded on the death of his father to the senior representation of the families of Heaton-Armstrong, Armstrong of Mangerton, Mount Heaton and Farney Castle, Macdonnell of New Hall, and Heaton of Yorkshire; *m* 1885, the Baroness Bertha Maxmiliana Zois-Edelstein, *o* surv. *d* of 4th Baron Zois-Edelstein, of Austria; two *s* one *d. Educ:* abroad and privately. Visited nearly all our Colonies, and travelled very extensively; though a Liberal in politics, contested Mid-Tipperary in 1892 against the separation of Ireland from England; stood as a Loyalist in favour of granting local self-government to the greatest possible extent to Ireland. *Publication:* Calculation of the Sun's Meridian Altitude. *Recreations:* big game shooting, billiards, motoring. *Address:* 5 Cornwall Gardens, SW. *TA:* Heatonarm, London. *T:* Western 7151. *Clubs:* Union, Royal Automobile. *Died 20 July 1917.*

HEAVEN, Rev. Hudson Grosett, MA; Lord of the Manor and sole landowner of Lundy Island; Vicar of Lundy Island since 1886; *b* 1826; *s* of late W. H. Heaven, of Lundy Island; unmarried. *Educ:* Trinity Coll., Oxford (BA 1851, MA 1852). Deacon, 1852; Priest, 1854; Curate of Knowle St Giles, and Assistant Master, Ilminster Grammar School, 1852-54; Assistant Master Taunton College School, 1855-58; Head Master, 1858-64; Curate of Lundy Island, 1864-86. *Address:* Blenheim, Torrington, North Devon. *Club:* Junior Conservative. *Died 28 Feb. 1916.*

HEAVISIDE, Arthur West, ISO 1904; *b* 1844; *m* 1869, Isabel Sarah Bell. Retired Superintending Engineer to HM Post Office; Inventor of the Bridge system of telephony and original investigator of wireless telegraphy. *Address:* 8 Elmswood Gardens, Acton Hill, W3. *Died 22 Sept. 1923.*

HEAVISIDE, Oliver, FRS 1891; mathematical physicist and electrician; *b* 18 May 1850; *s* of Thomas Heaviside; unmarried. Hon. PhD Göttingen. Hon. Mem., AAAS; Lit. Phil. Soc., Manchester. Faraday Medal, IEE. *Address:* Homefield, Lower Warberry, Torquay. *Died 4 Feb. 1925.*

HEBB, R. G., MA, MD; FRCP; Consulting Physician and Physician Pathologist to Westminster Hospital; Consulting Pathologist to Queen Charlotte's Hospital; Lecturer on Pathology at Westminster Hospital Medical School; Reader in Morbid Anatomy, University of London; editor Journal of Royal Microscopical Society; *m* 1903, Henrietta Frances, *o d* of late Nathaniel Sharp. *Address:* 50 Ridgmount Gardens, WC. *Died 12 May 1918.*

HEBBLETHWAITE, Percival, MA; *b* 28 Oct. 1849; *m* 1877; two *s* three *d. Educ:* Rossall School; King's College, London; Trinity College, Cambridge (Foundation Scholar, 1871; Latin Verse Prizeman, 1871, 1872; Fifth Classics, 1873). Vice-Master, Royal Institution School, Liverpool, 1875-78; Private Tutor, 1878-82; Assistant Lecturer in Classics, University College, Liverpool, 1882-98; Lecturer in Classics and Hon. Assistant Professor, 1898-1904; Secretary, 1900-4; Registrar, University of Liverpool, 1904-13. *Address:* Birch Road, Oxton, Cheshire. *T:* Birkenhead 1964. *Died 23 Feb. 1922.*

HEBERDEN, Charles Buller, Hon. DCL; Principal of Brasenose College, Oxford, since 1889; Fellow of Winchester College, 1914; *b* 1849; *s* of Rev. W. Heberden. *Educ:* Harrow; Balliol College, Oxford (Exhibitioner, 1868). First class Classical Mods and Lit. Hum. Fellow and Lecturer of Brasenose, 1872; Tutor, 1881; Proctor, 1881; Vice-Principal, 1883; member of Hebdomadal Council, 1896, 1902, and 1906-14; Vice-Chancellor, Oxford University, 1910-13. *Address:* Brasenose College, Oxford. *Club:* Oxford and Cambridge. *Died 30 May 1921.*

HEBERDEN, Surg. Capt. George Alfred, DSO 1900; Medical Officer, Kimberley Light Horse; *b* 27 April 1860; *s* of late Rev. George Heberden; *m* 1895, Winifred, *d* of late Rev. Henry Cottam. *Educ:* Malvern College; Jesus College, Cambridge; St George's Hospital, London. BA Cantab 1882; MRCS, LRCP 1888. District Surgeon of Predasdorp, 1888-89; Surgeon Cape Govt Railway, 1890-92; Dist Surgeon Kenhardt, 1893-94; Barkly West, 1895; Medical Officer to Mounted Forces during siege of Kimberley (despatches, DSO). JP, Barkly West. *Address:* Victoria West, Cape Colony. *Club:* Kimberley. *Died 23 Jan. 1916.*

HEBERDEN, William Buller, CB 1898; JP Devon; *b* 6 July 1838; *e s* of late Rev. W. Heberden, Vicar of Broadhembury, Devon. *Educ:* Harrow; Christ Church, Oxford; Hon. Fourth in Classics and Mathematics, 1860. Entered Inland Revenue Department, 1861; appointed Assistant Secretary, 1887; Sec. 1894; retired, 1898. *Address:* Elmfield House, Exeter. *Clubs:* MCC; Devon and Exeter, Exeter. *Died 30 Nov. 1922.*

HÉBERT, Louis Philippe, CMG 1903; sculptor; French-Canadian; *b* Prov. Quebec, 27 Jan. 1850; *m* 1879, Marie, *d* of Thomas Roy, Montreal. *Educ:* at common schools of his native village. In early days became clerk in a country store; went to Rome as Papal Zouave; obtained prize at Provincial Exhibition, Montreal, for wood-carving in 1873; afterwards studied in Paris; won prize given by Dominion Government for full-length statue of George Cartier 1882. Knight of Legion of Honour, 1901. *Principal Works:* statues, among which are those to Maisonneuve, in Montreal; *monuments*—Queen Victoria, Ottawa; Hon. Joseph Howe, Halifax; Sir Leonard Tilly, St John; Mgr de Laval, Quebec; Hon. John Young, Montreal; King Edward VII, Montreal; to South African Soldiers, Calgary. *Address:* 309 Elm Avenue, Montreal. *Died 13 June 1917.*

HEBRARD, Emile A.; editor of Le Temps, 1915-25; *b* Paris, 1862. *Address:* 5 rue des Italiens, Paris. *Died April 1927.*

HEDDERWICK, Thomas Charles Hunter, JP; MA; Barrister Middle Temple, North Eastern circuit; Metropolitan Police Magistrate for North London since 1910; *b* Scotland, 6 April 1850; 2nd *s* of late Robert Hedderwick (Queen's printer and publisher, Glasgow; founder of old Glasgow Weekly Citizen newspaper in the Liberal interest, 1843), and of Anna M. W. Hunter, Dumfries; *m* 1884, Jemima, *o* surv. *c* of James Neilson, Biggar Park, Biggar, Lanarkshire; two *d. Educ:* Universities of Glasgow and Leipsic. Barrister Middle Temple, 1876; in the Tichborne Appeal Case for "the Claimant"; founded the Bar Committee. Contested (L) South Lanarkshire 1892, Northern Burghs 1895, 1896, 1900, Newbury Division, Berks, 1910; MP (L) Northern Burghs, 1896-1900; member of Select Committee on Election Law, 1898, of Select Committee on Pensions for the Aged Deserving Poor, 1899, and of the Board of Visitors for HM Convict Prison, Aylesbury, 1902; acting Deputy-Chairman, County of London Sessions, 1907-10. *Publications:* The Old German Puppet Play of Dr Faust, a translation with notes, 1887; A Manual of Parliamentary Election Law, 1892 (new edn 1900); The Sale of Foods and Drugs, 1894 (new edn 1900); contributions of a literary character to various periodicals. *Recreations:* golf, book collecting. *Address:* The Manor House, Weston Turville, Wendover; Biggar Park, Biggar, NB. *Clubs:* Reform, Eighty. *Died 6 Feb. 1918.*

HEDLEY, John, MVO 1910; late Royal Artillery; *b* 21 Jan. 1834. Served Crimea, 1854-56 (Crimean and Turkish medals, clasps for

Sebastopol and Inkerman). Secretary, Royal Choral Society, 1872–1910. *Address:* Laxton Vicarage, Howden, Yorkshire.
Died 18 May 1916.

HEDLEY, Lt-Col John Ralph, DSO 1916; Northumberland Fusiliers (TF); commanding 5th Battalion Border Regiment (TF); *b* Woolley, Wantage, 21 March 1871; *y s* of John Hedley, Woolley, formerly of The Leaguer House, Stamfordham, Northumberland; *m* Ada Marie, 2nd *d* of late T. H. Bambridge, JP, Eshott Hall, Felton, Northumberland; one *s* one *d. Educ:* privately; Royal Grammar School, Newcastle. In business, Newcastle, 1885–1910; Chairman of Unionist Association, 1909–10; of Northern Conservative Club, 1906–10; founded Salisbury Club for training young men to speak in public; invited twice to stand for Parliament but declined; on permanent staff Valuation Department, Inland Revenue, in charge of quarter of million acres, Hull District, 1910; Chairman Hull and East Riding Club, 1913–14. Commission in 3rd Vol. Batt. Northumberland Fusiliers, 1901; promoted to field rank, Sept. 1912; called up on mobilisation of TF Aug. 1914; went abroad with unit, 1915; served in France, 1915–16 (DSO, despatches twice). *Recreations:* cricket, tennis, shooting, hunting. *Address:* Westgate House, Hornsea, East Yorks; Twyford, Alnmouth, Northumberland. *T:* Hornsea, PO 30. *Clubs:* Northern Conservative, Newcastle; Hull and East Riding, Hull.
Died July 1917.

HEFFERNAN, Sir John Harold, KCB 1911 (CB 1891); Royal Navy; *b* 1834; *m* 1861, Eliza Sarah (*d* 1914), *d* of late W. Hilton, Ollerton Lodge, Knutsford; three *s* two *d.* Assistant engineer, 1855; gold medal, Atlantic Telegraph, 1858; served Alexandria, then promoted to Inspector of Machinery, and to Chief Inspector of Machinery in 1885; retired, 1892.
Died 17 Sept. 1921.

HEGAN, Col Edward, CB 1908; *b* 19 Jan. 1855; *s* of late John Hegan, 20 Queen's Gate, SW; *m* 1882, Sarah, *o d* of late Lt-Col W. H. Goodair, JP, of Ashton Park, Ashton-on-Ribble. *Educ:* Harrow. Entered army, 1876; Captain, 5th Dragoon Guards, 1882; Major, 1887; Lt-Col 1899; Bt Col, 1903; Col 1906; Commandant School of Auxiliary Cavalry, Aldershot, 1882–84; ADC to GOC Western District, 1889–90; DAAG, Cork, 1890–93; DAQMG, Tirah, 1897; special service, South Africa, 1890–1900; AAG, South Africa, 1900; Commandant Cavalry Depot, 1899–1904; staff officer for Imperial Yeomanry, 1906–8; Colonel in charge Cavalry Records, 1909–11; served S Africa, 1891; Tirah, 1897–98 (despatches, medal with 2 clasps); South Africa, 1899–1900 (Queen's medal, 3 clasps); retired 1911. *Club:* Naval and Military.
Died 4 Dec. 1922.

HEGER, Dr Paul, MD; Hon. LLD St Andrews; Hon. Professor; *b* Brussels, 13 Dec. 1846; *s* of Professor Constantin Heger; *m* Léonie Van Mons (*decd*); one *s* two *d. Educ:* Brussels; Vienna; Leipzig. Professor of Physiology at University of Brussels, 1873–1907; practised medicine until he undertook, in 1889, the post of Principal and Director of the Institute of Physiology founded in that year by M Ernest Solvay, Parc Léopold, Brussels. *Publications:* Archives Internationales de Physiologie (with Prof. L. Fredericq); numerous reports and essays on the work of the laboratory of the Institut Solvay. *Address:* 23 Rue des Drapiers, Brussels. *T:* 22235.
Died Nov. 1925.

HEINEMANN, William; publisher; *b* Surbiton, 18 May 1863. Founded the publishing house which bears his name in 1890. President of the Publishers' Association of Great Britain and Ireland, 1909–11; President of the National Booksellers' Provident Society, 1913–20. *Publications:* The First Step, a play in 3 acts, 1895; Summer Moths, a play in 4 acts, 1898; War, a play in 3 acts, 1901. *Recreations:* travelling, play-writing. *Address:* 32 Lower Belgrave Street, SW1. *T:* Victoria 6426; 21 Bedford Street, WC2. *T:* Gerrard 5675. *Clubs:* Conservative, National, Bath, etc.
Died 5 Oct. 1920.

HELLARD, Frederick, ISO 1915; late a Secretary of HM's Woods, Forests, etc; *b* 11 April 1850; *s* of late C. B. Hellard, Portsmouth, Solicitor and formerly Mayor of that town; *m* 1877, Harriette M., *d* of late John Williamson; one *s* four *d. Educ:* private schools. Admitted a Solicitor, 1872; entered the Solicitor's branch of the Office of Woods, 1879; Principal Clerk to one of the Commissioners, 1885, and subsequently a Secretary; retired 1915, but rejoined and served again till 1919. *Address:* Wayside Cottage, New Milton, Hants.
Died 16 May 1925.

HELLEU, Paul-César; Chevalier de la Légion d'honneur; peintre et graveur; *b* Vannes, 17 déc. 1859. *Œuvres:* nombreux portraits aux

Salons de la Société Nationale des Beaux-Arts; tableau au Musée du Luxembourg. *Address:* 45 rue Emile Ménier, Paris.
Died March 1927.

HELLIER, John Benjamin, MD London; MRCS; Emeritus Professor of Obstetrics, University of Leeds, and Consulting Obstetric Physician, Leeds General Infirmary, Leeds Maternity Hospital and Hospital for Women; *b* Seacombe, Cheshire; *s* of Rev. Benjamin Hellier, formerly of Headingley College; *m* Eliza, *y d* of H. B. Harrison, JP, Manchester; two *s* two *d. Educ:* Kingswood; Leeds School of Medicine; University College, London. Graduate University, London, 1876; First-Class Honours Medicine; University Scholar and Gold Medallist in Obstetric Medicine; in practice as consulting specialist in Obstetrics and Gynæcology in Leeds; Honorary Fellow Glasgow Obstetrical and Gynæcological Society; late President of North of England Obstetrical and Gynæcological Society. *Publications:* many contributions to literature of obstetrics and gynæcology, and pædiatrics. *Recreations:* touring, literature. *Address:* Chapel Allerton, Leeds; 27 Park Square, Leeds. *TA:* Dr Hellier, Leeds. *T:* Leeds 25878.
Died 8 Nov. 1924.

HELM, Henry James, ISO 1903; FIC, FCS; late Deputy Principal of the Government Laboratory, London; *b* 19 March 1839; *s* of Henry Helm, cotton manufacturer, Padiham, Lancashire; *m* 1867, Lucilla, *d* of John Smith, Padiham. *Educ:* Private School, Burnley; Grammar School, Whalley. Entered Inland Revenue Service, 1859; passed by competition into Inland Revenue Laboratory, 1861, which became the Government Laboratory, 1894; and retired under the age limit, 1904; Juror at the Paris Exhibition, 1900, St Louis, 1904, and at Brussels, 1910. *Address:* Simonstone, Bromley, Kent.
Died 24 March 1918.

HELMER, Col (Temp. Brig.-Gen.) Richard Alexis, CMG 1918; Canadian Permanent Staff; Director-General of Musketry since 1916; Acting-Director of Military Training since 1914; *b* 12 Oct. 1864; *s* of Nathaniel Helmer and Melissa Johnson; *m* 1885, Elizabeth I. Hannum. *Educ:* Ottawa and Toronto, Ontario. Licentiate Chemist of Provinces Ontario and Quebec; joined 43rd Battalion Canadian Militia, 1883; served therein until 1906; transferred to Permanent Force of Canada as Deputy-Assistant Adjutant-General for Musketry, 1906; AAG 1908; Director of Musketry, 1911; Commandant, Canadian School of Musketry, 1907; Adjutant Canadian Rifle Team, Bisley, 1899; Canadian Palma Team, Sea Girt, 1903; Ottawa, 1907; Commandant, Camp Perry, 1912. Alderman, City of Hull, Quebec, for twelve years, twice elected Mayor. *Address:* Department of Militia and Defence, Ottawa, Canada. *Club:* Laurentian, Ottawa.
Died 1 Feb. 1920.

HELMSLEY, Viscountess; (Muriel Frances Talbot); 3rd *d* of 19th Earl of Shrewsbury; *m* 1st, 1876, Viscount Helmsley (*d* 1881), *e s* of 1st Earl of Feversham; one *s* (one *d* decd); *mother* of 2nd and *grandmother* of 3rd Earl of Feversham; 2nd, 1885, Hugh Darby Annesley Owen (*d* 1908). Founder and President LMS (Women's Branch); Chairman of Council National Society of Day Nurseries; President Islington and Brixton Unionist and Conservative Association; Hon. Secretary Women's Institute Training College Branch for Nurses; Executive Committee Lambeth Infirmary (Rescue Branch); Chairman Douglas Day Nursery; Executive St Clement Danes Day Nursery. *Address:* 48 Pont Street, SW1. *T:* Kensington 4909.
Died 2 March 1925.

HEMPHILL, 2nd Baron, *cr* 1905; **Stanhope Charles John Hemphill,** DL, JP; KC 1906; MA; *b* Cashel, 13 March 1853; *s* of 1st Baron Hemphill and Augusta, *d* of late Hon. Sir Francis Stanhope, *s* of 3rd Earl of Harrington; *S* father, 1908; *m* 1913, Hon. May Hamilton, 2nd *d* of 9th Baron Belhaven and Stenton. *Educ:* Shrewsbury School; Trinity College, Dublin (1st Classical Prize, Honours Moderatorship, and Medallist). Called to Bar, Middle Temple, 1877; Irish Bar, 1878. *Heir: brother* Capt. Hon. Fitzroy Hemphill, *b* 21 Nov. 1860. *Address:* 8 Lower Sloane Street, SW. *T:* Victoria 3053; Clifton House, Shankill, Co. Dublin. *Clubs:* Reform, National Liberal; University, Royal Irish Yacht, Dublin.
Died 26 March 1919.

HEMPHILL, Ven. Samuel, DD, LittD; MRIA 1893; Rector of Drumbeg, near Belfast, 1920; Archdeacon of Down, 1923; Examining Chaplain to Archbishop of Armagh, 1920, and to Bishop of Down, 1923; *b* Clonmel, 5 July 1859; *e s* of late Robert Hemphill, Springhill, Co. Tipperary; *m* 1885, Flora Margaret, *d* of Rev. Alexander Delap, Rector of Valencia, Co. Kerry; three *s* four *d. Educ:* Clonmel; Tipperary; Dublin University. Professor of Biblical Greek, Dublin University, 1888–98; Select Preacher in Dublin University, 1892–93, 1899; Canon of St Patrick's Cathedral, Dublin, 1909–14; Chancellor of Christchurch Cathedral, Dublin, 1919–20. *Publications:* The *Diatessaron* of Tatian, 1888; My Neighbour, 1897; The Satires of Persius translated, 1900; A History of the Revised Version of the New Testament, 1906. *Address:* Drumbeg Rectory, Dunmurry, Co. Antrim.   *Died 12 Jan. 1927.*

HEMSLEY, William Botting, LLD; FRS, FLS; VMH; late Keeper of Herbarium and Library, Royal Botanic Gardens, Kew; Hon. Member Natural History Society, Mexico; *b* Easthoathley, Sussex, 29 Dec. 1843. *Educ:* privately. Entered Kew, 1860. Corr. Mem., Deutscher Botan. Gesellschaft; Hon. Member, Royal Horticultural Soc., Royal Soc. of NSW, and NZ Inst. *Publications:* Handbook of Hardy Trees, Shrubs, and Herbaceous Plants, 1873 and 1877; Botany of the "Challenger" Expedition; Botany of Salvin and Godman's Biologia Centrali-Americana; Flora of China; Flora of Tibet; Flora of Seychelles (Journal of Botany, 1916–17); Flora of Aldabra (Kew Bulletin, 1919); numerous articles, translations, and reviews, largely relating to geographical botany and insular flora; etc. *Address:* 9 Walmsley Road, Broadstairs, Kent.

                                         Died 7 Oct. 1924.

HEMY, Charles Napier, RA 1910 (ARA 1898); RWS 1897; marine painter; *b* Newcastle-on-Tyne, 24 May 1841; *e s* of late Henri F. Hemy, distinguished musician, and Margaret, *d* of Angus Macdonald; *m* 1881, Amy Mary, *d* of W. G. Freeman, Falmouth; six *s* four *d*. *Educ:* Newcastle Grammar School; St Cuthbert's College, Durham; art studies, Newcastle Art School, under W. Bell Scott, as a boy, and Antwerp Academy, 1867, afterwards pupil of Baron Henri Leys. Made three voyages to sea as a youth; joined the Dominicans at Lyons at 19, but left at 22, and decided to become a painter; at 24 exhibited first picture at the Royal Academy; dissatisfaction with the results of these attempts resulted in going to Antwerp to study under Baron Leys; returned to England, 1870; lived in London till 1881, exhibiting at Royal Acad., Grosvenor, New Gallery; left London and built Churchfield, at Falmouth, 1882, where most of his subsequent pictures were painted. *Principal pictures:* Homeward (Birmingham Corporation); Oporto; Silent Adieu; Pilchards (Chantrey Bequest); Lost, 1897; Smugglers, 1899; Home Wind (Australian Government); Birds of Prey, 1901 (Leeds Corporation); The Crew, 1902; Youth, 1903; The Lifeboat; Haul Aft; London River (Chantrey Trustees); The Crab Merchant (Union Club, Sydney), 1904; Caught Out, 1907; Plymouth, Through Sea and Air, 1910; Life, The Trawler, Home at Last, 1913; Life, 1914; The Black Flag, 1915. *Recreation:* yachting on board the "Van der Meer". *Address:* Churchfield, Falmouth. *Clubs:* hon. member Royal Yacht Squadron, and marine painter to the club; hon. member Royal Cruising Yacht.

                                       Died 30 Sept. 1917.

HENDERSON, Amos; Professor of Education and Principal of Mapperley Hall Hostel, University College, Nottingham, since 1905; *b* 18 July 1864. *Educ:* Borough Road College, London; University College, Nottingham. Second Master People's College, Nottingham, 1885–90; Normal Master, Department of Education, University College, Nottingham, 1890–1905. *Publication:* Some Notes on Teaching. *Recreations:* cricket, tennis, golf. *Address:* Mapperley Hall, Nottingham. T: 2291.   *Died Oct. 1922.*

HENDERSON, Rev. Archibald, TD 1911; MA, DD (Glasgow); Senior Minister of the South United Free Church, Crieff; *b* 9 Aug. 1837; *s* of Rev. Dr Henderson, Glasgow; *m* 1863, *d* of Principal Candlish; two *s* three *d*. *Educ:* Glasgow University; Glasgow Free Church College; New College, Edinburgh; University of Göttingen. Ordained in Crieff, 1862; Member of Crieff School Board, 1873–1906; Chairman, 1892–1906; Junior Principal Clerk of Free Church General Assembly, 1888; Senior Clerk, 1907–16; Convener of the Foreign Mission Committee, 1900–4; nominated for Moderatorship of General Assembly, 1907, but declined office; Moderator of General Assembly, 1909; Joint-Convener of Committee on Conference with Church of Scotland, 1908–26; Hon. Chaplain to Territorial Forces, Scotland, 1910; Principal of Glasgow College of United Free Church of Scotland, 1918–21. Long Service Medal; DD St Andrews University, 1911. *Publication:* Historical Geography of Palestine. *Address:* Crieff. T: 78. *Club:* Scottish Liberal, Edinburgh.

                                       Died 11 April 1927.

HENDERSON, Lt-Gen. Sir David, KCB 1914 (CB 1909); KCVO 1919; DSO 1902; Director-General, League of Red Cross Societies, Geneva; late Argyll and Sutherland Highlanders; Colonel, Highland Light Infantry since 1918; *b* 11 Aug. 1862; *s* of late David Henderson, Glasgow; *m* 1895, Henrietta Caroline, *d* of Henry R. Dundas. Entered army, 1883; Captain, 1890; served Soudan, 1898 (despatches, brevet of Major, British medal, Khedive's medal with clasp); South Africa,

1899–1900 (wounded, despatches twice, DSO, brevet Lieut-Colonel; Queen's medal, four clasps, King's medal, two clasps); European War, 1914–17 (promoted Maj.-Gen. and Lt-Gen.); Director-General of Military Aeronautics, 1913–18. KGStJ 1920; Commander Legion of Honour, 1915; Grand Officer, 1919; Grand Officer Order of the Crown of Belgium; Grand Crown of the Sacred Treasure of Japan, and of the White Eagle of Russia; Grand Officer of the Order of the Crown of Italy. *Publication:* The Art of Reconnaissance, 1907. *Address:* 22 Hans Crescent, SW1. *T:* Victoria 449. *Club:* Naval and Military.

                                       Died 17 Aug. 1921.

HENDERSON, Vice-Adm. Frank Hannam, CMG 1900; Royal Navy, retired; *b* 2 June 1850; *s* of John Henderson, JP, Felderland, near Sandwich, Kent; *m* 1888, Agnes Jane, *d* of John Burgess, Derry. *Educ:* privately. Promoted to Lieutenant for capture of slave dhow with 180 slaves off coast of Arabia; Lieut for transport duties Ashantee War, 1874 (medal); Senior Lieut of "Eclipse" during Egyptian War, 1882 (medal, Khedive's star); commanded several expeditions on each coast, Africa; Humane Society's medal and Jubilee medal; in command of African West Coast Division during rebellion in Sierra Leone, 1898 (despatches, CMG). *Recreations:* golf, etc. *Address:* 15 St Mark's Road, Anglesey, Gosport. *Clubs:* Constitutional; Royal Naval, Portsmouth.

                                       Died 26 June 1918.

HENDERSON, Lt-Col Hon. Harold Greenwood, CVO 1919; Military Secretary to the Duke of Devonshire since 1916; *b* 29 Oct. 1875; *e s* of 1st Baron Faringdon; *m* 1901, Lady Violet Charlotte Dalzell, *y d* of 12th Earl of Carnwath; three *s* one *d*. *Educ:* Eton. Served 1st Life Guards, of which regiment was Adjutant; SA War (medal, two clasps, invalided home after a severe attack of enteric fever); retired, 1st Life Guards, 1906. Contested (C) N Berks, 1906; MP (C) Abingdon division Berkshire, 1910–16; Lt-Col commanding 1/1st Berks Yeomanry, Sept. 1914–Oct. 1915; DAAG War Office, 1916. *Recreations:* hunting, shooting, fishing. *Address:* 18 Arlington Street, SW; Buscot Park, Faringdon. *Clubs:* Carlton, Marlborough.

                                       Died 1 Nov. 1922.

HENDERSON, John M'Donald; MP (L) Aberdeenshire, West, 1906–18; chartered accountant and barrister-at-law; *b* 1846; *m* 1872, Kate Mary, 2nd *d* of Thomas Francis Robins; one *s* one *d*. *Educ:* Gordon's College, and Marischal College, Aberdeen. *Address:* White House, Felixstowe; Cambisgate, Wimbledon, SW. T: PO Wimbledon 119. *Club:* Reform.

                                       Died 20 Nov. 1922.

HENDERSON, John Robertson, CIE 1918; MB, CM; FLS; FRSE; *b* Melrose, 21 May 1863; *s* of Edward Henderson; *m* 1st, 1888, Alice Roberta (*d* 1915), *d* of late David Sinclair, Madras; one *s* one *d*; 2nd, 1921, Eliza Beatrice, *d* of late W. J. Adie, of Voe, Shetland. *Educ:* Dulwich College; Dollar Academy; Edinburgh University. Professor of Zoology, Madras Christian College, 1886–1911; Superintendent Government Museum and Principal Librarian Connemara Public Library, Madras, 1911–19. Fellow Madras University; President Caledonian Society of Madras, 1917–18. *Publications:* Report on the Challenger Anomura, 1888; papers chiefly on Indian crustacea and on South Indian numismatics. *Recreations:* fishing, field natural history. *Address:* 14 Murrayfield Avenue, Edinburgh.

                                       Died 26 Oct. 1925.

HENDERSON, Lt-Col Malcolm, DSO 1917; the Royal Scots; 2nd *s* of J. Henderson, Clifton, Ashbourne, Derbyshire. *Educ:* Repton; RMC Sandhurst. 1st Commission, 1903; Lieut 1907; Adjutant the 2nd Royal Scots, Feb. 1911–14; Captain, 1914; Brevet Major, 1916; Bt Lt-Col 1919; served European War, 1914–18 (Legion of Honour, Croix Chevalier, DSO, St Maurice and Lazarus Chevalier). *Clubs:* Naval and Military, Caledonian.

                                       Died 1 March 1923.

HENDERSON, Maj.-Gen. Philip Durham, CSI 1876; Unemployed Supernumerary List; *b* 19 Aug. 1840; 2nd *s* of late Maj.-Gen. R. Henderson, RE; *m* 1864, Rose, 2nd *d* of late Lt-Gen. P. Cherry of the Madras Cavalry; two *s* two *d*. *Educ:* private school. Joined 2nd Madras Cavalry, 1857; Attaché, 1870; Under Secretary to the Foreign Dept of the Govt of India, 1872; officer on special duty in Cashmere, 1874; General Superintendent of operations for the suppression of Thuggee and Dacoity, 1878; Resident in Mysore, 1892; left India, 1895. Decorated CSI for services on Staff of HM the King, then Prince of Wales, during his visit to India. *Address:* 47 Warwick Road, SW.   *Died 19 April 1918.*

HENDERSON, Robert, CB 1904; *b* 1842; 3rd *s* of Robert Henderson, Kinneff, Kincardineshire; *m* 1st, Jane Skene (decd), *d* of Capt. James

Dow, Port-Glasgow; 2nd, Mary Lewin, *o d* of W. S. Trevitt, of Holdingham, Lincolnshire, and *g d* of late W. Lewin, CE and JP, Boston. *Educ:* Parish School, Kinneff; Grammar School, Aberdeen; King's College, Old Aberdeen. Entered the Service of HM Customs, 1862; Collector, 1871; held that position at Ardrossan, Cowes, Shoreham, Gloucester, Newry, Dover, Folkestone, Southampton, Belfast, Glasgow, and London; Secretary, 1900; Commissioner, 1909; retired 1910. *Address:* The Hermitage, Beckenham.

Died 1 May 1925.

HENDERSON, Maj.-Gen. Sir Robert Samuel Findlay, KCMG 1919; CB 1917; MB Edin.; *b* Calcutta, 11 Dec. 1858; *s* of Rev. Robert Henderson, Senior Chaplain, Bengal. *Educ:* Bedford Grammar School; Fettes College; St Mary's Hospital, London; Edinburgh Univ. MB, CM, 1882. Entered Army Medical Service, 1884; served Sudan, 1885 (medal with clasp, bronze star); Burmah, 1886–91 (despatches, medal 3 clasps); Chin-Lushai Expedition, 1890 (1 clasp); NW Frontier, 1891–98 (medal with clasp); S African War, 1901–2 (Queen's medal 5 clasps); European War, 1914–17 (CB); retired 1917; Sec. to R. V. H. Netley, 1907; to Dir of Med. Services, India, 1908–12; Honorary Physician to the King, 1911; Asst Dir of Med. Services, Quetta Division, 1914; 17th Division, 1915; Director-General, New Zealand Medical Services, 1915–19, with rank of Temp. Surg.-General; Hon. Major-General, 1917; retired, 1919. *Address:* Holt & Co., 3 Whitehall Place, SW1. *Club:* Junior United Service.

Died 5 Oct. 1924.

HENDERSON, T. F.; *b* Lathones, Fifeshire, 24 May 1844; 2nd *s* of Rev. Archibald Henderson and Catherine Finlayson. *Educ:* University of St Andrews (Hon. LLD 1914). For several years on the staff of the Encylopædia Britannica; contributor of numerous Scottish lives to Dictionary of National Biography, and of several chapters to the Cambridge History of English Literature. *Publications:* The Casket Letters and Mary, Queen of Scots, 1889, 2nd edn 1890; Old-World Scotland, 1893; Centenary Burns (with W. E. Henley), vols I–IV, 1896–97; History of Scottish Vernacular Literature, 1898, 2nd edn 1900, 3rd edn 1910; Anthology of Scottish Verse, 1899; annotated edn of Scott's Border Minstrelsy, vols I–IV, 1902; Life of Robert Burns, 1904; James I and VI (Goupil Historical Series), 1904; Life of Mary Queen of Scots, 2 vols, 1905; The Auld Ayrshire of Robert Burns, 1906; selected edition of Burns's Poems (Englische Textebibliothek), Heidelberg, 1906; annotated edition of Macaulay's History of England, 1907; Scotland of To-day (with Mr Francis Watt), 1907, 2nd edn 1908, 3rd edn 1913; The Ballad in Literature, 1912; The Royal Stewarts, 1914. *Address:* The Wraes, by Bridge of Weir, Renfrewshire.

Died 25 Dec. 1923.

HENDLEY, Brig.-Gen. Charles Edward, CB 1916; commanding Ambala Brigade; *b* 26 Dec. 1868; *s* of late Surgeon-General John Hendley, CB. *Educ:* Trinity College, Stratford-on-Avon. East Kent Militia, Welsh Regiment, and 81st Pioneers, IA; served Burma, 1886–87 (medal, 2 clasps); NE Frontier of India, 1892–93 (clasp, despatches); Tirah Expedition, 1897–98 (medal, 3 clasps); European War, Indian Expeditionary Force, Dardanelles, 1915 (despatches twice, CB); staff appointments, DAAG, Brigade-Major, AQMG. *Club:* United Service.

Died 10 Jan. 1920.

HENDLEY, Col Thomas Holbein, CIE 1891; VD; Indian Medical Service; retired; *b* 1847; *e s* of T. Hendley; *m* 1872, Jane Elizabeth, *d* of Rev. John Dawson Hull, Vicar of Wickhambrook, Suffolk; one *s. Educ:* privately, and St Bartholomew's Hospital. MRCS, LRCP 1869. 27 years under Foreign Dept, of which 24 were as Residency Surgeon, Jeypore, the last 3 also as Admin. Med. Officer, Rajputana; Inspector Gen. of Civil Hosps, Bengal, 1898–1903; and officiating NW Provinces and Oudh, 1897; acting President Plague Commission, Calcutta, 1898; Fellow Calcutta University, 1899–1903; and Member of Syndicate, 1899; Vice-President Asiatic Society of Bengal and Trustee Indian Museum, 1899–1903; Hon. Associate St John of Jerusalem, 1904; KGStJ 1909; Chairman Executive Committee, Jeypore Exhibition, 1883; Member of Executive Council and a Governor of Imperial Institute, 1891–92, and organised its first exhibition (Indian Art Metal Work), 1892; President, Decennial (2nd) Art Conference at Lahore, 1894; Member Judging Committee Delhi Exhibition, 1903; Chairman, Indian Section Festival of Empire, 1911; Hon. Vice-Pres. (Tropical sect.), International Congress of Hygiene, 1894. *Publications:* author of several works on Indian art; Rulers of India and Chiefs of Rajputana, 1897; Medico-Topographical Histories of Jeypore and Rajputana, etc. *Address:* 4 Loudoun Road, NW.

Died 2 Feb. 1917.

HENDRIE, Col Sir John Strathearn, KCMG 1915; CVO 1907; *b* Hamilton, Canada, Aug. 1857; *e s* of William and Margaret Hendrie;

m 1885, Lena Maud, *d* of Peter R. Henderson, Kingston, Ont; one *s* one *d. Educ:* Hamilton School; Upper Canada College. Mayor of Hamilton, 1901–2; Member Ontario Legislature, 1902–14; Lieut-Governor of Ontario, 1914–19; Member Battlefields Commission; Minister without Portfolio, 1905–14; joined Canadian Militia, 1883; Col Canadian Field Artillery Militia, RO; director in several manufacturing and financial companies. *Recreations:* fishing, shooting. *Address:* Strathearn, Hamilton, Ont. *Clubs:* Hamilton Tamahaac, Country, Hamilton; York, Toronto, Ontario Jockey, Albany, Toronto.

Died 18 July 1923.

HENEAGE, 1st Baron, *cr* 1896; **Edward Heneage**, PC 1886; JP, DL; High Steward of Grimsby; Trustee Lincolnshire Agricultural Society and Mablethorpe Convalescent Home; *b* 29 March 1840; *e s* of George Fiesche Heneage, Hainton Hall, Lincoln, and Frances, *d* of late Michael Tasburgh, Burghwalls Hall, near Doncaster; *m* 1864, Lady Eleanor Cecilia Hare, *d* of 2nd Earl of Listowel; three *s* four *d* (inc. twin *d*) (and two *d* decd). *Educ:* Eton. 1st Life Guards, 1857–63; succeeded to family estates, 1864. MP (L) Lincoln, 1866–68; (L) Grimsby, 1880–86, (LU) 1886–92, 1893–95; was Vice-Chairman of Lindsey Quarter Sessions; Chancellor of Duchy of Lancaster, 1886; Vice-President of Committee of Agriculture, 1886; retired from office and joined Liberal Unionist party, 1886; Chairman of Liberal Unionist Council from 1893–98; was Vice-Chairman of Agricultural Chamber, 1870; Chairman, 1871; President of Fisherman's Provident Association (Grimsby Branch); Member of Central Council; Chairman of South Wold Hunt Club till 1904; owner of about 10,800 acres. *Recreation:* prior to 1880 owned Freeman and other racehorses and steeplechasers. *Heir: s* Hon. George Edward Heneage, *b* 3 July 1866. *Address:* Hainton Hall, Lincoln. *Clubs:* Brooks's, Turf.

Died 10 Aug. 1922.

HENEGAN, Lt-Col John, DSO 1893; Commandant, 10th Gurkha Rifles; *b* 29 Jan. 1865. Entered army, 1884; Captain, 1895; Major, 1904; Lt-Col 1909; served Burmah, 1886–89 (medal with two clasps); Northern Chin Hills, 1892–93 (despatches, DSO). *Address:* Maymyo, Burma.

Died 19 April 1920.

HENEY, Thomas William; *b* Sydney, 5 Nov. 1862; *e s* of T. W. Heney, Cooma, Monaro, NSW; *m* 1898, Amy Florence, *e d* of Hon. Henry Gullett, MLC; one *s* two *d. Educ:* state schools and privately. Entered newspaper service, 1878, and thereafter connected with journalism, city and country; Editor Sydney Morning Herald, 1903–18; in England, 1910 and 1918, with Australian Press Delegation; Editor Brisbane Telegraph, 1921–23; Sydney Daily Telegraph, 1924–26; attended Empire Press Conference, Melbourne, Oct. 1925; Melbourne, 1927, working at Australian Official War History. *Publications:* Fortunate Days (poems), 1886; In Middle Harbour (poems), 1890; The Girl at Birrell's (novel), 1896; A Station Courtship (novel), 1898–99; magazine contributions, etc. *Address:* Field Place, Exeter, NSW. *Club:* Warrigal, Sydney.

Died Aug. 1928.

HENLEY, 4th Baron (Ire.), *cr* 1799; **Frederick Henley;** Baron Northington (UK) 1885; *b* 17 April 1849; *e s* of 3rd Baron Henley and Julia Peel, *d* of Dean of Worcester; *S* father, 1898; *m* 1900, Augusta Frederica (*d* 1905), *d* of Herbert Langham and *sister* of Sir Herbert Hay Langham, 12th Bt. Attaché in the Diplomatic Service, 1868–73. Owner of about 5,450 acres. *Heir: brother* Hon. Anthony Ernest Henley, *b* 3 July 1858. *Address:* Watford Court, Rugby.

Died 23 Dec. 1923.

HENLEY, 5th Baron (Ire.), *cr* 1799; **Anthony Ernest Henley;** Baron Northington (UK) 1885; *b* 3 July 1858; *s* of 3rd Baron Henley and Julia Peel, *d* of Dean of Worcester; *S* brother, 1923; *m* 1st, 1882, Georgiana (*d* 1888), *d* of late Lt-Col R. M. Williams; 2nd, 1889, Emmeline, *d* of G. Maitland; one *d*. Owner of about 5,450 acres. *Heir: half-brother* Hon. Francis Robert Henley, *b* 11 April 1877. *Address:* Watford, Rugby.

Died 23 Oct. 1925.

HENLEY, Brig.-Gen. Hon. Anthony Morton, CMG 1919; DSO 1916; Director, Arthur Capel and Co., shipowners and coal exporters; *b* 4 Aug. 1873; 3rd *s* of 3rd and *heir-pres.* to 5th Baron Henley; *m* 1906, Sylvia Laura, 3rd *d* of 4th Baron Sheffield; three *d* (and one *d* decd). *Educ:* Eton; Balliol College, Oxford. Called to Bar, 1897; enlisted IY 1899; served with Scots Greys, 1900–7; with 5th Lancers, 1907–14; Gen. Service, 1914–17; commanding 127th Infantry Brigade, 1917–19 (despatches, CMG, DSO, Brevet Major and Col). *Address:* 9 Oxford Square, W2. *Clubs:* Brooks's, Wellington.

Died 17 May 1925.

HENNELL, Col Sir Reginald, Kt 1902; CVO 1910; DSO 1887; OBE 1919; Lieutenant The King's Body-Guard of the Yeomen of the Guard; *b* 11 June 1844. Joined Bombay Infantry, 1861; Lieut 1863; Capt. 1871; Major, 1881; Col 1887; retired, 1889; served Abyssinian Expedition, 1867–68 (medal); Afghan War, 1879–80 (services acknowledged by Government, medal); Burmah Campaign, 1886–87 (specially mentioned in despatches, DSO, medal and clasp); Col-Commanding 1st Vol. Batt. Middlesex Regt 1891, retired 1901; one of HM's Honorable Corps of Gentlemen-at-Arms, 1892; Exon of HM's Royal Body-Guard of the Yeomen of the Guard, 1894; Clerk of the Cheque and Adjutant of this Guard, 1895; Hon. Colonel, 3rd Cadet Battalion, Middlesex Regt, 1911. *Publications:* History of the Yeomen of the Guard, 1485–1904; Our Birthright; Looking Ahead; and other military essays. *Address:* 47 Coleherne Court, SW5. *Club:* United Service. *Died 22 May 1925.*

HENNESSY, Rt. Hon. Sir David Valentine, Kt 1915; JP; Lord Mayor of Melbourne, 1912–17, record for the city; *b* Melbourne, Jan. 1855; *s* of James Hennessy, of Waterford, Ireland; *m* Mary (CBE, Médaille de la Reconnaissance Française, Medal of Queen Elizabeth), *d* of late Michael Quinlan, Ballarat; one *s* three *d*. *Educ:* Model High Schools and Fitzroy College, Melbourne. Entered municipal life, city of Brunswick, 1892; Mayor, 1894; Member of Melbourne City Council from 1895; MP South Carlton for 4½ years; President of the Overseas Club, Melbourne; Member of the Royal Colonial Institute, London and Victoria League; Chairman and Director of several companies; Member British Empire League, Melbourne; Commander, Order of the Crown of Belgium, 1920; Order of St Sava, 1916. *Address:* White Lodge, Toorak Road, S Yarra, Melbourne, Australia. *Club:* Athenæum, Melbourne. *Died 16 June 1923.*

HENNESSY, Richard M., KC 1902; *b* 1854; *s* of John C. Hennessy and Mary Kenifeck. Called to Irish Bar, 1877; Inner Bar, 1902; Bencher King's Inns, 1913. *Address:* 16 Hume Street, Dublin. *Died 24 Oct. 1926.*

HENNESSY, William John; painter; *b* Thomastown, Co. Kilkenny, Ireland. Member National Academy, and Hon. Member Water Colour Society, NY; Member Society of Oil Painters, and Pastel Society, London; Member Union Internationale des Beaux-Arts et des Lettres, Paris; painter of figures and landscape subjects; lived alternately in France and England, but mostly in Calvados, Normandy, and in Sussex, and always in the country.

HENNIKER, Hon. Mrs Arthur, (Hon. Florence Ellen Hungerford Henniker-Major); novelist; *b* 1855; *d* of late Baron Houghton, and *sister* to 1st Marquis of Crewe; *m* 1882, Maj.-Gen. Hon. Arthur Henry Henniker-Major, CB (*d* 1912), 3rd *s* of 4th Baron Henniker. President of Society of Woman Journalists, 1896. *Publications:* Sir George, 1891; Foiled, 1893; Outlines, 1894; In Scarlet and Grey, 1896; Sowing the Sand, 1898; Contrasts, 1903; 4 Act Play, The Courage of Silence, King's Theatre, London, 1905; Our Fatal Shadows, 1907; Second Fiddle, 1912. *Address:* 2 Hyde Park Square, W2. *T:* Paddington 237. *Died 4 April 1923.*

HENNIKER-HUGHAN, Admiral Sir Arthur John, 6th Bt, *cr* 1813; CB 1919; Royal Navy, retired; MP (C) Galloway since 1924; *b* 24 Jan. 1866; *s* of Sir Brydges Powell Henniker, 4th Bt and Justina Louisa, *y d* of Thomas Hughan, of Airds, NB; succeeded to the property of his maternal grandmother on the death of his aunt, Mrs Houghton-Hughan, and took additional name of Hughan, 1896; *S* brother, 1908; *m* 1904, Inger Margueretta (*d* 1923), *o d* of Graham Hutchison of Balmaghie, Kirkcudbright; three *d*. Rear-Adm. 1916; Vice-Adm. 1920; retired, 1920; served in World War as Captain of HMS Ajax, Grand Fleet, 1914–16; ADC to King George V, 1914–16; Admiral Superintendent Devonport Dockyard, 1916–19; promoted Admiral, retired list, 1925. *Heir: cousin* Robert John Aldborough Henniker [*b* 26 May 1888; *m* 1914, Lucy Mabel, *d* of late Edward Swan Hennessy of Hazelbrook, Roscommon]. *Address:* The Airds, Parton, Kirkcudbright. *Club:* Naval and Military. *Died 4 Oct. 1925.*

HENNIKER-MAJOR, Hon. Edward Minet; British Vice-Consul at St Malo, 1888; retired on pension, 1919; *b* 3 Feb. 1848; 2nd *s* of 4th Baron Henniker; *m* 1869, Eveline Talavera, *widow* of W. Harvey, and *e d* of late Capt. Henri de St Maur, French Army. *Educ:* Eton. *Address:* 10 Havre des Pas, Jersey. *Died 20 Dec. 1924.*

HENRICI, Olaus M. F. E., PhD, LLD; FRS; Emeritus Professor of Mechanics and Mathematics, City and Guilds (Engineering) College; *b* 1840; *m e d* of late Rev. John Kennedy, DD; one *s*. Past Pres. of

London Mathematical Society. *Publications:* Skeleton Structures, especially in their Application to the Building of Steel and Iron Bridges, 1866; Congruent Figures, 1879; Vectors and Rotors, 1903; various papers on Mathematics. *Address:* Hiltingbury Lodge, Chandlers Ford, Hants. *Died 10 Aug. 1918.*

HENRIQUES, Henry Straus Quixano, KC 1921; *b* 8 Nov. 1866; *e s* of late E. M. Henriques, JP, Manchester; *m* 1894, Henrietta (*d* 1922), 2nd *d* of late Ferdinand Sichel; one *s* one *d*. *Educ:* Manchester Gram. School; Worcester Coll., Oxford (Sen. Class. Scholar), MA, BCL. Vinerian Law Scholar, 1891; Common Law Scholarship at the Inner Temple, 1892; Examiner for the degree of BCL, 1897; Member of the Northern Circuit; President of the Jewish Board of Deputies; Vice-President and Ex-President of the Jewish Historical Society of England; President of the St George's-in-the-East Jewish Settlement and of the West London Synagogue of British Jews; on the Executive Committees of the Grotius Society and International Law Association. *Publications:* The Law of Aliens and Naturalisation; The Jews and the English Law; The Return of the Jews to England; Jewish Marriages and the English Law; part of the treatise on Ecclesiastical Law in Halsbury's Laws of England. *Address:* 4 Harcourt Buildings, Temple, EC4. *TA:* 69 Temple. *T:* Central 9945; 176 Gloucester Terrace, W2. *T:* Paddington 2505. *Clubs:* Union, Maccabæans. *Died 12 Nov. 1925.*

HENRY, Sir Charles Solomon, 1st Bt, *cr* 1911; JP; MP (L) Wellington Division of Shropshire, 1906–18; Wrekin Division, since 1918; *b* 28 Jan. 1860; 2nd *s* of late J. S. Henry of Adelaide; *m* 1892, Julia, *e d* of late Leonard Lewisohn of New York. *Educ:* St Marylebone and All Souls Grammar School in connection with King's College; University of Göttingen. Established the firm of C. S. Henry and Co., 1882, which was converted into a Limited Liability Company, 1902; contested Chelmsford Division of Essex in Liberal interest, 1900. *Recreations:* riding, golf, motoring. *Heir:* none. *Address:* 5 Carlton Gardens, SW1. *TA:* Liegeoise; Parkwood, Henley-on-Thames. *T:* Hurley 5; Brooklands, Wellington, Salop. *T:* Wellington 4. *Clubs:* National Liberal, Royal Automobile, British Empire, Portland, Devonshire. *Died 27 Dec. 1919 (ext).*

HENRY, Rt. Hon. Sir Denis Stanislaus, 1st Bt, *cr* 1922; PC Ireland, 1919; KC, Ireland; Lord Chief Justice of Northern Ireland since 1921; Attorney-General for Ireland, 1919–21; Solicitor-General, Ireland, 1918; *b* 7 March 1864; 6th *s* of late James Henry, Cahore, Draperstown; *m* 1910, Violet, 3rd *d* of Rt Hon. Hugh Holmes; two *s* three *d*. *Educ:* Mount St Mary's Coll., Chesterfield; Queen's College, Belfast. Called Irish Bar, 1885; QC 1896; Bencher of King's Inns, 1898. JP, DL, Co. Londonderry; Commissioner Charitable Bequests, 1912; LLD (hon.) Queen's, Belfast. Contested (U) North Tyrone, 1906 and 1907; MP (U) Derry, 1916–21. *Heir: s* James Holmes Henry, *b* 22 Sept. 1911. *Address:* The Rath, Draperstown, Co. Derry. *Clubs:* Constitutional; University, Dublin; Ulster, Belfast; Northern Counties, Londonderry; Royal Ulster Yacht. *Died 1 Oct. 1925.*

HENRY, Lt.-Gen. George, CB 1903; Royal Engineers, retired list; *b* 23 Aug. 1846; *s* of Rev. T. Henry; *m* 1874, Mary Helen, *d* of late Surg.-Gen. H. H. Massy, CB. Entered army 1868; Captain, 1880; Major, 1887; Lieut-Col 1892; Col 1894; Major-Gen. 1901; Lieut-Gen. 1907; QMG India, 1900–3; Command 7th (Meerut) Division, India, 1903–8; Col Commandant RE 1916; served Afghan War, 1878–80 (medal); Burmese Expedition, 1885 (despatches, medal with clasp); Chin-Lushai Expedition, 1889–90, commanding RE (despatches, Brevet Lieut-Col, clasp). *Address:* c/o Cox & Co., Charing Cross, SW1. *Died 19 Nov. 1922.*

HENRY, William Alexander, KC (Nova Scotia) 1907; LLB; member of the legal firm of Henry, Stewart, Smith & McCleave, Halifax, NS; *b* Antigonish, Nova Scotia, 19 March 1863; *s* of Hon. William Alexander Henry, Judge of Supreme Court of Canada, and Christianna McDonald; *m* 1892, Minna H. Troop; one *s* one *d*. *Educ:* Halifax Grammar School; Lycée de Tours; Merchiston Castle School, Edinburgh; Dalhousie University, Halifax, NS (LLB 1886); Harvard University, Cambridge, Mass, US. Admitted to Nova Scotia Bar, 1887; President, Nova Scotia Barristers' Soc., 1917 and 1918. Played in Harvard Univ. football, cricket, and lacrosse teams, 1881–82, 1883–84; member of Gentlemen of Canada Cricket Team in Great Britain, 1887; played for Canada *v* United States at cricket, 1886, 1888, 1892, 1896. *Recreations:* golf, badminton; formerly cricket, football, baseball, hockey, running, jumping, lacrosse, lawn tennis. *Address:* 16 South Street, Halifax, Nova Scotia. *TA:* Henry, Halifax. *Clubs:* Halifax, Saraguay, Brightwood Golf, Halifax Golf, Gorsebrook Golf. *Died 11 Dec. 1927.*

HENSHALL, John Henry, RWS 1897 (ARWS 1883); *b* 11 April 1856; *s* of Benjamin Henshall, Manchester; married. *Educ:* S Kensington; Royal Academy Schools. Medals, SK; Royal Academy; Chicago International Exhibition; Paris Universal Exhibition and Brussels International Exhibition; exhibited Royal Academy, Royal Society of Painters in Water Colours, Salon, and leading exhibitions; pictures purchased by Birmingham, Leeds, Hull, Manchester, Bristol, Preston and Blackpool Corporations for permanent collections. *Recreations:* motoring, yachting. *Address:* The Cottage, Bosham, Sussex.
Died 18 Nov. 1928.

HENSLOW, Rev. George, MA; FLS, FGS; FRHS, VMH; late Professor of Botany to Royal Horticultural Society; President of Ealing Natural History Society, 1882–1904; *b* 1835; *s* of late Rev. J. S. Henslow, Prof. of Botany, University of Cambridge, and Rector of Hitcham, Suffolk; *m* 1st, Georgina (*d* 1875), *d* of late Rev. J. Bailey; 2nd, 1882, Katharine (*d* 1919), *d* of late Robert Forster, of Southwell, and *widow* of Richard Yeo, Ealing; one *s*. *Educ:* Sawston Parsonage, Cambs; Grammar School, Bury St Edmunds; Christ's College, Camb. (1854, Scholar and Medallist; 4th Sen. Opt.; 2nd class Divinity; 1st class Natural Science Tripos). Ordained, 1858; Curate of Steyning, Sussex; Headmaster, Hampton Lucy Grammar School, Warwick, 1861–65; Headmaster, Grammar School, Store Street, London, 1865–72; Curate, St John's Wood Chapel, 1868–70; Asst Minister of St James, Marylebone, 1870–87; Examiner Natural Science Tripos, Camb., 1867; Examiner in Botany to College of Preceptors, 1874–1912; Lecturer on Botany at St Bart's Med. School, 1866–90; at Birkbeck, Queen's College, etc. *Publications:* Origin of Floral Structures; Origin of Plant Structures; Floral Dissections; Botany for Beginners; How to Study Wild Flowers; The Making of Flowers; South African Flowering Plants; The Story of Wild Flowers; Poisonous Plants; Medical Works of XIV Century; The Uses of British Plants; Introduction to Plant-Ecology; The Heredity of Acquired Characters in Plants; British Wild Flowers; Origin and History of our Garden Vegetables; Floral Rambles in Highways and By-ways; theological—Evolution and Religion; Christian Beliefs reconsidered in the Light of Modern Thought; The Argument of Adaptation; Christ, no Product of Evolution; The At-one-ment, or the Gospel of Reconciliation; Spiritual Teachings of Bible Plants; Present-Day Rationalism Critically Examined; Plants of the Bible; The Spiritual Teaching of Christ's Life; The Vulgate, the source of False Doctrines; Spirit-Psychometry; Proofs of the Truths of Spiritualism; The Religion of the Spirit-World. *Recreation:* gardening. *Address:* Danehurst, Branksome Wood Road, Bournemouth.
Died 30 Dec. 1925.

HENSMAN, Howard; author and journalist; *b* Manchester; *o s* of Howard Hensman; *m* 1904; one *s* one *d*. *Educ:* privately. Contributor to most journals, magazines, and reviews on social, military, naval, Indian, and South African topics. *Publications:* A History of Rhodesia, 1900; Cecil Rhodes: A Study of a Career, 1901; When and Where of Famous Men and Women, 1908. *Recreations:* yachting, boating and punting, photography, cricket, cycling, lawn-tennis, all out-door sports. *Died 12 June 1916.*

HEPBURN, Sir Thomas Henry, Kt 1912; JP Devon; *b* 6 June 1840; *s* of Thomas Hepburn, JP, of Clapham Common, Surrey; *m* 1st, 1871, Alice, *d* of Rev. Dr Gotch of Bristol; 2nd, 1875, Josephine, *d* of John Robinson of Backwell House, Somerset; three *s* three *d*. *Educ:* Amersham School; University College, London; BA, London University, 1860. Engaged in paper-making from 1862; at St Mary Cray, Kent, for 11 years, and afterwards at Hele, Bradninch, Devon; Chairman of the Hele Paper Co., Ltd, established in 1892; concerned with Local Govt from 1884; member Devon County Council, 1888; Alderman, 1905; Vice-Chairman, 1913; Chairman, 1916; Chairman of the Finance Committee; member of the Mid-Devon Advisory Committee for the appointment of JPs; a Governor of University College, Exeter, Exeter School and Hele's School, Exeter, and Blundell's School, Tiverton. *Address:* Bradninch, near Cullompton, Devon. *TA:* Hepburn, Bradninch. *T:* Exeter 6. *M:* T334. *Clubs:* Reform; Devon and Exeter, Exeter.
Died 2 Feb. 1917.

HEPWORTH, Captain Melville Willis Campbell, CB 1902; RD 1910; Royal Naval Reserve; retired; *b* 27 April 1849; *s* of late Rev. Robert Hepworth, BA, Cheltenham. *Educ:* Bromsgrove School. Served in HM's Indian Marine, principally in Mercantile Marine, but also in RN; a Younger Brother of Trinity House; appointed Marine Superintendent of Meterological Office, 1899; Expert Assessor to International Conference on Safety of Life at Sea, 1913. *Publications:* Notes on Maritime Meteorology; The Seaman's Handbook of Meteorology (official); The Effect of the Labrador Current upon the Surface Temperature of the North Atlantic, and of the latter upon the Temperature and Pressure over our Islands; the Gulf Stream, and many other papers and memoirs on meteorology, oceanography, and navigation. *Address:* 2 Amherst Road, Ealing. *T:* Ealing 1303.
Died 25 Feb. 1919.

HERBERT, Sir Arthur (James), GCVO 1908 (KCVO 1905; CVO 1905); *b* 22 Aug. 1855; 2nd *s* of J. A. Herbert, of Llanarth, Monmouthshire; *m* Helen L. Gammell, Providence, Rhode Island, USA; one *s*. *Educ:* Christ Church, Oxford; MA. Entered Diplomatic Service, 1879; Secretary at HM's Embassies at Petrograd and Washington, and to Legations at Buenos Ayres, Tehran, Brussels, Berne, Stockholm; attached to Sir Peter Lumsden's mission for demarcation of Afghan frontier, 1884–85; received allowance for knowledge of Russian and Persian; Secretary of Legation, Copenhagen, 1901; Consul-General Buda-Pesth, 1902; Chargé d'Affaires Darmstadt and Carlsruhe, 1903–5; HM's Minister at Christiania, 1905–10; appointed Minister to Mexico, 1911, but did not proceed. Master of the Monmouthshire Hounds from 1907. *Address:* 1 Hill Street, Knightsbridge, SW7. *T:* Western 3901; Coldbrook, Abergavenny, Monmouthshire. *Clubs:* St James', Oxford and Cambridge, Brooks's, Ranelagh, Travellers'.
Died 31 Aug. 1921.

HERBERT, Hon. Aubrey Nigel Henry Molyneux, JP, DL; FRGS; MP (U) Southern Division of Somerset, 1911–18; Yeovil Division since 1918; *b* 3 April 1880; 2nd *s* of 4th Earl of Carnarvon and Elisabeth Catharine, *d* of Henry Howard; *m* 1910, Hon. Mary Vesey, *o c* of 4th Viscount de Vesci; one *s* three *d*. *Educ:* Eton; Balliol, Oxford. After leaving University entered the Diplomatic Service and was appointed Hon. Attaché at Tokio, and afterwards Constantinople. Contested S Somerset in Conservative interest, Jan. 1910 and Dec. 1910; Parliamentary Sec. to the Chief Secretary for Ireland; travelled extensively both in Near and Far East, including Japan, China, Turkey, Macedonia, Balkans, Yemen. Lieut Irish Guards, Aug. 1914; wounded and prisoner, France, Sept. 1914; Capt. on General Staff Mediterranean Forces, Dec. 1914; Capt. with Forces, 1915; served in Egypt; 1st landing in Dardanelles and Suvla (White Eagle of Serbia); Temp. Lt-Col Adriatic Mission, Dec. 1915; served in Mesopotamia, 1916 (despatches); also Salonica; served in Italy, 1917–18. *Publications:* Eastern Songs, 1911; Mons, Anzac, and Kut, 1919. *Address:* Pixton Park, Dulverton, Somersetshire. *T:* Dulverton 5; 28 Bruton Street, W. *T:* Mayfair 2292. *M:* AA 3311, Y 965. *Clubs:* Travellers', Bath, St James', Athenæum.
Died 26 Sept. 1923.

HERBERT, Lt-Col Charles, CSI 1909; *b* 16 May 1854; *e s* of Maj.-Gen. Charles Herbert; *m* 1882, Edith Helen, *d* of Edward Sharpe Marriott; three *d*. Entered army, 45th Regt, 1874; Extra ADC to Viceroy of India, 1878–82; Adjutant Deoli Irregular Force, 1880; Magistrate of Abu, 1882; Assistant Commissioner, Ajmer, 1889; officiating Political Agent in Eastern States, Rajputana, 1891–92; Political Agent, Kotah, 1894; Eastern States of Rajputana, 1900; Resident, Gwalior, 1901; in charge of ex-Ameer, 1904; Resident Jaipur, 1905–9. *Address:* Wyvern Cottage, Frant, Sussex.
Died 24 June 1919.

HERBERT, Col Edward William, CB 1902; late King's Royal Rifles; retired; *b* 22 March 1855; *e s* of Hon. Robert C. Herbert, 4th *s* of 2nd Earl of Powis; *m* 1887, Beatrice Anne, *d* of Sir Hedworth Williamson, 8th Bt; two *s* two *d*. Entered army, 1874; Captain, 1883; Major, 1884; Lieut-Col 1898; Colonel, 1902; commanding Rifle Depot, Winchester, 1904. Served Zulu War, 1879 (medal with clasp); Soudan, 1884 (brevet Major, medal with clasp, Khedive's Star); South Africa, 1901–2 (despatches, medal with 2 clasps, CB). *Address:* Herbert Park, Armidale, New South Wales. *Clubs:* Carlton, Naval and Military.
Died 28 Dec. 1924.

HERBERT, Hilary A., LLD; lawyer in Washington, DC, USA; *b* South Carolina; *s* of Thomas E. and Dorothy T. Herbert; *m* 1867, Ella B. Smith (*d* 1885), Selina, Alabama; one *s* one *d*. *Educ:* Universities of Alabama and Virginia. Col 8th Alabama Confederate Volunteers; disabled at Wilderness; practised law at Greenville and Montgomery, Alabama; for sixteen years representative in Congress from Alabama, Secretary US Navy, 1893–97. *Publications:* Why the Solid South, a History of Reconstruction; The Abolition Crusade and its Consequences; magazine articles. *Recreations:* fishing, hunting. *Address:* 1612, 21st Street, Washington, DC. *Clubs:* Metropolitan, Army and Navy, Washington.
Died 6 March 1919.

HERBERT, Sir Jesse, Kt 1911; JP; FRGS; Political Secretary to Liberal Chief Whip; Hon. Treasurer Liberal Central Association; *b* Reading, 1851; 3rd *s* of late Jesse Herbert, Reading, and Jane Anne, *d* of late

James Knight, Reading; *m* 1888, Eveline, *d* of Charles Warner, St George's Square, London; three *s* one *d*. *Educ:* Reading; London University (matriculated 1872). Called to Bar, Middle Temple; First Mayor of Royal Borough of Sutton Coldfield; Professor of International Law at Canton University; Legal Adviser to South China Government. *Recreations:* chess, painting, fishing. *Address:* 21 Abingdon Street, SW. *TA:* Animation, London. *T:* Victoria 2119; Sudbury Hill, Harrow. *T:* PO Harrow 164; The Shameen, West Mersea, Essex.
Died 26 Dec. 1916.

HERBERT, William de Bracy; barrister-at-law; Recorder of Newcastle-under-Lyme, since 1927; *b* 14 March 1872; *e s* of William Hawkins Herbert, JP, Painswick, Glos; *m* 1899, Frances Winifred, *d* of late Major Thomas Berington. *Educ:* Harrow; Trinity College, Cambridge (MA, LLM). Called to Bar, Inner Temple, 1893; Editor of Law Times, Law Times Reports, Cox's Criminal Cases, and Paterson's Practical Statutes; Secretary of Prime Minister's Committee as to persons not of British or allied parentage in Government offices, 1918–19; Secretary of Ministry of Health enquiry into London Lock Hospitals, 1928. *Publications:* Law of Banks and Bankers; Law of Fixtures and Repairs; Editor of Evans on Commission Agents and Saunders on Affiliation. *Address:* 4 Elm Court, Temple, EC. *T:* Central 1350; Windsor House, Bream's Buildings, EC. *T:* Holborn 3682. *Clubs:* Savile, MCC.
Died 10 Nov. 1928.

HERDMAN, Robert Duddingstone, ARSA 1908; *b* 1863; 2nd *s* of Robert Herdman, RSA; *m* 1896, Edna, *d* of Henry Norman of Leicester; one *s* one *d*. *Educ:* Edinburgh Academy and University; studied Art at the RSA school, studios in Paris, and the galleries of Madrid and Holland. Chairman of the Society of Scottish Artists, 1898; exhibited figure subjects and portraits chiefly in Edinburgh, London, Paris, Vienna, Munich, etc. *Recreation:* mechanics. *Address:* St Bernard's Tower, Bruntsfield Crescent, Edinburgh.
Died 9 Jan. 1922.

HERDMAN, Sir William Abbott, Kt 1922; CBE 1920; DSc; Hon. DSc Harvard, Durham, Sydney, and Western Australia; Hon. LLD Edinburgh; FRS 1892; FLS; Professor of Natural History, University of Liverpool, 1881–1919; Professor of Oceanography, 1919–21; *b* Edinburgh, 8 Sept. 1858; *e s* of Robert Herdman, RSA; *m* 1st, 1882, Sarah Wyse Douglas (*d* 1886); two *d*; 2nd, 1893, Jane Brandreth Holt (*d* 1922); one *d* (one *s* decd). *Educ:* Edin. Academy and University. Graduated 1879; asst to Sir Wyville Thomson in "Challenger" Expedition office; Demonstrator of Zoology in Edinburgh University, 1880; President Zoological Section British Association, 1895; General Secretary British Association, 1903–19; President of British Association, 1920; President of Linnean Society, 1904–8; Foreign Secretary Royal Society, 1916–20; (along with others) established a Marine Biological Station at Port Erin, Isle of Man, and a Sea-Fish Hatchery at Piel, near Barrow; Honorary Director of Scientific Work to the Lancashire Sea-Fisheries Committee; sent to Ceylon in 1901–2 to investigate the Pearl-Oyster Fisheries for the Government. *Publications:* Report upon the Tunicata collected during the voyage of the "Challenger," 3 vols 1882–89; The Invertebrate Fauna of the Firth of Forth; (with others) The Fauna of Liverpool Bay, 5 vols 1886–1900; Oysters and Disease, 1896–99; The Phylogenetic Classification of Animals; Fishes and Fisheries of the Irish Sea, 1902; Report to the Government on the Ceylon Pearl-Oyster Fisheries, Royal Society, 5 vols, 1903–6; Spolia Runiana I–V and about fifty other papers on Zoological subjects. *Recreations:* yachting (steam yacht Runa); much interested in early archæology. *Address:* Croxteth Lodge, Liverpool. *T:* Wavertree 691; Rowany, Port Erin, Isle of Man. *TA:* University, Liverpool. *M:* O 7646. *Clubs:* Athenæum; University, Athenæum, Liverpool; Royal Mersey Yacht.
Died 21 July 1924.

HERDT, Louis A., DSc; FRSC; MIEE; Officier d'Académie France; electrical engineer; Professor of Electrical Engineering, McGill University, Montreal, since 1909; Hon. Secretary, American Institute of Electrical Engineers; *b* Trouville, France, 1872; widower; two *s*. *Educ:* McGill University, Montreal; Ecole Supérieure d'Electricité, Paris; Institut Electrotechnique, Montefiore, Liège, Belgium. On Staff of Electrical Dept McGill University from 1899; also carried on a consulting practice; Consulting Electrical Engineer for the City of Winnipeg on a large Hydro Electric Development; Technical Expert, Ottawa Electric Co., Ottawa, Canada, City of Montreal, Montreal, Canada, Dominion Government, Canada, etc; Chairman Canadian National Committee, International Electrotechnical Commission; Chairman Montreal Electric Service Commission; Vice-Chairman Montreal Tramways Commission. *Publications:* Predetermination of Alternator Characteristics, Proceedings AIEE, 1902; Use of Electricity on Canals, Proceedings Canadian Soc. Civil Engrs, 1904; Oscillographic Researches, Proceedings Canadian Soc. Civil Engrs, 1904; Armature Reaction-Alternators, Electrical Review, 1906; Chart Calculation; Transmission Lines; Electrolytic Lightning Arresters; Electrolysis in Water Mains; Constant Voltage Operation of a High Voltage Transmission System; The Problem of the Electrical Railways, Electrical News. *Address:* Electrical Department, McGill University, Montreal, Canada. *Clubs:* Engineers', Montreal, Montreal.
Died March 1926.

HERIOT, Maj.-Gen. Mackay A. H. J.; *b* 1839; *s* of William Mackay Heriot, Major, Royal Marines; *m* 1867, Rosa, *d* of Thomas Fisher, MD of Canterbury, New Zealand; two *s* one *d*. *Educ:* private tutor. Served in China Expedition, 1857–59–60; was at the capture of Taku Forts and final surrender of Pekin, storming of Canton, etc; Colonel Commandant, Plymouth Division, Royal Marine Light Infantry, 1889–1902; commanded Plymouth Volunteer Brigade, 1893–1901. *Recreations:* fishing, hunting, shooting. *Address:* 19 Campden Hill Gardens, Kensington, W. *T:* Park 599. *Club:* Flyfishers'.
Died 18 Nov. 1918.

HERKLESS, Very Rev. Sir John, Kt 1917; DD; LLD; Vice-Chancellor and Principal of the University of St Andrews, and Principal of the United College of St Salvator and St Leonard since 1915; *b* Glasgow, 9 Aug. 1855; *y s* of William Herkless, engineer, Glasgow. *Educ:* Glasgow High School; Glasgow University; Jena University. Tutor in English Literature, Queen Margaret College, Glasgow; Assistant-Minister, St Matthew's Parish Church, Glasgow, 1881–83; Minister of the parish of Tannadice, 1883–94; Regius Professor of Ecclesiastical History, St Andrews Univ., 1894–1915; Provost of St Andrews, 1911–15; Chairman of Fife County Insurance Committee, 1913–15. *Publications:* Cardinal Beaton, Priest and Politician, 1891; Richard Cameron (Famous Scots Series), 1896; The Church of Scotland (Our Churches, and why we belong to them), 1897; Francis and Dominic, 1901; Introductions and Notes to Hebrews, etc, in Temple Bible, 1902; The Early Christian Martyrs, 1904; The College of St Leonard, 1905; The Archbishops of St Andrews, vol. i 1907, vol. ii 1909, vol. iii 1910, vol. iv 1913, vol. v 1916; The Robert Lee Lecture, 1913. *Recreation:* golf. *Address:* The University House, St Andrews. *Clubs:* Royal and Ancient, St Andrews; University, Edinburgh.
Died 11 June 1920.

HERMAN, E., (Mrs M. Herman); author and journalist; *m* Rev. M. Herman, FRGS, a minister of the Presbyterian Church of England. *Educ:* London. Regular contributor to British and American journals and periodicals; Asst Editor of Everyman, 1913; Editor of The Presbyterian, 1913 until its suspension on account of the War; Assistant-Editor of The Challenge, 1921–22. *Publications:* Eucken and Bergson: their Significance for Christian Thought, 1912, 5th edition, 1914; The Meaning and Value of Mysticism, 1915, 3rd edition, 1922; Christianity in the New Age, 1919; Creative Prayer, 1921, 2nd edition, 1922; article Quietism in Hastings' Encylopædia of Religion and Ethics, vol. x, 1918; (under pseudonym of *Hugh Sinclair*) Voices of To-day: Studies of Representative Modern Preachers, 1912. *Recreations:* country rambles, walking; Celtic mythology, poetry, and folklore. *Address:* 42 Upper Clapton Road, E5. *Club:* Writers'.
Died 2 Dec. 1923.

HERON, Rev. James, DD; Professor of Ecclesiastical History, Church Polity, and Pastoral Theology, Assembly's College, Belfast, Presbyterian Church in Ireland; *b* 5 Dec. 1836; closely related to late Capt. Mayne Reid, both being *g g s* of Rev. Thomas Mayne, who came from Scotland to Co. Down in the middle of the 18th century; *m* 1862. *Educ:* Royal Academical Institution, Belfast; Queen's College, Belfast; Assembly's College, Belfast; New College, Edinburgh. Graduated in the old Queen's University. Ordained in Muckamore, 1861; installed in Kilrea, Co. Derry, 1869; removed to Dundela, a Belfast suburban congregation, 1874; unanimously called by the General Assembly to succeed Dr W. D. Killen in the Chair of Church History, 1889; Moderator of General Assembly of Irish Presbyterian Church, 1901. *Publications:* The Church of the Sub-Apostolic Age; The Celtic Church in Ireland; A Short History of Puritanism; with numerous minor works and articles. *Recreation:* reading. *Address:* Assembly's College, Belfast.
Died 18 April 1918.

HERON-MAXWELL, Mrs Beatrice Maude Emilia; author, journalist, dramatist; *d* of late E. B. Eastwick, CB, MP, FRS; *m* 1st, Lane Huddart of Brynkir, Carnarvonshire; two *d*; 2nd, Spencer Horatio Walpole Heron-Maxwell, *s* of Sir John Heron-Maxwell, 6th Bt of Springkell. *Educ:* home. Vice-President of the Society of Women Journalists; Member of Institute of Journalists. *Publications:*

Adventures of a Lady Pearl Broker; What may Happen; A Woman's Soul (with her sister, Florence Eastwick); The Queen Regent; Anne's Sister and The Fifth Wheel (with Florence Eastwick); Through A Woman's Eyes (essays) in War Museum Library, 1917; The Cup of Trembling (with Florence Eastwick); The Tenth Step; The Silken Noose; and over 700 short stories and serials in leading magazines; and verses illustrated by herself in Pall Mall Magazine, Pearson's, etc; *plays*—The Moon Spell; The Scarlet Terror; The Housekeeper (with Mr Metcalfe Wood); St James's Theatre and on tour; The Long Arms; The Call of Birth; An Englishman's Lie; The Caravanners; Fear; Gerrard Double One Double O; The Bull's Eye; The Advocate; The Blue Room; Doña Quixota; film play, Atonement. *Recreations:* theatres, bridge, petits jeux. *Club:* Ladies' Army and Navy.
Died 7 March 1927.

HERON-MAXWELL, Capt. Sir Ivor Walter, 8th Bt, *cr* 1683, of Springkell; MC; *b* 15 Nov. 1871; *e s* of Sir John Robert Heron-Maxwell, 7th Bt and Caroline, *d* of Richard Howard-Brooke, Castle Howard, Avoca, Co. Wicklow; *S* father, 1910; *m* 1910, Norah, *d* of Hon. Francis Parker; one *s* three *d. Educ:* Harrow; Trinity College, Cambridge (MA). Served European War, 1916–18 (MC). *Heir: s* Patrick Ivor Heron-Maxwell, *b* 26 July 1916.
Died 19 Feb. 1928.

HERRICK, Col Henry, CMG 1919; DSO 1917; late Royal Army Medical Corps; *b* 1872. Served South African War, 1902 (medal); European War, 1914–17 (despatches, DSO); retired pay, 1927.
Died 10 May 1928.

HERRIES, Hon. Sir William Herbert, KCMG 1920; late Minister of Native Affairs, Customs, and Marine; Minister for Railways and Native Affairs, Government of New Zealand, 1912–19; *b* London, 19 April 1859; *s* of H. C. Herries, Barrister-at-Law, and Leonora Emma, *d* of H. Wickham; *m* 1889, Catherine Louisa (*d* 1912), *d* of E. F. Roche, late of Johnstown, Ireland, and Shaftesbury, NZ; no *c. Educ:* Eton College; Trinity College, Cambridge (BA). Left England for New Zealand, 1881; farming in North Island of New Zealand, near Te Aroha, Auckland province; entered NZ Parliament, 1896, and sat continuously for Bay of Plenty and afterwards Tauranga electorate. *Address:* Wellington, NZ. *Clubs:* Athenæum; Northern, Auckland; Wellington, Wellington.
Died 22 Feb. 1923.

HERRING, Lt-Col William, JP Norfolk; *b* 1839; *o s* of late William Herring, JP, of St Faith's House, Norwich, and Maria Elizabeth (*d* 1896), *d* of late George Robinson, of Knapton House, Norfolk; *m* 1876, Jessie, *d* of William Welsby, JP. Hon. Col 3rd Batt. King's (Liverpool) Regt; Lt-Col retired; late Major 27th Inniskillings; patron of one living. *Address:* Narborough House, Narborough, Norfolk.
Died 16 May 1917.

HERSCHEL, Col John, FRS 1871; FRAS 1872; Royal Engineers; Member of Senate, Calcutta University; late Deputy-Superintendent Great Trigonometrical Survey of India; *b* Cape of Good Hope, 29 Oct. 1837; 3rd and *y s* of Sir John F. W. Herschel, 1st Bt, and *brother* of 2nd Bt; *m* 1867, Mary Cornwallis (*d* 1876), *d* of Rev. F. Lipscomb, Rector of Welbury, Yorks, and *widow* of D. Power, QC. *Educ:* Clapham Grammar School, under late Rev. C. Pritchard; Addiscombe, where he passed through at head of his term. Entered Bengal Engineers, 1856; landed India, Jan. 1859, and after 6 months at Rurki was appointed to Great Trigonometrical Survey, in which department he served till date of his retirement, 1886; was employed by Royal Society to observe total eclipse of sun, 1868 (and again 1871), spectroscopically, and was among the earliest to view the coloured flames through the prism (also without eclipse, shortly after the earlier of these) and thus help to lay foundation of our present vastly extended knowledge of sun's constitution; he also observed many of southern nebulæ with same instruments; the results of these observations printed in Proceedings of Royal Society, vols xvi, xvii, etc. *Address:* Observatory House, Slough, Bucks.
Died 31 May 1921.

HERSCHEL, Sir William James, 2nd Bt, *cr* 1838; Civil Service, India, 1853–78; one of the Secretaries to the Board of Revenue, Calcutta; Commissioner of Dacca, 1872; Cooch Behar, 1874; *b* 9 Jan. 1833; *s* of Sir John F. W. Herschel, 1st Bt; *S* father, 1871; *m* 1864, Anne Emma Haldane (*d* 1873), *d* of A. Hardcastle, Hatcham House, Surrey; two *s* one *d* (and one *d* decd). *Educ:* Clapham Grammar School; Haileybury; MA Oxford. Discovered the use of finger prints, 1859, and after proving their individuality and their persistence for fifteen years, initiated the modern system of identification for civil purposes in Bengal, 1878. *Publications:* A Gospel Monogram; The Origin of

Finger-Printing. *Recreations:* scientific. *Heir: s* Rev. John Charles William Herschel, FRAS, Vicar of Braywood, 1914 [*b* 22 May 1869; *m* 1908, Catharine Margaret, *y d* of Col E. T. Browell, RA. *Educ:* Winchester; Christ Church, Oxford (MA); Wells Theological College. Ordained, 1906; Curate of Bracknell, 1906–8; Wooburn, 1908–10; Crowthorne, 1910]. *Address:* Rectory House, Warfield, Berks.
Died 24 Oct. 1917.

HERTSLET, Harry Lester, MVO 1902; *b* 1856; *y s* of late G. T. Hertslet, CVO; *m* 1882, Marion, *d* of late C. Matthews of Fouchers, Essex. Entered Lord Chamberlain's Department, 1874; Chief Clerk Lord Chamberlain's Department, 1901–8; retired, 1908; Jubilee medal, 1887, bar, 1897; one of the Gold Staff Officers in Westminster Abbey at Coronation of King Edward VII (medal), and George V (medal). *Address:* The Old Rectory, Itchenor, near Chichester. *TA:* Birdham, near Chichester.
Died 6 Aug. 1925.

HERVEY, Arthur; composer and writer on music; *b* Paris, 26 Jan. 1855; *o s* of late C. J. V. Hervey of Killiane, Wexford; *m* Clare, *d* of late Sir Edmund Harrison, and *widow* of late J. H. Webster. *Educ:* The Oratory School, near Birmingham. At first intended to enter the Diplomatic Service, but finally decided to devote himself to music; studied under Berthold Tours. For some time musical critic to Vanity Fair, and musical critic, Morning Post, 1892–1908. Orchestral compositions: Dramatic Overture; Youth, a concert overture composed for Norwich Festival; Two Tone Pictures, composed for Cardiff Festival; The Gates of Night, a descriptive ballad for voice and orchestra, composed for Gloucester Festival; In the East, tone poem composed for Cardiff Festival; Prelude, Ione, Philharmonic Society, 1907; Summer, tone poem composed for Cardiff Festival of 1907; Life Moods, Variations for Orchestra, Brighton Festival of 1910; Ilona, opera, 1914, etc; a large number of songs, including three albums of German Lieder, and many to English, French, or Italian words; also much music for the piano, violin, and violoncello. *Publications:* Masters of French Music; French Music in the XIX Century; Alfred Bruneau; Franz Liszt and his Music, 1911; Meyerbeer; Rubinstein; Saint-Saëns, 1921; contributions to supplement of Encyclopædia Britannica. *Recreations:* music, reading, walking. *Address:* 1 Norfolk Crescent, Hyde Park, W2. *T:* 6389 Paddington. *Club:* St James'.
Died 10 March 1922.

HERZOG, Rt. Rev. Edward, DD; Bishop of the Old Catholic Church in Switzerland; *b* 1841. Ordained priest of Roman Catholic Church, 1867; retired, with Dr von Döllinger and others, from communion with Rome on the definition of papal infallibility by Pius IX, 1870; assisted in the inauguration of the Old Catholic movement; consecrated as first Old Catholic Bishop for Switzerland by the Old Catholic Bishop Reinkens of Bonn, who was consecrated by the Archbishop of Utrecht, 1876. *Address:* 39 Willadingweg, Bern.
Died March 1924.

HESKETH, Lt-Col James Arthur, CMG 1917; DSO 1915; Assistant Engineer, Western Lines, Canadian Pacific Railway; *b* 1863. *Educ:* Royal Military College, Canada. Served European War, 1914–19 (despatches, CMG, DSO). *Address:* Winnipeg, Canada.
Died 26 Jan. 1923.

HESKETH, Sir Thomas George Fermor-, 7th Bt, *cr* 1761; late Ensign Rifle Brigade; Hon. Colonel 5th and 6th Battalions Liverpool Regiment; *b* 9 May 1849; *s* of Sir Thomas George Fermor-Hesketh, 5th Bt and Anna Maria Arabella Fermor, *d* of 4th Earl of Pomfret; *S* brother, 1876; *m* 1880, Florence, *d* of W. Sharon, San Francisco; two *s*. Owner of about 15,200 acres. *Heir: s* Thomas Fermor-Hesketh, *b* 17 Nov. 1881. *Address:* 9 Montagu Square, W1; Park Hall, Towcester; Eydon Hall, Byfield, Northants. *Clubs:* Carlton, Junior Carlton.
Died 19 April 1924.

HESLOP, Richard Oliver, JP; MA; FSA; iron and steel merchant; Consul for The Netherlands; *b* Newcastle-upon-Tyne, 14 March 1842; *s* of late Joseph Heslop of Wide Open Dykes and The Mount, Co. Cumberland, and Elizabeth, *d* of Capt. Henry Brough Oliver, 8th (King's) Regt of Foot; *m* 1867, Margaret Webster, *d* of late Cuthbert Harrison of Newcastle; two *s* one *d. Educ:* Royal Grammar School, Newcastle. Hon. MA Dunelm, 1901. A Vice-President, Newcastle Society of Antiquaries; a Vice-President of the Surtees Society, and President of the Literary and Philosophical Society, Newcastle. *Publications:* Northumberland Words, a Glossary (English Dialect Society, 1892); A Bibliography of the Northumberland Dialect (English Dialect Society, 1896); papers contributed to various societies on philological, historical, and archæological subjects. *Address:* 12 Eskdale Terrace, Newcastle-upon-Tyne.
Died 3 March 1916.

ESPELER, Hon. Wilhelm; late German Consul; retired; *b* Baden-Baden, Germany, 29 Dec. 1850; *m* Katherine Keutshie; one *s*. *Educ:* Karlsruhe; Baden. Miller and distiller for 14 years up to 1872, at Waterloo, Ontario; afterwards Immigration Commissioner for the Dominion of Canada at Winnipeg; Speaker of the Legislature of the Province of Manitoba, 1902–6; member of the Royal Trust Company of Canada, and member of the Winnipeg Board; also member of the Board of the North of Scotland Mortgage Company, Winnipeg branch. *Address:* Winnipeg, Manitoba, Canada. *T:* Main 8400. *M:* 4146. *Club:* Manitoba, Winnipeg.

ETHERINGTON, Ivystan; artist; *s* of Henry Mellor Hetherington (formerly of the Bank of England); *m* 1912, Edith May Madeleine, *d* of late Alfred Howlett. *Educ:* home; University Coll. School. From Heatherley's School of Art became a student at the Royal Academy, and first exhibited there, 1877; frequently exhibited at the Grosvenor and New Galleries. *Pictures:* When Autumn wreathes its Spell around the Year; An Old-fashioned Summer; Osiers, Langdale Farm; The Manor Garden; A Misty Moonrise; The Silent Marsh; With rushing Wind and gathering Storm, etc. *Recreations:* various. *Address:* 18 Loudoun Road, St John's Wood, NW. *Club:* Arts.
Died 23 Dec. 1917.

EWAT, Col Sir John, Kt 1919; JP; MB, CM (Edin.); medical practitioner; Captain (retired) of Cape Garrison Artillery; late MLA for Woodstock, Cape Province, 1904–10 and 1910–20; *b* Sarawak, Borneo, 26 Dec. 1863; *s* of late Capt. John Hewat, Dock Superintendent, Cape Town; *m* 1886, Lily, *d* of late A. Teesdale, Liverpool; two *s* two *d*. *Educ:* Edinburgh; SA College, Cape Town. Chief Whip Union Party; Government Nominee School Board, Cape Division; Vice-Pres. SA National Union; SA Delegate to Coronation King George V; Chairman SA Delegates to War Zone, 1915; Chairman SA Branch Empire Parliamentary Association; Chief MO General Life and Accident Insurance Co.; a Steward of the SA Turf Club; President of the Cape Colony Athletic and Cycling Union; JP Cape. Medals—Coronation, Union, Boer War; General Service, 1914–19, despatches, 1914 Star; Officer of the Crown of Belgium. *Address:* Woodstock, Cape Colony. *Clubs:* Sports; City, Civil Service, Cape Town.
Died 21 Aug. 1928.

EWBY, Louis John, CB 1912; *b* 1871; *s* of late J. P. Hewby; unmarried. *Educ:* St Paul's School; Magdalen College, Oxford. Served as a clerk in the Treasury, 1895–1908; Treasury Remembrancer and Deputy Paymaster for Ireland, 1908; returned to the Treasury as a Principal Clerk, 1912; Assistant Secretary, 1919; retired, 1921. *Address:* 29 Ladbroke Grove, W. *Clubs:* Oxford and Cambridge; University, Dublin.
Died 3 Jan. 1925.

EWITT, Edgar Percy, KC 1912; LLD; *s* of late William Henry Hewitt, Lancaster Gate, Hyde Park, and Shanklin, Isle of Wight, afterwards of Purlieu, Hythe, Southampton; *m* 1898, Mabel, *d* of late George Fuller Sandys; one *s* two *d*. Called to Bar; passed first in the 1st class of Honours for LLB at University of London and was awarded Law Scholarship, 1888; LLD London, 1890; Bencher, Lincoln's Inn, 1916. *Publications:* Hewitt on the Statutes of Limitations; The Taxes on Land Values; edited 4th edn of Kerr on Injunctions, and 9th edn of White and Tudor's Leading Cases. *Address:* 46 Harrington Gardens, SW7. *T:* Kensington 4327; 14 Old Square, Lincoln's Inn, WC2. *T:* Holborn 0419. *Clubs:* Carlton, 1900, United, 1912.
Died 24 Dec. 1928.

EWITT, Sir Frederic (William), Kt 1911; MVO 1902; MA, MD Cantab; MRCS; FRSM; Anæsthetist to His Majesty the King; Physician-Anæsthetist to St George's Hospital; Consulting Anæsthetist and Emeritus Lecturer on Anæsthetics at the London Hospital; *b* 2 July 1857; *s* of late George Frederick Hewitt of Badbury, Wilts; *m* 1891, Eve, *d* of late George Clare; one *s* two *d*. *Publications:* Anæsthetics and their Administration, 4th edition, 1912; and articles on anæsthetics in Treves's System of Surgery and other works. *Address:* 24 Harcourt House, Cavendish Square, W. *Club:* Savile. *T:* Paddington 869.
Died 6 Jan. 1916.

EWITT, Lt-Col Sir Joseph, 1st Bt, *cr* 1921; Kt 1919; JP Barnsley; Hon. Lieutenant-Colonel in the Army; solicitor and colliery owner; *b* 14 Oct. 1865; *s* of Alfred Hewitt; *m* 1891, Margaret Eliza, *d* of George Guest of Barnsley; one *s* four *d* (and one *s* decd). *Heir: s* Joseph Hewitt, *b* 8 Sept. 1907. *Address:* Ouslethwaite Hall, Barnsley, Yorks; The Crescent, Filey, Yorks. *Clubs:* Junior Carlton, Constitutional.
Died 8 Feb. 1923.

EWITT, Sir Thomas, Kt 1904; KC; JP for Devon and London; Sheriff of Devon, 1908; barrister-at-law; *b* 1837; 3rd *s* of Halford

Wotton Hewitt, JP Lichfield; *m* 1st, 1864, Elizabeth Jane, *d* of Mrs Keppel of Snettisham Hall, Norfolk, and her 1st husband, R. R. Wilson; 2nd, 1869, Fanny Dugard, *d* of John R. Powles, Eastwood Park, Greta Bridge, Yorks; three *s* one *d*. *Educ:* Lichfield Grammar School; High School, Darmstadt; Inner Temple. Captain 40th Middlesex RV (Gray's Inn), 1866–70; Captain National Reserve, London Division, 1913; late Counsel and Clerk to Commissioners of Taxes for City of London; QC 1899; practised chiefly in Revenue cases; President London Arbitration Court, 1901–6; contested NW Cornwall, 1906; Mayor of the Royal Borough of Kensington, 1912–13; for 23 years Director, and 20 years Chairman of The Ocean Accident and Guarantee Insurance Corporation; Chairman of Lynton and Barnstaple Railway Co.; Director of Lynton Cliff Railway Co. *Publications:* Westminster Papers, edited, 1862–64; Hewitt on Corporation Duty, 1892. *Address:* 9 Queen's Gate, SW7. *T:* Kensington 415; The Hoe, Lynton, Devon. *Clubs:* Reform, Albemarle, Ranelagh.
Died 8 Jan. 1923.

HEWLETT, Maurice Henry; writer; *b* 22 Jan. 1861; *e s* of Henry Gay Hewlett of Shaw Hill, Addington, Kent; *m* 1888, Hilda Beatrice, 2nd *d* of late Rev. George William Herbert, Vicar of St Peter's, Vauxhall; one *s* one *d*. *Educ:* London International College, Spring Grove, Isleworth. Barrister 1891; Keeper of Land Revenue Records and Enrolments, 1896–1900. Academic Committee, RSL, 1910. JP, County Alderman, Wilts. *Publications:* Earthwork out of Tuscany, 1895; The Masque of Dead Florentines, 1895; Songs and Meditations, 1897; The Forest Lovers, 1898; Pan and the Young Shepherd, 1898; Little Novels of Italy, 1899; Richard Yea-and-Nay, 1900; New Canterbury Tales, 1901; The Queen's Quair, 1904; The Road in Tuscany, 1904; Fond Adventures; The Fool Errant, 1905; The Stooping Lady, 1907; Half-way House, 1908; Open Country, 1909; Artemision: Idylls and Songs, 1909; Rest Harrow, 1910; Brazenhead the Great, 1911; The Agonists, 1911; The Song of Renny, 1911; Mrs Lancelot, 1912; Helen Redeemed and Other Poems; Lore of Proserpina, 1913; Ben-dish: A Study in Prodigality, 1913; A Lovers' Tale, 1915; The Little Iliad, 1915; Frey and his Wife; Gai Saber: tales and songs, 1916; The Song of the Plow, 1916; Thorgils of Treadholt, 1917; Peridore and Paravail, 1917; The Village Wife's Lament, 1918; Flowers in the Grass (poems) 1920; In a Green Shade, 1920; Wiltshire Essays, 1922. *Address:* Broadchalke, Salisbury. *Club:* Athenæum.
Died 15 June 1923.

HEXT, Rear-Adm. Sir John, KCIE 1897 (CIE 1889); retired; *b* 14 Oct. 1842; *s* of Rev. J. Hext; *m* 1st, 1874, Lilian Mary (*d* 1893), *d* of David Mitchell; 2nd, 1902, Jean (*d* 1913), *d* of Rev. W. Davidson. *Educ:* Marlborough. Entered RN 1857; Ashantee, 1873; Egyptian War, 1882; Director of Royal Indian Marine, 1883 to Feb. 1898. *Address:* St Benets, Newton Abbot, Devon.
Died 8 May 1924.

HEYDON, Hon. Louis Francis; MLC since 1887; *b* Sydney, 1848; *m* Mary, *d* of Edward Gell; one *s* one *d*. MLA, 1881; Minister of Justice, NSW, 1884. *Address:* 117 Pitt Street, Sydney, NSW.
Died 17 May 1918.

HEYGATE, Capt. Richard Lionel, JP; late Master of Foxhounds, North Herefordshire; *b* 1859; 2nd *s* of Major Edward Nicholas Heygate (*d* 1896), RE; *m* 1895, Eleanor Mary, *d* of E. J. Evans; two *d*. Captain RA, 1889–96; Major, 1915. *Address:* The Wells, Bromyard. *Club:* Naval and Military.
Died 26 Nov. 1926.

HEYGATE, Col Robert Henry Gage, DSO 1896; late Lieutenant-Colonel commanding 1st Border Regiment; *b* London, 26 July 1859; 2nd *s* of Sir Frederick W. Heygate, 2nd Bt of Bellarena. *Educ:* Eton; Sandhurst. Entered army, 1878; Major 1896; employed on staff Egyptian Army, 1893–98; served Egyptian Campaign, 1896–98 (despatches); Dongola Campaign, 1896, including engagement at Firket (DSO, Khedive's medal, two clasps); in operations, 1897–98 (British medal, 4th class Osmanieh, clasp); South Africa, 1899–1900 (wounded Colenso, despatches, Queen's medal, 2 clasps); retired 1909. *Address:* Bellarena, Co. Derry. *Club:* Naval and Military.
Died 28 Aug. 1923.

HEYWOOD, Sir Arthur Percival, 3rd Bt, *cr* 1838; JP Counties of Derby and Stafford; *b* 25 Dec. 1849; *s* of Sir Thomas Percival Heywood, 2nd Bt and Margaret (*d* 1894), *d* of late Thomas Heywood of Hope End, Herefordshire; *S* father, 1897; *m* 1872, Margaret Effie, *e d* of Rt Rev. G. H. Sumner of Guildford, sometime Bishop; three *s* six *d* (and one *d* decd). *Educ:* Trinity Coll., Camb., MA. High Sheriff, Derbyshire, 1899. *Publication:* Bell Towers, 1914. *Heir: s* Graham Percival Heywood, JP, DL, *b* 14 July 1878. *Address:* Doveleys,

Rocester, Staffs. *TA:* Rocester; Claremont, near Manchester; Duffield Bank, near Derby. *Club:* Athenæum.

Died 19 April 1916.

HEYWOOD, Bertram Charles Percival, TD; JP; MA; *b* 10 Nov. 1864; 2nd surv. *s* of Sir Thomas Percival Heywood, 2nd Bt, of Claremont, Lancashire, and Doveleys, Rocester; *m* 1889, Florence Maud, *d* of late E. David Meynell, of Kirk Langley, Derby. *Educ:* Winchester; Trinity College, Cambridge. Served in SA War as Capt. commanding 1st Vol. Co. Manchester Regt (Queen's medal with three clasps); Hon. Capt. in Army, 1901; commanded 2nd VB (later 6th Batt.) Manchester Regt, 1902–6; Manchester Infantry Brigade, 1906–11. *Address:* Wootton Lodge, Ashbourne. *Club:* Arts.

Died 27 Oct. 1914.

HEYWOOD, James Barnes, ISO 1905; formerly Secretary to the Treasury, New Zealand; *m. Address:* Abbey Hill, Winchester, Hants.

Died 2 Aug. 1924.

HEYWORTH, Brig.-Gen. Frederic James, CB 1915; DSO 1900; *b* 25 March 1863; *m* 1913, Mrs Hatfeild-Harter. Entered army, 1883; Captain, 1896; Major, 1900; Lt-Col 1908; Col 1911; served Soudan, 1885 (medal with clasp, Khedive's star); South Africa, 1899–1902 (despatches, DSO, Queen's medal, 6 clasps, King's medal, 2 clasps); European War, 1914–15 (despatches, CB). *Address:* Biddlesden Park, Brackley. *Clubs:* Guards, Turf.

Died 10 May 1916.

HIBBERT, Col Godfrey Leicester, CB 1917; CMG 1919; DSO 1900; late The King's Own; *b* 31 Jan. 1864; *s* of Leicester Hibbert of Crofton Grange, Orpington; *m* 1902, Mabel, *y d* of late Lieut-Gen. E. Faunce. *Educ:* Cheltenham College. Entered army, 1884; Captain, 1891; Major, 1900; served South Africa, 1900–2 (despatches, Queen's medal, 3 clasps); European War, 1915–18 (despatches, CMG). *Club:* Naval and Military.

Died 28 March 1924.

HIBBERT, Sir Henry Flemming, 1st Bt, *cr* 1919; Kt 1903; JP; DL; LLD (Victoria); FRGS; FZS; Chairman Lancashire County Council, 1921–27; *b* 4 April 1850; *e s* of Isaac Hibbert; *m* 1883, Marion, *d* of E. Reuss; three *d.* Mayor of Chorley, 1889–91; Freeman of London, 1903, and of Borough of Chorley; MP (U) Chorley Division, Lancs, 1913–18; late member of Consultative Committee of Board of Education; Member of Science in Education Committee. *Heir:* none. *Address:* Dalegarth, Chorley, Lancs. *TA:* Hibbert Chorley. *T:* Chorley 24. *Club:* Constitutional.

Died 15 Nov. 1927 (ext).

HICHENS, Rev. Frederick Harrison, MA; Honorary Canon Canterbury Cathedral since 1897; *b* East Dulwich, 22 April 1836; *s* of Robert Hichens, stockbroker, and Jane Snaith; three *s* two *d. Educ:* Chudleigh Grammar School; King's College, London; Exeter College, Oxford (scholar). Deacon, 1861; Priest, 1862; Curate of Sunningdale, Berks, 1861–63; Speldhurst, Kent, 1863–79; resident at Clifton, Bristol, 1879–85; Rector of Hackington (or St Stephens), Canterbury, 1885; removed from Kent to Cornwall; composed many hymns, chants, and kyries, some of which were used at Canterbury Diocesan Choral Festivals. *Recreation:* music. *Address:* Pennance House, Falmouth, Cornwall.

Died 13 Oct. 1921.

HICHENS, Rev. Thomas Sikes, MA; Hon. Canon Peterborough, 1899. *Educ:* Exeter College, Oxford. Vicar of Guilsborough, 1864–1902. *Address:* Woodlane House, Falmouth.

Died 24 March 1916.

HICKEY, Emily Henrietta; poet and prose-writer; lecturer on English Language and Literature; *b* Macmine Castle, Co. Wexford, 12 April 1845; 2nd *d* of Rev. Canon Hickey, and *g d* of "Martin Doyle." *Educ:* home; private school; lectures at University College, and Cambridge Correspondence Classes. Cambridge University 1st Class Honours Certificate with various marks of Distinction (Higher Local Examination). Co-founder, with Dr Furnivall, of the Browning Society, 1881. *Publications:* A Sculptor, and other Poems, 1881; Strafford, by Robert Browning (edited and annotated), 1884; Verse Tales, Lyrics, and Translations, 1889; Michael Villiers, Idealist, and other Poems, 1891; Poems, 1896; Our Lady of May and other Poems, 1902; Havelok the Dane (from Old English), 1902; The Dream of the Holy Rood, 1903; Thoughts for Creedless Women, 1905; A Parable of a Pilgrim, etc, Selections from Walter Hylton (edited), 1907; Lois, 1908; Our Catholic Heritage in English Literature, 1910; Litanies of the Most Holy Rosary, 1910; George Leicester, Priest,

1910; Prayers from the Divine Liturgy, 1910; Later Poems, 1913; Devotional Poems, 1922; Jesukin and other Christmastide Poems, 1924; several short stories; many literary papers; contributed to many English and American magazines. *Address:* c/o National Bank Ltd, High Street, NW1.

Died 9 Sept. 1924.

HICKLEY, Victor North, CIE 1913; VD; late Commandant Behar Light Horse; *b* 31 Dec. 1858; *s* of late Thomas Allen Hickley, Walton-on-Thames; *m* 1886, Alice, 3rd *d* of late John Haig; one *d. Educ:* Eton; Exeter College, Oxford. *Recreations:* polo, other sports. *Address:* c/o H. S. King and Co., 65 Cornhill, EC3. *Club:* Junior Army and Navy.

Died 16 Feb. 1923.

HICKS, Rt. Rev. Edward Lee; Bishop of Lincoln since 1910; *b* Oxford, 18 Dec. 1843; *m* 1876, Agnes Mary, *d* of Rev. Edwin Trevelyan-Smith, sometime Vicar of Cannock; two *s* two *d. Educ:* Magdalen College School, Oxford; Brasenose Coll., Oxford (Scholar) BA 1866; 1st Class in Classics in Moderations and in Greats; Chancellor's University Prize (Latin Essay), 1867; Craven University Scholar. Fellow and Tutor of Corpus Christi Coll., Oxford, 1866; Rector of Fenny Compton, near Leamington, 1873; 1st Principal of Hulme Hall, Manchester, 1886; Canon Residentiary of Manchester Cathedral and Rector St Philip's, Salford, 1892–1910; Rural Dean of Salford; Vice-President and late Hon. Sec. of United Kingdom Alliance; Select Preacher at Oxford; Examining Chaplain to Bishop of Manchester; Hon. Fellow of CCC Oxford. *Publications:* Greek Inscriptions in the British Museum, 1874, 1886, 1890; Manual of Greek Historical Inscriptions, 1882, 2nd edn 1901; Henry Bazely the Oxford Evangelist, 1886; Inscriptions of Cos (with W. R. Paton), 1891; Addresses on the Temptation, 1903; Building in Troublous Times (visitation charge), 1912; various articles in the Hellenic Journal. *Recreations:* music, temperance agitation, reading. *Address:* Old Palace, Lincoln.

Died 14 Aug. 1919.

HICKS, Rev. Herbert S., VD; MA; Rural Dean of Tynemouth; Hon. Canon of Newcastle; *b* Sturmer Rectory, Essex; his father was Lieut. RN before taking orders, and was a midshipman on HMS Conqueror at the battle of Trafalgar; *m* Minnie, *d* of late Rev. W. Syer, Rector of Kedington, Suffolk; one *s* five *d. Educ:* private schools. MA St Catharine's Coll., Cambridge. Ordained by Bishop of Manchester to Curacy of St Peter, Halliwell, 1858; Curate of Whixoe, Suffolk, 1860; Vicar of St Peter's, North Shields, 1860; Vicar of Tynemouth Priory, 1881–1910; Senior Chaplain to TRGA Vol., 1881–1902. *Publications:* Sermons; History of England in Rhyme; History of Tynemouth Priory. *Recreations:* interested in all outdoor sports and recreations. *Address:* The Orchard, Great Cornard, Sudbury, Suffolk. *M:* CF 7343. *Club:* Conservative, Sudbury.

Died 11 Nov. 1928.

HICKS, William Edward; editor Western Daily Press since 1891; *b* 1852. *Educ:* private school; University College, Bristol. Journalist; Worcester Herald, 1872; Western Daily Press, 1872–77; editor Bristol Evening News, 1877–83; leader-writer and assistant editor Western Daily Press, 1883–91; contributed literary and political articles to various magazines; ex-president Clifton Shakespeare Society. *Recreations:* cricket, golf, cycling, the drama. *Address:* 8 All Saints' Road, Clifton, Bristol. *T:* 492. *Club:* Bristol Liberal.

Died 7 Feb. 1921.

HICKS BEACH, William Frederick; *b* 16 July 1841; *y s* of Sir Michael Hicks Beach, 8th Bt of Williamstrip Park, Glos, and Netheravon House, Wilts; *heir pres.* to baronetcy held by great-nephew, Earl St Aldwyn; *m* 1st, 1865, Elizabeth Tyrwhitt-Drake (d 1901); four *s* three *d* (and one *s* decd); 2nd, 1903, Susan Christian. *Educ:* Eton; Christ Church, Oxford. Magistrate for Gloucestershire from 1879; Chairman of Cheltenham Bench for 8 years; Master of Cotswold Hounds for 8 years, and Chairman of Hunt Committee; Chairman of Board of Guardians for 46 years; Alderman of County Council and Chairman of its Public Health Committee; Chairman of Board of Diocesan Finance; Chairman RDC for 46 years, etc; Patron of one Living; Lord of the Manors of Great Witcombe, Cranham, and Buckle Wood; MP (U) Tewkesbury Division of Gloucestershire, 1916–18; presented with the Freedom of Borough of Cheltenham, 1922. *Address:* Witcombe Park, near Gloucester.

Died 7 Sept. 1923.

HICKSON, Mrs Murray; *see* Kitcat, Mabel.

HICKSON, Robert Rowan Purdon, ISO 1910; JP; MInstCE; Consulting Engineer in connection with Harbour Work, Suva, Fiji; President of the Sydney Harbour Trust since 1901; Chairman of the Managing Committee, Government Dockyard, Biloela, Sydney;

NSW; *b* Dingle, Co. Kerry, 15 Sept. 1842; *s* of Rev. George Hickson; *m* 1866, Sophia, *d* of Rev. Hamilton Haire; five *s* two *d. Educ:* private schools; St Columba College, Dublin. Articled to James Barton, MInstCE, Engineer-in-Chief of the principal works in the north of Ireland, 1860; Harbour Engineer, Barrow-in-Furness Railway Company, 1871; Engineer-in-Chief for Harbours and Jetties, South Australia, 1876; Engineer-in-Chief and Commissioner for Roads and Bridges, 1889; Engineer-in-Chief for Public Works, 1895; Under Secretary and Commissioner for Roads; retired, 1913. *Recreations:* motoring, aquatic sports. *Address:* Belcoo, Lindfield, New South Wales. *TA:* Lindfield. *T:* J 1206. *M:* 206. *Club:* Australian, Sydney.
Died 21 June 1923.

HICKSON, Maj.-Gen. Sir Samuel, KBE 1919; CB 1915; MB; late Royal Army Medical Corps; *b* 14 Nov. 1859; 4th *s* of late Capt. R. M. Hickson, of Dingle, Co. Kerry; *m* 1903, Elizabeth Constance, widow of R. Fry and *y d* of late Rev. Canon Bolsher, Cork. *Educ:* Trinity College, Dublin. Major, 1897; Lt-Col 1905; Bt Col and Hon. Surgeon to the King, 1913; served South Africa, 1896–97 (despatches, medal with clasp); S African War, 1899–1901 (despatches, Bt Lt-Col, Queen's medal 2 clasps, King's medal 2 clasps); European War, 1914–18 (despatches, CB, 1914 Star).
Died 22 March 1928.

HIERN, William Philip, JP; FRS 1903; FLS; botanist and mathematician; Devon County Alderman; *b* Stafford, 19 Jan. 1839; *s* of late J. G. Hiern and Ann, *d* of James Webb; *m* 1868, Martha Bamford. *Educ:* St John's College, Cambridge (Fellow, 1863–68). Gave attention to Systematic Botany and to Mathematics; made contributions to the Flora of Tropical Africa, British India, S Africa, etc. *Publications:* Monograph of Ebenaceæ, 1873; Catalogue of African Plants, collected by Dr F. Welwitsch, 1853–61; Dicotyledons, 1896–1900. *Address:* The Castle House, Barnstaple, Devon.
Died 29 Nov. 1925.

HIGGENS, Charles, LRCP, FRCS; Senior Consulting Ophthalmic Surgeon, Guy's Hospital; Ophthalmic Surgeon to the French Hospital; late Ophthalmic Surgeon, County of London War Hospital. *Publications:* A Manual of Ophthalmic Practice; Hints on Ophthalmic Out-patients Practice; Notes on 925 Extractions of Cataract, Lancet, 1894; on 130 Consecutive Extractions of Cataract without a Failure, Lancet, 1907; other papers on cataract and other eye affections in medical journals. *Address:* 52 Brook Street, W1. *T:* Mayfair 4820. *Club:* Bath.
Died 28 Dec. 1920.

HIGGINS, Clement; *b* 10 Jan. 1844; *y s* of W. Mullinger Higgins of Wrexham; *m* 1870, Augusta Mary, *o c* of Richard Wright of West Bank, near Mansfield; two *s* one *d. Educ:* Downing College, Camb. (MA, Foundation Scholar, Natural Science Tripos). Called to Bar, Inner Temple, 1871; formerly went North Wales, Chester, and Glamorganshire Circuit; Recorder of Birkenhead, 1882–1907. *Publications:* A Digest of Patent Cases; The Law and Practice of Patents for Inventions; The Pollution and Obstruction of Water Courses; joint-author of the Electric Lighting Act of 1882. *Address:* 3 Paper Buildings, Temple, EC; Winterdyne, Bournemouth West.
Died 4 Dec. 1916.

HIGGINS, Henry Vincent, CVO 1905; solicitor; *b* 18 April 1855; *e s* of late Matthew James Higgins ("Jacob Omnium" of The Times), and Emily Blanche, *y d* of Sir Henry Tichborne, 8th Bt; *m* 1st, 1876, Lady Hilda Jane Sophia Finch Hatton (*d* 1893), *y d* of 11th Earl of Winchilsea and Nottingham; two *s*; 2nd, 1894, Marie Louise, *d* of George Parsons of Columbus, Ohio, USA, and widow of late W. L. Breese of New York. *Educ:* Oratory School, Edgbaston; Merton College, Oxford. Lieut 1st Life Guards, 1876–83; Chairman of the Grand Opera Syndicate and Director of the Carlton and Ritz Hotels Companies, London, and Ritz Hotel, Paris. *Address:* 1 Upper Berkeley Street, W1. *T:* Mayfair 3338; 7 Bloomsbury Square, WC. *Clubs:* Turf, Guards, Beefsteak, Garrick.
Died 21 Nov. 1928.

HIGGINS, Rt. Rev. Michael, DD; VG; Canon Theologian of Tuam Chapter since 1905; RC Auxiliary Bishop of Tuam since 1912; *b* Ballyheane, Castlebar, Co. Mayo, Sept. 1863. *Educ:* St Jarlath's College, Tuam; St Patrick's College, Maynooth. Student to the Dunboyne Establishment, 1887; Priest, 1888; spent 13½ years doing Missionary work, 11½ years as Curate and 2 years as Parish Priest; 11 years teaching in St Jarlath's College, 4 as Professor and 7 as President; Hon. DD of the Propaganda College, Rome, 1904; Parish Priest of Cummer, 1910; one of the members of the first Governing Body of University College, Galway. *Address:* St Mary's, Castlebar, Co. Mayo.
Died 20 April 1918.

HIGGINSON, Gen. Sir George Wentworth Alexander, GCB 1903 (KCB 1889; CB 1871); GCVO 1922; JP; DL Bucks; retired, 1893; *b* 21 June 1826; *o s* of Gen. George Higginson and Lady Frances, *d* of 1st Earl of Kilmorey; *m* 1858, Hon. Florence (*d* 1912), *d* of late Baron Castletown of Upper Ossory; one *s* one *d. Educ:* Eton. Ensign Grenadier Guards, 1845; in which regiment served thirty years; was with it during whole of Crimean War, and twice promoted for service in the field; commanded Brigade of Guards and Home District, 1879–84; Lieut-Governor of the Tower of London, 1888–93. Knight of the Legion of Honour; Knight Grand Cross of the Crown of Italy; Crimean medal with 4 clasps. *Publication:* Seventy-One Years of a Guardsman's Life, 1916. *Address:* Gyldernscroft, Marlow-on-Thames. *Clubs:* Carlton, Guards.
Died 1 Feb. 1927.

HIGGS, Col Frederick William, CBE 1919; TD; MD, BS; MRCP; Medical Officer, Ministry of Health; Assistant Director of Medical Services, 47th (2nd London) Division, Territorial Army; *b* Harlesden, Middlesex, 18 May 1881; *e s* of Augustus William Higgs, LRCP, of Chelsea, originally of East Hagbourne, Berks, and Jane Fell Parker; *m* 2nd *d* of John Walter Scott, MRCS, formerly RN, of Chandlers Ford, Hants; two *d. Educ:* St George's Hospital. Obtained Medical Qualification, 1904; William Brown Exhibitioner; Home Surgeon and Physician, Medical Registrar and Tutor, Assistant Curator, Demonstrator of Pathology and Materia Medica, etc, St George's Hospital, 1904–12; Physician to Belgrave Hospital for Children, 1907–12; Divisional Medical Officer, LCC School Medical Service, 1912–20. Served Queen's Westminster Volunteers, 1897–1901; joined Territorial Force, 1909; served as MO to 2nd London Division RE and in 2nd London CCS; commanded Ambulance Train (Home), CCS (France); ADMS 66th Division (Belgium) (despatches thrice, CBE); ADMS 47th Div.; Military Member of County of London Territorial Army Association, and Representative of City and County of London Territorial Army Associations on the Central Joint Voluntary Aid Detachment Council (War Office); Assistant District Commissioner, Sutton Rover Scouts. *Publications:* contributions to medical journals on children's diseases, tuberculosis, etc. *Recreation:* archæology. *Address:* Dell Quay, Sutton, Surrey; Ministry of Health, SW1.
Died 26 March 1924.

HIGHMORE, Sir Nathaniel Joseph, GBE 1920; KCB 1913; Kt 1907; *b* 13 Nov. 1844; *s* of William Highmore, MD (*d* 1883), of Sherborne; *m* 1881, Annie Louisa, Order of Mercy, 1918, *d* of late John Lane Cutcliffe, JP, Stoke Damerel; one *d. Educ:* Sherborne School. Entered Inland Revenue Department, 1864; Barrister Middle Temple, 1881; assistant solicitor Inland Revenue, 1890–1903; solicitor for HM's Customs, 1903–13, and HM's Excise, 1909–13; retired, 1913; on the panel of Chairmen of Courts of Arbitration under the Conciliation Act 1896; resumed duty at the Custom House, 1914, as representative of the Board of Customs and Excise on the Committee on Trade with the Enemy; Secretary to the War Trade Department, 1915–19. *Publications:* The Excise Laws; The Stamp Laws; The Customs Laws, and other works on revenue law. *Address:* Harbybrowe, Worcester Park, Surrey. *T:* Malden 69.
Died 16 April 1924.

HILBERS, Ven. George Christopher, VD; MA; FRNS; Rector of St Thomas, Haverfordwest, since 1874. *Educ:* Exeter Coll., Oxford. Archdeacon of St David's, 1888–1900. *Address:* St Thomas Rectory, Haverfordwest. *Club:* Oxford and Cambridge.
Died 3 Nov. 1918.

HILDEBRAND, Arthur Hedding, CIE 1888; Superintendent and Political Officer, South Shan States, 1887–1902; *b* 1843; *m* 1879, Alice Mary, *d* of Oliver Gourley Miller, Dundee. *Address:* Ilsington Lodge, Puddletown, Dorset.
Died 1 Jan. 1918.

HILDYARD, Gen. Sir Henry John Thoroton, GCB 1911 (KCB 1900; CB 1897); Colonel Highland Light Infantry; *b* 5 July 1846; *s* of late Thomas Blackborne Thoroton Hildyard, MP, of Flintham Hall, Newark; *m* 1871, Annette, *d* of late Admiral J. C. Prevost; three *s. Educ:* Royal Naval Academy, Gosport. Royal Navy, 1859–64; entered army 1867; Capt. HLI 1876; Major, 1882; Bt Lieut-Col 1882; Col 1886; temporary Maj.-Gen. 1898; Maj.-Gen. 1899; served with Egyptian Expedition, 1882, as DAA&QMG; present at Kassassin and Tel-el-Kebir (despatches, medal and clasp, bronze star, 4th class Osmanieh, Brevet Lieut-Col); was DAAG and AAG at Headquarters; AAG Aldershot and Commandant Staff College, 1893–98; commanded 3rd Brigade, Aldershot, 1898–99; 2nd Brigade, South Africa, 1899–1900 (despatches); command 5th Division, South Africa, 1900–1 (despatches, medal and five clasps, KCB); Director-General of Military Education, 1903–4; Lieut-Gen. on Staff commanding troops, South Africa, 1904–5; General Officer Commanding in Chief,

S Africa, 1905–8; retired, 1911. *Address:* 20 Eccleston Square, SW. *T:* Victoria 1232. *Club:* United Service.

Died 25 July 1916.

HILL, 4th Viscount, *cr* 1842; **Rowland Richard Clegg-Hill,** JP; Bt 1726–27; Baron Hill of Almarez and of Hawkstone, Salop, 1814; *b* 12 Feb. 1863; *s* of 3rd Viscount and Mary, *d* of William Madax; *S* father, 1895; *m* 1890, Annie, *d* of William Irwin, Tanrago, Co. Sligo. Capt. 3rd Batt. Royal Warwickshire Regt, 1884–88; Member LCC, 1910–18; Alderman, 1921; Home Service duties, 1915–18. *Heir: brother* Hon. Francis William Clegg-Hill, *b* 4 Nov. 1866. *Address:* 61 Cadogan Square, SW1. *Club:* Wellington.

Died 19 Dec. 1923.

HILL, 5th Viscount, *cr* 1842; **Francis William Clegg-Hill;** Bt 1726–27; Baron Hill of Almarez and of Hawkstone, Salop, 1814; *b* 4 Nov. 1866; *s* of 3rd Viscount Hill and Mary, *d* of William Madax; *S* brother, 1923; *m* 1905, Caroline, *d* of Captain F. Corbett of Greenfields, Presteign. *Educ:* Radley. *Heir: half-brother* Lieut-Col Hon. Charles Rowland Clegg-Hill, DSO, *b* 5 May 1876. *Club:* Wellington.

Died 6 July 1924.

HILL, Alfred John, CBE 1919; JP; MInstCE, MIMechE, MInstT; Past President of Institute of Locomotive Engineers; Whitworth Scholar; *b* Peterborough, 1862; *s* of late Thomas Hill; *m* 1892, Margaretta, *d* of late John Bressey, Bournemouth; no *c*. *Educ:* privately. Entered the Locomotive Carriage and Waggon Works of the Great Eastern Railway at Stratford, 1877; promoted by various stages until in 1912 appointed Head of Department (title altered to Chief Mechanical Engineer in 1915); during War was Chairman of Southern Group of Railways for manufacture of munitions, and was sent by HM Govt to USA on special mission connected with the supply of railway material. *Publications:* papers to Instn of Civil Engineers on the Use of Cast Steel in Locomotives, and Repairs and Removals of Railway Rolling Stock (for the first awarded a Miller prize, and for the second a Watt medal and Crampton prize). *Recreation:* golf. *Address:* 12 Marina Court Avenue, Bexhill-on-Sea. *T:* Bexhill 560. *Club:* Union.

Died 14 March 1927.

HILL, Arthur, CIE 1903; Chief Engineer for Irrigation (retired), Bombay Presidency; *b* 11 Jan. 1858; *s* of Rev. A. Hill, Leicester. *Educ:* Coopers Hill. Entered Public Works Department as assistant engineer, 1880. *Address:* Babbacombe Cliff, Torquay.

Died 25 April 1927.

HILL, Arthur, ISO 1909; *b* 7 Feb. 1854; *s* of late J. Harding Hill; *m* 1883, Dorothy, *d* of late J. Rance Chapman. Was attached to the Marine Department of the Board of Trade for over 47 years. *Address:* Collina, Westleigh Avenue, Leigh-on-Sea.

Died 5 Sept. 1927.

HILL, Capt. Arthur Blundell George Sandys; late Rifle Brigade; *b* 13 May 1837; *e s* of Lord George Augusta Hill and Cassandra Jane, *y d* of Edward Knight of Godmersham Park, Kent; *heir-pres.* to 5th Baron Sandys; *m* 1871, Helen Emily, 3rd *d* of Richard Chenevix Trench, DD, Archbishop of Dublin; three *s* two *d* (and two *d* decd). Capt. Rifle Brigade; served Indian Mutiny (battle of Cawnpore, siege and capture of Lucknow), Doab and Oude Campaigns, and with Camel Corps in Central India; Inspector of Prisons in Ireland; succeeded to Gweedon estates, Donegal, 1878. *Address:* The Ashes, Hothfield, Kent.

Died 16 June 1923.

HILL, Arthur George, MA, DLitt; FSA; author and antiquary; *b* 12 Nov. 1857; *e s* of Thomas Hill of Belsize Avenue, Hampstead, and Sophia, *y d* of late Rev. Charles Thorold. *Educ:* Westminster; Jesus College, Cambridge (MA). University of Lille, Docteur ès Lettres (DLitt). Director of Wm Hill & Son and Norman & Beard, Ltd, Organ Builders; travelled throughout Europe in the pursuit of archæology, particularly in Spain, also in Palestine. *Publications:* Churches of Cambridgeshire, 1878; Tourists Guide to the County of Cambridge, 1880; The Organ Cases and Organs of the Middle Ages and Renaissance, two large folio volumes, 1883 and 1891, illustrated by the author; The Architectural History of the Christian Church, 1908; Christian Art in Spain, 1913; numerous papers in Archæologia and the Transactions of other societies, English and foreign. *Recreations:* travel, drawing, music, languages, fine art, especially architecture. *Address:* 41 Pall Mall, SW1. *T:* Gerrard 7103. *Clubs:* United University, Oxford and Cambridge Musical.

Died 16 June 1923.

HILL, Ven. Arundel Charles, DD; Archdeacon of Elgin, Canada, since 1894; *b* 22 May 1845; *s* of late Rev. B. C. Hill, MA (TCD),

Rector of York, County of Haldimand, Ontario, 1838–70. *Edu* University College, Toronto; Huron College, London. Ordain 1869; Curate of St Paul, London, 1869–70; St James', Toron 1870–73; Church of Ascension, Hamilton, 1873–75; Incumbent Burford, 1875–78; Rector of Strathroy, 1878–85; Rector of Trin Church, St Thomas, 1885–1915; Canon of Huron, 1885–19(Degree of DD conferred by Western University, London, Ont, 19 promoted to rank of Hon. Major and Chaplain of 25th Regime Elgin Infantry, St Thomas, 1908; Captain and Chaplain, 1898; retired list of officers retaining rank of Major. *Address:* Shelburr Ontario, Canada.

Died 22 Aug. 192

HILL, Brig.-Gen. Augustus West, CB 1900; The Duke Cambridge's Own (Middlesex Regiment); commanded a Divisio 1908–10; *b* 4 May 1853; *s* of Henry Worsley Hill, Capt. RN; *m* 187 Alice, *d* of Hon. George Vane, CMG, Treasurer of Ceylon; two Educ: Keir House, Wimbledon; Cheltenham Coll. Joined 57th For 1873; Captain, 1880; Major, 1885; Lieut-Col 1895; Brevet Col 19(served Zulu War, 1879, including relief of Echowe and capture Cetewayo (medal with clasp); served Boer War, 1900–1, includi relief of Ladysmith, operations in Upper Natal, Orange River Colon and Transvaal (despatches, medal with 7 clasps, CB); retired 19 *Club:* Army and Navy. *Died 4 Feb. 192*

HILL, Ernest George; Principal, Muir College, University Allahabad since 1913, and Professor of Chemistry; Meteorologist United Provinces Government; *b* 1872; *s* of Rev. George Hill, D Nottingham; *m* 1896, Margaret Brend, *d* of Rev. Eustace Rog Conder, DD, of Leeds; no *c*. *Educ:* Leeds; Magdalen College, Oxfor Honour School, Natural Science, 1895; ScD Dublin, 1906; appoint to Indian Educational Service as Professor of Chemistry, Muir Colleg Allahabad, 1895; Fellow of Allahabad University, 1896; since wh Dean of Faculty of Science and member of Syndicate; Director Education Section of United Provinces Exhibition, 1910. *Publicatio* numerous papers in scientific journals. *Recreations:* polo, cricket, go *Address:* Muir College, Allahabad, India. *Club:* East India Unit Service. *Died 28 June 191*

HILL, Sir G. Rowland, Kt 1926; Past President of the Rugby Footb Union, for which he was for many years Hon. Secretary; *b* Queer House, Royal Hospital Schools, Greenwich, 21 Jan. 1855; *s* of la Rev. James Hill, DD, of the Royal Hospital Schools. *Educ:* Chris Hospital. Late Record Keeper in the Principal Probate Registr Somerset House; Chairman of the Borough of Greenwi Conservative Association from 1887. *Clubs:* Junior Carlton, Sport

Died 25 April 192

HILL, Headon, (*nom de plume* of **Francis Edward Grainger** novelist; *b* Lowestoft, Suffolk, 1857; *e s* of late Rev. J. Grainger, M formerly Asst Master at Eton College, and Vicar of Penn, Buck married. *Educ:* Eton. In the army a few years; went to India, Egyp and the United States of America; afterwards engaged in journalis in London. *Publications:* over sixty novels, incl. Clues from Detective's Camera, 1893; Cabinet Secrets, 1893; Zambra Th Detective, 1894; The Rajah's Second Wife, 1894; By A Hair Breadth, 1897; The Spies on the Wight, 1899; The Plunder Shi 1900. *Club:* Authors'. *Died 2 Feb. 192*

HILL, Henry William; *b* Eton, 1850; *s* of late Henry Hill; *m* 2n 1892, Fanny, *d* of late Henry Lee Hogg of Cleobury Mortime Followed commercial pursuits for many years; a church worker, takir part in catholic movement in the Church of England; retired fro business, 1899, to become Lay-organising Secretary, English Churc Union; Secretary, 1902–20; Vice-President, 1920; organised sever large demonstrations, including that of the Lancashire men in Londc against the Education Bill, 1906; the Welsh procession in Londc 1912; the Hyde Park protest against the Welsh Disestablishment Bi 1913; and Victoria Park protest, 1914; Member of Canterbury Hou of Laymen, 1900–20; Member National Assembly Church England, 1920; re-elected, 1925; Diocesan Reader (Southwark an London); Director Fidelity (Church) Trust; Treasurer of the Guil of All Souls; Secretary, Marriage Defence Council, 1920. *Publicatio* much in the press on social and ecclesiastical subjects. *Address:* Mo End, Hambledon, Godalming.

Died 11 April 192

HILL, Lt-Col Hugh, MVO 1906; DSO 1915; FRGS; *b* 16 May 187 *Educ:* Rugby; Sandhurst; Staff College, Quetta. Entered Royal Wel Fusiliers, 1895; Capt. 1903; Major, 1913; Adjutant, 1904–7; serve S Africa, 1899–1900 (Queen's medal, two clasps); European War Brigade-Major to Jullundur Brigade and DAA&QMG 5th Arm Corps Headquarters, 1914–15 (despatches twice, DSO, promote

Brevet Lt-Col); extra ADC to the Prince and Princess of Wales during their tour in India, and when as King and Queen they were in India for the Durbar. *Address:* 45 Argyll Road, Kensington, W; The Thatched Cottage, Beaconsfield, Bucks.

Died 10 Sept. 1916.

HILL, James Bastian, FGS; Geological Adviser, Ministry of Health; *b* 28 Dec. 1861; *s* of late George Hill; *m* 1886, Lucia Mary (*d* 1912), *d* of late D. R. Comyn; one *d*. *Educ:* private schools; University College, London; Royal School of Mines. Served in Royal Navy, 1877-83; present at bombardment of Alexandria, 1882 (Egyptian medal one clasp, Khedive's star); on the Staff of HM Geological Survey of Great Britain, 1884-1911. *Publications:* numerous geological memoirs and papers. *Recreations:* shooting, fishing. *Address:* Ministry of Health, Whitehall, SW. *Club:* Junior Army and Navy.

Died 18 Dec. 1927.

HILL, James J., LLD Hon., Yale; *b* near Guelph, Upper Canada, 16 Sept. 1838. *Educ:* Rockwood Academy. In steamboat offices in St Paul, 1856-65; agent, North-Western Packet Co. 1865; later established general fuel and transportation business on his own account; head of Hill, Griggs, and Co. 1869-75; established The Red River Transportation Co. 1870; formed North-Western Fuel Co., 1873; organised syndicate which secured control of St Paul and Pacific Railroad from Dutch owners of the securities, 1877; reorganised system as St Paul, Minneapolis, and Manitoba Railroad; General Manager, 1879-81; Vice-President, 1881-82; President from 1882; it became part of Great Northern system, 1890, of which he was President to April 1907; Chairman of Board of Directors, 1907-12; retired from active work. *Publication:* Highways of Progress. *Address:* Great Northern Railway Building, St Paul, Minnesota, US.

Died 29 May 1916.

HILL, James Stevens, RI; *b* 1854. *Address:* 1A Steele's Studio, Haverstock Hill, NW. *Died 12 June 1921.*

HILL, Col Joseph, CB 1904; 3rd Battalion Northamptonshire Regiment; *b* 29 Dec. 1850; *s* of Charles Hill of Wollaston and Mariette, *d* of John Berkeley Monck, MP, of Coley Park, Reading; *m* 1883, Katherine, *d* of George Miller of Brentry, Glos; one *s* one *d*. *Educ:* Eton. JP, DL, Northamptonshire; High Sheriff, 1885. Served South Africa, 1902 (Queen's medal, 2 clasps); County Commandant, Northamptonshire. *Recreations:* hunting, cricket. *Address:* Wollaston Hall, Wellingborough. *Club:* Badminton.

Died 19 May 1918.

HILL, Col Peter Edward, CB 1907; Royal Artillery, retired; *b* 7 June 1834; *m* 1863, Emily Mary, *d* of William Clarke, MD. *Educ:* Cheltenham; RMA Woolwich. Entered army 1853; Col 1883; served Crimea, 1854-56 (medal, three clasps, 5th Medjidie, Turkish medal); Indian Mutiny, 1858-59 (medal); Afghan War, 1878-79 (despatches, medal). *Address:* Paxton House, Bath Road, Reading.

Died 13 July 1919.

HILL, Reginald Duke, DL, JP; High Sheriff of Essex, 1911; Master East Essex Foxhounds; *b* 4 Jan. 1866; *s* of late James Duke Hill of Terlings Park, Harlow, Essex; *m* 1893, Flora, *o d* of Major Francis Tower of Thremhall Priory, Essex, and *widow* of Osgood Beauchamp Hanbury of Holfield Grange; two *s*. *Address:* Holfield Grange, Coggeshall, Essex. *T:* 9 Coggeshall. *Club:* Boodle's.

Died 16 Jan. 1922.

HILL, Lt-Col Walter de Marchot, CBE 1919; MRCS, LRCP; *b* Bedford, 12 Feb. 1877; *s* of Major-Gen. W. Hill and Charlotte Miller, *d* of Beauchamp Colclough Urquhart, Meldrum and Byth, Scotland; *m* Margaret Ethel, *d* of Robert Reed of Bristol; one *d*. *Educ:* Bairlodge; St Bart's Hospital. Master of Electrical Engrg, Bliss School of Electricity, Washington, USA, 1905; House Surgeon, House Physician, Seaman's Hospital, Greenwich; MO 23 Fusiliers, 1914; MO 82 Brigade RFA, 18th Div., 1915; in command Special Military Surgical Hospital, Shepherd's Bush, 1916; Assistant Inspector of Military Orthopædics and Liaison Officer, Ministry of Pensions, War Office, 1919; Adviser in Special Orthopædic Surgery, Ministry of Pensions, 1922; Associate of the Order of St John of Jerusalem; 1914-15 Star. *Publications:* Treatment of Rheumatoid Arthritis; The Organisation and Administration of a Military Orthopædic Hospital in Jones's Orthopædic Surgery of Injuries, 1921. *Recreation:* golf. *Address:* 26 Thomas Street, W1. *T:* Mayfair 4841. *Club:* Wellington.

Died 20 June 1927.

HILL, William, BSc, MD London; Consulting Surgeon for Diseases of the Ear, Nose, and Throat, St Mary's Hospital, London; Endoscopic Surgeon (for Diseases of the Gullet), Metropolitan Ear and Throat Hospital; *s* of late George Hill of Tregassick, Cornwall; *m* Flora Hastings, *d* of David Robert Comyn. *Educ:* King's and University Colleges, London; St Mary's Hospital; formerly Senior Entrance Science Scholar; Scholar in Pathology. Assistant Curator of Museum and Assistant Lecturer on Anatomy, St Mary's Hospital; Registrar and Pathologist, Central London Throat and Ear Hospital; and Teacher of Botany, University College School, etc; Past President of the Harveian Society of London, of Section of Laryngology, Royal Society of Medicine, and of Section of Oto-rhino-laryngology, British Medical Association. *Publications:* Introductory Lecture on Occultism and Quackery in Medicine, 1902; many papers on professional subjects published in various medical journals. *Address:* Weymouth Street, Portland Place, W1. *T:* Langham 2408. *Clubs:* Savage; Royal Temple Yacht. *Died 24 Nov. 1928.*

HILLIER, Edward Guy, CMG 1904; of the Hong Kong and Shanghai Banking Corporation; *b* 1857; *s* of late Charles Batten Hillier, HBM Consul to Siam; *m* 1st, 1894, Ada (*d* 1917), *d* of late Frederick Everett, Erith, Kent; one *s* two *d*; 2nd, 1919, Eleanor, *d* of late Dr Timothy Richard, of Shanghai, China. *Educ:* Blundell's School, Tiverton; Trinity College, Cambridge. Entered the service of the Hong Kong and Shanghai Banking Corporation, 1883; Agent of the Bank in Peking, 1891; engaged in negotiation of various Chinese Government loans issued between 1895 and 1913; British Delegate on the Commission of Bankers for the Chinese Indemnity, 1902. Failure of sight in 1896 resulted in total blindness. *Address:* Peking, China.

Died 12 April 1924.

HILLIER, Frederick James; Director, Daily News and the Star; Chairman, Technical Committee, Newspaper Proprietors' Association; *b* Southampton, 1869; *m* 1890, Anne Henry; three *s*. Night Editor, Morning Leader and Daily News until 1913; News Editor, Daily News, until 1918. *Address:* 19-22 Bouverie Street, EC4. *T:* Central 313. *Died 1920.*

HILLIER, Joseph Hillier, MVO 1910; Controller of Supplies, HM Office of Works, 1905-10. *Address:* Seafield Cottage, Seafield Road, Broadstairs.

HILLIER, Sir Walter Caine, KCMG 1897; CB 1903; Adviser to Chinese Government, 1908-10; Adviser to Military Authorities in China, 1900 (despatches, medal); *b* Hong Kong; 1849; *s* of Charles Batten Hillier, late Consul at Bangkok; *m* 1906, Marion Ellen, *d* of late Sir Charles Umpherston Aitchison, KCSI. *Educ:* Bedford Gram. School; Blundell's School, Tiverton. Student Interpreter in China, 1867; Asst Chinese Sec. Peking, 1879-85; Chinese Secretary, 1885-89; Consul-General, Corea, 1889-96; Professor of Chinese, King's College, London, 1904-8. *Publications:* The Chinese Language, and How to Learn it, 1907; English-Chinese Dictionary, 1910. *Address:* The Oaks, Bracknell, Berks.

Died 9 Nov. 1927.

HILLINGDON, 2nd Baron, *cr* 1886; **Charles William Mills;** Bt 1868; DL; partner in Glyn, Mills and Co., Bankers; *b* 26 Jan. 1855; *e s* of 1st Baron and Lady Louisa Lascelles, *e d* of 3rd Earl of Harewood; *S* father, 1898; *m* 1886, Hon. Alice Marion Harbord, 2nd *d* of 5th Baron Suffield; one *s* (and two *s* decd). MP (C) West Kent, 1885-92. Owner of about 4,500 acres. *Heir: s* Hon. Arthur Robert Mills [*b* 19 Oct. 1891; *m* 1916, Hon. Edith Mary Winifred Cadogan, *d* of late Viscount Chelsea]. *Address:* Hillingdon Court, Uxbridge; Wildernesse, Sevenoaks. *Died 6 April 1919.*

HILLS-JOHNES, Lt-Gen. Sir James, VC 1858; GCB 1893 (KCB 1881; CB 1872); LLD University of Wales, 1917; *b* 20 Aug. 1833; *s* of late James Hills, Neechindipore, Bengal, India, and Charlotte, *d* of Signor Angelo Savi, Moisgunge; *m* 1882, Elizabeth, *d* and co-heir with her sister Mrs Johnes, of late John Johnes, Dolaucothy, Carmarthenshire; assumed in 1883 by Royal licence additional name and arms of Johnes. *Educ:* Academy, Edinburgh; Military College, Edinburgh; Addiscombe. Entered Bengal Artillery, 1853; served throughout Indian Mutiny, 1857-58; present at Hindun River, Badlee-Ka-Serai, Nujjefghur, siege and storming of Delhi, 1857; Lucknow, 1858; Bareilly, Allygunge and Mohamdee, 1858; dangerously wounded, 1857 (VC, Brevet Majority, medal and two clasps); ADC to Viceroy (Lord Canning), 1859-62; Assistant Resident, Nepal, 1862-63; commanded 8-inch mortar battery throughout Abyssinian campaign, 1867-68; present at capture of Magdala (Bt Lt-Col, medal); served throughout Lushai campaign, 1871-72 (CB, medal and clasp); served as AAG Kandahar Field Force, 1878-79; joined Sir F. S. Roberts' column in Kurrum Valley, 1879; accompanied it to Kabul; present at battle of Charasiab and occupation of Kabul; Military Governor, city of Kabul, 1879-80; assumed command 3rd Division Northern Afghanistan Field Force, 1880; directed operations of cavalry action at Padkoa Shana Logar Valley (received vote of thanks of Houses of Parliament, 5th May 1881, KCB, medal and clasp). JP, DL Carmarthenshire; Hon. Colonel 4th Batt. the Welsh Regt; Chairman Carmarthenshire County Association. *Address:* Dolaucothy, Llanwrda, RSO, South Wales. *TA:* Pumpsaint. *Clubs:* United Service, Junior Constitutional.

Died 3 Jan. 1919.

HIME, Lt-Col Rt. Hon. Sir Albert Henry, KCMG 1900 (CMG 1886); PC 1902; Hon. LLD Dublin, Edin. and Camb.; *b* Kilcool, Co. Wicklow, Ireland, 29 Aug. 1842; 7th *s* of late Rev. Maurice C. Hime and Harriette, *d* of late Rev. Bartholomew Lloyd, Provost of Trinity Coll., Dublin; *m* 1866, Josephine Mary, *d* of late J. Searle of Plymouth; five *s* two *d. Educ:* Portora Royal School, Enniskillen; by private tutor; Trinity Coll., Dublin; Royal Military Academy, Woolwich. Entered Royal Engineers, 1861, became Captain 1874, and Major 1881; retired with honorary rank of Lieut-Col 1883; was employed in Bermuda, under the Colonial Government, 1869-71, in the construction of a causeway and swing-bridge connecting the island of St George with the main island, for the successful completion of which works received the thanks of the Legislature and the acknowledgments of the Secretary of State for the Colonies; Colonial Engineer of Natal, 1875; member of Executive and Legislative Councils, 1876, retired when Natal assumed responsible government, 1893; served Zulu War, 1879 (medal with clasp); employed on survey of boundary between Orange Free State and Natal in 1884-85; thanked by Secretary of State for Colonies for successfully carrying out that survey; MLA Pietermaritzburg, 1897; Minister of Lands and Works and Minister of Defence, Natal, 1897-99; Prime Minister and Minister of Lands and Works and Minister of Defence, 1899, resigned 1903. Decorated for services generally and specially for assistance rendered to Imperial Government in connection with the war in South Africa. *Recreations:* sport of all kinds, but especially fishing. *Address:* Lymbrook, Marlow, Bucks. *Clubs:* Marlow; Victoria, Pietermaritzburg.   *Died 13 Sept. 1919.*

HIND, C. Lewis; writer; *b* 1862; *s* of late Charles Hind, JP; *m* 1907, Henriette Richardson Hitchcock. *Educ:* privately; Christ's Hospital. Sub-editor of the Art Journal, 1887-92; editor Pall Mall Budget, 1893-95; editor of the Academy, 1896-1903. *Publications:* The Enchanted Stone, 1898; Things Seen (printed for private circulation), 1899; Life's Little Things, 1901; Adventures among Pictures, 1904; Life's Lesser Moods, 1904; Days with Velasquez, 1905; Rembrandt, 1905; The Education of an Artist, 1906; Days in Cornwall, 1907; The Diary of a Looker-on, 1908; Turner's Golden Visions, 1910; The Post Impressionists, 1911; The Consolations of a Critic, 1911; Brabazon: His Art and Life, 1912; The Soldier Boy, 1916; The Invisible Guide, 1917; What's Freedom? (also the play of Freedom, with Lyall Swete, produced at the Century Theatre, New York), 1918; Things Seen in America (printed for private circulation), 1920; Art and I, Authors and I, 1921; More Authors and I, 1922; Life and I, 1923; Landscape Painting: From Giotto to Turner, vol. i, 1923; From Constable to the Present Day, vol. ii, 1924; The Uncollected Work of Aubrey Beardsley; Life and You; One Hundred Second-Best Poems; Naphtali: Being Influences and Adventures while Earning a Living by Writing, 1925; From My Books: An Anthology; One Hundred Best Poems; The Great Painters; In Art and Life; One Hundred Best Books, 1927. *Address:* 24 Queen Anne's Gate, Westminster, SW1. *T:* Victoria 857. *Clubs:* Arts, Authors'.

Died 31 Aug. 1927.

HINDE, George Jennings, PhD; FRS, FGS. *Publications:* Fossil Sponge Spicules from the Upper Chalk, Munich, 1880; Catalogue of Fossil Sponges in British Museum, 1883; Report on the Materials from the Borings at the Funafuti Atoll, 1904; other papers on fossil sponges, radiolaria, and corals. *Address:* 24 Avondale Road, South Croydon.

Died 18 March 1918.

HINDLE, Frederick George; solicitor; Clerk to Darwen Borough Justices since 1882; MP (L) Darwen Division of Lancashire, Jan.-Dec. 1910; *b* Darwen, 15 Jan. 1848; *m* 1876, Helen, *d* of Thomas Gillibrand, cotton manufacturer, Darwen; one *s. Educ:* Grammar School, Blackburn; Senior Prizeman at Examination as Solicitor in 1870. Practised in Manchester and at Darwen; contested (L) Darwen Division, 1906; Dec. 1910. Served 19 years as an officer in East Lancashire Volunteers and retired with rank of Major. *Publication:* The Legal Status of Licensed Victuallers, 1883. *Recreations:* golf, motoring, etc. *Address:* Astley Bank, Darwen. *T:* 3 Darwen.

Died 1 March 1925.

HINDS, John; HM's Lieutenant and Custos Rotulorum, County of Carmarthen, since 1917; *b* Cwnin Farm, near Carmarthen, 26 July 1862; *s* of late William Hinds and *d* of David Jones Penronw, Llanpumpsaint; *m* 1893, Lizzie, *d* of R. Powell, Cefntrefna, Llandovery; one *d. Educ:* Academy of late Alcwyn Evans, Carmarthen. Went to London, 1881; engaged at various drapery establishments; founded Hinds & Co. (Limited); Chairman of the Drapers' Fire Insurance Corporation; Past President of the Drapers' Chamber of Trade; Ex-President of the Blackheath Liberal Association; President West Carmarthen Liberal Association; Chairman of the Welsh Liberal Federation; Member of Board of Management of the Warehousemen, Drapers, and Clerks' School; Treasurer of Council of Honourable Society of Cymmrodorion; Treasurer of National Eisteddfod Association; Ex-President Baptist Union of Wales; Past Master of several Freemasons' lodges; and Past Senior Deacon of the Grand Lodge of England; Ex-President of the London Welsh Literary Union, and a Member of the Charitable Aid Society; MP (L) West Carmarthenshire, 1910-18; Carmarthen Division (Coalition L), 1918-23. Mayor of Carmarthen, 1925-26. *Address:* 14 Clarendon Court, W9. *T:* Paddington 8506; Neuadd-Deg, Carmarthen. *T:* Carmarthen 89. *M:* BX 5424. *Clubs:* Reform, National Liberal.

Died 23 July 1928.

HINE, George T.; architect in private practice; *b* Nottingham, 1841; *e s* of late T. C. Hine, FSA; *m* Florence Deane, *y d* of late E. Cooper of Failand House, Somersetshire; one *s* one *d. Educ:* privately in England and abroad. Articled to his father and practised for many years with him as an architect; in 1890 came to London and practised exclusively as an asylum architect; Consulting Architect to HM Commissioners in Lunacy. FRIBA and late member of Council; FRICS. *Publications:* several works on asylum construction and hygiene. *Recreations:* hunting, shooting. *Address:* 35 Parliament Street, Westminster, SW; 37 Hertford Street, Mayfair, W. *TA:* Asyla, London. *T:* 4415 Gerrard; Old Farm, near Berkhamsted, Herts. *Clubs:* Union, St Stephen's, Constitutional, Ranelagh, etc.

Died 25 April 1916.

HINGLEY, Sir George Benjamin, 2nd Bt, *cr* 1893; Chairman N. Hingley and Sons, Ltd, and Harts Hill Iron Co., colliery proprietors and ironmasters, Netherton, Dudley, and Brierley Hill; High Sheriff for Worcestershire, 1900; *b* 9 Sept. 1850; *s* of Hezekiah Hingley of Grassendale Park, Liverpool (*e b* of Sir Benjamin Hingley, 1st Bt), and Fanny Georgina, *d* of William Thompson, Liverpool; *S* uncle, 1905. *Heir:* none. *Address:* High Park, near Droitwich. *Club:* Union.

Died 19 Aug. 1918 (ext).

HINGSTON, George, ISO 1903; Collector of Customs, Glasgow, 1902-4; *b* 29 Sept. 1839; *s* of late Alfred Hingston; *m* 1873, Clara Gertrude, *d* of late Charles Hingston. *Educ:* Marlborough Coll. Entered HM Customs, 1858. *Address:* Degany House, Crown Hill, Devonshire.   *Died 7 Dec. 1925.*

HINKSON, Henry Albert, MA; author and barrister; Resident Magistrate for South Mayo since 1914; *b* Dublin, 18 April 1865; *m* 1893, Katharine Tynan; two *s* one *d. Educ:* Dublin High School; Trinity Coll., Dublin (Scholar); Germany. MA in Classical Honours, Royal University of Ireland, 1890; Barrister of the Inner Temple; formerly Senior Classical Tutor at Clongowes Wood College, Kildare. *Publications:* Dublin Verses (edited), 1895; Golden Lads and Girls, 1895; O'Grady of Trinity, 1896; Up for the Green, 1898; When Love is Kind, 1898; The King's Deputy, 1899; The Point of Honour, 1901; Sir Phelim's Treasure, 1901; Fan Fitz-Gerald, 1902; Silk and Steel, 1902; Copyright Law, 1903; The Wine of Love, 1904; The Splendid Knight, 1905; Golden Morn; The Castaways of Hope Island, 1907; Father Alphonsus, 1908; The King's Liege, 1909; The House of the Oak, 1911; The Considine Luck; Glory of War, 1912; Gentleman Jack, 1913; many short stories. *Recreations:* tennis, golf, shooting. *Address:* Brookhill, Claremorris, Co. Mayo. *TA:* Claremorris. *Club:* Savage.   *Died 11 Jan. 1919.*

HINTON, Lt-Col Godfrey Bingham, CMG 1915; Royal Field Artillery; *b* 19 March 1871. Entered army, 1890; Captain, 1899; Major, 1905; Lt-Col 1914; Adjutant Volunteers, 1897-1902; served European War, 1914-15 (despatches, CMG).

Died 21 March 1918.

HIRSCH, Emil G., LHD, LLD, DCL, DD, AM; Rabbi of Chicago Sinai Congregation since 1880; Professor of Rabbinics in the University of Chicago; Commissioner of Charities of the State of Illinois; Editor of the Reform-Advocate (a weekly); *b* Luxemburg, May 1851; *s* of Dr Samuel Hirsch, Rabbi, and Louise Mickolls; *m* 1878, Matilda, *d* of Dr David Einhorn and Julia Ochs; two *s* three *d. Educ:* Luxemburg (Gymnasium); University of Pennsylvania; Berlin; Hochschule für Wissenschaft des Judentunk, Berlin. Rabbi at Baltimore, 1877; Louisville, 1878–80; Elector at Large during Presidential Election for McKinley, 1896; President of Chicago Public Library; Member of the State Board of Charities; Chaplain of Illinois Naval Reserve; Vice-President of Parliament of Religions, Chicago, 1893; of Congress of Religion, 1894; often acted as Arbitrator in disputes between Labour and Employers; Orator at many public gatherings in the US. *Publications:* one volume of selected addresses; The Crucifixion from the Jewish Point of View; Translator and Editor of Olath Tamid, a Jewish Prayer-book; many contributions to Jewish and other religious publications; Editor of the Biblical Department of Jewish Encyclopedia. *Recreation:* travel. *Address:* 4608 Drexel Boulevard, Chicago. *TA:* Rabbi. *T:* Drexel 628. *Clubs:* Standard, Press, Quadrangle, Literary, the Book and Play, Society for Biblical Research, Chicago. *Died 7 Jan. 1923.*

HISLOP, Hon. Thomas William; Officer of Legion of Honour; barrister and solicitor; member of Legislative Council of New Zealand; *b* Edinburgh, 1850; *s* of John Hislop, LLD, FRS, Edinburgh, and Johanna, *d* of Major Horn of Stirkook, Caithness; *m* A. Simpson of New South Wales; two *s* three *d. Educ:* Shaw's Grammar School, Otago; High School and University, Dunedin. Commenced practice of law at Oamaru, 1871; returned MHR Waitaki District, 1875; and again, 1879; resigned 1880; re-elected 1885, 1887, and 1889; Colonial Secretary, 1887; afterwards Minister of Education; resigned, 1891; joined firm Brandon, Hislop & Brandon, barristers, Wellington; Mayor, Wellington, 1904–8; advocated and carried through purchase for city of Electric Works for lighting and power; initiated Zoological Gardens; carried out tramway system and drainage for suburbs, also a scheme for gradual paving of streets out of revenue instead of borrowing; while Minister of Education initiated amendment of Land Act giving option of tenure to purchaser of Govt Lands, also bills regulating hours of shops and factories, shipping, seamen, and many other social measures and legal reforms. *Publications:* frequent contributor to daily papers; pamphlets on social and political subjects. *Recreations:* tennis, swimming, motoring. *Address:* Sayes Court, Wellington, New Zealand. *T:* 75. *M:* 67. *Club:* Wellington, Wellington. *Died 2 Oct. 1925.*

HISSEY, James John; author; *o s* of James Hissey of Longworth, Berks; *m* 1st, 1880, Elizabeth (Bee), *e d* of Sir Thomas Bouch, CE, and Lady Bouch, Edinburgh; 2nd, 1890, Katherine Mary, *e d* of Richard Ridcock of Woolwich; three *s* two *d. Publications:* An Old-Fashioned Journey; A Drive Through England; On the Box Seat; A Tour in a Phaeton; Over Fen and Wold; Untravelled England; An English Holiday; The Charm of the Road; A Leisurely Tour in England; and other works on British topography. *Recreations:* sketching from nature, motoring, photography, engineering. *Address:* Trevin Towers, Eastbourne, Sussex. *T:* Eastbourne 249. *M:* HC 27. *Clubs:* Authors', Royal Automobile, Thatched House, Royal Societies; Devonshire, Eastbourne. *Died 5 March 1921.*

HITCHCOCK, Rev. William Maunder, MA; Hon. Canon of Durham, 1874; retired; *b* 18 July 1835; *s* of George Hitchcock; *m* 1858, Margaret Ellen (*d* 1918); three *s* one *d. Educ:* King's College, London; Wadham College, Oxford. BA 1858; MA 1861. Deacon, 1858; Priest, 1859; Curate of St James', Cheltenham, 1858–59; Perpetual Curate of Bussage, Gloucestershire, 1859–61; Curate of Edgbaston, 1861; Perpetual Curate of Shildon, Co. of Durham, 1862–66; Rural Dean of Chester-le-Street, 1872–80; Rector of Whitburn, Co. Durham, 1866–81; Rural Dean of Wearmouth, 1880–81; Vicar of Romford, Co. Essex, 1881–88; Vicar of East Farleigh, Co. Kent, 1888–93; Private Chaplain to Bishop of Durham, 1862–66, Examining Chaplain, 1866–79. *Died 18 Sept. 1921.*

HJELT, Edvard Immanuel; Vice-Chancellor at the University of Helsingfors; *b* Wichtis, Finland, 28 June 1855; *s* of Otto E. A. Hjelt, Professor of Medicine; *m* 1878, Ida Ostroem; two *s* five *d. Educ:* Lyceum; University, Helsingfors (PhD 1879). Docent of Chemistry, 1880, Professor of Chemistry, 1882–1907, and Rektor, 1899–1907, at the University of Helsingfors; Vice-Pres. Senate of Finland, 1907–9; Hon. LLD University of Aberdeen, 1906; Membre de Société des Sciences de Finlande and Academie Royale des Sciences de Suède. *Publications:* numerous research papers on Organic Chemistry; Principles of Organic Chemistry; continued with Brühl and Aschan the Ausführliches Lehrbuch der Chemie von Roscoe-Schorlemmer; Aus J. Berelius and G. Magnus Briefwechsel; Berelius, Liebig, Dumas, ihre Stellung zur Radikaltheorie; Geschichte d. organ. Chemie; and other biographical works. *Address:* Helsingfors. *T:* 337. *Died 2 July 1921.*

HOARE, Lt-Col Arthur Fanshawe, CB 1911; VD; MA; Assistant Master, Haileybury College, 1879–1914; *b* 14 Aug. 1854; *s* of Rev. Arthur Malortie Hoare and Maria Faithfull Fanshawe; *m* 1894, Gertrude J. Hoare; four *s* one *d. Educ:* Twyford School; Marlborough College; Balliol College, Oxford. Brackenbury History Scholar; Organising Secretary of Public Schools Brigade Camp, 1887–1909. *Publications:* a few essays on military subjects. *Address:* 10 Staverton Road, Oxford. *Died 25 May 1925.*

HOARE, Edward Wallis, FRCVS; practising veterinary surgeon; *b* 9 Oct. 1863; *s* of late Capt. William Jesse Hoare of Carrigrohane Castle, Co. Cork (late 7th Royal Fusiliers); *m* 1899, Emily, BA, NUI, *d* of late H. L. Helen, Dublin; one *s* five *d. Educ:* privately; New Veterinary College, Edinburgh (MRCVS 1886, and passed the Fellowship Examination, 1892). Lecturer in Veterinary Science, University College, Cork; late Member of the Board of Examiners, Royal College of Veterinary Surgeons; late External Examiner in Veterinary Jurisprudence, Toxicology, and Sanitary Law, University of Liverpool; Hon. Member of the American Veterinary Medical Association; Editor of the Veterinary News. *Publications:* A System of Veterinary Medicine, in 2 volumes, 1916; Veterinary Therapeutics, 3rd edition 1916; various papers on veterinary science. *Recreation:* horticulture. *Address:* 18 Cook Street, Cork; Clover Hill, Blackrock. *TA:* Hoare VS, Cork. *T:* 65 Y. *Died 26 Nov. 1920.*

HOARE, Rev. John Gurney, MA; Surrogate; Hon. Canon of Norwich; Hon. Life Governor of Church Missionary Society; *b* Holloway, 16 March 1847; 2nd *s* of late Rev. Edward Hoare, Hon. Canon of Canterbury and Vicar of Holy Trinity, Tunbridge Wells, and Maria, *d* of Sir Benjamin C. Brodie, 1st Bt; *m* 1873, Alice, *d* of late John Woodfall, MD; two *s* three *d. Educ:* Tonbridge School; Trinity College, Cambridge; BA (Classical tripos) 1869, MA 1872. Winner of high jump, University sports, 1869, 1870. Ordained deacon, 1873; priest, 1874; Curate of Christ Church, Sculcoates, Hull, 1873; Sunderland, 1873–75; Holy Trinity, Tunbridge Wells, 1875–77; Vicar of St Dunstan, Canterbury, 1877–88; of Aylsham, Norfolk, 1888–1922. *Publications:* Righteousness and Life; Lessons on Joshua and Judges; From Adam to Abraham; Christ revealed in Type, Title, and Prophecy; Life in St John's Gospel; The Foundation Stone of Christian Faith; editor of Great Principles of Divine Truth. *Recreations:* books, gardening, golf, cycling. *Address:* Belaugh House, Wroxham, Norfolk. *Died 26 Feb. 1923.*

HOARE, Rt. Rev. Joseph; RC Bishop of Ardagh and Clonmacnoise; consecrated 1895; *b* Ballymahon, Co. Longford, 1842; *s* of John Hoare and Maria Donohoe. *Educ:* Mount Melleray, Longford, and Maynooth. Curate of Longford, 1867; president of St Mel's, 1874; parish priest of Street, 1881; parish priest of Carrick-on-Shannon, 1887. *Address:* Bishop's House, St Michael's, Longford, Ireland. *Died 14 April 1927.*

HOARE, Rev. Richard Whitehead; Hon. Canon of Canterbury since 1910; Fellow of King's College, London, 1912; *b* London, 1840; *m* 1872, Isabella Anna Maria Neale of Croydon; two *s* two *d. Educ:* home. Deacon, 1863; Priest, 1864; Assistant Curate at All Saints, Clapham Park, 1863–65; St Barnabas, Kennington, 1865–66; St Saviour's, Croydon, 1866–69; Minister-in-charge of the new parish of St Michael and All Angels, Croydon, 1871; Vicar of St Michael and All Angels, Croydon, 1883–1918. *Address:* 14 Aberdeen Road, Croydon. *Died 22 Feb. 1924.*

HOARE, William Douro, CBE 1920; Director Bank of England since 1898; Lieutenant City of London; *b* 1 Aug. 1862; *s* of late Richard Hoare of Marden Hill, Hertford, and Susan, *d* of Col Tomkinson of Willington Hall, Tarporley, Cheshire; *m* 1891, Ida Mary, *d* of late Lachlan M. Rate of Milton Court, Dorking, and 9 South Audley Street, W. *Educ:* Winchester, 1875–80; Trinity Coll., Camb., 1880–83 (MA). *Address:* Guessens, Welwyn; 8 and 9 Austin Friars, EC. *T:* London Wall 6756; 88 St James's Street, SW1; North Lodge, Cromer, Norfolk. *TA:* Taurus, London. *Clubs:* Brooks's, Argentine, Beefsteak. *Died 10 April 1928.*

HOBART, Sir Robert Henry, 1st Bt, *cr* 1914; KCVO 1902; CB 1885; *b* 13 Sept. 1836; *e s* of late Hon. and Very Rev. Henry Lewis Hobart, DD (Dean of Windsor and Wolverhampton, Registrar of the Order of the Garter, 4th *s* of George, 3rd Earl, and Albinia, Countess of Buckinghamshire); *m* 1869, Hon. Julia Trollope, *d* of 1st Baron Kesteven; one *s* one *d. Educ:* Charterhouse; Trinity Hall, Cambridge (LLB). Private Secretary to Marquis of Hartington (8th Duke of Devonshire) as Sec. of State for War (twice), Postmaster-Gen., Chief Sec. for Ireland, and Sec. of State for India, 1863–74, and 1880–85;

to four Secretaries for Scotland, 1886–87, 1892–95; Secretary to the Earl Marshal (Duke of Norfolk) for the purposes of the coronation of their Majesties King Edward VII and Queen Alexandra, 1901–2 (Coronation Medal); Gold Stick Officer at the Coronation of their Majesties King George V and Queen Mary, 1911 (Coronation Medal). Official Verderer of the New Forest, 1906; DL and JP Co. Middlesex; JP Co. London and Southampton; MP (L) New Forest, 1906–10. *Heir: s* Claud Vere Cavendish Hobart, *b* 12 March 1870. *Address:* Langdown, Hythe, Southampton. *T:* Hythe 25, Southampton. *Clubs:* Travellers', National Liberal.

Died 4 Aug. 1928.

HOBBINS, Robert, ISO 1909; *b* 3 Dec. 1844; 3rd *s* of late Rev. F. C. T. Hobbins, Vicar of Bedingham, Norfolk; *m* 1873, Jane, *o d* of Arthur Jones of Priors Lee, Shifnal, Shropshire; one *d. Educ:* Norwich Grammar School. Formerly Collector of Customs at Southampton and Belfast. *Address:* 2 Lavington Road, West Ealing, W.

Died 21 Sept. 1922.

HOBHOUSE, Sir Charles Parry, 3rd Bt, *cr* 1812; JP; *b* Calcutta, 2 Jan. 1825; 3rd *s* of Henry William Hobhouse, 3rd *s* of Sir Benjamin Hobhouse, 1st Bt; *S* uncle, 1869; *m* 1st, 1855, Edith Lucy (*d* 1867), *d* of Sir Thomas E. M. Turton, 2nd Bt; one *s* five *d* (and one *d* decd); 2nd, 1868, Anna Maria, *d* of Alexander Sawers, merchant, Calcutta; one *s* three *d* (and one *d* decd). *Educ:* East Sheen, Dr Pinckney; Rugby; Dr Arnold; EIC Haileybury. Bengal Civil Service, 1844–71; member Bengal Council and Imperial Legislative Council, East Indies; Judge of High Court, Calcutta. Owner of 1,600 acres. *Recreation:* captain cricket club, Calcutta. *Heir: s* Rt Hon. Charles Edward Henry Hobhouse, *b* 30 June 1862. *Address:* Manor House, Monkton Farleigh, Bradford-on-Avon, Wilts. *TA:* Bathford.

Died 30 Dec. 1916.

HOBHOUSE, Rev. Walter, DD; Canon of Gloucester, 1913–20; Examining Chaplain to the Bishop of Birmingham since 1905; *b* 1862; 2nd *s* of late Rt Rev. Bishop Hobhouse and first wife, Mary, *d* of Gen. Hon. John Brodrick; *m* 1st, 1887, Mary Violet (*d* 1901), *y d* of Edmund M'Neill, DL, Craigdunn, Co. Antrim, Ireland; one *s* one *d*; 2nd, 1904, Edith (*d* 1921), *y d* of Rev. William Owen, Vicar of Damerham, Wilts; one *s* two *d. Educ:* Eton (Newcastle Scholar, 1880); New College, Oxford (Scholar, 1880–84; 1st class Moderations, 1881; 1st class Lit. Hum. 1884; Chancellor's Prize English Essay, 1885; Chancellor's Prize Latin Essay, 1886; *proxime accessit* Ireland scholarship, 1883–84). Fellow and Lecturer of Hertford College, 1884–87; Student and Tutor of Christ Church, Oxford, 1887–94; Headmaster of Durham School, 1894–99; editor of the Guardian, 1900–5; Bampton Lecturer at Oxford for 1909; Hon. Canon and Chancellor of Birmingham Cathedral, 1905–13; Archdeacon of Aston, 1912–13, of Gloucester, 1917–19. *Publications:* Theory and Practice of Ancient Education, 1885; The Spiritual Standard and other Sermons, 1896; Otium Didascali, 1898; The Church and the World in Idea and in History (Bampton Lectures, 1909). *Recreations:* golf, travel. *Club:* Athenæum. *Died 30 Oct. 1928.*

HOBSON, Sir Albert John, Kt 1922; JP Sheffield; Chairman of Thomas Turner and Co., Ltd; Director of the Birmingham Small Arms Co., Smallheath, Birmingham; Chairman of William Jessop and Son, Ltd, steel manufacturers, Brightside Works, Sheffield; Vice-Chairman of the High Speed Steel Alloys Co., Widnes; and Chairman of J. J. Saville and Co., Ltd, steel manufacturers, Sheffield; *s* of Alderman John Hobson, scissors manufacturer, and Thyrza A. Carr, *d* of Alderman John Carr, a member of the first Council of the borough, later city, of Sheffield; *m* Maude L. (decd), 2nd *d* of late G. H. Faber, MP. Ex-Master Cutler; ex-Pres. of Association of British Chambers of Commerce, London, 1920; Pro-Chancellor and LLD of the Sheffield University; Chairman of the Council for University Superannuation, London; President, Fisher Institution (Pension Charity); Alderman of the City of Sheffield; Lord Mayor, Sheffield, 1911–12. *Recreations:* politics, public work generally. *Address:* Esholt, Ranmoor, Sheffield. *TA:* Esholt, Sheffield. *T:* Sheffield 1721. *M:* WA 1295. *Clubs:* Devonshire, Junior Constitutional; Sheffield, Sheffield.

Died 20 April 1923.

HOBSON, Ven. Edward Waller, MA; Archdeacon of Armagh since 1915; Examining Chaplain to Lord Primate of All Ireland; *b* 5 Dec. 1851; *s* of late Canon John Meade Hobson, MA; *m* 1891, Frances Maria, *d* of late Robert Westley Hall-Dare, of Theydon Bois, Essex, and Newtownbarry, Ireland; no *c. Educ:* Atherstone School, Warwickshire; Royal School, Dungannon; Trinity Coll., Dublin University (ex-Royal Scholar, ex-University Scholar, First Honours and Silver Medallist). Curate of The Mariners' Church, Kingstown, Co. Dublin, 1876–78; Portadown, Ireland, 1878–81; Rector of Moy,

Co. Tyrone, 1881–95; Rector of Derryloran (Cookstown), Ireland, 1895–96; Portadown, Ireland, 1896–1915; Librarian Public Library, Armagh, from 1915. *Recreation:* formerly football; played for All Ireland (Rugby Union) against All England, 1875. *Address:* The Library, Armagh. *Died 17 April 1924.*

HODDER-WILLIAMS, Sir (John) Ernest, Kt 1919; CVO 1921; publisher; *b* Bromley, Kent, 16 Sept. 1876; *e s* of John Williams, Bromley, Kent; *g s* of Matthew Henry Hodder; *m* 1st, Ethel Oddy (*d* 1918); 2nd, Lilian, 2nd *d* of J. R. Pakeman. *Educ:* City of London School; University College, London; Paris; Berlin. Chairman of the firm of Hodder & Stoughton, Ltd, of London, book publishers and newspaper proprietors; Chairman Wakley & Son, Ltd, proprietors of The Lancet; Member of the City of London Corporation. KGStJ. Officer of the Crown of Italy, 1920, Commander, 1921; King Albert's Medal, 1920. *Publications:* The Life of Sir George Williams, Founder of the YMCA; (with E. C. Vivian) The Way of the Red Cross (Preface by Queen Alexandra). *Address:* 23 Cadogan Place, SW1. *T:* Sloane 3540; St Paul's House, Warwick Square, EC4. *T:* City 3704. *Clubs:* Devonshire, Whitefriars. *Died 8 April 1927.*

HODDING, Col John, CIE 1903; VD; Chief Manager of the Estates of The Hon. Sir Khajeh Salimollah, KCSI, Nawab Bahadur of Dacca; formerly commanding Behar Light Horse; *b* 1854; *m* 1880, Mary, *d* of Thomas Macgregor, Inverness. *Address:* Dacca, Eastern Bengal, India. *Club:* Sports. *Died 21 March 1919.*

HODGE, Albert H., RBS; sculptor; *b* 1875; Scotch; *m* Jessie Dunn Dunlop; one *s* one *d. Educ:* Glasgow. Trained at the Glasgow School of Art, in architecture (gold medal, silver medal, and 4 bronze medals); in the National Competition, also passed; 1st place in the United Kingdom in Architectural designs examination; exhibited works at the Royal Academy; executed groups of sculpture for town halls, Hull, Cardiff, Glamorgan, Deptford; public statues—Queen Victoria, Glasgow; Robert Burns, Stirling. *Recreations:* golf, angling. *Address:* 50 Bedford Gardens, Kensington, W. *Club:* Arts.

Died 27 Jan. 1918.

HODGE, Rev. Canon Edward Grose, MA; FES; Canon of Birmingham, 1919; *m* Florence Amy, *y d* of Col J. T. Smith, RE, FRS; two *s. Educ:* Trinity Hall, Cambridge. Ordained to the curacy of St Matthew's, Bayswater, 1878; after seven years was asked to organise the Diocese of London for the CETS; Vicar of Holy Trinity, Leicester, 1890; Vicar of St James', Holloway, 1893; Rector of Holy Trinity, S Marylebone, 1897, and became Rural Dean; Vicar of Paddington, 1911–19, and Rural Dean; Rector and Rural Dean of Birmingham, 1919–25; Prebendary of St Paul's Cathedral, 1911–19; Whitehead Professor at the London College of Divinity, 1895–1919; Proctor in Convocation and Member of the National Assembly, 1921–25; a member of most of the larger Church Patronage Trusts, the great Church Societies, and many Diocesan Committees. *Publications:* pamphlets on Church Finance; series of papers on Confirmation. *Recreations:* natural history, chiefly entomology; golf. *Address:* Halfacre, Woking. *Died 2 April 1928.*

HODGES, Rt. Rev. Edward Noel, DD; Rector of St Cuthbert's, Bedford, 1907–16; Archdeacon of Bedford, 1910–14; Assistant Bishop of St Albans, 1914–24; *b* 1849; *m* 1877, Alice, *d* of Capt. Shirreff, Moray, NB; one *s* two *d. Educ:* Queen's College, Oxford. Ordained 1873; Tutor Mission College, Islington, 1873–77; Principal, Noble College, Masulipatam, 1877–86; Trinity College, Candy, 1886–89; Bishop of Travancore and Cochin, 1890–1904; Assistant Bishop of Durham, 1904–6; Assistant Bishop of Ely, 1907–14; retired, 1924. *Address:* Silverburn, Hoddesdon, Herts.

Died 18 May 1928.

HODGES, Ven. George, MA; Hon. Canon of Ely, 1898–1912; Canon Residentiary since 1912; Commissary to the Bishop of Ely since 1903; Archdeacon of Sudbury since 1902; *b* 1851; *s* of Rev. George Hodges, Vicar of St Andrew's, Hastings; *m* Agnes Helena (*d* 1916), *e d* of William Sanders, MD; six *s* one *d. Educ:* St John's Coll., Cambridge; private tuition. BA 1873; MA 1888; ordained to curacy of Milton-next-Sittingbourne, 1878; Curate of Stoke-by-Nayland, 1877; Vicar of Stoke-by-Nayland, 1881–88; Vicar of St James's, Bury St Edmunds, 1888–1912; Rural Dean of Thingoes, 1888–1902; Examining Chaplain to Bishop of Ely, 1906–14; to Bishop of S Edmundsbury, 1914; nominated to St James's, Piccadilly, 1894, but the Marquis of Bristol lost the patronage, and he was not instituted; preached before Queen Victoria in the private chapel, Windsor, 1892. Select Preacher before the University of Cambridge, 1894; late Chaplain of 3rd Suffolk Vol. Batt.; Past Provincial Grand Chaplain of Suffolk PM Lodge, 1908; Grand Chaplain in the Grand Lodge

of England, 1908; Chaplain to the High Sheriff of Cambs, 1919. *Address:* Archdeacon's Lodgings, Ely. *Club:* Constitutional.
Died 30 Aug. 1922.

HODGES, Hon. Sir Henry Edward Agincourt, Kt 1918; Puisne Judge of the Supreme Court, Victoria, since 1889; Chancellor of Diocese of Melbourne since 1889; *b* Liverpool, Oct. 1844; *m* 1878, Margaret, *d* of George Knox; one *s* two *d*. *Educ:* Church of England Grammar School and University of Melbourne. Went to Australia, 1854. *Address:* Homeden, Toorak, Melbourne, Victoria. *Club:* Melbourne. *Died 8 Aug. 1919.*

HODGETT, Rev. Richard; Pastor, Ballymena Baptist Church since 1922; Lecturer, Irish Baptist College; *b* Dungannon, Co. Tyrone, 30 April 1884; *s* of Edward and Mary Hodgett; *m* 1912, Mary Elizabeth Kerr; two *s* three *d*. *Educ:* The Irish Baptist College. Pastor, Phibsborough Baptist Church, Dublin, 1912–14; Sharkill Road Baptist Church, Belfast, 1914–22; President, Baptist Union of Ireland, 1925–26. *Publications:* The Spirit Filled Church; The Doctrines and Practices of The Irish Baptists. *Address:* The Manse, Mount Street, Ballymena, Co. Antrim. *TA:* Hodgett Ballymena. *M:* IA 6530.
Died 26 Sept. 1927.

HODGINS, Lt-Col Frederick Owen, DSO 1917; Royal Canadian Engineers; *b* Ottawa, 6 Oct. 1887; 2nd *s* of Major-General W. E. Hodgins; *m* 1921, Rebecca Kathleen, *e d* of Henry Blakeney, Ottawa; one *d*. *Educ:* Royal Military Coll. of Canada (graduated with honours, 1907). Lieut Royal Canadian Engineers, 1907; Major, 1915; Bt and Temp. Lt-Col, 1918; went to France with 1st Canadian Division, Feb. 1915; served continuously till formation of Canadian Army Corps, Sept. 1915; Staff Officer to Chief Engineer, Sept. 1915–Feb. 1917; Staff Capt., War Office (Directorate of Fortifications and Works (aviation)), Aug. 1917–March 1918; specially employed, Headquarters Canadian Army Corps, March 1918–Aug. 1918; on re-organisation Canadian Engineers, 1918–19; Staff Officer to GOC Canadian Engineers and Chief Engineer Canadian Army Corps, specially employed Militia Headquarters, Ottawa, 1919; passed Staff College, Camberley, 1920; General Staff Officer, Military District No 3, Kingston, Ont, 1921 (despatches thrice, DSO). Associate Member, The Engineering Institute of Canada. *Recreation:* golf. *Address:* 1 Villa St Clare Apartments, Barrie Street, Kingston, Ont. *Clubs:* Junior Naval and Military; Country, Ottawa; Frontenac, Kingston; Cataraqui Golf and Country, Kingston. *Died 13 Nov. 1924.*

HODGINS, Rev. Joseph Rogerson Edmond Cotter, MA; Rector of Whitstone, Exeter, 1917; Vicar of St James's, Birkdale, 1905–17; Hon. Canon of Liverpool, 1896; Proctor in Convocation for Archdeaconry of Liverpool, 1906; Rural Dean of North Meols, 1913–17; *s* of late Rev. E. P. Hodgins, DD, Vicar of St Stephen's, Edge Hill, and Margaret Anne, *d* of Rev. Prebendary J. R. Cotter, MA (*g s* of Sir James Cotter, 1st Bt, MP); *m* 1880, Theresa Georgina Adelaide, *d* of Robert Conway Hickson, JP, of Fermoyle, Co. Kerry (High Sheriff, 1855); one *s* three *d*. *Educ:* Liverpool College; Emmanuel College, Camb. (Foundation Scholar, Thorpe Scholar, Hubbard exhibitioner and prizeman). BA (26th wrangler); 1873; MA 1876. Ordained Deacon, 1874; Priest, 1875, by Bishop of Chester; Curate of St Jude's, West Derby, 1874–75; Curate of St Luke's, Liverpool, 1875–81; Vicar of St Cyprian, Edge Hill, 1881–1905; Rural Dean of Liverpool (South), 1902–5; Surrogate, 1887. *Publications:* The Sunday School in relation to the Daily Life of the Young; While there's Life there's Hope, etc. *Recreations:* cricket, boating, golf. *Address:* Whitstone Rectory, Exeter. *Died May 1919.*

HODGSON, Rev. Francis Greaves; Rector of Aldwincle, Northamptonshire, since 1891; Hon. Canon of Peterborough Cathedral since 1901; Rural Dean of Higham; *b* 8 Sept. 1840; *s* of F. R. Hodgson, Oakley, near Manchester; *m* 1868, Fanny Satterfield (*d* 1917), *d* of James Bellhouse, Victoria Park, Manchester; two *s* two *d*. *Educ:* Rugby; Exeter College, Oxford; Cuddesdon College. Curate at Buxton, 1867–70; Rector of Pilton, 1870–91. *Address:* Aldwincle, St Peter's Rectory, Thrapston. *TA:* Aldwincle. *Club:* Royal Societies.
Died 12 June 1920.

HODGSON, Rev. Francis Roger, MA; *m*; no *c*. *Educ:* Rugby School; Corpus Christi College, Oxford. Deacon, 1877; Priest, 1878; Missionary Incumbent (UMCA) of St John the Evangelist, Mbweni, Zanzibar, 1877–89; Curate of Higher Mediety of Malpas, 1878–79; Archdeacon of Zanzibar, 1882–89; Vicar of Frithelstock, 1890–93; UMCA Secretary for West of England and Wales, 1893–1909; for South of England and Oxford, 1909–18; Curate in charge of St Anne's, Saunton, 1920. *Address:* St Anne's, Saunton, N Devon.
Died 4 Nov. 1920.

HODGSON, Sir Frederic Mitchell, KCMG 1899 (CMG 1891); VD 1897; *b* 22 Nov. 1851; *s* of late Rev. O. A. Hodgson, Rector of East Stoke, Wareham; *m* 1883, Mary Alice, Lady of Grace of the Order St John of Jerusalem (author of The Siege of Kumassi), *d* of late W. A. G. Young, CMG, Governor of Gold Coast; one *d*. Was in Secretary's Office, Post Office Dept, 1868–82; Postmaster-General, British Guiana, 1882–88; Colonial Sec., Gold Coast, 1888–98; administered the Govt on several occasions; Governor, 1898–1900; Governor and Commander-in-Chief, Barbados, 1900–4; Governor British Guiana, 1904–11. Formerly Capt. in 24th Middlesex RV; Capt. British Guiana RV, 1886–88; Major commanding Gold Coast RV, which he raised in 1892; Major comdg Barbados Volunteer Force, which he raised in 1901. KGStJ. *Address:* 21 Rosary Gardens, South Kensington, SW7. *T:* Kensington 6047. *Clubs:* Conservative, Ranelagh, West Indian. *Died 6 July 1925.*

HODGSON, George Bryan, JP; Joint General Manager, Press Association; *b* 29 July 1863; *s* of John Hodgson of Toft Hill, Bishop Auckland; *m* 1888, Mary, *d* of Thomas Forster of Benwell. *Educ:* privately. Editor, Shields Daily Gazette, 1892–1917; Assistant Manager, Press Association, 1917–18. President Institute of Journalists, 1911–12. *Publications:* The Life Story of James Annand; The Borough of South Shields; The Banks of Tyne, etc. *Address:* Byron House, 85 Fleet Street, EC4. *Club:* Authors'.
Died 31 March 1926.

HODGSON, Rt. Rev. Henry Bernard, DD; first Bishop of St Edmundsbury and Ipswich since 1914; *b* Barton Hall, Penrith, 10 March 1856; *s* of George Courtenay Hodgson, Vicar of Barton, and Elizabeth Buckham; *m* 1882, Penelope, *d* of Admiral Richard Laird Warren; three *s* one *d*. *Educ:* Shrewsbury School; Queen's College and Christ Church, Oxford. 1st class Mods, 1876; 1st class Final Classical School, 1878; student of Christ Church, 1878–85; assistant master Elizabeth College, Guernsey, 1879–81; Deacon, 1879; Priest, 1880; Vicar of Staverton, Northants, 1881–85; Headmaster of Birkenhead School, 1885–86; Vicar of Thornbury, Gloucestershire, 1886–97; Rural Dean of Norham, 1897; Vicar of Berwick-on-Tweed, 1897–1914; Archdeacon of Lindisfarne, 1904–14; Honorary Canon of Newcastle Cathedral and Examining Chaplain to the Bishop, 1900–14. *Address:* Bishop's House, Ipswich.
Died 28 Feb. 1921.

HODGSON, Rev. Prof. James Muscutt; Principal and Baxter Professor of Theology in the Theological Hall of the Congregational Churches of Scotland, 1894–1916; *b* Cockermouth; *e s* of late John Hodgson of Rose Bank, Cockermouth; *m* Emily A., *e d* of late Charles Williams, JP, of Salisbury. *Educ:* Cockermouth Grammar School; Glasgow University (MA, DD); Lancashire Independent College. DSc Edinburgh University. Congregational Minister, Uttoxeter, Staffs, 1865–75; Professor of Apologetics and Comparative Religion at Lancashire Independent College, Manchester, 1875–94. *Publications:* Religion—the Quest of the Ideal; Theologia Pectoris: Outlines of Religious Faith and Doctrine, founded on Intuition and Experience; Philosophy and Faith; Philosophy and Revelation; Facts and Ideas in Theology. *Address:* Bryn Glas, Conway, North Wales.
Died 12 March 1923.

HODGSON, Ven. Robert; Archdeacon of Stafford, 1898–1910; Prebendary of Lichfield since 1894; *b* Hoxne, Suffolk, 11 July 1844; *e s* of Rev. John Hodgson, Vicar of Hoxne; *m* 1st, 1870; 2nd, 1878. *Educ:* Eton (gained a Foundation scholarship, 1858); Oriel Coll., Oxford (MA). Scholar and Exhibitioner, 1863; 1st Class in Moderations, 1864; 3rd Class in Lit. Hum., 1867. Curate of Stoke-upon-Trent, 1868–72; Vicar of Christ Church, West Bromwich, 1872–83; Rural Dean of Handsworth, 1893–98; Vicar of Walsall and Rural Dean, 1883–92; Proctor for Archdeaconry of Stafford, 1895; Rector of Handsworth, 1892–1904; Canon-Residentiary of Lichfield, 1907. *Recreations:* gardening, golf. *Address:* Lombard Croft, Lichfield. *Died 29 Jan. 1917.*

HODGSON, Robert Kirkman, JP; *b* 1850; *o s* of late Kirkman Daniel Hodgson, MP, of Ashgrove, Kent, and Frances, *d* of late John Laforey Butler of Southgate; *m* 1875, Lady Honora Janet (Nora), 3rd *d* of 9th Earl of Cork; one *s* one *d* (and two *s* killed in action). *Educ:* Eton; Trinity College, Cambridge; MA. *Address:* Gavelacre, Longparish, Hampshire; 77 Eaton Square, SW1. *T:* Victoria 480. *Clubs:* Athenæum, Brooks's, Travellers'.
Died 26 May 1924.

HODGSON, Ven. Thomas; Archdeacon of Huntingdon since 1915; Vicar of St Neot's since 1912; Rural Dean, 1902. *Educ:* Hatfield Hall; Durham University (Foundation Scholar). Ordained, 1878; Curate of St Andrew, Bishop Auckland, 1878–79; Asst Master, St George's School, Brampton, 1879–83; Curate, 1883–90; Head-Master, Huntingdon Grammar School, 1884–90; Rector of Eynesbury, 1890–1912; Hon. Canon, Ely, 1911. *Address:* The Vicarage, St Neot's, Huntingdon. *Died 28 Sept. 1921.*

HODGSON, Rev. William, MA; Vicar of Aston, Birmingham, since 1917; Hon. Canon of Birmingham, 1917; Examining Chaplain to Bishop of Sodor and Man, 1916; *s* of late Rev. William Hodgson (Vicar of Christ Church, Colne, Lancs, 1837–74, and Curate of Haworth, Yorks, under Rev. Patrick Brontë, 1835–37 (father of Charlotte and Emily Brontë)); *m;* two *s* three *d. Educ:* University of London, Int. BA 1883; Merton College, Oxford, BA (1st Class Theological School), 1887; MA 1891. Deacon, 1887; Priest, 1888; Curate at St Peter-le-Bailey, Oxford, 1887–90; Curate in charge of St Michael's, Claughton, 1890–93; Vicar of St Mary and St Paul, Widnes, 1893–98; Emmanuel Church, Everton, Liverpool, 1898–1901; St John, Waterloo, Liverpool, 1901–12; Vicar of St Andrew, Southport, 1912–17; Hon. Canon of Liverpool, 1916. *Address:* Aston Vicarage, Birmingham.

Died 25 Dec. 1919.

HODGSON, William Hope; 2nd Lieutenant Royal Field Artillery; *b* 15 Nov. 1877; 2nd *s* of Rev. Samuel Hodgson. *Educ:* abroad. Some years at sea as an officer in Mercantile Marine; commenced writing, 1902; first book published, 1907; commissioned July 1915 (RFA); gazetted out of the army, 10 June 1916, owing to ill-health due to injuries received on active service; eventually regained health and was recommissioned, 18 March 1917. *Publications:* The Boats of the Glen Carrig, 1907; The House on the Borderland, 1908; The Ghost Pirates, 1909; The Night Land, 1912; Carnacki the Ghost Finder, 1913; Men of the Deep Waters, 1914; The Luck of the Strong, 1916; Captain Gault, 1917. *Address:* Lisswood, Borth SO, Cardigan, Wales; Chalet Mathilde, Sanary, Var, France.

Died 17 April 1918.

HODSDON, Sir James (William Beeman), KBE 1920 (CBE 1919); JP; MD, FRCSEd; President of Royal College of Surgeons, Edinburgh, 1914–17, Vice-President, 1917–19; Consulting Surgeon, Royal Infirmary, Edinburgh; *b* 1858; *s* of late Francis E. Hodsdon; *m* 1889, Joan, *d* of late William Raffin, Edinburgh. *Educ:* Sherborne School; Queen's College, Belfast; University and School of Medicine, Edinburgh; London; Vienna; Paris. Representative of RCS Edinburgh on General Medical Council; Member of the Dental Board of the United Kingdom; late Senior Surgeon, Royal Infirmary, Edinburgh; late Senior University Lecturer on Clinical Surgery; late Chairman of Committee of Management of Scottish Conjoint Board; Chairman of Governing Board, School of Medicine of Royal Colleges; late Examiner in Surgery, RCS Edin.; late Major RAMC (T), 2nd Scottish General Hospital (CBE, despatches twice). Late Lecturer in Surgery, Surgeons' Hall, Edinburgh; Examiner in Surgery, Universities of Edinburgh and Durham and Queen's University of Belfast. *Publications:* papers on various surgical subjects. *Recreations:* fishing, shooting, curling, golfing. *Address:* 6 Chester Street, Edinburgh. *T:* 2330. *Clubs:* Royal Societies; University, Edinburgh.

Died 28 May 1928.

HODSON, Col Frederic Arthur, CBE 1919; Commandant Northern Rhodesia Police, 1912–19; retired with rank of Colonel, 1919; *b* 20 Oct. 1866; *s* of late M. Storr Hodson, Crayhe, Easingwold, Yorkshire; unmarried. Enlisted 65th Regt, 1st Batt. Yorks and Lancs Regt, 1889; transferred 84th Regt 2nd Batt., Natal, 1892; served through Matabeleland Rebellion with Mounted Infantry Company Yorks and Lancs Regt, 1896; joined British South Africa Police, S Rhodesia, Nov. 1896; South Africa War, 1900–1 (Queen's and King's medal); Sub-Inspector BSA Police, 1902; seconded to Barotse Native Police, North-Western Rhodesia, with rank of Captain, 1903; Major, 1906; Second in Command Barotse Native Police, 1906; Lieut-Colonel Commandant Northern Rhodesia Police, 1912; temporary rank Colonel 1916 to end of Campaign; OC Lines of Communication General Northey's Column; commanded Forces North Eastern Border, German East Africa Campaign, 1914–16 (despatches, CBE). *Recreations:* tennis, golf. *Address:* The Cottage, Fulford, York. *T:* Fulford 34. *Clubs:* Sports; Yorkshire, York.

Died 31 Jan. 1925.

HODSON, Col George Benjamin, CB 1911; DSO 1902; Assistant Quartermaster-General Indian Army; *b* 3 Oct. 1863; *m* 1910, Dorothy Clara, *d* of Mr Murray of 42 Clanricarde Gardens, SW; one *d.* Entered army, 1882; Captain, 1893; Major, 1901; Lt-Col 1905; Colonel, 1909; served Egypt, 1882 (medal, bronze star); Burmese Expedition, 1885–87 (despatches, medal with clasp); Hazara, 1891 (clasp); NW

Frontier, India, 1897–98 (despatches, medal and clasp); Southern Nigeria, 1902; Aro Expedition (despatches, medal with clasp, DSO). *Address:* Lahore, Punjab, India. *Club:* United Service.

Died 25 Jan. 1916.

HODSON, Sir Robert Adair, 4th Bt, *cr* 1789; Lieutenant-Colonel commanding 4th Battalion Royal Irish Fusiliers, retired 1907; Hon. Colonel 1907; *b* 29 Sept. 1853; *s* of Sir George Frederick Hodson, 3rd Bt and Meriel Anne, *d* of Rev. Richard Neville; S father, 1888; *m* 1911, Emily Frances Louisa, *e d* of late Colonel G. Beresford, RA, of Woodhouse, Co. Waterford. *Educ:* Haileybury College. Owner of about 1,000 acres. *Heir: nephew* Edmond Adair Hodson, *b* 22 March 1893. *Address:* Holybrooke, Bray, Co. Wicklow.

Died 3 Jan. 1921.

HOERNLE, Augustus Frederic Rudolf, CIE 1897; MA (Oxford); PhD (Tübingen); *b* Agra (East India), 19 Oct. 1841; 2nd *s* of late Rev. T. C. Hoernle, CMS; *m* 1877, Sophie, *d* of R. Romig of Bonn (Germany); one *s. Educ:* public school in Esslingen and Stuttgart; Universities of Basel, Tübingen, and London. Church Missionary in Mirat, 1865; Professor in Jay Narain's Coll., Benares, 1870; returned to England, 1874; Principal Cathedral Mission College, Calcutta, 1877; joined Indian Educational Service, 1881; Principal of the Calcutta Madrasah, 1881; retired 1899; specially interested in archaeology, epigraphy, palæography, etc. Decorated for linguistic, numismatic, and archæological research. *Publications:* Comparative Grammar of the North Indian Languages; Comparative Dictionary of the Bihari Language; Edition of the Bower Manuscript, of Chanda's Prakrit Grammar, of the Seventh Anga of the Jains; Report on the British Collection of Central Asian Antiquities; Studies in the Medicine of Ancient India: Part I Osteology; History of India; numerous contributions to the Journal of Royal Asiatic Society, the Asiatic Society of Bengal, the Indian Antiquary, etc. *Address:* 8 Northmoor Road, Oxford.

Died 12 Nov. 1918.

HOEY, William, MA, DLit QUI; MA Oxon; MRAS; *b* Dungannon, 2 July 1849; *s* of late Rev. W. Hoey; *m* 1882, Eleanor, *d* of late Nathaniel Ferguson, of Mount Pottinger House, Belfast; three *s. Educ:* Grammar School, Drogheda; Connexional School, Dublin; Queen's College, Belfast. Entered Indian Civil Service, 1870; proceeded to India, 1872; appointed to Oudh, and subsequently NWP; Commissioner of Gorakhpur, 1897; Fellow of Allahabad University; Member of Provincial Numismatic Committee; retired, 1900; Lecturer on Indian History and Hindustani, Dublin University, 1903; Lecturer on Hindustani, Oxford University, 1906. *Publications:* Trades and Manufactures of Northern India; Translation of Oldenberg's Buddha: His Life, his Doctrine, his Order, from the German, and of The Life of Asafuddaulah, and Memoirs of Delhi and Fyzabad from the Persian; Urdu Praxis; Going East; contributions to the journals of the Royal Asiatic Society and Asiatic Society of Bengal. *Recreations:* interested in Indian history, archæology and numismatics, and in Persian. *Address:* 8 Bradmore Road, Oxford.

Died April 1919.

HOFFERT, Hermann H., DSc (London); FPhysS; HM Inspector (Divisional) of Schools Board of Education, Technological Branch; *b* Liverpool, 25 Dec. 1860; *o surv. s* of late Henry A. Hoffert, of German descent, naturalised Englishman; *m* 1891, Annie, *e d* of late E. Ward, of Reading, Berks; two *s* two *d. Educ:* Crediton Grammar School; Weymouth Collegiate School. Royal College of Science and Royal School of Mines, 1876–81; Associate Royal School of Mines in Geological, Metallurgical, and Mining Divisions, with De la Beche medal in mining; Neill Arnott medal for Experimental Physics, London University; DSc in Experimental Physics, 1885; Assistant and afterwards Demonstrator of Physics, Royal College of Science; Inspector of Schools under the Science and Art Department, 1893; in charge of the North-Western Division of England for Inspection of Science and Technical Schools under the Board of Education. *Publications:* papers to Physical Society of London on colour-combining apparatus and intermittent lightning flashes. *Recreations:* cycling, tennis, photography.

HOFMEYR, George Morgan, BA (Cape University); Rector of Grey University College, Bloemfontein, since 1928; *b* Montagu, Cape Colony, 3 July 1867; *s* of Rev. S. Hofmeyr, DD, and Anna Morgan, *d* of Rev. George Morgan; *m* Anna E., *d* of Prof. P. J. G. de Vos; one *s* one *d. Educ:* Victoria College, Stellenbosch. Devoted more than seven years to teaching; admitted as an Attorney-at-law, Notary Public, and Conveyancer of the Transvaal High Court, 1897; practised at Johannesburg and Germiston until 1906; served as Registrar and Treasurer to the Victoria College; Secretary for Education Union

of South Africa, 1910–27; retired, 1927. *Recreations:* gardening, etc. *Address:* Grey University College, Bloemfontein, South Africa.
Died 31 Oct. 1928.

HOGAN, Henry Charles; Member of National Assembly of the Church of England; *b* 29 Sept. 1860; 2nd *s* of late Cole Hogan; *m* 1883, Emma Maud Mary, *o d* of late George Alexander Stead; three *s* one *d*. *Educ:* privately. Entered ecclesiastical journalism 1881; Sub-Editor of the Record, 1881–1905; Editor of the Layman, 1905–8; Editor of the Record from 1908, also Editor of the Churchman from 1914, and of other Church and homiletical publications; late Hon. Secretary of Church of England Young Men's Society; Life Governor Cheltenham Training College; Vice-President Church Pastoral Aid Society; Chairman Barbican Mission to the Jews. *Recreation:* change of work. *Address:* 10 Longley Road, Tooting Graveney, SW17. *T:* Streatham 2980. *Died 31 Dec. 1924.*

HOGAN, James Francis; author, journalist; *b* Tipperary, 29 Dec. 1855; while an infant, parents emigrated to Australia and settled near Melbourne; unmarried. *Educ:* St Patrick's College, Melbourne. Entered Education Department, Victoria, 1873; joined literary staff of Melbourne Argus, 1881; settled in London, 1887. MP (AP) Mid Division of Tipperary, 1893–1900. *Publications:* An Australian Christmas Collection, 1886; History of the Irish in Australia, 1887; The Australian in London, 1888, The Lost Explorer, 1890; The Convict King, 1891; Robert Lowe, Viscount Sherbrooke, 1893; The Sister Dominions, 1895; The Gladstone Colony, 1898. *Recreations:* walking, touring, music, the drama. *Died 9 Nov. 1924.*

HOGAN, Rt. Rev. Mgr John F., DD; President, St Patrick's College, Maynooth, since 1912; *b* Coolreagh, Co. Clare, 1858. *Educ:* Ennis Diocesan College; St Sulpice, Paris; Freiburg in Breisgau. Ordained, 1882; spent some years for special studies in France and Germany; Professor of Modern Languages at Maynooth, 1886; edited Irish Ecclesiastical Record for close on twenty years; gave evidence on Irish University Education before the Robertson Commission; took part in organising reception of King George and Queen Mary, 1911; Senator of the National University of Ireland, 1913; Pro-Vice-Chancellor, 1914; Domestic Prelate of His Holiness the Pope, 1914. *Publications:* The Life and Works of Dante; Irish Catholics and Trinity College; Maynooth College and the Laity; many historical and theological essays in various reviews. *Address:* St Patrick's College, Maynooth. *TA:* Maynooth, Ireland.
Died 24 Nov. 1918.

HOGARTH, David George, CMG 1918; MA; DLitt Oxon; Hon. LittD Cantab; FBA 1905; Keeper of the Ashmolean Museum since 1909; President of the Royal Geographical Society since 1925; *b* Barton-on-Humber, 23 May 1862; *e s* of Rev. George Hogarth, Vicar; *m* 1894, Laura Violet, *y d* of Charles Uppleby, Barrow Hall; one *s*. *Educ:* Winchester; Magdalen College, Oxford. Craven Fellow, 1886; Tutor of Magdalen, 1886–93; Director, British School at Athens, 1897–1900; Statutory Commissioner under the Oxford and Cambridge Universities Act, 1923; Fellow of Magdalen College, Oxford; Radcliffe Trustee; Schweich Lecturer, 1924; FRSA, FRGS (Founder's Gold Medal, 1917); Vice-Pres. Hellenic Soc. Comdr RNVR, 1915–19, and Director of Arab Bureau, Cairo, 1916; Order of Nile 3rd class, 1917; Order of Nahda (Hejaz) 2nd class, 1919; explored Asia Minor, Syria, etc, and conducted excavations in Cyprus, Egypt, Crete, Syria and Melos. *Publications:* Devia Cypria, 1890; Modern and Ancient Roads in Eastern Asia Minor, 1892; A Wandering Scholar in the Levant, 1896; Philip and Alexander of Macedon, 1897; Authority and Archæology, 1899; The Nearer East, 1902; The Penetration of Arabia, 1904; The Archaic Artemisia of Ephesus, 1908; Ionia and the East, 1909; Accidents of an Antiquary's Life, 1910; The Ancient East, 1914; Carchemish I, 1914; The Balkans, 1915; Hittite Seals, 1920; Arabia, 1922; The Wandering Scholar, 1925; Kings of the Hittites (Schweich Lectures), 1926; *posthumous publication:* C. M. Doughty, A Memoir, 1928. *Address:* 20 St Giles, Oxford; Ashmolean Museum, Oxford. *T:* Oxford 3219. *Clubs:* Athenæum, Savile. *Died 6 Nov. 1927.*

HOGBEN, George, CMG 1915; MA; FGS; *b* 14 July 1853; *e s* of Rev. G. Hogben, Congregational Minister, and Mary B. McLachlan; *m* 1885, Emily Frances, *y d* of late Edward Dobson, MICE; two *s*. *Educ:* Congregational School, Lewisham; University School, Nottingham; Birkbeck Institution; St Catharine's College, Cambridge (Mathematical Sizarship); Gold Medallist, Royal Geographical Society, 1871; Haberdashers' Co's and Goldsmiths' Co's Exhibitions; 1st Class Mathematical Honours (Wrangler), 1877. In Accountant and Controller-General's Dept, Inland Revenue, 1872–73; Mathematical

Master, Aldenham School, 1877–81; subsequently at High School, Christchurch, N Zealand; Head-Master, Timaru High School, 1889–99; Inspector-General of Schools, NZ, 1899–1914, and late Director of Education (title changed); President of many learned societies; Member of the General Council of Education for NZ; Fellow of Senate, University, NZ, 1903–15. *Publications:* Methode Naturelle: Mathematical Geography; Earthquakes and other Earth Movements; many pamphlets. *Recreations:* bowling, seismology, proportional representation. *Address:* Wellington, New Zealand. *Club:* Civil Service, Wellington. *Died 25 April 1920.*

HOGG, Rev. Andrew Albert Victor; Rector of Gowran since 1906; Prebendary Killamary since 1907; Chancellor of Ossory, 1925; *b* 9 Jan. 1864; *s* of Rev. Dr Hogg, Rector of Cavan, and Ann Caroline Brushe; unmarried. *Educ:* Trinity College, Dublin. Ordained, 1891; Vicar of St John, Kilkenny, 1901–6; Minor Canon of St Canice's Cathedral, 1905–6; Rural Dean of Odagh, 1906; Member of Diocesan Council, 1907; Secretary of Diocesan Synod, 1920; Member of the Senate TCD, 1892; FRSAI, 1897. *Recreations:* tennis, gardening. *Address:* St Mary's Rectory, Gowran, Co. Kilkenny.
Died 11 Nov. 1927.

HOGG, Sir Frederick Russell, KCIE 1888; CSI 1887; Indian Civil Service, retired 1889; *b* Paris, 28 Oct. 1836; 5th *s* of Rt Hon. Sir James Weir Hogg, 1st Bt, and Mary, *d* of Samuel Swinton, Swinton; *m* 1st, 1857, Emily, 3rd *d* of Gen. Eckford; two *s* one *d* (and two *d* decd); 2nd, 1885, Harriett Venn, *d* of late William Stephens Dicken; one *s* (and one *s* decd). *Educ:* Eton; Haileybury Coll. Arrived at Calcutta in 1857; Postmaster-Gen., Punjab, 1863; Bombay, 1867; Bengal, 1868; Deputy-Director-General Post Office of India, 1869; Director-General Post Office of India, 1880; late partner in firm of Messrs Hogg, Curtis, Campbell, and Company. *Recreations:* took second prize for diving at Eton; won mile swimming race at Haileybury; Captain of term four-oar boat at college; used to play cricket, football, rackets, lawn-tennis; generally fond of all games and of shooting. *Address:* 6 Bickenhall Mansions, W. *Club:* Oriental.
Died 4 Sept. 1923.

HOGG, Maj.-Gen. George Crawford, CB 1896; *b* 13 Sept. 1842; *m* 1878, Henrietta Isabella, *d* of C. N. Minchin; three *s*. *Educ:* Cheltenham College. Entered Bombay Cavalry, 1858; Maj.-Gen. 1897; served Afghan War, 1878–80 (despatches several times, medal); QMG Bombay Army, 1891–95; commanding Deesa District, 1895–1900; Colonel 34th Prince Albert Victor's Own Poona Horse, 1904; transferred to unemployed supernumerary list, 1904. *Address:* Ablington, Cheltenham. *Club:* New, Cheltenham.
Died 12 Oct. 1921.

HOGG, Sir Stuart Saunders, Kt 1875; *b* Calcutta, 17 Feb. 1833; 4th *s* of Rt Hon. Sir James Weir Hogg, 1st Bt, MP; *m* 1860, Selina Catherine, *e d* of Sir Thomas Erskine Perry; two *s* one *d* (and two *d* decd). *Educ:* Eton. Entered Indian Civil Service, 1853; served in Punjaub, where he was Assistant-Commissioner during time of Mutiny; served as civil officer attached to flying column under Gen. John Nicholson (despatches); transferred later to Oude, and subsequently down to Bengal, where he was Magistrate and Collector of Burdwan, and afterwards Chief Commissioner of Police and Chairman of the Municipality, Calcutta. *Address:* Villa Céline, Beaulieu-sur-Mer, France. *Club:* East India United Service.
Died 23 March 1921.

HOGGE, James Myles, MA; MP (L) East Edinburgh, 1912–24; associated with B. Seebohm Rowntree in social investigation, etc; *b* Edinburgh, 19 April 1873; *m* 1905, Florence R. Metcalfe, Malton, Yorkshire; one *s* two *d*. *Educ:* Edinburgh Normal School and Edinburgh University; Moray House Training College; New College, Edinburgh. Began as pupil teacher in Edinburgh; 1st class King's Scholar, Moray House Training College, Edinburgh; Licentiate of United Free Church of Scotland; engaged in settlement work in Edinburgh slums; joined B. Seebohm Rowntree, Joseph Rowntree, and Arthur Sherwell, in social investigation; joint editor, Scottish Students' Song Book, British Students' Song Book; President, Edinburgh University Liberal Association; Senior President, Edinburgh Students' Representative Council; editor, Student, Edinburgh University; founded Young Scots' Society. Joint Chief Whip, Independent Liberal Party, 1918–22. President National Federation of Discharged Sailors and Soldiers, 1919–20. *Publications:* War Pensions and Allowances; Betting and Gambling; The Facts of Gambling; Licensing in Scandinavia; Aims and Achievements of Liberalism; Scotland Insured; Scots Home Rule; Pensions and Separation Allowances; A Book of Consolation. *Recreation:* work. *Club:* Press. *Died 27 Oct. 1928.*

HOGUE, Hon. James Alexander; *b* Clarence Town, New South Wales, 2 Sept. 1846; 3rd *s* of late Fitzarthur Hogue and Elizabeth Mackay; *m* Jessie, 4th *d* of late John Robards, Clarence Town; five *s* four *d*. *Educ:* National Schools, and Newcastle Grammar School. After leaving school learnt printing; acquired knowledge of shorthand; became newspaper reporter; joined Sydney Evening News staff, 1875; Sub-Editor five years, Editor ten years; Minister of Public Instruction and Labour, 1898–99; Colonial Secretary, 1904–7; MLA, Glebe, 1894–1910; Minister of Public Instruction and Minister for Labour and Industry, 1907–10; Trustee, National Park, NSW; Councillor, Royal Australian Historical Society. *Publications:* newspaper and magazine articles, etc. *Recreations:* music, bowls. *Address:* Mosman, Sydney, NSW. *Clubs:* Athenæum, Tattersall's, Sydney.

Died 2 Aug. 1920.

HOHLER, Henry Booth, JP, DL; *b* 1835; 2nd *s* of Rev. Frederick Williams Hohler, Rector of Winstone and Colesborne, Gloucestershire, and Jane Harriet, *e d* of late Thomas Theobald, of Greys Thurrock, Essex; *m* 1st, 1856, Henrietta Wilhelmina (*d* 1902), *o d* of late Robert Lawes of Kingston Hill, Surrey; 2nd, 1914, Ida Marion, *y d* of late Rev. William and Mrs Stracey-Clitherow, formerly of Boston House, Middlesex. High Sheriff, Kent, 1901. *Address:* Fawkham Manor, Kent. *Club:* Junior Carlton.

Died 14 Feb. 1916.

HOLBOROW, Col William Hillier, CMG 1896; late MLC of New South Wales; commanded a regiment of New South Wales Infantry; *b* 1841; *s* of late Daniel Holborow of Cromall, Gloucester; *m* 1864, Maria Amelia, *d* of late William Town, NSW. *Address:* Gadshill, Croydon, New South Wales.

Died 10 July 1917.

HOLCROFT, Sir Charles, 1st Bt, *cr* 1905; *b* 16 July 1831; 4th *s* of late Thomas Holcroft of Brierley Hill, Staffs; unmarried. Took a prominent part in establishing Birmingham University. Hon. LLD Birmingham 1909. *Heir:* none. *Address:* The Shrubbery, Summerhill, Kingswinford, Staffs.

Died 11 March 1917 (ext).

HOLDEN, Captain Edward Charles Shuttleworth, DSO 1900; JP; Lieutenant-Colonel, Derbyshire Yeomanry Cavalry; *b* 7 Jan. 1865; *o c* of Charles Shuttleworth Holden; *m* 1906, Aimee Marguerite (*d* 1913), *y d* of late Vicomte de Labrosse and *widow* of William R. Cookson of Binfield Park, Berks; one *s*. Served South Africa, 1899–1900 (despatches, DSO); resigned, 1910. *Address:* The Cottage, Doveridge, Derby. *Clubs:* Boodle's, Carlton.

Died 17 May 1916.

HOLDEN, Sir Edward Hopkinson, 1st Bt, *cr* 1909; MP (L) Heywood Division, Lancs, 1906–10; Chairman of the London City and Midland Bank, Ltd; *b* Tottington, near Manchester, 11 May 1848; *s* of late Henry Holden of Tottington, Lancashire; *m* 1877, Annie, *y d* of William Cassie, late of Aberdeen; two *s*. *Educ:* Summerseat; Owens College, Manchester. *Recreation:* golf. *Heir: e s* Harry Cassie Holden [*b* 20 Oct. 1877; *m* 1905, Edith Ross, *d* of John Pryor. *Educ:* Trinity Hall, Cambridge. Barrister-at-law of the Inner Temple, 1901; BA, LLB]. *Address:* 5 Threadneedle Street, EC. 19 New Cavendish Street, W. *T:* Paddington 2023; The Grange, Thorpe, Chertsey, Surrey. *Clubs:* Reform, National Liberal.

Died 23 July 1919.

HOLDEN, Sir Edward Thomas, Kt 1907; JP; *b* 1831; *m* 1st, 1854, Caroline (*d* 1901), *e d* of Robert Glass, Edinburgh; 2nd, 1902, Helen Sarah, 2nd *d* of F. H. Yates of Great Barr; one *s*. MP (L) Walsall, 1891–92; three times Mayor of Walsall, and member of the Town Council for over sixty years. *Address:* Glenelg, Walsall.

Died 13 Nov. 1926.

HOLDEN, Sir John Henry, 1st Bt, *cr* 1919; Managing Director Tunncliffe & Hampson, Ltd; Mayor of Leigh, 1911–13; Military Representative Leigh Area during the war; *b* 25 Jan. 1862; *s* of John Holden; *m* 1885, Emma, *d* of Thomas Cawkwell; three *s* two *d* (and two *s* one *d* decd). *Heir: s* George Holden, *b* 16 April 1890. *Address:* The Firs, Leigh, Lancs. *T:* Leigh 1; 7 Argyle Road, Southport. *T:* Southport 1181.

Died 4 May 1926.

HOLDEN, Rev. Robert; *b* 16 Sept. 1853; 4th *s* of Rev. A. A. Holden of Nuthall Temple, Nottingham; *m* 1880, Alice, *d* of John Trotter of Dyrham Park, Barnet; two *s* two *d*. *Educ:* Brentwood. Rector of Nuthall, 1879–1914. *Recreation:* gardening. *Address:* Nuthall Temple, near Nottingham. *T:* Bulwell 77. *M:* NN4343.

Died 10 May 1926.

HOLDER, Rear-Adm. Henry Lowe; *b* 1832; *m* 1868, Isabella, *d* of late Gen. J. S. Fraser, of Ardachie, Inverness. Entered Navy, 1852; Commander, 1864; Capt. 1871; retired, 1873; Rear-Adm. 1888; served Russian War, 1854–55 (Crimean and Turkish medals, Sebastopol clasp, 5th Class Medjidie); Straits of Simonoseki, 1864 (promoted, specially mentioned). *Address:* 5 Sussex Place, Southsea.

Died 5 Jan. 1924.

HOLDER, Sir John Charles, 1st Bt, *cr* 1898; JP, Birmingham; JP, DL, Worcestershire (High Sheriff, 1908); *b* Birmingham, 10 Dec. 1838; *o s* of late Henry Holder, of Birmingham and Malvern; *m* 1872, Geraldine Augusta, *d* of John Williams Knipe, of Worcester; four *s* six *d*. *Educ:* Camp Hill; privately. Chairman of Building Committee of New General Hospital, which cost upwards of £200,000, and was opened free of debt by Princess Christian, 1897; Treasurer of Birmingham Bishopric Endowment Fund; took an active part on Council of Birmingham University; presented to Birmingham Corporation Art Gallery La Petite Classe, by J. Geoffroy; The Marseillaise, by Gustave Doré; Dominicans in Feather (a group of Penguins), by H. Stacy Marks; The Sea Shall Give up Her Dead, by Sir Frederick Leighton; The Wizard, by Burne Jones; Rosa Trixplex, by Rossetti. Possessed pictures by Alma-Tadema, Langley (Disaster), Sidney Cooper, Vicat Cole, Frank Hollt, Kate Greenaway, William Geets, Leader, Keeley Halswelle, Rossetti, Henry Moore, Miss Kemp Welch, David Cox, Ansdell, etc. KGStJ. *Heir: s* Henry Charles Holder [*b* Edgbaston, 1 May 1874; *m* Evelyn, *d* of Sir Robert Ropner, 1st Bt; two *s* three *d*. *Educ:* Repton; Brasenose Coll. Oxford (BA)]. *Address:* Pitmaston, Moseley, Worcestershire. : 3080. *Clubs:* Union; Conservative, Birmingham.

Died 26 April 1923.

HOLDER, Rt. Rev. Mgr Joseph; Provost; Protonotary Apostolic *ad instar* VGMR, Diocese of Dunkeld (RC). *Address:* St Joseph's Rectory, Dundee. *Died 22 June 1917.*

HOLDERNESS, Sir Thomas William, 1st Bt, *cr* 1920; GCB 1917 (KCB 1914); KCSI 1907 (CSI 1898); BA; ICS; *b* 11 June 1849; *m* 1885, Lucy Shepherd, *d* of G. R. Elsmie, CSI, ICS; one *s* one *d*. *Educ:* Cheltenham; University College, Oxford. Indian Civil Service, 1872; Member of Famine Commission, 1897; Sec. to Government of India, Revenue and Agricultural Department, 1898–1901; received Kaiser-i-Hind medal, 1st class, 1899; Secretary Revenue Statistics and Commerce Department, India Office, 1901–12; Permanent Under-Secretary of State, India Office, 1912–19. *Publications:* Narrative of the Indian Famine, 1896–97; fourth edition revised of Strachey's India, 1911; Peoples and Problems of India, 1912; article, India Supplementary Volumes, Encyclopaedia Brittanica. *Heir: o s* Ernest William Elsmie Holderness, *b* 13 March 1890. *Address:* Flagcourt, Tadworth, Surrey. *T:* Burgh Heath 29. *Club:* Athenæum.

Died 16 Sept. 1924.

HOLDICH, Lt-Col Godfrey William Vanrennen, DSO 1916; RA; *b* 1882; *s* of Sir Thomas Hungerford Holdich; *m* 1909, Winifred, *d* of Arthur Fraser. *Educ:* Wellington. Served European War, 1914–18 (despatches, DSO, Order of the Nile and of Crown of Italy, Batt. Lieut-Col).

Died 13 April 1921.

HOLDSWORTH, Lt-Col John Joseph, CIE 1899; *b* 1844; *s* of late John Hall Holdsworth, MD; *m* 1st, 1871, Lucy (*d* 1880), *d* of late John Hall Bridgman, JP, of Lehra, Gorakhpur, India; 2nd, 1883, Maria Teresa (*d* 1898), *d* of late William James Howard of Sea Point Manor, Blackrock, Dublin; one *d*. Commandant Gorakhpur Light Horse; late Lt-Col commanding United Provinces Light Horse; a landed proprietor in India; Hon. ADC to the Viceroy of India (Baron Curzon of Kedleston), 1899. *Address:* Lehra, Gorakhpur, UP, India. *Club:* East India United Service.

Died 29 June 1920.

HOLE, William, RSA 1889 (ARSA 1878); RE; painter and etcher; *b* Salisbury, 7 Nov. 1846; *o c* of Richard Brassey Hole, MD, and Anne Burn Fergusson; *m* 1876, Elizabeth, *o d* of James Lindsay, WS; three *s* two *d*. *Educ:* Edin. Acad. Served apprenticeship as a civil engineer in Edinburgh; travelled in Italy before settling down; sketches commended by artists in Rome; adopted Art as a profession, 1870; studied in Royal Scottish Academy School; practised etching, both original and interpretative, in addition to painting, and later turned his attention to mural decoration. *Principal paintings:* End of the '45, 1879; Prince Charlie's Parliament, 1882; The Night's Catch, 1883; The Fill of the Boats, 1885; "If Thou hadst known," 1887; The Canterbury Pilgrims, 1889; The Ascension; The Life of Jesus of Nazareth, a series of 80 water-colour pictures completed 1906. *Original etchings:* "Quasi Cursores," 1884; The Canterbury Pilgrims, 1888; Illustrations of Burns's Poems, 1896; "Pro Nobis," 1897.

Interpretative etchings: The Mill (after J. Crome), 1888; The Sawyers (after Millet), 1890; Jumping Horse (after Constable), 1890; He is Coming (after M. Maris), 1889; Admiral Pulido Pareja (after Velasquez), 1893. *Mural paintings:* The Chancel of St James's Church, Edinburgh, 1896; Series of Historical Paintings in the National Portrait Gallery of Scotland, 1900; ditto in the Municipal Buildings, Edinburgh, 1903. *Address:* 13 Inverleith Terrace, Edinburgh.

Died 22 Oct. 1917.

HOLFORD, Lt-Col Sir George (Lindsay), KCVO 1910 (CVO 1901); CIE 1890; CBE 1919; Equerry-in-Waiting to HM, 1901–14; *b* 2 June 1860; *s* of late Robert Stayner Holford and Mary Ann, *d* of General James Lindsay, MP; *m* 1912, Susannah West, *d* of late Arthur Wilson of Tranby Croft, and *widow* of J. Graham Menzies. *Educ:* Eton. Joined 1st Life Guards, 1880; Equerry to Duke of Clarence, 1888–92; Lt-Col 1st Life Guards from 1908; Equerry-in-Waiting to Prince of Wales, 1892–99; Equerry-in-Waiting to King Edward to 1910; then Equerry-in-Waiting to Queen Alexandra; Extra Equerry to King George, 1910; commanded Reserve Regt 1st Life Guards during the war. Owned about 16,400 acres, and the Dorchester House Picture Gallery. *Address:* Weston Birt House, Tetbury; Dorchester House, Park Lane, W1. *T:* Gerrard 4479. *Clubs:* Carlton, Marlborough, White's.

Died 11 Sept. 1926.

HOLFORD, James Price William Gwynne; DL County of Brecon; Chairman Conservative Association for Breconshire; *b* 25 Nov. 1833; *m* 1891, Mary Eleanor, 3rd *d* of P. R. Gordon Canning, Hartpury, Gloucester; one *d. Educ:* Eton; Christ Church, Oxford. MP (C) Breconshire, 1870–90. *Address:* Buckland Bwlch SO, Breconshire; Treholford and Cilgwyn, Carmarthenshire. *Clubs:* Carlton, Junior United Service, Wellington.

Died 6 Feb. 1916.

HOLIDAY, Henry; *b* London, 17 June 1839; *s* of George Henry Holiday, teacher of classics and mathematics, and Climène Gerber of Mulhouse, Alsace; *m* 1864, Catherine (*d* 1924), *d* of Rev. T. Raven; one *d. Educ:* home. Went to Leigh's, 1854; student at RA, 1854; early impressed with imagination and beauty of Pre-Raphaelite pictures; kindly received by Millais, Rossetti, and Holman Hunt; formed lifelong friendship with Holman Hunt and Burne-Jones; while at RA formed sketching club with Albert Moore, Marcus Stone, and Simeon Solomon; first picture at RA, Durlestone Bay, painted 1857, hung on line in 1858 and sold first day; the Burgess of Calais painted 1858, RA 1859, recently presented to Guildhall Gallery; Dante's First Meeting with Beatrice when a Child, painted 1859, rejected 1860, hung on line 1861; subsequent time largely occupied with decorative work, mural painting, stained glass, mosaic, etc, but found time for painting and sculpture; exhibited at RA and Grosvenor—Diana, Adam, The Duet, Sleep (a life-size statue), Aspasia, Dante and Beatrice (bought by Corporation of Liverpool), etc; invented a new form of enamel in relief, to extend the use of the material to large scale work, 1899. *Publications:* a series of articles on wood engraving in the Magazine of Art; Stained Glass as an Art, 1896; Reminiscences of my Life, 1914; edited Aglaia, the journal of the Healthy and Artistic Dress Union. *Recreations:* chiefly mountain-climbing (English) and music; followed progress of science with interest, and accompanied Sir Norman Lockyer's eclipse expedition to India in 1871. *Address:* Wansfell, 18 Chesterford Gardens, Hampstead, NW3. *TA:* Henry Holiday, Hampstead. *T:* Hampstead 1030.

Died 15 April 1927.

HOLLAND, Sir Arthur, Kt 1913; JP, DL; MA; senior partner of Arthur Holland and Company, ship-owners and insurance brokers, 2 East India Avenue, EC; *b* Liverpool, 13 July 1842; 2nd *s* of Charles Holland, merchant; *m* 1868, Barbara, *o d* of Frederick Schwann of Gloucester Square, Hyde Park; five *s* one *d. Educ:* privately; Trinity College, Cambridge. Honours in Mathematical Tripos, 1864; entered office of Lamport and Holt, 1864; partner, 1870; on death of Mr Lamport fresh arrangements were made; active in politics and local affairs at Wimbledon, where he resided from 1874; first chairman of the Urban District Council of Wimbledon; 2nd Mayor of Wimbledon, 1906–7; contested Wimbledon Division of Surrey, 1910. *Publications:* pamphlets on social and political questions. *Recreation:* golf. *Address:* Holmhurst, Wimbledon, SW20. *TA:* Spartan, London. *T:* Wimbledon 367. *M:* P 2617 and P 7524.

Died 8 Jan. 1928.

HOLLAND, Lt-Gen. Sir Arthur Edward Aveling, KCB 1918 (CB 1915); KCMG 1919; DSO 1900; MVO 1903; RFA; MP (C) Borough of Northampton since 1924; Commandant, Royal Military Academy, Woolwich, 1912–14; *b* 13 April 1862; *y s* of Major-General Arthur Butcher; assumed surname of Holland in lieu of Butcher, 1910; *m* 1906, Mary Kate Duval, *o d* of Lewis Duval Hall, JP, DL; one *d.* Entered Army, 1880; Captain, 1888; Major, 1898; Lt-Col 1905; Colonel, 1910; served Burmah, 1885–89 (medal with two clasps); South Africa, 1900–1 (despatches twice, medal with four clasps, DSO); European War, France and Flanders, 1914–18; commanded Artillery, 8th Division, 1914–15; Artillery, 3rd Army, 1916; 1st Division, 1915–16; 1st Army Corps, 1917–18 (despatches eight times, CB, prom. Maj.-Gen., KCB, prom. Lieut.-Gen., KCMG). Commandeur Légion d'Honneur; Commandeur l'Ordre de Leopold; Belgium Croix de Guerre. *Address:* 45 Carlisle Mansions, Westminster, SW; Hanslope Lodge, Stony Stratford. *T:* Franklin 6240; Wolverton 22. *Clubs:* Naval and Military, Ranelagh.

Died 7 Dec. 1927.

HOLLAND, Bernard Henry, CB 1904; *b* 23 Dec. 1856; *e s* of late Rev. F. J. Holland, Canon of Canterbury, and Mary Sibylla, *d* of Rev. Alfred Lyall of Harbledown; *m* 1895, Florence Helen, *d* of Rev. W. A. Duckworth; one *s* two *d. Educ:* Eton; Trinity Coll., Cambridge (MA). Called to Bar, Inner Temple, 1882; The Charity Commission Office, 1884–90; Private Sec. to Duke of Devonshire, 1892–94; Sec. to various Royal Commissions, 1891–1908; Private Secretary to Secretary of State for Colonies, 1903–8; Alderman of London County Council, 1910–20; Sub-Commissioner for National Service for East Kent area, 1917; Member of Kent Education Committee, 1921; Chairman of the Kent and Canterbury Hospital Board, 1922. *Publications:* Selection from Crabbe's Poems, 1899; Onyx, 1899; Imperium et Libertas, a study in Politics, 1901; Life of the Duke of Devonshire, 1911; Verse, 1912; The Fall of Protection, 1913; The Lancashire Hollands, 1917; Memoir of Kenelm Digby, 1919; Belief and Freedom, 1923. *Address:* Harbledown Lodge, Canterbury. *Club:* Athenæum.

Died 25 May 1926.

HOLLAND, Comdr Gerald Edward, CMG 1916; CIE 1900; DSO 1890; Temporary Colonel RE; Dock and Marine Superintendent, London and North Western Railway, Holyhead; *b* Dublin, 21 Oct. 1860; 2nd *s* of late Denis Holland of Dublin; *m* 1896, Mary (*d* 1913), *e d* of late Edmund Dwyer Gray, MP, of Vartry Lodge, Ballybrack, Ireland; one *s* two *d. Educ:* Ratcliffe College, Leicestershire. Joined Royal Indian Marine, 1880; Lieut 1882; Commander, 1893; served with Burma Expeditionary Forces, 1887–89 (medal, 2 clasps), Chin-Lushai Expedition, 1880–90 (clasp, despatches, DSO); commanded Royal Indian Marine troopship "Warren Hastings" when that vessel was unfortunately lost on Reunion Island at 2AM on 14 Jan. 1897; tried by Court-Martial; result, a simple reprimand; commendatory order containing warm praise published simultaneously with Court-Martial finding by Viceroy and Governor-General in Council; served on Naval Transport Staff, Durban, 1899–1900; as Divisional Officer, ditto, 1900–1 (despatches thrice, medal, clasp, CIE); Principal Port-Officer, Rangoon, Burma, 1901–4; retired from Royal Indian Marine, 1905; served European War, 1914–16 (despatches twice, CMG). Officier Ordre de Leopold of Belgium. *Recreations:* cricket, golf, yachting, motoring. *Address:* Bryn-y-Mor, Holyhead. *M:* P 1374. *Club:* Oriental.

Died 26 June 1917.

HOLLAND, Lt-Col Guy Lushington, MVO 1911; in command of Pioneer Depot; *b* 21 Feb. 1861; *s* of Maj.-Gen. H. W. Holland. Entered Army, 1883; Captain, ISC, 1894; Major, Indian Army, 1901; Lieut-Col, 1908; served Sikkim Expedition, 1888 (despatches, medal with clasp); Chitral, 1895 (medal with clasp); China, 1900 (medal); Waziristan, 1901–2 (clasp). *Address:* 21 Havelock Road, Croydon.

HOLLAND, Rev. Henry Scott, MA; DD Aberdeen; DLitt Oxford, 1907; editor of The Commonwealth; Regius Professor of Divinity, Oxford, and Canon of Christ Church, since 1910; *b* 27 Jan. 1847; *s* of George Henry and Hon. Charlotte D. Holland, Gayton Lodge, Wimbledon. *Educ:* Eton; Balliol Coll. Oxford. First class Lit. Hum. 1870. Senior student, Christ Church, 1870–84; tutor, 1872; ordained, 1872; Select Preacher to University of Oxford, 1881–82, 1894–96; Censor of Christ Church, 1882–84; Canon, Truro, 1882–84; Exam. Chaplain to Bishop of Truro, 1882–1904; Canon of St Paul's 1884–1910; Precentor, St Paul's Cathedral, 1886–1910. *Publications:* Logic and Life; Creed and Character; Christ and Ecclesiastes; On Behalf of Belief; Pleas and Claims; God's City; Personal Studies, 1905; Vital Values, 1906; article on Justin Martyr in Smith's Eccles. Dict.; Apostolic Fathers; Life of Jenny Lind; Old and New; Fundamentals, pamphlet, 1909; Fibres of Faith, 1910; A Bundle of Memories, 1915; So as by Fire, 1916; Essay in Lux Mundi, and in volumes on Church Reform, and on Good Citizenship. *Recreations:* cycling, formerly rowing, racquets, football, swimming. *Address:* Oxford.

Died 17 March 1918.

HOLLAND, Maj.-Gen. Henry William, CB 1869; retired; *b* Bombay, 1825; *e s* of late Major Henry Colson Holland of Bombay Army; *m* 1st, 1850, Ellen (*d* 1863), *d* of James Farquharson, Bombay CS; 2nd, 1870, May (*d* 1881), *d* of late R. H. Ellis, Dublin, and *widow* of Col Giles Keane; 3rd, Laura Marie (*d* 1920). *Educ:* Cheltenham; Woolwich. Joined 13th Bombay Native Infantry, 1841; Captain, 1856; Major, 1861; Lieutenant-Colonel, 1867; Colonel, 1868; Major-General, 1877 (retired); appointed a SA Commissary-General, 1847; served in Abyssinian War as Controller of Supply and Transport, 1867–68 (despatches, brevet of Col, medal, and CB); was Commissary-General of Bombay Army, 1870–77. *Address:* 21 Havelock Road, Croydon.   *Died 20 Sept. 1920.*

HOLLAND, Captain Herbert Christian, MVO 1905; Chief Constable of Derbyshire since 1897; *b* 16 July 1858; *s* of Edward Holland, JP, DL, MP (Evesham), of Dumbleton Hall, Evesham; *m*; four *s. Educ:* Eton; Radley; Sandhurst. 8th and 15th Hussars; served Afghan War, 1879–80; Boer War, 1881; Egyptian War, 1882 (wounded); Capt. Derbyshire Yeomanry. JP Derbyshire. *Address:* The Wheathills, Kirk Langley, Derby. *TA:* Holland, Kirk Langley. *T:* 2 Kirk Langley. *Clubs:* Boodle's, Pratt's.   *Died 3 May 1916.*

HOLLAND, Major Hugh, DSO 1919; late General Staff Officer 2, War Office; *b* 20 Jan. 1884; 2nd *s* of Dr J. F. Holland, St Moritz, Switzerland; *m* 1911, Dorothy, *d* of the late J. A. F. Bennett of North Breache Manor, Ewhurst, Surrey; one *s. Educ:* Tonbridge School; Royal Military Academy, Woolwich. Joined Royal Artillery, 1903; retired, 1910; served European War, 1914–18 (despatches, DSO). *Publications:* contribs to various periodicals. *Recreations:* golf, tennis, winter sports. *Address:* 4 Paulton's Square, Chelsea, SW. *Club:* Sports.   *Died 15 Jan. 1922.*

HOLLAND, Adm. Swinton Colthurst, JP; FRGS; *b* 8 Feb. 1844; *m* 1881, Eva A. Williams; one *s* two *d.* Entered RN 1857; Rear-Admiral, 1899; Vice-Admiral, 1903; Admiral, 1907; ADC to Queen, 1895; Commodore in Charge, Hong Kong, 1896; Superintendent of Chatham Dockyard, 1899–1902; retired 1908. *Address:* Langley House, Chichester.   *Died 8 June 1922.*

HOLLAND, Sir (Thomas) Erskine, Kt 1917; KC 1901; DCL, LLD; FBA 1901; Fellow, All Souls College, Oxford, since 1875; *b* 17 July 1835; *e s* of Rev. T. A. Holland, Rector of Poynings, Sussex; *m* 1st, 1871, Louise (*d* 1891), *d* of M Jean Delessert; four *s* one *d* (and two *s* decd); 2nd, 1895, Ellen, *widow* of the Rev. Stephen Edwardes. *Educ:* Brighton Coll.; Balliol and Magdalen Colls, Oxford. Demy of Magdalen; 1st Class, final classical school; Fellow of Exeter Coll., 1859–71; Chancellor's Prizeman, 1860. Barrister, Lincoln's Inn, 1863; Bencher, 1907. Vinerian Reader in English Law, Oxford University, 1874; Professor of International Law and Diplomacy, 1874–1910, then Emeritus; Assessor (sole judge) of the Chancellor's Court, 1876–1910. Mem., Royal Commission on the Supply of Food, etc, in Time of War, 1903–5; British Plenipotentiary at the Geneva Conference, 1906. DCL Oxford; Hon. LLD Bologna, Glasgow, Dublin, Brussels; Hon. Professor and Hon. Member of the University of Perugia; Hon. Member of the University of Petrograd, of the Juridical Society of Berlin, and of the American Society of International Law; Hon. Citizen of Sanginesio; Correspondent of the Academies of the Moral and Political Sciences of the Institut de France, of the Istituto di Bologna, and of Padua and Brussels; Member of the Institut de Droit International (President, 1913); Corresponding Member of the Institut Américain de Droit International. Commander of the Order of the Crown of Italy; Grand Commander of the Rising Sun of Japan. *Publications:* An Essay on Composition Deeds, 1864, 1865; Essays on the Form of the Law, 1870; The Institutes of Justinian, as a recension of the Institutes of Gaius, 1873, 1881; Albericus Gentilis, a lecture, 1874; tradotto da Aurelio Saffi, 1884; Alberici Gentilis De Iure Belli, 1877; The Elements of Jurisprudence, 1880 (Swiney Prize, 1894), 13th English edition, 1924; The European Concert in the Eastern Question, 1885; The Admiralty Manual of Naval Prize Law, 1888; Studies in International Law, 1898; The War Office Manual of the Laws and Customs of War on Land, 1904; Neutral Duties in a Maritime War, 1905; The Laws of War on Land, 1908; A Valedictory Retrospect, 1910; Proposed Changes in the Law of Prize, 1911; R. Zouch Ius Feciale, 1911; Io. de Lignano De Bello, 1917; Letters to the Times on War and Neutrality, Ed. iii, containing the letters of forty years (1881–1920), 1921. *Address:* Poynings House, Oxford; 3 Brick Court, Temple, EC. *Club:* Athenæum.   *Died 24 May 1926.*

HOLLEY, Maj.-Gen. Edmund Hunt, JP, Devon; Lord of Manor of Okehampton; Colonel Commandant RA; *b* 24 May 1842; 4th *s*

of J. H. Holley, late of Oaklands, Okehampton; *m* 1879, 2nd *d* of Rev. H. E. Hayter-Hames; one *s* two *d. Educ:* Carshalton; Woolwich. Obtained commission in Royal Artillery, 1860; commanded a battery in Soudan Campaign, 1884 (despatches, received brevet promotion); was Colonel on Staff commanding RA, Cork District, 1894–98; succeeded to the family estates on the death of his eldest brother, 1898. *Recreations:* hunting, shooting. *Address:* Oaklands, Okehampton, Devon. *Club:* United Service.   *Died 9 April 1919.*

HOLLINGDRAKE, Sir Henry, Kt 1921; JP Cheshire; engineer; *b* 15 April 1872; *s* of late Robert Hollingdrake and Emma Hollingdrake of Edgeley House, Stockport; *m* 1898, Esther Emily, *d* of late Thomas Lewis and late Elizabeth Elstub Lewis of Dynas Powis, Glam; one *s* one *d. Educ:* Manchester Grammar School. Formed and was Chairman of the Stockport and District Prisoners of War Committee; formed the Stockport and District Comforts Fund; Member of the Cheshire Prisoners of War Aid Society; Member of the Lancashire and Cheshire Civilian Prisoners Relief Fund; rendered considerable service in connection with organizing transport for the conveyance of wounded in Cheshire; Member of the Soldiers and Sailors Families Association. *Address:* The Cleeve, Porlock, Somerset. *TA:* Hollingdrake, Porlock.   *Died 2 May 1923.*

HOLLINGS, Herbert John Butler; JP, DL; *b* 1855; *e s* of John Hollings, JP, of Wheatley Hall, Yorks, and The Watchetts, and Mary Jane Hope, *e d* of late Rev. Canon Mitton; *m* 1886, Nina Augusta Stracey, *d* of Gen. John Hall Smyth, CB; one *s* one *d. Educ:* Winchester; Oxford (BA 1878). Called to Bar, Inner Temple, 1880; patron of 1 living. *Address:* The Watchetts, Frimley, Surrey. *Clubs:* Constitutional, Junior Constitutional.   *Died 6 March 1922.*

HOLLINGTON, Alfred Jordan; JP; FRHS; Lieutenant of City of London; textile merchant; senior partner in the firm of Hollington Bros; *b* 12 May 1845; *s* of Thomas and Ann Hollington; *m* 1st, 1875, Alice, *d* of William Dear, Hyde Park Corner; two *s* four *d*; 2nd, 1890, Alice, *d* of Henry Clarke, JP, Hampstead. *Educ:* City of London School. Member of Corporation of London; Chairman of many committees; Member of 1st LCC; Chairman of Improvements Committee; Chairman of Wholesale Clothiers' Federation; Member of the London Textile Association and London Chamber of Commerce. PM of Lodge of Felicity, No 58; one of the founders and PM of Bishopsgate Lodge; PM of Tinplate Workers Co.; PM of Gold and Silver Wire Drawers' Co.; Member of Loriners' Co. *Recreations:* breeder of horses and shorthorn cattle; grower of orchids. *Address:* Forty Hill, Enfield, Middlesex. *TA:* Enfield. *T:* Enfield 142.   *Died 3 Dec. 1926.*

HOLLINS, Sir Frank, 1st Bt, *cr* 1907; JP; Chairman of Horrockes, Crewdson and Co., Ltd, cotton-spinners; *b* 16 April 1843; *s* of late Edward Hollins of Pleasley, Mansfield; *m* 1875, Dora Emily, OBE, 3rd *d* of Caleb Cox; four *s* two *d.* Heir: *s* Arthur Meyrick Hollins [*b* 16 July 1876; *m* 1908, Mary Prudence, *d* of late John Thwaites]. *Address:* Greyfriars, near Preston.   *Died 27 Jan. 1924.*

HOLLIS, William Ainslie, MA, MD; FRCP; an Ex-President, British Medical Association; Consulting Physician, Royal Sussex County Hospital; ex-President, Brighton and Sussex Medico-Chirurgical Society; ex-President, Brighton and Hove Natural History and Philosophical Society; *b* Lewisham, Kent, 1839; *m d* of Charles Lever; one *s* two *d. Educ:* Brighton College; Trinity College, Cambridge; St Bartholomew's Hospital, London. House Physician to St Bartholomew's Hospital when the appointment was first made. *Publications:* numerous medical and scientific papers in current periodicals. *Recreations:* cycling, cactus culture. *Address:* Salisbury Lodge, Salisbury Road, Hove, Brighton. *T:* 646 PO Brighton. *Clubs:* New University; Hove.   *Died 26 March 1922.*

HOLLOWAY, Maj.-Gen. Benjamin, CIE 1915; Indian Army; *b* 27 Aug. 1861; *s* of Lt-Col E. V. P. Holloway of Charlbury, Oxon; *m* 1901, Muriel Aimée Becher; four *s.* Entered Indian Army, 1883; Captain, 1892; Major, 1901; Lt-Col 1907; Col 1912; DAQMG, India, 1900; Asst Secretary, Military Dept, Govt of India, 1901–6; Commandant 29th Lancers, 1909; Deputy Secretary, Army Dept, Govt of India, 1912, Secretary, 1914; GOC Southern Brigade, 1916; served Burma, 1885–86 (despatches, medal with clasp). *Address:* Wellington, Nilgiris, India.   *Died 12 May 1922.*

HOLLOWAY, Sir Henry, Kt 1917; JP; Governing Director of Holloway Brothers (London) Ltd, contractors; *b* 5 Aug. 1857; 4th *s* of late Thomas Holloway, Lavington; *m* 1881, Annie Jane, *e d* of late John Gollop, Clapham, SW; seven *c. Educ:* privately. Founded the business of Holloway Brothers (London), Ltd, in conjunction with his late brother, Thomas Holloway. JP, 1882; Past President of the Institute of Builders; Past President of the London Master Builders' Association. *Address:* Bridge Wharf, Grosvenor Road, SW1. *TA:* Antefixa, Churton, London. *T:* Victoria 8560. *Club:* Reform.

Died 5 Aug. 1923.

HOLME, Charles; Vice-President, Japan Society; founder and for 25 years editor of the Studio; *b* Derby, 7 Oct. 1848; *s* of George Holme, silk manufacturer, Derby; *m* 1873, Clara, *d* of George Benton; one *s* three *d. Educ:* Derby (private school). East India merchant, 1868–86; travelled in Russia, Asia Minor, China, Japan, etc. Chevalier, Rising Sun of Japan. *Publications:* reviews, magazine articles and lectures upon the fine and decorative arts. *Recreation:* farming. *Address:* Upton-Grey House, near Basingstoke, Hants. *TA:* Upton-Grey.

Died 14 March 1923.

HOLME, Charles Henry; of Rawburn, Berwickshire; *b* 1853; *e s* of Bryan Holme Holme, of Paull Holme, Yorks, and Catharine Margaret, *d* of Gen. Hon. Sir Patrick Stuart, GCMG, of Eaglescarnie; *m* 1886, Eva Magdalen, *d* of Rev. Canon and Hon. Mrs Machell; three *s* two *d. Educ:* Bath College; RIE College, Coopers Hill. Served the Govt of India in PW Dept, 1876–99; MInstCE. *Address:* Rathburne, Duns, Berwickshire. *Club:* New, Edinburgh.

Died 12 Feb. 1928.

HOLME, George A.; *b* 28 March 1848; *s* of S. Holme, Holmestead, Liverpool; *m* 1886, Ada Laura, *e d* of Thomas Allen Hickley of Elm Grove, Walton on Thames. *Educ:* Repton School; University College, Oxford; 3rd Class Classical Mods, 1869; 3rd Class Law and History, 1871; BA 1871. Solicitor, 1876; Examiner in Common Law for Final Law Exam. (Honours); Chancery Taxing Master, 1901; Master of Supreme Court of Judicature, 1903. *Address:* 238 Royal Courts of Justice, Strand, WC; Angle, Harrow on the Hill. *T:* 186 PO Harrow. *Clubs:* United University; Northwood Golf; Vincent's, Oxford.

Died 9 Nov. 1917.

HOLMES, Arthur Bromley, MEng (Liverpool); MInstCE; *b* 8 June 1849; *s* of late Arthur East Holmes of Derby; *m* Elizabeth, *d* of late Richard Stone. *Educ:* Repton School. Served apprenticeship with Andrew Handyside and Co., Ltd, engineers, Derby, and was afterwards employed by them in the management of their business as constructors of bridges, roofs, and other steel and iron structures, and ultimately held the position of works manager; commenced business as consulting engineer in Liverpool in partnership with J. C. Vaudrey, 1882; one of the founders of the Liverpool Electric Supply Co., 1883; Engineer and Manager of that Company till its purchase by the Corporation of Liverpool, 1896; City Electrical Engineer, 1896–1903; one of the Founders and Engineers of the Birmingham Electric Supply Company; Consulting Engineer to the Liverpool Corporation, 1903–13. *Publications:* books and papers on electrical subjects. *Address:* 2 Princes Gate East, Liverpool. *T:* Royal Liverpool 481. *Club:* Athenæum, Liverpool.

Died 27 Dec. 1927.

HOLMES, Ven. Bernard Edgar; Chaplain SAMR (Lieutenant-Colonel, retired); *b* 1860; 7th *s* of John Holmes, Somerfield, Maidstone; *m* Grace Pauline, *e d* of late Sir Jacob Barry. *Educ:* St John's College, Cambridge (MA). Ordained, 1883; Curate of West Felton, Salop, 1883–87; Priest-Vicar of Truro Cathedral, 1888–90; Chaplain of Colonial Forces, 1892; Chaplain to the Forces, S Africa, 1897–1902; Canon of Grahamstown, 1907–21; Rector of King William's Town, 1891–1921; Rural Dean, 1892–1921; Archdeacon of King William's Town, 1910–21; British Chaplain at Rome, 1920–24. *Publication:* The Source of Civic Power. *Recreations:* golf, gardening. *Address:* c/o Standard Bank of S Africa, 10 Clement's Lane, EC4.

Died 7 July 1928.

HOLMES, Sir George (Charles Vincent), KCB 1911 (CB 1904); KCVO 1906 (CVO 1903); Chairman of Board of Public Works, Ireland, 1901–13; Hon. MINA; *b* 9 October 1848; 3rd *s* of Robert Holmes, of Moycashel, Co. Westmeath; *m* 1880, Louisa, *d* of late Charles Greenstreet Addison, barrister-at-law, London; one *s. Educ:* Downing College, Cambridge. Obtained an Entrance Scholarship, 1870, and Whitworth Engineering Scholarship, 1871; educated as an engineer at the Crewe Locomotive Works of the L&NWR; Resident Engineer to the building of great iron Rotunda of the Vienna International Exhibition of 1873; Member of the International Jury of this Exhibition, section of Prime Movers; Secretary of the Institution of Naval Architects, 1878–1901. *Publications:* Text-Book

of the Steam Engine; Marine Engines and Boilers, and Ancient and Modern Ships (both Handbooks of the Victoria and Albert Museum, South Kensington); also wrote Official Reports on Prime Movers for the Royal British Commission of the Vienna International Exhibition of 1873. *Recreations:* fishing, shooting. *Club:* St James'.

Died 13 Feb. 1926.

HOLMES, Brig.-Gen. Hardress Gilbert, CMG 1916; CBE 1919; JP; *b* 7 July 1862; 2nd *s* of Bassett Holmes, DL, JP, of St David's; *m* 1908, Alys Maude Josephine, *d* of late John Lloyd, Gloster, King's Co.; one *d.* Entered army, 1885; Major, 1905; retired, 1908; served NW Frontier, India, 1897–98 (medal 2 clasps); S Africa, 1899–1902; commanded Mounted Infantry Regt and a Column (despatches twice, Bt Major, Queen's medal 5 clasps, King's medal 2 clasps); rejoined army at beginning of the European War; commanded 9th Batt. the Yorkshire Regiment, BEF, 1914–16; Brig.-Gen. 1916; retired pay, 1920; served 1914–19 (despatches 4 times, CMG, CBE, Bt Lt-Col). High Sheriff Co. Tipperary, 1910. *Recreations:* hunting, shooting, fishing. *Address:* St David's, Nenagh, Co. Tipperary. *Clubs:* Naval and Military; Kildare Street, Dublin.

Died 4 Sept. 1922.

HOLMES, Rev. Henry Comber; Hon. Canon of York; Rector of Birkby since 1876, and Vicar of Hutton, Bonville, since 1885; *s* of late Rev. William Rusbridge Holmes; married; one *d. Educ:* Winchester; Exeter College, Oxford; BA, 1868; MA, 1872. Ordained, 1870; Curate of East Retford, Notts, 1870; Blyth, 1874; Rural Dean of Northallerton, 1897; Chaplain to 1st VB Yorks Regt, later 4th Batt. Yorks Regt, 1882–1915; member of North Riding Territorial Association. *Address:* Birkby Rectory, Northallerton. *T:* Great Smeaton.

Died 16 June 1920.

HOLMES, Rt. Hon. Hugh, PC 1885; Lord Justice of Appeal, Ireland, 1897–1915; *b* 17 Feb. 1840; *s* of late William Holmes, Dungannon; *m* 1869, Olivia (*d* 1901), *d* of J. W. Moule. *Educ:* Trinity Coll. Dublin. Called to Irish Bar, 1865; Solicitor and Attorney-General for Ireland, 1878–80; MP (C) Dublin Univ., 1885–87; Judge of High Court of Justice, Ireland, 1887–97. *Address:* 3 Fitz-William Place, Dublin. *Club:* Carlton.

Died 19 April 1916.

HOLMES, Thomas; late Police Court Missionary, North London Police Court; *b* Walsall, 1846; *s* of William Holmes, ironmoulder; *m* 1872, Margaret, *d* of Ralph Brammar, carpenter, Rugeley; five *s. Educ:* National School, Rugeley. For many years an iron worker; owing to an accident and subsequent illness had to give up his trade; taught night school, etc, for some years; in 1885 appointed Police Court Missionary at Lambeth Police Court; in 1889 transferred to North London Court; lecturer on criminology and social subjects; Associate Society for Study of Inebriates; established Home of Rest for women engaged in the Home Industries; The Home Workers' Aid Association, of which Hon. Organiser, 1903; and intended to devote the remainder of his life to the housing of London's poorest toilers, and hoped to improve the conditions under which home workers live and labour. *Publications:* Pictures and Problems from London Police Courts; Known to the Police; London's Underworld; articles in contemporary reviews; Editor of The London Homeworker. *Address:* 12 Bedford Road, Tottenham.

Died 26 March 1918.

HOLMES, Rev. Thomas Scott, DD, MA; FRHistS; Chancellor and Canon Residentiary of Wells Cathedral; Examining Chaplain to the Bishop of Bath and Wells; *b* 20 Aug. 1852; *s* of Rev. I. Holmes, BA, of Anfield, Liverpool; *m* 1880, Katharine, *d* of E. A. Freeman, DCL, of Somerleaze, Wells; one *d. Educ:* Royal Inst. School, Liverpool. Foundation Scholar and Prizeman, Sidney Sussex College, Cambridge; BA, Sen. Opt., 1875; MA 1878; BD 1909; DD 1910. Tutor, St Aidan's College, Birkenhead, 1875; Vice-Principal, Wells Theological Coll., 1877–80; Vicar of Wookey, Somerset, 1879–1900; Prebendary of Wells, 1895; Rural Dean of Axbridge, 1897–1900; Birkbeck Lecturer in Ecclesiastical History, Trinity Coll. Cambridge, 1906–8; Proctor in Convocation for the Chapter of Wells, 1909. *Publications:* History of the Parish of Wookey; Glastonbury Costumaria; Bruton and Montacute Cartularies; Bp R. de Salopia's Register, 2 vols (Somerset Record Society); Bishop Giffard and Bishop Bowett's Register, 1 vol.; Historical and Legendary Glastonbury; History of Wells and Glastonbury, 1908; The First Six Centuries of the Church in Gaul, 1910; an account of the Ecclesiastical Records and Plate of the Diocese of Bath and Wells, 1914; Register of Bishop Nicholas Bubwith, 1914; Register of Bishop John Stafford, 1916. *Address:* East Liberty, Wells, Somerset.

Died 10 Feb. 1918.

HOLMES, Col William, CMG 1916; DSO 1901; commanded 5th Infantry Brigade, Australian Expeditionary Force, Dardanelles, 1915; *b* 12 Sept. 1862; *s* of late Captain William Holmes, General Staff, NSW Military Forces; *m* 1887, Susan Ellen (*d* 1912), *d* of Lieut Henry Green, Reserve of Officers, NSW, late RHA; one *s* one *d*. 2nd Lieut (1st NSW Inf. Regt), 1886; 1st Lieut, 1890; Captain, 1894; Major, 1900; Bt Lt-Col, 1920; Lt-Col, 1905; Col, 1912; commanded 6th Australian Inf. Bde; served with 1st NSW Contingent, S African Campaign, 1899–1900; Relief of Colesburg, advance on Bloemfontein with Clement's Column, with Ian Hamilton's Column from Bloemfontein to Thabanchu, Hout Nek, Winburg, Ventersburg, Kroonstad, Lindley, Heilbron, Doorn Kop, Roodepoort, Johannesburg, Pretoria, Diamond Hill; wounded, 1900, and invalided (despatches, S African War medal, with four clasps); European War, 1914–16 (despatches, CMG); commanded Australian Naval and Military Force which occupied German New Guinea, 1914; British Administrator, 1914–15; ADC to the Governor-General of Australia, 1904–11. *Address:* Bondi, New South Wales, Australia.
Died 5 July 1917.

HOLMES-À-COURT, Hon. Edward Alexander; late Chief-Constable of Oxfordshire; *b* 23 Oct. 1845; 5th *s* of 2nd Lord Heytesbury; *m* 1880, Adelaide Sophie, *y d* of Hugh Hamersley of Pyrton Manor, Oxfordshire; one *s* two *d*. Lt-Col the King's LI, retired. *Address:* The Rosary, Freshwater Bay, Isle of Wight.
Died 23 June 1923.

HOLROYD, Sir Charles, Kt 1903; Hon. LittD Leeds; RE; FSA; Director of National Gallery, 1906–16; Keeper, National Gallery of British Art (Tate Gallery), 1897–1906; *b* Leeds, 9 April 1861; *s* of William Holroyd, merchant of that town, and Lucy Woodthrope of Aveley, Essex; *m* 1891, Fannie Fetherstonhaugh, *d* of Hon. John Alexander Macpherson of Melbourne; one *s*. *Educ:* Leeds Grammar School; Yorkshire College of Science; The Slade School of Fine Art, University College, London. Medal for Painting from Life, 1st prizes for Landscape Painting, Etching and Composition; Travelling Studentship for two years, spent in Italy. Assistant to Professor Legros at the Slade School for four years; frequently exhibited pictures at the Royal Academy, the Royal Institute of Painters in Water Colours, etc, and etchings in the Royal Society of Painter Etchers. Member of the Art Workers' Guild. *Publications:* Etchings, including the Monte Olivetto Series, and the Icarus Series, etc; Michael Angelo and his Works; Life of A. Legros for the Supplement to Encyclopædia Britannica. *Recreation:* gardening. *Address:* Sturdie House, Beechwood Avenue, Weybridge. *T:* Weybridge 305. *Clubs:* Athenæum, Arts, Burlington Fine Arts.
Died 17 Nov. 1917.

HOLROYD, Hon. Sir Edward Dundas, Kt 1903; *b* 25 Jan. 1828; *s* of Edward Holroyd, Senior Commissioner London Bankruptcy Court, 1831–69, and *g s* of Sir George Sowley Holroyd, Justice of the Court of King's Bench, described by Lord Brougham as "high amongst the greatest of any age"; *m* 1862, Anna Maria Hoyles, *d* of Henry Compton; two *s* three *d*. *Educ:* Winchester (Queen's gold medal for Latin and English Essays, 1845, 1846); Trinity College, Cambridge (1st Cl. Class. Tripos, MA 1854). Called to the English Bar, Gray's Inn, 1855; Melbourne Bar, 1859; Tasmanian Bar, 1867; offered a Judgeship, 1872 and 1873, but declined; QC 1879; Justice of the Supreme Court of Victoria, 1881–1906; retired 1906. President of Athenæum and Savage Clubs, Melbourne. *Address:* Fernacres, St Kilda, Melbourne, Victoria. *Club:* Junior Conservative.
Died 5 Jan. 1916.

HOLT, Sir Edward, 1st Bt, *cr* 1916; CBE 1920; twice Lord Mayor of Manchester; *b* 9 Sept. 1849; *e s* of Joseph Holt; *m* 1879, Elizabeth, *d* of Joseph Brooks, Cheatham, Manchester; one *s* three *d* (and one *s* decd). Heir: *s* Edward Holt, *b* 16 April 1883. *Address:* Woodthorpe, Prestwich, Lancs; Blackwell, Windermere.
Died 11 April 1928.

HOLT, Henry; author, publisher; editor Unpartizan (lately Unpopular) Review, 1914–21; *b* Baltimore, Md, 3 Jan. 1840; *s* of Dan and Ann E. Holt; *m* 1st, 1863, Mary Florence (*d* 1879), *d* of J. Selby West of New York; 2nd, 1886, Florence, *d* of Charles Corey Taber of New York; three *s* three *d*. *Educ:* Yale (AB 1862); Columbia (LLB 1864); Hon. LLD University of Vermont, 1901; Hon. Phi Beta Kappa Johns Hopkins Univ., 1914. Began publishing business with G. P. Putnam, 1863; subseq. President Henry Holt & Co.; Trustee Simplified Spelling Board; Trustee American Geographical Soc., 1892–1909; Fellow American Association for Advancement of Science; first Chairman New York University Settlement Society; first Chairman University Club Library; Member Harvard Visiting Committee on Philosophy and Psychology; lectured at Yale, Columbia, University of Vermont, and Union Theological Seminary. *Publications:* Calmire: Man and Nature, 1892; Talks on Civics, 1901; Sturmsee; Man and Man, 1905; On the Civic Relations, 1907; On the Cosmic Relations, 1914, second edition, enlarged, under title The Cosmic Relations and Immortality, 1919; Sixty Years a Publisher, 1924; The Hopeful Borderland, 1925; and sundry review articles. *Recreations:* music, landscape gardening. *Address:* 19 West 44th Street, New York; 57 East 72nd Street, NY; Fairholt, Burlington, Vermont. *Clubs:* Authors' (Presiding Officer, 1908–11), Century, City, University, Yale, New York; Ethan Alen, Country, Burlington.
Died 13 Feb. 1926.

HOLT, L. Emmett, MD, LLD; Emeritus Professor of Diseases of Children, Columbia University, and Physician-in-Chief to the Babies' Hospital, New York; Secretary Board of Scientific Directors, Rockefeller Institute of Medical Research. *Address:* 155 West 58th Street, New York.
Died 14 Jan. 1924.

HOLT, Sir Vesey (George Mackenzie), KBE 1920; JP Kent; a managing partner in Glyn Mills, Currie, Holt & Co., bankers and army agents; *b* 1854; *e s* of late Vesey Weston Holt; *m* 1880, Mabel Mary, *e d* of late Walter Drummond; four *s* one *d*. *Educ:* private schools. *Address:* 67 Cadogan Place, SW1; Mount Mascal, Bexley, Kent. *Clubs:* Arthur's, Travellers', Union.
Died 6 Dec. 1923.

HOLT, William R.; journalist and special correspondent; *b* Rochdale, 1870; *m* Mary (Minnie) Holt, Rochdale; two *s* one *d*. *Educ:* St Peter's, Rochdale. Trained as newspaper man on the Rochdale Observer, where his first important work was in connection with the death and burial of John Bright; was under Sullivan on the Birmingham Daily Mail; came to London, 1897; was in Belgrade immediately after assassination of King Alexander and Queen Draga, and attended the Skuptshina at which King Peter was elected to the throne; under fire during labour riots in Belgium, also in Sidney Street!; went to Constantinople for the jubilee of Sultan Abdul Hamid; accomplished a rapid transit journey by going from London to Washington and back, and interviewing President Taft, within twelve days. *Club:* Press.

HOLTZE, Maurice, ISO; PhD; Director Botanic Gardens, Adelaide, S Australia, 1892–1918; *b* Hanover, 9 July 1840; *s* of C. Holtze, Chief Inspector of Orphan Houses; *m* Evelampia, *d* of Surgeon-Captain Simon Mesenzoff, Russian Army; two *s* one *d*. *Educ:* Hildesheim; Marburg. Studied Horticulture and Botany at Royal Gardens, Hanover, and Imperial Gardens, Petrograd; went to Australia, 1872; Curator Botanic Gardens, Port Darwin, Northern Territory, 1876. *Address:* American River, Kangaroo Island, S Australia.
Died 12 Oct. 1923.

HOLWELL, Captain Raymond Vernon Doherty-, DSO 1915; RE; *b* 18 July 1882. Entered army, 1901; Captain, 1911; served European War, 1914–15 (despatches, DSO).
Died 9 Jan. 1917.

HOME, 12th Earl of, *cr* 1604; **Charles Alexander Douglas-Home,** KT 1899; DL, JP; Baron Home, 1473; Baron Dunglass, 1604; Baron Douglas (UK), 1875; Lord-Lieutenant of Lanarkshire, 1890–1918; Maj.-Gen. Royal Company of Archers; *b* The Hirsel, Coldstream, 11 April 1834; *s* of 11th Earl and Lucy, *e d* of 2nd and last Baron Montagu of Boughton; *S* father, 1881; *m* 1870, Maria, *o d* of Capt. Charles Conrad Grey, RN; one *s* four *d*. *Educ:* Eton; Trinity Coll. Camb. Lord-Lieut of Berwickshire, 1879–90. Heir: *s* Lord Dunglass, *b* 29 Dec. 1873. *Address:* The Hirsel, Coldstream, Berwickshire; Douglas Castle and Bothwell Castle, Lanarkshire. *Clubs:* Carlton, Travellers'.
Died 30 April 1918.

HOME, Col Frederick Jervis, CSI 1892; Royal Engineers (Retired List, 1895); *b* Calcutta, 22 Oct. 1839; *o surv. s* of late Maj.-Gen. Richard Home, Bengal Army; *m* 1868, Constance Stanley (*d* 1894), *e d* of John Stanley M'Gowan; two *s* one *d*. *Educ:* Kensington Proprietary Grammar School; HEIC Military Seminary, Addiscombe. Corps of Bengal Engineers, 1858; proceeded to India, 1860; Irrigation Branch of the Public Works Department, 1861–94; Inspector-General of Irrigation and Deputy-Secretary to the Government of India, Public Works Dept, 1890–94. Decorated for services in the Irrigation Department, India. *Address:* Aveland, Crieff, Perthshire. *TA:* Crieff.
Died 5 Nov. 1919.

HOME, Maj.-Gen. Hon. William Sholto; *b* 25 Feb. 1842; 4th *s* of 11th Earl of Home. Entered Grenadier Guards, 1860; Lieut and Capt. 1863; Capt. and Lieut-Col 1871; Major-Gen. 1895; served Egypt, 1882 (medal with clasp, 4th class Osmanieh, Khedive's star);

Suakin, 1885; Soudan, 1895 (clasp). *Address:* Cliveden Chambers, 105 Mount Street, W. *Died 22 Dec. 1916.*

HOMOLLE, Jean Théophile; Administrateur Général de la Bibliothèque Nationale depuis 1913; *b* Paris, 19 déc. 1848; *s* of Eugène Homolle, Dr en Médecine, et Florence Morlière; *m* Léonie Marthe Congnet; two *s* two *d. Educ:* Paris. Elève de l'Ecole Normale Supérieure, 1869-73; membre des Ecoles fr. d'Athènes et de Rome, 1874-78; Maître de Conférences à l'Université de Nancy, 1878-84; Professeur Suppléant au Collège de France, 1884-90; Directeur de l'Ecole française d'Athènes, 1891-1904, 1912-13; Directeur des Musées Nationaux, 1904-11; Membre de l'Académie des Inscriptions, 1892; Membre de l'Académie des Beaux-Arts, 1910. *Publications:* Les Archives de l'Intendance Sacrée à Délos; De antiquissimis Dianae simulacris Deliacis; Collaboration au Bulletin de Correspondance Hellénique depuis 1877; Direction de la publication des Fouilles de Delphes, et de Délos; Monuments figurés de Delphes. *Récréations:* promenade à pied, jardinage. *Address:* 8 rue des Petits Champs, Paris. *T:* Gutenberg 62-66. *Died June 1925.*

HONE, Nathaniel, RHA. *Address:* St Dolough's Park, Rahene, Co. Dublin. *Died 14 Oct. 1917.*

HOOD, Captain Basil; dramatic author; *b* 5 April 1864; *y s* of late Sir Charles Hood. *Educ:* Wellington College; Royal Military College, Sandhurst. Gazetted Lieutenant in Princess of Wales's Own (Yorkshire) Regt 1883; served 12 years; promoted Captain, 1893; afterwards half-pay; 3 years in 3rd Batt. same regiment; retired, 1898. Author of The Gypsies; Gentleman Joe; The French Maid; Dandy Dan; Duchess of Dijon; Orlando Dando; Her Royal Highness; The Rose of Persia; Ib and Little Christina, first serious play; The Emerald Isle; Sweet and Twenty; Merrie England, 1902; My Pretty Maid; A Princess of Kensington; dramatic versions of Hans Andersen's Tales; English versions of Merry Widow, Dollar Princess, The Count of Luxemburg, A Waltz Dream, and Gipsy Love; The Pearl Girl, 1913. *Recreations:* reading, travelling. *Address:* 88 St James's Street, SW. *Clubs:* Naval and Military, Garrick, Beefsteak.

Died 7 Sept. 1917.

HOOD, David Wilson, CBE 1919; MInstCE; Engineer-in-Chief, Trinity House; *b* 18 March 1874; 2nd *s* of late J. Hood, JP, Lilliesleaf, Roxburghshire; unmarried. *Educ:* Daniel Stewart's College and University, Edinburgh. *Address:* 5 Beech Mansions, W Hampstead, NW. *TA:* Dioptric, Fen, London. *T:* Hampstead 7564. *Club:* Caledonian. *Died 29 Oct. 1924.*

HOOD, Donald William Charles, CVO 1901; MD (Cantab); FRCP; Governor and Member Committee of Management of Bethlem and Bridewell Royal Hospitals; Consulting Physician and Member Board of Management of Earlswood Royal Institution; Vice-President West London Hospital; Senior Physician West London Hospital; in practice as consulting physician; *b* Market Lavington, Wilts, 23 June 1847; *e s* of late Sir Charles Hood, Lord Chancellor's Visitor in Lunacy; *m* 1871, Alice, *d* of John Wickham Flower of Park Hill, Croydon; one *s* three *d. Educ:* Harrow; Caius College, Cambridge. Late Examining Physician Foreign Office; late Manager Royal Institution of Great Britain; late Examiner in Medicine, Cambridge Univ. Decorated, 1901, for services rendered in connection with the Duke of Abercorn's and Georgina Countess of Dudley's fund for the relief of wounded and sick officers during the Boer War. *Recreations:* fishing, shooting. *Address:* 64 Boundary Road, St John's Wood, NW8. *T:* Maida Vale 2372. *Club:* Athenæum.

Died 15 March 1924.

HOOD, Rear-Adm. Hon. Horace Lambert Alexander, CB 1911; DSO 1904; MVO 1906; Naval Secretary to First Lord of the Admiralty since 1914; *b* 2 Oct. 1870; 2nd surv. *s* of 4th Viscount Hood; *m* 1910, Ellen, *d* of late A. E. Touzalin, and *widow* of George Nickerson; two *s.* Joined "Britannia," 1883; "Temeraire," 1885; "Calliope," 1889 (Hurricane at Samoa); obtained five first-class certificates, Beaufort Testimonial, Goodenough Medal, and Ryder Prize; Lieut, 1890; served Soudan Expedition, 1897-98 (Medjidieh, 4th class, despatches, medal, promoted to Commander); Captain, 1903; Rear-Admiral, 1913; served in "Hyacinth" in Somaliland Expedition, 1903 (despatches, medal, DSO); ADC to the King, 1912; in command of Royal Naval College, Osborne, 1910-14; served European War, 1914-15 (despatches). *Address:* East Sheen Lodge, Sheen, Surrey, SW. *T:* Richmond 72. *Clubs:* Naval and Military, Roehampton. *Died 31 May 1916.*

HOOD, Hon. Sir Joseph Henry, Kt 1920; MA, LLB; Judge of Supreme Court, Victoria, since 1890; *b* 1 June 1846. *Educ:* Melbourne

University. Called to Bar, 1868; member of Council, Univ. of Melbourne, from 1891. *Address:* Supreme Court, Melbourne, Victoria. *Died 29 Jan. 1922.*

HOOKINS, Rev. William; President of the Methodist New Connexion, 1903-4; *b* Bridgwater, 10 Oct. 1845; *m* Ellen Jane Fisher, Oldbury; four *s* three *d. Educ:* St Mark's College Schools; Ranmoor College, Sheffield. Entered Ministry, 1870; Superintendent of Irish Missions, 1890-93. *Address:* 2 Crown Hill Park, Torquay. *Died 14 Feb. 1917.*

HOOLE, Lt-Col and Hon. Col James, CMG 1900; 3rd Battalion Yorkshire Regiment; *b* 1850; *s* of late Francis Hoole of Moor Lodge, Sheffield, and of Edgefield, Bradfield, Yorks; *m* 1882, Mary Violet, *o d* of Rev. R. Hickman, of Birdinghay, Warwicks; three *s* two *d.* Served South Africa, 1900-1 (despatches, Queen's medal, three clasps). JP Oxfordshire, 1896; Lord of Manor of Headington. *Address:* Manor House, Headington, Oxford.

Died 8 Aug. 1917.

HOOPER, Rev. William, DD; missionary, CMS; translator, Mussoorie, India, since 1892; *b* 27 Sept. 1837; *s* of retired Lieut RN, and *d* of Thomas Bramston, MP; *m* 1st, 1862; 2nd, 1891; four *s* one *d. Educ:* Cheltenham Preparatory School; Bath Grammar School; Wadham College, Oxford; Hebrew Exhibition; Sanskrit Scholarship; 1st class in Lit. Hum.; BA, 1859; MA, 1861. Went to India, CMS, 1861; Benares, 1861-66; Calcutta, 1867-68; Vicar of Cressing, Essex, 1870-72; Benares, 1873; Lahore, 1874-79; Benares, 1881; Allahabad, 1882-87; Canon of Lucknow, 1906-19; Vicar of Mount Albert, New Zealand, 1889-90. *Publications:* translation of Old Testament in Hindi; Commentary on Epistle to Hebrews in English and Hindi; Hindi translation of Commentary on Epistle to Philippians; four lectures on Palestine; sermons on the Lord's Prayer; tract on the Lord's Day; Outline of Hinduism, in Hindi; Doctrine of Salvation as set forth in Christianity, Hinduism and Islam; Helps to Hindustani Idiom; The Hindustani Language; Hindi translation of St Clement's (of Rome) Epistle; Hebrew-Urdu Dictionary; Greek-Hindi Dictionary; Greek Grammar in Hindi; Urdu translation of Book of Common Prayer; Urdu Manual on the Holy Communion; Notes on the Bible; many sermons, lectures, etc. *Address:* Mussoorie, India.

Died 3 Oct. 1922.

HOOPER, Col Sir William Roe, KCSI 1903 (CSI 1897); *b* 12 Jan. 1837; *s* of John William Hooper of Bathwick; *m* 1859, Lucy Fanny (*d* 1919), *d* of Henry Benson Cox; one *d.* Served in India, 1859-95; President India Office Medical Board, 1895-1904; Hon. Surgeon to the King. FRCS. KGStJ. *Address:* Abertarff, Blackford Road, Edinburgh. *Died 29 Sept. 1921.*

HOPE, Adrian Elias, VD; *b* 8 April 1845; *e s* of late Capt. Adrian John Hope and Countess Rapp; *m* 1st, 1867, Lady Ida Duff, 2nd *d* of 5th Earl of Fife; three *d*; 2nd, 1876, Mildred Henrietta (*d* 1914), *e d* of Sir Francis Scott, 3rd Bt; two *d.* Late Hon. Col 1st London Rifle Volunteers. *Address:* 9 Clifton Place, Hyde Park, W2. *T:* Paddington 7147. *Clubs:* Carlton, Bachelors', Marlborough, St James', Royal Thames Yacht; Royal Yacht Squadron, Cowes.

Died 18 Nov. 1919.

HOPE, Sir Alexander, 15th Bt, *cr* 1628; JP Midlothian; *b* 22 Oct. 1824; *s* of Sir John Hope, 11th Bt and Anne, *d* of Sir John Wedderburn, 6th Bt; *S* brother, 1898. *Educ:* Haileybury. Bengal CS, 1845-75. Heir: *n* Major John Augustus Hope, *b* 7 July 1869. *Address:* Pinkie House, Musselburgh, NB. *Club:* New, Edinburgh.

Died 7 March 1918.

HOPE, Sir Edward Stanley, KCB 1908 (CB 1895); *b* 1 Feb. 1846; *e* surv. *s* of late George W. Hope of Luffness, East Lothian, formerly MP for Windsor, and the Hon. Caroline Georgiana, *d* of 2nd and last Lord Montagu of Boughton; *m* 1881, Constance Christina, *d* of Sir John Leslie, 1st Bt and Lady Constance Leslie of Glasslough, Ireland; one *s* one *d. Educ:* Eton; Christ Church, Oxford. Barrister, Inner Temple; Charity Commissioner for England and Wales, 1879-99; Registrar of Privy Council, 1899-1909; Lunacy Commissioner (unpaid), 1908-14. *Address:* Coulsdon Grange, Surrey. *T:* Purley 547. *Clubs:* Travellers', Turf.

Died 15 Feb. 1921.

HOPE, George Everard, JP, DL; Captain Grenadier Guards; *b* 4 Nov. 1886; *o c* of late Henry Walter Hope, and Lady Mary Catherine Constance, *sister* of 5th Earl of Rosebery; *m* 1911, Margaret, *d* of late John Cockton, JP, of Kirkborough, Cumberland; one *s* one *d. Address:* 65 Lowndes Square, SW; Luffness Castle, Aberlady, NB; Rankeillour

House, Springfield, Fife. *Clubs:* Wellington, Travellers'.
Died 10 Oct. 1917.

HOPE, Graham; *d* of Col W. Hope, VC, and *sister* of late Adrian Hope. Acted as Organising Secretary of the Women's Unionist and Tariff Reform Association for nearly four years. *Publications:* A Cardinal and his Conscience; My Lord Winchenden; The Triumph of Count Ostermann, 1903; The Gage of Red and White, 1904; The Lady of Lyte, 1905; Amalia, ⸺ The Honour of X, 1908.
Died 20 April 1920.

HOPE, James Edward; ⸺ Nov. 1852; *s* of James Hope of Belmont, Midlothian, and the H⸺n. Gertrude Elphinstone; *m* 1880, Sophia, *d* of Admiral Sir William Edmondstone 4th Bt, of Duntreath Castle; two *s* one *d*. *Educ:* Harrow; Oxford. Registrar of Estate Duties for Scotland till 1903. Member of Royal Company of Archers, King's Body Guard for Scotland. JP, Midlothian. *Address:* Belmont, Murrayfield, Midlothian. *T:* 4065 Edinburgh. *M:* S 1331. *Clubs:* Carlton; New, Edinburgh.
Died 8 Dec. 1917.

HOPE, Lt-Col Sir John (Augustus), 16th Bt, *cr* 1628; OBE 1918; MP (U) Midlothian, 1912–18; (CoU) North Midlothian and Peebles, Dec. 1918–22; *b* 7 July 1869; *s* of late Rev. Canon Charles Augustus Hope, Rector of Barwick in Elmet, Yorks; *S* uncle, 1918; *m* 1913, Hon. Mary Bruce, OBE, *e d* of 6th Lord Balfour of Burleigh; three *s* one *d*. Contested (U) Midlothian, 1910. Entered army, 1889; Major, 1905; served South Africa, 1901–2 (Queen's medal, 4 clasps); European War, with the 9th Batt. King's Royal Rifles (wounded); OBE; Lieut-Col, Reserve of Officers. *Heir: s* Archibald Philip Hope, *b* 27 March 1912. *Address:* Pinkie House, Musselburgh, NB. *Clubs:* Naval and Military, Carlton; New, Edinburgh.
Died 17 April 1924.

HOPE, John Owen Webley, CMG 1918; Senior Commissioner, Kenya Colony; *s* of late Rear-Adm. Charles Webley Hope; *b* 1875. *Club:* Caledonia⸺.
Died 15 Sept. 1927.

HOPE, Robert Charles, FSA; *b* Derby, 1855; *m* Mary, *d* of late Joseph Edgerley Purser, Dublin; two *s* one *d*. *Educ:* Derby School; Peterhouse, Cambridge. Late of Lincoln's Inn; Hon. Consul in Italy for the Univs of Scotland; resided in Scarborough, 1875–1900; then in Geneva and Florence; hon. secretary of the Yorkshire Lawn Tennis Association and County Club for first two years; founder and hon. sec. of the North of England Lawn Tennis Club and Filey LTC; invented the net adjuster and folding umpire's chair used at all first-class tournaments; manager and stage director of the Scarborough Dramatic Club for twelve years; conductor of the Scarborough Orchestral Society, 1899–1901, and of the Choral and Orchestral Society, 1890; manager and stage director of English Dramatic Club in Geneva, 1901–3, and of the English Dramatic Club, Florence, from 1907; travelled in America, Canada, China, Japan, Ceylon, S Africa, and Europe generally. *Publications:* Holy Wells of England; Mediæval Music; The Temples and Shrines of Nikko, Japan; The Leper in England; A Dialectal Glossary of Place-Nomenclature; The Church Plate in Rutland; English Goldsmiths, etc; composer of Church Service in D; editor of The Popish Kingdome or Reigne of Antichrist, by Barnabe Googe. *Recreations:* music, drama. *Address:* Wood Hall, Dulwich, SE21. *T:* Sydenham 0488.
Died 18 Dec. 1926.

HOPE, Col Thomas; JP, DL; late Captain Bombay Staff Corps; *b* 3 Feb. 1848; 2nd *s* of late Hon. Charles Hope, and Lady Isabella Helen Douglas, *d* of 5th Earl of Selkirk; *m* 1909, Mary Louisa, *d* of General Horace Albert Browne, Indian Army, and *widow* of Col W. G. Cumming, RE. MP (C) Linlithgow, 1893–95. *Address:* Summerhill, Dumfries. *Club:* New, Edinburgh.
Died 28 March 1925.

HOPE, Sir William Henry St John, Kt 1914; LittD, Hon. DCL (Durham); FSA; Assistant Secretary of the Society of Antiquaries, 1885–1910; *b* 23 June 1854; *s* of Rev. William Hope and Hester, *d* of Rev. J. B. Williams; *m* 1st, 1885, Myrrha Fullerton (*d* 1903); one *s*; 2nd, 1910, Mary, *d* of John Robert Jefferies. *Educ:* St John's Coll., Hurstpierpoint; Peterhouse, Cambridge. KGStJ. *Publications:* The Stall Plates of the Knights of the Garter, 1901; The Abbey of St Mary-in-Furness, 1902; Heraldry for Craftsmen and Designers, 1913; A Grammar of English Heraldry, 1913; Windsor Castle, its Architectural History, 1913; joint author of The Chronicles of the Collegiate Church of All Saints, Derby; and of The Corporation Plate and Insignia of Office of the Cities and Towns of England and Wales; numerous papers in various transactions on archæological subjects. *Address:* Galewood, Great Shelford, Cambridge.
Died 18 Aug. 1919.

HOPE, Lt-Col William Henry Webley, CMG 1913; RA; Directo⸺ of Inspection, Royal Small Arms Factory, Enfield; *b* 1871; *s* of lat⸺ Rear-Adm. Charles Webley Hope; *m* 1900, Florence, *d* of late Charl⸺ Walter Hill of Clapham, Sussex; one *s*. *Educ:* Royal Military Academy Woolwich. *Address:* Royal Small Arms Factory, Enfield.
Died 13 May 191⸺

HOPKINS, Arthur Antwis, JP; Metropolitan Police Magistrate, Bo⸺ Street, since 1913; *b* 2 June 1855; *e s* of late John Satchell Hopkins Edgbaston, Birmingham; *m* 1880, Ada, *y d* of late Rev. James Butler DCL, All Souls Coll. Oxford. *Educ:* Rugby School; Trinity Coll Camb. (MA). Barrister, 1879; Metropolitan Police Magistrate Lambeth, 1890–1913. *Address:* 63 North Gate, NW. *Clubs:* Unite⸺ University, Portland.
Died 6 July 191⸺

HOPKINS, Paymaster-in-Chief David Bertie Lyndsay, MVC 1904; Paymaster-in-Chief, RN (retired) 1911; *b* 14 Jan. 1862; *s* o⸺ late David Hopkins; *m* 1891, Annie Jeanette, *d* of late Archibal⸺ Menzies. Asst Clerk, 1878; Paymaster, 1894; Fleet-Paymaster, 1902 Clerk to Secretary in Minotaur during Egyptian War, 1882 (Egyptia⸺ medal, bronze star); Secretary to Commanders-in-Chief China Australia, Mediterranean and Portsmouth Stations. *Address:* Th⸺ Corner, Horley, Surrey.
Died 21 March 1925

HOPKINS, Everard; artist; contributor to Punch, Illustrated Londo⸺ News, Black and White, etc; *b* Hampstead, 5 Feb. 1860; *y s* of Manle⸺ Hopkins, Hawaiian Consul. *Educ:* Charterhouse; Slade School of Art Gower Street. Slade Scholar, 1878; Assistant Editor of the late Pilo⸺ newspaper. *Publication:* novel, Lydia. *Recreations:* cycling, tennis, golf *Address:* 85A Linden Gardens, W2. *T:* Park 1104. *Club:* Savile.
Died 17 Oct. 1928

HOPKINS, Rt. Rev. Frederick C., SJ; titular Bishop of Athribis; Vica⸺ Apostolic of British Honduras since 1899; *b* 1844; *s* of William Hopkins, Birmingham. *Educ:* Ratcliffe College; Oscott. Attende⸺ Birmingham Hospital Medical School; MRCS, London; entered the Society of Jesus, 1868; edited the Angelus (a Belize Catholic Church magazine), 1888–99. *Address:* Bishop's House, Belize, British Honduras.
Died 11 April 1923

HOPKINS, John Castell, FSS, FRGS, PRSL; author The Canadian Annual Review of Public Affairs, 1901–20; Managing Director, The Canadian Review Co., Ltd; *b* Sunset Park, Dyersville, Iowa, US, 1 April 1864; *s* of late John Castell Hopkins of The Cliffs, Duncan⸺ BC, and *g s* of late John Castell Hopkins, JP, Rowchester House⸺ Berwickshire; *m* 1907, Anne Beatrice Bonner, Toronto; two *d*. *Educ* Bowmanville; Toronto. Associate Editor Toronto Daily Empire⸺ 1890–93; seven years in Imperial Bank of Canada; Founder of the 1st Branch Imperial Federation League in Ontario; Hon. Secretary of the League in Canada for some years; a Founder and ex-President of the Empire Club of Toronto; Pres. in 1891–92 of the Ontario and Toronto Conservative Associations. *Publications:* 30 volumes in Canadian and British History or Biography; many pamphlets on public topics; Editor of Canada: An Encyclopædia of the Country, in 6 Vols; special contributor to NY Tribune, London Times, Sheffield Telegraph, Glasgow Herald; many magazine articles. Canadian contributor to Appleton's Encyclopædia, the Americana, and others. *Recreations:* golfing, reading novels. *Address:* 121 Farnham Avenue, Toronto, Canada. *Clubs:* Albany, Royal Canadian Yacht, Rosedale Golf, Toronto.
Died Nov. 1923.

HOPKINS, Sir John Ommanney, GCB 1899 (KCB 1892); JP; Admiral 1896; *b* 1834; *s* of Rev. W. T. Hopkins, Rector of Nuffield, Oxon; *m* 1st, 1875, Magdalen (*d* 1876), *d* of Metcalfe Larken; 2nd, 1882, Minna, *d* of Admiral Sir Sydney Colpoys Dacres, GCB; one *s* one *d*. *Educ:* Marlborough Coll. In Black Sea, 1854–55; at Sebastopol; private secretary to First Lord of the Admiralty, Earl of Northbrook, 1881–83; ADC to the Queen, 1881–85; Director of Naval Ordnance, 1883–86; Admiral Superintendent of Portsmouth Dockyard, 1886–88; Naval Lord of the Admiralty and Controller of the Navy, 1888–92; Commander-in-Chief North American and West India Station, 1892–95; Commander-in-Chief on the Mediterranean Station, 1896–99; medal and clasp for Sebastopol. *Recreations:* riding, shooting, fishing, cycling. *Address:* Greatbridge House, Romsey, Hants. *TA:* Romsey. *Clubs:* United Service; Royal Naval, Portsmouth; Union, Malta.
Died 30 July 1916.

HOPKINS, Livingston; cartoonist and part proprietor Sydney Bulletin; *b* Bellefontaine, Ohio, USA, 1846; *s* of Daniel and Sarah Hopkins; *m* 1875, Miss Commager of Ohio; five *c*. Left school at the age of fourteen; after various experiments in commerce, journalism, etc, the opportunity came for cultivating long-existing taste for humorous illustration; went to New York in 1870, and between that and 1883 contributed to most of the current American illustrated publications of that period; engaged by the Sydney Bulletin for three years (1883), which term renewed from time to time led to share in the business; retired. *Recreations:* music, fiddle-making, mechanics, and outdoor amusements. *Address:* Raglan Street, Mosman, near Sydney, NSW. *T:* Mosman 1117. *Clubs:* Imperial Service, Sydney; Recreation, Mosman.

Died 21 Aug. 1927.

HOPKINS, Tighe; writer; *b* 8 Dec. 1856; *o s* of late Rev. W. R. Hopkins, Vicar of Moulton, Cheshire; *m* 1881, Ellen (*d* 1914), *o d* of late Rev. H. J. Crump, and *step-d* of late Mortimer Collins, novelist; one *d. Educ:* St John's, Leatherhead; Oundle Grammar School. *Publications:* 'Twixt Love and Duty, 1886; For Freedom, 1888; Nugents of Carriconna, 1890; Incomplete Adventurer, 1892; Lady Bonnie's Experiment, 1895; Kilmainham Memories, 1896; Pepita of the Pagoda (Arrowsmith's Annual), 1897; Dungeons of Old Paris, 1898; An Idler in Old France, 1899; The Silent Gate: A Voyage into Prison, 1900; Man in the Iron Mask, 1901; The Women Napoleon Loved, 1910; Some forty chapters in London Stories, 1911; Wards of the State, an Unofficial View of Prison and the Prisoner, 1913; Romance of Fraud; Prisoners of War, 1914; Romance of Escapes, 1916; Your Unsuspected Self, 1917; Literary Staff of the Daily Chronicle, Nation; Carleton's Traits and Stories in Red Letter Library; De Quincey in Newnes's Classics; has written largely on Penal Reform. *Recreations:* cycling, walking. *Address:* Frayne, Herne Bay.

Died 14 Feb. 1919.

HOPKINS, William Joseph, MVO; *b* 22 Aug. 1863; *s* of Joseph Hopkins, Salisbury, Wilts; *m* Harriett Jane, *d* of John Barber, Southampton; three *s* two *d. Educ:* Salisbury Grammar School. Joined Metropolitan Police, 1885; served in all ranks; Superintendent of K Limehouse Division, D Marylebone Division, and A Whitehall Division; retired. Officier de l'Ordre Leopold II of Belgium; 1st and 2nd Jubilee, Edward VII and George V Coronation medals; Chairman of County Society — Wiltshiremen in London. *Recreations:* swimming, amateur theatricals. *Address:* 399 Fulham Palace Road, Fulham, SW6. *Club:* Stadium. *Died June 1927.*

HOPKINSON, Bertram, CMG 1917; MA; FRS 1910; MICE; Professor of Mechanism and Applied Mechanics, Cambridge University since 1908; Professorial Fellow, King's College, 1914; *b* 11 Jan. 1874; *e s* of late Dr John Hopkinson, FRS; *m* 1903, Mariana, *e d* of Alexander Siemens; seven *d. Educ:* St Paul's School; Trinity College, Cambridge. Called to Bar, 1897; on death of Dr J. Hopkinson, 1898, started business as a consulting engineer in partnership with Chas Hopkinson and Ernest Talbot; jointly with partners was responsible for the design of the electric tramways at Leeds and Newcastle-on-Tyne and numerous other works. *Publications:* edited Original Papers by Dr J. Hopkinson, with a memoir; author of several scientific and technical papers, read before the Royal Society, Institution of Civil Engineers, and other bodies. *Recreations:* sailing, walking, rowing, ski-ing. *Address:* 10 Adams Road, Cambridge. *T:* 108 and 268 Cambridge.

Died 26 Aug. 1918.

HOPKINSON, Edward, DSc (London), MA (Cambridge); MInstCE, MIMechE (Past President), MIEE; MP (CU) Clayton Division of Manchester since Dec. 1918; *b* Manchester, 28 May 1859; 4th *s* of late John Hopkinson, sometime Mayor of Manchester, and Alice, *d* of late John Dewhurst, Skipton; *m* Minnie, *e d* of late John Campbell of Rathfern, Co. Antrim; one *s* one *d. Educ:* Owens College, Manchester; Emmanuel College, Cambridge (Scholar and Fellow). Mechanical and electrical engineer; designed the electrical equipment of the Bessbrook and Newry Tramroad, also the original City and South London Railway, opened 1890, for papers on which he received the Telford and George Stephenson medals and premiums of the InstCE; Chairman David Lewis Colony for Epileptics; Member of Executive Committee Manchester Steam Users' Association; a Director of Mather & Platt Ltd, and of the Chloride Electrical Storage Co., Ltd; Indian Industrial Commission, 1916–18. *Publications:* technical papers in Trans of the Royal Society and Proc of the InstCE and InstMechE. *Recreations:* travelling, climbing. *Address:* Ferns, Alderley Edge, Cheshire. *T:* Alderley Edge 20. *Clubs:* Athenæum, Reform, Alpine. *Died 15 Jan. 1922.*

HOPKINSON, John, FLS, FGS, FZS, FRMS, FRMetSoc, AssocInstCE; Secretary Ray Society since 1902; Director St Albans Gas Co.; Income Tax Commissioner (St Albans); *b* Leeds, 1844; *m* Kate, *d* of Thomas Willshin of Kingsbury, St Albans; two *d. Educ:* Leeds; London; Berkhamsted. In business (J. & J. Hopkinson,

pianoforte manufacturers), 1860–1913; founded Herts Natural History Society 1875, editor from 1875, Hon. Secretary 1875–91, President 1891–93; Treasurer Ray Society, 1899–1902; founded the Conference of Delegates to British Association in 1880 (first Chairman), and chiefly instrumental in founding the Herts County Museum at St Albans, built in 1898, establishing a Meteorological Observatory at the Museum in 1900 by presenting the instruments; Conservative; Church of England. *Publications:* Bibliography of the Tunicata, 1912; British Freshwater Rhizopoda (with J. Cash and G. H. Wailes), 3 vols published; numerous papers in Geological Magazine, Annals Natural History, British Association Reports, Trans Herts Natural History Society, etc; several articles in works on Yorks, Herts, and Beds. *Recreations:* mountain walking, photography (especially geological). *Address:* Weetwood, Watford. *Died 5 July 1919.*

HOPLEY, Hon. William Musgrove; Senior Judge, Southern Rhodesia, since 1914; *b* 1858; *e s* of Frederick Hurlingh Hopley, MLA, and Wilhelmina Johanna von Abo; *m* 1882, Annie Catherine, *e d* of Hon. John Van der Byl, MLC; one *s* one *d. Educ:* St Andrew's Coll. Grahamstown; Diocesan College, Rondebosch, Cape Colony; Pembroke College, Cambridge. MA, LLM, 1st class Law Tripos, 1877. Called to Bar, Inner Temple, and joined Cape Bar, 1878; practised at Cape Town and Grahamstown till 1883; at Kimberley from 1883; Crown Prosecutor for Griqualand West, 1885–92; QC 1890; Puisne Judge of the Supreme Court, Cape Colony, March 1892, and assigned to the High Court of Griqualand; on staff of Field Marshal Lord Roberts as legal adviser at Bloemfontein, March, April, May, 1900; assigned to Supreme Court, Cape Town, temporarily 1904 and permanently 1907; late Puisne Judge, Cape Colony; retired on pension from the Bench of the Supreme Court of S Africa, CPD, 30 Sept 1914. *Address:* Judges Chambers, Salisbury, Rhodesia. *Clubs:* Civil Service, Cape Town; Salisbury, Salisbury.

Died March 1919.

HOPTON, Rev. Preb. Michael; *b* 1838; 2nd *s* of Rev. W. Parsons Hopton, Bishops Frome, Bromyard; *m* 1872, Mary Lucy (*d* 1910), 4th *d* of Sir William Rouse Boughton, 10th Bt, Downton Hall, Salop; one *d. Educ:* Harrow; Trinity Coll. Camb. (MA). Vicar of Staunton Long, 1866–76; Canon of Frome, 1876–1903; Prebendary of Hereford Cathedral, 1901. JP Herefordshire; late Hon. Sec. to Hereford Three Choirs Festival, the Clergy Widows and Orphan Charity; Hon. Treasurer Clergy Pension Fund for Hereford Diocese; Hon. Treasurer Diocesan Board of Finance. *Address:* Holmer Hall, Hereford. *TA:* Hereford. *Died 20 April 1928.*

HOPWOOD, Aubrey; author; *b* Edinburgh, 4 April 1863; 2nd *s* of late John Turner Hopwood of Ketton Hall, Stamford. *Educ:* Cheam School; Charterhouse. Lieut Northamptonshire Regiment, 1882; travelled round the world, 1889; Secretary of Arthur's Club, 1893–1907. *Publications:* Down by the Suwanee River, 1897; The Sleepy King, 1898; The Bunkum Book, 1900; Rhymes without Reason, 1903; The Old English Sheep Dog, 1905; author of lyrics for A Runaway Girl, The Lucky Star, Alice in Wonderland, Bluebell, The Cherry Girl, The Merry-go-Round, The Lady Wrangler, You and I, and many songs for music. *Recreations:* shooting, fishing. *Address:* The Beeches, Malmesbury. *T:* Malmesbury 33. *Clubs:* Authors', Garrick, Orleans. *Died 25 Oct. 1917.*

HOPWOOD, Avery; playwright; *b* Cleveland, Ohio; *s* of James Hopwood and Jule Pendergast. *Educ:* University of Michigan, AB, 1905. Went to New York as Special Correspondent for Cleveland Leader, 1905. *Publications:* (plays) This Woman and This Man; Seven Days (with Mary Roberts Rinehart); Judy Forgot; Nobody's Widow (produced in England as Roxana); Fair and Warmer; Sadie Love; Our Little Wife; Double Exposure; The Gold Diggers; The Bat, and Spanish Love (both with Mary Roberts Rinehart); The Girl in the Limousine; Ladies' Night; The Demi-Virgin; Why Men Leave Home; Little Miss Bluebeard; The Alarm Clock; The Best People (with David Gray); Naughty Cinderella; The Garden of Eden, etc. *Address:* c/o Farmers' Loan and Trust Co., 475 5th Avenue, New York, NY. *Clubs:* Lambs, University of Michigan, Coffee-House, New York. *Died 1 July 1928.*

HOPWOOD, Charles Augustus, CB 1897; *b* 27 Dec. 1847; *s* of late Rev. Canon Hopwood and Lady Ellinor Mary, *d* of 13th Earl of Derby; *m* 1888, Georgie Florence Louisa, *d* of late George Lear Curtis. Entered Foreign Office, 1872; Assistant Clerk, 1894; Senior Clerk, 1899; retired, 1906. *Address:* 18 Beaufort Gardens, SW3. *T:* Western 1719. *Died 21 March 1922.*

HORE, Col Charles Owen, CMG 1900; late Lieutenant-Colonel 2nd Battalion Royal Garrison Regiment; retired, 1907; *b* 2 Sept. 1860;

m 1889, Dulcibella Eden, *d* of General George T. Radcliffe. *Educ:* Cheltenham College. Late South Staffs Regiment; served Egypt, 1882, 1884–85, 1898; South Africa, 1899–1900 (despatches thrice, Queen's medal, 8 clasps). *Address:* 23 South Eaton Place, SW. *Club:* Army and Navy.   *Died 14 Feb. 1916.*

HORE, Maj.-Gen. Walter Stuart; retired, 1899; Bombay Infantry; *b* 1843; *s* of late Capt. William Hore, Bengal Army; *m* 1876, *d* of General W. S. Hatch, RA; one *s* one *d*. *Educ:* Cheltenham College. Served Abyssinian Campaign, 1867–68 (medal); Hon. Colonel 120th Rajputana Infantry; JP Herefordshire. *Address:* Lemore, Eardisley, Herefordshire.   *Died 1 April 1918.*

HORLICK, Sir James, 1st Bt, *cr* 1914; DL, JP; High Sheriff, Gloucestershire, 1902; Lord of the Manor of Cowley; *b* 30 April 1844; *m* 1873, Margaret Burford; two *s* (and one *s* decd). *Educ:* privately. For many years actively engaged in promoting the interests of Horlick's Malted Milk Co., of which concern the founder and Chairman; latterly took great interest in the agricultural matters of Gloucestershire, and in country pursuits. *Recreations:* shooting, motoring. *Heir: s* Ernest Burford Horlick [*b* 29 Feb. 1880; *m* 1902, Jane, *d* of late Col Cunliffe Martin; one *s* two *d*. *Educ:* Wellington College; Christ Church, Oxford]. *Address:* 2 Carlton House Terrace, SW1. *T:* Regent 2458; Kidbrooke Park, Forest Row, Sussex. *TA:* Horlick, Charles, London. *Clubs:* Bath, Constitutional, Carlton.   *Died 7 May 1921.*

HORN, David Bayne, CIE 1905; FCH; MICE; Irrigation, Marine, and Railway Branches, Public Works Department, Government of Bengal (retired); *b* 1851; *s* of late David Horn of Middle Douglie, Perthshire, and latterly of Dollar. *Educ:* RIE College. Appointed Assistant Engineer, Bengal, 1874; Executive Engineer, 1882; Under-Secretary, Public Works Department, 1885–86; Superintending Engineer, 1896; Member Legislative Council, Bengal, 1902; Chief Engineer and Secretary to Government, 1902–6; retired, 1906. *Club:* Oriental.   *Died 3 Jan. 1927.*

HORN, William Austin; *b* 24 Feb. 1841; *s* of late E. K. Horn; *m* Penelope, *d* of late W. C. Belt, Barrister-at-Law, Middle Temple; five *s* two *d*. *Educ:* St Peter's College; Worcester College, Oxford. For fifty years engaged in development of outlying portions of the British Empire in Australia, Ceylon, Malay States, India, Papua; several minor exploring expeditions in Australia, 1868–79; explored scientifically Central Australia in 1894; holder of Australian record for long ride on horseback, 164 miles in 22½ hours; represented district of Flinders in S Australia, for which State a JP for 52 years; Governor of Middlesex Hospital; Chairman of Knula Selangor Rubber Co., British New Guinea Develt Co., and Robinson River Rubber and Coconut Co.; Director of Bank of Adelaide, London. *Publications:* Results of Horn Scientific Exploration; Notes by a Nomad; Bush Echoes. *Recreations:* shooting, golf. *Address:* 5 Onslow Gardens, SW. *T:* Kensington 6695; Old Stoke Lodge, Stoke Charity, Hants. *Clubs:* Carlton, Junior Carlton.   *Died 23 Dec. 1922.*

HORNABROOK, Ven. Charles Soward; Archdeacon of Adelaide since 1918; Priest in Charge of St Mary Magdalene, Adelaide, since 1908; Canon of Adelaide, 1911; *m.* Ordained, 1889; Curate of Tarree, 1889–92; St John's, Adelaide, 1892–94; Rector of Kapunda, 1894–1901; Port Adelaide, 1901–5; general licence, Diocese of Adelaide, 1908; Archdeacon of Mt Gambier, 1908–11. *Address:* Adelaide, South Australia.   *Died 25 Sept. 1922.*

HORNBY, Albert Neilson; *b* Blackburn, 10 Feb. 1847; *s* of late W. H. Hornby. *Educ:* Harrow. Played cricket with marked success for 31 years—first for Harrow against Eton, 1864, and then for Lancashire, which he captained for many years. *Recreations:* cricket, football, fox-hunting, shooting. *Address:* Parkfield, Nantwich. *Clubs:* MCC; Lancashire County Cricket.   *Died 17 Dec. 1925.*

HORNBY, Sir (William) Henry, 1st Bt, *cr* 1899; JP, DL; MP (C) Blackburn, 1886–1910; head of W. H. Hornby & Co., cotton spinners and manufacturers; *b* 29 Aug. 1841; *s* of late William Henry Hornby, MP for Blackburn; *m* 1887, Letitia, *d* of Capt. W. R. Clayton Browne; one *s* three *d* (and one *s* decd). Served as a Naval Cadet in 1855 in the Baltic during the Crimean War. *Heir: s* Henry Russell Hornby [*b* 12 Sept. 1888; *m* 1913, Dorothy Elma, *o d* of Maj.-Gen. Sir W. Fry; one *s*. Was on active service in France]. *Address:* 34 Ennismore Gardens, SW7. *T:* Kensington 5269. *Club:* Carlton.   *Died 22 Oct. 1928.*

HORNE, Sir Andrew (John), Kt 1913; FRCPI; *b* Ballinasloe, Co. Galway, 18 Aug. 1856; *m* 1884, Margaret (*d* 1920), *d* of late Francis Norman, solicitor, Rutland Square, Dublin; two *s* two *d*. *Ed* Clongowes Wood College; Vienna. On obtaining medical degre was elected assistant to the Master, Rotunda Hospital; FRCPI 188 Vice-Pres., 1894–96, Pres., 1908–10; elected Master of Natio Maternity Hospital on its foundation, 1894; was Vice-President obstetrical section of British Medical Association held at Swans President obstetrical section Royal Academy of Medicine, Irelan Extern Examiner in Obstetrics, University of Dublin. *Publicatio* various papers on medical subjects. *Recreations:* golf, tennis, huntir *Address:* 94 Merrion Square, Dublin. *T:* Dublin 1476. *Clubs:* Ro Societies; Stephen's Green, Dublin.   *Died 5 Sept. 192*

HORNE, Frederic, OBE 1918; JP; Small Holdings Commission Ministry of Agriculture and Fisheries; retired, 1924; *b* Cuckfie Sussex, 14 Aug. 1868; *s* of late Charles Horne, MA, and Harr Silvester, *d* of Leonard Simpson; *m* Jean Picken, 2nd *d* of late Andre Thomson, The Manor, Shifnal; one *s* one *d*. *Educ:* Newpo Shropshire; Adams Grammar School. After leaving school, studi farming in Bucks, and Shropshire, and owing to ill-health went Central Queensland, 1881; returned after seven years, and farm for fifteen years at Hinnington, Shifnal; was for some years Vic Chairman of the Shropshire Chamber of Agriculture; contested Ludlow Division of Shropshire, 1904 and 1906, and Barkston A Division of Yorks, twice in 1910; formerly on Committee of Natior Liberal Club. *Publications:* several pamphlets dealing with Ru Depopulation, Land Reform, and Food Supply in time of Wa *Address:* Dickley-Wood, Harrietsham, near Maidstone, Kent. *Clt* National Liberal.   *Died 2 Feb. 192*

HORNE, Herbert P.; architect, writer, and connoisseur. Built Chur of the Redeemer, Bayswater Road, the new buildings in Brewhou Court, Eton College, the Baptistery, St Luke's, Camberwell, a various private houses. Contributed to the Saturday Review Fortnightly Review, Monthly Magazine, Burlington Magazine, Rev Archéologique, Rassegna d'Arte, etc; editor of the Hobby Hors 1887–91. *Publications:* Diversi Colores, 1891; The Binding of Book 1894; Life of Leonardo da Vinci by Vasari, done into English, wi a commentary, 1903; Condivi's Life of Michelangelo, done in English, 1904; Sandro Botticelli, 1908. *Address:* Palazzo proprio, Via dei Benci, Florence, Italy. *Club:* Burlington Fine Arts.   *Died 23 April 191*

HORNE, John, LLD; FRS; FRSE, FGS; *b* Campsie, Stirlingshire, Jan. 1848; *s* of late James Horne, Newmill, Campsie; *m* Anna Leylar (*d* 1926), *d* of late Henry Taylor and Anna M. Harringto Pernambuco, Brazil, and *step-d* of Robert Arbuckle, MD, Brazil, a of Auchenhay, Kirkcudbrightshire; two *s* one *d*. *Educ:* High Scho and Univ., Glasgow. Entered Geol Survey of Scot. 1867; Wollasto Fund, Geological Society, 1888; Murchison Centenary Fund (wi Dr Peach), 1892; Neill Medallist, Royal Society, Edinburgh, 189 Murchison Medallist, Geological Society (with Dr Peach), 189 Assistant Director, Geological Survey, Scot. 1901; retired fro Geological Survey, 1911. President (geological section), Britiš Association, Glasgow, 1901; President, Royal Society, Edinburgl 1915–19. Hon. LLD Aberdeen, 1902; Hon. LLD St Andrews, 191 Hon. LLD Edinburgh, 1920; Wollaston Medal, Geological Socie (with Dr Peach), 1921. Hon. Member of the Physical and Natur History Society, Geneva, 1920; Corresponding Member of th Geological Society of Belgium, 1922; Foreign Hon. Member American Academy of Arts and Sciences, 1925. *Publications:* Th Silurian Rocks of Scotland (with B. N. Peach, FRS, and J. J. H. Tea FRS); parts of several Geological Survey Memoirs, and various pape in jls and trans of scientific societies. *Recreations:* travelling in ne geological fields, reading. *Address:* 20 Merchiston Gardens, Edinburg   *Died 30 May 192*

HORNE, Lancelot Worthy, CBE 1918; MVO 1920; Superintende of the Line, London & North Western Railway, 1914; retired 192 when grouping of railways took place; *b* 1875; *e s* of late Octavi Horne and Harriet, *d* of late John Rowland Gibson, FRCS; unmarrie *Educ:* Shrewsbury. Entered service of L&NWR in General Manager office, 1893; transferred to office of Superintendent of Line, 189 has been Superintendent in charge of the Chester and Holyhead, th Birmingham and the London Districts; also Goods Manager Liverpool District; Assistant to Superintendent of the Line, 191 Major Engineer and Railway Staff Corps. *Recreations:* shooting, fishin *Address:* The Manor House, Cheddington, Bucks. *Club:* Conservative   *Died 7 March 192*

HORNER, Andrew Long, KC 1904; MP (U) South Tyrone sinc Jan. 1910; Crown Prosecutor, Co. Cavan; *b* Limavady, 1863; *m* 190

Annie M., *y d* of late John Robb, JP, Belfast; two *s* one *d*. *Educ:* Foyle College, Londonderry; Queen's University, Belfast. Member of North-West Irish Circuit; Bencher King's Inns, Dublin, 1912. Contested (U) South Tyrone, 1906. *Address:* 34 Fitzwilliam Place, Dublin. *Clubs:* Constitutional, Carlton.

Died 26 Jan. 1916.

HORNER, Egbert Foster, MusD; FRCO; Director of Examinations, Trinity College of Music, London; *b* London, 1864; *m* Emily Anna Charlesina, *d* of late Charles Fox, Tunbridge Wells; one *s* one *d*. *Educ:* pupil of Sir Frederick Bridge. MusB Durham University, 1895; MusD 1900. Organist of St John's Church, Westminster, 1890–1919; Examiner for Degrees in Music, University of Durham, 1924–27; Professor of Harmony and Counterpoint, Trinity College of Music; Examiner for Degrees in Music, University of Birmingham, 1927–28; Dean of the Faculty of Music, University of London, 1928; Examiner for Degrees in Music, University of London, 1928. Vice-President, Union of Graduates in Music; Member of the Court of Assistants, Royal Society of Musicians; Member of the Board of Studies in Music, Member of the Faculty of Music, and Recognised Teacher in Music, University of London. *Publications:* organ music, church music, etc. *Address:* 6 Alexandra House, St Mary's Terrace, W2.

Died 8 Oct. 1928.

HORNER, Sir John (Francis Fortescue), KCVO 1907; JP, DL; barrister; High Sheriff of Somerset, 1885; Commissioner of Woods and Forests, 1895–1907; *b* 28 Dec. 1842; *m* 1883, Frances, OBE, 4th *d* of William Graham, MP; two *d*. *Educ:* Eton; Balliol College, Oxford, MA. *Address:* 16 Lower Berkeley Street, W1. *T:* Langham 1660; Manor House, Mells, Frome. *Clubs:* United University, Athenæum, Brooks's.

Died 31 March 1927.

HORNING, Lewis Emerson; Professor of Teutonic Philology, University of Toronto (Victoria College), since 1905; *b* 2 April 1858; *s* of James Horning and Eliza Macklem, of United Empire Loyalist descent; *m* 1885, Beatrice Lillian, *d* of Charles Nixon; one *s* two *d*. *Educ:* Brantford Collegiate Institute, Victoria College; Postgraduate at Breslau, Goettingen, and Leipzic. Matriculated, 1880; four scholarships, BA, 1884. Taught Peterboro Collegiate Institute, 1884–86; Adjunct Professor Classic and Modern Languages, Victoria College, 1886–89; abroad, 1889–91; PhD Goettingen, 1891; Professor of German Language and Literature and of Old English, 1891–1905; public lecturer on literature, politics, and history. *Publications:* various High School and College textbooks; translation of Witkowski, History of German Drama in 19th Century; numerous magazine articles on Canadian literature, present day politics, etc; bibliography of Canadian (English) fiction with L. J. Burpee. *Recreation:* gardening. *Address:* Victoria College, Toronto, Canada.

Died 6 Jan. 1925.

HORNUNG, Ernest William; novelist and journalist; *b* Middlesbrough, 7 June 1866; *y s* of late John Peter Hornung, Middlesbrough; *m* 1893, Constance, *d* of late Charles Altamont Doyle, and *g d* of John Doyle ("H. B."). *Educ:* Uppingham School. In Australia, 1884–86; literary work ever since. *Publications:* A Bride from the Bush, 1890; Under Two Skies, 1892; Tiny Luttrell, 1893; The Boss of Taroomba, The Unbidden Guest, 1894; The Rogue's March, Irralie's Bushranger, 1896; My Lord Duke, 1897; Young Blood, Some Persons Unknown, 1898; The Amateur Cracksman, Dead Men Tell No Tales, 1899; The Belle of Toorak, Peccavi, 1900; The Black Mask, 1901; The Shadow of the Rope, 1902; No Hero, Denis Dent, 1903; Stingaree, A Thief in the Night, 1905; Mr Justice Raffles, 1909; The Camera Fiend, 1911; Fathers of Men, 1912; Witching Hill, 1913; The Thousandth Woman, The Crime Doctor, 1914; Notes of a Campfollower, 1919; The Young Guard (verse). *Address:* Midway Cottage, Partridge Green, Sussex. *Clubs:* Savile, Royal Automobile, MCC. *Died 22 March 1921.*

HORSFALL, Jeremiah Garnett, CIE 1890; Indian Civil Service (retired); *b* Fairfield Hall, Bolton Abbey, Yorkshire, 1840; *y s* of late Jeremiah Horsfall, JP; *m* 1875, Mary Isabella, 2nd *d* of late F. J. Howson of Huntingdon. *Educ:* Giggleswick; Christ's College, Cambridge (Scholar; BL). Entered Madras Civil Service, 1862; retired, 1890. Decorated for famine work in Ganjam District, 1888. *Address:* Hollenden, Exmouth, Devon.

Died 28 March 1920.

HORSFALL, Sir John Cousin, 1st Bt, *cr* 1909; County Alderman, West Riding of Yorkshire County Council; *b* 8 Dec. 1846; *s* of John Foster Horsfall, Oxenhope, near Keighley; *m* 1st, 1870, Elizabeth Ann (*d* 1887), *d* of James Hartley, Ilkley; three *d* (one *s* decd); 2nd, 1889, Sarah Emily, *d* of John Crossley Fawcett Greenfield, Brearley, near

Halifax; one *s* one *d* (and two *s* decd). *Educ:* privately, Rev. J. B. Grant, The Vicarage, Oxenhope; Commercial College, Rippenden, near Halifax. Worsted spinner, Glusburn, near Keighley; built Institute in Glusburn village, used for various purposes: Baptist religious worship and Sunday school, technical and art classes and lectures, recreation and library, swimming and slipper baths. *Heir:* s John Donald Horsfall, Captain TF Reserve [*b* 1 June 1891; *m* 1914, Henrietta, *d* of W. Musgrave, Shorbridge House, Eastbourne. *Address:* Beanlands, Crosshills, near Keighley]. *Address:* Hayfield, Crosshills, near Keighley. *TA:* Horsfall, Crosshills. *T:* Crosshills 20 and 30. *M:* C 7006, C 8095. *Clubs:* National Liberal; Union, Bradford.

Died 18 Oct. 1920.

HORSLEY, Gerald Callcott, FRIBA; Past-President Architectural Association; *b* 31 Oct. 1862; *y s* of late John Callcott Horsley, RA; *m* 1895, Susan, *d* of late Peter Black, Glasgow. *Educ:* Kensington School. Articled pupil to R. Norman Shaw, RA, 1879; became student of the Royal Academy; Owen Jones travelling student of Royal Institute of British Architects (1887, 1888). Designed many buildings, including St Paul's Girls' School, Brook Green, W; St Chad's Church, Longsdon; Framewood, Stoke Poges; Coverwood, Surrey; additions, Balcombe Place; offices for Universities Mission to Central Africa, Westminster, Harrow, and Pinner Stations for London and North-Western Railway. *Publications:* various papers and addresses on the Art of Architecture; a contributor to Architecture; A Profession of an Art, 1895. *Recreations:* sketching, golf. *Address:* 2 Gray's Inn Square, WC; 28 Bedford Gardens, Kensington, W. *T:* Central 2507. *Club:* Athenæum. *Died 2 July 1917.*

HORSLEY, Rev. J. W., MA Oxon; Vicar of Detling, Kent, 1911–21; Hon. Canon of Southwark; late Hon. Secretary, Southwark Diocesan Temperance Society; Borough Councillor and Chairman of Health Society of Southwark; Mayor of Southwark, 1910; Chairman of Clergy Friendly Society since 1882; *b* 14 June 1845, at Dunkirk, near Faversham, whereof his father , Rev. J. W. Horsley, MA Oxon, the first incumbent; *m* Mary Sophia, *e d* of Capt. Codd, Governor HM Prison, Clerkenwell; two *s* four *d*. *Educ:* King's School, Canterbury; Pembroke College, Oxford. Curate, Witney, Oxon (with Bishop Jacob), 1870; Curate, St Michael's, Shoreditch; Chaplain, HM Prison, Clerkenwell, 1876–86; Vicar, Holy Trinity, Woolwich; Rector of St Peter's, Walworth, 1894–1911. Member of Royal Commission on Venereal Disease, 1914. Clerical Sec. Waifs and Strays Society. Freemason, Grand Chaplain, 1906. *Publications:* Practical Hints on Parochial Missions (in conjunction with his brother-in-law, Bishop Dawes); Jottings from Jail; Prisons and Prisoners; I remember, 1911; How Criminals are Made and Prevented, 1912; Commentary of the Litany, 1915; and many papers and pamphlets. *Recreations:* natural history in most branches, especially botany and conchology; social reform, especially as regards temperance and sanitation. *Address:* c/o Detling Vicarage, Kent. *Club:* Swiss Alpine.

Died 25 Nov. 1921.

HORSLEY, Reginald Ernest, JP; MD; FRCSEd; author; *b* Sydney, NSW, 1863; *s* of late Capt. Charles Henry Horsley, 51st Madras NI, HEIC, Provost Royal Burgh of Crail, and Ex-officio Admiral of the Forth; *m* Mary, *d* of late William Inglis, of Kirkmay. *Educ:* Sydney Grammar School; Trinity College, Melbourne University; Universities of Edinburgh and Berlin. Was on editorial staff of Challenger Expedition Commission; was Assistant, Ear and Throat Wards, Edinburgh Royal Infirmary; Surgeon, Edinburgh (New Town) Ear and Throat Hospital; Aurist to the Edinburgh Institution for the Education of the Deaf and Dumb; Lecturer on Biology at Stonyhurst College affiliated Medical School; retired in 1903 from the profession of medicine; then engaged in literary work; travelled extensively in Australia, New Zealand, South Sea Islands and USA. *Publications:* The Yellow God; The Blue Balloon; Stonewall's Scout; Hunted through Fiji; In the Grip of the Hawk; The Romance of New Zealand (Romance of Empire); The Red Hussar, Hunting U-Boats, etc. *Recreations:* travelling, natural history. *Address:* Kirkmay House, Crail, Fife. *Died 22 July 1926.*

HORSLEY, Sir Victor Alexander Haden, Kt 1902; BS, MD (Halle); FRS 1886; FRCS; Surgeon to National Hospital for Paralysis and Epilepsy, 1886; Emeritus Professor of Clinical Surgery and Consulting Surgeon at University College Hospital since 1906; *b* Kensington, 14 April 1857; *s* of late John Callcott Horsley, RA; *m* 1887, Eldred, 3rd *d* of Sir Frederick Bramwell, 1st Bt; two *s* one *d*. *Educ:* Cranbrook School; Univ. Coll. Hospital. Professor-Superintendent of Brown Institution, 1884–90; Secretary to Royal Commission on Hydrophobia, 1885; Fullerian Professor at Royal Institution, 1891–93; Professor of Pathology, University College, 1893–96. 1st Medallist of the Lannelongue International Prize in Surgery, 1911; Royal

Medallist of the Royal Society; LLD and DCL Montreal and M'Gill Univ.; Foreign Associate of the Academy of Medicine, Paris, of the Academy of Wissenschaft, Berlin; Member of the Science Society of Sweden in succession to Lord Lister; Member of Learned Societies in Rome, Petrograd, Buda Pesth, Vienna, Philadelphia, etc. In 1884 he proved by experiment that the disease myxœdema was caused by the absence of the thyroid gland, and was subsequently awarded the Cameron gold medal and the Fothergill gold medal; was 1st Chairman of the Representative Meeting of the British Medical Association. A keen supporter of all Progressive measures and of National Sick Insurance; contested (L) University of London; he was prospective candidate of Market Harborough on temperance and woman suffrage lines, though on these grounds he was afterwards refused the support of the officials; Vice-Chairman of the LCC Sub-Committee of Enquiry into the Medical Inspection and Treatment of School Children, and Vice-President of the English League for the Taxation of Land Values. *Publications:* many papers, principally on the nervous system, in the Phil. Trans, Roy. Soc., Brit. Med. Journal, etc. *Address:* 25 Cavendish Square, W. *T:* Mayfair 2413. *Clubs:* Athenæum, National Liberal.   *Died 16 July 1916.*

HORT, Edward Collett, FRCPEd; consulting physician; *b* 1868; *s* of late Professor Hort, sometime Hulsean Professor in the University of Cambridge; *m* 1896, Ethel Augusta, *d* of late Rev. A. P. Gordon; two *d. Educ:* Emmanuel College, Cambridge; Guy's Hospital. Member Advisory Council for Medical Research, National Health Insurance Commission; Member Pathological Society, Great Britain and Ireland; Member Association Physicians; Fellow Royal Society of Medicine; Fellow of Royal Academy of Medicine, Ireland. Author of a new method of diagnosing Cancer by examining the blood, and of a new method of treating Gastric and Duodenal Ulcer with serum and dry protein; engaged in research work in private laboratory at Lister Institute. *Publications:* Rational Immunization in the Treatment of Pulmonary Tuberculosis, 1909; Autotoxæmia and Infection, Proc. Roy. Soc., 1910; Gastric Ulcer, BMJ, 1908, 1909, 1910; Diagnosis of Cancer by Examination of the Blood, ibid., 1909; Bacterial Vaccines and Rational Immunization, Pract., 1909; Normal Serum Therapy, Lancet, 1908; Use and Abuse of Tuberculin, Quart. Journ. of Medicine, 1911; Immune and Normal Serum Therapy, BMJ, 1911; Obscure Cases of Fever without Physical Signs, ibid.; The Dangers of Saline Injections, British Medical Journal, 1911; A Critical Study of Experimental Fever, Proc. Royal Society, 1912; Micro-organisms and their Relation to Fever, Journal of Hygiene, 1912; Salvarsan Fever and other Forms of Injection Fever, Proc. Royal Society Medicine, 1912; Fever, its Causes and Treatment, Lecture to Medical Graduates College, Medical Press, 1912; Vaccines and Fever, BMJ, 1913; The Etiology of Typhus Fever, Journ. of Hygiene, 1914; The Causal Organism of Typhus Fever, Journ. of Hygiene, 1914, BMJ, 1915; Hæmic Infections of the Urine, BMJ, 1914; The Sterility of Normal Urine, Journ. of Hygiene, 1914; The Etiology of Epidemic Cerebrospinal Fever, BMJ, 1915. *Recreations:* music, fishing. *Address:* 8 Harley Street, W1. *T:* Gerrard 2319; Thornlea, Harrow. *T:* Harrow 29.
                                                     Died 15 Oct. 1922.

HORTON, Major James; *b* 21 Jan. 1845. Served in 4th Dragoon Guards, 1860–87; Inspector of Saddlery, Royal Dockyard, Woolwich, 1887–1911; invented service saddle employed South African War; also the service 1910 riding saddle with automatic self-adjusting side bars, which has been patented. *Recreation:* painting. *Address:* Mentmore Lodge, Copers Cope Road, Beckenham, Kent.
                                                     Died 14 Nov. 1925.

HORTON, Lt-Col James Henry, DSO 1904; MRCS, LRCP; Major IMS; *b* 27 Dec. 1871. *Educ:* Guy's Hospital; Arthur Durham prize, 1891; Member and Cert. Medical Psychol Association. House Physician Guy's Hospital, 1895; entered IMS 1902; served East Africa, 1903 (despatches, DSO); Captain, 1905; Major, 1913; Indian Frontier War, 1908; Balkan War, 1912; Indian Expeditionary Force, Mesopotamia, 1914–15. *Address:* Personal Assistant to the Surgeon-General with the Govt of Bombay, Poona, India. *Club:* Junior Naval and Military.   *Died July 1917.*

HORTON-SMITH, Richard Horton, KC; MA; Bencher, late Senior Trustee, and Treasurer of Lincoln's Inn; Lincoln's Inn representative Governor of Tancred's Charities; Chairman of HM's Commissioners for Land Tax for the Holborn District; a Vice-President of the SPCK; *b* 4 Dec. 1831; *e s* of late Richard Smith of the City of London, and of The Lodge, Littlehampton, Sussex, and Elizabeth, *d* of late William Lumley; *e b* of Sir Lumley Smith, KC; *m* 1864, Marilla, *e d* of late John Baily, QC; two *s* two *d. Educ:* University College Sch.; University Coll. London; St John's Coll. Camb. 4th Classic and Senior Opt. 1856; Members' Latin Essay Prize,

1857; Fellow St John's Coll. 1859; Founder Raymond Horton-Smith Prize, 1900 (Camb. Univ.). Classical Lecturer, King's Coll. Lond. 1857. Called to Bar, 1859; QC 1877. Member of Original Liberal Unionist Committee for Maintenance of the Union, 1886; late Vice-Chairman of Committee University College Hospital, and subseq. on those of Brompton Hospital for Consumption, and Public Dispensary, Drury Lane (Chairman); late on Council, and also Committee of Hosp., King's Coll. London. *Publications:* Joint-Editor, De G. J. & S. (Chanc. Reports), 1862–65; Joint-Author (with De Gex), Arrangements between Debtors and Creditors, 1867–8–9; Theory of Conditional Sentences in Greek and Latin, 1894; various papers relative to the drama, etc. *Recreations:* literature, music (Director and VP, RAM; Hon. Counsel Philharmonic Society, and VP late Bar Musical Society), freemasonry (PJGW, PGSN). *Address:* 53 Queen's Gardens, Hyde Park, W. *T:* Paddington 2786. *Clubs:* Athenæum; Pitt, Cambridge.   *Died 2 Nov. 1919.*

HOSE, Rt. Rev. George Frederick, DD; *b* 3 Sept. 1838; *m* 1867, Emily Harriet, *d* of J. Kerbey, MRCS, HEIC. *Educ:* St John's Coll. Camb. (MA). Ordained 1861; Curate of Roxton and Gt Barford, Beds, 1861–65; Curate of Holy Trinity, Marylebone, 1865–68; Chaplain of Malacca, 1868–72; Chaplain of Singapore, 1872–81; Archdeacon of Singapore, 1874–81; Bishop of Singapore, 1881–1908. *Address:* The Manor House, Normandy, Guildford. *TA:* Hose, Normandy, Surrey.   *Died 26 March 1922.*

HOSIE, Sir Alexander, Kt 1907; MA; LLD; FRGS; *b* 16 Jan. 1853; *s* of late Alexander Hosie; *m* 1st, 1887, Florence Lindsay (*d* 1905); one *s*; 2nd, 1913, Dorothea (author of Two Gentlemen of China, 1924), *o d* of Rev. W. E. Soothill, Professor of Chinese, Oxford University. *Educ:* Grammar School, Old Aberdeen; King's College and University, Aberdeen. Student Interpreter in China, 1876; employed on special service at Chungking, 1882; 2nd Asst, 1886; 1st Asst, 1891; Consul at Wuchow, 1897; Kiu-kiang, 1900 (did not proceed); Consul-General for Province of Szechuen, 1902; Tientsin, 1908–12; Commercial Attaché to the British Legation in China, 1905–9; British Delegate to the Shanghai International Opium Commission, 1909; appointed personally to investigate the production of Opium in China, 1910; Coronation Medal, 1911; retired, 1912; Special Attaché to the British Legation, 24 Nov. 1919–11 Feb. 1920. *Publications:* Three Years in Western China; Manchuria, its People, Resources, and Recent History; On the Trail of the Opium Poppy, 1914; Szechwan, its Products, Industries and Resources, 1922; Editor of Philips' Commercial Map of China, 1922. *Address:* Coleford, Sandown, IW.   *Died 10 March 1925.*

HOSKIN, John, KC; LLD, DCL; one of the Board of Governors of University of Toronto; *b* Holsworthy, Devon, May 1836; *s* of Richard Hoskin; *m* 1866, Mary Agnes, *d* of late Walter Mackenzie, Barrister-at-Law, of Castle Frank, Toronto. *Educ:* London. Went to Canada, 1854; called to Bar, 1863; QC 1873; Bencher of Law Society of Upper Canada, 1876; sometime Treasurer; for many years Senator of Toronto University (Hon. LLD 1889); DCL (hon.) Trinity University; Chairman of Board of Trustees of University of Toronto until its reorganisation in 1906; Chairman of the New Board of Governors, 1906; Guardian *ad litem*, and Official Guardian of Infants, 1874–1904; Advisory Counsel to his Successor in Office from 1904; on the directorate of the Bank of Commerce, of the British American Assurance Company, of The Canada Life Assurance Co., and the Western Assurance Co.; President of the Canadian Landed and National Investment Company; a Director, late President Toronto General Trusts Company; a Director of the Toronto Gas Company, Vice-President the Western Assurance Company and British American Assurance Company. *Address:* Toronto. *Club:* York, Toronto.   *Died 6 Oct. 1921.*

HOSKING, Hon. Sir John Henry, Kt 1925; late Chairman of War Pensions Appeal Board; *b* Penzance, 1854; *m* 1890; two *s* one *d*. Went to Auckland, NZ, 1856. Barrister and Solicitor, 1875; KC 1907; Judge, Supreme Court, Wellington, 1914–25. *Address:* 24 Sefton Street, Wellington, New Zealand.
                                                     Died 30 May 1928.

HOSKINS, William, ISO 1907; *b* 2 Dec. 1842; *s* of Elias Hoskins; *m* 1879, Dulcinee, *d* of Henry Blick. Was Controller of Accounts and Stores for Prison Commissioners. *Address:* Glenroy, Southbourne Road, Bournemouth.   *Died 8 Nov. 1928.*

HOSKYNS, Rt. Rev. Sir Edwyn, 12th Bt; *cr* 1676; Bishop of Southwell, since 1904; *b* 22 May 1851; 4th *s* of Canon Sir John Leigh Hoskyns, 9th Bt; *S* brother, 1923; *m* 1883, Mary Constance Maude, *d* of Robert Benson; one *s* two *d. Educ:* Jesus College, Cambridge

(Fellow). Ordained, 1874; Curate, Welwyn, Herts; Quebec Chapel, 1879–81; St Clements, North Kensington, 1881–86; Rector, St Dunstan, Stepney, 1886–95; Vicar of Bolton, 1895–1901; Hon. Canon of Manchester from 1899; Rector of Burnley, 1901–4; Bishop of Burnley, 1901–5. *Heir: s* Edwyn Clement Hoskyns, *b* 9 Aug. 1884. *Address:* Bishop's Manor, Southwell.

Died 2 Dec. 1925.

OSKYNS, Sir Leigh, 11th Bt, *cr* 1676; *b* 14 Feb. 1850; 3rd *s* of Canon Sir John Leigh Hoskyns, 9th Bt, and Emma, *d* of late Admiral Sir John Strutt Peyton, KCH; *S* brother, 1914; *m* 1882, Frances Hester Frederica, *d* of John Samuel Bowles, Milton Hill, Berks; three *d* (one *s* decd). *Educ:* Haileybury; Trinity College, Oxford. Barrister-at-Law; formerly Crown Prosecutor, Kimberley. JP and High Sheriff for Oxfordshire, 1907. *Heir: b* Rt Rev. Edwyn Hoskyns, Bishop of Southwell, *b* 22 May 1851. *Address:* 78 Cadogan Square, SW1. *Clubs:* Arthur's, New University.

Died 12 Sept. 1923.

OSKYNS, Rear-Adm. Peyton, CMG 1900; MVO 1896; RN; commanded special service ships, Portsmouth; *b* Aston Tyrrold, Berks, 15 Sept. 1852; 5th *s* of Canon Sir John Leigh Hoskyns, 9th Bt, and Emma, *d* of Sir John Strutt Peyton, KCH; *m* 1882, Grace Macduff, *d* of D. M. Latham, JP, DL, Gourock House, Renfrewshire; two *s* two *d*. *Educ:* Haileybury; HMS "Britannia." Joined Navy, 1866, as Naval Cadet; retired 1907; served in the Sierra Leone rebellion, 1898 (despatches). Decorated: CMG for services in the Sierra Leone rebellion; MVO for services to Prince Henry of Battenberg, who was taking passage in HMS "Blonde" after Ashanti Expedition of 1895, and died *en route* to Sierra Leone. *Recreations:* shooting, fishing, golf. *Address:* The Brookside, Bedhampton, Havant. *Club:* United Service.

Died 20 Dec. 1919.

OSMER, James Kendall; author; *b* 29 Jan. 1834. *Educ:* graduated at Harvard, 1855; AB, AM 1867. Minister in Deerfield, Mass, 1860–66; Prof. of Rhetoric and Eng. Lit. at Antioch College, Ohio, 1866–72; Prof. of Eng. and History, University of the State of Missouri, 1872–74; PhD Univ. of Mo 1874; Prof. of Eng. and Germ. Lit., Washington Univ., St Louis, Mo, 1874–92; LLD 1897. President American Library Association, 1902–3; Librarian Minneapolis Public Library, 1892–1904, Emeritus from 1926; Member Minnesota Historical Society, Corresponding Member of Massachusetts Historical Society; Colonial Society of Mass, New England Historical and Genealogical Society; Fellow of the American Academy of Arts and Sciences, 1915; LLD Harvard University, 1925. *Publications:* Color Guard, 1864; Thinking Bayonet, 1865; Short History of German Literature, 1878; Life of Samuel Adams, 1884; Story of the Jews, 1885; Life of Young Sir Henry Vane, 1888; Short History of Anglo-Saxon Freedom, 1890; How Thankful was Bewitched, 1894; Life of Thomas Hutchinson, Royal Governor of Massachusetts Bay, 1896; History of the Mississippi Valley, 1901; History of the Louisiana Purchase, 1902; Appeal to Arms; Outcome of the Civil War, 1907; edited Journal of John Winthrop, 1908; The Last Leaf, 1912. *Address:* Public Library, Minneapolis, Minnesota, USA.

Died 11 May 1927.

OSTE, Sir William Graham, 4th Bt, *cr* 1814; 2nd Lieutenant, 2nd Rifle Brigade; *b* 12 Aug. 1895; *s* of Sir William Henry Charles Hoste, 3rd Bt and Alice, *d* of James Healy, of Sydney; *S* father, 1902. *Educ:* Royal Naval College, Osborne; Dartmouth; Harrow; Royal Military College, Sandhurst. Served European War, 1914–15 (wounded). *Heir:* none. *Address:* 48 Berkeley Square, W.

Died 9 May 1915 (ext).

OTHAM, 6th Baron, *cr* 1797; **Frederick William Hotham;** Bt 1621; *b* 19 March 1863; *s* of late Rev. William Francis Hotham and Emma, *d* of John Carbonell; *S* cousin, 1907; *m* 1902, Benita, *d* of late Thomas Sanders; two *d*. Owner of about 15,000 acres. Possessed the portrait of the famous Mrs Siddons, the actress, in The Fatal Marriage. *Heir: c* Henry Frederick Hotham, *b* 13 Aug. 1899. *Address:* Dalton Hall, Beverley; 32 Prince's Gate, SW7. *T:* Kensington 2290; Bucklands, Churt, Farnham. *T:* Hindhead 74. *Clubs:* Junior Constitutional; Yorkshire, York.

Died 7 Oct. 1923.

OTHAM, Sir Charles Frederick, GCB 1902 (KCB 1895; CB 1882); GCVO 1901; Admiral of the Fleet, 1903–13; *b* 20 March 1843; *m* 1872, Margaret (*d* 1918), *d* of David Milne-Home of Wedderburn, Berwickshire; one *s* one *d* (and one *s* decd). Served New Zealand, 1860–64 (despatches, medal, severely wounded); Bombardment of Alexandria, 1882 (medal, clasp, bronze star, 3rd class Osmanieh); late Naval ADC to the Queen; Lord of Admiralty, 1889; Commander-

in-Chief, Pacific Station, 1890–92; at Nore 1897–99; at Portsmouth, 1899–1903. *Address:* 67 Eccleston Square, SW1. *T:* Victoria 3469. *Clubs:* Army and Navy; New, Edinburgh; Yorkshire, York.

Died 22 March 1925.

HOTHFIELD, 1st Baron, *cr* 1881; **Henry James Tufton,** DL, JP; Bt 1851; Lord-Lieutenant of Westmorland since 1881 and Vice-Admiral of the coast of Cumberland and Westmorland; *b* Paris, 4 June 1844; *e s* of Sir Richard Tufton, 1st Bt, and Adelaide Amelie Lacour; *S* father as 2nd Bt, 1871; *m* 1872, Alice (*d* 1914), 2nd *d* of late Rev. William James Stracey-Clitherow; two *s* one *d* (and one *s* decd). *Educ:* Eton; Christ Church, Oxford. Lord-in-Waiting, 1886; Mayor of Appleby, 1895–96. *Heir: s* Hon. John Sackville Richard Tufton, *b* 8 Nov. 1873. *Address:* 2 Chesterfield Gardens, W1. *T:* Mayfair 7056; Appleby Castle, Westmorland; Skipton Castle, Yorkshire. *Clubs:* Carlton, Garrick.

Died 20 Oct. 1926.

HOUGH, Edwin Leadam, CBE 1920; late Senior Official Receiver in Bankruptcy, High Court of Justice; *b* Carlisle, 22 Oct. 1852; *e s* of Edwin Hough; *m* 1878, Emma, *d* of Joseph Chambers, Oxford, Lt-Col HM Bengal Army. *Educ:* Rossall; Queen's Coll., Oxford. Solicitor in Carlisle, 1878–90; Official Receiver Carlisle District, 1884; Official Receiver in High Court, 1890; retired, July 1919. *Recreations:* fishing, golf. *Address:* Kildonan, Enfield. *T:* Enfield 320.

Died 14 May 1928.

HOUGH, John Stanley, KC; Member of firm of Hough, Campbell & Ferguson, Barristers, Solicitors, etc, Winnipeg; *b* County of Prince Edward, Province of Ontario, 29 Sept. 1856; *m* 1896, Julia Frances Chaffey; one *s* one *d*. *Educ:* University of Toronto; Osgoode Hall. Called to Bar and admitted as Solicitor, 1882; in practice ever since in City of Winnipeg; Member Canadian Board of Royal Exchange Corporation, and Member of Advisory Board of Royal Trust Company; President of Winnipeg General Hospital. *Recreations:* golf, yachting. *Address:* 280 Roslyn Road, Fort Rouge, Winnipeg, Canada. *T:* Fort Rouge 6448. *M:* 3434 for Manitoba. *Clubs:* Bath; Mount Royal, Manitoba; St Charles Country, Winnipeg.

Died June 1928.

HOUGH, Sydney Samuel, FRS 1902; FRAS; HM Astronomer, Royal Observatory, Cape of Good Hope, since 1907; *b* 11 June 1870; *m* 1906, Gertrude Annie, *y d* of late J. H. Lee of Halstead, Essex. Formerly Fellow of St John's College; Isaac Newton student in the University of Cambridge; Fellow Royal Society of South Africa. *Publications:* various mathematical memoirs relating to astronomical subjects in Phil. Trans of the Royal Society and elsewhere. *Address:* Royal Observatory, Cape of Good Hope. *TA:* Astronomer, Cape Town. *Club:* Civil Service, Cape Town.

Died 8 July 1923.

HOUGHTON, Rev. Edward James, MA; Hon. Canon of Worcester Cathedral; Rural Dean and Vicar of Blockley since 1879; *b* Lytham, Lancashire, 28 May 1838; *s* of Edward Houghton and Sarah Jane Villiers; *m* Hannah Maria Walford (*d* 1916), The Grange, Alvechurch; three *s* three *d*. *Educ:* Rossall; Christ Church, Oxford. 2nd Master of Twyford School, under Rev. G. W. Kitchin, later Dean of Durham, and Curate of Twyford, 1860–63; Senior Curate of Alvechurch, 1863–66; Lecturer and Curate in charge of St Philip's, Birmingham, 1866; Vicar of Boston Spa, Yorks, 1866–71; Diocesan Inspector of Schools, Worcester, 1871–79. Diocesan Secretary, Society for Promoting Christian Knowledge; Hon. Secretary, Worcester Diocesan Joint Committee on Education, 1882–1903; Joint Hon. Secretary, Worcester Diocesan Council for Promoting Higher Religious Education in Secondary Schools; one of the examiners appointed by the Board of the National Society; Acting Chaplain of the 2nd Vol. Battalion of the Gloucestershire Regiment; retired after 20 years service; Hon. Secretary, Worcester Archidiaconal Board of Education, 1882–1900. *Publications:* Confirmation Address; Latin Sermon, Oxford. *Recreations:* captain of Rossall Cricket Eleven 2 years, Christ Church Eleven. *Address:* Blockley Vicarage, RSO, Worcestershire. *TA:* Blockley. *Clubs:* Constitutional, MCC; Worcester County.

Died 21 Oct. 1919.

HOULDSWORTH, Sir William Henry, 1st Bt, *cr* 1887; DL; landed proprietor; *b* Manchester, 20 Aug. 1834; *s* of late Henry Houldsworth, Coltness, Lanarkshire; *m* 1862, Elisabeth, *d* of Walter Crum, Thornliebank, Renfrewshire; two *s* three *d* (and one *s* decd). *Educ:* St Andrews University. Member: Royal Commission on Depression of Trade; Gold and Silver Commission; Royal Commission on Liquor Licensing Laws, 1896; Delegate of Great Britain to Monetary Conference, Brussels, 1890; Labour Conference, Berlin, 1892. MP (C) NW Manchester, 1883–1906. *Recreations:* golf, shooting, music.

Heir: s Henry Hamilton Houldsworth, *b* 17 Sept. 1867. *Address:* Coodham, Kilmarnock, NB. *Clubs:* Conservative, Carlton.

Died 18 April 1917.

HOULT, Joseph, JP; steamship owner of Liverpool; late City Councillor and Chairman of the Watch Committee; Magistrate for Liverpool; *b* 1847; *s* of late John Hoult of Liverpool; *m* 1872, Julia (*d* 1901), *d* of late James Murray of Edinburgh; one *s* three *d*. MP (C) Wirral Division of Cheshire, 1900–6. *Recreations:* fishing, shooting. *Address:* The Rocklands, Thornton Hough, Cheshire; Bowscar, Penrith. *Clubs:* Carlton, 1900; Liverpool Conservative.

Died 19 Oct. 1917.

HOUNDLE, Henry Charles Herman Hawker, CBE 1918; ISO 1903; *b* 1851. Chief Clerk, Local Government Board, Whitehall. *Address:* 3 Paper Buildings, Temple, EC4.

Died 30 Sept. 1919.

HOUSTON, Sir Robert Paterson, 1st Bt, *cr* 1922; MP (C) Liverpool, W Toxteth, 1892–1924; shipowner; head of Houston line of steamers; *b* Liverpool, 31 May 1853; *m* 1924, Dame Fanny Lucy, DBE, *d* of late Thomas Radmall and *widow* of 9th Baron Byron. *Educ:* Liverpool College and privately. *Heir:* none. *Address:* Beaufield, St Saviour's, Jersey, CI. *Clubs:* Carlton, Royal Thames Yacht.

Died 14 April 1926 (ext).

HOUSTON-BOSWALL-PRESTON, Thomas Alford; *b* 21 July 1850; *s* of Sir George Houston-Boswall, 2nd Bt; *heir pres.* to nephew, Sir Thomas Randolph Houston-Boswall, 5th Bt; assumed additional name of Preston by Royal Licence, 1886; *m* 1883, Alice Mary, *d* of late William Cunard; two *s* one *d*. *Address:* Tweed Hill, Berwick-on-Tweed. *Clubs:* Travellers', Orleans New.

Died 3 Jan. 1918.

HOVELL, Lt-Col Hugh De Berdt, DSO 1900; *b* 15 April 1863; 3rd *s* of late Dennis De Berdt Hovell of Boreham Holt, Elstree, Herts. *Educ:* Wellington College; Sandhurst. Entered 2nd Batt. Worcestershire Regiment, 1884; served South Africa, 1900–2 (despatches, Queen's medal 3 clasps, King's medal 2 clasps, DSO); Royal Humane Society's medal, 1891; commanded and trained 2nd Batt. Worcestershire Regt before the war, on Sir John Moore's and Sir Charles Napier's methods of command, for Gheluvelt, 1914; enlisted in his old 2nd Batt., 1915; served as private with his old comrades (1915 Star, War and Victory medals); originated in 1886 the use of telephones on rifle-ranges, and in 1888 the use of field telephones. *Publications:* Soldiers' Shooting; Soldiers' Training. *Club:* Junior United Service. *Died 27 Nov. 1923.*

HOVELL, T(homas) Mark, FRCS; medical attendant to the late Emperor Frederick III of Germany (Companion of Crown Order); Consulting Aural Surgeon, London Hospital; Consulting Surgeon, Hospital for Diseases of Throat, Golden Square; Aural Surgeon, British Home for Incurables; *e surv s* of late Dennis De Berdt Hovell and Mary, *d* of A. De Horne; *m* 1905, Hon. Margaret Cecilia Bateman-Hanbury, *d* of 2nd Baron Bateman; one *s*. *Publication:* A Treatise on Diseases of the Ear, 2nd edn; papers on throat, nose, and ear. *Address:* 105 Harley Street, W1. *T:* Paddington 1171; Lemsford House, Lemsford, near Hatfield. *T:* Hatfield 81.

Died 30 June 1925.

HOW, Ven. Henry Walsham; *b* Whittington, Shropshire, 17 May 1856; *s* of late Bishop Walsham How, of Wakefield; *m* 1886, Katharine, *d* of Prebendary Hutchinson, of Blurton, Staffs; three *s* one *d*. *Educ:* Marlborough; Wadham College, Oxford; Leeds Clergy School. Curate, Stoke-on-Trent, 1879–85; St Anne's, Haughton, Lancs, 1885–86; Rector, 1886–89; Vicar of Mirfield, Yorks, 1889–1902; Chaplain to Bishop of Wakefield, 1891–97; Vicar of Meltham, 1902–17; Hon. Canon of Wakefield, 1899–17; Rural Dean of Huddersfield, 1905–17; Proctor in Convocation, 1905–17; Archdeacon of Halifax and Canon of Wakefield, 1917–23. *Publications:* edited The Closed Door, Addresses by Bishop Walsham How; editor of Wakefield Diocesan Calendar, 1891–1906. *Address:* Elmhurst, Pickersleigh Road, Malvern Link. *Club:* Royal Societies.

Died 29 Nov. 1923.

HOWARD OF GLOSSOP, 2nd Baron, *cr* 1869; **Francis Edward Fitzalan-Howard,** DL, JP; *b* 9 May 1859; *s* of 1st Baron and Augusta, *e d* and *heir* of Hon. George Henry Talbot; *S* father, 1883; *m* 1st, 1883, Clara (*d* 1887), *d* of J. Greenwood of Swarcliffe, Ripley, Yorks; one *s* one *d*; 2nd, 1891, Hyacinthe, *d* of late William Scott-Kerr, of Chatto and Sunlaws, Roxburghshire; one *d* (one *s* decd). *Educ:* Oratory School, Edgbaston. *Heir:* s Hon. Bernard Edward Fitzalan-Howard,

b 10 May 1885. *Address:* Glossop Hall, Derbyshire; Dorlin Hou Acharach, Argyllshire, NB. *Clubs:* Bachelors', White's.

Died 22 Sept. 19.

HOWARD, Sir Ebenezer, Kt 1927; OBE 1924; JP; Director of F Garden City Limited and Welwyn Garden City Limited; shortha writer; President International Federation for Housing and To Planning; *b* City of London, 29 Jan. 1850; *s* of Ebenezer How of London and Ann Tow of Colsterworth; *m* 1st, 1879, Elizab Ann Bills of Coventry; one *s* three *d*; 2nd, 1908, Edith Annie Hayw of Letchworth. *Educ:* private schools, Sudbury, Cheshunt and Ipswi Stockbrokers' and merchants' offices; short time private secreta Dr Joseph Parker; solicitor's office; in 1872 went to Nebraska, US afterwards to Chicago; practised as stenographer in courts there; joir staff of Gurney & Sons, official shorthand writers to Houses Parliament, 1877; afterwards became partner of William Treadw spent spare time preparing scheme social reform, especially seek solution of twin problems of overcrowded city and depopula country; in 1899 formed Garden City Association (which in t formed "First Garden City Limited") to carry out a large comprehensive scheme of town planning; career closely associa with town-planning movement. *Publication:* To-morrow, a Peace Path to Real Reform, 1898; in subsequent editions called Garden Ci of To-morrow. *Recreation:* new fields of activity. *Address:* 3 Gra Inn Place, WC1; 5 Guessens Road, Welwyn Garden City. Cl National Liberal. *Died 1 May 19.*

HOWARD, Sir (Edward) Stafford, KCB 1909 (CB 1900); JP, C *b* Greystoke Castle, Cumberland, 28 Nov. 1851; 2nd *s* of He Howard, Greystoke; *m* 1st, 1876, Lady Rachel Campbell (*d* 190 *d* of 2nd Earl Cawdor; one *s* two *d*; 2nd, 1911, Catharine Meri *d* of late Sir Arthur Cowell-Stepney, 2nd Bt and Hon. Lady Cow Stepney of The Dell, Llanelly; one *s* one *d*. *Educ:* Harrow; Trir College, Cambridge (BA Classical Tripos). Barrister, Inner Temp MP (L) East Cumberland, 1876–85; Thornbury Division Gloucestershire, 1885–86; Under-Secretary for India in Gladstone's Government, 1886; Commissioner of HM's Woo Forests, and Land Revenues, 1893–1912; an Ecclesiasti Commissioner from 1914. *Address:* Cilymaenllwyd, Llanelly, S Wa *Clubs:* Travellers', Bath, Cavendish.

Died 8 April 19

HOWARD, Captain (Temp.-Major) Guy Robert, DSO 19 Royal Flying Corps; late Essex Regiment, 2nd Battalion (Spec Reserve); *b* 5 Feb. 1886; *s* of Col W. Howard. Served European W 1914–15 (wounded, despatches, DSO); while in command of a Pat of the 2nd Battalion, made a valuable reconnaissance through a thi wood. *M:* LM 9741. *Clubs:* Junior United Service, Royal Flyi Corps. *Died 24 Oct. 19*

HOWARD, Sir Henry, GCMG 1916 (KCMG 1899); KCB 1907 (C 1874); *b* 11 Aug. 1843; *s* of late Sir Henry F. Howard, GCB; *m* 18 Cecilia (*d* 1907), *d* of late Geo. W. Riggs of Washington, DC; c *s* three *d*. Attaché on Diplomatic Service, 1865; 3rd Secretary, 18 2nd Secretary, 1873; 1st Secretary, 1885; Secretary of Embassy, 18 Minister Plenipotentiary, 1894; Envoy Extraordinary and Minis Plenipotentiary, 1896; served in the United States of America, Netherlands, Guatemala, Greece, Denmark, China, Russia, France; British Minister at the Hague and Luxemburg, 1896–19 Minister Plenipotentiary in British Mission to the Pope, 1914– Jubilee Medal, 1897; Coronation Medal, 1902. *Club:* Traveller *Died 4 May 19*

HOWARD, Col Henry Richard Lloyd, CB 1900; late Colo Cheshire Royal Engineers Railway Battalion; Hon. Colo Denbighshire Hussars, Imperial Yeomanry; late a Gentleman-Arms; late Major, 16th Lancers; *b* 9 July 1853; *s* of Rev. R. H. How and Julia Elizabeth, *d* of late William Ripley; *m* 1881, Violet M (*d* 1913), *d* of the late Captain H. B. Hankey, RN, of West Lei Havant; one *s* one *d*. *Educ:* Eton; Christ Church, Oxford. Contest (C) Flintshire, 1895, 1900, and 1910; Flint Boroughs, 1910. CC St Asaph Div. of Flintshire; served Zulu War, 1879 (medal with clas commanded 9th Batt. Imperial Yeomanry, South Africa, 1900 (despatches, medal with 4 clasps, CB). *Recreations:* hunting, shooti fishing. *Address:* Wygfair, St Asaph. *TA:* Howard, Meriadog. *T:* Trefnant. *M:* DM 19. *Club:* Naval and Military.

Died 22 Dec. 19

HOWARD, Hon. Hugh Melville, DL; *b* 28 March 1883; *s* of 6 Earl of Wicklow and 2nd wife, Fanny Catherine, *e d* of Richard Rob Wingfield; *m* 1908, May, *o c* of Benjamin Aymar Sands of New Yo and Southampton, Long Island; one *s* one *d*. *Educ:* Eton; Trin

College, Oxford, MA. Contested (U) E Wicklow, Dec. 1910. *Address:* Bellevue, Delgany, Co. Wicklow. *Clubs:* Bachelors'; Kildare Street, Dublin.
Died 17 Feb. 1919.

HOWARD, Joseph, JP; one of HM's Lieutenants for the City of London; *b* 1834; *s* of late John Eliot Howard, FRS, Tottenham; *m* 1859, Ellen, *d* of H. Waterhouse; five *s* two *d*. *Educ:* University College, London. Barrister, Lincoln's Inn, 1856. MP (C) Tottenham, Middlesex, 1885–1906. *Address:* 18 Kensington Court, W8. *T:* Western 4863; Winchester House, EC. *Club:* Carlton.
Died 2 March 1923.

HOWARD, Robert Jared Bliss, MD; FRCS; *s* of Robert Palmer Howard; *m* 1888, Margaret Charlotte Smith, later Baroness Strathcona and Mount Royal (2nd in line); two *s* two *d* (and one *s* decd). *Educ:* M'Gill University; London Hospital. Fellow Royal Society of Medicine. *Address:* 46 Green Street, Park Lane, W1. *T:* Mayfair 4300.
Died 9 Jan. 1921.

HOWARD, Robert Mowbray, JP, DL; BA; *b* 1854; 3rd *s* of Henry Howard (*d* 1875), of Greystoke Castle, Cumberland, and of Thornbury Castle, Gloucestershire, and Charlotte Caroline Georgiana (*d* 1896), *e* of late Henry Lawes Long, of Hampton Lodge; *m* 1st, 1881, Louisa Georgina (*d* 1910), *e d* of late Rev. Walter Sneyd, of Keele Hall, Staffordshire; one *s* one *d*; 2nd, 1912, Audrey Cecilia Campbell (*d* 1918), 3rd *d* of late Charles Hallyburton Campbell, BCS; 3rd, 1927, Louisa Felicia, *o d* of late William Earle Welby, of Bainton House, Stamford. *Educ:* Trinity College, Cambridge. *Address:* Ignors, Compton, Guildford. *Club:* Arthur's.
Died 2 Oct. 1928.

HOWARD, T. Henry; Commissioner; Chief of the Staff of the Salvation Army, 1912–19; *b* Walsall, 12 July 1849; *m* M. Wassell, of Sedgeley; three *s*. *Educ:* privately; Tipton, Staffs; Ilkeston. Entered the Salvation Army as an officer, 1881; Commissioner for Australasia, 1884; appointed to the direction of the Field Work in the United Kingdom, 1892; became Principal of the International Training College in Clapton, and subsequently Foreign Secretary; placed on Retired List, 1919. *Publications:* Standards of Life and Service; numerous spiritual articles in the Salvation Army press. *Address:* 101 Queen Victoria Street, EC. *T:* Dalston 2375.
Died 1 July 1923.

HOWARD, Walter; actor, manager, dramatic author; *b* Leamington, 1866. *Educ:* Stratford-on-Avon. First appearance as an actor at Stratford-on-Avon, 1889; London, 1896; New York, 1914. *Plays:* The Wearin' o' The Green, 1896; A Life's Revenge, 1898; For the King, 1899; Two Little Drummer Boys, 1899; Man and Wife, 1900; Why Men Love Women, 1901; Two Little Sailor Boys, 1901; Under the Russian Flag, 1902; The Midnight Wedding, 1905; Her Love Against the World, 1906; The Prince and the Beggar Maid, 1908; Second to None, 1908; The Boy King, subsequently re-named The Ragged Prince, 1910; The Life Guardsman, 1911; The Soldier Princess, 1912; The Story of the Rosary, 1913; The Silver Crucifix, 1915; Seven Days' Leave, 1917; Boy of my Heart, 1920. *Address:* 23 Haymarket, SW1. *T:* Regent 1147. *Clubs:* Green Room, Devonshire, Eccentric. *Died 6 Oct. 1922.*

HOWARD-BROOKE, Col Richard Edward Frederic, of Castle Howard, Ovoca, Co. Wicklow, and Roskelton, Queen's County; JP Hampshire; *b* 1 Nov. 1847; 3rd *s* of late Richard Howard-Brooke; *m* 1878, Alice Eliza *d* of late Samuel King of The Castle, St Helens, Isle of Wight. *Address:* Faircroft, Ryde, Isle of Wight. *TA:* Ryde Wight. *T:* Ryde 75. *Clubs:* United Service; Royal Victoria Yacht, Ryde.
Died 13 Jan. 1918.

HOWARD-VYSE, Howard Henry, JP, DL; *b* 7 March 1858; *e s* of Col R. Howard-Vyse and Julia Agnes, *d* of 1st Lord Hylton; *m* 1882, Mabel Diana, *o d* of late Rev. G. Granville Sykes Howard-Vyse; one *s*. *Educ:* Eton. Royal Horse Guards, 1879–83. *Address:* Stoke Place, Slough, Bucks. *TA:* Vyse, Wexham. *Clubs:* Naval and Military, Turf.
Died 29 May 1927.

HOWARTH, William James, CBE 1919; MD, BCh, DPH Victoria University of Manchester; FRSanI, FRIPH; Medical Officer of Health, City of London. *Educ:* Manchester Grammar School and Owens College. Formerly House Surgeon at Manchester Royal Infirmary and Loughborough General Hospital; held the position of Medical Officer of Health of Bury, Lancs, Derby (10 years), and the County of Kent (5 years); in Kent was also School Medical Officer, and Executive Officer for tuberculosis work, and control of midwives; appointed to the City Corporation, 1912. Milroy Lecturer, Royal

College of Physicians, 1917; Fellow, Past-President and Vice-President of the Incorporated Society of Medical Officers of Health, and Past-President of the Metropolitan, Midland, and Home Counties Branches; Chairman Meat Preservation Committee of the Food Investigation Board; member of the Meat Inspection Committee, and of the Insanitary Areas Sub-Committee of the Ministry of Health; representative of the Ministry of Health on the Sanitary Inspectors' Examination Board; University nominee, Board of Management, Low Temperature Research Station, Cambridge; formerly Chief Rationing Officer under London and Home Counties Rationing Scheme. *Publications:* The Organisation and Administration of the Medical Inspection of Scholars, in Kelynack's Medical Inspection of Schools and Scholars; The Treatment of Enlargements of the Thyroid Gland, and some Observations on the Functions of that Organ; various contributions to Public Health literature. *Address:* Guildhall, EC2; 30 Westbourne Gardens, Folkestone, Kent.
Died 15 June 1928.

HOWE, Hon. James Henderson; MLC Northern District since 1897; a Member of the Council of School of Mines; *b* Scotland, 4 March 1839; *m* 1864, Harriette, *d* of Richard Keynes. Went to Australia, 1856; MHA, Stanley, 1881 and 1884; Gladstone, 1887, 1890, and 1893; Commissioner of Crown Lands, 1885–87, 1890, 1892–93; Commissioner of Public Works, 1889–90; a Member of Convention, 1897; succeeded in carrying an Amendment to the Constitution Bill for Invalid and Old Age Pensions. *Address:* Mambray, St Peter's, Adelaide. *Club:* Australasian National.
Died 5 Feb. 1920.

HOWELL, Col (temp. Brig.-Gen.) Arthur Anthony, CMG 1915; TD 1916; MRCS 1886; LRCPE 1891; 3rd London Regiment (Royal Fusiliers) (TF); *b* 1862; 3rd *s* of late Very Rev. David Howell, Dean of St David's; *m* 1895, Charlotte Isabel, *d* of late John Firth, of Abbeydale, Sheffield. *Educ:* Shrewsbury School; London Hospital. Joined the 3rd Vol. Batt. Royal Fusiliers as a Lieut 1896; served South African War with the CIV as a Captain, receiving Queen's medal and four clasps; Lt-Col Commanding 3rd Batt. The London Regt Royal Fusiliers (TF) 1910–16; served European War, 1914–16 (CMG, despatches twice, Order of St Anne); appointed to command 1st London Reserve Brigade, 1916, with temp. rank of Brig.-Gen.; promoted Colonel in TF 1917. *Address:* St David's, Worplesdon Hill, Brookwood, Surrey. *T:* Woking 503.
Died 15 Jan. 1918.

HOWELL, Rev. G.; Hon. Canon of Liverpool; Rural Dean of Walton since 1910. Ordained 1874; Assistant Curate, Christ Church, Everton, 1874–79; Vicar, 1879–1916. *Recreation:* walking. *Address:* Christ Church Vicarage, Everton.
Died 16 Aug. 1918.

HOWELL, Hon. Hector Mansfield; Chief Justice of Manitoba since 1909; *b* Ontario, 17 Sept. 1842; *m* 1875, Harriette Lally; one *s* three *d*. *Educ:* Albert College. Called to Bar of Ontario, 1871; Manitoba Bar, 1879; QC, 1884; Chief Justice of the Court of Appeal for Manitoba, 1906. *Address:* 66 Carlton Street, Winnipeg. *Clubs:* Manitoba, St Charles' Country, Hunt, Winnipeg.
Died April 1918.

HOWELL, Lt-Col Herbert Gwynne, DSO 1915; OBE 1919; late RFA; *b* 15 Nov. 1879; *s* of late Major M. G. Howell, Llanelwedd Hall, Radnorshire; *m* Annable, *d* of Capt. Martin, late The Buffs, of Dunmore, Galway, Ireland; one *s* one *d*. Entered army, 1900; Captain, 1911; employed with West African Frontier Force, 1904–9; served Bechuanaland, 1897 (medal with clasp); South Africa, 1900–2 (despatches twice, Queen's medal 4 clasps, King's medal 2 clasps); N Nigeria, Dakkakerri Campaign, 1908; European War, Cameroons, 1914–16 (DSO, despatches 3 times); Egypt, 1916–18; Palestine Campaign, Battle of Gaza and Capture of Jerusalem (despatches, OBE); retired pay, 1923. *Recreations:* polo, big game hunting. *Address:* Llanelwedd Hall, Builth, Wales; 26 South Park, Sevenoaks, Kent. *Clubs:* Army and Navy, Sports.
Died 16 Nov. 1925.

HOWELL, John Aldersey, DSO 1917; MC; *b* 13 Aug. 1888; *s* of Rev. J. A. Howell, MA, Vicar of Penmaenmawr, and Alice Mary, *d* of Canon C. F. Royds, Chester Cathedral; *m* 1922, Angel Helen Sibell, *o d* of Brig.-Gen. Hugh Archdale, CB, CMG; one *d*. *Educ:* Rossall. Stage, started with F. R. Benson; acted in London prior to War. Served in Cheshire Regt during the war, 2nd in Command of 10th Batt.; invalided with the hon. rank of Major, 1918 (DSO, MC, despatches). *Recreation:* golf. *Address:* 23 Chepstow Crescent, W11. *Club:* Savage. *Died 4 Aug. 1928.*

HOWELL, Mortimer Sloper, CIE 1886; *b* Bath, 3 Feb. 1841; *o s* of late John Warren Howell, MRCS; *m* 1895, Laura Sabina (*d* 1909); *d* of late Rev. Edward Wilton, West Lavington, Wilts; one *d. Educ:* Christ's Hospital; Corpus Christi Coll. Oxford. Emeritus Fellow of the Universities of Calcutta and Allahabad; Hon. LLD Edin. Entered Indian Civil Service, 1862; retired, 1896; was then Judicial Commissioner of Oudh. Decorated for official services and attainments in Oriental Literature. *Publication:* Grammar of the Classical Arabic Language, after the method of the native Grammarians. *Recreations:* Arabic literature, cycling, boating, golf. *Address:* Woodbury, Clevedon, Somerset. *T:* Clevedon, 53 Y. *Club:* East India United Service. *Died 9 Sept. 1925.*

HOWELL, Brig.-Gen. Philip, CMG 1915; 4th (Queen's Own) Hussars; *b* 7 Dec. 1877; *s* of late Lt-Col Horace Howell; *m* 1911, Rosalind, *d* of late H. E. Buxton, Fritton, Norfolk; one *d.* Entered Indian army, Queen's Own Corps of Guides, 1897; Captain, 1906; Major, 4th Hussars, 1913; Lt-Col 1914; Staff-Capt., Intelligence, India, 1904–6; passed Staff College, 1907; Brig.-Maj. to IG Cavalry, India, 1908; General Staff Officer, 3rd grade, War Office, 1909–11; General Staff Officer, 2nd grade, Staff College, 1912–13; Brig.-Gen., General Staff, 1915; served NW Frontier, India, 1908 (medal with clasp); European War, 1914–15 (despatches four times, CMG). *Died 10 Oct. 1916.*

HOWELL-PRICE, Lt-Col Owen Glendower, DSO 1917; MC; Australian Forces; *b* Australia. *Educ:* Sydney. Served European War, 1915–17 (despatches, MC, DSO). *Address:* Candahar Barracks, Tidworth.

HOWELLS, William Dean, Hon. DLitt Oxon; man of letters; *b* Martin's Ferry, Belmont County, Ohio, 1837; *s* of William Cooper and Mary Dean Howells; *m* 1862, Elinor G. Mead; one *s* two *d. Educ:* self-taught. MA Harvard and Yale; LittD Yale; DLitt Oxon; LittD Columbia; LLD Adelbert; LittD Princeton. Printer, 1848–58; journalist, 1858–61; United States Consul at Venice, 1861–65; editor of the Atlantic Monthly, 1866–81; author of travels, novels, essays, plays, criticisms, poems, from 1859. *Publications:* some seventy books of the kinds indicated; among others: A Foregone Conclusion; A Chance Acquaintance; Their Wedding Journey; A Counterfeit Presentment; The Lady of the Aroostook; Out of the Question; The Undiscovered Country; April Hopes; The World of Chance; The Landlord of Lion's Head; The Son of Royal Langbrith; Venetian Life; Italian Journeys; Tuscan Cities; Modern Italian Poets; The Rise of Silas Lapham; Indian Summer; The Shadow of a Dream; An Imperative Duty; The Albany Depôt, 1897, and 24 other farces; An Open-Eyed Conspiracy, 1898; The Story of a Play, 1898; The Ragged Lady, 1899; Their Silver Wedding Journey, 1899; Literary Friends and Acquaintance, 1900; A Pair of Patient Lovers, Heroines of Fiction, 1901; The Kentons, Literature and Life, 1902; Questionable Shapes, 1903; Letters Home, 1903; Miss Bellard's Inspiration, 1905; London Films, 1905; Certain Delightful English Towns, 1906; Through the Eye of the Needle, 1907; Fennel and Rue, 1908; Roman Holidays, 1908; Seven English Cities, 1909; The Mother and the Father, 1909; Imaginary Interviews, 1910; My Mark Twain, 1910; New Leaf Mills, Familiar Spanish Travels, 1913; The Seen and Unseen in Stratford-on-Avon, 1914; Years of my Youth, 1916; The Daughter of the Storage, 1916; The Leatherwood God, 1916. *Recreations:* theatre, reading, walking, gardening. *Address:* c/o Harper Bros, New York. *Clubs:* Century, New York; Tavern, Boston.

Died 11 May 1920.

HOWEY, Maj.-Gen. William; Bengal Infantry; *b* 7 Aug. 1838; *m* 1860, Annie Isabella, *d* of Major Henry Christian Talbot of Stone, Kent. Entered army, 1858; Maj.-Gen. 1894; unemployed supernumerary list, 1894; served Indian Mutiny, 1858–59 (medal). *Address:* Naval and Military Hotel, Harrington Road, South Kensington, SW7. *Died 18 July 1924.*

HOWIE, Rev. Robert, DD; Moderator of the General Assembly of the United Free Church of Scotland in 1902; *b* parish of Kilwinning, 4 Feb. 1836; *s* of John Howie (personally related to Howie of Lochgoin, author of Scots Worthies), and Mary Stevenson; *m* 1st, 1861, Catherine Coulson Davy (*d* 1910), related to Sir Humphry Davy and Dr Walter Coulson of London; 2nd, 1911, Martha Elder Dunsmore, Principal of Emgwali Training School, S Africa. *Educ:* Irvine Academy; Glasgow Univ.; Glasgow FC Coll.; Edinburgh FC Coll. Minister of Wynd Free Church, Glasgow, 1860–64; Trinity Free Church Congregation, 1864–72; St Mary's Free Church, Govan, 1872–1906, of which minister emeritus. As the Senior Minister connected with what was known as the Wynd Mission, and as Convener of the Church Extension Committee of the Free Church

Presbytery of Glasgow, more or less identified with movements resulting in the erection of upwards of forty new churches, and involving an outlay of upwards of £300,000; Convener of Home Mission and Church Extension Committee of Free Church and then of United Free Church during the ten years ending May 1906; Convener of Committee on Statistics of the said Churches during thirteen years. *Publications:* volume—The Churches and Churchless in Scotland; Plea for Equity in the Scottish Churches' Case; and sundry publications of a more ephemeral and controversial character, in defence of the orthodox views in regard to Holy Scripture. *Recreations:* travelled a good deal in different countries on the Continent, in Egypt, Palestine, India, and America. *Address:* 15 Clarendon Place, Stirling, Scotland. *Died 4 March 1918.*

HOWISON, George Holmes, MA, LLD; Professor of Philosophy, emeritus, at the University of California; *b* Montgomery County, Maryland, 1834; *e s* of Robert and Eliza (Holmes) Howison; *m* 1863, Lois Thompson Caswell, of Norton, Massachusetts. *Educ:* Marietta College, Ohio (BA 1852; MA 1855); Lane Theological Seminary, Cincinnati (1852–55); studied, later, at University of Berlin. Engaged in various educational offices in academies and public schools, as instructor, town superintendent, and headmaster, in Ohio and Massachusetts, 1855–64; Asst Prof. of Mathematics, Washington Univ., St Louis, 1864–67; Tileston Prof. of Political Economy, 1867–69; Senior Master in the English High School, Boston, 1869–71; Prof. of Logic and the Philosophy of Science, Massachusetts Institute of Technology, 1871–79; Lecturer on Ethics, Harvard Univ., 1879–80; student in Europe, chiefly at the University of Berlin, 1880–82; Lecturer on Logic and Metaphysics, University of Michigan, 1883–84; Mills Professor of Philosophy, University of California, 1884–1909. Editor of the Philosophical Publications of the University of California, and of the Publications of the Philosophical Union; Member American Editorial Board Hibbert Journal, London. Fellow American Association Advancement of Science; Member American Historical Association, American Political Science Association, New York Academy of Political Science, National Geographic Society, St Louis Philosophical Society; Hon. Member Philosophical Union, University of California, and of American Philosophical Association, 1915. LLD, Marietta, 1883; Michigan, 1909; California, 1914. *Publications:* Treatise on Analytic Geometry, 1869; The Limits of Evolution, and other Essays in Philosophy, 1901, 3rd edn, enlarged, with Reply to Prof. James Ward, 1916; Philosophy, its Fundamental Conceptions and its Methods (in Congress of Arts and Science, Vol. i, St Louis Universal Exposition), 1906; The Conception of God (jointly with Professors Royce, Le Conte, and Mezes), 1897. *Address:* 2631 Piedmont Avenue, Berkeley, California.

Died 31 Dec. 1916.

HOWLAND, William Bailey; President The Independent, New York, since 1913; publisher The Outlook, New York, 1890–1913; *b* Ashland, NY, 1849; *m* 1873, Ella M. Jacobs; two *s.* Founded Outing Magazine, 1882; Treasurer Congregational Home Missionary Society, 1893–1907; Trustee Chautauqua Institution; President Commissioners State Reservation at Niagara Falls; Treasurer Society for Italian Immigrants; Treasurer American Civic Association; President National Institute of Efficiency. *Address:* 119 W 40th Street, New York City. *Clubs:* Royal Societies; Manor House, Bedon; National Arts, Republican, City, Italian, Lake Placid, New York.

Died 27 Feb. 1917.

HOWLETT, Richard, FSA; *b* 17 Aug. 1841; *s* of S. B. Howlett of War Office; *m* Alice (*d* 1901), *d* of James Holderness Featherstone; two *s. Educ:* King's College School; Corpus Christi College, Cambridge. Barrister, Middle Temple, 1871; served in the Civil Service Commission, 1862–1906, retiring as Assistant Secretary of that Department. *Publications:* edited for the Master of the Rolls Series the Chronicles of William of Newburgh and Robertus de Monte, the Gesta Stephani, and several other 12th century chronicles. *Address:* c/o R. R. Howlett, 1 Sunnyside, Wimbledon.

Died 4 Feb. 1917.

HOWORTH, Sir Henry Hoyle, KCIE 1892; DCL; FRS 1893; FSA; Trustee and Hon. Librarian of the Chetham College; Trustee of British Museum since 1899; Member of the Royal Commission on Ancient Monuments; *b* Lisbon, 1 July 1842; *o s* of late Henry Howorth, Lisbon, merchant, and Elizabeth Beswiche, Rochdale; *m* 1869, Katherine (*d* 1921), *e d* of late J. P. Brierley, Lauriston, Rochdale; three *s. Educ:* Rossall. Barrister, Inner Temple, 1867; took an active part for many years in Lancashire politics and public life; wrote a large number of political letters in The Times; president Royal Archæological Institute and the Viking Society; Vice-President Asiatic and Numismatic Societies. MP (C) South Salford, Lancashire,

1886-1900. *Publications:* A History of the Mongols; Chinghis Khan and His Ancestors; The Mammoth and the Flood; The Glacial Nightmare and the Flood; Ice and Water; St Gregory the Great; St Augustine of Canterbury; The Golden Days of the Early English Church, 1916; more than a hundred scientific memoirs on geological, archæological, historical, and ethnological subjects, and a number of communications to the Reviews. *Address:* 45 Lexham Gardens, W8. *T:* Western 1748. *Clubs:* Carlton, Athenæum, Burlington Fine Arts.
Died 15 July 1923.

HOWSE, Francis, JP County of London; one of HM's Lieutenants for City of London; *b* 20 June 1851; 4th *s* of Thomas Howse, late of Silvermere, Woodberry Down, N; *m* 1876, Bessie, 2nd *d* of Charles Gatliff, late of Lakefield, Woodberry Down, N; three *s* two *d. Educ:* Clapham Grammar School. Admitted a solicitor, 1878; member of London School Board, 1891–94, also 1897; member of Hackney Borough Council, 1900–3; Under-Sheriff for City of London, 1904–5; Mayor of Hackney, 1905–6; Alderman, Walbrook Ward, City of London, 1906–9; Trustee of the Hackney Benevolent Society, the Stoke Newington Dispensary, the British Asylum for Deaf and Dumb Females, Clapton; Church-warden of St Thomas, Clapton Common, for 27 years. *Recreation:* angling. *Address:* 112A Holland Road, Kensington, W14. *Club:* City Carlton.
Died 13 Sept. 1925.

HOWSON, G. W. S.; Head Master, Gresham's School, Holt, Norfolk, since 1900; *s* of W. Howson, Head Master of Penrith School; *g s* of Rev. J. Howson, 2nd Master Giggleswick School; unmarried. *Educ:* Giggleswick School. Scholar Merton College, Oxford, 1879; 1st Class Final Honours School of Natural Science, 1883; MA 1886. Assistant Master, Newton College, 1883–86; Assistant Master, Uppingham School, 1886–1900. *Recreations:* riding, fives, trout-fishing. *Address:* Gresham's School, Holt, Norfolk. *TA:* Holt, Norfolk. *Club:* Cavendish.
Died 7 Jan. 1919.

HOYLE, Hon. Henry Clement, MLA; *b* 28 Nov. 1852; *m* 1877; three *s* four *d. Educ:* Convent School, Balmain, NSW; private study. Apprenticed to engine smithing and went through engineering trades; took prominent part in establishing trades unionism in NSW; being strong protectionist, was foremost in advocacy of manufacture of requirements of NSW within the State, and took prominent part in every movement from 1870 to advance democracy of Australia; at age of 22 was a member of Trades and Labour Council of NSW, and was President of eight-hours conference of Iron Trades; instrumental in inaugurating Association of Employees of Government Railways and Tramways of the State, and was first President of the Association; entered Parliament, 1891, in protectionist interest; defeated at 1894 general elections, and engaged in commercial pursuits for some years, re-entering Parliament in 1910; became Parliamentary Secretary of the State Labour Party in 1913; Assistant Colonial Treasurer and Minister for Railways of New South Wales, 1914. *Recreations:* cricket, reading. *Address:* Leoncliffe, New South Head Road, Vaucluse, Sydney, NSW.
Died 20 July 1926.

HOYLE, J. Rossiter, JP City of Sheffield; MICE; Master Cutler, Sheffield 1912–13; Director, Thomas Firth & Sons, Ltd, steel and gunmakers; *b* Manchester, 1856; *s* of William Jennings Hoyle of Manchester and Newcastle-on-Tyne; *m* 1883, Augusta, *e d* of Alexander Muir of Manchester and Liverpool. Member of Council of Mechanical Engineers' Institute; Director of the Projectile and Engineering Co., Ltd; two years President of Sheffield Society of Engineers and Metallurgists. *Address:* Norfolk Works, Sheffield; 8 The Sanctuary, Westminster, SW1.
Died 14 March 1926.

HOYLE, William Evans, MA, DSc; FZS, MRCS; *b* Manchester; *s* of William Jennings Hoyle, Manchester and Newcastle-on-Tyne; *m* 1st, 1883, Edith Isabel Sharp (*d* 1916), Manchester; one *d*; 2nd, 1918, Florence Ethel Mabel, *d* of late T. Hurry Riches, JP, and *widow* of J. H. Hallett, JP, of Radyr Chain; one *d. Educ:* Owens Coll., Manchester; Christ Church, Oxford; St Bartholomew's Hospital. Demonstrator of Anatomy, Owens College; Naturalist on Challenger Expedition Editorial Staff; Director Manchester Museum, 1889–1909; late Vice-Pres. and Hon. Librarian, Manchester Literary and Phil. Society; ex-President Section D, British Association; Corresponding Member, Academy of Sciences, Philadelphia; ex-Pres., Museums Association; ex-Pres., Conchological Society, Great Britain and Ireland; Director of the Welsh National Museum, 1909–24. *Publications:* papers on museums and zoology, chiefly Cephalopoda. *Address:* Glenroy, Blundell Avenue, Porthcawl. *T:* Porthcawl 186.
Died 7 Feb. 1926.

HOYLES, Newman Wright, KC; Hon. LLD; Principal, Law School, Osgoode Hall, Toronto, 1894–1923; *b* St John's, Newfoundland, 14 March 1844; *e s* of late Sir Hugh William Hoyles, Chief-Justice of Newfoundland; *m* 1873, Georgina M., *d* of late Lewis Moffatt of Toronto; one *s* two *d. Educ:* Upper Canada Coll., Toronto; King's Coll., Windsor, Nova Scotia; Trinity Coll., Camb. (BA 1867). Called to Ontario Bar, 1872; QC 1889; a member of the Church of England; President Corporation and Chairman of the Council of Wycliffe College, Toronto; President (Hon.) of the Upper Canada and Canadian Bible Societies; Vice-President British and Foreign Bible Society; a member of the Senate of the University of Toronto; Vice-President of the Church Missionary Society of England; President of Havergal College, Toronto. *Publications:* numerous articles in legal magazines. *Recreation:* rowing. *Address:* 567 Huron Street, Toronto. *T:* Hillcrest 0488. *Club:* University of Toronto (Hon. President).
Died 6 Nov. 1928.

HOZUMI, Baron Nobushige, LLD; Baron, *cr* 1915; Vice-President of the Privy Council, Japan; Barrister of Middle Temple; Honorary Professor of the Imperial University of Tokyo; President of the Imperial Academy; Judge of the Permanent Court of Arbitration, Hague; *b* 11 July 1855; *m* 1882, *d* of Baron Shibusawa. *Educ:* Tokyo University; Middle Temple (1st Class Scholarship); Berlin University. Member House of Peers, 1890–92; with two colleagues drafted present Japanese Civil Code. *Publications:* Ancestor Worship and Japanese Law (English); The New Japanese Civil Codes as Material for the Study of Comparative Jurisprudence (English); Hoten-ron, or Treatise on Codification (Japanese); Inkyo-ron, or Treatise on Retirement from House-headship (Japanese); Gonin-gumi, or the System of Mutual Help and Supervision among Five Families (Japanese); Horitsu Shinka Ron or The Evolution of Law, 2 vols (Japanese), etc. *Address:* 9 Haraikala Machi, Ushigome, Tokyo.
Died 1926.

HUBBARD, Bey Robert Richard, RD; Commander, RNR (retired); Captain, Imperial Ottoman Navy; *b* Ramsgate, 13 March 1843; 3rd *s* of late John Hubbard and Mary Hill, of Canterbury; *m* 1st, 1886, Lizzie (*decd*), 2nd *d* of Rev. George Sydenham, Vicar of Farewell, Staffordshire, and later of Montreal, Canada; one *s*; 2nd, 1912, Agnes, *d* of late Henry Cornelius, Mountrath, Queen's County, Ireland. *Educ:* private school. Entered Mercantile Marine, 1857; master of sailing ships, 1866–70; joined steamships, 1870; served as an officer and in command of all classes of steamers; entered Royal Naval Reserve as Sub-Lieutenant, 1877; Lieutenant, 1886; retired Commander, 1898; served as Lieutenant of HMS Arethusa, Benbow, Forth, and Venus, 1893–97. While in command of HM hired cruiser Kimberley towed gunboat Gadfly from Portsmouth to Simon's Bay (6,000 miles), war with Russia imminent, 1884 (despatches); also conveyed on deck of the same steamer for the relief of General Gordon, HM Nile steamer Albert from Chatham to Alexandria, 1885; was in Port Morant, Jamaica, during Negro rebellion, 1864; served in the Transport Service at the Cape during the Kaffir, Zulu, and Boer Wars, 1872–81; commanded tourist steamer Barracouta, 1886–90; Ceylon, 1894; and Norse-King, 1898; twice visited the West India Islands under the auspices of the Secretary of State for the Colonies in the interest of the development of the minor industries, and submitted to the Colonial Governments his scheme for faster communication with the United States and Great Britain; rescued a large number of people from drowning and shipwreck (medal and clasp, two diplomas, Liverpool Shipwreck and Humane Society; Medal d'Honneur and Diplome from the French Government; silver binocular glasses and vote of thanks from the Canadian Government); Founder of the Annual National Service for Seafarers in St Paul's Cathedral, 1905; Founder of the National Maritime Club, 1909; acted as Senior Officer in convoying two Turkish transports from Southampton to Constantinople, 1906; Order of the Osmanieh, 4th class; Order of the Medjidieh, 4th class; was offered and accepted service in the Imperial Ottoman Navy with the rank of Captain, and was appointed to HIMS Tirri-Mujgan; FRGS; FRS of St George; Younger Brother, Trinity House. *Publications:* Turkish Characteristics; In the Forbidden Mosque; Service under the Sultan; French Humanity; A Story of a Rescue in Mid Ocean; Wrecks and their Remedy; The Power of Bacsheesh in Turkey; In the Hands of the Turks; The Merchant Service a National Maritime Service; short stories. *Recreations:* boat-sailing, rowing, swimming.
Died 21 Dec. 1926.

HUBBARD, William Egerton, JP; Russia merchant; *e s* of late William Egerton Hubbard of Leonardslee, Sussex; *m* 1st, Jane Clifford, *d* of late Rev. Carey Borrer, Rector of Hurstpierpoint; 2nd, Mary Emily, *d* of late Thomas Jesson of Clarendon Terrace, Brighton; one *s* one *d. Educ:* Eton; Trinity Coll., Camb. (BA). Entered firm of John

Hubbard & Co. of 17 St Helen's Place, EC, 1865; Director London, County, and Westminster Bank; commanded company of 2nd Sussex RV, 1872–87; retired Hon. Major; took part in various philanthropic works; was Chairman Reformatory and Refuge Union; Treasurer National Refuges for Homeless and Destitute Children. *Address:* 5 South Park, Sevenoaks. *Died 10 Jan. 1918.*

HUDON, Lt-Col Joseph Alfred George, CMG 1902; retired, 1903; *b* Quebec City, 7 June 1858; *s* of F. E. Hudon and H. Couillard Dupuis; *m* 1881, Alphonsine, *d* of Charles Joncas, Quebec; two *s* two *d. Educ:* elementary school; Seminary and Commercial Academy, Quebec. Joined Militia, 1878; Royal Canadian Artillery, 1883; served North-West Rebellion, 1885 (medal with clasp); South Africa, 1900, command of C Battery Royal Canadian Artillery (despatches, medal with clasps, CMG). *Address:* Kingston, Ontario, Canada. *T:* 120. *Died 22 Sept. 1918.*

HUDSON, H. Lindsay, (Harry Lindsay); schoolmaster, journalist, novelist; *b* Belfast, of Yorkshire parentage; *m* Sarah Elizabeth (Bessie), *y d* of James Rosson of Liverpool; three *s* one *d.* Early life spent in Liverpool; certificated teacher and headmaster of schools at Gotherington, Gloucestershire, Wheelock, Cheshire, and Blaenavon, Monmouthshire; first editor of The Methodist Weekly; first essay in journalism, A Modern Pedagogue, appeared in Tit-Bits; wrote serial stories for the Liverpool Weekly Courier. *Publications:* Rhoda Roberts, a Welsh Mining Story, 1895; Robert Forward, 1896; Methodist Idylls, 1897; The Jacobite, a Romance of the Conspiracy of the Forty, 1898; More Methodist Idylls, 1899; An Up-to-Date Parson, 1899; Mab, 1900; Judah Pyecroft, Puritan, 1902; The Story of Leah, 1902; The Rockingstone Schoolmaster, 1903; The Cark of Coin, 1903; Gypsy Roy, 1904; On the King's Service, 1905; serials and short stories for various periodicals, 1906–10; The Stowaways, 1910; serial stories for various journals; The Surging Life, 1914; Number One Fisher Street, 1917; The Sabistons of Silverstones, 1920. *Recreations:* reading, walking, photography. *Address:* Trevethyn, Glossop, Derbyshire. *Died 4 Sept. 1926.*

HUDSON, Rev. Joseph, MA; Hon. Canon Carlisle; *b* 12 July 1834; *e s* of Rev. Joseph Hudson, MA, Vicar of Chillingham, Northumberland; *m* 1st, 1857, Mary Anne, *d* of John Unsworth of The Thorne, Penrith; 2nd, 1880, Emily Valence, *widow* of Rev. H. W. Cookson, DD, Master of Peterhouse, Cambridge; four *s* four *d. Educ:* Durham School; Peterhouse, Camb. *Address:* Crosby House, Carlisle. *TA:* Crosby House, Crosby-on-Eden. *M:* AO 1853. *Died 14 Nov. 1919.*

HUDSON, Major Robert Arthur, DSO 1916; 1/8th PWO (West Yorks) Regiment (Leeds Rifles), TF; *b* Gildersome, near Leeds, 16 June 1880; 3rd *s* of late Robert and Hannah Hudson of St Ives, Wood Lane, Headingley, Leeds; *m* Mary Vere, *e d* of Mark Senior, Ossett; one *s* one *d. Educ:* Giggleswick Grammar School. Took a commission in the 3rd Vol. Batt. PWO West Yorks, 1898; entered business of Robert Hudson, 1897; subseq. a Permanent Director of Robert Hudson, Ltd, Portable Railway Manufacturers, Gildersome, near Leeds; Hon. Colonel of the 1st (Leeds) Batt. Ripon Regiment of the Church Lads' Brigade; served European War, 1914–15 (DSO). *Recreations:* golf, motoring, Territorial and Church Lads' Brigade work. *Address:* 64 Headingley Lane, Leeds. *T:* Headingley 193. *M:* U 86. *Died Oct. 1917.*

HUDSON, Sir Robert (Arundell), GBE 1918; Kt 1906; JP London, and Suffolk; *b* 30 Aug. 1864; *e s* of late Robert Hudson, of Lapworth, Warwickshire, and Jessie (*d* 1921), *d* of late J. Kynoch, of Peterhead; *m* 1st, 1889, Ada (*d* 1895), *d* of late Henry Hammerton, of Coventry; one *d*; 2nd, 1923, Viscountess Northcliffe, GBE, RRC, *widow* of Viscount Northcliffe. Chairman of the Joint Finance Committee of the British Red Cross Society and the Order of St John; KGStJ; Chevalier of the Legion of Honour; a Trustee of Westminster Abbey Fund; Joint Treasurer of Westminster Hospital; Treasurer of the Sulgrave Manor Board; Trustee of Cassel Hospital, Swaylands; Member of the Imperial War Graves Commission, and of the Voluntary Hospitals Commission; Director of Sun Insurance Office and Sun Life Assurance Society; Patron of the living of Theydon Mount with Stapleford Tawney. *Publication:* edited the late Robert Hudson's Memorials of a Warwickshire Parish. *Address:* Hill Hall, Theydon Mount, Epping, Essex. *T:* Epping 21. *Clubs:* Marlborough, Reform, Burlington Fine Arts. *Died 25 Nov. 1927.*

HUDSON, William Henry; Staff Lecturer in Literature to the Extension Board of London University; *b* London, 2 May 1862; *s* of Thomas Hudson, FSS; *m* 1890, Florence Amy Leslie of London.

Educ: privately. Engaged in journalism in London; for several years private secretary to Herbert Spencer; Assistant Librarian, Cornell University, New York, 1890–92; Professor of English Literature, Stanford University, California, 1892–1901; Professorial Lecturer in the University of Chicago, 1902–3. *Publications:* The Church and the Stage, 1886; Introduction to the Philosophy of Herbert Spencer, 1894 (new edn 1904); Studies in Interpretation, 1896; Idle Hours in a Library, 1897; The Study of English Literature, 1898; The Sphinx and other Poems, 1900; The Meaning and Value of Poetry, 1901; Life of Sir Walter Scott, 1901; The Famous Missions of California, 1901; The Strange Aventures of John Smith, 1902; Rousseau and Naturalism in Life and Thought, 1903; Introduction to Sartor Resartus in Everyman's Library, 1908; Herbert Spencer (in Philosophies, Ancient and Modern), 1909; An Introduction to the Study of Literature, 1910 (new edn 1913); Keats and his Poetry, 1911; Gray and his Poetry, 1911; Lowell and his Poetry, 1911; Milton and his Poetry, 1912; Introduction to Dryden's Essays in Everyman's Library, 1912; The Story of the Renaissance, 1912; An Outline History of English Literature, 1913; Schiller and his Poetry, 1913; Wordsworth and his Poetry, 1913; The Man Napoleon, 1915; A Quiet Corner in a Library, 1915; France: The Nation and its Development, 1917; Whittier and his Poetry, 1918; Johnson and Goldsmith and their Poetry, 1918; A Short History of English Literature in the 19th Century, 1918; editor of The Vicar of Wakefield, 1898; Sir Roger de Coverley Papers, 1899; Bacon's Essays, 1901; Dryden's Essay of Dramatic Poesie, 1904; Spenser's Faery Queene, Book i, 1904; Shakespeare's Henry V; Macaulay's Essay on Clive, 1910; Macaulay's Essay on Warren Hastings, 1911; Representative Passages from English Literature, 1914; The Elizabethan Shakespeare; the Poetry and Life Series. *Died 12 Aug. 1918.*

HUDSON, William Henry; *b* 4 Aug. 1841; *s* of Daniel Hudson and Catharine Kemble; *m* 1876, Emily Wingrave (*d* 1921). *Publications:* The Purple Land, 1885; Argentine Ornithology, 1888–89; The Naturalist in La Plata, 1892; Birds in a Village, 1893; Idle Days in Patagonia, 1893; British Birds, 1895; Birds in London, 1899; Nature in Downland, 1900; Birds and Man, 1901; El Ombú, 1902; Hampshire Days, 1903; Green Mansions, 1904; A Crystal Age, 1906; A Little Boy Lost, 1907; The Lands End, 1908; Afoot in England, 1909; A Shepherd's Life, 1910; Adventures among Birds, 1913; Far Away and Long Ago, 1918; History of My Early Life, 1918; Birds of La Plata, 1919; Birds in Town and Village, 1919; The Book of a Naturalist, 1919; Dead Man's Plack, 1921. *Died 18 Aug. 1922.*

HÜGEL, Anatole, Baron von, KCSG; MA; Hon. ScD; FRAI, FRGS; *b* Florence, 1854; *y s* of Charles, Baron von Hügel, Austrian Minister at Florence and Elizabeth, *d* of late Gen. Francis Farquharson (East India Co., etc) and *niece* of late Gen. Sir James Outram, 1st Bt; *m* 1880, Eliza Margaret, *e d* of late William Froude, FRS. *Educ:* Jesuit Colleges of Kalksburg (Vienna) and Stonyhurst. Curator of the University Museum of Archæology and of Ethnology, Cambridge, 1883–1921; travelled and collected in Australasia, and spent three years (1875–77) with the natives of Fiji; Founder and first President of the Cambridge University Catholic Association, 1895–1922; President of St Edmund's House, Cambridge, 1917–20. *Publications:* contribs to Encyclopædia Britannica and to archæological, ethnological, and ornithological societies and journals. *Recreation:* gardening. *Address:* Croft Cottage, Cambridge. *T:* Cambridge 632. *Club:* Athenæum. *Died 15 Aug. 1928.*

HÜGEL, Friedrich, Baron von, Hon. LLD, St Andrews; Hon. DD, Oxford; Baron of Holy Roman Empire; *b* Florence, 8 May 1852; *s* of Baron Karl von Hügel, Austria, and Elizabeth, *niece* of Gen. Sir James Outram, 1st Bt; *m* 1873, Lady Mary Catherine Herbert, *e d* of 1st Baron Herbert of Lea, and *sister* of the 13th and 14th Earls of Pembroke; two *d* (and one *d* decd). *Educ:* his father's Embassies in Florence and Brussels, under advice of Alfred von Reumont, the historian. Rendered deaf, and some fifteen years incapable of sustained mental work, by typhus fever, 1871; settled in England spring 1871; worked at Greek and Hebrew; devoted life to historical criticism as applied to biblical documents, to psychology and philosophy as applied to religious experience, and to the consolidation of such studies amongst his fellow Roman Catholics; much intercourse with W. G. Ward, 1873–82. A naturalized British subject. *Publications:* paper on Pentateuch criticism at Friburg Catholic Scientific Conference, 1897; The Papal Commission and the Pentateuch, with Prof. Charles Briggs, 1906; The Mystical Element of Religion, 2 vols, 1908, 1909, new edn 1923; Eternal Life, 1912, 1913; The German Soul, 1916; Essays and Addresses, 1921; numerous articles on Biblical Criticism and Philosophy of Religion in English, American, French, and Italian Reviews; *posthumous publication:* Some Notes on the Petrine Claims,

1930. *Address:* 13 Vicarage Gate, Kensington, W8.
Died 27 Jan. 1925.

HUGGINS, Lt-Col Ponsonby Glenn, CB 1909; DSO 1887; late 81st Pioneers (Indian Army); *b* 21 Jan. 1857; 4th *s* of late H. J. Huggins, Chief-Justice, Sierra Leone, and Letitia, *d* of late William Laborde; *m* 1st, 1883, Elizabeth Sophia (*d* 1893), *o d* of Commander W. Grierson, RN; one *s* one *d*; 2nd, 1912, Margaret Rose, *d* of late J. E. M. Wylie and *widow* of G. F. W. Grierson. *Educ:* private schools, Würtemberg and Switzerland; Royal Naval School, New Cross; RMC, Sandhurst. Entered army, 1876; Lt-Col 1902; served Afghan War, 1878–79 (medal); Burmah, 1885–89 (despatches, DSO, medal with two clasps); Chin Hills, 1892–93 (clasp); Tirah, 1897–98 (despatches, medal with two clasps). *Address:* c/o Parry, Murray & Co., 54 Old Broad Street, EC2.
Died 4 Jan. 1925.

HUGHES, Captain Arthur Beckett, CBE 1919; RN (retired); *b* 1873; *s* of late Rev. John Edward Hughes of Cheswardine, Salop, and Mary Anne Chadwick of Daresbury Hall, Cheshire; unmarried. *Educ:* Park House, Reading; Naval Academy, Stubbington. Entered RN 1887; Lieutenant, 1896; Commander, 1907; Captain, 1915; served S African War, 1899–1902, as lieutenant of Philomel (medal); European War, 1914–19 (despatches, CBE); second in command of Ocean, when that ship, together with Irresistible, was sunk during the attack on the Chanak Forts 18 March 1915; retired, 1922. *Club:* United Service.
Died 8 April 1925.

HUGHES, Elizabeth Phillipps, MBE 1917; LLD; on the governing body of the University of Wales, of the University College, Cardiff, etc; Member of the Glamorgan Education Committee, etc; *b* Carmarthen, 22 June 1851; *d* of Dr John Hughes, Carmarthen. *Educ:* Hope House, Taunton; Ladies' College, Cheltenham; University of Cambridge. On the staff of the Ladies' College, Cheltenham, for five years; student of Newnham College, 1881–85; Moral Sciences Tripos Class I, History Tripos Class II. Principal of the Cambridge Training College for Secondary Teachers, 1885–99; went round the world, lectured a good deal in America, Japan, etc, 1899–1902; Professor of English for six months in three colleges in Japan; settled in Wales and undertook a good deal of unpaid public work, educational, insurance, tuberculosis, etc; Bardic name Merch Myrddin; sat on three Government Departmental Committees, and witness before several Royal Commissions; work in connection with the Red Cross; started the first Red Cross Women's Camp, helped to start the first Red Cross Hospital in S Wales in the late war. *Publications:* chiefly educational pamphlets and sections in educational books. *Recreations:* travelling, alpine climbing, etc. *Address:* Penrheol, Barry, S Wales.
Died 19 Dec. 1925.

HUGHES, Col Emilius, CB 1887; CMG 1879; retired list, Army Service Corps; *b* London, 6 June 1844; *y s* of Philip Hughes of War Office; *m* 1st, 1864, Mary Sandys Emily (*d* 1869), *d* of late Lt-Col M. Louis, RHA; 2nd, 1872, Ada Elizabeth (*d* 1904), *d* of Henry Grainger of High Ireby, Cumberland; one *s* four *d*. *Educ:* King's Coll., London. Joined Commissariat Department, 1862; served in South African War, 1878–79; operations against Sekukuni; Zulu Campaign, in Commissariat charge with Sir Evelyn Woods' Flying Column; action at Kambula and Battle of Ulundi (despatches, medal with clasp; CMG); promoted Commissary; Transvaal Campaign 1881. Newcastle Field Force (despatches); Egyptian Expedition 1882, senior Commissariat officer 2nd Division, including Battle of Tel-el-Kebir (medal with clasp, bronze star; 3rd class Medjidieh; promoted Lieut-Colonel); Soudan Expedition, 1884–85; with Force up the Nile, as Senior Commissariat Officer (despatches, clasp, promoted Colonel); Headquarters, 1885–87; AAG Dublin District, 1887–91; AAG, Malta, 1891–95; retired 1895. Chairman, Church of England Soldiers' and Sailors' Institutes Association, Church House, Westminster, 1922. *Address:* Allens, Plaxtol, Sevenoaks. *TA:* Colonel Hughes, Plaxtol. *T:* Plaxtol 18.
Died 30 July 1926.

HUGHES, Col George Arthur, DSO 1898; late Colonel Royal Army Medical Corps; retired, 1905; *b* 18 May 1851; 5th *s* of late James Hughes, Curragh Priven, Rathcormac, Co. Cork. *Educ:* Trinity Coll. Dublin. BA; MB; MCh. Entered army, 1877; served Afghan War, 1878; Bechuanaland Expedition, South Africa, 1884; Ashanti Expedition, 1896; Soudan Expedition, 1898 (despatches, DSO). *Club:* Army and Navy.
Died 13 April 1926.

HUGHES, Herbert, CB 1911; CMG 1901; *b* 25 April 1853; *s* of James Hughes; *m* 1884, Loetitia, *d* of H. Birkinyoung; three *d*. Colonel Commanding 3rd West Riding Brigade, Territorial Force, 1908–12; Member, Territorial Forces Advisory Committee at War Office,

1908–12; Lord Mayor of Sheffield, 1905–6. Decorated for Territorial service and services at International Industrial Conferences, 1886–1900; Commander of Royal Order of the Sword of Sweden. *Address:* Ashdell Grove, Sheffield. *T:* 440 Sheffield. *Club:* Junior Carlton.
Died 16 Jan. 1917.

HUGHES, John Williams Gwynne-, JP, DL; Lord-Lieutenant of Carmarthenshire since 1913; *b* 22 Nov. 1858; *e s* of late John Williams Morgan Gwynne-Hughes, and 2nd wife, Mary, *d* of late W. Lewis; *m* 1880, Emily Beatrice, *y d* of late George Henfrey; one *d*. *Educ:* Cheltenham; Jesus College, Cambridge. High Sheriff, Carmarthenshire, 1888; CC Carmarthenshire (Chairman 1903). *Recreations:* shooting, fishing. *Address:* Tregeyb, near Llandilo, Carmarthenshire.
Died 2 Jan. 1917.

HUGHES, Rev. Llewelyn Robert, MA; Rector of Llandudno since 1902; Canon of Bangor Cathedral since 1919; *s* of late Robert Hughes of Aberllefenny, Merionethshire; *m* 1890, May E., *d* of late Charles Sweetapple; two *s*. *Educ:* Queen's College, Oxford. Curate of Ffestiniog, 1883–85; of Carnarvon, 1885–88; Vicar of Portmadoc, 1888–1902; member of the Governing Body of the Church in Wales; Treasurer of the Bangor Diocesan Board of Finance; Chaplain to the Forces, 1914–19 (despatches); formerly Chaplain to Volunteer and Territorial Forces. *Publications:* Essays on Church and Educative Subjects; sermons; articles in Church periodicals. *Recreations:* travelling, architecture. *Address:* The Rectory, Llandudno. *Club:* Royal Societies.
Died 15 Jan. 1925.

HUGHES, Myra Kathleen, ARE; Member Water Colour Society of Ireland; *d* of late Sir Frederic Hughes, KLS, DL, of Rosslare Fort, Co. Wexford, and Lady Hughes. *Educ:* privately. Studied at the Westminster School of Art under Mr Mouat Loudan; Engraving and Etching School, Royal College of Art, under Sir Frank Short, RA, PRE, and Miss Pott, RE. Exhibited in the Royal Academy; Salon, Paris; Royal Hibernian Academy, etc; exhibitions of Etchings in New Dudley Galleries, 1909; Dublin, 1910. *Publications:* Illustrations in Art Journal, Studio, etc; various plates of old London and Old Dublin, Norway, Palestine, etc. *Address:* Little Nutcombe, Hindhead, Surrey.
Died 21 Aug. 1918.

HUGHES, Hon. Lt-Gen. Hon. Sir Sam, KCB 1915; MP Canada; Minister of Militia and Defence, 1911–16; *b* Darlington, Co. Durham, Ont, 8 Jan. 1853; *s* of John Hughes, a native of Tyrone, Ireland, and Caroline Laughlin, of Scotch-Irish-Huguenot descent; *m* 1st, 1872, Caroline J. (*decd*) *d* of late Major Preston, Vancouver, BC; 2nd, 1875, Mary, *d* of H. W. Buck, ex-MP West Durham; one *s* two *d*. *Educ:* public schools; Toronto Model and Normal Schools; Toronto Univ. Lecturer in English Language, Literature and History in Toronto Collegiate Institute until 1885, when he purchased the Lindsay Warder, which he edited until 1897; identified with amateur athletics; in the Active Militia from his thirteenth year; declined position of Deputy Minister of Militia in 1891, and of Adjt-General, Canada, 1895; Lt-Col commanding 45th Batt., 1897; took part in the Queen's Jubilee celebration, 20 June 1897 (medal); president of the Dominion of Canada Rifle Association; president, Small Arms Committee, Canada; chairman, Board of Visitors, Royal Military College, Kingston; Railway Intelligence Officer, Headquarters Staff; served in the Fenian Raids, 1870 (medal); from 1872 advocated and made personal offers of Colonial Military Assistance to the Empire in Imperial Wars; personally offered to raise corps for the Egyptian and Soudanese campaigns, the Afghan Frontier War, and the Transvaal War; visited Australia and New Zealand in 1897–98 in the interest of Colonial Assistance in Imperial Wars; served South African War, 1899–1900 (despatches several times); European War, in France, 1914–15; raised Canadian contingents for European War, 1914–16; contested House of Commons for N Victoria, 1891; elected 1892, 1896, and 1900; Victoria and Haliburton 1904, 1908, and 1911. Member of the Orange Order, Foresters, and Masonic Order; Methodist; Conservative. *Address:* Lindsay, Ont. *Clubs:* Rideau, Country, Hunt, Ottawa.
Died 24 Aug. 1921.

HUGHES, Spencer Leigh; MP (L) Stockport since 1910; parliamentary journalist; *b* 21 April 1858; *s* of late Rev. James Hughes; *m* 1881, Ellen Wayland (*d* 1916), *d* of late James Groves, Newport, Isle of Wight; one *d*. *Educ:* Woodhouse Grove School, near Leeds. Connected with Ransomes, Sims, and Jefferies, Ltd, the Ipswich engineers, for ten years; with the Morning Leader from its start, and with the Star from 1891. *Publications:* The English Character, 1912; The Art of Public Speaking, 1913; Things that don't Count, 1916; Press, Platform, and Parliament, 1918; Parliamentary Tales in the Windsor and Cassell's Magazines. *Recreation:* attempting to catch fish. *Address:* 40 Lexham Gardens, Kensington, W8. *T:* Victoria 6168.

Clubs: National Liberal, Eighty, Wigwam.

Died 22 Feb. 1920.

HUGHES, Sir Thomas, Kt 1898; JP Liverpool; head of firm Thomas Hughes and Son, timber importers; Hon. Freeman of the City of Liverpool; *b* Liverpool, 3 Aug. 1838; *e s* of Thomas Hughes, timber merchant; *m* 1866, Katherine, *d* of John Stott; two *s* five *d. Educ:* Liverpool Institute. Elected member City Council, 1878; re-elected three times without opposition; elected Alderman, 1891; Mayor of Liverpool, 1889; Lord Mayor, 1897; Chairman of Parliamentary Committee for the Creation of Greater Liverpool. *Recreation:* fishing. *Address:* Springwood, Linnet Lane, Liverpool. *TA:* Planks. *T:* Royal 1575. *Club:* Conservative, Liverpool.

Died 31 Oct. 1923.

HUGHES, Thomas M'Kenny, MA; FRS, FES, FSA; Woodwardian Professor of Geology, Cambridge University; Chevalier St Maur and St Laz; *m* Mary Caroline (*d* 1916), *d* of Rev. G. F. Weston. *Publication:* Cambridge, in Cambridge County Geographies. *Address:* Ravensworth, Cambridge. *Club:* Athenæum.

Died 9 June 1917.

HUGHES, Sir Walter Charleton, Kt 1906; CIE 1900; MInstCE; *b* 22 Sept. 1850; *m* 1889, Evelyn Isabel Rose, *e d* of late Col H. S. Hutchinson, ISC; two *s* one *d. Educ:* private schools; King's College, London. Fellow of King's College, London, and Fellow (appointed) of the University of Bombay. Joined Indian Public Works Department, 1868; Secretary to the Government of Bombay, PWD, 1887–92; Chairman Board of Trustees for the Port of Bombay, 1892–98 and 1900–10; additional member Bombay Legislative Council, 1897–1910; Chairman Bombay Improvement Trust, 1898–1900. *Address:* Dartmouth House, 2 Queen Anne's Gate, SW. *Club:* National, Byculla, Royal Bombay Yacht, Bombay.

Died 30 March 1922.

HUGHES, Walter Tatham, ISO 1905; Assistant Secretary to the Commissioners, Royal Hospital, Chelsea; *b* Aug. 1849; *s* of Rev. Henry Hughes, MA, Vicar of All Saints, Gordon Square, London, and Anne Amelia, *d* of Thomas James Tatham, JP, DL; *m* Charlotte, *d* of Francis Wheatley Preston, of Tenbury, Worcestershire; two *d. Educ:* Blackheath; Marlborough; France. Appointed to the Royal Hospital, Chelsea, 1867. *Address:* 12 Somerset Place, Lansdown, Bath.

Died 22 July 1917.

HUGHES-HALLETT, Col James Wyndham, CB 1900; CVO 1905; DSO 1896; commanding Gordon Volunteer Infantry Brigade, 1906; commanding 72nd and 79th Regimental Districts, 1902; retired, 1906; *b* Petham, Kent, 15 Sept. 1852; 3rd surv. *s* of late Rev. J. Hughes-Hallett of Higham, Canterbury and Dunmow, Essex, and Mary Frances, *d* of late Gen. Sir Thomas Gage Montresor, KCKH; *m* 1893, Alice, *d* of late Capt. Henry William Landers. *Educ:* Haileybury; Sandhurst. Entered army 1872; served during Afghan War, 1878–79, present at capture of Peiwar Kotal (despatches, medal with clasp); Captain 72nd Highlanders, 1880; with Egyptian Expedition 1882, including Tel-el-Kebir (despatches, medal with clasp, and bronze star); Major, Seaforth Highlanders, 1890; with Chitral relief force, 1895, in command of his regiment (despatches, medal with clasp, and DSO); South Africa, 1899–1902, in command of regt and temporarily in command of Highland Brigade (wounded, despatches thrice, CB and Brev. Col). *Recreations:* shooting, cricket. *Address:* 22 Campbell Avenue, Murrayfield, Edinburgh. *T:* Central 2220. *Clubs:* Naval and Military, Sports.

Died 2 June 1927.

HUISH, Marcus Bourne, LLB Camb.; Barrister, Inner Temple; editor Art Journal, 1881–93; *e s* of Marcus Huish and Margaret Bourne; *m* Catherine, *e d* of T. E. Winslow, QC; one *s.* Chairman Japan Society; Cavaliere Order Crown of Italy; Chevalier Order Sacred Treasure, Japan. *Publications:* Greek Terra Cotta Statuettes; Year's Art; Japan and its Art; The Seine and the Loire; Meryon; Samplers and Tapestry Embroideries; Happy England; His Majesty's Water-colours; American Pilgrims Way. *Recreation:* golf. *Address:* 21 Essex Villas, Kensington, W8. *T:* Park 3263. *Club:* New University.

Died 4 May 1921.

HULBERT, Rev. Charles Augustus, MA; Rector of Castor, Peterborough, since 1911; Hon. Canon of Peterborough, 1899; Surrogate, 1901; *b* 23 May 1838; *e s* of Rev. Canon C. A. Hulbert, Vicar of Almondbury, Yorkshire; *m* 1st, Louisa, *d* of Rev. B. Powell, JP, Vicar of St George's, Wigan; 2nd, Julia Margaret, *d* of Rev. F. P. Seymour, MA, Rector of Havant; three *s. Educ:* Caius College, Cambridge. Curate of Holy Trinity, Tunbridge Wells, 1861–65;

Bowdon, Cheshire, 1865–67; Incumbent of Slaithwaite, Yorks, 1867–79; Vicar of St Stephen's, Leeds, 1879–81; Rector of Nether Broughton, Leicestershire, 1881–1901; Rural Dean of Framland III, 1885–1901; Vicar of Towcester, Northamptonshire, 1901–11. *Address:* The Rectory, Castor, Peterborough.

Died 24 March 1919.

HULETT, Hon. Sir (James) Liege, Kt 1902; JP; ex-MLA, Natal; Member of Senate of Union Parliament, 1910–20; *b* 17 May 1838; *o s* of late J. L. Hulett of Gillingham, Kent, and Natal; *m* 1860, Mary Ann, *o d* of late B. Balcomb; six *s* two *d.* Entered Natal Legislative Council as Member for Victoria County, 1883; nominated to executive council, 1889; upon advent of responsible government in 1893 elected for old constituency to Legislative Assembly; retained seat until union, 1910, having served as Minister of Native Affairs and Speaker; Chairman and Managing Director of Sir J. L. Hulett and Son, Ltd, tea and sugar growers, manufacturers, and refiners. *Address:* The Manor House, Mentone Road, Durban, Natal.

Died 5 June 1928.

HULL, Arthur Eaglefield, MusD Oxon; FRCO; Editor Monthly Musical Record; Editor-in-Chief International Dictionary of Modern Music and Musicians; Principal of College of Music, Huddersfield; organ recitalist; *b* Market Harborough, 1876; 2nd *s* of S. Hull, Byfield, Market Harborough; *m* 1906, Bertha Constance Barrett, FRCO, 2nd *d* of Alfred Slapps Barrett of Bishop's Stortford; one *s* one *d. Educ:* privately. Principal Huddersfield College of Music, 1908; founder Huddersfield Chamber Music Society, later Huddersfield Music Club, 1900; editor Monthly Musical Society from 1913; founder British Music Society, 1918 and Hon. Director, 1918–21; founder and first editor of The Music Bulletin, 1918; founder London Contemporary Music Centre (later also the British Section of International Society for Contemporary Music), 1920; founder Composers' Advisory Board, 1920. *Publications:* Modern Harmony, 1915 (Spanish edn 1921, German edn 1926); Organ-playing: its technique and expression (6th edn 1922); monograph on Scriabin (3rd edn 1923); Music: Classical, Romantic and Modern, 1926; Handbook to Bach's Complete Organ Works, 1928; composer of songs, pianoforte pieces, organ music. *Address:* 19 Berners Street, W1. *T:* Regent 2481; Melbourne House, Huddersfield. *T:* Huddersfield 1094. *Club:* Oxford and Cambridge Musical.

Died 4 Nov. 1928.

HULL, Maj.-Gen. Sir Charles Patrick Amyatt, KCB 1918 (CB 1916); Commanding Wessex Division Territorial Forces since 1919; *b* 3 July 1865; *s* of late H. C. Hull, Barrister-at-law; *m* 1901, Muriel, *d* of late R. R. Dobell, Quebec, Canada; one *s* two *d. Educ:* Charterhouse; Trinity College, Cambridge (BA). Joined Royal Scots Fusiliers, 1887; Brevet-Col 1915; Col 1916; in India till 1896; ADC to the Viceroy, 1895–96; served South African War as Adjutant of 2nd Batt. RSF (severely wounded, Brevet-Major); on Staff, 1903–7 and 1909–12; Lt-Col to command the 4th Batt. Middlesex Regt 1912; served European War, 1914–18 (CB, prom. Maj.-Gen., KCB). Russian Order of St Vladimir 4th class, with swords. *Recreations:* hunting, polo, shooting, and fishing. *Club:* Naval and Military.

Died 24 July 1920.

HULL, Prof. Edward, LLD; FRS; consulting geologist; *b* Antrim Ireland, 21 May 1829; *e s* of late Rev. John Dawson Hull, Vicar of Wickhambrook, Suffolk; *m* 1857, *d* (*d* 1901), of late Dr C. T. Cooke Cheltenham; two *s* four *d. Educ:* Trinity Coll. Dublin (MA). Appointed to Geological Survey of United Kingdom, 1850; Scot District Surveyor, 1867; Ireland Director, 1869; Prof. of Geology in the Royal College of Science; retired 1890. President Royal Geological Society, Ireland, 1873; conducted a scientific expedition through Arabia Petraea and Palestine, sent out by Committee of Palestine Exploration Fund, 1883–84; a member of Royal Commission on Coal Reserves, 1891; Secretary to the Victoria Institute in 1900. *Publications:* A Treatise on Building and Ornamental Stones of Great Britain and Foreign Countries, 1872; The Coal Field of Great Britain, 5th edn 1905; contributions to: The Physical History of the British Isles, 1882; Mount Seir, Sinai, and Western Palestine 1885; Memoir on the Physical Geology of Arabia Petraea and Palestine, 1886; Physiology (Physical Geography), 1888; Physical Geology and Geography of Ireland, 2nd edn 1891; Volcanoes, Past and Present (Contemporary Science Series), 1892; Our Coal Resources at the Close of the Nineteenth Century, 1897 Reminiscences of a Strenuous Life, 1910; Monograph on the Sub oceanic Physiography of the North Atlantic Ocean, 1912. *Recreation* music—the organ. *Address:* 14 Stanley Gardens, W. *Club* Constitutional.

Died 19 Oct. 1917.

HULTON, Sir Edward, 1st Bt, *cr* 1921; formerly Newspaper Proprietor; *b* 3 March 1869; *s* of Edward Hulton, of Ashton-on-Mersey; *m* Millicent, *d* of John Warriss; one *d* (one *s* decd). *Heir:* none. *Address:* 51 Great Cumberland Place, W1. *T:* Paddington 5168; Downside, Leatherhead, Surrey.

Died 23 May 1925 (ext).

HULTON, Rev. Henry Edward; Hon. Canon of Chelmsford Cathedral since 1914; St Alban's, 1900-14; *b* 21 June 1839; *e* surv. *s* of late William Adam Hulton (Judge of HM County Courts), Hurst Grange, Preston, Lancashire, and Dorothy Ann, *d* of late Edward Gorst. *Educ:* Cheltenham College; Trinity College, Oxford (BA 1862, MA 1864). Ordained Deacon, 1863; Priest, 1865; Curate of Sonning, 1863-69; Vicar of All Saints', Dunsden, 1870-76; Vicar of Great Waltham, 1876-1906; Rural Dean of Chelmsford, 1886-1913. *Address:* Boreham Manor, Chelmsford. *Club:* New University.

Died 24 Dec. 1922.

HULTON-HARROP, William Edward Montagu, JP, DL; *b* 30 Aug. 1848; 2nd *s* of late Rev. Arthur Hyde Hulton and Elizabeth Margaret, 2nd *d* and *co-heir* of Jonah Harrop, DL, of Bardsley; *g s* of late William Hulton, DL, of Hulton Park, whose name he assumed; *m* 1878, Margaret Henrietta Elizabeth, *e d* of late Calverly Bewicke, of Close House, Northumberland; four *s* two *d.* *Educ:* Magdalene College, Cambridge. High Sheriff, Shropshire, 1885. *Address:* Lythwood Hall, Shrewsbury. *Club:* New University.

Died 7 April 1916.

HUMBLE-CROFTS, Rev. William John, MA Oxon; Rector of Waldron, Sussex; Prebendary of Chichester; Rural Dean of Dallington; Surrogate; *b* 9 Dec. 1846; *s* of Rev. M. M. Humble, Rector of Sutton Scarsdale, Derbyshire; *m* Bridget, *d* of Rev. Taylor White, Rector of Norton Cuckney, Notts; two *s* two *d.* *Educ:* Exeter College, Oxford. Second Class Moderations, Oxford, 1868. *Publications:* various poems and letters. *Recreations:* cricket, rowing, tennis, fencing; Captain of the Magnus School, Newark-on-Trent, and stroke of the Magnus boat; played cricket for Derbyshire County, and for the Gentlemen of Yorkshire, Derbyshire, and Notts, and Free Foresters, and Exeter College. *Address:* Waldron Rectory, Sussex. *M:* O 4423.

Died July 1924.

HUME, Alexander Williamson, JP; Editor Hobart Critic since 1911; Councillor Municipality of Clarence; *b* 20 May 1850; *s* of late Alexander Hume, Linlithgow, Scotland; *m* 1873, Amelia, 2nd *d* of late Alex. Clark of Hobart; one *s* two *d.* *Educ:* Hutchins School, Hobart. Engaged in law for nine years; took up journalism, 1879; joined Hobart Mercury, 1883; leader of staff Tasmanian News, 1887-1900; Editor Tasmanian News, 1900-11. *Publication:* Old Time Reminiscences of Tasmania. *Recreations:* in youth cricket, aquatics, football, then gardening. *Address:* Lindisfarne, Hobart, Tasmania. *TA:* Hobart Critic, Argyle Street.

Died 16 Feb. 1925.

HUME, George Haliburton, MD; DCL; FRCSE; Consulting Surgeon to Royal Victoria Infirmary, Hospital for Sick Children, Maternity Hospital, City Asylum, Newcastle-on-Tyne and Barrasford Sanatorium; *b* Berwickshire, 17 Sept. 1845; *m* 1878, Frances Diana, *e d* of Minchin Jackson, Canada; two *s* four *d.* *Educ:* Kelso Grammar School; Edinburgh University. Practised as a surgeon in Newcastle 1868-1914; for some years was Lecturer on Physiology in the University of Durham College of Medicine; retired from the post of Senior Surgeon to the Royal Infirmary, 1905; took a prominent part in promoting the building of the Royal Victoria Infirmary, opened 1906. *Publications:* papers on surgical subjects in medical journals; The Evolution of Surgical Principles, address at British Medical Association, Newcastle, 1893; History of the Newcastle Infirmary. *Address:* Gosforth, Newcastle-on-Tyne.

Died 8 May 1923.

HUMMELL, Rt. Rev. Francis Ignatius; Vicar Apostolic of the Gold Coast and titular Bishop of Trapezopolis since 1906; *b* Alsace, 1870. *Educ:* Ecole des Missions, Clermont; African Missions Seminary, Lyons. Missionary on the Niger, 1896-1906. *Address:* Cape Coast Castle, British West Africa.

Died 13 March 1924.

HUMPHREYS, Rev. Alfred Edward, MA; Vicar of St Michael, Stonebridge Park, Willesden, since 1907; Hon. Canon of Norwich Cathedral since 1901; *b* Oswestry, Salop, 1843; *m* 1883, H. A., *d* of T. J. Boileau, Judge, HEICS, Madras. *Educ:* King Edward School, Birmingham; Trinity College, Camb.; Browne Medal for Greek Ode and Davies Classical Univ. Scholarship. Scholar, Fellow, Assistant Tutor, Lecturer in Divinity, at Trinity Coll. 1862-77; Examiner, Proctor, and Preacher in the Univ. 1866-87; Vicar of St Matthew's, Cambridge, 1877-87, and Chaplain of Cambridge Union, 1884-87; Vicar of Hempton, Norfolk, 1887-95; Rector of Fakenham, Norfolk, 1887-1907. *Publications:* Commentary on 1 and 2 Timothy and Titus (Cambridge Bible), 1895; Christ's Daily Orders, 1898; Commentary on Philippians, 1900; Commentary on Caesar, Bell. Gall. Bk vi, 1900; Christ our Overlord, 1900; The Plain Truth about the Education Act, 1902; Fair Play, an Appeal for Justice in Tithe Rating, 1904. *Recreations:* rowing, cycling. *Address:* St Michael's Vicarage, Stonebridge Park, NW.

Died 17 Aug. 1922.

HUMPHREYS, Major Dashwood William Harrington, DSO 1904; *b* 6 Feb. 1872. Entered army, 1894; Captain 1903; served Thibet, 1903-4 (slightly wounded, despatches, DSO); ADC to Political Resident, Aden. *Address:* Aden Brigade, Aden.

Died 17 Feb. 1917.

HUMPHREYS, Eng. Rear-Adm. Sir Henry, KCMG 1919; CB 1916; RN; *s* of late Major D. Humphreys, RA; *m* A. Josephine, *d* of late Edward Eckersley, RN. Gained Royal Humane Society's Bronze Medal, 1897; served European War, Dardanelles, 1914-16 (despatches, CB, Officer Legion of Honour); retired list, 1921. *Address:* 4 Penlee Gardens, Stoke, Devonport.

Died 27 May 1924.

HUMPHREYS, Noel Algernon, ISO 1902; *b* London, 12 Sept. 1837; *e s* of Henry Noel Humphreys, author and artist; *m* 1880, Gertrude, 2nd *d* of Thomas Spencer Cobbold, MD, FRS; two *s* one *d.* *Educ:* private. Junior Clerk in Registrar-General's Office (England), 1856; engaged on preparation of census statistics, based upon the five census enumerations, 1861-1901; Secretary in the Census Office, 1890-93; Assistant Registrar-General, 1898-1900; late Hon. Secretary of the Royal Statistical Society; Member of the Departmental Committee on the Financial Aspect of Old Age Pensions, 1898; Chief Clerk in Registrar-General's Office (England), 1898-1905. *Publications:* edited, for Royal Statistical Institute, the Vital Statistics of Dr William Farr, DCL, FRS; contributed many papers on various branches of vital statistics to the Journal of the Royal Statistical Society and to the periodical press. *Address:* Glenside, East Liss, Hants.

Died 6 March 1923.

HUMPHREYS, Very Rev. Robert, MA; Dean of Killaloe since 1886; Incumbent of Ballinaclough 1891-1911. *Educ:* Trinity College, Dublin. Ordained 1853; Curate of Bromcliffe, 1855-57; Borrisokane, 1857; Broadford, 1857; Kilfenora, 1857-64; Lisdoonvarna, 1864; Prebendary of Killaloe, 1864-81; Incumbent of Quin, 1881-91; Dean of Kilfenora, 1884-86; Member of General Synod of Church of Ireland; Member of Representative Body of Church of Ireland. *Address:* Beechlands, Shankill, Co. Dublin.

Died March 1917.

HUMPHRY, Alfred Paget, MVO 1909; JP, DL; County Alderman, Cambridgeshire; Member of Council, National Rifle Association; Member of Cambridge Territorial Force Association; *b* Cambridge, 20 June 1850; *o s* of Sir George Murray Humphry, MD, FRS, and Mary, *d* of D. R. M'Nab, Epping Place, Epping, Essex; *m* 1st, 1876, Elizabeth, *d* of T. Boycott, MD; 2nd, 1887, Clara Edyth, *d* of C. Murchison, MD, FRS; three *s* two *d.* *Educ:* Rugby; Trinity Coll. Camb. Barrister, Lincoln's Inn, 1875. Winner of Queen's Prize, Wimbledon, 1871; member of various national rifle teams, 1872-83; Exec. Officer, National Rifle Association, 1881-91; Lt-Col commanding Cambridge University RV, 1886-89; Member of War Office Small Arms Committee, 1900-5; Senior Esquire Bedell, Cambridge University, 1877-1913; Bursar, Selwyn College, 1884-1900; Steward, Trinity College, Camb., 1887-97. *Publication:* History of the National Rifle Association. *Address:* Horham Hall, Thaxted, Essex; Trinity College, Cambridge. *Clubs:* Athenæum; Cambridge County.

Died 6 Oct. 1916.

HUMPHRY, Mrs C. E.; journalist; *d* of late Rev. James Graham, Londonderry Cathedral; *m* 1881; one *d.* *Educ:* Dublin. *Publications:* Manners for Men; Etiquette for Every Day; Three Cookery Books. *Recreations:* reading, gardening, the play. *Address:* Carrig-Cleena, Maidenhead.

Died 2 April 1925.

HUMPHRY, Laurence, MA, MD (Camb.); FRCP; Physician to Addenbrooke's Hospital, Cambridge; Lieutenant-Colonel RAMC (T), 1st Eastern General Hospital; formerly Assessor to the Regius Professor of Physics; Lecturer in Medicine in the University; Examiner in Medicine, Conjoint Board, London; *b* 1856; *s* of J. T. Humphry, barrister-at-law, London, and J. O. M'Nab of Epping; *m* 1889, Isabel

Lucy, d of Prof. Sir George Stokes, 1st Bt, MP. *Educ:* Haileybury College; Trinity College, Cambridge; St Bartholomew's Hospital. BA Nat. Sci. Trip., 1st Part, 1876; 1st Class Final MB, 1880. Resident Medical Officer City of London Chest Hospital, 1881-83; teacher of Pathology Cambridge University, 1884; Examiner in Medicine, Cambridge University, on several occasions; President Cambridge Medical Society, 1899-1900; Examiner in Medicine, Royal Army Med. Corps. President Cambridge and Huntingdon Branch, BMA, 1905. *Publications:* Manual of Nursing; article, Congenital Malformation of Heart, Allbutt's System of Medicine; contrib., Severe Symptoms following Puncture of Hydatid Cysts of Liver, Lancet, 1887; The Parathyroid Glands in Graves' Disease, *ibid*, 1905; Rupture of Coronary Artery, *ibid*, 1898; Aneurysm of the Aorta communicating with the Sup. Vena Cava, BMJ, 1910; Case of Acromegaly; Pressor substances in Urine (with Dr Dixon), *ibid*, 1910; Multiple Embolic Aneurysms of the Pulmonary Artery, Jl of Pathology and Bacteriology, vol. xvii, 1912; The Urinary Diastase Test and Loewi's Reaction in Pancreatic Lesons, BMJ, 1914. *Address:* Lensfield, Cambridge. *T:* 414.   *Died 5 Feb. 1920.*

HUNEKER, James Gibbons; critic; *b* Philadelphia, 1860; Irish-Hungarian descent; *g s* of Jas Gibbons, Irish poet, former vice-president, Fenian Brotherhood. *Educ:* Paris. Studied music with distinguished masters; adopted journalism as a profession; former musical, art, and dramatic editor of the New York Sun; music editor, New York Times; corresponding member Hispanic Society, New York; member Academy Natural Sciences, Philadelphia; member Institute Arts and Letters. *Publications:* Mezzotints in Modern Music, 1899; Chopin: the Man and his Music, 1900; Melomaniacs, 1902; Overtones, 1904; Iconoclasts, 1905; Visionaries, 1905; Egoists, 1909; Promenades of an Impressionist, 1910; Franz Liszt, 1911; The Pathos of Distance, 1913; New Cosmopolis, 1915; Ivory, Apes, and Peacocks, 1915; Unicorns, 1917; Bedouins, 1920; Steeplejack, 1920. *Address:* The World Office, New York. *Club:* Authors'.   *Died 9 Feb. 1921.*

HUNT, Edmund Langley, CMG 1902; LRCPI, LRCSI; *b* 22 April 1868. *Educ:* Kingsley College; Royal College of Surgeons, Ireland. Civil Surgeons SA Field Force, 1899-1902; Medical Officer on personal staff Com.-in-Chief, Feb. 1902 to termination of war (despatches, 2 medals, 6 clasps); Medical Officer, Anglo-German Boundary Commission to Lake Chad, N Nigeria, 1903-4 (despatches, received thanks of Mr Secretary Lyttleton and Government of Northern Nigeria, the thanks of the Emperor of Germany, and the Insignia of 3rd class, Crown of Prussia); MO, WAMS, 1905; received thanks of Sec. of State for services in connection with outbreak of plague at Accra, Gold Coast, 1908; transferred to Ceylon as Inspecting Medical Officer (IMO), 1912; promoted Assistant PCMO and IGH, 1915; transferred on promotion to Jamaica as SMO, 1920. *Address:* Kingston, Jamaica, West Indies.

Died 30 Sept. 1925.

HUNT, Capt. George Percy Edward, DSO 1900; RN; *m* Cecilia Teresa, *d* of late Rt Hon. Sir Cecil Clementi Smith. Served South Africa, 1899-1900 (DSO); retired, 1913. *Address:* The Great House, Almeley, Herefordshire.   *Died 22 Aug. 1917.*

HUNT, Major Gerald Ponsonby Sneyd, CMG 1916; Royal Berks Regiment; *b* 24 July 1877; *m* 1911, Helen Pennal, *sister* of Sir Archibald Dunbar, 9th Bt. Served S African War, 1899-1902 (Queen's medal 3 clasps, King's medal 2 clasps); European War, 1914-16 (despatches, CMG).   *Died 23 March 1918.*

HUNT, Rev. Henry de Vere, MA; Canon of Clonfert and Kilmacduagh, 1913; Rector of Ahascragh since 1888; *b* 12 March 1856; *s* of late Major Henry Leslie Hunt, Adjutant, 7th West York Rifle Volunteers, formerly of 67th Regt; *m* 1882, Mary Caroline, *d* of late Rev. Peter William Browne, Rector of Blackrod, Lancashire; one *s* three *d*. *Educ:* Bedford Grammar School; Clare College, Cambridge. Ordained, 1882; Curate of Wavertree, 1882-84; Littleton, Middlesex, 1884-86; Incumbent of Ennisnag, Kilkenny, 1886-88. *Address:* Ahascragh Rectory, Ballinasloe.

Died 27 Jan. 1919.

HUNT, Rev. H. G. Bonavia, MusD; FRSE; Vicar of Burgess Hill, Sussex; *b* 1847. *Educ:* privately; King's College, London; afterwards student in the Musical Faculty, Christ Church, Oxford; MusB Christ Church, Oxon, 1876; MusD Trinity College, Dublin, 1887. Member of the Senate, 1890; sub-editor and editor of the Quiver, 1865-1905; editor of Cassell's Magazine, 1874-96; editor and founder of Little Folks from commencement to 1876; founder and first Warden of Trinity College, London, 1872-92; founder and first Warden of the

Kilburn Grammar School, 1897-1904; Teacher of Musical History University of London, 1900-7. Ordained by Bishop of Winchester to curacy of Esher, 1878; afterwards curate of St Philip's, Regent Street, and St James's, Piccadilly; Vicar of St Paul's, Kilburn *Publications:* A Concise History of Music, 19th edn 1915; sermons anthems, and services. *Recreations:* cycling, musical composition *Address:* Burgess Hill Vicarage, Sussex. *T:* Burgess Hill 67. *Club:* Roy Societies.   *Died 27 Sept. 1917*

HUNT, Rev. Thomas Hankey; *b* Hatton, near Runcorn, Cheshire 1842; *m* 2nd *d* of late Rev. Dr William Antliff, President of the Methodist Conference, 1863-65; three *s* one *d*. Member of the Council of Forty of the United Kingdom Alliance, and of the National Temperance Federation; edited the Primitive Methodist World from 1883 until its amalgamation with the Leader, 1909; Sec. Sunday School Union, 1892-97; Pres. of the Primitive Methodist Connexion 1903-4; Sec. of Primitive Methodist Temperance Society 1897-1914, Pres., 1906-15; Secretary of the Liverpool District Education Committee; Director of the Primitive Methodist Leader *Publications:* The Liquor Problem, and How to Solve It; The Christian Citizen and Temperance Reform; Martin Luther: A Study for Protestants; Sunday School Reform, a Problem for the Times (Morse Lecture, 1908), etc. *Address:* 152 South Bank Road, Southport.

Died 1 Aug. 1921

HUNT, Major William Morgan, DSO, MC; Royal Artillery; *b* 1881 *s* of Langford Hunt, CE, of Owen Doon, and Augusta Morgan Entered Army, 1900; served Mesopotamia, 1914-16, No 23 MJ (twice wounded, despatches thrice); North-West Frontier, India Mohmand Expedition, No 8 MB, 1917-18 (despatches); Afghanistan 1919 (despatches). *Recreations:* rowing, football, boxing, big game shooting. *Address:* Owendoon House, Bawnboy, Co. Cavan.

Died 19 July 1925

HUNT-GRUBBE, Adm. Sir Walter James, GCB 1899 (KCB 1882 CB 1874); JP Hants; *b* 1833; *s* of Rev. James A. Hunt-Grubbe; *r* 1867, Mary (*d* 1908), *d* of William Codrington, Wroughton Wiltshire; one *s* two *d*. Entered Navy, 1845; served on W Coast of Africa, 1845-48, 1854-57, 1863-66, in suppressing slave trade Commander, 1861, for operations on River Gambia; Capt. 1866; in charge of Ascension Island, 1866; in command of Naval Brigade in Ashantee War (severely wounded), 1874; ADC, 1879-84; in command of N Division of Mediterranean fleet at Alexandria, 1882 Commander-in-Chief of Cape and W Coast of Africa Station 1885-88; Admiral Superintendent of Devonport Dockyard, 1888-91 President Royal Naval College, Greenwich, 1894-97. *Club:* United Service.   *Died 11 April 1922*

HUNTER, Sir Charles Roderick, 3rd Bt, *cr* 1812; MP (C) Bath 1910-18; Inspector of Musketry, Imperial Yeomanry, 1900; late Captain Rifle Brigade, retired, 1890; *b* 6 July 1858; *s* of Sir Claudius Stephen Paul Hunter, 2nd Bt and Constance, *d* of William Ives Bosanquet; *S* father, 1890; *m* 1887, Agnes, *d* of Adam S. Kennard Crawley Court, Hants; one *s* decd. *Educ:* Eton. *Heir:* none. *Address* 36 Draycott Place, SW3. *T:* West 6970. *Clubs:* Carlton, Travellers *Died 24 June 1924 (ext)*

HUNTER, Captain Douglas William, DSO 1916; MB, ChB Glas. DPH Camb.; RAMC, AIF. *Educ:* Glasgow University. Served European War, 1914-17 (DSO). *Address:* 10 Hallfield Road, Bradford *Died 25 March 1918*

HUNTER, Maj.-Gen. George Douglas, CB 1917; CMG 1916 DSO 1896; MRCS, LSA; Army Medical Service (retired); Director of Medical Services, British East African Expeditionary Forces, Dec 1915-March 1918; *b* 28 Aug. 1860; 2nd *s* of late Brig. Surgeon George Yeates Hunter, Indian Army; *m* 1895, Elfrida Hannah, *d* of late T W. U. Robinson of Houghton-le-Spring, Durham; one *s* one *d* Entered RAMC, 1884; Surg.-Major, 1896; served Nile Expedition 1884-85 (medal with clasp, Khedive's star); Soudan Frontier Field Force, 1885-86; Soudan, 1888-89 (clasp); Dongola Expeditionary Force, 1896 (despatches, DSO, British medal, Khedive's medal with two clasps); operations of 1898, including the battle of Khartoum (despatches, clasp to Khedive's medal, 4th class Osmanieh); Lt-Col 1904; Principal Medical Officer, Egyptian Army, 1905-8 (2nd class Medjidieh); European War, 1914-18 (despatches, CMG, CB) *Address:* Cadbury, Yatton, Somerset.

Died 15 April 1922

HUNTER, G(eorge) Sherwood, RBA 1889; *b* Aberdeen, NB, 1882 2nd *s* of James Hunter, granite merchant of that city; *m* Constance Mary, *d* of Ed. Montague Suart, HEIC. *Educ:* Edinburgh, Paris, Rome

Painted in Scotland, Holland, Spain, Italy, France, Egypt and Palestine; medals Crystal Palace, 1896, 1898; Hon. mention, Paris International, 1900. *Address:* The Malt House, Newlyn, Penzance.

Died 18 June 1920.

UNTER, Hamilton, CMG 1900; *b* 1845; *s* of Walter John Hunter, HEICS, formerly of Baughurst House, Hants; *m* 1882, Isabella Jane, *d* of late Sir John Gorrie; two *d*. Magistrate for Taviuni, Fiji, 1874; Stipendiary Magistrate, Cakandrovi, 1875; Chief Police Magistrate, Fiji, 1877; Deputy Commissioner for W Pacific, 1881; Acting Registrar-Gen. 1892; Official Receiver in Bankruptcy, 1894; Registrar Supreme Court, and Curator Intestate Estates, 1895; Judicial Commissioner to visit Islands, 1896; Acting Consul, Samoa, 1899; Consul at Tonga, 1901. *Address:* 18 South Parade, Southsea. *Club:* Royal Corinthian Yacht, Southsea.

Died 19 Jan. 1923.

UNTER, Rev. John, DD (Glas.) 1893; late Minister of Trinity Church, Glasgow; *b* Aberdeen, 14 July 1849; *m* 1883, Marion, *e d* of D. Martin, York; one *s*. *Educ:* Aberdeen; Nottingham; Springhill College, Birmingham, later Mansfield College, Oxford. Ordained Minister of the Congregational Church at York in succession to the Rev. James Parsons, 1871; Minister of Wycliffe Church, Hull, 1882; Trinity Church, Glasgow, 1887–1902; was elected the first Nonconformist President of the Theological Society of the University of Glasgow, 1895; King's Weigh House Church, Grosvenor Square, London, 1901; returned to the pastorate of Trinity Church, Glasgow, 1904–13. *Publications:* Devotional Services for Public Worship; Hymns of Faith and Life; A Plea for a Worshipful Church; Angels of God, and other sermons; The Coming Church; De Profundis Clamavi, a volume of Discourses preached on special occasions, 1908; God and Life, a volume of sermons delivered in the United States and elsewhere, 1910; and many contribs to religious and other jls. *Recreation:* walking. *Address:* 8 Prince Arthur Road, Hampstead, NW.

Died 15 Sept. 1917.

JNTER, Maj.-Gen. John Gunning, CB 1913; Indian Army (retired); *b* 1 Nov. 1859; *s* of late Col Alexander Hunter, Indian Army; *m* 1st, 1885, Louisa, *d* of late Donald McCallum, Perth; 2nd, 1921, Helen Barbara, *widow* of John Slater, Chorley Wood, Herts. *Educ:* Cheltenham; Sandhurst. First Commission, 70th Foot, 1878; served throughout Afghan War, 1878–79, with 70th Foot, including its march to Kandahar and to the vicinity of the Helmund River; transferred to Indian Army; served as Commandant, 10th Jâts, and vacated on completion of 7 years' tenure of command and after 25 years' service in the corps; served through the Burma War, 1887–90 (official thanks, Chief Commissioner, and despatches); served throughout the Chin-Lushai Expedition (Burma Column), commanded march and attack on Hanta (despatches); served as Brigade Commander at Home and in France in European War, 1914–17 (despatches); promoted to permanent rank of Maj.-Gen.; Special Appointment under the War Office, Sept. 1917 to the signing of peace; retired 1919; Colonel, late Jâts, 1922; awarded a Good Service Pension, 1922. *Address:* La Collinette, Morgat, Brittany. *Club:* East India United Service.

Died 11 June 1926.

JNTER, Lt-Col John Muir, CSI 1899; OBE 1920; Indian Staff Corps, late Royal Artillery; *b* Mauritius, 31 May 1844; *s* of Capt. Hugh Hunter, RN, and Elizabeth Mather; *m* 1870, Emily Jean, *d* of J. Patison Thom, Assistant Secretary India Office, London. *Educ:* Royal Naval School, Newcross; King's Coll. School, London; abroad and private tuition; Royal Mil. Academy, Woolwich. Political Agent in Kathiawar, Bombay Presidency, India, to 1901; Hon. Sec., War Pensions Committee; Hon. Sec., Sailors' Vegetable Fund. *Address:* c/o Bank of England, Burlington Gardens, W.

Died 13 Dec. 1920.

JNTER, Sir Thomas, Kt 1911; DL; LLD; WS; Town Clerk, Edinburgh, 1895–1918; *b* 16 June 1850; *s* of late Robert Hunter, Hawick. *Educ:* Hawick Academy; Edinburgh University. *Address:* 6 Albany Street, Edinburgh; House, Inverarbour, Inverleith Place, Edinburgh. *Clubs:* Royal Societies; University, Edinburgh.

Died 25 Aug. 1919.

JNTER, Sir (William) Bernard, Kt 1916; Managing Governor, Imperial Bank of India; *b* 1868. Late Secretary and Treasurer, Bank of Madras. *Address:* 2 Princes Street, EC.

Died 12 May 1924.

'NTER, William Henry, MICE, MASCE, etc; civil and consulting Engineer; Consulting Engineer to the Manchester Ship Canal Co. since 1910; to the Marine Board of Launceston, Tasmania; to the

Greenock Harbour Trust, etc; *b* 1849; *s* of late Henry Hunter, Sunderland; *m* 1st, 1880, Eliz. Jane (*d* 1893), *o d* of late Councillor Grainger of Sunderland; 2nd, 1895, Florence, 2nd *d* of late William Clayton, New Ferry, Birkenhead; one *s* two *d*. *Educ:* private schools; College of Physical Science, Newcastle-upon-Tyne. After pupilage on Harbour and Dock Works, Sunderland, became, in 1872, Resident Engineer on Hylton and Monkwearmouth Railway (Durham), then Assistant Engineer on the reconstruction of Weaver Navigation (Cheshire); engaged in pioneer and parliamentary work for the Manchester Ship Canal, river Dee, etc, 1882–87; Chief Assistant Engineer on the design and construction of the Ship Canal, 1887; Chief Engineer, 1895; Member of the Board of Consulting Engineers for the Panama Canal, 1905; a Past President of the Manchester Association of Engineers, etc. *Publications:* Rivers and Estuaries; many papers published in Technical Transactions, in the Proceedings of the Navigation Congresses, etc. *Recreations:* resting and reading. *Address:* 42 Spring Gardens, Manchester; Bank House, Woodley, Cheshire. *T:* City 1956, Manchester. *Clubs:* Whitehall; Brasenose, Engineers', Manchester.

Died 27 Feb. 1917.

HUNTINGTON, Sir Charles (Philip), 3rd Bt, *cr* 1906; late Lieutenant 3rd Battalion Royal Irish Regiment (Reserve); *b* 17 Jan. 1888; 5th *s* of Sir Charles Philip Huntington, 1st Bt and Jane Hudson, *d* of Walter Sparkes of Merton, Surrey; *S* brother, 1907; *m* 1st, 1909, Delia Dorothy (who obtained a divorce, 1922), *d* of late Daniel John O'Sullivan of the Grange, Killarney, Co. Kerry; 2nd, 1925, Madeleine, *y d* of late Capt. William Birch, RN, of Kilcool, Co. Wicklow. *Educ:* Eton; King's College, Cambridge. Entered at the Inner Temple, 1908; called to Bar, 1911; served European War, 1914–18 (wounded). *Heir:* none. *Recreations:* golf, motoring. *Address:* The Chauntry, Burnham Abbey, Bucks. *T:* Burnham 102. *Club:* Garrick.

Died 28 Jan. 1928 (ext).

HUNTINGTON, Henry Edwards; *b* Oneonta, NY, 17 Feb. 1850; *s* of Solon Huntington and Harriet Saunders; *m* 1st, 1873, Mary E. Prentice; 2nd, 1913, Arabella D. Huntington. *Educ:* private and public schools. In hardware business in Oneonta and New York; lumberman, St Albans, Va, 1874–80; superintendent of construction, Chesapeake, Ohio and South Western Railway, 1880–84; VP and General Manager Ohio, and Big Sandy RR and Ohio Valley Rly, 1886; Assistant to President Southern Pacific Co., 1892; First VP Southern Pacific Co., 1900; Chairman and Director of many companies. *Address:* San Gabriel, California, USA.

Died 23 May 1927.

HURLE, Col Edward Forbes Cooke-, DSO 1918; JP Hants, 1922; late Major Somerset Light Infantry, and Colonel Territorial Force; *b* 1866; 3rd surv. *s* of late J. Cooke-Hurle, Brislington Hill, near Bristol; *m* 1st, 1903, Grace (*d* 1908), *d* of late T. Davey, Bannerleigh, Leigh Woods, Bistol; one *d*; 2nd, 1913, Muriel Penelope, *d* of Major Maitland of Bartley Manor, Southampton; one *s*. Served European War, 1914–18 (DSO). *Address:* Northerwood Farm, Lyndhurst, Hants.

Died 21 Dec. 1923.

HUSBAND, Thomas Fair, ISO 1911; Civil Servant since 1881; *b* Wigtown, Scotland, 5 Sept. 1862; 7th *s* of James William Husband and Margaret Fair Anderson; *m* 1895, Mary Sophia, *y d* of Samuel Gilliland and Frances Knox, Brook Hall, Co. Derry; one *d*. *Educ:* Wigtown Normal School; Edinburgh University (MA 1881). *Publication:* (with M. F. A. Husband) Punctuation, its Principles and Practice, 1905. *Recreation:* open air. *Address:* 60B Belsize Park Gardens, NW3. *T:* Hampstead 3132. *Clubs:* National Liberal; Edinburgh University.

Died 24 Jan. 1921.

HUSON, Thomas, JP; RI, RE, RCA; analytical chemist, painter, etcher, and engraver; *b* Liverpool, 18 Jan. 1844; *e s* of late George Canning Huson, analytical chemist; *m* 1873, *d* of W. Fabian; four *d*. *Educ:* privately in Liverpool. An analytical chemist in Liverpool, 1864, carrying on at same time profession of painter, etcher and engraver; later retired from profession of chemistry, and devoted his time to art pursuits. *Publications:* Six landscape mezzotints, 1880; Round about Snowdon (in conjunction with Jas J. Hissey), 1894; Round about Helvellyn, 1895; Photoaquatint and Photogravure, 1897; and many etchings and engravings. *Recreations:* music, violin and viola, photography, mechanical pursuits, turning, carpentry. *Address:* Pen-y-Garth, Bala, North Wales. *TA:* Huson, Bala. *Club:* Royal Societies.

Died 2 Feb. 1920.

HUSSEY, Col Arthur Herbert, CB 1915; CMG 1918; late Royal Artillery; *b* 2 June 1863; 3rd *s* of late Edward Hussey, of Scotney Castle, Sussex. Entered army, 1882; Captain, 1891; Major, 1900; Lt-Col, 1908; Col, 1912; commanding RA Northumbrian Division, Northern Command, 1913; served S African War, 1902 (Queen's medal 4 clasps); European War, 1914–18 (despatches twice, CB, CMG). Order of Danilo (Montenegro), 2nd Class, 1917. *Club:* Naval and Military.   *Died 27 May 1923.*

HUSSEY-WALSH, Lt-Col William; late Reserve of Officers; *b* 1863; *s* of Walter Hussey-Walsh, of Cranagh and Mul Hussey; *m* 1892, Mary, *d* of Mrs Fazakerley Evered, of Wadhurst Castle, Sussex; one *d. Educ:* France; Austria; Oratory School, Edgbaston; Sandhurst. Entered Cheshire Regt, 1884; served Burma War, Chin-Lushai Expedition, on preliminary Chinese Boundary Commission, and during Wuntho Rebellion; paid Attaché Intelligence Branch, Burma, 1890 (Simla despatches) retired as Captain, 1899; joined 4th Batt. Essex Regt shortly after outbreak of S African War, and employed with SA Constabulary, 1901–6; Recruiting Staff Officer, SAC, Cape Town, 1903–6; Major (RO), 1903; Secretary to the British Branch of the Spanish Red Cross Soc. during war in Morocco, 1909 (Order of St John Lateran); raised and trained 26 (3 Tyneside Irish) Northumberland Fusiliers and 2nd GB Royal Welsh Fusiliers for service abroad, 1914–15; Commandant of Cairo Citadel, 1916; Western Frontier Force, Egypt, 1917–18 (despatches); Base Commandant, Beirut, Syria, (graded AAG), 1918–9, and at Port Said, 1919–20; Hon. Secretary for the Levant of the Officers' Association (Lord Haig's Appeal), with headquarters at Cairo, 1920; collected in the spring of 1921 £10,900 in Egypt, the Sudan and Palestine; on Council of Naval and Military Emigration League. Order of the Nile, 1919; Officer of Crown of Italy and of French Legion of Honour, 1920; Médaille d'Honneur, France (1st Class), 1921. Fellow, United Service Institute; FRCI. *Recreations:* all aquatic sports, riding, shooting, lawn tennis. *Address:* 24 Ennismore Gardens, SW7. *T:* Western 4025. *Club:* Naval and Military.

Died 2 Jan. 1925.

HUTCHINS, Sir David Ernest, Kt 1920; JP (Cape); FRGS; Chief Conservator of Forests, British East Africa (retired); *b* 22 Sept. 1850; *m* Violet B., *d* of Frederic J. Walker, The Priory, Bathwick, Bath; no *c. Educ:* Blundell's, Tiverton; School of Forests, Nancy. Served ten years in the Indian Forest Service; twenty-three in that of S Africa, and four in that of British East Africa; had a unique acquaintance with the extra-tropical forest of Africa, which extended in patches from the extreme south of the African coast to the Equator, altitude compensating latitude; specially studied extratropical trees; sent on a special mission to explore the forest girdling Mount Kenia, 1908; passed two months in the Alpine region, under the Equator, of snowy Kenia; visited Cyprus and reported to the Colonial Office on its forestry, 1909; made a forest tour through each of the Australian States, and prepared a study on Australian Forestry for the West Australian Government, 1914–15; made an offical tour through the New Zealand Forests, and reported to the New Zealand Government, 1916; Brachlyaena Hutchinsii, one of six most valuable trees in the extra-tropical forest of Africa, has been so named at Kew. *Publications:* various works on African Forestry; Report on Forests of British East Africa, illustrated, 1909; Forests of Mount Kenia, 1907; S African Forestry, visit of British Association to S Africa, 1905; Extra-tropical Forestry, illustrated, 1906; Report on Transvaal Forestry, illustrated, 1903; on Rhodesia, 1904; The Cluster-pine at Genadendaal; Tree-planting in Cape Colony, etc; Cyprus Forestry, 1909; A Forest Tour in Australia; Report on Forestry to W Australian Government, 1914–15; British Forestry; Journal of a Forest Tour (in Germany). *Recreations:* mountaineering, cycling, running, gardening. *Address:* Medo House, Cobham, Kent. *Club:* Authors'.

Died 1920.

HUTCHINS, Horace Albert, KC; Practising Advocate since 1898; *s* of Rodney Hutchins and Harriet Hulbert; *m* 1892, Arvilla Lyndon, *d* of late James H. Moran, St Martin's, New Brunswick, shipbuilder, and Hannah Cochrane; no *c. Educ:* St Francis College, Richmond; McGill University, Montreal. Admitted to the Bar, 1884; QC 1898. *Recreations:* riding, golf. *Address:* 204 St Catherine Street, W Montreal. *TA:* Hutlese. *T:* Main 2118; Westmount 308.

Died 13 Oct. 1923.

HUTCHINS, Sir Philip Perceval, KCSI 1891 (CSI 1888); *b* London, 28 Jan. 1838; 5th *s* of William Hutchins, and Isabella, *d* of Honoratus Leigh Thomas, sometime President of the College of Surgeons; *m* 1860, Fanny Annie, *d* of B. T. Norfor. *Educ:* Merchant Taylors' School; EIC College, Haileybury. Joined Madras Civil Service, 1857; district judge of Madura, 1872–82; called to the Bar, Inner Temple, 1875; judge of the Madras High Court, 1883; member of Council, Madras, 1886; member of the Governor-General's Council, 1888–98; joined India Office, 1893, as Judicial and Public Secretary; Member of Council of India, 1898–1908. *Publication:* An Indian Career, 1858–1908. *Recreations:* cricket, cycling, bowls. *Address:* Danesfort,

Camberley. *TA* and *T:* Camberley 67. *Club:* East India Uni Service.   *Died 21 May 19*

HUTCHINSON, Col Charles Alexander Robert, DSO 19 FRGS; Indian Army, retired; *b* Bulandshahr, India, 31 May 187: *s* of late Surg.-Gen. J. A. C. Hutchinson, IMS; *m* 1916, Barbara A Betsy, 2nd *d* of late James Fowler Allan, Aberdeen; one *d. E* Bedford School; Sandhurst. 2nd Lieut 18th Royal Irish Regime 1891; Indian Army (3rd Sikhs, Frontier Force), 1896; 41st Dog 1900; entered the Indian Staff College, 1906; Brigade Major, Ass Brigade, 1908–12; served NW Frontier of India, 1897; Tochi (me and clasp), Samana (clasp), Tirah (clasp); actions of Dargai, Sampa, Pass, Arhanga Pass, operations against Khani Khel Chamkannis a in Bazar Valley, 1897; Abor Expedition, 1911–12, General S Officer (despatches, Brevet Lieut-Colonel, medal and clas European War, 1914 (very severely wounded, despatches, DS retired, 1920. *Recreations:* rowing, tennis, golf, photography, wat colour painting.   *Died 25 July 19*

HUTCHINSON, Lt-Gen. Henry Doveton, CSI 1903; Indian arr retired; Colonel 3rd (Queen Alexandra's Own) Gurkha Rifles, 19 *b* 13 Sept. 1847; *e s* of late Dr T. Cayley Hutchinson, Dep. Inspec Gen. of Hospitals; *m* 1874, Annie Alice Campbell (*d* 1924), *siste* Sir James Frederick Stuart-Menteth, 4th Bt; two *s.* Served Sikh Campaign, 1887–88; Relief of Chitral, 1895 (medal and clasp); Ti Campaign, 1897–98 (2 clasps); raised for service the 2nd battal 3rd Gurkha Rifles, 1891; commanded troops in Chitral after Bri occupation, 1896; Director of Military Education in Ind 1896–1901; Special duty (China Expedition) in the India Offi 1901–2; Assist Military Secretary (for Indian Affairs), 1902–4; Direc of Staff Duties, War Office, 1904–8. *Publications:* Military Sketch Made Easy (5th edn); Field Fortification (5th edn); The Story Waterloo; The Story of 1812; The Story of Corunna; The Campa in Tirah, 1897–98, etc. *Clubs:* United Service, Pilgrims.

Died 21 Nov. 19

HUTCHINSON, Rev. Henry Neville, MA Camb.; FGS, FR(FZS; *b* Chester, 1856; *e s* of Rev. T. Neville Hutchinson, late Scie Master at Rugby, and Sarah K. Turner, Winson, Birmingham; *m* 19 Bertha, *d* of late Daniel Sydney Hasluck, Olton Court, Warwic *Educ:* Rugby; St John's College, Cambridge. Student-Master at Clif College, 1879–80; Curate to St Saviour's, Redland Park, 1884; priv tutor to sons of Earl of Morley, 1886–87; travelled for health; be literary work in London, 1891. *Publications:* Autobiography of Earth, 1890; The Story of the Hills, 1891; Extinct Monsters, 18 Creatures of Other Days, 1894; Prehistoric Man and Beast, 18 Marriage Customs in Many Lands, 1897; Primæval Scenes, 18 Living Races of Mankind (ed and part author), 1900; The Liv Rulers of Mankind, 1901. *Recreation:* country rambles. *Address:* St John's Wood Park, NW8. *T:* Primrose Hill 3297. *M:* XR 11 *Club:* Royal Societies.   *Died 30 Oct. 19*

HUTCHINSON, Lt-Col Hugh Moore, CMG 1918; DSO 19 York and Lancaster Regiment; late Connaught Rangers; *b* 18 Ju 1874; *s* of late Rev. S. Hutchinson, MA; *m* 1914, Eileen Millice *y d* of Minton Goode; one *s. Educ:* Cheltenham College; Sandhu Entered army, 1894; served Sierra Leone, 1898–99 (medal with cla South Africa, 1899–1901; relief of Ladysmith (dangerously wound 5 wounds, 23 Feb. 1900); operations in Transvaal, Free State, a Cape Colony (severely wounded, 3 wounds, 14 July 1901, despatch DSO, medal and 6 clasps); attached Egyptian army, 1902– commanded 12th Sudanese, 1906–12; Egypt, 1902; commanded Egyptian Battalion on cholera duty (4th class Medjidieh); Sud operations against Nyam-Nyams (medal and clasp), 1904–5; Sud operations against Talodi Arabs, 1906 (clasp); Sudan, 1911; operatio in Southern Kordofan (medal with clasp, 3rd class Osmanie European War, 1914–18 (American Distinguished Service Med 1914 Star, severely wounded, CMG).

Died 26 Dec. 19

HUTCHINSON, Col James Bird, CSI 1904; Indian Arm unemployed super-numerary list, 1902–5; Member of Council of Governor Punjab; *b* 22 March 1844; *m* 1869, Annie Charlotte, *d* Maj.-Gen. Hugh Rose; four *s* two *d. Educ:* Blackheath Propriet School; Cheltenham College. Joined South Lancashire Regt, 18 served with 5th Ghoorka Rifles, 1865–68; Commissioner a Superintendent, Lahore, 1894–99; Governor, Aitchison Coll., Laho 1900–5. JP Surrey. *Address:* Waverley Drive, Camberley.

Died 6 Sept. 192

HUTCHINSON, John; *b* Ballingham, Hereford; *s* of Geo. Hutchins (brother-in-law of the poet Wordsworth); *m* 1871, Helen Tayl *d* of Edward Meredith, MD, of Bath. *Educ:* at Chelsea, under the Rev. Derwent Coleridge; Paris. Many years engaged in educational work at Harrow, Hereford, Doncaster, and other schools; FEIS; FCP; Keeper of the Library of the Hon. Society of the Middle Temple, 1880–1909; retired, 1909. *Publications:* Ariconia, or Recollections of Wyeside, a poem, 1853; Herefordshire Biographies, 1890; Men of Kent, 1892; Llandrindod Legends and Lyrics (under pseudonym Ladylift), 1895; The Legend of Hereford Cathedral, a poem, 1897; Notable Middle Templars, 1902; Middle Temple Records: An Inquiry into the Origin and Early History of the Inn, 1904; The Sonnets of Shakespeare, 1912; Literary Legends, 1913; contrib. to Dictionary of National Biography and periodical literature. *Recreations:* fishing, ruralising, and (*olim*) cricket, etc. *Address:* Dullatur House, Hereford. *Clubs:* United; Hereford Constitutional.

Died 4 April 1916.

HUTCHINSON, Hon. Sir Joseph Turner, Kt 1895; Chief Justice of Supreme Court of Ceylon, 1906–11; *b* 1850; *m* 1897, Constance Mary, *d* of J. Lucas of Stapleton House, Upper Tooting. *Educ:* St Bees School; Christ's Coll., Cambridge (Scholar; MA 1876). Barrister, Middle Temple, 1879; Chief Justice, Gold Coast Colony, 1889; Chief Justice of Grenada, 1895–97; Chief Justice of Cyprus, 1897–1906. *Address:* Braystones, Beckermet, Cumberland. *Club:* Reform.

Died 20 Jan. 1924.

HUTCHINSON, Teasdale H.; agriculturist; *b* 31 May 1837; *m* 1880, a *niece* of J. B. Booth of Killerby; two *s* (one killed in the War) two *d*. *Educ:* Durham Grammar School. Commenced farming, 1865; twice won Royal Agricultural Society's prize for best managed farm in Yorkshire; won many prizes for shorthorns and hunters. *Recreations:* hunting, riding. *Address:* Manor House, Catterick, Yorks. *TA:* Catterick.

Died 27 May 1928.

HUTCHINSON, Maj.-Gen. William Francis Moore, RA; *b* 3 Feb. 1841. Entered army, 1857; Maj.-Gen. 1898; retired, 1901; DAG, RA, Headquarters, 1897–99; Commandant, Staff College, 1899–1901. *Address:* Bendemeere, Old Wish Road, Eastbourne.

Died 22 April 1917.

HUTCHISON, Sir George Aitken Clark, Kt 1928; MP (U) North Midlothian, 1922–23 and since 1924; *b* Renfrew, 6 July 1873; *s* of late Rev. John Hutchison, DD, Bonnington United Free Church, Leith, and Jane, *d* of late John Clark, Paisley; *m* 1902, Margaret, *d* of late John Blair, WS, Edinburgh; three *s*. *Educ:* Edinburgh Academy; Edinburgh University. Advocate, 1896; KC 1922; contested (U) Argyllshire in 1906, 1910 (Jan.) and 1910 (Dec.); North Midlothian, 1923. JP Argyllshire; Honorary Sheriff-Substitute of Argyll at Oban; Director of Royal Victoria Tuberculosis Hospital Trust, Edinburgh; served Recruiting Staff and Ministry of National Service; Director of Hospital for Diseases of Women, Edinburgh; Vice-Commodore of Royal Clyde Yacht Club and Rear-Commodore Royal Northern and Royal Eastern and Royal Forth Yacht Clubs. *Recreations:* tennis, yachting, horticulture. *Address:* Island of Eriska, Ledaig, Argyllshire; 24 Hans Place, SW1. *T:* Sloane 4320. *M:* SB91, SB 560. *Clubs:* Carlton, Junior Carlton, 1900; New, University, Conservative, Edinburgh; Conservative, Glasgow; numerous Yacht.

Died 22 Dec. 1928.

HUTCHISON, Very Rev. Michael Balfour; Dean of Glasgow since 1903; Rector of St Ninian, Glasgow, 1870–1920; Examining Chaplain to Bishops of Glasgow since 1881; *b* Isle of Cumbrae, Buteshire, 18 July 1844; *s* of John Hutchison (*b* 1765), Burgess of Glasgow and merchant there; *m* 1869, Margaret, *o d* of Rev. James Stewart, Rector of Holy Trinity, Paisley; two *s* two *d*. *Educ:* High School and University of Glasgow; Worcester and Lincoln Colleges, Oxford (BA 1867, MA 1870, DD 1905). Ordained, 1867; Curate of St Stephen, Norwich, 1869–70; Holy Trinity, Paisley, 1870; Diocesan Inspector of Schools, 1879–90. *Publication:* vol. of Translations of Hymns into Latin Verse. *Address:* The Deanery, Glencairn Drive, Pollokshields, Glasgow. *Clubs:* Glasgow Literary, Provand's Lordship.

HUTCHISON, Sir Thomas, 1st Bt, *cr* 1923; JP, DL; LLD; Consul for Belgium in Leith; a Brigadier of King's Body Guard for Scotland, Royal Company of Archers; *b* 16 Dec. 1866; *e s* of late Robert Hutchison, Carlowrie Castle, Kirkliston; *m* 1894, Jane Moir Ogilvy, *d* of late Alexander Ogilvy Spence, banker; one *s*. *Educ:* Collegiate School, Edinburgh; Edinburgh University. Director of Commercial Bank of Scotland Ltd; Director of J. G. Thomson & Co. Ltd, Wine Merchants; Chairman Longmorn Glenlivet Distillery Co. Ltd; Lord Provost of Edinburgh, 1921–23. *Recreations:* shooting, golf, archery. *Heir: s* Eric Alexander Ogilvy Hutchison, *b* 28 Feb. 1897. *Address:* 12 Douglas Crescent, Edinburgh; Hardiston, Kinross-shire. *Clubs:*

Junior Constitutional; Caledonian United Service, Edinburgh.

Died 12 April 1925.

HUTCHISON, William, MA, LLB; Solicitor in Glasgow; MP (U) Glasgow (Kelvingrove) since 1922; *b* Greenock; *s* of William Hutchison, Printer Lithographer; *m* Agnes Hood, *d* of William Grant, Dunoon; one *d*. *Educ:* Greenock Academy (dux); Glasgow University. Most distinguished student of his year in Law, Civil Law Prizeman and others. Contested (C) Bridgeton Division of Glasgow, 1910; stood down for Coalition Liberal, 1918. *Address:* 10 University Gardens, Glasgow. *TA:* Appellants, Glasgow. *T:* Western Glasgow, 1854. *Clubs:* Constitutional, St Stephen's; Conservative, Art, Glasgow.

Died 1 May 1924.

HUTSON, Ven. Eyre; Rector, All Saint's, St Thomas, Danish West Indies, since 1872; HBM Consular Chaplain; Archdeacon of Virgin Islands; *b* Barbados, 6 Sept. 1830; *s* of Rev. John Hutson, also a native; *m* 1858, Sarah Agnes Curil, a native; four *s* two *d*. *Educ:* Codrington College, Barbados (Scholar). Ordained 1853; Acting Chaplain, Soc. Chapel; Curate, St Fernando, Trinidad; St Thomas', and Holy Innocents, Barbados; as Senior Archdeacon three times administered the diocese during the vacancy. MA Emeritus; Knight of Dannebrog. *Recreation:* parish work. *Address:* St Thomas, Danish West Indies.

HUTTON, Arthur Hill; Metropolitan Police Magistrate, 1906–15; *b* 17 March 1859; *o* surv. *s* of late John Hill Hutton of Houghton Hall, Houghton-le-Spring, Co. Durham; *m* 1892, Sarah Elizabeth, *niece* and adopted *d* of late John Edward Taylor of 20 Kensington Palace Gardens, W. *Address:* Houghton Cottage, Walton Heath, Surrey. *T:* Burgh Heath 258. *Clubs:* Union, Garrick.

Died 12 Jan. 1923.

HUTTON, Lt-Gen. Sir Edward (Thomas Henry), KCB 1912 (CB 1894); KCMG 1900; DL; retired; Colonel Commandant The King's Royal Rifle Corps; Hon. Colonel 6th Light Horse (NSW Northern Rivers Lancers), and 15th Light Horse (NSW Mounted Rifles), and 6th Reserve Battalion, King's Royal Rifle Corps; *b* Torquay, 6 Dec. 1848; *s* of Edward Thomas Hutton, Beverley, Yorks; *m* 1889, Eleanor, *o d* of Lord Charles Paulet, and *g d* of 13th Marquess of Winchester. *Educ:* Eton. Joined 60th Rifles 1867; Col, 1892; Maj.-Gen. (temporary), NSW, 1893–96; Canada, 1898–1900; South Africa, 1900; Lt-Gen. 1907; served Zulu War, 1879; battle of Gingihlovo (despatches, medal); Boer War, with Mounted Infantry, 1881; Egyptian War, 1882; Mil. Sec., and in command of Mounted Infantry, including the reconnaissance in force, 5 Aug., and other operations at Alexandria; battle of Tel-el-Kebir (horse killed, despatches, Brevet Major, medal and star); Nile Expedition, 1884–85, in command of Mounted Infantry; also on the staff; raised and commanded Mounted Infantry at Aldershot, 1888–92; ADC to the Sovereign, 1892–1901; commanded the Military Forces, NSW, 1893–96; president Military Conferences in Australia, 1896; Assistant Adjutant-General, Ireland, 1896–98; Gen. in Command of the Dominion Militia, 1898–1900; commanded the Mounted Troops, other than Cavalry, on the flank of Lord Roberts's advance, and subsequently an independent column in the operations in the Eastern Transvaal (despatches, medal and 5 clasps); commanded and organised the Military Forces of Australia, 1901–4; Gen. of Administration Eastern Command and commanding 3rd Division, 1905–6; organised and commanded 21st Division, 3rd Army, 1914–15. 2nd Class Japanese Order of the Rising Sun. *Publications:* Brief History of the KRRC; pamphlets upon military and other questions. *Recreations:* cricket, shooting, hunting. *Address:* Fox Hills, Chertsey. *TA:* Longcross. *T:* Long Cross 11. *Club:* United Service.

Died Aug. 1923.

HUTTON, Rev. Henry Wollaston, MA; Prebendary of Lincoln Cathedral since 1877; *b* Gate Burton, Lincolnshire, 6 Nov. 1835; *s* of Rev. H. F. Hutton, of Spridlington, Lincolnshire; *m* 1860, Frances Annie, *d* of John Bromhead, of Reepham and Lincoln; one *s* one *d*. *Educ:* Southwell; Rugby; privately; Oxford. Curate of Southwell, 1859–61; Rector of St Mary Magdalene, Lincoln, 1862–77; Priest-Vicar, Lincoln, 1861–1913; Alderman of Lindsey (Lincolnshire) County Council from 1889. JP Lincolnshire. *Address:* Vicars' Court, Lincoln. *T:* 243 Lincoln.

Died 9 Oct. 1916.

HUTTON, John, JP, DL; County Alderman; *b* Solberge, 10 Jan. 1847; *e s* of John Hutton and Caroline, *d* of Thomas Robson, Holtby Hall, Yorkshire; *m* 1870, Hon. Caroline Shore, *e d* of 2nd Lord Teignmouth; one *s*. *Educ:* Eton; Christ Church, Oxford. MP (C) Northallerton, 1868–74; MP (C) Richmond Div. NR Yorkshire, 1895–1906; Chairman of North Riding Quarter Sessions, 1892–99; and of the County Council 1895–1915; formerly a representative of York Diocese in House of Laymen; formerly a Captain in North York

Rifles (Militia). *Publications:* Northallerton Farm Account Book; The Columnar Farm Account Book, pamphlets, etc. *Address:* Sowber Gate, Northallerton. *TA:* Northallerton. *T:* Northallerton 25. *Clubs:* Constitutional; Yorkshire, York.

Died 19 Dec. 1921.

HUXTABLE, Lt-Col Robert Beveridge, CMG 1918; DSO 1917; Australian Army Medical Corps; *b* 1867; *m* 1898, Teresa, *d* of M. F. Shine, Dungarvan, Ireland. *Educ:* Otago; Edinburgh University, MB, CM. Served European War, 1915–18 (despatches, CMG, DSO).

Died 11 May 1920.

HUYSHE-ELIOT, Hon. Reginald Huyshe; MLC Ceylon; *b* 18 March 1868; *e s* of late R. ffolliott Eliot, JP, DL, and Mary Milborough, *o d* of late General George Huyshe, CB; assumed additional name of Huyshe by Deed Poll, 1912; *m* 1893, Annie Buckland, *d* of G. B. Fletcher, Tapio, NSW; two *s. Educ:* privately; HMS Worcester. Commission, RNR; engaged in tea and rubber planting in Ceylon for past thirty years; Assistant Commissioner for Government of Ceylon at St Louis Exhibition, 1904; Member of Legislative Council from 1914, representing planting interests. *Address:* Norwood House, Norwood, Ceylon. *Clubs:* Badminton, Oriental, Royal Automobile.

Died 7 Jan. 1920.

HYDE, Lt-Col Dermot Owen, CBE 1919; DSO; MB; RAMC; OC British Station Hospital, Maymyo, Burma; *b* 1 Dec. 1877; *s* of Lt-Col Robert Hyde, AMS, and Jean *d* of Gen. Sir Patrick Craigie, KCB; *m* 1908, Hilda Edith Richmond, *d* of Lt-Col F. de R. Mauduit; two *s. Educ:* Trinity College, Dublin, BA, MB, DPH. Received a commission in RAMC, 1900; visited Australia, New Zealand and Tasmania with Imperial Representative Corps; served S African War with Kavanagh's Column and Calwell's Column; appointed in 1911 to West Riding Division TF, and worked on the Mobilisation Schemes of the medical units, including the Territorial General Hospitals of Leeds and Sheffield; proceeded with the Division to France and completed in 1916 five years as DADMS of an Infantry Division; commanded a Field Ambulance with the 5th Division during the Somme battle; OC No 1 Casualty Clearing Station, 1917; ADMS 21st Division, 1918–19; appointed for three years Senior Medical Officer Bermuda, and served as a Member of the Board of Health of the Colony; returned to England, 1922, and proceeded to the Dardanelles, being appointed ADMS to 18th Division. *Recreations:* tennis, golf. *Address:* No 2 British Infantry Lines, Maymyo, Burma; Glyn, Mills & Co., 3 Whitehall Place, SW1.

Died 19 April 1928.

HYDE, James Wilson, ISO 1904; *b* Paisley, 6 Feb. 1841; *s* of John Hyde and Mary Wilson; *m* 1877, Joanna Stuart Gibb, Glasgow; one *d. Educ:* Parish School, Govan; Free Church Normal Seminary, High School, Mechanics' Institution, and School of Design, Glasgow. Appointed Clerk, PO Glasgow, 1860; Money Order Office, London, 1864; Secretary's Office, London, 1870; Controller, Sorting Office, GPO, Edinburgh, 1878–1906; retired. *Publications:* The Royal Mail, its curiosities and romance; A Hundred Years by Post; The Post in Grant and Farm. *Recreations:* literature, music, painting. *Address:* c/o Chief Clerk, Sorting Office, General Post Office, Edinburgh.

Died 1 May 1918.

HYDE, William De Witt, LLD, DD; President of Bowdoin College since 1885; *b* Winchendon, Mass, 23 Sept. 1858; *s* of Joel and Eliza Hyde; *m* 1883, Prudence M. Phillips; one *s. Educ:* Phillips' Exeter Acad.; Harvard Coll. and Andover Seminary. *Publications:* Social Theology; Practical Ethics; Practical Idealism; God's Education of Man; Jesus' Way; The College Man and the College Woman; Self-Measurement; The Teacher's Philosphy; The Five Great Philosophies of Life; The Quest of the Best; The Gospel of Good Will. *Address:* Brunswick, Me, USA.

Died 29 June 1917.

HYMAN, Hon. Charles Smith, PC (Can.) 1904; late Minister of Public Works for Canada; resigned, 1906; *b* London, Ontario, 1854; *s* of Ellis W. Hyman and Annie Niles, *d* of late William Niles, MLA, Canada; *m* 1st, 1876, Elizabeth (*d* 1917), *d* of late John Birrell of London, Ont; 2nd, 1918, Alexandra, *d* of late Alexander Bremner, London, Ont. *Educ:* Hellmuth College, London, Ont. Was Alderman and Chairman of Finance Committee of London, 1882–83; President Board of Trade, 1881–82, and Mayor in 1884; Secretary Dominion Liberal Convention, 1893; first returned to Parliament, 1891; elected London, 1900 and 1904; was Chairman of Select Standing Committee of House of Commons on Railways, Canals, and Telegraph Lines; Chairman of the Redistribution Committee of 1903; sworn of the Privy Council and made a Member of the Cabinet without portfolio, 1904; Acting Minister of Public Works, 1904–5. *Address:* Idlewild,

London, Ont. *Clubs:* London, London; Toronto, Toronto; Rideau, Ottawa; St James's, Montreal; Union, St John.

Died 9 Oct. 1926.

HYNDMAN, Henry Mayers; *b* London, 7 March 1842; *e s* of late John Beckles Hyndman, MA Trinity Coll. Cambridge, barrister-at-law (donor £150,000 to build and endow churches East End London), and Caroline Seyliard Mayers; *m* 1st, 1876, Matilda Ware (*d* 1913); 2nd, 1914, Rosalind Caroline, *o d* of Major Travers, Tortington House, Arundel. *Educ:* privately; Trinity Coll. Camb (BA). Sussex County Eleven, 1863–68; correspondent Pall Mal Gazette, War, 1866; friends, Mazzini, Garibaldi and Saffi, 1867; article Cavour, Fortnightly Review, 1868; Australia, New Zealand Polynesia, America, 1869–71; wrote the leaders Melbourne Argu for free education during winning fight, 1869; journalist, 1871–74 visited America, 1874–80 at intervals; founded Social Democratic Federation, 1881; member Irish Land League, and Central Executive Land League of Great Britain, 1881–84; founded weekly paper Justice 1884; active in leading unemployed agitation; debated St James's Hal Socialism against Bradlaugh, 1884; tried Old Bailey for part in Wes End Riots, acquittal, 1886; active agitator for social remedies, 1887–95 stood general election Social-Democratic candidate for Burnley, 1895 delegate and chairman at International Socialist Congress, London 1896; Eight Hours, 1890; vigorous agitator against South African War 1899–1900; took very active part establishing new "International" at International Socialist Congress, Paris, 1900; constant writing an speaking for justice to India, 1900 onwards; active agitator agains Transvaal War, 1901–2; member of International Socialist Bureau 1900–10; Agitation, London and Provinces, 1903–4; Warnings agains German Menace, 1905–14; contested (Social Democratic Foundation Burnley, 1906 and 1910 (twice); Member National Worke Committee (War Emergency), 1914–19; helped to Constitut National Socialist Party against Anti-National Socialist Groups, 1916 Member of Food Consumers' Council, 1918–20. *Publications:* India Policy and English Justice, 1874; Bankruptcy of India, 1878, book 1886; England for All, 1881; Nationalisation of Land in 1772 an 1882; Historical Basis of Socialism, 1883; Emigration Fraud Expose 1884; Socialism and Slavery, reply to Herbert Spencer; A Commun for London, 1888; Mr Gladstone and the Eight Hours Law Commercial Crises of the 19th Century, 1892; Economics o Socialism, 1896; The Record of an Adventurous Life, 1911; Furthe Reminiscences, 1912; The Future of Democracy, 1915; Th Awakening of Asia, 1919; Clemenceau: The Man and His Time 1919; The Evolution of Revolution, 1920; Debate, Duke o Northumberland, Industrial Unrest, Committee Room, House o Commons, 1921; Marx Made Easy, 1921. *Recreations:* cricke racquets. *Address:* 13 Well Walk, NW3. *T:* Hampstead 3554.

Died 22 Nov. 192

HYNDMAN-JONES, Sir William Henry, Kt 1906; Chief-Justi Straits Settlements, 1906–14; *b* 9 Aug. 1847; *m* 1882. Edu Marlborough; Trinity College, Cambridge; LLB 1870. Called to Ba Lincoln's Inn, 1878; acting Senior Police Magistrate, an Commissioner to inquire into administration and working of Poli Force, Barbadoes, 1880; acting Judge of Court of Appeal, 188 Magistrate, 1st District, St Lucia, 1881; Member of Executive ar Legislative Council, 1881; Delegate to West Indian Telegraf Conference, 1882; acting Chief Justice of St Lucia and Tobago, 188 acting Attorney-General, 1883; acting Chief Justice of St Lucia ar Tobago; Member of Windward Court of Appeal, 1886; Magistra and Member of Executive and Legislative Council, Grenada, 188 Resident Magistrate for Westmoreland, Jamaica, 1888; St Thoma Ye-East, 1890; St Catherine, 1891; City and Parish of Kingston, 189 acting Puisne Judge, 1893; acting Attorney-General and Member Privy Council, 1895; Supernumerary Resident Magistrate for Jamaic 1896; Puisne Judge, Straits Settlements, 1896; acting Judic Commissioner for Federated Malay States in addition to other duti 1903; Judicial Commissioner, FMS, 1904; Chief Judic Commissioner, 1906; Chairman of Committee to draft Civil an Criminal Procedure Codes, SS; President of Statue Law Revisi Commission, SS; President of Commission to inquire into the sta of Johore Bahru Prison. *Club:* Albemarle.

Died 20 Aug. 192

HYSLOP, Rev. Archibald Richard Frith, MA; Vicar and Rural De of Kingston-on-Thames, Surrogate; Hon. Canon of Southwa Cathedral; Examining Chaplain to the Bishop of St Andrews; *b* July 1866; *s* of late Archibald Hyslop, JP, of Lotus, Dumfries; *m* 1 1893, Alice Sophia (*d* 1901), *d* of late Dr Maynard of Rangoon; 2r 1902, Elizabeth Lucy, 2nd *d* of Rev. W. Done Bushell, of Harro one *s* one *d. Educ:* St Paul's School (Captain, 1884–85); King's Colle Cambridge (Scholar). Carus Prize, 1887; honourably mentione

Porson Prize, 1888, and Chancellor's medals, 1889. Assistant Master in Harrow School, 1892–1902; ordained deacon, 1900; priest, 1901; Warden of Glenalmond, 1902–13; Canon of St Ninian's, Perth, 1909–13; Rector of Stoke, Coventry, 1913–18. *Publication:* (ed) Euripides' Andromach (Macmillan's Classical Series). *Recreations:* golf, figure-skating. *Address:* Vicarage, Kingston-on-Thames. *T:* Kingston 0648.   *Died 19 Oct. 1926.*

HYSLOP, Col James, DSO 1900; Deputy Director Medical Services, Union of South Africa; President Natal Medical Council, etc; *b* 3 March 1856; *s* of Thos Hyslop, Wood Park, Kirkcudbrightshire; *m* 1st, 1882, Clementina Flemming Cullen Elphinstone Brown; 2nd, Barbara, *widow* of Sir James Steel, 1st and last Bt. *Educ:* Hutton Hall; Edinburgh University; Berlin, Vienna, Munich. MB, CM, Edinburgh University. Formerly PMO, Natal Militia; Physician Superintendent, Natal Mental Hospital; Assistant Medical Officer, Border Counties Asylum, Melrose; Assistant Physician, Royal Edinburgh Asylum, Morningside; Delegate from Natal Government to Conference of South African States and Colonies on Plague, held at Pretoria, 1899; Chairman Plague Conference held at Durban, 1899. Decorated for services in South African War, 1899–1901; Natal Native Rebellion, 1906 (despatches). *Publication:* Investigation Anatomy of Central Nervous System. *Address:* The Huts, Pietermaritzburg, Natal. *Club:* Victoria, Pietermaritzburg.   *Died 5 Oct. 1917.*

HYSLOP, Sir Thomas, Kt 1911; JP; *b* Bank House, New Cumnock, Scotland, 9 Oct. 1859; *s* of John Hyslop, of Bank, and Agnes Kirkland; *m* Margaret Torrance; one *s* three *d*. *Educ:* Ayr Academy. In business in Glasgow, 1876–82, when proceeded to Natal, where engaged in farming; President Natal Farmers' Conference, 1899–1903; Member Invasion Losses Inquiry Commission, 1899–1903; Member for Umgeni Division, 1902–10; joined Hime Ministry as Treasurer, 1903; one of Natal delegates to Bloemfontein Customs Conference, 1903; delegate to Johannesburg Intercolonial Railway Conference, 1905, and Maritzburg Customs Conference, 1906; Treasurer in Smythe Ministry, 1905 and 1906; one of the Natal delegates to the National Convention in 1908 and 1909, which drafted the South African Constitution; with other delegates proceeded to London in 1909 to afford information in connection with the Draft South Africa Act to HM's Ministers; Member of the Financial Relations Commission provided for in the South Africa Act, 1911; Member of the Board of Railways and Harbours of the Union of South Africa from 1914. *Address:* Commercial Road, Maritzburg, Natal. *Clubs:* Victoria, Maritzburg; Pretoria, Pretoria.

Died Dec. 1919.

I

IBAÑEZ, Vicente Blasco; Spanish novelist; Commandeur de la Legion d'Honneur; *b* 1867; *m* 1st (wife *d* 1925); 2nd, 1925, Dona Elena Ortuzar Bulnes. *Publications:* The Shadow of the Cathedral; The Four Horsemen of the Apocalypse; Sonnica; The Dead Command; Blood and Sand; The Fruit of the Vine; Mare Nostrum; Woman Triumphant; Enemies of Woman; The Mayflower; The Torrent; The Temptress; In the Land of Art; La Bodega; Alfonso XIII Unmasked, 1925; Queen Calafia; The Old Woman of the Movies; The Mad Virgins; A Novelist's Tour of the World, 1927; The Pope of the Sea; The Mob. *Address:* Villa Fontana Rosa, Menton, AM, France. TA: Fonrosa, Menton.   *Died 28 Jan. 1928.*

IDDESLEIGH, 2nd Earl of (UK), *cr* 1885; **Walter Stafford Northcote;** Bt 1641; Viscount St Cyres, 1885; *b* 7 Aug. 1845; *e s* of 1st Earl and Cecilia, *d* of Thomas Farrer; *S* father, 1887; *m* 1868, Elizabeth Lucy, *e d* of Sir Harry Stephen Meysey-Thompson, 1st Bt; one *d* (and one *s* two *d* decd). *Educ:* Eton; Balliol College, Oxford. Private secretary to his father, 1867–68 and 1874–77; member of Inland Revenue Board, 1877–92. Owned about 2500 acres in Devonshire. *Publications:* Belinda Fitzwarren, 1901; Luck o' Lassendale, 1902; Charms, 1904; Dowland Castle, 1907; Ione Chaloner. *Heir: nephew* Henry Stafford Northcote [*b* 19 Nov. 1901. *Educ:* Rugby; Magdalen College, Oxford]. *Address:* Pynes, near Exeter.   *Died 26 May 1927.*

IDINGTON, Hon. John; Judge, Supreme Court, Canada, 1905, retired 1927; *b* 14 Oct. 1840; *m* Maggie, *d* of George Colcleugh; four *s* four *d*. *Educ:* Galt Grammar School; Toronto Univ., LLB; gold medallist, 1864. Barrister, 1864; QC 1876; Judge, High Court of Justice, Ontario, 1904. *Address:* 325 Stewart Street, Ottawa. *Club:* Rideau, Ottawa.   *Died 7 Feb. 1928.*

IDRIS, Thomas Howell Williams, JP Merioneth and London; High Sheriff for Merioneth, 1912–13; MP (L) Flint Boroughs, 1906–10; chemist and mineral water manufacturer; *b* Pembrokeshire, 5 Aug. 1842; 2nd *s* of Benjamin Williams; assumed additional surname of Idris by deed poll, 1893; *m* 1873, Emeline, *d* of John Trevena, Pembroke Dock; five *s* one *d*. *Educ:* National School; privately. Member of London County Council from formation to 1906; Mayor of St Pancras Borough, 1903–4; Director First Garden City, Ltd; President Pharmaceutical Conference, 1903 and 1904; President of Public Pharmacists Association; Fellow of Chemical Society; Member of Society of Chemical Industry; Freeman of City of London. *Publications:* Notes on Essential Oils (1st and 2nd editions); various papers on chemical subjects. *Recreations:* gardening, forestry. *Address:* 120 Pratt Street, Camden Town, NW. *T:* North 521 and 522; Dolycae, Cader Idris, Corris RSO, Merionethshire. *TA:* Idris, London. *M:* XN 853. *Club:* National Liberal.

Died 10 Feb. 1925.

ILBERT, Sir Courtenay Peregrine, GCB 1911 (KCB 1908); KCSI 1895 (CSI 1885); CIE 1882; Clerk of the House of Commons, 1902–21; *b* 12 June 1841; *m* 1874, Jessie, *d* of Rev. C. Bradley and *niece* of Dean Bradley; five *d*. *Educ:* Marlborough College; Balliol College, Oxford (Scholar, Fellow, Bursar); Hertford, Ireland, Craven, Eldon Scholar. Barrister, Lincoln's Inn, 1869; Legal Member of Council of Governor-General of India, 1882–86; President of Governor-General's Council, 1886; Vice-Chancellor of Calcutta Univ. 1885–86; Assistant Parliamentary Counsel to the Treasury, 1886–99; Parliamentary Counsel to the Treasury, 1899–1901; Chairman of Statute Law Committee; Member of Council of Marlborough College; of Board of Governors of London School of Economics; Vice-Pres. of London Library. JP Bucks. *Publications:* The Government of India, 1898; Legislative Methods and Forms, 1901; Parliament, 1911; The Mechanics of Law-making, 1914. *Address:* 24 Pelham Crescent, South Kensington, SW7; Troutwells, Penn, Bucks. *T:* Kensington 2751. *Club:* Athenæum.

Died 14 May 1924.

ILIFFE, Frederick, MA, MusD (Oxon); *b* 1847; *e s* of John Iliffe; *m* Katherine (*d* 1915), *d* of Frederich Willson Marvel, Kibworth. *Educ:* Kibworth Grammar School; privately. Organist of St Barnabas' Church, Oxford, 1879–83; St John's College, 1883; Organist to the University of Oxford, 1900–25; conductor of Queen's College Musical Society, 1883–1904, a number of male-voice cantatas being composed by eminent musicians expressly for its concerts; Examiner for Musical Degrees University of Oxford, 1908. *Publications:* Oratorio—Visions of St John the Divine; eight-part Motet—Sweet Echo (Milton), composed for the Cheltenham Festival Society, 1893; cantatas—Morning, 1896; Evening, 1899; Power of Song, 1901; Via Crucis (a Lenten Cantata), 1905; various anthems, services, and part songs; Analysis of J. S. Bach's Das Wohltemperierte Clavier (forty-eight preludes and fugues). *Recreations:* canoeing, fishing, gardening. *Address:* 13 Warnborough Road, Oxford.

Died 2 Feb. 1928.

ILSLEY, Most Rev. Edward, DD; *b* Stafford, 11 May 1838. *Educ:* Sedgley Park; Oscott College. Ordained, 1861; for 12 years Assistant Priest, Longton; Rector of Olton Seminary, 1873–83; Canon of Birmingham RC Cathedral, 1876; Bishop of Fesse, 1879–88; Bishop of Birmingham, 1888–1911; Archbishop of Birmingham, 1911–21; retired, 1921. Governor of Birmingham University; Pres. of Birmingham Catholic Diocesan Schools Association; retired from all duty. *Address:* Oscott College, Birmingham. *T:* 890 East.

Died 1 Dec. 1926.

INAYAT-KHAN, Pir-o-Murshid; poet, musician and philosopher; Representative General of the Sufi Movement; *b* Baroda, 1882; *g s* of Moula Bux, the founder of Indian Music Notation; *m* 1913, Ameena Begum; two *s* two *d*. *Educ:* Gayan Shala (Academy of Music at Baroda). Began public career as musician at the age of 18 and received Gold Medals from the citizens of Madras, Bangalore, Mysore, Rangoon, Travancore, Coimbatore, Bombay, and Calcutta; endeavoured to introduce a uniform system of music for all India, and in recognition of his work in this direction the Sangit Samilani of Bengal named him The Morning Star of the Renaissance of Indian Music; received the title of Tansen from Nizam of Hyderabad;

initiated a Sufi, 1906, by Sayed Abu Hashim Madani and thereafter made a pilgrimage to all the holy men of India; began to travel, 1910; lectured in America, Russia, France, Switzerland, Holland, Belgium, Germany, England, Italy, Scandinavia, and made the headquarters of his Movement in Geneva. *Publications:* A Sufi Message of Spiritual Liberty; Diwan of Inayat-Khan; Songs of India; Hindustani Lyrics: In an Eastern Rosegarden; Gayan; The Inner Life; The Way of Illumination; The Mysticism of Sound; The Soul, Whence and Whither; The Unity of Religious Ideals; Sufi Mystic Philosophy; Vadan. *Recreations:* music, travelling. *Address:* 51 Rue de la Tuilerie, Suresnes, Seine, France.								*Died 5 Feb. 1927.*

INCHES, Sir Robert Kirk, Kt 1915; Lord Provost of the City of Edinburgh; *b* 16 Feb. 1840; *s* of Robert Inches and Sarah Johns; *m* 1868; two *s* two *d. Educ:* Royal High School, Edinburgh. King's Clockmaker for Scotland; Senior Partner of Hamilton & Inches, Goldsmiths, Edinburgh; Lord Provost, Past Bailie and Judge of Police; Treasurer Edinburgh Merchant Company; Chairman Royal Tradesmen; Member of the Court of the Clockmakers' Co., London; DL County of City of Edinburgh; Extraordinary Director of the National Bank, and Scottish Widows' Fund; Senior Elder of St Giles' Cathedral, Edinburgh. *Address:* Srathearn House, Edinburgh. *Clubs:* Junior Constitutional; Scottish Conservative, Edinburgh.
Died 19 July 1918.

INFIELD, Henry John, JP; newspaper proprietor. Has for more than 30 years taken an active interest in newspapers and other publications, and been closely associated with many and varied commercial undertakings. Started the first halfpenny Morning Daily Newspaper in the United Kingdom at Brighton, 1868; converted the halfpenny daily into an enlarged penny paper, the Sussex Daily News, in 1873, at the same time issuing an evening edition at a halfpenny; established the Southern Weekly News, 1876; published the Evening Argus, a halfpenny paper, 1880; and the Morning Argus, a halfpenny morning paper, in 1896; converted his business into the Southern Publishing Co. Ltd, of which he was chairman and permanent director; Chairman of Ingram and Royle, Ltd, London, importers and exporters of natural mineral waters; of Brighton Theatre Royal, Ltd; and of The Brighton Grand Hotel Co. Ltd; Director, Brighton West Pier Co.; Brighton, Hove, and Preston United Omnibus Co. Ltd; Hanningtons, Ltd, Brighton; and a member of the Southern Counties Board of the Liverpool and London and Globe Insurance Company, Ltd. *Recreation:* motoring. *Address:* 130 North Street, Brighton. *Clubs:* Reform, Royal Automobile; New, Brighton.								*Died 24 July 1921.*

INGHAM, Rt. Rev. Ernest Graham, MA, DD; Vicar of St Jude's, Southsea, since 1912; *b* 1851; *s* of late Hon. S. S. Ingham, Speaker of House of Assembly, Bermuda. *Educ:* Bishop's College School, Lennoxville, Canada; St Mary Hall (later Oriel College), Oxford. Organizing Secretary CMS for West Yorks, 1878–80; Vicar of St Matthew's, Leeds, 1880–83; Bishop of Sierra Leone, 1883–97; Rector of Stoke-next-Guildford, 1897–1904; Rural Dean, 1904; Home Secretary Church Missionary Society, 1904–12; Proctor in Convocation for Diocese of Winchester. *Publications:* Sierra Leone after a Hundred Years, 1894; From Japan to Jerusalem, 1911; Sketches in Western Canada, 1913. *Address:* St Jude's Vicarage, Southsea.
Died 9 April 1926.

INGHAM, Robert Wood; His Honour Judge Ingham, DL, JP; Judge of County Court, Circuit 22, since 1892; *b* 1846; 2nd *s* of Sir James Taylor Ingham; *m* 1876, Mary, *d* of Rev. J. D. Penrose; four *s* one *d.* Barrister, Inner Temple, 1873. *Address:* Sugwas Court, Hereford.								*Died 10 Jan. 1928.*

INGILBY, Sir William, 3rd Bt, *cr* 1866; of Ripley Castle, Yorkshire, and Harrington Hall, Spilsby, Lincoln; *b* 13 Dec. 1829; *y s* of Rev. Sir Henry John Ingilby, 1st Bt and Elizabeth, 2nd *d* of Day Hort Macdowall; *S* brother, 1911; *m* 1874, Eleanor Isabella, *d* of late Henry Macdowall of Garthland, Co. Renfrew; two *s* (twins). *Educ:* Addiscombe. Formerly Lieut in Bengal Horse Artillery; JP West Riding, Yorkshire. *Heir:* *s* William Henry Ingilby [Bt Lt-Col Scots Guards, *b* 28 Dec. 1874; *m* 1906, Hon. Alberta Diana, 3rd *d* of 1st Baron Swansea; one *s*]. *Address:* Ripley Castle, Harrogate. *T:* Ripley 3. *Club:* Boodle's.								*Died 17 Dec. 1918.*

INGLEBY, Holcombe, JP; MA; *b* 18 March 1854; 2nd *s* of late Clement Mansfield Ingleby, LLD; *m* 1886, Harriet Jane, *d* of late C. F. Neville-Rolfe; one *s* one *d. Educ:* Corpus Christi College, Oxford. Mayor of King's Lynn, 1909–10 and 1919–22; High Sheriff of Norfolk, 1923; edited the Red Register of Lynn. MP (C) King's Lynn, 1910–18. *Address:* Sedgeford Hall, Norfolk. *T:* Snettisham 3. *TA:* Sedgeford. *Clubs:* Athenæum; Norfolk, Norwich.								*Died 6 Aug. 1926.*

INGLEFIELD, Adm. Sir Frederick Samuel, KCB 1911; DL, JP Derbyshire; FRGS; a Younger Brother of the Trinity House; *b* 1854; *s* of late Col S. H. S. Inglefield, RA; *m* 1903, Cecil, *d* of J. G. Crompton, DL, JP, of Flower Lilies, Derbyshire; two *s.* Entered navy, 1868; Rear-Admiral, 1906; retired voluntarily, June 1916; served Egypt, 1882 (medal, bronze star); Suakim, 1884–85 (clasp); Assistant Director of Naval Intelligence, 1902–4; Naval ADC to King Edward, 1905–6; a Lord of Admiralty, 1904–7; commanded 4th Cruiser Squadron, 1907–9; Admiral commanding Coast Guard and Reserves, 1909–12. Grand Officer of the Crown of Italy, 1910 (Messina, 1908). *Address:* Flower Lilies, Windley, Derbyshire; 15 Beaufort Gardens, SW3. *Clubs:* United Service; Derby County.
Died 8 Aug. 1921.

INGLES, Rev. David, MA; Vicar of Witham, 1886–1915; Hon. Canon of St Albans, 1893; *b* 23 May 1836; *m* Clementina Louisa (*d* 1918); six *d. Educ:* Trinity College, Cambridge. Curate of Chorleywood, 1861–62; Stoke-on-Trent, 1862–64; Cookham Dean, 1864–67; Frogmore End, 1867–70; Vicar of Apsley End, Herts, 1872–74; Halstead, 1874–86. *Recreations:* in Cambridge University Boat, 1860, which won; in First Trinity Boat, Henley, 1860, which won Grand Challenge and Stewards Cups; won University Sculls, 1858, University Pairs, 1859; Captain of the Sheringham Golf Club, 1903–4. *Address:* The Priory, Brentwood, Essex.
Died 14 Jan. 1921.

INGLIS, Captain Arthur McCulloch, DSO 1916; Gloucestershire Regiment (attached Tank Corps, as temp. Major); *b* 14 July 1884. *Educ:* Cheltenham College. Lieut 3rd Batt. Wiltshire Regt, 1901; in St Helena till the end of S African War; joined 2nd Batt. Gloucestershire Regt, 1906; ADC to Sir Henry L. Galway, Governor of Gambia, 1911; joined the Gambia Co. West African Frontier Force, 1913; served on the GOC's Staff (Gen. Dobell) in Cameroons till May 1916; joined the Tank Corps, July 1916, thereafter in France (DSO). *Recreations:* games, shooting. *Address:* Inglisby, Prestbury, Gloucestershire. *Clubs:* Army and Navy, Sports.
Died 12 May 1919.

INGLIS, Col Henry Alves, CMG 1918; retired pay; late RA; *b* 5 Oct. 1859; *s* of Thomas Inglis, MD, HEICS; *m* 1899, Ethel, *d* of George Robinson of Green Lane, Dalston, Cumberland. Entered army, 1879; retired, 1910; served Afghan War 1879–80, including relief of Kandahar (medal and clasp, bronze star); Zhob Valley Expedition, 1884; commanded RA, Weymouth, 1914–18. JP Cumberland. *Address:* Green Lane, Dalston, Cumberland.
Died 17 Feb. 1924.

INGLIS, Lt-Col Sir Robert William; Kt 1910; VD; President of the Stock Exchange Rifle Club; *b* 22 July 1843; 5th *s* of late Rev. Robert Inglis, MA, Edzell, Forfarshire; *m* 1st, 1869, Ellen Rose (*d* 1916); no *c*; 2nd 1919, Rebecca, *y d* of late Frederick William Fairclough, Southwark. *Educ:* Free Church Normal School, Edinburgh. Member of the Stock Exchange, 1872; dinner chairman of Benevolent Fund, 1895; member of the General Purposes Committee, 1895; Chairman, 1907–17; Member of Benevolent Fund Committee, 1896; Chairman since 1907; Queen's Edinburgh Rifle Volunteers, 1859–66; Ensign London Irish Rifles, 1872; promoted to Lieutenant, Captain, and Major, and retired with rank of Lieut-Col and right to wear the uniform, 1891; erected, endowed, and presented the Inglis Memorial Hall, Edzell, with 8500 volume Library and Parish Council Rooms, 1898; built and endowed the Rifle and Revolver Club, Borers' Passage, Devonshire Square, E, for use of the Stock Exchange Rifle Club, and the city banks rifle clubs, insurance offices, etc, 1903–4. *Recreations:* shooting, fishing. *Address:* Craigendowie, Reigate.
Died 10 April 1923.

INGPEN, Arthur Robert, KC; LLB; 4th *s* of Robert Frederick Ingpen; married. *Educ:* London University. Called to Bar, Middle Temple, 1879, and Lincoln's Inn (*ad eundem*); QC 1900; Bencher of Middle Temple, 1907. *Publications:* joint editor with late Lord Justice Vaughan Williams of the 10th edn of Williams on the Law of Executors and Administrators (2 vols); author of A Concise Treatise on the Law relating to Executors and Administrators; joint-author of titles Copyholds and Copyright and Literary Property in The Laws of England, edited by Lord Halsbury; joint-editor of the 7th edn of Seton on Judgments and Orders (3 vols); editor of Master Worsley's Book on the History of the Middle Temple; author of Middle Temple Bench Book, and of An Ancient Family: a Genealogical Study. *Address:* 12 New Square, Lincoln's Inn, WC. *T:* Central 9858. *Club:* Junior Carlton.								*Died 5 Sept. 1917.*

INGRAM, John H., author; *b* London, 16 Nov. 1849. Has travelled over various parts of Europe, and is conversant with the languages and literatures of several countries. *Publications:* Flora Symbolica, 1868; edited Poe's Works with Memoir, 1874; Life of E. A. Poe, 1880; Philosophy of Handwriting, 1879; The Bird of Truth, from Spanish of Fernan Caballero, 1881; Claimants to Royalty, 1882; Eminent Women Series, edited, 1883, etc; Haunted Homes, 1883, 2nd series, 1884; Oliver Madox-Brown, a Biography, 1884; Poe's Tales and Poems, with Biographical Essay, 1884; Poe's Poems and Essays, with new Memoir (Tauchnitz edition), 1884; Poe's Tales (Tauchnitz edition), 1884; The Raven, edited with Commentary, 1885; Poe's complete Poetical Works, annotated, with Memoir, 1888; E. B. Browning's Poetical Works, with Memoir, 1886; Life of E. B. Browning, 1888; annotated edition of Lockhart's Life of Burns, 1890; Darley's May Queen, with Biographical Sketch, 1892; Christopher Marlowe and his Associates, 1904; Poe's Poems, with sketch of the author, 1909 (The Muses Library); Chatterton, a Biography, 1910; Marlow and his Poetry, 1914; Chatterton and his Poetry, 1915; contributor to leading reviews of Europe and America. *Address:* 1 Hollingbury Terrace, Preston, Brighton.
Died Feb. 1916.

INGRAM, Thomas Allan, MA, LLD; Editor, Hazell's Annual, since 1913; *b* Castlederg, 26 July 1870; *e s* of Wm Ingram, Letterkenny, Co. Donegal; *m* Alice E., *y d* of R. J. Martin; one *s* three *d*. *Educ:* Elphin Grammar School; Trinity College, Dublin. Departmental Editor, Law and Economics, Encyclopædia Britannica, 1903–12; formerly in business; Alderman of the Woolwich Borough Council; Governor of the Woolwich Polytechnic; etc. *Publications:* Adam Smith on Free Trade and Protection; Woolwich Records (joint author); many articles in Encyclopædia Britannica, monthlies (Fortnightly, etc.), and daily press. *Recreations:* freemasonry, gardening, photography. *Address:* 17 Warwick Square, EC4; 27 Wrottesley Road, Woolwich.
Died 28 July 1922.

INGRAM, Captain Thomas Lewis, DSO 1916; MC; MA Cantab; MRCS, LRCP; RAMC attached 1st King's Shropshire Light Infantry; *b* Brighton, 1875; *e s* of T. Lewis Ingram, of The Priory, Wimbledon Common, SW; *m* 1909, Lilian, *e d* of late Lt-Col Donnithorne, Scots Greys; one *s* one *d*. *Educ:* Monkton Combe, Bath; Trinity College, Cambridge; London Hospital. Served S African War as trooper in 34th Co. Imperial Yeomanry (Middlesex) (Queen's medal with three clasps). MRCS, LRCP 1903; House Surgeon at Poplar Hospital, 1903–4; Senior House Surgeon Westminster Hospital, 1905; Medical Practice at Welford, near Rugby, 1906–14; Commission RAMC Sept. 1914; served European War, 1914–16 (wounded, despatches, Military Cross, DSO). *Recreations:* hunting, fishing, shooting. *Address:* Welford, near Rugby. *TA:* Welford. *T:* Welford 4. *M:* LC 7260.
Died Sept. 1916.

INGRAM, Sir William James, 1st Bt, *cr* 1893; late Managing Director, Illustrated London News and Sketch Ltd; *b* 27 Oct. 1847; *s* of late Herbert Ingram, MP Boston, originator of Illustrated London News, and Anne (who *m* 2nd, Sir Edward Watkin, 1st Bt), *d* of William Little, Eye; *m* 1874, Mary, *d* of Hon. Edward Stirling, Adelaide; three *s*. *Educ:* Winchester; Trinity Coll., Camb. Barrister, Inner Temple, 1872. MP (L) Boston, 1874–80, 1885–86, and 1892–95. *Heir: s* Herbert Ingram [*b* 26 Sept. 1875; *m* 1908, Hilda Vivian, *d* of late Col Carson Lake, New York; one *s* one *d*. *Address:* Tayside, Westgate-on-Sea. *Clubs:* Devonshire, Bath]. *Address:* The Bungalow, Westgate-on-Sea; 65 Cromwell Road, SW; 198 Strand, WC. *Club:* New University.
Died 18 Dec. 1924.

INMAN, Arthur Conyers, MA, MB, BCh (Oxon); Superintendent of the Laboratories of the Brompton Hospital for Diseases of the Chest, London, since 1907; *b* 1879; *e s* of Rev. H. T. Inman, MA (Cantab), 69 Warwick Road, Kensington, SW; *m* 1st, 1909, Dorothy Marguerite (*d* 1917), *o c* of F. J. Wethered, MD; 2nd, 1919, Colette, *y d* of M. Frey, Paris. *Educ:* Haileybury; St Edward's School, Oxford; Wadham College, Oxford; St Thomas' Hospital, London; Marburg; Dresden; Paris. BA (Oxon), Honour Schools of Nat. Science, 1900; MA, MB, BCh (Oxon), 1904. Held resident appointments at St Thomas' Hospital and Brompton Hospital; Hilfärztlicher Externat, Pathological Dept Dresden; worked at the Pasteur Institute, Paris, in the laboratories of late Prof. Metchnikoff; went on special duty to Nepal in 1909 and 1920. Hon. Capt. RAMC, Specialist Bacteriologist in BEF during European War. *Publications:* numerous contributions on scientific subjects in English, American, German, and French scientific journals. *Recreations:* travelling, golf. *Address:* 27 Cornwall Gardens, SW1. *T:* Western 2023; Kensington 2075. *Clubs:* Oxford and Cambridge, MCC.
Died 9 June 1926.

INMAN, Rev. Canon Edward, MA; Canon and Prebendary of Salisbury Cathedral; *s* of T. Gibson Inman, Barrister, JP; *m* 1867, Eleanora M., *d* of Rev. S. Slade-Gully, Rector of Berrynarbor, Devon, MA, JP of Trevennen House, Cornwall; two *s* two *d*. *Educ:* Oriel College, Oxford. Rector of W Knoyle, Wilts, 1872–82; Vicar of Gillingham, Dorset, with Motcombe, Enmore Green, E Stour, W Stour, and Milton, 1882–91; Vicar of Potterne, Wilts, and Rural Dean of Potterne, 1891–1900. *Address:* Sandecotes Lodge, Parkstone, Dorset. *TA:* Parkstone.
Died 14 May 1924.

INNES, Sir James, 13th Bt, *cr* 1628; *b* 20 Jan. 1846; *s* of Sir James Milne Innes, 11th Bt and Elizabeth, *d* of Alexander Thurburn of Keith; *S* brother, 1912. *Heir: n* James Bourchier Innes, *b* 27 Oct. 1883. *Address:* Edengight House, Keith, Banffs. *Club:* Junior Constitutional.
Died 7 Jan. 1919.

INNESS, George; painter; *b* Paris, France, 5 Jan. 1854; *s* of George Inness; *m* Julia G. Roswell-Smith. *Educ:* under his father in Rome; Paris. Exhibited annually at Paris Salon; hon. mention, Paris Salon, 1896, and gold medal, 1900; Officier Academie des Beaux Arts, Paris, 1902; ANA 1895; NA 1899. *Publication:* Art, Life, and Letters of George Inness, 1917. *Address:* Tarpon Springs, Florida; Cragsmoor, Ulster Co., NY, USA.
Died 27 July 1926.

INVERCLYDE, 3rd Baron, *cr* 1897; **James Cleland Burns**, Bt 1889; JP Lanarkshire, Renfrewshire, and County of City of Glasgow; DL Renfrewshire; Lord-Lieutenant Dunbartonshire; *b* 14 Feb. 1864; 2nd *s* of 1st Baron and Emily, *d* of G. C. Arbuthnot of Mavisbank; *S* brother, 1905; *m* 1891, Charlotte Mary Emily, *y d* of late Robert Nugent-Dunbar of Machermore Castle, Co. Kirkcudbright; one *s* two *d*. *Educ:* Repton. Hon. Colonel Clyde Royal Garrison Artillery; Hon. Colonel, 1st Cadet (Dumbartonshire) Battalion, Argyll and Sutherland Highlanders; Commander, RNVR; Principal Director Shipping Firm of G. & J. Burns, Ltd; Chairman Burns SS Company, Limited; a Director Cunard Steamship Company, Ltd; Deputy-Chairman, The Clydesdale Bank, Limited; and Director of Clyde Steamship Owners' Association; President Chamber of Shipping of United Kingdom, 1899; Chairman of Glasgow Shipowners' Association since 1900; Hon. Member Advisory Committee on New Lighthouse Works, etc; Member of Lloyd's Register General Committee, London, and Local Committee, Glasgow; Associate Member of Council, Institution of Naval Architects; Associate Member Institution of Engineers and Shipbuilders in Scotland; Warden of the Worshipful Company of Shipwrights; Chairman Glasgow City Mission; Commodore Royal Clyde Yacht and Royal Largs Yacht Clubs; Vice-Commodore Royal Northern Yacht Club; President Dumbartonshire Volunteer Force. *Heir: s* Hon. John Alan Burns, *b* 12 Dec. 1897. *Recreations:* shooting, yachting, curling, lawn-tennis, President Scottish Hockey Association. *Address:* Castle Wemyss, Wemyss Bay, Renfrewshire. *T:* Wemyss Bay 4; Hartfield, Cove, Dunbartonshire. *T:* Kilcreggan 7; 10 Berkeley Square, W1. *T:* Mayfair 3048. *TA:* Inverclyde, c/o Burns, Glasgow. *Clubs:* Travellers', Carlton, Royal Thames Yacht; Royal Yacht Squadron, Cowes; Ulster, Belfast; Western, Glasgow; New, Edinburgh.
Died 16 Aug. 1919.

IPSWICH, Viscount; **William Henry Alfred Fitzroy**; Lieutenant 5th (Reserve) Battalion Coldstream Guards; *b* 24 July 1884; *e s* of Earl of Euston and *g s* of 7th Duke of Grafton; *m* 1913, Auriol, *o c* of Major James Brougham, Potters Pury House, Northants; one *s* one *d* (and one *d* born posthumously). *Educ:* Harrow; Trinity College, Cambridge. *Heir: s* John Charles William Fitzroy, *b* 1 Aug. 1914. *Address:* Whittlebury, Towcester; 11 Alfred Place West, SW. *Club:* Guards.
Died 23 April 1918.

IREDELL, Lt-Gen. Francis Shrubb; *b* 1837; *s* of late Lt-Col F. M. Iredell; *m* 1867, Katharine Helen, *d* of John Green, Dublin, and *g d* of Hon. Edward Massy of Chester, and of Ballynort, Co. Limerick; one *s* two *d*. *Educ:* Cheltenham College. Served Indian Mutiny, 1857–58; Kathiawar, 1860–61; Afghan War, 1880–81; Lt-Gen. Indian Army, US List, 1893; Colonel, 114th Mahrattas, 1903. *Address:* Vernon Lodge, Preston Park, Brighton. *Club:* Junior Conservative.
Died 10 Nov. 1924.

IRELAND, Most Rev. John; RC Archbishop of St Paul since 1888; *b* Ireland, 11 Sept. 1838. *Educ:* Cathedral School, St Paul; Petit Séminaire, Meximeux; Grand Séminaire, Hyères, France. Ordained Priest, 1861; co-adjutor Bishop, St Paul, 1875. *Publication:* The Church and Modern Society, 1896. *Address:* 977 Portland Avenue, St Paul, Minn, USA.
Died 25 Sept. 1918.

IRELAND, Col Sir Robert Megaw, KBE 1919; CB 1911; CMG 1900; Army Pay Department; retired, 1911; *b* 5 June 1849; *s* of R. S. Ireland, MD; *m* 1872, Evaline Alice, *d* of Col Eardley Howard, BSC; two *s* four *d*. Served South Africa, 1899–1902 (despatches, Queen's medal, 6 clasps, King's medal, 2 clasps, CMG). *Address:* Montrose, Yarborough Road, Southsea.

Died 3 Sept. 1919.

IRVINE, Lt-Col Acheson Gosford, ISO 1903; *b* 1837; *y s* of late Lt-Col J. G. Irvine, many years Principal ADC to Governors-General of Canada. *Educ:* Quebec. Lt-Col (retired) Canadian Militia; served Fenian Raids, Canada, 1866 and 1870; with Red River Expedition, 1870, as Major 2nd Battalion or Quebec Rifles (medal with three clasps); North-West Rebellion, 1885 (medal); commanded Dominion Troops in Manitoba, 1871–74; was a member of Lt-Governor's Administrative Council of NW Territories of Canada, 1882–87; a Vice-President of the American Prison Association; Assistant Commissioner North-West Mounted Police, Canada, 1875; Commissioner, 1880, and Warden of Manitoba Penitentiary, 1892; first President Manitoba Rifle Association (which he organised), 1871; President of Red River Expedition Association, 1895; Warder, Kingston Penitentiary, 1913. *Club:* Frontenac, Kingston, Canada.

IRVINE, Alexander Forbes, DL, JP; *b* 17 Aug. 1881; *e s* of late Francis Hugh Forbes Irvine and Mary Agnes, *o d* of John Ramsay of Barra, NB; *m* 1905, Dorothy Isabel, 2nd *d* of late Col Henry Crawford of Rothie Norman, Aberdeenshire; five *s*. *Educ:* Winchester; New College, Oxford (Hons Modern History). *Address:* Drum Castle, Drumoak SO, Aberdeenshire.

Died 29 April 1922.

IRVINE, Adm. Sir St George Caufield D'Arcy-, KCB 1902 (CB 1882); *b* 23 May 1833; *m* 1868, Katherine, *o d* of late Vice-Adm. Sir Horatio Austin. Entered RN 1845; Admiral, 1897; served Nicaragua; China; Crimea, 1854–55 (Crimean and Turkish medals, Sebastopol clasp, Baltic medal); Turco-Russian War, 1878; bombardment Alexandria, 1882 (CB, Egyptian medal, Khedive's bronze star). *Address:* 2 Hans Crescent Mansions, SW. *Club:* United Service.

Died 2 July 1916.

IRVING, Charles John, CMG 1881; retired Government officer; *b* 7 Feb. 1831; *m* 1866, Mary Jane, *d* of Charles Tompkins; three *s* one *d*. Colonial Land and Emigration Office, 1852–53; clerk, Audit Office, 1853–64; special clerk, Audit Office, Mauritius, 1864–67; auditor-general, Straits Settlements, 1867–79; resident councillor, Malacca, 1879–82; Penang, 1882–87. *Address:* Sarlsdown, Exmouth.

Died 23 Feb. 1917.

IRVING, David Daniel; MP (Lab) Burnley since Dec. 1918; *b* 1854; *m* 1882, *d* of Henry Brock, Bristol. Was in Mercantile Marine and a railway servant; Secretary and agent to the Burnley Socialist Party for over twenty years. Contested (Lab) Accrington, 1906, Burnley North-West Manchester, 1908, Rochdale Jan. and Dec. 1910. *Address:* 80 Glen View Road, Burnley, Lancs.

Died 25 Jan. 1924.

IRVING, Henry Brodribb; actor-manager; *b* London, 5 Aug. 1870; *e s* of late Sir Henry Irving and Florence, *d* of Surg.-Gen. O'Callaghan; *m* 1896, Dorothea, *d* of John Forster Baird, barrister-at-law (Miss Baird appeared as Trilby at the Haymarket Theatre, 1895, and left the stage in 1912); one *s* one *d*. *Educ:* Marlborough College; New College, Oxford; MA. Appeared first on stage at Garrick Theatre in School, 1891; called to Bar, Inner Temple, 1894; lessee Shaftesbury Theatre, 1908; Queen's Theatre, 1909–11; Australian tour, 1911–12; South African tour, 1912–13; lessee of Savoy Theatre since 1913. *Publications:* The Life of Judge Jeffreys, 1898; French Criminals of the 19th Century, 1901; Occasional Papers, 1906; The Trial of Franz Müller, 1911; Trial of Mrs Maybrick, 1913; A Book of Remarkable Criminals, 1918. *Address:* 10 Sudbury Hill, Harrow. *T:* Harrow 164; The Mill, Whitstable. *Clubs:* Athenæum, Garrick, Beefsteak.

Died 17 Oct. 1919.

IRVING, Sir Henry Turner, GCMG 1888 (KCMG 1878; CMG 1874); *b* 1833; *m* 1884, Emma Patty (*d* 1903), *d* of Sir David Barclay, 10th Bt, and *widow* of Sir Henry Franks Frederic Johnson, 3rd Bt. Entered Colonial Office, 1854; Colonial Secretary of Jamaica, 1866–69; of Ceylon, 1869; Governor of Leeward Islands, 1873–74; of Trinidad, 1874–80; of British Guiana, 1882–88. *Address:* The Gap, Westhill, Ottery St Mary, Devon. *Died 22 Nov. 1923.*

IRVING, Hon. Paulus Æmilius, DCL; Puisne Judge, Victoria, British Columbia; *b* 3 April 1857; 3rd *s* of Sir Æmilius Irving, Toronto; *m* 1883, Diana, *d* of Hon. W. Hamley; two *s* two *d*. *Educ:* Trinity College School, Port Hope; Trinity College, Toronto. BA, 1877; MA, BCL, 1880. Called to Bar of Ontario, 1880; British Columbia 1882; Deputy Attorney-General, BC, 1883–90; Puisne Judge of Supreme Court of British Columbia, 1897; as special commissioner he settled mining disputes in Atlin, BC, 1899; his services on that occasion were acknowledged in the speech from the throne (vide BC Sessional papers, 1890); promoted to Court of Appeal, 1909. *Address:* Halwyn, 29 Richardson Street, Victoria, BC. *Clubs:* Union, Victoria, BC; Vancouver, Vancouver, BC.

Died 4 Feb. 1916.

IRVING, Rev. Robert, MA; Vicar of Christ Church, Sefton Park, Liverpool, since 1877; Hon. Canon of Liverpool since 1896; Bracken Hill, near Longtown, 1840; *y s* of Wm Irving; *m* 1872, Anne Maria, *d* of Peter Tasker, merchant, Liverpool; two *s* one *d*. *Educ:* Sedbergh; Christ's Coll. Camb. Graduated, 1863; first class ordinary BA. Deacon, 1864; Priest, 1866; Curate of St Matthias, Salford 1864–66; St Saviour, Liverpool, 1866–71; Curate and Ev. Lect Walton-on-the-Hill, 1871–73; in charge of St Mary, Wavertree Liverpool, 1873–77; Hon. Sec. Local Charities since 1878; Member of Toxteth School Board before its dissolution; Examiner for Liverpool School Board, 1876 and 1877; Rural Dean, Toxteth, 1908 President Liverpool Clerical Society. *Publications:* sermons on Future Punishment, Working Men's Clubs, sundry papers. *Recreations:* cricket, boating, football, cycling. *Address:* 25 Ivanhoe Road, Sefton Park, Liverpool. *Died 22 Oct. 1922.*

IRVING, Rev. Thomas Henry; Vicar of Hawkshead and Rural Dean of Ambleside since 1909; Hon. Canon of Carlisle, 1913; *b* 21 Dec. 1856; *s* of Rev. James Irving and Isabella Lawson; *m* Margaret Anne, 2nd *d* of late James Varley, The Croft, St Helens; two *s* one *d*. *Educ:* St Bees; St John's College, Cambridge. Curate of Farlam, 1879 Kendal, 1885; Vicar of Lindale in Cartmel and Rural Dean of Cartmel 1889. *Address:* Hawkshead Vicarage, Ambleside.

Died 11 Nov. 1926.

IRWIN, Sir Alfred (Macdonald Bulteel), Kt 1910; CSI 1904; *b* 20 Dec. 1853; *s* of Ven. Henry Irwin, BD, Archdeacon of Elphin; *m* 1884, Alice Kathleen (*d* 1899), *d* of Christopher French, JP, DL, of Clooniquin, Co. Roscommon; one *s* two *d*. *Educ:* Kingstown School Co. Dublin. Indian Civil Service, Panjab, 1876; Burma, 1877; Deputy Commissioner, 1886; Commissioner, 1898; Acting Judge, Lower Burma Chief Court, 1902; Member of Legislative Council, Burma, 1903; Acting Judicial Commissioner, Upper Burma, 1903; Judge Lower Burma Chief Court, 1905–9; Acting Chief Judge, 1908 retired, 1909. *Publications:* The Burmese Calendar, 1901; The Burmese and Arakanese Calendars, 1909. *Address:* 49 Ailesbury Road, Dublin *T:* Ballsbridge 110. *Club:* University, Dublin.

Died 1 Feb. 1921.

IRWIN, Col De la Cherois Thomas, CMG 1901; Hon. ADC to Earl of Minto and Earl Grey, Governors-General; late Hon. Secretary Canadian Patriotic Fund Association; retired, Royal Canadian Artillery; *b* Armagh, Ireland, 31 March 1843; *m* 1867, Isabella (*d* 1926), *d* of Robert Hamilton of Hamwood, Quebec; three *s* one *d*. *Educ:* privately; Royal Military Academy, Woolwich. Entered Royal Artillery, 1861; retired as Lt-Col 1882; entered Canadian Military Service, 1872; retired, 1909; RM Staff College, 1871–72 commandant Royal School of Artillery, 1873–82; Inspector of Artillery for Dominion of Canada, 1882–98; commanding Royal Canadian Artillery, 1883–97; President Dominion Artillery Association, 1900–1; President St John Ambulance Association 1923–24; Hon. Col Commandant Canadian Artillery, 1925 *Recreations:* Ottawa Golf Club, Rideau Curling Club, Denholm Angling Club. *Address:* 170 Cooper Street, Ottawa; Carnagh, Co Armagh, Ireland. *Club:* Rideau, Ottawa.

Died 19 March 1928.

IRWIN, Henry, CIE 1888; MICE; *b* 1841; *m* 1871, Henrietta Helen *d* of Rev. Robert Irwin. Joined Public Works Department, India 1868; consulting architect to Government, 1889; retired, 1896. *Address:* Loch End, Ootacamund, India.

Died 5 Aug. 1922.

IRWIN, Lt-Gen. John Staples, CB 1906; Mid Ulster Artillery Dungannon; *b* 29 Sept. 1846. *Address:* Dungannon, Co. Tyrone.

Died 4 Oct. 1917.

IRWIN, Thomas Lennox; secretary of Strand and St George's Registration Associations since 1885; member of Grand Council of the Primrose League; chairman of Finance Committee, 1904–5, and of General Purposes Committee, 1915; *b* Brompton, 9 Sept. 1846; *e s* of late Thos Irwin of the Exchequer and Audit Department, and Agnes, *d* of late William Jerdan of the Literary Gazette; *m* 1882, Elizabeth, *d* of late Wm Freeman, Lincoln's Inn. *Educ:* Cholmeley School, Highgate. Barrister, Lincoln's Inn, 1875; Secretary of Westminster Conservative Association, 1874–85. *Publication:* Pocket Guide to the Corrupt Practices Act, 1883. *Recreations:* cricket, football, lawn tennis, golf. *Address:* 6 Longfield Road, Ealing, W; Parliament Mansions, Victoria Street, SW1. *Club:* Junior Carlton.

Died 27 Aug. 1918.

ISAACS, Godfrey Charles; Managing Director Marconi's Wireless Telegraph Co. Ltd; 4th *s* of Joseph M. Isaacs; *m*; two *s*. *Educ:* London; Hanover and Brussels Universities. At an early age entered his father's firm of fruit and ship brokers; this business afforded occasion for considerable travel in almost all European countries, the opportunity of acquiring foreign languages and becoming acquainted with the characteristics of peoples of the Continent; in several years of a busy and active life acquired considerable business and financial experience; upon retiring from his father's firm, he continued to take considerable interest in business at home and abroad, until in 1910, at the invitation of Mr Marconi, consented to take the managing direction of Marconi's Wireless Telegraph Co. Ltd. *Recreation:* golf. *Address:* Lyne Grove, Virginia Water, Surrey. *T:* Chertsey 36. *M:* LC 1174; LE 8474.

Died 17 April 1925.

ISHERWOOD, John Henry Bradshaw-, JP; *b* 27 Aug. 1841; *e s* of late Thos Bradshaw-Isherwood and Mary Ellen, 2nd *d* of Rev. Henry Bellairs; *m* Elizabeth (*d* 1921), *d* of Thomas Luce, Malmesbury; three *s* one *d*. *Educ:* Rugby; Cambridge. Late Lieutenant 84th Regiment. *Address:* Marple Hall, Marple, Cheshire. *TA:* Marple.

Died 9 May 1924.

ISHIBASHI, Kazunori, ROI; RP; Member of the Imperial Art Society of Japan; *b* Matsuye, Japan. *Educ:* Buddhist Temple, Kyoto. Became pupil of the late Taki Katei, Imperial Court Artist, 1892; entered Army School, 1899; went through Boxer Campaign, 1890 (Sun Rising Order, Class 6). Studied Royal Academy School five years; exhibited RA first time, 1908; Paris Salon first time, 1911; Associate Société Nationale des Beaux-Arts, 1922; member Société Nationale des Beaux-Arts, 1923. *Address:* 11 Doria Road, Parson's Green, SW. *Club:* Chelsea Arts.

Died 2 May 1928.

ISMAY, Rev. William, MA; Vicar of Eckington, 1877–1919; Hon. Canon of Worcester since 1913, and Rural Dean of Pershore since 1908; *b* 10 May 1846; *m*; one *s* two *d*. *Educ:* Emmanuel College, Cambridge. Ordained, 1871; Curate of St Stephens, Canonbury, 1871–73; St Marks, Hamilton Terrace, 1873–77. *Address:* St Barnabas, Newland, Malvern.

Died 11 May 1922.

ISRAEL, John William, ISO 1910; Auditor General for the Commonwealth of Australia since 1901; *b* Launceston, Tasmania, 4 July 1850; *s* of John Cashmore Israel and Adelaide Maria Israel; *m* 1883, Jane M'Donald of Ulverstone, Tasmania; one *s*. *Educ:* Abraham Barrett's Academy, and Church of England Grammar School, Launceston. Audit clerk in the office of the Launceston and Western Railway Company, Launceston, 1870; after the Railway was transferred to the Government of Tasmania promoted to the position of Stationmaster, Launceston, and subsequently to office of Accountant of Tasmanian Government Railways; transferred to position of chief clerk of the Government Audit Office, Hobart, Tasmania, 1882; later deputy Auditor; Auditor-General for Tasmania, 1895; was Hon. Treasurer of late Royal Geographical Society of Australia, Victorian Branch; many years President of the Board of Benevolence, Grand Lodge of Freemasons, Tasmania; also was First Principal of Royal Arch Chapter; Past Senior Grand Warden of Grand Lodge of Victoria; first honorary member of the Australasian Corporation of Public Accountants. *Recreations:* gardening, reading. *Address:* Eshcol, Sackville Street, East Kew, Victoria. *TA:* Commonwealth Audit Office. *T:* Central 9978.

Died 30 May 1926.

IVEAGH, 1st Earl of, *cr* 1919; **Edward Cecil Guinness,** KP 1897; GCVO 1910; FRS 1906; LLD; Viscount Elveden 1919; Viscount Iveagh 1905; Baron Iveagh 1891; Bt 1885; *b* 10 Nov. 1847; 3rd *s* of Sir Benjamin Lee Guinness, 1st Bt and Elizabeth, *d* of Edward Guinness; *brother* of 1st Baron Ardilaun; *m* 1873, Adelaide (*d* 1916), *d* of late Richard Samuel Guinness, MP, Deepwell, Co. Dublin; three *s*. *Educ:* Trinity Coll., Dublin (Hon. LLD 1891). Chancellor Dublin University, 1908. *Heir: s* Viscount Elveden, *b* 29 March 1874. *Address:* 5 Grosvenor Place, SW1. *T:* Victoria 4567; Kenwood, Hampstead Lane, NW3. *T:* Mountview 2664; 80 St Stephen's Green, Dublin;

Elveden Hall, Suffolk; Farmleigh, Castleknock, Co. Dublin. *Clubs:* Athenæum, Carlton, Turf; Kildare Street, Dublin.

Died 7 Oct. 1927.

IVERACH, Rev. James, MA, DD; Principal since 1905 and Professor of New Testament Language and Literature, since 1907, United Free Church College, Aberdeen; *b* Caithness, 1839; 3rd *s* of James Iverach, Halkirk, Caithness; *m* Margaret, *d* of Donald Macdonald, Thurso; one *s* four *d*. *Educ:* Univ. and New Coll. Edinburgh. Ordained at West Calder, 1869; translated to Ferryhill, Aberdeen, 1874; Prof. of Apologetics, etc, UF Church College, Aberdeen, 1887–1907; Moderator United Free Church, 1912–13. *Publications:* Life of Moses; Life and Times of St Paul; Is God Knowable?; Evolution and Christianity; The Truth of Christianity; Theism, in the light of present Science and Philosophy; Descartes, Spinoza, and the New Philosophy, etc; was for years a contributor to the Spectator. *Recreation:* golf. *Address:* 12 Ferryhill Place, Aberdeen. *Club:* Scottish Liberal, Edinburgh.

Died 6 Aug. 1922.

IYENGAR, S. Kasturi Ranga, BA, BL; FJI; proprietor and editor, The Hindu, since 1905; *b* 1859; *s* of Sesha Iyengar, Revenue Official, Tanjore Dist; *m* Kanakammal, *d* of Gopala Iyengar, landlord, Tanjore; two *s* two *d*. *Educ:* The Presidency College, Madras. Sub-Registrar; resigned and studied for the Bar under the late Sir V. Bashyam Iyengar; practised at Coimbatore and at Madras, 1885–1905; connected with Indian national political organisations; Member of the All-India Congress Committee and President of the Madras Provincial Congress Committee; a member of the Indian Press Deputation in 1918, and visited the Western Front and Great Britain. *Recreations:* chess, indoor games. *Address:* 100 Mount Road, Madras. *TA:* Hindu, Madras. *T:* 305. *M:* 2650. *Club:* Cosmopolitan, Madras.

Died 12 Dec. 1923.

IZAT, Alexander, CIE 1898; MICE; Director of Bengal and North-Western Railway Company; *b* 1844; *m* 1873, Margaret Dewar, *d* of James Rennie; four *s* two *d*. Entered Indian Public Works Department, 1863, as Assistant-Engineer, Hyderabad; transferred to Railway Branch, 1870, and served in various parts of India, being instrumental in initiating and carrying out many metre-gauge extensions; services lent to Bengal and North-Western Railway as Agent and Chief Engineer, 1883, and continued in that capacity, carrying through many important extensions, until retirement from India, 1904; joined Board of Directors, 1902. *Address:* Balliliesk, Dollar, NB.

Died 2 Jan. 1920.

J

JACK, Alexander G. Mackenzie, CBE 1920; JP; MInstCE; retired; *b* 1851; *s* of Alex. Jack, Avoch, Scotland; *m* Marian, *d* of J. Herdman Bey, Constantinople; one *s* four *d*. *Educ:* Presbyterian Schools, Woolwich. Served apprenticeship in Engineering Dept, Woolwich Arsenal; engineer in US Navy; Supt Imperial Arsenal, Tientsin; General Manager, Managing Director, and Deputy Chairman from 1888 to retirement in 1921, of Hadfields, Ltd, Sheffield. *Recreations:* outdoor exercises, study of the Chinese language, violin. *Address:* Rock Hills, Brincliffe, Sheffield; 51 West Kensington Mansions, W14. *T:* Sheffield 754. *Clubs:* Constitutional; Sheffield, Sheffield.

Died 2 Aug. 1927.

JACK, Robert Logan, LLD; FGS, FRGS, MIMM; consulting geologist and mining engineer; *b* Irvine, Ayrshire, 1845; *s* of Robert Jack; *m* 1877, Janet, *d* of Dr James Simpson, Fintry, Stirlingshire; one *s*. *Educ:* Irvine Academy; Edinburgh University. Assistant Geologist, Geol Survey of Scotland, 1866–77; Govt Geologist of Queensland, 1877–99; Explorations in N Queensland before settlement took place and had some narrow escapes, having been speared by the natives; took prominent part in mining development of Colony and in inception of artesian water supply; President Geological Section Australasian Assoc. for Advancement of Science at first meeting in Sydney; President Royal Society, Queensland, 1896; represented Queensland at Greater Britain Exhibition, London, 1899; resigned 1899 and led an expedition in Korea and China in the interests of an English Company; the Boxer movement led to the withdrawal of the party from China into Burma across the Yangtse, Salwen, Mekong, and Irrawadi and the mountainous regions inhabited by Lolo and Tibetan tribes; Member of Council Geol Soc. London, 1902–3; returned to London, 1901; practised his profession there till 1903, and subsequently in Western Australia and New South Wales; held several Royal Commissions in Western Australia. *Publications:* numerous official publications; Mineral Wealth of Queensland; Explorations in the Cape York Peninsula; Artesian Water in the Western Interior; Handbook of Queensland Geology; (with Robert Etheridge) Geology and Palæontology of Queensland and New Guinea; The Back-Blocks of China, 1904; Report of the Royal Commission on the Collie Coalfield, Western Australia, 1905; Report on the Probability of Obtaining Artesian Water in the Kimberley District, Western Australia, 1906; Report of Royal Commission on Miners' Lung Diseases, Western Australia, 1911; Northmost Australia, 1922. *Address:* Norwich Chambers, Hunter Street, Sydney.

Died Nov. 1921.

JACK, William, MA, LLD, DSc; FRSE; *b* Stewarton, Ayrshire, 29 May 1834; *s* of Robert Jack, Irvine; *m* Agnes Jane Nichol (*d* 1901), *d* of J. P. Nichol, LLD, Professor of Astronomy, University of Glasgow; two *s. Educ:* Glasgow and Cambridge. Formerly Fellow of Peterhouse, Camb.; HM Insp. of Schools in SW district of Scotland, 1860–66; Professor of Natural Philosophy, Owens Coll. Manchester, 1866–70; editor Glasgow Herald, 1870–76; publisher (Macmillan and Co.), 1876–79; Professor of Mathematics, Glasgow University, 1879–1909. Assistant Commissioner Primary Education (Ireland) Commission, 1878; served on Queen's Colleges (Ireland) Commission, 1882. *Address:* 5 St John's Terrace, Hillhead, Glasgow.

Died 20 March 1924.

JACK, William Robert, MD Glasgow, BSc; FRFPSG; Visiting Physician, Glasgow Royal Infirmary; Lecturer in Clinical Medicine, Glasgow University; *b* 1866; *e s* of late Prof. William Jack; *m* 1904, Helen, *d* of Alexander Montgomery, Hamilton. Educ: Fettes College, Edinburgh; Glasgow University; continental medical schools. *Publications:* Wheeler's Handbook of Medicine, 2nd to 7th edns; various contribs to Glasgow Medical Jl. *Address:* 16 Woodside Place, Glasgow. *T:* Charing 1216.   *Died 11 July 1927.*

JACKSON, Benjamin Daydon, PhD; Secretary of the Linnean Society, 1880–1902; General Secretary, 1902–26; Curator of the Linnean Collections since 1926; Secretary to Departmental Committee of HM Treasury on Botanical Work, 1900–1; *b* London, 3 April 1846; *m* 1884, Jane, *y d* of late Charles Hunt, Manchester. *Educ:* private schools. Hon. PhD Upsala; Knight of the Swedish Order of the Polar Star, 1907. *Publications:* Life of John Gerard, 1877; Life of Dr William Turner, 1878; Guide to the Literature of Botany, 1881; Vegetable Technology, 1882; Pryor's Flora of Herts (edited), 1887; Index Kewensis (engaged nearly 14 years on its preparation), 1893–95; Supplement to the same (with Th. Durand) 1901–6; Glossary of Botanic Terms, 1900, 3rd edn 1916; Life of George Bentham (English Men of Science), 1906; New Genera and Species of Cyperaceae, by late C. B. Clarke (edited), 1908; Illustrations of Cyperaceae, by the same (edited), 1909; Darwiniana, 1910; Index to the Linnean Herbarium, 1912; Catalogue of Linnean Specimens of Zoology, 1913; Notes on a Catalogue of the Linnean Herbarium, 1922; Linnæus: the Story of his Life, 1923; many shorter articles, chiefly on botany, botanic history and bibliography. *Recreation:* change of work. *Address:* Burlington House, Piccadilly, W1; 21 Cautley Avenue, Clapham Common, SW4.   *Died 12 Oct. 1927.*

JACKSON, Hon. Cecil Gower, JP; Judge, Native High Court, Natal, since 1910; *b* 1872; *s* of Rev. N. Jackson; *m* 1904, Catherine Annie, *d* of R. Burkitt of Alford, Lincolnshire; no *c. Educ:* privately; silver medal Natal Lit. Ex. 1891. Held first appointment in Natal Civil Service, 1888; clerk of court in various Magisterial Offices and deputy clerk of Peace, and acted frequently as Magistrate 1894–1901; Assistant Magistrate, Ladysmith, Mazinto and Newcastle, 1902–3; Civil Magistrate, Durban, 1904; Magistrate, Weenen, 1905; Magistrate for special purposes, Mahlabatun, 1908 and Nongoma, 1909; Commissioner to revise sentences on native rebels, 1909. Served SA War, 1899–1902, and Native Rebellion, 1906. *Address:* Maritzburg, Natal. *Club:* Victoria, Maritzburg.

Died 15 April 1920.

JACKSON, Sir Charles James, FSA; *b* Monmouth, 24 May 1849; *s* of late James Edwin Jackson of Monmouth. Called to Bar, Middle Temple, 1888. Worked as a member of the Silver Committee of the Red Cross Society during the war. Admitted to the Freedom and Livery of the Worshipful Company of Goldsmiths of London prior to being admitted to the Freedom of the City of London, 1922. JP

Glamorgan. *Publications:* English Goldsmiths and their Marks; Illustrated History of English Plate. *Address:* 6 Ennismore Gardens, SW. *Clubs:* Junior Carlton, Ranelagh.

Died 23 April 1923.

JACKSON, Sir Cyril, KBE 1917; MA; *b* 6 Feb. 1863; *s* of late Laurence M. Jackson of South Park, Bodiam. *Educ:* Charterhouse; New College, Oxford. Barrister, Inner Temple; Toynbee Hall, 1885–95; Central Sec. Children's Country Holidays Fund, 1888–96; Member of London School Board, 1891–96; Inspector-General of Schools, and Permanent Head of Education Department, West Australia, 1896–1903; Chief Inspector, Board of Education, 1903–6; reported to the Manx Government on the Education of the Island, 1906; Expert Investigator on Unemployment in England and Ireland and on Boy Labour to the Royal Commission on the Poor Law, 1906; Acting Agent-General for Western Australia, 1910–11; Member London County Council, Limehouse Division, 1907–13; Chairman Education Committee, 1908–10, and 1922; Chairman LCC Unemployment Committee, 1921–23; Vice-Chairman, LCC, 1911; Alderman, LCC, 1913–16, and 1919; Chairman, LCC, 1915; Member of Senate London University, 1908–21; Governor Imperial College of Science, 1908–16 and since 1919; Member of Special Committee Home Office on Van Boys, 1912; on Distribution of Public Work, 1913; Chairman of London Intelligence Committee on Unemployment and Distress, Local Government Board, 1914; Chairman of Advisory Committee on National Register, 1915; Vice-Chairman War Pensions, etc, Statutory Committee, 1916, 1917; Member of Central Tribunal, 1915–16 and 1917–19; one of the Chairmen of the Committee on Production and Court of Arbitration, 1918–19; Member of Port of London Authority, 1915–16 and 1919; Representative of Board of Education at Conferences in USA (St Louis, 1904, Washington, 1919); Member of Royal Commission on Indian Services, 1923; Chairman, Groceries Trade Board, Labour Ministry, 1924; Member of Admiralty Committee on Officers' Pensions, 1924; Director (West End Board) of the Eagle Star and British Dominions Insurance Company. *Publications:* Unemployment and Trade Unions; Outlines of Education in England; The Religious Question in Public Education (with Michael Sadler and Athelstan Riley); articles in Edinburgh and other reviews. *Address:* Ballards Shaw, Limpsfield; 12 St James's Place, SW1. *T:* Gerrard 4009. *Club:* Savile.

Died 3 Sept. 1924.

JACKSON, Frank Stather; Judge of the Mayor's and City of London Court since 1921; *b* Torquay, Nov. 1853; *s* of J. H. Jackson, Salisbury; *m* Edith, *y d* of late James Easton, 44 Princes Gardens, SW. *Educ:* Sherborne. Admitted Solicitor, 1875; called to Bar, 1884; Registrar of the Mayor's Court, 1890; Assistant Judge of Mayor's Court, 1900. *Publication:* The Mayor's Court Practice (with Lewis Glyn, KC). *Recreation:* golf. *Address:* 18 Brunswick Gardens, W8; Lord Mayor's Court, EC. *Clubs:* St Stephen's, St George's; Richmond Golf.

Died 17 Oct. 1922.

JACKSON, Frederick Hamilton, RBA 1889; *b* 1848; *y s* of N. Jackson, of Hamilton, Adams and Co., wholesale booksellers. *Educ:* private schools. Entered his father's house of business, but gave it up to follow art; student and first-class medallist, Royal Academy Schools; exhibitor RA New Gallery, and other leading Galleries since 1870; Master of Antique School, Slade School, University College, under Sir Edward John Poynter, 1st Bt, PRA and M. A. Legros; founder of the Chiswick School of Art in 1880, in conjunction with E. S. Burchett, Perspective Lectr at the Schools, South Kensington; member of Art Workers' Guild, 1887; Society of Decorative Designers (committee) from its formation; Vice-Pres. 1903; Cantor Lecturer, 1907; late examiner to the Board of Education in principles of design; gave of late years special attention to decoration and design, writing and lecturing also upon technical and archæological subjects; practised, in addition to easel picture-painting, in oil and water colour, ecclesiastical decoration, including mosaic in the east end of St Bartholomew's, Brighton, the apse of St Basil's, Deritend, Birmingham, and design for many purposes. *Publications:* Hand-books for the Designer and Craftsman; Intarsia and Marquetry, and Mural Decoration; True Stories of the Condottieri; A Little Guide to Sicily; The Shores of the Adriatic, the Italian side and the Austrian side; Rambles in the Pyrenees and the adjacent districts. *Recreations:* principally travel, and in turning from one form of art production to another or to literary work, and gardening. *Address:* The Fair Haven, 15 Melrose Road, Southfields, SW.

Died 13 Oct. 1923.

JACKSON, Rt. Hon. Frederick Huth, PC 1911; partner in Frederick Huth and Co.; Director Bank of England; President of the Institute of Bankers, 1909–11; one of HM's Lieutenants for the City of London;

b London, 26 April 1863; *e s* of Thomas Hughes Jackson, The Manor House, Birkenhead; *g s* of late Sir Wm Jackson, 1st Bt; *m* 1895, Clara, *e d* of Rt Hon. Sir Mountstuart E. Grant Duff; one *s. Educ:* Harrow; Balliol Coll., Oxford. BA Oxford 1887 (Honours School History); MA 1890. *Address:* 64 Rutland Gate, SW7. *T:* Western 3191; Possingworth, Cross-in-Hand, Sussex; La Maison du Diable, Aix les Bains, France. *Clubs:* Athenæum, Oxford and Cambridge, Reform, New University.   *Died 3 Dec. 1921.*

JACKSON, Henry, OM 1908; LittD; Hon. LLD St Andrews, Aberdeen, and Glasgow; Hon. DLit Oxford; Hon. LittD Manchester and Sheffield; FBA; Regius Professor of Greek, Cambridge, since 1906; Fellow of Trinity College, Cambridge, since 1864, Vice-Master, 1914–19; Foreign hon. member of American Academy of Arts and Sciences; *b* Sheffield, 12 March 1839; *e s* of late Henry Jackson, surgeon, and late Frances Swettenham; *m* 1875, Margaret Edith, *d* of late Canon F. V. Thornton; two *s* three *d. Educ:* Sheffield Collegiate School; Cheltenham Coll.; Trinity Coll. Camb. BA 1862. Assistant Tutor, 1866; Prælector in Ancient Philosophy, 1875–1906; LittD 1884; Member of the Council of the Senate, 1882–86, 1888–92, 1892–96, 1900–2, 1902–6; Fellow of Winchester College, 1905–17. *Publications:* Translations (with R. C. Jebb and W. E. Currey); 1878; Aristotle's Nicomachean Ethics, Bk v, 1879; On some Passages in the Seventh Book of the Eudemian Ethics, 1900; Texts to illustrate the History of Greek Philosophy from Thales to Aristotle, 1901; Plato's Later Theory of Ideas, in Journal of Philology, Nos 20, 22, 25, 26, 28, 30, 49; articles on Greek Philosophers in Encyclopædia Britannica; papers in the Journal of Philology, and in Transactions and Proceedings of the Cambridge Philological Society, etc; About Edwin Drood, 1911. *Address:* Trinity College, Cambridge; Sunny Hill, St Stephen's Road, Bournemouth. *Club:* Athenæum.
Died 25 Sept. 1921.

JACKSON, Rev. Henry Latimer, DD; Rector of Little Canfield since 1911; *b* 1851; *o s* of late John Henry Jackson of Richmond, Surrey; *m* 1st, Annie (*d* 1906), *d* of late Robert Fell of Corbridge-on-Tyne; two *s* two *d*; 2nd, Caroline Harriot Leili (*d* 1921), *d* of late Walter Watson of Guildford; 3rd, 1923, Eleanor Hyde, 2nd *d* of late Mathias Sidney Smith Dipnall, of Christ's Hospital, and *widow* of W. H. Woodroffe, of British Guiana. *Educ:* Highgate Grammar School; Germany; Christ's College, Cambridge. Ordained to Curacy of St Neots, Hunts; then in charge of Houghton, Hunts; Rector of St James's, Sydney, and Fellow and Lecturer of St Paul's College, University of Sydney, of which MA *ad eund*, 1885; appointed to Crown Living of St Mary's, Huntingdon, 1895; Hulsean Lecturer at Cambridge, 1912; Select Preacher, 1906 and 1920; Lecturer in Modern and Medieval Dutch Literature, 1918; Lady Margaret Preacher, 1919; FRHistS. *Publications:* On the Path of Progress, 1901; Born of the Virgin Mary, 1903; The Fourth Gospel and some recent German Criticism, 1906; The Synoptic Problem (in Cambridge Biblical Essays), 1909; The Eschatology of Jesus, 1913; The Problem of the Fourth Gospel, 1918; Mediævalist and Modernist, 1919; A Manual of the Dutch Language (with B. W. Downs), 1921; articles in Hastings' Dictionary of Christ and the Gospels. *Recreations:* motoring, cycling, foreign travel. *Address:* Little Canfield Rectory, Dunmow, Essex. *T:* Dunmow 49Y1.

Died 21 March 1926.

JACKSON, Captain Henry Mather-; *b* 27 Feb. 1894; *e s* of Sir Henry Mather-Jackson, 3rd Bt; *m* 1920, Florence, *d* of late Granville W. Garth, New York; one *d. Educ:* Eton; RMC. Served European War, 1914–19; Capt. 9th Lancers. *Address:* Hellidon House, Daventry, Northants. *T:* Daventry 18. *Club:* Buck's.

Died 2 April 1928.

JACKSON, Sir John, Kt 1895; CVO 1911; JP; MP (U) for Devonport, 1910–Dec. 1918; LLD; FRSE; one of the largest contractors for Public Works; *b* York, 4 Feb. 1851; *y s* of late Edward Jackson, York; *m* 1876, Ellen Julia, *y d* of late George Myers, London; five *d. Educ:* York; Univ. of Edinburgh. Trained civil engineer; was contractor for last section of Manchester Ship Canal; Foundations Tower Bridge, Dover Harbour, and other works of magnitude; completed the Admiralty Docks at Keyham, Devonport; the Admiralty Harbour, Simon's Bay, South Africa, and Singapore Harbour, the great railway across the Andes from Arica on the Pacific Coast to La Paz, the capital of Bolivia; and the Great Barrage across the Euphrates at Hindia, near Babylon; carried out Mesopotamia Irrigation Works, Harbour Works in Canada and other places, and other large works; was a member of the Royal Commission appointed to enquire into the War in South Africa. Held highest Chilian Order of Merit and Spanish Order Grand Cross of Naval Merit. *Recreations:* yachting, cycling, motoring, Commodore Royal South-Western

Yacht Club. *Address:* 51 Victoria Street, Westminster, SW1; 48 Belgrave Square, SW1. *T:* Victoria 153; Henley Park, Henley-on-Thames. *T:* Henley 48. *Clubs:* Carlton, Junior Carlton, Royal Automobile; United Service, Edinburgh; Royal Yacht Squadron, Cowes; Royal Western Yacht, Plymouth.

Died 14 Dec. 1919.

JACKSON, John Brinckerhoff; *b* Newark, New Jersey, 19 Aug. 1862; *s* of late Frederick Wolcott and Nannie Nye Jackson; *m* 1886, Florence A., *d* of Matthew Baird of Philadelphia, Penn. *Educ:* private schools at Newark; United States Naval Academy, Annapolis, Maryland. Graduated, 1883; served for two years in American European Naval Squadron, principally in the Mediterranean; Ensign, 1885; resigned from Navy, 1886. Studied law, and was admitted to the Bar in New York, 1889; Hon. AM, Princeton University; Second Secretary of Legation, Berlin, 1890; Secretary of Embassy, 1894; served frequently as Chargé d'Affaires; Minister to Greece, Roumania and Servia, Bulgaria and Montenegro, 1902–7; Persia, 1907–9; Cuba, 1909–11; Roumania, Servia and Bulgaria, 1911–13; Volunteer Assistant at the American Embassy in Berlin, 1914, and Special Agent of the Department of State at same, Jan. 1915; visited England in 1915 to inspect places where German prisoners of war were interned, and after return to Germany was engaged in work connected with British prisoners until Feb. 1917; Delegate to the International Maritime Law Conference at Hamburg, 1902; rep. the United States at Coronation of King Peter of Servia, 1904; Delegate to First International Archæological Congress at Athens, 1905; American Representative at Olympic Games at Athens, 1906; Special Ambassador at the coming of age of the Crown Prince of Bulgaria, 1912. Member of NY Bar Association. *Recreations:* golf, swimming. *Address:* US Government Despatch Agency, 53 Victoria Street, Westminster, SW1. *Clubs:* Union League, University, Army and Navy, New York; Rittenhouse, Philadelphia; Metropolitan, Washington; Casino, Berlin; Imperial Yacht, Kiel; Jockey, Bucharest.

Died 20 Dec. 1920.

JACKSON, Sir Keith George, 4th Bt, *cr* 1815; late Lieutenant 83rd Foot; *b* 2 Aug. 1842; *s* of Sir Keith Alexander Jackson, 2nd Bt and Amelia, *d* of George Waddell; *S* brother (who was murdered at Delhi), 1857; *m* 1875, Alice, *d* of late Charles Francis Montrésor, BCS; two *s. Educ:* Ordnance School, Carshalton; Magdalene College, Cambridge. *Heir: s* Robert Montrésor Jackson [*b* 11 March 1876; *m* 1913, Katherine, *y d* of late John Abry of The Glen and Barden Park, Tonbridge; one *s*]. *Address:* La Paz, Entre Rios, Argentine.

Died 3 Sept. 1916.

JACKSON, Maunsell Bowers, KC; barrister; Clerk of the Crown for Ontario since 1864; *b* Co. Wexford, Ireland; *s* of Benjamin Jackson; *m* 1868, Claire Edith Cull; two *s* three *d. Educ:* Toronto Academy. Called to bar, Ontario, 1855. *Address:* Drumsnab, Castle Frank Road, Rosedale, Toronto, Canada. *T:* North 2349.

Died 29 March 1922.

JACKSON, Col Sir Robert Whyte Melville, KCMG 1918 (CMG 1900); KBE 1919; CB 1908; *b* 3 June 1860; *o s* of late Robert Jackson, Registrar-General of Shipping; *m* 1887, Frances, *d* of Capt. Hugh MacTernan, JP, DL, of Heapstown House, Sligo; one *s* two *d. Educ:* Marlborough. Entered 2nd Batt. Royal Inniskilling Fusiliers, 1881; Army Ordnance, 1886; Capt. Royal Inniskilling Fusiliers, 1870; Major, 1897; Lt-Col, 1901; Col, 1907; Brig.-Gen., 1915; served S Africa, 1900–1 (despatches twice, brevet of Col, Queen's medal 3 clasps, King's medal 2 clasps, CMG); Chief Ordnance Officer Cape Colony, 1903–5; Director Royal Army Clothing Factory, Pimlico, 1907–Feb. 1915; was made Director of Ordnance for Mediterranean Exped. Force (despatches thrice, KCMG, KBE). Order of the White Eagle, Serbia, 1916. *Recreations:* yachting, shooting. *Address:* 50 Hurlingham Court, SW6. *T:* Putney 295.

Died 25 Feb. 1928.

JACKSON, Sir Robert William, Kt 1882; CB 1874; Deputy Surgeon-General retired, 1882; *b* 1826; *m* 1st, 1860, Anne (*d* 1888), *d* of John Jones Simpson; 2nd, 1891, Gertrude, *d* of Robert P. Daye; three *s* one *d*. Entered Army Med. Department, 1854; served Crimea, 1854–56; Indian Mutiny, 1857–58; Ashanti War, 1874; Zulu War, 1880; Egyptian Campaign, 1882. *Address:* Eglinton, New Grove Avenue, Sandymount, Dublin.

Died 12 May 1921.

JACKSON, Col Sydney Charles Fishburn, CMG 1919; DSO 1889; *b* Dedham Grove, near Colchester, 21 April 1863; *s* of late Commander W. T. F. Jackson, RN; *m* 1898, Lucy Beatrice, 2nd *d* of late Sir W. H. Drake, KCB; two *s. Educ:* Wellington; Royal Military

College, Sandhurst. Gazetted RI Rifles, Sept. 1882; transferred to Hampshire Regiment, Oct. 1882; Capt. 1890; Major, 1901; Lieut-Col 1904; Brevet Col 1910; Subst. Colonel, Dec. 1914; retired, 1920; served Burma Campaign, 1885–89 (medal with two clasps, despatches twice, DSO); Zhob Valley Expedition, 1890; ADC to GOC Upper Burma Field Force, 1886–89; ADC to GOC Quetta District, 1889–93; ADC to HE the C-in-C in India, 1893–94; Station Staff Officer 1st class, Punjab, April 1897; DAAG Bombay Command Headquarters, 1897–1902; DAA and QMG 6th Division, 1906–10; served with Somaliland Field Force, 1903–4, in command of detachment Hampshire Regt (despatches, medal with 2 clasps, brevet of Lieut-Colonel); AQMG Eastern Command, 1917–18; AA and QMG Gibraltar, 1918–20; European War 1914–18, in command of 1st Hampshire Regt (despatches, severely wounded, 1914 Star, British War Medal, Victory Medal, CMG). *Recreations:* hunting, golf, rowing. *Club:* Army and Navy.   *Died 27 June 1928.*

JACKSON, Sir Thomas Graham, 1st Bt, *cr* 1913; MA; RA 1896 (ARA 1892); architect; *b* Hampstead, 21 Dec. 1835; *s* of Hugh Jackson, solicitor, and Eliza, *d* of Thomas Graham Arnold, MD; *m* 1880, Alice Mary (*d* 1900), *y d* of William Lambarde, JP, DL, of Beechmont, Kent; two *s*. *Educ:* Brighton College; Wadham College, Oxford (Scholar, 1854). Fellow Wadham College, 1864; vacated Fellowship by marriage, 1880; Hon. Fellow, 1882; Hon. DCL Oxford, 1911; Hon. LLD Camb. 1910. Associé de l'Académie Royale de Belgique, 1910. Pupil of Sir George Gilbert Scott, RA, 1858–61. *Works:* at Oxford: new Examination Schools of University; Restoration of Bodleian Library, St Mary's and All Saints Churches; new buildings for Brasenose, Lincoln, Corpus, Trinity, Balliol, and Hertford Colleges, new Radcliffe Library, Electric Laboratory, Somerville Hall, City High School and High School for Girls, etc; new Sedgwick Memorial Museum, Archæological Museum, Physiological and Psychological Laboratories, and new Law Library and Law School at Cambridge; restorations at Eltham Palace, Rushton Hall, Longleat, Great Malvern Priory, Portsmouth Church, Grimsby Church, Bath Abbey, Trinity Church, Coventry, Christchurch Priory, Hospital of St Cross, and Winchester Cathedral; new churches at Annesley, Hornblotton, Wimbledon, Stratton, Aldershot, Northington, Curdridge, and Narberth; new buildings for the following public schools—Eton, Westminster, Rugby, Harrow, Radley, Uppingham, Brighton, Giggleswick, Aldenham, Cranbrook, Sandwich; new buildings for Inner Temple, Drapers' Hall; several private homes. *Publications:* Modern Gothic Architecture, 1873; Dalmatia, the Quarnero, and Istria, 1887; Wadham College, Oxford: its History and Buildings (with illustrations), 1893; The Church of St Mary the Virgin, Oxford: its History and Architecture; Reason in Architecture, 1906; Byzantine and Romanesque Architecture, 1913; Gothic Architecture in France, England, and Italy, 1915; A Holiday in Umbria, 1917; The Renaissance of Roman Architecture, 1921–22; Memories of Travel, 1923. *Heir: s* Hugh Nicholas Jackson, Major RFA, late Lieut. RW Fusiliers; *b* 21 Jan. 1881. *Recreations:* boating, gardening, music, travel. *Address:* 49 Evelyn Gardens, S Kensington, SW. *Clubs:* Athenæum, Royal Societies.
                                                                        Died 7 Nov. 1924.

JACKSON, William Henry, CMG 1914; retired civilian; 3rd *s* of late Lt-Col Thomas Jackson, Harbledown Lodge, Harbledown, Kent; *m*; two *s* five *d*. *Educ:* King's School, Canterbury; RIEC, Coopers Hill. Entered Ceylon Civil Service, 1879; Police Magistrate, Colombo, 1892; Assistant Government Agent, 1895; Chairman of the Colombo Harbour Board, Principal Collector of Customs, and Member Legislative Council, 1901; Controller of Revenue and Member Executive Council, 1911; retired, 1913. *Recreations:* cricket, golf.   *Died 14 Dec. 1920.*

JACOB, Rt. Rev. Edgar, DD Oxon; Hon. DD Durham; Bishop of St Albans, 1903–19; *b* Crawley Rectory, near Winchester, 16 Nov. 1844; *s* of late Ven. Philip Jacob, Archdeacon and Canon of Winchester, and of Anna, *e d* of late Hon. and Rev. Gerard T. Noel, Canon of Winchester. *Educ:* Winchester; New College, Oxford (Scholar). Curate of Taynton, Oxon, 1868; Witney, 1869–71; charge of St James's Bermondsey, 1871–72; domestic chaplain to Bishop (Milman) of Calcutta, 1872–76; charge of Wilberforce Memorial Mission, S London, 1877; Vicar of Portsea, 1878–96; Hon. Canon of Winchester, 1884–96; hon. chaplain to the Queen, 1887–90; chaplain-in-ordinary, 1890–96; examining chaplain to Bishop (Browne) of Winchester, 1876–91; chaplain to Bishop (Thorold) of Winchester, 1891–95; to Bishop (Davidson) of Winchester, 1895–96; Rural Dean of Landport, 1892–96; Proctor in Convocation for Hants and Isle of Wight, 1895–96; Select Preacher, Oxford, 1895–96; Bishop of Newcastle, 1896–1903. *Publication:* The Divine Society (Cambridge

Lectures on Pastoral Theology), 1890. *Address:* Verulam House, St Albans. *Club:* Athenæum.
                                                                        Died 25 March 1920.

JACOB, Sir (Samuel) Swinton, KCIE 1902 (CIE 1890); CVO 1911; AICE, Hon. Assoc. RIBA; IA; late Chief Engineer Jaipur State, Rajputana, India; *b* 14 Jan. 1841; *s* of Col W. Jacob, Bombay Artillery; *m* 1874, Mary, *d* of Robert Brown, Edinburgh. *Educ:* Cheam School; Addiscombe HEIC College. Gained commission in Bombay Artillery. Lieut 1858; joined Indian Staff Corps, 1862; Capt., 1870; Major, 1878; Lt-Col, 1884; Colonel, 1888; served in PWD, 1862–96; 1st grade Exec. 1881; 1st class Supt Engineer, 1893; officiated as Supt Engineer and Secretary to the AGG for Rajputana, and CI on several occasions; services lent by the Govt of India in the Foreign Dept to the Maharajah of Jaipur in Rajputana, 1867; served at Aden, 1861–66 (thanked by Secretary of State); received thanks Govt of India for exertions during famine in Rajputana, 1868–69; commended by Govt of India for services in the PWD of the Jaipur State, 1872; again thanked 1873 and 1890; served as Asst Field Engineer with the Aden Force, 1865–66; blown up in the destruction of an Arab fort, 6 Jan. 1866. Attended coronation of King Edward VII as Political Officer with HH the Maharajah of Jaipur, bringing him and his suite from India and back to Jaipur, 1902; appointed by Govt of India on special duty as Consulting Engineer for Irrigation in Rajputana, 1902–5. In architectural work in India, among other works, designed the following: the Sandeman Memorial Hall at Quetta; Secretariat Offices for the Govt of India at Simla; the Victoria Memorial Hall at Peshawar; the Bank of Madras at Madras; the Albert Hall at Jaipur; the Jubilee Clock Tower at Jacobabad; St Stephen's College at Delhi; the Public Offices at Jodhpur and at Dholpur; the Hospital at Bharatpur; College for the Begum of Bhopal; a Palace for the Maharajah of Kotah; a Palace and other buildings for the Maharajah of Bikaner; the Church at Jaipur; the RC Church at Ajmere; the new Daly College at Isdore and subsidiary buildings; the Marble Canopies over the Statues of the late Queen Victoria at Lahore, Lucknow, and Ajudhya; Drinking Fountains at Calcutta and Bombay; Marble Altars, Fonts, Pulpits, etc, in different parts of India. Decorated for services as Engineer to the Jaipur State; for publication of the Jaipur Portfolios, title conferred by the French Govt Officer de l'Académie des Beaux Arts; Kaiser-i-Hind gold medal; Coronation medals for England and India. *Publications:* Jaipur Portfolios of Architectural Details; a work on Jaipur Enamels, letterpress by Surgeon-Col T. H. Hendley, CIE. *Address:* c/o H. S. King and Co., 9 Pall Mall, SW.
                                                                        Died 4 Nov. 1917.

JACOB, Lt-Colonel Walter Henry Bell, DSO 1919; late Royal Garrison Artillery; *b* 13 June 1871; *s* of Thomas Walter Jacob, Irish, late of War Office, and Louisa, *d* of late William Bell, English; *m* 1st, Mildred Jessie (*d* 1920), 2nd *d* of late Capt. Horatio Paul; 2nd, 1922, Adah Louisa, *d* of late T. Harbridge Jones. *Educ:* St Paul's School; Royal Military Academy, Woolwich. 2nd Lieut Royal Garrison Artillery, 1889; served South African War (Queen's medal and 2 clasps); European War (DSO, Serbian White Eagle with swords 4th class, Italian Croce di Guerra); retired pay, 1921. *Recreations:* polo, boating. *Address:* 20 Dietro La Chiesa, Sliema, Malta.
                                                                        Died 24 March 1925.

JACOB, Maj.-Gen. William; Indian Army; *b* 14 Dec. 1837; 2nd *s* of late Lt-Col W. Jacob, Bombay Artillery; *m* 1861, Eliza, *d* of Rev. G. A. Jacob, Teignmouth; two *s* two *d*. Entered army, 1855; Maj.-Gen. 1894; unemployed list, 1897; served Indian Mutiny, 1858 (medal with clasp); Afghan War, 1880–81 (despatches, medal). *Address:* Brookands, Tavistock, Devon.
                                                                        Died 9 March 1917.

JACOBS, Joseph; author and journalist; *b* Sydney, NSW, 29 Aug. 1854; *m* Georgina, 2nd *d* of late T. Horne; two *s* one *d*. *Educ:* Sydney Grammar School, St John's Coll. Camb. (Senior Moralist, 1876). Visited Spain for historical purposes, 1888; United States on a lecturing tour, 1896; corresponding member of Royal Academy of History, Madrid, and of the Brooklyn Institute; sometime editor of Folk Lore, Literary Year-Book, Jewish Year-Book; late Secretary of the Russo-Jewish Committee; President of the Jewish Historical Society; Literary Editor of the Jewish Encyclopedia; Editor, American Hebrew; Director, Bureau of Jewish Statistics, 1914. *Publications:* English Fairy Tales, 1890; Studies in Jewish Statistics, 1890; Celtic Fairy Tales, 1891; Indian Fairy Tales, 1892; Tennyson and In Memoriam, 1892; Jews of Angevin England, 1893; More English Fairy Tales, 1893; More Celtic Fairy Tales, 1894; Studies in Biblical Archæology, 1894; Æsop's Fables, 1894; Literary Studies, 1895; Reynard the Fox, 1895; As Others Saw Him (a Jewish Life of Christ), 1895; Sources of the History of the Jews in Spain, 1895; Jewish Ideals, 1896; Wonder Voyages, 1896;

Story of Geographical Discovery, 1898; Europa's Fairy Book, 1915; also translated Balthasar Gracian's Art of Worldly Wisdom from the Spanish, 1892, and Tales from Boccaccio, 1899; likewise published editions of North's Fables of Bidpai, 1887; Caxton's Æsop, 1889; Painter's Palace of Pleasure, 1891; Howell's Familiar Letters, 1892; Day's Daphnis and Chloe, 1890; Introduction to Job, the Arabian Nights, Morris's Old French Romances, Goldsmith's Comedies, and Thackeray's Esmond, all in 1896; Austen's Emma and Chamisso's Peter Schlemihl, 1898. *Recreations:* chess, novels, cycling, book collecting (8000 vols). *Address:* 11 Greystone Terrace, Yonkers, NY. *Clubs:* Maccabeans, New Vagabonds'; Authors', New York.

Died 3 Feb. 1916.

JAFAR, Raja Sir Saiyid Abu, KCIE 1922 (CIE 1918). *Address:* Pirpur, Fyzabad District, UP, India. *Died 14 Feb. 1927.*

JAFFRAY, Sir John Henry, 3rd Bt, *cr* 1892; *b* 9 Dec. 1893; *s* of Sir William Jaffray, 2nd Bt and Alice Mary, *d* of Francis Galloway; *S* father, 1914. *Educ:* Eton; Trinity Hall, Cambridge. 2nd Lieut Worcestershire Yeomanry, since 1914. *Heir:* *b* William Edmund Jaffray, 2nd Lieut King's Dragoon Guards, *b* 29 July 1895. *Address:* Skilta, Studley, Warwickshire.

Died 23 April 1916.

JAFFREY, Francis, FRCS; LRCP Lond; Consulting Surgeon to St George's Hospital; Consulting Surgeon to the Belgrave Hospital for Children; Hon. Secretary Fowey Cottage Hospital; *b* Adelaide, South Australia, 1861. *Educ:* privately; St George's Hospital. Formerly Demonstrator and Lecturer on Anatomy and Surgery in St George's Hospital Medical School; and visiting Surgeon to the Atkinson Morley Convalescent Hospital, Wimbledon. *Publications:* articles in medical papers, and an article on the general treatment of Dislocations in the System of Treatment edited by Latham and English. *Recreations:* sea-fishing, yachting, shooting. *Address:* Cliff Lawn, Fowey. *Club:* Royal Fowey Yacht. *Died 20 May 1919.*

JAIPUR, Maharaja of; Lt-Gen. HH Saramad-i-Rajhai-Hindustan Raj Rajendra Shree Maharajadhiraj; Sir Sawai Madho Singh Bahadur, GCSI 1888; GCIE 1901; GCVO 1903; GBE 1918; Donat of the Order of the Hospital of St John of Jerusalem, 1912; LLD Edin. 1908; Hon. Lieutenant-General; Hon. Colonel of 13th Rajputs (Schekhawati) Regiment, 1904; Member of the First Class of the Order of the Crown of Prussia, 1910; *b* 1861; *S* 1880. Salute, twenty-one guns. The Maharaja is head of Kuchhwaha clan of Rajputs, tracing descent from Rama, the celebrated king of Ayodhya (modern Oudh). The modern capital, Jaipur, was built in AD 1728 by Maharaja Jai Singh, the ancient capital being Amber, founded in AD 1150. The administration is carried on by a council consisting of ten members, the Maharaja exercising the supreme civil and military authority within his territories. The State of Jaipur comprises an area of 15,579 square miles, and has a population of 2,658,666. The State maintains a Transport Corps, organised in 1890, the strength of which is 1 superintendent, 8 officers, and 695 non-commissioned officers and men. The Maharaja, apart from being a wise and capable administrator, took a deep interest in all matters affecting the welfare of the British Empire. Among his many princely liberalities may be mentioned his subscription of Rs 1,600,000 towards founding a permanent Famine Fund for India, Rs 100,000 towards the Transvaal War Fund, Rs 400,000 added to the Famine Fund in memory of the Queen-Empress Victoria, Rs 250,000 towards the All India Victoria Memorial, Rs 300,000 for the promotion of the Imperial Institute, London, and Rs 75,000 towards King Edward's Hospital Fund; in commemoration of the visit of the Prince of Wales to Jaipur in 1905 he gave an additional Rs 300,000 to the Famine Fund; on the occasion of the Delhi Durbar of January 1903, his senior Maharanee, Her late Highness Maharanee Jadanjee, subscribed Rs 100,000 to the Famine Fund, and added to the same fund another Rs 100,000 in honour of the visit of the Princess of Wales in 1905; to the Women's Medical College, Hospital and Nursery School, Delhi, he gave Rs 300,000; to Prince of Wales's Relief Fund Rs 100,000; to Imperial Indian Relief Fund Rs 100,000; his total contributions in connection with the Great War amounted to Rs 2,383,622. Was a very catholic Hindu in his religion, and when invited in 1902 to be present at the coronation of King Edward VII he travelled to England in a strict orthodox style with 125 of his officers and attendants, a whole ship being chartered for the voyage, and all eatables and drinking-water being brought from India. *Heir:* Maharaj-Kumar Man Singh (adopted 24 March 1921). *Address:* Jaipur, Rajputana, India.

Died 7 Sept. 1922.

JAMAL, Sir Abdul Karim Abdul Shakur, Kt 1920; CIE 1915; merchant; *b* 1862; *m*; four *s* five *d*. *Educ:* Jamnager (Kathiawar);

Rangoon. Proprietor of the firm Jamal Bros & Co., Ltd; founder and half owner of Indo-Burma Petroleum Co., Ltd; Member Burma Legislative Council. *Address:* Jamal Manzie, Rangoon, Burma.

Died 2 Sept. 1924.

JAMES, Captain Arthur Keedwell Harvey; *see* Craven, A. S.

JAMES, Charles Canniff, CMG 1911; MA, LLD; *b* Napanee, Ontario, 14 June 1863; *s* of late Charles James, JP, and Ellen Canniff (UEL); *m* 1887, Frances L., *d* of James Crossen of Cobourg, Ontario; one *s*. *Educ:* Napanee High School; University of Victoria College (University of Toronto). Graduated, 1883; Master in Cobourg Collegiate Institute, 1883–86; Professor of Chemistry at Ontario Agricultural College, Guelph, Ontario, 1886–91; Deputy Minister of Agriculture for the Province of Ontario, Canada, 1891–1912; Special Commissioner on Agricultural Instruction, Canadian Department of Agriculture, 1912–13; Ex-President of Ontario Historical Society; Fellow of Royal Society of Canada. *Publications:* Text-book on Agriculture; various pamphlets on agricultural work; Bibliography of Canadian Poetry (English); contributions to the History of Ontario. *Recreation:* golf. *Address:* 144 St George Street, Toronto. *Clubs:* National, University, Lambton Golf and Country, Toronto. *Died 25 June 1916.*

JAMES, Edmund Janes, AM, PhD, LLD; President, State University of Illinois, 1904–20; President Emeritus since 1920; *b* Jacksonville, Illinois, 21 May 1855; *s* of Rev. Colin D. James and Amanda K. Casad; *m* 1879, Anna Margaret, *d* of Rev. Wm Roderick Lange of Halle am Saale, Prussia; two *s* one *d*. *Educ:* North-Western Univ.; Harvard Univ.; Universities of Halle, Leipsic, and Berlin. LLD Queen's Univ., Harvard Univ., North-Western Univ., and Univ. of Michigan. Principal of Public High School, Evanston, Illinois, 1877–79; of the Model High School, Normal, Illinois, 1879–82; Professor of Public Finance and Administration in the University of Pennsylvania in Philadelphia, 1883–96; Professor of Public Administration and Director of Extension Division, University of Chicago, 1897–1901; President North-Western University, 1902–4; founder and for eleven years Pres. American Academy of Political and Social Science; founder and for six years Pres. of the American Society for the Extension of University Teaching at Philadelphia; past Vice-Pres. of American Association for the Advancement of Science; Vice-Pres. of American Social Science Association; Pres. Board of Trustees of the Illinois State Historical Library; Chairman Illinois State Highway Commission; Delegate of United States Government to Pan-American Congress at Rio Janiero, 1906; Hon. Sec. of State Geological Commission; of State Tax Commission; Pres. of American Economic Association, 1910–11. *Publications:* Translation of the Panegyricus of Isocrates; History of American Tariff Legislation; The City Government of Philadelphia; The Modern Municipality and the Gas Supply; City Administration in Germany; The City Charters of Chicago; Government Regulation of Railways; Our Legal Tender Decisions; The Education of Business Men in Europe; the Origin of the Land Grant Act of 1862; and more than one hundred papers, essays, and monographs on educational, political, and social questions. *Recreations:* wheeling, mountain climbing, horseback riding, golf, occasional trips to Europe. *Address:* Urbana, Illinois. *Clubs:* Harvard, New York; University, Washington; University, Union League, Chicago, Cliff-Dwellers, Chicago; Evanston; University, Champaign; University, Urbana. *Died 17 June 1925.*

JAMES, Sir Edward Burnet, Kt 1908; JP; *b* 7 May 1857; *s* of late Stephen James of Bristol and Chew Magna, Somerset, and Mary, *d* of late George Bush, Bristol; *m* 1883, Mabel Amelia, *d* of Sir George William Edwards, JP; one *s* one *d*. Councillor (Bristol), 1891–1913; Alderman, 1906–13; High Sheriff, 1900–1; Lord Mayor, 1904–5 and 1907–8; Master of Society of Merchant Venturers, 1895; Chairman, Bristol South Conservative Association, 1905–7; President, Colston Dolphia Society, 1906–7. *Address:* Springfort, Stoke Bishop, Bristol. *T:* Stoke Bishop, Bristol, 65. *Club:* Constitutional, Bristol.

Died 27 Dec. 1927.

JAMES, Francis Edward, RWS; water-colour painter; Member New English Art Club; *s* of Rev. Henry James, Rector of Willingdon, Sussex; *m* Anna Georgiana, *widow* of late Phillip Scholfield of Maltby Hall, and *d* of Captain Gooch, RN. *Educ:* private school. *Address:* 42 South Street, Torrington, North Devon.

Died 25 Aug. 1920.

JAMES, Henry, OM 1916; author; *b* 15 April 1843; *s* of late Rev. Henry James. *Educ:* France; Switzerland; Harvard Law School. Became a naturalized Englishman, 1915. *Publications:* Watch and Ward, 1871; A Passionate Pilgrim, 1875; Roderick Hudson, 1875; Transatlantic

Sketches, 1875; The American, 1877; French Poets and Novelists, 1878; The Europeans, 1878; Daisy Miller, 1878; An International Episode, 1879; Life of Hawthorne, 1879; A Bundle of Letters, 1879; Confidence, 1879; Diary of a Man of Fifty, 1880; Washington Square, 1880; The Portrait of a Lady, 1881; Siege of London, 1883; Portraits of Places, 1884; Tales of Three Cities, 1884; A Little Tour in France, 1884; The Bostonians, 1886; Princess Casamassima, 1886; Partial Portraits, 1888; The Aspern Papers, 1888; The Reverberator, 1888; A London Life, 1889; The Tragic Muse, 1890; Terminations, 1896; The Spoils of Poynton, 1897; What Maisie Knew, 1897; In the Cage, 1898; The Two Magics, 1898; The Awkward Age, 1899; The Soft Side, 1900; A Little Tour in France, 1900; The Sacred Fount, 1901; The Wings of the Dove, 1902; The Ambassador, 1903; The Golden Bowl, 1905; English Hours, 1905; The American Scene, 1907; The High Bid, 1909; Finer Grain, 1910; The Outcry, 1911; A Small Boy and Others, 1913; Notes on Novelists, 1914. *Club:* Athenæum.

Died 28 Feb. 1916.

JAMES, Sir Henry Evan Murchison, KCIE 1901; CSI 1898; *b* 20 Jan. 1846; 3rd *s* of late William Edward James, Barrock Park, Cumberland; unmarried. *Educ:* Durham School. Asst Collector, 1865; Under-Secretary to Govt of Bombay, 1873; Postmaster-General, Bombay, 1875; Postmaster-General, Bengal, 1880; Director-General of the Post Office, 1886; Collector and Commissioner of Ahmedabad, 1889–91; Commissioner in Sind, 1891–1900; member of the Gov.-General's Legislative Council, 1895–97; officiating member of Council, Bombay, 1898–99; retired 1900; Member of Port-of-Spain Commission, 1903; Member of Council, Central Asian Society, Indian Section, Royal Society of Arts; FRGS. *Publication:* Long White Mountain, or Travels in Manchuria, 1888. *Address:* Glenshee, Cambridge Park, Twickenham. *T:* Richmond 123. *Clubs:* Carlton, East India United Service. *Died 20 Aug. 1923.*

JAMES, John Arthur, MVO 1909; JP; *b* 24 Feb. 1853; *m* 1885, Mary Venetia, *d* of late Rt Hon. George A. F. C. Bentinck. JP Warwick. *Address:* 3 Grafton Street, W; Coton House, Rugby. *Clubs:* Carlton, Travellers', Turf, Marlborough, Bachelors'.

Died 30 April 1917.

JAMES, Lt-Col Walter Haweis; late Royal Engineers; *b* 9 July 1847; *y s* of late H. C. James and Elizabeth Jane Page; *m* 1871, Fanny Eugenia Mabel Caunter, *o d* of Rev. G. Akehurst; three *s* one *d*. *Educ:* privately; RM Academy, Woolwich. Entered Royal Engineers, 1867; Captain, 1879; passed Staff College with Honours, 1877; served in the Intelligence Dept, War Office, and as Dep.-Asst Quartermaster-General, Zulu War; retired, 1880; re-employed, 1901; appointed to War Office as assistant to Permanent Under-Secretary, and promoted Major; Lieut-Col 1903. Contested (C) West St Pancras, 1885; Member of London County Council, 1889–92; Chairman of Sanitary Committee and Whip of the Moderate Party; many years a member of the Grand Council of the Primrose League; Vice-Chairman, 1899; recalled to the Army, 14 Sept. 1914; served in the Censor's Department till 31 May 1918 as 2nd Grade SO; retired then, having reached age limit. *Publications:* Modern Strategy; The Waterloo Campaign; numerous articles in the magazines and newspapers. *Recreations:* shooting, tennis. *Address:* 6 St Mary's Mansions, W2. *Club:* Authors'. *Died 13 Jan. 1927.*

JAMES, Col William Reginald Wallwyn, CMG 1916; retired 1917; *b* 23 Oct. 1860; *s* of Edward Wallwyn James; *m* 1889, Aline, *d* of Rev. Canon Hayman; one *s*. *Educ:* Royal Military Academy, Woolwich; Lieut RA, 1880; substantive Colonel, 1912; served S Africa, 1901 (clasp); European War, 1914–1916 (despatches, CMG). *Club:* United Service. *Died 6 Nov. 1925.*

JAMESON, John, JP, DL; Chairman and Managing Director, John Jameson & Son, Ltd; *e s* of late John Jameson of St Marnock's, and Anne, *d* of William Haig, Provost of St Andrews, NB; *m* 1870, Elizabeth, *e d* of late Thomas Collins Banfield. *Educ:* Trinity Coll. Dublin (MA). High Sheriff, Co. Dublin, 1880. Owned 4600 acres. *Address:* St Marnock's, Malahide, Co. Dublin.

Died 25 Feb. 1920.

JAMESON, Lt-Col John Eustace-; Commanding 24th (Reserve) Battalion the London Regiment since 1914; *b* Ireland, 22 March 1853; 3rd *s* of James Jameson, Anfield, Co. Dublin, and Alice, *d* of Alicia Eustace, and *g d* of Viscount Baltinglass; *m* Mary, *d* of J. B. Cabbell, Cromer Hall, Cromer. *Educ:* Wimbledon; Sandhurst. Late 18th Royal Irish, 20th Hussars, and Queen's Own Worcestershire Hussars; Lt-Col commanding the 24th (Reserve) County of London Battalion, The London Regiment (The Queen's), which he raised, 1 Sept. 1914; raised and commanded the 3/24th Battalion, London Regiment (The

Queen's) from 22 May 1915; attached to the Staff in Dublin as AAG (Advisory), 1 Aug. 1916; attached to the Staff (Irish) Division in Flanders from 5 Dec. (despatches). Late HM Inspector of Factories; manager of William Jameson and Co., distillers, Dublin. MP (N) W Clare, 1895–1906. *Recreations:* Hurlingham, All Ireland, and Wanderers' Polo Clubs. *Address:* 37 Cranley Gardens, SW. *Clubs:* Naval and Military, Reform.

Died 22 Dec. 1919.

JAMESON, Rt. Hon. Sir Leander Starr, 1st Bt, *cr* 1911; CB 1894; PC 1907; President British South Africa Company; MP Harbour Division, Capetown, 1910–12; *b* Edinburgh, 9 Feb. 1853; *s* of late R. W. Jameson, WS. *Educ:* London Univ.; MD 1877; MB and BS 1875; MRCS Eng. 1875. Administrator of Rhodesia, British South Africa Company, 1891–95; led raid on Transvaal, 29 Dec. 1895; battle of Krugersdorp, 1 Jan.; surrendered to Boers, 2 Jan. 1896; tried in London, and sentenced to 10 months' imprisonment, May 1896; released in December owing to ill-health; served S Africa, 1899–1900; elected member of Cape Legislative Assembly for Kimberley, 1900; appointed Director of De Beers Consolidated Company, 1900, and of the British South Africa Company, 1902; Premier, Cape Colony, 1904–8. *Heir:* none. *Address:* 2 Great Cumberland Place, W. *T:* Paddington 1453. *Clubs:* Beefsteak, Orleans.

Died 26 Nov. 1917 (ext).

JAMIESON, George, CMG 1897; Director of the British and Chinese Corporation, Chinese Central Railways and Yangtse Valley Company; *b* 1843; *m* 1873, Margaret, *d* of late Patrick Inkson of Berrleys, Banffs; one *s* three *d*. Entered Consular Service, 1864; Barrister, Middle Temple, 1880; Consul and Judge of Supreme Court, Shanghai, 1891; Consul-Gen., 1897–99. *Publications:* various papers on the Revenue and Statistics of China; prize essay on Bimetallism. *Address:* 43 Onslow Square, SW7. *T:* Kensington 2226. *Clubs:* Reform, Thatched House.

Died 30 Dec. 1920.

JAMIESON, William Allan, LLD, MD, CM; FRCPE; Surgeon to the King's Bodyguard for Scotland, the Royal Company of Archers; Consulting Physician for Diseases of the Skin, Edinburgh Royal Infirmary; Consulting and Visiting Physician to the Edinburgh City Hospital for Infectious Diseases, 1886–91; *b* Dreghorn Manse, Ayrshire, 1 April 1839. *Educ:* Irvine Academy; University of Glasgow (Arts); University of Edinburgh and Vienna (Medicine). Royal Household Jubilee Medal, 1897; Coronation Medal, 1911. President, Royal College of Physicians, 1909–10. KGStJ. *Publications:* a Manual of Diseases of the Skin, 4th edition, 1894; The Care of the Skin in Health, 1912; many contributions on Dermatology and allied subjects. *Recreations:* archery, cycling, travel. *Address:* 35 Charlotte Square, Edinburgh. *T:* 3154. *Club:* University, Edinburgh.

Died 21 April 1916.

JANE, Fred. T.; naval author and journalist, etc; *b* 6 Aug. 1870; *e s* of Rev. John Jane, Vicar of Upottery, Devon; *m* 1st, 1892, Alice, *d* of late Hamilton Beattie; one *d*; 2nd, 1909, Edith Frances Muriel, *o d* of late Captain Henry Chase Carré, RN; one *d*. *Educ:* Exeter School. Inventor of the Naval War Game; naval correspondent for the Engineer, Scientific American, and Standard; contested Portsmouth as Navy Interests Candidate, 1906. *Publications:* Blake of the "Rattlesnake", 1895; The Incubated Girl, 1896; To Venus in Five Seconds, 1897; The Lordship, the Passen, and We, 1897; The Violet Flame, The Port Guard Ship, 1899; Fighting Ships (naval annual); The Torpedo in Peace and War, 1898; The Jane Naval War Game (naval kriegspiel), 1898; The Imperial Russian Navy, 1900; Ever Mohun, 1901; Hints on Playing the Jane Naval War Game, 1902; The Jane Coast Operations War Game for the Instruction of Garrison Artillery in Coast Defence, 1903; The Imperial Japanese Navy, 1904; Heresies of Sea Power, 1906; The Ought-to-go, 1907; A Royal Bluejacket, 1908; All the World's Aircraft (Annual), 1910; How to play the Naval War Game, 1912; The British Battle Fleet, 1912; Your Navy as a Fighting Machine, 1914; various small war handbooks, 1914; The World's Warships, 1915. *Recreations:* motoring, scouts. *Address:* Hill House, Bedhampton, Havant, Hants. *TA:* Jane, Bedhampton. *T:* 115 Havant. *M:* BK 97, BK 264, BK 1616.

Died 8 March 1916.

JANES, Emily. *Educ:* private school. Diocesan Secretary, Girls' Friendly Society, St Albans diocese, 1877–78; voluntary parish work at Apsley, 1865–80; a Matron, Magdalen Hospital, Streatham, 1880–81; Private Secretary to Miss Ellice Hopkins, 1882–86, these years being spent in petitioning for the Amendment of the Laws for the Protection of Girls; Hon. Org. Sec. Ladies' Associations for the Care of Girls, 1886–95; Secretary of the National Union of Women Workers (later the National Council of Women), which had grown out of conferences and associations she had helped to organise from 1895 until 1917, when she resigned; Founder, Distaff Guild, Hampstead Garden Suburb, 1923. *Publications:* A Threefold Cord (a Magazine for Charitable Workers), 1891–93; editor, the Englishwoman's Year-Book, 1899–1908; The Associated Work of Women in Philanthropy—a paper in the Baroness Burdett Coutts' book, Woman's Mission; occasional magazine articles. *Recreations:* reading, music, conversation. *Address:* Dunclutha, Hastings, Sussex.

Died 26 Oct. 1928.

JANJIRA, HH Nawab Sir Sidi Ahmad Khan Sidi Ibrahim Khan, GCIE 1906; *b* 1862; descendant of the Sarul Khan family; *S* 1879; *m* 1st, Ahmedbib (*d* 1885); 2nd, 1886, Nazli Begum, of the Fyzee family of Bombay; 3rd, 1913, Kalsumbibi, a grand-daughter of the Nawab's great uncle; one *s*. The State has an area of 324 square miles and a population of 88,717; entitled to a salute of 13 guns. *Heir: s* Sidi Mahamad Khan, *b* 7 March 1914. *Address:* Janjira, Kolaba, Bombay. *Died 2 May 1922.*

JANVRIN, Rev. William Langston Benest, MA; Rector of Cradley, Malvern, since 1917; Prebendary in Hereford Cathedral; *b* London, 15 Aug. 1853; *s* of William and Jane Matilda Janvrin, both of Jersey; *m* 1879, Maud Madeleine Beavis; three *s* one *d. Educ:* Clare College, Cambridge. Ordained 1878; Priest, 1879; Curate of S Saviour's, S Pancras, London; Sherington, Bucks; Perpetual Curate in Beverley Minster, Yorkshire; Vicar of Southwold, Suffolk; Vicar of S Peter's, Hereford. *Address:* Cradley Rectory, Malvern. *TA:* Cradley. *T:* Ridgway Cross 5. *M:* CJ 9457.

Died 26 Dec. 1927.

JAPP, Francis Robert, MA, LLD; FRS; Emeritus Professor of Chemistry, Aberdeen University; *b* Dundee, 8 Feb. 1848; *y s* of James Japp, minister of Catholic Apostolic Church; *m* 1879, Elizabeth, *o d* of F. Tegetmeyer; two *d. Educ:* Universities of St Andrews, Edinburgh, Heidelberg and Bonn. Research Assistant and, later on, Lecturer on Chemistry in Normal School of Science, S Kensington (Royal Coll. of Science), 1878–90; Foreign Secretary of Chemical Society, 1885–91, and Vice-President, 1895–99 and 1915–18; Longstaff Medallist of Chemical Society, 1891; President Chemical Section, British Association, 1898; Vice-President of the Institute of Chemistry of Great Britain and Ireland, 1901–4. *Publications:* Inorganic Chemistry, jtly with Prof. Sir Edward Frankland, FRS, 1884; and numerous researches published in Journal Chemical Society from 1879. *Address:* 25 Ellerker Gardens, Richmond, Surrey.

Died 1 Aug. 1925.

JARDINE, David Jardine, of Applegarth; JP Dumfriesshire; FRGS; *b* 4 Aug. 1847; *s* of James Jardine of Dryfeholm, Tinwald, and Torthorwald, Dumfriesshire, and Larriston, Roxburghshire; *m* 1886, Angela, *d* of Sir Charles Tilston Bright, MP, late of Badsworth Hall, Yorkshire, and Carbrook Hall, Yorkshire; one *d* (one *s* decd). *Educ:* Trinity Coll., Cambridge. MA. Barrister. After leaving the university travelled in India, Java, China, Japan, Australia, New Zealand, Tasmania, America, Canada, Egypt, and South Africa. Spent four years in India shooting big game. Member Royal Company of Archers (King's Bodyguard for Scotland). *Recreations:* fond of racing, trains with Peacock at Middleham, Yorkshire; won the Royal Hunt Cup at Ascot with "Refractor", 1899, and Northumberland Plate with "Sir Harry", 1909. *Address:* Jardine Hall and Dryfeholm, Lockerbie, Dumfriesshire; Larriston Hall, Roxburghshire; 9 Upper Grosvenor Street, W1. *T:* Mayfair 3934. *Clubs:* Carlton, Boodle's.

Died 23 Aug. 1922.

JARDINE, Sir John, 1st Bt, *cr* 1916; KCIE 1897; Hon. LLD Aberdeen; MP (L) Roxburghshire, 1906–18; Judge of High Court, Bombay, 1885; Acting Chief Justice, 1895; retired 1897; *b* England, 27 Sept. 1844; 3rd *s* of William Jardine, JP, Dunstable; *m* 1880, Minnie Dunbar, *d* of Jabez Hogg, MRCS; six *s. Educ:* Christ's College, Cambridge. Chancellor's Gold Medal English Verse, Cambridge, 1864. Entered Bombay CS 1864; Political Officer in Native States of Kattywar, 1871; Secretary for trial of the Gaekwar of Baroda, 1875; Secretary to Treaty with Portugal and Law Officer to Government of India, 1877; Judicial Commissioner of Burma, 1878; President Burma School Board, 1881; Chief Secretary to Bombay Government, holding the Political, Secret, Educational, Persian, and Judicial portfolios, 1885. Fellow University of Bombay, 1872; sometime Dean of Arts and Dean of Law; Vice-Chancellor, 1895; President Royal Asiatic Soc. Bombay. Contested (L) Roxburghshire, 1900. *Publications:* Notes on Buddhist Law, with translations of the Burmese Law of Manu; Preface to Dr E. Forchhammer's King Wagaru's Code; editor of Customary Law of the Chin Tribe, and of Father Sangermano's Burmese Empire 100 Years Ago. *Recreation:* travel. *Heir: e s* Capt. John Eric Birdwood

Jardine, 5th Queen's West Surrey Regt, *b* 30 Sept. 1890. *Address:* Applegarth, Godalming. *Clubs:* Reform; Scottish Liberal, Edinburgh; Byculla, Bombay. *Died 26 April 1919.*

JARDINE, Major Sir John Eric Birdwood, 2nd Bt, *cr* 1916; 5th Battalion, The Queen's Regiment; *b* London, 30 Sept. 1890; *e s* of Sir John Jardine, 1st Bt, KCIE, LLD, and Minnie Dunbar, *d* of Jabez Hogg, FRCS; *S* father, 1919; unmarried. *Educ:* Charterhouse; Corpus Christi Coll., Oxford, BA 1914. Commissioned in 5th Batt. The Queen's Royal W Surrey Regt 1911; served in India, 1914–15, and in Mesopotamia, 1915–19 (despatches); Captain, 1916; Major, 1921. *Heir: b* Capt. Colin Arthur Jardine, *b* 24 Sept. 1892. *Recreations:* soldiering, books, tennis, bridge. *Address:* Black Gates, West Byfleet, Surrey. *Club:* New University.

Died 24 March 1924.

JARDINE, Sir Robert William Buchanan, 2nd Bt, *cr* 1885; *b* 21 Jan. 1868; *s* of Sir Robert Jardine, 1st Bt and Margaret, *d* of John Buchanan Hamilton, Leny, Perthshire; *S* father, 1905; *m* 1894, Ethel Mary, OBE, *d* of late Benjamin Piercy, of Marchwiel Hall, Wrexham, and Macomer, Sardinia; one *s* one *d* (and one *s* decd). *Educ:* Eton; Magdalene College, Cambridge. *Heir: s* John William Jardine, [*b* 7 March 1900; *m* 1921, Jean, *yr d* of Lord Ernest Hamilton; MFH Dumfreisshire]. *Address:* Castlemilk, Lockerbie, NB; 24 St James's Place, SW1. *T:* Regent 980; The Kremlin, Newmarket. *Clubs:* Arthur's, Carlton, Turf. *Died 30 Jan. 1927.*

JARMAN, John Robert, ISO 1909; a Sub-Inspector, Board of Education, 1875–1909, in Sunderland and Durham districts; *b* 27 June 1844; *m* 1873, Ellen Frances, *d* of Robert Halls. *Address:* 13 Tunstall Vale, Sunderland. *Died 19 April 1922.*

JARRETT, Col Henry Sullivan, CIE 1895; Colonel on the Supernumerary List; *b* 17 June 1839; 2nd *s* of late Thomas Jarrett, Speldhurst, Kent, and Eliza, *d* of late Capt. Chambers, 89th Foot; *m* 1874, Agnes Delacour, *d* of late Francis Beaufort, Bengal Civil Service; three *s. Educ:* Prior Park, Bath. First commission, 1856; served in India during the Mutiny (medal); also in the Mahsud-Waziri Expedition, 1860 (medal and clasp); and the second Yusufzai Expedition as ADC to Sir Neville Chamberlain and Sir John Garvock (clasp); Secretary and Member, Board of Examiners, Fort-William, Calcutta; and Asst-Secretary, Legislative Dept, Govt of India, 1870–94. Decorated for general services. *Publications:* History of the Caliphs; Institutes of the Emperor Akbar; Heine's Book of Songs into English verse; Stratheir. *Recreations:* fishing, shooting. *Address:* South Lodge, Imberhorne, East Grinstead. *Club:* United Service.

Died 15 April 1919.

JARVIS, Lt-Col Arthur Leonard Fitzgerald, ISO 1905; *b* 17 June 1852; *s* of late George Murray and Elizabeth Arnold Jarvis; *m* 1906, Frances Geraldine, *d* of late Capt. C. L. J. Fitzgerald, 1st WI Regt; one *s*. Entered Canadian Government Service, 1868; Private Secretary to Postmaster-General, 1882; to Minister of Agriculture, 1885–92; Secretary, Department of Agriculture, 1896; commanded the Governor-General's Foot Guards, 1899–1904; Assistant Deputy Minister of Agriculture, 1908; retired 1925. General Service Medal with one clasp, Long Service Medal, and Long Service Decoration. *Club:* Rideau. *Died March 1927.*

JASTROW, Morris, Jr, PhD, LLD; Professor of Semitic Languages in the University of Pennsylvania since 1885; *b* 13 Aug. 1861; *s* of Marcus Jastrow (*d* 1903) and Bertha Wolffsohn (*d* 1908); *m* 1893, Helen Bachman; no *c. Educ:* public and private schools, Philadelphia, 1866–81; University of Pennsylvania, 1881–85 (AB); Breslau and Leipzig Universities, 1881–84; Paris (Collège de France, Ecole des Hautes Etudes, Ecole des Langues Orientales Vivantes), 1884–85; Strasburg University, 1885. President of the American Oriental Society, 1914–15; President of the Society of Biblical Literature, 1916; Member of American Philos. Society; US Delegate to various Congresses; Haskell Lecturer at Oberlin College, Oberlin, O, 1913; Lewison Lecturer (Free Synagogue of New York), 1915, etc. *Publications:* Religion of the Babylonians and Assyrians, 1898; two grammatical treatises of Abu Zakariyya Hayyug, 1897; A Fragment of the Babylonian Dibbarra Epic, 1891; The Study of Religion, 1902; Die Religion Babyloniens and Assyriens, 1902–12; Atlas of Illustrations for the Religion of Babylonia and Assyria, 1912. Editor: (with memoir) Selected Essays of James Darmesteter (trans. by Helen Bachman Jastrow), 1895; series Handbooks on the History of Religion; Semitic Dept, International Encyclopedia; Editor of Rand, M'Nally and Co's Linguistic Map of Europe and the Near East, 1919; Aspects of Religious Belief and Practice in Babylonia and Assyria, 1911; Hebrew and Babylonian Traditions, 1914; Babylonia-Assyrian Birth-Omens and their Cultural Significance, 1914; The Civilization of Babylonia and Assyria, 1915; The War and the Baghdad Railway, 1917; The War and the Coming Peace, 1918; Zionism and the Future of Palestine, 1919; A Gentle Cynic, 1919; The Eastern Question and its Solution, 1920; The Book of Job, 1920; in conjunction with A. T. Clay, An Old Babylonian Version of the Gilgamesh Epic, 1920; numerous articles and monographs in American and European periodicals and serials. *Recreations:* walking, chess, reading novels. *Address:* 248 S 23rd Street, Philadelphia, Pa, USA. *T:* Locust 2481. *Club:* Franklin Inn, Philadelphia.

Died June 1921.

JAYNE, Rt. Rev. Francis John DD; *b* 1845; *s* of John Jayne, JP, and Elizabeth Haines; *m* 1872, Emily, *d* of Watts J. Garland, Lisbon; three *s* three *d*. *Educ:* Rugby; Wadham Coll., Oxford. Hody Greek Exhibition, 1st class Mods, Greats, Law and History; Fellow of Jesus College, 1868; Senior Hall and Houghton Greek Testament Prizeman, 1870. Curate, St Clement's, Oxford, 1870–71; Tutor, Keble College, 1871–79; Preacher at Whitehall, 1875–77; Principal, St David's Coll. Lampeter, 1879–86; Select Preacher, Oxford, 1884; Vicar, Leeds, 1886; Bishop of Chester, 1889–1919. *Address:* The Quarry, Oswestry, Salop. *Club:* Athenæum.

Died 23 Aug. 1921.

JEANS, Sir Alexander Grigor, Kt 1918; Managing Director and Editor of the Liverpool Post and Mercury and of the Liverpool Echo since 1904; *b* Elgin, 27 June 1849; *s* of Robert Jeans, JP, Elgin; *m* 1877, Ellen (*d* 1889), *d* of Thomas Gallon, Birkenhead; four *s* one *d*. *Educ:* Elgin Academy. Connected with the Liverpool Post since 1872; Manager, 1879; was Chairman of the Liverpool Reform Club, the Press Association, and the Cheshire Automobile Club; twice Captain of Wallasey Golf Club. *Recreations:* golf, motoring. *Address:* Inchbroom, Bidston Road, Birkenhead. *T:* Birkenhead 664. *Clubs:* National Liberal; Liverpool Reform, Liverpool Exchange.

Died 6 March 1924.

JEANS, Hon. Maj.-Gen. Charles Gilchrist, CB 1917; retired; late Army Ordnance Department; *b* 4 Aug. 1854. Entered Army, 1873; Col 1908; retired, 1913. *Died 5 Jan. 1920.*

JEANS, Sir Richard Walter, Kt 1922; late Director and General Manager, Bank of Australasia, and Chairman Australasian Bank Managers' Committee; *b* 2 July 1846; *m* 1902, Lucia Ellinor, *d* of Robert Fremuth, Dantzig. *Address:* Ridgeway, Langley Avenue, Surbiton, Surrey. *T:* Kingston 525. *M:* LO 5410. *Clubs:* Constitutional, Australasian.

Died 13 April 1924.

JEANS, William; journalist, retired; *b* Edinburgh. *Educ:* Elgin Academy; Edinburgh University. Was a journalist all his life; entered the Press gallery, 1863, and was there continuously till 1911, with the exception of the years 1866–67–68, which he spent in the press in Melbourne, Victoria; was for over 40 years the London editor and Parliamentary correspondent of the Dundee Advertiser, and during the same period also represented at Westminster the Leeds Mercury, the Yorkshire Observer, and the Liverpool Daily Post. Published a volume of Parliamentary Reminiscences covering the period from 1863 to 1886. *Recreation:* golf. *Address:* Deanfield, Belmont Road, Reigate. *Club:* National Liberal.

Died 5 Feb. 1916.

JEFFERS, Le Roy, FRGS; librarian, author, lecturer; *b* Ipswich, Mass, Aug. 1878; *s* of Charles P. Jeffers and Elizabeth B. Stalker; *m* 1918, R. E. Miller. Manager for the Booklovers Libraries, 1901–4; Manager, Book Order Office, New York Public Library, for its system of 52 branch Libraries, since 1905; also in main reading-room for evening service, 1906–14; visited European Libraries, 1908; Member American Library Association, New York Library Club; published through ALA comparative lists of books issued in various editions, showing the most economical method of purchasing desirable editions for library use; Lecturer on the Natural Wonders of the United States and Canada, and on Mountaineering in North America; Librarian American Alpine Club; Organiser and Secretary, Bureau of Associated Mountaineering Clubs of North America; Member National Institute of Social Sciences; California Academy of Sciences. *Publications:* The Call of the Mountains, 1922; contributor on mountaineering, travel, psychology, and library economy to periodicals. *Address:* 476 Fifth Avenue and 106 Central Park West, New York. *Clubs:* Alpine, Authors'; Explorers, American and Canadian, French Alpine; Adirondack Mountain, Appalachian Mountain, Fresh Air, Green Mountain, Harvard Travellers, Sierra.

Died 25 July 1926.

JEFFERSON, Frederick Thomas; Head of Kenrick & Jefferson, West Bromwich; Chairman and Managing Director of the Britannic Assurance Corporation; *b* 1854; *m* 1917, Millie Robinson, Brighton. *Address:* Lapworth Hall, Warwickshire.

Died 15 Nov. 1920.

JEFFERY, Edward Turner; President, Denver and Rio Grande Railway since 1891; *b* Liverpool, 6 April 1843; *m* 1877, Virginia Osborne, *d* of James C. Clarke, MA, Frederick Maryland. Emigrated to America 1850; entered employ of Illinois Central Railroad Co., 1856; general superintendent, 1877; general manager, 1885; resigned, 1889. *Address:* 165 Broadway, New York City, NY.

Died 24 Sept. 1927.

JEFFERY, Walter, MJI; Managing Editor, Evening News, Sunday News, and Woman's Budget, Sydney, NSW; *b* Portsmouth, 1861. *Educ:* Portsmouth. Went to sea, 1876; and was in different parts of the world until 1884; then began journalism, and arrived in Sydney in 1886; a Trustee of the Public Library of NSW, Sydney. *Publications:* A Century of Our Sea Story, 1900; The King's Yard, etc. *Recreation:* student of early Australian history and English naval history. *Address:* S. Bennett Ltd, 49 Market Street, Sydney, Australia.

Died 14 Feb. 1922.

JEFFREY, Rev. Norman Stuart; Hon. Canon of Manchester. *Address:* Rylea, Thornton-le-Fylde, Preston.

Died Sept. 1919.

JEFFREYS, Adm. Edmund Frederick, CVO 1903; RN; *b* 1 Oct. 1846; *s* of late General E. R. Jeffreys, CB. Entered Navy, 1860; Capt. 1885; Beaufort Testimonial, 1874; served Egyptian war, 1882; Asst Director of Torpedoes, 1889–93; Director of Naval Ordnance, Admiralty, 1897–1901; late Senior Officer, Coast of Ireland, 1901–4. *Club:* United Service. *Died 19 March 1925.*

JEFFREYS, Brig.-Gen. Patrick Douglas, CB 1896; OBE 1919; late 1st Battalion The Connaught Rangers; retired; *b* 29 July 1848; 2nd *s* of late Gen. Edmund Richard Jeffreys, CB; *m* 1897, Maude Maynard, *o d* of late Sir Richard Oldfield. *Educ:* Marlborough College. Entered army, 1866; served Zululand, 1879 (medal with clasp); Burmah, 1886–87 (despatches, medal with clasp); Zhob Field Force, 1890 (despatches); commanded, with temporary rank of Brigadier General, 2nd Brigade of Malakand Field Force during operations on NW Frontier, 1897–98, including operations in Bajour, in the Mamund country, and in Buner (despatches twice, medal with clasp); Commanded East Group, Kent Vol. Regt, 1915–19. JP and CC Kent. *Address:* Doddington Place, Sittingbourne, Kent. *T:* Doddington, Kent. *Club:* United Service.

Died 12 April 1922.

JELF, Sir Arthur Richard, Kt 1901; *b* Pankow, near Berlin, 1837; *s* of late Rev. Richard William Jelf, DD, Principal of King's College, London, and Emmy, Countess Schlippenbach of Prussia, Maid of Honour to the Queen of Hanover; *m* 1867, Jane, *y d* of late Rev. William Clark King, Vicar of Norham; three *s* three *d*. *Educ:* Eton; Christ Church, Oxford (2nd class Mods, 2nd class Greats, hon. 4th Mathematics). Barrister, Inner Temple, 1863; QC 1880. Recorder of Shrewsbury, 1879–1901; Judge of King's Bench Division of High Court of Justice, 1901–10. *Address:* Oak House, Carlton Road, Putney Hill, SW. *T:* Putney 1184. *Club:* Athenæum.

Died 24 July 1917.

JELLICORSE, Rev. William, MA; Prebendary of Wellington in Hereford Cathedral since 1891. *Address:* Maryvale, Ludlow.

Died 8 July 1920.

JENKINS, Rev. David; Hon. Canon of Truro. *Address:* Tideford Vicarage, St Germans, Cornwall.

Died 18 Dec. 1926.

JENKINS, Lt-Col Francis, CMG 1918; Officier de la Légion d'Honneur; Secretary Southern Provinces and Colony of Nigeria since 1921; *b* 31 May 1877; *s* of H. L. Jenkins of Clanacombe, Kingsbridge, Devon; *m* 1914, Margaret Campbell, *d* of late Capt. W. T. Fraser, 42nd Highlanders, and Mrs Fraser of Moorside, Cookham; two *d*. *Educ:* Harrow; RMC, Sandhurst. First commission Coldstream Guards, 1896; Capt. 1904; Major, 1911; temp. Lt-Col 1916; seconded for service with the West African Frontier Force, 1903–6, 1908–10, and 1911–19; Staff Officer for West African Frontier Force at the Colonial Office, 1911–16; served South Africa with Coldstream Guards, 1900–2 (Queen's medal 5 clasps, King's medal 2 clasps); West Africa, with Northern Nigeria Regt, 1903 (African Gen. Service medal and clasp); European War, with Nigeria Regt, Nigerian Frontier (mention, CMG); retired from Army, 1919; Colonial Secretary, Barbados, 1919–21. *Address:* Lagos, Nigeria. *Clubs:* Guards, Travellers', Sports.   *Died 8 Nov. 1927.*

JENKINS, Herbert; author; Managing Director of the publishing house of Herbert Jenkins Ltd; *s* of George J. Jenkins, Norwich; unmarried. *Educ:* Greyfriars College. In spare moments snatched from the commerce of books, contributed articles, stories, etc, to reviews and periodicals; founded the publishing house of Herbert Jenkins Ltd. *Publications:* The Life of George Borrow, 1911; Bindle, 1916; The Night Club, 1917; Adventures of Bindle, 1918; John Dene of Toronto, 1919; Malcolm Sage, Detective, 1920; Mrs Bindle, 1921. *Recreation:* walking. *Address:* 3 York Street, St James's, SW. *TA:* Booklover. *T:* Gerrard 7846.

Died 8 June 1923.

JENKINS, Huntly E.; barrister. *Address:* 1 Brick Court, Temple, EC4. *T:* Central 1596; 21 Craven Hill, W2. *T:* Paddington 4852.

Died 1 Nov. 1923.

JENKINS, Hon. John Greeley; *b* Pennsylvania, US, 8 Sept. 1851; 4th *s* of Evan Jenkins and Mary Davis of South Wales; *m* 1883, Jeannie Mary, *o d* of W. H. Charlton of Adelaide; one *s* one *d*. *Educ:* public schools in America; Wyoming Seminary, Pa. Worked on father's farm until 1872; travelled in Canada and United States for publishing company, 1872–78; arrived Adelaide, Australia, 1878; entered Town Council, Unley, 1885; Mayor, 1888; Member of Parliament for District of Sturt, 1887–1902; Torrens, 1902–5; served on several Royal Commissions; Minister of Education, 1891–92; introduced the Free Educational Bill, which was passed 1891; Minister for Works, 1892 and 1894–99; Chief Secretary, 1899–1901; Premier and Chief Secretary, 1901–5; Agent-General for S Australia, 1905–8; attended several important conferences between premiers of States and Commonwealth; during his premiership introduced and passed an amendment to the Constitution, reducing the number of members of Parliament and materially lessening the expense of Government; always strong advocate land settlement and progressive legislation; was for several years Deputy Grand Master of SA Grand Lodge; represented Commonwealth Government, International Telegraph Conference, Lisbon, 1908; Member of Council and Hon. Treasurer of the London Chamber of Commerce; Vice-President of the British Empire Products organisation; Vice-Chairman British Imperial Council of Commerce; attended International Congress of Commerce in Boston, 1912, and Paris, 1914; and International Trade Conference in Atlantic City, 1919, Paris, 1920; on the Directorate of the International Chamber of Commerce, Vice-President and on the Council of the Royal Colonial Institute; Member of the Council, the Empire Cotton Growing Corporation; Member of Council, British Empire Exhibition, 1924. *Publications:* Australian Products; Social Conditions of Australia; Edited Australasian Section Encyclopedia Americana. *Recreations:* walking, gardening. *Address:* 12a Windsor Court, Bayswater, W; 27 Clement's Lane, EC4. *T:* Central 4727. *TA:* Starproof, London. *Club:* City Carlton.

Died 22 Feb. 1923.

JENKINS, Rt. Hon. Sir Lawrence Hugh, KCIE 1903; Kt 1899; PC 1916; *b* 22 Dec. 1858; 2nd *s* of R. D. Jenkins, JP, Cilbronnau, Cardigan; *m* 1892, Catherine Minna, 2nd *d* of late Andrew Brown Kennedy; one *s*. *Educ:* Cheltenham College; Oxford University. Called to Bar, Lincoln's Inn, 1883; Bencher of Lincoln's Inn, 1909; Judge of Calcutta High Court, 1896–99; Chief Justice of the High Court of Judicature, Bombay, 1899–1908; Member of Council of India, 1908–9; Member of the Judicial Committee of the Privy Council since 1916; Chief Justice, High Court, Bengal, 1909–15; Chairman of Quarter Sessions, Cardiganshire. Past District Grand Master of Freemasons for Bombay and Bengal. *Address:* Cilbronnau, near Cardigan.   *Died 1 Oct. 1928.*

JENKINS, Brig.-Gen. (Hon.) Noble Fleming, CMG 1916; CBE 1919; *b* 29 Oct. 1860; *s* of late D. J. Jenkins, MP Penryn and Falmouth; *m* 1st, 1886, Mabel (*d* 1918), *d* of late Major General J. F. Richardson, CB; three *d*; 2nd, 1919, Edith Muriel, *d* of Major L. B. Edgar; one *s* two *d*. *Educ:* Rugby; Sandhurst. Captain Border Regt, 1888; served South African War, 1899–1901; rejoined 3rd Border Regt on outbreak of war; served European War, 1914–18 (despatches, CMG, CBE). Deputy-Secretary of the SPG. *Address:* 32 Greycoat Gardens, SW1. *T:* Victoria 3207.   *Died 19 Aug. 1927.*

JENKINS, William Henry Phillips, JP, DL; *b* 1842; *o surv. s* of late John Jenkins of Caerleon, Co. Monmouth, and Elizabeth, *d* and co-heiress of late Henry Phillips of Llantarnam House, Co. Monmouth;

m 1st, 1872, Lady Caroline Anne (*d* 1912), *y d* of 6th Earl of Jersey; 2nd, 1914, Kathleen, 2nd *d* of late John H. Abernethy. *Educ:* Rugby; Merton College, Oxford. *Address:* Frenchay Park, Bristol. *Clubs:* Boodle's, New University.

Died 26 Dec. 1916.

JENKINS, Rev. William Owen, DD (Oxon); Principal, The Diocesan College, Rondebosch, SA; Canon and Chancellor of St George's Cathedral, Cape Town; Examining Chaplain to the Archbishop of Cape Town; *b* 1863; *s* of late W. Jenkins, of Abercastell, and Mary, *e d* of late Daniel Owen of Ty Gwyn, Pembs; *m* 1891, Margaret Collinson (*d* 1915), *e d* of late W. G. Steel of Carlisle; two *s* four *d*. *Educ:* Haverfordwest School; Classical Exhibitioner of Jesus Coll. Oxford. BA (Classical Honours), 1885. Chaplain of St Andrew's Coll. Grahamstown, 1888–91; Rector of East London East (S Africa), 1891–94; Rector and Rural Dean of Graaff Reinet, 1894–99; Member of Provincial Synods, 1898, 1904, 1909, 1915, and of Provincial Standing Committee, 1910–15; Examiner in Divinity and Philosophy and Member of Council Cape Univ. *Publications:* The Incarnation in St Paul's Theology; The Christian Hope of Immortality; Lilies, Corner Stones, and Pearls; The Philosopher as Statesman, A Study in Plato's Republic. *Address:* Rondebosch, SA.

Died 19 July 1919.

JENKINSON, Sir Edward George, KCB 1888 (CB 1884); *b* 1835; *m* 1865, Annabella (*d* 1915), *d* of Capt. T. Monk Mason, RN. *Educ:* Harrow; Haileybury Coll. Indian Civil Service, 1856–80; served Indian Mutiny; late Private Secretary to Lord Spencer, Lord-Lieut of Ireland, 1882–84.   *Died 1 March 1919.*

JENKINSON, Francis John Henry, Hon. DLitt, Oxford; Librarian, University Library, Cambridge, since 1889; *b* 20 August 1853; *s* of John Henry Jenkinson; *m* 1902, Margaret Clifford, *o d* of late Ludovick C. Stewart. *Educ:* Marlborough; Trinity Coll., Cambridge (Fellow and late assistant tutor). *Address:* Southmead, Chaucer Road, Cambridge.   *Died 21 Sept. 1923.*

JENNER, George Francis Birt, CMG 1902; *b* Paris, 26 May 1840; *e s* of Albert Lascelles Jenner, Wenvoe Castle, Glamorgan, and Henrietta Morris, *e d* of Sir John Morris, 2nd Bt, Sketty Park, Glamorgan; *m* 1867, Stephanie Emilianoff, *d* of Alexis Emilianoff, Ragatova, in the Government of Orel, Russia. *Educ:* abroad. Entered Diplomatic Service, 1857; Attaché, Washington, 1859; accompanied Lord Lyons in attendance on the Prince of Wales when in Canada and US, 1860; Turin, 1860; Athens, 1862; Dresden, 1866; Berne, 1866; Constantinople, 1867; Teheran, 1868; Acting Consul-General at Tabreez, 1868; Berne, 1872; Stockholm, 1876 (Acting Charge d'Affaires, 1879); Secretary of Legation and Oriental Secretary, Tehran 1882; Secretary of Legation, Mexico, 1884 (Chargé d'Affaires, 1885); Buenos Ayres, 1887 (Chargé d'Affaires, 1888–89); Chargé d'Affaires, Lima, 1891–92; Minister Resident and Consul-General, Bogota, 1892–97; transferred to Central America, 1897; retired on a pension, 1902. Jubilee medal, 1897. *Address:* Les Alouettes, Cannes. *Club:* St James's.   *Died 1 Dec. 1924.*

JENNINGS, Arthur Seymour, FJI, FIBD; Founder and Editor of The Decorator, and Paint and Wallpaper; Chairman and Managing Director, Trade Papers Publishing Co. Ltd; Past President, Incorporated Institute of British Decorators; author and journalist since 1882; expert and Lecturer in Decoration, Paints, Colours, and Varnishes; *b* Camberwell, SE, 3 Jan. 1860; *s* of William Jennings, leather technologist; *m* 1885, Jennie Marguerite, *d* of Thomas Higenbotham, Yonkers, NY, USA; one *d*. Educated as architect; late Lecturer, Science and Art Department, Board of Education; late Associate Editor, Scientific American and Oils, Colours, and Drysalteries; member of Technical and Scientific Circle; Consulting Examiner, City and Guilds of London Institute; Weekly Newspaper Proprietors' Association; member Society of Authors; member Paint and Varnish Committee, British Engineering Standards Association; honorary Life member, International Association of Master Painters and Decorators, of the United States and Canada; member of Council, Oil and Colour Chemists' Association; member Research Association of British Paint, Colour and Varnish Association. *Publications:* The Modern Painter and Decorator; The Decoration and Renovation of the Home; The House Beautiful; Painting by Immersion and by Compressed Air; Wall Papers and Wall Coverings; Paint and Colour Mixing; The Builders' Pocket Book; Motor and Coach Painting; The Painters' Pocket Book; Commercial Paints and Painting, Paints and Varnishes, etc. *Recreations:* freemasonry, music. *Address:* 4 Brunswick Square, Hove, Brighton. *T:* Hove 6641. *TA:* Polystyle (Holb.), London. *T:* Holborn 4776. *Club:* Authors'.

JENNINGS, Brig.-Gen. Herbert Alexander Kaye, CIE 1916; RA; retired list; *b* 1862; *s* of Maj.-Gen. C. J. Jennings; *m* 1893; one *d*. *Educ:* Wellington College; RMA Woolwich. Entered RA 1882. *Address:* Simla, India. *Club:* Naval and Military.

Died 15 Jan. 1921.

JENNINGS, James George, CIE 1919; MA; Director of Public Instruction, Bihar and Orissa; *b* 14 June 1866; *s* of James Jennings; *m* 1894, Maud Walrond, *d* of Gateward Coleridge Davis, Barrister-at-Law; three *d*. *Educ:* Ashby-de-la-Zouch Grammar School; privately; Lincoln College, Oxford. Indian Educational Service, 1892; Professor of English Literature, Government College, Benares, 1892; Government College, Allahabad, 1895; Inspector of Schools, United Provinces, 1906; Principal, Government College, Allahabad, 1907; Director of Public Instruction, Bihar and Orissa, 1913–17 and 1920–21; Vice-Chancellor, Patna University, 1917–20; Member of the Legislative Council, Bihar and Orissa, 1913–16 and 1917–20; Additional Member (temporary) of the Viceroy's Legislative Council, 1917; Fellow of Allahabad University, 1895–1913; Hon. Fellow since 1913; ex officio Fellow of Calcutta University, 1913–17. *Publications:* Addresses to Students, 1918; Essay on Metaphor; Select Passages on Duty to the State; Selections from Marcus Aurelius Antoninus; Sakuntala, adapted from Kalidasa; From an Indian College. *Address:* 16 Charlbury Road, Oxford. *Club:* East India United Service.

Died Jan. 1921.

JENNINGS, Rev. Canon John Andrew; Canon of Christ Church Cathedral, 1913; Wallace Lecturer in Divinity, Trinity College, Dublin, since 1902; Rector of Harold's Cross, Dublin, since 1901; Rural Dean, 1905; *b* 1855; *o s* of John Jennings, Blackrock, Co. Dublin; *m* 1881, Jane Charlotte, *y d* of Rev. Samuel McCutcheon, Longford; two *s* one *d*. *Educ:* Trinity College, Dublin. Downes' Divinity Prize, 1st; BA 1880; MA 1883. Ordained, 1880; priested, 1881; Curate of St Peter's Drogheda, 1880; Rector of Portnashangan (Meath), 1881; Rector of Donaghpatrick (Meath), 1882; Rector of St Mary's, Dublin, 1896. Hon. Chaplain to Lord Lieut 1901, and to all subsequent Lord Lieuts; member of Senate, TCD; member of General Synod of Church of Ireland; member of Dublin Diocesan Council; governor of King's Hospital (Blue Coat School); trustee of Mageough Home; Professor of Pastoral Theology, Trinity College, Dublin, 1912–17; Select Preacher, Dublin University, 1914, 1915, 1916, 1917, and 1921. *Publications:* Modern Elocutionist, 1879, many editions; Wayside Restings (poems), 1880; six volumes of Readings, 1880–96, many editions; editor of Church of Ireland Parish Magazine, circulation 13,000 monthly, 1888–98; Unto the Perfect Day, 1883; Liturgical Reading, 1883; Reverence, 1891; The True Order, 1907; various articles, sermons, and verses. *Recreations:* sketching, photography. *Address:* Harold's Cross Rectory, Dublin.

Died Dec. 1923.

JENNINGS, Col Robert Henry, CSI 1904; RE; *b* 13 Oct. 1852; *e s* of late Robert Jennings, Woodlawn, Cork; *g s* of late Lieut T. Jennings, RN, Lakeville, Cork; *m* 1892, Bessie, *d* of late Archibald Gray and Mrs Gray, 37 Holland Park, W and St Mary's Tower, Birnam, Perthshire; one *s* one *d*. *Educ:* Royal Military Academy, Woolwich. Travelled much in Europe and the East; entered RE 1872; Colonel, 1903; served Afghan War, 1879–80; Chief Political Officer, Sir C. Macgregor's Force Mari Expedition (despatches, medal); Chief Political Officer, Toba Column, 1882; made exploration, Persia, Baluchistan, Helmund, 1884–85 (thanked by Commander-in-Chief; high approval Government of India); Army Staff till 1890; Consul to HBM, Basra, Turkish Arabia, 1892; Resident, Jeypore, 1898; Indore, 1899–1902; Western Rajputana States, 1903–5; on special duty representing HE the Viceroy as host of King of Afghanistan's eldest son during latter's tour in India, 1904–5; decorated for special services, 1904. Member, RSA; FRBS. *Publications:* numerous articles in Gazetteer of Baluchistan, 1891, of Persia, 1892; description of country and routes, between Baghdad, Nejf, and Karbela, in Mesopotamia, 1892; and Baluchistan and Persia, 1886, with scientific appendices and illustrated Diary. *Recreations:* shooting, fishing, literary works, politics. *Address:* 20 Roland Gardens, SW. *Clubs:* Junior United Service, Authors'.

Died 21 Nov. 1918.

JENNINGS, Gen. Sir Robert Melvill, KCB 1909 (CB 1896); *b* 20 Nov. 1841; *s* of Rev. M. J. Jennings, MA; *m* 1873, Dame Agnes Mary (*d* 1920), *d* of Rev. J. S. Gilderdale; one *s* one *d*. Entered Bengal Cavalry, 1859; Maj.-Gen. 1895; Lt-Gen. 1900; General, 1904; served North-West Frontier, India, 1863–64 (medal with clasp); Egyptian war, 1862 (despatches, brevet of Col, 4th class Osmanieh, Khedive's star); Hon. Colonel 6th PW Cavalry. *Address:* c/o H. S. King & Co., 9 Pall Mall, SW1.

Died 16 Aug. 1922.

JENNINGS, William Thomas, JP; Member, House of Representatives New Zealand, since 1902; *b* Auckland, New Zealand, 1 Jan. 1854; father from Lancaster, and mother from Fermanagh, maiden name M'Ivor; *m* 1886, Dora Mary Brannigan, of Australia. *Educ:* St Paul's and St Peter's Schools, Auckland. Was apprenticed to his uncle, the then proprietor of the New Zealander, daily paper, and learned the printing business; was manager Dunedin Age, evening paper, and filled responsible positions in other offices throughout the colony; late Member Legislative Council, New Zealand; was enthusiastic volunteer for number of years, attaining position Acting-Lt Hobson Rifles, and subseq. Hon. Lieut Auckland Engineer Corps; took part in three annual contests NZ Rifles Association's shooting tournaments; active member friendly societies for over 20 years, attaining positions President Hibernian Society, and Grand District President United Ancient Order of Druids; President Typographical Union, and President Tailoresses' Union, Auckland. *Publications:* written for various newspapers and periodicals. *Address:* Parliamentary Buildings, Wellington, NZ.

Died 6 Feb. 1923.

JERDAN, Rev. Charles, MA, DD (Edin), LLB (Lond.); senior minister of Sir Michael Street United Free Church, Greenock, since 1884; *b* 25 March 1843; *s* of David Jerdan and Elisabeth Smiles; *m* 1st, 1870, Jane Forbes (*d* 1902), *d* of George Paterson, Glasgow; one *s*; 2nd, 1905, Agnes, *d* of John Haddow Carmichael, Greenock. *Educ:* Edinburgh University; Divinity Hall of United Presbyterian Church. Ordained at Dennyloanhead, Stirlingshire, 1867, and minister there till 1878; minister of Tay Square Church, Dundee, 1879–84; junior Principal Clerk of United Free Church General Assembly, 1907; Senior Clerk, 1916–20; served on many important committees of United Presbyterian and United Free Church Supreme Courts. *Publications:* Messages to the Children, 1897; For the Lord's Table, 1899; For the Lambs of the Flock, 1901; Gospel Milk and Honey, 1905; Pastures of Tender Grass, 1909; Manna for Young Pilgrims, 1912; Seed-Corn and Bread, 1915; The Wells of Salvation, 1919; Scottish Clerical Stories and Reminiscences, 1920; The One Saving Name, 1922; contributions to the Pulpit Commentary, Hosea, Hebrews, James. *Address:* 68 Union Street, Greenock.

Died 1926.

JERMYN, Sir Alfred, Kt 1919; *b* 4 June 1845; *s* of William and Harriott Jermyn; *m* Ellen, 3rd *d* of late James Horatio Bobby of Diss, Norfolk; eight *c*. *Educ:* King Edward VI Grammar School, Wymondham. Until 1915 senior partner in the firms of Jermyn & Perry and Jermyn & Sons of King's Lynn, Hunstanton and Oakham, drapers; Founder and Chairman of Berry & Stanton, Ltd, Sheerness; Jermyn, Smart & Smith, Ltd, New Brompton; Chairman and Director Hobbie's Manufacturing Co. Ltd, Dereham and London; Chairman and Director Foster & Bird Ltd, King's Lynn; also of the East Coast Steamship Co. Ltd, of King's Lynn, Hull and Newcastle; Director of Savage's Engineering Co. Ltd, and of the King's Lynn Docks and Railway Co. Ltd; formerly member of the Norfolk County Council for 15 years; Commissioner of Taxes (Land and Income); Chairman and Governor of High School for Girls; Governor of King Edward VII Grammar School, King's Lynn; JP and Alderman of the Borough; Mayor of King's Lynn, 1898; Member of the Wheelwrights' Company, City of London; Member of Philanthropic Lodge of Freemasons, and of the Foresters, Rechabites, Shepherds, and Good Templar Societies; widely known in Wesleyan Methodist and Free Church circles; President of the West Norfolk Federation of Free Church Councils. *Recreations:* public service, golf. *Address:* Burleigh House, King's Lynn. *T:* 34. *Club:* West Norfolk, King's Lynn and County, King's Lynn.

Died 27 June 1921

JERNINGHAM, Charles Edward Wynne; JP County of London; Member of the Cable Censors' Committee at the Press Bureau, 1914; *b* 26 March 1854; *y s* of Charles William Edward Jerningham, late of Painswick, Gloucestershire, and Emma, *d* of Evan Wynne Roberts of Grove House, Surrey; *heir-pres.* to the baronetcy of Jerningham. *Educ:* Beaumont and Stonyhurst; for some time Senior Philosophe at the latter. Was the last to receive a nomination for the Grenadier Guards before the adoption of the competitive examination system. For twenty-two years wrote the Letter from the Linkman in Truth over the signature of Marmaduke, and for fourteen years contributed a weekly article to the Graphic over the same signature. Editor, Vanity Fair, 1912. With Sir Reginald Beauchamp—the originator—helped to found the Self-Help Emigration Society; Member, Executive Council of the Commons and Footpaths Protection Society, and the Coal-Smoke Prevention Association; corresponding Member of the Archæological Society of France; founded The Art Collectors' Protection Association; and with W. Lacon Threlford, The Institute of Linguists, 1910. In 1906 presented to the nation the collection of prints of the Royal London Parks now permanently exhibited at the London Museum. Catholic; Radical. *Publications:* joint author (with Mr Ralph Nevill) Piccadilly to Pall Mall, 1908; The Maxims of Marmaduke, 1910; The Bargain Book, 1911. *Recreations:* a collector of old English glass, composer of waltzes and songs. *Clubs:* St James's, Bachelors', New, Ranelagh, etc.

Died 7 Feb. 1921.

JEROME, Jerome Klapka; writer; *b* Walsall, 2 May 1859; *o* surv. *s* of Rev. Jerome Clapp Jerome; *m* 1888, Georgina Henrietta Stanley, *d* of Lieut Nesza of the Spanish Army; one *d*. *Educ:* Marylebone Grammar School. Clerk; schoolmaster; actor; journalist; editor of The Idler (with Robert Barr), 1892–97; of To-Day, 1893–97. *Publications:* On the Stage and Off, 1888; Idle Thoughts of an Idle Fellow, 1889; Three Men in a Boat, 1889; Diary of a Pilgrimage, 1891; Novel Notes, 1893; John Ingerfield, 1894; Barbara, 1886; Fennel, 1888; Sunset, 1888; New Lamps for Old, 1890; Ruth, 1890; Wood Barrow Farm, 1891; Prude's Progress, 1895; Rise of Dick Halward, 1896; Sketches in Lavender, 1897; Letters to Clorinda, 1898; The Second Thoughts of an Idle Fellow, 1898; Three Men on the Bummel, 1900; Miss Hobbs, 1900; Paul Kelver, 1902; Tea Table Talk, 1903; Tommy & Co., 1904; Idle Ideas in 1905; Susan in Search of a Husband, 1906; The Passing of the Third Floor Back, 1907; The Angel and the Author, 1908; Fanny and the Servant Problem, 1908; They and I, 1909; The Master of Mrs Chilvers, 1911; Esther Castways, 1913; The Great Gamble, 1914; Malvina of Brittany, 1917; Cook, 1917; All Roads lead to Calvary, 1919; Anthony John, 1923; My Life and Times, an Autobiography, 1926. *Address:* 41 Belsize Park, Hampstead, NW.

Died 14 June 1927.

JEROME, Thomas Stroud, ISO 1903; Chief Inspector of Works, War Office. *Address:* War Office, SW.

Died 1 April 1917.

JERRED, Sir Walter (Tapper), KCB 1918 (CB 1912); Assistant Secretary, Local Government Board, since 1910; *b* 1864; *m* 1901, Gertrude, *d* of John Kirkbank-Lamin. LLB, MA. Barrister, Middle Temple. *Address:* Local Government Board, SW.

Died Oct. 1918.

JERROLD, Laurence; *b* London, 1873; *e s* of Evelyn (*e s* of Blanchard, *e s* of Douglas Jerrold) and Florence Yapp; *m* 1908, Germaine, *d* of late Paul Leprince-Ringuet, Paris; two *s* one *d*. *Educ:* Paris Univ. (Bachelor of Letters and Philosophy). Founded at 20 with other Jeunes, a Jeune Revue: The Magazine International, in which he published translations into French of the most Whitmanish of the Leaves of Grass, and which started a new French literary movement in praise of Nature and Life, and thereupon died; wrote in French on English literature (Revue Blanche; Humanité Nouvelle, etc); and in English on French literature and life (political questions, drama, art, music, in English and American reviews and in special journalistic correspondence); chief Paris correspondent of the Daily Telegraph. *Publications:* The Real France, 1911; The French and the English, 1913; France To-day, 1916. *Address:* 45 Rue Ampère, Paris; Les Peupliers, Petites Dalles, Seine Inférieure, France.

Died Oct. 1918.

JERSEY, 8th Earl of, *cr* 1697; **George Henry Robert Child Villiers;** Viscount Grandison, 1620; Viscount Villiers and Baron Hoo, 1691; DL, JP Oxon, and JP Middlesex; CA Oxfordshire and Middlesex; High Steward of City of Oxford; *b* 2 June 1873; *e s* of 7th Earl of Jersey and Margaret, Countess of Jersey; *S* father, 1915; *m* 1908, Lady Cynthia Almina Constance Mary Needham, *o d* of 3rd Earl of Kilmorey; two *s* two *d*. *Educ:* Eton; New College, Oxford. Owned about 19,400 acres. *Heir: s* Viscount Grandison, *b* 15 Feb. 1910. *Address:* Osterley Park, Isleworth; Middleton Park, Bicester; Baglan House, Briton Ferry, S Wales. *Clubs:* Carlton, Turf, Bachelors', Jockey.

Died 31 Dec. 1923.

JERVOISE, Sir Eustace James Clarke, 6th Bt, *cr* 1813; late Captain South Lancashire Regiment; *b* 14 March 1870; *s* of Alan Arthur Clarke Jervoise, *nephew* of Rev. Sir Samuel Clarke Jervoise, 1st Bt, and Helen Jane, *d* of Major J. Cruickshank; *S* uncle, 1911. *Heir: half-b* Dudley Alan Lestock Clarke-Jervoise [*b* 27 Nov. 1876; *m* 1908, Grace Estre, *y d* of Walter Ellison of Eastbrook, Wellingborough. *Address:* Evesham Cottage, Hailsham]. *Address:* Idsworth, Horndean, Hants.

Died 11 May 1916.

JERWOOD, Rev. Thomas Frederick; Hon. Canon of Peterborough since 1915. Rural Dean of Rothwell II, 1900–21; Rector of Little Bowden, 1874–1924. *Address:* 8 Webster Gardens, Ealing, W5.

Died 29 Dec. 1926.

JESSE, Richard Henry; President of University of Missouri 1891–1908, Emeritus Professor of Ancient and Mediæval History, 1909; *b* Ball Farm (birthplace of Washington's mother), Lancaster, Co. Va, 1 March 1853; *s* of W. T. Jesse and Mary Claybrook; *m* 1882, Addie Henry Polk of Princess Anne, Md; three *s* three *d*. *Educ:* Hanover Academy; University of Virginia; Europe. LLD, Tulane University, 1891; University of Wisconsin, 1904; South Carolina College, 1905; Missouri Valley College, 1906; Washington University, 1907; University of Missouri, 1908. Instructor in French and Mathematics, Hanover Academy, 1875–76; Dean of Academic Department, University of Louisiana, 1878–84; Professor of Latin, Tulane University, New Orleans, 1884–91. A member of the Committee of Ten, 1891 (National Educational Association); Chairman, Section Higher Education, NEA, 1898; President State Teachers Association of Missouri, 1899; President Southern Association Colleges and Secondary Schools, 1903 and 1905; awarded medal for services to Education; President of National Association of State Universities, 1905–6; delegate from United States to first International Congress of Radiology in Belgium, 1905; offered retirement on Carnegie Foundation; offer accepted after July 1, 1908. *Publications:* Missouri Literature (with E. A. Allen); papers in transactions of various societies, etc. *Died 1921.*

JESSEL, Albert Henry, KC 1906; *b* 31 Oct. 1864; *y s* of late Henry Jessel and Julia, *d* of late Louis Cohen; *m* Ella, 3rd *d* of late George C. Raphael; three *s* three *d*. *Educ:* Clifton; Balliol College, Oxford (MA). Called to Bar, 1889; practised in Chancery Division; Vice-President of United Synagogue; late President South London Jewish Schools, and Hon. Sec. Jewish Voluntary Schools Association; contested (C) Accrington Division, Lancs, January 1910; Central Hackney, December 1910. *Publications:* joint editor of volume on Companies in Encyclopædia of Forms and Precedents; article on Executors and Administrators in the Encyclopædia of the Laws of England. *Recreations:* riding, shooting, golf. *Address:* 6 Gloucester Square, W. *T:* 3322 Paddington. *Clubs:* Carlton, Junior Carlton, United, Cecil, 1900. *Died 2 Jan. 1917.*

JESSEL, Sir Charles James, 1st Bt, *cr* 1883; JP, DL; MA; Chairman of the Imperial Continental Gas Association; *b* London, 11 May 1860; *e s* of late Rt Hon. Sir George Jessel, Master of the Rolls; *m* 1890, Edith, 2nd *d* of late Rt Hon. Sir Julian Goldsmid, 3rd Bt, MP; two *s* two *d*. *Educ:* Rugby; Balliol Coll. Oxford (MA). Barrister, Lincoln's Inn, 1885; did not practise. *Recreation:* shooting. *Heir: s* George Jessel, MC, Capt. TF Reserve [*b* 28 May 1891; *m* 1923, Muriel, *d* of late Col J. W. Chaplin, VC, and *widow* of Major F. Swetenham]. *Address:* 31 Hill Street, W1. *T:* Grosvenor 1696; Ladham House, Goudhurst, Kent. *Clubs:* Garrick, Brooks's, Beefsteak.

Died 15 July 1928.

JESSON, Charles; late Organiser of the Musicians' Union; MP (Co.Lab) for Walthamstow W, Dec. 1918–Nov. 1922; *b* Leicester, 1 June 1862; *s* of John William Jesson, boot and shoe manufacturer; *m* 1889, Emily Roberts; one *d*. *Educ:* public schools in Leicester. Served as musician in the Army. Mem., LCC, 1906–19. *Recreation:* politics. *Address:* 33 Meteor Road, Westcliffe-on-Sea, Essex. *T:* Southend 1100. *Died 21 Sept. 1926.*

JESSOP, Lt-Comdr John de Burgh, DSO 1917; RN, retired; *b* 28 Aug. 1885; *o s* of late William de Burgh Jessop of Overton Hall, Derbys, and Judith, 2nd *d* of Sir John Gay Newton Alleyne, 3rd Bt; *m* 1917, Ethel Joane, *d* of Capt. C. H. Hill, late Gloucester Regt; one *d*. Served European War, 1914–18.

Died 23 March 1924.

JESSOP, Walter Hamilton Hylton, FRCS; JP; Senior Ophthalmic Surgeon and Lecturer on Ophthalmic Medicine and Surgery, St Bartholomew's Hospital; Ophthalmic Surgeon, Foundling Hospital; Examiner in Ophthalmology, Queen's University, Belfast; President, Ophthalmological Society, UK; *b* 1853. *Educ:* Bedford; Caius College, Camb. MA, MB. Late Hunterian Professor of Comparative Anatomy and Physiology, Royal College of Surgeons. *Publications:* Manual of Ophthalmic Surgery and Medicine. *Address:* 73 Harley Street, W; *T:* Paddington 1077; The Mill House, Sutton Courtenay, Berks. *T:* Abingdon 87. *M:* 6453LC; 7557LB. *Clubs:* Reform, Burlington Fine Arts; Berkshire. *Died 16 Feb. 1917.*

JETTÉ, Sir Louis Amable, KCMG 1901; LLD; Chief Justice of the Court of King's Bench, Quebec, 1909; retired 1911; *b* L'Assomption, PQ, 15 Jan. 1836; *s* of late Amable Jetté, merchant, and Caroline Gauffreau, *g d* of a St Domingo planter; *m* 1862, Berthe, *d* of Toussaint Laflamme. Called to the Bar, 1857; engaged in journalism; elected to House of Commons for Montreal (East), 1872, re-elected in 1874;

appointed Judge Superior Court, 1878; re-appointed, 1908; Chief Justice Province of Quebec, 1909–11; Professor of Civil Law, Laval University, 1878; LLD; subsequently Dean of the Faculty at Montreal. Member of the Alaskan Boundary Tribunal, 1903; Lieutenant-Governor of the Province of Quebec, 1898–1908. Commander of the Legion of Honour of France, 1898. *Address:* 71 d'Auteuil Street, Quebec. *Clubs:* St James's, Montreal; Garrison, Quebec.

Died May 1920.

JEUNE, John Frederic Symons-, JP Co. Oxon; Examiner of Standing Orders for the Houses of Lords and Commons; barrister, Inner Temple; *b* 10 Dec. 1849; 2nd *s* of late Rt Rev. Francis Jeune, Bishop of Peterborough, and *b* of late Lord St Helier, PC, GCB; *m* 1873, Frances Susannah, *d* of Richard Hanmer Bunbury, Capt. RN; one *s* one *d* (and one *s* decd). *Educ:* Rugby. Late Lt W Somerset Yeomanry. KGStJ. Assumed additional name and arms of Symons under the will of his great-uncle, Rev. B. P. Symons, DD, Warden of Wadham College, Oxford. *Address:* Runnymede House, Old Windsor. *Clubs:* Travellers', Windham, Wellington, Beefsteak.

Died 8 Feb. 1925.

JEVONS, Shirley Byron; editor of The Sportsman, 1903–11; *b* Doncaster; *s* of late John William Jevons, founder and proprietor of the Nottingham Daily Express; *m* 1887, Mary Wigley of Nottingham. *Educ:* Makepeace Hall College, Yorkshire. Served in the Army. Sub-editor Birmingham Daily Gazette, 1885–90; dramatic critic and assistant editor of the Sportsman, 1890–1903; retired, 1923. *Publications:* Private Lawrie and his Love; Baffled; The Livingstone Mystery; and other tales. *Recreation:* study. *Address:* Flat 7, Orchard House, SE5.

Died 6 Oct. 1928.

JODHPUR, HH Raj Rajeshwar Maharaja Dhiraj Maharaja Sri Sir Sumer Singhji Sahib Bahadur of, KBE 1918; Rajhai-Hind; *b* 14 Jan. 1898; *s* of late Maharaja Sir Sirdar Singhji Sahib Bahadur; ascended the gaddi 5 April 1911; *m* sister of HH the Jamsahib of Nawanagar; one *d*. *Educ:* Wellington College. Placed the whole of the resources of the State at the disposal of the British Government during European War; served at the head of the Jodhpur Lancers at the front; made an Hon. Lieut in the British Army; head of the great Rathore clan of Rajputs, a branch of the great Solar race of antiquity; the State of Marwar over which he ruled is the largest State in Rajputana. *Recreations:* polo, hunting. *Address:* Jodhpur, Marwar State, India.

Died 3 Oct. 1918.

JOGLEKAR, Rao Bahadur Ramchandra Narayan, ISO 1913; BA; Chief Land Officer Tata Hydro-electric Department Bombay; Collector, Baroda State, 1917–20; sometime General Adviser to the Chief of Inchalkaranji; *b* Satara, 8 Dec. 1858; *e s* of late Narayan Bhikaji Joglekar, retired Deputy Collector; four *s* four *d*. *Educ:* Deccan Coll., Poona. Held non-gazetted appointments in Nasik, Satara, Ahmednagar, Poona, and Sholapur Districts, 1883–99; Deputy Collector, 1899; Deputy Collector, 1st grade, and Native Assistant to the Commissioner, Central Division, 1901–16. *Publications:* The Court-Fee Manual; Alienation Manual; the annotated Bombay Land Revenue Code, Act 5 of 1879, revised and brought up to 1 Oct. 1920 and Watan Act. *Address:* 203 Kala Haud, Shukrawar, Peth, Poona City. *Club:* Dekkan Gymkhana.

Died 16 April 1928.

JOHNS, Rev. Claude Hermann Walter, LittD, DD; *b* Banwell, Somersetshire, 4 Feb. 1857; *e s* of late Rev. Walter Pascoe Johns, and Eleanor, *d* of Charles Gilbert, of Mutford Hall; *m* 1910, Agnes Sophia, *d* of late Rev. John Griffith, LLD. *Educ:* Faversham Grammar School; Queens' College, Cambridge (School and College Exhibitioner, Foundation Scholar); 27 Wrangler 1880; MA 1885; LittD 1909; Hon. DD 1915. Second Master Horton College, Tasmania, 1880–84; Paston Grammar School, 1885–87; Tutor at St Peter's College, Peterborough, 1887–92; ordained 1887; Curate of St Botolph's Helpston, 1887–88; St John's, Peterborough; St Mark's, Peterborough; Assistant Chaplain of Queens' College, Cambridge, 1892–1901; Edwardes Fellow of Queens' College, 1903–09; Lecturer in Assyriology at Queens' College, 1895–1909; at King's College, London, 1904–10; Rector of St Botolph's Parish, Cambridge, 1892–1909; Hon. Fellow, Queens' College, 1915; Master of St Catharine's College, Cambridge, 1909–19, and *ex officio* Canon Residentiary of Norwich. *Publications:* Assyrian Deeds and Documents of the 7th century BC; An Assyrian Doomsday Book; The Oldest Code of Laws; Babylonian and Assyrian Laws, Contracts and Letters; The Year Names of the First Dynasty of Babylon; The Bohlen Lectures on the Religious Significance of Semitic Proper Names; History of Assyria; History of Babylonia; The Schweich Lectures on the relations between the Laws of Babylon and the Laws of the

Hebrew Peoples; numerous articles and notes on Assyriology a Biblical Archæology in scientific journals and dictionaries. *Recreatio* cricket, football, tennis, collector of insects, ferns, and birds' eggs Tasmania. *Address:* Rathmines, Barnes Close, Winchester.

Died 20 Aug. 192

JOHNS, Col Sir William Arthur, Kt 1914; CB 1917; CIE 19 AMICE; temporary Colonel in army; Superintending Engineer sir 1906; *b* 6 Dec. 1858. *Educ:* St Columba's, Ireland; Uppingham; R College. Entered India PWD, 1880; employed with Seistan Bound Commission, 1902–3; Frontier Surveys, 1912–13; served German E Africa, 1915–17 (despatches, CB). *Address:* Sunnylands, Carrickferg Ireland. *Club:* East India United Service.

Died 2 June 191

JOHNSON, Rev. Arthur Henry, MA; Chaplain of All Souls Colle Oxford and Fellow, 1869–74 and since 1906; Modern Histc Lecturer at University College, Oxford, since 1885; *b* 8 Feb. 184 2nd *s* of Captain George J. Johnson, of Castlesteads, Cumberlar and Frederica, *yr d* of Sir Frederick Hankey, KCMG; *m* 1873, Bert Jane, *y d* of Robert Bentley Todd, MD (Oxon), FRS; two *s*. *Ed* Eton; Exeter College, Oxford. Priest, 1872; Chairman of the Mode History Board, 1893–1912; Hon. Secretary to Curators of t University Parks, 1911–24; Ford Lecturer for 1909; Modern Histc Lecturer to Pembroke College, 1874–84, St John's College, 1875–8 Wadham College, 1875–84, Trinity College, 1876–1903, Hertfo College, 1876–1903, Worcester College, 1883–85, Corpus Chri College, 1884–85, Balliol College, 1884–90, Merton Colleg 1884–1923. *Publications:* Europe in the XVI Century; T Enlightened Despot; The Disappearance of the Small Landowne The History of the Drapers' Company; Letters of Charles Grevi and Henry Reeve. *Recreations:* Oxford running Blue; fishing, shootir hunting. *Address:* All Souls College, Oxford; 5 South Parks Roa Oxford. *M:* BY 9892.

Died 31 Jan. 192

JOHNSON, Bertha Jane, MA (Oxon) by decree, 1920; Poor La Guardian since 1894; *b* London, 1846; *y d* of late Robert Bentl Todd, MD (Oxon), FRS, sometime Professor of Anatomy a Physiology, King's College, London; *m* 1873, Rev. Arthur Johnson, MA, Fellow and Chaplain and tutor, All Souls Colleg Oxford; two *s*. *Educ:* home; Slade School of Art. Artist, portra exhibited at Royal Academy, etc; Member of Council of La Margaret Hall, Oxford, 1879–1926; for many years Vice-Chairm of Oxford Charity Organisation Society; Member of the origir Committee of the Association for the Education of Women Oxford; Hon. Secretary with supervision of Home Students, 1883–9 Principal of Home Students, 1894–1910; Principal of the Society Oxford Home Students, appointed by the University, 1910–21; the original Committee of Lady Margaret Hall; Hon. Secretar 1880–1914; member of Education Committee, Oxfordshire Coun Council, 1903–22, and co-opted Member of its Examining Boa till 1924. *Address:* 5 South Parks Road, Oxford. *Club:* Universi Women's.

Died 24 April 192

JOHNSON, Ven. Charles, JP; Archdeacon of Zululand ar Missionary at St Augustine's; *b* Barnesley, Yorkshire, 3 Sept. 185 *s* of Wm Johnson; *m d* of Canon Jenkinson; five *s* five *d*. *Edu* Maritzburg College; private tuition. Began mission work as missiona at Springvale, Natal; after work in other places, was sent to the peop of Hlubi, the well-known Basuto chief, then in Natal, who ask that he might go with him to that part of Zululand which had bee given to him as a reward for his services in the Zulu war; first bega the Memorial Mission on the battlefield of Isandhlwana; after a yea went to a place about 10 miles away, nearer the chief's own hous this place was then called St Augustine's, Rorke's Drift; the peop were all heathen and very ignorant; had 67 native teachers under hir and established 38 out-stations round his central place, besides a larg number of places where services were held, called preaching centre had about 8000 baptized Christians, and 1700 under regul instruction. *Publications:* various Zulu books and translations. *Addre* St Augustine's, Zululand. *TA:* Vaut's Drift, Natal.

Died 1 Nov. 192

JOHNSON, Claude Goodman; Managing Director of Rolls-Royc Ltd, London, Derby, Bombay; Managing Director of Automobil Rolls-Royce (France), Ltd, Paris; Managing Director of Rolls-Royc of America, Incorporated; *b* 1864; *s* of late William Goodma Johnson, Science and Art Department, South Kensington. *Educ:* Paul's School; Art School, South Kensington. Principal clerk, Imperi Institute, from its inception for 10 years; first Secretary Roy Automobile Club, 5½ years; as such, organised the first pure automobile Exhibition held in this country, 1899; the 1000 mile reliability trial of automobiles, 1900, and the campaign throughout the country with a view to educating County Councils as to the utility and safety of motor vehicles; Joint Manager with late Hon. Charles S. Rolls, of C. S. Rolls & Co.; this Co. acquired the whole of the output of motor cars designed by Mr F. H. Royce of Royce, Ltd (the Rolls-Royce cars); these subsequently became Rolls-Royce, Ltd. *Address:* Adelphi Terrace House, WC2. *T:* Gerrard 7161; Villa Vita, Kingsdown, Deal. *T:* Kingsdown, Deal 12. *Clubs:* Royal Thames Yacht, Ranelagh, Royal Automobile.

Died 11 April 1926.

JOHNSON, Cyrus, RI; *b* 1 Jan. 1848. *Educ:* Perse Grammar School, Cambridge. First exhibited in RA 1871, genre and then landscape; and as a portrait painter in 1877; among his sitters were Mrs Luttrell (1877), Mrs Perceval, W. H. C. Plowden, FRS, Sir John Duckworth, the Rev. Edward Thring, R. Neville Grenville, Rt Hon. Edward Gibson, Lord Ebury, Canon Kynaston, Dr Merry, Lord Halsbury, Sir George Macfarren, and Sir Bryan Donkin. *Address:* 8 Margravine Gardens, Baron's Court, W6. *Club:* Arts.

Died 27 Feb. 1925.

JOHNSON, Rev. Frank; Editor of Sunday School Chronicle and Times since 1899; British Congregationalist and Examiner, 1909–12; Publications Secretary National Sunday School Union since 1911; Founder and Editor of the Graded Quarterlies (Primary, Junior, Intermediate, and Senior); Hon. Sec. British International Lessons Council since 1913; *m* 1894, Alice, *d* of William Cottom, of Birmingham; one *s* two *d*. *Educ:* Wolverhampton; London University; New College (Pye Smith Scholar of latter and Associate of the Theological Senatus). Schoolmaster for two years; Assistant Master, Model School, Borough Road Training College; minister of Congregational Church, Stone, Staffs, 1893–99, during which period held the post of Secretary to Staffs Congregational Union; minister, Hemel Hempstead Congregational Church, 1916–18. *Publications:* Under Cross and Crescent, 1904; Faith and Vision, 1906; Bible Teaching by Modern Methods, 1907; Life of Sir Francis F. Belsey, 1914; The Disciples' Prayer, 1914; The Way of Success, 1925; contributed largely to his own and various other periodicals. *Recreations:* rose culture, cycling, music. *Address:* 57 and 59 Ludgate Hill, EC4. *Died 13 Sept. 1927.*

JOHNSON, Maj. Frederick Henry, VC 1915; BSc (1st Hons Lond); temp. Major while in command of a Field Co., 231st Field Co. RE; *b* Streatham, 15 Aug. 1890; *s* of Samuel Rogers Johnson; unmarried. *Educ:* Whitgift Middle School; St Dunstan's College, Catford; Battersea Polytechnic; University of London. Worked as engineering apprentice and improver, 1907–11; Whitworth Exhibitioner, 1910; Day Student at Battersea Polytechnic, 1911–14; Chairman, Students' Council, editor of Polytechnic Magazine, 1914; graduated in Engineering, University of London, as internal student, 1914; Member of London University OTC, 1914; temp. 2nd Lieut RE 1914; served European War, 1914–16 (wounded on Hill 70, despatches, VC). *Recreations:* cycling, rowing. *Address:* 24 Cranworth Gardens, Brixton, SW. *Died Dec. 1917.*

JOHNSON, George William, CMG 1905; MA; Principal Clerk in Colonial Office, 1900–17; *b* 5 July 1857; *e s* of late W. H. F. Johnson, MA, JP, of Llandaff House, Cambridge; *m* 1883, Lucy, 6th *d* of late James Nutter of Cambridge; two *s* two *d*. *Educ:* his father's school; Perse Grammar School; Trinity Coll., Camb. (Foundation Scholar 1877), 8th Wrangler and 3rd class Classical Tripos, 1880. Appointed 2nd class Clerk Colonial Office, 1881. *Publications:* Dickens Dictionary of Cambridge; editor of the Christian Socialist, 1891; occasional reviews in the Spectator, etc; (in conjunction with his wife) Memoir of Josephine E. Butler, 1909; The State and Sexual Morality, 1920. *Recreations:* reading, chess. *Address:* 22 Westbourne Park Villas, W2. *T:* Park 1948. *Club:* National Liberal.

Died 13 Feb. 1926.

JOHNSON, Sir Henry James, Kt 1911; solicitor; *b* 14 June 1851; *s* of Manuel John Johnson, Radcliffe Observer, Oxford, and Caroline, *d* of Prof. J. A. Ogle, Oxford; *m* 1884, Pauline, *d* of Julius Hinterhuber, Salzburg; one *s*. *Educ:* Winchester; Oxford, MA. President, Law Society, 1910–11; firm, Waltons and Co., 101 Leadenhall Street, EC. *Address:* 55 Sloane Gardens, SW. *T:* Victoria 3481. *Clubs:* United University, Savile. *Died 1 March 1917.*

JOHNSON, Rt. Rev. James, DD (Durham), MA; Assistant Bishop of Western Equatorial Africa since 1900. *Educ:* Freetown Grammar School; Fourah Bay College, Sierra Leone. Catechist, CMS, 1858; Tutor CMS Grammar School, 1860; Catechist, Christ Church, 1861; ordained, 1863; Missionary Curate of Christ Church till 1873; Native

Missionary in charge of St Paul's Church, Lagos, Yoruba Country, 1874; Superintendent of interior Yoruba Mission, 1877; Pastor of St Paul's Church, Lagos, 1881; Secretary Native Church Committee and Church Missions; Diocesan Inspector; Bishop's Examining Chaplain; Member of Bible Translation Committee; Member of Legislative Council and Board of Education, 1886. *Publication:* Yoruba Heathenism. *Address:* Lagos, West Africa.

Died 18 May 1917.

JOHNSON, Rt. Rev. Joseph Horsfall, DD, STD; Bishop of Los Angeles, California, USA; *b* 7 June 1847; *s* of Hon. Stephen Hotchkiss Johnson and Eleanor Horsfall; *m* 1881, *d* of Hon. Isaac Davis of Worcester, Mass; one *s*. *Educ:* private schools. Graduate in Arts, 1870, Williams College, General Theological Seminary, New York, 1873. Rector successively of Holy Trinity, Highland, NY; Trinity, Bristol, RI; St Peter's, Westchester, NY City; Christ Church, Detroit, Michigan. *Publications:* pamphlets and sermons. *Address:* Cathedral House, 615 S Figueroa Street, Los Angeles, California.

Died 18 May 1928.

JOHNSON, Brig.-Gen. Ronald Marr, CMG 1919; DSO 1917; late RFA; *b* 4 Nov. 1873; *s* of late Thomas Marr Johnson and Mrs A. Gunning Keen; *m* 1904, Gladys, *d* of Maj.-General Sir John Leach, KCVO; one *s*. *Educ:* Fonthill; Radley; RMA, Woolwich; Staff College, Quetta. Served China, 1900; European War, 1914–18; retired pay, 1923. *M:* PD 5677. *Clubs:* Army and Navy; Royal St George's Golf. *Died 15 Nov. 1925.*

JOHNSON, Lt-Col Thomas Gordon Blois-, CMG 1916; CIE 1918; Commandant 22nd Punjabis; *b* 27 Jan. 1867; 4th *s* of late Major W. T. Johnson. *Educ:* United Service College, Westward Ho; Sandhurst. Entered army, 1888; Indian Staff Corps, 1890; served NW Frontier of India, 1897–98; Relief of Malakand; operations in Bajaur Mohmand (medal, 2 clasps); Tirah, 1897–98 (clasp); NW Frontier of India, 1902; operations against Darwesh Khel-Waziris; commanded a detachment despatched to quell the rising in Bastar Native State; Mesopotamian Campaign, 1915 (severely wounded at Kut-El-Amara, CMG). *Recreations:* riding, sailing, golf, Champion of Northern India (Coulmarg, Kashmir), 1904, shooting. *Club:* Junior United Service.

Died 6 Nov. 1918.

JOHNSON, Lt-Col T. Pelham, DSO 1916; ASC; Officer Commanding 15th Division Train, BEF, France; *b* Stratford Rectory, Saxmundham, 16 June 1871; *s* of Rev. F. A. Johnson, BA, and Ellen, *d* of Richard Garrett of Carlton Hall, Saxmundham; *m* Lilian Dora, *e d* of late Col Henry Vere Hunt, Indian Staff Corps; one *d*. *Educ:* Woodbridge Grammar School; Queens' College, Cambridge; Royal Military College, Sandhurst. First Commission to Bedfordshire Regt, 1892; India, 1893–95; served Chitral campaign, 1895 (medal and clasp); transferred to ASC, 1896; served in East Africa and Uganda, 1898–1903 (East and Central African medal, 1900; African General Service medal, 1899–1900, despatches); served in South Africa, 1904–9; went to France with 4th Division, Aug. 1914; took 15th Div. Train to France, July 1915 (despatches 4 times, DSO). Croix de Chevalier du Mérite Agricole, April 1917.

Died June 1918.

JOHNSON, William, MBE 1918; MP (L-Lab) Nuneaton Division of Warwickshire, 1906–18; Member, Police Committee and Standing Joint-Committee since 1890; Member, Foleshill Board Guardians and Rural District Council since 1902; *b* Chilvers Cotton, 1849; father, collier; grandfather, collier; *m d* of a Butty collier; four *s* one *d*. *Educ:* Collycroft School. Factory worker twenty years, with brief intervals colliery worker with father; General Sec. and Agent, Warwickshire Miners' Association, 1885–1916; Treasurer of Midland Miners' Federation; County Councillor for Bedworth since 1889; Alderman, 1915; Education Committee, Warwickshire County Council, 1903; Chairman of Bedworth Parish Council since 1894; Governor of Nicholas Chamberlain's Charity. JP Warwickshire. *Publications:* Essay: Mazzini's Duties of Man; Machinery *v* Human Labour, based on Pattison's Mental Science. *Recreations:* cricket, music. *Address:* Bedworth, Warwickshire. *T:* Bedworth 8Y. *Club:* National Liberal.

Died 20 July 1919.

JOHNSON, Rev. William Cowper, MA; Hon. Canon Norwich, 1901. *Educ:* Trinity College, Cambridge. Curate of St Mary's, Nottingham, 1870–72; St Giles in the Fields, 1872–75; Flitton, Beds, 1875; Vicar Pulloxhill, Beds, 1875–80; Rural Dean of Hingham, 1896; Rector of Yaxham, 1880–1915. *Address:* 6 Christ Church Road, Newmarket Road, Norwich.

Died 6 April 1916.

JOHNSON, Rt. Hon. Sir William Moore, 1st Bt, *cr* 1909; PC 1881; *b* 1828; *s* of late Rev. William Johnson, Chancellor Diocese of Cloyne, Cork; *m* 1884, Susan, *d* of Richard Bayly, JP, Green Park, Kilmalloch, Limerick. *Educ:* Trinity Coll. Dublin (MA). Irish Barrister 1853; Law Adviser to the Crown in Ireland, 1868–74; QC 1872; Solicitor-General for Ireland, 1880–81; Attorney-General, 1881–83; MP Mallow, 1880–83; Judge High Court of Justice, King's Bench Division, Ireland, 1883–1909; Judge High Court of Admiralty (Ireland), 1893–1909. *Heir:* none. *Address:* 26 Lower Leeson Street, Dublin. *Clubs:* Reform; Dublin University; St George Yacht, Kingstown.   *Died 9 Dec. 1918 (ext).*

JOHNSON, Ven. William Percival; Archdeacon of Nyasa since 1896; Central Africa Itinerant Missionary. *Educ:* Bedford School; University College, Oxford (MA; DD 1911). Ordained, 1876. *Address:* Universities' Mission, Likoma, Nyasaland.
Died 11 Oct. 1928.

JOHNSTON, Andrew, JP, DL; *b* 23 May 1835; *s* of Andrew Johnston, MP for St Andrews Boroughs, and Priscilla, *e d* of Sir Thomas Fowell Buxton, 1st Bt, MP; *m* 1858, Charlotte, *e d* of Rev. George Trevelyan. *Educ:* Rugby; Univ. Coll. Oxford. MP (L) South Essex, 1868–74. High Sheriff, 1880–81; Chairman of Quarter Sessions, 1880–1910; Chairman Essex County Council, 1889–1915; Director Commercial Union Assurance Co., Ltd; New River Co., Ltd. *Address:* Forest Lodge, Woodford Green, Essex.
Died 28 Feb. 1922.

JOHNSTON, Col Charles Arthur, CB 1917; DSO 1917; MB; DPH (London); Indian Medical Service (retired); *b* 28 Feb. 1867; *m* Isabel Mary, *d* of late Dr J. H. Honeyman; one *s*. Capt. 1890; Major, 1902; Lt-Col 1910; Col 1920; served Manipur, 1891 (medal with clasp); Burma, 1891–92 (despatches, clasp); Tirah, 1897–98 (medal with clasp); China, 1900 (medal); European War, 1914–18 (DSO, CB, despatches twice); retired, 1920. *Address:* 6 Grosvenor Street, W1. *Club:* Junior United Service.
Died 23 April 1926.

JOHNSTON, Lt-Col Charles Evelyn, DSO 1918; MC 1918; *b* 29 May 1878; *e s* of Reginald Eden Johnston, of Terlings, Harlow, Essex; *m* 1905, Pleasance, *y d* of Col W. J. Alt, CB; three *s* one *d*. *Educ:* Eton; New College, Oxford (MA). Member of E. Johnson & Co. Ltd, 20 King William Street, EC; Director London Joint City and Midland Bank, London and Brazilian Bank, San Paulo Railway, Indemnity Mutual Marine Assurance, Brazilian Warrant Co. Lieut-Col London Regt (TAR); served European War, 1914–18 (despatches, DSO, MC). *Recreation:* Oxford VIII 1899 and 1900. *Address:* Little Offley, Hitchin; 160 St James' Court, SW. *Clubs:* Oxford and Cambridge, Leander, City of London.
Died 27 Aug. 1922.

JOHNSTON, Ven. Charles Francis Harding, MA; *b* Barnstaple, 6 Oct. 1842; *s* of Rev. G. Johnston, and Elizabeth, *d* of James Gordon Morgan, MD; *m* Kate, *d* of Richard Mallam, MRCS, Kidlington; two *s*. *Educ:* Barnstaple Grammar School; Christ's College, Cambridge (Wrangler, 2nd Classical Tripos). In Inland Revenue Dept, Somerset House, 1859–62; Civil Service Commission, 1862–63; Master, Trinity College, Glenalmond, 1867–68; ordained, 1867; Chaplain of HMIE, 1869–90; Domestic Chaplain to Bishop of Bombay, 1869–75; Archdeacon of Bombay, 1888–90; Curate of All Saints, Oxford, 1890–91; Vicar of Headington Quarry, Oxford, 1891–1916. *Publication:* Editor St Basil on the Holy Spirit, revised text, 1892. *Address:* Thelwall Vicarage, Warrington.
Died 22 Aug. 1925.

JOHNSTON, Brig.-Gen. Francis Earl, CB 1915; the Prince of Wales's (North Staffs Regiment); *b* 1 Oct. 1871; *m* Morna (*d* 1915). Served expedition to Dongola, 1896 (Egyptian medal with clasp, medal); S African War, 1900–2 (despatches twice, Queen's medal, 3 clasps; King's medal, 2 clasps); Dardanelles, 1914–15 (CB).
Died 8 Aug. 1917.

JOHNSTON, Sir George, 10th Bt, *cr* 1626, of that ilk, and of Caskieben; *b* 21 April 1845; *s* of late Robert Johnston, descended from a brother of the 5th Bt; *S* kinsman, Sir William Johnston, 1917; *m* 1876, Agnes Elizabeth, *d* of Rev. R. J. Sparkes. Sometime coffee planting in Ceylon. *Heir:* cousin Thomas Alexander Johnston, *b* 15 Dec. 1857. *Address:* Garlands, Ewhurst, Guildford.
Died 11 May 1921.

JOHNSTON, George Jameson, MA, MB; FRCSI; Visiting Surgeon and Clinical Lecturer, Royal City of Dublin Hospital; Professor of

and Examiner in Surgery, Royal College of Surgeons in Ireland; Consulting Surgeon Royal Hospital for Incurables, Dublin, and Masonic Orphan Boys' School; *b* 18 April 1866; *s* of Ronald Johnston, Mullaghmore, Co. Tyrone; unmarried. *Educ:* Royal School, Dungannon; School of Physic, Trinity College, Dublin. Ex-Demonstrator of Anatomy and Operative Surgery, School of Physic, TCD; ex-Assistant Surgeon Richmond Hospital; ex-Examiner in Anatomy Conjoint Board, RCPSI; Examiner in Surgery Conjoint Fellowship and Dental Boards, RCPI and RCSI; ex-Examiner in Clinical Surgery, Univ. Dublin; and in Surgery, National University of Ireland; ex-Member of Council Royal Coll. of Surgeons in Ireland; ex-Temp. Lt-Col RAMC in charge of Surgical Division of a base hospital, BEF; ex-Visiting Surgeon Dublin Castle Red Cross Hospital; mentioned for war work. *Publications:* papers on various surgical subjects. *Recreations:* golf, philately. *Address:* 13 Lower Fitzwilliam Street, Dublin. *T:* 1862. *Club:* Hibernian United Services, Dublin.
Died 8 Oct. 1926.

JOHNSTON, Sir Harry (Hamilton), GCMG 1901; KCB 1896 (CB 1890); JP; DSc Cambridge; Gold Medallist Zoological, Royal Geographical, and Royal Scottish Geographical Societies; Hon. Member Italian Geographical Society, and Royal Irish Zoological Societies; Trustee of the Hunterian Collection, Royal College of Surgeons; Hon. Life Member of the New York Zoological Society; *b* Kennington, London, 12 June 1858; *s* of John Brookes Johnston and Esther Laetitia Hamilton; *m* 1896, Hon. Winifred Irby, OBE, *d* of 5th Lord Boston, and *step-d* of Sir Henry Percy Anderson, KCB. *Educ:* Stockwell Grammar School; King's Coll., London; student Royal Academy of Arts, 1876–80. Medallist S Kensington School of Art, 1876; Hon. Member RWS. Silver medallist Zoological Society, 1896. Studied painting at RA and also in France; travelled in North Africa, 1879–80; explored Portuguese West Africa and River Congo, 1882–83; commanded Scientific Expedition of Royal Society to Mt Kilimanjaro, 1884; HM Vice-Consul in Cameroons, 1885; Acting Consul in Niger Coast Protectorate, 1887; Consul for province of Mozambique, 1888; expedition to Lakes Nyasa and Tanganyika (founding of the British Central Africa Protectorate), 1889; Commissioner and Consul-General, BCA, 1891; Consul-Gen., Regency of Tunis, 1897–99; Special Commissioner, Commander-in-Chief and Consul-General for Uganda Protectorate, etc, 1899–1901. War Medal, 1914–18. *Publications:* essays on the Tunisian Question, 1880–81; River Congo, 1884; Kilimanjaro, 1885; History of a Slave, 1889; Life of Livingstone, 1891; various blue-books and reports on West Africa, Central Africa, North Africa, and East Africa, 1888–1901; British Central Africa, 1897; A History of the Colonisation of Africa by Alien Races, 1899–1913; The Uganda Protectorate, 1902; British Mammals, 1903; The Nile Quest (History of the Exploration of the Nile), 1903; Liberia, 1906; George Grenfell and the Congo, 1908; A History of the British Empire in Africa, 1910; The Negro in the New World, 1910; The Opening-up of Africa, 1911; Views and Reviews, 1912; Common Sense in Foreign Policy, 1913; Phonetic Spelling, 1913; Pioneers in West Africa, Canada, India, Australasia, Tropical America, and South Africa (6 vols), 1911–13; A Gallery of Heroes and Heroines, 1915; The Truth about the War, 1916; The Black Man's Part in the War, 1917; The Gay Dombeys (a novel), 1919; Comparative Study of the Bantu and Semi-Bantu Languages, vol. i, 1919; vol. ii, 1922; Mrs Warren's Daughter, 1920; The Backward Peoples, 1920; The Man who did the Right Thing, 1921; The Veneerings, 1922; Little Life-Stories, 1923; The Story of My Life, 1923; Relations, 1925. *Recreations:* painting, biological studies, music. *Address:* St John's Priory, Poling, Arundel.
Died 31 July 1927.

JOHNSTON, Rev. Hugh William; Rector of North Cray since 1864; Hon. Canon of Canterbury, 1904. *Educ:* Trinity Coll. Cambridge. Ordained 1861; curate of Chaddesley-Corbet, Worcestershire, 1861–63; Salehurst, Sussex, 1863–64; Rural Dean, East Dartford, 1894–1913.
Died 1 Sept. 1918.

JOHNSTON, Rt. Hon. Sir James, Kt 1918; PC Ireland, 1919; Member of Senate of Northern Ireland; *b* 29 Nov. 1849; *m* 1876, Jeannie, *d* of George Cleland, of Ballywoolen, Co. Down. High Sheriff of Belfast, 1912; Lord Mayor, 1917 and 1918. *Address:* Belvoir Park, Newtownbreda, Co. Down. *Clubs:* Constitutional; Ulster Reform, Belfast.
Died 13 April 1924.

JOHNSTON, Rt. Rev. James Steptoe, DD; *b* 9 June 1843; *s* of James and Louisa C. B. Johnston; *m* 1865, Mary M. Green; two *s* two *d*. *Educ:* Oakland College, Miss; University of Va. Four years in Confederate Army (Lee's), Co. I. 11th Miss Regt till 1862; after that 2nd Lt Stuart's Cavalry. Deacon, 1869; priest, 1871; Rector of St James Church, Port Gibson, Miss, 1870–76; Ascension Church, Mt Stirling,

Ky, 1876–80; Trinity Church, Mobile, Ala, 1880–88; Bishop of West Texas, 1888–1914. *Publications:* sermons and articles in church and secular papers. *Address:* 517 E Myrtle Street, San Antonio, Texas.
Died 4 Nov. 1924.

JOHNSTON, Sir John Barr, Kt 1899; merchant; *b* 9 Aug. 1843; *e s* of John Johnston, Beragh, Co. Tyrone, Ireland; *m* 1877, Isabel, *d* of Alexander Weir, Ballindrait, Co. Donegal; one *s* three *d*. Alderman and Justice of the Peace for the City of Londonderry; Mayor of Londonderry, 1897–98; JP and Grand Juror for County Tyrone; High Sheriff of the County of the City of Londonderry, 1900. *Address:* Londonderry.
Died 12 Feb. 1919.

JOHNSTON, Rev. John Octavius, MA; Cathedral Chancellor, Lincoln; *b* Barnstaple, 1 Nov. 1852; *y s* of Rev. George Johnston and Elizabeth, *d* of James Gordon Morgan, MD, Barnstaple; *m* Harriette Louisa, *d* of Dalton Mallam, Oxford; two *s* one *d*. *Educ:* Barnstaple Grammar School; Keble Coll., Oxford, 1874–79. BA 1878; 2nd class Classics, 1st class Theology; Senior Hall Houghton Greek Testament Prize, 1880; MA 1881. Curate of Kidlington, Oxon, 1879–81; Principal of St Stephen's House, Oxford, 1881–84; Theological Tutor of Merton College, 1883–95; Chaplain, 1885–95; Vicar of All Saints', Oxford, 1885–95; Examiner in Honour School of Theology, 1890–92; Examining Chaplain to the Bishop of Oxford, 1880–1913; Vicar of Cuddesdon and Principal of Cuddesdon Theological College, 1895–1913; Honorary Canon of Christ Church, 1902–13; Proctor in Convocation for the Diocese of Oxford, 1902–17; Proctor for Lincoln Chapter, 1918. *Publications:* joint-editor of Three Anti-Pelagian Treatises of St Augustine; Dr Liddon's Life of Dr Pusey; Dr Pusey's Spiritual Letters; Life and Letters of H. P. Liddon, DD; Men of God. *Address:* Sub-deanery, Lincoln.
Died 6 Nov. 1923.

JOHNSTON, Reginald Eden, JP; Director, Bank of England; *b* 1847; *s* of Edward Johnston, 23 Queen's Gate Terrace, SW; *m* 1875, Alice (*d* 1907), *d* of Rev. C. Eyres, Great Melton, Norfolk; two *s* three *d*. *Address:* Terlings, Harlow. *Club:* Union.
Died 20 Nov. 1922.

JOHNSTON, Robert Mackenzie, ISO 1903; FSS; Registrar-General and Government Statistician. Fellow and Member of Council of the Royal Society of Tasmania; Member of Council and of Senate of the University of Tasmania; Fellow and Past President of Section F (Economics and Statistics) of the Australasian Association for the Advancement of Science; FRGSA; Hon. Foreign Corresponding Member of the Geological Society of Edinburgh. *Publications:* Systematic Account of the Geology of Tasmania; numerous publications relating to the Natural History of Tasmania. *Address:* Hobart, Tasmania.
Died 20 April 1918.

JOHNSTON, Robert Matteson, MA Cantab; Inner Temple, barrister-at-law; Professor of Modern History, Harvard University, since 1919; editor of The Military Historian and Economist; *b* Paris, 11 April 1867; *s* of W. E. Johnston, MD. *Educ:* schools, England, France, USA; Pembroke College, Cambridge. Engaged in business until 1900; first lectured at Harvard University, 1904; Professor of History, Bryn Mawr College, 1907; Assistant Professor History, Harvard, 1908–19. Secretary of the Military Efficiency Association. Major US army, attached to General Staff, AEF, 1918–19. *Publications:* The Roman Theocracy and the Republic, 1901; Napoleon, a short biography, 1904; The Napoleonic Empire in Southern Italy, 1904; Memoirs of Malakoff, 1906; The French Revolution, a short history, 1906; Leading American Soldiers, 1907; The Corsican, 1910; The Holy Christian Church, 1911; Mémoire de Marie Caroline, reine de Naples, 1912; Bull Run, 1913; Arms and the Race, 1915. *Recreations:* fencing, motoring. *Address:* Littlewood, Norfolk, Mass, USA. *Clubs:* Savile; Harvard, Boston.
Died 1 Jan. 1920.

JOHNSTON, Samuel; inventor; *b* Shelby, Orleans Co., NY, 9 Feb. 1835; *m* 1856, Arsula S. Vaughan, Cattaraugus Co., NY. *Educ:* common schools. Inventor of corn planters, rotary and disk harrows, self-rakes for harvesters, mowing machines, corn harvesters, self-raking reapers, platform reapers and binders, cold-rolling rolling-mills, roller reamers, roller forging mills; also a metal-working process by which finished articles are produced in duplicate from ores or metals; a method of veneering hard metals with soft or *vice versa*. Discoverer of a method of coking fuels of all kinds in particles so fine that they float in air, and the fuel is transported in pipes or burned within the apparatus to the desired temperature up to one equalling the electric furnace, or making it into water gas; a continuous roasting and smelting furnace which separates and recovers the various impurities of ores and recovers the metals; a method of treating the chimney gases and

converting them to heat; an apparatus for filling all forms of moulds for sand-moulding and making cores, giving uniform texture to the moulds or core—saving 90 per cent of labour. *Address:* 420 Ashland Avenue, Buffalo, NY.

JOHNSTON, Sir William, 9th Bt, *cr* 1626; JP; *b* 31 July 1849; *s* of Sir William Bacon Johnston, 8th Bt and Mary, *d* of William Tye; S father, 1865; unmarried. *Educ:* Merchiston Castle School, Edinburgh. Was in Oriental Bank, China; later Director of the Ceylon Tea Plantations Co., Ltd, London. *Recreations:* fencing, shooting, gardening. *Heir: kinsman* George Johnston, *b* 21 April 1845. *Address:* The Ranche, Buckhurst Hill, Essex. *Clubs:* Caledonian; Royal Northern, Aberdeen.
Died 22 Nov. 1917.

JOHNSTON, Vice-Adm. Charles; retired list; *b* 1843; *s* of James Johnston; *m* 1878, Janet, *d* of George Schonswar, JP, DL, Co. Gloucester; one *s* five *d*. *Educ:* Naval Academy, Gosport; HMS Illustrious. Specially promoted to Captain for services in Madagascar when in command of HMS Dryad; gained Gold Medal of the United Service Institution, 1884. *Publications:* articles on Naval Prize Law. *Address:* Mouswald Place, Ruthwell RSO, Dumfriesshire.
Died 2 Dec. 1927.

JOHNSTONE, Sir Donald (Campbell), Kt 1915; Chief Judge, Chief Court, Punjab, since 1915; *b* 23 Feb. 1857; *s* of Maj.-Gen. H. C. Johnstone, CB; two *s* one *d*. *Educ:* Edinburgh Academy. Passed into Indian Civil Service, 1877; proceeded to India, 1879; Secretary Revenue Board, Punjab, 1887–91; Sessions Judge, Punjab, 1894–1905; Puisne Judge, Chief Court, Punjab, till April 1915. *Address:* Chief Court, Lahore, Punjab.
Died 26 Nov. 1920.

JOHNSTONE, James William Douglas, CIE 1911; Inspector-General of Education, Gwalior State, Central India, 1894–1911; *b* Murree, Punjab, 30 Aug. 1855; *e s* of late Maj.-Gen. Henry Campbell Johnstone, CB, of the Indian Staff Corps. *Educ:* Edinburgh Academy and University. Appointed to Punjab Educational Dept, 1877; transferred to Foreign Dept of Govt of India, on appointment as Head-master, Mayo College, Ajmere; appointed principal Daly College, Indore, 1885; was official representative of Central India for collecting art products for Colonial and Indian Exhibition of 1886; services lent by Government of India to Gwalior State for employment as tutor to HH Maharaja Scindia, 1890; on HH's attaining his majority, was appointed Inspector Gen. of Education in the State, 1894; was also Census Comdr, Gwalior State, 1900–2 and 1910–11, in addition to ordinary duties; was employed on famine duty in 1897 and 1900; accompanied His Highness to England in 1902, to be present at the Coronation of King Edward, and received Coronation medal; was political officer with the Maharaja of Gwalior at King George V's Coronation (medal); RGS, and a Fellow of the Allahabad University; was a member of the Majlis-i-Khas or State Council, Gwalior State; retired 1911. *Publications:* Census Report of Gwalior State, 1901; Gwalior, 1905. *Recreations:* golf, tennis, shooting. *Address:* Queen Anne's Mansions, SW. *T:* Victoria 5510. *Clubs:* East India United Service; Royal and Ancient, St Andrews, NB.
Died 18 Oct. 1925.

JOHNSTONE, Lieut John Andrew, RFA and RFC; *b* 11 May 1893; *e s* of late Maj. James Henry L'Estrange Johnstone, MVO, JP, RE, and Amy Octavia, *y d* of late Andrew Wauchope. *Address:* The Hangingshaw, near Selkirk.
Died 20 May 1915.

JOHNSTONE, Col Montague George, DSO 1900; Hon. Colonel and late Colonel Commanding 3rd King's Own Yorkshire Light Infantry; *b* 21 March 1848; 2nd *s* of late Gen. Montague Cholmeley Johnstone and Louisa, *d* of late Lt-Gen. Sir Henry Somerset, KCB, KH, and *g d* of Lord Charles Somerset; *m* 1880, Agnes (*d* 1923), *widow* of Capt. Johnston Stansfeld and *yr d* of late Joseph Harrison, JP, DL, of Galligreaves and of Samlesbury Hall, Lancashire, Lord of the Manor of Hadley, Essex; two *s* one *d*. *Educ:* Cheltenham College. Formerly Maj. 2nd Dragoons (Royal Scots Greys); an extra ADC to Lord Lieut of Ireland, 1880 (Duke of Marlborough); served on Headquarters Staff in Bechuanaland Expedition, 1884–85; in former year assisted in raising the 2nd Mounted Rifles (Carrington's Horse), and in South Africa, 1900–1 (despatches, medal with 3 clasps, DSO and Lt-Colonelcy); employed by Master of the Horse and by Colonial Office, also was Commandant of Lambeth Palace Camp during Coronation of King Edward VII; commanded his present regiment during its embodiment in the Mediterranean, 1902; was a Lt-Col Reserve of Officers; commanded 1st Westminster Battalion, National Reserve; held several military appointments and belonged for many years to the King's Bodyguard for Scotland; employed by the War Office, on the Staff, 1914–18. Coronation medal, 1911. *Address:* 66 Beaufort Mansions, Chelsea, SW. *T:* Kensington 2968. *Club:* Naval and Military.   *Died 12 June 1928.*

JONES, Lt-Col Alfred Stowell, VC 1857; JP Berks; CE; MInstCE; Consulting Engineer for Sewage Disposal; *b* Liverpool, 24 Jan. 1832; *s* of late Archdeacon J. Jones; *m* 1863, Emily (*d* 1918), *y d* of late John Back, Aldershot Place, Surrey; one *s* one *d. Educ:* Liverpool Coll.; Staff Coll., Sandhurst. Entered 9th Lancers, 1852; served throughout siege of Delhi as DAQMG to the cavalry (despatches thrice, promoted Captain and Brevet-Major); wounded at Agra by bullet through bridle-arm and 22 sabre cuts, 10 October 1857; graduated at Staff Coll., 1861; Staff, Cape of Good Hope, 1861–67; retired, 1872; Manager of all Sewage Works of the 1st Army Corps, Aldershot, 1895–1912; retired 1912. Decorated: for taking a nine-pounder plus gun from the enemy, 8 June 1857. *Publications:* Will a Sewage Farm Pay? (three editions), 1874–87; Natural and Artificial Sewage Treatment, 1902; many papers in professional journals. *Address:* Ridge Cottage, Finchampstead, Berks. *Club:* Junior United Service.   *Died May 1920.*

JONES, Rev. Basil M., MA; Vicar of Llanfair, near Ruthin, with Jesus Chapel, since 1870; Chaplain of HM Prison, Ruthin, since 1904; *e s* of Rev. James Jones, MA, Rector of Llanfwrog, Denbighshire; *m* Emily (*d* 1910), *y d* of Francis Willis, MD, of Shillingthorpe, Lincs; two *s* two *d. Educ:* Ruthin and Newport Salop Grammar Schools; Jesus Coll., Oxford (Scholar), BA 1863; MA 1866. Deacon, 1866; Priest, 1867; Curate of Llanwenarth, 1866; Llanfwrog, 1868; Prebendary of St Asaph, 1899; Chaplain to the High Sheriff of Denbighshire, 1878; Governor of County School for Girls at Ruthin, 1900; Vice-Chairman, 1907; Chairman of Parish Council of Llanfair, 1907; Rural Dean of Dyffryn Clwyd, 1916. *Publications:* occasional sermons and addresses. *Address:* Llanfair Vicarage, Ruthin.   *Died 9 March 1925.*

JONES, Maj. Bryan John, DSO 1916; Leinster Regiment; *b* 13 May 1874; *e surv. s* of Colonel T. J. Jones, late Royal Artillery, of Lisnawilly, Dundalk, and Margaret Gertrude, *d* of late Sir Theophilus Shepstone, KCMG; *m* 1911, Grace, *o d* of late S. H. Stephens, County Inspector, Royal Irish Constabulary. *Educ:* privately. First Commission in Leinster Regiment, 1894; served South African War, 1900–2 (despatches, Queen's and King's medals); European War, 1914–18 (despatches, DSO, thrice wounded). *Publications:* contributor of articles on Irish archæology and folklore to various periodicals. *Recreations:* riding, gardening, military history, Irish subjects. *Address:* Lisnawilly, Dundalk.   *Died 20 Sept. 1918.*

JONES, Chester, JP; Metropolitan Police Magistrate, Bow Street, since 1920; *b* 1854; 4th *s* of John Henry Jones of Elmwood, Streatham, SW; *m* 1888, Ellen, *d* of late John Shyane. *Educ:* University College, London; Trinity Hall, Cambridge; BA 1876. Called to Bar, Middle Temple, 1879; Police Magistrate, Thames, 1907–11; Old Street, 1911–14; Lambeth, 1914–20; presided over many Home Office Enquiries on Industrial Matters; Member of Vice-Regal Commission on loss of Dublin Crown Jewels. *Recreation:* yachting. *Address:* 3 Marine Parade, Brighton. *Clubs:* New University, United University.   *Died 9 July 1922.*

JONES, Rt. Hon. Sir David Brynmor, Kt 1906; PC 1912; KC; LLB, Hon. LLD (Wales); a Master in Lunacy since 1914; *b* 12 May 1852; *e s* of late Rev. Thomas Jones, Swansea, Chairman Congregational Union of England and Wales; *m* 1892, Florence (*d* 1920), *widow* of A. de M. Mocatta, and *d* of Maj. Lionel Cohen. *Educ:* University School and College, London. Barrister, Middle Temple, 1876; QC 1893; Bencher, 1899; Reader, 1911; Judge of County Courts, 1885; resigned, 1892. MP (L) Stroud Division of Gloucestershire, 1892–95, Swansea District, 1895–1914. Member Welsh Land Commission, 1893; Chairman County Court Departmental Committees, 1893 and 1899; Chairman Metropolitan Police Commission, 1906; Member Welsh Church Commission, 1907; Member Venereal Diseases Commission, 1913; Recorder of Merthyr Tydfil, 1910–14; Recorder of Cardiff, 1914–15; Member Court of Referees, 1896–1914, and a Chairman of Standing Committees, House of Commons, 1906–14. Hon. Counsel to and Member of Court of University of Wales; a Vice-President and Chairman of Council of the Cymmrodorion Society. JP Glamorganshire. *Publications:* Essay on Home Rule and Imperial Sovereignty, 1886; edited The Divine Order and other Sermons, by the Rev. Thomas Jones, with an introduction by Robert Browning, 1884; Address on Welsh History in the Light of Recent Research, 1891; The Welsh People (with Principal Rhys), 1900, etc. *Recreations:* travel, sculling, tennis. *Address:* 27 Bryanston Square, W.

T: Paddington 2091. *Clubs:* Reform, Devonshire, Ranelagh.   *Died 6 Aug. 1921*

JONES, Rev. Donald, BD (Durham); Principal of Bede College, Durham, 1903–25; Lecturer in the University of Durham; *b* 1857; *s* of Thomas Evan Jones of The Precincts, Canterbury; *m* 1923, Mary Edith Macray, Whitefield, Cumberland, *d* of Rev. Dr Macray, Recto of Ducklington, Oxfordshire. *Educ:* The King's School, Canterbury; Lichfield Theological College. Assistant Master at the King's School, Canterbury, and Victoria College, Jersey, 1877–86; Deacon, 1887; Priest, 1888; Curate of Aughton, Lancashire, 1887–89; Priest-Vicar in Lichfield Cathedral, and Vice-Principal and Lecturer at the Theological College, Lichfield, 1889–1903. *Publications:* An Analytical Sketch of Jewish History and a First Index to Early Church History. *Recreations:* golf, cycling, fishing.   *Died Aug. 1925*

JONES, Miss E. E. Constance; DLitt (Hon) Wales; Mistress of Girton College, Cambridge, 1903–16, Vice-Mistress, 1896–1903, and Resident Lecturer in Moral Sciences, 1884–1903; *d* of J. Jones, MD, JP, of Langstone Court, Herefordshire, and Llancayo House Monmouthshire, and Emily Edith, *d* of Thomas Oakley, JP, of Lydar House, Monmouth; kin to Dr David Lewis, first Principal of Jesus College, Oxford. *Educ:* at home; Miss Robinson's, Alstone Court Cheltenham; Girton Coll., Camb. First Class in Moral Science Tripos, 1880. Examiner in Logic in the Cambridge Higher Local 1902–3–4; Governor of the Univ. College of Wales, Aberystwyth; Member of the Aristotelian Society, and the Soc. for Psychical Research, etc. *Publications:* trans. (with Miss E. Hamilton) Lotze Mikrokosmus; Elements of Logic as a Science of Propositions; General Logic; Primer of Logic (2nd edn 1913); Primer of Ethics; A New Law of Thought and its Logical Bearings; vol. on Girton College in Beautiful Britain series; The Three Great Questions: an outline of Private and Public Duty, 1915; article, Henry Sidgwick in Hastings Encyclopædia of Religion and Ethics, 1920; various articles and reviews; was entrusted with carrying through the press the 6th and 7th editions of late Prof. Sidgwick's Methods of Ethics and with editing his Lectures on the Ethics of Green, Spencer and Martineau and National and International Right and Wrong (a reprint of two essays from Practical Ethics). *Recreations:* architecture, languages *Address:* Meldon House, Weston-super-Mare; Ar-y-Bryn, Llanddew Skyrrid, Abergavenny. *Club:* Writers'.   *Died 17 April 1922*

JONES, Maj. Evan Rowland; author and writer, first editor and proprietor of The Shipping World, and the publications of the Shipping World Company; *b* Penylan Farm, by Tregaron Cardiganshire, 1840; *s* of William Jones and Mary, *d* of Evan Rowlands, of Wenallt, Cardiganshire; *m* 1867, Kate Alice, *d* of William Evans, of Llanwnda, Carnarvonshire; no *c. Educ:* public and private schools, military classes, and by private tutors. Went to America at age of 15; organised the Welsh citizens of Milwaukee into the Lincoln Anti-Slavery Society, 1860; enlisted (under age) for the American War in 5th Wisconsin Regiment, 1861; served on Non-Commissioned Staff and as Second Lieut, Captain, and Brevet Major filled the office of Judge Advocate of a Brigade Court Martial 1864–65; held a position in Department of State, Madison, until appointed by President Grant in 1869 American Consul for the NE Coast, resident in Newcastle upon Tyne; Consul for South Wales resident at Cardiff, 1884–92; reported upon the whole Consular System by instructions from the Department of State. MP (L Carmarthen Boroughs, 1892–95. Member of Council and Court of Governors of University College of South Wales and Monmouthshire; President of Cymmrodorion Society. *Publications* Lincoln, Stanton, and Grant; Historical Sketches; Four Years in the Army of the Potomac; Heroes of Industry; Life of (his friend) Joseph Cowen; papers on economic subjects; Una Montgomery. *Recreations* formerly tennis, riding, swimming; then walks, books. *Address:* The Pryors, Hampstead, NW3. *T:* Hampstead 5092. *TA:* Shipping World London. *T:* Gerrard 2381. *Clubs:* Savage, National Liberal.   *Died 16 Jan. 1920*

JONES, Francis, MSc; FRSE, FCS; *b* Edinburgh, 1845; *s* of Francis and Esther Jones; *m* Jessie Ferguson, *d* of Thomas Chapman Edinburgh; one *s* five *d. Educ:* Edinburgh Institution; Edinburgh University; Heidelberg University. Research Assistant to Prof. Roscoe 1866; Demonstrator in Chemistry, Owens College, Manchester 1870–71; Senior Chemistry Master, The Grammar School Manchester, 1872–1919; Vice-President of the Literary and Philosophical Society of Manchester, and President, 1909–11 *Publications:* Junior Course of Practical Chemistry; Questions on Chemistry; German Science Reader; The Air of Rooms: An

Examination of the effect produced on the air of rooms by the use of gas, coal, electric light, etc, for heating and lighting purposes; Address on the History of the Introduction of Science in Schools and Colleges; various papers read before the Chemical Society of London and Manchester Literary and Philosophical Society on Boron Hydride, Stibine, Volatility of Sulphur, Action of Alkalies on Glass, etc. *Recreations:* golf, photography. *Address:* 17 Whalley Road, Whalley Range, Manchester.   *Died 22 Oct. 1925.*

JONES, Lt-Col Frank Aubrey, DSO 1900; late Welsh Regiment; *b* 4 Aug. 1873. Entered army, 1895; served Sierra Leone, 1898–99 (wounded, medal with clasp); South Africa, 1899–1902 (severely wounded; despatches; Queen's medal, 3 clasps; King's medal, 2 clasps; DSO).   *Died 11 July 1916.*

JONES, Hon. George; Member Legislative Council of New Zealand since 1895; editor and proprietor of The Oamaru Mail; *b* Hutt Valley, New Zealand, 24 Oct. 1844; *s* of George Jones of Shropshire and London, and Ann Eliza Adams of London; *m* Dorothy Tweedy of Sunderland; four *s* four *d*. *Educ:* common schools; Rev. Mr Scales' Academy; Rev. G. O. Vance's Grammar School, Geelong. Served part apprenticeship as printer at Heath and Cordell's of that time; then employed for a year at Government Printing Office at Brisbane. At age of 17 worked as journeyman compositor on the Rockhampton Bulletin; arrived in Christchurch, NZ, 1863, and was successively employed in the Standard, the Lyttelton Times, and the Press; entered into business as printer and publisher in Christchurch in 1866, eventually taking in as partner the late George Tombs, afterwards of Whitcombe and Tombs; subsequently went to Auckland and started the Waikato Times and Auckland Echo; on the demise of the Echo, in conjunction with Messrs Reed and Brett, established the News in Dunedin, in the Provincialist interest; purchased the Oamaru Mail, 1877; was brought into political prominence through a State prosecution which was consequent on his libelling Attorney-General Sir F. Whitaker, when he appeared at the Bar of the House, and subsequently in the Supreme Court, by whom he was acquitted; sat in House of Reps, 1880–81; resigned owing to ill-health; an advocate of liquor prohibition. As a boy was a member of the first musical society in Australia shortly after its establishment, and took a prominent part in music throughout that country and New Zealand. *Recreations:* music, gardening. *Address:* Mail, Oamaru. *T:* 143, 159, 27.   *Died Dec. 1921.*

JONES, Harry; Parliamentary Correspondent, Daily News; barrister-at-law, Middle Temple; *b* Llanelly, South Wales, 27 March 1866; *m* 1895, Emily Margaret, *d* of Thomas Mainwaring; one *s*. Assistant-editor South Wales Daily News; acting editor Weekly Sun; editor Evening Sun; managing editor Western Daily Mercury; deputy editor Daily Chronicle. *Publications:* Liberalism and the House of Lords; War Letters of a Public Schoolboy, 1918. *Recreations:* golf, walking. *Address:* 29 Half Moon Lane, Herne Hill, SE. *T:* Brixton 726. *Clubs:* National Liberal; Dulwich and Sydenham Golf.   *Died 11 Jan. 1925.*

JONES, Sir Henry, CH 1922; Kt 1912; MA, LLD; DLitt Wales 1905; FBA 1904; Professor of Moral Philosophy, University of Glasgow, since 1894; *b* Llangernyw, North Wales, 30 Nov. 1852; *m* 1882, Annie Walker, Kilbirnie, Ayrshire; two *s* one *d* (and two *s* one *d* decd). *Educ:* University of Glasgow (MA 1879). Hon. LLD St Andrews, 1895. Professor of Philosophy and Political Economy at University College of North Wales, Bangor, 1884–91; Professor of Logic and Metaphysics at University of St Andrews, 1891–94; Hibbert Lecturer on Metaphysics at Manchester College, Oxford. *Publications:* Browning as a Religious and Philosophical Teacher, 1891; The Philosophy of Lotze, 1895; Idealism as a Practical Creed, 1909; The Working Faith of the Social Reformer, 1910; Social Powers, 1913; Philosophical Landmarks, 1917; Principles of Citizenship, 1919; A Faith that Enquires, 1922; *posthumous publication:* Old Memories, 1923. *Address:* The University, Glasgow; Noddfa, Tighnabruaich, Argyllshire.   *Died 4 Feb. 1922.*

JONES, Sir Henry, Kt 1919; *b* Hobart, 1862; *m* 1883, Alice, *d* of W. Glover, Manchester. Founder and Managing Director of H. Jones & Co. Ltd; Chairman of Directors of Henry Jones Co-operative Ltd, Melbourne; Director of Tongkah Harbour Tin Dredging Co.; part owner Bendena Station, Queensland. *Address:* Old Wharf, Hobart, Tasmania.   *Died 29 Oct. 1926.*

JONES, Rev. Canon Henry David, VD; MA; Canon Residentiary of Chichester since 1900; *b* 1842; *e s* of Robert Jones, DL, of Middlesex, and of Glanbrane Park, Llandovery; *m* 1st, Emily, *e d* of W. Leetham, JP, Hull; 2nd, Elizabeth Lucy (*d* 1918), 3rd *d* of Rev.

James Kirkpatrick, of Holydale, Keston, Kent; five *s* two *d*. *Educ:* Shrewsbury School; St John's College, Cambridge (Exhibitioner, 1861; BA, 1864; MA, 1868). Curate of St James', Kingston-upon-Hull, 1865–67; St Gabriel's, Pimlico, 1867–69; Aberaman, Glamorganshire, 1869; Rector of St Mary's, Aberdeen, 1869; Chaplain at Genoa, 1874; Curate of St Michael's, Bournemouth, 1875; Prebendary of Colworth in Chichester Cathedral, 1891–1903; of Gates, 1903; Treasurer, 1911; Precentor, 1918; Rural Dean of Hastings, 1889–1905; Rector of Upper St Leonards, 1879–1915. *Address:* The Chantry, Chichester.

Died 26 April 1925.

JONES, Henry Festing; author; *b* 1851; 2nd *s* of Thomas Jones, QC, of the Northern Circuit, barrister-at-law, and Ellen, *o c* of Rev. William Carmalt of Putney School. *Educ:* private tuition; Rottingdean; Radley; Trinity Hall, Cambridge. Articled to a solicitor, 1873; met Samuel Butler, author of Erewhon, 1876; admitted a solicitor, 1876; retired from the law, 1887, and joined Butler, assisting him in his work and travelling with him in Italy. *Publications:* about 20 songs and 6 four-part songs, words by various poets, 1886–1907; King Bulbous: a Comic Opera for schools and classes, words by P. H. Crib, 1897; Diversions in Sicily, 1909; Castellinaria and other Sicilian Diversions, 1911; The Note Books of Samuel Butler, 1912; Samuel Butler, Author of Erewhon, a Memoir, 1919 (James Tait Black Prize); Mount Eryx and other Diversions of Travel, 1921; several pamphlets about Butler; in collaboration with Butler—Gavottes, Minuets, Fugues, etc, for the piano, 1885; Narcissus, a Cantata, 1888; Ulysses, an Oratorio, 1904; (with A. T. Bartholomew) joint-editor of the Shrewsbury Edition of the complete Works of Samuel Butler. *Recreation:* sketching. *Address:* 120 Maida Vale, W9. *T:* Maida Vale 2652. *Club:* New University.

Died 23 Oct. 1928.

JONES, Capt. Henry Michael, VC 1857. Entered army, 1849; served in Crimea; severely wounded at Alma; Capt. 1855; dangerously wounded at Redan; left army, 1857; entered Diplomatic Service, 1858; Consul-Gen. at Tabreez, 1868; at Christiania, 1875; Philippopolis, 1880; Minister Resident at Bangkok, 1889; Minister Resident at Lima, 1894, and at Quito, 1895–98; retired. Knight of the Legion of Honour. *Clubs:* United Service, Junior United Service.

Died 18 Dec. 1916.

JONES, Rt. Rev. Herbert Edward; Suffragan Bishop of Lewes since 1914; Archdeacon of Chichester since 1914; *b* 6 April 1861; *s* of Sir Willoughby Jones, 3rd Bt, of Cranmer Hall, Norfolk; *m* 1888, Madeleine, *d* of Edward Long Fox, MD, Clifton; one *s* one *d*. *Educ:* Trinity College, Cambridge. Curate of St Andrews, Westminster, 1884–86; Rector of Knebworth, 1888–97; Rector of Petworth, 1897–1906; Examining Chaplain to the Bishop of Chichester, 1903–7; Vicar of Hitchin, 1907–13; Hon. Canon of St Albans; Examining Chaplain to the Bishop of St Albans. *Address:* 2 Eaton Gardens, Hove, Sussex.   *Died 19 Feb. 1920.*

JONES, Howard Parker, MA, PhD; M'Leed Professor of Modern Languages, Dalhousie University, Halifax, Nova Scotia, since 1906; *b* 27 Sept. 1863; 3rd *s* of St Clair Jones of Weymouth, Nova Scotia; *m* 1893, Isabel, *y d* of Thomas Ridd, Barnstaple, England; one *s* two *d*. *Educ:* The Collegiate School and King's College, Windsor, Nova Scotia (BA 1884, MA 1891); PhD Heidelberg University, 1886. Professor of Modern Languages, King's College, Windsor, NS, 1888–92; Instructor in German at Cornell University, Ithaca, NY, 1893–98; Professor of Modern Languages at Hobart College, Geneva, NY, 1898–1906. Honorary member of the Phi Beta Kappa Society. *Publications:* A German Reader; articles in various periodicals. *Recreations:* croquet, rowing. *Address:* King Street, Dartmouth, Nova Scotia.   *Died 29 April 1924.*

JONES, Sir James Edward, Kt 1914; JP; merchant; *b* 14 July 1843; *s* of Ellis and Ann Jones, Castlemere, Rochdale; *m* 1869, Hannah Hoyle, Crossfield, Rochdale; two *d*. *Educ:* Rochdale; Collegiate School, Sheffield. *Recreations:* golf, riding, driving. *Address:* Sparthfield, Rochdale. *T:* Rochdale 114. *Club:* Reform, Manchester.

Died 8 Jan. 1922.

JONES, Sir John Bowen Bowen-, 1st Bt, *cr* 1911; DL, JP; *b* 25 Dec. 1840; *s* of John Jones of the City of London, merchant, and Ann Bowen; *m* 1863, Elizabeth Margaret (*d* 1904), *e d* of Evan Bowen, Ensdon House, Montford, Shropshire; no *c*. Mem., Royal Commn on Horse Breeding. Pres., Royal Agric. Soc. Heir: none. *Address:* Council House Court, Shrewsbury.

Died 6 June 1925 (ext).

JONES, Rev. Josiah Towyn; MP (Co.L) East Carmarthen, 1912–18, Llanelly (Carmarthen), 1918–22; Governor of Cardiff and Aberystwyth Universities; Member Carmarthen County Council; Chairman of the Welsh Congregational Union, 1919–20; late Welsh Whip and Lord of the Treasury; *b* 28 Dec. 1858; *m* 1885, Mary Howells, Plas Cadwgan, Swansea Valley; two *d.* Worked on farm as a boy; went to sea, served as cabin-boy. Entered Presbyterian College, Carmarthen, 1876; ordained Congregationalist Minister, Dowlais, 1880; Minister Cwmaman, 1884–1904; retired, 1906; Organiser for Welsh Congregational Union and member of Welsh Central Board; late member Carmarthen CC and Education Committee. *Address:* 22 Marine Terrace, New Quay, Cardiganshire. *Club:* National Liberal.   *Died 16 Nov. 1925.*

JONES, Kennedy; *see* Jones, W. K.

JONES, Capt. Kingsmill Williams, DSO 1915; Medical Officer to The Buffs (1st Battalion); *b* 11 March 1875; *s* of late Percival Jones, Dublin. *Educ:* Wesley College, Dublin; Trinity College, Dublin (Mathematical Scholar). BA Dublin 1898; MA, MD, DPH 1903; MB, BCh, BAO 1901; LM (Rotunda Hosp. Dub.), 1901. Elected Member of Manchester City Council 1913. Went to France with his unit, 18th Field Ambulance, 6th Div. BEF Sept. 1914 (twice wounded, DSO, despatches). *Publication:* Delirium in Febrile Conditions, 1908. *Recreation:* rowing. *Address:* 2 Syndall Street, Stockport Road, Manchester. *T:* City 4568. *Club:* Arts, Manchester.
                                          Died Aug. 1918.

JONES, Rev. Lewis; Congregational Minister; Minister of Tynycoed and Bethlehem, Abercrave, Swansea Valley; *b* 6 April 1842 at a farmhouse called Rhydybod, Llanuwchllyn, Merionethshire; *s* of David and Jane Jones, farmers; *m*; one *s* one *d.* *Educ:* Bala College; Glasgow University. Ordained as Congregational Minister at Tynycoed and Bethlehem Chapels, Abercrave, 1867; resigned, 1919; took prominent part in Denominational Associations; special Preacher and President of Congregational Union of Wales; served on School Board; Chairman of Ystradgynlais Tribunal; a strict total abstainer and non-smoker; President of the Bible Society branch of the district; an extensive sphere of labour of mixed farmers and labourers; five Sunday Schools under his care; rebuilt the chapels and built three new schools, and cleared all the debt. *Publications:* Paul in Europe; Israel of the Old Testament; Is there a Word from the Lord? (special sermon); Church Independency in the Light of History; articles in periodicals. *Address:* Cœdmor, Llantwit Major, Glam.
                                          Died Aug. 1928.

JONES, Rt. Rev. Llewellyn, DD; Bishop of Newfoundland and Bermuda since 1878; *b* Liverpool, 11 Oct. 1840; *m* 1881, Elizabeth Alice (*d* 1903), *d* of Hon. Sir Adams G. Archibald, KCMG, Lt.-Gov. of Nova Scotia; two *s* one *d.* *Educ:* Cheltenham; Harrow; Trinity Coll. Cambridge (MA). Ordained, 1864; Rector of Little Hereford, 1874–78. *Address:* St John's, Newfoundland; Hamilton, Bermuda.
                                          Died 9 Jan. 1918.

JONES, Rev. Lloyd Timothy; Hon. Canon of Peterborough. *Address:* All Saints Vicarage, Northampton.
                                          Died 3 Jan. 1920.

JONES, Brig.-Gen. Lumley Owen Williames, DSO 1915; 2nd Battalion Essex Regiment; *b* 1 Dec. 1876. *Educ:* Winchester. Entered army, 1897; Captain, 1905; Adjutant, 1912; Bt Lt-Col 1916; employed with West Africa Frontier Force, 1904–8; served South Africa, 1901–2 (Queen's medal, 4 clasps); West Africa, 1905–6 (medal with clasp); European War, 1914–18 (despatches thrice, DSO, Bt Col); Legion of Honour. *Address:* Cefn Bryntalch, Abermule, Montgomeryshire.   *Died 14 Sept. 1918.*

JONES, Hon. Sir Lyman Melvin, Kt 1911; Chevalier of the Legion of Honour, 1914; Member (L) of Senate of Dominion of Canada since 1901; *b* Ontario, 21 Sept. 1843; of Welsh-Scotch descent; *s* of Norman Jones and Therese Jane Patterson; *m* 1873, Louise, *d* of Thomas Irwin; one *d.* Alderman of City of Winnipeg and Chairman of Finance Committee, 1886; Mayor of Winnipeg and Vice-President of Board of Trade, 1887; re-elected Mayor, 1888; Provincial Treasurer, Manitoba, 1888; represented Consituency of Shoal Lake; re-elected 1888 to represent North Winnipeg; resigned office, 1889, though retaining seat in Legislature until end of term, and returned to Eastern Canada to devote his time to private business; upon amalgamation of the Massey and Harris Companies in 1891 became Managing Director of consolidated Companies; President since 1902; President, Bain Wagon Co., Ltd., Woodstock, and Johnston Harvester Co., Batavia, NY, USA; Vice-President, Ontario Jockey Club;

Director Canadian Bank of Commerce; Director, Blackstone Mutual Fire Insurance Co. and Merchants' Mutual Fire Insurance Co., Providence, RI, USA; Verity Plow Co. Ltd. *Recreations:* golf, motoring. *Address:* Llawhaden, St George St, Toronto, Canada. *TA:* Melvin, Toronto. *Clubs:* National, York, Toronto Hunt, Royal Canadian Yacht, Toronto; Rideau, Ottawa; Manitoba, Winnipeg.
                                          Died 15 April 1917.

JONES, Lt-Col Michael Durwas Goring-, CMG 1916; DSO 1918; 2nd Durham Light Infantry; *b* 13 Jan. 1866. Lieut 1886; Capt. 1896; Major, 1908; Lt-Col 1915; Adjutant Indian Vols 1901–6; served European War, 1914–18 (despatches, CMG, DSO).
                                          Died 19 May 1919.

JONES, Maj. Percy Arnold Lloyd-, DSO 1915; RAMC; *b* 17 Oct 1876. Served one year in ranks; Lieut RAMC, 1904; Capt. 1908; served South Africa, 1900 (Queen's medal, 3 clasps); European War, 1914–16 (despatches twice, DSO).
                                          Died 29 Dec. 1916.

JONES, Sir Philip Sydney, Kt 1905; MD; FRCS; *b* 15 April 1836; 2nd *s* of David Jones, Sydney; *m* 1863, Hannah Howard, *d* of Rev. G. Charter; three *s* four *d.* *Educ:* private schools; University College, London. MD, University of London, 1860; FRCS 1861. Fellow of Senate, University of Sydney; Vice-Chancellor, 1904–5; Hon. Consulting Physician, Royal Prince Alfred and Sydney Hospitals; President, Inter-Colonial Medical Congress, 1892. *Recreations:* travel, croquet. *Address:* Llandilo, Strathfield, New South Wales. *Club:* Union, Sydney.   *Died 18 Sept. 1918.*

JONES, Rev. Richard Thomas; Vicar of Glanogwen, Bethesda, since 1898; Canon of Bangor Cathedral since 1910. *Educ:* Lampeter. Ordained, 1885; Curate Pwllheli, 1895–8; Vicar of Nevin, 1888–98. *Address:* Glanogwen Vicarage, Bethesda, N Wales.
                                          Died 1 April 1917.

JONES, Maj.-Gen. Robert Owen, CB 1885; RE; *b* 14 Nov. 1837; *s* of late William Jones, Bryn Tegid, and Ann, *d* of Owen Owen, Dolgadfa; *m* 1878, Harriette (*d* 1922), *d* of Rt Hon. Sir James Parker Deane, PC, QC, DCL; four *d.* *Educ:* Cowbridge; Woolwich. Commissioned in Royal Engineers, 1856; served Ashanti War, 1873–74; engineer in charge of communications from the Prah to the coast; Boundary Commissioner, 1884–85; retired, 1887. JP County Merioneth. *Address:* Bryn Tegid, Bala, N Wales. *Club:* Junior United Service.   *Died 19 Feb. 1926.*

JONES, Rev. Canon Thomas; Canon of St David's Cathedral, 1908; *b* 14 June 1839; *m* 1865; two *s* one *d.* *Educ:* St David's College, Lampeter. Ordained 1862; Curate of Llanelly, Brecon, 1862; Llanfigon, 1864; Llandyssuil, Cardigan, 1865; Vicar of Llanwnen, W Silian, 1868; Llywel, Brecon, 1878; Rector of Penboyr, Carmarthen, 1889; retired, 1914. *Address:* Millbank, Lampeter, Cardiganshire. *TA:* Lampeter.   *Died 1927.*

JONES, Thomas Ridge, MD Aberdeen; consulting physician, Victoria Hospital for Children; *b* 1840; *s* of Thomas and Ellen Jones, Rhyl, North Wales; *m* 1876, Ruth, *d* of Joseph Ridge, MD, FRCP; four *s* one *d.* *Educ:* Liverpool Institute and privately; Middlesex; St George's Hospitals; Aberdeen University. Was awarded 1st prize in each subject, except botany, and the Governor's Prize for Clinical Medicine and Surgery, given to the most distinguished student at the Middlesex Hospital; for twenty-six years Physician, and for last fifteen years Consulting Physician to the Victoria Hospital for Children. FRSM. *Publications:* On the Recent Outbreak of Smallpox at St George's Hospital, St George's Hospital Report, vol. v; Lymphatic Leukæmia, Pathological Society, 1878; Observations on Cerebral Hæmorrhage from Forty Fatal Cases (serial), BMJ, 1863–64; Colalepsy, ibid. 1863; On Anæsthetics (serial), ibid. 1872. *Recreations:* riding, mountaineering. *Address:* 4 Chesham Place, SW. *T:* 746 Victoria; Iford Manor House, near Lewes, Sussex. *Clubs:* Reform, Wellington.
                                          Died 4 April 1924.

JONES, W. Lewis, MA; Professor of English Language and Literature, University College of North Wales, since 1897; *b* 1866; *s* of William Jones, of Llangefni, Anglesey; *m* 1901, Edith, *d* of Elias Owen, Menai Bridge; one *d.* *Educ:* Friars School, Bangor; Queens' Coll., Camb. (Scholar). Graduated Classical Tripos, 1885; Members' (University) Prizeman for English Essay, 1887. Assistant Lecturer in English, Univ. Coll. of N Wales, 1891; Examiner in English in the University of Glasgow, 1903–6; Examiner in English in the University of Birmingham, 1909–11; Vice-Principal of University College of N Wales, 1903–5. Member of Court and of Senate of University of

Wales. *Publications:* editor of Caniadau Cymru (an anthology of Welsh poetry), 1897, second edn 1907; articles in Quarterly Review, Modern Language Review, Transactions of Cymmrodorion Society and other periodicals; The University of Wales (with W. Cadwaladr Davies) in College Histories, 1905; King Arthur in History and Legend, 1911; Land of my Fathers (a patriotic anthology), 1915; contributor to Cambridge History of English Literature. *Recreations:* golfing, cycling. *Address:* Ceinwen, Bangor, N Wales.

Died 2 Feb. 1922.

JONES, Walter, JP; MIME; founder of Jones & Attwood, Ltd, heating and hydraulic engineers; *b* 1846; *m* 1876, *e d* of Thomas Noke. *Publications:* Heating by Hot Water; National and Municipal Finance; Capital and Labour, etc. *Address:* The Uplands, Stourbridge. *T:* Stourbridge 381.   *Died 25 Aug. 1924.*

JONES, Lt-Col Walter Dally, CMG 1917; *b* 21 May 1855; *y s* of late John Jones of The Clock House, Wandsworth, SW; *m* 1886, Marion Isabella, 2nd *d* of late Col Frank Crossman, 12th Bengal Cavalry; three *d*. *Educ:* Harrow; Trinity College, Cambridge. 2nd Lieut 99th Duke of Edinburgh's Lanarkshire Regt 1878; Captain Wiltshire Regt 1885; passed Staff College, 1889; DAAG Gibraltar, 1891–98; retired 1901. Secretary Wiltshire TF Association, 1908–12; Assistant Secretary Committee of Imperial Defence, Nov. 1914; Senior Assistant Secretary War Cabinet, Dec. 1916; served S African War, 1879, Zulu Campaign, Defence of Eshowe (medal with clasp); S African War, 1899–1900, Press Censor on Gen. Rt Hon. Sir Redvers Buller's Staff, Relief of Ladysmith (despatches twice, Queen's medal with 6 clasps, brevet of Lieut-Col). Chevalier of the Legion of Honour, 1916. *Address:* 53 Belgrave Road, SW. *Clubs:* Army and Navy, Garrick, Beefsteak.   *Died 20 Feb. 1926.*

JONES, Lt-Col Walter Thomas Cresswell, CB 1921; DSO 1900; Royal Marine Light Infantry; *b* 31 Jan. 1874; *s* of late Rev. George Jones; *m* 1909, Hildred, *e d* of A. St Clair Buxton; one *s* three *d*. *Educ:* Bradfield College, Berks; Rev. J. Scott Ramsay, Army Tutor. Served with Naval Brigade, S Africa (despatches thrice, DSO); Dardanelles, 1915 (despatches). *Address:* Forton Barracks, Gosport, Hants.

Died 16 Aug. 1923.

JONES, Sir William Hollingworth Quayle, Kt 1892; *b* 6 Feb. 1854; *e s* of late Rev. C. W. Jones, Vicar of Pakenham, and Rural Dean of Thedwastre, Suffolk; *m* 1st, 1884, Alice (*d* 1890), *d* of Charles Kent of Woodcot, Oxford; 2nd, 1893, Claire (whom he *div.* 1905), *d* of E. Berdoe-Wilkinson; 3rd, 1906, May Bradley (whom he *div.* 1910), 5th *d* of late William Dyer. *Educ:* Caius Coll., Camb (BA 1876; MA 1879). Barrister, Middle Temple, 1877; Acting Judge Gold Coast, 1882; Queen's Advocate, Gold Coast, 1883; Chief Justice of the West African Settlements, 1887; title subsequently changed to Chief Justice of Sierra Leone, retired invalided, 1895; was Deputy Governor on various occasions, and acting Governor, Sierra Leone, 1892; belongs to SE Circuit; appointed in 1897, 1898, 1899, 1900, 1901, 1902, 1903, 1904 and 1905 to act as a Chairman at Courts of London Sessions during absence of 1st, the Chairman, and 2nd, the Deputy Chairman, also Feb. 1906, as Deputy for the Chairman under the Quarter Sessions (London) Act, 1896. Formerly Captain in the West Suffolk Militia, retired 1889; was reappointed Captain, 3rd Batt. Suffolk Regiment, 1896; Hon. Major 1899; retired, 1900, with rank of Major. JP Suffolk. *Address:* Barton Mere, Bury St Edmunds. *Club:* New University.

Died 6 Jan. 1925.

JONES, (William) Kennedy; MP (U) Hornsey Division of Middlesex since 1916; *b* Glasgow, 4 May 1865; *m* 1892, Hetty, *d* of James Staniland, Birmingham; one *s* three *d*. *Educ:* High School, Glasgow. Joint Founder Daily Mail, Daily Mirror; Editor Evening News, 1894–1900. Contested (Ind.) Wimbledon, April 1916; Director-General (unpaid) Food Economy Dept, Ministry of Food, 1917; Chairman Select Committee on Transport (Metropolitan Area), 1919; Chairman, Advisory Committee Ministry of Transport (London Traffic), 1920. *Address:* 8 King's Bench Walk, EC4. *T:* City 7007. *Clubs:* Constitutional, Royal Automobile, Royal Thames Yacht, Royal Aero.   *Died 20 Oct. 1921.*

JONES-PARRY, Rear-Adm. John Parry, JP Cheshire; retired; inventor of non-recoil carriage, and mantle to protect crew; *b* 7 Oct. 1829; *s* of late Rev. J. Jones-Parry; *m* 1st, 1861, Catherine (*d* 1865), *d* of J. de Winton; two *s* one *d;* 2nd, 1898, Marion, *d* of H. Roome. *Educ:* sea. Served at Odessa and Sebastopol; a gunnery officer on board HMS "Terrible" stationed in the Black Sea from beginning to end of the war; retired 1873. *Address:* Edern, Parkwood Road, Boscombe.

Died 18 April 1920.

JONES-VAUGHAN, Maj.-Gen. Hugh Thomas, CB 1894; JP Carnarvonshire; *b* 1841, Glanywern, Merionethshire; *e s* of late Rev. Canon Thomas Jones and Catherine, *d* of Liston Vaughan; *m* 1883, Eva, *e d* of Evan Owen, Hengwrtucha, Dolgelly; one *s*. *Educ:* RMC Sandhurst. Passed Staff College, 1871; Maj.-Gen. 1899; served in the Indian Mutiny, 1857–58; present at the actions of Chanda, Ummeerapore and Sultanpore; final siege and capture of Lucknow (medal and clasp); Afghan War, 1878–79–80, as Brigade-Major with 1st division Peshawur Field Force; capture of Ali Musjid; and in expeditions to the Bazar and Lugman valleys; Brigade-Major in the Zaimusht Expedition, and at assault and capture of Zawa (three times mentioned in despatches, Brevet of Lt-Col, medal and clasp); AAG Western District, 1887–92; appointed Col on the Staff with temporary rank of Major-General, 1894; General Officer commanding troops, Straits Settlements, 1894–99; Distinguished Service Record, 1899; Col, Loyal North Lancashire Regiment, 1909. *Recreations:* shooting, hunting, rowing. *Address:* Tyddynllydyn, Rhydyclafdy, Carnarvon. *Club:* United Service.   *Died 11 April 1916.*

JONNART, Celestin Auguste; French Ambassador Extraordinary to the Vatican; member of French Academy, 1923; *b* Flechin, Pas-de-Calais, 1857. Rendered eminent service to France in politics and in the Colonies in the diplomatic service. *Address:* French Legation to the Holy See, Rome.   *Died 30 Sept. 1927.*

JOPP, Col John, CB 1894; Indian Army; *b* 13 March 1840; *m* 1886, Annie Florence Mead, *d* of late Surg.-Maj. John Memsie, IMS. Entered army, 1856; Col, 1886; served Aden, 1858; Abyssinian War, 1868 (medal); Afghan War, 1879–80 (medal, despatches); Political Resident, Aden, and commanding 2nd Class District, 1890–95; ADC, 1895–97.   *Died 16 June 1923.*

JORDAN, Edwin Oakes, PhD; Andrew MacLeish Distinguished Service Professor Emeritus of Bacteriology, University of Chicago; *b* 28 July 1866; American parentage; *m* 1893; two *s* one *d*. *Educ:* Mass Institute of Technology; SB 1888; PhD, Clark Univ., 1892; ScD, Univ. of Cincinnati, 1920. Member International Health Board, 1920–27; Board of Scientific Directors of the Rockefeller Foundation, 1930–34; Editor of The Journal of Infectious Diseases, The Journal of Preventive Medicine, The Newer Knowledge of Bacteriology and Immunology, 1928; President: American Society of Bacteriologists, 1905; American Epidemiological Society, 1930–31; Chicago Institute of Medicine, 1932–33; Nat. Acad., 1936. Sedgwick Medal, 1935. *Publications:* trans. Hueppe, Bacteriology; A Text-Book of General Bacteriology (11th edition); Food Poisoning (2nd edition), 1931; Epidemic Influenza, 1927; special monographs in Jl of the American Medical Association, Jl of Infectious Diseases, Jl of Experimental Medicine, Jl of Hygiene, etc. *Recreations:* travel, golf. *Address:* University of Chicago, Chicago, Ill.

Died 2 Sept. 1926.

JORDAN, Rt. Hon. Sir John (Newell), GCMG 1920 (KCMG 1904; CMG 1897); GCIE 1911; KCB 1909; PC 1915; Member of the League of Nations Advisory Committee, Geneva; *b* Balloo, Co. Down, Ireland, 5 Sept. 1852; *m* 1885, Annie Howe, *d* of Dr Cromie, Clough, Co. Down; three *s* (and one *d* decd). *Educ:* Royal Belfast Academical Institution; Queen's College, Belfast. 1st class Honours. Appointed Student Interpreter in China, 1876; Assistant Chinese Secretary to HBM Legation, Peking, 1889; Chinese Secretary, 1891; Consul-General, Corea, 1896–98; Chargé d'Affaires, 1898–1901; Minister Resident at Seoul, 1901; HBM Minister Resident at Court of Corea, 1901–6; HBM Envoy Extraordinary and Minister Plenipotentiary, Peking, 1906–20. Jubilee Medal, 1897; Coronation Medal, 1902. *Publications:* translations of the Peking Gazette. *Recreation:* riding. *Address:* 12 Portinscale Road, SW15.

Died 14 Sept. 1925.

JORDAN, Rev. Louis Henry, BD; Special Lecturer on the History and Comparison of Religions; *b* Halifax, Canada, 27 July 1855; *s* of late William Jordan, merchant, Halifax; *m* 1890, Catherine Pollok, 2nd *d* of Hon. James McDonald, Chief-Justice of Nova Scotia. *Educ:* Dalhousie University, Halifax (Lord Dufferin Gold Medallist, being premier member of the Graduating Class of 1857); Edinburgh (Medallist in Philosophy, 1882); Princeton; Oxford; Marburg; Leipsic; Berlin. Minister of St Andrew's Church, Halifax, 1882–85; Erskine Church, Montreal, 1885–90; St James Square Church, Toronto, 1894–1900; Lecturer on Church Polity, Montreal Theological College, 1887–89; Special Lecturer on Comparative Religion, University of Chicago, 1902; all the years since 1890 (excepting pastorate in Toronto) were devoted to travel, reading and lecturing, in different parts of the world. *Publications:* Comparative Religion: its Genesis and Growth, 1905; Comparative Religion: a Survey of its Recent Literature, 1906, 1910, 1914; Comparative Religion: its Method and Scope, 1908; The Study of Religion in the Italian Universities (with Professor Labanca), 1909; Modernism in Italy: its Origin, its Incentive, its Leaders and its Aims, 1909; Comparative Religion: its Adjuncts and Allies, 1915; contributions to the Review of Theology and Philosophy, Expository Times, Hibbert Jl, Princeton Theological Review, American Jl of Theology, Biblical World, etc. *Recreation:* foreign travel. *Club:* Authors'.

Died 4 Oct. 1923.

JORDAN, William George; author and educator; *b* New York City, 6 March 1864; *s* of Henry and Mary Moat Murdock; *m* 1922, Nellie B. Mitchell. *Educ:* The College of the City of New York. Editor of Book Chat, 1884; Editor of Current Literature; retired from this position to lecture on his new system of education; Managing Editor of The Ladies' Home Journal, 1897; Editor-in-Chief of the Saturday Evening Post, 1898; Editor of the Search-Light, 1905. In 1907 wrote a pamphlet on the House of Governors, which led, in 1908, to a meeting of the Governors of all the States in Washington, and the organization of the State Executives for annual meetings as a House. *Publications:* The Kingship of Self-Control; The Majesty of Calmness; The Power of Truth; Mental Training; A Remedy for Education; The Crown of Individuality; Little Problems of Married Life; The Wood Carver; The Power of Purpose; What every American should know about the League of Nations; Feodor Vladimir Larrovitch, a memoir; The Trusteeship of Life; The Vision of High Ideals; educational works. *Recreation:* book collection. *Address:* 317 East Seventeenth Street, New York. *Clubs:* Authors', Dutch Treat, The Musketeers, New York. *Died 20 April 1928.*

JOSA, Ven. Fortunato Pietro Luigi; Rector of St Endellion since 1917; *b* 5 June 1851; *m* Beatrice Mary, *d* of A. Cleaver of Nottingham; one *s* three *d*. *Educ:* Collegio Romano, Rome; St Augustine's College, Canterbury; St Boniface, Warminster. Ordained, 1874; Sub-Warden of the Bishop's College for Training Schoolmasters, 1874; Assistant Curate of St Philip's; East Indian Missionary, Non Pareil, 1876; Rector of Holy Trinity, 1884; Canon of the Cathedral, 1892–1914; Rural Dean of Demerara, 1893–95; Government Examiner in Oriental Languages, 1878; Vicar-General Diocese of Guiana, 1912–14; Archdeacon of Demerara, 1910–14; Vicar of Christ Church, Demerara, 1890–1914. *Publications:* The Apostle of the Indians; The Life of St Francis of Assisi; Manual of the Hindi Lanuage; English Church History of the West Indian Province; The Tale of a Roaming Catholic; and many pamphlets in English and Hindi, etc. *Recreations:* golf, philately. *Address:* The Rectory, St Endellion, Port Isaac, N Cornwall. *Club:* Corona. *Died 19 Dec. 1922.*

JOSEPH, Delissa, FRIBA 1889; in practice as an architect since 1882; *b* Jan. 1859; *e s* of late Isaac Solomon Joseph; *m* 1887, Leah (Lily), *d* of late Joseph Solomon. *Educ:* Durham House School and Jews' College. Member of Council of Royal Institute of British Architects, 1922–23, of City of London Conservative Association, of United Synagogue, of Jews' College, and of Anglo-Jewish Association; exhibited Architectural Works at Royal Academy, held a one-man show at Suffolk Street Galleries, 1924. *Principal works:* whole of Fitzgeorge Avenue, Chelsea Embankment Gardens, and Rangoon Street; Adelaide Court, Rutland Court, Chelsea Court, Castlenau Gardens, Exeter Mansions, Stanhope Court, Brookfield House, Oxford Circus House, Bartlett House, Peninsular House, West India House, St George's House, Bush Lane House, Chesterfield House; Hotel Rembrandt, Coburg Court Hotel, Jermyn Court Hotel, Park View Hotel, Park Gate Hotel; seven Synagogues; thirteen superstructures of Tube Stations, and buildings in St Paul's Churchyard, Old Jewry, Walbrook, Langham Place, Great St Helen's, Kingsway, Fleet Street, Cheapside, St Swithin's Lane, Tottenham Court Road, Oxford Street, Hanover Street, Albemarle Street, etc. *Publications:* Higher Buildings for London and Building Heights and Ancient Lights, RIBA Journal; numerous letters to the Times on Higher Buildings for London. *Recreations:* motoring, golfing, reading, smoking. *Address:* 2 Basinghall Avenue, EC2. *T:* London Wall 1138; 4 Cornwall Mansions, 33 Kensington Court, W8. *TA:* Rebuilding London. *Club:* Maccabaeans. *Died 10 Jan. 1927.*

JOSHI, Rev. Canon D. L.; Canon of St Thomas' Cathedral, Bombay; Hon. Chaplain to Bishop of Bombay; Marathi Priest-in-charge, Emmanuel Church, Bombay; *b* 8 May 1864; *s* of late Rev. Lucas M. Joshi and Karunabai; *m* Anubai, *d* of late D. Nana; one *s*. *Educ:* Robert Money School, Bombay; College of Science, Poona; Divinity School, Poona. Left Civil Engineering for Theology, 1882; after being a schoolmaster, ordained, 1893; for sixteen years in charge of the CMS Marathi Church in Bombay. *Publications:* Editor of Dharmadipika,

an Anglo-Marathi Magazine; translator of Walker's Commentary on Philippians; Oxenden's Family Prayers; and several other books and booklets; engaged on the revision of the Marathi Bible. *Address:* Molesworth, Girgaum, Bombay. *TA:* Testimony, Bombay. *Died Oct. 1923.*

JOULAIN, Rt. Rev. Henry, OMI; DD; Bishop of Jaffna since 1893; *b* St Romans, 24 Sept. 1852; *s* of James Joulain and Mary Morillon. *Educ:* Petit Séminaire de Mont Morillon; Grand Seminary of Poitiers. Priest, 1875; Assistant parish-priest at St Andre de Niort, 1876–80; entered Congregation of Oblates of Mary Immaculate, 1880; sent to Ceylon same year; Missionary till 1893. *Address:* Jaffna, Ceylon. *TA:* Bishop, Jaffna. *Club:* Jaffna Catholic (Hon. Pres.). *Died 7 Feb. 1919.*

JOURDAIN, Lt-Col Charles Edward Arthur, DSO 1900; Commanding 2nd Battalion Loyal North Lancashire Regiment; *b* 7 May 1869; *s* of late Rev. F. Jourdain; *m* 1912, Alexia Grace, *y d* of Captain Frederick Papillon, RN. Entered army, 1888; Captain, 1895; Major 1906; Lt-Col 1913; served South Africa, 1899–1902 (despatches, DSO); European War, 1914–17. *Club:* Junior United Service. *Died 29 July 1918.*

JOURDAIN, Eleanor Frances; Principal, St Hugh's College, Oxford, since 1915; *d* of late Rev. Francis Jourdain, Vicar of Ashburne, Derbyshire. *Educ:* home; Lady Margaret Hall, Oxford (Scholar); second class in the Final Honour School of Modern History, 1886. Assistant Mistress in High Schools (Tottenham and Clifton); Headmistress of the School for Girls, Corran, Watford, 1892; Vice-Principal, St Hugh's College, Oxford, 1902; obtained the Degree of Doctor of the University of Paris for a thesis on the Divina Commedia, 1904; MA Oxon 1920; Taylorian Lecturer in French, Oxford, 1920; Fellow of the Huguenot Society; Member of the Aristotelian Society; on the Council of the Dante Society. *Publications:* Le Symbolisme dans la Divine Comédie de Dante; The Theory of the Infinite in Modern Thought; An Introduction to the Study of the French Classical Drama; Methods of Moral Instruction and Training of Girls in France (a contribution to a volume edited by Prof. Sadler); Dramatic Theory and Practice in France, 1690–1808, etc. *Address:* St Hugh's College, Oxford. *T:* Oxford 782. *Club:* University Women's. *Died 6 April 1924.*

JOWETT, Rev. John Henry, CH 1922; MA, DD Edinburgh, 1910; New York, 1911; Minister of Westminster Chapel, 1918–23; *b* 1864; *s* of Josiah and Hannah Jowett; *m d* of Francis Winpenny, Barnard Castle. *Educ:* Hipperholme Grammar School; Edinburgh University; Oxford University. Minister of St James's Congregational Church, Newcastle upon Tyne, 1889–95; Carr's Lane, Birmingham, 1895–1911; Pres. Free Church Council, 1910; Minister of Fifth Avenue Presbyterian Church, NY, 1911–18. *Publications:* Apostolic Optimism; From Strength to Strength; Meditations for Quiet Moments; Brooks by the Traveller's Way; Thirsting for the Springs; The Passion for Souls; Silver Lining; The Transfigured Church; The Preacher: his Life and Work; Things that Matter Most; Daily Meditations; The Eagle Life; The Friend on the Road. *Recreation:* walking. *Address:* 10 Chichester Road, Croydon. *Died 19 Dec. 1923.*

JOWITT, Frederick McCulloch, CBE 1918; JP; *b* 1868; *m* 1900, Helen Dorothy, *d* of W. T. Benson, Montreal. *Address:* Hollins Hall, Ripley, Leeds. *Club:* Reform. *Died Sept. 1919.*

JOY, George William; artist; *b* Dublin, 7 July 1844; *s* of W. Bruce Joy, MD; *m* 1877, Florence, *d* of Thomas Masterman; four *d*. *Educ:* Harrow. Studied Kensington; Royal Academy; Paris (under Charles Jalabert and Bonnat). Served 21 years in Artists' Corps, representing them at Wimbledon, Bisley, etc; also shot 6 times in International Match for Ireland. *Pictures:* Domenica; Chess-players; Laodamia; Young Nelson's First Farewell; Wellington at Angers; Prince Charlie and Flora Macdonald; The King's Drum shall never be beaten for Rebels, in Russel-Cotes Municipal Art Gallery, Bournemouth; Princess Alice of Albany, for Queen Victoria; Reverie, for New Zealand Government; Truth, to German Government; Joan of Arc, sold to French Government; Lear and Cordelia, and The Death of General Gordon, in Leeds Municipal Art Gallery; The Danaids; The Drummer of the Peninsular; Christ and a Little Child, at Church House, Westminster; A Merchantman Seeking Goodly Pearls; A Dinner of Herbs, in Oldham Municipal Art Gallery; Britannia; The King's Daughter; Dreams on the Veldt; Griselda; The Sword; A Dream of Fair Women; A Herald, temp. Edward III, Eve; Tancred and Clorinda, 1910; Card Houses; and many portraits, including Sir Theodore Martin, Countess Cranbrook, Countess Farrers, Lady Craig

as a child, R. Bowerman; also impressionist flower pictures and studies, etc; obtained Gold Medals at Paris, Munich and Berlin; also the Chicago Medal. *Publication:* autobiographical sketch in The Work of George W. Joy, 1904. *Recreations:* music, rifle shooting, cricket. *Address:* Woodside, Purbrook, Hants. *T:* Waterlooville 79. *Club:* Arts.
Died 28 Oct. 1925.

JOYCE, Thomas Heath; *b* London, 9 July 1850; *s* of Thomas Joyce, Freshford, Somerset; editor and proprietor of the Atlas; *m* 1st, 1874, Ellen Margaretta (*d* 1916), *d* of George Murphy; 2nd, Emma, *d* of late W. Frances Knight, Overton, Hants; two *s*. *Educ:* mainly abroad. Joined staff of the Graphic at its start in Dec. 1869; editor of Daily Graphic, 1890–91, and joint-editor with Hammond Hall, 1891–1906; editor of the Graphic, 1891–1906. FRGS. *Publications:* miscellaneous journalistic and magazine contributions; trans. Victor Hugo, History of a Crime. *Recreations:* travel, walking, photography; journeyed round the world, 1907. *Clubs:* Whitefriars; Royal Albert Yacht, Southsea.
Died 13 May 1925.

JOYNER, Robert Batson, CIE 1898; MICE; FRGS; *b* 1 March 1844; 3rd *s* of late Henry St John Joyner, and Frances, *e d* of Alfred Batson, Ramsbury, Wilts; *m* 1879, Margaret Vye, *e d* of late N. Milne; one *s* two *d*. *Educ:* privately. Appointed by Sec. of State to Bombay Public Works Department, 1868; constructed Mutha Canal Irrigation Work and Poona Water Supply; twice thanked by Government for work done in Great Famine, 1876–77; designed and constructed Gokak Canal Works and other large schemes; employed in designing and constructing works for utilising Falls of Gokak, 1886–87, services being specially lent by Government of India; sent to Sindh to specially report on irrigation matters, 1889; appointed Superintending Engineer of that Province, 1891; and 1st Class Superintending Engineer, 1894; had charge of Famine Relief Works, 1896–98; specially thanked by Government. Decorated for work in India. *Publications:* Report on Utilisation of River Indus and Irrigation Management of Province of Sindh; paper on Proper Management of Indian Famines; Bombay Hydro-Electric Works design. *Recreations:* rowing, polo and pig-sticking formerly; latterly photography, sketching, cycling, etc. *Address:* Woody Bay, N Devon. *Died 30 July 1919.*

JUDD, George William, ISO 1913; Superintendent of Preventive Service, Karachi, since 1881; *b* 11 Nov. 1854; *s* of Captain George William Judd, Ordnance Department; *m* 1878, M. F. S. Malvery, *d* of late editor and proprietor of Our Paper, published at Karachi; four *s* three *d*. *Educ:* K.E. and I.E. School, Karachi. Entered Commissioner's Office, 1872; silver medal, Delhi Durbar. *Recreations:* cricket, shooting, fishing. *Address:* Andrew Road, Keomari, Karachi. *T:* 107.

JUDD, John Wesley, CB 1895; LLD; FRS; FGS; Emeritus Professor of Geology in the Imperial College of Science and Technology, 1915; *b* Portsmouth, 18 Feb. 1840; *m* 1878, Jeannie Frances, *d* of John Jeyes; one *s* one *d*. *Educ:* Camberwell; Royal School of Mines. Geological Survey of England and Wales, 1867–70; Inspector of Schools, 1871; President Geological Society, 1887–88; Prof. of Geology, 1876–1905; Dean of Royal College of Science, London, 1895–1905. *Publications:* Geology of Rutland, 1875; Volcanoes: What they are and what they teach, 1878; The Student's Lyell, 1896 and 1911; The Coming of Evolution, 1910; and many scientific memoirs in the Transactions of the Royal and other Societies. *Recreations:* geological exploration, gardening. *Address:* 30 Cumberland Road, Kew; Beachside, Walmer, Kent. *Died 3 March 1916.*

JUDGE, Mark Hayler, ARIBA; senior partner Mark H. Judge & Son; retired, 1921; chief surveyor to Sanitary Assurance Association since 1880; *b* Battle, Sussex, 26 Feb. 1847; *e s* of late George Hayler, Battle, and Mary, *e d* of late John Brignall, Wittersham, Kent; adopted surname of Judge, 1861; *m* 1875, Emily, *e d* of late John Harwood Simpson, MInstME, Stokesley, Yorks; one *s* two *d*. *Educ:* St Mary's National School, Hastings; Parker's Endowed School, Hastings. Founded Sunday Society, 1875; hon. secretary Sunday Society for Opening Museums, etc, on Sundays, since 1875; Director of Artizans', Labourers', and General Dwellings Co., Ltd, since 1877; member of Vestry of Paddington, 1886–92; chairman Metropolitan Board of Works Enquiry Committee, 1886–89; curator Parkes Museum of Hygiene, Univ. Coll., 1878–82; secretary International Medical and Sanitary Exhibition, Kensington, 1881; trustee Paddington Free Public Library; Founder University Extension Guild, 1903; Hon. Sec. Further Strand Improvement Committee since 1903; founded British Constitution Association, 1905; Chairman Sandgate and Shorncliffe Sir John Moore Centenary Memorial Committee; Chairman Committee on War Damage, instituted 1915. *Publications:* Sanitary Arrangements of Dwelling-Houses, 1884; Sanitary

Architecture, 1901; Communal and Individual Responsibility as regards Health Conditions, 1909; and other works on hygiene, including articles in reviews on cognate subjects and individualism; Political Socialism—A Remonstrance (Editor); The War and the Neutral Powers—International Law, 1914.
Died 25 Jan. 1927.

JUDSON, Harry Pratt, LLD; President of the University of Chicago, 1907–23; President Emeritus since 1923; *b* Jamestown, NY, 20 Dec. 1849; *s* of Rev. Lyman P. Judson and Abigail C. Pratt; *m* 1879, Rebecca A. Gilbert, Troy, NY; one *d*. *Educ:* Williams College. AB 1870; AM 1883; LLD 1893; LLD Queen's University, Canada, 1903; State University of Iowa, 1907; Washington University, 1907; Western Reserve, 1909; Harvard, 1909; University of Michigan, 1911; North-Western University, 1913; Dalhousie University, Halifax, NS, 1919. Teacher and Principal, High School, Troy, NY, 1870–85; Prof. of History, University of Minnesota, 1885–92; Prof. of Political Science and Head Dean of the Colleges, University of Chicago, 1892–94; Prof. and Head Dept of Political Science, and Dean of Faculties arts, literature and science, 1894–1907; acting President, 1906–7. Co-editor American Historical Review, 1895–1902; member General Education Board, 1906; member of the Rockefeller Foundation, 1918–23; Chairman, Commission on Medical Education in China, Rockefeller Foundation, 1914; Chairman, University of Chicago War Service, 1917–18; Director American Persian Relief Commission, 1918–19. Knight Royal Prussian Order of the Crown, 1904; Officer Legion of Honour, 1913; First Class Order of the Lion and Sun (with brilliants), Persia, 1919; Commander of the Order of St Sava, 1921; gold medal, National Institute of Social Sciences, 1920. *Publications:* History of the Troy Citizens Corps, 1884; Caesar's Army, 1885; Caesar's Commentaries (co-editor), 1885; Europe in the Nineteenth Century, 1894, 1898, revised, 1901; The Growth of the American Nation, 1895, 1900; The Higher Education as a Training for Business, 1896; The Mississippi Valley (in Shaler's United States of America), 1894; The Young American, 1895; The Government of Illinois, 1900; The Essentials of a Written Constitution (Decennial Publications, The University of Chicago, vol. iv); Our Federal Republic, 1925. *Recreations:* golf, fly-fishing. *Address:* The University of Chicago, Chicago. *Clubs:* Quadrangle, University, Union League, Cliff Dwellers, Chicago; University, Washington; Century, New York.
Died 4 March 1927.

JULER, Henry Edward, FRCS; *b* Suffolk; *s* of H. C. Juler, MD; *m*; two *s* three *d*. *Educ:* London; Paris; Berlin; St Mary's Hospital Medical School. House Surgeon, Female Lock Hospital; Medical Superintendent of St Mary's Hospital; Demonstrator of Anatomy, St Mary's Hospital Medical School; Pathologist, Royal Westminster Ophthalmic Hospital; Consulting Ophthalmic Surgeon, St Mary's Hospital; Consulting Ophthalmic Surgeon to the Royal Westminster Ophthalmic Hospital, and to the London Lock Hospitals. *Publications:* A Handbook of Ophthalmic Science and Practice; and other works on the Eye. *Recreations:* fond of horse exercise, golf, motor cars. *Address:* 24 Cavendish Square, W1. *T:* Mayfair 1633.
Died 23 April 1921.

JULIAN, Maj.-Gen. Sir Oliver Richard Archer, KBE 1921 (CBE 1919); CB 1916; CMG 1900; late Army Medical Service; *b* 26 July 1863; *s* of Captain Thomas Archer Julian, late 52nd Regt, of Broomhill, Ivybridge; *m* 1888, Lily, *d* of late Sampson Taylor Rowe. Entered army, 1887, Major, 1899; served South Africa, 1899–1902 (despatches twice; Queen's medal 4 clasps—Talana, Defence of Ladysmith, Laing's Nek, Belfast; King's medal 2 clasps; CMG); Zakka Khel Expedition, 1908; Mohmand Expedition, 1908 (despatches, Bt Lt-Col); European War, France and Belgium, 1915–17 (despatches, CB); DDMS Western Command, 1917–19 (CBE); DMS, Mesopotomia, 1919–21 (despatches, KBE); Physician and Surgeon, Royal Hospital, Chelsea, 1913–15; retired pay, 1921. *Address:* Ivydene, South Molton, Devon. *Died 13 June 1925.*

K

KADOORIE, Sir Ellis, Kt 1917; merchant, of Hong-Kong; *b* Baghdad, 7 Dec. 1865; *s* of Silas Kadoorie and Remah Eleazar; unmarried. *Educ:*

privately. *Recreation:* racing. *Address:* 10 Ice House Street, Hong-Kong. *Clubs:* Hong-Kong; Shanghai.   *Died Feb. 1922.*

KAGWA, Sir Apolo, KCMG 1925; Principal Minister, 1914–26; formerly Regent of Buganda. Visited England, 1902. *Address:* Mengo, Uganda.   *Died 21 Feb. 1927.*

KAINE, Hon. John Charles; MLC Stadocona division, Quebec; in Cabinet, without portfolio, since 1906; *b* 18 Oct. 1854; *m* 1st, 1879, Theresa Maria Tucker; 2nd, 1904, Helen Smith. *Address:* 5 Ste Ursule Street, Quebec.   *Died 23 April 1921.*

KAMBAL, Miralai (Col) Beshir Bey, DSO 1917; Inspector Kordofan Arab Tribes since 1900; *b* Halfayet El-Melouk, Khartoum North District, Khartoum Province, 1855; descendant of Malik Shawish Kambal, last King of Dongola till 1817; *m* 1870; six *s* fourteen *d. Educ:* in his own house at Halfayet El-Melouk. Under the former Sudan Government—service rendered in Khartoum, Sennar, Red Sea Coasts, Expedition of Darfur with Gordon Pasha in 1876, Kassala and Abyssinian frontiers with the following ranks in the Irregular troops: Bulukbashi, Head of 25 Irregular Cavalry; Bimbashi, Head of 100 Irregular Cavalry; Sangak, Head of 200, 300 and 400 Irregular Cavalry; under Dervishes Rule, 1885–98—under captivity in Omdurman, 1885–90; Bahr-el-Jebel, 1891–93; Omdurman, 1894–95; passed in prison in Omdurman 1896–98; mentioned in Ten Years' Captivity in the Sudan, by Father Ohrwalder, and Fire and Sword, Slatin Pasha, as well as in Arabic publications of Ibrahim Fawzi Pasha and Naoum Bey Shoukair; under Sudan Government, 1899–1918—OC Irregular Battalion and then as Sub-Governor Kordofan, 1899. 4th Medjidie, 4th Osmanieh, English and Egyptian Sudan medals with clasps of Djebel-Dayer Talodi, Djebel Nimi; Victoria medal, 1912. *Recreations:* the only recreation he enjoyed was cultivation during three months' leave every year. *Address:* El-Obeid, Kordofan, Sudan.   *Died 6 Sept. 1919.*

KANE, Adm. Sir Henry Coey, KCB 1911 (CB 1891); retired 1899; *b* 1843; *s* of Sir Robert Kane, FRS, Fortlands, Killiney. Sub-Lieutenant RN 1863; Naval Attaché to Maritime Courts, 1883–87; Director of Naval Ordnance, 1894–97. *Address:* 201 Ashley Gardens, SW. *T:* Victoria 7711. *Club:* United Service.

Died 30 Jan. 1917.

KANE, Captain Robert Romney Godred, DSO 1915; Royal Munster Fusiliers; *b* 11 Oct 1888; *s* of late Judge R. R. Kane, 4 Fitzwilliam Place, Dublin, and Glendree, County Clare; unmarried. *Educ:* Oratory School, Edgbaston; Sandhurst. Entered army 1908; joined the 1st Batt. Royal Munster Fusiliers in India (Rawal Pindi); was in India and Burma till Aug. 1914; served European War, on Staff in Gallipoli from the first landing till 13 July 1915 (twice wounded); on Staff in France, 1915–16 (DSO; Chevalier, Legion of Honour; despatches). *Recreations:* hunting, polo, big and small game shooting. *Address:* 201 Ashley Gardens, SW. *Club:* Junior Army and Navy.   *Died 1 Oct. 1918.*

KANE, William Francis de Vismes, DL, JP; MRIA; member Diocesan Council, Diocese of Clogher, Church of Ireland; *b* Exmouth, 19 April 1840; *o s* of Joseph Kane, of Dublin, and Withycombe Grange, Devon, and Eliza, *d* of Col the Count de Vismes, Coldstream Guards; *m* 1st, 1863, Emily, *d* of Rev. C. J. Hamilton; one *d*; 2nd, 1902, Hon. Louisa Catherine, *d* of 1st Lord Bateman, and *widow* of late Col Green Wilkinson, Scots Guards. *Educ:* Brighton College; Dublin Univ. (MA). High Sheriff, Co. Monaghan, 1865 and 1909; sometime a Director and Chairman of the Grand Canal Co., Ireland, in which he initiated large reforms. *Publications:* Handbook of European Butterflies; a Catalogue of the Lepidoptera of Ireland; articles on entomology, and microscopic crustaces, etc, in various scientific magazines. *Recreations:* archæology, horticulture, natural history, microscopy. *Address:* Drumreaske, Monaghan. *TA:* Ballinode.   *Died 18 April 1918.*

KANTARAJ URS, Sir Mysore, KCIE 1921; CSI 1914; Dewan (Chief Minister) of Mysore, 1918–22; retired 1922; *b* 20 Sept. 1870; *s* of Narasaraj Urs and Kempanaja Ammanni, of the Kalale family, Mysore; *m* Maharajakumari Jayalakshmi Ammanni, *e sister* of Maharaja of Mysore; one *d. Educ:* Maharaja's Coll., Mysore; The Christian Coll., Madras. Assistant Commissioner, 1894; Asst Private Secretary to HH the Maharani Regent, 1895–99; Special Asst Commissioner, Bangalore, 1899; Deputy Commissioner, Mysore District, also President, Mysore City Municipal Council, 1902; Chairman, Mysore City Improvement Trust Board, 1908; Excise Commissioner in Mysore, 1912; Chairman, Industries and Commerce Committee, 1912–16; Member of the Executive Council, Mysore, 1913–18;

visited Japan, March–Aug. 1916; Chairman, Agricultural Committee, 1916–18; created Rajaseva Dhurina (Gandabherunda Order), Oct. 1916. *Recreations:* riding, tennis. *Address:* Jayalakshmi Vilas, Mysore, India. *Clubs:* United Service (Hon.); Bangalore, Ursu, Mysore.

Died 3 Oct. 1923.

KAPP, Dr Gisbert; *b* Mauer, near Vienna; father of German family, mother of Scotch; *m* 1884, Therese Mary Krall; two *s. Educ:* Polytechnic School, Zürich. In practical engineering work, partly in England, partly abroad, since 1876; Manager to the works of Messrs Crompton and Co., Chelmsford, 1882–84; set up as Consulting Engineer in Westminster, 1884; went to Berlin and became General Secretary to the German Association of Electrical Engineers and Lecturer of Electrical Engineering at Charlottenburg, 1894; Professor of Electrical Engineering, the University, Birmingham, 1905–18. Telford Medallist, 1886–88; Hon. DEng Karlsruhe and Dresden; Past President Institution of Electrical Engineers; President of the Engineering Section British Association, 1913. *Publications:* for 11 years editor of Elektrotechnische Zeitschrift; Electric Transmission of Power; Transformers; Dynamo Machines; Construction of Electric Machinery; Alternating Currents; Principles of Electrical Engineering and their Application; various papers at the Institutions of Civil and Electric Engineers. *Recreations:* golfing, yachting. *Address:* Selly Park, Birmingham.   *Died 10 Aug. 1922.*

KARAULI, HH Maharaja Dhiraj Sir Bhanwar Pal, Deo Bahadur, Yadukul Chandra Bhal, GCIE 1897 (KCIE 1894); *b* 24 July 1864; *S* 1886; recognized as head of Jadon Rajputs (Lunar dynasty), and as the lineal descendant of Sri Krishna, the god; married, six wives; no *c. Educ:* Mayo College, Ajmere. A patron of learning, especially Sanskrit. The State has an area of 1,242 square miles and a population of over 150,000; entitled to a salute of 17 guns; received Coronation medal, 1912. *Recreation:* shooting. *Address:* Karauli, Rajputana.

Died 3 Aug. 1927.

KARKARIA, R. P.; *b* Bombay, 16 May 1869; *m* cousin; no *c. Educ:* St Xavier's School and College. BA 1888; Senior Fellow and Professor St Xavier's College, Bombay, 1891; Principal and Professor of English Language and Literature, Collegiate Institutions, 1898; Examiner in History and Philosophy, Bombay University; was the first to give in India a series of lectures on the Great War—its historical causes, course, etc—which he began in Bombay in September 1914; contributed to a Parsi paper during 1915–16, a Calendar of Eminent Parsis for every day in the year; organised with Bombay Jashan Committee the Historical Celebration at Sanjan, 1916, of the 1,200th anniversary of Parsis' first arrival in India at that place. FRHistS, MRAS. *Publications:* discovered the Anstey MS of, and edited 1892, with notes, Carlyle's hitherto Unpublished Lectures on European Literature and Culture, originally delivered in 1838; Parnell's Poems, and Golden Treasury, Book IV; India—Forty Years of Progress and Reform, 1896; India since the Mutiny, Historical Sketch of the Parsis, Shivaji, Akbar, and other Essays; Bibliography of Bombay; European Travellers in Gujarat; translated Parsi Sacred Book, the Pahalavi Dinkard; Cicero's De Natura Deorum and a Teleogical Treatise of the Avesta; Zoroaster and Comte—some Zoroastrian traits in Positivism; Purim and Farwardigan—in the Hoshang Memorial Volume, 1909; The French Revolutionary and the Parsi Calendars: a study in chronology—in the Cama Memorial Volume; Firdausi: his Editors and Translators; Proselytism among the Parsis and among the Jews: a Historical Parallel; Death of Shivaji, 1905; edited Lord Curzon's Farewell Speeches in India, with Essays on his Vice-royalty, 1906; Mahmud Begurra, Sultan of Gujarat; edited Dean Church's Dante, with Introduction, 1906; The Scientific Study of Mahratha History, 1907; Lord Curzon's Indian Vice-royalty, 1908; Essays in English History, 1908; Charm of Bombay, an Anthology with notes, 1914. *Recreations:* book-hunting, coin-collecting, visiting historical places in Western India. *Address:* Gowalia Tank, Grant Road, Bombay, 7.

Died 13 May 1919.

KASHMIR and JAMMU, Maharaja of; Lt Gen. HH Sir Pratap Singh Indar Mahindar Bahadur, Sipar-i-Saltanat, GBE 1918; GCIE 1911; GCSI; LLD Punjab University; Hon. Colonel 47th Dogras; *b* 1850; the third of his line, and *g s* of the founder of the dynasty, Maharaja Ghulab Singh; *S* 1885. Area of 84,432 square miles; population of 3,320,518; entitled to a salute of twenty-one guns within the limits of his State, and twenty-one guns in the rest of India; British Government conferred additional powers on the Maharaja in 1905; HH signalised this by inaugurating public works of importance, a motor road *via* Banihal Pass to Srinagar, etc; the Govt again conferred full powers on the Maharaja in 1921. *Recreations:* religious and historical discussion. *Address:* Srinagar, Kashmir; Jammu, Punjab.

Died 23 Sept. 1925.

KATO, Viscount Takaaki, Viscount, 1916; Baron, 1911; Hon. GCMG; Prime Minister of Japan since 1924; *b* 3 Jan. 1860; *m* 1886, Haruji, *sister* of Baron Hisaya Iwasaki; one *s* one *d. Educ:* Univ. of Tokio. Private Sec. to the Minister for Foreign Affairs, 1888–90; Director of Banking Bureau and Director of Taxation Bureau, Finance Department, 1891–94; Envoy Extraordinary and Minister Plenipotentiary at the Court of St James's, 1894–99; Minister for Foreign Affairs, 1900–1 and 1906; Ambassador of Japan at the Court of St James's, 1908–13; Minister for Foreign Affairs, Jan. 1913; resigned, Feb. 1913; Leader of the Kensei Kwai since 1913; Minister for Foreign Affairs, 1914–15; Member of the House of Peers, 1915. *Address:* Shimo-Nibancho, Tokio, Japan.
Died 28 Jan. 1926.

KATO, Adm. Baron Tomasaburo, Juhnii; Insignia of the First Class of the Order of the Paulownia and Rising Sun, Insignia of the First Class of the Order of the Sacred Treasure, and Insignia of the Second Class of the Order of the Golden Kite; Japanese Prime Minister and Minister of Marine since June 1922; *b* Hiroshima, Japan, 1859. Entered navy at age of 12; midshipman, 1888; Captain, 1899; Professor at the Naval College; Construction Supervisor in the Navy Department; Chief of Staff of Standing Squadron, 1902; of the Kamiura Fleet; of the combined Fleet under Admiral Togo in the Russo-Japanese war of 1904–5; Vice-Minister of Marines, 1906; Commander-in-Chief, Kure Naval Station, 1909–14; also served in the Navy Department; Commander-in-Chief of the First Fleet when war broke out in 1914; promoted to Admiral, 1915; Minister of Marine in 1918 in the Terauchi Cabinet; created Baron in recognition of war services; one of the three chief Japanese Delegates, Washington Conference, 1921–22. *Address:* Ichichome, Nagatacho, Kohjimachi-Ku, Tokio, Japan. *Died 24 Aug. 1923.*

KAUFMANN, Rev. Moritz, MA; Rector of Ingworth since 1892, and Vicar of Calthorpe, Norfolk, since 1893; *b* 7 Oct. 1839; *s* of Leopold and Babetta Kaufmann, of Gross-sachsen, Weinheim, in the Grand Duchy of Baden; *m* Mary Josephine, *d* of William Pilkington and Eliza Campbell Watson, of Cloughton, Birkenhead; three *s* one *d. Educ:* Grammar School of Weinheim; Trinity College, Dublin. Respondent, Prizeman in Hebrew, Syriac, Chaldee, and modern languages; English Composition Prize awarded by the late Prof. Dowden. After serving several cures at home and abroad he was tutor at St Aidan's Theological College, Birkenhead, 1877–83; subsequently curate in charge of Erpingham, 1884–92; Donnellan Lecturer for the University of Dublin, 1899–1900. *Publications:* Utopias or Social Schemes of Improvement from Sir Thomas More to Karl Marx; Christian Socialism; Charles Kingsley, Christian Socialist and Social Reformer; Socialism and Communism in their Practical Application; Socialism and Modern Thought; Social Development under Christian Influence; The Housing of the Working Classes and of the Poor, in Social Problems Series, etc; contributor to Cambridge Modern History; Pascal's Thoughts, translated and selected (Devotional Works). *Recreations:* country walks, perusal of fiction. *Address:* Ingworth, Norwich. *TA:* Aylsham. *Club:* New Athenæum.
Died 8 March 1920.

KAULBACH, Ven. James Albert, MA, DD; Rector of Truro, Nova Scotia, since 1903; Archdeacon of Nova Scotia and Canon of St Luke's Cathedral since 1889; Examining Chaplain since 1896; *b* Lunenburg, NS, 30 Aug. 1839; 3rd *s* of J. H. Kaulbach, High Sheriff of Lunenburg, NS; *m* 1876, Mary Sophia, *d* of James F. Bradshaw, Quebec; one *s. Educ:* Collegiate School and King's College, Windsor, NS. Ordained Deacon, 1864; Priest, 1865; Curate at River John, 1864–70; Vicar of Truro, Nova Scotia, 1870–1903. *Address:* Truro, Nova Scotia. *Club:* Clericus, Halifax, NS. *Died 25 Feb. 1913.*

KAVANAGH, Rt. Hon. Walter MacMurrough, PC Ireland 1916; JP, DL; *b* Jan. 1856; *e s* of Rt Hon. Arthur McM. Kavanagh; *m* 1887, Helen Louisa, *d* of Colonel J. S. Howard; two *s. Educ:* Eton; Christ Church, Oxford. High Sheriff, Co. Carlow, 1884. MP (N) Carlow, 1908–10. *Address:* Borris House, Borris, Co. Carlow. *Clubs:* Reform; Sackville Street, Dublin. *Died 18 July 1922.*

KAY, Lt-Col Sir William Algernon Ireland, 6th Bt, *cr* 1803; CMG 1918; DSO 1914; King's Royal Rifle Corps; *b* 21 March 1876; *s* of Sir William Algernon Kay, 5th Bt and Emily, *d* of late Thomas James Ireland, Ousden Hall, Suffolk; *S* father, 1914. Entered army, 1896; Captain, 1901; Major, 1914; Adjutant Volunteers, 1906–8, and Territorials, 1908–9; served Sierra Leone, 1898–99 (medal with clasp); South Africa, 1899–1902 (despatches; Queen's medal, 4 clasps; King's medal, 2 clasps); European War, 1914–18 (DSO, Bt Lt-Col, CMG). Heir: none. *Club:* Naval and Military.
Died 4 Oct. 1918 (ext).

KAY-SHUTTLEWORTH, Hon. Edward James, BA; *b* 16 March 1890; *y s* of 1st Baron Shuttleworth; *m* 1914, Sibell, 2nd *d* of C. R. W. Adeane; one *s* one *d. Educ:* Eton; Balliol College, Oxford. Barrister, Inner Temple, 1913; temporary commission, 7th Service Batt. Rifle Brigade since 1914; served European War, 1915.
Died 10 July 1917.

KAY-SHUTTLEWORTH, Hon. Lawrence Ughtred, JP Lancashire, 1912; Private Secretary (unpaid) to the Rt Hon. Walter Runciman, 1913–14; Temporary 2nd Lieutenant Royal Field Artillery; *b* 21 Sept. 1887; *e s* of 1st Baron Shuttleworth; *m* 1913, Selina Adine, *d* of Col Hon. Francis Bridgeman; two *s* one *d. Educ:* Eton; Balliol College, Oxford; BA 2nd Class (History Honour School), 1910. Called to Bar, Inner Temple, 1913; contested Altrincham Div. of Cheshire, 1913. *Address:* 7 Queensberry Place, SW. *T:* Kensington 5402; Gawthorpe Hall, Burnley; Barbon Manor, Kirkby Lonsdale. *Clubs:* Brooks's, Reform, Cobden, Eighty.
Died 30 March 1917.

KAYE, Lt-Col James Levett; temporarily employed at War Office since 1916; *b* 27 Dec. 1861; *s* of James Kaye, Barrister of Lincoln's Inn; *m* Edith Mary, *o d* of late Stephen Harvey-James, Indian Civil Service; no *c. Educ:* Winchester; Sandhurst. Entered army, 1882; served with the Royal Berkshire Regt in Egypt and Gibraltar till 1885, including Suakin campaign, 1885; joined Indian Army and served with 25th Punjab Infantry, 5th Bengal Cavalry and Central India Horse; joined the Political Department of the Government of India, 1889; Settlement Commissioner in Kashmir, 1895–1904; Political Agent, Alwar, 1905; Resident at Indore, 1907; Resident in Mewar, Rajputana, India, 1911–16. *Recreations:* shooting, motoring, golf. *Address:* Whitehall Court, SW. *Club:* East India United Service.
Died 17 Nov. 1917.

KAYE, Sir Joseph Henry, 1st Bt, *cr* 1923; *b* 6 Sept. 1856; *s* of late Henry Kaye of Lindley, Huddersfield; *m* 1885, Emily, *d* of Alfred Crowther, JP, of Greenroyd, Huddersfield; one *s. Educ:* locally. Woollen and worsted cloth manufacturer; Chairman of Kaye & Steward, Ltd, Huddersfield; Chairman of Gledhill Bros & Co., Ltd, Huddersfield; Director of Lloyd's Bank; Director of London Midland and Scottish Railway; Past President of Huddersfield Chamber of Commerce; Past Chairman, Huddersfield Fine Cloth Manufacturers' Association; Trustee of the Huddersfield Royal Infirmary; JP County Borough of Huddersfield, etc; President of the Huddersfield Conservative Association; Member of the Royal Commission in 1916–17 on the Textile Trades after the war; Prominent Member of Committee of the Huddersfield War Hospital, 1915–19. *Recreations:* foreign travel, formerly mountaineering etc, golf. Heir: *s* Captain and Flight-Commander Henry Gordon Kaye, *b* 24 Feb. 1889. *Address:* Norwood, Huddersfield. *T:* Huddersfield 2099. *Clubs:* Carlton, Junior Carlton, Constitutional. *Died 24 Dec. 1923.*

KEABLE, Robert; novelist; *b* 6 March 1887; *s* of Rev. Robert Henry Keable and Margaret Charlotte Hopkins, late of Pavenham Vicarage, Bedfordshire. *Educ:* Whitgift Grammar School; Magdalene College, Cambridge (Open Latimer-Neville History Exhibitions and School Scholarships); BA, 1st Class History Tripos, 1908; MA 1914; Westcott House Clergy Training School. Ordained, 1911; Curate of Bradford Parish Church, Yorks, 1911–12; The Universities Mission to Central Africa, 1912–14; Rector Leribe, Basutoland, 1914–20; Chaplain to the S African Forces on service in France, 1917–18; resigned orders, 1920; first novel published, 1921; Assistant Master, Dulwich College, 1921; Dunstable Grammar School, 1922. *Publications:* Darkness and Light, 1913; Songs of the Narrow Way, 1914; The Loneliness of Christ, 1914; A City of the Dawn, 1915; The Adventures of Paul Kangai, 1915; The Perpetual Passion, 1916; The Drift of Pinions, 1917; This Same Jesus, 1918; Standing By, 1919; Pilgrim Papers, 1920; Simon Called Peter, 1921; The Mother of All Living, 1921; Peradventure, 1922; Recompense, 1924; Numerous Stories, 1925; Tahiti: Isle of Dreams, 1925; Lighten our Darkness (in USA, Ann Decides), 1927; contributor to various magazines; *posthumous publication:* Monty Mad, 1928. *Recreations:* travel, swimming, rowing, shooting. *Address:* c/o A. P. Watt & Son, 10 Norfolk Street, Strand, WC2. *Died Dec. 1927.*

KEANE, Lt-Col Richard Henry, CBE 1919 (OBE 1918); *b* 3 May 1881; 3rd *s* of late Sir Richard Francis Keane, 4th Bt, of Cappoquin, Co. Waterford; *m* 1906, Alice, *y d* of late Sir Lumley Smith, Judge of the City of London Court; one *s* two *d. Educ:* Clifton; Royal Agricultural College, Cirencester. Joined Royal Naval Division, 1915; transferred to the Army, 1916; commanded 15th Batt. (Transport Workers) South Lancs, 1917–19 (OBE, CBE). *Address:* Fortwilliam, Glencairn, Co. Waterford, Ireland. *Died 22 Nov. 1925.*

KEARNS, Maj. Reginald Arthur Ernest Holmes, CMG 1916; Army Service Corps, Territorial Forces. Served European War, 1914–16 (despatches, CMG); DAQMG 1916.

Died 24 Nov. 1918.

KEARNS, Col Thomas Joseph, CB 1913; CMG 1917; Serjeant-at-Arms City of London since 1907; and commanding Army Service Corps, 1st London Division Territorial Force; *b* 6 Jan. 1861; *o s* of late Philip Kearns, Belfast; *m* Haidee Ida, *o d* of late Henry Holmes, Toronto; no *c. Educ:* Dagmar House School, Hatfield, Herts. Served in ranks until commissioned Riding Master Army Service Corps, 1896; retired on appointment as City Marshal, London, 1904. Served South African War, 1879; Zulu Campaign (medal with clasp); Ashantee Expedition, 1895–96 (star, honourably mentioned); South African War, 1899–1902; on staff (despatches thrice, Queen's medal with six clasps, King's medal with two clasps); European War, 1914–19 (despatches five times); Diamond Jubilee Medal; Coronation Medals, King Edward VII and King George V; 1914–15 star; Officer of the Order of Leopold II, Belgium. *Address:* Mansion House, EC. *Club:* Royal Automobile.

Died 30 June 1920.

KEARTON, Richard, FZS; field naturalist, author and lecturer; *b* Thwaite in Swaledale, Yorks, 2 Jan. 1862; 2nd *s* of late John Kearton, yeoman farmer, and Mary, *e d* of Richard Hunter of Winton, Westmorland; *m* 1889, Ellen Rose Cowdrey; three *s* two *d. Educ:* Muker National School. Farmer in Swaledale, Yorks, until 1882; sub-manager of Publicity Department, Cassell & Co., publishers; retired, 1898. *Publications:* Birds Nests, Eggs and Egg Collecting; British Birds' Nests: How, Where and When to Find and Identify Them, illustrated entirely by photos taken direct from Nature; With Nature and a Camera, being the Adventures and Observations of a Field Naturalist and an Animal Photographer; Wild Life at Home: How to Study and Photograph It; Our Rarer British Breeding Birds; Our Bird Friends; Strange Adventures in Dickybird Land (a Book of Natural History Fiction for Children); A Photographically Illustrated Edition of White's Selborne, 1902; Wild Nature's Ways; The Adventures of Cock Robin and his Mate; Pictures from Nature; Nature's Carol Singers; The Fairyland of Living Things; Kearton's Nature Pictures; The Adventures of Jack Rabbit; Baby Birds at Home; Wonders of Wild Nature; At Home with Wild Nature; Wild Bird Adventures; The Pocket Book of Birds (with Howard Bentham); A Naturalist's Pilgrimage; contributor to various papers and magazines. *Address:* Ashdene, Caterham Valley, Surrey.

Died 8 Feb. 1928.

KEARY, Charles Francis; novelist and writer on history and philosophy. *Educ:* Marlborough; Trinity Coll., Cambridge. Formerly on the staff of the British Museum. *Publications:* A Wanderer, 1888; A Mariage de Convenance, 1889; The Two Lancrofts, 1893; Herbert Vanlennert, 1895; The Journalist, 1898; Twixt Dog and Wolf, 1901; High Policy, 1902; Bloomsbury, 1905; The Mount, 1909; The Brothers: a masque (verse), 1902; Rigel: a mystery (verse), 1904; Religious Hours (verse), 1916; The Dawn of History (ed), 1879; Outlines of Primitive Belief, 1882; The Mythology of the Eddas, 1882; The Vikings in Western Christendom, 1890; Norway and the Norwegians, 1892; The Pursuit of Reason, 1911; and other writings on antiquarian subjects; contributed to the Edinburgh, Nineteenth Century, Fortnightly, and other reviews and magazines. *Club:* Savile.

Died 25 Oct. 1917.

KEATING, Most Rev. Frederick William, DD; RC Archbishop of Liverpool since 1921; *b* Birmingham, 1859. *Educ:* St Chad's Grammar School, Birmingham; Sedgley Park; Benedictine Coll., Douai; Olton Seminary. Ordained, 1882; Administrator of St Chad's Cathedral, Birmingham, 1898–1908; Bishop of Northampton, 1907–21. *Address:* Archbishop's House, Belvidere Road, Liverpool. *T:* Royal 465.

Died 7 Feb. 1928.

KEATINGE, Henry Pottinger, CMG 1913; MB; FRCS; Corresponding Member Royal Zoological Society; Hon. Fellow Royal Academy of Medicine in Ireland; Member of the Egyptian Institute; *b* 31 July 1860; *s* of Gen. R. H. Keatinge, VC, CSI. *Educ:* Uppingham; Guy's Hospital; Durham University College of Medicine. Served with Egyptian Army, 1884–90; Nile and frontier campaigns during that period (medal, three clasps; bronze star and 4th class Osmanieh; appointed to the Cairo School of Medicine, 1890; later as Director of it and of the Kasr el Ainy Hospital (2nd class Medjidieh) (despatches, Egypt, 1915); retired from Egyptian Government Service, 1919 (2nd class Order of the Nile). *Address:* 21 Regent Road, Jersey. *Clubs:* Garrick, Flyfishers'.

Died 21 June 1928.

KEBTY-FLETCHER, John Robert; MP (C) Altrincham Division Cheshire, Dec. 1910–1913; *b* Liverpool, 1868. *Educ:* Liverpool College; abroad. Linguist; past President of the Liverpool Produce Exchange. Contested (C) Rossendale Division, 1906 and 1910. *Address:* Hooton, Cheshire.

Died 12 July 1914

KEELING, Rev. William Hulton, MA Oxon; LLD Leeds; Head Master of Bradford Grammar School since 1871; *b* Blackley Rectory, Manchester, 1840; *e s* of Rev. William Robert Keeling; *m* 1874, Henrietta Frances (*d* 1905), *d* of Rev. Sydney Gedge; five *s* four *d. Educ:* Manchester Grammar School; Wadham College, Oxford. 1st cl. Classical Mods 1859; 2nd cl. Lit. Hum., 1862; VIth Form Master Bromsgrove School, 1863–65; VIth Form Master Rossall School 1865–67; Head Master Northampton Grammar School, 1867–71; Member of the Committee of the Head Masters' Conference, 1894–97 and 1899–1902. *Address:* Bradford Grammar School.

Died 30 March 1916

KEEN, Austin, Hon. MA (Cantab); FCS; Education Secretary to the Cambridgeshire County Council since 1894. *Educ:* University College of Wales, Aberystwyth. Science Master at Ardwyn School, 1881–8; Organising Secretary of the Huddersfield Technical School, 1882–9 Permanent Member of Executive (ex-Hon. Secretary and Chairman) of the Association of Directors and Secretaries of Education in Counties and County Boroughs; Member of the Education Committee of the County Councils Association; Member of the Court of Governors and of the Council of the University College of Wales, Aberystwyth; Co-opted Member of Cambridge University Board of Agricultural Studies; Member of the Joint Scholarship Board; Chairman of the East Anglian Musical Competition; Commissioner for National Savings in Cambridgeshire; Member of the Horticultural Advisory Committee of the Board of Agriculture etc; Hon. Local Sec. for Cambridgeshire for the Royal Automobile Club. *Publications:* Ten Years' Work in Cambridgeshire under the Technical Instruction Act; various papers on education administration and the training of teachers; The Catalogue of the Cambridgeshire County Library. *Recreations:* fruit-growing, shooting, croquet. *Address:* Cefn Llys, Cambridge. *TA:* Keen, Cefnllys, Cambridge. *T:* 176. M. CE 1725. *Clubs:* Royal Automobile; Cambridge Union Society.

Died 20 Jan. 1922

KEENE, Col Alfred, DSO 1887; *b* 17 April 1855; *s* of late H. G. Keene, CIE; *m* 1894, Janet Frances, *widow* of Col Ayrton Pullan. Entered army, 1874; Col 1904; retired 1905; served Afghan War, 1878–80 (despatches, medal); Burmah, 1885–86 (despatches, DSO, medal with clasp). *Address:* Down Close, The Ridgeway, Guildford.

Died 21 April 1918

KEENE, Charles James, CIE 1903; VD; Public Works Department India (Railways), retired 1905; Secretary, Madras and Southern Mahratta Railway, and Major Railway Rifles, retired 1912; *b* 25 May 1850; *m* 1881, Mary Victoria Josephine, *y d* of late Wellington Shego of Dublin; four *s* one *d. Address:* Ealing.

Died 9 April 1917

KEENE, Most Rev. James Bennett; Bishop of Meath (Church of Ireland) since 1897; *b* Dublin, 25 Oct. 1849; *y s* of Arthur Bennett Keene, MA; *m* 1913, Henrietta Sophia, *o* surv. *d* of Rev. W. Streatfeild. *Educ:* Rathmines School, and Trinity College, Dublin; First Honourman and Prizeman in Classics, 1867; first of the First Honourmen in Science, 1867, 1868, 1869; first Primate's Hebrew Prizeman, 1867, 1868, 1869; Mathematical Scholar and Lloyd Exhibitioner, 1870; Senior Moderator and Gold Medallist in Mathematics, Logic, and Ethics, 1871; Wall Biblical Scholar in Hebrew, Syriac and Chaldee, 1872; M'Cullagh Prize and Bishop Law's Mathematical Premium, 1872; Elrington Theological Prize, 1874; Extra Prize at Theological Exhibition and Divinity Testimonium (First Class), 1875. Rector of Navan, 1879; Prebendary of Tipper and Canon of St Patrick's; Examining Chaplain to the Bishop of Meath, 1885; Headmaster of Navan College; Diocesan Nominator and Secretary of Board of Education; Member of Senate TCD. *Address:* Bishopscourt, Ardbraccan, Navan; 26 Clyde Road, Dublin. *Clubs:* New Oxford and Cambridge; University, Dublin.

Died 5 Aug. 1919

KEENE, William, CBE 1918; MVO 1909; *b* Ewe Cote, Whitby, Yorks, 13 May 1851; 2nd *s* of late Rev. William Keene and Mary Loy, *d* of George Merryweather; *m* 1885, Louisa Catharine, *d* of late Rev. Frederick Pitman of Iddesleigh, Devon, and Mrs H. M. Northcote. *Educ:* Shrewsbury; Uppingham. Passed an examination 1887; Consul at Madeira, 1888; Consul for Island of Madeira and

its Dependencies, to reside at Funchal, 1894; Consul for Departments of the Nord (with exception of the town of Dunkirk), Pas de Calais, and Somme, to reside at Calais, 1894; Consul for Piedmont, and for the Provinces of Porto Maurizio, Genoa, Massa, Piacenza, Parma and Reggio to reside at Genoa, 1897; Consul General with the same district, 1900; Member of the British Commission for the Milan Exhibition, 1906; Member of the Superior Jury at Turin International Exhibition, 1911, and at the Genoa International Exhibition, 1914; retired on a pension, 2 Jan. 1918; received the Coronation medal, 1911. *Recreations:* all sports. *Address:* Villa Erin, San Remo, Italy. *T:* 224. *Clubs:* St James's, Constitutional, New Oxford and Cambridge.
Died 1 April 1920.

KEETON, Haydn, MusD Oxon; Organist and Master of the Choristers, Peterborough Cathedral, since 1870; *b* Mosborough, Derbyshire, 26 Oct. 1847; *s* of Edwin and Ruth Keeton; *m* 1st, 1872, Eliza, 2nd *d* of Thomas Southam, surgeon, Peterborough; one *s* one *d*; 2nd, 1908, Anne, *e d* of Thomas Southam. *Educ:* St George's Chapel, Windsor. Chorister boy at St George's Chapel, Windsor, 1858; articled pupil to Sir George Elvey, Organist of St George's Chapel, 1862–68; Organist of Datchet Church about 1865; Assistant Music Master at Eton College, 1868; MusB (Oxon), 1869; MusD, 1877; Organist of Aldin House, Slough, the Rev. J. Hawtrey's Preparatory School, 1869; conducted the Peterborough Orchestral Society for 25 years, and the Peterborough Choral Union for about 20 years; Examiner for Oxford University, 1895, and for Durham University, 1899, 1900, 1916; Examiner for the Royal College of Organists. *Publications:* chants, services, anthems, organ voluntaries, part-songs, and madrigal. *Recreation:* bridge. *Address:* Thorpe Road, Peterborough. *TA:* Peterborough. *Died 27 May 1921.*

KEILY, Rt. Rev. John, DD; RC Bishop of Plymouth since 1911; *b* 23 June 1854; *s* of Bartholomew and Margaret Keily, Limerick. *Educ:* Plymouth; Roulers; Bruges. Ordained, 1877; after various appointments, including the Cathedral, Rector of Holy Cross, Plymouth, for 25 years, Diocesan Inspector, and Member of Central Education Council, etc, became Canon of the Diocese; Bishop Assistant at the Pontifical Throne, etc, 1927. *Address:* Bishop's House, Cecil Street, Plymouth. *T:* 1479 Plymouth.
Died 23 Sept. 1928.

KEITH, Col James, DSO 1891; late Royal Artillery; *b* 5 Nov. 1842; *s* of William Keith, MD. Entered army, 1861; Captain, 1875; Major, 1881; Lieut Col, 1890; Colonel, 1894; served Afghanistan, 1878–79 (medal); Sikkim, 1878 (despatches, medal with clasp); Hazara, 1891 (despatches, DSO); Izazai, 1892. *Address:* Queen Anne's Mansions, SW. *Died 5 Feb. 1919.*

KEITH, Skene; *b* Edinburgh, 1858; *s* of Thomas Keith. *Educ:* Edinburgh University and in New York. Was a special Assistant Surgeon in the Edinburgh Royal Infirmary until removed to London, 1888; Consulting Surgeon to the Hounslow Hospital. *Publications:* Text-Book of Abdominal Surgery; Gynaecological Operations; Cancer, the Relief of Pain and Possible Cure. *Recreation:* gardening. *Address:* 7 Manchester Square, W.
Died 19 Aug. 1919.

KEKEWICH, Sir George William, KCB 1895 (CB 1892); DCL; MP (L) Exeter, 1906–10; *b* 1 April 1841; 4th *s* of late Samuel Trehawke Kekewich, MP S Devon, and Louisa, *d* of Lewis William Buck, MP N Devon; married. *Educ:* Eton; Balliol Coll., Oxford. 1st class Classics Moderations; 2nd class Classics Final Schools, Oxford. Examiner in Education Department, 1867; Senior Examiner, 1871; Secretary Education Department, 1890–1900; Secretary also of Science and Art Department, 1899–1900; Secretary of Board of Education, 1900–3; Hon. DCL, Durham, 1897; JP Middlesex. *Recreations:* salmon-fishing, gardening. *Address:* 6 Sackville Gardens, Hove. *Clubs:* Reform, National Liberal; Union, Brighton.
Died 5 July 1921.

KELK, Sir John William, 2nd Bt, *cr* 1874; JP; *b* 13 Jan. 1851; *s* of Sir John Kelk, 1st Bt; *S* father, 1886. *Educ:* Jesus Coll., Cambridge. Sheriff Co. Wilts, 1892; late Major Wilts Yeomanry Cavalry. *Heir:* none. *Address:* 40 Grosvenor Square, W1. *T:* Mayfair 3349. *Club:* Junior Carlton. *Died 22 March 1923 (ext).*

KELLAS, A. M., BSc; PhD; Lecturer on Chemistry, Middlesex Hospital Medical School. *Educ:* Aberdeen Grammar School; University and Heriot-Watt College, Edinburgh; University College, London; Heidelberg University. *Recreations:* mountaineering, travel; interested in geographical exploration. *Address:* 4 St Mark's Crescent, Regent's Park, NW. *Club:* Alpine. *Died 5 June 1921.*

KELLEHER, Stephen B.; Fellow of Trinity College, Dublin, since 1904; Erasmus Smith's Professor of Mathematics in the University of Dublin; *b* Cork, June 1875; *s* of late William Kelleher, Cork; *m* 1910, Isabel Marion Johnston, Londonderry; two *d. Educ:* Christian Brothers Schools, Cork. Entered Royal University of Ireland, 1892; MA 1896; studied at Queen's College, Cork, 1892–96; entered Trinity College, Dublin, 1898; BA 1902. *Address:* 46 Leeson Park, and 24 Trinity College, Dublin. *Club:* University, Dublin.
Died 18 Aug. 1917.

KELLETT, Sir Henry de Castres, 3rd Bt, *cr* 1801, of Lota; *b* 15 Sept. 1851; *e s* of late Henry de Castres Kellett (who was 3rd *s* of Henry de Castres Kellett, 3rd *s* of Richard Kellett, father of the 1st Bt); *S* cousin, 1886 (by special remainder) but did not assume the title until Feb. 1906; *m* 1880, Joan R. M., 2nd *d* of William Harrison of Richmond, Victoria; three *s* four *d*. Member of Kew Borough Council, Victoria, Metropolitan Fire Brigades Board, Victoria, and Tramways Trust, Victoria. *Heir: s* Henry de Castres Kellett [*b* 2 Oct. 1882; *m* 1905, Rubie Septima, 7th *d* of Easton Johnston]. *Address:* High Street, Kew, Victoria, Australia.
Died 20 June 1924.

KELLEY, Maj. Sir Frederic Arthur, Kt 1923; OBE 1919; MP (U) Rotherham, Dec. 1918–1923; *b* 6 May 1863; *m* 1888, *d* of Charles Henry Pickles. *Educ:* Tettenhall College, Wolverhampton; Giggleswick Grammar School. A National Service representative in South Yorkshire; for several years a member of the Sheffield City Council; contested Hallamshire and Spen Valley. JP West Riding Yorks, Sheffield, Harrogate. *Address:* Grey Cauds, Harrogate.
Died 29 May 1926.

KELLEY, Howard G.; President of the Grand Trunk Railway Company of Canada and the Grand Trunk Pacific Railway Co., 1917–22; *b* Philadelphia, Pa, 12 Jan. 1858; *s* of Edwin A. Kelley and Mary B. Peterson; *m* 1899, Cora J. Lingo, Denison, Texas. *Educ:* Polytechnic College, Pa. Entered Railway Service, 1881; Superintendent, Montana, 1884–87; Resident Engineer and Superintendent, bridges and buildings, St Louis SW Railway System, 1887–90; Chief Engineer, 1890–98; Minneapolis and St Louis Railway, 1898; Iowa Central Railway, 1900; Consulting Engineer St Louis SW Railway, 1898–99; President American Railway Engineering and Maintenance of Way Association, 1905–6; Chief Engineer Grand Trunk Railway System, 1907. *Address:* 731 Sherbrooke St, W, Montreal. *Club:* Engineers', Montreal.
Died 15 May 1928.

KELLOCK, Thomas Herbert, MA, MD, MCh (Camb.); FRCS, LRCP; Surgeon to and Lecturer on Surgery, Middlesex Hospital; Consulting Surgeon, Hospital for Sick Children, Great Ormond Street; Consulting Surgeon to the Yarrow Home, Broadstairs; and the Lord Mayor Treloar's Cripples' Hospital and College, Alton; Examiner in Surgery, University of Cambridge; *b* Totnes, Devon, 1863; *s* of T. C. Kellock, solicitor; *m* 1915, Margaret, *y d* of Alexander Brooke; one *s. Educ:* Totnes Grammar School; Emmanuel College, Cambridge (Exhibitioner); St Thomas's Hosp. Medical School. Honours in Mathematical Tripos, 1883; Cheselden Medallist, 1891. Medical Superintendent (3 years) at the Hospital for Sick Children, Great Ormond Street; Surgical Registrar and Tutor in Surgery, Middlesex Hospital; Captain RAMC(T). *Publications:* A Surgical Report of the Middlesex Hospital, 1897; also various contributions to medical jls and trans of medical societies. *Address:* 2 Upper Wimpole Street, Cavendish Square, W1. *T:* Langham 1465. *Club:* New University. *Died 19 Dec. 1922.*

KELLY, Rt. Rev. Denis; RC Bishop of Ross since 1897; *b* Kilnaneave, Nenagh, Co. Tipperary, 29 Feb. 1852; *e s* of William Kelly and Bridget, *d* of late James Butler. *Educ:* The College, Ennis; Collège des Irlandais, Paris. 1st prizeman in Classics, Mathematics, Mental Philosophy, Theology, Scripture and Canon Law; DD. Received priest's orders, 17 March 1877; appointed curate of Roscrea; after four months appointed Professor, later on Vice-President, and finally President of the Ennis College; Member of the Agricultural Board for Ireland, 1900–21; Royal Commissioner on Poor Laws and the Relief of Distress, 1906–9; Member of Cabinet Committee on Irish Finance, 1911; of National Education Committee of Inquiry (Ireland), 1913, etc. *Publications:* letters and pamphlets, mostly on educational topics. *Address:* Bishop's House, Skibbereen, Co. Cork.
Died 18 April 1924.

KELLY, Frederick Septimus; *b* Sydney, NSW, 29 May 1881; *s* of late T. H. Kelly. *Educ:* Eton; Balliol College, Oxford (Nettleship musical scholar; BA 1903; MA 1912). Stroked Eton eight, 1899;

rowed in Oxford eight, 1903; competed at Henley Regatta, 1902–6, winning, among other races, the Diamond Sculls in 1902, 1903, 1905; won Wingfield Sculls, 1903, and rowed in winning Leander eight at the Olympic Sports of 1908. Studied music, 1903–8, at Dr Hoch's Konservatorium, Frankfort o/M, under Professors Knorr (composition), and Engesser (pianoforte), and had some further lessons in composition from Mr D. F. Tovey; made formal début as pianist and composer in Sydney, 1911, and in following spring, 1912, gave a series of concerts in London. Sub-Lieutenant in the Royal Naval Division, 1914; sailed for the Mediterranean with the Hood Battalion, 1915; landed on Gallipoli Peninsula in April; wounded, June; returned to active service, July; Lieutenant, June 1915. *Publications:* article on sculling in The Complete Oarsman; *musical:* opus 1–7, consisting mostly of songs, and works for the pianoforte. *Recreations:* rowing, the usual games, motoring, travel. *Address:* Bisham Grange, Marlow. *T:* Marlow 38. *Club:* Union.

Died 13 Nov. 1916.

KELLY, Captain Hubert Dunsterville Harvey-, DSO 1915; late Squadron Commander Royal Flying Corps; late Royal Irish Regiment; *b* 9 Feb. 1891. Entered Army, 1910; Captain, 1915; served European War, 1914–18 (despatches, DSO).

Died 29 April 1917.

KELLY, Col James Graves, CB 1895; late Aide-de-camp to the Queen; Unemployed Supernumerary List; late Colonel on Staff, Sialkot; *b* 28 Nov. 1843; *m* 1st, 1873, Lavinia (*d* 1900), *d* of late R. MacMullen; four *d*; 2nd, 1901, Eleanor, *d* of late P. Riley. Entered army, 1863; Col 1895; served Hazara Expedition, 1891 (medal with clasp); Miranzai Expedition, 1891 (clasp); Chitral, 1895; Relief of Chitral; Commanded the Force from Gilgit (thanks of Govt of India, despatches, CB, brevet of Col, ADC to Queen, medal with clasp). *Club:* United Service.

Died 20 June 1923.

KELLY, John, ISO 1906; late Secretary and Assistant Registrar-General, Ireland, retired. *Address:* 2 Royal Terrace, West Kingstown.

KELLY, Sir Malachy, Kt 1912; Chief Crown Solicitor for Ireland, since 1905; *b* 25 May 1850; *s* of late Ignatius Kelly, Crown Solicitor, Co. Mayo, and Mary, *d* of late Peter Thoby; *m* 1894, Annie, *d* of Rt Hon. Sir Patrick Coll, KCB (*d* 1899); one *s* two *d*. *Educ:* privately. Admitted a Solicitor, 1871; Sessional Crown Solicitor, Co. Mayo, 1881–85; Crown Solicitor, 1885–1905. *Address:* Thorndale, Temple Road, Milltown, Co. Dublin; Maryland, Castlebar. *Club:* Stephen's Green, Dublin.

Died 25 March 1916.

KELLY, Mark Jamestown, FRGS; FSA; Consul-General of Honduras in London; resigned Consulate-General of Salvador, 1911, after fifteen years service; *b* 1848. As Financial Agent of Salvador in Europe carried out the financial arrangements which discharged the foreign debt of that Republic, and enabled the building of a railway system there, and negotiated a new loan for the country in London, 1908; appointed by Salvador Government to attend the International American Conference at Buenos Ayres as Delegate of the Republic, 1910; Chairman of the Salvador Railway Company of London; President of the Salvador Chamber of Commerce in London; identified with railway construction, formerly, in Ecuador. Chevalier Order of the Legion of Honour; Officer of Public Instruction of France. *Recreations:* collecting old china, travelling. *Address:* Beech House, Redhill, Surrey. *T:* Redhill 402. *Club:* City Carlton.

Died 13 Dec. 1916.

KELLY, Surgeon Peter Burrowes, DSO 1915; RN; Lieutenant-Surgeon Royal Naval College, Osborne, Isle of Wight; *b* 23 Sept. 1888; *s* of Gilbert Graves Kelly; *m*; one *d*. *Educ:* Dublin; London. Served Dardanelles, 1914–15 (wounded, despatches, DSO); at landing of Expeditionary Force. *Recreations:* Rugby, football, cricket, shooting. *Address:* The Abbey, Athy, Co. Kildare.

Died 6 April 1920.

KELLY, Rev. Thomas; Pastor St Francis de Sales' Church, Smith's Falls, since 1898; *b* Waterford. *Educ:* Catholic University High School, Waterford; St Vincent's College, Castleknock; St John's College, Waterford. Ordained, 1877; went to Canada as Private Secretary to late Archbishop Cleary, 1881; Rector, Cathedral of St Mary Immaculate, Kingston. *Address:* Smith's Falls, Ontario.

Died 4 June 1926.

KELLY, Rt. Rev. William Bernard; first Bishop of Geraldton since 1898; *b* 1855. *Address:* Bishop's House, Geraldton, Western Australia.

Died 26 Dec. 1921.

KELTIE, Sir John Scott, Kt 1918; LLD St Andrews; FRGS, FSS, FSAScot; Hon. Member Geographical Societies of Edinburgh, Paris, Berlin, Petrograd, Rome, Brussels, Amsterdam, Geneva, Marseilles, Lisbon, Philadelphia, etc; *b* Dundee, 29 March 1840; *m* 1865, Margaret Scott (*d* 1922); one *d*. *Educ:* Univ. of St Andrews and Edinburgh. Editorial staff of W. and R. Chambers, 1861; of Macmillan and Co., 1871–84; for several years sub-editor of Nature; editor of Statesman's Year Book since 1880; inspector of geographical education, RGS, 1884; Librarian RGS, 1885–92; Sec. Royal Geographical Society, 1892–1915; Joint Editor of Geographical Journal, 1915–17; retired, 1917. President Geographical Section, British Association, 1897; awarded Cullum Gold Medal (American Geographical Society), Gold Medals of Paris and Royal Scottish Geographical Societies, 1915, and Victoria Medal RGS, 1917. Commander of the Swedish Order of North Star, 1898, of the Norwegian Order of St Olaf, 1907; Finnish Order of the White Rose, 1921. *Publications:* History of Scottish Highlands and Clans, 1874; Report on Geographical Education, 1886; Applied Geography, new edn 1908; The Partition of Africa, 1894; The History of Geography (with O. J. R. Howarth), 1914; editor of The Story of Exploration; wrote largely on geographical and scientific subjects to the leading daily, weekly, and monthly periodicals. *Recreation:* golf. *Address:* 88 Brondesbury Road, NW6. *T:* Willesden 1040. *Club:* Royal Societies.

Died 12 Jan. 1927.

KEMBALL, Col Arnold Henry Grant, CB 1912; Lieutenant-Colonel 54th Canadian Infantry Battalion, since 1915; fruit-rancher; *b* 4 Jan. 1861; *s* of late Maj.-Gen. John Shaw Kemball; *m* 1895, Alvida Sundt; two *d*. *Educ:* Wellington College. Entered army, 1880; Captain ISC 1891; Major, Indian army, 1897; Lt-Col 1905; Col 1907; DAAG Malakand Field Force, 1897; DAQMG Tirah Force, 1897–98; served Hazara expedition, 1898 (medal with clasp); Hazara, 1891; Isazai, 1892; NW Frontier, 1897–98 (despatches, medal with clasp); Tirah, 1897–98 (despatches, clasp, brevet-major). *Address:* Kaslo, British Columbia.

Died 1 March 1917.

KEMNAL, Sir James, Kt 1920; FRSE; Managing Director of Babcock & Wilcox Ltd, London and Renfrew, Scotland; Chairman of Worthington, Simpson Ltd, London and Newark; Vice-President of Sociedad Española de Construcciones, Babcock & Wilcox, Bilbao; Director of French Babcock & Wilcox Co., Paris; Director of Power Securities Corporation, London; *b* London, 1864; *m* 1905, Linda Larita, *d* of Clement De Leuze, Nyallo, Victoria, formerly of Nice; one *s*. President of the British and Latin-America Chamber of Commerce; Member Institution Mechanical Engineers, Institution Naval Architects, Electrical Engineers, and other learned societies; Liveryman, Shipwrights Co. *Recreations:* yachting, fishing. *Address:* Kemnal Manor, Chislehurst. *TA:* Manor, Chislehurst. *T:* Sidcup 248. *Clubs:* St Stephen's, City Carlton, Conservative; Glasgow.

Died 8 Feb. 1927.

KEMP, Stephen, FRAM; Member of the Philharmonic Society; Professor of Pianoforte at the Royal Academy of Music, Royal College of Music, and Guildhall School of Music; *b* Great Yarmouth, 8 Nov. 1849; *s* of Robert and Jane Kemp; *m* 1st, 1880, Clara Beasley (decd); three *s* three *d*; 2nd, 1906, Gertrude Thorne. *Educ:* Great Yarmouth Grammar School; Royal Academy of Music (Free Scholarship). Toured through England and Wales as solo pianist with Lazarus Anemoic Union, 1871; in Norway with Svendsen the flautist, 1878; began giving annual chamber concerts at Prince's Hall, Piccadilly, 1885. Editor of Modern Music. *Address:* 80 Oxford Gardens, Notting Hill, W.

Died 30 Oct. 1918.

KEMP, Adm. Thomas Webster, CB 1917; CMG 1918; CIE 1905; *b* 27 Sept. 1866. Entered Navy, 1880; Lieutenant, 1890; Commander 1900; Senior Naval Officer, Persian Gulf, 1905; Rear-Adm. retired 1917; Vice-Adm. retired, 1922; Adm. retired, 1926; served China 1900. *Club:* United Service.

Died 13 Jan. 1928.

KEMPE, Sir Alfred Bray, Kt 1912; DCL (Hon., Durham); FRS; Chancellor, Diocese of London, since 1912; also Chancellor of the Dioceses of Southwell, St Albans, Peterborough, Chichester, and Chelmsford; Bencher of Inner Temple, 1909; *b* Kensington, 6 July 1849; 3rd *s* of late Rev. John Edward Kempe, Rector of St James', Piccadilly; *m* 1st, Mary (*d* 1893), 2nd *d* of late Sir William Bowman, 1st Bt; 2nd, 1897, Ida, *d* of His Honour Judge Meadows White, QC; two *s* one *d*. *Educ:* St Paul's School; Trinity Coll., Cambridge (MA). 22nd Wrangler. Barrister Inner Temple and Western Circuit, 1873; Treas. and Vice-Pres. of the Royal Soc., 1899–1919; Secretary Royal Commission on Ecclesiastical Courts, 1881–83; Chancellor of the Diocese of Newcastle, and Official to the Archdeacons of Essex

Southwark, and Kingston to 1912. *Publications:* How to Draw a Straight Line, 1877; A Memoir on the Theory of Mathematical Form (Philosophical Transactions), 1886. *Recreations:* mathematics, music. *Address:* 2 Paper Buildings, Temple, EC4. *T:* Central 179; 22 Pembridge Square, W. *T:* Park 1566. *Club:* Athenæum.

Died 21 April 1922.

KEMPE, Rev. Edward Wood, MA; Hon. Priest to the King, 1901; Vicar of Jesus Church, Forty Hill, Enfield, since 1874; *b* Hadley, Middlesex, 9 July 1844; *s* of late Rev. Prebendary John Edward Kempe, Rector of St James's, Piccadilly; *m* 1878, Margaret Millar (*d* 1909), *d* of W. H. Challis, of Enfield; two *s* three *d. Educ:* St Paul's School; Trinity Coll., Cambridge. Junior Optime, 1867. Curate of St Andrew's, Enfield, 1868–74; Priest in Ordinary to Queen Victoria, 1878–1901. Member of Edmonton Board of Guardians, 1882–1905; Member of Enfield Education Committee, 1903–7; Member of London Diocesan Conference since 1899. *Publication:* Enfield and its Environs, 1896. *Recreations:* music, drawing. *Address:* Forty Hill Vicarage, Enfield. *Died 12 May 1918.*

KEMPE, Sir John Arrow, KCB 1909 (CB 1900); BA; *b* 5 Jan. 1846; *s* of late Rev. John Edward Kempe, Rector of St James's, Piccadilly; *m* 1872, Mary Jane (*d* 1926), *d* of Rev. J. Edwards, Vicar of Barrow-on-Trent; three *s* three *d. Educ:* St Paul's School; Trinity College, Cambridge. Silver Medal, winning trial eight for University boat, 1866. Clerkship in Treasury, 1867; Assistant Private Secretary to Mr Disraeli, 1868; Private Secretary to Chancellor of Exchequer (Sir S. Northcote), 1874–80; to Sir R. Lingen, 1880–81; to Lord Frederick Cavendish, 1881; member of Commission on Agricultural and Dairy Schools, 1887–88; Principal Clerk in Treasury, 1888–94; Deputy Chairman Board of Customs, 1894–1904; Assistant Comptroller and Auditor, 1904; Comptroller and Auditor-General, 1904–11; member of Royal Commission on Electrical Communication with Lighthouses and Light Vessels, 1892–97; Chairman of Local Taxation Committee, 1911–14; Member of Royal Commission on the Civil Service, 1915. *Address:* Coram Court, Lyme Regis. *T:* Lyme Regis 12.

Died 4 April 1928.

KEMPSTER, Col Francis James, DSO 1887; late Assistant Adjutant-General, Madras; *b* 12 March 1855. Entered army, 1876; Col 1896; served Afghan War, 1880 (medal); Bechuanaland, 1884–85; Soudan Frontier Field Force, 1887 (despatches, DSO, 3rd class Medjidie, medal, Khedive's star); Suakim, 1888 (despatches, clasp); Soudan Frontier, 1889 (despatches, brevet of Lieut-Col, clasp); Ashanti, 1896 (despatches, ADC to Queen, star); NW Frontier, 1897 (despatches, medal with two clasps); retired, 1902.

Died 29 Dec. 1925.

KENDAL, William Hunter, (Mr Grimston); actor and manager; *b* London, 16 Dec. 1843; *m* 1869, Madge Robertson; two *s* three *d. Educ:* private school; tutor. Commenced his career on the stage in London at the Soho Theatre (later called the Royalty), 1861, Glasgow in 1862, where he remained till 1866, supporting such stars as Mr and Mrs Charles Kean, Helen Faucit, G. O. Brooks, etc; made his second appearance in London at the Haymarket Theatre, 31 Oct. 1866, in A Dangerous Friend, with Mr and Mrs Charles Matthews; remained there five or six years, playing such parts as Charles Surface, Captain Absolute, Romeo, Orlando, Pygmalion, etc; thence to Court Theatre for couple of seasons; from there to Old Prince of Wales Theatre for Diplomacy, London Assurance, and Peril; back to Court Theatre for a season; then became Lessee and Manager, in partnership with John Hare, at St James's Theatre, 1879–88, producing there The Queen's Shilling, The Squire, Impulse, The Ironmaster, A Scrap of Paper, Lady of Lyons, As You Like It, William and Susan, Ladies' Battle, etc; toured with Mrs Kendal in the United States of America and Canada from 1889–95 with phenomenal success. *Recreations:* fishing, shooting, riding, motoring, collecting pictures. *Address:* 12 Portland Place, W; The Lodge, Filey, Yorkshire. *M:* LD 3670, LD 7958. *Clubs:* Junior Carlton, Garrick, Beefsteak, Royal Automobile.

Died 6 Nov. 1917.

KENDALL, H. Bickerstaffe; editor of The Holborn Review, 1902–16; *b* Wakefield, 1844; *s* of Rev. Charles Kendall, President of Conference, 1881. *Educ:* Durham University. Connexional Editor, 1892–1901; President of Conference, 1901. *Publications:* Handbook of Primitive Methodist Church Principles and Polity; Christ's Kingdom and Church in the Nineteenth Century; The Origin and History of the Primitive Methodist Church; section Primitive Methodism in A New History of Methodism, 1909. *Address:* 29 Castlemain Road, Stourfield Park, Bournemouth.

Died 10 March 1919.

KENEALY, Noel Byron; editor of periodicals dealing with automobilism; 5th *s* of late E. V. Kenealy, LLD, QC; *m* 1905, Isabel, *e d* of late Col St Leger Shervinton, commdg Malagasy army. *Educ:* Slade, Herkomer, and Paris Schools. Founded the Hertfordshire Automobile Club and the British Motor Boat Club. Adviser on art matters; exhibited at Royal Academy. *Recreations:* motoring, golf. *Club:* Royal Automobile.

Died 18 Dec. 1918.

KENNAN, George, LittD; writer and lecturer; *b* Norwalk, Ohio, USA, 16 Feb. 1845; *s* of John Kennan and Mary Ann Morse; *m* 1879, Emeline, *d* of J. R. Weld. *Educ:* in common and high schools of Norwalk and Columbus, Ohio. Telegraph Operator, Norwalk, Ohio, 1857; Assistant Manager Western Union Telegraph Office, Cincinnati, Ohio, 1863–64; went to NE Siberia as explorer and telegraphic engineer, 1865; Superintendent of Construction, Middle Division Russo-American Telegraph Co. in Siberia, 1866–68; made an exploration of Eastern Caucasus, 1870–71; Night Manager of Associated Press at Washington, DC, 1877–85; made investigation of Russian exile system in Siberia, 1885–86; lectured throughout United States, 1889–98, and in Great Britain in 1894; reported the Spanish-American war in 1898 as special correspondent in Cuba of The Outlook (NY); expelled from Russia by order of the Minister of the Interior, 1901; went to Martinique, 1902, to report for The Outlook (NY) the eruption of Mont Pelée and the destruction of St Pierre; Special Correspondent in the Far East, 1904–6; staff writer, M'Clure's Magazine, 1906–8; and the Outlook since 1909. Received war medal, Japan, 1907; Order of The Sacred Treasure, Japan, 1908; Member of National Institute of Arts and Letters. *Publications:* Tent Life in Siberia, 1870, new edition, 1910; Siberia and the Exile System, 2 vols, 1890; Campaigning in Cuba, 1899; Folk Tales of Napoleon, 1902; The Tragedy of Pelée, 1902; A Russian Comedy of Errors, 1915; The Chicago and Alton Case, 1916; Misrepresentation in Railroad Affairs, 1916; E. H. Harriman's Far Eastern Plans, 1917; The Salton Sea, 1917; E. H. Harriman: A Biography, 2 vols, 1922; various articles. *Recreations:* yachting, cycling, flower-gardening. *Address:* Medina, NY, USA. *Club:* Authors', New York.

Died 10 May 1924.

KENNARD, Maj. Arthur Molloy, DSO 1900; commanding 179th Brigade Royal Field Artillery in France; *b* 7 July 1867; *s* of Arthur C. Kennard; *m* 1912, Evelyn Mary, *widow* of Charles H. Helbert and *o d* of Lord David and Lady Mary Kennedy; one *s.* Entered RA 1886; Captain, 1897; Major, 1900; served South Africa, 1899–1902 (despatches; Queen's medal, 3 clasps; King's medal, 2 clasps; DSO); promoted temp. Lt-Col of 95th Brigade Royal Field Artillery, 21st Div. Kitchener's 3rd Army, 1915; wounded, Battle of Loos, Sept. 1915. JP, DL Stirlingshire. *Address:* Kersehill, Falkirk, Scotland. *Club:* Naval and Military.

Died 2 Jan. 1917.

KENNARD, Rt. Rev. Monsignor (Canon) Charles H.; Canon of the Diocese of Clifton; Domestic Prelate of His Holiness Pius X; *b* 1840; *y s* of John Pierse Kennard of Hordle Cliff, Hants, and Sophia, *d* of Sir John Chapman. *Educ:* Harrow; University College, Oxford. Played against Cambridge at racquets three years in succession; holder of the gold racquet at Oxford, 1861; Member of the Harlequin and Perambulator Cricket Clubs. Received into the Catholic Church by Dr Newman, 1868; President of the Burnham and Berrow Golf Club. *Address:* Westleigh, Burnham, Somerset. *Clubs:* Oxford and Cambridge; RN Devon Golf.

Died 6 Aug. 1920.

KENNARD, Martyn Thomas; *b* 14 Sept. 1859; *s* of late H. Martyn Kennard, JP, DL; *m* 1903, Cora, *widow* of 4th Earl of Strafford. *Educ:* Eton; Christ Church, Oxford. Spent most of his life big game shooting, chiefly in India. *Clubs:* Marlborough, Turf.

Died 12 May 1920.

KENNARD, Captain Willoughby Arthur, DSO 1915; 13th Hussars; *b* 20 May 1881. Entered army, 1900; Captain, 1906; served S African War, 1899–1902 (Queen's medal, 4 clasps); European War, 1914–16 (despatches, DSO, severely wounded). *Clubs:* Cavalry, Bath, Orleans.

Died Oct. 1918.

KENNAWAY, Rt. Hon. Sir John Henry, 3rd Bt, *cr* 1791; CB 1902; PC 1897; Colonel 3rd Volunteer Battalion, Devon Regiment; President Church Missionary Society and London Society for promoting Christianity among Jews; *b* 6 June 1837; *e s* of Sir John Kennaway, 2nd Bt and Emily, *d* of Thomas Kingscote, Kingscote; *S* father, 1873; *m* 1866, Fanny, *d* of Archibald F. Arbuthnot; one *s* two *d. Educ:* Harrow; Balliol Coll., Oxford. First Class in Law and Modern History School. MP (C) East Devon, 1870–85, Honiton Div., Devon, 1885–1910; Father of House of Commons, 1908–10.

Owned about 4,100 acres. *Publication:* On Sherman's Track. *Heir:* s John Kennaway, b 7 April 1879. *Address:* Escot, Ottery St Mary, Devon. *Clubs:* Athenæum, National.

Died 6 Sept. 1919.

KENNAWAY, Sir Walter, Kt 1909; CMG 1891; Secretary to the Department of the High Commissioner for New Zealand in London, 1874–1909; b 1835; m 1864, Alicia, d of J. E. Jones; four s three d. Sec. of Public Works, Canterbury Prov., NZ, 1870–74. *Address:* Malda, Thicket Road, Anerley, SE.

Died 24 Aug. 1920.

KENNEDY, Sir Alexander (Blackie William), Kt 1905; created a Pasha by HM King Hussein, 1924; LLD (Glasgow and Birmingham); DEng (Liverpool); FRS 1887; Emeritus Professor of Engineering in University College, London; senior partner in firm Kennedy and Donkin, civil engineers; b Stepney, 17 March 1847; e s of late Rev. John Kennedy, DD, and Helen Stodart, *sister* of late Professor Blackie; m 1874, Elizabeth Verralls (d 1911), e d of late William Smith, LLD, Edinburgh; two s one d. *Educ:* City of London School; Royal College of Mines. Pupil to marine engineers, then in various engineering works; Professor of Engineering in University College, London, 1874–89, where established first engineering laboratory; designed electric works for lighting and power in Edinburgh, Manchester, Calcutta, Loch Leven, Japan, etc; Director of St James' and Pall Mall Electric Supply Company; Associate Member of Ordnance Committee, 1909; Member of Lord Parker's Committee on Wireless Telegraphy, 1913; Vice-Chairman of the (late) Anti-Aircraft Equipment Committee; Chairman of the Electric Railway Advisory Committee under the Ministry of Transport; Past President Instn of Civil Engrs, Past President Instn Mech. Engrs, and elected Hon. Member of both Institutions; President Camera Club; Hon. FRS Edin.; Hon. FRS, New South Wales. *Publications:* trans. Reuleaux, Kinematik, 1876; The Mechanics of Machinery, 1886; Moore's Alps in 1864, 1902; Yprès to Verdun, 1921; Petra, its History and Monuments, 1925. *Recreations:* music, mountaineering, photography, golf. *Address:* 7A The Albany, W1. *T:* Regent 5663; Broadway Court, SW1. *T:* Victoria 3601. *M:* XP 302. *Clubs:* Athenæum, Garrick, Alpine. *Died 1 Nov. 1928.*

KENNEDY, Maj.-Gen. Alfred Alexander, CB 1921; CMG 1915; Colonel 3rd (King's Own) Hussars; commanding the West Riding Area and the 49th (West Riding) Division, with headquarters at York, since 1923; b 10 Dec. 1870; s of late Myles Kennedy, Stone Cross, Ulverston; m 1898, Dora Campbell, d of W. T. Rowley, Birkdale, Lancashire; one s. *Educ:* Harrow; RMC, Sandhurst. Entered army, 1891; Capt. 1896; Major 1902; Lt-Col 1913; Brevet Col 1915; Maj.-Gen. 1919; served South African War, 1902 (Queen's medal, 3 clasps); European War, 1914–19 (despatches seven times, Bt Col, Maj.-Gen., CB, CMG, Officier Légion d'honneur). *Clubs:* Cavalry, Ranelagh.

Died 31 March 1926.

KENNEDY, Brig.-Gen. Charles Henry, CB 1914; Royal Marines; Commandant, Chatham Division, Royal Marine Light Infantry; b Wellington, Madras Presidency, India, 28 Feb. 1860; s of late Maj.-Gen. H. F. Kennedy, 60th King's Royal Rifle Corps; m 1891, Georgina Frances, d of William Loudon Gordon, Inspector-General of Hospitals and Fleets, RN; two s. *Educ:* Bath College. Joined Royal Marine Lt Infantry, 1880; served in the Royal Marine Battalion throughout the war, 1882, in Egypt; present at occupation of Port Said, the actions at Tel-el-Mahuta, Mahsaneh, Kassassin 28 Aug., Kassassin 9 Sept., Tel-el-Kebir (medal, Tel-el-Kebir clasp, and Khedive's star); commanded the Royal Marines at the storming of Illig, 1904, and capture of the Sultan and the Dervish garrison on the Somali coast, 1904 (mentioned in official report; General East African medal; Somaliland, clasp). *Recreations:* fishing, shooting, riding, etc. *Address:* Chatham. *Died 14 Nov. 1916.*

KENNEDY, Frederick Charles, CIE 1886; b 1849; m 1881, Mary, d of John Cuddie of Falkirk. Late manager of Irawaddy Flotilla Co. Ltd. *Club:* Oriental. *Died 17 April 1916.*

KENNEDY, George, KC 1902; MA, LLD; b Bytown (later Ottawa), 1 March 1838; s of Donald Kennedy and Janet Buckham; m 1883, Sarah Jackson Watson (d 1910); no c. *Educ:* Castleton Co. Grammar School; University of Toronto. First Classical Schoolmaster; subsequently first class Honours in Classics, Mathematics, Metaphysics and Ethics, Modern Languages and Natural Sciences; BA 1857, gold medal; MA 1860; LLB 1864. Called to Bar, Osgoode Hall, 1865; MD 1877; practised profession at Ottawa, 1866–71; Law Clerk of the Department of Lands, Forests and Mines of the province of Ontario, 1872; Law Examiner in University, 1878–80. Ex-President,

Hon. Member, and thirty years Editor of the Transactions of the Canadian Institute; Ex-President and Hon. Member of the Andrew's Society; Ex-President of the Caledonian Society; Ex-President of the Burns Literary Society. *Publications:* Scottish-Canadian Poets (joint editor); Alexander M'Lachlan's Poems (joint editor); Science and English Law; Digest of Crown Lands Cases; Analysis of the Public Land Laws of Canada, etc. *Clubs:* National, Madawaska, Toronto. *Died June 1916*

KENNEDY, Rev. James Houghton, DD; Rector of Stillorgan since 1897; Canon of St Patrick's Cathedral, Dublin, since 1913. *Educ:* Trinity College, Dublin (MA). Curate of Trory, 1866–67; Headford, 1869–70; Dalkey, 1870–73; Monkstown, 1873–78; Select Preacher University of Dublin, 1906, 1909, and 1913; Canon of Christ Church Cathedral, Dublin, 1900–13. *Publications:* Natural Theology and Modern Thought, 1891; Editor Second and Third Epistles to the Corinthians, 1900. *Address:* The Rectory, Stillorgan, Dublin.

Died 14 July 1924

KENNEDY, Brig.-Gen. John, CMG 1918; DSO 1916; Argyll and Sutherland Highlanders; b 1878; m 1919, Mrs C. R. Pawson. Entered Army, 1898; Major, 1915; served European War, 1914–18 (despatches, DSO and bar, CMG, Bt Col). *Club:* Army and Navy.

Died Oct. 1921

KENNEDY, Sir John Charles, 3rd Bt, cr 1836; DL, JP; b London, 23 March 1856; e s of Sir Charles Edward Bayly Kennedy, 2nd Bt, and Augusta, y d of Viscount Glentworth; S father, 1880; m 1879, Sydney, d of Sir James Macaulay Higginson, KCB; two s two d. *Educ:* Trinity Coll., Cambridge (BA). Lived at home after father's death, farming 400 acres. *Recreations:* hunting, shooting, cricket. *Heir:* s John Ralph Bayly Kennedy, b 9 April 1896. *Address:* Johnstown Kennedy, Hazlehatch, Co. Dublin. *Club:* Kildare Street, Dublin.

Died 22 March 1923

KENNEDY, Col John Murray, MVO 1905; VD; JP, DL; late Hon. Colonel 5th King's Own Scottish Borderers (Volunteers) (retired); b 5 April 1841; m 1880, Frances Eleanor Catherine, d of Lt-Col John James Brandling, CB, RA; one d. *Educ:* Cambridge University (BA). *Address:* Knocknalling, Dalry, Kirkcudbrightshire.

Died 24 March 1928

KENNEDY, Captain Macdougall Ralston, CMG 1912; DSO 1899; Director of Public Works, Soudan; Royal Engineers, retired, 1909; b 20 Dec. 1873; s of Rev. A. Kennedy; m 1904, d of Maj.-Gen. W. H. Ralston. *Educ:* Edinburgh Academy; RMA Woolwich. Entered army, 1893; served Crete, 1898 (despatches); Egypt, 1899 (DSO, 4th class Medjidie). *Recreations:* yachting, golfing, shooting.

Died 2 Nov. 1924

KENNEDY, Myles, JP, DL Co. Lancaster; High Sheriff, 1922; b 3 June 1862; e s of late Myles Kennedy, JP, of Stone Cross, Ulverston and Margaret, d of late A. B. Rowley; m cousin Ethel Campbell, 3rd d of late Joseph Rowley, JP, Co. Flintshire; two s two d. *Educ:* Harrow; Royal School of Mines. Chairman, North Lonsdale Iron and Steel Co. Ltd. *Recreations:* shooting, fishing, golf. *Address:* Stone Cross, Ulverston, Lancashire. *M:* B 4425 and TB 250. *Clubs:* Windham, Royal Automobile. *Died 9 Aug. 1928*

KENNEDY, Captain Myles Arthur Claude, DSO 1912; 8th Gurkha Rifles; b 12 Aug. 1885; o s of Col Claude Kennedy; m 1913, Nora Constance Marion, d of late W. L. Mumford, MD; one d. Entered army, 1905; Indian army, 1906; served Abor Expedition, 1912 (despatches, medal with clasp, DSO).

Died 2 Nov. 1918

KENNEDY, Hon. Lord; Neil J. D. Kennedy, MA (Aberdeen), LLD (Edin.); Chairman Scottish Land Court since 1912; b Rosehall, Sutherlandshire, April 1855; s of Rev. John D. Kennedy, Free Church, and Catharine Mackay, Inverness; m 1902, Hilda, y d of Walter Stevenson, Westhorpe, Hendon. *Educ:* High School, Inverness; Aberdeen and Edinburgh Universities; New College, Edinburgh. First bursar in Divinity, and Grierson Scholar in Law; called to Bar, 1877; KC (Scot.) 1906. Was recommended by the Faculty of Advocates for the Chair of Civil Law in Edinburgh University, 1889 and 1893; lecturer on Private International Law in Edinburgh University, 1898; Professor of Civil and Scots Law, University of Aberdeen, 1901–7; contested the county of Inverness in the Liberal interest, 1895; appointed a member of the Royal Commission on Registration of Titles, 1907; Sheriff of Renfrew and Bute, 1907–12; Chairman of Crofters' Commission and Member of the Congested Districts Board, 1908–12. *Publications:* many articles on literary and legal subjects in the Juridical Review and other legal publications. *Address:* 22 Ainslie Place, Edinburgh. *Clubs:* Scottish Liberal, Edinburgh; University, Aberdeen.   *Died 12 Feb. 1918.*

KENNEDY, Robert, DL; JP; MA, MD, DSc; St Mungo Professor of Surgery in the University of Glasgow and ex-officio Surgeon in the Royal Infirmary since 1911; *b* Glasgow, 20 Dec. 1865; *m* 1895, Janet Lyon (*d* 1922), *d* of John Miller, MD; one *d. Educ:* Univs of Glasgow, Edinburgh and Berlin. Graduated in Univ. of Glasgow with highest honours in Arts and Medicine; John Clark Scholar, 1886-87; George A. Clark Scholar, 1888-92. Surgeon to out-door department, Glasgow Victoria Infirmary, 1892-96, and of Western Infirmary, 1896-1900; Assistant Surgeon, Western Infirmary, 1900-10, and Lock Hospital, 1893-94; Examiner in Surgery, St Andrews University, 1901-4; Lecturer in Applied Anatomy, University of Glasgow, 1906-11; Surgeon and Lecturer in Clinical Surgery, Western Infirmary, 1910-11; Senior and Consulting Surgeon in Charge Orthopaedic Department, Scottish National Red Cross Hospital, Bellahouston, 1917-19; Director and Consulting Surgeon, Shakespeare Hospital (Ministry of Pensions), Glasgow, 1918-19; Surgeon-in-Chief, Bellahouston Hospital (Ministry of Pensions), Glasgow, 1919-22. *Publications:* On the Regeneration of Nerves, 1897; On the Restoration of Co-ordinated Movements after Nerve-Crossing with Interchange of Function of the Cerebral Cortical Centres, 1901; Experiments on the Restoration of Paralysed Muscles by means of Nerve Anastomosis, Parts I, II, and III, 1911, 1914, 1915; Phil. Trans, Suture et Anastomoses des Nerfs in Chipault's L'Etat Actuel de la Chirurgie Nerveuse, 3 vols, Paris, 1903; Suture of the Brachial Plexus in Birth Paralysis of the Upper Extremity, Brit. Med. Journal, 1903 and 1904; Operative Procedure in Nerve Injuries, British Jl of Surgery, 1918; numerous papers in various departments of surgery in the medical jls and trans of societies. *Address:* 14 Woodside Terrace, Glasgow. *T:* Ch. X 501.

          Died 3 June 1924.

KENNEDY, Robert Gregg, CIE 1907; *b* 1851; *m* 1889, Mabel Sarah, *d* of G. B. M. Wyse. *Educ:* RIE College. Entered service, 1873; Executive Engineer, 1881; Superintending Engineer, 1898; Chief Engineer and Commissioner to Sec. Central Provinces, 1903; Joint Sec. to Punjab Irrigation, 1904; Sec. (Irrigation) to Chief Commissioner NW Frontier Provinces, 1905; retired 1906. *Publication:* Report on Irrigation in the UP. *Address:* c/o British Linen Bank, West End Branch, Edinburgh.

          Died 2 March 1920.

KENNEDY, Lt-Col William Magill, CIE 1916; Indian Army, retired; in Civil Employ as Deputy Commissioner, Assam; *b* 1868; *s* of late Charles George Blagrave Kennedy, JP, of Mullantean, Stewartstown, Co. Tyrone; *m* 1922, Violet Hope, *e d* of Robert Ponsonby Staples, Lissan, Cookstown, Co. Tyrone. *Educ:* Royal School, Dungannon; Trinity College, Dublin. Joined the 4th Batt. Royal Inniskilling Fusiliers (Tyrone Militia), 1887; 2nd Batt. 1890; transferred to the Indian Staff Corps and posted to the 9th Madras Infantry, 1892; took part in Chin Hills Expedition, 1892-93; Assistant Commissioner, Assam, 1894; Deputy Commissioner, 1905; Commissioner of Excise and Salt and Inspector-General of Registration, Eastern Bengal and Assam, 1905-11; Member and Secretary of Assam Labour Enquiry Committee, 1906; Second Secretary to the Chief Commissioner of Assam, 1912-13; officiating Chief Secretary, 1913; Member of Legislative Council, Eastern Bengal and Assam, 1910-11; Assam Legislative Council, 1912-15; Tea Commissioner for India, 1917-19; Chairman, Assam Labour Board, 1915-20. *Recreations:* fishing, shooting, golf. *Address:* Mullantean, Stewartstown, Co. Tyrone; c/o King, Hamilton & Co., Calcutta. *Clubs:* East India United Service; Bengal, Royal Calcutta Turf, Calcutta.   *Died 22 Sept. 1923.*

KENNEDY, Adm. Sir William Robert, GCB 1911 (KCB 1897); *b* 4 March 1838; *s* of John Kennedy, Chargé d'Affaires, Naples; *m* 1868, Edith L., *d* of Capt. E. Stopford, RN; one *d. Educ:* Cheam; Dr Maldon's, Brighton. Navy Cadet, 1851; Sub-Lt 1857; Lieut 1857; Comdr 1867; Capt. 1874; Rear-Admiral 1889; Vice-Admiral 1896; Admiral 1901; served Crimea (two medals); China, 1856-59 (medal and clasps); Commander-in-Chief, East Indies, 1892-95; at the Nore, 1901-2. Royal Humane Society's medal. *Publications:* Sporting Adventures in the Pacific; Sport Travel in Newfoundland; Sporting in South America; Hurrah for the Life of a Sailor. *Recreations:* shooting, fishing. *Address:* Falconer's Hill, Daventry. *Club:* United Service.

          Died 9 Oct. 1916.

KENNEDY, Lt-Col Willoughby Pitcairn, CSI 1906; *b* 10 Dec. 1850; *e s* of Gen. Sir Michael Kavanagh Kennedy, KCSI; *m* 1887;

one *d.* Entered army, 1870; served Afghan War, 1880 (medal); Special Political Agent, Cambay, 1890-94; Administrator, Raj-Piplah estates, 1890-94; Navanagar estate, 1895; Political Agent Kathiawar, 1901; Agent to Governor there, 1902; retired 1906. *Address:* Lynedoch, W Byfleet, Surrey.   *Died 7 Aug. 1928.*

KENNEY, Col Arthur Herbert, CMG 1893; DSO 1900; Royal Engineers; late commanding Royal Engineers, Devon Sub-District; retired; *b* Plymouth, 4 Jan. 1855; 2nd *s* of late Captain E. H. Kenney, RN, and Charlotte Mary, *d* of late Captain Bignell, RN. *Educ:* private tuition; Royal Mil. Acad., Woolwich. Lieut RE, 1873; Captain 1885; Major, 1892; Lt-Col 1900; served in India, 1876-83; Egypt and Soudan, 1884-85; West Africa, 1890-92; Assistant Field Engineer, Kuram Valley, and Kabul Field Force, during Afghan War, 1879-80 (medal); Nile Expedition, 1884-85 (medal, two clasps, and Khedive's star), and was in charge of Boat Repairing Party River Column (despatches); South African War, 1899-1900 as OC Advance Depot RE, CRE 10th Division and CRE Gen. Ian Hamilton's Force (despatches, medal, 3 clasps, and DSO); re-employed from the retired list 1 Sept. 1914, as CRE of a Division till 31 July 1915, and as Commandant of a Training Centre till 30 May 1916 (despatches, 1915 Star, British War medal, Victory medal and oak leaf); was British Commissioner of the Anglo-French Commissions for delimiting the frontiers of the Colonies of the Gambia, and of Sierra Leone, 1890-92 (CMG). *Address:* 44 Preston Park Avenue, Brighton.

          Died 4 Sept. 1923.

KENNEY-HERBERT, Edward Maxwell, JP Bucks; late HM Divisional Inspector of Schools, Board of Education; *b* 10 Dec. 1845; *s* of Rev. A. R. Kenney-Herbert, Rector of Bourton-on-Dunsmore, Co. Warwick; *m* 1876, Lady Jane White, *d* of 3rd Earl of Bantry; one *s* one *d. Educ:* Rugby School; Merton College, Oxford. *Address:* 6 Woodfield Road, Ealing, W. *T:* Ealing 1215.

          Died 26 Jan. 1916.

KENNINGTON, T. B.; painter of portraits, genre pictures; *b* Great Grimsby, Lincolnshire. *Educ:* private school; Liverpool School of Art. Gold medal, South Kensington; scholarship medal while at Liverpool; two years at South Kensington, afterwards Paris under Bouguereau and Tony Fleury; formerly member NEAC, also RBA; Vice-President, Institute of Oil Painters; member of Royal British Colonial Society of Artists; Bronze medal, Paris, 1889 and 1900. *Recreation:* chess. *Address:* 8 Netherton Grove, Chelsea, SW. *Club:* Arts.

          Died 14 Dec. 1916.

KENNION, Rt. Rev. George Wyndham, DD *hon.* Glasgow; Bishop of Bath and Wells, 1894-1921; *b* 1845; *s* of George Kennion, MD, Harrogate and Catherine Elfrida, *d* of late T. J. Fordyce, of Ayton Castle, Berwickshire; *m* 1882, Henrietta, *d* of Sir Charles Dalrymple Fergusson, 5th Bt. *Educ:* Eton; Oriel Coll., Oxford (MA). Ordained 1869; Domestic Chaplain to Bishop of Tuam, 1869-70; Curate of Doncaster, 1870-71; Vicar of St Paul, Hull, 1873-76; Vicar of All Saints, Bradford, 1876-82; Bishop of Adelaide, 1882-94; Lecturer in Pastoral Theology, University of Cambridge, 1900; Ramsden Preacher Univ. Camb., 1901. *Recreations:* in former years boating and all school-boys' games, hunting, shooting; in Australia, riding, swimming, boating; then cycling, reading. *Address:* The Palace, Wells, Somerset. *Club:* Athenæum.   *Died 19 May 1922.*

KENNY, The Rt. Hon. William; Hon. Mr Justice Kenny, PC 1902; Judge of the King's Bench Division of the High Court of Justice, Ireland, since 1897; *b* Dublin, 14 Jan. 1846; *o s* of late Edward Kenny, solicitor, Ennis, Co. Clare; *m* 1873, Mary, *e d* of David Coffey, Master in Chancery. *Educ:* privately; Trinity Coll., Dublin (MA). Irish Bar, 1868; QC 1885; Bencher, King's Inns, 1890; member of Senate of University of Dublin; a leader at Chancery Bar; mainly instrumental in establishing the Liberal Union of Ireland after the defeat of Home Rule Bill of 1886, and in organising the memorable visit of Lord Hartington and Mr Goschen to Dublin in 1887; MP (U) Dublin (Stephen's Green), 1892-97; Solicitor-General for Ireland, 1895-97; elected MP 1892 by majority of 15; there being three candidates Nationalist vote was divided, but in 1895, when Nationalist vote was solid against him, he was elected by 456; a Nationalist again contested seat on his appointment as Solicitor-General when he retained it, hitherto deemed an impregnable Nationalist stronghold, with a practically undiminished majority; Judge for Probate and Matrimonial Business, 1919; Chairman Irish Railway and Canal Commission. *Address:* Marlfield, Cabinteely, Co. Dublin. *Club:* Kildare Street, Dublin.   *Died 4 Feb. 1921.*

KENRICK, John Arthur, JP; *b* 1829; *e s* of late Archibald Kenrick of Berrow Court and Anne, *d* of late William Paget of Loughborough,

Co. Leicester; *m* 1866, Clara, *d* of Rev. John Taylor. *Address:* Berrow Court, Edgbaston.   *Died 23 April 1926.*

KENRICK, Rt. Hon. William, PC 1899; JP; *b* 1831; *s* of late Archibald Kenrick, W Bromwich; *m* 1862, Mary, *d* of late J. Chamberlain, and *sister* of Rt Hon. Joseph Chamberlain [Mr Chamberlain's first wife was a sister to Mr Kenrick]; two *s* two *d*. *Educ:* private school, Hove; University Coll., London. Gold medal for chemistry, 1850. Was a hardware manufacturer; Alderman and Town Councillor (Mayor 1877), Birmingham; MP (UL) Birmingham, N Div., 1885–99. *Recreation:* landscape painting. *Address:* The Grove, Harborne, Birmingham. *Club:* Burlington Fine Arts.

Died 31 July 1919.

KENSINGTON, Sir Alfred, Kt 1914; *b* 26 April 1855; *s* of Arthur Kensington (*d* 1886); *m* 1881, Alice H. M., *d* of late Maj.-Gen. H. C. Johnstone, CB; two *s* one *d*. *Educ:* Marlborough; University Coll., Oxford. Entered Indian Civil Service, 1877; held various appointments in the Indian Civil Service in the Punjab, and under Government of India; Judge, Chief Court, Punjab, 1904; Chief Judge, 1914; retired, 1915. *Address:* 3 Buckingham Gate, SW1. *T:* Victoria 5861. *Club:* Albemarle.   *Died 2 Nov. 1918.*

KENSINGTON, William Charles, ISO 1909; JP; Permanent Under-Secretary for Lands and Immigration, New Zealand, 1901–12; *b* Werndu, Criccieth, N Wales, 3 Aug. 1845; *e s* of late Charles J. W. Kensington, Prince Hill, Worton, Wilts; *m* 1st, Emily Selena (*d* 1869), *d* of G. Owen Ormsby; 2nd, 1873, Amy (*d* 1906), *d* of Lt-Col Hon. W. H. Kenny, 73rd Regt; three *s* two *d*. *Educ:* Grosvenor School, Bath; King's School, Bruton, Somerset. Went NZ 1862; Ensign 1st Batt. New Zealand Militia, 1865, later Captain; served Maori War, 1863–65 (war medal); Captain Auckland Rifle Brigade, 1871. *Address:* Cheverell, Marton, Rangitreikei, NZ. *Club:* Marton.

Died 20 Aug. 1922.

KENT, Lt-Gen. Henry; Colonel, Middlesex Regiment, since 1900; *b* 3 Aug. 1825; *m* Caroline (*d* 1891), *d* of William Ward, Wolverhampton. Entered army, 1845; Maj.-Gen. 1883; retired, 1886; served Crimea, 1854–55 (medal with three clasps, 5th class Medjidie, Turkish medal); commanded 77th Regiment, 1868–80; 7th and 57th Regimental Districts, 1880–83. *Address:* Glenthorne, The Downs, Wimbledon, SW19. *Clubs:* United Service, Junior United Service, Army and Navy.   *Died 24 Feb. 1921.*

KENT, Prof. Thomas Parkes, MA; Professor of Mathematics in the University of Cape Town; *b* Nevis, West Indies; *e s* of Rev. Alfred Kent; *m* 1906, Constance, *y d* of Henry Beard of Cape Town and Kenilworth; three *s* one *d*. *Educ:* Kingswood School, Bath; Christ Church, Oxford (Scholar); Exhibitioner, London Univ., First Class Honours in Final School of Mathematics; Honours in Final, Natural Science School. Assistant Master at Fettes College, Edinburgh, and Cranleigh School, Surrey; Professor in Mathematics at the Diocesan College, Rondebosch, 1902; at the South African College, Cape Town, 1908. *Publications:* articles and verse in educational and other journals; The Flick of Fortune (novel). *Address:* Nevis, Claremont, near Cape Town. *Clubs:* Civil Service; Owl, Cape Town.

Died 4 Aug. 1923.

KENYON, 4th Baron, *cr* 1788; **Lloyd Tyrell-Kenyon,** KCVO 1907; TD; DL, JP; Bt 1784; Baron of Gredington, 1788; Aide-de-camp to King George V; Lord-in-Waiting, 1916; Lord Lieutenant of Denbighshire; *b* London, 5 July 1864; *o s* of late Hon. Lloyd Kenyon, and Fanny Mary Katherine, *d* of 1st Baron Harlech, Brogyntyn, Shropshire; *S* grandfather, 1869; assumed additional surname of Tyrell, 1912; *m* 1916, Gwladys Julia, *d* of late Col H. R. Lloyd Howard, CB; one *s* one *d*. *Educ:* Eton; Christ Church, Oxford. Late Col commanding Shropshire Imperial Yeomanry; Pres., North Wales University Coll.; Pro-Chancellor, University of Wales; Lord-in-Waiting, 1900–5; Col commanding 2/1 Welsh Horse, Dec. 1914–Dec. 1916; Chairman Advisory Committee on Milk, 1924; President National Museum of Wales; Chairman Agricultural Wages Board, 1924, etc. Owner of about 10,000 acres. *Recreations:* hunting, shooting. *Heir: s* Hon. Lloyd Tyrell-Kenyon, *b* 13 Sept. 1917. *Address:* 2H The Albany, Piccadilly, W1. *T:* Gerrard 2893; Gredington, Whitchurch, Shropshire; Peel Hall, Bolton, Lancs; Boreham House, Chelmsford. *Clubs:* Carlton, Turf.

Died 30 Nov. 1927.

KENYON, Edith C.; novelist; *b* Hooton Pagnell, Doncaster, Yorks; 3rd *d* of late John Kenyon, MRCS, and Ellen (Wilton), of Hooton Pagnell and Brynllwydwyn, N Wales. *Educ:* chiefly at home. Lived at Hooton Pagnell and in Wales; later for several years, in Bradford

with brother, Dr J. E. Kenyon; went to Hastings, 1895, and after three years to London; began writing early; several of her first novels were published in New York. *Publications:* Altogether 40 books; latest: A Queen of Nine Days, 1903; A Girl in a Thousand, 1904; Sir Claude Mannerley, 1905; Love's Golden Thread, 1905; Gladys's Repentance, 1906; The Adventures of Timothy, 1907; Two Girls in a Siege; Chats with Women, 1908; A Girl from Canada, 1911; The Wooing of Mifanwy, 1912; The Winning of Gwenora, 1913; Pickles: a Red Cross Heroine, 1916; The Blue Eyes of Nansi; In Another Woman's Shoes, 1919. *Recreations:* fiction, chess. *Address:* 14 Manor Road, Twickenham, SW.   *Died 21 June 1925.*

KENYON, James, JP; woollen manufacturer; Chairman of Liverpool Storage Co.; *b* Bury, 1846; *s* of James Kenyon of Crimble, near Bury; *m* 1875, Elise, *y d* of F. Genth of Burnage; four *s* one *d*. *Educ:* Bury Grammar School; Liverpool Collegiate. MP (C) Bury, Lancashire, 1895–1902. *Recreations:* shooting, cricket, racing. *Address:* Walshaw Hall, Bury, Lancashire. *Clubs:* Carlton, Conservative.

Died 25 Feb. 1924.

KENYON-SLANEY, Maj. Philip Percy, MC; MP (C) Tavistock since 1924; *b* 12 Feb. 1896; *er s* of late Percy Robert Kenyon-Slaney and Geraldine Ellen Georgina, *d* of Rev. George Whitmore. *Educ:* Bradfield College, Berks. Served Army, 1914–21 (European War, MC, despatches). Contested (C) Tavistock Division, 1923. *Recreations:* shooting, fishing, hunting. *Address:* Beechwood House, Plympton, Devon. *T:* Plympton 13Y2; 7 Chester Terrace, SW1. *T:* Sloane 3119 and 6240. *Club:* Junior Army and Navy.

Died 9 Sept. 1928.

KEOGH, Martin Jerome, LLD; Justice, Supreme Court of New York, 1896–1909 and 1910–12; *b* Ireland, 1855; *m* 1894, Katharine Temple Emmet, New Rochelle. *Educ:* New York University. Admitted to Bar, 1875; practised at New York, 1875–95. *Address:* New Rochelle, New York.

Died 24 Oct. 1928.

KEPPEL, Sir George Roos-, GCIE 1917 (KCIE 1908; CIE 1900); KCSI 1913; Member of the Council of the Secretary of State for India, 1920; Chief Commissioner and Agent to Governor-General North West Frontier Province, India, 1908–19; Hon. Colonel Khyber Rifles, 1909; *b* 7 Sept. 1866. Joined Royal Scots Fusiliers, 1886; Captain, 1895; Brevet Major, 1899; Bt Lt-Col 1907; transferred to Indian Staff Corps, 1897; served Burmese Expedition, 1885–89 (medal with two clasps); Tirah Expedition, 1897–98 (medal with three clasps); commanded operations against the Para Chamkannis, 1899 (CIE and Brevet of Major); Bazar Valley Field Force, 1908, as Chief Political Officer, and in command of a column (despatches, medal with clasp, KCIE); employed in France, 1914, as extra King's Messenger; operations on NW Frontier of India, 1915–17; Afghan operations, 1919 (despatches three times, GCIE); Military Governor Martial Law Area, NWFP, 1919 (despatches); Temp. Major-General, 1919; retired Dec. 1919; President, Indian Branch League of Mercy, 1915–19. Swedish Military Order of the Sword; KGStJ 1916. *Address:* Whitehall Court, SW1. *T:* Victoria 3160, ext. 35. *Clubs:* Marlborough, Wellington, United Service, Arts, Royal Automobile.

Died 11 Dec. 1921.

KEPPEL, Rear-Adm. Leicester Chantrey; retired; 2nd *s* of late Rev. Canon the Hon. Thomas Robert Keppel; *m* Emily (*d* 1913), *d* of George Robinson of Bagatelle Moka, Mauritius; one *s* three *d*. Served as midshipman in HMS Bellerophon, 1854; was actively engaged in embarking the army at Varna and landing at Old Fort; served at Eupatoria in defence of that town; at bombardment of Sevastopol, 1854, and bombarded Fort Constantine at 600 yards; served in HMS Magicienne, at bombardment in destruction of Friedericksham, 1855; in charge of boat under fire against Viborg, and lifted two infernal machines when under fire and cleared passage; in charge of mortar vessel at bombardment of Seveaborg, 1855; was engaged with Russian artillery at Ravenoari in Finland, 1855; engaged in suppression of Slave Trade on East Coast of Africa and captured several slave dhows under fire, 1861; served in expedition up Zambesi with Dr Livingstone; in command of gun-boats Janus and Insolent at Chefoo, 1867–69; kept Neinfe Rebels in check; obtained redress for outrages on British subjects at Jamone, Formosa, 1868 (received thanks of Commander-in-Chief and Her Majesty's Minister); punished piratical natives for attack on Sharp Peak River Min, Chefoo, and attacked Pington and subdued natives at Foochowfoo (received official thanks, 1869); West Coast of Africa—served in Niger Expedition when several piratical villages were destroyed, and severe punishment inflicted on river pirates, 1877 (despatches); as Commander in HMS Avou up Congo, commanded expedition for punishment of pirates, who had attacked and pillaged American vessel Joseph Nickeroon (received approval of Lord Derby, also approval from their Lordships for skill and gallantry with which the operations were conducted, as well as approval of the Secretary of State for Foreign Affairs); commanded HM Ships Constance and Cleopatra in China and Japan; Flag-Capt. to Commander-in-Chief at Nore, etc. *Address:* Guelderland, West Worthing. *Club:* Junior Naval and Military.

Died 22 Sept. 1917.

KER, Hon. John Errington, MRCS, LRCP; Superintending Medical Officer, Jamaica Government Medical Service, since 1904; Member Legislative Council of Jamaica; *b* Port Rush, Co. Antrim, 22 June 1860; *s* of late C. B. Ker, MICE, late resident engineer on the GIP, India; *m* Naomi, *d* of Henry Morley, Nottingham; no *c*. *Educ:* Clifton College; privately; France and Germany; St Thomas' Hospital, London; Rotunda, Dublin. House-Surgeon Birmingham General Hospital, 1887–88; Hertford British Hospital, Paris, 1888–89; Birmingham Homoeopathic Hospital, 1889; Assistant-Surgeon, Colonial Hospital, Gibraltar, District Medical Officer, Police Surgeon, etc, 1889; later on appointed Port Surgeon, Gibraltar; Civil Surgeon during the war, 1899–1900; attached to No 3 General Hospital, Rondebosch, Cape Colony, and Springfontein, ORC, and later to No 2 General Hospital, Pretoria, also to Railway Department (medal and 3 clasps). *Recreations:* riding, gardening, travelling. *Address:* Halfway Tree, St Andrews, Jamaica. *Club:* Jamaica.

Died 25 Oct. 1918.

KER, William Paton, FBA; MA; Fellow of All Souls College, Oxford, since 1879; Professor of Poetry, Oxford, since 1920; *b* 30 Aug. 1855; *s* of William Ker, merchant, Glasgow. *Educ:* Glasgow Academy; Glasgow University; Balliol College (Snell Exhibitioner). Taylorian Scholar, 1878; Professor of English Literature and History in the University College of South Wales, Cardiff, 1883–89; Professor of English Literature, University College, London, 1889–1922. *Publications:* Epic and Romance, 1897; The Dark Ages, 1904; Essays on Medieval Literature, 1905; Sturla the Historian, 1906; The Art of Poetry, 1920. *Address:* 95 Gower Street, WC. *Clubs:* Alpine, Athenæum, United University; Western, Glasgow.

Died 17 July 1923.

KERR, Hon. James Kirkpatrick, KC; PC Can.; Life Senator since 1903; *b* Puslinch, near Guelph, Ontario, Canada, 1 Aug. 1841; *s* of Robert Warren Kerr and Jane Hamilton, *d* of late James Kirkpatrick; *m* 1st, 1864, Anne Margaret, *d* of Hon. William Hume Blake, Chancellor of Upper Canada; 2nd, 1883, Adelaide Cecil, *d* of Rev. G. Stanley-Pinhorne, Cumberland, and *niece* of late Rt Hon. Alexander Staveley Hill of Oxley Manor, Staffordshire; one *s* four *d*. *Educ:* Dr Tassie's School, Galt, Ontario. Called to Bar, 1862; QC for Ontario, 1874, and Canada, 1881; Bencher of Law Society, 1879; contested (L) Centre Toronto, 1891. Vice-Pres. of Canadian General Electric Co., and director of several large industrial and other companies; President of Liberal Association for Ontario, 1892–1904; The Speaker of the Senate, Canada, 1909–11. Grand Master of Masonic Grand Lodge of Canada, 1874–77; Member of Supreme Council, 33rd Degree Ancient and Accepted Scottish Rite, for England, Canada and United States; Provincial Great Prior Masonic Knight Templar and Knight of Grand Cross of the Temple, 1883 (England and Wales). *Address:* Rathnelly, Toronto, Canada. *TA:* The Senate of Canada, Ottawa, and Kerdason, Toronto. *Clubs:* Toronto, York, Hunt, Ontario, Ontario Jockey, Toronto; Rideau, Ottawa.

Died 4 Dec. 1916.

KERR, John, MA, LLD; *b* 15 July 1830; *s* of John Kerr, Dalry, Ayrshire; *m* 1866, Elizabeth Jackson, *d* of Dr Thomas Jackson Graham, RN; five *s* four *d*. *Educ:* Dalry Parish School; Glasgow and Edinburgh Universities; Trinity College, Cambridge. Honours in Classics, 1858; Silver Goblet Declamation Prize, 1858; Historical Essay Prize, Life and Character of William III, 1859. Assistant Master in King Edward VI's School, Bury St Edmund's, 1859; HM Inspector of Schools in Scotland N district, 1860–78; Chief Inspector in SW district, 1878–88; Senior Chief Inspector of Schools and Training Colleges, 1888–96; Classical Examiner for degrees in Edinburgh University, 1867–70, in Glasgow University, 1872–75; in the course of forty-seven years examined the majority of the Secondary Schools in Scotland, and gave evidence before almost all important Education Commissions. *Publications:* Cambridge Burney Prize Essay, 1860; Memories Grave and Gay, 1902; Other Memories Old and New, 1904; Leaves from an Inspector's Log-book, 1913; Scottish Education, Primary, Secondary, and University from the 12th Century to 1913; a considerable number of magazine articles. *Recreations:* travelling, curling, fishing, golf. *Address:* 15 Royal Terrace, Edinburgh.

Died 1 Dec. 1916.

KERR, John; *b* 1852; *m* 1877, Helen Margaret, *d* of Thomas Melville of Kersehill, Stirlingshire; two *s* four *d*. MP (U) Preston, 1903–6. *Address:* Bramshill, Frinton-on-Sea, Essex.

KERR, Rev. John, MA (Edin.); Minister Church of Scotland, parish of Skelmorlie, 1876–78; Dirleton since 1878; Member of Editorial Committee, Church Service Society; Clerk to Synod of Lothian and Tweeddale, 1907–15; *b* Dumfries, 1852; *m*; two *s* four *d*. *Educ:* Glencairn School; Edinburgh University. Captain Scottish Curling Team which visited Canada and United States, 1902–3; Chaplain Royal Caledonian Curling Club, 1897–1913; Most Worshipful Past Grand Chaplain Grand Lodge of Scotland; Retired Chaplain (Lt-Col) 8th Royal Scots (TF). *Publications:* The History of Curling, the Jubilee volume of the Royal Caledonian Curling Club; The Golf-Book of East Lothian; Golf Song-Book; Curling in Canada and the United States; article Curling in Badminton volume on Ice Sports, and in World of Sport; Archery, Golf, and Curling in Scottish History and Life; Parish Councils in Country Parishes; Fellowship with the Father; Rich and Poor; The Renascence of Worship (Lee Lecture for 1905); North Berwick in Health Resorts Series. *Recreations:* curling, golf, travel. *Address:* Dirleton, RSO, East Lothian.

Died 8 Dec. 1920.

KERR, Lord Ralph Drury, KCB 1911 (CB 1879); *b* 11 Aug. 1837; 3rd *s* of 7th Marquess of Lothian and *heir pres.* to 10th Marquess; *m* 1878, Lady Anne Fitzalan Howard, *d* of 14th Duke of Norfolk; one *s* three *d* (and one *s* one *d* decd). Entered 10th Hussars, 1857; Maj.-Gen. 1890; retired, 1898; served Afghan campaign, 1879; Inspecting Officer for auxiliary cavalry, 1883–88; commanded Curragh District, 1891–96. *Address:* Woodburn, Dalkeith, NB.

Died 18 Sept. 1916.

KERR, Admiral of the Fleet Lord Walter Talbot, GCB 1902 (KCB 1896); *b* Scotland, 28 Sept. 1839; 4th *s* of 7th Marquis of Lothian, and Lady Cecil Talbot, *d* of 2nd Earl Talbot; *m* 1873, Lady Amabel Cowper (*d* 1906), *d* of 6th Earl Cowper; four *s* two *d*. *Educ:* Radley College. Entered Navy, 1853; served in Baltic, 1854–55; with Naval Brigade at relief and battle of Lucknow; Royal Humane Society medal for saving life; Capt. 1872; Rear-Admiral 1889; Vice-Admiral 1895; Admiral 1900; Private Secretary to First Lord of Admiralty, 1885–90; second in command Mediterranean, 1890–92; Junior Lord of Admiralty, 1892; 2nd Lord, 1894–95; commanded Channel Squadron, 1895–97; Senior Naval Lord of Admiralty, 1899–1900; Admiral of the Fleet, 1904. *Recreations:* cycling, photography, botany. *Address:* 58 Cromwell Road, SW7. *T:* Western 6248; Melbourne Hall, Derby. *Club:* Junior Carlton.

Died 12 May 1927.

KERR, Captain William, DSO 1916; MC; 2nd Battalion The Border Regiment; *b* 2 March 1877; *m* 1st, Ester Isobel; one *c*; 2nd, Emily, *daughters* of R. Dalton, Cummersdale, Carlisle. *Educ:* St Patrick's, Carlisle. Entered Army, 1895; served South African Campaign (Queen's medal, 7 clasps); European War, 1914–17; present at battles of Ypres, Neuve Chapelle, Festubert, Loos (wounded at Festubert, despatches thrice, Military Cross, DSO). *Address:* c/o R. Fulton, Cummersdale, Carlisle.

Died May 1918.

KERR, Captain William Alexander, VC 1857. Late Southern Mahratta Horse; served Indian Mutiny, 1857 (despatches, medal with clasp, VC). *Publications:* Riding; Riding for Ladies; Peat and its Products; Imperial Horse Supply; etc. *Address:* 73 Bouverie Road, W, Folkestone.

Died 21 May 1919.

KERRISON, Roger, JP; *b* 1842; *e s* of late Roger Allday Kerrison, Norwich, and Adelaide Thorpe, *d* of John Stokes; *m* 1st, 1867, Florence Lucy (*d* 1903), 3rd *d* of Rev. Sir Charles Clarke, 2nd Bt; two *d*; 2nd, 1905, Ellen, *d* of James Smith, Alterton. *Educ:* Harrow; Trinity College, Cambridge, MA. High Sheriff, Suffolk, 1900; late Lieut Norfolk Artillery Militia. *Address:* Colne House, Earls Colne, Essex. *Clubs:* Wellington, New University, Hurlingham; Royal Yacht Squadron, Cowes.

Died 6 March 1924.

KERSHAW, John Felix; late Judge of Court of Appeal, Cairo (Egyptian Government); *b* 20 Nov. 1873; *s* of late Sir Louis Kershaw, KC, late Chief Justice of Bombay; *m* Anne Winston, *d* of Overton Price and Anne Rodgers, Kentucky, USA; two *s* one *d*. *Educ:* Shrewsbury School; Balliol College, Oxford. Honours in History and Law, Oxford, 1895 and 1896. Called to Bar, 1897; practised NE Circuit; Judge, Khartoum, 1902; Judge, First Instance, Cairo, 1905; appointed to Native Appeal Court, 1913; President of Court of Enquiry, Australian Red Cross, 1915; President, Military Court (trading with the Enemy), throughout War; Legal Adviser (temp.

Lt-Col) to 20th Corps during troubles in Egypt, 1919, and later same to GHQ British Army in Egypt; Legal Adviser to Court of Enquiry, Alexandria Riots, 1921; President of Cairo Assize Court, and resigned, June 1926, in consequence of adverse verdict in case of instigators of Sirdar's murder. 2nd Class, Order of the Nile; 3rd Class, Medjidieh. *Publications:* Hints on Criminal Investigation, 1907; Reply to Charge of Atrocities Alleged against British Soldiers, 1919 (Blue Book); Causes of Alexandria Riots, 1921 (Blue Book). *Recreations:* rowing, shooting, tennis, racing, swimming, golf. *Address:* Zeenalek, Gezira, Cairo, Egypt. *M:* YL5348(GB). *Clubs:* White's; Gezira Sporting, Cairo.

Died 16 June 1927.

KESTELL-CORNISH, Rt. Rev. George Kestell; Anglican Bishop of Madagascar since 1919; Archdeacon of Madagascar, 1901–19; SPG Missionary since 1882; *b* 4 Sept. 1856; *e s* of late Rt Rev. R. K. Kestell-Cornish, Bishop of Madagascar; *m* 1885, Sarah Louisa Champernowne. *Educ:* Keble College, Oxford (MA 1885). Ordained 1880; Curate of St James', Great Grimsby, 1880–82; Principal, High School, Tanarive, Madagascar, 1884–90; Mahanoro, 1891–94 and 1899–1901; Principal, St Augustine's Theological College, Ambinanindrano, 1902–19. *Address:* La Mission Anglicane, Ambatobe, Tananarive, Madagascar.

Died 23 June 1925.

KESTEVEN, Sir Charles Henry, Kt 1920; Solicitor to Government of Bengal since 1919; *m* 1921, Annie Lauder (Nancy), *d* of late James Wilson. Solicitor to the Government of India, 1904–19. *Address:* Calcutta. *Clubs:* White's, Oriental.

Died 18 Jan. 1923.

KESWICK, Maj. Henry, JP; MP (U) Epsom Division of Surrey, 1912–18; *b* 20 Oct. 1870; *e s* of late William Keswick, MP; *m* 1900, Ida Winifred, *d* of late William Johnston, ICS; three *s*. *Educ:* Eton; Trinity Coll., Cambridge (MA). Entered Jardine, Matheson & Co. of Hong-Kong, China, and Japan. Captain in 3rd Batt. King's Own Scottish Borderers; served South African War. Chairman Municipal Council and of Chamber of Commerce, Shanghai; member Legislative and Executive Councils, Hong-Kong, and Vice-Chairman of the Hong-Kong Chamber of Commerce; Chairman of Directors of the Hong-Kong and Shanghai Banking Corporation, Hong-Kong and Whampoa Dock Company, and many other public companies; first Chairman of the Far Eastern Section of the London Chamber of Commerce; Member of the London Committee of the Hong-Kong and Shanghai Banking Corporation; Member of the Royal Company of Archers. At outbreak of war rejoined his old battalion, and was given command of the 3rd VB KOSB, which he relinquished on its disbandment. Member of County Council of Dumfriesshire; President of the Dumfriesshire Unionist Association. *Address:* Cowhill Tower, Dumfries. *Clubs:* Carlton; Scottish Conservative, Edinburgh.

Died 29 Nov. 1928.

KETCHEN, Maj.-Gen. Isaac, RA; *b* 13 Feb. 1839; 2nd *s* of Isaac Ketchen, JP, of Kingillie, Nairn; *m* 1872, Celia Catherine Caroline (*d* 1896), *d* of Col W. L. Twentyman; one *d*. Entered army, 1857; Maj.-Gen. 1890; retired, 1893; served Jowaki Expedition, 1876. *Address:* Hotel Rembrandt, Thurloe Place, SW7. *Club:* United Service.

Died 12 Jan. 1920.

KETTLE, Thomas Michael; Professor of Economics of Ireland, University College, Dublin, since 1910; Irish Bar; journalist; *b* 2 Feb. 1880; *s* of A. J. Kettle, farmer and a pioneer of the Land Movement, and Margaret, *d* of Laurence M'Court of St Margaret's, Co. Dublin; *m* 1909, Mary, *d* of David Sheehy, MP. *Educ:* Christian Brothers' School, N Richmond St, Clongowes; Univ. College, Dublin. MP (N) East Tyrone, 1906–10. *Publications:* The Philosophy of Politics; Handbook on Old Age Pensions Act, 1908; contrib. to various jls and reviews. *Address:* Clonmore, Glasnevin, Dublin.

Died 9 Sept. 1916.

KEY, Ellen; lived in her own house, built on a little piece of ground, owned by the state, in the country, Sweden; *b* Sundsholm, Province of Småland, Sweden, 11 Dec. 1849; *d* of Emil Key, and Countess Sophia Posse; unmarried. *Educ:* in parents' home. After father's loss of his fortune, commenced, 1880, to teach in Stockholm in the school of a friend; also to lecture at the working-men's institute, 1884; had begun in 1870 to write articles; left the school 1899 and the lectures 1903, and went abroad; made several lecturing tours and passed most of the time between 1899–1910 abroad. *Publications:* in English: The Century of the Child; Love and Marriage; The Morality of Women; Love and Ethics; The Woman Movement; Rahel Varnhagen; The Renaissance of Motherhood; War, Peace and the Future; The All Conqueror, 1924; *relevant publication:* (in English), Ellen Key, her Life

and her Work, a study by Louise Nyström-Hamilton; in her own and other languages wrote about thirty greater or smaller works. *Recreations:* nature, books, music, art. *Address:* Strand, Alvastra, Sweden.

Died April 1926.

KEY, Rev. Sir John Kingsmill Causton, 3rd Bt *cr* 1831; MA; *b* Wandsworth, 22 Aug. 1853; *e s* of Sir Kingsmill Grove Key, 2nd Bt and Mary Sophia, *d* of G. H. Hahn of the Orchard, Wandsworth; *S* father, 1899; *m* 1891, Emily, 3rd *d* of William Woodward of Hardwicke Bank, Tewkesbury. *Educ:* Clifton; Lincoln Coll., Oxford. BA 1877; MA 1878. Curate of St George's, Kidderminster, 1878–81; missionary of the Universities Mission to Central Africa, Zanzibar, 1882–1904; Rhodesia, 1912–14; Canon of Zanzibar, 1899; Vicar of Moulsford, 1915–21. *Heir: b* Kingsmill James Key, *b* 11 Oct. 1864. *Address:* Pemba, Southbourne-on-Sea, Hants.

Died 27 April 1926.

KEYES, Comdr Adrian St Vincent, CBE 1919; DSO 1915; RN; *s* of late Gen. Sir Charles Keyes, GCB; *b* 1882; *m* 1916, Eleanor, *d* of Lt-Col Walter-Campbell, The Ivy House, Hampton Court; one *s*. Served Dardanelles, 1914–18 (despatches, DSO); present at landing of Expeditionary Force in Gallipoli; retired.

Died 6 Oct. 1926.

KEYMER, Rev. Nathaniel, MA; a Canon Missioner in the Diocese of Southwell since 1888; a Proctor in Convocation for Diocese of Southwell 1906–16; *b* 13 April 1844; *e s* of Rev. Nathaniel Keymer, Head Master of Christ's Hospital, Hertford; *m* 1869, Susan Anne, *d* of Francis Eugenia Scoble Willesford; two *s*. *Educ:* Christ's Hospital; Kensington Grammar School; Pembroke College, Cambridge; Cuddesdon College. BA 1866; MA 1870. Deacon, 1867; Priest, 1868; Curate of Bingham, Notts, 1867–77; First Vicar of Middlestown, Wakefield, 1877; Rural Dean of Tuxford, 1884–1902; Rector of Headon, 1879–1911. *Publications:* Durham Mission Tune-Book, 1886; A Help to Intercession, 1874; Instructions on Confirmation, 1890; The Holy Eucharist in Type and Shadow, 1897; Instructions on the Holy Eucharist, 1918; Life in Christ, or What it is to be a Christian, 1918; The Anointing of the Sick for Healing, 1920. *Address:* Derby House, Nottingham. *T:* 1549.

Died 10 Dec. 1922.

KEYSER, Arthur Louis; *s* of late Alfred Keyser of Cross Oak, Berkhamsted, Herts. *Educ:* Clifton College; Steffisburg, Thun, Switzerland. Travelled in Australia, 1882; also visited New Zealand and New Guinea on board HMS Nelson when Admiral Sir James Erskine hoisted the British flag in New Guinea; Secretary to Governor of Fiji, 1884; entered service of Malay States, 1888; held various posts in Selangor, including that of Ulu Selangor; subsequently Collector and Magistrate, Jelebu, 1890–97; and officer in charge of the Negri Sembilan; Commissioner on board HMS Aeolus to the Keeling Cocos Islands and Christmas Islands, receiving thanks of Secretary of State for his report, 1897; in same year received similar thanks for saving life in Jelebu floods; seconded for service under Foreign Office; Acting Consul in Borneo-Brunei and Sarawak, 1898; Consul, 1899; transferred to Foreign Office; Consul at Berbera, Somali Coast, 1900; at Zaila, 1901; Somaliland medal, with clasp; HBM Consul for provinces of Cadiz, Cordova, Huelva and Seville, 1903–18; Consul-General, 1916–18; Consul-General, Ecuador, First Sec. HM Legation, Quito and Chargé d'Affaires during absence of HM Minister, 1918; retired, 1920. *Publications:* Description of Visit to New Guinea, also Java; several novels; People and Places, a Life on Five Continents, 1922; Trifles and Travels, 1928. *Recreations:* won lawn-tennis championship of Australia, 1882; of New South Wales, 1884. *Address:* Tangier, Morocco. *Clubs:* White's, Junior Carlton, Ranelagh, Royal Automobile.

Died 7 March 1924.

KEYSER, Col Frederick Charles, CB 1882; *b* London, 8 April 1841; *e s* of late Alfred Keyser of Cross Oak, Great Berkhampstead; *m* 1st, 1872, Louisa Frances Marshall (*d* 1909), *d* of late Lt-Gen. George C. Vialls, CB; 2nd, 1909, Mabel Laura, *d* of late B. L. Gordon, KCB. *Educ:* Totteridge; Neuwied, Germany; Royal Academy, Gosport. Gazetted Ensign to Royal Fusiliers, 1858; commanded 2nd Batt. 1885; Inspector of Signalling, Aldershot, 1889 (retired under age clause, 1898); Colonel, 1885; Afghan War, 1879–80; covering of retreat from Maiwand; defence of Kandahar, and Battle of 1 Sept. (despatches, medal with clasp); in command Signallers, Egyptian Expedition, 1862; commanded Corps of Signallers. Battles: Kassassin, severely wounded, Tel-el-Kebir (despatches, medal and clasp, Bronze Star, 3rd class Medjidie and CB). Commanded 3rd Battalion (now disbanded) Royal Northern Reserve Regt, 1900–1; appointed to Command Home Counties Volunteer Brigade, with rank of Brig-Gen., 1902. *Recreations:* racing, shooting, yachting. *Address:* 87 Prince of Wales Mansions, Battersea Park, SW. *Clubs:* United Service, Sports. *Died 4 April 1920.*

KHAIRPUR STATE, HH Mir Imam Baksh Khan, Ruler of, GCIE 1911. Population about 130,000. *Address:* Khairpur State, Bombay Presidency. *Died Feb 1921.*

KIBBLEWHITE, Ebenezer Job; Editor of the Weekly Times, 1884–1910, Building News and Engineering Journal, and English Mechanic and World of Science, 1878–1922; Director, Strand Newspaper Co., Ltd, 1894–1922; *b* London 7 Dec. 1846; *e s* of Ebenezer Heather Kibblewhite; *m* 1st, 1868; 2nd 1873; five *s. Educ:* Royal Asylum of St Anne's Society; Sion College. Commenced life as a pupil teacher, then in a solicitor's office, and afterwards became associated with John Passmore Edwards in journalistic work. *Publications:* The Gospel of Humanity; The Record of Our Race. *Recreations:* gardening, walking. *Address:* 10 Lancaster Place, Strand, WC. *T:* Gerrard 1291. *Died 2 Dec. 1924.*

KIDD, Benjamin; author; *b* 9 Sept. 1858; *m* 1887, Maud Emma Isabel, *d* of late John Perry, of Weston-super-Mare; three *s.* Occupied with the development of system of social philosophy outlined in his books. Formerly Member of the Inland Revenue Office. Travelled for economic studies, Eastern, Southern and Western United States, and Canada, 1898; South Africa, 1902; Special Correspondent of the Times. *Publications:* Social Evolution, 1894 (trans. German, 1895; Swedish, 1895; French, 1896; Russian, 1897; Italian, 1898; Chinese, 1899; Czech, 1900; Danish, 1900; Arabic, 1913); The Control of the Tropics 1898 (published in USA, Mr Joseph Chamberlain spoke of its effect on British colonial policy); Principles of Western Civilisation, 1902 (trans. Spanish 1903); prefatory article on Application of Doctrine of Evolution to Sociological Theory, 10th edn Enc. Brit. 1902, and of the article Sociology in 11th edn 1911; The Significance of the Future in the Theory of Organic Evolution (two lectures Royal Institution, London 1906); Individualism and After (Herbert Spencer Lecture, University of Oxford, 1908); The Two Principal Laws of Sociology, Bologna, 1909; articles Civilisation, Darwinism, Enc. Relig. and Ethics, 1910–11. *Clubs:* Athenæum, Savile. *Died 2 Oct. 1916.*

KIDD, Henry, JP, DL; *b* 1862; 2nd *s* of Robert Charles Kidd (*d* 1866), and Mary Jane, *y d* of Rev. George Mason, of Cuckney, Notts; *m* 1897, Lady Mary Kerr, *d* of 9th Marquis of Lothian; one *s* one *d.* Late Capt. Lothian and Berwick Imp. Yeo. 1896–1901; Lieut Imp. Yeo. S Africa, 1900. *Clubs:* St James's, Orleans. *Died 23 June 1923.*

KIDD, James; MP (U) Linlithgowshire, 1918–22 and since 1924; solicitor; *b* 11 March 1872; *m* 1899, Jessie, *d* of Thomas Turnbull. *Educ:* Carriden Public School; Edinburgh University. Parliamentary Secretary to the Scottish Board of Health, 1922. *Address:* Muiredge, Carriden, Bo'ness, Scotland. *Clubs:* Constitutional; Scottish Conservative, Edinburgh. *Died 2 March 1928.*

KIDSTON, Robert, JP Stirlingshire; LLD, DSc; FRS, FRSE, FGS, FRPSE; *b* at Bishopton House, Bishopton, Renfrewshire; *y s* of late Robert Alexander Kidston; *m* Agnes Marion Christian, *y d* of late Major Patrick Oliphant of Over Kinnedar, Fife; two *d. Educ:* Stirling High School; Univ. of Edinburgh. Foreign Member Kaiser. Mineral. Ges., Petrograd; Hon. Mem. Soc. Russe de Mineralogie, Petrograd; Foreign Mem. Soc. Géol. de Belgique; Murchison Fund, Geol Soc. London, 1887; Neill medal, Roy. Soc. Edin., 1890; Murchison medal, Geological Society, London, 1916. *Publications:* Catalogue of Palaeozoic Plants in the Geological Collection of the British Museum; Végétaux houil dans le Hainaut-Belge dans les Collections du Musée royal d'Histoire nat. à Bruxelles, 1911; and over 100 papers and memoirs on the Carboniferous Flora, published in Trans of Royal Societies, Edinburgh and London, Geological Society London, Linnean Society, Royal Physical Society, Edinburgh, Geological Soc. of Glasgow, Nat. Hist. Soc. Glasgow, Geol. and Polytechnical Soc. Leeds, Geol. Soc. of Manchester, Yorkshire Nat. Union, Bot. Soc. of Edinburgh, etc. *Recreations:* gardening, curling, fishing. *Address:* 12 Clarendon Place, Stirling. *T:* Stirling 156. *Died 13 July 1924.*

KIDSTON, Hon. William; Premier of Queensland, 1903–7, and since 1908; *b* Falkirk, 1849; widower. Emigrated to Australia, 1882; established a bookseller's and stationer's business at Rockhampton; MLA Rockhampton, 1896; Treasurer and Postmaster-General of Queensland, 1899; Treasurer, 1903. *Address:* Brisbane, Queensland. *Died 27 Oct. 1919.*

KIDSTON-KERR, Col Alex. Ferrier, CB 1896; JP, DL for Kinrossshire; retired; *b* 24 Sept 1840; 6th *s* of late Ven. Glen Kidston of Newton House, Newton, Lanarkshire; assumed the additional surname of Kerr on succeeding to entailed estate of Gairney, Kinrossshire; *m* 1873, Jean Howe, *d* of late James Howe M'Clure, Solicitor, Glasgow. *Educ:* Merchiston Castle School, Edinburgh; privately in France. Entered 42nd Royal Highlanders, 1858; Capt. 1873; Maj. 1881; Brevet Lt-Col 1884; Colonel 1888; served Ashanti War, 1874; Battle of Amoaful; capture and destruction of Becquah; Battle of Ordansu and capture of Coomassie (despatches, medal with clasp); Egyptian Expedition, 1882–84; Battle of Tel-el-Kebir (medal with clasp, bronze star, 4th class Osmanieh); Soudan, 1884; Battle of El Teb (despatches, 2 clasps); Brevet of Lieut-Col Soudan Expedition, 1884–85; Nile, action of Kerkeban (2 clasps); Jubilee Medal. *Recreations:* hunting, golf, shooting. *Address:* Gairney, Kinross; The Grange, Grange, Edinburgh. *TA:* The Grange, Edinburgh. *T:* Central 6829. *M:* 3579. *Clubs:* Army and Navy; New, Edinburgh. *Died 2 March 1926.*

KIKUCHI, Baron Dairoku, *cr* 1902; Privy Councillor, 1912; President of Imperial Academy, 1st class Order of Sacred Treasure, 2nd class Rising Sun; Rigakuhakushi (DSc Japan); Hon. LLD Glasgow, Manchester, and Rutger's; MA Cantab.; BA London; Hon. Professor of Imperial Universities of Tokyo and Kyoto; corresponding member of British Association for the Advancement of Science; *b* Yedo (now Tokyo), 17 March 1855; 2nd *s* of Dr Shûhei Mitsukuri (born Kikuchi, adopted into Mitsukuri family); *m* Tatsu, *d* of H. Fukuda; three *s* five *d. Educ:* Kaiseijo (Yedo); University College School, London; St John's College, Cambridge. Professor of Mathematics, Tokyo Imp. Univ., 1877–98; Vice-Minister of Education, 1897–98; President Imperial University, Tokyo, 1898–1901; Minister of Education, 1901–3; President of Peers' School, 1904–5; President, Kyoto Imperial University, 1908–12; Life member of the House of Peers, 1890; resigned, 1912; Member of the Imperial Academy since 1889; President of the Earthquake Investigation Committee. *Publications:* several books on Mathematics, etc; Education in Japan, in English. *Heir:* Taiji Kikuchi. *Address:* 124 Takehayacho, Koishikawa, Tokyo, Japan. *Died 19 Aug. 1917.*

KILBRIDE, Dennis; MP (N) Kildare South, 1906–18; tenant farmer; *b* 1848; *s* of Thomas Kilbride, Lugnacurran, Queen's Co. *Educ:* Clongowes. MP (N) South Kerry, 1887–95; MP (N) Co. Galway N, 1895–1900 (returned for both North Galway and South Kerry, elected to sit for North Galway). *Address:* Duke Street, Athy, Co. Kildare. *Died Oct. 1924.*

KILBURNE, George Goodwin, RI; painter (figure pictures); *b* Norfolk, 24 July 1839; *e s* of late Goodwin Kilburne, Hawkhurst, Kent; *m* 1st, 1862, *d* of late Robert Dalziel, painter, *niece* to the Bros Dalziel, to whom he was apprenticed; three *s* two *d;* 2nd, 1899, Edith Golightly; two *d. Educ:* Hawkhurst. On leaving school, five years apprenticed to Dalziel Bros, wood-engravers, London; worked at wood-engraving for one year more, then gave it up for painting; followed the profession of an artist ever since. Particular interest in hunting, and in ancient arms and armour, possessed good collection of arms and armour, principally swords. *Recreations:* hunting, cycling, golf. *Address:* Normanton, 16 Albion Road, Swiss Cottage. *Club:* Artists' Society. *Died 21 June 1924.*

KILLANIN, 2nd Baron, *cr* 1900; **Martin Henry Fitzpatrick Morris;** Bt 1885; PC Ire. 1920; JP Co. Cavan; HM Lieutenant and Custos Rotulorum, Co. Galway; Hon. LLD Royal University of Ireland; a Commissioner of National Education in Ireland; Governor, University College, Galway; a Director of the Bank of Ireland; Barrister, Lincoln's Inn; *b* 22 July 1867; *e s* of Baron Morris and Killanin, PC, and Anna, *d* of Hon. Henry George Hughes, a Baron of Court of Exchequer, Ireland; *S* father, 1901. *Educ:* Trinity College, Dublin (BA); essay gold medallist of Univ. Philosophical Society. Circuit Registrar and Private Sec. to his father, when Lord Chief Justice of Ireland, 1887–89; High Sheriff Galway, 1897; Senator, Royal Univ. of Ireland, 1900–7; Member of Irish Agricultural Wages Board, 1917–19; CC for Spiddal Division of Co. Galway, 1899–1920; contested (C) Borough of Galway, 1895; MP (C) Galway, 1900–1; served on Select Committee, House of Lords, on Chantrey Trust, 1904; Chairman of Viceregal Commission on Primary Education (Ireland), 1918–19. KGStJ. *Heir:* n Michael Morris, *b* 30 July 1914. *Publications:* an essay on Spiritual Realism, 1892; Transatlantic Traits, 1897; and contribs to the Nineteenth Century and other magazines. *Address:* Galvia, Lee on the Solent, Hampshire; Spiddal House, Co. Galway. *Clubs:* Athenæum; County, Galway. *Died 11 Aug. 1927.*

KILNER, Group-Captain Cecil Francis, DSO 1915; RAF; *b* 8 Oct. 1883; *s* of late W. A. Kilner, Kemsing, Kent. Entered RMLI 1902; Captain, 1913; served European War, 1914–18 (despatches, DSO and bar); promoted Wing-Comdr, 1918; Group-Captain, 1924.
Died 20 Oct. 1925.

KILNER, Rt. Rev. Francis Charles, DD; Suffragan Bishop of Richmond since 1913; Hon. Canon of Ripon and Rector of Stanhope, Co. Durham. *Educ:* Rugby School; Keble College, Oxford; Cuddesdon College. Ordained 1874; Curate of Christ Church, Bootle, 1874–79; Missioner, Diocese of Winchester, 1879–81; Vicar of Bingley, Yorks, 1892–1906; Rural Dean of South Craven, 1892–1906; Warden, Diocesan Home for Women Workers, 1900–6; Archdeacon of Craven, 1896–1913; Vicar of Gargrave, 1906–13. *Address:* The Rectory, Stanhope, Co. Durham.
Died 19 March 1921.

KILVERT, Sir Harry Vernon, Kt 1921; JP; *b* 28 June 1862; *s* of late Nicholas Kilvert, The Lodge, Ashton-upon-Mersey, Cheshire; *m* 1889, Annie Gertrude, *d* of Henry S. Pemberton. *Address:* The Lodge, Ashton Lane, Ashton, Cheshire.
Died 12 March 1924.

KIM, Tan Jiak, CMG 1911; unofficial member Legislative Council, Straits Settlements. *Address:* Singapore.
Died 22 Oct. 1917.

KIMBER, Sir Henry, 1st Bt, *cr* 1904; MP (C) Wandsworth (1st member), 1885–1913; Vice-Chairman of Capital and Counties Bank; Chairman of South Indian Railway Co.; founder or reconstructor of several colonial and other undertakings; *b* 13 July 1834; *s* of Joseph Kimber of Canonbury; *m* 1861, Mary Adelaide (*d* 1901), *d* of late Gen. Charles Dixon, RE; three *s* two *d* (and three *s* one *d* decd). *Educ:* private schools; tutors; University College, London. First Prizeman of Incorporated Law Society, 1858 and Second in Law at Univ. Coll. London. Solicitor, 1858; founded firm of Kimber and Ellis, later Kimbers, Williams and Co.; retired in favour of his sons, 1890; favourite work to rescue and reform commercial enterprise; one of the founders of New Rugby, Tenn, USA; six times contested Wandsworth, eight times elected, twice unopposed. *Recreations:* parliamentary and business; travelling, globe-trotting. *Heir: s* Henry Dixon Kimber, *b* 8 Nov. 1862. *Address:* Lansdowne Lodge, East Putney, SW15. *T:* Putney 154; Albany Chambers, Petty France, Westminster, SW1. *T:* Victoria 484; 79 Lombard Street, EC. *Clubs:* Carlton, City Carlton (of which a founder), St Stephen's, Ranelagh, Royal Automobile.
Died 18 Dec. 1923.

KINCH, Prof. Edward, FIC; Professor of Chemistry, Royal Agricultural College, Cirencester, 1881–1915; *b* 19 Aug. 1848; 3rd *s* of Charles Kinch; *m* 1889, Edith (decd), 3rd *d* of Rev. George Huntington. *Educ:* Grammar School, Henley-on-Thames; Royal College of Chemistry, Oxford Street, W. Chief-Assistant to Professor of Chemistry, RA College, 1869–73; on Teaching Staff, Royal College of Chemistry and Royal School of Mines, South Kensington, 1873–75; Superintendent of Minerals, India Museum, London, 1875–76; Prof. of Chemistry, Imperial College of Agriculture, Tokio, Japan, 1876–81. *Publications:* papers in Trans of the Asiatic Society of Japan, Jl of the Chemical Society, Mineralogical Magazine, Jl of the Royal Agricultural Society, Trans of the Surveyors' Institution, Agricultural Students' Gazette, etc. *Recreations:* rowing, gardening. *Address:* Komaba, Haslemere, Surrey. *Clubs:* Savile, Farmers'.
Died 6 Aug. 1920.

KING, Alfred John, BSc; *b* 14 Feb. 1859; 2nd *s* of late Alderman John King, formerly Mayor of Manchester; *m* 1888, Julia Constance, *d* of late Thomas Oliver of Bollington; two *s* one *d. Educ:* Oliver's Mount School, Scarborough; Owens College. Bleacher and finisher; Chairman, Bollington District Council, 1896–1906; member, Society of Friends; MP (L) Knutsford Div. of Cheshire, 1906–10. *Address:* Elleray, Windermere. *T:* Windermere 174. *Clubs:* Devonshire; Reform, Clarendon, Manchester.
Died 16 March 1920.

KING, Arthur Thomas, ISO 1903; Chief Clerk, National Debt Office; retired, 1910; *b* 30 Sept. 1845. *Address:* The Summit, Stevenage, Herts.
Died 26 March 1922.

KING, Sir Charles Albert, Kt 1912; CB 1907; Comptroller and Accountant-General of Post Office, 1901–19; *b* 1853; *s* of late Rev. W. King of Fordham, Essex. *Address:* 46 The Avenue, Beckenham. *T:* Bromley 444.
Died 1 Feb. 1922.

KING, Charles Macintosh, JP, DL; Convener of County of Stirling; Chairman of Stirlingshire Territorial Force Association; Joint Convener of the Smaller Livings Committee of the Church of Scotland; *b* 1836; *s* of John King of Campsie; *m* 1867, Jane Margaret, *d* of Dr Andrew Buchanan, Professor of the Institutes of Medicine in Glasgow University; two *s* three *d. Educ:* Glasgow High School and University. Hon. Colonel 4th Vol. Batt. Argyll and Sutherland Highlanders; Chairman of Campsie Parish School Board for forty-three years, etc. *Recreations:* walking, shooting. *Address:* Antermony House, Milton of Campsie. *Clubs:* County, Stirling; Western, Glasgow; Conservative, Edinburgh.
Died 11 Feb. 1920.

KING, Sir Charles Simeon, 3rd Bt, *cr* 1821; *b* 8 Dec. 1840; *s* of Rev. Sir James Walker King, 2nd Bt; *S* father, 1874; *m* 1891, Sophia Louisa, *d* and *heir* of late Robert Snow Bolton-Davis, Swerford Park, Oxon. A writer on religious and political subjects. *Publications:* edited, Henry's (Rev. William, FRS) Upper Lough Erne in 1739, 1892; A Great Archbishop of Dublin, William King, DD (1650–1729), 1906. *Heir:* none. *Address:* The Highlands House, St Leonards-on-Sea.
Died 3 April 1921 (ext).

KING, George; Director and one of the founders of The Sphere and The Tatler; Chairman of Technical Journals Ltd, proprietors of The Architect's Journal and The Architectural Review; *m* Sister Janet (*d* 1911), Royal Red Cross, *d* of Benjamin Wells, ARAM; two *d.* Winner of the £500 Prize Competition given by Tit-Bits for best scheme of National Old Age Pensions. *Recreations:* golf, fishing. *Address:* Vardin, Purley. *Clubs:* Devonshire, Constitutional.
Died 12 July 1922.

KING, Sir George Anthony, Kt 1924; Chief Master, Supreme Court Taxing Office since 1921; *b* 23 Oct 1858; *o s* of George Farquharson King, solicitor; *m* 1888, Mabel, *y d* of Rev. Henry Ralph Blackett; one *s. Educ:* Winchester; Corpus Christi College, Oxford. BA 1881; 2nd class Jurisprudence; MA 1884. Solicitor, 1885; Master of the Supreme Court, 1902–21; London Diocesan Reader, 1896; Member of the House of Laymen, 1906, and of the National Assembly; Treasurer Pan-Anglican Congress, 1908; Vice-President, BFBS and CMS; Treasurer, CEMS and RTS, and of National Mission of Repentance and Hope, 1916. *Publications:* In Our Tongues, 1900; Costs on the High Court Scale, 1910; joint-editor of the Annual Practice. *Address:* Penn Road House, Croydon. *T:* Croydon 574. *Club:* National.
Died 17 Jan. 1928.

KING, George Kemp, MVO 1911; Acting Principal, Territorial and Volunteer Forces Directorate, War Office, since 1917; Assistant Principal, Territorial Directorate, 1913–17; *b* 25 March 1880; *e s* of George King, Eltham, Kent; *m* 1917, Mary Lilian Wenonah, *e d* of Robert N. Helme, Netherleigh, Lancaster; one *s. Educ:* Christ's Hospital; St John's College, Cambridge (Foundation Scholar). Bracketed 13th Wrangler, 1902; 1st Class, Natural Sciences Tripos, Part I, 1903; BA, 1902. Clerk of the Higher Division, War Office, 1903; Editor, War Office List, 1905–6; Resident Clerk, 1906–13; Private Secretary to Sir Edward Ward, Permanent Under-Secretary of State for War, 1908–12; acted as Private Secretary to Mr (later Viscount) Haldane, when Secretary of State for War, April–Aug. 1908; Private Secretary to Col Seely, Secretary of State for War, 1912–13. *Address:* 1 K Montagu Mansions, Portman Square, W1.
Died 5 Aug. 1920.

KING, Sir Gilbert, 4th Bt, *cr* 1815; country gentleman; *b* 30 May 1846; *e s* of Sir Gilbert King, 3rd Bt; *S* father, 1895; *m* 1st, 1888, Charlotte (*d* 1892), *d* of Robert Heard, Pallastown, Co. Cork; one *d*; 2nd, 1897, Louisa, *d* of late Lt-Col Henry Baker Sweet. *Educ:* Blackheath Proprietary School; Trinity Coll. Dublin (MA). High Sheriff, Co. Roscommon, 1892; Co. Leitrim, 1894 and 1904; Co. Sligo, 1909. *Heir: cousin* George Adolphus King, *b* 3 Sept. 1864. *Address:* Charlestown, Drumana, Ireland.
Died 9 July 1920.

KING, Mrs Harriet Eleanor Baillie Hamilton; *d* of Adm. William Alexander and Lady Harriet Baillie Hamilton; *m* Henry Samuel King (*d* 1878), JP, of Manor House, Chigwell, Essex; seven *c.* Roman Catholic. *Publications:* Aspromonte, and other Poems; The Disciples; A Book of Dreams; Ballads of the North, and other Poems; The Prophecy of Westminster; The Foreshadowing of a Saint; The Hours of the Passion; Letters and Recollections of Mazzini. *Address:* 1 Woburn Square, WC.
Died 10 May 1920.

KING, Sir Henry Clark, Kt 1906; Solicitor and Notary Public and Commissioner, High Court, Madras; *b* 20 June 1857; *s* of Rev. C.

W. King, HM's Inspector of Schools, and Mary Anne King, *d* of Rev. Canon Douglas of Durham; *m* Ethel, *e d* of G. Alderson Smith of Wheatcroft, Scarborough; one *s* two *d*. *Educ:* Durham; Marlborough. Articled to A. S. Field of Leamington in 1875, and went to India in 1880 as assistant to Tasker and Wilson; afterwards senior partner in the firm of King and Josselyn, Madras; was one of the three secretaries appointed by the Presidency of Madras in connection with the reception of TRH the Prince and Princess of Wales at Madras, 1906. *Recreations:* Marlborough College XI 1874–75; Marlborough College XX 1874; for many years played for the Madras Presidency XI. *Address:* 26 First Avenue, Hove. *T:* 8838. *Clubs:* Durham County; Madras.   *Died 23 July 1920.*

KING, Rev. Henry Hugh; Rector of Falmouth since 1912; *b* 1869; *y s* of Ridley King, Architect, Ipswich and Leeds, and Eliza, *d* of James Fenton, CE, Low Moor, Bradford; *m* Enid Mary, *d* of Edward Anketell-Jones, of Ettrick, Victoria; two *d*. *Educ:* Royal Masonic School; Felsted; private tutors; Trinity College, Dublin. Crammed for Indian Civil Service; invalided by football accident; read for Holy Orders at Truro, Scholae Cancellarii; ordained 1895; remained in diocese ever since; held curacies at Hessenford and Penzance; Chaplain for 3 years to Lord St Levan; Vicar of Marazion for 7 years; Rural Dean of Penwith, 3 years; Chaplain at Santa Cruz, Teneriffe; Vicar of Bodmin, Cornwall, to 1912; Hon. Canon of Truro Cathedral; PGC Cornwall, 1912. *Recreations:* reading, illuminating, gardening. *Address:* The Rectory, Falmouth.   *Died 17 Aug. 1918.*

KING, John Charles, ISO 1911; late Assistant Colonial Secretary of Gibraltar; *b* 20 May 1847; *s* of David King, Perth, NB; *m* Louise, *d* of late J. Gregory Imossi, Gibraltar; one *s* one *d*. *Educ:* under private tuition abroad. Appointed to Gibraltar Civil Service 1866; Official Trustee, 1913. *Address:* Prince Edward's Road, Gibraltar.

Died 24 March 1918.

KING, Leonard William, MA, LittD; FSA; Assistant Keeper of Egyptian and Assyrian Antiquities, British Museum, since 1913; Professor of Assyrian and Babylonian Archaeology in the University of London; King's College, since 1915; *b* London, 8 Dec. 1869; 5th *s* of Robert King (*d* 1886) and Mary, *o d* of late John Henry Scarborough; *m* 1906, Anna, 3rd *d* of late Henry Anthony Burke of Tully, Co. Galway; one *s* one *d*. *Educ:* Rugby; King's College, Cambridge. Excavated at Konyunjik (Nineveh) for the British Museum, 1903–4; collected rock inscriptions in Assyria, Persia and Kurdistan, 1901, 1903–4; Lecturer in Assyrian, King's College, London, 1910–15. FRGS 1905. *Publications:* Babylonian Magic and Sorcery, 1896; Cuneiform Texts in the British Museum, 1896–1914; Assyrian Chrestomathy, 1898; Letters of Hammurabi, 1898–1900; Babylonian Religion and Mythology, 1899, and Assyrian Language, 1901 (Books on Egypt and Chaldaea, vols iv and v); Annals of the Kings of Assyria, 1902; Guide to the Babylonian and Assyrian Antiquities in the British Museum, 1900, 2nd edn 1908 (with Dr Wallis Budge); Seven Tablets of Creation, 1902; Sculpture and Inscription of Darius at Behistûn (with R. C. Thompson, MA), 1907; Egypt and Western Asia, Amer. edn 1906, Eng. edn 1907 (with H. R. Hall, MA); Studies in Eastern History, 1904–7; History of Sumer and Akkad, 1910; Boundary-Stones in the British Museum, 1912; Catalogue of the Kouyunjik Collection in the Brit. Mus. (Supplement), 1914; Gates of Shalmaneser; History of Babylon; also contributed to DNB; Enc. Bibl.; Enc. Brit. etc. *Address:* 29 St Edmund's Terrace, Regent's Park, NW; British Museum, WC.

Died 20 Aug. 1919.

KING, Sir Lucas White, Kt 1919; CSI 1898; LLD; FSA; *b* 28 Sept. 1856; *e s* of late Dep. Surg.-Gen. Henry King, Principal, Medical School, Madras; *m* 1891, Geraldine, *e d* of late Alfred Harmsworth, barrister-at-law, Middle Temple, and Mrs Harmsworth, of Poynter's Hall, Herts; one *s* three *d*. *Educ:* Ennis College and Dublin University. Exhibitioner and Honourman, Trinity Coll., Dublin, where he took the degrees of BA and LLB (1878), and LLD (1896). Entered Indian Civil Service 1878, and held, among others, the following appointments; Asst Resident, Mysore, 1887; First Asst to the AGG, Central India, 1888; Deputy Comr, Derah Ismail Khan, 1890–95; Political officer, Zhob Valley Field Force, 1890; Political officer, Waziristan Field Force, 1894 (despatches, medal and clasp); Boundary officer, Indo-Afghan Demarcation Commission, 1895; Deputy Comr, Peshawar, 1895; Deputy Comr, Kohat, 1897–1900; Political officer, Kohat-Kurram Field Force, and subsequently of the Tirah Expeditionary Force, 1897–98 (despatches, medal with three clasps, CSI); Deputy Commissioner, Kangra; Commissioner, Lahore; Salt Revenue, Northern India; Multan; Rawal Pindi; Coronation (Durbar) medal, 1902; resigned ICS, 1905. Professor of Oriental Languages, Dublin University, 1905–22. Member of the following societies:

Antiquaries of London, Antiquaries of Ireland, Royal Asiatic, First Edition. JP Co. Dublin, 1906–22. *Publications:* Memoirs of Bābur; Sa'di's Odes; Life of Tamerlane; brochures on Oriental Numismatics, and monograph on the Orakzai Country and Clans. *Recreations:* shooting, archaeology, Persian literature, first editions. *Address:* Craig Veigh, Aboyne, Aberdeenshire; 29 Abercorn Place, NSW. *Club:* Junior Carlton.   *Died 23 Aug. 1925.*

KING, Oliver; Professor of the Pianoforte, Royal Academy of Music, since 1893; *b* London, 1855. *Educ:* under Sir Joseph Barnby and W. H. Holmes; Conservatorium, Leipzig. Pianist to Princess Louise; in Canada during Governor-Generalship of Lord Lorne; gained Philharmonic Society's prize for best overture, 1883; Precentor, St Marylebone Church, 1884–6; made several tours as a solo player in Germany, Holland, England, Ireland, America and Wales. *Publications:* Symphony Night, 1880; overture Among the Pines, 1883; concerto for Pianoforte and Orchestra, 1885; violin concerto, cantatas, organ suites, piano solos, violin solos, many songs, duets, and trios, also part-songs, and fifty anthems and church-services, etc. *Recreation:* organ building. *Address:* 10 Rostrevor Road, SW.

Died about 1923.

KING, William Benjamin Basil; writer; *b* Charlottetown, Prince Edward Island, Canada, 26 Feb. 1859; *s* of William King, originally of Bucks, England; *m* Esther Manton Foote, Boston, USA. *Educ:* St Peter's School, Charlottetown; King's College, Windsor, Nova Scotia. *Publications:* Let Not Man Put Asunder; In the Garden of Charity; The Steps of Honour; The Giant's Strength; The Inner Shrine; The Wild Olive; The Street Called Straight; The Way Home; The Letter of the Contract; The Side of the Angels; The Lifted Veil; The High Heart; The City of Comrades; The Thread of Flame, The Empty Sack; The Dust Flower; The Conquest of Fear; The Happy Isles; Faith and Success; The High Forfeit; The Spreading Dawn, 1927. *Address:* 1 Berkeley Street, Cambridge, Mass, USA. *TA:* Basilking, Boston.   *Died 22 June 1928.*

KING, William Frederick, CMG 1908; LLD 1904; Chief Astronomer of the Department of the Interior of Canada since 1890; Member of Board of Examiners for Dominion Land Surveyors, since 1885; *b* Stowmarket, Suffolk, 19 Feb. 1854; *s* of William King and Ellen Archer; *m* 1881, Augusta Florence, *d* of John Allen Snow, of Ottawa; two *s* one *d*. *Educ:* Grammar School, Port Hope, Ontario; Univ. of Toronto. BA 1875, Gold Medallist in Mathematics. Dominion Land and Topographical Surveyor, 1876; Inspector of Surveys, Department of the Interior, 1881; Chief Inspector, 1886; HM Comr for the International Boundary between Canada and the United States under Treaties of 1892, 1903, 1906 and 1908; also under Agreements, entered into in 1899, 1901 and 1906; member of International Waterways Commission, 1904–7; Director of Dominion Astronomical Observatory from its opening in 1905; Superintendent of the Geodetic Survey of Canada, 1909. Fellow (and Hon. President since 1906) of the Royal Astronomical Society of Canada; FRSC (Pres., 1911–12); FAAAS. *Publications:* various scientific papers. *Address:* Observatory House, Ottawa. *Club:* Rideau, Ottawa.

Died 23 April 1916.

KING, Yeend, RI (Vice-President); *b* London, 21 Aug. 1855; *o s* of Henry King; *m* 1881, Edith Lilian, 4th *d* of T. L. Atkinson, mezzotint engraver; one *d*. *Educ:* Temple Choir School; Philological School. Apprenticed to Messrs O'Connors, glass painters, Berners Street, London; left after three years; first studied painting under William Bromley, RBA, afterwards in Paris under Bonnat and Cormon; on returning made specialty of landscape with figure; an exhibitor in RA since 1876. *Pictures:* From Green to Gold, bought for permanent collection, Liverpool; The Lass that Loves a Sailor; Sweet September; The Miller's Daughter; Hay in September, RA, 1896; The Garden by the River, purchased by Council of RA as trustees for the Permanent Collection, New South Wales, 1897; Milking Time, also purchased by the Council of RA under terms of Chantrey Bequest, 1898. *Medals:* Paris, Berlin, Chicago. *Recreation:* gardening. *Address:* 219 Maida Vale, W. *Clubs:* Arts, Savage, Wigwam, St John's Wood Arts.   *Died 10 June 1924.*

KING-HARMAN, Col Wentworth Henry, JP, DL; *b* 27 March 1840; 2nd *s* of late Hon. L. H. King-Harman and *d* of late J. R. Johnstone of Alva, NB; *m* 1863, Annie Kate, *d* of D. J. Smith, of Kingston, Canada; one *s* three *d*. *Educ:* Cheltenham, Royal Military Academy, Woolwich. Late RA. Entered Army, 1856; Captain, 1867; Major, 1875; Lt-Col 1882; Col, 1886; late Chief Government Inspector of Small Arms. *Address:* Newcastle, Ballymahon.

Died 1 April 1919.

KING-WOOD, William, CIE 1909; CBE 1919; Director Persian Section, Indo-European Telegraph Department; *b* 1 May 1867; *m* 1904, Daisy Grace, *o d* of Sir Hugh Adcock; three *s* one *d*. *Educ:* Dollar Academy, NB. Served in South Africa, 1899–1901 (medal, 3 clasps, despatches). *Recreations:* tennis, shooting, fishing. *Address:* Tehran, Persia. *Club:* Junior Naval and Military.

Died 27 Jan. 1921.

KINGSBURGH, Rt. Hon. Lord; Rt. Hon. Sir John Hay Athole Macdonald, GCB 1916 (KCB 1900; CB 1882); VD 1892; PC 1885; KC; JP, DL; LLD; FRS; FRSE; MIEE; Lord Justice-Clerk of Scotland, Lord President Second Division Court of Session, 1888–1915; a Brigadier-General, 1891, Adjutant-General, 1896–1902, Ensign-General, 1904, of the Royal Company of Archers, King's Body Guard for Scotland; *b* Edinburgh, 27 Dec. 1836; *s* of late Matthew Norman Macdonald Hume, WS, Ninewells, and Grace, *d* of Sir John Hay, 5th Bt, Smithfield and Haystoune; *m* 1864, Adelaide Jeanette (*d* 1870), *d* of Maj. John Doran, Ely House, Wexford; two *s*. *Educ:* Edin. Acad. and University (LLD 1884); Basle University. LLD St Andrews, 1911. Advocate, 1859; QC 1880; Sheriff of Ross, Cromarty and Sutherland, 1874–76; Sheriff of Perthshire, 1880–85; Commissioner of Northern Lighthouses, 1876–80 and 1885–88; Member of HM Prison Board, 1880–85; Member of HM Board of Supervision, 1880–85; Solicitor-General for Scotland, 1876–80; Dean of the Faculty of Advocates, 1882–85; Lord Advocate of Scotland, 1885–89. Member Committee of Privy Council on Education, 1885–89; Chairman Royal Commission on Boundaries of Glasgow, 1888; Member, HM Road Board; MP (C) Universities of Edinburgh and St Andrews, 1885–89; Col Commandant of Queen's RV Brigade, 1882–92; Brig.-Gen. Commanding the Forth Brigade, 1888–1901; Hon. Col Queen's Brigade, 1900; Hon. Col of Motor Volunteer Corps, 1903; Hon. Col Army Motor Reserve; Vice-President Royal United Service Institution; Vice-President National Rifle Association; President Royal Scottish Society of Arts, 1890–92. Royal Commemoration medals (two), 1897: one as Adj.-Gen. of the Royal Bodyguard, the other as Brig.-Gen. of Troops on duty at Royal Procession; Royal Coronation Medal; obtained many medals and diplomas for life-saving inventions, military works, and electrical inventions, including decorations from HM the King of the Belgians and the United States Government. It was through his exertions with the Postmaster-General and the Government that post-cards were introduced into Great Britain; inventor of a Holophote Course Indicator for preventing collisions at sea; a Military Field Telegraph; a Barothermotelemeter, and other electrical appliances. *Publications:* Common Sense on Parade, or Drill without Stays; Macdonald on Tactics; A New Form of Infantry Attack; A Treatise on the Criminal Law of Scotland; Prisoners on Oath; Our Trip to Blunderland; Electricity in the Household; Power Traction in War; Infantry in a New Century; The Future of Motor Traction; Infantry Training, Dress, and Equipment; The Making of the Infantry Soldier; Criminal Law and Procedure; The Volunteers in 1905; The Past and Future of Power Traction on Roads; Roads; Fifty Years of It, or the Experiences and Struggles of a Volunteer of 1859; Life Jottings of an Old Edinburgh Citizen, 1915; and numerous books, pamphlets and lectures on Tactics, Law, and Electricity. *Recreations:* captain of the Royal and Ancient Golf Club, 1887–88; president Scottish Amateur Athletic Association; Steward, Royal Automobile Club; golf, cricket, lawn-tennis, curling, electrical inventions and research, driving; President Scottish Automobile Club; strong supporter of autocar movement; the arbiter in disputes in international football matches. *Address:* 15 Abercromby Place, Edinburgh. *Clubs:* Constitutional, Royal Societies, Royal Automobile; New, Edinburgh; Golf, Wimbledon; New, Luffness. *T:* Edinburgh 196. *M:* S 1.

Died 9 May 1919.

KINGSFORD, Charles Lethbridge, MA; FBA 1924; *b* Ludlow, 25 Dec. 1862; 3rd *s* of late Rev. Sampson Kingsford, formerly Fellow of St John's College, Cambridge, and Vicar of St Hilary, Cornwall, and Helen, *d* of William Lethbridge of Kilworthy, Tavistock; *m* 1892, Alys, *d* of late C. T. Hudson, LLD, FRS. *Educ:* Rossall; St John's College, Oxford (Scholar). 2nd Moderations, 1st, Lit. Hum.; 2nd, Modern History; Arnold Essay, 1888. On editorial staff of Dictionary of National Biography, 1889; Examiner Education Department, 1890; Assistant Secretary, 1905–12; Private Secretary to Sir A. Boscawen, Ministry of Pensions, 1917–18; Vice-President of Society of Antiquaries, 1920–23; Ford Lecturer in English History at Oxford, 1923–24; Vice-President of the Royal Historical Society and the London Topographical Society. *Publications:* Song of Lewes, 1890; The Crusades (with late T. A. Archer), 1894; Henry V (Heroes of the Nations), 1902; Chronicles of London, 1905; Stow's Survey of London with Introduction and Notes, 1908; Sir Otho de Grandison (Transactions of Royal Historical Society), 1909; J. Pecham, De

Paupertate (with A. G. Little and F. Tocco), 1910; The First English Life of Henry V, 1911; English Historical Literature in the Fifteenth Century, 1913; The Grey Friars of London, 1915; The Story of the Middlesex Regiment, 1916; Stonor Letters (Camden 3rd Series), 1919; The Story of the Royal Warwickshire Regiment, 1921; Prejudice and Promise in Fifteenth-Century England (Ford Lectures), 1925; Calendar of MSS of Lord De L'Isle and Dudley, vol i (Royal Commission on Historical MSS), 1925; The Early History of Piccadilly, Leicester Square and Soho, 1925; numerous articles in Dictionary of National Biography; contributions to English Historical Review, Encyclopædia Britannica, 11th edn, Camden Miscellany, vols xii and xiii; Archæologia, London Topographical Record, Cambridge Mediaeval History. *Address:* 15 Argyll Road, Kensington, W8. *T:* Park 4117. *Club:* United University.

Died 27 March 1926.

KINGTON-BLAIR-OLIPHANT, Lt-Col Philip Lawrence, DSO 1916; Captain Reserve of Officers; Temporary Lt-Col commanding 11th Royal Irish Rifles since Aug. 1916; *b* 1867; *o s* of Philip Oliphant Kington-Blair-Oliphant of Ardblair, Perthshire; *m* 1901, Laura Geraldine Bodenham, 2nd *d* of Frederick Bodenham, Hereford; three *s* one *d*. *Educ:* Harrow. Gazetted 2nd Lieut Rifle Brigade, 1888; Capt. 1895; retired (Reserve of Officers), 1903; in 1914 joined the Ulster Volunteer Force, and was serving with that force at the outbreak of the War; on the formation of the Ulster Division he was appointed second in Command of the 11th Batt. Royal Irish Rifles (DSO for action in Battle of the Somme, despatches twice). *Publications:* several novels, under the name of Philip Lawrence Oliphant, among them The Little Red Fish, Maya, and The Tramp. *Address:* Ardblair Castle, Blairgowrie, Perthshire. *Club:* Authors'.

Died 8 April 1918.

KINKEAD, Richard John, JP Co. Galway; AB; MD Dublin; LRCSI; Professor of Obstetrics and Lecturer in Medical Jurisprudence and Hygiene, University College, Galway; Physician and Gynæcologist, late The Galway Hospital; Surgeon HM Prison, Galway; *b* Ballina, Co. Mayo; *s* of Rev. Francis Kinkead and Elizabeth, *d* of Robert Croften, JP, Croften Park, Ballina; *m* 1st, Alice, *d* of Thos S. Langley; 2nd, Emily, *widow* of Col Poulett Somerset, CB, MP, and *d* of John Hubert Moore; four *d*. *Educ:* Rossall Coll.; Arlington House, Portarlington; Royal Coll. of Surgeons, Ireland, and Univ. of Dublin. Silver medals, Medicine and Surgery. Practised in Tuam, 1865–77; Hon. Secretary Tuam Diocesan Synod; Professor, 1876; Ex-Member Governing Body, Univ. Coll., Galway; Examiner National University, Ireland, and of late Queen's University in Ireland; Past President Irish Medical Association; Fellow Royal Acad. of Medicine, Ireland; Provincial Grand Master South Connaught; Member Representative Church Body. *Publications:* Financial Scheme and Supplemental Scheme, Diocese of Tuam; Our Homes; The Irish Medical Practitioner's Guide; Insanity, Inebriety and Crime; Our Senses and How they Serve us; The Use and Abuse of Alcohol; numerous contributions to medical and other journals. *Recreations:* none. *Address:* University College, Galway; Forster House, Galway. *TA:* Kinkead, Galway. *T:* 3 Galway. *Club:* Galway County.

Died 18 March 1928.

KINLOCH, Maj.-Gen. Alexander Angus Airlie, CB 1893; DL, JP; retired pay; *b* Sidmouth, 27 Dec. 1838; *e s* of late Col John Grant Kinloch of Logie and Kilrie, and Agnes, *d* of F. Garden Campbell of Troup and Glenlyon; *m* 1867, Constance Emma Mary (*d* 1916), *d* of late Frederic Beckford Long; five *s* one *d*. *Educ:* Royal Military Academy, Woolwich. Entered Rifle Brigade, 1855; exchanged to King's Royal Rifle Corps, 1871; DAAG for musketry, India, 1870–77; DAQMG during Afghan war, and afterwards in India; mentioned in despatches; Brevets of Major and Lt-Col; medal and 2 clasps; commanded 2nd and 4th Batt. KRR, and afterwards three 2nd class districts in India, and 1st Brigade Chitral Relief Force (medal and clasp); retired under age clause, 1895, with honorary rank of Maj.-Gen. in recognition of services in the Army. Decorated for service in the field. Owner of about 2,000 acres. *Publication:* large game shooting in Thibet, the Himalayas, Northern and Central India. *Recreations:* shooting, fishing, hawking. *Address:* Logie, Kirriemuir, NB.

Died 17 Jan. 1919.

KINNAIRD, 11th Baron, *cr* 1682; **Arthur FitzGerald Kinnaird,** Baron Kinnaird of Rossie (UK) 1860; KT 1914; DL, JP; FRGS; Lord High Commissioner to the Church of Scotland 1907, 1908 and 1909; Hon. Colonel of late Tay Division RE (Vol.) Submarine Miners from 1893; *b* 16 Feb. 1847; *s* of 10th Baron and Mary, *d* of William Henry Hoare, The Grove, Mitcham, Surrey; S father, 1887; *m* 1875, Mary Alma, *d* of Sir Andrew Agnew, 8th Bt; two *s* one *d* (and three *s* one *d* decd). *Educ:* Eton; Trinity Coll., Cambridge (MA). President

Football Association; Director of Barclay's Bank Limited, bankers; President, YMCA; Owner of about 11,900 acres. *Heir: s* Master of Kinnaird, *b* 31 July 1880. *Address:* 10 St James's Square, SW1. *T:* Regent 685; Rossie Priory, Inchture, Perthshire. *Clubs:* Athenæum; New, Edinburgh.   *Died 30 Jan. 1923.*

KINNEAR, 1st Baron, *cr* 1897; **Alexander Smith Kinnear;** PC 1911; Judge of the Court of Session, Scotland, 1882–1913; *b* Edinburgh, 3 Nov. 1833; *s* of John Kinnear and Mary, *d* of Alexander Smith, banker, Edinburgh. *Educ:* Glasgow and Edinburgh Universities. Barrister, Scotland, 1856; QC 1881; Dean of Faculty of Advocates, 1881. *Heir:* none. *Address:* 2 Moray Place, Edinburgh. *Clubs:* Athenæum, Brooks's.

Died 20 Dec. 1917 (ext).

KINNEAR, John Boyd, of Kinloch (late of Kinnear); landowner; *b* 1828; *e s* of C. Kinnear of Kinloch, and Christian Boyd Greenshields; *m* 1st, 1852, Sarah Harriet (*d* 1866), *o d* of G. Frith; 2nd 1868, Teresa, 4th *d* of Clemente Bassano of Venice. *Educ:* home; Univs of St Andrews and Edinburgh. Called to Scottish Bar, 1850; Political Secretary to Lord Advocate, 1852–56; called to English Bar, 1856; leader-writer on Daily News, Morning Star, London Review and Pall Mall Gazette, 1860–70; served as volunteer in Italian war of 1866; owing to bad health lived in island of Guernsey, 1870–84; MP (RU) E Div. of Fife, 1885–86; 1882–1905 farmed about 600 acres of his own land, applying the latest knowledge of chemistry and physiology with successful results, and giving to his workpeople an interest in the form of profit-sharing. No special recreations apart from the subjects above indicated. Owner of about 900 acres. *Publications:* besides several law books, Principles of Reform, Political and Legal, 1864; Principles of Property in Land, 1880; Principles of Civil Government, 1887; Foundations of Religion, 1905; Teaching of the Lord, 1906; articles—Land in Enc. Brit., 9th edn, and Chamber's Cyclopaedia; articles on Farming Tenure and Game Laws in Dictionary of Political Economy; and several pamphlets on Corn-Laws, the Eastern and Irish questions, Laws affecting women, etc. *Address:* Kinloch, Collessie, Fife.

Died 10 Nov. 1920.

KINNOULL, 13th Earl of, *cr* 1633; **Archibald Fitzroy George Hay,** DL, JP; Viscount Dupplin and Lord Hay, 1627, 1633, 1697; Baron Hay (GB) 1711; Lieutenant 1st Battalion Black Watch, retired; *b* London, 20 June 1855; *s* of 12th Earl and Emily, *d* of 7th Duke of Beaufort; *S* father, 1897; *m* 1st, 1879, Josephine Maria (*d* 1900), *d* of John Hawke, solicitor, London; one *s* decd; 2nd, 1903, Florence Mary, *y d* of late Edward Darell; two *d* (and twin *s* decd). Formerly Col of Egyptian Gendarmerie; served with staff of Baker Pasha in Egypt. *Heir: g s* Lord Hay of Kinfauns, *b* 30 March 1902. *Recreations:* shooting, fishing, all games, music etc. *Address:* 74 Eaton Place, SW. *T:* 4575 Kensington; Balhousie Castle, Perth. *M:* LN 6033. *Clubs:* Carlton, Orleans.   *Died 7 Feb. 1916.*

KINO, Maj. Algernon Roderick, DSO 1915; late East Yorkshire Regiment; *b* 17 June 1880; *m* 1907, Alice Elsie, *d* of H. G. Beard. Entered army, 1900; Captain, 1910; Major, 1915; served European War, 1914–18 (despatches, DSO).

Died 10 Feb. 1924.

KIPPEN, William James, JP, DL; KC 1919; Chairman, Standing Joint Committee, Dumbartonshire; Ex-Convener, Western Divisional Council, Scottish Unionist Association; *o s* of James Hill Kippen of Busby and Westerton. *Educ:* Clifton College; Trinity College, Oxford (BA); Edinburgh University (LLB). Advocate, 1890. *Recreations:* country pursuits. *Address:* Westerton, Balloch, Dumbartonshire.

Died 1 Dec. 1928.

KIRALFY, Imre; author; Kt Commander Royal Order of Leopold; Kt Commander of the Portuguese Order of Villa Viçosa; and of the Imperial Japanese Order of the Sacred Treasure; Officier de l'Instruction Publique of France; *m* Marie, *d* of John Graham, Carlisle; five *s* one *d*. Created and was Commissioner-General of the following International Exhibitions held in London: Franco-British Exhibition, 1908, the Imperial International Exhibition, 1909, the Japan-British Exhibition, 1910; the Coronation Exhibition, 1911, the Latin-British Exhibition, 1912; Anglo-American Exposition, 1914; Director-General of the Empire of India Exhibition, 1895; India and Ceylon Exhibition, 1896; Victorian Era Exhibition, 1897; Universal Exhibition, 1898; Greater Britain Exhibition, 1899; Woman's International Exhibition, 1900; Military Exhibition, 1901; Paris in London Exhibition, 1902; Fire Exhibition, 1903; also British Commissioner-General of the Liège Universal Exposition, 1905; author of Nero, 1888–91; Venice in London, 1891–93; Columbus,

1892–93; America, 1893; India, 1895–96; Our Naval Victories, 1898; China, or the Relief of the Legations, 1901; created and designed The Great White City and the Stadium for the Olympic Games, London, 1908. *Publications:* Babylon; Rome; Nero; The Bride of the Sea; Columbus; America; India; China, etc. *Recreation:* photography. *Address:* Tower House, Cromwell Road, SW. *T:* Western 1440. *TA:* Kiralfy, London. *Clubs:* British Empire, Constitutional.

Died 27 April 1919.

KIRBY, Col Norborne, CIE 1917; retired; *b* 19 Sept. 1863; 5th *s* of late Rev. H. T. Murdoch Kirby, Mayfield, Sussex; *m* 1898, *c* Evelyn Rivers, *d* of Rev. R. R. Kirby, Ventnor; three *s* one *d*. *Educ:* Cheltenham College; RIE College, Cooper's Hill. Lieut RE 1886; Capt. 1895; Maj. 1903; Lt-Col 1911; Col 1915; served NE Frontier, India, 1892–93 (medal with clasp). *Address:* The Towers, Ventnor, I of W.   *Died 6 April 1922.*

KIRK, Sir Amos Child, Kt 1922; JP; Alderman of City of Cardiff since 1920; Lord Mayor of Cardiff, 1918–19; *b* Leeds, 14 Jan. 1856; *s* of George and Sarah Ann Child Kirk; *m* 1881, Mary Elizabeth, *d* of Charles and Ann Garland, Leeds; one *s* two *d*. *Educ:* St Mark's National School, Woodhouse, Leeds. Agent, Liverpool Victoria Insurance Offices, 1876; Director, 1908; Divisional Manager for South Wales, for above office; Councillor, City of Cardiff, 1907. *Recreation:* literature. *Address:* Clifton House, Newport Road, Cardiff. *T:* Cardiff 1577. *Clubs:* Conservative, Central, Cardiff.

Died Oct. 1928.

KIRK, Sir John, GCMG 1886 (KCMG 1881; CMG 1879); KCB 1890; FRS 1887; MD, LLD, DSc, DCL; Member of Government Committee for Construction of Uganda Railway since 1895; Foreign Secretary, Royal Geographical Society, 1894–1911; *b* Scotland, 19 Dec. 1832; 2nd *s* of Rev. John Kirk, Arbirlot, Forfarshire; *m* 1867, Helen (*d* 1914), *d* of Charles Cooke; one *s* three *d*. *Educ:* Edinburgh Univ. Served in Turkey during Russian War; Chief Officer on Dr Livingstone's Govt Expedition to Africa, 1853–64; Political Agency, Zanzibar, 1886; HM Agent and Consul-General; retired from Consular Service, 1887; British Plenipotentiary at Brussels to African Conference, 1889–90; HM Special Commissioner to Niger Coast, 1895. Vice President: Royal Society, 1894–95; Linnean Society, 1882–83. *Address:* Wavertree, Sevenoaks, Kent. *Club:* Athenæum.

Died 15 Jan. 1922.

KIRK, Sir John, Kt 1907; JP County of London, 1909; *b* Kegworth, Leicestershire, 10 June 1847; *m* 1872, Elizabeth, *d* of George Ayris; four *s* three *d*. *Educ:* Castle Donnington Grammar School. Spent part of boyhood in France; at sixteen became clerk to Pure Literature Society; then Assistant Secretary to Ragged School Union, 1873–79; Secretary Open Air Mission; Secretary, 1879, Director, 1907, and then Treasurer of Shaftesbury Society and Ragged School Union; organised Pearson's Fresh Air Fund, and other Press Funds; FCIS. *Publications:* contribs to journalism. *Recreations:* reading, foreign travel; visited most European countries, Canada, Australasia, America and South Africa; interest in child cripples and children generally. *Address:* 32 John Street, Theobald's Road, WC1. *T:* Museum 1951; Westcott, Surrey. *T:* Westcott 16. *Club:* National Liberal.

Died 3 April 1922.

KIRKE, Henry, JP; MA, BCL (Oxon); retired civilian; *b* 4 June 1842; *m* 1864, Agnes, *d* of Admiral Sir S. Lushington, GCB; two *s* six *d*. At different times Sheriff of Demerara; Police Magistrate of Georgetown; Judge of Supreme Court in British Guiana; Attorney-General of Jamaica; Special Commissioner for British Guiana at Calcutta International Exhibition, 1883–84, etc. *Publications:* Twenty-five years in British Guiana; From the Gun-room to the Throne; The First English Conquest of Canada. *Address:* The Haywards, Middle Wallop, Hants.   *Died 9 July 1925.*

KIRKMAN, Hon. Thomas; was Member of the late Legislative Council, Natal; *b* Dec. 1843; 2nd *s* of late Rev. T. P. Kirkman, MA, FRS, Rector of Croft, near Warrington; unmarried. *Educ:* Rossall School. In various subordinate positions in Manchester for eight years; went to Natal in 1868 with brother John; settled on Government grant of land in Alexandra County; was fourteen years in Volunteer force, and had eight months' active service during Zulu War, 1879; elected a Member of Legislative Assembly for Alexandra County at inauguration of responsible Government, 1893; appointed to Upper House, 1897, re-appointed, 1907; FRMS 1898. *Recreation:* microscopical studies. *Address:* Croftlands, Esperanza, Natal, S Africa. *Clubs:* Quekett Microscopical; Victoria, Pietermaritzburg.

Died 29 Oct. 1919.

KIRKPATRICK, Hon. Andrew Alexander; Minister of Mines, Minister of Marine and Minister of Immigration, South Australia, 1924–27; *b* London, 4 Jan. 1848; *m* 1878, Catherine Maria Cooper; three *s* four *d*. Arrived in South Australia, 1861; was Chairman of the United Labour Party, the Trades and Labour Council, and the Eight Hours' Celebration Union; MLC Southern District, 1891–97; Central District since 1900; Chief Secretary and Minister of Industry, 1905–9; Agent-General for South Australia, 1904–14. His mother accompanied Florence Nightingale to the Crimea. *Address:* Adelaide, S Australia.   *Died Aug. 1928.*

KIRKPATRICK, Francis, ISO 1903; JP; *b* 21 Dec. 1840; *s* of late Alexander Kirkpatrick of Crumlin Road, near Belfast, Ireland; *m* 1867, Agnes Mackie, *d* of late Henry Longfield Black of Newry, Ireland; two *s* four *d*. *Educ:* Edenderry National School, Crumlin Road, near Belfast. Arrived in New South Wales, 1858; obtained an appointment as Cadet in the Audit Department of the Civil Service; transferred to the Treasury from that Department, 1864; appointed successively Book-keeper, Accountant, 1872, Consulting Accountant and Chief Inspector of Accounts, 1888; Under-Secretary for Finance and Trade, The Treasury, New South Wales, 1891; retired from the Civil Service of New South Wales after 46 years' service, 1904. *Address:* 4 Parkview Road, Manly, near Sydney, New South Wales.

Died 10 June 1921.

KIRKPATRICK, Lt-Col Henry Pownall, DSO 1902; late 2nd in command of 16th Queen's Lancers; *b* 18 April 1862; *e s* of late Edward Kirkpatrick, Tyldesley, Lancs, and Agnes, *y d* of late James Pownall, Pennington Hall, Leigh, Lancashire; *m* 1898, Ruby, *o c* of Major W. B. Morris, 7th Hussars. *Educ:* Uppingham; Brasenose College, Oxford. *Clubs:* Naval and Military, Cavalry, Boodle's.

Died 30 Aug. 1919.

KIRKPATRICK, John, MA (Cantab), Dr jur (Heidelb.); LLB (Edin.); Hon. LLD (Glasgow and Edin.); advocate; Officier de l'Instruction Publique; *b* 1835; *s* of late John Kirkpatrick, Advocate, formerly Chief Justice of Ionian Islands; *m* 1st, Louisa, *sister* of late Prof. J. Henslow of Cambridge; 2nd, 1907, Alma, *d* of late Gen. Davidson Smith. Secretary of Senatus and Dean of Law Faculty, 1886–97; Professor of History in Edinburgh University, 1881–1909. One of founders, then Hon. Member of Franco-Scottish Society; Hon. Secretary of Edinburgh Vacation Courses. *Publications:* Digest of Scottish Law of Evidence; many historical and legal papers; account of Octocentenary Festival of Bologna; translator of Baedeker's guide-books, 1861–81; editor of Lord Mackenzie's Roman Law, Fischer's Scots in Sweden; author of Handbook of Idiomatic English, 1912, and War Studies, 1915. *Recreations:* modern languages, travel.   *Died 12 Jan. 1926.*

KIRKWOOD, Maj. John Hendley Morrison, DSO 1917; JP; *b* 11 May 1877; *o s* of late J. M. Kirkwood of Yeo, Devon, and Glencarha, Co. Mayo; *m* 1902, Gertrude, *d* of Sir Robert Park Lyle, 1st Bt; two *s* one *d*. *Educ:* Harrow. Was in 7th Dragoon Guards; served S Africa, 1899–1901 (wounded, medal, 5 clasps, despatches); Captain in the Royal North Devon Hussars; served with 4th Dragoon Guards, 1914–15 (wounded); with 1st Life Guards and Household Batt. (DSO) and commanded 1st Batt. Royal Irish Rifles. MP (C) SE Essex, 1910–12. *Address:* Yeo, Fairy Cross, SO, N Devon. *Clubs:* Turf, Carlton.   *Died 7 Feb. 1924.*

KIRKWOOD, William Montague Hammett; Legal Adviser, His Imperial Japanese Majesty's Government, Tokyo, 1885–1902; *b* 1850; 4th *s* of late John Townsend Kirkwood of Yeo Vale, N Devon, and Gore Court, Kent; *m* 1st, Harriet Alice, *d* of Hugh Darby Owen of Betty's Hall, Montgomeryshire; 2nd, Ethel, *d* of Edward Morris. *Educ:* Marlborough College. Old Marlburian Scholar. Member of Inner Temple; Her Majesty's Crown Advocate in Japan and Legal Adviser, British Legation and Consulates, 1882–85; assisted in drafting the Japanese Constitution and Codes of Law; travelled extensively through the Far East; spent several months amongst the head-hunting tribes of Formosa in 1897, and was engaged to organise the administration of that island when ceded to Japan; was Adviser to the first US Phillipine Commission, and received the thanks of Congress for his services; was a censor in the War Office during the War, and Commandant of Boy Scout Camps working for the Flax Branch of the Board of Agriculture; Commissioner of Boy Scouts for Kensington. Knight Grand Cross of the Rising Sun; Knight Grand Cross of the Sacred Treasure; Japanese Constitution Medal. *Address:* 12 Egerton Gardens, SW. *T:* Western 3823.

Died 28 March 1926.

KISHANGARH, Lt-Col HH Umdai Rajhae Buland Makan Maharajadhiraj Maharaj Sir Madan Singh Bahadur, KSCI 1911;

KCIE 1909; *b* 1 Nov. 1884; *S* his father, the late Maharaja Sir Sardul Singh Bahadur, GCIE, 1892; *m* 2nd *d* of present chief of Udaipur, and *y sister* of HH the Maharani of Bhavnagar; two *d*. *Educ:* privately; served as Member of the Imperial Cadet Corps and European War, 1914–15 (despatches). The State has an area of 858 square miles and a population of over 90,000. *Recreations:* polo, tennis, coursing, pigsticking, shikar. *Address:* Kishengarh, Rajputana, India.

Died Oct. 1926.

KITCAT, Mabel, (Mrs S. A. P. Kitcat); pen name, Mrs Murray Hickson; *d* of His Hon. Judge Greenhow, late of Leeds (for 29 years Recorder of Berwick-on-Tweed); *great n* of Harriet and James Martineau; *m* Sidney A. P. Kitcat. *Educ:* Birklands, Highgate. Began to write for pleasure and in leisure hours; continued to write for the same reason and in the same way; wrote a good deal about cricket, both tales and articles; wrote articles, verses, short stories, for Longmans' Magazine, The Gentlewoman, Vanity Fair, The Bystander, and many other publications. *Publications:* A Latter-Day Romance; Concerning Teddy; Chronicles of Teddy's Village; Shadows of Life; (with Keighley Snowden) a play, The Whip Hand. *Recreations:* amateur theatricals, gardening, reading, motoring. *Address:* Warling Dean, Esher, Surrey.

Died 12 Nov. 1922.

KITCHENER OF KHARTOUM, 1st Earl *cr* 1914, of Broome; Horatio Herbert Kitchener, KG 1915; KP 1911; GCB 1898 (KCB 1896; CB 1889); OM 1902; GCSI 1909; GCMG 1902 (KCMG 1894; CMG 1886); GCIE 1908; PC 1914; Baron, 1898; Viscount, 1902, of Khartoum; of the Vaal, Transvaal, and Aspall, Suffolk; Viscount Broome, 1914, of Broome, Kent; Baron Denton, 1914, of Denton, Kent; Secretary of State for War since 1914; Colonel Commandant Corps RE 1906; Colonel Irish Guards, 1914; Field-Marshal, 1909; *b* Crotter House, Ballylongford, Co. Kerry, 24 June 1850; *s* of late Lt-Col H. H. Kitchener, of Cossington, Leics, and Frances, *d* of Rev. J. Chevallier of Aspall Hall, Suffolk. *Educ:* RM Academy, Woolwich. Entered Royal Engineers 1871; Major-General, 1896; Palestine Survey, 1874–78; Cyprus Survey, 1878–82; commanded Egyptian Cavalry, 1882–84; Nile Expedition, 1884–85 (despatches, brevet Lieut-Col, medal with clasp, 2nd cl. Medjidie, Khedive's star); Governor of Suakim, 1886–88 (despatches, clasp); Soudan Frontier, 1889, including engagement at Toski (despatches, CB, and clasp); Adjutant-Gen. Egyptian army, 1888–92; Sirdar, 1890; commanded Dongola Expeditionary Force, 1896 (promoted Major-Gen., KCB, 1st cl. Osmanieh, British medal, Khedive's medal with two clasps); commanded Khartum Expedition, 1898 (thanks of Parliament, raised to Peerage, grant of £30,000, GCB, two clasps of Khedive's medal); Chief of Staff of Forces in South Africa, 1899–1900; Commander-in-Chief, 1900–2 (despatches, promoted Lieut-General and General, received Viscounty, grant of £50,000, thanks of Parliament); Commander-in-Chief, India, 1902–9; Member of Committee of Imperial Defence 1910; HM's Agent and Consul-General in Egypt, 1911–14; Lord Rector of Edinburgh University, 1914; Grand Cordon Order of Leopold. *Publications:* contributions to Blackwood's Magazine. *Heir: b* Lt-Col Henry Elliott Chevallier Kitchener, *b* 5 Oct. 1846. *Address:* York House, St James's Palace, SW; Broome Park, Canterbury. *Clubs:* Athenæum, United Service, Junior United Service.   *Died 5 June 1916.*

KITCHIN, Ven. Arthur, MA; Vicar of Hardingstone, Northants, since 1913; *b* 14 March 1855; 3rd *s* of late Joseph Kitchin of Dunsdale, Westerham, Kent; *m* Edith Ann, *y d* of late Thomas Everard of New Hall Park, Thurlaston, Leicestershire; one *s* three *d*. *Educ:* Westminster; Christ Church, Oxford. Deacon, 1878; Priest, 1879; Curate of Bexley Heath, Kent, 1878–82; Gulval, Cornwall, 1882–83; Chaplain (Bengal Ecclesiastical Establishment), St James', Calcutta, 1883; St Paul's Cathedral, Calcutta, 1884–89; Mussoorie, 1889–92; St Thomas', Calcutta, 1894–1905; officiating Archdeacon of Calcutta, 1887, 1900 and 1902; Furlough, 1892–94, 1899, and 1905; Exam. Chaplain to the Bishop of Calcutta, 1902–5; Archdeacon of Calcutta, 1903–7; Rector of Rushden, 1905–13; Rural Dean of Higham Ferrers I, 1906–13. *Address:* Hardingstone Vicarage, Northants.

Died 17 Feb. 1928.

KITSON, Col Charles Edward, DSO 1916; Colonel in charge of Record Office, Lichfield, since 1925; *b* 3 Nov. 1874; *s* of late Col J. E. Kitson, CB; *m* 1905; one *d*. *Educ:* Wellington College. Joined Kent Artillery Militia, 1891; 2nd Royal West Kent Regt, 1893; served South African War (Queen's medal 3 clasps, King's medal 2 clasps); European War (Bt Lt-Col, DSO); commanded 2nd Bn The Queen's Own Royal West Kent Regiment, 1920–24. *Club:* Army and Navy.

Died 11 Oct. 1928.

KITTSON, Rev. Henry, MA, DCL; Canon, Christ Church Cathedral, Ottawa; Canon Missioner Diocese of Ottawa; *b* 15 Nov. 1848; *s* of Norman Kittson; *m* 1875, Flora Grant (decd); one *s* two *d*. *Educ*: Berthier Grammar School; Bishop College University, Lennoxville, Quebec. Missionary in Diocese of Montreal, 1871–82; Rector of St John's Church, St Paul, Minn, US, 1882–86; Rector, Church of Advent, Montreal, 1886–1901. *Publications*: Church History from Archives; A Study of Early Canadian Church; sermons and papers. *Recreations*: chiefly yachting and canoeing. *Address*: Berthier, Quebec, Canada.   *Died 23 July 1925.*

KLEIN, Edward Emanuel, MD; FRS; late Lecturer on advanced Bacteriology, Medical School, St Bartholomew's Hospital; connected with Medical Department of Local Government Board since 1871, in carrying out pathological and bacteriological inquiries; *b* 1844; *m* 1877, Sophia Amelia (*d* 1919). *Publications*: several text-books on Histology and Bacteriology; numerous reports on Pathological and Bacteriological subjects in the Reports of the Medical Officer of the Local Government Board, 1871–1907; The Bacteriology and Etiology of Oriental Plague, 1906. *Recreation*: gardening. *Address*: 13 Wilbury Villas, Hove, Sussex.   *Died 9 Feb. 1925.*

KLOTZ, Otto, LLD, DSc; FRAS, FRSC; Hon. Fellow, New Zealand Institute; Director Dominion Observatory; *b* Preston, Ont, 31 March 1852; *m* 1873, Marie Widenmann; three *s*. *Educ*: Univ. of Toronto; Univ. of Michigan. Early days Surveyor and Explorer in Canadian North-West; exploratory survey to Hudson's Bay, 2,000-mile canoe trip, 1884; Astronomer since 1885; connected with Alaska Boundary Survey, 1893–94; completed first astronomic girdle of the world, wiring the British Empire together astronomically, 1903–4; Chairman Carnegie Library, 1910–12; President of the Canadian Club, 1912–13; of the University Club, 1914–15; Delegate for Canada at International Seismological Meeting at The Hague, 1907; at Zermatt, 1909; at Manchester, 1911; and at Petrograd, 1914; Chairman National Committee of Canada, International Astronomical Union, 1920; President American Seismological Society, 1920–21; Delegate for Canada at Rome, International Astronomers' Union, May 1922. *Publications*: numerous papers on Astronomy, Gravity, Terrestrial Magnetism and Seismology. *Recreation*: golf. *Address*: 437 Albert Street, Ottawa, Canada. *Clubs*: Authors'; Rideau, Rivermead, University, Ottawa.   *Died Dec. 1923.*

KNAGGS, Sir Samuel William, KCMG 1920 (CMG 1908); *b* 25 Dec. 1856; *s* of Robert Knaggs, MRCSE; *m* 1893, Violet Grey, *d* of J. A. Harragin, SIP; one *s* four *d*. *Educ*: Royal College, Trinidad. Entered Trinidad Service, 1876; Chief Commissioner, Port of Spain, 1899; Receiver-General, Trinidad, 1901; Colonial Secretary, Barbados, 1903; Colonial Secretary, Trinidad and Tobago, 1907; administered the Government of Barbados in 1903, 1904, 1905, 1906 and 1907; and of Trinidad and Tobago in 1907, 1908, 1909, 1910, 1912, 1913, 1915 and 1916; retired 1918.
                                    Died 31 Dec. 1924.

KNAPP, Charles Welbourne; President the St Louis (Missouri) Republic; member of Board of Directors Associated Press; *b* St Louis, Missouri, 23 January 1848; *s* of John Knapp. *Educ*: St Louis (Mo) University; AB 1865; AM 1867; LLD 1904; Columbia College (NY), and Univ. of Kentucky Law School, LLB 1867. *Recreation*: golf. *Address*: The Republic, St Louis, Mo. *Clubs*: Noon-day, Commercial, Round Table, Aztec, Gridiron.
                                    Died 6 Jan. 1916.

KNATCHBULL, Maj. Reginald Norton, DSO 1900; 2nd Battalion The Leicestershire Regiment; *b* 7 Feb. 1872; *s* of Col Norton Knatchbull, late Derbyshire Regt; *m* 1906, Winifred, *d* of W. F. Peel; one *d*. Entered army, 1891; Capt. 1900; Major, 1908; served S Africa, 1899–1900 (despatches, Queen's medal, 5 clasps, DSO); European War, 1914–15 (wounded).   *Died Aug. 1917.*

KNATCHBULL, Sir Wyndham, 12th Bt, *cr* 1641; *b* 9 Aug. 1844; 2nd *s* of Sir Norton Knatchbull, 10th Bt and Mary, *e d* of Jesse Watts-Russell of Ham Hall, Stafford; *S* brother, 1871; *m* 1902, Margaret Elizabeth, *widow* of John Dillon Browne. MP East Kent, 1875–76. *Heir*: *c* 4th Baron Brabourne, *b* 27 Nov. 1863. *Address*: Mersham Hatch, Ashford, Kent. *Clubs*: Carlton, Junior Carlton.
                                    Died 30 July 1917.

KNATCHBULL-HUGESSEN, Herbert Thomas, MA; *b* Mersham Hatch, near Ashford, Kent, 1 Dec. 1835; *y b* of 1st Baron Brabourne and 4th *s* of late Rt Hon. Sir Edward Knatchbull, 9th Bt, MP and 2nd wife, Fanny Catherine, *e d* of Edward Knight of Godmersham Park, Kent, and Chawton House, Hants. *Educ*: Eton; Trinity College,

Oxford. MA 1859; Barrister 1860. MP (C) North-East Kent, 1885–95. *Recreation*: cricket. *Club*: Carlton.
                                    Died 15 May 1922.

KNECHT, Edmund, PhD (Zurich), MScTech (Manchester); FIC; Associate Professor of Technological Chemistry, Manchester University, Manchester; Editor, Journal of Dyers and Colourists; *b* Liverpool, 1861; 3rd *s* of late Gustav Knecht, BSc. *Educ*: private tuition; Zurich University; Swiss Federal Polytechnic. Demonstrator in Chemistry at the Polytechnic, 1883–84; Head of Chemistry and Dyeing Department, Bradford Technical College, 1884–90; Lecturer in Chemistry, Manchester Technical College, 1890–1902; Prof. of Tinctorial Chemistry, Municipal School of Technology, 1902–9. *Publications*: (with Eva Hibbert) New Reduction Methods in Volumetric Analysis, 1925; numerous contributions to current scientific and technical literature, and Encyclopædia Britannica; several books on bleaching, dyeing, textile printing and analytical chemistry. *Recreations*: golf, cycling. *Address*: Marple Cottage, Marple.
                                    Died 8 Dec. 1925.

KNEELAND, Abner W., BA, MA, BCL, PhD; retired Professor of English Language and Literature in Macdonald College, Province of Quebec; *b* 22 May 1853; *s* of Gardner Kneeland, contractor, and Susan Goddard; *m* four *s* two *d*. *Educ*: Victoria and McGill Universities. Began teaching, 1877; Principal of a public school in Montreal, 1879; Prof. of English in M'Gill Normal School, 1892; Member of the Council of Public Instruction for the Province of Quebec, 1890; Chairman of the Text-book Committee for PQ, 1890–1914. Liberal; Methodist; a Member of the Senate of Wesleyan Theological College and of the Board of Governors L'Institute Methodiste Française, Montreal. *Publications*: wrote for The Montreal Daily Star, Weekly Witness, The New Outlook, etc; articles on Travel, Civics, Forestry, Fertilization, Education, Religion, Physiography; and contributed many poems to various magazines and newspapers. *Recreations*: fishing, horticulture. *Address*: Macdonald College, PQ, Canada. *T*: Ste Anne de Bellevue 267. *TA*: Ste Anne de Bellevue, PQ.
                                    Died 20 Nov. 1928.

KNEEN, Thomas; Clerk of the Rolls, Isle of Man. *Address*: Douglas, Isle of Man.   *Died 23 Nov. 1916.*

KNEEN, William, RBA, 1897–1904; artist, painter; member New English Art Club, 1899–1904; and Society of Painters in Tempera; Art Master at Westminster School; *b* Isle of Man, 1 Dec. 1862; 4th *s* of late John Kneen, Isle of Man, and Elizabeth Cleator; *m* 1901, Winifred Ida Mary, *e d* of late J. P. Leech, Kensington; one *d*. *Educ*: Isle of Man; the Grammar School, Manchester; under Professor Fred. Brown. Exhibited usually at the New English Art Club; the International Society of Sculptors, Painters and Gravers; The Goupil Gallery Salon. *Recreation*: reading. *Address*: Westridge, Marchmont Road, Richmond, Surrey. *T*: Richmond 2695. *Club*: Chelsea Arts.
                                    Died Oct. 1921.

KNIGHT, Edward Frederick; Morning Post special war correspondent in South Africa; barrister, journalist, author; *b* 23 April 1852; *e s* of Edward Knight, Papcastle, Cumberland. *Educ*: Westminster; Caius Coll., Cambridge (BA). On staff of Morning Post. Travelled in South America, Turkey, South Africa, Central Asia, etc. Called to Bar, 1879. Times correspondent in Hunza-Nagar Campaign, 1891 (throughout which served as officer, medal and despatches); Matabeleland, 1893–95; Madagascar, 1895; Sudan Campaign, 1896; Greece, 1897; Sudan, 1897–98; Cuba, 1898; Spain, 1899; Morning Post correspondent, South Africa, 1899–1900 (severely wounded Belmont, right arm amputated); with Ophir Tour round the World, 1901–2; South Africa, 1902–3; with Kuroki's Army in Russo-Japanese War, 1904; Turkey, 1908. *Publications*: Albania and Montenegro; The Cruise of the Falcon; The Threatening Eye; Sailing (All England Series of Sports); The Falcon on the Baltic; The Cruise of the Alerte; Save Me from My Friends; Where Three Empires Meet; Madagascar in War Time; Rhodesia of To-day; Letters from the Sudan; A Desperate Voyage; Small Boat Sailing; With the Royal Tour; South Africa after the War; Over Sea Britain; The Awakening of Turkey; Reminiscences, 1923, etc. *Recreation*: yachting; undertook voyages in command of small sailing yachts, Falcon, Alerte, etc, to South America, West Indies, the Baltic, etc.
                                    Died 3 July 1925.

KNIGHT, Sir Henry Edmund, Kt 1883; JP; Alderman City of London; *b* 25 March 1833; *s* of John William Knight, St Marylebone and St Albans; twice *m*; five *s* five *d*. *Educ*: City of London School. Member of Corporation of London, Cripplegate Ward, 1867; Alderman, 1874; Sheriff of London and Middlesex, 1875; Lord

Mayor, 1882; Member of Court of Lieutenancy for City of London; a Governor of the Royal Hospitals. *Address:* 41 Hill Street, W; Stainhill Park, Hampton-on-Thames. *Club:* City Liberal.

Died 21 Nov. 1917.

KNIGHT, Rt. Rev. Henry Joseph Corbett, DD; Bishop of Gibraltar since 1911; Fellow and Lecturer of Corpus Christi College, Cambridge, and Principal of the Clergy Training School, 1901–11; *s* of late Rev. J. L. Knight; *m* 1st, Clara Gwyn Kerslake (*d* 1911); 2nd, 1915, Bridget, 3rd *d* of late Horace Swete, MD. *Educ:* Islington Proprietary School; St Catharine's College, Cambridge (Scholar). BA; 1st Class Classical Tripos, 1882; 1st Class Theol. Tripos, 1884; Scholefield and Evans (University) Prizes, 1884; MA 1885. Deacon, 1885; Priest, 1886; Classical and Theological Lecturer of Selwyn College, Cambridge, 1884–95; Tutor, 1885–95; Rector of Marnhull, 1895–1901; Examining Chaplain to Bishop of Salisbury, 1896; Commissary for the Bishops of Wellington and Rangoon; Hulsean Lecturer, 1905–6; Preacher before the University, 1887, 1895, 1905, 1913, 1919; Examiner in Theological Tripos, 1888, 1896; Member of the Board of Examiners, SPG, 1906. Sub-Prelate of the Order of St John of Jerusalem, 1913. *Recreations:* chiefly cycling. *Address:* 23 Old Park Road, Hitchin. *Died 27 Nov. 1920.*

KNIGHT, Captain John Peake, DSO 1914; Lieut Royal Field Artillery; *b* 3 Aug. 1890. Entered army, 1910; served European War, 1914–15 (despatches; DSO).

Died 31 Aug. 1916.

KNIGHT, Chief Engr T. H., CIE 1917; MINA; RIM; Inspector of machinery, Bombay Dockyard. *Address:* Royal Indian Marine Dockyard, Bombay. *Died 18 Oct. 1918.*

KNIGHT, William Angus, LLD (Glasgow); Professor of Moral Philosophy University of St Andrews, 1876–1902; Examiner to Civil Service Commission since 1878; *b* Scotland, 22 Feb. 1836; 2nd *s* of late Rev. Geo. Fulton Knight, Mordington, Berwickshire; *m* Mary (*d* 1915), *d* of David Landale, St Mary's, Kirkcaldy; one *s* one *d. Educ:* Circus Place School, High School, and University, Edinburgh. Examiner to University of St Andrews, 1871–73; Examiner to University of London, 1888–93, 1894–99; Examiner in Victoria University, 1892–95; Examiner to University of New Zealand, 1878, etc. Commander of the Order of the Saviour of Greece, 1910. *Publications:* Poems from the Dawn of English Literature to the Year 1699, 1863; Colloquia Peripatetica, or Deep Sea Soundings, 1870; Studies in Philosophy and Literature, 1879; (ed) Spinoza Essays, 1882; (ed) Philosophical Classics for English Readers, 15 vols, 1880–90; Hume, in same series, 1886; Memorials of Coleorton, 1887; Wordsworth's Poetical Works and Life, 11 vols, 1881–89; Transactions of the Wordsworth Society, 8 vols, 1880–86; Principal Shairp and His Friends, 1888; Essays in Philosophy, Old and New, 1890; Selections from Wordsworth, 1889; (ed) The White Doe of Rylstone, 1891; Wordsworth's Prose, 1893; Stories and Rhymes of Golf, 1893; (ed) University Extension Manuals, 25 vols, 1891–99; The Philosophy of the Beautiful: Its History, 1891; Its Theory, 1893; Aspects of Theism, 1894; The Christian Ethic, 1894; The English Lake District, as Interpreted in the Poems of Wordsworth, 1878–91; Through the Wordsworth Country, 1892; Wordsworthiana, 1889; (ed) Rectorial Addresses delivered at the University of St Andrews, 1894; (ed with Biographical Introduction) The Literature of the Georgian Era, by Prof. Minto, 1894; Memoir of John Nichol, Professor of English Literature in Glasgow University, 1895; The Works of William Wordsworth and Dorothy Wordsworth, 12 vols, 1896–97; Nugæ Viatoria, 1897–1903; Lord Monboddo and some of his Contemporaries, 1900; Dove Cottage 1800–1900; Varia, being Studies on Problems of Philosophy and Ethics, 1901; Inter Amicos, 1901; Pro Patria et Regina, 1901; Early Chapters in the History of the University of St Andrews and Dundee, 1902; Some Nineteenth Century Scotsmen, 1902; Andreapolis, 1902; Official Catalogue of the Contents of Dove Cottage, 1902; Catalogue of Portraits of Philosophers, Poets, etc, presented to the University of St Andrews, 1902; Retrospects, 1903; Reciprocity in Trade, the Empire's Safeguard, 1903; (ed) The Poems of Coleridge; Biographical Sketch of Sir Thomas Thornton, 1905; Prayers, Ancient and Modern, 1905; Letters of the Wordsworth Family, 1907; (ed) The Poems of Sir Walter Scott; Memorials of Thomas Davidson, 1907; The Poets on Christmas, 1907; Things New and Old, Sunday Addresses, 1909; A Psalter for Daily Use, 1909; Coleridge and Wordsworth in the West Country, their Friendship and Surroundings; The Golden Wisdom of the Apocrypha, 1910; A Book of Sacred Verse, 1910; The Glamour of Oxford, 1911; An Easter Anthology, 1912; The Browning Centenary, 1912; Prayers, Ancient and Modern, 1912; Pro Patria et Rege, Poems on War, British and American, two series, 1915.

Recreations: mountaineering, golf, rod, gun. *Address:* Greta Lodge, Keswick. *Clubs:* Athenæum; Royal and Ancient Golf, St Andrews.

Died 4 March 1916

KNIGHT-ADKIN, Harry Kenrick; Hon. Secretary Diocesan Board of Missions 1921–25; Public Preacher and Hon. Canon of Bristol 1922; *b* 1851; *e s* of Rev. Henry Adkin; took name of Knight-Adkin by deed poll, 1910; *m* Georgina Elizabeth, *o c* of James Peter Knight, Cheltenham; three *s* one *d. Educ:* Northleach Grammar School; Univ of London, BA 1877. Private Tutor Cheltenham, 1870–77; Assistant Master New College, Eastbourne, 1877–78; Curate of St John's, Cheltenham, 1879–84; Vicar of Cold Salperton, 1884–97; Rector o Crudwell (Wilts), 1898–1909; Vicar of Hankerton (Wilts), 1902–10; Rector of Horfield Bristol and OCF Horfield Barracks, 1910–21 Freemason, PM, 82, 2888, PPGC (Gloucestershire), PPJGW (Wilts). *Publications:* Sermon, Religion and Science; pamphlet, Mathematica Formulae. *Recreation:* gardening. *Address:* 69 Alma Road, Clifton Bristol. *Died 5 Jan. 1927*

KNOLLYS, 1st Viscount, *cr* 1911; **Francis Knollys,** 1st Baron o Caversham, 1902; GCB 1908 (KCB 1897; CB 1876); GCVO 1901 KCMG 1886; ISO 1903; PC 1910; Private Secretary to King Edward when Prince of Wales, 1870–1901, and 1901–10; to King George 1910–13; Lord-in-Waiting to Queen Alexandra since 1910; *b* 16 July 1837; 2nd *s* of late Gen. Rt Hon. Sir William Thomas Knollys, KCB, and Elizabeth, *d* of late Sir John St Aubyn, 5th Bt; *m* 1887, Hon. Ardyn Mary Tyrwhitt (*d* 1922), *d* of Sir Henry Tyrwhitt, 3rd Bt, and Emma Harriet, Baroness Berners; one *s* one *d.* Groom-in-Waiting to King Edward when Prince of Wales, 1886–1901; Gentleman Usher to Queen Victoria, 1868–1901. *Heir: s* Hon. Edward George William Tyrwhitt Knollys, *b* 16 Jan. 1895. *Address:* St James's Palace, SW; Blount's Court, Henley-on-Thames.

Died 15 Aug. 1924.

KNOLLYS, Rev. Erskine William, MA; Hon. Canon of Canterbury, 1905; *b* 31 July 1842; *e s* of Canon W. F. E. Knollys; *m* Caroline, *d* of Prebendary J. E. Kempe; three *s* two *d. Educ:* Radley; Brasenose College, Oxford. Deacon, 1866; Priest, 1867; Diocesan Inspector of Schools; Vicar of Addington, Surrey; Rector of Great Chart; Vicar of South Norwood; of Folkestone, 1898; Rural Dean of the Deanery of Elham, 1909. *Address:* Charlton, Goodrich, Ross-on-Wye. *TA:* Goodrich, Ross. *M:* CG 4891.

Died 23 Nov. 1923.

KNOLLYS, Maj. Louis Frederic, CMG 1877; *b* 26 Feb. 1847; 3rd *s* of late Canon W. F. E. Knollys; unmarried. *Educ:* Radley; Marlborough. Joined 32nd Light Infantry, 1866; Major in the Cameronians (Scottish Rifles), 1881; ADC to the Governor of Mauritius, 1872; ADC Fiji, 1875; Commandant Armed Native Constabulary, Fiji, 1877; ADC to the Governor of New Zealand, 1880; ADC to the Governor of Ceylon, 1883; Inspector-General of Police and Prisons, Jamaica, 1886; Inspector General of Police, Ceylon, 1891; Inspector-General of Police and Prisons, Ceylon, 1898; Provisional Member of the Legislative Council, Ceylon, 1899; retired, 1902. Commanded an expedition to suppress a rising in the mountains in Fiji, and restored order, 1876 (CMG). *Address:* The Graig, Ross, Herefordshire. *Died 15 Dec. 1922.*

KNOTT, Cargill Gilston, DSc, LLD (St Andrews); FRSE; General Secretary, Royal Society of Edinburgh; Reader in Applied Mathematics Edinburgh University since 1892; *b* Penicuik, Scotland, 30 June 1856; *s* of Pelham Knott; *m* 1885, Mary, *e d* of Rev. J. M. Dixon, Paisley; one *s* three *d. Educ:* Arbroath High School; Edinburgh University. Assistant to Chair of Natural Philosophy, Edinburgh University, 1879–83; Prof. of Physics, Imperial University, Japan, 1883–91; conducted Magnetic Survey of Japan, 1887. Fourth Order of the Rising Sun, 1891; awarded Keith Prize (Roy. Soc. Edin.) for original work on magnetic strains, 1897; Thomson Lecturer, UF Church College, Aberdeen, 1905–6 (Earthquakes), and 1913–14 (Radio-activity); Hon. Secretary of Napier Tercentenary Celebration, Edinburgh, 1914, and Editor of the Memorial Volume. *Publications:* Electricity and Magnetism; Physics; Physics of Earthquake Phenomena; Memoir of Professor P. G. Tait; Four-Figure Mathematical Tables; article Pneumatics, Encyclopædia Britannica; Light in Supplement; Photometry in 11th edn; revised Kelland and Tait's Quaternoins (3rd edn 1904); Earthquake Waves in Dictionary of Applied Physics, 1922; papers on Electricity, Magnetism, Seismology, Elasticity, etc. *Recreations:* golf, chess. *Address:* 42 Upper Gray Street, Edinburgh. *T:* 7640. *Died 26 Oct. 1922.*

KNOTT, John, AM, MD, ChB, DPH (Dublin); FRCSI, MRCPI, MRIA; practising physician, scientist, author, critic; *b* Kingsland, Co.

Roscommon, 5 June 1853; *o s* of William Knott. *Educ:* Kingsland National School; Schools of Surgery, RSCI; first prize at every competitive examination, and First Senior Exhibition with gold medal; both Mapother medals, and gold medal of the Pathological Society; licentiate of the RCPI and RCSI; Univ. of Dublin (two Moderatorships and medals). House-Surgeon and House-Physician at the Houses of Industry Hospitals for a year respectively; visited the Universities of Heidelberg, Leyden, Paris, Vienna, Buda Pesth, Cracow, Bologna, and Moscow; for several years Senior Demonstrator of Anatomy, and afterwards College Anatomist, Schools of Surgery, RCSI; formerly Examiner in Physics, Conj. Exam. RCP & SI; also Examiner in Biology, afterwards in Pathology and in Physiology, Apothecaries' Hall, Ireland. *Publications:* Pathology of the Oesophagus (gold medal of the Pathological Society), 1878; Mapother's Physiology, 3rd edn (wholly re-written), 1882; Use of Organic Acids in Gout and Rheumatism, 1887; The Fever of Over-exertion, 1887; Hey's Internal Derangement of the Knee-joint, 1905; Dupuytren's Contraction of the Palmar Fascia, 1905; Dies Caniculares, 1907; Spontaneous Combustion, 1908; Aconite, Queen-Mother of Poisons, 1908; Heat Waves and Ocean Currents; The Gulf Stream Myth, 1909; Normal Ovariotomy, Female Circumcision, Clitoridectomy and Infibulation, 1908; The Origin of Syphilis and the Invention of its Name, 1909; Iron, Metallic and Magnetic, Medicinal and Philosophical, 1909; Phthiriasis, 1910; Sir Walter Raleigh's Royal Cordial, 1910; The Last Illness of Lord Byron, 1910; The King's Evil and its Cures, 1911; Introduction to Eugenics, 1911; The Last Illness of Napoleon Bonaparte, 1912; Influenzal and other Therapeutics, 1918; etc. *Recreations:* travel, study of art, ethnology, or comparative religion; listening to music. *Address:* 2 Sallymount Terrace, Ranelagh, Dublin. *TA:* John Knott, Ireland. *Clubs:* Authors', Royal Societies.
Died Jan. 1921.

KNOWLES, Maj.-Gen. Sir Charles Benjamin, KCB 1903 (CB 1881); *b* 14 Aug. 1835; *s* of late John Knowles of The Lawn, Rugby; *m* 1892, Constance Mary, OBE, Lady of Grace, Order of St John of Jerusalem, *d* of late James Elmslie, and *widow* of Rev. George Elliott. Entered army, 1855; Maj.-Gen. 1890; served Crimea, 1855 (wounded, medal with clasp, Turkish medal); Afghan War, 1878–80 (despatches twice, CB, medal with two clasps). *Address:* Eastfields, Camberley, Surrey. *Club:* Army and Navy.
Died 29 July 1924.

KNOWLES, Sir Charles George Frederick, 4th Bt, *cr* 1765; Vice-Admiral (retired), 1894; *b* 14 March 1832; *s* of Sir Francis Charles Knowles, 3rd Bt; *S* father, 1892; *m* 1st, 1861, Elizabeth, *d* of late John Chapman; two *d* (and two *s* one *d* decd); 2nd, 1882, Mary (*d* 1890), *d* of C. Thomson, Halifax, Nova Scotia; three *s* two *d*. Entered RN 1845; served in Burmese War, 1853; commanded Niger Expedition, 1864. *Heir: s* Francis Howe Seymour Knowles [*b* 13 Jan. 1886; *m* 1914, Kathleen, *d* of late W. Lemon]. *Educ:* Oriel College, Oxford]. *Address:* 3 Moreton Road, Oxford. *Club:* United Service.
Died 3 March 1918.

KNOWLES, Rev. Francis; Honorary Canon of Christchurch Cathedral, New Zealand since 1894; Secretary and Treasurer to the Church Property Trustees of the Diocese of Christchurch; *b* 5 Aug. 1830; *s* of William Barnard Knowles and Elizabeth Andsley; *m* 1st, 1855, Charlotte (*d* 1890), *d* of Nathaniel and Mary Wiles, Cheltenham; two *s*; 2nd, 1891, Annie, *widow* of Rev. Charles Alabaster, MA. *Educ:* Stebonheath House Academy, Stepney, London. Associate College of Preceptors, London, 1848; Assistant Master, The Proprietary School, Cheltenham, 1847–50; Scripture Reader, Halesworth, Suffolk, 1850; Deacon, 1857; Priest, 1859; Vicar of Lyttelton, 1859–72; Merivale, 1872–76; Balclutha, 1876–78; Gladstone, 1878–79; Diocesan Registrar, Christchurch, since 1879. *Recreations:* walking, general reading. *Address:* Christ's College, Christchurch, NZ. *T:* Christchurch 1267.
Died 11 Sept. 1916.

KNOWLES, Frederick Arthur, CMG 1914; FRCI; *b* 17 April 1872; *e s* of late Col F. Knowles, 2nd Lancers, Indian Army; *m* 1914, Elsie Anna, *o d* of late Richard Seeman; one *s* one *d*. *Educ:* Wellington. Assistant Collector, Uganda Protectorate, 1898; served in Uganda, 1898 (medal); 1st Class Magistrate, 1902; Sub-Commissioner, 1906; Sessions Judge, N and W Provinces, 1908; Provincial Commissioner and Sessions Judge, Buganda Kingdom, 1908; N and W Provinces, 1911; Acting Chief Secretary during 1911; Provincial Commissioner, Buganda Kingdom, 1913–16; retired Sept. 1916. *Address:* St Chad's, Woodfield Road, W5. *T:* Ealing 476.
Died 22 Sept. 1922.

KNOWLES, Lt-Col John George, CIE 1913; VD; Commandant Surma Valley Light Horse; Hon ADC to Viceroy and Governor-General, Cachar; tea planter. *Address:* Surma Valley, Cachar, Assam.
Died 28 Feb. 1919.

KNOWLES, Sir Lees, 1st Bt, *cr* 1903; CVO 1909; OBE 1920; TD; DL; MA, LLM; *b* 16 Feb. 1857; *e s* of late John Knowles; *m* 1915, Lady Nina Ogilvie-Grant, OBE, DJStJ, *y d* of 10th Earl of Seafield. *Educ:* Rugby; Trinity Coll., Cambridge (MA, LLM, 1882). President Cambridge University Athletic Club, 1878; an Amateur-Champion Athlete. Endowed three annual three-yearly Exhibitions for Rugby boys, and one yearly for a graduate in his fourth year, at Trinity Coll., Cambridge. Hon. Sec. to Guinness Trust for Housing the Poor, 1889; Private Secretary (unpaid) to Mr Ritchie, President of the Local Government Board, 1887–92, to President of the Board of Trade, 1895–1900; 2nd Church Estates Commissioner (unpaid), 1896–1906; Trustee of the London Parochial Charities; Hon. Secretary to the Lancashire Conservative MP's Association. Barrister Lincoln's Inn, 1882. Contested (C) Leigh Division, 1885; MP (C) Salford, W, 1886–1906. Lt-Col TF, retired 1908; late Commandant, 7th and 8th Batts Lancs Fus (Terr.); Vice-Chairman of Lancs Territorial Army Association, and Chairman of that of East Lancs; KGStJ; Member of Merchant Taylors' Company and the Plumbers' Company; formerly on Council of Rossall School; a Governor of Chetham's Hospital, Manchester; Past-President of the Hackney Horse Society; Lord of the Manor of Turton. *Publications:* A Day with Corps-Students in Germany; The War in the Peninsula; The Battle of Minden, etc; (ed) Letters of Capt. Engelbert Lutyens, St Helena, 1820–23, 1915; The British in Capri, 1906–8, 1918; A Gift of Napoleon, 1921; Fun, Fact and Extract; The Taking of Capri, 1923. *Heir:* none. *Address:* Westwood, Pendlebury; Turton Tower, Lancs; 4 New Square, Lincoln's Inn, WC; 4 Park Street, W1. *T:* Grosvenor 1293. *Clubs:* Carlton, Junior Carlton; Union, Constitutional, Manchester.
Died 7 Oct. 1928 (ext).

KNOWLES, Lilian Charlotte Anne, LittD; Professor of Economic History, University of London; *d* of late Philip Tomn and Mrs Tomn of Killagorden, Truro; *m* 1904, C. M. Knowles, barrister-at-law; one *s*. *Educ:* Truro High School; the Continent; Girton College, Cambridge. History Tripos, First Class, 1893; Law Tripos (Part I), First Class, 1894; LittD Trinity College, Dublin, 1906. Trained under Archdeacon Cunningham; lecturer in Modern Economic History at the London School of Economics and Political Science, 1904; Reader in Economic History in the University of London, 1907; Member of the Departmental Committee on the rise in the cost of living to the working classes, 1918; Member of the Royal Commission on the Income Tax, 1919–20; Member of the Council of the Royal Economic Society; Member of the Council of the Royal Historical Society; Dean of the Faculty of Economics in the University of London, 1920–24. *Publications:* The Industrial and Commercial Revolutions in Great Britain in the Nineteenth Century; The Economic Development of the Overseas Empire, 1763–1914; various papers on economic history subjects; (ed English edn) The Referendum in Switzerland, by Simon Deploige; editor of series of Girton College Studies. *Address:* 47 St Mary's Mansions, Paddington, W; Killagorden, Truro, Cornwall. *Club:* University of London.
Died 25 April 1926.

KNOWLES, Robert Millington, JP, DL; *b* 1843; *e s* of late James Knowles, JP, of Eagley Bank, and Mary Elizabeth, *d* of late Robert Millington of Ordsall; *m* 1st, 1867, Ellen Marsden (*d* 1872), *e d* of late John Haslam, JP, of Bolton; 2nd, 1875, Hon. Alice Catherine Brooks (*d* 1892), *e d* of 1st Lord Crawshaw; two *d*. *Educ:* University College, London. High Sheriff, Notts, 1885; Hon. Major late S Notts Yeomanry. *Address:* Colston Bassett Hall, Bingham, Nottinghamshire. *Clubs:* Wellington, Brooks's.
Died 28 Nov. 1924.

KNOWLING, Hon. George; *b* Exeter, 15 Sept. 1841; *s* of George and Elizabeth Knowling; *m* Elizabeth Upham of Silverton, Devon; three *s* four *d*. *Educ:* Marlborough House School, Exeter. Went Newfoundland, 1858; succeeded uncle in business, 1886; member of Legislative Council, 1898. *Address:* Thornlea, Riverhead, St John's, Newfoundland. *TA:* Knowling, St John's. *T:* 405, 405A, 527. *Club:* City, St John's.
Died Nov. 1923.

KNOWLING, Rev. Richard John, DD; Canon of Durham and Professor of Divinity in the University of Durham since 1905; Professor of New Testament Exegesis in King's College, London, 1894–1905; *b* Devonport, 16 Sept. 1851; *e s* of Prebendary Knowling, Vicar of Wellington, Somerset; *m* 1893, Ellen (*d* 1914), *e d* of Maj.-Gen. Raban. *Educ:* Blundell's School, Tiverton; Balliol College,

Oxford. Fellow of King's College, London, 1899; Emeritus Professor, 1905; Examiner for Hall-Houghton Prizes at Oxford, 1897, and for Denyer and Johnson Scholarships, 1905; Select Preacher at Cambridge, 1895; Boyle Lecturer, 1903–5; Examining Chaplain to Archbishop of Canterbury, 1903, and to Bishop of Exeter, 1903–16; Examiner for BD in University of London, 1905–6. *Publications:* Witness of the Epistles; Acts of the Apostles, in Expositor's Greek Testament; Our Lord's Virgin Birth; Epistle of St James (Westminster Commentaries); cont to Smith and Wace's Dict. of Christian Biog., the Critical Review, Enc. Brit. 10th edn, Biblical World; Critical Questions, 1903; The Testimony of St Paul to Christ (Boyle Lectures), 1905; Manchester Cathedral Lectures, 1907; Messianic Interpretation, 1910; articles in Hastings' Dictionary of Christ and the Gospels, 1906. *Address:* Durham.

Died 4 July 1919.

KNOX, Maj. Arthur Rice, DSO 1900; retired; *b* 8 March 1863; *s* of late Maj.-Gen. T. Knox, RA. *Educ:* Cheltenham College. Entered RA, 1883; Captain, 1892; Major, 1900; served South Africa, 1899–1900 (despatches, Queen's medal, 5 clasps, DSO); European War, 1914–15 (wounded).   *Died 22 April 1917.*

KNOX, (Edmund Francis) Vesey, KC 1906; *b* 23 Jan. 1865; *s* of late Vesey Knox, of Shimnah, Newcastle, Co. Down; *m* 1st, 1891, Anne (*d* 1907), *d* of W. Lloyd; two *s* one *d*; 2nd, 1917, Agnes, *d* of Julian Beerbohn and *widow* of R. Nevill. *Educ:* Keble Coll., Oxford. Fellow of All Souls College, 1886–93; Barrister, Gray's Inn, 1889; Bencher, 1906; Treasurer, 1913; in practice at the Parliamentary Bar; MP (N) W Cavan, 1890–95; MP (N) Londonderry, 1895–98. *Address:* 25 Carlyle Square, Chelsea, SW3; Shimnah, Newcastle, Co. Down; Goldsmith Building, Temple, EC4. *T:* Central 639. *Club:* Reform.

Died 15 May 1921.

KNOX, Sir George Edward, Kt 1906; ISO 1915; LLD Allahabad; Judge High Court, North West Provinces, India, since 1890; *b* 14 Nov. 1845; *m* 1868, Katherine Anne Louise, *d* of late Major William Loch, 1st Bombay Lancers. *Educ:* Merchant Taylors' School; University College, London. Entered ICS 1864; Legal Remembrancer, 1887. KGStJ 1915. *Publications:* Digest of Criminal Law of the Bengal Presidency; Digest of Civil Procedure; The Legal Remembrancer, 1879–82; Treatise upon the Indian Stamp Law. *Address:* Braemar, Naini Tal, India.

Died 20 July 1922.

KNOX, Sir James, Kt 1905; JP Co. Ayr; Director, Linen Thread Co., Ltd; *b* 4 Jan. 1850; *s* of James Knox of Riverside, Kilbirnie, and Janet Muir, Beith; *m* 1875, Anne Eliza (*d* 1919), *o d* of James McCosh of Merksworth, Dalry; two *d*. *Address:* Place, Kilbirnie, Ayrshire. *Clubs:* New, Western, Glasgow.   *Died 30 Sept. 1926.*

KNOX, Richard; Lieutenant-Colonel, retired 1888; *b* 23 Dec. 1848; *e s* of late Lt-Gen. Richard Knox, 18th Hussars, and Mary, *d* of Gen. Bryce M'Master, HEICS; *m* 1882, Mary Eliza, *o c* of late Clement Milward, QC; one *s*. Joined 18th Hussars 1867; exchanged as Captain to 13th Hussars, 1878. *Address:* Holt Hatch, Alton, Hants.

Died 4 Feb. 1918.

KNOX, Robert, MB, CM, MD Edin.; MRCS, MRCP, LRCP, FRPS, MIEE; DMRE Cantab.; late Honorary Radiologist, King's College Hospital; Director, Electrical and Radiotherapeutic Department, Cancer Hospital (Free), Fulham Road, SW; Consulting Radiologist, Great Northern Central Hospital; Consulting Radiologist, Chelsea Hospital for Women; Honorary Consulting Radiologist, Queen Alexandra Hospital, Millbank; Honorary Radiologist, Royal Sea-bathing Hospital; *b* Leith. *Educ:* Edinburgh University; Guy's Hospital. Fellow of the Royal Society of Medicine, Past Pres., Electro-therapeutic Section; Fellow of the Medical Society of London; Member, British Medical Association; Vice President, British Institute of Radiology; Past Pres. Röntgen Society; Hon. Fellow American College of Radiology; Hon. Mem. American Röntgen Ray Society, Radium Society, New York Röntgen Society, Scandinavian Röntgen Society. Joint editor British Journal of Radiology. *Publications:* Radiography, X-Ray Therapeutics and Radium Therapy, 2nd edn, 1917, 3rd edn, 1919, 4th edn, 1924; Radiography of the Gall Bladder, Acta Radiologica, 1924; article on Radium Therapy in Eden and Lockyer's Gynæcology; various articles on X-Rays and Radium in medical journals. *Address:* 38 Harley Street, W1. *T:* Langham 1568; 15 South Grove, Highgate, N6. *T:* Mountview 0068.

Died 21 Sept. 1928.

KNOX, Maj.-Gen. Sir William George, KCB 1900 (CB 1889); Colonel Commandant RA; *b* 20 Oct. 1847; 2nd *s* of late Gen. T.

E. Knox, CB; *m* 1889, Alice, *d* of Sir Robert Dundas, 1st Bt. *Educ* RM Academy, Woolwich. Royal Artillery, 1867; Abyssinia Campaign, 1867–68 (medal); Ashanti Campaign, 1874, includin Battles of Amoaful, Ordashu, capture of Coomassie (medal and clasp Afghan Campaign, 1878–79, including capture of Ali Musj (despatches, medal and clasp); Zulu and Transvaal Campaign, 187 capture of Sekikuni's stronghold (despatches, Brevet of Major, med and clasp); Turkish War medal from Sultan of Turkey for servic with Red Crescent Society in winter Balkan Campaign, Russo Turkish War, 1877, and present at several actions; defence Ladysmith and operations in ORC (despatches 5 times, Queen medal, 4 clasps, King's medal, 2 clasps, KCB); commanding RH Curragh to 1899; late commanding 23rd Brigade, South Africa; la GOC 8th Division, Irish Command. *Recreations:* hunting, shootin fishing. *Address:* 24 Portman Square, W. *T:* Mayfair 1532; Sherbor St John, Hants. *Club:* Naval and Military.

Died 14 Dec. 191

KNOX LITTLE, Rev. Canon William John, MA; Canon Worcester since 1881; Sub-Dean, 1902; Proctor for Chapter i Convocation of Canterbury, 1888–1911; Vicar of Hoar Cros 1885–1907; *b* 1889; *s* of John Little, Stewartstown, Co. Tyrone; Annie, *d* of Henry Gregson, Moorlands, Lancs; six *s* four *d*. *Edu* Trinity Coll., Cambridge. Asst master Sherborne School; curate Chri Church, Lancaster; curate of Turweston, Bucks; curate of S Thomas's, Regent St; Rector of St Alban's, Cheetwood, Mancheste 1875–85. Acting Chaplain to Brigade of Guards and subsequentl to Household Cavalry during part of S African War (despatche Queen's medal and clasps). *Publications:* Meditations on the Thre Hours' Agony of Our Blessed Redeemer, 1877; Characteristics an Motives of the Christian Life, 1880; Mystery of the Passion, 188 Witness of the Passion of Our Most Holy Redeemer, 1884; Th Broken Vow, a Story of Here and Hereafter, 1887; The Child Stafferton, 1888; The Journey of Life; The Light of Life, 188 Sunlight and Shadow in the Christian Life, 1889; The Waif from th Waves; A Story of Three Lives, 1890; The Christian Home—i Foundation and Duties, 1891; The Perfect Life, 1899; Sketches an Studies in South Africa, 1899; Manual of Devotion for Lent, 190 Holy Matrimony, 1900; A Treasury of Meditation; Confirmation an Holy Communion, 1901; The Conflict of Ideals in the Church England, 1905. *Address:* The College, Worcester.

Died 3 Feb. 1918

KOEBEL, W. H.; author and traveller; *b* 1872; *e s* of late Oscar Koebe of Murley Grange, Bishopsteignton, Devon; *m* Eleanor, *y d* of lat Anthony Garstin of New Zealand; one *d*. *Educ:* privately; and i France, Switzerland, Germany. Undertook special commissions fo South America for The Times, Sphere, Standard, etc, 1918; proceede on a special mission to South America for the British Government receiving the thanks of the War Council, 1921; founded and edite the Anglo South American Handbook. *Publications:* The Great Sout Lane; Argentina, Past and Present; Modern Chile; The Romance o the River Plate; British Exploits in South America; Portugal, its Lan and People; In the Maoriland Bush; South America; Uruguay; The South Americans, from the social and industrial point of view Paraguay; Madeira, Old and New; In Jesuit Land; Modern Argentina Central America; Hodson's Voyage; The Singular Republic; The Anchorage; The Butterflies' Day; The Return of Joe; The Seat o Moods, etc; Editor-in-Chief of the Encyclopædia of South America 1913; contributor to many newspapers and magazines. *Recreations* sports, games, bibliography. *Address:* 23 Gilston Road, The Boltons SW. *Clubs:* St James', Argentine, Authors'; Barnstaple and North Devon.   *Died 20 June 1923*

KOHLER, Kaufmann, PhD; President of the Hebrew Union College Cincinnati, Ohio, 1903; President Emeritus, 1921; *b* Fürth, Germany 10 May 1843; *s* of Moritz Kohler and Babette Loewemayer; *m* 1870 Johanna, *d* of Rev. Dr David Einhorn; two *s* two *d*. *Educ:* Univs o Munich, Berlin, Leipzig and Erlangen. Rabbi of the Beth E Congregation in Detroit, 1869; Minister of Sinai Temple, Chicago Ill, 1871–79; of Temple Beth El, New York, 1879–1903; hon minister for life from 1903, being relieved of active ministerial work in order to accept the Presidency of the Hebrew Union Coll. in Cincinnati; introduced Sunday services, in addition to the regular Saturday service, during ministry in Chicago, being their first introduction into Jewish pulpits in America; convened the Pittsburg Conference, 1885; President for many years of the New York Board of Jewish Ministers; Hon. Pres. of Central Conference of American Rabbis, 1903; editor in charge of the departments of Theology and Philosophy of the Jewish Encyclopædia. *Publications:* Der Segen Jacobs 1869; On Capital Punishment according to Jewish Law, 1869; On the Song of Songs, 1878; Ethical Basis of Judaism, 1887; Jewish Ethics;

Moses and Jesus; Church and Synagogue in their Mutual Relations; Backwards or Forwards; Lectures on Reform Judaism, 1885; The Testament of Job; On the Psalms; A Guide to Instruction in Judaism; Principles of Jewish Theology upon a Historical Basis, 1910 (German); Hebrew Union College and other Addresses, 1916; Jewish Theology, Historically and Systematically Considered, 1918; Heaven and Hell in Comparative Religion, with special reference to Dante's Divine Comedy, 1923; edited Collected Writings of Rev. Dr David Einhorn, 1880; editor of weeklies Sabbath Visitor, 1881–82, and Jewish Reformer, 1886. *Recreations:* theatre, symphony concerts, walks. *Address:* 2 W 88th Street, New York City.

Died 28 Jan. 1926.

KOHLSAAT, Herman H.; proprietor and editor Chicago Record Herald; *b* Edwards County, Illinois, 22 March 1853; *s* of Reimer Kohlsaat, Brunsbuttel, Holstein, Denmark, Officer in Danish Army, and Sarah Hall, Surrey, England; *m* 1880, Mabel E., *d* of E. Nelson Blake, leading member and former President Chicago Board of Trade; two *d*. *Educ:* public and private schools, Galena and Chicago. Bought the Chicago Inter-Ocean, 1891; sold it, 1894; purchased the Times-Herald and Evening Post, 1895. Republican; took active part in election of President M'Kinley and in drafting gold plank in Republican platform of 1896. *Clubs:* Chicago, Chicago, Union League, Press. *Died 17 Oct. 1924.*

KOLHAPUR, Maharaja of, HH Sir Shahu Chhatrapati, GCIE 1911; GCSI 1895; GCVO 1903; LLD Camb.; MRAS; Hon. Colonel in British Army, 1915; Hon. Colonel 103rd Mahratta Light Infantry; direct descendant of Shivaji, the founder of the Maratha Empire; *b* 26 June 1874; adopted on 17 March 1884, from the Kagal Jabagirdar's family, being the natural born son of Jayasingrao Ghatge Sarjarao Vazarat Ma-ab, Jabagirdar of Kagal; *m* Lakshmibai Saheb, *g d* of a sister of HH the late Ganapatrao Gaikwad, Maharaja of Baroda; one *s* one *d*. *Educ:* privately under a European tutor and guardian, Mr S. M. Fraser; Rajkumar Coll., Rajkote. Administered the affairs of the Kolhapur State from 2nd April 1894. Decorated for loyalty, good government, and in recognition of the dignity of the house. Had a salute of 21 guns. *Recreations:* polo, shikar, and other manly sports. *Address:* Kolhapur, Bombay Presidency, India.

Died 6 May 1922.

KOUROPATKIN, Alexei Nicholaevitch; General of Infantry since 1901; ADC to the Russian Emperor, 1902–17; *b* 17 March 1848; nobleman of Government Pskov; *m*; one *s*. *Educ:* after having finished the courses of the I Corps of Cadets and of the I Military School, Emperor Paul I, ended with the diploma of the first Category at the Academy of the General Staff of army, Emperor Nicholas I. Member of honour at the Academies; of the General Staff of army, Emperor Nicholas I; of Engineering, Emperor Nicholas I; of Military Jurisprudence, Emperor Alexander II; of artillery, Grand Duke Michael, and at the Imperial Academy of Military Medicine. Officer from 1866; attached to the General Staff of army from the year 1874; Col 1878; Maj.-Gen. 1882; Lt-Gen. 1890; sent to foreign countries for scientific purposes, 1874–75; officer of the General Staff of army, district Turkestan, 1876–77; Bulgaria, 1877–78; chief of the Asiatic bureau of the Main Staff of army, 1878–79; assistant-professor of Military Statistics at the Academy of the General Staff of army, Emperor Nicholas I; commander of the rifle-brigade, Turkestan, 1879–83; General for treating the questions of Strategy at the Main Staff of army, 1883–90; Governor of the Trans-Kaspian district and commander of the troops of this district, 1890–98; head of the Ministry of War, 1898; served in Turkestan against Buchara, 1867–68; in Algeria in the expedition of French troops, 1874; in Turkestan against Kokand, 1876; in Bulgaria against the Turks, 1877–78; in Middle Asia against Akhal-Teke, 1880–81, where he commanded the main detachment and stormed Geok-Tepe (twice wounded); commanded Russian Forces in first part of Russo-Japanese War, 1904. Order of St Stanislaus of the 3rd class with swords and knot; Order of St Anne of the 3rd class with swords and knot, and the rank of Lt, 1869; the rank of Second Captain, 1870; the rank of Captain and the Order of St Georges of the 4th class, 1876; Order of St Woldemar of the 4th class with swords and knot and the rank of Lt Col, Order of St Stanislaus of the 2nd class with swords and "the Golden Arm", 1877; the rank of Col and the Order of St Anne of the 2nd class with swords, 1878; Order of St Woldemar of the 3rd class with swords, 1879; Order of St Georges of the 3rd class, 1881; the rank of Maj.-Gen. 1882; Orders of St Stanislaus and St Anne of the 1st class; Order of St Woldemar of the 2nd class; Orders of the White Eagle and St Alexander Nevsky; (French) Légion d'honneur, grande croix, grande croix d'officier, croix de commandeur et croix de chevalier; (Mecklenburg-Schwerin) Crown of the Wends; (Servian) Cross of officer of the Order Takova and the golden medal for courage;

(Roumania) Great Cross of the Order of Star and the Iron Cross; (Montenegro) the golden medal "for courage", and the Order of Daniel of the 1st class; (Persian) Image of the Shah with diamonds, and the golden ribbon with knot, and the Order of Lion and Sun of the 2nd class; (Bucharia) Orders of Tskender-Salis, of the Crown and of the Star of the 1st class with diamonds; (Tunis) Great Cross of officer of the Order Nishan Tphtikhar; (Japan) Order of the Rising Sun of the 1st class. *Publications:* Algeria, 1877; Kashgaria (gold medal of Imperial Russian Geographical Society), 1879; The Operations of the Troops of General Skobeleff during the War of Russia with the Turks 1877–1878, 1885; The Blockade of Plevna, 1885; The Crossing of the Balkan by the Detachment of General Skobeleff and the Battle near the Village Sheinovo, 28 Dec. 1877, 1889; The Conquest of Turkomania and the Expedition against Akhal-Teke in the years 1881–1882, with the Description of the Battles in the Middle Asia from the year 1839 till the year 1876, 1899; Russia for Russians; the Past and Future Problems of the Russian Army, 1910. *Address:* St Sbg Tavritcheskaia 3, Petrograd; (in summer) Tcheschourino, Gouv. de Pskow, Russia. *Died 10 Feb. 1921.*

KRAUS, Adolf; lawyer; *b* 1849; *m*; three *s* one *d*. *Educ:* Rokycan, Bohemia. Was President Board of Education, City of Chicago; Corporation Counsel, City of Chicago; President, Civil Service Commission; Former owner and editor Chicago Times. Knight of the Order of Francis Joseph; was International President, Order of B'nai B'rith, for twenty years. *Recreation:* golf. *Address:* East End Park Hotel, Chicago. *TA:* Kragos, Chicago. *Clubs:* Covenant, Athletic, Standard, Chicago. *Died 22 Oct. 1928.*

KRETSER, Edward de, ISO; JP; *b* 31 July 1854; *s* of Peter Cornelius de Kretser; *m* 1877, Alice Grace Anjou. *Educ:* Colombo Academy, later Royal College. Clerk, Colonial Secretary's Office, 1872; Chief Clerk, 1892; Director of the Widows' and Orphans' Pension Fund from 1897; a Manager of the Public Service Mutual Guarantee Association from 1901; Secretary Ceylon Savings Bank from 1908; ex-officio Secretary of the Public Service Mutual Provident Association, 1892–1900, and President from 1901; Auditor of the Departmental Funds of the Police Dept; Assistant Auditor-General, Ceylon Civil Service, 1901–7; Assistant Controller of Revenue, 1907–21; retired on pension, 1921. *Address:* Gracelyn, Bambalapitiya, Colombo. *M:* 6.345. *Died 6 Oct. 1925.*

KRISHNAN, Hon. Mr Justice Cheruvari, MA (Cantab); Dewan Bahadur; Judge, High Court of Judicature, Madras, since 1920; Barrister-at-law; *b* Cannanore, North Malabar, India, in the Cheruvari Tarwad, Nov. 1868; *m* 1895, Kinathi Madhavi of Tellicherry; two *s* five *d*. *Educ:* High School, Cannanore; Presidency College, Madras; Christ's College, Cambridge. Took degree at Cambridge in Natural Science. Called to Bar, Middle Temple, 1891; enrolled as Advocate, High Court of Madras, 1892; entered Government Service as Assistant Chemical Examiner and acting Professor of Chemistry, Presidency College, Madras; resigned and returned to practice, 1893; elected Fellow of the Madras University; Judge of the Court of Small Causes, Madras, 1906; acted as Chief Presidency Magistrate, 1911; Chief Judge of the Court of Small Causes, Madras, 1912; received the title of Dewan Bahadur; acted as Judge of the High Court, 1916, and subsequently several times. *Recreations:* cricket, tennis, billiards. *Address:* Shenstone Park, Chetput, Madras. *T:* 208. *M:* 6531 and 8004. *Club:* Cosmopolitan, Madras.

Died 9 Feb. 1927.

KROPOTKIN, Prince Peter Alexeievitch; geographer; *b* 9 Dec. 1842; *s* of Prince Alexei Petrovitch and Ekaterina Nikolaevna Kropotkin (*b* Sulima). *Educ:* Corps of Pages, Petrograd, 1857–62; Petrograd Univ. 1869–73. Gold Medal of Russian Geographical Society for journey across North Manchuria in 1864; Aide-de-Camp to military Governor of Transbaikalia; Attaché for Cossack's Affairs to Governor-General of Eastern Siberia; crossed North Manchuria from Transbaikalia to the Amur, 1864; up the Sungari to Kirin, 1864; Secretary to Physical Geography Section of Geographical Society; explored the glacial deposits in Finland and Sweden, 1871; joined International Working Men's Association, 1872; arrested and confined in fortress St Peter and St Paul, 1874; escaped from military hospital, 1876; came to England; founded at Geneva the anarchist paper Le Révolté; expelled from Switzerland, 1881; condemned at Lyons to five years' imprisonment, 1883; liberated, 1886. *Publications:* (in Russian in Memoirs of Russian Geographical Society) Report of the Olekma and Vitim Expedition, with Catalogue of Heights in East Siberia, 1874; Researches on the Glacial Period, vol. i 1876, General Sketch of the Orography of East Siberia, 1876 (French trans., with additions, Brussels, 1904); in Russian and French Prisons, 1886; Russia, in Enc. Britannica, 9th and 10th edns; Russia, Asia, and France, in

Chambers' Enc., last edition; Recent Science in Nineteenth Century, 1892–1901; Paroles d'un Révolté, 1884; La Conquête du Pain, 1888; L'Anarchie, sa Philosophie, son Idéal, Paris, 1896 (Eng. trans. 1897); La Science moderne et l'Anarchie, 1912; The State, its Part in History, 1898; Fields, Factories, and Workshops, 1899, 2nd edn, 1901, 8th edn, 1912; Memoirs of a Revolutionist, 1900 (French, German, Dutch, Swedish, Danish, Spanish, Italian, Russian trans), 3rd edn 1908; Mutual Aid, a Factor of Evolution, 1902, cheap edn 1915; Modern Science and Anarchism, 1903, revised edn 1912; The Orography of Asia, with maps, 1904; The Desiccation of Asia (Geographical Jl), 1904 and 1914; Ideals and Realities in Russian Literature, 1905, cheap edn 1916; The Conquest of Bread, 1906, new edn, 1913; The Great Revolution 1789–1793, 1908; Terror in Russia, 1909. *Recreations:* bookbinding, carpentry. *Died 8 Feb. 1921.*

KUENEN, Johannes Petrus, PhD, LLD; Professor of Physics, University, Leiden, Holland; *b* Leiden, Holland, 11 Oct. 1866; *e s* of Professor Abraham Kuenen, Theological Professor, University, Leiden; *m* Dora Wicksteed, 3rd *d* of Rev. R. H. Wicksteed, Childrey, Berks; three *s* two *d*. *Educ:* Grammar School and University of Leiden, PhD; gold medal for prize essay. Demonstrator and Lecturer, University, Leiden; Professor, University College, Dundee, 1895–1907. *Publications:* Books on Heat; Theory of Mixtures; Equation of State; various scientific papers. *Recreations:* cycling, gardening, boating. *Address:* Leiden, Holland.

Died 25 Sept. 1922.

KUROKI, General Count, Hon. GCMG 1906; *b* Satsuma, 1844. A Kagoshima Samurai; commanded Left Column in war with China; General, 1903; served Russo-Japanese War; victorious at Yalu, Kiu-lien-ling, etc. *Address:* Tokyo, Japan.

Died 4 Sept. 1923.

KUSEL, Baron de, (Selig) Bey; *b* Liverpool, 12 June 1848; *m* 1876, Elvira, *e d* of Cleto Chini of Leghorn and Cairo; one *d*. *Educ:* Cheltenham. Bey, 1882; present at Bombardment of Alexandria (war medal, Khedive's Star); was Controller-general of Egyptian Customs and of the Gunpowder Department; Inspector-General of the Coastguards; Egyptian Delegate on International Sanitary Board of Egypt. Kt Commander of Villa Vicosa and of Order of Christ; Commander of the Medjidie, Osmanieh, and Nichan-ifihar; Chevalier of Crown of Italy; Capt. East Surrey Regt (retired). *Publication:* An Englishman's Recollections of Egypt, 1915. *Address:* Tanglelands, Dormanspark, Surrey. *Club:* Junior Army and Navy.

Died 1917.

KUTLEHR, Raja Ram Pal of, CSI 1904; head of an ancient family of Rajputs who formerly ruled, according to the local traditions, for over two hundred generations; judicial powers were granted in 1873; *b* 22 Nov. 1849; *s* of Raja Narain Pal; *m* 1st, *sister* of Raja Sham Ser Singh of Rampur Bushahr State; 2nd, *d* of Raja Mahendra Sein of Keental State, Simla; one *s*. *Educ:* Shastri (nagri). Persian and English Sub-Registrar of Kutlehr, 1867; Judicial Powers granted, 1875; Judicial Powers, First Class, 1877; a Sanad for good conduct and morality, 1877; a letter of thanks for offer of military service in Afghan war, 1879; silver and gold medal Delhi Coronation Durbar, 1903; numerous Sanads for services during European War; life member of St John Ambulance Association. *Address:* Kutlehr, Kangra, Punjab.

Died 21 Nov. 1927.

KUYPER, A., DD, LLD; *b* Maassluis, 29 Oct. 1837; *m* 1863, I. H. Schaay (*d* 1899); four *s* three *d*. *Educ:* University of Leiden. Candidatus philologiæ, Doctor Theologiæ. Golden medal from the University of Groningen for paper on Calvini et Lasci de ecclesia sententiarum comparatio. Pastor of the Reformed Church at Beest, 1863; Utrecht, 1868; Amsterdam, 1870; member of the States-General for Gonda, 1874–77; for Sliedrecht, 1894–1901; Prime-minister after the elections of July 1901; Minister of State, 1907, 1910; Member of States General, 1908; Member of Senate, 1913. Founded Free University, Amsterdam, 1880; professor, Free University; lecturer, Encyclopædia, Dogmatics, Hebrew, Exegesis NT, Dutch Literature, Esthetics; founded the daily The Standard and became its chief editor 1872, the Heraut (weekly), 1878; founded Reformed Free Churches, 1886; lectured in America in twenty places; Stone lecturer, 1898. Commander of Order of Dutch Lion, 1912; Grand Cross of Order of Leopold of Belgium, of Medjidie of Turkey; of Christ, Portugal; Hon. Doctor of Laws, Princeton, New Jersey; Hon. Doctor of Technical Science, Delft; Hon. Doctor of Philology, Hope College, Holland, Mich; Hon. Doctor of Jurisprudence, University of Leuven, 1910; Hon. President of Netherland Press Association, 1897; President of the Netherland Council for Internationalism, 1911; Hon. Member of the Flemingue Royal Academy of Literature, Ghent, 1906.

Publications: Joannes a Lasco opera, 2 vols; edited Encyclopædia Theologiæ, 3 vols; E voto Dordraceno, 4 vols; The Work of the Holy Spirit, 3 vols; Calvinism; From the Scriptures; Political Platform of the Anti-Revolutionary Party; The Incarnation; Socialism and Christianity; The Evolution; The South African Crisis; Common Grace, 3 vols; Varia Americana, 1899; Around the Old World, etc, 2 vols; and many other publications; Anti-revolutionary Politics, vols. Two hundred and fourteen volumes altogether. *Address:* The Hague, 5 Kanaalstraat. *T:* 710.

Died 8 Nov. 1920.

KYLLACHY, Hon. Lord; William Mackintosh, JP, DL; MA, LLD; *b* 9 April 1842; *e s* of late William Mackintosh, Inshes House, Inverness-shire; *m* 1869, Jane (*d* 1909), *d* of David Stevenson, CE; two *s* one *d*. *Educ:* Edinburgh Academy and University; Hon. LLD 1889. Advocate, 1865; Procurator, Church of Scotland, 1880; Sheriff of Ross, Cromarty, and Sutherland, 1881; QC and Dean of Faculty of Advocates, 1886; raised to Bench as Lord Kyllachy, 1889; Judge of the Court of Session and Justiciary, retired, 1907. *Address:* Kyllachy, Tomatin, Inverness-shire; 6 Randolph Crescent, Edinburgh. *Clubs:* Brooks's; New, Edinburgh. *Died 9 Dec. 1918.*

KYNNAIRD, Viscount; Sigismondo Maria Giuseppe; Duca di Mondragone; *b* 20 June 1886; *e s* of 10th Earl of Newburgh; *m* 1910, Teresa, *d* of Principe Ugo Boncompagni Ludovisi, *e s* of Principe di Piombino. *Address:* 10 Via Virginio Orsini, Rome.

Died 4 Nov. 1918.

L

LA BILLOIS, Hon. Charles H.; *b* Dalhousie, Restigouche, County, New Brunswick, 18 Dec. 1856; *s* of Joseph H. La Billois, for many years a merchant and postmaster in Dalhousie; his grandfather came from Brittany and was a surgeon under Napoleon Bonaparte, reaching America in 1816; his grandparents, on his mother's side, came from Ireland after the Rebellion; *m* Charlotte, *y d* of John M'Naughton, lumber merchant, of Quebec; two *s* two *d*. *Educ:* Grammar School, Dalhousie; Model School, Carleton, Province of Quebec. Returned to the House of Assembly, New Brunswick, to represent Restigouche, his native county, at the General Election, 1882, and re-elected at every election since; appointed a Member of the Executive Council, 1891, under leadership of Hon. A. G. Blair. Commissioner of Agriculture, 1897; Acting Commissioner, Board of Works, 1900; Chief Commissioner, Board of Works, 1900. *Address:* Dalhousie, New Brunswick. *Died 22 Nov. 1928.*

LABORDE, Edward Daniel, CBE 1922; ISO 1903; *b* 20 Sept. 1863; *s* of late Edward Laborde, CMG, Administrator of several West Indian Colonies. Chief Clerk to Governor Windward Islands, 1885; Private Secretary to Governor Sir Walter Sendall, 1888; Chief of Police St Vincent, 1889; Supervisor of Customs, 1897; Acting Colonial Secretary, Member Executive and Legislative Council, 1901; Chief of Police and Inspector of Prisons, St Lucia, 1902; Acting Administrator of St Vincent, 1904; Acting Administrator and Colonial Secretary, St Lucia, 1905; Treasurer, Island of Grenada, 1915; Acting Administrator, St Lucia, 1907; has acted as Administrator, Colonial Secretary, Grenada, on various occasions; Administrator, Government of St Lucia, June 1921–Aug. 1922, when he retired. London Representative of St Lucia and Hon. Treasurer for West Indian and Atlantic Colonies at British Empire Exhibition; Member of West Indian Conference, 1926. *Club:* West Indian.

Died 29 June 1928.

LABORI, Fernand; Avocat à la Cour d'Appel de Paris, ancien bâtonnier; ancien député de l'Arrondissement de Fontainebleau; *b* Reims, France, 18 April 1860; *s* of Adolphe Labori, Inspecteur Principal hon. aux Chemins de Fer de l'Est; *m* 1893, Marguerite Okey; three *d*. *Educ:* Reims; two years in Germany and England; Paris. Called to Bar, 1884; has taken part in many famous cases, including the Zola Case, the Dreyfus Appeal, and the Humbert Case. Fondateur de la Revue du Palais et de la Grande Revue; Ancien rédacteur en chef de la Gazette du Palais; Membre du Conseil de l'Ordre, 1905; bâtonnier de l'Ordre des Avocats à la Cour de Paris, 1911–13;

Publication: The Répertoire encyclopédique du droit français, 12 vols. *Address:* 12 rue Pigalle, Paris.   *Died 14 March 1917.*

LACE, John Henry, CIE 1913; Chief Conservator, Burma, 1908, retired 1913. Joined India Forest Department, 1881; Conservator, 1902; retired 1913.   *Died 9 June 1918.*

LACON, Captain Henry Edmund, JP County of Suffolk; *b* 6 July 1849; *o s* of late Henry James Lacon, Captain RN, of the Goldrood, Ipswich, *y s* of Sir Edmund Lacon, 2nd Bt, of Ormesby Hall, Norfolk; *m* 1890, Hon. Margaret Erskine, *o d* of 5th Baron Erskine of Spratton Hall, Northampton. *Educ:* Harrow. Late Captain in the 71st Highland Light Infantry. *Address:* The Lodge, Bramford, Ipswich.
Died 18 March 1924.

LACOSTE, Hon. Sir Alexandre, Kt 1892; PC (Canada) 1892; LLD, DCL; Chief Justice, Quebec, 1891–1907; *b* Boucherville, Canada, 12 Jan. 1842; *s* of Hon. Louis Lacoste, senator (member of an old Languedoc family which settled in Canada) and Mary Antoinette Thaïs Proulx; *m* 1866, Marie Louise, *d* of Leon Globensky of Montreal; three *s* seven *d*. *Educ:* St Hyacinthe Coll.; Laval Univ., Quebec. Barrister, 1863; QC 1880; Bâtonnier of the Bar, Montreal, 1879–81; Professor of Law, Laval University; Member of Legislative Council, 1882–84; Member of Senate, 1884–91; Speaker, 1891; Administrator for the Province of Quebec, 1898; resigned, 1907. *Address:* 71 St Hubert Street, Montreal. *Club:* Mount Royal, Montreal.
Died 16 Aug. 1923.

LADD, Prof. George Trumbull, LLD; Clark Professor of Metaphysics and Moral Philosophy in Yale University (Emeritus); *b* 19 Jan. 1842; *m* 1st, 1869, Cornelia Ann Tallman; 2nd, 1895, Frances Virginia Stevens; two *s* one *d*. *Educ:* Western Reserve College; Andover Theological Seminary. Preached, Edinburgh, Ohio, 1869–71; Pastor, Spring St Congl Church, Milwaukee, Wis, 1871–79; Prof. of Philosophy, Bowdoin Coll., 1879–81; Yale, 1881–1905 (Emeritus, 1905); Lecturer, Andover Theol. Sem., 1879–81; at Doshisha and Summer School, Japan, 1892; and in 1899 and 1906–7, before the Imperial Universities and Commercial Colleges of Japan; and in 1899–1900 at Bombay, under the auspices of the Bombay University, and in Calcutta, Madras, and elsewhere in India; several times lecturer at Harvard, and conducted Graduate Seminary in Ethics in 1895–96; Delegate to World's Congress of Psychologists at Paris, 1900; Guest and Unofficial Adviser of Prince Ito, in Korea, 1907. Decorated Order of the Rising Sun, 3rd class, 1899; 2nd class, 1907; Gold Medallist of the Imperial Educational Soc. of Japan, 1907; several times admitted to audience with the Emperor of Japan; Founder of American Psychological Association, and President in 1893; Member American Phil. Soc., American Oriental Soc.; Society of American Naturalists; Vice-Pres. Amer. Soc. of Associated Sciences, 1911–12. *Publications:* Principles of Church Polity, 1882; Doctrine of Sacred Scripture, 2 vols, 1884; Lotze's Outlines, trans. 6 vols, 1887; Elements of Physiological Psychology, 1887 (revised edn with Prof. R. S. Woodworth, 1911); What is the Bible?, 1888; Introduction to Philosophy, 1889; Outlines of Physiological Psychology, 1890; Philosophy of Mind, 1891; Primer of Psychology, 1894; Psychology, Descriptive and Explanatory, 1894; Philosophy of Knowledge, 1897; Outlines of Descriptive Psychology, 1898; Essays on the Higher Education, 1899; A Theory of Reality, 1899; Lectures to Teachers (in Japanese only), 1899; Philosophy of Conduct, 1902; Philosophy of Religion, 2 vols, 1905; In Korea with Marquis Ito, 1908; Knowledge, Life, and Reality, 1909; Rare Days in Japan, 1910; What Can I Know?, 1914; What Ought I to Do?, 1915; What Should I Believe?, 1915; What May I Hope?, 1915; The Secret of Personality, 1917; Intimate Glimpses of Life in India, 1919. *Recreations:* music, gardening. *Address:* New Haven, Connecticut. *T:* Center 3333.
Died Aug. 1921.

LAFFAN, Rev. Robert Stuart de Courcy, MA; Rector of St Stephen, Walbrook with St Benet Sherehog since 1899; *b* 18 Jan. 1853; *e s* of late Lt-Gen. Sir Robert Michael Laffan, KCMG; *m* Bertha Jane (*d* 1912), *d* of Frederick Grundy, and *widow* of Surg.-Gen. Leith-Adams. *Educ:* Winchester; Merton Coll., Oxford (Exhibitioner); 1st class Mods 1876; BA (1st Lit. Hum.), 1878; MA 1884. Deacon, 1882; Priest, 1883; Senior Classical Master and Chaplain, Derby School, 1880–84; Headmaster, King Edward the VI's School, Stratford-on-Avon, 1884–95; Select Preacher to University of Oxford and Select Preacher to University of Cambridge for 1898 and 1899; Principal of Cheltenham College, 1895–99; Chaplain to 12th London Batt. (Rangers), 1904–12; rejoined Aug. 1915; in charge of St George's Garrison Church, Aldershot, 1916–19; Member of International Olympic Committee from 1899, and of Technical Education Board LCC, 1900–4; Member of Council, Shakespeare Memorial

Association, Stratford-on-Avon; Member of British Olympic Council from 1905. Officer of Order of Redeemer (Greece), 1907; Officier de l'Instruction Publique (France), 1907; Commander II Class of the Swedish Royal Order of Wasa, 1912. *Publication:* Aspects of Fiction, 1885. *Address:* 1 Brunswick House, Palace Gardens Terrace, Kensington, W8. *T:* Park 2524.
Died 16 Jan. 1927.

LAFLEUR, Paul Theodore, MA; Professor of Comparative Literature, McGill University, since 1907; Molson Professor of English, 1920. *Educ:* High School, Montreal; McGill University. *Address:* 215 Peel Street, Montreal. *Club:* University, Montreal.
Died 9 Feb. 1924.

LA FOLLETTE, Robert Marion; Senator; *b* Primrose, Wisconsin, 14 June 1855; *s* of Josiah La Follette and Mary Ferguson; *m* 1881, Belle Case of Baraboo, Wis. *Educ:* University of Wisconsin; LLD. Admitted to Bar, 1880; District Attorney Dane Co., 1880–84; Member of Congress, 1885–91; took prominent part in framing McKinley Bill; Governor of Wisconsin, 1901–3, 1903–5, 1905–7; elected US Senator, 1905 for term 1905–10, and resigned Governorship; re-elected United States Senator three terms, 1910–19. *Publication:* Autobiography—A Personal Narrative of Political Experiences, 1913. *Address:* Maple Bluff Farm, Madison, Wis; 2112 Wyoming Avenue, Washington, DC, USA.
Died 18 June 1925.

LAING, Malcolm Alfred; Lord-Lieutenant of Orkney and Shetland since 1892; late Captain 14th Hussars; *b* 20 May 1846; *s* of Samuel Laing, late Chairman Brighton Railway Co. *Educ:* Harrow; Sandhurst. Passed 1st out of Sandhurst, 1864; gazetted 14th Hussars, 1865; Captain, 1870; retired, 1873. *Recreations:* shooting, fishing, racing, golf. *Address:* 18 Queen Street, Mayfair, W. *T:* 3092 Gerrard; Crook, Orkney. *Clubs:* Turf, Arthur's, Jockey.
Died 10 Dec. 1917.

LAIRD, Thomas Patrick, CA; Professor of Accounting and Business Method, University of Edinburgh; senior partner of Moncreiff and Horsburgh, CA, Edinburgh; *b* 1860; *m* 1st, Mary Jane, *d* of Rev. James Macgregor; 2nd, Caroline Grizel, *d* of James Edward Barclay; one *s* one *d*. *Educ:* Sharp's Institution and Academy, Perth. Admitted Member Society of Accountants, Edinburgh; Secretary of that Society, 1916–20; Member of the University Court, University of Edinburgh; Chairman of British Assets Trust Ltd. *Address:* 35 Inverleith Row, Edinburgh; 46 Castle Street, Edinburgh. *TA:* Monarch, Edinburgh. *T:* Central 999. *Club:* Northern, Edinburgh.
Died 11 June 1927.

LAKE, Sir Arthur Johnstone, 8th Bt, *cr* 1711; *b* 15 Oct. 1849; *s* of Edward Lake and Clara, *d* of Sir William Johnstone, 7th Bt; *S* cousin, 1916; *m* 1884, Emily Burton (*decd*); one *d* (and two *d* decd). *Heir:* *c* Atwell Henry Lake, Lt RN, *b* 13 Feb 1891.
Died 10 Nov. 1924.

LAKE, Sir St Vincent Atwell, 7th Bt, *cr* 1711; *b* 3 Jan. 1862; *s* of St Vincent David Lake and Frances, *d* of Peter Partington; *S* uncle, 1897; *m* 1885, Elizabeth Daisy (*d* 1900), *d* of Charles Day. *Heir:* *c* Arthur Johnstone Lake [*b* 15 Oct. 1849; *m* 1884, Emily Burton (decd); three *d*].
Died 12 Nov. 1916.

LAKING, Sir Guy Francis, 2nd Bt, *cr* 1902; CB 1914; MVO; FSA; Keeper of the King's Armoury; Keeper of the Armoury of the Wallace Collection; Keeper, Secretary and Accounting Officer of the London Museum, Lancaster House, St James, since 1911; *b* 21 October 1875; *s* of Sir Francis Laking, 1st Bt and Emma (*d* 1905), *d* of Joseph Mansell; *S* father, 1914; *m* 1898, Beatrice, *d* of Charles Mylne Barker; one *s* one *d*. *Educ:* Westminster School. Went to the Architectural Museum, Westminster, to learn drawing; was going to be artist, but joined the firm of Christie, as took such deep interest in pictures and works of art. KGStJ; Knight Commander of the Charles III of Spain; Knight of the Crown of Italy; Officer of the Leopold of Belgium; Officer of St John the Lateran. *Publications:* The Armoury at Windsor Castle, 1904; The Armoury of the Knights of St John, 1905; The Furniture of Windsor Castle, 1905; The Sèvres Porcelain of Buckingham Palace, 1907; articles upon art subjects in Magazine of Art, The Art Journal, etc; the *catalogue raisonné* of the European and Eastern Armour at Hertford House, etc. *Recreations:* riding, drawing, reading; all matters connected with the stage. *Heir:* *s* Guy Francis William Laking, *b* 3 Jan. 1904. *Address:* Meyrick Lodge, Avenue Road, Regent's Park, NW; York Gate House, Broadstairs. *Clubs:* Marlborough, Conservative, Garrick.
Died 22 Nov. 1919.

LALAING, Count de, Hon. GCVO 1915; *b* London, 1856; *e s* of late Count and of Julia Maria Vibart; *S* father, 1881; *m* Christine, *d* of Baron du Tour de Bellinchave, grand master of the ceremonies at the Dutch Court; one *s* one *d*. *Educ:* Brussels (LLD). Entered Belgian Foreign Office, 1879; 2nd Secretary, Vienna, 1881; Chargé d'Affairs, Bucharest, 1883; Attaché au Cabinet du Roi, 1884; 1st Secretary, Berlin, 1886; the Hague, 1887; Councillor in London, 1889; Minister, Rio de Janeiro, 1893; Bucharest, 1896; Envoy Extraordinary and Minister Plenipotentiary, 1898; Berne, 1899; London, 1903–15. Commander, Order of Leopold; Grand Cross, Order of the Crown of Belgium; Grand Cross of the Star of Roumania, and of the Crown of Italy, etc. *Recreations:* golf, shooting. *Address:* 15 West Halkin Street, Belgrave Square, SW1. *T:* Victoria 3919; 43 Rue Ducale, Brussels; Santbergen, Flandre orientale, Belgium. *Clubs:* Travellers', Royal Automobile, Bachelors'; Cercle du Parc, Brussels.

Died 13 Nov. 1919.

LALL, I. C., OBE 1918; ISO; MA; *b* 27 April 1863; *s* of Chandu Lall, Educational Department, Lahore; *m* 1888, Georgina, 3rd *d* of A. Athim, EA Commissioner in the Punjab; two *s* three *d*. *Educ:* Baring High School, Batala; Government Coll., Lahore. BA Calcutta University, 1884; MA Punjab University, 1885. Entered the Punjab Provincial Civil Service, 1885; Settlement Officer, 1902–12; Deputy Commissioner, Gujerat, 1912; retired from service, 1918. *Recreations:* tennis, riding. *Address:* Lahore, Punjab.

Died 27 March 1922.

LAMB, Sir Archibald, 3rd Bt, *cr* 1795; DL; late Major 2nd Life Guards; Major Imperial Yeomanry; served South Africa; *b* 5 Nov. 1845; *s* of Charles James Savile Montgomerie Lamb and Anna Charlotte, *d* of Arthur Grey; *S* grandfather, 1860; *m* 1875, Louisa, *y d* of Sir Henry Estridge Durrant, 3rd Bt and *widow* of J. R. Fenwick. *Educ:* Eton; Trinity Coll., Camb. Owner of about 2,700 acres. *Heir:* *b* Lt-Col Charles Anthony Lamb, *b* 21 March 1857. *Address:* Beauport, Battle, Sussex. *Club:* Carlton. *Died 6 Nov. 1921.*

LAMB, Rev. Benjamin; Hon. Canon of Ripon. *Address:* Belford, Devonshire Place, Bath. *Died 19 Jan. 1925.*

LAMB, Edmund, MA (Oxon); FCS, FRGS; County Councillor, West Sussex; *b* 8 July 1863; 2nd surv. *s* of late Richard Westbrook Lamb, JP and DL of West Denton, Northumberland, and Georgiana, *d* of Stephen Eaton of Ketton Hall, Co. Rutland, and *g s* of Joseph Lamb, JP and DL of Temon, Co. Cumberland; *m* 1893, Mabel, *o d* of Stephen Winkworth, Holly Lodge, Campden Hill, W, and *g d* of Thomas Thomasson, the friend and supporter of Cobden and Bright; one *d*. *Educ:* Oratory School, Edgbaston, Birmingham; Merton Coll., Oxford (honours degree); University Coll., London. A colliery proprietor in Northumberland, and a landowner in Northumberland and Sussex. MP (L) Leominster Div. of North Herefordshire, 1906–10. MIME. *Recreations:* horse breeding, farming. *Address:* Borden Wood, Liphook, Hants; Holly Lodge, Campden Hill, W8. *T:* Park 4791. *Clubs:* Oxford and Cambridge, Union, Bath. *Died 3 Jan. 1925.*

LAMB, Sir Richard Amphlett, KCSI 1911 (CSI 1909); CIE 1901; *b* 4 April 1858; *s* of late William Lamb, Indian Vet. Department; *m* 1901, Kathleen, 2nd *d* of Lt-Col J. P. Barry, IMS; four *s*. *Educ:* Highgate Grammar School. Joined ICS 1879; served as assistant collector and magistrate; as forest settlement officer, Khandesh; as Deputy Commissioner, Burmah, 1887–90 (medal with clasp); subsequently assistant collector, acting collector, and collector and magistrate, Bombay; Chairman Poona Plague Committee, 1897; Secretary and Acting Chief Sec. to Govt of Bombay, 1904; Commissioner Central Division, 1905; Member, Indian Excise Committee, 1905–6; Chief Secretary, 1907; Member of Executive Council, Governor of Bombay, 1910; retired 1915. Kaiser-i-Hind medal (1st class), 1900. *Address:* Tudor House, Broadway, Worcs. *Clubs:* East India United Service; Club of Western India, Poona.

Died 27 Jan. 1923.

LAMBART, Lt-Col Sir Gustavus Francis, 1st Bt, *cr* 1911; CVO 1903; late Major and Lt-Col 5th Leinster Regiment; *b* 25 March 1848; *e s* of Gustavus W. Lambart of Beau Parc, Co. Meath; *m* 1911, Kathleen Moore Brabazon; one *s*. Formerly Chamberlain to Duke of Marlborough; Comptroller to HE The Earl of Dudley, 1902–3; Chamberlain, 1904; Secretary to Order of St Patrick. *Heir:* *s* Oliver Francis Lambart, *b* 6 April 1913. *Address:* Beau Parc, Co. Meath. *Clubs:* Carlton; Kildare Street, Dublin.

Died 16 June 1926.

LAMBART, Richard, DSO 1914; *b* 26 June 1875; *s* of late Maj. Fred Lambart, Scots Fusiliers; *m* 1913, Faith Bevan. *Educ:* Radley. Entered army, 1914; served European War, 1914–15 (despatches, DSO). *Address:* 30 Milner Street, Cadogan Square, SW. *Club:* Roy Automobile. *Died 6 Jan. 1924.*

LAMBERT, Agnes; *b* Milford Hall, Salisbury; *y d* of late Rt Hon. Si John Lambert, KCB, Permanent Secretary of the Local Governmen Board, and Ellen, *d* of Henry Shorto, of Salisbury. *Publications:* School Bank Manual; edited The Free Trade Speeches of Charle Pelham Villiers; numerous articles in the Nineteenth Century, Dubli Review, and other periodicals. *Recreations:* music, gardening. *Addres* Milford House, Elms Road, Clapham Common, SW.

Died Nov. 1917

LAMBERT, Alfred Uvedale Miller, JP; MA; FRHistS, FSA; MFF Burstow Foxhounds, 1900–5; *y s* of late Henry Thomas Lambert JP of Sandhills, Bletchingley, Surrey and Georgina Emily, *d* of lat Rev. Sir Thomas Combe Miller, 6th Bt (*d* 1902), of Froyle Park Hants; *m* 1st, 1894, Violet (*d* 1894), *d* of late Walter James Marshall JP, DL of Patterdale Hall, Westmorland; 2nd 1904, Cecily *o d* of lat Gerard Hoare, JP, MFH Burstow Foxhounds, of Stansted House Godstone; one *s*. *Educ:* Eton; Trinity Coll., Camb. 2nd Lieu Middlesex Yeomanry Cavalry, 1891–95. *Publications:* Blechingley Parish History, 1921. *Address:* South Park Farm, Bletchingley, Surrey *Club:* Windham. *Died 6 June 1928*

LAMBERT, Adm. Sir Cecil Foley, KCB 1920; *b* 28 May 1864; 3r *s* of late Sir Henry Edward Francis Lambert, 6th Bt and *heir-pres*. t Sir John Foley Grey, 8th Bt; *m* 1896, Rosina, *d* of Francis Drake Served Egypt, 1882 (medal and star); 4th Sea Lord Admiralty 1913–19; Director of Personnel, Air Ministry, 1919–21; additiona member of the Air Council, 1920–21; Vice-Admiral, 1921; retire list, 1921; Adm. retired list, 1926. *Address:* 8 Palace Street, SW1. *Club* Orleans. *Died 29 Feb. 1928*

LAMBERT, Francis L., ISO 1903; *b* Roscommon, Ireland, 28 Feb 1838; *m* 1865, Josephine Amelia, 3rd *d* of late B. H. Hickey, Anerley two *s* one *d*. *Educ:* privately. Entered Excise Department, 1858; passe into Government Laboratory, 1862, obtaining a prize for proficienc in Practical and Theoretical Chemistry; returned to Excise Branch and having passed through all the grades, reached the highest post that of Chief Inspector of Inland Revenue, from which he retired in 1902. *Recreations:* historical and scientific studies, gardening. *Address* 17 Heathhurst Road, Sanderstead.

Died 31 July 1925

LAMBERT, Rev. Frederick Fox, MA; Hon. Canon of St Albans 1898. *Educ:* Corpus Christi College, Oxford. Curate o Kidderminster, 1866–68; Vicar of Loversall, 1868–72; Chaplain t the Marquis of Salisbury, 1872–77; Claremarket Mission, 1877 Bedington, 1878–79; Rector of Clothall, 1879–91; Vicar of Cheshunt 1891–1911. *Address:* Aston Dene, Stevenage.

Died 25 April 1920

LAMBERT, Sir George Thomas, Kt 1903; CB 1897; Director o Greenwich Hospital; *b* 9 Nov. 1837; *y s* of late Henry Lambert, MP and Catherine, *d* of Wm Talbot of Castle Talbot; descended from 2nd Earl of Shrewsbury. *Educ:* Downside Coll., Bath; London Univ. matriculated in first class, 1856. Acted as private secretary to members of the Government in several administrations, including the 16th Earl of Derby, Sir George Trevelyan, Earl of Camperdown, Sir Massey Lopes and Lord Brassey. *Address:* 7 Park Place, St James's, SW. *Clubs:* White's, Arthur's. *Died 20 Nov. 1918*

LAMBERT, Sir John, KCIE 1893 (CIE 1882); Member of Legislative Council, 1892; retired, 1897; *b* 1838; *m* 1869, Annie, *d* of Lt-Gen. F. D. Atkinson. Entered Bengal Police, 1863, as Assistant and District Superintendent; Visitor Jail and Lunatic Asylumns, 1872; Deputy Commissioner of Police, Calcutta, 1874; Foreign Dept, 1882–84; Acting Commissioner, Calcutta, 1885–86; Commissioner, 1889. *Address:* 81 Harcourt Terrace, SW. *T:* Kensington 4178. *Club:* Oriental. *Died 31 Aug. 1916.*

LAMBERT, Col (temp. Brig.-General) Thomas Stanton, CB 1918; CMG 1918; Commander 13th Infantry Brigade; *b* 27 Jan. 1871; *s* of late Rev. R. U. Lambert, MA, Vicar of Christ Church, Bradford-on-Avon, Wiltshire and Agnes, *d* of Archdeacon Stanton, Burbage, Wilts; *m* Geraldine Rachel Foster; two *s* one *d*. *Educ:* Charterhouse; RMC, Sandhurst. East Lancashire Regt 1891; India, 1897–1904; Staff College, Camberley, 1905–7; Staff Captain, Harrismith, ORC, S Africa, 1907–9; War Office, 1911–14; served with BEF, Aug. 1914–Nov. 1914 with 4th Div.; present at Le Cateau, Nery, Marne, Aisne, Ploegsteert (severely wounded); commanded 1st Batt. East

Lancashire Regt at Marne and Aisne; DAAG 37th Div., March–May 1915; commanded 2nd Batt. East Lancashire Regt, June–Oct. 1915; Bridoux Salient (Loos operations), 26–28 Sept. 1915; Acting AAG, GHQ Oct.–Dec. 1915; commanded 69th Infantry Brigade, 1916–18, including capture of Contalmaison, and actions of Le Sars, and Hill 60, Menin Road, Cameron Covert (Polygon Wood); Italy, 1917–18; commanded 32nd Division, 1918–19; Operations of 4th Army, Aug.–Nov. 1918, including actions at Damery, Huleuille, passage of Somme at Brie and St Christ, Holnon Wood, Hindenburg Line, Sequehart, passage of Oise and Sambre Canal at Ors, relief of Avesnes; commanded 1st King's Brigade, Lancashire Division, Army of the Rhine; commanded Dublin Brigade, Oct.–Dec. 1919. *Recreations:* tennis, riding, winter sports. *Club:* United Service.

Died 20 June 1921.

LAMBERT, Lt-Col Walter Miller, DSO 1887; JP Dorset; *b* 8 May 1843; *y s* of Richard Lambert of Lyston Hall, Essex, and Charlotte, *d* of John Campbell; *m* 1878, Frances, *o c* of F. B. Courtenay; one *s* two *d*. *Educ:* Cheltenham College. Entered Royal Marine Artillery, 1860; Lt-Col 1886; served Burmah, 1885–86 (despatches, DSO, medal with clasp). *Recreation:* fishing. *Address:* 25 Princess Road, Bournemouth. *Died 25 Jan. 1924.*

LAMBERT, Rev. William Henry, MA; *b* 1833; 5th *s* of Sir Henry John Lambert of Aston House, Oxon; *m* 1866, Georgiana Joyce (*d* 1920), 3rd *d* of Robert Biddulph of Ledbury; one *s*. *Educ:* Eton; Merton College, Oxford. Ordained, 1857; Curate of St Mary's, Bridgnorth, 1857–58; Rector of Stoke Edith with Westhide, 1858–1905; Rural Dean of Weston, 1886–96 and 1904–11; Prebendary of Hereford Cathedral, 1887–1918; Pres. of the Woolhope Naturalists Field Club, 1893. *Address:* Fenton House, Hereford. *Died 23 Feb. 1924.*

LAMBOURNE, 1st Baron, *cr* 1917; **Amelius Richard Mark Lockwood,** PC 1905; GCVO 1927 (CVO 1905); JP, DL; Lord-Lieutenant of Essex, since 1919; Vice President RSPCA; President Royal Horticultural Society; President of the Bribery and Secret Commissions Prevention League Incorporated; *b* 17 Aug. 1847; *e s* of late Gen. Mark Wood; assumed surname of Lockwood, 1876; *m* 1876, Isabella (*d* 1923), 2nd *d* of Sir John Ralph Milbanke, 8th Bt, Minister at Munich and The Hague. *Educ:* Eton. Entered Coldstream Guards, 1866; retired, 1883; Provincial Grand Master of Essex Freemasons, 1902. MP (C) Epping Division of Essex, 1892–1917. *Heir:* none. *Address:* 5 Audley Square, W1. *T:* Grosvenor 1972; Bishop's Hall, Romford, Essex. *T:* Chigwell 16. *TA:* Audlesque, London; Bishop's Hall, Chigwell Row. *M:* LC 5677; F1625; A8290. *Club:* Carlton. *Died 26 Dec. 1928 (ext).*

LAMBTON, Lt-Col Francis W., JP Pembrokeshire; retired; *b* Naples, 1834; 3rd *s* of William Henry, *y b* of 1st Earl Durham, and Henrietta Lambton, *co-heiress* of Cuthbert Ellison, jr, of Durham; *m* 1866, Lady Victoria Alexandrina Elizabeth Campbell (*d* 1909), *e d* of 2nd Earl Cawdor; four *s*. *Educ:* Eton. Served in the Crimea in the Scots Guards, 1854 to end of war. *Recreations:* all sorts of sports. *Address:* Brownslade, near Pembroke. *Club:* Travellers'.

Died 6 Oct. 1921.

LAMBTON, Lt-Col George Charles, DSO 1900; OBE 1919; late Worcestershire Regiment; *b* 10 Nov. 1872; 4th *s* of late Lt-Col Francis W. Lambton and Lady Victoria Alexandrina Elizabeth Campbell (*d* 1909), *e d* of 2nd Earl Cawdor. *Educ:* Wellington. Entered KRRC 1892; Worcestershire Regt 1895; Captain, 1900; served S Africa, 1899–1902, with 5th Mounted Infantry (despatches, Queen's medal four clasps, King's medal two clasps, DSO); European War, 1914–15 (despatches twice, Bt Lt-Col); retired pay, 1922. *Address:* Brownslade, near Pembroke. *Died 30 Aug. 1927.*

LAMPLUGH, George William, FRS 1905; *b* Driffield, East Yorkshire, 8 April 1859; *m* 1887; two *s* one *d*. *Educ:* private schools. Mercantile occupation until 1892; joined the Staff of the Geological Survey as Assistant-Geologist; District Geologist, 1901; President Geological Society, 1918–20; Assistant Director, HM Geological Survey of Great Britain, 1914–20 (retired). *Publications:* numerous geological, geographical, etc, papers and memoirs. *Address:* 13 Beaconsfield Road, St Albans.

Died 9 Oct. 1926.

LAMY, Etienne Marie Victor; homme de lettres; Membre, et depuis 1913 Secrétaire Perpétuel, de l'Académie Française; Officier de la Légion d'Honneur; *b* Cize Jura, 2 June 1845. *Educ:* Collège Stanislas. Docteur en droit, 1870; Député de Jura, 1871–81. *Publications:* Le Tiers Parti, 1868; Rapport sur le Budget de la Marine, 1878; Discours,

1879; La République en 1883; L'Armée et la Démocratie, 1889; La France du Levant, 1898; La Femme de demain, 1899; Aimée de Coigny, 1900; Etudes sur le Second Empire, 1900; Témoins de jours passés, 1909 (2e Série, 1913); Au Service des idées et des lettres, 1909; Quelques Œuvres et quelques Ouvriers (2 séries), 1910 et 1913. *Address:* 3 Place d'Jéna, Paris; Château de Vannoz par Champagnole, Jura; L'Estagnol, Antibes. *Died 9 Jan. 1919.*

LANCASTER, William Joseph Cosens, AMICE; civil engineer, British Admiralty Service; *b* Weymouth, 23 May 1851; *o s* of Capt. William Lancaster; *m* 1878; one *s*. *Educ:* Royal Naval Coll., Greenwich (medallist). Went to sea at age of 15; obliged to abandon the profession in consequence of extreme shortsight; adopted profession of civil engineer, making specialty of sea and harbour work; travelled in Baltic and Mediterranean, East and West Indies, East, West and South Coasts of Africa, etc; began to write sea stories, under pseudonym of "Harry Collingwood," 1878. *Publications:* The Secret of the Sands, 1879; Under the Meteor Flag, 1884; The Pirate Island, 1884; Voyage of the Aurora, 1885; Pirate Island, 1885; The Congo Rovers, 1886; Log of the Flying Fish, 1887; The Rover's Secret, 1888; Missing Merchantman, 1889; Doctor of the Juliet, 1892; Cruise of the Esmeralda, 1894; The Pirate Slaver, 1895; Jack Beresford's Yarn, 1896; Log of a Privateersman, 1896; The Homeward Voyage, 1897; An Ocean Chase, 1898; The Castaways, 1899; A Pirate of the Caribbees, 1900; Dick Leslie's Luck; Across the Spanish Main, 1906; With Airship and Submarine; Geoffrey Harrington's Adventures, 1907; A Middy in Command; Under the Chilian Flag; Blue and Grey, 1908; The Cruise of the Thetis, 1909; Harry Escombe; A Middy of the Slave Squadron; Overdue, 1910. *Recreations:* yachting (especially yacht racing), yacht designing, swimming, shooting, riding, painting in water colours, photography, cycling, music. *Club:* Whitefriars'.

Died June 1922.

LANDON, Perceval; barrister-at-law; special correspondent, dramatist and author; *b* 29 March 1869; *s* of late Rev. Edward Henry Landon and Caroline, *d* of late Rev. and Hon. Arthur P. Perceval; unmarried. *Educ:* Hertford College, Oxford; BA 1893. Called to Bar, Inner Temple, 1895; special correspondent for The Times, SA War, 1899–1900; private secretary to Governor of New South Wales, 1900; special correspondent Daily Mail, Delhi Durbar, China, Japan, Siberia, 1903; special correspondent The Times, expedition to Lhasa, 1903–4; special correspondent the Daily Telegraph, Prince of Wales' visit to India, 1905–6; Persia, India and Nepal, 1908; Russian Turkestan, 1909; Egypt and Sudan, 1910; NE frontier of India, Delhi Durbar, 1911; Mesopotamia and Syria, 1912; Scandinavia, British and French lines, 1914–15; Italian Lines, 1917; Peace Conference, Paris, 1919; Constantinople, 1920; India, Mesopotamia, Syria, Palestine, 1921; Prince of Wales' Tour, India and Japan, 1921–22; China, North America, 1922; Peace Conference, Lausanne, 1923; China, Nepal, Egypt, 1924; China, 1925; on staff Daily Telegraph. Silver Medal of the Royal Society of Arts, 1915. *Publications:* Heliotropes, 1903; Lhasa, 1905; Under the Sun, 1906; 1857: The Story of the Indian Mutiny, 1907; Raw Edges, 1908; The House Opposite; For the Soul of the King (trans. from the French), 1909. *Address:* 1 The Studios, Gunter Grove, Chelsea, SW. *T:* Kensington 8846. *Club:* Beefsteak.

Died 23 Jan. 1927.

LANDOR, A. Henry Savage, MRI; FRGS; Hon. Corresponding Member, Ecole d'Anthropologie de Paris; Hon. Member and Gold Medallist Geographical Society, Marseilles; Hon. Member Italian Anthropological Society; Founder Member of International Anthropological Institute, Paris; painter, sculptor, explorer; *b* Florence; 2nd *s* of late Charles Savage Landor; *g s* of Walter Savage Landor. *Educ:* Liceo Dante, Instituto Tecnico, Florence; Atelier Thaddeus, and Atelier Julian, Paris. Travelled in the East several years; also United States of America, etc. First white man to reach both sources of the great Brahmaputra River and establish their exact position (Tibet, 1897); first white man to settle the geographical problem that no range higher than the Himalayas existed north of the Brahmaputra River in Tibet; first white man to explore Central Mindanao Island, where he discovered the "white tribe" (Mansakas); held under Duke of Abruzzi's expedition world's record in mountaineering, having reached an altitude of 23,490 ft on Mount Lumpa (Nepal), 1899; accompanied Allied troops on the march to Pekin, 1900; was the first Anglo-Saxon to enter the Forbidden City, side by side with the doyen General Linievitch on the day of Allies' entry; went from Russia to Calcutta overland, across Persia, Afghanistan, and Beluchistan, 1901–2; spent one year cruising in the Philippine and Sulu Archipelagos, visiting some 400 islands, 1903; was in the American War against the Malanaos (Mindanao Island), 1903; also in the war between Sultans Abdul Aziz and Mulai Hafid in Morocco; witnessed Belgian campaign, battles of Malines, Termonde, siege and

bombardment of Antwerp, Ostende, Nieuport, Roulers, Ypres; visited French and British Fronts, 1914; bombardment Arras; visited Austro-Italian Front, 1916; made extensive journey in Albania, Macedonia and Greece, 1918, visiting Italian, French, Serbian and English front lines, thus completing inspection of entire Western Front in Europe, from Antwerp to Salonica; crossed Africa in its widest part, 1906; crossed South America from Rio de Janeiro to Lima, traversing unexplored Central Brazil and over the Andes, 1910–12. Inventor of two types of improved armoured cars, of a new type of rigid airship, of a device for destroying barbed-wire entanglements, and of an armoured motor-cycle with mitrailleuse. *Publications:* Alone with the Hairy Ainu, or 3,800 Miles on a Pack-saddle; Corea, or the Land of the Morning Calm; A Journey to the Sacred Mountain of Siao-ou-tai-shan; In the Forbidden Land, 1898; China and the Allies, 1901; Across Coveted Lands, 1902; The Gems of the East, 1904; Tibet and Nepal, 1905; Across Widest Africa, 1908; The Americans in Panama, 1910; An Explorer's Adventures in Tibet, 1910; Across Unknown South America, 1913; Mysterious South America, 1914. *Address:* c/o Grindlay, 54 Parliament Street, SW1; Calappiano, Empoli per Vinci, Italy; 10 Via Farini, Florence, Italy. *Club:* Royal Aero.
Died 26 Dec. 1924.

LANDOUZY, Louis Joseph; Professeur de clinique médicale et Doyen de la Faculté de Médecine de Paris; Médecin de Hôpitaux (Hôpital Laënnec); Membre de la Société de Biologie, de l'Académie de Médecine et de l'Institut; *b* Reims (Marne); de père et de grandpère, médecins; *m* Louise, fille de feu le chirurgien A. Richet, de l'Institut; no *c*. *Educ:* éducation classique, au lycée de Reims (Marne); éducation médicale, Ecole de médecine de Reims, puis Faculté de Médecine et Hôpitaux de Paris. *Publications:* La Pleurésie, dite *a frigore*, fonction de Tuberculose; La Typhobacillose; Asthme et tuberculose; Tuberculose chez les enfants du premier âge; Tuberculoses professionnelles; Hérédité de la tuberculose: A. Hérédité de graine; B. Hérédité terrain: dystrophisme tuberculeux: études cliniques et experimentales; Tuberculose: maladie sociale; Cent ans de Phtisiologie, 1808–1908; Empoisonnements non professionnels par l'Aniline; Localisations angiocardiaques typhoïdiques; Atrophies myopathiques: myopathie type Landouzy Déjerine; Paralyses dans les Maladies aiguës; Enquête sur l'alimentation d'une centaine d'ouvriers et d'employés parisiens, 1905, avec D. H. Labbé; Education alimentaire rationnelle, 1911; Tableaux muraux d'Education alimentaire, rationnelle, hygiénique et économique, 1906; Les Sérothérapies, 1898; Glossaire médicale, 1902, avec Dr Jayle; Pneumococcie, Pneumonie and Pleurésie, in Traité de Médecine de Brouardel et Gilbert; Crénothérapie, cures hydro-minérales, avec A. Gautier, Moureu et de Launay, 1910; Eléments d'Anatomie et de Physiologie médicales, avec Dr L. Bernard, 1913; avec Dr Jean Heitz, Le Substratum scientifique de la Balnéothérapie, etc: Congrès de Physiothérapie, Berlin, 1913, Congrès international de Médicine, Londres, 1913; Fièvres typhoïde et paratyphoïdes, Presse Médicale, 1914; La Guerre et la Réforme du Soldat tuberculeaux, in Revue d'Hygiéne, 1915; La Syphilis avant la guerre, in Bulletin de l'Académie de Médicine, 1915 et 1916; Médicine Allemande et Médicine Française, in Les Allemands et la Science, 1916, etc. Rédacteur en chef de la Revue de Médecine; Directeur scientifique de la Presse Médicale. *Récréations:* voyages, tableaux, livres. *Address:* 15 rue de l'Université, Paris.
Died 10 May 1917.

LANDRY, Col Hon. Auguste Charles Philippe Robert; Senator since 1892; Speaker of the Senate since 1911; *b* 15 Jan. 1846; *m* 1st, 1868, Wilhelmina (*d* 1903), *d* of late Etienne Couture, St Gervais, PQ; 2nd, 1908, Marie Clara Amelie, *d* of late Hon. Elisée Dionne, MLC. *Educ:* Quebec Seminary; Laval University. MP (C) Montmagny, 1878–87. *Address:* Notre Dame de Quebec. *Club:* Garrison, Quebec.
Died 20 Dec. 1919.

LANDRY, Maj.-Gen. Joseph Phillippe, CMG 1917; *b* 1870; *s* of late Hon. Phillippe Landry, President of the Senate of Canada; *m* 1896, Blanche, *d* of late Hon. Sir Alexandre Lacoste, PC, LLD. *Educ:* Quebec and Ottawa Universities; Lille University; McGill University. Barrister, Canada, 1896; served European War, 1914–18 (despatches twice, CMG). *Club:* Garrison, Quebec.
Died July 1926.

LANDRY, Hon. Sir Pierre Armand, Kt 1916; Chief Justice of the King's Bench Division of the Superior Court of New Brunswick; *b* 1 May 1846; *m* 1870; six *s* one *d*. *Educ:* St Joseph's University (MA); Laval. Barrister, New Brunswick, 1870; QC 1881; MLA, 1870–74, 1878–83; Chief Commissioner of Public Works, 1878–82; Provincial Secretary, 1882–83; Member Canadian House of Commons for seven years; Judge Supreme Court of New Brunswick, 1893. *Address:* Dorchester, New Brunswick.
Died 28 July 1916.

LANE, Col Clayton Turner, CIE 1895; JP, DL; Supernumerary List, Indian Army; *b* 20 Feb. 1842; 3rd *s* of late James Lane of Knockeevan, Camberley; *m* 1867, Nicola Arbuthnot, *d* of late William Allardyce of Aberdeen; four *s* two *d*. *Educ:* private school. Ensign, Bengal Army, 1858; Asst and District Supt of Police, Punjaub, 1863; Berar, 1865; Inspector-General of Police, Hyderabad Assigned District, 1877; Deputy-Comr, 1895; US List 1896. *Address:* Downfold, Guildford. *T:* 280 Guildford.
Died 11 June 1920.

LANE, Sir Harry Philip Parnell, Kt 1925; CBE 1918; MVO 1913; Chief Constable of Lancashire since 1912; *b* 1870; *m* 1903, Flora Emma, *d* of late Capt. E. R. Peel, Rockferry, Cheshire. *Address:* Ellet Hall, Lancaster. *Clubs:* Flyfishers'; County, Lancaster.
Died 24 April 1927.

LANE, James Ernest, FRCS; Senior Surgeon, London Lock Hospital; Consulting Surgeon, St Mary's Hospital; Major RAMC (T). Formerly Member of the Council and of the Court of Examiners of the Royal College of Surgeons of England; Member of Royal Commission on Venereal Diseases. *Publications:* editor of Heath's Practical Anatomy, 9th edn; many articles on the treatment of venereal diseases. *Address:* 47 Queen Anne Street, W1. *T:* Langham 1035.
Died 4 Nov. 1926.

LANE, John; publisher; *b* West Putford, N Devon, 14 March 1854; *e s* of Lewis and Mary Grace Lane; *m* 1898, Annie E. King. *Educ:* Chulmleigh. Joint-founder with Mr Elkin Mathews of the Bodley Head Publishing business, 1887; dissolved partnership, 1894; since conducted the Bodley Head publishing business in Vigo Street, London; Founder of the Yellow Book, 1894, and art editor of it from vol. iv. *Publications:* edited and wrote Introduction, Life of Sir Thomas Bodley, 1894; Sir Caspar Purdon Clark, 1905; edited Memoirs of the Count de Cartrie, 1906. *Recreation:* collecting objets d'art. *Address:* 8 Lancaster Gate Terrace, W2. *TA:* Bodleian, London. *T:* Paddington 7177. *Clubs:* Reform, Cocoa-Tree, Whitefriars, Pilgrims, Sette of Odd Volumes; Union, Brighton; National Arts, New York.
Died 2 Feb. 1925.

LANE, Mrs John, (Annie E. Lane); *b* Geneva, Switzerland; *o c* of late Julius Eichberg, Boston, USA, Superintendent of Music in the Public Schools of Boston, and Director of the Boston Conservatory of Music; *m* 1st, Tyler Batcheller King, LLD, Boston; 2nd, 1898, John Lane (*d* 1925), London, publisher. *Educ:* Boston. Author of the words of the American national hymn To Thee O Country, set to music by Julius Eichberg. *Publications:* Kitwyk; The Champagne Standard; According to Maria; Talk of the Town; Maria Again; War Phases according to Maria; translations—Balthasar and Honey Bee, from the French of Anatole France; Peterkins, from the German of Ossip Schubin; articles in The Fortnightly Review, The Nineteenth Century, Blackwood's, The Atlantic Monthly, The Century, Lippincott's Magazine, etc. *Recreation:* music. *Address:* 8 Lancaster Gate Terrace, W2. *T:* Paddington 7177.
Died 23 Jan 1927.

LANE, John Henry Hervey Vincent, JP, DL; *b* 1867; *e s* of late John Henry Bagot Lane, JP, DL, of King's Bromley Manor and Lily Hill and Susan Anne, *d* of late Henry William Vincent of Lily Hill; *m* 1902, Hon. Grace Louisa Edwardes, 3rd *d* of 4th Baron Kensington two *s* five *d*. *Educ:* Eton. Captain 4th Batt. South Staffordshire Regt patron of King's Bromley. Owner of 2,500 acres. *Address:* King's Bromley Manor, Lichfield. *Clubs:* Carlton, Travellers', Wellington
Died 22 Feb. 1917

LANE, John Macdonald; late Commissioned Officer, Indian Navy retired; *b* 1840; *s* of James Lane, late of Knockevan, Camberley; *m* 1872, *d* of late Rev. W. Powell; three *s* (one killed in War) two *d* *Educ:* private school; Naval College, Southsea. Joined Indian Navy 1856; passed final exams, qualified for command of Man-of-War 1861; took part in Persian War, 1856 (medal and clasp); Indian Mutiny, 1857; abolition of slavery on Arabian Coast, 1858; service abolished, 1862; joined Indian Telegraph Dept, 1862; with Bhootan Expedition, 1864; constructed line to Darjeeling and through Assam to Gowhatty, 1864; latter country completely undeveloped; surveyed for line to Bankok *via* Tenasserim River, and shot the rapids, 188?; laid sea cable, Kenery Island, Bombay Harbour, to main land, 1885 retired 1890 with rank of Chief Superintendent. *Publications:* Created and Created; Varied Life by Sea and Land; A Revolution in Diet; Nation's Loss of Beauty. *Recreations:* fishing, gardening, etc. *Address:* Dudley House, Montpelier Road, Twickenham.
Died 19 Jan. 1927

LANG, Col Arthur Moffatt, CB 1908; RE (retired); *b* 15 Nov. 1832; *e s* of Arthur Lang, ICS of Westhill, Harrow, and Sarah, *o d* of Gen. R. Tickell, CB; *m* 1st, 1858, Sarah (*d* 1889), *d* of Gen. F. B. Boileau, RA; 2nd, 1893, Edith Mina (*d* 1903), *y d* of Rev. Owen C. Seymour Lang, MA, of Bentley, Hants; 3rd, 1905, Ida F. C., *d* of James C. Richardson, JP, Glanrafon, Glamorganshire. *Educ:* Rugby; Cheltenham; Military College, Addiscombe. Entered Army, 1852; Lt-Col 1877; Col 1881; retired, 1888; served Indian Mutiny, 1857-58; siege, assault of Delhi, Agra, relief of Lucknow, Cawnpore, seige and capture of Lucknow (despatches four times, medal 3 clasps); held appointments in PWD and MWD, India, including Principal of Roorkee Engineering College, Deputy Inspector-Gen. for Fortifications, Chief Engineer in Baluchistan, in Burmah, in North-West Provinces. *Address:* Box Grove Lodge, Guildford, Surrey.
Died 6 Aug. 1916.

LANG, Lt-Col Godfrey George, DSO 1916; late 2nd Battalion West Yorkshire Regiment; *b* 24 April 1867; *e s* of late George Lukis Lang, ICS and Louisa Astell; *m* 1899, Isabel Frances Emily, *y d* of late R. P. Ebden, CB; one *d*. *Educ:* Clifton College; Bedford Grammar School, Sandhurst. Entered Army, 1887; Captain, 1894; Major 1907; Lt-Col 1916; served NW Frontier India, 1907 (medal with clasp); European War (despatches twice, DSO); retired pay, 1921. *Recreations:* polo, cricket, hunting, golf, shooting, fishing. *Address:* c/o Cox and Co., Charing Cross, SW1.
Died 29 July 1923.

LANG, Sir Peter Redford Scott, Kt 1921; Regius Professor of Mathematics, University of St Andrews, 1879; retired, 1921; Colonel 1st Fifeshire Volunteer Artillery and TF; retired, 1914; *b* Edinburgh, 8 Oct. 1850. *Address:* Mansefield, St Andrews. *Clubs:* Royal and Ancient, St Andrews; Scottish Conservative, Edinburgh.
Died 5 July 1926.

LANG, William Lindsay Holmes; Joint Editor, The Financial News since 1921; *b* Glasgow, 27 April 1888; *o s* of William Lang, LDS, Glasgow, and Margaret Lindsay, Possil Park; *m* Felicia, 4th *d* of late William Lindsay, JP, last Provost of Broughty Ferry; one *d*. *Educ:* various schools, including Dundee High School and Harris Academy. Apprenticed to Scots Law on staff of The Times, 1906-8; legal practice, politics and journalism, 1908-12; Editor Manchester Weekly Times, 1912-15; Naval Service with Grand Fleet 1915-19; Founder and Editor of The Dolphin (organ of the Imperial Merchant Service Guild), and leader writer and literary critic to the Liverpool Courier, 1919-21. *Publications:* A Sea Lawyer's Log, 1919; several monographs on political and economic questions; articles to philosophical periodicals throughout the world. *Recreations:* football (formerly), cricket, tramping, reading, the theatre. *Address:* 55 Holland Park Avenue, W11. *Club:* Royal Societies.
Died 19 May 1928.

LANG, Col William Robert, JP; DSc; FRSC; Director of Military Studies, since 1919, Professor of Chemistry, 1900-19, University of Toronto; *y s* of late John Lang, Dowanhill, Glasgow; *m* 1909, Edith, *y d* of A. J. Hollington, JP, of Forty Hill, Enfield, one of HM's Lieutenants for City of London; one *s* three *d*. *Educ:* Univs of Glasgow and Paris; on staff of former, 1890-1900. FCS, FIC; TD; late Major of RE (T); Col Canadian Militia (COTC); 5 years' war service, General Staff, CEF (GSO 1st Grade) (mentioned for valuable services, thanked by Army Council). *Publications:* some fifty original papers in English, French and American scientific journals; also Part II of The Guide, by Gen. Sir W. D. Otter, KCB. *Address:* The University of Toronto, Canada. *Clubs:* Caledonian; York, Toronto; Scottish Conservative, Edinburgh.
Died 20 Nov. 1925.

LANGBRIDGE, Rev. Frederick; Rector of St John's and Canon of St Munchin's, St Mary's Cathedral, Limerick; Chaplain, District Asylum; *b* Birmingham, 17 March 1849; *m* 1878, Jane, *d* of John Wilson, Kendal; three *d*. *Educ:* King Edward VI's School, Birmingham; St Alban Hall; Merton College, Oxford (MA). DLitt, TCD, 1907. *Publications: poems:* Gaslight and Stars, 1892; Sent Back by the Angels, 1885; Poor Folk's Lives, 1887; A Cracked Fiddle, 1892; A Cluster of Quiet Thoughts, 1896; The Scales of Heaven, 1896; Clear Waters, 1897; Little Tapers, 1899; The Distant Lights, 1902; Ballads and Legends (Collected Issue of narrative poems); The Peaks of Proud Desire; The Power of Red Michael, 1909; Restful Thoughts for Dusty Ways, 1912; *novels:* The Dreams of Dania, 1897; Love has no Pity, 1901; also many books for children and for boys; editor, What to Read, 1889; Poets at Play, 1888; Ballads of the Brave, 1890; *plays* (with Freeman Wills): The Only Way; Rouget de L'Isle; After All; (sole author) The Chevalier de St George; The Devil's Trap; (with A. H. Ferro) The Children of Kings. *Recreations:* billiards, croquet, chiefly reading. *Address:* St John's Rectory, Limerick.
Died 19 Jan 1922.

LANGDALE, Henry Joseph, JP, DL; *b* 2 June 1853; *e s* of Charles Joseph Langdale (*d* 1895) and Henrietta (*d* 1898), *e d* and co-heir of late Henry Grattan, MP, of Celbridge Abbey, Co. Kildare. *Educ:* Beaumont. Late Capt. 4th Batt. Royal Irish Fusiliers (Militia). *Address:* Houghton Hall, Sancton, E Riding, Yorks.
Died 11 Sept. 1923.

LANGDON, Rev. Alfred; Prebendary of Lincoln. *Address:* The Vicarage, New Sleaford.
Died 16 Nov. 1925.

LANGDON, Col Harry, CB 1911; VD; TD; retired; *b* 29 March 1855; 3rd *s* of John Langdon, Huyton Park, Liverpool; *m* Elizabeth Day, *y d* of John Hind Talbot, Liverpool; three *s* four *d*. *Educ:* Liverpool Institute; High School. Governing Director J. Langdon and Sons, Ltd, Government contractors, Liverpool. Commanded the Royal Naval Artillery Volunteers, 1878-92; transferred to Mersey Div. Submarine Miners as Capt. 1893; Major, 1894; Lt-Col, 1905-8; transferred to Lancs Fortress RE (T) as Lt-Col and Honorary Colonel, 1908. *Recreations:* shooting, riding, yachting. *Address:* Oxton Hall, Oxton, Cheshire. *TA:* Military, Liverpool. *T:* Birkenhead 619. *Clubs:* Royal Mersey Yacht, Lyceum, Liverpool.
Died 7 July 1925.

LANGELIER, Hon. Charles, KC; Judge of Court of Sessions of the Peace, Quebec, since 1910; *b* 23 Aug. 1852; *m* 1882, Marie Lucile La Rue; one *d*. *Educ:* Laval Univ., Quebec (Doctor in Law, Dufferin medal). One of the Governors of Laval University; President of the Licence Commission for the city of Quebec. Admitted to Bar, 1875; QC 1897; sat one Parliament as Member of the House of Commons of Canada, and eleven years as Member of the Quebec Legislature; Minister of the Crown as Secretary of the Province, 1890; Sheriff of Quebec, 1900. *Publications:* Souvenirs Politiques, two vols, 1878-96; The Criminal Procedure, 1916. *Address:* 111 Grande Allée, Quebec. *T:* 966. *Club:* Garrison, Quebec.
Died 7 Feb. 1920.

LANGFORD, 4th Baron, *cr* 1800; **Hercules Edward Rowley,** KCVO 1900; Representative Peer for Ireland since 1884; Lieutenant-Colonel Grenadier Guards (retired); *b* 1 June 1848; *e s* of 3rd Baron and Louisa Augusta, *e d* of Edward Michael Conolly, MP; *S* father, 1854; *m* 1st, 1889, Georgina (*d* 1901), 6th *d* of Sir Richard Sutton, 4th Bt; one *s* (and one *s* one *d* decd); 2nd, 1915, Margaret Antonia, *e d* of Rev. W. M. Carruthers, of Little Munden, Herts. *Educ:* Eton. Ensign Grenadier Guards, 1867; State Steward to Viceroy of Ireland, 1886-92. *Heir: s* Hon. John Hercules William Rowley, *b* 16 Dec. 1894. *Address:* Summerhill House, Enfield, County Meath. *Clubs:* Carlton; Kildare Street, Dublin.
Died 29 Oct. 1919.

LANGFORD, 5th Baron, *cr* 1800; **John Hercules William Rowley;** *b* 16 Dec. 1894; *e s* of 4th Baron and Georgina (*d* 1901), 6th *d* of Sir Richard Sutton, 4th Bt; *S* father, 1919. *Heir: u* Hon. William Chambré Rowley, *b* 30 Aug. 1849. *Address:* Summerhill House, Enfield, County Meath.
Died 29 Sept. 1922.

LANGFORD, Surgeon Martyn Henry, DSO 1915; RN. Served Dardanelles, 1914-15 (despatches, DSO); was serving in the Inflexible when she was mined, and attended the wounded under great difficulties.
Died 15 Dec. 1918.

LANGLER, Sir Alfred, Kt 1927; sole executor of the Hackett Estate, and governing director of the West Australian Newspaper Co. Ltd since 1917; *b* Ipplepen, Devonshire, 1865. Some time on the literary staffs of different Devonshire journals, and a contributor to various London papers; on the editorial staff of the Register, Adelaide, 1890-95; joined the West Australian literary department, 1895; after some years, in addition to his literary work, became actively concerned in the business management of the paper; editor-in-chief of the West Australian and Western Mail, 1916-23; Australian delegate to Second Imperial Press Conference, Ottawa, 1920; Chairman Western Australian Committee Third Imperial Press Conference, 1925. JP for Western Australia. *Address:* West Australian Office, Perth, WA. *Club:* Weld, Perth.
Died 26 March 1928.

LANGLEY, John Newport, FRS 1883; ScD Cambridge; Hon. LLD St Andrews; Hon. ScD Dublin; Hon. MD Groningen; Hon. Dr Strasbourg; Fellow of Trinity College, Cambridge, 1877; Professor of Physiology, Cambridge, since 1903; Editor Journal of Physiology; *b* 2 Nov. 1852; 2nd *s* of John Langley and Mary, *e d* of Richard Groom; *m* 1902, Vera Kathleen, *d* of Frederick G. Forsyth-Grant of Ecclesgreig, Kincardineshire; one *d*. *Educ:* Exeter Grammar School and privately; St John's College, Cambridge (Scholar). 1st class Natural Sciences Tripos. Lecturer Trinity College, Cambridge, and University Lecturer, 1884–1903. Royal Medallist of Royal Society, 1892; Baly Medal, RCP, 1903; Andreas Retzius Medal, Swedish Soc. Physic., 1912; Mem. Council Royal Society, 1897–98; Vice-Pres. 1904–5; Mem. Council Cambridge Univ., 1898–1900; President Section I Brit. Assoc., 1899; President Neurol. Soc. of Great Britain, 1893; Corr. Mem. Société de Biologie, Paris; Phys. Med. Soc. Florence; Imp. Mil. Acad. of Med., Petrograd; Hon. Mem. Soc. de Neurol. Kasan; KK Gesell. d. Aertze, Vienna; Swedish Society of Physicians; (Gesell.) Deutsch. Nervenärtze; Soc. de Biol., Buenos Aires; and of Amer. Physiol. Soc.; For. Mem. Acad. Roy. de Méd. de Belgique; Kong. Danske Vidensk. Selskab. Copenhagen; R. Accad. d. Lincei, Rome; k. Svenska Vetensk.-Akad., Stockholm; k. Vetensk. Soc. Upsala; Bavarian Acad. Sci. Munich; Member Soc. Belge de Biol., Soc. Roy. de Sci. Med. et Nat. de Bruxelles, and Portuguese Soc. Nat. Sci. *Publications:* Autonomic Nervous System, Pt I, 1921; numerous scientific papers. *Recreations:* gardening, golf, skating. *Address:* Hedgerley Lodge, Cambridge. *T:* Cambridge 445. *M:* ER 1665 and 3011. *Club:* Athenæum.

Died 5 Nov. 1925.

LANGLEY, Walter, RI; painter; *b* Birmingham, 1852; *m* 1896. *Educ:* National School, Birmingham. Served apprenticeship as lithographer, studying art in local School of Art in evenings; obtained National Scholarship and studied at South Kensington 2 years; finally took up painting as profession; settled in Newlyn, Cornwall, 1882; gold medal for painting at Paris and Chicago; painted an autograph portrait, by invitation of the Directorate, for the gallery of the Uffizi, Florence. *Exhibited:* RI (water colours)—Among the Missing; Departure of the Fleet; Disaster; After the Storm, etc; RA (oil paintings)—Never morning wore to evening but some heart did break; Motherless; Bread-winners; Wandering Musicians; Between the Tides, etc.

Died 1922.

LANGLEY, Sir Walter Louis Frederick Goltz, KCMG 1912; CB 1899; Assistant Under-Secretary of State in the Foreign Office since 1907; *b* 22 Feb. 1855; *m* 1894, Gertrude Mary (*d* 1895), *d* of William Ramsay; one *s*. Was private secretary to successive Parliamentary Under Secretaries of State for Foreign Affairs, 1887–98. *Address:* 10 Warwick Square, SW. *Club:* Travellers'.

Died 30 Sept. 1918.

LANGMAN, Sir John Lawrence, 1st Bt, *cr* 1906; *b* 24 June 1846; *s* of late Joseph Langman, Plymouth and London, and Eleanor James, *d* of John Lawrence, Aberdeen; *m* 1868, Mary (*d* 1904), *d* of late James Marks; one *s* (one *d* decd). Equipped and maintained the Langman Field Hospital in South African War, 1900 (despatches, Queen's medal with three clasps); KGStJ. *Heir:* *s* Archibald Lawrence Langman, *b* 2 Sept. 1872. *Address:* 97 Eaton Square, SW1. *T:* Sloane 3233. *Club:* Devonshire. *Died 3 Oct. 1928.*

LANSDELL, Rev. Henry, DD; FRGS, MRAS; *b* Tenterden, 10 Jan. 1841; *e* *s* of Henry and Julia Lansdell; *m* Mary, *d* of Charles Colyer, of Farningham and Greenhithe, Kent. *Educ:* at home; St John's Coll. Highbury. Ordained 1867; curate, Greenwich, 1868; and in charge of St Peter's, Eltham, 1885–86; Reader, St Germans, Blackheath, 1881–82; Lecturer, St James's, Plumstead, 1891; Chaplain of Morden College, Blackheath, 1892–1912; travelled in every country of Europe and Asia, 5 countries of Africa, and across America, 1870–1904; visited 170 foreign mission stations in Europe, Asia and Africa, 1888–90; prospected for missionary purposes, took photographs, and collected specimens of fauna in Russian and Chinese Turkestan. Part owner of about 700 acres. *Publications:* originator and editor Clergyman's Magazine, 1875–86; Through Siberia, 1882; Russian Central Asia, 1885, abridged into Through Central Asia, 1887; Chinese Central Asia, 1893; The Sacred Tenth, 1906; The Tithe in Scripture, 1908; Princess Ælfrida's Charity, Parts i–vii. *Recreation:* literary composition. *Address:* Dimsdale, 4 Pond Road, Blackheath Park, SE3. *TA:* Lansdell, Blackheath. *T:* 1594 Lee Green.

Died 5 Oct. 1919.

LANSDOWNE, 5th Marquess of (GB), *cr* 1784; **Henry Charles Keith Petty-Fitzmaurice,** KG; GCSI 1888; GCMG 1884; GCIE 1888; PC 1895; DCL (Hon. Oxford), LLD; 26th Baron of Kerry and Lixnaw, 1181; Baron of Keith and Nairne, 1681; Earl of Kerry, Viscount Clanmaurice, 1723; Viscount Fitz-Maurice and Baron Dunkeron, 1751; Earl of Shelburne, 1753; Baron Wycombe, 1760; Earl of Wycombe and Viscount Calne, 1784; Trustee of National Gallery since 1894; late Lord-Lieutenant of Wilts; *b* 14 Jan. 1845; *e* *s* of 4th Marquis and Emily Jane Mercer Elphinstone de Flahault, *e* *d* of Comte de Flahault and Baroness Keith and Nairne; *S* father

as Marquess, 1866, mother as Baron Nairne, 1895; *m* 1869, Lady Maud Evelyn Hamilton, CI, GBE, CH, *d* of 1st Duke of Abercorn; one *s* two *d* (and one *s* decd). Lord of Treasury, 1869–72; Under Secretary for War, 1872–74; Under-Secretary for India, 1880; Gov.-Gen. of Canada, 1883–88; Gov.-Gen. of India, 1888–93; Secretary for War, 1895–1900; Foreign Secretary, 1900–5; Minister without Portfolio, 1915–16. *Heir:* *s* Earl of Kerry, *b* 14 Jan. 1872. *Address:* 65 Brook Street, W. *T:* Mayfair 6999; Bowood Park, Calne, Wiltshire; Derreen, Kenmare, Co. Kerry. *Clubs:* Brooks's, Travellers'.

Died 3 June 1927.

LANSING, Robert; Diplomatist and Adviser in International Law; *b* Watertown, NY, 17 Oct. 1864; *s* of John Lansing and Maria L. Dodge; *m* 1890, Eleanor, *d* of John W. Foster (a former Secretary of State). *Educ:* Amherst. LLD Amherst, 1915; Princeton, 1917; Columbia, 1918; University of State of NY, 1919. Admitted to Bar, 1889; Counsel for US Behring Sea Arbitration, 1892–93; Counsel for US Behring Sea Claims Commission, 1896–97; Solicitor for US Alaskan Boundary Tribunal, 1903; Counsel North Atlantic Coast Fisheries Arbitration, 1909–10; Agent of US, American and British Claims Arbitration, 1912–14; Counsellor for Department of State, 1914–15; Secretary of State, USA, 1915–20; Commissioner to Peace Conference at Paris, 1918–19; Counsel for Chile in Tacna-Africa Arbitration, 1923–24. *Publications:* Government, its Origin, Growth and Form in the United States (joint), 1902; The Peace Negotiations, 1921; Notes on Sovereignty, 1921; The Big Four of the Peace Conference, 1921. *Address:* 1323 18th Street, Washington, DC. *Clubs:* Metropolitan, Chevy Chase, Congressional Country, Washington.

Died 30 Oct. 1928.

LANTERI, Edward, RBS; Professor of Sculpture, Royal College of Art, since 1880; *b* Burgundy; naturalised Englishman, 1900. *Educ:* Ecole des Beaux Arts, Paris, under Cavelier, Aimé, Millet and Guillaume. Was assistant to Sir Edgar Boehm for twenty years; Exhibitor at the Royal Academy from 1876. *Principal works:* Bust Portraits: King Edward VII; late Duchess of Leinster; late M Waddington, French Ambassador; Paul Cambon, French Ambassador; Admiral Lord C. Beresford; Sir W. Richmond, RA; Sir Archibald Geikie, OM (Geological Museum); Alfred Stevens (Tate Gallery); Paysan (Musée du Luxembourg, Paris, Tate Gallery, and Preston Museum); *statues:* Omphale, marble acquired by King Edward VII; Peace (Victoria and Albert Museum); Sir Samuel Sadler, Middlesbrough; *statuettes:* Fencing Master; Sir A. Harris; Sir Edgar Boehm, RA; *groups:* The Duet, marble acquired by A. Carnegie; The Fisherman and the Mermaid. *Publication:* Modelling: a Guide for Teachers and Students (3 volumes). *Address:* Royal College of Art, S Kensington, SW. *Died 1917.*

LAPWORTH, Charles, FRS; FGS; LLD, MSc; *b* Farringdon, 1842; *o* *s* of James Lapworth; *m* Janet, *d* of Walter Sanderson, Galashiels; two *s* one *d*. Certificated Teacher, Culham, 1862–63; Galashiels, NB, 1864–75; Madras College, St Andrews, 1875–81; Prof. of Geology and Physiography, Birmingham University, 1881–1913; MSc; Emeritus Professor, 1914; Consulting Geologist on matters of mining and civil engineering—Water Bills of Birmingham, Gloucester, Harrogate, Leicester, etc. Hon. LLD Univ. Aberdeen, 1883; Univ. Glasgow, 1912; Bigsby Medallist (1887) and Wollaston Medallist (1889) of the Geological Society; Royal Medallist Royal Society (1891); Wilde Medallist Manchester Phil. Soc. 1905; President, Section C, Brit. Assoc., 1892; Pres. Geol. Soc., 1902–4; Member of Council Royal Society, 1895–96; Member Royal Coal Commission, 1902–4. *Publications:* scientific papers and memoirs in Geology and Palæontology, dealing mainly with researches among Graptolites and the Lower Palæozoic Rocks; editor Page's Textbooks, Geology and Physical Geography; editor Monograph, British Graptolites, Palæontographical Soc. 1900–8; Intermediate Textbook of Geology, 1899. *Recreations:* field geology, music. *Address:* 38 Calthorpe Road, Edgbaston, Birmingham. *TA:* Geology, Birmingham.

Died 13 March 1920.

LARCOM, Arthur, CB 1904; Senior Clerk in HM Foreign Office; barrister-at-law; *b* 9 Nov. 1847; 4th *s* of Maj.-Gen. Rt Hon. Sir Thomas Aiskew Larcom, 1st Bt; *m* 1884, Sophie (*d* 1913), *d* of Alexander Perceval of Temple House, Co. Sligo. *Educ:* Oriel College, Oxford; MA 1872. Appointed to a Clerkship in the Foreign Office, 1871; Acting 3rd Secretary to the Legation at Tehran, 1875–77; Acting Oriental Secretary, Tehran, 1879–81; Acting 2nd Secretary, Tokio, 1884–87; Senior Clerk and Head of US Dept in FO, 1899; HM Agent before the International Court of Arbitration at The Hague in the matter of the Venezuelan Claims, 1903. *Address:* Villa Miramare, San Remo, Italy. *Clubs:* Travellers', Oxford and Cambridge.

Died 19 March 1924.

LARCOMBE, Thomas, ISO 1903; appointed to the War Office, 1857; retired, 1903; *b* 14 Jan. 1842; *s* of late William Larcombe; *m* 1st, 1876, Elizabeth Ellen (*d* 1903), *e d* of Richard James, 207 Adelaide Road, South Hampstead; 2nd, 1905, Agnes, *y d* of William Adam Oldaker, 54 Ladbroke Road, Holland Park, Kensington. Twice elected head of the poll as Member of Local Board and District Council, Hampton, Middlesex; served as Vice-Chairman of the Council, and Chairman of Finance and Education Committees; elected Trustee of Hampton Charities, and Representative Governor of Hampton Grammar School; for many years President of Hampton (Middlesex) Liberal Association; Member of Northbrook Society. *Recreation:* travel. *Address:* 15 Oakwood Court, Kensington, W. *Club:* National Liberal. *Died 14 Dec. 1916.*

LARDNER, James Carrige Rushe, KC 1921; MP (N) North Monaghan, 1907–18; *b* 1879; *s* of Hugh Lardner, Swan Park, Monaghan; *m* 1920, Rita, *d* Sir Joseph Downes, South Hill; two *s*. *Educ:* St MacCarten's College, Monaghan; Clongoweswood College, Co. Kildare. Barrister, King's Inns, Dublin, and Gray's Inn, London; Bencher, King's Inns, 1924. Director Dublin South Eastern Railway Co.; Member of Committee to consider on Medical Benefits under National Insurance Act (Ireland). *Address:* 22 Ailesbury Road, Dublin. *T:* Ballsbridge 261. *Clubs:* Devonshire; Royal Dublin, Stephen's Green, Dublin. *Died 3 May 1925.*

LARGE, Captain Edwin Ryder, DSO 1917; OBE 1919; RD 1923; FRGS; RNR; *b* 31 Dec. 1878; 3rd *s* of late A. R. Large, Woolston, Hants; *m* Elsa Marguerite, *y d* of late Thomas King, Minister of Education, South Australia; two *s*. *Educ:* Woolston College, Hants. Entered Mercantile Marine, 1893; Younger Brother of Trinity House, 1913; served in Calcutta Naval Volunteers, 1895–96; various periods of service in HM Fleet; served European War, 1914–19; attached to Gallipoli Expedition (1915–16) from First Landing until Final Evacuation (despatches); successful gunnery actions against enemy submarines (DSO, monetary awards); presentation from Admiral Sir Lewis Bayly, Commander-in-Chief, Coast of Ireland; Appreciation of High Commissioner for Australia for services under Australian Government; Appreciation of Lords Commissioners of Admiralty on three occasions; General Service and Mercantile Marine War Medals; Lloyd's Silver Medal for Meritorious Services; Lloyd's Silver Medal for saving life at sea; Royal Humane Society's Bronze Medal for jumping overboard at sea and rescuing a seaman; whilst commanding HMT Karroo, acted as Commodore of Convoys; represented the Mercantile Marine at the Admiralty, on Mercantile Marine Awards Committee, Feb. 1918–Feb. 1919; OBE for services in connection with inquiries into submarine attacks on British merchant vessels. FRCI; Captain RNR 1926. *Address:* 42 Corringham Road, Golders Green, NW11. *T:* Speedwell 2500. *TA:* Rydelar, London. *Clubs:* Cocoa Tree; Royal Bombay Yacht; Sind. *Died 10 Nov. 1928.*

LARIVIÈRE, Hon. Alphonse Alfred Clément; *b* Montreal, 24 July 1842; 3rd *s* of late Abraham C. La-rivière of Montreal, and Adélaide Marcil of Longueuil. *Educ:* St Mary's College, Montreal. Elected President of the Board of Arts and Manufactures for the Province of Quebec, the Institut des Artisans Canadiens, and the Cercle St Pierre of Montreal; President of the Selkirk County Agricultural Society; Superintendent of the Catholic Schools; Joint Secretary of the Board of Education, and a member of the Council of the University of Manitoba; contested St Anne in the Manitoba Legislative Assembly, 1874; elected for St Boniface, 1878, 1879, 1881; Provincial Secretary, 1881; Minister of Agriculture, Statistics and Health, 1883–86; Provincial Treasurership, 1886; elected to represent Provencher in the Dominion House, 1889; three times re-elected; was called to the Senate, 1911. *Address:* St Boniface, Manitoba, Canada. *Died 20 Sept. 1925.*

LARKWORTHY, Falconer, FIB; late Chairman of Ionian Bank, Ltd; Director Commercial Union Assurance Co., Ltd, and Palatine Insurance Co.; *b* Weymouth, 22 March 1833; *s* of Dr Ambrose Larkworthy, Bombay, and Amelia *d* of John Cooke, shipowner, Calcutta; *m* 1st, Mary, *d* of Captain Balston, Cape Town; 2nd, Elizabeth, *d* of J. W. Clover, The Wood, Aylsham, Norfolk; three *s* three *d*. *Educ:* High School, Liverpool. Colonial and international banker; political economist; strong advocate of a new national and international currency and exchange system. Church of England. Commander of the Order of the Saviour (Greece). *Publications:* Ninety-one years, Being the Reminiscences of Falconer Larkworthy (ed Harold Begbie), 1924; numerous papers on Currency and Exchange. *Address:* 35 Belsize Avenue, NW3. *T:* Hampstead 492. *Died 14 May 1928.*

LARNACH, James Walker, JP; *b* 10 June 1849; *e surv. s* of late Donald Larnach of Brambletye, Sussex; *m* 1889, Lady Isabel Lettice Theodosia (*d* 1904), *d* of 9th Earl of Cork; one *d*. *Educ:* Eton; Trinity College, Cambridge (MA). Hon. Major late Suffolk Hussars Yeomanry Cavalry; High Sheriff Oxfordshire, 1904. Won the Derby with Jeddah, 1898. *Address:* Brambletye, Sussex; Lanwades Hall, Suffolk. *Clubs:* Jockey, Turf, Marlborough, Junior Carlton, Windham. *Died 24 Jan. 1919.*

LA ROCQUE, Rt. Rev. Paul, DD, DCL; RC Bishop of Sherbrooke since 1893; *b* Marieville, PQ, 28 Oct. 1846. *Educ:* Collèges Ste Thérèse and St Hyacinthe. Ordained, 1869; Rector Cathedral St Hyacinthe, 1884–93. *Address:* Bishop's House, Sherbrooke, Province of Quebec. *Died Aug. 1926.*

LASCELLES, Rt. Hon. Sir Frank (Cavendish), GCB 1897; GCMG 1892 (KCMG 1886); GCVO 1904; PC 1894; *b* 23 March 1841; 5th *s* of late Rt Hon. William Saunders Sebright Lascelles, MP, and Caroline, *e d* of 6th Earl of Carlisle; *m* 1867, Mary Emma (*d* 1897), *e d* of late Sir Joseph F. Olliffe, MD, Physician to British Embassy, Paris; one *d* (two *s* decd). Entered Diplomatic Service, 1861; 2nd Secretary Diplomatic Service, 1871; Agent and Consul-General, Bulgaria, 1879; Minister, Roumania, 1886; Persia, 1891; Ambassador to Russia, 1894; to Germany, 1895–1908. *Address:* 14 Chester Square, SW1. *T:* Kensington 1287. *Clubs:* Travellers', St James', MCC. *Died 2 Jan. 1920.*

LASCELLES, Hon. Frederick Canning; *b* 8 May 1848; 2nd *s* of 4th Earl of Harewood and 1st wife, Elizabeth Joanna, *e d* of 1st Marquess of Clanricarde; *m* 1878, Frederica Maria (*d* 1891), *d* of late Hon. Sir Adolphus Liddell, KCB; one *s* four *d* (and one *s* decd). Commander RN; retired. *Address:* Sutton Waldron House, Blandford. *Died 31 Dec. 1928.*

LASCELLES, Hon. Gerald William, CB 1914; BA; FZS; Deputy Surveyor, New Forest, 1880–1914; President of Land Agents' Society, 1911; *b* 26 Oct. 1849; 3rd *s* of 4th Earl of Harewood; *m* 1875, Constance Augusta Mary Fitzclarence, *o c* of late J. Burton Phillipson of Bramshaw House, Lyndhurst, Hants, and of Sunninghill, Berks; one *s* one *d* (and two *s* decd). *Educ:* Eton; Magdalene College, Cambridge. *Publications:* Badminton vol. on Falconry; ditto Shooting vol. (part of); Thirty-five Years in the New Forest, 1915; portions of Fur and Feather Series; various articles, mainly on sport. *Recreation:* manager of Old Hawking Club since 1872. *Address:* Tillington House, Petworth. *Clubs:* Carlton, St James', Beefsteak, Authors'. *Died 11 Feb. 1928.*

LASH, Zebulun Aiton, KC; LLD; barrister-at-law; *b* St John's, Newfoundland, 29 Sept. 1846; *s* of William Lash, banker; *m* 1871, Elizabeth Ann, *d* of late Judge Miller of Galt, Ontario; three *s* one *d*. *Educ:* Dundas Ontario Grammar School; University of Toronto. Called to Bar of Ontario, 1868; QC 1879. Lecturer to Law Society, 1872–76; practised law in Toronto, Ontario, till 1876; Deputy of the Minister of Justice of Canada, 1876–82; returned to Toronto; Bencher of Law Society, 1883; re-elected till after 20 years of service became Bencher for life by statute. Hon. LLD, University of Toronto, 1910; Vice-Chairman, Board of Governors of University of Toronto; President, Great North Western Telegraph Co.; Vice-President, Canadian Bank of Commerce; Director and Senior Counsel, Canadian Northern Railway Co.; Vice-President, National Trust Co.; Director, Bell Telephone Co., and other companies. *Publications:* Defence and Foreign Affairs: a suggestion for the Empire; pamphlets and articles on legal subjects. *Recreations:* fishing, shooting, canoeing. *Address:* 59 Admiral Road, Toronto, Canada. *TA:* Lash, Toronto. *T:* Hillcrest 3846. *M:* 1560 and 1561, Ontario, 1917. *Clubs:* York, Toronto, University, Toronto; Rideau, Ottawa; Mount Royal, Montreal. *Died 24 Jan. 1920.*

LASSETTER, Brig.-Gen. Harry Beauchamp, CB 1902; CMG 1917; late Commander 2nd Australian Light Horse Brigade; *b* 19 March 1860; *s* of late F. Lassetter, of Sydney; *m* 1891, Elizabeth Anne, *d* of late J. M. Antill; one *s*. *Educ:* Eton; Cheltenham; RMC, Sandhurst. Joined HM 38th Regt as 2nd Lt 1880; Lt 80th Regt 1881; Captain, 1887; proceeded to NSW, 1888 (with local rank of Major); raised and trained Mounted Rifles in the Colony; Lt-Col, 1894; went to England with detachment Queen Victoria's 60th Jubilee, 1897; commanded the Colonial escort in the Queen's procession; served Nile Expedition (medal with clasp, bronze star); South Africa in command of New South Wales Mounted Rifles, 1902 (despatches, medal and clasp, CB); European War 1915–17 (CMG). *Address:* Sydney, New South Wales. *TA:* Lassetter, Sydney. *Club:* Naval and Military. *Died 17 Feb. 1926.*

LATHAM, Charles; Professor of Mining, University of Glasgow, since 1907; *b* Birkdale, Lancashire, 1868; 2nd *s* of late James Beven Latham; *m* Nellie, 2nd *d* of William White, Nottingham; one *d. Educ:* Wigan High School; Rivington Grammar School; School of Mines, Wigan. Articled to Moss Hall Coal Co., Wigan; Assistant General Manager, Moss Hall Coal Co., 1891–93; Director of Mining, University College, Nottingham, 1893–1902; Dixon Lecturer in Mining, University of Glasgow, 1902–7; Examiner in Mining, University of Manchester, 1908. MInstME. *Publications:* Colliery Winding Machinery; Coal Cutting by Machinery; Detection and Estimation of Inflammable Gases in Mine Air by means of Flame Caps. *Recreations:* golf, cycling, fishing. *Address:* 16 Queensborough Gardens, Glasgow, W. *Club:* College, Glasgow. *Died 27 Sept. 1917.*

LATHAM, Peter Wallwork, MA, MD; FRCP; Consulting Physician Addenbrooke's Hospital, Cambridge (Physician, 1863–99); *b* Wigan, Lancashire, 21 Oct. 1832; *e s* of John Latham, physician; *m* 1st, 1862, Jamima Burns (*d* 1877), *y d* of John M'Diarmid, Dumfries; one *d*; 2nd, 1884, Marianne Frances, *d* of J. F. Bernard, MD, Clifton, and Marianne, *sister* of the brothers Sir Henry Lawrence, KCB and John, 1st Lord Lawrence. *Educ:* Neuwied, Germany; Glasgow University; Caius College, Cambridge (Scholar 1855); St Bartholomew's Hospital, London. 19th Wrangler, 1858; 1st in Natural Sciences Tripos, 1859; with distinction in Chemistry, Physiology, Comp. Anatomy, Botany, and Mineralogy. Fellow of Downing College, 1860; Councillor of the Royal Coll. of Physicians, 1886–87; Censor, 1887–89; Senior Censor, 1894–95; Harveian Orator, 1888; Downing Professor of Medicine, Cambridge, 1874–94; formerly Assistant Physician to the Westminster Hospital. *Publications:* among others: On the Early Symptoms of Phthisis, 1864; On Nervous or Sick Headache, 1873; On the Formation of Uric Acid in Animals, 1884; On Some Points in the Pathology of Rheumatism, Gout, and Diabetes (Croonian Lectures), 1886; The Harveian Oration, 1888; On Blood Changes in Disease; articles in Quain's Dictionary of Medicine. *Address:* 15 Royal York Crescent, Clifton, Bristol. *Clubs:* Royal Societies; Cambridge County. *Died 29 Oct. 1923.*

LATHBURY, Daniel Conner; journalist; *b* 11 April 1831; *m* Bertha, *y d* of late Professor Bonamy Price. *Educ:* King's College, London; Brasenose College, Oxford (MA). President of the Union. Barrister, Lincoln's Inn, but has never practised; joint-editor of The Economist, 1878–81; editor of The Guardian, 1883–99; editor of The Pilot from its foundation to its death, 1900–4. Editor of Correspondence on Church and Religion of W. E. Gladstone, 1910. *Address:* Hascombe, Godalming. *Club:* Athenæum.
Died 14 June 1922.

LATHROP, Rose Hawthorne, (Mother Mary Alphonsa Lathrop); superioress Dominican Community of Third Order, and directress of Charitable Home; *b* Lenox, Mass, 20 May 1851; *d* of Nathaniel Hawthorne; *m* 1871, George Parsons Lathrop, author. Devoted to betterment of cancerous and destitute men and women unable to find care in any existing hospital. Established in 1898 St Rose's Free Home for Cancer, 426 Cherry Street, New York, and in 1901 Rosary Hill Home, Hawthorne, Westchester Co., New York, for country annexe; built new City Home for 90 patients, St Rose's, Corlaer's Park, and Jackson Street, New York, 1912. *Publications:* (poems) Along the Shore; A Story of Courage; Memories of Hawthorne. *Address:* 71 Jackson Street, near Corlaer's Park, New York. *Died 9 July 1926.*

LATIMER, Rev. William Thomas, MA, DD; Senior Minister of Eglish Presbyterian Church, Dungannon, since 1872; *o s* of Rev. John Latimer, Ballynahatty, Omagh, Co. Tyrone; *m* Frances, *d* of Andrew Macbeth, mill-owner, Ballindrait, Strabane; one *s* one *d. Educ:* Queen's College, Belfast (Queen's University). BA; MA Belfast; DD, Belfast and Derry United Theolog. Faculty. *Publications:* The Doctrines of the Plymouth Brethren (seventh edition), 1908; The Life and Times of Rev. H. Cooke, DD, LLD, Belfast, 1888 (new edition, 1899); A History of the Irish Presbyterians, 1893 (second edition, 1902); Popular History of the Irish Presbyterian Church, 1897 (Guild edition, 1897); Ulster Biographies, 1897; Presbyterianism in Omagh, Belfast, 1913; Tom Eccles, the Robber, 1913; many historical articles and reviews in the Journal of the Royal Society of Antiquaries, the Northern Whig, the Witness, Belfast, the Irish Presbyterian, and in other periodicals. *Recreations:* walking, reading, etc. *Address:* Eglish Manse, Dungannon, Co. Tyrone.
Died 19 July 1919.

LA TOUCHE, Sir James John Digges, KCSI 1901 (CSI 1896); Member of Council of India, 1907–14; *b* 16 Dec. 1844; *s* of William Digges La Touche, Dublin; *m* 1873, Julia, *d* of T. W. Rothwell. *Educ:*

Trinity Coll. Dublin. Entered ICS 1867; Lt-Gov. of the United Provinces of Agra and Oudh, 1901–6; retired, 1906.
Died 5 Oct. 1921.

LA TOUCHE, Robert Percy O'Connor, JP of Harristown, Co. Kildare; *b* 12 July 1846; *o s* of John La Touche and Maria, *o d* of Robert Lambart Price of Trengwainton, Cornwall; *m* 1870, Lady Annette Louisa Scott, 2nd *d* of 3rd Earl of Clonmell. *Address:* Harristown, Brannockstown, Co. Kildare. *Clubs:* Marlborough; Kildare Street.
Died 13 March 1921.

LATULIPE, Rt. Rev. E. A.; Bishop of Haileybury since 1915; *b* St Anicet, county of Huntingdon, PQ, 3 Aug. 1859; *s* of Antoine Latulipe and Lucie Bonneville. *Educ:* Montreal College and Grand Seminary, Montreal. Ordained 1885; Professor in Montreal College, 1885; Curate in the Parish of St Henri, 1886–88; Chaplain, Motherhouse of the Sisters of St Ann, 1888–91; Chaplain Provincial Monastery of the Good Shepherd, Montreal, 1891–94; Rector of the Cathedral, Pembroke, Ontario, 1894–1906; Parish Priest at Haileybury, Ontario, 1906–8; Vicar Apostolic of Temiscamingue, 1908–15. *Publications:* Visite pastorale chez les Sauvages du Lac Barrière et du Grand Lac Victoria; Pastoral Letters. *Address:* Haileybury, Ontario. *Died 14 Dec. 1922.*

LATYMER, 5th Baron, *cr* 1341; **Francis Burdett Thomas Coutts-Nevill,** JP; MA, LLM Cambridge; barrister, Inner Temple; [the Barony had been in abeyance 300 years when terminated in his favour; took family name of Coutts-Nevill by Royal Licence, 1914, his heir retaining original name]; *b* 18 Sept. 1852; *s* of late James Drummond Money and Clara Maria Burdett, *d* of late Sir Francis Burdett, 5th Bt; *m* 1875, Edith Ellen, *e d* of late Charles Churchill, Weybridge Park; one *s* four *d. Educ:* Eton; Trinity College, Cambridge. *Publications:* Poems, 1896; The Revelation of St Love the Divine, 1898; The Alhambra, and other poems, 1898; The Mystery of Godliness, 1900; The Poet's Charter, 1903; Musa Verticordia, 1905; The Romance of King Arthur; The Book of Job, 1907; Psyche, 1911; Ventures in Thought, 1914. *Heir:* s Hon. Hugh Burdett Money-Coutts [*b* 13 Aug. 1876; *m* 1900, Hester Frances, 4th *d* of late Maj.-Gen. John Cecil Russell, CVO; three *s* one *d*]. *Address:* 15 Hanover Square, W1. *Died 8 June 1923.*

LAUDER, Charles James, RSW; Member of Royal Institute Fine Arts, Glasgow; *s* of James Thompson Lauder, artist, portrait painter, and Rachael, *d* of Peter Currie, Greenock; *m* 1st, Mary M'Callum, Glasgow; 2nd, Gertrude Annie Ashton, artist, London. *Educ:* village school, Maryhill, Glasgow. Bred to designing; studied art under Heath Wilson, School of Design, Glasgow; Medallist Crystal Palace, 1884; painted much in Venice and in various cities of Italy, France, and Holland; lived 15 years at Richmond on Thames; painted on the Thames from Hampton Court to the Pool; pictures shown in several one-man shows in London and Glasgow. *Publications:* Picturesque London; Hampton Court; Royal Richmond. *Recreations:* reading (mainly history), gardening. *Address:* Asolo, Thorntonhall, Lanarkshire. *T:* Clarkston 205. *Club:* Art, Glasgow.
Died April 1920.

LAUDER, Sir Thomas North Dick-, 9th Bt, *cr* 1688; late Lieutenant 60th Rifles; *b* 28 April 1846; *e s* of Sir John Dick-Lauder, 8th Bt and Lady Anne Dalrymple, 2nd *d* of 9th Earl of Stair; *S* father, 1867. KJStJ. *Heir:* b George William Dalrymple [*b* 4 Sept. 1852; *m* 1882, Jane Emily Clifford, *d* of W. P. Woodward; one *s. Address:* Gorton House, Hawthornden, Edinburgh. *Club:* New, Edinburgh]. *Address:* Fountain Hall, Pencaitland, Haddington; Grange House, Edinburgh. *Clubs:* Army and Navy, Junior Carlton; New, Edinburgh.
Died 19 June 1919.

LAUDERDALE, 13th Earl of, *cr* 1624; **Frederick Henry Maitland,** DL, JP; Baron Maitland, 1590; Viscount Lauderdale, 1616; Viscount Maitland, Baron Thirlestane and Boltoun, 1624; Baronet of Nova Scotia, 1672; Representative Peer for Scotland since 1889; retired Lieutenant-Colonel Bengal Staff Corps, 1886; Lord-Lieutenant of Berwickshire, 1890–1901; *b* 16 Dec. 1840; *s* of Gen. Frederick Colthurst Maitland, *g s* of 4th *s* of 6th Earl and Anne, *d* of Stephen Williams; *S* cousin, 1884; *m* 1st, 1864, Charlotte, *d* of Lt-Col B. W. A. Sleigh, 77th Regt; two *s* one *d* (and one *s* decd); 2nd, 1883, Ada, *d* of Rev. H. T. Simpson, Rector of Adel, Yorkshire; one *d*. Served in 8th and in 4th Hussars, 1861–74; served under Foreign Dept Government of India, 1869–86. Hereditary Royal Standard Bearer for Scotland, 1670 to 1910. *Heir:* s Viscount Maitland, *b* 12 April 1868. *Address:* Lauriston, Hollington Park, St Leonard's-on-Sea. *T:* Hastings 82; Thirlestane Castle, Lauder, Berwickshire. *Clubs:* Carlton, United Service. *Died 1 Sept. 1924.*

LAURIE, Rev. Sir (John Robert Laurie) Emilius, 3rd Bt, *cr* 1834; *b* 16 May 1823; *s* of Sir John Bayley, 2nd Bt; *S* father, 1871; assumed name of Laurie on succeeding to Maxwelton, 1886, under the will of his *great uncle* Sir Robert Laurie; *m* 1855, Marianne Sophia (*d* 1909), *d* of late Edward R. Rice, MP, of Dane Court, Kent; three *s* one *d* (and one *s* decd). *Educ:* Eton; Trinity Coll. Camb. Vicar of Woburn; St John's, Paddington; Rector of St George's, Bloomsbury. *Heir: s* Claude Villiers Emilius Laurie, *b* 25 Nov. 1855. *Address:* Maxwelton House, Thornhill, NB; 14 Hyde Park Street, W. *Club:* National.
Died 3 Dec. 1917.

LAURIE, Ranald Macdonald, DSO 1917; TD, DL; Member of Stock Exchange; Lieutenant-Colonel late commanding 2nd East Anglian Brigade RFA (T); *b* 1869; *s* of R. P. Laurie, CB, MP for Canterbury and Bath, and Amy, *d* of Sir Ranald Martin, CB; *m* 1894, Florence Albreda, *d* of Hon. Greville Vernon; one *s*. *Educ:* Eton; Christ Church, Oxford. Served European War in France, Egypt, and Palestine, 1914–19 (DSO, Order of the Nile 3rd Class, despatches). *Address:* Ford Place, Grays, Essex. *Clubs:* Carlton, United University.
Died 21 Oct. 1927.

LAURIER, Rt. Hon. Sir Wilfrid, GCMG 1897; PC 1897; KC; DCL; LLD; *b* St Lin, Quebec, 20 Nov. 1841; *o c* of late Carolus Laurier, PLS, and Marcelle Martineau; *m* 1868, Zoë, *d* of G. N. R. Lafontaine of Montreal. *Educ:* L'Assomption Coll; M'Gill University; BCL of M'Gill, 1864. Roman Catholic. Barrister, 1864; QC 1880. Entered Parliament 1871; re-elected 1874; member of Federal Assembly, 1874; Minister of Inland Revenue in the Mackenzie Ministry, 1877; defeated at General Election of 1878, but was immediately afterwards elected for Quebec East; was re-elected at the General Elections in 1878, 1882, 1887, 1891, and 1911; Leader of Liberal Party, 1891; Premier of Canada, 1896–1911 (the first French Canadian to hold that post). *Address:* 335 Laurier Avenue, Ottawa. *Clubs:* Rideau, St James's, National, Union, Ottawa.
Died 17 Feb. 1919.

LAVERACK, Frederick Joseph; *b* Leeds, 1871; *s* of George and Elizabeth Laverack; *m* Rose, *e d* of Robert Roberts, Leeds; one *s* two *d*. *Educ:* Ranmoor College, Sheffield; privately. Studied law, but afterwards became a Congregational minister with pastorates in Yorkshire and Fulham; joined the late Sir Arthur Pearson in 1916 and organised The Blinded Soldiers' Children Fund, raising £100,000; reorganised Chaplain's Dept, National Institute for the Blind; Joint Sec. Greater London Fund for the Blind; late Director of Association for the General Welfare of the Blind; very successful in raising large funds for charitable purposes; a well-known organiser and business expert; in much request as a speaker and lecturer. Contested (L) Brixton Nov. 1922; MP (L) Brixton Division of Lambeth, Dec. 1923–Oct. 1924. *Publications:* Life's Asides; These Sayings of Mine; many articles. *Recreations:* reading, chess, motoring. *Address:* Invergordon, 48 Harold Road, Upper Norwood, SE19. *T:* Sydenham 4773. *Club:* National Liberal.
Died 11 April 1928.

LAVERGNE, Hon. Mr Justice Joseph; a Judge of the Court of the King's Bench for the Province of Quebec since 1906; *b* 29 Oct. 1847; *s* of late Louis David Lavergne, JP, and Marie Geneviève Delagrave; *m* 1876, Maria Louise Emilie, *d* of late J. G. Barthe, MP, barrister and writer; one *s* one *d*. *Educ:* St Ann's College, PQ. Admitted at Bar, 1871; practised law for twenty-six years in partnership with Sir Wilfrid Laurier in Arthabaska; was Mayor of town of Arthabaska, and Warden of County of Arthabaska for some years; during same period edited a weekly newspaper, and was a member of Canadian House of Commons, 1887–97, representing the constituency of Drummond and Arthabaska; Judge of Superior Court for district of Ottawa, 1897; Montreal, 1901; King's Bench, 1906. *Publications:* Le Journal d'Arthabaska; L'Union des Cantons de l'Est. *Recreations:* books, billiards, cards. *Address:* Court House, Montreal; 340 Kensington Avenue, Westmount, PQ, Canada. *T:* Westmount 422. *Club:* Rideau, Ottawa.
Died Jan. 1922.

LAVISSE, Ernest; Membre de l'Académie française; Professeur à l'Université de Paris; Directeur de l'Ecole normale supérieure; Directeur de la Revue de Paris; Corresponding Fellow of the British Academy; *né* au Nouvion-en-Thiérache (Aisne), 17 déc. 1842. *Educ:* Paris, au lycée Charlemagne; à l'Ecole normale supérieure. Professeur aux lycées de Nancy, Versailles et Henri IV (Paris), 1865–75; maître de conférences à l'Ecole normale supérieure, 1875–80; Professeur à la Faculté des Lettres de l'Université de Paris. *Publications:* Publications pédagogiques: Questions d'éducation nationale; Etudes et étudiants; Publications historiques: Etudes sur l'histoire de Prusse; la Jeunesse du Grand Frédéric; le Grand Frédéric avant l'avènement; l'Allemagne impériale; Trois Empereurs d'Allemagne; vue générale de l'histoire

de l'Europe; a dirigé en collaboration avec M A. Rambaud la publication d'une grande "Histoire générale"; a dirigé la publication d'une "Histoire de France jusqu'à la Révolution française," et y a écrit deux volumes sur Louis XIV. *Address:* rue de Médicis 51, Paris.
Died 18 Aug. 1922.

LAW, Lt-Col Alfred; Chief Constable of Hertfordshire since 1911; *b* 1871; *y s* of Maj.-Gen. Samuel Crozier Law and Annie Emily Cotgrave, *d* of Col Charles Hogg; *m* 1896, Katherine, *y d* of Edward Rotheram, of Crossdrum, Oldcastle, Co. Meath; one *s* one *d*. *Educ:* Wellington; Sandhurst. Joined 2nd Batt. North Staffordshire Regiment, 1890; Adjutant, North Down Rifles, 1899–1904. Called to Bar, Middle Temple, 1909; rejoined army, April 1915; appointed AA & QMG, South Midland Division. *Address:* The Dell, Hertingfordbury, Herts. *TA:* Hertingfordbury. *T:* Hertford 149.
Died 8 Nov. 1928.

LAW, Rt. Hon. Andrew Bonar, PC 1911; JP Dumbartonshire; LLD Glas.; MP (U) Central Division, Glasgow, since Dec. 1918; Lord Rector, Glasgow University since 1919; *b* New Brunswick, 16 Sept. 1858; *s* of Rev. James Law, MA, of New Brunswick, and Eliza, *d* of William Kidston of Glasgow; *m* 1891, Annie Pitcairn (*d* 1909), *d* of Harrington Robley of Glasgow; two *s* two *d* (and two *s* decd). *Educ:* New Brunswick; Gilbertfield School, Hamilton; High School, Glasgow. MP (U) Blackfriars Div. of Glasgow, 1900–6; MP (U) Dulwich Div. of Camberwell, 1906–10; contested (U) Manchester, NW, 1910; MP (U) Bootle Division, Lancs, 1911–18; Parliamentary Secretary to the Board of Trade, 1902–6; Leader of Opposition in House of Commons, 1911–15; Secretary of State for the Colonies, 1915–16; Chancellor of the Exchequer, 1916–18; Lord Privy Seal, 1919–21 (resigned); Plenipotentiary, Peace Conference, 1919; Leader of the House of Commons, 1916–21 (resigned); Member of the War Cabinet, 1916–19; Leader of Unionist Party, 1911–21 (resigned); Prime Minister and First Lord of the Treasury, 1922–23. Formerly Chairman of Glasgow Iron Trade Association; was a member of William Kidston and Sons, iron merchants, Glasgow, and William Jacks & Co., iron merchants, Glasgow. *Recreations:* golf, chess, tennis. *Address:* 24 Onslow Gardens, SW1.
Died 30 Oct. 1923.

LAW, Sir Archibald Fitzgerald, Kt 1908; Chief Judicial Commissioner, Federated Malay States, since 1906; *b* 1853; *m* 1883, Louisa Alice, *d* of E. P. Squarey, Downton, Wilts. *Educ:* Oriel College, Oxford. Called to Bar, Inner Temple, 1879; Assistant Commissioner, Cyprus, 1880; President of District Court, Famagusta, 1883; Director of Survey and Principal Forest Officer, 1886; MLC, 1887; Queen's Advocate, 1892; Puisne Judge, Straits Settlements, 1893. *Address:* Stourbridge, Wimborne, Dorset. *Club:* Oxford and Cambridge.
Died 26 July 1921.

LAW, Mary; violinist; *b* London 1889; *d* of Edward Gibbon Law. *Educ:* Guildhall School of Music; London; Chicago. Made début, 1900. *Recreation:* riding. *T:* London Wall 5753.
Died 1919.

LAW, Rev. Robert, DD; Professor of New Testament Literature and Exegesis, Knox College, Toronto; *b* 1860; *s* of James Law, farmer, East Mains, Broxburn, West Lothian; *m* Ralphina Melville, *d* of Rev. Robert Brown, Markinch, Fife; five *s* one *d*. *Educ:* Daniel Stewart's College, Edinburgh; Edinburgh and Tübingen Universities; United Presbyterian Theological Hall. Minister of United Presbyterian (and United Free) Church in Mearns, 1885–91; Kilmarnock, 1891–97; Bridge of Allan, 1897–1901; Lauriston Place Edinburgh, 1902–9; Kerr Lecturer, 1905; DD Edinburgh University, 1911. *Publications:* The Tests of Life: a Study of the First Epistle of St John, being the Kerr Lectures for 1909 (third edition, 1914); The Emotions of Jesus, 1914; The Grand Adventure, 1916; various encyclopaedia and magazine articles. *Address:* 70 St Albans Street, Toronto. *T:* North 5732.
Died 7 April 1919.

LAWES, Edward Thornton Hill, MA, BCL; barrister-at-law; Recorder of Salisbury, 1908–18; *b* 1869; *e s* of late Henry Fricker Lawes, barrister-at-law; *m* 1907, Eleanor Stokes, 2nd *d* of late Samuel Sandars of Chalfont Grove, Bucks, and 7 De Vere Gardens, W. *Educ:* Clifton; Corpus Christi Coll., Oxford. Called to Bar, Lincoln's Inn, 1894; Western Circuit, Revising Barrister, 1904. *Publications:* (ed jtly with author) Wills on Evidence, 2nd edn; The Law of Compensation for Industrial Diseases, 1909. *Address:* Ennox Lodge, Hinton Charterhouse, Bath.
Died 13 Oct. 1921.

LAWLESS, Col Hon. Edward; *b* 13 Sept. 1841; *s* of 3rd Baron Cloncurry; *b* and *heir-pres.* of 4th Baron Cloncurry; *m* 1880, Mary

Elizabeth, *d* of late Rev. Benjamin Burton. Formerly Capt. Rifle Brigade; Hon. Col Royal Dublin Fusiliers. *Address:* Bryanstown, Maynooth, Co. Kildare. *Died 24 April 1921.*

LAWRENCE OF KINGSGATE, 1st Baron, *cr* 1923; **Charles Napier Lawrence;** Chairman of North British and Mercantile Insurance Company and Antofagasta and Bolivia Railway; *b* 27 May 1855; 3rd *s* of 1st Baron Lawrence; *m* 1881, Catherine Sumner of New York. *Educ:* Marlborough College. Formerly a merchant; Chairman, London and North-Western Railway, 1921-24; Chairman, London Midland and Scottish Railway, 1923-24; served on Royal Commissions, St Louis Exhibition, and Shipping Bounties and Rebates; Chairman of Royal Commission on Insurance Acts of 1911, 1912, which sat 1924-26. *Heir:* none. *Recreations:* shooting, golf. *Address:* 23 Eaton Square, SW1. *T:* Victoria 441. *Clubs:* Brooks's, Garrick, St James', Athenæum.

Died 17 Dec. 1927 (ext).

LAWRENCE, Hon. (Alfred) Clive, CBE 1918; HM Procurator General and Solicitor to the Treasury since 1923; *b* Oct. 1876; *e s* of 1st Baron Trevethin; *m* 1924, Mildred, *yr d* of late Rev. Edward Parker Dew, Breamore, Hants; one *d*. *Educ:* Haileybury; Trinity Hall, Camb. Barrister, Middle Temple, 1902; S Wales Circuit; Revising Barrister, 1914; Junior Counsel to Ministry of Labour, March 1919; Solicitor to Ministry of Labour, August 1919; Director of Intelligence Branch, Procurator-General's Dept, 1914-19. Officer of the Order of St Maurice and St Lazarus, Italy, 1919. *Recreations:* shooting, fishing, golf. *Address:* 15 Grove End Road, NW8. *Clubs:* Travellers', Garrick.

Died 13 March 1926.

LAWRENCE, Sir Joseph, 1st Bt, *cr* 1918; Kt 1902; JP Co. Surrey; Chairman of Linotype and Machinery Ltd and of International Linotype Ltd; Director of Mergenthaler Linotype Co., New York; Commissioner of Lieutenancy for City of London; Alderman of Surrey County Council; *b* 23 Sept. 1848; *s* of late Philip Lawrence, Zante, Ionian Isles; *m* 1873, Margaret Alice, *d* of late Joseph Jackson, Southport; one *d*. *Educ:* privately; Owens Coll. Manchester. Captain of 40th Lancashire Vols, 1873-78; was one of the principal and earliest pioneers of the Manchester Ship Canal; took an active part in the passage of the Patents Acts 1902-7; Sheriff of City of London, 1900-1. Contested (C) Cardiff, 1900; MP (C) Monmouth Boroughs, 1901-6. Conservative and Imperialist. *Heir:* none. *Address:* Oaklands, Kenley, Surrey. *Clubs:* Carlton, City Carlton, Constitutional.

Died 24 Oct. 1919 (ext).

LAWRENCE, Roger Bernard, KC 1913; Vice-Chancellor of the Co. Palatine of Lancaster, 1919; *s* of late Philip Henry Lawrence, barrister; *m* Clara Mabel, *d* of the Rev. Philip Henry Wicksteed; two *s* two *d*. *Educ:* London University; BA. Barrister, Lincoln's Inn; Bencher, 1919. *Address:* The Beeches, Poplar Road, Oxton, Birkenhead; 9 Cook Street, Liverpool. *Clubs:* Reform, Athenæum, Liverpool; Union, Manchester. *Died 8 Dec. 1925.*

LAWRENCE, Rev. Thomas Joseph, JP; MA, LLD; Hon. Canon of Salisbury, 1919; Rector of Upton Lovel, Wilts, since 1902; *b* Chesterton, near Cambridge, 23 April 1849; *m* Elizabeth Anna, *d* of Edward Ede, JP, of Plymouth; one *s* one *d*. *Educ:* Perse Grammar School, Cambridge; Downing Coll. Camb. (Scholar and prizeman). Whewell Univ. Scholar; Senior Moral Sciences Tripos; Senior Law and History Tripos. Fellow and Tutor of Downing Coll., 1873-76; ordained 1874; Vicar of Tadlow, Cambs, 1877-88; Deputy-Professor of International Law at Camb. 1883-85; Professor of International Law in the Univ. of Chicago, USA, 1892-98; Rector of Nailstone, Leicestershire, 1894; Rector of Girton, Cambs, 1895-1902; Hon. Fellow of Downing College, 1908; Assistant-Chaplain, Chapel Royal, Savoy, 1894-1909; Lecturer on International Law at Royal Naval College, Greenwich, and at Royal Naval War College, Portsmouth, 1884-1909; Preacher before the University of Cambridge on several occasions; Member of the Institut de Droit International; Reader in International Law in the University of Bristol. *Publications:* Disputed Questions in Modern International Law, 1884; Handbook of Public International Law, 1885, 10th edn, revised and brought up to date, 1918; Principles of International Law, 1895, 6th edn, brought up to date, 1915; contributions to History of the Nineteenth Century, 1902, and to King's College Lectures on Colonial Problems, 1913; War and Neutrality in the Far East, 1904; International Problems and Hague Conferences, 1908; Documents Illustrative of International Law, 1914. *Recreation:* gardening. *Address:* Upton Lovel Rectory, Wilts. *Died 16 Aug. 1919.*

LAWRENCE, Maj.-Gen. William Alexander; Indian Army; *b* 5 July 1843; *m* 1884, *d* of G. F. White; one *s*. Entered army, 1861; Maj.-Gen. 1897; retired list, 1902; served Afghan War, 1878-80 (despatches, medal with clasp, brevet Lt-Col). *Address:* 23 Pembroke Gardens, Kensington, W8. *T:* Western 3034.

Died 8 July 1924.

LAWRIE, Allan James, KC 1924; Deputy Chairman County of London Quarter Sessions since 1911; *b* 1873; *e s* of late J. D. Lawrie of Monkrigg, East Lothian; *m* Ethel, *y d* of late Judge Adams; three *s*. *Educ:* Fettes College, Edinburgh; Trinity College, Oxford. Called to Bar, Lincoln's Inn, 1899; contested (L) Holderness Division, Yorkshire, 1900; Treasury Counsel, Middlesex Sessions, 1908. *Recreations:* shooting, fishing, golf. *Address:* 36 Scarsdale Villas, W8. *T:* Western 1681; Sessions House, Newington, SE. *Clubs:* Brooks's, National Liberal, Eighty, Public Schools.

Died 1 Feb. 1926.

LAWS, Rev. George Edward; Vicar of Congresbury, Somerset; Hon. Canon of Bristol. Deacon, 1879; Priest, 1880; Curate, St John, Upper Holloway, 1879; St Matthew, Luton, 1882-83; Emmanuel, Clifton, 1884-87; Vicar of St Clement's, Bristol, 1887-1905; St Peter, Bristol, 1905. *Address:* The Vicarage, Congresbury, Somerset.

Died Dec. 1923.

LAWSON, Abercrombie Anstruther, DSc; FRSE; FLS; Professor of Botany, University of Sydney, since 1912; 4th *s* of late William Lawson, Fife, Scotland. *Educ:* University of Glasgow; Bonn. Travelled in Europe, 1906-7; student at Bonn, 1906; Lecturer in Botany, Glasgow University, 1907-12. *Publications:* Memoirs; On the Morphology of the Gymnosperms and Cytology. *Recreations:* golf, mountain climbing, travelling. *Address:* The University, Sydney, NSW. *Club:* Australian, Sydney.

Died 26 March 1927.

LAWSON, Alexander; Professor of English Literature at St Andrews, 1897-1920; *b* Lowvalleyfield, Culross, 18 Sept. 1852; *o s* of late Alexander Lawson and Catharine MacQuarrie. *Educ:* Geddes School, Culross; Univs of St Andrews and Heidelberg. MA with 1st class Honours in Philosophy, 1874; Tyndall-Bruce Scholar, 1874; Ramsay Scholar, 1875; BD 1877; Assistant to Professor Thomas Spencer Baynes, LLD, during session 1876-77. Assistant Clergyman successively in St Michael's, Dumfries, and Maxwell Parish, Glasgow; ordained Collegiate Minister of Elgin, 1882; Examiner in English and Philosophy in University of St Andrews, 1886-89; Chairman of Elgin Parochial Board, 1889-93; presented to Parish of Deer, Aberdeenshire, by Presbytery of Deer and inducted 1898; Dean of the Faculty of Arts, St Andrews, 1902-7. Hon. DD of Edinburgh Univ. 1905. *Publications:* Letters on Golf, 1889; A Book of the Parish of Deer, 1896; Poems of Alexander Hume, edited for Scottish Text Society, 1902; Kingis Quair, 1910; edited a St Andrew's Treasury of Scottish Verse, 1920; literary articles in various journals, 1888-97. *Recreations:* golf, bridge, piquet. *Address:* 4 Gillespie Terrace, St Andrews, NB. *Club:* Scottish Conservative, Edinburgh.

Died 22 Jan. 1921.

LAWSON, Rev. Frederick Pike; Hon. Canon of Peterborough. *Address:* Sudborough Rectory, Thrapston.

Died 3 Nov. 1920.

LAWSON, Major Frederick Washington, DSO 1918; Engineer for Metropolitan Water Supply and Sewerage, Perth, Western Australia; *b* Launceston, Tasmania, 12 June 1869; *m* 1892, Christina Vernon; three *s* one *d*. *Educ:* public schools, Victoria. Served articles Mechanical Engineering with J. Buncle & Sons, Melbourne; entered Public Service of NSW, 1892; attached to Water Supply, Drainage, and Irrigation Branch of Public Works Dept; transferred to Public Works Dept, Western Australia; engaged on water supply and drainage works. Served with Australian Engineers in France (promoted Major, despatches, DSO). MICE; MInstME; MRSanI; Vice-President Inst. Engineers Aust.; Member Faculty Engrng, WA University. *Publications:* technical papers, Institute of Engineers, Australia. *Recreations:* interested in all sports. *Address:* King's Park, Perth, Western Australia. *T:* 4556. *Clubs:* Naval and Military, Masonic, Perth.

Died 17 Nov. 1924.

LAWSON, Henry Hertzberg; *b* near Grenfell, New South Wales, 17 June 1867; *s* of Peter Hertzberg Larsen, a Norwegian, and Louisa Albury, of New South Wales. Went to London, 1900; returned to Sydney, 1903; contributed verse and prose to the Bulletin. *Publications:* Short Stories in Prose and Verse, 1895; In the Days when the World was Wide, and Other Verse, 1896; While the Billy Boils, 1898; Verses, Popular and Humorous, 1900; The Country I Come From, 1901; Joe Wilson and His Mates, 1901; Children of the Bush, 1902; On

the Track and Over the Sliprails; When I Was King and Other Verses, 1905; The Rising of the Court; The Skyline Riders, and other works.
Died 3 Sept 1922.

LAWSON, H. S., MA Cantab; Headmaster of Buxton College; temporary Second Lieutenant RFA (T); *b* Weston-in-Gordano, Somerset, 19 Oct. 1876; *s* of late Rev. Robert Lawson of Camerton, Somerset, and *d* of late John Mason Neale; *m* 1908, J. K., *d* of late O. J. Trinder of Tadorne, Surrey; two *s* one *d*. *Educ*: Haileybury; Peterhouse, Cambridge. Ministry of Education, Cairo; Wellington College, Berks; Wolverhampton Grammar School; Tutor to sons of Earl of Morton. *Recreations*: cricket, football, golf. *Address*: Buxton College, Derbyshire. *T*: Buxton 122. *M*: LD 6271. *Club*: New Oxford and Cambridge.
Died 5 Feb. 1918.

LAWSON, Sir John Grant, 1st Bt, *cr* 1905; JP and DL; *b* Yorkshire, 28 July 1856; 2nd *s* of late Andrew Lawson, Aldborough, Yorkshire, and Isabella, *d* of John Grant, Nuttall Hall, Lancashire; *m* 1902, Sylvia, *y d* of Charles Hunter, Selaby Hall, near Darlington; two *s* one *d*. *Educ*: Harrow; Christ Church, Oxford (MA). MP (C) Thirsk and Malton Division, York, 1892-1906. Parliamentary Charity Commissioner, 1895-1900; Secretary of Local Government Board, 1900-5; Chairman of Ways and Means and Deputy Speaker, 1905. *Recreation*: hunting. *Heir*: *s* Peter Grant Lawson, *b* 28 July 1903. *Address*: Middlethorpe Lodge, York; Nuttall Hall, Lancashire. *Clubs*: Carlton; Yorkshire, York.
Died 27 May 1919.

LAWSON, Thomas William; banker and broker, yachtsman, author, farmer; *b* Charlestown, Mass, 26 Feb. 1857; *s* of Thomas Lawson and Anna Maria Loring; *m* 1878, Jeannie Augusta Goodwillie. *Educ*: public schools, Cambridge, Mass. In business as Banker and Broker. *Publications*: The Krank, 1887; History of the Republican Party, 1888; Secrets of Success, 1888; Collection of Poems and Short Stories from Magazines, 1888; Lawson History of the America Cup, 1902; Frenzied Finance, 1905; Friday the Thirteenth, 1907.
Died 7 Feb. 1925.

LAWSON, Victor F.; newspaper editor and publisher; *b* Chicago, 9 Sept. 1850. *Educ*: Phillip's Academy, Andover, Mass. Took charge of his father's interest in a printing establishment, 1872; bought Chicago Daily News, 1876; started morning edition, 1881; sole proprietor, 1888; changed name of morning issue to the Chicago Record (later Chicago Herald and Examiner); ex-President of the Associated Press; established Daily News Fresh-Air Fund, which maintained the Lincoln Park Sanatorium for sick poor children; inaugurated popular movement for establishment of Postal Savings Banks in America. Hon. Doctor of Laws, University of Michigan, 1923, and Columbia University, New York, 1924. *Address*: 15 North Wells Street, Chicago. *Clubs*: Royal Automobile; Commercial, Chicago, University, Union League, Mid-day, Chicago Athletic, Press, Onwentsia, South Shore Country, Saddle and Cycle, Wayfarers, Chicago; Century, New York.
Died 19 Aug. 1925.

LAYARD, George Somes; author and reviewer; *b* 4 Feb. 1857; *s* of Rev. C. C. Layard; *m* Eleanor Byng, *d* of Thomas Gribble; one *s* one *d*. *Educ*: Harrow; Trinity Coll., Camb. BA Cambridge. Barrister-at-law; Western Circuit; member of the Inner Temple; one of the Malvern Hills Conservators, 1900-2; inventor of a system for the federation of private libraries, and originator (in the Nineteenth Century) of a scheme which had its development in the London distributing kitchens. *Publications*: Charles Keene; Mrs Lynn Linton; Portraits of Cruikshank, by himself; Tennyson and his Pre-Raphaelite Illustrators; His Golf Madness, and other Queer Stories; Society Straws; The Gentle Art of Booklending (privately printed); Dolly's Governess; Kate Greenaway (with M. H. Spielmann); Sir Thomas Lawrence's Letterbag; Suppressed Plates, 1907; A Great Punch Editor (Shirley Brooks), 1907; Wax: a novel, 1909; Peter Layard: a memoir (privately printed), 1919; Pierre Lombart's Headless Horseman, 1922; contributor to Dictionary of National Biography and Times Supplement of Encyclopædia Britannica. *Recreations*: book-hunting, print-collecting, croquet. *Address*: 5 Pelham Place, SW7. *T*: Kensington 6894.
Died 30 May 1925.

LAZIER, Stephen Franklin, KC; MA, LLB; head of firm of Lazier and Lazier, Barristers, Hamilton, Ont; *b* Picton, Prince Edward Co., Ont, Canada, 1 July 1841; *s* of Benjamin Franklin Lazier and Leonora Clark; *m* Alice Maude Mary Lister of Hamilton, Ontario, Canada; two *s* two *d*. *Educ*: Dundas Grammar School; University of Victoria College, Ontario. Ex-President Ontario Bar Association; President Hamilton Law Association; for over 25 years School Trustee of Hamilton Board of Education; for 23 years Recording Steward of

Hamilton Centenary Methodist Church; four times Delegate to Methodist General Conference; Trustee for 35 years of Centenary Methodist Church; Ex-President Hamilton Branch of Bible Society; Ex-Chairman Board of Education, Hamilton; Ex-President Hamilton Young Men's Christian Association. *Recreations*: travelling, motoring. *Address*: 131 Charles Street, Hamilton, Ontario, Canada. *T*: 520 Hamilton, Ontario. *M*: 33534. *Club*: Hamilton, Hamilton.
Died Sept. 1916.

LEA, Hugh Cecil; newspaper proprietor; *b* 27 May 1869; *s* of Carl Adolph Lea and Elizabeth Maria, *d* of late Thos Matthews. *Educ*: Boulogne; Reims; Munich. MP (L) E St Pancras, 1906-10. Member, LCC, 1910-13. *Address*: 14 Grafton Street, Bond Street, W1. *Club*: Reform.
Died 29 Jan. 1926.

LEA, Col Samuel Job, CB 1899; retired pay; *b* Hoylake, Cheshire, 13 July 1851; *s* of Rev. J. Lea, Vicar of Shocklach, Cheshire, and Jane Bell, Perth; *m* 1872, Annie (*d* 1912), *d* of T. Parker of Aldford, Cheshire. *Educ*: private schools. Entered army, 1872; Lt-Col, 1890; served in Egypt, 1882; Nile Expedition, 1884-85; Soudan, 1885-86; (Egypt), medal with clasp, 4th class Medjidie and Khedive's star; (Nile), two clasps; DAAG Ireland, 1897-1900; special service South Africa, 1900-1 (despatches, Queen's medal, 2 clasps). Decorated for service abroad. *Recreations*: hunting, shooting, fishing. *Address*: 20 Beach Road, Fairbourne, N Wales.
Died 29 June 1919.

LEACH, Charles, DD; MP (L) Colne Valley, West Riding of Yorkshire, 1910-16; *b* in a Yorkshire village, near Halifax, 1 March 1847; *m* 1867, Mary Jane, *y d* of Charles Fox. *Educ*: private tutors; Ranmoor Theological College, Sheffield. Trained and educated for the Non-conformist ministry; carried on his ministry at Sheffield, Birmingham, Manchester, and London; founded the Queen's Park College and Institute in West London, subseq. carried on by the London County Council; wrote a large number of books and stories; travelled on the Continent, in Syria, Turkey, Canada, and America, and made nine visits to Palestine and Egypt; recognised as one of the founders of the Sunday afternoon movement; retired from the Pastorate and became a Parliamentary candidate; one of the founders and later Vice-Chairman of the Abstainers and General Insurance Co., Ltd. *Publications*: Is my Bible True; Sunday afternoons with Working Men; How I reached the Masses; Bethesda Chapel; The Romance of the Holy Land, etc. *Recreations*: cycling, story writing. *Address*: Springfield, Canonbury Park South, N.

Died 24 Nov. 1919.

LEACH, Maj.-Gen. Sir Edmund, KCB 1907 (CB 1885); Colonel Queen's Own Regiment, 1904-21; *b* 28 Nov. 1836; 6th *s* of late Henry Leach of Corston, Pembroke; *m* 1869, Frances Elizabeth, 2nd *d* of late W. H. Ince; two *s*. *Educ*: Sandhurst. Entered Queen's Own Regiment, 1854; Captain, 1864; Major, 1866; Lt-Col, 1872; Lt-Col commanding 1st Batt. Queen's Own (Royal West Kent) Regt, 1883; Col 1884; Maj.-Gen. 1894; retired 1898; served Crimea, 1855-56; New Zealand War, 1863-66 (despatches thrice, medal, Bt Major); Egyptian War, 1882 (medal, 4th class Osmanie, Khedive's star); Nile Expedition, 1885 (despatches, CB); was AAG Eastern District, 1886-91; commanded troops Barbados, 1894-95. *Address*: 27 Thurloe Square, SW.
Died 7 Aug. 1923.

LEACH, Frederick, ISO 1902; *b* 28 July 1843; *s* of late Henry Leach, JP, DL, of Corston, Pembrokeshire; unmarried. Late Senior Clerk, War Office. *Address*: The Holt, Lindfield, Hayward's Heath; 7 Stanford Road, Kensington Court, W.
Died 27 Feb. 1916.

LEACH, Rev. Henry, MA; Hon. Canon, Gloucester, 1897; *m* Lucy (*d* 1913), *o d* of late William Peel, Ackworth Park, Yorks. *Educ*: Emmanuel College, Cambridge. Master Ipswich Grammar School, 1853-58; Curator of St Thomas's, Portman Square, 1858-63; Vicar of All Saints, Horton, Bradford, 1864-76; Framfield, Sussex, 1876-83; St Peter's, Kensington, 1883-86; Rector of Ash Church, Gloucester, 1886-98; Vicar of Staunton-on-Arrow, Herefords, 1900-3. *Address*: Southover, East Grinstead, Sussex.
Died 4 June 1921.

LEACH, Sir John, KCVO 1904; *b* 3 May 1848; *s* of late Thomas Leach, Seaford Lodge, Ryde, Isle of Wight; *m* 1st, 1878, Agnes Jane (*d* 1921), *d* of late Henry Beck of Herne Bay, Kent; 2nd, 1923, Marian, *d* of late Francis Norvall. *Educ*: Royal Military Academy. Commissioned Royal Artillery 1869; served in Afghan Campaign, 1879, and Bazaar Valley Expedition (medal); Major, RHA, 1890; Lt-Colonel, RHA, 1896; Col on the Staff RA (Brigadier-General) Bengal, 1900-4; Maj.-Gen., 1904; appointed to command Coast Defences, Plymouth, 1905. *Club*: Naval and Military.
Died 2 Jan. 1927.

LEACH, Rear-Adm. Robert Owen; *b* 1832; *m* 1869, Mary, *d* of late Captain William Donaldson Davies. Entered Navy, 1846; Lieut 1854; Commander, 1863; Captain, 1869; retired, 1873; Rear-Adm., 1886; served Baltic (medal); New Zealand (medal). *Address:* Conway House, Charlton Kings, Cheltenham.

Died 21 Dec. 1920.

LEACHMAN, Col Gerard Evelyn, CIE 1916; DSO 1918; Royal Sussex Regiment; Political Officer, Ramadi, Mesopotamia; *b* 27 July 1880; *s* of Dr Leachman, Fairley, Petersfield. *Educ:* Charterhouse. Entered army, 1900; Capt. 1910; Major, 1915; served S Africa, 1899–1902 (despatches, Queen's medal 4 clasps, King's medal 2 clasps); European War (Mesopotamia), 1914–17 (Bt Lt-Col, CIE, DSO). Gill Medal, RGS, 1911, for travels in NE Arabia; Macgregor Medal for Exploration, 1910. *Club:* United Service.

Died 12 Aug. 1920.

LEAF, Walter, LittD, DLitt; Chairman, Westminster Bank; Fellow of London University; Member of the LCC (E Marylebone), 1901–4; *b* Norwood, 28 Nov. 1852; *e s* of Charles John Leaf, FLS, FSA, and Isabella Ellen, *d* of late John Tyas of The Times; *m* 1894, Charlotte Mary, *d* of late J. A. Symonds; one *s* one *d*. *Educ:* Harrow; Trinity College, Cambridge (Minor Scholar, 1869; Scholar, 1871; Fellow, 1875; Hon. Fellow, 1920); Craven Univ. Scholar, 1873; BA, Senior Classic (bracketed), 1874; MA, 1877; LittD, 1888; DLitt (Oxford), 1904. Entered firm of Leaf, Sons & Co., 1877; Chairman Leaf & Co. Ltd, 1888–92; one of founders and first Members and Vice-President of London Chamber of Commerce; Deputy Chairman, 1885–86; Chairman, 1887; Deputy Chairman Committee of London Clearing Banks, 1917; Chairman, 1918–19; President of the Inst. of Bankers, 1919–21; Member of Council and Chairman of British National Committee, International Chamber of Commerce; President of the Chamber, 1925–26. President of Hellenic Society, 1914–19; Pres. of the Classical Association, 1921. Vice-President Alpine Club, 1902-3-5. *Publications:* The Story of Achilles (with J. H. Pratt), 1880; The Iliad of Homer trans. into English Prose (with A. Lang and E. J. Myers), 1882; The Iliad, ed with English Notes and Introduction, 1886–88, 2nd edn 1900–2; Companion to the Iliad, 1892; A Modern Priestess of Isis (trans. from Russian), 1894; Versions from Hafiz, an Essay in Persian Metre, 1898; Troy, a study in Homeric Geography, 1912; Homer and History, 1915; Little Poems from the Greek, 1922; Strabo on the Troad, 1923; numerous papers in Jl of Philology, Hellenic Studies, Geographical Jl, etc. *Recreations:* mountaineering, cycling, photography, travelling, skating, motoring. *Address:* 6 Sussex Place, Regent's Park, NW1. *T:* Paddington 3270. *Clubs:* Athenæum, Alpine, Skating. *Died 8 March 1927.*

LEAH, Samuel Dawson, ISO 1904; Chief-Inspector of Excise, Inland Revenue Department, 1902; retired 1906; *b* 30 Jan. 1844; *y s* of late Edward Leah, Wellington, Salop; *m* 1884; one *s* one *d*. *Educ:* Admaston, Salop; High Ercal Grammar School, Salop. Entered Inland Revenue Department, 1869; Assistant Chief Inspector of Excise, 1898. *Recreation:* literature. *Address:* 18 Applegarth Road, Brook Green, W.

Died 2 May 1916.

LEAHY, Arthur Herbert; Emeritus Professor of Mathematics, University of Sheffield; *b* Corfu, 25 May 1857; *e s* of late Col Arthur Leahy, RE, Flesk, Killarney, and Harriet, *d* of B. M. Tabuteau, Dublin; *m* 1913, Margaret, *o d* of W. J. Chichele Nourse; one *s* one *d*. *Educ:* Temple Grove; Uppingham; Trinity College, Dublin; Pembroke College, Cambridge. BA as 9th Wrangler, and 3rd class Class. Tripos, 1881; MA 1884. Instructor, RMA, Woolwich, 1882–83; Mathematical Master, Bradfield College, 1883–85; Fellow of Pembroke College, 1887; Bursar, 1888–92; Mathematical Lecturer, 1887–92; Professor of Mathematics in the University of Sheffield, and in Firth College, Sheffield, 1892–1922; Dean of Faculty of Pure Science, 1905–11, Dean of the Faculty of Arts, 1919–22; Public Orator, 1912–22. President of Sheffield Literary and Philosophical Society, 1909; Vice-President Section A, British Association, 1910. *Publications:* papers on oscillatory actions in ether, on functions connected with spherical harmonics, and other mathematical subjects; The Courtship of Ferb, 1902; Heroic Romances of Ireland, 1905. *Recreation:* Ancient Irish Literature. *Address:* Flesk, 3 Goda Road, Littlehampton, Sussex. *Died 16 May 1928.*

LEAN, Maj.-Gen. Kenneth Edward, CB 1911; *b* 28 May 1859; *s* of late James Lean, BCS; *m* 1887, Nina, *d* of Captain G. Quin, late 79th Highlanders. *Educ:* Clifton College. Entered Army, 1879; Captain, 1887; Major, 1897; Lt-Col 1904; Col 1908; Brig.-Gen. 1912; served S Africa, 1879–81 (medal with clasp); Burma, 1885–86 (medal with clasp); commanded 5th Mounted Infantry and Independent Mobile Column, South Africa, 1899–1902; present at actions of

Belmont, Grasspan, Modder River, Majesfontein, Johannesburg, Diamond Hill, Wittebergen, and Bothaville (despatches, Brevet Lt Col, Queen's medal 5 clasps, King's medal 2 clasps); European War, 1914–18. *Address:* Fairfield, Walmer, Kent. *Club:* United Service.

Died 13 Nov. 1921.

LEANE, Col Edwin Thomas, CBE; VD; *b* Prospect, South Australia, 25 Aug. 1867; *s* of T. J. Leane; *m* Katie Mary, *d* of James Machin, Adelaide, SA; three *s* three *d*. *Educ:* public school, North Adelaide. Joined S Australian Militia Garrison Artillery, 1888; commissioned 3rd Regiment (Infantry), 1890; served S African War, 1899–190.. (King's medal 2 clasps, Queen's medal 3 clasps, despatches); at outbreak of European War joined 12th Batt. AIF with rank of Captain; Major 1915; Dep. ADOS 2nd Australian Division, 1915–16; Lt-Colonel 1916; ADOS, AIF Headquarters, London, 1916–17; ADO. Australian Army Corps, 1917–18; ADOS, AIF, France, and CC Australian Army Ordnance Corps and temp. Col, 1918; Col, 1918 proceeded to London as Director of Ordnance Services Repatriation and Demobilisation Dept AIF, 1918; returned to Australia Nov. 191.. (CBE, Belgian Croix de Guerre, VD, despatches 6 times) Administrator and Chief Magistrate, Norfolk Island, 1924–26; Deput.. Administrator, Northern Territory, Feb–May 1925. *Recreations:* rifl.. shooting, horticulture. *Clubs:* Imperial Service, Sydney; Naval an.. Military, Royal Automobile, Stock Exchange, Melbourne.

Died Aug. 1928

LE BAS, Sir Hedley Francis, Kt 1916; Governing Director, Caxto.. Publishing Co. Ltd; *b* Jersey, 19 May 1868; *s* of late Capt. T. A. L.. Bas; *m* 1900, Mary, *d* of Joseph Barnes, Dorchester; one *s* one *d*. *Edu..* Jersey. At 18 years of age enlisted in the 15th Hussars, in whic.. regiment he served seven years in the ranks. Founded the Caxto.. Publishing Co., 1899. KGStJ 1910. Joint Hon. Secretary Prince o.. Wales' Fund; Member of National War Savings Committee; Hon.. Treasurer English Golf Union; Hon. Organiser Lord Kitchene.. National Memorial Fund. *Publication:* (ed) Lord Kitchener Memoria.. Book. *Recreations:* golf, swimming (Royal Humane Society Awar.. for saving life). *Address:* Chussex, Walton Heath, Tadworth. *Club..* Reform, Aldwych; Walton Heath Golf.

Died 25 March 1926

LE BLANC, His Honour Sir Pierre Evariste, KCMG 1916; KC.. 1893; Lieutenant-Governor of Quebec since 1915; *b* 10 Aug. 1854.. *y s* of late Joseph Le Blanc of St Martin and late Adèle Bélanger o.. Ste Thérèse; *m* 1886, Hermine, *d* of late Théodose Beaudry and lat.. Catherine Vallée of Montreal; one *s* two *d*. *Educ:* Jacques-Cartie.. Normal School; McGill University, Montreal. Called to Bar a.. Montreal, 1879. A member of the Quebec Legislature, 1882–1908.. Speaker of the Legislative Assembly, 1892–97; Leader of the.. Opposition, 1904–8. LLD Laval University, 1915. *Address:* Montreal.. Spencer Wood, Quebec. *Clubs:* St James, Mount-Royal, Montrea.. Hunt, Jockey, Montreal; Garrison, Quebec.

Died 20 Oct. 1918

LEBOUR, George Alexander Louis, MA, DSc; FGS; Professor o.. Geology since 1879 and Vice-Principal since 1902, Armstrong.. College (formerly Durham College of Science), Newcastle upo.. Tyne; *b* 1847; *s* of Alexander Lebour, artist; *m* Emily, *d* of Dr W.. Hodding of London. *Educ:* Royal School of Mines. On H.. Geological Survey, 1867–73; Lecturer in Geological Surveying i.. Durham College of Science, 1873–79; Murchison Medallist of th.. Geological Society, 1904; Member of several Research Committee.. of the British Association; Sub-editor for Foreign Geology of th.. Geological Record, 1874–80. *Publications:* Geology o.. Northumberland and Durham, 3 editions, 1878–89; Geological Ma.. of Northumberland, 1877; more than 100 papers on Carboniferou.. Geology, Heat-conductivity of Rocks, Underground Temperature.. and many reviews on scientific subjects; Geology of Durham i.. Victoria County History, etc; papers on relations between Publi.. Health and Geology; Reports on Foreign and British Coal-fields.. *Address:* Armstrong College, Newcastle upon Tyne; Radcliffe House.. Corbridge-on-Tyne. *Died 7 Feb. 1918*

LE BRAZ, Anatole; Professor of French Literature, University o.. Rennes; Officier Légion d'Honneur; Docteur ès Lettres; *b* Duault.. Côtes-du-Nord, 2 April 1859. *Educ:* Lycée St Louis; Faculté de.. Lettres de Paris. Professor of Philosophy, College of Etampes.. 1884–86; Professor Lycée of Quimper, 1886–1900; Lecturer a.. Harvard, 1906; United States and Canada, 1907, 1912, and 1915.. *Publications:* Soniou Breiz-Izel; La Chanson de la Bretagne, 1892.. Pâques d'Islande; Le Sang de la Sirène; Le Gardien du Feu; La Terr.. du Passé; Au Pays des Pardons; La Légende de la mort chez les Bretons.. armoricains; Vieilles Histoires du pays Breton; Le Théâtre celtique..

Les contes du soleil et de la brume; Au Pays d'exil de Chateaubriand; Ames d'Occident. *Address:* 12 Rue José-Maria de Heredia, Paris, VIIᵉ.
Died March 1926.

E BRETON, Clement Martin, OBE 1918; KC 1904; Recorder of Sudbury, 1918; barrister-at-law, South Eastern Circuit; *b* 1852; 2nd surv. *s* of late Very Rev. William Corbet le Breton, MA, Dean of Jersey. *Educ:* Victoria Coll., Jersey; Royal Military Coll. Jersey; Royal Military Coll. Sandhurst. Honours, Ensign, Northumberland Fusiliers, 1870; Lt 1871; retired, 1874. Barrister, Inner Temple, 1879; Military Services (Civil Liabilities) Commissioner, 1916; Arbitrator in Industrial Disputes for Ministry of Labour, 1917; Chairman Shirt-making and Tailoring Trade Boards, 1918; *Address:* 1 Harcourt Buildings, Temple, EC; 19 Half Moon Street, W. *Clubs:* Orleans, Reform.
Died 1 July 1927.

ECK, David Calder, KC 1912; Barrister, Middle Temple; *b* 1857; 2nd *s* of late Rev. Alexander Leck, Kilmacolm, Renfrewshire; *m*; two *s*. *Educ:* Glasgow University, LLB. *Address:* 5 Paper Buildings, Temple, EC4; Ravenshoe, Burgh Heath. *T:* Burgh Heath 230.
Died 18 March 1927.

ECKY, Col Frederic Beauchamp, DSO 1900; retired; late Royal Horse Artillery; *b* 11 Oct. 1858; *s* of John Frederick Lecky, DL, of Ballykealey, Tullow, Co. Carlow, Ireland; unmarried. *Educ:* Uppingham School; RMA, Woolwich. Entered Royal Artillery, 1878; Captain, 1886; Major, 1896; served in Egyptian Expedition, 1882; present at Battle of Tel-el-Kebir (medal and clasp and bronze star); South Africa, 1900–1 (despatches, Queen's medal 6 clasps, King's medal 2 clasps, DSO). *Club:* Naval and Military.
Died 15 Nov. 1928.

ECOCQ, Charles; composer; *b* Paris, 3 June 1832. *Educ:* Conservatoire national de musique. Officier de la Légion d'Honneur; membre de la société des Auteurs et Compositeurs dramatiques; membre de la société des Artistes musiciens. Works, operettas: Fleur de Thé, 1868; les Cent vierges, 1871; La Fille de Mme Angot, 1872; Giroflé, Girofla, 1874; le Petit Duc, 1878; le Jour et la Nuit, 1881; le Cœur et la Main, 1882; Plutus, 1886; Ali-Baba, 1887; le Cygne, 1899; Yetta, 1903. *Address:* 28 rue de Surène, Paris.
Died Oct. 1918.

EDGER, Edward; proprietor and editor of The Era; retired, 1905. *Educ:* Collegiate and Commercial School, Denmark Hill, Surrey. *Recreation:* collector of armour, antique marquetry, old silver and oak furniture, old delft, oriental china, and bric-à-brac. *Address:* The Three Gables, Fitz-John's Avenue, NW3. *T:* Hampstead 441; Villa Plage, Royal Parade, Eastbourne.
Died 24 Sept. 1921.

EDLIE, James Crawford, OBE 1918; MA, BCL; barrister-at-law; Deputy-Clerk of the Privy Council, 1909–21; *b* 29 April 1860; *o* surv. *s* of late Alexander Holmes Ledlie, of Calcutta. *Educ:* Heidelberg University; Lincoln College, Oxford. 1st Class Lit. Hum., 1884; Taylorian Scholar (German), 1883. Entered the Judicial Department of the Privy Council Office, 1893; Chief Clerk of the Judicial Department, 1902–9. *Publication:* (trans.) Sohm's Institutes of Roman Law. *Address:* Verney House, Kilternan, Co. Dublin.
Died 18 Nov. 1928.

EE, Hon. Charles Alfred; *b* 13 Nov. 1842; *m* 1865 (widower 1915); three *s* two *d.* MLA Tenterfield, 1884–1920; was Father of NSW Parliament, retired 1920; Minister for Justice, 1898–99; Minister for Public Works, 1904–10. *Address:* Tenterfield, New South Wales.
Died 15 Aug. 1926.

EE, Gordon Ambrose de Lisle, CB 1920; CVO 1926; Clarenceux King of Arms since 1926; *b* Aberdeen, 11 July 1864; 2nd *s* of Rev. Dr F. G. Lee, of All Saints', Lambeth; *m* 1888, Rose (*d* 1922), *d* of Robert Wallace, Secretary to the Earl Marshal. *Educ:* St Mary's College, Harlow; Westminster School. An artist and designer in black and white, 1885–89; Blue-mantle Pursuivant of Arms, 1889–1905; York Herald of Arms, 1905–22; Norroy King of Arms, 1923–26; Sec. to the Deputy Earl Marshal (Lord Fitz Alan of Derwent); Sec. to the Earl Marshal of England (Duke of Norfolk), 1911–17; Deputy Registrar of the Heralds' College in 1899; Member of Council, Japan Society, 1909–15. Arranged and superintended the heraldry, ceremonial and ecclesiology in Mr Tree's revivals of Richard II and Much Ado about Nothing, and of Raymond Rôze's opera, Joan of Arc; part author and producer of the Chelsea Pageant, 1908. *Publications:* B. Margaret of Salisbury, a Sketch of the Life and Times of the Last of the Plantagenets, 1887; Lives of V. Philip Howard, Earl of Arundel, Queen Mary Tudor, and St Philip Neri; (with Mr K.

Tomita) Japanese Treasure Tales, 1906; (ed) The Episcopal Arms of England and Wales, 1906; Some Notes on Japanese Heraldry, 1909. *Recreations:* the play, the study of Japanese art, antiquities, etc. *Address:* Zenda, Cumberland Road, Kew Gardens, Surrey; Heralds' College, EC4.
Died 12 Sept. 1827.

LEE, Sir Henry Austin, KCMG 1902; CB 1892; Counsellor of Embassy in Diplomatic Service; late Commercial Attaché for France, Belgium, and Switzerland; *b* 6 April 1847; *s* of George A. Lee of Frogmore, Guernsey, and Ceylon Civil Service; *m* 1892, Madeleine de Wolff, *d* of B. Franklin Smith of New York. *Educ:* Elizabeth College, Guernsey; Pembroke College, Oxford (MA, Hon Fellow). Entered Foreign Office, 1870; transferred to Diplomatic Service, 1892; attached to the Marquis of Salisbury's Special Embassy to Constantinople, 1876–77; Assistant Private Secretary to the Earl of Beaconsfield, at the Congress of Berlin, 1878; at various times Private Secretary to Sir Charles Dilke, Lord Fitzmaurice, Viscount Bryce, Sir James Fergusson, MP, Earl of Lytton, Marquis of Dufferin and Ava. *Recreation:* shooting. *Address:* 14 bis Avenue du Trocadero, Paris; Isle of Jethou, near Guernsey. *Clubs:* Arthur's, Brooks's, St James'.
Died 7 Nov. 1918.

LEE, Maj.-Gen. Henry Herbert, CBE 1918; JP, DL; *b* 1838; *m* 1873, Constance (*d* 1890), *e d* of G. Lyall of Headley Park, Surrey. *Educ:* Marlborough. Served Abyssinia, 1868 (despatches, medal); Egypt, 1885; rep. Diocese of Llandaff in House of Laymen. *Address:* The Mount, Dinas Powis, Cardiff. *Club:* United Service.
Died 19 March 1920.

LEE, Rev. James Wideman, DD; *b* Rockbridge, Georgia, USA, 28 Nov. 1849; *e s* of Zachry J. Lee and Emily H. Wideman; *m* 1875, Emma Eufaula, *d* of Rev. L. L. Ledbetter of Cedartown, Ga; three *s* three *d.* *Educ:* Bawsville Academy; Grantville High School; Emory Coll., Oxford, Ga. Ordained to ministry, Methodist Episcopal Church, South, 1876; pastor of churches in Georgia at Rockmart, Long Cane, Carrolton, Dalton, Rome, and Atlanta; pastor St John's Church, St Louis, Mo, 1893, 1901–5 and 1911–15; head of an expedition to Palestine, 1894; Presiding Elder St Louis District, 1897–1901 and 1915, 1916; Chaplain, Barnes' Hospital, and Assistant to the Trustees, 1917; Pastor Trinity Church, Atlanta, Ga, second time, 1905–9; Pastor Park St Church, second time, 1910. *Publications:* The Making of a Man, 1892, trans. Japanese 1893, Chinese 1904, Korean 1908; Christ the Reason of the Universe, in an Address before the World's Parliament of Religions, held in Chicago, 1893; The Earthly Footsteps of the Man of Galilee, 1895; Henry W. Grady, Editor, Orator, and Man, 1897; edited and illustrated The Self-interpreting Bible, 1897; Illustrated History of Methodism, 1900; History of Jerusalem, 1904; The Real Uncle Remus, 1908; Abraham Lincoln, 1909; Religion of Science, 1912 (trans. Japanese, 1916); Magnetizing the Commonplace, A Lesson in Human Geography, 1914; Robert Burns, or The Geography of Genius, 1915; Climate and Unity, 1916; The Bible and Life, 1916; The Inner and Outer Half of Man, 1917. *Recreation:* travelling. *Address:* 5043 Washington Avenue, St Louis, Mo, USA. *T:* Forest 4262.
Died 4 Oct. 1919.

LEE, John, CBE 1923; Director of Automatic Telephone Manufacturing Co. and of other companies; Controller of the Central Telegraph Office, 1919–27; *b* 1867; *m* 1902, Mary Emily, *d* of H. R. Nickson, Birkenhead; one *s* one *d.* *Educ:* Belfast; MA; MComSc. Lecturer at various Industrial Conferences at Oxford and Cambridge; delegate to International Telegraph Conference, Paris, 1925. *Publications:* Modern Telegraph Practice; Economics of Telegraphs and Telephones; Plain Economics; Management, a Study of Industrial Organisation; The Social Implications of Christianity; The Principles of Industrial Welfare; Christian Social Duty; An Introduction to Industrial Administration; Letters to an Absentee Director; Editor of the Dictionary of Industrial Administration. *Address:* Mulgrave Lodge, Sutton, Surrey. *T:* Sutton 337. *Club:* National Liberal.
Died 24 Dec. 1928.

LEE, Rev. Richard, MA Cambridge; *ad eundem,* MA Dublin; *s* of late Rev. Richard Lee, Ex. Sch. TCD. *Educ:* Christ's Hospital; Jesus Coll. Camb. Foundation Scholar; Rustat Scholar; 1st (bracketed) 2nd class Classical Tripos, 1869. Assistant Master at Christ's Hospital, 1871–76; Curate of Holy Trinity, Finchley, 1873–75; Lecturer of St Benet, Paul's Wharf, 1875–76; Head Master of Christ's Hospital, London, 1876–1902; Fellow (Hon.) of College of Preceptors, 1921.
Died 27 Feb. 1922.

LEE, Richard Henry; *o s* of late John Henry Lee of 15 Collingham Gardens, SW; *g g s* of James Lee of Pinchinthorp, Yorkshire; *m* Rosina, y d of late Charles Wigg of Hoole Bank, Chester. *Address:* Yarner, Bovey Tracey, S Devon. *Died 8 Sept. 1923.*

LEE, Sir Sidney, Kt 1911; FBA 1910; engaged, at King George's request, on full biography in two volumes of King Edward VII from original papers (vol. i (from Birth to Accession) appeared in March 1925; vol. ii (the Reign)); editor of Dictionary of National Biography, 1891–1917; *b* London, 5 Dec. 1859. *Educ:* City of London School; Balliol College, Oxford. Clark Lecturer in English Literature, Trinity College, Cambridge, 1901–2; Lecturer at Lowell Institute, Boston, USA, 1903; Lecturer for the Common University Fund at Oxford, 1909; Professor of English Language and Literature in the University of London (East London College), 1913–24; Dean of Faculty of Arts, University of London, 1918–22; Emeritus Professor of English, 1924. President of English Association, 1917. Hon. DLitt Oxford, 1907; Hon. LLD Glasgow, 1907; Hon. LittD Victoria University, Manchester, 1900; Foreign Member, American Academy of Arts and Sciences; Corresponding Member, Massachusetts Historical Society; Member of Royal Commission on Public Records from 1910; Chairman of the Executive, Shakespeare's Birthplace Trust, Stratford-on-Avon, from 1903; Registrar of Royal Literary Fund, 1907; Trustee of National Portrait Gallery, 1924. *Publications:* Stratford-on-Avon from the Earliest Times to the Death of Shakespeare, 1885, new edn 1906; Lord Herbert of Cherbury's Autobiography, with a continuation of his Life, 1886, new edn 1906; A Life of William Shakespeare, 1898 (illustrated edn 1899, popular edn 1900, 1907, 1915, revised 1925); A Life of Queen Victoria, 1902 (new edn 1904); Shakespeare First Folio Facsimile, with Introduction, and Census of Extant Copies, 1902; Elizabethan Sonnets, 1904; Great Englishmen of the 16th Century, 1904, 1925; Shakespeare's Poems and Pericles, 1905; Shakespeare and the Modern Stage, 1906; America and Elizabethan England in Scribner's Magazine, 1907; The French Renaissance in England, 1910; Principles of Biography, 1911; Shakespeare and the Italian Renaissance, 1915; Comment on Prefatory Pages of First Folio, 1923; editor, A Year's Work in English Studies (English Association), 1921, 1922, 1923, 1924. *Address:* 108A Lexham Gardens, Kensington, W8. *T:* Western 7183. *Club:* Athenæum. *Died 3 March 1926.*

LEE-DILLON, Hon. Harry (Lee Stanton), FSA; *b* 25 July 1874; *o c* of 17th Viscount Dillon; *m* 1st, 1904, Brenda Mary (marr. diss. 1911), *e d* of Thomas Smith, LSA, MRCS; one *d*; 2nd, 1913, Kathleen Clare, 2nd *d* of late James Atchison, Civil Engineer, of Cardigan, Lavender Bay, Sydney, NSW. *Educ:* Charterhouse; Sandhurst. Late Lieut Rifle Brigade. *Address:* 146 Rue de la Paix; Boulogne, France. *Clubs:* White's, Army and Navy. *Died 7 Feb. 1923.*

LEE WARNER, Philip Henry; *b* 1877; *e s* of late Sir William Lee Warner, GCSI, Hon. LLD Cantab; *m* 1907, Mary King, 2nd *d* of General Thomas Sherwin, Boston, Mass; one *s* two *d*. *Educ:* Rugby; University College, Oxford; Honours Mod. History. Partner Chatto & Windus, Publishers, 1905; incorporated the Medici Society Ltd, 1908; Managing Director and Publisher to above, 1908–21, when resigned; Chairman, Charles Whittingham and Griggs (Printers) Ltd (from incorporation), 1919–21; Managing Director, 1922; incorporated (and became Managing Director) Martin Hopkinson & Co. Ltd, Publishers, 1923. *Address:* 14 Henrietta Street, Covent Garden, WC2. *T:* Gerrard 8321; The Manor House, Bletchingley, Surrey. *T:* Bletchingley 11. *TA:* Bletchingley. *Clubs:* Athenæum, Arts. *Died 28 Jan. 1925.*

LEEBODY, Prof. John R., MA, DSc; FIC; President Magee Presbyterian College; *b* 1840; 2nd *s* of Rev. H. Leebody, Ballindery, Co. Antrim; *m* 1866, Mary Isabella Welsh (*d* 1911), *d* of John Welsh, Kirkcubbin, Co. Down; two *s* two *d*. *Educ:* Royal Acad. Institute, Belfast; Queen's College, Belfast; Queen's University (First Science Scholar in College and First Honourman and Gold Medallist in mathematics and physics in the University). Professor of Mathematics and Physics in Magee College, 1865. *Publications:* Religious Teaching and Modern Thought, 1889; various magazine and review articles. *Recreations:* fishing, shooting, golf. *Address:* Magee Presbyterian College, Derry. *Died 21 Aug. 1927.*

LEECH, Henry Brougham, LLD; *b* 15 Nov. 1843; 2nd *s* of Rev. John Leech, DD, late of Mitchelstown, Co. Cork; *m* 1875, Annie Louise, *d* of William Garbois of Dublin; five *s* one *d*. *Educ:* Trinity College, Dublin and Cambridge; Fellow of Gonville and Caius College, 1873. Called to the Irish Bar, 1871; Professor of Jurisprudence and International Law, University of Dublin, 1878–88; Lecturer in Hindoo and Mohammedan Law, 1881; Deputy Regius Professor of Feudal and English Law, 1883–84; Regius Professor of Laws,

1888–1908; Registrar of Deeds in Ireland, 1891–1908; Registrar ‹ Titles in Ireland, 1893–1908; Associé de L'Institut de Dro‹ International, 1893; Member of the American Acad. of Political an‹ Social Science, 1902. *Publications:* Essay on Ancient International Law 1878; Registration of Titles *v* Registration of Assurances, 1891; Th‹ South African Republics, their History and International Positio‹ 1901; The Irish University Question: its History and its Solutio‹ 1905; A Handbook for Unionist Speakers, 1910; The Continuity ‹ the Irish Revolutionary Movement, 1847–1912; Prolusiones Emeri‹ 1919, being Translations into Latin and Greek Verse; and othe‹ pamphlets and essays. *Address:* 19 Porchester Square, W2. *Club‹* Authors', Junior Constitutional. *Died 2 March 192‹*

LEECH, Sir Stephen, KCMG 1919; *b* 8 July 1864; 2nd *s* of late Joh‹ Leech of Gorse Hall, Dukinfield, Cheshire. *Educ:* Eton; Magdale‹ Coll., Oxford. Entered HM's Diplomatic Service as Attaché, 188‹ 3rd Secretary, 1890; 2nd Secretary, 1894; 1st Secretary, 190‹ Counsellor of Embassy, 1907; Minister Resident, 1909; Envc‹ Extraordinary and Minister Plenipotentiary, 1913; employed at Berli‹ Brussels, Constantinople, Lisbon, Rome, Copenhagen, Christiani‹ Peking, Cuba, Hayti and Santo Domingo; retired, 1920. *Addres‹* Parkhill, Lyndhurst, Hampshire. *Club:* Travellers'. *Died 12 May 192‹*

LEEDS, 10th Duke of, *cr* 1694; **George Godolphin Osborne;** B‹ 1620; Viscount Latimer, Baron Osborne, 1673; Earl of Danby, 167‹ Viscount Osborne of Dunblane, 1675; Marquis of Carmarthen, 168‹ Baron Godolphin, 1832; Prince of the Holy Roman Empire; MF‹ Bedale; *b* 18 Sept. 1862; 2nd *s* of 9th Duke and Fanny, 2nd *d* of 4‹ Baron Rivers (*ext.*); *S* father, 1895; *m* 1884, Lady Katherine Franc‹ Lambton; one *s* four *d*. *Educ:* Eton; Trinity College, Cambridge. M‹ (C) Lambeth Brixton Division, 1887–95; Treasurer of the Househol‹ 1895–1901; LCC (City of London) from 1898. Owner of abo‹ 24,300 acres. *Recreation:* owner of yacht "Corisande." *Heir: s* Marqu‹ of Carmarthen, *b* 12 March 1901. *Address:* 11 Grosvenor Crescen‹ SW1; Hornby Castle, Bedale, Yorkshire. *Clubs:* Carlton; Royal Yac‹ Squadron, Cowes (Commodore). *Died 10 May 192‹*

LEEDS, Sir Edward Templer, 5th Bt, *cr* 1812; *b* 11 Oct. 1859; 2r‹ *s* of Sir Edward Leeds, 3rd Bt and 2nd wife, Fanny, *o d* of Maj.-Ge‹ Templer, EICS; *S* half-brother, 1894; *m* 1906, Charlotte August‹ *d* of Rev. Edward Crow, MA. *Heir: c* Reginald Arthur St John Leed‹ *b* 13 May 1899. *Address:* 1 Queen's Parade, Cheltenham. *Died 31 May 192‹*

LEEDS, Lt-Col Thomas Louis, CMG 1918; DSO 1917; la‹ Commandant 59th Scinde Rifles (Frontier Force); *b* 25 July 186‹ 3rd *s* of late Edward Montagu Leeds and Jessie, *d* of Thomas Spea‹ Kirkcaldy; *m* 1904, Clara Guion, *d* of Col Kilburn, USA Army; or‹ *d*. *Educ:* Sherborne. Joined 3rd Batt. Derbyshire Regt, 1889; 1st Ba‹ Sherwood Foresters (Derbyshire Regt), 1891; transferred to Indi‹ Army, 1894; joined 6th Punjab Infantry, PFF (later 59th Rifles, FF‹ 1896; served in China, Zakka Khel, and Mohmand Expeditio‹ (medal and clasp for China), 1900; Zakka and Mohmand Expeditio‹ 1908; France, Sept. 1914–Dec. 1915 (despatches, Bt Lt-Co‹ Mesopotamia, 1916 (despatches 4 times, DSO, CMG, 3rd class Ord‹ of St Stanislas); retired, 1921. *Recreations:* fishing, golf. *Address:* Am‹ Hall, Washbrook, near Ipswich. *Club:* United Service. *Died 8 July 192‹*

LEEDS, William Henry Arthur St John; late Commissioner IC‹ Burma; *b* 3 March 1864; *s* of Henry Leeds and Adelaide Louisa, of William Davis; *c* and *heir-pres.* to Sir Edward Templer Leeds, 5‹ Bt; *m* 1898, Edith Mabel, *d* of late Maj.-Gen. Muspratt William‹ two *s* one *d*. *Address:* 10 Cranley Gardens, SW. *T:* Kensington 547‹ *Club:* East India United Service. *Died 22 Aug. 191‹*

LEEFE, Gen. John Beckwith, RMA; *b* 6 June 1849; *m* 1880, Jul‹ Mary, *d* of Capt. J. G. Gurney. Entered RMA 1867; Captain, 187‹ Major, 1886; Lt-Col 1896; Col 1902; Maj.-Gen. 1905; Lt-Gen. 190‹ Gen. 1912; Professor of Fortification, RN College, 1883–90; serve‹ S Africa, 1900 (Queen's medal with clasp); retired 1914. *Addres‹* Foxwood, Farnham, Surrey. *Died 30 March 192‹*

LEEKE, Rev. Edward Tucker; Canon since 1877, and Sub-Dea‹ of Lincoln Cathedral since 1898; *b* 1841; *s* of Rev. William Leek‹ Vicar of Holbrooke, near Derby; *m* 1880, Dora, *d* of Rt Re‹ Christopher Wordsworth, Bishop of Lincoln; five *s* two *d*. *Edu‹*

Trinity College, Cambridge (Fellow). Ordained, 1867; Assistant Tutor, Trinity College, 1864–68; Curate of St Andrew the Less, Cambridge, 1868–69; Vicar, 1869–77; Chancellor of Lincoln Cathedral and Examining Chaplain to Bishop of Lincoln, 1877–98; Chaplain, Lincoln Hospital, 1887–1902, 1906–7; Vicar of St Nicholas, W St John, Lincoln, 1902–19. *Address:* The Chancery, Lincoln.
Died 23 May 1925.

EEKE, Rt. Rev. John Cox, DD, MA; Sub-Dean of Southwark since 1905; *b* Holbrooke, Derbyshire, 1843; *s* of Rev. W. Leeke; *m* Alice, *d* of John Meynell of Meynell Langley, Derbyshire; two *s* one *d. Educ:* private tuition; Trinity College, Cambridge. Curate of Wanstead, 1867–70; Holbrooke, 1870–74; Rector of Kidbrook, Blackheath, 1875–1901; St Mark's, Plumstead, 1901–5; Rural Dean of Woolwich, 1892–1905; Hon. Canon of Rochester, 1900–5; Bishop of Woolwich (Suffragan), 1905–18. *Recreations:* various. *Address:* Stone Cross House, Byfield, Northants. *Died 28 Nov. 1919.*

EES, Sir Harcourt James, 4th Bt, *cr* 1804; *b* 24 April 1840; *s* of Sir John Lees, 3rd Bt and Maria Charlotte, *d* of Edward Sullivan; *S* father, 1892; *m* 1st, 1860, Charlotte (who divorced him 1872), *d* of W. M'Taggart; two *s* two *d* (and three *s* decd); 2nd, 1872, Harriet Helen Constance (who divorced him 1887), *d* of Henry Morgan Howard; two *s* two *d*; 3rd, 1899, Louise Hayes. Late Lieut 60th Rifles. *Heir: s* Arthur Henry James Lees, *b* 18 Jan. 1863. *Address:* Upperton and Co., 14 Lincoln's Inn Fields, WC. *Died 22 March 1917.*

EES, Sir John M'Kie, KBE 1919; KC 1901; *b* 13 Nov. 1843; *o* surv. *s* of Walter Lees, Glasgow; *m* 1st, 1873, Eliza (*d* 1875), *e d* of Sir John Gillespie; 2nd, 1881, Alice Susan, 3rd *d* of James Clark, of Crossbasket, Lanarkshire; three *s. Educ:* Ayr and Edinburgh Academies, and Edinburgh University; MA, Edinburgh, 1864; LLB, 1867. Examiner to Glasgow University for Degrees in Law, 1874–80; and to Edinburgh University, 1877–80. Called to Bar, 1867; Sheriff-Substitute of Lanarkshire at Airdrie, 1872–75, and at Glasgow, 1875–91; Sheriff of Stirling, Dumbarton, and Clackmannan, 1891–1917; and of Forfarshire, 1917–22; Commissioner of Northern Lighthouses, 1917; Convener of the Sheriffs of Scotland, 1907–19. *Publications:* Sheriff Court Styles; Small Debt Handbook; Pleading in Sheriff Court; Analysis of Small Debt Amendment Act; Forms of Interlocutors, etc. *Recreations:* golf, cycling, fishing. *Address:* 4 Darnaway Street, Edinburgh. *T:* Central, Edinburgh 1873. *Club:* University, Edinburgh. *Died 5 Nov. 1926.*

EES, Thomas Orde Hastings, JP; MA; Barrister-at-Law; *b* 1846; *s* of Rev. John and Lady Louisa Lees (*d* of 11th Earl of Huntingdon); *m* Grace, *d* of Joshua Wigley Bateman of Guilsborough, Northamptonshire (secretary to the Duchy of Cornwall). *Educ:* Royal Naval School; Newcross; Royal Academy, Gosport; MA, Trinity College, Dublin. Obtained a cadetship in the Royal Irish Constabulary, 1868; served as DI in counties Longford, Mayo, Louth, and Tipperary; appointed Chief Constable of Northamptonshire, 1875; called to the Bar (Middle Temple), 1881; for some years went Midland Circuit; contested (C) Northampton 1886, opposing Messrs Labouchere and Bradlaugh; the first Chief Constable of Isle of Wight, 1890; retired 1899; received special thanks and jubilee medal for services rendered Court at Osborne, 1896–97. *Publications:* The Constable's Pocket Book, and other technical works; Editor of Snowden's Police Officers' Guide. *Recreations:* field sports, travel, ornithology (FZS). *Address:* Guilsborough, Northamptonshire; 3 Temple Gardens, EC. *Club:* Junior Carlton. *Died 30 Sept. 1924.*

E FANU, William Richard; Secretary and Treasurer to the Governors of Queen Anne's Bounty; *b* 1861; unmarried. *Educ:* Haileybury; St John's College, Cambridge. *Address:* The Albany, Piccadilly, W. *Club:* Arts. *Died 22 March 1925.*

EFROY, A. H. F., KC; MA; Professor of Roman and English Law and General Jurisprudence, and Special Lecturer on English Constitutional law, Colonial law, and Federal law, University of Toronto; *b* Toronto, 21 June 1852; *s* of late General Sir John Henry Lefroy, KCMG, etc, and Emily Merry, *d* of late Sir John Beverley Robinson, 1st Bt, Chief Justice of Upper Canada; *m* 1884, Mary Theodora, *d* of Henry Seton Strathy of Toronto, Banker; two *s* (3rd *s* Frazer Keith Lefroy, 2nd Lieut RFA, killed on Western Front, 7 April, 1917). *Educ:* Rugby; New Coll. Oxford. 2nd Class Honours in Literae Humaniores, 1873; called to English Bar, 1877; called to Bar of Upper Canada, 1878; has since then practised as barrister and solicitor in Toronto. *Publications:* Legislative Power in Canada, 1897–98; Canada's Federal System, 1913; article on The Dominion of Canada, in *Corpus Juris*, 1917; Canadian Constitutional Cases;

contributor to Nelson's Encyclopædia of Canada; joint translator with J. H. Cameron of A Short History of Roman Law, by P. F. Girard, 1906; editor of the Canadian Law Times, and writer of numerous articles in the Law Quarterly Review. *Recreations:* golf, bicycling. *Address:* 163½ Church Street (Athena Building), Toronto. *Clubs:* New University; Toronto, Toronto. *Died 8 March 1919.*

LEFROY, Rev. Frederick Anthony, MA; Hon. Canon of Gloucester Cathedral; *b* 19 Dec. 1846; *s* of Very Rev. Jeffrey Lefroy, Rector of Ahaderg, Dean of Dromore, Ireland, and Helena, *d* of Rev. F. S. and Lady Helena Trench; *m* 1881, Henrietta (*d* 1920), *d* of George Gurney, Shincliffe, Eastbourne; three *s* two *d. Educ:* Harrow; Trinity College, Cambridge. Curate of St George's, Brandon Hill, Bristol, 1870–76; Vicar, 1876–92; Examining Chaplain to Bishop of Gloucester and Bristol, 1891; Vicar of South Petherton, Somerset, 1892–1902; Vicar of Haresfield, Glos, 1902–17; Examining Chaplain to the Bishop of Gloucester. *Address:* Glassfall Lodge, Cheltenham. *Club:* Constitutional. *Died 25 Dec. 1920.*

LEFROY, Rt. Rev. George Alfred, DD; Bishop of Calcutta since 1913; *b* Co. Down, Aug. 1854; *s* of Very Rev. Jeffrey Lefroy, Dean of Dromore, *g s* of Chief Justice Lefroy (of the Queen's Bench, Ireland). *Educ:* Marlborough and Trinity Coll. Cambridge; 1st class in Theological Tripos. Ordained 1879; joined the Cambridge Mission in Delhi same year; became head of United SPG and Camb. Mission in Delhi, 1891; Bishop of Lahore, 1899–1912. *Address:* The Palace, Calcutta. *Died 1 Jan. 1919.*

LEFROY, Harold Maxwell-, MA; FES, FZS; Professor of Entomology, Imperial College of Science and Technology, South Kensington, since 1912; *b* 20 Jan. 1877; 4th *s* of C. J. Maxwell-Lefroy and Elizabeth Catherine M'Clintock, Itchel Manor, Crondall, Hants; *m* 1904, Kathleen Hamilton, *d* of William O'Meara of British Guiana; one *s. Educ:* Marlborough College; King's College, Cambridge. 1st class Natural Science Tripos, 1898. Entomologist to Imperial Department of Agriculture for the West Indies, 1899–1903; Imperial Entomologist for India, 1903–12; Hon. Curator, Insect House, Zoological Gardens, from 1913; Imperial Silk Specialist, India, 1915–16; Temp. Lieut-Col Mesopotamia E Force, 1916; attached Royal Commission on Wheat Supplies, 1917–18. *Publications:* Indian Insect Pests, 1906; Indian Insect Life, 1910; Manual of Entomology, 1923; many contribs to West Indian Bulletin, Agricultural Jl of India; Memoirs of the Agricultural Department of India, etc. *Address:* Imperial College of Science, S Kensington, SW. *TA:* Lefroy, Scientist, Southkens, London. *T:* Kensington 6444.
Died 14 Oct. 1925.

LEGARD, Albert George; sometime Divisional Inspector of Schools for Wales; retired; *b* 31 May 1845; *y s* of George Legard, Westhorpe House, Scarborough; *m* 1875, Mildreda (*d* 1920), *d* of Matthew R. Bigge of Islip Grange, Northants. *Educ:* Durham School; Balliol College, Oxford. 1st Class Classical Moderations, 1866; 1st Class Lit. Hum. 1868. One of HM Inspectors of Schools, 1871; Sheffield District, 1871–72; Leeds District, 1872–96; sometime Member of Welsh University Court, and Member of South Wales University College Council, and Governor of various schools. *Recreations:* riding, walking. *Address:* 5 Kensington, Bath.
Died 18 Feb. 1922.

LEGARD, Sir Algernon Willoughby, 12th Bt, *cr* 1660; *b* 14 Oct. 1842; *s* of Henry Willoughby Legard, 2nd *s* of Sir Thomas Legard, 7th Bt, and Charlotte Henrietta, *d* of Henry Willoughby; *S* cousin, 1901; *m* 1872, Alicia Egerton, *y d* of Rev. George Brooks, late Rector of Hampden, Bucks. *Educ:* Marlborough; Trinity Coll., Camb. *Heir: nephew* Digby Algernon Hall Legard, *b* 7 Dec. 1876. *Address:* 18 Victoria Road, Kensington, W8. *Club:* Boodle's.
Died 9 Sept. 1923.

LEGARD, Rev. Cecil Henry, MA, LLB; Rector of Cottesbrooke, 1887–1914; *b* 28 Nov. 1843; *s* of Henry Willoughby Legard; *heir presumptive* to Sir Algernon Willoughby Legard, 12th Bt; *m* 1873, Emily (*d* 1915), *d* of James Hall; one *s* one *d. Educ:* Magdalene College, Cambridge. Vicar of Boynton, Yorks, 1870–79; Aylesby, Great Grimsby, 1879–80; Rector of Healing, Lincolnshire, 1880–87; Curate of Riby, Lincolnshire, 1884–87. *Address:* Langham Lodge, Cottesbrooke, Northampton. *Clubs:* Arthur's; Yorkshire, York.
Died 20 Feb. 1918.

LE GEYT, Maj.-Gen. Philip Harrison; Indian Army; *b* 22 Dec. 1834. Entered army, 1851; Maj.-Gen. 1892; retired list, 1892; served Persian Expedition, 1856–57 (medal with clasp); Indian Mutiny,

1858–59; served in Political Dept as Assistant Political Agent, Kathiawar and Cutch, 1863; Mahi Kantha, 1872–80; Political Superintendent, Palanpur, 1880; returned to Europe, 1889. *Address:* Littledale, 45 Blackwater Road, Eastbourne.

Died 23 May 1922.

LEGG, Captain Sir George Edward Wickham, KBE 1920; MVO 1902; Secretary, Soldiers', Sailors', and Airmen's Families Association, since 1896; *b* 13 July 1870; 3rd *s* of late Rev. W. Legg, Rector of Hawkinge, Kent; *m* 1895, Kathleen (Lady of Grace, Order of St John of Jerusalem), *d* of late Col Sir James Gildea, GBE, KCVO, CB; one *s*. *Educ:* Radley; Trinity College, Cambridge; RMC, Sandhurst. Joined South Staffordshire (80th) Regt, 1891; and subsequently the 3rd Batt. Royal West Kent Regt (Militia); Capt. in the Reserve of Officers, 1905–20. Member of the Council of St Peter's College, Radley, from 1914. KGStJ 1899; Chevalier, Légion d'Honneur, 1919. *Publications:* editor of the Radley College Register: (2nd edn), 1847–1904, (3rd edn), 1847–1912. *Address:* 14 Pembroke Gardens, Kensington, W8. *T:* Western 0509. *Died 1 Sept. 1927.*

LEGG, John Wickham, Hon. DLitt Oxon; FSA; Chairman of the Council of the Henry Bradshaw Society for Editing Rare Liturgical Texts, 1895–1915; *b* 28 Dec. 1843; *m* 1872, Eliza Jane (*d* 1908), *d* of Richard Houghton; one *s*. *Educ:* University Coll., London. MRCS 1866; FRCP 1876. Tutor to late Duke of Albany, 1866–67; Demonstrator of Morbid Anatomy, 1874; Lecturer on Pathological Anatomy and Assistant Physician at St Bartholomew's Hospital, London, 1878–87; Bradshaw Lecturer at the Royal College of Physicians of London, 1883; Member of the Canterbury House of Laymen, 1909–13. *Publications:* edited numerous volumes for Henry Bradshaw Society; Breviarium Romanum Quignonianum for Cambridge University Press, 1888; Sarum Missal from three early MSS for Clarendon Press, Oxford, 1916; English Church Life from 1660 to 1833, 1914; Collected Essays, Liturgical and Historical, 1917; Church Ornaments and their Civil Antecedents, 1917; contribs to Archaeologia, Proceedings of Royal Society, Archaeological Jl, Jl of Theological Studies, Trans of Bibliographical Society. *Address:* 82 Woodstock Road, Oxford. *Died 28 Oct. 1921.*

LEGGE, Col Hon. Sir Harry Charles, GCVO 1920 (KCVO 1910; CVO 1901); Equerry-in-Waiting to the Queen, 1893, and to the King, 1901–15; Paymaster of the King's Household, 1915–20; Extra Equerry to the King, 1915; Secretary and Registrar of the Order of Merit since 1907; *b* Patshull, Staffordshire, 4 Nov. 1852; 2nd *s* of 5th Earl of Dartmouth; *m* 1884, Amy Gwendoline, *d* of Gustavus and Lady Fanny Lambart, Beau Parc, Ireland; one *d* (one *s* decd). *Educ:* Eton. Coldstream Guards, 1872–99; Adj. 1st Battalion, 1878–85; Soudan Campaign, Brevet Major, 1885; Groom-in-Waiting to Queen Victoria, 1889. *Recreations:* none. *Address:* Fulmer Gardens, Slough. *TA:* Stoke Poges. *T:* Fulmer 8. *Club:* Carlton.

Died 20 Jan. 1924.

LEGGETT, Major Eric Henry Goodwin, DSO 1915; Royal Artillery; *b* 31 Dec. 1880. Entered army, 1899; Captain, 1907; Major, 1914; employed with Malay States Guides, 1905–8; Staff Captain RA 4th Division Eastern Command, 1911–13; Brigade-Major, 1913–14; served European War, 1914–15 (despatches, DSO).

Died 30 July 1916.

LE GRAVE, Rev. William, DSO 1902; Chaplain to the Forces, RC; retired 1903; *b* 5 Sept. 1843. *Educ:* St Edmund's Coll., Ware. Ordained, 1867; taught mathematics at above college, 1866–78; became Chaplain to the Forces, 1878; served in Malta, Bermuda, Ashanti Expedition, 1895–96; Senior RC Chaplain in South Africa, 1899–1900 (despatches twice, DSO). *Address:* 30 Park Road, Abingdon, Berks. *Died 20 April 1922.*

LEHFELDT, Robert Alfred, BA Cantab, DSc London; FRSSAf; Professor of Economics, University of the Witwatersrand, Johannesburg, since 1917; *b* Birmingham, 7 May 1868; *s* of late Dr F. C. Lehfeldt. *Educ:* St John's College, Cambridge. Demonstrator of Physics, Firth College (later University of) Sheffield, 1890–96; Professor of Physics, East London College, London, 1896–1906; Professor of Physics, SA School of Mines and Technology, 1906–17; Correspondent for S Africa of the Royal Economic Society. *Publications:* Text-Book of Physical Chemistry, 1902; Electro-chemistry, 1906, in Sir William Ramsay's series on Physical Chemistry; Economics in the Light of War, 1916; Gold, Prices, and the Witwatersrand, 1919; Restoration of the World's Currencies, 1923; Money (World's manual series), 1926; numerous papers. *Address:* PO Box 1176, Johannesburg, South Africa. *TA:* University, Johannesburg. *Club:* Royal Societies. *Died Sept. 1927.*

LEHMANN, Liza, (Elizabeth Nina Mary Frederika), (Mr▪ **Herbert Bedford);** soprano, retired on marriage, 1894; appointe▪ Vocal Professor at the Guildhall School of Music, 1914; compose▪ *b* London, 1862; *d* of Rudolf Lehmann, artist, and Amelia Lehmann composer of songs; *g d* of Robert Chambers, publisher; *m* 1894 Herbert Bedford, composer, artist and author. Studied singing unde▪ her mother and Signor Randegger; composition under Raunkilde Rome; Freudenberg, Wiesbaden; and Hamish MacCunn, Londor made professional début as soprano at a Monday Popular Conce▪ in 1885, and from then until marriage sang at principal concerts i▪ the kingdom. *Publications:* song-cycle for four solo voices, wit▪ pianoforte accompaniment, entitled In a Persian Garden, the wor▪ being from the Rubaiyát of Omar Khayyám; a setting for bariton solo, chorus and orchestra of Scott's Young Lochinvar; two musica dualogues (words by Austin Dobson), The Secrets of the Heart, an▪ Goodnight, Babette; Endymion (Longfellow), Scena for soprano an▪ orchestra; In Memoriam (words selected from Tennyson), a song cycle for a solo voice with pianoforte accompaniment; The Daisy Chain (Twelve Songs of Childhood); More Daisies; Once Upon Time (a Fairy Cantata); Sergeant Brue (a musical farce, book by Owe▪ Hall); Romantic Suite, for Violin and Piano; The Vicar of Wakefiel▪ (light romantic opera); The Golden Threshold, an Indian song-garlan▪ (cantata); Nonsense Songs from Alice in Wonderland (song-cycle)▪ Practical Hints for Students of Singing; also many separate songs *Recreation:* gardening. *Address:* 40 Warwick Avenue, Paddington, W *T:* Paddington 6873. *Died 19 Sept. 1918*

LE HUNTE, Sir George Ruthven, GCMG 1912 (KCMG 1903▪ CMG 1898); *b* 20 Aug. 1852; *s* of George Le Hunte of Wexford▪ *m* 1884, Caroline Rachel, *d* of John Clowes of Burton Court Herefordshire; one *s* one *d*. *Educ:* Eton; Trinity College, Cambridge BA 1873; MA 1880. Barrister, Inner Temple, 1881; Private Secretar▪ to Sir Arthur Gordon, KCMG (Lord Stanmore), first Governor o▪ Fiji, 1875; served in various offices in Fiji, 1875–87; Judicia Commissioner for High Commission Western Pacific, 1883; Presiden▪ of Dominica, 1887–94; Colonial Secretary, Barbados, 1894–97▪ Colonial Secretary, Mauritius, 1897; Lieut-Governor British New Guinea, 1898–1903; Governor South Australia, 1903–8; Governo▪ and Commander-in-Chief of Trinidad and Tobago, 1908–15; retired▪ Jan. 1916. Decorated for Colonial service. *Recreations:* general. *Address▪* Sandridge, Crowborough, Sussex.

Died 29 Jan. 1925

LEIGH, Egerton, JP, DL; *b* 13 July 1843; *s* of late Egerton Leigh, DL▪ and Lydia Rachel, *d* and *co-heir* of late John Smith Wright of Bulcote Lodge, Notts; *m* 1st, 1874, Lady Elizabeth Mary (*d* 1880), *e d* of 3r▪ Earl of Bantry (*ext*); one *d*; 2nd, 1889, Violet Cecil Mary, 2nd *d* o▪ Col Alfred Tippinge, of Longparish House, Whitchurch, Hants; one *s* one *d*. High Sheriff, Co. Chester, 1882; was Captain 1st Roya▪ Dragoons. *Address:* 20 Cadogan Place, SW1. *T:* Victoria 7591. *Clubs* Arthur's, Cavalry. *Died 18 Oct. 1928*

LEIGH, Lt-Col Henry Percy Poingdestre, CIE 1892; Indian Army Unemployed Supernumerary List, 1907; retired; late Commissioner▪ Punjab; *b* Jamaica, 28 Dec. 1851; *e s* of late Col Henry Leigh, 98th Regt and APD, and Ursula, *d* of late J. Davison; *m* 1879, Annie, *d* of late W. R. Maxwell, 95th Regt; one *s* three *d*. *Educ:* private school▪ RMA, Woolwich. Joined Royal Artillery, 1871; Indian Staff Corps. 1877; served in 2nd and 16th Bengal Cavalry; entered Punjab Commission, 1879; special duty in Kurrum Valley, 1886; 1st and 2nd Miranzai expeditions as political officer, 1891 (despatches, medal and clasp, CIE). *Club:* Bath and County, Bath.

Died 25 Feb. 1928

LEIGH, Hon. and Very Rev. James Wentworth, DD; FSA; Dean▪ of Hereford, 1894–1919; Provincial Grand Master of Freemasons for Herefordshire; *b* Paris, 21 Jan. 1838; 3rd *s* of 1st Lord Leigh; *m* 1871▪ Frances (*d* 1910), *d* of Pierce Butler, Georgia, USA, and Frances A. Kemble; one *d* (and one *s* one *d* decd). *Educ:* Harrow; Trinity College, Cambridge. *Publication:* Other Days, 1921. *Recreations:* formerly cricket and riding, etc. *Address:* Brent House, 63 Pont Street, SW. *Clubs* Royal Societies, Wellington. *Died 5 Jan. 1923*

LEIGH, Roger, JP; *b* 27 April 1840; adopted *s* of Sir Robert Holt Leigh▪ 1st Bt (*ext*), of Hindley Hall; *m* 1st, 1861, Elizabeth Jane (*d* 1884)▪ *d* of late Captain Thomas Eden Blackwell, Argyllshire Highlanders; three *d*; 2nd, 1885, Agatha Elizabeth, *o d* of late Alfred Shaw. *Educ:* Christ Church, Oxford; Trinity Coll., Camb. MP Rochester▪ 1880–85. *Address:* Hindley Hall, Wigan; 3 Queen's Parade, Bath. *Died 29 Feb. 1924.*

LEIGH, Hon. Rupert; employed under the War Office since 1915; *b* 10 Dec. 1856; *brother* and *heir-pres.* to 3rd Baron Leigh; *m* 1906, Beatrice Mary, 2nd *d* of late D. R. Smith; one *s. Educ:* Wellington Coll. Late Major, 4th Dragoon Guards; served Afghanistan, with 15th Hussars, 1878-79 (medal); Egypt, 1882 (medal with clasp, bronze star); Bechuanaland, 1884-85; NW Frontier India, 1897 (medal with 2 clasps); ADC to two Governors of New South Wales, 1890-94; Military Secretary to Governor of Bombay, 1900. *Address:* 7 Beaufort Gardens, SW. *Club:* Naval and Military.
Died 14 Aug. 1919.

LEIGHTON, Major Sir Bryan Baldwin Mawddwy, 9th Bt, *cr* 1692; JP for Shropshire; Colonel Westmorland and Cumberland (late Shropshire) Imperial Yeomanry since 1914; passed through Upavon Flying School and gazetted Flying Officer Royal Flying Corps, 1914; *b* 26 Nov. 1868; *e s* of Sir Baldwin Leighton, 8th Bt and Hon. Eleanor Leicester Warren, *d* of 2nd Lord de Tabley; *S* father, 1897; *m* 1890, Margaret Frances, *d* of late John Fletcher, Saltoun Hall, Haddingtonshire; one *s* (and one *s* decd). Joined Americans in Spanish-American war; served South Africa, 1896-97, also 1900-1; served Bechuanaland, 1896-97 (medal and clasp); present in Manchuria, Russo-Japanese War; with the Turkish Army in Thrace, Balkan Campaign; served European War. Owner of about 4,100 acres. *Heir: o surv. s* Richard Tihel Leighton, Yeomanry and RFC (missing, Aug. 1917), *b* 13 Feb. 1893. *Address:* 8 Wellington Court, Knightsbridge, SW. *T:* Kensington 3478; Loton Park, Shrewsbury. *Clubs:* Bachelors', Carlton.
Died 19 Jan. 1919.

LEIGHTON, Edmund Blair, RI; artist; *b* London, 21 Sept. 1853; *s* of Charles Blair Leighton, artist; *m* 1885, Katherine, *e d* of late W. Nash; one *s* one *d. Educ:* University Coll. School. Student Royal Academy, and exhibitor there every year from 1887. Collector of old musical instruments, arms, old furniture, etc. *Works:* Boyhood of Alfred the Great, 1913; *photogravures and engravings:* Lay thy Sweet Hand in mine, etc; The Question; Just by Chance; Two Strings; Goodbye; Next-door Neighbours; In 1816; Sorrow and Song; Launched in Life; Waiting for the Coach; The New Governess; In Time of Peril; Elaine; God Speed; The Accolade; Home; Adieu; Alain Chartier and Queen Margaret of Scotland, RA, 1903; Ribbons and Laces, etc; Vox Populi, 1904; A Foundling, 1905; Vows, 1906; Tristram and Isolde, 1907; The Dedication, 1908; The Shadow, 1909; Pelléas and Mélisande, 1910; To the Unknown Land, 1911; A Hostage, 1912; Boyhood of Alfred the Great, 1913; St Elizabeth of Hungary, 1915; Affections, 1916; Maternity, 1917; Crusaders, RA, 1918; Evicted, Suppression of Religious Houses in 1540, RA, 1919; Mated, RA, 1920. *Address:* 14 Priory Road, Bedford Park, W. *Club:* Arts.
Died 1 Sept. 1922.

LEINSTER, 6th Duke of, *cr* 1766; **Maurice FitzGerald;** Baron of Offaly, 1205; Earl of Kildare, 1316; Viscount Leinster (GB), 1747; Marquess of Kildare, 1761; Earl of Offaly, 1761; Baron Kildare, 1870; Premier Duke, Marquess, and Earl, of Ireland; *b* Kilkea Castle, Co. Kildare, 1 March 1887; *s* of Gerald, 5th Duke, and Hermione, *d* of 1st Earl of Feversham; *S* father, 1893. *Educ:* Eton. *Heir: brother* Lord Edward FitzGerald, *b* 6 May 1892. *Address:* Carton, Maynooth, Co. Kildare.
Died 4 Feb. 1922.

LEIPER, William, JP; RSA 1896 (ARSA 1891); FRIBA 1881; architect, retired; *b* Glasgow, 21 May 1839; *s* of Wm Leiper and Jane Mellis. *Educ:* High School, Glasgow, and private school. Pupil of Boucher and Cousland, architects; afterwards with Wm White, FSA, and J. L. Pearson, RA; designed Dowanhill, Camphill, and Hyndland churches; also St James' Church, Kilmacolm; Sun Fire Offices, Glasgow; Messrs Templetons' factory; Kinloch-Moidart; Kelly, Cairndhu, Cornhill, Ballimore, Glendaruel, Auchenbothie, and other mansions; Dumbarton and Partick Burgh buildings; also designed the decorations for Imperial Yacht "Livadia," and the decoration of the Banqueting Hall, Municipal Buildings, Glasgow; silver medal, Paris Exhibition, 1900. *Recreations:* painting, sketching. *Address:* Terpersey, Helensburgh.
Died 28 May 1916.

LEISHMAN, John G. A.; late American Ambassador to Germany; *b* Pittsburgh, Penn, 28 March 1857, of Scotch-Irish descent; *m* 1880, Julia Crawford; one *s* two *d. Educ:* public schools. Former President of the Carnegie Steel Co., from which office he resigned to accept the nomination tendered by President McKinley as American Minister to Switzerland, 1897; Ambassador to Turkey, 1901-9; Rome, 1909-11. *Clubs:* Union League, New York Yacht, New York; Metropolitan, Washington; Duquesne, Pittsburgh, Pittsburgh; Travellers', Paris; Cercle d'Orient, Club de Constantinople, Constantinople; Caccia, Rome; Union, Berlin.
Died 27 March 1924.

LEISHMAN, Maj.-Gen. John Thomas; Royal Artillery, retired; *b* 1835; 2nd *s* of James Leishman, Bromrigg, Dollar, and Dymchurch; *m* 1860, Annie (*d* 1910), *d* of late Capt. Weir, 6th Dragoons; one *s* two *d. Educ:* Edinburgh University; Addiscombe College. Commissioned (Bombay Artillery), 1855; served with Sir Hugh Rose's force in the Hyderabad District, 1859; transferred to Royal Artillery, 1861; Captain, 1864; Major, 1872; Colonel, 1884; retired as Major-General, 1885. *Recreations:* interested in church, school, and hospital work. *Address:* Chatsworth, Craneswater Park, Southsea. *Club:* Royal Albert Yacht, Southsea.
Died 5 Aug. 1920.

LEISHMAN, Lt-Gen. Sir William Boog, KCMG 1918; KCB 1924 (CB 1915); Kt 1909; MB, CM; FRS 1910; FRCP; FRFPS Glasgow; MRCPE; Hon. LLD Glasgow University and McGill University, Montreal; Director-General Army Medical Service since 1923; Hon. Physician to the King, 1912; *b* 6 Nov. 1865; *s* of late Prof. William Leishman; *m* 1902, Maud Elizabeth, *e d* of late Lt-Col Edward Gunter; one *s* three *d. Educ:* Westminster; Glasgow University. Surgeon, AMS, 1887; Major, RAMC, 1899; Bt Lt-Col, 1905; Lt-Col, 1911; Brevet Col, 1912; Colonel, 1915; Major-General, 1918; Lt-Gen. 1923; served Waziristan Expedition, 1894-95 (medal with clasp); European War, 1914-18 (despatches thrice, KCMG, CB, Commander Legion of Honour, Distinguished Service Medal, USA). Asst Prof. of Pathology, Army Med. School, Netley, 1900-3; Professor of Pathology, Royal Army Medical College, 1903-13; late Examiner in Pathology, University of Oxford; and in Tropical Medicine, University of Cambridge; Harben Lecturer, 1910; Linacre Lecturer, Cambridge, 1925; President, Society of Tropical Medicine and Hygiene, 1911-12; Member of the Yellow Fever Commission, W Africa, 1913-15; the Medical and Sanitary Advisory Committee for Tropical Africa, Colonial Office, 1913; the Medical Research Council, 1913-23; Chairman, Foot and Mouth Disease Research Committee, Ministry of Agriculture, 1924; Member of the Scientific Advisory Committee of British Empire Cancer Campaign, 1924. KGStJ. *Publications:* contribs to medical and scientific literature. *Address:* War Office, SW; Wyberton, Park Hill Road, Croydon. *Clubs:* Athenæum, Junior United Service.
Died 2 June 1926.

LEITCH, Hon. James; Judge, Supreme Court of Ontario, Appelate Division, since 1913; *b* South Branch, Stormont Co., Ont, 2 June 1850; Scotch descent; *s* of William and Nicholas Bryden Leitch; *m* 1876, Elizabeth, *d* of E. Strickland, merchant, Buckingham, Quebec; one *s* four *d. Educ:* private tutor; Williamstown and Cornwall Grammar Schools. Called to Ontario Bar, 1876; QC 1889; practised profession in Cornwall, Ont; Reeve of Cornwall, 1884; Mayor, 1885, 1886; President of Bar Association, united counties of Stormont, Dundas, and Glengarry, 1904-5; Member of High School Board, 1887-1906, Chairman, 1903-6; Life Governor and a Director, Cornwall General Hospital; Candidate for election to Ontario Legislature for Stormont, 1886 and 1890; Candidate for election to House of Commons of Canada for Stormont, 1896; Chairman, Ontario Railway and Municipal Board, 1906-12; Judge of the Supreme Court of Ontario, 1912; a Conservative; a Presbyterian. *Address:* Toronto. *Clubs:* Cornwall, Lambton Golf and County.

LEITCH, Rev. Matthew, DD, DLit; President and Professor of Biblical Criticism, Assembly's College, Belfast, Presbyterian Church in Ireland. *Address:* College Park, Belfast.
Died 30 April 1922.

LEITH OF FYVIE, 1st Baron, *cr* 1905; **Alexander John Forbes-Leith,** JP, DL, Aberdeenshire; *b* 6 Aug. 1847; *e s* of Admiral John Leith and Margaret Forbes of Blackford; *m* 1871, Mary Louise, *d* of D. A. January of St Louis, USA; one *d* (one *s* decd). Entered RN 1860; Lieut 1869; retired, 1871; served New Zealand War, 1864-65; received Humane Society's Silver Medal for Saving Life, 1866. *Recreations:* yachting, shooting, motoring. *Heir:* none. *Address:* Fyvie Castle, Aberdeen. *TA:* Alleith, Fyvie. *T:* Fyvie 8; Hartwell House, near Aylesbury. *T:* Stone 2; 23 St James' Place, SW1. *T:* Gerrard 6134. *Clubs:* Carlton, Coaching, Naval and Military, Marlborough; Royal Yacht Squadron, Cowes; New, Edinburgh.
Died 14 Nov. 1925 (ext).

LEITH, Major Thomas, JP, DL; *b* 1830; *m* 1874, Lady Mary Isabella Dalzell, *sister* of 12th Earl of Carnwath. *Educ:* Royal Military Academy, Edinburgh. Formerly in Bombay Staff Corps, and ADC to Sir Bartle Frere, Governor of Bombay; served with the Bombay Fusiliers at the storming of Moltan, 1848; with Sind Horse in Persian Expedition, 1857, and Indian Mutiny. *Address:* Petmathen, Oyne, Aberdeenshire. *Clubs:* Wellington; Royal Northern, Aberdeen.
Died 30 Jan. 1920.

LEITH-BUCHANAN, Sir Alexander Wellesley George Thomas, 5th Bt, *cr* 1775; *b* 5 Dec. 1866; *s* of Sir George Hector Leith-Buchanan, 4th Bt and Eliza, *d* of Thomas Tod, Drygrange, Roxburghshire, NB; *S* father, 1903; *m* 1888, Maude Mary, *d* of late Alexander Grant; two *s*. JP, DL Dunbartonshire; Vice-Chairman Territorial Army Association, County of Dumbarton; Lt-Col commanding 9th Batt. Argyll and Sutherland Highlanders, 1911–17. *Heir: s* George Hector Macdonald Leith-Buchanan, *b* 30 Jan. 1889. *Address:* Ross Priory, Dumbarton, Scotland.   *Died 29 April 1925.*

LEMAN, Count Georges, GCMG; Lieutenant-General in the Belgian Army; *b* Liège, 8 Jan. 1851; one *s* one *d*. *Educ:* Athenæum, Brussels; Military School, Brussels. Officer in the Engineer Service; Commander-in-Chief of the Military School; Military Governor of the fortress of Liège, which he defended in 1914; Grand Cross, Legion of Honour; Grand Cross, Order of Leopold. *Publications:* works on mathematics, mechanics, fortification, etc. *Address:* 60 quai St Léonard, Liège, Belgium.   *Died 17 Oct. 1920.*

LE MARCHANT, Sir Denis, 3rd Bt, *cr* 1841; *b* 8 June 1870; *s* of Sir Henry Denis Le Marchant, 2nd Bt and Hon. Sophia Strutt, *e d* of 1st Lord Belper; *S* father, 1915; *m* 1915, Katherine, *d* of William Mackay, of Bonar Bridge, NB. *Educ:* Trinity Hall, Cambridge. *Heir: brother* Brig.-Gen. Edward Thomas Le Marchant, *b* 23 Oct. 1871. *Clubs:* Travellers', Wellington.
                                                             Died 29 April 1922.

LEMASS, Peter Edmund, ISO 1903; LRCSI 1880; *b* Dublin, 6 March 1850; *s* of late P. J. Lemass; *m* 1883, Maria Patricia, *d* of late Michael Scallan, Dublin; one *s* three *d*. *Educ:* public and private schools; Ledwich School of Medicine; St Vincent's Hosp., Dublin. Studied surgery and medicine, 1875–80; was Senior Secretary to Board of National Education, Ireland, till 1915, when he retired. *Recreations:* walking, music, theatres. *Address:* 3 Clifton Terrace, Monkstown, Co. Dublin.   *Died 20 March 1928.*

LE MESSURIER, Col Augustus, CIE 1886; *b* 23 June 1837; *m* 1871, Kathleen, *d* of Maj.-Gen. Moxon, BSC. Entered army, 1856; Col 1885; served Okamundel Field Force, 1859; Abyssinian Campaign, 1866 (despatches, medal); Afghan War, 1879–80 (Brevet of Lieut-Col, medal); Hazara Expedition, 1891 (medal with clasp). *Address:* 57 Mount Avenue, Ealing. *T:* Ealing 1164. *Clubs:* United Service, Sports.   *Died 19 Feb. 1916.*

LE MESURIER, Captain Charles Edward, CB 1916; RN; Commodore, 2nd class. Served European War, 1914–17, including Jutland Bank (despatches, CB).
                                                              Died 10 Nov. 1917.

LE MESURIER, Col Frederick Augustus, CB 1893; LLB; Royal Engineers; *b* Newbury, 17 March 1839; *y s* of F. H. Le Mesurier, Comdr RN, and Jane, *d* of T. C. Maunsell of Thorpe Malsor; *m* 1866, Louisa, *d* of John Denis Browne, MP for Co. Mayo; one *s* two *d*. *Educ:* Royal Naval School, New Cross; RMA, Woolwich. LLB Univ. of London. Barrister, Middle Temple. Entered Royal Engineers, 1857; Superintendent Public Works, Trinidad, 1861–63; Inspector of Army Signalling, 1875–80; Commandant of Pretoria, 1880–81; organised and trained a battalion of rifles to take part in defence of town against Boers (despatches, Bt-Lt-Col); CRE base at Suakin, 1885 (despatches, medal with clasp and bronze star); Chief Engineer Ireland, 1889–94. Decorated for services in S Africa and Suakin. *Address:* 31 St Margaret's Road, Oxford.   *Died 9 June 1926.*

LEMMON, Col Sir Thomas Warne, KCB 1922 (CB 1897); Colonel 3rd Battalion (Militia) East Surrey Regiment; *b* 1838; *s* of late William Lemmon of Gatcombe House, Hants; *m* 1st, 1864, Emma Louisa (*d* 1885), *d* of late Thomas Warne; 2nd, 1886, Ellerie, *d* of late James Bayliss; one *s*. Appointed Ensign North Middlesex Regt, 1860; Brig.-Gen. 1900; transferred to 1st Royal Surrey Militia, 1866; commanded 3rd East Surrey Regt as Lt-Col, 1887–98, when appointed Hon. Colonel of Battalion; received Jubilee commemoration medal. *Recreations:* shooting, riding. *Address:* Burleigh, Brimscombe, Gloucestershire. *Club:* Junior United Service.
                                                              Died 8 Jan. 1928.

LE MOINE, Juchereau de St Denis, ISO 1906; Sergeant-at-Arms of the Senate of Canada; *b* 13 July 1850; *s* of Robert Auguste Le Moine of Chateau Richer, Quebec, and Emma Juchereau du Chesnay; *m* 1875, Margaret Louisa Mackey; two *d*. *Educ:* Quebec Seminary; St Mary's College, Montreal. Served on gunboat La Canadienne, also in Ottawa troop of Cavalry; was Captain and Quartermaster in 5th Princess Louise Dragoon Guards. *Address:* 505 Wilbrod Street,

Ottawa. *T:* 1239. *M:* 151, 229. *Clubs:* Golf, Country, Hunt, Connaught Park, Jockey, Ottawa.   *Died 1922.*

LEMON, Sir James, Kt 1909; JP; MICE, FRIBA, FSI, FGS; Past-President of the Institution of Municipal and County Engineers, and Hon. Treasurer; retired Civil Engineer; *b* Lambeth, 15 Jan. 1833; *s* of James Lemon and Sophia Glannon; *m* 1859; no *c*. *Educ:* private school, Westminster. Seven years assistant to the late Sir Joseph Bazalgette, Metropolitan Board of Works; Borough Engineer, Southampton, 1866–78; Consulting Engineer, 1878–81; went into private practice, Southampton and Westminster, 1878; served the offices of Councillor, Alderman, and Mayor, Southampton; Mayor, two years; Member of County Council of Hants, six years; FRSanI. *Publications:* professional reports; Reminiscences of Public Life in Southampton, two vols. *Recreation:* bowls. *Address:* 11 The Avenue, Southampton. *Clubs:* National Liberal; South Hants, Gladstone, Southampton.   *Died 10 May 1923.*

LENG, Christopher David, JP; Director Sir W. C. Leng & Co.; *b* 1861; *e s* of late Sir Wm C. Leng of Oaklands, Sheffield; *m*; one *s* one *d*. *Educ:* Collegiate School; Lausanne. *Recreations:* hunting, motoring, golf. *Address:* Sandygate, Sheffield. *T:* 656. *M:* W 6, W 7, W 1894. *Club:* Junior Constitutional.
                                                              Died 1 Jan. 1921.

LENNARD, Lt-Col Sir Henry Arthur Hallam Farnaby, 2nd Bt, *cr* 1880; JP, DL; *b* 7 Nov. 1859; *s* of Sir John Farnaby Lennard, 1st Bt and Julia, *d* of late Henry Hallam, FRS; *S* father, 1899; *m* 1894, Beatrice, *d* of Albemarle Cator of Woodbastwick Hall, Norfolk; one *s* three *d*. *Educ:* Eton; Christ Church, Oxon. Owner of about 1,200 acres. *Heir: s* Stephen Arthur Hallam Farnaby Lennard, *b* 31 July 1899. *Address:* Wickham Court, West Wickham, Kent. *Clubs:* Arthur's, Travellers'.   *Died 26 Feb. 1928.*

LENNARD, Sir Thomas Barrett-, 2nd Bt, *cr* 1801; *b* 29 Dec. 1826; *s* of Thomas Barrett-Lennard and Mary, *d* of Bartlett Bridger Shedden; *S* grandfather, 1857; *m* 1853, Emma (*d* 1916), *d* of late Rev. Sir John Page Wood, 2nd Bt; two *s* four *d* (and one *s* one *d* decd). *Educ:* St Peter's Coll., Camb. (MA). Owner of about 6,000 acres. *Heir: s* Thomas Barrett-Lennard, JP, DL [*b* 25 Oct. 1853; *m* 1884, Mary, *d* of late Canon Price. *Educ:* Harrow. Barrister, Middle Temple. *Address:* Horsford Manor, Norwich. *Clubs:* Brooks's, Travellers']. *Address:* Belhus, Aveley, Essex; 7 Lewes Crescent, Brighton. *Clubs:* United University, Farmers'.
                                                              Died 17 Jan. 1919.

LENNARD, Sir Thomas Barrett-, 3rd Bt, *cr* 1801; JP, DL; *b* 25 Oct. 1853; *s* of Sir Thomas Barrett-Lennard, 2nd Bt and Emma (*d* 1916), *d* of late Rev. Sir John Page Wood, 2nd Bt; *S* father, 1919; *m* 1884, Mary, *d* of late Canon Price. *Educ:* Harrow. Barrister, Middle Temple; a Chairman of Quarter Sessions, Norfolk. Owner of about 4,000 acres. *Heir: b* Richard Fiennes Barrett-Lennard, *b* 17 May 1861. *Address:* Horsford Manor, Norwich. *Club:* Brooks's.
                                                              Died 19 Sept. 1923.

LEON, Sir Herbert Samuel, 1st Bt, *cr* 1911; JP; *b* 11 Feb. 1850; 2nd *s* of late George Leon; *m* 1st, 1873, Esther (*d* 1875), 2nd *d* of late Edward Henry Beddington; one *s* one *d*; 2nd, 1880, Fanny, 3rd *d* of David Hyam, MP (N) Div. of Bucks, 1891–95; one *s* one *d*. *Educ:* privately. Alderman of Bucks County Council; Chairman of Finance Committee. *Heir: s* George Edward Leon [*b* 7 May 1875; *m* 1899, Mildred Ethel, *d* of late L. J. Jennings, MP; one *s* one *d*. *Address:* 48 Brompton Square, SW]. *Address:* Bletchley Park, Bletchley, Bucks. *T:* Bletchley 31; 7 Cleveland Row, St James's, SW1. *T:* Regent 749. *Clubs:* Devonshire, Reform, Portland.
                                                              Died 23 July 1926.

LEONCAVALLO, Ruggiero; composer; *b* Naples, 8 March 1858. *Educ:* Naples Conservatoire. *Works:* I Pagliacci, 1892; Medici, 1893; Chatterton, 1896; La Bohème, 1897; Zazà, 1900; Roland von Berlin, 1904; Maià 1910; Malbruk, 1911.
                                                              Died 9 Aug. 1919.

LE-POER-TRENCH, Col Hon. William, CVO 1912; late Royal Engineers; *b* 17 June 1837; *s* of 3rd Earl of Clancarty and Lady Sarah Juliana Butler, *d* of 3rd Earl of Carrick; *m* 1864, Harriet (*d* 1909), *o c* of Sir William Martins; one *s* (and one *s* decd). Entered RE 1854; Capt., 1861; Major, 1872; Col 1879; served in China, 1857–58 (despatches, medal with clasp); in charge of operations to connect the triangulation of England with Germany through France and Belgium, 1860–61. MP (C) Co. Galway, 1872–74; contested Whitechapel in 1886 and 1893; Chairman of Poor Law and Lunacy

Inquiry Commission, Ireland, 1877–79. JP for London, Westminster, Middlesex, and Bucks. *Address:* St Huberts, Gerrard's Cross, Bucks. *Clubs:* Carlton, Constitutional, United Service.

Died 16 Sept. 1920.

LE QUEUX, William Tufnell; novelist; traveller; Ex-Consul of Republic of San Marino; *b* London, 2 July 1864; *e s* of William Le Queux, Châteauroux, Indre. *Educ:* privately in London; Pegli, near Genoa. Studied art in Paris; forsook the Quartier Latin; made a tour through France and Germany on foot; became journalist and special correspondent; foreign editor of Globe, 1891; resigned to devote time to novel writing, 1893; travelled in Algeria, Morocco, Kabylia, the Areg region of the Sahara, etc; journeyed through Macedonia, Turkey, Montenegro, Serbia, Albania, 1907; Arctic, 1908; Sudan, 1909; correspondent of Daily Mail during Balkan war; collector of mediæval manuscripts, codices, and monastic seals, of which he possessed a large and valuable collection; had intimate knowledge of secret service of Continental Powers; consulted by the Government on such matters; forecast the war in his book The Invasion, 1908; lectured on Spies and Spying. Commander of Orders of St Sava of Serbia, Danilo of Montenegro, Crown of Italy, San Marino Order. *Publications:* Guilty Bonds, 1890; Secrets of Monte Carlo, 1899; An Observer in the Near East, 1907; German Spies in England, 1915; Rasputin, the Rascal Monk; The Secret Life of the Ex-Tsaritza, The Intriguers, 1920; Landru, 1921; Things I Know, 1923; Where the Desert Ends, 1923; The Crystal Claw, 1924; The Broadcast Mystery, 1924; Hidden Hands, 1925; The Blue Bungalow, 1925; The Fatal Face, 1926; The Chameleon, 1927; Blackmailed, 1927; and many other books. *Recreations:* revolver practice, ski-ing in Switzerland, the study of Egyptology and criminology, experiments in wireless telephony (Member of the Institute of Radio Engineers; President of Wireless Experimental Association; was first wireless experimenter to broadcast). *Address:* c/o Camelot Press, 34 Strand, WC. *Clubs:* Devonshire; Swiss Alpine. *Died 13 Oct. 1927.*

LE SAGE, Sir John Merry, Kt 1918; Lieutenant of the City of London; late Managing Editor, Daily Telegraph; retired June 1923; *b* Clifton, 23 April 1837; *s* of John Le Sage, Clifton; *m* Elizabeth Lord Martin. *Educ:* Clifton; Bath; London. After a brief provincial career was engaged on the staff of the Daily Telegraph, and served for many years under the direction of the late J. M. Levy and Lord Burnham; acted as special correspondent in France, Germany, Italy, Russia, Egypt, America, Canada; with the German army in the campaign of 1870–71; and with Lord Wolseley's Force in Egypt in 1882; was in Paris during the whole period of the Commune; managing editor for many years. *Recreation:* cricket. *Address:* 25 Ranelagh Avenue, Hurlingham, SW6. *T:* Putney 1089.

Died 1 Jan. 1926.

LESCHER, Joseph Francis; Baron of the old Kingdom of France by grant, Louis XIII, of Kertsfeld, Alsace; Hereditary Count of the Holy Roman Empire by Brief of Pope Pius X; JP counties of Essex, Middlesex, and London; DL Essex; *b* 6 Aug. 1842; *m* Mira Charlotte, *d* of Capt. Hankey, 9th Lancers, and Charlotte, *d* of the Marquis d'Etampes; two *d. Educ:* Stonyhurst College. High Sheriff of Essex, 1885–86. *Recreations:* travel, hunting, shooting. *Address:* Boyles Court, near Brentwood, Essex. *Clubs:* Reform, St George's.

Died 8 Jan. 1923.

LESLIE, Lt-Col Archibald Stewart, CMG 1918; TD; JP, DL; Yeomanry; *b* 1873; *m* 1910, Margaret Isobel, *d* of Col E. W. Horne; four *s. Educ:* Oxford University. Late Secretary, Grouse Disease Inquiry; served European War, 1914–18 (despatches, CMG). *Address:* Kininvie, Banffshire; 1 Eton Terrace, Edinburgh. *T:* 6793. *Club:* New, Edinburgh. *Died 1 May 1928.*

LESLIE, Sir Bradford, KCIE 1887; Civil Engineer; Chairman of the Southern Punjab Railway Co. Ltd; original designer and builder of large bridges in Bengal, including the highway bridge over the river Hooghly at Calcutta; *b* 18 Aug. 1831; *s* of late Charles R. Leslie, RA; *m* 1855, Mary Jane Eliza (*d* 1886), *d* of late W. Honey, MInstCE; one *s* one *d* (and three *d* decd). Fellow of University of Calcutta; Officier de l'instruction publique, France. *Address:* 171 Maida Vale, W9. *T:* Maida Vale 2661.

Died 21 March 1926.

LESLIE, George Dunlop, RA 1876 (ARA 1868); *b* London, 2 July 1835; *y s* of Charles R. Leslie, RA; married; four *s* two *d. Educ:* Mercers' School. Student at Royal Academy, 1856; figure and landscape painter. *Publications:* Our River, 1881; Letters to Marco, 1894; Riverside Letters, 1896; The Inner Life of the Royal Academy, 1914. *Pictures:* Mid-summer Morn, 1904; The Deserted Mill, 1905.

Recreations: gardening, boating. *Address:* Compton House, Lindfield, Sussex. *Club:* Athenæum. *Died 21 Feb. 1921.*

LESLIE, Sir John, 1st Bt, *cr* 1876; DL; late Lieutenant 1st Life Guards; *b* 16 Dec. 1822; *e s* of late Charles P. Leslie, Glasslough, Co. Monaghan, MP, and his 2nd wife, Christiana, *d* of George Fosberry, Clorane, Co. Limerick; *m* 1856, Lady Constance Damer, *sister* of 4th Earl of Portarlington; one *s* four *d. Educ:* Harrow; Christ Church, Oxford (BA). MP (C) Co. Monaghan, 1871–80. Owned about 44,500 acres. *Heir: s* Col John Leslie [*b* 7 Aug. 1857; *m* 1884, Leonie Blanche, *d* of Leonard Jerome of New York; three *s. Address:* 46 Great Cumberland Place, W. *Club:* Turf]. *Address:* Glaslough, Co. Monaghan; 22 Manchester Square, W. *Clubs:* Carlton, Athenæum, Travellers'. *Died 23 Jan. 1916.*

LESLIE, Robert Murray, MA, BSc, MD (Edinburgh); MRCP; Senior Physician, Prince of Wales General Hospital; Physician, Royal Hospital for Diseases of the Chest, London; Civil Physician, Bermondsey Military Hospital; Physician, Canning Town Hospital for Women and Children; Lecturer on Medicine, NE London Post-Graduate College; Deputy Chairman and Examiner, Incorporated Institute of Hygiene; Chairman of Council, Women's Imperial Health Association of Great Britain; *b* 23 June 1866; *s* of Alexander Leslie, JP Ross-shire, and Isabella Murray, Old Meldrum, Aberdeenshire; *m* 1920, Gwladys Olive, *y d* of Capt. Knox Keith, RN. *Educ:* George Watson's College, Edinburgh; Universities of Edinburgh and London. Sir Edward Baxter Scholar, Natural Science, 1889; Ettles Scholar, 1892; University Medallist in Medicine and Obstetric Medicine and Stark Scholar in Clinical Medicine, 1892; FRSM; Member of Eugenics and other Scientific Societies; late Assistant to Professor of Pathology and Professor of Clinical Medicine, University of Edinburgh; Senior Resident Physician, Edinburgh Royal Infirmary; and House Physician, Brompton Hospital for Consumption; Assistant to Examiners in Medicine, London University; Senior Medical Registrar and Lecturer on Practical Medicine, King's College Hospital; President, NE London Clinical Society; Officier d'Académie Française. *Publications:* The Health of a Woman, 1917; Hæmorrhage from the Lungs, in Encyclopædia Medica, 1917; Disordered Action of the Heart, in Clinical Journal, 1919; Vaccine Treatment of Influenza and Pneumonia, in Medical Press, 1919. *Recreations:* travel, mountaineering, golf. *Address:* 143 Harley Street, W1. *T:* Mayfair 397. *Clubs:* Royal Automobile, Albemarle, Roehampton.

Died 29 March 1921.

LESLIE-ELLIS, Lt-Col Henry, JP and DL Co. Wicklow; High Sheriff, 1902; FSA, FRGS; *b* 10 Feb. 1852; *e s* of late Robert Francis Ellis Leslie-Ellis of Magherymore, Co. Wicklow; *m* 1894, Margaret, *d* of Rev. S. Rolleston, Rector of St Minver, Cornwall; three *s* one *d. Educ:* Harrow; Sandhurst. Late Major Inniskilling Dragoons, and Lieut-Col Royal Bucks Hussars; joined Inniskilling Dragoons, 1872; served Boer War, 1881–82; was Staff Officer to Colonel Curtis's column to Potchefstroom, 1882; later, Adjutant and second in command, Royal Bucks Hussars. *Recreations:* hunting, travel; collector of Greek, Roman, and English gold coins. *Address:* Magherymore, Wicklow. *Clubs:* Army and Navy, Wellington; Kildare Street, Dublin.

Died 1919.

LE SOUËF, W. H. Dudley; Director Zoological Gardens since 1901, and Manager Royal Park, Melbourne; *b* Victoria, Australia; English parentage; *s* of A. A. C. Le Souëf; *m* 1888, Edith E. Wadeson, England; three *s* three *d. Educ:* Melbourne; Crediton Grammar School, Devon. Travelled extensively in various parts of the world in the interests of his Society; took part in the Zoological Congress at Boston, USA, and in the Ornithological Congress in Cambridge, England; Member, British Ornithologists' Union; British Ornithologists' Congress; Corresponding Member, Zool Soc.; Washington Park Zool Soc.; SNG, Frankfort; Corres. Fellow, Amer. Ornithol Union; Past-President and Hon. Member Royal Australian Ornithological Union; Life Vice-President and Member Melbourne Camera Club. *Publications:* Wild Life in Australia; Animals of Australia (jointly); Birds of Australia (jointly); Description of Birds' Eggs from North Australia (Ibis, 1896–98); Visit to Albatross Island (Ibis, 1893); Mound-building Birds of Australia (Ibis, 1899); Visit to Queensland (Vict. Nat. 1891); many papers on ornithology and on geographical subjects; many photos, mostly of natural history subjects, in many publications; Ascent of Mount Peter Botte. *Address:* Zoological Gardens, Parkville, Melbourne. *Died 6 Sept. 1924.*

LESSARD, Maj.-Gen. François Louis, CB 1900; *b* 9 Dec. 1860; *m* 1882, Florence, *d* of Thomas Conrad Lee, Quebec; three *d. Educ:* Collège St Thomas, PQ; Commercial Academy, Quebec. 2nd Lieut Quebec Garrison Artillery, 1880; transferred to 65th Batt. Infantry,

Montreal, 1884; appointed to Cavalry School Corps, 1884; Rebellion, Canadian North-West, 1885 (medal); Captain Royal Canadian Dragoons, 1888; Major, 1894; Lieut-Col 1898; served S African War, 1899-1901 (despatches, medal 5 clasps); Brevet Colonel, 1901; Adjutant-Gen. Canadian Militia, 1907-12; GOC 2nd Division, 1912-15; Substantive Colonel, 1907; Brigadier-General, 1911; Major-General, 1912; Inspector-General Eastern Canada, 1915; GOC Mil. Dist No 6 and OC Halifax Fortress Command, 1917-18; ADC to Governor-General of Canada, 1901-11. *Address:* Meadowvale, Ontario. *Clubs:* Junior Army and Navy; Hunt, Toronto.

Died Aug. 1927.

LESTER, Rev. Henry Arthur; Director, Bishop of London's Sunday School Council; *s* of Edward Lester of Bedford; *m* Alice, *d* of John Perrin of Thurnham, Kent; three *s* one *d*. *Educ:* Bedford Modern School; Oxford University. BA 1895, Honours Mod. History; MA 1899; ordained, 1896. Assistant Chaplain and Tutor, St John's Training College, Battersea, 1896-98; Vice-Principal Warrington Training College, 1898-1911; University Extension Lecturer of Manchester and Liverpool Universities. *Publication:* Sunday School Teaching. *Recreation:* golf. *Address:* 108 Muswell Hill Road, N10.

Died 24 July 1922.

LE STRANGE, Hamon, FSA; *b* 25 Nov. 1840; *e s* of Henry L. Styleman le Strange, of Hunstanton Hall, Norfolk, and Jamesina, *d* of John Stewart, MP, of Belladrum, Inverness-shire; *m* Emmeline, *d* of William Austin, of Boston, Massachusetts; three *s* three *d*. *Educ:* Eton; Christ Church, Oxford. 1st class in Law and Modern History. 3rd Secretary in HM Diplomatic Service at Mexico, Paris, and Washington, 1865-71; Chairman of Quarter Sessions for Norfolk; County Alderman; Provincial Grand Master of Freemasons; Chairman of Eastern Sea Fisheries Joint Committee. *Publications:* Norfolk Official Lists; History of Freemasonry in Norfolk; Le Strange Records, 1100-1310. *Address:* Hunstanton Hall, Norfolk. *Club:* Athenæum.

Died 25 March 1918.

LE STRANGE, Roland, JP, DL; *b* 5 March 1869; *e s* of late Hamon Le Strange and Emmeline, *d* of William Austin, of Boston, Massachusetts; *m* 1891, Hon. Agneta Frances Delaval, *o d* of 18th Baron Hastings; two *s*. Late Lieut PWO Norfolk Artillery. *Address:* Hunstanton Hall, Norfolk.

Died 20 Feb. 1919.

LESUEUR, Daniel; Officier de la Légion d'honneur; femme de lettres; ex-vice-présidente de la Société des Gens de Lettres; Présidente du Denier des Veuves des Gens de Lettres; *b* à Paris; *m* Henry Lapauze, Conservateur du Palais des Beaux-Arts de la Ville de Paris, Officier de la Légion d'honneur. *Educ:* en France et en Angleterre. *Publications:* poésies: trad. de Lord Byron; romans: Marcelle; Un Mystérieux Amour; Amour d'aujourd'hui; Névrosée; Une Vie tragique; Passion slave; Justice de femme; Haine d'amour; A force d'aimer; Invincible Charme; Lèvres closes; Comédienne; Au delà de l'amour; L'Honneur d'une femme; Fiancée d'outre-mer; Le Cœur chemine; La Force du passé; L'Or sanglant; Fleur de joie; Lys royal; Le Meurtre d'une âme; Le Marquis de Valcor; Madame de Ferneuse; Le Fils de l'Amant; Madame l'Ambassadrice; Nietzschéenne; Le Droit à la Force; Flaviana Princesse; Chacune soir Rêve; Une Ame de Vingt ans; Au Tournant des Jours; Sociologie; L'Evolution féminine. *Recreations:* sports, équitation. *Address:* Petit Palais, Champs Elysées, Paris. *T:* Elysées, 17.88; La Valcorie, Parmain (Seine-et-Oise). *T:* 15.

Died 3 Jan. 1921.

LETCHWORTH, Rev. Arnold, MA; Hon. Canon of Southwark Cathedral; *b* 6 July 1840; *s* of Henry Finch and Maria Elizabeth Letchworth; *m* 1886, Mary Frances Oldman. *Educ:* Kensington Proprietary Grammar School; Exeter College, Oxford. Deacon, 1864; Priest, 1865; Curate, Christ Church, Folkestone, 1864-66; Saltburn-by-Sea, 1867-69; Vicar, St John's, Kingston-on-Thames, 1870-1915. *Address:* 12 St Augustin's Road, Bournemouth.

Died 18 Jan. 1923.

LETCHWORTH, Sir Edward, Kt 1902; FSA; late Grand Secretary of Freemasons; *b* 18 March 1833; *e s* of late Henry Finch Letchworth, Oak Hill, Surbiton; *m* 1902, Mary Constance, *widow* of Thomas Blaikie of Aberdeen. Formerly a solicitor, and for many years one of the Chief Stewards of Her Majesty's Manors; was a promoter of the Volunteer movement in 1859, and served as Captain in both the 33rd and 40th Middlesex Volunteer Corps, 1860-67; Governor of the Foundling and St Bartholomew's Hospitals. *Address:* 14 Cornwall Gardens, SW. *T:* 2093 Kensington; Freemasons' Hall, WC; Lynn Court, 30 Broadwater Down, Tunbridge Wells, Kent. *Clubs:* Junior Carlton, Garrick.

Died 8 Oct. 1917.

LETCHWORTH, Rev. Henry Howard, MA; Hon. Canon of Canterbury, 1911; *b* 24 Aug. 1836; 2nd *s* of late Henry Finch Letchworth of Oak Hill, Surbiton; *m* 1885, Mary Georgina, *d* of late Lt J. Strettell, RN, and *widow* of Frederick Fortreath Smart; three *s*. *Educ:* Kensington Grammar School; Oriel College, Oxford. Deacon, 1859; Priest, 1860; held various curacies; Vicar, Holy Trinity, Southampton, 1885; Rector, Exton, Hants, 1886; Vicar, St Peter's, Maidstone, 1889; Vicar, Detling, 1898-1911; Rural Dean of Sutton, 1904-11. *Address:* 62 Old Dover Road, Canterbury.

Died 18 Oct 1921.

LETHBRIDGE, Alan Bourchier; author and writer on Russian affairs; *b* Sandhill Park, Taunton, 21 Jan. 1878; *s* of Sir Wroth Lethbridge, 4th Bt and Ann Williams, *d* of Thomas Benyon; *m* 1912, Marjorie Colt, *o d* of General Byrne, United States Army (retired). *Educ:* Eastman's Naval Academy; Sherborne; Heidelberg. Intended for the Navy, failed medically; a year tea-planting in Ceylon and then travelled extensively—S America, the Near East, Russia and Europe generally; political officer in Northern Nigeria, 1903-7; visited Siberia and later Canada and the United States; after marriage lived chiefly in Russia; during European War was attached to the Foreign Office, having previously served as interpreter; subsequently transferred to the Ministry of Information; Fellow of United States Geographical Soc.; Special Correspondent, Daily Telegraph, in West Africa, 1919; Fellow Royal Historical Society. *Publications:* The New Russia; The Soul of the Russian; Germany as it is To-day; West Africa—the Elusive, etc. *Recreations:* travel, books, carnations. *Address:* 2316 Nineteenth Street, Washington, DC. *Clubs:* Wellington; Royal Dorset Yacht.

Died 25 Feb. 1923.

LETHBRIDGE, Lt-Col Sir Alfred Swaine, KCSI 1896 (CSI 1890); JP Hants; *b* Tirhoot, Bengal, 30 Sept. 1844; *s* of W. F. Lethbridge, Woolborough, Devonshire, and Susan, *d* of Robert Swaine, Musbury, Devonshire; *m* 1899, Edith Seymour, *widow* of George Bellett, and *d* of H. F. Waring of Lyme Regis, Dorset. *Educ:* King's Coll., London; Aberdeen (MD). Entered Bengal Medical Service, 1867; Lt-Col 1887; served in Burmah and Bengal; Additional Member of Council of Viceroy of India, 1895-97; retired April 1898. *Address:* Windhover, Bursledon, Hants.

Died 11 March 1917.

LETHBRIDGE, Sir Roper, KCIE 1890 (CIE 1878); Kt 1885; DL; JP, Devon, and JP Kent; Lord of the Manor of Exbourne; patron of one living; President of Anti-Tea-Duty League; President of the Devonshire Association for 1901; member of the Exeter Diocesan Board of Education, and of the Standing Committee of the Exeter Diocesan Conference; Chairman of Council of the Devon and Cornwall Record Society; Vice-President of the Okehampton Agricultural Society; Commissioner for Income Tax appeals, Okehampton; Vice-President of Tariff Reform League, and Chairman of Devonshire Branch of League; *b* Devonshire, 23 Dec. 1840; *e s* of late E. Lethbridge; *m* 1st, 1865, Eliza (*d* 1895), *d* of W. Finlay, and *g g d* of Henry, 11th Baron Teynham; one *s* one *d*; 2nd, 1897, Emma, *d* of John Neave and *widow* of late Frederick Burbridge, Micklefield, Herts. *Educ:* Plymouth and Mannamead Coll.; Exeter Coll., Oxford (Scholar), MA; graduated in double Classical and Mathematical Honours. Barrister, Inner Temple, 1880; Bengal Education Service, 1868-76; Secretary Simla Education Commission, 1877; Indian Political Agent, 1878; a founder and one of the original Committee of the Imperial Federation League, 1884; candidate for Whitby, 1884; MP (C) North Kensington, 1885-92. Editor Calcutta (Quarterly) Review, 1871-78. *Publications:* The Golden Book of India; History of India; History and Geography of Bengal; Selections from Modern English Literature; High Education in India; India and Imperial Preference; Life of Ramtann Lahiri, the Bengali Reformer; The Indian Offer of the Imperial Preference; many other educational and political books and pamphlets. *Address:* Exbourne Manor, Exbourne, Devon. *TA:* Lethbridge, Exbourne. *Club:* Carlton.

Died 15 Feb. 1919.

LETT, Rev. Henry William, MA; MRIA; Rector of Aghaderg, Co. Down, since 1886; Chancellor of Dromore Cathedral; Rural Dean and Member of the Diocesan Council and General Synod of the Church of Ireland; *b* 1838; *s* of Rev. Canon Charles Lett, Rector of Finvoy, of Tincurry, County Wexford, and Elizabeth Mary, *d* of Lt-Col Marcus Corry, DL, of Ballyhomra; *m* 1865, Louisa Kathleen, *d* of John Tandy, of Dublin; one *s* three *d*. *Educ:* Trinity College, Dublin. Curate of Derryaghy, Co. Antrim, 1861; Incumbent of Meigh and Curate of Camlough, Co. Armagh, 1863; Rector of Montiaghs, Co. Armagh, 1875. *Publications:* Descriptive Notes of all the Hepatics found in the British Islands, 1902; Census Report on the Mosses of Ireland, 1915. *Address:* Aghaderg Glebe, Loughbrickland, Banbridge, Co. Down.

Died 26 Dec. 1920.

LETTS, Edmund Albert, DSc (Hon.); FRSE, FCS, FIC, FRSanI; Emeritus Professor of Chemistry in the Queen's University, Belfast; *b* Sydenham, Kent, 27 Aug. 1852; 3rd *s* of Thomas Letts of Clare Lodge, Sydenham, and South View, Isle of Wight, and of Emma Horwood, 3rd *d* of Frederick Barry of Boxhill, Surrey. *Educ:* Bishop Stortford School; King's College, London; Universities of Vienna and Berlin. Chief Assistant, Chemical Laboratory, University of Edinburgh, 1872; First Professor of Chemistry in University College, Bristol, 1876; Keith Prizeman, RSE, 1890. *Publications:* (with Dr Adeney) Appendix VI to 5th Report of the Royal Commission on Sewage Disposal, and (with Eric H. Richards) Appendix III to 7th Report of *ditto*; On the Pollution of Estuaries and Tidal Waters; Some Fundamental Problems in Chemistry—Old and New; various papers on scientific subjects. *Address:* Queen's University, Belfast; 6 Dunelin, Malone Road, Belfast. *Died 19 Feb. 1918.*

LEUCHARS, Col Hon. Sir George, KCMG 1915 (CMG 1903); DSO 1907; *b* 16 April 1868; *m* 1891, Marion, *d* of late W. Mackenzie, MA. Served S Africa, Umvoti Mounted Rifles, 1899–1902 (despatches, Queen's medal 4 clasps, CMG); Native Rebellion, Natal, 1906; Bt Col OC Troops, Natal (medal and clasp, DSO); represented Umvoti Co. Natal Parliament, 1893–1906; Minister of Native Affairs and Public Works, 1903–5; returned to Union Parliament, Umvoti Division, 1910; JP; Minister of Commerce and Industries, Union of S Africa, 1911; Minister Public Works and Acting Minister Posts and Telegraphs, 1912; resigned, 1912; OC Troops, Natal, 1914–15. *Address:* Bracken, Greytown, Natal. *Died Feb. 1924.*

LEUDESDORF, Charles, MA; Fellow of Pembroke College, Oxford, since 1873; Registrar of the University of Oxford since 1906; *b* Manchester, 30 Jan. 1853; *s* of Henry Leudesdorf, Manchester; unmarried. *Educ:* private school; The Owens College, Manchester; Worcester College, Oxford. Exhibitioner, 1869, Scholar, 1870–73; Mathematical Lecturer, Pembroke College, 1873–1906; Proctor, 1887; Secretary to Boards of Faculties, 1889–1906. *Publications:* A translation of Cremona's Elements of Projective Geometry, 1885; various papers on mathematical subjects in the Proceedings of the London Mathematical Society. *Address:* 8 Bardwell Road, Oxford. *T:* Oxford 309. *Died 10 Aug. 1924.*

LEVANDER, F. W., FRAS 1871; Editor of the British Astronomical Association since 1900; Librarian, 1895–1906; on Council, 1895–1911; President, 1906–8. *Address:* 30 North Villas, Camden Square, NW. *Died 20 Dec. 1916.*

LEVER, Col Sir Arthur Levy, 1st Bt, *cr* 1911; JP Essex; *b* 17 Nov. 1860; *s* of late Joseph Levy of Leicester; added the name of Lever for family reasons, by Deed Poll 1896, by Royal Licence 1911; *m* 1896, Beatrice (*d* 1917), 3rd *d* of late Philip Falk; one *s. Educ:* University College School; privately and abroad. Member of the Royal Commission on Coast Erosion and Afforestation, 1906–11; MP (L) Harwich Division NE Essex, 1906–10; contested South Wolverhampton, 1910; MP (NL) Central Hackney, 1922–23. Member of the London War Pensions Committee; Deputy Director of Recruiting for South-Eastern Region, 1917; served in European War first as Major 2/1st Batt. The London Regiment, Royal Fusiliers, and subsequently on Headquarters' Staff, Southern Command, with rank of Colonel (temp.) and retired as Colonel. *Recreations:* hunting, outdoor sports. *Heir: s* Tresham Joseph Philip Lever, *b* 3 Sept. 1900. *Address:* 20 Hans Crescent, SW1. *T:* Victoria 202; The Grange, Knockholt, Kent. *T:* Knockholt 14. *Clubs:* Reform, Bath, Ranelagh. *Died 23 Aug. 1924.*

LEVERHULME, 1st Viscount, *cr* 1922, of the Western Isles; **William Hesketh Lever,** FRGS; Bt 1911; Baron 1917; Chairman of Lever Brothers, Ltd, and founder of Port Sunlight; *b* Bolton, Lancashire, 19 Sept. 1851; *m* 1874, Elizabeth Ellen (*d* 1913), *d* of Crompton Hulme of Bolton; one *s. Educ:* Bolton Church Institute. Entered father's business in Bolton, 1867; removed to Wigan, 1877, and afterwards to Warrington and Wirral; Congregationalist. Contested (R) Wirral, 1900; Birkenhead 1892, 1894, and 1895; MP (L) Wirral Div., Cheshire, 1906–10; High Sheriff, Lancs, 1917; Junior Warden for Grand Lodge of England, 1918; Mayor of Bolton, 1918–19. Hon. RI; Hon. FRIBA; Hon. LLD Edin.; Grand Officer, Order of Léopold II, Belgium. *Heir s* Hon. William Hulme Lever, *b* 25 March 1888. *Address:* Borve Lodge, Leverburgh, Harris, Scotland; The Hill, North End, NW3. *T:* Hampstead 1324; The Bungalow, Rivington, near Bolton. *Clubs:* Reform, National Liberal, Royal Automobile, Caledonian. *Died 7 May 1925.*

LEVESON GOWER, Major Lord Alastair St Clair Sutherland-, MC; Royal Horse Guards; *b* 24 Jan. 1890; *only brother* and *heir-pres.*

of 5th Duke of Sutherland; *m* 1918, Elizabeth Helene, *d* of Warren Gardener, Demarest, New York. Late Lieut Lovat's Scouts Yeomanry; served European War, 1914–18 (wounded, despatches, MC). *Died 28 April 1921.*

LEVESON GOWER, Arthur Francis Gresham, FSA; *b* 25 April 1851; *y s* of late Wm Leveson Gower of Titsey Place, Surrey, and Emily, 3rd *d* of Maj.-Gen. Sir Francis Hastings Doyle, 1st Bt; *m* 1881, Caroline Frederica (*d* 1895), *y d* of late George Savile Foljambe of Aldwark, Yorks, and Osberton, Notts; two *d. Educ:* Eton; Christ Church, Oxford; BA 1874, MA 1877. Entered Diplomatic Service, 1876; 3rd Sec. 1879; 2nd Sec. 1881; Sec. of Legation, 1895; employed at Constantinople, Rio de Janeiro, Vienna, Berlin, Berne, Belgrade, Athens; Secretary of Legation at the Hague, 1898–1905; retired, 1905. KJStJ; one of three representatives of Order on occasion of German Emperor's visit to Palestine, 1898; admitted to Freedom of City of London, 1913; a Special Constable, Headquarters Central Department Section XI, stationed at Buckingham Palace during the war. *Address:* Hadleigh House and Clifford Lodge, Windsor. *Clubs:* Athenæum, Travellers'. *Died 26 Dec. 1922.*

LEVETT, Ernest Laurence, KC 1891; MA; *m* Mary Jeudwine (*d* 1912). Called to the Bar, Lincoln's Inn, 1873; Bencher; retired from practice; late Fellow of St John's College, Cambridge. *Address:* 78 Cambridge Terrace, Hyde Park, W; North Bank, Alnmouth, Northumberland. *Died 3 Oct. 1916.*

LEVEY, Charles Joseph, ISO 1904; Resident Magistrate; *b* Grahamstown, Cape Colony, 1846; *m* 1876, Sarah Randall. *Educ:* Lovedale Seminary, Cape Colony. Commanded a column of Tembus in Transkeian War (medal); Hon. Lieut-Colonel DDV Guard, Dordrecht, Cape Colony; Commandant, Dordrecht, in Boer War, 1900; captured rebel chief Sandillis in Kafir rebellion, Cape Colony; fortified and successfully defended Residency, Southeyville, Cape Colony, 1879; commanded native volunteers against chiefs Stock and Mfanta, Cape Colony, 1880; Political Officer with Colonel Wavell's column in Tembu War, 1880; Clerk to British Resident, Fingoland, Cape Colony, 1880; Political Agent with emigrant Tembus, 1875; Magistrate, Southeyville, 1877; Magistrate, Xalanga, 1883; Civil Commissioner and Resident Magistrate, Wodehouse, Cape Colony, 1900; succeeded Lord Cecil, Imperial Commissioner, Western Transvaal, 1901; Resident Magistrate, Marico, Transvaal Colony, 1902. *Address:* Malmani Kloof Road, Seapoint, Capetown, SA. *Died 9 Oct. 1920.*

LEVEY, George Collins, CMG 1878; *b* Devonshire, 1835; *s* of late George Levey, Camberwell Grove; *m* 1st, 1863, Euphemia Dalton (*d* 1874), *e d* of Charles Whybrow Ligar, Surveyor-General of Victoria; 2nd, 1877, Mary Elizabeth (*d* 1908), *d* of George Parker, Washington, and *widow* of late Hon. J. E. Bouligny, Member of Congress for City of New Orleans. *Educ:* University Coll. London. First person in Victoria to employ machinery in quartz-crushing; travelled all over Europe, 1859–61; MLA Normanby, 1861–68; editor and proprietor of Melbourne Herald, 1863–68, which paper he issued at 1d, and thus founded cheap journalism in Australia; editor and contributor to Melbourne Age, 1869–81; Secretary to Commissioners for Victoria at the Exhibitions in London, Paris, Vienna, Philadelphia, Melbourne, 1873, 1876, 1878, 1880–81; Executive Commissioner, Amsterdam, 1883; Secretary Royal Commission, Hobart Exhibition, 1894–95; Secretary Adelaide Exhibition, 1887; Colonial Committee of Royal Commission to Paris Exhibition, 1900. *Publications:* Handbooks to Australasia and River Plate; Australian Encyclopædia. *Address:* Royal Colonial Institute. *Died 13 April 1919.*

LEVY, Joshua Moses; retired General Foreign Merchant; *b* Gibraltar, 19 Dec. 1854; *e s* of Moses de Joshua Levy and Esther Pariente; unmarried. *Educ:* Northwick College. Elder and Past Warden, Spanish and Portuguese Jews' Synagogue; Member London Committee of Deputies of the British Jews; Member Council Jews' College; Committee of Delegates of Sir Moses Montefiore's Endowment at Ramsgate; Member London Chamber of Commerce; Member of Council British Merchants' Morocco Association; Member Council of League of British Jews. *Recreations:* travelling, horse riding. *Address:* 98 Sutherland Avenue, W9. *Clubs:* Maccabeans; Ramsgate, Ramsgate. *Died 2 March 1922.*

LEVY, Major Walter Henry, DSO; *b* 1 Nov. 1876; *e s* of late Henry Levy, 11 Hyde Park Place, W, and Annette, *d* of E. H. Beddington; *m* 1903, Nellie, *e d* of 1st Viscount Bearsted; one *s* three *d. Educ:* Rugby. Director of M. Samuel & Co., Ltd, Gresham Life Assurance Society Ltd, Gresham Fire and Accident Society Ltd; travelled extensively; served European War in France and Belgium, 1914–18 (despatches twice, DSO). *Recreations:* shooting, rowing. *Address:* 54 Lowndes Square, SW1. *T:* Kensington 3337. *Clubs:* Carlton, Wellington, Ranelagh. *Died 9 June 1923.*

LEWIN, Lt-Col Thomas Herbert, JP; *b* 1 April 1839; *s* of G. H. Lewin, barrister; *m* 1876, Margaret, 3rd *d* of late John R. McClean, MP for East Staffordshire, and *widow* of Ralph, *e s* of late Sir George Elliot, 1st Bt, MP for Durham; one *s* two *d*. *Educ:* private schools; Addiscombe College. Major Indian Army, 1877; retired, 1878, Lt-Col; served Indian Mutiny, 1854–57; defence of Cawnpore, siege of Lucknow (medal with clasp); Lushai Expedition, 1871–72 (medal with clasp). *Publications:* A Fly on the Wheel, or How I helped to govern India; Life and Death; Wild Tribes of the South-East Frontier. *Recreations:* lawn tennis, billiards, music. *Address:* Parkhurst, Abinger Common, Dorking. *Club:* United Service.
Died 12 Feb. 1916.

LEWIS, Mrs Agnes Smith; *b* 1843; *e* twin *d* of John Smith, Irvine, Ayrshire; *m* 1887, Rev. Samuel Savage Lewis (*d* 1891), Fellow of Corpus Christi College, Cambridge. *Educ:* Irvine Academy till the age of 12; private schools (Birkenhead and London) till the age of 18; afterwards entirely by the private tuition of distinguished university graduates. Hon. DPhil Halle; LLD St Andrews; DD Heidelberg; LittD Dublin. Discoverer (Feb. 1892) of the Syro-Antiochene, or Sinaitic Palimpsest, the most ancient known MS of the Four Gospels in Syriac, and of other valuable Oriental MSS; Gold Medallist of Royal Asiatic Society, 1915. *Publications:* before marriage—Eastern Pilgrims; Effie Maxwell; Glenmavis; Brides of Ardmore; Monuments of Athens (translation); Glimpses of Greek Life and Scenery; Through Cyprus; after marriage—Life of Rev. S. S. Lewis; Introduction to the Four Gospels from the Sinaitic Palimpsest; Some Pages of the Sinaitic Palimpsest retranscribed; A Translation of the Syriac Gospels; In the Shadow of Sinai; co-editor of The Story of Ahikar; The Palestinian Syriac Lectionary of the Gospels; and of Palimpsest Fragments of Palestinian Syriac; Studia Sinaitica I, Catalogue of the Sinai Syriac MSS; VI, A Palestinian Syriac Lectionary from the Pentateuch Prophets, etc; IX, X, Select Narratives of Holy Women from the Sinai Palimpsest, with a Translation; The Transitus Mariæ, in Syriac; Horse Semiticæ, III, IV; Acta Mytholgica Apostolorum, in Arabic, with translation; Codex Climaci Rescriptus; The Old Syriac Gospels, or Evangelion da Mepharreshe; co-editor of, Leaves from Three Ancient Qur'ans, 1914; Margaret Atheling and other Poems, 1917. *Recreation:* travel. *Address:* Castle-brae, Chesterton Lane, Cambridge. *M:* CE 2078. *Died 29 March 1926.*

LEWIS, Angelo, (Prof. Hoffmann), MA; author, editor, journalist; *b* London, 23 July 1839; *m* 1864, Mary Ann Avery; one *d*. *Educ:* North London Collegiate School; Wadham College, Oxford. Barrister, Lincoln's Inn, 1861; practised until 1876; on staff of Saturday Review, under J. Douglas Cook; contributor to Chambers' Journal, the Cornhill, Temple Bar, London Society, St Paul's, and many other serials; winner of prize of £100 offered by Youth's Companion, Boston, for best short story for boys; took up conjuring as a hobby, and in 1876, under *nom de plume* of Professor Hoffmann, produced Modern Magic, the first English book of any importance on the subject; the popularity of this book led to the production of others, as below; inventor of card games, Quinto, Schnapps, Bimbo, Frisco, Queen Mab, San Tan, Zigzag, Knock Out and Boss. *Publications:* Modern Magic, 1876; More Magic, 1890; Later Magic,1903; Drawing-room Amusements; Conjurer Dick; Tricks with Cards; Home Gymnastics; Puzzles, Old and New; The Book of Card and Table Games; Baccarat, Fair and Foul; Every Boy's Book of Sport and Pastime; The Modern Hoyle; Hoyle Modernised; The Secrets of Conjuring and Magic (Robert-Houdin); The Secrets of Stage Conjuring (Robert-Houdin); The Sharper Detected and Exposed (Robert-Houdin); Drawing-room Conjuring; Magic at Home; The Game of Skat; The Book of Patience Games; Dominoes; The Chess Games of Greco; King Koko, 1904; Magical Tit-bits, 1910; Latest Magic, 1918; Handbooks on Piquet, Ecarté, Bridge, Auction Bridge, Rubicon Bézique, Hearts, Heartsette, Ombre, Five Hundred, and Quinto; also Progressive Whist and Euchre. *Recreations:* chess, billiards. *Address:* Manningford, Upper Bolebrook Road, Bexhill-on-Sea. *Club:* Whitefriars. *Died 23 Dec. 1919.*

LEWIS, Arthur Cyril Wentworth; Editor The Straits Times, Singapore, Federated Malay States, since 1927; *b* Nottingham, 4 Oct. 1885; *e s* of Arthur Lewis, Felbrigge, Roughton, Norwich, and Margaret (*decd*), *d* of Rev. W. H. Cornforth; *m* 1923, Josette Eugenie Nöel of Le Faouét, Morbihan, Brittany. *Educ:* Felstead; Exeter College, Oxford. BA (History Honours), 1908. Entered journalism on Nottingham Daily Express, 1909; Literary Editor Sheffield Telegraph, 1910–13; on staff of The Times, 1914–23; special

correspondent, Denmark and Morocco, and Chief Correspondent of The Times in Paris, 1921–22; Editor, The Englishman, Calcutta, 1923–27; served in World War, 1914–19, France, Egypt, Palestine, and Salonika; Lieut-Colonel, ADAP & SS. *Recreations:* travelling, lawn tennis, golf. *Address:* The Straits Times, Singapore, FMS. *Clubs:* New University, Authors', Press; Bengal, Calcutta.
Died 15 March 1928.

LEWIS, Arthur Hornby, DL, JP; *b* 1843; *e s* of James Owen Lewis of St Anne's Mount, Aigburth, Lancs; *m* 1879, Helen, *e d* of James Reid Stewart, DL, JP, of Calder Park, Lanarkshire, NB. High Sheriff of Cheshire, 1905–6. *Recreations:* shooting, hunting. *Address:* Danesfield, Great Marlow, Bucks; 29 Park Lane, W1; Chaseley, Eastbourne, Sussex. *Club:* Conservative.
Died 22 Sept. 1926.

LEWIS, Brig.-Gen. Bridges George, CB 1918; DSO 1900; late Commanding 1st Battalion East Lancashire Regiment; *b* 3 March 1857; *s* of Rev. G. B. Lewis; *m* 1st, 1879, Mary (*d* 1917), *d* of Rev. Canon Burn-Murdoch; one *s* one *d*; 2nd, Laura Montgomery, *d* of Rev. W. Glenn; one *s* two *d*. *Educ:* Uppingham; Sandhurst. Entered army, 1878; Captain, 1885; Adjutant 2nd Batt., 1887–91; Major, 1895; served South Africa, 1900–1 (despatches, Queen's medal four clasps, DSO); European War, 1914–18 (CB, despatches); Temp. Brig.-Gen. Comd 56th Infantry Brigade, 2nd New Army, Sept. 14. JP Co. Carlow. *Address:* Sandbrook, Tullow, Co. Carlow.
Died 24 April 1925.

LEWIS, Col David Francis, CB 1893; Aide-de-camp to the King; *b* Buttington, near Welshpool, 21 Oct. 1855; *e s* of late Rev. D. P. Lewis and Louisa, *y d* of late Capt. F. Hallowes, RN, of Glapwell Hall, Derbyshire; *m* 1910, Edith Marion, *o* surv. *d* of late Henry Smith, JP, DL, of Summerhill Court, Staffs. *Educ:* private school; Sandhurst, 1875. Joined 2nd Bn The Buffs, 1876–90; promoted Major in Cheshire Regt; served Zulu War, 1879 (wounded, despatches); Egyptian Army, 1886–1900 (medal with clasp, Khedive's star, 3rd Class Medjidie); Sudan, 1896–99 (Egyptian medal 8 clasps, Queen's medal, Brevets Lt-Col and Col, CB, ADC to the Queen, despatches 6 times, thanks of both Houses of Parliament); was in command at action of Rosaires; was Times Correspondent with the French Army, Morocco, 1907, and with the Spanish Army round Melilla, 1909; Spanish Order of Military Merit; raised 16th Batt. Royal Warwickshire Regt, Oct. 1914; County Comdt Warwickshire Vol. Corps (despatches). JP Warwickshire and Gloucestershire. *Recreation:* hunting. *Address:* Hungerdown, Seagry, Chippenham, Wilts. *T:* Seagry 3. *Club:* Naval and Military.
Died 2 Feb. 1927.

LEWIS, Lt Donald Swain, DSO 1915; Royal Engineers and Royal Flying Corps; *b* 5 April 1886. Entered army, 1904; served European War, 1914–15 (DSO). *Died 10 April 1916.*

LEWIS, Edgar Samuel; Editor and Director Daily Mail, Hull, and Hull Times, Co. Hull, since 1890; *b* Worcester, 22 Dec. 1853; 2nd *s* of Edmund Lewis, Deputy-Clerk of Peace; *m* 1878, Emma Bourner Sprigg; one *s* one *d*. *Educ:* Worcester Upper and Middle School. Journalist; Editor Westmorland Gazette, 1883–89; Preston Herald, 1889–90. *Publication:* A Bonny Westmorland Lass. *Address:* 22 Whitefriargate, Hull. *T:* 4304 Hull.
Died 16 April 1922.

LEWIS, Sir George James Graham, 2nd Bt, *cr* 1902; Head of firm Lewis and Lewis, solicitors; *b* 12 Sept. 1868; *s* of Sir George Henry Lewis, 1st Bt and Elizabeth, *d* of Ferdinand Eberstadt; *S* father, 1911; *m* 1896, Marie, *d* of Emil Hirsch; one *s* two *d*. *Educ:* Harrow; Balliol College, Oxford. Admitted a solicitor, 1894. *Heir: s* George James Ernest Lewis, *b* 25 Feb. 1910. *Address:* 21 Montagu Square, W1. *T:* Mayfair 166; The Grange, Rottingdean, Sussex; (office) Ely Place, Holborn, EC1. *T:* Holborn 536. *M:* A 193. *Clubs:* Bath, Royal Automobile. *Died 8 Aug. 1927.*

LEWIS, Harold; Literary Editor of the Globe until its cessation, Feb. 1921; *b* Bath, 22 June 1856; *e s* of William Lewis, JP; *m* Isabella (*d* 1913), *d* of Wakefield Simpson of Whitby; two *s* two *d*. *Educ:* Grosvenor School, Bath. BA London, 1879. On staff of Bath Herald till June 1883; specially interested in the condition of the poor and in children's education; editor of the Bristol Mercury, 1883–1901; staff of Nottingham Guardian, 1901–14. MJI. *Publications:* The Church Rambler; The Original Bath Guide; various pamphlets and articles on archæological questions. *Recreations:* Captain, 1886–96, 2nd Gloucester VRE; a lover of the drama. *Address:* 31 Epperstone Road, West Bridford, Nottingham. *Died 30 Sept. 1924.*

LEWIS, Sir Henry, Kt 1911; JP; b 21 Nov. 1847; s of Thomas Lewis, MP for Anglesey; m 1872, Annie, d of Rev. Roger Edwards, DD; two s two d. Educ: Friars School, Bangor; The College, Bala. Alderman of City of Bangor; Co-opted Member of North Wales Counties Training College; Member of Council of University College of N Wales. Publications: History of Friars School, and other local histories. Recreations: motoring, walking. Address: Pendyffryn, Bangor. T: 94. M: CC 3941.   Died 16 Nov. 1923.

LEWIS, Col Henry, OBE 1919; JP, DL; Joint Master of Foxhounds, Tredegar and Pentyrch; b 1847; e s of Henry Lewis (d 1881), and 1st wife, Anne, d of late Walter Morgan; m 1879, Mabel, d of Capt. P. F. Durham. Hon. Col late 1st Royal Devon Imperial Yeomanry. Address: Green Meadow, Tongwynlais, Cardiff. Club: Cavalry.   Died 9 July 1925.

LEWIS, Isaac; partner in Lewis and Marks; Director, Johannesburg Consolidated Investment Co.; Swaziland Corporation; South African Breweries, Ltd; Victoria Falls and Transvaal Power Co., Ltd; b Neustadt, Province of Kovno, Russia, 1849; m Sarah Ann (d 1919). Went to South Africa, 1870. Address: Vereeniging, South Africa.   Died 29 March 1927.

LEWIS, James Henry, DCL, MusD; FEIS; Principal, Victoria College of Music, London; Warden and Licensed Lay Chaplain to the Incorporated Guild of Church Musicians, London; b 23 Feb. 1856; m 1881, Annie, d of late William Roff, Malvern; one s four d. Educ: Malvern. Trained for the musical profession; composer of numerous pianoforte solos, songs, organ music, anthems, services, etc. Freeman of the City of London and Liveryman of the Worshipful Company of Basketmakers. Publications: many text-books, etc, including Harmony, Counterpoint, Double Counterpoint and Canon, Fugue, Elements of Music, History of Church Music, Dictionary of Musical Terms, Pronouncing Vocabulary of Musical Terms, The Material of Melody, and Early Steps in Musical Art. Recreation: photography. Address: Thornton Lodge, Twickenham, SW; Victoria College of Music, 158 Holland Park Avenue, W11.   Died 20 Nov. 1924.

LEWIS, Hon. John, CMG 1923; MLC since 1898; Director of Bagot, Shakes & Lewis, Ltd, Stock and Station Agents, Adelaide, SA; pastoralist; b Brighton, SA, 12 Feb. 1842; s of late James Lewis; m 1876, Martha Ann Brook; four s two d. Educ: private school, Brighton. Pioneer and explorer; crossed the Continent from Adelaide to Darwin in 1872; explored in the Northern Territory in 1872 and 1873; JP for 50 years; on Licensing Bench for 42 years; for seven years President of the Royal Geographical Society (SA Branch); for three years President of the Horticultural and Floricultural Society; on various Councils and Boards, including Pastoralists' Association, Aborigines' Friends' Association, South Australian Soldiers' Fund, Adelaide Children's Hospital, Botanic Garden, etc. Publication: Fought and Won: Autobiography, 1922. Recreations: took a keen interest in all sport, including horse racing; owned Wee Gun, winner of the Adelaide Cup in 1919. Address: Benacre, Glen Osmond, South Australia.   Died 25 Aug. 1923.

LEWIS, John Christopher, ISO 1910; JP; Commissioner of Affidavits; retired Civil Service Officer; b Barbados, 1842; m 1871; three s two d. Educ: Barbados. Entered Civil Service, Trinidad, 1861; 5th Clerk GPO, 1868; Acting 2nd Clerk, 1868; Postmaster San Fernando, 1869, and 1899; Member of Municipal Council, 1903; Mayor of San Fernando, 1904; re-elected, 1905; Manager of the Government Boys' and Girls' Central School from 1890. Travelled in the West Indies and British Guiana, and visited America, Canada, The Azores, France, Great Britain, Sweden, Finland and Russia. Publications: Christ the Saviour of the World; Kathleen. Address: Lewisville, San Fernando, Trinidad, BWI.   Died 11 June 1918.

LEWIS, John Hardwicke; water-colour painter; b Hyderabad, Deccan, 1840; e s of Frederic Christian Lewis, jun. (known as the "Indian Lewis," for his many canvasses of Durbars, etc, at all the native Courts in India); m 1st, Ellen, d of Rev. Dr Wm Andrews; 2nd, Elizabeth Eugenie, d of Wm Steele, artist; two s two d. Educ: privately, after 2½ years at Kensington Grammar School. Studied oil painting in Paris under Thomas Couture; painted portraits and genre in London, and exhibited many years at the Royal Acad. prior to 1885; from 1889 lived at Veytaux in Switzerland, and devoted all his time to Swiss landscape painting in water-colours; the interval between 1885 and 1889 was spent in California. Publications: illustrated Our Life in the Swiss Highlands, by Addington Symonds; The Upper Engadine, by Rev. Spencer C. Musson; three books on the Lake of Geneva, by

Gribble; La Côte d'Emeraude, Brittany, by Spencer C. Musson. Recreations: writing, reading. Address: Veytaux, Switzerland.   Died 3 Oct. 1927.

LEWIS, John Penry, CMG 1911; Ceylon Civil Service, retired; b 17 Sept. 1854; 2nd s of late Rev. John Lewis; m 1894, Violet Marion, d of late Joseph Anderson of Ankerwyke, Wraysbury; one s two d. Educ: Mill Hill School; Queen's University, Ireland; BA 1876; MA 1882. A Member of the Middle Temple; Ceylon Civil Service, 1877-1910; retired as Government Agent, Central Province, and Member Executive and Legislative Councils, 1910; was Superintendent of Pearl Fisheries, Ceylon, 1904, 1905, and 1906; first Special Officer under Waste Lands Ordinance, 1907-10; Church of England. Publications: compiled A Manual of the Vanni Districts, 1895; Tombstones and Monuments in Ceylon, 1913; Ceylon in Early British Times, 1913; papers to Folklore, Architectural Review, Journal of Ceylon Branch of Royal Asiatic Society. Recreations: sketching, archæology, etc. Address: Canford Cliffs, Dorset. TA: Canford Cliffs. Club: Authors'.   Died 20 Sept. 1923.

LEWIS, Very Rev. Julius; Dean of Ballarat since 1915. Educ: Moore College, NSW. Ordained, 1875; curate of Hamilton, 1876-79; Portland, 1879-81; Christ Church Cathedral, Ballarat, 1881-84; Canon, 1887-88; Vicar of Maryborough, 1884-88; Incumbent of St Jude's, Melbourne, 1888-97; Archdeacon of Tamworth, 1897; Vicar of Tamworth, 1897-1902; of Armidale, 1902; Canon Residentiary St Peter's Cathedral, Armidale; Archdeacon of Armidale, 1902-14. Address: The Deanery, Christ Church Cathedral, Ballarat, Victoria.   Died 1920.

LEWIS, Thomas, FRAS; Assistant, Royal Observatory, Greenwich; Secretary, Royal Astronomical Society. Awarded Lalande Prize by French Academy, 1907. Publications: Memoir on Double Stars; Joint-Editor, The Observatory. Address: Royal Observatory, Greenwich. Club: Royal Astronomical.   Died 5 June 1928.

LEWIS, Thomas Arthur; Barrister; MP (Co.L) University of Wales, since Nov. 1922, Pontypridd Division of Glamorgan, Dec. 1918-July 1922; Junior Lord of the Treasury, unpaid, 1922; b 21 Sept. 1881; s of Rev. J. M. Lewis, Cemaes, Pembrokeshire, and Phœbe, d of Thomas Griffiths, Pantygroes, Pembrokeshire; m 1919, Marjorie, d of late William Culross, Adelaide, S Australia; one d. Educ: University College, Cardiff. Joined Inns of Court OTC, 1915; commissioned April 1916; served Salonica, 1916-18. Parliamentary Private Secretary to Capt. Hon. F. Guest, MP, Chief Government Whip, Feb. 1919; called to Bar, Middle Temple, 1919. Address: Cemaes, Pontypridd. Club: National Liberal.   Died 18 July 1923.

LEWIS, Sir Thomas William, Kt 1918; JP, DL; Stipendiary Magistrate, Cardiff, 1887-1923; b 1852; y s of late Thomas William Lewis, JP, of Abercanaid House, Merthyr; m 1st, Elizabeth Agnes, d of late Robert Tidman, Ipswich; 2nd, Henrietta Catherine, d of late Rev. H. Willmott, Rector of Kirkley. Barrister, Middle Temple, 1879. Address: Gilestone Manor, near Cardiff. Club: Oxford and Cambridge.   Died 28 April 1926.

LEWIS, Rev. Canon William; Canon Residentiary of Llandaff Cathedral, 1903-14; Rector of Ystradyfodwg since 1869. Curate of Nantyglo, 1862-64; Pentredach, 1864-68; perpetual Curate of St John Baptist, Llandrisant; Precentor of Llandaff, 1891; Rural Dean of Rhondda, 1895; Examining Chaplain, Bishop of Llandaff, 1905-14. Address: Ystradyfodwg, Pentre, RSO.   Died 27 Jan. 1922.

LEWIS, William George, ISO 1908; a Commissioner of Customs and Excise, 1910; retired, 1912; b 1844. Address: Evesham Lodge, Reigate. T: Reigate 367.   Died 27 July 1926.

LEWIS, William James, FRS 1909; Professor of Mineralogy, Cambridge, since 1881; Fellow of Oriel College, Oxford; b 16 Jan. 1847; s of Rev. J. Lewis, late of Bonvilston; unmarried. Educ: Jesus Coll., Oxford (MA). 1st Math. Mods; 1st Math. Final Schools; 1st Natural Science Schools; Senior Math. Scholar. Publications: treatise on Crystallography, 1899; North Wraxhall, 1913. Address: Trinity College, Cambridge.   Died 16 April 1926.

LEWTAS, Lt-Col John, CBE 1918; late Commissioner of Medical Services, Ministry of National Service; b Liverpool; s of Dr T. Lewtas; m Annie Chambers, d of Henry Threlfall Wilson, The Cranes, Surbiton; one s. Educ: Liverpool College; Edinburgh University; St Thomas' Hospital Medical School. Entered the Indian Medical

Service, 1875; served with the Guides in the Afghan campaigns of 1878–79 and 1880 (despatches twice, medal 2 clasps); Lecturer on Ophthalmology, and Ophthalmic Surgeon Medical College Hospital, Calcutta; Surgeon to the Mayo Hospital; late Fellow of the Calcutta University. *Publications:* various contributions to medical journals. *Recreation:* fishing. *Address:* 15 Cheyne Place, SW3. *T:* Kensington 5093.
Died 23 Sept. 1920.

LEWTHWAITE, Sir William, 1st Bt, *cr* 1927; DL, JP Cumberland, since 1875; County Alderman, Cumberland; *b* 29 Oct. 1853; *s* of Wm Lewthwaite, JP, DL, of Broadgate, and Mary, *d* of Wm Challinor of Leek, Co. Stafford; *m* 1881, Helena Jane, *d* of Charles Challinor of Basford Hall, Co. Stafford; one *s* one *d*. *Educ:* Rugby; Trinity College, Cambridge. *Heir:* *s* William Lewthwaite, *b* 20 June 1882. *Address:* Broadgate, Broughton-in-Furness. *TA:* The Green.
Died 13 Dec. 1927.

LEWTON-BRAIN, Lawrence, BA; FLS; Director of Agriculture, Federated Malay States, since 1910, and of Straits Settlements since 1919; *b* 1879; *s* of J. Lewton-Brain of The Rookery, Yaxham, Norfolk; *m* 1904, Annie, *d* of late W. O'Meara of Ossory and Colonial Civil Service, British Guiana; three *s*. *Educ:* Firth College, Sheffield; St John's College, Cambridge (Foundation scholar and Hutchinson student). Demonstrator in Botany, Cambridge University, 1900; Mycologist and Agricultural Lecturer to the Imperial Department of Agriculture for the WI, 1902; studied the diseases of sugar-cane, cacao, cotton, and other tropical plants, also the breeding and hybridization of the sugar-cane; proceeded to Hawaii and became Assistant Director of the Division of Pathology and Physiology of the Hawaiian Sugar Planters' Association, Experiment Station, 1905; Director of the Division, 1907; worked on sugar-cane and its diseases, the bacteria of sugar, etc. *Publications:* The Anatomy of the Leaves of British Grasses (Trans Linnean Soc.), 1902; numerous bulletins and papers on the botany and pathology of tropical cultivated plants, 1902–10. *Recreations:* tennis, photography. *Address:* Kuala Lumpur, Federated Malay States. *TA:* Agriculture, K. Lumpur. *M:* SL 17.
Died 24 June 1922.

LEY, Sir Francis, 1st Bt, *cr* 1905; JP; *b* 3 Jan. 1846; *o s* of late George Phillips Ley of Burton-on-Trent, and Sarah, *d* of John Pott, Yoxall, Staffs; *m* 1st, 1870, Georgina Townsend (*d* 1886), *d* of late Capt. George Willis of Aislaby Hall, Yorks; one *s* two *d*; 2nd, 1888, Alison Catherine, *d* of late John Jobson, JP, of Spondon, Derbys; one *s* (and one *s* decd). *Educ:* privately. Lord of the Manors of Epperstone and Kirkoswald, Lazonby, Staffield, and Glassonby in Cumberland; High Sheriff, Notts, 1905; founded in 1874, and Governing Director of Ley's works in Derby; ex-President Nottingham General Hospital, Derbyshire Children's Hospital, Notts County Cricket Club, and Notts Agricultural Society. KGStJ. Owner of about 6,500 acres of agricultural property. *Heir:* *s* Henry Gordon Ley, Major Notts Imp. Yeo. [*b* 12 March 1874; *m* 1899, Rhoda, *d* of Herbert Prodgers, JP, of Kington, St-Michael's House, Wilts; two *s* one *d*. *Address:* Willington House, Derbyshire]. *Recreations:* salmon fishing, shooting. *Address:* Epperstone Manor, Notts; Lealholm Lodge, Grosmont, Yorks. *Clubs:* Royal Automobile; Nottinghamshire County.
Died 27 Jan. 1916.

LEY, William Henry; *b* London 26 Dec. 1847. *Educ:* Winchester College. Became a clerk in journal office, House of Commons, 1868; became Clerk of the Journals, 1895; retired 1908. *Address:* 36 St George's Road, SW1. *Club:* Wellington.
Died 21 July 1919.

LEYCESTER, William Hamilton; one of the Magistrates of the Police Courts of the Metropolis since 1912; at Bow Street since 1922; *b* 1864; *s* of William Leycester, for many years chief of The Times Parliamentary Staff; *m* Frances Eliza, *d* of J. C. Warne, Captain 24th Regiment (SW Borderers). *Educ:* King's College School; Peterhouse, Cambridge (Scholar), 18th Wrangler, 1888. Called to Bar, 1888; practised chiefly at the London Sessions and Central Criminal Court, where he was one of the Treasury Counsel. *Club:* Garrick.
Died 23 Oct. 1925.

LEYLAND, Christopher John, JP Northumberland; *b* 19 Sept. 1849; *e s* of late John Naylor of Leighton Hall, Montgomeryshire; *m* 1st, 1874, Everilda Elizabeth (*d* 1890), *d* of late Ralph Creyke, Rawcliffe, Yorkshire; one *d*; 2nd, 1892, Helen Dora, *e d* of Digby Cayley, Norton Grove, Yorkshire; three *s* three *d*. Entered Navy, 1862; retired Sub-Lieutenant in 1872; Director, The Parsons Marine Steam Turbine Co. Ltd; Parsons Foreign Patents Co. Ltd; Cleveland Shipbuilding Co. Ltd. *Address:* The Mead, Beal, Northumberland. *Club:* Carlton.
Died 21 Oct. 1926.

LEYLAND, John; writer on naval, international, and historical subjects; *s* of Francis A. Leyland, author of The Brontë Family; *m* Fanny Julia, (*d* 1921), *d* of T. Duncan; two *s*. Has written for the Times, Daily Chronicle, Observer, Nineteenth Century, Quarterly and Edinburgh Reviews, Country Life, New York Herald, and other English and American papers and magazines; editor of the Army and Navy Gazette, 1904–9; of The Navy 1910–12; author of articles and statistics in the Naval Annual from 1896; edited the volume, 1901, 1915, and 1916; part editor, 1906 and 1914; attached to Admiralty War Staff, 1917–18; Hon. Member RUSI. *Publications:* The Blockade of Brest, 1803–1805 (Navy Records Society); The Royal Navy, its Influence in English History and the Growth of Empire; The Achievement of the British Navy in the World War; (with Comdr C. N. Robinson, RN) In the Queen's Navee and For the Honour of the Flag. *Address:* Crimsworth Dene, Forest Hill. *T:* Sydenham 923.
Died 5 Jan. 1924.

LEYTON, Albert Sidney Frankau, MA, MD, ScD; FRCP, DPH; Director of Clinical Laboratory, Addenbrooke's Hospital, Cambridge; *b* London, 5 Jan. 1869; *m* 1909, Helen Gertrude, *widow* of Robert S. Stewart, MD; two *s*. *Educ:* City of London School; Gonville and Caius Coll. Camb. Lecturer on Experimental Medicine, Univ. of Liverpool; Director of the Liverpool Cancer Research; former Professor of Pathology, University of Leeds; Asst Physician, Hospital for Consumption; Goulstonian Lecturer, Royal Coll. of Physicians; Member of the Physiological and Pathological Societies. *Publications:* author of scientific and medical papers, chiefly on the nervous system, cancer, and enteric fever; Essentials of Morbid Histology. *Address:* The Chestnuts, Great Shelford, near Cambridge. *T:* Shelford 46; *TA:* Leyton, Great Shelford. *M:* FC 1066.
Died 21 Sept. 1921.

LIAS, Rev. Chancellor John James; Chancellor of Llandaff Cathedral; *b* 30 Nov. 1834; *s* of Charles Lias, silver plate manufacturer, London; *m* 1st, 1865, Miss E. Attenborough; 2nd, 1890, Miss Mortlock; five *s* one *d*. *Educ:* King's College, London; Emmanuel College, Camb. (Foundation Scholar); MA. Was compelled, from ill-health, to give up reading for Mathematical Honours at Cambridge; ordained, 1858, to curacy of Shaftesbury, Dorset; by another breakdown in health forced to give up regular clerical work for five years; Curate of Folkestone, 1865–66; Vicar of Eastbury, 1866–68; Minor Canon of Llandaff Cathedral, 1868–71; Professor of Modern Literature at St David's College, Lampeter, 1871–80; Vicar of St Edward's, Cambridge, 1880–92; Preacher at the Chapel Royal, Whitehall, 1884–86; Examining Chaplain to the Bishop of Llandaff, 1887–1900; Rector of East Bergholt, 1892–1903; also formerly Hulsean Lecturer and Lady Margaret Preacher, Cambridge; member of Council of the Imperial Federation League from foundation until it was dissolved. *Publications:* Rector and His Friends (Dialogues), 1868; Doctrinal System of St John, 1875; Commentaries on Joshua (Pulpit Commentary), Judges, 1st and 2nd Corinthians (Cambridge Bible for Schools), 1st Epistle to St John; Hulsean Lectures on the Atonement, Are Miracles Credible?, Miracles, Science and Prayer, Principles of Biblical Criticism, Nicene Creed; articles in Encyclopædia Britannica, Murray's Bible Dictionary, and Murray's Shorter Dictionary of Ecclesiastical Biography; papers read before the Victoria Institute, etc. *Recreations:* music, light reading. *Address:* The Lodge, Abington, Cambridge.
Died 16 March 1923.

LIBERTY, Sir Arthur Lasenby, Kt 1913; DL, JP, CC Bucks; Founder and Chairman of Liberty and Co. Ltd, and promoter of other industries connected with the decorative arts; *b* Chesham, Bucks, 13 Aug. 1843; *e s* of the late Arthur Liberty, of Chesham; *m* 1875, Emma Louise, *d* of late Henry Blackmore, of Exmouth. *Educ:* University School, Nottingham. Member of Council of London Chamber of Commerce; Member of Advisory Committee Royal School of Art Needlework; Vice-President of the Silk Association of Great Britain and Ireland; a Director of the British Produce Supply Association; Past Master of the Glass-Sellers' Company; President of the English Monumental Inscriptions Society; Chairman of Council of the Bucks Architectural and Archæological Soc., and of the Bucks Association for loan of Pictures to Country Schools; County Council Representative on the Bucks Territorial Association; Member of the Royal Institute; Fellow of the Asiatic Society of Japan; Member of the Organising Council of the Japan Society; FRHistS; FSS; Past President of the Sette of Odd Volumes; Juror at Paris International Exhibition, 1900; member of London Committee of the Milan Exhibition, 1906; Lord of the Manor of The-Lee, Bucks; High Sheriff for the county of Bucks in 1899; Chairman of The-Lee Parish Council; travelled in the Far East; awarded medals for papers read before the Society of Arts in 1890 and 1900. *Publications:* Springtime in the Basque Mountains; De Libertat; Pictorial Records of Japan; A Day in Tangier; The Treasure Hunt. *Recreations:* travelling, sketching, shooting. *Address:* Lee Manor, The-Lee, Bucks. *TA:* The-Lee. *T:* The-Lee 2; 28 Warwick Street, Regent Street, W. *M:* BH 1258, BH 1356. *Club:* Devonshire.

Died 11 May 1917.

LICHFIELD, 3rd Earl of, *cr* 1831; **Thomas Francis Anson,** DL, JP; Viscount Anson and Baron Soberton, 1806; Director National Provincial Bank of England, Ltd; Bank of Australasia, etc; *b* 31 Jan. 1856; *s* of 2nd Earl and Lady Harriet Georgiana Louisa Hamilton, *d* of 1st Duke of Abercorn; *S* father, 1892; *m* 1878, Lady Mildred Coke, *d* of 2nd Earl of Leicester; three *s* three *d*. *Educ:* Harrow; Trinity College, Cambridge; BA. Owner of about 20,000 acres in Staffordshire. *Heir: s* Viscount Anson, *b* 9 Dec. 1883. *Address:* 38 Great Cumberland Place, W. *T:* Mayfair 3716; Shugborough Park, Stafford. *Club:* Brooks's.   *Died 29 July 1918.*

LIDDELL, Adolphus George Charles, CB 1908; *b* 29 June 1846; *s* of Hon. Sir Adolphus Frederic Octavius Liddell, KCB and Frederica Elizabeth Lane-Fox; unmarried. *Educ:* Eton; Balliol Coll., Oxford. 2nd Class Lit. Hum., 1869. Called to Bar, 1871; North Eastern Circuit; Secretary to Royal Commission on Municipal Corporations, Reformatory and Industrial Schools, and Trawling; Revising Barrister for S Division of West Riding of Yorks, 1884–86; Counsel to the Mint on the Durham and Northumberland Sessions; Chief Clerk, Crown Office in Chancery, 1886; Assistant Secretary, Lord Chancellor's Department 1888–1919; Private Secretary to Lord Chancellor 1909–15. *Publication:* Notes from the Life of an Ordinary Mortal, 1911. *Address:* 6 Seville Street, Lowndes Square, SW. *Clubs:* Travellers', Wellington.   *Died 12 Aug. 1920.*

LIDDELL, Charles; *b* 1856; *y s* of John Liddell of Benwell Hall, Northumberland; *m* 1894, Madeline, *d* of late J. A. Dease, Turbotston, W Meath; one *d*. *Educ:* Ushaw College, Co. Durham; High Sheriff for Cumberland, 1917. *Address:* Warwick Hall, Carlisle. *TA:* Warwick Bridge.   *Died 9 July 1922.*

LIDDELL, Colin, ISO 1913; *b* 8 Feb. 1862; *s* of Walter George Liddell, sugar planter. Entered Public Service, 1881; Surveyor-General, Jamaica, 1894. *Address:* Hazeldean, South Camp Road, Kingston, Jamaica.   *Died Oct. 1916.*

LIDDELL, Sir Robert Morris, Kt 1916; DL; Managing Director, William Liddell & Co., Ltd, of Donacloney, Belfast, London, New York, etc; *b* 20 July 1870; *s* of William Liddell; *m* 1896, Charlotte Walton, *d* of late John Arnott Taylor of Belfast; three *s* three *d*. *Educ:* Christ College, Finchley. Hon. Treasurer the UVF Hospital Fund, and the UVF Patriotic Fund. Ex-High Sheriff, Co. Down. *Address:* Banoge House, Donacloney, Co. Down. *TA:* Bangoe, Donacloney, Co. Down. *Clubs:* Constitutional; Union, Belfast.

Died 16 April 1928.

LIDDELL, T. Hodgson, RBA; landscape painter; *b* Edinburgh, 1860; *y s* of W. H. Liddell; *m* 1885, May, *e d* of late Henry Pitman; three *s*. *Educ:* Royal High School, Edinburgh. Travelled in China, and held exhibition of water-colours painted there, at the Fine Art Society, 1909; author and illustrator of China, its Marvel and Mystery. Principal pictures exhibited in RA and other galleries: Sabbath of Still Rest; An Old Waterway; A Fen Flood; Springtime; A Bend of the Avon; Borderland (and at St Louis); The Estuary at Aberdovey, 1904 (purchased) for the M'Kelvie Gallery, Auckland, NZ); Cleeve Mill, and Mill Pool, 1905. *Recreations:* travelling, riding, shooting.

Died June 1925.

LIDDLE, Robert W.; Organist and Rector Choir Southwell Cathedral since 1888; *b* Durham, 1864; married; no *c*. *Educ:* Durham. Organist St Baldred's, North Berwick, 1886–88; Conductor Mansfield Harmonic Society, 1898; Orchestral Society, 1906; Organist and Choirmaster St Peter's Church, Mansfield, 1904; Conductor Newark and District Orchestral Society, 1908; Manager and 1st violin of the Liddle String Quartette. *Publications:* Evening Services; Anthems: O Send Out Thy Light, Save Lord and Hear Us, As for Me, etc; Hymn tunes and Chants. *Recreation:* the practice and performance of chamber music. *Address:* Vicar's Court, Southwell, Notts.

Died 30 Dec. 1917.

LIFFORD, 6th Viscount, *cr* 1781; **Archibald Robert Hewitt;** Baron Lifford, 1768; *b* 14 Jan. 1844; *s* of 4th Viscount and Lady Mary Acheson, *d* of 2nd Earl of Gosford; *S* brother, 1913; *m* 1878, Helen Blanche, *d* of late C. S. Geach; one *s* two *d* (and one *s* decd). Entered

Navy, 1858; retired Capt. 1890. *Heir: s* Lt-Col Hon. Evelyn James Hewitt, DSO, *b* 18 Dec. 1880. *Address:* Hill House, Lyndhurst, Hants.

Died 21 May 1925.

LIGHTFOOT, Rev. John, DSc, MA, MusB; Vicar of Cross Stone since 1882; Hon. Canon of Wakefield, 1910; *b* Tunstall, 18 Dec. 1853; *s* of Peter and Catherine Lightfoot; *m*; five *d*. *Educ:* University of Edinburgh; Theological College, Lichfield. Ordained, 1875; Curate, Heath Town, Bradford, Halifax. *Publications:* Studies in Philosophy; Text Book, XXXIX Articles; Pastor Meus Dominus; Logic and Education; Theory of Music; Elementary and Intermediate Algebra; Advanced Arithmetic; The Complete Arithmetic; Alexander the Great; Short Methods in Arithmetic; Graphic Algebra, etc. *Recreation:* golf. *Address:* Cross Stone, Todmorden.

Died 9 Aug. 1917.

LIGHTFOOT, Rev. John Alfred; Vicar of Haile, Cumberland, since 1926; *b* 18 May 1861; *s* of George Lightfoot of Birkby, Maryport, Cumberland; *m* Marianne F., *d* of David Marshall Lang, Lay Sec. of Church Missionary Society. *Educ:* Merchant Taylors' School, London; Hertford Coll., Oxford (BA 1883, MA 1887). Deacon, 1885; Priest, 1886; Tutor and Asst Chaplain of St John's Hall, Highbury, 1886–93; Afternoon Lecturer at Christ Church, Highbury, 1886–91; Curate of St Augustine's, Highbury, 1892–93; Vicar of St Stephen's, Canonbury, 1893–99; Principal of the Church Missionary College, Islington, 1899–1917; Vicar of Christ Church, Chislehurst, 1917–25; Examining Chaplain to Bishop of Durham, 1901–12. *Recreations:* lawn tennis, cycling. *Address:* Haile Vicarage, Beckermet, Cumberland.

Died 2 Jan. 1928.

LILLEY, Capt. James Lindsay, DSO 1900; Victorian Mounted Rifles; *b* 1871; *m* 1913, Olive Agatha Hope, *y d* of late Rev. C. E. Cummings and Mrs Geoffrey ffolkes of Smytham, Little Torrington, Devon. Served South Africa, 1900–1 (despatches, Queen's medal 3 clasps, DSO).   *Died 1 Dec. 1923.*

LILLY, William Samuel, JP; MA; barrister; Secretary to Catholic Union of Great Britain since 1874; *b* 10 July 1840; *e s* of late William Lilly, Windout House, near Exeter; *m* 1907, Anna Marie, *d* of M. Félix Emery of Geneva. *Educ:* Peterhouse, Cambridge. Hon. Fellow of Peterhouse. Under-Secretary to Govt of Madras, 1869. *Publications:* Ancient Religion and Modern Thought, 1884; Chapters in European History, 1886; A Century of Revolution, 1889; On Right and Wrong, 1890; On Shibboleths, 1892; The Great Enigma, 1893; A Manual of the Law specially affecting Catholics (with Sir J. P. Wallis), 1893; The Claims of Christianity, 1894; Four English Humorists of the Nineteenth Century, 1895; Essays and Speeches, 1897; First Principles in Politics, 1899; A Year of Life, 1900; Renaissance Types, 1901; India and its Problems, 1902; Christianity and Modern Civilisation, 1903; Studies in Religion and Literature, 1904; Idola Fori, 1910; Many Mansions, 1907; The New France, 1913. *Recreations:* riding, rackets, cycling. *Address:* 36 Fitzgeorge Avenue, West Kensington, W. *T:* Hammersmith 1486. *Club:* Athenæum (elected under Rule 2, 1887).

Died 29 Aug. 1919.

LIMA, Sir Bertram Lewis, KBE 1918; Captain in the Canadian Army; Chairman of the Daily Mirror, Sunday Pictorial, Glasgow Daily Record, and Leeds Mercury newspaper companies; *b* 1883. *Address:* 1 Duchess Street, Portland Place, W. *T:* Mayfair 1741.

Died 24 Feb. 1919.

LINCOLNSHIRE, 1st Marquess of, *cr* 1912; **Charles Robert Wynn-Carrington,** KG 1906; GCMG 1885; PC 1881; Earl Carrington, 1895; Baron Carrington, 1796; Viscount Wendover, 1895; Joint-Hereditary Lord Great Chamberlain of England; *b* 16 May 1843; *m* 1878, Hon. Cecilia Margaret Harbord, *e d* of 5th Lord Suffield; five *d* (one *s* decd). *Educ:* Eton; Trinity Coll., Camb. (BA). MP (L) High Wycombe, 1865–68; Captain Royal Bodyguard, 1881–85; Governor, New South Wales, 1885–90; Lord Chamberlain of the Household, 1892–95; Pres. Board of Agriculture, 1905–11; Lord Privy Seal, 1911; Mem., LCC; Lord-Lieut of Bucks, 1915–23. Liberal. Protestant. Owner of 23,000 acres. *Heir:* (to Barony) *b* Hon. Rupert Clement George Carington, *b* 18 Dec. 1852. *Address:* Daws Hill Lodge, High Wycombe, Bucks. *T:* High Wycombe 67; 53 Princes Gate, SW7. *T:* Kensington 74. *Clubs:* Brooks's, National Liberal.

Died 13 June 1928.

LINDLEY, Baron, *cr* 1900 (Life Peer); **Rt. Hon. Nathaniel Lindley,** Kt 1875; PC; FRS 1897; Hon. LLD Edin. and Camb.; DCL Oxford; *b* Acton Green, Middlesex, 29 Nov. 1828; *o s* of John Lindley, PhD, FRS, Professor of Botany, Univ. Coll. London; *m* 1858, Sarah (*d* 1912), *e d* of Edward John Teale, Leeds; four *s* two *d* (and one *s* two *d* decd). *Educ:* Univ. Coll. London. Barrister, Middle Temple, 1850; QC 1872; Judge of Court of Common Pleas, 1875; Lord Justice of Appeal, 1881–97; Master of the Rolls, Oct. 1897–1900; Lord of Appeal in Ordinary, 1900–5. *Publications:* Introduction to the Study of Jurisprudence; Treatises on the Law of Partnership and Companies. *Address:* The Lodge, East Carleton, Norwich.

Died 9 Dec. 1921.

LINDLEY, Rear-Adm. George Robert, CB 1893; retired; *b* 5 July 1850; *s* of late Robert Charles Lindley of Mansfield, and Elizabeth, *d* of Chas Delmar of Elmstone, Kent; *m* 1896, Kate Louisa, *d* of late James Windebanks of Southsea; one *s* two *d. Educ:* Dover; on board HMS "Britannia." Entered Navy 1863; served on board HMS "Achilles" during the Egyptian War (medal and Khedive's star); commanded a Naval brigade landed in Witu territory, East Coast of Africa, in 1893 (CB, South African medal and clasp). *Address:* Watersend, Temple Ewell, Dover.

Died 1 Aug. 1918.

LINDLEY, Maj.-Gen. Hon. John Edward, JP Norfolk and Suffolk; late Colonel, Royal Dragoons; *b* 15 Sept. 1860; *e s* of late Baron Lindley; *m* 1887, Isabel, *d* of late Francis Morgan Nichols, Lawford Hall, Essex; one *d.* DAAG Aldershot, 1893–96; Jersey, 1899; Commandant, School of Instruction, Imperial Yeomanry, 1901–3; AAG, NE District and Northern Command, 1903–5; Commandant Cavalry School, 1905–7; Brigadier-General Commanding 3rd Cavalry Brigade, 1907–10; Commanded Welsh Division, 1913–15; served S Africa, 1899–1900 (Queen's medal 2 clasps); Gallipoli, 1915. *Address:* The Maultway House, Camberley, Surrey. *Club:* Naval and Military.

Died 7 April 1925.

LINDLEY, Sir William Heerlein, Kt 1911; MICE, FGS; Dr ing *hc*; Consulting Engineer; *b* 30 Jan. 1853; *s* of William Lindley, Civil Engineer; *m* Fanny H. Getz of Frankfurt-on-Main; one *s* two *d. Educ:* Mr Thompson's School, Kidbrook House, Blackheath; Mr George Valentine's School, Blackheath; private tuition; matriculated London University, 1869. His father's resident engineer on Budapest Waterworks, 1870–73; Engineer-in-Chief of the City of Frankfurt-on-Main, 1873–95, for sewage and water-works, harbour works and regulation of River Main, electrical supply works, streets, and roads, town planning and other engineering works and for the technical administration; at same time and till present, consulting engineer for designing and execution of various municipal works in other towns. Was a member of the Commission for the regulation of the Danube at Vienna and for the water supply of Amsterdam; President of the Engineering Standards Commission of the German Gas and Waterworks Engineers; President of Commission on Vagabond Currents from Electric Tramways and Rules for Abating same; Member of International Committee on Pipe-Screw Thread; and Assistant Commissioner of Royal Commission on Canals and Waterways. *Works:* water-works—Warsaw (with his father), Bucharest, Crajova, Ploesti Pitesti, Baku; designed new water supply of Petrograd from Lake Ladoga, 1912; sewage works—Elberfeld, Warsaw, Homburg, Mannheim, Hanau, Wurzburg, Prague, Crajova, Samara; Electrical Supply Works, Elberfeld. *Recreations:* mountaineering, riding. *Address:* c/o Institution of Civil Engineers, Great George Street, SW. *Died 30 Dec. 1917.*

LINDSAY, 11th Earl of, *cr* 1633; **David Clark Bethune,** JP; Lord Lindsay of The Byres, 1445; Baron Parbroth, 1633; Viscount Garnock; Baron Kilbirny, Kingsburne, and Drumry, 1703; *b* 18 April 1832; *s* of David Aytone Lindsay and Jane Emilia, *d* of John Aytone of Kippo, Fifeshire; S cousin, 1894; *m* 1866, Emily Marian, *d* of Robert Crosse, Doctors' Commons, and *widow* of Capt. Edmund Charles Barnes, 91st Regt; two *s* one *d. Educ:* St Andrews, Edinburgh Universities. Owner of about 2,300 acres. *Heir: s* Viscount Garnock, *b* 18 May 1867. *Address:* Wormiston House, Crail; Kilconquhar Castle, Kilconquhar, Fifeshire. *Died 20 March 1917.*

LINDSAY, David; *b* Goolwa, South Australia, of Scotch parents, 20 June 1856; *m* 1881, Annie Theresa Stuart; four *s* one *d. Educ:* private schools. Entered Survey Department, South Australia, 1872; Junior Surveyor Northern Territory, 1878; Surveying and Control of Public Works till 1882; explored Arnhem Land, NT, 1883; exploring in north-west of South Australia, 1884; exploring and surveying from the Southern boundary to the Gulf of Carpentaria, 1885–86; rode across Australia from North to South with only a small black boy as companion, 1888; surveying, exploring, and prospecting in the MacDonnell Ranges, Central Australia, 1889–90; leader of the Elder Scientific Exploring Expedition; crossed the great Victoria District, 550 miles in 35 days, the 42 camels having only 7½ gallons of water each for the whole journey, during the journey discovered and reported the existence of a great auriferous area—on this report prospectors went out and found the great goldfield of West Australia; overlanded a mob of camels from Port Augusta to Coolgardie, 1891–93; stayed in the goldfields till 1895, assisting in the exploration and exploitation of that great mineral belt; visited London in connection with mining, 1895–96; since which time been intimately associated with the development of the mining industry in various states of Australia; was a member of the Commonwealth Royal Commission to advise as to railways and new ports to develop the Northern Territory, 1913; exploring in Northern Territory, 1916–20. *Publications:* Journals of Exploration; Territoria. *Address:* 56 Market Street, Sydney, NSW. *Died 18 Dec. 1922.*

LINDSAY, Harry; *see* Hudson, H. L.

LINDSAY, Col Henry Arthur Peyton, CB 1924; CSI 1921; CMG 1915; CBE 1919; Indian army, retired; *b* 29 Jan. 1868; *m* Charlotte Eliza, *d* of late Maj. F. Stewart. Entered West India Regt, 1887; Capt. Indian Army, 1898; Major, 1905; Lt-Col 1913; Col, 1916; served NW Frontier, India, 1897–98 (medal with clasp); European War, 1914–18 (despatches, CMG, Bt Col); retired, 1924.

Died 30 Dec. 1926.

LINDSAY, Rev. Dr James; philosopher, theologian, and man of letters; *e s* of late John Cowan Lindsay; *m* 1908, Margaret, *e d* of late James Cook, Glasgow, and *widow* of R. Barclay Shaw, of Annick Lodge and Knockgerran, Ayrshire. *Educ:* under his father; Glasgow University. MA 1878; BSc 1879; BD 1882; DD 1899; FRSL 1910; FRSE 1889; FGS 1888; MRAS 1897. Declined Principalship of Calcutta College, 1882; University Extension Lecturer, 1886–87; Corresponding Member of Royal Academy of Sciences, Letters, and Arts, Padua, 1894; Member Aristotelian Society, 1897; Examiner to the Associated Theological Colleges, British and Colonial—Philosophy, 1897–99, and Honours Theology, 1899; Hugh Waddell Lecturer, Queen's University, Canada, 1899–1900; Member of International Congress of Psychology, Paris, 1900; Associate Editor of Bibliotheca Sacra from 1903; Associate Philosophical Society of Louvain, 1903; Member of the Kant Society, Halle, 1904; Member of International Congress of Philosophy, Heidelberg, 1908; Request by German Commission to write on present English Philosophy declined, 1910; Member of Goethe-Gesellschaft, and of English Goethe Society, 1913. *Publications:* Progressiveness of Modern Christian Thought, 1892; Essays, Literary and Philosophical, 1896; Significance of the Old Testament for Modern Theology, 1896; Recent Advances in Theistic Philosophy of Religion, 1897; Momenta of Life, 1901; Studies in European Philosophy, 1909; The Fundamental Problems of Metaphysics, 1910; The Psychology of Belief, 1910; New Essays, Literary and A Critical Essay on European Literature, 1913; A Philosophical System of Theistic Idealism, 1917; Seven Theistic Philosophers, 1920; Great Philosophical Problems, 1922. *Address:* Annick Lodge, Irvine; Broadstone, Stranraer.

Died 25 March 1923.

LINDSAY, Sir John, KBE 1924; Kt 1915; Town Clerk of Glasgow, 1912–27; *b* Glasgow, 16 Dec. 1860; *s* of late Alex. Lindsay, Marine Engineer; *m* 1893, Charlotte Elizabeth (*d* 1922), 3rd *d* of late David Douglas, retired Valuator, Arbroath; one *s* one *d. Educ:* Gorbals and Hutchesontown Sessional Schools; Glasgow University. Entered the service of the Sheriff Clerk of Lanarkshire, 1875; Assistant Clerk of Police, Glasgow, 1891; Clerk of Police and Town Clerk Depute (Police Department); DL for the County of the City of Glasgow; JP for the Counties of the Cities of Glasgow, Dundee and Aberdeen, and Counties of Lanark, Dumbarton and Argyll; Honorary Sheriff-Substitute of Lanarkshire. *Publications:* Treatises on the Statutory Police Law of Glasgow; Municipal Glasgow: its evolution and enterprises; etc. *Recreation:* bowling. *Address:* St Mungo, Pollokshields, Glasgow. *T:* Central 6400. *Died 23 Sept. 1927.*

LINDSAY, William Alexander, CVO 1924; KC; JP, DL; MA; Peerage-Counsel; Clarenceux King of Arms since 1922; *b* 8 June 1846; *e s* of late Hon. Colin Lindsay and Lady Frances Howard, *d* of 4th Earl of Wicklow; *m* 1870, Lady Harriet Gordon, *d* of 5th Earl of Aberdeen; three *s* two *d* (and three *s* decd). *Educ:* Eton; Cambridge; MA 1871. Member of Lloyd's, 1868; Barrister, Middle Temple, 1873; QC 1897; Bencher, 1906; Norroy King of Arms, 1919–22 (previously Windsor Herald and Portcullis Pursuivant); Royal Commissioner to inquire into Corrupt Practices, 1880; contested Burnley, 1874, 1876, 1894, 1896; Huddersfield, 1880; Forfarshire, 1885. FSA. *Publications:* articles on Earldom of Mar, the O'Briens, and various genealogical subjects; the Stewart and Guelph Pedigrees; The Royal Household, 1837–97; Charters of Inchaffray; contributor to Encyclopædia Britannica and Lord Halsbury's Laws of England. *Address:* 17

Cromwell Road, SW7. *T:* Western 3595; Goldsmith Building, Temple, EC4; College of Arms, EC4. *T:* Central 485. *Clubs:* Athenæum, Carlton. *Died 13 Sept. 1926.*

LINDSAY-HOGG, Sir Lindsay, 1st Bt, *cr* 1905; JP; late Member of East Sussex County Council; *b* 10 March 1853; *s* of late William Hogg of Oakleigh, Pembury, near Tunbridge Wells, and Lancaster Gate, London, Consul for the Hanseatic States; assumed name of Lindsay-Hogg, 1906; *m* 1880, Alice, *d* of John Christian Cowley of Heathfield, Addington, Surrey, and Julia, *e d* of late Sir William Baynes, 2nd Bt; two *d* (and one *s* one *d* decd). *Educ:* Harrow. MP (C) Southern and Eastbourne Div. of Sussex, 1900–6. Owner of property in Sussex. *Recreations:* coaching and any kind of sports; has done much towards the Rifle Clubs and the formation and improvement of the agricultural and other societies throughout England, and president of a large number. *Heir: g s* Anthony Henry Lindsay-Hogg [*b* 1 May 1908; *e s* of late William Lindsay Lindsay-Hogg and Nora Cicely, *d* of late Capt. J. J. Barrow of Holmewood, nr Tunbridge Wells, Dornoch, NB, and 35 Hyde Park Gardens, W. *Address:* Hayward's Grange, Rotherfield, Sussex]. *Address:* Rotherfield Hall, Jarvis Brook, Sussex. *T:* Rotherfield 7. *Club:* Carlton. *Died 25 Nov. 1923.*

LINDSELL, Henry Martin, CB 1904; *b* 7 May 1846; *e s* of Lt-Col Lindsell, JP, DL, of Fairfield, Biggleswade, Beds, and Emma, *d* of Rev. Martin Hogge, Vicar of Southacre, Norfolk; unmarried. *Educ:* Harrow (Head of the School); Trinity College, Oxford (scholar). 1st class Mods; 2nd class Litteræ Humaniores; MA Oxon. Called to the Bar, Inner Temple, 1874; appointed Examiner to the Education Department, 1876; Advising Counsel, 1891; Principal Assistant Secretary (Legal), 1903 (retired). JP and CC Beds; Chairman of Quarter Sessions. *Address:* 67 Albert Hall Mansions, SW; Shortmead, Biggleswade, Beds. *Club:* United University. *Died 30 Jan. 1925.*

LINES, Rt. Rev. Edwin S., DD Yale, 1897, Berkeley Divinity School, 1904, Princeton, 1911, Rutgers, 1917; Bishop of the Diocese of Newark, USA, since 1903; *b* Naugatuck, Connecticut, 23 Nov. 1845; *m* 1880, Mary L. Morehouse; two *s. Educ:* The Cheshire School; Yale University; Berkeley Divinity School. Rector Christ Church, West Haven, Conn, 1874–79; St Paul's Church, West Haven, Conn, 1879–1903; Member, Board of Missions, 1901–25; sometime Member of National Churches Council, Educational and Social Service Boards, etc. *Publications:* a number of historical papers and addresses, lectures, and contributions to periodicals. *Address:* 21 Washington Street, Newark, NJ, USA. *Clubs:* Graduates, New Haven; Nassau, Princeton. *Died 25 Oct. 1927.*

LINKLATER, John Edmund; Barrister-at-Law; Registrar in Bankruptcy, High Court of Justice since 1887; *b* 14 Nov. 1848; *s* of late John Linklater, Solicitor of Walbrook, EC; *m* 1876, Emma, *d* of late Walter Lindesay Willson; two *d. Educ:* Eton; Christ Church, Oxford (BA, SCL, 1871; MA, 1874). Called to Bar, Inner Temple, 1872. *Address:* 3 Collingham Road, SW. *T:* Western 1225. *Club:* New University. *Died 11 Jan. 1917.*

LINTON, Sir James Dromgole, Kt 1885; PRI; ROI; Hon. Member Royal Scottish Water Colour Society; Hon. Associate of the Royal Institute of British Architects; *b* London, 26 Dec. 1840; *o s* of late James Linton, London, and Jane Scott, Carlisle; *m* 1867, Harriet Maria, *d* of late Henry Allen; three *s* five *d. Educ:* Cleveland House, Barnes. President of the Royal Institute of Painters in Water Colours, 1884–99, and from 1909. Corresponding member of the Society of Water Colour Painters, Vienna; Hon. President of the Royal Society of Miniature Painters. KSJ; Officier of the Order of Leopold, Belgium; Jubilee Medal, 1897. *Address:* 4 The Mall, Parkhill Road, Haverstock Hill, NW. *Club:* Savage. *Died 3 Oct. 1916.*

LIPSETT, Maj.-Gen. Louis James, CB 1918; CMG 1915; Royal Irish Regiment, attached to Canadian Forces; *b* 15 June 1874; *o surv. s* of late Richard Lipsett and Mrs Lipsett, The Cottage, Merthyr-Tydfil. Entered army, 1894; Capt. 1901; Maj. 1913; DAA and QMG, 1905–7; ADC to Maj.-Gen. 2nd Div. Aldershot, 1907–8; General Staff Officer, 2nd Grade, Canadian Forces, 1911; served NW Frontier, India, 1907–8 (medal 2 clasps); European War, 1914–18 (despatches, Bt Lt-Col and Col, CB, CMG). *Club:* Army and Navy. *Died 14 Oct. 1918.*

LISH, Joseph J.; Past President, Society of Architects (London), and a Gold Medallist of the Society of Architects; *m* Nancy Bentley Hozier Roberton, *d* of late Edward M'Leod of Natal, SA, and *g d* of late John Roberton of Lauchope, Lanarkshire; two *s* two *d. Publications:* (ed

and jt author with W. H. Hudleston and Prof. A. Meek) The Dove Marine Laboratory, containing a history of the Dove family and their descendants; Cullercoats and Marine Biology; articles upon Reinforced Concrete and Portland Cement, showing the position this country can claim to have occupied in the origination and development of these materials. *Address:* Croftlands, Thornthwaite, near Keswick. *Died 17 Jan. 1923.*

LISLE, 6th Baron, *cr* 1758 (Ire.); **George William James Lysaght;** *b* 29 Jan. 1840; 2nd *s* of 5th Baron and Henrietta, *d* of John Church; *S* father, 1898; *m* 1868, Amy Emily, *d* of late Ayliffe Langford, Ventnor, Isle of Wight; one *d* (one *s* decd). *Educ:* private tutors; Plymouth Grammar School. Formerly Lt in Devon Militia Artillery, and in Jackson's Forest Rangers Waikato Militia; served Maori War, 1864–65. Owner of about 7,000 acres in Counties Cork and Limerick. *Heir: g s* John Nicholas Horace Lysaght, *b* 10 Aug. 1903. *Address:* West End, Mallow, Co. Cork. *Died 16 March 1919.*

LISTER, Joseph Jackson, FRS; late Fellow of St John's College, Cambridge; *s* of late Arthur Lister, FRS; *m* 1911, Dorothea Charlotte Edith, *d* of late George Selwyn Marryat. *Publications:* articles on Foraminifers, Mycetozoa, etc, in Lankester's Treatise on Zoology; part author of chapters on Arthropoda in Sedgwick's Students' Textbook of Zoology, and of various zoological memoirs. *Address:* Merton House, Grantchester, near Cambridge; St John's College, Cambridge. *Club:* Savile. *Died 5 Feb. 1927.*

LISTER, Thomas David, CBE 1920; late Physician to Mount Vernon Hospital for Consumption, and to Royal Waterloo Hospital for Children; Member of Senate of London University, elected in 1919 by Medical Graduates in Convocation; Head Office Medical Adviser of the Royal Exchange Assurance Corporation, Friends' Provident Institution, and North British and Mercantile Insurance Company (West End); Consulting Physician to the National Union of Teachers; Consulting Physician to the Post Office Sanatorium Society; Consulting Physician to the Association of Local Government Officers; Consulting Physician for Chest Cases to the Prince of Wales' Hospital for Officers, St Marylebone, 1917–19; *b* London, 30 Jan. 1869; *s* of late Francis Wilson Lister and Elizabeth Wishart, *o d* of David Roy, of Glasgow; *m* Louise Edna Bertha, *e d* of Eugen Ritter, London. *Educ:* Aske's School (Haberdashers' Company); Guy's Hospital. MD Lond. 1894; FRCS 1894, MRCP 1900; FRSM. House Surgeon at Guy's, 1893–94; Pathologist to East London Hospital for Children, 1897–1900; Member and Hon. Advisory Physician to Council of National Association for Establishment and Maintenance of Sanatoria for Workers suffering from Tuberculosis, and as Chairman of Sites and Buildings Sub-committee drafted the scheme of the Benenden Sanatorium; Pres. and Treas. of Assurance Medical Society; an invited member of Panel Committee of the County of London and of the Hospital Saturday Fund Board of Delegates. *Publications:* Industrial Tuberculosis, 1910; section (jointly) on Heart and Lungs in Knocker's Medico-Legal Aspects of Accidents; contributions to transactions and medical journals on Life Assurance, Children's Diseases, Consumption, and allied subjects. *Address:* Nenthorn, Henley-on-Thames. *Club:* Royal Societies. *Died 30 July 1924.*

LISTER, Rev. Thomas Llewellyn, VD; MA; Hon. Canon of Llandaff, 1909–22; Rural Dean of Newport, 1905. *Educ:* Jesus College, Oxford (MA). Ordained 1862; Curate of St Woolos, Newport, 1862–75; Vicar of St Mark's, Newport, 1895–1916. *Address:* 31 Fields Road, Newport, Mon. *Died 25 July 1926.*

LISTER-KAYE, Sir John Pepys, 3rd Bt, *cr* 1812; DL; Groom-in-Waiting to King Edward VII, 1908–10; late Lieutenant Royal Horse Guards; *b* 18 Feb. 1853; *s* of Lister Lister-Kaye and Lady Caroline Pepys, 3rd *d* of 1st Earl of Cottenham; *S* grandfather, 1871; *m* 1881, Natica, *d* of Antonio Yznaga del Valle, New York, USA; one *s* decd. *Educ:* Eton; Trinity Coll., Camb. *Heir: b* Cecil Edmund Lister-Kaye, *b* 16 Jan. 1854. *Address:* Overton Lodge, Wakefield. *Clubs:* Marlborough, Carlton, Turf, Guards. *Died 27 May 1924.*

LISTOWEL, 3rd Earl of, *cr* 1822; **William Hare,** KP; PC; JP; Baron Ennismore, 1800; Viscount Ennismore, 1816; Baron Hare (UK), 1869; Captain Scots Guards (retired 1856); *b* Convamore, 29 May 1833; *e s* of 2nd Earl and Maria Augusta, 2nd *d* of late Vice-Adm. William Windham; *S* father, 1856; *m* 1865, Lady Ernestine Mary Brudenell-Bruce, *y d* of 3rd Marquess of Ailesbury; one *s* two *d* (and one *s* decd). Lieut Scots Guards, 1852; severely wounded at the Alma; Lord-in-Waiting, 1880. *Heir: s* Viscount Ennismore, *b* 12 Sept. 1866.

Address: Kingston House, Prince's Gate, SW; Convamore, Ballyhooly, Co. Cork. *Club:* Brooks's; Royal Yacht Squadron, Cowes.

Died 5 June 1924.

LITTLE, Mrs Archibald; *b* Madeira; *y d* of late Calverley Bewicke of Hallaton Hall, Leicestershire, and Mary Amelia Hollingsworth; *m* 1886, Archibald Little (*d* 1908), Pioneer of Upper Yangtse and author of The Far East and Through the Yangtse Gorges. Worked on many philanthropic committees in England; then founder, organizing Secretary, and finally President of the Tien Tsu Hui, or Anti-foot-binding Society of China; Vice-President of the Women's Conference at Shanghai, 1900; delivered lectures before the Geographical Societies of Glasgow, Edinburgh, Aberdeen, Dundee, Manchester, Liverpool, Newcastle, South Shields, also at Glasgow Exhibition; read a paper of Mr Little's before the British Association at Glasgow. *Publications:* Intimate China; The Land of the Blue Gown; Round About my Peking Garden; Li Hung Chang, his Life and Times; A Marriage in China; Out in China, a Novelette; A Millionaire's Courtship; Fairy Foxes, a Chinese Legend; Mother Darling, written to establish the rights of mothers to their own children; A Noble Army and a Holy War; many novels, among these Margery Travers; Onwards! but Whither; The Last of the Jerninghames; and many magazine and newspaper articles; edited Mr Archibald Little's Across Yunnan; also Gleanings from Fifty Years in China. *Recreations:* travel, sightseeing. *Club:* Ladies' Empire.

Died 31 July 1926.

LITTLE, James, MD Edin.; MRIA; FRCPI; Hon. LLD Edinburgh; Hon. Physician to His Majesty in Ireland, 1908; Regius Professor of Physic, Dublin University, since 1898; *b* Newry; *s* of Archibald Little and Mary, *d* of Richard Coulter; *m* Anah (*d* 1914), *d* of Robert Murdoch, Dublin; two *s* one *d*. *Educ:* Armagh Royal School; Medical School, TCD, and University, Edinburgh; MD Hon. Causa, Dublin. In 1866 became Physician, Adelaide Hospital; Professor of Practice of Medicine, Royal College of Surgeons, Ireland; president of the Royal College of Physicians, Ireland, and of the Royal Academy of Medicine, Ireland, and consulting physician to four Dublin hospitals, and Crown Representative for Ireland on General Medical Council. *Publications:* First Steps in Clinical Study; Chronic Diseases of the Heart. *Recreations:* field sports. *Address:* 14 St Stephen's Green, Dublin. *Clubs:* Athenæum, Junior Carlton; Kildare Street, Dublin.

Died 23 Dec. 1916.

LITTLEJOHN, Harvey, MA, MB, BSc (Public Health); FRCS, FRSE; Professor of Forensic Medicine since 1906, and late Dean of the Faculty of Medicine, Edinburgh University; *s* of the late Sir Henry Duncan Littlejohn. *Educ:* Edinburgh University; Vienna; Berlin; Paris. Formerly MOH, Sheffield; President, Section of Forensic Medicine, International Medical Congress, 1913; Major RAMC (T) Commanding Medical Unit OTC; President Medico-Legal Society of London. *Publications:* Illustrations of Forensic Medicine, and numerous papers on Forensic Medicine and Public Health. *Address:* 11 Rutland Street, Edinburgh. *T:* 2106. *Clubs:* Savile; University, Edinburgh. *Died 15 Aug. 1927.*

LITTLEJOHN, Robert; Director of the African Banking Corporation since 1900; Member of Tariff Commission. General Manager African Banking Corporation, 1891-1900. *Address:* 8 Cavendish Square, W1. *Clubs:* Constitutional, Caledonian, Gresham.

Died 24 May 1920.

LITTLER, Captain Charles Augustus, DSO 1916; 12th Battalion Australian Imperial Forces; *b* Launceston, Tasmania, 26 March; *s* of Augustus Littler and Hannah Murray; *m* 1892, Helen Cotgrave Thomas; three *s*. *Educ:* Edinburgh College. Trained as a Banker; several years Commercial Agent for Tasmania in Far East; travelled largely in Java, Malay States, Philippines, China, Borneo, Manchuria, Japan, and Siberia; served with Russians and Americans in the field; explored the interior of Mindanao, Southern Philippines, and spent much time amongst the wild people; a member of many economic, traffic, harbour, and tariff commissions. Served European War, 1915-16 (DSO). *Address:* Silwood, Devonport West, Tasmania.

Died 3 Sept. 1916.

LITTLEWOOD, Bt-Col Harry, CMG 1917; JP; Hon. MSc (Leeds); FRCS 1886; LRCP 1884; Examiner in Surgery, University of Cambridge; Consulting Surgeon, General Infirmary, Leeds; *b* Norfolk, 13 April 1861; 2nd *s* of late Charles F. Littlewood, Hempstead Hall, Norfolk, and Mary, *d* of Augustine Worts, Lessingham, Norfolk; unmarried. *Educ:* Norwich; University College, London; University College Hospital. Atkinson-Morley Surgical Scholar, 1884; late Senior Surgeon and Chairman of the Faculty, Leeds Infirmary, and President

of the Leeds and West Riding Medico-Chirurgical Society; Consulting Surgeon to the Victoria Hospital, Keighley, and Malton Cottage Hospital; late Professor of Surgery and Lecturer on Practical and Operative Surgery in the University of Leeds, and Resident Surgical Officer to the Leeds Infirmary; late House Surgeon, House Physician, and Resident Obstetric Officer, University College Hospital and Senior Demonstrator of Anatomy, University College, London; and Clinical Assistant, Royal London Ophthalmic Hospital; Examiner in Surgery in the National University of Ireland. Gazetted to the Territorial Force, RAMC, as Surgeon Lt-Col 2nd Northern Division General Hospital, Leeds, 1908; Administrator 2nd Northern General Hospital, Leeds, 1915-19. Lord of the Manor of Hempstead, Norfolk; KGStJ. *Publications:* contribs on surgical subjects to medical societies and medical jls. *Recreations:* farming, motoring. *Address:* Erpingham Lodge, Ingworth, Norfolk. *TA:* Aylsham, Norfolk. *M:* U 790.

Died 19 Dec. 1921.

LIVEING, Edward, MD (Cantab); FRCP; Registrar of the Royal College of Physicians, 1889-1909, Emeritus Registrar, 1909; Consulting Physician, St Marylebone General Dispensary; *b* Nayland, Suffolk, 8 Feb. 1832; 2nd *s* of Edward Liveing and Catherine, *o d* of Geo. Downing, Barrister, Lincoln's Inn; *m* 1st, 1854, Frances (*d* 1885), *o d* of Lt Henry Torlesse, RN, Police Magistrate at Hobart; three *s* two *d*; 2nd, 1898, Harriet Susan, *e d* of Rev. J. Wilson Brown, Rector of Stowlangtoft, Suffolk, and Hon. Canon of Ely. *Educ:* King's College, London; Gonville and Caius College, Cambridge; BA Math. Honours, 1858; MB 1859; MD 1870. FRCP 1874. Examiner in Medicine, University of Cambridge, 1870-71; Fellow and late Member of Council, King's College, London; formerly Assistant Physician to King's College Hospital. *Publication:* On Megrim, a contribution to the pathology of Nerve Storms. *Address:* 52 Queen Anne Street, Cavendish Square, W.

Died 2 April 1919.

LIVEING, George Downing, JP; MA; ScD; FRS 1879; President of St John's College, Cambridge, since 1911; *b* Nayland, Suffolk, 21 Dec. 1827; *e s* of Edward Liveing and Catherine, *o d* of George Downing, Lincoln's Inn; *m* 1860, Catherine (*d* 1888), 2nd *d* of Rowland Ingram, Rector of Little Ellingham, Norfolk. *Educ:* St John's College, Cambridge (MA, Hon. ScD 1908); Fellow, 1853-60, and from 1880; 11th Wrangler 1850; 1st in Natural Sciences Tripos, 1851. Lecturer on Natural Science, St John's Coll., Camb. 1853; Professor of Chemistry, Staff and Royal Military Colleges, 1860; Professor of Chemistry, Cambridge, 1861-1908; started the first laboratory for students in Cambridge, 1852; active in organizing. *Publications:* many papers on Spectroscopy, Crystallisation, etc; On the Transmutation of Matter, Camb. Essays, 1st ser. 1855; Chemical Equilibrium the Result of Dissipation of Energy, 1885; (jtly with Mr Warren) Report on University Colleges, 1897; (jtly with Sir J. Dewar) Collected Papers on Spectroscopy, 1915. *Recreations:* field geology, gardening. *Address:* St John's College, Cambridge.

Died 26 Dec. 1924.

LIVEING, Robert, AM and MD Cantab; Consulting Physician to the Skin Department, Middlesex Hospital; *b* Nayland, Suffolk, 30 March 1834; *s* of Edward Liveing, MRCS; *m* Adelaide (*d* 1906), *d* of Adm. Edward Hawker; one *s* one *d*. *Educ:* Christ's Coll., Cambridge (Scholar). Math. Hons 1856. Fellow of King's Coll. London; formerly Lecturer on Anatomy and Physician to Middlesex Hospital; Gulstonian Lecturer, 1873; Vice-President Alpine Club, 1869 and 1870. *Publications:* Handbook on Diseases of the Skin; Notes on the Treatment of Skin Diseases; Lectures on Leprosy. *Recreations:* travelling, gardening. *Address:* 11 Manchester Square, W. *Club:* Alpine. *Died 22 Feb. 1919.*

LIVERSIDGE, Archibald, MA Cambridge, LLD Glasgow; FRS 1882; FIC, FCS, FGS, FRGS; Hon. FRSE 1900; ARSM; Emeritus Professor of Chemistry in the University of Sydney (Professor, 1873-1908), and First Dean of the Faculty of Science, 1879-1904; Vice-President Chemical Society, 1910-13; Vice-President Society of Chemical Industry, 1909-12; *b* Turnham Green, 17 Nov. 1847; *s* of late John Liversidge, Bexley, Kent; unmarried. *Educ:* private school and tutors; Royal School of Mines and Royal College of Chemistry, Royal Exhibitioner, 1867; Christ's College, Cambridge (Scholar in Natural Science). Instructor in Chemistry, Royal School of Naval Architecture, 1867; Univ. Demonstrator in Chemistry, Camb., 1870; Hon. Sec. of the Royal Soc. NSW, 1875-89; President, 1886, 1890, and 1901; Member Phil. Society, Cambridge, Physical Society, London; Mineralogical Societies, Great Britain and France; Hon. Member: Royal Society NSW, 1908; Royal Society Victoria, 1892; New Zealand Inst., 1890; Royal Historical Society, London, 1877; K. Leop.-Car. Akad. Halle, 1894; Corr. Mem. New York Acad. Sci.

1899; Royal Society, Tasmania, 1875; Queensland, 1886; Soc. d'Acclim. Mauritius, 1876; Edinburgh Geological Society, 1893; Trustee of the Australian Museum, 1874–1908; Member of the First Board of Technical Education, Sydney; originated the Faculty of Science, 1879, and the School of Mines, Sydney University, 1890; the Australasian Association for the Advancement of Science, 1885; the Sydney Section of the Society of Chemical Industry, 1902; and was first Chairman, 1903–5; a member of the original Board of three of the Technological Museum, Sydney, 1879; Hon. Sec. Australasian Association for the Advancement of Science, 1888–1909, Hon. Member, 1902, President, 1888–90, Vice-President from 1890; a Vice-President British Association, 1896. *Publications:* The Minerals of New South Wales; Report upon Technical Education and Museums; and over 100 papers, researches, etc, upon Chemistry and Mineralogy, published by the Royal Soc. London, Chemical Soc., Royal Soc. NSW. *Address:* Fieldhead, Coombe Warren, Kingston Hill, Surrey. *T:* Kingston 1775. *Clubs:* Athenæum, Carlton.

Died 26 Sept. 1927.

LIVESEY, James; Senior member, Livesey, Son & Henderson, Civil and Mechanical Engineers; *b* 1831; *s* of Joseph Livesey, Preston. *Educ:* Preston. Commenced his career on the Caledonian Railway; served pupilage at locomotive works of Beyer and Peacock, Manchester; Locomotive Superintendent, and Assistant Engineer on construction work, Isabel Segunda Railway in Spain, Santander to Alar del Rey, 1859; one of the earliest advocates of the use of steel, and devoted considerable time to its manufacture and general application; reported for the Buenos Ayres and Great Southern Railway on the advantages of steel rails over iron, and his recommendations were adopted 1869; laid out and arranged a new and extensive steel works for the Freedom Iron and Steel Company of Pennsylvania; the first pair of reversing engines ever made were sent to these works; designed and erected a large and novel grain elevator at Carcarana, on the River Plate, in Argentina; commissioned by the Canadian Government to visit the United States of America to make an exhaustive examination of the principal railways in that country, and to report thereon; Consulting Engineer to the Buenos Ayres Great Southern Railway and afterwards to many railways in all parts of the world; inventor of the iron and steel permanent way, largely adopted in South America, India, Egypt, etc, and of the patent switch lock, which prevents a signalman splitting a train when passing over the facing points, and which the Government ordered to be adopted on all the railways in the United Kingdom; inventor of the newspaper folding machine (fifty-six years ago), later incorporated in the printing machine by which all newspapers are folded. *Address:* 4 Whitehall Court, SW1. *Clubs:* Royal Thames Yacht, Hurlingham.

Died 3 Feb. 1925.

LIVINGSTONE, Matthew, ISO 1902; *b* 1837; *s* of John Livingstone, Hilltown, Dundee; *m* Elizabeth Jane Stirling, *o d* of John Adam Ewart, late Chief Assistant Keeper of the Register of Sasines; two *d*. *Educ:* Dundee; Edinburgh University. Appointed Chief Clerk of the General Register of Sasines for Scotland, 1871; Chief Assistant Keeper, 1891; Deputy Keeper of the Records of Scotland, 1892–1903. *Publications:* Guide to the Public Records of Scotland, 1905; Editor of The Register of the Privy Seal of Scotland, 1908. *Address:* Sidlaw, 32 Hermitage Gardens, Edinburgh.

Died 26 April 1917.

LLANGATTOCK, 2nd Baron, *cr* 1892; **John Maclean Rolls,** JP, DL; *b* 25 April 1870; *e s* of 1st Baron Llangattock and Georgiana, *d* of Sir Charles Fitzroy Maclean, 9th Bt of Morvaren; *S* father, 1912. *Educ:* Eton; Christ Church, Oxford; BA 1893; MA, BCL, 1896. Barrister Inner Temple, 1896; Captain and Hon. Major (retired) 1st Monmouthshire Volunteer Artillery; Major 2/4th Welsh, RFA (T), 1915; High Sheriff, Monmouth, 1900; Mayor of Monmouth, 1906–7; owner of property in Monmouthshire; of land in Southwark, Newington, Camberwell, Bermondsey. *Heir:* none. *Address:* The Hendre, Monmouth. *T:* Monmouth 26. *M:* AX 57, 60, 202. *Clubs:* Carlton, Junior Constitutional, Royal Automobile.

Died 1 Nov. 1916 (ext).

LLEWELYN, Sir John Talbot Dillwyn-, 1st Bt, *cr* 1890; JP, DL; *b* 26 May 1836; *e s* of John Dillwyn-Llewelyn, FRS, Penllergare, Swansea, and Emma, *d* of Thomas Mansell Talbot, Margam; *m* 1861, Julia (*d* 1917), *d* of Sir Michael Hicks-Beach, 8th Bt; one *s* two *d* (and one *s* decd). *Educ:* Eton; Christ Church, Oxford (MA). MP (C) Swansea, 1895–1900; late Director GW Railway; was Chairman Quarter Sessions of Glamorganshire, and an Alderman of the County Council. Owner of about 14,900 acres. *Heir:* *s* Charles Leyshon Dillwyn-Venables-Llewelyn, *b* 29 June 1870. *Recreations:* was some years captain of the South Wales cricket eleven; and President of the

Welsh Rugby Football Union. *Address:* Penllergare, Swansea. *Clubs:* Athenæum, Carlton.

Died 6 July 1927.

LLEWELYN, Sir Leonard (Wilkinson), KBE 1917; late Controller of Non-Ferrous Metals, Ministry of Munitions; *b* 11 June 1874; *s* of late Llewelyn Llewelyn, JP, High Sheriff, Monmouthshire, 1913, and *d* of Geo. Wilkinson; *m* 1st, 1899, Edith (*d* 1913), *d* of late Edward Jones, JP, DL, of Snatchwood Park, Pontypool, Monmouthshire; one *s* three *d*; 2nd, 1922, Mrs Elsie Louise Jones, Glen Usk, Caerleon, Newport, Mon. *Educ:* Monmouth Grammar School; Cheltenham; Heidelberg. Director of Duffryn Aberdare Colliery Co. Ltd, Cambrian Collieries, Glamorgan Collieries, Fernhill Collieries, John Lysaght Ltd, Sankey and Sons Ltd, Harwood Bros Ltd, Phœnix Patent Fuel Ltd, Arrow Fuel Ltd, Consolidated Cambrian Collieries, D. Davis and Sons, Welsh Navigation Colliery Co.; Managing Director of North's Navigation Collieries (1889) Ltd, Celtic Collieries Ltd, Crown Preserved Coal Co. Ltd, Frenchwood Mill Co. Ltd, and other large steel and colliery undertakings. Contested North Monmouthshire General Election, 1918. High Sheriff Monmouthshire, 1920; JP Cos Glamorgan and Monmouth. Officer of the Légion d'Honneur; Officer of the Order of Leopold; Officer of the Order St Stanislav; Silver Medal of the Royal Humane Society. *Recreations:* polo, horse-breeding, golf. *Address:* Malpas Court, Newport, Mon. *T:* Newport 2887; Glen Usk, Caerleon, Mon. *Clubs:* Junior Carlton, Bath, Sports.

Died 13 June 1924.

LLEWELYN, Sir Robert Baxter, KCMG 1898 (CMG 1889); *b* 1845; *s* of John Llewelyn; *m* 1873, Theodora Louisa, *d* of Charles Harvey of Campbeltown; two *d*. Extra Clerk Colonial Office, London, 1868; Registrar Colonial Secretary's Office, Jamaica, 1869; Private Secretary to Sir J. P. Grant, 1873; Clerk of Privy Council, Jamaica, 1877; Commissioner for Turks Islands, 1878; Administrator of Tobago, 1885; of St Vincent, 1888; of St Lucia, 1889; of the Colony of the Gambia, 1891–1900; Governor of Windward Islands, 1900–6. *Club:* Junior Carlton.

Died 19 Feb. 1919.

LLOYD, Charles Harford, MA, MusD Oxon; Hon. RAM, and FRCO; Organist, Choirmaster, and Composer at HM Chapel Royal, St James's Palace, 1917; *b* Thornbury, Gloucestershire, 1849; *y s* of late Edmund Lloyd, Solicitor. *Educ:* Thornbury Grammar School; Rossall School; Magdalen Hall (Hertford College), Oxford; Open Classical Scholarship; 2nd Class Mod.; 2nd Class Final Theol. Sch. First President of Oxford University Musical Club; Organist of Gloucester Cathedral, 1876; Organist of Christ Church Cathedral, Oxford, 1882; Precentor and Musical Instructor, Eton College, 1892–1914; conducted, while at Gloucester, the Three-Choir Festivals of 1877 and 1880; at Oxford, the Choral and Orchestral Societies; at Eton, the Windsor and Eton Choral and Orchestral Societies; at various times Examiner in Music in the Univs of Oxford, Cambridge, London, and Durham; Member of Council Royal College of Music and Past President of Royal College of Organists; Grand Organist of English Freemasons, 1917. *Musical publications:* Hero and Leander, Song of Balder, Andromeda, Longbeards' Saga, Song of Judgment, Alcestis, etc, anthems, services, organ pieces, Trio for Pianoforte, Clarionet, and Bassoon, Characteristic Pieces for Violin and Pianoforte, etc. *Recreations:* figure skating, cycling, boating, golf. *Address:* Hillcrest, Slough. *T:* Slough 182. *Club:* United University.

Died 16 Oct. 1919.

LLOYD, Edward; singer; *b* 7 March 1845; *s* of Richard Lloyd (*d* 1850), vicar choral in Westminster Abbey, and Miss Hopkins; *m* 1921, Mrs Clement Walter Hann. *Educ:* Grey's School, Southwark. Choir, Westminster Abbey, 1852–60; tenor, St Andrew's, Well St, and Chapel Royal; first appeared Gloucester Musical Festival, 1871; sang at all principal festivals. *Recreations:* golfing, walking, tennis.

Died 31 March 1927.

LLOYD, Lt-Col Fitzwarren, CIE 1914; VD; late Commandant, Assam Valley Light Horse; *b* 16 Aug. 1859; *s* of late Col Lloyd, Aston Hall, Oswestry; *m* 1891; no *c*. *Educ:* Eton. *Address:* Grindlay & Co., 54 Parliament Street, SW1.

Died 15 Feb. 1923.

LLOYD, Lt-Gen. Sir Francis, GCVO 1918 (CVO 1909); KCB 1911 (CB 1900); DSO 1898; a Commissioner Duke of York's Royal Military School since 1920; Colonel Royal Welch Fusiliers, 1915; Hon. Colonel 13 County of London, Kensington Battalion, 1920; retired pay, 1920; *b* 12 Aug. 1858; *s* of Col Richard Thomas Lloyd and Lady Frances, *d* of Thomas Robert, 10th Earl of Kinnoull; *m* 1881, Mary, *d* of George Gunnis Leckie, Stirling. *Educ:* Harrow. Joined 33rd Duke of Wellington Regt, 1874; transferred Grenadier Guards,

1874; Capt. 1885; Major, 1892; Lt-Col 1898; Col 1902; Brig.-Gen. 1904; Maj.-Gen. 1909; Lt-Gen. 1917; Suakim Expedition as Signalling Officer Guards Brigade, 1885; battle of Hasheen (medal with clasp, Khedive's star, despatches); Nile Expedition, 1898; battle of Khartoum (despatches, DSO, British medal, Khedive's medal); South Africa, 1900-2 (severely wounded, despatches, CB, South African medals, Queen's and King's); commanded 2nd Batt. Grenadier Guards, and subsequently 1st Batt. Grenadier Guards; commanded 1st Guards Brigade, 1904-8; Welsh Division TF, 1909-13; London District, 1913-19. Food Commissioner for London and Home Counties, 1919-20. Danish Order of Dannebrog, II Class; Grand Cross St Sava (Serbia); Grand Officer Crown of Belgium; White Eagle, Russia; KGStJ 1916; one of HM Lieutenants for the City of London; JP, DL Salop; JP Essex. *Address:* Aston Hall, Oswestry, Shropshire. *TA:* Queenshead; Rolls Park, Chigwell, Essex. *T:* Chigwell 7. *Club:* Carlton.   *Died 26 Feb. 1926.*

LLOYD, Sir Horatio, Kt 1890; Recorder of Chester since 1866; Chairman of Quarter Sessions, Cheshire, since 1883; *b* 29 Sept. 1829; *s* of late Edward Watson Lloyd, Prothonotary and Clerk of the Crown; *m* 1856, Harriette(*d* 1902), *d* of late Honoratus Leigh Rigby, Hawarden, Flintshire; three *s*. *Educ:* Rossall, and privately. Bar, 1852; Counsel to HM's Mint and Post Office, and revising barrister; Judge of County Courts, Chester, 1874-1906; Royal Commissioner to inquire into Welsh Sunday Closing Acts, 1889. *Publications:* The Law of Quarter Sessions, 1875; Chitty's Statutes, 1865-80; papers on archæological subjects. *Recreations:* aquatics, watercolour painting. *Address:* 8 Stanley Place, Chester. *Club:* Royal Societies.
                                                    Died 24 Dec. 1920.

LLOYD, Howard, JP Worcestershire; was Director of Lloyd's Bank Ltd; *b* 16 Aug. 1837; 3rd *s* of Isaac Lloyd; *m* Marabella, 3rd *d* of John Eliot Howard, FRS; seven *s*. *Educ:* private schools. For 31 years General Manager of Lloyd's Bank Limited. *Address:* Grafton Manor, Bromsgrove. *TA:* Bromsgrove. *T:* Bromsgrove 52. *Clubs:* New Oxford and Cambridge; Union, Conservative, Birmingham.
                                                    Died 17 Sept. 1920.

LLOYD, Rev. Iorwerth Grey, MA; FSA; Prebendary or Canon of Llandewi Aberarth in St David's Cathedral; a Surrogate for Diocese of St David's; *b* 22 Oct. 1844; *e s* of late Rev. Henry Robert Lloyd, MA, Rector of Cliffe-at-Hoo, Kent, and Harriet, 4th *d* of Hon. and Rt Rev. Edward Grey, DD, sometime Bishop of Hereford and Prebendary of Westminster Abbey; *m* 1871, Nina, 3rd *d* of late Charles Eastland de Michele, sometime HBM Consul at Petrograd; three *s* three *d*. *Educ:* Durham School; Exeter College, Oxford (3rd class in Law and Modern History, 1867). Curate of Ashford, Kent, 1868-69; Cliffe-at-Hoo, 1869-71; Coulsdon, 1871-79; Chaplain to 3rd Marquis of Ailesbury, 1878-86; Vicar of Hersham, Surrey, 1879-83; Wiston, Pembrokeshire, 1883-87; Clarbeston, 1885-87; Rector of Bosherston, Pembrokeshire, 1887-1903; Rural Dean of Castlemartin, 1893-1903; formerly a Member of Croydon (Surrey) Board of Guardians, and afterwards Chairman of Walton-on-Thames School Board; Vicar of Slebech with Minwear and Newton North, Pembrokeshire, 1903-19; Rural Dean of Dungleddy to 1919; Hon. Sec. to Building Committee of St David's Diocesan Board, 1911-18. *Publications:* Parish Church of Cliffe in the Archæologia Cantiana, vol. xi; Preparation for Confirmation, a paper read before the Clergy of the Rural Deanery of Castlemartin in the St David's Diocesan Gazette, No 20. *Recreation:* fly-fishing. *Address:* 5 Staverton Road, Oxford.   *Died 24 Dec. 1920.*

LLOYD, Col Sir Morgan George, KCB 1911 (CB 1897); commanding 3rd Battalion the Royal Irish Regiment, 1885-1903; Hon. Colonel; *b* 1843; *s* of Owen Lloyd of Lisadurn, Co. Roscommon, JP and DL, and Harriet, *d* of Arthur French of French Park, Co. Roscommon, and *sister* of 1st, 2nd and 3rd Barons de Freyne and Rt Hon. Fitzstephen French, MP; *m* 1870, Emily Olivia (*d* 1912), 2nd *d* of Thomas Bell, Brookhill, Co. Wexford, Ireland; one *s* two *d*. *Educ:* private school; Royal Military Coll. Sandhurst. Late King's Dragoon Guards. Decorated for length of service in the Militia. *Recreations:* shooting, golf, etc. *Address:* Raheen, Tenby, S Wales.
                                                    Died 25 June 1917.

LLOYD, Col Robert Oliver, CB 1919; JP and DL, Pembrokeshire; Chairman Pembrokeshire Territorial Force Association, 1909-20; *b* 20 March 1849; 4th *s* of Rev. Canon Charles Lloyd, late Rector of Chalfont, St Giles, Bucks; *m* 1877, Mary Isabella (*d* 1912), *d* of Maj.-Gen. D. G. Pollard of Castle Pollard, Westmeath; one *s* one *d*. *Educ:* Marlborough College; Royal Military Academy, Woolwich. Joined Royal Engineers, 1870; served in India, 1872-1901; on active service in Burmah, 1885-88 (severely wounded, despatches, medal with 2

clasps); promoted Colonel in the Army, 1899; Chief Engineer Bombay Army, Poona, 1899-1901; retired, 1902. *Recreations:* racing, polo, cricket, shooting. *Address:* 16 Forest Road, Branksome Park, Bournemouth, W. *Club:* Pembroke County, Haverfordwest.
                                                    Died 29 July 1921.

LLOYD, Col Thomas, CB 1897; JP Cardiganshire and Pembrokeshire; *b* 12 June 1853; *e s* of late Edmund Lloyd, and *g s* of late Thomas Lloyd of Coedmore, Lord-Lieut of Cardiganshire. *Educ:* Clifton Coll.; Shrewsbury School. Commanded Cardigan Royal Garrison Artillery Militia, 1887-1904. *Recreations:* riding, rowing, fishing. *Club:* United Service.
                                                    Died 12 June 1916.

LLOYD, Maj.-Gen. Thomas Francis, JP, DL, Co. Limerick; retired; *b* 21 April 1839; *s* of Thomas Lloyd of Beechmount, JP for counties of Clare, Limerick, and Tipperary, DL for Co. Limerick, *g s* of Thomas Lloyd of Beechmount, DL, MP for Co. Limerick; *m* 1870, Mary Henrietta, *d* of Christian Allhusen of Stoke Court, DL Bucks. *Educ:* Cheltenham Coll. Ensign, 98th Regt (Prince of Wales's), 1855; served in NW Frontier campaign, 1860; action of Poluteen, forcing the Burrarah Pass, and taking of the stronghold Makin (medal and clasp); commanded the 98th P of W Regt for 5½ years; commanded the 2nd Regimental District 5 years, and was Asst Adjt and QMG Cork District for 4 years, when he was promoted Maj.-Gen.; High Sheriff, 1894; Colonel-in-Chief, North Staffordshire Regiment, 1911. Owner of 1,500 acres. *Address:* Beechmount, Rathkeale, Co. Limerick. *Club:* United Service.
                                                    Died 8 Nov. 1921.

LLOYD, William Harris, MD; Hon. Surgeon to the King since 1901; *b* 1836; *s* of William Lloyd of Waterford, and of Kyle, Templemore, Co. Tipperary; *m* 1870, Phœbe, *d* of late Lt-Gen. Vincent; two *d*. Served China, 1857-58; Inspector-General of Hospitals and Fleets, 1890; retired, 1896. *Address:* 4 Alfred Place West, S Kensington, SW. *Club:* United Service.   *Died 2 April 1923.*

LLOYD-BAKER, Granville Edwin Lloyd, JP, DL, Gloucester; County Councillor, 1889-1910; *e s* of T. B. Lloyd Baker of Hardwicke Court, and Mary, *o c* of Nicholas Lewis Fenwick of Besford Court, Worcestershire; *m* 1868, Catherine (*d* 1890), 4th *d* of Hon. Arthur Lascelles of Norley, Cheshire; one *s* five *d*. *Educ:* Eton; Christ Church, Oxford. High Sheriff, Gloucestershire, 1898; served in various committees in the County Council and as Magistrate; Chairman of the Reformatory Committee, and of the Visiting Justices of the Prison. *Publications:* Dairying in Denmark; The Metayer System in Italy; French Agricultural Schools; Old Age Pensions, an Ounce of Fact; Large and Small Holdings in Denmark. *Recreation:* travelling. *Address:* Hardwicke Court, near Gloucester. *TA:* Lloyd-Baker, Hardwicke. *T:* Hardwicke District 2. *Club:* Carlton.
                                                    Died 3 Oct. 1924.

LLOYD OWEN, David Charles, JP Warwickshire; MD (Birm.) 1902; MB, BCh 1901; FRCSI 1880; MRCS 1865; *s* of Rev. D. Owen, originally of Darowen, Mont. *Educ:* Birmingham; Paris. Past Acting Honorary and Consulting Honorary Surgeon to the Birmingham and Midland Eye Hospital, Children's Hospital, and General Hospital; Vice-Chairman of the British Ophthalmic Hospital at Jerusalem; Past Vice-President of the Ophthalmological Society of Great Britain; one of the founders and First President of the Midland Ophthalmological Society; Past President of the Ophthalmological Section of the British Medical Association; Past President of the Midland Medical Society. KGStJ. *Publications:* numerous books and papers on subjects connected with his speciality, including Ophthalmic Therapeutics, Pain in Eye Diseases, Hereditary Nystagmus, etc; translations of Giraud Teulon on Vision, etc. *Recreations:* archæology, genealogy. *Address:* Bron-y-Graig, Harlech, N Wales.   *Died 25 Dec. 1925.*

LOANE, Miss M.; *d* of late Captain J. Loane, RN. *Publications:* The Queen's Poor; The Next Street but One; From Their Point of View; An Englishman's Castle; Neighbours and Friends; The Common Growth; Shipmates. *Address:* 22 Elmdale Road, Clifton.
                                                    Died 23 Feb. 1922.

LOBB, John, FRGS, FRHistS; Senior Bridgemaster of the City of London; Chairman of the Law and City Courts Committee of the Corporation of the City of London for 1905; on the Editorial Staff of the Sun Evening Newspaper, 1891-1903; *b* Tower Hamlets, 7 Aug. 1840; *e s* of late John and Louisa Lobb; *m* 1st, 1863, Ann, *o d* of Rev. Samuel Bruton of Kingswood, Gloucester; two *s* three *d*; 2nd, 1884, 2nd *d* of Henry Moon of Clayhidon, near Wellington, Devon; three *s* one *d*. *Educ:* privately. Called to the Primitive

Methodist ministry, 1862; resigned for commercial sphere; editor and proprietor of the Kingsland Monthly Messenger, 1871–73; became manager of the Christian Age, 1872–90; chief proprietor, 1880–90; Chairman of the Epping Forest Committee, 1899; member of the Court of Common Council for the Ward of Farringdon Without, 1887–1905; for 15 years member of the London School Board; 9 years Chairman of the Stores Committee; Chairman of the Finance Committee; Guardian of the City of London Union for 18 years; Chairman of the Lunatic Visiting Committee for 5 years; member of the Metropolitan Asylum Board for 3 years; Chairman of the Freemen's Orphan School for 2 years; 12 years Governor of Lady Holles's Trust, and St Bride's Foundation; a Governor of the Haberdashers' Schools and Sir John Cass's Institute; Member of the Institute of Journalists from 1886; during 1905–13 travelled 80,000 miles, lectured to 220,000 persons on Spiritualism; visited Mexico and the USA, 1909. *Publications:* Story of the Life of Rev. Josiah Henson; The Life and Times of Frederick Douglas, 1886; Life of the Rev. T. de Witt Talmage, DD, 1879; Talks with the Dead, 1906; The Busy Life after Death, 1908; The Banished Christ and the Bible; A Sketch of the Life of Sarah Flower Adams, 1910; Startling Revelations from the Heaven Worlds, 1920. *Address:* 14 Emmanuel Road, Balham, SW12. *Died July 1921.*

LOCH, Sir Charles Stewart, Kt 1915; BA; Tooke Professor of Economic Science and Statistics, King's College, London, 1904–8; Secretary to the Council of the London Charity Organisation Society, 1875–1914; resigned 1914; *b* Bengal, 4 Sept. 1849; 5th *s* of late George Loch, Indian Civil Service, judge, High Court, Calcutta and Louisa Gordon, his first wife; *m* 1876, Sophia E., *e d* of late Edward Peters, ICS; one *s* one *d*. *Educ:* Trinity Coll., Glenalmond; Balliol Coll., Oxford. Clerk, Royal College of Surgeons, 1873–75; member Royal Commission on Aged Poor, 1893–95; Dunkin Trust Lecturer, Manchester Coll., Oxford, 1896 and 1902; Guy medal, Royal Statistical Society, 1899; a Member of the Institut International de Statistique; Member of the Royal Commission on the Care and Control of the Feeble-minded; Member of the Royal Commission on the Poor Laws. Hon. DCL, Oxford; Hon. LLD, St Andrews. *Publications:* Charity and Charities in Encyclopædia Britannica, 1902; Charity Organisation; Old Age Pensions and Pauperism; Charity and Social Life, 1910; *poems:* Things Within, 1922; articles on charitable, social, and economic subjects, published in Aspects of the Social Problem, 1895, Methods of Social Advance, 1904, the Statistical and Economic Journals, and elsewhere. *Address:* Little Bookham, Surrey. *Died 23 Jan. 1923.*

LOCHHEAD, John, RBA; *b* Glasgow; father a publisher in that city; *m* 1893, *y d* of late Sir Daniel Macnee, PRSA; one *s*. *Educ:* Glasgow. Started studies in Edinburgh at Life School there; afterwards travelled in France, Holland, Belgium, Switzerland, etc, for further study; exhibitor at New Salon, Munich, Budapest, Berlin and America; represented in the National Gallery, Berlin, and Fine Art Society, Prague; also exhibitor at all the important picture exhibitions in Britain. *Chief Pictures:* Decking the May Queen; Summertime in the Fen Country; The Evening Hour; All Things Bright and Beautiful; Country Content; By the Ferry, Summertime; A Garden of Sunbeams. *Publications:* A Riverside Idyll; illustrated Quiet Folk, by R. Menzies Fergusson, DD. *Recreations:* travelling, golf, walking; also viewing and collecting various phases of art, and art objects. *Address:* Abinger, West Kilbride, Ayrshire; Studio, 113 St Vincent Street, Glasgow. *Club:* Glasgow Art. *Died June 1921.*

LOCHHEAD, William, BA, MSc; FAAS; Professor of Biology, Macdonald College-McGill University, since 1906; President Quebec Society Protection of Plants since 1908; *b* 3 April 1864; *s* of W. Lochhead and Helen Campbell; *m* 1889, Lilias Grant; one *s*. *Educ:* McGill and Cornell Universities. Scholarships every year of University course, 1881–85; Fellowship in Cornell University, 1886–87; attended Cornell (post graduate), 1886–87, 1894–95, and several summer sessions; Teacher of Science in Perth, Galt, and London Collegiate Institutes, 1887–94, 1895–98; Professor of Biology, Ontario Agricultural College, 1898–1906. President Quebec Pomological Society, 1916–17; President Ont Entomological Society, 1902–4; Editor, Journal of Agriculture for Quebec, 1908–20. *Publications:* Bulletins—The San Jose and Allied Scales; The Hessian Fly; The Pea Weevil; Nature Studies; Spray-Calendar; Heredity and Genetics; Class Book of Economic Entomology. *Recreations:* tennis, bowling. *Address:* Macdonald College, Quebec, Canada. *T:* 38. *Clubs:* University, Montreal; Gamma Alpha Society, Cornell. *Died 26 March 1927.*

LOCK, B. Fossett; His Honour Judge B. Fossett; County Court Judge, Circuit 16 (East Riding of Yorkshire and parts of North and West Ridings), since 1913; *b* 13 Dec. 1847; 3rd *s* of Henry Lock of Dorchester, solicitor; *m* 1879, Jane Elizabeth (*d* 1920), 2nd *d* of Rev. J. P. Hammond, Vicar of Sopley, Hants; one *s* one *d*. *Educ:* Dorchester Grammar School; Eton (King's Scholar); King's Coll., Camb. (Scholar). BA 1871 (aegrotat, Classical Tripos); MA 1877. Called to Bar (Lincoln's Inn), 1873; joined the Chancery Bar, Western Circuit and Dorset Sessions; Hon. Secretary of Positivist Society, 1880–86; held Commission in the Royal Naval Artillery Volunteers, 1890–92; Hon. Secretary of the Selden Society, 1895–1913; Examiner to the Council of Legal Education, 1896–1906; Chairman of Committee of the Social and Political Education League, 1887–1913; Chairman of the central Legal Aid Society; Member of Admiralty Volunteer Committee; a Vice-President of the Dorset Men in London; a member of the Council of the Selden Society; and of the Yorkshire Archæological Society. *Publications:* Joint Editor of the Annual Practice, 1910–11; Memoir of Professor Maitland, in the Dictionary of National Biography; sundry articles and pamphlets on the Defence of Poor Prisoners and Legal Aid for the Poor, etc. *Recreations:* sailing, rowing, walking, sketching. *Address:* The Toft, Bridlington, Yorkshire. *TA:* Bridlington. *T:* Bridlington 99; 11 New Square, Lincoln's Inn, WC. *Clubs:* Royal Societies; Royal Cruising; Royal Yorkshire Yacht. *Died 11 Aug. 1922.*

LOCK, Rev. John Bascombe, MA; Fellow and Bursar of Gonville and Caius College, Cambridge; *b* Dorchester, 18 March 1849; *s* of late Joseph Lock, Dorchester; *m* 1873, Emily, 3rd *d* of late Edwin Baily, Cirencester; three *s* one *d*. *Educ:* Grammar School, Bristol; Caius Coll., Camb. (scholar 1868). 3rd wrangler Mathematical Tripos, 1872; moderator and examiner in Mathematical Tripos, 1876–77. Curate of Horningsea, 1872; assistant master at Eton, 1872–84; Lecturer on Mathematics and assistant tutor at Caius College, 1884–89; member of Financial Board, of the Press, University Buildings, Syndicates and of the Building Committee in the University of Cambridge; late Chairman of Addenbrooke Hospital. *Publications:* many mathematical books for schools and colleges; chiefly Arithmetic, Trigonometry, and Mechanics. *Recreations:* motoring, formerly rowing, bicycling, lawn-tennis, fives, skating. *Address:* Herschel House, Cambridge. *T:* Cambridge 150. *M:* CE 2629. *Died 8 Sept. 1921.*

LOCKHART, Sir Simon Macdonald, 5th Bt, *cr* 1806; MVO 1897; retired; *b* 13 March 1849; *s* of Sir Norman Macdonald Lockhart, 3rd Bt and Margaret, *d* of John M'Lean; *S* brother, 1870; *m* 1898, Hilda Maud, 2nd *d* of Col A. H. M. Macdonald Moreton, late Coldstream Guards. *Educ:* Eton. Served Egyptian Campaign, 1882; Colonel 1st Life Guards, 1892–98; Brig.-Gen. on Staff commanding cavalry at Curragh, 1900–1. *Heir:* none. *Address:* The Lee, Lanark. NB. *Clubs:* Carlton, United Service; Royal Yacht Squadron, Cowes. *Died 25 March 1919 (ext).*

LOCKYER, Sir (Joseph) Norman, KCB 1897 (CB 1894); FRS 1869; Hon. LLD Glasgow, Aberdeen, and Edinburgh; Hon. ScD Cambridge and Sheffield; Hon. DSc Oxford; Director of Hill Observatory, Salcombe Regis, Sidmouth; Director of Solar Physics Observatory, South Kensington, 1885–1913; *b* Rugby, 17 May 1836; *s* of Joseph Hooley Lockyer and Anne, *d* of Edward Norman, Cosford; *m* 1st, 1858, Winifred (*d* 1879), *y d* of William James, Trebinshon, near Abergavenny; four *s* two *d* (and three *s* decd); 2nd, 1903, Thomazine Mary, *y d* of late Samuel W. Browne, of Bridgwater and Clifton, and *widow* of Bernard E. Brodhurst, FRCS. *Educ:* private schools; Continent. Appointed to War Office, 1857; editor of Army Regulations, 1865; Secretary, Duke of Devonshire's Royal Commn on Science, 1870; transferred to Science and Art Department, 1875. Pres. of British Assoc. for Advancement of Science, 1903–4; Rede Lecturer at Cambridge, 1871; correspondent of Institute of France, 1875 (Janssen Medal); chief of English Govt Eclipse Expeditions, 1870, 1871, 1882, 1886, 1896, 1898, 1900, 1905; observed the eclipse of 1878 in the United States. *Publications:* Elementary Lessons in Astronomy, 1870; contributions to Solar Physics, 1873; Spectroscope and its Applications, 1873; Primer of Astronomy, 1874; Studies in Spectrum Analyses, 1878; Star-gazing Past and Present, 1878; Chemistry of the Sun, 1887; Movements of the Earth, 1887; Meteoritic Hypothesis, 1890; Dawn of Astronomy, 1894; Rules of Golf, 1896; The Sun's Place in Nature, 1897; Recent and Coming Eclipses, 1897; Inorganic Evolution, 1900; Stonehenge, and other British Stone Monuments Astronomically Considered; Education and National Progress, 1906–1907; Surveying for Archæologists, 1909; Tennyson as a Student and Poet of Nature, 1910, etc. *Recreations:* tennis, golf (St George's Club). *Address:* 16 Penywern Road, SW5; Salcombe Regis, Sidmouth. *TA:* Phusis, London; Lockyer, Sidmouth. *T:* Western 5383. *Club:* Athenæum. *Died 16 Aug. 1920.*

LODER, Sir Edmund Giles, 2nd Bt, *cr* 1887; JP; *b* 7 Aug. 1849; *e* *s* of Sir Robert Loder, 1st Bt and Maria Georgiana, 4th *d* of Hans Busk; *S* father, 1888; *m* 1876, Marion, *d* of W. E. Hubbard, Leonardslee, Horsham; one *d* (one *s* decd). *Educ:* Eton; Trinity Coll., Camb. (MA). High Sheriff, Northampton, 1888. *Heir: g s* Giles Rolls Loder, *b* 10 Nov. 1914. *Address:* Leonardslee, Horsham, Sussex. *Club:* Athenæum.   *Died 14 April 1920.*

LODGE, Henry Cabot; *b* Boston, USA, 12 May 1850; *m* 1872, Anna Cabot Davis; two *s* one *d. Educ:* Harvard (PhD); Harvard Law School (LLB). Suffolk Bar, 1876; Member of Congress (Republican), 1887–93; Senator from 1893; served two terms Member of House of Representatives, Mass; elected to 50th, 51st, 52nd, and 53rd Congresses. LLD Harvard; Williams, 1893; Yale, 1902; Clarke, 1902; Amherst College, 1914; Union College, 1915; Princeton, 1916; Dartmouth, 1917; Brown, 1918; President Massachusetts Historical Society; Fellow Royal Historical Society, 1917. *Publications:* Essays on Anglo-Saxon Land Law; Life and Letters of George Cabot, 1877; A Short History of the English Colonies in America, 1881; Alexander Hamilton, 1882, Daniel Webster, 1883, George Washington, 1889 (in American Statesmen series); Studies in History, 1886; Speeches, 1892; Hero Tales from American History (with Theodore Roosevelt), 1895; History of Boston, 1891; Historical and Political Essays, 1892; Certain Accepted Heroes, 1897; The Story of the American Revolution, 1898; Ballads and Lyrics; Story of the Spanish War, 1899; A Fighting Frigate and other Essays and Addresses, 1902; One Hundred Years of Peace, 1913; The Democracy of the Constitution; War Addresses, 1917, etc. *Address:* Nahant, Mass, USA.
                                                    Died 9 Nov. 1924.

LOEB, Prof. Jacques; Member Rockefeller Institute for Medical Research, New York, since 1910; *b* 7 April 1859; *m* 1890, Anne L. Leonard; two *s* one *d. Educ:* Ascanisches Gymnasium, Berlin; Universities of Berlin, Munich, Strassburg (MD 1884); Hon. DSc Cantab 1909; Hon. MD Geneva, 1909; Hon. PhD Leipzig, 1909; Hon. DSc Yale, 1923; Doctor (Hon.) Strassburg, 1923. Assistant in Physiology, Univ. of Wurzburg, 1886–88; Strassburg, 1888–90; Stazione zoologica, Naples, 1890–91; Associate in Biology, Bryn Mawr Coll., Bryn Mawr, Pa, 1891–92; Asst Professor of Physiology, Univ. of Chicago, 1892–95; Associate Professor, 1895–1900; Professor, 1900–3; Professor of Physiology, Univ. of California, 1903–10. Member, Nat. Acad. of Sciences; American Philosophical Society; American Physiological Society; American Society Biol. Chemists; Corr. mem., Académie des Sciences de l'Institut de France; Academy of Sciences, Cracow; Med. Gesellsch., Budapest; Bataafsch Genootschap der Proefondervindelijke Wijsbegeerte te Rotterdam; Foreign Fellow Linnean Society, London; For. Mem. Acad. Royale des Sciences de Belgique, Brussels; Hon. mem. Royal Institution of Gt Britain; Société de Biologie, Paris; Acad. Royale de Med. de Belgique, Brussels; Soc. Impériale des Amis des Sciences Naturelles, Moscow; Cambridge Philosophical Society, England; Med. Geselslch. Wien; Assoc. mem. Société Royale des Sciences Medicales et Naturelles, Brussels; Société Belge de Biologie; Fellow Amer. Acad. Arts and Sciences. *Publications:* Animal Heliotropism and its Identity with the Heliotropism of Plants, 1890; Physiological Morphology, Part I Heteromorphosis, 1891; Physiological Morphology, Part II Organisation and Growth, 1892; Comparative Physiology of the Brain and Comparative Psychology, 1900; Studies in General Physiology, 1905; The Dynamics of Living Matter, 1906; Investigations on Artificial Parthenogenesis, 1906; The Mechanistic Conception of Life, 1912; Artificial Parthenogenesis and Fertilisation, 1913; The Organism as a Whole, 1916; Forced Movements, Tropisms, and Animal Conduct, 1918; Proteins and the Theory of Colloidal Behaviour, 1922. *Address:* Rockefeller Institute, 66th Street and Avenue A, New York.   *Died 12 Feb. 1924.*

LOEWENSTEIN-WERTHEIM, HSH Princess; Lady Anne Savile; *b* 1866; *d* of 4th Earl of Mexborough; *m* 1897, HSH Prince Ludwig Karl zu Loewenstein-Wertheim-Freudenberg (*d* 1899). *Address:* 8 Upper Belgrave Street, SW.
                                                    Died 31 Aug. 1927.

LOFTIE, Rev. Arthur Gershom; Rector of Wetheral and Warwick, Cumberland, 1904–16; Hon. Canon of Carlisle Cathedral, 1908; Chaplain to the High Sheriff of Cumberland, 1912; *b* Nice, 22 Oct. 1843; *s* of John Henry Loftie, JP, Co. Down and Co. Armagh, Ireland, of Tanderagee, Co. Armagh; *m* 1874, Jamesina Roberta, *y d* of James Robert Grant of the Hill, Cumberland; no *c. Educ:* Portarlington School; Trinity College, Dublin. Ordained to Curacy of Arthuret, Cumberland, 1867; Vicar of Beckermet, St Bridget's, W Cumberland, 1871; collated to Rectory of Great Salkeld, Cumberland, near Penrith, 1894; a Member of the Cumberland and Westmorland Archæological

and Antiquarian Society; Hon. Chaplain to the Bishop of Carlisle, 1920. *Publications:* Calder Abbey, its Ruins and History, 2nd edn, 1892; Great Salkeld, its Rectors and History, 1900; editor of The Rural Deanery of Gosforth; Diocese of Carlisle, its Churches and Endowments, 1889; compiled a Catechism for Children, 1872; fourth edn translated into Hindustani, 1881. *Recreations:* archæology, architecture, gardening. *Address:* Undermount, Rydal, near Ambleside, Westmorland.   *Died Oct. 1922.*

LOGAN, Brig.-Gen. David Finlay Hosken, CB 1917; CMG 1916; RA; *b* 28 Dec. 1862; *s* of late David Logan, Chief Engineer, South Indian Railway, and Jean Hosken; *m* Ethel Mayzod Evans; one *d. Educ:* private school, Reading; RMA, Woolwich. 1st Commission, 1883; Adjutant, 1st Glamorgan VA; Adjutant, Cape Garrison Artillery; served South Africa (King's and Queen's medals); European War, 1914–17 (despatches, CB, CMG); Humane Society's bronze medal; Brig.-Gen. 1916. *Recreations:* golf, fishing. *Address:* c/o Cox & Co., 16 Charing Cross, SW1. *Club:* United Service.
                                                    Died 17 June 1923.

LOGAN, John William, JP; AMICE; MP (L) Harborough Division, Leicestershire, 1891–1904, and 1910–16; *b* Newport, Mon., 1845; *s* of John Logan, The Maindee, Newport, Mon. *Educ:* Gloucester Collegiate School. *Recreations:* hunting, shooting, fishing. *Address:* East Langton Grange, Market Harborough. *Clubs:* Reform, Cobden.
                                                    Died 25 May 1925.

LOGUE, His Eminence Cardinal Michael; RC Archbishop of Armagh since 1888; Roman Catholic Primate of All Ireland since 1887; *b* Co. Donegal, 1840. Formerly Bishop of Raphoe (cons. 1879) and coadjutor to the late Primate, 1887; created Cardinal, 1893. *Address:* Ara Cœli, Armagh.
                                                    Died 19 Nov. 1924.

LÖHR, Hervey, ARAM; composer, pianist, and conductor; *b* Leicester, 13 June 1856; *s* of George Augustus Löhr. *Educ:* privately; Royal Academy of Music, under Sir Arthur Sullivan, W. H. Holmes, and Dr Prout (Lucas Medal (twice), Potter Exhibition, Santley Prize for accompaniment). Associate of Philharmonic Society; Member Royal Society of Musicians. Compositions: five symphonies; a grand opera (Kenilworth); oratorio (The Queen of Sheba); trio for piano and strings; quartet and quintet for piano and strings; two string quartets; pianoforte music, songs, part-songs, Church music, etc.
                                                    Died 16 Jan. 1927.

LOMAS, Surg.-Capt. Ernest Courtney, CB 1916; DSO 1901; MB; FRCSE; RN; *b* 24 Dec. 1864; *m* 1901, Eleanor Mary Ruthven, *d* of Robert Howden, East Lothian. *Educ:* Owens College, Manchester. MB, ChB, Vict.; MRCS 1888; FRCSE 1907. Surgeon, RN 1891; landed with Naval Brigade; attached Ladysmith Relief Column, South African War, 1899–1900 (despatches, medal with 2 clasps, DSO); specially promoted Staff-Surgeon, 1900; Fleet-Surgeon, 1904; Surgeon-Capt., 1918; SMO of Hospital Ships Maine and Rohilla, when these vessels were totally wrecked, 1914; SMO Hospital Ship Garth Castle, 1915 (CB for services during the War); retired, 1919. *Address:* Boggs, Pencaitland, East Lothian.
                                                    Died 24 Feb. 1921.

LOMAS, John; prominent Anglican Churchman in the jurisdiction of North and Central Europe, and estate owner in Switzerland; *b* Manchester, 2 Nov. 1846; *s* of George Lomas; *m* 1875, Maria Thurston, *d* of Christopher Gabriel, Norfolk House, Streatham Hill; three *s* two *d. Educ:* Manchester Grammar School; Victoria University, Manchester. Editor of the Anglican Church Magazine, 1886–1912; General Secretary of North and Central Europe Church Conferences from 1912; President and Director of various educational, charitable, social, and commercial undertakings. *Publications:* Sketches in Spain from Nature, Art, and Life; In Spain; Don Luis; numerous magazine articles; also Church music, Communion offices, anthems, etc. *Recreation:* church and organ music. *Address:* St Jean, Territet, Switzerland. *TA:* Lomas, Territet. *T:* Montreux 225. *Clubs:* Constitutional, Church Imperial; Montreux International.
                                                    Died 1 March 1927.

LOMAX, John A.; Member of Society of Oil Painters; *b* 1857; *s* of John Lomax, Manchester; *m* Lily, *d* of James Lings, of Manchester. *Educ:* Stuttgart; Munich. *Works:* How the Old Squire caught the Big Sack; To bring the Roses back; Overtaken; The Elopement; Reconciliation; Run to Earth, etc. *Recreations:* tennis, billiards, cycling, golf. *Address:* 17 Marlborough Road, St John's Wood, NW. *Clubs:* Arts, St John's Wood Arts.   *Died 13 Dec. 1923.*

LONDESBOROUGH, 2nd Earl of, *cr* 1887; **William Francis Henry Denison**, KCVO 1908; Baron Londesborough, 1850; Viscount Raincliffe, 1887; *b* 30 Dec. 1864; *e s* of 1st Earl and Lady Edith Frances Wilhelmina Somerset, *y d* of 7th Duke of Beaufort, KG; *S* father, 1900; *m* 1887, Lady Grace Augusta Fane, *e d* of 12th Earl of Westmorland; two *s* one *d*. DL East Riding of Yorkshire; late Lieut Yorks Hussars; late Hon. Col 2nd Vol. Batt. East Yorks Regt; Hon. Col 5th (Cyclist) Batt. East Yorks Regt. Owner of about 52,700 acres. *Heir: s* Viscount Raincliffe, *b* 17 July 1892. *Address:* Blankney Hall, Lincoln; Londesborough Park, Market Weighton; Londesborough Lodge, Scarborough; The Island, Walton on the Hill, near Epsom; 7 Chesterfield Gardens, W. *T:* Mayfair 5606. *Clubs:* Marlborough, Orleans. *Died 30 Oct. 1917.*

LONDESBOROUGH, 3rd Earl of, *cr* 1887; **George Francis William Henry Denison;** Baron Londesborough, 1850; Viscount Raincliffe, 1887; *b* 17 July 1892; *e s* of 2nd Earl and Lady Grace Augusta Fane, *e d* of 12th Earl of Westmorland; *S* father, 1917. Owner of about 52,700 acres. *Heir: b* Hon. Hugo William Cecil Denison, *b* 13 Nov. 1894. *Address:* Blankney Hall, Lincoln; Londesborough Park, Market Weighton. *Died 12 Sept. 1920.*

LONDON, Jack; writer; *b* San Francisco, 12 Jan. 1876; *s* of John London; *m* 1st, 1900, Bessie Maddern; two *d*; 2nd, 1905, in Chicago, Charmian Kittredge. *Educ:* Univ. of California. Sailor, gold-miner, tramp, writer, socialist, lecturer, journalist, etc. In his search for adventures among the scum marine population of San Francisco Bay he soon lost his ideal romance and replaced it with the real romance of things; he became, in turn, a salmon fisher, an oyster pirate, a schooner sailer, a fish patrolman, a longshoreman, and gay-faring adventurer; when he was seventeen he shipped before the mast as able seaman; went to Japan and seal-hunting on the Russian side of Behring Sea, among other things, and served at divers times in various forecastles; he became possessed of an interest in sociology and economics; swayed partly by this, and partly by the fascination of the enterprise, he tramped over the United States and Canada, many thousands of miles, and having more than one jail experience because he possessed no fixed place of abode, and no visible means of support; later on he repeated his vagabond career in the East End of London; he went over Chilcoot Pass with the first of the Klondike rush of 1897; went as war correspondent to Japan, Korea, and Manchuria, 1904; war correspondent, Mexico, 1914; started on a seven years' cruise around the world in a fifty-foot ketch-rig yacht, 1906. *Publications:* The Son of the Wolf, 1900; The God of His Fathers; A Daughter of the Snows; The Children of the Frost; The People of the Abyss; The Cruise of the Dazzler; The Call of the Wild; The Kempton-Wace Letters; The Faith of Men; The Sea Wolf, 1904; The War of the Classes; The Game, 1905; Tales of the Fish Patrol, 1905; Moon-Face; Scorn of Women, 1906; White-Fang, 1906; Love of Life, 1907; Iron Heel; The Road, 1908; Before Adam, 1908; Martin Eden, 1909; Lost Face, Revolution, Theft, Burning Daylight, 1910; Adventure, 1911; The Cruise of the Snark, 1911; South Sea Tales, 1911; When God Laughs, 1912; A Son of the Sun, 1912; The House of Pride, 1912; Smoke Bellew Tales, 1912; The Night Born, 1913; The Abysmal Brute, 1913; John Barleycorn, 1913; The Valley of the Moon, 1913; John Barleycorn; The Strength of the Strong; The Mutiny of the Elsinore, 1914; The Jacket, 1915; The Little Lady of the Big House, 1916; The Acorn Planter (play); The Turtles of Tasman; Jerry and Michael; The Human Drift; Hearts of Three. *Recreations:* kite-flying, yacht-sailing, fencing, boxing, horseback riding, swimming, agriculture. *Address:* Glen Ellen, Sonoma County, California. *Club:* Bohemian, San Francisco.
Died 22 Nov. 1916.

LONG, 1st Viscount, *cr* 1921, of Wraxall; **Walter Hume Long,** PC; JP; FRS 1902; Hon. LLD Birmingham; Lord-Lieutenant for Wilts; Colonel commanding Royal Wilts Imperial Yeomanry (Prince of Wales's Own), 1898–1906; *b* Bath, 13 July 1854; *e s* of late Richard Penruddocke Long (MP Chippenham, 1859–65; N Wilts, 1865–68), Rood Ashton, Wilts, and Dolforgan, Montgomeryshire, and Charlotte, *d* of Rt Hon. William Wentworth Fitz-William-Hume Dick (MP Wicklow, 1850–80); *m* 1878, Lady Dorothy Blanche (Doreen), 4th *d* of 9th Earl of Cork and Orrery; one *s* one *d* (and one *s* two *d* decd). *Educ:* Harrow; Christ Church, Oxford (Hon. Student). MP (C) North Wilts, 1880–85; Devizes Division, 1885–92; Parliamentary Secretary to Local Government Board, 1886–92; MP (C) West Derby, Liverpool, 1892–1900; President Board of Agriculture, 1895–1900; President of Local Government Board, 1900–5; MP (C) South Bristol, 1900–6; MP (C) South Dublin, 1906–10; MP (CU) Strand Division, 1910; for St George's, Westminster, 1919–21; Chief Secretary for Ireland, 1905–6; President Local Government Board, 1915–16; Secretary of State for the Colonies, 1916–18; First Lord of the Admiralty, 1919–21; Chairman of Harrow Governors, 1924. *Publication:* Memories, 1923. *Recreations:* cricket, hunting. *Heir: g s* Walter Francis David Long, *b* 14 Sept. 1911. *Address:* Rood Ashton, Trowbridge, Wilts. *Clubs:* Carlton, Cavalry.
Died 26 Sept. 1924.

LONG, George Bathurst, MVO 1910; HM Privy Purse, 1901–11; Comptroller's Office, 1874–1901; *b* 28 July 1855; *s* of late Walter Bathurst Long, Special Commissioner, Somerset House; *m* 1883, 2nd *d* of John Kenshole of Heavitree, Exeter; one *d*. *Educ:* St Paul's School. *Address:* Clarehurst, Baldslow Road, Hastings. *Clubs:* Junior Conservative; Hastings, St Leonards and County Conservative, Hastings. *Died 2 Jan. 1917.*

LONG, Sir James, Kt 1910; JP; late Chairman of Cork Harbour Commission; Member of the Governing Body, University College, Cork; *b* Nov. 1862; *m* 1884, Mary (*d* 1923), *d* of William Elliott of Plymouth; two *s* two *d*. *Address:* Spy Hill Villa, Queenstown, Co. Cork. *Died 17 Sept. 1928.*

LONG, John Luther; *b* 1861. *Publications:* The Darling of the Gods; Madame Butterfly, 1898; Miss Cherry Blossom of Tokyo; The Fox Woman, 1900; The Prince of Illusion, 1901; Naughty Nan; Heimweh, and other Stories, 1906; *plays:* Adrea; Lady Betty Martingale; Crowns, 1923; *novels:* War; Seffy. *Address:* 250 Ashbourne Road, Elkins Park Branch, Philadelphia, Pa, USA.
Died 31 Oct. 1927.

LONG, Lt-Col Walter, CMG 1916; DSO 1902; Royal Scots Greys; temp. Lt-Col 6th Battalion Wiltshire Regiment since 1915; *b* 26 July 1879; *e s* of Rt Hon. W. H. Long, MP; *m* 1910, Sibell, *e d* of Hon. Francis Johnstone. *Educ:* Harrow. Entered army, 1899; Captain, 1902; Major, 1915; ADC to Maj.-Gen. Scobell, 1st Cavalry Brigade, Aldershot; Adjutant of the Scots Greys, 1906–9; served South African campaign, 1899–1902 (despatches, Queen's medal, 2 clasps, King's medal, 2 clasps, DSO); European War, 1914–15 (despatches twice, CMG); Order of St Stanislas (3rd Cl.). *Recreations:* hunting, polo, shooting, cricket. *Clubs:* Cavalry, Bath.
Died 27 Jan. 1917.

LONG, Lt-Col and Hon. Col William, CMG 1900; 4th Battalion Somerset Light Infantry; retired; *b* 22 Jan. 1843; *e s* of William Long, FSA, JP, of Wrington, Somerset, and Elizabeth Hare, *o c* of late James Hare Jolliffe, of Bathford, Somerset; *m* 1867, Anna Mary, *e d* of late Henry Hunter, Capt. 5th Dragoon Guards; one *s* seven *d*. *Educ:* Eton. Served South Africa, 1900–2 (despatches, Queen's medal with clasp, King's medal 2 clasps, CMG); DL and JP, Somerset; High Sheriff, 1899. Provincial Grand Master of Somerset, and of Mark Master Masons, Somerset. *Address:* Newton House, Clevedon. *Club:* Junior United Service. *Died 9 May 1926.*

LONGE, Col Francis Bacon, CB 1910; JP; late RE; of Spixworth Park, Norwich; *b* 31 Oct. 1856; *m* 1905, May, *d* of late Deputy Surg.-Gen. John Meane. *Educ:* Cheltenham Coll.; Royal Military Academy, Woolwich. Lieut Royal Engineers, 1876; transferred to Indian Establishment, and posted to the Bengal Sappers and Miners, 1878; appointed to Survey of India, 1880; Substantive Colonel in army, 1905; served with Kurram, Kabul, and Kandahar Field Forces, 1879–81; Kabul-Kandahar march, 1880 (despatches twice, received thanks of Governor-General, medal 3 clasps, and bronze star); with Suakim Expeditionary Force, 1885 (medal and clasp, Egyptian Star); Wuntho Expedition (Upper Burma), 1891 (medal and clasp); served as Survey Officer with the Chin-Manipur and Burma-China Boundary Commissions, 1894 and 1897–98, respectively, and as a Member of the Indian Survey Committee of 1904–5; Surveyor-General of India, 1904–11; Hon. ADC to the Viceroy and additional Member of the Legislative Council of the Governor-General, 1909–10. *Address:* c/o Cox & Co., Charing Cross, SW1. *Club:* Junior United Service. *Died 2 June 1922.*

LONGFELLOW, Ernest Wadsworth; artist; *b* Cambridge, Mass, 1845; *s* of the poet Henry Wadsworth Longfellow. Pupil of Couture, Paris. *Works:* Morning on the Ægean; Evening on the Nile; Italian Phifferari; A Wind came up out of the Sea; Stirling Castle; Misty Morning; various portraits. *Address:* Century Association, 7 W 43rd Street, New York. *Died 24 Nov. 1921.*

LONGFORD, Joseph Henry; Emeritus Professor of Japanese, King's College, London University, 1916; Vice-President, Japan Society, London, 1922; *b* 25 June 1849; *s* of late Charles Longford of Blackrock, co. Dublin, and of Mary, *d* of late Capt. Ralph Manning, 24th Regt; *m* Alice, *d* of late Walter Johnston, Trench Hall, Northumberland;

one *s* two *d*. *Educ:* Royal Academical Institution and Queen's College, Belfast; BA Queen's University in Ireland; DLitt Queen's University of Ulster, 1919. Entered HM Consular Service in Japan as Student Interpreter, 1869; served for 33 years, travelling during this period throughout the whole of the Japanese Empire, from the Kurile Islands in the extreme north to Formosa in the extreme south; successively HM Consul and Judge of HM Consular Courts at Tokio, Hiogo, Hakodate, Tainan, Tamsui, and Nagasaki; retired on a pension in 1902; called to Bar, Middle Temple, 1889; Professor of Japanese, King's College, London, 1903–16; nominated on HM's behalf as one of the suite of Prince Komatsu, the official representative of the Emperor of Japan at King Edward's Coronation (Coronation medal); received from Emperor of Japan, silver wedding medal, Order of the Rising Sun, and, on occasion of visit to London of Crown Prince, Order of the Sacred Treasure; Chairman of Japan Society, London, 1921–22. *Publications:* Penal Code of Japan, 1877; Japan (Living Races of Mankind), 1905; The Regeneration of Japan (Cambridge Modern History), 1910; The Story of Old Japan, 1910; The Story of Korea, 1911; Japan of the Japanese, 1911; The Evolution of New Japan, 1913; Japan (Spirit of the Allied Nations), 1915; Japan (Harmsworth Encyclopedia), 1920; Japan (Nations of Today), 1923; contributions to the Transactions of the Asiatic Society of Japan, and of the Japan Society, London, and, principally on Japanese subjects, to the Quarterly, Fortnightly and National Reviews, The Nineteenth Century and other Reviews, and to the Press; numerous Reports, principally on industrial subjects in Japan, issued by the Foreign Office. *Recreations:* boating, walking, cricket (spectator), bridge. *Address:* 10 Esmond Road, Bedford Park, W. *T:* Chiswick 2387. *Clubs:* Reform; Royal Irish Yacht. *Died 12 May 1925.*

LONGHURST, Sir Henry Bell, Kt 1902; CVO 1910; LDSRCS; Hon. Surgeon-Dentist to HM the King; *b* London, 20 Jan. 1835; *s* of late James Longhurst; *m* 1865, Mary (*d* 1923), *d* of late Samuel Wilmot, Nottingham; six *s* two *d*. *Educ:* private school; Univ. College, London. *Recreations:* shooting, fishing, gardening. *Address:* Grove House, Park Road, Hampton Hill, Middlesex.

Died 5 Aug. 1926.

LONGLEY, Hon. James Wilberforce; statesman, jurist, and littérateur; a Judge of the Supreme Court of Nova Scotia since 1905; *b* Paradise, Nova Scotia, Canada, 4 Jan. 1849; *m* 1st, 1877, Annie, *y d* of N. Brown; two *s* one *d*; 2nd, 1901, Lois E., *y d* of late George Fletcher; three *s*. A lecturer and public speaker, and a regular contributor to the magazines; a Liberal in politics, and an advanced thinker on social and religious questions; graduated from Acadia University, 1871; admitted to the Bar of Nova Scotia, 1875; first elected to Parliament, 1882; entered Government, 1884; Attorney-General, 1886–1905, having sat in Parliament without interruption from 1882; QC 1892; DCL 1897; LLD 1905; FRSC 1898. *Publications:* Love; Socialism, its Truths and Errors; The Greatest Drama; A Material Age; Canada and Imperial Federation; Religion in 19th Century; Life of Joseph Howe, etc. *Address:* 18 Green Street, Halifax, NS. *TA:* Halifax, NS. *T:* 1599. *Died 16 March 1922.*

LONGSTAFF, George Blundell, JP, London and Devon; MA, MD, Oxon; FRCP, FSA, FLS, FCS, FGS; *b* 12 Feb. 1849; *s* of George Dixon Longstaff, MD, of Wandsworth, and Maria, *d* of Henry Blundell of Hull; *m* 1st, 1875, Sara Leam (*d* 1903), *d* of Ed. Dixon of Southampton; two *s* one *d*; 2nd, 1906, Mary Jane Donald, FLS, FGS. *Educ:* Rugby; New Coll., Oxford (Scholar, First Class in Natural Science); St Thomas' Hospital (Mead medal). Devoted much time to municipal and philanthropic work; served on many committees of the Charity Organisation Society; a Guardian of the Poor; LCC for Wandsworth, 1889–1903; as Chairman of its Building Act Committee took a principal part in drafting and getting through Parliament the London Building Act, 1894; sometime Vice-President of the Royal Statistical and Entomological Societies. *Publications:* Studies in Statistics, 1891; The Langstaffs of Teesdale and Weardale, 1907; Marriage and the Church, 1910; Butterfly Hunting in Many Lands, 1912. *Recreations:* travelling, botany, entomology, skating. *Address:* Highlands, Putney Heath, SW. *TA:* Roehampton. *Clubs:* Savile, Conservative, Skating.

Died 7 May 1921.

LONGSTAFF, Llewellyn Wood, FRGS (formerly on Council), FZS, FRMetS; Lieut-Colonel formerly commanding 1st Volunteer Battalion, East Yorkshire Regiment; retired 1880; Surrey National Reserve; Divisional Vice President, Red Cross; *b* 23 Dec. 1841; *e s* of late G. D. Longstaff, MD and Maria, *d* of H. Blundell, JP; *m* 1873, Mary L., *d* of late Thomas W. Sawyer of Southampton; four *s* three *d*. *Educ:* Wandsworth Proprietary School; by Tutor on the Continent; Royal School of Mines. Twice President of the Hull Incorporated

Chamber of Commerce and Shipping; by his support made practicable the British National Antarctic Expedition, 1899–1904. *Recreations:* voyaging, travelling. *Address:* Ridgelands, Wimbledon, SW. *TA:* Swordsmen Wim, London. *T:* Wimbledon 749 and 1837. *Clubs:* Royal Societies, Royal Yorkshire Yacht.

Died 20 Nov. 1918.

LONGUEVILLE, Thomas; *b* 29 April 1844; *e* and *o* surv. *s* of Thomas Longueville of Prestatyn, Trelogan, and Penyllan; *m* 1868, Mary Francis, *o* surv. *c* of Alexander Robertson of Balgownie; three *s* one *d*. *Educ:* Christ Church, Oxford. Cornet in the North Shropshire Yeomanry, 1865–68; for some years a partner in Croxon's Bank, Oswestry; JP Co. Salop; for 20 years a constant contributor to The Saturday Review; also frequent contributor to other journals and magazines. *Publications:* The Life of a Prig; A Life of Sir Kenelm Digby; Rochester and other Literary Rakes; Policy and Paint; A Life of James II; Turenne; Vices in Virtues, etc. *Recreations:* incapacitated from taking any; formerly painting, hunting, and attending races. *Address:* Llanforda, Oswestry. *Died 18 Aug. 1922.*

LONSDALE, Rev. Henry, MA; Hon. Canon of Carlisle, 1901. *Educ:* Magdalene College, Cambridge (Scholar). MA. Deacon, 1875; Priest, 1876; Vicar of Thornthwaite, 1881–89; Upperby, 1889–1904; Corbridge-on-Tyne, 1904–17. *Address:* Arlaw Banks, Winston, Darlington. *Died 17 June 1926.*

LONSDALE, James Rolston; MP (U) Mid-Armagh since Jan. 1918; *b* 31 May 1865; *s* of James Lonsdale, DL, of the Pavilion, Armagh; *brother* of 1st Baron Armaghdale; *m* 1902, Maud, *d* of John Musker, Shadwell Court, Norfolk. *Educ:* Royal School, Armagh; Trinity College, Dublin. High Sheriff of Co. Armagh, 1907; a Unionist. *Address:* 12 Sussex Square, W2. *Clubs:* Carlton, Bachelors'.

Died 23 May 1921.

LORAINE, Sir Lambton, 11th Bt, *cr* 1664; JP; Rear-Admiral (retired); *b* Northumberland, 17 Nov. 1838; *S* father, 1852; *m* 1878, Frederica Mary Horatia, *d* of Charles Acton Broke, and *co-heiress* of the Brokes of Nacton; one *s* two *d* (and one *s* decd). *Educ:* Burlington House School, Fulham (extinct); a short time at Cambridge. *Recreations:* usual recreations of country and town. Heir: *s* Percy Lyham Loraine, *b* 5 Nov. 1880. *Address:* 7 Montagu Square, W; Bramford Hall, near Ipswich. *TA:* Loraine, Bramford. *Clubs:* United Service, Naval and Military.

Died 13 May 1917.

LORAINE, Rev. Nevison; Prebendary of St Paul's Cathedral, and Canon non-residentiary; Vicar of Grove Park-West, W, since 1870; *b* Northumberland; *s* of Nevison and Jane Loraine; *m* Agnes May (*d* 1915), *d* of John and Hannah Howard; three *s* one *d*. *Educ:* Northumberland Grammar School; Croft House; Private Tutors; College of Divinity. Ordained 1860; Curate of St Giles in the Fields, 1860–61; Incumbent of Holy Trinity, Liverpool, 1861–70; Fairchild Lecturer, 1899; Golden Lecturer, 1908–9; Biblical Examiner, London Reading Union, 1884. *Publications:* Discourses on the Lord's Prayer; The Voice of the Prayer Book; Home Reunion, pub. Letter to Archbishop of Canterbury; The Eastern Question, an Ecclesiastical Political Brochure; The Sceptic's Creed; The Church and Liberties of England; The Battle of Belief; Half-Hours with Busy Men; Golden Lectures; sundry reviews, articles, lectures, etc. *Recreations:* travel, literature, athletics, motoring. *Address:* Grove Park Vicarage, Chiswick. *TA:* Prebendary Loraine, Chiswick. *M:* LC 3957.

Died 10 Sept. 1917.

LORD, Herbert Owen; Master, Cotswold Hounds since 1904; *b* 2 Nov. 1854; 2nd *s* of Captain Arthur Owen Lord, 72nd Highlanders (Seaforth), and Lucy Sophia, *d* of late Henry Taylor, TCS; *m* Mary Ollivant, *e d* of late William Dugdale, JP, DL, of Simonstone Hall, Lancashire, and Lilley Brook, Charlton Kings; two *d*. *Educ:* Eton. *Recreations:* hunting, shooting, golf, cricket, etc. *Clubs:* Boodle's, Orleans, Pratt's, Bath, Sandown, Roehampton.

Died 2 April 1928.

LORD, John King; Professor Emeritus of Latin Language and Literature; Trustee Dartmouth College, United States, America; *b* 21 Oct. 1848; *s* of John King Lord and Laura Esther Smith; *m* Emma Fuller Pomeroy; three *s* one *d*. *Educ:* Dartmouth College, 1868. *Publications:* New Hampshire in 9th edn Enc. Brit.; also in Johnson's Cyclopædia; Cicero: Laelius; Livy: Books i, xxi, xxii; Atlas of the Geography and History of the Ancient World; editor, Chase's History of Dartmouth College, and the Town of Hanover, vol. i; wrote History of Dartmouth College, vol. ii. *Address:* Hanover, New Hampshire, USA. *T:* W 44. *Died 26 June 1926.*

LORD, Sir Riley, Kt 1900; *b* Accrington, 24 Feb. 1838; *s* of late George Lord, Accrington; *m* 1857, Mary (*d* 1894), *d* of John and Susannah Haggas, Keighley. Represented the Prudential Life Assurance Co. for over 44 years; entered Newcastle-upon-Tyne Council, 1885; Sheriff of Newcastle, 1892–93; Mayor, 1895–96 and 1899–1900; during first mayoralty inaugurated Victoria Diamond Jubilee Fund to build new Infirmary; raised £100,000, another £100,000 was bequeathed by John Hall for same purpose, and £100,000 more contributed by Lord Armstrong; foundation stone of Royal Victoria Infirmary laid 20 June 1900 by Prince of Wales on behalf of the Queen, and opened by His Majesty 11 July 1906; JP Newcastle-upon-Tyne and Northumberland. *Address:* Highfield Hall, Gosforth, Newcastle-upon-Tyne.   *Died 17 Aug. 1920.*

LOREBURN, 1st Earl, *cr* 1911; **Robert Threshie Reid;** Baron 1906; GCMG 1899; Kt 1894; JP; DCL, Oxon; *b* 3 April 1846; 2nd *s* of Sir James John Reid, Mouswald Place, Dumfries, and Mary, *d* of Robert Threshie, Barnbarroch, Kirkcudbrightshire; *m* 1st, 1871, Emily Douglas (*d* 1904), *d* of Capt. Arthur Cecil Fleming; 2nd, 1907, Violet Elizabeth, *e d* of W. F. Hicks-Beach of Witcombe Park, Glos. *Educ:* Cheltenham College; Balliol College, Oxford. First Class in Moderations and in Lit. Hum.; Demy of Magdalen Coll.; Scholar of Balliol Coll.; Ireland Univ. Scholar, 1868. Barrister 1871; QC 1882. MP (L) Hereford, 1880–85; MP (L) Dumfries, 1886–1905; Solicitor-Gen. 1894; Attorney-General, Oct. 1894; University Counsel, Oxford, 1899–1906; Lord Chancellor, 1905–12. Decorated for his services in connection with the Venezuelan Boundary Arbitration Commission. *Publications:* Capture at Sea, 1913; How the War Came, 1919. *Recreations:* Oxford University XI, 1866–68; represented Oxford v Cambridge at racquets, 1865–67. *Heir:* none. *Address:* 8 Eaton Square, SW; Kingsdown, Dover. *Clubs:* Brooks's, National Liberal.
Died 30 Nov. 1923 (ext).

LORIMER, John Campbell, KC; MA, LLB; Advocate; Sheriff-Principal of Aberdeen, Kincardine, Banffs, since 1911; *s* of Rev. Dr John Gordon Lorimer, Glasgow, and Jane, *d* of Rev. Dr John Campbell, Tolbooth Church, Edinburgh; *m* 1875, Jemima Margaret, *d* of Rev. Prof. Bannerman, DD, of Abernyte, Perthshire. *Educ:* Glasgow Academy; Glasgow and Edinburgh Universities. Scottish Bar, 1866; Counsel for Inland Revenue, Scotland, 1882–86; Advocate Depute, 1886 and 1892–95; Parliamentary Counsel to Secretary for Scotland, 1900–8; KC 1903; Member of Court University of Edinburgh, 1901–9; Sheriff-Principal of Ayr, 1908–11; Director, Century Insurance Company. *Publications:* Lectures on Company Law; New Death Duties (commentary on); Appendix on the Law of Scotland to Lord Lindley's Law of Partnership. *Recreation:* formerly mountaineering. *Address:* 9 Gloucester Place, Edinburgh. *Club:* Royal Northern, Aberdeen.   *Died 20 Jan. 1922.*

LORIMER, Sir William, Kt 1917; *b* 4 Nov. 1844; *s* of William Lorimer and Margaret Kirkhope Whigham; *m* 1st, 1869, Jane (*d* 1902), *d* of Alex. Smith; 2nd, 1913, Mary Elizabeth, *d* of John Sieber, of Irwell Springs, Lancashire; four *s* four *d*. *Educ:* Sanquhar, Dumfriesshire. For practically the whole of his business life connected with the locomotive industry; for many years managing partner of the firm of Dubs & Co., of Glasgow, later absorbed in the North British Locomotive Co., of which Chairman from its formation in 1903; Chairman for over twenty years of the Steel Co. of Scotland, and a Director of the Glasgow and South Western Railway; a member of the Dominions Royal Commission since it was appointed in 1912, and in that capacity visited all the self-governing Dominions. LLD of the University of Glasgow and a member of the University Court. *Address:* Kirklinton, Langside, Glasgow. *Clubs:* Reform; Western, Glasgow.   *Died 9 April 1922.*

LORT PHILLIPS, Lt-Col John Frederick, JP, DL; *b* 1854; *e s* of Richard Ilbert Lort Phillips (*d* 1860) and Frederica Maria Louisa, *e d* of late Baron de Rutzen of Slebech Hall, Pembrokeshire; *m* 1895, Hon. Maude, late Maid of Honour to Queen Victoria, 2nd *d* of late Haughton Charles Okeover of Okeover, Staffordshire, and *widow* of Sir Andrew Barclay Walker, 1st Bt of Osmaston Manor, Derbyshire. High Sheriff, Pembrokeshire, 1880. *Address:* Lawrenny, Kilgetty, Pembrokeshire.   *Died 15 May 1926.*

LOTE, Thomas Alfred, JP; MFH Teme Valley; *b* 1863; *s* of Henry Lote, Croydon; *m* 1890, Hannah, *d* of George Townsend, Shrewsbury. *Address:* Brook House, Knighton.

LOTI, Pierre, (Louis Marie Julien Viaud); Captain French Navy; French novelist; member of the French Academy since 1891; *b* Rochefort, 14 Jan. 1850; *s* of M. Viaud. Entered Navy, 1867; 2nd Lieutenant, 1873; Lieutenant "Oceania," 1881; served Pacific,

Tonkin campaign, China; Comdr Legion of Honour 1910, Grand Cross, 1921. *Publications:* Aziyadé, 1876–77; Le mariage de Loti (1st called Rarahu), 1880 (trans. 1890); Le roman d'un Spahi, 1881 (trans. 1890); Fleurs d'ennui, 1882; Mon frère Yves, 1883 (trans. 1887); Les trois dames de la Kasbah, 1884; Pêcheur d'Islande, 1886 (trans. 1888); Madame Chrysanthème, 1887 (trans. 1888); Propos d'exil, 1887; Japonneries d'automne, 1889; Au Maroc, 1890; Roman d'un enfant, 1890 (trans. 1891); Le livre de la pitié et de la mort, 1891 (trans. 1892); Fantôme d'orient, 1892 (trans. 1892); Le désert: Ramuntcho; La Galilée, Jérusalem; and others; Figures et choses qui passaient, 1898; L'Inde sans les Anglais, 1903; La Troisième jeunesse de Mme Prune, 1905; Disenchanted, 1906; Pélerin d'Angkor, 1912. *Address:* L'Académie Française, Paris.
Died 10 June 1923.

LOTON, Sir William Thorley, Kt 1923; Director W Australian Bank since 1882; *b* England, 1839. Went to Western Australia, 1863; founded firm of Padbury, Loton & Co.; was Member Legislative Council. *Address:* Weld Chambers, St George's Terrace, Perth, W Australia.   *Died 22 Oct. 1924.*

LOUCH, Ven. Thomas; *b* Hadleigh, Suffolk, 1848; *s* of Thomas Frederick Louch, of HM Inland Revenue, and Mary Ann, *d* of Charles Steane; *m* 1889, Mary Grace, *d* of George Baston, JP, Geraldton, Western Australia; one *s* one *d*. *Educ:* Sandbach Grammar School; Owens College; St Aidan's Theological College. Resided in Cork (Ireland), 1852; Sandbach (Cheshire), 1854; Manchester, 1862; St Aidan's College, Birkenhead, 1877; Curate of Holy Trinity, Warrington, 1879–81; St Stephen's, Poplar, London, 1881–86; Rector of Geraldton, Western Australia, 1886–1900; Rector of Albany, 1900–22; Archdeacon of the Bunbury Diocese, 1905–22; Examining Chaplain to the Bishop of Bunbury; Administrator of the Bunbury Diocese, 1917 and 1920; Hon. Chaplain to the Defence Forces, 1890–1910, retiring with the rank of Lieutenant-Colonel. *Address:* Albany, Western Australia. *Clubs:* Albany, Western Australia.
Died 19 Oct. 1927.

LOUCKS, Rev. Edwin; late Rector of Pictou, Diocese of Ontario, Canada; Canon of St George's Cathedral, Kingston, Ontario; *b* 1 March 1829; *m* 1864; three *s* three *d*. *Educ:* Bishop's College, Lennoxville, Quebec. Curate in sole charge at Lennoxville; Senior Curate, Christ Church, Ottawa, Ontario; retired. *Address:* 37 Division Street, Kingston, Ontario.   *Died 20 July 1919.*

LOUDAN, Mouat, RP; Member National Portrait Society and Art Workers' Guild, etc; *b* of Scottish parentage in London, 1868; *m* 1898; two *s*. *Educ:* Dulwich College. Entered Royal Academy Schools, where worked for four years, obtaining medals for drawing, painting, modelling, also the gold medal and travelling studentship; after this studied in Paris; here of late years devoted himself almost entirely to portraiture. *Recreations:* mechanics, cabinet work, etc; golf. *Address:* 48 Circus Road, NW.
Died 26 Dec. 1925.

LOUDON, James; President of the University of Toronto, 1892–1906, and Professor of Physics, 1887–1906; *b* Toronto, 1841, of Irish parentage; *m* 1872, Julia, *d* of John Lorn M'Dougall of Renfrew; three *s* one *d*. *Educ:* The Toronto Grammar School, Upper Canada College and Univ. of Toronto. BA, MA, LLD, Univ. of Toronto; LLD Queen's, Princeton, Johns Hopkins, McMaster, and Glasgow Universities; DCL, Trinity University (Toronto); FRSC; Pres. RSC (1901–2). Math. Tutor in Univ. Coll. Toronto, 1863; Classical and Math. Tutor, 1864; Math. Tutor and Dean of Residence, 1865; Prof. of Mathematics and Natural Philosophy, 1875. *Publications:* various mathematical and physical papers in Jl of Canadian Institute, the Philosophical Magazine, the American Jl of Math. and the Trans of Roy. Soc. of Canada. *Address:* 83 St George Street, Toronto, Canada. *T:* Coll. 1259, Toronto.   *Died 28 Dec. 1916.*

LOUDOUN, 11th Earl of, *cr* 1633; **Charles Edward Hastings Abney-Hastings,** DL, JP; Baron Botreaux, 1368; Baron Hungerford, 1426; Baron de Moleyns, 1445; Baron Hastings (England) 1461; Baron Loudoun, 1601; Baron Donington (UK), 1880; *b* 5 Jan. 1855; *s* of Countess of Loudoun and 1st Baron Donington (*d* 1895); *S* mother, 1874; *m* 1880, Hon. Alice Mary Elizabeth Fitzalan-Howard (*d* 1915), 3rd *d* of 1st Lord Howard of Glossop. Owner of about 33,000 acres. *Heir:* to earldom: *niece* Edith Maud Rawdon-Hastings, *b* 13 May 1883; to barony of Donington: *brother* Gilbert Theophilus Clifton-Hastings-Campbell, *b* 29 May 1859. *Address:* Willesley Hall, Ashby-de-la-Zouche; Loudoun Castle, Galston. *TA:* Galston. *Clubs:* Carlton, Marlborough; Royal Yacht Squadron, Cowes.   *Died 17 May 1920.*

LOUGH, Rt. Hon. Thomas, PC 1908; Parliamentary Secretary to the Board of Education, 1905–8; MP (L) Islington, W, 1892–1918; HM Lieutenant of Co. Cavan since 1907; tea merchant in London since 1880; *b* Ireland, 1850; *s* of Matthew Lough, Killynebber House, Cavan, and Martha, *d* of William Steel; *m* 1880, Edith, *d* of late Rev. John Mills. *Educ:* Royal School, Cavan; Wesleyan Connexional School, Dublin. Contested (L) Truro, 1886; founder Home Rule Union, 1887; London Reform Union, 1892. *Publications:* England's Wealth, Ireland's Poverty, 1896; The Brussels Sugar Convention, 1903; Ten Years' Tory Rule in Ireland, 1905; Parliament during the War, 1917. *Recreation:* golf. *Address:* 97 Ashley Gardens, SW1. *T:* Victoria 7646; Drom Mullac, Killeshandra, Co. Cavan. *T:* Victoria 7646. *Clubs:* Reform, National Liberal, Eighty; Stephen's Green, Dublin; Royal Irish Yacht, Kingstown.

Died 11 Jan. 1922.

LOUGHEED, Hon. Sir James Alexander, KCMG 1916; PC Canada; KC; Leader of Opposition in Senate of Canada; *b* 1 Sept. 1854; *m* 1884, *e d* of late William L. Hardisty of Hon. Hudson's Bay Co.; four *s* one *d*. *Educ:* Toronto, Canada. Practised law, Toronto, 1881; moved to North-West Territories, 1883; QC 1889; called to Senate of Canada, 1889; Minister of the Interior, 1920–21; Leader of Government in Senate, 1911–21. *Address:* Calgary, Alberta, Canada. *TA:* Lougheed, Calgary. *Clubs:* Rideau, Ottawa; National Toronto; Ranchmen's, Calgary.

Died Nov. 1925.

LOUISSON, Hon. Charles, JP; Member Legislative Council, New Zealand; *b* London, 1842; *s* of George Louisson, merchant; *m* 1877, Hannah, *d* of Maurice Harris, JP, of Christchurch, NZ; two *s* two *d*. *Educ:* Gravesend, England. Emigrated to Victoria, 1855; settled in NZ 1865; served as a city councillor for ten years; twice presented with silver service, etc, by citizens; Mayor of Christchurch, NZ, 1888, 1889, 1898, 1899; Commissioner for NZ, 1888, at the International Exhibition in Melbourne; District Grand Master for Canterbury, NZ, for Scotch Masonic Constitution from 1889–99. *Recreations:* Member, Canterbury Jockey Club; President, NZ Metropolitan Trotting Club. *Address:* 214 Gloster Street, Christchurch. *T:* 726. *Club:* Canterbury, Christchurch. *Died 19 April 1924.*

LOUSADA, Duc de; Commander Francis Clifford de Lousada, RN; *b* 17 Oct. 1842; 3rd *s* of late Marquis de Lousada and Marianne, *d* of Sir Charles Wolseley, 7th Bt; *S* brother, 1905; *m* 1879, Emily Florence, *widow* of Sir Eardley G. C. Eardley, 4th Bt. *Address:* 4 Lancaster Street, Hyde Park, W. *T:* Paddington 2357. *Club:* Naval and Military. *Died 5 Feb. 1916.*

LOUŸS, Pierre; *b* 10 Dec. 1870; *g n* of Duke of Abrantès; *g g s* of Sabatier, president of the Institut de France and surgeon in ordinary to Napoleon the First; *brother* of French Ambassador to Russia; *m y d* of late José-Maria de Heredia, poet, member of the Académie Française. *Educ:* Lycée Janson de Sailly, Paris. Six visits to North Africa; when aged 19, founded the review La Conque, to which Swinburne, Leconte de Lisle, Heredia, Verlaine, Mallarmé, Maeterlinck, and Moréas were contributors; his book Aphrodite had the greatest circulation ever reached by any living writer in France—350,000 copies were printed, not including translations; ten dramas and operas were written under this title and subject, and several of them played in Russia, Austria, Argentina, France, etc, including one at the Opéra Comique, Paris, with music by Camille Erlanger. *Publications:* Astarté, 1892; Les Chansons de Bilitis, 1895; Aphrodite, 1896; La Femme et le Pantin, 1898; Les Aventures du Roi Pausole, 1901; Sanguines, 1903; Archipel, 1906; Psyché, 1909; several translations from the Greek (Meleagros, Lucian). *Recreations:* bibliophilism (ancient books), musical composition, painting, etching, etc; Persian cats; Greek, Egyptian, and Japanese collections. *Address:* 29 Rue de Boulainvilliers, Paris. *T:* 683–64. *Died 4 June 1925.*

LOVELAND, Richard Loveland, DL (Middlesex); JP London and Middlesex; KC; *b* London, 18 July 1841; *o surv. s* of late John Perry Loveland, JP, Middlesex, and Harriet Hannah, *o d* of late Richard Errington, Beaufront, Hexham, Northumberland; *m* Maria Elizabeth Oddie (*d* 1913), 5th *d* of Rev. P. H. Nind, Vicar of Woodcote-cum-Southstoke, Oxon; two *s* three *d*. *Educ:* Kensington Grammar School; Pembroke College, Oxford. Barrister, 1865; Deputy-Chairman of Middlesex Sessions, 1889–96; Deputy-Chairman of the County of London Sessions, 1896–1911. KGStJ. *Publications:* editor of Sir John Kelying's Crown Cases; Shower's Cases in Parliament; Hall on the Seashore Rights; Griffith and Loveland on the Judicature Acts, etc. *Address:* Bury House, Alverstoke, near Gosport, Hants.

Died 21 Sept. 1923.

LOVELL, Sir Francis Henry, Kt 1900; CMG 1893; LLD; FRCS; Dean of the London School of Tropical Medicine; *b* 1844. Chief Medical Officer of Mauritius and member of the Legislative Council, 1878–93; Surgeon-General and member of the Executive and Legislative Councils of the Colonies of Trinidad and Tobago, 1893–1901; retired from the Colonial service, 1901. *Address:* London School of Tropical Medicine, Royal Albert Dock, E.

Died 28 Jan. 1916.

LOVELL, Mark; *see* Tollemache, David.

LOVERSEED, John Frederick; MP (L) Sudbury Division of West Suffolk, 1923–24; *b* 22 Dec. 1881; *s* of late Henry Loverseed, builder and contractor, Nottingham; *m* 1910, Katherine Annie, *d* of Wm Thurman, Grantham; one *s*. *Educ:* Southwell Grammar School; Gosberton Hall. Farming, 1899–1905; Agent to Sir R. Winfrey, MP, 1908–13; to Major S. G. Howard, 1922; Capt. and Adjt 5th Batt. Suffolk VTC, 1914; Military Rep. Tribunals West Suffolk, 1916; County Councillor, West Suffolk, 1919; Town Councillor, Sudbury, 1919; Mayor of Sudbury, 1921–23; Chairman of Governors, Sudbury Grammar School; Governor of East Anglian School, Bury St Edmunds; of King Edward's Grammar School, Bury St Edmunds; of Girls' Secondary School, Sudbury; Governor Court of Guardians, Sudbury; West Suffolk Education Committee and Standing Joint Committee; Member of Wesleyan Methodist Conference, 1924. JP Suffolk, 1924. *Recreations:* cricket, tennis, bowls. *Address:* Newland, Queen's Road, Sudbury, Suffolk. *TA:* Loverseed, Sudbury, Suffolk. *T:* Sudbury 9. *Club:* National Liberal.

Died 14 Aug. 1928.

LOVETT, Col (Brig.-Gen.) Alfred Crowdy, CB 1915; *b* 22 Nov. 1862; *m* 1903, Fannie, *e d* of Col E. W. Rumsey, of Trellick, Monmouth. Entered army and gazetted to Gloucestershire Regt 1883; Capt. 1891; Major, 1903; Lt-Col 1911; Col 1915; Instructor RMC, 1901–6; served European War, 1914–17 (despatches, CB). *Club:* Army and Navy. *Died 27 May 1919.*

LOVETT, Maj.-Gen. Beresford, CB 1889; CSI 1873; FRGS, FRSA; *b* 16 Feb. 1839; *s* of late Rev. Robert Lovett of Marbœuf Chapel, Paris, and Rector of Pickwell, Leicestershire; *m* 1876, Agnes (*d* 1914), *d* of W. Turnbull Blewitt; one *d*. After passing through Addiscombe Military College entered RE 1858; Maj.-Gen. 1892; employed in Persia, 1866–70, in the Telegraph Dept, and 1870–72 on the Special Mission to Seistan, for which service was given the CSI; served Jowaki-Afreedee Expedition, 1878 (medal with clasp); Afghan War, 1878–79 (brevet of Lieut-Col, medal with clasp); HM Consul in Persia, 1880–83; Hazara Expedition, 1888 (CB, clasp); retired, 1894. *Address:* Hillside, 58 Harvey Road, Guildford. *Clubs:* East India United Service; County, Guildford.

Died 12 Sept. 1926.

LOVETT-CAMERON, Rev. Charles Leslie, MA; *b* 26 Jan. 1843; *s* of late Rev. J. H. Lovett-Cameron, Vicar of Shoreham, Kent; *m* 1876, Caroline, *d* of Edward A. Holden, DL, of Aston Hall, Derbyshire. *Educ:* Eton; Merton College, Oxford (Scholar); 1st Class Mod. 1865; BA (2nd Class Lit. Hum.) 1867; MA 1869. Deacon, 1876; Priest, 1877. Assistant Master at Eton College, 1868–80; Vicar of Stratfield Mortimer, 1880–1913; Rural Dean of Reading, 1903–11; Hon. Canon of Christ Church, Oxford, 1907; Treasurer of the Berks Clergy Charity, 1897–1916; interested in archæology and horticulture. *Address:* Abbeycroft, Mortimer, Berks.

Died 24 Jan. 1927.

LOVIBOND, Joseph Williams, JP City of Salisbury and Co. Wilts; FRMS; Chairman of John Lovibond & Sons, Ltd, and of The Tintometer Ltd; Lord of the Manor of Lake, Wilts; *b* 1833; 3rd *s* of John Locke Lovibond of Long Sutton, Somerset, Greenwich, and Starts Hill, Kent; *m* Charlotte, *d* of Edward Steer, Crockham Hill, Kent; three *d*. *Educ:* privately. Entered Mercantile Marine, 1846; California gold miner, 1849; Lovibond's Brewery, Greenwich, 1854; Mayor of Salisbury, 1878–90; Silver Medallist, St Louis Exposition, 1906, for a new theory of Light and Colour, also two bronze medals for its practical application, all awarded by the International Juries; Inventor and Patentee of apparatus for measuring and recording colour sensations, also a gold and two silver medals at the Brussels Exhibition, 1910; holder of three medals awarded by the Royal Sanitary Association for apparatus dealing with Sanitary Hygiene and with Colour Education. *Publications:* Light and Colour Measurement; Colour Phenomena; a pamphlet on Free Trade; The Teachers' Handbook of Colour. *Recreation:* trout-rearing. *Address:* The Pleasaunce, Lake, near Salisbury. *Died 1918.*

LOW, Charles Rathbone, FRGS; Commander Indian Navy; *b* Dublin, 30 Oct. 1837; *s* of Maj. J. H. Low, 39th Bengal Native Infantry; *m* Catherine, *d* of General Boileau, RE, FRS. Went to sea, 1853; served in Indian and China Seas, Persian Gulf, Red Sea, and East Coast of Africa, in suppression of piracy and the slave trade. First Librarian and Asst Sec. Royal United Service Institution, 1865–68; represented the Indian Navy at the Thanksgiving Service in St Paul's for the Recovery of the Prince of Wales, 1872; in the Abbey at the Jubilee Service of Queen Victoria, 1887; in the Funeral Procession of Her late Majesty; at the Coronation of King Edward VII; in the Funeral Procession of His late Majesty; and at the Coronation of King George V; in 1856 saved a seaman from drowning in the Hooghly, and was congratulated by the Governor-General, Lord Canning. *Publications:* Tales of Old Ocean, 1866; Land of the Sun, 1870; History of the British Navy, 1872; Life of Field-Marshal Sir G. Pollock, 1873; Life and Voyages of Captain James Cook, 1876; History of the Indian Navy, 1877; Life of Lord Wolseley, 1878; The First Afghan War, 1879; Soldiers of the Victorian Age, 1880; History of Maritime Discovery, 1881; Life of Lord Roberts, 1883; History of the British Army, 1889; Great African Travellers, 1890; Her Majesty's Navy, 1892; Britannia's Bulwarks, 1895; The Olympiad, 1903; also many minor works, and hundreds of magazine articles and contributions to The Times. *Address:* Lowville, Bournemouth; 27 Russell Road, Kensington, W. *T:* Park 2864. *Club:* Junior Naval and Military.

Died 7 Feb. 1918.

LOW, Hon. Sir Frederick, Kt 1909; **Hon. Mr Justice Low;** a Judge of High Court of Justice, King's Bench Division, since 1915; *b* 21 Nov. 1856; *s* of late Stephen Philpot Low, DL, JP, Kent; *m* 1882, Katherine, 4th *d* of late Charles Thompson; one *s* two *d*. *Educ:* Westminster; privately. Admitted a Solicitor, 1878; called to Bar, Middle Temple, 1890; KC, 1902; Bencher, 1911; SE Circuit. Contested Salisbury (L), 1900; Battersea, Clapham Division, 1906; MP (L) Norwich, 1910–15. Commissioner of Assize, Western and Midland Circuits, 1913–15; Recorder of Ipswich, 1906–15. Captain in the 4th VB Royal West Surrey Regiment and 22nd Middlesex RV, 1880–90. *Address:* 51 Sloane Gardens, SW. *T:* Victoria 434; 373 Royal Courts of Justice, Strand, WC. *Clubs:* Anthenæum, Reform.

Died 4 Sept. 1917.

LOW, George Macritchie, FFA, FRSE; Manager and Actuary of the Scottish Equitable Life Assurance Society 1900–20; a Director, National Bank of Scotland, 1904–18; Member of the Royal Company of Archers (King's Body Guard for Scotland); *b* Edinburgh, 1849; *m* 1891, Charlotte Ellen (*d* 1916), *d* of late David McLaren, merchant. *Educ:* Edinburgh. Secretary, 1875, and Manager, 1883, of the Edinburgh Life Assurance Company; President of the Faculty of Actuaries in Scotland, 1900–3 and 1915–19. *Publications:* article, Life Insurance, in the 9th Edition of the Encyclopædia Britannica; various papers and addresses on actuarial and other cognate subjects. *Recreations:* golf, fishing. *Address:* 11 Moray Place, Edinburgh. *T:* 2796. *M:* SG 4099. *Clubs:* University, Edinburgh; Honourable Company of Edinburgh Golfers, Muirfield.

Died 29 Nov. 1922.

LOW, Sir James, 1st Bt, *cr* 1908; Kt 1895; DL, JP; Managing Director of Lindsay and Low Limited, Dundee; *b* 10 Feb. 1849; *s* of William Low; *m* 1890, Katherine, *d* of Wm Munro; one *s* two *d* (and one *s* decd). Lord Provost of Dundee, 1893–96. *Heir: s* Walter John Low, *b* 27 May 1899. *Address:* Kilmaron Castle, near Cupar, Fifeshire.

Died 30 June 1923.

LOW, Lt-Col Robert Balmain, DSO 1896; late Hodson's Horse, Indian Army; *b* 7 Oct. 1864; *e s* of Gen. Sir Robert Cunlife Low, GCB; *m* 1st, 1899, Mabel Violet, *d* of Maj.-Gen. O'Grady Haly, CB; 2nd, 1918, Leslie Dumville (*d* 1919), *d* of Francis C. D. Smythe of Cambridge Gardens, W, and *widow* of Alex. G. Macmillan. Entered Army, 1885; Captain 1896; Major, 1903; served Lushai Expedition, 1889 (clasp); Hazara Expedition, 1891 (medal with clasp); Chitral Relief Force, 1895 (despatches, DSO, medal with clasp); Tirah Expedition, 1897–98 (two clasps); China, 1900–1; Provost-Marshal and Headquarters Camp Commandant (despatches, brevet majority, medal with clasp). *Address:* Ambala, India.

Died 20 April 1927.

LOW, Robert Bruce, CB 1919; MD, DPH; Assistant Medical Officer, Local Government Board (retired); Inspector of Examinations under the General Medical Council; *b* Edinburgh, 1846; *s* of John Low; *m* 1874, Henrietta Jane, *d* of Samuel Spencer of Howsham, Lincolnshire; two *s* four *d*. *Educ:* Royal High School and University of Edinburgh; Post Graduate Studies at St Thomas' Hospital, London, and at Universities of Würzburg and Berlin. After graduation in 1867

was House Surgeon at Royal Infirmary, Edinburgh; and after a year's post-graduate study, practised as a rural general practitioner for nineteen years, fifteen of which were in North Yorkshire; was Deputy Coroner for North Riding; MOH for Helmsley Rural District; Medical Inspector to the Local Government Board, 1887; Assistant Medical Officer, 1900; late Examiner in Sanitary Science, State Medicine and Public Health at the Universities of Cambridge, Edinburgh, Glasgow, and Leeds; served on the War Office Anti-Typhoid Inoculation Committee, 1904–12; Member of Council of the Epidemiological Section of the Royal Society of Medicine; Fellow of the Society of Tropical Medicine. *Publications:* Reports on the Progress and Diffusion of Plague, Cholera, and Yellow Fever throughout the World, 1896–1918; Reports on the Epidemiology of Exanthematic Typhus Fever 1914, Cerebrospinal Fever 1915, Acute Anterior Poliomyelitis 1916, Smallpox 1918, etc; German Methods of Isolating Smallpox Cases, 1903; The State Animal Vaccine Establishments of Germany, 1905; The Tenure of Office and Appointment of Medical Officers of Health, 1886. *Address:* 98 York Mansions, Battersea Park, SW11.

Died 12 May 1922.

LOW, Hon. Seth, LLD; *b* 18 Jan. 1850; married. *Educ:* Brooklyn Polytechnic Institute; Columbia University. Mayor of Brooklyn, 1881–85; contested Greater New York, 1897; President of Columbia University, New York, 1889–1901; Mayor of New York City, 1902–3; President, National Civic Federation, New York; President, Chamber of Commerce of State of New York, 1914–16. *Address:* Bedford Hills, NY.

Died 18 Sept. 1916.

LOW, William Malcolm, JP, DL; *b* 1835; *e s* of General Sir John Low, GCSI, KCB, Clatto, Co. Fife, and Augusta, *d* of John Talbot Shakespear; *m* 1872, Lady Ida Feilding (*d* 1915), *d* of 7th Earl of Denbigh. *Educ:* Haileybury College. Indian Civil Service, 1856–76; received special letter conveying thanks of Her Majesty for services in the field during Indian Mutiny; retired from ill-health, as Commissioner of the Nerbudda Districts. MP (C) Grantham, 1886–92. *Recreations:* gardening, fishing, boating. *Address:* 22 Roland Gardens, SW. *Clubs:* Carlton; New, Edinburgh.

Died 14 June 1923.

LOWE, Lt-Col Arthur Cecil, CMG 1918; DSO 1900; HAC; *b* 1868; *s* of Henry W. Lowe of Holywood House, Walton-on-Thames; *m* 1910, Amy Louisa, 2nd *d* of late S. W. Partridge, Lynn Court, Tunbridge Wells. Served South Africa, 1900 (despatches, Queen's medal, 3 clasps, DSO). *Address:* 7 East India Avenue, EC.

Died 24 Nov. 1917.

LOWE, Arthur Labron, CBE 1919; MA, LLB; *b* Edgbaston, 1861; *y s* of late Henry Lowe, of Southfield, Norfolk Road; *m* 1st, 1890, Mary Letitia (*d* 1918), *d* of late A. Bruce Mitchell, Edgbaston; three *d*; 2nd, 1923, Emma Mary, *y d* of late Rev. G. A. Smallwood, Ashby-de-la-Zouch, Leicestershire. *Educ:* Clifton College; Clare College, Cambridge. Admitted Solicitor, 1887; member of firm of Johnson, Barclay, Johnson & Lowe, 1900–5; Registrar, Birmingham County Court and District Registrar of the High Court of Justice there from 1905; Joint Editor of Costs and Fees Section of Annual County Court Practice; member of the Standing Committee for framing County Court Rules; elected a Fellow of the College of Teachers of the Blind, 1914; member of the Advisory Committee on the Welfare of the Blind, Ministry of Health, from 1919; Pres. Association of County Court Registrars, 1910–20; President Birmingham Law Society, 1916–18; Chairman of Birmingham Branch British Red Cross Society from its formation to 1922; Chairman of Committee, Birmingham Royal Institution for the Blind, 1902–13; Chairman of the Midland Counties Association for the Blind, 1916–24. *Recreations:* farming, gardening. *Address:* Monkspath Hall, Shirley, Warwickshire; 52 Westfield Road, Edgbaston. *T:* Edgbaston 432. *Club:* Union, Birmingham.

Died 7 Feb. 1928.

LOWE, Rev. Joseph; Hon. Canon of Newcastle. *Address:* Haltwhistle.

Died 22 Aug. 1920.

LOWELL, Amy, LittD; author; *b* Brookline, Mass, 9 Feb. 1874; *d* of Augustus Lowell and Katharine Bigelow Lawrence. *Educ:* private schools. Phi Beta Kappa Poet, Tufts College, 1918; Columbia University, 1920; Hon. LittD Baylor University, 1920; Hon. Member Phi Beta Kappa Society, Columbia, 1920; Member Poetry Society America; NE Poetry Club; Member American Geographical Society; NE Woman's Press Association; Boston Proof-Readers' Association. *Publications:* A Dome of Many-Coloured Glass, 1912; Sword Blades and Poppy Seed, 1914; Six French Poets, 1915; Men, Women, and Ghosts, 1916; Tendencies in Modern American Poetry, 1917; Can

Grande's Castle, 1918; Pictures of the Floating World, 1919; Legends, 1921; (with Florence Ayscough) Fir-Flower Tablets: Poems translated from the Chinese, 1921; A Critical Fable, 1922; John Keats, 1924. *Address:* Sevenels, Brookline, Mass, USA. *Clubs:* Lyceum; Colony, MacDowell, PEN, The Poets, New York; Chilton, Boston.

Died 12 May 1925.

LOWELL, Percival, AB cum laude, Harvard, 1876; non-resident Professor of Astronomy, Massachusetts Institute of Technology, since 1902; Director of the Lowell Observatory, Flagstaff, Arizona; *b* Boston, USA, 13 March 1855; *s* of Augustus Lowell and Katharine Bigelow, *d* of Abbott Lawrence, Minister Plenipotentiary to Great Britain, 1851; *m* 1908, Constance Keith, of Boston. *Educ:* Harvard College (2nd year Honours in Mathematics; Bowdoin prize medallist). Counsellor and Foreign Secretary to Korean Special Mission to US, and guest of Korean Government in Söul, 1883; lived in Japan at intervals, 1883–93; Phi Beta Kappa Poet at Harvard, 1889; established Lowell Observatory, 1894; undertook Eclipse Expedition to Tripoli, 1900; sent Expedition to the Andes to photograph the planet Mars, 1907; made discoveries on the planets, especially Mars, and formulated theory of its habitability. Fellow American Academy Arts and Sciences; Member: Royal Asiatic Society of Great Britain and Ireland; American Philosoph. Society; Société Astronomique de France; Astronomische Gesellschaft; Société Belge d'Astronomie; Hon. Mem. Sociedad Astronomica de Mexico; Hon. Fellow Royal Astronomical Society of Canada. LLD Amherst College, 1907, Clark University, 1909. Janssen Medallist of the Société Astronomique de France, 1904, for researches on Mars. *Publications:* Chosön, 1885; The Soul of the Far East, 1886; Noto, 1891; Occult Japan, 1894; Mars, 1895; Annals of the Lowell Observatory, vol. i 1898; vol. ii 1900; vol. iii 1905; The Solar System, 1903; Mars and its Canals, 1906; Mars as the Abode of Life, 1909; The Evolution of Worlds, 1910. *Address:* 53 State Street, Boston, USA. *Clubs:* Royal Societies; Somerset, Union; Saint Botolph, Boston; Century, Aero, Authors', New York; Imperial, Tokio, Tokio. *Died 13 Nov. 1916.*

LOWNDES, Maj.-Gen. Thomas. Joined Madras Army, 1854; Political Agent, Bhamo, 1872–73; Inspector-General of Police, Rangoon, 1875–86. *Address:* 71 Oxford Terrace, W2. *Club:* Constitutional. *Died 15 Feb. 1927.*

LOWNDES, William Selby-, JP; *b* 13 Nov. 1836; *e s* of late William Selby-Lowndes and 1st wife, Lucy, *d* of late Isaac Rawlins Hartman; *m* 1867, Jessie Mary, *d* of Lt-General Lechmere Worrall, and *widow* of Eyre Coote of West Park, Hants; one *s*. Master of the Whaddon Chase Hunt; patron of three livings. *Address:* Whaddon Hall, Stony Stratford. *Died 3 Nov. 1920.*

LOWRY, Charles, JP; MA; Headmaster, Tonbridge School, 1907–22; *b* 19 Oct. 1857; *s* of Rev. C. H. Lowry of Stanwix House, Carlisle; *m* 1883, Frances Maria, *d* of Rev. C. C. Lowndes of Windermere; one *s* two *d*. *Educ:* Eton; Corpus Christi College, Oxford. Asst Master at Wellington College, 1883; Eton College, 1883–1900; Headmaster Sedbergh School, 1900–7. *Recreations:* rowing, golf. *Clubs:* Cavendish; Leander. *Died 13 Dec. 1922.*

LOWRY, Adm. Sir Robert Swinburne, KCB 1913; *b* Zante, 4 March 1854; *e s* of late Lt-Gen. R. W. Lowry, CB; *m* 1893, Helena, *d* of T. Greer, Sea Park, Belfast, and Grove House, Regent Park; one *s* one *d*. *Educ:* HMS "Britannia," Dartmouth. Entered Navy Dec. 1867; Lieut 1875; served in "Serapis" during Prince of Wales's trip to India in that year; Gunnery Lieut 1880; Commander, 1890; commanded HMS "Ganges"; received Royal Humane Society's bronze medal for saving life, 1873; thanks of French Government with a piece of Sèvres china for exertions in rescuing the corvette "Seigneley" when ashore at Jaffa, 1892; Captain, 1896; Asst Director of Naval Intelligence, 1897–1900; Flag-Captain to Rear-Admiral Lord C. Beresford in HMS "Ramillies"; Captain of HMS "Hood," 1902; Capt. RNE College, Devonport; Capt. HMS "Russell" and ADC to the King; Rear-Admiral in the Channel Fleet, 1907; Pres. Royal Naval War College, 1907–8; commanded 2nd Cruiser Squadron, 1908–10; Vice-Admiral 1911; Admiral 1913; Admiral Commanding in Scotland, 1913–16; Commander-in-Chief, Rosyth, 1916; retired, 1917; Chairman Committee on Naval Education, 1916–17; Chairman Admiralty Committee on Mercantile Marine, 1917–18. *Recreations:* shooting, fishing, cycling, golf. *Address:* Wickham Lodge, Wickham, Hants. *Club:* United Service. *Died 29 May 1920.*

LOWRY-CORRY, Adm. Hon. Armar; *b* 25 May 1836; *s* of 3rd Earl of Belmore; *m* 1868, Geraldine (*d* 1905), *d* of late James King-King, MP, of Staunton Park, Herefordshire; five *s* three *d* (and three

s one *d* decd). Entered Navy, 1849; Admiral, 1894. *Address:* 15 Warwick Square, SW. *Club:* United Service.

Died 1 Aug. 1919.

LOWRY-CORRY, Col Hon. Henry William; late commanding Coldstream Guards; *b* 30 June 1845; *s* of 3rd Earl of Belmore; *m* 1876, Hon. Blanche Edith Wood (*d* 1921), *d* of 1st Viscount Halifax; one *s* two *d* (and one *s* decd). MP (C) Co. Tyrone, 1873–80. Served Egypt, 1885 (medal with clasp, Khedive's star); JP and late Chairman of Quarter Sessions for W Suffolk; Chairman Suffolk TAA. *Address:* Edwardstone Hall, Boxford, Suffolk. *Club:* Travellers'.

Died 6 May 1927.

LOWTHER, Rt. Hon. Sir Gerard Augustus, 1st Bt, *cr* 1914; GCMG 1911 (KCMG 1907); CB 1904; PC 1908; *b* 16 Feb. 1858; 2nd *s* of late Hon. William Lowther, *brother* of 3rd Earl of Lonsdale, and Hon. Charlotte Alice, *d* of only Baron Wensleydale; *m* 1905, Alice, *d* of Atherton Blight of Philadelphia, USA; two *d* (and one *d* decd). *Educ:* Harrow. Entered Diplomatic Service, 1879; served in Madrid, Paris, Constantinople, Vienna, Sofia, Bucharest, Tokio, Budapest; Secretary of Embassy, Washington; Envoy Extraordinary and Minister Plenipotentiary for Chile, 1901–4; Minister at Tangier, 1904–8; HBM Ambassador at Constantinople, 1908–13. *Heir:* none. *Address:* 23 Belgrave Square, SW. *T:* Victoria 6495. *Clubs:* Travellers', St James's, Prince's. *Died 5 April 1916 (ext).*

LOYD, Archie Kirkman, KC; DL; MP (U) North or Abingdon Division of Berks, 1895–1905, and 1916–18; *b* 1847; *s* of late Thomas Kirkman Loyd and Annie, *d* of late James Haig; *m* 1885, Henrietta, *d* of late E. L. Clutterbuck, Hardenhuish, Wilts; three *s*. Barrister, 1868; Midland Circuit; Bencher Middle Temple, 1894; retired from Bar, 1895. Alderman Berks County Council; VP of Council of British Red Cross Society. *Address:* Downs House, East Hendred, Berks; 60A Cadogan Square, SW1. *T:* Kensington 4052. *Clubs:* Carlton Windham, 1900; Berks County.

Died 1 Dec. 1922.

LUARD, Lt-Col Charles Eckford, CIE 1923; Indian Army, retired; *b* 11 Oct. 1869; *s* of late Col C. H. Luard, RE; *m* 1903, Alice Margaret, *d* of James Todd, Aberdeen; two *s* one *d*. *Educ:* Marlborough; Christ Church, Oxford, MA. Indian Army (8th Gurkhas); Political Dept, Govt of India; Political Agent, Bhopal; sometime Private Secretary to Maharajah of Indore; retired, 1925. University Member Oxford City Council. *Publications:* History of States in Central India; joint author of Official History of the King-Emperor's Visit to India; Bibliography of Central India History, etc; Census of Central India, 1901, 1911, and 1921. *Address:* Woodsend, Boars Hill, Oxford. *T:* Oxford 24. *M:* FC 7952. *Died 17 May 1927.*

LUARD, Major Edward Bourryau, DSO 1915; 1st Battalion, King's (Shropshire Light Infantry); *b* 20 Sept. 1870; *s* of late Lt-Gen. R. G. A. Luard, CB; *m* 1905, Louise Henrietta Smith. Entered army, 1891; Captain, 1900; Major, 1910; served S African War, 1899–1902 (Queen's medal, 3 clasps); European War, 1914–15 (DSO). *Club:* Sports. *Died 24 April 1916.*

LUBBOCK, Frederic; Chairman London Board, Bank of New Zealand; Chairman London Merchant Bank, Ltd; Director London Assurance Corporation; Director British Bank of South America, Ltd; *b* 1 May 1844; 6th *s* of Sir John W. Lubbock, 3rd Bt; *m* 1869, Catherine, *o d* of John Gurney of Earlham Hall, Norfolk; six *s* one *d*. *Educ:* Eton. *Address:* 26 Cadogan Gardens, SW3. *T:* Kensington 2604; Emmets, Ide Hill, Sevenoaks. *Club:* Arthur's.

Died 22 June 1927.

LUBBOCK, Hon. Harold (Fox-Pitt); *b* 10 June 1888; *s* of 1st Baron Avebury and 2nd wife Alice Augusta Laurentia Lane, *d* of General Augustus Henry Lane Fox-Pitt-Rivers; *m* 1914, Dorothy, *e d* of Henry William Forster; one *s* one *d*. *Educ:* Eton; Trinity College, Cambridge; MA. Capt. West Kent Yeomanry. *Address:* 48 Grosvenor Street, W.

Died 4 April 1918.

LUBBOCK, Montagu, MD (London and Paris); FRCP; formerly Assistant Physician to the West London Hospital, Physician to Out-patients, Charing Cross Hospital, and Assistant Physician to the Children's Hospital, Great Ormond Street; *b* 24 May 1842; 5th *s* of late Sir John W. Lubbock, 3rd Bt, of High Elms, Kent, and Harriet Hotham, *d* of Col Hotham; *m* 1st, 1872, Lora (*d* 1882), *y d* of Capt. Geo. Hotham, RE; one *s*; 2nd, 1888, Nora (*d* 1918), *e d* of Nottidge Charles Macnamara, FRCS, of the Lodge, Chorley Wood, Herts. *Educ:* Eton College; football and cricket elevens; boating eight; won the running, hurdle race, and fives contests; President of the Debating

Society. Upon leaving Eton, was Captain of the 11th Kent Volunteers in 1859. Was in the City for a short time; became MD Paris; returning then to England, he became MD London, thereafter in practice as a physician in London. *Publications:* contributed articles to medical works and papers to medical journals. *Recreations:* walking, golf. *Address:* 127 Mount Street, Berkeley Square, W. *Club:* Athenæum.
Died 8 April 1925.

LUBBOCK, Hon. Norman; *b* 16 Dec. 1861; 2nd *s* of 1st and *brother* and *heir-pres.* of 2nd Baron Avebury; *m* 1919, *cousin* Edith Harriet, *e d* of late Sir Nevile Lubbock, KCMG. *Address:* Fishleigh House, Hatherleigh, N Devon. *Died 11 Nov. 1926.*

LUCAS OF CRUDWELL, 8th Baron *cr* 1663 **AND DINGWALL,** 11th Lord *cr* 1609; **Auberon Thomas Herbert,** PC 1912; Royal Flying Corps; *b* 25 May 1876; *o* surv. *s* of Hon. Auberon Herbert and Lady Florence Amabel, *d* of 6th Earl Cowper; *S* uncle, 1905; *co-heir* to Barony of Butler. *Educ:* Bedford Grammar School; Balliol Coll. Lieutenant Hants Yeomanry; Under-Secretary of State, War Office, 1908–11; Under-Secretary of State for Colonies, 1911; Parliamentary Secretary, Board of Agriculture, 1911–14; President of the Board of Agriculture, 1914–15. *Recreation:* ornithology. *Heir-pres.: sister* Hon. Nan Ino Herbert, *b* 13 June 1880. *Address:* 32 Old Queen Street, SW. *T:* Victoria 938; Picket Post, Ringwood. *Clubs:* Brooks's, Travellers'. *Died 3 Nov. 1916.*

LUCAS, Rev. Arthur, MA; Hon. Canon of Rochester; *b* 1851; *s* of W. S. Lucas, of St Bartholomew's Hospital; *m* 1884, Lilian (*d* 1920), 4th *d* of Ven. Arthur Davenport, Archdeacon of Hobart, Tasmania. *Educ:* Uppingham; Clare College, Cambridge (Scholar and Exhibitioner). Assistant Master and Chaplain, Tonbridge School, 1878–1910; Acting Headmaster, 1907. *Recreations:* travel, golf. *Address:* 3 Bina Gardens, SW5. *T:* Kensington 1590.
Died 18 Feb. 1921.

LUCAS, Sir Arthur, Kt 1919; *b* 1845; *s* of Louis Lucas; *m* 1893, Juliana Violet, *d* of Alfred G. Henriques, JP, Brighton. *Educ:* University College School and College, London. Civil Engineer; AMICE and MIME; pupil of Sir John Hawkshaw; Director of Imperial Continental Gas Association; and Deputy Chairman of Continental Union Gas Co.; Vice-President of the Hospital for Sick Children, Great Ormond Street; Chairman of the Hospital Convalescent Home, Swanley. *Address:* 27 Bruton Street, W1. *T:* Gerrard 5108. *Clubs:* Athenæum, Burlington Fine Arts. *Died 9 Jan. 1922.*

LUCAS, Charles James; *b* 25 Feb. 1853; *s* of late Charles Thomas Lucas and Charlotte Emma, *d* of C. Tiffin; *m* 1881, Mildred Frances, *y d* of Eric Carrington Smith of Ashfold, Sussex; two *s*. *Educ:* Harrow. Lt-Col (retired) Engineer and Railway SC VD; one of HM Lieutenants for City of London; High Sheriff for Sussex, 1904–5; DL, JP Sussex. *Address:* Warnham Court, Horsham. *TA:* Lucas-Warnham. *T:* Broadbridge Heath 9. *Clubs:* Carlton, Royal Automobile.
Died 17 April 1928.

LUCAS, Col Francis Alfred, VD; *b* 7 June 1850; *m* 1887, Alice, *y d* of late Viscount de Stern. Contested (C) Louth Div. of Lincs, 1895; MP (C) Lowestoft Div. of Suffolk, 1900–6; contested Kennington, Jan. and Dec. 1910. Supply and Transport Officer, S London Vol. Brigade, 1890–1900; commanding Harwich Vol. Brigade, 1900–6; 41 years' service in Reserve Forces; Deputy Chairman, Alliance Assurance Co., Ltd. JP Suffolk. *Address:* Stornoway House, Cleveland Row, SW. *TA:* Sobriety, London. *T:* Regent 3935. *Clubs:* Athenæum, Carlton, St James's, Garrick.
Died 11 Dec. 1918.

LUCAS, Francis Herman, CB 1911; CVO 1917; Financial Secretary, India Office; *b* 1878; *m* 1903, Helen Mary, *e d* of late Morris Smith, Dalbeattie, Kirkcudbrightshire; one *s* three *d*. *Educ:* Winchester College (Scholar); Trinity College, Cambridge (Scholar). Entered India Office, 1901; Assistant Private Secretary to Lord George Hamilton, 1902–3; to Rt Hon. St John Brodrick, MP, 1903–5; and to Rt Hon. John Morley, MP, 1905–7; Principal Private Secretary to Viscount Morley, 1909–10, to the Marquess of Crewe, 1910–15, and to Rt Hon. Austen Chamberlain, MP, 1915–17. *Address:* 50 Oakley Street, Chelsea, SW3.
Died 13 April 1920.

LUCAS, Brig.-Gen. Frederic George, CB 1918; CSI 1919; CIE 1921; DSO 1898; *b* Falmouth, 20 Oct. 1866; *e s* of late Frederic Lucas, Paymaster, RN; *m* 1920, Ethel Fanny Whitelock, *widow* of Lt-Col A. J. Menzies, DSO; one *d*. *Educ:* Royal Naval School, New Cross; Royal Acad. Gosport (Burney's); Royal Military College, Sandhurst.

Joined East Lancashire Regt, 1886; Indian Staff Corps, 1888; Captain, 1897; Bt Major 1898; Major, 1904; Lt-Col 1911; Col 1917; served Hazara Expedition, 1891 (medal and clasp); Isazai Expedition, 1892; commanded the Gurkha Scouts, Tirah Expedition, 1897–98 (despatches twice, brev. of Maj. and DSO, medal with two clasps); Waziristan, 1901–2 (despatches, clasp); Bazar Valley, 1908 (despatches, medal and clasp); European War, including Mesopotamia, 1914–18 (Bt Col, CB, CSI, Légion d'Honneur, Croix d'Officier); Afghanistan, 1919 (despatches, clasp); Waziristan, 1919–20 (despatches, CIE, 2 clasps); retired, 1921. *Clubs:* United Service, Alpine.
Died 5 Oct. 1922.

LUCAS, John Seymour, RA 1898 (ARA 1886); FSA; historical and portrait painter; *b* London, 21 Dec. 1849; *s* of Henry Lucas; *n* of John Lucas, portrait painter; *m* 1877, Marie Élizabeth (*d* 1921), *d* of Louis Dieudonne de Cornelissen and Marianne Bath. *Educ:* Royal Academy School of Art. Practised as painter of genre and historical pictures, and portraits; visitor at Royal Academy Schools of Art, from 1886; Examiner Department of Science and Art, South Kensington; painted (1898) fresco for Royal Exchange, representing William the Conqueror granting the first charter to the City of London, presented by the Corporation of London; commissioned by King Edward VII to paint the reception of the Moorish Embassy, 1901, and in 1914 commissioned to paint for the House of Commons, a large fresco of The Flight of the Five Members, 1642. *Engraved works:* Armada in Sight; The Surrender of Don Pedro de Valdez to Drake on board the "Revenge"; Eloped; The Toper; The Smoker; The Loving Cup, etc. *Address:* New Place, Woodchurch Road, NW; Blythborough, Suffolk. *Died 8 May 1923.*

LUCAS, Keith, .ScD; FRS 1913; Fellow and Lecturer in Natural Sciences, Trinity College, Cambridge; *b* Greenwich, 8 March 1879; *s* of Francis Robert and Katharine Lucas; *m* 1909, Alys, *d* of Rev. C. E. Hubbard; three *s*. *Educ:* Rugby; Trinity College, Cambridge. Fellow of Trinity College, 1904; ScD Cambridge, 1911; Croonian Lecturer, Royal Society, 1912. *Publications:* papers on Physiology of Nerve and Muscle in Journal of Physiology. *Address:* Fen Ditton, Cambs; Trinity College, Cambridge. *T:* Cambridge 739 and 580.
Died 5 Oct. 1916.

LUCAS, Marie Élizabeth Seymour; *b* Paris, 28 April 1855; *d* of Louis Dieudonne de Cornelissen and Marianne Bath (lineally descended from Antonius Cornelissen of Antwerp, patron of the Fine Arts, and friend of Van Dyck, who painted his portrait; a daughter of Rubens married into the Cornelissen family); *m* 1877, John Seymour Lucas. *Educ:* at home; London; Germany; Royal Academy. *Paintings:* Types of English Beauty; We are but Little Children weak; Weighed and found Wanting, etc. *Address:* New Place, Woodchurch Road, West Hampstead. *Died 25 Nov. 1921.*

LUCAS-TOOTH, Sir (Archibald) Leonard (Lucas), 2nd Bt, *cr* 1906; Major Hon. Artillery Company; *b* 3 June 1884; *s* of Sir Robert Lucas Lucas-Tooth, 1st Bt and Helen, *d* of Frederick Tooth, of Goderich, Sydney; *S* father, 1915; *m* 1916, Rosa Mary, *y d* of Charles A. Bovill, 60 Pont Street, SW; two *d* (of whom one was born posthumously). *Heir:* none. *Address:* Holme Lacy, Herefordshire; Kameruka, Co. Auckland, New South Wales.
Died 12 July 1918 (ext).

LUCCHESI, Andrea Carlo, RBS; sculptor; *b* London (City), 19 Oct. 1860. *Educ:* Euston Coll.; West London; School of Art; Royal Academy Schools. Began life as a sculptor's moulder and drifted into carving and afterwards modelling; exhibited at Royal Academy and other exhibitions from 1881. *Address:* 1 and 2 Camden Studios, Camden Street, NW. *Clubs:* Savage, St John's Wood Arts.
Died 9 April 1925.

LUCE, Rev. Edward; Rector of St Saviour, Jersey; Canon of Winchester; *b* 1851; *s* of late Francis Edward Luce of St Lawrence, Jersey, and Louisa, *d* of late John Orange of St Brelade; *m* 1882, Catherine Wynne, *d* of late John Este Vibert of the Grange, St Mary, Jersey; one *s* four *d*. *Educ:* Victoria College, Jersey; Pembroke College, Oxford. Deacon, 1874; held in succession the Rectories of St John, St Mary, and St Saviour in the Island of Jersey; Vice-Dean of Jersey from 1898; a member of the States of Jersey, and on several occasions deputed by that body to represent them before His Majesty's Privy Council. *Recreations:* agricultural pursuits; was for many years President of the Royal Agricultural and Horticultural Society of Jersey. *Address:* St Saviour's, Jersey. *Died 1 July 1917.*

LUCK, Gen. Sir George, GCB 1909 (KCB 1897; CB 1879); *b* 24 Oct. 1840; family to which he belonged resided at Malling, Kent;

m 1867, Ellen Georgina, *d* of Maj.-Gen. Frank Adams, CB. *Educ:* private schools. Joined army, 1858; Capt. Inniskilling Dragoons, 1867; Lt-Col 15th Hussars, 1879; Brig.-Gen. commanding Sind District, 1884; Inspector-General of Cavalry in India, 1887–93; commanding Quetta District, 1893; Inspector-General of Cavalry in Great Britain and Ireland, 1895–98; commanding Bengal Army, 1898–1902; commanded 15th Hussars in Afghan and Boer wars; in command of Bengal Army, 1898–1903; Colonel of the 15th the King's Hussars, 1904; General, 1905; HM's Lieutenant the Tower of London, 1905–7. *Address:* Landford Lodge, Salisbury. *Club:* Army and Navy.
Died 10 Dec. 1916.

LUCK, Richard; Recorder of Richmond, Yorks, since 1920; *b* 14 Sept. 1847; *s* of late Ald. Richard Luck, JP, Mayor of Darlington, 1872. *Educ:* Queen Elizabeth Grammar School, Darlington; St John's College, Cambridge (11th Senior Optime; MA, LLM). Called to Bar, Inner Temple, 1871; North Eastern Circuit; President Darlington Conservative and Unionist Club. *Address:* Central Chambers and Osborne Villa, Darlington. *TA:* Richard Luck, Darlington. *T:* chambers 2416; residence 2417. *Died Nov. 1920.*

LUCKES, Eva C. E., CBE 1917; Matron, London Hospital, Whitechapel, E1. Lady of Grace of the Order of St John of Jerusalem; member of the British Red Cross Society; Royal Red Cross (1st class). *Publications:* General Nursing, ninth and revised edition, 1914; Hospital Sisters and their Duties, fourth and revised edition, 1912. *Address:* London Hospital, Whitechapel, E1. *T:* Avenue 5020.
Died 16 Feb. 1919.

LUCKMAN, Ven. William Arthur Grant, VD; *b* 25 June 1857; *e s* of Rev. W. Grant Luckman; *m* Sophia Carolina, *d* of Rev. Prebendary Ommanney of Chew Magna, Somerset. *Educ:* Keble College, Oxford (MA). Ordained, 1881; Master of Boys' High School, Allahabad, 1882–86; Chaplain of St Paul's Cathedral, 1881–91 and 1893–94; Naini-tal, 1891–93; St John, Calcutta, 1893–95; Canon of Calcutta, 1900–7; Archdeacon, 1907–11. *Address:* The Rectory, Colinton, Midlothian. *Clubs:* East India United Service, Oriental.
Died 8 Jan. 1921.

LUCY, Sir Henry, Kt 1909; JP; "Toby, MP" of Punch; *b* Crosby, 5 Dec. 1845; *m* Nancy, *d* of John White, headmaster, Crescent School. *Educ:* Crescent School, Liverpool; Paris. Apprenticed to Liverpool merchant; joined staff Shrewsbury Chronicle as chief reporter, 1864; went to Paris to study language and literature, 1869; returned to London, joined staff of new morning edition Pall Mall Gazette, 1870; joined Daily News as special correspondent, chief of Gallery staff, and writer of Parliamentary summary, 1873; editor of the Daily News, 1886; resigned, preferring earlier vocation in Press Gallery, 1887; began to contribute Cross Bench articles in the Observer, 1880; joined the staff of Punch, creating the character of "Toby, MP" from whose Diary the Essence of Parliament, commenced by Shirley Brooks, was extracted, 1881; retired, 1916. *Publications:* Handbook of Parliamentary Procedure; Men and Manner in Parliament, 1875; Gideon Fleyce, a novel, 1882; East by West, 1884; A Diary of Two Parliaments: The Disraeli Parliament, 1880, and the Gladstone Parliament, 1885; A Diary of the Salisbury Parliament, 1892; A Diary of the Home Rule Parliament, 1895; Faces and Places, 1895; Mr Gladstone, a Study from Life, 1896; The Miller's Niece, 1896; A Diary of the Unionist Parliament, 1901; Peeps at Parliament, 1903; Later Peeps at Parliament, 1905; The Balfourian Parliament, 1906; Memories of Eight Parliaments, 1908; Sixty Years in the Wilderness, 1909 (second series, 1912); Nearing Jordan (third series), 1916; The Diary of a Journalist, 1920, second vol. 1922, third vol. 1923; Lords and Commoners, 1921. *Recreation:* travel; made journey round the world, crossing US, visiting Japan, returning through India, 1883–84; visited the Cape, 1894; West Indies, 1902; United States, 1903. *Address:* Whitethorn, Hythe, Kent. *Club:* National Liberal.
Died 20 Feb. 1924.

LUDLOW, 2nd Baron, *cr* 1897, of Heywood; **Rt. Hon. Henry Ludlow Lopes,** JP Wilts and Northampton; DL Wilts; *b* Wiltshire, 30 Sept. 1865; *s* of 1st Baron Ludlow and Cordelia Lucy, *e d* of Erving Clark, Efford Manor, Devon; *m* 1st, 1903, Blanche (*d* 1911), *widow* of 7th Lord Howard de Walden; 2nd, 1919, Alice Sedgwick, *widow* of Sir Julius Wernher, 1st Bt. *Educ:* Eton; Balliol College, Oxford; BA, 1885 (2nd class Honours); MA, 1890. Barrister; Capt. Royal Wiltshire Imp. Yeomanry; LCC; Pres. of Cancer Hospital; late Treasurer of St Bartholomew's Hospital; European War, 1917–18, Staff; MFH Hertfordshire Hounds. *Recreations:* shooting, hunting, stalking, coaching. *Heir:* none. *Address:* Bath House, Piccadilly, W; Luton Hoo, Luton, Beds. *Clubs:* Carlton, Marlborough, Bachelors'.
Died 8 Nov. 1922 (ext).

LUKIN, Maj.-Gen. Sir Henry Timson, KCB 1918 (CB 1916); CMG 1902; DSO 1900; Permanent Force, Union of South Africa (retired); *b* 24 May 1860; *s* of R. H. Lukin, Barrister-at-Law; *m* 1891, Lily, *d* of M. H. Quinn, Fort Hare, SA. *Educ:* Merchant Taylors' School. Served South African War, 1879; Zulu Campaign; attached to Cavalry Brigade in advance on Ulundi; present at battle (severely wounded, medal with clasp); operations in Basutoland, 1881 (medal and clasp); Field Adjutant Bechuanaland Field Force, Langeberg Campaign, 1896–97 (despatches several times); South African War; Lieut-Colonel 1900; commanded artillery, Wepener siege, 1900; commanded 1st Colonial Division, Cape Colony, 1901 (despatches thrice, Queen's medal four clasps, King's medal two clasps, DSO); Colonel Commanding Cape Mounted Riflemen, 1903–12; Commandant-General Cape Colonial Forces, 1904–12; Inspector-General Permanent Force Union of South Africa, 1912; served South-West Africa, 1914–15; European War, 1915–18; commanded South African Infantry Brigade, Egypt and France, 9th Division, BEF, and 64th Division (Order of the Nile, 3rd Class, KCB, Commandeur Légion d'Honneur); Hon. Major-General in the Army, 1919. *Recreations:* golf, polo, tennis. *Address:* Ascot, Kenilworth, Cape, South Africa. *Clubs:* Windham; Civil Service, Cape Town.
Died 16 Dec. 1925.

LUKIS, Surg.-Gen. Hon. Sir Charles Pardey, KCSI 1911 (CSI 1910); VD 1915; MD Lond.; FRCS; Director-General Indian Medical Service since 1910, and Member of the Viceroy's Legislative Council, India; Hon. Surgeon to HM, 1913; *b* 9 Sept. 1857; *s* of late W. H. Lukis; *m* 1885, Lilian, *e d* of late Col John Stewart, CIE, RA, of Ardvorlich; two *s* three *d*. *Educ:* St Bartholomew's Hospital. Late Principal and Professor of Medicine, Medical College, Calcutta; and first Physician, College Hospital; served Waziri Expedition, 1881; Zhob Valley Expedition, 1884. Chairman Executive Committee, Indian Council, St John Ambulance Association; Commissioner for the St John Ambulance Overseas Brigade within the Empire of India, 1915; Hon. Surg. to HE the Viceroy of India, 1905; Good Service Pension, 1910; KGStJ 1911. *Publications:* A Manual of Tropical Hygiene; Editor of The Indian Journal of Medical Research, Ghosh's Materia Medica, and Waring's Bazaar Medicines of India. *Address:* Home Department, Government of India, Simla. *Clubs:* East India United Service; Bengal, Calcutta; United Service, Simla.
Died 24 Oct. 1918.

LUMHOLTZ, Carl; explorer and author; *b* near Lillehammer, in the central part of Norway, 1851. *Educ:* Lillehammer Latin og Realskole; University of Christiania. Sent by the Museums of Christiania University to Australia as zoological collector, 1880–84; camped for nearly a year with the blacks of the coast range near Cardwell, Queensland; discovered the tree kangaroo of Australia and other mammals; turned to anthropology and travelled seven years among the Indians of Mexico, mostly in the little known Sierra Madre of Northern Mexico; his faculty to gain the confidence of the natives was largely due to his ability of learning and rendering their songs; between the years 1914 and 1917 he spent two years travelling in Dutch Borneo, making a journey through the central part of the island; subseq. planned an expedition to New Guinea (Dutch part), 1920. *Publications:* Among Cannibals, 1889; Unknown Mexico, 1902; New Trails in Mexico, 1912; Through Central Borneo, two years travel in the Land of the Headhunters, 1920; Symbolism of the Huichol Indians; Decorative Art of the Huichol Indians, published as Memoirs of the American Museums of Natural History. *Recreations:* ski-ing, skating, dancing. *Address:* Christiania, Norway; c/o Norwegian Consulate General, New York.
Died 5 May 1922.

LUMLEY, Col Francis Douglas, CB 1902; CBE 1919; late Middlesex Regiment; *b* 13 Nov. 1857; *m* 1886, Leonora Constance (*d* 1893), *d* of Arthur Kenyon. Entered army, 1875; Captain, 1884; Major, 1893; Lieut-Col 1901; Brevet Colonel, 1904; Substantive Col 1907; Commanding No 10 District, 1908–11; served South Africa, 1899–1902 (despatches, CB, medal with five clasps); European War, 1914–19 (despatches). *Club:* Naval and Military.
Died 4 Dec. 1925.

LUMLEY, Brig.-Gen. Hon. Osbert (Victor George Atheling), CMG 1917; *b* 18 July 1862; *brother* and *heir* of 10th Earl of Scarbrough, and *brother* of late Lady Bolton, and of Lady Bradford, Lady Zetland, and Lady Grosvenor; *m* 1892, Constance Eleanor, OBE, *e d* of late Captain Eustace John Wilson-Patten, 1st Life Guards, and Emily Constantia, *d* of Rev. Lord John Thynne (she *m* 2nd, 3rd Marquess of Headfort); one *s* one *d* (and one *s* one *d* decd). Formerly ADC and Military Private Secretary to Lord-Lieutenant of Ireland (Marquess of Zetland), ADC to Major-General Sir R. Thynne, KCB, commanding NE District, and Colonel-in-Charge, Cavalry Records (Hussars), 1910–14. *Address:* 50 Cadogan Square, SW1. *T:* Victoria 2095. *Died 14 Dec. 1923.*

LUMLEY, Theodore, JP; Member Special Local Tribunal for London; Consul-General for Monaco in London; Knight of the Order of St Charles. *Educ:* Paris. Solicitor; Prizeman, Law Society, 1868; Commissioner for the Strichen and Auchmedden Estates, Aberdeenshire; Solicitor to the Government of Portugal and of the Imperial Persian Legation in London; Hon. Solicitor, Royal General Theatrical Fund, and St Peter's Hospital; conducted the Langworthy case and many other *causes célèbres*; member of the Court of Assistants of the Company of Turners; member of the firm of Lumley and Lumley, 37 Conduit Street, W1, 15 Old Jewry Chambers Bank, EC; 821 Boulevard Haussmann, Paris. *Address:* 25 Upper Grosvenor Street, W1. *TA:* Lumbulns, London. *T:* Gerrard 3582. *Clubs:* Devonshire, Royal Automobile, Royal Aero, Royal Motor Yacht. *Died 2 July 1922.*

LUMSDEN, Gen. Sir Peter Stark, GCB 1885 (KCB 1879; CB 1873); CSI 1870; DL and JP for the Counties of Aberdeen and Banff; *b* 9 Nov. 1829; *s* of late Col T. Lumsden, CB, Belhelvie Lodge, Aberdeenshire; *m* 1862, Mary, *d* of J. Marriott. *Educ:* Military Coll. Addiscombe. Entered Indian Army, 1847; served in the Quartermaster-Gen.'s Department in frontier campaign in the NW of India, 1851–54; on special military mission to Afghanistan, 1857–58; in Central India campaign, 1857–58; in China at capture of Taku Forts and occupation of Pekin, 1860; with Bhootan Field Force, 1865; as Deputy Quartermaster-Gen., 1864–68; as Quartermaster-Gen. of the Army, 1868–73; Acting Resident, Hyderabad, 1873; Adj.-Gen. of the Army, 1874–79; Chief of the Staff in India, 1879; ADC to the Queen, 1870–81; British Commissioner for demarcation of NW boundary of Afghanistan, 1884–85; member of the Council of India, 1883–93. *Publication:* Lumsden of the Guides, 1899. *Address:* Buchromb, Dufftown, NB. *Club:* United Service. *Died 9 Nov. 1918.*

LUND, Niels M., ARE; *b* 30 Nov. 1863. *Educ:* Royal Academy of Arts, London; Paris. Honourable mention and Gold Medallist, Paris Salon, 1894–95. First exhibited at RA, 1887; Salon, 1894; Pictures in the Luxembourg, Paris, and other public Galleries. *Address:* 169 Adelaide Road, NW. *Died 28 Feb. 1916.*

LUSCOMBE, Ven. Popham Street; authorised to officiate in Diocese of Sydney. *Educ:* Moore Theological College, NSW; Queens' College, Camb. (MA). Incumbent of Wollombi, 1879–93; Gresford, 1893; Canon of Christ Church Cathedral, Newcastle; Rector of Waratah, 1901–11; Dungog, 1911–22; Archdeacon of Northumberland, 1908–11; Rector of Paterson, 1922–24; Archdeacon of Gloucester, NSW, 1911–24. *Address:* Kanawha, West Ryde, New South Wales. *Died 6 Feb. 1927.*

LUSHINGTON, Alfred Wyndham, CIE 1915; *s* of James Law Lushington, ICS; *m* Elizabeth Alice, *d* of Capt. S. Cordue, Bagshot, Surrey; one *s* two *d*. *Educ:* Malvern College. Joined India Forest Dept, 1882. Imperial Forest Service, Conservator of Forests, Madras, 1905 (retired). *Address:* Dyces House, Waltair, India. *Died 26 March 1920.*

LUTTMAN-JOHNSON, Lt-Col Frederic, DSO 1900; late Lieutenant-Colonel commanding and Hon. Colonel 3rd Leinster Regiment; *b* 22 Jan. 1845; *s* of Rev. H. W. R. Luttman-Johnson of Binderton, Chichester. Entered army, York and Lancaster Regiment, 1865; retired 1900; served South Africa, 1900–2 (despatches, Queen's medal, 3 clasps, King's medal, 2 clasps, DSO); JP West Sussex. *Address:* Redhill House, Petworth, Sussex. *Club:* Army and Navy. *Died 11 Aug. 1917.*

LUTTRELL, Hugh Courtenay Fownes; *b* Woodlands, W Somerset, 10 Feb. 1857; *s* of late George Fownes Luttrell and Elizabeth, *d* of Sir Alexander Hood, 2nd Bt, MP; *m* 1904, Dorothy Hope Wedderburn, *e d* of Sir William Wedderburn, 4th Bt; two *s* four *d*. *Educ:* Cheltenham Coll. Capt. in Rifle Brigade; ADC to Lord Cowper and Lord Spencer, Viceroys of Ireland; ADC to General Sir John Adye, Governor of Gibraltar; Captain and Hon. Major 3rd Battalion Duke of Cornwall's Militia, 1887–96. MP (L) Tavistock Division of Devonshire (W Devon), 1892–1900 and 1906–10. *Recreations:* gardening, painting. *Address:* Ward House, Bere Alston, Devon. *Died 14 Jan. 1918.*

LUTWYCHE, Hudson Latham, JP, DL; *b* Homefield Houses, Lancashire, 10 July 1856; *o surv. s* of late Hudson Lutwyche, Kynaston,

Ross, Herefordshire; *m* 1888, Alice Metta, *o d* of Otis Hopkins, Milwaukee, USA; one *s*. *Educ:* Rugby; Cheltenham College. Captain 3rd Batt. Royal Lancaster Regiment; travelled a good deal; took great interest in county business, especially in all matters of sport; High Sheriff, Herefordshire, 1889. *Recreations:* hunting, shooting, fishing, all field sports. *Address:* Kynaston, Ross, Herefordshire. *TA:* Hoarwithy. *Clubs:* Boodle's, St James'. *Died 19 July 1925.*

LÜTZOW, Count, PhD of the Bohemian University of Prague; Hon. FRSL; FRGS; DLitt Oxon; Chamberlain of HM the Emperor of Austria since 1881; *m* Anna, *y d* of late Baron von Bornemann, minister of Mecklenburg in Paris. *Educ:* Vienna and Innsbruck Universities. Member of Austrian Parliament, 1885–89; Member of Royal Society of Sciences, Bohemia, and of the Bohemian Academy of Francis Joseph; Ilchester Lecturer, Oxford, 1904; lectured at American Universities, 1912. *Publications:* Bohemia, an Historical Sketch; History of Bohemian Literature, 1899; Prague (Mediæval Towns Series); The Labyrinth of the World (ed and trans. from the Bohemian of Comenius), 1901; The Historians of Bohemia, 1904; The Life and Times of Master John Hus, 1909; The Hussite Wars, 1914; many literary and political articles. *Recreations:* racing, hunting, fencing. *Address:* Château de Zampach, Hnátnice, Bohemia. *TA:* Lützow Hnátnice, Bohemia. *Clubs:* Jockey, Vienna; Bohemian Art (Ümelecky, Klüb) Chicago. *Died 13 Jan. 1916.*

LUXFORD, Major Rev. John Aldred, CMG 1916; Chaplain to the Forces, 3rd class, NZ Chaplain Department. Served SA War, 1902 (Queen's medal with clasp); European War, 1914–16 (despatches, CMG). *Address:* Christ Church, New Zealand. *Died 1921.*

LUXMOORE, Henry Elford, MA; retired ex-Senior Assistant Master, Eton College; 2nd *s* of Rev. Henry Luxmoore, Vicar of Barnstaple, Devon. *Educ:* Stoke Poges; Eton College (KS 1852–59); Pembroke College, Oxford (Rouse Scholar); 1st Class Mods, 1862; 1st Class Lit. Hum., 1864. Assistant Master at Eton, 1864–1904; Bucks County Council and Education Committee; ex-Chairman Eton Society for Improvement of Cottage Accommodation; Oxford Diocesan Board; ex-Master of Guild of St George, 1922–26; Advisory Committee, St Albans Diocese. *Publications:* mainly pamphlets, English Manners, Tudor and Stuart; Noblesse Oblige; Eton Chimneys; Layman's Argument; Confirmation; Ut casti sint; Addresses to Guild of St George; Reproductions of water-colour drawings; "Eton from a Backwater"; contributions to Nat. Biog. Hortic. Journal, Quarterly Review. *Recreations:* ethics and economics, rural reconstruction, art, gardening. *Address:* Baldwin's End, Eton, Bucks. *TA:* Eton. *Club:* Savile. *Died 11 Nov. 1926.*

LUZZATTI, Luigi; Member Chamber of Deputies, 1870–1921; Senator, 1921; Professor of Public Law, University of Rome; *b* Venice, 1 March 1841. *Educ:* Gymnase and Lycée, Venice; University of Padua. Professor of Political Economy, Technical Institute, Milan, 1863; Professor of Constitutional Law, University of Padua, 1866; General Secretary to Minister of Agriculture, 1869–73; Chancellor of the Exchequer, 1891, 1896, 1903, 1906, 1920; Minister of Agriculture, Industry, and Commerce, 1909; President of the Council of Ministry and Home Minister, 1910; Member of the Institute of France and Grand Cross of the Legion of Honour, 1898; Minister of State, 1906. Knight of Savoia's Order; Grand Cross of Sts Mauritius and Lazarus; Grand Cross de l'ordre de Leopold, Belgique, etc. *Publications:* La Diffusion du Crédit et les Banques populaires, 1863; L'Eglise et l'Etat en Belgique avec applications à l'Italie, 1866; La Liberté de conscience et de science, 1910 (traduite en français, en allemand, en japonais, etc); Pro italico nomine; Reports on Popular Banks instituted by him in Italy; A Book on Small Property, 1913; Scienza e patria, 1916; Sul filosofo dalmata Giorgio Politeo, 1919; Grandi Italiani, Grandi Sacrifizi per la Patria, 1924; articles on social, financial, and religious questions; Dio nella Liberta, 1926, etc. *Address:* Via Vittorio Veneto 84, Rome. *T:* 10-51. *Died 29 March 1927.*

LYALL, Sir Charles James, KCSI 1897 (CSI 1893); CIE 1880; MA Oxon; Hon. LLD Edin.; Hon. PhD Strassburg; Hon. DLitt Oxford; FBA; Fellow of King's College, London; *b* 9 March 1845; *s* of late Charles Lyall, 55 Sussex Gardens, W; *m* 1870, Florence Lyall, *d* of Henry Fraser; two *s* five *d*. *Educ:* King's College School; King's College; Balliol College, Oxford. Entered BCS 1867; Asst Magistrate Meerut, Bulandshahr, and Allahabad Districts, 1867–71; Under-Secretary to Govt NW Provinces, 1871–72; Asst Under-Secretary, Foreign Department, 1872; Under-Secretary to Govt of India in

Revenue, Agriculture, and Commerce Department, 1873–80; Secretary to Chief Comr of Assam, 1880–83; Judge and Comr Assam Valley Districts, 1883–84; Secretary to Govt of India in Revenue and Agricultural Department, 1886; again Secretary to Chief Comr Assam, 1887; Judge and Commissioner of Assam Valley Districts, 1888–89; Secretary to Govt of India in Home Department, 1889–94; Chief Commissioner, Assam, 1894; Chief Commissioner Central Provinces, India, 1895–98; Secretary Judicial and Public Department, India Office, 1898–1910. *Publications:* Translations of Ancient Arabic Poetry, 1885; edition of Ten Ancient Arabic Poems, 1894; articles in Enc. Brit., 9th and 11th editions; edition of two ancient Arabic *Dīwāns*, with translation, 1913. *Address:* 82 Cornwall Gardens, SW7. *T:* Western 7083. *Club:* Athenæum.

Died 1 Sept. 1920.

LYALL, David Robert, CSI 1891; *b* Ochterlony House, Forfarshire, NB, 24 Nov. 1841; *e s* of late David Lyall; *m* 1866, Laura Agnes, *d* of late Maj.-Gen. W. J. B. Knyvett; two *s* three *d*. *Educ:* Edinburgh Academy; Capt. of the XI and Football XX. Entered Bengal Civil Service, 1861; Inspector-General of Police LP, 1883–87; Comr of Chittagong, 1887–91; Comr of Patna, 1891–92; member of Board of Revenue and of Legislative Council, Bengal, 1892–96; retired 1896; Civil Political officer with Chin Lashai Expedition, 1888 (medal and clasp, CSI); President of Committee to inquire into Military and Public Works Expenditure, Simla, 1894; Superintendent of the Cooch Behar State, 1896–99. *Recreations:* cricket, racquets, pig-sticking, shooting. *Address:* Netherclay House, Bishop's Hull, Taunton. *TA:* Bishop's Hull. *Clubs:* East India United Service; Somerset County.

Died 3 Jan. 1917.

LYALL, Sir James Broadwood, GCIE 1888; KCSI 1892; retired officer Indian Civil Service; director Hand in Hand Insurance Company; *b* England, 4 March 1838; *s* of Rev. Alfred Lyall, Rector of Harbledown, Kent, and Mary, *d* of James Broadwood, Lyne, Sussex; *m* 1874, Katherine, *d* of Rev. J. Cautley. *Educ:* Eton; Haileybury Coll. Appointed Bengal CS, 1857; landed in India, 1858; joined Punjab Commission, 1859; Resident in Mysore and Chief Commissioner of Coorg, 1883–87; Lieut-Governor of the Punjab, 1887–92; visited China, Japan, Canada, and US, 1892; member Royal Commission on Opium, 1893; revisited India in that capacity; President Indian Famine Commission, 1898. *Publications:* only official. *Recreations:* golf, cycling, shooting. *Address:* Statenborough House, Eastry, Dover. *Club:* Athenæum.

Died 4 Dec. 1916.

LYE, Lt-Col Robert Cobbe, DSO 1904; 34th Sikh Pioneers; *b* 27 Nov. 1865. Entered army, 1885; Capt. 1896; Major, 1903; served Burmah, 1885–87 (slightly wounded, despatches, medal with clasp); Miranzai Expedition, 1891; Chitral, 1895 (medal with clasp); NW Frontier, India, 1897–98 (clasp); Thibet, 1903–4 (severely wounded, despatches, DSO). *Address:* Sialkot, India.

Died 28 June 1917.

LYELL, 1st Baron, *cr* 1914, of Kinnordy; **Leonard Lyell;** Bt, 1894; DL; *b* 21 Oct. 1850; *e s* of late Col Henry Lyell and Katherine, *d* of Leonard Horner, FRS, and *nephew* of Sir Charles Lyell, 1st Bt, the geologist; *m* 1874, Mary, *d* of Rev. J. M. Stirling; one *d* (and one *s* one *d* decd). MP (L) Orkney, 1885–1900. *Heir: g s* Charles Antony Lyell, *b* 14 June 1913. *Address:* Kinnordy, Kirriemuir, Forfarshire. *Club:* Athenæum.

Died 18 Sept. 1926.

LYELL, Hon. Charles Henry; MP (L) South Edinburgh, 1910–17; *b* 18 May 1875; *o s* of 1st Lord Lyell of Kinnordy; *m* 1911, Rosalind Margaret, *e d* of Vernon J. Watney; one *s* one *d*. *Educ:* Eton; New College, Oxford. MP (L) East Dorset, 1904–10; Parliamentary Private Secretary to Rt Hon. Sir Edward Grey, 3rd Bt, MP, Secretary of State for Foreign Affairs, 1906 and to Rt Hon. H. H. Asquith, Prime Minister, 1910. JP Forfarshire; Lt Forfar and Kincardine Artillery Militia, 1900–8; Vice-Chairman County Territorial Association, Forfarshire, 1908; gazetted Capt. in Fife RGA, Sept. 1914; Major in Highland Battery, Fife RGA, May 1915. *Recreations:* shooting, motoring. *Address:* 1 Cadogan Gardens, SW; Kinnordy, Kirriemuir, NB. *Clubs:* Brooks's, Reform.

Died 18 Oct. 1918.

LYELL, William Darling, MA; Advocate; Sheriff-Substitute of Lanarks, since 1912; *b* Edinburgh, 12 Jan. 1860; *s* of David Lyall, Solicitor before the Supreme Courts of Scotland; *m* 1st, 1891, Helen (*d* 1903), *d* of James Earl Moreton, FRCS; 2nd, 1907, Viola, *d* of John Williams, Carmarthen. *Educ:* Edinburgh University. Admitted to the Bar of Scotland, 1882; appointed an Extra Advocate Depute, 1889; Sheriff-Substitute of Dumfries and Galloway, 1890–1900; Renfrew

and Bute, 1900–12. *Publication:* The House in Queen Anne Square, 1920; The Justice-Clerk, 1923. *Address:* 29 Park Circus, Glasgow *T:* Charing Cross, Glasgow, 1278. *Clubs:* Caledonian; Scottish Conservative, Edinburgh; Western, Glasgow.

Died 5 March 1925.

LYLE, Sir Harold, KBE 1925; CMG 1916; *b* Newcastle-on-Tyne 17 Jan. 1873; *m* Rose Hilda Sawer; one *s* one *d*. Student Interpreter Siam, 1893; Vice-Consul at Bangkok, 1902; Consul at Chiengmai, 1907; called to Bar, Middle Temple, 1910; British Consul-General, Bangkok, with local rank of First Secretary of Legation, 1913; retired, 1924. *Address:* Longfield, Kingswear, S Devon.

Died 16 July 1927.

LYLE, Henry Samuel, MRCS; Senior Surgeon Liverpool Hospital for Cancer and Skin Diseases since 1899; *b* Bideford, 24 Oct. 1857; *s* of late D. Lyle of Bideford; *m* Millicent, *widow* of G. O'Brien of Liverpool; no *c*. *Educ:* Bideford Grammar School. Entered Liverpool Royal Infirmary School of Medicine, 1874; subsequently went to King's College, London, qualified as MRCS, 1880; Assistant Surgeon to Liverpool Hospital for Cancer and Skin Diseases, 1892–99. *Publications:* Treatment of Ringworm; Treatment of Vesicular Eczema; Case of Cancer cured by X-Rays; Relations between Cancer and Chronic Inflammation; Improved Mouth Gag. *Address:* 209 Upper Parliament Street, Liverpool. *T:* Royal 5008. *Club:* Liverpool Chess.

Died 29 March 1916.

LYLE, Sir Robert Park, 1st Bt, *cr* 1915; Chairman and Managing Director Abram Lyle & Sons, Limited, Sugar Refiners, London, when this firm and Henry Tate & Sons, Limited amalgamated in 1921, became Chairman of Tate & Lyle Limited; Chairman British Sugar Refiners' Association; Member of the Royal Commission on the Sugar Supply; *b* 17 Oct. 1859; 6th *s* of late Abram Lyle, JP, of Oakley, Greenock, and Mary, *d* of late William Park, Greenock; *m* 1882, Agnes, 4th *d* of the late William Jamieson, Shipowner, Greenock; one *d* (and one *d* decd). *Educ:* Madras College; St Andrews. On leaving school joined the family business in Greenock; became a partner in 1882, and was more particularly identified with the shipowning branch of the firm; transferred to London, 1897, to take up position as a Managing Director of the sugar refining business; became Chairman, 1908. Served over twenty years in 1st Vol. Batt. Argyll and Sutherland Highlanders; retired with rank of Major, 1897. FZS; Associate Institute Naval Architects. *Heir:* none. *Address:* 81 Cadogan Square, SW1. *T:* Kensington 1289. *Clubs:* Caledonian, Royal Thames Yacht, Ranelagh.

Died 11 July 1923 (ext).

LYNCH, George, FRGS; author and war correspondent; *b* Cork, Ireland, 27 March 1868. *Educ:* under John Henry, Cardinal Newman. Travelled and explored in deserts of Western Australia, in the Pacific Islands, etc; acted as war correspondent for the London Daily Chronicle during the Spanish-American war; represented the Illustrated London News during the Boer war; wounded at the battle of Reitfontein, in the early part of the siege of Ladysmith; captured by the Boers while making an attempt to go from Ladysmith to General Buller's force; kept prisoner for a month in Pretoria; liberated; invalided home after enteric fever; acted as war correspondent for the Daily Express and the Sphere in the China campaign and relief of the Legations; acted as special correspondent for London Daily Mail, United States; for the New York Journal, Macedonia, 1903; and London Daily Chronicle, Japan and Manchuria with Japanese army, 1904; in Petrograd during the disturbances of spring, 1905; correspondent for the Illustrated London News and Westminster Gazette during World War; invented gloves for handling barbed wire and several patents adopted by the War Office and Admiralty; travelled six times around the world. *Publications:* The War of the Civilisations; Realities; Impressions of a War Correspondent; The Path of Empire; Old and New Japan. *Recreations:* war-corresponding, yachting, fox-hunting, taking out patents. *Address:* 248 Gloucester Terrace, Hyde Park, W2. *T:* Park 3918. *Clubs:* Savage, City of London.

Died 29 Dec. 1928.

LYNCH, John Gilbert Bohun; author and caricaturist; *b* London, 21 May 1884; *o s* of late Trueman Lynch and Renira, *d* of late Capt. G. B. Martin, CB, RN; *m* twice; one *s* one *d*. *Educ:* Haileybury; University College, Oxford. *Publications:* Glamour, 1912; Cake, 1913; Unofficial, 1915; The Complete Gentleman, 1916; The Tender Conscience, 1919; Forgotten Realms, 1920; A Perfect Day, 1923; Menace from the Moon, 1924; Respectability, 1927; The Complete Amateur Boxer, 1913; Knuckles and Gloves, 1922; Max Beerbohm in Perspective, 1921; The Prize Ring, 1926; A History of Caricature, 1926; The Italian Riviera, 1927; Collecting, 1928; Decorations and Absurdities (with Reginald Berkeley); edited Isles of Illusion; A Muster of Ghosts, 1924; contributed to Home Chat, Quarterly Review, Answers, London Mercury, Chums, Fortnightly Review, and other periodicals. *Address:* Northlew Manor, Beaworthy, N Devon. *Club:* Savage.   *Died 2 Oct. 1928.*

LYNCH, Sir John Patrick, Kt 1911; JP Co. Dublin; President Incorporated Law Society of Ireland, 1905–6; Vice Chairman, Dublin Castle Red Cross Hospital; Governor of the House of Industry Government Hospitals; *b* 1858; *e* surv. *s* of late Standislaus John Lynch, JP, member of the Irish Land Commission; *m* 1896, Frieda, *d* of late William Ottmann, of Irving Place, New York; three *d. Educ:* Clongowes Wood College. *Address:* Belfield, Booterstown, Co. Dublin. *TA:* Okandl, Dublin. *T:* Ball's Bridge, No 2. *M:* IK 212 and 1244. *Clubs:* Stephen's Green, Dublin; Royal Irish Yacht.
                                Died 4 March 1921.

LYNCH, Richard Irwin; Curator, Botanic Garden, Cambridge, 1879–1919; *b* St Germans, 1850. Entered Kew, 1867; held responsible positions, 1870–79; Associate Linnean Society, 1881; awarded Veitch Memorial medal in silver, 1901, in gold, 1924; Hon. MA Cantab, 1906; Victoria Medallist of Honour, 1906; Associate Royal Botanic Society; Corresponding Member Royal Horticultural Society; raised many Hybrids, especially the Gerberas cultivated on Riviera; raised (at Kew) the universal window plant Campanula isophylla alba. *Publications:* Book of the Iris; Papers in Journal Royal Horticultural Society; Journal Linnean Society; the Gardeners' Chronicle, etc. *Recreation:* photography. *Address:* Granta, Upper Walnut Road, Chelston, Torquay.   *Died 7 Dec. 1924.*

LYNDEN-BELL, Col Edward Horace Lynden, CB 1915; MB; Army Medical Staff; *b* 18 Dec. 1858; *e s* of Maj.-Gen. T. Lynden-Bell of Brook Hill, Co. Wexford; *m* 1891, Mary Haigh, *e d* of Major Guyon, Royal Fusiliers. Major, 1895; Lt-Col 1903; Colonel, 1912; Deputy Director of Medical Services, London District, 1912; served Burma, 1885–89 (medal, 2 clasps); European War as DDMS, 1914–17 (CB). KStJ. *Club:* Junior United Service.
                                Died 1 Sept. 1922.

LYNE, Rev. Leonard Augustus; Hon. Canon of Gloucester; Hon. Diocesan Missioner. *Address:* St Mark's Vicarage, Gloucester.
                                Died 18 Dec. 1919.

LYNN-JENKINS, Frank; sculptor; HM Examiner for the Board of Education, S Kensington; *b* Torquay, 1870; *m* 1901, Phœbe, *d* of Charles and Henriette Le Févre; no *c. Educ:* Weston College. Studied at Lambeth School of Modelling; Royal Academy student. Won several prizes and medals, and British Institution Exhibition; exhibited at Royal Academy, Paris Salon, and numerous International Exhibitions, from 1895; silver medallist Paris Exhibition, 1900; executed many important decorative schemes (Lloyd's Registry, United Kingdom Prov. Assoc., etc), also portrait statues and busts; formerly, for several years, collaborated with Prof. Gerald Moira in many large decorative schemes in coloured relief; member of Art Workers' Guild, and Royal Society of British Sculptors (one of the founders of the latter). *Publications:* occasional contributor to contemporary Art magazines. *Recreations:* golf, music. *Club:* Chelsea Arts.   *Died Sept. 1927.*

LYON, Sir Alexander, Kt 1906; DL; Lord Provost of Aberdeen, 1905–8; *b* 20 Feb. 1850; *m* 1875, Elsie, *d* of late William Inglis; one *s* four *d. Educ:* Aberdeen. *Address:* 10 Queen's Road, Aberdeen.
                                Died 26 April 1927.

LYON, Adm. Herbert; *b* 28 Dec. 1856; 4th *s* of A. W. Lyon, JP, Abbotsclownholme, Rocester, Stafford; *m* Frances Violet Inglis, *d* of late Maj.-Gen. T. Inglis, CB, RE; one *d. Educ:* Mr Malden's School, Windlesham House, Brighton; the Rev. H. Burney's, Royal Academy, Gosport. Entered navy as Cadet, 1870; Midshipman, 1872; Sub-Lieut, 1876; Lieut, 1880; Commander, 1894; Captain, 1900; Rear-Admiral, 1910; served as midshipman in Charybdis in the Lingi and Lukut river expeditions, Straits of Malacca, Perak (medal and clasp); as Sub-Lieut (medal and clasp) in Zulu War, relief of Ekowe, Battle of Ginginhlovo; as Captain of Retribution at the blockade of Venezuela; last appointment Commodore at Hong-Kong. Foreign Orders: Crosses of Naval and Military 3rd class Order of Merit (Spain), gold and silver medal 2nd and 3rd class of the Nichau-Imtiaz (Turkey), Collar Order of the Commander of the Order of Redeemer (Greece). *Recreations:* polo, shooting, fishing, hunting. *Address:* Stoke Cottage, Devonport. *T:* 26X Devonport. *M:* CO 527. *Clubs:* Royal Naval, MCC.
                                Died 6 March 1919.

LYONS, Sir Joseph, Kt 1911; DL County of London; Chairman J. Lyons and Co., Ltd; *b* London; *s* of late Nathaniel Lyons, of Newmarket and London; *m* Psyche, *d* of late Isaac Cohen. *Educ:* borough Jewish schools and private academy. For some years followed the profession of an artist, exhibiting at various exhibitions; after which became a caterer and then the head of J. Lyons and Co. Ltd; Director of Trafford Park Estates, Manchester; Chairman Hancocks, Ltd, NZ; Vice-Chairman Trafford Park, Ltd; Chairman Strand Palace Hotel, Ltd. *Publication:* (part author) Master Crime and Treasures of the Temple. *Recreations:* painting, writing, motoring. *Address:* 26 West Kensington Gardens, W. *T:* Hammersmith 168. *M:* LD 8200. *Clubs:* Royal Automobile, Eccentric.
                                Died 21 June 1917.

LYONS, Rt. Hon. William Henry Holmes, PC 1922; *b* 1843; *m* 1888, Lily, *e d* of late George Evans, Gortmerron House, Co. Tyrone; two *d. Educ:* Harrow. Grand Master of Grand Orange Lodge of Ireland, and Grand Master of Imperial Grand Black Chapter of the British Commonwealth; Chairman of South Antrim Constitutional Association; Sheriff of Antrim, 1904. *Address:* Newlands, 30 Deramore Park, Belfast. *T:* Malone 456. *Club:* Ulster, Belfast.
                                Died 26 March 1924.

LYSAGHT, Hon. Horace George, JP for Co. Cork; *b* 16 Feb. 1873; *e s* of 6th Baron Lisle, of Mount North; *m* 1899, Alice Elizabeth, *d* of Sir John Wrixon Becher, 3rd Bt; three *s* one *d* (and two *d* decd). *Address:* Newmarket Cottage, Co. Cork.
                                Died 30 Sept. 1918.

LYSTER, Cecil Rupert Chaworth, MRCS; FRSM; Medical Officer in charge of Electrical Department of Middlesex Hospital since 1902; MO in charge of Electrical Massage and X-Ray Department, 2 AM Hospital, Millbank; Surgeon to the Bolingbroke Hospital, SW, since 1902; *b* 14 Dec. 1859; *e s* of Alfred Chaworth Lyster and Elizabeth, *d* of Capt. Charles Leighton Kennett; *m* 1903, Edith (*d* 1919), *d* of late George J. Thompson; no *c. Educ:* privately. Charing Cross Hospital Resident Medical Officer; Resident Obstetrical Officer Charing Cross Hospital, 1881–82. Travelled in America and the Continent; Medical Superintendent and Hon. Secretary to Bolingbroke Hospital, SW, 1885–1903; made a special study of Electro-Therapeutics. Vice-Pres. of Radiological Section of Royal Society of Medicine. *Publication:* The Treatment of Disease by Different Forms of Rays. *Recreation:* yachting. *Address:* 50 Gordon Mansions, WC1. *T:* Museum 2502; 70 Wimpole Street, W1. *T:* Mayfair 1769.   *Died 26 Jan. 1920.*

LYSTER, Lt-Gen. Harry Hammon, VC 1858; CB 1881; *b* 24 Dec. 1830; *s* of Anthony Lyster of Stillorgan Park, Dublin. Served throughout Central India campaign, 1857–58; Afghan campaigns, 1878–79; commanded 3rd Ghoorka Regt, 1879–87; ISC on US List, 1892; served as special constable in 1847, in London during the time of the Chartist Riots. *Address:* 1 St Mark's Square, Gloucester Gate, NW1. *T:* Hampstead 4997.   *Died 1 Feb. 1922.*

LYSTER, Thomas William, MA; Librarian, National Library of Ireland, 1895–1920; *b* Co. Kilkenny, 17 Dec. 1855; *s* of Thomas Lyster, Rathdowney and Jane Smith, Roscrea. *Educ:* Wesleyan School, Dublin; Dublin University. First Senior Moderatorship at degree. Assistant Librarian, National Library of Ireland, 1878–95; Examiner in English under Intermediate Education Board, 1880, and several subsequent years; Vice-President of Library Association, 1899. *Publications:* translator, with notes, revision, and enlargement, of Düntzer's Life of Goethe, 1883; editor of English Poems for Young Students, 1893, 5th edition 1904; critical papers in The Academy, etc; papers on library technique and theory. *Address:* 10 Harcourt Terrace, Dublin.   *Died 12 Dec. 1922.*

LYTTELTON-ANNESLEY, Lt-Gen. Sir Arthur Lyttelton, KCB 1923; KCVO 1903; Kt 1903; Hon. Colonel 11th Prince Albert's Own Hussars; *b* 2 Sept. 1837; *e s* of Arthur Lyttelton-Annesley, JP, DL, of Arley Castle, Staffordshire, and Camolin Park, County Wexford; unmarried. *Educ:* Harrow. Joined 11th Hussars, 1854; was present at siege and capture of Sevastopol (medal and clasp, Turkish medal); King Edward's and King George's Coronation medals; Knight Commander of the Order of Christ of Portugal, and Kaiser-i-Hind medal; served ten years in India with the 11th, and commanded the regiment for some years, and brought it home; was Aide-de-Camp to Field-Marshal HRH the Duke of Cambridge; was Assistant Adjutant-General of the Forces; Adjutant-General of the Bombay Army; commanded the troops in Scotland for five years; was awarded the good service pension for distinguished and meritorious service; representative in the female line of the Annesleys, Earls of Anglesey,

Earls of Mount Norris, and Viscounts Valentia, and of George, 1st Lord Lyttelton; was on the Staff of Prince of Wales, 1875–76, and returned to England with HRH through Egypt, Spain, and Paris. *Recreations:* travelling, boating, yachting, reading, gardening. *Address:* Templemere, Weybridge. *Club:* Carlton.

Died 16 Feb. 1926.

LYTTON, Lady Constance (Georgina); *b* Vienna, 12 Feb. 1869; *d* of 1st Earl of Lytton. *Educ:* home. Childhood and youth spent chiefly abroad; in 1908, aged 39, realised that women, together with men, participate in life's responsibilities, and should have an equal share in self-government; that the Government had always prevented this; became a Suffragette; four times imprisoned, two hunger-strikes; at the first of these was released because of heart condition, at the second (Walton Jail, Liverpool), disguised as a working woman, heart condition not noticed, and she was forcibly fed; May 1912 had a stroke; invalided since then. *Publications:* No Votes for Women, pamphlet, 1909; Prisons and Prisoners, 1914. *Recreations:* my friends, music, flowers. *Address:* Homewood, Knebworth, Herts. *TA:* Knebworth. *T:* Knebworth 5.

Died 22 May 1923.

LYVEDEN, 3rd Baron, *cr* 1859; **Courtenay Percy Robert Vernon;** Lieutenant RNVR (Transport Service); President of British Committee, Study of Foreign Municipal Institutions; has been a member of dramatic profession since 1882; *b* Grafton Underwood, Kettering, 29 Dec. 1857; *s* of Rev. Hon. Courtenay John Vernon and Alice Gertrude, *d* of late Rev. M. FitzGerald S. Townshend; *S* uncle, 1900; *m* 1st, 1890, Fanny Zelie (*d* 1924), *d* of Major Charles Hill of Wollaston Hall, Wellingboro; one *s* one *d*; 2nd, 1925, Ada, *d* of Arthur Hodgkinson. *Educ:* Eton. For some years Capt. 1st Royal Lanark Militia. Owner of about 4,200 acres. *Recreations:* boating, hunting, shooting. *Heir: s* Hon. Robert Fitzpatrick Courtenay Vernon, *b* 1 Feb. 1892. *Club:* Royal Thames Yacht.

Died 25 Dec. 1926.

M

MAASDORP, Hon. Christian George; Puisne Judge of Supreme Court, Cape Colony, 1885–1910; appointed Judge President of Cape Provincial Division of Supreme Court by first Union Ministry, 1910; *b* Malmesburg, 1848; 3rd *s* of G. H. Maasdorp, MD; *m* 1876, Ella Elizabeth, *d* of late Hon. C. W. Hutton; three *s* two *d*. *Educ:* Graaff Reinet College; Cape University (MA). Called to Bar, Inner Temple, 1871. *Address:* Hillside, Church Street, Rondebosch, Cape Town.

Died May 1926.

MABERLY, Col Charles Evan, DSO 1900; Royal Horse Artillery; retired; *b* 5 April 1854; *s* of late Maj.-Gen. Evan Maberly, CB, of Avonmouth House, Christchurch. *Educ:* RMA, Woolwich. Served Nile Campaign, 1884–85 (Egyptian medal, clasp, bronze star); South Africa, 1899–1900 (severely wounded, despatches, Queen's medal with clasp, DSO). *Address:* 98 Piccadilly, W1. *T:* Mayfair 4779. *Clubs:* St James's, Naval and Military, Pratt's, Arthur's, Boodle's; Kildare Street, Dublin. *Died 7 Sept. 1920.*

MABIE, Hamilton Wright; editor and writer; associate editor of The Outlook since 1879; *b* Cold Spring-on-Hudson, New York; *m* 1876. *Educ:* Williams Coll.; Columbia University; LLD Union College; BA, MA, LHD, Williams College; LLB Columbia University; LLD Western Reserve University. Practised law six or seven years; abandoned it for editorial and literary work. *Publications:* Norse Stories; My Study Fire (first series); Under the Trees and Elsewhere; Short Studies in Literature; Essays in Literary Interpretation; My Study Fire (second series); Essays on Nature and Culture; Essays on Books and Culture; Essays on Work and Culture; The Life of the Spirit; William Shakespeare, Poet, Dramatist, and Man; A Child of Nature; Parables of Life; In Arcady; Backgrounds of Literature; Works and Days; The Great Word; Christmas To-day; Introductions to Notable Poems; American Ideals, Character and Life; Japan, To-day and To-morrow, 1914. *Recreations:* cycling, golf. *Address:* 381 Fourth Avenue, New York City. *Clubs:* Century, Authors', Aldine, Graduates, Alpha Delta Phi, Canoe Brook. *Died Jan. 1917.*

MACALISTER, Alexander, LLD, MD, DSc, MA; FRS, FSA; Professor of Anatomy, Cambridge University, since 1883; Fellow of St John's College; *b* Dublin, 9 April 1844; 2nd *s* of Robert Macalister and Margaret Anne, *y d* of Col James Boyle, Dungiven; *m* 1866, Elizabeth (*d* 1901), *d* of James Stewart, Perth. *Educ:* Trinity Coll. Dublin. Demonstrator of Anatomy, College of Surgeons, 1860; Professor of Zoology, University of Dublin, 1869; Professor of Anatomy and Chirurgery, Dublin, 1877. *Publications:* Introduction to Animal Morphology, 1876; Morphology of Vertebrate Animals, 1878; Text-Book of Human Anatomy, 1889; Evolution in Church History, 1879; Memoir of James Macartney, 1900; besides numerous papers and smaller text-books for students in Zoology and Physiology. *Recreation:* travel. *Address:* Torrisdale, Cambridge.

Died 2 Sept. 1919.

MacALISTER, Sir John Young Walker, Kt 1919; OBE 1920; FSA, FRGS; FJI; Secretary and Editor, Proceedings of Royal Society of Medicine; *b* 1856; *s* of Donald MacAlister, Tarbert, Cantyre; *m* 1874, Elizabeth, 2nd *d* of George Batley, Blackhall, Edinburgh; two *s*. *Educ:* High School, Liverpool; Edinburgh University. Studied medicine for three years; compelled by ill-health to give it up; sub-librarian, Liverpool Library; librarian of Leeds Library; engaged in journalism in connection with Leeds Mercury and Yorkshire Post; 1st librarian, Gladstone Library, 1887; founded The Library, 1889; Hon. Secretary Library Association, 1887–98; President, 1914–19; promoted Consolidating and Amending Library Act, 1892; Chairman of Editing Committee of 7th International Congress of Hygiene; Hon. Sec. Gen. and Organiser of the 2nd Internat. Library Conference, 1897; Commissioner for Paris Exposition, 1900; member of Committee of Internat. Congress on Tuberculosis, 1901; in 1905 formulated scheme for amalgamating the Medical Societies of London, which led to the amalgamation of all the leading societies, with a new Charter under the name of The Royal Society of Medicine; Member of Committee of Japan Exhibition, London, 1910, of College of Ambulance, Village Centre (Enham, Hants), Federation of Medical Societies and Society for prevention of Venereal Diseases, People's League of Health; Founder and first Chairman of the University of London Press, 1910; Hon. Sec. Surgical Advisory Committee, War Office; Organiser and Hon. Sec. Emergency Surgical Aid Corps for Admiralty, War Office, and Metropolitan Police. *Recreation:* sleeping. *Address:* 33 Finchley Road, NW8. *T:* Hampstead 2448. *Clubs:* Athenæum, Garrick, Savage (Hon. Life Member), Bath.

Died 1 Dec. 1925.

MACALPINE, Sir George Watson, Kt 1910; JP; LLD M'Master (Toronto); Chairman of the Altham Colliery Company, Ltd; Great Harwood Colliery Company, Ltd; Accrington Brick and Tile Company, Ltd; Whinney Hill Plastic Brick Company, Ltd; Vice-President of the British and Foreign Bible Society; Ex-President of the Baptist Union; *b* Paisley, 10 March 1850; *m* 1877, Marianne, *y d* of James Barlow, JP, Accrington; four *s* one *d*. *Educ:* John Neilson and Grammar Schools, Paisley. *Publication:* The Days of the Son of Man. *Recreation:* golf. *Address:* Broad Oak, Accrington. *T:* Accrington 2743. *M:* N 4476, etc. *Club:* National Liberal.

Died 18 April 1920.

MACANDREW, Maj.-Gen. Henry John Milnes, CB 1918; DSO 1900; Indian Army, 5th Cavalry; *b* 7 Aug. 1866; *s* of late Sir Henry Macandrew, Aisthorpe, Inverness; *m* 1892, Esther, *y d* of Henry Ritchie Cooper, JP of Ballindalloch, Stirlingshire; one *s* one *d*. *Educ:* The Inverness College. Joined 2nd Batt. Cameron Highlanders, 1884; transferred to Lincoln Regt, 1886; joined 5th Bengal Cavalry, 1889; served as Brigade Transport Officer 2nd Brigade Tirah Expeditionary Force 1897; Brigade Transport Officer Khyber Force, 1898 (Indian Frontier medal with 2 clasps, despatches); served in Kitchener's Horse, South Africa, Feb–June 1900; Intelligence Officer, Delagoa line, July–Sept. 1900; DAAG Intelligence, General Clement's Column, Sept. 1900–Feb. 1901; Feb.–May 1901 DAAG Intelligence to Gen. Hon. Neville Lyttelton, and Gen. Bruce Hamilton May 1901–June 1902; as DAAG Intelligence Army Headquarters Staff, S Africa (S African medal and 4 clasps, King's medal and 2 clasps, DSO, despatches twice); European War, 1914–18 (despatches, CB); Brigade Major to the Inspector-General of Cavalry in India, 1903–5. *Recreation:* gentleman rider across country and on flat. *Address:* Aisthorpe, Inverness, Scotland. *Club:* Cavalry.

Died 16 July 1919.

M'ARDLE, John Stephen, JP; MCh RUI (hc); FRCSI, etc; Professor of Surgery, University College, Dublin, since 1910; Lecturer on Surgery and Senior Surgeon, St Vincent's Hospital, Dublin, since 1886; Consulting Surgeon, Children's Hospital, Temple Street; Consulting Surgeon, Maternity Hospital, Holles Street; *b* Dundalk,

1859; *m*; two *s* two *d*. *Educ*: St Mary's College, Dundalk. House Surgeon, St Vincent's Hospital, 1879–81; Demonstrator of Anatomy, Cecelia Student Medical School, 1880; Staff Surgeon, St Vincent's, 1881; Professor of Surgery, Catholic University, 1900. Member of Senate National University of Ireland; Member of Governing Body, Dublin University College. *Publications*: The Surgery of the Abdomen, 1888; Hydrocele and its Treatment, 1888; Diseases of Joints, 1889; Clinical and Operative Surgery, 1900; Renal Surgery, 1895; Operative Surgery, 1905. *Recreations*: shooting, farming. *Address*: 72 Merrion Square, Dublin; Ballytregue, Wicklow. *T*: Dublin 293. *M*: IK 463–464.   *Died 14 April 1928.*

MACARDLE, Sir Thomas Callan, KBE 1920; JP, DL; Chairman: Macardle, Moore & Co. Ltd; The Dundalk Brewery; Dundalk and Newry Steampacket Co., Ltd; Dundalk Race Co., Ltd; Kinahan Bros, importers and bonders, Ltd; Alpha Trust Ltd; President Dundalk Chamber of Commerce; *b* 14 Jan. 1856; *s* of E. H. Macardle, JP, Cambrieville, Dundalk, and Margaret Callan, Tullagee, Co. Louth; *m* 1888, Minnie, *d* of Lt-Col James Clarke Ross, late Scots Greys; two *s* two *d*. *Educ*: St Mary's College. High Sheriff, County Louth, 1917. *Address*: St Margaret's, Dundalk, Co. Louth, Ireland. *TA*: Macardle, Dundalk. *T*: Dundalk 50. *M*: IY 54. *Clubs*: Stephen's Green, Dublin; Dundalk.   *Died 18 Dec. 1925.*

MACARTHUR, Rt. Rev. James, Assistant Bishop-in-charge of the Isle of Wight since 1921; Archdeacon of Isle of Wight since 1906; *b* 7 June 1848; *m* 1879, Emily Harriette (*d* 1905), *d* of Richard Gardnor, solicitor and high bailiff, Carmarthen; one *d*. *Educ*: Glasgow Univ. (MA 1868). Hon DD Oxon, 1898. Late Fellow, University of Bombay. Called Scottish Bar, 1871; Inner Temple, 1874; Cuddesdon Theological College, 1877–78; ordained, 1878; curate, St Mary, Redcliffe, 1878–80; Rector, Lamplugh, Cumberland, 1880–87; Vicar, St Mary's, Tothill Fields, 1887–92; Vicar, All Saints, South Acton, 1892–98; Rural Dean of Ealing, 1894–98; Bishop of Bombay, 1898–1903; Bishop Suffragan of Southampton, 1903–20. *Address*: Luccombe Hill, Shanklin, Isle of Wight. *TA*: Shanklin. *T*: Shanklin 42. *Club*: Athenæum.   *Died 2 Feb. 1922.*

MACARTHUR, Mary R.; Secretary, Women's Trade Union League and National Federation of Women Workers; Hon. Secretary Central Committee on Women's Employment; Member, National Insurance Advisory Committee; *b* 13 Aug. 1880; *m* 1911, William C. Anderson, MP (*d* 1919); one *d*. *Educ*: Glasgow and Germany. *Recreation*: playgoing. *Address*: 42 Woodstock Road, Golder's Green, NW4. *T*: Finchley 2234.   *Died 1 Jan. 1921.*

M'ARTHUR, William Alexander, DL; *b* Sydney, 1857; *s* of Alexander M'Arthur, MP; *m* 1890, Florence Creemer, *d* of J. C. Clarke, MP. MP (R) E Riding of York (Buckrose Div.) 1886–87; unseated on scrutiny; MP (GL) Cornwall Mid, St Austell, 1887–1908; a Junior Lord of Treasury, 1892–95; one of the Liberal Whips. *Clubs*: Garrick, Devonshire.   *Died 7 June 1923.*

MACARTNEY, John William Merton, CB 1911; CVO 1921; late Colonel commanding Royal Guernsey Light Infantry; *b* 15 Nov. 1850; *e s* of William Merton Macartney, barrister, who was *e* surv. *s* of Rev. Arthur Chichester Macartney, formerly Vicar of Belfast and Templepatrick; at one time Captain in Royal Artillery; the representative of the Macartneys of Blacket who migrated from Kirkcudbright to Co. Antrim, 1629; *m*; three *s* two *d*. *Educ*: HMS Britannia. Joined 54th Foot as Ensign, 1869; Captain in Dorsetshire Regiment, 1881; Major, 1889; Lt-Col 1900; served in India, Egypt, Burmah, and at home; DAAG Rawal Pindi, 1884–86; Guernsey and Alderney Dist, 1900–3; Secretary to the Government in the Island of Guernsey, 1913; resigned command, 2nd RGLI, 1913. *Publications*: History of Development of Tactics; Studies of Waterloo. *Recreations*: much interested in rifle-shooting; member NRA. *Address*: Elmgrove, Guernsey. *TA*: Guernsey. *T*: 2333.

Died 24 May 1925.

MACARTNEY, Rt. Hon. Sir William (Grey) Ellison-, KCMG 1913; PC 1900; JP; *b* Dublin, 7 June 1852; *e s* of late John William Ellison-Macartney and Elizabeth Phœbe, *e d* of Rev. John Grey Porter; *m* 1897, Ettie, *e d* of late John Edward Scott, Outlands, Devonport; one *s* one *d*. *Educ*: Eton; Exeter College, Oxford (BA 1st cl. Honours). MP (U) S Antrim, 1885–1903; Parliamentary Sec. to the Admiralty, 1895–1900; High Sheriff, Co. Antrim, 1908; Deputy-Master, Royal Mint, 1903–13; Governor of Tasmania, 1913–17; Western Australia, 1917–20; Chairman, Governors of the People's Palace, Mile End Road, and of Council of the East London College, University of London. *Address*: 48 Elm Park Road, Chelsea, SW3. *T*: Kensington 5957. *Club*: St Stephen's.   *Died 4 Dec. 1924.*

MACBEAN, Maj.-Gen. Forbes, CB 1900; CVO 1905; ADC to the King, 1907–11; *b* 3 Jan. 1857; *s* of late Col Forbes Macbean, 92nd Highlanders; *m* 1889, Mary Katherine Fishburn, *d* of late Capt. W. T. Forbes Jackson, RN. *Educ*: Uppingham. Entered 92nd Highlanders, 1876; Capt. 1884; Major, 1893; Brevet Lieut-Col 1898; served Afghan War, 1879–80; present at engagements in and around Kabul; present on march from Kabul to Kandahar (medal with three clasps and bronze star); served with 92nd Highlanders, Transvaal Campaign, 1881; with 1st Batt. in Tirah Campaign, 1897–98 (severely wounded, despatches, medal with two clasps, Brevet Lt-Col); S African War, 1899–1902 (despatches, CB, medal with five clasps, King's medal with two clasps, Bt-Col); commanded 1st Batt. Gordon Highlanders, 1900–4; Highland Territorial Division, 1908–11; Bareilly Brigade, 1911–15. *Club*: Army and Navy.   *Died 20 Feb. 1919.*

McBEE, Silas; Editor of the Churchman, 1896–1912; founder and editor of The Constructive Quarterly since 1912; *b* Lincolnton, NC, 14 Nov. 1858. *Educ*: Univ. of the South; Hon. DCL. *Publication*: An Eirenic Itinerary. *Address*: 244 Madison Avenue, New York.

Died 3 Sept. 1924.

MACBETH, Rev. John, LLD; Rector of Killegney and Rossdroit since 1873; Precentor of Ferns Cathedral; *b* 21 May 1841; *s* of Robert Macbeth, of Kilcreevy, Co. Armagh; *m* 1869, Isabella Jemima (*d* 1914), *y d* of Richard Star, of Ballytore, Co. Kildare; one *s* four *d*. *Educ*: Trinity College, Dublin. Held Curacies of Maryborough and of Ferns; was in 1873 presented to his present living; has added a chancel to Killegney Church, restored St Peter's Church, Rossdroit, built a schoolhouse, and enlarged the Glebe House; an examiner under the Intermediate Board of Education, and also under the Board of Religious Education of the General Synod. *Publications*: The Story of Ireland and her Church; Notes on the Book of Common Prayer; Notes on the Thirty-nine Articles; numerous pamphlets. *Recreations*: a frequent speaker on temperance and foreign missions; did much to advance the cause of religious instruction in the secondary schools, and was founder of the Ferns Exhibition with that object. *Address*: Killegney Parsonage, Enniscorthy. *TA*: Clonroche, Co. Wexford.

Died 23 Sept. 1924.

M'BRIDE, Hon. Sir Peter, Kt 1915; Agent-General for Victoria in London 1913–22; formerly Minister of Mines, Minister of Forests, Minister of Railways, and Acting Chief Secretary, State of Victoria, Australia; *b* Dunolly, Victoria, 9 Feb. 1867; *m*; one *s* one *d*. *Educ*: Wesley College, Melbourne. Member of Parliament of Victoria from 1897; Cabinet rank from 1909. Order of St Sava; Belgian Order of the Crown; Grande Officier of the Order of Leopold II (Belgian). *Recreations*: racing, tennis. *Address*: c/o Melbourne Place, Strand, WC. *TA*: Yarra, Estrand, London. *T*: City 8656. *Clubs*: Royal Automobile, Junior Naval and Military, Consitutional, British Empire, Sports, City Carlton, Australian, Royal Thames Yacht; Phyllis Court, Henley; Athenæum, Royal Yacht, Melbourne.

Died March 1923.

M'BRIDE, Sir Richard, KCMG 1912; KC 1905; LLD California 1913; barrister-at-law; Agent General for British Columbia in London since 1916; *b* New Westminster, BC, 15 Dec. 1870; 2nd *s* of Arthur H. M'Bride; *m* 1896, Margaret, *y d* of Neil M'Gillivray; five *c*. *Educ*: Public and High Schools, New Westminster; Dalhousie University, Halifax, Nova Scotia (LLB 1890). Barrister British Columbia, 1892; contested Westminster District for Canadian House of Commons, 1896; returned as member for Dewdney in local elections, 1898, 1900 and 1903; Victoria City, 1907; Victoria City and Yale, 1909; Victoria, 1912; Minister of Mines; Prime Minister, British Columbia, 1903–16; Conservative. *Address*: British Columbia House, 1 and 3 Regent Street, SW.   *Died 6 Aug. 1917.*

McBRYDE, Hon. Duncan Elphinstone; Member of the Legislative Council, Victoria, since 1893; *b* Argyllshire, Scotland, 1853; *m* Ellen, *d* of late Archibald Menzies, Melbourne; two *d*. *Educ*: private school. Left Scotland for Australia; arrived in Melbourne Jan. 1872; directed his attention to pastoral pursuits, finally bought Mount Poole Station, New South Wales; about 1885, silver lead mining in the Broken Hill district (about 200 miles from Mount Poole), was largely engaging public attention; bought an interest in the Broken Hill Proprietary Company, of which he was a Director for 30 years; Director of the Commercial Bank of Australia; one of the original shareholders of the Silverton Tramway Company; was Minister for Public Works. JP for Victoria and New South Wales; Presbyterian. *Recreations*: gardening, fishing, motoring. *Address*: Kamesburgh, Wallace Avenue, Toorak, Victoria. *T*: Brighton 1007. *M*: 284 and 1060. *Club*: Australian, Melbourne.   *Died Nov. 1920.*

M'CABE, Sir Daniel, Kt 1916; JP; DL; Lord Mayor, Manchester, 1914–15; Director of Manchester Ship Canal; Alderman of the City of Manchester; *b* 1852. Knight of St Sylvester. *Address:* 104 Rochdale Road, Blackley, Manchester.

Died 29 Sept. 1919.

MACCALL, Hon. Maj.-Gen. Henry Blackwood, CB 1896; commanding 2nd Class District, India, 1901–2; retired; *b* 15 Aug. 1845; *s* of late Col George Maccall; *m* 1885, Grace Mabel, *d* of P. J. Farquharson, Langton House, Blandford. Entered army, 1864; Col 1895; served Izazai Expedition 1892; Chitral Relief Force, 1895 (despatches, CB, medal with clasp). *Club:* Army and Navy.

Died 22 July 1921.

M'CALL, Hon. Sir John, Kt 1911; MD, LLD; Agent-General for Tasmania in London since 1909; Member of House of Assembly and Member of the Executive Council; Warden of Leven Municipality and Chairman of Leven Harbour Trust; *b* Devonport, Tasmania, 20 Aug. 1860; *s* of late Hon. John Hair M'Call; *m* twice; three *s* one *d*. *Educ:* Glasgow University. Gave a large amount of time to service of the public, both in Local Government and Parliament; was Chief Secretary in Propsting Government and Pres. of Central Board of Health; President of the Australian Natives Association in London; Medical Officer in charge of Australian Officers' Hospital in London. *Recreations:* practically none. *Address:* 56 Victoria Street, SW; 30 Nevern Mansions, SW. *T:* Western 3562. *Clubs:* British Empire, Australasian.

Died 27 June 1919.

McCALLUM, Col Sir Henry Edward, GCMG 1904 (KCMG 1898; CMG 1887); RE; Governor of Ceylon, 1907–13; *b* Yeovil, 28 Oct. 1852; *e s* of Maj. H. A. M'Callum, RMLI, and Eleanor, *d* of Major Brutton, RMLI; *m* 1897, Maud, 3rd *d* of Lt-Col Creighton, RMLI; one *s* three *d*. *Educ:* privately; Royal Military Academy, Woolwich. Passed from Woolwich first out of fifty-two cadets, 1871, Pollock medallist, 1871, Fowke medallist, 1874; Chatham, 1871–74; Superintendent Telegraphy Southern District, 1874; Inspector-General Fortifications office, 1874–75; Private Secretary to Sir William Jervois, Governor Straits Settlements, 1875–77; several times mentioned in despatches, Perak medal and clasp; Superintendent Admiralty Works, Hong-Kong, 1877–78; Singapore, 1878–79; Royal Arsenal, Woolwich, 1879–80; Deputy Colonial Engineer, Penang, 1880–84; Colonial Engineer and Surveyor-General, Straits Settlements, member Executive and Legislative Councils, 1884–97; Commandant Singapore Volunteer Artillery, 1888–97; Special Commissioner in Pahang, Malay Peninsula, to suppress outbreak (received thanks of HM Government), 1891; Governor and Commander-in-Chief, Lagos, 1897–99; special mission to Hinterland in connection with French aggression in Lagos (received thanks of HM Government), 1898 (West African medal and clasp); Governor of Newfoundland, 1898–1901; ADC to HM, 1900–1; Governor of Natal, 1901–7 (South African medal with four clasps; Natal Rebellion Medal). Decorated: CMG, construction of fortifications, Singapore; KCMG, special services, Lagos Hinterland; GCMG, special services in South Africa. *Recreations:*cricket, shooting, fishing, golf. *Address:* Lauriston, Crawley Ridge, Camberley. *Club:* Junior United Service.

Died 24 Nov. 1919.

M'CALLUM, Sir John Mills, Kt 1912; JP Co. Renfrew; MP (L) Paisley since 1906; *b* 1847; *s* of late John M'Callum, senior, of J. and J. M'Callum, dyers, Paisley; *m* 1875, Agnes, *d* of Stephen Oates, JP, ship-broker, Grimsby. *Educ:* John Neilson Institution, Paisley. Chairman of firm of Isdale and M'Callum, Ltd, soap-makers, Paisley; from early manhood took active interest in the social and religious progress of the town and was closely associated with the Paisley Liberal Club; he was for a number of years a member of the Town Council, and served a period on the magisterial bench. *Address:* Southdene, Castlehead, Paisley. *T:* 409. *Clubs:* National Liberal; Scottish Liberal, Edinburgh; Glasgow Liberal.

Died 10 Jan. 1920.

McCALMONT, Maj.-Gen. Sir Hugh, KCB 1900 (CB 1885); CVO 1903; *b* 9 Feb. 1845; *e s* of late James McCalmont, Abbeylands, Co. Antrim, and Emily, *d* of late James Martin, Ross, Co. Galway; *m* 1885, Hon. Rose Elizabeth Bingham, 3rd *d* of 4th Baron Clanmorris; one *s*. *Educ:* Eton. MP (C) North Antrim, 1895–99. Entered army, 1865; Capt. 1869; Major, 1878; Lt-Col 1885; Maj.-Gen. 1896; served Red River Expedition 1870 (despatches, medal); Gold Coast, 1873 (medal); Armenia, 1877 (brevet of Major, medal); ADC to Sir Garnet Wolseley, South Africa, 1879 (despatches, Brevet Lt-Col, medal with clasp); expedition against Marris, 1880 (despatches); Egypt, 1882, including Kassassin twice, Tel-el-Kebir, and capture of Cairo (despatches, medal with clasp, 3rd class Medjidie, Khedive's Star);

Nile Expedition, 1884–85 (despatches, brevet of Col, CB and clasp); commanded Cork District, 1898–1903; retired, 1906; Colonel, 7th Hussars, 1907. *Recreations:* hunting, shooting, cycling, etc. *Address:* 5 Carlos Place, W1; Mount Juliet, Thomastown, Co. Kilkenny. *Clubs:* Carlton, Army and Navy, Bachelors; Kildare Street, Dublin; Royal St George Yacht, Kingstown.

Died 2 May 1924.

McCANN, Pierce; MP (SF) East Tipperary since 1918.

Died 6 March 1919.

McCARTHY, Sir Frank, Kt 1923; CBE; journalist. *Address:* Rangoon, Burma.

Died 13 Feb. 1924.

M'CARTHY, James Desmond, CMG 1891; Colonial Surgeon, 1880; Chief Medical Officer, Gold Coast, 1884; retired, 1893; *b* Oct. 1839; *s* of John M'Carthy, Cork; *m* 1895, Clara Augusta, *d* of Horatio Bethune Leggatt, Hants. Surgeon RN, 1872–74. Served Ashanti Expedition, 1873 (despatches, medal and clasp); Assistant Surgeon, Lagos, W Africa, 1877. Decorated for services on Gold Coast. *Publications:* report on Ventilation and Analysis of Air in HMS "Devastation"; various sanitary reports and papers, including analysis of water-supply of Gold Coast and Lagos; paper on Disposal of Sewage in Tropical Climates, read before the Congress of the Royal Institute of Health, Dublin, Aug. 1898. *Recreations:* yachting, shooting. *Address:* Pitmore Cottage, Sway, Hants.

Died 29 July 1923.

M'CARTHY, Jeremiah, MA, MB; FRCS; Consulting Surgeon London Hospital. *Educ:* Trinity College, Dublin; London Hospital. Was Lecturer on Surgery London Hosp. Medical College. *Address:* 1 Cambridge Place, Victoria Road, W.

Died 26 April 1924.

McCARTHY, Michael John Fitzgerald; barrister-at-law; author; *b* Midleton, Co. Cork; *s* of Denis McCarthy and Catherine Fitzgerald of Clonmult; *m* 1887, Margaret, *d* of John Ronayne of Donickmore. *Educ:* Vincentian Seminary, Cork; Midleton College, Co. Cork; Trinity College, Dublin. BA 1885; called to the Bar, 1889; took no part in public life until the appearance of Five Years in Ireland, 1901; since then was writer and speaker against the power exercised by the Roman Catholic Church in politics and in education. Stood for Stephen's Green Parliamentary Division of Dublin, 1904, but retired to avoid a split in the Unionist vote; started and conducted Christian Defence Effort in opposition to Papal aggression. *Publications:* Five Years in Ireland, 1895–1900, 1901, tenth edition, 1903; Priests and People in Ireland, 1902, fifth edition, 1905, popular edition, 1908; Rome in Ireland, 1904; Gallowglass, or Life in the Land of the Priests, 1904; Catholic Ireland and Protestant Scotland, 1905; The Coming Power, a Contemporary History of the Far East, 1905; Church and State in England and Wales, 1906; Irish Land and Irish Liberty, 1910; The Nonconformist Treason, 1912; The Irish Revolution, vol. i, 1912; The Dictators, 1913; many Letters to Parliament, and other publications in opposition to Home Rule, 1913–20; The British Monarchy and the See of Rome, 1924; The Irish Papal State, 1925; Church and Empire Breaking, 1927; Anglo-Catholic Bolshevism, 1927; The Bishops and the House of Commons, 1928. *Recreations:* reading, observing, walking. *Address:* 13 Alwyne Mansions, Wimbledon, SW.

Died 26 Oct. 1928.

M'CARTHY, Robert Henry, CMG 1906; JP; *b* 9 May 1856; *s* of Jeremiah M'Carthy of Cork; *m* 1877, Mary Emily, *d* of Richard Beamish, of Ballinora, Co. Cork; one *d*. *Educ:* privately. Imperial Customs, 1875–95; formerly Collector of Customs and Member of the Executive and Legislative Councils of Trinidad; retired, 1908; Special Services: Missions in connection with commercial treaties to Washington, 1899 and 1900; Ottawa and Caracas, 1900; to Barbadoes West Indian Conferences on Quarantine, 1904 and 1907; and in 1908 Conference at Barbadoes on West Indian trade with Canada; Reported upon and reorganised Malta Customs, 1908–10; technical adviser Royal Commission on Trade between Canada and the West Indies, 1909 and 1910. *Recreations:* billiards, chess, golf. *Address:* Lampton, Hounslow.

Died 12 March 1927.

McCARTHY, Tim; Editor Irish News, Belfast, since 1906; *e s* of late Denis McCarthy of Cloghroe, Cork; *m* Katie, *d* of late Denis M'Lynn Sligo. *Educ:* National Schools; privately. Reporter and Editor Cork Herald and Cork Weekly Herald; Sub-Editor, News Editor and Leader writer Evening Sun; Sub-Editor and Leader Writer Dublin Evening Telegraph; Acting-Editor Irish People (organ of the United Irish League); sentenced to imprisonment, 1902–3; editor series of Provincial papers in Ulster, 1904–6. *Publications:* many articles in

magazines; a short History of the Irish Brigade in France. *Recreations:* walking, travelling in Ireland. *Address:* 131 Antrim Road, Belfast.
Died 30 Dec. 1928.

MACCARTHY, Rt. Rev. Welbore, DD; *m* 1872, Emily Fearon, *d* of William Delves; two *d. Educ:* St Aidans, Birkenhead; Trinity Coll., Dublin. Curate of Preston-Patrick, 1867-68; Ulverston, 1868-71; Christ Church, Battersea, 1871-72; Balham, 1872-73; Chaplain at Jhansi, 1874-75; Rangoon, 1875-77; St Paul's Cathedral, Calcutta, 1877-82; Bishop's Commissary, 1879-82, and 1891-98; Mussoorie, 1882-84; Meerut, 1884-85; Shahjehanpore, 1885-87; Lucknow, 1888-89; Chaplain, St Paul's Cathedral, Calcutta, 1889-98; Archdeacon of Calcutta, 1892-98; Rector of Ashwell, 1898-1901; Vicar of Gainsborough, 1901-5; Prebendary of Lincoln Cathedral, 1901; Rural Dean of Corringham, 1901; Vicar of Grantham, 1905; Rural Dean of North Grantham and Prebendary of Empingham in Lincoln Cathedral, 1905; Rector of North and South Stoke and Rural Dean of Beltisloe, 1910-18; Bishop of Grantham (Suffragan to Lincoln), 1905-18. *Address:* 20 Somerset Road, West Ealing. *Club:* Oriental. *Died 21 March 1925.*

MACCARTIE, Lt-Col Frederick Fitzgerald, CIE 1898; JP; MB; IMS; retired; *b* 6 Aug. 1851; *s* of late Justin Maccartie of Carrignavar, Cork; *m* 1881, Julie Charlotte, *d* of Capt. J. A. Vanrenen; two *d.* Surgeon, 1878; Lt-Col 1898; served Afghan War, 1878-80 (medal). *Address:* Carrignavar, Co. Cork. *Clubs:* Bombay Yacht; Cork County.
Died Nov. 1916.

M'CAUGHEY, Hon. Sir Samuel, Kt 1905; Member of Legislative Council, New South Wales since 1899; *b* Ballymena, Ireland, 1835; unmarried. Went to Australia 1876; presented twenty battle-planes to the State. *Address:* North Yanco, Yanco, NSW. *Club:* Union, Sydney. *Died 28 July 1919.*

McCAULEY, Ven. George James; Archdeacon of Sierra Leone and Canon of St George's Cathedral since 1916. Ordained 1863; Assistant Native Missionary at Wilberforce, 1863-67; Pastor of Wellington, 1867-80; Pastor of Kissy, 1880-94; Assistant Colonial Chaplain for six months at the Gambia, 1882; Pastor of St John's, Brookfield, 1900-8; Pastor of Christ Church, 1908-11. Hon. MA, University of Durham, 1912. *Address:* Freetown, Sierra Leone.
Died 5 Jan. 1917.

M'CAUSLAND, Lt-Gen. Edwin Loftus; *y s* of late Rev. W. H. M'Causland; *m* Georgina, *o c* of Very Rev. James Mitchell, DD; two *s* one *d. Educ:* privately. Joined Royal Marine Light Infantry, 1876; took part in Egyptian War, 1882; severely wounded at Tel-el-Kebir (medal and clasp, Khedive's bronze star); Commandant Chatham Division, 1909-10; Maj.-Gen., 1910; retired pay, 1922. *Recreations:* golf, sketching. *Address:* Solent Lodge, Lee-on-Solent, Hants. *Club:* Cocoa Tree. *Died 12 Oct. 1923.*

McCAUSLAND, Maj.-Gen. William Henry, RA; *b* 11 May 1836; *m* Mary (*d* 1915). Entered army, 1854; Maj.-Gen. 1889; retired, 1890; served China War, 1860 (medal with clasp).
Died 17 Nov. 1916.

MACCAW, William John MacGeagh, FRGS; MP (U) West Down, 1908-18; *b* 1850; *s* of Rev. William MacCaw, DD, and Sarah, *d* of John MacGeagh, JP; *m* Eleanor Elizabeth (*d* 1918), *d* of Walter Hardy, solicitor; two *s* two *d. Educ:* privately. Lived for twenty years in India; travelled extensively in the East and in Europe; contested (U) East Tyrone, Jan. and July 1906. *Recreations:* golfing, shooting. *Address:* 103 Eaton Square, SW1; Rooksnest Park, Godstone, Surrey. *Clubs:* Carlton, Oriental, City of London.
Died 3 March 1928.

McCAWLEY, Hon. Thomas William; Chief Justice of the Supreme Court of Queensland since 1922, and President of the Court of Industrial Arbitration since 1917; *b* Toowoomba, Queensland, 24 July 1881; *s* of late James McCawley; *m* 1911, Margaret Mary, *d* of late Thomas O'Hogan; three *s* one *d. Educ:* St Patrick's Boys' School, Toowoomba. Entered Public Service of Queensland, 1898; First Clerk, Dept of Justice, 1905; called to Bar, 1907; Crown Solicitor, 1910-17; Under-Secretary for Justice, 1915-17; Judge of the Supreme Court of Queensland, 1917; Member of Senate of University of Queensland. *Address:* Windermere Road, Ascot, Brisbane.
Died 16 April 1925.

M'CLELAN, Hon. Abner Reid; *b* 1831; *y s* of late Peter M'Clelan, a Justice of the Court of Common Pleas; *g s* of Peter M'Clelan, who, with Miss Wilson, whom he subsequently married, came to Nova Scotia from Londonderry, Ireland; remoter ancestry from Galloway, Scotland; *m* Anna B., *d* of late W. J. Reid, Collector of Customs at port of Harvey. *Educ:* Mount Allison, Sackville (DCL). LLD Univ. of New Brunswick. Elected to Provincial Parliament of New Brunswick, 1854, and each subsequent election till 1867, when he resigned seat and office of Chief of Public Works in the Government to enter the Dominion Senate; appointed Lieut-Gov. 1896; always a Liberal in politics, favouring free trade and a closer union with Great Britain and the Empire. *Address:* Riverside, Albert County, NB (place of his birth). *Club:* Union, St John.
Died 30 Jan. 1917.

M'CLELLAN, Rev. John B., MA; Hon. Member Surveyors' Institution; late Principal Royal Agricultural College, Cirencester. Formerly Fellow of Trinity College, Cambridge, and Rural Dean of North Camps, Diocese of Ely. *Publications:* New Translation of New Testament, vol. i, from a Revised Greek Text, with Harmony of the Four Gospels, Notes, and Dissertations; Treatise on the Election and Consecration of Bishops. *Address:* Ruthven, The Avenue, Kew Gardens, SW. *Died 24 April 1916.*

M'CLELLAND, Prof. John Alexander, FRS 1909; MA, DSc (RUI), MA (Camb.), ScD (Dublin); Professor of Experimental Physics, University College, Dublin; Commissioner of National Education, Ireland; *b* 1870; *s* of Wm M'Clelland of Dunallis, Coleraine; *m* 1901, Ina, *d* of J. Esdale; two *s* three *d. Educ:* Academical Institution, Coleraine; Queen's College, Galway, Royal University; First Science Scholar, Galway; Special Prizeman, MA degree (RUI) 1893; 1851 Exhibition Scholarship, 1894; Junior Fellowship (RUI) 1895, Fellowship, 1901; Trinity College, Cambridge (Research degree, Cambridge, 1897). Prof. of Physics, University College, Dublin, 1900; Member of Senate of National University of Ireland and of Governing Body of University College, 1908; Secretary of Royal Irish Academy; member of Advisory Council for Scientific and Industrial Research. *Publications:* papers on physical subjects in various journals. *Recreation:* golf. *Address:* Rostrevor, Orwell Road, Rathgar, Dublin.
Died 13 April 1920.

McCLELLAND, Sir Peter Hannay, KBE 1918; *b* 1856; *s* of Thomas McClelland and Margaret Davidson. *Educ:* Wigtown Normal School; George Watson's Coll., Edinburgh. A partner of Duncan, Fox & Co., Liverpool, London and South America; a Liveryman of the Girdlers' Guild; a Life Governor of the Royal Scottish Corporation; Director of the South American Export Syndicate, Ltd. *Recreations:* motoring, horsemanship. *Address:* Eaton House, 66A Eaton Square, SW1. *T:* Victoria 6648; Springfield, Northaw, Herts. *Clubs:* Royal Automobile, Argentine. *Died 14 Jan. 1924.*

McCLINTOCK, Very Rev. Francis George le Poer; Rector of Drumcar since 1886; Dean of Armagh since 1908; Chaplain to Lord-Lieutenant since 1908. *Educ:* Trinity College, Cambridge (MA). Curate of Kilsaran, 1878-79; Rector, 1879-86. *Address:* Drumcar, Dunleer SO, Co. Louth. *Died 3 Feb. 1924.*

M'CLURE, Rev. Edmund, MA; MRIA; Secretary of the Society for Promoting Christian Knowledge, 1875-1915; Hon. Canon, Bristol; *b* Ireland of Scotch parentage; *m* twice; two *s* one *d. Educ:* Trinity College, Dublin; Germany. Curate in Belfast for ten years; travelled in Australia, South Seas, South America, and United States, etc; acquainted with French, German, Dutch, Danish, Spanish, Italian, Celtic, Latin, Greek, Hebrew, Aramaic, Syriac and other languages. *Publications:* a chapter of English Church History, 1888; a Star Atlas (2nd edn 1901), translated and adapted from German of Professor Klein; Historical Church Atlas, 1897; (joint) History of SPCK, 1898; British Place-Names in their Historical Setting, 1909; Modern Substitutes for Traditional Christianity, 1913; 2nd edn with additional section on Modernism, 1914; Spiritualism, Historical and Critical Sketch, 1916; translator: Hommel's Hebrew Tradition, 1897; Prof. Kittel's Babylonian Excavations and Early Bible History, new edn 1903; Prof. Pellat's (from French), The New State of Matter, 1905; Dr Troelstra's De Naam Gods in den Pentateuch, 1912; Pfarrer Dahse's Is a Revolution in Pentateuch Criticism at hand? 1912. *Recreations:* study was his chief recreation; chiefly interested in recent scientific research and in linguistic questions concerning the Bible. *Address:* 80 Eccleston Square, SW1. *T:* Victoria 3418; St Leonard's, Malvern Link. *M:* LA 8401. *Club:* Reform.
Died 18 Nov. 1922.

McCLURE, Sir John David, Kt 1913; Headmaster of Mill Hill School since 1891; *b* 9 Feb. 1860; *s* of late John McClure, JP, Wigan; *m* 1889, *d* of late J. Johnstone, Holcombe, Lancs; one *s* two *d. Educ:* privately; Owens Coll. Manchester; Trinity Coll. Cambridge; LLD, MA

(Cantab.); DMusLond. Assistant Master, Hinckley Grammar School, 1878–82; entered Trinity College, Cambridge, of which College afterwards Exhibitioner and Prizeman; graduate in Mathematics and Law. Lecturer under the Camb. Univ. Extension Syndicate, 1885–91; Prof. of Astronomy, Queen's Coll. London, 1888–94; Barrister Inner Temple, 1890; elected by the Graduates in Arts to the Senate of the newly constituted University of London, 1900, but resigned owing to ill-health, 1901; Joint Hon. Secretary IAHM, 1904–13; Chairman of the Congregational Union of England and Wales, 1919–20. *Recreations:* travel, curling. *Hobby:* music. *Address:* Mill Hill School, NW. *TA:* Millhillian, London. *T:* 208 PO Finchley. *Club:* Savile.

Died 18 Feb. 1922.

M'CLYMONT, Rt. Rev. James Alexander, CBE 1919; VD; DD (Edin.); Editor of Church of Scotland Guild Text-Books and Guild Library; Convener of Committee on Chaplains to HM Forces; Principal Clerk of the General Assembly; Moderator of General Assembly of Church of Scotland, 1921–22; Principal Chaplain of Church of Scotland in this country with rank of Brigadier General, 1917–19; Trustee of Iona Cathedral; *b* Girvan, Ayrshire, 26 May 1848; 4th *s* of late Samuel M'Clymont, JP, Milburne, Girvan; *m* 1886, Agnes, 5th *d* of late Thomas Smith, JP, Ashwood, near Dundee. *Educ:* Girvan Grammar School; Ayr Academy; Edinburgh University; Tübingen. *Publications:* Beck's Pastoral Theology of The New Testament (joint-translation with Rev. T. Nicol); The New Testament and its Writers, an Introduction to the Books of the New Testament; volume on St John's Gospel in The Century Bible; text of Greece (Beautiful Books series); New Testament Criticism, its History and Results (Baird Lecture, 1910–11). *Recreations:* travelling, curling, golfing. *Address:* 22 Murrayfield Drive, Edinburgh. *Clubs:* Authors'; Conservative, Edinburgh.

Died 19 Sept. 1927.

McCOMB, Col Robert Brophy, CB 1900; ASC; retired; *b* 22 Nov. 1855. Entered army, 1874; Col, 1900; served Egyptian War, 1882 (medal and Khedive's star); Bechuanaland Expedition, 1884–85; Zululand, 1888; South Africa, 1899–1902, as Asst Adjt-Gen. (despatches, Queen's medal, King's medal, two clasps, CB). *Address:* c/o Lloyds Bank, Ltd (Cox's Branch), 6 Pall Mall, SW1.

Died 18 Nov. 1925.

M'CONAGHEY, Lt-Col Allen, CIE 1911; *b* 31 March 1864. Entered army, 1884; Captain ISC 1895; Major, Indian Army, 1902; Lt-Col 1910; Political Assistant Quetta-Pishin, 1896; Political Agent, Sinjawi, 1902; Chagai, 1904; Kalat, 1904; Deputy Commissioner, Sibi, 1905; Political Agent, Zhob, 1906; Political Agent and Deputy Commissioner in Quetta-Pishin, 1907–19; retired 1919. *Club:* United Service.

Died 31 May 1925.

McCONNELL, John Wanklyn, JP, Ayrshire and Manchester; MA (Cantab.); Chairman Fine Cotton Spinners and Doublers Association, Limited; Director, The Williams Deacon's Bank, Ltd; *b* 14 Feb. 1855; *s* of William McConnel of Manchester and Knockdolian, Ayrshire and Margaret Bradshaw Wanklyn; *m* 1885, Edith, *yr d* of Rev. R. H. Cobbold, Rector of Ross, Herefordshire; no *c. Educ:* Repton; Caius College, Cambridge. Called to Bar, Lincoln's Inn, 1880; Managing Director and Chairman of McConnel Co. Ltd, Fine Spinners, until its incorporation in the Fine Spinners Association; interested in cotton growing since 1907; served on the Empire Cotton Growing Committee. *Publications:* A Century of Fine Cotton Spinning; various pamphlets on Cotton Growing. *Recreations:* fishing, shooting, golf, etc. *Address:* Knockdolian, Colmonell, Ayrshire; 6 St James's Square, Manchester. *Clubs:* British Empire; Union, Manchester; Prestwick and Formby Golf.

Died 25 May 1922.

M'CONNELL, Sir Robert John, 1st Bt, *cr* 1900; DL; *b* 6 Feb. 1853; *s* of Joseph M'Connell of Clogher; *m* 1st, 1874, Mary (*d* 1896), *d* of Charles Smylie; three *s* one *d* (and two *s* three *d* decd); 2nd, 1897, Elsie, *d* of George Hewson (whom he *div.* 1904). Was created a baronet on the occasion of Queen Victoria's visit to Belfast; Lord Mayor of Belfast, 1900. *Heir: s* Joseph McConnell [*b* 17 Sept. 1877; *m* 1900, Lisa, *d* of late Jackson M'Gown; two *s* one *d. Address:* Glen Dhu, Belfast]. *Address:* Glen Dhu, Belfast. *Club:* Constitutional.

Died 22 April 1927.

McCORKILL, Hon. John Charles, DCL, University of Bishops College; LLD, Laval University; a Puisne Judge, Superior Court, Montreal, since 1906; *b* 31 Aug. 1854; *s* of Robert and Margaret McCorkill; *m* 1884, Apphia Mary, *y d* of late Hon. Elijah Leonard. *Educ:* St John's High School; McGill Normal School and McGill College, Montreal. Advocate, 1878; KC 1899; MPP (L) Missisquoi, 1897; Legislative Councillor, District of Bedford, 1898–1903; MPP

Co. Brome, Quebec, 1903–6; Treasurer of the Province and Member of the Executive Council, 1903–6; Major (retired) Fifth Royal Scots, Montreal. *Recreation:* golf. *Address:* Braeside, 189 Grande Allee, Quebec. *Clubs:* Garrison, Quebec; St James's, Montreal.

Died 10 March 1920.

McCORMICK, Rev. James; Rector of Moyrus-Roundstone, since 1878; Canon of Tuam since 1892; *m; six s* one *d. Educ:* Trinity College, Dublin (MA, DD). Ordained, 1876; Curate of Tuam, 1876–78; Superintendent, Irish Church Mission; Member of the General Synod, Church of Ireland, from 1890; Diocesan Nominator from 1903; Member of Diocesan Council from 1889. *Address:* Roundstone, SO, Co. Galway.

Died 6 May 1921.

McCORMICK, Very Rev. Joseph Gough, DD; Dean of Manchester since 1920; *b* London, 1874; *s* of late Rev. Joseph McCormick, DD, Rector of St James's, Piccadilly, and Frances Harriett, *d* of Col and Hon. Mrs Haines; *m* Alison Mary, *d* of Rev. E. Conybeare; two *s* two *d. Educ:* Exeter School; St John's College, Cambridge (Winchester Prizeman). Ordained 1897; Curate at Great Yarmouth; Vicar of St Paul's, Princes Park, Liverpool, 1901; Vicar of St Michael's, Chester Square, 1909–20; Hon. Chaplain to the King, 1915; Chaplain to the King, 1918; Proctor in Convocation for the Diocese of London, 1919; Chaplain to IZ 1923; Vice-President Lancs Co. Cricket Club, 1924. *Publications:* Plain Words on Vexed Questions; Christ and Common Topics. *Recreation:* cricket, Norfolk County XI, from 1899. *Address:* The Deanery, Manchester. *Club:* New Oxford and Cambridge.

Died 30 Aug. 1924.

M'CORMICK, Robert; Ambassador of the United States to France, 1905–7; *b* Rockbridge, Co. Virginia; *s* of William Sanderson M'Cormick and Mary Ann Grigsby; *m* 1876, Katharine Medill, *d* of Joseph Medill, Chicago. *Educ:* University of Virginia. Secretary United States Legation, London, 1889–92; Official Representative in London of Chicago Columbian Exposition, 1892–93; United States Minister to Austria-Hungary, 1901–2, when raised to rank of Ambassador; at Petrograd, 1902–5. *Recreations:* shooting, riding, golf, etc. *Address:* American Embassy, Paris. *Clubs:* St James's; Chicago, Washington Park, Chicago Golf, Chicago; Union, University, Players, New York; Metropolitan and County, Washington; Jockey, Petrograd.

Died 18 April 1919.

MACCRACKEN, Henry Mitchell, DD, LLD; Chancellor Emeritus, 1910; Chancellor of New York University, 1885–1910; *b* Oxford, Ohio, 28 Sept. 1840; *e s* of late Rev. John Steele Maccracken; *m* Catherine, *o d* of Rev. Thomas Swan Hubbard, Vermont; three *s* one *d. Educ:* Miami University, Oxford, Ohio; Princeton Theological Seminary; Germany. In charge of Presbyterian parishes in Columbus, Ohio and Toledo, Ohio, 1863–81; Chancellor of University of Pittsburgh, Pa, 1881–84. *Publications:* Lives of Church Leaders; Book of the Hall of Fame, which foundation he organised, 1900. *Address:* University Heights, New York City. *T:* Tremont 4332.

Died 24 Dec. 1919.

M'CRAE, Sir George, Kt 1908; DSO 1917; JP for County of the City of Edinburgh; MP (L) Stirling and Falkirk District of Burghs, 1923–24; *b* 29 Aug. 1860; *m* 1880, Eliza Cameron Russell (*d* 1913); four *s* (one killed in the War) five *d. Educ:* Edinburgh Lancastrian School; Heriot-Watt College, Edinburgh. Entered Town Council of Edinburgh, 1889; elected Treasurer of the city, 1891; Chairman of Finance Committee, 1891–99; was successful in promoting various financial and other reforms in the City Council; MP (L) East Edinburgh, 1899–1909; Vice-President and Chairman of the Local Government Board for Scotland, 1909; Chairman Scottish Board of Health, 1919–22. Hon. Col Territorial Force (VD) and Hon. Lt-Col in the Army. Raised a Battalion of 1550 in twelve days in 1914, and two reserve companies of 250 men each later; this Battalion became the 16th (S) Battalion The Royal Scots, which he commanded in European War (despatches twice, DSO). *Publications:* Lectures on Municipal Finance, etc. *Recreations:* riding, golf. *Address:* Torluish, North Berwick. *Club:* Reform.

Died 27 Dec. 1928.

McCRAITH, Sir James William, Kt 1918; JP; *b* 19 March 1853; *s* of William McCraith, Kirkcudbrightshire, and Sarah, *d* of James Yorke, Northamptonshire; *m* 1876, Maria Elizabeth, *d* of Thomas and Elizabeth Dickinson of Holly Mount, Notts; three *s* one *d. Educ:* King's School, Grantham. Chairman City of Nottingham Unionist Association; Trustee Nottingham Savings Bank; ex-President Nottingham Law Society; ex-President Notaries of England and Wales. *Recreations:* shooting, golf, tennis. *Address:* The Park, Nottingham. *T:* 852. *Club:* Carlton.

Died 9 July 1928.

M'CRAITH, Sir John Tom, Kt 1904; JP; *b* 8 Nov. 1847; *s* of late W. M'Craith. Director of Nottingham and Notts Banking Co.; Trustee, Nottingham Savings Bank; Chairman of Nottingham and County Constitutional Club; Alderman of the City of Nottingham; Vice-Chairman of the Nottinghamshire Territorial Assoc. *Address:* Park Terrace, Nottingham.   *Died 5 Dec. 1919.*

McCRAKEN, Sir Robert, Kt 1922; Chairman of Steel Brothers & Co. Ltd; *b* 4 Nov. 1846; *s* of James McCraken of Ardwell, Ayrshire; *m* 1890, Pauline, *d* of late Edouard Chrestien; three *d. Educ:* Ayr Academy. *Address:* 23 Kensington Palace Gardens, W8. *T:* Park 3962. *Clubs:* Oriental, Ranelagh.   *Died 3 Nov. 1924.*

McCUBBIN, Frederick; Australian artist; landscape and portrait painter; Drawing Master at the National Gallery, Melbourne, since 1884; *b* West Melbourne, 25 Feb. 1855; *s* of A. McCubbin, Garvin, Ayrshire; *m* 1889, Annie Moriarty. *Educ:* St Paul's, Swanston Street, and Wilmot's School, West Melbourne. First Examiner in Drawing Matriculation, Melbourne University, from 1900; exhibited at Paris Salon, 1897, and at the Grafton Galleries, London. *Pictures:* Down on his Luck (Perth Gallery); A Bush Burial (Geelong Gallery); The Pioneers and Winter Evening (Melbourne Gallery); On the Wallaby Track (Sydney Gallery); Ti-tree Glade, and portrait of the artist (Adelaide Gallery). *Address:* Carlsberg, Kensington Road, South Yarra, Melbourne, Australia.   *Died 22 Dec. 1917.*

McCUBBIN, Lt-Col Thomas, CMG 1901; JP; late Durban Light Infantry. Served South Africa, 1899–1901, in command of Durban Light Infantry (despatches twice, Queen's medal with clasp, CMG). *Address:* Durban, Natal.   *Died 15 Dec. 1925.*

MACCULLAGH, Sir James Acheson, Kt 1896; JP; Medical Inspector Local Government Board; *b* Dublin, 4 Oct. 1854; *e s* of late John MacCullagh, RM; *m* 1880, Ida M'Clelland. *Educ:* Ennis Coll.; Dublin University (BA, MD) (Stip. Cond.). House Surgeon Londonderry City and County Infirmary. Mayor of Londonderry thrice. *Recreations:* president NW Football Association, president Londonderry Cycling Club, capt. Londonderry Cricket Association. *Address:* Lisgorm, Galway. *Club:* County, Galway.
                                                    Died July 1918.

McCULLOCH, Allan Riverstone; Zoologist of the Australian Museum, Sydney, since 1906; Specialist in ichthyology; *b* 20 June 1885; *s* of Herbert Riverstone McCulloch and Ella Maud Backhouse; unmarried. *Educ:* Sydney. Entered service of the Australian Museum as a Voluntary Cadet, 1898; joined the salaried staff, 1902; fishes trawled by the Federal Investigation Vessel Endeavour and the collection of the Australian Museum provided most of the material for his studies; engaged on a Catalogue of Australian Fishes; elected to the Councils of the Linnean and Zoological Societies of NSW and the Great Barrier Reef Committee; the gathering of natural history and ethnological collections carried him far into Western Papua, the New Hebrides, and along the Australian coastline from south of Tasmania to the Torres Straits. *Publications:* fifty odd papers dealing with fishes, and others with mammals, reptiles, and crustaceans of Australia, in the publications of various scientific societies and institutions of Australia; more generally known as a writer of popular articles in semi-scientific journals. *Recreations:* keen on drawing and painting; and a little music when time permitted; also managed a fair amount of travelling around on anything from warships to pearling-luggers along the Australian coasts and South Seas. *Address:* Australian Museum, College Street, Sydney.
                                                    Died 1 Sept. 1925.

M'CULLOCH, Rev. James Duff, DD; Minister of Hope Street Free Church, Glasgow, since 1889; Senior Minister since 1921; Principal of Free Church College, Edinburgh, since 1905; *b* 1836; 5th *s* of late Andrew M'Culloch and Catherine Ross; *m* 1870, Anne Isabella, 3rd *d* of late Rev. George Davidson of Latheron; five *s* three *d. Educ:* Fearn FC School; Tain Royal Academy; Edinburgh Univ.; New Coll. Edinburgh. Minister of the Free Church at Latheron, 1867–89; Moderator of the General Assembly of the Free Church of Scotland, 1901. *Address:* Free Church College, Edinburgh; Torbeg, 52 Eastwood Mains Road, Giffnock, Glasgow. *T:* Giffnock 127.
                                                    Died 11 Dec. 1926.

MACCUNN, Hamish; composer of music and conductor; *b* Greenock, Scotland, 22 March 1868; twin 2nd *s* of James MacCunn, formerly shipowner, Greenock; *m* 1889, Alison Quiller, *o d* of late John Pettie, RA; one *s. Educ:* various schools in Greenock; private tutors; Royal College of Music, London; Scholar, 1883–87; studied composition under Dr C. H. H. Parry; also pianoforte and viola.

Conductor with the Carl Rosa Opera Company, The Moody-Manners Opera Company, and of light operas, etc, at the Savoy, Adelphi, Lyric, Apollo, Prince of Wales', Queen's and Daly's theatres, and with Mr Thomas Beecham at Covent Garden and His Majesty's Theatres, 1910; Conductor of Stock Exchange Orchestra, 1913–14. *Publications:* overtures, etc—The Land of the Mountain and the Flood, Chior Mhor, The Ship o' the Fiend, The Dowie Dens o' Yarrow, and Highland Memories; dramatic cantatas, etc—Lord Ullin's Daughter, Bonny Kilmeny, The Cameronian's Dream, Queen Hynde, The Lay of the Last Minstrel, The Death of Parcy Reed, The Wreck of the Hesperus, Kinmont Willie, Livingstone the Pilgrim (with Rev. Silvester Horne—Livingstone Centenary Meeting, Albert Hall, 1913); Lamkin, The Jolly Goshawk; music in English productions of Earl and the Girl, Talk of the Town, A Waltz Dream, and Autumn Manœuvres; operas—Jeanie Deans (with Joseph Bennett); Diarmid (with the Duke of Argyll); The Pageant of Darkness and Light (with John Oxenham and Hugh Moss); Orient Exhibition, 1908; songs, about 100; part songs, about 20; and various other miscellaneous works. *Recreations:* fishing, golf, billiards. *Address:* 6 Abbey Court, NW. *T:* 2066 PO Hampstead.
                                                    Died 2 Aug. 1916.

M'CUTCHEON, George Barr; author; *b* Indiana, USA, 26 July 1866; *s* of John Barr and Clara Glick M'Cutcheon; *m* 1904, Marie Van Antwerp Fay. *Educ:* Purdue University. City editor, Lafayette Evening Courier, 1893–1901. *Publications:* Graustark; Castle Craneycrow; The Sherrods; Brewster's Millions; The Day of the Dog; Beverly of Graustark; The Purple Parasol; Nedra; Cowardice Court; Jane Cable; The Flyers; The Daughter of Anderson Crow; The Husbands of Edith; The Man from Brodney's; The Alternative; Truxton King; The Butterfly Man; The Rose in the Ring; What's-his-Name; Mary Midthorne; Her Weight in Gold; The Hollow of her Hand; A Fool and his Money; Black is White; The Prince of Graustark; Mr Bingle; The Light that Lies; From the Housetops; Green Fancy; Shot with Crimson; The City of Masks; Sherry; Anderson Crow, Detective; West Wind Drift; Quill's Window; The Court of New York, 1920; Yollop; Viola Gwyn; Oliver October; East of the Setting Sun; Romeo in Moon Village; Kindling and Ashes; The Inn of the Hawk and Raven; Blades; various magazine stories and serials. *Address:* c/o Dodd, Mead & Co., 443 Fourth Avenue, New York City.
                                                    Died 23 Oct. 1928.

MacDERMOT, Captain Ffrench Fitzgerald, (The MacDermot-Roe); late Captain 4 Brigade South Irish Division, RA; *b* 26 May 1848; *s* of William Ffrench MacDermot-Roe; *m* 1st, Marian (*d* 1885), *d* of Robert Reid, RIC; 2nd, 1891, Agnes Kathleen, *d* of Bernard Daly. Descended from the Princes of Leinster; held the above ancient chieftain title, and was also the Lord of Moylurg, as recorded in the history of the county of Roscommon; head of the Protestant branch of the MacDermot sept or clan. It was the Princess Eva, daughter of Dermot, Prince of Leinster, who married Richard St Clair, Earl of Pembroke, of Chepstow Castle, near Bristol, an alliance which led to the conquest of Ireland in the reign of King Henry II, given in English history. The Macdermot family suffered heavily in days gone by through confiscation and suppression of their titles, particularly during the reign of Queen Elizabeth and later on in Cromwell's time, when their estates and castles were taken from them and bestowed upon Colonel King, an officer of the Parliamentary forces. The head of the family is the Macdermot, Prince of Coolavin Roe (or rua), signifying red, a nom de guerre of Feudal times. *Address:* Villa Elise, Pont de la Russe, Monte Carlo. *Club:* Royal Societies.
                                                    Died 8 Nov. 1917.

MacDERMOT, Rev. Henry Myles Fleetwood; *b* 24 March 1837; *s* of Theodosia and Henry MacDermot, MD; *m* Mary Emily Langdon; eight *s* three *d. Educ:* home. Ordained, 1860; Curate, 1860–80; Rector of St Joseph, Grove, 1880–82; St Michael and All Angels, Kingston, 1882–85; St Mark, Craigton 1885–1911; Chaplain to Archbishop of West Indies; Chaplain to the Forces at Newcastle Jamaica; Canon and Tutor of Ch. Theological College, Jamaica; retired, 1914. *Recreations:* reading, chess. *Address:* 788 Shuter Street, Montreal.
                                                    Died 28 Sept. 1918.

M'DERMOTT, Peter Joseph, CMG 1918; ISO 1905; Under Secretary, Chief Secretary's Department, Queensland; *b* 1858; *m* 1895, Mary Fleming. Entered Public Service, 1872. *Address:* Chief Secretary's Dept, Brisbane.   *Died 9 Nov. 1922.*

MACDONALD OF EARNSCLIFFE, 1st Baroness, *cr* 1891, of Earnscliffe in the Province of Ontario; **Susan Agnes Macdonald;** [was created a peeress in own right on death of her husband in consideration of his public services]; *b* 1836; *d* of Hon. T. J. Bernard,

PC Jamaica; *m* 1867, Rt Hon. Sir John Alexander Macdonald, PC, GCB, LLD, DCL, Prime Minister of Canada, 1867–73, and 1878–91; one *d*. *Heir:* none. *Address:* Earnscliffe, Ottawa.

Died 5 Sept. 1920 (ext).

MACDONALD, Alexander, MA; Ruskin Master of Drawing in the University of Oxford. *Address:* Ruskin Drawing School, Beaumont Street, Oxford. *T:* Oxford 44.

Died 16 Oct. 1921.

M'DONALD, Sir Andrew, Kt 1897; *b* 1836; *s* of Thomas M'Donald, Kirkhill, Midlothian; *m* 1857, Isabella, *d* of late William Fisher, Lanark; one *s*. Master of Edinburgh Merchant Co., 1888–89; Lord Provost of Edinburgh, 1894–97. *Address:* 40 Lauder Road, Edinburgh; Toftcombs, Biggar, NB. *Died 15 July 1919*.

MACDONALD, Sir Archibald John, 4th Bt, *cr* 1813; *b* 2 Feb. 1871; *s* of Sir Archibald Keppel Macdonald, 3rd Bt and Catharine Mary, *d* of late John Coulthurst, and *widow* of Hon. Edward T. Stonor; *S* father, 1901; *m* 1900, Constance Mary, *d* of Rev. Henry Martyn Burgess. *Heir:* none. *Recreations:* golf, motoring, shooting, fishing, tennis. *M:* AA 1797, 1069.

Died 11 Oct. 1919 (ext).

MACDONALD, Augustine Colin; Lieutenant-Governor of Prince Edward Island; *b* Panmure, Prince Edward Island, 30 June 1837; *s* of Hugh Macdonald, who came to Prince Edward Island in 1805 from Moidart, Invernesshire, and Catherine, *d* of A. Macdonald of Rhue Arisaig, Invernesshire; *m* Mary Elizabeth, sixth *d* of late Hon. John Small Macdonald, Charlottetown; three *s* four *d*. *Educ:* Grammar School, Georgetown; Central Academy, Charlottetown, PEI. First returned to Local Assembly, 1870; sat for three sessions; elected to represent King's Co. on the Province entering Confederation; and sat for twenty sessions in Parliament at Ottawa. *Address:* Charlottetown, Prince Edward Island.

Died July 1919.

M'DONALD, Hon. Charles; MP, Speaker House of Representatives, Commonwealth Parliament, Australia, 1910–13 and 1914–17; *b* Melbourne, Victoria; *s* of late Charles Thomas Young M'Donald of Charters Towers, Queensland; *m* 1892, *e d* of Alfred Tregear, Charters Towers, Queensland; one *d*. *Educ:* State School, Victoria and NSW. Watchmaker by trade; connected with the labour movement in Queensland since its inception; President Australian Labour Federation, 1890–92; MLA of Queensland for district of Flinders, 1893–1901; returned to first House of Representatives, 1901 (Commonwealth Parliament); Chairman of Committees of House of Representatives, 1907–10; a Fellow of the Art Society of Queensland. *Recreations:* golf, a keen lover of all kinds of sport. *Address:* Hughenden, Studley Avenue, Kew, Melbourne. *T:* Hawthorn 497.

Died Nov. 1925.

MACDONALD, Maj.-Gen. Sir Donald Alexander, Kt 1918; CMG 1908; ISO 1903; Quartermaster-General Canadian Militia, 1904–17; *b* 31 Oct. 1845; *s* of late Alexander Eugene Macdonald, Deputy-Clerk of the Crown and Registrar of the Surrogate Court of Cornwall, Canada; *m* 1876, Mary, 2nd *d* of Hon. Mr Justice Hugh Richardson, formerly of the Superior and Supreme Court of the North-West Territories of Canada; one *d*. *Educ:* County High School. Joined Militia, Rifle Company of Cornwall as Ensign, 1863; Lieut 59th Regt 1865; Capt. 1866; Adjt 59th Regt 1869; Major, 1871; Lieut-Col 1877; Col 1900; Brig.-Gen. 1907; Maj.-Gen. 1912; served during Fenian Raids, 1866; Red River Expedition, 1870 (medal, two clasps); North-West Rebellion, 1885 (medal); Long Service Decoration; sometime Chief Superintendent Military Stores; Director-General of Ordnance, Canada, 1903–4; third military member Militia Council. *Address:* Chateau Laurier, Ottawa, Canada. *T:* Q 3625, Q 1919. *Clubs:* Ottawa, Canada, Rideau, Golf, Country, Ottawa; Royal Canadian Yacht, Toronto. *Died 3 May 1920*.

MACDONALD, Rev. Frederic William; President of the Wesleyan Methodist Conference, 1899; *b* 25 Feb. 1842; *s* of Rev. G. B. Macdonald; *m* Mary (*d* 1909), *y d* of late Benjamin Cork of Burslem. *Educ:* St Peter's Collegiate School and Owens College, Manchester. Entered Wesleyan ministry, 1862; joint editor of London Quarterly Review, 1871–75; represented British Methodist Conference at General Conference of Methodist Episcopal Church of America, 1880; appointed Professor of Theology, Handsworth College, 1881; appointed Secretary of Wesleyan Missionary Society, 1891; visited Australia and New Zealand, 1903. *Publications:* Life of Fletcher of Madeley; Life of William Morley Punshon; Latin Hymns in the Wesleyan Hymn Book; In a Nook with a Book; As a Tale that is

Told, 1919. *Recreations:* those of a book-lover. *Address:* 18 Wellington Road, Bournemouth. *Died 16 Oct. 1928*.

MACDONALD, Rev. Frederick William, JP; Hon. Canon of Salisbury; late Rural Dean of Wylye; late Alderman of County Council of Wiltshire; *b* 1848; *s* of W. Macdonald, MA, Archdeacon of Wiltshire and Residentiary Canon of Salisbury; *m* 1874, Frances Lucy Matthews Pimperne, Dorsetshire; no *c*. *Educ:* Marlborough College; Somerset College, Bath; Oxford. Travelled Australian Colonies, South America, Europe; Curate of Coggs, Oxon, 1874–76; Brizenorton, Oxon, 1876–77; Vicar of Stapleford, Wilts, 1877–95; Rector of Wishford, Wilts, 1895–1924. In Freemasonry—Past Grand Chaplain of England; late Provincial Grand Mark Master for Wiltshire. *Publications:* brochures on local government; educational matters. *Recreations:* fishing, golf, freemasonry. *Address:* Pinehurst, Clevedon, Somerset. *Died 24 Nov. 1928*.

M'DONALD, Hugh Campbell, CMG 1914; Resident and District Magistrate; *b* 12 Oct. 1869; *s* of Donald Wm M'Donald, JP, and Sarah Bisset, *niece* of late General Bisset; *m* 1st, 1901, Jean, *d* of James Bladon, Edenbridge; two *s*; 2nd, 1919, Elsie May, *y d* of T. J. Wall, Southampton, and *widow* of Capt. F. Hardie, RAMC; one *d*. *Educ:* South Africa. Joined Sir Harry Johnston's Administration, Nyasaland, 1894; Judicial Officer, Lower Shire District, 1897; Resident 1st Grade, 1907. *Address:* Zomba, Nyasaland.

Died 16 March 1921.

MACDONALD, James Alexander; Managing Editor, The Globe, Toronto, 1902–16; *b* Middlesex Co., Ontario, Canada, 22 Jan. 1862; *s* of late John A. Macdonald, a native of Pictou Co., Nova Scotia; *m* 1890, Grace Lumsden Christian; two *s* one *d*. *Educ:* Hamilton and Toronto, Ontario; Edinburgh. Graduated at Knox Coll. Toronto, 1887; ordained to ministry of the Presbyterian Church, and inducted pastor of Knox Church, St Thomas, Ontario, 1891; resigned pastoral charge, 1896; entered journalism in Toronto as first editor of The Westminster; Member of Board of Governors of the University of Toronto from 1906; Member first Imperial Press Conference, London, 1909; President of Westminster Co., Toronto; Vice-Pres. Toronto Conservatory of Music. Hon. LLD Glas. and Oberlin. *Publications:* From Far Formosa, volume on life-work of late Dr G. L. MacKay; The Significance of Lincoln; What a Newspaper Man saw in Britain; Democracy and the Nations. *Address:* The Globe, Toronto. *Club:* Ontario, Toronto.

Died 14 May 1923.

MACDONALD, Maj.-Gen. Sir James Ronald Leslie, KCIE 1904; CB 1900; DL (Aberdeenshire) 1914; LLD; Colonel Commandant Royal Engineers since 1924; *b* 8 Feb. 1862; *s* of Surgeon-Major James Macdonald, MD, FRCSE (retired); *m* 1894, Alice Margaret, *y d* of Gen. George Pringle, ISC. *Educ:* Grammar School, Aberdeen; Aberdeen University. Entered RE 1882; Capt 1890; Brevet Major, 1895; Brevet Lt-Col 1899; Major, 1899; Brevet Col 1900; Col 1905; Brig.-Gen. commanding Presidency Brigade, India, 1905; served with Hazara Expedition, 1888 (despatches, medal and clasp); Chief Engineer Preliminary Survey for Uganda Railway, 1891–92; Uganda, 1892; Nouma Expedition, 1893; acting Commissioner Uganda Protectorate, 1893; commanded operations against rebels, Uganda, 1893 (acknowledgment of Govt, medal); Chief Staff Officer Unyoro Expedition, 1893–94 (medal, brevet of Major, Brilliant Star of Zanzibar, 2nd class); chief command of operations in Uganda, 1897–98; commanded at action of Lubwa's Hill, siege of Lubwa's Fort, engagements of Kizalera, Kijembo, etc (medal with 2 clasps, brevet of Lt-Col, thanks of Govt); commanded Juba Expedition, 1898–99; Director of Railways, China Expeditionary Force, 1901 (despatches, brevet of Col, medal); commanded operations in Thibet, 1903–4, including engagements at Guru, Niani, Tsechen, capture of Gyantse and advance to Lhasa (medal and clasp, KCIE); commanding Presidency Brigade, 1905–7; commanding Lucknow Infantry Brigade, 1907–9; commanding troops in Mauritius, 1909–12. Decorated for services in Uganda and Thibet. *Publication:* Soldiering and Surveying in British East Africa. *Address:* c/o Grindlay & Co., 54 Parliament Street, SW1.

Died 27 June 1927.

MACDONALD, James Smith; Editor, Farmer and Stockbreeder since 1895, and Agricultural Correspondent of the Morning Post; Director in firm of Macdonald & Martin, Ltd; formerly acting editor of Farming World; *b* 1873; *s* of late William Macdonald, editor North British Agriculturist; *m* 1900, Jeannie, *d* of George Kerr, Edinburgh; two *s*. *Educ:* George Watson's College, Edinburgh; attended science course affecting agriculture and live stock. Holder of first-class certificates; written extensively on agricultural and live stock subjects in home and foreign publications from experience in Great Britain and abroad. Chairman Institute of Journalists (London District), 1918. *Recreation:* golf. *Address:* The Rookery, 7 Dorset Road, Merton Park, SW19. *T:* PO Wimbledon 767. *Clubs:* Farmers', Aldwych.

Died 9 Dec. 1923.

MACDONALD, John, ISO 1907; Collector of Inland Revenue at Edinburgh, 1902–7; *b* 1843; *e s* of Robert B. W. MacDonald, Glen Urquhart, Inverness; *m* 1887, Annie, *e d* of Roderick Finlayson, Tain, Ross-shire; two *s* two *d*. *Educ:* local schools. Entered Inland Revenue Department, 1867; held several offices in the country and Somerset House. *Publications:* one of the editors of Ham's Inland Revenue Year-Book from first publication to 1907; Smuggling in the Highlands. *Recreation:* angling. *Address:* 66 Polwarth Terrace, Edinburgh.

Died 19 Feb. 1928.

MACDONALD, Col John Andrew, of Glenaladale, CB 1897; Hon. Colonel and late Lieutenant-Colonel commanding 3rd (Militia) Battalion, Queen's Own Cameron Highlanders; *b* Borrodale, Inverness-shire, 29 July 1837; *e s* of late Angus Macdonald of Glenaladale and Mary, *d* of Hugh Watson, Torsonce, Midlothian; *m* 1st, 1862, Helen (*dsp* 1864), *d* of Edward Chaloner, Liverpool; 2nd, 1901, Margaret Mary Teresa, *widow* of George Edmund Wicksted, and *y d* of late Sir Edward Blount, 8th Bt. *Educ:* Ushaw Coll. near Durham. Decorated: Diamond Jubilee. *Address:* Glenfinnan, Inverness-shire, NB; Betley Hall, Crewe. *Clubs:* Caledonian; New, Edinburgh. *Died 25 Feb. 1916.*

MACDONALD, Rt Hon. Sir John Hay Athole; *see* Kingsburgh, Rt. Hon. Lord.

MACDONALD, John Ronald Moreton of Largie, JP, DL for Argyll; landed proprietor; *b* 1873; *s* of late Charles Moreton Macdonald, of Largie and Elizabeth Hume Campbell, of Glendaruell; *m* 1906, Daisy, *d* of late Gen. Eyre Crabbe, CB; two *s* two *d*. *Educ:* Eton; Magdalen College, Oxford (MA). Chiefly resident on his own property since he inherited it in 1894, and occupied in its management, in local affairs, in county business, and in literary work. *Publications:* A History of France, 1916; contribs to Cambridge Modern History, and other historical essays. *Address:* Largie Castle, Tayinloan. *Clubs:* Travellers', Cavendish; New, Edinburgh.

Died 10 Sept. 1921.

MACDONALD, Ranald Mackintosh, CBE 1919; NZ Red Cross Service, England; *b* 1860; *e s* of late W. K. Macdonald, Orari, NZ; *m* 1885, Gertrude, *d* of George Gould, NZ; three *s* two *d*. Mechanical Engineer, NZ Railways; Managing Director Christchurch Tramways; Christchurch City Council; Canterbury Agricultural and Pastoral Association, CJC; Director several companies. *Recreation:* motoring. *Address:* Hambledon, Christchurch, NZ. *Clubs:* Royal Automobile, Junior Athenæum; Christchurch, Christchurch, NZ.

Died 21 Oct. 1928.

MACDONALD, Lt-Col Reginald Percy, DSO 1889; reserve of officers; late Hampshire Regiment; *b* 10 June 1856; *e s* of Maj. Gen. J. C. Macdonald; *m* 1890, *d* of Thomas Chard, Ramsgate and *widow* of Alex. Murray of Old Polmaise, Stirling. *Educ:* Clifton Coll. Served in Royal Pembroke Artillery Militia, 1875 and 1876; joined 67th Hampshire Regt, 1878; promoted Captain, 1884, Major, 1892; Lieut-Col, 1903; gazetted 2nd in command, 1897; voluntarily retired, 1897; served in Afghan War, 1879–80, with the 67th Regt (medal); served in Burma Expedition, 1885–87, with the 2nd Batt. Hampshire Regt, including the surrender of Mandalay (medal with clasp); also with the 1st Batt. Hampshire Regt, 1887–89, including the expedition to Mogaung (despatches, DSO, and clasp); South Africa, 1899–1900. *Recreations:* all sports.

M'DONALD, Rev. Walter, DD; Prefect of the Dunboyne Establishment, St Patrick's College, Maynooth; *b* 1854, of tenant farmer stock, at Emil, Piltown, Co. Kilkenny. *Educ:* St Kieran's College, Kilkenny; St Patrick's College, Maynooth. Priest 1876; professor of St Kieran's College, Kilkenny, where for five years he taught philosophy, theology, and English literature; Professor of Theology at St Patrick's College, Maynooth, 1881. Founded The Irish Theological Quarterly, 1906, of which he was chief editor for three years, when he retired. *Publications:* Motion: its Origin and Conservation (this book was condemned by the S Congregation of the Index at Rome, and withdrawn from circulation by order of that body); The Principles of Moral Science; Some Ethical Questions of Peace and War with Special Reference to Ireland, 1919. *Recreation:* walking. *Address:* St Patrick's College, Maynooth, Ireland.

Died 2 May 1920.

MACDONALD, Sir William Christopher, Kt 1898; Governor of M'Gill University, Montreal, to which he gave large endowments; Director of the Bank of Montreal; Governor of Montreal General Hospital; merchant; *b* Glenaladale, Prince Edward Island, 1831; *y s* of late Hon. Donald Macdonald, President Legislative Council of Prince Edward Island. *Educ:* Central Academy, Charlotte Town, Prince Edward Island. *Address:* 449 Sherbrooke Street, West, Montreal, Canada. *Club:* Mount Royal, Montreal.

Died 11 June 1917.

MACDONALD, William Rae; actuary; Albany Herald since 1909; Carrick Pursuivant, 1898–1909; *b* Edinburgh, 25 Dec. 1843; *o s* of William Rae Macdonald of Mont Albion, Surinam, South America, and his wife, Isabella Johnston; *m* 1880, Annie S. Johnston. *Educ:* Edinburgh Institution. Fellow Faculty of Actuaries in Scotland. *Publications:* On the Calculus of Finite Differences, 1876; On the Theory of Logarithms, 1885; a translation from the Latin of The Construction of the Wonderful Canon of Logarithms, by John Napier of Merchiston, with a bibliographical account of the various editions of his works, 1889; article on John Napier in the Dictionary of National Biography, 1894; The Heraldry of Elgin, in the Proceedings of the Society of Antiquaries of Scotland, 1899–1900; Heraldry in Churchyards between Tain and Inverness, in the Proceedings of the Society of Antiquaries of Scotland, 1901–2; Scottish Armorial Seals, 1904. *Recreations:* heraldic and archæological investigation. *Address:* Neidpath, 4 Wester Coates Avenue, Edinburgh.

Died 1923.

MACDONELL, Angus Claude, KC; DCL; Senator; barrister-at-law, of Osgoode Hall, Toronto; *b* Toronto, 23 June 1861; *s* of Angus Duncan Macdonell, a United Empire Loyalist, and Pauline Rosalie De-La-Haye (French descent); unmarried. *Educ:* Toronto Model School; Trinity University. Member House of Commons, 1904–17; Conservative; a Catholic. *Recreations:* aquatics, general field athletics. *Address:* Toronto. *Clubs:* Toronto, Albany, Toronto Hunt, Royal Canadian Yacht, Argonaut Rowing, Ontario Jockey, Empire, Toronto; Rideau, Ottawa.

Died April 1924.

MacDONELL, Edgar Errol Napier, CMG 1918; *b* 10 Oct. 1874; *s* of late Rt Hon. Sir Hugh MacDonell, GCMG, PC; *m* 1906, Violet, *o d* of Frank Forrester; one *d*. *Educ:* Eton. Served at the Consulate of Lisbon, 1896; Vice-Consul and Agent for British Central Africa to reside at Chinde, 1898; Acting Consul, Beira, 1900; Consul at Moçambique, 1900; Acting Consul-General, Lourenço Marques, 1901–2; Consul for Liberia, 1902; Consul for Continental Greece, 1906; Consul for Roumania, 1910; Consul-General, Portuguese East Africa, 1912; received Queen's S African War Medal; appointed Chief Liaison Officer to Portuguese GEA Expeditionary Force, with rank of Staff Major, 1917 (Commendador of the Portuguese Order of Aviz, despatches); subsequently promoted Staff Colonel; HBM Consul-General for States of Rio de Janeiro, 1921; retired on pension, 1924. *Recreations:* shooting, fishing, sports generally. *Club:* Eccentric.

Died 4 Dec. 1928.

MACDONELL, Sir John, KCB 1914 (CB 1898); Kt 1903; LLD, MA; FBA 1913; King's Remembrancer, 1912–20, and Master of Supreme Court, 1889–1920; *b* 1846; *s* of James Macdonell of Rhynie, Aberdeenshire; *m* 1873, Agnes, 3rd *d* of Daniel Harrison of Shirly House, Beckenham, Kent; two *d*. *Educ:* Aberdeen and Edinburgh Universities. Barrister Middle Temple, 1873; appointed Revising Barrister for Middlesex, 1884; one of the Counsel to the Board of Trade and London Chamber of Commerce; Membre de l'Institut International de Statistique; late Vice-President of the Royal Statistical Society; President of Grotius Society; editor of State Trials, 1887; editor of Civil Judicial Statistics from 1894, of the Criminal Judicial Statistics, 1900, and of the Journal of Comparative Legislation; elected Associate of the Institut de Droit International, 1900; Member, 1912; Member of Board of Studies of Economics, London University, and the first Dean of the Law Faculty of that University; Quain Professor of Comparative Law, University College, London, 1901–20; President of Society of Public Teachers of Law, 1912–13; Member of Royal Commission on Shipping Combinations and of Sub-Commission to South Africa, and of Lord Gorell's Committee on High Court and County Courts; Chairman of Committee of Enquiry into Breaches of the Laws of War; Vice-President of Medico-Legal Society. *Publications:* Survey of Political Economy; The Land Question; The Law of Master and Servant; (ed) Smith's Mercantile Law; articles in reviews, magazines, periodical press. *Recreations:* golf, bicycle. *Address:* 31 Kensington Park Gardens, W; 173 Royal Law Courts, WC. *Clubs:* Athenæum, Reform.

Died 17 March 1921.

MACDONNELL, 1st Baron, *cr* 1908, of Swinford; **Antony Patrick Macdonnell**, GCSI 1897 (KCSI 1893; CSI 1888); KCVO 1903; PC 1902; PC (Ire.) 1903; DLitt, DCL (Oxon); *b* 7 March 1844; *m* 1878, Henrietta, *d* of Ewen MacDonell (Keppoch); one *d*. *Educ:* Queen's Coll., Galway. Entered Indian Civil Service, 1865; Acting Chief Commissioner in Burmah, 1889; Chief Commissioner of Central Provinces, 1891; Acting Lt-Governor, Bengal, 1893; Member of Council of Viceroy of India, 1893–95; Lt-Governor of NW Provinces and Chief Commissioner of Oudh, 1895–1901; Member of the Council of India, 1902; Under-Secretary of State in Ireland, 1902–8; Member of the Irish Convention, 1917–18. *Heir:* none. *Address:* 3 Buckingham Gate, SW1. *T:* Victoria 5861. *Clubs:* Reform; St Stephen's Green, Dublin.

Died 9 June 1925 (ext).

MACDONNELL, Henry, CB 1897; Inspector-General of Hospitals and Fleets; *b* 1839; *s* of late Wm Macdonnell of Dublin; *m* 1886, Francis Alice, *e d* of late Sir William R. Holmes, Consular Service, of Kilrea, Ireland. *Educ:* Dublin; LRCSI 1860; LRCPI 1861. Entered RN as Surgeon, 1861; became Staff-Surgeon, 1874; Fleet-Surgeon, 1882; Deputy Inspector-General, Hospitals and Fleets, 1890; Inspector-General, 1897; served at bombardment of Alexandria, 1882, and during subsequent Egyptian War (medal with clasp, bronze star); served as Deputy Inspector-General at Haslar, Malta, and Chatham Hospitals; Inspector-General, Haslar, 1898–99; retired 1899. Decorated on the occasion of Her Majesty's Diamond Jubilee; awarded the Jubilee Medal of 1897. *Address:* Keith House, Villiers Road, Southsea. *Died 31 Aug. 1922.*

McDONNELL, Col John, CB 1900; RA; retired 1903; *b* 28 May 1851; *s* of Luke J. McDonnell, DL, Merrion Square, Dublin; *m* 1890, Pauline, *d* of late Col Hannay, and *widow* of late Captain Milford, RWF; one *s*. *Educ:* Stoneyhurst College; RMA. Joined RA, 1872; Captain, 1881; Major, 1889; Lt-Col, 1897; Col, 1901. Served Afghan War, 1879–80 (medal); Boer War, 1900 (commanded the Artillery, 6th Division); severely wounded at Klip Kraal (medal with two clasps, CB, despatches); Commandant, Royal Hibernian Military School, 1914–19. *Address:* 18 Clyde Road, Dublin. *Clubs:* Kildare Street, Dublin; Royal St George Yacht, Kingstown.

Died 25 Aug. 1928.

M'DONNELL, Richard Grant Peter Purcell, CIE 1905; late Burma Police Department. Inspector of Police, 1886; District Superintendent, 1896; Commissioner Rangoon Town Police, 1899–1908; retired, 1908. *Club:* East India United Service.

Died 24 April 1927.

MACDONNELL, Col William, CB 1891; retired; *b* 7 June 1831; *s* of William Macdonnell; *m* 1878, Annie Jessie, *d* of Col C. J. Cox of Fordwich, Kent. *Educ:* privately in Dublin. Ensign, 1848; and served in the 55th, 14th, and 88th Regiments; joined the Army Pay Department as Staff Paymaster, 1878; became Chief Paymaster, 1881; sometime Chief Paymaster Home District. Decorated for long and meritorious service. *Recreation:* riding. *Address:* Via Castilfidardo, 47, Rome. *Died 12 July 1919.*

MACDONNELL, Rt. Rev. William Andrew; Bishop of Alexandria since 1906; *b* 1853. *Educ:* Ottawa University; Grand Seminary, Montreal. Ordained, 1881. *Address:* The Palace, Alexandria, Ont. *Died 10 Nov. 1920.*

M'DOUALL, William, MRAS; *b* Owsden Rectory, Suffolk, 13 April 1855; *e s* of late Rev. W. S. M'Douall, Rector of Owsden; unmarried. *Educ:* Uppingham School, 1868–73. Joined Indo-European Government Telegraph Department in Persian Gulf in June 1875, and proceeded to Bushire; stationed at various places in Persian Gulf until 1890, when services transferred to consular service, and appointed to open new Vice-Consulate at Mohammerah, on the Karun River, 1904; Consul 1904; Consul, Kermanshah, 1909; Hamadan, 1916; retired 1918; Mesopotamia Civil Administration, 1918–21; Assistant Political Officer, Badrah; Anglo-Persian Oil Co., 1923. *Address:* Khaniqin, Iraq.

Died 2 Nov. 1924.

M'DOUGALL, John, CMG 1912; JP; Commissioner, Customs Department, Ottawa, Canada, since 1896; *b* Blue Mountain, Pictou, NS, 13 March 1848; *m* Margaret Jane Macleod of Westville, NS; two *s*. *Educ:* Grammar School, New Glasgow, NS. MP Pictou, 1881–96. *Address:* 149 Daly Avenue, Ottawa.

Died 14 June 1919.

MACDOUGALL, Brig.-Gen. Alexander, CMG 1918; Canadian Forestry Corps; *b* 1878; *s* of late J. T. MacDougall, CMG. Served European War, 1915–18 (Legion of Honour).

Died Jan. 1927.

MACDOUGALL, Maj.-Gen. James Charles, CMG 1916; *b* Toronto, 16 July 1863; *s* of Alex. Duncan MacDougall, Barrister, of Osgoode Hall, Toronto, and *g s* of Captain Duncan MacDougall, 79th Cameron Highlanders; *m* 1889, Josephine, *d* of George Macaulay Hawke, Toronto; one *s*. *Educ:* Collegiate Institute and Royal Military College, Kingston, Ontario. Joined Canadian Permanent Force (Royal Canadian Regt), 1885; Lt-Col same Regt 1910; served South Africa (Queen's medal with clasp); held various staff appointments in Canada and was acting Adjutant-General at the beginning of European War; joined first Canadian Contingent as Military Secretary to GOC; commanded Canadian Training Division, Shorncliffe, Kent, 1915 and 1916; brought to the notice of the Secretary of State for War, for valuable services rendered in connection with the War; employed on special duty, 1917–18; retired, 1919. *Clubs:* Caledonian; Royal Bermuda Yacht. *Died 30 Jan. 1927.*

MACDOUGALL, Sir James Patten, KCB 1914 (CB 1906); DL, JP, Vice-Convener (1901–4, 1910), Argyllshire; MA Oxon; Keeper of the Records of Scotland, Deputy Clerk Register, and Registrar-General since 1909; Vice-President and Chairman of Local Government Board for Scotland, 1904–9; *b* 29 May 1849; *e s* of John Patten, WS, and of Jane Maxwell Campbell, *e d* of D. MacDougall of Gallanach, Argyllshire; assumed surname of MacDougall on succeeding to his mother in 1891; *m* 1884, Alice Mary, *e d* of late Maj. Horne of Stirkoke, Caithness-shire; no *c*. *Educ:* Edinburgh Academy; Christ Church, Oxford. Called to Bar, Inner Temple, 1873; Advocate, Scottish Bar, 1874. Legal Secretary to Lord Advocate, 1886, and 1892–94; Legal Member of Local Government Board, 1894–1904; Chairman of Departmental Committee on Poor Law Medical Relief in Scotland, 1902; Member of Royal Commission on Poor Laws and Relief of Distress, 1905; a Boundary Commissioner for Scotland, 1917. *Address:* Gallanach, Oban, NB; 39 Heriot Row, Edinburgh. *Clubs:* Brooks's; New, Edinburgh; Royal Highland Yacht, Oban; Honourable Company of Edinburgh Golfers, Muirfield.

Died 10 March 1919.

M'DOUGALL, Sir John, Kt 1902; late Chairman London County Council; *b* 1844; *s* of Alexander M'Dougall, Manchester, and Jane Shemwell of Youlgrave; *m* 1st, 1867, Lucy Armstrong; two *s* three *d*; 2nd, 1882, Ellen Mary, *d* of George Lidgett, JP, Blackheath; one *s* two *d*. *Address:* Clifton House, Greenwich Park, SE. *T:* 205 Deptford. *Club:* National Liberal.

Died 8 May 1917.

MACDOUGALL, Lt-Col Stewart, of Lunga, Argyll; JP and DL Co. Argyll, and County Councillor; landed proprietor; *b* 1854; 2nd but *o surv. s* of John MacDougall of Lunga and Richmond Margaret, *d* of Don. Stewart; *m* Wilhelmina, 2nd *d* and *co-heiress* of Wm Liddell of Sutton and Keldy Castle, Yorkshire; three *d*. *Educ:* at home. Entered 93rd Highlanders, 1876; served Egyptian Campaign, 1882 (seriously wounded Tel-el-Kebir, despatches, medal and clasp and Khedive's Star); Adjutant 4th Batt. Argyll and Sutherland Highlanders, 1884–89; retired as Major, 1892; Lt-Col in command 10th Batt. Gordon Highlanders, 1914; Gentleman-at-Arms in Household of HM from 1900; received Coronation medals. *Recreations:* shooting, golf, hunting, and all outdoor sports, yachting. *Address:* Lunga, Ardfern, Argyll. *TA:* Lunga, Ardfern; Engine Court, St James's Palace, SW. *Clubs:* Carlton, Naval and Military; New, Edinburgh.

Died 21 July 1916.

M'EACHRAN, Duncan, JP; FRCVS, VS Edin.; LLD and DVS McGill; *b* Campbeltown, Argyllshire, Oct. 1841; *o s* of David M'Eachran and Jean Blackney; *m* 1868, Esther, 3rd *d* of Timothy Plaskett of St Croix, West Indies. *Educ:* Edinburgh. Was invited to join in the establishment of a course of lectures in connection with the Board of Agriculture of Ontario at Toronto, 1862; removed to Montreal, where he inaugurated the Montreal Veterinary College in connection with the Medical College of McGill University, 1866, which, 1890, became the Faculty of Comparative Medicine and Veterinary Science, of which he became Dean, and held that position till his retirement, 1903; organised the Cattle Quarantine System of Canada, 1876; after twenty-six years he resigned the active duties of the position and became Honorary Veterinary Adviser to the Government; represented Canada at scientific congresses at Baden Baden, at London (Tuberculosis Congress, 1901), and in all international discussions and agreements bearing on animal diseases; was largely instrumental in raising the Strathcona Horse, sent to South

Africa during the Boer War; President of the New Walrond Cattle Ranch in the Rocky Mountain region of Canada. *Publications:* Handbook on the Diseases of Horses, 1866; Notes of a Trip to Bow River, 1881; Notes of a Visit to the Scientific Institutions of France, Germany, and Denmark, 1898; numerous scientific bulletins on Contagious Diseases for the information of agriculturists and stock-breeders, issued by the Government. *Recreations:* principally spending two or three months annually on the foothills of the Rocky Mountains, where in early days he hunted buffalo and other game; devoted himself to the breeding of high-class agricultural horses. *Address:* Ormsby Grange, Ormstown, PQ. *Clubs:* Authors'; St James's, Montreal, Ranchman's, Calgary.   *Died 13 Oct. 1926.*

McEVOY, Ambrose, ARA 1924; ARWS 1926; *b* 1878; *s* of Captain A. McEvoy; *m* 1902, Mary Spencer, *d* of Col Spencer Edwards of Freshford, Bath; one *s* one *d.* Studied at the Slade School; Member of the New English Art Club, International Society of Painters, National Portrait Society, etc; Royal Society of Portrait Painters. Works have been acquired by the Luxemburg Gallery, National Gallery of British Art (Tate Gallery), Manchester Art Gallery, Ottawa Gallery, National Gallery of Canada, Municipal Gallery of Johannesburg, and other Galleries. *Address:* 107 Grosvenor Road, SW1. *T:* Victoria 5901; Duffield Cottage, Duffield, Derbyshire. *T:* Duffield 116.   *Died 4 Jan. 1927.*

MACEWAN, David, MD, CM Edin., LLD St Andrews University; Emeritus Professor of Surgery, University College, Dundee (University of St Andrews); Consulting Surgeon, Dundee Royal Infirmary; *b* Kinross-shire, 1846; *m* 1st, Bertha Elizabeth, *e d* of Rev. Robert Templeton, Grahamstown, South Africa; 2nd, Margaret, *d* of late R. S. Stronach, Hillhead, Glasgow. *Educ:* Perth Academy; University of Edinburgh. *Publications:* papers to medical journals. *Address:* 2 Airlie Place, Dundee.

Died 31 March 1927.

MACEWAN, Peter, FCS; Editor of The Chemist and Druggist; corresponding member Société de Pharmacie, Paris; *b* Lockee, Forfarshire, 29 May 1856; *m* Euphemia, *d* of R. Thomson, Edinburgh; three *s* two *d. Publications:* The Art of Dispensing; Pharmaceutical Formulas, etc. *Recreation:* golf. *Address:* 64 Southwood Lane, Highgate, N. *T:* Hornsey 1760; 42 Cannon Street, EC. *Clubs:* National Liberal; Highgate Golf.   *Died 16 May 1917.*

MACEWEN, Dr Alexander R.; Moderator, General Assembly, United Free Church, 1915; Professor of Church History, New College, Edinburgh, since 1901; *b* Edinburgh, 1851; *s* of Rev. Alexander MacEwen, DD, Glasgow, and Eliza Robertson, Dunfermline; *m* 1885, Margaret, *d* of R. H. Begg, Moffat; two *s* one *d. Educ:* Glasgow Academy (Medallist); Glasgow Univ.; Balliol College, Oxford; Göttingen University; UP Theological College. Foundation Bursar, Jeffrey Greek Medallist, Muirhead (Latin) and Moral Philosophy First Prizeman at Glasgow; Snell Exhibitioner and Arnold Historical Essayist at Oxford; MA (Honours) of Oxford; BD and Hon. DD of Glasgow. Deputy Professor of Greek, Assistant Professor of Latin, Classical Examiner for Degrees at Glasgow University; UP minister at Moffat, at Anderston, and at Claremont Church, Glasgow; Chairman of Moffat School Board; member of Glasgow School Board; Governor of Hutcheson's Schools; Secretary of Christian Unity Association; director of other trusts and societies; educational, charitable, and religious. *Publications:* Memoir of Alexander MacEwen, DD, 1876; Roman Satiric Poetry, 1877; St Jerome, 1878; Life of Principal Cairns, 1894; The Eastern Church in Greece, 1890; The Erskines, 1900; Antoinette Bourignon, Quietist, 1910; A History of the Church in Scotland, vol. i, 1913; various articles and reviews. *Recreations:* riding, travel. *Address:* New College, Edinburgh.   *Died 26 Nov. 1916.*

McEWEN, Robert Finnie, DL, JP Co. Berwick; JP Co. Ayr; FSA (Scot.); Member of the King's Bodyguard in Scotland; *b* 1861; *o s* of late Rev. John McEwen, MA, of Kirkmichael; and Isabella, *d* of Wm Finnie of Kilmarnock; *m* 1893, Mary Frances, *e d* of late Henry Dundas; one *s* one *d. Educ:* Edinburgh University, MA; Cambridge, BA. Called to Scottish Bar, 1888; member of Council, Royal College of Music, London, from 1906. *Publications:* Church music, songs and part songs. *Recreations:* shooting, fishing, music. *Address:* Marchmont House, Greenlaw, Berwickshire; Bardrochat, Colmonell, Ayrshire. *Clubs:* Carlton; New, Edinburgh.

Died 31 March 1926.

MACEWEN, Sir William, Kt 1902; CB 1917; MD; FRS 1895; Hon. Surgeon to HM in Scotland; Surgeon-General RN for Scotland; President British Medical Association, 1922; Professor of Surgery,

Glasgow University, since 1892; *b* 22 June 1848; *m* 1873, Mary Watson, *d* of late Hugh Allan of Crosshill, Glasgow; three *s* three *d.* Hon. LLD, Glasgow and Liverpool Universities; DCL Durham, 1921; Hon. FRCS, England and Ireland; Hon. DSc, Oxon and Trinity College, Dublin. Hon. Member Imperial Medical Academy, St Petersburg; of Royal Medical Academy of Rome; of American Surgical Society, and of German Surgical Congress; President International Surgical Society, 1920–23; corresponding member Surgical Society of Paris. *Publications:* Osteotomy, 1880; On Pyogenic Infective Disease of the Brain and Spinal Cord; Meningitis, Abscess of the Brain, Infective Sinus Thrombosis, 1893; On Hernia and its Radical Cure; On a Method of Cure of Aneurism; On Transplantation of Bone by Bone Grafting; On the Growth of Bone; The Growth and Shedding of the Antler of the Deer, 1921. *Address:* 3 Woodside Crescent, Glasgow; Garrochty, Kingarth, Bute. *T:* National 194, Charing Cross, Glasgow.   *Died 22 March 1924.*

M'FADDEN, Edward; *b* 23 April 1862; *s* of M. M'Fadden, JP, Mem. of County Council, and B. M'Gahan. *Educ:* admitted Solicitor in 1886. Chairman County Council, Donegal, 1899, 1900 and 1901; Chairman Letterkenny Urban Council, 1898–1902; Nationalist; MP (N) Donegal East, 1900–6. *Address:* Letterkenny, Co. Donegal. *Club:* National Liberal.   *Died 12 Oct. 1922.*

MACFADYEN, William Allison, MA Oxon; LLD Cape; Professor of Philosophy at the Transvaal University College since 1912; *b* 24 Feb. 1865; *s* of Rev. J. A. Macfadyen, MA, DD, of Manchester, England; *m* 1893, Marian, *d* of Rev. Dr Roberts, Professor of Latin, St Andrews University, NB; one *s* one *d. Educ:* Manchester Grammar School; Brasenose College, Oxford. Vice-Principal of Graaff Reinet College, Cape Colony, 1889–91; at the Bar, Capetown, 1891–92; joined Pretoria Bar, S Africa, 1892; Docent in English Literature and Philosophy, 1893–99; Official Translator of Laws of Transvaal and Free State, 1900–1; Assistant Director of Education, Transvaal, 1901–2; at the Transvaal Bar and Lecturer in Law, 1902–6; Professor of Law, Rhodes University College, Grahamstown, 1906–11; Chairman of Senate, 1907–10; Acting Professor of English and Philosophy, Grey University College, Bloemfontein, 1911–12. *Publications:* Official Translation of Laws; Political Laws of Transvaal; two vols Law Reports; essays and lectures. *Address:* PO Box 14, Pretoria, SA. *Club:* Pretoria, Pretoria.

Died Oct. 1924.

MACFALL, Haldane; Major (retired); *b* 24 July 1860; *e s* of late Lt-Col D. Chambers Macfall; *m* Mabel, *d* of Admiral Sir James Hanway Plumridge, KCB, MP, of Hopton Hall, Suffolk. *Educ:* Norwich Grammar School; Sandhurst. Gazetted to West India Regiment, 1885; served in Jamaica and West Africa; retired as Lieutenant, 1892; in the European War—Captain, The Essex Regiment, Jan. 1915; Major (2nd in command), The Sherwood Foresters. Awarded Civil List pension for distinction in literature, 1914. Exhibited Royal Academy, International and elsewhere. *Publications: (pseudonym* Hal Dane): The Wooings of Jezebel Pettyfer, 1897 (called The House of Mirth and The House of the Sorcerer in America); The Masterfolk, 1903; Whistler, 1905; Irving, Ibsen, part author of Rouge, 1906; Old English Furniture (Connoisseur), Boucher, Fragonard, Vigée Le Brun, 1908; Beautiful Children, 1909; The French Pastellists of the Eighteenth Century, 1909; History of Painting (8 volumes), 1910; The Splendid Wayfaring, 1913; The Nut in War, 1914; Battle, 1914; Germany at Bay, 1917; Beware the German's Peace, 1918; The Book of Lovat, 1928; The Three Students, 1926, and The Perfect Lady, and Life of Beardsley—decorated; Songs of the Immortals and Persuasions to Joy, 1927. *Recreations:* the playhouse; books; designing covers and decorations for books; the study of life and people. *Address:* The White House, Challoner Crescent, West Kensington, W14. *T:* Western 2294. *Club:* Whitefriars.   *Died 25 July 1928.*

MACFARLAND, Robert Arthur Henry, MA; Headmaster of Campbell College, Belmont, near Belfast, since 1907; *s* of John MacFarland of Omagh, Co. Tyrone, and *g s* of Rev. William Henry, DD, of Newtownards, Co. Down, and Letterkenny, Co. Donegal; unmarried. *Educ:* Royal Academical Institution, Belfast; Queen's College, Belfast; Gonville and Caius College, Cambridge (Foundation Scholar). BA with First Class Honours in Mathematical Science in Queen's University, Ireland, 1880; Ninth Wrangler in Mathematical Tripos, 1883. Chief Master of the Army Class at Repton School, 1889–1907; commanded the Contingent of the Officers' Training Corps at Repton School, 1900–3, and Campbell College Contingent, 1915–20. *Recreations:* golf, cycling. *Address:* Campbell College, Belfast. *T:* Knock 102. *Club:* Ulster Reform, Belfast.

Died 11 April 1922.

MACFARLANE-GRIEVE, William Alexander, JP Roxburgh, Cambridge and Berwick; MA and SCL Oxford; MA Cambridge; FSA Scot; *b* 1844; *o* surv. *s* of William Macfarlane, MD, FRCS, RN, and Margaret Verner (Jane), *o d* of George Grieve, of Eastfield, Berwickshire. *Educ:* Royal High School, Edinburgh; Universities of Edinburgh and Bonn; Balliol College and St John's College, Oxford (Scholar); 2nd class in Classical Moderations, 1865, name appearing in the class list as Comyn-Macfarlane; BA and SCL 1866. A Master at St Peter's College, Radley, 1867–68; in residence at Oxford engaged in literary work, 1869–72; on succeeding to the Edenhall entail ceased to use the surname of Comyn and assumed the surname and arms of Grieve, both by Royal Licence; of Lincoln's Inn; owner of about 9,000 acres of land in the counties of Roxburgh, Cambridge, and Berwick; member of Licensing Committee, Co. Cambridge; a Commissioner of Supply for the Counties of Roxburgh and Berwick; Lord of the Manors of Eleswell and Impington Ferme-part; patron of one living; for many years actively engaged in agriculture and forestry. *Recreations:* book-collecting, farming and stock-breeding, sylviculture (medal of RASE 1911), heraldry, music. *Address:* Impington Park, Cambridgeshire; Penchrise Peel, via Hawick; Edenhall House, near Kelso. *Clubs:* Conservative, New University, Constitutional; Cambridge County; Oxford County; Border, Hawick; Scottish Conservative, Edinburgh.

Died 8 March 1917.

MACFETRIDGE, Ven. Charles; Rector of Kilgariffe since 1874; Archdeacon of Ross since 1904. *Educ:* Trinity College, Dublin. Ordained, 1869; Curate of Christ Church, Cork, 1869–73; Kinsale, 1873–74. *Address:* Clonakilty, Co, Cork.

Died 14 Jan. 1920.

MACGIBBON, Rev. James, MC; DD; Minister of Glasgow Cathedral since 1916; *b* Edinburgh, 1865; *s* of George Ramsay MacGibbon; *m* 1906, Margaret, *d* of late Robert Robin, Castlehill, Hamilton; three *s*. *Educ:* George Watson's College, and University of Edinburgh. MA 1884; BD 1887; Assistant to Very Rev. Sir James Cameron Lees, St Giles's Cathedral, Edinburgh, 1887–90; Minister of Blackford, Perthshire, 1890; Collegiate Minister of Hamilton, 1901; served as Chaplain to the BEF in France, 1915–16 (despatches, Military Cross); DD Glasgow University, 1920. *Recreations:* walking, cycling. *Address:* 6 Bute Gardens, Glasgow, W. *T:* Western 4357. *Clubs:* Conservative, Edinburgh; New, Glasgow.

Died 18 Nov. 1922.

MACGILL, Maj. Campbell Gerald Hertslet, MVO 1911; TD; *b* 1876; *o s* of late Campbell MacGill, of Stratford-sub-Castle, Salisbury; *m* 1910, Evelyn Ross, *y d* of late Allan Burnett, of Blackheath; one *s* three *d*. Entered the Board of Green Cloth, 1898; Assistant Sec., 1908; Establishment Officer of the King's Household, 1922; Coronation medals, 1902 and 1911; one of the Gold Staff Officers at the Coronation of King George V; late Major of the London Rifle Brigade; Adjutant 2nd Battalion London Rifle Brigade, Sept. 1914–June 1915; Staff Capt., July 1915–May 1916; Brig.-Maj., Group B, 1st Lond. Div., 1916. *Address:* 8 Prince of Wales Mansions, Battersea Park, SW11. *T:* Latchmere 4515.

Died 22 Nov. 1922.

MACGILL, Adm. Thomas, CB 1897; RN; *b* Clapham, 16 Aug. 1850; 2nd *s* of late Rev. Thomas MacGill; *m* 1884, Maria, *d* of J. West. *Educ:* Western College, Brighton. Naval Cadet, 1863; Lieutenant, 1874; Commander, 1885; Captain, 1892; served as Lieut of Humber during Egyptian War, 1882 (medal and star); also at Suakim, 1884 (clasp, Suakim); Harbourmaster at Suakim, 1885 (clasp, despatches, and promoted Commander); Captain of Phœbe, employed against chief M'baruk, capture of stronghold Mwele, E Africa (medal, despatches); served in Benin Expedition, 1897 (despatches, clasp, CB); Captain in charge, Bermuda Dockyard. *Club:* Royal Naval, Portsmouth.

Died 16 April 1926.

MACGILLIVRAY, Hon. Angus; Judge of the County Court; *b* Bailey's Brook, Picton Co., NS, 22 Jan. 1842; *e s* of John and Catharine MacGillivray, and *g s* of Angus MacGillivray of Inverness-shire, Scotland; *m* 1st, Maggie (*d* 1879), *d* of Alexander McIntosh; 2nd, Mary E., *e d* of John Doherty of New York; three *s* four *d*. *Educ:* common schools; St Francis Xavier College, Antigonish. MA. Studied law under late Hugh M'Donald (afterwards Judge Supreme Court); admitted barrister and attorney, 1874; elected to House of Assembly, NS, 1878 and 1882; Speaker of Nova Scotia Legislature, 1883–86, and in 1886 became member of the Fielding Ministry; resigned, March 1887, and ran against Sir John Thompson, Minister of Justice for House of Commons, Canada; defeated by 40 votes; elected House of Assembly, 1887, and became member of Govt; resigned, 1891,

and again unsuccessfully opposed Sir John Thompson; appointed MLC of Nova Scotia, 1892; resigned, 1895, and elected for House of Assembly, 1895; member of the Murray Ministry, 1896; re-elected 1897 and 1901; Lecturer on Constitutional History in St Francis Xavier University; Judge of the County Court for one of the Judicial Districts of the Province, 1902. *Address:* Antigonish, Nova Scotia.

Died 4 May 1918.

MACGILLIVRAY, William, JP; Writer to the Signet since 1870; senior partner of the firm of Lindsay, Howe & Co., WS, Edinburgh, since 1907; *b* 1823; *e s* of Alexander MacGillivray of Stonehaven; *m* 1868, Margaret Dods, Musselburgh; three *s*. *Educ:* Stonehaven; Edinburgh University. Clerk to George Monro, Advocate, Edinburgh; Court Manager, Dundas & Wilson, CS, Edinburgh; partner of Messrs Lindsay, Howe & Co., WS, Edinburgh, 1870; Director of John Watson's Educational Institution, Edinburgh; also of the Orphan Hospital, Dean; Director of the British Linen Bank, Edinburgh; and of the Edinburgh Life Assurance Company. *Publications:* Rob Lindsay and his School, 1905; Auld Drainie and Brownie, 1906; The Story of Little Janet, 1907; The Elder and His Wife, 1910; Cotbank and its Folks, 1911; all collected into one volume under title Memories, 1912; Tante Claire, her Life and her Wisdom, 1908; Life of Professor MacGillivray, Aberdeen, 1910; Men I Remember, 1913. *Recreations:* literature, natural history. *Address:* 4 Rothesay Place, Edinburgh. *T:* Central 378. *Club:* University, Edinburgh.

Died 23 Nov. 1917.

McGILLYCUDDY, Denis Donough Charles, (The McGillycuddy of the Reeks), JP; *b* 14 May 1852; *e* surv. *s* of late Richard McGillycuddy of The Reeks, and Anna, *d* of Capt. John Johnstone, 23rd Welsh Fusiliers, of Mainstone Court, Co. Hereford; *m* 1881, Gertrude Laura, *y d* of Edmond Howd Miller of Ringwood, Passaic Co., New Jersey, US; one *s*. Was in RN. *Heir:* *s* Maj. Ross Kinloch McGillycuddy, *b* 26 Oct. 1882. *Address:* The Reeks, Killarney; Bauncluone, Beaufort, Co. Kerry.

Died 16 March 1921.

M'GILP, Maj. Clyde, DSO 1917; Officer Commanding 1st Battery, NZF Artillery; *b* NZ, 12 Oct. 1885; *s* of A. M'Gilp, Birkenhead, Auckland, NZ; unmarried. *Educ:* Auckland. At the age of 17 served in South Africa as a trooper; on return to NZ entered Artillery (Volunteer) as a gunner, passed through all ranks; commanded the Battery as Major, 1909; commanded Battery in Egypt, Gallipoli, and France (despatches twice, DSO); total service, 17 years. *Address:* c/o The Director of Base Records, NZ Military Forces, Wellington, New Zealand.

Died 1918.

M'GINNESS, Brig.-Gen. John R.; USA, retired; planter; *b* near Dublin, 17 Sept. 1840; *e* surv. *s* of Francis M'Ginness and Annie Hartford; unmarried. *Educ:* United States Military Academy, West Point, NY. First Lieutenant Ordnance, 1863; Captain, 1869; Major, 1881; Lieut-Col 1898; Col 1902; Brig.-General, retired 1904; served at various arsenals in United States; Asst Ordnance Officer and Chief Ordnance Officer, Department of the South, 1864; breveted Capt. and Major for gallant and meritorious conduct at siege of Charleston and vicinity, 1864; Asst Ordnance Officer, War Department, 1864–69; served on plains with General Sherman, 1866; Chief of Ordnance of Philippine Islands, 1898–1901. *Publications:* Official reports as Commandant of Rock Island and various other arsenals in the United States. *Recreations:* riding, walking, tennis, golf, snowshoeing, hunting big game, etc. *Address:* c/o War Department, Washington, USA. *Clubs:* Union League, Hamilton; Army and Navy, Washington; Army and Navy, Catholic, Manhattan, New York; Westover, Norfolk, Va; Union, Cleveland.

Died 17 Dec. 1918.

M'GOUN, Archibald, KC; MA, BCL; Professor of Civil Law, M'Gill University, Montreal, since 1888; *b* Montreal, 1853; *s* of Archibald M'Goun, a native of Douglas, Lanarkshire, Scotland, and Jane Mackay, *d* of Samuel Mackay of Ayr, Scotland; *m* 1887, Abigail, *d* of Thomas Mackay of Toronto; one *s* one *d*. *Educ:* M'Gill Univ., Montreal; L'Ecole de Droit, Paris, France. Twice President University Literary Society 1884–85; one of the founders of the Imperial Federation League in Canada, 1885; delegate to Imperial Federation Council in London, 1886; Vice-President of League (later the British Empire League) in Canada; Fellow Royal Colonial Institute; Chairman of meeting, Montreal, to promote Free Trade within the Empire, 1907; President Graduates' Society, M'Gill University, 1887; course of lectures on Constitutional Law, 1897; lectures on Corporations and on Agency and Partnership; QC 1899; Attorney as practising advocate for various commercial corporations; Pres. Montreal Economic and Statistical Society, 1907. *Publications:* Federation of the Empire,

Address as President of University Literary Society, 1884; Economic Study, Commercial Union with the United States, with a word on Imperial Reciprocity, 1886; A Federal Parliament of the British People, 1890; article on Imperial Reciprocity in Canadian Encyclopædia; articles in The Commonwealth, Ottawa, 1900–1; A Revenue Tariff within the Empire, 1905. *Recreations:* experiments in Phonetics; articles in an International Phonetic Alphabet Neotype, based on Ellis's Palæotype; member Victoria Rifles Reserves. *Address:* British Empire Building, Montreal; Dunaven, Bellevue Avenue, Westmount.   *Died 5 June 1921.*

McGOWEN, Hon. James Sinclair Taylor; Prime Minister and Colonial Treasurer, New South Wales, 1910–13; *b* at sea, 16 Aug. 1855, of English parentage; *m*; six *s* two *d. Educ:* at private and denominational schools. Began work at an early age; was boiler-maker's apprentice, Sydney, 1870; afterwards at Atlas Works, and Railway Department till 1910; Member for Redfern, 1891–1920; Secretary and President Boiler-makers' Society; President Eight-Hour Demonstration Committee. *Recreations:* formerly cricket, subseq. fishing and bowls. *Address:* 177 Pitt Street, Redfern, NSW.
Died April 1922.

M'GRATH, Sir Joseph, Kt 1911; LLD; *b* 25 Aug. 1858; *m* 1893, Eleanor Mary, *d* of Patrick McAlister, Dublin; one *s* two *d. Educ:* St Stanislaus' College, Tullabeg, Tullamore. Called to Irish Bar, 1892; Registrar and Member of the Senate of the National University of Ireland, 1908; one of the Secretaries of the Royal University of Ireland; Life Governor of the Royal Veterinary College of Ireland; a Vice-Chairman of the National Society for the Prevention of Cruelty to Children; Hon. Secretary of the Clongowes Union from foundation in 1897; a Vice-President of the Royal Dublin Society. *Address:* 11 Clyde Road, Dublin.   *Died 15 March 1923.*

MACGREGOR, Sir Evan, GCB 1906 (KCB 1892; CB 1882); ISO 1902; JP; *b* 31 March 1842; 3rd *s* of late Sir John Atholl Bannatyne MacGregor, 3rd Bt, and Mary, *d* of late Admiral Sir Thomas Masterman Hardy, 1st Bt, GCB; *m* 1884, Annie Louise (*d* 1922), *d* of late Col W. A. Middleton, CB; one *d. Educ:* Charterhouse. Permanent Secretary to Admiralty, 1884–1907. *Address:* Aynsome, Cartmel, Lancs. *Club:* Caledonian.
Died 21 March 1926.

MACGREGOR, Gregor, BA; member of London Stock Exchange; *b* 31 Aug. 1869; *s* of late Donald MacGregor, JP, and Euphemia Watt, Ardgartan, Arrochar, NB; *m* 1902, Ruby, *e d* of late T. W. N. Oliver, 26 Brunswick Terrace, Brighton; two *s. Educ:* Cargilfield, Edin.; Uppingham; Jesus College, Cambridge. Cambridge XI 1888–91; went to Australia with Lord Sheffield's XI 1891–92; Middlesex XI 1892–1907; played for England *v* Australia, all matches, 1890 and 1893. *Recreations:* cricket, golf; football formerly (Cambridge XV and Scottish International). *Address:* 39 Craven Hill Gardens, W. *T:* Paddington 2754. *Clubs:* Sports, MCC; Honourable Company of Edinburgh Golfers, Muirfield.   *Died 20 Aug. 1919.*

MACGREGOR, Col Henry Grey, CB 1889; *b* Belfast, 15 Jan. 1838; *y s* of late Gen. Sir D. Macgregor, KCB (*d* 1881), and Elizabeth, *d* of late Sir William Dick, Bt; *m* 1863, Rosetta (*d* 1891), *d* of late Rt Hon. Sir Joseph Napier, 1st Bt. *Educ:* Trinity Coll., Cambridge. Joined 17th Regt 1858; passed through Staff College, 1865; special service, Zulu War, 1878–79; AQMG and DAQMG Transvaal War, 1880–81; DAQMG Egyptian expedition, 1882; AAG Suakim expedition, 1885; Instructor RM Coll., 1867–69; ADC Gen. Officer commanding SE Dist, 1869–71; Garrison Instructor, 1872–77; DAAG Northern Dist, 1883–85; ADC to the Queen, 1886–95; AAG of Army, 1890–95; retired from Army, 1895; despatches, Zulu War, twice, 1879 (promoted Major); despatches, Egyptian expedition, 1882 (promoted Lieut-Col); despatches, Suakim expedition, 1885. Decorated for Zulu War, 1879 (medal and clasp); Egyptian expedition, 1882 (medal, bronze star, and 4th class Osmanieh); Suakim expedition, 1885 (clasp). *Address:* 4 Brechin Place, South Kensington, SW. *Club:* National.
Died 13 Oct. 1925.

M'GREGOR, Rt. Rev. Mgr James; Rector of Blairs College since 1899; *b* Keith, 1860. *Educ:* Blairs College; Scots College, Rome. Priest, 1883; Curate at Aberdeen Cathedral, 1883–91; Priest in Charge of Dufftown Mission, 1891–95; Administrator, Aberdeen Cathedral, 1895–99; Domestic Prelate to the Pope, 1908; Canon of Aberdeen Chapter, 1912. *Address:* Blairs College, Aberdeen.
Died 10 Feb. 1928.

McGREGOR, His Honour James Drummond; Lieutenant-Governor of Nova Scotia since 1910; *b* New Glasgow, NS, 1 Sept.

1838; *s* of Roderick McGregor and Janet Chisholm; *m* 1st, 1867, Elizabeth McColl, of Guysboro (*d* 1891); one *s*; 2nd, 1894, Roberta Ridley of Peterborough. Merchant and shipowner; senior partner in firms of R. McGregor & Sons and J. D. & P. A. McGregor; twice elected to Local Legis. and once defeated; contested House of Commons, 1900; twice Mayor of New Glasgow; summoned to the Senate, 1903; a Presbyterian. *Address:* Government House, Halifax, NS.   *Died 4 March 1919.*

MACGREGOR, Robert, RSA 1889; *b* 1848; married. *Address:* 62 Hanover Street, and Kenmure Cottage, Portobello, Edinburgh. *Club:* Scottish Arts, Edinburgh.   *Died 9 Nov. 1922.*

MACGREGOR, Hon. Robert Malcolm; Member Provincial Parliament of Nova Scotia for Pictou County since 1904; also Member Executive Council of the Province since 1911; *b* 9 Jan. 1876; *s* of late Lieut-Governor James D. MacGregor and first wife, Elizabeth M'Coll; *m* 1905, Laura MacNeil; one *s* two *d. Educ:* Dalhousie College, BA. Director Nova Scotia Steel and Coal Co., Ltd; Director Bank of Nova Scotia; Director Eastern Trust Company. *Recreations:* curling, tennis. *Address:* New Glasgow, Nova Scotia. *Club:* Halifax, Halifax.   *Died 10 Sept. 1924.*

MACGREGOR, Robert Roy, ISO 1902; Secretary of the Congested Districts Board for Scotland, 1897–1912; *b* 3 Nov. 1847; *e s* of late Rev. Alexander MacGregor, MA, West Parish, Inverness; *m* 1875, Henrietta (*d* 1906), *d* of late Rev. Thomas Davidson of Abbey St Bathans, Berwickshire; two *s* one *d. Educ:* Aberdeen and Edinburgh Universities. Entered HM Exchequer, Edinburgh, by competition, 1867; secretary to Committee on System of Land Registration in Scotland, and three other committees on various subjects, 1888–96; author of several works. *Recreation:* golf. *Club:* Conservative, Edinburgh.   *Died 5 Jan. 1922.*

MACGREGOR, Rt. Hon. Sir William, GCMG 1907 (KCMG 1889; CMG 1881); CB 1897; PC 1914; MD Aberdeen; Hon. DSc Camb.; Hon. LLD Edin.; LLD Aberdeen; LLD Queensland; FFPS Glas.; First Chancellor, University of Queensland; *b* Scotland, 1847; *e s* of late John MacGregor; *m* 1883, Mary, *d* of R. Cocks; one *s* three *d. Educ:* Aberdeen; Glasgow. Formerly Resident Surgeon and Resident Physician Glasgow Royal Infirmary, and Royal Lunatic Asylum, Aberdeen; Asst Government Medical Officer, Seychelles, 1873; Surgeon Civil Hospital, Port Louis, Mauritius, 1874; Chief Medical Officer, Fiji, 1875; was Receiver-General and Administrator of the Government, and Acted as High Commissioner and Consul-General for the Western Pacific; Administrator of British New Guinea, 1888; Lt-Governor, 1895; Governor of Lagos, 1899–1904; Governor of Newfoundland, 1904–9; Governor of Queensland, 1909–14. Fellow of Royal Geographical Societies of England and Scotland and Berlin, and of Royal Anthropological Society of Italy; Albert medal, 2nd class, and Clarke gold medal, for saving life at sea; Watson gold medal, 1872; also Founder's medal Royal Geographical Society of England; and Mary Kingsley Medal, 1910. Declared Queen Victoria's sovereignty over British New Guinea, 4 Sept. 1888. Represented the West African Colonies and Protectorates at the Coronation, 1902; KGStJ; retired 1914. *Address:* Chapel on Leader, Earlston, Scotland. *Club:* Athenæum.   *Died 3 July 1919.*

MACGREGOR, William York, RSA 1921; *b* Finnart, Dumbartonshire, 1855; *s* of John Macgregor, shipbuilder, Glasgow. *Educ:* Glasgow Academy. Studied Art in Glasgow, and afterwards for some years was a pupil of M. Legros at the Slade School, University College, London. *Address:* Albyn Lodge, Bridge of Allan, NB. *Clubs:* Scottish Arts, Edinburgh; Glasgow Art, Glasgow.
Died Sept. 1923.

M'GRIGOR, Brig.-Gen. Charles Roderic Robert, CB 1904; CMG 1916; late commanding 3rd Battalion King's Royal Rifles; *b* 5 Sept. 1860; *s* of Sir Charles M'Grigor, 2nd Bt; *m* 1892, Ada Rosamond, *d* of late Robert Bower of Welham, Yorkshire; one *s* one *d. Educ:* Eton. Officer; served Griqualand East (medal, clasp); Boer War, 1882 (medal, clasp, and Khedival Star); Suakin Expedition, 1884 (two clasps); Suakin Expedition, 1885 (clasp, Medjidieh, and Brevet); South African War, 1899–1902 (despatches twice, Queen's medal six clasps, King's medal two clasps, and Brevet); Brig.-General in charge of Administration, Western Command, 1909; various positions on Staff; served European War, 1914–16 (CMG). *Recreation:* shooting. *Club:* Naval and Military.
Died 9 July 1927.

M'GRIGOR, Captain Sir James Rhoderick Duff, 3rd Bt, *cr* 1831; *b* London, 27 April 1857; *s* of Sir Charles Rhoderic M'Grigor, 2nd

Bt; *S* father, 1890; *m* 1890, Helen, *d* of J. G. Meiggs, an American; one *s* one *d. Educ:* Eton; Christ Church, Oxford. Entered army (85th Light Infantry), 1877; transferred to Rifle Brigade, 1878; retired as Capt. 1890. *Recreations:* shooting, fishing. *Heir: s* Charles Colquhoun M'Grigor, Rifle Brigade [*b* 26 April 1893; *m* 1919, Amabel, *o d* of E. L. Somers Cocks, 47 Wilton Crescent, and Bake, St Germans]. *Address:* 58 Sloane Street, SW1. *Clubs:* Junior United Service, Travellers'. *Died 4 Feb. 1924.*

McGUINNESS, Joseph; MP (Sinn Fein), Longford Co. since Dec. 1918; draper. MP South Longford, 1917.
Died 31 May 1922.

McGUIRE, Hon. Thomas Horace, LLD Hon.; Chief Justice of Supreme Court, North-West Territories; retired, 1903; *b* Kingston, 21 April 1849; *m* 1877, Mary Victory, *e d* of late John Cunningham, Kingston. *Educ:* Collegiate Institute and Queen's University, Kingston. First Chief Justice of this Court. Formerly the Court (by statute) consisted of "Five Puisne Judges", but by Act of 1900 the Court consists of "a Chief Justice and four Puisne Judges". Chairman of the Educational Council of Province of Saskatchewan, and Member of Senate of Provincial University; President of Board of Trade. *Address:* Prince Albert, Sask, Canada.
Died 13 July 1923.

MccGWIRE, Maj.-Gen. Edward Thomas St Lawrance; *b* 13 March 1830. Entered army, 1849; Maj.-Gen. 1886; retired, 1890. *Address:* 32 Royal Crescent, W.
Died 16 March 1917.

McHARDY, Lt-Col Sir Alexander Burness, KCB 1911 (CB 1900); FSA; late RE; *b* 11 June 1842; *s* of late David McHardy, Cranford, Aberdeen; *m* 1865, Elise (*d* 1906), *o d* of late Sir John and Lady Anderson; one *s* two *d. Educ:* Aberdeen University. Served in the Royal Engineers, 1862–77, and for part of that time acted as Surveyor-General, Hong Kong; in 1877 transferred from Home District to Prison Department, England; served on Committee on Metropolitan Police Stations, 1881; Secretary Dept Committee on Employment of Convicts, 1882; appointed Surveyor of Prisons, 1882; Sec. Royal Commission on Irish Prisons, 1884; in 1886 appointed Prison Commissioner, Scotland; served on Dept Committee on Prisoners Awaiting Trial, 1889, and on Dept Committee on Habitual Offenders, 1894; chairman Prison Commission, Scotland, 1896–1909, and chairman of Dept Committee on Inebriates Acts, 1898. *Address:* 3 Ravelston Park, Edinburgh; Crauford, Aberdeen.
Died 10 Aug. 1917.

MACHELL, Percy Wilfrid, CMG 1906; *b* 5 Dec. 1862; *s* of late Rev. Canon Richard Machell and Hon. Emma Willoughby, *sister* of 8th Lord Middleton; *m* 1905, Countess Victoria Alice Leopoldine Ada Gleichen, *d* of late HSH Prince Victor of Hohenlohe Langenburg (Lady Valda Machell); one *s. Educ:* Clifton; Sandhurst. Joined 56th Regiment as Lieutenant, 1882; Captain 1888; temporary Major, 1893; retired (Reserve of Officers), 1896; served with the Nile Expeditionary Force, 1884–85 (medal with clasp, bronze star); joined Egyptian Army, 1886; in command at capture of Fort Khormoussa, 1888 (4th class Osmanieh); operations round Suakin and action of Gamaizah, 1888 (horse shot, clasp); Soudan, 1889–91; Toski Expedition; Brigade-Major No 2 column; capture of Tokar (clasp, and clasp on bronze star, 4th class Medjidie); commanded 12th Soudanese Battalion, 1891–95; Inspector-General, Egyptian Coastguard, 1896; Adviser to the Ministry of the Interior, Egypt, 1898–1908; Grand Cordon of Medjidie, 1902. Alderman, LCC, 1912–13; JP Westmorland, 1913; Lieut-Col commanding the Lonsdale Batt. Border Regiment, 1914. *Address:* Crakenthorpe Hall, Appleby, Westmorland. *Club:* Naval and Military. *Died July 1916.*

MACHUGH, Rt. Rev. Charles, DD; RC Bishop of Derry since 1907; *b* 1855. *Educ:* Maynooth. Professor St Colomb's Diocesan Seminary, 1890–1905; Parish Priest at Strabane, 1905–7; Vicar-General, Derry. *Address:* Bishop's House, Derry.
Died 12 Feb. 1926.

MACHUGH, Lt-Col Robert Joseph; War Correspondent on staff of the Daily Telegraph. Represented that paper in the Cuban Campaign during the Spanish-American War, 1898; in the Boer War, South Africa, 1899–1901; in the Russo-Japanese War, 1904; during the latter war he was attached to the staff of General Baron Kuroki and accompanied the First Japanese Army from Korea to the Shaho; was present at the battles of the Yalu, Mo-tien-ling Pass, To-wan, An-ping, and Liaoyang (medal with clasp); accompanied the Serbian Army in the Balkan War of 1912 (Commander Order of St Sava),

Mexico early in 1913, and witnessed the revolution; travelled extensively in United States, Canada, West Indies, Africa (South and East), Europe, Mexico, China and Japan; joined the last 1st City of London Royal Garrison Artillery, 1895; transferred to the Territorial Army, 1908; commanded the 6th London Brigade, Royal Field Artillery, with which he served as Lieut-Col in France; a member of the Q Club. *Publications:* The Siege of Ladysmith; Modern Mexico; introductions to various works, and numerous contributions on military and historical subjects in the magazines.
Died 6 July 1925.

McILLREE, John Henry, ISO 1910; late Assistant Commissioner Royal North-West Mounted Police; *b* Jamaica, 28 Feb. 1849; *s* of late Surg.-Gen. McIllree of the British Army; *m* 1884, Lily, *d* of J. Winter Humphrys of Ballyhaise House, Co. Cavan, Ireland; one *s* one *d. Educ:* Halifax School; Windsor University, NS; Sandhurst. Member of the Royal North-West Mounted Police from its formation, 1873; retired, 1911; 1885 Rebellion Medal. *Recreations:* shooting, fishing, golf. *Clubs:* Union of BC, Victoria Golf.
Died 17 May 1925.

MACINNES, Lt-Col Duncan Sayre, CMG 1917; DSO 1900; RE; General Staff Officer, Staff College; *b* 19 July 1870; *s* of late Hon. Donald Macinnes, of Hamilton, Canada; *m* 1902, Millicent, *d* of F. Wolferstan-Thomas; one *s* one *d.* Entered army 1891; Captain, 1902; Major, 1911; Bt Lt Col, 1915; served Ashanti, 1895–96 (star); South Africa, 1899–1900 (despatches twice, Queen's medal, 3 clasps, King's medal, 2 clasps, DSO); European War, 1915–17 (CMG). *Address:* The Ridge, Camberley, Surrey. *Club:* Army and Navy.
Died 23 May 1918.

McINNIS, Lt-Col Edward Bowater, CMG 1890; *b* 22 May 1846; *m* 1889, Maud Susanna, *d* of Capt. Wearing, RM and *g d* of (Temp.) Gen. Wearing, RM, ADC (of Trafalgar). Major, Lt-Col 1887; served Afghan War, 1878–80 (despatches); march to Candahar and battle of Candahar (despatches, medal with two clasps, bronze decorations); Adjutant 9th Lancers; Inspector-General of Police, Gold Coast, and British Guiana, 1891; commanded Militia, British Guiana, 1892–1902; on special duty to Urnan Venezulean frontier, 1896; commanded the Cavalry of the Colonial Forces at Queen Victoria's Diamond Jubilee, 1897; proceeded on Special Mission to Malta, 1909–10, to inquire into the organization of police of that island; acted as Political Officer and ADC the Sultans of Perak and Kedah during the Coronation of King George. *Clubs:* Army and Navy; Radnor, Folkestone. *Died 4 April 1927.*

M'INROY, Col Charles, of The Burn and Arnhall, NB, CB 1894; DL (Kincardineshire); JP Kincardine and Forfar shires; unemployed Supernumerary List, Indian Army; *b* 3 March 1838; *s* of late J. P. M'Inroy, Lude, Blair Atholl, and *nephew* of late Lt-Col W. M'Inroy of The Burn and Arnhall, Vice-Lt of Kincardineshire; *m* 1862, Emelia Katherine, *e d* of late Alex. Hamilton, LLB, WS; two *s* two *d. Educ:* private and Wimbledon School. Entered army 1855; Lieut 1858; Capt. 1867; Major, 1875; Lieut-Col 1881; Col 1885; served Indian Mutiny, 1857–59; present at surrender of Kirwee, at Sahao (despatches), Girwàsa (despatches); commanded in cavalry actions of Maharàjpore, Jakoli, (thanked in despatches), and Mow Mahoni (medal and clasp for Central India); Abyssinian Campaign, 1868 (despatches and medal); Egyptian War, 1882, present at Kassassin and Tel-el-Kebir (medal with clasp, Khedive's star); Burmah Expedition, 1885–86; principal Commissariat Officer in Upper Burmah, 1888–89 (medal with two clasps). *Recreations:* fishing, shooting, curling (vice-pres. Royal Caledonian Curling Club, 1896–97), golf. *Address:* The Burn, Edzell, Brechin. *TA:* Burn Edzell. *Club:* New, Edinburgh.
Died 4 Feb. 1919.

MACINTYRE, John, JP; DL; MB, CM; LLD Glasgow University; FRSE, FRMS, FRFPSG; MIEE; Hon. Lt-Commander RNVR; late University Lecturer on Diseases of the Nose and Throat, Glasgow University; Consulting Surgeon for Diseases of the Nose and Throat, and Consulting Medical Electrician, Glasgow Royal Infirmary; Vice-President of Medical Faculty and Emeritus Professor of Laryngology, Anderson College of Medicine, Glasgow; *b* 2 Nov. 1859; *m* 1892, Agnes Jean, *d* of late Henry Reid Hardie. *Educ:* Glasgow University; Vienna. Held various appointments, such as assistant and afterwards Dispensary Surgeon to the Glasgow Royal Infirmary; Demonstrator of Anatomy in the School of Medicine attached to that hospital. Fellow of the British Laryngological, Rhinological, and Otological Association, London, and President, 1893 and 1900; Fellow of the London Laryngological Society, Röntgen Society, London; Hon. Member of the British Electro-Therapeutic Society, London. Senior Editor British Journal of Laryngology; President of West of Scotland

Branch British Medical Association. Membre de la Société d'Otologie, de Laryngologie, et de Rhinologie, Paris; Corresponding Member of the American Laryngological Association. KGStJ. *Publications:* numerous papers on surgery, X-rays, electrical and physical science in relation to medicine, and demonstrations upon these subjects before the Royal Societies of London and Edinburgh, International Medical Congresses, and British Medical Association, published in the different Transactions and Proceedings of the societies or in the Lancet, British Medical Journal, Nature, and other scientific journals published at home or abroad. *Recreations:* yachting, naval volunteering. *Address:* 179 Bath Street, Glasgow. *T:* Nat. 162 Douglas, Glasgow. *Clubs:* Services; College Art, Glasgow.

Died 29 Oct. 1928.

M'IVER, Sir Lewis, 1st Bt, *cr* 1896; MP (UL) Edinburgh W, 1895–1909; Hon. Colonel of Forth Royal Garrison Artillery; *b* 6 March 1846; *s* of John M'Iver, Madras; *m* 1884, Charlotte, *d* of Nathaniel Montefiore; two *d*. *Educ:* Bonn University. Barrister 1878; Indian Civil Service, 1868–84; MP (L) Torquay Division, Devon, 1885–86; contested (UL) South Edinburgh, 1892. *Heir:* none. *Address:* 25 Upper Brook Street, W1. *T:* Mayfair 1209. *Clubs:* Ranelagh, Brooks's, Baldwin, St James', Royal Automobile.

Died 9 Aug. 1920 (ext).

MACK, Sir Hugh, Kt 1908; JP; Chairman of Directors of Hugh Mack & Co., Ltd, Belfast, Wholesale Woollen and Manchester Warehousemen; *b* 18 Nov. 1832; 3rd *s* of David Mack of Lisburn; *m* 1st, 1863, Emma, *d* of late William Gilbert of Belfast; 2nd, 1868, Margaret, *d* of late James Moore of Drumbadmore, Co. Fermanagh; three *s* four *d*. *Educ:* Lisburn. Founded business of which subseq. Chairman, 1859; Vice-President Ulster Liberal Association. *Address:* Dalboyne, Lisburn.   *Died Sept. 1920.*

MACK, Hon. Jason Miller; President of Legislative Council of Nova Scotia since 1920; *b* 17 March 1843; *m* 1878, Minnie, *o d* of Daniel Kellaher, Liverpool, NS. *Educ:* Normal School and King's College, University, Windsor. Barrister, 1869; KC 1907; MLC since 1907; Minister without portfolio, which position he resigned later; DCL King's College, 1921. *Address:* Liverpool, Nova Scotia.

Died Jan. 1927.

MACKARNESS, Ven. Charles Coleridge, DD; Examining Chaplain to the Archbishop of York; Canon of York since 1896; Fellow of Denstone College since 1901; *b* 22 July 1850; *e s* of late Bishop Mackarness of Oxford; *m* 1882, Grace Emily, *e d* of Rev. Canon Milford, formerly Rector of East Knoyle, Wilts; four *s* two *d*. *Educ:* Winchester; Exeter College, Oxford. BA, 2nd class Final Classical School, 1873; MA 1876; BD and DD 1914; Assistant Curate of St Mary's, Reading, 1874–79; Chaplain, Censor, and Theological Lecturer in King's College, London, 1879–81; Vicar of Aylesbury, 1882–89; Rural Dean of Aylesbury, 1887–89; Vicar of St Martin's, Scarborough, 1889–1916; Archdeacon of the East Riding, 1898–1916. *Publications:* The Message of the Prayer-Book, 1887; The Poetry of Keble as a Guide to the Clergy, 1891; Memorials of the Episcopate of Bishop Mackarness, 2nd edn, 1892; Faith and Duty in time of War (sermons), 1916. *Recreations:* formerly in Winchester Cricket XI, 1868; Capt. of Exeter Coll. Oxford XI, 1873; member of Oxford Univ. Association Football XI, 1873; cycling. *Address:* 1 Polstead Road, Oxford.   *Died 1 March 1918.*

MACKARNESS, Frederic Coleridge, MA; **His Honour Judge Mackarness;** County Court Judge, Circuit 50 (Sussex) since 1911; *b* 31 Aug. 1854; *s* of Rt Rev. J. F. Mackarness, Bishop of Oxford; *m* 1882, Amy (*d* 1916), *d* of Rev. Richard Chermside. *Educ:* Marlborough; Keble College, Oxford. Called to Bar, Middle Temple, 1879; Advocate of Cape Supreme Court, 1882; Revising Barrister for London, 1889; Recorder of Newbury, 1894; Professor of Roman-Dutch Law Univ. Coll. London, 1905–6; MP (L) Newbury Div. Berks, 1906–10. *Address:* 21 Montpelier Square, SW7. *T:* Kensington 2412; Kingsmead, Bramber. *Club:* Reform.

Died 23 Dec. 1920.

MACKAY, Alexander Grant, KC; MA; Minister of Municipal Affairs and Minister of Health since 1918; MPP Athabasca District, Alberta; Member of the Legislature of the Province of Alberta since 1913; Leader of the Liberal Opposition in the Legislature of the Province of Ontario, 1907–11; *b* 7 March 1860; Scotch parentage; unmarried. *Educ:* Toronto University. Four years High School Principal; Member Legislature of Province of Ontario, 1902–13; Minister of Crown Lands, Ontario, 1904–5. *Address:* Edmonton, Canada.

Died April 1920.

MACKAY, Ebenezer, BA, PhD; M'Leod Professor of Chemistry in Dalhousie University since 1896; *b* Plainfield, Pictou County, Nova Scotia, 1864; *s* of Angus Mackay, a native of Rogart, Sutherlandshire. *Educ:* Pictou Academy; Dalhousie University; Johns Hopkins University. Principal of Schools, New Glasgow, NS, 1886–92; Fellow, Johns Hopkins University, 1895. *Address:* Dalhousie University, Halifax, NS. *Club:* Halifax.   *Died 6 Jan. 1920.*

MACKAY, Ven. John Alexander, DD; Archdeacon of Saskatchewan and Superintendent of Indian Missions; *b* Hudson's Bay Territories, 1838; *s* of William Mackay, an officer of the Hon. Hudson's Bay Company, and Mary Bunn; *m* 1864, Margaret Drever of Winnipeg; one *s* four *d*. *Educ:* by Rev. E. A. Watkins and Rev. J. Horden, afterwards Bishop Horden, missionaries of the CMS; St John's College, Winnipeg, under Bishop Anderson. Ordained deacon, 1862; priest, 1863; for fifty-nine years missionary among the Cree Indians in the Canadian North-West. *Publications:* translation of Oxenden's Pathway of Safety; A Manual of Family Prayer; Psalms and Hymns, all in Cree; revision of the Bible in Cree for the British and Foreign Bible Society; Revision Hordon's Cree Grammar and Hunter's Translation of Book of Common Prayer in Cree. *Address:* Prince Albert, Saskatchewan, NWT, Canada.

Died Nov. 1923.

MACKAY, Hon. Robert; Senator since 1901; *b* Scotland, 1840; *m* 1871, *d* of late George Baptist, Three Rivers, PQ; four *s* two *d*. Went to Canada, 1855; director of many companies. *Address:* Kildonan Hall, 681 Sherbrooke Street W, Montreal. *Clubs:* St James's, Mount Royal, Canada, Montreal; Rideau, Ottawa.

Died 16 Dec. 1916.

M'KAY, William D., RSA 1883 (ARSA 1877); LLD Edin.; *b* Gifford, East Lothian, 1844; *e s* of Peter M'Kay, parish schoolmaster there. *Educ:* parish school, Gifford. Entered at Trustees' Academy, Edinburgh, 1860; afterwards studied at the Royal Scottish Academy's School. Librarian, 1896; Secretary, 1907; practised the landscape and landscape with figures department of Art. *Publications:* George Manson and his works, in collaboration with P. W. Adam, RSA, and late John M. Gray, 1880; The Scottish School of Painting, 1906; Raeburn's Technique, special article for The Studio, Feb. 1908; in collaboration with Frank Rinder, The Royal Scottish Academy, 1826–1916, 1917. *Address:* 1 Warrender Park Crescent, Edinburgh. *Club:* Scottish Arts, Edinburgh.   *Died 10 Dec. 1924.*

M'KEAN, Captain George Burdon, VC 1918; MC; MM; late Corps of Military Accountants; *b* Bishop Auckland, Co. Durham, 4 July 1890; *s* of James M'Kean, merchant, and Jane Ann Henderson. *Educ:* Robertson College and University of Alberta, Edmonton. Went to Canada alone, 1905; lived and worked on a cattle ranch, and later on a farm owned by brother, until 1911, when he entered Robertson College; registered with the University of Alberta as a student in Arts and Medicine, 1912; enlisted in Canadian Expeditionary Force, 1915; Sergeant, 1916; France, 1916; Commission, 1917; Captain, 1919 (twice wounded, VC, MC, MM); retired pay, 1926. *Publication:* Scouting Thrills, 1919. *Recreations:* tennis, football. *Address:* c/o Lloyds Bank, Ltd, Cox and King's Branch, 6 Pall Mall, SW1.

Died Nov. 1926.

McKEE, Rev. Robert Alexander, MA; Vicar of Farnsfield, 1882–1923; Canon of Rampton in Southwell Cathedral, 1915; Rural Dean of Southwell, 1910; *b* Ward House, Co. Leitrim, 1847; *e s* of Rev. James McKee, DD, late Vicar of Wymynswold, Co. Kent; *m* 1872, Mary, 2nd *d* of John Jeffery, Northampton; four *s* two *d*. *Educ:* St John's College, Cambridge; Deacon, 1871; Priest, 1872; Curate of Atherton, 1871–73; Curate in charge of St Anne, Hindsford, 1873–77; Vicar of Lumb-in-Rossendale, 1877–82; Secretary to the Board of Education for the County of Notts, 1897; Secretary to the Notts Church Schools' Association, 1903; Secretary to the Southwell Diocesan Education Committee, 1904; Organising Secretary of SPG for the Archdeaconry of Nottingham, 1903. *Address:* Bickerton Vicarage, Malpas, Cheshire.

Died 19 Feb. 1926.

MACKEEN, Hon. David; Senator since 1896; *b* 20 Sept. 1839; *m* 1st, 1867, Isabel (decd), *d* of late Henry Poole, Derby, England; 2nd, 1877, Francis M. (decd), *d* of late William Lawson, Halifax, NS; 3rd, 1888, Jane K., *e d* of late John Crerar, Halifax, NS. *Address:* Maplewood, Halifax, NS. *Clubs:* Halifax, Halifax; Rideau, Ottawa.

Died 13 Nov. 1916.

MACKELLAR, Hon. Sir Charles Kinnaird, KCMG 1916; Kt 1912; MB, CM; Member of the Legislative Council of New South Wales since 1886; President of the State Children Board New South Wales for 14 years; *b* Sydney, NSW, 5 Dec. 1844; *s* of Frederick Mackellar, MD, of Sydney, NSW; *m* 1877, Marion, *d* of Thomas Buckland of Sydney; two *s* one *d*. *Educ:* Sydney Grammar School; University of Glasgow. Representative of the Jennings Dibbs Government, and Minister for Mines, 1886; Member of the Senate of the Commonwealth, 1900; sometime President of the Board of Health and Medical Adviser to the Government of NSW. *Address:* Rosemount, Ocean Street, Woollahra, Sydney. *Club:* Australian, Sydney. *Died July 1926.*

M'KENDRICK, John Gray, LLD (Hon. Aberdeen and Glasgow), MD; FRS, FRSE, FRCPE; MRI; Professor of Physiology, Glasgow University, 1876-1906, then Emeritus; formerly Examiner in Physiology, University of London, Victoria University, University of Birmingham, Universities of Oxford, Cambridge, Durham, and Aberdeen (1916); *b* Aberdeen, 1841; *o s* of James M'Kendrick, merchant, Aberdeen; *m* 1867, Mary (*d* 1898), *d* of W. Souttar, Aberdeen; two *s* two *d*. *Educ:* Aberdeen and Edinburgh Universities (MD, ChM Aberdeen). Formerly Assistant to Professor of, and Lecturer on, Physiology, Edinburgh; Fullerian Professor of Physiology at Royal Institute of Great Britain; twice delivered the Thomson Lectures at the Free Church College of Aberdeen; formerly one of the lecturers in connection with the Gilchrist Trust; served on the Councils of the Royal Society and of Royal Society of Edinburgh; President of Physiological Section of British Association; subseq. spent most of the year at Maxieburn, Stonehaven. *Publications:* Animal Physiology, 1876; Lectures on the History of Physiology, 1879; A Text-Book of Physiology, 1888; Life in Motion, or Muscle Nerve, 1892; Physiology, 1896; Life of Helmholtz, 1899; Boyle (Oxford) Lecture on Hearing, 1899; Science and Faith, 1899; Christianity and the Sick, 1901; and various papers on physiological acoustics and experimental phonetics. *Address:* Maxieburn, Stonehaven. *T:* Stonehaven 8. *Died 2 Jan. 1926.*

MACKENZIE, Col Sir Alfred Robert Davidson, KCB 1907 (CB 1886); late Bengal Cavalry; *b* 30 Sept. 1835. Entered army, 1854; Colonel 1882; served Indian Mutiny, 1857-58 (medal with 2 clasps); Afghan War, 1879-80 (despatches, medal with clasp, bronze decoration). *Club:* East India United Service. *Died 8 May 1921.*

M'KENZIE, Lt-Col Archibald Ernest Graham, DSO 1916; Commanding 26th (New Brunswick) Battalion Canadians since 1916; *b* Campbellton, New Brunswick, Canada, 21 Jan. 1878; *s* of Archibald M'Kenzie; *m* 1904, Charlotte B., *d* of James M. Troy, Newcastle, NB. *Educ:* University of New Brunswick (BA 1902; MA 1904); King's College, BCL 1907. After graduation Principal of Harkin's Academy, Newcastle, New Brunswick; admitted to Bar of New Brunswick in 1907, and commenced practice in Campbellton; contested (L) the County of Restigouche, 1912; always took deep interest in militia, being Adjutant of Batt. at outbreak of war. *Recreations:* fishing, curling. *Address:* Campbellton, NB, Canada. *Clubs:* Union, St John; Campbellton. *Died 8 Sept. 1918.*

MACKENZIE, David James; advocate; *b* 8 March 1855; *s* of Thomas Mackenzie, Ladyhill, Elgin; *m* 1886, Margaret Jane, *d* of George Wilson, MD, Huntly, Aberdeenshire. *Educ:* schools in Elgin and Aberdeen; Universities of Aberdeen and Edinburgh. Admitted a Member of the Faculty of Advocates, 1879; appointed Sheriff-Substitute of Caithness, Orkney, and Zetland at Lerwick, 1885; transferred to Wick, 1891; to Kilmarnock, 1902, and to Lanarkshire at Glasgow, 1914; retired, 1920. FSAScot 1887. *Publications:* Byways among Books, 1900; Poems, 1920, etc; a contributor to various magazines, including Blackwood's, All the Year Round, Good Words, and Chambers's. *Recreations:* reading, book-hunting, scribbling with pen and pencil. *Address:* Deansford, Bishopmill, Elgin. *Died 27 May 1925.*

M'KENZIE, Donald Duncan, KC; Judge of Supreme Court of Nova Scotia since 1923; MPPC; *b* Lake Ainslie, Nova Scotia, 8 Jan. 1859; *s* of Duncan M'Kenzie and Jessie M'Millan; *m* 1891, Florence N. M'Donald of Sydney Mines, NS; one *s*. *Educ:* Sydney Academy. Admitted to the Nova Scotia Bar, 1889; elected to the Local Legislature of Nova Scotia, 1900; resigned, 1904; elected to House of Commons; re-elected 1908, 1911, 1917, and 1921; Leader of Liberal Opposition, House of Commons, Ottawa, 1919-21; Solicitor-General, Canada, 1921-23. Presbyterian. *Recreations:* quoits, horses, fishing. *Address:* Halifax, Nova Scotia. *Died June 1927.*

MACKENZIE, Ven. Gaden Crawford; Archdeacon of Perth, Huron, since 1905. *Educ:* Trinity College, Toronto (Hon. DCL). Ordained, 1869; Incumbent of Dysart, 1869-70; Curate, 1870-72; Chaplain, 1872-73; Rector of Kincardine, 1873-79; Gracechurch, Brantford, 1879-1905. *Address:* Brantford, Ontario. *Died 20 March 1920.*

MACKENZIE, J. Hamilton, ARSA 1923; RSW 1910; ARE 1910; President Glasgow Art Club, 1923-25; *b* Glasgow, 1875; *m* Margaret Thomson Wilson, artist (*decd*). *Educ:* Glasgow School of Art (Haldane Travelling Scholarship); R. Instituto de Belli Arti, Florence. Exhibits at Glasgow Institute, RSA, etc; Fleeting Shadows was purchased by Glasgow Corporation Art Gallery, 1913. Army Service, RASC, Motor Transport, 1915-19—rank, Private; East Africa, 1916. *Publications:* amongst his etchings: Cathedral of St Francis, Assisi; L'Ancien Greffe and Cathedral Tower, Bruges. *Address:* 204 West Regent Street, Glasgow; Studio, 104 West George Street, Glasgow. *Clubs:* Glasgow Art; Scottish Arts, Edinburgh. *Died 29 March 1926.*

MACKENZIE, J. J., BA, MB; FRS Canada; Professor of Pathology and Bacteriology, University of Toronto, since 1900; *b* 1865; a Canadian by birth, of Scottish parentage; *m* 1892, Agnes Kathleen, *d* of W. Vesey-Rogers, Dublin. *Educ:* Univ. of Toronto; Univs of Leipzig and Berlin. Sometime Fellow in Biology, Univ. of Toronto; subsequently Bacteriologist to the Ontario Provincial Board of Health; wrote on bacteriological and pathological subjects; member of the American Public Health Association, the Society of American Bacteriologists, and American Association of Pathologists and Bacteriologists; Past President, Royal Canadian Institute. Served European War attached to No 4 Canadian General Hospital (University of Toronto) in Greece. *Address:* 56 Wychwood Park, Hillcrest, Toronto. *T:* Hillcrest 7007. *Clubs:* Royal Societies; Toronto Golf, York, Toronto. *Died 1 Aug. 1922.*

MACKENZIE, Sir James, Kt 1915; MD Edin.; LLD, Aberdeen and Edinburgh; FRCP; FRS 1915; Consulting Physician to the King in Scotland; Consulting Physician to the London Hospital; *b* 12 April 1853; *s* of Robert Mackenzie, Scone; *m* 1887, Frances, *d* of George Jackson, Boston; one *d*. *Educ:* Perth Academy; Edinburgh University. After graduation (1878) appointed House Physician and Assistant to Professors of Clinical Medicine, Royal Infirmary, Edinburgh; in medical practice in Burnley, 1879-1907; in consulting practice in London, 1907-18. Oliver-Sharpey Lecturer, Royal College of Physicians, 1911; Schorstein Lecturer, London Hospital, 1911; Gibson Memorial Lecturer, Edinburgh College of Physicians, 1914. *Publications:* The Study of the Pulse, etc, 1902 (German trans); Diseases of the Heart, 1908, 3rd edn 1913 (German, French, and Italian trans); Symptoms and their Interpretation, 3rd edn 1918 (German, Italian, Danish and Spanish trans); Principles of Diagnosis and Treatment in Heart Affections, 1916 (Italian trans); The Future of Medicine, 1919; numerous papers to scientific journals. *Address:*53 Albert Hall Mansions, Kensington Gore, SW7. *Died 26 Jan. 1925.*

MACKENZIE, Kenneth James Joseph, MA, ASI, etc; Reader in Agriculture in the University of Cambridge and Consultant to the Institute of Animal Nutrition; *b* 1867; *s* of late Major A. C. C. Mackenzie, RE, and Melesina, *d* of late J. H. Woodward; unmarried. *Educ:* Fort Augustus College; the SEA College, Wye; BDFA Institution, Reading; abroad. Late Professor of Agriculture, SEASC; Member of the Agricultural Board of Studies and Examiner, London University; late Editor of the Journal and Governor of the Royal Agricultural Society of England; chairman of the Cambridgeshire and Isle of Ely Chamber of Agriculture and many other agricultural societies, and judged all sorts of classes at agricultural shows; represented the British Government on the International Exhibition at Brussels, 1910; and went in 1918 to France on behalf of the War Office and YMCA to lecture to the BEF concerning the home food supply, etc. *Publications:* Cattle, 1919, a reconstructive work on animal husbandry; many articles in the various agricultural periodicals, and wrote in all classes of publications upon the feeding of England during the war. *Address:* Christ's College, Cambridge. *T:* Cambridge 913. *Clubs:* Savile, Farmers'. *Died 5 June 1924.*

McKENZIE, Marian, FRAM; leading contralto vocalist and teacher; *b* Plymouth; *e d* of Capt. Joseph McKenzie; *m* Richard Smith Williams (*d* 1926). *Educ:* privately at Plymouth; musical education under Dr Samuel Weekes, Plymouth; Royal Acad. of Music, under Cavaliere Alberto Randegger, etc. Parepa Rosa Scholar; Westmoreland Scholar, RAM; bronze, silver, and gold medallist, RAM; principal contralto of the Handel and Bach Festivals, and of the Leeds, Birmingham,

Norwich, Chester, etc, Festivals, and of the Welsh Eisteddfodd, also of HM State concerts and the Viceregal Court; Associate Philharmonic Society; member Royal Society of Musicians. *Recreation:* bridge. *Address:* 83 Carlisle Mansions, Victoria Street, SW1. *T:* Victoria 5353.
Died 16 June 1927.

McKENZIE, Hon. Robert Donald, OBE 1919; JP; *b* Maldon, Victoria, Australia, 19 March 1865; 2nd *s* of Hugh McKenzie, JP; *m* 1895, Emma Mary, *e d* of James Widgery, Sydney, NSW; three *s* one *d. Educ:* St Paul's Grammar School, Melbourne. Arrived in West Australia with the advent of gold discoveries, 1892; a pioneer of Kalgoorlie; largely interested in mining and commercial pursuits; first Senior Councillor of Kalgoorlie, afterwards Mayor; Member of Legislative Council for North-East Province, 1904–16; served on three Royal Commissions in connection with mining industry in West Australia; founded Kalgoorlie Chamber of Commerce, elected first President, 1910–11; Hon. Minister and Member of the Executive Council of West Australia, 1910–11; hon. Red Cross work in France, 1915–18 (despatches). *Recreations:* golf, bowls. *M:* CT1. *Clubs:* Perth, Hannans, Kalgoorlie, Masonic, Perth.
Died 1928.

MACKENZIE, Col Robert Holden, FSA 1887; FSAScot 1904; Gentleman of the King's Body-Guard for Scotland; late Major Worcestershire Regiment and Colonel commanding 4th (Special Reserve) Battalion the Cameronians (Scottish Rifles); raised the 1st (Highlanders) Cadet Battalion the Royal Scots in Edinburgh in 1911. Was in HMS Lively when that vessel was wrecked and lost, while attached to Royal Commission on the Highland Crofters, 1883; ADC to Sir Walter Sendall, GCMG, Governor of the Windward Islands, 1885–86; to Sir Henry Bulwer, GCMG, Governor of Natal and afterwards Cyprus, 1886–89; to Lieut-General Sir F. M. Colvile, KCB, 1891–93; and to Major-General Sir A. E. Turner, KCB, Inspector-Gen. of Auxiliary Forces, 1900–1; served operations in Soudan, 1889; South African War, 1900–2; a member of Council of the Royal United Service Institution, and for some years on the Staff of the Royal Military Tournament. Esq.OStJ. *Publications:* The Trafalgar Roll; papers and contributions to Dictionary of National Biography, Scottish Historical Review, Cornhill, Chambers' Journal, Macmillan's, United Service, Cavalry, and other magazines. *Recreations:* Military and Scottish History and Antiquities. *Clubs:* United Service; New, Edinburgh.

MACKENZIE, Maj.-Gen. Roderick, JP and DL for Aberdeenshire; *b* 1830; *s* of late Major Forbes Mackenzie; *m* 1878, Caroline, *d* of J. A. Beaumont; one *d. Educ:* Military Academy, Woolwich. Served in the Royal Artillery throughout the Crimean War. Knight of the Legion of Honour; 5th class Medjidie. *Address:* Foveran House, Aberdeenshire; 14 Charles Street, Berkeley Square, W. *T:* Mayfair 5772. *Clubs:* Carlton, United Service, Turf; New, Edinburgh.
Died 19 May 1916.

MACKENZIE, W. G., ARHA. *Educ:* Old School of Art, Belfast (National Scholarship); London, under E. J. Poynter, RA; Julian's, Paris. Specimens of his painting from the figure were purchased by the authorities of South Kensington and elsewhere, and used as examples in the Government Schools of Art; Adjudicator at the School of Art, Belfast. *Works:* Portrait of late C. C. Connor (last Mayor of Belfast), City Hall, Belfast; Presentation Portrait of Sir Crawford McCullagh, ex-Lord Mayor of Belfast, Royal Hibernian Academy, Dublin. *Address:* Studio, Clarence Place, Belfast.

MACKENZIE, Sir William, Kt 1911; President of the Canadian Northern Railway; member of Mackenzie, Mann & Co.; *b* Kirkfield, Ont., 30 Oct. 1849, of Scottish parentage; Presbyterian; *m* 1872, Margaret (*d* 1917), *d* of John Derry, KGStJ; two *s* six *d. Address:* Benvenuto, 350 Avenue Road, Toronto. *Clubs:* Toronto, Toronto; St James's, Montreal; Manitoba, Winnipeg; Rideau, Ottawa.
Died 5 Dec. 1923.

MACKENZIE, William Dalziel, JP, DL; *b* Renfrewshire, 1840; *e s* of Edward Mackenzie, of Fawley Court, JP, DL Oxon, and Mary Dalziel; *m* 1st, 1863, Mary Anna (*d* 1900), *e d* of Henry Baskerville, of Crowsley Park, Oxon; 2nd, 1902, Mary Catherine (*d* 1924), 2nd *d* of Adam S. Gladstone, and *widow* of Sir Francis G. Stapleton, 8th Bt; one *s* four *d. Educ:* Harrow; Magdalen Coll., Oxford, MA. Barrister-at-law, Inner Temple, 1863; Conservative candidate, Reading, 1874; later at Truro and Woodstock; JP Oxon (High Sheriff, 1873), Bucks Cos Dumfries, Kirkcudbright, Inverness; DL; Lt-Col late Queen's Own Oxfordshire Hussars, Imperial Yeomanry; Director of L&NWR Co., 1873–82. *Publications:* On Agricultural Depression

and Fiscal Question, etc. *Recreations:* farms largely, estate improvements, planting, etc. *Address:* House of Farr, Inverness; Fawley Court, Henley-on-Thames. *T:* Henley 201. *Clubs:* Carlton, Cavalry, Constitutional, Caledonian.
Died 4 Dec. 1928.

MACKENZIE, Lt-Col William Scobie, DSO 1917; OBE 1920; RAOC; *m* 1906, Geraldine, *d* of late Col Francis Moore; three *s* two *d.* Served European War, 1914–18 (despatches, DSO). *Address:* Forthside House, Stirling.
Died 1 Sept. 1926.

McKEOWN, Robert John; MP (U) North Belfast, Northern Parliament; Director, Milfort Weaving and Finishing Co Ltd, Belfast and other companies; *b* Coagh, Co. Tyrone, 12 May 1869; *m* 1899, Elizabeth J., *d* of John McVea, Whitehead; two *s* one *d. Educ:* Moneymore Intermediate School; private tuition. Chairman of the Irish Power-loom Manufacturers Association, 1914–20; member of the Flax Control Board, London, during the War; Parliamentary Secretary for the Ministry of Education and also for the Ministry of Commerce; President of the Ulster Reform Club, 1920, and Chairman of the Ulster Liberal Unionist Association, 1921. *Recreations:* golf, boating. *Address:* Cliff Lodge, Whitehead, Co. Antrim. *T:* Whitehead 12. *M:* OI 7643. *Clubs:* Constitutional; Ulster Reform, Belfast; Co. Antrim Yacht.
Died 9 April 1925.

McKEOWN, Walter, CBE 1919; BA, MD, MRCS Eng.; Col CAMC; President of the Academy of Medicine, Toronto; *b* Toronto, 10 Feb. 1866; *m* 1892, Minnie, *e d* of late John Woods, Toronto; one *s* two *d. Educ:* Upper Canada College and University, Toronto; Middlesex Hospital. Continuously in practice in Toronto from 1891; Associate Professor of Clinical Surgery, University of Toronto; Surgeon-in-Chief, St Michael's Hospital, Toronto; served in NW Rebellion, 1885; European War, CEF, 1915; Member of the Royal Commission on Pensions appointed by Dominion Government, 1922. *Recreation:* music. *Address:* 140 Wellesley Crescent, Toronto.
Died 6 Sept. 1925.

McKERRELL, Brig.-Comdr Augustus de Ségur, CB 1908; *b* 28 Aug. 1863; *s* of late Robert McKerrell. *Educ:* Cheam; Eton; RMC Sandhurst. Joined the Cameron Highlanders, 1884; Captain 1892; Major 1899; Bt Lt-Col 1899; Bt-Col 1904; employed with Egyptian army, 1893–1903; served Soudan, 1884–85 (medal with clasp, bronze star); Soudan, 1885–86; Dongola, 1896 (Egyptian medal); Nile Expedition, 1897 (clasp), 1898 (despatches, brevet Lt-Col, clasp and medal), 1899 (clasp, 3rd class Medjidie and 3rd Osmanieh); Governor, Dongola, 1900–2; Berber, 1902–3; commanded 2nd Batt. Cameron Highlanders, 1910–12. *Address:* Headquarters, Black Watch Infantry Brigade, Dundee. *Club:* Naval and Military.
Died 24 April 1916.

MACKESY, Col Charles Ernest Randolph, CMG 1917; CBE 1919; DSO 1917; JP; retired; landowner; *b* Dublin, 1861; *s* of Captain E. R. Mackesy, late 97th Regt; *m* Jessie (*d* 1920), *d* of Thomas Adam, Kilmarnock; three *s. Educ:* France; Switzerland; Germany. Took first prize on several occasions for all-round athletics; spent several years in Western USA; since 1891 in NZ; 20 years Vol. and Terr. Officer; left with main body, 1914, in command of Auckland MR; served 5½ years abroad; several times in command of Mounted Brigade; Military Governor and Administrator East of Jordan (despatches five times, CMG, CBE, DSO); served on County Council and Harbour Boards. *Publications:* pamphlets on Chronology, etc. *Address:* The Hill, Whangarei, Auckland, New Zealand.
Died 20 Nov. 1925.

MACKEY, Brig.-Gen. Hugh James Alexander, CMG 1917; DSO 1915; MVO 1901; late RFA; *b* 19 March 1876; *s* of late Capt. Hugh A. Mackey, RA; *m* 1904, Violet Alice, *e d* of Henry Edgar Rodwell; three *d.* Entered RA 1896; Captain, 1902; Major, 1912; Adjutant, RMA, 1909–13; Lt-Col, 1917; Col, 1921; served European War, 1914–19, including Mesopotamia (despatches six times, DSO, CMG, Order of St Stanislas, 1914 Star, GS and Victory medals); retired pay, 1921. *Address:* c/o Lloyds Bank, Cox's Branch, 6 Pall Mall, SW1. *Club:* Army and Navy.
Died 1 May 1927.

MACKEY, Hon. Sir John Emanuel, Kt 1921; MA, LLB; MLA Gippsland West, 1902; Speaker of the Legislative Assembly, Victoria, since 1917; *b* 7 Aug. 1865; *m* Zella, *y d* of late Hon. William Bates, Minister of Trade and Customs; two *s* two *d.* Was Minister of Lands; Chief Secretary; Minister for Labour; Solicitor-General; Barrister-at-law; Lecturer on Equity, University of Melbourne; Member of the Council of the University of Melbourne, Trustee and Treasurer of the Melbourne Public Library and National Gallery; Member of the Board of Visitors of the Melbourne Observatory; Chairman of

Trustees of the Melbourne Cricket Ground. *Address:* Selborne Chambers, Melbourne, Victoria, Australia.

Died April 1924.

MACKIE, Charles H., RSA 1917 (ARSA 1902); RSW 1902; *b* 1862; *s* of Captain William Mackie, 2nd Regt (Queen's Royals); *m* 1891, 2nd *d* of Provost Walls, Dunfermline; one *s*. *Educ:* Edinburgh University; Royal Scottish Academy Schools. Painter of landscapes, portraits, and mural decorations; Chairman of Society of Scottish Artists, 1900–1; exhibited at Munich, Venice, Berlin, Buda-Pesth, Dresden, and Amsterdam International Exhibitions; received Gold Medal at Amsterdam, 1912, also RA, RSA, Pittsburg, PA, etc. *Publications:* several wood-block colour prints. *Recreations:* golf, bicycling. *Address:* Coltbridge Studio, Murrayfield, NB. *Club:* Scottish Arts.

Died 12 July 1920.

MACKIE, Rev. George M., MA, DD; Missionary to the Jews and Minister of Anglo-American Congregation, Beyrout, since 1880; *b* Banchory-Ternan, near Aberdeen, 1854; *s* of Rev. James Mackie. *Educ:* graduated in Arts at Aberdeen Univ. with honours in Ment. Phil.; entered Edinburgh Divinity Hall as First Bursar, 1876, and shortly after completing his theological studies offered himself as a missionary on behalf of Israel. In his Arabic and Hebrew studies, while chiefly seeking to qualify himself for the work of an evangelist, by long residence in the East and contact with Jews, Moslems, and Oriental Christians, he become deeply conscious of the family background of the Bible and of the helpfulness of Oriental life and folklore in explaining its meaning. In 1901 the degree of DD was conferred upon him by Aberdeen University. Contributed various articles on such matters to Hastings' Bible Dictionary and the Expository Times; author of the text-book, Bible Manners and Customs, belonging to the Guild Library Series of the Church of Scotland. *Recreations:* golf, sketching. *Address:* Beyrout, Syria.

Died 1922.

MACKIE, John Beveridge, FJI; editor and proprietor Dunfermline Journal, Dunfermline Express, West Fife Echo, Rosyth and Forth Mail; *b* Dunfermline, 2 June 1848; 3rd *s* of John Mackie and Janet Syme; *m* 1885, Lilias, *d* of late James Robb, editor of Scottish Farmer; two *s* three *d*. *Educ:* Free Abbey Acad. Dunfermline. Reporter Dunfermline, Cupar-Fife, Edin. and Glasgow; sub-editor Glasgow Herald, 1870–77; with his brothers William and Robert conducted Daily Review, Edin., 1877–86; leader-writer Newcastle Daily Leader, 1886–89; editor of North-Eastern Daily Gazette, 1890–1903. *Publications:* Life and Work of Duncan M'Laren, 1888; Modern Journalism, 1894; Memories; Pitcairnie: a Tale of the Press-Gang; Friends of the People; Pittencrieff Glen, its History, Antiquities, and Legends; Essays on Influence; Margaret, Queen and Saint; Dunfermline Men of Mark; Dunfermline Born Princes and Princesses; Idylls of Dunfermline; The Model Member: Sir Henry Campbell-Bannerman's Forty Years Connection with the Stirling Burghs, 1914; Andrew Carnegie: his Dunfermline Ties and Benefactions, etc. *Address:* Park Place, Dunfermline. *TA:* Journal, Dunfermline. *T:* 11.

Died 22 May 1919.

MACKIE, Sir Peter Jeffrey, 1st Bt, *cr* 1920; FSA; JP; *b* 26 Nov. 1855; *e s* of Alexander Mackie; *m* 1889, Jessie, *d* of Thomas Abercrombie; two *d*. Chairman White Horse Distillers, Ltd; travelled extensively and wrote on Tariff Reform, Empire Federation, and other political subjects; Unionist; Episcopal; owner of 12,000 acres. *Publications:* Empire; The Keeper's Book (16 editions). *Recreations:* all sports. *Heir:* none. *Address:* Corraith, Symington, Ayrshire. *T:* Troon 19. *TA:* Symington, Kilmarnock; Glenreasdell, Whitehouse, Argyll. *Clubs:* Caledonian; County, Ayr.   *Died 22 Sept. 1924 (ext).*

MACKIE, Sir Richard, Kt 1909; JP; ship owner and coal exporter; *b* Dunfermline, April 1851; *m* 1876, Isabella, *d* of late Laurence Thomson, St Andrews; two *s* two *d*. *Educ:* Dunfermline. Came to Leith, 1865; entered an office of Shipbrokers and Coal Exporters; in the same office from above date and acquired the business, 1873; carried on the firm of Mackie, Koth and Co., from 1873 as Shipbrokers and Coal Exporters; established the firm of Richard Mackie & Co., Steamship Owners, 1882; senior partner of both firms; Provost of Leith, 1899–1908. Italian and Swedish Vice-Consul; Knight of the Polar Star Sweden; Cavaliere of the Crown of Italy. *Recreations:* golf, bowling, yachting. *Address:* Trinity Grove, Leith. *TA:* Mackie, Leith. *T:* Granton 223. *M:* WS 1, WS 2. *Clubs:* Junior Constitutional, Conservative, Edinburgh; Royal Forth Yacht, Merchants', Leith.   *Died 30 June 1923.*

MACKINLAY, Lt-Col George; *b* 1847; 2nd *s* of late John Mackinlay, MRCS; *m* 1871, Lucy Teshmaker, *d* of late David Graham Johnstone,

JP; one *d*. *Educ:* Kensington Grammar School; RM Academy, Woolwich. Joined RA 1866; served in the Punjab and in Malta six years; Instructor, RM Academy, Woolwich, seven years; passed Artillery College; Observer, transit of Venus Expedition to Jamaica, 1882; retired, 1889; took part in Missionary work in Galicia, Spain, 1892–94; rejoined the army at Woolwich during Boer War, 1900–2; retired half-pay Lt-Col; Assistant Inspector of Steel under the Admiralty in Yorkshire, 1915–16, during World War; Vice-President of the Victoria Institute. *Publications:* The Text Books of Gunnery, 1883 and 1887; The Magi, how they recognised Christ's Star (in which it was first demonstrated that 8 BC was the date of the Nativity), 1907; Recent Discoveries in St Luke's Writings (in which the existence of three parallel narratives in St Luke's Gospel was first pointed out), 1921. *Address:* Coverley, 4 Thornlaw Road, West Norwood, SE27.

Died 1 Oct. 1928.

MACKINNON, Hon. Donald Alexander, KC; LLB; MP for Queen's County, Prince Edward Island, since 1921; *b* 21 Feb. 1863, of Scottish parentage; *m* 1892, Louisa Owen (*d* 1912), of Georgetown; one *s* one *d*. *Educ:* Prince of Wales College; Dalhousie University, Halifax; LLB. Admitted to the Bar of PEI 1887; QC 1900; President Law Society of PEI 1901; a Member of House of Assembly of PEI 1893; re-elected 1897 for Murray Harbour Electrical District; Attorney-General in Provincial Cabinet; MP East Queen's, PEI, to House of Commons, Canada, 1900–4; Lieut-Governor of PEI, Canada, 1904–10; Hon. Colonel, 82nd Regiment, 1909; President Law Society of PEI, 1916; Vice-President, British and Foreign Sailors Society for PEI; Chief of Caledonian Club; Commissioner for Boy Scouts, PEI; appointed Honourable for life, 1927. *Publications:* The Constitution (PEI); History of Queen's County; PEI in 1950; joint editor of Past and Present Prince Edward Island. *Address:* Charlottetown, Prince Edward Island. *TA:* Fingon. *T:* 64.

Died April 1928.

MACKINNON, Sir Lauchlan Charles, Kt 1916; *b* Corry, Broadford, Isle of Skye, 12 April 1848; *s* of late Alex. K. Mackinnon and Barbara, *d* of Capt. Reid; *m* 1876, Emily Grace Mackinnon (*d* 1923); one *s* two *d*. *Educ:* Bath; Finchley College, London. Went to Australia, 1870; General Manager of the Argus and Australasian, 1880–1920; proprietor of the Mackinnon share on the death of the original proprietor, Lauchlan Mackinnon, 1888. *Address:* Downes, Crediton, Devon. *Clubs:* Reform, Oriental; Melbourne, Australian, Melbourne.

Died 3 Dec. 1925.

M'KINNON, Rev. W.; Minister, Gairloch; ex-Moderator General Assembly Free Church of Scotland, 1908; *b* Strath, Skye, 1843. *Educ:* Free Church School, Strath; Normal Training College, University, and Free Church College, Glasgow. Minister at Ballachulish, 1878; North Uist; Glenmoriston. *Address:* Gairloch, Scotland.

Died 13 Feb. 1925.

MACKINTOSH, Rt. Rev. Mgr Alexander; Catholic Priest, Fort William; *b* Inverness-shire, 1854 (Gaelic-speaking Highlander). *Educ:* Blair's College, Aberdeen; Douai; Paris; St Peter's Seminary, Glasgow. Ordained, 1877; Canon Theologian of Argyll and the Isles since 1907; Vicar General, 1917–18; Vicar Capitular (*sede vacante*), 1918–19; Protonotary Apostolic and Domestic Prelate, 1920. *Address:* The Presbytery, Fort William, Scotland.

Died 4 May 1922.

MACKINTOSH, Charles Rennie, FRIBA; IA; architect; artist; *b* Glasgow, 7 Jan. 1869; *y s* of William Mackintosh; *m* 1900, Margaret, *d* of John Macdonald. *Educ:* Glasgow School of Art; Paris. Greek Thomson Scholar, 1889; travelled in France and Italy. *Works:* public, ecclesiastic, and domestic, executed in Scotland, England, Belgium, Germany, Austria, Italy, and Russia. Corresponding member of Künstler Osterreiche, Vienna. *Publication:* Meister der Inner Kunst. *Recreations:* travel, research. *Address:* 2 Haus Studios, 43A Glebe Place, Chelsea, SW3.   *Died 10 Dec. 1928.*

MACKINTOSH, Most Rev. Donald A.; Archbishop of Chersona, and Coadjutor-Archbishop of Glasgow, with the right of succession, since 1912; Provost of the Chapter; *b* 1845. *Educ:* France; Blairs College, Aberdeen. Ordained Priest, 1871; Vicar-General of the Archdiocese of Glasgow, 1909–12. *Address:* 5 Westbourne Gardens, Kelvinside, Glasgow.   *Died 13 Oct. 1919.*

MACKINTOSH, Rev. William Lachlan, MA Oxon; Rector of St Michael and All Angels, Inverness, since 1910, and Canon of the Cathedral since 1911; *b* Ballifeary (then Eilenach), Inverness, 31 Aug. 1859; *e s* of late Eneas Mackintosh, JP and DL of Balnespick, Inverness-shire (*d* 1893), and Isabella Lachlan, *d* of Isaac Barker of Itonfield,

Cumberland. *Educ:* Marlborough College; Pembroke College, Oxon; Ely Theological College. Deacon, 1886; Priest, 1887; Assistant Curate, Wantage, Berks, 1887–91; Canon Residentiary of Inverness Cathedral with the charge of the Mission Chapel of the Holy Spirit, 1891; succeeded to the property of Balnespick and Clune, Inverness-shire, on the death of his father, 1893; resigned his Canonry in order to work entirely at the Mission, 1902; endowed the Mission Chapel, so that it became an incumbency (St Michael and All Angels), 1910. *Publications:* The Will of God in Daily Life, 1895; The Life of Archbishop Laud, 1907. *Recreation:* ecclesiology. *Address:* St Michael's Lodge, Abban Street, Inverness; Balnespick, Tomatin, Inverness-shire. *Club:* Highland, Inverness.

Died 20 April 1926.

M'KISACK, Henry Lawrence, MD; FRCP (London); Consulting Physician; *b* Carrickfergus, 27 Oct. 1859; *s* of late James M'Kisack, Belfast, and Eleanor Sophia, *d* of late Hill Willson of Purdysburn and Carrickfergus; *m* Emily (*d* 1927), *d* of late Henry Matier, Dunlambert, Belfast; one *s* one *d. Educ:* Hillbrook, Holywood; Alfred House, Broadstairs; Queen's College, Belfast; post-graduate study in Dublin, London and Birmingham. Graduated MB in RUI with honours in 1887; Consulting Physician, Royal Victoria Hospital, Belfast; Ulster Volunteer Force Hospital; Lisburn and Hillsborough District Hospital, and to the Ministry of Pensions (Ulster Region); Pres. of Ulster Branch British Medical Association, 1914–15; President of Ulster Medical Society, 1911–12; University Clinical Lecturer, Queen's University, Belfast; Fellow of Royal Society of Medicine, Member of Association of Physicians of Great Britain and Ireland, and of other Medical Associations; Director of Henry Matier and Co., Ltd, Belfast. *Publications:* Dictionary of Medical Diagnosis, 2nd edition; Aids to Case-Taking, 2nd edition; various papers on medical subjects. *Address:* 88 University Road, Belfast. *T:* Belfast 829. *Clubs:* Royal Societies; Ulster, Belfast.

Died 26 March 1928.

MACKLIN, Albert Romer; His Honour Judge Macklin; Judge of County Court Circuit No 37 (West London, Barnet, St Albans, and Chesham), since 1919; *b* 14 Nov. 1863; *s* of late Albert Macklin and Mary, *d* of Frank Romer; *m* 1889, Martha Kate, *d* of Benjamin John Warren, Deal; one *s* one *d. Educ:* City of London School; Caius College, Cambridge. 1st Class Classical Tripos, Part I, 1884; 1st Class Law Tripos, 1886; Chancellor's Medal for English Verse, 1886; Tancred Law Studentship; BA, LLB, 1886. Called to the Bar, 1889; joined South-Eastern Circuit; Revising Barrister, 1907–14; Legal Adviser to War Trade Department, Dec.–Dec. 1915; CC Judge Circuit 11, 1916–19. *Publication:* (with Lord Justice Vaughan Williams) the Article of Libel and Slander in Lord Halsbury's Laws of England. *Address:* 138 Gloucester Terrace, Hyde Park, W2.

Died 18 Aug. 1921.

MACLACHLAN, Lt-Col Alexander Fraser Campbell, DSO 1902; 3rd Battalion, King's Royal Rifle Corps; *b* 23 July 1875. *Educ:* Eton; Magdalen College, Oxford. BA 1897. Entered army, 1899; served South Africa, 1899–1902 (wounded, despatches, medal, four clasps, and King's medal); European War, 1914–17 (despatches, Bt Lt-Col). *Address:* Newton Valence, Alton, Hants.

Died 22 March 1918.

MACLACHLAN, Brig.-Gen. Ronald Campbell, DSO 1916; commanding 8th Battalion Rifle Brigade since 1914; *b* 24 July 1872; *s* of Mrs Maclachlan, Newton Valence, Alton, Hants; *m* Elinor Mary, *d* of J. C. Cox, Sydney, and *widow* of Hon. Sidney Trench. *Educ:* Cheam; Eton; RMC, Sandhurst. Hon. MA Oxford University. Entered army, 1893; Capt. 1900; Major, 1910; Lt-Col 1915; served S Africa, 1899–1900 (despatches, Queen's medal, 4 clasps); Tibet Expedition, 1903–4 (medal); European War, 1914–16 (DSO). *Address:* Newton Valence, Alton, Hants. *Club:* Army and Navy.

Died 11 Aug. 1917.

MACLACHLAN, Col Thomas Robertson, CMG 1915; 92nd Punjabis; *b* 8 April 1870. Served Thibet, 1903–4 (despatches, medal with clasp); NW Frontier, India, 1908 (medal with clasp); European War, Mesopotamia, 1914–17 (CMG, Bt Col).

Died 30 Oct. 1921.

McLAGAN, Archibald Gibson, CIE 1922; of Pumpherston, Mid Calder, Scotland; senior partner in Turnbull, Gibson & Co.; *b* 2 June 1853; *y s* of late Charles Gibson, Pitlochry, Perthshire; *m*; one *s* two *d. Educ:* Church of Scotland School, Pitlochry; Perth Grammar School. Three years in a Liverpool merchant and shipping office; several years in India with a mercantile firm; returned from India for private family reasons and joined Turnbull, Gibson & Co. *Recreation:*

fishing mostly. *Address:* 21 Bury Street, St Mary Axe, EC3. *TA:* Affreter, Ald, London. *T:* Avenue 5701. *M:* YN 8218. *Club:* Oriental.

Died 15 May 1928.

M'LAREN, Hon. Francis (Walter Stafford); Flight Lt RFC; MP (L) Spalding Division, Lincs, since 1910; *b* 6 June 1886; *s* of 1st Baron Aberconway; *m* 1911, Barbara, *d* of Sir Herbert Jekyll, KCMG; two *s. Educ:* Eton; Balliol College, Oxford. Parliamentary Secretary to Rt Hon. Lewis Harcourt; Lieut RNVR since 1914; on active service Dardanelles campaign with RN Armoured Car Squadron. *Address:* 8 Little College Street, SW. *T:* Victoria 3400. *Clubs:* Bachelors', Queen's.

Died 30 Aug. 1917.

MACLAREN, James Anderson, KC 1922; Member of Scottish Bar; *b* Glasgow, 13 Sept. 1866; father, one of the magistrates of Glasgow; *m* 1st, 1905, Margaret, *d* of Robert Young, Crieff, Perthshire; three *s* two *d*; 2nd, 1926, Janet (*d* 1928), *d* of James Davie, Dunfermline. *Educ:* Glasgow and Edinburgh Universities. Called to Scottish Bar, 1888; served South African War (Queen's medal with 5 clasps); settled for a time at Crieff, Perthshire, when became a magistrate of that borough and member of the Crieff School Board; returned to the Bar, 1909. *Publications:* Court of Session Practice—the standard work; Bill Chamber Practice; Expenses in the Supreme and Sheriff Courts. *Recreation:* walking.

Died 23 May 1926.

McLAREN, Sir John, KBE 1919; JP; MInstCE, MInstME; Chairman of J. & H. M'Laren, Ltd, Engineers, Leeds; *s* of Henry M'Laren of Hylton Castle, Sunderland, and Jean, *d* of John Buchanan, Gilchorn, Arbroath; *b* 1 April 1850; *m* 1881, Jane, *d* of James M'Cracken, Glenapp; one *s* three *d. Educ:* privately. Served on Royal Commission on International Exhibitions, Brussels, 1910; Turin and Rome, 1911; President Chamber of Commerce, Leeds, 1918–19; Chairman of the Management Board, and Board of Control of the National Ordnance Factories, Leeds, 1915–19. *Publications:* contributor of papers to the Institution of Civil Engineers, Mining Engineers, Farmers' Club, etc. *Recreations:* shooting, fishing, etc. *Address:* Highfield House, Headingley, Leeds. *TA:* McLaren, Leeds. *T:* Headingley 292. *Clubs:* British Empire, Farmers', Leeds.

Died 12 Oct. 1920.

MACLAREN, Hon. John James, DCL, LLD; Justice of Appeal, 1902–23; *b* Lachute, Quebec; *s* of late John Maclaren, a native of Callander, Scotland; *m* 1st, 1870, Margaret G. Mathewson (*d* 1875); 2nd, 1878, Mary E. Mathewson (*d* 1906); one *s* two *d. Educ:* Victoria University; BA and Prince of Wales' Gold Medallist, 1862; LLB 1868; LLD 1886; McGill University, BCL 1868; DCL 1887. Was British Secretary of British and American Joint Commission on Oregon Claims, 1867–69; Advocate, Quebec, 1868; QC 1878; Member of Bar Council and Law Examiner; removed from Montreal to Toronto, 1884; Barrister, Ontario, 1884; Hon. Lecturer on Comparative Jurisprudence, University of Toronto, 1886–90; Vice-Chancellor, Victoria University, and a Regent since 1870; Senator of University of Toronto since 1891; President of the World's Sunday School Convention at Tokyo, Japan, 1920. *Publications:* Bills, Notes, and Cheques, 1st edn, 1892, 5th edn 1916; Banks and Banking, 1st edn 1896, 4th edn 1914; Roman Law in English Jurisprudence, 1887. *Address:* Osgoode Hall, Toronto, Canada.

Died July 1926.

MACLAREN, Maj. Kenneth, DSO 1900; 13th Hussars; retired; *b* 18 Oct. 1860; *m* 1st, Leila Evelyn (*d* 1904); one *d*; 2nd, 1910, Ethel Mary Wilson. *Educ:* Harrow School. Entered army, 1880; Captain, 1887; served North-West Frontier, India, 1897–98 (despatches, medal with clasp); S Africa, 1899–1900 (severely wounded, despatches, Queen's medal 3 clasps, DSO). *Address:* Dunmar, Tighnabruaich, Argyllshire. *Club:* Naval and Military.

Died 20 Sept. 1924.

McLAREN, Rev. William David, MA; *b* 31 Jan. 1856; *s* of David McLaren and Helen Muir. *Educ:* Edinburgh University. Congregational Minister, Northampton, 1883–94; disabled by partial blindness; Biblical Lecturer, Free Churches' Council of England, 1898–1906; on Staff Congregational College, Melbourne, 1906–17. *Publications:* Our Growing Creed, 1912; articles, etc. *Address:* c/o National Provincial Union Bank, Putney, SW.

Died 11 Nov. 1921.

McLAUGHLIN, Sir Henry, KBE 1919; Chairman McLaughlin & Harvey, Ltd, Belfast, Dublin, and London; *b* 21 March 1876; *s* of W. H. McLaughlin, DL, of Macedon, Co. Antrim; *m* 1899, Ethel, *d* of W. S. Mollan, Belfast; two *d. Educ:* Belfast Royal Academy; Mount Radford, Exeter. Past President Building Employers'

Association, Dublin; Hon. Director Irish Recruiting, 1915–16; Director Red Cross Our Day Fund (Ireland), 1917; Member Lord French's Recruiting Council, 1918. *Recreations:* breeder of Scottish deerhounds, golf, swimming, tennis. *Address:* Riversdale, Monkstown, Co. Dublin. *Clubs:* National; St Stephen's Green, Dublin.

Died 21 Nov. 1927.

M'LAURIN, Duncan, RSW; Hon. Member of the Glasgow Art Club; *b* Glasgow, 1848; *s* of Duncan M'Laurin, Bank Agent; unmarried. *Educ:* High School of Glasgow; Glasgow School of Design; Heatherly's Academy, London. Painting, Cattle by Stream, bought by the Corporation of Glasgow; painting, Home from the Plough, bought by the Scottish Modern Arts Association. *Address:* Bloomfield, Helensburgh. *Died 25 Jan. 1921.*

MACLAURIN, Richard Cockburn, MA, ScD, LLD; President, Massachusetts Institute of Technology, since 1909; *b* Lindean, Scotland, 1870; *s* of Rev. R. C. Maclaurin, MA; *m* 1904, Margaret Alice Young; two *s.* *Educ:* Auckland Grammar School; St John's College, Cambridge. New Zealand University Scholar; Foundation Scholar, St John's Coll. Cambridge, Class I div. i part ii Mathematical Tripos; studied Strassburg University, 1895; Smith's Prizeman (Mathematics), Cambridge University, 1897; M'Mahon Studentship (Law), St John's College, 1897; Member Lincoln's Inn; Yorke Prizeman (Law), Cambridge University, 1898; Fellow of St John's College, 1897–1903. Prof. Mathematics, Victoria College, New Zealand Univ., 1898–1905; Dean Faculty of Law, NZ, 1905–7; Prof. Mathematical Physics, Columbia Univ., New York, 1907–9. LLD (Cambridge), 1905; ScD (Cambridge), 1908; ScD (Dartmouth), 1909; LLD (Wesleyan), 1909; LLD (Harvard), 1910; LLD (Denison), 1914. *Publications:* Title to Realty; The Theory of Light; Light; numerous papers published by Royal Society, Philosophical Magazine, Revue Scientifique, Cambridge Philosophical Society, etc. *Recreation:* travelling. *Address:* Cambridge, Mass. *Clubs:* St Botolph, University, Tavern, Union, Engineer's Commercial, Boston; Technology New York; Cosmos, Washington.

Died 15 Jan. 1920.

MACLAVERTY, Edward Hyde East, ISO 1907; late Senior Collector of Revenue, Jamaica; *b* 19 March 1847; *s* of Rev. Colin Maclaverty, MA; *m* 1875, Elizabeth, *d* of late Edward Claver Smith of Spanish Town, Jamaica. *Address:* Dulce Domum, Kingston, Jamaica. *Died 5 Oct. 1922.*

MACLEAN, Rev. Alexander Miller, CMG 1916; DD (Edin.); Minister of the First Charge of the Abbey of Paisley since 1910; Chaplain in Ordinary to His Majesty for Scotland since 1914; *b* Argyllshire, 1865; *e s* of late Rev. Lachlan Maclean, Minister of North Knapdale; *m* 1890, Mary, *o c* of Robert Brown, Edinburgh; one *d.* *Educ:* Royal High School and University, Edinburgh. Graduated in Arts, 1884, in Divinity in 1887; ordained Minister of Turriff, Aberdeenshire, 1889; translated to Cramond, Midlothian, 1896; Peebles, 1906; represented the Church of Scotland in India and inaugurated the Scots Church of St Andrew, Simla, 1904; promoted in 1911 a scheme of restoration and improvement of surroundings of Paisley Abbey for which nearly £70,000 was subscribed; Vice-Convener of the Highland Committee of the Church of Scotland, 1914; Chaplain (successively) to the 5th Gordons, Edinburgh City Artillery, and Renfrewshire RE; served at the Front with the British Expeditionary Force, 1914–16, also 1918–19 (despatches, CMG). *Publications:* With the Gordons at Ypres; Queen Victoria and her Time; Paisley Abbey Restoration; articles in various magazines and newspapers. *Recreations:* fishing, golfing, curling. *Address:* The Abbey Manse, Paisley. *TA:* Paisley. *T:* Paisley 2527.

Died 6 March 1925.

MACLEAN, Allan, CMG 1916; Consul-General, Valparaiso, since 1913; *b* 13 March 1858. Consul at Dar-al-Baida, 1893; Bilbao, 1906; Dantzig, 1910. *Address:* Valparaiso, Chile.

Died Oct. 1918.

MACLEAN, Charles Donald, MA, MusD; *b* Cambridge, 27 March 1843; *e s* of late Rev. A. J. Macleane. *Educ:* Shrewsbury; Exeter Coll., Oxford (scholar); studied music under Ferd. Hiller of Cologne. Indian Civil Service (Madras), 1865–93, and was there Inspector of Schools, Cantonment Magistrate, Supervisor Government Press, Small Cause Court Judge, Sub-Secretary Board of Revenue, Under-Secretary to Government, Government Translator in Tamil and Canarese, Judge and Collector in Chingleput, Madras, Nellore, Neilgherry, Salem districts; various special duties, etc; Organist Exeter College, Oxford, 1863–65; Organist and Music-director, Eton Coll. 1871–75; Organist, Crystal Palace, 1880; Lecturer; many orchestral works performed at

Crystal Palace and elsewhere; Vice-President Orchestral Association and Musical Association of Great Britain, and Royal College of Organists; member Philharmonic Society, and Society of British Composers; General Secretary and English Editor of the International Musical Society. *Publications:* Madras Manual of Administration, 3 vols, Polyglot report of London Congress, History of Modern English Music in Paris Encyclopedie, and many contributions to Press. *Recreation:* Captain, National Reserve. *Address:* 61 Drayton Gardens, South Kensington, SW. *T:* Western 2087. *Clubs:* Athenæum, United University, Services, Playgoers.

Died 23 June 1916.

MACLEAN, Maj.-Gen. Charles Smith, CB 1881; CIE 1888; Indian Staff Corps; *b* 15 Dec. 1836; *m* 1869, Margaret, *d* of Peter Bairnsfather. Entered army, 1853; Maj.-Gen. 1893; served Indian Mutiny, 1857 (severely wounded, medal with clasp); China, 1860 (medal with two clasps); Afghan War, 1878–80 (despatches several times, Brevet Lt-Col, CB, medal with clasp); Mahsood-Wuzeeree Expedition, 1881; Consul-General for Khorassan and Sistan, 1889–91.

Died 15 July 1921.

M'LEAN, Hon. Sir George, Kt 1909; CMG 1909; JP; Member of Legislative Council, NZ, since 1882; *b* Elgin, NB, 10 Sept. 1834; *y s* of James M'Lean and Jane Proctor of Scotston Hill, Co. Elgin; *m* 1867, Isabel, *d* of Hon. Matthew Holmes, MLC, Wellington; one *s* five *d.* *Educ:* Elgin Grammar School; St Andrews. Came out to Melbourne about 1852; joined Oriental Bank, 1859; appointed Manager of Bank of New Zealand, Dunedin, 1862; became member of mercantile firm, Cargills and M'Lean, 1868, returned member of Provincial Council for Waikonaiti; Provincial Treasurer, 1869; returned member of House of Representatives for Waikonaiti; Postmaster-General, 1876; and a member of two later ministries. *Address:* Hazelwood, Dunedin, NZ. *TA:* Dunedin. *T:* 238. *Club:* Fernhill, Dunedin. *Died 17 Feb. 1917.*

MACLEAN, Lt-Col Henry Donald Neil, DSO 1900; late KOSB; *b* 24 June 1872. Entered army, 1893; Capt. 1900; served North-West Frontier, India, 1897–98 (medal with two clasps); South Africa, 1899–1902 (despatches, Queen's medal 3 clasps, King's medal 2 clasps, DSO); European War, 1914–17 (despatches, Bt Lt-Col); retired pay, 1922. *Died 25 Aug. 1926.*

McLEAN, Col James Reynolds, CBE 1918; Deputy Director General of Recruiting; *b* 1872; *m* 1900, Emma Margaret, *d* of Lawrence Steele, Southampton. *Educ:* Edinburgh and Cambridge Universities. *Address:* Greenaleigh, Fydian Road, Cardiff.

Died 3 July 1921.

MACLEAN, John Cassilis Birkmyre, CB 1917; Surgeon Rear-Admiral, retired; *b* 28 Aug. 1849; *s* of Rev. A. Maclean, DD; *m* 1892, Maude, *e d* of late E. Hewlett, The Priory, Totnes; one *s.* *Educ:* Aberdeen University. Entered RN 1872; retired, 1907; present at bombardment of Alexandria and in Egyptian Campaign, 1882 (specially promoted). *Address:* 12 Penlee Gardens, Devonport. *T:* Devonport 360. *M:* CO 7136. *Club:* Royal Western Yacht.

Died 25 Dec. 1925.

McLEAN, John Roll; proprietor of the Cincinnati Enquirer; *b* Cincinnati, 17 Sept. 1848. *Educ:* public schools, Cincinnati; Harvard. Bought interest of his father, Washington McLean, in Cincinnati Enquirer, afterwards purchasing the other interests; prominent in State and National Democratic politics; Democratic candidate for governor, Ohio, 1899; Ohio Member Democratic National Committee. *Address:* Washington. *Died 9 June 1916.*

MACLEAN, Kaid, Gen. Sir Harry Aubrey de Vere, KCMG 1901 (CMG 1898); *b* 15 June 1848; *s* of Andrew Maclean (of the Macleans of Drimmin); *m* 1st, Catherine Coe (whom he divorced 1905); three *d*; 2nd, 1913, Ella, *d* of late Gen. Sir Harry Prendergast, VC. Formerly in 69th Foot; became Instructor to the Moorish Army under the late Sultan, and accompanied him in his expeditions; Colonel of Sultan of Morocco's Bodyguard; captured by Raisuli, July 1907, while on a mission from the Sultan, and held a prisoner for seven months. Decorated for services rendered to British Government. *Address:* Tangier, Morocco. *Clubs:* Junior Carlton, Caledonian, St Stephen's, Royal Automobile. *Died 4 Feb. 1920.*

MACLEANE, Rev. Douglas, MA; Public Preacher, Salisbury Diocese; Canon of Salisbury since 1910; Proctor in Convocation since 1906; *b* Bath, 1856; *s* of Rev. Arthur Macleane (Editor of Bibliotheca Classica; First Principal of Brighton College); *brother* of Bishop of Moray and Ross, and of late Charles Maclean, MusD, ICS; *m* 1887,

Augusta S. Wightwick; two d. Educ: Christ's Hospital (2nd Grecian); Scholar and Fellow, Pembroke College, Oxford. Curate of Great Witley, Worcester, 1879–82; Domestic Chaplain to Earl of Craven, 1882–85; Fellow of Pembroke, Oxford, 1882–91; Rector of Codford St Peter, Wilts, 1885–1914; Vicar of Branksome Park, Dorset, 1915–22; Diocesan Warden of Sacred Study since 1907; Examining Chaplain to Bishop of Moray since 1904; Fellow of SS Mary and Andrew, Taunton, since 1911; President, East Dorset Branch of ECU, 1914–25; of Sarum District Union, 1923. Publications: A History of Pembroke College, Oxford, 1897; Oxford College Histories (Pembroke), 1900; The Great Solemnity of the Coronation, 1902; Reason, Thought, and Language, 1906; Our Island Church, 1909; Lancelot Andrewes, 1910; Statutes of Salisbury Cathedral (co-editor), 1913; Equality and Fraternity, 1924; many contributions to reviews and magazines; on staff of Saturday Review and Church Times. Recreation: rowed in College boat. Address: The Close, Salisbury. TA: Salisbury. Club: Authors'.   Died 31 Aug. 1925.

MACLEAR, Lt-Col Harry, DSO 1915; 2nd Battalion East Lancs Regiment; b 16 Feb. 1872. Entered army, 1891; Captain 1900; Major, 1910; special service Somaliland Field Force, 1903–4; employed with West African Frontier Force, 1905–7; Provost Marshal Mohmand Field Force, 1908; served Chitral, 1895 (medal with clasp); NW Frontier, India, 1897–98 (clasp); East Africa, 1903–4 (medal with clasp); European War, 1914–15 (DSO).
                                                                   Died 15 March 1916.

McLEARN, Sir William, Kt 1900; Head of William McLearn and Co., Railway Contractors; b 1837. Mayor of Londonderry 1899 and 1900; Chm. Technical School Cttee; also representing the Londonderry Borough Council on the Agriculture and Technical Instruction Board for Ireland. Address: Carrickmore, Londonderry.
                                                                   Died 14 April 1918.

M'LEISH, Col Duncan, CMG 1900; CBE 1919; VD; commanded 3rd Brigade Australian Light Horse (Victorian Mounted Rifles); b 20 July 1851; 2nd s of Duncan and Catherine M'Leish, formerly of Scotland; unmarried. Educ: private tuition. Entered Victorian Mounted Rifles, 1886; served with that corps up till leaving for service in South Africa, 1899; Major, 1900; returned to Australia, 1900, and rejoined his old regiment; commanded 2nd Batt. Australian Horse, 1902 to end of war; returned to Australia shortly afterwards; Lt-Col 1903; retired list, 1911; served European War, 1914–16. Address: Glenmore, Yea, Victoria, Australia. Clubs: Naval and Military; Melbourne Stock Exchange.   Died 17 April 1920.

M'LELLAN, C. M. S.; playwright; b Bath, Maine, USA, 1865. Educ: Boston. Editor and dramatic critic in New York until 1897, then lived in England; plays produced in London: Leah Kleschna, Glittering Gloria, On the Love Path, The Jury of Fate; and The Strong People, 1910; wrote under the name of Hugh Morton the libretti of The Belle of New York, An American Beauty, The Girl from Up There, and Nelly Neil, produced in London; and In Gay New York, The Whirl of The Town, Yankee Doodle Dandy, Puritania, The Honeymooners, and The Telephone Girl.
                                                                   Died 22 Sept. 1916.

M'LENNAN, Lt-Col Bartlett, DSO 1917; Officer Commanding 42nd Canadian Battalion The Royal Highlanders of Canada; b Montreal, 10 Nov. 1868; y s of late Hugh M'Lennan; unmarried. Educ: Lyall School, Sorel; Royal Military College, Kingston. In business in Montreal; Director Montreal Telegraph Co., Canada Sugar Refining Co., Canadian Explosives Co., Mundeth & Co. Ltd; went to France, Oct. 1915, with 42nd Canadian Batt. (despatches twice, DSO); Lt-Col 1917. Recreations: hunting, polo. Address: 50 Ontario Avenue, Montreal, Canada. Clubs: Bath; Mount Royal, Montreal.
                                                                   Died 3 Aug. 1918.

MACLENNAN, Hon. Farquhar Stuart; Puisne Judge Superior Court and Deputy Local Judge in Admiralty. Address: Montreal, Canada.   Died 18 June 1925.

M'LENNAN, John Ferguson, KC 1905; Advocate; Sheriff of Caithness, Orkney, and Zetland since 1905; b Inverness, 3 Oct. 1855; o s of late Malcolm M'Lennan, Procurator-Fiscal of Caithness, and author of Peasant Life in the North; unmarried. Educ: Inverness Academy; Grammar School, Old Aberdeen; Universities: Aberdeen (MA), 1875; Edinburgh (LLB), 1879; Forensic Prizeman, 1878; Edinburgh University Endowment Association Law Fellowship, 1879. Scotch Bar, 1881. Address: 20 Heriot Row, Edinburgh. Clubs: Royal Societies; Northern, Scottish Arts, Edinburgh.
                                                                   Died 1 June 1917.

MACLEOD, Adm. Angus, CVO 1904; b 11 June 1847; m 1st, Rose, d of R. Hickson, and widow of J. R. Pollock; 2nd, Jane Margaret (d 1906), d of Captain J. B. Forster, 62nd Wiltshire Regiment; one s. Entered navy, 1860; Lieut 1868; Commander, 1881; Captain, 1888; Rear-Admiral, 1901; Vice-Admiral, 1905; Admiral, 1910; served Gold Coast, 1874 (slightly wounded, despatches, Ashantee medal, Coomassie clasp); Senior Naval Officer, Gulf of Siam, 1893; ADC to Queen Victoria and to King Edward VII, 1899–1901; Director of Naval Ordnance, Admiralty; Senior Officer, Coast of Ireland, 1904–6; retired, 1910. Address: 87 Victoria Street, SW; Holmisdal, Glendale, Isle of Skye. Clubs: United Service, National.
                                                                   Died 29 April 1920.

M'LEOD, Clement Henry, FRS Canada; Professor of Geodesy, M'Gill University, Montreal, since 1888; Vice-Dean of the Faculty of Applied Science, 1908. Educ: M'Gill University. Consulting Engineer; Superintendent of the Observatory, M'Gill College; Fellow of M'Gill University; Member: Canadian Society of Civil Engineers; American Astronomical Society. Determined difference of longitude, in co-operation with Greenwich Observatory, Montreal and Greenwich, in 1892, and other longitudes in Canada; various astronomical expeditions. Publications: publications in the Trans of the Royal Society of Canada, astronomical, meteorological, and physical subjects; Trans Canadian Soc. of Civil Engineers; meteorological reports. Address: M'Gill College, Montreal, Canada.
                                                                   Died 26 Dec. 1917.

M'LEOD, Hon. Donald; late Member Legislative Assembly, Victoria; b Caithness; m; four s four d. Educ: John Knox's Grammar School, Melbourne. Went to Victoria as a child, 1850; trained as a chemist; followed agricultural and mining pursuits for many years; Town Clerk, Daylesford, and Official Assigner Insolvency, etc, for twenty-five years; MP Daylesford, 1899; Hon. Member Irvine Government, 1902; Minister Mines and Forests, 1904; Acting Minister of Water Supply and Acting Treasurer, 1909; Chief Secretary and Minister of Health, Victoria, 1915–18; Member of the Executive Council of Victoria; of Melbourne University Council; President Daylesford Hospital, etc. Address: 244 Beaconsfield Parade, Middle Park, Melbourne. T: Windsor 2905. Clubs: Stock Exchange, Freemasons, Melbourne.   Died about 1918.

MACLEOD, Very Rev. Donald, VD; DD; Chaplain in Ordinary to the King in Scotland; acting editor of Good Words, 1872–1905; Emeritus Minister of Parish of The Park, Glasgow; b Campsie, Stirlingshire; s of Rev. Norman Macleod, DD, Dean of the Chapel Royal, Celtic Scholar and Author; brother of Rev. Norman Macleod, DD, Dean of Chapel Royal and Dean of the Thistle, first editor of Good Words, and author; m Isabella, d of James Anderson of Highholm, Renfrewshire; three s one d. Educ: different schools; Univ. of Glasgow (BA). Travelled two years; first parish Lauder; subsequently Linlithgow; Moderator of the Assembly of the Church of Scotland, 1895–96; Convener of the Home Mission Committee of the Church of Scotland, 1888–1900. Publications: Memoir of Norman Macleod, DD; Sunday Home Service; Christ and Society; The Doctrine and Validity of the Ministry and Sacraments of the National Church of Scotland, Baird Lecture, 1903; many contributions to Good Words; lectures on the Reformation, the Parochial System, and Dr Chalmers, in the St Giles' Series. Address: 8 Tipperlinn Road, Edinburgh. Clubs: Western, Glasgow; University, Edinburgh.
                                                                   Died 11 Feb. 1916.

M'LEOD, Gen. Sir Donald James Sim, KCB 1913 (CB 1898); KCIE 1906; DSO 1887; Colonel 28th Light Cavalry; retired, 1906; b India, 22 Feb. 1845; 2nd s of Lt-Gen. W. C. M'Leod; m 1877, Camilla, e d of Maj. J. Nicholas; one s one d. Educ: Kensington Proprietary School. Joined Madras Cavalry, 1861; served on Army Staff, India, 1877–88; DQMG Madras Army, on service in Burma, 1886–87 (medal DSO); commanding 3rd Madras Lancers, 1890–93; AAG District, 1893–95; Brig.-Gen. commanding a 2nd Class District, 1895–1900; Maj.-Gen. commanding 1st Class District, 1901–3; Lt-Gen. commanding Burma Division, 1903–6. Address: 99 Barkston Gardens, SW5. T: Western 2789. Club: United Service.
                                                                   Died 16 Jan. 1922.

McLEOD, Hon. Sir Ezekiel, Kt 1917; Chief Justice, Supreme Court, New Brunswick, since 1914; b 29 Oct. 1840. Educ: High School, Cardwell, King's Co., NB; Harvard. Called to Bar, 1868; QC 1882; Member Provincial Legislature, 1882–86; Attorney-Gen., 1882–83; Member House of Commons, 1891–96; a Senator of the University of New Brunswick; late Judge, Supreme Court, and Judge, Vice-Admiralty, New Brunswick. Address: St John, New Brunswick.
                                                                   Died 11 June 1920.

M'LEOD, Hon. Harry Fulton, KC 1910; BA; represented York County in New Brunswick Parliament, 1908; Solicitor-General for Province, 1908; Provincial Secretary and Receiver-General, New Brunswick, 1911; resigned from NB Government Dec. 1913; MP 1913, and as supporter of Union Government and Conscription, 17 Dec. 1917; *b* Fredericton, NB, 14 Sept. 1871; United Empire Loyalist descent; *s* of Rev. J. M'Leod, DD; *m* 1909, Ina F., *d* of Lt-Col G. W. Mersereau; one *s* two *d*. *Educ:* Fredericton Collegiate School; University NB (first Honour Man and Gold Medallist). Admitted to Bar of NB 1895; contested NB Parliament, 1903; Mayor of Fredericton, 1907–8. Grand Master LCL of New Brunswick, 1906–7; Lieut-Col of 71st York Regiment since 1909; O/C 12th Batt. 1st Division Canadian Expeditionary Force, Aug. 1914–July 1916; Colonel, with command Divisional troops, Shorncliffe, England, July 1916. *Address:* Fredericton, NB, Canada. *Clubs:* Fredericton City, Fredericton Bicycling and Boating; Union, St John, NB; Laurentian, Ottawa. *Died 7 Jan. 1920.*

M'LEOD, Herbert, Hon. LLD St Andrews; FRS, FCS; Hon. Director Royal Society Catalogue of Scientific Papers; *b* Stoke Newington, 19 Feb. 1841; *o s* of Bentley M'Leod. *Educ:* Stockwell Grammar School; private school at Deal. Assistant Chemist in the School of Mines, 1860–71, under Professors A. W. Hofmann and E. Frankland; Professor of Chemistry, Royal Indian Engineering College, Cooper's Hill, 1871–1901; President of Section B, British Association, 1892; formerly Examiner in Chemistry in the Universities of Oxford, London, Birmingham and Cambridge, and to the Pharmaceutical Society; contributed papers to the Royal, Chemical and Physical Societies. *Address:* 109 Church Road, Richmond, Surrey. *Died 1 Oct. 1923.*

MACLEOD, James John, CIE 1896; Indigo planter, Tirhoot, India; *b* Snizort, Isle of Skye, 9 Nov. 1841; 4th surv. *s* of Rev. Roderick Macleod of Snizort. *Educ:* Edinburgh Institution and University of Edinburgh. Lt-Col Behar Light Horse. Decorated as a leading planter and a prominent member of the Behar Light Horse; officiated commandant on several occasions. *Recreations:* steeplechase-riding, polo, pig-sticking. *Address:* Lalseriah, Segowlie, Chumparun, India. *Club:* Bengal, Calcutta. *Died 24 Feb. 1919.*

MACLEOD, John, ISO 1902; late HM Inspector of Schools; retired; *b* Bonar Bridge, 1 Nov. 1839; *s* of Roderick Macleod; *g g g s* of Roderick Macleod of Assynt, and *c* Elizabeth, *d* of Macleod of Assynt; *m* 1st, 1876, Jane Emily, *d* of Lt-Colonel Myers, 71st HLI; one *s* one *d*; 2nd, 1908, Katharine Louisa, *e d* of late Wadham Locke Sutton of Rossway, Herts; one *d*. *Educ:* Glasgow University. Was successively Professor of Mathematics in King's College, NS; Assistant to the Professor of Mathematics in the University of Glasgow; Mathematical Instructor in the Royal Military Academy, Woolwich; elected Fellow of the Mathematical Society of London, 1872. *Publications:* Reminiscences; numerous original theorems in pure geometry. *Recreation:* golf; was twice elected Captain of the Moray Golf Club. *Address:* Fairfield, Nairn. *Died 5 July 1927.*

MACLEOD, Col Kenneth, MD; FRCSE; Hon. Physician to the King; Indian Medical Service (retired); *b* North Uist, Inverness-shire, 23 July 1840; *s* of Rev. Norman Macleod, relative of Rev. Norman Macleod, DD, Glasgow; twice married; four *s* six *d*. *Educ:* Aberdeen and Edinburgh Univs. AM, LLD, Aberdeen University; Fellow of University of Calcutta; Hon. FRCS. Graduated in Edinburgh with distinction, 1861; Assistant Medical Officer, Durham County Asylum, 1861–65; entered Indian Medical Service, 1865; retired, 1892; held successively appointments of Civil Surgeon of Jessore, medical charge of 6th Bengal Light Infantry; Member and Secretary, Cattle Plague Commission; Secretary, Medical Department, Professor of Anatomy and of Surgery, Calcutta Medical College; appointed Member of Medical Board, India Office, 1893; appointed Professor of Military Medicine, Army Medical School, Netley, 1897. *Publications:* Medico-legal Experience in Bengal, 1876; Operative Surgery in the Calcutta Medical College Hospital, 1885; Epidemic Dropsy, 1893; Nerve Splitting and Stretching, 1894; numerous communications to medical periodicals and societies, and official reports; editor, Indian Medical Gazette, 1870–92. *Recreation:* golf. *Address:* Duncaple, Westend, Hampshire. *TA:* Westend, Southampton. *Died 17 Dec. 1922.*

M'LEOD, Norman F.; *b* Madras, India, June 1856; *s* of Gen. W. C. M'Leod, Madras Army; unmarried. *Educ:* Clifton College; RIE College, Cooper's Hill. Public Works Department, United Provinces, India, 1878; Superintending Engineer, 1903; Chief Engineer and Secretary to Government Irrigation, 1905–11; Member of Legislative Council, United Provinces, 1909–11; retired, 1911. *Address:* c/o H. S. King & Co., Pall Mall, SW1. *Club:* East India United Service. *Died 20 April 1921.*

McLEOD, Brig.-Gen. William Kelty, CSI 1919; late RA; *b* 1862; *s* of late Lt-Gen. W. K. McLeod; *m* 1920, Mary Forrester, *d* of late James Lumsden, Huntingtowerfield, Perth; one *d*. *Educ:* Trinity College, Glenalmond; Royal Military Academy, Woolwich. Served NW Frontier of India, 1897–98 (medal with clasp); European War, 1914–19 (despatches, CSI). *Address:* Greenbank, Perth. *T:* Perth 114. *Died 22 Nov. 1928.*

McMAHON, Col Bernard William Lynedoch, CMG 1917; CVO 1925; Equerry to Princess Louise, Duchess of Argyll; *b* 10 Oct. 1865; *s* of Maj. William McMahon, late 14th Light Dragoons; unmarried. *Educ:* Wellington College. Durham Light Infantry, 1885–1915; served S African war, 1899–1902 (Queen's medal with four clasps, King's medal with two clasps, Brevet of Major); Commandant School of Musketry; served European War (1914 Star, British War Medal, Victory Medal, CMG). *Address:* The Mount, Penshurst, Kent. *TA:* Penshurst. *Club:* Junior United Service. *Died 23 Dec. 1928.*

M'MAHON, Sir Lionel, 4th Bt, *cr* 1815, of the City of Dublin; *b* 30 June 1856; *s* of Sir Beresford Burston McMahon, 2nd Bt and Maria Catherine, *sister* of Sir Thomas Bateson, Bt (1st Baron Deramore); *S* brother, 1905; *m* 1888, Annie Cecilia Austin-Cooke (*d* 1923). *Educ:* Rugby. Late Lt 58th Regt; Barrister-at-law, Inner Temple, 1888; DL Co. Tyrone; High Sheriff, Co. Tyrone, 1914. *Heir:* none. *Address:* Mountfield Lodge, Omagh, Co. Tyrone. *Died 20 Feb. 1926 (ext).*

MACMANUS, Joseph Edward; First Acting Editor of the Daily Mail, 1896–98; Editor of The Morning, 1898; Assistant Director for Great Britain of Le Figaro, Paris, 1905. Author of many short plays, verses and songs. Qualified as a Solicitor, but never practised. *Recreations:* sailing, motoring. *Address:* 35 Eldon Chambers, Fleet Street, EC. *T:* Bearable, London. *Clubs:* Press, Amateur Camping. *Died 17 June 1921.*

MACMASTER, Sir Donald, 1st Bt *cr* 1921; KC; DCL; Barrister Quebec, 1871; Ontario, 1882; Lincoln's Inn, 1906; MP (U), Chertsey Division, Surrey, since 1910, (Co U) since 1918; *b* Williamstown, 3 Sept. 1846; *o s* of Donald Macmaster and Mary Cameron; *m* 1st, 1880, Janet (*d* 1883), *d* of Ranald Sandfield Macdonald, Lancaster, Ont.; 2nd, 1890, Ella Virginia, *d* of Isaac Deford, Baltimore, Md; two *d*. *Educ:* Grammar School, Williamstown, Ont.; M'Gill University, Montreal. BCL; Elizabeth Torrance gold medal, prize essayist and valedictorian, 1871; DCL 1894. QC 1882; served as Crown prosecutor in several Canadian *causes célèbres*, and as Arbitrator between Newfoundland Government and Reid-Newfoundland Railway, 1904–5; Counsel for United States Government in Gaynor and Green Extradition Inquiry and Appeals thereon to Judicial Committee of Privy Council, before which he practised his profession; appointed on Royal Commission to inquire into matters concerning good government of Quebec, 1892; Pres. of Montreal Bar, 1904; twice elected Pres. of McGill Soc. and President of St Andrews Society, Montreal; member for Glengarry in Ontario Legislature, 1879–82; MP (C) Canadian House of Commons, 1882–86; Unionist candidate for Leigh Division of Lancashire, 1906; Member of the Speaker's Conference for reform of representation and franchise. *Publication:* Monograph, The Seal Arbitration at Paris, 1894. *Recreations:* golf, travel. *Heir:* none. *Address:* 57 Sloane Gardens, SW1. *Clubs:* Carlton, Constitutional; St James's, Montreal. *Died 3 March 1922 (ext).*

M'MICHAEL, Solon William, ISO 1903; Chief and General Inspector of Customs for Dominion of Canada since 1894, and Member of the Board of Customs for Canada since 1895; *b* Waterford, Ontario, 18 Nov. 1848; *e s* of late Aaron M'Michael, JP; *m* Josephine, *d* of Charles Shoemaker, Muncy, Penn., USA; one *s* one *d*. *Educ:* Simcoe Grammar School. Appointed to Customs, 1873; Financial Inspector of Customs for Dominion, 1885. *Address:* 101 St George Street, Toronto, Canada. *TA:* M'Michael, Toronto. *T:* College 6069. *M:* 20200. *Club:* National, York Downs Golf and County, Toronto. *Died 24 Sept. 1923.*

McMILLAN, Alec, MA; 2nd *s* of late John McMillan, JP, Castramont, Stewartry of Kirkcudbright; *m* 1888, Nellie, *d* of James Fortescue Harrison, JP (MP 1874–80), author of The Evolution of Daphne and other novels, author and composer of Night Winds and other songs. *Educ:* Aldenham School; Brasenose College, Oxford. Exhibitioner,

Merton College, Scholar, Brasenose College, 1864; 1st class Classical Moderations, 1866. In ICS, 1868–94; Under-Secretary to Government, NWP and Oudh, 1874–77; District Judge, Meerut, 1884; Agra, 1886; Cawnpore, 1890; Lucknow, 1892; Barrister, Inner Temple, 1883; Professor of Indian Jurisprudence and Indian History, King's College, London, 1899–1902; HM Consul for the Alpes Maritimes and Monaco, 1902–10; originated Memorial Scheme that eventuated in erection of Queen Victoria Memorial Hospital at Nice. *Publications:* Divers Ditties, 1895; Portentous Prophets and Prophetesses, 1898; Mainly About Robert Bruce, 1901; Essence of Ecclesiastes, in Metre of Omar Khayyám (under nom de plume Alastair Buchanan), 1904. *Club:* Hurlingham.

Died 11 June 1919.

McMILLAN, Rev. Charles D. H.; Vicar of Malmesbury with St Mary, Westport, since 1907; Hon. Canon of Bristol Cathedral, 1911; Rural Dean of Malmesbury, 1912; *s* of late Charles S. McMillan, of Bristol; *m* 1890, Alice Mary, *e d* of late Samuel Mackenzie, of Bayswater. *Educ:* King's School, Bruton; Wadham College, Oxford. BA 1888 (2nd Class Modern History); MA 1892. Curate of Stanley, Yorks, 1889–91; Wakefield Cathedral, 1891–92; Vicar of St John's Church, Wakefield, 1892–1907; Hon. Canon of Wakefield Cathedral, 1906–7; Chairman of Wakefield School Board, 1901–3. *Publication:* The Sleeping Cardinal and other Sermons. *Address:* Malmesbury.

Died 6 May 1919.

MACMILLAN, Rev. Donald, MA, DD; Clerk to Synod of Glasgow and Ayr since 1913; Hastie Lecturer in the University of Glasgow, 1906–9; *b* Skipness, Argyllshire, May 1855; *m* 1889, Edith, 2nd *d* of John H. Worthington, Manchester; two *s*. *Educ:* Glasgow University; Jena. Ordained to parish of Wanlockhead, 1883; translated to parish of Auchtertool, 1886; translated to Kelvinhaugh Parish, Glasgow, 1891; retired, 1923; editor of Church of Scotland Sabbath School Magazine, 1899–1900; editor of Saint Andrew, 1899–1905; Pres. of the Knox Club, 1911; Convenor of Church of Scotland's Pension Fund for Ministers, 1917; Senior Grand Chaplain Grand Lodge of Scotland, 1918; Vice-Convener of Aged and Infirm Ministers Fund and Pension Fund, 1921. *Publications:* (ed) late Professor Hastie's Outlines of Pastoral Theology, 1904; John Knox, A Biography, 1905; George Buchanan, A Biography, 1906; Life of the Rev. Dr George Matheson, 1907; The Aberdeen Doctors 1610–38, 1909; A Short History of the Scottish People, 1911; Life of Professor Flint, 1914; Patriotism and Religion, 1917; Socialist and Proletarian Sunday Schools: A Menace to the Church, 1923; The Life of Professor Hastie, 1926; articles on theological subjects to various journals, magazines and reviews. *Recreation:* golf. *Address:* Knapdale, Forest Row, Sussex. *Club:* Conservative, Glasgow. *Died 27 March 1927.*

MACMILLAN, Michael, DLitt; Fellow Bombay University; Wilson Philological Lecturer, 1882, 1891, 1895, 1901, 1905; English Lecturer, Birmingham University, 1905–20; *b* Newton-Stewart, NB, 23 Jan. 1853; *m* 1879, Tilly, *d* of Rev. Stephen Balmer, Portpatrick. *Educ:* Rugby; Marlborough; BNC, Oxford (scholar). 1st class Classical Moderations; 2nd class Final Classical Schools; BA 1876. Joined Bombay Educational Department, 1878, as Professor of Logic and Moral Philosophy at Elphinstone College; Principal of Elphinstone Coll., Bombay, 1900–7, and Professor of English Literature, 1891–1907; Delegate of Bombay Asiatic Society to Hanoi Congress, 1902. *Publications:* Simple Essays; Essays for the Young; Questions and Answers on Elementary Logic; Annotated editions of Marmion, Rokeby, Paradise Lost I–IV, Vicar of Wakefield, Southey's Nelson, Ivanhoe, Pope's Homer's Iliad, Pride and Prejudice, Othello, Julius Cæsar, Twelfth Night, Kenilworth, Vanity Fair; School History of India; Promotion of General Happiness; Globe Trotter in India Two Hundred Years Ago, and other Indian studies; Tales of Indian Chivalry (translated into Marathi, Gujarati, Kanarese, and Telugu); Princess of Balkh; In Wild Mahratta Battle; The Last of the Peshwas; Bruce of Bannockburn (Modernized Version of Barbour); with D. B. Hakim, Handbook of English Grammar and Composition; with A. Barrett, English Idioms, Indian English Corrected, and Notes on the Siege of Corinth. *Recreations:* played Rugby XV Oxford *v* Cambridge, 1876; walking, cycling. *Address:* University, Birmingham.

Died 28 Aug. 1925.

MACMILLAN, Rev. Robert Alexander Cameron, MA, DPhil; Minister of St John's Presbyterian Church, Kensington, since 1913; *b* 11 May 1883; *s* of Rev. John Macmillan, Minister of Lochbroom, Ross-shire; unmarried. *Educ:* High School and University of Glasgow. Ordained 1909; transferred to Johannesburg, 1911; Doctor of Philosophy, 1912. *Publication:* The Crowning Phase of the Critical Philosophy—A Study in Kant's Critique of Judgement, 1912. *Address:* 98 Holland Road, W. *Died 11 April 1917.*

M'MILLAN, Hon. Sir William, KCMG 1901; *b* Londonderry, Ireland , 14 Nov. 1850; *s* of Rev. Gibson M'Millan, Wesleyan minister; *m* 1st, 1877, Ada Charlotte, *d* of Frederick Graham; 2nd, 1892, Helen, *d* of Rev. William Gibson; one *s* four *d*. *Educ:* Wesley College, Dublin; private school, London. Arrived Australia, 1869; member of firm of W. & A. M'Arthur, London and Sydney; President of Sydney Chamber of Commerce, 1886, entered New South Wales Parliament, 1887; Colonial Treasurer, 1889; Member of Federal Conference, 1890; Delegate to Federal Convention, 1891 and 1897; Member of House of Representatives Federal Parliament, 1901–3. *Address:* Althorne, Woollahra, Sydney, New South Wales. *Clubs:* Devonshire; Australian, Sydney; Melbourne, Melbourne.

Died 21 Dec. 1926.

McMILLAN, William Bentley, CBE 1918; JP; Provost of Greenock since 1909; Hon. Sheriff Substitute for Renfrew and Bute; *b* 5 Nov. 1871; *s* of late Matthew and Mary McMillan; *m* Margaret Campbell, *d* of late Duncan and Jessie Campbell; one *s* two *d*. *Educ:* Motherwell. Entered Corporation, 1894; Member Northern Lighthouses Trust, etc. *Recreations:* public work, yachting, golf. *Address:* The Criags, Greenock. *TA:* Provost McMillan, Greenock. *T:* Greenock 477. *M:* VS No 1. *Clubs:* Greenock, Royal Gourock Yacht; Royal Clyde Yacht; Scottish Automobile; Scottish Constitutional.

Died 1 June 1922.

McMILLAN, Sir William Northrup, Kt 1918; FRGS, CMZS; Hon. Member of Legislative Council, British East Africa; Captain 25th (Service) Battalion Royal Fusiliers (Frontiersmen); *b* St Louis, Missouri, USA, 19 Oct. 1872; *s* of William and Eliza McMillan, of Hamilton, Ontario, Canada; *m* 1894, Lucie Fairbanks Webber, of Northampton, Mass, USA; no *c*. *Educ:* Pottstown, Pennsylvania, USA Ranching, New Mexico, 1890–93; business, St Louis, USA, 1893–98; business, London, 1898–1901; exploration and big-game hunting in Africa, 1901–5; ranching in British East Africa from 1905. Member of the Order of the Cross of Solomon, and Star of Ethiopia. *Publications:* maps and pamphlets for Royal Geographical Society. *Recreations:* big game hunting, fishing, shooting, yachting. *Address:* Nairobi, Colony of Kenya; 19 Hill Street, Berkeley Square, W1. *T:* Mayfair 6647. *TA:* McMillan, Nairobi. *Clubs:* St James's, Ranelagh, Royal Automobile; Union League, Manhattan, New York; Tuna, California. *Died 22 March 1925.*

MACNAB, Brig.-Gen. Colin Lawrance, CMG 1918; *b* Halifax, Nova Scotia, 2 Dec. 1870; *m* Beatrice Marian, *d* of Rev. W. B. Bliss, Wicken, Essex; two *s*. *Educ:* St Edward's; Oxford; Westminster. Joined 1st Border Regt, 1891; Asst. Adjutant, 1894–97; Adjutant, 1897–1900; Captain, Northumberland Fusilliers, 1900; Major, The Royal Sussex Regt 1903; commanded Royal Sussex Regt 1911–15; Brig.-Gen. Mesopotamia, 1915; France, 1916–17; served South African War (despatches); European War (despatches twice, CMG). *Recreations:* fishing, shooting. *Address:* Littlebury, Saffron-Walden, Essex. *TA:* Littlebury, Essex. *Club:* United Service.

Died 13 Oct. 1918.

M'NAB, Hon. Robert, MA, LLB, LittD; Minister of Justice and Marine, New Zealand; *b* 1864. *Educ:* Invercargill Grammar School; Otago University. Called to Bar, 1889; MHR, Mataura, 1893–96 and 1898–1908; MP Hawkes Bay, 1914; Minister for Lands, 1906. *Publications:* Murihiku, 1909; The Old Whaling Days, 1913; From Tosman to Marsden, 1914; editor Historical Records of New Zealand. *Address:* Wellington, New Zealand. *Died 17 Feb. 1917.*

MacNACHTAN, Col Neil Ferguson, CVO 1912; Clerk and Treasurer, United Counties Northumberland and Durham; *b* 5 Feb 1850; *s* of Edmund A. MacNachtan; *m* 1st, Jeannie Hervey Lawder; 2nd, Edith Isabell Radclyffe; one *s* two *d*. *Educ:* Cobourg Grammar School; Victoria College. Enlisted in Cobourg Garrison Artillery, 1868; commanded same, 1891–1900; commanded 14th Battery Canadian Field Artillery, 1901–6; commanded 10th Brigade Canadian Field Artillery, 1907–12; retired as Colonel; commanded Canadian Artillery team which competed with British Territorial Artillery in England, 1911 (CVO). *Recreations:* of late years, shooting and fishing. *Address:* Cobourg, Ontario, Canada. *T:* Residence 229; Office 36.

Died 10 Dec. 1928.

MACNAGHTEN, Sir Arthur Douglas, 7th Bt *cr* 1836; 2nd Lieutenant, 8th Battalion, Rifle Brigade; *b* 25 Jan. 1897; *s* of Hon. Sir Edward Charles Macnaghten, 5th Bt, KC and Edith Minnie, *d* of Thomas Powell; *S* brother, July 1916. *Heir:* uncle Hon. Francis Alexander Macnaghten, *b* 18 May 1863.

Died 15 Sept. 1916.

This entry did not appear in Who's Who.

MACNAGHTEN, Sir Edward Henry, 6th Bt *cr* 1836; 2nd Lieutenant, The Black Watch, Royal Highlanders; *b* 12 Feb. 1896; *e s* of Hon. Sir Edward Charles Macnaghten, 5th Bt and Edith Minnie, *d* of Thomas Powell; *S* father, 1914. *Heir: b* Arthur Douglas Macnaghten, *b* 25 Jan. 1897. *Address:* 26 Sussex Square, Hyde Park, W; Dundarave, Bushmills, Ireland.

Died 1 July 1916.

MACNAGHTEN, Rev. Henry Alexander, MA; Rector of Tankersley, 1886–1918; Hon. Canon of Sheffield, 1914–18; *e s* of late Elliot Macnaghten and 1st wife, Isabella, *o d* of late John Law; *b* 1850; *m* 1st, 1873, Louisa (*d* 1921), *d* of Ross D. Mangles; two *s* one *d*; 2nd, 1925, Evelyn Vere, *o d* of late William Lewis Boyle and Mrs Boyle, Evelyns, Hingham. *Educ:* Eton; King's College, Cambridge. Ordained priest, 1874; Curate of St Mary, Beverley, 1876–77; Vicar of Wentworth, Yorkshire, 1877–82; Prescott, Lancs, 1882–86. *Address:* 2 Manson Place, SW7.

Died 17 July 1928.

MACNAGHTEN, Sir Melville Leslie, Kt 1907; CB 1912; *b* 16 June 1853; *y s* of late Elliot Macnaghten of Ovingdean, Sussex, sometime Chairman of the East India Company; *m* 1878, Dora, *e d* of Rev. Dr Sanderson, Canon of Chichester; two *s* two *d*. *Educ:* Eton. Manager of family estates, Bengal, 1873–88; Chief Constable of Criminal Investigation Department, Scotland Yard, 1889–1903; appointed to represent police on Hon. H. H. Asquith's Committee to enquire into the identification of Criminals, 1893–94; late Assistant Commissioner of Metropolitan Police; Chief of the Criminal Investigation Department, 1903–13. Knight Commander of the White Military Order of Spain, and Second Class Commander of the Order of Dannebrog. *Publication:* Days of My Years, 1914. *Address:* Queen Anne's Mansions, St James's Park, SW. *T:* Victoria 7598. *Club:* Garrick.

Died 12 May 1921.

M'NAIR, Lt.-Gen. Edward John; Bengal Infantry; *b* 9 July 1838; *m* Catherine Louisa Spry Dyas (*d* 1910). Entered army, 1856; Lt.-Gen. 1891; retired list, 1892; served Indian Mutiny, 1857 (medal with clasp for Delhi); Hazara Campaign, 1868 (medal with clasp); Afghan War, 1879–80 (despatches, medal). *Address:* 9 St James's Square, Bath.

Died 15 April 1921.

McNAIR, Captain Eric Archibald, VC 1916; 9th (Service) Battalion Royal Sussex Regiment. *Educ:* Charterhouse; Magdalen College, Oxford. Served European War, 1914–17 (VC). *Address:* c/o Chartered Bank of India, Australia and China, 38 Bishopsgate, EC. *Club:* Bath.

Died Aug. 1918.

MACNAMARA, N. C., FRCS, FRCSI; Fellow of Calcutta University; late Professor, Ophthalmic Medicine, Calcutta; Vice-President of the Royal College of Surgeons; Surgeon and Founder of Mayo Hospital, Calcutta; *m d* of Hon. Henry Vincent Bayley, BCS. Consulting Surgeon to Westminster Hospital and of the Royal Westminster Ophthalmic Hospital; Vice-President of the British Medical Association; Member of the War Office Committee on Army Medical Service, and Government Committee on Leprosy; Chairman of the Committee of British Medical Association on Medical Education and of Teaching University for London; Surg.-Maj. Bengal MS and of Staff in Sonthal Rebellion; also of Tirhout Volunteers in Indian Mutiny. *Publications:* Origin and Character of the British People; Story of an Irish Sept; Human Speech, 1908; The Evolution of Purposive Living Matter, vols 95 and 97 of International Scientific Series, 1910; Hunterian Oration, 1901; Diseases of the Eyes, 5th edn; Hist. of Asiatic Cholera, 3rd edn; Diseases of Bones and Joints, 3rd edn; Instinct and Intelligence, 1915, etc. *Address:* The Lodge, Chorleywood, Herts. *Club:* Athenæum.

Died 21 Nov. 1918.

MACNAMARA, Walter Henry; a Master of Supreme Court; Secretary and Registrar of Railway and Canal Commission; Registrar to Court under Benefices Act (1898); *b* 1851; *e s* of late Henry Macnamara, Barrister and Railway Commissioner; *m* 1882, Florence (*d* 1917), *d* of F. de Mauduit. *Educ:* Repton; Christ Church, Oxford. Barrister 1874. One of delegates appointed by Foreign Office to represent Great Britain at International Railway Congress in Paris, 1900; Washington, 1905; Berne, 1910; Vice-President of the Norwegian Club. *Address:* Apsley Cottage, Banstead, Surrey; The Hut, Birchington, Thanet; Royal Courts of Justice, WC2. *Club:* Reform.

Died 17 Sept. 1920.

M'NAUGHT, William Gray, MusDoc; FRAM; Assistant Inspector of Music Education Department, 1883–1901; Examiner Society of Arts; editor of Messrs Novello & Co's School Music and other Series; *b* Mile End, 30 March 1849; 2nd *s* of Donald M'Naught, Greenock;

m 1878, Clara Weybret Waller; two *s* one *d*. *Educ:* private school, Stepney; Royal Acad. of Music, 1872–76. Music Director Bow Bromley Institute, 1876–1900; Adjudicator at competitions, etc. *Publications:* editor The Musical Times and School Music Review. *Recreation:* general reading. *Address:* Annandale, Woodside Park, Finchley, N12. *T:* 950 PO Finchley.

Died 13 Oct. 1918.

McNAUGHT, William Kirkpatrick, CMG 1914; Hon. Colonel 109th Regiment Infantry Canadian Militia; President American Watch Case Co., Ltd, 509 King Street West, Toronto; Member Hydro-Electric Commission of the Province of Ontario; Member of the Land Transport Commission of Canada appointed by Department of Militia and Defence; Member of the Royal Commission on Unemployment for the Province of Ontario; Chairman Industrial Commission of Province of Ontario; *b* Fergus, Ontario, 6 Sept. 1845; *s* of John McNaught and Sarah Kirkpatrick of Penpont, Scotland; *m* 1872, Caroline Eliza, *d* of Ladds William Lugsdin, Toronto; three *s* one *d*. *Educ:* Public and Grammar Schools, Brantford; Bryant and Stratton Commercial College, Toronto. Began as invoice clerk; elected for North Toronto to Ontario Legislature, 1906; re-elected, 1906 and 1911; founded The Trader and Canadian Jeweler and edited it for 26 years; Ex-President and Chairman of Art Committee of Canadian National Exhibition. Liberal-Conservative; Baptist. *Publications:* Lacrosse and How to Play it; Canadian Pioneers; Ontario's True National Policy in regard to Black and White Coal; The Milk Question; Why a Protective Tariff Policy is necessary for Canada; Imperial Federation; Canada First in the Empire. *Recreations:* lacrosse, rowing, sailing, rifle shooting. *Address:* 614 Huron Street, Toronto, Canada. *Clubs:* National, Royal Canadian Yacht, Toronto.

Died Feb. 1919.

MACNAUGHTAN, Sarah; author; 4th *d* of late Peter Macnaughtan, JP. *Educ:* at home. Worked at music and painting; travelled in South America, South Africa, Canada and United States, Turkey, Macedonia, Palestine, Egypt, Greece, India, Kashmir, Nepal, Burma, etc; helped with Red Cross Society's work (comforts for sick and wounded) in S Africa; wrote books, articles, etc; Belgian Order of Leopold. *Publications:* Selah Harrison, 1898; The Fortune of Christina M'Nab, 1901; The Gift; A Lame Dog's Diary; The Expensive Miss du Cane; Three Miss Graemes; Us Four; The Andersons; Peter and Jane; Four Chimneys; Some Elderly People, 1915; A Woman's Diary of the War. *Address:* 1 Norfolk Street, Park Lane, W. *T:* Mayfair 4049.

Died 24 July 1916.

MACNAUGHTON-JONES, Henry, MD, MCh, QUI; MAO (*honoris causa*), RUI; FRCSI; FRCSE; Consulting Surgeon; *b* Cork; *s* of William Thomas Jones, MD and Helen Macnaughton Jones; *m* Henrietta, 3rd *d* of William Verling Gregg, of Cork; three *c*. *Educ:* Queen's College, Cork. Demonstrator of Anatomy, Queen's College, Cork, at age of 19; ten years Demonstrator and Lecturer on Descriptive Anatomy in this college; Professor of Midwifery, 1876; Examiner in Midwifery (obstetrics and gynæcology) in the Royal University of Ireland, 1881; did duty in eight of the Poor Law dispensary districts of Cork city, resigned in 1872; eleven years physician to the Cork Fever Hospital; surgeon to the County Hospital; in 1868 founded the Cork Eye, Ear and Throat Hospital; in 1872 founded the Cork Maternity; in 1874 was principal mover in the foundation of the Women and Children's Hospital, later the Victoria Hospital; founded the Premier Branch of the British Medical Association in Ireland; came to London, 1883; thrice President of the Irish Medical Schools and Graduates Association; twice President of the British Gynæcological Society; hon. member Obstetrical Societies, Belgium, Leipzig, Munich, Rome; Vice-President and President Obstetrical and Gynæcological section of the Royal Society of Medicine for 1909–10 and 1910–11; President of the Irish Association (in London), 1909–10; Hon. President International Congresses of Obstetrics and Gynæcology, Amsterdam, Rome, Paris, Petrograd and Berlin; Raconteur for Great Britain and Ireland, International Congress of Obstetrics and Gynæcology, Berlin, 1912. *Publications:* Diseases of Women (2 vols), 9th edn, 1904; Diseases of the Ear and Nasopharynx, 6th edn, 1902; Noises in the Head and Ear; Surgical Essays; Affections of the Hip, Knee and Ankle, 1885; Practical Points in Gynæcology, 1890; Hints to Midwives. *Recreations:* rowing, writing verse (A Piece of Delf and Other Fragments, 1st and 2nd series; The Dawn of Life and other Poems; The Thames, etc). *Address:* 13 Harley Street, W; *T:* Mayfair 2243; The Rest, 6 Ravenscroft Park, Barnet; *T:* Barnet 451. *TA:* Macnaughton-Jones, London.

Died 16 April 1918.

MacNEECE, Maj.-Gen. James Gaussen, CB 1911; Director Medical Services, Indian Army; *b* 27 Feb. 1856; *s* of Rev. James MacNeece,

MA, late of Clonfeacle Rectory, Moy and Mulnagore Lodge, Dungannon, Co. Tyrone; *m* Josephine Alice, 2nd *d* of Nicholas Coulthurst, Malabar, Southsea; no *c*. Major RAMC 1890; Lt-Col 1898; Col 1907; Surg.-Gen. 1910; PMO Malta, 1905; India, 1910; DDMS Southern Command, 1912; Director Med. Services, Indian Army, 1915–16; served Bozdar Field Force, 1881; Zhob Valley Expedition, 1884; Afghan War, 1878–80 (medal with clasp); S Africa, 1900–1 (despatches, Queen's medal, three clasps); Maj.-Gen. on Retired List, 1918. Commander St Maurice and St Lazarus (Italy). *Address:* 9 Spenser Road, Southsea, Hants. *Club:* Junior United Service. *Died 13 Dec. 1919.*

M'NEIL, Daniel, KC 1907; barrister-at-law; *b* Hillsborough, Inverness County, 31 Jan. 1853; 2nd *s* of Malcolm M'Neil and Ellen Meagher; *m* 1881; two *s* three *d*. *Educ:* Hillsborough High School; College of St Francis Xavier, Antigonish. Admitted to Bar of Nova Scotia, 1879; elected to represent his native county in 1886 in the Local Legislature of this province, and also in 1890; a member of the Government of Nova Scotia, 1886–93; contested his native county in 1901 and 1906. *Address:* Inverness, County of Inverness, Nova Scotia. *T:* 8 Inverness. *Club:* Inverness. *Died 16 Nov. 1918.*

MACNEILL, John Gordon Swift, KC; MP (N) S Donegal, 1887–1918; Professor of Constitutional Law and of the Law of Public and Private Wrongs since 1909, Clerk of Convocation since 1910, and Dean of Faculty of Law, National University of Ireland, since 1912; *b* Dublin, 11 March 1849; *o s* of Rev. John Gordon Swift MacNeill, MA, and Susan Colpoys, *d* of Rev. Henry Tweedy, MA, and formerly Lieut 7th Dragoon Guards; unmarried. *Educ:* Trinity College, Dublin (Three First Honours Classics); Christ Church, Oxford (Classical Exhibition); 2nd class Classical Mods, 1870; 2nd class Final School Law and Modern History, 1872; MA 1875. Auditor of Irish Law Students' Debating Society, 1875; First Place and First Exhibition at Final Examination for call to Irish Bar, 1875; called to Irish Bar, 1876; Professor of Constitutional and Criminal Law, King's Inns, Dublin, 1882–88; was severely criticized and caricatured for protesting in the House of Commons against the cession of Heligoland to Germany, 1890; proposed motion disallowing votes of directors of Mombasa Railway which resulted in defeat of Unionist Government, 1892; QC 1893; was commended by Sir Henry Campbell-Bannerman, as Premier, in the House of Commons for his success in procuring, after years of agitation, the abolition of flogging in the Royal Navy, 1906; by repeated motions in the House of Commons established the principle that the position of Minister of the Crown is incompatible with the holding of directorships in Public Companies; proposed motion with reference to the conduct of the trial of the Great Yarmouth Election Petition, 1906; one of the seven members of the House of Commons who constituted the Committee of Privileges, 1908; by persistent questions to Ministers in the House of Commons from November 1914, pressed the Government to introduce the legislation embodied in The Titles Deprivation Act 1917. *Publications:* The Irish Parliament, what it was and what it did, 1885; English Interference with Irish Industries, 1886; How the Union was carried, 1887; Titled Corruption, 1894; The Constitutional and Parliamentary History of Ireland, 1917; Studies in the Constitution of the Irish Free State, 1925; What I have Seen and Heard, 1925. *Recreations:* pedestrianism, pet dogs, travel, original research, visits to places of archæological, historic or architectural interest; collections of old plate, china and historic relics. *Address:* 17 Pembroke Road, Dublin, Barra, Baily, Co. Dublin. *Club:* National Liberal. *Died 24 Aug. 1926.*

M'NEILL, Captain Malcolm, CMG 1916; DSO 1902; late Argyll and Sutherland Highlanders; temp. Lieutenant-Colonel commanding a Service Battalion; *b* 30 Jan. 1866; *s* of late Lt-Col A. C. M'Neill, CSI (Madras Army). Entered army, 1885; Captain, 1894; served Waziristan, 1894–95, assistant superintendent of signalling (medal and clasp); Tochi Valley, 1897 (medal and clasp), Somaliland, 1901 (DSO, despatches, medal and clasp); retired, 1906; served European War, 1914–16 (despatches CMG). *Publications:* In Pursuit of the Mad Mullah; Service and Sport in the Somali Protectorate, 1902. *Recreations:* big game hunting, fishing, shooting. *Address:* Dun-Grianach, Oban. *Clubs:* Junior United Service, New, Edinburgh. *Died 3 June 1917.*

McNEILL, Sir Malcolm, Kt 1904; CB 1901; late Chairman of the Local Government Board for Scotland; retired; *b* 15 Nov. 1839; *y s* of Captain McNeill, Colonsay, Gigha and Ardlussa; *m* 1st, 1864, Clara Elizabeth, *y d* of Robert Buchanan of Ardoch; 2nd, 1871, Susan Carruthers (*d* 1914), *e d* of Archibald McNeill, PCS; two *s* two *d*. *Educ:* Eton; Sandhurst. Retired from army, 1861 and entered the Civil Service, 1867, under the Board of Supervision for the Relief of the

Poor and of Public Health in Scotland; became Secretary of the Board of Supervision, 1892; of the Local Government Board, 1894; and Vice-president and Chairman, 1897. *Recreations:* golf, wood-carving. *Address:* 53 Manor Place, Edinburgh. *T:* Edinburgh 1025. *Club:* New, Edinburgh. *Died 4 May 1919.*

McNUTT, Hon. Peter; Minister without Portfolio, Prince Edward Island; *b* Darnley, 5 April 1834; *s* of late Hon. Peter S. McNutt of Darnley, Prince Edward Island, whose father, James McNutt, a native of Londonderry, Ireland, came to Prince Edward Island as private secretary to Governor Patterson in 1770; *m* 1861, Anna Stewart McNutt of Malpeque, Prince Edward Island. *Educ:* Darnley; Prince of Wales College, Charlottetown. Was Commissioner of Small Debts until the County Courts were established; a Coroner for Prince County since 1863; High Sheriff of County, 1875–77; first returned at a bye-election in 1882 to Legislative Council; re-elected at General Elections, 1882 and 1897, for 4th District of Prince County, and again at General Election, 1900, to the Legislative Assembly; member of the Executive Council of Prince Edward Island, without portfolio, continuously since Oct. 1897; merchant and farmer, Presbyterian, Liberal. *Address:* Malpeque, Prince Edward Island. *Died Nov. 1919.*

MACNUTT, Hon. Thomas; Member of the Dominion House of Commons for Saltcoats, Saskatchewan, 1908–25; *b* Campbelton, NB, 3 Aug. 1850; *s* of Charles S. MacNutt, of Scotch descent, and Emily Allison Sims, English; *m* 1885, Margaret M'Fadyen; two *s* one *d*. *Educ:* Collegiate and Commercial College, Ottawa. Went west on staff of special survey, 1874; spent three years at that work, then took up land and farming thereafter, doing considerable work in meantime in connection with colonisation and immigration; was contractor and later Inspector of Public Works for Territorial Government; President Saltcoats District Telephone Company and Agricultural Society; Director of several local institutions; Justice of the Peace and Coroner for many years; served in Militia during Fenian raid, 1866, and Rebellion, 1885 (Service Medal and Ontario Land Grant); defeated for old Territorial Assembly, 1892; elected, 1902; for New Sask. Legislature in 1905; Speaker of Saskatchewan Legislative Assembly, 1905–8; re-elected 1908, but resigned; Presbyterian; Independent. *Address:* Saltcoats, Sask. *Died Feb. 1927.*

MACONOCHIE, Archibald White; Managing Director of Maconochie Bros, Ltd, London, Lowestoft, Fraserburgh and Stornoway; *b* 1855; *m;* one *s* three *d*. *Educ:* Shrewsbury. Member of Tariff Commission, 1904; MP (LU) for East Aberdeenshire, 1900–6; contested (C) East Aberdeenshire, 1906; Partick Division, Lanarks, 1910–11; Wednesbury Division of Staffordshire, 1918. *Address:* 8 Porchester Gate, Hyde Park, W2. *T:* Park 4619. *Clo* Maconochie, Milleast, London; Cudham Hall, Cudham, Kent. *M:* LF 7687. *Died 3 Feb. 1926.*

MACONOCHIE, Sir Evan, KCIE 1921; CSI 1918; ICS, retired; *b* 8 July 1868; *s* of Alexander Maconochie, late of the Home Office, Whitehall; *m* 1899, Margaret Lucy, *d* of late Sir Denzil Ibbetson, KCSI; three *s* one *d*. *Educ:* Sherborne School; New College, Oxford. Joined Bombay Civil Service, 1889; served as Assistant Collector and Settlement Officer; Under-Secretary to Govt of India Dept of Rev. and Agriculture, 1897–1900; Private Secretary to Maharaja of Mysore, 1902–9; Collector and Commissioner of Division; Agent to the Governor in Kathiawar, 1915–22; JP Devon. *Publication:* Life in the Indian Civil Service, 1926. *Recreations:* shooting, fishing, golf. *Address:* Upway, Seaton, Devon. *Club:* East India United Service. *Died 4 Dec. 1927.*

MACOUN, James Melville, CMG 1912; FLS; Head of Biological Division, Geological Survey of Canada since 1917; *b* Belleville, Ontario, 7 Nov. 1862; *e s* of Prof. John Macoun, Dominion Naturalist, and Ellen Terrill Macoun; *m;* one *d*. *Educ:* Albert University, Belleville. Assistant Botanist and Naturalist to Geological Survey of Canada, 1883–1917; travelled over whole Dominion in that capacity; Joint-Secretary of British Fur-Seal Commission, 1891; British Agent in Behring Sea, 1892; at Paris Arbitration, 1893, as fur-seal expert; one of the British Fur-Seal Commissioners, 1896–98; represented Canada at Paris Exposition, 1900, as Forestry Commissioner; assisted Ambassador Bryce and Sir Joseph Pope at settlement of fur-seal question at Washington, 1911; elected Corresp. Member of Zoological Society of London, 1893, and Fellow of the Linnæan Society of London, 1914. *Publications:* numerous reports of the Geological Survey and other departments; Flora of the Pribyloff Islands; Catalogue of Canadian Birds. *Recreation:* walking. *Address:* Department of Mines, Ottawa. *TA:* Ottawa. *T:* Q 8527. *Club:* University. *Died 8 Jan. 1920.*

MACOUN, John, MA; FRSCan; Naturalist to Dominion of Canada; *b* Maralin, County Down, 17 April 1831; *m* 1862, Ellen Tyrrell; two *s* three *d*. *Educ*: self-educated. Emigrated to Canada, 1850; farmed in the bush till 1857; taught in public schools until 1874; while still teaching in public schools became Professor of Botany in Albert College, Belleville, Ont, 1868; Professor of Natural History, 1875–79; explorer for the Dominion Government, 1879; placed on Civil List with title of Dominion Botanist, 1881; Dominion Naturalist and Assistant Director of the Geological Survey of Canada, 1886. *Publications:* The Great North-West; Catalogue of Canadian Plants; Catalogue of Canadian Birds; many reports and short papers. *Recreation:* field work in the summer. *Address:* Sidney, Vancouver Island, Canada. *T:* 129.   *Died 18 July 1921.*

M'PEAKE, James Young; Vice-Chairman National Magazine Co. Ltd; Editor of Nash's Magazine since 1915; *b* Belfast, 18 Dec. 1868; *e s* of Robert M'Peake, Belfast; *m* Gertrude, 3rd *d* of Denis Sheils, Skerries, Co. Dublin; two *s*. *Educ*: St Malachy's College, Belfast. In 1890 joined staff Dublin Daily Express, of which successively Sub-Editor and Editor; Editor Dublin Evening Mail, 1900–12; Managing Director London Budget, 1912–14. *Recreation:* golf. *Address:* 40 Montagu Mansions, W1. *T:* Mayfair 4743. *M:* XE 9707. *Clubs:* Savage; Highgate Golf.   *Died 19 Sept. 1924.*

MACPHAIL, Rev. William Merry, MA; General Secretary of the Presbyterian Church of England since 1907; Moderator of the Synod of the Presbyterian Church of England, 1916–17; *b* Newcastle, 31 Oct. 1857; 3rd *s* of late Dugald Macphail, author of well-known Gaelic songs; *m* 1882, Sarah Stone, 3rd *d* of late William Goldie, of Ashmore, Dorsetshire; one *s* two *d*. *Educ*: Sherborne; George Watson's College, Edinburgh; Edinburgh University; Glasgow Free Church College. Took the MA degree with Honours in Mental Philosophy at Edinburgh University; holder of the Hamilton Fellowship and the Ferguson Scholarship in Mental Philosophy; Ministerial Assistant at the West Free Church, Rothesay, 1881–82, and at Mayfield Free Church, Edinburgh, 1882; Minister of Mayble Free Church, Ayrshire, 1882–85; Streatham Presbyterian Church, London, SW, 1885–1907; Clerk of the Synod of the Presbyterian Church of England, 1895–1908. *Publication:* The Presbyterian Church, its Doctrine, Worship and Polity. *Recreation:* golf. *Address:* 58 Blenheim Gardens, Cricklewood, NW; Offices of the Presbyterian Church of England, 7 East India Avenue, EC. *TA:* Byterian Led. London. *T:* Central 10116.   *Died 23 Sept. 1916.*

MACPHERSON, Lt-Colonel Archibald Duncan, CIE 1926; *b* 14 Jan. 1872; *s* of late Sir William and Lady Macpherson; *m* 1911, Viva Tertia Pevensey Duke; three *s*. *Educ*: Charterhouse; Sandhurst. Joined 77th Middlesex Regt, 1891; 2nd (Sam Brown's) Cavalry PFF, 1893; Political Department of the Government of India, 1898; retired, 1927. *Address:* c/o Grindlay & Co., Ltd, 54 Parliament Street, SW1. *Club:* Junior Naval and Military.   *Died 27 Aug. 1928.*

MACPHERSON, Sir Arthur George, KCIE 1889; *b* 26 Sept 1828; *y s* of Hugh Macpherson, MD; *m* 1860, Frances Caroline (*d* 1918) *d* of late William Martin; four *s* one *d*. *Educ*: Aberdeen; Edinburgh. Barrister, Inner Temple, 1852; Legislative Secretary, Government of Bengal, 1862–64; Under-Secretary of India, 1864; Judge of High Court at Calcutta, 1864–77; legal adviser to Secretary of State for India, 1879–82; Judicial Secretary, India Office, 1882–93. *Address:* Tenerife, Trefusis Terrace, Exmouth.

Died 22 Jan. 1921.

MACPHERSON, Charles, MusD Dunelm (*honoris causa*); FRAM, FRCO; Hon. Member American Guild of Organists; Organist of St Paul's Cathedral since 1916; President, Royal College of Organists, 1920–22; Professor of Harmony, Royal Academy of Music; an Examiner for the Associated Board of the RAM and RCM; *b* Edinburgh, 10 May 1870; *e s* of late Charles Macpherson, Burgh Architect to City of Edinburgh and Mrs Macpherson (afterwards *m* Rev. W. Fancourt, MA, St Mungo's, West Linton, Peeblesshire); *m* 1910, Sophia Menella, *y d* of Rev. W. C. E. Newbolt; one *s*. *Educ*: St Paul's Choir School; Royal Academy of Music; Charles Lucas Medallist (for Composition), 1893. Organist of St David's, Weem, Aberfeldy, NB, 1887–89; of private chapel at Luton Hoo, Beds (the late Madame de Falbe), 1889–95; Sub-organist, St Paul's Cathedral, 1895–1916; conductor of the London Church Choir Association since 1914; Hon. Conductor of Choir at opening ceremony and Thanksgiving Service, 24 May, at the British Empire Exhibition, Wembley, 1925. *Publications:* various musical compositions for church use, also orchestral and other secular works; A Short History of Harmony; lectures, etc. *Recreations:* sketching, golf. *Address:* 8 Amen Court, St Paul's, EC4.   *Died 28 May 1927.*

McPHERSON, Col David William, CMG 1917; Canadian Army Medical Corps; Officer commanding Ontario Military Hospital, 1916; *b* Toronto, of Scotch parents, 13 June 1869; *m* 1905, Margaret, *d* of late William and Margaret Sloane, Quebec. *Educ:* Wellesley Public School and Toronto Collegiate; Toronto University, MB; MD, CM Trinity University; Fellow of the American College of Surgery, 1913. Practised Surgery in Toronto and was Surgeon to Grace Hospital, Toronto; when Canadian Army Medical Corps was established, 1899, joined as Lt and worked his way up to Lt-Col in command of No 11 Canadian Field Ambulance; DADMS Canadian Military District No 2, 1913; offered services for France, 6 Aug. 1914; organised No 2 Canadian Field Ambulance, came overseas as Commanding Officer, Sept. 1914, went to France with the 1st Canadian Division, Feb. 1915; through 2nd Battle of Ypres; Officer commanding Canadian Convalescent Hospital, Epsom, 1915 (temp. Col 5 Dec. 1916, despatches thrice, CMG). *Address:* 556 Bathurst Street, Toronto, Canada.   *Died 1923.*

MACPHERSON, Rev. Ewen George Fitzroy, CMG 1915; CBE 1919; BA; Rector of Chawton since 1926; late Chaplain to the Forces, 1st Class; *b* 31 Oct. 1863. *Educ:* Durham University. Ordained, 1888; Curate of Medomsley, 1888–92; Chaplain to Forces Portsmouth, 1892–94; Curragh Camp, 1894–99; Natal, 1899–1900; Johannesburg, 1900–4; Winchester, 1904–9; Gibraltar, 1909–13; served South Africa, 1899–1902 (despatches, Queen's medal 6 clasps, King's medal 2 clasps); European War, 1914–19 (despatches, CMG); Asst Chaplain-General, Southern Command, 1916; Western Command, 1920–22; Vicar of Reculver with Hoath, 1922. *Address:* Chawton Rectory, Hants.
Died 28 Nov. 1926.

MACPHERSON, George; JP and DL County of Stafford; JP County of Worcester; *b* 1851; 3rd *s* of G. Macpherson, JP of Gibston, Aberdeenshire; *m* 1st, 1880, Emma Stone (*d* 1889), 3rd *d* of late H. Addenbrooke of Sutton Coldfield; 2nd, 1894, Hilda Mary, *o d* of late E. Bindon Marten, CE; one *d* (and one *s* decd). *Educ:* Chanonry House, Aberdeen. Commenced business at Tudhoe Iron Works, Co. Durham; became partner in firm of Philip Williams & Sons, Coal and Ironmasters, Tipton; Director of the London and North-Western Railway and Barclay Bank Ltd; Chairman Birmingham Canal Co. and SS Mond Gas Co; Chairman of the S Staffs Ironmasters' Association and the Midland Wages Board. *Recreations:* fishing, shooting. *Address:* The Lloyd House, near Wolverhampton. *T:* Wolverhampton 866; Edinglassie Lodge, Glass, Huntly, NB. *M:* E 454, E 1103. *Club:* Caledonian.

Died 24 April 1924.

MACPHERSON, Hector, FRSE; author and journalist. *Publications:* Mr Gladstone, His Political Career, 1892; Thomas Carlyle, 1896, and Adam Smith, 1899, in Famous Scots Series; Herbert Spencer, 1900; new and condensed edition of Adam Smith's Wealth of Nations, 1903; Books to Read, and How to Read Them, 1904; The Scottish Church Crisis, 1904; Scotland's Battles for Spiritual Independence, 1905; A Century of Intellectual Development, 1907 (trans. Japanese); A Century of Political Development, 1908 (trans. Japanese); Intellectual Development of Scotland, 1911; Scotland's Debt to Protestantism, 1912; The Jesuits in History, 1914 (trans. Hungarian). *Address:* 5 Merchiston Bank Avenue, Edinburgh.

Died Oct. 1924.

MACPHERSON, Maj.-Gen. Sir William (Grant), KCMG 1918 (CMG 1902); CB 1915; Colonel Commandant RAMC since 1925; late Army Medical Service; *b* Kilmuir, Ross-shire, 27 Jan. 1858; 3rd *s* of late Rev. W. Macpherson of Kilmuir Easter, Ross-shire; *m* 1st, 1884, Elizabeth Anne (*d* 1907), 2nd *d* of late James Clunas of New Orleans, USA, and Nairn, NB; 2nd, 1910, Geraldine Ethel, *y d* of late Gen. Sir John Doran, KCB. *Educ:* Fettes College, Edinburgh; Edinburgh, Tübingen and Leipzig Universities. MA (Honours, Classics and Greek Travelling Scholar), MB Edinburgh University; LLD (Edin. Univ.); DPH Cambridge University. Editor-in-Chief Official Medical History of the War, and author of several articles and works on military medical subjects. Served at the War Office as a Deputy Assistant and Deputy Director-General of the Army Medical Service, and as a member of the Advisory Board for Medical services and of the Army Sanitary Committee; was in medical charge of Sir Charles Euan Smith's Mission to Fez, 1892, and of Sir A. Nicolson's Mission to Morocco City, 1896; represented HM Govt and War Office at several International Conferences; Hon. Secretary of Central British Red Cross Committee from formation till 1902; on special duty S Africa, 1902-3, and Panama and Cuba, 1908; Senior Medical Officer, N China Command, and attached to Japanese Army in the Field, Russo-Japanese War, 1904–5; one of the British Plenipotentaries at the Conference for the Revision of the Geneva

Convention, 1906; attached to Directorate of Military Operations, War Office, 1906–10; PMO Malta, 1910; Asst Director Medical Services, 4th Quetta Division, and Lecturer Medical Services, Staff College, Quetta, 1911–14; served European War, 1914–18, as Director of Medical Services 1st Army and as Deputy Director-General, GHQ; also as Director of Medical Services British Force in Macedonia, 1915–16 (despatches nine times, KCMG, CB); formerly Hon. Physician to HM. FRGS; FRSocMed. KGStJ. 3rd Class Sacred Treasure of Japan; Commander, Legion of Honour and Crown of Italy; Japanese Red Cross Society's decoration for meritorious services and Japanese war medal; USA Distinguished Service Medal. *Address:* 14 Evelyn Gardens, SW7. *Clubs:* Savile, Junior United Service. *Died 15 Oct. 1927.*

MACQUOID, Katharine Sarah; novelist; writer of travel books; *b* Kentish Town, 26 Jan. 1824; 3rd *d* of late Thomas Thomas and Phœbe Gadsden; *m* 1851, Thomas Robert Macquoid, RI (*d* 1912); two *s*. *Educ:* home. *Publications:* first short story appeared in Welcome Guest, 1859; Piccalilli, 1862; A Bad Beginning, 1862; Chesterford, 1863; Hester Kirton, 1864; By the Sea, 1865; Elinor Dryden, 1867; Charlotte Burney, 1867; Wild as a Hawk (Marjorie), 1868; Forgotten by the World, 1869; Rookstone, 1871; Patty, 1871; Miriam's Marriage, 1872; Pictures across the Channel, 1872; Too Soon, 1873; Through Normandy, 1874; My Story, 1874; The Evil Eye, 1875; Diane, 1875; Lost Rose, 1876; Through Brittany, 1877; Doris Barugh, 1877; Pictures and Legends from Normandy and Brittany, 1878; The Berkshire Lady, 1879; In the Sweet Spring Time, 1880; Beside the River, 1881; Little Fifine, 1881; In the Ardennes, 1881; A Faithful Lover, 1882; Her Sailor Love, 1883; About Yorkshire, 1883; Under the Snow, 1884; Louisa, 1885; A Strange Company, 1885; At the Red Glove, 1885; A Little Vagabond, 1886; Joan Wentworth, 1886; Sir James Appleby, 1886; Mère Suzanne, 1886; At the Peacock, 1887; Puff, 1888; Elizabeth Morley, 1889; Roger Ferron, 1889; Pepin, 1889; Cosette, 1890; The Haunted Fountain, 1890; At an Old Chateau, 1891; Drifting Apart, 1891; The Prince's Whim, 1891; Maisie Derrick, 1892; Miss Evon of Eyoncourt, 1892; Berris, 1893; In an Orchard, 1894; Appledore Farm, 1894; His Last Card, 1895; In the Volcanic Eifel, 1896, and In Paris, 1900 (jointly with Gilbert S. Macquoid); The Story of Lois, 1898; A Ward of the King, 1898; His Heart's Desire, 1903; Pictures in Umbria, 1905; A Village Chronicle, 1905; Captain Ballington, 1907; Molly Montague's Love Story, 1911; many stories in magazines and newspapers. *Recreation:* visits from my friends. *Address:* The Edge, 8 Lucien Road, Tooting Common, SW. *Died 24 June 1917.*

MACQUOID, Percy, JP; RI; artist designer and decorator; *b* 1852; *s* of late T. R. Macquoid; *m* 1891, Theresa I., *d* of Thos Dent. *Educ:* Marlborough; Royal Academy Schools. *Publications:* A History of English Furniture; Costume, Furniture and Domestic Habits in Shakespeare's England, 1916; Theatrical Designs for Scenery and Costume in Paolo and Francesca, Nero, The School for Scandal, Antony and Cleopatra, Romeo and Juliet, Joseph and his Brethren, False Gods, Henry VIII, If I were King, The Aristocrat, Mary Rose, The Dover Road and other plays, etc. *Address:* The Yellow House, 8 Palace Court, Bayswater, W2. *T:* Park 2400; Hoove Lea, Hove. *Clubs:* Garrick, Arts; Union, Brighton.

Died 20 March 1925.

MACRAE, Col Alexander William, CIE 1911; JP Hampshire; Hon. Colonel Malabar Volunteer Rifles; *b* 15 June 1858; *s* of Dr Charles Mackenzie Macrae. *Address:* Kerala, Yateley, Hants.

Died 1 Feb. 1920.

MACRAE, Charles Colin, JP; *b* 6 Aug. 1843; *s* of A. C. Macrae, MD, Inspector-General of Hospitals; *m* Cecilia, *d* of Samuel Laing, once Finance Minister of India and for many years MP for Orkney and Shetland. *Educ:* Eton; University College, Oxford. Called to Bar, 1868; practised for 8 years in Calcutta, where he was Secretary to the Legislative Council, Govt of Bengal; then practised in this country at the Common Law and Parliamentary Bar, and before the Privy Council, and was standing Counsel to the India Office, retired 1889; Chairman of the London, Brighton, and South Coast Rly Co., London Caledonian Trust, British and China Corporation, and Director of the Gresham Life and Fire Insurance Societies, and various other companies. *Publications:* The Law of Divorce in India; The Indian Contract Act, with notes. *Recreations:* shooting, fishing, golf, sketching. *Address:* Ravenshall, Bournemouth West. *TA:* Pavy, London. *T:* Bournemouth 1500. *Clubs:* Windham, City of London; Bournemouth. *Died 28 Nov. 1922.*

MACRAE, Sir Colin George, Kt 1900; *b* 30 Nov. 1844; *m* 1877, Flora Maitland (*d* 1921), 3rd *d* of John Colquhoun, 1 Royal Terrace,

Edinburgh; one *s* one *d. Educ:* Edinburgh Academy and University; MA. Writer to HM Signet, 1871; JP for Counties of Edinburgh, Forfar and Dumbarton; Chairman of School Board of Edinburgh, 1890–1900. Decorated for services to education. *Recreations:* shooting, fishing, cycling, etc. *Address:* Glenflora, Colinton. *TA:* Macrae, Edinburgh. *T:* 2495 Edinburgh Central. *Club:* New, Edinburgh.

Died 9 Dec. 1925.

MACRAE, Robert Scarth Farquhar, CIE 1917; CBE 1919; Indian Police, retired; Chief Police Officer, Port of London Authority's Police, since 1925; *b* 18 May 1877; *s* of late John Macrae, Procurator-Fiscal of Orkney, and Mrs Garson of Grindelay, Orphir, Orkney; *m* 1911, Beatrix Reid, *d* of late Andrew McGeoch, Glasgow; one *s* one *d. Educ:* Trinity College, Glenalmond; St Andrews University. Somaliland Expeditionary Force, 1903–4; Political officer, Somaliland, 1904–5; Comr of Police, Baroda, 1912–16; Controller of Native Craft, Mesopotamia Expeditionary Force, 1916–19; Dep. Inspector General of Police, Bihar and Orissa, 1919–25; retired, 1925. *Address:* 88 Finchley Road, NW3. *Died 20 Feb. 1926.*

MACRAY, Rev. William Dunn, MA, Hon. LittD; FSA; Rector of Ducklington, 1870–1912; antiquary, author and editor; *b* 1826; *m* 1856, Adelaide Otilia Alberta (*d* 1905), 2nd *d* of Otto Schmidt of Berlin; three *s* two *d. Educ:* Magdalen Coll. School and Magdalen Coll. Oxford (Fellow). Asst in Bodleian Library, 1840–1905. *Publications:* editor of numerous works for the Record Office, Rolls Series, Clarendon Press, Roxburghe Club; Catalogues of the Rawlinson and Digby MSS in Bodleian Library, 1862–98; Index to the Catalogue of Ashmolean MSS, 1867; Annals of the Bodleian Library, 1868, 1890; Calendar of the Clarendon State Papers in the Bodleian, 1867–76 (vols ii. iii); edited Clarendon's History of the Rebellion (6 vols) for the Oxford University Press, 1888; Register of Fellows of Magdalen College, 8 vols, 1894–1915; Breviarium Bothanum, 1901, etc. *Address:* Bloxham, Oxfordshire; Magdalen College, Oxford. *Died 5 Dec. 1916.*

MACRITCHIE, David, FSA Scot and Ireland; FRAI; author; *b* Edinburgh, 16 April 1851; *y s* of William Dawson MacRitchie, MD, surgeon in the Hon. East India Company's Service and Elizabeth Elder, *d* of John MacRitchie of Craigton, Perthshire, Writer, Edinburgh; unmarried. *Educ:* Edinburgh Southern Academy, Edinburgh Institution and Edinburgh University. Became a member of the Society of Chartered Accountants, Edinburgh, but soon thereafter turned his attention to ethnology and antiquarian research, largely from the point of view of traditional lore; wrote on the subject of dwarf races, in tradition and in fact; on the archaic underground dwellings of the British Isles; and on the history and character of the gypsies; in 1888 he founded the cosmopolitan Gypsy Lore Society, the quarterly Journal of which he edited in collaboration with his friend Francis Hindes Groome until 1892, when the society became dormant; on its revival, in 1907, he was made first President; one of the founders, 1906, of the St Andrew Society, Edinburgh, its aim to define Scotland's position in history. *Publications:* Ancient and Modern Britons, 1884; The Gypsies of India, 1886; The Testimony of Tradition, 1890; The Ainos, a work chiefly drawn from Japanese sources, 1892; Fians, Fairies and Picts, 1893; Scottish Gypsies under the Stewarts, 1894; The Savages of Gaelic Tradition, 1920; in 1897 he edited and published the Diary of a Tour through Great Britain in 1795, by his grandfather, the Rev. William MacRitchie, Perthshire; contributed a number of articles to magazines and scientific journals and to the Harmsworth Encyclopædia of Religion and Ethics, and the Encyclopædia of Occultism. *Recreation:* travel. *Address:* 4 Archibald Place, Edinburgh. *Club:* Scottish Arts, Edinburgh.

Died 14 Jan. 1925.

M'ROBERT, Sir Alexander, 1st Bt *cr* 1922; KBE 1919; Kt 1910; LLD Aberdeen; FRGS; Chairman of British India Corporation, Limited, Cawnpore; *b* 21 May 1854; *e s* of John M'Robert, Douneside, Tarland, NB; *m* 1st, 1883, Rachel, *d* of Dr William Hunter Workman, of Worcester, Massachusetts, USA; three *s. Educ:* Public Schools, Newhills, NB; Royal College of Science. Before going to Cawnpore in 1884, held the appointment of Neil Arnott Lecturer in Experimental Physics, Mechanics' Institution, Aberdeen; and was Lecturer in Chemistry in Robert Gordon's College, Aberdeen; invested with the Order of Honour of Afghanistan, 1918. President of the Upper India Chamber of Commerce for nine years, and represented that body in the Legislative Council of the United Provinces of Agra and Oudh for five successive terms of two years each; represented Chamber at the Congresses of Chambers of Commerce of the Empire at Montreal 1903, London 1906 and 1912, Sydney 1909, and Toronto 1920; Fellow of the University of Allahabad in the Faculty of Science since 1904; Member of

Committee of Management, Government Engineering College, Roorkee, since 1900; Governor of Agricultural College, Cawnpore; Lt-Col Commanding Cawnpore Volunteer Rifles (VD), 1899–1912; pioneered the movement for providing sanitary dwellings for factory workers in India; travelled extensively all over the world. *Heir: s* Alasdair Workman M'Robert, *b* 11 July 1912. *Address:* The Shieling, Cawnpore. *TA:* M'Robert, Cawnpore. *Clubs:* Bath, Oriental, National Liberal; Cawnpore; Royal Northern, Aberdeen.

Died 22 June 1922.

McSWEENY, George, KC 1911; HM Third Serjeant-at-Law in Ireland, 1913; Second Serjeant since 1919; Crown Counsel for Co. Cork; *b* 1865; *m* 1919, Kathleen, *widow* of late F. D. Matthews, Bombay; one *d. Educ:* National Schools; University College, and Trinity College, Dublin. Called to Irish Bar, 1896. *Address:* Lochlin, Howth, Co. Dublin. *T:* Howth 62.

Died 14 Nov. 1923.

MacSWINEY, Terrence Joseph; MP (SF) Mid Cork since Dec. 1918; *b* 1880. Lord Mayor of Cork, 1920.

Died 25 Oct. 1920.

M'TAGGART, John M'Taggart Ellis, LittD; Hon LLD St Andrews; FBA 1906; Fellow since 1891 and Lecturer, 1897–1923, of Trinity College, Cambridge; *b* 3 Sept. 1866; *s* of late Francis Ellis M'Taggart, Judge of County Courts and late Caroline Ellis; *m* 1899, Margaret, *d* of late Joseph Bird, Auckland, New Zealand. *Educ:* Clifton College; Trinity College, Cambridge. *Publications:* Studies in the Hegelian Dialectic, 1896; Studies in Hegelian Cosmology, 1901; Some Dogmas of Religion, 1906; A Commentary on Hegel's Logic, 1910; The Nature of Existence, vol. i, 1921. *Recreation:* novel-reading. *Address:* Trinity College, Cambridge. *Club:* Savile.

Died 18 Jan. 1925.

McTAGGART, Captain W. B., DL, JP; *m* 1st, Letitia, *d* of A. Thompson of Blackrock, Dublin; 2nd, Louisa, *d* of Admiral Joseph Grant Bickford, RN; one *s. Educ:* Harrow. Joined 14th Hussars, 1868; retired 1879; Chairman, Mysore Gold Mining Co. Ltd, etc; Master of the Surrey Staghounds fourteen years, resigned 1915. *Publications:* Absolute Relativism, and many philosophical treatises and essays. *Recreations:* hunting, shooting, fishing. *Clubs:* Naval and Military, Carlton.

Died 9 Nov. 1919.

M'VAIL, Sir David Caldwell, Kt 1910; MB; FRFPS Glasgow; Hon. FRCPI; Ex-Professor of Clinical Medicine, St Mungo's College; Hon. Consulting Physician to Glasgow Royal Infirmary; Crown Member for Scotland General Medical Council, 1892–1912; *b* Kilmarnock, 6 Oct. 1845; *s* of late James M'Vail; *m* 1877, Lily Neilson, *d* of late Thomas N. Brown; one *s* one *d. Educ:* Anderson's College; Glasgow University. Was the Annual Lecturer to the Faculty of Physicians and Surgeons of Glasgow, 1882—on the Mechanism of Respiration. Member of the Court of Glasgow University since 1891. *Publications:* various papers on Pulmonary, Cardiac and Physiological subjects. *Address:* 3 St James's Terrace, Glasgow. *T:* 443 Hillhead, Glasgow. *Clubs:* Liberal, Glasgow University.

Died 4 Nov. 1917.

McVAIL, John Christie, MD, LLD; FRFPS; DPH Cambridge; (retired); late Member Scottish Board of Health; late Deputy Chairman National Health Insurance Commission, Scotland; Crown Member for Scotland, General Medical Council, 1912–22; *b* Kilmarnock, 22 Oct. 1849; *s* of late James McVail; *m* Jessie Shoolbred, *d* of late John Rowat, Kilmarnock; two *s* two *d. Educ:* Anderson's College; Glasgow University. Practised medicine in Kilmarnock, 1873–91; was physician to Infirmary, Medical Officer of Health and Crown Examiner in Medico-legal cases for North Ayrshire; late Member Council British Medical Association; late County Medical Officer, Stirlingshire and Dunbartonshire; late Member, Highlands and Islands Medical Service Board; late Examiner in Medical Jurisprudence and Public Health, Universities of Edinburgh, Glasgow, and St Andrews; then Univ. of Aberdeen and Scottish Conjoint Board; ex-President Society Medical Officers of Health of Great Britain and Incorporated Sanitary Association of Scotland, and of Glasgow and West of Scotland Branch, British Medical Association; Lane Lecturer, Cooper Medical College, San Francisco, 1906; later President Epidemiological Section, Royal Society of Medicine; Medical Investigator Royal Commission on Poor Laws, 1907 (Appendix Report, vol. xiv); Milroy Lecturer, Royal College of Physicians, London, 1919; Jenner Medallist Royal Society of Medicine, 1922; Stewart prize, British Medical Assoc. 1922; Member of Court of Governors, London School of Hygiene and Tropical Medicine, 1924. *Publications:* Evidence before Royal Commission on

Vaccination, vol. vi of Report; The Prevention of Infectious Diseases, 1907; numerous writings on public health subjects, especially on Smallpox and Vaccination; Ethics of Preventive Medicine, published in Public Health, 1901; County Health Reports; Half a Century of Smallpox and Vaccination, 1919; The British Medical Association: Its Constitution and Government, a Historical Survey, 1924. *Address:* 44 Rotherwick Road, Golders Green, NW11. *T:* Speedwell 1567.

Died 29 July 1926.

MACVICAR, Hon. John; Mayor, City of Des Moines; Commissioner-General International Municipal Congress and Exposition, Chicago, 1911; *b* Galt, Ontario, 1859; *s* of John MacVicar, Scotland, and Mary M'Ewen, Scotland; *m* 1884, Nettie M. Nash; one *s* two *d. Educ:* Public Schools, Erie, Pennsylvania. Recorder Town of North Des Moines, Ia, 1888; Mayor, 1889; Mayor, City of Des Moines, Ia, 1896–1900, and from 1916; Pres. League of American Municipalities, 1897; Member of the City Council and Superintendent of Department of Streets and Public Improvements, Des Moines, under Commission form of city government, 1908–12; Plattsburg Training Camp, 9th Regiment, 1916; commissioned Captain Quartermaster, Officers' Reserve Corps, USA, 7 Feb. 1917; assigned to active duty as Assistant to the Quartermaster, Fort Douglas, Utah, 18 May 1917; discharged 6 March 1919; Superintendent, Department Public Safety, Des Moines, 1922–23. *Publications:* several articles on municipal affairs. *Address:* Des Moines, Iowa, USA.

Died 15 Nov. 1928.

M'VITTIE, Surg.-Gen. Charles Edwin; Surgeon-General 1895; Hon. Physician to HM since 1910. Served Afghan War, 1880 (medal); Burmese Expedition, 1886–87 (despatches, medal with 2 clasps).

Died 27 Feb. 1916.

MACWATT, Hay, MA, LLB; Sheriff-Substitute of Ross and Cromarty and Sutherland (retired 1912); *b* 1855; 2nd *s* of David MacWatt, late Procurator-Fiscal of Clackmannanshire; *m* 1897, May, *d* of late R. C. MacWatt, MD, Medical Officer of Health for Berwickshire. *Educ:* Edinburgh Collegiate School; Edinburgh University. Called to Scots Bar, 1881; Sheriff-Substitute of Argyll 1897–1904. *Address:* Elsick House, Strathpeffer, Ross-shire. *T:* Strathpeffer 42. *Club:* University, Edinburgh.

Died 13 Oct. 1920.

McWEENEY, Edmond J., MA, MD, MCh, MAO, Royal University of Ireland; FRCPI; DPH of the Conjoint Royal Colleges in Ireland; Professor of Pathology and Bacteriology at University College, Dublin; *b* Dublin, 9 March 1864; *s* of Theophilus M'Weeney, journalist (Freeman's Journal), of Beaumont, Rathgar, Co. Dublin, and Margaret, *d* of late Jonathan Kendellen of Castlebar, Co. Mayo; *m* 1891, Emilie, *d* of late Simon Brazil of Kingstown, Co. Dublin. *Educ:* Coll. St Bertin, St Omer (France); Catholic University, Dublin. Entered at the first Matric. Exam. held by the then newly created Royal University of Ireland, Nov. 1881, and gained exhibition; scholar (£150) in Mod. Lit. 1882; BA with 1st Hon. and £50 Prize and Studentship (£500) in Mod. Lit. 1884; MA 1885. Meanwhile worked at medicine and graduated MB with hons and exhibition, 1887; MD 1891; devoted himself to Pathology and Bacteriology, and worked in Vienna 1888 under Kolisko, and in Berlin 1889 under C. Fraenkel and von Esmarch; in 1894 gained the studentship in these subjects (£400); appointed Pathologist to the Mater Misericordiæ Hospital, Dublin, 1889; and Bacteriologist to the Irish Local Govt Board, 1900, which positions he continued to hold; President of Pathological Section, Royal Academy of Medicine, in Ireland; Consulting Pathologist to the Troops in Ireland. *Publications:* translator and joint-author of Tappeiner's Chemical Methods of Clinical Diagnosis, as well as of numerous papers on human and vegetable pathology and bacteriology in various medical journals and in the transactions of the Royal Academy of Medicine in Ireland. *Recreations:* golf, cycling, swimming, botanising (Fungi). *Address:* 84 St Stephen's Green, S Dublin. *T:* 2017.

Died 20 June 1925.

M'WHAE, Hon. Sir John, Kt 1924; Agent-General for Victoria in London, 1922–24; late Member for Melbourne City, Legislative Council, Victoria, 1909–22; Minister of Public Works, Bowser Administration; Member of Executive Council in the State of Victoria; Hon. Minister Lawson Administration; for 30 years Member Stock Exchange of Melbourne; six years chairman of latter; *b* Ballarat, 1858; of Scotch parentage; *m* E. H. Douch, Williamstown, Australia; three *s* two *d. Educ:* Dumfries Academy; Ballarat Grammar School. Started life in Union Bank of Australia; afterward Member of the Ballarat and Melbourne Stock Exchanges; connected with pastoral properties in Victoria, Queensland. *Address:* 314 Collins Street, Melbourne. *TA:* M'Whae, Melbourne. *Clubs:* Australian, Stock Exchange, Melbourne.

Died 17 Sept. 1927.

McWHINNIE, Hugh, FJI; *b* farm of Merkland, Kirkoswald, Ayrshire; *m* Elizabeth, *d* of George Hoyle, Ashton-under-Lyne; two *s. Educ:* Parochial School, Dailly; Kirkoswald. Joined the Oldham Standard as a reporter; subsequently became connected with the Liverpool Albion, and later joined the Liverpool Courier; Editor of the Demerara Daily Colonist for 3 years; connected with the Editorial Department of the Liverpool Daily Post for 17 years; Editor of Bristol Daily Mercury and Bristol Evening Echo, 1901-4; was on literary staff of the Tribune; then for 17 years Managing Director of the North Devon Press, Ltd, North Devon Herald. *Recreations:* cycling, horticulture, mechanics. *Address:* Rozelle, Victoria Road, Barnstaple. *T:* 6 Barnstaple. *Club:* Press.   *Died 1923.*

M'WILLIAM, Andrew, CBE 1919; DMet; ARSM; Consulting Metallurgist, formerly Metallurgical Inspector to Indian Government; Assistant Professor of Metallurgy in the University of Sheffield; *s* of John A. M'William and Agnes M'Pherson; *m* 1900, Georgina Beebee, *d* of George Croome, of Gloucestershire; one *s. Educ:* Allan Glen's School, Glasgow; Royal School of Mines; Associate of the Royal School of Mines, 1887; 1st Class in Metallurgy. Demonstrator in Metallurgy in Sheffield Technical School, 1887-91; Chemist and Steel Manager in works, 1891-94; Lecturer in Metallurgy to Staffs CC 1894-96; manager of danger area to British Explosives Syndicate, 1896; Lecturer in Metallurgy, University College, Sheffield; visited Sweden for general tour of steel works, 1899; again in 1907 to study electric melting; went to Spitsbergen for a Sheffield syndicate to investigate coal and mineral prospects, 1908; late Consulting Metallurgist to the Tata Iron and Steel Co., Jamshedpur, India; Member Iron and Steel Institute and Institute of Metals; Hon. Member and President, Sheffield Society of Engineers and Metallurgists; Hon. Life Fellow of Permanent Way Institution; Capt. and OC [E] Co. Chota Nagpur Light Horse. *Publications:* General Foundry Practice (with Dr Longmuir); many papers on original investigations to Iron and Steel Institute, Institute of Metals, Society of Engineers and Metallurgists, Odontological Section of the Royal Society of Medicine; popular series Notes on Metals in local newspaper; reviews and articles in Nature and elsewhere. *Address:* 221 Upperthorpe, Sheffield.

Died 5 April 1922.

MADDEN, Archibald Maclean, CMG 1908; *b* 31 May 1864; *e s* of late Surg.-Gen. Charles D. Madden, CB, Hon. Surgeon to the King; *m* 1902, Cecilia Catherine, *e d* of late Canon A. P. Moor, of Truro; three *s. Educ:* Cheltenham; Trinity College, Cambridge (BA). Clerk, Librarian's Depart, Foreign Office, 1890-93; Acting Vice-Consul, Dar-al-Baida, 1894; employed on Special Service in Morocco, 1894 and 1895; Acting Consul, 1894; Clerk to Legation, Tangier, 1894; accompanied Sir Ernest Mason Satow's special mission to Fez, 1894-95; Sir Arthur Nicolson's (later Lord Carnock) special mission to Morocco, 1896; Acting Consul, Tangier, 1896 and 1898; Vice-Consul, 1897; Vice-Consul, Mogador, 1900-7; Consul, Dar-al-Baida (Casablanca), 1907-14; present at bombardment and siege of Casablanca and Franco-Spanish military occupation, Aug. 1907; HBM Consul at Bilbao, 1914; in Foreign Office, 1923-25, when he retired. *Address:* 53 Sisters Avenue, SW11.

Died 15 Oct. 1928.

MADDEN, Rt. Hon. Dodgson Hamilton, PC (Ire.) 1889; MA, LLD and LittD (Hon.) Trinity College Dublin; Judge of High Court of Justice, Ireland (King's Bench Division), 1892; retired, 1919; Vice-Chancellor of Dublin University, 1895-1919; *b* 28 March 1840; *o s* of Rev. Hugh Hamilton Madden, MA, Chancellor of Cashel; *m* 1st, 1868, Minnie (*d* 1895), *d* of Lewis Moore, DL, Cremorgan, Queen's Co.; 2nd, 1896, Jessie Isabelle, *d* of Richard Warburton, DL, Garryhinch, King's Co. *Educ:* Trinity College, Dublin (Classical Scholar and Medallist; Gold Medallist in Ethics and Logics). Barrister, Ireland, 1864; QC 1880; third Serjeant-at-Law, 1887; Solicitor-General for Ireland, 1888; Attorney-General, 1889-92; MP (C) for Dublin University, 1887-92. *Publications:* Treatise on Registration of Deeds, etc, 1868, 2nd edn 1901; Practice of Land Judges Court, 1870, 3rd edn 1888; The Diary of Master William Silence: a Study of Shakespeare and of Elizabethan Sport, 1897, new edn 1907; Some Passages in the Early History of Classical Learning in Ireland, 1907; Shakespeare and his Fellows, an attempt to decipher the Man and his Nature, 1916; A Chapter of Mediæval History: The Fathers of Literature, of Sport, and Horses, 1923. *Recreations:* riding, fishing, literature. *Address:* The Orchard, East Sheen, Surrey. *Clubs:* University, Kildare Street, Dublin.

Died 6 March 1928.

MADDEN, Hon. Sir Frank, Kt 1911; Speaker of Legislative Assembly, Victoria, since 1904; *b* Cork, 1847; *m* Annie Eliza, *d* of late Hon. Goodall Francis. *Educ:* London; Beauchamp; Melbourne. Went to Australia, 1857; MLA Eastern Suburbs, 1884-1904; Boroondara since 1904. *Address:* Mooroolbeck, Studleigh Park, Kew, Melbourne.

Died Feb. 1921.

MADDEN, Hon. Sir John, GCMG 1906 (KCMG 1899); Kt 1893; Chief Justice of Supreme Court, Victoria, since 1893; Lieutenant-Governor, 1899; Chancellor of Melbourne University, 1897; administered Government of Victoria, Jan. 1900-Oct. 1901; *b* 16 May 1844; *m* 1872, Gertrude Frances, *d* of F. J. S. Stephen; one *s* five *d. Educ:* Melbourne University (BA 1863; LLD 1866; Hon. DCL Oxford, 1906); Hon. LLD Aberdeen. Called to Australian Bar, 1866. *Address:* Cloyne, St Kilda, Melbourne; Yamala, Frankston, Victoria. *Club:* Melbourne, Melbourne.

Died 9 March 1918.

MADDEN, Hon. Walter, JP; Member Victorian Executive Council; Chairman and Managing Director National Trustees Executors and Agency Company, Melbourne; Vice-Chairman, National Mutual Life Association of Australasia Limited; *b* Cork, Ireland, 1848; *s* of John and Margaret Madden; unmarried. *Educ:* Clapham; France; Melbourne. Began as a midshipman on board HMS Victoria, and for a time was engaged in marine survey of Victorian coast; then became land surveyor in Victorian public service; entered Parliament, 1880; Minister of Lands, 1881-82; was member for the Wimmera District and Chairman of the Country party in the Legislative Assembly; took a prominent part in dealing with land, water-supply, railway, and rabbit questions; was Vice-President of Royal Commission on vegetable products, which was appointed on his motion in 1886; was member of Royal Commission with reference to the Transfer of Land Statute and the Management of the Titles Office, and of the Royal Commission on Irrigation and Water-Supply. *Recreations:* no special recreations. *Address:* Queen Street, Melbourne. *TA:* National, Melbourne. *T:* 1784. *Clubs:* Melbourne Australian, Reform.

Died 3 Aug. 1925.

MADDISON, Rev. William, MA; Vicar of Gosforth, Newcastle-on-Tyne, since 1893; Hon. Canon of Newcastle, 1908; *b* 1853; *s* of Thomas Maddison; *m* 1879, Elizabeth, *o d* of George Blagdon of Redhill, Durham; two *s* two *d. Educ:* Durham School (KS and Head of School); University College, Durham (Classical Scholar, 1872-75; BA 1st Class Classics, 1875); Fellow of the University, 1875. Deacon, 1876; Priest, 1877; Curate of East Rainton, 1876; Bedlington, 1879; Vicar of Blyth, 1882-87; St Augustine's, Tynemouth, 1887-93; Chaplain to City of Newcastle Asylum, 1893-1906. *Address:* Gosforth Vicarage, Newcastle-on-Tyne.

Died 8 July 1920.

MADDOCK, Sir Simon, Kt 1922; JP, DL; Chairman Urban Council of Rathmines; Member County of Dublin County Council; Member of Council, Royal Dublin Society; Council Dublin Chamber of Commerce; Director Johnston, Mooney & O'Brien, Limited; James H. Webb & Co. Limited; Housing of the Very Poor Association, Ltd; Governor Meath Hospital, National Children's Hospital and Westmoreland Government Hospital; *b* 4 May 1869; *s* of late Benjamin Maddock, 52 Dartmouth Square, Dublin; *m* 1901, Randalina Augusta Caroline, *d* of Colonel J. D. Johnstone, DL, and Hon. Mrs Augusta Johnstone of Snow Hill, Lisbellaw, Co. Fermanagh; one *d. Educ:* High School, Dublin. *Address:* Mount Jerome House, Dublin. *T:* Rathmines 269. *Clubs:* Constitutional; Hibernian United Service, Dublin.

Died 15 Dec. 1927.

MADELEY, Earl of; Richard George Archibald John Lucien Hungerford Crew-Milnes; *b* 7 Feb. 1911; *e s* and *heir* of 1st Marquess of Crewe.   *Died 31 March 1922.*

MADEN, Sir John Henry, Kt 1915; JP for Lancashire; CC; MP(L) Rossendale, NE Lancs, 1892-1900, and (Coal.) 1917-18; *b* 11 Sept. 1862; *s* of late Henry Maden; *m* 1891, Alice, *d* of late Joshua Meller, Lytham, Lancashire; one *s. Educ:* Grammar School, Manchester. First Freeman of Bacup; Mayor of Bacup, 1896-97, 1900-10 and 1917. *Recreations:* golf, billiards, etc. *Address:* Rockcliffe House, Bacup, Lancashire. *TA:* Magpie, Manchester. *T:* Bacup 121. *Clubs:* Reform, Devonshire, National Liberal.

Died 18 Feb. 1920.

MADGE, Sir William Thomas, 1st Bt *cr* 1919; *b* Plymouth, 6 Oct. 1845; *m* 1st, 1865, Mary Helen Webber (*d* 1891); two *d* (and two *s* decd); 2nd, 1892, Judith Ketchell. Six years on the Western Morning News at Plymouth; joined The Globe in London in 1866; soon became publisher, and subsequently manager; resigned in 1908 after

42 years' active service; became Proprietor, 1912–14; started The People Newspaper (Limited), the first Conservative Sunday penny paper, 1881; jointly with the late Sir George Armstrong, 1st Bt, acquired the whole paper, which soon became a phenomenal success under his management; in 1914 became sole proprietor, retiring in 1922; ran the Sun, 1904–6; was responsible for the historic journalist coup, in the publication in The Globe of 30th May 1878, of the Salisbury-Schouvaloff Treaty; appeared at the Bar of the House of Commons in Aug. 1901, with the then editor, in connection with a leading article reflecting on the Irish Party. *Recreations:* motoring, an ardent politician. *Heir: g s* Frank William Madge, *b* 24 March 1897. *Address:* Broughton Lodge, Putney, SW15; Devonia, St Margaret's Bay, Kent. *T:* Putney 2012 and St Margaret's Bay 27. *M:* YL7167, XP3514. *Clubs:* Constitutional, United.

Died 29 Jan. 1927.

MAFLIN, Maj. George Hamilton, ISO 1913; VD; Chief Inspector Customs Preventive Service, Calcutta. *Address:* Customs Service, Calcutta.

MAGNAY, Sir William, 2nd Bt *cr* 1844; *b* 30 Nov. 1855; *s* of Sir William Magnay, 1st Bt and Amelia, *d* of Thomas Clarke; *S* father, 1871; *m* 1879, Margaret, *d* of Matthew Soulsby; two *s* one *d* (and one *s* two *d* decd). *Publications:* The Fall of a Star, 1897; The Pride of Life; The Heiress of the Season, 1899; The Man-Trap, 1900; The Red Chancellor, 1901; The Man of the Hour, 1902; Count Zarka, 1903; The Master Spirit, 1906; The Mystery of the Unicorn, 1907; The Duke's Dilemma, 1907; The Amazing Duke, 1907; The Red Stain, 1908; The Powers of Mischief, 1909; The Long Hand, 1911; Paul Burdon, 1912; The Players, 1913; The Fruit of Indiscretion, 1913; The Price of Delusion, 1914; The Black Lake, 1915. *Heir: s* Christopher Boyd William Magnay [*b* 27 March 1884. *Educ:* Harrow; Pembroke College, Cambridge]. *Address:* 8 Gloucester Place, Portman Square, W. *T:* Mayfair 3653. *Club:* Union.

Died 8 Jan. 1917.

MAGNUS, Katie, (Lady Magnus); *b* 2 May 1844; *d* of late E. Emanuel, JP, Southsea; *m* 1870, Sir Philip Magnus, 1st Bt, MP; two *s* one *d. Educ:* home. *Publications:* First Makers of England; Minor Moralities and Heresies; Outlines of Jewish History; Jewish Portraits; Picture Stories from the Bible; Book of Verse; Boys of the Bible; Little Miriam's Bible and Holiday Stories; numerous contributions in prose and verse to Westminster Gazette; articles in National Review, Spectator, and other magazines, etc. *Address:* 16 Gloucester Terrace, W2; Tangley-Hill, Chilworth, Surrey. *TA:* Chilworth, Surrey.

Died 2 March 1924.

MAGRATH, Maj.-Gen. Beauchamp Henry Whittingham; Indian Army; *b* 4 Feb. 1832; *m* 1871, Manie, *d* of H. Greene, Bray, Co. Wicklow. Entered army, 1849; Maj.-Gen. 1890; unemployed list, 1890. *Address:* Mountjoie, London Road, Camberley, Surrey. *Club:* Junior Constitutional.

Died 13 Nov. 1920.

MAGUINNESS, Rev. John Thomas; Hon. Canon of Ripon. *Address:* Lagg Cottage, Maxwell Road, Bournemouth.

Died 20 Oct. 1920.

MAGUIRE, James Rochfort, CBE 1918; MA; *b* 1855; *s* of Rev. John Maguire, Rector of Kilkeedy, Co. Limerick; *m* 1895, Hon. Julia Beatrice, *e d* of 1st Viscount Peel. *Educ:* Cheltenham; Merton Coll., Oxford. Formerly Fellow of All Souls Coll., Oxford. Barrister, Inner Temple, 1883; MP (N) N Donegal, 1890–92; W Clare, 1892–95; Chairman of the British South Africa Company since 1923; Chairman of the Rhodesian Railways, Ltd. *Address:* 3 Cleveland Square, SW1. *T:* Regent 382.

Died 18 April 1925.

MAGUIRE, Most Rev. John A., DD; RC Archbishop of Glasgow since 1902; *b* Glasgow, 8 Sept. 1851. *Educ:* St Mungo's Academy, and St Aloysius College, Glasgow; Stonyhurst College; Glasgow University; Propaganda, Rome. Assistant Cathedral, Glasgow, 1875; Diocesan Secretary, 1879; Incumbent of Partick, 1883; Canon, 1884; Vicar-General, 1885; Provost of Chapter, 1893; Auxiliary Bishop (titular of Trocmadae), 1894. *Address:* 160 Renfrew Street, Glasgow.

Died 14 Oct. 1920.

MAHAFFY, Arthur William, OBE 1919; Administrator of Dominica since 1915; *b* 22 Oct. 1869; *s* of late Sir John Pentland Mahaffy, GBE, CVO, Provost of Trinity College, Dublin, and Frances, *d* of William MacDougall of Drumleck, Howth, Ireland; *m* 1903, Enid, *d* of Captain Boyd of the Devonshire Regiment and Australia; two *s* one *d. Educ:* Marlborough; Magdalen College, Oxford; Trinity College,

Dublin. Second Lt Royal Munster Fusiliers, 1892–95; Govt Agent Gilbert Islands, 1896; Assistant to Resident, British Solomon Islands, 1897; Deputy Commissioner W Pacific and Magistrate W Solomon, 1898; Colonial Secretary Fiji, 1904; Assistant High Commissioner W Pacific, 1908; Member of Anglo-French Conference on New Hebrides, 1914. *Publications:* occasional contribs to Blackwood. *Recreations:* rowing, fishing, shooting and cricket; all outdoor sports; winning Varsity Four, Oxford (record time, 6 mins 30 secs), 1889; winning Trial viii, 1890; rowed at Henley several years; captain of Dublin Univ. Boat Club three years in succession. *Address:* Government House, Dominica, BWI. *TA:* Accentors, Dominica. *Clubs:* New University, Leander; Dominica.

Died 28 Oct. 1919.

MAHAFFY, Rev. Gilbert; Canon of Christ Church Cathedral, Dublin, 1905–16; Incumbent of Booterstown, Co. Dublin, 1913–16. *Educ:* Royal Belfast Academical Institution; Trinity College, Dublin (MA). Ordained 1873; Curate of Strabane, 1873–75; St George's, Dublin, 1875–79; Monkstown, 1879–86; Incumbent of St Paul, Dublin, 1886–94; St Mary, 1894–96; St Peter's, 1896–1913; Prebendary of St Michael's, 1914–16. *Address:* 27 Wellington Place, Clyde Road, Dublin.

Died 20 Dec. 1916.

MAHAFFY, Sir John Pentland, GBE 1918; CVO 1904; JP Co. Dublin; MA, DD; MusD Dublin; Scholar, Graduate, late Fellow and Professor of Ancient History, late Precentor of the College chapel, Vice-Provost 1913, then Provost, Trinity College, Dublin; Commissioner of Intermediate Education, Ireland; President Royal Irish Academy, 1911–16; Member of the Irish Convention, 1917–18; *b* Switzerland, 26 Feb. 1839; *y c* of Rev. Nathaniel B. Mahaffy and of Elizabeth Pentland; *m* 1865, Frances, *d* of William MacDougall, Howth; two *s* two *d. Educ:* home, but in Switzerland and Germany, where his parents resided, till age of 11. Corresp. Member: Imperial Academy of Vienna; Royal Academy, Berlin; Lincei, Rome; Hon. Member: Academy of Sciences, Utrecht; Parnassus, Athens; Archaeol. Soc. of Alexandria; Royal Soc. of Bavaria. High Sheriff, Co. Monaghan, 1901–2 and 1918–19. Hon. Fellow, Queen's Coll., Oxford. Hon. DCL Oxford; Hon. LLD St Andrews and of Athens, 1912; Hon. PhilD Louvain, 1908. Knight Commander of the Order of the Redeemer in Greece. Owner of property in Co. Monaghan where he sat on the Grand Jury. *Publications:* trans. Kuno Fischer's Commentary on Kant, 1866; Twelve Lectures on Primitive Civilisation, 1868; Prolegomena to Ancient History, 1871; Kant's Critical Philosophy for English Readers, 1871; Greek Social Life from Homer to Menander, 1874, 7th edn 1900; Greek Antiquities, 1876, subseq. a school-book in France, Russia and Hungary; Rambles and Studies in Greece, 1876, 5th edn 1905; Greek Education, 1879; A History of Classical Greek Literature, 1880; Report on the Irish Grammar Schools, 1880–81; The Decay of Modern Preaching, 1882; The Story of Alexander's Empire, 1890; Greek Life and Thought from Alexander to the Roman Conquest, 1887; The Art of Conversation, 1889; The Greek World under Roman Sway; Greek Pictures, 1890; Problems in Greek History, 1892; Sketch of the Life and Teaching of Descartes; edited Duruy's Roman History, 1883–86; Alexander's Empire, 1887; The Petrie Papyri deciphered and explained; 3 vols (viii, ix, xi) of the Cunningham Memoirs, published by the Royal Irish Academy, 1891–1905; Empire of the Ptolemies, 1896; Petrie's History of Egypt, vol. iv; An Epoch in Irish History, 1904; The Silver Age of the Greek World, 1906; What have the Greeks done for Modern Civilisation? Lowell Lectures, 1909. *Recreations:* played cricket for many years in Gentlemen of Ireland, after playing for his College; shot in Irish Eight at Wimbledon; game-shooting, salmon fishing, music. *Address:* Provost's House, Dublin; Earlscliff, Baily, Ireland. *Clubs:* Athenæum; Fellows Trinity College Dublin.

Died 30 April 1919.

MAHDI HUSAIN, Khan, Wahud-ud-Daula, Azod-ul-Mulk, Nawab Mirza, Khan Bahadur, CIE 1911; *b* 1834. *Educ:* India; Arabia. Travelled extensively in Arabia, Persia, Afghanistan, Baluchistan, and Europe; visited Mecca, Medina, Kaymiani. Kaiser-i-Hind gold medal, 1907. *Publication:* Takhullus. *Recreations:* riding, shooting. *Address:* Tirminigaz, Lucknow, UP.

MAHER, Maj.-Gen. Sir James, KCMG 1918; CB 1916; late AMS; *b* 27 Dec. 1858; *m* 1902, Gertrude, *d* of J. F. Browne, BCS. Entered RAMC 1885; Maj.-Gen. 1918; served Soudan, 1885 (medal with clasp, bronze star); Ashanti, 1895–96 (honourably mentioned, prom. Surgeon-Major, star); European War, 1914–18 (KCMG, CB); Director Medical Services Headquarters, Egypt, 1916–17; retired pay, 1917. *Address:* The Moorings, Boundary Road, Worthing.

Died 7 Jan. 1928.

MAHON, Sir William Henry, 5th Bt, *cr* 1819; DSO 1900; JP, DL; late Colonel commanding 4th West Yorkshire Regiment; *b* 31 Dec. 1856; *s* of Sir William Vesey Ross Mahon, 4th Bt and Jane, *d* of Rev. Henry King; *S* father, 1893; *m* 1905, Hon. Edith Dillon, 2nd *d* of 4th Lord Clonbrock; *two s one d* (and one *s* one *d* decd). Served South African War, 1900–2 (despatches). *Heir: s* George Edward John Mahon, *b* 22 June 1911. *Address:* Castlegar, Ahascragh, Co. Galway. *Clubs:* Carlton; Kildare Street, Dublin.

Died 13 Aug. 1926.

MAHONY, Rt. Rev. Mgr John Mathew, JCD; VG; Dean of Hamilton Diocese, Ontario, 1906, and Vicar-General since 1909; Rector of Cathedral since 1899; *b* Hamilton, Ont., 1862. *Educ:* Hamilton; St Jerome's College, Berlin; Grand Seminary, Montreal; Laval University. Ordained, 1894; Privy Chamberlain to the Pope, 1908; Domestic Prelate, 1912. *Address:* 56 Mulberry Street, Hamilton, Ontario.   *Died 8 May 1918.*

MAHONY, Maj. Michael Joseph, DSO 1916; MD, RUI; Hon. Physician, St Vincent's Hospice for the Dying; *s* of Richard Mahony, Tramore. *Educ:* Castleknock College, Dublin. Major RAMC; served South African War, 1900–1 (Queen's medal four clasps); European War, 1914–18 (despatches, DSO, immediate award, Somme 1916, TD). Médaille de Reconnaissance Française (en argent). *Address:* 33 Derby Lane, Stoneycroft, Liverpool.

Died Dec. 1927.

MAIDEN, Joseph Henry, ISO; JP; FRS 1916; FLS; Director of the Botanic Gardens, Sydney; retired, 1924; Government Botanist, NSW; *b* St John's Wood, London, 25 April 1859; *e s* of Henry Maiden; *m* 1883, Jeanie, *y d* of John Hammond of Manchester; *four d. Educ:* City of London Middle Class School, and as assistant to late Prof. Frederick Barff, MA. First Curator Technological Museum, NSW, 1881; late Superintendent of Technical Education; Consulting Botanist, Forest Department, and Department of Agriculture; hon. or corresponding member of a large number of scientific societies; Linnean Medal, 1915. *Publications:* Useful Native Plants of Australia; Illustrated Flowering Plants and Ferns of New South Wales; Manual of the Grasses of New South Wales; Wattles and Wattle-barks; Forest Flora of New South Wales; Critical Revision of the genus Eucalyptus; Sir Joseph Banks, the Father of Australia, etc. *Address:* Botanic Gardens, Sydney.   *Died 16 Nov. 1925.*

MAIN, Lt-Comdr Frank Morgan, DSO 1915; RD; RNR; served on patrol duty, European War, 1914–17 (despatches, DSO).

Died 21 Oct. 1924.

MAINWARING, Col Charles Salusbury, JP, DL, Co. Denbigh; JP Merioneth and Carnarvon; Colonel late 1st Volunteer Battalion Royal Welsh Fusiliers; *b* 7 July 1845; *e s* of T. Mainwaring, MP for Denbigh; *m* 1901, Gertrude, *d* of Thomas Loverock; *one s one d. Educ:* Eton; Christ Church, Oxford; MA 1870. Served in Denbighshire Yeomanry, Royal Denbigh Militia and Denbighshire Volunteers; commanded the Battalion, 1890–99; was the first Commanding officer to receive the Q distinction for passing in all military subjects. Contested (C) West Denbighshire, 1885. *Recreations:* agriculture, garden; County Council; Welsh University Court; education. *Address:* Galltfaenan, Trefnant, RSO; Cerrigydruidion, N Wales. *Clubs:* Carlton, Junior Carlton, Boodle's, Hurlingham.

Died 14 June 1920.

MAINWARING, Hon. Maj.-Gen. Rowland Broughton, CMG 1899; retired; *b* 11 Sept. 1850; *s* of Rev. C. H. Mainwaring of Whitmore, Stafford; *m* 1880, Evelyn Louisa Jane, *d* of late Capt. Mervyn Archdale. *Educ:* Marlborough. Entered army, 1871; Col 1899; served Gold Coast, 1873 (Ashanti medal); Burmese expedition, 1885–86; commanded expedition from Bhanio, Mogoumg, 1886 (medal with clasp); served Hazara expedition, 1891 (clasp); commanded 2nd Batt. Royal Welsh Fusiliers, Crete, 1898 (Bt of Col, CMG); AAG Portsmouth, 1899; AAG S Africa, 1899–1900 (despatches, Queen's medal 2 clasps); commanded 23rd Regimental Dist, 1900–6; 68th Welsh Div., 1915–17. *Address:* The Lodge, Bembridge, Isle of Wight. *TA:* Bembridge. *T:* Bembridge 47. *Club:* Army and Navy.   *Died 22 Nov. 1926.*

MAIR, Alexander, MA; Professor of Philosophy, University of Liverpool, since 1910; *b* Glasgow, 1870; *m* 1903, Isabel Hewitt, Bangor; *one s four d. Educ:* Edinburgh University. Graduated MA (1st Class Hons in Philosophy), 1898. Assistant Lecturer in Philosophy and English Literature, University College of North Wales, 1899; Assistant Lecturer in Philosophy, Liverpool, 1900; Independent Lecturer in Philosophy, Liverpool, 1904; Dean of the Faculty of Arts,

Liverpool, 1908–11; Examiner in Philosophy, Aberdeen 1904–8; Edinburgh, 1909–12; President of University Club, Liverpool, 1921; President of Liverpool Psychological Society, 1924; President of Association of University Teachers, 1925. *Publications:* Belief, Hallucination, Enc. of Religion and Ethics; Philosophy and Reality, 1911; various articles and reviews. *Recreations:* walking, golf. *Address:* 26 Parkfield Road, Liverpool. *Club:* University, Liverpool.

Died 8 Oct. 1927.

MAIR, Prof. Alexander W., LittD Aberdeen 1911; Professor of Greek, Edinburgh University, since 1903; *m* 1906; *five s six d. Educ:* Aberdeen Univ., 1889–93 (1st Class Honours Classical Literature, Liddell Prize for Verse Composition, 1890, 1891, 1892, 1893; Simpson Prize for Greek, 1893); Fullerton Scholar, 1893; Ferguson Scholar, 1894; Caius College, Cambridge University, 1893–98 (1st Division 1st Class Classical Tripos, Part I, 1896; 1st Class with Special Distinction Class. Tripos, Part II, 1898); Craven Scholar, 1897; Sir W. Browne Medal, 1897; Senior Chancellor's Medallist, 1898; Schuldham Plate, 1898. Fellow Gonville and Caius, 1899–1905; Lecturer Aberdeen University, 1898–99; Lecturer Edinburgh Univ. 1899–1903; Classical Examiner to London University, 1919–23. *Publications:* Hesiod, Introduction, Translation and Appendices, 1908; Callimachus, 1921; Lycrophron, 1921; in Hastings' Encyclopædia of Ethics, etc, articles on Hesiod, Pindar, Life and Death, Sin, Suicide, Worship; much verse contributed to various magazines. *Recreation:* golf. *Address:* 9 Corrennie Drive, Edinburgh. *T:* 52632.

Died 13 Nov. 1928.

MAIR, Charles, LLD (Hon.) Queen's University, Kingston, Ontario, 1904; author; for many years in Canadian Government Civil Service; superannuated, 1921; Canadian Government Immigration Agent in charge of the Fort Steele District of East Kootenay, BC; *b* Canada, 21 Sept. 1838; *s* of late James Mair, Scotland; *m* 1869, Eliza L. Mackenney, *niece* of late Sir John Schultz; *one s three d. Educ:* Grammar School, Perth, Canada; Queen's University, Kingston. Paymaster for Dominion Government to men engaged in opening immigration road from Fort Garry to Lake of the Woods, 1868; prisoner in the hands of the insurrectionists, 1869–70; sentenced to death, but escaped, and joined expedition from Portage la Prairie to Fort Garry; one of the founders of the "Canada First" party; was acting Quartermaster of the Governor-General's Body Guard, the Toronto Cavalry Regiment, commanded by Lt-Col George T. Denison in Riel's North-West Rebellion of 1885; ex-Fellow Royal Society of Canada. *Publications:* Dreamland and other poems, 1868; Tecumseh, 1886; Through the Mackenzie Basin, a Narrative of the Athabasca and Peace River Expedition of 1899; The American Bison, an article contributed to the Royal Society of Canada. *Address:* 1601, 15th Ave W, Calgary, Alberta, Canada.   *Died July 1927.*

MAIR, George Herbert, CMG 1920; Assistant Director on League of Nations Secretariat since 1919; *b* 8 May 1887; *e s* of late Fleet Surgeon G. Mair, RN; *m* 1911, Maire O'Neill; *one s one d. Educ:* Aberdeen University (MA, Seafield Gold Medal); Christ Church, Oxford (Scholar, BA 1st Cl. Mod. Hist.). Joined editorial staff Manchester Guardian, 1909, and acted as leader writer, special correspondent, literary editor and political correspondent in London, 1911–14; Assistant Editor Daily Chronicle, 1914, but resigned to devote full time to Government work first under Home Office and later with Foreign Office (News Dept), Department of Information and Ministry of Information; Assistant Secretary Ministry of Information, 1918; Director of Press Section British Peace Delegation, Paris, 1919. Chevalier of the Legion of Honour, 1919. *Publications:* Edition of Wilson's Arte of Rhetorique, 1908; English Literature: Modern, 1911, enlarged edn, 1914; articles in many papers and reviews. *Recreation:* walking. *Address:* 34 Walpole Street, SW3. *T:* Victoria 4999. *Clubs:* Garrick, Savile, St James's.

Died 2 Jan. 1926.

MAIR, John Bagrie, OBE 1920; MVO 1909; KPM 1922; JP Morayshire; Chief Constable of Morayshire; *b* Drumblade, Aberdeenshire, 8 May 1857; *s* of late John Mair, farmer, Pitscurry, Huntly; *m* 1883, Jessie, *e d* of William Blackley, High Blantyre, Lanarkshire; *three s three d. Educ:* Longhill School; privately. At the age of 21 years appointed a constable in the Lanarkshire Constabulary; a Sergeant in the Burgh of Johnstone, 1883; a Detective Inspector in the Burgh of Paisley, 1885; a Superintendent in the Burgh of Elgin, 1890; Chief Constable of County and Burgh of Elgin, 1892; in charge of the Police arrangements when Royalty visited this county on 14 different occasions; received valuable presents from King George when Prince of Wales. *Recreations:* golf, fishing, curling. *Address:* Maida View, Elgin. *T:* 18. *M:* SO 505. *Clubs:* Moray Golf, Elgin, Elgin.

Died 26 Jan. 1927.

MAIR, Very Rev. William, MA, DD; retired Parish Minister; *b* Savoch, 1830; *s* of Rev. James Mair, MA, schoolmaster; *m* 1866, Isabella, *d* of David Edward of Balruddery. *Educ:* Savoch Parish School; Aberdeen Grammar School; Marischal College and University, Aberdeen. Minister at Lochigelly, 1861–64; Parish Minister of Ardoch, 1864–69, of Earlston, 1869–1903; Moderator of the Church of Scotland, 1897; retired to Edinburgh, 1903. *Publications:* A Digest of Laws and Decisions, Ecclesiastical and Civil, relating to the Constitution, Practice and Affairs of the Church of Scotland, 4th edn 1911; Speaking, 4th edn 1908; The Truth about the Church of Scotland, 1891; Jurisdiction in Matters Ecclesiastical, 1896; Loyalty: The Christ our King, address to the General Assembly, 1897; pamphlets on Union of Scottish Churches—Churches and the Law, 1904; The Scottish Churches, two papers, 1907; The Scottish Churches: National Religion, 1907; The Scottish Churches: The Hope of Union, 1909; The Scottish Churches: External Relations, 1912; The Scottish Churches, Jan. 1914; The Scottish Churches, Jan. 1915; My Young Communicant, 1906; several other pamphlets; My Life, 1911; Action Sermons, 1917; The Scottish Churches, 1918. *Address:* 145 Mayfield Road, Edinburgh. *T:* 5076.

Died 27 Jan. 1920.

MAIRIS, Gen. Geoffrey; late Royal Marines; *b* 23 May 1834; *y s* of late Major V. H. Mairis, formerly 78th Highlanders and 6th Dragoon Guards, of Marston and Collingbourne, Wilts, and Elizabeth, *y d* and *co-heiress* of late Thomas Edwards, The Manor House, West Lavington, Wilts, and *g s* of late Rev. William Mairis, DD, of Exeter College, Oxford, Rector of Wallingford, Berks, Vicar West Lavington, Wilts, Prebendary of Wells Cathedral, and Chaplain to late Duke of Kent; *m* 1867, Barbara, 3rd *d* of late Richard Brouncker of Boveride, Dorset. Entered army, 1852; General, 1896; retired, 1899; served Crimea, 1854–55, including battle of Balaclava and siege of Sevastopol (medal with 2 clasps, 5th Cl. Medjidie, Turkish medal); China, 1857–61, including storm and capture of Taku Forts and occupation of Pekin (wounded, despatches, medal with 2 clasps); Zulu War, 1879; Commanded Battalion, Ireland, 1881–82; Depôt, 1883–85; 1st Division (Chatham), 1885–86. *Recreations:* shooting, hunting. *Address:* 51 St Aubyn's, Hove, Sussex. *Club:* United Service.

Died 22 April 1917.

MAITLAND, Rev. Adam Gray, LLD; Hon. Canon of Worcester. Deacon, 1878; Priest, 1879; Vicar of Dudley, 1892–1918.

Died 16 Aug. 1928.

MAITLAND, Dalrymple, JP; CP; Speaker of House of Keys since 1909; Chairman of the Isle of Man Steam Packet Co. Ltd; Isle of Man Railway Co.; Isle of Man Banking Co. Ltd; Director of the Liverpool Daily Post and Mercury; *b* Liverpool, 1848; *s* of John Maitland, Editor and one of the Proprietors of the Liverpool Mercury, and Agnes, *d* of James Dalrymple, Isle of Man; *m* 1879, Fanny, *d* of Charles Caley, Merchant, Douglas, Isle of Man. *Educ:* private schools, Liverpool and Douglas. On leaving school went into business with William Dalrymple at the Union Mills, Isle of Man, as Woollen Manufacturer and Corn Miller; retired from business, 1887; one of the members for Middle Sheading, House of Keys, since 1890. *Address:* Brook Mooar, Union Mills, Isle of Man. *Clubs:* National Liberal; Junior Reform, Liverpool; Ellan Vannen, Douglas.

Died 25 March 1919.

MAITLAND, Air-Cdre Edward Maitland, CMG 1919; DSO 1917; AFC 1919; BA; FRGS; RAF; senior Airship Officer; took part in R 34's Atlantic crossing, 1919; *b* 21 Feb. 1880; *e s* of late Arthur Maitland, MA, JP. *Educ:* Haileybury; Trinity Coll. Camb. 2nd Lt, The Essex Regt 1900; Adjutant 3rd Batt. 1906–9; appointed to Balloon School, South Farnborough, 1909; Air Battalion, 1910; Commanding Officer, No 1 Squadron, RFC (Airships), on formation of Royal Flying Corps, 1913; early in 1914, when the Admiralty took over the Army Airships, was gazetted to the Royal Naval Air Service, as Wing Commander; Wing-Captain, 1915; Brig.-Gen. on formation of Royal Air Force, April 1918; served in South African War, 1901–2, Transvaal and Orange River Colony (medal and 4 clasps); served with Expeditionary Force, Belgium, early in 1914 with observation balloons co-operating with British fleet; American Distinguished Service Medal, 1917; American Navy Distinguished Service Cross, 1921. *Publication:* Log of the R 34. *Recreations:* ballooning, ski-running, tennis. *Address:* 16 Chelsea Court, SW. *T:* Western 1887. *Clubs:* White's, Orleans, Bath, Garrick.

Died 24 Aug. 1921.

MAITLAND, Sir Herbert Lethington, Kt 1915; MB; *b* 12 Nov. 1868; *s* of late Duncan Mearns Maitland and Emily, *d* of John Dalgetty; *m* 1898, Mabel Agnes, *d* of Samuel Cook; two *s.* *Educ:* Newington

College and Sydney University, MB, MCh. Surgeon, Sydney Hospital; Lecturer in Clinical Surgery, Sydney University. *Address:* 147 Macquarie Street, Sydney, Australia.

Died 23 May 1923.

MAITLAND, William James, CIE 1887; late Deputy Government Director of Indian Guaranteed Railways; *b* 22 July 1847; *s* of late Augustus Maitland, and *g s* of late Sir Alexander Maitland, 2nd Bt, of Clifton Hall, Midlothian; *m* 1878, Agnes (*d* 1908), *e d* of late Ralph Neville-Grenville of Butleigh Court, Glastonbury; one *d* (and one *s* decd). *Educ:* Edinburgh Academy. *Address:* 18 Lennox Gardens, SW. *T:* 5000 Kensington; Witley Manor, Witley, Surrey. *Clubs:* Carlton, Travellers'.

Died 8 May 1919.

MAITLAND, William Whitaker, CVO 1921; OBE 1918; Secretary to the Government, Jersey, CI, since 1904; *b* 15 June 1864; *e s* of Rev. John Whitaker Maitland of Loughton Hall, Essex, and Venetia, *d* of Sir Richard Digby Neave, 3rd Bt, of Dagnam, Essex; *m* 1902, Lindisfarne, *d* of Archdeacon of Northumberland, and Lady Louisa Hamilton; one *s* one *d.* *Educ:* Harrow; Trinity Hall, Cambridge. In Ceylon, 1889–1902; Lord of the Manor of Loughton and patron of one living. *Recreations:* shooting, fishing. *Address:* Government Office, Jersey; Loughton Hall, Essex. *T:* Loughton 112. *Clubs:* Junior Carlton; Badminton.

Died 5 Nov. 1926.

MAITLAND-KIRWAN, Lionel, of Gelston and Collin; *b* Dalgan Park, Co. Mayo, Ireland, 16 April 1849; *s* of Charles Lionel Maitland-Kirwan, DL, of Co. Mayo, Ireland, and Matilda Elizabeth Maitland-Kirwan of Gelston Castle, Castle Douglas, NB; *m* Agnes, *y d* of Willwood Herries Maxwell of Munches, Dalbeattie, NB; one *s* two *d.* *Educ:* tutor and crammer, Southsea. *Recreations:* shooting, fishing. *Address:* Collin, Castle Douglas, Kirkcudbrightshire. *T:* Auchencairn 7. *TA:* Auchencairn. *Clubs:* Junior Carlton; New Edinburgh.

Died 5 June 1927.

MAJOR, Albany Featherstonehaugh, OBE 1918; FSA; Principal, War Office (retired); Hon. Secretary, Committee on Ancient Earthworks (Congress of Archæological Societies); *b* 3 Dec. 1858; *e s* of late Charles Messenger Major and Emily, *e d* of late William Storey Featherstone; *m* 1901, Margit, *e d* of Albert Grön, Sandefjord, Norway. *Educ:* Dulwich College. Appointed to Admiralty, 1878; transferred to War Office (after open competition), 1884. Hon. Secretary, Viking Club 1894–1904; Hon. Editor, 1904–9; Hon. Vice-President, 1917; President, Croydon Natural History and Scientific Society, 1919–20. *Publications:* A Throw of the Dice; An Ancient Tale Retold, 1884; Sagas and Songs of the Norsemen, 1894; Stories from the Northern Sagas (joint editor), 1899; Early Wars of Wessex: being Studies from England's School of Arms in the West, 1913. *Recreation:* field archæology. *Address:* 30 The Waldrons, Croydon. *Club:* Authors'.

Died 7 Dec. 1925.

MAJOR, Dr Charles Immanuel Forsyth, FRS 1908; FZS, etc; scientist and explorer; *b* 1843; *s* of Charles Forsyth Major, scholastic divine—a younger son of Capt. John Major and Ann, *d* of Capt. John Forsyth, Royal Navy. Member and corresponding member of various British and foreign scientific societies; and author of numerous scientific publications in England and abroad. *Address:* British Museum, South Kensington, SW; Bastia, Corsica.

Died 25 March 1923.

MAJOR, Francis William, CMG 1917; ISO 1910; *b* 1863; *s* of Charles Henry and Frederica Frances Sage Major; *m* 1895, Eleanor Laura Louisa, *d* of William Rowland Pyne; no *c.* *Educ:* The Philberds, Maidenhead, Berks. Treasury, Trinidad, 1885; secretary to Road and Crown Lands Commission, Agricultural Contracts Commission, and Civil Service Commission, Trinidad, 1887–90; private secretary to Sir W. Robinson, 1888; assistant Comptroller of Customs, 1891; assistant Treasurer, 1891; Comptroller of Customs, 1895; Receiver-General Bermuda, and member Executive and Legislative Council, 1899; prepared scheme (which was approved by Secretary of State) for improvement of financial administration of Bermuda; Commissioner of Customs, 1908–22, MLC and Currency Officer, Kenya; Government Representative, Homeward Loading Sub-Committee, 1917; Chairman, Port Advisory Board, Mombasa, 1920. Served European War, 1914–18 (despatches); received thanks of Admiralty for services rendered; Croix de Chevalier, Belgium. *Recreations:* ordinary. *Address:* Mombasa, British East Africa.

Died 7 Aug. 1923.

MAKGILL, Sir George, 11th Bt, *cr* 1627, of Kemback; *b* 12 Dec. 1868; *e s* of Sir John Makgill, 10th Bt and Margaret Isabella, *d* of Robert Haldane, of Cloanden, Perthshire; *S* father, 1906; *m* 1891, Frances

Elizabeth, *e d* of Alexander Innes Grant, of Merchiston, Otago, NZ, and Frances Anne, *e d* of Col Henry Rutherfurd, Bengal Artillery; two *s* two *d*. *Educ:* privately. Wrote novels, magazine articles and stories, chiefly of Colonial life. *Publications:* Outside and Overseas; Cross Trials; Blacklaw, Felons, etc. *Heir: s* John Donald Alexander Arthur Makgill, late Lt Coldstream Guards, *b* 31 Dec. 1899. *Address:* Kemback, near Cupar, Fife; Yaxley Hall, Eye, Suffolk. *T:* Eye 7. *Clubs:* Authors', Caledonian; New, Edinburgh.

Died 17 Oct. 1926.

MALCOLM, Sir James William, 9th Bt, *cr* 1665; *b* 29 March 1862; *s* of James Malcolm, *g g g s* of 1st Bt and Adeline, *e d* of James Attye; *S* cousin, 1901; *m* 1885, Evelyn Alberta, 3rd *d* of late Albert George Sandeman, and *g d* of late Viscount de Moncorvo; two *s* two *d*. *Educ:* Magdalene College, Cambridge. Administrative Assistant Ministry of Munitions, 1916; late Captain Pembroke Artillery Militia; JP Counties Norfolk and Suffolk. *Heir: s* Michael Albert James Malcolm [*b* 9 May 1898; *m* 1918, Hon. Geraldine M. Digby, *d* of 10th Baron Digby; one *s* one *d*. *Educ:* Eton. Lieut Scots Guards, Special Reserve; served European War, 1914–18; wounded in France, 1918]. *Address:* Itchin, Stoke House, Alresford, Hants. *TA:* Alresford, Hants. *T:* Alresford 79. *Clubs:* Boodle's, Royal Automobile.

Died 30 April 1927.

MALCOLMSON, Maj.-Gen. John Henry Porter, CB 1897; retired; *b* 20 Oct. 1832; *m* 1860, Ada Jessie (*d* 1907), *d* of E. B. Meyer. *Educ:* private school; Addiscombe. Joined Bombay Artillery, 1849; served in the Indian Mutiny and Afghan campaign, 1878–80. Decorated for the rearguard action at Kushki na Khud in 1879. *Recreations:* participated in cricket, boating, hunting, cycling and shooting big and small game. *Club:* Junior United Service.

Died 30 June 1920.

MALDEN, Charles Edward, MA; Recorder of Thetford since 1885; *b* Chertsey, 1845; *e s* of late Henry Malden and Georgina, *d* of Col Drinkwater-Bethune; *m* 1877, Sarah Fanny, 2nd *d* of late Sir Richard Mayne, KCB; two *s* two *d*. *Educ:* Univ. Coll. School; Ipswich School; Trinity Coll. Camb. (Scholar and Prizeman); 1st class Classical Tripos, 1867. Barrister, Inner Temple, 1870; in practice on South-Eastern Circuit; Revising Barrister, 1884; Commissioner Civil Liabilities, 1916–20. *Address:* 15 Collingham Place, SW5. *T:* Western 4323.

Died 29 Nov. 1926.

MALET, Sir Charles St Lo, 6th Bt, *cr* 1791; *b* 1 Nov. 1906; *s* of Sir Edward St Lo Malet, 5th Bt and Louise Michelle, *d* of Phillibert Dubois; *S* father, 1909. *Heir: b* Harry Charles, JP [*b* 21 Sept. 1873; *m* 1906, Mildred Laura, *d* of Capt. H. S. Swiney, Gensing House, St Leonards; one *s* two *d*. Formerly in Cape Mounted Rifles and Capt., 8th Hussars; served South Africa, 1899–1902 (Queen's medal, four clasps, King's medal, two clasps). *Address:* Wilbury, Salisbury]. *Address:* St Lo, Westcliff Road, Broadstairs; 34 Corso d'Italia, Rome.

Died 21 Nov. 1918.

MALET, Guilbert Edward Wyndham; Royal Artillery, retired 1879; *b* 12 July 1839; *e s* of W. W. Malet, Priest, and Eliza, 2nd *d* of E. J. Esdaile, JP, of Cothelestone House, Somerset; *m* 1st, Florence, *d* of C. W. Wilshere, JP, of The Frythe, Welwyn; 2nd, Gertrude, *e d* of Sir P. Cunliffe Owen, KCB; four *s* two *d*. *Educ:* Winchester. Lieut, Bengal Artillery, 1858; Royal Artillery, 1861; Royal Horse Artillery, 1865; Capt. and Adjt, 22nd Brigade RA, 1872; RHA, 1874; Major, 1879; Capt. 1st Herts RV, 1880–86; founder of the Army Guild, Holy Standard, 1873, and S Helena, 1875; Secretary, WI Section, R Colonial and Indian Exhibition, 1886; founder of Military and Naval Exhibitions, Chelsea, and Director of RME, 1890 (surplus £10,100, for Soldiers' Church Institutes); Secretary, European Commission, Chicago Exposition, 1893, of Soldiers and Sailors Help Society, 1899, of Capetown Cathedral Memorial Fund, 1902, of S Stephen's College Delhi Building Fund, 1913, Cambridge-Delhi Mission. KGStJ. *Publications:* History of J Battery Royal Horse Artillery; Soldiers' and Sailors' Friends Handbook. *Address:* 52 Penywern Road, SW5; Austin House, Frome.

Died 15 Oct. 1918.

MALING, Captain Irwin Charles, CMG 1892; *b* 2 Feb. 1841; 2nd *s* of late Commander Robert Saunders Maling, RN, sometime HM Salt Commissioner, India; *m* 1868, Emily Ann, *o d* of late Rev. Benjamin Whitelock, MA, of Groombridge, Kent. *Educ:* Wimbledon School and Royal Military Acad., Neustadt, Austria. Formerly in 89th, 35th and 23rd Regts; retired 1879; served during Indian Mutiny, 1858–59 (medal); was private sec. and ADC to Sir A. E. Kennedy, CB, Gov.-in-Chief of W African Settlements (successfully carried out several special missions to native chiefs), 1868–70; private sec.

to Marquess of Normanby, GCMG (successively Gov. of Queensland and New Zealand), 1871–79; Colonial Sec. and Registrar-Gen. Grenada, 1879–89, and Administrator of St Vincent, 1889–93; administered Govt of Grenada, 1880, 1882, 1884, 1885 and 1886–87; acted as Colonial Sec. of Leeward Islands and Pres. of Antigua, 1888, and as Administrator of Leeward Islands, 1889; retired from official life, 1893. *Recreations:* shooting, fishing. *Address:* 5 St John's Park, Blackheath, SE. *Club:* Junior United Service.

Died 13 June 1918.

MALINS, Sir Edward, Kt 1919; JP Co. Warwick; JP City of Birmingham; MD Edin., MSc Birm.; FRCP Lond; Consulting Obstetric Physician to the General Hospital, Birmingham; Professor of Midwifery, University of Birmingham; *b* Liverpool, 22 Dec. 1841; *s* of Samuel Malins, MD; *m* 1869, Mary (*d* 1920), *d* of Henry Owen, CE; five *s* one *d*. *Educ:* King Edward's School, Birmingham; Univ. of Edin. Appointed Medical Officer to Hospital for Women, Birmingham, 1876, and to the Lying-in Charity; Obstetric Physician to the General Hospital, 1877. Pres. Midland Medical Society, 1882; Pres. Birm. Branch Brit. Med. Assoc. 1901; Pres. Univ. Graduates' Club, 1876; President Birmingham Debating Society, 1880; President Obstetrical Society of London, 1903–4; Governor of King Edward's School; Bailiff, 1900; Examiner in Midwifery, Roy. Coll. Physicians, London; University of Manchester, etc. *Publications:* various papers in connection with diseases of women and midwifery. *Recreations:* contributions to literature; arts; Church work, etc. *Address:* 50 Newhall Street, Birmingham. *TA:* Malins, Birmingham. *T:* 2114.

Died 23 July 1922.

MALLOCK, Major Charles Herbert, DSO 1917; Special Reserve, RFA; *b* 15 May 1878; *e s* of late Richard Mallock and 1st wife, Mary Jones, *d* of T. A. H. Dickson, Liverpool; *m* 1906, Margaret Iris, 4th *d* of John Bazley-White; three *s*. JP; CC. Patron of one living and Lord of the Manor of Cockington. Served S Africa, 1901 (Queen's medal, 4 clasps); European War, 1914–17 (DSO). *Address:* Cockington Court, Torquay.

Died 5 Nov. 1917.

MALLOCK, William Hurrell; *b* 7 Feb. 1849; *s* of William Mallock, and Margaret, *e d* of Ven. R. H. Froude, Archdeacon of Totnes (*sister* to J. A. Froude the historian). *Educ:* private tuition; Rev. W. B. Philpot, Littlehampton; Balliol Coll., Oxford. Third Class in Moderations; Second Class Final Classical Schools; Newdegate prize poem, 1872. Never adopted any profession, though at one time intended for diplomacy; spent a considerable portion of his life since leaving Oxford in London and Devonshire; also in South of France and Italy; travelled and resided in Cyprus and East of Europe. *Publications:* The New Republic, 1877; religion and philosophy—Is Life Worth Living?; The New Paul and Virginia; Studies of Contemporary Superstitions; economic and social science—Social Equality; Property and Progress; Labour and the Popular Welfare, 1893; Classes and Masses, 1896; Aristocracy and Evolution, 1898; Doctrine and Doctrinal Disruption, 1900; Religion as a Credible Doctrine, 1902; The Reconstruction of Belief, 1905; The Nation as a Business Firm, 1910; Social Reform, 1914; The Limits of Pure Democracy, 1918; novels—A Romance of the Nineteenth Century; The Old Order Changes; A Human Document; The Heart of Life; The Individualist; The Veil of the Temple, 1904; two small volumes of verses; Lucretius on Life and Death, a Poem; An Immortal Soul, 1908; Capital, War, and Wages, 1918; Memoirs of Life and Literature, 1920; his main object in his political and economic writings to expose the fallacies of Radicalism and Socialism; his philosophic writings aimed at showing that science taken by itself can supply man with no basis for religion. *Club:* Bachelors'.

Died 2 April 1923.

MALTBY, Lt-Comdr Gerald Rivers, MVO 1902; RN; *b* 1851; *s* of late Rev. Henry Joseph Maltby, Canon of Durham; *m* 1876, Hersey Eliza Cecilia (*d* 1906), *d* of late Adm. Sir George Elliot, KCB. Entered Navy, 1866; retired, 1876; served Ashanti, 1874 (despatches, promoted, medal and clasp). Assistant Hon. Secretary General Committee RN Exhibition, 1891; Hon. Secretary Royal Naval Fund, 1892; Secretary Royal United Service Institution, 1893–98; Assistant Secretary Imperial Institute, 1898–1902. *Address:* 54 St George's Square, SW1. *T:* Victoria 2089. *Clubs:* United Service, Naval and Military.

Died 3 April 1922.

MALTHUS, Col Sydenham, CB 1879; JP for Surrey; *b* 29 May 1831; *m* 1867, Henrietta, *e d* of late Rev. T. Maberly. Entered army, 1852; Colonel (retired), 1880; commanded 94th Regiment in Zulu war, 1879, present at Ulundi (medal). *Address:* Dalton Hill, Albury, Guildford. *Club:* Constitutional.

Died 26 May 1916.

MAN, Edward Garnet, JP; barrister; *b* 8 Feb. 1837; *s* of Henry Man, Commander RN, of Halstead Hall, Kent; *m* 1867, Catherine, *d* of J. Matthews of 21 Manchester Square and Halliford, Middlesex; four *s* five *d*. Barrister, 1866; formerly Asst Commissioner and JP Bengal; served with 3rd Sikh Irregular Cavalry during mutiny; Government Advocate, Burmah; Special Correspondent, Times, in Perak War; JP Surrey and Kent; Chairman of Kent County Bench (Elham); Diocesan Lay Reader, Canterbury. *Publications:* Our Trade and Commerce; Santalia and the Sonthals; Papal Aims and Papal Claims. *Recreations:* riding, driving, cycling. *Address:* Halstead, Riviera, Sandgate, Kent. *T:* 39 Sandgate. *Clubs:* St Stephen's, United; Radnor, Cinque Ports.   *Died 15 Nov. 1920.*

MANBY, Sir Alan (Reeve), KCVO 1918 (MVO 1901); Kt 1903; Physician Extraordinary to the King; late Surgeon Apothecary to the King and the Household at Sandringham; also to HM Queen Alexandra; late Physician Extraordinary and Surgeon Apothecary to King Edward VII; *b* 4 June 1848; *s* of late Frederic Manby, East Rudham, Norfolk; *m* 1876, Charlotte Annie, *d* of late Edmund Farrer, Petygards Hall, Swaffham, Norfolk; one *s* one *d*. *Educ:* Epsom; Guy's Hospital. MD Durham, MRCS, LSA; FRCS; FRSM. Surgeon Apothecary to the Prince and Princess of Wales at Sandringham, and to Duke of York, 1885; in attendance on Prince and Princess of Wales during Colonial tour, 1901. Member (Pres. 1892–93) Norfolk and Norwich Medical Chir. Society; President East Anglian Br. BMA 1896; Vice-President Obs. Section BMA Oxford, 1904; Vice-President Therapeutical Section, BMA, Toronto, 1906. Kt Commander 2nd Class Danish Royal Order of Dannebrog, 1903. Inventor of various instruments. *Publications:* various papers, British and American Medical Journals, etc. *Address:* East Rudham, Norfolk. *TA:* East Rudham. *T:* 2 East Rudham. *M:* AH 1051.   *Died 29 Sept. 1925.*

MANCE, Sir Henry Christopher, Kt 1885; CIE 1883; LLD; PPIEE; MInstCE; inventor of the heliograph; Director, West African Telegraph Co.; *b* 1840; *s* of late Henry Mance, Brockley; *m* 1874, Annie, *d* of John Sayer, of Yatton; three *s* two *d*. *Educ:* privately. Entered service of Indian Government, Persian Gulf Telegraph Department, 1863; became engineer and electrician of the line; was Capt. in Sind Volunteers; retired from the service, 1885. Mem., Physical Society. *Publications:* various papers on electrical subjects; Mance's Method, etc. *Address:* 25 Linton Road, Oxford. *Club:* Thatched House.   *Died 21 April 1926.*

MANCINELLI, Luigi; conductor and composer; pupil of Mabellini of Florence; *b* 6 Feb. 1848. Twenty years conductor at Covent Garden, London. Grand Collar of San Ehiago of Portugal; Commander of the Crown of Italy. *Works:* operas, Ero e Leandro, Isora di Provenza, Paolo and Francesca; two Masses; Ouverture Romantica, 1910; several oratorios, including Isaia, and orchestral suites; a great number of songs; La Prière des Oiseaux, from Rostand's Chantecler, for small orchestra (for private performances), contralto voice and girls' chorus; three act opera, 1916, fantasia lirica on Shakespeare's Midsummer Night's Dream, and six songs, including one on Shelley's Indian Serenade; two symphonic and choral orchestral poems, Frate Sole and Giuliano l'Apostata, both illustrated with a vision on the stage. *Address:* Rome, via Scipioni 287.   *Died 2 Feb. 1921.*

MANDER, Captain John Harold, OBE 1920; Chief Constable of Norfolk, 1915; *b* The Mount, near Wolverhampton, 1869; *s* of late Charles B. Mander; *m* 1894, Elinor, *d* of late J. P. A. Lloyd-Philipps of Dale Castle, Milford Haven, and Mabys, Cardiganshire; two *d*. *Educ:* Rugby; Trinity Hall, Cambridge. Lt 3rd N Stafford Regt, 1888–90; gazetted Duke of Cornwall's Light Infantry, 1890; Captain, 1899; served S African War, 1899–1900 (despatches); Adjutant 4th VB Durham LI, 1901–5; Brigade Major, Durham LI Brigade, 1904–5; Chief Constable, Isle of Ely, 1906–15. *Recreations:* shooting, cricket, golf, etc. *Address:* Thorpehurst, Thorpe St Andrew, Norwich. *T:* Norwich, Thorpe 5. *Club:* Naval and Military.   *Died 9 Dec. 1927.*

MANDERSON, Maj.-Gen. George Rennie, CB 1881; Royal Bengal Artillery; *b* 17 Feb. 1834; *m* 1st, 1873 (*d* 1875), *d* of late Sir W. H. Walker; 2nd, 1880, Harmine, *d* of late C. Herring-Cooper. Entered army, 1851; Major-General 1885; served Burmah, 1852–53 (despatches, medal with clasp); Indian Mutiny, 1857 (despatches, medal with three clasps); Jowaki campaign, 1877–78 (despatches, clasp); Afghan war, 1878–79 (despatches, CB, medal and clasp). *Address:* Fullands, Taunton, Somerset.   *Died 8 Jan. 1918.*

MANFIELD, Harry, JP; CA; MP (L) Mid-Northants, 1906–18; *b* 1 Feb. 1855; *e s* of late Sir Philip Manfield; *m* 1909, Louisa, *d* of late Sir John Barran, 1st Bt, of Chapel Allerton Hall, Leeds. *Address:* Moulton Grange, Northants. *Clubs:* Reform, National Liberal, Eighty, Bath.   *Died 9 Feb. 1923.*

MANGAN, Rt. Rev. John, DD; RC Bishop of Kerry since 1904; *b* Listowel, Co. Kerry, 1852; *s* of John Mangan, Bedford, Listowel. *Educ:* Maynooth College. Served for a few years in the Liverpool Mission; Professor at St Michael's College, Listowel; Parish Priest of Glengariffe, Sneem, and Kenmare; was Archdeacon of Aghadoe and Vicar-General of Kerry. *Address:* The Palace, Killarney, Co. Kerry.   *Died 1 July 1917.*

MANIFOLD, Hon. Sir Walter Synnot, Kt 1920; JP Queensland; President of Legislative Council of Victoria, Australia, 1919–23; *b* 30 March 1849; *s* of late Thomas Manifold of Waiora, Danderong Road, Melbourne, pastoralist, and Jane Elizabeth M., *d* of late Walter Synnot, HM 66th Regiment, 2nd *s* of Sir Walter Synnot, of Ballymoyer, County Armagh; *m* 1885, Fanny M., *d* of late Alexander John Smith, Commander, RN; no *c*. *Educ:* Church of England Grammar School; University, Melbourne. Solicitor, 1875; pastoralist in North West Queensland, pastoralist at Wollaston, Warrambool, Victoria, 1886–1914; Member of Legislative Council of Victoria for Western province, 1901–24. *Address:* Kyalite, Toorak Road, Toorak, Victoria. *T:* U 2465. *Clubs:* Melbourne; Warrambool; Hamilton.   *Died 15 Nov. 1928.*

MANN, Rt. Rev. Mgr Horace K., DD; Rector of the Collegio Beda, Rome, since 1917; *b* London, 27 Sept. 1859; *s* of Robert K. Mann, Hull, and Jane Mountain, Yorkshire. *Educ:* St Cuthbert's College, Ushaw. Taught for some years at Ushaw; ordained priest for the diocese of Hexham and Newcastle, 1886; assistant master at St Cuthbert's Grammar School; Headmaster, 1890–1917. Corresponding Member Royal Historical Academy of Spain; Member of the Accademia d'Arcadia, and of the R Società Rom. di Storia Patria. *Publications:* The Lives of the Popes, from the life of St Gregory I (590–604) to Gregory IX (1227–1241), thirteen vols; Life of Hadrian IV, the English Pope. *Address:* Collegio Beda, Via S Noccolo da Tolentino, 67, Roma. *Clubs:* Authors'.   *Died 1 Aug. 1928.*

MANNERS, 3rd Baron *cr* 1807; **John Thomas Manners,** JP; late Captain 3rd Hampshire Regiment; *b* 15 May 1852; *s* of 2nd Baron and Lydia Sophia, *d* of Vice-Adm. William Bateman Dashwood; *S* father, 1864; *m* 1st, 1885, Constance (*d* 1920), *d* of Col Henry E. H. Fane, MP, of Clovelly Court, Devonshire; one *s* twin *d* (and one *s* one *d* decd); 2nd, 1922, Mrs Claud Guinness, Christchurch. *Educ:* Trinity Coll., Cambridge (MA). Entered Grenadier Guards 1875; retired, 1883. *Heir: s* Hon. Francis Henry Manners, late Capt. Grenadier Guards; *b* 21 July 1897. *Address:* Avon Tyrrell, Christchurch; 38 Great Cumberland Place, W1. *T:* Paddington 2279. *Club:* Carlton.   *Died 19 Aug. 1927.*

MANNERS, J. Hartley; dramatic author; *b* London, 10 Aug. 1870; *m* Laurette Taylor. *Educ:* private schools. An actor, 1898–1905; first appearance Bijou Theatre, Melbourne; last, California Theatre, San Francisco; in America, 1902–14. *Publications: (plays)* The Cross-Ways; As Once in May; The Girl in Waiting; The Panorama of Youth; A Queen's Messenger; A Woman Intervenes; The Wooing of Eve; Peg o' my Heart; Zira; A Marriage of Reason; Happiness; The Day of Dupes; Just as Well; The Harp of Life; Out There; One Night in Rome; The National Anthem; All Clear; God of my Faith; God's Outcast. *Clubs:* Devonshire; Lotos, New York.   *Died 19 Dec. 1928.*

MANNERS, Major Lord Robert William Orlando, CMG 1917; DSO 1900; King's Royal Rifle Corps; Reserve of Officers; Brigade Major; *b* 4 Feb. 1870; 4th *s* of 7th Duke of Rutland; *m* 1902, Mildred Mary, *d* of Rev. Charles Buckworth, *widow* of Major H. E. Buchanan Riddell; one *d*. Served Isazai, 1892; South Africa, 1899–1902 (despatches, Queen's medal with 6 clasps, King's medal with 2 clasps, DSO); European War, 1914–17 (wounded, CMG). *Address:* Knipton, Grantham. *Club:* Wellington.   *Died 8 Sept. 1917.*

MANNERS-SUTTON, Francis Henry Astley; Private Secretary to the Duke of Devonshire since 1908; *b* 10 Feb. 1869; *e s* of late Hon. Graham Manners-Sutton, 2nd *s* of 3rd Viscount Canterbury; *c* and *heir-pres.* to 5th Viscount. Colonial Civil Service, 1891–93; was Private Secretary to late Lord James of Hereford; attached War Staff, Admiralty. *Address:* 4 Down Street, Piccadilly, W. *Clubs:* Carlton, St James's.   *Died 7 March 1916.*

ANSEL, Col Alfred, DSO 1891; late commanding Northern Section RA, Plymouth; retired; *b* 5 Feb. 1852; *s of* late Captain W. H. Mansel. Entered army, 1872; Lt-Col 1898; served Naga Expeditionary Force, 1879–80 (despatches, medal with clasp); Mahsood-Wuzeeree expedition, 1881; Burmah, 1886–87 (despatches, two clasps). *Address:* Plymouth.   *Died 7 July 1918.*

ANSFIELD, Cyril James, MVO 1909; Deputy Surgeon-General RN Hospital, Haslar; *b* 19 June 1861; *y s* of late Rev. Edward Mansfield, BA, Vicar of Highnam, near Gloucester. *Educ:* Cheltenham College; Aberdeen University. MB CM. Entered Royal Navy, 1885; MD Aberdeen, 1896; Medical Officer in charge RN College, Osborne, 1905–9, during the time Prince of Wales was a cadet. *Recreations:* golf, shooting, fishing. *Address:* Haslar. *Clubs:* Junior United Service; Royal Naval, Portsmouth.   *Died 7 May 1916.*

ANSFIELD, Walter; Financial Editor of the Daily Chronicle, 1907–15; Echo and Evening Chronicle, 1915; controlled City pages of Westminster Gazette, 1908–12; *b* 1870; *y s* of Charles E. Mansfield, a former City Editor of the Morning Post; *m* 1893, Helen, *y d* of Robert Hall, Chester; one *d.* Assistant Financial Editor of the Morning Post for several years. *Publications:* many works of fiction, partly in collaboration under the nom de plume of Huan Mee; at one time contributor to Punch and other journals; part author of musical plays produced in London and Australia. *Recreations:* cycling, billiards. *Address:* 9 West Lodge Avenue, West Acton, W. *Club:* Eccentric.   *Died 30 April 1916.*

ANSON, Edward, BA; Registrar of the High Court in Bankruptcy for companies and winding up; Barrister, Middle Temple; *b* 1 Aug. 1849; father, London physician; *m* 1st, 1880, *widow* of Rev. W. P. Manson (*d* 1891); four *s* two *d;* 2nd, 1914, Eileen, *d* of George Beck. *Educ:* St Paul's School; Brasenose College, Oxford; Scholar and Hilmeian Exhibitioner; graduated with honours (Lit. Hum.). Called to Bar, 1878. *Publications:* joint editor with Sir John Macdonnell, CB, of the Journal of Comparative Legislation; Law of Trading Companies; Law of Debentures; Practical Guide to Company Law; Builders of our Law, 2nd edn; contrib. to Encyclopædia Britannica, and Encyclopædia of the Laws of England. *Recreation:* cycling. *Address:* High Court of Justice, Bankruptcy Buildings, WC.   *Died 29 Nov. 1919.*

ANSON, James Alexander; editor of Cassell's Encyclopædia (vols vii to x) and of The Makers of British Art Series; *b* Alloa, 18 Aug. 1851; *e s* of James Bolivar Manson, editor of Edinburgh Daily Review (*d* 1868), and Jane (*d* 1913), *d* of Robert Graham; *m* Margaret Emily, *y d* of Charles Deering; four *s* two *d* (and one *s* killed in action at Richebourg, 1915). *Educ:* High School and Univ. of Edinburgh. Member of editorial staff of Cassell, Petter, and Galpin, 1870–94; chief editor, Cassell and Company, 1894–1900; editorial staff The Times Supplement to the Encyclopædia Britannica, 1900–5; Harmsworth Educational Staff, 1908–10; dramatic critic, Weekly Dispatch, 1890–92; literary editor of the Daily Chronicle, 1891. *Publications:* In Memoriam edition of Burns's Poetical Works, in 2 vols 1896, in 1 vol. 1901; Valour for Victoria, 1901; Sir Edwin Landseer, RA, 1902; Indoor Games, 1906; Daily Sea Trips, 1906; The Bowler's Handbook, 1906; The Slums and Auld Reekie, 1907; Curiosity Land for Young People, 1908; Indoor Amusements, 1911; The Complete Bowler, 1912; contributor of articles on Bowls to the Field over the pen-name of Jack High, and of articles on Royal Bowls to the Sunday Times. *Recreations:* bowls, whist, chess, dominoes; captain of Herne Hill Bowling Club, 1885–1910; Hon. Member of English Bowling Association; Member of the Old Edinburgh Club. *Address:* 4 Cornwall Avenue, Church End, Finchley. *Clubs:* Savage, Edinburgh University (London).   *Died 8 Feb. 1921.*

ANSON, John, ISO 1903; late Controller of Money Order Department, General Post Office; *b* 9 Oct. 1842; *m* 1875, Marion, *d* of John de Putron, Guernsey. *Address:* 3 George Place, Guernsey.   *Died 6 June 1923.*

ANSON, Sir Patrick, GCMG 1912 (KCMG 1903; CMG 1900); MD, LLD (Aberdeen and Hongkong); FRS 1900; FRCP (London); Hon. DSc Oxon; late Physician and Medical Adviser to Colonial Office; distinguished as a Parasitologist; first to enunciate hypothesis (since proved correct by Maj. Ross) that the mosquito was the host of the malarial parasite at one stage of its existence, and thus an active agent in diffusing the disease; *b* 3 Oct. 1844; *s* of John Manson of Fingask, Aberdeen; *m* 1875, Henrietta Isabella, *d* of Capt. J. P. Thurburn; one *s* three *d. Publications:* Goulstonian Lecturers, 1896;

Tropical Diseases, 1907; various scientific papers. *Address:* The Sheiling, Clonbur, Co. Galway.   *Died 9 April 1922.*

MANTON, 1st Baron *cr* 1922, of Compton Verney, Co. Warwick; **Joseph Watson,** JP; *b* 10 Feb. 1873; *s* of George Watson (*d* 1905), JP and Mary Anne (*d* 1906), *d* of Thomas Walker Hornsby; *m* 1898, Frances Claire, *d* of Harold Nickols; four *s. Educ:* Repton; Clare Coll., Cambridge. Chairman: Joseph Watson and Sons Ltd; Olympia Agricultural Co.; Dir, London and North Western Railway. *Heir:* *s* Hon. George Miles Watson, *b* 21 June. 1899.   *Died 13 March 1922.*
This entry did not appear in Who's Who.

MANTON, Sir Henry, Kt 1912; *b* Dec. 1835; *s* of Alderman Henry Manton; *m* Mary, *d* of William Woodroffe of Normanton-on-Soar, Leicestershire, yeoman farmer; two *s* three *d. Educ:* King Edward's School, Birmingham. In trade as silversmith; City Councillor from 1881; JP City of Birmingham since 1892; Deputy Chairman of Justices, 1911–13; Guardian of the Poor since 1876; Acting President Poor Law Unions Association, 1910–13. *Publications:* sundry pamphlets on poor law and social subjects. *Recreation:* social work. *Address:* Rowington, Norfolk Road, Edgbaston, Birmingham. *TA:* Mantonia. *T:* Edgbaston 1116. *Club:* Liberal, Birmingham.   *Died 12 Oct. 1924.*

MANVELL, Rev. Arnold Edward William, MA; Vicar of Peterborough since 1920; Hon. Canon of Peterborough Cathedral, 1925; *b* Dover, 1868; *s* of W. Manvell; *m* 1903, Gertrude Theresa, *d* of C. Baines, Leicester; one *s. Educ:* Dover College; Oxford University; Wycliffe Hall, Oxford. Ordained, 1892; Curate of Sherborne Abbey, Dorset, 1892; Priest in Charge, St James', Leicester, 1897; Vicar of St Barnabas, Leicester, 1904; Chaplain, Leicester Mental Hospital, 1906; Chaplain to Peterborough Workhouse, 1920. *Address:* The Vicarage, Peterborough.   *Died 3 May 1927.*

MANVERS, 4th Earl *cr* 1806; **Charles William Sydney Pierrepont,** DL; Viscount Newark and Baron Pierrepont, 1796; Captain, Notts Yeomanry Cavalry; Lieutenant-Col and Hon. Colonel 4th Battalion Sherwood Foresters; *b* 2 Aug. 1854; *s* of 3rd Earl, and Georgina, *d* of Augustin, Duc de Coigny; *S* father, 1900; *m* 1880, Helen *d* of Sir Michael Shaw-Stewart, 7th Bt; one *s* three *d. Educ:* Eton. MP (C) Nottinghamshire, 1885–95 and 1898–1900; formerly Lieut Grenadier Guards. Owner of about 38,000 acres. *Recreation:* Master of the Rufford Hunt from 1900. *Heir:* *s* Viscount Newark, *b* 25 July 1888. *Address:* 6 Tilney Street, W1. *T:* Mayfair 5954; Thoresby Park, Ollerton, Nottinghamshire; Holme Pierrepont, Nottingham.   *Died 17 July 1926.*

MAPLESON, Henry, VD; JP; DL; Colonel Royal Field Artillery (retired); President Société Internationale de Musique; *b* London, 17 Feb. 1851; *s* of Col J. H. Mapleson, DL, JP. *Educ:* St Mary's College; Bonn University. Originally destined for the army, on leaving Univ. of Bonn, underwent a course of training at Woolwich, where he successfully passed his examination for the Royal Artillery; abandoning the idea of the army as a calling, was gazetted to the Reserve of Officers in order to enable him to follow his father's profession as Director of Italian Opera in London, New York, etc; made tour of the world and visited the principal cities of both hemispheres; was shipwrecked in the Gulf of Mexico and was one of the five survivors who reached New Orleans; organised by Command of King Edward VII the fête given by His Majesty at the British Embassy, Paris, in honour of the President of the French Republic (M Loubet) on 3 May 1903; Royal Victoria Decoration for officers of 20 years' service; Chevalier Legion of Honour, France; Grand Army of Republic Medal, USA; Coronation Medal, King and Queen of Spain; Orders of Leopold, Belgium; Isabella la Catholique, Spain; Sauveur, Greece; de Wasa, Sweden and Norway; Medjidie, Turkey, and Sainte Anne, Russia; received a public subscription of £3,000 with a testimonial and service of plate as a recognition of his public services, 1908. Performed active duties as a Recruiting Officer during the European War, and received letter of appreciation from Army Council. *Publications:* contribs to several English and American magazines; a musical, dramatic and art critic. *Recreations:* riding, driving, hunting, shooting, yachting. *Club:* Junior Army and Navy.   *Died 26 Sept. 1927.*

MAPPIN, Sir Frank, 2nd Bt, *cr* 1886; *b* 6 Sept. 1846; *s* of Sir Frederick Thorpe Mappin, 1st Bt and Mary, *d* of J. Wilson, Sheffield; *S* father, 1910. Retired Captain and Hon. Major, 1st West York Yeomanry Cavalry; JP. *Heir:* *b* Wilson Mappin [*b* 14 Jan. 1848; *m* 1876, Emily Kingsford, *d* of George Wilson, Tapton Hall, Eccleshall; one *d* (twin *s* decd)]. *Address:* Birchlands, Sheffield. *Clubs:* Reform, National Liberal.   *Died 30 May 1920.*

MAPPIN, Sir Wilson, 3rd Bt, *cr* 1886; *b* 14 Jan. 1848; *s* of Sir Frederick Thorpe Mappin, 1st Bt and Mary, *d* of J. Wilson, Sheffield; *S* brother, 1920; *m* 1876, Emily Kingsford, *d* of George Wilson, Tapton Hall, Eccleshall; one *d* (twin *s* decd). *Heir: g s* Charles Thomas Hewitt Mappin, *b* 7 March 1909. *Address:* Thornbury, Fulwood Road, Sheffield. *Died 8 June 1925.*

MARAIS, Rev. Johannes Izak, BA, DD; Professor of Natural Theology and Speculative Philosophy, Theological College, Stellenbosch, since 1877; *b* Cape Town, 1848, of Huguenot parentage; *m* 1876, *d* of Oloff Fehrsen, MD; two *s* three *d*. *Educ:* private schools; South African College, Cape Town (Gold Medallist, 1866); Theological College of the Dutch Reformed Church, Stellenbosch; Universities of Edinburgh and Utrecht. BA of the University of the Cape of Good Hope; Hon. DD of St Andrews. Minister of the Dutch Reformed Church, Hanover, Cape Colony, 1873–77; Member of Council of the University of the Cape of Good Hope from 1884; President of Council, Victoria College, Stellenbosch, and Lecturer in Hebrew from 1883; Examiner in Old Testament, University of Cape of Good Hope. *Publications:* contrib. to International Bible Dictionary; Government Report on Bishop Grundtvig and the People's High School in Denmark. *Address:* Victoria College, Stellenbosch, South Africa. *Died 1919.*

MARCH, George Edward, CMG 1881; *b* 1834; *m* 1st, 1858, Florence, *d* of late Wentworth Beaumont; 2nd, 1873, Virginia (*d* 1877), *d* of late Gen. Gabriel, CB; 3rd 1883, Margaret Mary, *d* of late A. T. Roberts of Coeddu, Flint. Clerk in Librarian Dept Foreign Office, 1855; transferred to Treaty Dept, 1860; Supt Treaty Dept 1873; Acting Sec. of Legation and Diplomatic Sec. to Gen. Sir Alfred Horsford, British delegate at Conference on Rules of Military Warfare at Brussels, 1874; secretary to Royal Commission on Extradition, 1877; retired on pension, 1881. *Address:* 61 Cadogan Square, SW. *Died 29 May 1922.*

MARCHAMLEY, 1st Baron, *cr* 1908, of Hawkstone; **George Whiteley;** PC 1907; JP; *b* 30 Aug. 1855; *s* of George Whiteley, Halifax; *m* 1881, Alice (*d* 1913), *d* of W. Tattersall, Quarry Bank, Blackburn; two *s* two *d*. MP (C) Stockport, 1893–1900; Patronage Secretary of Treasury, 1905–8; MP (L) West Riding, Pudsey Div. of Yorks, 1900–8. *Heir: s* Hon. William Tattersall Whiteley, *b* 22 Nov. 1886. *Address:* 29 Prince's Gardens, SW7. *T:* Kensington 5299. *Club:* Reform. *Died 21 Oct. 1925.*

MARCHANT, Maj.-Gen. Alfred Edmund, CB 1900; ADC; retired list; *b* 26 Feb. 1863; *s* of late W. L. Marchant, of Adelaide, South Australia; *m* 1st, Mary Collett, *d* of late S. C. Homersham; 2nd, 1897, Edith Mary, *d* of late A. P. Turner, Jersey; two *d*. Joined Royal Marines, 1881; ADC to the King, 1910; served Soudan, 1884–85 (wounded, M'Neill's Zeriba, medal with two clasps, Khedive's star); HMS Calliope during severe hurricane at Samoa; South Africa, 1899–1900 (CB, despatches thrice, Queen's medal 7 clasps); Antwerp, 1914; Coronation medal. *Clubs:* Junior United Service, Sports. *Address:* Milton House, Fareham. *Died 21 Jan. 1924.*

MARCHMONT, Arthur Williams; novelist; *b* Southgate, Middlesex, 1852; *s* of late Rev. Henry Marchmont; *m* 1892. *Educ:* privately; Pembroke College, Oxford, BA. Entered Lincoln's Inn, 1888. After leaving Oxford engaged in journalism, at first in London, and subsequently in provinces, editing in succession the North Eastern Daily Gazette and Lancashire Daily Post; contributing meanwhile constantly to reviews and magazines; abandoned journalism for fiction, 1894. *Publications:* Isa, 1887; By Right of Sword, 1897 (dramatized and produced in America, 1902); A Dash for a Throne, 1898; The Greatest Gift, 1899; In the Name of a Woman, 1900; For Love or Crown, 1901; Sarita the Carlist, 1902; When I was Czar, 1903; By Snare of Love; The Queen's Advocate, 1904; A Courier of Fortune (produced as play), 1905; By Wit of Woman, 1906; In the Cause of Freedom; The Man who was Dead, 1907; A Millionaire Girl; My Lost Self, 1908; An Imperial Marriage, 1909; At the Call of Honour; The Case of Lady Broadstone, 1910; Elfa; In the Name of the People, 1911; The Ruby Heart of Kishgar; The Mystery of Eagrave Square, 1912; Under the Black Eagle; When Love Called, 1913; The Heir to the Throne, 1914; The Lady Passenger; A Tight Corner, 1915; Because of Misella, Her Sentinel, 1916; The Unguarded Hour, 1918; The Man Without a Memory, 1919; His Majesty, 1920; When the Empire Crashed, 1921; By Hand Unseen, 1922. *Recreations:* golf, travel. *Address:* 33 Bloomfield Road, Bath. *T:* 283. *Club:* Authors'. *Died 1 July 1923.*

MARDEN, Orison Swett; author; founder and editor of Succe Magazine; *b* Thornton, NH, about 1850; *s* of Louis and Mart (Cilley) Marden; *m* 1905, Clare Evans; one *s* two *d*. *Educ:* Coll. Liberal Arts, Boston Univ. (BS AB, AM, BO, LLB), and Harva Univ (MD). President, The Aldine Club; National Institute of Soc Sciences. *Publications:* Pushing to the Front, or Success und Difficulties, 1894; Rising in the World, or Architects of Fate; Ho to Succeed, 1896; Success, 1897; The Secret of Achievement, 189 Character the Grandest Thing in the World, 1899; Cheerfulness a Life Power, 1899; The Hour of Opportunity, 1900; Good Mann and Success, 1900; Winning Out, 1900; Elements of Business Succe 1900; Talks with Great Workers, 1901; How They Succeeded, 19C An Iron Will, 1901; Economy, 1901; Stepping Stones, 1902; T Young Man Entering Business, 1903; Stories from Life, 1905; T Making of a Man, 1905; Choosing a Career, 1905; Every Man a Kir 1906; Success Nuggets, 1906; The Power of Personality, 1906; T Optimistic Life, 1907; He Can Who Thinks He Can, 1908; Peac Power and Plenty, 1909; Do It To A Finish, 1910; Not the Salar but the Opportunity, 1910; Be Good to Yourself, 1910; Getting C 1910; The Miracle of Right Thought, 1910; Self Investment, 191 The Joys of Living; The Exceptional Employee; The Progressi Business Man; Training for Efficiency, 1913; I Had a Friend; Hir for Young Writers; Keeping Fit, 1914; Women and Home; T Crime of (Sex) Silence, 1915; The Victorious Attitude; Making L a Masterpiece; Selling Things; Everybody Ahead, 1916; How to G What You Want, 1918; Published Success Magazine; Thrift, 191 Ambition and Success, 1919; You Can, But Will You, 1920; Succe Fundamentals; Masterful Personality, 1921; Round Pegs in Squa Holes; Self-Discovery; Prosperity, How to Attract It, 1922; Maki Yourself, 1923; Inspiration Magazine, 1923. *Address:* 251 4th Avenu New York City; Glen Cove, Long Island, New York. *T:* Gramer 6221. *Died 10 March 192*

MARESCAUX, Vice-Adm. Gerald Charles Adolphe, CB 191 CMG 1915; *b* 1860; *s* of late Laurence M. Marescaux, Agra Ban Karachi; *m* 1894, Kathleen Louisa Rose, 2nd *d* of late Maj.-Gen. B. Dennis, RA, Ennel Lodge, Mullingar; *two s*. *Educ:* Royal Nav Academy, Gosport. Entered navy, 1873; Lieutenant, 188 Commander, 1896; Captain, 1903; Rear-Adm. 1913; District Capta North of Ireland Coast Guards, 1910–12; Captain-in-Charg Portland, 1913; received thanks of English and Dutch Governmen also from Colonial Governor (Gambia) for various services; serv European War, 1914–19 (despatches thrice, CMG, CB); Command of the Legion of Honour; DAQMG, Base Commandant; temp. Lieu Colonel, 1914–17; temp. Colonel , 1917; retired 1915. *Addre* Inchiholohan, Kilkenny. *Club:* Junior Constitutional. *Died 3 Sept. 192*

MARGOLIOUTH, Rev. G., MA; Biblical and Oriental scholar an writer; *b* (of Jewish parents) Wilkowiczky, Russian Poland, 4 De 1853; *m* 1886, Marian, *d* of John Fearon, of Cockermouth. *Edu* Düsseldorf; University of Bonn; Cuddesdon College, Oxon; Queer College, Cambridge. Ordained, 1881; naturalised British subje 1887; Semitic Languages Tripos in Honours (Ægrotat), 189 Tyrwhitt Hebrew Scholar (1st class), 1891. Appointment at the Briti Museum (in charge of Hebrew, Syriac and Ethiopic MSS), 18 (retired 1914); founded the Text and Translation Society for t publication of Oriental works, 1900, and served as Hon. Secretar 1900–3; Member of the Aristotelian Society, 1905–8; Examiner Hebrew and Aramaic in the University of London, 1909–13 and sin 1917; Member of the Board of Studies in Theology, 1914. *Publicatio* Descriptive List of the Hebrew and Samaritan MSS in the Briti Museum, 1893; The Superlinear Punctuation, 1893; The Liturgy the Nile, Palestinian-Syriac and English, 1896; The Palestinian-Syri Version of the Holy Scripture, four recently discovered portion 1896; Ibn-al-Hiti's Arabic Chronicle of Karaite Doctors, 189 Descriptive List of Syriac and Karshuni MSS in the British Museu 1899; Catalogue of the Hebrew and Samaritan MSS in the Briti Museum, vol. i 1899; vol. ii 1905; vol. iii, section 1, Kabbalah, 190 sections 2–7, 1912; sections 8–9, 1915; Original Hebrew Ecclesiasticus, xxxi, etc, 1899; Hebrew Babylonian Affinities, 189 The Problem of Immortality, 1904; articles in the Contempora Review, the Jewish Quarterly Review, etc. *Recreations:* country l and general literature. *Address:* 4 Albany Villas, Hove, Sussex. *Died 14 May 192*

MARILLIER, Frank William, CBE 1920 (OBE 1919); *b* 22 No 1855; *s* of Rev. J. F. Marillier, MA, late Vicar of Much Dewchurc Hereford; *m* 1891, Katherine Maud Brooke; two *d*. *Educ:* Brist Grammar School. Engineering pupil to the late Maj. J. Pearson, la Bristol and Exeter Railway, Bristol, 1872; draughtsman, Great Weste Railway, 1876; Works Manager GWR Depôt, Saltney, Chester, 189

Carriage and Wagon Superintendent, GWR, Swindon, 1914; during the war Chairman of the Ambulance Trains Committee; retired from GWR 1921; Town Council; Churchwarden Swindon Parish Church; Director Swindon Permanent Building Society. *Publications:* Sundry Railway Papers; Steam Heating on Trains, etc. *Recreations:* cycling, motoring, golf, tennis, croquet, billiards. *Address:* Deva, Westlecott Road, Swindon, Wilts. *TA:* Marillier, Deva, Swindon. *M:* HR 2445. *Club:* North Wilts Golf.   *Died 14 June 1928.*

MARIS, Matthew; painter; *b* The Hague, 1839. *Educ:* Hague Art School; Antwerp. Travelled in Germany and Switzerland, 1860; enrolled in Municipal Guard of Paris, 1870. *Works:* Souvenir d'Amsterdam; The Little Daughter of the Artist, Swan: A Fairy Tale.
Died 22 Aug. 1917.

MARJORIBANKS, Hon. Coutts; *b* 6 Dec. 1860; 2nd *s* of 1st Baron Tweedmouth and *heir-pres.* to 3rd Baron; *m* 1895, Agnes Margaret, *d* of late Col Kinloch, RA, and *widow* of Commander Jasper E. T. Nicolls, RN; one *d* (one *s* decd). Formerly Lieut Cameron Highlanders. *Address:* Invercraig, Kalemalka Lake, Vernon, British Columbia.   *Died 1 Nov. 1924.*

MARKER, Richard; JP Devon and Dorset; DL Devon; *b* 10 Aug. 1835; *s* of Rev. T. J. Marker, Rector of Gittisham, Devon; *m* 1865, Hon. Victoria Alexandrina, *d* of 9th Baron Digby; one *s* one *d* (and one *s* decd). *Educ:* Harrow. *Address:* Combe, Honiton. *Clubs:* Travellers', Wellington.   *Died 8 March 1916.*

MARKHAM, Adm. Sir Albert Hastings, KCB 1903; RN; retired 1906; *b* Bagnères, 11 Nov. 1841; 4th *s* of Capt. John Markham, RN, and Marianne, *d* of John Brock Wood; *m* 1894, Theodora, *d* of F. T. Gervers, Amat, Ross-shire; one *d*. *Educ:* home; Eastman's RN Academy, Southsea. Entered RN 1856; served 8 years on China station; took active part in operations leading to fall of Pekin, and suppression of Taiping rebellion; Lieut, 1862; served on Mediterranean and Australian stations; received an expression of their Lordships' approval for his activity in suppressing so-called labour traffic in South Sea Islands; Commander, 1872; commander of Alert in Arctic Expedition, 1875–76, when he succeeded in planting Union Jack in highest northern position reached to then, viz 83° 20' 26"; for this promoted to capt. and received gold watch from Royal Geographical Society; Flag Captain in Pacific, 1879–82; Capt. of Naval Torpedo School at Portsmouth, 1883–86; Commodore Training Squadron, 1886–89; ADC to the Queen; Rear-Admiral and 2nd in command of Mediterranean Squadron, 1892–94; Commander-in-Chief at the Nore, 1901–4; during periods of professional unemployment made various voyages of exploration to Davis Strait, Lancaster Sound, Novaya Zemlya and Hudson's Bay; received thanks of Canadian Government for his valuable services in the exploration of Hudson's Strait and Bay; on Council of British Empire League, Navy Records and Hakluyt Societies. *Publications:* The Cruise of the Rosario, 1873; A Whaling Cruise to Baffin's Bay, 1874; The Great Frozen Sea, 1877; Northward Ho! 1878; The Life of John Davis the Navigator, 1882; A Polar Reconnaissance, 1880; Life of Sir John Franklin, 1890; Life of Sir Clements R. Markham, 1917; a frequent contributor to Good Words, North American Review, Youth's Companion, Badminton Magazine and other Serials. *Recreations:* fond of all kinds of sport; made large collections in natural history. *Address:* 19 Queen's Gate Place, SW. *T:* Western 336. *Club:* United Service.
Died 28 Oct. 1918.

MARKHAM, Sir Arthur Basil, 1st Bt, *cr* 1911; JP; MP (L) for Mansfield Division of Nottinghamshire since 1900; *b* 25 Aug. 1866; *s* of late Charles Markham of Tapton House, Derbyshire, and Rosa, *d* of Sir Joseph Paxton; *m* 1898, Lucy *d* of Capt. A. B. Cunningham, late RA; three *s* one *d*. *Educ:* Rugby. Formerly Captain, 3rd Sherwood Foresters; JP Leicestershire and Derbyshire. *Heir: s* Charles Markham, *b* 28 Aug. 1899. *Address:* 48 Portland Place, W. *T:* Mayfair 610; Newstead Abbey, Mansfield; Beachborough Park, Shorncliffe. *Club:* Reform.   *Died 7 Aug. 1916.*

MARKHAM, Brig.-Gen. Charles John, CBE 1919; retired Army Officer; *b* 21 June 1862; *s* of Rev. C. W. Markham; *m* 1893, Isabella Cameron, *d* of Col Gardner, RMA; one *s*. *Educ:* Westminster; RMC, Sandhurst. Gazetted to King's Royal Rifle Corps, 1882; served in India, Burma, England, Gibraltar, Malta, S Africa and Egypt; commanded 1st Batt KRRC, 1904–8; 42nd Infantry Brigade, 14th Light Division, Sept. 1914–July 1915 at home and in France; 205th Infantry Brigade, 68th Division, at home, Sept. 1915–March 1917; served Manipur Expedition, 1891; NE Frontier, 1891–92; European War, 1914–19 (CBE). *Address:* 52 Campden House Court, W8. *T:* Park 4397. *Club:* Naval and Military.   *Died 7 July 1927.*

MARKHAM, Sir Clements Robert, KCB 1896 (CB 1871); DSc Cambridge and Leeds; FRS 1873; late President Royal Geographical Society, International Geographical Congress, 1894–99, Hakluyt Society, 1889–1909, and Geographical, Elizabethan and Royal Society Clubs; one of the Governors of Westminster School and Trustee of Dr Busby's charities; *b* Stillingfleet, Co. York, 20 July 1830; *s* of Rev. David F. Markham, Vicar of Stillingfleet and Canon of Windsor, and Catherine, *d* of Sir William Mordaunt Milner, 4th Bt, Nunappleton, Co. York; *m* 1857, Minna, *d* of Rev. J. H. Chichester, Rector of Arlington, Co. Devon; one *d*. *Educ:* Cheam; Westminster School. Entered the Navy in 1844; served in the Arctic Expedition of 1850–51; left the Navy 1852; travelled in Peru, 1852–54; introduced the cultivation of the quinine-yielding chinchona trees from Peru into British India, 1859–62; geographer to the Abyssinian Expedition; Secretary to the Royal Geographical Society, 1863–88; Secretary to the Hakluyt Society, 1858–87; Assistant Secretary in the India Office, 1867–77. *Publications:* Life of the Great Lord Fairfax; The Fighting Veres; History of Peru; Threshold of the Unknown Region; Memoir of the Indian Surveys; History of Persia; History of the Abyssinian Expedition; Missions to Tibet; Lives of Columbus, John Davis and Major Rennell; Travels in Peru and India; Ollanta, an Inca drama, translated from the Quichua; The Paladins of Edwin the Great, 1896; Richard III: His Life and Character, 1907; Quichua Dictionary, 1908; Life of Sir Leopold M'Clintock, 1909; The Story of Majorca and Minorca, 1909; The Incas of Peru, 1910, and other works; edited twenty-two volumes for the Hakluyt Society, two for the Navy Records Society, one for the Roxburghe Club. *Recreations:* travelling, topographical research. *Address:* 21 Eccleston Square, SW. *Clubs:* Athenæum, Royal Societies.
Died 30 Jan. 1916.

MARKHAM, Lt.-Gen. Sir Edwin, KCB 1897; Colonel-Commandant Royal Horse Artillery; *b* 28 March 1833; *s* of W. Markham, Becca Hall, Yorks; *m* 1877, Evelyn, *d* of Admiral Hon. Sir Montagu Stopford; two *s* one *d*. Served in Crimea, 1854–55; and India, 1857–58; Deputy-Adjt-General RA Headquarters, 1887–92; Lt-Governor, Jersey, 1892–95; Inspector-General of Ordnance at Headquarters, 1895–98; Governor of Military College, Sandhurst, 1898–1902. *Address:* 51 Brunswick Place, Brighton.
Died 31 March 1918.

MARKIEVICZ, Constance Georgine; Member Dail Eireann for Dublin City, South, since 1923; Secretary for Labour, 1921–22; MP (SF), St Patrick's, Dublin, Dec. 1918–22; *b* 4 Feb. 1868; *d* of Sir Henry William Gore-Booth, 5th Bt and Georgina Mary, *d* of Col Charles John Hill; *m* 1900, Casimir Dunin de Markievicz; one *d*. Took part in Dublin Rebellion, 1916; sentenced to death; subsequently commuted to penal servitude for life; released, 1917.
Died 15 July 1927.

MARKS, Barnett Samuel, RCA; *b* Cardiff, 8 May 1827; *s* of Mark Lyon Marks and Anne Michael; *m* 1858, Zipporah (*d* 1905), *d* of Michael Marks; two *s* four *d*. *Educ:* private school in Cardiff. Studied art from earliest days as a portrait painter and organised classes for artisans in the subject of drawing; president for some years of the Cardiff Hebrew Congregation; part founder of the Cardiff and Ealing Free Public Libraries; one of the earliest volunteers; a vice-president of the Industrial Committee of the Jewish Board of Guardians; Past Master of the Buckingham and Chandos Lodge of Freemasons; president of Art Section (1883) of the Cymmrodorion Society in connection with the National Eisteddfod of Wales. *Portraits:* HM King Edward VII (as Prince of Wales); Maharajah of Kuch Behar; 7th Earl of Shaftesbury, KG; 1st Earl of Lathom, GCB; 1st Lord Rothschild, GCVO; Lord James Crichton-Stuart; Baroness Charlotte de Rothschild; Dr Lloyd, Bishop of Bangor; Very Rev. F. W. Farrar, Dean of Canterbury; Chief Rabbi Dr N. M. Adler; Very Rev. Dr Hermann Adler, CVO, Chief Rabbi; Sir Morgan Morgan and Lady Morgan; Sir John and Lady Monckton; Sir Edward Hill, MP; Sir Philip Magnus, MP; Sir T. Marchant Williams; Sir Edward Montague Nelson, KCMG; Sir Horace Brooks Marshall, etc; also painter of genre works. *Publications:* Presidential Address (in official publication) before the Art Section of the Cymmrodorion Society in connection with the National Eisteddfod of Wales, 1883; Fleeting Shadows, Fair Maidens three (words set to music by F. Helena Marks). *Address:* 10 Matheson Road, West Kensington, W.
Died 6 Dec. 1916.

MARKS, Harry Hananel; editor and chief proprietor of The Financial News; *b* London, 9 April 1855; 5th *s* of late Rev. Prof. D. W. Marks, and Cecilia, *d* of late Moseley Wolff, Liverpool; *m* 1884, Annie Estelle Marks (*d* 1916); one *s* one *d*. *Educ:* Univ. College, London; Athenée Royale, Brussels. Journalist in United States, 1871–83; LCC for East

Marylebone, 1889; contested (C) North-East Bethnal Green, 1892; LCC for St George's in the East, March 1895; MP (C) St George, Tower Hamlets, 1895–1900; MP (C) Isle of Thanet Div. of Kent, 1904–10. Major (officer commanding) 1st Cadet Batt. The Buffs (East Kent Regiment). JP Kent. *Publications:* Leaves from a Reporter's Note-Book, 1881; The Metropolitan Board of Works, 1888; The Case for Tariff Reform, 1905. *Address:* 6 Cavendish Square, W. *T:* Gerrard 3503; Callis Court, St Peter's, Thanet. *M:* D 600. *Clubs:* Carlton; Cinque Ports, Royal Temple Yacht.

Died 22 Dec. 1916.

MARKWICK, Col Ernest Elliott, CB 1905; CBE 1919; retired, Army Ordnance Department; *b* 19 July 1853; *e s* of late William Markwick of East Acton, W; *m* 1882, Amy, *o c* of late F. M. Murton; two *s* one *d. Educ:* private school; King's College School. Entered the late Control Department of the Army, 1872; served Zulu War, 1879; Boer War, 1880–81; siege of Pretoria (despatches); Bechuanaland Expedition, 1884–85 (hon. mentioned and specially promoted); Chief Ordnance Office Cork District, 1887–93; Gibraltar, 1893–98; Western District, 1898–1903; 2nd Army Corps, 1903–4; Assistant Director of Ordnance Stores, Southern Command, 1905; ADOS, Irish Command, 1914–19. FRAS; Past President of the British Astronomical Association. *Address:* c/o Glyn, Mills, Currie, Holt & Co., 3 Whitehall Place, SW1.

Died 4 July 1925.

MARLING, Sir William Henry, 2nd Bt *cr* 1882; DL, JP; *b* Stroud, 1 July 1835; *s* of Sir Samuel Stephens Marling, 1st Bt and Margaret Williams, *d* of William Bentley Cartwright; *S* father, 1883; *m* 1860, Mary Emily (*d* 1918), *d* of John Abraham Longridge, Lancashire; four *s. Educ:* Trinity Coll. Camb. *Heir: s* Col Percival Scrope Marling, *b* 6 March 1861. *Address:* Stanley Park, Stroud, Gloucestershire. *T:* 35 Stroud. *Died 19 Oct. 1919.*

MARRABLE, Brig.-Gen. Arthur George, CB 1916; King's Own Yorkshire Light Infantry; *b* 26 April 1863; *s* of late George Marrable, HM's Paymaster. *Educ:* Rugby; Oxford. psc; served Burma, 1886–89 (medal 2 clasps); NW Frontier of India, 1897–98 (severely wounded, medal 2 clasps); S African War, 1899–1902 (despatches twice, Queen's medal 4 clasps, King's medal 2 clasps, Bt Major); Bt Lt-Col; European War, 1914–16 (despatches thrice, Bt Col, 1914 Star, General Service Medal, Victory medal, Officer Legion of Honour, Commander Order of the Crown (Belgium), Croix de Guerre, Belgium). *Clubs:* United Service, Junior Constitutional.

Died 31 Dec. 1925.

MARRABLE, Mrs; President Society of Women Artists; *d* of Lieut Cockburn, 17th Lancers; *g c* of Mrs Dunlop of Dunlop, Burn's first patroness; her uncle, Ralph Cockburn, was one of the original members RWS; *m* Frederick Marrable, architect, *s* of Sir Thomas Marrable; one *s. Educ:* Queen's College, under Henry Warren, Alfred Newton, RWS, and Prof. C. Welsch; Rome. Member Royal Belgian Society; Member Verein der Schripstellerin und Kunstlerinnen in Wien. Travelled much in Italy, Austria and Switzerland; was for many years the only English artist in the Engadine; painted pictures for King Edward, King George, Her Majesty the Queen, late Duchess of Teck, etc; exhibited in the RA, RBA, New Gallery, Women Artists, and in Rome, Belgium, America and Australia. *Recreations:* reading, travelling in beautiful scenery, music. *Address:* 12 Zetland House, Cheniston Gardens, Kensington, W.

Died 21 May 1916.

MARRIOTT, Ernest; artist and author; *b* Manchester, 9 July 1882; *s* of Rhodes Marriott. Studied under Walter Crane at Manchester Municipal School of Art; for ten years acted as Librarian to the Portico Library; travelled considerably in Europe, and made many paintings of Continental scenes; for two and a half years acted as Chief Assistant to Gordon Craig in Florence at the School for the Art of the Theatre; produced a number of caricatures, book-plate designs, book illustrations, and theatre-scene designs; a collector of oriental paintings, Japanese prints and carvings; organised and arranged picture exhibitions at Zürich, Cologne, Warsaw, and at several towns in England; delivered lectures on art, and contributed poetry, verses, articles, and criticisms to many journals; during the war acted as Hon. Quartermaster of an Auxiliary Military Hospital. *Publications:* Jack B. Yeats, his Pictorial and Dramatic Art; Giovanni Segantini; A Catalogue of Works on Architecture; Continental Vignettes; Illustrations to Stories from Don Quixote; Bruges and the Ardennes; On the Zuider Zee, etc; verses for children under the *nom de plume* of Timothy Quince. *Address:* 9 Albert Square, Manchester.

Died 8 March 1918.

MARRIOTT, Very Rev. John Thomas; Incumbent of All Saints Bathurst, NSW and Dean of Bathurst, 1882–1912. *Educ:* University of Giessen (PhD); Trinity College, Toronto (Jure Dignitatis DD); Melbourne University (MA 1887); Fellow Australian College of Theology, 1900. Headmaster Andover Grammar School, 1867–72; Curate of Edmondthorpe, Leicestershire, 1872–76 and 1878–79; Headmaster Wymondham Grammar School, 1872–79; Incumbent of St Saviour, Redfern, 1880–81; St Luke, Burwood, 1881–82. *Address:* Oakwood, Burgess Hill, Sussex.

Died 15 April 1924.

MARRIOTT, Maj. Richard George Armine, DSO 1900; JP Essex; *b* 26 Jan. 1867; *s* of late Humphrey R. G. Marriott of Abbot's Hall Shalford, Essex; *m* 1912, Eileen Anita, *o d* of Brig.-Gen. R. A. Hickson; one *s* three *d. Educ:* Harrow. Entered army (The Buffs), 1887; Captain 1896; Major, 1905; served South Africa, 1899–1902 (severely wounded, despatches, Queen's medal 3 clasps, King's medal 2 clasps, DSO); retired pay, 1907. *Address:* Arthington, Torquay, Devon.

Died 15 Dec. 1924.

MARRIOTT, William, FRMetSoc; Corresponding Member Hertfordshire Natural History Society; Assistant Secretary of Royal Meteorological Society, 1872–1915; *b* 9 Aug. 1848; *s* of William Marriott; *m* Jane S. Old. *Educ:* Colfe's Grammar School, Lewisham; University College, London. Engaged at Royal Observatory Greenwich, 1869–72; Inspector of the Stations of Royal Meteorological Society, 1878–1911; appointed Lecturer on Meteorology, 1905. *Publications:* Hints to Meteorological Observers, seven edns; Some Facts about the Weather, two edns; numerous papers on meteorological subjects; editor of the Meteorological Record, 1881–1911; (with J. S. Fowler) Our Weather. *Address:* 70 Victoria Street, Westminster, SW. *T:* 2721 Victoria.

Died 28 Dec. 1916.

MARSDEN, Capt. George, DSO 1900; 3rd (SR) Battalion The Cheshire Regiment; late South African Light Horse; *b* 9 Feb. 1874; *s* of late Capt. Richard Marsden, RNR, JP; *m* 1904, Mary Julia, *o d* of late George Booker of Kenogue, Co. Louth, Ireland; two *d. Educ:* St Paul's School. Joined 3rd West Yorkshire Regiment; passed school of instruction, Chelsea; resigned commission; joined Perth (Western Australia) Artillery; employed on special mission to inquire into the condition of the aborigines of W Australia, 1896–97; appointed ADC to Governor of W Australia (Sir Gerard Smith, KCMG); resigned, 1899; joined South African Light Horse, 1899 (despatches thrice). Decorated for services in South African Boer War. *Club:* Sports.

Died 24 Sept. 1916.

MARSDEN, R. Sydney, DSc, MD, ChM, DPH (Edin. etc); LAH (Dublin) *hc*, 1911; Medical Officer of Health for Birkenhead; *b* Sheffield, 1856; *s* of late Robert Marsden; *m* Beatrice Eva, *e d* of Rev. C. Cotterell Ward, MA (Cantab), Rector of Salford, Oxon; one *d. Educ:* Universities of Edinburgh, Göttingen, Berlin and Paris. FRSE, FRPS, MRIA, FInstChem, etc. President, Royal Medical Society, 1881; thrice President Med. Soc., and President Lit. and Sci. Soc., Birkenhead; Lectr on Chem. Univ. Coll. Bristol, 1879; received grants for original research from Govt Research Fund, the Royal and Chem. Societies of London, and frequently called to give evidence before Royal Commissions and Select Parliamentary Committees; was the first person to produce the "Diamond" artificially. *Publications:* The Artificial Preparation of the Diamond, 1881; A Short Account of Edinburgh University Tercentenary Festival, 1884; History of Birkenhead Literary and Scientific Society, 1907: Genealogical Memoirs of the Family of Marsden (with B. A. and J. A. Marsden), 1914; numerous papers on Chemistry and Physics to the Transactions and Proceedings of Royal and other learned Societies, British and Foreign, and also many papers to the Medical Journals, and contributions to the literature of sanitary science; an acknowledged authority on all matters dealing with public health. *Recreations:* gardening, collecting pictures, china, books, bijoutry, etc. *Address:* 6 Cearns Road, and Town Hall, Birkenhead. *T:* 668 Birkenhead.

Died March 1919.

MARSDEN, Sir Thomas Rogerson, Kt 1918; CBE 1918; JP; Managing Director of Platt Brothers & Co. Ltd, Oldham. *Address:* Brookhurst, Alexandra Road, Oldham.

Died 24 Jan. 1927.

MARSDEN, Lt-Col William, MA Cambridge; late Royal Irish Fusiliers, and South Lancashire Regiments; *b* 1841; *e s* of Canon Marsden of Grey Friars, Colchester; *m* 1873, Katharine, *d* of B. Rigby Murray of Parton, NB; two *s* one *d.* Captain Instructor, School of Musketry, 1873–75; DAAG Southern and Western Districts,

1875–80; DAAG School of Musketry, 1880–83; Head of Range Department, National Rifle Association, 1876–81; appointed Secretary, 1890; Member of Council, 1881–1909; Vice-President, 1909. *Address:* Cedar Court, Farnham, Surrey.

Died 3 June 1925.

MARSH, Maj.-Gen. Frank Hale Berwick; Bengal Infantry; *b* 26 July 1841; 2nd *s* of late Col Hippisley Marsh and Louisa, *e d* of Gen. Sir Robert Henry Cunliffe, 4th Bt; *m* Sophia Frederica Augusta (*d* 1918), *d* of Col R. Taylor; one *s* five *d.* Entered army, 1859; Maj.-Gen. 1897; returned England, 1897; served NW Frontier of India Campaign, 1863 (despatches, medal with clasp); Abyssinian Expedition, 1867–68 (medal). *Address:* Acton Lodge, 12 Radnor Park West, Folkestone.

Died 25 Jan. 1923.

MARSHALL, Alfred, MA and Hon. DSc Oxon and Camb.; Hon. LLD Edin. and Bristol; FBA; *b* London, 26 July 1842; *m* 1877, Mary, *d* of Rev. Thomas Paley. *Educ:* Merchant Taylors' School; St John's Coll., Camb. Title to probationary classical Fellowship at St John's Coll., Oxford, 1861; Second Wrangler, 1865; Fellow of St John's College, Cambridge, 1865–77 and 1885–1908; Principal of Univ. Coll., Bristol, 1877–82; Lecturer at and Fellow of Balliol Coll., Oxford, 1883–84; Professor of Political Economy, Cambridge Univ., 1885–1908; Emeritus Professor, 1918; Member of Royal Commission on Labour, 1891. Vice-President of the Royal Economic Soc.; Foreign Member or Fellow of the Institute or Academies of France and Sweden, and of Rome, Milan and Turin; Hon. Fellow of Balliol College and of St John's College, Cambridge; Hon. Dr Jur Cracow and Christiana. Prix Emile de Laveleye of the Belgian Academy, 1921. *Publications:* Economics of Industry (in conjunction with his wife), 1879; Principles of Economics, vol. i, 1890, translated into several languages; Elements of Economics, vol. i, 1891; Memorandum on the Fiscal Policy of International Trade, published as a White Paper, 1903; Industry and Trade, 1919; Money, Credit and Commerce, 1923, etc. *Address:* Balliol Croft, 6 Madingley Road, Cambridge. *T:* Cambridge 286. *Died 13 July 1924.*

MARSHALL, Col Sir Arthur Wellington, Kt 1898; DL, JP for Huntingdonshire; Hon. Colonel, late Lieutenant-Colonel commanding 5th Battalion (Militia) King's Royal Rifle Corps; *b* 18 July 1841; *s* of James Marshall of Goldbeaters, Middlesex; *m* 1867, Constance (*d* 1915), *d* of late W. H. Desborough of Hartford, Hunts; three *s* one *d.* Sheriff of the counties of Cambridge and Huntingdon, 1890. *Address:* The Towers, Buckden, Huntingdon.

Died 1 Dec. 1918.

MARSHALL, Charles Devereux, FRCS; Surgeon to the Royal London (Moorfields) Ophthalmic Hospital; Ophthalmic Surgeon to the Victoria Hospital for Children, Chelsea; Surgeon (late Lieutenant) Royal Naval Volunteer Reserve; *b* 8 Dec. 1867; *s* of William Marshall, solicitor, Southsea; unmarried. *Educ:* University College, London. Held various appointments at University College Hospital and at the Royal London Ophthalmic Hospital. *Publications:* Diseases of the Eyes; many papers relating to scientific subjects, chiefly ophthalmological, published in various journals and books. *Recreation:* yachting. *Address:* 112 Harley Street, W. *T:* 181 Mayfair; 28 Merton Road, Southsea. *Clubs:* Royal Cruising, Primrose, Royal Albert Yacht.

Died 24 Sept. 1918.

MARSHALL, George Balfour, MD, CM (Edin.); FRFPS (Glas.); Consultant Gynæcological Surgeon, Glasgow Royal Infirmary; Professor of Obstetrics and Gynæcology, St Mungo's Medical College, Glasgow; Examiner in Obstetrics and Gynæcology for the Fellowship of the Royal Faculty of Physicians and Surgeons, and for the Triple Qualification of the Edinburgh and Glasgow Colleges; *b* Edinburgh, 1863; *e s* of T. R. Marshall; *m* 1901, Anna Morrison, 3rd *d* of John Stewart, Greenhill House, Paisley; two *s* one *d. Educ:* George Watson's College and University (graduated with honours), Edinburgh; Jena; Berlin; Doctor of Medicine, Edinburgh, with honours, 1894. Settled in Glasgow, 1894; on Gynæcological Staff of the Glasgow Royal Infirmary, 1896; Visitor to the Examinations of the Pharmaceutical Society of Great Britain. Past Pres. Glasgow Obstetrical and Gynæcological Society. *Publications:* Manual of Midwifery; numerous papers on gynæcological and obstetrical subjects. *Recreations:* fishing, photography. *M:* GB 8383. *Address:* 19 Sandyford Place, Glasgow. *T:* 4337 Douglas. *Died 31 Jan. 1928.*

MARSHALL, Sir James Brown, KCB 1911 (CB 1902); Director of Dockyards and Dockyard Work, 1906–17; *b* 23 Feb. 1853; *s* of Samuel Marshall, Berwick; *m* Alice E., *d* of late Joseph Paraoh, Bedhampton. *Educ:* Royal School of Naval Architecture and Royal Naval College, Greenwich. Entered Royal Dockyard, Portsmouth, 1867; since

engaged in progressive positions at the Royal Dockyards and Admiralty. *Address:* Mornington Hall, West Cowes, Isle of Wight.

Died 22 July 1922.

MARSHALL, Rev. James M'Call, MA; Rector of Croft, Darlington, since 1894; a Governor of St Peter's School, York; Vice-President of Surtees Society; *b* 1838; *s* of late James Marshall, of Harper's Hill; *m* Annette, *d* of late Joseph Blakemore of Edgbaston; four *s* two *d. Educ:* Manchester School and Trinity Coll., Oxford (1st class Mod., 1st class Lit. Hum., BA 1862). Ordained, 1874; Fellow of Brasenose Coll., Oxford, 1863–66; Lecturer, 1863–65; also of Wadham Coll., 1864–65; Assistant Master, Clifton Coll., 1865–69; 2nd Master, Dulwich College, 1869–84; Member of Council, Girls' Public Day School Co., 1876–84; Headmaster, Durham School, 1884–94. Strong supporter of women's education. *Publications:* edited Greek Irregular Verbs; The Odes and Epodes of Horace, 1874. *Recreations:* gardening, travelling. *Address:* Croft Rectory, near Darlington.

Died 10 Jan. 1926.

MARSHALL, Rev. John Turner, MA; DD; President Baptist College, Manchester, 1898–1920; Lecturer in Biblical Languages; *b* Farsley, near Leeds, 13 May 1850; *s* of Jonathan Marshall; *m* 1877, Hettie, *d* of W. G. Cooper, Burnley; one *d. Educ:* Tottington Boarding School; Rawdon, Owens and Manchester Baptist Colleges. Appointed Classical Tutor of the Baptist College, Manchester, 1877. Lecturer on the History of Christian Doctrine in the University of Manchester, 1904; President of the Baptist Union of Great Britain and Ireland, 1909; Dean of Faculty of Theology in Manchester University, 1915. *Publications:* Job and his Comforters; wrote a series of articles in the Expositor 1891, to show that the divergences of the Synoptic Gospels are, in many cases, due to variant translation of a common Aramaic original; contributed numerous articles to the Critical Review, the Expository Times, and Hastings' Dictionary of the Bible; Commentaries on Job and Ecclasiastes. *Recreation:* an occasional round of golf. *Address:* 23 Ladybarn Road, Fallowfield, Manchester.

Died 23 June 1923.

MARSHALL, Brig.-Gen. John Willoughby Astell, CB 1905; late Brigadier-General commanding Troops, Jamaica; *b* 13 March 1854. Entered army, 1876; Captain, 1887; Major, 1893; Lt-Col, 1898; served W Africa (despatches, medal with clasp), 1892; Gambia (despatches, Brevet Major), 1892; Ashanti (star), 1895–96; Sierra Leone (despatches, Brevet Col), 1896–99; retired, 1911. *Address:* 206 Gloucester Terrace, Hyde Park, W.

Died 14 Nov. 1921.

MARSHALL, John Wilson, MA; Professor of Greek and Vice-Principal University College of Wales, Aberystwyth; *s* of Alexander Marshall, MD, Kilmarnock. *Educ:* Glasgow University; Balliol College, Oxford. Captain, Officers' Training Corps (retired). *Address:* University College of Wales, Aberystwyth.

Died 30 March 1923.

MARSHALL, Sir (Joseph) Herbert, Kt 1905; JP County and Borough of Leicester; *b* 13 June 1851; *s* of late James Marshall of Leicester; *m* 1873, Clara Ann, *d* of late Vittore Albini of Garzeno, Como, Italy; two *s* two *d. Educ:* privately. Hon. Representative of the Royal Academy and the Royal College of Music; Mayor of Leicester, 1896–97; Member of the Council of the National Union; President Leicester Borough Conservative Association; Vice-President, Leicestershire Automobile Club; Musical Director, Leicester Philharmonic Society; twice contested Harborough Division, Leicestershire. *Recreations:* travelling, motoring, politics, Freemasonry. *Address:* Ratcliffe Lodge, Knighton, Leicester. *TA:* Duetto, Leicester and London. *T:* 2021 Leicester; Mayfair 1330, London. *M:* BC 6. *Clubs:* Carlton, Junior Conservative.

Died 1 Sept. 1918.

MARSHALL, Lt-Col Noel George Lambert; Chairman of the Canadian Red Cross during European War, President, 1922; *b* London, England, 30 Dec. 1852; *s* of Kenric R. and Charlotte A. Marshall; *m* 1879, Harriette Isobel, *d* of John Hogg, MP; two *s. Educ:* Toronto Grammar Schools. Chairman the Standard Fuel Co. of Toronto; President Dominion Automobile Co., and Faramel, Ltd; Chartered Trust and Executor Co.; Director Standard Bank Western Canadian Flour Mills, and Canadian Northern Prairie Lands Co.; Conservative Anglican; devoted a large portion of his life to public service and a member of the Boards of many charitable institutions; a member of the Ontario Parole Commission for sixteen years (sometime Chairman). KGStJ; Commander of the Order of the Legion of Honour of France; Commander of the Order of the Crown of Italy; Grand Officer of the Order of St Sava, Serbia. *Address:* 623

Sherborne Street, Toronto, Canada. *Clubs:* York, Toronto Hunt, National, Toronto. *Died 9 Dec. 1926.*

MARSHALL, Col Sir Thomas Horatio, Kt 1906; CB 1892; *b* Hartford Beach, Cheshire, 5 Jan. 1833; *o s* of Thomas Marshall, barrister-at-law, and of Agnes Phœbe, *d* of Digby Legard of Wotton Abbey, Co. Yorks; *m* 1st, 1857, Laura Anne (*d* 1858), *d* of Rev. Martin Stapylton; one *s;* 2nd, 1862, Lucy Martina (*d* 1916), *d* of Rev. Edward Nugent Bree; four *s* two *d. Educ:* Eton; Exeter Coll., Oxford (MA). 3rd (Militia) Batt. Cheshire Regt, 1862–88; retired as Major and Hon. Lt-Col; 3rd Volunteer Battalion Cheshire Regt, 1860–98 (Lt-Col commanding, 1865–98); Hon. Col 1898; Earl of Chester's Yeomanry Cavalry, 1852–62. JP for Counties of Cheshire, Anglesey and Carnarvon; patron of one living. Decorated for service in Auxiliary Forces. *Recreations:* hunting, shooting, rowing, golf. *Address:* Bryn-y-Coed, Bangor, N Wales. *TA:* Bangor. *Club:* Junior Carlton. *Died 29 March 1917.*

MARSHALL, Thomas Riley, LLD; Vice-President of the United States, 1913–21; *b* North Manchester, Ind., 14 March, 1854; *m* 1895, Lois I. Kimsey, Angola, Ind. *Educ:* Wabash College. Admitted to Bar, 1875; Governor of Indiana, 1909–13. *Address:* Columbia City, Indiana, USA. *Died 1 June 1925.*

MARSHALL, Major W. R., DSO 1915; 15th Battalion Canadian Forces. Served European War, 1914–15 (DSO).
Died May 1916.

MARSHALL, Lt-Col William Thomas, VC 1884; Secretary Fife County Territorial Association; *b* 5 Dec. 1854. *Educ:* privately. Joined 19th Hussars, 1873; commissioned, 1885; served Egyptian War, 1882–84, present at battle of Tel-el-Kebir (medal with clasp and Khedive's star); Soudan Expedition, 1884, present in engagements at El Teb and Tamai (despatches, VC, two clasps); served South Africa, 1899–1900, operations in Natal including actions at Lombard's Kop, Defence of Ladysmith, Laing's Nek (Queen's medal with four clasps); late Camp Quarter-master, Aldershot, 19th (Queen Alexandra's Own Royal) Hussars, retired 1907; mentioned in despatches, 6 Aug. 1917, for valuable services rendered in connection with the War. *Address:* St Helen's, Kirkcaldy, Fife, NB. *T:* 246. *TA:* Kingdom, Kirkcaldy. *Died 11 Sept. 1920.*

MARSHALL-HALL, Sir Edward, Kt 1917; QC 1898; Recorder of Guildford since 1916; *b* Brighton, 16 Sept. 1858; *y s* of late Dr Alfred Hall, FRCP, and Julia Elizabeth, *d* of James Sebright; *m* Henriette Kroeger; one *d. Educ:* Rugby (Mathematical prizeman); St John's College, Cambridge. BA 1882; Barrister, Inner Temple, 1883; Bencher, 1910; practised in London and on the South-Eastern Circuit and Sussex Sessions; MP (C) Southport Div. of Lancs, 1900–6; East Toxteth Div., Liverpool, 1910–16. *Recreations:* shooting, golf. *Address:* 3 Temple Gardens, EC4. *T:* Central 700; 5A Wimpole Street, W1; Overbrook, Brook, Godalming. *Clubs:* Carlton, Garrick, Beefsteak, MCC. *Died 24 Feb. 1927.*

MARSHAM, George, CBE 1920; DL, JP; *b* 10 April 1849; *s* of Rev. George Marsham, Allington Rectory, Maidstone. *Educ:* Eton; Merton College, Oxford. Kent County Council; Chairman, 1900–10; Chairman Royal Insurance Co., Maidstone Branch; Maidstone Gas Co.; Director, Royal Insurance Co., Maidstone Waterworks Co.; President, Mote Cricket Club; Committee West Kent General Hospital (Chairman for over 30 years); Churchwarden for over 30 years; Member Kent County Cricket Club Committee. *Recreation:* cricket. *Address:* Hayle Cottage, Maidstone. *T:* Maidstone 90. *Clubs:* Junior Carlton, MCC. *Died 2 Dec. 1927.*

MARSHAM, Rev. Hon. John; *b* 25 July 1842; 2nd *s* of Charles, 3rd Earl of Romney; *m* 1866, Penelope Jane, *y d* of Rev. W. Wheler Hume, St Leonards-on-sea; four *s* six *d* (and one *s* decd). *Educ:* Eton; Oxford; Cambridge; Cuddesdon. Ordained, 1866; Rector of Barton Segrave, 1868–1908; Rector and Arch Priest of Haccombe, Devon, 1908; retired, 1911. *Recreations:* cricket, shooting. *Address:* St Clair, Seaford, Sussex. *Died 16 Sept. 1926.*

MARSTON, Robert Bright, FZS; FJI; Member of Japan Society; *b* London, 30 May 1853; *s* of late Edward Marston; *m* 1881; four *s* (two killed in France) three *d. Educ:* Croydon, Bonn, Islington Proprietary School. In the publishing business for over 50 years; for nearly 50 years editor of the Fishing Gazette; founder of the Fly-Fishers' Club, 1884, President, 1897 and 1910; late Hon. Sec. Publishers' Association; editor Publishers' Circular; Chairman Thames Angling Preservation Society; Member Government Fresh-Water Fish Committee, 1917; Member of the Joint Committee of the Ministry of Agriculture and the Ministry of Transport, 1919–22; Member Executive Council Fisheries Organisation Society. *Publications:* War, Famine, and our Food Supply, 1897; Walton, and some Earlier Writers on Angling; editor of the 100th edition of The Compleat Angler; of Angling, and How to Angle; translator of Liesegang's Carbon Process of Photography; Tissandier's History and Handbook of Photography; Rohlff's Travels in Morocco; Mechanical Traction in War; Articles on Food Supply in War Time in the Nineteenth Century, etc. *Recreations:* salmon, trout and general angling; archery; shooting; cycling; formerly captain of football and cricket clubs; amateur photography. *Address:* Surrey Lodge, 160 Denmark Hill, SE5. *Club:* Fly-Fishers'. *Died 2 Sept. 1927.*

MARTELLI, Ernest Wynne, KC 1908; **His Honour Judge Martelli;** County Court Judge for Hampshire since 1916. Called to Bar, Lincoln's Inn, 1888; Bencher, 1913. *Address:* 14 Ladbroke Road, W. *Died 2 May 1917.*

MARTI, Prof. Karl, Dr theol., ordentlicher Professor für das Alte Testament an der Universität, Bern, since 1895; zugleich auch Professor für semitische Philologie since 1901; *b* Bubendorf (Baselland), 25 April 1855; *m* 1879, Fräulein Lina Rieder von Basel; one *s* eight *d. Educ:* Pädogoguin von Basel, 1870–73; Universität zu Basel (Kautzsch, Socin), Göttingen (Ritschl), und Leipzig (Fleischer, Delitzsch), 1873–78. Licentiat der Theologie (Basel), 1879; zum Doctor theologiae honoris causa ernannt von der theolog. Fakultät zu Basel, 1895. Das Examen für den Pfarrdienst in der reformierten Kirche der Konkordatskantone der Schweiz bestanden, 1877; Pfarrer in Buus (Baselland), 1878–85; Pfarrer in Muttenz (Baselland), 1885–95; gleichzeitig von 1881 an, zuerst als Privatdozent, dann von 1894 an als ausserodentlicher Professor, an der Universität Basel thätig. *Publications:* der Prophet Jeremia von Anatot, 1889; der richtige Standpunkt zur Beurteilung der abweichenden theologischen Anschauungen, 1890; der Prophet Sacharja, der Zeitgenosse Serubbabels, 1892; der Einfluss der Ergebnisse der neuestenttest. Forschungen aug Religionsgeschichte und Glaubenslehre, 1894, ins Schwedische übersetzt von K. O. Tellander, 1894; August Kayser's Theologie des Alten Testaments, 2. Aufl, 1894; 3. Auflage unter dem Titel: Geschichte der israelitischen Religion, 1897, 5. Aufl, 1907; kurzgefasste Grammatik der biblisch-aramäischen Sprache, 1896, 2 Aufl. 1911; das Buch Jesaja (Tübingen, 1900), das Buch Daniel erklärt (Tübingen, 1901) und Dodekapropheton I. (Tübingen, 1903), II. (Tübingen, 1904) im kurzen Hand-Commentare zum Alten Testament, der seit 1897 von mir herausgegeben und 1904 vollständig geworden ist; various articles (Chronology of Old Testament and others) in Ency. Bib.; Die Religion des Alten Testaments unter dem Titel: The Religion of the Old Testament: Its Place among the Religions of the Nearer East, London, 1907; ins Japanische übersetzt, Tokyo 1914; Stade's Nachfolger in der Herausgabe der Zeitschr. für die alttestament. Wissenschaft, 1907–23; Stand und Aufgabe der alttestamentlichen Wissenschaft in der Gegenwart, Rektoratsrede, Bern, 1912; Herausgeber der Studien zur semit, Philol. u. Religionsgesch. zu Wellhausens 70. Geburtstag, Giessen, 1914; zur Beiträge zur alttest. Wissenschaft zu Karl Buddes 70 Geburtstag, Giessen, 1920. *Address:* Bern, Marienstrasse 25. *TA:* Prof. Marti. Bern. *T:* 3774. *Died 22 April 1925.*

MARTIN, Lt-Gen. Sir Alfred Robert, KCB 1910 (CB 1902); Colonel of the 5th Royal Gurkha Rifles; *b* 30 March 1853; *e s* of late Col D. W. Martin; *m* 1882, Bessie Charlotte St George, 2nd *d* of late Surg.-Gen. Sir Annesley C. C. De Renzy, KCB; two *s* three *d. Educ:* Harrow. Entered army (34th Cumberland Regiment), 1871; 5th Gurkha Rifles, 1877; Captain, 1886; Major, 1894; Lt-Col 1900; Col 1899; Maj.-Gen. 1904; Lt-Gen. 1909; served against Jowaki-Afreedees, 1877–78 (medal with clasp); Afghan War, 1878–80 (despatches three times, medal with four clasps, bronze star); served expedition against Atekzai tribe, 1880; Marri tribe, 1880; Hazara, 1888 (clasp); Miranzai, in command of 1st Batt. 5th Gurkha Rifles (despatches, brevet of Major, clasp); served Isazai expedition; Waziristan, 1894–95 (despatches, brevet Lieut-Col, clasp), Tochi expedition, 1897; Tirah, 1897–98 (despatches, medal with two clasps); held several Staff appointments, including AMS for Indian affairs, Horse Guards; Brigade Commander, India, 1904–6; Adjutant-General in India, 1906–8; Divisional Commander, India 1908–12; retired, 1912; awarded Distinguished Service Award. *Address:* Saint Peters, Farringdon, near Alton, Hants.
Died 27 Oct. 1926.

MARTIN, Arthur Anderson, MD, ChB; FRCSE; Senior Surgeon, Palmerston North Hospital, New Zealand. Late Field Ambulance, 5th Division, 2nd Army; late Surgical Specialist, No 6 General

Hospital, Rouen, France, British Expeditionary Force; late Civil Surgeon, South African Field Force, 1901 (medal 4 clasps); retired Captain, New Zealand Medical Corps. *Publications:* A Surgeon in Khaki, 1915. *Address:* The Hospital, Palmerston North, New Zealand.
Died Oct. 1916.

MARTIN, Cornwallis Philip Wykeham-, JP; CC; *b* 19 March 1855; *o s* of Philip Wykeham-Martin (*d* 1878) and Elizabeth (*d* 1893), *d* of late John Ward; *m* 1876, Anna Bertha (*d* 1923), *e d* of Major William Pitt Draffen. *Educ:* Eton; Merton College, Oxford. Late Captain 1st Kent RV. *Address:* Leeds Castle, Maidstone; Chacombe Priory, Banbury; Packwood Hall, Knowles, Warwicks. *Club:* United University.
Died 23 Feb. 1924.

MARTIN, Col Cunliffe, CB 1881; retired; *b* 3 Feb. 1834; 5th *s* of late Sir Ranald Martin, CB; *m* 1870, Frances Mary, *d* of late T. R. Colledge, MD, FRSE; three *s* four *d*. *Educ:* Cheltenham College. Joined 1st Bengal Light Cavalry, 1852; served with the Governor-General's bodyguard in the suppression of the Santhal rebellion, 1855; with 14th Light Dragoons, 1857 (severely wounded, despatches, medal and clasp); as ADC to late FM Sir Donald Stewart in Expedition to Abyssinia, and with 12th Bengal Cavalry at taking of Magdala, 1868 (medal, despatches); commanded Central India Horse, Afghan War, in operations in Besud and Khama Valleys, 1880, in march from Kabul to Kandahar and battle of Kandahar under Earl Roberts (despatches thrice, medal and clasp, star and CB). *Address:* Delmar, Cheltenham. *TA:* Cheltenham. *T:* 1041. *Club:* New, Cheltenham.
Died 10 July 1917.

MARTIN, Capt. Edward Harington, CMG 1917; RN. Captain-Supt., Halifax Dockyard, Nova Scotia. *Address:* Halifax Dockyard, Nova Scotia.
Died 26 May 1921.

MARTIN, Col Ernest Edmund, CMG 1916; CBE 1919; FRCVS, DVH; Deputy Director of Veterinary Services; *b* 20 June 1869; 2nd *s* of late T. J. Martin of Osborne House, Taunton; *m* 1913, Alexine Aimée Samuelson. *Educ:* Queen's College, Taunton. Served S Africa, 1902 (Queen's medal 2 clasps); European War, 1914–18 (despatches, CMG). *Club:* Junior Naval and Military.
Died 23 Aug. 1925.

MARTIN, Col George Blake Napier, CB 1881; RA (retired); *b* 28 Feb. 1847; *m* 1889, Evelyn Henrietta, *o d* of late Col Henry Clement Swinnerton-Dyer, RA. Entered army, 1866; Capt. 1878; Major, 1884; Lt-Col 1893; Col 1897; served Egypt, 1882, including Tel-el-Kebir (despatches, brevet of Major, medal with clasp, 4th class Medjidie, Khedive's Star); Nile, 1884–85 (two clasps); Burmah, 1886 (medal with clasp).
Died 20 Jan. 1917.

MARTIN, Sir George Clement, Kt 1897; MVO 1902; MusD; Hon. MusD Oxford; Hon. RAM; FRCO; Organist St Paul's Cathedral since 1888; *b* 11 Sept. 1844; *m* 1879, Margaret, *d* of T. M. Cockburn. *Educ:* privately. Organist, Lambourn; Dalkeith. Compositions mainly for the Church. *Recreations:* shooting, bicycling, photography, golf. *Address:* 4 Amen Court, St Paul's, EC. *T:* City 160. *TA:* Martin, St Paul's. *Club:* Constitutional.
Died 23 Feb. 1916.

MARTIN, Rev. Canon Henry, MA; *b* 1844; *s* of Rev. R. M. Martin, Vicar of Thorpe, Surrey, and Charlotte, *d* of J. R. Buttemer; *m* 1st, 1874, Constance Clare Lawton (*d* 1905), *d* of Maj.-Gen. Trafford, Plas Panthoel, Carmarthenshire; two *s* one *d*; 2nd, 1906, Frances Eliza Mary, *d* of Maj.-Gen. Griffith, Maesgwyn, Winchester; one *s* one *d*. *Educ:* Merchant Taylors' School; Oxford. Graduated with Honours in Theology, 1872. Classical Master Elizabeth College, Guernsey, 1872–73; Curate All Saints, Guernsey, 1873; Vice-Principal Cheltenham Training College, 1873–78; Curate of Christ Church, Cheltenham, 1876–78; Principal, Training College, Winchester, 1878–1912; Hon. Canon of Winchester, 1898; Hon. Lt-Col (retired) 1st Vol. Batt. Hampshire Regt; VD. *Recreations:* bicycling, golf, mountaineering. *Address:* Clifton Mount, Winchester. *TA:* Canon Martin, Winchester. *T:* 121. *Clubs:* Alpine, Swiss Alpine, New Oxford and Cambridge, Hampshire County.
Died 27 July 1919.

MARTIN, Rev. Henry, MA; Hon. Canon of Durham, 1899; Vicar of Kelloe since 1916; *b* Dore, 1844; *s* of Rev. Richard Martin of Killaloe; *m* 1874, Mary, *d* of W. J. Lunn, MD, Hull; six *s* five *d*. *Educ:* Sheffield Collegiate School; Clare College, Cambridge (scholar, prizeman), senior optime, 1867. Curate, Chapel en le Frith; Earls Heaton; St Paul's, Hull; Vicar, St John's, Sunderland, 1875–85; Vicar, Stockton-on-Tees, 1885–1916; Rural Dean of Stockton, 1903;

Proctor, York Convocation, 1903–18; served on Soothill, Sunderland, and Stockton School Boards; Chairman, Durham Dio. CETS; Commissary to Bishop of Barbados, 1906. *Recreations:* bicycling, gardening. *Address:* Kelloe Vicarage, Coxhoe, Co. Durham. *M:* J1551.
Died 13 June 1923.

MARTIN, Howard, PPSI; Official Arbitrator under the Acquisition of Land Compensation Act 1919, since 1920; *s* of late Rev. Samuel Martin of Westminster; *m e c* of late C. E. Smith, of Silvermere, Cobham, Surrey, and Colwood Park, Bolney, Sussex; three *s* three *d*. *Educ:* University College School, London; private tuition. Articled as a pupil to Robert Jacomb Hood, CE, and afterwards employed for some years as assistant engineer on the construction of new railways in Surrey and Sussex and the Newhaven Harbour works; joined as partner a firm of surveyors in Croydon, 1870; joined the late Herbert Thurgood, surveyor, in partnership at 27 Chancery Lane, 1882; practised there as surveyor, land agent, etc, till 1920; Member of Council of Surveyors Institution since 1892; President, 1908–9. *Publications:* a number of contribs to the Transactions of the Surveyors Institution on professional subjects. *Recreations:* golf, hunting, reading, music. *Address:* South Lawn, Reigate. *T:* Redhill 278; 12 Great George Street, Westminster, SW1. *T:* Victoria 5322. *Club:* St Stephen's.
Died 19 Jan. 1924.

MARTIN, Hon. Joseph, KC; *b* Milton, Ontario, Canada, 24 Sept. 1852; *s* of Edward and Mary Ann Martin; *m* 1881, Mrs Elizabeth Jane Eaton (*d* 1913), Ottawa, Canada; no *c*. *Educ:* Canadian and Michigan Public Schools; Toronto University. Barrister in Canada since 1882; Canadian QC 1899; Member of Legislature, Manitoba, 1882–92; Attorney-General and Minister of Education, Manitoba, 1888–91; Member of Dominion of Canada House of Commons for Winnipeg, 1893–96; Member of Legislature, British Columbia, 1898–1903; Attorney-General and Minister of Education, British Columbia, 1898–99; Premier of British Columbia, 1900; contested (L) South-West Warwickshire, 1909; MP (L) East St Pancras, 1910–18. Took active part in Manitoba against Canadian Pacific Railway monopoly, Abolition of French as official language and of separate schools, and in favour of introduction of Torrens System of Land Registry; strong Free Trader and advocate of unrestricted reciprocity between United States and Canada. *Publications:* owned and edited daily newspapers in Vancouver, Canada, for some time. *Clubs:* Royal Automobile; Vancouver, Vancouver.
Died 2 March 1923.

MARTIN, Sir Richard, Kt 1921; JP; ex-Mayor of Swansea. *Address:* c/o Town Hall, Swansea.
Died 16 Sept. 1922.

MARTIN, Rev. Richard; Prebendary of Exeter Cathedral since 1894; *b* Staverton Vicarage, Devon, 1 March 1836; 3rd *s* of Rev. William Martin and Jane Champernowne of Dartington Hall; *m* Eliza Rose (*d* 1919). *Educ:* Marlborough; Corpus Christi College, Oxford. Curate of Swymbridge, 1859–61; Rector of Challacombe, 1861–80; Vicar of Swymbridge, 1880–87; Ilfracombe, 1887–1905; Rural Dean of Shirwell, 1871–87; Barnstaple, 1894–1905; Proctor in Convocation, 1895; Sub-Dean of Exeter Cathedral, 1911. *Recreations:* rowed in the Oxford boat against Cambridge, 1857. *Address:* Carlton Close, Exmouth.
Died 20 Feb. 1927.

MARTIN, Sir Richard Biddulph, 1st Bt *cr* 1905; banker; Chairman Martin's Bank, Ltd; *b* London, 12 May 1838; *m* 1864, Mary Frances, *o d* of late Adm. Richard Crozier, KTS, Westhill, Isle of Wight. *Educ:* Hardenhuish; Harrow; Exeter College, Oxford (MA). Chairman Assets Realisation Co., Debenture Corporation, and Anglo-American Debenture Corporation; formerly Chairman British North Borneo Company; Director Sun Fire and Life Offices, etc; Fellow and formerly President of Institute of Bankers, of which he was one of the founders; President (1906) and Treasurer of the Royal Statistical Society; Fellow of the Anthropological Institute; FRGS; Hon. Secretary to the Metropolitan Hospital Sunday Fund; Treas. of St Mark's Hospital for Fistula, and of the Royal National Orthopædic Hospital, of the Childhood Society, and of Association for Promoting Welfare of Feeble-Minded; Prime Warden of the Fishmongers' Company, 1906. MP (LU) Tewkesbury, 1880–85; Mid or Droitwich Division of Worcestershire, 1892–1905; JP for Co. of Kent, Co. of Worcester, and Co. of Gloucester; a Lieut of City of London. *Heir:* none. *Recreations:* photography, formerly archery, sketching. *Address:* Overbury Court, Tewkesbury; 10 Hill Street, Mayfair, W. *T:* 2946 Gerrard. *Clubs:* Athenæum, Windham, Ranelagh; Travellers', Paris. *M:* AB 1434; AB 670.
Died 23 Aug. 1916 (ext).

MARTIN, Col Rowland Hill, CB 1898; CMG 1901; retired; *b* 30 Oct. 1848; *s* of late Col A. P. Martin of Fleetlands, Fareham; *m* 1902,

Emily, widow of John Nugent, CSI. *Educ:* Cheltenham College. Entered Army, 1869; Colonel, 1896; served Bechuanaland Expedition, 1884–85; Nile, 1898 (despatches, Queen's medal, Egyptian medal with clasp, CB); commanded 21st Lancers in charge at Omdurman; South Africa, 1902 (despatches, Queen's medal with clasp, CMG); late commanding 21st Lancers, 1892–98. JP Hants. *Club:* Cavalry. *Died 31 Jan. 1919.*

MARTIN, Sidney, MD; FRS; Physician to University College Hospital; Professor of Clinical Medicine, University College Hospital; *b* Jamaica, 8 April 1860; 2nd *s* of late John Ewers Martin, Jamaica; *m*; one *d*. *Educ:* University College, London. Pathologist and Assistant Physician, Victoria Park Chest Hospital; Pathologist and Medical Tutor, Middlesex Hospital; Assistant Physician, Hospital for Consumption, Brompton. *Publications:* Diseases of the Stomach, 1895; Appendix to Report of Royal Commission on Tuberculosis, 1896; A Manual of Pathology, 1903; papers on Medical and Scientific Subjects in Proc. Roy. Soc.; etc. *Address:* 51 Wimpole Street, W1. *T:* Paddington 1705. *Died 22 Sept. 1927.*

MARTIN, Stapleton, MA; *b* 1846; 2nd *s* of Marcus Martin, Barrister, and Harriett Mary, *o c* of John Stapleton of Calcutta; *m* 1895, Helen Gertrude, 2nd *d* of Walker Busfeild, JP, of Charlton, Somerset; two *s* three *d*. *Educ:* privately; Christ's College, Cambridge. Called to Bar, Middle Temple, 1871. *Publications:* Izaak Walton and his Friends, 1903; various articles and pamphlets. *Recreations:* hunting, billiards. *Address:* The Firs, Norton, Worcester. *Clubs:* Oxford and Cambridge; MCC. *Died 26 Sept. 1922.*

MARTIN, Sir (Thomas) Carlaw, Kt 1909; JP; LLD (St Andrews); FRSE; Director Royal Scottish Museum, 1911–16; *b* 1850; *m* 1879, Isobel Laurie Spence. *Educ:* Edinburgh Univ. Edited Scottish Morning Journals, 1890–1910; Chairman Scottish Agricultural Commission to Canada, 1908; to Australia, 1910–11. *Address:* 18 Blackford Road, Edinburgh. *Clubs:* National Liberal; Scottish Liberal, Edinburgh. *Died 26 Oct. 1920.*

MARTIN, Col Thomas Morgan, CMG 1916; late Acting Commissioner New South Wales District, St John Ambulance Brigade, Overseas; *b* 30 Nov. 1854; *s* of John W. Martin, LLD, Blackrock, Dublin, and Grace Morgan; *m* Mary, *d* of Dr J. Marshall, Dromore, Co. Tyrone; three *s* three *d*. *Educ:* Rev. R. North's School, Dublin; Trinity College, Dublin. Practised for five years in Piltown, Ireland, and for forty-two years in Sydney, NSW; served South African War, 1899–1900. With the 1st NSW Field Hospital, and as Secretary to Surg.-Gen. Williams PMO, Gen. Ian Hamilton's, and later Gen. Hunter's Forces; served European War, first in Egypt, afterwards in France, 1915–16 (CMG); OC No 2 Australian Auxiliary Hospital (Southall), 1917; Col AAMC Reserve; late Officer Commanding No 2 Australian General Hospital. *Recreation:* golf. *Address:* 21 Oxford Street, Sydney, NSW. *Club:* Imperial Service, Sydney. *Died 23 May 1928.*

MARTIN, Victoria Claflin Woodhull; financier and reformer; editor and proprietor, The Humanitarian Magazine; writer; *b* Homer, Ohio, US, 23 Sept. 1838; 7th *c* of Reuben Claflin and Roxanna Hummel; *m* 1st, Canning Woodhull (*d* 1873); 2nd, John Biddulph Martin (*d* 1897); one *s* one *d*. Banker; memorialised Congress in 1870 for Women's Suffrage; lectured throughout US on Finance, Women's Suffrage, Religious and Scientific Improvement of Human Race; nominated for Presidency of US in 1872 by the Equal Rights Party; organised conventions for the discussion of social reform; carried on a continuous propagandist work in the interests of the working classes both in America and Europe for over 30 years. *Publications:* The Origin, Tendencies, and Principles of Government; Social Freedom; Garden of Eden Stirpiculture; Rapid Multiplication of the Unfit; The Human Body the Temple of God; Argument for Woman's Electoral Rights, etc. *Recreations:* scientific agriculture, psychical research, motoring, collecting works of art. *Address:* Bredon's Norton, near Tewkesbury, Worcestershire. *TA:* Bredon. *T:* 2 Bredon. *M:* AB 110. *Club:* Ladies' Automobile. *Died 9 June 1927.*

MARTIN, W. A. P., DD, LLD; ex-President of Imperial University, Peking; *b* Livonia, Indiana, 10 April 1827. *Educ:* Indiana State Univ.; Presbyterian Theol. Seminary. Arrived China, 1850; stationed as Missionary at Ningpo; went as Interpreter with US Minister, Reid, to Tientsin, where new treaties were made after storming of forts by British and French 1858; went with US Minister, Ward, to Peking; witnessed defeat of Allies at Taku, 1859; accompanied Mr Ward to Japan, then under Shogun; made President and Professor of International Law in Imperial College, Peking, 1867; held position 25 years, and resigned on account of health; appointed by Imperial Decree President of New University, 1898; in Siege in Peking, shut up eight weeks in HBM's Legation, 1900; President Viceroy's University, Wuchang, 1902–5. *Publications:* In Chinese—Evidences of Christianity; Natural Philosophy; Mathematical Physics; Mental Philosophy, with preface by Li Hung Chang; Translations of four Text-books of International Law, Wheaton, Woolsey, Bluntschli, and Hall. In English—A Cycle of Cathay; The Lore of Cathay; The Siege in Peking; Chinese Legends and other poems; The Awakening of China, 1907. *Recreation:* verse-making. *Address:* A. P. Mission, Peking, China. *Died 17 Dec. 1916.*

MARTIN, Sir William, Kt 1919; JP; FSAScot; *b* 24 Feb. 1856; *m* 1880, Helen Amelia Dyer; three *s* two *d*. *Educ:* Glasgow University. Hon. Representative Royal Humane Society; Member, Scottish National War Savings Committee; President of Toynbee House, Glasgow; Hon. Vice-President, National Citizens Council; Vice-Chairman Westerton Garden Suburb. *Recreations:* literature, walking. *Address:* 24 Atholl Gardens, Kelvinside, Glasgow. *T:* Douglas 3440; Oakvale, Hunter's Quay, Argyll. *Club:* Liberal, Glasgow.
Died 13 Sept. 1924.

MARTIN-LEAKE, Vice-Adm. Francis, CB 1922; DSO 1917; RN (retired); *s* of late Stephen Martin Leake of Thorpe Hall, Essex, and Marshalls, Ware, Herts; *b* 1869; unmarried. Served European War, 1914–19; commanded cruiser Pathfinder, 1914 and Achilles in Grand Fleet, 1915–17; Chief of Staff to Admiral Commanding at Queenstown, 1918–19; Rear-Admiral retired, 1921; Vice-Adm. retired, 1926. *Address:* Marshalls, Ware, Herts. *M:* NK3229. *Club:* United Service. *Died 21 Jan. 1928.*

MARTINEAU, George, CB 1902; *b* 24 Sept. 1835; *s* of George Martineau of Tulse Hill; *m* 1861, Ida, *d* of late Major Roderick Mackenzie of Kincraig; three *s* one *d*. *Educ:* University College, London. Adviser to British Delegates at International Conferences on Sugar Bounties, Brussels, 1875, 1898, 1902 and Paris 1876, 1877; Assistant British Delegate to International Sugar Commission, 1903–5. *Publications:* Free Trade in Sugar, 1889; The Statistical Aspect of the Sugar Question, 1899; The Brussels Sugar Convention, 1904; Sugar: Cane and Beet, 1917; A Short History of Sugar, 1856–1916, a Warning; Sugar from several Points of View, 1918; magazine articles. *Address:* Gomshall Lodge, Gomshall, Surrey.
Died 5 Feb. 1919.

MARTYN, Edward; dramatist; *b* Masonbrook, Co. Galway, 31 Jan. 1859; *e s* of late John Martyn, JP of Tulira, Co. Galway, and late Anne, *d* of late James Smyth, JP, of Masonbrook. *Educ:* Belvedere, Dublin; Beaumont, Windsor; Christ Church, Oxford; chiefly self-educated; a Catholic and Nationalist. One of the original founders of the Irish Dramatic Movement in 1899; Founder of the Palestrina Choir of men and boys at Dublin for the reform of liturgical music, in same year, which in 1903 became the Schola Cantorum of that Archdiocese; organised a reform of church architecture, stained glass, etc, 1903; was President of Sinn Fein from 1904 until he resigned in 1908; founded at Dublin, 1914, The Irish Theatre, for the production of native non-peasant plays, plays in the Irish language, and translations of Continental master dramas; promoter of Gaelic League and other educational improvements for Ireland; a Governor of the Galway College of the National University. *Publications:* Morgante the Lesser; Preface to Robert Elliot's Art and Ireland; Ireland's Battle for her Language; the following plays—The Heather Field, 2 acts; Maeve, 2 acts; The Tale of a Town, 5 acts; The Placehunters, 1 act; Romulus and Remus, 1 act; Grangecolman, 3 acts; The Dream Physician, 5 acts; The Privilege of Place, 3 acts; Regina Eyre, 4 acts; poems; many articles on Art, Politics, etc. *Recreation:* Mr George Augustus Moore. *Address:* Tulira, Ardrahan, Co. Galway; 15 Leinster Street South, Dublin. *M:* IM262. *Club:* Kildare Street, Dublin.
Died 5 Dec. 1923.

MARZBAN, Jehangier B., CIE 1920; JP; proprietor of the Jame Jamshed, the leading Anglo-Vernacular daily of Bombay (30 years); *b* Bombay, 1848; grandfather was the first founder of Vernacular Journalism (128 years ago) in the Presidency; *m*; three *s* two *d*. *Educ:* Elphinstone College, Bombay. Assistant Manager of the Times of India (7 years); Manager of the Bombay Gazette (9 years); proprietor Advocate of India (5 years); late Chairman Consumption Home at Deolali. *Publications:* thirty books on travels, wit and humour, and fiction. *Address:* Jame Jamshed Printing Works, Bombay, India.
Died Dec. 1928.

MASEFIELD, Col Robert Taylor, CB 1897; JP, DL, Salop; *b* Ellerton Hall, Newport, Shropshire, 1839; *e s* of late Robert Masefield, Ellerton Hall; *m* 1864, Emily, *d* of T. Rylands of Banshee House, Newport,

Salop. *Educ:* privately. Joined 31st Regt, 1860; served Chinese War, 1860–62 (medal and clasp); occupation of Pekin (medal and clasp); Lt-Col commanding 2nd Volunteer Batt. King's Shropshire Light Infantry, 1876–1904; Hon. Col 1904. *Recreations:* all country sports. *Address:* Springhayes, Woodbury, S Devon.

Died 1 Nov. 1922.

MASHAM, 2nd Baron, *cr* 1891; **Samuel Cunliffe-Lister,** JP; (title taken from the town of Masham, chiefly his property); *b* 2nd Aug. 1857; *s* of 1st Baron and Anne, *d* of John Dearden, Hollins Hall, Halifax; *S* father, 1906. *Educ:* Harrow; Oxford University. Protestant. Conservative. Possessed some first-class pictures—Gainsborough, Sir Joshua Reynolds, Romney, etc. Owner of about 24,000 acres; Manningham Mills (chief shareholder). *Heir: b* Hon. John Cunliffe-Lister, *b* 9 Aug. 1867. *Address:* Swinton, Masham, Yorks.

Died 24 Jan. 1917.

MASHAM, 3rd Baron, *cr* 1891; **John Cunliffe-Lister;** *b* 9 Aug. 1867; *s* of 1st Baron and Anne, *d* of John Dearden, Hollins Hall, Halifax; *S* brother, 1917; *m* 1906, Elizabeth Alice, *d* of W. R. Brockton. Protestant. Conservative. Possessed some first-class pictures—Gainsborough, Sir Joshua Reynolds, Romney, etc. Owner of about 24,000 acres; Manningham Mills (chief shareholder). *Heir:* none. *Address:* Swinton, Masham, Yorks.

Died 4 Jan. 1924 (ext).

MASHAM, William George, ISO 1904; late first-class clerk, Board of Education; *b* 1843. *Address:* 70 Norwood Hill, SE.

Died 14 Feb. 1916.

MASHITER, Col Sir George Coope, (formerly Helme), KCB 1909 (CB 1898); CMG 1900; *b* Warley Lodge, Essex, 25 Nov. 1843; 2nd *s* of Thomas Mashiter (*ne* Helme) of Manor House, Little Bookham, Surrey and Hornchurch Lodge, Essex; *m* 1874, Florence Sophia, 2nd *d* of Rev. J. Pearson of East Horneon, Essex. *Educ:* Winchester; Sandhurst. Joined 10th Foot, 1862; Captain, 1876; Major, 1881; exchanged to Wiltshire Regiment, 1883; Lt-Col half-pay, 1888; retired, 1889; Jubilee Decoration, 1897; served South Africa, in command of 6th Batt. Middlesex Regt, 1900–2 (despatches, Queen's medal with clasp, King's medal 2 clasps, CMG); Lt-Col, retired pay, from 1889; Lt-Colonel (and Hon. Colonel) commanding 6th Battalion Duke of Cambridge's Own Middlesex Regt 1889–1904; Colonel commanding West Yorkshire Vol. Inf. Brigade, 1906–7; Colonel commanding 1st West Riding Brigade, Territorial Force, 1907–9; Hon. Col 6th Batt. West Yorkshire Regt from 1907; Hon. Col 6th Batt. Middlesex Regt since 1921; JP, DL Wilts. *Recreations:* hunting, shooting. *Address:* Rowden Lodge, Chippenham, Wilts. *T:* Chippenham 78. *Club:* Naval and Military.

Died 11 Aug. 1927.

MASKELYNE, John Nevil; Lessee of St George's Hall, London; *b* Cheltenham, 22 Dec. 1839; *s* of John Nevil and Harriett Maskelyne of Cheltenham; *m* 1861, Elizabeth (*d* 1911); two *s* one *d*. *Educ:* Cheltenham. Appeared as conjurer at age 16; exposed Davenport Brothers' Cabinet and Dark Seance, 1865; first appeared London, 1873; at Egyptian Hall, Piccadilly, to 1904. *Publications:* Modern Spiritualism; Sharps and Flats; The Supernatural?; etc. *Recreations:* music, hill-climbing. *Address:* St George's Hall, Langham Place, W. *TA:* Maskelyne, London. *T:* 1545 Mayfair. *Clubs:* Junior Constitutional, Aero. *Died 18 May 1917.*

MASON, Alfred John, ISO 1903; Superintendent of Deposit, Reference and Binding Department, Local Government Board, 1866–1913; *b* 26 May 1853; *s* of late Charles Mason; *m* 1874, Alice Sophia, *d* of William and Sophia Fernes.

Died 5 Sept. 1918.

MASON, Rev. Arthur James, DD; *b* 4 May 1851; 3rd *s* of G. W. Mason, Morton Hall, Notts; *m* 1899, Margaret, *d* of late Rev. G. J. Blore, DD; two *s* one *d*. *Educ:* Repton School; Trinity College, Cambridge. Fellow of Trinity College, 1873–84; Assistant Tutor, 1874–77; Canon of Truro, 1877–84; Vicar of All Hallows, Barking, 1884–95; Fellow of Jesus College, 1896–1903; Lady Margaret Professor of Divinity, Cambridge University, 1895–1903; Hon. Fellow of Jesus College, 1909; Vice-Chancellor, Cambridge, 1908; Master of Pembroke College, Cambridge, 1903–12; Hon. Fellow since 1912; Canon of Canterbury since 1895; Hon. Chaplain to HM. *Publications:* The Persecution of Diocletian, 1875; Commentary on Thessalonians and 1st Epistle of St Peter, 1879; The Faith of the Gospel, 1887; The Relation of Confirmation to Baptism, 1893; The Conditions of our Lord's Life upon Earth, 1896; Thomas Cranmer, 1898; Historic Martyrs of the Primitive Church, 1905; Memoir of

Bishop Wilkinson, 1909; Memoir of Bishop Collins, 1912; The Church of England and Episcopacy, 1914; What Became of the Bones of St Thomas, 1920; edited the Five Theological Orations of Gregory of Nazianzus; History of the Papacy in the 19th Century, by Bishop Nielsen. *Address:* The Precincts, Canterbury.

Died 24 April 1928.

MASON, Hon. Sir Arthur Wier, Kt 1922; Puisne Judge, Supreme Court, Transvaal, 1902; Judge President since 1923; *b* 1860; *s* of Rev. Frederick and Maria Mason of Durban; *m* 1890, Ellen Lavinia (*d* 1912), *d* of John Harwin of Maritzburg; one *s* one *d*. *Educ:* New Kingswood School, Bath; New College, Eastbourne. BA(Lond.). Admitted to Bar in Natal as Solicitor, 1881, and as Advocate from 1884; a Puisne Judge of the Supreme Court, Natal, 1896; Commissioner of the Special Court (for treason cases), 1900; and President, 1901; Delimitation Commissioner, 1919; Chairman, 1923. *Address:* Supreme Court, Pretoria. *T:* 238.

Died 8 June 1924.

MASON, Charlotte Maria Shaw; Principal of the House of Education, Ambleside; Director of the Parents' Union School; Editor of the Parents' Review; *b* Bangor, 1 Jan. 1842; *d* of Joshua Mason, merchant, Liverpool; spinster; churchwoman. *Educ:* home. After a short training and some experience in schools of various grades, and in a Training College (Chichester), perceived certain principles leading to a reformed theory and practice of education; to further such reform, wrote several volumes; lectured; founded the Parents' National Education Union, 1887; the House of Education, 1891; the Parents' Union School, 1891; the Parents' Review, 1890, etc; lived to see a pretty wide adoption of her principles and methods in Elementary Schools, Secondary Schools, and home schoolrooms. *Publications:* Home Education; Parents and Children; School Education; Some Studies in the Formation of Character; Ourselves; The Forty Shires; The Ambleside Geography Books (vols i, ii, iii, iv, v), (revised and brought up to date 1922); The Saviour of the World (a Life of Christ in verse): vol. i, The Holy Infancy; vol. ii, His Dominion; vol. iii, The Kingdom of Heaven; vol. iv, The Bread of Life; vol. v, The Great Controversy, vol. vi, The Training of the Disciples; The Basis of National Strength (series of Letters to The Times) and A Liberal Education for All (three pamphlets, dealing with Elementary, Continuation and Secondary Schools); articles in magazines. *Recreations:* reading, driving. *Address:* Scale How, Ambleside. *Died 16 Jan. 1923.*

MASON, Rev. Edmund Robert, MA (Oxon); Hon. Canon of Ely Cathedral; 2nd *s* of Henry Mason and Isabella Russell of Deptford; *m* 1883, Lilly Marian Williams, *e d* of Ebenezer R. Williams of Handsworth; two *s* one *d*. *Educ:* privately; Queen's College, Oxford (BA, 3rd Class Theological School). Ordained, 1871; Curate of St George's, Edgbaston, Birmingham, 1871–76; Association Secretary of the Church Missionary Society, 1876–81; Vicar of Christ Church, Birmingham, 1881–88; Prebendary of Lichfield Cathedral, 1881–88; Commissary to Bishop of Sierra Leone, 1883–97; Vicar of Oxton, Notts, 1888–97; Vicar of Luton, Beds, 1897–1910; Rural Dean, 1905–10; Chaplain to the High Sheriff of Bedfordshire, 1907; Select Preacher, Cambridge, 1911–12. *Publications:* sermons and papers, chiefly on missionary subjects, contributed to the press. *Address:* Foxley, Barton Road, Cambridge.

Died 6 July 1922.

MASON, Rev. George Edward; *b* 20 Oct. 1847; *s* of George William Mason of Morton Hall, Retford; unmarried. *Educ:* Repton; Trinity College, Cambridge. Curate at St John's, Red Lion Square, London; then presented by late Duke of Portland to living of Whitwell, Derbyshire; resigned the living after having held it for 34 years, 1908; resigned at same time Hon. Canonry of Southwell Cathedral; Principal of St Bede's College, Umtata, Cape Colony, 1908; resigned, 1920. Long Service Medal (King Edward) as Hon. Chaplain to the 4th Battalion Notts and Derbyshire Regiment. *Publications:* Round the Round World on a Church Mission; Claudia, the Christian Martyr.

Died 30 March 1928.

MASON, Lt-Col James Cooper, DSO 1900; banker; Commanding 10th Regiment Royal Grenadiers Militia of Canada; *b* Toronto, 11 Jan. 1875; *e s* of late Brig.-Gen. Hon. James Mason, Senator; *m* 1904, Jean Florence, *d* of late Alexander MacArthur. *Educ:* Toronto Collegiate Institute. Served as Lieut and Capt. Royal Canadian Regt, South Africa, 1899–1900 (severely wounded) (despatches, brevet of Major, DSO, medal and three clasps). *Address:* 268 St George Street, Toronto, Canada. *Clubs:* Royal Canadian Yacht; Scarborough Golf.

Died 6 Aug. 1923.

MASON, Robert, JP; MP (Co.L), Wansbeck Division of Northumberland, 1918–22; Alderman, Northumberland; b Belford, Northumberland, 17 Dec. 1857; m 1884, Rosa Elizabeth Thompson; two s three d. Address: Marden House, Whitley Bay, Northumberland. T: Whitley Bay 83. M: TY7 and TY8. Clubs: National Liberal; Liberal, Union, Pen and Palette, Newcastle-upon-Tyne.
Died 1 Aug. 1927.

MASON, Sir Thomas, Kt 1909; JP, DL County of City of Glasgow; AICE London. Deacon Convener of the City of Glasgow, 1889–90; Dean of Guild of the City of Glasgow, 1906–8; President of the Incorporated Old Men and Women's Home; Chairman of the Clyde Navigation Trust; Chairman of the General Board of Control for Scotland; Caledonian Canal Commissioner. Address: Craigie Hall, Bellahouston, Glasgow.
Died 26 April 1924.

MASPERO, Sir Gaston Camille Charles, Hon. KCMG 1909; Egyptologist; b Paris, 1846; m 1st, 1871, Harriet Yapp; 2nd, 1880, Louise d'Estournelles Constant de Rebecque; two s one d. Educ: Lycée Louis-le-Grand; Ecole normale, Paris. Professeur d'Egyptologie Ecole des Hautes Etudes, 1869; Docteur ès Lettres, 1873; Professor of Egyptian Philology and Archæology, Coll. of France, 1874; Director of the Boulaq Museum, succeeding Mariette Bey, 1881–86; Académie des Inscriptions, 1883; Director of Excavations, Egypt, 1899–1914; Secrétaire perpétuel Académie des Inscriptions, 1914; Hon. Fellow Queen's College, and Hon. DCL Oxford, 1887. Publications: in English—Egyptian Archæology, 1889; Life in Ancient Egypt and Assyria, 1891; Dawn of Civilisation, 1894; The Struggle of the Nations, 1896; The Passing of the Empires, 1900; New Light on Ancient Egypt, 1908; Egypt, Ancient Sites and Modern Scenes, 1910; Art in Egypt, 1912. Address: Palais Mazarin, 25 Quai Conti, Paris; Le Pavillon, Milon-la-Chapelle, Seine-et-Oise.
Died 30 June 1916.

MASSEY, Rev. Edwyn Reynolds, MA; Rural Dean of Claydon, 1893; Hon. Canon of Christ Church, 1915; Surrogate for Buckinghamshire Archdeaconry; b 28 April 1847; 3rd s of Rev. Thomas Massey, Rector of Hatcliffe, Lincs; m 1879, Jessie Margaret Hawkins; four s three d. Educ: Newark-on-Trent; Exeter College, Oxford (Exhibitioner). 1st Class Mods; BA 1870; MA 1872. Deacon, 1871; Priest, 1872; Curate of Summertown, 1871–74; Vice-Principal of Lichfield Theological College, 1874–80; Tyrrell Diocesan Chaplain, 1876–79; Vicar of Merton, Oxon, 1880–93; Diocesan Inspector of Schools, 1888–93; Rector of Marsh Gibbon, Bucks, 1893; Editorial Secretary of Oxfordshire Archæological Society, 1905–11. Publications: contributor to Revised Marginal References to the Revised Version of the Bible, 1898; various articles in magazines, etc. Recreations: bowls, cycling, archæology.
Died 19 Sept. 1923.

MASSEY, Rev. John Cooke, MA; Rector of Risley, Derbyshire, 1892–1927; b 1 Feb. 1842; 2nd s of Rev. Thomas Massey, Rector of Hatcliffe, Lincs; m 1869, Elizabeth, 2nd d of Andrew Irwin; one s five d. Educ: Pocklington Grammar School; Exeter College, Oxford. Lieutenant in King's Own Staffordshire Regiment, 1862–66; ordained, 1866; Curate of Rugeley, Staffordshire, 1866–69; South Normanton, Derbyshire, 1869–71; Rector, 1871–92; Rural Dean of Alfreton, 1883–92; Ilkeston, 1899–1909; Hon. Canon of Southwell Cathedral, 1885; Hon. Diocesan Inspector of Schools in Religious Knowledge; late Chairman of Southwell Diocesan Sunday School Committee; Editor of Southwell Diocesan Magazine, 1894–1901. Publications: several sermons, etc; articles for Press. Recreation: cycling. Address: Chislehurst, 37 Marlborough Road, Bournemouth West, Hants.
Died 21 Aug. 1928.

MASSEY, Rt. Hon. William Ferguson, PC 1914; Hon. LLD Edinburgh, 1917; Member for Franklin, New Zealand Parliament, from 1896 (C, 1896–1904, Reform Party since 1904); Prime Minister of New Zealand since 1912; b Limavady, Co. Derry, 26 March 1856; s of John Massey and Marian Ferguson; m 1882, Christina, CBE, e d of Walter Paul, Auckland, NZ; three s two d. Educ: public school and secondary schools at Londonderry. Went out to New Zealand, 1870, to join his parents, who had emigrated with the Nonconformist settlers, 1862; followed farming pursuits, and eventually settled at Mangere, near Auckland; was early associated with Local Government, and at different times held positions of Member of Road Board, Chairman of School Committee, President of Auckland Agricultural and Pastoral Association, President of Farmers' Club, etc; entered New Zealand Parliament as Member (C) for Waitemata, 1894; Chief Opposition Whip, 1895; Leader of the Opposition, 1903; held office as Minister of Finance, Railways, Lands, Labour, Agriculture, Industries and Commerce; a Representative of New

Zealand at Imperial War Cabinet and Conference, 1917–18; at Plenipotentiary Peace Conference, Paris, 1919; at Imperial Conference, 1921; and at Imperial and Economic Conferences, 1923; Grand Officer Legion of Honour, France; Grand Officer of the Order of the Crown of Belgium. Publications: pamphlets and miscellaneous articles. Recreations: general interest in all sport. Address: Wellington, New Zealand. TA: Wellington. Clubs: Northern, Auckland, Auckland; Wellington, Wellington.
Died 10 May 1925.

MASSIE, John, MA; Hon. DD (Yale); JP County of Oxford; MP (L) Cricklade Division, Wiltshire, 1906–10; Yates Professor of New Testament Exegesis, Mansfield College, Oxford, 1886–1903; b 3 Dec. 1842; e s of Rev. R. Massie, Newton-le-Willows; m 1876, Edith Mary, 2nd d of late Alexander Ogilvie, 4 Great George Street, SW, and Sizewell House, Suffolk. Educ: Atherstone Grammar School; St John's Coll., Cambridge (Scholar); Corpus Christi Coll., Oxford (incorporated, 1886). Classical Prof., Spring Hill Theological College, Birmingham, 1869–86; also Prof. of New Testament Exegesis, 1871–86; Councillor and Alderman of Leamington, 1878–87; Vice-Chairman of Council of Leamington High School for Girls since 1890; Assistant Commissioner to Royal Commission on Secondary Education, 1894; Member of Executive of National Liberal Federation, 1894–1906 and since 1910; Treasurer, 1903–6; President of Liberation Society; President of Oxford and District Free Church Council 1896–1921; Member of Council and Education Board of Mansfield College; President National Education Association, and of Body of Protestant Dissenting Deputies; Chairman of Council, 1918–21, and Chairman of Education Committee, Congregational Union; Chairman of Oxfordshire Committee under War Pensions Act, 1916–21; and of Higher Education Sub-Committee of Oxfordshire County Council. Publications: contributions to Hastings' Dictionary of the Bible, Cheyne's Encyclopædia Biblica, and other theological publications; commentary on I and II Corinthians in Century Bible, 1902; articles on educational and other subjects in various reviews and magazines; pamphlets on Drift towards Dogmatic Teaching in Schools, 1893; Clericalism and Primary Education, 1895; The Proposed University for Roman Catholics in Ireland, 1899; etc. Recreations: outdoor games, fly-fishing, music. Address: Charlton Lea, Old Headington, Oxford. TA: Headington. T: 10 Oxford. Clubs: Reform, National Liberal.
Died 11 Nov. 1925.

MASSIE, Brig.-Gen. Roger Henry, CB 1919; CMG 1919; b 2 July 1869; e and o surv. s of Edward Massie, of Coddington, Cheshire; m 1902, Cecil Dorothea, e d of late Maurice J. Hall, of The Willows, Middleburg, Cape Colony; one s two d. Educ: Stubbington House, Fareham; Royal Military Academy, Woolwich. Commissioned in RA 1888; served Soudan, 1896; Indian Frontier and Tirah, 1897–98; S Africa, 1899–1902; Staff-Capt. DAAG (Intelligence) and DAQMG, S Africa, 1901–5; France and Belgium, 1916–18; CRA Portsmouth, 1919–20; Brig.-Gen. commanding Heavy Artillery, Canadian Corps, BEF, 1917–18; commanded Royal Garrison Artillery, Western Command, 1920–22; retired pay, 1922. Address: Wick Vale, Finchampstead, Berks. T: Eversley 59. Club: Army and Navy.
Died 23 Feb. 1927.

MASSINGBERD, Stephen Langton, JP; DL; Lord of Manor of Gunby and Patron of Welton-cum-Gunby, Lincolnshire; b 12 May 1869; o s of late Edmund Langton and Emily (d 1897), e d and heiress of late Charles Langton Massingberd; m 1895, Margaret (d 1906), 2nd d of Vernon Lushington, KC, 36 Kensington Square, W; no c. Educ: Charterhouse; Trinity College, Cambridge (History Tripos, 1891). Assistant Secretary to the Royal Statistical Society of London, and Editor of the Society's Journal, 1895–98; Member of the Lindsey County Council from 1904; Alderman, 1922; Vice-Chairman Spilsby Board of Guardians from 1908; Chairman from 1914; late Major 3rd Batt. the Lincolnshire Regt; served in South Africa, 1902, and in France 1916–18 (despatches). Address: Gunby Hall, Burgh, Lincolnshire. M: BE 908.
Died 21 May 1925.

MASSINGHAM, Henry William; journalist; b Old Catton, Norwich, 25 May 1860; s of Joseph Massingham, Norwich, and Marianne Riches; m 1st, 1887, Emma Jane (d 1905), d of late Henry Snowdon of Norwich; five s one d; 2nd, 1907, Ellen, d of the same. Educ: Norwich Grammar School, under Dr Jessopp. On staff of Norfolk News and Daily Press, Norwich; subsequently editor of National Press Agency; assistant editor and editor of the Star; literary editor, special Parliamentary representative, assistant editor, and editor of the Daily Chronicle; special Parliamentary representative of the Daily News; editor of the Nation, 1907–23; Commander of the Order of the Redeemer (Greece). Publications: The London Daily Press (articles for Leisure Hour), 1892; introduction to Labour and Protection (symposium), 1903; to Winston Churchill's Liberalism and the Social Problem, 1909; and to Works of Mark Rutherford, 1923; many articles in the magazines. *Recreation:* travel. *Address:* 21 Bedford Square, WC1.

Died 28 Aug. 1924.

MASSON, Frederic; ci-devant Bibliothécaire au Ministère des Affaires Etrangères, destitué en 1880; Secrétaire perpetuel de l'Académie Française; Fondateur de l'Assistance Mutuelle des Veuves, de la Guerre; Président de la Maison Chinoise; Administrateur de l'Hôpital de l'Institut (Fondation Dosne, Hôtel Thiers); *b* Paris, 1847; *m* M. Cottin. *Publications:* Napoléon et les Femmes; Napoléon chez lui, 1894; Cavaliers de Napoléon; Josephine Imperatrice, 1898; Napoléon et sa Famille, 1897-1912; Napoléon et son Fils, 1908, etc. *Address:* 15 rue de la Baume, Paris; Clos des Fées, Asnières-sur-Oise, Seine-et-Oise.

Died 19 Feb. 1923.

MASSON, John, MA, LLD; Senior Classical Lecturer in Edinburgh Provincial College; *s* of Rev. John Masson, of Dundee. *Educ:* Dundee High School; Universities of St Andrews, Leipzig, Berlin, and Paris. Rector of Waid Academy, Anstruther; Examiner in Classics in St Andrews University; Classical Lecturer in University College, Dundee. *Publications:* collaborated in Professor Lewis Campbell's large edition of Sophocles, to which he contributed a chapter on The Manuscripts of Sophocles; Book on the Atomic Theory of Lucretius, 1884; Lucretius, Epicurean and Poet, 1907-9; Selections from the Georgics, 1921; articles on Lucretius and Sophocles in British Quarterly Review, Journal of Philology, Classical Review, and Quarterly Review (Jan. 1897, on "Epicurus and his Sayings"; articles on classical literature in Chambers's Encyclopædia. *Recreations:* walking, fly-fishing. *Address:* 123 Mayfield Road, Edinburgh.

Died 17 Dec. 1927.

MASSY, 7th Baron, *cr* 1776; **Hugh Somerset John Massy;** *b* 15 Feb. 1864; *s* of 6th Baron and Lady Lucy Maria Butler (*d* 1896), *d* of 3rd Earl of Carrick; *S* father, 1915; *m* 1886, Ellen Ida Constance (*d* 1922), *d* of Charles William Wise, Rochestown, Tipperary; two *s* three *d* (and one *d* decd). *Heir: s* Hon. Hugh Hamon Charles George Massy [*b* 13 July 1894; *m* 1919, Margaret, *d* of late Richard Leonard of Meadsbrook, Ashbourne, Co. Limerick, and *widow* of Dr Moran, Tara, Co. Meath; one *s*]. *Address:* Killakee, Rathfarnham, Co. Dublin. *TA:* Rathfarnham.

Died 20 Oct. 1926.

MASSY, Col Harry Stanley, CB 1903; late Commandant 19th Bengal Lancers and Assistant Adjutant-General; *b* 12 July 1855; 3rd *s* of late Major Henry William Massy of Grantstown Hall, Tipperary; *m* 1894, Geraldine Aileen, *d* of George Massy of Glenville, Limerick; one *s* one *d*. Entered army, 1874; Capt. 1885; Major, 1894; Lieut-Col 1900; served against Jowaki Afreedees, 1877-78 (medal with clasp); Afghan War, 1878-80 (wounded, medal with clasp, despatches); Burmah, 1886-88 (despatches, clasp); 2nd Miranzai Expedition, 1891 (clasp); NWF India, 1897-98 (despatches, medal with two clasps). *Recreation:* aviation. *Address:* Grantstown Hall, Tipperary. *T:* Richmond 1554.

Died 10 Oct. 1920.

MASSY-BERESFORD, John George; JP Peeblesshire and Fermanagh; DL; *b* 7 Feb. 1856; *s* of Very Rev. J. M. Massy-Beresford, Dean of Kilmore, and Emily Sarah Massy-Beresford of Macbichill; *m* 1892, Hon. Alice Elizabeth Mulholland, *y d* of 1st Baron Dunleath and Frances Louisa, *d* of Hugh Lyle; two *s* one *d*. *Educ:* Malvern; Jesus Coll., Cambridge (BA 1879). High Sheriff, Co. Fermanagh, 1900; served in Lanarkshire Yeomanry Cavalry, 1876-84; British Red Cross in France, 1915-16. *Recreations:* hunting, yachting, shooting, fishing. *Address:* St Hubert's, Belturbet, Ireland. *TA:* Belturbet. *M:* IL6. *Clubs:* Royal Automobile; Royal St George Yacht, Kingstown.

Died 27 July 1923.

MASTERMAN, Rt. Hon. Charles Frederick Gurney, PC 1912; MA; MP (L) Rusholme Division of Manchester, 1923-24; *b* 25 Oct. 1873; 4th *s* of late Thomas William Masterman of Rotherfield Hall, Sussex, and Margaret Hanson, *d* of Thomas Gurney; *m* 1908, Lucy Blanche, *e d* of Rt Hon. Gen. Sir Neville Lyttelton; one *s* two *d*. *Educ:* Weymouth Coll.; Christ's College, Cambridge. First class in Natural Sciences Tripos, 1895; 1st class in Moral Sciences, 1896; President of the Union, 1896; Fellow of Christ's College, 1900; wrote for Nation, Athenæum etc; was Literary Editor Daily News; Sec., Children's Country Holiday Fund, London, 1900-3; Guardian of the Poor, Camberwell, 1901-4; Lecturer, Cambridge and London University Extension Societies; contested Dulwich as Liberal Candidate, 1903; Parliamentary Secretary Local Government Board, 1908-9; MP (L) West Ham (North), 1906; unseated on petition, 1911; MP (L) South West Bethnal Green, 1911-14; Under-Secretary of State, Home Department, 1909-12; Financial Secretary to Treasury,

1912-14; late Chairman of National Insurance Commission; Chancellor Duchy of Lancaster, 1914-15; Director of Wellington House (Propaganda Dept), 1914-18. *Publications:* Tennyson as a Religious Teacher, 1899; From the Abyss, 1902; In Peril of Change, 1905; F. D. Maurice, 1907; The Condition of England, 1909; The New Liberalism, 1920; How England is Governed, 1921; England after War, 1922; contributed to The Heart of the Empire (essays), 1901. *Address:* 46 Gillingham Street, SW1. *T:* 1036 Victoria. *Clubs:* Reform, National Liberal.

Died 17 Nov. 1927.

MASTERS, Rev. James Hoare; Canon Residentiary of Chichester Cathedral; Prebendary of Wisborough in Chichester Cathedral; Custos and Chaplain of St Mary's Hospital, Chichester; *s* of Captain Masters, RN, of Ryde, Isle of Wight; *m* 1859, Margaret, *d* of John Atkinson of Leeds, Solicitor; one *s*. *Educ:* Clapham Grammar School; Emmanuel College, Cambridge. Curate of Limpsfield, Surrey, and All Saints, Southampton; Vicar of Lower Beeding, Horsham, for 21½ years, 1861-83; Rector of Slinfold, Horsham, 1883-1902; Rural Dean for 30 years; Surrogate in the Diocese of Chichester. *Address:* The Close, Chichester. *Club:* Constitutional.

Died 6 Jan. 1918.

MASTERS, Rev. William Caldwall, MA; Rector of Stanton Fitzwarren, Wiltshire, 1885-1919; Hon. Canon of Bristol, 1912; *b* 1843; *s* of Rev. J. Smalman Masters (MA, Jesus College, Oxford; Incumbent of Christ Church, Shooter's Hill, Kent); *m* 1870, Ellen (*d* 1918), *sister* of J. Ashfordby-Trenchard, of Stanton Fitzwarren and of Nyn Park, Herts; two *s* one *d*. *Educ:* St Mary Magdalen College, Oxford. Curate of St Mary's, Hitchin, Herts, 1866-69; Vicar of Long Marston and Assistant Priest of Tring, Herts, 1870. *Publications:* Some Notes on the Ancient Church of St Leonard, Stanton Fitzwarren, and otherwise, dedicated to the Lord Bishop of Bristol, Dr G. Forrest Browne; Two Addresses, etc, dedicated to the same; Christian Architecture; The Soldier and the Cross, an address at the dedication of the Churchyard Soldier's Cross, Stanton Fitzwarren, Jan. 1916; In Memoriam, E. M., 1919. *Recreations:* literature, mediæval architecture, wood-carving and designing. *Address:* 29 York Gardens, Clifton, Bristol.

Died 19 Aug. 1924.

MATHER, Rt. Rev. Herbert, DD; Chancellor of Hereford Cathedral, 1906; *b* 1840; *m* 1872. *Educ:* Trinity Coll., Cambridge. Ordained Deacon, 1866; Priest, 1867; Vice-Principal Carmarthen Training College, 1865-67; Principal, 1867-68; Curate of Newland, 1868-70; Chaplain to Bishop of Newfoundland and Incumbent of St John's Cathedral, 1870-72; Chaplain to Bishop of Nova Scotia, 1872-73; Rector of All Saints, Huntingdon, 1874-77; Vicar of Loddington, 1877-93; Rural Dean of Gartree, 1886-89; Provost of St Andrew's Cathedral, Inverness, 1891-97; Bishop of Antigua, 1897-1904; Assistant Bishop to Bishop of Hereford, 1905-12; Rector, Hampton Bishop, Hereford, 1908-12; in charge of diocese of Accra, 1912-13. *Address:* Trevathan, Beckenham, Kent.

Died 30 July 1922.

MATHER, James Marshall; nonconformist minister; *b* Darlington, 9 May 1851; *s* of John Mather and Sarah, 2nd *d* of James Marshall, Darlington; *m* Helena, 2nd *d* of S. R. de Ville, Staffordshire; one *s* one *d*. *Educ:* Lincoln. Pupilled to a firm of architects, Lincoln, in which city his father was the minister of a large Nonconformist church; when out of his articles, studied for and entered same ministry, and lived since in Lancashire. *Publications:* Life and Teachings of John Ruskin (nine editions); Popular Studies in Nineteenth Century Poets; Lancashire Idylls; The Sign of the Wooden Shoon; By Roaring Loom; Rambles round Rossendale (2 series). *Recreations:* walking, the novels of Balzac. *Address:* 7 Granville Avenue, Broughton Park, Manchester.

Died May 1916.

MATHER, Rt. Hon. Sir William, Kt 1902; PC 1910; JP; MICE, MIMechE; *b* 1838; *s* of late William Mather, of Manchester, and Amelia, *d* of late James Tidswell, of Manchester; *m* 1863, Emma, *d* of Thomas Watson, of Highbury; one *s* four *d*. *Educ:* private schools, and in Germany. Late Chairman of Mather and Platt, Ltd; Manchester; established the system of 8 hours' day at Mather & Platt's, Ltd, Salford Works, in 1893; system continued at their Park Works; a Governor and member of Council of Owens College, and of Victoria University of Manchester; a Trustee of the Gordon College, Khartoum; interested himself largely in the question of cotton growing in the Sudan; Ex-Pres. of the British Science Guild; President of Textile Institute; member of the Royal Commission Exhibitions Branch, Board of Trade; investigated Technical Education in America and Russia for Royal Commission on Technical Instruction, 1883; engaged in promoting technical education for many years; Chairman of Froebel Educational Institute of London; Chairman of British Education

Section of Franco-British Exhibition, 1908; was member of the Committee appointed by the Minister of War in 1901 to report on the reorganisation of the War Office; a Liberal; MP S Div. of Salford, 1885–86; Gorton Div. of Lancashire, SE, 1889–95; Rossendale Div. of Lancashire, NE, 1900–4; Hon. LLD Princeton Univ., 1905; Victoria Univ. of Manchester, 1908. *Address:* Manchester; Bramble Hill, New Forest, Hampshire. *Clubs:* Reform, Brooks's, Devonshire.
Died 18 Sept. 1920.

MATHERS, Edward Peter; newspaper proprietor, editor, author; *b* Edinburgh, 19 Aug. 1850; *s* of late David Mathers, publisher, newspaper proprietor; *m* 1885, Mary Augusta, *d* of late Robert Horace Powys, *cousin* of 4th Baron Lilford; one *s* four *d*. *Educ:* High School, Edinburgh; Edinburgh Institution. English journalist till 1878; emigrated then to South Africa and held positions in the Press, founding and editing the Natal Advertiser; in early eighties travelled throughout Transvaal goldfields; wrote about them, being the only journalist who foretold their greatness; returned to England, 1888; founded his weekly paper, South Africa, and inaugurated annual South African dinners in London, being Chairman of Committee; Life Member of Royal Geographical Society and Royal Colonial Institute. *Publications:* Trip to Moodie's; Goldfields Revisited; Golden South Africa; South Africa and How to Reach it; Zambesia, England's El Dorado in Africa. *Recreation:* travel. *Address:* 10 Stanley Crescent, W11. *TA:* Eddies, London. *T:* Park 119. *Club:* Ranelagh.
Died 13 Oct. 1924.

MATHERS, Helen, (Mrs Henry Reeves); novelist; *b* Misterton, Crewkerne, Somerset, 26 Aug. 1853; 3rd *d* of late Thomas Mathews, Misterton, and Maria Buckingham; *m* Henry Albert Reeves (*d* 1914), orthopædic surgeon. *Educ:* Chantry School, Frome. *Publications:* Comin' thro' the Rye; Cherry Ripe; My Lady Greensleeves; Sam's Sweetheart; Story of a Sin; Eyre's Acquittal; A Man of To-Day; The Lovely Malincourt; The Sin of Hagar; Venus Victrix; Murder or Manslaughter; Found Out; Blind Justice; Bam Wildfire; The Juggler and the Soul; Becky; Cinders; Honey; Griff of Griffiths Court; Side-Shows; The Ferryman; Tally Ho!; Pigskin and Petticoat; Gay Lawless; Love, the Thief. *Recreation:* needlework. *Club:* Ladies' Park.
Died 11 March 1920.

MATHERS, Hon. Thomas Graham; Chief Justice of the King's Bench, Manitoba, since 1910; *b* 1859; *s* of late Christopher Mathers and Rachel Graham, both of North of Ireland ancestry; *m* 1892, Jessie, *d* of late Richard Waugh, journalist; one *s* one *d*. *Educ:* Lucknow and Kincardine, Ont. Came to Manitoba, 1883; called to the Bar of Manitoba, 1889; Head of Law Department, Manitoba Government Railways, 1888–90; Puisne Judge of the King's Bench, 1905; Agent Minister of Justice for Manitoba and Counsel for the several departments of the Dominion Government, 1896–1905; Alderman of Winnipeg, 1898–99; Chairman Board of License Commissioners, 1899–1900; contested Mayoralty, 1900. *Recreations:* golf, shooting. *Address:* 16 Edmonton Street, Winnipeg, Man. *T:* 936 Main. *M:* 440. *Clubs:* Manitoba, Winnipeg; Brandon, Brandon; St Charles Country, St Charles.
Died 16 Aug. 1927.

MATHESON, Annie; *b* Blackheath, 1853; *d* of late Rev. James Matheson, of Nottingham. *Publications: poems:* As Months Go By; Religion of Humanity; Love's Music; Love Triumphant; Selected Poems; Snowflakes and Snowdrops; Roses and Loaves; Maytime Songs; Hal's Book; *prose:* Leaves of Prose; Story of a Brave Child (Joan of Arc); Florence Nightingale; A Plain Friend; Our Hero of the Golden Heart; editor and joint author of By Divers Paths; anthologist and editor of: Sayings from the Saints; A Little Book of Courage; Songs of Love and Praise; A Daybook for Girls; originator and editor of Rose and Dragon books, including Young Citizen series. *Club:* Lyceum.
Died 16 March 1924.

MATHESON, Charles Louis, KC (Ireland), 1891; MA; Recorder of Belfast and County Court Judge, Antrim, since 1919; *b* Dublin, 3 Feb. 1851; 2nd *s* of Robert N. Matheson, Clerk of the Privy Council, Ireland, and Victorine, *d* of Jean Phillipe Jossevel, Juge du Pays, of Moudon, Switzerland; *m* Elinor, *o d* of Charles Tuthill, Barrister-at-Law, of Newstead, Roebuck, Co. Dublin; two *s* three *d*. *Educ:* Rathmines School; Trinity Coll., Dublin (First Honours). Auditor of the College Historical Society, 1874; Irish Barrister, 1874; HM First Serjeant at Law in Ireland, 1913–19. *Address:* 62 Merrion Square, Dublin. *T:* Dublin 1550. *Club:* University, Dublin.
Died 20 May 1921.

MATHESON, Sir Kenneth (James), 2nd Bt, *cr* 1882; DL, JP; *b* London, 12 May 1854; *e s* of Sir Alexander Matheson, 1st Bt and 2nd wife, Lavinia Mary, *sister* of 8th Lord Beaumont; *S* father, 1886;

m 1913, Ada Juliana, *d* of late George E. B. Lousada, and *widow* of Daniel C. Stiebel. *Educ:* Harrow; Christ Church, Oxford. *Heir:* half-*brother* Alexander Percival Matheson [*b* 6 Feb. 1861; *m* 1884, Eleanor, *d* of late Rev. Kyrle Ernle Aubrey Money; four *d* (three *s* decd). *Address:* Anderun, Littlehampton. *Clubs:* National Liberal, Hurlingham]. *Address:* Follaton, Totnes, Devon; 43 Grosvenor Square, W1. *T:* Mayfair 6030; 19 Sussex Square, Brighton. *Club:* Carlton.
Died 25 Jan. 1920.

MATHESON, Rt. Hon. Sir Robert Edwin, Kt 1907; PC Ireland, 1910; LLD; Barrister-at-law; *b* 6 May 1845; *e s* of late R. N. Matheson, Clerk of the Privy Council for Ireland; *m* 1866, Cherrie M. Hardy (*d* 1918); one *s* four *d*. *Educ:* Rathmines; Trinity College, Dublin. Studied law at King's Inns, Dublin, and Middle Temple, London; called to the Irish Bar, 1875; Secretary General Register Office, Dublin, 1877; Assistant Registrar-General, 1879–1900; Registrar-General for Ireland, 1900–9; Commissioner of Irish Census, 1881, 1891, 1901; Hon. LLD Royal University, 1901; Examiner in Vital Statistics, etc, Dublin University, 1901–9; President Statistical Society of Ireland, 1905–6. *Publications:* Digest of the Irish Marriage Law; Varieties and Synonyms of Surnames and Christian Names in Ireland; Report on Surnames in Ireland; Insects, Fungi, and Weeds injurious to Farm Crops; Housing of People of Ireland, 1841–1901; Results of Census of 1901, etc. *Address:* 44 Belgrave Square, Monkstown, Co. Dublin.
Died 10 Jan. 1926.

MATHEW, Charles James, CBE 1917; KC 1913; MP (Lab) Whitechapel and St George's Division of Stepney, since 1922; Member London County Council (P) St George's in the East, 1910–19; Alderman since 1919; *b* 24 Oct. 1872; *y s* of late Rt Hon. Sir James Charles Matthew, Lord Justice of Appeal; *m* 1896, Anna, *d* of late James Archbold Cassidy of Monasterevan, Co. Kildare; two *s* one *d*. *Educ:* The Oratory School, Birmingham; Trinity Hall, Cambridge (BA). Called to the Bar, Lincoln's Inn, 1897; Bencher, Lincoln's Inn, 1918. *Address:* 75 Albert Hall Mansions, SW7. *T:* Kensington 5272; 10 Old Square, Lincoln's Inn, WC2. *T:* Holborn 1586. *Club:* Athenæum.
Died 8 Jan. 1923.

MATHEW, Frank; novelist and barrister-at-law; *b* Bombay, 1865; *s* of late Frank Mathew, CE; *nephew* of late Sir James Charles Mathew; *m* 1899, Agnes, *d* of James Tisdall Woodroffe, Advocate-General of Bengal; two *s*. *Educ:* Beaumont College; King's College School; London Univ. Inglis Scholarship, King's College, London, 1886; Stephen Endowment, 1887. *Publications:* Father Mathew: his Life and Times, 1890; At the Rising of the Moon; Irish Stories and Studies, 1893; The Wood of the Brambles, 1896; A Child in the Temple, 1897; The Spanish Wine, 1898; Defender of the Faith, 1899; One Queen Triumphant, 1899; Love of Comrades, 1900; The Royal Sisters, 1901; Ireland, 1905; An Image of Shakespeare, 1922. *Address:* 1 Hernes Road, Oxford.
Died 25 Oct. 1924.

MATHEWS, Sir Charles Willie, 1st Bt, *cr* 1917; KCB 1911; Kt 1907; Director of Public Prosecutions since 1908; Barrister-at-Law, Western Circuit; *b* New York, 16 Oct. 1850; *s* of William West and Elizabeth West, actress (stage name, Lizzie Weston); step *s* of late Charles James Mathews, the comedian, whose surname he assumed by deed poll; *m* 1888, Lucy, *d* of Lindsay Sloper; no *c*. *Educ:* Eton. Called to the Bar, Middle Temple, 1872; Bencher, 1901; joined Western Circuit; Junior Counsel to the Treasury at the Central Criminal Court, 1886; Senior Counsel, 1888; contested Winchester (GL), 1892; Recorder of Salisbury, 1893–1908; Hon. Member of the Jockey Club. *Heir:* none. *Address:* 88 Sloane Street, SW1. *Clubs:* Turf, Garrick, Beefsteak.
Died 6 Jan. 1920 (ext).

MATHEWS, George Ballard, MA; LLD Glasgow; FRS; *b* London, 23 Feb. 1861. *Educ:* Ludlow Grammar School; University College, London; University of Cambridge. Assistant-Lecturer in Pure Mathematics at the University College of N Wales, Bangor; Professor of Mathematics there, 1884–96; late Fellow of St John's College, Cambridge; Examiner in Mathematics for the Universities of Ireland (National) and Manchester. *Publications:* Theory of Numbers, part I; A Treatise on Bessel Functions (conjointly with Prof. A. Gray, FRS, LLD); Tract on Algebraic Equations; Projective Geometry; articles on Universal Algebra and on Number in the Encyclopædia Britannica; and various papers on mathematical subjects. *Address:* 7 Menai View Terrace, Bangor.
Died 19 March 1922.

MATHEWS, Rev. William Arnold, MA; Hon. Canon of Carlisle; *b* Hatfield, Yorkshire, 1839; *s* of William Mathews, MD, JP; *m* 1866, Caroline Sara Georgina, *d* of William H. Stuart of Lennoxville, Canada; five *s* four *d*. *Educ:* Uppingham; Corpus Christi College, Oxford. Ordained, by Bishop Jackson of Lincoln; Curate of St Peter's,

Old Radford, Nottingham, 1862; Vicar of Laughton, Lincolnshire, and a Diocesan Inspector of Schools, 1865; Vicar of Dacre, Cumberland, 1871; Rector of Skelton, Cumberland, and Rural Dean of Greystoke, 1877; Vicar of St Mary's, Carlisle, 1879; Appleby, 1883; Rural Dean of Appleby, 1886; Proctor in Convocation for the Archdeaconry of Carlisle; Rector of Bassingham, 1896–1913; Vicar of St Wendron, Helston, 1913–23. *Publications:* The National Church of a Christian Nation; Constitutional Church Reform, 1886; The Witness of the World to Christ, 1889. *Recreations:* fishing, carpentry. *Address:* 27 Rockliffe Road, Bath.

Died 28 Nov. 1925.

MATSUMURA, Jinzo, DSc; Hon. LLD (Aberdeen); Professor of Botany and Director of Botanic Gardens, Imperial University, Tokio; *b* 1856 (Samurai); *m* 1879; one *s*. *Educ:* began self-study in botany, 1877; Universities of Würzburg and Heidelberg, 1886–88. Assistant Professor, Imperial University, Tokio, 1883; Professor, 1890; retired, 1922. *Publications:* Nippon Shokubutsu mei-i, or Nomenclature of Japanese Plants in Latin, Japanese, and Chinese, 1884; Catalogue of Plants in the Herbarium of the College of Science, Imperial University, 1886; Names of Plants and their Products in English, Japanese, and Chinese, 1892; Ito and Matsumura—Tentamen Floræ Lutchuensis, 1899; Shokubutsu mei-i: Enumeration of selected scientific names of both native and foreign plants, with romanised Japanese names, and in many cases Chinese characters, 1900; Conspectus of the Leguminosæ found growing wild or cultivated in Japan, Loochoo, and Formosa, 1902; Revisio Alni Specierum Japonicarum, 1902; Index Plantarum Japonicarum sive Enumeratio Plantarum omnium ex insulis Kurile, Yezo, Nippon, Sikoku, Kiusiu, Liukiu, et Formosa hucusque cognitarum systematice et alphabetice dispositu: Cryptogamæ, 1904; Phanerogamæ, 1905; Matsumura and Hayata—Enumeratio Plantarum in insula Formosa sponte crescentium, 1906; Chinese Names of Plants, 1915; A Classified Etymological Vocabulary of the Japanese Language Ancient and Modern, 1915; An Etymological Vocabulary of the Yamato Language, 1921. *Address:* 16 Akebonocho, Hongo, Tokio, Japan.

Died 4 May 1928.

MATTHEW, Frederic David, Hon. DLitt Oxford; *b* 14 Oct. 1838; *m* 1874, Gertrude, *e d* of late Rev. J. W. v. R. Hoets; four *s* three *d*. *Educ:* King's College School. Co-founder with the late Dr Frederick James Furnival of the Wyclif Society. *Publications:* edited English Works of Wyclif for Early English Text Society, 1880; Life of John Wyclif, 1884. *Address:* 70 Belsize Park Gardens, NW.

Died 23 Jan. 1918.

MATTHEW, Reginald Walter, CMG 1921; Director in the Department of Overseas Trade; *b* 14 Sept. 1879; *e s* of late Walter E. Matthew, Archdeacon of Colombo; *m* 1908, Dorothy, *y d* of late George Chambers, of Clarendon Road, Holland Park. *Educ:* St Paul's School; Jesus College, Oxford. Entered War Office, 1903; transferred to Board of Trade, 1904; Secretary to Committee on Supply and Training of British Boy Sailors, 1906; Secretary, Merchant Shipping Advisory Committee, 1910–14; Secretary to British Delegation at International Conference on Unification of Maritime Law, Brussels, 1909, 1910, and 1912; Private Secretary to Mr Harold John Tennant, Parliamentary Secretary, Board of Trade, 1909–10; and to following Presidents—Mr Sydney Buxton, 1911–13; Mr John Burns, 1914; Mr Walter Runciman, 1914–16; Sir Albert Stanley, 1917; joined Department of Overseas Trade, Dec. 1917; Chevalier, Legion of Honour, 1918. *Recreation:* lawn tennis. *Address:* 21 Riverview Gardens, Castelnau, Barnes, SW13.

Died 8 Nov. 1928.

MATTHEWS, Col Godfrey Estcourt, CB 1911; CMG 1915; *b* 17 June 1866. Entered Royal Marines, 1884; Captain, 1894; Major, 1902; Lieut-Colonel, 1910; Col 1915; served in Nile Expedition, 1897 (medal with clasp), 1898 (despatches twice, brevet of Major, two clasps, medal), 1899 (clasp); employed with Egyptian army from 1907; served with Plymouth Batt., RN Division, in Gallipoli, 1915. *Club:* Naval and Military.

Died 13 April 1917.

MATTHEWS, Joseph Bridges, KC 1913; Recorder of Tewkesbury, 1912–23, and of Dudley from 1923; *s* of John Matthews, late of Worcester; *m* Florence Louisa, *e d* of Henry William Batson, late of Worcester; two *d*. *Educ:* Worcester Cathedral School. Solicitor at Worcester, 1884–95; Sheriff of Worcester, 1895–96; called to the Bar, Middle Temple, 1896; Bencher, 1924; Oxford Circuit; Bronze Medal Royal Humane Society. *Publications:* Law Relating to Married Women; Covenants in Restraint of Trade; Moneylending: joint editor of Pritchard's Quarter Sessions, 2nd edn; editor of Hayes and Jarman

on Wills, 12th and 13th edns. *Address:* Bickley Court, Kent; 2 Paper Buildings, Temple, EC4. *T:* Temple 57; Holborn 1835.

Died 5 Aug. 1928.

MATTHEWS, Col Valentine, CBE 1918; VD; MRCS, LSA; late Royal Army Medical Corps (Volunteers); late Temporary Lieutenant-Colonel in Army; organised arrangements for meeting, housing, feeding and transport of travelling soldiers on leave; late Senior Surgeon Westminster General Dispensary; Inspector of Rest Houses, London District; *b* 14 Feb. 1855; *s* of William Matthews; *m* Maude, *d* of J. H. Garlant; one *s*. *Educ:* St Paul's School; King's College, London. Medical Registrar, House Physician, and Assistant Demonstrator of Anatomy, King's College Hospital. First Jefe (Hon.) No 3 Ambulance, Cruz Roja, Madrid; Hon. Life Member St John Ambulance Association; late County Director Voluntary Aid Detachment, Territorial Force Association, County of London. *Publications:* (with Capt. J. Harper) Handbook for Volunteer Medical Officers; various communications to medical journals. *Recreations:* fishing, sculling, etc. *Address:* 29 Onslow Square, SW7. *T:* Kensington 225. *Club:* Reform.

Died 6 Oct. 1921.

MATTHEWS, Sir William, KCMG 1906 (CMG 1901); consulting engineer for harbour and dock works; *b* 8 March 1844; *s* of late John Matthews of Penzance, and Alice, *d* of Thomas Richards. *Educ:* privately in Cornwall. A civil engineer and a member of the firm of Coode, Matthews, Fitzmaurice & Wilson, consulting engineers for harbours to the Crown Agents for the Colonies; chief engineers of the National Harbour at Dover; consulting engineers for harbours and docks at Colombo, Singapore, and other ports; advisers on these and kindred subjects to the Admiralty, Board of Trade, and Colonial governments; consulting engineers to the Mersey Conservancy, the Humber Conservancy, the Tyne Commissioners; Member of a Committee appointed by the Admiralty in 1901 to inquire into the naval works at Gibraltar; appointed by the Admiralty in 1900 to report upon the Naval Harbour at Malta; Member of Royal Commission on Coast Erosion, 1906; of International Technical Commission on Suez Canal, 1908; of Royal Commission on Oil Fuel, 1912; MICE 1876; President, Institution of Civil Engineers, 1907; Officer of Order of Leopold (Belgium), 1894. *Address:* 14 Strathray Gardens, Hampstead, NW. *T:* 1939 Hampstead; 9 Victoria Street, Westminster, SW1. *TA:* Penlee, London. *T:* 47 Westminster. *Clubs:* Junior Carlton, St Stephen's.

Died 8 Jan. 1922.

MATTHEY, Col Edward, CB 1902; Lieutenant-Colonel and Hon. Colonel late London Rifle Brigade; *b* 1836; *s* of late John Matthey; *m* 1861. *Address:* 31a Weymouth Street, W. *TA:* Eked, London.

Died 21 Oct. 1918.

MATZ, Bertram Waldrom; publisher; Editor of The Dickensian; *b* London, 5 March 1865; *m*; one *s* two *d*. A Founder and President of the Dickens Fellowship, and its first Hon. Secretary, 1902–3; Editor of the National Edition of Dickens's Works; Dickens's Miscellaneous Papers, Plays, and Poems; first Editor of The Odd Volume. *Publications:* Charles Dickens: the Story of his Life and Writings; Thomas Carlyle: a brief Account of his Life and Work; The Dickens Birthday Book; The Humour of Pickwick; The Sayings of Sam Weller; The George Inn, Southwark; The Dickens Calendar; The Inns and Taverns of Pickwick; Dickensian Inns and Taverns; Character Sketches from Dickens; Dickens in Cartoon and Caricature, etc; the memorial edition of Forster's Life of Dickens; contributor to the Fortnightly Review, Bookman, Strand, and various magazines and newspapers on Dickens, Meredith and other subjects. *Address:* 29 Woodfield Avenue, Streatham, SW16.

Died 17 July 1925.

MAUDE, Ven. Charles Bulmer; Archdeacon of Salop, 1896–1917; *b* 1848; *s* of late Edmund Maude of Middleton, Yorks; *m* 1878, Geraldine *d* of late Alexander Donovan, JP, DL, of Framfield Place, Sussex. *Educ:* Exeter Coll., Oxford (MA). Vicar of S Cyprian, Kimberley, 1875–81; Wilnecote, 1881–86; Leek, 1886–96; S Chad's, Shrewsbury, 1896–1906. *Address:* The Castle, Ludlow. *TA:* Ludlow.

Died 11 May 1927.

MAUDE, Edith Caroline, CBE 1920; *b* 1865; *d* of late Major Henry Whitby Briscoe, RA, of Tinvane, Co. Tipperary; *m* 1894, Gerald Edward Maude (Barrister-at-law, and late Major 4th Battalion East Surrey Regiment), *s* of late Captain Hon. Francis Maude, RN and 2nd wife, Georgiana, *d* of Gervase Parker Bushe; one *s*. Secretary of the Shipwrecked Mariners' Society since 1896; Hon. Secretary Soldiers' and Sailors' Families' Association (Kennington and S Lambeth Branch), 1911–18; President since 1918 and Hon. Secretary (County of London Branch); Member of Council, Women's Holiday Fund, Association for the Welfare of the Blind; Chairman of Evelyn

Convalescent Cottage, Upper Wargrave, and of Committee of Royal Home for Soldiers' Daughters, Hampstead, etc. *Address:* 14 Cranley Place, SW7. *T:* Kensington 1610.

Died 6 Oct. 1922.

MAUDE, Lt-Gen. Sir Frederick Stanley, KCB 1916 (CB 1915); CMG 1901; DSO 1900; late Coldstream Guards; *b* 24 June 1864; *y s* of late Gen. Sir Frederick Francis Maude, VC, GCB, and Catherine Mary, *d* of Very Rev. Sir George Bisshopp, 8th Bt; *m* 1893, Cecil Cornelia Marianne St Leger, *d* of late Col Rt Hon. Thomas Edward Taylor, MP, of Ardgillan Castle, Co. Dublin; one *s* two *d. Educ:* Eton; Sandhurst. Entered army, 1884; Capt. 1896; Major, 1899; Lt-Colonel, 1907; Colonel, 1911; Maj.-Gen. and Divisional Commander, 1915; passed Staff College, 1896; served Soudan, including engagement at Hasheen, and destruction of Tamai, 1885 (medal with clasp, Khedive's star); Adjutant 1st Batt. Coldstream Guards, 1888–92; Brigade Major, Brigade of Guards, 1897–99; served South African War, 1899–1901, including advance on Kimberley; operations in the Orange Free State, actions at Poplar Grove, Driefontein, Karee Siding, Vet River and Zand River; and operations in the Transvaal, actions near Johannesburg, Pretoria, Diamond Hill and Belfast; operations in Cape Colony (despatches, Queen's medal with six clasps, DSO); Brigade Major, Guards Brigade, 1900–1; Military Secretary to Governor-General of Canada, 1901–4; Private Secretary to Secretary of State for War, 1905; DAA&QMG Plymouth, 1906–8; General Staff, 2nd London Division, Territorial Force, 1908–9; Assistant Director Territorial Force, War Office, 1909–12; Chief of General Staff, 5th Division, 1912–14; General Staff, War Office, 1914; Staff, 3rd Army Corps, 1914; Brig.-Gen. 1914, and commanding 14th Infantry Brigade; European War, 1914–15 (wounded, despatches seven times, CB); commanding 33rd Division, afterwards 13th Division, 1915; Temp. Lt-Gen. in command of Tigris Army Corps, July 1916; Commander-in-Chief in Mesopotamia, August 1916; Lt-Gen., Feb. 1917; Officer of the Crown of Italy, March 1917. *Address:* Mardale, Watford, Herts; 6 Lower Sloane Street, SW. *Club:* Guards'.

Died 18 Nov. 1917.

MAUDE, Isabel Winifred Maude Emery; *see* Emery, Winifred.

MAUDE, Major Ralph Walter, DSO 1919; Secretary, Guards' Club; *b* 1873; *y s* of Captain Charles Henry Maude and Hon. Georgiana Henrietta Emma, *d* of 2nd Baron Sudeley; *m* 1905, Alice (whom he divorced 1914), *d* of N. W. Thomson; one *s. Educ:* Charterhouse. Journalist from the age of twenty-one till outbreak of European war; for a long period closely associated with the late Charles Norris Williamson, journalist and author; contributor to most of the leading publications; joined Army 1914, and was first attached to 2/8th Gurkhas, with whom he served as interpreter throughout first year of war; afterwards sent to General Headquarters for instruction as Asst Paymaster under the later Commissioner of Police; subsequently Asst Paymaster, Bethune, Dieppe, Rouen, Amiens, and Cologne (DSO, French Croix de Guerre, despatches thrice). *Publication:* The Haymarket Theatre (with eldest brother, Cyril Maude). *Recreations:* the society of congenial companions, fishing. *Address:* Guards' Club, Brook Street, W1. *T:* Mayfair 870. *Club:* Junior Naval and Military.

Died 17 Jan. 1922.

MAUDSLAY, Walter Henry; *b* 23 Sept. 1844; *g s* of Henry Maudslay, engineer; *m* 1st, 1869, Emily (*d* 1885), *e d* of Charles Lucas of Warnham Court, Sussex; one *s;* 2nd, 1889, Violet, *e d* of Bevil Granville of Wellesbourne, Warwickshire and Northchurch, Herts. *Educ:* Brighton College; Trinity Hall, Cambridge. For 33 years a member of the firm of Maudslay, Sons & Field, Marine Engineers, Lambeth; for 35 years (since its establishment) a Director of the Employers' Liability Assurance Corporation, Ltd; for several years Chairman, in the South of England, of the Iron Trades Employers Association, and later Vice-President of the Federated Employers of Great Britain; Managing Director since its establishment of The Birmingham Aluminium Casting 1903 Co., Ltd, and also Chairman since 1913; for 40 years Member of the Committee and subsequently Treasurer of the General Lying-In Hospital, Lambeth. *Recreations:* shooting, fishing. *Address:* 69 Cadogan Gardens, SW3. *T:* Kensington 1013; Nausidwell, near Falmouth, Cornwall. *Club:* Wellington.

Died 25 Aug. 1927.

MAUDSLEY, Henry, MD, LLD; FRCP; physician; *b* Rome, near Settle, Yorkshire, 1835; 3rd *s* of late Thomas Maudsley; *m* Ann Caroline, *y d* of late John Conolly, MD, DCL, Lawn House, Hanwell. *Educ:* Giggleswick School; privately; University Coll. London (MD 1857). Medical Superintendent of Manchester Royal Lunatic Hospital, 1859–62; physician, West London Hospital, 1864–74; Professor of Medical Jurisprudence in University Coll. London, 1869–79;

Goulstonian Lecturer, RCP, 1870; editor, Jl of Mental Science, 1862–78. *Publications:* Responsibility in Mental Disease, 1874; Physiology of Mind, 1876; Pathology of Mind, 1879, 2nd edn 1895; Body and Will, 1883; Natural Causes and Supernatural Seemings, 1886, 3rd edn 1897; Life in Mind and Conduct, 1902; Heredity, Variation and Genius, 1908; Organic to Human, Psychological and Sociological, 1917. *Address:* Heathbourne House, Bushey Heath, Herts. *Clubs:* Reform, Savile. *Died 23 Jan. 1918.*

MAUNDER, Edward Walter, FRAS; Secretary, Victoria Institute, 1913–18; Superintendent, Solar Department, Royal Observatory, Greenwich, 1873–1913 and 1916–19; *b* 12 April 1851; *y s* of Rev. George Maunder, Wesleyan minister; *m* 1st, 1875, Edith Hannah Bustin; 2nd, 1895, Annie Scott Dill Russell; three *s* two *d. Educ:* University College School, and King's College, London. Entered Royal Observatory, Greenwich, as assistant, 1873; elected Fellow, Royal Astronomical Society, 1875; on the Council, 1885–89 and 1891–92; Secretary, 1892–97; Vice-President, 1897; founded British Astronomical Association, 1890; President, 1894–96; eclipse expeditions—West Indies, 1886; Lapland, 1896; India, 1898; Algiers, 1900; Mauritius, 1901; Labrador, 1905. *Publications:* Royal Observatory, Greenwich, its History and Work; Astronomy without a Telescope, 1902; The Astronomy of the Bible, 1908; (with Mrs Maunder) The Heavens and their Story, 1908; Science of the Stars, 1912; Are the Planets Inhabited?, 1913; Sir William Huggins, and Spectroscopic Astronomy, 1913; edited, Indian Eclipse of 1898; Total Solar Eclipse of 1900; The Observatory, 1881–87; The Journal and Memoirs of the British Astronomical Association, 1890–94; and 1896–1900; Astronomical Department of Knowledge, 1895–1904. *Address:* 8 Maze Hill, Greenwich Park, SE. *Club:* Royal Societies. *Died 21 March 1928.*

MAUNG KIN, Hon. Sir, KCIE 1924; Home Member of the Executive Council of the Governor of Burma since 1923; *b* Aug. 1872; *o s* of U Po Kyaw, ATM; *g s* of U Aung, KSM, ATH; *m* Ma Than May, *d* of U. Po, rice-miller; one *s* one *d. Educ:* Government College, Rangoon. Called to the Bar, 1896; Law Lecturer at Government College, 1902; Assistant Public Prosecutor, Rangoon, 1905; Assistant-Govt Advocate, Burma, 1912; Chief Judge, Small Cause Court, Rangoon, 1913–14; Judge of the Chief Court, 1915; officiated as Chief Judge of the Chief Court, 1920; Judge of the High Court of Judicature at Rangoon, 1922. *Recreations:* tennis, riding. *Address:* Windermere Park, Rangoon, Burma; Sherwood, Maymyo, Burma. *Clubs:* Orient, Paperchase, Rangoon; Country, Maymyo. *Died 22 Oct. 1924.*

MAUNG PE, ISO 1913; KSM 1901; was Additional Judge, Court of Small Causes, Rangoon, Burma; *b* 30 July 1858; *s* of U Zan, of Bassein, Burma; *m;* two *s* one *d. Educ:* Rangoon. Held ministerial appointments under Government from 1877; was on special duty in the Office of the Deputy Superintendent of Census of Burma, and was gazetted as an Extra Assistant Commissioner, 1881; Township Officer, Pegu; Akunwoon of the Bassein District; served as Township Officer in the Districts Henzada and Thongwa, 1883–87; Assistant Town Magistrate of Rangoon, 1887; Township Officer in Magwe and Tharrawaddy Districts, 1890; in charge of Myanaung Sub-Division in the Henzada District, 1895; Magistrate of Eastern Sub-Division, Rangoon, 1896. *Address:* 47 Crisp Street, Rangoon. *Died 15 May 1924.*

MAUNSELL, General Sir Frederick Richard, KCB 1897 (CB 1873); unemployed; *b* Co. Wicklow, Ireland, 4 Sept. 1828; *s* of Rev. D. H. Maunsell, Balbriggan, Ireland; *m* 1863, Maria Alexandrine (*d* 1883), *d* of Don Manuel Velez, New Granada; three *s* three *d. Educ:* King Edward's School, Birmingham; Grosvenor College, Bath; Addiscombe College. Served at siege of Mooltan, battle of Goojerat (medal and two clasps), 1848–49; battle of Budli Serai, sieges of Delhi and Lucknow, Oudh Campaign (medal and two clasps), 1857–58; Afghan Campaign (medal and one clasp), 1878; Lieutenant, RE, 1846; Captain, RE, 1858; Major, 1858; Lieut-Colonel, 1869; Colonel, 1874; Major-General, 1878; Lieut-General, 1884; Col Comdt, 1886; General, 1887; Hon. Colonel 1st KGO Sappers and Miners, 1904. *Address:* 32 Ashley Gardens, SW; Laleham, Middlesex. *Club:* United Service. *Died 29 Oct. 1916.*

MAUREL, Victor; singer; *b* Marseilles, 17 June 1848; *m. Educ:* Paris Conservatoire under Fauré. Covent Garden since 1873; Simon Boccanegra, 1881; created Iago in Verdi's Otello, and Falstaff, 1893. *Died 23 Oct. 1923.*

MAURICE, Lt-Col David Blake, DSO 1900; late Royal Berkshire Regiment; *b* 24 Dec. 1866; *e s* of late Oliver Calley Maurice, JP,

London Street, Reading, and Manton Grange, Marlborough, Wilts; *m* 1903, Cecilia Evelyn, *e d* of James Simonds, JP, Redlands, Reading. *Educ:* Uppingham (in cricket XI and Rugby XV). Entered 3rd Royal Berks, 1885; 1st Royal Berks, 1889; Adjutant, 1st Royal Berks, 1894–98; served in Mounted Infantry and Staff, S Africa, 1889–1901 (despatches, Queen's medal five clasps, DSO); Adjutant QVB West Yorkshire Regt, 1903–6; commanded Depôt Royal Berks Regt, 1908–12. *Died 4 Dec. 1925.*

MAVOR, James, PhD; FRSC; Professor of Political Economy in the University of Toronto, 1892–1923; Emeritus, 1923; *b* Stranraer, 8 Dec. 1854; *s* of late Rev. James Mavor, MA, and Mary Ann Taylor Bridie; *m* 1883, Christina, *d* of P. B. Watt, London; two *s* one *d*. *Educ:* High School and University of Glasgow. Assistant editor of Industries, editor Scottish Art Review; University Extension Lecturer in Political Economy; Professor of Political Economy, St Mungo's College, Glasgow, 1888; travelled extensively in America, in the Far East, and in Russia. *Publications:* Wages Theories and Statistics, 1888; Economic Theory, and History Tables and Diagrams, 1890; Scottish Railway Strike, 1891; Currency Reform, 1891; Economic Study, and Public and Private Charity, 1892; Report on Labour Colonies in Germany, etc, to HM Board of Trade, Parliamentary Paper, 1893; English Railway Rate Question, 1894; edited Handbook of Canada, 1897; Notes on Art, 1898; Report on Immigration into Canada from Europe (to Canadian Government), 1900; Report on Workmen's Compensation Acts (to Provincial Government of Ontario), 1900; Papers on Municipal Affairs, 1904; Report to HM Board of Trade on the North-West of Canada, Parliamentary Paper, 1905; Taxation of Corporations in Canada, 1909; Railway Transportation in America, 1909; Taxation in Upper Canada, 1913; Economic Survey of Canada, 1914; Applied Economics, 1914; An Economic History of Russia, 1914 (new edition 1925); My Windows on the Street of the World, 1923; The Russian Revolution, 1926. *Recreation:* chess. *Address:* 145 Isabella Street, Toronto. *Clubs:* Savile; Toronto, York, Arts and Letters, Toronto; City, New York. *Died Nov. 1925.*

MAW, William Henry, LLD; FRGS, FRMS; President, Institution of Civil Engineers; Past President, Institution of Mechanical Engineers, and Royal Astronomical Society; Joint editor of Engineering since 1866; *b* Scarborough, 6 Dec. 1838; *s* of W. M. Maw, Scarborough; *m* 1867, Emily, *d* of Thomas Chappell; three *s* five *d*. Professional training in works of Great Eastern Railway, 1855–65; Member of Royal Commission for St Louis Exhibition, 1904; Member of the Advisory Panel, Munitions Inventions Department, Ministry of Munitions of War. *Publications:* Recent Practice in Marine Engineering; Double-Star Observations (Memoirs RAS), etc; joint-author of The Waterworks of London, and Road and Railway Bridges. *Recreations:* astronomy, microscopy. *Address:* 18 Addison Road, Kensington, W14. *T:* Park 2208; Outwood, Surrey; 35 and 36 Bedford Street, WC2. *TA:* Engineering, Westrand, London. *T:* Gerrard 3663 and 8598. *Clubs:* Royal Thames Yacht, Garrick. *Died 19 March 1924.*

MAXIM, Sir Hiram Stevens, Kt 1901; CE, ME; late of the firm Vickers Sons and Maxim; civil, mechanical and electrical engineer; inventor of the automatic system of firearms; *b* Maine, USA, 5 Feb. 1840; *er s* of Isaac Weston Maxim and Harriett Boston, *d* of Levi Stevens; naturalised British citizen; *m* 1st, Louisa Jane Budden; one *s* two *d*; 2nd, 1881, Sarah, *d* of late Charles Haynes. *Educ:* Maine. Chief Engr, United States Electric Lighting Co., 1878; moved to London; Maxim Gun Co., 1884, later Vickers Sons and Maxim; Maxim gun adopted for use in army, 1889, and in RN, 1892; conducted extensive experiments with a view of ascertaining how much power was required to perform artificial flight, and prepared various scientific papers for publication; Chevalier of the Legion of Honour. *Recreations:* reading scientific books, studying the abstract sciences. *Publication:* My Life, 1915. *Address:* Sandhurst Lodge, High Road, Streatham, SW. *Died 24 Nov. 1916.*

MAXWELL, Col Francis Aylmer, VC 1900; CSI 1911; DSO 1898; 18th Bengal Lancers; Military Secretary to Lord Hardinge, 1910–16; *b* 7 Sept. 1871; *s* of T. Maxwell, Guildhall; *m* 1906, Charlotte Alice Hamilton, 3rd *d* of late P. H. Osborne of Currandooley, NSW; two *d*. Joined Royal Sussex Regt, 1891; Captain, 1901; Major, 1909; Bt Lt-Col, 1915; served Waziristan, 1895 (medal with clasp); Chitral, 1895 (despatches, medal with clasp); North-West Frontier, India, 1897–98 (despatches, DSO, three clasps); South Africa, 1900–2 (medal with 6 clasps, King's medal with 2 clasps, VC; Brevet Major); European War, 1914–17 (Bar to DSO; Temp. Brig.-Gen.). Decorated for gallantry in saving Q Battery at Koorn Spruit. *Address:* The Grange, Guildford. *Club:* Cavalry. *Died 21 Sept. 1917.*

MAXWELL, Hamilton, RSW; *b* Glasgow, 27 Dec. 1830; parents Scotch. *Educ:* High School, Glasgow. Trained to business at an early age; sailed to Melbourne, Australia, 1852; had some experience of the Bush and gold digging and returned home, 1856; lived two years in Derbyshire in charge of farm, colliery and brickwork; went to Bombay, 1859; Sheriff of Bombay and Chairman of the Bank of Bombay, 1878; returned to Scotland, 1881; since then a professional artist; had a studio in Paris, 1893–1908; made many water colour drawings of ancient towns and villages in France, Italy and Germany; a Vice-President Royal Institute of the Fine Arts, Glasgow; President of the Glasgow Art Club, 1909; 33rd degree of Scottish Freemasonry. *Publication:* Artist's Wanderings, in Glasgow Herald, signed HM. *Recreations:* shooting, fishing, golf, cricket, painting. *Address:* 8 St James' Terrace, Hillhead, Glasgow. *Club:* Glasgow Art. *Died 5 Feb. 1923.*

MAXWELL, Col Hon. Henry Edward, DSO 1900; The Black Watch; *b* 27 Nov. 1857; *s* of late Hon. Richard Thomas Maxwell, *brother* of 10th Baron Farnham; *m* 1887, Edith Augusta Emily, *d* of Col Robert Godolphin Cosby of Stradbally Hall, Queen's Co.; one *s* one *d*. Entered army 1876; Captain, 1885; Major, 1895; Lt-Col, 1903; Brevet-Col, 1906; served South Africa, 1899–1902 (wounded, despatches, Queen's medal, 4 clasps, King's medal, 2 clasps, DSO); JP; DL; High Sheriff, Co. Cavan, 1910. *Address:* Arley, Mount Nugent, County Cavan. *Clubs:* Naval and Military; Kildare Street, Dublin; Royal St George Yacht. *Died 2 March 1919.*

MAXWELL, Lt-Col Henry St Patrick, CSI 1892; late Deputy Commissioner 1st grade, Assam; *b* 17 March 1850; *s* of Gen. William Maxwell, RA; *m*; one *d*. Entered army, 1869; Lt-Col 1895; served Daffla Expedition, 1874–75 (despatches); against Naga Hill tribes, 1879–80 (despatches, medal with clasp); Akha Expedition, 1883–84 (despatches); Manipur, 1891 (despatches, clasp). *Address:* 20 Oakley Avenue, Ealing, W. *Club:* United Service. *Died 15 Aug. 1928.*

MAXWELL, Lawrence, BS, AM, LLB, LLD; lawyer, Cincinnati; *b* Glasgow, 4 May 1853; *s* of Lawrence and Alison Crawford; *m* 1876, Clara Barry Darrow; two *d*. *Educ:* University of Michigan; Cincinnati Law School. Admitted to the Bar, 1875; Solicitor-General of the US, 1893–95; Lecturer, Cincinnati Law School, 1896–1916; Non-Resident Lecturer, Law Department University of Michigan, 1909–16; Chairman of Section of Legal Education of American Bar Association, 1905; Chairman Bar Committee on Revision of the Equity Rules of Supreme Court, USA, 1911; Commemoration Orator at the 75th anniversary of the founding of the University of Michigan, 1912; President, Cincinnati Musical Festival Association. *Recreation:* music. *Address:* Union Central Building, Cincinnati, Ohio, USA. *TA:* Maxwell, Cincinnati. *Clubs:* Queen City (Pres., 1915–24), Commercial, Country, University, Optimists, Cincinnati; Metropolitan, Washington; University, New York. *Died 18 Feb. 1927.*

MAXWELL, Richard Ponsonby, CB 1903; late Senior Clerk, Foreign Office; *b* 21 Oct. 1853; *s* of late Rev. Charleton Maxwell. *Educ:* Winchester; St John's Coll., Cambridge. Entered FO 1877; acting 3rd Secretary in Diplomatic Service, 1880; assisted British Agent on Behring Sea Arbitration, Paris, 1893; Private Secretary to Sir Thomas Henry Sanderson, 1894–96; Assistant Clerk, 1896; Secretary to British Plenipotentiaries at Peace Conference, The Hague, 1899; acting Secretary of Legation, 1899; acting Senior Clerk, 1900; retired, 1913. *Address:* 3 Whitehall Court, SW1. *Clubs:* Travellers'; Kildare Street, Dublin. *Died 23 May 1928.*

MAXWELL, Lt-Gen. Sir Ronald Charles, KCB 1915 (CB 1900); KCMG 1918; Colonel Commandant Royal Engineers, since 1920; *b* 26 Dec. 1852; *s* of late Lieut-Col Charles Francis Maxwell; *m* 1903, Emily Mary, *e d* of T. F. Burnaby Atkins of Halstead Place, Kent. Entered army 1872; Captain, 1884; Major, 1891; Lt-Col 1899; Colonel, 1902; Major-General, 1909; Lieut-General, 1916; retired list, 1919; served Afghanistan, 1879–80 (medal with clasp, bronze star); S Africa, 1900–2 (despatches, Queen's medal 3 clasps, King's medal 2 clasps, CB); AAG, War Office, 1902–6; Brig.-Gen. i/c Administration Western Command, 1906–9; Maj.-Gen. i/c Administration Southern Command, 1909–11; commanding East Coast Defences, 1911–14; served European War, 1914–18; Inspector-General of Communications in France, 1914; Quartermaster-General to the Armies in France, 1915–17 (despatches, KCB, KCMG); Grand Officer Legion of Honour, 1915; Grand Officer of the Crown, Belgium, 1915; Commandeur de l'Ordre de Mérite Agricole, 1917. *Address:* Poplars, Burghfield Common, near Reading. *Club:* Naval and Military. *Died 20 July 1924.*

MAXWELL, Captain Sir William, KBE 1919; traveller, publicist; War Correspondent, formerly of The Standard and The Daily Mail. Accompanied Lord Kitchener in the march on Khartoum; present at the battle of Omdurman (medal with clasp); accompanied the German Emperor through the Holy Land and Syria; was at first Peace Conference at The Hague; was besieged in Ladysmith; on relief of garrison went to Kimberley; was with Lord Roberts' army in every engagement from the capture of Bloemfontein to Lydenburg and Komati Poort; saw Kruger at Delagoa Bay; accompanied the Duke and Duchess of York in their tour through Australia, Canada, and the Colonies; travelled in Morocco, interviewed Sultan Abdul Aziz at Fez; accompanied Mr Chamberlain in his South African tour, 1902-3; also King Edward in his yacht to Lisbon, Gibraltar, Malta, Naples, Rome; with General Kuroki's army from the battle of the Yalu to the battle of the Sha-ho; with General Nogi at the last assaults on and surrender of Port Arthur (Order of Rising Sun); joined the Daily Mail, 1905; accompanied the Prince of Wales in Indian tour; present at coronation of the Shah of Persia; travelled through Persia and along line of projected German railway from Persian Gulf to Constantinople; present at Delhi Durbar; journeyed up the Yang-tsi and from Hankow to Pekin during the revolution; in Pekin during the mutiny; made report on Borkum and German island defences; with the Bulgarians in the Balkan War; represented Daily Telegraph in beginning of European War, 1914-15; with the Belgians till the Germans entered Brussels; was taken prisoner by a British cavalry patrol outside Mons; present at battles of Marne and Aisne; received commission as Captain attached to Imperial General Staff; attached to Headquarters Staff in the Dardanelles Expedition; afterwards head of section in Secret Service; Director of public companies; Chevalier of the Legion of Honour. *Publications:* With the Ophir round the Empire, 1902; Sixteen Famous Battles; With the Japanese from the Yalu to Port Arthur; Canada of To-day. *Address:* Wraysbury, Bucks. *Clubs:* St James's, Royal Automobile.

Died 23 Dec. 1928.

MAXWELL, Sir William Francis, 4th Bt, *cr* 1804; DL, JP; *b* 19 June 1844; 2nd *s* of Sir William Maxwell, 3rd Bt and 1st wife, Mary, *d* of John Sprot; *S* father, 1886; *m* 1884, Jessidora, *o d* of late John Anthony Macrae of Macrae, LLD; one *d*. Owned about 6,400 acres. *Heir:* none. *Address:* Cardoness, Gatehouse, Kirkcudbrightshire. *Clubs:* Carlton; New, Edinburgh.

Died 26 Jan. 1924 (ext).

MAXWELL, Admiral William Henry; JP Sussex; retired list; *b* 13 June 1840; *s* of Lt-Col Charles Francis Maxwell, 82nd Regt; *m* 1871, Catherine Penelope, *d* of Colonel F. T. Maitland; one *s*. *Educ:* various. Entered the Navy, 1854; served in HMS Euryalus as midshipman, the Baltic, during war with Russia, 1854-56, and HMS Boscawen, Cape Station, 1857-60; Lieutenant in HMS Lyra, East Coast of Africa, 1860-62, suppressing slave trade; HMS Sutlej, in Pacific, 1863-66; Commander HMS Octavia, 1868-69, Abyssinian Expedition, East Indies; HMS Dryad, 1869, captured a slaver on Madagascar coast, freed 200 slaves; HMS Excellent, School of Gunnery, 1869-72; Captain HMS Emerald, Australian Station, 1878-82; HMS Neptune, Channel Fleet, 1883-85; Commodore Hong Kong, 1887-88; ADC to the Queen, 1887-88; Rear-Admiral, 1889; Vice-Admiral, 1895; retired, 1895; retired Admiral, 1900; Conservator of the Thames, 1896-1906. *Address:* Holywych House, Cowden, Kent. *Club:* United Service.

Died 1 July 1920.

MAXWELL, William Henry, MA, PhD, LLD; City Superintendent of Schools; Emeritus Superintendent City of New York since 1898; *b* Stewartstown, Ireland, 5 March 1852; *m* 1877, Marie A. Folk; one *s* one *d*. *Educ:* Royal Academical Institution, Belfast; Queen's Colls, Galway and Belfast. Teacher, Victoria Coll., Belfast, 1872-74; journalist, NY, 1877, 1880; teacher, Public Schools, Brooklyn, NY, 1880-82; Asst Superintendent of Schools, Brooklyn, 1882-87; Superintendent of Schools, Brooklyn, NY, 1887-98. *Publications:* a series of text-books on English grammar and composition. *Recreations:* pedestrianism, bicycling, golf. *Address:* 500 Park Avenue, New York. *T:* 5580 Plaza, New York. *Clubs:* Century Association, City, New York.

Died 3 May 1921.

MAXWELL-STUART, Herbert Constable; JP, DL; *b* 1842; *e s* of late Hon. Henry Constable Maxwell-Stuart, of Traquair, and Juliana, *d* of Peter Middleton, of Stockeld Park, Co. York. *Address:* Scarthingwell Hall, Tadcaster; Traquair House, Innerleithen, NB; Terregles, Dumfries, NB.

Died 13 April 1921.

MAY, Sir Arthur William, KCB 1914 (CB 1911); KHP 1913; FRCS; Surgeon-Vice-Admiral Royal Navy, retired; *b* 13 June 1854; *s* of late Rev. Henry Thomas May, Fellow of New College, Oxford; *m* 1892,

Adelaide Gibson, *d* of William Baldock, Cooling Castle, Kent. *Educ:* Sherborne School; King's College Hospital. Entered Royal Naval Medical Service, 1878; served Egyptian War, 1882; Suakim Expedition, 1884; Nile Expedition for relief of General Gordon, 1884-85, Camel Corps; Deputy Director-General Medical Dept, RN, 1905-9; Director-General, 1913-17; DL, JP Cornwall; Knight of Grace St John of Jerusalem; 1st Class Order of Sacred Treasure, Japan; Commander of the Order of Leopold, Belgium. *Address:* Tremeer, St Tudy, Cornwall. *M:* AF 509. *Club:* Army and Navy.

Died 20 April 1925.

MAY, Sir Francis Henry, GCMG 1919 (CMG 1895); BA, LLD, DCL; *b* Dublin, 14 March 1860; 4th *s* of late Rt Hon. George Augustus Chichester May, Lord Chief-Justice of Ireland, and Olivia, 4th *d* of Sir Mathew Barrington, 2nd Bt, of Glenstal, Co. Limerick; *m* 1891, Helena, *d* of late Gen. Sir George Digby Barker, GCB; four *d*. *Educ:* Harrow; Trinity College, Dublin (1st Honourman and Prizeman Classics and Modern Languages; BA 1881). Appointed, after competitive exam., to Hong-Kong Cadetship, 1881; Asst Protector of Chinese, 1886; Private Sec. to Governor Sir William Des Vœux, to Acting Governor Sir Francis Fleming, and to Acting Governor Lieut-Gen. Digby Barker, 1889-91; Asst Colonial Sec. 1891; Acting Colonial Treas. 1892; member Legislative Council, 1895; Captain Superintendent of Police, 1893-1902, and Superintendent Victoria Gaol and Fire Brigade, Hong-Kong, 1896-1902; Colonial Secretary, Hong-Kong, 1902-10; administered the Government of Hong-Kong during 1903, 1904, 1906-7 and 1910; Governor of Fiji and High Commissioner Western Pacific, 1910-12; Governor of Hong-Kong, 1912-19; Knight of Grace of St John of Jerusalem; JP, Suffolk. *Publications:* Guide to Cantonese Colloquial; Yachting in Hong-Kong. *Recreations:* hunting, polo, shooting, rifle-shooting, fishing, yachting. *Address:* Clare Priory, Suffolk. *Club:* Windham.

Died 6 Feb. 1922.

MAYCOCK, Sir Willoughby Robert Dottin, KCMG 1913 (CMG 1905); *b* 7 July 1849; *o s* of late Colonel Dottin Maycock, formerly of 6th Inniskilling Dragoons; *m* Emma Leah (*d* 1919), *o d* of John Prigge. Served temporarily in Exchequer and Audit Department, 1870-72; obtained a clerkship in the Foreign Office, 1872; attached to Royal Commission for negotiation of a treaty of commerce with France, 1881 and to Rt Hon. Joseph Chamberlain's special mission to Washington, 1887; received a Royal Commission as Acting Second Secretary in HM Diplomatic Service, 1887; Assistant in Treaty Department of Foreign Office, 1897; Superintendent, 1903-13; joint editor of British and Foreign State Papers; received Jubilee medal, 1897; Coronation medals, 1902 and 1911; retired on pension, 1913; entered 2nd Middlesex Rifle Militia, 1870; promoted to rank of Captain, 1873; resigned, 1880; Director of the Pilbara Copper Fields, Ltd. *Publication:* With Mr Chamberlain in the United States and Canada, 1887-88. *Recreations:* field sports, cycling, music, drama. *Address:* 80 St George's Square, SW. *Clubs:* St James's, Roehampton; Epsom; Sandown Park.

Died 22 Nov. 1922.

MAYDON, Hon. John George; late Member of Union Parliament, Legislative Assembly; *b* Morhanger, Bedfordshire, Oct. 1857; *s* of John Maydon, of Morhanger and Salden, Bucks; *m*; two *s* two *d*. *Educ:* City of London School, under Dr E. A. Abbott. Entered shipping office of Natal Direct Line in Mark Lane; went to Natal to volunteer for the Zulu War, throughout which he served with the Durban Mounted Rifles; spent a year in the OFS, then returned to England for a year, at the end of which came out again to Natal to manage the affairs of the Natal Direct Line of Steamers in SA; entered the first Natal Parliament under Responsible Government, 1893; was in England on holiday at the outbreak of the Boer War in 1899, and immediately sailed to offer his services in SA, which were not accepted, and he proceeded to the front as newspaper correspondent, being present at all the battles of the western campaign from Magersfontein to the capture of Bloemfontein; called back to Natal in May 1901, he re-entered Parliament and led an attack on the Natal Government which led to Colonel Hime's resignation, and Sir George Sutton forming a ministry in which he became Colonial Secretary, shortly after taking also the portfolio of Railways and Harbours; sent by his Government to London in 1905 to represent it at the Shipping Conference on Rebates; elected Greyville, Durban, for Union Parliament. *Publications:* Natal, its History, Government, and Products, 1896; French's Cavalry Campaign. *Recreations:* hunting, shooting. *Address:* Netherley, Maritzburg. *Clubs:* City Carlton, Junior Constitutional; Durham, Maritzburg.

Died Aug. 1919.

MAYGAR, Lt-Col Leslie Cecil, VC 1901; DSO 1917; 8th Australian Light Horse Regiment; *b* 26 May 1871. *Educ:* privately. Served South

Africa, 1901–2 (Queen's medal, 3 clasps, VC); European War, 1915–17 (DSO). *Address:* Strathearn, Longwood, Victoria, Australia.
Died Nov. 1917.

MAYNARD, Lt-Col Frederic P., MB; FRCS; Indian Medical Service, 1887; retired; Ophthalmic Surgeon, Crewe Memorial Cottage Hospital; School Oculist, Cheshire County Council. *Educ:* St Bartholomew's Hospital; Paris, etc.; late Fellow Calcutta University; Professor of Ophthalmic Surgery, Medical College, and Ophthalmic Surgeon, College Hospital, Calcutta; Surgeon-Superintendent, Mayo Native Hospital, Calcutta; Medical Officer and Naturalist, Baluch-Afghan Boundary Commission. Editorial Staff, British and American Journals of Ophthalmology; Fellow of Royal Society of Medicine, London; Member of Ophthalmological Society of London and North of England Ophthalmic Society. *Publications:* Manual of Ophthalmic Operations (2nd edn); Manual of Ophthalmic Practice. *Address:* Prudential Chambers, Market Street, Crewe. *T:* Crewe 223; Threotynerode, Audlem, Cheshire. *Club:* Bengal United Service, Calcutta.
Died 30 Sept. 1921.

MAYNARD, John Percy Gordon; DL; *s* of William Joseph Maynard; *m* 1874, Haida, *d* of Weldon Molony, and *g d* of Sir Anthony Weldon, Bt; two *s* one *d.* Master of Ward Union Hounds, with which pack he hunted continuously for last 35 years of his life. *Recreations:* hunting, racing. *Address:* Ratoath Manor, Co. Meath. *Club:* Sackville Street, Dublin.
Died 13 March 1918.

MAYNE, Ven. Joseph; Incumbent of Larah, 1894–1923; Archdeacon of Kilmore, 1910–23; *b* 18 Oct. 1843. *Educ:* Trinity College, Dublin (MA). Ordained, 1874; Incumbent of Garrison, 1874–78; Killasnett, 1878–90; Killenkere, 1890–94. *Address:* 6 Crofton Mansions, Dunleary, Co. Dublin.
Died 7 March 1927.

MAYO, 7th Earl of, *cr* 1785; **Dermot Robert Wyndham Bourke,** KP 1905; PC (Ire) 1900; DL, JP; Baron Naas, 1766; Viscount Mayo, 1781; Representative Peer for Ireland, 1890; Senator Irish Free State, 1921; Cornet, 10th Hussars, 1870; Lieutenant County Kildare; Lieutenant Grenadier Guards, retired 1876; *b* 2 July 1851; *s* of 6th Earl and Blanche Julia, *d* of 1st Baron Leconfield; *S* father, 1872; *m* 1885, Geraldine Sarah, *d* of late Hon. Gerald Henry Brabazon Ponsonby. *Educ:* Eton. Conservative; Church of Ireland. *Publications:* Sport in Abyssinia; De Rebus Africanis; The War Cruise of the Aries; History of the Kildare Hunt. *Recreations:* fox-hunting, promoting the agricultural and industrial welfare of Ireland; collector of English china and miniatures. *Heir:* cousin Major Walter Longley Bourke, *b* 28 Nov. 1859. *Address:* Palmerstown, Straffan, Co. Kildare. *Clubs:* White's, Stratford; Kildare Street, Dublin.
Died 31 Dec. 1927.

MAYO, Arthur, VC 1857; *b* Oxford, 18 May 1840; 5th *s* of Herbert Mayo, FGS, Cheshunt, Herts, and Sarah Harman, Theobalds, Cheshunt; *m* 1865, Ellen, *d* of Joseph Baker; five *c. Educ:* Berkhamsted School, Herts. Went on voyage in Wellesley East Indiaman, 1855–56; entered Indian Navy, 1857; served in steam frigate Punjaub, and with Indian Navy Brigade ashore, June 1857–Jan. 1860, when invalided home; entered Magdalen Hall, Oxford, 1862; BA 1865; ordained, 1866; Assistant Curate, St Peter's, Plymouth; was received into the Roman Catholic Church, 1867.
Died 18 May 1920.

MAYOR, Rev. Joseph Bickersteth, MA; Emeritus Professor of King's College, London; Hon. Fellow of St John's College, Cambridge; *b* 1828; *s* of Rev. Robert Mayor and Charlotte Bickersteth (*sister* of Henry Bickersteth, Lord Langdale, and of Edward Bickersteth of Watton); *m* 1863, Miss A. J. Grote (*niece* of George Grote, the historian, and of John Grote, Professor of Moral Philosophy at Cambridge); two *s* two *d. Educ:* Rugby, 1841–47; St John's College, Cambridge, 1847–63; BA 1851; 2nd in 1st class of Classical Tripos. Fellow and Lecturer, 1852; Tutor, 1860; Deacon, 1859; Priest, 1860; Headmaster of Kensington Proprietary School, 1863–68; Professor of Classics at King's College, London, 1870–79; Hon. LittD Dublin. *Publications:* Greek for Beginners, 1869; Cicero de Natura Deorum, 3 vols, 1880–85; Guide to the Choice of Classical Books, 3rd edn 1885; Supplement to ditto, 1896; Sketch of Ancient Philosophy, 1881; Chapters on English Metre, 2nd edn 1901; Epistle of St James with Introduction, Notes and Commentary, 3rd edn 1910, with further studies, 1913; Clement of Alexandria, Seventh Book of the Stromateis, edited from Dr Hort's Notes, with English translation, Commentary, and Dissertations, 1902; Handbook of Modern English Metre, 1903, 2nd edn 1912; The World's Desire and other Sermons, 1906; Epistle of St Jude and Second Epistle of St Peter, with Introduction, Notes, and Commentary, 1907; part author of the book entitled Virgil's

Messianic Eclogue, 1907; Tolstoi as Shakespearian Critic in RSL Transactions for 1908; Select Readings from Psalms, with Essay on the Growth of Revelation, 1908; editor of Prof. Grote's posthumous works, viz. Examination of the Utilitarian Philosophy, 1870, Treaties on Moral Ideals, 1876, Exploratio Philosophica, Part II, 1900; editor of Classical Review, March 1887–Dec. 1893. *Address:* Queensgate House, Kingston Hill, Surrey.
Died 29 Nov. 1916.

MEAD, Percy James, CSI 1921; CIE 1914; Chief Secretary to the Government, Bombay; *b* 15 Nov. 1871; *s* of late Lt-Col Clement John Mead, late Bengal Royal Artillery; *m* 1st, 1904, Frances Alexandra, *d* of George Cowie; 2nd, 1913, May Gertrude, *d* of late Canon Maddock; two *s* two *d. Educ:* Haileybury; King's College, Cambridge. Entered Indian Civil Service, 1894; Under-Secretary to Govt of Bombay, Revenue and Finance, 1901; Talukdari Settlement Officer, 1905; Superintendent, Census Operations, 1910; Junior Collector, 1911; Senior Collector, 1916; Director of Industries, 1917; Chief Secretary to Government, 1919. *Recreations:* cricket, tennis, golf, etc. *Address:* c/o Grindlay & Co., 54 Parliament Street, SW1. *Club:* East India United Service.
Died 7 April 1923.

MEADE, Rev. Hon. Sidney; Canon of Salisbury since 1891; *b* 29 Oct. 1839; 3rd *s* of 3rd Earl of Clanwilliam and Elizabeth, *d* of 11th Earl of Pembroke; *m* 1868, Lucy Emma, 2nd *d* of late John Henry Jacob, of The Close, Salisbury; one *s* one *d* (and one *d* decd). *Educ:* Oxford. Ordained, 1866; Curate of S Mary's, Reading, 1866–69; Rector of Wylye, Wilts, 1869–82; Assistant Curate of Christ Church, Bradford-on-Avon, 1882–1901. *Address:* Frankleigh House, Bradford-on-Avon, Wilts.
Died 11 Feb. 1917.

MEAGHER, Michael; MP (N) North Kilkenny, 1906–18; farmer; *b* 27 Feb. 1846; *s* of Patrick Meagher, JP, Tullaroan, and Mary Josephine O'Dwyer, Graystown Castle, Co. Tipperary; *m* 1881, Johanna, *o d* of William Corcoran, Ballingarry, Co. Tipperary. *Educ:* St Patrick's College, Mountrath, Queen's Co. Took part in the Fenian rising, 1867. *Address:* Chestnut Villa, Tullaroan, Co. Kilkenny.
Died Dec. 1927.

MEARA, Rev. Henry George Jephson; Hon. Canon of Oxford. *Address:* Steventon Vicarage, Berks.
Died 4 June 1921.

MEARNS, Andrew Daniel, JP; Director, The Cunard Steamship Co., Ltd and America-Levant Line, Ltd; Chairman, Liverpool Steamship Owners Association, 1922; President, Liverpool Shipping Staffs Association, 1922; *b* 6 March 1857; *s* of late Captain Daniel Mearns of Montrose; *m* Laura Cannington, *d* of late Edwin Phillips, Liverpool; one *s* two *d. Educ:* Russell's Academy, Belfast. *Recreation:* golf. *Address:* Uplands, Burbo Bank Road, Blundellsands. *TA:* Cunard, Liverpool. *T:* Crosby 39. *M:* TC 4097.
Died 6 Dec. 1925.

MEARS, Thomas Lambert, MA, LLD London; Barrister-at-law; Member of the Senate (retired 1915) and Representative of the University of London on the Essex Education Committee, and on the Territorial Force Association for the County of London; Lieutenant-Colonel formerly commanding 5th Middlesex Rifle Volunteers; *b* New York, of English parents; *m* 1875, Alice Catherine, *e d* of late J. H. Westcar Peel of Watlington, Oxfordshire; two *s* one *d. Educ:* King's and University Colleges. AKC, London; called to the Bar, Inner Temple, 1868; South-Eastern Circuit; for many years Reporter to the Law Reports of Admiralty cases in the Court of Admiralty and Court of Appeal; Fellow of Geographical and Zoological Societies, and Fellow and Member of Council of Botanical Society; Member of the Royal Institution of Great Britain; a Governor and Member of the Board of Management of the Middlesex Hospital; twice circumnavigated the globe, visiting N and S America, Sandwich Islands, Australia, Tasmania, New Zealand, Ceylon, Burma, Siam, China, Japan, etc. *Publications:* an Analysis of Ortolan's Roman Law; a translation with notes of the Institutes of Gauis and Justinian; editor of the several handbooks of Travel, and of editions of Practical Forms and Forms of Agreement, and joint-author of the last edition of Admiralty Law and Practice. *Address:* 1 St Andrew's Place, Regent's Park, NW.
Died 10 Jan. 1918.

MEASE, Very Rev. Charles William O'Hara, MA; Incumbent of Castleknock since 1903; Dean of the Chapel Royal, Dublin, since 1913; Chaplain to the Household of the Lord Lieutenant; *b* Dublin, June 1856; *y s* of late Andrew Mease, FRCSI; *m* 1896, Martha Gertrude, *d* of late Alfred Billing, JP, Helsby, Cheshire; one *d. Educ:* Armagh and Cavan Royal Schools; Trinity College, Dublin (Royal Scholar); 1st Honourman in Classics; MA, Divinity Testimonium.

Ordained, 1881; Curate of Monaghan, 1881–83; Incumbent Killoughter, 1883–84; Curate St Stephen's, Dublin, 1884–88; Rector, Killiskey, 1888–93; Dean's Vicar St Patrick's Cathedral, Dublin, 1893–1902. *Recreations:* tennis, golf. *Address:* Mount Hybla, Castleknock, Dublin. *T:* 24 Castleknock. *Club:* University, Dublin.
Died 21 May 1922.

MECREDY, Richard James, BA: Director R. J. Mecredy and Co. Ltd; Mecredy, Percy and Co., Ltd; Editor Motor News; Joint Editor, with Sir James Campbell Percy, of Irish Cyclist; *b* Ballinasloe, 18 May 1861; *s* of Rev. James Mecredy, DD; *m* 1887; three *s* three *d*. *Educ:* Portora School, Enniskillen; Trinity College, Dublin. Apprenticed to T. T. Mecredy; solicitor, 1882; abandoned the law for journalism, 1886; became proprietor of Irish Cyclist, 1886, jointly with brother Alec, and edited it from that time; started Motor News, 1900; one of the first to recognise the merits of the pneumatic tyre; Director of the first Dunlop Company; went off the Board when the Company was refloated. *Publications:* Encyclopædia of Motoring; Health's Highway; Road Books of Ireland; etc. *Recreations:* touring, cycling, motoring, camping; principal hobby, scenery. *Address:* Vallombrosa, Bray, Co. Wicklow. *T:* 26 Bray; Motor News, Dublin. *T:* Dublin 2453. *Club:* Irish Automobile, Dublin.
Died April 1924.

MEDLICOTT, William Norton; Southwark Local War Pensions Committee, 1919–22; *b* Birmingham; *s* of Thomas and Eliza Medlicott; *m* 1894, Margaret, *d* of John Macmillan of Stoke-on-Trent; two *s* one *d*. Assistant editor Birmingham Daily Gazette, 1889; editor Manchester Evening Mail, 1890–92; managing editor Staffordshire Evening and Weekly Post, 1893–94; Church Family Newspaper, 1895–1911, editor 1905–11; Secretary Ada Leigh Homes, Paris, 1913–17. *Address:* 19 Gloucester Place, Greenwich, SE10.
Died 17 May 1923.

MEDLYCOTT, Rev. Sir Hubert James, 6th Bt, *cr* 1808; *b* 9 Dec. 1841; *s* of Sir William Coles Medlycott, 2nd Bt and Sarah Jeffery, *d* of Rev. Edward Bradford; *S* brother, 1908; *m* 1870, Julia Ann, *d* of Rev. Charles Thomas Glyn; one *s* two *d*. *Educ:* Harrow; Trinity College, Cambridge. Ordained, 1866; Curate, Brington, Northants, 1866–70; Vicar of Milborne-Port, 1870–83; Hill, Glos, 1883–86. *Heir:* *s* Hubert Mervyn Medlycott [*b* 29 Sept. 1874; *m* 1906, Nellie Adah, *d* of Hector E. Monro, Edmonsham, Dorset, two *s*. *Educ:* Harrow; Trinity College, Cambridge (BA). Major Dorset Yeomanry. *Address:* Milborne Port, Sherborne]. *Address:* 31 Chester Street, SW1. *T:* Victoria 7347; Ven House, Sherborne, Dorset. *Club:* Wellington.
Died 25 May 1920.

MEE, Arthur, (Idris); journalist; *b* Aberdeen, 1860; *o s* of late George S. Mee (sometime editor Bradford Observer); *m* 1888, Claudia, *d* of late David Thomas, Llanelly. Connected with the Welsh press since 1876; one the editorial staff of the Western Mail since 1892; also edited the Western Mail Almanac, Literary Supplement, Illustrated Guide to Cardiff, Cambrian Notes. *Publications:* Llanelly Parish Church, its History and Records, 1888; Observational Astronomy, 1893, 2nd edn 1897; (ed) Who's Who in Wales, 1920; and a number of astronomical and astrological brochures. *Address:* Tremynfa, Llanishen. Cardiff.
Died 15 Jan. 1926.

MEESON, Engr-Comdr Edward Hickman Tucker, DSO 1915; Royal Navy; *b* 20 Dec. 1877; *s* of Frederick Richard Meeson, Eastbourne; *m* 1908, Glady May, *d* of George Robert Gordon Joy, Solicitor; one *d*. *Educ:* Westminster; Royal Naval Engrg College. Assistant Engineer, 1899; Engineer Lieut 1904; Engineer Lieut-Commander, 1912; served in HMS Laurel in action off Heligoland Bight (DSO and specially promoted to Engineer Commander 1 June 1915). *Address:* 32 Arundel Road, Eastbourne.
Died 31 May 1916.

MEHARRY, Rev. J. B., BA, DD; ex-Moderator, Presbyterian Church of England. *Educ:* Queen's Colleges, Belfast and Galway; Assembly's College, Belfast. *Publications:* From Natural to Spiritual; The Principles of Presbyterianism; The Advantages of Presbyterianism as a Form of Church Government; The Christian Priest.
Died 20 Jan. 1916.

MEHTA, Khan Bahadur, Sir Bezonji Dalabhoy, Kt 1912. *Address:* Nagpur, India. *Died 5 May 1927.*

MEIKLE, Andrew; Editor Wolverhampton Express and Star; *b* Dunfermline, Fifeshire, 24 May 1847; 3rd *s* of James Meikle, handloom weaver; *m* 1878, *o d* of Robert Parker, Leicester; no *c*. *Educ:* Roland Street School, Dunfermline. Served seven years'

apprenticeship as compositor in Dunfermline Press, subsequently became reporter on that paper; afterwards reporter on the Teviotdale Record, Jedburgh; Bolton Guardian; chief reporter Bolton Chronicle; editor Somerset County Herald; editor and manager Warrington Examiner; and for 38 years associated with the Wolverhampton Express and Star and allied papers owned by the Midlands News Association, Ltd. *Recreations:* cards, walking. *Address:* 33 Merridale Road, Wolverhampton. *T:* Wolverhampton 953. *Club:* Wolverhampton Liberal.
Died 14 Aug. 1922.

MEISSAS, Gaston; Member of the Société of Géographie. *Publications:* Marseilles; part author Paris, in 9th edition Ency. Brit. *Address:* Avenue Bosquet 3, (VIIᵉ) Paris.

MELDON, Sir Albert, Kt 1910; *b* 25 May 1845; *s* of late James Dillon Meldon, JP, 24 Merrion Square, Dublin and Coolarne, Athenry, Co. Galway; *m* 1st, 1873, Mary (*d* 1914), *d* of late Bernard Doherty of Buncrana, Co. Donegal; 2nd, 1917, Lily, *d* of Andrew Levins Moore, JP, of Ashton, Co. Dublin; three *s*. *Educ:* Stonyhurst Coll., Lancashire. Called to the Bar, 1868; Resident Magistrate, 1883–1910, and voluntarily during the war 1915–17 (received thanks of Government six times); DL, JP Co. Wicklow, and County Director RCJ and SJAB. *Address:* Vevay, Bray, Co. Wicklow. *T:* Bray 36. *M:* TI 133. *Clubs:* Stephen's Green, Royal Irish Automobile, Dublin.
Died 27 Nov. 1924.

MELHADO, Carlos, CMG 1911; Member Executive Council, British Honduras; represented Colony of British Honduras at the Corporation, 22 June 1911; *b* 30 April 1852; *m* 1874, Florence Irene Stevenson; three *s* two *d*. *Address:* Belize, British Honduras.
Died 15 Oct. 1922.

MELINE, Felix Jules; Deputy for the Vosges; Avocat à la Cour; Leader of Moderate and Protectionist Republicans; *b* Remiremont, Vosges, 20 May 1838. *Educ:* Faculté de Paris. Elected to National Assembly (Vosges), 1872; re-elected for Remiremont, 1876; Minister of Agriculture, 1883–85; President of the Council, 1888; Premier, 1896–98; Candidate for Presidency, 1899. *Address:* Rue de Commaille 4, (VIIᵉ) Paris. *Died Dec. 1925.*

MELITUS, Paul Gregory, CSI 1912; CIE 1894; Indian Civil Service; *b* 1858; *s* of G. P. Melitus; *m* 1906, Janet Douglas, *d* of James Douglas Cowan. *Educ:* Marlborough; Wren and Gurney; Balliol College, Oxford. Entered ICS 1878; Assistant Magistrate, etc, Bengal, 1880; Asst and Deputy Comr and Assistant Secretary to Chief Commissioner, Assam, and Acting Postmaster-General, Bengal, 1886–91; Under-Sec. Home Dept, Govt of India, 1891; Deputy Sec., 1893; Sec. to Chief Comr, Assam, 1894; Judge and Commissioner, Assam Valley Districts, 1898; Member, Board of Revenue, Eastern Bengal and Assam, 1905; retired, 1913. *Address:* 17 Gwydyr Mansions, Hove, Sussex. *Club:* East India United Service.
Died 23 Feb. 1924.

MELLIS, Rev. James, MA Edinburgh; Minister Emeritus since 1910; *b* Manse of Tealing, Forfarshire, 1843; *e s* of Rev. David Barclay Mellis and Mary, *d* of Rev. John Campbell, DD, Tolbooth Parish, Edinburgh; *m* 1872, Jane Anne, *d* of Rev. John Roxburgh, DD, Glasgow; one *s* two *d*. *Educ:* privately; High School, University, and New College, Edinburgh; Erlangen. Licensed preacher, 1867; ordained Free Church, Carnbee, Fife, 1869; Clerk of Free Synod of Fife; translated to Southport, 1879; Clerk of the Presbytery of Liverpool, 1894–1919; served on numerous Church Committees; Joint-Convener of Committee on Intercourse with other Churches, 1896–1910; President of Southport Free Church Council, 1898–99 and 1917–18, and Past Vice-President of the District Council; Convener of Welsh-English Committee, 1906–24; Moderator of Synod of Presbyterian Church of England, 1910; on Board of Southport Infirmary, 1882–1919, Vice-Chairman, 1895–1919; present at Coronation of King George V in Westminster Abbey, 1911. *Publications:* Occasional Sermons and Appreciations; From My Study; Reflections and Recollections, 1913; Talks and Tales, 1919; Quiet Reflections, 1924. *Address:* The Elms, Normans Place, Altrincham, Cheshire.
Died 13 Sept. 1925.

MELLIS, Col William Andrew, CB 1919; Aberdeen Territorial Force Association, County of Aberdeen; *b* 1848; *s* of Major George Mellis, Huntly; *m* 1875, Margaret, *d* of Jas Kewart, Clunmore. Late Gordon Highlanders. *Address:* Territorial Force Assocation, Aberdeen.
Died 4 June 1925.

MELLISH, Lt-Col Henry, CB 1917; JP, DL Notts; Alderman and Vice-Chairman, Nottinghamshire County Council; Chairman,

Nottinghamshire Education Committee and Nottinghamshire Territorial Association; Chairman, Quarter Sessions (Retford Division); *b* 31 Oct. 1856; *s* of late Lt-Col William Leigh Mellish and Margaret Anne, *d* of Sir Samuel Cunard, 1st Bt; unmarried. *Educ:* Eton; Balliol College, Oxford. 1st class moderations (mathematics), 1877; 1st class science, 1879; held a commission in Notts Volunteers and Territorial Force, 1876–1912; commanded 4th (Notts) VB Sherwood Forresters, 1901–5; President, Royal Meteorological Society, 1909–10. *Recreation:* rifle shooting (represented England in match for Elcho Shield at Wimbledon and Bisley on over twenty occasions). *Address:* Hodsock Priory, Worksop. *T:* North Carlton 3. *Club:* New University. *Died 2 Feb. 1927.*

MELLISS, Col Sir Howard, KCSI 1897 (CSI 1893); late Inspector-General of the Imperial Service Troops of India; *b* 2 April 1847; *s* of George Melliss, Talbot Square, London, and St Helens; *m* 1877, Edith Mary, *d* of General Conran, RHA. *Educ:* privately; RMC Sandhurst. Served in the 33rd (Duke of Wellington's) Regt, and Royal Scots Fusiliers; was present at the storming and capture of Magdala, 1868; was on special service, Baroda; in Intelligence Branch, QMG's Dept, Simla; AQMG of the Indian Division in Egypt, 1882; on Staff of Bombay army as Brigade-Major and AQMG; was Military Attaché to Admiral Sir Frederick Richards in Burmah, 1885; was organiser and afterwards Inspector-General of Imperial Service troops in India; Abyssinian, Burma, Indian Frontier, Jubilee, and Egyptian medals; Knight Commander of Star of India; in receipt of distinguished service pension; Order of Medjidie, Egyptian Bronze Star. *Address:* 6 Buckingham Palace Gardens, SW1. *Club:* Naval and Military. *Died 21 June 1921.*

MELLOR, Francis Hamilton, CBE 1918; JP, Cheshire and Lancashire; KC; County Court Judge, Manchester, since 1911; late Chairman of the Conciliation Boards under the Coal Mining Minimum Wage Act for Lancashire, Cheshire, and North Staffordshire; of the Conciliation Boards connected with the Lancashire and Yorkshire Railway Companies, and also the Cheshire Lines and Wirral Railway Co.; *b* 13 May 1854; 10th *s* of late Rt Hon. Sir John Mellor; *m* 1886, Mabel Lucy, *e d* of Herbert Knowles of Barnagore, Calcutta; one *d*. *Educ:* Cheltenham College; Trinity College, Cambridge (MA). Called to the Bar, Inner Temple, 1890; was a member of General Council of Bar, 1898–1911; Recorder of Preston, 1898–1921; Chairman of Salford Hundred Appeal Tribunal. *Publication:* part author of Short and Mellor's Crown Office Practice. *Address:* Heathfield, Knutsford, Cheshire. *Clubs:* New University, MCC; Union, Manchester. *Died 26 April 1925.*

MELLOR, Sir James (Robert), Kt 1911; LLM Cantab; late Senior Master of the Supreme Court, King's Remembrancer, and King's Coroner; Master of the Crown Office, King's Bench, 1874; Registrar of the Court of Criminal Appeal, 1908; retired, 1912; *b* 4 May 1839; 3rd *s* of late Rt Hon. Sir John Mellor; *m* 1868, Anne Jane (*d* 1921), *e d* of Thomas Shaw; three *s* four *d*. *Educ:* Trinity Hall, Cambridge (LLB 1863, LLM 1866). Called to the Bar, Inner Temple, 1865. *Address:* Eastgate, Tenterden, Kent. *Died 19 Feb. 1926.*

MELLOR, John Edward, CB 1919; late Chairman Denbighshire Territorial Force Association; *b* Ashton-under-Lyne, Lancashire, 1852; *s* of late Thomas Walton Mellor (MP for Ashton under Lyne, 1868); *m* 1st, Miss Andrew (*d* 1889), of Ashton-under-Lyne; 2nd, 1895, Miss Rhodes of Hadfield, Derbyshire; one *s* one *d*. *Educ:* Rossall. JP for Lancaster, Chester, and Denbighshire; DL and Vice-Lieutenant for Denbighshire; late Hon. Col 9th Training Battalion, Manchester Regiment. *Recreations:* shooting, fishing. *Address:* Tan-y-Bryn, Abergele, North Wales. *TA:* Mellor, Abergele. *T:* Abergele 4. *M:* CA 993. *Club:* Carlton. *Died 20 Aug. 1925.*

MELLOR, John James; JP, DL; Hon. Colonel, retired, 1st Volunteer Battalion Lancashire Fusiliers; Chairman of J. & J. J. Mellor, Ltd, Bury, and of the Brook Mills Co. Ltd, Heywood, cotton spinning and manufacturing concerns; *b* Oldham, 12 August 1830; *y s* of late Jon. Mellor, of Hope House; *m* Jennette, *o c* of late Robert Clegg, Clayton-le-Moors. *Educ:* private schools and private tutors. From 1851 largely interested in cotton-spinning and manufacturing and in railway working and administration; devoted to scientific and engineering work; MP (C) for the Radcliffe-cum-Farnworth Division of Lancashire, 1895–1900; an officer of volunteers 27 years, and for many years commanding officer of the regiment. *Address:* The Woodlands, Whitefield, near Manchester. *Died 12 Jan. 1916.*

MELLOR, Captain William, DSO 1915; Royal Navy (retired); *b* 20 Aug. 1874; *s* of John Mellor, Blundellsands; *m* 1920, Emily Constance, *d* of late John Whitmore, JP of Kilsallaghan, Dublin; one *s*. Served Dardanelles, 1914–15, in charge of trawler mine-sweepers (DSO, despatches). *Address:* Oaklands, Blundellsands, Liverpool. *Club:* United Service. *Died 10 May 1928.*

MELLOWES, William Joseph, (Liam); MP (SF) North Meath and East Galway, Dec. 1918–22 (but did not take his seat). *Died 8 Dec. 1922.*

MELLY, George Henry, OBE 1920; Director Lamport & Holt, Ltd, Liverpool, London, Manchester, New York, Rio de Janeiro, and Buenos Aires; *b* 5 March 1860; *s* of George Melly, 90 Chatham Street, Liverpool; *m* Elizabeth, *d* of Edward Edmonds, London; no *c*. *Educ:* Rugby. Director Liverpool and London and Globe Insurance Co. Ltd; Thames and Mersey Marine Insurance Co. Ltd; Liverpool and London War Risks Insurance Association Ltd; Excess Values (Liverpool and London); War Risks Insurance Association Ltd; Royal Mail Steam Packet Co. (Liverpool Local Board); Archibald McMillan & Son Ltd; Dumbarton, Liverpool, Brazil and River Plate Steam Navigation Co. Ltd. *Address:* 101 Royal Liver Buildings, Liverpool. *T:* Bank 8880; The Lane Cottage, Freshfield. *T:* Formby 254. *M:* CM 6943. *Clubs:* City of London, Windham; Palatine, Racquet, Liverpool. *Died 20 Oct. 1927.*

MELROSE, James, CB 1904; JP for Portsmouth; Chief Inspector of Machinery, Royal Navy (retired); *b* 1841; *s* of James Melrose, engineer, of Hawick; *m* 1880, Jane Foot, *d* of Capt. John Milton. *Educ:* Devonport; Stoke Grammar School. Entered Navy as Assistant Engineer, 1861; Sanitary Comr and Chm. Bd of Health, Gibraltar, during cholera epidemic, 1884; served with distinction through all ranks in engineering branch up to time of retirement, 1901; after that specially employed at the Admiralty conducting experimental investigations on oil fuel, north country coal, etc. *Address:* Winton House, South Hayling. *Club:* Hayling Island Golf. *Died 18 July 1922.*

MELROSE, John, CBE 1920; JP; *b* May 1853; *s* of John Melrose, engineer; *m* 1876, Grace French, *d* of David Taylor. *Educ:* Hawick High School. Engineer in Hawick; Provost of Hawick, 1902–19. *Address:* Hopehill, Hawick. *T:* Hawick 64. *Clubs:* Scottish Conservative, Edinburgh; Border, Hawick. *Died 7 April 1927.*

MELVILL, Maj.-Gen. Charles William, CB 1919; CMG 1918; DSO 1917; General Officer Commanding New Zealand Military Forces since 1924; *b* 5 Sept. 1878; *y s* of late Lieutenant Teignmouth Melvill, VC, 24th Regiment, and Mrs Melvill of Lanarth, Bournemouth; *m* 1911, Rita, 3rd *d* of William Burnett, Te Tarata, Dunedin, NZ, and *niece* of General Sir Charles Burnett, KCB; no *c*. *Educ:* Wellington College. 2nd Lieut S Lancs Regt, 1897; left as Capt. and Adjt, 1906; on Staff of NZ Forces, 1911; Staff College, Camberley, 1913; psc; went to France with S Lancs Regt, Sept. 1914 (wounded); Chief Instructor School of Instruction, Western Command, Jan.–May 1915; Brigade Major Tay Defences, May–Sept. 1915; GSO to NZ Forces, Gallipoli, 1915; remained till evacuation; Brig. Major, NZ Rifle Brigade, Egypt; commanded 4th Batt. NZ Rifle Brigade, 1916–17 (including Somme); Commander 1st NZ Inf. Brig. till Feb. 1919 (despatches four times; Officer of Order of the Crown of Belgium, 1917; Croix de Guerre, 1918); GOC Wellington Military District, 1919–21; Central Command, NZ, 1921–24. *Recreations:* fishing, shooting, polo. *Address:* GHQ, Wellington, NZ; Lanarth, Bournemouth. *Club:* Junior Naval and Military. *Died Sept. 1925.*

MELVILLE, 6th Viscount, *cr* 1802; **Charles Saunders Dundas,** ISO 1902; Baron Dunira, 1802; *b* 27 June 1843; *s* of Rev. Hon. Charles Dundas (Rector of Epworth, Lincs), 4th *s* of 2nd Viscount, and Louisa, *d* of Sir William Boothby, 9th Bt; *S* brother, 1904; *m* 1st, 1872, Grace Selina Marion (*d* 1890), *o c* of William Scully; four *s* two *d* (and two *s* decd); 2nd, 1891, Mary (*d* 1919), *d* of late George Hamilton, MD, Falkirk; 3rd, 1920, Margaret, *e d* of late William James Todd, Edinburgh, and *g d* of late Samuel Bishop Todd, Belfast. Consul, Santos, 1869; Canary Islands, 1877; Stettin, 1882; Consul-General, Hamburg, 1885; Kingdom of Norway, 1897–1907. *Heir: s* Hon. Henry Charles Clement Dundas, *b* 25 June 1873. *Address:* Melville Castle, Lasswade, Edinburgh. *Died 21 Sept. 1926.*

MELVILLE, Sir George, KCMG 1900 (CMG 1891); *b* Aberdeen, 1 July 1842; *s* of late George Melville of Culross, NB; *m* 1869, Marie

Elise Louise, *d* of late Capt. FitzLanders of Charlton Hall, Northumberland; two *d* one *s*. *Educ:* Edinburgh Acad., and by private tutors. Entered Imp. Civil Service, after competitive examination, June 1862; Lieut Kent Artillery Militia, 1873; transferred to the Colonial Civil Service, Nov. 1874, when appointed to act as Treasurer of Sierra Leone; acted also as Colonial Secretary of that colony, 1875; Assistant Government Secretary of British Guiana, 1879; acted on several occasions as Government Secretary; in 1889 appointed Colonial Secretary of British Honduras; administered the Government, 1890–91; administered the Government of the Falkland Islands, 1893; Colonial Secretary of the Bahamas, 1894; administered the Government, 1894–95; Colonial Secretary, Leeward Islands, and Island Sec., Antigua, 1895–1902; administered the Government of the Leeward Islands, 1895–97, 1899–1902; Administrator of St Lucia, 1902–5, administered the Government of the Windward Islands, 1903; retired on pension, 1905. Decorated for services while officer administering the Government of British Honduras. *Address:* c/o Cox & Co., Charing Cross, SW1. *Club:* Constitutional.

Died 24 Feb. 1924.

MELVILLE, Lt-Col Harry George, MD; FRCSE; Indian Medical Service; Professor of Materia Medica, Lahore Medical College; *b* Edinburgh, 24 March 1869; *s* of late Francis Suther Melville, DCS, Edinburgh; *m* 1903, Isobel, *y d* of late Alexander Lawson, JP of Burnturk, Fife, NB; one *d*. *Educ:* Collegiate School and University Edinburgh (MB, CM 1890). MD 1906; FRCSE 1900. Joined Indian Medical Service, 1892; Medical Officer, 5th Punjab Cavalry, 1896; served Waziristan, 1894–95 (medal and clasp); Punjab Frontier, 1897 (medal and two clasps); Tirah, 1897–98; appointed to Lahore Medical College, 1901; Fellow, Punjab University. *Publications:* contributions to medical journals. *Recreations:* polo, riding, golf, shooting. *Address:* c/o H. S. King & Co., 9 Pall Mall, SW. *Club:* East India United Service; United Service, Simla; Punjab, Lahore.

Died 7 Dec. 1918.

MELVILLE, Robert Dundonald; KC 1914; Professor of Civil Law, Royal School of Law, Cairo, 1906–24; *b* 16 July 1872; 4th *s* of late Francis Suther Melville, DCS, Edinburgh. *Educ:* Collegiate School; University of Edinburgh. MA 1893; LLB 1896; Forensic Prizeman, 1894. Called to the Scottish Bar, 1897; Order of the Nile, 1921. *Publications:* A Manual of the Principles of Roman Law, 1915, 3rd edn 1921; (jtly) A Treatise upon the Law of Arbitration in Scotland; and "Burgh Government"; many articles on legal, historical and general subjects to various periodicals. *Recreations:* golf, tennis. *Address:* c/o Mitchell & Baxter, WS, Edinburgh. *Clubs:* Royal Automobile; Scottish Conservative, Edinburgh; Turf, Cairo; Union, Alexandria.

Died 7 Sept. 1927.

MELVILLE, William, MVO 1903; JP; *b* 1852; *s* of late James Melville of County Kerry. Entered the Metropolitan Police, 1872; was for several years on the Continent and took an active part in the suppression of Anarchism; accompanied Queen Victoria, King Edward VII and other members of the Royal Family in various Continental tours; also in attendance on several foreign sovereigns while visiting this country; late Chief of the Special Police Service, New Scotland Yard; Chevalier of the Order of Francis Joseph of Austria; Knight of Order of St Silvester of Holy Roman Empire, 1908; Chevalier of the Order of Dannebrog, Denmark; Order of Christ, Portugal; Crown of Italy; Officier de la Légion d'Honneur; Commander of the Order of Isabel la Católica, Spain. *Address:* Kenmare, Orlando Road, Clapham, SW. *Club:* National Liberal.

Died 1 Feb. 1918.

MENDEL, William, DL; *b* 19 June 1854. *Educ:* privately. Director Harrod's Stores, Ltd; D. H. Evans and Co. Ltd; Paquin, Ltd. *Address:* 31 Hans Mansions, SW. *T:* Kensington 3210. *Clubs:* Reform, Royal Automobile.

Died 6 Jan. 1917.

MENTETH, Sir James Stuart-, 3rd Bt, *cr* 1838; *b* 29 July 1841; *e s* of Thomas Loughnan Stuart-Menteth (2nd *s* of 1st Bt) and Isabella Maria, 2nd *d* of James Tobin, Dublin; *S* uncle, 1870; *m* 1872, Helen Gertrude, *d* of Darwin E. Fay of Fulton, NY; two *d*. *Heir: cousin* Lt-Col James Frederick Stuart-Menteth, late 2nd Dragoon Guards [*b* 26 Feb. 1846; *m* 1st, 1868, Frances Octavia Moore (*d* 1887), *d* of Gen. Sir James Wallace Sleigh, KCB; three *s* one *d* (and two *s* decd); 2nd, 1888, Elizabeth Alyson, *d* of Capt. Edward Algernon Blackett, RN, of Wylam; one *s* three *d*. *Address:* Rownhams Mount, near Southampton]. *Address:* Canandaigua, New York.

Died 28 Oct. 1918.

MENTETH, Lt-Col Sir James Frederick Stuart-, 4th Bt, *cr* 1838; late 2nd Dragoon Guards; *b* 26 Feb. 1846; *s* of William Stuart-Menteth

(4th *s* of 1st Bt), and Sarah, *d* of Col Hamilton; *S* cousin, 1918; *m* 1st, 1868, Frances Octavia Moore (*d* 1887), *d* of Gen. Sir James Wallace Sleigh, KCB; three *s* one *d* (and two *s* decd); 2nd, 1888, Elizabeth Alyson, *d* of Capt. Edward Algernon Blackett, RN, of Wylam; one *s* three *d*. *Heir: s* William Frederick Stuart-Menteth [*b* 18 June 1874; *m* 1921, Winifred Melville, *d* of Daniel Francis and *widow* of Capt. Rupert George Raw, DSO; one *s*]. *Address:* Rownhams Mount, near Southampton. *Club:* Army and Navy.

Died 7 Sept. 1926.

MENZIES, Rev. Allan, BD, DD; Professor of Divinity and Biblical Criticism, St Mary's College, St Andrews, since 1889; *b* Edinburgh, 23 Jan. 1845; 3rd *s* of Prof. Allan Menzies, Edinburgh University, and Helen, *d* of Alexander Cowan, of Valleyfield; *m* Mary Elizabeth, *d* of Rev. John Adamson Honey, DD, Inchture, Perthshire; two *d*. *Educ:* Edinburgh Acad.; German schools; Edinburgh and St Andrews Univs (MA). Minister of Abernyte, Perthshire, 1873. *Publications:* National Religion, 1888; History of Religion, 1895; The Earliest Gospel, 1901; Second Corinthians, 1912; translated Baur's First Three Centuries of Christianity; The Apostle Paul; Pfleiderer's Philosophy of Religion; editor of supplementary issue of the Ante-Nicene Fathers; editor of Review of Theology and Philosophy. *Recreations:* swimming, boating, golf, cycling. *Address:* St Andrews, Fifeshire; St Mary's, Innellan, Argyllshire. *Club:* Royal and Ancient, St Andrews.

Died 8 May 1916.

MENZIES, Captain Arthur John Alexander, DSO 1915; MB; Royal Army Medical Corps; *s* of late Alexander Menzies, Lankat Estate, Sumatra; *m* 1916, Ethel Fanny Whitelock, *y d* of late Rev. D. L. Boyes, Melrose. Served European War, 1914–17 (DSO). *Address:* c/o Holt & Co., 3 Whitehall Place, SW.

Died 9 Aug. 1918.

MENZIES, James Acworth, MA (Dunelm), MD (Edin.); Professor of Physiology, University of Durham, since 1915; *s* of late Rev. R. Menzies, Riding Mill, Northumberland; *m* Florence E., *d* of late Rev. A. McLaren, DD, Manchester; one *d*. *Educ:* Edinburgh University (MB, CM 1890; MD, Gold Medallist, 1894). Demonstrator of Physiology, Owens College, Manchester, 1890–96 and 1898–99; House Surgeon, Royal Eye Hospital, Manchester, 1896–97; Honorary Ophthalmic Surgeon, Rochdale Infirmary, 1905–11; Lecturer on Physiology, University of Durham College of Medicine, 1911–15. *Publications:* (with Professor Bainbridge) Essentials of Physiology; papers in Journal of Physiology, British Medical Journal, Ophthalmoscope, etc. *Recreation:* golf. *Address:* University of Durham College of Medicine, Newcastle-upon-Tyne.

Died 9 July 1921.

MERCADIER, Elie; Officer of the Legion of Honour; Director of the Agence Havas in London; *b* Monestier, Tarn, 1844. *Educ:* Toulouse. *Address:* Agence Havas, 113 Cheapside, EC.

Died 30 Sept. 1916.

MERCER, Maj.-Gen. Sir David, KCB 1918 (CB 1915); Adjutant-General Royal Marine Forces since 1916; *b* London, 1 July 1864; *s* of late D. D. Mercer; *m* 1893, Katherine Frances, *d* of late W. F. Lawrence, Boston, USA; two *s* one *d*. *Educ:* Dulwich College. Entered RMLI 1883; Adjutant Portsmouth Division, 1891–95; Staff-Officer, Depot RM, Deal, 1899–1903; DAAG, RM, 1903–8; AAG, RM, 1911–14; Brig.-General commanding 1st RN Brigade, RN Division, 1914–16; served throughout the operations in Gallipoli (despatches twice, CB), and elsewhere, 1915–18 (KCB, Commander Legion of Honour). *Recreations:* golf, fishing, shooting. *Address:* 7 Bickenhall Mansions, W1. *T:* Mayfair 1685. *Clubs:* United Service; Huntercombe Golf.

Died 1 July 1920.

MERCER, Col Edward Gilbert, CMG 1916; late Commanding 1st London Regiment (Royal Fusiliers); *b* 1873; *s* of late Edward John Bush Mercer, Bath; unmarried. *Educ:* King's School, Gloucester; Magdalen College, Oxford (MA). Assistant Master at Harrow School and Commandant Harrow School OTC; served S African War with 2nd Batt. Royal Fusiliers (Queen's medal 4 clasps); European War, 1914–18 (despatches, CMG). *Address:* West Hill House, Harrow-on-the-Hill. *Clubs:* New University, Oxford and Cambridge Musical.

Died 19 Dec. 1926.

MERCER, Rt. Rev. John Edward, DD *hc* Oxon; Canon Residentiary Chester Cathedral, since 1916; Archdeacon of Macclesfield, 1919; *b* Bradford; *s* of Rev. Edward Mercer; *m* 1st, 1882, Josephine Archdall; 2nd, 1916, H. Ethel Bennion. *Educ:* Rossall School; Lincoln College, Oxford. Ordained, 1880; Curate of Tanfield, 1880–82; Penshaw, 1882–83; Rossall School Missioner, Newton Heath, 1883–89; Rector of St Michael, Manchester, 1889–97; St James, Gorton, 1897–1902; Bishop of Tasmania, 1902–14; first Moorhouse Lecturer, Melbourne. *Publications:* What is the World External to Mind?; The Soul of Progress; Social Equality; The Spiritual Evolution of the Race; The Science of Life and the Larger Hope; Nature Mysticism; The Problem of Creation, etc. *Address:* Lumley House, Chester.

Died 27 April 1922.

MERCIE, Jean Marius Antonin; Grand Grand Officer, Legion of Honour; sculptor and painter; Professor Ecole des Beaux-Arts; President Société Artistes Français; *b* Toulouse, 29 Oct. 1845. Member of the Institute; Grand Prix de Rome. *Works: sculpture:* David avant combat; David après le combat; Gloria Victis; Quand même; tombeaux du roi Louis Philippe (Dreux, France), Baudry, Thiers, Michelet (Père Lachaise, Paris), Pellegrini (Buenos Ayres); *monuments:* Général Lee (Washington), Francis Scott Key (Baltimore), etc; *picture portraits:* Vénus; Galathie et Pygmalion, etc. *Address:* 15 avenue Observatoire, Paris.

Died 14 Dec. 1916.

MERCIER, Charles Arthur, MD; FRCP, FRCS; Physician for Mental Diseases to Charing Cross Hospital; Examiner in Mental Diseases at the London University; *b* 1852; *s* of late Rev. L. P. Mercier; *m* 2nd, 1913, Mary, *y d* of late Donald MacDougall. *Educ:* Merchant Taylors' School; London Hospital. Cabin boy, warehouseman, clerk, medical student; medical officer of various asylums. *Publications:* Sanity and Insanity; Nervous System and the Mind; Lunacy Law for Medical Men; Psychology, Normal and Morbid; Text-book of Insanity, Criminal Responsibility, etc. *Recreations:* mechanics, chess, photography, motoring. *Address:* 34 Wimpole Street, W. *T:* Paddington 986. *M:* A 4422. *Clubs:* Savile, Casual.

Died 2 Sept. 1919.

MERCIER, Cardinal Desiré; Archbishop of Malines and Cardinal since 1907; *b* Braine l'Alleud, 1851; a Belgian. Professor of Philosophy at Louvain University, 1882–1906; Founder of the Institute of Philosophy and the Revue Neo-scholastique. *Publications:* Criteriologie Metaphysique Générale; Les Origines de la Psychologie Contemporaine; A Manual of Modern Scholastic Philosophy, 1917; A mes Séminaristes; Retraite Pastorale; La Vie Intérieure. *Address:* Malines, Belgium.

Died 23 Jan. 1926.

MEREDITH, Rev. Richard; Prebend of Tullowmagimma and Canon of Leighlin Cathedral since 1906; *s* of Richard Duke Meredith, BA, TCD. *Educ:* Trinity College, Dublin (MA and Div. Testl). Ordained, 1869; Curate of Clonenagh, 1869–76; Incumbent of Killaban, 1876–1919; Rural Dean of Aghade, 1913. *Address:* 28 Corrig Avenue, Kingstown, Co. Dublin.

Died Dec. 1928.

MEREDITH, Rt. Hon. Richard Edmund, PC (Ire) 1907; *b* 18 Nov. 1855; *s* of late William Rice Meredith, solicitor; *m* 1880, Annie, *d* of late John Pollock, solicitor; three *s* two *d*. Barrister, Hilary 1879; appointed QC 1892; elected a Bencher of King's Inns, 1894; Judge of the Supreme Court of Judicature in Ireland, and Judicial Commissioner of the Irish Land Commission, 1898–1906; Master of the Rolls in Ireland, 1906–12. *Address:* 32 Molesworth Street, Dublin. *Clubs:* University, Dublin; Royal St George Yacht, Kingstown.

Died 28 Jan. 1916.

MEREDITH, William Appleton, JP Norfolk; MB, CM; FRCS; Consulting Surgeon Samaritan Free Hospital, London; *b* 3 March 1848; *e s* of Samuel Ogden Meredith of Philadelphia; naturalised a British subject in 1886; *m* Caroline, *d* of late Henry Atkinson Green of Boston, USA. *Educ:* abroad; University College, London; University of Edinburgh (MB, CM). *Publications:* various papers on abdominal surgery. *Address:* Little Massingham Manor, King's Lynn, Norfolk.

Died 6 Oct. 1916.

MEREDITH, Hon. Sir William Ralph, Kt 1896; LLD; Chief Justice of Ontario since 1912; *b* 31 March 1840; *s* of John Walsingham Cooke Meredith, London, Ontario, and Sarah, *d* of Anthony Pegler; *m* 1862, Mary, *d* of Marcus Holmes, Ontario; three *d* (one *s* decd). *Educ:* London, Ontario; University of Toronto (LLB, LLD). Called to the Bar of Upper Canada, 1861; QC 1875; Member (C) of Legislative Assembly for London, Ontario, 1872–94; Chief Justice of the Common Pleas Div., High Court of Justice of Ont, 1894–1912; Chancellor of the University of Toronto. *Address:* Toronto, Ontario. *Club:* Toronto.

Died 22 Aug. 1923.

MEREDYTH, Sir Henry (Bayly), 5th Bt, *cr* 1795; JP; *b* 14 Jan. 1863; *e s* of Henry William Meredyth (*d* 1878) and Harriet Anne, *e d* of Rev. William Le Poer Trench; *S* grandfather, 1889; *m* 1st, 1886, Kathleen (whom he divorced, 1894), *o c* of late Robert O'Hara,

Raheen, Co. Galway; one *s* decd; 2nd, 1897, Mildred Beatrice (*d* 1912), *d* of Edmund B. Liebert; one *d*. Late Lieut 4th Brig. N Irish Division RA, and West Somerset Yeomanry. Owned over 20,000 acres. *Heir:* none. *Address:* Hollymount, Co. Down. *Clubs:* Carlton, Bachelors', Cavalry; Kildare Street, Dublin.

Died 30 Sept. 1923 (ext).

MEREWETHER, Rev. Wyndham Arthur Scinde, MA: Canon of Salisbury Cathedral since 1919; Rural Dean of Wilton; *b* 12 Sept. 1852; *s* of H. A. Merewether, QC; *m* 1888, Harriot Edith Fox (*d* 1928), *d* of Wilson Fox, MD, FRS, Physician-in-Ordinary to Queen Victoria. *Educ:* Winchester; Oriel College, Oxford. Curate of Bradford-on-Avon, 1876–80; St George, Hanover Square, 1880–86; Vicar of North Bradley, Wilts, 1886–1908; Bradford-on-Avon, 1908–14; St Thomas, Salisbury, 1914–22. *Recreations:* cricket (Winchester XI, 1870–71); Oxford *v* Cambridge Association football, 1874. *Address:* 38 The Close, Salisbury.

Died 3 Dec. 1928.

MERK, William Rudolph Henry, CSI 1887; LLD; Indian Civil Service; *b* Simla, India, 12 Dec. 1852; *e s* of Rev. J. N. Merk; *m* 1894, Rosamond, *d* of Albert Savory of Kirkham Abbey, Yorks, and Sun Rising, Banbury. *Educ:* private schools in Switzerland and Germany; King's Coll., Aberdeen. Passed 3rd for ICS; joined in India, 1875; on political duty in Afghan War, 1879–81; Under-Sec. Punjab Govt, 1882–84; with Afghan Boundary Commission, 1884–87; Deputy-Commissioner, Peshawar, 1887–92; with Black Mountain Expedition, 1888; in charge of Kurram, 1892–94; Commissioner, Peshawar, 1896–98; Chief Political Officer, Mohmand Field Force, 1897; Chief Sec. Punjab Government, 1898–99; Commissioner, Derajat, 1900–1; in charge of Mahsud Waziri blockade, 1900–2; Commissioner, Multan, 1903; Chief Commissioner Andaman and Nicobar Islands, 1904–6; Commissioner, Delhi, 1906–7; Multan, 1908; member, Legislative Council, Govt of India, 1909; Financial Commissioner Punjab; Chief Commissioner of NW Frontier Province; retired from service, 1910. Decorated for services with Afghan Boundary Commission. *Recreations:* riding, shooting, fishing, etc. *Address:* c/o Lloyds Bank, Ltd, 9 Pall Mall, SW1. *Club:* East India United Service.

Died 15 Jan. 1925.

MERRIMAN, Rt. Hon. John Xavier, PC 1909; JP; MLA, Union of South Africa, since 1910; Member of Cape Parliament for Victoria West; surveyor and farmer; *b* Street, Somersetshire, 15 March 1841; *s* of Nathaniel James Merriman, later Bishop of Grahamstown, and Julia Potter; *m* 1874, Agnes (*d* 1923), *d* of Hon. Joseph Vintcent, MLC. *Educ:* Rondebosch Diocesan College; Radley, near Oxford. Went to South Africa, 1849 and 1861; entered politics, 1869; Member of Cape Parlt for Namaqualand, Wodehouse; joined Molteno Ministry, Cape, 1875–78; Scanlen Govt, 1881–84; Commissioner of Crown Lands, 1875–78, 1881–84; Treasurer-General, 1890–93; member of Cape Jameson Raid Committee; drew up Report, 1896; Treasurer-General, 1898–1900; Prime Minister and Treasurer, 1908–10; Member of National Convention for Union, 1908. *Address:* Schoongezigt, Stellenbosch, Cape Colony. *Clubs:* Reform; Civil Service, Cape Town.

Died 2 Aug. 1926.

MERRIMAN, Col William, CIE 1890; Royal Engineers; retired; *b* Kensington, 2 April 1838; 5th *s* of late Dr John Merriman of Kensington and Marlborough; *m* 1872, Emily Jane Anna Elizabeth, *e d* of late Col Fitzroy Molyneux Henry Somerset, RE; one *s* three *d*. *Educ:* Kensington School and Addiscombe College. Commission in RE (Bombay), 1856; served in India, South Africa (Boer Campaign); Headquarters Staff, Bombay, etc; Fellow of Bombay University. Decorated for services in connection with the Coast Defences of Bombay, Karachi, Aden, etc. *Recreations:* cricket, football, hunting, shooting, rowing, golf, etc. *Address:* Creffield, Colchester. *TA:* Colchester. *Clubs:* East India United Service, Sports; Byculla, Bombay.

Died 11 March 1917.

MERRY, Rev. William Walter, DD Oxon; Rector of Lincoln College, Oxford, since 1884; *b* Worcestershire, 6 Sept. 1835; *o s* of late Walter Merry and Elizabeth Mary Byrch; *m* 1862, Alice Elizabeth (*d* 1914), *o d* of late Joseph Collings, Jurat of Royal Court of Guernsey; two *s* two *d*. *Educ:* Cheltenham; Balliol College, Oxford (MA). Scholar; 1st class Mods, 1855, 2nd class Lit. Hum. 1857; Chancellor's Prize, Latin Essay, 1858; deacon, 1860; priest, 1861; Curate, All Saints, Oxford; Select Preacher, Oxford Univ., 1878–79, 1889–90; Whitehall Preacher, 1883–84; Member of the Hebdomadal Council, 1896–1908; Vice-Chancellor, 1904–5; Public Orator University of Oxford, 1880–1910; life member of the Council of Cheltenham College; Hon. DLitt Victoria Univ. of Manchester; Hon. LLD Aberdeen. *Publications:* Greek Dialects, 1875; Selected Fragments of

Roman Poetry, 1891 (2 edns); Orationes tum Creweianae tum Gratulatoriae, 1909; edited Homer's Odyssey, vol. I 1870, vol. II 1878; completed James Riddell's edition of Odyssey, books i–xii, 1876; edited plays of Aristophanes: Clouds, 1879 (3 edns); Acharnians, 1880 (4 edns); Frogs, 1884 (3 edns); Knights, 1887 (2 edns); Birds, 1889 (3 edns); Wasps, 1893; Peace, 1900. *Address:* Lincoln College, Oxford.
Died 5 March 1918.

MERZ, John Theodore, PhD; Vice-Chairman Newcastle-upon-Tyne Electric Supply Co. Ltd; director of several companies; former Member of Senate University of Durham; *b* Manchester, 1840; *s* of Philip Merz; *m* 1873, Alice Mary Richardson; two *s* one *d*. *Educ:* Darmstad; Giessen, Göttingen, Heidelberg, and Bonn Universities. Hon. DCL Durham; Hon. LLD Aberdeen. *Publications:* Leibnitz (Philosophical Classics), 1884; History of European Thought in the Nineteenth Century: vol. i, 1896, 3rd edn, 1907; vol. ii, 1903, 2nd edn, 1912; vol. iii, 1912; vol. iv, 1914; Religion and Science, 1915; A Fragment on the Human Mind, 1919. *Recreations:* bibliophily, gardening. *Address:* The Quarries, Newcastle-upon-Tyne. *Clubs:* Reform; Union, Newcastle.
Died 21 March 1922.

MESSEL, Rudolph, PhD; FRS 1912; Manager, Royal Institution; President, Society of Chemical Industry, and Past Foreign Secretary of same; Member Board of Studies in Chemistry, University of London; Member of Governing Body, Imperial College of Science and Technology, London; Managing Director of Spencer, Chapman & Messel, Ltd; *b* Darmstadt, Germany, 14 Jan. 1848; *s* of L. Messel, banker; unmarried. *Educ:* Darmstadt; Universities of Zürich, Heidelberg, Tübingen. DSc nat. Tübingen. Came to England, 1870; assistant, J. C. Calvert; later appointed assistant to Sir Henry Roscoe, both at Manchester; entered into chemical industry and introduced numerous new processes; was the first, prior to Winkler, to devise conjointly with Squire, a successful process for the manufacture of sulphuric anhydride by the catalytic process; Past Vice Pres., Chemical Soc. *Publications:* various, mainly in relation to industrial chemistry. *Recreations:* art, literature. *Address:* 147 Victoria Street, SW1. *T:* Victoria 2400; Silvertown, Essex. *Clubs:* Devonshire, Savage.
Died 18 April 1920.

MESSENT, Philip Glynn, CIE 1914; MInstCE; Consulting Engineer (with A. J. Barry, K. A. Wolfe Barry, and J. Lumsden Rae) to the Trustees of the Port of Bombay, and Consulting Engineer (with A. J. Barry and K. A. Wolfe Barry) to the Trustees of the Port of Aden, 2 Queen Anne's Gate, Westminster, SW; *b* 1862; *e s* of late Philip J. Messent, MInstCE and Elizabeth, *d* of late Joseph Glynn, FRS, MInstCE. *Educ:* Charterhouse. Articled pupil and assistant to Philip J. Messent, MInstCE, Chief Engineer to the Tyne Improvement Commissioners, 1880–84; Assistant Engineer to the Bombay Port Trust, 1884–99; Chief Engineer to the Bombay Port Trust, 1899–1922; carried out many important works, including the Alexandra Dock (50 acres) and the Hughes Dry Dock, 1,000 ft long and 100 ft wide at entrance; extensive reclamations and Bombay Port Trust Railway. *Address:* 6 Grosvenor Hill, Wimbledon, SW19. *T:* Wimbledon 1112. *Clubs:* Northern Counties; Byculla, Royal Bombay Yacht, Bombay; Club of Western India, Poona.
Died 4 Aug. 1925.

MESSER, Adam Brunton, MD Edin.; Hon. Physician to the King; Inspector-General of Hospitals and Fleets, Royal Navy (retired); *y s* of late Adam Messer of Blainslie; *m* Elizabeth Mary, *y d* of late Capt. Belches, RN. *Educ:* Edinburgh Academy; Universities of Edinburgh and Paris. Joined Royal Navy, 1859; specially promoted for distinquished service in New Zealand War, 1863–64; Member of Royal Anthropological Institute; Coronations of Edward VII and George V, New Zealand War, and Sir Gilbert Blane's gold medals. *Address:* Kinclune, Carlisle Road, Eastbourne. *Club:* Caledonian United Service, Edinburgh.
Died 11 Oct. 1919.

METAXA, Count Andrea; *b* 23 March 1844; *m* 1871, Louisa Elizabeth (*d* 1896), *d* of late Thomas White of Congelow, Yalding, Kent; one *d*. *Educ:* Cheltenham. Special war correspondent, 1870. *Publications:* Round the Wight in an Open Canoe; Journal of a Tour in the Mediterranean; Walking Tour through the Isle of Wight, 1870. *Recreations:* rowing, public and political speaking on Eastern Question, Women's Suffrage Bill, Deceased Wife's Sister's Bill, and Married Woman's Property Act. *Heir: g s* Andrea-Richard-Dudley, *b* 20 Jan. 1902. *Address:* 4 Park Place, St James's, SW.
Died 15 March 1921.

METAXAS, Dimitry George, Hon. GCVO 1906; Greek Minister to Rome, 1908; *b* Syra, Greece; 2nd *s* of George L. Metaxas, lawyer; *m* 1st, Helene C. Cantacuzéne (*d* 1909); one *d*; 2nd, 1915, Amelie

Mavrogordato. *Educ:* Athens. Diplomatic service at the Foreign Office, Constantinople, Rome, Berlin, Belgrade, London; Secretary, Conference, Berlin, 1880; and during negotiations, Prevesa, for delimiting new Greco-Turkish frontiers; Envoy Extraordinary and Minister Plenipotentiary of King of the Hellenes to Great Britain, 1895–1908.
Died 1 Feb. 1928.

METCALFE, Sir Charles Herbert Theophilus, 6th Bt, *cr* 1802; civil engineer; *b* 8 Sept. 1853; *o c* of Sir Theophilus John Metcalfe, 5th Bt and 1st wife, Charlotte, *d* of Lieut-Gen. Sir John Low, KCB; *S* father, 1883; unmarried. *Educ:* Harrow; University Coll., Oxford (MA 1881). Articled to Fox and Sons; employed in construction of railways in Ireland, Lancs, Cheshire and Southern Africa. *Heir: cousin* Theophilus John Massie Metcalfe, *b* 19 June 1866. *Address:* Winkworth Hill, Hascombe, Godalming. *Club:* Carlton.
Died 29 Dec. 1928.

METCALFE, Hon. Thomas Llewellyn; Justice of Court of King's Bench, Manitoba, since 1909; *b* St Thomas, Ontario, 21 Feb. 1870; unmarried. *Educ:* Portage la Prairie. Came West, 1876; early life farming and ranching; admitted Manitoba Bar, 1894; afterwards to Bar of Saskatchewan and Alberta; practised at Winnipeg; was Counsel for prisoner in Molson's Bank Robbery Case; Member Royal Commission last Revision Dominion Statutes; also Fisheries Commission, 1909. *Recreations:* active generally; special—polo, riding. *Address:* Court House, Winnipeg. *T:* Fort Rouge 328. *M:* 655. *Clubs:* Manitoba; St Charles Country; Polo, Hunt.
Died 2 April 1922.

METCALFE, Rev. W. M., DD (St Andrews, 1892); FSAScot; Minister of South Parish, Paisley; Assessor to Lord Rector of University of St Andrews, 1892–99; Clerk to the Presbytery of Paisley; *b* York, 14 Sept. 1840; *s* of John and Hannah Metcalfe; *m* Cecilia, *d* of James and Cecilia Simpson, Dundee; two *s* three *d*. *Educ:* New Coll., London. Minister of Tighnabruaich; Editor Scottish Review, 1882–1900. *Publications:* The Natural Truth of Christianity, 1880; The Reasonableness of Christianity, 1882; Pinkerton's Vitæ Antiquæ Sanctorum Scotiæ, 1889; Ancient Lives of Scottish Saints, 1895; Legends of the Saints in the Scottish Dialect of the Fourteenth Century, 1896; The John Neilston Institution: its First Fifty Years, 1902; Charters and Documents relating to the Burgh of Paisley, 1902; The Legends of SS Ninian and Machor in the Scottish Dialect of the Fourteenth Century, 1904; History of the County of Renfrew, 1905; A History of Paisley, 1909; Supplementary Dictionary of the Scottish Language, 1910; The Lordship of Paisley, 1912; Specimens of Scottish Literature (1325–1835), 1913; Robert Henryson's Poems, 1916; many articles on literary and other topics. *Recreations:* reading, golfing. *Address:* South Manse, Paisley.
Died 8 Aug. 1916.

METCHNIKOFF, Elie; Professor at the Pasteur Institute, Paris; *b* 1845. *Educ:* Gressen, Göttingen and Munich. Prof. of Zoology and Anatomy, Odessa, 1873–82; apptd Dir of bacteriol lab., Odessa, 1886; went to Ecole Normale, Paris, 1888. Membre de l'Académie de Médecine; Foreign Member of the Royal Society of London and of the Académie des Sciences; awarded Nobel Prize for Medicine or Physiology (with Prof. Paul Ehrlich), 1908. *Publications:* Intra Cellular Digestion, 1882; The Comparative Pathology of Inflammation, 1892; The Nature of Man, 1903; Immunity in Infective Diseases, 1906; Optimistic Essays, 1907; The Prolongation of Human Life, 1910. *Address:* rue Dutot 18 (XVᵉ), Paris.
Died 15 July 1916.

METHUEN, Sir Algernon Methuen Marshall, 1st Bt, *cr* 1916; MA; head of Methuen & Co., Ltd, publishers; *b* Southwark, 23 Feb. 1856; 3rd *s* of John Buck Stedman, FRCS, Godalming, and Jane Elizabeth, *d* of Richard Marshall; assumed surname of Methuen, Aug. 1899, Royal licence 1916; *m* 1884, Emily Caroline, *d* of Edwin Bedford, Ladbroke Terrace, W. *Educ:* Berkhampstead School; Wadham College, Oxford (BA 1878, MA 1881). Head of High Croft Preparatory School, Milford, 1880–95; founded Methuen and Co., June 1889; JP Surrey, 1909; contested (L) Guildford Division, Surrey, 1910. *Publications:* A Simple Plan for a New House of Lords, 1911; An Anthology of English Verse, 1921; Shakespeare to Hardy, 1922; An Alpine ABC, 1922; *pamphlets:* Peace or War in South Africa, 1901, enlarged edn as The Tragedy of South Africa, 1905; England's Ruin, 1905; also some school books. *Heir: none. Address:* New Place, Haslemere, Surrey. *Clubs:* Reform, National Liberal.
Died 20 Sept. 1924.

METTAM, Prof. A. E.; Principal of Royal Veterinary College of Ireland since 1900; Professor of Bacteriology and Pathology since

1900; President of the Royal College of Veterinary Surgeons, 1911–12–13. Professor of Anatomy and Histology, Royal Dick Veterinary College, Edinburgh, 1890–1900; George Heriot Research Fellow Edinburgh University, 1896; Past President of the Scottish Microscopical Society; Examiner in National University of Ireland and in the Universities of London and Manchester; member Royal Irish Academy. *Address:* Royal Veterinary College, Dublin.

Died Nov. 1917.

MEULEMAN, Most Rev. Brice, SJ; Catholic Archbishop of Calcutta since 1902; *b* Ghent, 1 March 1862. *Educ:* St Barbe's Coll., Ghent. Joined the Society of Jesus, 1879; after three years' philosophical and scientific studies at Louvain, joined the Jesuit Mission in Bengal, 1886; taught philosophy for six years in St Xavier's College, Calcutta and theology for three years in St Mary's Seminary, Kurseong; nominated Superior of the Jesuit Mission in Bengal, 1900. *Address:* Calcutta.

Died 15 July 1924.

MEXBOROUGH, 5th Earl of, *cr* 1766; **John Horace Savile,** DL, JP; Baron Pollington, 1753; Viscount Pollington, 1766; *b* 17 June 1843; *s* of 4th Earl and 1st wife, Rachel Katherine (*d* 1854), *d* of 3rd Earl of Orford; *S* father, 1899; *m* 1st, 1867, Venetia Stanley (*d* 1900), *d* of Sir Rowland Stanley Errington, 11th Bt; one *d* decd; 2nd, 1906, Donna Sylvia Cecilia Maria (*d* 1915), *d* of the Nobile Carlo de Ser Antoni of Lucca and Naples, and *widow* of Captain Claude Clerk, CIE. *Educ:* Eton; Trinity Coll., Cambridge (MA 1863). Contested the first election by ballot ever held in the United Kingdom, Pontefract, Yorks. Buddhist. Owned about 7,600 acres. *Heir:* half-brother Hon. John Henry Savile, *b* 27 Sept. 1868. *Recreations:* gardening, reading. *Address:* Albert Court, Kensington Gore, SW; Cannizaro, Wimbledon Common, SW. *T:* Wimbledon 103; Methley Park, Leeds. *M:* A 1956. *Clubs:* Carlton, Hurlingham, Lords, Travellers'.

Died 4 June 1916.

MEYER, Arthur; Director of the Gaulois; publicist; *b* Paris, 16 June 1845; *m* Marguerite de Turenne, *g d* of Duke de Fitz-James. *Publications:* Ce que mes yeux ont vu, 1911; Ce que je peux dire, 1912; Ce qu'il fait taire (play), 1914; numerous articles. *Recreations:* collected books, drawings, autographs. *Address:* rue Drouot 4, Paris. *TA:* Arthur Meyer, Paris. *T:* 212, 21. *Clubs:* Cercle interallié, Paris.

Died 2 Feb. 1924.

MEYER, Sir Carl Ferdinand, 1st Bt, *cr* 1910; JP, Essex; Lieutenant of the City of London; Director of the National Bank of Egypt; Chairman of the London Committee of De Beers; *b* Hamburg, 23 Dec. 1851; *s* of Siegmund Meyer, Hamburg, and Elise Rosa, *d* of Reuben Hahn; naturalised British citizen, 1877; *m* 1883, Adèle, *d* of Julius Levis, of Belsize Grove, Hampstead; one *s* one *d*. *Educ:* abroad. *Recreations:* music, shooting. *Heir:* *s* Frank Cecil Meyer [*b* 7 May 1886; *m* 1920, Marjorie, 2nd *d* of Frederick Seeley, Hale, Cheshire]. *Address:* 12 Park Crescent, Portland Place, W1. *T:* Langham 2116; Shortgrove, Newport, Essex. *Club:* Junior Carlton.

Died 18 Dec. 1922.

MEYER, George von Lengerke; Secretary of the United States Navy, 1909–13; *b* Boston, USA, 24 June 1858; *s* of George Augustus Meyer and Grace Helen, *d* of William Parker, Boston, and *g d* of Bishop Parker, Massachusetts; *m* 1885, Alice, *d* of Charles H. Appleton and Isabella, *d* of Jonathan Mason, Boston; one *s* two *d*. Graduated, Harvard, 1879; Member of the City Government of Boston, 1889–92; Member of the Massachusetts Legislature, 1892–97; Speaker of the House of Representatives, 1894–97; Chairman of the Massachusetts Board, Paris Exposition Commissioners, 1898; Member, Republican National Committee from Massachusetts, 1898–1904; United States Ambassador to Italy, 1900–5, to Russia, 1905–7; Postmaster-General, 1907–9; Chevalier Grand Cross, Grand Cordon of SS Maurizio e Lazzaro, Italy; of Alexander Nevsky, Russia; of Rising Sun, Japan; LLD Harvard, 1911. *Recreations:* fishing, shooting, hunting. *Address:* Hamilton, Mass. *Clubs:* Somerset, Boston; Knickerbocker, New York; Metropolitan, Washington.

Died 10 March 1918.

MEYER, Kuno, PhD; Professor of Celtic at the University of Berlin since 1911; Member of the Royal Prussian Academy; *b* Hamburg, 20 Dec. 1858; *y s* of Dr Edward Meyer, Classical Master at the Johanneum. *Educ:* Gelehrtenschule of the Johanneum, Hamburg. Studied Germanic and Celtic Philology at the University of Leipzig, 1879–83; Lecturer in Teutonic Languages at University College, Liverpool, 1884, Professor, 1895–1915; founded the Zeitschrift für Celtische Philologie, 1895, and jointly with Whitley Stokes, the Archiv für Celtische Lexikographie, 1898; founded the School of Irish Learning, Dublin, 1903; Hon. DLitt Wales, Oxford, and St

Andrews. *Publications:* Eine irische Version der Alexandersage, 1883; The Battle of Ventry, 1884; The Irish Odyssey, 1885; A German Grammar (Parallel Series), 1888; The Vision of MacConglinne, 1892; The Age and Origin of Shelta, 1892; The Voyage of Bran, 1894; Hibernica Minora, 1895; Early Relations of the Brython and Gael, 1896; King and Hermit, 1901; Liadain and Curithir, 1902; Four Songs of Summer and Winter, 1903; The Law of Adamnan, 1904; Ancient Irish Poetry, 1911; contributions to Irish Lexicography, etc. *Address:* Niebuhrstrasse 11A, Charlottenburg.

Died 11 Oct. 1919.

MEYER, Paul; Commandeur de la Légion d'Honneur; member of the Institute of France; Associate of the British Academy; directeur de l'Ecole Nationale des Chartes, Paris; professeur honoraire au Collège de France; *b* Paris, 17 Jan. 1840. *Educ:* Lycée Louis le Grand; Ecole des Chartes. *Publications:* (ed) Romania, 1872; many publications concerning the Romance languages and literatures. *Address:* 16 Labourdonnais, Paris.

Died 1917.

MEYER, Sir William Stevenson, GCIE 1918 (KCIE 1909; CIE 1901); KCSI 1915; Indian Civil Service, retired 1918; High Commissioner for India since 1920; *b* 13 Feb. 1860; *er s* of Rev. Theodore Jonah Meyer (minister of Presbyterian C of E) and Jane Ann, *d* of William Stevenson; *m* 1895, Mabel Henrietta (*d* 1914), *d* of late Major William W. Jackson, IA; one *s* decd, one *d* decd. *Educ:* Blackheath; University College School, London; University College, London. Entered ICS 1881; Assistant Secretary to Madras Government, 1886–89; Secretary Board of Revenue, 1890–94; Deputy Secretary Government of India, Financial Department, 1896–1901; Editor, Imperial Gazetteer of India, 1902–4; Financial Secretary, Government of India, 1905–9; Chief Secretary, Government of Madras, 1909; Member of Royal Commission on Decentralization in India, 1907–9; a British Delegate to International Opium Conference, The Hague, 1911–12; Member of Lord Nicholson's Committee on the Indian Army, 1912–13; President, Central Recruiting Board, India, 1917–18; Ordinary Member of Council of Governor-General of India, 1913–18; led Indian delegns, 1st and 2nd Assemblies of League of Nations, 1920–21. *Publication:* Administrative Problems of British India, 1910 (translation and revision of J. Chailley, L'Inde Britannique). *Address:* St James's Court, Buckingham Gate, SW1. *Clubs:* Reform, Overseas.

Died 19 Oct. 1922.

MEYERHEIM, Robert Gustav, RI 1898; belonged to family of Berlin artists of same name; a native of Dantzic. *Educ:* Academy at Carlsruhe under Professor Gude; Düsseldorf under Professor Oswald Achenbach; settled in England 1875, taking up water-colour in addition to oil-painting. *Address:* Lindeneck, Wimblehurst Road, Horsham.

Died 16 May 1920.

MEYNELL, Alice Christiana Gertrude; poet and essayist; *b* 22 Sept. 1847; *yr d* of late Thomas James Thompson and Christiana, *d* of Thomas Edward Weller; *m* 1877, Wilfrid Meynell; eight *c*. *Educ:* by her father, who, having completed his own education at Trinity Coll., Cambridge, married early and devoted himself to his two daughters, of whom the elder was Lady (Elizabeth) Butler, the battle-painter (wife of Lt.-Gen. Sir William Francis Butler). Spent much of her early life in Italy. *Publications: verse:* Preludes (volume of poems written in girlhood), 1875; Poems (the same republished with some changes and additions), 1893; The Rhythm of Life, 1893; The Poetry of Pathos and Delight (anthology of Coventry Patmore's poetry), 1895; The Colour of Life, 1896; The Flower of the Mind: a General Anthology of English Poetry, 1897; Later Poems, 1901; Selections from the Poets; A Selection from the verses of John B. Tabb, 1906; Collected Poems, 1913; A Father of Women, and other Poems, 1917; *essays:* The Children, 1896; The Spirit of Place, 1898; Ceres' Runaway, 1910; Hearts of Controversy, 1917; The Second Person Singular, and other Essays, 1921; *prose:* John Ruskin, 1900; Mary, Mother of Jesus, 1912; also contributor to a number of periodicals; The School of Poetry (posthumous). *Recreation:* music. *Address:* 2A Granville Place, W; Greatham, Pulborough, Sussex.

Died 27 Nov. 1922.

MEYNELL, Edgar; Recorder of Doncaster since 1921; *b* 6 Sept. 1859; *o surv. s* of late Judge Meynell; unmarried. *Educ:* The Oratory, Edgbaston. Called to the Bar, Middle Temple, 1884; joined the North Eastern Circuit; was a Revising Barrister in Hull and the East Riding of Yorkshire, 1892–1912. *Address:* Old Elvet, Durham. *T:* Durham 133. *Clubs:* Union; Northern Counties, Newcastle-upon-Tyne; Durham County, Durham.

Died 4 July 1923.

MEYNELL, Everard; author, journalist; *b* 1882; 2nd *s* of Wilfrid Meynell; *m* 1907, Grazia Carbone, singer, Buffalo, USA; two *s* two *d. Publications:* Life of Francis Thompson; Corot and his Friends, etc; contributor to Illustrated London News, Dublin Review, etc. *Address:* Greatham, near Pulborough, Sussex.

Died 7 Jan. 1926.

MEYRICK, Sir George Augustus Eliott Tapps-Gervis-, 4th Bt, *cr* 1791; *b* 9 March 1855; *s* of Sir George Eliott Meyrick Tapps-Gervis-Meyrick, 3rd Bt, and Fanny, *d* of Christopher Harland; *S* father, 1896; *m* 1884, Jacintha, *d* of Charles Paul Phipps; two *s* two *d*. *Heir: s* George Llewellyn Tapps-Gervis-Meyrick, *b* 23 Sept. 1885. *Address:* Hinton Admiral, Christchurch, Hants; Bodorgan, Anglesey.

Died 12 May 1928.

MEYRICK, James Joseph, CB 1882; FRCVS; *b* London, 6 Sept. 1834; *o s* of late Theobald Meyrick of Ballinasloe, Ireland; *m* 1881, Elizabeth Henrietta, *d* of late James Westbeare. *Educ:* City of London School; Royal Veterinary College, London. Gazetted Veterinary Surgeon to Royal Artillery, 1860; became Vet.-Surgeon, 1st class, 1870, and Inspecting Vet.-Surgeon, 1881; served Canada, 1862–67 (including Fenian raids, 1866, medal); India, 1868–80; Egypt, 1882–83; superintended Government horse-breeding operations in Punjab, 1878–80 (thanks of Government of India and Punjab Government); Egyptian Campaign, 1882 (despatches, medal, Egyptian medal, 3rd class Osmanieh). Decorated for services in Egyptian Campaign. *Publications:* Stable Management and Prevention of Disease among Horses in India; Veterinary Manual for Use of Salootris and Native Horse-owners in India (translated into Hindustani; published and distributed by Indian Government). *Recreations:* shooting, painting. *Address:* 45 The Chase, Clapham Common, SW4.

Died 14 Feb. 1925.

MEYSEY-THOMPSON, Col Richard Frederick; late Rifle Brigade; *b* 17 April 1847; 2nd *s* of Sir Harry Stephen Meysey-Thompson, 1st Bt, and Elizabeth Anne, *d* of Sir John Croft, 1st Bt; *m* 1879, Charlotte, *y d* of Sir James Walker, 1st Bt; one *s* one *d*. *Educ:* Eton. Commanded 4th West Yorkshire Regiment; Local Director of Barclays Bank, York; Member of York Race Committee; formerly member of Irish National Hunt Steeplechase Committee; Medal for Ashanti campaign, and clasp for Coomassie, and also Royal Humane Society's Medal. *Publications:* A Fishing Catechism; A Shooting Catechism; A Hunting Catechism; The Course, The Camp, The Chase; The Horse. *Address:* Westwood Mount, Scarborough. *T:* Scarborough 367. *Clubs:* Army and Navy; Yorkshire County, York.

Died 1 Sept. 1926.

MIALL, Louis Compton, DSc; FRS; *b* Bradford, 1842; *m* Emily (*d* 1918), *d* of Joseph Pearce; three *c*. Professor of Biology, University, Leeds, 1876–1907; Fullerian Professor of Physiology in the Royal Inst., 1904–5; President Zoological Section, British Association, 1897; Education Section, 1908. *Publications:* Special Memoirs on Natural History, Object Lessons from Nature, 1891; Natural History of Aquatic Insects, 1895; Round the Year, 1896; Thirty Years of Teaching, 1897; Injurious and Useful Insects, 1902; House, Garden, and Field, 1904; The Early Naturalists, 1912, etc. *Address:* Thornycroft, Ben Rhudding, Leeds. *Died 21 Feb. 1921.*

MICHAEL, Albert Davidson, FLS, FZS, FRMS, FRHS, FRGS, etc; *b* 5 May, 1836; *s* of J. Michael, Solicitor, London; *m* 1865, Anne Smith. *Educ:* King's College, London. Practised as a solicitor in London; also known in connection with the Conservative organisation in Surrey; late President of the Royal Microscopical Society, and the Quekett Microscopical Club; late Vice-Pres. of the Linnean Society, and member of the Scientific Committees of the Zoological and Royal Horticultural Societies; Vice-President of Ray Society, etc. *Publications:* numerous books and papers on the acarina and on microscopical subjects published by the Ray, Linnean, Zoological and Royal Microscopical Societies, Das Tierreich and in other English, French, Belgian and German scientific publications. *Recreations:* the microscope, travel, gardening. *Address:* The Warren, Studland, Dorset.

Died 29 May 1927.

MICHELHAM, 1st Baron, *cr* 1905, of Hellingly; **Herbert Stern;** KCVO 1912; Bt 1905; a Baron of Portugal; *b* 28 Sept. 1851; *s* of late Baron Hermann de Stern (in Kingdom of Portugal) and Julia, *d* of late Aaron Asher Goldsmid; *m* 1898, Aimée Geraldine (despatches twice, Order of Mercy, Mons Star, Médaille d'Or, Légion d'Honneur), *d* of Octavius Bradshaw; two *s*. Senior Partner in firm of Herbert Stern and Co., 33 Cornhill, EC, and Paris; DL of City of London; Alderman, LCC, 1906–12. *Heir: s* Hon. Herman Alfred Stern, *b* 5 Sept. 1900. *Address:* 26 Princes Gate, SW. *T:* Kensington 502; Strawberry Hill, Twickenham; Imber Court, Thames Ditton; 23 rue Nitot, Paris. *Club:* Carlton. *Died 7 Jan. 1919.*

MICHELHAM, Lady; (Aimée Geraldine); Lady President of the League of Mercy; *d* of Octavius Bradshaw; *m* 1st, 1899, 1st Baron Michelham (*d* 1919), *s* of Baron Hermann de Stern and Julia, *d* of Aaron Asher Goldsmid; 2nd, 1926, Frederick, *s* of late Frederick Almy, of Cedarhurst, Long Island, NY. Order of Mercy, Legion of Honour, Médaille des Epidémies, 1914 Star, despatches twice. *Address:* 20 Arlington Street, SW1. *T:* Regent 603; The Mansion, Strawberry Hill. *T:* Richmond 164; 23 rue Nitot, Paris.

Died 1 Jan. 1927.

MICHELL, Rev. Francis Rodon; Vicar of Ash, next Sandwich, Canterbury; *b* Ilfracombe, 6 Aug. 1839; *e s* of John Michell, solicitor, and Mary Elizabeth Bryan; *m* 1866, Adelaide Lachlan, *d* of Lieutenant Maclean, 67th Regt Bengal NI; four *s* four *d*. *Educ:* Penzance Grammar School; St Augustine's College, Canterbury. Ordained, 1862; sent to Pekin by the SPG as their first ordained missionary; when mission closed in 1864 he went to Shanghai, China, and thence in 1866 to Calcutta; Chaplain on the Bengal Ecclesiastical Establishment, 1867; Archdeacon of Calcutta and Examining Chaplain to the Bishop of Calcutta, 1887; Fellow of the University of Calcutta, 1889; retired from the Service, 1892. *Recreations:* carpentering, bookbinding. *Address:* Ash Vicarage, Canterbury. *Club:* Primrose.

Died Aug. 1920.

MICHELL, John, ISO 1903; HM Consul-General St Petersburg, 1894–1903; *b* Cronstadt, 20 Aug. 1836; *s* of John Michell of Bodmin and Amelia, *d* of T. Bishop of St Petersburg; *m* Louisa, *d* of R. C. Dangar of St Neots; three *s*. *Educ:* abroad. Home, Civil, and Consular Services; clerk in the Admiralty, 1860; Vice-Consul, St Petersburg, 1866; assisted late Capt. Glascott, RN, in verifying the Turco-Persian boundary Maps, 1867–69; Consul-General for Northern, North-Eastern, and Central Russia, 1886; Consul-General, 1894; received Jubilee decoration. *Address:* Hotakka, Ayrupää Railway Station, Wiborg, Finland. *Died 11 Sept. 1921.*

MICHELL, Hon. Sir Lewis Loyd, Kt 1902; CVO 1910; JP; Director British South Africa Co., Rhodesia Railways and Mashonaland Railway; *b* Plymouth, 11 Aug. 1842; *s* of John Michell, solicitor, of Ilfracombe, and Mary Bryan; *m* 1871, Maria Agnes, *d* of Edward Philpott, Civil Commissioner, Uitenhage, Cape Colony; four *s* three *d*. *Educ:* Christ's Hospital. Bolitho's Bank, Penzance; London and South African Bank; for 30 years with the Standard Bank of S Africa, latterly as General Manager; was President of the Martial Law Board and Treasurer of Lord Milner's Relief Fund during the Boer War; late Minister without portfolio, Cape Colony; Chairman of De Beers Consolidated Mines; Member of the Legislative Assembly for Cape Town; Fellow of the Bankers' Institute, South Africa; Fellow Royal Colonial Institute. *Publication:* Life of Cecil Rhodes, 1910. *Address:* Rondesbosch, Cape Province. *Died 29 Oct. 1928.*

MICHELSON, Christian; former Prime Minister, Norway; *b* 1857. Admitted to the Bar, 1879; became partner in a Bergen shipping firm; Chairman of Board of Aldermen, Bergen; returned to Storthing for Bergen, 1891; went back to business and municipal life, 1894; and again returned to Storthing for Bergen, 1903; member of Cabinet under M Hagerup's Premiership, 1905; Chief of Provisional Norwegian Government after separation of Union with Sweden, 7 June–25 Nov. 1905; again Prime Minister to 1907. *Address:* Fjösanger, Norway.

Died 28 June 1925.

MICHIE, James Coutts, ARSA; artist; *b* 29 July 1861; 3rd *s* of late Henry Michie; *m* 1900, Mrs MacCulloch. *Educ:* Edinburgh, Rome, Paris. Received medal in Paris Salon, 1898; acted on the Executive Committee for Franco-British Exhibition, 1907, and for Rome, 1911; travelled in France, Italy, Spain, Morocco, living in Tangier for several years. *Recreations:* cycling, billiards. *Address:* 184 Queen's Gate, SW. *T:* Kensington 241; Oak Hall, Haslemere. *Clubs:* Arts; University, Aberdeen. *Died 18 Dec. 1919.*

MICHIE, Robert James, MA; leader-writer Bristol Times and Mirror; *b* Banffshire, 3 Aug. 1856; *m* 1900, Annie Crawford Smith. *Educ:* schools in Scotland and Newcastle-on-Tyne; University of Aberdeen (Honours in Philosophy and Classics). Entered journalism, 1881; on sub-editorial staffs successively of Reading Mercury till 1890 and Birmingham Daily Gazette till 1897; editor of Western Morning News, Western Weekly News, and Naval and Military Record, 1897–1902. *Recreation:* gardening. *Address:* Times and Mirror Office, Bristol. *Died 31 Dec. 1928.*

MICHOLLS, E. Montefiore, MA; barrister-at-law; *b* 27 July 1852; *s* of late Horatio L. Micholls; *m* Ada, *d* of late Maurice Beddington,

JP; two *s* two *d. Educ:* Rugby; New College, Oxford. Called to the Bar, 1877; Chairman of the Executive Committee of the National Society for Epileptics; Manager of elementary schools in the East End of London, and of two industrial schools; and on the committees of other charitable and educational societies. *Recreations:* fishing, shooting, golf. *Address:* 11 Queen's Gate, SW7. *T:* Kensington 747.

Died 11 Sept. 1926.

MICKS, William Lawson; *b* 25 Jan. 1851; *s* of late Sir Robert Micks, sometime Secretary to Board of Inland Revenue, and Ellen, *d* of James Lawson of Waterford; *m* Isabel, *d* of late Rev. Canon Meyrick, Rector of Blesinton, Co. Wicklow; three *s* one *d. Educ:* Kilkenny College; Trinity College, Dublin. Entered Irish Church Temporalities Commission as Clerk, 1872; Registrar, 1878; Assistant-Secretary Irish Land Commission on its formation, 1881; transferred to temporary post of Comptroller under the Arrears of Rent (Ireland) Act 1882, 1882; reverted to former post, 1883; a General Inspector under Local Government Board for Ireland, 1885; acted as a Commissioner on the County Donegal Light Railway Commission, 1890; first Secretary of Congested Districts Board for Ireland, 1891; was a Commissioner on the Local Government Board for Ireland, 1898–1910; was seconded to act as Chairman of the Viceregal Poor Law Reform Commission for Ireland, 1903, which reported in 1906; nominated to be a member of the Viceregal Committee of Inquiry into the Agriculture and Technical Instruction (Ireland) Act 1899, and the administration of that Act, 1906; dissented from his colleagues and submitted a Minority Report in 1907; hon. member of Congested Districts Board for Ireland, 1909, Permanent Member, 1910; retired from the public service on pension, 1924. *Publication:* History of the Congested Districts Board, 1925. *Address:* 3 Palmerston Villas, Palmerston Park, Dublin.

Died 4 April 1928.

MIDDLEMORE, Sir John Throgmorton, 1st Bt, *cr* 1919; MP (LU) Birmingham, North, 1899–1918; *b* 9 June 1844; 4th *s* of William Middlemore, Hawkesley, and Mary, *d* of Thomas Groom, Edgbaston; *m* 1st, 1878, Marian (*d* 1879), *d* of Richard Bagnall, Worcester; 2nd, 1881, Mary, *d* of late Rev. Thomas Price, Selly Oak, Birmingham; one *s* four *d* (and two *d* decd). *Educ:* Edgbaston; Bowdoin Coll., Brunswick USA. Trained as surgeon (profession not taken up because of ill-health). Founder of the Children's Emigration Homes, Birmingham, and of the Middlemore Home, Halifax, Nova Scotia; member of Birmingham City Council, 1883–92; JP Birmingham and Worcestershire. *Heir: s* William Hawkslow Middlemore, *b* 10 April 1908. *Address:* Lark Hill, Worcester.

Died 17 Oct. 1928.

MIDDLETON, 9th Baron, *cr* 1711; **Digby Wentworth Bayard Willoughby,** DL, JP; Bt 1677; Alderman, East Riding of Yorkshire County Council; President Buckrose Conservative Association; Chairman, Advisory Council on Light Horse Breeding to Board of Agriculture, 1911; *b* 24 Aug. 1844; *s* of 8th Baron and Julia Louisa, *o d* of Alexander William Bosville, Thorpe and Gunthwaite, Yorkshire; *S* father, 1877; *m* 1869, Eliza Maria Gordon, *o d* of Sir Alexander Penrose Gordon-Cumming, 3rd Bt. *Educ:* Eton. Scots Guards, 1864; Lieut and Capt. 1867; retired, 1869; late Hon. Col ER Yorkshire Volunteer Artillery; late MFH Lord Middleton's Hunt, ER Yorks. Owned about 99,600 acres; possessed minerals in Notts. *Recreations:* forestry, sport. *Heir: brother* Hon. (Godfrey) Ernest (Percival) Willoughby, *b* 18 June 1847. *Address:* Wollaton Hall (built by John of Padua), Nottingham; Birdsall House, and Settrington House, York; Middleton Hall, Tamworth; Applecross, RSO, Ross-shire. *Clubs:* Carlton, Junior Carlton.

Died 28 May 1922.

MIDDLETON, 10th Baron, *cr* 1711; **(Godfrey) Ernest (Percival) Willoughby,** Bt 1677; *b* 18 June 1847; *s* of 8th Baron and Julia Louisa, *o d* of Alexander William Bosville, Thorpe and Gunthwaite, Yorkshire; *S* brother, 1922; *m* 1881, Ida Eleanora Constance (*d* 1924), *d* of George W. H. Ross; two *s* four *d* (and two *s* decd). *Educ:* Eton. Formerly Captain 9th Lancers; owned about 99,600 acres; possessed minerals in Notts. *Heir: e* surv. *s* Major Hon. Michael Guy Percival Willoughby, *b* 21 Oct. 1887. *Address:* Wollaton Hall (built by John of Padua), Nottingham; Birdsall House and Settrington House, York; Middleton Hall, Tamworth; Applecross, RSO, Ross-shire; The Green, Brompton, RSO, Yorkshire. *Clubs:* Army and Navy; Yorkshire, York.

Died 11 Nov. 1924.

MIDDLETON, Reginald Empson, MInstCE, MIMechE, FSI, FRSanI, FRMS; late Joint Engineer to the Staines Reservoirs Joint Committee, Engineer of Higham Ferrers and Rushden Water Board, Huntingdon, Welwyn, etc; *b* 30 May 1844; *s* of Rev. Joseph Empson Middleton, Vice-Principal of St Bees College and Vicar of Belton,

Leicestershire; *m* E. A., *d* of Henry White of Silverdale, Sydenham, SE; four *s* two *d. Educ:* St Bees Grammar School, Cumberland; Charterhouse. Articled to Robert Stephenson & Co., Newcastle-on-Tyne; engaged in the locomotive department of Whitehaven, Cleator, and Egremont Railway, and of the Great Eastern Railway, afterwards on the Moldo-Wallachian bridges; Resident Engineer Solway Junction Railway and Cadiz Waterworks, etc; District Engineer Honduras Interoceanic Railway; engaged on Southport and Ventor Piers, Whitby and Redcar Railway; engineer in charge of survey department, Forth Bridge Works; Consulting Engineer for Waterworks at Dauntsey, Honiton, Stoney Stanton, Wymington, Glamorgan County Council, etc, and for several sanitation works; Assistant Commissioner to Royal Commission on London Water Supply, 1891–93; Joint Engineer for New River Water Company's Bill, 1896; Highland Water Power Bill, 1899; Charing Cross, Hammersmith and District Railway Bills, 1901, 1902, etc; Chief Engineering Witness for London Water Companies before the Royal Commission on London Water Supply, 1898–99; appeared for and advised the Metropolitan Water Companies and a large number of water companies, corporations, and councils; was engaged for some of the London waterworks companies in connection with arbitration for purchase. *Publications:* pamphlets on Triangulation at the Forth Bridge; London (Welsh) Water Supply; Village Water Supplies; The Pollution of Water and its Correction; Pollution of Rivers; the Relative Value of Percolation Gauges; The Desirability of making Watershed Areas and Sanitary Districts Coterminous; a Treatise on Surveying (part author), 4th edition 1920. *Recreation:* rowing (Tyne Amateur Rowing Club, Kingston Rowing Club; Tyne Grand Challenge Cup, Clydesdale Cup; Steward's Plate, Durham; Plate, York; Garland Challenge Cup and Championship, Tyne). *Address:* 90 Kensington Park Road, W11.

Died 1 July 1925.

MIFFLIN, Lloyd, LittD; *b* Columbia-on-the-Susquebanna, Pennsylvania, 15 Sept. 1846; *s* of J. Houston Mifflin, portrait painter and author of vol. of lyrics. *Educ:* Washington Classical Institute; private tutors; studied in Europe, 1871–73. In early life devoted himself to landscape painting; a pupil of Moran, NA, and of Herzog, Germany; health failing, gave up art, retired to country and devoted himself to literature, especially to the sonnet, of which he wrote more than five hundred. *Publications:* The Hills, 1896; At the Gates of Song, 1897; The Slopes of Helicon, and Other Poems, 1898; Echoes of Greek Idyls, 1899; The Fields of Dawn and Later Sonnets, 1900; Castalian Days, 1903; The Fleeing Nymph and Other Verse, 1905; Collected Sonnets of Lloyd Mifflin, 350, 1905; My Lady of Dream, 1906; Toward the Uplands, 1908; Flower and Thorn, 1909; As Twilight Falls, 1916. *Recreations:* painting, riding, driving, the pursuit of literature. *Address:* Norwood, near Columbia, Pennsylvania, USA.

Died 16 July 1921.

MILBANK, Sir Powlett Charles John, 2nd Bt, *cr* 1882; JP, DL; Lord-Lieutenant of Radnorshire, 1895; Master of Foxhounds, Radnorshire and West Herefordshire, since 1902; *b* Edinburgh, 1 May 1852; *o* surv. *s* of Sir Frederick Acclom Milbank, 1st Bt, and Lady (Alexina Harriet Elizabeth) Milbank, *d* of Sir Alexander Don, 6th Bt; *S* father, 1898; *m* 1875, Edith Mary, *d* of Sir Richard Green-Price, 1st Bt; one *s* three *d. Educ:* Eton. MP (C) Radnorshire, 1895–1900. *Heir: s* Frederick Richard Powlett Milbank, *b* 7 Sept. 1881. *Address:* Barningham Park, Barnard Castle, Yorks; Norton Manor, Norton, RSO, Radnorshire. *TA:* Norton, Prestign; Barningham, Barnard Castle. *Clubs:* Carlton, Bachelors'.

Died 30 Jan. 1918.

MILBURN, Sir Charles Stamp, 2nd Bt, *cr* 1905; *b* 5 Dec. 1878; *s* of Sir John Davison Milburn, 1st Bt and Clara Georgiana, *d* of late William Charles Stamp, Tulse Hill, Surrey; *S* father, 1907. *Educ:* Christ's College, Cambridge (MA 1904). *Heir: brother* Leonard John Milburn, *b* 14 Feb. 1884. *Address:* Guyzance, Acklington, Northumberland; Wardrew House, Gilsland, Northumberland; Milburn House, Newcastle-on-Tyne.

Died 16 July 1917.

MILBURN, James Booth; Editor of The Tablet since April 1920; *b* York, 1860; *e s* of late W. C. Milburn, York; *m* 1895, Caroline, *yr d* of late W. Moody (of the Bank of England), Manchester; *s* one *d. Educ:* St Cuthbert's College, Ushaw. Master at Ushaw and afterwards at St Bede's College, Manchester; Assistant Editor of The Tablet, 1895–1920. *Publications:* The Oxford Movement, 1895; A Martyr of Old York, 1902; Joan of Arc, 1905; The Restoration of the Hierarchy, The Rise of the Christian School, 1907; numerous articles in the Dublin Review, the Ushaw Magazine and The Tablet. *Address:* The Retreat, Field Lane, London Road, Brentford.

Died 21 April 1923.

MILDMAY, Major Sir Henry Paulet St John-, 6th Bt, *cr* 1772; JP County of Hampshire; *b* 28 April 1853; *e s* of Sir Henry Bouverie Paulet St John-Mildmay, 5th Bt and Hon. Helena Shaw-Lefevre, 2nd *d* of Viscount Eversley, GCB. Late Grenadier Guards; served Egyptian War, 1882 (medal with clasp, Khedive's star); Suakin Expedition, 1885 (despatches, Brevet Major, clasp). Owned about 10,900 acres. *Heir: brother* Gerald Anthony Shaw-Lefevre St John-Mildmay [*b* 30 Oct. 1860; assumed by Royal licence additional surnames of Shaw and Lefevre, 1900; *m* 1892, Isabel Emily, 2nd *d* of Rev. C. A. St John-Mildmay of Hazelgrove; one *s* one *d* (and one *s* decd). *Address:* Dockham House, Coates, Cirencester. *Clubs:* Travellers', Isthmian]. *Address:* Dogmersfield Park, Winchfield, Hants.

Died 24 April 1916.

MILDMAY, Lt-Col Herbert Alexander St John-, MVO 1911; Gentleman-at-Arms; *b* 20 July 1836; *s* of Capt. George William St John-Mildmay, RN and Mary, *d* of Peter Baillie, sometime MP, and *widow* of John Morritt, Rokeby Park; *m* 1884, Susan Margaret Stacpole, *d* of late Hon. John Lothrop Motley, US Minister at Court of St James's. Late Rifle Brigade; served Crimea, 1855 (medal with clasp, Turkish medal); NW Frontier of India, 1864 (medal). *Address:* 31 Gloucester Street, SW1. *T:* Victoria 5447.

Died 21 Oct. 1922.

MILES, Col Charles Napier, CB 1900; MVO 1901; High Steward for Malmesbury since 1892; *b* 9 April 1854; *e s* of Col. Charles William Miles of Burtonhill, Malmesbury; *m* 1880, Emily Georgina, *d* of late John W. Gooch Spicer. *Educ:* Eton (played against Harrow, 1871-72). Entered 1st Life Guards as Lieut 1875; Capt. 1882; Major, 1895; served Egyptian Campaign, 1882 (medal and clasp, Khedive's bronze star); commanded Household Cavalry Regt, from July till their return to England, in the South African War, 1900 (despatches: Queen's medal, 3 clasps: CB); Lieut-Col 1st Life Guards, 1895-1902; retired 1906; Lord of the Manor of Burtonhill; Patron of one living. *Address:* Ingelburne Manor, Malmesbury. *T:* 44 Malmesbury; Cardigan. *Clubs:* Arthur's, Pratt's, Carlton, Orleans.

Died 25 May 1918.

MILES, Lt-Gen. Sir Herbert (Scott Gould), GCB 1914 (KCB 1908; CB 1900); GCMG 1916; GBE 1918; CVO 1903 (MVO 1897); *b* 31 July 1850; *s* of Maj.-Gen. William Miles, *m* 1877, Alice, CBE, *y d* of late Joseph Parker of Brettenham Park, Suffolk; two *d*. *Educ:* Wellington College; Royal Military College, Sandhurst. Entered army, 1869; Colonel, 1893; AAG, Aldershot, 1893-98; Commandant of the Staff College, 1898-99; served South Africa (DAG), 1899-1900 (despatches twice, Queen's medal 6 clasps, CB); Commandant, Staff College, Camberley, 1900-3; General Commanding Troops Cape Colony, 1903; Director of Recruiting and Organisation, Headquarters, 1904; QMG to the Forces, 1908-12; Governor and Commander-in-Chief, Gibraltar, 1913-18; Colonel, Royal Munster Fusiliers; Governor, Wellington College; Commissioner, Chelsea Hosp.; Grand Officer Legion of Honour; Grand Officer Crown of Italy; Grand Cross of Isabel la Católica of Spain. *Address:* Satis House, Yoxford, Suffolk. *Clubs:* Army and Navy, Marlborough, Travellers'.

Died 6 May 1926.

MILES, Lt-Gen. Nelson Appleton; late Commanding United States Army; *b* Westminster, Mass, 8 Aug. 1839. Entered army as volunteer, 1861, attaining rank of Maj.-Gen. of Volunteers, grade by grade, and at age of 25 commanded an army corps; entered regular army at close of Civil War; rose by regular grades to be Lieut-Gen., succeeding to command of US army, 5 October 1895; conducted successfully several campaigns against hostile Indians on Western frontiers, notably against Sitting-Bull, Chief Joseph, and Geronimo; was in command of US troops at Chicago during the riots in 1894; represented US army at seat of Turko-Grecian war, and also at Queen Victoria's Diamond Jubilee, 1897; commanded army during war of 1898 with Spain, and during war in the Philippines; Harvard University conferred degree of LLD. *Publications:* Personal Recollections, or From New England to the Golden Gate; Military Europe; Serving the Republic; also many magazine articles and military reports. Washington, DC. Died 15 May 1925.

MILEY, Col James Aloysius, CSI 1897; *b* 22 Oct 1846; 2nd *s* of late James Miley; *m* 1868, Kate, *d* of William Watson. *Educ:* private schools, Ireland and France; RMC, Sandhurst. Appointed 12th Foot, 1865; Indian Army, 1870; Regiment duty till 1875; Departmental Staff till 1898; Military Accountant-General and *ex-officio* Dep. Secretary for Finance, Military Department, Government of India, 1893-1902. *Address:* 7 Sloane Street, SW. *T:* Victoria 2625. *Clubs:* Naval and Military, Portland. Died Feb. 1919.

MILFORD HAVEN, 1st Marquess of, *cr* 1917; **Admiral of the Fleet Louis Alexander Mountbatten;** GCB (mil.) (KCB (mil.)); GCB (civil) 1887; GCVO; KCMG; PC 1914; DL Isle of Wight; LLD; Earl of Medina, 1917; Viscount Alderney, 1917; Personal Aide-de-camp to King George V; *b* Gratz (Austria), 24 May 1854; *e s* of Prince Alexander of Hesse and Countess Julia Theresa von Haucke; *g s* of Louis II, Grand Duke of Hesse; naturalised British subject as Prince Louis of Battenberg; in 1917 he relinquished at the King's request his German titles, assumed by Royal Licence the surname of Mountbatten, and was created a Peer as above; *m* 1884, his cousin, Princess Victoria, *d* of Louis IV, Grand Duke of Hesse, KG, and of Princess Alice, Queen Victoria's daughter; two *s* two *d*. Entered Royal Navy as Naval Cadet, 1868; Sub-Lieut 1874; Lieut 1876; Comdr 1885; Capt. 1891; Commodore, 1902; served in Egyptian War, 1882 (medal and Khedive's star); Director of Naval Intelligence, 1902-5; Rear-Admiral, 1904; Commanding Second Cruiser Squadron, 1905-7; second in Command Mediterranean, 1907-8; Commander-in-Chief Atlantic Fleet, 1908-10; Commanding 3rd and 4th Divisions Home Fleet, 1911; Second Sea-Lord of Admiralty, 1911-12; First Sea-Lord of Admiralty, 1912-14, when he resigned; Adm., retired 1919; Adm. of the Fleet, retired 1921; Elder Brother of Trinity House; Rede Lectr, Cambridge Univ., 1918; Fellow Royal Numismatic Society and Royal Geographical Society; Protestant. *Publications:* Men-of-War Names; British Naval Medals. *Heir: s* Earl of Medina, *b* 6 Nov. 1892. *Address:* Kent House, East Cowes, IW. *Clubs:* United Service, Naval and Military, Bachelors', Bath, Athenæum.

Died 11 Sept. 1921.

MILLAIS, Sir John Everett, 3rd Bt, *cr* 1885; *b* 28 Nov. 1888; *o s* of Sir Everett Millais, 2nd Bt and Mary St Lawrence, *o d* of William Edward Hope Vere of Craigie Hall, Midlothian and Blackwood, Lanarkshire; *S* father, 1897. *Educ:* HMS Britannia. Served in HMS Amethyst, 1914; Lieut-Commander, RN (retired); JP Kent, 1919. *Heir: uncle* Geoffrey William Millais [*b* 18 Sept. 1863; *m* 1901, Madeleine Campbell, *d* of Col Charles Halliburton Grace; two *s* one *d*]. *Address:* Leacon Hall, Warehorne, Ashford, Kent. *Clubs:* Junior Naval and Military, Royal Automobile.

Died 30 Sept. 1920.

MILLAR, A. H., JP; LLD (St Andrews), 1909; FSAScot 1882; FRSA; FLA 1914; Chief Librarian and Curator, Dundee Free Library and Museum, since 1908; *b* Glasgow, 25 Nov. 1847; *y s* of Andrew Millar, manufacturer and Mary Browning; *m* 1st, Margaret (*d* 1912), *d* of James Small, manufacturer, Kinross; one *s*; 2nd, 1919, Margaret, *d* of David Smart, chemist, Port Glasgow. *Educ:* St Peter's School, Glasgow and privately; studied music at Andersonian University, Glasgow. Highest certificates in Theory and History of Music from John Hullah, and in Original Composition from Sir George A. Macfarren; was Assistant to Colin Brown, Professor of Music, Andersonian Univ., 1869; began to write art-criticism for Art Journal, 1879; joined staff of Dundee Advertiser, Jan. 1881, as leader-writer, art-critic, and reviewer, also writing historical serials for People's Journal and People's Friend; Literary Editor, 1889-1908, music critic and art critic, 1886-1908, Dundee Advertiser; Editor of Valentine's Shire Series of Illustrated County Histories; President Scottish Library Association, 1912-13, 1913-14 and 1914-15; was on staff of Dictionary of National Biography and wrote 100 articles for it. *Publications:* The History of Rob Roy, 1883; The Castles and Mansions of Ayrshire, 1885; The Black Kalendar of Scotland (first series), 1885; Miniature Series of Historical Works, 1886-92; Quaint Bits of Glasgow, 1887; The Roll of Eminent Burgesses of Dundee, 1513-1887, 1887; The Castles and Mansions of Renfrewshire and Buteshire, 1889; The Glamis Book of Record, 1890; The Historical Castles and Mansions of Scotland, 1890; Fife, Pictorial and Historical: its People, Castles, Mansions and Burghs, 1895; Contemporary Writers, 1895-97; Bygone Glasgow, 1896; Book of Glasgow Cathedral (with Archbishop Eyre, George Eyre Todd, and others), 1898; Compt-Buik of David Wedderburn of Dundee, 1586-1632; Glasgow in the "Forties" by William Simpson, RI, edited with biography, 1899; Scottish Burgh Life, 1903; Mary, Queen of Scots, her Life-Story, 1905; Story of Robert the Bruce, 1908; Scottish Forfeited Estates Papers, 1909; The First History of Dundee, 1918; Haunted Dundee, 1923; Glimpses of Old and New Dundee, 1925; James Bowman Lindsay, Pioneer of Wireless Telegraphy, 1926; Gregarach: the Strange Adventure of Rob Roy's Sons, 1926. *Address:* Albert Institute, Dundee. Died 27 Feb. 1927.

MILLAR, James Gardner, KC 1909; Sheriff of Lanarkshire since 1908; *b* Glasgow, 1 May 1855; *s* of John Millar, merchant, Glasgow, one of the Magistrates of the City; unmarried. *Educ:* Glasgow High School; Glasgow University (MA); Edinburgh University (LLB); LLD (Glasgow). Called to the Bar, 1881; Sheriff Court Depute, 1894; Extra

Depute on Western Circuit, 1895; acted as interim Sheriff-Substitute in Ayr, Kilmarnock and during winter of 1904–5 in Glasgow; Legal Secretary to Lord Advocate, 1905; Sheriff-Substitute of the Lothians and Peebles at Edinburgh, 1906–8. *Recreations:* golf, fishing. *Address:* 5 Park Circus, Glasgow. *Clubs:* National Liberal; University, Scottish Liberal, Edinburgh; Western, New, Glasgow.

Died 28 June 1917.

MILLER, Vice-Adm. Charles Blois, CB 1916; *b* 22 March 1867; *s* of Sir Alexander Edward Miller, CSI, KC, LLD, of Ballycastle, Co. Antrim, and Elizabeth Furley Miller; *m* 1919, Ethel Margaret, *d* of Rt Hon. John Young, PC, and *widow* of John Stevenson. *Educ:* Lockers Park, Hemel Hempstead. Entered HMS Britannia, 1880; served in HMS Northumberland during Egyptian Campaign of 1882 (medal, bronze star); Commander, 1903; Captain, 1908; served European War, including Battle of Jutland Bank (CB), 1916; retired list, 1924. *Recreations:* general. *Address:* Crowmarsh Battle, Wallingford. *Clubs:* Naval and Military; Naval, Portsmouth.   *Died 14 July 1926.*

MILLER, Sir Denison Samuel King, KCMG 1920; JP; Governor, Commonwealth Bank of Australia since 1912; *b* Fairy Meadow, near Wollongong, New South Wales, 8 March 1860; *s* of the late Samuel King Miller, Headmaster Demliquin Public School, New South Wales; *m* Laura Constance, *e d* of late Doctor John Theophilus Heeley; four *s* two *d*. *Educ:* Demliquin Public School. Joined Bank of New South Wales, 1876; rose to position of Accountant in the Head Office; General Managers' Inspector, 1907; Metropolitan Inspector, 1909; one of the founders of the Institute of Bankers of New South Wales, and for some time its Honorary Treasurer; Chairman of the Executive of the Hospital Saturday Fund, and Life Governor of the Sydney Hospital, and Royal Alexandra Hospital for Children, Sydney; took an active part in all patriotic and charitable organisations. *Recreation:* golf. *Address:* Cliffbrook, Coogee, New South Wales. *TA:* Commonwealth Bank, Sydney. *T:* Randwick 205. *M:* 2086. *Clubs:* Australian, Royal Sydney Yacht, Australian Golf, Sydney.

Died 6 June 1923.

MILLER, Fred, MA; Managing Editor Daily Telegraph since 1923; *b* Dundee, June 1863; *e surv. s* of late Dr James W. Miller, Dundee; *m* 1887, Jane Cairns, *e d* of James Johnston, drysalter, Dundee; one *s* three *d*. *Educ:* Dundee Institution; Royal High School, Edinburgh; Edinburgh University. Joined staff of Daily Telegraph in 1883; Chief Sub-Editor, 1895–1900; Assistant Editor, 1910–23. *Address:* 102 Dartmouth Road, NW2. *T:* Willesden 1557.

Died 5 Nov. 1924.

MILLER, George, ISO 1903; JP; *b* Sydney, 19 Dec. 1842; *s* of George Miller (formerly a Deputy Assistant Commissary-General, who settled in the Colony in 1836, and was afterwards Managing Trustee of the Savings Bank of NSW); unmarried. *Educ:* St Philip's Grammar School, Sydney; Upton Park Academy, Slough, Bucks; Brighton College. Clerk, NSW Civil Service, 1860; was for 2 years Private Secretary to the Hon. Charles Cowper, when Premier and Chief Secretary; and for 1 year Private Secretary to the Hon. William Forster, when Chief Secretary; resigned, 1865, to engage in squatting pursuits in Queensland; appointed to Education Department, NSW, 1867, of which he was Chief Clerk for 15 years and Acting Under Secretary for two periods of 18 months and 10 months respectively; was appointed Comptroller General of Prisons, 1890; Under Secretary of Justice, 1896; Under Secretary combined Departments of Attorney-General and of Justice, 1901–5; retired from service, 1905. Decorated for faithful service. *Recreations:* cycling, sculling. *Clubs:* Australian, Union, Sydney.   *Died 8 Feb. 1923.*

MILLER, Henry, CIE 1917; *b* 1859; *s* of late William Charles Miller, Liverpool; *m* 1892, Frances Margaret Adams. *Educ:* Uppingham. Engineer; tea planter. Late Member of Council, Assam. *Address:* Halton, Adelaide Road, Walton-on-Thames.

Died 11 April 1927.

MILLER, Hon. Sir Henry John, Kt 1901; Speaker of the Legislative Council, New Zealand, 1892–1903; Member since 1903; *b* 9 Sept. 1830; 2nd *s* of Rev. Sir Thomas Combe Miller, 6th Bt, and Martha, *e d* of Rev. Thomas Holmes; *heir-pres.* to Sir Charles John Hubert Miller, 8th Bt; *m* 1864, Jessie, *d* of John Orbell, of Hawkesbury, Waikonati, NZ; five *s* one *d* (and one *d* decd). *Address:* Legislative Council, Wellington, NZ; Fernbrook, Oamaru, Otago, NZ.

Died 9 Feb. 1918.

MILLER, Sir John Alexander, 3rd Bt, *cr* 1874; DSO 1900; DL; *b* 27 Sept. 1867; *s* of Sir William Miller, 1st Bt and Mary Anne, *d* of late John Farley Leith; *S* brother, 1906; *m* 1st, 1889, Inez Mary (who

divorced him 1901), *e d* of late Capt. William Mitchell Innes; 2nd, 1901, Ada Mary (whom he divorced 1906), *o c* of Francis Henry Paget; 3rd, 1907, Eveline Frances, *e d* of John Blencowe Cookson, CB. *Heir:* none. *Address:* Manderston, Duns, Berwickshire.

Died 16 Feb. 1918 (ext).

MILLER, Sir Leslie Creery, Kt 1914; CBE 1919; Chief Judge in Mysore, 1914–22; *b* 28 June 1862; *s* of late Sir Alexander Edward Miller, CSI, KC; *m* 1886, Margaret Julia, OBE, *d* of Robert Lowry; no *c*. *Educ:* Charterhouse and Trinity College, Dublin. Entered Indian Civil Service, 1881; served Madras as Assistant Collector and Magistrate; Manager Pittapur estate, 1891–92; Principal Assistant and District Magistrate, 1895; Collector and Magistrate, 1899; District and Sessions Judge, 1900; Judge High Court of Madras, 1906–14. *Address:* Glen Morgan Estate, Pykara PO, Nilgiri Hills, *Club:* East India United Service.   *Died 17 Feb. 1925.*

MILLER, Philip Homan, ARHA 1890; painter of portraits and figure subjects and contributor to leading illustrated papers; *b* Londonderry; *s* of Rev. J. H. Miller, headmaster, Foyle College, and Margaret Irwin; *m* Sophia, *d* of Rev. J. P. Holmes, Corbeg, King's Co. *Educ:* under brother, Prof. Dr T. Miller; Queen's College, Belfast; Royal College of Surgeons, Dublin. Studied architecture and painting, and entered Royal Acad. schools, gaining 1st prize figure-drawing from life; began exhibiting Royal Acad., 1879; some 40 drawings of noted members in White's Club his work; he suggested the club for Irish artists in London, and became Hon. Sec. *Recreation:* gardening. *Address:* 1 Campden Hill Road, W; Moyleen, Great Marlow.

Died 23 Dec. 1928.

MILLER, Willet G., MA, LLD; FRSC, FGS; Provincial Geologist of Ontario since 1902; *b* of Canadian parents in the Province of Ontario; not married. *Educ:* Port Rowan High School; University of Toronto; post-graduate student at the American Universities, Chicago and Harvard, and at Heidelberg, Germany. Fellow, 1890–93, and Examiner in Mineralogy and Geology, Univ. of Toronto, 1893–95; Lecturer, and later Professor, in Geology in Queen's University, Kingston, Canada, 1893–1902; Assistant in field geology, Geological Survey of Canada, in the region north of Lake Huron, 1891–93; in charge of field work in geology in Eastern Ontario for the Bureau of Mines, 1897–1901; Member Royal Ontario Nickel Commission, 1915–17; Canada's Representative on Imperial Mineral Resources Bureau, 1918–22; LLD, hon, Queen's University, Kingston, 1907; and University of Toronto, 1913; President Canadian Mining Institute, 1908–10; Life Member Geological Society of America, Geological Society of London, British Association for Advancement of Science, Canadian Mining Institute, American Institute of Mining Engineers, and Hon. Member and Gold Medallist, 1914, of the Institution of Mining and Metallurgy; Member Washington Academy of Sciences; Society of Economic Geologists; American Association for Advancement of Science. *Publications:* writings chiefly on the pre-Cambrian and economic geology of Ontario; papers and reports on corundum-bearing rocks, iron ores, gold deposits, cobalt-silver ores, etc, in Annual Reports of Ontario Bureau of Mines, American Geologist, Journal of Geology, Canadian Mining Institute, etc. *Recreations:* canoeing, exploring. *Address:* Department of Mines, Toronto. *Clubs:* National, Victoria, Rosedale Golf, Toronto.

Died Feb. 1925.

MILLER, Rev. William, CIE 1884; MA, LLD, DD; Principal of Madras Christian College, Madras, 1863–1908; Hon. Principal since 1908; *b* Thurso, 13 Jan. 1838; *s* of William Miller, Thurso; unmarried. *Educ:* Bellevue Academy; Marischal College, Aberdeen; New College, Edinburgh. Member of the Legislative Council of Madras, 1893–97 and 1899–1902; Moderator of the Assembly of Free Church of Scotland, 1896–97; Vice-Chancellor of the University of Madras, 1901–4; Kaiser-i-Hind Gold Medal, 1907. *Publications:* Our Scandinavian Forefathers, 1862; The Plan of History, 1863; The Greatest of the Judges, 1878; The Least of All Lands, 1888; criticisms on several of Shakespeare's Plays; and many addresses and lectures. *Address:* Burgo Park, Bridge of Allan, Scotland.

Died 15 July 1923.

MILLER, Major William Archibald, DSO 1916; MC; MB; Royal Army Medical Corps; Special Reserve; *s* of late Rev. Robert Miller, MA, FEIS. *Educ:* George Watson's College, and University, Edinburgh. Served European War, 1914–17 (DSO, MC and bar, despatches). *Address:* Anneville, 9 Canaan Lane, Edinburgh. *Club:* United Sport.   *Died 1925.*

MILLEVOYE, Lucien; Député de Paris 16e arrondissement (quartier de l'Etoile) depuis 1898 (nationale Libérale); s'était signalé à la

Chambre par de nombreux et importants discours sur la politique extérieure, sur les vieux arts et sur les questions sociales; *b* Grenoble, 1 Aug. 1850; fils d'Alfred Millevoye, ancien premier président de la cour d'appel de Lyon; petit-fils du poéte Charles Millevoye, l'auteur célèbre de l'Anniversaire, et de la Chute des feuilles; *m*. Magistrat à Lyon; il donna sa démission, refusant d'exécuter les décrets de 1880 contre la liberté religieuse; ami du Général Boulanger, il fit une ardente campagne politique de 1888 à 1890; Député d'Amiens de 1889 à 1893; prépara par une longue série de conférences l'alliance franco-russe; rédacteur a La Patrie depuis 1896. *Recreations:* escrimait à l'épée et au pistolet, de nombreux duels (les plus connus sont eux contre Goldmann, correspondant de la Gazette de Francfort; Berteaux, ancien ministre de la guerre; Comte de Noailles, son dernier concurrent; grand amateur de musique; s'occupait beaucoup de questions artistiques (a présenté un rapport très remarqué sur l'opéra). *Address:* 16 rue Spontini, Paris.

Died 25 March 1918.

MILLS, Hon. Algernon Henry; managing partner Glyn, Mills, Currie & Co.; *b* 13 Feb. 1856; 2nd *s* of 1st Baron Hillingdon and Lady Louisa Isabella Lascelles, *e d* of 3rd Earl of Harewood; *m* 1880, Lady Mary Frances Seymour (*d* 1895), *o d* of 4th Earl of Portarlington; one *s*. Director Sun Insurance Office, Central London Railway Co., and Great Western Railway. *Address:* Wood Norton, Evesham.

Died 21 Oct. 1922.

MILLS, Charles A., ARHA. *Address:* 55 Millmount Avenue, Drumcondra, Ireland.

MILLS, Hon. Charles Houghton; MLC; *b* Nelson, New Zealand, 1844; *s* of late Richard Mills of Portsmouth; *m* Margaret, *d* of John Morison of Nelson; two *s* four *d*. *Educ:* public schools, Nelson and Wellington, in which was pupil-teacher for four years. Subsequently engaged in mercantile pursuits; master mariner's certificate; member of House of Representatives for Waimea, Picton, district of Marlborough, 1890; Waimea, Sounds, 1893; Wairau, 1896; Chairman of Public Petitions Committee; Government Whip, 1893–1900; member of the Seddon Ministry, 1900–6; Member of Hall-Jones Government until the Ward Ministry was formed, when he retired; called to Legislative Council, 1909. *Address:* Leitrim Street, Blenheim, New Zealand. *T:* 2443. *Died 3 April 1923.*

MILLS, Prof. Edmund James, DSc London; Hon. LLD Glasgow; FRS 1874; FIC; Emeritus Professor of Technical Chemistry at Glasgow Royal Technical College; *b* London, 8 Dec. 1840; *s* of Charles F. and Mary Anne Mills; *m* Amelia, *d* of late William Burnett, London. *Educ:* Cheltenham Grammar School; Royal School of Mines. Assistant to the late Dr John Stenhouse, FRS, 1861; Chemical Tutor at Glasgow University, 1862–65; appointed Professor of Technical Chemistry, Glasgow, 1875. *Publications:* many original memoirs and essays on chemistry; amongst them—Destructive Distillation, 1877 (4th edn); Fuel and its Applications 1889; also My Only Child (poems), 1895; The Secret of Petrarch, 1904. *Address:* 64 Twyford Avenue, West Acton, W3. *Club:* Athenæum.

Died 21 April 1921.

MILLS, Capt. Hon. Geoffrey (Edward); Royal Naval Volunteer Reserve; Naval Provost Marshal, London; *b* 15 March 1875; *y s* of 1st Baron Hillingdon and Lady Louisa Isabella Lascelles, *e d* of 3rd Earl of Harewood; *m* 1st, 1901, Grace Victoria (whom he divorced 1914), *d* of late Hon. Hungerford T. Boddam, Judge of the High Court, Madras; two *s* (and one *s* one *d* decd); 2nd, 1917, Hilda Susan Ellen, *y d* of Sir Daniel Cooper, 2nd Bt, and *widow* of late Viscount Northland. Late Lieut West Kent Imperial Yeomanry. *Address:* 28 Welbeck Street, W1. *Club:* White's.

Died 14 Aug. 1917.

MILLS, Brig.-Gen. George Arthur, CB 1900; *b* 28 March 1855; *s* of Captain George Longley Mills, Bombay Army; *m* 1885, Helen Henrietta, *d* of John Garland Baker, of Mahagastotte, Ceylon; one *d*. *Educ:* Clifton College. Gazetted to Royal Madras Fusiliers (102nd), 1873; ADC to General Officer Commanding Ceylon, 1879–82; Captain, 1880; Egyptian Army and served in Egypt, 1885–87; Major 1st Royal Dublin Fusiliers, 1888; Lieut-Col 1898; Lieut-Col commanding 1st Bn Royal Dublin Fusiliers till 1902; served with 1st Bn during South African War, 1899–1902; severely wounded (left hand and arm disabled) at the battle of Alleman's Nek, 1900 (despatches four times); commanded No XI District, 1906–10; retired 1910; Commanding 7th Reserve Brigade, 1914; Combatant Member Travelling Medical Board to 20 Jan. 1917; landed in France, 17 Oct. 1917; Area Commandant Vraignes; March 1918, OC Corps Troops, Cavalry Corps; April 1918, Special Service 4th Army, BEF, France;

Headquarters 4th Army Staff, B Branch, 1912–19 (despatches, War and Victory medals); served in Gibraltar, Ceylon, Egypt (medal and Khedive's Star), India, Baluchistan, and South Africa, 1899–1902 (despatches 4 times, Queen's medal 5 clasps, King's medal 2 clasps, CB). *Recreations:* racing (India), pig-sticking (won Guzerat pig-sticking cup in 1897), shooting (big and small game), fishing, hunting, polo, etc. *Address:* Bridge House, Padworth, Reading. *Club:* Junior Naval and Military.

Died 19 Sept. 1927.

MILLS, Harry Woosnam; Director, Times of Ceylon Co., Ltd; London Representative, Times of Ceylon; *b* 1873; *m* 1901, Kathleen (*d* 1923), *y d* of George Nagington, Comberley Hall, Staffs; three *s* one *d*. In Colombo since 1901, previously 2 yrs in Paris; 3 yrs in India on Civil and Military Gazette. *Publications:* The Pathan Revolt in North-West India; The Tirah Campaign; Ceylon: a Traveller's Paradise. *Address:* Firgrove House, West End, Southampton. *Clubs:* Sports; Colombo. *Died March 1925.*

MILLS, Col Herbert James, CB 1887; retired; *b* 13 Aug. 1836; *s* of late John Mills and Louisa Hubbard; *m* 1st, Elizabeth Ann (*d* 1874), *d* of Robert Jolly of Woolwich; 2nd, Alice Ethel Gausden, *widow* of H. J. Money. *Educ:* private tuition. Served in Canada, 1869–74; with Egyptian Expedition, 1882–84 (despatches, medal, bronze star, 3rd class Medjidie); Soudan, as Senior Ordnance Officer, 1884 (despatches twice); assistant to Director of Artillery at War Office, 1886–91; Senior Ordnance Officer for Southern District, 1891–94. Decorated: for Egyptian Campaign. *Recreations:* music, athletics. *Address:* 17 Clifton Gardens, Maida Vale, W9. *Died 2 May 1927.*

MILLS, James, MA, LLD; *b* Co. of Simcoe, Province of Ontario, of Irish parentage, 24 Nov. 1840; *m* 1869, Jessie Ross of Cobourg, Ontario; one *s* five *d*. *Educ:* public schools of Ontario; Bradford Grammar School, Simcoe County; Victoria University, Cobourg (BA (Prince of Wales's Gold Medal for highest General Proficiency), 1868; MA 1871; LLD (Hon.) 1892). After graduation taught at an academy in the Province of Quebec for one year; taught the Latin and Greek Classics in the Cobourg Collegiate Institute for three years; went to Brantford, Ontario, as headmaster of High School, 1873; President Ontario Agricultural College, Guelph, 1879–1904; organised the Farmers' Institutes of Ontario, and took charge of them for ten years; organised and controlled the provincial Travelling Dairies; was Director of the three Dairy Schools of the Province; and as Chairman of Board of Directors of the Fruit Experiment Stations of Ontario assisted in testing the suitability or non-suitability of different varieties of fruit to the varying conditions of soil and climate throughout the Province; Member of the Board of Regents of Victoria University for 20 years, and of the Senate of the University of Toronto for 16 years; Member of the Board of Railway Commissioners for Canada, 1904–14; Librarian and Supervising Officer for the Commission, 1914. *Publication:* First Principles of Agriculture. *Address:* Railway Commission Offices, Ottawa, Canada. *Clubs:* Country, Ottawa.

Died Dec. 1924.

MILLS, Joseph Trueman; JP, DL for Leicestershire; High Sheriff in 1880; JP for Bedfordshire, Buckinghamshire, Hertfordshire, and Norfolk; Director of Weymouth and Portland Railway, Union Assurance Society, and New River Co.; *b* 15 Jan. 1836; 2nd *s* of J. Remington Mills, JP, of Tolmers, Herts and L. Matilda, *d* of Joseph Trueman of Walthamstow; *m* 1858, Eliza Anna, 4th *d* of James Layton, JP, Baldock, Herts; one *s* three *d*. *Educ:* privately. *Recreations:* hunting, shooting. *Address:* Stockgrove, Leighton Buzzard. *Club:* City.

Died 17 Jan. 1924.

MILLS, Lawrence Heyworth, DD New York; Hon. MA Oxon; Professor of Zend Philology, Oxford, since 1898; *b* NY, 1837; *s* of late P. L. Mills and Elizabeth Caroline Kane; *m* Maria Bowen, *d* of Robert Paige Swann of Leesburg, Virginia; three *s* one *d*. *Educ:* New York University; Theological Seminary, Fairfax, co. of Virginia. Came to Oxford, 1887, on the invitation of Professor M. Müller, and resident there from that time. *Publications:* Sacred Books of the East, vol. xxxi, 1887, translated into Gujrati by Palanji Madan, Bombay; Gâthas, with Zend, Pahlavi, Sanskrit, and Persian texts, commentary, etc, Leipzig, 1892–94; 2nd edn, Gâthas, verb. and metrical, 1900; 3rd vol., Gâthas, Dictionary, 1st issue, 1902 (printing of Dictionary, third vol. Gâthas, recommenced 1910; suspended for the editing and translating of the Pahlavi commentaries in ZDMG, and JRAS; Dictionary of Gâthas, completing them, pp 1196, subventioned by Secretary of State for India in council, 1914); Zarathushtra, Philo, the Achaemenids, and Israel, vol. i 1904, vol. ii 1906; Daniel and Revelations compared with Avesta (university lectures), 1907; Yasna I with Avesta, Sanskrit, Pahlavi, and Persian texts, first three translated with full original Sanskrit equivalents of the Avesta, 1910; Our Own Religion in Ancient Persia (university lecture), 1913; Lore in Avesta in Catechetical Dialogues, published by Trustees of the Sir J. J. Translation Fund of Bombay, 1916; The Creed of Zarathushtra, a treatise written for the Zoroastrian Association of Bombay, 1916; The Fundamental and Dominant Presence of Zoroastrian Thought in the Jewish Exilic, Christian and Muhammad Religions, and in the Greek and Gnostic Philosophies with their Modern Successors, 1917; The Vital Necessity of the Persian Theology to all Biblical Study; The Great Utility of Avesta Study to that of the Veda; articles: Zoroastrianism and the Bible, Nineteenth Century Rev. (trans. Gujrati and Italian); Zeitschrift, German Oriental Soc.; Asiatic Quarterly Rev., etc. *Recreations:* advanced research; formerly fencing, and small boat yachting on open sea. *Address:* 218 Iffley Road, Oxford. *TA:* Prof. Mills, Oxford.

MILLS, Rev. William, MA; Rector of Bennington since 1881; Hon. Canon of St Albans, 1912. *Educ:* Trinity College, Dublin. Deacon, 1875; Priest, 1876; Curate of Coleshill, 1875–76; Upton, 1876–79; Little Marlow, 1879–81. *Address:* Bennington Rectory, Stevenage.
Died 6 April 1922.

MILLS, Rt. Rev. William Lennox, DD, LLD, DCL; Bishop of Ontario since 1901; *b* Woodstock, Ontario; *s* of William Mills; *m* Katharine Sophia, *d* of late Stanley Clark Bagge of Montreal; one *s*. *Educ:* Woodstock Grammar School; Huron Coll., London, Ont; graduate of the Western University, London, 1872; BD and DD of the Univ. of Trinity College, Toronto, in course 1884–94, DCL (*Honoris Causa*); LLD Queen's University, Kingston (*Honoris Causa*); DD Bishop's Coll., Lennoxville (*ad eundem*). Ordained Deacon, 1872; Priest, 1873; Incumbent of Trinity Church, Norwich, Ontario, 1872; Rector of St Thomas' Church, Seaforth, Ontario, 1874; Rector of the Crown Rectory of St John's, Province of Quebec, 1875; Rector of Trinity Church, Montreal, 1882; Examining Chaplain to the Bishop of Montreal, and Lecturer in Ecclesiastical History in the Montreal Diocesan Theological College, 1883; Canon of Christ Church Cathedral, Montreal, 1884; Archdeacon of St Andrew's, Diocese of Montreal, 1896; Bishop Coadjutor of Ontario, with title of Bishop of Kingston, 1900. *Address:* Bishop's Court, Kingston, Ontario, Canada. *Died 4 May 1917.*

MILLSPAUGH, Rt. Rev. Frank Rosebrook, DD; Bishop of Kansas since 1895; *b* Nichols, NY, 12 April 1848; *s* of Cornelius Madden Millspaugh and Elvira Rosebrook; *m e d* of Rt Rev. R. H. Clarkson, Bishop of Nebraska; one *s* two *d. Educ:* Faribault, Minn; Shattuck Hall; Seabury Divinity School. Lay Reader at seventeen; Deacon, 1873; Priest, 1874; Missionary with seven stations, Minnesota, 1873–76; Dean of Trinity Cathedral, Omaha, 1876–86; President Standing Committee; Delegate General Covention; Rector St Paul's, Minneapolis, Minn, 1886–94; Dean Grace Cathedral, Topeka, Kansas, 1894–95. *Recreation:* fishing. *Address:* Bishop's House, Topeka, Kansas. *Club:* Country, Topeka. *Died Nov. 1916.*

MILMAN, Sir Francis John, 4th Bt, *cr* 1800; Lieutenant Royal Artillery, retired 1870; *b* 10 Aug. 1842; *s* of Sir William Milman, 3rd Bt, and Matilda Frances, *e d* of Rev. John Pretyman; *S* father, 1885; *m* 1870, Katharine Grace, *d* of Stephen Charles Moore, DL, JP, Barne, Clonmel; six *s* one *d. Educ:* Woolwich. Entered RA 1864; Hon. Major and Adjt 2nd Brig. Welsh Division RA, 1879–87. *Heir: s* Francis Milman [*b* 27 Oct. 1872; *m* 1898, Georgina Maude Emma, *o c* of late Thomas Ripon Wallis]. *Died 2 June 1923.*

MILNE, Alan Hay, CMG 1911; BA Cantab; late (retired 1917) Secretary of the Liverpool Chamber of Commerce, the Liverpool School of Tropical Medicine, the Liverpool Merchants' Mobile Hospital (Incorporated), the Union of Tobacco Manufacturers of Great Britain and Ireland; *b* 1869; *y s* of late Very Rev. A. J. Milne, LLD, of Fyvie, Moderator of the General Assembly of the Church of Scotland; unmarried. *Educ:* Fettes College, Edinburgh; Pembroke College, Cambridge (Scholar). Member, Navy Committee for Export of Coal to France and Italy; Postmaster-General's Telephone Advisory Committee for Liverpool. *Publications:* Ulysses or de Rougemont of Troy; The Life of Sir Alfred Lewis Jones. *Address:* c/o Bank of Liverpool. *Died 21 Jan. 1919.*

MILNE-HOME, David William; JP; DL Berwickshire; Hon. Colonel South-East of Scotland Royal Field Artillery; Member of Berwickshire County Council, and of Berwickshire County Association (Territorial); Major Special Reserve of Officers; employed with the Royal Garrison Artillery since Oct. 1914; *b* 30 April 1873; *s* of late Colonel David Milne-Home, Royal Horse Guards, and Jane, 3rd *d* of Sir Thomas Buchan-Hepburn, 3rd Bt; *m* 1904, Margaret Florence, *o c* of late Captain Arthur Pole, 13th Hussars, and Mrs Pole,

7 Tedworth Square, SW; three *d. Educ:* privately. Served in the South-East of Scotland Artillery from 1894 till the regiment was disbanded, 1909; as ADC and Private Secretary to Sir Hubert E. H. Jerningham, KCMG, Governor of Trinidad and Tobago, 1897–1900; succeeded to entailed estates of Wedderburn, Paxton, and Billie on death of his father, 1901. *Recreations:* shooting, fishing, gardening, forestry. *Address:* Paxton House, Berwick-on-Tweed; Caldra, Duns; Grange, Reston; Wedderburn Castle, Duns. *TA:* Home, Paxton. *M:* SH 144. *Clubs:* Carlton, Bath; New, Edinburgh.
Died 27 July 1918.

MILNER, 1st Viscount, *cr* 1902; **Alfred Milner,** KG 1921; GCB 1901 (KCB 1895); GCMG 1897; Baron 1901; *b* 23 March 1854; *s* of Charles Milner, MD and Mary Ierne, *d* of Maj.-Gen. John Ready, Governor of Isle of Man, and *widow* of St George Cromie; *m* 1921, Violet Georgina, *d* of late Admiral Frederick Augustus Maxse, and *widow* of Lord Edward Herbert Gascoyne-Cecil of Great Wigsell, Bodiam, Sussex. *Educ:* Germany; King's College, London; Balliol College, Oxford (MA; 1st class Classical). Barrister Inner Temple, 1881; mainly engaged in journalism (Pall Mall Gazette, etc), 1882–85; contested Harrow Division, 1885; Private Secretary to George Goschen (Chancellor of the Exchequer), 1887–89; Under-Secretary for Finance in Egypt, 1889–92; Chairman Board of Inland Revenue, 1892–97; Governor of the Cape of Good Hope, 1897–1901; Governor of Transvaal and Orange River Colony 1901–5, and High Commissioner for South Africa, 1897–1905; Member of War Cabinet (Minister without portfolio), 1916–18; Secretary of State for War, 1918–19; Secretary of State for the Colonies, 1919–21; Fellow of New College, Oxford; Hon. DCL Oxon; Hon. LLD Cambridge. *Publications:* England in Egypt, 1892; The Nation and the Empire, 1913; Questions of the Hour, 1923. *Heir:* none. *Address:* 14 Manchester Square, W1. *T:* Langham 1488; Sturry Court, near Canterbury. *Clubs:* Athenæum, Brooks's, New University.
Died 13 May 1925 (ext).

MILNER, Brig.-Gen. George Francis, CMG 1918; DSO 1902; 5th Lancers; Brigade Commander Lowland Mounted Brigade, 1913–14; Inspector of Cavalry since 1914, and commanding 1st Reserve Cavalry Brigade; *b* 10 July 1862; *s* of Henry Beilby William Milner (2nd *s* of Sir William Mordaunt Sturt Milner, 4th Bt), and Charlotte Henrietta, *d* of Most Rev. Marcus Beresford, Archbishop of Armagh; *m* 1910, Phyllis Mary Lycett, *d* of Edward Lycett Green of Ken Hill, King's Lynn; two *s. Educ:* Eton. Joined 17th Lancers, 1883; promoted into 1st Life Guards, 1893; commanded 5th Lancers, 1909; served South African War, 1900–2, as Brigade-Major to Brigadier-Gen. Robert George Broadwood; also in command of 12th Imperial Yeomanry with rank of Lieut-Colonel (despatches, Queen's medal five clasps, King's medal two clasps, DSO); European War, 1914–18 (CMG, despatches twice); Crown of Prussia, 2nd class. *Clubs:* Turf, Bachelors'. *Died 20 June 1921.*

MILNER, James Donald, FSA; Director, Keeper, and Secretary National Portrait Gallery since 1916; *b* 20 Nov. 1874; *e s* of late James Milner; *m* 1902, Lily Bruton; one *s* two *d.* Entered National Portrait Gallery, 1893; Clerk, 1895; Acting Assistant Keeper, 1896. *Publications:* Catalogue of Portraits of Botanists in the Museums of the Royal Botanic Gardens, 1906; contributions to the Second Supplement of the Dictionary of National Biography. *Address:* National Portrait Gallery, St Martin's Place, WC2.
Died 15 Aug. 1927.

MILNER-BARRY, E. L., MA; Professor of German and Teutonic Philology in the University College of North Wales; Lieutenant Royal Naval Volunteer Reserve, employed as Naval Intelligence Officer and Interpreter; *s* of late Rev. E. Milner-Barry, Vicar of Scothorne, Lincoln; *m o d* of Dr William Henry Besant, FRS, and Margaret Elizabeth, *d* of Rev. Prof. R. Willis. *Educ:* Universities of Kiel and Berlin; Caius College, Cambridge (Scholar; First-Class Medieval and Modern Languages Tripos, 1889). Assistant and Housemaster at Mill Hill School, 1891–1907; for many years an active member of the Modern Language Association, Vice-Chairman of Committee, 1907–10; examiner in German to the Univ. of London, 1897–1903; in the Univ. of Cambridge, 1898–99, 1911–12; in the University of Oxford, 1914–15; in the University of Leeds, 1914–16; occasional examiner for the Civil Service Commission, etc. *Publications:* editions of Scheffel's Trompeter von Säkkingen; Hackländer's Geheimer Agent; contributor to the Morning Post, the Guardian, etc. *Recreations:* golf, travel. *Address:* Plas Lodwic, Bangor, North Wales.
Died 7 May 1917.

MILNER-WHITE, Sir Henry, Kt 1918; JP; MA, LLD; *b* 19 Dec. 1854; *y s* of late Robert White, Egypt House, Cowes; *m* 1st, 1883,

Kathleen Lucy (d 1890), γ d of Charles Meeres, MRCS, Sandown, IW; 2nd, 1894, Annie Booth (Nita), o c of late Robert Teasdale, JP, Darlington, and widow of W. Hubert Hall; two s. Educ: Pembroke College, Cambridge. Barrister Inner Temple, 1886; Chairman Eastleigh Petty Sessional Division; President of Board of Trade Inquiry, 1921, on foundering of British India SS Huntspill; Treasurer of University College, Southampton, and Representative of the University of Cambridge, on the Council; Member of County of Hampshire and the Isle of Wight Territorial Force Association from its formation, 1908; Chairman and Managing Director of Edwin Jones & Co., Ltd, Southampton; Member of Board of Finance and other Diocesan Committees; Member of the House of Laity, National Assembly; was General Lay Secretary Church Congress at Southampton, 1913; President for three years Southampton Chamber of Commerce; Delegate to Chicago Exhibition, 1893; Life Governor, Vice-President, Trustee, and Member of Committee of Management, Royal South Hants and Southampton Hospital; Chairman Executive Committee Red Cross Hospitals, Highfield, Southampton, throughout the War, 1914–19; Chairman Southampton Record Society. Recreation: travel. Address: The Deepdene, Southampton. Club: Carlton.   Died 16 April 1922.

MILNES, Alfred, MA, DLit (London); b Bolton, 16 April 1849; 2nd s of late Benjamin Milnes; m 1876, Helena Emily, d of late C. J. A. Goldberg, West Malling, Kent; four d. Educ: private school; Lincoln College, Oxford; University of London. Formerly Rector's Scholar of Lincoln Coll., Oxford; Head Master Imperial Naval School, Tokio, Japan, 1876–78; Assistant Clerk to Senate of University of London, 1878–97; Clerk, 1897–1901; External Registrar, 1901–15; University Extension Staff Lecturer on Economics and Political Science; Hon. Member of the Cobden Club. Publications: Elementary Notions of Logic; Problems and Exercises in Political Economy; From Gild to Factory; Economic Foundations of Reconstruction; Economics for To-day; Economics of Fairy Lore; editor of Johnson's Select Works; editor of Butler's Hudibras. Address: 44 Goldhurst Terrace, South Hampstead, NW6. T: Hampstead 4660. Clubs: National Liberal, London University.   Died 1 Nov. 1921.

MILROY, Hugh, ISO 1902; SSC; of Chapel, Kirkcudbrightshire; b Galloway, 13 Feb. 1840. Educ: Galloway; Edin. Univ. Joined the Civil Service, 1862; admitted a Solicitor before the Supreme Court, 1866; appointed a Commissioner of Supply for Kirkcudbrightshire, 1895; JP 1899; late Chief Clerk, Crown Office, Edinburgh. Recreations: shooting, fishing, golf. Address: West Grove, West Ferry Road, and Crown Office, Edinburgh.   Died Oct. 1919.

MILVAIN, Sir Thomas, Kt 1913; CB 1912; KC; LLM; Judge Advocate General since 1905; b 4 May 1844; 5th s of late Henry Milvain, of North Elswick Hall, and Jane Aitken, e d of Edward Davidson; m Mary Alice, 3rd d of John Henderson, Durham; one s one d. Educ: Durham School; Trinity Hall, Cambridge (LLB 1866, LLM 1871). Called to the Bar, Middle Temple, 1869; QC 1888; MP (C) Durham City, 1885–86, 1886–92, when defeated; contested Cockermouth Division of Cumberland, 1895; Maidstone, 1901; Chancellor of the County Palatine of Durham and Sadberg, 1892; Recorder of Bradford 1892–1905; MP (C), Hampstead, 1902–5. Recreations: shooting, fishing, golf. Address: Eglingham Hall, Alnwick; 3 Plowden Buildings, Temple, EC. Clubs: Carlton, New, University.
Died 23 Sept. 1916.

MINCHIN, Maj.-Gen. Frederick Falkiner, CB 1917; retired; b 17 March 1860; m 1st, 1887, Marjorie (d 1904), d of late Gen. H. D. Abbott, CB; two s one d; 2nd, 1905, Caroline, d of John Lloyd of Astwick Manor, Herts; two s one d. Entered RA 1879; Capt. 1887; Major, 1897; Lt-Col 1904; Col 1911; served Burma, 1889 (medal with clasp); Inspector Ordnance Dept, 1896–1903; Chief Inspector, 1903–7; Member Ordnance Board, 1908–11; Director of Ordnance Inspection, India, 1911–15; Military Adviser, Ministry of Munitions, 1915. Recreations: fishing, shooting. Address: Annagh Coolbawn, Borrisokane, Co. Tipperary. TA: Annagh, Coolbawn, Ireland.
Died 11 July 1922.

MINCHIN, Col William Cyril, CB 1917; b 1856; s of Major James White Minchin; m 1st, E., d of James Broughton Ballard, of Glenbrook, Co. Cork; 2nd, Beryl, widow of Henry Harker; no c. Joined 77th Regiment, 1875; APD 1884; served in the Nile Expedition, 1898. Address: Trinity Gardens, Folkestone. Club: Junior United Service.   Died 9 March 1924.

MINNS, Capt. Allan Noel, DSO 1916; MC; LMSSA; Royal Army Medical Corps; b Thetford, Norfolk, 23 March 1891; s of Dr Allan G. Minns; unmarried. Educ: Guy's Hospital. Served European War,

Mesopotamia, 1915–17 (despatches, DSO, MC); served in Mesopotamia attached 1st Rifle Brigade, 18th Division, Baizi. Address: Alexandra House, Thetford.   Died 6 April 1921.

MIRBEAU, Octave; b Treviers, Calvados, 16 Feb. 1850. Educ: Jesuites du Collège du Vannes. Publications: Les Lettres de ma Chaumière; Contes de ma Chaumière; Le Calvaire; L'Abbé Jules; Sebastian Roch; Le Jardin des Supplices; Le Journal d'une Femme de Chambre; Les Vingt-et-un Jours d'un Neurasthénique; Farces et Moralités; La 628 E 8; Dingo; plays: Les mauvais Bergers; Les Affaires sont les Affaires; Le Foyer; L'Epidémie; la Porte feuille; Vieux ménage; Scrupules. Address: Château de Cheverchemont, Eriel sur Seine, Seine-et-Oise. T: 22.   Died 16 Feb. 1917.

MIREHOUSE, William Edward; Barrister-at-Law; Recorder of the Borough of Wenlock since 1889; Revising Barrister since 1888; b 29 Oct. 1844; γ s of Rev. William Squire Mirehouse, Hambrook Grove, county of Gloucester, and Rector of Colsterworth, county of Lincoln; m 1904, Ethel, o d of the late Horace Shearly of Billingshurst, Sussex; two d. Educ: Harrow; Clare College, Cambridge (BA 1867; MA 1870). Barrister Lincoln's Inn, 1870; member of Oxford Circuit. Recreations: played in Harrow cricket eleven, 1863; played in Harrow football eleven, 1862; hunting, shooting. Address: Hambrook Grove, near Bristol; 4 Pump Court, Temple, EC. Club: New University.   Died 17 June 1925.

MITCHELL, Rt. Rev. Anthony, DD; Bishop of Aberdeen and Orkney since 1912; b Aberdeen, 24 Oct. 1868; s of John Mitchell; m 1893, Elizabeth, d of Leslie Valentine, Inverurie; one s one d. Educ: Grammar School, Aberdeen; King's College, Aberdeen University; Jenkins prize for Classical Philology, 1889; Black prize, and Seafield Gold Medal for Latin, 1890; Blackwell Essay, 1893; MA (1st Class Honours in Classics) 1890; BD (Honours) 1903; Caius College, Cambridge; Edinburgh University; Episcopal Theol College, 1890; Jamieson Bursary, Urquhart Greek Prize, and Luscombe scholarship, 1890; Ordained, 1892; Curate of St Mary's Cathedral, Edinburgh, with charge of Church of Good Shepherd, Murrayfield, 1892; Hebrew Lecturer, Edinburgh Theological College; Curate, St John's, Dumfries, 1893; Rector, St Andrew's, Glasgow, 1895; Diocesan Missioner of Glasgow and Galloway, 1902; Rector of St Mark's, Portobello, 1904; Principal, and Pantonian Professor of Theology, Theological College of the Episcopal Church in Scotland, 1905; Canon of St Mary's Cathedral, Edinburgh, 1905, and Chancellor, 1912; Examining Chaplain to Bishop of Edinburgh. Publications: Tatters from a Student's Gown (verse), 1890; History of the Episcopal Church in Scotland, 1907; Story of the Church in Scotland, 1908; Biographical Studies in Scottish Church History, 1914. Address: Bishops Court, Aberdeen. T: 1545.
Died 17 Jan. 1917.

MITCHELL, Major Charles Johnstone, DSO 1917; Oxfordshire and Buckinghamshire Light Infantry Reserve of Officers; b 20 Sept. 1879; 2nd s of Col H. L. Mitchell, RA, 28 Cornwall Gardens SW, and Mary Arabella Susan, e d of C. D. Reynolds of Ramslade, Bracknell; m 1906, Maud Elsie, γ d of Charles Arthur Galton, ICS; one s. Served European War, 1914–17 (DSO). Address: 28 Cornwall Gardens, SW. Club: Army and Navy.
Died 16 Oct. 1918.

MITCHELL, Edmund; novelist; b Glasgow, 1861; m 1886; four s one d. Educ: Elgin Academy; Aberdeen University (MA and gold medallist for English Literature). Followed the profession of journalism in India, Australia and America, and travelled widely as a special correspondent; Senior Lieut Bombay Vol. Artillery, 1888–89. Publications: The Temple of Death, 1894; Towards the Eternal Snows, 1896; Chickabiddy Stories, 1899; Plotters of Paris, 1900; The Lone Star Rush, 1901; Only a Nigger, 1901; The Belforts of Culben, 1902; The Despoilers, 1904; In Desert Keeping, 1905; Tales of Destiny, 1913; dramatic work: The Telephone, 1901. Recreations: chess, reading. Address: 1815 North Normandie Avenue, Los Angeles, California.
Died 31 March 1917.

MITCHELL, J. Campbell, RSA 1919; b Campbeltown, Argyllshire, 1865. Educ: Grammar School, Campbeltown. Painted landscape and seascape; represented in the New Pinakothek, Munich, by A Scottish Moorland; in Corporation Art Gallery, Aberdeen, by Aberlady; in Walker Art Gallery, Liverpool, by Springtime, Midlothian; in Public Gallery, Auckland, New Zealand, by On the Kintyre Coast; and in the Smith Institute, Stirling, by The Haunt of the Curlew. Address: Duncree, Corstorphine, Midlothian. T: Corstorphine 65. M: SG 3022. Clubs: Scottish Arts, Edinburgh.
Died 16 Feb. 1922.

MITCHELL, John; JP for County of the City of Dundee; FJI; editor Dundee Courier since 1887; *b* Perth, 16 April 1860; three *s* one *d*. *Educ:* St Leonard's School, Perth; Glasgow University. Telegraphist in Dundee Post Office; joined Scotsman reporting staff, 1882; President of Institute of Journalists, 1910–11; Temporary Major Dundee Volunteer Regiment. *Recreations:* riding, cycling, bowling, curling. *Address:* 4 Prospect Place, Dundee. *T:* Dundee 1858. *M:* TI 3962. *Clubs:* Eastern, New, Dundee; King James VI, Perth.
Died 7 Nov. 1923.

MITCHELL, John Ames; editor of Life; *b* New York, 17 Jan. 1845; *m* 1885. *Educ:* Harvard Scientific School, 1864; studied architecture in Paris, 1867–70. Practised as architect in Boston until 1876, but gradually drifted into artistic and decorative work, illustrating books, etc, and went to Paris again for study and remained four years; during that time produced several etchings, receiving an honourable mention at the Paris Exposition; studied drawing and painting in Julian's atelier, and with Albert Maignan; went to New York, 1880; started Life, 1883, and edited that journal from its first issue. *Publications:* Croquis de l'Exposition, 1879 (a series of etchings); The Summer School of Philosophy at Mount Desert, 1881; The Romance of the Moon, 1886; The Last American, 1889; Life's Fairy Tales, 1893; Amos Judd, 1895; That First Affair, 1896; Gloria Victis, 1897; The Pines of Lory, 1901; The Villa Claudia, 1904; The Silent War, 1906; Dr Thorne's Idea, 1910; Pandora's Box, 1911; Drowsy, 1917. *Recreations:* literature, motoring; summer on his estate at Ridgefield, Conn. *Address:* 17 West Thirty-First Street, New York. *T:* 3680 Madison Square.
Died 29 June 1918.

MITCHELL, Sir Thomas, Kt 1906; CVO 1906; *b* Belfast, 1844; *m d* of late Thomas Goble, Worthing. *Educ:* HM Dockyard, Chatham. Draughtsman, Chatham Dockyard, 1871; at Admiralty three years; foreman of Portsmouth Dockyard during building of Trafalgar; Admiralty overseer, Palmer's Shipyard, Jarrow, 1889–91, where he superintended the building of the Resolution and Revenge; Constructor, Hong-Kong Dockyard, 1891–95; Senior Constructor, Devonport Dockyard, 1895–99; Chief Constructor, Bermuda, 1899–1902; Sheerness, 1902–3; then at Chatham; manager of Constructive Department, Portsmouth, during building of Dreadnought (thanks of Admiralty) and Bellerophon (Kt); retired 1907. *Address:* 37 Salisbury Road, Craneswater Park, Southsea.
Died 1 April 1919.

MITCHELL, Col Thomas, CB 1902; Magistrate County of Surrey; Hon. Colonel 5th Volunteer Battalion East Lancashire Regiment; *b* 1839; *s* of John Mitchell, Fearnes Hall, Lancashire; *m* 1881, Margaret, *d* of John Lord, JP, of Bacup, Lancashire, and Mooswald Place, Dumfries; one *s* one *d*. *Educ:* Preston Grammar School; afterwards private tutor. Joined the 4th Lancashire Rifles, 1859. *Recreations:* athletics, hunting, shooting, travelling. *Address:* Wimbledon Lodge, Eaten Gardens, Hove, Sussex. *Clubs:* Junior Carlton, Constitutional.
Died 2 June 1921.

MITCHELL-THOMSON, Sir Mitchell, 1st Bt, *cr* 1900; JP Peeblesshire; DL, JP, Edinburgh; FRSE; FSSA; Lord Provost of Edinburgh, 1897–1900; *b* 15 Dec. 1846; *y s* of late Andrew Thomson of Seafield, Alloa, and Janet, *e d* of William Mitchell, Alloa; assumed by Royal licence additional surname of Mitchell, 1900; *m* 1st, 1876, Eliza Flowerdew (*d* 1*d* of late William Lowson of Balthayock, Perthshire; one *s*; 2nd, 1880, Eliza Lamb, *y d* of late Robert Cook, shipowner, Leith; two *d*. *Educ:* Alloa and Edinburgh. Member Royal Company of Archers; Director of the Bank of Scotland, the Scottish Widows' Fund and Caledonian Railway; KGStJ. *Heir: s* William (Lowson) Mitchell-Thomson [*b* 15 April 1877; *m* 1909, Madeleine, *d* of Sir Malcolm Donald McEacharn]. *Address:* Inglismaldie, Laurencekirk, Kincardineshire. *T:* Central 306, Edinburgh. *Clubs:* Carlton, Junior Carlton, Constitutional.
Died 15 Nov. 1918.

MITCHINSON, Rt. Rev. John, DCL, DD; Master of Pembroke College, Oxford, and Canon of Gloucester since 1899; Assistant Bishop of Peterborough, 1881–1914; of Gloucester, 1904–5; Hon. Fellow of St Chad's, Denstone, and of St Andrew, Taunton; *b* Durham, 23 Sept. 1833; *o s* of John Mitchinson; unmarried. *Educ:* Durham School; Pembroke Coll., Oxford (Scholar). 1st class (Classics) Moderations, 1853; 1st class Lit. Hum. and 1st class Nat. Sci. Oxford, 1854–55; Fellow of Pembroke Coll., Oxford; President of the Union. Assistant Master in Merchant Taylors' School, 1858–59; Headmaster of the King's School, Canterbury, 1859–73; Hon. Canon of Canterbury, 1871–99; Select Preacher, Oxford, 1872–73, 1893–94, 1903–4; Ramsden Preacher, Cambridge, 1883, and Oxford, 1900, 1913; Bishop of Barbados and the Windward Islands, 1873–81;

Coadjutor to Bishop of Antigua, 1879–82; Rector of Sibstone, 1881–99; Archdeacon of Leicester, 1886–99; Hon. Fellow of Pembroke College, Oxford, 1882–99. *Address:* Pembroke Coll. Oxford; Cathedral Gardens, Gloucester.
Died 25 Sept. 1918.

MITFORD, Maj.-Gen. Reginald Colville William Reveley; retired list; *b* Waterloo Manor, Hants, 23 Feb. 1839; *y s* of John Mitford, barrister-at-law, and *g s* of the historian of Greece; *m* 1865, Margaret A., *d* of late H. Moore. *Educ:* Rugby School. Appointed Ensign in the Indian Army, 1855; served Indian Mutiny (severely wounded, despatches and GGO, recommended by Lord Clyde for VC, 23 Oct. 1858); two NW Frontier Expeditions; Afghan War; retired, 1886; travelled in China, Japan, N America, civilised Europe, Germany and Austria. *Publications:* To Cabul with the Cavalry Brigade; Orient and Occident; edited Forbes Mitchell's Reminiscences of the Great Mutiny. *Recreations:* sketching, travelling, shooting. *M:* 6943 LK. *Clubs:* Wellington, Hurlingham.
Died 21 Aug. 1925.

MITFORD, Capt. Robert Osbaldeston-, JP; FRGS, FZS; late 73rd Regiment (2nd Battalion Black Watch); *b* 25 Nov. 1846; *e s* of late Edward Ledwich Osbaldeston Mitford and Janet, *d* of late Ven. Benjamin Bailey, Archdeacon of Ceylon; assumed additional name of Osbaldeston, 1912; *m* 1875, Annie, 2nd *d* of late Maj.-Gen. Charles Stuart Lane; three *s* five *d*. *Educ:* Eton; Sandhurst. Lord of the Manors of Mitford, Molesdene, Pigdon, etc; patron of the living. *Address:* Mitford Castle, Northumberland. *TA:* Osbaldeston, Mitford. *T:* Morpeth 52. *M:* LK 6943 and NL 2165. *Clubs:* Naval and Military, Royal Automobile.
Died 27 Dec. 1924.

MITRA, S. M., MRAS; Hindu author; settled in England since 1905; *b* 30 Nov. 1856; unmarried. Connected with the Indian press for thirty years—English, Urdu, and Bengali writer; ten years Proprietor and Editor of the Deccan Post; lectured under London University, British Navy League, Central Asian Society, East India Association, etc; selected by Calcutta Sahitya Parishad in 1901 to revise transliteration of Arabic and Persian words and phrases in vogue in Bengali language; opposed in 1907 anti-British Bengal boycott movement in The Times; often wrote in reviews; represented India at the International Free Trade Congress in London, 1908; represented Hindu medicine at the International Congress of Medicine, London, 1913. *Publications:* in English: Life of Sir John Hall; Position of Women in Indian Life (with HH the Maharani of Baroda); Indian Problems; British Rule in India; Anglo-Indian Studies; Peace in India—how to attain it; Moslem-Hindu entente-cordiale; Imperial Preference and India; Hindupore (an Anglo-Indian romance); Voice for Women— without votes; Yoga Mental Culture; revised Anglo-Indian terms in Standard Dictionary; in Urdu: Zibeh ul baqar; in Bengali: Nayati Prabandha, etc. *Recreations:* Hindu psychotherapy, reciting Persian poetry. *Address:* Royal Asiatic Society, 74 Grosvenor Street, W1.
Died 15 Nov. 1925.

MITTAG-LEFFLER, Gösta, Dr Phil; Professor of Mathematics, University of Stockholm, 1881–1911; Editor of the international mathematical journal, Acta Mathematica; possessor of probably the greatest existing library for mathematics; *b* Stockholm, 16 March 1846; *s* of Member of Parliament, Rector J. O. Leffler and Gustava Mittag; *brother* of late authoress Anne-Charlotte Leffler (in her first marriage, Edgren, in her second marriage, Duchessa di Cajanello); *brother* of the philologist Frits Läffler; *m* 1882, Signe (*d* 1921), *d* of General J. af Lindfors, Finland. Prof. and Mrs Mittag-Leffler bequeathed by will all their property, including the library and their estate at Djursholm, to an International Mathematical Institution, bearing the name Makarna Mittag-Lefflers Matematiska Stiftelse; Foreign Member Royal Society; Hon. Member Philosophical Society, Cambridge, London Mathematical Society, Royal Institution, Manchester Literary and Philosophical Society, Royal Irish Academy; member of nearly all the learned societies of Europe, including Institute of France, Società Italiana (detta dei XL), Accademia dei Lincei, Academies of St Petersburg, Göttingen, Belgium, Stockholm, Christiania, Copenhagen, Helsingfors, etc; Hon. Doctorates from Bologna, Oxford, Cambridge, Christiania, Aberdeen, St Andrews. *Publications:* Sur la représentation analytique des fonctions monogènes uniformes d'une variable indépendante, 1884; Sur la représentation analytique d'une branche uniforme d'une fonction monogène, 1900–20; Niels Henrik Abel (Revue du mois), 1907; a great number of dissertations in higher analysis. *Recreation:* travelling. *Address:* Djursholm, Sweden. *T:* Stockholm 755.11; Djursholm 809.
Died July 1927.

MITTON, Rev. Henry Arthur, MA; Master of Sherburn House, Durham, 1874–1913; resigned, 1913; *b* 24 Jan. 1837; *e s* of Rev. Canon

Mitton, Vicar of St Paul's, Manningham; *m* 1861, Annie Eliza (*d* 1903), *e d* of Rev. Theodore Dury, Rector of Westmill, Herts; four *s* four *d*. *Educ:* Bradford school; Christ's College, Cambridge (head of Modern History, univ. exam., under Sir James Stephen, 1858; BA 1859). Ordained by Bishop of Ripon, 1860; Curate sole charge of Heaton, Bradford, 1860–64; Incumbent of St Barnabas', Heaton, 1864–68; selected by the Bishop of Durham from outside his own diocese to be Vicar of Bishop-Auckland, 1868; broke down from fever and overwork, 1874; appointed by Bishop Baring to Sherburn House, one of the very few ancient leper foundations (later Brethren and Sisters) remaining in England. *Publications:* Lectures, in answer to Dr Parker, on the Book of Common Prayer; short account of Christ's Hospital, Sherburn, etc. *Recreations:* angling, pedestrianism. *Address:* The Rectory, Bowness-on-Solway, Carlisle.

Died 1 July 1918.

MIVART, Dr Frederick St George, MD Louvain; FRCSE; late Medical Inspector HM Local Government Board; *b* London; *s* of Dr St George Mivart, FRS; *m* 1877, Marie Sophie, *d* of D. Maurigy of Brancolar, Nice, France; one *s* one *d*. *Educ:* Beaumont; Catholic College of Higher Studies, Kensington; St Mary's Hospital, London; Louvain University; Royal Infirmary, Edinburgh; Paris and Vienna. FZS; Fellow of the Royal Society of Medicine; Fellow of the Royal Sanitary Institute; conducted scientific and other enquiries on behalf of the Local Government Board. *Address:* 15 Stafford Terrace, Kensington, W8. *T:* Park 1877. *Club:* Reform.

Died 5 Nov. 1925.

MOBERLY, Winifred Horsbrugh, MA; Principal of St Hilda's College, Oxford, since 1919; *b* April 1875; *d* of Col Charles Morris Moberly, Indian Staff Corps; unmarried. *Educ:* Winchester and Sydenham High Schools; Lady Margaret Hall, Oxford (scholar). Bursar at Lady Margaret Hall, Oxford, 1910–12; organiser of Training Schemes for Unemployed Women for the Central Committee on Women's Employment, 1914–15; Administrator of the "Millicent Fawcett Hospitals" in Russia and Galicia, 1915–17; Area Secretary, YWCA for the Women's Army Auxiliary Corps in Calais, 1917–18; Lecturer in USA for War Workers' Campaign, Oct. and Nov. 1918. *Address:* St Hilda's College, Oxford. *Club:* University Women's.

Died 6 April 1928.

MOCKLER, Col Percy Rice, CMG 1918; JP Oxon; retired pay; *b* Sept. 1860; *y s* of late Edward Mockler, of Rockville, Co. Cork, and Julia, *d* of J. B. G. Ferryman, of Leckhampton, Glos; *m* 1896, Augusta, *e d* of late Thomas Fielden Campbell, 26 Devonshire Place, W. *Educ:* Cheltenham College; RMC, Sandhurst. Joined 6th Foot (Royal Warwickshire Regt), 1879; served Burmah Expedition as a Brigade Transport Officer, 1885–87 (despatches, medal and clasp); retired, 1906; re-employed European War, 1914–18 as a Colonel-in-charge of Records (despatches, CMG). *Recreations:* gardening; formerly football, polo, racquets. *Address:* Peppard House, Rotherfield Peppard, Oxon. *Club:* Army and Navy.

Died 11 March 1927.

MOFFAT, Rev. John Smith, CMG 1890; retired on pension; *b* Kuruman, Bechwanaland, 10 March 1885; *s* of late Rev. Robert Moffat, DD, and Mary, *d* of late James Smith; *m* 1858, Emily (*d* 1902), *d* of late J. S. Unwin, Brighton. *Educ:* private school, Newcastle-on-Tyne; Cheshunt Coll.; New Coll., London. Missionary in Matabeleland, 1859–65; Bechwanaland till 1879; Commissioner on western border of the Transvaal during British occupation, 1880–81; Resident Magistrate, Maseru, Basutoland, 1882–84; Resident Magistrate, Taungs, Bechwanaland, 1885–87; Assistant Commissioner in Bechwanaland Protectorate and Matabeleland, 1887–95; Resident Magistrate, Taungs, 1895–96. Decorated for special diplomatic services in Matabeleland. *Publication:* The Lives of Robert and Mary Moffat. *Recreation:* honorary missionary work. *Address:* Cape Town.

Died 28 Dec. 1918.

MOFFATT, Alexander; Sheriff-Substitute of Stirlingshire at Falkirk since 1904; of Linlithgowshire since 1917; *b* 31 Aug. 1863; *s* of Alexander Moffatt, shipowner, Glasgow, and Lilly, *d* of John Millar of Greenock; *m* 1888, Blanche Helen Isabel (*d* 1913), *d* of Alexander M'Ritchie, supt engineer Peninsular and Oriental Steamship Co., London; one *s* one *d*. *Educ:* Park School, Glasgow; Universities of Glasgow and Edinburgh (MA, LLB, of former). Advocate at Scottish Bar, 1888; Sheriff-Substitute of Shetland, 1900–4; contested (C) Paisley, 1895; volunteer officer, 1880–88 and 1900–5; Major-Commandant 7th VB Gordon Highlanders, 1904. *Publications:* articles on Copyright, Salvage, Ports and Harbours, Pilots and others in Green's Encyclopædia of Scots Law; occasional contributions to legal journals. *Recreations:* yachting, shooting, walking. *Address:* Arnotdale,

Falkirk. *T:* Falkirk 150. *Clubs:* Junior Army and Navy; University Scottish Conservative, Edinburgh; Stirling County, Stirling.

Died 29 March 1921.

MOGGRIDGE, Ernest Grant, CB 1919; late Assistant Secretary Ministry of Transport; *b* 18 June 1863; *s* of late Edward Moggridge; unmarried. *Educ:* privately. Entered Home Civil Service (Class I), 1886; Secretary's Office, General Post Office; transferred to Board of Trade, 1892; Secretary to Royal Commission on Electrical Communication with Lighthouses and Light-vessels, and to Committee on International Code of Signals; Private Secretary to Permanent Secretary to Board of Trade; Asst Secretary for Marine Department of Board of Trade, 1913–16. *Clubs:* Union, Windham.

Died 1 Feb. 1925.

MOIR, Byres, MD Edin.; Consulting Physician to the London Homœopathic Hospital and Bromley Cottage Hospital; *b* 1853; *s* of Patrick Moir Byres, of Tonley, Aberdeenshire; *m* Evelyn, *d* of Col Collings Bonamy, Guernsey; two *s* one *d*. *Educ:* Manchester Grammar School; Owens College, Manchester; Edinburgh University. After qualification studied in Paris; Surgeon to Orient Line; House Surgeon and Physician to London Homœopathic Hospital. *Publications:* contributions to medical journals. *Address:* Weymouth Court, 1 Weymouth Street, W1. *T:* Langham 2334.

Died 4 July 1928.

MOLE, Harold Frederic, FRCS, LRCP; Surgeon, Bristol Royal Infirmary; *b* 1866; *s* of late Frederic M. Mole of Edgbaston; *m* 1913, Harriet, *d* of late Reuben Holmes of Heanor, Derbyshire. *Educ:* Bristol; St Bartholomew's Hospital. Late Junior House Surgeon and Anæsthetist, Junior House Physician, House Physician and House Surgeon and Senior Resident Officer, Bristol Royal Infirmary; Assistant Surgeon and Surgeon-in-charge of the Aural Department, Bristol Royal Infirmary. *Publications:* Two cases of Intubation in Adults; Two cases of Ruptured Tubal Pregnancy; Two cases of Ruptured Intestine; the Aural Complication of Influenza; contributed to Bristol Medico-Chirurgical Journal. *Address:* 24 College Road, Clifton, Bristol. *T:* 1349. *Club:* Clifton.

Died 21 Dec. 1917.

MOLESWORTH, Sir Guilford Lindsey, KCIE 1888 (CIE 1879); late Consulting Engineer to the Government of India for State Railways; retired, 1889; *b* 3 May 1828; *y s* of Rev. John Edward Nassau Molesworth, DD, Vicar of Rochdale, and 1st wife, Harriet, *d* of William Mackinnon; *m* 1854, Maria Elizabeth (*d* 1919), *d* of John Thomas Bridges, of St Nicholas Court, Thanet, and Harriet Elizabeth, *d* of Sir Robert Affleck, 4th Bt; one *s* two *d* (and three *s* one *d* decd). *Educ:* King's School, Canterbury; College of Civil Engineers, Putney. Served apprenticeship under Sir William Fairbairn, and pupillage under Mr Dockray, Engineer-in-Chief, London and North Western Railway; Chief Assistant Engineer on London, Brighton, and South Coast Railway; in Arsenal at Woolwich during Crimean War; Mechanical Engineer Ceylon Railway, 1859; subsequently Agent and Chief Engineer; Chief Resident Engineer Ceylon Govt Railway in 1862; Director-General of Railways to Ceylon Govt and Director of Public Works in 1867; Consulting Engineer to the Govt of India, 1871; President of the Institution of Civil Engineers, 1904. Afghan War medal; Burma War medal and clasp; thanks of Government for services performed during the Afghan War in the enemy's country; property in Swords, near Dublin, 850 acres. *Publications:* Conversion of Wood by Machinery; Pocket-book of Engineering Formulæ; Metrical Tables; Decimal Coinage; Light Railways; Gauge of Railways in India; Land as Property; Imperialism and Free Trade; Text-book of Bi-metallism; The Divorce of Silver and Gold; Political Economy in its Relation to Strikes; Reason and Instinct in Ants; Iron Manufacture in India; Silver and Gold (prize essay); Masonry Dams; Graphic Statics; Our Empire under Protection and Free Trade; Economic and Fiscal Facts and Fallacies; Life of John Edward Nassau Molesworth, DD; A Spy of the Huns, etc. *Address:* Manor House, Bexley, Kent. *Clubs:* St Stephen's, Royal Societies.

Died 21 Jan. 1925.

MOLESWORTH, Mrs Mary Louisa; *b* Holland, 1839; *e d* of Charles Augustus Stewart, *o s* of Maj.-Gen. Stewart, Strath, NB, and Agnes Janet, *d* of John Wilson, Transy, Fife; *m* 1861, Major Richard Molesworth (*d* 1900) (late Royal Dragoons), *s* of Anthony Oliver Molesworth and 2nd wife, Grace Jane Crofton, and *nephew* of 7th Viscount Molesworth; one *s* three *d* (and two *s* one *d* decd). *Educ:* home, and partly in Switzerland. Spent several years in France and Germany. *Publications:* early novels—She was Young and He was Old, etc, under name of Ennis Graham; books for the young—Carrots; Cuckoo Clock; Herr Baby; A Charge Fulfilled; Little Old Portrait;

and many others; later novels—Hathercourt Rectory; The Red Grange; Neighbours, etc; Lives of the Saints for Children; Stories for Children in Illustration of the Lord's Prayer, 1897; Meg Langholme, 1897; Miss Mouse and her Boys, 1897; The Laurel Walk, 1898; The Magic Nuts, 1898; The Boys and I; The Old Pincushion; The Grim House, 1899; This and That; The House that Grew; The Wood Pigeons and Mary; Peterkin; The Story of a Year, 1910. *Recreation:* wrote stories as amusement when very young. *Address:* 155 Sloane Street, SW.   *Died July 1921.*

MOLINEUX, Rev. Arthur Ellison; Hon. Canon of Canterbury. *Address:* The Vicarage, Minster, Ramsgate.
Died 22 Dec. 1919.

MOLINEUX, Rev. Charles Hurlock; Hon. Canon of Southwell. *Address:* Staveley Rectory, Chesterfield.
Died 26 Aug. 1927.

MOLLISON, James W., CSI 1911. Superintendent of Farms, Bombay, 1890; Deputy Director of Agriculture, 1897; Inspector-General of Agriculture in India, 1901; retired, 1912.
Died 4 Oct. 1927.

MOLLOY, Bernard Charles; *b* 1842; *s* of late Kedo Molloy and Maria Teresa (late of Hawke House, Sunbury), *d* of James Tracy Lynam. Barrister Middle Temple, 1872; formerly Capt. in French Army; special gold medal Franco-German War; Private Chamberlain Court of the Vatican; MP (N) Birr, King's Co., 1880–1900. *Address:* 5 Paper Buildings, Temple, EC. *T:* Holborn 1268. *Club:* Reform.
Died 26 June 1916.

MOLONY, Rev. Henry William Eliott, MA; Hon. Canon of St Albans, 1914. *Educ:* All Souls College, Oxford; Leeds Clergy School. Ordained, 1882; Curate of St John's, Hammersmith, 1882–85; St Saviour, Hoxton, 1885–91; Vicar of Great Ilford, 1892–1912; Rural Dean of Barking, 1907–12; Rector of Stevenage, 1912–18. *Address:* Windsor Road, Parkstone, Dorset.
Died 23 Aug. 1919.

MOLSON, Major John Elsdale, JP West Sussex; MD; MP (U) Gainsborough, 1918–23; *b* 6 Aug. 1863; *s* of late Samuel Elsdale Molson, Montreal, Canada; *m* Mary, *d* of A. E. Leeson, MA, MD; three *s* one *d*. *Educ:* Cheltenham College; Emmanuel College, Cambridge. Contested NE Bethnal Green, Jan. and Dec. 1910; served in RAMC(T) in England and Egypt, Aug. 1914–Dec. 1918. *Recreations:* shooting, motoring, golf. *Address:* Goring Hall, Worthing. *T:* Goring-by-Sea 8; 21 St James' Court, Buckingham Gate, SW. *T:* Victoria 2360. *TA:* Molson, Goring-by-Sea. *M:* BP 8141. *Clubs:* Carlton, Oxford and Cambridge.
Died 28 Nov. 1925.

MOLYNEUX, Rev. Sir John Charles, 9th Bt, *cr* 1730; LLB; Vicar of Portesham, Dorchester, Dorset, since 1886; *b* Ireland, 27 June 1843; *s* of Rev. Sir John William Henry Molyneux, 8th Bt, and Louisa Dorothy, *d* of John Christian, Deemster of I of M; *S* father, 1879; *m* 1st, 1873, Fanny, (*d* 1893), *d* of Edward Jackson, Walsoken House, Wisbech; one *s* three *d* (and two *s* decd); 2nd, 1895, Ada Isabel Hepzibah (*d* 1925), *d* of Rev. A. F. Wynter, Rector of Barnardiston, Suffolk. *Educ:* Bradfield College; Christ College, Cambridge. Ordained 1867. *Heir:* *s* William Arthur Molyneux [*b* 26 July 1877; *m* 1924, Constance Cochrina Hood, of Invergeldie, Comrie, Perthshire, *d* of Mrs Stanley Clay, Rose Hill, Sevenoaks]. *Address:* Portesham Vicarage, Dorchester.
Died 26 Aug. 1928.

MOMBER, Captain Edward Marie Felix, DSO 1916; Royal Engineers; Temporary Major, Officer Commanding 176 Tunnelling Company, Royal Engineers; *s* of Frederick Ernest Momber and Eugénie Ardoin. *Educ:* Stubbington House; Cheltenham College (head of both Schools); RMA Woolwich. Commissioned RE, 1907; SME Chatham, 1909; 11th Field Company RE, Aldershot, 1912; Capt. Oct. 1914; 25th Fortress Company RE, Hong Kong; and Adjutant RE till beginning of war; Adjt to Siege Companies RE, Chatham, Nov.–Dec. 1914; served European War, 1914–16, in France; formed 176 Tunnelling Company RE, April 1915 (Military Cross, despatches, DSO); Temp. Major, Dec. 1915. *Recreations:* Rugby—for RMA, Woolwich, SME Chatham, Captain Aldershot Command, played for United Services, Portsmouth, also Army, Hampshire County, cap; rowing—Royal Engineers Yacht Club, on Medway and at Henley, Captain Hong Kong RC; fencing—represented RMA, Woolwich, and won sabres competition, cadet at Olympia in 1907; gymnastics—colours for RMA, Woolwich against

Sandhurst, 1907; holder of about 40 cups for swimming, field-sports, and rowing; hunting, rider in point-to-point.
Died 20 June 1917.

MONACO, Prince of, Albert Honoré Charles; *b* Paris, 13 Nov. 1848; *S* father, Prince Charles III, 1889; *m* 1st, 1869, Lady Mary Victoria Douglas-Hamilton (marr. annulled 1880; she *m* 2nd, Count Tassilo Festetics de Tolna, GCVO); 2nd, 1889, Alice (*née* Heine, Duchesse de Richelieu, *b* New Orleans, 10 Feb. 1858). Catholic. *Heir:* by 1st marriage, Prince Louis Honoré Charles Antoine, *b* Baden-Baden, 12 July 1870. *Recreation:* oceanographic studies. *Address:* The Palace, Monaco; Château Marchais, par Liesse, Aisne, France; 10 avenue du Président Wilson, Paris.
Died 26 June 1922.

MONCK, 5th Viscount, *cr* 1800; **Henry Power Charles Stanley Monck,** JP, DL; Baron Monck, 1797; Baron Monck (UK), 1866; *b* Dublin, 8 Jan. 1849; *e s* of 4th Viscount and Elizabeth Louise Mary Monck, 4th *d* of 1st and last Earl of Rathdowne; *S* father, 1894; *m* 1874, Lady Edith Caroline Sophia Scott, *d* of 3rd Earl of Clonmell; one *d* (two *s* decd). *Educ:* Eton; Christ Church, Oxford (BA, SCL). Lieut Coldstream Guards, 1871; served in Egyptian campaign, 1882; and expedition to Suakin, Feb. to May 1885 (medal with 2 clasps, bronze star); Captain, retired, 1885. Church of England; Conservative; owned about 14,200 acres in Cos Wicklow, Kilkenny, Wexford, Westmeath, and City of Dublin. *Recreations:* shooting, cricket, racquets. *Heir:* *g s* Henry Wyndham Stanley Monck, *b* 11 Dec. 1905. *Address:* Charleville, Enniskerry, Co. Wicklow. *Clubs:* Carlton, Kildare Street, Dublin.
Died 18 Aug. 1927.

MONCKTON, Arthur; JP; *b* 20 July 1845; 2nd *s* of late General Henry Monckton and Anne, *o d* of John Groome Smythe of Hilton; *m* 1896, Lady Gertrude Bouverie, *d* of 4th Earl of Radnor; two *s* two *d*. *Educ:* Eton; Christ Church, Oxford. After leaving Oxford went to the Royal Agricultural College, Cirencester, and for a few years acted as Land Agent to his brother, Francis Monckton, Stretton Hall (MP for West Staffordshire, 1871–85); resigned after an attack of rheumatic fever. *Recreations:* gardening, magic lantern exhibitions. *Address:* Normanston Hall, Lowestoft. *TA:* Lowestoft.
Died 2 May 1917.

MONCKTON, Edward Philip; barrister; Recorder of Northampton since 1890; County Councillor King's Cliffe Division, Northamptonshire; *b* Bareilly, India, 18 July 1840; *e s* of Edward Henry Cradock Monckton, HEICS, and later of Fineshade Abbey, Northamptonshire, and 2nd wife, Maria Catherine, *y d* of H. W. Tydd; *m* 1866, Christabel (*d* 1899), *d* of Rev. C. D. Francis, Vicar of Tysoe, Warwickshire; seven *s* three *d*. *Educ:* private schools; Trinity Coll., Cambridge (MA). FSA; Barrister-at-Law, Inner Temple, 1868; Midland Circuit; Lieut-Col 3rd Northamptonshire Regt (retired 1895); member of House of Laymen; High Sheriff of Rutland, 1883–84; MP (C) N Northampton, 1895–1900; JP Northamptonshire, Rutland, Liberty of Peterborough; Chairman of Quarter Sessions, Liberty of Peterborough. Owned about 3,200 acres. *Recreations:* rowing, cricket, hunting, shooting, geology, science. *Address:* Fineshade Abbey, Stamford; Laundimer House, Oundle, Northamptonshire. *Clubs:* Carlton, Junior Carlton, Cavendish.
Died 17 April 1916.

MONCKTON, Francis; JP, DL Staffordshire; late Hon. Major Staffordshire Yeomanry Cavalry; *b* 7 March 1844; *e s* of General Henry Monckton and Anne, *o d* of John Groome Smythe; *g s* of 1st Viscount Galway; *m* 1889, Evelyn Mary, *d* of Algernon Charles Heber-Percy of Hodnet Hall, Co. Salop; one *s* three *d* (and two *s* decd). *Educ:* Eton; Christ Church, Oxford. MP (C) West Staffordshire, 1871–85; High Sheriff, 1895. *Club:* Carlton.
Died 30 Sept. 1926.

MONCKTON, Lionel; composer; musical critic, Daily Telegraph; *b* 1862; *s* of late Sir John Monckton; *m* Gertie Millar. *Educ:* Charterhouse; Oxford. *Publications:* songs in Gaiety plays. *Address:* 69 Russell Square, WC1. *T:* Central 9235. *Clubs:* Conservative, Eccentric, Green Room.
Died 15 Feb. 1924.

MONCRIEFF, Hon. James William, DL Kinross-shire; WS; *b* 16 Sept 1845; 3rd *s* of 1st Baron Moncreiff and Isabella, *o d* of Robert Bell, Scotland; *m* 1872, Mary Lillias (*d* 1910), *e d* of late George Mitchell Innes of Bangour, Linlithgowshire; four *s* (and one *s* decd). *Address:* 6 Ainslie Place, Edinburgh. *Clubs:* Brooks's; New, Edinburgh.
Died 30 Jan. 1920.

MONCRIEFF, Alexander Bain, CMG 1909; MICE; civil engineer; Member American Society Civil Engineers; *b* Dublin, 22 May 1845;

m 1877, Mary Bonson Sunter. *Educ:* Belfast Academy. Went to South Australia, 1875; Engineer for Harbours and Jetties, 1888–1909; Chairman of South Australian Supply and Tender Board, 1895–99; Engineer-in-Chief, South Australia; President Institute of Surveyors, 1901, and of Public Service Association of South Australia, 1904; Railways Commissioner, 1909–16; Chairman of the Municipal Tramways Trust, Adelaide; retired, 1922. *Address:* 12 Alexandra Avenue, Rose Park, Adelaide, South Australia.

Died 11 April 1928.

MONCRIEFF, Lt-Gen. George Hay, VD; Colonel, The Royal Scots; retired, 1900; *b* 22 Aug. 1836; *s* of late General George Moncrieff; *m* 1871, Flora Caroline, *sister* of Sir Archibald Lamb, 3rd Bt and *d* of Charles James Savile Montgomerie Lamb and Anna Charlotte Grey. *Educ:* Leamington College, Sandhurst. Scots Guards, 1854–86; served Crimea, 1855–56 (despatches, medal and clasp (Sebastopol) and Turkish medal); Assistant Military Sec., headquarters, 1887–90; commanded Curragh Brigade, 1890–91; commanded Dublin District, 1891–95. *Recreation:* golf. *Address:* 38 Thurloe Square, SW; Greenside, Sunningdale. *Clubs:* Guards', United Service.

Died 15 Oct. 1918.

MONCRIEFF, Robert Hope; author and editor; *b* Edinburgh, 1846. *Educ:* Edinburgh, and privately in England. Took some steps towards the Scottish Bar, but "penned a stanza", etc, at an early stage, and served a time as a school teacher. *Publications:* The World of To-day; Bonnie Scotland; and some 200 volumes of fiction, history, school-books, guide-books, etc, under various aliases, chiefly as Ascott R. Hope. *Club:* Athenæum. *Died 10 Aug. 1927.*

MONET, Claude; artist; *b* Paris, 14 Nov. 1840. A soldier in Africa for two years; studied under Gleyre; visited England, 1870. *Principal works:* Views of Argenteuil, 1872; Cathedrals, 1874; Views of Vetheuil, 1875; of Pourville and cliffs of Etretat, 1881; of Bordighera, 1886; of the Creuse, 1889; Le Meules, 1891; Cathedrals, 1894; Le Bassin des Nymphéas, 1900. *Address:* Giverny, Vernon, Eure, France.

Died 5 Dec. 1926.

MONET, Hon. Dominique; Puisne Judge since 1908; President of the Court of King's Bench, Crown Side, since 1920; *b* 2 Jan. 1865; *m* 1887, Marie Louise La Haye. *Educ:* L'Assomption Collège; Laval University. Advocate, 1889; KC 1905; MP (L) Napierville, 1891–96; Laprairie and Napierville, 1896–1904; Napierville, 1904–5; Minister of Public Works, 1905. *Address:* Montreal, Province of Quebec.

Died Feb. 1923.

MONETA, Ernesto Teodoro; President of the Società Internazionale per la Pace; Unione Lombarda; *b* Milan, 1838. Received the Nobel Prize, 1907; took part in the Milan uprising, 1848; General Staff Officer in Garibaldi's Army, 1860; Officer in the Italian Army, 1861–67; Director of the Secolo, 1867–96; founded the Unione Lombarda, 1888; came under the influence of Hodgson Pratt in 1886, and from that time worked energetically in forming Peace Societies throughout Northern Italy; attended most of the International Peace Congresses, and was President of the fifteenth, held at Milan, 1906; Member of Carnegie Consultative Council, and Member Emeritus of Institute Internat. de la Paix; edited the fortnightly review, La Vita Internazionale, the Almanacco Pro Pace and the Storia delle guerre, delle insurrezioni, e della pace nel secolo XIX. *Address:* 21 Portici Settentrionali, Milan. *Died 10 Feb. 1918.*

MONEY, Col Charles Gilbert Colvin, CB 1898; Colonel, retired; *b* 7 Sept. 1852; *s* of Gilbert P. Money, Bengal Civil Service; *m* 1881, Sophie Louisa, *d* of Alexander Johnston, Bengal Civil Service. *Educ:* Harrow. Served in 5th Fusiliers, afterwards called the Northumberland Fusiliers, from 1872; commanded 1st Batt. Northumberland Fusiliers in Soudan campaign, 1898 (despatches, CB, medals and clasp for Khartoum); occupation of Crete, 1898–99; South Africa, 1899–1901 (despatches, Queen's medal 5 clasps, Brevet Col); commanded 24th Regimental District, 1902–5; and Colonel in charge of Records, South Midland grouped Regimental District, 1905–7. *Address:* 7 Lypiatt Terrace, Cheltenham. *Died 29 Feb. 1928.*

MONEY, Walter, FSA; *b* The Dene, Donnington, Berks, 21 Aug. 1836; *m* Charlotte Ann (*d* 1922), *d* of Mrs Gillmore, Herborough House, Newbury; one *s* one *d*. *Educ:* private school. Local secretary for Berks, Soc. of Antiquaries, and of British Arch. Association; Correspondent of the National Trust; presented site and raised the funds for the erection of the Memorial to Lord Falkland on the battlefield of Newbury; originator of the Didcot, Newbury, and Southampton, and the Lambourn Valley Railways, the Newbury District Hospital and other local institutions. *Publications:* The History

of Newbury; The History of Hungerford; The History of Speen—the Roman *Spinæ*; Church Goods in Berkshire; The Two Battles of Newbury, 1643–44 (1st and 2nd edns); The Story of the Siege of Donnington Castle; The Siege of Basing; A Royal Purveyance in the Elizabethan Age; A Popular History of Newbury and the Neighbourhood, 1905; many memoirs on historical and archæological subjects. *Address:* Shawdene House, Donnington, Newbury.

Died 18 Oct. 1926.

MONEY-KYRLE, Ven. Rowland Tracy Ashe; Archdeacon of Hereford since 1923; Canon of Hereford since 1925. *Educ:* New College, Oxford; Wells Theological College. Curate of Portsea, 1890–95; Ross, 1895–98; Rector of Ribbesford, 1898–1902; Vicar of Kentish Town, 1902–10; Rector of Ross, 1910–26. *Address:* Cathedral Close, Hereford.

Died 26 Dec. 1928.

MONIER-WILLIAMS, Major Craufurd Victor, DSO 1919; MC; Assistant-Manager, Owen & Dyson, Ltd, Rother Iron Works, Rotherham; *b* Chessington, Surrey, 18 Feb. 1888; *s* of M. F. Monier-Williams, Stoke d'Abernon, Cobham. *Educ:* Rugby School. Served European War with the Territorial Force, 49th Division, being seconded from his regiment, 5th York and Lancaster to the Signal Service, RE, France, 1915–18; attained rank of Lieut-Col; Assistant-Director of Signals (DSO, MC, despatches four times). *Address:* Rother Iron Works, Rotherham. *Died 14 May 1922.*

MONIER-WILLIAMS, Monier Faithfull; solicitor; Chairman of the English and Scottish Law Life Association; Chairman of the British Law Insurance Company; on the Board of Eagle Star and British Dominions Insurance Company; and on the Board of the Solicitors' Law Stationers Society, Ltd; *b* 15 April 1849; *e s* of late Sir Monier Monier-Williams, KCIE (Boden Professor of Sanscrit in the University of Oxford), and Julia, *d* of Rev. F. J. Faithfull; *m* Emma Georgina, *d* of late Gordon Wyatt Clark, DL, JP, of Mickleham Hall, Dorking; two *s* one *d*. *Educ:* Rugby. *Address:* 25 Old Court Mansions, Kensington, W8; Nutlea, Nelson Road, Bognor. *Clubs:* Conservative, City of London, Alpine. *Died 13 Nov. 1928.*

MONOD, Théodore; retired pastor of the Reformed Church of France; *b* 1836; *s* of late Frédéric Monod, the founder of l'Union des Eglises Evangéliques de France; *m*; four *s* two *d*. *Educ:* University of Paris. Bachelier ès Sciences; Licencié ès Lettres; studied law, 1855–58; at New York became a Christian, 1858; studied theology in the Presbyterian Seminary, Allegheny City, 1858–60; Founder and Pastor of the Second Presbyterian Church of St Anne, Kankakee Co., Illinois, 1860–63; Pastor of the Chapelle du Nord, Paris, 1864–75; Home Missionary among the French Protestant Churches, 1875–77; Pastor of the Reformed Church of Paris, 1877–1906. *Publications:* Regardant à Jésus, 1862; De quoi il s'agit, 1875; Le Don de Dieu; Le Libérateur, Journal mensuel, 1875–79; Crucifiés avec Christ; Jésus Laïque; Poésies; Loin de Nid, 1882; Au Vent la Voile, 1898; *in English:* The Gift of God, and Life More Abundant (republished together in one volume, The Gift and the Life, 1912); Denying self, etc; several hymns, in French and in English; addresses given at Mildmay, Keswick, and other meetings. *Address:* 5 rue Renault, à Saint-Maudé (Seine). *Died 1921.*

MONRO, Alexander, CIE 1904; MA; *b* 21 May 1847; *s* of late Henry Monro; *m* 1879, Evelyn Agnes, *o d* of Arthur Dingwall. *Educ:* Sherborne; Oriel Coll., Oxford (Scholar). Called to the Bar, Inner Temple, 1872; went to India as Inspector of Schools, 1879; Fellow of Madras University, 1885; Director of Public Instruction, Central Provinces, 1888–1904; acting Director of Public Instruction, Madras, 1893–4; retired from the Indian Educational Service, 1904; Member of Legislative Council, Madras, 1893–94; Mayor of Godalming, 1909–10 and 1910–11. *Recreations:* cycling, golf. *Address:* Crawford, Frith Hill, Godalming. *Died 20 Sept. 1916.*

MONRO, James, CB 1888; *b* 1838; *s* of George Monro, solicitor, Supreme Court, Edinburgh; *m* 1863, Ruth, *d* of William Littlejohn, banker, Aberdeen. *Educ:* High School, Edinburgh; Universities of Edinburgh and of Berlin. Served Bengal Civil Service, 1857; held the offices of Magistrate, Civil and Sessions Judge, Inspector-General of Police, Commissioner Presidency Division, etc; Assistant Commissioner Metropolitan Police, 1884; Chief Commissioner, 1888; resigned, 1890; returned to Bengal, and founded the Ranaghat Medical Mission. *Address:* 15 Bolton Road, Chiswick, W4.

Died 28 Jan. 1920.

MONTAGU, Rt. Hon. Edwin (Samuel), PC 1914; MP (Coalition L) Chesterton Division of Cambridgeshire, 1906–22; a Trustee of the British Museum, 1920; *b* 6 Feb. 1879; 2nd *s* of 1st Baron Swaythling and Ellen, *d* of Louis Cohen, Bitterne, Hants; *m* 1915, Hon. (Beatrice) Venetia Stanley, *d* of 4th Baron Stanley of Alderley and 4th Baron Sheffield; one *d*. *Educ*: Clifton; City of London School; Trinity College, Cambridge (BA 1902, MA 1905). Pres. of the Union, 1902. Parliamentary Secretary to Chancellor of Exchequer, 1906–8; to Prime Minister, 1908–10; Parliamentary Under-Secretary of State, India, 1910–14; Chancellor Duchy of Lancaster, 1915; Financial Secretary to Treasury, 1914–16; Minister of Munitions and Member of War Committee, 1916; Secretary of State for India, 1917–22. *Posthumous publication*: An Indian Diary, 1930. *Address*: 4 Gordon Place, Bloomsbury, WC6. *T*: Museum 7387.

Died 15 Nov. 1924.

MONTAGU, General Sir Horace William, KCB 1905 (CB 1869); Senior Colonel Commandant Royal Engineers; *b* Swaffham, Norfolk, 16 May 1823; 3rd *s* of late Rev. George Montagu, Rector of South Pickenham, and Emily, *d* of Rev. W. Yonge; *m* 1859, Catherine Frances, *d* of late Gen. Poole Valancey England, RA; three *s* four *d*. *Educ*: Shrewsbury. Joined RE Corps, 1842; landed Crimea and present at battles of Alma and Inkerman and siege of Sevastopol; taken prisoner 22 March during a sortie, but was exchanged, and returned, 3 Aug., to the siege, six weeks before Sevastopol fell (Crimean medal with three clasps; Kt of the Legion of Honour; Sardinian Order of Merit; Turkish war medal and 5th class of Medjidie; Brevets of Major and Lieut-Col); returned to England 1856, and was subsequently commanding Royal Engineers at Sheerness, Colchester, and at Halifax, Nova Scotia. *Address*: 15 Oxford Road, Colchester.

Died 14 Nov. 1916.

MONTAGUE, Charles Edward; author; *b* 1 Jan. 1867; 3rd *s* of late Francis Montague, of St Margaret's, Twickenham, and Rosa McCabe; *m* 1898, Madeline, *o d* of Charles Prestwick Scott of Manchester (editor of The Manchester Guardian); five *s* two *d*. *Educ*: City of London School; Balliol Coll., Oxford. Director of the Manchester Guardian Limited and a Governor and hon. graduate of the University of Manchester; served in army in France, Belgium and Germany, 1915–19 (despatches thrice); Royal Humane Society Bronze Medal for saving life from drowning. *Publications*: A Hind Let Loose, 1910; Dramatic Values, 1911; The Morning's War, 1913; Disenchantment, 1922; Fiery Particles, 1923; The Right Place, 1924; Rough Justice, 1926; Right off the Map, 1927; *posthumous*: Action, 1928; A Writer's Notes on His Trade, 1930. *Recreation*: mountaineering. *Address*: Kitt's Quarries, Burford. *Club*: Alpine.

Died 28 May 1928.

MONTEAGLE OF BRANDON, 2nd Baron *cr* 1839; **Thomas Spring Rice,** KP 1885; DL; *b* 31 May 1849; *s* of Hon. Stephen Edmond Spring Rice and Ellen Mary, *d* of late Serjeant Frere; *S* grandfather, 1866; *m* 1875, Elizabeth (*d* 1908), *d* of Most Rev. Samuel Butcher, Bishop of Meath; one *s* (and one *s* one *d* decd). *Educ*: Harrow; Cambridge. BA; Senior Optime in Mathematics, 1872. *Heir*: *s* Hon. Thomas Aubrey Spring Rice, *b* 3 Nov. 1883. *Clubs*: Athenæum; Kildare Street, Dublin. *Died 24 Dec. 1926.*

MONTEITH, Col John, CB 1906; *b* 24 June 1852; 2nd *s* of Robert Thomson Monteith and Charlotte Eliza Steele; *m* 1902, Evelyn, *o d* of late Hon. Henry Leslie Pepys. *Educ*: Elizabeth College, Guernsey; Sandhurst. Entered army, 1872; Capt. ISC, 1884; Major, 1892; Lieut-Col Indian Army, 1898; Bt Col 1902; served Afghan War, 1879–80 (despatches thrice, medal with clasp); Soudan Expedition, 1885 (medal with clasp, bronze star); Zhob Valley, 1890; DAAG, 1902–4; retired, 1910; served as a Commandant on Lines of Communication in France during European War, 1914–17. *Address*: Villa Forster, Dinard, France. *Died 2 June 1928.*

MONTGOMERY, Sir Basil Templer Graham-, 5th Bt *cr* 1801, of Stanhope; DL and JP, Kinross; *b* 1 March 1852; *s* of Sir Graham Graham-Montgomery, 3rd Bt and Alice, *d* of late J. Hope Johnstone; *S* brother, 1902; *m* 1st, 1880, Mary (marr. diss. 1905), *y d* of Sir Thomas Moncreiffe, 7th Bt; one *d* (one *s* decd); 2nd, 1905, Theresa Blanche, *e d* of late Col Verschoyle, Grenadier Guards. *Educ*: Trinity College, Glenalmond; Rugby. Joined the 60th Rifles, 1872; served on the staff of General Barton, CB, in Afghanistan, 1878–79 (medal); retired from the army, 1880. A Gentleman of the King's Body Guard for Scotland; Lt-Colonel and County Commandant Kinross-shire Volunteers. Owned 6,000 acres. *Heir*: *b* Rev. Charles Percy Graham-Montgomery [*b* 6 Sept. 1855; *m* 1887, Minnie Gertrude Compton, *d* of Maj.-Gen. Chamberlain Walker, Bombay Staff Corps; two *s*]. *Address*: Kinross House, Kinross, NB; 25 Bruton Street, W1. *T*: Mayfair 81. *Club*: Turf. *Died 4 Oct. 1928.*

MONTGOMERY, Florence Sophia; novelist; *b* 1843; *d* of Admiral Sir Alexander Leslie Montgomery, 3rd Bt, and Caroline Rose, *d* of James Campbell, Mddx. Began by telling stories to her younger sisters; was induced to publish by the novelist Whyte Melville. *Publications*: A very Simple Story, 1866; Peggy, and other Tales, 1868; Misunderstood, 1869; Thrown Together, 1872; The Children with the Indiarubber Ball, 1872; Thwarted, 1873; Wild Mike and his Victim, 1874; Seaforth, 1878; The Blue Veil, 1883; Transformed, 1886; The Fisherman's Daughter, 1888; Colonel Norton, 1895; Tony, 1897; Prejudged, 1900; An Unshared Secret, and other stories, 1903; Behind the Scenes in a Schoolroom, 1914. *Address*: 56 Cadogan Place, SW. *Died 8 Oct. 1923.*

MONTGOMERY, Rt. Hon. Hugh de Fellenberg, PC (Ire.) 1924; DL; Senator Northern Ireland; *b* 14 Aug. 1844; *o s* of H. R. S. Montgomery of Blessingbourne and Maria, *y d* of Emanuel de Fellenberg, of Hofwyl, Berne, Switzerland; *m* 1870, Mary Sophia Juliana, *y d* of Hon. and Rev. John Maude, Rector of Enniskillen; five *s* (and three *s* one *d* decd). *Educ*: privately; Christ Church, Oxford. *Address*: Blessingbourne, Fivemiletown. *M*: JI 1919. *Clubs*: Ulster, Belfast; University, Dublin. *Died 8 Oct. 1924.*

MONTGOMERY, Walter Basil Graham, OBE 1920; *b* 1881; *o s* of Sir Basil Templer Graham-Montgomery, 5th Bt, and 1st wife, Mary Katherine, *d* of Sir Thomas Moncreiffe, 7th Bt; *m* 1912, Fanny (whom he divorced, 1914), *o c* of late Theodore M. Zarifil. *Educ*: Eton; Trinity Hall, Cambridge. DL, JP, County Councillor, Kinross-shire; Provost of Kinross. *Address*: 25 Bruton Street, W1; Kinross House, Kinross. *Died 23 March 1928.*

MONTGOMERY, Maj.-Gen. William Edward; *b* 18 July 1847; *m* 1891, Alberta, *d* of late Gen. Rt Hon. Sir Henry Ponsonby, GCB. Entered army, 1866; Maj.-Gen. 1895; Lieut-Col 1st Batt. Scots Guards, 1885–94; retired, 1900; served South African War, 1879 (despatches, medal with clasp). *Address*: Grey Abbey, Newtownards, Co. Down. *Died 11 June 1927.*

MONTGOMERY-MOORE, Gen. Sir Alexander George, KCB 1900; JP Belfast and DL Tyrone; High Sheriff, Co. Tyrone, 1904; Colonel 4th Hussars; *b* 6 April 1833; *s* of Alexander James Montgomery-Moore of Garvey, Co. Tyrone; *m* 1887, Hon. Jane Colborne, *d* of 1st Baron Seaton. *Educ*: Eton. ADC to Commander of Forces, Ireland, 1856–60; commanded 4th Hussars, 1868–80; AAG, Dublin District, 1880–85; commanded Belfast District, 1886; SE District, 1887; troops in Canada, 1893; Aldershot, 1899. Owned 3,500 acres. *Address*: Gipsy Lodge, Norwood, SE. *Clubs*: Carlton, United Service. *Died 17 Jan. 1919.*

MONTROSE, 5th Duke of *cr* 1707; **Douglas Beresford Malise Ronald Graham,** KT 1879; Chancellor, Order of the Thistle, since 1917; ADC to HM the King; *cr* Baron Graham before 1451; Earl of Montrose, 1505; Marquis of Montrose, 1645; Duke of Montrose, Marquis of Graham and Buchanan, Earl of Kincardine, Viscount Dundaff, Baron Aberuthven, Mugdock, and Fintrie, 1707; Earl and Baron Graham (Peerage of England), 1722; Lord-Lieutenant of Stirlingshire since 1885; Hereditary Sheriff of Dumbartonshire; Lord High Commissioner, Church of Scotland, 1916–17; Lord Clerk Registrar of Scotland since 1890; *b* 7 Nov. 1852; 3rd *s* of 4th Duke and Caroline Agnes, *y d* of 2nd Lord Decies; *S* father, 1874; *m* 1876, Violet Hermione, GBE, 2nd *d* of Sir Frederick Graham, 3rd Bt of Netherby, Cumberland; three *s* two *d*. *Educ*: Eton. Joined Coldstream Guards, 1872; transferred to 5th Lancers, 1874; retired 1878; late Colonel commanding 3rd Batt. Argyll and Sutherland Highlanders; served South African War (medal and two clasps). In politics a Tory. Owned 115,000 acres. *Recreations*: all outdoor sports. *Heir*: *s* Marquis of Graham, *b* 1 May 1878. *Address*: Buchanan Castle, Glasgow. *TA*: Dundaff, Drymen. *Clubs*: Carlton, United Service; Royal Yacht Squadron, Cowes. *Died 10 Dec. 1925.*

MONTY, Hon. Rodolphe, PC Canada; KC 1909; senior partner, Monty, Duranleau, Ross Angers & Monty, Advocates, Montreal, Quebec; *b* Montreal, 30 Nov. 1874; *s* of Jacques Monty, St Cesaire, Quebec, and Adele Beauchemin, of Beloeil, Quebec; *m* 1899, Eugenie, *d* of Dr Arthur Dorval; six *s* three *d*. *Educ*: Ste Marie de Monnoir Coll.; Laval Univ. (BA); McGill Univ. (LLD). Called to Quebec Bar, 1897; in partnership with A. Duranleau, 1898–1921, firm was changed to later title; Sec. of State, Canada, 1921; President Law Students Society, Laval, 1895–96; Member Council of Bar for nine years; Treasurer Council of Bar for two years; Examiner for the Bar for five years; subseq. Bâtonnier of the Bar of Montreal and General Bâtonnier of the Province of Quebec, Canada; President of La Société de Repatriment and de Colonisation de la Province de

Quebec; Conservative; Catholic. *Recreation:* golf. *Address:* 4238 Delorimer Avenue, Montreal, Quebec. *Clubs:* St Denis, Delorimier, Canadian, Laval Sur Le Lac Golf, Montreal.

Died 1 Dec. 1928.

MOODY, Lt-Col Arthur Hatfield, CBE 1919; TD; JP; FJI; *b* 21 Jan. 1875; *o s* of George Moody of Stourbridge, journalist and newspaper proprietor; *m* 1905, Mary H. A., *e d* of C. Holroyd-Doveton; one *s* two *d*. *Educ:* King Edward's School, Stourbridge; Wolverley. Proprietor and Editor of the Worcestershire and Staffordshire County Express, Stourbridge; Fellow and Past Vice-President of Institute of Journalists; President Staffordshire and Warwickshire Newspaper Society, 1921; President Midland Newspaper Federation, 1923; Mayor of Stourbridge, 1921–24; Deputy Mayor, 1919–21 and 1924–25; County Councillor for Worcestershire; Member Worcestershire Territorial Association; Hon. Member Institute of Municipal Accountants, 1923; took a prominent part in obtaining Charter of Incorporation for Stourbridge in 1914; an original Alderman of the Borough; Supply Officer, 1st Mounted Brigade, and (under Forage Committee of War Office) District Purchasing Officer for Berks and Oxon; Deputy Administrator for Eastern Area; Administrator of Eastern Area; Administrator of Northern Area; and Administrator of West Midland Areas (mentions twice, Brevet Major, CBE, TD). *Publications:* Through Vigo's Golden Gates; articles upon local government, trade, and travel. *Address:* Norton Close, Stourbridge, Worcestershire. *T:* 100 Stourbridge. *M:* NP 6461. *Died 7 Feb. 1926.*

MOODY, Maj.-Gen. Sir John Macdonald, Kt 1906; *b* 24 June 1839; *s* of late John Moody, RN; *m* 1873, Isabella, 3rd *d* of Rev. J. Mainwaring of Boden Hall, Cheshire. Entered Royal Marines, 1855; Col-Commandant RMLI, 1899–1902; took much interest in recruiting for both the sea and land forces, and in the employment of ex-sailors and soldiers; Vice-Chairman of the National Employment Society for Reserve and Discharged Soldiers, etc; member of Defence Committee of the London Chamber of Commerce and of Council of Marine Society (Training Ship "Warspite"); took much interest in the Boys' Brigade, of which he was a Vice-President; also member of London Council, and Hon. President City and East London Battalion; a Director of the Sailors' Home, Well Street. *Address:* 29 Upper Berkeley Street, W1. *T:* 4880 Mayfair. *Club:* Junior United Service. *Died 13 Sept. 1921.*

MOODY, William H.; Associate Justice of Supreme Court of United States, 1906–10; Secretary of the Navy, 1902; Attorney-General, 1904–6; *b* Newbury, Mass, 23 Dec. 1853; *s* of Henry L. Moody and Melissa A. Emerson; descended from William Moody of Ipswich, England, who settled at Newbury, Mass, 1634. *Educ:* Schools of Salem and Danvers; Phillip's Academy, Andover, Mass, graduating 1872; graduated at Harvard, 1876. Studied law under late Richard Dana; admitted to Bar in 1878; District Attorney for Eastern Massachusetts, 1890–95; elected to 54th Congress from Sixth Massachusetts District, 1895; re-elected to 55th, 56th and 57th Congresses; prosecuted the "beef trust" and "peonage" cases in the Supreme Court. *Recreations:* fond of horseback riding, base-ball, and other out-door sports. *Address:* Washington, DC; Haverhill, Mass. *TA:* Boston, Mass. *T:* Main 197. *Clubs:* Metropolitan, Washington; Chevy-Chase, Maryland; University, Boston; Pentucket, Haverhill.

Died 2 July 1917.

MOOKERJEE, Sir Asutosh; Saraswati, Sastravachaspati; Kt 1911; CSI 1909; MA, DL, DSc, PhD; one of His Majesty's Judges in the High Court of Judicature, Fort William, in Bengal, since 1904; Vice-Chancellor of the University of Calcutta, 1906–14, and 1921–23; *b* 29 June 1864; *s* of Dr Ganga Prasad Mookerjee of Calcutta; *m* 1886, Jogmaya, *d* of Ram Narain Bhattacharjee of Krishnaghur; four *s* three *d*. *Educ:* South Surburban School; Presidency College; City College. MA 1885; Premchand Roychand Student, 1886; DL 1894; DSc (Hon.) 1908. Fellow and Syndic of Calcutta University since 1889; Tagore Professor of Law, 1897; enrolled a Vakil of Calcutta High Court, 1888; Professor of Mathematics at Ind. Assoc. for Cultivation of Science, 1887–92; Representative of University on Council of Lieut-Governor of Bengal, 1899–1903, and of Calcutta Corporation on same Council and Additional Member of Council of Governor-General of India, 1903–4; Bengal Member of Indian University Commission, 1902; Member on Calcutta University Commission, 1917–19. FRAS, FRSE, FRIA and Fellow of other learned Societies British and Foreign; President, Asiatic Society Bengal, 1907–9 and 1921–23; Chairman, Trustees Indian Museum since 1909; Founder-President, Calcutta Mathematical Soc. since 1908; President, Council of the Imperial Library, Calcutta; President of the First Indian Science Congress, 1909; Twin President, Bengali Literary Conference, 1916

and 1918. *Publications:* Geometry of Conics, 1892; Law of Perpetuities, 1899; Vyavahara Matrika of Jimntavahana, 1912; Addresses Academic and Literary, 1915; numerous papers on Mathematics in Journals and Transactions of Learned Societies. *Recreation:* walking. *Address:* 77 Russa Road North, Bhowanipur, Calcutta. *T:* Calcutta 646.

Died 25 May 1924.

MOON, Henry E., ISO 1903; late Staff Clerk, Privy Council Office. *Address:* St Mary's Grove, Chiswick, W4.

Died 28 June 1920.

MOOR, Rt. Hon. Sir Frederick (Robert), KCMG 1911; PC 1907; DCL, LLD; MLA; Premier of Natal, 1906–10; *b* 12 May 1853; *e s* of Frederick William Moor and Sarah Annabella, *d* of Robert Ralfe; *m* 1878, Charlotte Mary St Clair, *d* of William James Dunbar-Moodie; three *s* three *d* (and one *d* decd). *Educ:* Hermannsburg School, Natal. Commenced life as a diamond digger at Kimberley, 1872; subsequently owned claims in Kimberley mine; twice elected by fellow-diggers as member of Kimberley Mining Board; returned to Natal, 1880, settling down as a farmer, which occupation he continued to follow; member Legislative Assembly, 1886–1910; was one of the party who carried Responsible Government for the Colony; Minister for Native Affairs, 1893–97 and 1899–1901; declined office under Sir Henry Binns, 1897; one of Natal delegates to Customs Union Conference at Cape Town, 1898, also Bloemfontein and Maritzburg, 1906; Natal delegate to inaugural festivities of Australian Commonwealth; Acting Prime Minister for Colony of Natal during Sir Henry Hime's visit to England for Coronation ceremony; Chairman of Natal Industries Commission, 1905–6, of Customs Convention, 1908; called to form a Ministry in 1906; attended Colonial Conference of Premiers in London, 1907; Minister of Commerce and Industries, United South Africa, 1910; Senate as one of the members especially deputed to look after native interests, 1910–20; received Freedom of Cities of London, Manchester, and Bristol. *Address:* Greystone, Estcourt, Natal. *Club:* Victoria, Pietermaritzburg. *Died 18 March 1927.*

MOOR, George Raymond Dallas, VC 1915; Lieutenant Hampshire Regiment; Aide-de-camp on General's Staff; *b* Melbourne, 22 Oct. 1896; 2nd *s* of W. H. Moor, late Auditor-General, Transvaal, and *nephew* of late Sir Ralph Moor, KCMG. *Educ:* Cheltenham College. Entered army, 1914; served European War (Dardanelles), 1914–18 (VC for personal bravery near Krithia). *Address:* c/o Cox & Co., 16 Charing Cross, SW1. *Died 3 Nov. 1918.*

MOORE, Rev. Alfred Edgar, MA; Canon of Lincoln; Warden of Browne's Hospital, Stamford, since 1918; late Vicar of Horncastle and Rural Dean; married. *Address:* Browne's Hospital, Stamford.

Died 29 June 1924.

MOORE, Rev. Canon Arthur John, MA; Vicar of Holywood, Co. Down, since 1897; Chancellor of Down Cathedral; *b* 1853; *s* of late Rev. Theodore Octavius Moore, MA; *m* 1878, Ruth Isabella O'Neill; no *c*. *Educ:* Foyle College, Londonderry; Trinity College, Dublin. Curate of Shankill, Lurgan, 1876; Incumbent of St Jude's Church, Ballignafeigh, Belfast, 1879–86; Christ Church, Lisburn, 1886–94; Rector of Coleraine, 1894–97. *Address:* The Vicarage, Holywood, Co. Down. *Died 8 Sept. 1919.*

MOORE, Col Athelstan, DSO 1902; Royal Dublin Fusiliers; employed with New Zealand Military Forces; *b* 9 July 1870; *m* Nora Kathleen; one *s*. Entered army, 1899; served South Africa, 1899–1902 (despatches, Queen's and King's medals with 4 clasps); N Nigeria, 1908 (medal with clasp). *Address:* 81 Church Road, Richmond, Surrey. *Died 14 Oct. 1918.*

MOORE, Dr Benjamin, FRS 1912; Professor of Bio-Chemistry, Oxford University, since 1920; Medical Research Staff, National Health Insurance. *Educ:* Queen's College, Belfast; Leipzig University. Five years on staff of University College; then went to Yale University; late Lecturer in Physiology, Charing Cross Medical School; Professor of Bio-Chemistry, Liverpool University, 1902–14. *Publications:* The Dawn of the Health Age; The Origin and Nature of Life; Biochemistry, a Study of the Origin, Reactions and Equilibria of Living Matter, 1921. *Address:* Oxford. *Died 3 March 1922.*

MOORE, Maj.-Gen. Charles Alfred; Bombay Cavalry; *b* 12 Nov. 1839; *m* 1873, Mary Henrietta, *d* of late J. F. Moir. Entered army, 1856; Maj.-Gen. 1895; retired, 1900; served Indian Mutiny, 1858–60 (medal and clasp); Abyssinian War, 1867–68 (despatches twice, medals). *Address:* Glenarbuck, The Park, Cheltenham.

Died 30 June 1925.

MOORE, Adm. Charles Henry Hodgson; *b* 22 March 1858; *s* of late Maj.-Gen. C. W. Moore; *m* Fanny Ponsonby, *d* of late A. Dalrymple; one *s* one *d*. Entered Navy, 1871; Commander, 1895; Captain, 1900; Rear-Adm. 1910; retired, 1913; Vice-Admiral, 1915; Admiral (retired), 1919. *Address:* Austhorpe, Grassington Road, Eastbourne.   *Died 17 March 1920.*

MOORE, Maj.-Gen. Claude Douglas Hamilton, CB 1925; CMG 1918; DSO 1915; Royal Warwickshire Regiment; General Officer Commanding 42nd (East Lancashire) Division Territorial Army, since 1927; late Commanding Infantry Brigade Ahmednagar, India; *b* 9 Feb. 1875; *m* 1912, Gladys Jesse Chamberlain. *Educ:* Cambridge University (MA). Entered Army, 1898; Capt. 1901; Major, 1914; DAA&QMG, North China, 1912; served S African War, 1899–1901 (Queen's medal 4 clasps); European War, 1914–18 (despatches eight times, DSO, CMG, Bt Lt-Col and Col, Fifth Class Order of the Rising Sun for services at Tsingtao, Third Class Order of the Nile, Legion of Honour, France); Maj.-Gen. 1925. *Club:* Junior Army and Navy.
Died 14 Sept. 1928.

MOORE, Rev. Courtenay, MA; VPRSAI; *b* 25 March 1840; *s* of Alexander Moore of Rossnashane, Co. Antrim; *m* 1869, Jessie Mona Duff, *d* of Capt. B. Duff, Gordon Highlanders (*s* of Garden Duff of Hatton Castle, Aberdeenshire), and Louisa, *e d* of 5th Baron Duffus; two *s* two *d*. *Educ:* Trinity College, Dublin. Catechetical Premiums; Honourman in Ethics; A Respondent at Degree Examination; A Divinity Testimonium of the First Class. Deacon, 1865; Priest, 1866; Curate of Brigown, 1865; Rector of Farahy, 1871; of Castletown-Roche, 1875; of Brigown, Mitchelstown, 1882–1920; Canon of Cloyne, 1885; Rural Dean, 1893; Precentor of Cloyne Cathedral, 1909. *Publications:* two Irish novels: Con Hegarty; Jer. Sharkey; several theological pamphlets; St Patrick's Liturgy, 3rd edn; Prayers for the Faithful Departed, 3rd edn; A Chapter of Irish Church History; many articles in Cork Archæological and Historical Journal. *Recreations:* cycling, archæologizing.   *Died June 1922.*

MOORE, Rev. Edward, DD; Hon. DLitt Dublin; FBA 1906; Canon of Canterbury since 1903; Hon. Fellow of Pembroke College and of Queen's College, Oxford; *b* Cardiff, 28 Feb. 1835; *s* of John Moore, MD, and 2nd wife, Charlotte Puckle; *m* 1st, 1868, Katharine Edith (*d* 1873), *d* of John Stogdon, Exeter; one *s* two *d*; 2nd, 1878, Annie (*d* 1906), *d* of Adm. John Francis Campbell Mackenzie; one *s* two *d*. *Educ:* Bromsgrove Grammar School; Pembroke College, Oxford (Exhibitioner). Double 1st class Moderations, 1855; double 1st class in Classics and Mathematics, 1857. Fellow and Tutor, Queen's College, Oxford, 1862–64; Principal of St Edmund Hall, Oxford, 1864–1913; Corr. Mem., Accademia Della Crusca, 1906. *Publications:* Aristotle's Ethics, bks i–iv, 5th edn 1896; Aristotle's Poetics, with notes, 1875; The Time References in the Divina Commedia, 1887; Contributions to the Textual Criticism of the Divina Commedia, 1889; Dante and his Early Biographers, 1890; Tutte le Opere di Dante Alighieri (The Oxford Dante), 1894; Studies in Dante, 1896, 2nd Series, 1899, 3rd Series, 1903; Gli Accenni al Tempo nella Divina Commedia, Florence, 1900. *Address:* The Precincts, Canterbury.
Died 2 Sept. 1916.

MOORE, Sir Edward Cecil, 1st Bt, *cr* 1923; *b* 22 Nov. 1851; *s* of Edward Moore, FCA; *m* 1st, 1876, Sarah Ann (*d* 1887), *d* of Horatio Brown Mead; one *s* (and one *s* decd); 2nd, 1893, Florence Mary Georgianna, *d* of James Harverson; two *s* one *d*. Alderman, Bishopgate Ward, since 1912; Sheriff, 1914–15; Lord Mayor of London, 1922–23. *Heir: g s* Edward Stanton Moore, *b* 28 Dec. 1910. *Address:* 1 Lancaster Gate Terrace, W2. *Club:* City Carlton.

Died 7 Dec. 1923.

MOORE, Col Edward James, CB 1911; VD; Territorial Force Reserve; late 20th Battalion London Regiment; *b* 25 May 1862; *m* 1891, Helena, *d* of Isaac Crookenden of Blackheath. *Address:* Park End, Blackheath Park, SE3. *T:* Lee Green 233.

Died 7 March 1925.

MOORE, Ven. Edward Marsham; Rector of Uppingham, 1907–20. *Educ:* Christ Church, Oxford; Cuddesdon Theological College. Curate of Ashborne, 1867–72; Vicar, 1872–76; Rector of Benefield, 1876–1907; Archdeacon of Oakham, 1906–18; Hon. Canon Peterborough, 1899–1906. *Address:* Vale House, Loose, Maidstone. *Club:* Oxford and Cambridge.

Died 5 Sept. 1921.

MOORE, Francis William; dramatic author; *b* Finsbury, 27 June 1849; 2nd *s* of late Henry Moore, Croydon, and Frances Isabella Riddle; unmarried. *Educ:* privately. *Publications:* Humorous Pieces in Prose

and Verse, 1893; Original Plays and Duologues, chiefly Humorous, 1893; The Kingdom of Arcadee, 1895; When George the Fourth was King, 1896. *Recreation:* rose-growing. *Address:* Maythorne, 1 Park Hill Rise, Croydon. *T:* 25.   *Died 14 Dec. 1927.*

MOORE, George Arbuthnot; *b* Birkenhead, 16 March 1857; *s* of Charles Moore of Easterlands, Somerset; *m* 1881, Lucy Olivia, 3rd *d* of William Whitmore St George, of Clifton Park, Birkenhead; one *s* one *d*. *Educ:* Birkenhead School; Stuttgart; Wurtemburg. Appointed a member of the Advisory Committee to the Department of Overseas Trade by Sir Arthur Steel Maitland at its inception; a member of the Interim Provisional Council to the Board of Trade by Sir A. Stanley; Chairman of the Council of the Liverpool Chamber of Commerce, 1918–19; Chairman of the Taxation and Finance Committee of the Council of the Association of British Chambers of Commerce, 1921–23, and a Liverpool representative on the Council of that Association. *Recreations:* shooting, farming, mechanics, lawn tennis, squash racquets. *Address:* Rowler, Brackley, Northants. *M:* CM 348 and M 6244. *Clubs:* St Stephen's, Royal Automobile.
Died 3 Dec. 1923.

MOORE, Rev. Henry Dodwell, MA; Canon or Prebendary of Lincoln since 1903; Vicar of Honington, Lincolnshire, 1867–1916; Rural Dean, 1879–1915; *b* 1838; 2nd *s* of late Philip Charles Moore, a Proctor in Doctors Commons; *m* 1867, Augusta Rosina (*d* 1901), *d* of Sir Arthur James Rugge-Price, 5th Bt, of Richmond, Surrey; three *s* five *d*. *Educ:* Pembroke College, Oxford. BA (2nd Class Mathematics), 1862; MA 1865. Deacon, 1863; Priest, 1864; Curate of Barkingside, Essex, 1863–65; St Michael's, Bromley, E, 1865–67; Curate in charge of Wisborough Green, Sussex, 1867; an Inspector of Schools in Diocese of Lincoln, 1870–83; Secretary of the Grantham Clerical Society, 1896–1915. *Address:* The Hollies, Brant Broughton, Newark. *TA:* Brant Broughton.

Died 2 Aug. 1919.

MOORE, Sir John Samuel, KCB 1911 (CB 1902); Paymaster-in-Chief, Royal Navy; retired 1891; *b* 1831; *e s* of John Percy Moore, MD, and Elizabeth, *d* of Samuel Porter, Saltash, late Lieut 10th (Lincoln) Regt; *m* 1861, Mary Anne, *d* of Thomas Spearman, Heywood, Paymaster-in-Chief, RN; one *s*. *Educ:* private schools. Entered Royal Navy, 1846; served on the Cape station during Kaffir War, 1849–52 (medal); present at the capture of the forts at Bomarsund in the Baltic, 1854 (medal); present at the operations against Sebastopol, Kertch, and Yenikale, and capture of Kinburn (Crimean and Turkish medals, Sebastopol clasp); secretary to Commodore in India during the Mutiny, 1857–58; and secretary to Commodore, East Indian station, 1859–60; secretary to Commander-in-Chief, Mediterranean station, during Egyptian War, 1882 (specially mentioned in despatches, Egyptian medal, Alexandria clasp, Khedive's bronze star, Medjidie 3rd class); Fleet Paymaster HM yacht Victoria and Albert, 1883–91. *Recreations:* gardening, fishing. *Address:* Alverstoke, Hants.   *Died 21 Nov. 1916.*

MOORE, Louis Herbert, BA; General Manager of the American Press Telegram Company, and London correspondent of the Washington Star; *b* Brooklyn, New York, 1 Nov. 1860; *m* Alice, *d* of late Theodore Mace of Montclair, New Jersey; one *d*. *Educ:* Public Schools, Boston, Mass; St Stephen's College, Annandale, New York. Travelled extensively in Europe; was European Manager of the United and Associated Press of America, 1889–97; represented his Association at most of the notable events in Europe during that time, including the funeral of Alexander III at St Petersburg, the coronation of Nicholas II, at Moscow, and the Armenian troubles at Constantinople; in 1900 organised the foreign service of the Daily Express and was Foreign Editor of that paper for two years. *Recreations:* travel, golfing, amateur photography. *Address:* 66 Burton Court, Sloane Square, SW. *TA:* Luisaient, London. *T:* 840 Victoria. *Club:* Savage.
Died 19 Jan. 1918.

MOORE, Sir Norman, 1st Bt, *cr* 1919; MD (Cantab); FRCP; Consulting Physician to St Bartholomew's Hospital, London; President of Royal College of Physicians of London, 1918–22, and Representative of the College in General Medical Council; Hon. Fellow of St Catharine's College, Cambridge; *b* Higher Broughton, Lancashire, 8 Jan. 1847; *o s* of Robert Ross Rowan Moore and Rebecca, *d* of B. C. Fisher; *m* 1st, 1880, Amy (*d* 1901), *d* of William Leigh Smith of Crowham, Sussex; one *s* one *d* (and one *s* decd); 2nd, 1903, Milicent, *d* of Maj.-Gen. John Ludlow. *Educ:* Owens College, Manchester; St Catharine's Coll., Cambridge. BA 1869; MA 1872; MD 1876; Hon. LLD. House Physician, St Bartholomew's Hospital, 1872–74; Casualty Physician, 1875–77; Assistant Physician, 1883–1902; Physician, 1902–11; Lecturer on Comparative Anatomy,

1874–85; Lecturer on Pathology, 1887–93; Lecturer on Principles and Practice of Medicine, 1893–1911; Fellow of Royal College of Physicians, 1877; Harveian Orator, 1901; Senior Censor, 1908; Harveian Librarian, 1910–18; Pres., 1918–20; Rede Lecturer, Cambridge, 1914. *Publications:* several medical treatises; the Harveian Oration for 1901; 459 lives (chiefly of medical writers) in Dictionary of National Biography; FitzPatrick Lectures on the History of Medicine; The History of St Bartholomew's Hospital; Life of Charles Waterton, 1871; translation of the Concise Irish Grammar of E. Windisch; essay on History of Medicine in Ireland; Loss of the Crown of Loegaire Lurc (Irish text and translation). *Heir:* s Alan Hilary Moore [b 23 Jan. 1882; m 1922, Hilda Mary, d of Rt Rev. Winfrid O. Burrows, Bishop of Chichester]. *Address:* 67 Gloucester Place, Portman Square, W1. *T:* Mayfair 537; Hancox, Battle, Sussex. *T:* Battle 1Y5. *Club:* Athenæum.   *Died 30 Nov. 1922.*

MOORE, Rev. Obadiah; St George's Cathedral; Acting Pastor of Bishop Crowther Memorial Church (St Clement's), Cline Town, Freetown, though retired; b York, Sierra Leone, 23 Dec. 1848; of Mendi and Dahomian descent; m 1st, 1878, d of Rev. W. Quaker, one of three Foundation Pastors of the Sierra Leone Native Pastorate Church; 2nd, 1894, d of Hon. T. J. Sawyerr, merchant, etc, MLC, Sierra Leone; three s two d. *Educ:* Wesleyan Village School; Church Elementary School, Kent, Sierra Leone; CM Grammar School, Freetown; CMS College, Fourah Bay, 1867–70; Monkton Combe Collegiate School, Somerset, England, 1875–76. Junior Tutor, CMS Grammar School, 1870; Senior Tutor, 1871–75; in England, 1875–76; returned to Grammar School, 1876; ordained 1877; first Pastor, Sierra Leone Native Church at Bonthe, Sherbro District, 1880–82; Native Principal, CMS Grammar School, Freetown, 1882–1906; Canon, St George's Cathedral, Freetown, 1898; retired from active service, 1906; visited England four times. *Recreation:* boating. *Address:* Freetown, Sierra Leone, West Africa.

Died 27 Feb. 1923.

MOORE, Lt-Col Richard St Leger, CB 1902; DL, JP; Master Kildare foxhounds, 1883–97; former President, Irish Amateur Athletic Association; b Kilbride Manor, Co. Wicklow, 12 July 1848; e s of Richard Moore, and g s of Rt Hon. Lord Chief Justice Moore; m 1873, Alice Geraldine, d of Joseph Pratt Tynte, Tynte Park, Co. Wicklow; one s three d. *Educ:* Harrow. Served in 9th Lancers, 12th Lancers, and 5th Lancers, 1866–81; since 1881 lived at home as a country gentleman; High Sheriff, 1899; commanded 17th Batt. Imp. Yeo., South Africa, 1900 (despatches, CB). Owned 2,500 acres. *Recreations:* hunting, shooting, fishing, cricket, tennis, polo, boxing, fencing, running. *Address:* Killashee, Naas, Co. Kildare, Ireland. *M:* IO 424. *Clubs:* Army and Navy, Cavalry, Hurlingham; Kildare Street, Dublin.

Died 18 Oct. 1921.

MOORE, Thomas, MVO 1911; b 1858. In charge of Police, Great Central Railway; Supt Executive and Statistical Branches Metropolitan Police Office. *Address:* 8 Berridge Road, East Nottingham.

Died 20 May 1920.

MOORE, Sir Thomas O'Connor, 11th Bt, cr 1681; b 5 Nov. 1845; s of Sir Richard Emanuel Moore, 10th Bt and Mary Anne, e d of Andrew Ryan O'Connor, barrister, Mt Pleasant, Co. Dublin; S father, 1882; m 1908, Katherine Mathilda Howard, d of late Capt. J. G. Elphinstone, HEICS. *Heir:* none. *Address:* 36 Wellington Road, St Luke's, Cork.   *Died Jan. 1926 (ext).*

MOORE, Vice-Adm. W. Usborne; b 1849; s of late John Alldin Moore, barrister; m 1877, Gertrude Usborne; one s three d. *Publications:* The Cosmos and the Creeds; Glimpses of the Next State; The Voices. *Address:* 8 Western Parade, Southsea. *Club:* United Service.   *Died 15 March 1918.*

MOORE, William H.; b Utica, NY, 25 Oct. 1848; s of Nathaniel F. Moore and Rachel A. Beckwith; m 1879, Ada Small. Entered Amherst College, 1867; admitted to the Bar, Wis, 1872; settled in Chicago, and made a specialty of Corporation Law; with his brother, James H., reorganised the Carnegie Steel Co., later forming the four great corporations known as the "Moore group", with a combined capital of $187,000,000, all subseq. absorbed in the US Steel Corporation; also promoted other large industrial corporations, including the Diamond Match Co., National Biscuit Co., American Tin Plate Co., American Steel Hoop Co., etc; Director US Steel Corporation. *Address:* E 54th Street, New York.

Died 11 Jan. 1923.

MOORMAN, Frederic William, BA, PhD; Professor of English Language, University of Leeds, since 1912; b 8 Sept. 1872; s of late

Rev. A. C. Moorman; m 1898, Frances B. Humpidge; two s one d. *Educ:* Caterham School; University College, London; University College of Wales; Strasburg University. Assistant Lecturer in English Language and Literature, University College of Wales, Aberystwyth, 1895; Lecturer and Assistant Professor at Yorkshire College and University of Leeds, 1898. *Publications:* William Browne and the Pastoral Poetry of the Elizabethan Age, 1897; The Interpretation of Nature in English Poetry from Beowulf to Shakespeare, 1905; An Introduction to Shakespeare, 1906; Robert Herrick: a Biographical and Critical Study, 1910; The Place-Names of the West Riding of Yorkshire, 1911; The May King, 1914; Yorkshire Dialect Poems (anthology), 1916. *Recreations:* birdwatching, gardening, cycling. *Address:* 2 Hollin Lane, Headingley, Leeds.

Died 8 Sept. 1919.

MOORSOM, Lt-Col Henry Martin, MVO 1903; KPM 1909; b 1839; s of Capt. W. S. Moorsom; m 1877, Edith Arabella Louisa Florence, d of late William Thomas Bristow Lyons, Brook Hill, Co. Antrim. Entered Rifle Brigade, 1855; retired, 1877; served Indian Mutiny, 1857–58 (medal with clasp); Canada, 1866 (medal with clasp); Chief Constable, Lancs, 1880–1909. *Address:* Court Manor, Westmeon, Petersfield. *Club:* Army and Navy.

Died 29 Dec. 1921.

MOORSOM, James Marshall, KC; JP; b 1837; 4th s of Vice-Admiral and Mary Maude Moorsom; g s of Admiral Sir Robert Moorsom, KCB, who commanded the Revenge at the battle of Trafalgar; m 1877, Emma Catherine Browne of Tallantire; two s. Called to the Bar, Inner Temple, 1863; QC 1885; Bencher, 1892; Treasurer, 1914. MP (L) for Yarmouth, 1892–95. *Address:* Fieldside, Keswick, Cumberland; Inner Temple, EC. *Clubs:* Oxford and Cambridge, MCC.   *Died 26 March 1918.*

MORANT, Adm. Sir George Digby, KCB 1901; retired; b Ireland, 8 Aug. 1837; e s of late George Morant, Grenadier Guards, Shirley House, Carrickmacross, Ireland, and Lydia, 3rd d of late John Hemphill, Rathkenny, Co. Tipperary; m 1866, Sophia Georgina (d 1911), y d of late Col George William Eyres, Grenadier Guards; two s four d. *Educ:* Dr Burney's Royal Naval Academy. Entered RN, 1850; Captain, 1873; Admiral, 1901; commanded HM ships Grasshopper, Enterprise, Cockatrice, Valorous, Achilles, Victor Emmanuel (as Commodore); superintended Pembroke Dockyard, and as superintending fittings of contract-built ships under Naval Defence Act, and as Admiral Superintendent of Chatham Dockyard, 1892–95; Inspector of Irish Lights, 1875–78; war medals for Burmah, Baltic, Crimea (two clasps), China. *Recreations:* reading, drawing, shooting, fishing. *Address:* 31 Redcliffe Square, SW10. *T:* Western 1628. *Club:* United Service.   *Died 13 Feb. 1921.*

MORANT, Sir Robert Laurie, KCB 1907 (CB 1902); 1st Secretary of the Ministry of Health since 1919; b 7 April 1863; s of late Robert Morant, Hampstead, and Helen, d of Rev. Henry Lea Berry; m 1896, Helen Mary, d of late Edwin Cracknell of Wetheringsett Grange, Suffolk; one s one d. *Educ:* Winchester; New College, Oxford. Educational work of various kinds; tutor to Royal Family of Siam, and organiser of public education in that country; subsequently social and educational work in East London; Assistant Director of Special Inquiries and Reports in Education Department, Whitehall, 1895; Private Secretary to Sir John Gorst, and subsequently Assistant Private Sec. to Duke of Devonshire; Permanent Secretary, Board of Education, 1903–11; Chairman of Insurance Commission, 1912–19. *Publication:* Regulations for Secondary Schools, 1904. *Address:* 17 Thurloe Square, SW7. *T:* Kensington 5616.

Died 13 March 1920.

MOREL, Edmund Dene; MP (Lab) Dundee since 1922; Secretary and part founder of the Union of Democratic Control, and Editor of Foreign Affairs; b 10 July 1873; s of Edmond Morel-de-Ville and Emmeline de Horne; m 1896, Mary Richardson; four s one d. *Educ:* Eastbourne. Author and journalist; founded Congo Reform Association, 1904; took a leading part in movement against Congo misrule, and published many pamphlets on the subject; visited the States and inaugurated similar movement there, 1904; published with Pierre Mille, the French African explorer, Le Congo léopoldien; member of West African Lands Committee (Colonial Office), 1912–14; Liberal candidate, Birkenhead, Oct. 1912–Oct. 1914; resigned upon outbreak of war; Hon. Secretary Congo Reform Association, 1904–12; Editor African Mail for ten years; a Vice-President of the Anti-Slavery Society; Labour candidate for Dundee, 1921–22; Silver medal Society of Arts for paper on British in Nigeria. *Publications:* Affairs of West Africa; The British Case in French Congo; King Leopold's Rule in Africa; Red Rubber; Great Britain and the

Congo; Nigeria; Morocco in Diplomacy; Ten Years of Secret Diplomacy; Truth and the War; Africa and the Peace of Europe; The Black Man's Burden; Thoughts on the War; The Peace, and Prison; Pre-War Diplomacy; Diplomacy Revealed. *Address:* Kings Langley, Herts.   *Died 12 Nov. 1924.*

MORESBY, Adm. John; explorer and author; retired, 1888; Admiral, 1893; *b* 15 March 1830; *s* of late Adm. of the Fleet Sir Fairfax Moresby and Eliza Louisa, *y d* of John Williams, Bakewell; *m* 1859, Jane (*d* 1876), *d* of Philip Scott; one *s* four *d*. Discovered (1873) finest harbour in New Guinea, on which Port Moresby now stands; also 25 large inhabited islands, and more than 100 smaller ones, and explored over 600 miles of previously unknown coast line; served in the Baltic, 1854–55 (medal); China, 1861; Japan, 1864; Senior Officer, Bermuda, 1879–81. *Publications:* Discoveries and Surveys in New Guinea; A Cruise in Polynesia and Visits to the Pearl-Shelling Stations in Torres Straits, 1876; Two Admirals, 1909. *Address:* Blackbeck, Fareham.
Died 12 July 1922.

MORETON, Lord; Henry Haughton Reynolds-Moreton, DL, JP; *b* 4 March 1857; *e s* of 3rd Earl of Ducie and Julia, *d* of James Haughton Langston, Sarsden; *m* 1888, Ada Margarette, *d* of late Dudley Robert Smith, Belgrave Square, W. MP (L) W Gloucestershire, 1880–85. *Address:* 37 Park Lane, W1. *T:* Mayfair 4462; Sarsden House, Kingham, Oxford. *Clubs:* Brooks's, Travellers'.
Died 28 Feb. 1920.

MORETON, Hon. Sir Richard (Charles), KCVO 1913 (CVO 1913; MVO 1907); DL; HM's Marshal of the Ceremonies, 1887–1913; *b* London, 21 Jan. 1846; 7th surv. *s* of 2nd Earl of Ducie and Elizabeth, *d* of 2nd Lord Sherborne; *m* 1868, Janie, *e d* of late Thomas Ralli, and Lady of the Bedchamber to HRH the Duchess of Albany; one *d*. Cadet RN. *Address:* Crookham House, Crookham, Hants. *T:* Fleet 60. *TA:* Church-Crookham.
Died 2 March 1928.

MORGAN, Alfred Kedington, FSA; ARCA; Art Master at Rugby School and Hon. Curator of the Art Museum; *b* S Kensington, 23 April 1868; *e s* of Alfred Morgan, artist; *m* Gertrude Ellen Hayes, ARE; no *c*. *Educ:* The Royal College of Art. Student in training, RCA; Art Master at Cheltenham Grammar School; Peripatetic Art Master to the School Board for London, and afterwards LCC; Assistant Examiner in Geometrical Drawing to the Board of Education; Art Master at Aske's School, Hatcham; sometime ARE (resigned); Member of National Art Collections Fund; Exhibitor at Royal Acad. and other public exhibitions. *Recreation:* music. *Address:* The Art Museum, Rugby. *M:* NX 427.
Died 14 April 1928.

MORGAN, Lt-Col Anthony Hickman, DSO 1894; DL, JP Co. Cork; *b* 1858; *e s* of late Capt. Anthony Morgan of Bunalun, Skibbereen, Co. Cork (late Capt. 95th Regiment), and Eliza Tymons of Riverstown, Co. Clare; *m* 1896, Mary, *d* of late C. E. Bagnell of Clonkennan, Limerick. Entered Army Medical Department, 1881; retired, 1896; served Egyptian War, 1882 (medal, Khedive's star); Gambia, 1891–92 (medal with clasp); West Coast Africa, 1893–94 (despatches); Gambia, 1894 (despatches, DSO, clasp); served on board hospital ship Princess of Wales, South Africa, 1889–90, as Officer commanding troops and PMO (despatches, medal and clasp); High Sheriff, County of Cork, JP, 1904. KGStJ; FRGS; FZS; MSI. Contested (C) Isle of Wight, 1906. *Address:* 14 Grosvenor Place, SW1. *T:* Kensington 2123; Hollybrook House, Skibbereen, Co. Cork. *Clubs:* Army and Navy, Carlton, Hurlingham; Royal St George's Yacht; Royal Northern Yacht; Royal Yacht Squadron, Cowes; Royal Cork Yacht; Royal Highland Yacht, Oban.
Died 29 Sept. 1924.

MORGAN, Hon. Sir Arthur, Kt 1907; President, Legislative Council, Queensland, since 1906; Lieutenant-Governor of Queensland, 1908; *b* Rosenthal, Warwick, Queensland, 19 Sept. 1856; 4th *s* of James Morgan, formerly Member for Warwick; *m* 1880, Alice Augusta, *e d* of Henry Edward Clinton; five *s* three *d*. *Educ:* Public School, Warwick. Elected to Municipal Council, 1885; Mayor, 1886, 1887, 1888, 1889 and 1898; MLA, Warwick, 1887, 1888, 1893, 1898, 1899, 1902; Chairman of Committees of the Legislative Assembly, 1891; Chairman Royal Commission on Local Government, 1896; Speaker of the Legislative Assembly, 1898–1903; Premier, Chief Secretary, and Minister for Railways, 1903–6. *Publication:* Discovery and Development of the Downs, 1902. *Recreations:* shooting, fishing. *Address:* Clinton, Paddington, Brisbane. *T:* Brisbane 311. *Clubs:* Johnsonian, Brisbane; Warwick, Warwick; Pioneers, Sydney.
Died Dec. 1916.

MORGAN, Major Cecil Buckley, DSO 1900; late West India Regiment; *b* 18 Nov. 1860; *s* of Thomas Morgan, FSA, Streatham; *m* 1894, Maude Mary, *d* of Richard Keeling of Penkridge, Staffs. Entered army, 1884; Major, 1898; served Niger Territories, 1892–93 and 1895 (twice wounded); Sierra Leone; 1898–99 (severely wounded, despatches, DSO, medal with clasp). *Address:* Uitenhage, Roodewal, Orange River Colony.
Died 29 March 1918.

MORGAN, David John, JP; partner in Morgan, Gellibrand and Co., Russian merchants; *b* 1844; *m* 1867, Emily, *d* of A. Bigland of Liverpool. *Educ:* Forest School, Walthamstow; Switzerland. MP (C) South-west or Walthamstow Div. of Essex, 1900–6. *Address:* Bentley Mill, Brentwood, Essex. *Clubs:* Carlton, City.
Died 28 Feb. 1918.

MORGAN, Brig.-Gen. Sir Hill Godfrey, KBE 1919; CB 1902; CMG 1918; DSO 1896; *b* 20 June 1862; *s* of late Capt. Hill Faulconer Morgan, 28th Foot; *m* 1886, Fanny, *d* of late J. Bousfield of Grassmere, Craneswater Park, Southsea. Joined 1st Gloucestershire Regt (28th) from Militia (1883) as a Lieut and transferred to Army Service Corps, 1888, as Captain; Major, 1898; served Dongola Expeditionary Force, 1896–98 (despatches, DSO, 4th class Medjidie, British medal, Khedive's medal with two clasps); Nile expedition, including Khartoum (despatches, 4th class Osmanieh, clasp); Director of Supplies, Natal, 1899–1900, and Director of Supplies, South Africa, 1900–2 (despatches five times, Brevet Lieut-Col, Queen's medal six clasps, King's medal two clasps, CB); Lt-Col 1904; Bt-Col 1917; retired, 1906; Asst Director of Supplies, Central Force, Home Army, 5 Aug. 1914; Military Member Organising Committee Farmers' County Committees, 9 Dec. 1914; Administrative Member Forage Committee, 27 May 1915; Temp. Brig.-Gen., 18 Aug. 1917; mentioned for valuable services in connection with War, 6 July 1918. *Clubs:* Junior United Service, Ranelagh.
Died 4 Jan. 1923.

MORGAN, Rev. John; Archdeacon of Bangor, 1902–20; Rector of Trefdraeth, 1902–20. *Educ:* Sidney Sussex College, Cambridge (Sen. Opt.). Curate, Bangor, 1868–70; Curate, Llanberis, 1870–72; Vicar of Corris, Merrions, 1872–76; Rector of Dowlais, 1876–80; Vicar, Bangor, 1880–85; Rector of Llandudno, 1885–1902. *Address:* c/o The Vicarage, Carnarvon.
Died 1 Jan. 1924.

MORGAN, John Hammond, CVO 1901; MA Oxon; FRCS; Consulting Surgeon to Charing Cross Hospital, late Professor of School; Consulting Surgeon to Hospital for Sick Children; *b* 19 Aug. 1847; *s* of John Morgan, FRCS; *m* 1874, Isabel, 2nd *d* of W. C. Lucy of Brookthorpe, Gloucestershire. *Educ:* Harrow; Trinity College, Oxford. Examiner in Surgery, University of Oxford. Member of Council, RCS; late Pres., Med. Soc. of London. Was President of Oxford University Athletic Club; winner of Inter-University 3 mile race in 1868–69–70; attached as Surgeon to several London Hospitals. Hon. Surg., 14th Middlesex RV; Medical Chief of Croix Rouge Hospital for Wounded Soldiers at Nevers, 1917. KGStJ; Médaille de Reconnaissance de la République Française. Decorated for services in connection with Duke of Abercorn's Fund for sick and wounded officers. *Publications:* Catalogue of Museum of Charing Cross Hospital; Lettsomian Lectures, 1897; many papers on surgical subjects. *Recreations:* fishing, shooting, travel. *Address:* 3 Connaught Square, W2. *T:* Paddington 6250; Hilliers, Bucklesbury, Reading. *Clubs:* Athenæum, New University, Beefsteak.
Died 11 Oct. 1924.

MORGAN, Lt-Col Stuart Williams, DL, JP; Master of Foxhounds, Brecon; *b* 1867; *e* surv. *s* of John Williams Morgan and Ellen, *d* of W. H. Lee, Edgbaston; *m* 1893, Blanche (*d* 1898), *o d* of P. K. Budworth of Greensted Hall, Essex; one *s* decd. *Educ:* Cheltenham Coll. Late Lt-Col 3rd Batt. S Wales Borderers. *Address:* Bolgoed, Brecon.
Died 16 Nov. 1922.

MORGAN, Walter J., RBA. *Address:* 17 Radnor Road, Handsworth, Birmingham.
Died 31 Oct. 1924.

MORGAN, Sir Walter Vaughan, 1st Bt, *cr* 1906; Alderman of City of London; one of HM Lieutenants for the City; Treasurer of Christ's Hospital; *b* 3 May 1831; 6th *s* of Thomas Morgan of Glasbury and Marianne, *d* of William Vaughan of Brecon; unmarried. *Educ:* Christ's Hospital. Entered service of National Provincial Bank of England, 1846; retired as Chief Cashier at Manchester, 1856, to join his brothers in London in founding the firm of Morgan Brothers, merchants and newspaper proprietors, and the Morgan Crucible Company; the firm consisted of six brothers, who continued in partnership for thirty years, and still so continued, except that death reduced the number to two; one of the proprietors of The Chemist and Druggist and The Ironmonger Journals. Sheriff of City of London, 1900–1; Lord Mayor of the City of London, 1905–6. Orders of Saviour of Greece; St Maurice and St Lazare, Italy; and Rising Sun, Japan; Commander of the Legion of Honour; Kt Commander of the Order of St Olav. Heir: none. Recreation: Freemason of many years' standing; Grand Treasurer of the Grand Lodge of England, 1897–98; and Past Grand Warden, 1906. Address: 2 Whitehall Court, SW. Clubs: Reform, Gresham.

Died 12 Nov. 1916 (ext).

MORGAN, Rev. William, MA, DD; b 1862; s of an Aberdeenshire farmer; m 1903, e d of late Peter Esslemont, MP for East Aberdeenshire, and afterwards Chairman of the Scottish Fishery Board. Educ: Aberdeen University; United Presbyterian College, Edinburgh; Halle. For 18 years Minister of the United Free Church, Tarbolton, Ayrshire; acted as Examiner in Philosophy, Aberdeen University (hon. DD 1910); Professor of Systematic Theology and Apologetics, Queen's Theological College, Kingston, Canada, 1912; delivered in Glasgow the Kerr Lectures, 1914, and the Dudleian Lecture, Harvard University, 1921. Publications: The Religion and Theology of Paul; also contributed largely to current periodical literature.   *Died 16 Jan. 1928.*

MORGAN, William Pritchard; b 1844; s of late W. Morgan, Pillgwenlly, Newport, Mon. Solicitor; practised in Queensland; returned to England, 1883; interested in gold mining property in Wales and China. MP (GL) Merthyr Tydfil, 1888–1900. Address: Byways, Engelfield Green, Surrey; Plas Tyddyngladis, near Dolgelley, N Wales.   *Died 5 July 1924.*

MORISON, Alexander Blackhall, MD, FRCP; Consulting Physician, Royal Northern Hospital, London and to Mount Vernon Hospital; b 1850; s of Alexander C. Morison, surgeon, Bengal MI, HEICS; m Elizabeth Stewart, e d of Duncan Maclachlan, Edinburgh. Educ: Universities of Edinburgh, Berlin, and Würzburg. Graduated, University of Edinburgh, 1872; after study on Continent, settled in practice in London; specialized in Medicine; appointed Physician to Great Northern Central Hospital, Paddington Green Children's Hospital, and St Marylebone General Dispensary. Morison Lecturer, Royal College of Physicians, Edin., 1897–98. FRCPE 1889; FRCP 1903; Fellow, Royal Society of Medicine and of Medical Society of London; Corresponding Member, Edinburgh Medico-Chir. Society; President, National Medical Union, etc. Publications: Disorders of the Heart; The Nervous System and Visceral Disease; On the Nature, Causes, and Treatment of Cardiac Pain; The Blackhalls of the Ilk and Barra; Hereditary Coroners and Foresters of the Garioch (New Spalding Club). Recreations: antiquarian research, fishing, sketching, golf. Address: 14 Upper Berkeley Street, W1. T: Paddington 2168. TA: Benachie, London. Club: Caledonian.

Died 23 Dec. 1927.

MORISON, Hon. Donald, KC; b 22 April 1857; m 1883, Catherine E., e d of Robert Trapnell, Co. Donegal; one s one d. Admitted to the Bar, 1881; MHA for Bonavista District, Newfoundland, 1888–97 and 1906–13; Attorney-General, 1894; Judge of Supreme Court, 1898–1902, when returned to active practice of the legal profession; Attorney-General, 1909–13; one of the Counsel for Great Britain at North Atlantic Fisheries Arbitration at the Hague, 1910. Address: St John's, Newfoundland. TA: Morison, Newfoundland.

Died 24 April 1924.

MORLAND, Gen. Sir Thomas Lethbridge Napier, KCB 1915 (CB 1903); KCMG 1917; DSO 1902; General Officer Commanding-in-Chief, Aldershot Command, 1922–23; Aide-de-camp General to the King since 1922; b 9 Aug. 1865; s of Thomas Morland, Montreal, and Helen Elizabeth, d of Gen. Henry Servante; m 1890, Mabel Eleanor Rowena (d 1901), e d of Admiral Henry Craven St John of Stokefield, Thornbury; two d. Entered army, 1884; Captain, 1893; Major, 1899; served Nigeria, 1897–98 (despatches, Brevet Major, medal with clasp); Nigeria, 1901, 1902, 1903 (CB); European War, 1914–18 (despatches twice, KCB, promoted Lt-Gen.); King's Royal Rifle Corps; Inspector-General, West African Frontier Force, 1905–10; Brigadier-General commanding 2nd Infantry Brigade, Aldershot, 1910–13; commanded 2nd London Division Territorial Force, 1914; General, 1923. Club: Naval and Military.

Died 21 May 1925.

MORLEY OF BLACKBURN, 1st Viscount, cr 1908; **John Morley,** PC 1886; OM 1902; MA, LLD, DCL; FRS; Hon. Fellow, All Souls, Oxford; Chancellor of Victoria University, 1908–23; b Blackburn, 24 Dec. 1838; s of late Jonathan Morley, surgeon; m 1870, Mary,

d of Thomas Ayling. Educ: Cheltenham College; Lincoln College, Oxford. Hon. LLD, Glasgow, 1879; Cambridge, 1892; St Andrews, 1902; Edinburgh, 1904; Hon. DCL, Oxford, 1896. Barrister, Lincoln's Inn, 1873; MP (L) Newcastle-on-Tyne, 1883–95; twice Chief Secretary for Ireland with seat in Cabinet, 1886, and 1892–95; Bencher of Lincoln's Inn, 1891; Trustee of British Museum, 1894; MP (L) Montrose Burghs, 1896–1908; Member of Historical Manuscripts Commission; Secretary of State for India, 1905–10; Lord President of the Council, 1910–14. Publications: Edmund Burke, 1867; Critical Miscellanies, 1871, second series, 1877; Voltaire, 1871; Rousseau, 1873; The Struggle for National Education, 1873; On Compromise, 1874; Diderot and the Encyclopædists, 1878; Burke (English Men of Letters series), 1879; The Life of Richard Cobden, 1881; Walpole (English Statesmen series), 1889; Studies in Literature, 1891; Oliver Cromwell, 1900; Life of Gladstone, 4 vols, 1903; Recollections, 1917. Heir: none. Address: Flowermead, Wimbledon Park, SW. Club: Athenæum.

Died 23 Sept. 1923 (ext).

MORLEY, Rt. Hon. Arnold, PC 1892; b 18 Feb. 1849; s of Samuel Morley, MP for Bristol, and Rebecca, d of Samuel Hope, Liverpool; m 1911, Elsie (d 1912), widow of Daniel Runyon, of New York. Educ: Trinity Coll., Cambridge (MA); took an ægrotat degree in Mathematical honours, having been 9th in the 3 days. Barrister, Inner Temple, 1873; MP (L) Nottingham, 1880–85; (L) Nottingham East, 1885–95; Patronage Secretary and Chief Liberal Whip, 1886–92; Postmaster-General, 1892–95; acted as counsel for Home Office in Colliery Accident Inquiries, 1880–85; Chairman of Dominions Commission, 1912; passed as extra master, the examination of the Board of Trade, with one hundred marks. Recreations: shooting, fishing, stalking, cycling, yachting; owned steam yacht "Yarta"; rowed in 1st Trinity 1st boat, head of the river, 1870. Address: 7 Stratton Street, Picadilly, W. T: Gerrard 3806. Clubs: Brooks's, Turf, National Liberal; Royal Yacht Squadron, Cowes.

Died 16 Jan. 1916.

MORLEY, Charles; Editor of the Pall Mall Magazine, 1905–11. Publications: Studies in Board Schools; London at Prayer, 1909. Address: c/o Pall Mall Magazine, Newton Street, Holborn, WC.

Died 20 April 1916.

MORLEY, Charles; b 1847; s of late Samuel Morley, MP, and b of late Rt Hon. Arnold Morley. Educ: Trinity Coll., Cambridge (BA 1870; MA 1874). Hon. Secretary to Royal College of Music; was a partner in firm of Messrs I. and R. Morley, Wood Street, EC. MP (GL) Brecknockshire, 1895–1906. Recreations: music, driving. Address: Shockerwick, Bath; 46 Bryanston Square, W. Clubs: Athenæum, Reform, Brooks's, National Liberal, Travellers'.

Died 27 Oct. 1917.

MORLEY, Edward Williams; b Newark, NJ, 29 Jan. 1838; s of Rev. Sardis Brewster Morley and Anna Clarissa Treat; m 1868, Isabella Ashley Birdsall of Winsted, Connecticut. Educ: Williams College. Professor of Chemistry, Western Reserve University at Cleveland, Ohio, 1868–1906; Professor Emeritus since 1906. Member National Academy of Sciences, 1897; Foreign Member Chemical Society, London; Hon. Member Royal Institution; Hon. Member American Chemical Society; Past President AAAS, and of American Chemical Society; Hon. President, Eighth International Congress Applied Chemistry, 1912; ScD Yale, 1909; LLD Western Reserve University, 1891; Williams College, 1901; Lafayette College, 1907; University of Pittsburgh, 1915; Davy Medallist, 1907; Elliot Cresson Medallist, 1912; Willard Gibbs Medallist, 1917. Publications: On the Densities of Oxygen and of Hydrogen, and on the Ratio of their Atomic Weights; and about forty other papers. Recreations: automobile, camera. Address: West Hartford, Connecticut. M: 4179 C.

Died 24 Feb. 1923.

MORLEY, Rt. Rev. Samuel, MA, DD; b 1841. Educ: London Univ.; Pembroke Coll., Cambridge (MA). DD, Archbishop of Canterbury, jure dignitatis. Late Chaplain of St John's Church, San Remo; Chaplain of Assouan, Egypt and Archdeacon of Church of England in Egypt; ordained, 1868; Curate of Ilkeston, Derbyshire, 1868–70; Curate of Sandgate, 1871–75; Chaplain of Secunderabad, India, 1875–78; Domestic Chaplain to the Bishop of Madras, 1878–96; consecrated Bishop in Tinnevelly and Madura in St George's Cathedral, Madras, 28 Oct. 1896, by the Bishops of Calcutta, Madras, and Travancore; retired, 1903. Address: Sillwood, Upper Bridge Road, Redhill, Surrey.

Died 6 Nov. 1923.

MORRIS, (Charles) Greville; artist; b 1861; m Harriet Maud Catherine, d of Rev. Maurice Edward Jenkins (formerly Vicar of

Egton, Yorks), Christ College, Cambridge. *Educ:* Cheltenham College; received art training at Paris. *Address:* Kenython, Parkstone, Dorset.   *Died 13 Jan. 1922.*

MORRIS, Comy-Gen. Sir Edward, KCB 1882 (CB 1879); JP City and County of Dublin; *b* 1833; *s* of late Robert Morris, Rosbercon House, Co. Kilkenny; *m* 1858, Elizabeth Dorcas (*d* 1875), *d* of William Bishop Mant; one *d*. Entered Commissariat Dept, 1854; served Crimea, 1854–56 (medal with clasp and Turkish medal); Zulu War, 1879 (medal with clasp, despatches twice); Egypt, 1882 (despatches twice, medal with clasp, Egyptian Star and 2nd class of the Medjidie); Commissary-General, 1881–86; retired, 1886. *Club:* Junior United Service.   *Died 15 Feb. 1923.*

MORRIS, Rev. Ernest Edwin, TD; RD; JP; MA; Vicar of Ashbourne and Hon. Canon of Southwell; Income Tax Commissioner and Assessor under Clergy Discipline Act, etc; *b* 30 Aug. 1856; *s* of late Henry Morris of Shrewsbury; *m* Josephine, *d* of late Richard Knott Bolton, MA, of Carrickmines, Co. Dublin, and Fenny Bentley, Derbyshire; three *s* two *d*. *Educ:* Shrewsbury; Jesus College, Cambridge; Ely Theological College. Formerly Vicar of Blackwell; Chaplain to High Sheriff; Chaplain to 6th Batt. Derbyshire Territorial Infantry; Chairman of Governing Body of Queen Elizabeth's Grammar School; Member of County Licensing Committee; Derbyshire Territorial Association, etc. *Address:* The Vicarage, Ashbourne, TA: Vicar, Ashbourne.   *Died 7 July 1924.*

MORRIS, Sir Henry, 1st Bt, *cr* 1909; MA, MB London; FRCS; President Royal Society of Medicine, 1910–12; President Royal College of Surgeons, 1906–9; Consulting Surgeon and Emeritus Lecturer on Surgery, Middlesex Hospital; Past-Representative of Royal College of Surgeons on and Treasurer of the General Medical Council, 1905–17; Founder and Vice-President of Imperial Cancer Research Fund; *b* 7 Jan. 1844; *e s* of late William Morris, surgeon, of Petworth, Sussex, and Louisa Amelia, *d* of James Andrews; *m* 1878, Louise Sarah, *d* of Rev. William Bowman. *Educ:* Epsom College; University College; Guy's Hospital. Formerly Surgeon to, and Lecturer on Anatomy and Surgery, Middlesex Hospital Medical College; Examiner in Surgery, University of London, and in Anatomy, University of Durham; Chairman of the Court of Examiners RCS for six years; delivered Cavendish Lecture, 1893; Hunterian Lectures, 1898; Bradshaw Lecturer, Royal College of Surgeons, 1903; Annual Oration, Medical Society of London, 1905, On the Financial Relations between the London Hospitals and their Medical Schools; Hunterian Oration on John Hunter as a philosopher, Feb. 1909, delivered before the Prince and Princess of Wales; Bradshaw Lecture on Cancer and its Origin; Sir Mitchell Banks Memorial Lecture, University of Liverpool, 1908; Hon. FRCSI; Foreign Corr. Mem., Société de Chirurgie; Hon. Mem., Medical Soc., State of New York; Trustee, Hunterian Museum, London. *Publications:* The Anatomy of the Joints of Man; Surgical Diseases of the Kidney and Ureter; Injuries and Disease of the Genital and Urinary Organs; Injuries of the Lower Extremity; Injuries and Diseases of the Abdomen; Editor of Morris's System of Anatomy, 4th edition; The Treatment of Inoperable Cancer; "Suggestion" in relation to the Treatment of Disease, 1910; Looking Back, or from Superstition to Research—Christian Science Refuted, 1909; contributor to Playfair's Gynæcology and Allbutt's Medicine; various articles in The Outlook during the period of the 1914–18 War. *Heir:* none. *Address:* 42 Connaught Square, W2. *T:* Paddington 725.

                                                   Died 14 June 1926.

MORRIS, Sir Malcolm Alexander, KCVO 1908; FRCSE, FZS; Chairman of British Federation of Medical and Allied Services; President of Institute of Hygiene; Vice-President of National Council for Combating Venereal Diseases; Member of Committee of Radium Institute; *b* 17 Aug. 1849; *y s* of John Carnac Morris, FRS, MCS; *m* 1872, Fanny, *d* of Thomas Cox, Dorchester, Oxon. *Educ:* St Mary's Hospital; Berlin; Vienna. Surgeon to the Skin Department, St Mary's Hospital and Seamen's Hospital; Lecturer on Skin Diseases, London School of Clinical Medicine; President of the Harveian Society; representative of National Association for the Prevention of Tuberculosis at the Berlin Congress 1899; Secretary-General, British Congress of Tuberculosis, 1901; President Dermatological Section Royal Society of Medicine; President Dermatological Section International Medical Congress, London, 1913; Member Royal Commission on Venereal Diseases, 1913–15; Fellow of Royal Sanitary Institute. *Publications:* Skin Diseases, 1894, sixth edn 1917; Light and X-Rays in Skin Diseases, 1907; The Nation's Health, 1917; Story of English Public Health, 1919. *Address:* 11 Marlborough Place, NW8. *T:* Hampstead 1070. *Clubs:* Reform, MCC.

                                                   Died 19 Feb. 1924.

MORRIS, Rev. Richard; Hon. Canon of Rochester, 1908. *Educ:* Trinity College, Dublin. Ordained, 1868; Curate of Doon, 1869; Castle Terra, 1869–72; Vicar of St Mark's, New Brompton, 1872. *Address:* Vittoria Walk, Cheltenham.

                                                   Died 25 Jan. 1923.

MORRIS, Sir Robert Armine, 4th Bt, *cr* 1806; DL, JP; *b* 27 July 1848; *s* of Sir John Armine Morris, 3rd Bt, and Catherine, *d* of Ronald Macdonald; *S* father, 1893; *m* 1885, Lucy Augusta (*d* 1902), *d* of Thomas Cory, Sketty House, Swansea; one *s* four *d* (and one *s* decd). Major 3rd Batt. Welsh Regt, 1882–84. Owned about 3,000 acres. *Heir:* *s* Tankerville Robert Armine Morris, late Lieut 1st Batt. Gloucestershire Regt, *b* 9 June 1892. *Address:* Sketty Park, Swansea. *Club:* Carlton.   *Died 20 Feb. 1927.*

MORRIS, Rev. Rupert Hugh, DD (Oxon); FSA; Vicar of St Gabriel's, Pimlico; Prebendary of Mathry ("Golden Prebend") in St David's Cathedral; *b* Holywell, Flintshire, 1844; *s* of William Morris, JP, formerly editor of Y Cymro, a Welsh Church newspaper; *m* Fanny Ada, *d* of Lt-Gen. C. E. Gold (late Colonel of 65th). *Educ:* Ruthin Grammar School; Jesus College, Oxford (Scholar and Powis Scholar). 2nd class Classics, Moderations; 2nd class Classics, Final Exam. Lit. Hum. Assistant Classical Master, Rossall School, 1865–69; Curate of Poulton le Fylde, 1867–69; Principal of Training College for S Wales and Monmouthshire, 1869–76; Lecturer of St Peter's, Carmarthen; Secretary of St David's Diocesan Board of Education, 1870–76; appointed by Bishop Thirwall to Stall in St David's Cathedral for educational work; Curate of St Mary's, Park Street, Grosvenor Square, London, W, 1876–78; Vicar, 1878–82; Headmaster of Godolphin School, 1876–84; Chaplain and Librarian to Duke of Westminster, 1884–95; Vice-President of Cambrian Archæological Association. *Publications:* Chester in the Times of Plantagenets and Tudors, 1893; History of the Diocese of Chester, 1895; Rules for Paraphrasing, etc. *Address:* St Gabriel's Vicarage, 4 Warwick Square, SW.

                                                   Died 8 Jan. 1918.

MORRIS, Samuel; JP; merchant and shipowner; *b* 1846; *s* of late George Morris, Fiddown, Co. Kilkenny, and Catharine, *d* of James Aylward; *m* 1874, Catharine, *d* of James Feehan, Tybroughny; six *s* three *d*. *Educ:* O'Shea's Grammar Sch., Carrick-on-Suir; Dublin. MP (N) Co. Kilkenny, S, 1894–1900; JP counties of Tipperary and Waterford, and city of Waterford. *Address:* Newrath House, Waterford. *T:* 57 and 193 Waterford; 10 Carrick-on-Suir.

                                                   Died Aug. 1920.

MORRIS, Rev. Silas, MA; Principal, Baptist College, Bangor, since 1896; *b* 1862; *m* 1892, Miss M. H. Williams, Pontardulais; one *s*. *Educ:* Elementary Schools, Dafen (near Llanelly, Carmarthenshire) and Pontardulais; Aberavon Academy, Pontypool College, and N Wales University College (upon entering which last he took the highest entrance Scholarship, 1884); graduated London University MA (in Classics), 1888). Classical Tutor at North Wales Baptist College, Llangollen, 1886; removed to Bangor, 1892; Editor of Seren Gomer, 1893–1904. *Address:* Baptist College, Bangor.

                                                   Died 25 July 1923.

MORRIS, Lt-Col Thomas Henry; CBE 1918; JP, DL; *b* 3 Feb. 1848; *e s* of William Morris, JP, DL, The Lodge, near Halifax, Yorks; *m* 1909, Florence Ethel, *y d* of Richard Crompton, Bury; no *c*. *Educ:* Rugby. Chairman, Halifax Commercial Banking Co. JP, DL W Riding Yorks. *Address:* Bolton Lodge, Bolton Percy, Yorks. TA: Bolton Percy. *T:* 16 Tadcaster. *M:* WY1. *Club:* Union.

                                                   Died 26 Nov. 1927.

MORRIS-AIREY, Harold, CBE 1919; Technical Adviser, HM Signal School, Royal Naval Barracks, Portsmouth; *b* 1880; *o s* of William M. Airey, Crumpsall, Manchester; *m* 1917, Eva, *d* of late William Prescott, Manchester; three *s*. *Educ:* Owens College, Manchester; University of Bonn. Was Lecturer in Physics at the Universities of Bonn, Manchester, and Durham; carried out experimental work in Wireless Telegraphy at Armstrong College, Newcastle; at the outbreak of war offered services to Admiralty, and in 1915 was appointed to the Wireless Telegraphy Department in HMS Vernon as Lieut RNVR; took part in early development of wireless apparatus in naval aircraft; promoted to Lt-Commander; was appointed in charge of development of Naval Wireless Transmission with rank of Lieut-Col, RM, 1918; appointed wireless expert to Admiralty, 1920. *Publications:* papers on electricity and optics in various scientific journals. *Recreation:* motoring. *Address:* 16 Villiers Road, Southsea. *T:* Portsmouth 5802. *M:* BK 6705.

                                                   Died 19 June 1927.

MORRISBY, Major Hon. Arthur; JP; Acting Clerk Legislative Council, 1916–18; granted the title of Honourable for life by the King, 1916; Coroner for Tasmania since 1911; *b* Sandford, Tasmania, 29 Dec. 1847; *s* of late John Morrisby of Clarence, Tasmania; *m* 1875, Isabel Snowden (*d* 1880), of Hobart; one *s. Educ:* Mornington School, near Bellerive, Clarence. Member Clarence Municipality, 1890–92; Member and Chairman First Town Board, Zeehan, West Coast, Tasmania; Chairman, 1892–94 and 1896–1900, Member to 1902; Chairman Board of Advice, Cemetery Trust, 1892–1902; Member of Licensing Bench, Marine Board of Strahan, Macquarie Harbour, 1898–1902; Minister without portfolio, 1903–4; formed, and was appointed Captain of the Zeehan Rifle Company, 1st Batt. Tasmanian Infantry, 1896; served in S African War in command of E Squadron 3rd Batt. Australian Commonwealth Horse, and retired with rank of Major (medal with clasp); elected by Parliament as a Member of the Council of the University of Tasmania; elected Lay Representative, Anglican Synod of Tasmania, 1907; Chairman of Committee of Synod, 1911–16; Chairman of Committee, 1919; Member of the Diocesan Council, 1914; Member of the Legislative Council of Tasmania for Gordon, 1899–1916; Chairman of Committees, 1907–16; appointed by Government as a Royal Commissioner to open Parliament, 1914. *Recreations:* rifle shooting and sporting shooting, rowing. *Address:* Bellerive, near Hobart, Tasmania. *Club:* Military, Hobart.

Died 16 Sept. 1925.

MORRISON, Brig.-Gen. Colquhoun Grant, CMG 1915; late 1st Dragoons; *b* 28 Jan. 1860; *m* 1914, Vera, *d* of Col H. A. Sawyer. Entered army, 1879; Captain, 1889; Major, 1897; Lt-Col, 1908; Col, 1911; Instructor RMC, 1891–97; DAAG Jersey, 1899–1901; served S Africa (Queen's medal, 3 clasps), and Commandant and Area Administrator, 1901–2; DAAG Orange River Colony and Cape Colony, 1906–9; specially employed, War Office, 1911; AA&QMG Gibraltar, 1912–14; served European War, 1914–15 (CMG). *Club:* Army and Navy. *Died 23 May 1916.*

MORRISON, Maj.-Gen. Sir Edward Whipple Bancroft, KCMG 1919 (CMG 1917); CB 1918; DSO 1900; *b* 6 July 1867; *s* of Alexander R. Morrison, Hamilton, Ont; *m* 1911, Mrs Emma Fripp of Ottawa. Served South Africa, 1899–1900 (despatches, Bt Capt., Queen's medal 3 clasps, DSO), commanded 8th Artillery Brigade CFA, 1909–13; Director of Artillery Headquarter Staff, 1913–14; OC 1st Artillery Brigade, CEF, 1914–15; served Second Ypres, Festubert, Givenchy; GOC II Canadian Divisional Artillery, 1915–16, St Eloi, Third Ypres and Somme; GOC Canadian Corps Artillery, 1916–19; Vimy, Hill 70, Lens, Paschendaele, 1917, Amiens, Arras, Queant-Drocourt Line, Canal du Nord, Bourlon Wood; capture of Cambrai, Valenciennes, Mons, 1918; Army of Occupation in Germany, 1919 (KCMG, CMG, despatches, CB, Major-General, 1918); Inspector-General of Artillery, 1919; Master-General of the Ordnance, 1920; President of Canadian Artillery Association, 1921. *Publication:* With the Guns. *Address:* 21 M'Leod Street, Ottawa, Canada. *Club:* Rideau, Ottawa.

Died May 1925.

MORRISON, Col F. L., CB 1916; VD; 5th Battalion Highland Light Infantry (Territorial Force); *b* 24 Oct. 1863. *Educ:* Glasgow University (MA, LLB). Writer. *Address:* Ashcraig, Great Western Road, Glasgow.

Died 22 Dec. 1917.

MORRISON, George Ernest; Political Adviser to the President, Chinese Republic, since 1912; Times Correspondent, Indo China, Siam, Peking, 1895–1912; *b* Geelong, Victoria, Australia, 4 Feb. 1862; *s* of late Dr G. Morrison; *m* 1912, Jennie Wark, *d* of Robert Robin; three *s. Educ:* Melbourne and Edinburgh Universities (MD, CM). Crossed Australia on foot from the Gulf of Carpentaria to Melbourne, Christmas, 1882–83; speared in New Guinea, Oct. 1883; graduated, 1887; crossed from Shanghai to Rangoon by land, 1894; as special for the Times travelled from Bangkok in Siam to Yunnan city in China and round Tonquin, 1896; and in 1897 crossed Manchuria from Stretensk in Siberia to Vladivostok; was in Peking during siege of Legations, June–Aug. 1900; was present at the triumphal entry into Port Arthur, January 1905; in 1907 crossed China from Peking to the French border of Tonquin; represented Times, Portsmouth Peace Conference, 1905; rode from Honan city in Central China across Asia to Andijan in Russian Turkestan, 3,750 miles in 175 days, 1910; travelled in every province of China except Tibet; 1st Class Order Excellent Crop (China). *Publication:* An Australian in China: being the Narrative of a Quiet Journey across China to Burma, 1895. *Address:* Peking. *Club:* Oriental. *Died May 1920.*

MORRISON, Very Rev. George Herbert, DD; Minister of Wellington Church, Glasgow, since 1902, and Moderator of the

United Free Church General Assembly, 1926; *b* 2 Oct. 1866; *s* of Doctor Thomas Morrison, Rector, Free Church Training College, Glasgow; *m* 1st, 1894, Agnes Gray Orr (*d* 1902); 2nd, 1904, Christine Marie Auchinvole, Glasgow; one *s* two *d* (younger son killed, 1918). *Educ:* Glasgow Academy and Glasgow University. Sub-Editor of the New English Dictionary, Oxford, 1888–89; Assistant to Dr Alexander Whyte, Edinburgh, 1893–94; Minister of First Free Church, Thurso, 1894–98; St John's Free Church, Dundee, 1898–1902. *Publications:* edited the Memoirs of Thomas Boston, and Hugh Macdonald's Rambles round Glasgow; many volumes of sermons and addresses; a constant contributor to the Religious Press. *Recreations:* walking, field-botany. *Address:* 29 Lilybank Gardens, Glasgow, W2. *T:* Glasgow 1516 W.

Died 14 Oct. 1928.

MORRISON, Col John, MVO 1910; OBE 1918; VD; JP; late commanding 13th (the Sutherland and Caithness Highland) Battalion Seaforth Highlanders; Vice-Lieutenant of Sutherland. *Address:* Rhives, Golspie, Sutherland. *Died 1 March 1919.*

MORRISON, R. E., RCA; portrait painter; *b* Peel, Isle of Man, 31 Dec. 1851; *s* of John Morrison, builder; *m* 1879; one *s. Educ:* Peel; Liverpool School of Art; London; Académie Julien, under Bougeureau and Tony Robert Fleury, Paris. Followed the profession of portrait painter in his adopted city, Liverpool, where he resided for more than forty years; painted many noted people in Liverpool and throughout the northern counties. *Recreation:* landscape sketching. *Clubs:* Arts; University, Artists', Liverpool.

MORRISON, Walter, JP; *b* 21 May 1836; *s* of James Morrison, of Morrison, Dillon, and Co., and Mary Anne, *d* of John Todd, of same firm. *Educ:* Eton; Balliol Coll., Oxford (1st class Lit. Hum. 1857). MP (L) Plymouth, 1861–74; contested City of London, 1880; MP (LU) Skipton Division, 1886–92 and 1895–1900; Chm., Central Argentine Railway, 1887; Chairman of Governors, Giggleswick Sch.; a Founder, Palestine Exploration Fund; Hon. DCL Oxford, 1921. Owned about 13,900 acres. *Publications:* some occasional papers. *Address:* Malham Tarn, Langcliffe, Settle; 77 Cromwell Road, SW. *Club:* United University. *Died 18 Dec. 1921.*

MORROW, Albert; *b* Comber, Co. Down, 1863; *m* 1901, Catherine Macnamara; one *s* one *d. Educ:* Belfast; Royal College of Arts, London. Started on the English Illustrated Magazine, 1884; illustrated books and magazines from then onwards; had hundreds of posters reproduced, both theatrical and commercial, Answers posters, Lloyd's News posters, and for Cassell & Co.; exhibited for seven consecutive years in the Royal Academy. *Recreations:* principally walking, sketching landscape. *Died Oct. 1927.*

MORSON, Walter Augustus Ormsby, KC (Canada); barrister; Member of Legislative Assembly (C) Prince Edward Island, since 1902; *b* Hamilton, PEI, 24 Dec. 1851; *m* 1891, May Elizabeth Des Brisay. *Address:* Charlottetown, Prince Edward Island.

Died Sept. 1921.

MORTIMER, Rev. Christian; Canon of Lichfield, 1890–1914. *Educ:* Clare Coll., Cambridge (MA; Junior Optime). Ordained 1859; curate of Eaton-Bishop, Herefordshire, 1859–64; Middle, Salop, 1864–68; Vicar of Grinshill, 1868–71; Ash, Salop, 1871–80; Rector of Pitchford, Salop, 1880–90; Diocesan Inspector, 1871–88; Preb. of Dassett-Parva, 1885–90; Examining Chaplain to Bishop of Lichfield, 1890–91. *Address:* Poundfields, Old Woking, Surrey.

Died 23 Aug. 1916.

MORTIMER, George Frederick Lloyd; KC 1919; Recorder of Rotherham since 1905; *b* 1866; *m* 1893, Mary Isabella Edith, *d* of Sir Thomas Wrightson, 1st Bt and Elizabeth, *e d* of Samuel Wise. *Educ:* Birkenhead School; Balliol College, Oxford (1st class Lit. Hum., 1889). President Oxford Union Society; Bencher of Inner Temple, 1924. *Address:* 4 Harcourt Buildings, Temple, EC4. *TA:* 69 The Temple. *T:* Central 8435; 3 Cheyne Place, SW3. *Club:* New University. *Died 5 Sept. 1928.*

MORTIMER, Lt-Col James, CMG 1916; 5th Battalion Yorkshire Regiment (Territorial Force). Served S African War, 1900–1 (Queen's medal, 4 clasps); European War, 1914–16 (despatches, CMG). *Address:* Grove Cottage, Driffield, E Yorks.

Died 15 Sept. 1916.

MORTIMER, Col Sir William Hugh, KCB 1911 (CB 1900); *b* 13 Dec. 1846; *s* of A. J. Mortimer, British Paymaster-General, English German Legion; *m* 1877, Evelyn Maude Mary, *e d* of George Harries of Trevacoon and Rickerton, Pembrokeshire; three *d*. Entered army as Ensign 41st Welsh Regiment; Army Pay Department, 1878; served Egyptian Campaign, 1882 (medal with clasp); Tel-el-Kebir (bronze star); South Africa, 1899–1902, first as Chief Paymaster Natal Forces, and afterwards as Chief Paymaster of Forces South Africa (despatches twice, CB, Queen's medal, 4 clasps, King's medal, 2 clasps); Chief Paymaster, Army Pay Department, retired 1906. *Address*: Quarrymill, Dyke Road, Brighton.   *Died 24 Oct. 1921.*

MORTIMORE, Lt-Col Claude Alick, DSO 1916; late Royal Field Artillery; *b* 28 Dec. 1875; *s* of late Alexander Mortimore; unmarried. *Educ*: Uppingham. Served S Africa, 1900–2 (Queen's medal 4 clasps, King's medal 2 clasps); European War, 1914–18 (DSO, Chevalier Légion d'Honneur, Bt Lt-Col); retired pay, 1922. *Address*: 17 Sussex Mansions, SW7. *T*: Kensington 1411. *Club*: United Service.
Died 7 April 1927.

MORTIMORE, Frederick William, MVO 1916; Paymaster-Captain, Royal Navy (retired); *b* 27 Oct. 1858; 2nd *s* of late Richard Mortimore of Cullompton, Devon; unmarried. *Educ*: Sherborne School. Entered Navy, 1875; retired, 1914. *Address*: Riseholme, Elm Road, Horsell, Woking. *Club*: Junior United Service.
Died 12 May 1928.

MORTON, Sir Alpheus Cleophas, Kt 1918; MP (L) Sutherlandshire, 1906–18; architect and surveyor; *b* 1840; 2nd *s* of late Francis Morton of Old Sodbury, Gloucestershire; *m* 1874; three *s* five *d*. *Educ*: privately in Canada. Member of Corporation of London since 1882; contested Hythe Burghs, 1885; Christchurch, Hants, 1886; Bath, 1900; MP (L) Peterborough, 1889–95; Deputy-Alderman of the Ward of Farringdon Without; Chairman of the Metropolitan Paving Committee; member of City and Guilds Institute; Guardian of City of London; Governor of St Bartholomew's Hospital; Member of the City Lieutenancy. *Address*: 124 Chancery Lane, WC; 47 Gauden Road, Clapham, SW4. *Clubs*: National Liberal; Scottish Liberal, Edinburgh.   *Died 26 April 1923.*

MORTON, General Boyce William Dunlop; Indian Army; *b* 24 Aug. 1829; *m* 1855. Entered army, 1848; Lt-Gen. 1892; unemployed list, 1887; served Cossyah and Jyntiah Hills Campaign, 1861–63 (despatches); in civil employ, 1864–84; Deputy Commissioner of seven districts in succession, including Darjeeling, 1867–73. *Publications*: Some Indian Experiences; What Follows; What I Believe. *Address*: 2 Priory Parade, London Road, Cheltenham.
Died 15 Aug. 1919.

MORTON, Edward; dramatist, critic, and journalist; *m* Rosamond, *d* of Capt. Thomas Devereux Bingham, Wartnaby Hall, Leicestershire. *Publications*: Travellers' Tales, 1892; Man and Beast (with I. Zangwill), 1893; Miss Impudence, comedy in one act, produced at Terry's Theatre, 1892; San Toy, or The Emperor's Own, comic opera (music by Sidney Jones), produced at Daly's Theatre, 1899. *Club*: Authors'.
Died 6 July 1922.

MORTON, Paymaster Rear-Adm. James Elliot Vowler, CB 1918; Royal Navy; *b* Chittlehamholt Parsonage, N Devon, 27 Oct. 1861; *e s* of late Rev. James Henry Morton, MA, Trinity College, Dublin; unmarried. *Educ*: St John's Foundation School, Leatherhead. Entered Royal Navy, 1878; served in N America and West Indies, Australia, China, W Coast of Africa, Pacific and Mediterranean Stations; Fleet Paymaster, 1902; on board HMS Charybdis at the Blockade of Venezuela Coast and action at Puerto Cabello; in 1911 when in HMS Carnarvon, took part in the Investiture of the Prince of Wales at Carnarvon Castle (Coronation medal); served in HMS Tiger, 1914–18; present at the battles of Dogger Bank, 1915, and Jutland, 1916; Paymaster-in-Chief 1916; Paymaster Rear-Adm., 1920; Russian Military Order (2nd class) of St Stanislaus; Officer of the Legion of Honour. *Recreations*: shooting, fishing. *Address*: Crescent Mansions, Plymouth.   *Died 21 Sept. 1924.*

MORTON, James H., ARCA; artist; *b* Darwen, 1881; *s* of James and Elizabeth Morton. *Educ*: elementary schools and Higher Grade School, Darwen (Huntingdon Scholarship and Local Exhibition); Royal College of Art (RCA Scholarship). Taught art in Darlington for twelve months; subsequently designing and painting; Exhibitor at the Royal Academy, International, Liverpool Exhibitions. *Recreations*: walking, botany. *Address*: 30 Sudell Road, Darwen.
Died 5 Nov. 1918.

MORTON, Levi Parsons, LLD; *b* Shoreham, Vermont, USA, 16 May 1824; *s* of Rev. Daniel Oliver and Lucretia Parsons Morton; descendant of George Morton of Bawtry, Yorks, financial agent in

London of the Mayflower Pilgrims who arrived at Plymouth, Mass on ship "Ann", 1623; *m* 1st, Lucy Kimball (*d* 1871); 2nd, 1873, *d* of W. L. Street; five *c*. *Educ*: Shoreham Academy. Founded the Banking Houses of L. P. Morton and Co., Morton, Bliss, and Co., New York, and Morton, Rose, and Co., Morton, Chaplin, and Co., London, and the Morton Trust Co., New York; Member of Congress from New York, 1878–81; United States Minister to France, 1881–85; Vice-President of the United States, and President of the Senate, 1889–93; Governor of the State of New York, 1895 and 1896; Dartmouth College, 1891, and Middleburg College, 1893, bestowed on him LLD. Owned 1,000 acres. *Address*: Ellerslie, Rhinecliff-on-Hudson; 681 Fifth Avenue, New York. *Clubs*: Century, Union, Metropolitan, Union League of New York Lawyers, Republican, Downtown.   *Died 16 May 1920.*

MORTON, Thomas Corsan; artist; Curator, Kirkcaldy Museum and Art Gallery, Fifeshire; late Keeper, National Galleries of Scotland; *b* Glasgow, 1859; *s* of James Morton, MD, LLD, and Elizabeth Corsan; *m* 1890, Amelie Lydiard Robertson; one *s* one *d*. *Educ*: High School, Glasgow. Studied art at the Slade School, London, under Professor Alphonse Legros, and thereafter at Paris under Messieurs Boulanger and Lefevbre; afterwards settled in Glasgow, and later in Edinburgh, but subsequently resident in Kirkcaldy. *Recreations*: walking, reading. *Address*: 44 Townsend Place, Kirkcaldy, Fifeshire. *Club*: Glasgow Art.
Died 24 Dec. 1928.

MORVI, HH Thakur Saheb Sir Waghji Ravaji, GCIE 1897; *b* 7 April 1858; *S* 1870. *Educ*: Rajkumar College. The state had an area of 822 square miles and a population of about 90,000. *Address*: Morvi, Kathiawar, Bombay.   *Died July 1922.*

MOSCHELES, Felix; *b* London, 8 Feb. 1833; *o s* of late Ignaz Moscheles, composer, godson of Felix Mendelssohn. *Educ*: London and Leipsic; studied painting in Paris and Antwerp. Exhibited first pictures in Antwerp and at the Paris Salon; later in the Academy, Grosvenor and New Galleries; very active in the cause of International Arbitration and Peace; wrote pamphlets and many articles on the subject; member of committees of different Peace Societies; President and Chairman of the International Arbitration and Peace Association; President of the London Esperanto Club; Member of the International Peace Bureau, Bern. *Publications*: Felix Mendelssohn's Letters to Ignaz and Charlotte Moscheles; In Bohemia with Du Maurier; Fragments of an Autobiography, 1902. *Recreations*: propaganding, lecturing. *Address*: 80 Elm Park Road, SW. *T*: Western 1051. *Club*: National Liberal.   *Died 22 Dec. 1917.*

MOSELY, Alfred, CMG 1900; LLD; *b* 13 Oct. 1855; *s* of late Abraham Mosely, formerly of Clifton, Bristol; *m* 1881, Florence Louisa, *d* of Thomas Roberts; two *s* four *d*. *Educ*: privately; Bristol Grammar School. Served with the Princess Christian Hospital, South Africa; Member of Tariff Commission, 1904; organised Industrial and Educational Commissions to America, 1902 and 1903 respectively, and Commission of several hundred School Teachers to United States and Canada, 1906–7; and arranged reception of 1,000 Canadian and US school teachers on a return visit to this country, 1908–9; Knight of Grace of the Order of St John of Jerusalem. *Publications*: reports and pamphlets on industrial and educational matters and economics. *Address*: West Lodge, Hadley Wood, Barnet. *TA*: West Lodge, Cockfosters. *Club*: Constitutional.
Died 22 July 1917.

MOSER, Oswald, RI, ROI; *b* 1874; *m* 1911, Margot Murray. *Educ*: Skelsmergh House School, Highgate. Studied art at St John's Wood Art Schools; exhibited Dixisti (The Last Supper) at the Royal Academy and the Salon (mention honourable) and subsequently purchased by Lord Winterstoke for Bristol; gold medal and the diplôme d'honneur at the Paris autumn Salon; The Adoration of the Magi, exhibited at the Royal Academy, Paris Salon, and invited to the Royal Scottish Academy, 1914, and purchased by the Earl of Moray. *Recreations*: shooting, fishing, golf, tennis. *Address*: 33 Canfield Gardens, Hampstead, NW. *T*: Hampstead 5379. *Club*: St John's Wood Arts.
Died 30 Sept. 1916.

MOSHIER, Prof. H. H.; Major, 11th Canadian Field Ambulance; Professor of Physiology, University of Alberta, since 1914; *b* 11 Jan. 1889; *m* 1914, Ida Winifred Griffith; no *c*. *Educ*: Toronto University, Canada. House Physician, Toronto General Hospital, 1909–11; practised medicine at Calgary, 1911–14. *Publications*: papers on the Wasserman Reaction, Canadian Medical Association, 1911, and Vaccine Therapy, Alberta Medical Association, 1912. *Recreations*: golf, mountain climbing. *Address*: University of Alberta, Canada.
Died 29 Aug. 1918.

MOSLEY, Sir Alexander, Kt 1926; CMG 1901; JP; *b* 1847; *s* of Thomas Mosley, Gibraltar and Cheshire; *m* 1881, Mercedes, *y d* of late Francis Francia, JP, Gibraltar; one *s* four *d*. Partner in banking firm, Thomas Mosley & Co., Gibraltar. Formerly President Gibraltar Chamber of Commerce and Unofficial Member Executive Council, Gibraltar. *Address:* Gibraltar.

Died 17 April 1927.

MOSLEY, Sir Oswald, 5th Bt, *cr* 1781; Captain, Derbyshire Yeomanry (Territorial Force); *b* 29 Dec. 1873; *s* of Sir Oswald Mosley, 4th Bt and Elizabeth Constance, *d* of Sir William White; *S* father, 1915; *m* 1895, Katharine Maud, *d* of late Justinian H. Edwards Heathcote; three *s*. Owned about 3,800 acres. *Heir: s* Oswald Ernald Mosley [*b* 16 Nov. 1896; *m* 1920, Lady Cynthia Blanche Curzon, *d* of 1st and last Marquess Curzon of Kedleston; one *s* one *d*]. *Clubs:* Carlton, Turf, Pratt's; Kildare Street, Dublin.

Died 21 Sept. 1928.

MOSS, Rev. Henry Whitehead, MA; Prebendary of Hereford, since 1887; *b* Lincoln, 23 June 1841; *e s* of late Henry Moss, Lincoln; *m* 1887, Mary, *o d* of Rev. W. A. Beaufort, Egglestone Vicarage, Darlington; two *s* four *d*. *Educ:* Shrewsbury School; St John's Coll., Cambridge. Porson Prizeman, 1861, 1862, 1863; Craven University Scholar, 1862; Browne's Medallist, 1863; BA (Senior Classic), 1864; MA 1867. Lecturer and Fellow of St John's College, Cambridge, 1864; repeatedly elected a member of the Committee of the Headmasters' Conference, of which he was Chairman, 1899–1902; a selected speaker at the Church Congress, 1875 and 1896; Select Preacher before the Univ. of Cambridge, 1905; Headmaster of Shrewsbury School, 1866–1908. *Publications:* a contributor to Sabrinae Corolla and Florilegium Latinum. *Address:* Highfield Park, near Oxford. *Club:* Oxford and Cambridge.

Died 14 Jan. 1917.

MOSS, His Honour Judge Samuel, JP (Denbighshire); MA, BCL; County Court Judge, North Wales, Chester District (Circuit No 29), since 1906; barrister-at-law; *b* 13 Dec. 1858; 2nd *s* of late Enoch Moss, Broad Oak, Rossett, North Wales; *m* 1895, Eleanor, *d* of E. B. Samuel, The Darland, Wrexham; four *s* two *d*. *Educ:* privately; Worcester Coll., Oxford. Barrister Lincoln's Inn, 1880; formerly practised on North Wales and Chester Circuit; Assistant Boundary Commissioner for whole of Wales, 1887; MP (L) E Denbighshire, 1897–1906; formerly Alderman and first Vice-Chairman of Denbighshire CC, and 2nd Chairman; formerly member of Chester City Council. *Publication:* The English Land Laws, 1886. *Recreations:* cycling, riding, shooting. *Address:* 50 Hough Green, Chester; Accre Hall, Llandegla, near Wrexham, N Wales. *M:* FM 910.

Died 14 May 1918.

MOSSOP, Joseph Upjohn, DSO 1902; farmer; *b* Grey Town, Natal, 27 April 1872; *s* of James Mossop, an Englishman who came to Natal, 1840; *m* 1904, Clarissa, *d* of Henry Melvill Meek of Wakkerstroom District, Natal; three *s* one *d*. *Educ:* Grey Town; private tutor. Was a burgher of the Transvaal; despatch rider to Generals C. and Louis Botha and T. Smuts during early part of Boer War; surrendered to Gen. Rt Hon. Sir Redvers Buller, May 1900; caught and imprisoned by Boers; escaped and became guide to Generals Dartnell and Buller; made intelligence officer in Col Stewart's column of Johannesburg Mounted Rifles; joined Gen. Hamilton's column; assisted in capture of Gen. C. Emmett. *Address:* Brooklyn Farm, PO Machadodorp, Eastern Transvaal, South Africa.

Died 26 June 1928.

MOSTYN, Sir Pyers Charles, 10th Bt, *cr* 1670; *b* 13 Aug. 1895; *s* of Sir Pyers William Mostyn, 9th Bt and Anna Maria (*d* 1916), *d* of Thomas Aloysius Perry, Bitham House, Warwicks; *S* father, 1912. *Heir: cousin* Pyers George Joseph Mostyn, Lieut Royal Welsh Fusiliers, *b* 28 Sept. 1893. *Address:* Talacre, Prestatyn, Flints; The Mount, Constitution Hill, Parkstone, Dorset. *Club:* Wellington.

Died 16 Jan. 1917.

MOTT, Sir Frederick Walker, KBE 1919; MD, BS London; FRCP 1892; FRS 1896; Fellow of University College, London; Consulting Physician to Charing Cross Hospital; Pathologist to London County Asylums, retired 1923; Lecturer on Morbid Psychology, Birmingham University; *b* Brighton, 23 Oct. 1853; *s* of Henry Mott, Brighton, and Caroline, *d* of William Fuller; *m* 1885, Georgiana Alexandra, *d* of late George Thomas Soley; four *d*. *Educ:* University Coll. and Hospital, London (University Scholar and Gold Medallist; MB, BSc 1881; MD 1886). Late RAMC (Bt Lt-Col); Corresponding Member of Neurological and Psychiatrical Societies of France, Belgium and The Netherlands; Mem., Amer. Psychiatrical Soc.; Fullerian Prof.

of Physiology, Royal Instn; Croonian Lectr, RCP, 1900; Lettsomian Lectr, RCP, 1916 (The Effects of High Explosives upon the Central Nervous System); Fothergill Gold Medal and Prize, Med. Soc. of London, 1911; Moxon Gold Medal, RCP, 1919; Officer, Order of Star of Roumania. *Publications:* Nature and Nurture in Mental Development; Brain and the Voice; War Neuroses and Shell Shock; Editor, Archives of Neurology and Psychiatry; numerous contributions to medical journals and recent textbooks of medicine and in Encyclopædia Britannica; several original papers relating to neurology in the Proceedings and Philosophical Transactions of the Royal Society, and in Brain. *Recreation:* golf. *Address:* 25 Nottingham Place, W1. *T:* Mayfair 1426. *Clubs:* Athenæum (hon.), Savage.

Died 8 June 1926.

MOTTRAM, Rev. William; Emeritus Secretary of the Congregational Union Temperance Committee; *b* 29 March 1836; *s* of Thomas and Frances Louisa Mottram; *m* 1st, Lucy Hannah (*decd*), *d* of Thomas Mellor of Rangeflat House, Warslow; 2nd, Elizabeth, *d* of J. H. Fruen, Salisbury; three *s* two *d*. *Educ:* Waterhouses Trustees School; private tutors. Held pastorates in the west of England 1859–87; editor Tewkesbury Weekly Record, 1879–83; pastor at Borough Road Church and Superintendent of Lambeth Baths Mission, 1887–96; missioner, lecturer, and preacher in every county of England and Wales; lecture on Adam Bede raised £1,400 for charitable objects. *Publications:* The True Story of George Eliot in Relation to the Characters in Adam Bede; Manuals for Temperance Sunday; various sermons and periodical contributions. *Recreations:* travel, reading, hymnology, old English games. *Address:* 32 Selby Road, Anerley, SE2.

Died Aug. 1921.

MOUBRAY, John James, JP; HM Lieutenant for County of Kinross; *b* 1857; *o s* of Robert Moubray (*d* 1880), and Catherine Beveridge (*d* 1904), *d* of John Wilson, of Hillpark; *m* 1893, May Marianne, *e d* of William Calvert Booth, of Oran, Catterick, Yorkshire; three *s* four *d*. *Educ:* St John's Coll., Oxford (MA; Hon. Fellow). *Address:* Naemoor, Rumbling Bridge, Kinross-shire; Killerby, Catterick, Yorkshire. *Clubs:* Carlton, Boodle's.

Died 21 Oct. 1928.

MOULD, Percy; Chief Manager, The Mercantile Bank of India, Ltd, since 1913; 2nd *s* of late Col J. S. Mould, RMLI; *m* Edith Katherine, *d* of late Walter Langton of Barrow House, Keswick; one *s* two *d*. *Educ:* Portsmouth. Joined Mercantile Bank of India, Ltd, 1886. *Recreations:* golf, shooting. *Address:* Broadwater House, Tunbridge Wells. *T:* Tunbridge Wells 372. *M:* XF 4700. *Club:* Oriental.

Died 14 Nov. 1923.

MOULE, Ven. Arthur Evans, DD; Rector of Burwarton cum Cleobury North, 1908–14; late Archdeacon in the Missionary Diocese of Mid China; *b* 10 April 1836; 6th *s* of late Rev. Henry Moule, MA, Vicar of Fordington, Dorset; *m* 1861, Eliza Agnes, *y d* of late Rev. J. H. Bernau, Vicar of Belvedere, Kent, for twenty years missionary in British Guiana; six *s* three *d*. *Educ:* home; Malta College; CMS College, Islington. BD Lambeth given by Archbishop Tait; DD Lambeth, 1912. Left England for China, 1861; witnessed in Dec. 1861 the storming of Ningpo by the Taipings, their expulsion by Capt. Roderick Dew in May 1862, and the second siege of Ningpo by 100,000 Taipings in Sept. 1862; worked in and around Ningpo, 1861–69; in charge of the Mission, 1864–69, when his brother, afterwards Bishop in Mid-China, moved inland to Hangchow (first inland mission residence); in Ningpo again, 1871–76; Hangchow, in sole charge, 1876–79; witnessed founding of the Chüki Mission 80 miles south; after furlough, to Shanghai as Secretary of the Mission and Archdeacon; worked in Shanghai, 1882–94; in charge temporarily of the Cathedral of the Holy Trinity; invalided home, 1894, and retired by CMS, 1898; Rector of Compton Valence, Dorset, 1898–1902; rejoined CMS, 1902; work in Chehkiang and Kiangsu; at home, 1910, but in reserve; Vice-President of CMS. *Publications: English*—Four Hundred Millions; Chinese Stories; Story of Chehkiang Mission (4 editions); The Glorious Land; China as a Mission Field; The China Mission; Reasons of the Hope that is in us; New China and Old (3rd edition); Tufts and Tails; Young China; Songs of Heaven and Home (3rd edition); Half a Century in China; three essays on the Opium Question; The Splendour of a Great Hope; The Chinese People; City, Hill, and Plain; *Chinese*—Commentary on the Translation of the Thirty-nine Articles; Adams' Private Thoughts; Filial Piety (illustrated); Sermons on the Gospels (2 vols); A Letter to the Scholars of China; Goulburn on Personal Religion; Chinese Hymnal Companion; Sheet Tracts. *Address:* Junior School, Weymouth College, Weymouth.

Died 26 Aug. 1918.

MOULE, Charles Walter, MA; Senior Fellow and President, and formerly Lecturer, Tutor (1879–92), and Librarian (1895–1913) of Corpus Christi College, Cambridge; *b* 9 Feb. 1834; *s* of Rev. H. Moule, Vicar of Fordington, Dorset; *m* 1885, Mary Dora, *d* of Lieut-Col R. Cautley, 10th Bengal Cavalry; one *s* one *d*. BA 1857, when he was bracketed Senior Classic with the late Sir J. R. Seeley and two others; fifteen times Public Examiner for the Classical Tripos, besides examining for University Scholarships and Prizes. *Recreations:* long walks, walking-tours, sketching. *Address:* 13 Cranmer Road, Cambridge.   *Died 1 May 1921.*

MOULE, Rt. Rev. Handley Carr Glyn, DD; Bishop of Durham, since 1901; *b* Dorchester, 23 Dec. 1841; *y s* of Rev. Henry Moule, MA, Vicar of Fordington, and Mary Mullett Evans; *m* 1881, (Harriot) Mary (*d* 1915), *d* of Rev. C. Boileau Elliott, FRS, Rector of Tattingstone, Suffolk; one *d* (and one *d* decd). *Educ:* home; Trinity Coll., Cambridge. Carus Greek Testament Prize, 1862; Browne's Classical Medallist, 1863; Second Classic in the Tripos of 1864; BD 1894; DD 1895. Fellow of Trinity Coll., Cambridge, 1865–81; Assistant Master at Marlborough, 1865–67; ordained at Ely; Dean of Trinity Coll., 1873–76; 1st Principal of Ridley Hall, Cambridge, 1881–99; Norrisian Professor of Divinity, Cambridge, and Professorial Fellow of St Catharine's Coll., 1899–1901 (Hon. Fellow, 1902); Hon. Chaplain to Queen Victoria, 1898–1901; Chaplain in Ordinary to King Edward VII, 1901; Select Preacher at Cambridge, 1880, and frequently later; at Oxford, 1895. *Publications:* Six Sacred Poems, awarded Seaton's Prize at Cambridge between 1869–76; Commentaries on the Epistles to the Romans, Ephesians, Philippians, and Colossians, in the Cambridge Bible, and on Romans in the Expositor's Bible (between 1880 and 1894); Thoughts on Christian Sanctity, 1885; Outlines of Christian Doctrine, 1889; Veni Creator, 1890; Charles Simeon, in "English Leaders of Religion", 1892; Ridley on the Lord's Supper, a critical edition, 1895; In the House of the Pilgrimage (poems), 1896; Ephesian Studies, 1900; The Secret of the Presence (sermons), 1900; Thoughts for the Sundays of the Year, 1901; The School of Suffering (Memoir of a Daughter), 1905; Christus Consolator, 1915; Christ and Sorrow, 1916; The Call of Lent, 1917; Auckland Castle, 1918; many other religious works since 1885. *Recreation:* the telescope. *Address:* Auckland Castle, Bishop Auckland.   *Died 8 May 1920.*

MOULE, Horace Frederick D'Oyly, CSI 1897; late of Indian Civil Service; *b* 4 Nov. 1843; *s* of Rev. Horatio Moule, Rector of Wolverton, Somerset; *m* 1871, Banna (*d* 1913), *d* of late Gen. Richard Horsford, Bengal Artillery; two *s* two *d*. *Educ:* Cheltenham. Joined ICS, 1863; served in NWP and Oudh as magistrate and collector; Commissioner of Lucknow and Rohilkhund, and Member of Board of Revenue; JP Surrey. Decorated for public services. *Address:* 7 Hereford Square, SW7. *T:* Kensington 7482. *Clubs:* Reform, Wellington.   *Died 19 Dec. 1925.*

MOULTON, Baron, *cr* 1912 (Life Peer); **John Fletcher Moulton,** GBE 1917; KCB 1915; Kt 1906; PC 1906; MA; FRS 1884; Lord of Appeal in Ordinary and Member of Judicial Committee of Privy Council since 1912; *b* Madeley, 18 Nov. 1844; *s* of Rev. James Egan Moulton, Wesleyan minister, and Catherine, *d* of William Fiddian; *m* 1st, 1875, Clara (*d* 1888), *widow* of Robert William Thompson, Edinburgh; one *s*; 2nd, 1901, Mary May (*d* 1909), *d* of Major Henry Davis, of the Villa Floridiana, Naples; one *d*. *Educ:* New Kingswood School, near Bath; London Univ. (BA 1865); St John's College, Cambridge (Scholar). Whilst undergraduate at Cambridge entered for various Math. Exams and carried all before him; was Senior Wrangler and first Smith's Prizeman, Cambridge, 1868; in the same year took gold medal for maths, London Univ.; Fellow of Christ's Coll., Cambridge, 1868; resigned Fellowship, and came to London, 1873; Barrister Middle Temple, 1874; QC 1885; Judge, Court of Appeal, 1906–12; Treasurer, Middle Temple, 1910; MP (L) Clapham Division, 1885–86; South Hackney, 1894–95; Launceston Div. of Cornwall, 1898–1906; Fellow and Member of Senate of University of London; member of the Royal Commission on Civil Service Superannuation, Gas, etc; member of the Superior Jury at the last Paris Exhibition, and first Chairman of the Medical Research Committee under the National Insurance Act; President of the Institution of Gas Engineers, 1917–18; Chairman Advisory Committee to Home Office for Administration of the Cruelty to Animals Act, 1876; of Committee on Chemical Products, 1914; of Committee on High Explosives, 1914; Director General of Explosive Supplies in Ministry of Munitions, since 1914; Hon. LLD Cambridge; Edinburgh, 1911; Commandeur de la Légion d'Honneur and Grand Officier de l'Ordre de l'Etoile Noire; Commandeur de l'Ordre de Léopold de Belgique; Grand Cordon Order of the White Eagle of Russia. *Address:* 57 Onslow Square, SW7; Forest Green, Bank,

Lyndhurst. *TA:* Snatcher, London. *T:* Ken. 720. *Clubs:* Athenæum, Garrick, Savage, Royal Automobile.
                                      Died 9 March 1921.

MOULTON, Rev. Prof. James Hope, MA, DLit, DD, DCL, DTheol; Greenwood Professor of Hellenistic Greek and Indo-European Philology, Manchester University, since 1908; Tutor Wesleyan College, Didsbury, since 1902; *b* 11 Oct. 1863; *s* of Rev. William Fiddian Moulton, MA, DD (member of the New Testament Revision Company), and Hannah, *d* of Rev. Samuel Hope; *nephew* of Baron Moulton, FRS, and Professor Richard Green Moulton; *m* 1890, Eliza Keeling (*d* 1915), *d* of Rev. G. R. Osborn; one *s* one *d* (and one *s* decd). *Educ:* The Leys School, Cambridge; King's College, Cambridge. First Class in Classical Tripos, 1884 and 1886, with distinction in Philology; Chancellor's Medal for English Poem, 1885; entered Wesleyan Ministry, 1886; Classical Master, The Leys Sch., Cambridge; Fellow of King's College, Cambridge, 1888–94; lecturer and frequently examiner in Classical Tripos, Part II; Classical Lecturer at Girton and Newnham Colleges, 1887–1901; Gold Medal in Classics, London, and DLit; Hon. DD Edinburgh, 1909—the same degree his father received, 1874; Hon. DCL Durham, 1910; Hon. DTheol Berlin (on occasion of its centenary), and Gröningen (at its tercentenary, 1914). *Publications:* Grammar of New Testament Greek, vol. i, Prolegomena, 1906, 3rd edition 1908 (translated into German, 1911, with considerable additions); article, Zoroastrianism, in Hastings' Dictionary of the Bible; Early Religious Poetry of Persia (Cambridge Manuals), 1911; Early Zoroastrianism (Hibbert Lectures, 1912), 1913; Religions and Religion (Fernley Lecture, 1913); Vocabulary of the Greek Testament, Parts I and II, 1914–15, with Prof. Milligan of Glasgow; The Teaching of Zarathushtra, 1917; The Treasure of the Magi; numerous papers in Expositor, Expository Times, Classical Review, etc. *Recreations:* tennis, golf. *Address:* Didsbury College, Manchester. *T:* Didsbury 85.
                                      Died 9 April 1917.

MOULTON, Richard Green; Professor (Emeritus) of Literary Theory and Interpretation, University of Chicago, USA, 1892–1919; *b* 1849; *y s* of late Rev. James Egan Moulton; *m* Alice Maud, *y d* of late Skelton Cole of Sheffield. *Educ:* New Kingswood School, Bath; Clevedon College, Northampton; Christ's College, Cambridge. BA and Exhibitioner, London University; MA and scholar of Christ's College, Cambridge, 1877; PhD University of Pennsylvania, 1891. Lecturer in Literature to Cambridge University (Extension), 1874–90; Lecturer to the American Society for Extension of Univ. Teaching, 1890–91; Lecturer to the London Society for Extension of Univ. Teaching, 1891–92. *Publications:* Shakespeare as a Dramatic Artist; The Ancient Classical Drama; The Literary Study of the Bible, 2nd edn, enlarged and partly rewritten, 1899; The Modern Reader's Bible, new edn, 1907; A Short Introduction to the Literature of the Bible, 1901; The Moral System of Shakespeare, 1903, republished 1907 under title, Shakespeare as a Dramatic Thinker; World Literature, and its Place in General Culture, 1911; The Modern Study of Literature, 1915; The Bible at a Single View, 1918; The Modern Reader's Bible for Schools: New Testament Volume, 1920; Old Testament Volume, 1922. *Recreations:* walking, music especially. *Address:* Hallamleigh, Frant Road, Tunbridge Wells. *T:* Tunbridge Wells 958.
                                      Died 15 Aug. 1924.

MOUNET, Jean Sully; Knight of Legion of Honour, 1889; *b* Bergerac, Dordogne, 27 Feb. 1841. *Educ:* Conservatoire. First prize tragic acting, 1868; *début* at Odéon, Paris, 1868; served War of 1870. *Publication:* (drama) La Buveuse de Larmes. *Address:* Rue Guy Lussac, 1 (V⁰) Paris.   *Died 1 May 1916.*

MOUNT EDGCUMBE, 4th Earl of, *cr* 1789; **William Henry Edgcumbe,** GCVO 1897; PC 1879; DL; Baron Edgcumbe of Mount Edgcumbe, Co. Cornwall (UK), 1742; Viscount Mount Edgcumbe and Valletort, 1781; Keeper of Privy Seal to the Prince of Wales since 1907; Lord-Lieutenant of Cornwall since 1877; Vice-Admiral of Cornwall; Member of the Council of the Duchy of Cornwall since 1889; *b* London, 5 Nov. 1832; *s* of 3rd Earl and Caroline Augusta, *e d* of Rear-Adm. Feilding; *S* father, 1861; *m* 1st, 1858, Lady Katherine Elizabeth Hamilton (*d* 1874), 4th *d* of 1st Duke of Abercorn; one *s* three *d;* 2nd, 1906, Caroline Cecilia (*d* 1909), *d* of Hon. George Edgcumbe, and *widow* of 3rd Earl of Ravensworth. *Educ:* Harrow; Christ Church, Oxford. MP (C) Plymouth, 1859–61; Equerry, 1858; and afterwards Lord-in-Waiting to the Prince of Wales; Lord Chamberlain in HM Household, 1879–80; Lord Steward in HM Household, 1885–86, 1886–92; Brig.-Gen. Plymouth Vol. Brigade, 1878–82; Hon. Col 2nd POW Vol. Batt. Devonshire Regt; ADC to Queen Victoria, 1887–97; Provincial Grand Master, Freemasons of Cornwall, since 1869. Church of England;

Conservative. *Heir: s* Viscount Valletort [*b* 2 July 1865; *m* 1911, Lady Edith Villiers, *o d* of 5th Earl of Clarendon]. *Recreations:* sketching, landscape gardening. *Address:* Mount Edgcumbe, Plymouth; 3 Lowndes Square, SW. *T:* Victoria 1256. *Clubs:* Carlton, Travellers', Marlborough; Royal Yacht Squadron, Cowes.

Died 25 Sept. 1917.

MOUNT STEPHEN, 1st Baron, *cr* 1891; **George Stephen,** GCVO 1905; DL; Bt 1886; *b* 5 June 1829; *s* of William Stephen, Dufftown, Banffshire, and Elspet, *d* of John Smith, Knockando, Co. of Elgin; *m* 1st, 1853, Annie Charlotte (*d* 1896), *d* of Benjamin Kane; 2nd, 1897, Gian, DBE, *d* of late Captain Robert George Tufnell, RN. Went to Canada, 1850; became Director, Vice-President, and President of Bank of Montreal; President St Paul and Manitoba Railway; became head of the Canadian Pacific Railway till 1888; Conservative; Presbyterian. *Heir:* none. *Address:* 17 Carlton House Terrace, SW; Brocket Hall, Hatfield, Hertfordshire; Grand Metis, Quebec, Canada. *Clubs:* Carlton, Arthur's. *Died 29 Nov. 1921 (ext).*

MOUNTBATTEN, Major Lord; Leopold Arthur Louis, GCVO 1915 (KCVO 1911); *b* 21 May 1889; *yr s* of Princess Beatrice and late Prince Henry of Battenberg. *Educ:* Magdalene College, Cambridge. Served European War, 1914-18 (despatches).

Died 23 April 1922.

MOUNTGARRET, 15th Viscount (Ireland), *cr* 1550; **Edmund Somerset Butler;** Baron, 1911; *b* 1 Feb. 1875; *e s* of 14th Viscount Mountgarret and 1st wife, Mary Eleanor, *d* of St John Chiverton Charlton of Apley Castle, Shropshire; *S* father, 1912; *m* 1897, Cecily, *d* of late Arthur Grey, Sutton Hall, Easingwold. Owned about 14,700 acres. *Heir: half brother* Hon. Piers Henry Augustine Butler, *b* 28 Aug. 1903. *Address:* Nidd Hall, Yorks; Ballyconra, Kilkenny.

Died 22 June 1918.

MOWAT, Robert Anderson; *b* 1843; *o s* of late Joseph Mowat, Edinburgh; *m* 1871, Jessie (*d* 1922), *d* of late Thomas Clarkson, Edinburgh. *Educ:* Church of Scotland Normal School, Edinburgh; School of Arts, Edin.; University College, London. Passed a competitive examination and was appointed a Student Interpreter on the China Consular Establishment, 1864; Acting Interpreter at HBM's Consulate in Hankow during part of 1866; Acting Law Secretary of HBM's Supreme Court for China and Japan at Shanghai, 1867-68, when appointed to substantive post; called to Bar, Inner Temple, 1871; Acting Assistant Judge of the Supreme Court, 1876-78; Acting Judge, 1878; Assistant Judge and Registrar, 1878; Acting Chief Justice, 1879, 1881 and 1888-89; Judge of HBM's Court for Japan, April 1891, but remained, at the request of the Secretary of State, at Shanghai as Acting Chief Justice and Acting Consul-General till Oct. 1891, when he took up his post in Japan; retired on a pension, 1897. *Address:* 10 Grand Avenue Mansions, Hove. *T:* Hove 8853. *Died 7 June 1925.*

MOWATT, Rt. Hon. Sir Francis, GCB 1901 (KCB 1893; CB 1884); ISO 1902; PC 1906; a member of the Royal Commission of 1851; *b* 27 April 1837; *o s* of Francis Mowatt (formerly MP for Falmouth, and Cambridge) and Sarah Sophia, *d* of Captain Barnes, EIC Marine Service; *m* 1864, Lucy (*d* 1896), *d* of Andreas Frerichs, Cheltenham, and *widow* of Count Stenbock, of Kolk, Esthonia; three *s* three *d*. *Educ:* Winchester; St John's College, Oxford. Entered HM Treasury, 1856; Permanent Secretary to the Treasury, 1894-1903. *Address:* 41 Sloane Gardens, SW1. *T:* Victoria 5831. *Clubs:* Reform, Athenæum.

Died 20 Nov. 1919.

MOWBRAY, Rev. Sir Edmund George Lionel, 4th Bt, *cr* 1880; MA; *b* Mortimer, Berks, 26 June 1859; *s* of late Rt Hon. Sir John Robert Mowbray, 1st Bt, and Elizabeth Gray, *d* of George Isaac Mowbray, Mortimer, Bucks. *S* brother, 1916; *m* 1891, Caroline Elwes, *d* of late Gen. George T. Field, RA; one *s*. *Educ:* Eton; New College, Oxford (BA 1882; MA 1885). Deacon, 1883; Priest, 1884; Assistant Curate, St John the Evangelist, Westminster, 1883-86; travelled in America and South Africa, 1886-87; Curate, St Bartholomew's, Dover, 1887-90; Rector of Durley, Hants, 1890-92; Vicar of St Bartholomew's, Dover, 1892-1906; Licensed Preacher in Diocese of Ripon, 1906-8; Vicar of Freeland, Oxon, 1908-9; Vicar of St Michael's and All Angels, Brighton, 1909-17. *Heir: s* George Robert Mowbray, *b* 15 July 1899. *Address:* Warennes Wood, Mortimer, Berks. *Died 2 Feb. 1919.*

MOWBRAY, Major John Leslie, DSO 1915; Royal Artillery; *b* 19 July 1875. Entered army, 1900; Captain, 1911; Staff Captain, Headquarters India, 1909-13; Brigade-Major, 1914; served European War, 1914-15 (DSO). *Died 24 July 1916.*

MOWBRAY, Sir Reginald Ambrose, 3rd Bt, *cr* 1880; *b* 5 April 1852; *s* of Rt Hon. Sir John Robert Mowbray, 1st Bt and Elizabeth Gray, *d* of George Isaac Mowbray of Mortimer, Berks; *S* brother, 1916. *Educ:* Christ Church, Oxford (MA). *Heir: brother* Edmund George Lionel Mowbray [*b* 26 June 1859; *m* 1891, Caroline Elwes, *d* of Gen. George T. Field, Royal Artillery; one *s*]. *Address:* 90 Piccadilly, W; Warennes Wood, Mortimer, Berks.

Died 30 Dec. 1916.

MOWBRAY, Sir Robert Gray Cornish, 2nd Bt, *cr* 1880; JP, DL; Chairman of Quarter Sessions and Chairman of the County Council for Berkshire; *b* London, 21 May 1850; *e s* of Rt Hon. Sir John Robert Mowbray, 1st Bt and Elizabeth Gray, *d* of George Isaac Mowbray of Mortimer, Berks; *S* father, 1899. *Educ:* Eton; Balliol Coll., Oxford (1st class Final Classical Schools, 1872; MA 1875). Fellow of All Souls, 1873; President Oxford Union Society, 1873; Barrister, Inner Temple, 1876; went on the Oxford Circuit; Secretary to Royal Commission on Stock Exchange, 1877-78; contested Whitby, 1880, and Prestwich Div. of SE Lancs, 1885; MP (C) Prestwich Division of SE Lancashire, 1886-95, and Brixton Division of Lambeth, 1900-6; Parliamentary Private Secretary to Chancellor of Exchequer (George Joachim Goschen, later 1st Viscount Goschen), 1887-92; member of Royal Commn on Opium, 1893-95, of Royal Commn on Indian Expenditure, 1896; member of Court of the Goldsmiths' Company; Prime Warden, 1898-99 and 1914-15; director of University Life Assurance Society. *Recreation:* travelling. *Heir: brother* Reginald Ambrose Mowbray [*b* 5 April 1852. *Educ:* Christ Church, Oxford (MA)]. *Address:* 90 Piccadilly, W; Warennes Wood, Mortimer, Berks. *Clubs:* Athenæum, Carlton, Oxford and Cambridge.

Died 23 July 1916.

MOXON, Col Charles Carter, CMG 1916; DSO 1918; Hon. Colonel 5th Battalion Yorkshire Light Infantry (Territorial Force); *b* 1866; *s* of Richard Moxon, Pontefract; *m* 1904, Lucia Percival. *Educ:* Edinburgh Acad. MRCS, LRCP. Served S African War, 1900-1 (Queen's medal, 3 clasps); European War, 1914-18 (despatches, CMG, DSO). *Address:* Monk Fyston Lodge, South Milford SO. *T:* South Milford 4. *Died 20 March 1924.*

MOXON, Ven. Robert Julius; Archdeacon of Grafton, since 1897. Ordained, 1888; Vicar of Lower Clarence, 1888-92; Tenterfield, 1892-95; Inverell, 1895-96. *Address:* The Vicarage, Grafton, NSW.

MOYERS, Sir George, Kt 1887; DL (Dublin); JP Co. Dublin; LLD; *b* 11 May 1836; *s* of William Moyers, Fortfield House; *m* 1st, 1857, Ada Constance (*d* 1885), *d* of Peter Lambert, of Castle Ellen, Co. Galway; two *s* five *d;* 2nd, 1904, Lily Pakenham, *widow* of Thomas Aiskew Mooney, LLD. *Educ:* Bellevue House, Bristol; Trinity Coll., Dublin (BA 1856; LLB). Architect, civil engineer, and surveyor, first in London and subsequently in Dublin; Lord Mayor, 1881; entertained Earl Cowper Lord-Lieut (of Ireland, 1880-82) and Countess Cowper at Mansion House, Dublin, this being the last occasion upon which the representatives of the Sovereign were received there; opened the South City Markets to the public; Commissioner of Pembroke Township, 1869-1901; Chairman of Board, 1887-92; life Governor of the King's Hospital, Mercers' Hospital, the Meath Hospital and Co. Dublin Infirmary, the Old Men's Asylum, Dublin. *Recreations:* cricket, rifle shooting, yachting. *Address:* 27 Belgrave Square, Monkstown, Co. Dublin. *Clubs:* Junior Carlton, Constitutional; Leinster, Dublin. *Died 4 Nov. 1916.*

MOYES, William Henry; writer. Assistant editor of The Lady for four years; sub-editor on the Morning Post for three years, after having had charge of special editions; and Editor of The Local Government Journal and Officials Gazette for four years; contributed articles for many years on home, foreign, colonial, Parliamentary, and other problems to the daily and weekly Press, monthly magazines, etc. *Publications:* The God Stone; When Least Expected; The Mormon's Daughter; The Mystic's Legacy; Quest of the Twin Soul; and other novels and serial stories; The Beauties and Antiquities of Wiltshire; Cycling Tours on the Continent; Haunted Surrey; Superstitions of the Year; How to Succeed in Parliament; Oratory and Debating Skill at St Stephen's; Local Government in Parliament; The Mystery of Christ's Divine Humanity, etc. *Recreations:* cycling, cricket. *Address:* 3 Kenilworth Gardens, Southbourne Grove, Westcliff-on-Sea.

Died 22 Jan. 1926.

MOYSE, Charles E.; Molson Professor of English Literature, McGill University, Montreal, 1878-1920; Dean of the Faculty of Arts and Vice-Principal of McGill University, 1903-20; *b* Torquay, 9 March 1852; *s* of Charles W. Moyse and Mary Anne, *d* of John Jenkins of Exeter; *m* Janet McDougall, *d* of John Stirling of Montreal; two *s*.

Educ: Independent College, Taunton; University College, London. BA (London), 1874; Exhibitioner in English, 1st BA (1872); prizeman in Animal Physiology, 2nd BA (1874). Hon. President St James' Literary Society, Montreal; President Devonian Society of Montreal; LLD (Hon.) McGill, 1903; made an Honorary Freeman of the Borough of Torquay, July 1921; Editor, McGill University Magazine, 1901–5. *Publications:* The Dramatic Art of Shakespeare, 1879; Poetry as a Fine Art, 1883; Shakespeare's Skull (under the pseudonym of Belgrave Titmarsh), 1889; Ella Lee (verse), 1910; The Lure of Earth (verse), 1911; verse and literary articles in serial literature. *Address:* 324 Sherbrooke Street, West, Montreal. *T:* Uptown 3125. *Clubs:* University of London; University, Montreal.

Died July 1924.

MOYSEY, Maj.-Gen. Charles (John), CMG 1884; Royal Engineers (retired); *b* 12 June 1840; *s* of Rev. Frederick Luttrell Moysey and Arabella, *niece* of 3rd Viscount Bangor; *m* 1873, Frances Henrietta, 2nd *d* of Sir Peter Benson Maxwell; one *s* two *d*. *Educ:* Cheltenham Coll. Entered army, 1857; Maj.-Gen., 1897; served Zulu War, 1879, including Ulundi (despatches, Brevet Lieut-Col, medal with clasp); Assistant Inspector-General of Fortifications at headquarters, 1884–89; commanding RE Thames District, 1889–94. *Address:* Bathealton Court, Wiveliscombe, Somerset.

Died 14 Sept. 1922.

MOYSEY, Henry Luttrell, ISO 1903; FRCI; retired as Postmaster-General and Director of Telegraphs, 1906; *b* 10 Dec. 1849; *s* of late Rev. Frederick Luttrell Moysey of Bathealton Court, Wiveliscombe, Somerset; *m* 1875, Dora Kathleen, *d* of William Hervey O'Grady, JP, of Batticaloa, Ceylon; two *s* one *d*. *Educ:* Cheltenham College. Entered Ceylon Civil Service, 1870. *Address:* Cresswell House, Bexhill-on-Sea. *TA:* Loutre, Bexhill-on-Sea. *T:* 470 Bexhill.

Died 15 Aug. 1918.

MUDDIMAN, Sir Alexander Phillips, KCSI 1926 (CSI 1920); Kt 1922; CIE 1913; Governor of United Provinces of Agra and Oudh since 1927; Home Member of Executive Council of Governor-General and Leader of the Assembly, 1924–27; *b* 14 Feb. 1875; *s* of Alexander Phillips Muddiman, bookseller and publisher, and Anne Griffiths. *Educ:* Wimborne School. Entered Indian Civil Service, 1897; served in Behar in various capacities; Under-Secretary to the Government of Bengal, 1903; Registrar of the High Court at Fort William, 1905; Additional Member Legislative Council, 1915; Secretary to the Government of India Legislative Department, 1915–21; Officiating Law Member, 1919; President of the Council of State, India, 1920–24. *Address:* Governor's Camp, United Provinces, India. *Clubs:* Oriental, Travellers'.

Died 17 June 1928.

MUDFORD, W. H.; *b* 1839; *s* of proprietor of Kentish Observer and Canterbury Journal. Late editor and manager of The Standard; resigned editorship in 1900. *Recreations:* cycling, shooting, travel. *Address:* Westcombe Lodge, Wimbledon Common, SW. *Clubs:* Carlton, Junior Carlton. *Died 18 Oct. 1916.*

MUDHOLKAR, Hon. Rao Bahadur Rangnath Narsinh, CIE 1914; BA, LLB; President, Indian National Congress, 1912; Advocate Central Provinces and Berar; President Amraoti City Municipality; Member Central Provinces Legislative Council since 1914; *b* Bombay Presidency, 16 May 1857. *Educ:* Dhulia High School; Elphinstone College, Bombay (Fellow). Vakeel Bombay High Court; Secretary Indian Industrial Conference (President, 1908); Delegate of Indian National Congress to England, 1890; Chairman of several factories and commercial concerns; Member Imperial Legislative Council, 1910–12. *Address:* Amraoti, India.

Died Jan. 1921.

MUDIE-SMITH, Richard; journalist, editorial staff of Daily Chronicle; *b* 1877; *s* of Samuel Smith, of Seamer, Yorks, and Susan Elizabeth, *d* of James Mudie, of Arbroath, NB; *m* 1904, Mabel Wesley, *y d* of Edwin Hunt, *g g g d* of Charles Wesley; one *s*. *Educ:* Kent College, Canterbury. Fellow of the Royal Statistical Society. Assistant editor of Examiner, 1901; on staff of Daily News, 1902–6, and 1910–12; assistant editor of Nation, 1907; editor of the London Missionary Society's publications, 1907–9; organised and superintended a census of Public Worship in London and Greater London on behalf of the Daily News, 1902–3; organised an exhibition of Sweated Home Industries of the United Kingdom for the same paper, 1906, which resulted in the passing of the Trade Boards Act. *Publications:* The Religious Life of London; Thoughts for the Day; Sweated Industries; The Heart of Things: Passages from the Writings of F. W. Robertson; (with H. R. A.) The Lost Homes of England.

Address: 62 Rotherwick Road, Hampstead Garden Suburb, NW. *T:* 1539 Finchley. *Club:* National Liberal.

Died 23 Feb. 1916.

MUHRMAN, Henry; *b* Cincinnati, Ohio, 21 Jan. 1854; of German parentage; *m* 1880 (wife *d* 1900). *Educ:* The Cincinnati Public Schools. At the age of 15 became a lithographer; left Cincinnati, 1876 to study Art at Munich; returned to America, 1878; was elected a member of the New York Water-Colour Society and Society of American Artists; settled in London, 1883; painted mostly at Hampstead Heath and Kew Bridge; elected member of the International Society of Sculptors, Painters and Gravers, and the Pastel Society, London, also of the Secession Societies in Munich and in Berlin; represented in the Galleries of Dublin and Munich (Pinakothek), and largely in important private collections; received medals of the Munich Academy of Fine Arts, 1877; Chicago Universal Exposition, 1893; gold medals at the Munich (1897) and Dresden (1901) International Exhibitions; also gold medal at the St Louis Universal Exposition, 1904. *Address:* The Goupil Gallery, 5 Regent Street, SW.

Died 30 Aug. 1916.

MUIR, Col Charles Wemyss, CB 1902; CIE 1887; *b* 12 April 1850; *s* of Sir William Muir, KCSI, and Elizabeth, *d* of James Wemyss, BCS; *m* 1883, Alice, *d* of Horace Abel Cockerell, CSI; one *s* one *d*. Entered army, 1869; Lieut-Col 1895; Col 1899; served Afghan War, 1880 (medal); Soudan, 1885 (despatches, medal with two clasps, Khedive's star); Burmah, 1885–87 (medal with clasp); Tirah, 1897–98 (despatches, medal, three clasps); European War. *Address:* Cox Green, near Maidenhead. *Club:* United Service.

Died 27 Dec. 1920.

MUIR, Rt. Rev. Pearson M'Adam, DD; Minister of Glasgow Cathedral, 1896–1915 (retired); Chaplain in Ordinary to King George V in Scotland since 1910; Acting Chaplain 8th Scottish Rifles; *b* Kirkmabreck Manse, Kirkcudbrightshire, 26 Jan. 1846; *y s* of Rev. John Muir, Minister of Kirkmabreck, and Gloriana M'Adam, *d* of John Pearson, Springhill, Muirkirk; *m* 1871, Sophia Anne (*d* 1907), *y d* of Very Rev. James Chrystal, DD, LLD (Minister of Auchinleck, and Moderator in 1879 of the Gen. Assembly of the Church of Scotland); two *s* three *d*. *Educ:* Kirkmabreck; Glasgow High School and University. Ordained and became Minister of Catrine, Ayrshire, in 1870; Minister of Polmont, Stirlingshire, in 1872; Minister of Morningside, Edinburgh, in 1880; Secretary of Church Service Society, 1888–1907; Convener of Colonial Committee, 1892–97; Lecturer on Pastoral Theology in Universities of Edinburgh and St Andrews, 1895–96, 1903–4, 1905–6; and in Universities of Aberdeen and Glasgow, 1896–97, 1902–3, 1904–5; Moderator of the General Assembly of Church of Scotland, 1910–11. *Publications:* Samuel Rutherford (in the St Giles' Lectures on Scottish Divines, 1881–82); The Church of Scotland: A Sketch of its History, 1890; Monuments and Inscriptions in Glasgow Cathedral (in Book of Glasgow Cathedral, edited by G. E. Todd), 1898; Religious Writers of England, 1901; Modern Substitutes for Christianity (Baird Lecture), 1909; Seventh Jubilee of the General Assembly, 1910. *Address:* West Manse, Cambuslang, Lanarkshire. *Died 13 July 1924.*

MUIR, Sir Richard David, Kt 1918; a Bencher of the Middle Temple since 1909; Recorder of Colchester since 1911; *b* 1857; *s* of late Richard Muir and Anne Burleigh, of Greenock; *m* 1889, Mary Beatrice, *d* of late William Leycester (barrister-at-law, and chief of the Times Parliamentary corps); one *s* one *d*. *Educ:* King's College, London. Was engaged on Times staff, Press Gallery, House of Commons; called to Bar, Middle Temple, 1884; Counsel to the Treasury at the North London Sessions; Junior Counsel to the Treasury at the Old Bailey; a Senior Counsel to the Treasury, 1901; Senior Treasury Counsel at Central Criminal Court, 1908. *Address:* 30 Campden House Court, W8. *T:* Park 504; 3 Temple Gardens, EC4. *Club:* Garrick. *Died 14 Jan. 1924.*

MUIR, Ward; author and journalist; *b* 1878; *s* of Rev. J. J. Muir; *m* Dorothea Lang; one *d*. *Educ:* Merchant Taylors', Crosby; Brighton College. *Publications:* novels, essays, and magazine contributions. *Recreations:* landscape photography, trout-fishing. *Address:* 44 Mecklenburgh Square, WC1. *T:* Museum 6972. *Clubs:* Savage, Camera, Whitefriars. *Died 9 June 1927.*

MUIR-MACKENZIE, Sir John William Pitt, KCSI 1909 (CSI 1906); Indian Civil Service, retired; *b* 19 March 1854; 6th *s* of Sir John William Pitt Muir-Mackenzie, 2nd Bt, of Delvine, Dunkeld, Perthshire, NB, and Sophia Matilda, *d* of James Raymond Johnstone, Alva; *m* 1st, 1876, Frances Louisa (*d* 1895), *d* of Lt-Gen. Montague Cholmeley Johnstone; two *s* two *d* (and one *d* decd); 2nd, 1898, Rhoda (*d* 1900), *d* of William Watson, Oxon; 3rd, 1904, Marie Thérèse, *e d* of Henry Windsor Villiers Stuart, Dromana, Cappoquin, Co. Waterford, Ireland. *Educ:* Eton, 1866–69; private tuition; Rev. Alfred Green, St David's, Pembrokeshire. Passed exam. into Indian Civil Service, 1874; served in India, 1876; deputed to study agriculture at the Royal Agricultural College, Cirencester, 1883 (Member, Royal Agricultural College); to Reunion and Mauritius in connection with coolie labour questions, 1893; was Under Secretary and officiated as Secretary to the Govt of India in the Revenue and Agricultural Depts; subsequently Director of Agriculture; Chief Sec. to the Govt of Bombay and Commissioner in Sind; Member of Indian Irrigation Commission; Member of the Executive Council of the Government of Bombay, 1905–10; temporary Governor, 1907; retired from ICS, 1910; MRAS (by examination). *Recreations:* golf, music. *Address:* 22 Draycott Place, SW. *T:* Kensington 1153. *Clubs:* East India United Service; Byculla, West of India, Bombay.

Died 25 Oct. 1916.

MUIR-MACKENZIE, Montague Johnstone; Official Referee since 1905; *b* 29 Sept. 1847; 5th *s* of Sir John William Pitt Muir-Mackenzie, 2nd Bt, of Delvine, Perthshire, and Sophia Matilda, *d* of James Raymond Johnstone, Alva, NB; *m* 1888, Hon. Sarah Napier Bruce, *d* of 1st Baron Aberdare; one *d*. *Educ:* Charterhouse; Brasenose College, Oxford (Scholar; 1st class in Moderations and Final Schools). Fellow of Hertford Coll., Oxford, 1874–88; Barrister, 1873; Secretary to Lord Chief-Justice Coleridge, 1873–77; Recorder of Deal, 1892; Recorder of Sandwich and Bencher of the Middle Temple, 1894; Standing Counsel to the Board of Trade, and other public bodies; Hon. Sec. of the Royal College of Music. *Publications:* Mackenzie on Bills of Lading; Chalmers and Mackenzie on the Judicature Acts; Mackenzie and Lushington on the Laws of Registration; Mackenzie and Clarke on the Bankruptcy Acts; Notes on the Temple Organ. *Address:* 21 Hyde Park Gate, SW; Royal Courts of Justice, WC. *Clubs:* United University, National, Ranelagh.

Died 18 April 1919.

MUIR-MACKENZIE, Sir Robert Cecil, 5th Bt, *cr* 1805; Lieutenant 5th Battalion Durham Light Infantry; *b* 17 Oct. 1891; *o s* of Lt-Col Sir Robert Smythe Muir-Mackenzie, 4th Bt and Anne Elizabeth Augusta, *d* of Captain Charles Kinnaird Johnstone Gordon, Aberdeenshire; *S* father, 1918; *m* 1914, Kate Brenda Blodwen, *d* of late Henry Jones, Cardiff; one *s*. *Heir:* s Robert Henry Muir-Mackenzie, *b* 6 Jan. 1917. *Died 12 April 1918.*

MUIR-MACKENZIE, Lt-Col Sir Robert Smythe, 4th Bt, *cr* 1805; late Royal Artillery; *b* 27 Nov. 1841; 2nd *s* of Sir John William Pitt Muir-Mackenzie, 2nd Bt, and Sophia Matilda, 5th *d* of James Raymond Johnstone of Alva, Clackmannan; *S* brother, 1909; *m* 1872, Anne Elizabeth Augusta (*d* 1908), *d* of Captain Charles Kinnaird Johnstone Gordon of Craig, Aberdeenshire; one *s* two *d* (and one *d* decd). *Heir:* s Robert Cecil Muir-Mackenzie [*b* 17 Oct. 1891; *m* 1914, Kate Brenda Blodwen, *d* of late Henry Jones, Cardiff; one *s*]. *Address:* Marldon House, Paignton.

Died 2 Feb. 1918.

MUIRHEAD, Alexander, DSc (London); FRS. *Address:* The Lodge, Shortlands, Kent. *TA:* Muirheads, London. *T:* Bromley 750.

Died 13 Dec. 1920.

MUIRHEAD, John, RBA, RSW; *b* Edinburgh, 1863; 2nd *s* of John Muirhead, architect and builder; *m* Margaret Neale, *e d* of James Cooper, dentist, Edinburgh. *Educ:* Royal High School, Edinburgh. Commenced studies at Board of Manufacturers' School, Edinburgh, 1880; exhibited first pictures, Royal Scottish Acad., 1881, and afterwards painted a great deal in France, Belgium and Holland; exhibited Royal Acad., Royal Inst. of Painters in Water Colours, New English Art Club, Liverpool, Manchester, International Rome, Pittsburg USA, Munich, Dresden, and many other art centres; illustrated Hilaire Belloc's River of London. *Publication:* Photogravure of picture, Declining Day and Ebbing Tide. *Recreations:* fishing, cycling. *Address:* 148 Gipsy Hill, SE19; Monument Cottage, Houghton, Hunts. *Club:* The Three Arts.

Died 21 Nov. 1927.

MULCAHY, Hon. Edward; twice Minister of Lands, Works, and Mines, Tasmania; Commonwealth Senate, 1903–10 and 1919–20; *b* Limerick, 28 March 1850. Went to Tasmania, 1854. *Educ:* primary schools, Hobart. *Address:* Tara, Melville Street, Hobart, Tasmania.

Died 23 Oct. 1927.

MULES, Rt. Rev. Charles Oliver, DD; *b* 1837; *s* of Rev. J. H. Mules, Vicar of Ilminster; *m* 1870, Laura (*d* 1925), *d* of Capt. F. H. Blundell,

Nelson; three *s* one *d*. *Educ:* Cheltenham; Trinity Coll., Cambridge (Senior Optime; MA). Ordained, 1864; Archdeacon of Waimea; Bishop of Nelson, New Zealand, 1892–1912. *Address:* 25 Trafalgar Square, Nelson, New Zealand.

Died 9 Oct. 1927.

MULHOLLAND, Rosa; *see* Gilbert, Rosa, (Lady Gilbert).

MULJI, Rao Sahib Sir Vasanji Trikamji, Kt 1911; JP; Hon. Magistrate; Member Bombay Cotton Exchange; Member Bombay Panjrapole, etc; *b* 8 July 1866.

Died 12 Jan. 1925.

MULLEN, Benjamin Henry, MA; Director of Museums and Libraries, Salford, since 1892; *b* Dublin, 19 Jan. 1862; *s* of late Benjamin Mullen, Warrenpoint, Clontarf; *m* Essie, *d* of late Henry Gibson, JP, Ardnardeen, Clontarf. *Educ:* Bective College, Dublin; Foyle Coll., Londonderry; Trinity Coll., Dublin (Mus. Ex.; BA 1884; MA 1887). Assistant in Art and Ethnographical Department, National Museum of Ireland, Dublin, 1884–92; Lecturer on Manchester University Extension Staff, Lecturer under the Ogden Trust; Freeman of City of Dublin. *Publications:* numerous articles on art, archæology, and ethnography. *Address:* Royal Museum and Libraries, Peel Park, Salford. *Died 23 Oct. 1925.*

MULLER, W. Max, PhD (Leipsic); Professor of Exegesis at the Religious Education Seminary, Philadelphia, since 1890; Assistant Professor of Egyptology, University of Pennsylvania; *b* Gleissenberg, Bavaria, 15 May 1862; *s* of F. Müller, teacher; *brother* of Dr Ernst Müller, politician and member German Reichstag; *m* 1889; two *s* one *d*. *Educ:* Gymnasium of Nürnberg; studied at Universities of Erlangen, Leipsic, Berlin, Munich (theology, classical and Oriental philology; one of the last students of G. Ebers, the Egyptologist). Went to America, 1888; lived at New York; visited the Orient, 1900, etc; chief studies: points of contact between Egyptology and the Bible; African languages. *Publications:* Asien und Europa nach den ägyptischen Denkmälern, 1893; Die Liebespoesie der alten Agypter, 1899; Egyptian Mythology, 1918; Egyptological Researches, 1906–, for the Carnegie Institution, Washington, etc. *Recreations:* bicycling, other exercise. *Address:* 4325 Sansom Street, Philadelphia, Pa, USA.

Died 12 July 1919.

MULLINGER, James Bass, BA; late University Lecturer in History, Cambridge; Emeritus Librarian and Lecturer in History, St John's College, Cambridge; late President Cambridge Antiquarian Society; *b* Bishop Stortford, Herts; 2nd *s* of John Morse Mullinger and Mary, 2nd *d* of Rev. James Bass. *Educ:* University College; St John's College, Cambridge (MA). Graduated in double honours (third class in Classical Tripos, and second class in Moral Sciences), 1866; Le Bas Prizeman, 1866; Hulsean, 1867; Kaye, 1875. Lecturer at Bedford Coll., London, 1881–83; Lecturer to Teachers' Training Syndicate at Cambridge on History of Education, 1885–95; Birkbeck Lecturer on Ecclesiastical History to Trinity Coll., Cambridge, 1890–94; Hon. LittD Cambridge. *Publications:* Cambridge Characteristics in the Seventeenth Century, 1867; The Ancient African Church, 1869; The New Reformation, 1875 (a narrative of the Old Catholic Movement, by "Theodorus"); The Schools of Charles the Great, 1876; The University of Cambridge from the Earliest Times of the Decline of the Platonist Movement, 3 Vols, 1873–1911, Vol. IV, 1916; An Introduction to English History (in conjunction with late S. R. Gardiner), 1881, 1883, 1894, 1903; The Age of Milton (with Canon Masterman), 7th edn, 1913; History of St John's College, Cambridge, 1901; also numerous historical articles in Encyclopædia Britannica, Dictionary of Christian Antiquities, Dictionary of National Biography, Encyclopædia of Religion and Ethics, Cambridge Modern History, and History of English Literature. *Recreations:* architecture, visiting places of historic interest, chess. *Address:* St John's College, and 68 Lensfield Road, Cambridge.

Died 22 Nov. 1917.

MULLINS, Major Charles Herbert, VC 1900; CMG 1900; Imperial Light Horse; barrister; *s* of Canon Mullins; *m* 1902, Norah Gertrude, *d* of S. Haslam, Brooklands, Uppingham; two *s* one *d*. Served South Africa, 1900 (despatches, VC, CMG). Decorated for gallantry at Elandslaagte. *Address:* Enduline, Parktown, Johannesburg.

Died 23 May 1916.

MULLINS, Lt-Col George Lane; Australian Army Medical Corps; Officer Commanding No 4 Australian General Hospital; Hon. Organising Secretary, Red Cross Society, New South Wales Division; Red Cross Director, New South Wales; Hon. Consulting Physician, St Vincent's Hospital, Sydney; Hon. Director, Department of Special

Therapeutics, Sydney Hospital, etc; *b* Sydney, 24 Aug. 1862; *s* of late James Mullins, JP, of Sydney, and Elizabeth Lane; *m* 1891, Mary Ellen, *d* of late Patrick Burke, JP, of Orange, NSW; four *s*. *Educ:* St Mary's College, Lyndhurst, Sydney; Sydney Grammar School; Dublin University (MA, MD). Filled positions at St Vincent's Hospital, Sydney, of Assistant Physician, Hon. Physician, Consulting Physician and Medical Officer in charge of Electro-Therapeutic Department; held following positions in Commonwealth Military Forces— Adjutant, Staff Officer Medical Services, Acting PMO, Chief Instructor Officers' School of Instruction, Examiner in Military Sanitation, etc; Deputy Chairman, Lecturer, Examiner, St John Ambulance Association, NSW; was Commissioner, St John Ambulance Brigade in the Commonwealth (10 years); Knight of Grace, Order of St John of Jerusalem in England; Conspicuous Service Medal, Order of St John; Life Member Red Cross Society of Japan; Consulting Medical Officer, Consulate-General of France (NSW); Vice-President Inter-colonial Medical Congress, 1896, 1899; travelled extensively in Europe. *Publications:* History of Smallpox and Vaccination in New South Wales, 1898; A Course of First Aid, 3rd edn 1914; Camps and Camp Hygiene, 1908; Medical Electricity, 1915. *Recreations:* Red Cross work, motoring. *Address:* 205 Macquarie Street, Sydney; St Meldan's, Rose Bay, Sydney. *Club:* University, Sydney.   *Died 20 March 1918.*

MUMMERY, John Howard, CBE 1920; DSc (Penn), LDS FRCS; retired; *b* 18 Jan. 1847; *s* of John R. Mummery, late of 10 Cavendish Place, W; *m* 1st, 1873, (Mary) Lily, *d* of Dr William Lockhart, Shanghai and Blackheath; 2nd, 1907, Lilian B., *e d* of Thomas Parker, Nottingham; three *s* two *d*. *Educ:* University College and Hospital, London. Examiner Dental Board of the United Kingdom; late Lecturer on Bacteriology at Royal Dental Hospital; member of the committee on the causes of dental disease of the Medical Research Council; Honorary Fellow Royal Society of Medicine. *Publications:* The Microscopic Anatomy of the Teeth; several papers in the Philosophical Trans of the Royal Society, especially on the distribution of nerves to the dentine. *Recreation:* golf. *Address:* 79 Albert Bridge Road, SW11. *T:* Latchmere 4065.

Died 30 Aug. 1926.

MUNCASTER, 5th Baron, *cr* 1783; **Josslyn Francis Pennington,** VD; Bt 1676; Baron UK 1898; Lord Lieutenant, County of Cumberland since 1876; Hon. Colonel Cumberland Volunteers; *b* Hamilton Place, London, 25 Dec. 1834; *s* of 3rd Baron Muncaster and Frances Catherine, *y d* of Sir John Ramsden, 4th Bt; *S* brother, 1862; *m* 1863, Constance Ann, *d* of Edmund L'Estrange, Tynte, Co. Sligo. *Educ:* Hatfield private school; Eton. Army, Capt. 90th Light Infantry; served in Crimea, 1854–56; in trenches and two attacks on Redan and storming party (medal and clasp, Turkish medal); afterwards Capt. Rifle Brigade; late Col East York Militia; late Lieut in Yorkshire Hussars; MP (C) W Cumberland, 1872–80, and Egremont Div. of Cumberland, 1885–92; Protestant; Conservative; owned about 15,000 acres, and minerals in Lancashire. *Recreation:* country life. *Heir:* none. *Address:* Muncaster Castle, Cumberland. *Clubs:* Army and Navy, Carlton.   *Died 30 March 1917 (ext).*

MUNDAY, Luther; *b* 1857; *m d* of General English, CB. *Educ:* by his father, a schoolmaster. Planter and estate owner, Ceylon, 1878–84; Member of Executive Committee, People's Palace, 1887; Secretary Lyric Club, 1887–93; founder Green Park Club, and others; produced 43 plays, and organised 400 charitable and other entertainments; director of two London theatres, and acted as manager-in-chief to Sir Charles Wyndham and Sir Herbert Beerbohm Tree; Delegate on Board of Governors Waterloo Hospital; Hon. Treasurer Animals' Hospital; Lecturer, and Member of First Committee, Shakespeare Memorial National Theatre; cartoon artist and sculptor. *Recreation:* doing nothing. *Publication:* A Chronicle of Friendships. *Address:* 37 Half Moon Street, W; Littlewick Green, Berks. *T:* Littlewick Green 13. *Club:* Isthmian.   *Died 29 March 1922.*

MUNDY, Alfred Edward Miller, JP; *b* 28 Nov. 1849; *o s* of late Alfred Miller Mundy and Jane, 2nd *d* of late Rear-Admiral Sir John Hindmarsh, KH; *m* 1st, 1873, Ellen Mary (whom he divorced, 1881; she *m* 2nd 1882, 20th Earl of Shrewsbury), *y d* of late Charles Rowland Palmer-Morewood, Alfreton Hall, Co. Derby; one *d*; 2nd, 1883, Catharine Louisa, 3rd *d* of Sir John William Cradock-Hartopp, 4th Bt; one *s* three *d*. *Educ:* Christ Church, Oxford. High Sheriff, Derby, 1891. *Address:* Shipley Hall, Derby. *Club:* Royal Yacht Squadron, Cowes.   *Died 15 April 1920.*

MUNDY, Admiral Godfrey Harry Brydges, CB 1917; DSO 1919; MVO 1903; *b* 11 Aug. 1860; *e s* of Maj.-Gen. Pierrepont Henry Mundy; *m* 1890, Rose, 9th *d* of late Sir Robert Miller Mundy, KCMG;

one *s* one *d*. Entered Royal Navy 1873; Commander, 1896; Captain, 1902; Rear-Adm. 1912; Vice-Adm. 1917; Adm. 1920; served Egyptian War, 1882 (medal, Khedive's bronze star); Admiral Superintendent Pembroke Dockyard, 1908–11, Devonport Dockyard, 1913–16; retired, 1917; Vice-Admiral North Atlantic Convoy, 1917–18. *Club:* Naval and Military.

Died 7 Oct. 1928.

MUNRO, Sir Henry, Kt 1906; JP Inverness-shire; *b* 1842; *m* 1870, Margaret, *d* of John Fraser, Inverness. Was a member Royal Commission Highlands and Islands, 1892, commonly known as the Deer Forests Commission; three times elected Pres. of Inverness Chamber of Commerce; bank director and a director of other public companies; member of the Extra Parliamentary Panel for Scotland under the Private Legislation Procedure (Scotland) Act of 1899; was a member of the Scottish Land Enquiry Committee which reported on the Land Question in Scotland, 1914. *Address:* Ness Mount, Inverness.   *Died 23 Dec. 1921.*

MUNRO, Sir Hugh Thomas, 4th Bt, *cr* 1825; JP, DL; *b* 16 Oct. 1856; *e s* of Sir Campbell Munro, 3rd Bt, and Henrietta Maria, *d* of John Drummond; *S* father, 1913; *m* 1892, Selina Dorothea (*d* 1902), *d* of Maj.-Gen. Thomas Edmond Byrne, Royal Artillery; one *s* two *d* (and one *d* decd). Private Secretary to late Sir George Pomeroy Colley, Governor of Natal, 1880; served as volunteer in Basuto campaign, 1880–81 (medal and clasp); contested (C) Kirkcaldy District of Burghs, 1885; was long on Central Council of Conservative Party in Scotland, and chairman of Tay Divisional Committee of National Union of Conservative Associations for Scotland, and chairman of Forfarshire Unionist Organisation; member of County Council for Forfarshire from its formation; member of School Board, etc; FRGS. *Publications:* many articles on mountaineering, notably a catalogue universally accepted as the standard of all the Scottish mountains. *Recreations:* shooting, mountain climbing, travel. *Heir:* *s* Thomas Torquil Alfonso Munro, *b* 7 Feb. 1901. *Address:* Lindertis, Kirriemuir, NB. *TA:* Munro, Craigton. *M:* LN 842 and SR 919. *Clubs:* Wellington, Royal Automobile, Alpine; New, Scottish Mountaineering, Edinburgh.

Died 19 March 1919.

MUNRO, Col Lewis, CBE 1919 (OBE 1919); retired pay; *b* 25 July 1859; *s* of late Captain Lewis Munro, HEICS; *m* 1885, Maud, *d* of late C. Breed Eynaud, Malta; no *c*. *Educ:* Clifton College; RMC, Sandhurst; Staff College. Joined 37th Regt, 1880; Adjutant 1st Hampshire Regt, 1882; Brigade Major, Gibraltar, 1892, Aldershot, 1898; served Boer War, 1899–1901, as Brigade Major Infantry Brigade, and afterwards DAAG Headquarters; Aden Hinterland Expedition, 1902; commanded 2nd Hampshire Regt, 1906–9; retired as substantive Colonel, 1910; employed throughout European War as Assistant to Maj.-Gen. i/c Admin and AQMG, Eastern Command, and subsequently under the Air Ministry (despatches three times, CBE). *Recreations:* shooting, fishing, golf. *M:* HC 4861. *Clubs:* Army and Navy, MCC.   *Died 11 Nov. 1927.*

MUNRO, Robert, MA, MD, LLD; FRSE; *b* Ross-shire, 21 July 1835; *m* 1875, Anna (*d* 1907); *d* of late William Taylor, Kilmarnock. *Educ:* Tain Royal Academy; University of Edinburgh. Doctor at Kilmarnock till 1886, when he retired to devote more attention to archæological and anthropological pursuits; Secretary Society of Antiquaries of Scotland, 1888–99; President of Anthropological Section of British Association, 1893; Rhind Lecturer on Archæology, 1888, Dalrymple Lecturer on Archæology, 1910 (University of Glasgow); Munro Lecturer on Anthropology and Prehistoric Archæology, 1911 (University of Edinburgh); Hon. Member of the Royal Irish Academy, of the Royal Society of Antiquaries of Ireland, Société Royale des Antiquaires du Nord, Société d'Architecture de Bruxelles, Friesch Genootschap, etc; Associé étranger de la Société d'Anthropologie de Paris; Corr. Mem. of the Anthrop. Societies of Berlin, Vienna, and the Numismatic Society of Philadelphia. *Publications:* Ancient Scottish Lake-Dwellings, 1882; The Lake-Dwellings of Europe, 1890 (French edn 1908); Rambles and Studies in Bosnia-Herzegovina and Dalmatia, 1895, 2nd edn 1900; Prehistoric Problems, 1897; Prehistoric Scotland and its place in European Civilisation, 1899; Man as Artist and Sportsman in the Palæolithic Period, 1904; Archæology and False Antiquities, 1905; Munro Lectures (Palæolithic Man, and Terremare), 1912; Prehistoric Britain, 1914; Darwinism and Human Civilization, with special reference to the origin of German Military Kultur, 1917; From Darwinism to Kaiserism, 1919; numerous contributions to medical and scientific journals. *Recreation:* travel. *Address:* Elmbank, Largs, Ayrshire. *Club:* Authors'.   *Died 18 July 1920.*

MUNRO, Sir Thomas, GBE 1920 (KBE 1917); Kt 1914; JP, DL; County Clerk of Lanarkshire; Clerk to County of Lanark Education

Authority; Clerk to the Lanark District Board of Control; *b* Moorfarm House, Tain, 1866; *s* of late Thomas Munro, solicitor, Dingwall and Tain, and Helen (*d* 1889), *d* of late Hector Mackenzie, JP, Ullapool; *m* 1897, Jean Russell, *d* of late James Smart, Balgreen, Hamilton; two *d*. *Educ:* privately; Milne's Institution, Fochabers; Edinburgh University. Formerly chief adviser Labour Regulation Department of Ministry of Munitions, and Member of the Munition Council; adviser to Demobilisation Branch of Ministry of Labour; a member of HM Commission Dilution of Labour for Clyde and Tyne Districts; Assessor to Central Board of Control (Liquor Traffic); Chairman under appointment by the Govt of the Provisional Joint Industrial Committee and acted as Chairman of several other Government Commissions and Committees during the War. *Address:* 2 Rothesay Place, Edinburgh. *TA:* 281, 282 and 283, Hamilton. *M:* V 777. *Clubs:* Caledonian, National; University, Edinburgh.

Died 11 April 1923.

MUNSEY, Frank Andrew; owner and publisher of the Sun and the Evening Telegram, New York; *b* Mercer, Maine, USA, 21 Aug. 1854; unmarried. *Educ:* common schools of Maine. Began in country store in Maine; became manager of Western Union Telegraph Office, Augusta, Maine; came to New York in 1882; started The Golden Argosy, a juvenile weekly (later the adult Argosy-Allstory Weekly); and launched Munsey's Weekly, 1889; converted into Munsey's Magazine, 1891; made addresses on publishing and advertising; lectured on journalism at Yale University, 1902. *Publications:* A Tragedy of Errors; Derringforth; Under Fire; Afloat in a Great City; The Boy Broker. *Recreations:* yachting, golf, horseback riding, automobiling. *Address:* 280 Broadway, New York City. *TA:* Munsey, New York. *Clubs:* Union League, New York Yacht, Riding, Lotos, Pilgrims, Turf and Field, Merchants', New York; Chevy Chase, Metropolitan, Washington.

Died 22 Dec. 1925.

MUNSTER, 4th Earl of, *cr* 1831; **Aubrey FitzClarence;** Viscount FitzClarence, Baron Tewkesbury, 1831; *b* 7 June 1862; *s* of 2nd Earl and Wilhelmina, *d* of Hon. John Kennedy-Erskine; *S* brother, 1902. Was Gentleman Usher to Queen Victoria and King Edward VII. *Heir:* nephew Geoffry William Hugh FitzClarence, *b* 17 Feb. 1906. *Address:* 2 Warwick Square, SW1. *T:* Victoria 2884. *Clubs:* Bachelors', St James's, Carlton. *Died 1 Jan. 1928.*

MUNSTERBERG, Dr Hugo; Professor of Psychology since 1892, and Director of Psychological Laboratory, Harvard; *b* Dantzig, 1 June 1863; *m* Selma Oppler, Strasburg. *Educ:* Dantzig Gymnasium; Leipsic; Heidelberg. Assistant Professor University of Freiburg, 1887-91. *Publications:* Psychology and Life, 1899; American Traits, 1902; The Americans, 1904; Principles of Art Education, 1905; Eternal Life, 1905; Science and Idealism, 1906; On the Witness Stand, 1907; Psycho-Therapy, 1908; The Eternal Values, 1909; Psychology and the Teacher, 1909; Psychology and Industrial Efficiency, 1913. *Address:* 7 Ware Street, Cambridge, Massachusetts, USA.

Died 15 Dec. 1916.

MUNTZ, Frederick Ernest, JP, DL; landed proprietor; *b* 14 June 1845; *e s* of late G. F. Muntz, JP, DL; *m* 1869, Georgiana Jane, *e d* of late A. Borrowman of Edinburgh; one *s*. *Educ:* Corpus Christi College, Cambridge (BA 1871). Called to the Bar, Lincoln's Inn, 1873. High Sheriff, Warwickshire, 1902; Capt. Hon. Major late 3rd Batt. Devonshire Regt; Lord of the Manor of Tanworth in Arden; contested Rugby Division of Warwickshire, 1899; Patron of Tanworth in Arden. *Address:* Umberslade, Hockley Heath, Warwickshire. *TA:* Hockley Heath. *T:* Tanworth in Arden 9. *Clubs:* Carlton, Oxford and Cambridge, Hurlingham. *M:* AC 44, AC 740, AC 2834. *Died 25 Nov. 1920.*

MUNTZ, Sir Gerard Albert, 2nd Bt, *cr* 1902; President of the Institute of Metals, 1910 and 1911; Vice-President of the Institute of Mechanical Engineers; *b* 27 Nov. 1864; *s* of Sir (Philip) Albert Muntz, 1st Bt, and Rosalie, *d* of Philip Henry Muntz; *S* father, 1908; *m* 1st, 1893, Katherine Blanche (whom he divorced, 1907), *d* of James Prinsep; three *d*; 2nd, 1909, Henrietta Winifred, 3rd *d* of late Lt-Col F. L. Graves, Royal Artillery; one *s* two *d*. Chairman Non-Ferrous Metal Committee (Board of Trade), 1916-17; Chairman Metallurgical Committee (Ferrous and Non-Ferrous) Department of Scientific and Industrial Research, 1916-19; Member of Copper, Zinc, Lead, Sectional Committees of Imperial Mineral Resources Bureau, 1920; Member of Council of British Non-Ferrous Metals Research Association from 1920; Consultant Director of Muntz's Metal Co. Ltd (Managing Director, 1896), and Elliott's Metal Co. Ltd; Chairman of the Brass and Copper Tube Association, 1911-21. *Heir:* s Gerard

Philip Graves Muntz, *b* 13 June 1917. *Address:* Tiddington House, near Stratford-on-Avon. *Club:* St Stephen's.

Died 22 Oct. 1927.

MURDOCH, Prof. James, MA; Professor of Oriental Studies, University of Sydney, since 1919; *b* Kincardineshire, Scotland, 1856. *Educ:* Universities of Aberdeen, Oxford, and Göttingen. Asst Prof. of Greek, Aberdeen Univ., 1880-81; Headmaster Maryborough Grammar School, Qld, 1881-85; 2nd Master Brisbane Grammar School, 1885-88; from 1888 mostly resident in Japan for purposes of study and research. *Publications:* History of Japan: vol. i, 1911; vol. ii, 1902; vol. iii (1650-1868) in the Press; vol. iv (1868-1912) on the stocks. *Address:* University of Sydney, Australia.

Died 30 Oct. 1921.

MURE, William John, CB 1897; JP Co. Edinburgh; MA; advocate, Edinburgh; *b* 1845; *s* of late David Mure, Judge of the Court of Session, Scotland; *m* 1878, Emily May (MBE 1920), *d* of John Brown Innes, WS, Edinburgh; one *d*. *Educ:* Loretto; Harrow; Trinity College, Cambridge. Called to Scotch Bar, 1871; Legal Secretary to the Lord Advocate, 1885-86, 1886-92, and 1895-96. *Address:* 39 Lennox Gardens, SW1. *T:* Kensington 6107. *Clubs:* Carlton, Wellington; New, Edinburgh.

Died 9 Nov. 1924.

MURFREE, Mary Noailles, (pen-name **Charles Egbert Craddock**); novelist; *b* Murfreesboro, Tennessee; *d* of late William L. Murfree, lawyer; *g g d* of Colonel Hardy Murfree of Murfreesboro, North Carolina (he served with conspicuous gallantry throughout the American Revolution, 1775-82; the town of Murfreesboro, Tennessee, was named in his honour). In 1878 began to contribute fiction to magazines under pen-name of "Charles Egbert Craddock", real identity not known until 1885. *Publications:* In the Tennessee Mountains, 1884; Where the Battle was Fought, 1884; Down the Ravine, 1885; The Prophet of the Great Smoky Mountains, 1885; In the Clouds, 1886; The Story of Keedon Bluffs, 1887; The Despot of Broomsedge Cove, 1888; In the Stranger-People's Country, 1891; His Vanished Star, 1894; The Phantoms of the Footbridge, 1895; The Mystery of Witch-face Mountain, 1895; The Juggler, 1897; The Young Mountaineers, 1897; The Story of Old Fort London, 1899; The Bushwhackers, 1899; The Champion, 1902; A Spectre of Power, 1903; The Storm Centre, 1905; The Frontiersmen, 1905; The Amulet, 1906; The Windfall, 1907; The Fair Mississippian, 1908; The Ordeal, 1912; The Raid of the Guerrilla, and other Stories, 1912; The Story of Duciehurst, 1914. *Address:* Murfreesboro, Tennessee, USA. *Died 1 Aug. 1922.*

MURIE, Dr James, MD Glasgow, LLD St Andrews; *b* 1830. Was naturalist to Consul Petherick's expedition to Gondokoro; pro-sector to Zoological Society; assistant librarian and secretary to Linnean Society. *Address:* Canvey Cottage, Leigh-on-Sea, Essex.

Died 21 Dec. 1925.

MURLAND, William; JP Northamptonshire; *b* 1855; *s* of J. W. Murland, Nutley, Booterstown, Co. Dublin; *m* 1887, Mary Geraldine Fitzgerald; two *s*. *Educ:* Trinity College, Dublin. Called to the Irish Bar, 1878; High Sheriff, Northamptonshire, 1913. *Address:* Badby House, Daventry, Northants; 28A Cadogan Place, SW1. *T:* Victoria 3722. *M:* 3722. *Club:* Junior Carlton.

Died 2 March 1926.

MURPHY, George Fitzgerald, JP Co. Meath; BA; *b* 1850; *e s* of late James George Murphy of The Grange, and Mary, *d* of late Col Fitzgerald of Geraldine Co., Kildare; *m* 1884, Lady Mary Louisa Plunkett, *e d* of 10th Earl of Fingall. High Sheriff, County Meath, 1908. *Address:* The Grange, Dunsany. *Clubs:* Orleans; Sackville Street, Dublin. *Died 13 Nov. 1920.*

MURPHY, Rev. Hugh Davis, DD; Rector of St George's, Belfast, since 1880; Chaplain to the Lord-Lieutenant of Ireland; *b* Co. Antrim, 8 June 1849; *m* Francesca Barbara, *d* of late Rev. Richard Burgess, BD, Rector of Upper Chelsea and Prebendary of St Paul's; four *s* one *d*. *Educ:* Trinity Coll., Dublin. BA 1873; MA 1884; BD 1890; DD 1891; Prizeman, English Literature; Downes Prizeman, Written Sermon. Ordained, 1874; Curate of Ballinderry, 1874-75; Assistant Chaplain, Bethesda Church, Dublin, 1875-77; Curate of St George's, Belfast, 1878; Member of the General Synod of the Church of Ireland; Rural Dean of North Belfast; Chaplain in Belfast to the Actors' Church Union; Canon of St Patrick's Cathedral; a Prince Mason, and three times Provincial Grand Chaplain of the Masonic province of Antrim. *Publications:* A Forgotten Gospel; The State of the Soul between Death and the Resurrection; poems in various periodicals. *Recreations:*

gardening, shooting, Continental travel, modern literature. *Address:* 39 Wellington Park, Belfast.

Died 8 March 1927.

MURPHY, Sir James Joseph, 1st Bt, *cr* 1903; Kt 1902; DL (City of Dublin); steamship owner; Partner, Palgrave, Murphy and Co; *b* 24 Jan. 1843; 2nd *s* of late Michael Murphy, JP and Margaret, *d* of Philip Lawless; *m* 1869, Bridget Jane, *d* of late Francis Norman; five *d* (two *s* decd). Chairman, Royal Bank of Ireland; President of Chamber of Commerce, Dublin, 1902-3-4. *Heir:* none. *Address:* Yapton, Monkstown, Co. Dublin. *T:* Kingstown 8. *TA:* Yapton, Kingstown. *Clubs:* Constitutional; Royal Irish Yacht, Kingstown; St Stephen's Green, Dublin. *Died 16 Feb. 1922 (ext).*

MURPHY, James Keogh, MA, MD, MCh (Cantab); FRCS; consulting surgeon; Surgeon to the Miller General Hospital for South East London; Surgeon to Paddington Green Children's Hospital; General Medical Editor to the Oxford University Press and Hodder & Stoughton; *b* 12 Sept. 1869; *e s* of late Rt Hon. Mr Justice (James) Murphy, PC, LLD, and Mary, *d* of late Rt Hon. Mr Justice (W. M.) Keogh; *m* 1895, Mabel Roney, *d* of late Joshua K. Schofield of Cambria Kersal, Manchester; one *s*. *Educ:* Charterhouse (Senior Scholar); Caius College, Cambridge (Scholar; 1st Class Natural Science Tripos); St Bartholomew's Hospital. Demonstrator of Anatomy to the University of Cambridge for three years; completed medical education at St Bartholomew's and obtained the Laurence Scholarship and large Gold Medal; the post of External Assistant at the Rotunda Hospital, Dublin, by competitive examination; returned to St Bartholomew's and acted as House Physician; a family practitioner for five years in Princes' Square; returned to St Bartholomew's, having obtained the Fellowship of the Royal College of Surgeons whilst in practice, to devote himself especially to surgery; there acted as Demonstrator of Anatomy for three years, and devoted himself to the work of his hospital appointments. *Publications:* The Records and Lessons of a Series of 3,000 Midwifery Cases (Practitioner); The Radical Treatment of Tubercular Disease of the Ankle and Tarsus, read at BMA, published BMJ and Lancet; editor with Mr D'Arcy Power of A System of Syphilis, in six volumes; editor of the Practitioner's Encyclopaedia of Medicine, Surgery, and Midwifery, 2nd edn 1913; editor and translator Kirmisson's Handbook of the Surgery of Children, etc. *Recreations:* motoring; Surgeon Royal Naval Volunteer Reserve. *Address:* 17 Devonshire Place, W. *T:* 1998 Park; 16 Pembridge Crescent, W. *T:* 878 Mayfair; 8961 City. *TA:* Oxymoron, London. *M:* LK 9914. *Club:* Constitutional.

Died 13 Sept. 1916.

MURPHY, Very Rev. John. *Address:* West Calder, NB.

MURPHY, Rt. Rev. John Baptist Tuohill, SSP; STD, LLD; RC Bishop of Port Louis (Mauritius), since 1916; *b* Mein House, Knocknagoshil, 24 June 1854; *s* of Bartholomew Murphy, gentleman-farmer, and Johanna Tuohill. *Educ:* Blackrock College, Dublin; Holy Ghost College, Paris. Won an Exhibition and Medal for Greek Verse at the Catholic University, Dublin. Assistant Master at St Mary's College, Trinidad, for five years; ordained Priest, 1878; Dean of Studies, Rockwell College, 1879-86; President Pittsburg College, 1886-99; Blackrock College, 1899-1904; Trinity Park, Bath, 1904-6; Provincial, USA, 1906-10; Ireland and England, 1910-16. *Publications:* several volumes of sermons; articles in various reviews; brochures on special subjects. *Address:* The Palace, Port Louis, Mauritius.

Died 17 April 1926.

MURPHY, John Harvey; KC 1920; *b* 1862; *o s* of late John Patrick Murphy, KC, of the Middle Temple, and *g s* of late Patrick Mathias Murphy, QC, of Dublin; *m* 1891, Lucy, *e d* of late Edward C. Clarke; one *s* one *d*. *Educ:* Downside School, Bath; Trinity Hall, Cambridge. Called to the Bar, Middle Temple, 1887; practised on SE Circuit, Herts and Essex Sessions, and Probate and Divorce Court. *Publications:* Chief Reporter to The Times in Probate and Divorce Court, June 1895-Sept. 1909. *Recreations:* books, the drama, fishing, miniature rifle-shooting. *Address:* Lowood, College Road, Upper Norwood, SE19. *T:* Sydenham 1319; 3 Temple Gardens, Temple, EC4. *T:* Central 700. *Clubs:* Reform, Royal Automobile.

Died 20 Dec. 1924.

MURPHY, Martin, ISO 1903; CE; DSc; Government Inspecting Engineer on the Western Division of the National Trans-Continental Railway, Canada, since 1906; *b* Ballendaggen, Enniscorthy, 11 Nov. 1832; *s* of Thomas Murphy, Ballinduggan, Co. Wexford; *m* 1861, Maria Agnes, *d* of Cornelius Buckley and Mary (*née* McCarthy), Banteer, Ireland; eight *s* three *d*. Resident Engineer, Dublin, Wicklow, and Wexford Railway, 1862-67; went to Canada, 1868; Provincial

Government Engineer of Nova Scotia, 1875-1903; President Canadian Society of Civil Engineers, 1902-3. *Address:* Edmonton, Alberta, Canada. *Died Jan. 1926.*

MURPHY, Martin Joseph, JP; MP (N) East Waterford, 1913-18; *b* 1862. High Sheriff, City of Waterford, 1889-90; JP Co. Waterford. *Address:* Atlantic, Tramore, Co. Waterford. *Club:* National Liberal.

Died 4 Sept. 1919.

MURPHY, Sir Michael, 1st Bt, *cr* 1912; *b* 9 March 1845; *s* of Michael Murphy of 21 Merrion Square, Dublin, JP; *m* 1877, Mary (*d* 1882), *d* of James and Mary Freeman of Rathmines, Co. Dublin; one *s* one *d* (and one *s* decd). Head of the firm of Michael Murphy, Ltd, steamship owners, of Dublin, Liverpool, Swansea and Cardiff; member of the Board of Superintendence of the Belfast Banking Company, Ltd; also ex-chairman of the Dublin Port and Docks Board; was largely instrumental in reviving the shipbuilding industry in Dublin. *Heir: s* George Francis Murphy [*b* 31 March 1881; *m* 1913, Frances Mary, *d* of late Richard Davoren. *Address:* Hawthorn, Shrewsbury Road, Dublin]. *Address:* Wyckham, Taney, Dundrum, Co. Dublin. *Clubs:* Reform; St Stephen's Green, Dublin.

Died 10 April 1925.

MURPHY, Patrick Charles, MD; Senator of Canada since 1912; physician and surgeon; *b* Kinkira, PEI, 14 Sept. 1868; *m* 1st, 1893 (wife *d* 1901); 2nd, 1904 (wife *d* 1912); four *s* three *d*; 3rd, 1915. *Educ:* native district, Summerside High School; New York University (graduated in medicine at head of class, 1893). Began practice of medicine in PEI; President Maritime Medical Association at Halifax, NS, 1904; organised the Tignish Trading Co., 1904. *Publications:* contributor to contemporary medical literature and current political literature. *Address:* Tignish, Prince Edward Island.

Died March 1925.

MURPHY, Sir Shirley Forster, KBE 1919; Kt 1904; FRCS; Lieutenant-Colonel Royal Army Medical Corps (Territorial Force); late Medical Officer of Health, Administrative County of London; Member of Royal Commission on Tuberculosis; *b* 21 May 1848; *s* of late George Murphy; *m* 1880, Ellen Theodora, *d* of Henry S. King; two *d*. *Educ:* University College School; Guy's Hospital. Vice-President Royal Sanitary Institute, Society of Medical Officers of Health, Epidemiological Section Royal Society of Medicine, and Royal Statistical Society; late Examiner in Public Health, Royal Colleges of Physicians and Surgeons; Bisset Hawkins Medallist, Royal College of Physicians and Jenner Medallist, Royal Society of Medicine. *Address:* 9 Bentinck Terrace, Regent's Park, NW8. *T:* Hampstead 958. *Clubs:* Athenæum, Savile.

Died 27 April 1923.

MURPHY, William Martin, JP; *b* 29 Dec. 1844; *e s* of late Denis William Murphy of Bantry, Co. Cork, and Mary Anne, *d* of late James Martin of Castletown Bere, Co. Cork; *m* 1870, Mary Julia (*d* 1900), *d* of late James Fitzgerald Lombard, JP, of South Hill, Co. Dublin; three *s* three *d*. MP (NL) Dublin (St Patrick's Division), 1885-92; contested Kerry S, 1895; Mayo N, 1900; carried out several railway and electric tramway and lighting undertakings in the United Kingdom, and constructed railways in the Gold Coast Colony, West Africa; Chairman Dublin United Tramways Company, and a director of the Great Southern and Western Railway of Ireland; founded in 1905 the Irish Independent, the only halfpenny daily morning paper in Ireland; President Dublin Chamber of Commerce, 1912-13; principal promoter and Chairman of Committee of Irish International Exhibition held in Dublin, 1907; prominent in opposition to Syndicalist Strikes in Dublin, 1913; Chairman Finance and General Purposes Committee, Dublin Castle Red Cross Hospital, from February 1915. *Address:* Dartry, Rathmines, Co. Dublin. *TA:* Railways, Dublin; Arenaceous, London. *T:* Rathmines 33, Dublin. *Clubs:* Reform; Royal Irish Yacht, Kingstown.

Died 26 June 1919.

MURPHY, Col William Reed, DSO 1890; FZS; Lieutenant-Colonel Indian Medical Service; retired; *b* 23 Oct 1849; unmarried. *Educ:* Clongoweswood College, County Kildare; Trinity College, Dublin; Royal College of Surgeons, Ireland (took all prizes during student course there and at Meath Hospital). Took 1st prize at Netley on entering Indian Medical Service, 30 March 1872; served with Indian Contingent, Malta and Cyprus, 1878; Afghanistan, 1878-80 (despatches, medal and clasp); received special thanks from the Brig.-Gen. commanding the Cavalry Brigade at the cavalry action of Pat Kao Shana, for conduct in action at great personal risk (London Gazette, 22 Oct. 1880); Hazara, 1888 (despatches, Indian medal, and clasp); Lushai, 1888-89 (clasp); PMO Lushai Column, Chin Lushai

Field Force, 1889–90 (despatches, mentioned by Government of India, clasp, DSO); Chitral Relief Force, 1895 (medal and clasp); PMO Kurram–Kohat Force, 1897 (despatches, 2 clasps); PMO Kurram M Column, Tirah Field Force, 1897–98 (despatches, clasp); granted Indian Army Good Service Pension, 1918; Member of the Royal Institution of Great Britain. *TA:* Ejus, London. *T:* Regent 683. *Clubs:* East India United Service, Junior Naval and Military.

Died 7 Aug. 1927.

MURRAY OF ELIBANK, 1st Baron, *cr* 1912; **Alexander William Charles Oliphant Murray,** PC 1911; Director, S. Pearson and Son; *b* 12 April 1870; *e s* of 1st Viscount and 10th Baron Elibank and Blanche Alice, *e d* of Edward John Scott, Southsea, Hants; *m* 1894, Hilda Louisa Janey Wolfe (*half-sister* of late Lt-Gen. Sir James Wolfe Murray), *d* of James Wolfe Murray, Cringletie, Peebles-shire and 2nd wife, Louisa Grace, *d* of Sir Adam Hay, 7th Bt; no *c. Educ:* Cheltenham. Late Lieut Lothians and Berwickshire Yeomanry Cavalry; contested West Division Edinburgh, May 1895; also Peebles and Selkirk, July 1895; and city of York by-election, 1900; MP (L) Midlothian, 1900–5, Peebles and Selkirk, 1906–10, and Midlothian, 1910–12; Comptroller HM's Household and Scottish Liberal Whip, 1906–10; Under Secretary of State for India, 1909; Chief Liberal Whip, 1909–12; Parliamentary Secretary to Treasury, 1910–12. *Address:* Elibank, Walkerburn, Scotland. *Clubs:* Brooks's, Reform, Bachelors', Marlborough.

Died 13 Sept. 1920 (ext).

MURRAY, Albert E., RHA, FRIBA, FRIAI; architect; ex-President of the Royal Insitute of the Architects of Ireland; Professor of Architecture, Royal Hibernian Academy; *b* 14 May 1849; 2nd *s* of late William George Murray, RHA, Avonmore, Co. Dublin, and M. A., *d* of James Craig of Armagh; *m* 1902, Amy H., *o d* of Andrew Johnston, Dublin; one *s* one *d. Educ:* privately. Extensive practice, and consultant to many hospitals, which latter work a special study; Professor of Architecture in the Royal Hibernian Academy; Hon. Sec. to Royal Institute of Architects of Ireland, 1883–1901; Examiner in Architecture in National Univ., Ireland; Examiner in the Diploma of Public Health, Royal College of Physicians, 1887–96; Hon. Sec. Military Lodge (Masonic) of Ireland since 1883; Governor of Mercers Hospital, Dublin; on visiting Committee of Dublin Hospital Sunday Fund; Freeman of the City of Dublin. *Recreations:* yachting, fishing, golf, sketching. *Address:* 37 Dawson Street, Dublin. *T:* 676; 2 Clyde Road, Dublin. *T:* Ballsbridge 507. *Clubs:* Junior Constitutional; Royal Irish Yacht, Northern Counties, Londonderry.

Died 20 March 1924.

MURRAY, Major Alexander Penrose; *b* 13 July 1863; *e s* of George Joseph Murray of Ayton, Fife and Augusta Anne, *d* of Rev. George Deane, Rector of Bighton, Hants; *m* 1st, 1891, Nina (*d* 1894), *d* of Col Alexander Solovtsoff; one *s*; 2nd, 1895, Ethel Chorley, *d* of Maj.-Gen. Arthur Hill; one *s. Educ:* Eton. 2nd Lieut Royal Aberdeenshire Highlanders, 1881; Lieut Gordon Highlanders, 1883; Capt. 1893; served Eastern Soudan, 1884, present at battle of El Teb (medal, clasp, and Khedive's star); retired from army, 1895; Vice-Consul at Odessa, 1891; Acting Consul at Batoum, 1891–92; transferred to Sebastopol, 1892; Consul-General for the Governments of Poland, Kovno, Grodno, Minsk, and Vilna, to reside at Warsaw, 1897; received the Jubilee Medal, 1897; served with 1st Batt. Gordon Highlanders South African War, 1899–1901 (severely wounded); operations in the Orange Free State, including actions at Houtnek (Thoba Mountain) and Zand River; operations in the Transvaal, including actions near Johannesburg and Pretoria; operations in the Transvaal, west of Pretoria (despatches, Queen's medal with three clasps); Consul-General, Hayti, 1908–11; Consul St Pierre Miquelon, 1912–13; retired, 1913; served European War 1914–17 with Gordon Highlanders (hon. rank of Major); received the Royal Humane Society's silver medal for saving life from drowning. *Address:* 16 Polwarth Grove, Edinburgh.

Died March 1926.

MURRAY, Maj.-Gen. Anthony Hepburn; Royal Artillery; *b* 31 Oct. 1840; *m* 1871, Mary Madeline, *d* of Gen. G. Radcliffe. Entered army, 1857; Maj.-Gen. 1896; retired, 1897. *Address:* St Enodoc, Wellington College, Berks. *Club:* Naval and Military.

Died 27 May 1917.

MURRAY, Col Arthur Mordaunt, CB 1909; MVO 1908; FRGS; *b* Southfleet, Kent, 20 Jan. 1852; *s* of Rev. George Edward Murray and Penelope Frances Elizabeth Pemberton, *y d* of Brig.-Gen. Austin; *m* 1st, 1895, Isabel (*d* 1896), *d* of Richard Laurence Pemberton of Hawthorn Towers, Co. Durham; one *d*; 2nd, 1898, Mabel, *d* of John Nicholson of Seaforth, Lancashire; two *s* one *d* (and one *s* decd). *Educ:*

Uppingham School; Royal Military Academy, Woolwich. Received a commission in Royal Artillery, 1873; served as Assistant-Superintendent of Transport in the 1st Division Peshawur Valley Field Force, 1878–79 (despatches); appointed to Royal Horse Artillery, 1880; Captain, 1882; Brigade-Major RA Egypt, 1885–87; Major, 1889; Assistant Military Secretary to GOC South Africa, 1895; Lt-Col, 1898; Assistant-Commandant Royal Military Academy, Woolwich, 1900; Bt Col, 1902; sent on a mission to Japan, 1906; Commandant Duke of York's Royal Military School, Chelsea, 1907–9; Member Royal United Service Institution, Whitehall. *Publications:* Imperial Outposts, 1907; Fortnightly History of the War, 1914–16; awarded the gold medal of the Royal Artillery Institution for an essay on Fire Discipline, 1892; silver medal of the same Institution for The Tactics of Massed Batteries in the Field. *Recreation:* travelling. *Address:* 4 Albert Place, Kensington, W8. *T:* Western 2686. *Club:* Reform.

Died 23 May 1920.

MURRAY, Charles Oliver, RE; artist and etcher; *b* Denholm, Roxburghshire; 3rd *s* of late Thomas Murray; *m* 1869, Elizabeth, *e d* of late Archibald Campbell, Glasgow. *Educ:* Minto School; Edinburgh School of Design; School of the Royal Scottish Academy. Gained Keith prize there and National Medallions Queen prize; silver and gold medals for anatomical studies and drawing from the antique in the national competitions, awarded at International Exhibitions: London, 1884; silver medal, Munich, 1893; gold medal, Paris, 1900; silver medal for etching; elected to Royal Society of Painter Etchers on its foundation, exhibiting there and at Royal Academy, yearly since 1876; engaged in drawing illustrations for books and magazines for several years, afterwards as an etcher, original and interpretive; etched pictures by many distinguished artists, and many original plates, landscape, architectural and figure subjects. *Publications:* in addition to above plates, etchings illustrating Keats's Eve of St Agnes, Border Ballads, etc. *Recreations:* reading, travelling. *Address:* 10 Avondale Road, South Croydon. *Club:* Art Workers' Guild.

Died 11 Dec. 1924.

MURRAY, Col Sir (Charles) Wyndham, KCB 1917 (CB 1902); Kt 1905; late Member of Honourable Corps of Gentlemen-at-Arms; Gentleman Usher of the Scarlet Rod in the Order of the Bath, 1913–28; *b* 22 Feb. 1844; *s* of late Rev. Thomas Boyles Murray, Prebendary of St Paul's, and Helen, *d* of Sir W. Douglas, KH; *m* 1890, Emma Cecilia (*d* 1922), *d* of Edward Walker, and *widow* of Major Konarski. *Educ:* Marlborough College. Gloucestershire Regiment, 1862; Staff College, 1872; DAQMG Cork, 1875; Intelligence Branch, QMG Dept, Dublin, 1877; Brig.-Major 1st Brigade, 1878; Military Attaché, Turkey, 1878 (despatches); ADC and DAQMG Zululand, 1879 (despatches, Brevet-Major, medal with clasp); Staff Officer, Kabul, 1880 (medal); Staff Officer, Pishin Outposts, Afghanistan, 1881 (despatches); DAQMG Egypt, 1882 (despatches, medal with clasp for Tel-el-Kebir, Brevet Lt-Col, 4th class Osmanieh, Khedive's Star); DAQMG Bechuanaland, 1884–85 (despatches); Military King's Messenger, France, 1915–16 (War Medal, 1914–15 Star, Victory Medal); MP (C) Bath, 1892–1906; late Chairman Japan Society; 3rd Class Order of Rising Sun, Japan; Grand Cross, St John of Jerusalem. *Recreations:* shooting, yachting. *Address:* 10 Rutland Gate, SW7. *T:* Kensington 4473; 147 King's Road, Brighton. *M:* A 393. *Clubs:* Carlton; Royal Yacht Squadron, Cowes.

Died 1 Nov. 1928.

MURRAY, David, MA, LLD; FSA, FSAScot; a solicitor in Glasgow; *b* Glasgow, 15 April 1842; *s* of David Murray (*d* 1848), solicitor in Glasgow and Ann Hunter Guthrie (*d* 1901); *m* 1872, Frances Porter (*d* 1919), *e d* of late Arthur Francis Stoddard of Broadfield, Renfrewshire; three *d. Educ:* Merchiston Castle, Edinburgh; University of Glasgow. Dean of the Faculty of Procurators in Glasgow, 1895–98; President of the Archæological Society of Glasgow, 1895–98; Vice-President of the Society of Antiquaries of Scotland, 1900–3; President of the Royal Philosophical Society of Glasgow, 1904–7; Rhind Lecturer in Archæology for 1908; President Glasgow Bibliographical Society, 1912–13, 1915–20; a Member of the University Court of the University of Glasgow. *Publications:* The York Buildings Company, a Chapter in Scotch History, 1883; The Law relating to the Property of Married Persons, 1891; An Archæological Survey of the United Kingdom; The Preservation and Protection of our Ancient Monuments, 1896; Museums, Their History and Their Use, 1904; Early Burgh Organisation in Scotland, vol. i, Glasgow, 1924; Memories of the Old College of Glasgow; Some Chapters in the History of the University, 1927; and numerous others. *Recreations:* travelling, yachting, book-collecting. *Address:* 13 Fitzroy Place, Glasgow; Moorepark, Cardross, Dunbartonshire. *Clubs:* Reform, Royal Societies; Western, Glasgow; University, Edinburgh; Royal Northern Yacht.

Died 2 Oct. 1928.

MURRAY, Dr Donald, JP; MB, CM Glasgow; MP (L) Western Isles, Inverness, Dec. 1918–22; Medical Officer of Health for Burgh of Stornoway and School Medical Officer for Lewis and the western portion of Ross-shire; *b* Stornoway, 21 Oct. 1862; *s* of Alan Murray; *m* 1898, Janet Catherine Grace, *d* of Alexander Macpherson, Stornoway. *Educ:* Glasgow University. President of the Glasgow Univ. Medico-Chirurgical Society, 1890; and of the University Liberal Club, 1889–90; JP Ross and Cromarty. *Address:* 4 St Alban's Road, NW5. *Club:* National Liberal.

Died 6 July 1923.

MURRAY, Col Frank, DSO 1904; 8th Ghoorka Rifles; *b* 10 June 1864. Entered Army, 1885; Capt. 1896; Major, 1903; served Burmah, 1885–89 (medal with two clasps); Waziristan, 1894–95 (clasp); Thibet, 1903–4 (despatches, DSO). *Address:* Shillong, Assam.

Died 18 April 1917.

MURRAY, Ven. Frederic Richardson, LTh, MA, DD; Rector of St Mary's, Belize, since 1888; Archdeacon of Belize since 1904; *b* 1 Sept. 1845; *m* Mary Jane, *d* of late Rev. John Dolphin, BA Oxon, Vicar of Lower Guiting, Glos; three *s* five *d*. *Educ:* Spencer's, Newcastle-on-Tyne; Stepney Grammar School, London; Clare College, Cambridge; Scorton, Yorks; Hatfield Hall, Durham. Ordained, 1868; Priest, 1869; Curate of Grimley, 1868–70; Shepton-Beauchamp, 1870–71; Ruyton-XI-Towns, 1871–72; St Andrew's, Deal, 1872–73; SPG Missionary, Newfoundland, 1873–81; Chaplain to Bishop Feild, 1873; Rector of Twillingate, 1873; Rural Dean Notre Dame Bay, 1873; Incumbent St John's Cathedral, 1877; Rector of St Mary's Heart's Content, 1879; offered St George's, Halifax, 1881; Rector and Minor Canon St Luke's Pro-Cathedral, Halifax, NS, 1881; Assistant Rector Parish Church, Kingston, 1888; Commissary Bishop of Jamaica, 1889; Bishop Holme, 1891; Bishop Ormsby, 1893; Bishop Bury, 1905; Bishop Farrar, 1912–15; Bishop Dunn, 1919–24; Headmaster Belize High School, 1890; Acting Rector of St John's, 1891; Archdeacon of Honduras, 1894; Canon, 1905–7; Administrator of the Diocese, 1911–17, 1920–23. *Address:* St Mary's Rectory, Belize, British Honduras.

Died 28 June 1925.

MURRAY, Sir George Sheppard, Kt 1906; *b* 26 June 1851; *s* of late Alexander Murray, Ceylon Civil Service; *m* 1888, Lucy Mary Johanna, *d* of late Nicholas Belfield Dennys; one *s* one *d*. Unofficial Member of the Legislative Council of Straits Settlements, 1888–1906. *Address:* Cleveland House, St James's Square, SW1. *T:* Gerrard 5884; Barretstown Castle, Ballymore Eustace, Co. Kildare. *Clubs:* Wellington, Junior Carlton, Sports, Royal Automobile.

Died 27 Oct. 1928.

MURRAY, Lt-Gen. Sir James Wolfe, KCB 1900; DL Peebles, 1907; *b* 13 March 1853; *e s* of late James Wolfe Murray of Cringletie, and 1st wife, Elizabeth Charlotte, *d* of John Whyte Melville; *m* 1st, 1875, Arabella (*d* 1909), *d* of W. Bray; two *s* three *d*; 2nd, 1913, Fanny Worswick, *d* of late James Scott Robson and *widow* of Sir Donald Horne Macfarlane. *Educ:* Glenalmond; Harrow; RMA, Woolwich. Entered RA, 1872; Colonel, 1899; served Ashanti, 1895, in command of Lines of Communication (Bt Lt-Col, star); Commanding Lines of Communication, Natal, 1899–1900 (despatches twice); Quartermaster-General in India, 1903–7; in Command of 9th (Secunderabad) Division, India, 1907–11; General Officer Commanding-in-Chief Scotland, 1913, S Africa, 1914; 1st Military Member of the Army Council, 1914–15; GOC-in-Chief Eastern Command, 1916–17; Russian Order of St Anne, 1st Class, with swords; Order of White Eagle. *Address:* Cringletie, Peebles. *T:* Peebles 69. *Clubs:* Army and Navy; New, Edinburgh.

Died 17 Oct. 1919.

MURRAY, Sir John, KCVO 1926 (CVO 1913); JP, DL; FSA, etc; head of publishing house of John Murray, founded 1768 by John Murray the first; Vice-Chairman Hospital for Sick Children; President of Publishers' Association, 1898–99; Chairman League of Remembrance; *b* London, 18 Dec. 1851; *s* of late John Murray, publisher, and Marion, *d* of Alexander Smith, Edinburgh; *m* 1878, Evelyn, *d* of William Leslie (late MP), of Warthill, Aberdeenshire; one *s* one *d* (and two *d* decd). *Educ:* Eton; Magdalen College, Oxford (MA). Captain of Royal Wimbledon Golf Club, 1884; Treasurer Roxburghe Club; JP, DL London; High Sheriff, 1908; DPh Univ. of Athens; Commandeur de l'Ordre Royal du Sauveur (Greece); Ordre de la Couronne (Belgium); edited Quarterly Review, 1922–28. *Publications:* Memoirs of John Murray III, 1919; (ed) Gibbon's Autobiography, 1897; (ed) Byron's Correspondence, 1922, and other works. *Recreations:* shooting, golf, cricket, riding, etc. *Address:* 50 Albemarle Street, W1. *TA:* Guidebook, London. *T:* Mayfair 738. *Clubs:* Athenæum, MCC, etc.

Died 30 Nov. 1928.

MURRAY, Keith William, FSA 1891; Portcullis Pursuivant of Arms since 1913; Carnarvon Pursuivant Extraordinary, 1911; *b* 1860; *s* of late William Powell Murray of Lincoln's Inn, barrister-at-law, a Registrar of the High Court in Bankruptcy, and Georgina Charlotte Daysh, *o d* of Hon. Arthur Richard Turnour, Commander RN; *m* Grace, *y d* of late Sir George Samuel Abercromby, 6th Bt, of Birkenbog and Forglen; one *d*. *Educ:* Marlborough. Studied civil and mechanical engineering, 1880–86; subsequently taking up the subjects of heraldry and genealogy; edited the Genealogist, 1889–94; afterwards contributed to that magazine and publications of a similar nature and to the Scots Peerage; some years in the London Scottish Rifle Volunteers; Gold Staff Officer at the Coronation of HM King Edward VII; Knight of Grace of the Order of St John of Jerusalem, 1912. *Recreations:* golf, fishing, shooting, etc. *Address:* College of Arms, Queen Victoria Street, EC. *T:* Central 1686; 37 Cheniston Gardens, Kensington, W. *Club:* Junior Carlton.

Died 11 Jan. 1922.

MURRAY, Sir Patrick Keith, 8th Bt, *cr* 1673; Captain Grenadier Guards (retired); *b* 27 Jan. 1835; *s* of Sir William Keith Murray, 7th Bt, and 1st wife, Helen Margaret Oliphant, *o c* of Sir Alexander Keith; *S* father, 1861; *m* 1st, 1870, Frances (*d* 1874), *d* of Anthony Murray, Dollerie, Perthshire; two *s* (one *d* decd); 2nd, 1876, Ioné Campbell Penney (*d* 1881), *d* of late Hon. Lord Kinloch, a Judge of Court of Session; two *s* one *d*. *Educ:* Trinity Coll., Cambridge. Entered army, 1854. *Heir: s* Capt. William Keith Murray, *b* 8 April 1872. *Address:* Ochtertyre, Crieff, Perthshire.

Died 10 Jan. 1921.

MURRAY, Richard, OBE 1920; MVO 1912; Principal Technical Assistant, Naval Store Department, Admiralty; *b* 19 June 1865; *s* of Richard Murray of Portsmouth; *m* 1886, Isabella, 5th *d* of late Thomas Sagar, Fleet Engineer, RN; one *s*. Joined Admiralty service, 1880. *Address:* Naval Store Department, Admiralty, SW.

Died 12 Sept. 1925.

MURRAY, Sir Robert, Kt 1914; Partner in Love and Stewart, Timber Merchants, Glasgow; *b* 1846; *m* Jane Stewart (*d* 1922). *Address:* 2 Hanover Terrace, Regent's Park, NW1. *T:* Paddington 1056.

Died 14 June 1924.

MURRAY, Col Robert Davidson, MB; Indian Medical Service, retired; *b* 30 Aug. 1851; *s* of William Murray, JP, Kilcoy, Ross-shire; *m* Mary McInnes, *e d* of Deputy-Surg.-Gen. George Mackay, MD, IMS, Madras; three *s* three *d*. *Educ:* Inverness Royal Academy; Aberdeen University. Graduated in Medicine with first-class honours at Edinburgh University, 1874; Senior Resident Physician Edinburgh Royal Infirmary, 1874–75; entered Indian Medical Service, 1875; held many important appointments under the Bengal Government, 1876–1904; First Resident Surgeon, Presidency General Hospital, and Superintendent of Asylums, 1882–86; served with the Burmese Expeditionary Force, 1886–87; commanded Field Hospital in Mandalay (medal and despatches); Civil Surgeon of Howrah, 1890–96; Professor of Surgery, Calcutta Medical College, and First Surgeon to the Medical College Hospital, 1898; PMO, Lahore District, 1904; Inspector General of Civil Hospitals, United Provinces of Agra and Oudh, 1905–10; Member of the Legislative Council of the Lieut-Governor, United Provinces, and the first Medical Officer to obtain a seat on Indian Legislature. *Publications:* numerous contributions to the Medical Press. *Address:* 5 Nevern Square, SW5. *T:* Western 2882. *Club:* East India United Service.

Died 12 Jan. 1920.

MURRAY, Maj.-Gen. Robert Hunter, CB 1896; CMG 1898; *b* 12 Aug. 1847; *y s* of late John Murray, JP, and *g s* of late John Murray of Wooplaw, Roxburghshire, NB; *m* 1887, Florence, *d* of late Captain H. W. Barlow, RE; one *s* one *d*. *Educ:* Edinburgh Academy. Ensign 72nd Highlanders, 1867; served throughout Afghan War, 1878–80, as Adjutant; severely wounded at Battle of Kandahar (medal with four clasps for Peiwar Kotal, Charasia, Kabul and Kandahar; and bronze star for Kabul-Kandahar March; Bt of Major); Egyptian Campaign, 1882, as Brig. Major of the Indian Contingent (medal with clasp, for Tel-el-Kebir, and Egyptian bronze star; Bt of Lieut-Col); Sudan Campaign, 1885, as asst to Chief of the Staff; actions of Hasheen, Tamai (clasp for Suakim); DAAG, Guernsey, 1889–92; Sudan Campaign, 1898, in command of the 1st Batt. Seaforth Highlanders (severely wounded, Egyptian Sudan medal with two clasps, medal); Colonel, 1892 (five times despatches); ADC to Queen Victoria; commanding 72nd and 79th regimental districts, 1899–1900; 1st Batt. Seaforth Highlanders to 1899; Maj.-Gen. commanding Infantry Brigade, Aldershot, 1900–2; commanding troops at Alexandria, 1902–4; Col Seaforth Highlanders, 1914–24. *Address:* The Red House, Yateley, Hants. *Club:* Army and Navy.

Died 17 Jan. 1925.

MURRAY, Major William, OBE 1919; MP (Coalition Unionist) Dumfries, Dec. 1918–22; *b* 31 Oct. 1865; *e s* of late Capt. John Murray, RN, of Murraythwaite, and Grace Harriet, *d* of Col William Graham; *m* 1892, Evelyn, *d* of John Bruce; three *d*. *Educ:* Magdalen College, Oxford. Contested Dumries Burghs, 1895 and 1900, and Dumfriesshire, Jan. and Dec. 1910; Member of Faculty of Advocates; Capt. 5th Batt. KOSB, 1899–1912. *Address:* Murraythwaite, Ecclefechan, Scotland; 98 Park Street, Mayfair, W1. *Clubs:* Carlton, Arthur's; New, Edinburgh. *Died 5 March 1923.*

MURRAY BAILLIE, Lt-Col Frederick David; *b* 1862; *er s* of late Col James William Murray Baillie, JP, RHG, of Cally and Broughton, and Elizabeth Florence, *d* of late Frederick R. Magenis; *m* 1900, Alexandra Helen Agnes, *o d* of late James Cavan-Irving, 5th Dragoon Guards, of Burnfoot; one *d*. *Educ:* Eton. Formerly Major 4th Hussars; Major and Hon. Lieut-Col, retired, late 2nd Co. of London Yeomanry; a Railway Transport Officer, 1914–17. *Address:* Ilston Grange, Leicester; Cally, Gatehouse, Kirkcudbright. *Clubs:* Boodle's, Cavalry. *Died 23 Dec. 1924.*

MURTON, Sir Walter, Kt 1899; CB 1894; *b* East Stour, Ashford, Kent, 6 April 1836; 2nd *s* of late Walter Murton, and Elizabeth, *d* of late Richard Coleman; *m* 1860, Mary (*d* 1895), *y d* of late John Callaway of Canterbury; two *s*. *Educ:* Tonbridge School. Admitted a solicitor, 1858; appointed Solicitor to the Board of Trade in 1875 from the first formation of the Legal Department; retired, 1900. A British Representative at Conference on German Claims arising from S African War, 1900; travelled in the Dominions and other countries, 1900–8. Decorated 1894 in recognition of services at the Board of Trade. *Publications:* Wreck Inquiries; Law and Practice. *Address:* Gipp's Close, Langton, Kent. *TA:* Langton Green. *Clubs:* Devonshire; Tunbridge Wells and Counties. *Died 20 June 1927.*

MUSCIO, Bernard; Challis Professor of Philosophy, University of Sydney, since 1922; *b* NSW, 1887; *s* of Bernard Muscio, Orchard Hills, NSW; *m* 1915, Florence Mildred, *e d* of Charles Fry, Sydney; no *c*. *Educ:* privately; Sydney University (BA 1910); Gonville and Caius College, Cambridge (BA Cambridge, 1913). University Demonstrator in Experimental Psychology, Cambridge, 1914; Investigator to the Industrial Fatigue Research Board, 1919–22. *Publications:* Lectures on Industrial Psychology, Sydney, 1917, 2nd edn London, 1921; various reports of investigations in industrial fatigue, published by the Industrial Fatigue Research Board; articles on philosophy and psychology in Mind, Monist, British Journal of Psychology, etc. *Address:* The University, Sydney, NSW. *Died 28 May 1926.*

MUSGRAVE, Charles Edwin, FICS; Secretary London Chamber of Commerce; Chevalier, Order of St Anne of Russia; Officer of the Crown of Roumania; *b* 17 April 1861; *e s* of late E. G. Musgrave, Stotfold, Beds. *Educ:* privately. Sub-Editor of The Citizen, 1881; entered service of London Chamber of Commerce, 1882; Assistant Secretary, 1884; Secretary, 1909; Secretary, Congress of Chambers of Commerce of the Empire, 1920, and of British Imperial Council of Commerce since formation, 1911, London Labour Conciliation and Arbitration Board, and Timber Trade Federation of United Kingdom; President Chartered Institute of Secretaries, 1921–22; Member, Court of Turners' Company; gave evidence before Royal Commissions, etc. *Publications:* (joint) Handbook, The Factory and Workshops Act, 1901; The London Chamber of Commerce, from 1881 to 1914. *Recreations:* rowing, touring, reading. *Address:* 97 Cannon Street, EC; Temple Chambers, EC4. *TA:* Convention, Cannon, London. *T:* City 1949. *Clubs:* Author's, Gresham. *Died 3 Aug. 1923.*

MUSGRAVE, Major Herbert, DSO 1915; Royal Engineers; *b* 11 May 1876; *y s* of late Sir Anthony Musgrave, GCMG; *m* 1915, Georgeanna, *o d* of Mark Hopkins; one *d*. *Educ:* Harrow. Entered army, 1896; Captain, 1905; with S African Constabulary, 1901–4; DAA&QMG, Malta, 1908–12; served S African War, 1899–1902 (despatches twice, Queen's medal 5 clasps, King's medal 2 clasps); European War, 1914–16 (wounded, DSO). *Address:* Hurstanclays, East Grinstead. *Club:* United Service. *Died 3 June 1918.*

MUSGRAVE, Sir Richard George, 12th Bt, *cr* 1611; DL, JP; *b* 11 Oct. 1872; *e s* of Sir Richard Courtenay Musgrave, 11th Bt and Adora Frances Olga (she *m* 2nd, the 3rd Lord Brougham), *d* of Peter Wells of Forest Farm, Windsor; *S* father, 1881; *m* 1895, Hon. Eleanor Harbord, 7th *d* of 5th Baron Suffield; one *s*. Owned about 6,900 acres. *Heir: s* Nigel Courtenay Musgrave, *b* 11 Feb. 1896. *Address:* 17 Charles Street, W1. *T:* Gerrard 2136; Eden Hall, Langwathby, Cumberland. *Died 21 May 1926.*

MUSPRATT, Edmund Knowles, JP; LLD; FCS, FIC; Chairman, British Insulated and Helsby Cables, Ltd; Vice-Chairman, United Alkali Co., Ltd; Member of Council, University of Liverpool; *b* Linacre, near Liverpool, 6 Nov. 1833; *s* of late James Muspratt, Seaforth Hall; *m* 1861, Frances Jane, *d* of Thomas Baines, Liverpool; three *s* four *d*. *Educ:* Pestallozian Institution, Worksop; Universities of Giessen and Munich. Formerly member of the firms James Muspratt & Sons and Muspratt Bros & Huntley, later incorporated in the United Alkali Co., Ltd; President, Society of Chemical Industry, 1885–86; President, Liverpool Chamber of Commerce, 1875; Member, City Council, Liverpool, 1877–86; Member, Lancashire County Council, 1889–1902; Pro-Chancellor, University of Liverpool, 1903–9; President, Financial Reform Association. *Publications:* My Life and Work; addresses to various Societies. *Recreations:* travelling, reading. *Address:* Seaforth Hall, near Liverpool.
Died 1 Sept. 1923.

MUSPRATT-WILLIAMS, Lt-Col Charles Augustus, CIE 1916; *b* 13 Sept. 1861; *s* of General Jackson Muspratt-Williams; *m* 1892, Ethel Annie, *d* of late Rear-Admiral A. J. Kennedy, RN; one *s* one *d*. *Educ:* Cheltenham College. Entered Army, 1881; Captain, 1889; Major, 1889; Lt-Col 1909; Assistant Superintendent, Gunpowder Factory, Kirkee, Small Arms Factory, Kirkee, Gun Carriage Factory, Bombay, 1887–90; Assistant Superintendent, Gunpowder Factory, Ishapur, 1890–91; Superintendent, 1892–98; Chief Inspector of Explosives with the Government of India, 1898–1920; retired, 1920. *Address:* c/o Lloyds Bank, Ltd, 9 Pall Mall, SW1. *Club:* Public Schools. *Died 6 May 1925.*

MUSTERS, John Patricius Chaworth, DL; JP; *b* Oxton, 1860; *e s* of late John Chaworth Musters and Caroline Anne, *e d* of late Henry Porter Sherbrooke of Oxton, Notts; *m* Mary Anne, *d* of George Sharpe; four *s* five *d*. *Educ:* Eton; Christ Church, Oxford. Farmer; colliery director; magistrate; High Sheriff, Notts, 1902; Patron of 2 livings; owner of Annesley, Wiverton, and Edwalton, all in Nottinghamshire. *Recreations:* farming, sport, ornithology. *Address:* Annesley Park, Nottingham. *TA:* Annesley, Woodhouse. *Clubs:* Carlton; Notts County, Nottingham.
Died 12 Dec. 1921.

MYER, Horatio; *b* Hereford, 1850; *s* of H. Myer; *m* 1877, Esther, *d* of Henry Joseph. Engaged in wool trade, 1869–75, and in shipping iron trade, 1876–84; iron founder, 1876–1903; Member for Kennington, LCC, 1889–1904; MP (L) North Lambeth, 1906–10. *Publication:* pamphlet, Taxation of Landlords. *Address:* 64 Maida Vale, W. *T:* Paddington 1667; Forthill, Henley. *Club:* National Liberal. *Died 1 Jan. 1916.*

MYERS, Hon. Sir Arthur, Kt 1924; JP (New Zealand); Director, National Bank of New Zealand, Ltd, London; Director, New Zealand Insurance Co.; *b* 19 May 1867; 2nd *s* of late Louis Myers, Auckland, NZ; *m* 1903, Vera Anita, OBE, *d* of late B. W. Levy; one *s* two *d*. *Educ:* Wellington College, New Zealand. Chairman Director The Campbell and Ehrenfried Co., Auckland, NZ; Member Royal Commission on Local Government (England); Lieut-Col New Zealand Military Forces (retired); Mayor of Auckland, 1905–8; Member New Zealand Parliament for Auckland City East, 1910–21; Member Mackenzie Ministry, 1912, holding portfolios Finance, Defence, and Railways; Member National Ministry New Zealand, 1915–19, holding portfolios Customs, Pensions, and Munitions; presented Myers Park and Kindergarten, Town Hall Clock and other benefactions to Auckland City. *Recreations:* golf, tennis, fishing. *Address:* 71 Upper Berkeley Street, W1. *T:* Paddington 1185. *Club:* Constitutional. *Died 9 Oct. 1926.*

MYLNE, Rt. Rev. Louis George, DD; Hon. Canon, Worcester, 1917; *b* Paris, 1843; *s* of Major C. D. Mylne, Bombay Army; *m* 1879, Amy, *d* of G. W. Moultrie; five *s*. *Educ:* Merchiston Castle School, Edinburgh; St Andrews University; Corpus Christi College, Oxford. Curate of N Moreton, Berks, 1867–70; Senior Tutor of Keble College, Oxford, 1870–76; Bishop of Bombay, 1876–97; Rector of Alvechurch, Worcestershire, 1905–17; Vicar of St Mary, Marlborough, 1897–1905; Prebendary of Woodford and Wilsford in Salisbury Cathedral, 1899–1905. *Publications:* English Church Life in India, 1881; Corporate Life of the Church in India, 1884; Counsels and Principles of the Lambeth Conference of 1888; Sermons preached in Bombay, 1889; Churchmen and the Higher Criticism, 1893; Hopes for Reunion, 1896; The Hidden Riches of Secret Places (in Mankind and the Church), 1907; Mission to Hindus, 1908; The Holy Trinity, 1916. *Address:* Redcliffe, Battenhall, Worcester.
Died 19 Feb. 1921.

N

NADIA, Maharaja of; Hon. Maharaja Kshaunish Chandra Ray Bahadur; Member Bengal Executive Council since 1924; *b* at the Palace, Krishnagar, 29 Oct. 1890; *s* of late Maharaja Kshitish Chandra Ray Bahadur; *m* Maharani Jyotirmoyee Daby, *d* of late Raja Ashutoshe Nath Ray of Cossimbazar; two *d*. *Educ:* privately. Came of the oldest aristocratic family in Bengal; created Maharaja at Coronation Durbar, Delhi, 1911; made Maharaja Bahadur, 1917; first non-official elected Chairman of Nadia District Board, 1920–24; Member of the Bengal Legislative Council, 1921–23. *Recreations:* photography, shooting. *Address:* The Palace, Krishnagar, Nadia, Bengal; 2 Bright Street, Ballygunje, Calcutta. *T:* Regent 198. *M:* 1114, 3303, 5308, and 11867. *Clubs:* Calcutta; Darjeeling Gymkhana.

Died May 1928.

NAESMYTH, Sir James Tolmé, 7th Bt, *cr* 1706; *b* 6 Aug. 1864; *s* of Sir Michael George Naesmyth, 6th Bt and Mary Ann, *d* of John Nicholls, late Clerk to the Lord Chancellor's Court, Westminster; *S* father, 1907. *Heir:* nephew Douglas Arthur Bradley Naesmyth, *b* 1 Jan. 1905. *Address:* Posso, Peeblesshire, NB.

Died 24 July 1922.

NAESMYTH, Sir Douglas Arthur Bradley, 8th Bt, *cr* 1706; *b* 1 Jan. 1905; *s* of late Donald Luttrell Kilve Naesmyth, MRCS (3rd *s* of 6th Bt), and Flora, *d* of late H. W. Burrage; *S* uncle, 1922. *Heir:* none.

Died Jan. 1928.

NAIRNE, Sir Perceval Alleyn, Kt 1915; FRGS; Solicitor, admitted 1864, firm Baker & Nairne; Solicitor to Worshipful Company of Drapers, London, to National Union of Teachers, to League of Mercy and to King George's Fund for Sailors; Chairman Seaman's Hospital Society and London School of Tropical Medicine; *b* 12 Feb. 1841; 5th *s* of Captain Alexander Nairne, HEICS, previously RN (Copenhagen, 1801); unmarried. *Educ:* Clapham Grammar School. Secretary Rochester and Southwark Diocesan Conferences in succession, 1886–1911; Order of Mercy. *Address:* 176 The Grove, Camberwell, SE; 3 Crosby Square, Bishopsgate, EC. *T:* 5841 Avenue.

Died 10 Dec. 1921.

NAISH, Redmond, ISO 1908; Accountant in National Education Office, Ireland; *b* 6 June 1848; *s* of late Carrol Naish, JP; *m* 1882, Mary, *d* of late Alderman Macdermot, Dublin. *Educ:* Tullabeg. Entered Department, 1868. *Address:* 66 Northumberland Road, Dublin.

NAISMITH, Lt-Col William John, DSO 1900; TD 1902; MD Edinburgh; FRCSE; *b* 8 Sept. 1847; *s* of John Naismith, MD, HEICS; *m* 1890, Edith Mary, *y d* of late William Rutherford Sanders, MD, FRCPE, Prof. of Pathology in the University of Edinburgh; one *s* two *d*. Surg.-Lt-Col Ayrshire Imperial Yeomanry; Surg. HM Prison of Ayr, Ayr Industrial Schools, and Ayrshire County Constabulary; Medical Officer, 6th Batt. Imperial Yeomanry; served South Africa, 1900–2 (despatches, Queen's medal 3 clasps, King's medal 2 clasps, DSO); retired. *Address:* 19 Queen's Gardens, St Andrews, Fife.

Died 3 Jan. 1926.

NANAK CHAND, Masheerud-dowla Rai Bahadur, CSI 1911; CIE 1901; Pensioner, 1st class, Sirdar and Jagirdar of Indore State; *b* 1860; *e s* of Masheerud-dowla Rai Bahadur Omeid Singh, tutor and adviser to Chief of Indore; two *s*. *Educ:* Delhi and Indore. Hindu by religion, Vaish by community; received his father's title of Masheerud-dowla Rai Bahadur from Indore State at age 13; Judicial Secretary to Minister, 1886; State Treasurer, 1886–91; Deputy Minister, 1891–95; Residency Vakil as well in 1893, and Minister, 1895–1913 (except for ten months); Kaiser-i Hind Medal, first-class, for services in the famine of 1898–99; after retiring he travelled round the world, and visited Ceylon, China, Japan, America, England, France, Switzerland and Italy. *Publications:* edited J'Khairkhah-i-Vaish, a monthly paper in Urdu, for four years; wrote Moortibhooshan and Vidhwa-Vivah, in Nagri, on idolatry and widow marriage; and Hinduism, in English. *Recreation:* tennis. *Address:* Santoshkuti, Indore; Mohalla Dassa, Delhi.

Died 29 March 1920.

NAND LAL, Diwan Bahadur Pandit, ISO 1911; *b* Amritsar, Nov. 1857; a Kashmiri Pandit of Lahore, Punjab; *s* of Pandit Janardhan Koul. *Educ:* Collegiate School, Amritsar. Served about 5 years in Financial Commissioner's Office, Punjab, and in Deputy Commissioner's Office, Lahore; transferred to Baluchistan; served for some years as Confidential Clerk and then as Head Clerk to new Quetta and Pishin

District; Subordinate Judge of Quetta, 1885; Extra Assistant Commissioner; for about 4 years was Personal Indian Asst to Agent to the Governor-General in Baluchistan; was Secretary to the Sandeman High School at Quetta; transferred to Central India as Extra Assistant to the Agent to the Governor-General, 1902; Second Assistant to Agent Governor-General, 1915; Assistant Political Agent, Bundelkhand, 1919; President of Victoria Library and Lady O'Dwyer Girls' School, Indore; retired after 50 years' service, 1924; made a Rai Saheb by Lord Curzon on the Queen's Birthday, 1899; made Rai Bahadur by Lord Minto, 1910; made Diwan Bahadur by Lord Reading, 1925. *Address:* Indore, India.

Died 28 May 1926.

NANJUNDAYYA, H. Velpanuru, CIE 1914; *b* 13 Oct. 1860; *e s* of Subbayya Garu; descended from a high-class Brahman family of Mysore; *m*; six *s* five *d*. *Educ:* Wesleyan Mission School, Mysore; Christian College, Madras; Madras University (Fellow, 1895). Graduated, 1880; obtained Law Degree, 1883. Advocate of the Chief Court of Mysore, but did not practise long; accepted a place as Munsiff and entered the service of the Mysore Government, 1885; Under Secretary to Government, 1895; Judge, Chief Court of Mysore, 1904; present at both the Delhi Durbars; subsequently Mem. of Council and Chief Judge Chief Court; retired from State Council, 1916; Vice-Chancellor, Mysore University. *Publications:* A Treatise on Law, and a Manual of Political Economy, in Kanada, the language of the Mysore State, and of the Ethnographic Survey of Mysore Castes. *Address:* Mallesvaaram, Bangalore, India.

Died 7 May 1920.

NANSON, Hon. John Leighton, MLA West Australia; barrister-at-law, Gray's Inn; *b* Carlisle, England, 22 Sept. 1863; *s* of late John Nanson, solicitor, Carlisle; *m* Janet Drummond, *d* of late A. Durlacher, Resident Magistrate, Geraldton, West Australia; one *d*. *Educ:* Carlisle Grammar School; King William's College, Isle of Man. For many years assistant editor of the West Australian, Perth, WA; subsequently called to the Bar; Minister for Lands, WA, 1901; Member Coolgardie Water Scheme Commission, 1902; Leader of Opposition, 1902–3; Minister for Works, 1904; Attorney-General, Minister for Education and Member of the Executive Council, West Australia, 1909–11. *Recreations:* usual. *Address:* 1 Ord Street, Perth, West Australia. *Club:* Weld, Perth.

Died 29 Feb. 1916.

NANTON, Sir Augustus Meredith, Kt 1917; Senior Winnipeg Partner in Osler, Hammond and Nanton, Investment Brokers; *b* Toronto, 7 May 1860; *s* of (Daniel) Augustus Nanton, barrister, Osgood Hall, Toronto, and Mary Louisa, *d* of Sheriff W. B. Jarvis of Toronto; *m* 1st, 1886, Georgina Hope Hespeler (*d* 1887); 2nd, 1894, Ethel Constance, *d* of late Thomas Clark, Winnipeg; three *s* three *d*. *Educ:* Toronto Model School. Vice-President, Dominion Bank of Great West; Life Insurance Co. President, Winnipeg Electric Railway Co.; Director and Chairman, Canadian Committee, Hudson's Bay Co.; Director and Member Executive Canadian Pacific Railway; Director, Royal Trusts Co., Manitoba Bridge and Iron Works, Cockshutt Plow Co., Ogilvie Flour Mills Co., Canada Starch Co., Guarantee Co. of North America. *Address:* Kilmorie, 229 Roslyn Road, Winnipeg. *Clubs:* Marlborough; Manitoba, St Charles' Country, Hunt, Winnipeg; Toronto, Toronto; Mount Royal, Montreal; Rideau, Ottawa.

Died 24 April 1925.

NAOROJI, Dadabhai, LLD (hon.) Bombay; first Indian Member of Parliament; *b* Bombay, 4 Sept. 1825; *s* of Mr Naoroji, a Parsi priest, and Manekbai; *m* 1838, Gulbai, *d* of Mr Sorabje, a Parsi priest; two *d*. *Educ:* Elphinstone School and College. First Indian Professor in India of Mathematics and Natural Philosophy, 1854; visited England, as partner in first Indian firm in England, 1855; Professor of Gujarati, and Life Governor, University College, London; obtained admission of Indians to the Civil Service, 1870; Prime Minister Baroda, 1874; Member of Corporation and Municipal Council, Bombay, 1875–76 and 1881–85; Member Legislative Council, Bombay, 1885–87; promoted Bombay Ripon Technical School, 1885; MP (L) Central Finsbury, 1892–95; great reception in India, 1893; President Indian National Congress, 1886, 1893, and 1906; President London Indian Society for many years; moved for inquiry into Indian affairs in House, 1894; defeated Government *re* Simultaneous Examinations, 1893; Member of Inter-Parliamentary Conference at The Hague, 1894; Member of Royal Commission on Indian Expenditure, 1895 (only Indian member of a Royal Commission); gave evidence to the Welby Commission, 1897; Member of British Committee of the Indian National Congress from beginning (1889); contested N Lambeth, 1906; addressed many public meetings on India. *Publications:* Poverty and Un-British Rule in India, 1901; The Rights of Labour, 1906; and papers on Poverty of India; England's Duties to India; Mysore; Expenses of the Abyssinian War; Indian Civil Service Clause in the Governor-General of India's Bill; Admission of Educated Natives into the Indian Civil Service; Wants and Means of India; Commerce of India; Financial Administration of India; Correspondence with Secretary of State on Condition of India, 1880; Note on General Education; Minute on Technical Education; Reply to Sir Grant Duff in Contemporary Review, 1887; and many papers on Indian social, political, and economic subjects; collection published, 1887; Correspondence with Lord George Hamilton, 1900–1. *Address:* The Sands, Vesava; Andheri, BB, and CI Railway, Bombay.

Died 2 July 1917.

NAPIER OF MAGDALA, 2nd Baron, *cr* 1868; **Robert William Napier;** *b* 11 Feb. 1845; *s* of 1st Baron and 1st wife, Anne Sarah, *d* of George Pearse, Medical Inspector-General at Madras; *S* father, 1890; *m* 1885, Eva Maria Louisa Langham (author of A Stormy Morning, How She Played the Game, Half a Lie, etc), *d* of 4th Baron Macdonald, and *widow* of Capt. Algernon Langham, Grenadier Guards; one *d. Educ:* privately. Entered Army, 1860, at age of 15; served in Bengal Army, 1861–82; Umbeyla campaign, 1864; Abyssinian campaign, 1868; retired as Lieut-Col in 1883. Protestant. *Heir: brother* Hon. James Pearse Napier [*b* 30 Dec. 1849; *m* 1876, Mabel Ellen (*d* 1907), *yr d* of Lt–Col Windsor Parker, Suffolk; two *d* (one *s* decd)]. *Address:* Lynedale, Isle of Skye.

Died 11 Dec. 1921.

NAPIER, Col Alexander, MD; RAMCT; retired; late Officer Commanding 4th Scottish General Hospital, Glasgow; in practice in Glasgow since 1876; Physician, Victoria Infirmary, Glasgow; Hon. Librarian and Fellow of Royal Faculty of Physicians and Surgeons, Glasgow; *b* Glasgow, 21 June 1851; *s* of Alexander Napier and Jane Struthers; *m* 1879, Elizabeth Harper; four *s* three *d. Educ:* High School, Glasgow; Universities of Glasgow and Berlin. Two years in practice in S Africa. *Publications:* translations: Physiology and Pathology of the Sympathetic System of Nerves (Prof. A. Eulenburg and Dr P. Guttmann), 1879; A Handbook of Physical Diagnosis, comprising the Throat, Thorax, and Abdomen (Dr P. Guttmann), 1879; Manual of Stretcher Drill. *Recreations:* loafing, rarely; golfing, occasionally; botanising, collecting old books, especially old English Bibles. *Address:* 10 Athole Gardens, Glasgow, W2. *T:* Western, 5411 Glasgow. *Club:* Conservative, Glasgow. *Died 5 Oct. 1928.*

NAPIER, Arthur Sampson, MA, DLitt, BSc, PhD; FBA; Merton Professor of English Language and Literature, Oxford University, since 1885; also Rawlinsonian Professor of Anglo-Saxon since 1903; Fellow of Merton College, Oxford; *b* Cheshire, 30 Aug. 1853; *e s* of late George Webster Napier, Alderley Edge, Cheshire; *m* Mary Ferrier, 2nd *d* of James Hervey, Alderley Edge; four *s* one *d. Educ:* Rugby School; Owens Coll., Manchester; Exeter Coll., Oxford (MA, DLitt); University of Berlin. Reader of English, University of Berlin, 1878–82; Professor of English Language and Literature, University of Göttingen, 1882–85; Corresponding Member, Royal Academy of Sciences, Göttingen; Hon. Member, American Academy, Boston; Hon. LittD Manchester; Hon. DLitt Groningen. *Publications:* Ueber die Werke des altenglischen Erzbischofs Wulfstan, 1882; Wulfstan-Sammlung der ihm zugeschriebenen Homilien, Berlin, 1883; History of the Holy Rood-tree (Early English Text Society), 1894; Crawford Collection of Early English Charters (in conjunction with Mr W. H. Stevenson, Oxford), 1895; Old English Glosses, 1900; The Franks Casket, 1901; contributions to the Zeitschrift für deutsches Alterthum, Anglia, Englische Studien, Archiv für das Studium der neueren Sprachen, American Modern Language Notes, Academy, etc. *Address:* Merton College, Oxford; Headington Hill, Oxford.

Died 10 May 1916.

NAPIER, Major Egbert; late 3rd Gordon Highlanders; Chief Constable of Norfolk; *b* Penbedw Hall, Flintshire, 12 Aug. 1867; *s* of Col Edward Napier, late 6th Dragoon Guards, and Marthe Louise, *d* of late W. B. Buddicom, Penbedw Hall, Flintshire; *m* Evangeline, *d* of J. G. Dreyer, Copenhagen, and Valschrivier, Orange River Colony; two *d. Educ:* Wellington College. Formerly on Staff of Commissioner of Metropolitan Police; served South African War, 1900–1; Brigade Major Kroonstad District and Adjutant of Driscoll's Scouts. *Died 19 Nov. 1916.*

NAPIER, Hon. Mark Francis, BA; barrister; *b* 21 Jan. 1852; *s* of 10th Baron Napier and Ettrick and Anne Jane Charlotte, *o d* of Robert Manners Lockwood; *m* 1878, Emily, *y d* of 7th and last Viscount Ranelagh; two *s* (and one *s* decd). *Educ:* Cambridge. Called to the Bar, Inner Temple, 1876; contested Roxburgh, 1886; MP (L) Roxburgh, 1892–95. *Address:* Puttenden Manor, Lingfield, Surrey.

Died 19 Aug. 1919.

NAPIER, Vice-Adm. Sir Trevylyan Dacres Willes, KCB 1919; (CB 1916); MVO 1903; Royal Navy; *b* 19 April 1867; 4th *s* of Admiral Gerard John Napier; *m* 1899, Mary Elizabeth, *d* of Admiral Sir Michael Culme-Seymour, 3rd Bt, and Mary Georgiana Watson; one *s* two *d. Educ:* privately. Entered Royal Navy as Naval Cadet, 1880; Midshipman, 1882; served in Egyptian War; Lieutenant, 1887; Commander, 1899; served in HM Yacht; Captain, 1903; commanded HMS Crescent, 1904–7, as Flag-Capt. to Admiral Sir John Durnford on Cape Station; commanded Royal Naval College, Dartmouth, 1907–10; HMS Bellerophon, 1910–12, and 2nd Light Cruiser Squadron, 1913; served European War, 1914–16, Battle of Jutland Bank (despatches); Naval ADC to King George V, 1913; in command of Light Cruiser Squadrons, 1914–17; Vice-Admiral, Light Cruiser Force, 1917–19. *Club:* United Service.

Died 30 July 1920.

NAPIER, Col William, CMG 1896; Member of the firm of Napier & Weir, merchants; *b* Scotland, 1861; *s* of David Napier. Served as trooper in Natal Carbineers for four years; entered service of BSA Co., 1891; joined Victoria Rangers as a subaltern, 1892; commanded a troop under Major Alan Wilson during advance into Matabeleland, 1893; present at all engagements which led to subjugation of Lobengula's forces; in command of whole of armed forces in Rhodesia, 1895; commanded all local forces engaged in suppressing Matabeleland rebellion, 1896, up to arrival of Sir Richard Martin (despatches, Matabele Medal for 1893); commanded A Squadron of the Southern Rhodesia Reserve Force for a few months, Boer War, 1899–1900. *Address:* Hillside, Bulawayo. *Clubs:* Junior Constitutional; Bulawayo.

Died 29 Jan. 1920.

NAPIER, Maj.-Gen. William John, CB 1917; CMG 1916; late Royal Artillery; *b* 10 Nov. 1863; 3rd *s* of late Hon. William Napier (2nd *s* of 9th Baron Napier), and Louisa Mary, *d* of John H. Lloyd, QC; *m* 1889, Maud Denison Gooch, *o d* of late Col Edward Nicol William Holbrook, RMLI; one *s*. Served S African War, 1899–1900 (Queen's medal 3 clasps); European War, 1914–18, Dir of Artillery, WO, promoted Maj.-Gen. (despatches, CMG, CB); retired pay, 1922. *Address:* 14 Carlyle Mansions, Cheyne Walk, Chelsea, SW3. *T:* Kensington 5858. *Clubs:* United Service, Royal Automobile, Ranelagh. *Died 18 Nov. 1925.*

NAPOLEON, HIH Prince (Victor Jerome Frederic); head of Napoleon family; *b* Palais Royal, Paris, 18 July 1862; *e s* of Prince Napoleon and Princess Marie Clotilde de Savoie; *m* 1910, HRH Princess Clementine of Belgium; one *s* one *d*. Expelled from France, 1886. *Address:* 241 Avenue Louise, Brussels; Château de Ronchinne, par Courrière, Province Namur; Domaine de Farnborough Hill, Farnborough, Hants. *Died 3 May 1926.*

NARSINGARH, Sahib Bahadur of; HH Shri Huzur Raja Sir Arjun Singhji; KCIE; *b* 10 Jan. 1887; *s* of Maharaj Moti Singhji Sahib of Dkuankher; belongs to the Paramar or Ponwar branch of Agnikul Rajputs; *S* 1897; *m* 1907, *d* of HH Rajah Sahib Bahadur of Sailana; one *s* three *d. Educ:* Daly College; Mayo College; Imperial Cadet Corps. Invested with full ruling powers, 1909; the State was 734 square miles in extent, and had a population of 101,426, the Chief receiving a salute of 11 guns. *Heir: s* Shri Maharaj Kumar Shri Vikram Singh Bahadur, *b* 21 Sept. 1909. *Address:* Narsingarh, Central India.

Died 22 April 1924.

NASH, Rev. Adam James Glendinning, MA; Rector of St Mildred, with St Margaret, City of London, since 1912; Hon. Canon of Ripon Cathedral, since 1900; Fellow of Sion College, 1912; Surrogate for the Master of the Faculties and the Vicar-General of Canterbury, 1912; Editor of the London Diocese Book since 1912; *s* of Joseph and Matilda Glendinning Nash. *Educ:* Queens' College, Cambridge (BA 1871, MA 1874). Deacon, 1871; Priest, 1872; Curate of St John's, Fitzroy Square, London, 1871–78; Assistant Thursday Morning Lecturer at St Peter-upon-Cornhill, London, 1877–81; Vicar-Designate of St Thomas, Finsbury Park, 1878–81; General Secretary of Bradford Church Congress, 1898; VP Cambridge Church Congress, 1910; Past Provincial Grand Chaplain of West Yorkshire Freemasons; Chaplain to the Mayor of Bradford; Vicar of St John's with St Hilda, Bradford, 1881–1912; Official Principal to Archdeaconry of Craven, 1894–1912; Proctor in the Convocation of York, 1895–1919; Assessor under Clergy Discipline Act; Hon. Secretary to Ripon Diocesan Conference, 1898–1912; Member of Bradford Governing Body of Ripon Diocesan Education Society. *Publications:* Confirmation Day Suggestions and Meditations, 1890, 1891, and 1892; Preparation for Confirmation, 1903; Summary of Foreign Marriage Law, 1904, 2nd edn 1910; Parish Church Anthem Book, 1905. *Address:* 4 Harley House, Regent's Park, NW1. *T:* Paddington 3100. *Died 13 Oct. 1920.*

NASH, Rev. Alexander, MA (Oxon); Hon. Canon of Gloucester Cathedral since 1901; Hon. Secretary of Diocesan Board of Finance (Maintenance Committee), and Diocesan Queen Victoria Clergy Fund; *b* Poonah, India, 1845; *s* of Lieut A. Nash, RE and HEIC, and Lucy Anne, *g d* of Sir Charles Blois, 6th Bt, Cockfield Hall, Suffolk; *m* 1868, Elizabeth, *e d* of W. W. Cowslade of Erleigh, Reading; four *s* four *d*. *Educ*: abroad; private schools; BNC, Oxford. Entered Holy Orders, 1868, and for seven years was Curate of Standish with Hardwicke; Rector of Quedgeley, Gloucester, 1876–89; Vicar of Standish with Hardwicke, 1889–1923. *Recreations*: rowed in BNC boat Head of River, 1867 and 1868; gardening. *Address*: Whiteknights, Tuffley, Gloucester. *Died 29 Aug. 1924.*

NASH, John Brady, MD Edin. and Sydney; MRCS; Member of Legislative Council, New South Wales, since 1900; Director Royal Prince Alfred Hospital, Sydney, 1917; Director Sydney Hospital, since 1905; Member of the Board of Health for New South Wales, 1918; Lieutenant-Colonel, unattached list, Australian military forces; *b* at sea, near Canary Islands, 19 May 1857; *s* of Dr Andrew Nash, JP, LRCP, etc, and Margaret Brady, both of Co. Cork; *m* 1888, Agnes M'Cormick of Newcastle, NSW; four *d*. *Educ*: St Patrick's Coll., Melbourne, Victoria; Sydney (Matriculated, 1877) and Edinburgh Universities. Took honours in most subjects; graduated, 1882; MD 1892; studied in London, Dublin, and Paris before returning to New South Wales in 1883; at Newcastle, New South Wales, 1883–1900; practising as a surgeon in Sydney since 1900; Hon. Consulting Surgeon, Coast Hospital, Sydney; Hon. Surgeon, State Hospital, Rookwood, Sydney; Hon. Surgeon to St Margaret's Hospital for Women, Sydney; Member Royal Commission on decline of the birthrate in New South Wales, 1903; for five years commanded the Irish Rifle Regiment in the Australian military forces; Lt-Col Australian Army Medical Corps, Australian Imperial Expeditionary Force, 1914–16; on service in Egypt, 1915; Anzac during October 1915 (an original Anzac). Lectured on literary, especially Shakespearian, subjects before the Shakespearian Society, and other bodies. *Publications*: numerous contributions on medical and surgical subjects to medical journals in Australia and to the Australian Medical Congresses. *Recreation*: literature. *Address*: 219 Macquarie Street, Sydney, New South Wales. *T*: 3681 City. *Clubs*: Australian, University, Sydney.

NASH, Joseph, RI. *Address*: The White House, Somerleyton, Suffolk. *Died 24 May 1922.*

NASH, Col Llewellyn Thomas Manly, CMG 1915; late Army Medical Staff; *b* 7 April 1861; *s* of Surg.-Major T. L. Nash, MD; *m* 1901, Editha Gertrude, *y d* of Rev. Charles Sloggett. Major, 1897; Lieut-Col 1905; served Miranzai Expedition, 1891 (despatches, medal with clasp); Hazara Expedition, 1891 (clasp); European War, 1914–18 (CMG, despatches twice). *Address*: 16 Queen's Road, Richmond, Surrey. *T*: Richmond 3048. *Club*: Junior United Service. *Died 9 Sept. 1928.*

NASIR-EL-MULK, Abdul Kassim Khan, GCMG 1897 (KCMG 1889); late Regent of Persia, 1911; *b* 1858. *Educ*: Teheran; Balliol College, Oxford. Sent on special mission to Europe, 1897; was Governor of Khurdistan. *Died Dec. 1927.*

NATHAN, Sir Nathaniel, Kt 1903; KC; *b* 1843; *e s* of late Jonah Nathan, Pembridge Square, W; *m* 1870, Helen (*d* 1906), *o d* of Thomas Turner, JP Doncaster. *Educ*: University College School and University College, London (BA 1863). Called to the Bar, 1866; joined Midland Circuit; practised at Birmingham, 1873–88; a resident magistrate in Jamaica, 1888; Magistrate for Kingston, 1891; served as Acting Judge of Supreme Court, Jamaica, till 1893, when appointed Senior Puisne Judge of Trinidad; Attorney-General of Trinidad, 1898; and acted as Chief Justice, 1901–3. *Publication*: Economic Heresies, 1909. *Address*: 77 St James' Court, SW. *Club*: Reform. *Died 18 Feb. 1916.*

NATHAN, Sir Robert, KCSI 1919 (CSI 1911); CIE 1903; BA; barrister-at-law; *b* 1866; *s* of late Jonah Nathan. *Educ*: St Peter's Coll., Cambridge. Entered Indian Civil Service, 1888 (retired, 1915), serving as assistant magistrate and collector, settlement officer, joint magistrate, etc; Under-Secretary to Government of India, Financial and Commercial Department, 1895; Home Department, 1897; Magistrate and Collector, 1900; Secretary to Indian Universities Commission, 1902; Deputy Secretary, Home Department, 1903; on special duty in the Home and Finance Departments, 1904; Private Secretary to the Viceroy, 1905; Commissioner, Dacca Division, Eastern Bengal, 1907; Officiating Chief Secretary to the Governor of Eastern Bengal and Assam, 1910; President Dacca, 1912, and Patna, 1913, Universities Committees. *Publications*: Official History of Plague in India; Progress

of Education in India, 1897–98, 1901–2; articles for the Imperial Gazetteer of India. *Address*: C3 The Albany, W1. *T*: Gerrard 7088. *Club*: East India United Service. *Died 26 June 1921.*

NATHUBHAI, Tribhovandas Mangaldas, JP; Hon. Magistrate, and Fellow of the University, Bombay; Sheth or head of the Kapol Banya community, resigned the presidentship after tenure thereof for twenty-five years, 1912; *b* 28 Oct. 1856; *s* of Sir Mangaldas Nathubhai, CSI (the first Hindu in India to get the honour of Knighthood); *m* 1st, 1875; 2nd, 1883; two *s* three *d*. *Educ*: St Xavier's College, Bombay. Was for twenty years an elected Member of the Bombay Municipal Corporation; an Honorary Magistrate ever since the establishment of Courts of Bench Magistrates in Bombay; nominated by Government a Member of the Bombay Provincial Advisory Committee for students proceeding to Europe; President, Trustee, or Member of the Committees of several Hindu public charity funds in Bombay; President of the Hindu Mahajan Committee; Patron of the Teachers' Association, Bombay, Sanitary Association, Bombay, and Hindu Gymkhana, Bombay; Patron of the Hindu Ambulance Corps; rendered eminent services during the first outbreak of plague in Bombay, which were recognised both by Government and the public; political representative of Bombay Hindus for the Coronation of King George V; much interested in the question of Moral Education. *Publications*: Moral Education and the Four Cardinal Truths; Foundations of Morality and Suggestions for a Moral Code; Hindu Castes and Customs; Search after Truth (Series 1 and 2); A Discourse on the Depressed Classes; Universal Brotherhood; Relative Position of Man and Woman; Moral Courts. *Address*: Sir Mangaldas House, Lamington Road, Bombay. *T*: Bombay 1457. *Clubs*: (Hon.) Ranelagh; Orient, Bombay; Western India Turf. *Died 6 April 1920.*

NAVILLE, Henri Edouard, DCL, LLD, Dr Phil, Dr Litt, Dr Theol; Hon. FSA; Fellow of King's College, London; Hon. Professor at the University of Geneva; *b* Geneva, 1844; *s* of Adrien Naville and Sophia Rigaud; *m* 1873, Marguerite, *d* of Count Alexandre de Pourtales; two *s* two *d*. *Educ*: Geneva; King's College, London; Universities of Bonn, Paris, and Berlin. Excavating in Egypt since 1883; member of several learned and religious societies; ex-President of the Evangelical Alliance; Foreign Associate of the Institute of France; Member of the historical philosophical class of the Videnskaps-Selskabet of Christiania; Foreign Member of the Academy of Buda-Pesth, and of the Academy of Vienna; Correspondent of the Academy of History of Madrid; Hon. Member International Committee of the Red Cross; Hon. Knight of Grace of the Order of St John of Jerusalem; Commander of the Crown of Italy; Officer of the Légion d'Honneur; Knight of the Red Eagle, 3rd class, Prussia; and of the Polar Star, Sweden. *Publications*: Textes relatifs au mythe d'Horus, 1870; La Litanie du soleil, 1875; Inscription historique de Pinodjem III, 1883; Das ägyptische Todtenbuch der XVIII[ten] bis XX[ten] Dynastie 1886; La Religion des anciens Egyptiens, 1906; The Papyrus of Iouiga, 1908; Archæology of the Old Testament, 1913; L'Evolution de la langue égyptienne et les langues sémitiques, 1920; l'Ecriture égyptienne, 1926; Papyrus funéraires de la XXIe Dynastie, 2 vols; for the Egypt Exploration Fund:—the Store City of Pithom, 1883; Goshen, 1886; the City of Onias, 1888; Bubastis, 1889; the festival-hall of Osorkon II, 1890; Ahnas el Medineh, 1891; the Temple of Deir el bahari, 6 vols; the Temple Deir el bahari of the XI Dynasty, 3 vols; The Cemeteries of Abydos, Pt I, 1914; Schweich Lectures: The Text of the Old Testament, 1916; The Law of Moses, 1920; La Haute Critique dans le Pentateuque, 1921. *Address*: Malagny, near Geneva. *Died 17 Oct. 1926.*

NAYLOR, James Richard, CSI 1890; JP; Indian Civil Service (retired); *b* 3 Sept. 1842; *s* of James Richard Naylor, Crown Office, House of Lords; *m* 1868, Eleanor (*d* 1909), step *d* of C. Hexton, of the Bombay Revenue Survey. Entered Bombay Civil Service, 1862; appointed Legal Remembrancer to Govt of Bombay, 1874; Member of Legislative Council, Bombay, 1884; acted as Member of Governor's Council, Bombay, 1887–88. *Decorated* for service to the Government of Bombay as Legal Remembrancer and Member of the Legislative Council. *Address*: Hallatrow Court, Bristol. *Died 13 May 1922.*

NAYLOR, Ven. William Herbert; Archdeacon of Clarendon since 1894; *b* 5 May 1846; *m*; six *s*. *Educ*: McGill University, Montreal (MA). Ordained, 1873; Curate of St Armand West, 1873–74; Rector, 1874–76; Incumbent, St Paul's, Shawville, 1874–1907; Rector, St James Church, Farnham, 1907–17; Rural Dean of Clarendon, 1883–94. *Address*: Philipsburg, Quebec, Canada. *Died 6 June 1918.*

NEALE, Sir Henry James Vansittart-, KCB 1902 (CB 1897); JP for Berks and Westminster; Assistant Secretary to the Admiralty, 1896–1903; *b* 30 Nov. 1842; *s* of late Edward Vansittart-Neale of Bisham Abbey, and Frances Sarah, *d* of J. N. Farrer of Ingleborough, York; *m* 1887, Florence, *d* of Arthur Shelley Eddis, QC, County Court Judge, Clerkenwell; two *d*. Pres., E Berks Agricl Assoc., 1905. Patron of one living. *Address:* Bisham Abbey, Marlow. *Club:* St Stephen's.   *Died 15 July 1923.*

NEEDHAM, Francis Jack, CIE, 1899; FRGS; *b* 14 Dec. 1842; *e s* of Hon. Francis Henry Needham (3rd *s* of 2nd Earl of Kilmorey), and Fanny Amelia, *y d* of Charles Hubbard. Entered HEICS, 1867; Assistant Supt of Police, 1876; Assistant Political Officer, Sadiya, 1882; Dep. Insp.-Gen., Bengal Police Dept, 1885–1905; Gill Memorial, RGS, 1887, for his services in exploring the Valley of the Lohil Brahmaputra between Assam and the Zaujul Valley in Tibet. *Publication:* Grammar of Miri, Singpho, and Kampti Languages. *Address:* Shillong, Assam.   *Died 11 Nov. 1924.*

NEEDHAM, Sir Frederick, Kt 1915; MD, MRCP, etc; HM Commissioner of the Board of Control since 1892; *b* 1832; 2nd *s* of James P. Needham; *m* 1st, Charlotte (*d* 1907), *d* of Rev. J. Shooter, Vicar of Bishop Wilton, Yorks; 2nd, 1913, Helen Millicent Sherwood, *d* of William Lewin Newman, York. *Educ:* St Peter's School, York; St Bartholomew's Hospital, London. Medical Superintendent of York Lunatic Hospital, 1858–74; Medical Superintendent of Barnwood Hospital for the Insane, Gloucester, 1874–92; Member of Royal Commission on Care and Control of Feeble-minded, 1905, etc.; formerly President of the Medico-Psychological Association of Great Britain and Ireland; of the York Medical Society; of the Gloucestershire Medical and Surgical Association; of the Psychological section of the British Medical Association; honorary member of the Medico-Legal Society of New York. *Address:* Imperial Hotel, Bournemouth.
Died 6 Sept. 1924.

NEEDHAM, Sir George William, Kt 1920; *b* 9 Nov. 1843; *s* of William Needham; *m* 1887, Sarah, *d* of John Ashworth; one *s. Educ:* Oldham High School. Vice-Chairman of Platt Bros & Co.; Vice-President of Oldham Chamber of Commerce and of Oldham Royal Infirmary; Governor of Oldham Grammar School and connected with various other institutions; President of the Oldham Branch of the St John's Ambulance Assoc., being a Knight of Grace. *Address:* Holly Bank, Oldham. *T:* 526. *M:* J 64. *Clubs:* Manchester Reform; Reform, Albion, Oldham.   *Died 29 Feb. 1928.*

NEEDHAM, Joseph, MB, CM Aberdeen; MRCP, MRCS, etc; Anæsthetist to third London General Hospital, to King George Hospital, and to the Weir Hospital; a Medical Officer, Board of Education, London County Council, and of Metropolitan Police; *b* London, 1853; *m* 1st, 1880, Jane Robinette, (*d* 1884), *e d* of Rev. J. A. Coghlan, MA, Vicar of Tetsworth, Oxon; 2nd, 1892, Alicia Adelaide; one *s. Educ:* privately; London Hospital Medical College; University of Aberdeen. London Hospital Medical Scholar, 1875; Highest Hons and Special Hons for Graduation Thesis, Aberdeen; and gained other Honours in Surgery, Chemistry, Anatomy, Physiology, Materia Medica, Botany, Gynæcology, etc. Formerly Assistant Professor of Anatomy, University of Aberdeen; Demonstrator of Histology, London Hospital Medical College and London School of Medicine for Women. King George V Coronation Medal. *Publications:* contributions to the medical and scientific Press. *Recreations:* music, study of archæology, cycling. *Address:* 150 Harley Street, W1; Clapham Park, SW. *T:* Brixton 291. *M:* LM 9377.
Died 2 Aug. 1920.

NEIL, Rev. John, DD; Minister of Westminster Presbyterian Church, Toronto, since 1884; Moderator of Assembly of Presbyterian Church in Canada; *b* Mono Centre, County of Dufferin, Ontario, 5 April 1853; parents from Scotland; *m* Louise B., *d* of Rev. Dr Bayne, Minister of Pictou, Nova Scotia. *Educ:* Public School, Mono; Jarvis Street Collegiate, Toronto; Toronto University (BA); Knox College, Toronto; Edinburgh University. DD Queen's University, Kingston, Ontario. Minister Campbellville, 1882–84; spent three months in England and France conveying greetings to chaplains and men, 1917–18. *Address:* 38 Charles Street E, Toronto. *T:* North 1757.
Died March 1928.

NEILSON, George, FSAScot; *b* Ruthwell, Dumfriesshire, 7 Dec. 1858; *s* of Capt. Edward Neilson, merchant marine, and Janet Paterson; *m* 1892, Jane, *d* of Thomas Richardson; one *d* (one *s* decd). *Educ:* Cummertrees, Dumfriesshire; King William's Coll., Isle of Man. Passed law agent, 1881; Procurator Fiscal of Police of Glasgow,

1891–1910; Stipendiary Magistrate of Glasgow, 1910–23; President Glasgow Juridical Society, 1889; President Glasgow Archæological Society, 1907–10; President Royal Philosophical Society of Glasgow, 1913–15; and of Sir Walter Scott Club, 1914–18; Rhind Lectr in Archæology, Soc. of Antiquaries of Scotland, 1912; Hon. LLD Glasgow Univ., 1903. *Publications:* Trial by Combat, 1890; Per li neam Valli, 1891; Peel, its meaning and derivation, 1899; Annals of the Solway, 1899; John Barbour, Poet and Translator, 1900; Huchown of the Awle Ryale, the Alliterative Poet, 1902; Acts of the Lords of Council 1496–1501 (joint editor), 1918. *Address:* Wellfield, Partickhill, Glasgow.   *Died 15 Nov. 1923.*

NEILSON, Col Walter Gordon, CMG 1916; DSO 1900; late Argyll and Sutherland Highlanders; *b* 1 Oct. 1876; *s* of late Col James Neilson, CB; *m* 1908, Ida Clementina, of Duntrune, Forfarshire, *o c* of late Frederic Graham Lacon, and former wife of John Alfred Wigan (who assumed by royal licence, 1896, additional surname of Graham); one *d. Educ:* Merchiston Castle School. Entered army, 1897; Bt Lt-Col, June 1918; Lt-Col, 1922; Col, 1924; passed Staff College; served South Africa, 1899–1902; advance on Kimberley, including actions at Modder River and Magersfontein; operations in the Orange Free State, and actions at Paardeberg; operations in the Transvaal, including the action at Zilikat's Nek, etc (twice wounded, despatches twice, Queen's medal 3 clasps, King's medal 2 clasps, DSO); European War, 1914–18 (despatches six times, CMG). *Address:* 15 Regent's Park Terrace, NW1. *T:* Hampstead 7238. *Club:* Army and Navy.
Died 29 April 1927.

NEITENSTEIN, Frederick William, ISO 1906; Comptroller-General of Prisons, New South Wales, 1896–1909; Deputy Public Service Commissioner; retired from Public Service, April 1910; *b* London, 8 Jan. 1850; *s* of Frederick John Neitenstein of London; *m* 1879, Marion, *d* of George Walker, MD, and Selina Campbell; one *d. Educ:* Sherman College, Kent; Paris and London, privately. Served in the English Mercantile Marine in Devitt and Moore's ships until entering the NSW Govt Service as Lieut of the training ship Vernon, 1873; Commander, 1878; Commander of training ship Sobraon, 1892; Magistrate for the State, 1890; at various times acted on various Boards (Member, Central Board for Old Age Pensions, and Public Service Supply Board), Royal Commissions, etc; reorganised the entire prison system, and engaged on reformatory work for the past 33 years; member Howard Association, London; voted special gratuity by Parliament for distinguished services; received thanks of government; Past Deputy Grand Master of Freemasons. *Publications:* Prevention and Treatment of Crime; various papers on reformatory and prison matters. *Recreation:* reform and philanthropic work. *Address:* Bank of New Zealand, Sydney, New South Wales. *Club:* Royal Colonial Institute.
Died 23 April 1921.

NELIGAN, Rt. Rev. Moore Richard; Rector of Ford since 1911; *y s* of late Rev. Canon Neligan, DD, late Incumbent, Christ Church, Leeson Park, Dublin; *m* 1894, Mary, *e d* of late Edmund Macrory, KC, of 19 Pembridge Square, W; two *s* two *d. Educ:* Reading School; Trinity College, Dublin (BA 1884; MA 1887; DD (*jure dignitatis*), 1902. Curate of St Paul's, Sculcoates, Hull; East Dereham, Norfolk; Christ Church, Lancaster Gate, W; Vicar of St Stephen's, Paddington, W; Bishop of Auckland, 1903–10. *Publications:* The Religion of Life; The Churchman as Priest; sermons, pamphlets. *Recreations:* cycling, riding, fishing. *Address:* Ford Rectory, Northumberland.
Died 24 Nov. 1922.

NELKE, Paul; Senior Partner of Nelke, Phillips & Co.; *b* Berlin, 5 Sept. 1860; *s* of Julius Nelke, banker; *m* Maria, *d* of C. Conrad; two *d. Educ:* abroad. *Recreation:* racing. *Address:* 10 Cadogan Square, SW1. *T:* Kensington 771; Wood Lee, Virginia Water.
Died 22 Dec. 1925.

NELSON, Rev. Canon Charles Moseley, MA; Registrar, University College, Auckland, New Zealand; *b* Southwark, London, 7 Oct. 1843; *e s* of Charles Coventry and Anne Nelson, of Southwark; *m* Georgiana Sophia, *y d* of James Coates (Private Secretary to Capt. William Hobson, RN, First Governor of New Zealand); two *s* two *d. Educ:* City of London School; Queens' College, Cambridge (minor scholar and foundation scholar; BA (2nd Class Classics), 1867; MA, 1871). Deacon, 1867; Priest, 1868; Curate of Phillack and Gwithian, Cornwall, and Diocesan Inspector of Schools, 1867–68; Vicar of St Paul's (Mother Church), Auckland, NZ, 1870–1908; Bishop's Examining Chaplain, 1870–1902; Canon, 1893; Clerical Representative and Clerical Secretary, General Synod, 1874, 1880, 1886, 1892; Acting Professor (Classics and English) at University College, Auckland, 1891; Governor, Auckland Grammar School,

1881–99; Governor, St John's College, Auckland, 1892–1910; Trustee, since 1897; Hon. Life Governor, Orphan Home Trust Board, Auckland, 1908, elected upon retiring from position of Chairman of the Board, which he had held many years; a Freemason of high standing in the craft. *Address:* University College, Auckland, NZ.   *Died 17 Feb. 1919.*

NELSON, Rt. Rev. Cleland Kinloch, DD; Bishop of Atlanta, 1907–17; *b* Cobham, Virginia, 23 May 1852; *s* of Keating S. Nelson; *m* M. Bruce Matthews of Maryland. *Educ:* St John's College, Annapolis, Maryland. Rector St John the Baptist, Germantown, Philadelphia, 1876; Rector Church of the Nativity, South Bethlehem, Penna, 1882–92; Bishop of Georgia, USA, 1892–1907. *Publications:* sermons and addresses. *Recreations:* gardening, architecture. *Address:* 731 Piedmont Avenue, Atlanta, Georgia; *T:* Ivy 119 and Main 842.   *Died 13 Feb. 1917.*

NELSON, Lieut David, VC 1915; L Battery, Royal Horse Artillery; *b* 27 Dec. 1886; *m* 1915. Served ten years in ranks; 2nd Lieut RA, 1914; Lieut 1915; served European War, 1914–15 (despatches twice, VC).   *Died 8 April 1918.*

NELSON, Sir Edward Montague, KCMG 1897; JP; DL; *b* 5 March 1841; *s* of late George Nelson, Warwick; *m* 1866, Mary Caroline, *d* of F. Wallis, FRCS; four *s* one *d. Educ:* privately. Sheriff of Middlesex, 1892. *Address:* The Lawn, Warwick; 3 Whitehall Court, SW. *Clubs:* Junior Carlton, etc.

Died 4 Feb. 1919.

NELSON, Sir William, 1st Bt, *cr* 1912; JP; *b* 8 Dec. 1851; 2nd *s* of James Nelson (*d* 1899), of Cooldrinagh, Co. Kildare, and Elizabeth (*d* 1896), *d* of late Richard MacCormack of Glainden, Co. Westmeath; *m* 1879, Margaret, *d* of late Michael Hope, of Gartlandstown, Co. Westmeath; three *s* five *d. Educ:* St Edward's College, Liverpool. *Recreations:* racing, hunting, fishing, golf. *Heir: s* James Hope Nelson [*b* 26 Feb. 1883; *m* 1913, Elizabeth (marr. diss. 1921), *d* of Dr Jules F. Vallee, St Louis, USA. *Educ:* Stonyhurst College]. *Address:* 16 Hill Street, Berkeley Square, W1. *TA:* Navarque. *T:* Mayfair 3919. *Club:* Bath.   *Died 7 July 1922.*

NESBIT, E(dith), (Mrs Hubert Bland); poet and novelist, and author of children's books; *b* London, 19 Aug. 1858; *y d* of John Collis Nesbit; *m* 1st, 1880, Hubert Bland (*d* 1914); two *s* two *d*; 2nd, 1917, Thomas Terry Tucker. *Educ:* France, Germany, London. *Publications:* Lays and Legends, 1886; Leaves of Life, 1888; Lays and Legends, 2nd series, 1892; Grim Tales, 1893; Something Wrong, 1893; A Pomander of Verse, 1895; In Homespun, 1896; The Marden Mystery, 1896; Songs of Love and Empire, 1897; The Secret of Kyriels, 1898; The Story of the Treasure-Seekers, 1899; Pussy and Doggy Tales, 1899; The Book of Dragons, 1900; The Would-be-Goods; Nine Unlikely Tales; Thirteen Ways Home, 1901; Five Children and It, 1902; The Red House, 1903; The Literary Sense, 1903; The Phœnix and the Carpet, 1904; The New Treasure Seekers, 1904; The Rainbow and the Rose, 1905; Oswald Bastable, 1905; The Enchanted Castle, 1906; Man and Maid, 1906; The Incomplete Amorist, 1906; The Railway Children, 1906; The House of Arden, 1908; Ballads and Lyrics of Socialism, 1908; Salome and the Head, 1909; These Little Ones, 1909; Daphne in Fitzroy Street, 1909; Harding's Luck, 1909; Fear, 1910; The Magic City, 1910; Ballads and Lyrics, 1910; Dormant; The Wonderful Garden, 1911; The Magic World, 1912; Wings and the Child, 1913; Wet Magic, 1913; Garden Poems, 1914; The Incredible Honeymoon, 1921; The Lark, 1922; Poems, 1922; in collaboration with Hubert Bland—The Prophet's Mantle, 1885; in collaboration with Oswald Barron—The Butler in Bohemia, 1894. *Address:* The Longboat, Jesson St Mary's, New Romney, Kent.

Died 4 May 1924.

NESBIT, Paris, KC; Barrister practising in the Supreme Court of South Australia; *b* 8 Aug. 1852; *s* of Edward Planta Nesbit; *m* 1st, Ellen Logue; three *s*; 2nd, Cecilia Elizabeth Hughes. *Educ:* Angaston and Tanunda, South Australia. Called to the Bar, 1874; QC 1893; for 10 years, 1883–93, drafted nearly all the principal South Australian Statutes. *Publications:* Translations from German Poets; The Beaten Side; numerous letters in local newspapers. *Recreations:* reading, motoring, bridge. *Address:* Barossa, St Peter's, Adelaide. *TA:* Nesbit, Adelaide. *T:* Central 212.

Died 31 March 1927.

NESBITT, Rev. Allan James; Rector of Hollymount since 1873; Canon of Tuam since 1887. *Educ:* Trinity College, Dublin (BA). Ordained, 1864; Curate of Westport, Castlebar, and Athenry. *Address:* Hollymount, SO, Co. Mayo.   *Died 19 May 1918.*

NETHERSOLE, Sir Michael, Kt 1917; CSI 1914; *b* 24 April 1859; *s* of John Nethersole; *m* Margaret, 3rd *d* of late Rt Hon. Sir Edward Nicholas Coventry Braddon, KCMG. *Educ:* Sutton Valence; RIE College. Entered India Public Works Dept, 1880; Executive Engineer, 1892; lent to Kashmir State, 1893–1900; Chief Engineer and Secretary to Government, United Provinces, 1900–11; Inspector General of Irrigation, 1912–17; retired 1917; Chief Hy. Engineer, Andra Valley Power Co., Tata Sons, Bombay. *Recreations:* riding, golf, all field sports, bridge. *Address: c/o* Tata Sons, Ltd, Navsari Buildings, Bombay. *Clubs:* East India United Service; Royal Bombay Yacht.   *Died 16 June 1920.*

NEUMANN, Sir Sigmund, 1st Bt, *cr* 1912; sole partner in S. Neumann & Co.; on Board of African Banking Corporation, and London Joint Stock Bank, Ltd; partner of Neumann, Lubeck, & Co., Bankers; *b* Bavaria, 1857; *s* of Gustav Neumann, Fuerth, Bavaria; *m* 1890, Anna Allegra, *d* of late Jacques Hakim, Alexandria; two *s* three *d. Heir: s* Cecil Gustavus Jacques Neumann, *b* London, 9 June 1891. *Address:* 146 Piccadilly, W; *T:* Gerrard 2782; Cecil Lodge, Newmarket; Glenmuick, NB; Bamham Hall, Norfolk.

Died 13 Sept. 1916.

NEVARES, Celso; Ex-Consul-General of Ecuador in London; *b* Ecuador, 13 June 1850; *m* an Englishwoman. Jubilee Medal, 1897; Coronation Medal. *Address:* Broad Lea, Beckenham, Kent. *T:* Bromley 1067.

NEVE, Arthur, FRCSE; Surgeon, Mission Hospital, Kashmir; *b* Brighton, 1858; *m* 1912, Betsy Sophia Havard. *Educ:* Brighton Grammar School; RCS and University, Edinburgh. President Indian Medical Missionary Association, 1908–10, Hon. Vice-President for life; Vice-President International Medical Congress, Bombay, 1909; Major RAMC (temp.), War Hospital, Dartford (despatches); 1st Class Medal Kaiser-i-Hind, 1900; Back Award, Royal Geographical Society, 1911. *Publications:* Guide-book to Kashmir and North Himalayas (10th edition); Picturesque Kashmir; Thirty Years in Kashmir, 1913. *Recreation:* Himalayan exploration.

Died 14 Oct. 1919.

NEVILL, Lord George Montacute, JP, DL; *b* 23 Sept. 1856; 3rd *s* of 1st Marquess of Abergavenny; *m* 1882, Florence Mary, *o d* of late Temple Soanes of Brenchley House, Kent; one *s* one *d* (one *s* decd). *Address:* 22 Palmeira Square, Hove, Sussex. *Clubs:* Carlton, Ranelagh; Union, Brighton.   *Died 10 Aug. 1920.*

NEVILL, Most Rev. Samuel Tarratt, DD; Bishop of Dunedin since 1871; Primate of New Zealand since 1902; *b* 13 May 1887; *s* of Jonathan Nevill and Mary, *d* of George Berrey; *m* 1st, 1863, Mary S. C. Penny of Mont le Grand, Exeter; 2nd, Rosalind Margaret, *d* of Rev. Geoff Fynes-Clinton of Anderson Bay, New Zealand. *Educ:* St Aidan's; Magdalene College, Cambridge (Hon. Fellow). Rector of Shelton, Staffordshire, 1864–71. *Publications:* Spiritual Philosophy; pamphlets, etc. *Address:* Bishopsgrove, Dunedin.

NEVILLE, Admiral Sir George, KCB 1909; CVO 1905 (MVO 1901); JP; County Councillor; *b* 18 March 1850; 2nd *s* of late Ralph Neville-Grenville of Butleigh Court, Glastonbury, and Julia Roberta, *d* of Sir Robert Frankland Russell, 7th Bt; *m* 1886, Fairlis Florence, 2nd *d* of late D. Lloyd Jones of Llandovery, Carmarthenshire, and Victoria, Australia; three *s. Educ:* Joined HMS Britannia, 1863; Sub-Lieut, 1869; Lieut, 1872; Commander, 1885; Captain, 1892; was twice round the world with HRH the Duke of Edinburgh in HMS Galates, and once as 1st Lieut of HMS Comus; served also under HRH the Duke of Edinburgh in HMS Sultan, Black Prince, Minotaur, Alexandra, and Vivid; commanded HMS Dolphin, Dido, Australia, and Mars, and local naval forces at Melbourne; 1st Cruiser Squadron, 1905–7; 3rd and 4th Divisions Home Fleet, 1909–11; retired, 1913. *Address:* Murtrey, Frome. *Clubs:* Naval and Military, Royal Automobile.   *Died 5 Feb. 1923.*

NEVILLE, Rev. Hon. Grey; Rector of Bluntisham, Huntingdonshire, since 1917; *b* 4 Dec. 1857; 2nd *s* of 6th Lord Braybrooke and Lucy Frances Le Marchant, *d* of John Le Marchant Thomas Le Marchant; *m* 1889, Mary Peele, *d* of late Rev. Francis Slater; two *s* five *d. Educ:* Eton; Magdalene College, Cambridge. Ordained, 1882; Curate of Hunstanton, 1882–83; St Giles's, Cambridge, 1884–85; Vicar of Waltham St Lawrence, Berks, 1885–1912; Rector of Christchurch, Cambs, 1912–17. *Address:* Bluntisham Rectory, St Ives, Hunts.

Died 28 Dec. 1920.

NEVILLE, Nigel Charles Alfred; stipendiary magistrate of South Staffordshire since 1885; *b* 10 April 1849; *o s* of late Thomas Neville of Shenstone House, Lichfield; *m* 1892, Julia Anne, *d* of late David Ballinger of Wolverhampton. *Educ:* Uppingham; St John's College, Cambridge (BA). Barrister, Inner Temple, 1873. *Address:* Shenstone House, Lichfield. *TA:* Shenstone.   *Died 12 April 1923.*

NEVILLE, Sir Ralph, Kt 1906; **Hon. Mr Justice Neville;** Judge of the High Court of Justice since 1906; *b* 13 Sept. 1848; *s* of Henry Neville, surgeon, Esher, and Mary Neville; *m* 1872, Edith Cranstoun, *e d* of late Henry T. J. Macnamara, one of Her Majesty's Railway Commissioners. *Educ:* Tonbridge School; Emmanuel College, Cambridge (MA; Hon. Fellow). Barrister 1872; QC 1888; Bencher of Lincoln's Inn; contested Kirkdale Div. of Liverpool, 1886; MP (L) Liverpool Exchange, 1887–95; sometime President of Garden City Association. *Address:* Royal Courts of Justice, WC; Banstead Place, Banstead, Surrey. *T:* Burgh Heath 192. *Clubs:* Athenæum, Reform.
Died 13 Oct. 1918.

NEVILLE, Col William Candler, DSO 1900; Colonel Cheshire Regiment; retired 1909; *b* 22 Jan. 1859; *s* of Major Robert Neville, late 51st Regiment, of Ahanure, Co. Kilkenny, and Rockfield, Co. Dublin; *m* 1892, Amy, *y d* of Colin G. Ross of Gruinards, Ross-shire; one *s* one *d. Educ:* Cheltenham College. Entered army, 1878; Captain, 1885; Major, 1896; served Burmese Expedition, 1887–88 (medal with clasp); S Africa, 1900–2 (despatches, medal with 4 clasps, DSO); commanding 22nd Regimental District, 1914. *Club:* Junior United Service.   *Died 28 June 1926.*

NEWALL, Col Stuart, CB 1900; New Zealand Mounted Infantry; *b* 9 May 1843; *s* of late Thomas Newall of Dumfries; *m* 1872, Georgina, *d* of George Roberts; one *s* four *d.* Served New Zealand, 1863–66 (medal); South Africa, 1899–1900 (despatches, Queen's medal, 2 clasps, CB). *Address:* Wellington, New Zealand.
Died 1920.

NEWBOROUGH, 4th Baron, *cr* 1776; **William Charles Wynn;** Bt 1742; *b* 4 Nov. 1873; *s* of Hon. Thomas John Wynn and (Sybil) Anna (Katherine), *d* of Edwin Corbett, HM minister at Athens; *S* grandfather, 1888; *m* 1900, Grace Bruce, *d* of Col Henry Montgomerie Carr of Kentucky. *Educ:* Heidelberg; Trinity Hall, Cambridge. *Heir: brother* Hon. Thomas John Wynn [*b* 22 Nov. 1878; *m* 1907, Vera Evelyn Mary, *d* of Capt. Philip Montagu, 12th Lancers, and *widow* of Henry L. Winch; one *d*]. *Address:* Bryn Llewellyn, Festiniog, Wales; 39 Park Lane, W. *T:* Mayfair 5949. *Clubs:* Bachelors', Travellers'.   *Died 19 July 1916.*

NEWCASTLE, 7th Duke of, *cr* 1756; **Henry Pelham Archibald Douglas Pelham-Clinton,** DL; JP; Earl of Lincoln, 1572; Lord High Steward of Retford; Master Forester of Dartmoor; Keeper of St Briavel's Castle; Member of London School Board, 1894–97; *b* 28 Sept. 1864; *s* of 6th Duke and (Henrietta) Adela, *d* of late Henry Thomas Hope of Deepdene, Surrey; *S* father, 1879; *m* 1889, Kathleen Florence May, OBE, *d* of late Major Henry Augustus Candy, 9th Lancers, and Hon. Mrs (Frances Kathleen) Candy, *d* of 3rd Baron Rossmore. *Educ:* Eton. Owned about 35,600 acres. *Heir: brother* Lord Henry Francis Hope Pelham-Clinton-Hope [*b* 3 Feb. 1866; assumed additional surname of Hope, 1887; *m* 1st, 1894, Mary Augusta (marr. diss. 1902), *d* of William Yohé; 2nd, 1904, Olive Muriel (*d* 1912), *d* of George Horatio Thompson, banker, Melbourne, and formerly wife of Richard Owen; one *s* two *d*]. *Address:* Clumber Park, Worksop; Forest Farm, Windsor Forest; 11 Berkeley House, Hay Hill, W1. *T:* Mayfair 4308. *Clubs:* Carlton, St James's, Garrick.
Died 30 May 1928.

NEWDEGATE, Anne Emily Newdigate-, (Lady Newdigate-Newdegate); 2nd *d* of late Very Rev. Thomas Garnier, Dean of Lincoln, and of Lady Caroline Elizabeth, *d* of 4th Earl of Albemarle; *m* 1858, Sir Edward Newdigate-Newdegate, KCB, (*d* 1902), of Arbury, Warwicks. *Publications:* Gossip from a Muniment Room; The Cheverels of Cheverel Manor; Cavalier and Puritan. *Address:* Medecroft, Winchester.   *Died 23 Dec. 1924.*

NEWLAND, Captain H. Osman, FRHistS; *s* of late Major O. Newland; *m* Lois, *d* of late F. N. Druitt; one *d. Educ:* Counter Hill, City of London, and Goldsmith's Institute. Introduced Study of Citizenship into London School Board and the LCC schools; compiled first course of Sociology in United Kingdom; special LCC lecturer in Sociology, Commercial History and English Literature; assisted found Sociological Society; Founder and Hon. Sec. British West African Association; explored Sierra Leone, 1912; assisted open new route Mont Blanc for Paris-Lyons-Mediterranean Railway, 1913; Recruiting, Sub-area Commander and Military Intelligence, 1917; Officer for Education, RAF, 1918–19. *Publications:* Short History of

Citizenship; Local Government Handbook to Education; The Model Citizen; Sierra Leone: Its People, Products, Secret Societies; The Ivory Coast; Coconuts, Kernels, Cocoa and other Vegetable Oils; Origin and Systems of Empire; Romance of Commerce; Soldiers of Empire (song), etc. *Recreations:* mountain-climbing, cycling, sculling, swimming, music. *Address:* The Trossachs, Herne Bay; 79 Mount Nod Road, SW16. *T:* Streatham 89. *Clubs:* Authors', New Oxford and Cambridge.   *Died 27 June 1920.*

NEWMAN, David, MD; FRFPSG; Consulting Surgeon to the Glasgow Royal Infirmary, and for many years Pathologist and Lecturer on Pathology to the same hospital; Medical Assessor, WC Act; *b* 1853; *e s* of Edward Newman, MD, Fleet Surgeon, RN, of Craig Ailey, Cove, Dunbartonshire, and Annabella, *d* of late David Smith of Whitevale House, Glasgow, and Farthingneuk, Dumfriesshire; *m* 1885, Jean, *d* of William Polson, JP Edgehill, Paisley; one *s* one *d. Educ:* Universities of Glasgow and Leipzig. Senior Fellow of the Association of Surgeons of Great Britain and Ireland; Fellow of the Royal Society of Medicine of London; Vice-President International Medical Congress, London Meeting; President Glasgow Medico-Chirurgical Society; President of the Clinical and Pathological Society of Glasgow; Member Assoc. International d'Urologie. *Publications:* Surgical Diseases of the Kidneys; Diagnosis of Surgical Diseases of the Kidneys; Malignant Disease of the Throat and Nose, etc; numerous papers to medical and surgical journals, and contributions to societies, especially relating to diseases of the kidneys and bladder. *Address:* Craig Ailey, Cove, Dunbartonshire. *Club:* Western, Glasgow.
Died 22 April 1924.

NEWMAN, Edward Braxton, ISO 1902; *b* 15 Dec. 1842; *s* of John Newman. Entered the Foreign Office, 1859; First Class Clerk, 1873; Assistant to Chief Clerk, 1890; retired, 1907. *Address:* 71 Chelsham Road, Clapham, SW.   *Died 20 March 1916.*

NEWMAN, Ven. Ernest Frederick, MA; Vicar of Marystowe since 1909, and Rector of Coryton since 1922; Archdeacon of Plymouth; *b* Coryton, Devon, 2 March 1859; *s* of Rev. W. S. Newman, Rector of Coryton; *m* Jessie, *d* of late Lieut E. Hathway, 10th Hussars; three *s. Educ:* Marlborough; Keble College, Oxford; Wells Theological College. Assistant Curate, St Mary's, Reading, 1884–86; Chaplain (ACS) Bengal, 1887–88; Chaplain to the Forces: Tower of London, 1889–94; Caterham, 1894–1900; South Africa, 1900–4 (despatches); Portsmouth, 1904–8; Rural Dean of Tavistock, 1917–20. *Address:* Marystowe Vicarage, Lew Down, Devon. *TA:* Chillaton. *M:* TA 7234.   *Died 28 April 1928.*

NEWMAN, Philip Harry, RBA, FSA; Remembrancer and Hon. Librarian, Royal Society of Literature; early Member of Society of Designers, and sometime Vice-President; retired; Member of Committee and sometime Hon. Treasurer of Artists' Benevolent Fund; *b* London, 1840; *e s* of Philip Robert Newman, merchant, and Margaret Eliza Barnfather; *m* 1860, Charlotte Isabella Gibbs (*d* 1920), art student; one *s* one *d. Educ:* London and Paris; student London University and St Martin's and Spitalfields Schools of Art; also in Paris. Designer of decorative works in painting, stained glass, and wall tiling pictures; frequent exhibitor at Royal Academy and RBA, etc; principal works in oil: Sardanapalus, Orpheus and Eurydice, My Father's House of Many Mansions, The Temptation, Solomon dedicating the Temple, Murder of Becket, The Quarries of Cheops; black and white illustrations, numerous; Judy, and A Shakespeare Reverie Tercentenary Tribute and Souvenir; decorative paintings and stained glass at Church of St Mary the Virgin, Aldermaston; Apse of Chapel, Royal Masonic Institute for Boys, Bushey, Herts; spirit fresco, Our Lord healing the Sick, St Peter's Church, Belsize Park, etc; designer of War memorials: Birkbeck College, FM School Chapel, Bushey, Herts, St Mary's Church, Aldermaston, Stamford Brook; writer and lecturer on art subjects; inventor of method of preserving ancient wall paintings, applied successfully at Canterbury, Aldermaston, and elsewhere. Hon. Member Artists' Society and Langham Sketch Club. *Publications:* contributions to Social History of England, and numerous papers in Transactions Royal Society of Literature and Archæologia; poems various. *Recreations:* music, billiards, sketching. *Address:* 5 Ravenscourt Square, W6.   *Died 21 Dec. 1927.*

NEWMARCH, Francis Welles, CSI 1914; Financial Secretary, India Office, since 1911; *b* 29 Dec. 1853; *e s* of late Rev. Charles Francis Newmarch, Rector of Leverton, Lincs. *Educ:* Balliol College, Oxford; Corpus Christi College (Scholar). 1st class in Classical Mods; 1st class, Lit. Hum. Entered India Office, 1877; Military Dept, till 1902; then Assistant Secretary Financial Dept; Secretary Public Works Dept. *Recreations:* mountaineering, walking. *Address:* India Office, SW. *Clubs:* Alpine, Constitutional, Wigwam.   *Died 2 Jan. 1918.*

NEWMARCH, Sir Oliver Richardson, KCSI 1894 (CSI 1888); Major-General, retired, 1887; *b* 31 Oct. 1834; *s* of late Dr Henry Newmarch and Violet, *d* of Col Sherwood, RA; *m* 1st, 1858, Mary Isabella (*d* 1867), *d* of Major Parke, 61st Regiment; four *d*; 2nd, 1874, Agnes Mary, *d* of late James Norman; one *s*. *Educ:* Charterhouse; Merton College, Oxford. Entered Bengal Army, 1855; served in Indian Mutiny (medal); Military Secretary Government of India, 1884; Military Secretary India Office, 1889–99. *Club:* United Service.
Died 16 Feb. 1920.

NEWNHAM-DAVIS, Lt-Col Nathaniel; author; Lieutenant-Colonel, retired; Captain Sup. Companies, Territorial Force; *b* London, 6 Nov. 1854; *e s* of Henry Newnham-Davis and Mary Newnham; unmarried. *Educ:* Harrow. Joined the Buffs, 1873; served through Griqualand West and Zulu campaigns with Imperial Mounted Infantry, 1877–79 (despatches twice, medal and clasp); served in Straits Settlements, China, India; attached three years to Intelligence Department, Simla; retired 1894; joined staff of the Sporting Times same year; resigned 1912; editor Man of the World, 1894–1900; editor Town Topics, 1914; on outbreak of war applied for re-employment in army; was appointed an officer of the military guard over prisoners of war at Alexandra Palace in 1915. *Publications:* Three Men and a God, 1896; An Ideal (Palace Theatre), 1896; Jadoo, 1898; Military Dialogues, 1898; Dinners and Diners, 1899; Baby Wilkinson's VC, 1899; The Transvaal under the Queen, 1899; Military Dialogues on Active Service, 1900; A Charitable Bequest (Criterion Theatre), 1900; The Gourmet's Guide to Europe, 1903; part author Lady Madcap (Prince of Wales's Theatre), 1904; A Day in Paris (Empire Theatre), 1908; New York (Empire Theatre), 1911; The Gourmet's Guide to London, 1914. *Recreation:* amateur theatricals. *Address:* 32 Clarence Gate Gardens, NW. *T:* Paddington 3722. *Clubs:* Naval and Military, Beefsteak, Garrick, Royal Eastern.
Died 28 May 1917.

NEWTON, Sir Alfred James, 1st Bt, *cr* 1900; JP; Alderman of the ward of Bassishaw since 1890; Governor of the Hon. The Irish Society, since 1906; Chairman Harrod's Stores, Ltd, and D. H. Evans & Co., Ltd; *b* Hull, 19 Oct. 1849; *s* of late George Beeforth Newton of Kottingham, East Yorks; *m* 1874, Elizabeth Jane (Lily), *e d* of late Joseph Watson of Mill House, Mitcham Common; one *s* one *d*. Lord Mayor of London 1900, when he founded City of London Imperial Volunteers, for which service the Baronetcy was conferred; Conservative Unionist and Churchman; formerly yeast merchant (merged with H. Love & Co.) and shipowner; contested West Southwark, 1900; Hon. Freeman Royal Borough of Scarborough, and of Londonderry; Orders of: Leopold, Belgium; Lion and Sun, Persia (highest grade); Grand Cordon of Servia; Order of Medjidie, 1st Class; Polar Star of Sweden. *Heir: s* Harry Kottingham Newton, *b* 2 April 1875. *Address:* Kottingham House, Burton-on-Trent; 17 Cumberland Terrace, Regent's Park, NW1. *TA:* Newtonio, London. *T:* North 508. *Club:* Bath.
Died 20 June 1921.

NEWTON, Ernest, CBE 1920; RA 1919 (ARA 1911); FRIBA; *b* 12 Sept. 1856; *s* of Henry Newton, Bickley, Kent, and Mary Lockyer; *m* 1881, Antoinette Johanna, *d* of William Hoyack, Rotterdam; three *s*. *Educ:* Blackheath; Uppingham. Articled to R. Norman Shaw, RA, 1873; after six years spent in his office, began practice on his own account; work almost entirely domestic architecture; principal works—Bullers Wood, Chislehurst; Redcourt, Haslemere; Steep Hill, Jersey; Glebelands, Wokingham; Ardenrun Place, Blindley Heath; House of Retreat and Chapel for the Sisters of Bethany, St Swithun's Church, Hither Green; President Royal Institute of British Architects, 1914–17 (Royal Gold Medallist, 1918); Hon. Membre de la Société Centrale de l'Architecture de Belgique; Officier d'Academie de France; Membre Correspondant de la Société des Architectes diplômés par le Gouvernement, France; Officier de l'Ordre de la Couronne, Belgium. *Publications:* A Book of Houses, 1890; A Book of Country Houses, 1903. *Recreation:* novel reading. *Address:* 4 Raymond Buildings, Gray's Inn, WC1. *T:* Chancery 7684; 17 Blomfield Road, W9. *T:* Paddington 4514. *Clubs:* Athenæum, Arts.
Died 25 Jan. 1922.

NEWTON, Hibbert Henry, JP; Clerk of the Parliaments and Clerk of the Legislative Council of Victoria since 1924; *b* Ballenglen, near Oakleigh, Victoria, 1861; *s* of late Hon. Hibbert Newton, barrister-at-law, Postmaster-General in the Nicholson Ministry; *m* Clara Violet, *o d* of late W. Ravenscroft Stephen; three *s* one *d*. *Educ:* All Saints' Grammar School, St Kilda; matriculated at Melbourne University. Entered the Public Service of Victoria as an officer of the Law Department in 1880; joined the staff of the Legislative Assembly in 1884; Clerk Assistant in 1902; Clerk of the Legislative Assembly, 1910; Clerk of the Parliaments, 1912; Chief Clerk Commonwealth

Celebrations Staff, 1901; Clerk of the Interstate Conferences of Premiers and Ministers, held at Melbourne in 1909, 1912, and 1914. *Address:* State Parliament House, Melbourne.
Died 2 Jan. 1927.

NEWTON, Rev. Horace, MA; Canon of York, 1885; *b* 7 Sept. 1841; *m*; five *d*. *Educ:* St John's College, Cambridge (Scholar). Ordained, 1865; Curate of St Mary, Nottingham, 1865–68; Vicar of Holy Trinity, Heworth, 1869–77; Driffields-Ambo, Yorkshire, 1877–92; Redditch, 1892–1905. *Address:* Holmwood, Redditch. *T:* Redditch 17. *M:* AB 1935. *Club:* Constitutional.
Died 12 Nov. 1920.

NEWTON, John; Secretary, Native Races and the Liquor Traffic United Committee, and Member of Committee; *b* 9 Feb. 1864; *m* 1st, 1887, Elizabeth Lees (*d* 1908); 2nd, 1912, Helena Bessie Ethel, 2nd *d* of E. R. Norris of Harlesden, NW; two *s* one *d*. Asst-master, elementary school; Parliamentary Agent, United Kingdom Alliance; resigned 1909; Member of Executive Committee, Anglo-Indian Temperance Association; Vice-Chairman Executive, Children's Protection League; Joint Hon. Secretary of the National Temperance Federation; Fellow of the Royal Colonial Institute. *Publications:* Life of Captain John Brown, of Harper's Ferry; W. S. Caine, MP, a Biography; Our National Drink Bill, its direct and indirect effects upon National Health, Morals, Industry, and Trade; contributed to various literary periodicals. *Recreation:* golf. *Address:* 178 Palace Chambers, SW.
Died 31 Aug. 1916.

NEWTON, William George, ISO 1914; late Deputy Controller HM Stationery Office, retired 1917; *b* 1859; *s* of late John Newton of Woolwich; *m* 1891, Blanche, *e d* of late George Thomas Jelley, of the War Department. Entered the Stationery Office, 1875; Private Secretary to Controller, 1879; Assistant Controller, 1904. *Address:* 17 Charlton Road, Blackheath, SE.
Died 7 April 1920.

NEWTON-BRADY, Sir Andrew, Kt 1911; Resident Magistrate, Belfast, since 1908; *b* 1849; *e s* of Sir Thomas Francis Brady, JP; assumed additional surname of Newton, 1870; *m* 1st, Annie, *d* of late Robert Mecredy, of Lissoughter Lodge, Recess, Co. Galway; 2nd, Julie, *d* of late Arthur Henry D'Esterre, MD; three *s* three *d*. *Educ:* France. Barrister-at-Law; Secretary to Royal Commission on Oyster Fisheries, 1869; and subsequently in the Irish Civil Service; appointed Resident Magistrate, Co. Galway, 1882; Co. Clare, 1894; received the thanks of Government on many occasions. *Recreations:* golf, fishing, shooting. *Address:* Mullafarry, Greystones, Co. Wicklow. *M:* RI 3453. *Club:* United Service, Dublin.
Died 20 March 1918.

NIBLETT, Robert Henry, ISO 1911; JP; MA; Deputy Collector, United Provinces, India; *b* 1859; *s* of Philip Niblett, JP; *m* 1885, Kathleen Allen, *d* of late Charles Howard; five *s* four *d*. MA (Honours) 1881; Headmaster, Boys' High School, Naini Tal, 1881; Assistant Editor, UP Gazetteer, 1882; joined UP Civil Service, 1884. *Address:* Myrtle Villa, Allahabad, UP, India.
Died 5 May 1918.

NICHOL, Robert; MP (Lab) East Renfrewshire, 1922–24; teacher in Allan Glen's School, Glasgow; *b* 12 Feb. 1890; *s* of James M. Nichol, engineer; *m* 1920, Saltie, *d* of late Bailie James Alston, Glasgow. *Educ:* Glasgow Univ. (MA 1910). *Address:* 4 Polayn Garth, Welwyn Garden City, Herts.
Died 16 April 1925.

NICHOL, Col Hon. Walter Cameron, LLD; Lieutenant-Governor of British Columbia, 1921–26; *b* Goderich, Ont, 15 Oct. 1866; *s* of Robert K. Addison Nichol and Cynthia Jane Ballard; *m* 1897, Quita Josephine March, *d* of Charles Greenwood Moore, MD, London, Ont; one *s* one *d*. Came to British Columbia, 1897; interested in mining and various industries in British Columbia; publisher and newspaper owner, retired; formerly Editor, Hamilton Herald, 1888–96; Hon. Colonel 16th the Canadian Scottish Regiment, Victoria, BC; an Officer of the Legion of Honour; Religion, Anglican. *Recreations:* driving, motoring, yachting, etc. *Clubs:* Vancouver Terminal City, Western, Royal Vancouver Yacht, Vancouver Rowing, Vancouver; Union, Oak Bay Golf, Colwood Golf, Royal Victoria Yacht, Victoria; Rainier Seattle Golf and County, Seattle.
Died 19 Dec. 1928.

NICHOLAS, Captain John, MVO 1902; Royal Artillery; Superintendent Royal Mews, Buckingham Palace, 1892-1913; *b* 30 Sept. 1851; 2nd *s* of John Nicholas of Ely, Cambridgeshire; *m* 1878, Mary Ann Newbolt (*d* 1906), *d* of James Egan of Dublin. Entered army, 1869; Riding Master and Hon. Lieut RA, 1888; Hon. Captain, 1898; retired, 1898. *Address:* Bushy Lodge, Hampton Court, Middlesex.   *Died 20 April 1920.*

NICHOLAS, Sir Walter Powell, Kt 1919; Solicitor; a member of the firm of Morgan, Bruce & Nicholas, Pontypridd; *b* 12 June 1868; 5th *s* of John Nicholas of Brynamman, Carmarthenshire; *m* 1897, Florence (JP County Glamorgan), *e d* of Edward Edwards of Risca, Monmouthshire; one *d*. *Educ:* privately; Alderman Davis Schools, Neath. Admitted Solicitor, 1894 (1st Class Honours; Law Society's Prizeman); Solicitor to the South Wales Miners' Federation; Clerk to the Rhondda Urban District Council, 1901, the Ystradyfodwg and Pontypridd Main Sewage Board, 1901, and the Pontypridd and Rhondda Joint Water Board, 1911; Chairman of the Insurance Committee for the County of Glamorgan since 1915; and of the Executive Committee of the Urban District Councils Association of England and Wales; Member of the Royal Commissions on Local Government and Mining Subsidence; Member of the Representative Body, Governing Body, and Electoral College of the Church in Wales, and Chairman of the Legal Committee of the Representative Body. *Recreation:* motoring. *Address:* The Garth, Trealaw, Glam. *TA:* Trealaw. *T:* Tonypandy 53. *M:* L 1273. *Club:* Royal Automobile.
                      Died 10 April 1926.

NICHOLL, Maj.-Gen. Sir Christopher Rice Havard, KCB 1921; *b* 15 Dec. 1836; 5th *s* of late Rt Hon. John Nicholl of Merthyr Mawr, Glamorgan; *m* 1868, Florence Emma, *d* of Rev. Charles R. Knight of Tythegston Court, Glamorgan; two *s* six*d*. *Educ:* Eton. Rifle Brigade, 1855; Maj.-Gen. 1890; retired, 1892; served Crimea, 1855–56 (medal with clasp, Turkish medal); Indian Mutiny, 1857–59 (medal with clasp); Ashanti War, 1874 (medal with clasp, brevet Lt-Col); commanded 3rd Battalion Rifle Brigade; Colonel Commandant 1st Rifle Brigade. *Recreations:* illuminating, travel, walking. *Address:* 11 Tedworth Square, SW3. *T:* Kensington 1065.
                      Died 31 March 1928.

NICHOLLS, Harry; comedian; *b* London, 1852; *m sister* of late Henry Pettitt, dramatic author; one *s* two *d*. *Educ:* City of London School. Went on stage at 18; first appearance in London Surrey Theatre; four years at Grecian Theatre; fourteen years principal comedian Drury Lane Theatre; *ditto* five years at Adelphi Theatre. Hon. Treasurer of the Actors' Benevolent Fund; a Trustee of the Actors' Orphanage Fund; Past Master of the Worshipful Company of Joiners and Member of the Court of Assistants. *Publications:* part author of Jane; A Runaway Girl; The Toreador, etc; author of many pantomimes (at Drury Lane and elsewhere); many comic songs, farces, etc. *Address:* 31 Birch Grove, W3. *Club:* Green Room.   *Died 29 Nov. 1926.*

NICHOLLS, Hon. Sir Henry Alfred Alford, Kt 1926; CMG 1896; MD; late Principal Medical Officer of Dominica, West Indies; *b* London, 27 Sept. 1851; *s* of Thomas William Nicholls of London; *m* 1877, Marion, 3rd *d* of John Corney Crompton, JP, of Dominica; four *s* six *d*. *Educ:* University, Aberdeen; St Bartholomew's, London. MB (Honours) and CM Aberdeen, 1873; MD Aberdeen, 1875; MRCS 1873. Medical Superintendent, Dominica Yaws Hospitals, 1877; Medical Officer Public Institutions, 1880; Health Officer, 1897; Senior Medical Officer, 1904; Crown nominee in Legislative Assembly, 1875–77; Official Member of Legislative Council, 1898; of Executive Council, 1915; Member of Executive Council of Leeward Islands, 1922; acted several times as Administer of Dominica; Chairman of Poor Law Board, 1885–91; Local Commissioner Colonial and Indian Exhibition, 1886; in 1891, appointed Special Commissioner to inquire into prevalence of Yaws in West Indies (thanked by Secretary of State for Report, which was published as a Blue-book); Chairman, Roseau Town Board, 1896–98; President Dominica Agricultural Society, 1906; represented Leeward Islands at WI Agricultural Conferences in Barbados, 1899, 1901, and 1902; Trinidad, 1905; represented the Colony at W Indian Quarantine Conference at Barbados, 1904, and at Imperial Health Conference, London, 1914; Commissioner for Dominica at Tropical Products Exhibition, London, 1914; Chairman, Road Commission, 1918; JP; FLS; CMZS; corr. and hon. mem. of several learned societies at home and abroad. *Publications:* Text-Book of Tropical Agriculture; Dominica, Illustrated and Described; numerous papers and pamphlets on medical, botanical, and agricultural subjects. *Recreation:* experimenting in tropical agriculture. *Address:* Kingsland House, Roseau, Dominica; St Aroment, Dominica, West Indies. *TA:* Nicholls, Dominica. *Clubs:* Authors', West Indian; Dominica.
                      Died Feb. 1926.

NICHOLS, Catherine Maude, RE, SM, NBA; painter, etcher, and author; *b* Norwich; *e d* of late W. P. Nichols, FRCS (Senior

Consulting Surgeon of the Norfolk and Norwich Hospital, and Bethel Hospital, Norwich; Mayor of Norwich, 1866). *Educ:* Norwich. Many sketching tours, chiefly England and France; travelled in France, Germany, and Switzerland; exhibited frequently at the Salon, Academy, Royal Painter-Etchers, Venice, Melbourne, etc; first Lady Fellow of the Royal Painter-Etchers; Membre de l'Union International des Beaux Arts, Paris; principal paintings—Earlham, Norwich; Strangers Hall, Norwich; Very Rev. Canon Fitzgerald; Brancaster Staithe; and many others; etched upwards of 200 plates. *Publications:* Lines of Thought and Thoughts in Lines, 1892; Old Norwich; Two Norfolk Idylls; Cromer Sketches; Doubts Dispelled; Zoroaster; Why I became a Catholic; Black and White Norwich; Haunts of George Borrow in and around Norwich: a series of four etchings, 1913; Six Dry Points after old Crome; contributed articles to various periodicals. *Recreations:* reading, the theatre. *Address:* The Studio, 73 Surrey Street, Norwich. *Club:* Forum.
                      Died 30 Jan. 1923.

NICHOLS, Rt. Rev. William Ford, DD; Bishop of California since 1893; *b* 9 June 1849; *s* of Charles H. and Margaret E. Nichols; *m* 1876, Clara Quintard; two *s* two *d*. *Educ:* Trinity College, Hartford, Connecticut; Berkeley Divinity School, Middletown, Connecticut. Deacon, 1873; Priest, 1874; Assistant Bishop of California, 1890; Private Secretary to Bishop Williams of Conn, 1871–76; Assistant, Holy Trinity, Middletown, Conn, 1873–75; Rector, St James', West Hartford, Conn, and Grace, Newington, Conn, 1875–77; Christ Church, Hartford, Conn, 1877–87; St James', Philadelphia, 1887–90; Member of Delegation from Connecticut to Seabury Centenary at Aberdeen, 1884; Professor of Church History, Berkeley Divinity School, 1885–87; Assistant Secretary, House of Bishops, 1886; Deputy to General Convention, 1889; declined election as Assistant Bishop of Ohio, 1888; acted for Presiding Bishop in transfer of The Church in Hawaii to the American Church, 1902; and in temporary charge again of District, 1920–21; First President Province of the Pacific (American Church), 1915; Hon. President Seamen's Church Institute of America; one of the Episcopal Canons of St George's Collegiate Church, Jerusalem; Hon. Life Member of Pacific Union Club, San Francisco. *Publications:* On the Trial of Your Faith; Character; Apt and Meet; A Father's Story of the Fire and Earthquake of 1906; Some World-Circuit Saunterings; various articles in reviews, etc. *Address:* 1215 Sacramento Street, San Francisco.
                      Died 5 June 1924.

NICHOLSON, 1st Baron, *cr* 1912, of Roundhay; **Field-Marshal William Gustavus Nicholson**, GCB 1908 (KCB 1898; CB 1891); Colonel Commandant, Royal Engineers; *b* 2 March 1845; *y s* of William Nicholson Phillips (assumed surname of Nicholson, 1827), Leeds, and Martha, *d* of Abram Rhodes, Yorks; *m* 1871, Victoria Ursula, *d* of Dominique d'Allier. Entered RE, 1865; Col 1891; served Afghan War, 1878–80 (despatches); Candahar Field Force, 1879 (despatches); march to Candahar (despatches, brevet of Major, medal, three clasps, bronze star); Egyptian War, 1882, including Tel-el-Kebir (4th class Osmanieh, Khedive's star); Burmese Expedition, 1886–87, as AAG Army Headquarters (despatches, brevet of Lieut-Col, medal with clasp); Tirah Expeditionary Force, 1897–98, as Chief of Staff (despatches, KCB, medal with two clasps); Adjutant-General in India, 1898–99; served South Africa as Military Secretary to Commander-in-Chief, and Director of Transport at Headquarters, 1899–1900 (despatches twice, promoted Maj.-Gen., medal with five clasps); Director-General of Mobilisation and Military Intelligence, War Office, 1901–4; Chief British Military Attaché, Japanese Army, 1904–5; QMG of the Forces, and 3rd Military Member of the Army Council, 1905–7; Chief of General Staff, then Chief of Imperial Gen. Staff, and 1st Military Member of the Army Council, 1908–12; Chairman of Commission on Indian Army Expenditure, Simla, 1912–13. *Heir:* none. *Address:* 51 Pont Street, SW. *Clubs:* Athenæum, United Service, Army and Navy.
                      Died 13 Sept. 1918 (ext).

NICHOLSON, Sir Charles Norris, 1st Bt, *cr* 1912; LLB, MA; MP (L) Doncaster since 1906; 2nd Church Estates Commissioner since 1910; Vice-Chairman of London War Pensions Committee under the statutory Committee, 1916; *b* 30 July 1857; *e s* of William Norris Nicholson, late one of the Masters in Lunacy, and Emily, *d* of James Stock Daniel; *m* 1882, Amy Letitia, *d* of George Crosfield of Warrington; two *d* (one *s* decd). *Educ:* Charterhouse; Trinity College, Cambridge. Called to the Bar, Lincoln's Inn; many years a Member of Board of Guardians, Shoreditch. *Heir: g s* John Norris Nicholson, *b* 19 Feb. 1911. *Address:* 35 Harrington Gardens, SW. *T:* Kensington 439. *Clubs:* Oxford and Cambridge, Ranelagh, Queen's, etc.
                      Died 29 Nov. 1918.

NICHOLSON, Brig.-Gen. John Sanctuary, CB 1902; CMG 1905; DSO 1897; CBE 1918; MP Abbey Division of Westminster since 1921, (Independent Anti-Waste Conservative) 1921–22, (U) since 1922; Captain 7th Hussars; *b* London, 19 May 1863; 2nd *s* of William Nicholson, Basing Park, Alton, Hants (sometime MP Petersfield), and Isabella Sarah, *d* of John Meek; unmarried. *Educ:* Harrow. Joined 7th Hussars, 1884; Comdt of BSA Police, 1896, raised corps; served Matabeleland, 1896 (despatches, DSO); South Africa, 1900 (despatches, Bt Lt-Col); Comdt. BSA Police, Rhodesia, South Africa, 1899–1900; Insp.-Gen. SA Constabulary, 1903–5; European War, 1914–15 (despatches); retired 1920. *Recreations:* hunting, shooting. *Address:* 2 South Audley Street, W. *Clubs:* Naval and Military, Cavalry. *Died 21 Feb. 1924.*

NICHOLSON, Joseph Shield, MA (London); ScD (Cambridge); FBA 1903; Professor of Political Economy, University of Edinburgh, 1880–1925; *b* Wrawby, Lincolnshire, 9 Nov. 1850; *s* of Rev. Thomas Nicholson, Congregational minister, and Mary Anne Grant; *m* 1885, Jeanie, *e d* of William Ballantyne Hodgson, LLD, late Prof. of Political Economy, Edinburgh University; two *d* (one *s* decd). *Educ:* King's Coll., London (BA 1870); University, Edinburgh; Trinity Coll., Cambridge (Scholar); Heidelberg. Cobden Prize, Cambridge, 1877 and 1880; MA London, 1877 (Gerstenberg Prize); ScD Cantab. Private tutor, Cambridge, 1876–80; Hon. LLD St Andrews and Edinburgh. *Publications:* Effects of Machinery on Wages, 1878; Tenant's Gain not Landlord's Loss, 1883; editor of Smith's Wealth of Nations, 1884; The Silver Question, 1886; Money and Monetary Problems, 1888; Principles of Political Economy: vol. i, 1893; vol. ii, 1897; vol. iii, 1901; Historical Progress and Ideal Socialism, 1894; Strikes and Social Problems, 1896; Banker's Money, 1902; Elements of Political Economy, 1903; The Tariff Question, 1903; The History of the English Corn Laws, 1904; Rates and Taxes as affecting Agriculture, 1905; Rents, Wages, and Profits in Agriculture and Rural Depopulation, 1906; A Project of Empire, 1909 (trans. Japanese); Lectures on Public Finance, 1906; The Neutrality of the United States, 1915; War Finance, 1918; Inflation, 1919; Revival of Marxism, 1920 (trans. Japanese); Tales from Ariosto, 1913; Life and Genius of Ariosto, 1914; romances—Thoth, 1888; A Dreamer of Dreams, 1889; Toxar, 1890. *Recreations:* fishing, golf, chess problems. *Address:* 3 Belford Park, Edinburgh. *Died 12 May 1927.*

NICHOLSON, Major Randolph, DSO 1919; MC; late Royal Horse Artillery; partner in W. C. Hunter & Co., 6th Avenue, Nairobi, Kenya Colony; *b* 8 April 1894; 4th *s* of F. Frederic Nicholson and Mrs Emily F. Nicholson, of Willoughton Manor, Lincoln; *m* 1921, Margery, 2nd *d* of William and Haydee Nathalie Ward-Higgs, of 29 Mincing Lane, EC, and 197 Cromwell Road, SW; one *s. Educ:* Felsted. With Borneo Co. Ltd, 1911–14; Regular Commission in RA, 1914; served European War, France and Belgium, 1915–19 (despatches, DSO, MC and bar); Egyptian Expeditionary Force, Syria, Palestine, and Egypt, 1919–20; on Staff 6 months during 1917; resigned, May 1920. *Recreations:* polo, tennis, golf, big-game shooting. *Address:* PO Box 96, Nairobi, Kenya Colony. *TA:* care Venator Nairobi. *T:* 89. *M:* B 6041. *Clubs:* Public Schools; Nairobi; Muthaiga Country. *Died 4 Aug. 1928.*

NICHOLSON, Maj.-Gen. Stuart (James), CB 1897; retired; *b* 20 Nov. 1836; *s* of late William Henry Nicholson of St Margaret's, Rochester; *m* 1870, Elizabeth, *d* of David Laing Burn of St Andrews, NB; one *s* two *d. Educ:* Charterhouse; Royal Military Academy, Woolwich. Entered Royal Artillery, 1855; Captain, 1863; Major, 1872; Lt-Col 1881; Col 1885; Maj.-Gen. 1895; ADC to Insp.-Gen. RA, 1864–69; Instr School of Gunnery, 1872–77; commanded Chesnut Troop RHA, 1877–81; Asst Director of Artillery, War Office, 1881–84; Member Ordnance Committee, 1884–85; commanded RA and NSW Artillery with Soudan Expedition, 1885 (despatches, medal with clasp, bronze star; promoted Colonel); Comdt and Supt School of Gunnery, Shoeburyness, 1887–92; Maj.-Gen. command RA Brigade, Malta, 1892–95; in command of RA Southern District, 1895–97; Colonel Commandant Royal Artillery, 1906; JP for Essex. *Publication:* ABC of Fair Trade. *Recreations:* fishing, golf. *Address:* 8 Hope Street, St Andrews. *Clubs:* United Service; Royal and Ancient Golf, St Andrews. *Died 10 April 1917.*

NICOL, John, CMG 1901; *b* Ramstone, Monymusk, Scotland, 1838; *m* 1862, Janet MacDonald, of Catrine, Ayrshire, Scotland; one *s* five *d.* Left Scotland for Durban, Natal, 1860; carried on business as builder and timber merchant for 34 years; for several years a volunteer in the Durban Field Artillery; joined the Durban Town Council in 1885; twice Deputy Mayor and four times elected Mayor of the borough; Justice of the Peace for eight years. *Address:* Banchory, Corrie Road, Durban. *Died 25 May 1920.*

NICOL, Rev. Thomas, DD; Moderator, General Assembly of the Church of Scotland, 1914; Professor of Divinity and Biblical Criticism, University of Aberdeen, since 1899; *b* 21 Oct. 1846; *m* 1878, Annie, *o* surv. *d* of late Rev. John Underwood, minister of Kirkcudbright; three *s* two *d. Educ:* Aberdeen, Edinburgh, and Tübingen Univs; MA of Aberdeen, 1868, with First Class Honours in Classics and Mental Philosophy, and with Simpson Greek Prize; Hutton Prize and Fullerton Scholarship; BD of Edinburgh, 1871; DD of Edinburgh, 1893. Ordained minister of Kells, Kirkcudbrightshire, 1873; translated to Tolbooth Parish, Edinburgh, 1879; Croall Lecturer, 1897–98; Convener from 1896 to 1911 of Church of Scotland Jewish Mission Committee; Editor of Church of Scotland Mission Record, 1886–1900; Baird Lecturer, 1906–7. *Publications:* (trans. with Rev. Dr James A. M'Clymont) Beck's Pastorallehren des Nenen Testaments (Pastoral Theology of The New Testament); Church of Scotland Sabbath School Teachers' Book, Grade I (edited); Recent Explorations in Bible Lands; Recent Archæology and the Bible (Croall Lectures, 1897–98); The Present Position and Prospects of Biblical Science (Introductory Lecture); The Four Gospels in the Earliest Church History (Baird Lectures, 1906–7). *Recreation:* golf. *Address:* 53 College Bounds, Old Aberdeen. *Died 7 Aug. 1916.*

NICOLET, Gabriel; Chevalier de la Légion d'Honneur; Member of Society of Oil-Painters of Royal Society of Portrait Painters; of the Royal West of England Academy; and of Société internationale des Aquarellistes; *b* Pons, Charente Inférieure, France, 5 March 1856; father, clergyman; *m* 1905, Amy Magnus. *Educ:* University of Liège; Royal Academy of Arts, Liège; Dusseldorf; Paris. Lived in England since 1885 and also in Paris; Bronze Medal, Universal Exhibition, Paris, 1889; Gold Medal, Paris Salon, 1895, HC; Silver Medal, Universal Exhibition, Paris, 1900. *Recreations:* riding, rowing, fencing. *Address:* 18 rue de l'Université, Paris. *Club:* Arts. *Died April 1921.*

NICOLL, James H., MC; JP Glasgow; MB Glasgow; Hon. Lieutenant-Colonel Royal Artillery; Consulting Surgeon to the Royal Hospital for Sick Children, Glasgow, Glasgow Ear and Throat Hospital, and to the Glasgow Lunacy Board's Asylum; Acting and Consulting Surgeon in various war hospitals in Britain and overseas; *b* Glasgow, 1865; *s* of Rev. James Nicoll, Glasgow; unmarried. *Educ:* Glasgow Academy and Univ.; London Hospital. After graduation in Glasgow, studied surgery for four years at the London Hospital and at various other hospitals in London and on the Continent; was Professor of Surgery, Anderson's College; Examiner in Surgery, University of Glasgow; Member of University Court, University of Glasgow, as representative of President (Raymond) Poincaré, Lord Rector of Glasgow University; Surgeon to the Western Infirmary, Glasgow; Hon. Secretary Glasgow Branch of British Medical Association; President Surgical Section of Glasgow Medico-Chirurgical Society. *Publications:* numerous publications on surgical subjects. *Recreations:* golf, fishing, walking. *Address:* 4 Woodside Place, Glasgow. *T:* Charing Cross 271, Glasgow; Central 271. *Clubs:* Royal Automobile; Western, New, Glasgow.

Died 15 Aug. 1921.

NICOLL, Sir William Robertson, CH 1921; Kt 1909; MA, LLD (Aberdeen and St Andrews); DD Halifax (NS); editor of: The British Weekly since 1886; The Bookman since 1891; The Expositor since 1885, etc; *b* Lumsden, Aberdeenshire, 10 Oct. 1851; *er s* of Rev. Harry Nicoll, Free Church minister, and Jane Robertson; *m* 1st, 1878, Isa, *o c* of Peter Dunlop, Skaithmuir, Berwickshire; one *s* one *d*; 2nd, 1897, Catherine, *d* of Joseph Pollard, High Down, Herts; one *d. Educ:* Grammar School, Aberdeen; University, Aberdeen (MA 1870; LLD 1890); LLD St Andrews, 1922; DD Halifax, NS, 1920. Free Church Minister of Dufftown, 1874–77; of Kelso, 1877–85. *Publications:* Life of James Macdonell, 1890; (ed with T. J. Wise) Literary Anecdotes of the Nineteenth Century, vol. 1, 1895, vol. 2, 1896; Professor Elmslie; The Lamb of God; The Incarnate Saviour; The Key of the Grave; Songs of Rest (Series i and ii); The Return to the Cross,1897; Sunday Afternoon Verses, 1897; Letters on Life, 1901; The Church's One Foundation, 1901; The Garden of Nuts, 1905; The Day Book of Claudius Clear, 1905; The Lamp of Sacrifice, 1906; My Father, 1908; Life of Ian Maclaren, 1908; The Round of the Clock, 1910; Emily Brontë, 1910; The Expositor's Dictionary of Texts, 1910; Sunday Evening, 1910; The Problem of Edwin Drood, 1912; A Bookman's Letters, 1913; Reunion in Eternity, 1918; Letters of Principal (Rev. James) Denney, 1920; Princes of the Church, 1921; (ed) The Expositor's Greek Testament; and numerous theological works. *Address:* Bay Tree Lodge, Hampstead, NW3; The Old Manse, Lumsden, Aberdeenshire. *Clubs:* Reform, Bath, Whitefriars. *Died 4 May 1923.*

NICOLLS, Maj.-Gen. Oliver Henry Atkins; Colonel Commandant, Royal Artillery, since 1904; *b* 24 July 1834; *m* 1st, 1875, Harriet (*d* 1881), *d* of Rev. C. Y. Crawley; 2nd, 1885, Mary (*d* 1891), *d* of E. Wolstenholme Lee. Entered army, 1853; Maj.-Gen. 1890; served Crimea, 1854–56 (medal with clasp, Turkish medal); Ferak Expedition, 1875–76 (despatches, medal with clasp, brevet Lt-Col); Commanding RA, North British District, 1887–90; RA Brigade, Malta, 1891–92; troops in Woolwich district, 1892–94; retired, 1896. *Address:* 4 East Pallant, Chichester. *Died 15 Oct. 1920.*

NICOLSON, Sir Arthur Thomas Bennet Robert, 10th Bt of that Ilk and Lasswade, *cr* 1629; DL, Orkney and Shetland; JP; Commissioner of Supply for Shetland; *b* Morphett Vale, Adelaide, 6 Nov. 1842; *s* of Sir Arthur Bolt Nicolson, 8th Bt, and Margaret, *d* of Rev. George Bisset, Aberdeenshire; *S* father, 1879; *m* 1881, Annie, *d* of late John Rutherford, Bruntsfield Place, Edinburgh, formerly of Australia; four *s* one *d*. *Educ:* Melbourne College. *Heir: s* Arthur John Frederick William Nicolson, advocate [*b* 8 June 1882. *Educ:* Edinburgh Univ. (MA, LLB)]. *Address:* Brough Lodge, Fetlar, and Grimista, Lerwick, Shetland. *TA:* Fetlar, Shetland. *Died 27 May 1917.*

NIECKS, Frederick, MusD; Reid Professor of Music, and Dean of the Faculty of Music, Edinburgh University, 1891–1914; *b* Düsseldorf, Germany, 3 Feb. 1845; *m* 1907, Christina, 3rd *d* of late Professor Sir John Struthers, MD, and Christina, *d* of James Alexander, surgeon, Wooler, Northumberland. *Educ:* private school and teachers at Düsseldorf; Leipsic University; musically by Dr Langhans, Grunewald, Leopold Auer (violin), and Tausch (pianoforte and composition), Düsseldorf and Cologne. Violinist and teacher of music at Düsseldorf till 1868; then settled in Scotland, where he was engaged in teaching music, and from 1875 as a writer on music, contributing largely to musical journals; Hon. LLD Edin. *Publications:* A Concise Dictionary of Musical Terms, with prefix, an Introduction to the Elements of Music, 1884; Chopin as a Man and Musician, 1888; A History of Programme Music (a contribution to the History of Musical Expression), 1907. *Recreations:* fine arts, literature. *Address:* 40 George Square, Edinburgh. *Died 24 June 1924.*

NIGHTINGALE, Thomas Slingsby, CMG 1915; Secretary, Office of High Commissioner Union of South Africa, London, since 1911; *b* Bedford, Cape Colony, 1866; *e s* of late Percy Nightingale (*g s* of Sir Charles Nightingale, 11th Bt, Kneesworth, Cambridgeshire), Inspecting Comr Cape of Good Hope, and Frances Emma, *e d* of Peter Brophy; *m* 1900, Doris Elizabeth, *d* of late Charles Stoughton Collison, of East Bilney, Norfolk; two *s* one *d*. *Educ:* Royal Naval School, New Cross; St George's School, Brampton. Entered Civil Service, Cape of Good Hope, 1883; served successively in: War Dept; Civil Commissioner and Resident Magistrate's Office, King William's Town; Customs Dept Cape Town, Kimberley, Port Elizabeth, East London; Resident Magistrate and Sub-Collector of Customs, Port Nolloth, Namaqualand, 1891–96; Chief Clerk Office of Agent-General, Cape of Good Hope, London, 1898; Secretary, 1905; frequently acted as Agent-General for varying periods up to May 1910 when upon establishment of Union became 1st Assistant-Secretary in Office of High Commissioner Union of S Africa; Acting High Commissioner, Nov. 1913 till Aug. 1914; Commissioner of Supreme Court of SA and Member of Advisory Committee of Imperial Education Conference; represented Union of SA as joint Delegate with Sir Richard Solomon at the International Radio-Tel. Conference, London, 1912. *Recreations:* golf, cycling. *Address:* Kneesworth, Limpsfield, Surrey. *TA:* Limpsfield. *Club:* Royal Societies'. *Died 20 June 1918.*

NIHALSINGH, Rev. Canon Solomon, BA; Evangelistic missionary; *b* 15 Feb. 1852; *s* of Thakur Himmat Singh, Mainpuri Chauhan, Rajput; a Jagirdar by birth; *m* 1870, *d* of Subahdar Sundar Singh, a Tilok Chandi Bais of Baiswara; three *s* three *d*. *Educ:* Govt High School, Lakhimpur; Canning College, Lucknow. Second master in the CMS High School, Lucknow; eventually Headmaster; Headmaster of the CMS High School, Jabbulpore, 1886; ordained 1891; sent to England as delegate of the UP and Oudh branch of the CMS to the Centenary Celebrations of the Church Missionary Society in London, 1899; Hon. Canon in All Saints Cathedral, Allahabad, 1906. *Publications:* An English Grammar for the use of the Middle Classes in Oudh; translation into English of the Urdu Entrance Course, Majmua-Sakhun, 1873–75; Khulasat-ul-Isaiah (in two parts); Risala-e-Saf Goi, or Plain Speaking; Verses on Temperance, in Urdu; Munajat Asi, or the Prayers of a Sinner; Verses on the Coronation of King Edward VII and George V, in Urdu; and a number of handbills in Hindi for free distribution. *Recreation:* theological study. *Address:* 2 Pioneer Road, Allahabad. *Died 8 May 1916.*

NILKANTH, Rao Bahadur Sir Ramanbhai Mahipatram, Kt 1927; BA, LLD; High Court Pleader; *s* of Rao Saheb Mahipatram Kupram Nilkanth, CIE; *m* 1889, Vidyagauro, *d* of Gopilal, MBE, BA, Kaiser-i-Hind Gold Medallist; two *s* five *d*. *Educ:* Elphinstone College, Bombay; Gujarat College, Ahmedabad. President of Ahmedabad Municipality; member of the Legislative Council, Bombay; Secretary of General Societies. *Publications:* brochure on marriage ritual; satire called Bhadram Bhadra; essays on literature and criticism; essay on humour, with humorous sketches. *Address:* Bhadra Ahmedabad, Bombay Presidency, India. *M:* 2690. *Club:* Gujarat, Ahmedabad. *Died March 1928.*

NILSSON, Madame Christine, (Comtesse de Miranda); Prima Donna; *b* Sweden, 20 Aug. 1843; *m* 1st, 1872, M Auguste Rouzaud (*d* 1882); 2nd, 1887, Comte de Miranda (*d* 1902). *Educ:* Halmstad; Stockholm, under Berwald. Went to Paris, 1860; studied under Français Wartel; made her *début* in Paris, 1864; first appearance in London, 1867; sang in the following operas: The Magic Flute; Martha; Don Juan; Faust; Robert the Devil. *Address:* 3 rue Clément Marot, Paris. *Died 22 Nov. 1921.*

NINNIS, Insp.-Gen. Belgrave, CVO 1912; Royal Navy, retired; 4th *s* of Paul Ninnis of St Austell, Cornwall; *m* Ada Jane, *d* of James Sutton of Streatham, Surrey; two *s* one *d*. *Educ:* privately. Joined Royal Navy, 1861; Naturalist to Northern Territory of South Australia Surveying Expedition, 1864–66; served in the Arctic Expedition, 1875–76, under Captain (Sir George) Nares; awarded Sir Gilbert Blane Gold Medal, CVO, MD, MRCS, LLM, FSA; Knight of Justice, Order of St John of Jerusalem. *Publications:* Remarks on the Ethnology, Natural History, and Meteorology of the Northern Territory of South Australia; On an Epidemic amongst the Esquimaux Dogs, Arctic Expedition, 1875–76. *Address:* The Elms, Leigham Avenue, Streatham, SW16. *T:* Streatham 1814. *Club:* Army and Navy. *Died 18 June 1922.*

NIPHER, Francis Eugene; Professor of Physics in Washington University, St Louis, 1874; Professor Emeritus, 1915; *b* Port Byron, NY, 10 Dec. 1847; *s* of Peter Nipher and Roxalana P. Tilden; *m* 1873, Matilda Aikins; one *s* four *d*. *Educ:* State University of Iowa. Secretary, Academy of Science of St Louis, 1875–85, President, 1885–90; President, St Louis Engineers' Club, 1890; Fellow American Association for Advancement of Science; Member American Physical Society; American Philosophical Society of Philadelphia; Société Française de Physique; Royal Society of Arts; in 1902 he showed that over-exposed photographic plates which are to reverse should be developed in the light instead of the dark room; discovered the causes of magnetic disturbances in the earth's field, and produced such disturbances in the field of a bar magnet surrounded by electrified air; showed that water in a vapour condition can be decomposed by an electric current; obtained experimental proof that electrification of masses of matter diminishes gravitational attraction; converted gravitational attraction between masses of matter into a repulsion, when the masses were wholly shielded from each other by metal; showed that the electrical potential of the earth is constantly subject to enormous local variations. *Publications:* Theory of Magnetic Measurements, 1886; Electricity and Magnetism (Math.), 1895; Introduction to Graphical Algebra, 1898; Experimental Studies in Electricity and Magnetism, 1914; many papers in Transactions Academy of Science of St Louis, including A Method of Measuring Pressure due to Wind at any Point on any Structure, and The Law of Contraction of Gaseous Nebulæ. *Address:* Kirkwood, St Louis County, Mo, US. *T:* Kirkwood 934 W. *Died 6 Oct. 1926.*

NISBET, Hume; author and artist; *b* Stirling, Scotland, 8 Aug. 1849. *Educ:* in Letters under Mr James Culross, LLD; in Art under Sam Bough, RSA. Left Scotland at sixteen; spent seven years travelling through Australia; on return was appointed Art Master in the Watt College and Old School of Arts, Edinburgh; held this position for eight years; resigned in 1885; travelled for Messrs Cassell through Australia and New Guinea, 1886; since then occupied as novelist, etc; revisited Australia and other parts in 1895; visited China and Japan, etc, 1905–6. *Publications:* 46 romances, including Bail Up, 1890; Bush Girl, 1894; The Great Secret and Tale of Tomorrow, 1895; In Sheep's Clothing, 1900, etc; 4 vols of poetry—Egypt, Memories of the Months, The Matador; Hathor, Colonial Tales, being vols i and ii of Poetic and Dramatic Works, in 8 vols; Travels; A Colonial Tramp; 5 books on art—Where Art Begins, etc; Life and Nature Studies, 1915. *Recreations:* travelling, studying Nature and humanity. *Address:* Dhooon Villa, Willingdon Road, Eastbourne. *Club:* Yorick.

NISBET, Rev. Matthew Alexander; Rector of Ickham since 1897; *b* Delhi, 1838; *s* of Matthew Nisbet, 48th Bengal Native Infantry; *m* 1875, Louisa J. Scobell, *d* of Rev. S. G. Scobell; three *d. Educ:* Cheltenham College; Jesus College, Cambridge (Scholar). Captain of College Boat; Captain of College Eleven (cricket); MA; MA *comitatus causa* Oxford. Curate of Longborough, 1861; Chipping Campden, 1867; Vicar of St Luke's, Gloucester, 1872; Chaplain to Volunteers; Chairman of Gloucester School Board, 1876–81; Rural Dean of Gloucester; Rector of Ringwould, 1881; Guardian and District Councillor; Hon. Sec. of the Canterbury Diocesan Education Society, 1885–1912; Hon. Sec. of the Canterbury Diocesan Sunday School Teachers' Association, 1887–1907; Hon. Canon of Canterbury, 1891; Chairman of the Finance Committee of the Diocesan Association; Member of Kent County Education Committee, 1904–13; Rural Dean of East Bridge. *Recreations:* walking, golf. *Address:* Ickham Rectory, Canterbury. *TA:* Wickhambreux. *M:* N 8918. *Clubs:* Constitutional; St George's, Sandwich; Cinque Ports, Deal; East Kent, Canterbury.

Died 5 Sept. 1919.

NISBET, Pollok Sinclair, ARSA; RSW 1879; *b* Edinburgh, 18 Oct. 1848; *s* of late John Nisbet, decorator, Edinburgh; *m* Hellen, *y d* of John Grieve of Loyal and Inglestone, Perthshire; one *s* one *d. Educ:* Edinburgh Institution. Travelled and painted extensively in Spain and Italy, and in Morocco, Tunis, and Algeria; studied in Rome and Venice. *Address:* Edinburgh. *Club:* Scottish Arts, Edinburgh.

NISBET, Col Robert Parry, CIE 1885; FRGS; Indian Army (retired); *b* 2 Nov. 1839; *s* of Harry Nisbet, Clifton; *m* 1865, Anne Claxton, *d* of John Delap Wilson, Hants. *Educ:* King's College, London. Called to the Bar at the Middle Temple, 1872; elected a Fellow of the University of London; he passed through all the grades of the Civil Commission, Panjab, and held many important posts; Deputy Commissioner of Lahore for five years; was also for the same term Deputy Commissioner and Superintendent of the Hill States at Simla; and on promotion was successively Commissioner of the Delhi, Derajat, Peshawar, and Rawal Pindi Divisions, Panjab; from Commissioner of Rawal Pindi he was in 1888 appointed to be HM's Resident in Kashmir, which post he held till he retired from the Service in 1892. *Address:* 229 Cromwell Mansions, Cromwell Road, SW. *T:* Kensington 3351.

Died 5 June 1916.

NISBETT, Lt-Col George Dalrymple More, JP; *b* 1850; *e s* of late John More Nisbett, of Cairnhill and of The Drum, and Lady Agnes (*d* 1900), 2nd surv. *d* of 9th Earl of Stair and 1st wife, Margaret, *d* of James Penny, Lancs. Brevet Lt-Col (retired), late Bedfordshire Regt. *Address:* The Drum, Gilmerton, Midlothian. *Clubs:* United Service, Junior United Service; New, Edinburgh.

Died 22 Sept. 1922.

NISSIM, Charles, JP; late Member of Governor of Bombay's Legislative Council; Hon. Presidency Magistrate for Bombay, 1904; President Bank of Bombay; Vice-President Jewish Association; Partner of the firm of David Sassoon and Co., merchants and bankers; *b* Bombay, 23 Nov. 1845; *m* Rachel (*decd*), 3rd *d* of late E. J. Abraham; one *s. Educ:* Elphinstone High School; David Sassoon Hebrew School. Left for China, 1862, returning, 1880; visited Europe several times, and Palestine; settled down in Bombay; JP, Fellow of University of Bombay, 1899; Director of several Joint Stock Companies; invited guest of HE the Governor to the Delhi Durbar; spoke English, French, German, Hebrew, Arabic, Hindustani, Guzrathi, Marathi, and Chinese. *Recreations:* reading, riding, swimming, chess. *Address:* 203 Knightsbridge, SW. *T:* Kensington 3290. *Clubs:* British Empire; Royal Bombay Yacht, Bombay.

Died 3 Nov. 1918.

NIVEN, Charles, MA, DSc; FRS; Professor of Natural Philosophy, Aberdeen University, 1880–1922; *m* Mary, *d* of late Sir David Stewart and Mary Irvine; one *s* two *d. Educ:* Aberdeen and Cambridge. Formerly Fellow of Trinity College, Cambridge, and Professor of Mathematics in Queen's College, Cork. *Publications:* papers in Proceedings and Transactions of the Royal Society and other periodicals. *Recreation:* fishing. *Address:* 6 Chanonry, Old Aberdeen. *Club:* Royal Northern, Aberdeen.

Died 11 May 1923.

NIVEN, James, MB, BChir Cantab; AM Aberdeen; MA Cantab; LLD Aberdeen; *b* 12 March 1851; widower; three *d. Educ:* Aberdeen and Cambridge Universities. Formerly Fellow of Queens' College, Cambridge; lately Medical Officer of Health for Manchester; formerly Medical Officer of Health, Oldham. *Publications:* Annual Reports; numerous papers. *Address:* 50 Granville Road, Fallowfield, Manchester.

Died Oct. 1925.

NIVEN, William, JP (Berks); FSA, ARE; *s* of late D. Graham Niven, RCS, of Pershore. *Educ:* private schools. Was articled to late Sir G. Gilbert Scott, RA, 1865; subsequently practised architecture for some years; etched plates of chiefly architectural subjects; for some years hon. editor of Records issued annually by the Architectural and Archæological Society for the County of Buckingham. *Publications:* Old Worcestershire Houses, 1873; Warwickshire, 1878; Staffordshire, 1882; City Churches, Destroyed or Threatened, 1887; Monograph of Aston Hall, 1884. *Recreations:* study of architecture and works of art, collector of old Wedgwood. *Address:* Marlow Place, Marlow.

Died 7 Nov. 1921.

NIVEN, Sir William Davidson, KCB 1903 (CB 1897); MA; FRS; late Director of Studies in Royal Naval College, Greenwich; *b* 1842; *s* of Charles Niven, Peterhead. *Educ:* Trinity College, Cambridge (Wrangler, Fellow). *Address:* Eastburn, Sidcup.

Died 29 May 1917.

NIXON, Alfred, FCA, FSAA, FCIS; late Principal, Municipal High School of Commerce, Manchester—Day and Evening Departments and School of Languages; *b* 17 March 1858; *m*; one *s* one *d. Educ:* University of Manchester. In practice for many years as a chartered accountant; headmaster to organize the Municipal Evening School of Commerce, 1889; during the war conducted special business training courses for 1,000 women; responsible under the Board of Education and the Ministry of Labour for the full-time training of 1,500 officers and disabled men; First President Incorporated Society of Commercial Teachers; Member of Council, Chartered Institute of Secretaries; late Member of Teachers' Registration Council representing commercial teachers; late Chairman of the Finance Committee of the Sale Administrative Education Committee; late Chairman of the Exchange Ward Liberal Committee; Past President of the Manchester Society of Incorporated Accountants. *Publications:* Accounting and Banking, and text-books on auditing, book-keeping, business practice, law and secretarial work; Editor of Longmans, Green & Co's Commercial Series. *Recreation:* social and political work. *Address:* Littlecroft, Queen's Road, St Anne's-on-Sea; 31 Victoria Buildings, Manchester. *T:* City 2050. *Club:* Reform, Manchester.

Died 27 Oct. 1928.

NIXON, Maj.-Gen. Arundel James; Colonel Commandant Royal Artillery, since 1921; *b* 31 May 1849; *m* 1876, Maria Lucy, *y d* of John Lawrence, Langstone Court, Monmouthshire. Entered Army, 1868; Maj.-Gen. 1906; commanded RA Gibraltar, 1906–10; retired, 1910. *Address:* Clone House, Ballyragget, Co. Kilkenny.

Died 9 April 1925.

NIXON, General Sir John (Eccles), GCMG 1919; KCB 1911 (CB 1902); *b* 16 Aug. 1857; *yr s* of Maj.-Gen. John Pigott Nixon, Bombay NI, and Ellen, *d* of G. Cooper, Brentford; *m* 1884, Amy Louisa, *y d* of James Wilson, Gratwicke, Billingshurst; one *s. Educ:* Wellington. Served in 25th, The King's Own, Borderers, and 18th Bengal Lancers; held staff appointments in India; served Afghan War, 1879–80; Zamusht Expedition, 1879 (despatches, medal); Mahsud Waziri Expedition, 1881; Chitral Relief Force, as DAQMG for Intelligence (despatches, medal and clasp, Brevet of Lieut-Colonel); North-West Frontier of India, 1897–98, as Chief Staff Officer, Tochi Field Force (despatches, clasp); commanded a cavalry brigade in South Africa, 1901–2 (despatches, medal, four clasps, CB); commanded Bangalore Brigade, 1903–6; Inspector-General of Cavalry in India, 1906–8; commanded 7th (Meerut) Division, 1908–10, and 1st Peshawar Division, 1910–12; commanded the Southern Army in India, 1912–15; commanded the Northern Army in India, 1915; commanded the Expeditionary Force in Mesopotamia, April 1915–Jan. 1916. *Publication:* Notes for Staff Officers on Field Service. *Recreations:* cricket, golf, racquets. *Club:* United Service.

Died 15 Dec. 1921.

NOBLE, Robert, RSA; *b* Edinburgh, 1857. *Educ:* Government School of Design. Exhibited first picture Royal Scottish Acad., 1877; visited Paris following year; afterwards studied at the Scottish Academy Life School, and later at Carolus Duran's Life School in Paris; exhibited Coming from Church, and the Linn Jaws, 1887, in the Royal Academy; gained silver medal for Landscape at Edinburgh International Exhibition; awarded Bronze Medal Paris International, 1900; was the 1st Chairman of the Society of Scottish Artists, and one of the hangers of the Franco-British Exhibition, London. *Address:* East Linton, Prestonkirk, NB. *Club:* Scottish Arts, Edinburgh.

Died 12 May 1917.

NOBLE, Wilson; *b* 21 Nov. 1854; *s* of late John Noble, JP, DL, of Park Place, Henley-on-Thames, and Lily, *d* of Capt. Ellis, Bengal

Artillery; *m* 1879, Marian Carolin, *d* of W. P. W. Dana of Boston, USA; four *d. Educ:* Eton; Trinity Coll, Cambridge (MA). Called to the Bar, Inner Temple, 1880. Contested Hastings, 1885; MP (C) Hastings, 1886–95; President of Röntgen Soc. of London, 1899–1900. *Recreations:* scientific pursuits (especially electricity and investigations in Röntgen rays), motoring. *Address:* Park Place, Henley-on-Thames. *Clubs:* Athenæum, Carlton.

Died 1 Nov. 1917.

NOEL, Lt-Col Hon. Edward; Deputy-Assistant-Adjutant-General Ceylon, 1899–1902; *b* 28 April 1852; 2nd *s* of 2nd Earl of Gainsborough and Ida Harriet Augusta, *e d* of 16th Earl of Erroll; *m* 1884, Ruth, *d* of late W. H. Lucas, of Trenifle, Cornwall; three *s. Educ:* Oscott College. Entered Rifle Brigade, 1872; Captain, 1880; Major, 1890; Lieut-Col 1898, on half-pay; served Ashanti War, 1873–74; NW Frontier, India, 1877–78; Burma, 1886–87–88. *Publications:* Natural Weights and Measures, 1889; International Time, 1892; Gustaf Adolf, the father of modern war, 1908. *Address:* Exton Park, Oakham. *Died 9 Nov. 1917.*

NOEL, Evan Baillie; Secretary of Queen's Club, West Kensington, since 1914; *b* 23 Jan. 1879; 2nd *s* of Eugene Frederic Noel, JP, and Ethel Maria Chapman; *m* 1906, Marjorie Dean Sweeting; one *s* one *d. Educ:* Evelyns, Hillingdon, Uxbridge; Winchester College; Trinity College, Cambridge. On the staff of The Times, 1903–14; Sporting Editor until 1909; went abroad for a year owing to ill-health; won Amateur Championship of Rackets, 1907, and MCC Silver Racket at tennis, 1908. *Publications:* A History of Tennis; First Steps to Rackets (with Hon. Charles Napier Bruce); Winchester College Cricket; and numerous articles on tennis, rackets, and other games in periodicals, daily newspapers, etc. *Recreations:* formerly cricket, tennis, rackets, and other ball games (not played for reasons of health); collecting books and prints on games, especially tennis; bridge. *Address:* 107 Comeragh Road, W14. *T:* Fulham 1421. *Clubs:* Bath, MCC, Prince's Tennis, Rackets. *Died 22 Dec. 1928.*

NOEL, Admiral Francis Charles Methuen; retired; *b* 1852; 3rd *s* of Col E. A. Noel (*d* 1899), DL, JP, of Clanna, Gloucestershire, and Sarah, *d* of late W. B. Darwin of Elston Hall, Notts; *m* 1886, Wilmot Juliana, *d* of T. Maitland Snow of Cleve House, Exeter; one *s* one *d. Educ:* Stubbington House; Royal Naval College. Commanded HMS Partridge in West Indies; commanded Scout in Red Sea, present at operations round Suakim (Khedive's medal); served with International Expedition, for relief of Kandamos, Crete; commanded Wallaroo during China War, 1900 (medal); was Deputy Commissioner for Western Pacific, and served on Anglo-French Commission in New Hebrides; was officially present at the inauguration of the Australian Commonwealth; commanded HMS Hood in home waters; awarded Captain's Good Service Pension; Rear-Admiral, 1907; Admiral on retired list, 1915; Assessor for Appeals in the House of Lords. *Recreations:* literary. *Address:* 33 Redcliffe Square, SW. *Club:* Junior United Service.

Died 30 Dec. 1925.

NOEL, Admiral of the Fleet Sir Gerard Henry Uctred, GCB 1913 (KCB 1902); KCMG 1898; Admiral of the Fleet, 1908–15; retired 1915; *b* 5 March 1845; 2nd surv. *s* of late Rev. Augustus William Noel, Rector of Stanhoe, Norfolk, and Lucy Elizabeth, *d* of Capt. Norris William Tonge, RN, Alveston; *m* 1875, Charlotte Rachel Frederica, *e d* of late Francis Joseph Cresswell and Charlotte, *d* of 4th Lord Calthorpe. Commanded Naval Guard at Cape Coast Castle, 1873 (promoted, medal, clasp); a Lord of the Admiralty, 1893–98; ADC to the Queen, 1894–96; Rear-Admiral Mediterranean Fleet, 1898–99; commanded Home Fleet, and Admiral-Superintendent, Naval Reserves, 1900–3; Commander-in-Chief, China Station, 1904–6; at the Nore, 1907–8; Gold Medal of Royal United Service Institution. *Address:* Fincham, Downham, Norfolk. *Club:* United Service. *Died 22 May 1918.*

NOEL, Rev. Canon John Monk, RD; *b* St James' Parish, Westminster, 4 June 1840; *m* 1868, Eliza Anne Le Messurier, St John's; one *s* four *d. Educ:* Archbishop Tenison's Grammar School, London; Queen's Theological College, St John's, Newfoundland. SPG Missionary to Newfoundland, 1860; Incumbent of Ferryland, 1864–67; Upper Island Cove, Conception Bay, 1868–76; Rector of St Paul's, Harbour Grace, Newfoundland, 1876–1913; Rural Dean of Conception Bay, 1895; Canon of St Boniface, St John Baptist Cathedral, 1897. *Recreation:* three month's holiday to England, July to Sept. 1908. *Address:* Harvey Street, Harbour Grace, Newfoundland.

Died 1921.

NOLAN, Sir Robert Howard, KBE 1923 (CBE 1918); Hon. Secretary NZ Soldiers' Club. *Address:* Remuera, New Zealand.

Died 13 July 1923.

NOPS, Walter, ISO 1902; *b* 1850; *m* 1883, Elizabeth Moule. Was in Secretary's Office, GPO, St Martin's-le-Grand, EC. *Address:* Elmdale, Bromley, Kent. *Died 26 Feb. 1918.*

NORBURY, Edwin Arthur, RCA; Director of the Norbury Sketching School and St James' Life School; Principal of The Henry Blackburn Studio; painter and illustrator; *b* Liverpool, 1849; 2nd *s* of late Richard Norbury, RCA, of Macclesfield; *m* 1873, Elvira, *e d* of D. C. Browne, of Norwich; two *d. Educ:* Dr Wand's School, Liverpool. At age of 15 began contributing to the Illustrated London News and Illustrated Times; afterwards joined the Graphic as Artist Correspondent, and sketched many passing events; resided chiefly in North Wales, 1875–90; was Vice-President and one of the Founders of the Royal Cambrian Academy; organised the first Technical Art Classes, and received an Exceptional Recognition from the Science and Art Departments; went to Siam to direct the Royal School of Arts and to give Art Instruction in the Raj. Kumara College, 1892; painted two pictures for the King of Siam of the Crown Prince's coming-of-age ceremonies; was Special Artist to the Graphic and Daily Graphic during the Franco-Siamese War of 1893; returned to London, 1896; exhibited at the Royal Academy, Royal Institute, etc, and chief American galleries. *Publications:* many illustrations of books, magazines, and papers, including The Kingdom of the Yellow Robe, The Arabian Nights, Animal Arts and Crafts, etc. *Recreations:* sketching, rowing, walking. *Address:* 241 King's Road, Chelsea, SW. *Club:* London Sketch. *Died 16 Oct. 1918.*

NORBURY, Insp.-Gen. Sir Henry (Frederick), KCB 1897 (CB 1879); MD; FRCS; RN; Hon. Surgeon to Kings Edward VII and George V; *b* 1839; *m* 1868, Mina Legge, *d* of E. G. Wade-Brown of Burton Bradstock, Dorset; three *s* five *d. Educ:* Oundle School; St Bartholomew's Hospital, London; University of Malta. Entered Royal Navy as Surgeon, 1860; promoted Staff Surgeon, 1872; Fleet Surgeon, 1879; Deputy-Inspector-General, 1887; Inspector-General, 1894; was landed in medical charge of the Naval Brigade during the Kafir War of 1877–78 (despatches); during Zulu War of 1879 was Principal Medical Officer of General Sir Charles Pearson's column; present at the battle of Inyezane and during defence of Ekowe; was afterwards Principal Medical Officer of the Naval Brigade with General Crealock's column (despatches several times; medal with three clasps); promoted; late Director-General of the Medical Department of the Navy; created a Military CB; KCB (Mil.) 1897; Knight of Grace of St John of Jerusalem in England, 1895; awarded the Blane Gold Medal 1879; Jubilee medal of Queen Victoria and Coronation medals of Kings Edward VII and George V. *Publication:* The Naval Brigade in South Africa. *Address:* St Margaret's, Eltham, SE9. *T:* Eltham 1333.

Died 10 Dec. 1925.

NORDAU, Max Simon, MD Paris, Budapesth; Officier d'Académie, France; author and physician; President Congress of Zionists; *b* Budapesth, 29 July 1849; *y s* of Gabriel Südfeld, Rabbi, Krotoschin, Prussia, and his 2nd wife; *m* Anna-Elizabeth, 2nd *d* of State-councillor Captain Julius Dons, Copenhagen, Denmark; one *d. Educ:* Royal Gymnasium and Protestant Gymnasium, Budapesth; Royal University, Budapesth; Faculty of Medicine, Paris. Wrote very early for newspapers; travelled for several years all over Europe; practised as a physician for a year and a half, 1878–80, at Budapesth; settled then at Paris, residing there ever since; Hon. Mem. of the Greek Acad. of the Parnassos; Foreign Member of the Royal Academy of Medicine of Madrid; LLD *hc* Athens; Comdr Royal Hellenic Order of St Saviour. *Publications:* Paris, Studien und Bilder aus dem wahren Milliardenlande, 1878; Seifenblasen, 1879; Vom Kreml zur Alhambra, 1880; Aus der Zeitungswelt (together with Ferdinand Gross), 1880; Paris unter der dritten Republik, 1881; Der Krieg der Millionen, 1882; De la castration de la Femme, 1882; Die conventionellen Lügen der Culturmenschheit, 1883; Ausgewählte Pariser Briefe, 1884; Paradoxe, 1885; Die Krankheit des Jahrhunderts, 1887; Seelenanalysen, 1891; Gefühlskomödie, 1892; Entartung, 1893; Das Recht zu lieben, 1894; Die Kugel, 1895; Drohnenschlacht, 1896 (The Drones must Die, 1899); La funzione sociale dell arte, 1897; Doctor Kohn, 1898; Zeitgenössische Franzosen, 1901; Morganatic, 1904; Mahâ-Rôg, 1905; On Art and Artists, 1907; Der Sinn der Geschichte, 1909; Zionistische Schriften, 1909; Märchen, 1910; Der Lebenssport, 1912; Franzosische Staatsmanner, 1916; Biología de la Etica (Spanish), 1918; Impresiosmes españolas (Spanish), 1920; Los Grandes del Arte español (Spanish), 1921; Moral and the Evolution of Man, 1922. *Recreations:* foil-fencing, swimming. *Address:* 14 Rue Henner, Paris.

Died 22 Jan. 1923.

NORDENSKJÖLD, Otto, PhD; Professor of Geography, University of Gothenburg; *b* 6 Dec. 1869; *m* Karen Berg; one *s* three *d*. *Educ:* University of Upsala. Arctic and Antarctic explorer; Leader of Scientific Expeditions to Terra del Fuego, 1895–97; Alaska and Yukon, 1898; the Antarctic Regions, 1901–4; West Greenland, 1909; South America and Patagonia, 1920; also to Spitzbergen, Iceland, etc; most important studies: former extension of land-ice in South America; remains of the extinct animal Neomylodon brought to Europe; Antarctic ice conditions; cretaceous fossils and tertiary vertebrates and plant remains discovered in the Antarctic; also Swedish petrology; Hon. Corresponding Member Royal Geographical Society, London; Hon. Member Geographical Society, Paris, Berlin, Vienna, Rome, Madrid, Budapest, Brussels, Amsterdam, and others. *Publications:* Antarctica: the Swedish Antarctic Expedition, 1901–4 (in 7 languages); Die Polarwelt (Swedish, German, French, Russian); La Terre de Feu; Südamerika; and many others. *Address:* Göteborg, Sweden. *Died 2 June 1928.*

NORFOLK, 15th Duke of, *cr* 1483; **Henry Fitzalan-Howard,** KG; PC; JP; Earl of Arundel, 1139; Baron Maltravers, 1830; Earl of Surrey, 1483; Baron FitzAlan, Clun, and Oswaldestre, 1627; Earl of Norfolk, 1644; Earl Marshal and Hereditary Marshal and Chief Butler of England; Premier Duke and Earl; Lieutenant-Colonel 4th Royal Sussex till 1912; Lord Lieutenant, Sussex, since 1905; *b* Carlton Terrace, 27 Dec. 1847; *s* of 14th Duke and Augusta Mary Minna Catherine, *d* of 1st Lord Lyons; *S* father, 1860; *m* 1st, 1877, Lady Flora Paulyna Hetty Barbara, (*d* 11 April 1887), *d* of 1st Baron Donington and Edith, Countess of Loudoun; one *s* decd; 2nd, 1904, Hon. Gwendolen Mary Constable-Maxwell, later 13th Baroness Herries; one *s* three *d*. Special Envoy to Pope Leo XIII, 1887; Mayor of Sheffield, 1895–96; first Lord Mayor of Sheffield, 1896–97; first Mayor of Westminster, 1899; Postmaster-General, 1895–1900; served South Africa, 1900; Kt Grand Cross, Order of Christ, Holy See. Owned about 49,900 acres. *Heir: s* Earl of Arundel, *b* 30 May 1908. *Address:* Norfolk House, St James's Square, SW; Arundel Castle, Sussex; Derwent Hall, Derbyshire; Beech Hill, Sheffield. *Clubs:* Carlton, Travellers', White's; Royal Yacht Squadron, Cowes. *Died 11 Feb. 1917.*

NORMAN, Rev. Alfred Merle, MA, LLD, DCL; FRS; FLS; Hon. Canon of Durham since 1885; late Rector of Houghton-le-Spring, Co. Durham, and Rural Dean; *b* 1831; *s* of John Norman, DL, Iwood House, Somerset. *Educ:* Winchester; Christ Church, Oxford. A marine zoologist and the author of very many publications on the subject; his extensive collections of the invertebrate fauna of the North Atlantic and Arctic Oceans were placed in the British Museum, and his scientific library was given to the University of Cambridge; Medallist of the "Institute" of France; Gold Medal, Linnean Society, 1906. Land-owner in Somersetshire. *Address:* The Red House, Berkhamsted, Herts. *Died 26 Oct. 1918.*

NORMAN, Arthur William, ISO 1910; BA, BSc (London); Assistant Secretary, Estate Duty Office, Inland Revenue, 1908–13; *b* 1 May 1850; *s* of late W. J. Norman; *m* 1883, Irene, *d* of late Rev. Gideon R. J. Ouseley; one *s* one *d*. *Educ:* private; University College, Gower Street, and King's College, WC. Graduated at London University in Arts and Science. Entered Inland Revenue Department, 1867. *Publications:* A Digest of the Death Duties, 3rd edn 1911; Death Duty Tables, etc. *Recreation:* walking. *Address:* Kilfinane, Seafield Road, Southbourne-on-Sea, Hants. *Died 24 Nov. 1928.*

NORMAN, Edward; banker; Chairman, Bank of Liverpool and Martin's Ltd, London Board, since 1919; *b* Bromley Common, Kent, 31 July 1847; *y s* of late George Warde Norman, of Bromley Common, Kent; *m* 1875, Eleanor Mary (*d* 1911), *y d* of Rev. Aretas Akers of Malling Abbey, Maidstone, Kent; one *d*. *Educ:* Eton. Clerk in House of Commons, 1870–81; Assistant Secretary to Public Works Loan Board, 1881–83; Partner in firm of Martin & Co., Bankers, 1883–91; Director of Martin's Bank, Ltd, 1891; Chairman of Public Works Loan Commission, 1908–21; Director of Guardian Assurance Company, Ltd, of Buenos Ayres, and Pacific Railway Company, Ltd, and of Commercial Bank of Spanish America, Ltd. *Recreations:* formerly lawn tennis, shooting, cricket, hunting, football. *Address:* Chelsfield House, Chelsfield, Kent; 68 Lombard Street, EC. *Club:* Windham. *Died 5 Feb. 1923.*

NORMAN, Commander F. M., (*pseudonym* **Martello Tower**), RN; author; *b* 1833; *s* of Robert C. Norman of Kent; unmarried. *Educ:* Harrow. Entered Royal Navy, 1848; retired as Commander, 1863; assisted to land allied armies in Crimea; served for 4 months with the original Naval Brigade before Sebastopol; wounded in a boat action in China, 1857; JP for, Hon. Freeman, and twice Mayor of Berwick-on-Tweed; Fellow of the Botanical Society of Edinburgh. Decorated: Inkerman and Sebastopol clasps, Crimea; Medjidie, 5th class; China, 1856–58. *Publications:* At School and at Sea; Martello Tower in China; History of HMS Havannah; Manual of School Drill (14 editions); Manual of English Grammar for School Teachers (5 editions); Guide to the Fortifications of Berwick-on-Tweed. *Recreations:* tastes and employments lay in the direction of natural history and of church work; held many honorary public offices; lectured and contributed a number of papers on natural history matters to Club Proceedings, and on other subjects to the Newcastle Diocesan Conference. *Address:* Cheviot House, Berwick-on-Tweed. *Died 6 Oct. 1918.*

NORMAND, Mrs Ernest, (Henrietta Rae); painter of classical pictures; *b* London, 30 Dec. 1859; *y d* of late T. B. Rae; *m* 1884, Ernest Normand (*d* 1923), the painter; one *s* one *d*. *Educ:* Queen's Square School of Art; Heatherley's; British Museum; Royal Academy Schools; Paris. Commended to study Art at the age of 13; exhibited first picture at the Royal Academy, 1880; represented at the Royal Acad. each succeeding year by important pictures; Medallist at Paris and Chicago Universal Exhibitions. *Principal paintings:* Ariadne, 1885; A Naiad, 1886; Eurydice, 1886; Doubts, 1887; Zephyrus and Flora, 1888; Death of Procris, 1889; Ophelia, 1890; La Cigale, 1891; Flowers Plucked and Cast Aside, 1892; Mariana, 1893; Psyche at the Throne of Venus, 1894; Apollo and Daphne, 1895; Summer, 1896; Isabella, 1897; Diana and Calisto, 1899; decoration in fresco for the Royal Exchange, subject: Sir Richard Whittington and his Charities, 1900; portrait of first Marquess of Dufferin and Ava, 1901; The Sirens, 1903; Songs of the Morning, 1904; In Listening Mood, 1905; portrait of The Lady Tenterden and Echo, 1906; Roses of Youth, 1907; Abelard and Heloïse, 1908; Hylas and the Water Nymphs, 1910; Spring's Awakening, 1913; portrait of Sir Robert Anderson, Bt, ex-Lord Mayor of Belfast, 1912; portrait of Lady M'Culloch, 1918; Nemesis, and a portrait of Frederick, third Marquess of Dufferin and Ava, 1919; portrait of the Rt Hon. Sir James Johnston, ex-Lord Mayor of Belfast, and a portrait of John Johnston of Lurgan, 1921; Summer, and portrait of Miss Moyna Macgill, 1922; portrait of Alderman Thomas Edward McConnell, MP, 1925. *Recreation:* gardening. *Address:* 4 Fox Hill Gardens, Upper Norwood, SE19. *T:* Sydenham 1949. *M:* YN 1806. *Club:* Lyceum. *Died 26 March 1928.*

NORREYS, Lord; Montague Charles Francis Towneley-Bertie; JP; DL; served with Yeomanry Cavalry, South Africa, 1900; Captain in the Army, since 1915, special service; *b* 3 Oct. 1860; *e s* of 7th Earl of Abingdon and 1st wife, Caroline Theresa, *e d* of Charles Towneley, Lancs; *m* 1885, Hon. Rose Riversdale (*sister* of 4th Baron Wolverton), *d* of Hon. Henry Carr Glyn and Rose, *d* of Rev. Denis Mahony; one *s* one *d*. *Heir: s* Hon. Montagu Edmund Henry Cecil Towneley-Bertie, Lieut Grenadier Guards [*b* 2 Nov. 1877. Served European War (wounded)]. *Address:* 35 York Terrace, Regent's Park, NW. *Club:* Turf. *Died 24 Sept. 1919.*

NORRIS, George Michael, ISO 1902; LLB; late First Class Clerk, Board of Education; *b* 11 Sept. 1841; *s* of late William Norris of Hornsey Lane; unmarried. *Educ:* at an Islington School. As Society of Arts' Prizeman received a nomination to compete for a clerkship in the Board of Education, 1864; reorganised the Birkbeck College; was a vice-presidential member of the governing body of the Birkbeck College, one of the first Hon. Secs of the London Society for the Extension of University Teaching, and a member of the City of London College Council. *Recreations:* reading, walking. *Died 11 Nov. 1922.*

NORRIS, William Edward; novelist; *b* 1847; *s* of late Sir William Norris, formerly Chief Justice of Ceylon. *Educ:* Eton. Barrister Inner Temple, 1874, but never practised. *Publications:* Heaps of Money, 1877; Mademoiselle de Mersac, 1880; Matrimony, 1881; No New Thing, 1883; My Friend Jim; Adrian Vidal, 1885; Chris, 1888; Major and Minor, 1888; The Rogue, 1889; Matthew Austin; Billy Bellew, 1895; The Dancer in Yellow, 1896; Clarissa Furiosa, 1897; Marietta's Marriage, 1897; The Fight for the Crown, 1898; The Widower, 1898; Giles Ingilby, 1899; An Octave, 1900; The Flower of the Flock, 1900; His Own Father, 1901; The Embarrassing Orphan, 1901; The Credit of the County, 1902; Lord Leonard the Luckless, 1903; Nature's Comedian, 1904; Barham of Beltana, 1905; Harry and Ursula, 1907; Pauline, 1908; The Perjurer, 1909; Not Guilty, 1910; The Rt Hon. Gentleman, 1913; Barbara and Company, 1914; Proud Peter, 1916; The Fond Fugitives, 1917; The Obstinate Lady, 1919; The Triumphs of Sara, 1920; Tony the Exceptional, 1921; Sabine and Sabina, 1922; Next of Kin, 1923; The Conscience of Gavin Blane, 1924; Trevalion, 1925. *Recreation:* golf. *Address:* Bellair, Torquay. *Clubs:* National, Windham. *Died 19 Nov. 1925.*

NORTH, Col Dudley, CB 1896; *b* 8 Oct. 1840; *o* surv. *s* of late Dudley North and Sarah, *d* of Major Lockyer of Lockyersleigh, New South Wales. *Educ:* Harrow. Joined 47th Regt, 1858; Capt. 1866; Special Service Officer, Gold Coast, 1873-74 (dangerously wounded, despatches, medal and clasp, Brevet Major); ADC to Governor of Malta, 1875-78; commanded the wing North Lancashire Regt with the Zhob Valley Expedition, 1884; AAG Canada, 1892-97; retired, 1897. *Address:* 23 Down Street, W. *Clubs:* Naval and Military, United Service. *Died 22 Nov. 1917.*

NORTH, Col Edward, CB 1917; FRCS; retired; late HM Army Medical Service; *b* Dec. 1856; unmarried. *Educ:* privately. Served S African War (despatches); European War, 1914-17 (despatches, CB). *Club:* Junior United Service. *Died 6 June 1927.*

NORTH, Frederic Dudley, CMG 1902; JP; Under Secretary Colonial Secretary's Department, West Australia, since 1902, and Comptroller-General of Prisons, since 1912; four times President of the Civil Service Association; Mayor of Cottesloe for four years in succession; President of Civil Service Club for 6th time; *b* 9 Nov. 1866; *e s* of Charles Augustus North and Rachel Elizabeth, *d* of Sir Francis Grant, PRA; *m* 1887, Flora Frances, *y d* of Edward Hamersley; two *s* two *d*. *Educ:* Rugby. *Address:* Catlidge, Cottesloe, Western Australia. *Clubs:* Carlton; Weld, Civil Service, Perth. *Died 22 Aug. 1921.*

NORTH, Sir Harry, Kt 1905; *b* 26 Dec. 1866; *e s* of late Col John Thomas North of Avery Hill, Eltham, Kent; *m* 1894, Jessie Louisa, *d* of late David Evans, JP, of Cliffden, Saltburn, and Middlesbrough, Yorks; one *s* two *d*. *Educ:* Jesus College, Cambridge. Captain and Hon. Major, 4th Batt. (Mil.) Royal Munster Fusiliers; retired, 1905; one of HM's Lieutenants for the City of London; Hon. Lt-Col City of London Royal Engineer Cadet Training Corps. *Address:* Lemon Well, Eltham, Kent. *T:* 187 Lee Green. *M:* LE 5236. *Clubs:* Carlton, Junior Carlton, Royal Automobile, Royal Thames Yacht. *Died 26 Nov. 1920.*

NORTH, John William, ARA 1893; RWS; *b* 1842. *Address:* Washford, Taunton. *Club:* Arts. *Died 20 Dec. 1924.*

NORTHBOURNE, 2nd Baron, *cr* 1884; **Walter Henry James,** DL, JP; Bt, 1791; Hon. Colonel 5th Battalion Durham Light Infantry, 1895-1921, and Cinque Ports Volunteer Artillery; *b* 25 March 1846; *s* of 1st Baron and Sarah Caroline, *d* of Cuthbert Ellison, Hebburn Hall, Durham; *S* father 1893; *m* 1868, Edith Emeline Mary, *d* of John Newton-Lane, King's Bromley Manor, Stafford; three *s* one *d* (and one *s* decd). *Educ:* Radley; Christ Church, Oxford (MA). MP (L) Gateshead, 1874-93. Owned about 6,700 acres. *Heir: s* Hon. Walter John James [*b* 2 Sept. 1869; *m* 1894, Laura Gwenllian, *e d* of Adm. Sir Ernest Rice, KCB; one *s* three *d* (and one *s* decd)]. *Address:* Betteshanger, Dover. *Club:* Travellers'. *Died 27 Jan. 1923.*

NORTHCLIFFE, 1st Viscount, *cr* 1917, of St Peter in the County of Kent; **Alfred Charles William Harmsworth;** Bt, 1904; Baron Northcliffe of the Isle of Thanet, 1905; newspaper proprietor; *b* Chapelizod, Co. Dublin, 15 July 1865; *e s* of late Alfred Harmsworth, of the Middle Temple, barrister-at-law, and Geraldine Mary, *d* of William Maffett, Pembroke Place, Co. Dublin; *m* 1888, Mary Elizabeth, GBE, RRC, *e d* of late Robert Milner, Kidlington, Oxford, and St Vincent, West Indies. Founded Daily Mail, 1896; chief proprietor, The Times, 1908; Chairman of the British War Mission to the USA, 1917; Chairman British War Mission, 1917-18; Director of Propaganda in Enemy Countries, 1918, and of the Civil Aerial Transport Committee, 1917; Hon. LLD, Rochester University, USA. *Heir:* none. *Publication:* At the War, 1916. *Address:* 1 Carlton Gardens, SW; Elmwood, St Peter's, Thanet; Buckthorn Hill, Crowborough, Sussex; Chapelizod, Co. Dublin. *Club:* Beefsteak. *Died 14 Aug. 1922 (ext).*

NORTHCOTE, Rev. Hon. John Stafford; Chaplain to King George V; Prebendary of St Paul's, since 1906; Hon. Secretary of London Diocesan Church Schools Association; Chairman of Grey Coat Hospital Schools; Fellow of King's College, London, 1913; *b* London, 3 Jan. 1850; 3rd *s* of 1st Earl of Iddesleigh and Cecilia Frances Farrer, CI; *m* 1881, Hilda Cardew (*d* 1908), 2nd *d* of Very Rev. Frederic William Farrar, Dean of Canterbury; one *s* two *d* (and two *s* decd). *Educ:* Eton; King's Coll. London (AKC 1878). Mechanical Engineer, at Beyer and Peacock's Locomotive Factory, Manchester, and at Sir W. G. Armstrong and Company, Newcastle, 1867-73; Inspector of Railway Material and Locomotive Engines under the Indian Government, 1873-76; ordained, 1878; Curate of St Margaret's,

Westminster, 1878-81; Rector of Upton Pyne, near Exeter, 1881-89; Vicar of St Andrew, Westminster, 1889-1916; Chairman of Council, Girls' Public Day School Trust. *Recreation:* Member of the first Rugby football team that played for Manchester. *Address:* 33 Rossetti Garden Mansions, SW3. *T:* Kensington 7098. *Died 5 June 1920.*

NORTHCOTT, Rev. William, MA; Vicar of Atherstone since 1888; Canon of Coventry, 1918; *b* 16 July 1854; *s* of James Northcott, late of Fir Lodge, Denmark Hill; *m* 1880, Nora Catherine Marie, *d* of Rev. G. F. Mathews, Vicar of Mancetter, and Rural Dean of Atherstone; four *s* four *d*. *Educ:* St John's College, Cambridge (Foundation Scholar; 2nd Class, Classical Tripos). Vicar of Hartshill, 1880-88; Chaplain Atherstone Union since 1908. *Publications:* occasional sermons and hymns. *Recreations:* chess, etc; formerly golf, lawn tennis, rowing, football. *Address:* The Vicarage, Atherstone. *Died 12 Oct. 1924.*

NORTHESK, 10th Earl of, *cr* 1647; **David John Carnegie,** DL; JP; Baron Rosehill, 1639; Captain 3rd Battalion Gloucestershire Regiment since 1888; a Representative Peer for Scotland; *b* 1 Dec. 1865; *s* of 9th Earl and Elizabeth, *d* of Admiral Sir George Elliot, KCB; *S* father, 1891; *m* 1894, Elizabeth Boyle, *d* of Maj.-Gen. George Skene-Hallowes; one *s* one *d*. *Educ:* Eton. ADC to Governor of Victoria, Earl of Hopetoun, 1889-91 and 1892-95. Owned about 10,000 acres. *Heir: s* Lord Rosehill, *b* 24 Sept. 1901. *Address:* 6 Hans Crescent, SW1. *T:* Victoria 1092; Ethie Castle, Arbroath, Forfarshire; Whitley Ridge, Brockenhurst, Hants. *Died 5 Dec. 1921.*

NORTHROP, Cyrus, LLD Yale, Wisconsin, Illinois, and South Carolina; President of University of Minnesota, 1884-1911, subsequently Emeritus; *b* Ridgefield, Conn, 30 Sept. 1834; *y c* of Cyrus Northrop and Polly B. (*née* Fancher); *m* 1862, Anna Elizabeth, *d* of Joseph D. Warren of Stamford, Conn; one *s* one *d*. *Educ:* Yale (BA, LLB, LLD). Clerk of Senate and House of Representatives of Connecticut, 1860-62; Editor of New Haven Daily Palladium, 1862-63; Professor of Rhetoric and English Literature in Yale College, 1863-84; Candidate for Congress, 1867. *Address:* Minneapolis, Minnesota, USA. *Clubs:* Congregational, Commercial, Publicity, University, Yale. *Died 3 April 1922.*

NORTHRUP, William Barton, KC Canada; MA; Clerk Canadian House of Commons, 1918-24. Barrister; Church of England. *Address:* Ottawa, Canada. *Clubs:* Rideau, Country, Ottawa; Royal Canadian Yacht, Albany, Toronto; Belleville, Belleville. *Died Oct. 1925.*

NORTHUMBERLAND, 7th Duke of, *cr* 1766; **Henry George Percy,** KG 1899; PC 1874; JP Surrey; DL; LLD; FRS; Earl of Northumberland, Baron Warkworth, 1749; Earl Percy, 1766; Earl of Beverley, 1790; Lord Lovaine, Baron of Alnwick, 1784; Trustee of the British Museum since 1900; Lord-Lieutenant of Northumberland; Chancellor of Durham; *b* 29 May 1846; *e s* of 6th Duke and Louisa, *d* of Henry Drummond, Albury Park, Surrey; *S* father, 1899; *m* 1868, Lady Edith Campbell (*d* 1913), *d* of 8th Duke of Argyll; three *s* five *d* (and four *s* one *d* decd). *Educ:* Oxford. Hon. Col 3rd Batt. Northumberland Fusiliers, and 1st Northumberland Artillery Volunteers; MP (C) N Northumberland, 1868-85; Treasurer of Household, 1874-75; President of Archæological Institute, 1884-92. *Heir: s* Earl Percy [*b* 17 April 1880; *m* 1911, Lady Helen Magdalen Gordon-Lennox, *d* of 7th Duke of Richmond and Gordon; two *s* two *d*]. *Address:* 2 Grosvenor Place, SW. *T:* Victoria 1462; Albury Park, Guildford; Alnwick Castle, Northumberland; Syon House, Brentford; Kielder Castle, North Tyne. *Clubs:* Athenæum, Carlton, St Stephen's, Travellers'; Northumberland and Northern Counties. *Died 14 May 1918.*

NORTON, 2nd Baron, *cr* 1878; **Charles Leigh Adderley;** *b* 10 March 1846; *e s* of 1st Baron and Hon. Julia Anne Eliza Leigh, *e d* of 1st Lord Leigh; *m* 1870, Caroline Ellen, *d* of Sir Alexander Beaumont Churchill Dixie, 10th Bt; three *s* four *d* (and two *s* two *d* decd). Formerly Assistant Local Government Board Inspector, and Private Sec. to his father as Pres. of Board of Trade. Church of England; Conservative; owned about 4,600 acres; Saltley estate came by marriage, *temp.* Charles I, with heiress of Arden family. *Heir: s* Hon. Ralph Bowyer Adderley, *b* 9 Oct. 1872; *m* 1899, (Mary) Louisa, *d* of Robert Watson, Ballydarton, Co. Carlow, and *widow* of Inglis Brady. *Address:* Wellington Lodge, Bredon, Worcestershire. *Died 4 Dec. 1926.*

NORTON, Major Alfred Edward Marston, DSO 1900; FRGS; *b* 13 July 1869; *s* of late John Norton of Golding Hall, Salop; *m* 1895,

Fannie Margaret Stacy. Served with S Australian Contingent, South Africa, 1900 (despatches, Queen's medal, 2 clasps, DSO); European War (Bt Lt-Col). *Club:* Naval and Military.

Died 8 June 1922.

NORTON, Edward, JP; Director of Royal Mail Steam Packet Co., Union Castle Steamship Co., and Nelson Lines; *b* 1841; 2nd *s* of late Edward Norton of Scole, Norfolk; *m* 1st, Edith, *d* of late Charles Lamport of Bindon House, Somerset; 2nd, Edith Sarah, *d* of late Rt Hon. Sir Alfred Wills of Saxholm, Bassett; four *s* two *d. Address:* Uplands, Fareham, Hants. *Club:* Union.

Died 20 May 1923.

NORTON, Ven. John George; Rector of Christ Church Cathedral, Montreal, and Rector of Montreal, Canada, since 1884; Archdeacon of Montreal since 1902; *b* 28 Oct. 1840; 2nd *s* of late William Norton, Hollybank, Arva, Co. Cavan, and Sarah A. Richmond; *m* 1st, 1873, Lucy Durham, *d* of late William Henderson, FRHS; 2nd, 1902, Amelia Josephine, *d* of late Stanley C. Bagg, Montreal; one *s* one *d. Educ:* Trinity College, Dublin (MA, DD). Ordained, 1865; Curate of Kilmacrenan, 1865–67; Mullabrack, 1867–69; St Nicholas, Durham, 1869–72; Vicar of St Giles, Durham, 1872–84; Archdeacon of St Andrews, PQ, 1900–2; Canon of Montreal, 1893–1902. *Publications:* Hearty Services or Revived Church Worship, 3rd edn 1888; Worship in Heaven and on Earth, 1884. *Address:* The Rectory, 441 University Street, Montreal.

Died Sept. 1924.

NORTON, Rt. Rev. John Henry, DD; (3rd) Bishop of Port Augusta since 1906; *b* Ballarat, Victoria, 31 Dec. 1855. *Educ:* private schools and colleges at Ballarat; with the Jesuits at Melbourne; St Kieran's College, Kilkenny; Propaganda, Rome. Received minor orders from Archbishop Goold at Melbourne, 1876; Deaconship at Rome, 1881; Priest at Rome by Cardinal Monaco la Valetta, 1882; affiliated to the Diocese of Adelaide, and arrived there, 1883; appointed to the Cathedral; first Resident Parish Priest of Petersburg, 1884; Diocesan Consultor; Vicar-General, 1896; Administrator of the Diocese, 1905. *Address:* Bishop's House, Petersburg, South Australia.

Died 22 March 1923.

NORTON, Prof. Richard; *b* Feb. 1872; *s* of Charles Eliot Norton, Professor of the History of Fine Arts at Harvard University, and Susan Sedgwick. *Educ:* private schools and Harvard University. Studied at American School of Classical Studies in Athens, and the University of Munich, 1892–95; Prof. of History of Fine Arts at Bryn Mawr, Penn 1895–97; Assistant Director American School of Archæology in Rome, 1897–99, Director, 1899–1907; Director of American Expedition to Cyrene, 1910 and 1911; 1914, organised the American Volunteer Motor Ambulance Corps, which served on the French front and was *cité* twice. *Publications:* Bernini and other Essays, 1915; articles on archæological and kindred subjects in the American Journal of Archæology, Journal of Hellenic Studies, Encyclopædia Britannica; catalogue of casts in Museum of Fine Arts at Portland, Oregon. *Recreations:* out-door sports. *Address:* c/o Brown, Shipley, and Co., 123 Pall Mall, SW. *Club:* Brook, New York.

Died 2 Aug. 1918.

NORTON, Robert, JP; DL; *b* 11 Oct. 1838; *s* of late William Norton of Burcote House, Co. Northampton; *m* 1st, 1867, Amelia Harriett (*d* 1900), *d* of late Rev. John Duncombe Shafto; two *s* two *d.* 2nd, 1903, Isabel, *d* of late Hugh Lee Pattinson. Called to the Bar at Middle Temple, 1865; MP (C) Tunbridge Div. of Kent, 1885–92; High Sheriff of Kent, 1910. *Address:* Downs House, Yalding, Maidstone; St Mary's, Boscombe, Hants. *Club:* Carlton.

Died 7 June 1926.

NORWOOD, Rev. Reginald, MA; Vicar of All Souls', Heywood, Manchester, since 1924; *b* 3 Jan. 1874; 5th *s* of late Rev. R. P. Norwood, BA, Vicar of Fritwell, Oxon; *m* 1902, Charlotte Eveline, *o d* of Rev. Canon O'Flaherty, Prebend of Kilbragh; one *s* one *d. Educ:* private school; Trinity College, Dublin (Senior Moderator and Gold Medallist; Prizeman in French, in German, and in Italian; Prize Essayist in French and in English). Formerly Headmaster of Inverness College, of Lutterworth Grammar School and of Sandringham School, Southport; Vicar of Wimbish, 1919; Originator of the Moderators' (War) Memorial, TCD, 1918. *Recreations:* formerly tennis, fives, Badminton, Rugby football. *Address:* All Souls' Vicarage, Heywood, Lancs.

Died April 1928.

NOTTER, Col J. Lane-, MA, MD; Royal Army Medical Corps (retired); *b* Carrigduve, Co. Cork; *s* of late Richard Notter of Rock Island and Carrigduve, Co. Cork, and Margaret, *d* of James Lane of

Riverstown, Co. Cork; *m* Fannie, *d* of Surgeon-General J. D. McIllree, AMS; one *d. Educ:* Trinity Coll., Dublin (Fellow Commoner). Entered Army Medical Service, 1866 (First Place); subsequently served in Canada and Malta as Assistant-Surgeon, Royal Artillery; Assistant-Professor, and subsequently Professor, of Military Hygiene, Army Medical School at Netley; on Special Duty at Headquarters, SA Field Force; ex-President Epidemiological Society of London; Fellow, Royal Society of Medicine; Governor of Wellington College, Berks; Fellow and Member of Council, Royal Sanitary Institute; late Examiner in Hygiene, Board of Secondary Education, South Kensington; Examiner in Public Health at Cambridge University, Leeds, and Liverpool Universities, Royal Colleges of Physicians and Surgeons, London, and Victoria Universities, and University of Wales; Hon. Member Hungarian Society of Public Health; Delegate to represent Foreign Office and War Office, and HM Plenipotentiary to sign the Convention at Venice, 1897; Hon. Associate Order of St John of Jerusalem; Delegate to following Congresses on behalf of War Office—Berlin, 1890; Chicago, 1893; Rome, 1894; Buda-Pesth, 1894. *Publications:* The Theory and Practice of Hygiene (with Col R. H. Firth); Hygiene, 9th edn 1908; Practical Domestic Hygiene, 5th edn 1907; editor, 8th edition Parke's Manual of Practical Hygiene; author of sections Air and Military Hygiene, in Murphy and Stevenson's Treatise on Hygiene and Public Health, 1892; Hygiene of the Tropics in Davidson's Diseases of Warm Climates; Enteric Fever in the European Army in India, its Etiology and Prevention, Transactions International Hygienic Congress, 1892; section Hygiene, Ency. Brit., Times edition, 1902; and various papers on hygiene and preventive medicine in other works and periodicals. *Recreations:* yachting, photography, travel. *Address:* 3 Kensington Mansions, Earl's Court, SW; Rock Island, Co. Cork. *Club:* Athenæum.

Died 24 Oct. 1923.

NOTTINGHAM, Rev. Edward Emil, MA; Rector of Sutton-upon-Derwent, York, since 1918; *b* 1866; *s* of late Edward Nottingham, Pilsgate, Stamford; *m* Ada Annie, *d* of late Skelton Smalley, Pilsgate, Stamford; one *s* two *d. Educ:* Stratford-on-Avon and Stamford Grammar Schools; St Catharine's Coll., Cambridge. Senior Classical Scholar and Librarian Scholar; 2nd class Classical Tripos, 1888. Second Master, King Alfred's School, Wantage, 1888–89; Loughborough School, 1889–94; Curate of Loughborough, 1893–94; Assistant Master and Chaplain of Eastbourne College, 1894–95; Vice-Principal, Training College, Chester, 1895–98; Principal of Diocesan Training College, York, 1898–1908; Vicar of Acaster Selby with Appleton Roebuck, 1910–18; Assistant Master, St Peter's School, York, 1917–18 (war work). *Recreations:* golf, travelling. *Address:* The Rectory, Sutton-on-Derwent, Yorks.

Died 10 March 1921.

NOVIKOFF, Mme Olga, ("OK"); Russian political writer; *b* Moscow, 1848; *d* of Alexis Kireeff, Hussar-Guards Officer of St George's Cross, and Alexandra Alabieff (mentioned in poems of Pushkin Lermontoff, etc); *m* Lieut-General John Novikoff (*brother* of the Ambassador at Vienna), Rector of St Petersburg University (*d* 1890). Began writing political articles in the hope of continuing the work of her brother who was killed in the Turkish War in defending the Slavonic cause, in addition to which she pleaded for Anglo-Russian alliance and friendship; nicknamed by Disraeli, MP for Russia, the title of Mr William Thomas Stead's biography; co-worker with Mr Gladstone in the Slavonic Cause. *Publications:* Is Russia Wrong?; Friends or Foes; Russia and England; Skobeleff and the Slavonic Cause; Russian Memories; many articles in Pall Mall Gazette, Westminster Gazette, in 1916–17, chiefly in the Asiatic Review and National Opinion; monthly reviews, and French and Russian reviews and papers; pamphlets: Searchlights on Russia; More Searchlights on Russia. *Address:* 4 Brunswick Place, Regent's Park, NW1. *T:* Langham 2619.

Died 21 April 1925.

NUGENT, Algernon John FitzRoy; *b* 5 Oct. 1865; *e s* of Albert Llewellyn Nugent, Baron Nugent (of the Austrian Empire), and Elizabeth, *e d* of Theodore Baltazzi, Constantinople; *m* 1895, Clara, *d* of Sir George Eliott Meyrick Tapps-Gervis-Meyrick, 3rd Bt; no *c. Educ:* Winchester; Trinity College, Cambridge. *Recreations:* captain of first Trinity Boat Club and stroke of the eight in 1887; a keen but only fair golfer; a keen musician; a breeder of Dandie Dinmont terriers, which he exhibited and judged. *Heir: brother* Albert Beauchamp Nugent, *b* 12 Feb. 1874. *Address:* Gally Hill, Crookham, Fleet, Hants. *TA:* Church, Crookham. *T:* Fleet 33. *Clubs:* Oxford and Cambridge, MCC; Leander, Henley-on-Thames.

Died 15 March 1922.

NUGENT, Sir Charles, 5th Bt, *cr* 1795; Count of Holy Roman Empire; Lieutenant 17th Lancers; retired, 1869; *b* 7 Feb. 1847; *s* of

Sir John Nugent, 3rd Bt, and Letitia Maria, *e d* of Charles Whyte Roche, Bally-gran, Co. Limerick; *S* brother, 1863; *m* 1871, Emily Ruth Eades, *e d* of Thomas Walker, Park Lane, W, and Berkswell Hall, Warwickshire; one *s* decd. Cornet of Regt, 1866. *Heir: g s* Hugh Charles Nugent, *b* 26 May 1904. *Address:* Ballinlough Castle, Co. Westmeath.							*Died 22 May 1927.*

NUGENT, Col (Temp. Col Comdt) Charles Hugh Hodges, CIE 1916; CBE 1920; MIME; *b* 11 Dec. 1868; *s* of late Col Sir Chares Butler Peter Nugent Hodges Nugent, KCB, RE, and Emma, *d* of Rev. R. A. Burney; *m* 1904, Jessie, *d* of late Maj.-Gen. Edward Wray, CB, RA. 2nd Lieut RE, 1888; Captain, 1899; Major, 1907; Lt-Col 1915; Col 1919; Inspector of Iron Structures at War Office, 1899–1905; original member of War Office Mechanical Transport Committee; Inspector of Machinery, Army Headquarters, Simla, from 1911; formerly member of Trials Committee Royal Automobile Club; raised and organised mechanical transport services in India, Aden, Mesopotamia, etc, 1914–18 (despatches); served with North-West Frontier Field Force against Afghans, 1919 (despatches); employed as Asst Commanding Royal Engineers, Presidency District; Deputy Director Military Works, United Provinces District, Meerut, India. *Clubs:* Junior United Service, Royal Automobile, Ranelagh; United Service, Simla.							*Died 2 Dec. 1924.*

NUGENT, Sir Edmund Charles, 3rd Bt, *cr* 1806; DL; JP; Captain Grenadier Guards; retired, 1862; *b* 12 March 1839; 2nd *s* of 2nd Bt and Hon. Maria Charlotte, 2nd *d* of Lord Colborne; *S* father, 1892; *m* 1863, Evelyn Henrietta (*d* 1922), *d* of Gen. E. F. Gascoigne; one *s* two *d* (and two *s* decd). Entered army, 1857; High Sheriff Norfolk, 1900. *Heir: g s* (George) Guy (Bulwer) Nugent [*b* 5 Nov. 1892; *m* 1921, May Esther, *y d* of Jesse Arthur Bigsby; one *s*]. *Address:* West Harling Hall, Attleborough. *Clubs:* Carlton, Travellers'.
								Died 4 Dec. 1928.

NUGENT, Sir Horace Dickinson, KBE 1923; CMG 1917; HM Consul-General at Chicago, 1909–23; *b* 26 Feb. 1858; *s* of William Tasker Nugent, late of the Foreign Office and HM Consular Service; *m* 1893, Antoinette, *y d* of late Clement Guion of New York; one *s*. *Educ:* Haileybury. Employed in Foreign Office, 1880–81; Vice-Consul attached to British Legation, Bucharest, Roumania, 1881–86; Junior Vice-Consul, New York, 1886–91; Senior Vice-Consul, 1891–92; Consul for Texas and New Mexico, 1892–1909; Coronation medal, 1911. *Recreations:* golf, fishing. *Club:* Royal Societies.							*Died 30 April 1924.*

NUGENT, Maj.-Gen. Sir Oliver Stewart Wood, KCB 1922 (CB 1917); DSO 1896; JP; DL; late 60th Rifles; *b* 9 Nov. 1860; *s* of late Major-General St George Mervyn Nugent and Emily, *d* of Rt Hon. Edward Litton; *m* 1899, Catherine Percy, *d* of late Thomas Evans Lees and of Mrs (Bernarda Maria Elisa) Lees (*née* Turnbull), of Beaucroft, Wimborne, Dorset; one *s* two *d*. *Educ:* Harrow. Entered King's Royal Rifles, 1883; Capt. 1890; Major 1899; served Hazara Expedition, 1891 (medal with clasp); Samana Expedition, 1891 (despatches, clasp); Izazai Expedition, 1892; Chitral Relief Force, 1895, including Malakand Pass (slightly wounded); engagement at Khar (despatches, DSO, medal with clasp); South Africa, 1899–1900 (dangerously wounded, despatches, Queen's medal 2 clasps); European War, 1914–18 (Maj.-Gen.); retired pay, 1920. *Address:* Farren Connell, Mount Nugent, Co. Cavan. *Clubs:* Army and Navy; Kildare Street, Dublin.						*Died 31 May 1926.*

NUGENT, Col Robert Arthur, CB 1884; CMG 1917; retired; *b* Bruges, Belgium, 1 Aug. 1853; 2nd *s* of late Robert Nugent and Emma, *d* of John Hunter; *m* 1876, Marion Henrietta Annie (*d* 1924), *y d* of Thomas Smith, of Weston-super-Mare, and *widow* of Frederick Hitchcock, of Four Courts, Dublin. *Educ:* The Athenée, Bruges; Hartley Coll., Southampton. Joined Control Department, 1872; Ashanti War, 1873–74 (medal); Egyptian Expedition, 1882–84: Tel-el-Kebir; El Teb; Tamai; Soudan Campaign, 1884–85: Abu Klea and Gubat (medal 5 clasps, 4th class Medjidie, bronze star, despatches); Brevet Colonel, 1898; Substantive Colonel, 1898; Assistant Director Military Transport, Woolwich Arsenal, 1914–18. Decorated: Suakim, 1884; Expedition under Sir Gerald Graham, VC. *Recreations:* golf; fishing. *M:* KL 4583. *Club:* United Service.
								Died 12 Aug. 1926.

NUNBURNHOLME, 2nd Baron, *cr* 1905; **Charles Henry Wellesley Wilson,** CB 1918; DSO 1900; late Major 2nd Volunteer Battalion, East Yorkshire Regiment; *b* 24 Jan. 1875; *s* of 1st Baron and Florence Jane Helen, *d* of Col William Henry Charles Wellesley; *S* father, 1907; *m* 1901, Lady Marjorie Cecilia Wynn-Carrington, *d* of 1st Marquess of Lincolnshire; two *s* one *d*. *Educ:* Eton. Served South

Africa, 1900 (Queen's medal, 4 clasps, DSO); European War, Captaii RGA; MP (L) Hull, 1906–7; HM Lieut East Riding of Yorkshire *Heir: s* Hon. Charles John Wilson, *b* 25 April 1904. *Address:* 4? Berkeley Square, W1. *T:* Mayfair 6591; Hunmanby Hall, Hunmanby E Yorks. *Clubs:* Bachelors', National Liberal.
								Died 15 Aug. 1924

NUNN, Rev. Henry Drury Cust; Vicar of Sharow, 1884; Rural Dean Hon. Canon of Ripon Cathedral, and Proctor in Convocation ii Archdeaconry of Ripon; *y s* of Rev. Thomas Nunn, Rector o Stansted, Kent; *m* 1st, Eliza Mary, *d* of R. S. Francis; 2nd, Helena Sophia (*d* 1909), *d* of Rev. Canon Worsley; three *s* one *d*. *Educ:* Corpu Christi College, Cambridge (Scholar and Divinity Prizeman, MA) Curate of St Andrew's, Leeds, 1868; Minor Canon and Vicar o Ripon, 1872; Surrogate. *Publication:* Sons of Heaven and Sons of Earth *Recreations:* cricket, sketching. *Address:* Sharow Cottage, Ripon.
								Died 7 Jan. 1922

NUTT, Alfred Young, MVO 1906; ISO 1911; late resident architeci HM Office of Works, Windsor Castle; *b* 1847; *s* of late W. Y. Nutt Rector of Cold Overton; *m* 1873, Mary, *d* of J. George; three *d* Entered Office of Works, 1867; surveyor to Dean and Canons oi Windsor, 1874; carried out exterior restoration work at St George'? Chapel and designed Jubilee celebration decorations at Windsor anc Eton, 1887–97; architect for Westminster Abbey annexe a Coronation of Edward VII, 1902; also for Coronation annexe, King George V, 1911; retired, 1912. *Address:* Morcott West, Slough, Bucks.
								Died 24 July 1924

NUTT, Col James Anson Francis. Entered army 1866; Capt. 1878. Major, 1884; Lieut-Col 1893; Col 1897; served Afghan War, 1880 (medal); commanded RA, North-West Frontier of India, 1898 (medal and clasp); commanded RA, Eastern District, 1899; commanded RA Natal Field Force, from Vaal Krantz to relief of Ladysmith (medal and two clasps). *Club:* Naval and Military.
								Died 23 Jan. 1924.

NUTTALL, Sir Edmund, 1st Bt, *cr* 1922; AMICE; head of the firm of Edmund Nuttall & Co., Civil Engineering Contractors of Traffoi Park, Manchester; *b* 29 May 1870; *s* of late James Nuttall oi Manchester; *m* 1895, Ethel Christine, 2nd *d* of Rev. Frederick Lillington, MA Oxon; two *s*. *Educ:* privately. Articled to the late Sir Edward Leader Williams, MInstCE, 1887; succeeded to his father's business, 1898; responsible for numerous engineering works oi national importance. *Recreations:* shooting, deep sea fishing. *Heir: s* Edmund Keith Nuttall, *b* 27 March 1901. *Address:* Chasefield Bowdon, Cheshire. *TA:* Tunnelling, Manchester. *T:* Altrincham 1317; Trafford Park 310. *M:* NB 5840. *Clubs:* St Stephen's; Constitutional, Manchester.

								Died 11 Oct. 1923.

NUTTALL, Most Rev. Enos, BD Lambeth, 1879; DD 1880; Bishop of Jamaica since 1880, and Archbishop of the West Indies since 1897; *b* 26 Jan. 1842; *e s* of James Nuttall, Yorks, and 1st wife, Alice, *d* of William and Martha Armistead, Yorks; *m* 1867, Elizabeth Duggan, *d* of Rev. Philip Chapman, Wesleyan minister; two *s* three *d*. Deacon and priest, Kingston, Jamaica, 1866; Island Curate of St George's, Kingston, 1866–80; Bishop in charge of Diocese, Honduras, 1881–91; Primate of West Indies, 1893. Hon. DD Oxon, 1897; Hon. DCL Durham; Hon. LLD Cantab, 1908. *Publications:* The Churchman's Manual, 1894; The Jamaica Day School Catechism, 1905; Devotions and Catechisms for Children and Young People; Lectures on the Life of the World to Come. *Address:* Bishop's Lodge, Kingston, Jamaica, West Indies.						*Died 31 May 1916.*

NUTTALL, Harry, JP Manchester and Cheshire; FRGS; President Manchester Ear Hospital; President Manchester Reform Club, 1907; MP (L) Stretford, Lancashire, 1906–18, retired; *b* Manchester, 1849; *s* of Joseph Nuttall of Manchester; *m* 1886, Edith Mary, *d* of William Smith, JP, Bolton-le-Moors, Lancashire; two *d*. *Educ:* privately. Owens College, Manchester. An import and export merchant at Manchester; contested Stretford, 1900; President, Manchester Chamber of Commerce, 1905; President Manchester Geographical Society, 1910–20. *Recreations:* golf, motoring. *Address:* Briarfield, Walton-on-the-Hill, Surrey; Bank of England Chambers, Manchester. *Clubs:* Reform; Manchester Reform.
								Died 25 Sept. 1924.

NUTTING, Sir John Gardiner, 1st Bt, *cr* 1902; JP Co. Dublin; DL Co. Dublin and of City; High Sheriff for Co. Dublin, 1895–96; *b* 24 July 1852; 2nd *s* of John Nutting, Redlands, Bristol; *g s* of Edward Nutting, Colchester, Essex; *m* 1879, Mary Stansmore, *d* of Restel R.

Bevis, Manor Hill, Claughton; Cheshire; three *s* two *d. Educ:* Clifton College; Germany. Chairman of E. and J. Burke, Ltd, of Dublin. *Recreation:* hunting (member of Meath and Kildare Hunts). *Heir: s* Harold Stansmore Nutting, Captain 17th Lancers [*b* 14 Aug. 1882; *m* 1913, Enid Hester Nina, *d* of F. B. Homan-Mulock, Ballycumber House, King's County; one *s.* Late ADC to Governor-General, Australia]. *Address:* St Helens, Booterstown, Dublin. *Clubs:* Carlton, Junior Constitutional; Sackville Street, Dublin.

Died 18 Feb. 1918.

NYS, Ernest, Hon. DCL Oxon; Conseiller à la cour d'appel; Professeur à l'Université de Bruxelles; membre de la Cour permanente d'arbitrage, The Hague; *b* Courtrai, Belgium, 27 March 1851. *Educ:* Universities of Ghent, Heidelberg, Leipzig, Berlin. Honorary Doctor of Laws of the Universities of Edinburgh and Glasgow; Member of the Institut de Droit international, Académie royale de Belgique, Académie roumaine de Bucarest, American Philosophical Society, Philadelphia, Reale Istituto Veneto, British Academy. *Publications:* La Guerre maritime, 1881; Le Droit de la Guerre et les Précurseurs de Grotius, 1882; L'Arbre des Batailles; Etudes de Droit international et de Droit politique; Recherches sur l'Histoire de l'Economie politique (translated into English by A. and N. Dryhurst); Les Origines du droit international, 1894; Le Droit international et les Principes, les Théories, les Faits, 1904; Idées modernes, droit international et franc-maçonnerie; Le Droit romain, le droit des gens et le Collège des docteurs en droit civil. *Address:* 39 rue Saint Jean, Bruxelles.

Died Sept. 1920.

O

OAKES, Sir Augustus Henry, Kt 1905; CB 1902; Librarian and Keeper of the Papers, Foreign Office, 1896–1904; retired, 1905; *b* 2 Nov. 1839; *e* surv. *s* of late Lieut-Col Richard Montague Oakes, 22nd Light Dragoons and 1st Life Guards, of Elmsfield, Harrow; *m* 1871, Jane Alice, 2nd *d* of late William Henry Cane, MD (surgeon, Bucks Yeomanry Cavalry and Royal Elthorne Militia), Uxbridge; one *s* two *d. Educ:* abroad. Appointed to a clerkship in the Foreign Office, after passing a competitive examination, 1858; an Assistant Clerk, 1889; a Senior Clerk and Librarian and Keeper of the Papers, 1896; a burgess of Newport, Pembrokeshire. *Publications:* chief compiler and editor of the British and Foreign State Papers, and the Collection of Commercial Treaties, 1897–1904; joint author of The Great European Treaties of the Nineteenth Century. *Address:* The Nook, Milford, near Godalming. *TA:* Milford, Surrey.

Died 17 Aug. 1919.

OAKES, Hon. Charles William, CMG 1922; MLC since 1925; Nationalist MP (for Eastern Suburbs) State Parliament, New South Wales, 1920–25; Chief Secretary and Minister for Public Health, 1922–25; *b* Wagga Wagga, New South Wales, 1861; English parents; *m* Elizabeth Gregory, New South Wales; one *s* one *d. Educ:* New South Wales State School. Apprenticed to the jewellery trade; in business afterwards on his own account for 26 years; Alderman Paddington Council, 1899–1904; MP (L) Paddington, 1891–1910; Hon. Minister in the Justice Department, 1907–10; Senator, New South Wales, 1913–15; elected State Member, NSW, for Waverley, 1917–20; Minister for Housing, Holman Cabinet, 1919–20; Member of Fuller Cabinet, 1922–25; Chairman of Prince of Wales Visit Committee to NSW, 1920. *Recreations:* sailing, numismatics, early Australian history. *Address:* Quondong, Balfour Road, Belle Vue Hill, Wollahra, Sydney, NSW. *T:* FM 1842, Sydney.

Died 3 July 1928.

OAKES, Sir Reginald Louis, 4th Bt, *cr* 1815; General Manager of the Cairo Electric Railways and Heliopolis Oasis Co.; *b* 29 Sept. 1847; *s* of late Henry Frederick Oakes and Mary Dovity, *d* of John Ward, Hunts; *S* grandfather, 1850; *m* 1882, Florence, *d* of Charles de Bels Brounlie, Vice-Consul at Turin. *Educ:* Ghent University. *Heir:* none. *Address:* Heliopolis, Egypt.

Died 11 Oct. 1927 (ext).

OATES, Francis Hamer, CB 1919; JP Notts (Chairman of Quarter-Sessions); Assistant Secretary Board of Education; barrister; *b* 1866;

2nd *s* of late William Henry Coape Oates, Langford Hall, Notts, and Sophia, 4th *d* of late L. Domenichetti. *Educ:* Harrow; Trinity College, Cambridge. *Address:* Besthorpe, near Newark. *Clubs:* Oxford and Cambridge, Boodle's.

Died 9 May 1923.

OATES, Frederick Arthur Harman, MVO 1922; FSA; Keeper of the King's Armoury since 1920; late Keeper, Secretary and Accounting Officer of the London Museum, SW1; *o s* of Frederick Oates, Whitby, Yorks; *m* 1887, Elizabeth, *d* of Robert Grimmer Martins of Worsted, Norfolk; two *s* three *d. Educ:* London City School and Private Tutor, Rev. R. Langridge. Lifelong antiquary; appointed by Trustees and Keeper as Assistant Secretary on the formation of London Museum, 1911, Keeper and Secretary, 1919; Accounting Officer; Fellow of British Numismatic Society, and of Meyrick Society; Hon. Curator of Swiss Cottage and Museum, Osborne, IW, 1925. *Publication:* Catalogue of a Collection of Finger Rings, 1917. *Recreations:* search for antiquarian objects, walking. *Address:* Henry VIII Gateway, Windsor Castle. *T:* Windsor Castle 360. *Club:* Athenæum.

Died 3 Oct. 1928.

OBAIDULLA KHAN, Nowabzada Hafiz Mohamad Bahadur, CSI 1912; Colonel-in-Chief, Bhopal Victoria Imperial Service Lancers; Hon. Major, British Army; *b* 3 Nov. 1878; 2nd *s* of the Begum, Ruler of Bhopal; *m* 1902; three *s* one *d. Educ:* at home by private tutors; learnt Koran by heart. Joined Bhopal Victoria Imperial Service Lancers, 1904; Commander-in-Chief of the State Forces, 1905; ADC to the Viceroy, 1906; Commission as Captain in HM's Army, 1908; accompanied Her Highness the Begum of Bhopal on pilgrimage to Mecca; Her Highness, who was escorted by Imperial Service Troops, was attacked by Beduin Arabs who fired on the cavalcade; but through his tactful arrangements they were successfully repulsed; took part in Coronation Durbars, 1903 and 1911; attended the Coronation Ceremony at Westminster Abbey, 1910; toured all over Europe; promoted Major, 1911; keen interest in education; Trustee of the Mohammedan Anglo-Oriental College at Aligarh; subscribed 60,000s to the College Funds. *Recreation:* very keen sportsman. *Address:* Jahan Numa Palace, Bhopal, Central India. *T:* 18. *Clubs:* Central Indian Residency, Indore; Bhopal Military.

Died March 1924.

O'BEIRNE, Hugh James, CB 1905; CVO 1908; JP, DL; Counsellor, Petrograd Embassy, since 1906; *b* Jamestown, Drumsna, Co. Leitrim, 7 Sept. 1866; *s* of late Hugh O'Beirne. *Educ:* Beaumont; Balliol College, Oxford. Attaché at Petrograd, 1892; 2nd Secretary, Washington, 1895–98; Secretary at British Embassy, Paris, 1900–6. *Address:* British Embassy, Petrograd; Jamestown, Drumsna, Co. Leitrim. *Club:* St James's.

Died 5 June 1916.

OBEYESEKERE, Hon. Sir (Solomon) Christoffel, Kt 1911; MLC; Vice-President of the Board of Agriculture, Ceylon; landed proprietor; Representative of the Low Country Sinhalese in the Legislative Council of Ceylon, since 1900; *b* 12 Feb. 1848; *s* of late D. B. F. Obeyesekere, Mudhjar of Talpe Pattoo, and Cornelia Susannah Dias Bandaranaike; *m* 1878, Ezline Maria, 2nd *d* of late Hon. James Alwis, MLC; one *s* three *d. Educ:* Colombo Academy (Queen's College); St Thomas' College. Passed the District Courts Proctor's Examination as 1st in order of merit, 1872; devoted his time more to cocoanut planting and improving his estates than practising at the Bar; Vice-President, Ceylon Branch of Royal Asiatic Society; Member of British Empire League; of Royal Colonial Institute; of Colombo Friend in Need Society; an incorporated Trustee of the Anglican Church in Ceylon; a Member of the Executive Committee of the Synod of the Church of England in Ceylon; President of Christian Literature Society, Ceylon; Member of the Committee of the British and Foreign Bible Society, Colombo; President of the Sinhalese Sports Club, Colombo; Member of the Ceylon Turf Club; Patron of the Ceylon Plumbago Merchants' Union; presented with the gold Victoria Diamond Jubilee Medal, 1897; visited England for Coronation of King Edward VII; presented with gold Coronation Medal of King Edward VII, 1902; and again as an authorised representative of Ceylon at the Coronation of King George V, presented with the Coronation Medal of King George V and Queen Mary, 22 June 1911. *Recreations:* shooting, tennis, cricket. *Address:* Hill Castle, Colombo, Ceylon. *TA:* Frelequet, Colombo. *Clubs:* Corona; Sinhalese Sports, Turf, Colombo.

Died 14 Oct. 1926.

OBRE, Henry, CBE 1919; JP; partner in the firm of Heatley & Co., 34 Leadenhall Street; *b* 17 April 1855; *e s* of Henry Obré of Fort Villa, Queenstown, Co. Cork; *m* Emma Eveline Wynn, *d* of late Lieut A. E. Wilby (61st) Gloucestershire Regt. *Educ:* privately; Queen's College, Cork. Entered the firm of Harris Bros & Co., and became a partner, 1892; retired in 1919 and joined Heatley & Co; Chairman of Baltic and Corn Exchange Red Cross Hospital, Calais, Paris Plage and Boulogne; Director of the Baltic and Mercantile Shipping Exchange, since 1911, and Trustee for the Baltic and Mercantile Shipping Benevolent Association. *Recreations:* fishing, golf. *Address:* The Manor House, Knebworth, Herts. *T:* Knebworth 15. *M:* H 7270. *Clubs:* Union, City of London, Royal Thames Yacht.

Died 12 July 1922.

O'BRIEN, Patrick; MP (N) Kilkenny since 1895; *b* 1853; *s* of James O'Brien, Tullamore, and Catherine, *d* of P. Byrne; unmarried. Mechanical and marine engineer; MP for N Monaghan, 1886–92; contested Limerick City, 1892. *Address:* House of Commons, SW. *Clubs:* National Liberal; Leinster, Dublin.

Died 12 July 1917.

O'BRIEN, Richard Barry; barrister and author; *b* Kilrush, Co. Clare, Ireland, 1847; *y c* of Patrick Barry O'Brien; *m* 1877, Kathleen Mary, *d* of Dr Teevan, of Kensington, W; five *s* two *d*. *Educ:* private tutors and Catholic University, Dublin. Called to the Irish Bar, 1874; to the English Bar, 1875; practised for a short time in England, then glided into politics and literature; one of the founders of the Irish Literary Society; Chairman from its foundation, 1892–1906, President, 1906–11; Director of National Bank in 1911; LLD of National University of Ireland. *Publications:* The Irish Land Question and English public opinion, 1879; The Parliamentary History of the Irish Land Question, 1880; Fifty years of Concessions to Ireland (2 vols), 1883–85; Irish Wrongs and English Remedies, 1887; Thomas Drummond, Life and Letters, 1889; The Life of Charles Stewart Parnell (2 vols), 1898; Life of Lord Russell of Killowen, 1901; A Hundred Years of Irish History, 1902; Irish Memories, 1904; England's Title in Ireland, 1905; Dublin Castle and the Irish People, 1909; John Bright—a Monograph, 1910; editor Autobiography of Theobald Wolfe Tone, 1893; editor Children's Study—Ireland, 1896; editor Speeches of John Redmond, MP, 1910. *Address:* 100 Sinclair Road, Kensington, W.

Died 17 March 1918.

O'BRIEN, William; journalist and author; MP (N) Cork City; 1910–18, when he withdrew from public life; *b* 2 Oct. 1852; *s* of James O'Brien, Mallow, Co. Cork, and Kate, *d* of James Nagle; *m* 1890, Sophie, *d* of Hermann Raffalovich, Paris. *Educ:* Cloyne Diocesan Coll.; Queen's Coll., Cork. Reporter on Cork Daily Herald, 1869–75; writer on Freeman's Journal, 1875–80; founded United Ireland newspaper, 1880; prosecuted nine times for political offences; spent more than two years in prison; elected to Parliament for native town as a nationalist, 1883; S Division Tyrone, 1885–86; NE Division Cork, 1887–92; elected MP (N) Cork City and NE Cork, 1892; MP (N) NE Division Cork Co., 1892–95; elected Cork City and NE Cork, 1910; was a member of the Land Conference of 1903, which settled the Land Question, and ever since then an advocate of the Policy of Conciliation for the union of all classes and creeds in Ireland with a view to Home Rule by Consent; founded the All-for-Ireland League, 1898, and an Independent Parliamentary Party with that object; withdrew from Parliament, with Mr Maurice Healy and the rest of his All-for-Ireland colleagues, at General Election, 1918. *Publications:* When we were Boys (novel, written in prison), 1890; Irish Ideas, 1894; A Queen of Men (novel), 1897; Recollections, 1906; An Olive Branch in Ireland and its History, 1910; Evening Memories, 1920; The Irish Revolution and How it Came About, 1923; Edmund Burke an Irishman, 1924; The Parnell of Real Life, 1926. *Address:* Bellevue, Mallow, Co. Cork.

Died 25 Feb. 1928.

O'CALLAGHAN, Col Denis Moriarty, CMG 1917; late Army Medical Staff; *b* 11 Dec. 1861; *y s* of late Rev. Robert O'Callaghan, LLD, The Rectory, Holton, Suffolk, and *o d* of Denis Moriarty, Dingle; *m* 1912, Katherine, *e d* of Mrs Sayer of Yewtree House, Westfield, Sussex; one *s*. Capt. RAMC, 1886; Major 1898; Lt-Col 1906; Col 1915; Adjutant Vol., 1894–95; served Ashanti, 1895–96 (Star); Nile Expedition, 1898 (despatches, two medals); S Africa, 1900–1 (Queen's medal 3 clasps); European War, 1914–1917 (despatches, CMG). *Recreations:* polo, hunting, golf. *Club:* Junior United Service.

Died 6 Nov. 1926.

O'CALLAGHAN, Most Rev. Thomas Alphonsus, DD; OP; RC Bishop of Cork; consecrated coadjutor, 1884; succeeded 1886; *b* Cork, 1839. *Educ:* Minerva College, Rome. Prior of St Clement's, Rome, 1881. *Address:* Farranferris, Cork.

Died 14 June 1916.

O'CONNELL, Captain James Ross; *b* 28 Aug. 1863; *y s* of Sir Maurice O'Connell, 2nd Bt, and Emily Clunes, *d* of Rear-Adm. Sir

Richard O'Conor, KCH. *Educ:* The Oratory, Edgbaston. Lieutenant, 85th Regiment 1884; Captain, 85th, 1892; served with the Dongola Expeditionary Force under Horatio Herbert Kitchener (later Earl Kitchener of Khartoum), 1896; with 3rd Egyptian Battalion, including engagement at Firkhet and operations at Hafir (despatches, 4th class Medjidie, British medal, and Khedive's medal with four clasps); with 12th Sudanese in the operations, 1898, including the battle of Khartoum (despatches, 4th class Osmanieh), Comm. 2nd Egyptian Batt.; and in 1899 in the operations in the final advance against the Khalifa (3rd class of the Medjidie); Governor of Kordofan, Sudan, to 1907. *Recreations:* shooting, fishing, golf. *Address:* Lakeview, Killarney. *Club:* United Service.

Died 25 Feb. 1925.

O'CONNELL, Sir Morgan Ross, 4th Bt, *cr* 1869; JP, DL, Co. Kerry; JP Co. Clare; Lord of the Manor of Ballycarbery; *b* 20 July 1862; *s* of Sir Maurice James O'Connell, 2nd Bt, and Emily Clunes, *d* of Rear-Admiral Sir Richard O'Conor; *S* brother, 1905; *m* 1884, Mary Pauline, *d* of Lt-Col James Francis Hickie, of Slevoyre, Co. Tipperary; three *s* one *d* (and one *d* decd). Owned 18,800 acres. *Heir: s* Maurice James Arthur O'Connell, Lieut 2nd Royal Fusiliers; *b* 24 Dec. 1889. *Recreations:* shooting, fishing, golfing. *Address:* Lakeview, Killarney, Co. Kerry. *Clubs:* Royal Automobile; Kildare Street, Dublin.

Died 27 April 1919.

O'CONNELL, Sir Peter Reilly, Kt 1908; JP Co. Antrim; MD; *s* of Patrick O'Connell, Maudabawn, Co. Cavan; *m* 1907, Jane Mary, *e d* of late Edward Hughes, JP, Belfast. *Educ:* St Patrick's College, Cavan; Catholic University, Dublin; Queen's College, Galway. MD, MCh Royal University, Ireland. Member of the Senate, Queen's University, Belfast; Lecturer and Examiner in Clinical Surgery in Queen's University, 1911–12; President of the Ulster Medical Association, 1910–11; Senior Surgeon, Mater Infirmorum Hospital, Belfast; High Sheriff, Belfast, 1907–8; DL for Co. of City of Belfast. *Address:* Oatlands, Stillorgan, Co. Dublin. *Died Sept. 1927.*

O'CONNOR, His Honour Arthur, KC; Judge of County Courts, Durham Circuit, 1901; Dorset Circuit, 1911–20; Barrister, Middle Temple, 1883; *b* 1 Oct. 1844; *e s* of William O'Connor, MD, Dingle, Co. Kerry; *m* Ellen, *e d* of W. Connolly. *Educ:* Ushaw. MP (N) Queen's County, 1880–85, when elected simultaneously for East Donegal; MP (N) E Donegal, 1885–1900; Chairman of Public Accounts Committee, 1895, 1896, 1897, 1898, 1899, and 1900; Deputy Chairman of Committees of the House; member of the panel of Chairmen of the Standing Committees on Trade and on Law; member of the Royal Commission on Trade Depression, 1885–86; on Civil Service Establishments, 1887; on Incidence of Local Taxation; Public Works Loan Commissioner since 1890; member of Home Office Committee on Prisons, 1894; Chairman of the Treasury Departmental Committee on the Stationery Department, 1896; one of the Panel of Chairmen of the Court of Arbitration under the Conciliation Act of 1896, and Chairman of the Leicestershire Joint District Board under the Coal Mines (Minimum Wages) Act 1912. *Address:* Dumsdale, Bournemouth.

Died 30 March 1923.

O'CONNOR, Col Arthur Patrick, CB 1900; FRCSI; late Army Medical Staff; *b* 9 Aug. 1856; *s* of late Charles A. O'Connor, Acres, Co. Roscommon; *m* 1890, Alice, *d* of Archdeacon Badnall, DD; one *s* one *d*. Entered army, 1880; Lieut-Colonel, 1900, Col, 1907; served Burmese Expedition, 1885–86 (medal with clasp); South Africa, 1899–1902 (despatches, CB, Queen's medal, 3 clasps, King's medal, 2 clasps). *Died 25 Jan. 1920.*

O'CONNOR, Rt. Hon. Charles Andrew, PC 1911; MA and Senior Moderator, Dublin University; ex-Auditor College Historical Society; *b* Roscommon, 1854; *s* of Charles Andrew O'Connor, solicitor, Roscommon; *m* Blanche, *d* of James Scully of Shanballymore, Co. Tipperary. *Educ:* St Stanislaus College, Tullamore; Trinity College, Dublin. Called to the Irish Bar, 1878; QC 1894; Bencher, King's Inns, 1896; Solicitor-General, Ireland, 1909–11; Attorney-General, 1911–12; Master of the Rolls in Ireland, 1912–24; Judge of Supreme Court, Irish Free State, 1924–25. *Address:* 48 Thurloe Square, SW7. *T:* Kensington 7024. *Clubs:* Reform, Athenæum; University, Dublin.

Died 8 Oct. 1928.

O'CONNOR, John; KC 1919; *b* 10 Oct. 1850; *s* of W. O'Connor and Julia, *d* of John Corbet; unmarried. MP (N) Tipperary, Jan.–Nov. 1885; MP (N) South Tipperary, 1885–92; North Kildare, 1905–18; contested Kilkenny City and S Tipperary, 1892. *Address:* 5 Frognal Mansions, Hampstead, NW3. *T:* Hampstead 1496. *Club:* National Liberal. *Died 27 Oct. 1928.*

O'CONOR, James Edward, CIE 1891; late Financial Department, India; *b* 1843; *s* of John O'Conor, Tallow, Co. Waterford; *m* 1868, Marian (*d* 1904). Registrar Dept of Agriculture and Commerce, 1873–5; Assistant Secretary, 1875; transferred as Assistant Secretary in Department of Finance and Commerce, 1879; on special duty for Melbourne Exhibition, 1880–81, and in England with Indian Currency Committee, 1898; Director-General of Statistics, India, 1895–1902; retired, 1902. *Publications:* reports on production, cultivation, and manufacture in India of tobacco, lac, ground nut, eucalyptus, and various other articles; also annual reviews of the trade of India, 1875–1902. *Address:* Francesco, Church Road, Upper Norwood, SE. *Club:* Reform.

Died 8 Jan. 1917.

O'CONOR, Sir John, KBE 1920; MA, MD, BCh; Senior Medical Officer, British Hospital, Buenos Aires, since 1894; *b* 21 Dec. 1863; *s* of late Abraham O'Conor, Carrick-on-Shannon, Ireland; *m* 1892, Grace Beatrice Richmond, *d* of late James Oxley, Welshmill, Frome; two *s* two *d. Educ:* Armagh; Trinity College, Dublin. House Surgeon, Royal Portsmouth Hospital, 1887–89; Resident Medical Officer, British Hospital, Buenos Aires, 1890. *Publications:* articles and papers in medical publications. *Recreations:* tennis, golf. *Address:* Mayfair, Freshwater Bay, Isle of Wight; 1042 Avenida Mayo, Buenos Aires. *Clubs:* Devonshire; Jockey, Buenos Aires; Royal Albert Yacht, Southsea. *Died 8 Oct. 1927.*

O'CONOR DON, Rt. Hon. Denis Charles Joseph O'Conor, PC Ireland; JP; BA, LLB; HM's Lieutenant and Custos Rotulorum for Co. Roscommon; *b* Conalis, 26 Oct. 1869; *e s* of late Rt Hon. Charles Owen O'Conor Don and Georgina, *d* of T. A. Perry, Bitham House, Warwickshire. *Educ:* St Gregory's College, Downside; London University. Member of both the English and Irish Bars. *Recreations:* shooting, motoring, etc. *Address:* Clonalis, Castlerea, Co. Roscommon. *M:* DI 47 and DI 56. *Club:* Reform.

Died 23 Feb. 1917.

ODDIE, John William, JP; MA; Senior Fellow of Corpus Christi College, Oxford; *b* 20 Aug. 1839; *o c* of Thomas Oddie, Hambleton, Lancs. *Educ:* Preston Grammar School; Wadham College, Oxford (BA (1st class Classics) 1865). Pupil and friend of Benjamin Jowett and John Ruskin; Classical Lecturer of Wadham, 1866; Fellow and Tutor of CCC, 1867; Dean, 1873; Vice-President, 1874; Public Examiner, 1874; Acting Head of CCC, 1879–80; represented the College on Oxford University Commission, 1879–80; resided at Lyzwick Hall (art school), Keswick, 1873–1910; JP Cumberland since 1879; showed watercolours in Manchester and Liverpool Autumn Exhibitions, in Agnew's galleries, and elsewhere. *Publications:* Vampelectrum: a Fairy Play; Choice Poems of Heinrich Heine, 1896; Ruskin at Corpus; curling songs and other contributions to periodicals. *Recreations:* painting, gardening, talking with pleasant people; formerly rowing, golfing, curling. *Address:* Strathmore, St Leonards-on-Sea.

Died 19 Jan. 1923.

ODDY, Sir John James, Kt 1916; mohair spinner and manufacturer; *b* 24 Feb. 1867; *s* of James Oddy; *m* 1892, Marion, *d* of John Ambler, Bradford; one *d. Educ:* Ley's School, Cambridge. MP (U) Pudsey Division, West Riding, Yorks, 1908–10. *Address:* The Hall, Ilkley, Yorks. *T:* Ilkley 311. *Clubs:* Carlton; Bradford; Leeds.

Died 20 Feb. 1921.

O'DEA, Rt. Rev. Thomas, DD; RC Bishop of Galway and Kilmacduagh since 1909; *b* 1858; *s* of M. O'Dea of Kilfenors, Co. Clare. *Educ:* Maynooth. Professor of Theology there, 1882–94, and Vice-President, 1894–1903; Bishop of Clonfert, 1903–1909; member of the Intermediate Board of Education, Ireland; of the Governing Body of University College, Galway; and of the Senate of the National University, Ireland. *Publications:* Maynooth and the University Question; an unpublished treatise on justice. *Address:* Mount St Mary's, Galway. *Died 9 April 1923.*

ODGERS, William Blake; KC 1893; MA, LLD; FRHistS; Recorder of Bristol since 1912; Director of Legal Studies at the Inns of Court since 1905; Professor of Law at Gresham College, EC since 1907; *b* Plymouth, 15 May 1849; *s* of Rev. W. J. Odgers, Unitarian minister, and Eliza, *d* of John Collins, Horton, Somerset; *m* 1877, Frances, *d* of Charles Hudson, formerly Coroner of Stockport; three *s* one *d. Educ:* Bath Grammar School (Exhibitioner); University Coll. London (Scholar); Trinity Hall, Cambridge (Exhibitioner, Scholar, Wrangler, Law Student, MA, LLD). Middle Temple, Barrister, 1873; Bencher, 1900; Western Circuit; Recorder of Winchester, 1897–1900; of Plymouth, 1900–12; Hon. LLD Tufts Coll., Mass. *Publications:* King Arthur and the Arthurian Romances, 1872; Odgers on Libel and Slander, 1881 (5 edns); Odgers on Pleading and Practice, 1891 (8 edns); An Outline of the Law of Libel, 1897; Odgers on Local Government, 1899 (2 edns); Powell on Evidence (10th edition); Odgers on the Common Law of England, 1911 (2 edns); Bullen and Leake's Precedents of Pleadings (7th edition), 1915. *Address:* 15 Old Square, Lincoln's Inn, WC2. *T:* Holborn 5744; The Gart, 34 Holden Road, North Finchley, N12.

Died 16 Dec. 1924.

ODLING, William, MA, MB; FRS; Fellow of Worcester College, Oxford; *b* London, 1829. Fullerian Professor of Chemistry, Royal Institution, 1868–72; Waynflete Professor of Chemistry, Oxford University, 1872–1912. *Publications:* Manual of Chemistry, Descriptive and Theoretical, 1861; Lectures on Animal Chemistry, 1866; Outlines of Chemistry, 1869; A Course of Six Lectures on the Chemical Changes of Carbon, 1869; Chemistry, 1884; Laurent's Chemical Method. *Address:* 15 Norham Gardens, Oxford. *Club:* Athenæum.

Died 17 Feb. 1921.

O'DOHERTY, Philip; MP (N) North Donegal, 1906–18; *b* 1871; *s* of Owen and Margaret O'Doherty. *Educ:* St Columba's College, Londonderry. Admitted a solicitor, 1895. *Address:* 11 East Wall, Londonderry. *T:* 'Derry 224.

Died 6 Feb. 1926.

O'DONNELL, Frank Hugh Macdonald; *b* 1848; *e s* of Captain MacDonald O'Donnell of Tirconnell, Donegal; unmarried. *Educ:* The Queen's University, Ireland (MA, with Gold Medal, 1869); several Continental teachers. An Irish Nationalist in Politics and Advocate of Self-Government for India with Indian Representation in Imperial Parliament; founded so-called Irish Active Policy, 1873; entered Parliament, 1874; collaborated with Messrs Charles Biggar and Stewart Parnell in general policy, until foundation of Land League, which he persistently opposed; organised along with Alexander MacDonald, MP, the opposition to flogging in the Army, which produced its abolition in 1879; founded the Farmers' Alliance, 1879; founded the Indian Constitutional Association, 1882; quitted Irish Parliamentary Politics, 1885; co-founder of the National Democratic League, 1899; President of the National Democratic League, 1904–6; many years resident in France, Germany, and Austria. *Publications:* The Message of the Masters; The Ruin of Irish Education and The Irish Fanar; The Stage Irishman of the Pseudo-Celtic Drama; Paraguay on Shannon; The Price of a Political Priesthood; The History of the Irish Parliamentary Party. *Recreations:* yachting, books. *Address:* 38 Tregunter Road, The Boltons, SW.

Died 5 Nov. 1916.

O'DONNELL, Maj.-Gen. Hugh, CB 1911; DSO 1889; Colonel on Staff, India; *b* 9 Feb. 1858; 2nd *s* of J. W. O'Donnell, PWD Military Works; *m* 1894, Susan, (*d* 1908), *d* of T. G. S. Garnett, JP, Shefferlands, near Lancaster. *Educ:* privately; Sandhurst. 2nd Lieut 8th King's, 1878; Lieut 24th Regiment, 1879; Captain, 1889; Major, 1898; Lieut Col, 1904; Bt-Col, 1907; Substantive Col in Army, 1907; Maj.-Gen., 1912; Indian Staff Corps, 1880; commanded 42nd (later 6th) Gurkha Rifles, 1899–1907; AAG for Musketry and Commandant School of Musketry, Northern Army, 1907–10; served with 24th Foot through Zulu War, 1879 (medal and clasp); raised and commanded Mogoung Levy (Police Batt.) throughout Burma Expedition, 1886–91; served through Mogoung Expedition, 1887–88; commanded Mogoung Field Force, 1888–89 (thanks of Govt of India and Commander-in-Chief in India, wounded, despatches, medal, 3 clasps, DSO); commanded Mogoung column in the Wuntho Expedition, 1890–91 (despatches); Major-General commanding Bannu Brigade, NWP, 1911–15. *Recreations:* ordinary games, etc. *Club:* United Service.

Died 2 Dec. 1917.

O'DONNELL, His Eminence Cardinal Patrick; RC Archbishop of Armagh since 1924; *b* Kilraine, Glenties, Co. Donegal, 1856; *s* of Daniel O'Donnell and Mary Breslin. *Educ:* Catholic University, Maynooth. Professor of Theology and Prefect of the Dunboyne Establishment, Maynooth; Rector of the Catholic University of Ireland; RC Bishop of Raphoe, 1888–1922; Titular Archbishop of Attalia and Coadjutor to Cardinal Logue, 1922–24; Cardinal, 1925. *Address:* Ara Coeli, Armagh.

Died 22 Oct. 1927.

O'DONOGHUE, David J.; biographer and editor; Librarian of University College, Dublin, 1909; *b* Chelsea, 22 July 1866; *m* Florence White; three *d.* Began to write for press in 1886, largely for Dublin papers; wrote chiefly on Irish literary subjects; Vice-President of National Literary Society, Dublin. *Publications:* Ireland in London (with F. A. Fahy), 1887; The Poets of Ireland, a Biographical

Dictionary, 1891–93, new and enlarged edn, 1912; Irish Humorists, 1892; Minor Irish Poets, 1893; Humour of Ireland, 1894; Reliques of Barney Maglone (introduction to), 1894; Irish Poetry of the Nineteenth Century, 1894; List of 1,300 Irish Artists, 1894; Fardorougha the Miser (introduction to), 1895; Writings of James Fintan Lalor, 1895; Life of William Carleton, 2 vols, 1896; edited Traits and Stories of the Irish Peasantry, 4 vols, 1896–97; Life and Writings of James Clarence Mangan, 1898; edited Works of Samuel Lover, 6 vols, 1898–99; also The Black Prophet, by Carleton, 1898; Bibliographical Catalogue of Collections of Irish Music, 1899; Richard Pockrich, an Irish Musical Genius, 1899; Life of Robert Emmet, 1902; Prose Writings of James Clarence Mangan, 1903; Poems of James Clarence Mangan, 1904; Sir Walter Scott's Tour in Ireland, 1905; Geographical Distribution of Irish Ability, 1906; Memoir of John Keegan, in collection of Legends and Stories, by Keegan, 1907; Essays of Thomas Davis, 1915; also author of numerous articles in Dictionary of National Biography, Catholic Cyclopædia, etc.
Died 1917.

O'DONOVAN, John, MVO 1920; ISO 1922; JP; *b* Lisard, Rosscarbery, Co. Cork, 22 May 1858; *s* of Florence O'Donovan and Mary Haggerty; *m* 1892, Josephine Whitaker, *widow*; three *s* one *d*. *Educ*: Mount Fachnanas National School, Rosscarbery, County Cork. Teaching Staff of School under Board of National Education, Ireland, 1872–75; emigrated to New Zealand, 1878; joined New Zealand police force as constable, 1879; studied law and passed the solicitors' law professional examinations under the University of New Zealand, 1892 and 1893; first instructor in police training college, Police Headquarters, Wellington; Serjeant, 1898; Sub-Inspector, 1902; Inspector, 1911; Superintendent, 1915; Commissioner, 1916–21; retired on superannuation with honorary rank and title of Commissioner, 1921; accompanied special police contingent which toured New Zealand with the King and Queen as Duke and Duchess of Cornwall, 1901; in command of a similar contingent on the occasion of the visit of the Prince of Wales to New Zealand, 1920. *Address*: c/o Police Headquarters, Wellington, New Zealand.
Died April 1927.

O'DWYER, Rt. Rev. Edward Thomas; RC Bishop of Limerick; consecrated 1886; *b* Holy Cross, Co. Tipperary, 1842. *Educ*: Maynooth. *Address*: The Palace, Corbally, Limerick.
Died 19 Aug. 1917.

O'DWYER, Surg.-Gen. Thomas Francis, MD (RUI); LRCS (Edin.); *m* Henrietta, *d* of Rev. J. Ringwood; one *s* one *d*. Entered army, 1864; retired, 1901; served Egyptian Expedition, 1882 (despatches, medal with clasp, bronze star, promoted Surg.-Maj.); Soudan Expedition, 1884–85; Secretary to PMO (despatches, clasp); late PMO South-Eastern District, Canada and Aldershot. *Address*: Rodney Cottage, Clifton, Bristol. *Club*: Clifton.
Died 5 Feb. 1919.

OELSNER, Herman; sometime Taylorian Professor of the Romance Languages in the University of Oxford (from foundation of Chair, 1909, till resignation, 1913); first holder of the Taylorian Lectureship in Old French and Romance Philology, 1905–9; *b* 1871; *y s* of late Isidor and Eliza Oelsner; *m* Ethel Mary Fisk. *Educ*: Dulwich College; Caius College, Cambridge. BA 1892; MA Cantab, 1898, and Oxon (by incorporation), 1906; PhD Berlin, 1896. Was recognised as Intercollegiate Lecturer in Romance in the University of Cambridge, 1898; temporarily Prof. of French Language and Literature in the University Coll. of N Wales, 1903–4; formerly Examiner in French and other Romance Languages, University of Cambridge; in French and Spanish, University of Oxford; in Italian, University of London and Royal University of Ireland; Member of the Council of the Philological Society; Romance Editor of The Modern Language Review, 1910–13. *Publications*: The Influence of Dante on Modern Thought, 1895 (Cambridge Univ. Le Bas Prize Essay, 1894); Dante in Frankreich, 1898; editions of Dante's Commedia (with Philip H. Wicksteed), 1899–1901; of Edward Fitzgerald's Six Dramas of Calderón, 1903, and of Dante's Vita Nuova, 1908; translations of Gaspary's History of Italian Literature to the Death of Dante, 1901, and (with A. W. Baker Welford) of Cervantes' Galatea, 1903; contributions on Romance subjects to numerous periodicals, and on Provençal and Italian Literature to the Ency. Brit. and to Nelson's Ency. *Club*: Savage. *Died 26 April 1923.*

O'FARRELL, Sir Edward, KCB 1917 (CB 1911); Kt 1915; *b* Dublin, 6 Dec. 1856; *s* of Michael Richard O'Farrell, barrister-at-law, late of Park, Youghal, Co. Cork; *m* 1895, Dorothy Flora, *d* of William Richardson-Bunbury, of Busselton, WA, and Amelia Georgina Molloy; one *d*. *Educ*: Trinity College, Dublin (Scholar, BA). Called

to the Irish Bar, 1882; Registrar to the Irish Land Commission till 1903; Registrar and Assistant Secretary to Estates Commissioners, 1903–8; Assistant Under-Secretary to Lord Lieut of Ireland, 1908–18; a Census Commissioner for Ireland, 1911; an Estates Commissioner, 1918–23. *Address*: Cuilnagreine, Carrickmines, Co. Dublin. *Club*: University, Dublin. *Died 13 Aug. 1926.*

O'FARRELL, Rt. Rev. Michael; Bishop of Bathurst, since 1920; *b* near Mullingar, 1865. *Educ*: Navan, Maynooth. Professor All Hallows' College, Dublin, 1892–98; Irish College, Paris, 1898–1903; mission work in Ireland, 1903–13; Vice-Rector, St John's College, University of Sydney, 1915–20. *Address*: Bishop's House, Bathurst, Australia.
Died 3 April 1928.

OGILVIE, Sir Andrew Muter John, KBE 1918; CB 1912; VD; *b* 1858; *s* of late Robert Annesley Ogilvie, CB; unmarried. *Educ*: University College, London. Private Secretary to successive Post-masters-General, 1891–99; Assistant Secretary, PO, 1903; a British delegate to International Telegraph Conference, Lisbon, 1908; Third Secretary, Post Office, 1911–14; Joint 2nd Secretary of the Post Office, 1914–19; Col (retired) RE (TF); Director of Army Signals (Home Defence), 1913–19; Member of Council, Institution of Electrical Engineers, 1913–16 and 1921–24. Officer, Belgian Order of Leopold, 1919. *Address*: 7 Sheffield Terrace, Kensington, W8. *T*: Park 60; Golf Cottage, St John's, Woking. *Clubs*: Union, Albermarle.
Died 26 Dec. 1924.

OGILVIE, George, BSc, MD; FRCP; Senior Physician to the French Hospital, and to the Hospital for Epilepsy and Paralysis, Maida Vale; *b* 1852; *m* 1893, Helen, *d* of Surgeon-General John Houston. *Educ*: Universities of Edinburgh, Paris, Würzburg, and Vienna. Graduated BSc (Edinburgh) in the Mathematical Sciences, 1875; also Neill-Arnott Prizeman; MD Edinburgh, 1876. Practised as a Physician, and medical adviser to the Standard and Scottish Widows' Cos; Fellow Royal Society of Medicine; Membre de la Société de Médecine de Paris; Chevalier de la Légion d'Honneur; Kt Order of Isabel la Catolica, Spain; Kt Order of Nossa Senhora de Villa Viçosa. *Publications*: contributions to the medical journals on Diseases of the Nervous System; Typhoid Fever; The Inheritance of Disease, Germ Infection in Tuberculosis; What is Specific Disease of the Nervous System?, 1904; Les descendants des tuberculeux: Hérédo-prédisposition, etc. *Address*: 22 Welbeck Street, Cavendish Square, W. *T*: 1018 Paddington. *Clubs*: Reform, Caledonian.
Died 13 Dec. 1918.

OGILVIE, Rt. Rev. James Nicoll, DD; Ex-Moderator, Church of Scotland; *b* 4 April 1860; *s* of Rev. Alexander Ogilvie, LLD, Aberdeen; *m* 1885, Elizabeth Johnston, *d* of I. Massie, Aberdeen; one *s*. *Educ*: Grammar School, Aberdeen; Aberdeen University (MA Hon. 1881); Edinburgh University (Gunning Fellow, 1883); Leipsic University (1883–84). Assistant Minister West Parish Church, Aberdeen, 1884; Chaplain, Indian Ecclesiastical Establishment, 1885; served twenty years Madras and Bangalore; Fellow Madras University, Examiner in History; retired as Presidency Senior Chaplain, Church of Scotland, 1904; Minister New Greyfriars Parish, Edinburgh, 1905, resigned 1919; Moderator General Assembly, 1918; Joint Convener Indian Churches Committee, Church of Scotland, 1907; Convener Foreign Mission Committee, 1909–25; Commissioner to African Missions, 1920, to Indian Missions, 1921. Hon. DD Aberdeen University, 1911; Baird Lecturer, 1915; Duff Lecturer, 1923. *Publications*: The Presbyterian Churches of Christendom; Castle Memories, Twenty Tales of Edinburgh Castle; The Greyfriars' Churches; The Apostles of India (Baird Lecture); Afric's Sunny Fountains: an Indian Pilgrimage; Our Empire's Debt to Missions (Duff Lecture). *Recreation*: golf. *Address*: Balgownie, Colinton, Edinburgh. *Club*: University, Edinburgh. *Died 9 June 1926.*

OGILVIE-GRANT, William Robert; Assistant Keeper of the Zoological Department, Natural History Museum, SW, 1913–18; *b* 25 March 1863; 2nd *s* of Hon. George Henry Essex Ogilvie-Grant and Eleanora, 4th *d* of late Sir William Gordon Gordon-Cumming, 2nd Bt; *m* 1890, Maud Louisa, *e d* of Vice-Admiral Mark Robert Pechell; one *s* three *d*. *Educ*: Cargilfield and Fettes College, Edinburgh; private crammer in Edinburgh; studied zoology and anatomy. Assistant, 2nd Class, Zoological Dept, British Museum, 1882; transferred to Natural History Museum, 1883; Assistant, 1st Class, 1893; studied ichthyology under Dr Albert C. L. G. Günther; in 1885 was placed in charge of the Ornithological Section during the absence in India of the late Dr Richard B. Sharpe, with whom he afterwards co-operated in raising the collection of Birds from comparative insignificance to its vast proportions of nearly 800,000 specimens, and in making it by far the finest in any museum in the world; did extensive work in the field, and made special collecting trips to Arabia, Sokotra, Abd-el-Kuri, the Madeira Group, Canaries, Salvage Island, Azores, etc, and secured many zoological and botanical species new to science; took a prominent part in organising many expeditions to explore unknown parts of the world (notably Ruwenzori, Snow Mountains, New Guniea, etc), and form zoological collections, and in raising the large funds necessary to defray the expenses; Editor of Bulletin of the Brit. Ornith. Club, 1904–14; Fellow Zoological Society (served on Council, 1905–10 and 1911–16); Fellow, Royal Society for Protection of Birds and of Avicultural Society (served on Councils of both Societies); joined 1st Batt. County of London Regt (Vol.) 1914; invalid since 1916. *Publications:* Catalogue of Birds in the British Museum, vols xvii (part), xxii, and xxvi (part); Allen's Nat. Library Handbook to the Game-Birds, vols i and ii, 1895–97; The Gun at Home and Abroad; British Game-birds and Wild-fowl, Nat. Hist., 1912; Reports on the BOU Expedn and Wollaston Expedn. to Dutch New Guinea, 1909–13 (1915), etc; large number of monographs and papers on Natural History subjects, chiefly ornithological, published in periodicals such as Ibis, Bulletin Brit. Ornith. Club, Trans and Proc. Zoological Soc., etc. *Recreations:* natural history in the field, gardening. *Address:* Farley Hill Cottage, near Reading.

Died 26 July 1924.

OGILVY, Mrs Nisbet-Hamilton, (Mary Georgiana Constance); *b* Dundas; *o c* of Rt Hon. Robert Adam Christopher Nisbet-Hamilton (Robert Adam Dundas, who had assumed surname of Christopher and then also of Nisbet-Hamilton), MP, and Lady Mary Bruce, *e d* of 7th Earl of Elgin; *m* 1888, Henry Thomas Ogilvy (assumed additional name of Nisbet-Hamilton) (*d* 1909), 2nd *s* of Sir John Ogilvy, 9th Bt of Inverquharity. Owned 22,000 acres. *Address:* Biel, Prestonkirk; Archerfield, Dirleton; Winton Castle, Pencaitland, East Lothian. *Died 25 June 1920.*

OGLE, Sir Henry Asgill, 7th Bt, *cr* 1816; Captain Royal Navy (retired); *b* Corfu, 12 Sept. 1850; 2nd and *e* surv. *s* of Gen. Sir Edmund Ogle, 6th Bt, RE, and Catharine Beverley, *d* of Henry St Hill; *m* 1917, Daisy, *e d* of T. L. Boyd, Vista Lieta, San Remo. *Educ:* Southsea. Entered Royal Navy, 1864. Gained £100 Scholarship at Greenwich, 1877, etc; served in West Indies, N America, Mediterranean, China, Cape, India, West Coast of Africa, Australia, etc; served with Naval Brigade in Natal; served at Admiralty and at Ordnance Committee, and a Deputy Commissioner of the Western Pacific. *Recreations:* member of Cyclists' Touring Club, riding, etc. *Heir:* *b* Lt-Col Edmund Ashton Ogle, *b* 13 Aug. 1857. *Address:* Capo di Monte, San Remo. *Clubs:* United Service; Royal Naval, Portsmouth.

Died 5 March 1921.

O'GRADY, Lt-Col John de Courcy, CB 1900; JP, DL; late the Connaught Rangers; *b* 1 Nov. 1856; 3rd *s* of Willaim de Courcy O'Grady, Chief of his name (The O'Grady); *m* 1892, Evelyn Wanda, *y d* of late Major-Gen. A. Mattei, CMG, and Mrs Mattei (*née* Ceneska Lesczinska). *Educ:* Windermere College; RMC Sandhurst. Entered army, 1878; Captain, 1881; Major, 1891; Lieut-Col 1900; retired 1903; served Zulu War; Secocoeni War (severely wounded, despatches); Boer War, 1879–81 (despatches, medal, and clasp); S African War, 1899–1901 (despatches, Queen's medal 5 clasps, CB); High Sheriff, Co. Limerick, 1914. *Recreations:* shooting, fishing. *Address:* Kilballyowen, Bruff, Kilmallock, Co. Limerick. *TA:* O'Grady, Bruff. *M:* TI 25. *Club:* County Limerick.

Died 30 Aug. 1920.

O'GRADY, Standish, BLitt; author and publicist; *b* 18 Sept. 1846; *s* of Thomas O'Grady and Susanna Dowe; *m* Margaret, *d* of Rev. William Fisher; three *s*. *Educ:* Tipperary Grammar School; Trinity Coll., Dublin. Scholar Classical; Silver Medallist in Ethics and Psychology; *do* Oratory in Undergraduate Philosophical Society; Gold Medallist as Essayist in the same. Relinquished the Bar for journalism in the first instance, and afterwards for literature, chiefly Irish history and Irish historical romance; his works in this department of literature generally believed to have been the starting point of the Celtic Renaissance. *Publications:* History of Ireland, Heroic Period, vols i and ii, republished as a romantic Trilogy: (1) The Coming of Cuculain; (2) In the Gates of the North; (3) Triumph and Death of Cuculain; History of Ireland, Critical and Philosophical, vol. i; The Flight of the Eagle; The Bog of Stars; Finn and His Companions; Ulrick the Ready; The Story of Ireland; Lost on Du-Corrig; The Chain of Gold; The Coming of Cuculain Cycle, 3 vols; editor of Pacata Hibernia, etc. *Recreations:* golf, cycling. *Address:* The Vicarage, Easton Maudit, Wellingborough, North Hants. *Died 18 May 1928.*

O'GRADY, Lt-Col Standish de Courcy, CMG 1918; DSO 1917; MB; Royal Army Medical Corps; *b* 27 July 1872; *e s* of late Capt.

S. de C. O'Grady and Charlotte, *d* of G. P. Houghton, Kilmarnock; *m* 1911, Esther Alice, *o d* of Col P. D. Vigors of Holloden, Co. Carlow; two *s* one *d*. Served East Africa, 1904 (despatches, medal and clasp); European War (despatches thrice, DSO, CMG). *Address:* c/o Holt & Co., 6 Whitehall Place, SW1.

Died 23 Dec. 1920.

O'GRADY, Rev. William Waller; Rector of Kilmocomogue since 1879; Canon of Cork since 1886; Treasurer of St Finn Barre's Cathedral, Cork, and Rural Dean of Glensalny West; *b* 7 April 1844; *s* of Rev. Thomas O'Grady (*nephew* of 1st Viscount Guillamore), and Helen, *d* of R. Dring; *m* Matilda Kate, *d* of John Christopher Delmege, Castle Park, Limerick; two *d*. *Educ:* Trinity College, Dublin (MA). Ordained, 1869; Curate of Drimoleague, 1869–70; Incumbent, 1870–79. *Address:* The Rectory, Bantry, Ireland.

Died 18 March 1921.

OGSTON, Frank, MD and CM, Aberdeen; Professor of Medical Jurisprudence, University of Otago, Dunedin, New Zealand; *b* 23 June 1846; *s* of Dr Francis Ogston, Professor of Medical Jurisprudence, University of Aberdeen; *m*; one *d*. *Educ:* Aberdeen; Vienna; Prague; Paris. Assistant to Professor of Medical Jurisprudence, Aberdeen University; lately Professor of Hygiene, Otago University; District Medical Officer of Health for the Otago Southland District of New Zealand; Member British Medical Association; Fellow of Society of Medical Officers of Health of England; Membre Corr. Etranger de la Société de Médécine Légale de France, etc. *Publications:* editor of Lectures on Medical Jurisprudence by Francis Ogston; Hints to Teachers on Medical Inspection of School Children, 1907. *Recreation:* golf. *Address:* 236 High Street, Dunedin, NZ. *Clubs:* Dunedin; Otago Golf. *Died 1917.*

O'HALLORAN, Joseph Sylvester, CMG 1895; Secretary Royal Colonial Institute, 1884–1909; *b* Adelaide, SA, 28 March 1842; *e s* of late Capt. William Littlejohn O'Halloran; *m* 1886, Alice Mary, *d* of late Henry Simpson, Ridge Park, Adelaide. *Educ:* private schools. Clerk, Audit Office, SA, 1859; Clerk, Executive Council and Court of Appeals, 1869; Private Secretary to Rt Hon. Sir James Fergusson, Bt, Governor SA, 1870; Asst Secretary, Royal Colonial Institute, London, 1881; Secretary Geographical Section of the British Association, Montreal, 1884; Aberdeen, 1885. *Publications:* contributed to the National Dictionary of Biography, Chambers's Encyclopædia, the Field, etc. *Recreations:* travelled extensively in the Colonies; for some years a volunteer, South Australia.

Died 25 Jan. 1920.

O'HALLORAN, Rev. Richard; a Catholic priest; Rector of the Catholic Church, Mattock Lane, Ealing, which he himself erected; founded several missions and erected schools and churches. *Educ:* Mill Hill. Ordained Deacon at Pro-Cathedral, Kensington, and Priest at Belmont Cathedral; incorporated a secular priest of the diocese of Westminster by Cardinal Manning. *Publications:* Rights of the Secular Clergy Vindicated; Cardinal and Priest. *Recreations:* gardening, flower culture. *Address:* The Catholic Church, Mattock Lane, Ealing, W.

Died Oct. 1925.

O'HANLON, Rt. Rev. Mgr. James, DD; Vicar-General of Birmingham and Provost of the Chapter since 1905; *b* 1840. Ordained 1865; Headmaster of St Chad's Grammar School, 1867–72; Prof. of Theology at Oscott, 1872–77; Rector of Olton Seminary, 1888–89; Domestic Prelate to the Pope. *Address:* 71 Hunter's Road, Birmingham. *Died 25 Feb. 1921.*

O'HARA, Rt. Rev. Henry Stewart, DD; *b* 6 Sept. 1843; *e s* of Rev. James O'Hara (former Rector of Coleraine), The Castle, Portstewart; *m* 1872, Hatton Thomasina, *y d* of Thomas Scott, DL, of Wilsboro, Londonderry. *Educ:* Collegiate School, Leicester; Trinity College, Dublin (BA 1865; MA 1868; DD *jure dignitatis*, 1900). Rector of Coleraine, 1869; Vicar of Belfast, 1894; Canon of St Patrick's Cathedral, Dublin, 1897; first Dean of Belfast, 1899; Bishop of Cashel and Emly, Waterford, and Lismore, 1900; resigned 1919. *Address:* Laurel Hill, Coleraine. *Club:* Ulster, Belfast.

Died 11 Dec. 1923.

O'HARA, Col James, CB 1917; *b* 16 Nov. 1865; *s* of late Col James O'Hara, DL, late Capt. 2nd DGs, of Lenaboy, Galway; *m* 1902, Margaret (*d* 1928), *e d* of late W. Chalmers Carmichael; one *s* one *d*. *Educ:* Wellington; RM College, Sandhurst. Served in 2nd Dragoon Guards (Queen's Bays), 1886–95; appointed to Army Pay Dept, 1895; served South African War, 1899–1902 (despatches twice, Queen's medal with 2 clasps, King's medal with 2 clasps); Col and Chief Paymaster, 1913; Command Paymaster, Northern Command; retired pay, 1925. *Address:* Lenaboy, Hucclecote, Gloucester. *Club:* Kildare Street, Dublin. *Died 23 Dec. 1928.*

O'HARA, John Bernard, MA; poet; *b* Bendigo, Victoria, 29 Oct. 1862; *s* of P. K. O'Hara; *m* 1910, Agnes Elizabeth Law, of Hamilton, Victoria; two *s* one *d*. *Educ:* Carlton College; Ormond College (Scholarship); Melbourne University (with first-class honours, Stawell Exhibition for Engineering and Mathematical Exhibition). Lecturer in Mathematics and Physics at Ormond College, 1886–89; Principal of South Melbourne College, 1889–1916. *Publications:* Songs of the South, 1891; Songs of the South (second series), 1895; Lyrics of Nature, 1899; A Book of Sonnets, 1902; Odes and Lyrics, 1906; Calypso and Other Poems, 1912; The Poems of J. B. O'Hara, 1918; At Eventide, 1922. *Recreations:* tennis, walking. *Address:* 98 Beaconsfield Parade, Albert Park, Melbourne. *T:* 4307 C. *Died 31 March 1927.*

O'HARE, Patrick; MP (N) North Monaghan, 1906–7; a Bailie, Glasgow; *b* 1849. *Address:* 25 Circus Drive, Dennistoun; Tullygillen House, Monaghan. *Died Nov. 1917.*

O'HIGGINS, Kevin Christopher; Minister for External Affairs, Irish Free State, since 1927; Member of Dáil for Dublin County since 1923; *b* 7 June 1892; *s* of late Thomas Francis O'Higgins, FRCSI, Stradbally, Leix, and Anne, *d* of Timothy Daniel Sullivan, poet; *m* 1921, Bridget May, *d* of Andrew Cole; one *s* two *d*. *Educ:* Clongowes; St Patrick's College, Carlow; National University of Ireland (BA). Minister for Economic Affairs, 1922; Minister for Home Affairs, later Vice President of Executive Council and Minister of Justice, 1922–27. MP (Sinn Fein) Queen's County, 1918–22. *Address:* Woodlands, Timoque, Stradbally, Queen's County. *Died 10 July 1927.*

OHNET, Georges; *b* Paris, 3 April 1848. *Educ:* Sainte Barbe; Lycée Bonaparte. Elected Président de la Société des auteurs dramatiques, 1902. *Publications:* Serge Panine, 1880; Le Maître de Forges, 1881; La Comtesse Sarah, 1883; Lise Fleuron, 1884; La Grande Marnière, 1885; Les Dames de Croixmort, 1885; Noir et Rose, 1887; Volonté, 1888; Le Docteur Rameau, 1889; Dernier Armour, 1890; L'Ame de Pierre, 1890; Dette de Haine, 1891; Le Lendemain des Amours, 1893; Le Droit de l'Enfant, 1894; Nemrod et Cⁱᵉ, 1895; La Dame en Gris; La Fille du Député, 1895; L'inutile Richesse, 1896; Vieilles Rancunes; Le Curé de Favières; Roi de Paris; An Fond du Gouffre, 1899; Gens de la Noce, 1900; La Ténébreuse; Le Brasseur d'Affaires; Le Crépuscule; La Marché a l'Amour; Marchand de Poison; Le Chemin de la Gloire; La Conquérant; La Dixième Muse; La Route rouge; L'Aventure de Raymond Dhautel; Pour tuer Bonaparte; La Serre de l'aigle; Le Revenant; Le Partisan; *plays:* Regina Sarpi; Marthe; Le Colonel Roquebrune; Les Rouges et les Blancs; dramatised several of his novels with great success. *Address:* 14 Avenue Trudaine, Paris. *Died 5 May 1918.*

O'KEEFE, Hon. Michael, MHA; Speaker, House of Assembly, since 1925; Member of Parliament (Lab) for Wilmot since 1912; *b* Westbury, Tasmania, 12 Sept. 1865; *e s* of Edmund O'Keefe and Josephine Thorne; *m* 1896, Beatrice Emily Dutton, *g d* of late Captain Dutton, RN, and late Rev. John Copeland Dixon, BA; two *s* two *d*. *Educ:* Selbourne, Beaconsfield. Farming and mining until 1912. *Recreations:* gardening, music, reading. *Address:* The Palms, Beaconsfield, Tasmania; Speaker's Room, Hobart, Tasmania. *T:* 41. *Died Oct. 1926.*

O'KELLY, James Joseph; MP (N) County Roscommon since 1895; *b* 1845; *s* of late John O'Kelly, Roscommon, and Bridget, *d* of John Lalor. *Educ:* Dublin University; Sorbonne. Served in French Army (Siege of Paris), in Cuba, USA against Indians; travelled in Mexico; war reporter, New York Herald; formerly War Correspondent of Daily News; MP Co. Roscommon, 1880–85; N Roscommon, 1885–92. *Publications:* The Mambi Land, a History of Personal Adventures with President Cespides in the Cuban Insurrection. *Address:* 17 Brewster Gardens, W. *Died 22 Dec. 1916.*

OKUMA, Prince Shigenobu; Prime Minister, Japan, 1914–16; *b* Saga, Hizen, 1838. A retainer of Lord Nabeshima; one of the founders of the new government; Finance Minister, 1869–81; Foreign Minister, 1888–89; Minister of Agriculture and Commerce, 1896–97; Prime Minister and Foreign Minister, 1898; founder and ex-leader of the Progressive party; founder and President of the Waseda University, Tokio; founder of the Japanese Women's University. *Recreation:* horticulture. *Address:* Waseda, Tokio. *T:* Bancho 177. *Died Jan. 1922.*

OLDERSHAW, William James Norman, CBE 1918; VD; Sugar Controller for the Commonwealth Government; *b* Melbourne, 24 April 1856; *s* of William Oldershaw. *Educ:* Wesley College, Melbourne. Devoted many years (40) to Rifle Shooting and Militia work; Emerald Hill Artillery, 1877; 1st Australian Infantry Regt, 1886; Lt-Col commanding, 1900; Hon. Secretary Australian War Contingent Association, London, 1914; special work as Commercial Adviser to Australian Government since 1915. *Recreation:* rifle shooting (won Queen's Prize, 1882, Melbourne). *Club:* Bombay. *Died 13 Oct. 1926.*

OLDFIELD, Sir Francis Du Pre, Kt 1923; Professor of Jurisprudence, Manchester, since 1924; Puisne Judge, Madras High Court, 1913–24; *b* 30 June 1869; *e s* of Canon C. Oldfield, Stamford; *m* 1898, Frances, *e d* of late Sir Richard Cayley and Sophia Margaret, *d* of Hon. David Wilson; one *s* one *d*. *Educ:* Marlborough; Trinity College, Cambridge. Entered the Indian Civil Service, 1890; Head Assistant, Madras, 1897; Sub-Collector and Joint Magistrate, 1904; District and Sessions Judge, 1908; Fellow, Madras University, 1916; Vice-Chancellor, 1918. *Address:* 53 Palace Court, W2. *Club:* East India United Service. *Died 14 Feb. 1928.*

OLDFIELD, Sir Richard Charles, Kt 1889; late Indian Civil Service; *b* 3 Nov. 1828; *e s* of Henry Swann Oldfield and Letitia, *d* of Col Richard Scott; *m* 1854, Maria S. (*d* 1885), *d* of Major Frederick Angelo; one *s* one *d*. *Educ:* Eton; Haileybury. Entered Bengal CS, 1848; served during Mutiny; wounded near Agra; Judge of the High Court of Judicature, Allahabad, 1873–87. *Club:* Oriental. *Died 26 Dec. 1918.*

OLDHAM, Ven. Algernon Langston, DD; Archdeacon of Ludlow, 1904–13; Prebendary of Hereford Cathedral; Rector and Rural Dean of Bridgnorth, 1882–1905; *s* of late James Oldham of Lucastes, Hayward's Heath, and Brighton; two *s*. *Educ:* Rugby; Trinity College, Oxford; Cuddesdon. Canon Residentiary of Hereford Cathedral, 1905–9. *Publication:* Why we are Churchmen. *Address:* The Elms, Shrewsbury. *Died 23 July 1916.*

OLDHAM, Charles H., BA; Professor of Commerce, University College, Dublin. *Address:* University College, Dublin. *Died 20 Feb. 1926.*

OLDHAM, Sir Ernest Fitzjohn, Kt 1921; senior partner of Vizard Oldham Crowder and Cash, 51 Lincoln's Inn Fields, WC2; Vice-President and Deputy-Chairman, Federation of British Industries; *b* 16 Jan. 1870; *s* of Frederick Jennings Oldham, Melton Mowbray; *m* 1899, Margaret Alice, *d* of late William Tatham, solicitor, Orpington, Kent; one *s* three *d*. *Educ:* Oakham. *Address:* 19 Palace Court, W2. *Clubs:* Carlton, Conservative, Royal Automobile, Ranelagh. *Died 22 Sept. 1926.*

OLDHAM, Col Sir Henry (Hugh), KCVO 1914 (CVO 1902); Kt 1897; Lieutenant of the Honourable Corps of Gentlemen-at-Arms since 1891; *b* 17 Sept. 1840; *o s* of late Henry Oldham, MD, and Sophia, *d* of James Smith; *m* 1868, Ella (*d* 1921), *d* of late Arthur Pigou, BCS; two *s* two *d*. *Educ:* Radley College; Royal Military College, Sandhurst. Entered army, 4 Nov. 1858; served in 48th Regt and Cameron Highlanders; appointed to Honourable Corps of Gentlemen-at-Arms, 1887; Clerk of the Cheque, same corps, 1887; served in China War (medal and two clasps), 1860; Cossyah and Jyntiah Hill Campaign (mentioned in despatches), 1863–64. *Address:* Cannington, Boscombe, Bournemouth. *Club:* United Serive. *Died 20 Sept. 1922.*

OLDHAM, William Benjamin, CIE 1893; late Indian Civil Service; *b* Monkstown, Co. Dublin, 16 April 1845; 2nd *s* of late Thomas Wilson Oldham, Dublin; *m* 1879, Maud Julia, 4th *d* of General Sir Anthony Blaxland Stransham, GCB; three *s*. *Educ:* Kingstown School; Trinity College, Dublin (Exhibitioner; Sizar; 1st Prize, Greek verse). Indian Civil Service, 1865; Orissa Famine, 1866–67; Bihar Famine, 1874; Madras Famine, 1877–78; Bengal Famine, 1897; and Frontier Service; Member of Bengal Board of Revenue to 1900; was Member of Bengal Legislative Council; Pres. of Bengal Sanitary Board; Col commanding Calcutta Vol. Rifles; ADC to the Viceroy of India. *Decorated* for Lushai Hills Campaign, 1892, when Inspector-General of Military Police. *Publications:* Some Ethnical and Historical Aspects of the Burdwan District; Hunting and Chasing in the Seventies. *Address:* Owlston, Talbot Avenue, Bournemouth. *TA:* Oldham, Bournemouth. *T:* 2230. *Clubs:* Carlyle, W Bournemouth. *Died 14 Oct. 1916.*

OLDRIEVE, William Thomas, HRSA, FRIBA; architect, Edinburgh; *b* 1853. *Educ:* Mansfield Grammar School. Assistant Surveyor in HM Office of Works, 1881; Architect for Provincial Post Office buildings in England and Wales, 1892; HM Principal Architect for Scotland, 1904; retired, superannuated, 1914; Member of the Royal Commission on the Ancient Monuments of Scotland; Secretary Ministry of Munitions for N and E Scotland, 1917–18; Munitions Works Board; Deputy Principal Surveyor for Scotland, 1918. *Address:* Oldrieve, Bell, and Paterson, 22 Ainslie Place, Edinburgh. *T:* 3859; 13 Braid Avenue, Edinburgh. *T:* Edinburgh 1772.
Died Jan. 1922.

OLDROYD, Sir Mark, Kt 1909; JP; woollen manufacturer; Chairman, M. Oldroyd & Sons; retired, 1920; Alderman; *b* 30 May 1843; *s* of late Mark Oldroyd, Dewsbury, and Rachel, *d* of Marmaduke Fox, Soothill; *m* 1st, 1871, Maria Tew (*d* 1919), *d* of William Mewburn; 2nd, 1920, A. J. Pattison (*d* 1926), of Gainsborough. Late Mayor of Dewsbury; MP (R) Dewsbury, 1888–1901; Director of Airedale Collieries, Ltd, Castleford. *Address:* Hyrstlands, Dewsbury.
Died 5 July 1927.

O'LEARY, Brig.-Gen. Tom Evelyn, CB 1914; CMG 1916; CBE 1919; *b* Aug. 1862; *s* of late Surg.-Gen. Thomas Conor O'Leary; *m* 1894, *d* of late Maj.-Gen. Francis William Ward, CB; one *d*. *Educ:* Beaumont. Entered army, 1884; served in the Irish Fusiliers; served Miranzai Expedition, 1891 (medal with clasp); Isazai Expedition, 1892; Chitral, 1895 (despatches, Brevet-Major, medal with clasp); South Africa, 1899–1902 (despatches twice, Brevet Lt-Col, Queen's medal 6 clasps, King's medal 2 clasps); European War, 1914–18 (despatches, CMG, CBE). *Address:* West End, Haslemere, Surrey. *TA:* Chiddingfold. *Club:* Army and Navy.
Died 16 Sept. 1924.

OLIPHANT, Philip Lawrence; see Kington-Blair-Oliphant, P. L.

OLIVEIRA, Francisco Regis de; Brazilian Ambassador at Lisbon since 1914; *m* Donna Amelia (*née* da Silva Guimarães). Entered upon his career forty years ago and became Secretary of Legation successively at Paris, Berlin, Vienna, and Montevideo, then Minister in turn in Paraguay, Spain, Russia, Italy, and Austria; Brazilian Minister in London; his grandfather accompanied Dom João VI when that king fled to Brazil on the invasion of Portugal by Napoleon, and subsequently took a prominent part in proclaiming the independence of the South American Colony. *Address:* Brazilian Embassy, Lisbon.
Died 23 Jan. 1916.

OLIVER, Charles Nicholson Jewel, CMG 1905; *b* 24 April 1848. Joined the Public Service, Department of Lands, 1866; Under-Secretary for Lands, New South Wales, 1880; Railway Commissioner, 1888; Chief Commissioner for Railways, 1897; retired, 1907. *Address:* Camira, Pennant Hills, near Sydney, New South Wales.
Died 14 June 1920.

OLIVER, Daniel, LLD; FRS; *b* Newcastle-on-Tyne, 6 Feb. 1830; *e s* of Daniel Oliver, Newcastle; *m* 1861, Hannah, *d* of James Wall, The Hills, Sheffield; one *s* two *d*. *Educ:* Friends' School, Brookfield, near Wigton, and at private schools. Emeritus Professor of Botany, University Coll. London, (Professor, 1861–88); Keeper of Herbarium and Library, Royal Gardens, Kew, to 1890; Royal Medal of Royal Society, 1884; Linnean Medal, 1893. *Publications:* works on elementary botany, and on African botany; special Memoirs in Trans Linnean Soc. London, etc. *Recreations:* painting, gardening. *Address:* 10 Kew Gardens Road, Kew.
Died 21 Dec. 1916.

OLIVER, Rev. George, BA; Rector of St John's, Longton, Staffs, since 1896; *b* 1848; *e s* of Alderman Oliver, Bath; *m* 1st, 1881, Miss Whitehouse of Sedgley, Staffs; 2nd, 1894, Miss V. Walker of Brighton; one *s* two *d*. *Educ:* Lansdowne College, Bath; New College, Oxford. Curate of St Mary's, Sedgley, 1876–80; Hallam Fields, Derbyshire, 1880–85; Vicar of St George's, Darlaston, 1885–96; Proctor in Convocation for Archdeanery of Stoke-on-Trent; Prebendary of Bishopshull in Lichfield Cathedral; Chairman of Stoke-on-Trent Board of Guardians; Chairman of Longton War Pensions Committee. *Recreations:* cricket, cycling. *Address:* St John's Rectory, Longton, Staffs.
Died 17 Dec. 1920.

OLIVER, Matthew William Baillie, OBE 1919; MA, MB, BCh Cambridge; FRCS, LRCP; Surgeon to the Central London Ophthalmic Hospital; Ophthalmic Surgeon to the Queen's Hospital for Facial Injuries, Sidcup, and the Royal National Orthopædic Hospital; Ophthalmic Surgeon to the Italian Hospital; Ophthalmic Surgeon to Queen Mary's Auxiliary Hospital, Roehampton; *s* of late

Robert Oliver of Strathwell, Whitwell, Isle of Wight. *Educ:* Cheltenham College; Trinity College, Cambridge; St Bartholomew's Hospital. Held various appointments at St George's Hospital for two years; held the appointments of Chief Assistant in the Ophthalmic department at St Bartholomew's Hospital and Asst Ophthalmic Surgeon to the Miller Hospital, Greenwich; served in the RAMC in France, Aug. 1914–May 1919 (despatches). *Publications:* various papers on surgical and ophthalmological subjects. *Recreations:* golf, tennis, swimming, motoring. *Address:* 128 Harley Street, W1. *T:* Langham 1939. *M:* DN 4193. *Clubs:* New University, Royal Automobile.
Died 10 Feb. 1926.

OLIVER, William, ISO 1903; late Senior Principal Clerk, Supreme Court Pay Office; *b* 27 May 1836; *s* of Rev. John Oliver; *m* 1st, 1868, Mary, *d* of Thomas Black, Highgate; 2nd, 1876, Fanny Biden, *y d* of Charles Biden Rogers, Kew, Surrey. *Address:* Fotheringay, Cumberland Road, Kew.
Died 20 Jan. 1917.

OLIVEY, Sir Walter Rice, KCB 1887 (CB 1882); Colonel and Chief Paymaster, retired 1889; *b* 1831; *e s* of late Hugh Oliver Olivey; *m* 1855, Elizabeth (*d* 1913), *d* of late R. Goodfellow, Falmouth; three *s*. *Educ:* Truro Grammar School; Falmouth Classical School. Ensign by purchase 91st Argyllshire Regt, 1851; served in New Zealand War (medal) and in Egyptian Campaign of 1882 as Chief Paymaster (CB and medal); also in Egyptian Campaign, 1884–85, as Chief Paymaster (clasp, and KCB); received distinguished service reward. *Recreations:* shooting, boating, an amateur mechanic. *Address:* 51 Blessington Road, Lee, SE. *TA:* Opetide, London. *Club:* Junior Constitutional.
Died 26 Nov. 1922.

OLIVIER, Rev. Dacres, MA; Prebendary of Salisbury; Hon. Chaplain to the Earl of Pembroke; *b* Potterne, 26 Oct. 1831; *s* of Col Olivier of Potterne, Manor House, Wilts, and Mary, *d* of Admiral Sir Richard Dacres; *m* Emma Selina (*d* 1908), *d* of Rt Rev. Robert Eden, Primus of the Scottish Episcopal Church; six *s* three *d*. *Educ:* Rugby; Christ Church, Oxford. Curate of Great Yarmouth and of Wilton, 1854–67; Rural Dean, 1885–97; Rector of Wilton, Wilts, 1867–1912. *Address:* The Close, Salisbury, Wilts; The Lea, Grasmere. *Club:* Constitutional.
Died 7 Jan. 1919.

OLLIVANT, Alfred; *b* 1874; 2nd *s* of Col E. A. Ollivant, Royal Horse Artillery, Elliotts, Nuthurst, Sussex, and Catharine, 2nd *d* of Professor J. J. Blunt; *g s* of Rt Rev. Alfred Ollivant, Bishop of Llandaff; *m* 1914, Hilda, *d* of Robert Wigram (*g s* of Sir Robert Wigram, 1st Bt), and Mary Edith, *d* of Samuel Solly, FRS; one *d*. *Educ:* Rugby; RM Academy, Woolwich (passed out Senior Gunner, Toombs' Memorial Scholar, and Winner of the Riding Prize). Commission in Royal Artillery, 1893; resigned, 1895. *Publications:* Owd Bob, 1898; Danny, 1903; The Gentleman, 1908; The Royal Road, 1912; The Brown Mare, 1916; Boy Woodburn, 1917; Two Men, 1919; One Woman, 1920; Boxer and Beauty, 1924. *Address:* 20 Evelyn Gardens, SW7. *Club:* Athenæum.
Died 19 Jan. 1927.

OLLIVANT, Brig.-Gen. Alfred Henry, CMG 1916; Royal Artillery; General Staff Officer, 1st grade, Supreme War Council; *b* 19 Oct. 1871; *s* of Colonel A. Ollivant, Indian Army, and *g s* of Rt Rev. Alfred Ollivant, late Bishop of Llandaff; unmarried. *Educ:* Winchester Coll.; Woolwich. Entered Royal Artillery, 1891; Captain, 1899; Major, 1911; Bt Lieut-Col 1914; Lt-Col, 1917; served with Somaliland Expeditionary Force, 1904 (medal with clasp); passed Staff College, 1908; General Staff Officer, 2nd grade, at Colonial Office, 1909–11; 3rd grade, at War Office, 1911–13; 2nd grade, at Admiralty, 1913–14; Bt-Col 1918; served European War with Royal Naval Division as General Staff Officer, 1st grade, at Antwerp, 1914 (despatches); Dardanelles, 1915–16 (despatches, CMG); BEF France, 1916–17 (Order of St Anne of Russia, 2nd Class, despatches). *Club:* Army and Navy.
Died 31 Aug. 1919.

OLLIVANT, Sir (Edward) Charles (Kayll), KCIE 1892 (CIE 1888); retired from Indian Civil Service; *b* 7 Feb. 1846; *s* of Rev. Edward Ollivant and Susan Maria, *d* of John James Kayll, IoM; *m* 1st, 1870, Lucy C. (*d* 1891), 2nd *d* of Judge Eddis, QC; 2nd, 1899, Edith Margaret, 2nd *d* of Rev. Thomas Sikes Hichens, Hon. Canon Peterborough Cathedral; one *s* one *d*. *Educ:* Marlborough. Entered ICS, 1868; Municipal Commissioner, Bombay, 1881–90; Political Agent, Kathiawar, 1890–95; Officiating Commissioner in Sind, 1895; Officiating Chief Secretary to Government of Bombay, 1896; Member of Council of Governor of Bombay, 1897–1902; Member of the Council of Marlborough College; Director of the BB&CIR. *Address:* 2 Westbourne Crescent, W2. *T:* Paddington 725.
Died 24 Dec. 1928.

OLMSTED, Rt. Rev. Charles Sandford, DD; Bishop of Colorado since 1902; *b* Olmstedville, NY, 8 Feb. 1853; *s* of Levi Olmsted and Maria Beach; three *s* one *d*. *Educ:* St Stephen's College and General Theological Seminary, NY. Missionary, Morley, NY, 1876–84; Rector, Cooperstown, NY, 1884–96; Archdeacon of Susquehanna, 1886–96; Rector, St Asaph, Bala, etc, 1896–1902. *Publications:* December Musings and Other Poems; Mediæval Poets. *Address:* The Elms, Saybrook, Connecticut, USA.

Died 21 Oct. 1918.

OLMSTED, Rt. Rev. Charles Tyler, DD, DCL; Bishop of Central New York since 1904; *b* 28 April 1842; *s* of Charles A. and Ardelia W. Olmsted; *m* 1876, Catharine Lawrence. *Educ:* Trinity College, Hartford, Conn. Deacon, 1867; Priest, 1868; Prof. of Mathematics, St Stephen's College, Annandale, 1866–68; Assistant Minister, Trinity Parish, New York, 1868–84; Rector, Grace Church, Utica, NY, 1884–99; Vicar, St Agnes' Chapel, Trinity Parish, New York, 1899–1902; Bishop Coadjutor, Central New York, 1902–4. *Publications:* The Rock Whence Ye are Hewn: a Course of Lectures on Early History of English Church; various sermons. *Address:* 1101 Park Avenue, Utica, NY. *T:* 250.

Died 26 March 1924.

OLNEY, Richard; *b* Oxford, Massachusetts, 15 Sept. 1835; *s* of Wilson Olney; descended from Thomas Olney, who came to America in 1635 from St Albans, Hertfordshire, England; on mother's side descended from Andrew Sigourney, a French Huguenot, who came to America in 1687 on revocation of Edict of Nantes; *m* 1861, Agnes Park Thomas. *Educ:* Leicester Academy (Leicester, Mass); Brown University, Providence, RI (graduated 1856); Harvard Law School (LLB 1858). LLD Harvard University, 1893; Brown University (Providence, RI), LLD 1893; Yale University, LLD 1901. Admitted to the Bar, Supreme Judicial Court, Suffolk County, Mass, 1859; served one term Mass Legislature, 1874; Attorney-General, United States, March 1893 to June 1895; Secretary of State of the United States, 10 June 1895 to 4 March 1897; declined to be nominated as Ambassador to Great Britain, March 1913; American Member of Commission under treaty between US and France, 1915. *Address:* 710 Sears Building, Boston, Mass. *Club:* Somerset.

Died 9 April 1917.

O'LOGHLIN, Hon. James Vincent, VD; *b* Gumeracha, South Australia, 25 Nov. 1852; *s* of pioneer colonist; *m* 1907, Blanche, *y d* of John Besley of Mt Gambier, SA; three *s* one *d*. *Educ:* Kapunda Classical and Commercial Academy. Spent earlier years in agricultural and pastoral pursuits, and in the wheat and milling trade; engaged in journalism; in 1884 started Terowi Enterprise, a successful up-country paper; subsequently became editor and managing director of the Southern Cross in Adelaide, with which paper still connected; in 1888 was elected member of Legislative Council, and was returned again in 1894 at head of the poll; in 1896 became Chief Secretary and Leader of the Upper House in the (Rt Hon. Charles Cameron) Kingston Government, the strongest and longest-lived administration which had held office in South Australia for S Australia in Federal Parliament, Session, 1907; elected Senior Member for Flinders, House of Assembly, 1910; Senator for SA, 1913–20; Lt-Colonel in the local forces; ex-Chief President Australian Natives Association; President of the Irish National Association, and for 14 years a trustee of the Savings Bank; served on several Royal Commissions, and was Chairman of the Public Service Royal Commission; volunteered for active service and took a contingent of the Australian Imperial Force to the Front, Aug. 1915, and again in 1916 (British Empire War Medal, 1914–18, Gallipoli Star, 1914–15, Victory Medal, 1914–18, Volunteer Decoration); Senator for South Australia, Federal Parliament, since 1922. *Address:* Hawthorn, South Australia. *Club:* Naval and Military.

Died 4 Dec. 1925.

O'LOGHLIN, Hon. Laurence, JP; *b* Salisbury, Jan. 1854; *m* Frances Morris; six *s* five *d*. *Educ:* Salisbury; Seven Hills Catholic College. District Councillor in the Port Germain District Council, SA; Member of Vermin Board; MP district of Frome, 1890–1914; for Burra Burra, 1914; Government Whip, 1894–96; Commissioner of Crown Lands, South Australia, 1896–1902; Minister of Lands, Agriculture, Mines, and Controlling Northern Territory, 1905–9; Minister of Public Works, 1909–10; Speaker, House of Assembly, 1912–15. *Address:* Pinnaroo, South Australia.

Died 27 Jan. 1927.

O'LOGHLIN, Very Rev. Robert Stuart, DD; Dean of Dromore; *b* 30 July 1852; *y s* of late Bryan O'Loughlin, of Carrigview, Co. Limerick, and Elizabeth, *d* of late George Smith, of Brisna, Co.

Limerick; *m* Florence Marie, *d* of late Hon. J. Burrowes, of New Orleans, USA; three *d*. *Educ:* Diocesan School, Limerick; Trinity College, Dublin. *Publications:* The Glory of God, and other Sermons; The Crisis in the Church of England; pamphlets on the Baptismal Controversy; The Priesthood of the Laity; The Doctrines of the Plymouth Brethren; and on other ecclesiastical and religious subjects. *Address:* Lurgan.

Died Feb. 1925.

OLPHERT, Sir John, Kt 1902; CVO 1903; DL; Gentleman Usher to three Lords Lieutenant of Ireland; HM Lieutenant County Donegal; *b* 2 Sept. 1844; *e s* of late Wybrants Olphert of Ballyconnel House, JP and DL; *m* 1869, Frances Susan, *o d* of late Robert Burrowes, MP; one *d*. *Address:* Ballyconnel House, Falcarragh, Co. Donegal.

Died 11 March 1917.

OLSEN, Dr Björn Magnusson; Professor of Icelandic Philology in the University, Reykjavik, Iceland; *b* 14 July 1850. *Address:* Reykjavik, Iceland.

Died 16 Jan. 1919.

O'MALLEY, Col William Arthur D'Oyly, CB 1909; Indian Army; *b* 6 Jan. 1853; *s* of William O'Malley; *m* 1885, Violet Eliza Caroline, *d* of Skipwith Henry Churchill Tayler, ICS. Entered Army, 108th Foot, 1873; Bengal Staff Corps, 1877; Captain, ISC, 1885; Major, 1893; Lt-Col, Indian Army, 1899; Brevet-Col 1903; served Mahsood Wuzuree Expedition, 1881 (despatches); Jakht-i-Suleiman Expedition, 1883 (despatches); Zhob Valley Expedition, 1890; Waziristan, 1894–95 (despatches, brevet Lt-Col, medal with clasp); NW Frontier, India, 1897–98 (medal with clasp); also 1902. *Address:* High View, Kintbury, Berks. *Club:* New, Cheltenham.

Died 3 April 1925.

O'MARA, Joseph; operatic tenor; managing director and principal tenor of The O'Mara Opera Co., Ltd; *b* Limerick, 1866; *y s* of James O'Mara; *m* 1896, *o d* of M. J. Power, late of Waterford. *Educ:* Jesuit College, Limerick. Made first appearance in public in opera Ivanhoe, 1891; continued there till close of Royal English Opera House; engaged in 1893 by Sir Augustus Harris, and was retained by him for three years, singing at Drury Lane and Covent Garden as principal tenor in all the grand operas; sang at all the principal concerts in London and the provinces; toured three years in USA. *Recreations:* cycling, yachting, tennis. *Club:* Savage.

Died 5 Aug. 1927.

O'MEARA, Capt. Bulkeley Ernest Adolphus, DSO 1900; Kimberley Town Guard; transferred to Intelligence Department, 1900; *b* Umballa, India, 1 Feb. 1867; *s* of late Alfred O'Meara, St Mark's, Simla, India; *m* 1899, Edith, *e d* of William and Anna Hines. *Educ:* Dulwich College; King's College School, Somerset House, London. Served as trooper in original Pioneer Force which annexed Rhodesia to the British Empire, 1889–91; Surveyor in De Beers Consolidated Mines, Ltd, Kimberley; served in South African War, 1899–1901, in Kimberley Town Guard; Intelligence Officer for Griqualand West, as far as Mafeking; Staff Officer Intelligence to Vryburg and Carnarvon Columns; Press Censor and Interpreter and Intelligence Officer at Oudtshoorn, under Acting Inspector-General Western (despatches four times); Govt Surveyor Cape and Transvaal Colonies, practising at Johannesburg. *Decorated* for Siege of Kimberley. *Recreations:* took part in all kinds of South African sports, including big game shooting in north. *Club:* Rand, Johannesburg.

Died 31 Aug. 1916.

O'MEARA, Lt-Col Charles Albert Edmond, CIE 1917; Indian Army, retired; *b* 7 Aug. 1868. 2nd Lieut East Lancs Regt, 1891; Capt. Indian Army, 1891; Major, 1901; Lt-Col 1911; Director and Superintendent, Army Clothing Dept, India, 1910; retired, 1922. *Club:* Junior Naval and Military.

Died 20 Jan. 1923.

O'MEARA, Stephen, LLD Hon.; Police Commissioner, City of Boston; editor and publisher Boston Journal, 1896–1902; *b* Charlotte-town, PEI, 26 July 1854; *m* 1878, Isabella M. Squire; three *d*. *Educ:* Boston Public Schools. Reporter, Boston Journal, 1872–79; city editor, 1879–81; managing editor, 1881–91; general manager; 1891–96; Hon. degree of AM from Dartmouth College, 1889. *Address:* 585 Beacon Street, Boston, Mass, USA. *Clubs:* Algonquin, Exchange, Press, Union, Boston.

Died 14 Dec. 1918.

OMMANNEY, Sir Montagu Frederick, GCMG 1904 (KCMG 1890; CMG 1882); KCB 1901; ISO 1903; King of Arms, Order of St Michael and St George, 1908, Secretary, 1900; Director British North Borneo Co. since 1910; Hon. Treasurer Royal Colonial

Institute, 1888–1912; a Vice-President of the Institute since 1912; b 4 April 1842; s of Francis Ommanney, Worcester Park, Surrey, and Julia, d of Thomas Metcalfe; m 1st, 1867, Charlotte Helen (d 1913), d of O. Ommanney; three s four d; 2nd, 1914, Winifred Rose, d of C. Harris St John of West Court, Finchampstead. Educ: Cheltenham; Woolwich. Entered Royal Engineers, 1864; Captain, 1878; Crown Agent for Colonies, 1877–1900; Permanent Under-Secretary of State for Colonies, 1900–7; late Director of London Assurance Co.

Died 19 Aug. 1925.

O'MORCHOE, Rev. Thomas Arthur, MA; otherwise The O'Morchoe, or chief of his Sept of Oulartleigh, Co. Wexford; Rector of Kilternan Parish, Diocese of Dublin, since 1894; b 22 March 1865; e s of Arthur MacMurrogh Murphy (who was The O'Morchoe (d 1918)) of Oulartleigh, Co. Wexford, and Susan Elizabeth, e d of Thomas Bradley, MD, of Kells Grange, Co. Kilkenny, and Sophia, d of Robert Wolfe of Tentower, Queen's Co.; m 1891, Anne, d of John George Gibbon, LLD, BL, of Kiltennell, Co. Wexford; four s three d. Educ: Trinity College, Dublin. Member of the Royal Dublin Society, and Royal Society of Antiquaries of Ireland; Member of Dublin County Committee of Agriculture and Technical Instruction, from foundation to 1920, and Board of Education of the General Synod of the Church of Ireland, 1906–11; late Editor of the Dublin University Missionary Magazine; engaged in historical research, and in particular the origins of Celtic history. Owned property in Co. Wexford. Publications: The Evidential Value of the Resurrection; articles on Reorganisation of Missionary Methods; A Register of Clerical Societies; The Chiefs of Ireland. Heir: e s Capt. Arthur Donel MacMurrogh O'Morchoe [b 3 June 1892. Educ: Trinity Coll., Dublin]. Address: The Rectory, Kilternan, Co. Dublin. T: Foxrock, 1x1. *Died 1921.*

O'NEILL, 2nd Baron, cr 1868; **Edward O'Neill**, JP, DL; b 31 Dec. 1839; s of 1st Baron and 1st wife, Henrietta, d of late Hon. Robert Torrens, Judge of Common Pleas, Ireland; S father, 1883; m 1873, Lady Louisa Katherine Emma Cochrane, d of 11th Earl of Dundonald; one s three d (and two s decd). Educ: Trinity College, Cambridge. MP (C) Co. Antrim, 1863–80. Heir: g s Shane Edward Robert O'Neill [b 6 Feb. 1907; s of late Hon. Arthur Edward Bruce O'Neill (e s of 2nd Baron), and Lady Annabel Hungerford Crew-Milnes, e d of 1st Marquess of Crewe (she m 2nd, Major James Hugh Hamilton Dodds]. Address: 12 Queen's Gate, SW7. T: Western 210; Shane's Castle, Antrim, Ireland. Club: Carlton.

Died 19 Nov. 1928.

O'NEILL, Charles, JP Lanarks; MP (N) South Armagh since 1909; Assistant Professor of Botany, St Mungo's College, 1897–99; b 1849; s of Hugh O'Neill, Glenravel, Co. Antrim; m 1874, Margaret, d of Michael McKillop, Airdrie. Educ: Glasgow University (MB and CM). Member of Coatbridge Town Council, Airdrie and Coatbridge Water Trust, etc; Senior Magistrate of Coatbridge; was elected three times for same Parliamentary constituency in one year (a unique circumstance); the only surviving Nationalist in Parliament associated with Isaac Butt at inception of Home Rule movement; contested S Armagh, 1900. Address: Glenravel House, Coatbridge. Clubs: National Liberal, Irish. *Died 1 Jan. 1918.*

O'NIAL, Surg.-Gen. John, CB 1881; LRCSI; retired, 1887; b 1827. Asst-Surgeon, 1852; Surgeon, 1859; Surgeon-Major, 1872; Surgeon-General, 1885; served Kaffir War, 1852–53 (medal); Afghan War as PMO (despatches, medal with clasp); Nile, 1884–85 (despatches, promoted, medal with clasp, Khedive's star); Soudan, 1885–86. Club: Naval and Military. *Died 1 Sept. 1919.*

ONIONS, Alfred, JP; MP (Lab) Caerphilly Division of Glamorganshire since 1919; Alderman Monmouthshire County Council, 1919; General Treasurer for South Wales Miners' Federation; Member of the Parliamentary Committee Trade Union Congress; b St George's, Salop, 30 Oct. 1858; s of Jabez Onions, miner; m 1887, S. A. Dix, d of a miner; two s one d. Educ: St George's Church School. Checkweigher Abercarn Colliery, 1887; Member of Mynyddyslwyn School Board, 1888; Bedwellty School Board, 1899; first Chairman of Risca Urban District Council; Member of Monmouthshire County Council 13 years. Address: Melrose Villa, Tredegar, Monmouthshire. T: Tredegar 7. *Died 6 July 1921.*

ONNES, Prof. (Heike) Kamerlingh, PhD, DSc; Emeritus Professor of Physics and Director of the Physical Laboratory, Leyden; b Groningen, 21 Sept. 1853. Liquefied helium; discovered the possibility of perpetual electric current through metals at certain temperatures; Foreign Member Royal Societies of London, Dublin, Edinburgh; Hon. Member Royal Institute of Great Britain, Chemical

Society; Nobel Prize for Physics, 1913. Address: Haagweg 19, Leyden, Holland. *Died 21 Feb. 1926.*

ONSLOW, Maj.-Gen. George Thorp, CB 1902; Royal Marine Light Infantry; b 17 July 1858; s of late Major Pitcairn Onslow, RM, of Dunsborough, Ripley, Surrey, and Adelaide, o d of Capt. Saltren Willett; m 1887, Ethel Paul, d of Rev. David Kitcat, Weston-Birt, Gloucestershire; two d. Educ: Clifton Coll.; Wellington College. Entered Royal Marines, 1875; Captain, 1884; Major, 1892; Lieut-Col, 1898; Colonel, 1902; Col Commandant, 1906–9; Colonel on Reserved List, 1909; Maj.-Gen. Retired List, 1919; served Soudan, 1884–85 (medal, two clasps, star); South Africa, 1900 (medal, CB); Inspector of Marine Recruiting, 1900–5. Address: 1 Iverna Gardens, Kensington, W8. Club: United Service.

Died 14 June 1921.

ONSLOW, Sir William Wallace Rhoderic, 5th Bt, cr 1797; DL, JP; Lieutenant 12th Regiment (retired); b Simla, 13 Aug. 1845; s of Sir Matthew Richard Onslow, 4th Bt, and 1st wife, Eliza Antonia, d of Gen. William Wallace; S father, 1876; m 1873, Octavia Katherine, d of Sir Arthur Knox-Gore, 1st Bt; two s three d (and two s decd). Educ: Marlborough. Entered 12th Regt 1864; Capt. 3rd Batt. Duke of Cornwall's Light Infantry, 1875–82. Owned about 10,000 acres. Heir: s Roger Warin Beaconsfield Onslow, late Lieut Suffolk Regt [b 29 April 1880; m 1905, Mildred, e d of Sir Robert Rodney Wilmot, 6th Bt; one s]. Address: Hengar, St Tudy, RSO, Cornwall. Clubs: Carlton, Naval and Military.

Died 13 Jan. 1916.

OPENSHAW, Mary; see Binstead, M.

OPPENHEIM, Lassa Francis Lawrence, MA, LLD; Whewell Professor of International Law in the University of Cambridge since 1908; Editor of the Series, Contributions to International Law and Diplomacy; b Germany, 30 March 1858; s of Aaron Oppenheim, Frankfort-on-Main; naturalised in England, 1900; m 1902, Elizabeth Alexandra, d of Lt-Col Phineas Cowan; one d. Educ: Lycée, Frankfort-on-Main; Universities of Göttingen, Heidelberg, Berlin, Leipzig. Lecturer in the Univ. of Freiburg (Baden), 1886; Extraordinary-professor, 1889; Professor in the University of Basle, 1891; Lecturer at the London School of Economics and Political Science (University of London), 1895; Associate of the Institute of International Law, 1908, Member, 1911; Hon. Member Real Academia de Jurisprudencia, Madrid; Corresponding Member of the American Institute of International Law. Publications: Die Rechtsbeugungsverbrechen, 1886; Zur Lehre von der Untersuchungshaft, 1888; Die Nebenklage, 1889; Das ärztliche Recht zu körperlichen Eingriffen an Kranken und Gesunden, 1892; Die Objekte des Verbrechens, 1894; Gerechtigkeit und Gesetz, 1895; Das Gewissen, 1898; International Law: a treatise, vol. i Peace, 1905, second edn, 1912; vol. ii War, 1906, second edn, 1912; The Science of International Law, 1908; International Incidents for discussion in Conversation Classes, 1909, second edn, 1911; The Future of International Law, 1911; The Panama Canal Conflict, 1913; The Collected Papers of John Westlake on Public International Law, 1914. Address: Trinity College, or Whewell House, 62 Grange Road, Cambridge. T: Cambridge 753. Club: Reform.

Died 7 Oct. 1919.

OPPENHEIM, Lt-Col Lawrie Charles Frith, CMG 1918; b 1871; s of Charles Oppenheim, 40 Great Cumberland Place, W, and Isabelle, d of W. P. Frith, RA; m 1908, Mary, d of J. Monteith of Carstairs, Lanark; one s. Educ: Harrow; Trinity College, Cambridge (BA). Served with Tirah Field Force, 1897–98; attached Northampton Regiment and present at actions of Dargai, Maidan, etc; Nile Expeditionary Force, 1898, present at Battle of Khartoum (medal with clasp); South African War, 1899–1902, with Thorney croft's Mounted Infantry and Scottish Horse (Queen's medal with seven clasps, King's medal with two clasps); joined Queen's Bays, 1900; specially employed, 1904–9, under War Office and Committee of Imperial Defence in compilation of Official History of South African War; attached 2nd Battalion Highland Light Infantry, 1914; Military Attaché, The Hague, Jan. 1915–April 1920; Military Attaché, British Legation, Berne, 1920–22; British Military Representative on Permanent Advisory Commission of League of Nations, Geneva, since 1922 (Brevet-Major, CMG, Bt Lt-Col, Chevalier Order of St Vladimir, Commander Order of Orange Nassau, Officier de l'Ordre de Léopold, Commander of the Portuguese Order of Aviz). Address: 40 Great Cumberland Place, W. Club: Brooks's.

Died July 1923.

OPPENHEIMER, Sir Bernard, 1st Bt, cr 1921; Chairman and Permanent Director South African Diamond Corporation, Ltd;

Chairman of London Committee and Permanent Director Pniels, Ltd; Chairman New Vaal River Diamond and Exploration Co., and of Kryn & Laby Metal Works, Ltd; Director of Blaauwbosch Diamonds, Ltd; *b* 13 Feb. 1866; *s* of Edward Oppenheimer; *m* 1890, Lena, *y d* of late Michael Straus; one *s* two *d*. Founded diamond-cutting factories for disabled soldiers at Brighton, Cambridge, Fort William and Wrexham. *Recreations:* farming, raising pedigree stock. *Heir: s* Michael Oppenheimer [*b* 26 Dec. 1892; *m* 1920, Caroline Magdalen, *d* of Sir Robert Grenville Harvey, 2nd and last Bt]. *Address:* 36 Curzon Street, W1. *T:* Gerrard 8337; Sefton Park, Stoke Poges, Bucks; Kimberley, S Africa.

Died 13 June 1921.

ORANGE, George James, CBE 1920; Managing Director since 1912 of Spottiswoode, Dixon & Hunting, Ltd, Regent House, Kingsway, WC, Advertising Agents and Consultants; *b* Chester, 1871; *e s* of late John G. Graves Orange of that city; *m* 1913, Viola Audrey, *d* of Walter Stanleigh Phillips, Beauchamps, Rochford, Essex; two *s* one *d*. Formerly assistant editor and leader writer Galignani Messenger, Paris; first Managing Director, Educational Book Co. Ltd, 1908–12; Joint Hon. Organiser Official Agents, National War Savings Committee, 1917–18; Hon. Director of activities, Chambers of Commerce, Chambers of Trade, Chambers of Agriculture and kindred organisations, Victory Loan Campaign, 1919; for some years a Member of the Institute of Journalists; Past President, Thirty Club of London; Past President, Athenæum Debating Society, Manchester; one of the founders, Aldwych Club; travelled extensively in America and Canada. *Recreation:* golf. *Address:* 57 Nassau Road, Barnes, SW. *T:* Hammersmith 1512. *Clubs:* Authors', Aldwych.

Died 16 March 1925.

ORANGE, William, CB 1886; MD, FRCP; retired civil servant; *b* Newcastle-on-Tyne, 1833; *s* of Rev. John Orange; *m* 1864, Florence Elizabeth (*d* 1913), *d* of Thomas Ingleman Hart, Sevenoaks. *Educ:* St Thomas's Hospital Medical School. Assistant Medical Officer Surrey County Lunatic Asylum, 1859–62; Deputy-Superintendent of Broadmoor Asylum at the date of its opening in 1862; Superintendent thereof, 1870–86; member of the Council of Supervision thereof, 1891–1904. *Decorated* for service at Broadmoor under the Home Office. *Publications:* sundry articles bearing upon insanity associated with crime. *Address:* 11 Marina Court, Bexhill-on-Sea, Sussex. *Died 31 Dec. 1916.*

ORANMORE and BROWNE, 3rd Baron (Ireland), *cr* 1836; 1st Baron Mereworth, of Mereworth Castle (UK), *cr* 1926; **Geoffrey Henry Browne Browne,** KP 1918; PC Ireland 1921; DL; JP; a Member of the Irish Convention, 1917–18; appointed a Commissioner of Congested Districts Board, 1919; elected a Senator for Southern Ireland, 1921; a Representative Peer for Ireland; *b* 6 Jan. 1861; *o s* of 2nd Baron and Christina, *d* of Alexander Guthrie of the Mount and Bourtree Hill, Ayrshire; *S* father, 1900; *m* 1901, Lady Olwen Verena Ponsonby, Lady of Grace of St John of Jerusalem, *e d* of 8th Earl of Bessborough; two *s* one *d* (and one *d* decd). *Educ:* Trinity College, Cambridge (MA). Knight of Grace of St John of Jerusalem; Grand Officer of Order of Crown of Roumania. Owned about 8,000 acres. *Heir: s* Hon. Dominick Geoffrey Edward Browne [*b* 21 Oct. 1901; *m* 1925, Mildred Helen, *e d* of Hon. Thomas Egerton; one *d*]. *Address:* 21 Portland Place, W1. *T:* Langham 1012; Mereworth Castle, Kent. *T:* Wateringbury 43; Castle MacGarrett, Claremorris, Co. Mayo. *Clubs:* Bachelors', Carlton.

Died 30 June 1927.

ORDISH, Thomas Fairman, FSA; *b* 1855; 2nd *s* of late Thomas Ordish, London, and Sarah, *e d* of late Fairman and Berthalina Mann, Attleborough, Norfolk; *m* 1880, Ada, *d* of late John Lamacraft, London; one *d*. *Educ:* privately; influenced by the late W. F. Ainsworth, FSA. Editor of the Antiquary, 1888–90; of The Bookworm, 1888; of the Camden Library, 1891–93; of the London Topographical Record, 1901–6; Communications on Folk-Drama, Folk-Lore Society, 1891–93; Chairman, Entertainment Committee Folk-Lore Congress, 1891; Organised London Topographical Society, 1898; Vice-President, 1906; Founded London Shakespeare Commemoration League, 1902; Director of Commemoration, 1903; Lectures on Shakespeare and London, 1903–14, *passim*. *Publications:* Early London Theatres, 1894; Shakespeare's London, 1897, 2nd edn, enlarged, 1904; contributed to Colbourn's New Monthly Magazine, 1874–77; Contributions to The Antiquary since 1880, including series on London Theatres and on Early English Inventions, 1885–87; to The Bibliographer, 1882; to The Bookworm, 1888; to Book-Song, 1893; on Improvement of Westminster to Cornhill Magazine, 1904; History of London Traffic to the Report of the Royal Commission on London Traffic, 1905; Chapter on Elizabethan London to London

vols of Memorials of Counties, 1908; Government and Extension of Washington, USA, and History of Metropolitan Roads to Reports of the London Traffic Branch of the Board of Trade, 1908, 1910; Roads out of London, edited from Ogilby's Survey for London Topographical Society, 1913; London as seen by Shakespeare; William Blake and London, Lond. Topog. Record, vols v, ix; on Keats and London, to the John Keats Memorial Volume, 1921. *Recreations:* gardening, conducting rambles in Old London. *Address:* Langdale, Cecil Park, Herne Bay, Kent.

Died 5 Dec. 1924.

O'REILLY, Rt. Rev. James; Parish Priest of St Joseph's, Penarth; Dean of St Illtyd's Conference and Vicar-General of the Archdiocese of Cardiff; *b* Tenode, Westmeath, Ireland, 10 June 1856. *Educ:* St Bernard's Grammar School, Granard; All Hallows College, Dublin. Priest, 1879; Assistant Priest, Swansea, 1879; Merthyr, 1881; Dowlais, 1881; took charge of the United Missions of Aberdare and Mountain Ash, 1882; resided in the former town for the next 28 years; Vicar General of the Diocese of Newport, 1911; Vicar Capitular and Domestic Prelate to Pope Benedict XV. *Recreation:* golf. *Address:* St Joseph's, Penarth, Glamorgan. *TA:* Penarth. *T:* Penarth 247.

Died 23 March 1928.

O'RIORDAN, Rt. Rev. Mgr. Michael, DPh, DD, DCL; Rector of the Irish College, Rome, since 1905; named Protonotary Apostolic by Pius X, 1907; *b* Co. Limerick, Ireland, 1857. *Educ:* The Irish College; The Propaganda and The Gregorian University, Rome. Ordained priest, 1883. *Publications:* A Criticism of Draper's History of the Conflict of Religion and Science; Life of St Columbanus, and of other Irish Saints in Italy; A Reply to Dr Starkie's attack on the Managers of Irish National Schools; Catholicity and Progress in Ireland; numerous articles in American, English, Italian and Irish Reviews. *Address:* Irish College, Rome.

Died 27 Aug. 1919.

ORLEANS, Duc d'; Louis Philippe Robert; Head of the Bourbon-Orléans House; *b* York House, Twickenham, 6 Feb. 1869; *e s* of late Comte de Paris, and *nephew* of Duc de Chartres; *m* 1896, Archduchess Maria Dorothea of Austria (*b* 14 June 1867). *Educ:* Municipal College, England; Collège Stanislas, France. Exiled from France, 1886; received commission 60th Rifles; served in India, 1888–89; went to Paris, but again expelled. *Address:* Anjou, near Brussels.

Died 28 March 1926.

ORMATHWAITE, 2nd Baron, *cr* 1868; **Arthur Walsh,** JP; Bt 1804; Captain 1st Life Guards, retired 1855; Hon. Colonel 3rd Battalion South Wales Borderers, since 1876; *b* 14 April 1827; *s* of 1st Baron and Lady Jane Grey, *y d* of 6th Earl of Stamford and Warrington; *S* father, 1881; *m* 1858, Lady Katherine Emily Mary Somerset (*d* 1914), *d* of 7th Duke of Beaufort, KG; five *s* three *d* (and two *s* decd). *Educ:* Eton; Trinity Coll., Cambridge. Entered Army, 1847; Lord-Lieut for Radnorshire, 1875–95; MP (C) Leominster, 1865–67; Radnorshire, 1868–80. Owned about 26,300 acres. *Heir: s* Hon. Sir Arthur Henry John Walsh [*b* 10 April 1859; *m* 1890, Lady Clementine Frances Anne Pratt, *o d* of 3rd Marquis Camden]. *Address:* Strettington House, Chichester. *Club:* Carlton.

Died 27 March 1920.

ORMEROD, Joseph Arderne, MA, MD Oxford; FRCP; Registrar Royal College of Physicians, London, since 1909; Consulting Physician to St Bartholomew's Hospital; Consulting Physician to National Hospital for Paralysed and Epileptic, Queen Square; *b* 7 April 1848; *e surv. s* of Ven. T. J. Ormerod (*e s* of George Ormerod, DCL, FRS, historian of Cheshire), Archdeacon of Suffolk, of Sedbury Park, Gloucestershire, and Tyldesley, Lancashire, and Maria, *e d* of Sir Joseph Bailey, 1st Bt, of Glanusk Park; *m* Mary Ellen, 3rd *d* of Edward Milner, FLS, of Dulwich Wood, Norwood; four *s* four *d*. *Educ:* Rugby; Oxford; St Bartholomew's Hospital. Scholar of CCC; Fellow of Jesus Coll., Oxford; Chancellor's Prizeman Latin Verse; 1st Class Classical Moderations, 2nd Class Literæ Humaniores, 1st Class Natural Science. Formerly Medical Registrar and Demonstrator of Morbid Anatomy to St Bartholomew's Hospital; Physician to the City of London Chest Hospital, Victoria Park; Physician to the King George Hospital, Stamford Street, SE; Examiner in Medicine to the University of Oxford, and to the Conjoint Board of RCP and RCS; Harveian Orator, Royal College of Physicians, 1908; Lumleian Lecturer, Royal College of Physicians, 1914; President of Neurological Section of the Royal Society of Medicine. *Publications:* articles in Clifford Allbutt's System of Medicine; and other contributions to medical literature, chiefly concerning diseases of the nervous system. *Address:* 25 Upper Wimpole Street, W1. *T:* Paddington 1772; Greenhill, Upham, Hants. *Club:* Athenæum.

Died 5 March 1925.

ORMONDE, 3rd Marquess of, *cr* 1825; **James Edward William Theobald Butler,** KP 1888; PC 1902; Earl of Ormonde, 1328; Viscount Thurles, 1525; Earl of Ossory, 1526; Baron Arklow, Baron Ormonde (UK), 1821; 27th Hereditary Chief Butler of Ireland; HM's Lieutenant of Kilkenny since 1878; Vice-Admiral of Leinster; Hon. Colonel 5th Battalion Royal Irish Regiment; *b* Kilkenny Castle, 5 Oct. 1844; *s* of 2nd Marquess and Frances Jane, *e d* of Hon. Sir Edward Paget, GCB, and 2nd wife, Lady Harriet, *d* of 3rd Earl of Dartmouth; *S* father, 1854; *m* 1876, Lady Elizabeth Harriet Grosvenor, *e d* of 1st Duke of Westminster, KG; two *d*. Unionist. *Educ:* Harrow. Joined 1st Life Guards, 1863; retired as Captain, 1873; commanded Royal East Kent Yeomanry, 1883–94; First Class Crown of Prussia. Owned in Ireland about 24,000 acres; in England about 2,500; and a picture gallery, Kilkenny Castle. *Recreation:* yachting. *Heir: b* Lord Arthur James Wellington Foley Butler [*b* 23 Sept. 1849; *m* 1887, Ellen, *d* of Gen. Anson Stager, US Army; two *s* two *d*]. *Address:* Kilkenny Castle; 32 Upper Brook Street, W1. *T:* Mayfair 4236; Ballyknockane Lodge, Clonmel. *Clubs:* Carlton, Cavalry; Royal Yacht Squadron, Cowes (Commodore); Kildare Street, Royal Irish, Royal St George's, Dublin.   *Died 26 Oct. 1919.*

ORMROD, Peter; late Major in 6th West Riding Regiment and Lieutenant-Colonel 2/4th Loyal North Lancashire Regiment; *b* 1869; *e s* of late James Cross Ormrod and Edith, *d* of John Hargreaves of Sillwood Park, Berkshire; *m* 1895, Gertrude Rose, *d* of John George Lyon of Pontefract; two *s* three *d*. Was Capt. 3rd Batt. Loyal North Lancashire Regiment; Lord of the Manor of Nether Wyresdale. *Address:* Picket Post, Ringwood, Hants.

Died 23 Oct. 1923.

ORMSBY, Rt. Rev. George Albert, DD; Archdeacon of Lindisfarne since 1914; Hon. Canon, St Nicholas Cathedral, Newcastle-on-Tyne; Examining Chaplain to the Bishop of Newcastle, 1914; Vicar of Eglingham, 1912; *b* Dublin, 16 Sept. 1843; *s* of late Rt Hon. Henry Ormsby, Chancery Judge of High Court of Justice in Ireland, and Julia, *d* of late Henry Hamilton, Tullyish House, Co. Down, Ireland; *m* 1871, Ellie, *d* of late Canon Scott, Vicar of New Seaham, Durham; six *s* two *d*. *Educ:* Trinity College, Dublin. BA 1865; Divinity testimonium, 1st Class, 1866; Prizeman in Hebrew, Syriac, and Chaldee, 1864–66; MA 1868; BD and DD *Jure Dignitatis*, 1893; *Ad eundem*, MA Durham, 1877; FRCI 1895. Curate of Eglingham, Northumberland, 1866–69; Rector of Jarrow, 1869–75; of Rainton, 1875–85; Vicar of St Stephen's, Walworth, London, 1885–93; chaplain to the Duke of Manchester, 1869–91; Lecturer in St Swithin's, London Stone, 1890–93; organising secretary for CETS, diocese of Rochester, 1889–93; Bishop of Honduras and Central America, 1893–1907; President of the YMCA, Paris Branch, 1909–12; Chaplain of British Embassy Church, Paris, 1907–12; Rural Dean of Glendale, 1912–14; Assistant Bishop in the Diocese of Newcastle, 1912–15; sub-prelate, Order of St John of Jerusalem in England, 1903. *Address:* Eglingham Vicarage, Alnwick, Northumberland. *Club:* National.   *Died 14 Feb. 1924.*

ORMSBY, Sir Lambert Hepenstal, Kt 1903; JP, DL, Co. Dublin; BA, MD, MB Dublin University; LRCPI; FRCSI; Colonel and Hon. Consulting Surgeon, New Zealand Expeditionary Force, 1915; *b* Onehunga Lodge, Auckland, New Zealand, 19 July 1850; *o s* of George Owen Ormsby, CE, Surveyor-General of the Colony of New Zealand; *m* 1st, 1874, Anastatia (*d* 1911), *o d* of John Dickinson; one *s* one *d*; 2nd, 1921, Geraldine, OBE, RRC, *o d* of William Mathews Hyerès, France. *Educ:* Grammar School, Auckland, NZ; Royal School, Dungannon; TCD and RCSI. Articled apprentice to the late Sir George Porter, 1st Bt, MD, FRCS; studied at the Meath Hospital and School of the Royal College of Surgeons in Ireland; late Senior Demonstrator and Surgical Teacher, Examiner in Surgery, RCSI; President, RCSI, 1902–4; Secretary, 1921; Member of the Senate, University of Dublin; Fellow and Member of the Council of the Royal College of Surgeons; late Representative of the College on General Medical Council; Senior Surgeon of the Meath Hospital and County Dublin Infirmary; Senior Surgeon National Children's Hospital; Consulting Surgeon to the Drummond Military School, Bray, Co. Wicklow; Hon. Consulting Surgeon to the Dublin Branch of the Institute of Journalists; Fellow of the Royal Medico-Chirurgical Society of London; Fellow of the Royal Academy of Medicine, Ireland; Chairman of the Board of Superintendence of Dublin Hospitals, and Governor of the Lock Government Hospital; was formerly Surgeon to the Royal Longford Rifles; Chairman of the Association for the Housing of the Very Poor, Dublin; Founder of the Dublin Red Cross Order of Nursing Sisters; inventor of Ormsby's Ether Inhaler; Pile Clamp; New Form of Rectal Speculum; Aseptic Glass Drainage-tube; New Form of Chest Bandage. *Publications:* Deformities of the Human Body; Medical History of the Meath

Hospital and County Dublin Infirmary; Surgical Operation Chart; Red Cross Nursing Chart; Lectures on Surgical Emergencies; Lectures on the Causes, Symptoms, and Treatment of Varicose Veins; Lectures on the Diseases of the Rectum; The Study of Diseases peculiar to Children. *Address:* 92 Merrion Square, Dublin. *TA:* Ormsby, Merrion Square, Dublin. *T:* 1088. *Clubs:* Constitutional; United Service, Dublin. *M:* RI 1296, RI 4163.   *Died 21 Dec. 1923.*

ORMSBY, Lt-Col Vincent Alexander, CB 1915; 3rd Queen Alexandra's Own (Gurkha Rifles); Indian Army; *b* 17 July 1865. Entered army, 1885; Captain Indian Army, 1896; Major, 1903; Lt-Col 1910; served NW Frontier, India, 1897–98 (medal, 2 clasps); Tirah, 1897–98 (clasp); European War, 1914–15 (CB).

Died 2 May 1917.

ORNSTEIN, John Isidore Maurice, CMG 1882; *b* 1854; *s* of Maurice Ornstein. Late Dep. Director General Customs; acting Under Secretary of State and Assistant Financial Adviser, Egypt (1st class Medjidie, 2nd class Osmanieh). *Address:* 1 Rue de Courcelles, Paris. *Club:* St James's.   *Died 22 April 1919.*

O'RORKE, Rev. Benjamin Garniss, DSO 1917; MA; Chaplain to the Forces since 1901; *b* 1875; *s* of W. J. O'Rorke, Nottingham; *m* Myra Roberta, *d* of late Rev. H. Mac-Dougall, Rector of St Michael's, Stamford, sometime Chaplain to the Forces; three *d*. *Educ:* Nottingham High School; Exeter College, Oxford; Wycliffe Hall, Oxford. Ordained, 1898; Curate of St Peter's, Tiverton, 1898–1901; served S African Campaign, 1901–2; Bloemfontein, 1901–5; Aldershot, 1902–4; Pretoria, 1905–9; Bordon Camp, 1909–14; Hon. Sec. Army Missionary Association, 1910–14; Commissary to the Bishop of Accra since 1913; went out with British Expeditionary Force, Aug. 1914; captured by the Germans during retreat from Mons; prisoner for ten months; returned to France, 1915 (despatches, DSO). *Publications:* African Missions, 1912; Our Opportunity in the West Indies, 1913; In the Hands of the Enemy, 1915; The Three Heroes, 1916. *Address:* c/o Sir Charles M'Grigor, Bt, & Co., 39 Panton Street, SW1.   *Died 25 Dec. 1918.*

O'RORKE, Hon. Sir (George) Maurice, Kt 1880; Speaker of House of Representatives, New Zealand; Member of Legislative Council since 1904; *b* 1830; *s* of Rev. John O'Rorke, Moylough, Co. Galway, and Elizabeth Dennis; *m* 1858, Cecilia Mary, *d* of late Alexander Shepherd (first Colonial Treasurer of New Zealand, 1842–56), of Auckland; one *s*. *Educ:* Trin. College, Dublin (BA 1852, MA and Hon. LLD 1896). Barrister Auckland, 1868; Member of House of Representatives; eight times elected Speaker of House of Representatives, 1862–92; Speaker of Auckland Provincial Council, 1865–76, and member of New Zealand Ministry, 1872–74; Member of the Senate of New Zealand University; Chairman of Council of Auckland University College, Auckland Grammar School Board. *Address:* Onehunga, Auckland, N Zealand.

Died 24 Aug. 1916.

ORPEN, His Honour Richard Theodore; Chief Justice of Barbados since 1925; *b* 13 Oct. 1869; *e s* of Right Rev. Raymond d'Audemar Orpen, DD (*y s* of Sir Richard Orpen of Ardtully, Kenmare, Ireland), formerly Archdeacon of Ardfert and Bishop of Limerick, and Sarah Lucinda, *d* of Daniel de Courcey MacGillycuddy, JP, of Tralee, Co. Kerry; *m* 1909, Victoria Maud, *d* of Alfred Henshaw, JP, of St Philips, Milltoun, Co. Dublin; no *c*. *Educ:* privately; Trinity College, Dublin. Science Scholar Moderator; BA with honours in Mathematics and Experimental Science. Called to the Bar, King's Inns, Dublin, 1898; Police Magistrate, Southern Nigeria, Aug. 1903; Acting Attorney-General, Aug. 1903–Jan. 1904; Acting Solicitor-General for various periods, 1905–10; Acting Puisne Judge, June–August 1905, June–July 1908, Sept.–Dec. 1909; Resident Magistrate, Jamaica, June 1910; Acting Judge, Kingston Court, June 1920–Feb. 1921; Acting Puisne Judge, Feb.–Aug. 1921, Nov. 1922–Sept. 1923, March–Aug. 1924, and Feb.–May 1925; Judge, Kingston Court, Dec. 1921. *Recreation:* golf. *Address:* Bridgetown, Barbados, BWI.

Died 1926.

ORR, His Honour James, KC; Chairman of Quarter Sessions and County Court Judge of Down since 1897; *b* Ballymena, Co. Antrim, 27 Oct. 1841; *e s* of late William Orr and Mary, *d* of late Robert Harrison; *m* Annie Disney, *d* of late Alexander Davison; four *s* one *d*. *Educ:* Bromsgrove Grammar School, Worcestershire; Jesus Coll., Cambridge (scholar). 2nd class Classical Tripos, 1864; MA. Irish Barrister 1867; QC Trinity, 1884; appointed County Court Judge of Monaghan and Fermanagh, June 1891. *Address:* 37 Upper Mount Street, Dublin. *Club:* University, Dublin.

Died 19 Jan. 1920.

ORR, Maj.-Gen. John William; Indian Army; *b* 7 Dec. 1829; *m* Charlotte (*d* 1910), *y d* of late Lt-Col Cubitt, RA, of Catfield, Norfolk. Entered army, 1850; Maj.-Gen. 1890; unemployed list, 1888; served Burmese War, 1852–53 (medal); late Mutiny, 1858–59 (medal with clasp). *Address:* 1 Merchiston Crescent, Edinburgh.
Died 1 April 1916.

ORR, Major Michael Harrison, DSO 1902; late 1st Alexandra, Princess of Wales' Own (Yorkshire Regt); *b* Ballymena, Co. Antrim, 23 Dec. 1859; *s* of late William Orr of Hugomont, Ballymena, Co. Antrim; unmarried. *Educ:* Trinity College, Stratford-on-Avon; Royal Military College, Sandhurst. Joined 19th Regt, 1880; served Egyptian War, 1884–86; Frontier Field Force in Egypt (Egyptian medal and Khedive's Star); South African campaign, 1899–1902, in the operations near Colesberg under General Sir John French (severely wounded, despatches); served in Lord Roberts's march from Bloemfontein to Pretoria; present at the engagements of Brandfort, Vet River, Zand River, and the operations near Johannesburg and Pretoria, also Diamond Hill and Belfast (despatches, DSO, South African medal 5 clasps, King's medal 2 clasps). *Recreations:* cricket, golf, cycling. *Address:* c/o Glyn, Mills & Co., 3 Whitehall Place, SW1. *Clubs:* Golfers'; Royal Portrush Golf.
Died 17 March 1926.

ORR-EWING, Sir Archibald Ernest, 3rd Bt, *cr* 1886; DL, JP Stirlingshire; *b* 22 Feb. 1853; 2nd *s* of Sir Archibald Orr-Ewing, 1st Bt, and Elizabeth Lindsay, *o d* of James Reid; *S* brother, 1903; *m* 1879, Hon. Mabel Addington, *y d* of 3rd Viscount Sidmouth; one *s* two *d* (and one *s* decd). *Educ:* Harrow. Late Captain 3rd Batt. Argyll and Sutherland Highlanders; Royal Archers (King's Body Guard for Scotland). *Heir: s* Col Norman Archibald Orr-Ewing, DSO [*b* 23 Nov. 1880; *m* 1911, Laura Louisa, *d* of Abraham John Robarts, Lillingstone Dayrell, Bucks, and Hon. Edith, *d* of 8th Viscount Barrington; two *s* one *d*]. *Address:* 7 Hereford Gardens, Park Lane, W. *Clubs:* Carlton, Boodle's, Hurlingham; Royal Yacht Squadron, Cowes; New, Edinburgh.
Died 21 April 1919.

ORR-LEWIS, Sir Frederick Orr, 1st Bt, *cr* 1920; President of Lewis Brothers, Ltd; President and Founder of Canadian Vickers, Ltd; Director of Merchants Bank of Canada, Montreal Cotton Company, and Bankers' Trust Company, Montreal; *b* Hamilton, Canada, 11 Feb. 1866; 2nd *s* of late William Thomas Lewis of Swansea, Co. Glamorgan and Montreal, Canada; *m* 1896, Maud Helen Mary, *o d* of William Booth, London, Ontario, Canada; one *s* two *d*. *Heir: s* (John) Duncan Orr-Lewis [*b* 21 Feb. 1898; *m* 1921, Marjory, *d* of James Milne]. *Address:* Whitewebbs Park, near Enfield, Middlesex; 20 Bleury Street, Montreal, Canada. *Clubs:* Junior Carlton, Wellington, Ranelagh; Mount Royal, St James', Forest and Stream, Jockey, Hunt, Mount Royal Golf, Montreal; Rideau, Ottawa.
Died 18 Nov. 1921.

ORSMAN, W. J., JP Co. of London; *b* 13 Aug. 1838; twice *m*; widower; one *s* one *d*. *Educ:* Cambridge. Assistant to Florence Nightingale in the Crimean War; entered GPO London, 1856; retired from the position of Supervisor of HM Mails, 1889; elected to LCC 1889; retired, 1895; Founder of the Golden Lane and Hoxton Costers' Christian Mission, 1861, and later the Consulting Superintendent; Member of the Council of the Ragged School Union and Shaftesbury Society; was one of the first Governors of the City Parochial Foundation. *Publications:* Golden Lane Mission Magazine, 12 vols, etc. *Recreations:* interested in costermongers and street-traders, and their donkey-shows; also in the evangelistic work at Costers' Hall, Hoxton, N; girls' and boys' Guilds, poor children's meals, holiday homes, etc. *Address:* 53 Forest Road, Tunbridge Wells.
Died 4 Jan. 1923.

OSBORNE, Rt. Rev. Edward William, DD; *b* Calcutta, 5 Jan. 1845; *s* of Rev. J. F. Osborne, Priest of the English Church. *Educ:* Gloucester, England. Deacon, 1869; Priest, 1870; Curate of Highworth, Wilts, 1869; Kenn, Devon, 1872; Society of St John the Evangelist (Cowley Fathers), 1875; worked in Boston, USA, 1877–89; S Africa, 1889–96; missions in India, 1897–98; worked in Boston, 1899–1904; consecrated Bishop Coadjutor of Springfield, 1904; succeeded as Bishop, 1906; resigned on account of ill-health, Oct. 1916. *Publications:* The Children's Saviour; The Saviour King; The Children's Faith; The Story of Daniel; Wonderful Things in the Church Catechism; Our Wonderful Faith; Woman—God's Gift to Man; Boys and Girls I have Known; Chapters for Church-goers. *Address:* 3915 Falcon Street, San Diego, California, USA.
Died 5 July 1926.

OSBORNE, Lord Francis Granville Godolphin; *b* 11 March 1864; *s* of 9th Duke of Leeds and Fanny Georgiana, *d* of 4th Baron Rivers;

m 1896, Ruth, *e d* of late Vice-Admiral Grieve, Commander Royal Navy. *Address:* Ord House, Berwick-on-Tweed. *Club:* Naval and Military.
Died 17 Oct. 1924.

OSBURN, Comdr Francis, Royal Navy; *b* 1834; 3rd *s* of late William Osburn, Royal Society of Literature, Egyptologist, Leeds; *m* 1859, Victoria Pauline, *d* of Captain Richard Bushelle, RN, Dover; five *s* four *d*. Entered Royal Navy as Naval Cadet, 1848; joined HMS Victory; served as Midshipman in HMS Desperate on relief expedition for Sir John Franklin, 1852; as Lieutenant in HMS Ajax during Russian War (Baltic medal); present at bombardment of Bomarsund; promoted and served in HMS Curacoa in Crimea; Stipendiary Magistrate, Jamaica, 1879; JP Dominion of Canada. *Address:* Winsley, Southbourne, Sussex.
Died 29 March 1917.

O'SHAUGHNESSY, Patrick Joseph; MP (N) West Limerick, 1900–18; *b* 1872; *s* of David O'Shaughnessy, Rathkeale, Co. Limerick, and Norah, *d* of John W. Power. *Educ:* Rathkeale; French College, Blackrock. *Address:* Rathkeale, Co. Limerick.
Died 29 Dec. 1920.

O'SHAUGHNESSY, Richard, CB 1903; MVO 1900; Commissioner of Public Works, Ireland, 1891–1903; *b* Oct. 1842; *s* of James O'Shaughnessy, MRCSE, DL, Limerick City; *m* 1867, Ellen, *d* of James Potter, Farm Lodge, Limerick. Graduated Trinity College, Dublin. Called to the Bar, Ireland, 1866; MP (HR) Limerick City, 1874–83; Registrar, Petty Sessions Clerks, 1883–91; Commissioner of Public Works, Ireland, 1891–1903. *Address:* 8 Palmerston Park, Dublin. *Club:* Stephen's Green, Dublin.
Died 17 Aug. 1918.

O'SHEA, Sir Henry, Kt 1916; JP; Lord Mayor, Cork, 1911–16; *b* 8 July 1858; *s* of Michael O'Shea; *m* 1882, Bridget, *d* of John Blewitte; four *s* six *d*. *Educ:* National School, Kilbrin. Member of Cork Corporation, 1898; High Sheriff, 1901; Alderman, 1908. *Address:* Old Court, Rochestown, Co. Cork.
Died 1926.

O'SHEA, Lucius Trant, MSc (Sheffield); BSc (London); Professor of Applied Chemistry in the University of Sheffield; *e s* of late Major Rodney Payne O'Shea, 20th Regiment of Foot, and late Elizabeth Caroline, *d* of late Admiral of the Fleet Sir Lucius Curtis, 1st Bt, KCB, and Mary Figg Greetham; *m* Mary, 2nd *d* of late F. M. Tindall; one *s* one *d*. *Educ:* Manchester Grammar School; Owens College, Manchester. Assistant Lecturer and Demonstrator in Chemistry in Firth College, Sheffield, 1880; Lecturer in Mining Chemistry, 1890; Fellow of the Chemical Society, and Member of the Society of Chemical Industry; Honorary Secretary of the Institution of Mining Engineers; went to South Africa in command of detachment of the 1st West York Royal Engineer Volunteers, 1901, and was attached to 17th Field Co. RE at Standerton; remained in South Africa till the declaration of peace (Queen's medal, 5 clasps; granted rank of Hon. Lieut in the army); Officer Commanding the University of Sheffield OTC, 1911–17. *Publications:* Elementary Chemistry for Coal Mining Students; papers read before learned societies; A Contribution to the History of the Constitution of Bleaching Powder; Retention of Lead by Filter Paper; Note on the Woolwich Testing Station; A Testing Station for Mining Explosives; The Safety of High Explosives, with Special Reference to Methods of Testing. *Recreations:* golf, volunteering. *Address:* The Department of Applied Science, The University, Sheffield. *T:* 335 Broomhill, Sheffield.
Died 18 April 1920.

O'SHEA, Lt-Col Timothy, DSO 1916; *b* 1856. Major and Quartermaster (retired pay) the King's Royal Rifle Corps; Lt-Col and Quartermaster 9th Batt. London Regt; retired; served Burma, 1891 (medal with clasp); South African War, 1902 (despatches, Queen's medal with 2 clasps); European War, 1914–18 (despatches twice, DSO, 1914 Star, Allies medal and Victory medal, Coronation medal (King George)). *Address:* 15 Berkeley Road, Crouch End, N8.
Died 7 July 1921.

OSLER, Sir Edmund Boyd, Kt 1912; Member Dominion House of Commons for West Toronto, 1896–1917; *b* Tecumceth Parsonage, Co. Simcoe, Ontario, 1845; 4th *s* of late Rev. Featherstone Lake Osler and Ellen Free Pickton; *m* 1873, Annie Farquharson (*d* 1910), *d* of late Francis James Cochran of Balfour, Aberdeenshire; three *s*three *d*. *Educ:* Grammar School, Dundas, Ont. Head of financial firm of Osler & Hammond, Toronto; President, Toronto Bond Trade, 1896; one of representatives of Canada at Congress of Chambers of Commerce, London, 1896; Director of and member of the Executive of Canadian Pacific Rly Co.; President of Dominion Bank of Canada; Chairman, Endowment Committee, Trinity University, and a member of Governing Body of Univ. of Toronto. *Address:* Craigleigh, Toronto, Canada. *Clubs:* York, Toronto, Toronto Golf, Toronto; Mount Royal, Montreal.   *Died 4 Aug. 1924.*

OSLER, Featherston, DCL (hon.) University of Trinity College; *b* 4 Jan. 1838; *e s* of late Rev. Featherstone Lake Osler, MA (Cantab), formerly of Falmouth, England, and Ellen Free Pickton; *m* 1861, Henrietta (*d* 1902), *d* of late Capt. Henry Smith, HEICS; three *s* three *d.* Barrister, 1860; Bencher Law Society of Upper Canada (elected), 1875–79, 1879, and *ex-officio* since 1910; Puisne Judge, Common Pleas, 1879–83; Justice of Appeal for Ontario, 1883–1910; declined appointment to Supreme Court of Canada, 1888 and 1909; Commissioner for revising Ontario Statutes, 1887, 1897, and 1907–14 (Chairman); Trustee of Corporation of Univ. of Trinity College, Toronto; Senator of University of Toronto (elected); President Toronto General Trusts Corporation since 1910. *Address:* 80 Crescent Road, Toronto. *Clubs:* York, Empire, Toronto.
                    Died 17 Jan. 1924.

OSLER, Sir William, 1st Bt, *cr* 1911; MD; FRS 1898; FRCP 1884; Student (Fellow) of Christ Church, Oxford; Regius Professor of Medicine, Oxford, since 1904; Hon. Professor of Medicine, Johns Hopkins University; *b* Bond Head, Canada, 12 July 1849; 6th *s* of late Rev. Featherstone Lake Osler and Ellen Free Pickton; *m* 1892, Grace, *e d* of late John Revere of Boston, Mass, and *widow* of Dr S. W. Gross, Philadelphia; one *s* decd. *Educ:* Trinity College School; Trinity College, Toronto; Toronto University; McGill University, Montreal; University Coll. London; Berlin and Vienna. Professor of the Institutes of Medicine, McGill University, 1874–84; Professor of Clinical Medicine, University of Pennsylvania, 1884–89; Professor of Medicine, Johns Hopkins University, 1889–1904. Hon. DSc Oxford, Cambridge, Dublin, Liverpool, and Leeds; LLD McGill, Toronto, Aberdeen, Edinburgh, Yale, Harvard, Johns Hopkins Universities; DCL Durham and Trinity University, Toronto; Hon. MD, Christiania; Hon. FRCP, Dublin; Foreign Associate of the Academy of Medicine, Paris; President of the Bibliographical Society, 1913–18; President of the Classical Association, 1918–19. *Publications:* Cerebral Palsies of Children, 1889; The Principles and Practice of Medicine, 1891, 8th edn 1912; Chorea and Choreiform Affections, 1894; Abdominal Tumours (lectures), 1895; Angina Pectoris and Allied States (lectures), 1897; Monograph on Cancer of the Stomach, 1900; Science and Immortality, 1904; Æquanimitas and other Addresses, 1904; Counsels and Ideals, 1905; editor of A System of Medicine, 2nd edn 1915; Thomas Linacre, 1908; An Alabama Student and other Biographical Essays, 1908; A Way of Life, 1914. *Heir:* none. *Recreation:* bibliography. *Address:* 13 Norham Gardens, Oxford. *Club:* Athenæum.   *Died 29 Dec. 1919 (ext).*

O'SULLIVAN, Most Rev. Charles; RC Bishop of Kerry and Aghadoe since 1917; *b* East Kerry, 1862. *Educ:* Killarney Seminary; Maynooth. Served Mission at Millstreet, 1887–1907; Dean of Kerry and Pastor of Tralee, 1907–17; Member of Congested Districts Board, 1918. *Address:* The Palace, Killarney.
                    Died 29 Jan. 1927.

O'SULLIVAN, Ven. Leopold, DD; Archdeacon of Killaloe since 1909; Rector of Clough-Jordan since 1877. *Educ:* Trinity Coll., Dublin. Ordained, 1870; Curate of Dunkerren, 1870–75; Canon of Killaloe, 1888–89. *Address:* The Rectory, Clough-Jordan, Co. Tipperary.   *Died 22 Oct. 1919.*

O'SULLIVAN-BEARE, Daniel Robert (The O'Sullivan-Beare); Consul-General at Rio de Janeiro, 1913–15, and since 1919; *b* 1865; *o s* of late The O'Sullivan-Beare. *Educ:* French schools; Dublin University (TCD) (graduate in Arts and in Medicine, First Senior Moderator, and Gold Medallist in Natural Science). Attached to Army Medical Department during Egyptian Campaign, 1885; subsequently travelled during several years in various parts of the world; was shipwrecked in Straits of Magellan; Medical Officer in the Gold Coast Colony, 1893; acting Medical Officer to Agency at Zanzibar, 1893–94; Vice-Consul for the Island of Pemba, East Africa, 1894; was engaged during several years in suppressing the slave trade; received personal rank of Consul, as reward for services in that connection, 1906; while in Africa, introduced to the notice of the medical profession a native remedy for cure of Blackwater Fever, which has since proved to be a specific for the disease in question; Consul at Bahia, Brazil, 1907; acting Consul-General at Rio de Janeiro, 1907–8; transferred, as Consul, to São Paulo, Brazil, 1907; seconded by Foreign Office for military service and gazetted Lt-Col, RAMC, Nov. 1915; served throughout the duration of the War; received the Order of the Brilliant Star of Zanzibar. *Recreations:* riding, tennis. *Address:* c/o H. S. King & Co., 9 Pall Mall, SW1. *Club:* Royal Thames Yacht.   *Died 13 June 1921.*

OSWALD, Richard Alexander, JP for Ayrshire, Kirkcudbright, and Dumfriesshire; DL for Ayrshire and Kirkcudbright; Vice-Lieutenant of Ayrshire; Convener of Ayrshire, 1901–13; *b* 1841; *e s* of late George Oswald and 1st wife, Lydia Margaret, *d* of late Frederick Homan of Ardenwood, Co. Kildare; *m* 1868, Maude, 2nd *d* of late James Hugh Smith Barry of Marbury Hall, Cheshire, and Fota, Co. Cork. *Educ:* Radley; Harrow. Late Lieut 29th Foot; owned 11,540 acres in Ayrshire, and 24,160 in Kirkcudbright. *Address:* Auchincruive, Ayr, NB; Cavens, Kirkcudbright, NB.
                    Died 13 April 1921.

OSWALD, William Digby, DSO 1902; *b* 20 Jan. 1880; *s* of T. R. Oswald; *m* 1905, Catherine Mary, *d* of late Rev. J. Scott Yardley; two *d.* Served South Africa with Railway Pioneer Regiment, 1902 (despatches, medal, 5 clasps, DSO).
                    Died 16 July 1916.

OUIMET, Hon. Joseph Alderic; *b* 20 May 1848; *m* 1874, Marie Thérèse (*d* 1897), *d* of late J. F. A. Chartier La Rocque, Montreal; three *s* three *d. Educ:* Victoria University, Cobourg, Ont. Advocate, 1870; QC 1880; MP (C) Laval, 1873–96; Speaker, 1887–91; Minister of Public Works, 1892–96; Puisne Judge, Court of King's Bench, 1896–1906. *Clubs:* Mount Royal, Canadian, Montreal.
                    Died 12 May 1916.

OULTON, George N., KC 1904; Bencher of King's Inns. Late Conveyancing Counsel to the Master of the Rolls; Scholar and Moderator, TCD. *Address:* 19 Upper Mount Street, Dublin.
                    Died 30 Dec. 1928.

OUTCAULT, Richard Felton; artist; *b* Lancaster, Ohio, 14 Jan. 1863; *s* of J. P. Outcault and Catherine Davis; *m* 1890, Mary Jane Martin, Lancaster, Ohio. *Educ:* McMicken University, Cincinnati. On staff New York Journal since 1905. *Publications:* Buster, Mary Jane and Tige, 1908; Buster Brown, the Busy Body, 1909; Real Buster and the only Mary Jane, 1909; Buster Brown in Foreign Lands, 1912; Buster Brown—the Fun Maker, 1912; Buster Brown and his Pets, 1913. *Address:* Flushing, Long Island, New York.
                    Died 25 Sept. 1928.

OUTRAM, Sir James, 3rd Bt, *cr* 1858; *b* 13 Oct. 1864; *o s* of Sir Francis Boyd Outram, 2nd Bt and Jane Anne (*d* 1903), *e d* of late Patrick Davidson, Inchmarlo, Kincardineshire; *S* father, 1912; *m* 1921, Lilian Mary, *d* of late Joseph Balfour, Athelstone House, Brighton. *Educ:* Haileybury; Pembroke College, Cambridge. *Heir:* brother Francis Davidson Outram, OBE, Bt Major (formerly) Royal Engineers [*b* 4 Aug. 1867; *m* 1st, 1893, Maud Charlotte (*d* 1913), *d* of late James Pope Kitchin, The Manor House, Hampton; one *d*; 2nd, 1915, Isabel Mary, *er d* of late Henry Charles Berry. *Address:* Lyss-na-Greyne, Aboyne, Aberdeenshire]. *Address:* 98 Bouverie Road West, Folkestone.   *Died 12 March 1925.*

OUTTRIM, Hon. Alfred Richard; late Member of the Legislative Assembly, representing Maryborough, Victoria, Australia; *b* Mile End Road, London, 30 March 1845; *s* of James Outtrim and Elizabeth Rosa Stephenson, both of London; *m* 1871, Jane Lavinia Tutcher; one *s* three *d. Educ:* Denominational School, Maryborough, Victoria. Left London Docks with members of the family in the sailing ship Eliza for Melbourne, 1852; held office in three Governments in Victoria; held eight portfolios, *viz.* Minister of Mines in the three Governments, Minister of Forests in two Governments, Minister of Water Supply in one Government, Minister of Defence in one Government, and Minister of Railways in one Government; Mayor of Maryborough, Victoria, twice; Member of the Borough Council for many years; acting Chairman of Committee of the Legislative Assembly, Victoria. *Recreation:* no time for recreation in his young days. *Address:* State Parliament House, Melbourne, Victoria, Australia.
                    Died Dec. 1925.

OUTTRIM, Frank Leon, ISO 1904; VD; JP; Lieutenant-Colonel Victorian Garrison Artillery Militia (retired); *b* London, 22 Aug. 1847; *s* of James Outtrim and Rosa Elizabeth Stephenson; *m* Frances Caroline, *o d* of Captain William Henry Litchfield, Williamstown, Victoria; one *s. Educ:* Church of England School, Maryborough, Victoria. Came to colony with parents, 1852; joined Public Service, 1863; filled various positions in Postal Department; selected for First Deputy Commissioner Income Tax, 1895; connected with local military forces for many years, and was Major in command of North Melbourne Battery Garrison Artillery for seven years, promoted Lieutenant-Colonel on retirement; Deputy Postmaster-Gen., State of Victoria, 1897; retired 1907. *Address:* Minyonge, 78 Holmes Road, Moonee Ponds, Melbourne, Victoria.   *Died 2 April 1917.*

OVENDEN, Very Rev. Charles T., DD; Dean of St Patrick's Cathedral, Dublin, 1911; Canon of St Patrick's Cathedral, Dublin, since 1889; *b* Enniskillen, 11 Sept. 1846; *s* of William C. Ovenden, MD, and Isabella Parkinson; *m* 1871, Isabella Mary, *d* of late John Robinson, JP, Uplands, Co. Wicklow; two *d*. *Educ*: Portora Royal School, Enniskillen; Mannheim, Germany; TCD. Ordained 1870 for Curacy of Magdalene Church, Belfast; Rector of Dunluce, Co. Antrim, 1872–79; Succentor of St Patrick's Cathedral, Dublin, 1879–84; Rector of Portrush, 1884–86; Chaplain to the Lord Lieutenant and Precentor of Clogher, 1886–1903; Dean of Clogher, 1903–11; Rector of Enniskillen, and Rural Dean, 1886–1911. *Publications*: edited 1st edition of the Cathedral Anthem Book of Words; In the Day of Trouble; To Whom shall we go?; The Church Navvy; The Enthusiasm of Christianity; The Face of Nature; Marvels in the World of Light; The Foundation of a Happy Life; Problems in Life and Religion; Deep Questions; Popular Science for Parochial Evenings; Modern Criticism of the Holy Scriptures; Morning and Evening Service with office of Holy Communion; anthems—I will always give Thanks; For the Rain cometh down; processional anthem—The Son of God goes forth to War. *Recreations*: oil-painting, music. *Address*: The Deanery, St Patrick's Close, Dublin. *TA*: The Deanery, Dublin. *T*: Dublin 2901. *M*: IK 4094. *Clubs*: Hibernian Catch, Friendly Brothers, Dublin. *Died 9 July 1924.*

OVEREND, Walker, MA, MD Oxon; Chief Assistant, X-Ray Department, St Bartholomew's Hospital; Hon. Radiologist to East Sussex Hospital, Hastings. Late Physician to Prince of Wales' Hospital, N. *Address*: 29 Eversfield Place, St Leonards.

Died 10 Feb. 1926.

OVERTON, Robert; author, dramatist, journalist; lecturer on literary and philosophical subjects; *b* 8 Dec. 1859; *y* surv. *s* of late Charles Overton, HM Customs, and Marler Sulyard Talbot. *Educ*: privately. Royal Defence Corps, late Honourable Artillery Company. *Publications*: Queer Fish; A Round Dozen; Ten Minutes; The Overton Reciters; Overton Entertainer; Water-Works; Nine and Three; After School; Lights Out; The King's Pardon; Far from Home; Friend or Fortune?; The Son of the School; The Orphan of Tor College; Decoyed across the Seas; A Chase Round the World; Dangerous Days; Saturday Island; The Three Skippers; The Secret of the Caves; The Clue of the Cloak; *dramas*: Hearts of Oak; Next of Kin; The Mills of God; No Quarter; *one-act plays*: The Man in Possession; Purgatory; Fortune Favours Fools; Splendid Silence; A Mad Marriage; The Lady Secretary; Santa Claus; Gertie's Convict; Mrs Seton's Secret; Two Negatives; pantomimes, operettas, monologues. *Recreations*: boating, field sports, voyaging in tramp steamships, chess. *Address*: c/o Sampson Low, Limited, 100 Southwark Street, SE1.

Died 28 Nov. 1924.

OWEN, Col Arthur Allen, MVO 1911; gentleman-at-arms; *b* 19 Jan. 1842; *m* Jennie (*d* 1905), *d* of Edwin Lewis, of Goldthorn Hill, Wolverhampton. Entered Army, 1859; Major, 1877; retired, 1881; served S Africa, 1877–79 (despatches, medal with clasp, brevet Lt-Col); Jubilee medal and clasp; Coronation medal of King Edward VII and King George V; Order of Mercy. *Address*: Polesdon, Datchet. *Club*: Naval and Military. *Died 29 April 1917.*

OWEN, Maj.-Gen. Charles Henry; *b* 1830; *s* of Henry Owen (*nephew* of Henry Owen Cunliffe of Wycoller); *m* Emily Linzee (*d* 1908), *d* of W. A. Hunt of Burleigh, near Plymouth; three *s* three *d*. *Educ*: RMA, Woolwich. Obtained a commission in the Royal Artillery, 1848; joined Royal Artillery as Lieutenant, 1849; served Crimean Campaign, 1854–55, at Inkerman, and in all the six bombardments, throughout the siege, and at the fall of Sebastopol (despatches, Chevalier Legion of Honour, 5th class Medjidie, Crimean medal and two clasps, Turkish war medal, Brevet Major for distinguished service in the field); Professor of Artillery at the RMA, Woolwich, 1859–73; Member of Ordnance Select Committee, and of the Committee on Ordnance; served in command of 2 or 3 field batteries from 1873, and commanded the Field Artillery at Aldershot, 1879; retired, full pay, 1881. Decorated for service in the Crimea. *Publications*: Motion of Projectiles, Lectures on Artillery, Modern Artillery (Class Book in the service); papers on military and scientific subjects in the Proceedings of the RA Institution, RUSI, and in the US Magazine. *Recreations*: art (member of the Water Colour Society of Ireland, and of the Lancashire and Cheshire Antiquarian Society); hunted regularly in England and Ireland. *Address*: Hanley, Camberley, Surrey. *TA*: Camberley. *Clubs*: Army and Navy; West Surrey, Camberley.

Died 6 Nov. 1921.

OWEN, Lt-Col Charles William, CMG 1887; CIE 1881; JP Sussex; LRCP, MRCS; *b* 28 Jan. 1853; *s* of A. S. Owen, Enfield, Mddx; *m*

1st, 1878, Mary Elizabeth (*d* 1920), *e d* of late Horace Barry; 2nd, 1921, Mabel Howard, *e d* of Rev. H. Hopley, Goodrest, Uckfield, formerly Vicar of Westham. Surgeon, 1876; Lt-Col 1896; served on Headquarter Staff, Afghan War, 1879–80 (despatches), including operations round Cabul, 1879 (slightly wounded, despatches, CIE, medal with two clasps); Egyptian War, on Headquarter Staff, IEF, 1882, including Tel-el-Kebir (medal with clasp, Khedive's Star); served on Afghan Boundary Commission (CMG); Mohmund Expedition, 1893, on Headquarter Staff (medal and clasp); formerly Surgeon to Commander-in-Chief in India, Lord Roberts; Medical Adviser to late HH Maharaja of Patiala; Vice-Chairman of Eastbourne Rural District Council and Member of Board of Guardians; Member of East Sussex Education Committee; Chairman of Hailsham Grouped Council Schools; Member of St John's Hospital; Land Tax Commissioner; County Director British Red Cross Soc., Sussex; Member East Sussex War Pensions Committee; Order of Hurmat, 1886, etc. *Recreations*: educationalist, amateur photographer, motorist. *Address*: The Horns, Hankham, Westham, Sussex. *TA*: Owen Hankham. *T*: Pevensy 1X1. *M*: AP 2371. *Clubs*: Services; The Lewes and County; Sussex County and Eastbourne Automobile, Eastbourne.

Died 23 May 1922.

OWEN, Sir Douglas, KBE 1917; Kt 1915; Barrister, Inner Temple; Lecturer London School of Economics, Army Class (Ocean Transport); Lecturer, Royal Naval War Colleges; Chairman, Advisory Committee State War Risks Insurance Office; Chairman of Coal Exports Committee; Member of Panel of Advisers on School Commercial Certificates, University of London; *b* 1850; 4th *s* of Dr W. B. Owen, Cleveland Square, W; *m* 1889, Elizabeth Charlotte, *d* of A. W. Surtees. *Educ*: King's College School; private. Represented Colonial Office at Shipping Freights Conference at Johannesburg, 1904; Hon. Secretary Mansion House Committee on Port of London, 1902; Member of Admiralty Small Committee of Experts *re* Naval Manœuvres, 1906; Member Lord Herschell's Special Committee on Marine Insurance Bill, 1895; Hon. Sec. Budget Protest League, 1909; Hon. Sec. and Treasurer Society for Nautical Research; Chairman, Paddington Green Children's Hospital, and member of House Committee, London Hospital; Chevalier de la Légion d'Honneur, France; Officier de l'Ordre de la Couronne, Belgium. *Publications*: (with Sir Mackenzie Chalmers, draughtsman of Bill) Digest of the Law of Marine Insurance; Declaration of War, a Survey of the Position of Belligerents and Neutrals in Maritime War; Ocean Trade and Shipping; London, the Port of the Empire; Ports and Docks. *Recreations*: literature, fishing, shooting. *Address*: 44 St George's Court, Gloucester Road, SW7. *T*: Kensington 3125. *Clubs*: Savile, Ranelagh.

Died 15 Nov. 1920.

OWEN, Edward Cunliffe, CMG 1886; Secretary to Metropolitan Electric Supply Co.; *b* 1857; *s* of late Col Henry Charles Cunliffe Owen, CB, RE; *m* 1882, Emma P., *d* of late Sir (Francis) Philip Cunliffe Owen, KCB. *Educ*: Wellington; Trinity Coll., Cambridge. *Address*: 16 Stratford Place, W. *Club*: Oxford and Cambridge.

Died 27 Dec. 1918.

OWEN, Henry, DL, JP; DCL Oxford; FSA; Treasurer of the National Library of Wales; Chairman of the Hon. Society of Cymmrodorion, and Pembrokeshire Quarter Sessions; High Sheriff, Pembrokeshire, 1902; Member of Royal Commission on Public Records. *Publications*: Gerald the Welshman; Old Pembroke Families; Owen's Pembrokeshire, etc. *Address*: Poyston, Haverford West. *Clubs*: Athenæum, Savile, New University.

Died 14 April 1919.

OWEN, Col Henry Mostyn, CB 1902; MVO 1904; Dragoon Guards; late Assistant Director Remounts; *b* 26 April 1858; *m* 1894, Hilda Mary, 3rd *d* of Sir Robert Gunter, 1st Bt; one *s* two *d*. Entered army, 1878; Captain, 1886; Major, 1895; Lieut-Col 1898; served with the Carabiniers, Afghanistan, 1879–80 (medal); South Africa, 1901–2 (despatches, Queen's medal 5 clasps, CB). *Address*: Hambleton House, Norton-Malton. *TA*: Malton 189. *Club*: Yorkshire, York.

Died 18 Nov. 1927.

OWEN, Sir (Herbert) Isambard, Kt 1902; MD, MA; FRCP; Hon. Fellow of Downing College, Cambridge; Hon. Fellow of the University of Bristol; Vice-Chancellor of the University of Bristol, 1909–21; *b* Bellevue House, near Chepstow, Mon, 28 Dec. 1850; *s* of the late William George Owen, Chief Engineer of the Great Western Railway; *m* 1905, Ethel, *d* of late Lewis Holland-Thomas of Caerffynnon, Merioneth; two *d*. *Educ*: King's School, Gloucester; Rossall; Downing College, Cambridge; St George's Hospital. Late Physician to and Lecturer in Medicine at St George's Hospital; Consulting Physician to and Hon. Governor of St George's Hospital;

Vice-Dean of Faculty of Medicine of Univ. of London, 1901–4; Member of General Medical Council, 1910–25; late Examiner in Medicine, Universities of Cambridge, London, and Durham, Royal Army Medical Corps, and Royal College of Physicians of London; Hon. Fellow and late Vice-President Medical Society of London; took the leading part in the establishment of the University of Wales, 1891–93, and in the reconstruction of the University of Durham, 1907–9; Senior Deputy-Chancellor, University of Wales, 1895–1910; late Vice-President of University Coll., Bangor; Member of Council of University Coll., Cardiff; Gov., University College, Aberystwyth; late Member of Central Welsh Board; late President of Teachers' Guild of Great Britain and Ireland, 1898–99; Principal of Armstrong College, Newcastle, 1904–9; Hon. Lieut-Col Volunteer Force. Hon. DCL Durham, 1905; LLD Wales *hc* 1911; Hon. LLD Bristol, 1912. *Publications:* various papers on education and on professional subjects. *Recreation:* chiefly cycling. *Address:* c/o Faithfull, Owen, Blair and Wright, Dacre House, Westminster, SW1. *Club:* Athenæum.
Died 14 Jan. 1927.

OWEN, Sir Hugh, GCB 1899 (KCB 1887; CB 1885); *b* 1835; *e s* of Sir Hugh Owen (knighted for services in connection with education in Wales); *m* 1865, Charlotte Elizabeth, *d* of late Charles Burt of Tufnell Park, N; two *s* three *d*. Barrister Middle Temple, 1862; Assistant Secretary of Local Government Board, 1876–82; Permanent Secretary, 1882–98; Chairman of the Commissioners under the London Govt Act, 1899–1907; one of the Commissioners forming the Court of Arbitration under the Metropolis Water Act, 1902; in consideration of his services in connection with public health and poor law administration was presented with the honorary freedom of the Plumbers' Company, which was followed by the freedom of the City of London, and was elected Honorary Fellow of the Royal Institute of Public Health, and a Lodge of Freemasons adopted the name of the Hugh Owen Lodge. *Publications:* Education Acts Manual; Municipal Corporation Act, 1882; and other legal works relating to duties of local authorities. *Address:* South Grove, Highgate, N; 1 Pump Court, Temple, EC.
Died 28 Jan. 1916.

OWEN, Jean A., (Mrs Owen Visger); author and journalist; *b* Staffordshire; *e d* of late Thomas Pinder, Burslem and Endon; *m* 1st, 1863, George Newton Owen; 2nd 1883, Harman Visger, Bristol; one *d. Educ:* Elgin, Scotland; Neuwied, Germany. Sailed for New Zealand, June 1863; lived near Auckland for five years; voyages to Tahiti, Hawaiian Islands, etc; in England again, 1869–72; through West Indies, across Panama, and again arrived in the Hawaiian Islands, 1873; from Honolulu (after Mr Owen's death) by San Francisco and New York to England again, 1876; shipwrecked in the RMS Douro off Cape Finisterre, 1882; travelled much in various parts of Europe, and made many voyages in the North and South Pacific; lived in Australia and Honolulu, 1910–13, when she returned to England. *Publications:* From San Francisco to New York, 1869; Our Honolulu Boys, 1877; Silver Linings, Ethel's Comforter, Under Palm and Pine, Sea Blossom, A Runaway, Make the Best of Yourself, Candelaria—between 1877 and 1883; After Shipwreck, 1882; Forest, Field, and Fell, 1892; The Country Month by Month, 1894; The Story of Hawaii, 1898; Birds in their Seasons, 1904; Facing the World, 1905; (with Otto Herman) Birds Useful and Hurtful, 1909; Love Covers All, 1911; Ruth Thornton, 1913; editor and collaborateur of On Surrey Hills, Drift from Longshore, and of all books that have been published under the signature of "A Son of the Marshes"—that title having been chosen by Mrs Visger to cover the collaborated work of a working naturalist in Surrey and herself. *Recreations:* the tending of plants, music, travel. *Club:* Writers'.
Died 30 July 1922.

OWEN, Rt. Rev. John; Bishop of St Davids since 1897; *b* 24 Aug. 1854; *s* of Griffith Owen, Ysgubor-wen-Llanengan, and Ann Jones; *m* 1882, Amelia Mary Elizabeth, *d* of Joseph Longstaff, Appleby, Westmorland; four *s* six *d. Educ:* Bottwnog Grammar School; Jesus College, Oxford (Scholar). Double 2nd class Honours in Moderations, 1874; 2nd class Mathematics Honours Finals; MA. Deacon, 1879; Priest, 1880; Welsh Professor and Classical Lecturer St David's College, Lampeter, 1879–85; Warden and Headmaster of Llandovery College, 1885–89; Dean of St Asaph, 1889–92; Principal of St David's College, Lampeter; Canon of St Asaph, 1892–97. *Publications:* various articles and addresses on the Church in Wales. *Address:* The Palace, Abergwili, RSO, Carmarthenshire. *TA:* Carmarthen. *Club:* Athenæum.
Died 4 Nov. 1926.

OWEN, Gen. Sir John Fletcher, KCB 1906 (CB 1902); *b* 9 April 1839; 3rd *s* of Rev. Canon J. Owen, JP, DL Carnarvonshire, MA (Rector of Llaniestyn, of Hendrevinws; unmarried. *Educ:* Rossall Hall; RMA Woolwich. Graduate of the Artillery Coll. (*pac*). Asst Supt Royal Gun Factories, 1877–78; served with (Sir Evelyn) Wood's Column

in Zulu War, 1879, commanding a mounted Gatling battery at battle of Ulundi (despatches, brevet of Lieut-Col); Commandant Mil. Forces South Australia, 1885–88; Commandant Camp and School Coast Defences, Golden Hill, 1889–90; Commandant Defence Forces, Queensland, 1891–94; Major-General on the Staff commanding Artillery Brigade, Malta, 1895–99; promoted to Lieut-General, February 1899; received Reward for Distinguished Service, Nov. 1899; President Ordnance Committee, 1902–4; General, 1904; Colonel Commandant, Royal Artillery, 1906. *Publications:* various professional papers and lectures. *Recreations:* shooting, fishing, cycling, etc. *Club:* United Service.
Died 10 June 1924.

OWEN, Rev. John Smith; Hon. Canon, Norwich. *Educ:* Trinity College, Dublin (MA, LLD). Curate of St Stephens, Norwich, 1863–69; Vicar of St Matthew's, Thorpe Hamlet, 1869–74; North Walsham, 1874–1905; Witton, 1905–16. *Address:* Lyndhurst, Mundesley-on-Sea.
Died 20 March 1922.

OWEN, Lt-Col Robert Haylock, CMG 1916; Australian Military Forces; *b* 1862; *s* of Colonel Percy Owen, VD, Royal Australian Artillery; *m* Hilda Grace, *d* of Thomas Irvine Rowell, CMG, MD; one *s* one *d. Educ:* Sydney Grammar School. Lieutenant Australian Soudan Contingent, 1883; Lieutenant to Major in HM South Lancashire Regt; Lt-Col and Chief Staff Officer New Zealand Forces; Lt-Col commanding 3rd Battalion AIF, Gallipoli Campaign (despatches twice, CMG). *Address:* Woodmancote, Dursley, Glos.
Died 5 April 1927.

OWEN, Lt-Col Sydney Lloyd, DSO 1916; late Royal Engineers; *b* 27 Feb. 1872; *e s* of late Dr and Mrs Lloyd Owen of Southsea. *Educ:* Portsmouth Grammar School; Royal Military Academy, Woolwich. Entered Army, 1891; served South African War, 1899–1902 (despatches, 2 medals and 7 clasps); European War, 1914–18 (despatches, DSO); retired pay, 1921. *Recreations:* cricket, football, golf, amateur theatricals. *Address:* Cox & Co., 16 Charing Cross, SW1. *Club:* United Service.

OWEN, Sir Thomas David, Kt 1921; *b* Halton, Cheshire, 18 Nov. 1854; unmarried. *Educ:* Brynford House School, Holywell, Flintshire. Served articles as Chemist and Metallurgical Chemist at Flint Chemical; Head Chemist to Works of John Hutchinson & Co., Chemical Works, Widnes; Manager of Grasselli Chemical Works, USA; joined father's firm in Liverpool, chemical merchants, of which firm became sole partner; Vice-President, Etablissement Union, Paris and Rouen, Chemical Manufacturers; member of Council of University College of North Wales, Bangor. *Recreations:* cricket, golf, bowls, motoring. *Address:* Fowell House, Albion Street, Wallasey, Cheshire. *TA:* Filtered, Liverpool. *T:* Wallasey 900, Central 421 Liverpool. *M:* HF 37. *Clubs:* New Brighton Cricket; Leasowe Golf.
Died 23 Sept. 1921.

OWEN, William, ISO 1902; late Chief Clerk, Exchequer and Audit Department; *b* 20 April 1837; *s* of Sir Hugh Owen (knighted for services in connection with education in Wales); *m* 1869, Charlotte Lydia, *d* of Joseph Pennington. Barrister Middle Temple, 1862. *Address:* 6 Clyde Road, St Leonards-on-Sea.
Died 17 March 1918.

OWEN-LEWIS, Lt-Col Arthur Francis, OBE 1918; DSO 1900; DL, Co. Monaghan; Inspector of Prisons for Ireland; late Yorkshire Regiment and Reserve of Officers; *b* 6 Aug. 1868; *e s* of late Henry Owen-Lewis, MP Co. Carlow, DL, of Inniskeen, Co. Monaghan; *m* 1896, Kathleen, *d* of late William Henry, of Tivoli, Co. Dublin. Entered Army, 1889; served South Africa, 1900–2 (despatches, Queen's medal 3 clasps, King's medal 2 clasps, DSO); European War, 1914–18 as GSO Irish Command and AQMG France (despatches twice, OBE). *M:* IY 212. *Clubs:* Army and Navy; United Service, Dublin.
Died 22 Dec. 1926.

OWEN-SMYTH, Charles Edward, CMG 1920; ISO 1903; Permanent Head, Works and Buildings of South Australia, 1886–1920; *b* Ferrybank, Co. Kilkenny, Ireland, 1 Jan. 1851; *s* of Stephen Smyth of Ferrybank, and Emma Gaynor, *g d* of William Lewys Owen of Egryn Abbey and Caerbelleran, Co. Merioneth; *m* 1889, Bessie Saunderson Laidlaw, *d* of late John Davidson, Galashiels; one *s* one *d. Educ:* Erasmus Smith School, Dublin. Entered the Public Service of South Australia, 1876; Architect in Chief Department, 1878; Founder of the Adelaide Branch Royal Society of St George, 1908; President League of Empire and All British League; Vice-President Navy League. *Recreation:* field shooting. *Address:* Egryn, Hazelwood Park, Marryatville, Adelaide, South Australia.
Died 1 Oct. 1925.

OWENS, Hon. William; Senator, Dominion of Canada, since 1896; *b* Argenteuil Co., 15 May 1840; *s* of Owen Owens, Denbigh, Wales, and Charlotte Lindley of Brentford, England; *m* 1st, 1862, Catherine M., *d* of O. Powers, La Chute, Quebec; one *d*; 2nd, 1890, Margaret C., *d* of John M'Martin, Chicago; one *s* one *d*. *Educ:* Argenteuil Co. Was for twenty-five years member of the firm of T. & W. Owens and Owens Brothers, operating general stores and lumber business at Stonefield and Montebello, Que, and later head of the Owens Lumber Co., also Riverside Stock Farm at Montebello; President of the Ottawa River Navigation Co., of the Ottawa Valley Railway, and of the Carillon and Granville Railway; Vice-President Central Railway of Canada; was Mayor, Councillor, and Postmaster of Chatham, PQ; Member (C) Legislative Assembly, 1881–91; Member Church of Engalnd; Conservative. *Address:* 4026 Dorchester Street, Montreal. *T:* 4026 Mount.   *Died 8 June 1917.*

OXENDEN, Sir Percy (Dixwell Nowell Dixwell-), 10th Bt, *cr* 1678; JP; *b* 6 June 1838; assumed additional surname Dixwell in 1890; *S* brother 1895; *m* 1868, Isabella, *d* of Hon. and Rev. Daniel Heneage Finch-Hatton and Lady Louisa Greville (2nd *d* of Countess of Mansfield by 2nd husband, Hon. Robert Fulke Greville); two *d* (and one *s* decd). *Educ:* Harrow; Christ Church, Oxford. Late Captain Royal East Kent Yeomanry. *Heir:* none. *Address:* Craigmore, Leigh-on-Sea, Essex.   *Died 12 July 1924 (ext).*

OXFORD AND ASQUITH, 1st Earl of, *cr* 1925; **Herbert Henry Asquith,** KG 1925; PC 1892; PC Ireland 1916; KC; BA; FRS; Viscount Asquith, of Morley, 1925; Member of Judicial Committee of Privy Council since 1925; Lord Rector Glasgow University, 1905; Rector Aberdeen University, 1908; High Steward of Oxford, 1927; Elder Brother Trinity House since 1909; *b* Morley, Yorkshire, 12 Sept. 1852; 2nd *s* of Joseph Dixon Asquith, Croft House, Morley, and Emily, *d* of William Willans, of Huddersfield; *m* 1st, 1877, Helen Kelsall (*d* 1891), *d* of Frederick Melland, of Manchester; three *s* one *d* (and one *s* decd); 2nd, 1894, Emma Alice Margaret, (Margot), *d* of Sir Charles Tennant, 1st Bt; one *s* one *d*. *Educ:* City of London School; Balliol Coll., Oxford (Scholar, Fellow; Craven University Scholar; 1st class Lit. Hum. 1874). Barrister, Lincoln's Inn, 1876; QC 1890; MP (L) East Fife, 1886–1918; MP (L) Paisley, 1920–24; Secretary of State for Home Dept, 1892–95; Ecclesiastical Commissioner, 1892–95; Chancellor of the Exchequer, 1905–8; Prime Minister and First Lord of the Treasury, 1908–16; Secretary of State for War, 1914; Hon. DCL Oxford and Durham; Hon. LLD Edinburgh, Glasgow, Cambridge, Leeds, St Andrews, Bristol; specially awarded War Star, 1914; War Medal, 1914–18; Victory Medal, 1919. *Publications:* Occasional Addresses (1894–1916), 1918; The Genesis of the War, 1923; Studies and Sketches, 1924; Fifty Years of Parliament, 1926; Speeches, 1927; Memories and Reflections, 1928. *Recreation:* golf. *Heir: g s* Viscount Asquith, *b* 22 April 1916. *Address:* 4 Bedford Square, WC1. *T:* Museum 6464; The Wharf, Sutton Courtney. *Clubs:* Brooks's, Athenæum, Reform.   *Died 15 Feb. 1928.*

OXLEY, Adm. Charles Lister, JP; *b* 1841; *e s* of Charles Christopher Oxley, Ripon Hall, and Mary, *d* of late Rev. W. J. D. Waddilove; *m* 1878, Emily (*d* 1897), *d* of Robert Kearsley, Highfield; two *s* five *d*. Served in attack on Peiho Forts; ADC to Queen Victoria, 1892–95. *Address:* The Hall, Ripon. *Club:* United Service.   *Died 21 July 1920.*

OYAMA, Iwao, Field-Marshal Prince, OM 1906; a Samurai of Satsuma; *b* Oct. 1842. Studied military tactics in Europe; attaché with Prussian army in Franco-Prussian War; served with the Imperial Forces during the Satsuma Rebellion, 1877; General, 1891; Minister of War, 1880–95; commanded the 2nd Army during the China–Japan War, 1895; Field-Marshal, 1898; Chief of General Staff, 1899–1906; Commander-in-Chief in Manchuria, Russo-Japan War, 1904–5. *Address:* Aoyama, Tokio.   *Died 11 Dec. 1916.*

P

PACKARD, Lt-Col Henry Norrington, DSO 1915; Royal Field Artillery; *b* 12 March 1870. Entered army, 1890; Captain, 1900; Major, 1908; served European War, 1914–15 (DSO).   *Died 12 April 1916.*

PADDISON, Sir George Frederick, KBE 1926; CSI 1923; MA Oxon; Indian Civil Service; Commissioner of Labour, Madras; *s* of C. F. Paddison, Ingleby, Lincoln; *m* Eleanor Letitia Roberts; two *s*. *Educ:* Richmond School, Yorks; Queen's College, Oxford. Indian Civil Service, Madras, since 1897. *Recreations:* shooting, lawn tennis. *Address:* Labour Commissioner's Office, Madras, India. *TA:* Labdep, Madras. *T:* 5260. *M:* 5780. *Club:* Madras.   *Died 24 Oct. 1927.*

PADDON, Rev. William Francis Locke, BA; Incumbent of Parish of the Gulf Islands, formerly Mission District of Mayne, British Columbia, 1896–1922; 3rd *s* of Rev. T. H. Paddon, sometime Vicar of High Wycombe, and Anne, *d* of Wadham Locke, Rowdeford, Wilts. *Educ:* Rugby; Marlborough; Wadham College, Oxford. Missionary CMS, Nazareth, 1868; Incumbent of Ballyconree and Priest, 1871; Incumbent of Roundstone, 1876–77; Kilmain, 1878–87; Prebend of Kilmeen, 1887; emigrated to BritishColumbia, 1889. *Address:* Mayne Island, British Columbia.   *Died 28 Aug. 1922.*

PAGE, Lt-Col Cuthbert Frederick Graham, DSO 1916; Royal Artillery; *b* 21 Jan. 1880; *m o d* of Col C. E. Wyncoll. Served Ashanti War, 1900 (medal); South African War, 1901–2 (medal); European War, 1914–16 (despatches, DSO, Bt Lt-Col, Italian Silver Medal for valour).   *Died 6 Nov. 1919.*

PAGE, Lt-Col F., DSO 1915; Hertfordshire Regiment (Territorial Force). Served South African War, 1900–1; European War, 1914–15 (wounded, DSO). *Address:* Hertford.   *Died Aug. 1917.*

PAGE, Frederick, JP; DCL, MA Dunelm, MD Edinburgh; FRCS; late Member of Senate, Durham University; Emeritus Professor of Surgery, Durham University; *e surv. s* of Frederick Page, MD, FRCS, Surgeon, Royal Portsmouth, Portsea and Gosport Hospital; *m* 1876, Margaret, *e d* of late John Graham and *niece* of late T. Graham, FRS, Master of Mint; one *s* two *d*. *Educ:* Edinburgh Univ.; Colonial Hospital, Perth, Western Australia. Late House Phys., Royal Infirmary, Edinburgh; Senior House Surgeon, Asst Surgeon, and Surgeon, Royal Infirmary, Newcastle-on-Tyne; Surgeon, Fleming Memorial Hospital for Sick Children, Newcastle; Registrar, College of Medicine, Newcastle-on-Tyne (Durham Univ.); Representative of Coll. of Med. in Armstrong Coll., Newcastle (formerly Univ. of Durham Coll. of Physical Science, Newcastle); Consulting Surgeon, Royal Infirmary, Fleming Memorial Hospital, Northumberland and Durham Eye Infirmary, Throat and Ear Hospital, The NER Co.; Surgeon, Northumberland Coal Owners' Mutual Protection Association, Newcastle; The Knight Memorial Hospital, Blyth; Med. Referee, Workmen's Compensation Act; External Examiner in Clinical Surgery, Edinburgh University; Lord of the Manor of Nethershall Tindalls-Soham, Cambridge, etc; Chairman of Visiting Justices HM's Prison and of the Discharged Prisoners' Aid Society; Chairman of the Licensing Committee for the City and County of Newcastle-upon-Tyne; an additional Land Tax Commissioner and member of the Lord Chancellor's Committee *in re* Justices of the Peace. *Publications:* Surgery of the Thyroid Gland; Results of Major Amputations treated Antiseptically in the Newcastle Infirmary, 1878–98; Excision of Varicose Aneurism of the Femoral Artery; Twelve Successful Cases of Ligature of Femoral Artery for Popliteal Aneurism, etc. *Recreations:* literature, the drama. *Address:* 20 Victoria Square, Newcastle-on-Tyne. *T:* 344, Nat. 7.   *Died 3 July 1919.*

PAGE, Gertrude, (Mrs Dobbin); authoress; *d* of John E. Page, JP, of Woburn Sands and Bedford; *m* George Alexander, *s* of Captain R. A. Dobbin, Indian Staff Corps, of Armagh, Ireland. *Publications:* Love in the Wilderness; The Edge of Beyond; The Silent Rancher; Paddy the Next Best Thing; Two Lovers and a Lighthouse; Winding Paths; The Rhodesian; The Great Splendour; Where the Strange Roads go down; The Pathway; Follow After; The Supreme Desire; Some There Are; The Veldt Trail; The Course of my Ship (with R. A. Foster-Melliar); Paddy the Next Best Thing, dramatised by Robert Ord and Gayer Mackay; The Edge o' Beyond, dramatised by Roy Horniman and R. Miller. *Address:* Salisbury, Rhodesia. *TA:* Pagina Bedford. *Club:* Empress.   *Died 1 April 1922.*

PAGE, Herbert William, JP Surrey; MA, MChir Cantab; FRCS; *b* 1845; *e s* of W. B. Page, JP Cumberland, FRCS; *m* 1905, Kathleen, *d* of Rev. Canon Houghton. Consulting Surgeon to St Mary's Hospital and to Cumberland Infirmary; ex-Member of Council, Royal College of Surgeons; ex-Consulting Surgeon Great Western Railway Co. and

London and North-Western Railway Companies; ex-Pres. Neurological Soc. of London; Assistant Surgeon Hessian Division of German Army in war of 1870-71; formerly Member of Court of Examiners, Royal College of Surgeons, and Examiner in Surgery, Universities of Oxford, Cambridge, and Birmingham. *Publications:* numerous contributions to medical and surgical literature. *Address:* Sedgecombe House, Farnham. *Club:* New University.

Died 9 Sept. 1926.

PAGE, Hon. James; MP; Federal Representative for Maranoa, Queensland, since 1901; *b* London, 1860; *s* of William Page; *m* 1881, Elizabeth Mary Sutherland; one *s*. Service with Royal Field Artillery, 1877-81; South African War, 1877-78-79 (medal with bar); came to Australia, 1883; followed pastoral pursuits in Queensland central district; JP Queensland. *Address:* Federal Parliament House, Melbourne; Brisbane, Queensland.

Died 3 June 1921.

PAGE, John Lloyd Warden; author; *b* Minehead, Somerset, 26 Aug. 1858; *e s* of late John Theodore Page, RN; *m d* of Rev. Charles Parsons, MA; one *d*. *Educ:* Grammar School, Tavistock. *Publications:* An Exploration of Dartmoor and its Antiquities, 1889; An Exploration of Exmoor and the Hill Country of West Somerset, 1890; The Rivers of Devon from Source to Sea, 1893; The Coasts of Devon and Lundy Island, 1895; Okehampton, Its Castle, etc, 1891; The North Coast of Cornwall, 1897; In Russia without Russian, 1898; The Church Towers of Somersetshire (in collaboration with E. Piper, RE); The Isle of Skye, 1898-1900; and magazine work. *Recreations:* boat-sailing, cycling tours, foreign travel. *Address:* Derrymore, Parkstone. *TA:* Parkstone. *Died Nov. 1916.*

PAGE, Thomas Nelson, BL, DL, LLD; Member of American Academy of Arts and Letters; *b* Oakland Plantation, Virginia, 23 April 1853; 2nd *s* of Major John Page (late CSA), and Elizabeth Burwell Nelson; *m* Florence (*d* 1921); two *d*. *Educ:* Washington and Lee University; University of Virginia. Practised law in Richmond, Va, 1875-93; United States Ambassador to Italy, 1913-19; delivered lectures on subjects connected with history of Southern States; wrote and published stories and essays. *Publications:* In Old Virginia, or Marse Chan and other stories, 1867; Two Little Confederates, 1888; On Newfound River, 1891; Among the Camps,1891; The Old South; Essays, Social and Historical, 1891; Elsket and other stories, 1892; Befo' de War; Poems in Negro Dialect (with A. C. Gordon), 1888; Pastime Stories, 1894; The Burial of the Guns, 1894; The Old Gentleman of the Black Stock, 1896; Red Rock, 1898; Santa Claus Partner, 1899; Social Life in Virginia before the War, 1901; Two Prisoners, 1903; A Captured Santa Claus, 1902; Gordon Keith, 1903; Bred in the Bone and other stories, 1904; The Negro: The Southerner's Problem, 1904; The Coast of Bohemia; Poems, 1906; Under the Crust (stories), 1907; The Old Dominion: Her Making and Her Manners, 1908; Robert E. Lee: Man and Soldier, 1908; Tommy Trot and his Visit to Santa Claus, 1908; John Marvel, Assistant, 1909; The Land of the Spirit, 1913; Thomas Jefferson, The Apostle of Liberty, 1918; Italy and the World War, 1921. *Recreations:* golf, living in the country. *Address:* Southborough, Mass, USA. *Clubs:* Metropolitan, Cosmos, Chevy Chase, Washington; Westmoreland, Richmond, Va; Southern Society, University, Century, Authors', New York; Tavern, Boston.

Died 1 Nov. 1922.

PAGE, Walter Hines; American Ambassador to England, 1913-18; member of publishing firm of Doubleday, Page and Co.; *b* North Carolina, USA, 15 Aug. 1855; *e s* of A. F. Page; *m* Alice, *d* of Dr John Wilson of Michigan; three *s* one *d*. *Educ:* Johns Hopkins University. Editor of the Forum (New York), 1890-95; The Atlantic Monthly (Boston), 1896-99; The World's Work (New York), 1900-13. LLD (Randolph-Macon College, Virginia, Tulane University, La, Aberdeen, Edinburgh, Sheffield, and Cambridge, England); DCL (Oxon). *Publications:* The Rebuilding of Old Commonwealths; The Southerner, a novel. *Address:* Garden City, Long Island, New York. *Clubs:* University, Authors', National Arts, New York. *Died 23 Dec. 1918.*

PAGET, Lt-Col Albert Edward Sydney Louis, MVO 1904; 11th Hussars; *b* 23 May 1879; *e s* of General Sir Arthur Henry Fitzroy Paget and Mary, *d* of Paran and Marietta Stevens. Entered army, 1900; Capt. 1909; ADC to Major-Gen., Infantry Brigade, S Africa, 1900-1; served S Africa, 1900-1 (Queen's medal, 4 clasps); ADC to Lord-Lieut of Ireland, 1905-6; Adjutant, 11th Hussars, 1906-8; ADC to GOC-in-C Eastern Command, 1908-12; served European War, 1914-15 (wounded, despatches, Bt Major). *Clubs:* Cavalry, Bachelors', Turf. *Died 2 Aug. 1917.*

PAGET, Admiral Sir Alfred (Wyndham), KCB 1911; KCMG 1905 (CMG 1899); DSO 1917; temporary Captain Royal Naval Reserve; *b* 20 March 1852; 2nd *s* of late Gen. Lord Alfred Henry Paget, CB (5th *s* of 1st Marquis of Anglesey), and Cecilia, *d* of G. T. Wyndham; *m* 1906, Viti, *e d* of Sir William MacGregor and Mary, *d* of R. Cocks; one *d*. Entered RN, 1865; Captain, 1896; Vice-Admiral, 1911; served Egyptian War, 1882 (medal, Khedive's star); Eastern Soudan, 1884-85; Suakim, 1888 (despatches, promoted Commander, clasp, 3rd class Medjidie); Naval Attaché to Paris, Petrograd, and Washington, 1896-99; China, 1900-1; Senior Officer, Coast of Ireland, 1908-11; Officer Legion of Honour. *Address:* 33 Seymour Street, W. *T:* Mayfair 5363. *Clubs:* United Service, Turf, Bachelors'.

Died 17 June 1918.

PAGET, General Rt. Hon. Sir Arthur (Henry Fitzroy), GCB, 1913 (KCB 1907; CB 1904); KCVO 1906 (CVO 1901); PC Ireland, 1912; King at Arms, Order of the British Empire, 1918; *b* 1 March 1851; *e s* of late Gen. Lord Alfred Henry Paget, CB, and Cecilia (*d* 1914), 2nd *d* and co-heir of G. T. Wyndham, Cromer Hall, Norfolk; *m* 1878, Mary (*d* 1919), *o d* of late Paran and Marietta Stevens; two *s* one *d* (and one *s* decd). Entered Scots Guards, 1869; Lt-Col 1882; Col 1895; Maj.-Gen. 1900; served Ashanti War, 1873 (medal with clasp); Soudan, 1885 (medal with clasp, Khedive's star); Burmah, 1887-88 (medal with clasp); Soudan, 1888-89, including action of Gemaizah (clasp); commanded 1st Scots Guards, South Africa; 20th Brigade (despatches, medal 6 clasps); 1st Div. 1st Army Corps, 1902-6; Eastern Command, 1908-11; Officer commanding the Forces in Ireland, 1911-17; Order of the Red Eagle (first class); Grand Cross of the Dannebrog; Legion of Honour (Grand Officer); Order of St Alexander Nevsky (Russia); Order of the White Eagle (Serbia). *Address:* Warren House, Coombe Wood, Kingston Hill. *T:* Kingston 0600. *Club:* Turf. *Died 9 Dec. 1923.*

PAGET, Very Rev. Edward Clarence, DD; Rector since 1900 and Dean of Calgary since 1901; *b* Swithland Rectory, Leicestershire, 14 Aug. 1851; 3rd *s* of Rev. E. J. Paget, and *g s* of Vice-admiral Sir Charles Paget, GCH; unmarried. *Educ:* Keble College, Oxford (First Class in Modern History; MA); Cuddesden College. Ordained 1875; Curate of Frampton Cotterell, 1875-77; Assistant Master, St Paul's Cathedral Choir School, 1877-78; Principal, Dorchester Missionary College, 1878-84; Asst Minister, Davenport Cathedral, Iowa, 1886-87; Rector of Holy Trinity, Muscatine, Iowa, 1887-99; Vicar of Revelstoke, BC, 1899-1900. *Publications:* A Year under the Shadow of St Paul's Cathedral; Ideal of Christian Priesthood; The True Motive of Missionary Work, 1882; Memoir of the Hon. Sir Charles Paget, 1913. *Address:* The Rectory, Calgary, Canada.

Died March 1927.

PAGET, Sir (George) Ernest, 1st Bt, *cr* 1897; DL; Lieutenant-Colonel Leicestershire Yeomanry, retired; Chairman Midland Railway, 1890-1911; *b* 10 Nov. 1841; *o s* of George Byng Paget and Sophia, *d* of William Tebbutt; *m* 1866, Sophia (*d* 1913), *d* of Col Charles Holden; one *s* one *d* (and one *s* decd). *Educ:* Harrow. Joined 7th Hussars, 1860; transferred to Royal Horse Guards, 1861, retired, 1867. *Heir: s* Cecil Walter Paget [*b* 19 Oct. 1874; *m* 1906, Lady Alexandra Louisa Godolphin Osborne, *d* of 9th Duke of Leeds]. *Recreation:* won the Cambridgeshire Stakes with Re-Echo, 1922. *Address:* Sutton, Bonington, Loughborough. *TA:* Kegworth Rail. *Clubs:* Turf, Carlton.

Died 30 Dec. 1923.

PAGET, Mary, (Lady Paget); *b* America; *o d* of late Paran Stevens and Mrs Marietta Stevens; *m* 1878, Gen. Rt Hon. Sir Arthur Henry Fitzroy Paget. *Educ:* New York; Paris. *Address:* 35 Belgrave Square, SW; Warren House, Coombe Wood, Kingston Hill. *TA:* Fitzroy, London. *T:* Victoria 1754. *Died 18 May 1919.*

PAGET, Stephen, FRCS; Consulting Aural Surgeon, Middlesex Hospital; Vice-Chairman Research Defence Society; *b* 17 July 1855; 4th *s* of Sir James Paget, 1st Bt, and Lydia, *d* of Rev. Henry North; *m* 1885, Eleanor Mary, 2nd *d* of Edward Burd, MD, of Shrewsbury; two *d*. *Educ:* Shrewsbury; Christ Church, Oxford; St Bartholomew's Hospital. FRCS 1885. *Publications:* The Surgery of the Chest, 1896; John Hunter, 1897; Ambroise Paré and his Times, 1510-1590, 1897; Essays for Students, 1899; Experiments on Animals, 1900, 3rd edn 1906; Memoirs and Letters of Sir James Paget, 1901; Selected Essays and Addresses by Sir James Paget, 1902; Chronicles of the Royal Medical and Chirurgical Society, 1905; The Young People, 1906, enlarged edn, as Essays for the Young People, 1910; Confessio Medici, 1908; The Faith and Works of Christian Science, 1909; I Wonder, 1911; For and Against Experiments on Animals, 1912; Another Device, 1912; Francis Paget, Bishop of Oxford (with Rev. J. M. C. Crum), 1912; Pasteur and After Pasteur, 1914; The New Parents'

Assistant, 1914; Essays for Boys and Girls, 1915; I Sometimes Think, 1916; Sir Victor Horsley, 1919; Henry Scott Holland, Memoir and Letters, 1921; I have Reason to Believe, 1922. *Address:* Furzedown, Limpsfield, Surrey. *T:* New Oxted 151.

Died 8 May 1926.

PAGET, Brig.-Gen. Wellesley Lynedoch Henry, CMG 1915; CB 1914; MVO 1904; *b* 2 March 1858; 6th *s* of late Col Leopold Grimston Paget and Mrs Leopold Paget, (Georgiana Theodosia), Park Homer, Wimborne; *m* 1888, Isabelle Louise, *d* of late W. H. Swire; one *s* one *d*. *Educ:* Wellington College; Woolwich. Lieut RA 1878; Adjutant Royal Horse Artillery, 1895–97; served in S African War, 1899–1900; commanded 2nd Brigade Division, RFA, 1900; Relief of Ladysmith and operations in Natal and the Transvaal; appointed to command A Battery (The Chestnut Troop), RHA, 1900; operations in NE Transvaal (despatches three times, Bt Lt-Col, Queen's medal with 6 clasps); European War, 1914–16 (despatches twice, CMG). *Recreations:* hunting, shooting, fishing. *Address:* Cheriton Manor, Templecombe, Somerset. *Club:* Army and Navy.

Died 11 June 1918.

PAGET, William Edmund; JP, Leicestershire; Lord of the Manor of Wymeswold; *b* 1879; *s* of late William B. Paget of Loughborough; *m* 1905, Barbara, 3rd *d* of late W. S. Hunter, Gilling Castle, York; one *s* one *d*. *Educ:* Winchester; Trinity College, Cambridge (BA). *Recreations:* hunting (Joint Master Quorn Hounds, 1919), shooting. *Address:* Nanpantan, Loughborough. *Club:* Windham.

Died 27 March 1928.

PAGET-COOKE, Sir Henry, Kt 1906; *b* 16 May 1861; *s* of late William Major Cooke (Metropolitan Police Magistrate), of Westbourne Terrace, W, and Bellecroft, Newport, Isle of Wight, and Maria Bartlett, *d* of late Dr Ashwell of Grafton Street, W; assumed additional surname of Paget; *m* 1891, Grace Bernard, *d* of late Arthur Hathaway, HEICS; one *s*. *Educ:* Cheltenham College. Admitted a Solicitor, 1886; joined firm of Russell-Cooke and Co., 1890, senior partner, 1903, his firm acting in most of the Parliamentary and Municipal Election Petitions since 1890; legal adviser to Princess Beatrice as Governor of the Isle of Wight, and to the Liberal Central Association; Coronation Medal, 1911. *Recreations;* Cheltenham College Eleven, 1879–80; won the Fives Championship Cup, open to the College, in 1880; golf, boating, shooting. *Address:* 25 Orsett Terrace, Hyde Park, W2. *T:* Paddington 1400; 11 Old Square, Lincoln's Inn, WC1. *TA:* Rusellanum, London. *T:* Holborn 1924. *Clubs:* Reform, Eighty.

Died 7 March 1923.

PAICE, Rev. Arthur; Vicar of St Mary, Lichfield, since 1918; Rural Dean of Lichfield, 1918; Prebendary of Lichfield Cathedral; *b* 8 Oct. 1857; *s* of Henry Charles and Eliza Paice of Egham, Surrey; *m* 1895, Mabel Frederica (*d* 1918), *d* of Rt Rev. Sir Lovelace Tomlinson Stamer, 3rd Bt, Lord Bishop Suffragan of Shrewsbury; no *c*. *Educ:* privately; Corpus Christi College, Cambridge; Westcott's Clergy Training School. BA 1881 (Theol. Tripos); MA 1884. Deacon, 1881; Priest, 1882; Curate St Matthew, Walsall, 1881–83; Curate of Hartshill, Stoke-on-Trent, 1883–87; Vicar, 1887–1901; Vicar and Rural Dean, S Matthew, Walsall, 1901–18; Proctor in Convocation, Archdeaconry of Stafford. *Recreations:* cricket, golf, tennis. *Address:* St Mary's Vicarage, Lichfield.

Died 3 July 1923.

PAIN, Rt. Rev. Arthur Wellesley, DD *jure dig.*; Hon. Secretary, Church Missionary Society of Australia and New Zealand since 1917; Canon of Sydney since 1918; *b* Felmersham, Beds, 21 Aug. 1841; *s* of Joseph and Mary Pain; *m* 1871, Annie Bisdee, *e d* of George Thorne of Sydney; three *s* three *d*. *Educ:* St Catharine's College, Cambridge. Ordained, 1866; Curate of Holbrook, Suffolk, 1866–67; Incumbent of Narellan, NSW, 1868–83; with Cabramatta, 1877–83; RD of Camden, 1872–83; Rector of St John, Darlinghurst, Dio. of Sydney, 1883–1902; RD of East Sydney, 1885–1902; Chaplain to Archbishop of Sydney, 1893–1902; Canon of Sydney, 1897–1902; Bishop of Gippsland, 1902–17. *Address:* Felmersham, Beecroft, New South Wales. *TA:* Beecroft.

Died 14 May 1920.

PAIN, Barry Eric Odell, BA; author; *b* 28 Sept. 1864; *s* of John Odell and Maria Pain, Cambridge; *m* 1892, Amelia Nina Anna (*d*1920), *d* of Rudolf Lehmann; two *d*. *Educ:* Sedbergh; Corpus Christi Coll., Cambridge (classical scholar). Was one of the best-known contributors to Granta, the University magazine at Cambridge; served in the anti-aircraft section, RNVR, 1915–16, afterwards on the London Appeal Tribunal. *Publications:* In a Canadian Canoe, 1891; Playthings and Parodies, 1892; Stories and Interludes, 1892; Graeme and Cyril, 1893;

Kindness of the Celestial, 1894; The Octave of Claudius, 1897; Wilmay and other Stories of Women, 1898; The Romantic History of Robin Hood, 1898; Eliza, 1900; Another Englishwoman's Love Letters, 1901; The One Before, 1902; Little Entertainments, 1903; Lindley Kays, 1904; Curiosities, 1904; The Memoirs of Constantine Dix, 1905; Wilhemina in London, 1906; First Lessons in Story Writing, 1907; The Shadow of the Unseen (with J. Blyth), 1907; The Gifted Family, 1909; Proofs before Pulping, 1909; The Exiles of Faloo, 1910; Here and Hereafter, 1911; Eliza Getting on, 1911; An Exchange of Souls, 1911; Exit Eliza, 1912; Stories in Grey, 1912; Stories without Tears, 1912; The New Gulliver, 1913; Eliza's Son, 1913; Mrs Murphy, 1913; One Kind and Another, 1914; The Short Story, 1915; Edwards, 1915; The Problem Club, 1919; The Death of Maurice, 1920; Marge Askinforit, 1921; This Charming Green Hat Fair, 1925; Essays of To-day and Yesterday, 1926. *Club:* Arts.

Died 5 May 1928.

PAIN, Brig.-Gen. Sir (George) William (Hacket), KBE 1919; CB 1900; the Queen's, Royal and the Worcestershire Regiments; MP (U) South Londonderry, since 1922; *b* 5 Feb. 1855; *s* of George Pain, 11th Hussars; *m* 1898, Saidie, *y d* of late Sidney Merton, Sydney. Entered army 1875; Captain, 1886; Major, 1894; Lieut-Col 1900; served Soudan, 1888 (medal with clasp, Khedive's star); Nile Frontier Field Force, 1889 (3rd class Medjidie); capture of Tokar, 1891 (3rd class Osmanieh, clasp to star); Dongola Expeditionary Force, 1896 (despatches, brevet of Lieut-Col, British medal, Khedive's medal two clasps); Nile Field Force, 1897; AAG to Egyptian Army to end of campaign; Brevet Colonel, 1901; South Africa, 1901–2 (despatches, CB, medal 3 clasps, King's medal 2 clasps); Col 1907; commanding a District, 1908–11; retired 1912; raised and commanded 108th Infantry Brigade, Ulster Division, 1914 (Bronze Star, 1915, General Service and Victory medals); commanded 15th Reserve Infantry Brigade in Belfast, 1916; Northern District Irish Command during Irish Rebellion, 1916–Nov. 1919; Divisional Commissioner Royal Irish Constabulary until truce, 1921 (despatches, KBE). *Recreations:* hunting, all field sports. *Clubs:* Royal Autombile, United Service; Kildare Street, Dublin.

Died 14 Feb. 1924.

PAINE, Major James Henry, DSO 1893; Royal Garrison Artillery, Native Mountain Artillery, India; *b* 8 Sept. 1870; *m* 1896, Caroline Mary, *d* of Dep. Insp.-Gen. Henry Piers, RN, and Ellen Sarah, *d* of John Colborn, Cork. *Educ:* Marlborough. Entered army, 1890; Captain 1899; served operations at Mekran, 1893 (despatches, DSO). *Address:* 26 Mountain Battery, Abbottabad, India.

Died 25 July 1918.

PAINTER, Sir Frederic George, Kt 1914; *b* 18 Dec. 1844; *s* of James Painter, Bristol; *m* 1911, Marion, *d* of Stuart Boyd Connolly, Manchester. Sheriff of City of London, 1913–14; Chevalier of the Legion of Honour; Commander of the Order of the Dannebrog; Order of the Crown of Belgium. *Address:* 8 The Boltons, SW10. *T:* Kensington 4829.

Died 9 June 1926.

PAKENHAM-MAHON, Capt. Henry, DL Co. Roscommon; late Scots Guards; *b* 13 July 1851; *o s* of Henry Sandford Pakenham-Mahon (*e s* of Hon. and Very Rev. Henry Pakenham, Dean of St Patrick's, Dublin, who was *brother* of 2nd Earl of Longford), and Grace Catherine, *d* of Major Denis Mahon; *m* 1890, May, *o d* of Col Sidney Burrard, Grenadier Guards; one *d*. *Educ:* Eton. Shot in the Rockies and up the Pacific coast; Member of several of the Royal societies, bibliographical, etc; greatly improved the extensive Strokestown estates and planted the country round, like his predecessors, since King Charles II granted Nicholas Mahon the lands and deer park. *Recreations:* shooting, farming, forestry, gardening. *Address:* Strokestown Park, Longford, Ireland; 33 Pont Street, SW1. *TA:* Strokestown. *T:* Kensington 2016. *Clubs:* Guards, Carlton; Kildare Street, Dublin.

Died 12 Jan. 1922.

PALADINI, Grande Ufficiale Prof. Carlo; Professor of English and Italian literature at the Reale Istituto Technico Galileo, and of literature relating to forestry at the Reale Istituto Superiore Forestale Nazionale, Florence; *b* near Lucca, 1864; *m* Maria Pagani, Milan; three *c*. *Educ:* almost entirely self-taught; learned reading and writing from the parish priest of his native village. At sixteen joined a party of sellers of plaster casts, with whom he wandered about the world; in the United States he took to journalism, and wrote for many of the chief periodicals; lived at New Orleans, Salt Lake City, then in Gautemala, British Honduras, Hawaii, and Hong Kong; on returning to Italy he contributed to the daily papers and reviews; Francesco Crispi sent him to accompany Gladstone on the English statesman's last visit to Italy, the result of this journey being a volume entitled Gladstone e Dufferin in Italia—Lord Dufferin being at this time British

Ambassador in Rome; was private secretary to two ministers of Public Instruction, Bianchi and De Marinis, also to the Prime Minister, Alessandro Fortis; Commendatore of the Crown of Italy, Cavaliere dei SS Maurizio e Lazzaro and Officier d'Académie of the French Republic. *Publications:* Novelle Cinesi, 1900; Intervisté (a series of Interviews with Gladstone, Cecil Rhodes, Chamberlain, Lord Salisbury, Jefferson Davis, Edwin Booth, etc), 1902; San Francesco d'Assisi nell' arte e nella storia lucchese, 1900; L'Isola di Montecristo, 1908; Il Turdus Musicus; Impero e Libertà nelle Colonoie inglesi, 1916; The United States, Wilson and Italy, 1918; Un occasione perduta; L'Alleanza anglo-italiana in Egitto, 1918; Lenin, 1920; Francesco Carrara cittadino lucchese e plebeo; Paese de vai lucchese de trovi; Il corvo di San Gemiguano; La volpe di Fiorini. *Recreations:* shooting, philately, art collection. *Address:* Villa Paladini, Massa Pisana, near Lucca, Tuscany.   *Died 10 July 1922.*

PALANPUR, HH Diwan Sir Shere Mahommed Khan, Lohani Zubdat-ul-Mulk, Nawab of, GCIE 1898 (KCIE 1893); *b* 1852; *S* father 1877. Hereditary title of Nawab and personal two additional guns, 1910; the State had an area of about 1,750 square miles and a population of over 200,000. *Address:* Palanpur, Bombay Presidency.
Died Nov. 1918.

PALEY, Frederick John, MD (London); MRCS, LRCP; Hon. Surgeon to Royal Sussex County Hospital, Brighton, since 1907, and in general practice; *b* Peterborough, 26 Sept. 1859; *s* of Frederick Apthorp Paley, LLD, MA, and Ruth, *d* of George Matthew Burchell of Scotsland, Bramley, Surrey; *m* 1892, Maude Cecil, *d* of George Cook Attfield, MRCS, of 17 Salisbury Road, Hove; two *s* one *d*. *Educ:* The Oratory School, Edgbaston; St Bartholomew's Hospital (qualified to practise, 1883). After holding positions of Resident Medical Officer at St George's Retreat, Burgess Hill, House Surgeon to the Women's Hospital, Brighton, and the Royal Sussex County Hospital, Brighton, commenced practice in Brighton, 1890; Hon. Surgeon to the Women's Hospital, 1890; Hon. Surgeon to Royal Sussex County Hospital, 1907; Hon. Consulting Surgeon to Royal Sussex County Hospital, 1922; President of the Brighton and Sussex Medico-Chirurgical Society, 1900, after holding office as Hon. Secretary in 1889 and 1890, and serving on the Council subsequently for four years; Lt-Col RAMC (TF) (despatches). *Recreation:* motoring. *Address:* 18 Brunswick Place, Hove. *T:* Hove 8891. *M:* CD 1961.
Died 12 Nov. 1924.

PALGRAVE, Sir Robert Harry Inglis, Kt 1909; JP Suffolk; FRS; Yarmouth Director of Barclay and Co., Bankers, Ltd; *b* Westminster, 11 June 1827; 3rd *s* of late Sir Francis Palgrave, KH, and Elizabeth, *d* of Dawson Turner, FRS; *m* 1859, Sarah Maria (*d* 1898), *d* of George Brightwen; one *d*. *Educ:* The Charterhouse. Taylor Prize Essay of the Statistical Society, 1871; was in 1875 one of three representatives of the English Issuing Country Bankers to give evidence on their behalf before the Select Committee of the House of Commons on Banks of Issue; editor of The Economist newspaper, 1877–83; President of Section F of the British Association, Southport, 1883; served on Royal Commission to inquire into the Depression of Trade and Industry, 1885; Lord of the Manor, and patron of the living of Henstead; received Hon. Freedom of Great Yarmouth, 1910; Kt Order of Wasa, Sweden. *Publications:* The Local Taxation of Great Britain and Ireland, 1871; Notes on Banking in Great Britain and Ireland, Sweden, Denmark, and Hamburg, 1873; An Analysis of the Transactions of the Bank of England for the years 1844–72, 1873; Bank Rate and the Money Market in England, France, Germany, Holland, and Belgium, 1844–1900, 1903; An Enquiry into the Economic Condition of the Country, 1904; editor of Dictionary of Political Economy, 3 vols, 1894–1914, Appendix, 1908; preparing a collected edition of the historical works of the late Sir Francis Palgrave. *Recreation:* gardening. *Address:* Henstead Hall, near Wrentham, Suffolk. *Club:* Athenæum.
Died 25 Jan. 1919.

PALK, Major Hon. Lawrence Charles Walter, DSO 1915; 1st Battalion the Hampshire Regiment; *b* 28 Sept. 1870; 2nd *s* of 2nd Baron Haldon and Hon. Constance Mary Barrington, *d* of 7th Viscount Barrington. *Educ:* Wellington College. Enlisted 8th HRI Hussars, 20 May 1890; 2nd Lieut Hampshire Regt, 1894; Captain, 1900; Major, 1914; served S African War, 1901–2 (Queen's medal, 5 clasps); European War, 1914–15 (despatches twice, DSO); Legion of Honour. *Clubs:* Army and Navy, Junior Naval and Military.
Died 1 July 1916.

PALLES, Rt. Hon. Christopher, PC 1892; PC Ireland 1872; JP; Lord Chief Baron of Exchequer in Ireland, 1874–1916; *b* 25 Dec. 1831; *s* of Andrew Christopher Palles, Little Mount Palles, Cavan, and

Eleanor, *d* of Matthew Thomas Plunkett, Rathmore, Co. Kildare; *m* 1862, Ellen (*d* 1885), *o d* of late Denis Doyle, Dublin; one *s*. *Educ:* Clongowes Wood College and Trin. Coll., Dublin (BA 1852). Irish Barrister, 1853; QC 1865; Solicitor-General for Ireland, 1872; Attorney-Gen., 1872–74; Hon. LLD Dublin and Cantab. *Address:* Mount Anville House, Dundrum, Co. Dublin. *Club:* University, Dublin.
Died 14 Feb. 1920.

PALMER, Capt. Alexander Edward Guy, DSO 1917; MC; Green Howards; *b* 1886; *e s* of Lt-Comdr C. B. Palmer (retired), RN; *m* 1919, Jeannie Léonie, *e d* of M Baratoux; one *d*. *Educ:* Eton. Served European War, 1914–18 (despatches, DSO). *T:* Yateley 25. *Club:* Junior United Service.
Died 9 Jan. 1926.

PALMER, Charles Felix; Recorder of Richmond, Yorkshire, since 1910; Assistant Recorder of Leeds since 1910; 2nd *s* of late Rev. F. Palmer. Called to the Bar, Middle Temple, 1884. *Address:* Shadwell Lane, Moor Allerton, Leeds.
Died 11 Dec. 1919.

PALMER, Charles Frederick; MP (Indep.) the Wrekin Divison of Salop since Feb. 1920; *b* 9 Sept. 1869; *m* 1894, Annie Dudley Smith; one *d*. Parliamentary Journalist on the Globe, 1886–1915; Editor of the Globe, 1912–15; Dramatic and Musical Critic of the People for 20 years; Assistant Editor of John Bull and joint Editorial control with Mr Bottomley, of the National News and Sunday Evening Telegram; one of the founders of the Society of Dramatic Critics, subseq. merged in the Critics Circle of the Institute of Journalists, and a member of the Committee of the Critics Circle; associated with Mr Kennedy Jones, in raising the £1,000,000,000 Victory Loan; originator of the idea which resulted in the formation of the Federation of British Industries. *Recreations:* work, tennis, gardening. *Address:* 21 Ridgmont Gardens, WC1. *T:* Museum 121. *Clubs:* Constitutional, Services.
Died 25 Oct. 1920.

PALMER, Rev. Charles Samuel, MA; Prebendary and Treasurer of Hereford Cathedral; *b* 29 May 1830; *s* of Rev. H. Palmer, Withcote Hall, Leicestershire; *m* 1854, Ellen, *d* of Rev. H. Douglas, Canon of Durham; one *d*. *Educ:* Exeter Coll., Oxford (MA 1855). Deacon, 1854; Priest, 1855; Proctor in Convocation for Chapter of Hereford, 1889–1916; Rector of Eardisley, 1866–1906; Canon of Hereford, 1892–1909. *Address:* Hampton Manor, Hereford.
Died 10 March 1921.

PALMER, Sir Edward Geoffrey Broadley, 10th Bt, *cr* 1660; JP; *b* 14 June 1864; *o s* of late Col Frederick Palmer and Mary, *o d* of William Henry Harrison; *S* cousin, 1909; *m* 1891, Sibyll Caroline, *e d* of late Capt. William James Smith Neill, RA; two *s* one *d*. *Educ:* Eton; Magdalene College, Cambridge (MA). Late Major 3rd Leicester Regt; JP Leicestershire; High Sheriff, Rutland, 1910. *Heir:* *s* Geoffrey Frederick Neill Palmer, Capt. Coldstream Guards [*b* 20 Sept. 1893. *Educ:* Repton; Trinity College, Cambridge]. *Address:* Withcote Hall, Oakham; Carlton Park, Northants; Carlton Curlieu Hall, Leicestershire. *Club:* Junior Carlton.
Died 15 May 1925.

PALMER, Sir Francis Beaufort, Kt 1907; *b* 7 July 1845; *s* of Rev. William Palmer (one of the originators of the Oxford Movement) and Sophia, *d* of Admiral Sir Francis Beaufort, KCB, FRS; *m* 1898, Georgiana Elizabeth, *d* of 8th Baron de Hochepied Larpent and Catherine Mary, *d* of Maj.-Gen. Sir Peter Melvill Melvill, KCB; three *s*. *Educ:* University College, Oxford. Called to the Bar, 1873; Bencher Inner Temple, 1907. *Publications:* Company Precedents; Private Companies; Company Law; Peerage Law in England; and other works. *Address:* 29 Bryanston Square, W. *T:* Paddington 1946; 5 New Square, Lincoln's Inn, EC. *Clubs:* Athenæum, Burlington Fine Arts.
Died 15 June 1917.

PALMER, Frederick Stephen, MD University College, Durham; FRCP; MRCS and LSA; Consulting Physician West End Hospital for Diseases of the Nervous System; *b* East Sheen, Surrey; *e s* of Henry Smith Palmer, MRCS and LSA, of East Sheen, Surrey; *m* Mary Georgiana, *d* of Charles Edward Fry of Compton House, Compton Bishop, Somersetshire; one *d*. Formerly Senior House Surgeon, Westminster Hospital, and Resident Medical Officer (4 years) Radcliffe Infirmary, Oxford; many years in general medical practice at East Sheen, Surrey; Fellow of Royal Society of Medicine, and Medical Society of London; Vice-President Medical Society of London; President and Hon. Secretary for the South Durham University Medical Graduates Association; ex-President of the West London Medico-Chirurgical Society; *Publications:* various contributions to medical journals and hospital reports. *Address:* 11 Wimpole Street,

W1. *T:* Mayfair 8412; 28 Kew Gardens Road, Kew, Surrey. *Club:* Royal Societies.
Died 21 April 1926.

PALMER, Rear-Adm. George; *b* 1829; *e s* of Rev. George Palmer, Rector of Sullington, Sussex; *m* 1859, Ellen Douglas of Cowes, Roxburghshire; two *s* two *d*. *Educ:* Royal Naval School. Entered navy as Naval Cadet in HMS Thunder, 1844; surveying in the West Indies to 1848; then in the Plumper, Encounter, Britannia Flagship in Mediterranean; Lieut in President Flagship in Pacific; severely wounded at Petropaulski; 1st Lieut of Amphitrite, then to the Monarch Flagship; 1st Lieut of the Edinburgh, then in command of the Procris gunboat; Inspecting Commander of Coast Guard, from N to S Foreland; Commander to Aurora, Captain Sir Leopold Maclintock; Commander of Rosario; Captain, 1870; retired, 1873. *Publications:* The Migration from Shinar; Scripture Facts and Scientific Doubts; Kidnapping in the South Seas. *Address: c/o* Countess of Moray, Kinfauns Castle, Perthshire.
Died 1 Jan. 1917.

PALMER, Rev. George Herbert; Hon. Doctor of Music; *b* 9 Aug. 1846; *er s* of Jonathan Palmer, Cambridge, and Elizabeth, *d* of Thomas Stevenson, Rainton, Yorks. *Educ:* Trinity College, Cambridge (BA). Ordained, 1869; Curate of St Margaret, Toxteth Park, Liverpool, 1869–76; priest-organist, St Barnabas, Pimlico, 1876–83. *Publications:* The Antiphoner and Grail, 1881; Harmonies to the Office Hymn Book, 1891; The Sarum Psalter, 1894, 6th edn 1920; Sarum Vespers, 1908; Antiphons to Magnificat and Nunc Dimitis, 1911; Requiem Services, 1903; The Hymner, 2nd edn 1905; Sarum Grails, Alleluias and Tracts from the Sarum Gradale, 1908; Introits, 2nd edn 1918; Sarum Diurnal, pt i 1918, pt ii 1921; Sarum Compline, 3rd edn 1922. *Address:* 18 Fairacres Road, Oxford.
Died 20 June 1926.

PALMER, Sir George Hudson, 5th Bt, *cr* 1791; *b* 9 Aug. 1841; 2nd *s* of Sir George Joseph Palmer, 3rd Bt and Emily Elizabeth, *y d* of George Peter Holford of Westonbirt, Gloucestershire; *S* brother, 1906. *Educ:* Eton; Balliol College, Oxford. *Heir: cousin* Frederick Archdale Palmer [*b* 25 Aug. 1857; *m* 1892, Lilian, *d* of late Gen. Edward Arthur Somerset, CB; two *s* (and one *s* decd). *Address:* Barton, Martinhoe, Devon]. *Address:* Wanlip Hall, Leicester. *Club:* St James's.
Died 22 Oct. 1919.

PALMER, Admiral Norman Craig, CVO 1913 (MVO 1909); Royal Navy; *b* 20 Aug. 1866; *s* of late E. C. Palmer; *m* 1895, Winifred Josephine Reid, *d* of Somerville Livingstone-Learmonth. Entered Navy, 1880; Lieut, 1888 (promoted for special service in capture of slave dhow, East Coast of Africa, 1888); Commander, 1899; Captain, 1904; Rear-Admiral, 1915; Vice-Admiral, 1919; First Superintendent of Physical Training, HM Navy, 1902–5; Naval ADC to King Edward VII and King George V while commanding HM Yachts, 1909–13; commanded HM ships Royal Arthur, Highflyer, Suffolk, Aboukir, Conqueror, 1913–14; Adm. retired, 1924. *Clubs:* United Service; Royal Yacht Squadron (hon.), Cowes.
Died 12 Jan. 1926.

PALMER, Mrs Potter, (Bertha Honoré); *b* Louisville, Ky; *d* of Henry H. Honoré; *m* 1871, Potter Palmer (*d* 1902). *Educ:* Convent School, Georgetown. Became social leader; elected President, Board of Lady Managers, World's Columbian Exposition, 1891; visited Europe and interested foreign Governments there in the Fair; appointed by President only woman member of National Commission for Paris Exposition, 1900; awarded Legion of Honour. *Address:* 100 Lake Shore Drive, Chicago.
Died May 1918.

PALMER, Ralph Charlton; *b* 1839; 3rd *s* of Colonel George Palmer, of Nazeing Park, Essex. *Educ:* Winchester; Balliol College, Oxford. Barrister Lincoln's Inn, 1864; Secretary to Public Schools Commission, 1868; Principal Secretary to Lord Chancellor Selborne, 1880; Clerk of the Crown in Chancery, 1880–85; Lord Chancellor's Legal Visitor in Lunacy, 1885–1910; Deputy Chairman Executive Committee of City and Guilds Institute for Advancement of Technical Education; Member of Senate, University of London, 1912–20; JP Essex, 1898. *Address:* Hubbards, Nazeing, Waltham Cross. *T:* 11 Nazeing; 9 Little Stanhope Street, Mayfair, W1. *Club:* United University.
Died 8 Sept. 1923.

PALMER, (William) Howard, JP Berks; Chairman, Huntley & Palmers, Ltd, Reading; *b* 1865; 3rd *s* of late Samuel Palmer of Northcourt, Hampstead, NW; *m* Ada Morgan, 4th *d* of late William Reed, Onslow Gardens, SW; one *s*. *Educ:* Cholmeley School, Highgate. High Sheriff for Berks, 1903. *Recreations:* hunting, shooting. *Address:* Heathlands, Wokingham, Berks; 22 Down Street, Piccadilly,

W1. *Clubs:* Junior Carlton, Royal Automobile, Ranelagh.
Died 17 March 1923.

PALMES, Rev. George, JP; MA; *b* 1851; *e s* of late Rev. W. L. Palmes and Marion, *e d* of A. Empson of Spellow Hill; *m* 1882, Eva Blanche, *y d* of Henry Dalbiac Harrison of Holbrook Park, Sussex; two *s*. *Educ:* Lincoln College, Oxford. Rector of Elston, Notts, 1887–93; Vicar of Naburn, 1904. *Address:* Naburn Hall, York.
Died 30 July 1927.

PANAGAL, Rajah of; Hon. Rajah Sir Panaganti Ramarayaningar, KCIE 1926; *b* 1866. *Educ:* Hindu High School, Triplicane; The Presidency College, Madras. Member of the Imperial Legislative Council, 1912–15, and Member of the Madras Legislative Council since 1920; invited to the Imperial War Conference, 1918; visited England as representative of the Landed Aristocracy, and gave evidence before the Parliamentary Joint Committee; appointed as Minister of the Madras Government, under the Reforms Act, 1920; Chief Minister to the Govt of Madras in charge of Local Self-Government Dept, 1921; title of Hereditary Rajah conferred in 1922; President of the South Indian Liberal Federation; elected Leader of the Justice Party; presided over the All-India Non-Brahmin Congress, Amraoti, 1925; Fellow of Madras University, 1919. *Address:* Tawker's Gardens, Royapettah, Madras.
Died Dec. 1928.

PANK, Sir John Lovell, Kt 1922; DL, Hertfordshire; JP, Herts and Middlesex; Alderman and Vice-Chairman, Herts County Council; *b* 1846. Chairman Herts Education Committee from formation; Chairman Barnet County Bench. *Recreation:* the mountains. *Address:* Somerset Road, New Barnet. *Club:* Junior Constitutional.
Died 18 Oct. 1922.

PANKHURST, Emmeline; Hon. Treasurer Women's Social and Political Union; *b* 4 July 1858; *d* of Robert Goulden, Manchester, and Sophia Jane Craine; *m* 1879, Richard Marsden Pankhurst (*d* 1898), LLD, Barrister-at-law; three *d* (two *s* decd). *Educ:* private schools, Manchester and Paris. Always active Suffragist, also worked in many Reform movements; co-founded Women's Social and Political Union, 1903; elected on School Board and Board of Guardians, Manchester; after abolition of School Board co-opted member of Education Committee; resigned all other work to devote life to winning votes for women; on outbreak of war devoted all her time to National Service; took active part in recruiting work and made many speeches on the war. *Publications:* My Own Story (autobiog.), 1914; Women's Suffrage pamphlets, etc; Poor Law Reform pamphlets.
Died 14 June 1928.

PANTON, Mrs Jane Ellen, FZS; *b* London, 18 Oct. 1848; *d* of William Powell Frith, RA; *m* 1869, James Panton, Wareham, Dorset; three *s* two *d*. Pioneer of Home Decoration and Management by Correspondence, and journalist, 1882–1900. *Publications:* One Year in His Life, etc, 1881; Country Sketches in Black and White, 1882; Jane Caldecott, 1882; Less than Kin, 1885; Listen! Poems for Children's Hour, 1885; Curate's Wife, 1886; Dear Life, 1886; From Kitchen to Garret, 1887, 11th edn 1897; Tangled Chain, 1887; By-paths and Cross-roads, 1889; Nooks and Corners, 1889; Homes of Taste, 1890; Having and Holding, 1890; Within Four Walls, 1893; Suburban Residences, 1896; The Way They Should Go, 1897; Simple Homes, 1898; A Dream House, 1898; A Short Cut to Comfort, 1907; Leaves from a Life, 1908, 5th edn 1908; A Cannibal Crusader, 1908; Fresh Leaves and Green Pastures, 1909; Leaves from a Garden, 1910; More Leaves from a Life, 1911; Most of the Game, 1911; Round about a Rectory, 1912; The Year's Mind, 1913; Leaves from a Housekeeper's Book, 1914; Leaves from the Countryside, 1914; The Building of Whispers, 1915; The River of Years, 1916; An Eclipse of the Sun—Leaves from my War Book, 1917; For Kitchen and Garret: Hints for the Lean Year, 1919. *Address: c/o* Miss Panton, 26 Southsea Avenue, Watford, Herts.
Died 13 May 1923.

PANZERA, Lt-Col Francis William, CMG 1911; FRSA; Reserve of Officers, retired; Commandant, Knockaloe Alien Dentention Camp, Peel, Isle of Man; late Resident Commissioner, Bechuanaland Protectorate; *b* 1851; *s* of J. G. I. A. Panzera, civil engineer, and *g s* of J. G. Panzera, formerly Minister of War, and afterwards British Consul, Naples; *m*; one *s* two *d*. Served for some years with Royal and Militia Artillery; appointed to serve as Acting Engineer with RE in Eastern District to raise, organise, and train Harwich Militia Division, and 1st Class Army Reserve (Submarine Miners) RE, 1888; commanded troops, Harwich and Landguard, 1890–91; nominated by War Office to serve under Colonial Office in South Africa, 1892; Government Engineer Officer and Superintendent Public Works,

Bechuanaland and Protectorate, and Engineer Officer, Bechuanaland Border Police, 1893; Member Protectorate Concessions Commission, 1893; commanded Imp. Base, Macloutsie; and southern line of Communications, under Colonel Goold-Adams, Matabele War, 1893–94 (promoted Major Reserve of Officers, medal); Magistrate, Macloutsie and Tati Districts, 1893–94; Secretary, Khama Southern Boundary Commission, 1894; Imp. Govt Engineer and Representative, Vryburg-Palapye Sect. (subsidised), Rhodesia Railways, 1894; Expert to Treasury for Jameson Trial, 1896; British Member and President British-Transvaal Joint Boundary Commission, 1897; Special Commissioner, Ngamiland, 1898–99; served throughout South African War, 1899–1902; DAAG, commanded artillery, etc, Defence of Mafeking; subsequently as DAAG on Staff of Dep. Insp.-Gen. of Communications; Assistant Commissioner of Bechuanaland Protectorate, 1901; and Commandant Northern Protectorate; Imperial Military Member Western Section War Losses Compensation Commission (despatches twice, medal with 2 clasps, King's medal with 2 bars, promoted Lt-Col Reserve of Officers). *Publications:* Questions and Answers on Gunnery; The Officering of the Artillery Militia. *Address:* Gatewick, Dovercourt, Essex. *Clubs:* British Empire, Junior Army and Navy; Royal Harwich Yacht.

Died 14 June 1917.

PAPE, Archibald Gabriel; Master of Foxhounds (Silverton), Master of Beagles (Stoke Hill); *b* Weymouth, 29 Sept. 1876; *s* of Gabriel Pape and Emily Julia Pape; *m* 1905, Lily Lynette Aplin; two *s. Educ:* Kingston School, Yeovil. *Address:* Hillcot, Stoke Hill, Exeter. *TA:* Stoke Hill, Exeter. *M:* TT 9775.

Died 3 Dec. 1927.

PAPILLON, Rev. Thomas Leslie; Hon. Canon of St Albans since 1907; Vicar of Writtle, Essex, 1884–1909; *b* Lexden, Essex, 12 April 1841; *s* of Rev. John Papillon, Rector of Lexden, and Frances Anne Prudentia, *d* of Rt Rev. John Leslie, Bishop of Kilmore, Ireland; *m* 1st, 1871, Edith Mary (*d* 1908), *d* of Rev. Charles B. Dalton, Prebendary of St Paul's and Vicar of Highgate; one *s* two *d*; 2nd, 1909, Laura Mary, *d* of Samuel Dickson, of Writtle. *Educ:* Marlborough; Balliol College, Oxford (Scholar). 1st class Moderations (Classics), 1862; 1st class Final Classical School, 1864; Hertford Scholar, 1862; Latin Verse Prize, 1863; Fellow of Merton College, 1865–70, and of New College, Oxford, 1870–84; Asst Master at Rugby, 1868–69; Tutor and Dean, New College, 1870–84; Junior Bursar, 1877–84; Moderator (Honours), 1877–79 and 1885–87; Whitehall Preacher, 1877–79; Examiner at Victoria Univ., 1892–94; at Leeds Univ., 1905; and at various times for Sandhurst, Woolwich, and the Civil Service; member of the Mosely Educational Commission to the United States, 1903. *Publications:* Commentary on Virgil, 1882, revised 1892; A Manual of Comparative Philology 3rd edn. 1882; edited Dean Bradley's Aids to Writing Latin Prose; articles on campanology in the Times supplement to Ency. Britannica (9th edn.), on bells in Encyc. Brit. (11th edn.) *Address:* 41 Brittany Road, St Leonards-on-Sea.

Died 28 Dec. 1926.

PAPPRILL, Rev. Frederick; Vicar of Holy Trinity, Leicester, since 1906; Hon. Canon of Peterborough, 1919; Hon. Canon, Leicester, 1922; *b* 9 April 1859; *s* of William Fogg Papprill; *m* 1889, Alice Jane Smith; two *s* three *d. Educ:* Thanet College, Margate. Ten years' experience in the commercial world in London; ordained, 1887; missionary on Afghan Frontier, 1887–1900; Simla, 1900–4; invalided home, 1904; Asst-Priest, Hoddesdon, 1904–6. *Recreations:* fishing, bowls. *Address:* Holy Trinity Vicarage, Leicester. *T:* 954.

Died 25 March 1924.

PARDO-BAZÁN, Countess Emilia; Spanish novelist and critic; Counsellor of Public Instruction (the first woman this honour was accorded to); *b* La Corunna, Galicia, 16 Sept. 1852; *o c* of Count Pardo-Bazán; title granted by King Alphonso XIII; *m* 1868, Don José Quiroga (*d* 1912), of Orense; one *s* two *d*. A well-known lecturer and speaker; the Hispanic Society of New York granted to her First Prize Medal of Literature and Art. *Decorations:* Banda de Damas Nobles de Maria Luisa; Pro Ecclesia et Pontifice. *Publications:* novels: Pascual Lopez, 1879; La Tribuna (The Tribune), 1882; La Cuestión Palpante, 1883; El Cisne de Vilamorta (The Swan of Vilamorta), 1885; Los Pazos de Ulloa (The Son of a Bondswoman), 1886; La Madre Naturaleza (Our Mother Nature), 1887; La Piedra Angular (Angular Stone), 1891; La Quimera (The Chimera), 1905; Dulce Dueño (Sweet Master), 1911; A Wedding Trip; Ulloa's Manor; Midsummer Madness; Morrina; A Christian Woman; The Trial; Thou wilt be King; Adan and Eva; Guzman's Child; Mystery; The Treasure of Gaston; The Black Syrene; Bucolique; Tales of Marineda; Into the Tramway; New Tales; Mystic Tales; Tales of the Patrie; Tales of Love; The Profound Soul; Tragic Tales (eight volumes of tales); The Naturalism; Novel and Revolution in Russia; From Galice; The Epic

Poets; The Holy Francis of Assisi; French Modern Literature: The Romantics, The Transition (critique and story); My Pilgrimage; From the Old Spain; From the Catholic Europe; Near the Tour Eiffel (travels); The Old Spanish Cookery (a volume); The Modern Spanish Cookery (a volume); theatre (five plays); short novels, polemics, essays, portraits and sketches. *Address:* Madrid, San Bernardo, 37. *Clubs:* Lyceum; Ateneo de Madrid; Sociedad Economica de Amigos del pais (the first to enter).

Died 12 May 1921.

PAREKH, Sir Gokuldas Kahandas, Kt 1921; Vakil High Court, Bombay, since 1871; *b* Umreth, Kaira, 24 Jan. 1847; *s* of Kahandas Kalidas Parekh, school master; *m* 1863, Parsanbai, *d* of Hargovandas T. Mehta. *Educ:* Elphinstone College, Bombay. Mathematical Teacher, High School, S'urat, 1867–68; Deputy Educnl Inspector, Gujarati Schools, Bombay, 1868–71; Head Master, Alfred High School, Mandvi and Inspector of Schools, Kachh, 1871; Deputy Inspector of Gujarati Schools, Bombay, 1871–80; Member of Bombay Legislative Council representing the Municipalities of the Northern Division, Bombay Presidency, 1897–1920. *Address:* New Queen's Road, Bombay, India.

Died March 1925.

PARENT, Hon. Simon Napoleon, KC; Chairman, Transcontinental Railway Commission; *b* 12 Sept. 1855; *s* of Simon Polycarpe Parent; *m* 1877, Marie Louise Clara, *d* of Ambroise Gendron; four *s* four *d. Educ:* Laval University. Admitted to practise law, 1881; member Quebec City Council, 1890–94; Mayor, 1894–1906; elected to Legislature, 1890–1905; Minister of Crown Lands, 1897–1906; Premier and Minister of Lands, Mines, and Fisheries, Quebec, 1900–5. *Address:* Ottawa, Ont. *Clubs:* Rideau, Laurentian, Garrison, Ottawa.

Died Sept. 1920.

PAREPARAMBIL, Rt. Rev. Dr Aloysius; Vicar Apostolic of Ernakulam; *b* Pulingundu, Travancore, 25 March 1847. *Educ:* Seminary. Priest, 1870; Professor of Latin, and subsequently Vice-Rector of a seminary; a parish priest in his native place for seven years; was always in office of counsellor and secretary to his Bishop, Dr Lavigne, SJ; Bishop, 1896; travelled through France, Belgium, and Italy, 1895, and 1905; Bishop of Tio, and Vicar Apostolic for the Syrian Catholics of the Vicariate of Ernakulam in the Malabar Coast. *Address:* Ernakulam, Malabar, India.

Died 9 Dec. 1919.

PARFITT, His Honour James John, KC 1908; BA; Judge County Court, Circuit No 41, Clerkenwell, since 1921; Bencher of Middle Temple, 1917; *b* Slwch Villa, near Brecon, S Wales, Dec. 1857; *m* 1900, Elizabeth Mary, 4th *d* of late F. W. Reynolds, of Hillside, Woolton, near Liverpool. *Educ:* Prior Park College, Bath; London University. Was for about 3 years a tutor in Cardinal Newman's School at Edgbaston; called to the Bar, 1887; practised on the Midland Circuit; formerly Junior Counsel to the Post Office on his Circuit and Standing Counsel to the Assay Authorities in Birmingham; Recorder of Northampton, 1916–18; County Court Judge, Leeds and Wakefield (Circuit 14), 1918–21; Sussex Circuit, 1921, and Commissioner at Manchester Assizes, July 1921; Commissioner of Assize on S Wales Circuit, Jan. 1924, and on Oxford Circuit, June and July 1924; played cricket for Surrey, 1881–82, for Somersetshire, 1883–85; formerly one of the Governors of Birmingham University, and formerly a member of the General Council of the Bar. *Recreations:* golf, bicycling, walking; formerly cricket. *Address:* Lamb Building, Temple, EC; 17 The Grange, Wimbledon, SW19. *T:* Wimbledon 2168.

Died 17 May 1926.

PARGITER, Frederick Eden, MA; *b* 1852; 2nd *s* of Rev. R. Pargiter; *m* Florence, *e d* of Henry Beverley, Judge of High Court, Calcutta; one *s* one *d. Educ:* Taunton Grammar School; Exeter College, Oxford (1st class Math. in Mods, 1871 and Finals, 1873; Boden Sanskrit Scholar, 1872). Entered ICS (Bengal), 1875; Under-Secretary, Government of Bengal, 1885; District and Sessions Judge, 1887; Judge of High Court, Calcutta, 1904; retired, 1906; Secretary Bengal Asiatic Society, 1884–85, President, 1903–5; Member of Council, Royal Asiatic Society, 1907–11, 1912–16, and 1921–25, Vice-President, 1916–21; Fellow of Calcutta University, 1905–6. *Publications:* Bengal Municipal Acts; Revenue History of the Sundarbans; Beverley's Land Acquisitions Acts; translation of the Markandeya Purana with Notes; Dynasties of the Kali Age; Ancient Indian Historical Tradition; Centenary Volume,(1923) of the Royal Asiatic Society; papers in Journals of Bengal and Royal Asiatic Societies, Epigraphia Indica, etc. *Address:* 12 Charlbury Road, Oxford.

Died 18 Feb. 1927.

PARISET, Georges; Agrégé d'histoire, 1988; LittD 1897; Professor of Modern History in the University of Nancy since 1891, of

Strasbourg since 1919; *b* 8 July 1865; *m* Jeanne Schmidt; four *c*. *Educ:* Sorbonne. *Publications:* Church and State in Prussia, 1713–40, 1897; The Anglo-Venezuelan Dispute about Guiana, 1900; La Révolution, le Consulat et l'Empire, Lavisse, Histoire de France Contemporaine 11–111, 1920–21; France under the Consulate and the Empire, in Cambridge Modern History, IX, 1906, etc. *Address:* 3 rue de la Monnaie, Strasbourg, France.

Died 25 Sept. 1927.

PARK, Col and Hon. Col James Smith, MVO 1905; VD; JP County of City of Glasgow; Member of Town Council, Glasgow, since 1914; late Commander 1st Lanarkshire Royal Engineers Volunteers and Scottish Group Telegraph Companies Royal Engineers Territorial Force; member of the Corporation and of the Territorial Force Association of the County of City of Glasgow; *b* Glasgow, 25 Dec. 1854; *s* of late Robert Ballantyne Park of Glasgow; unmarried. *Educ:* Western Academy and University, Glasgow. Late Managing Director at Glasgow of Allan Line, also principal owner and manager of The Park Steamship Company, Limited, and an underwriter at Lloyd's; Chairman, Dominion of Canada Investment and Debenture Company, Ltd; and J. Broadfoot & Sons, Ltd; Director of W. Beardmore & Co., Ltd, and R. and J. Dick, Ltd; and Forth and Clyde Junction Railway Company; member of the Board of Trade Committee on New Lighthouse Work; Director in many philanthropic and educational institutions; gave important evidence on behalf of shipowners before Royal and other commissions; raised and successfully contested very important points connected with shipping with the Board of Trade; was a member of Board of Trade Committee to consider question of Boy Sailors, and of War Office Committees regarding Auxiliary Forces; long an advocate of universal physical and military training. *Recreations:* riding, cycling, golf, and other athletics. *Address:* 20 Park Terrace, Glasgow, W; Auchenkyle, Monkton, Ayrshire. *TA:* Parque, Glasgow. *T:* Charing Cross 115, Glasgow. *Clubs:* Constitutional; New Conservative, Glasgow.

Died 1 Feb. 1921.

PARK, Sir Maitland Hall, Kt 1914; MA, LLD Glasgow, 1909; Chief Editor Cape Times, since 1902; *b* Cumbernauld, Dunbartonshire, NB, 10 Oct. 1862; *y s* of late Rev. Hugh Park, Established Church, Cumbernauld; *m* 1st, Alice, *d* of late Robert Orr, Helensburgh, NB; 2nd, 1892, Anna, *d* of Peter Baillie, Inverness; one *s*. *Educ:* Glasgow High School and University. Sub-Editor of the Glasgow Herald, 1885–86; joined staff Pioneer, Allahabad, NWP, India, 1886, as Assistant Editor, and remained as Assistant Editor, Acting Editor, and Chief Editor until 1902. *Recreations:* fishing, golfing, lawn tennis, bowling. *Address:* Fairlight, Orangezicht, Cape Town. *Clubs:* Imperial Colonies; Civil and City, Cape Town.

Died 15 March 1921.

PARK, Rev. Philip Lees; Hon. Canon of Gloucester Cathedral; *b* Plymouth, 7 April 1860; *s* of Thomas Park, surgeon, Royal Artillery, and Emma Lees; *m*; two *s* one *d*. *Educ:* Winchester; Trinity College, Oxford. Assistant Curate of Quebec Chapel, Marylebone, London, 1883–87; St Paul's, Clifton, Bristol, 1887–92; Vicar of Highnam, Gloucester, 1892–1922; Rural Dean of the North Forest, Dio. of Gloucester, 1909–22. *Publication:* Notes on the Occasional Prayers and Thanksgivings (Book of Common Prayer). *Address:* Parkfield Lawn, St Stephen's Road, Cheltenham. *TA:* Cheltenham.

Died 20 March 1925.

PARK, Rev. William, AM, DD, LLD; Senior Minister, Rosemary Street Presbyterian Church, Belfast; *b* Stewartstown, Co. Tyrone, 29 March 1844; *m* 1874, Susan, *y d* of Rev. John Edgar, DD; two *s* three *d*. *Educ:* Royal School, Armagh; Queen's College, Belfast; New College, Edinburgh; Assembly's College, Belfast. Ordained Minister of First Ballymena Presbyterian Church, 1866; installed as Minister of Rosemary Street Church, Belfast, 1873; Convener of Committee of General Assembly on Statistics for fifteen years; Convener of Continental Mission, two years; Convener and Joint Convener of Foreign Mission, sixteen years; Moderator of General Assembly, 1890–91; resigned the full charge of Congregation, 1923; President of the Alliance of Reformed Churches holding the Presbyterian System, for eight years, 1913–21; presided at the eleventh General Council of the same in Pittsburg (USA), Sept. 1921. *Publications:* ephemeral—sermons, etc. *Recreation:* walking. *Address:* Garthowen, Sans Souci Park, Belfast.

Died 5 June 1925.

PARK, Col William Urquhart, MVO 1905; VD; *b* 28 Jan. 1846; *s* of Thomas Park; *m* 1891, Margaret, *e d* of James W. Black, Greenock. *Educ:* Cambridge (MA). Lt-Col and Hon. Col 1st VB Argyll and Sutherland Highlanders, 1903–8. *Address:* 61 Finnart Street, Greenock.

Died April 1917.

PARKER OF WADDINGTON, Baron *cr* 1913 (Life-Peer); **Robert John Parker,** Kt 1906; a Lord of Appeal in Ordinary since 1913; *b* 25 Feb. 1857; *s* of late Rev. Richard Parker of Claxby, Alford, Lincs, and Elizabeth Coffin; *m* 1884, Constance, *d* of John Trevor Barkley; three *s* two *d*. *Educ:* Eton; King's College, Cambridge (BA 1880; MA 1883). Called to the Bar, Lincoln's Inn, 1883; Junior Counsel to the Treasury in Equity matters, 1900–6; Judge of the High Court, 1906–13. *Address:* 28 Wellington Court, SW; Aldworth, Haslemere. *Clubs:* Athenæum, United University.

Died 12 July 1918.

PARKER, Charles Sandbach, CBE 1917; of Fairlie; Chairman and Managing Director, Demerara Co., since 1908, and British Empire Producers' Organisation since 1916; *b* 1 Nov. 1864; *e s* of Samuel Sandbach Parker, Aigburth, Liverpool; *m* 1906, Harriette Dorothy, *y d* of E. G. B. Meads Waldo, of Stonewall Park, Kent; two *d*. *Educ:* Eton; University College, Oxford. Partner of Sandbach, Tinne & Co., Liverpool, and Sandbach, Parker & Co., Demerara, 1890–1908; Head of Russian Metals Dept, Commission Internationale de Ravitaillement, 1915–17; Member of Executive Committee, West India Committee, since 1898; of Trade and Industry Committee, Royal Colonial Inst., since 1917; Unionist Candidate for Barnstaple Division of Devonshire since 1910; contested Division, 1910 and 1911; Order of St Stanislav (Russia), 2nd class, with star, 1918. *Recreations:* cricket, golf, shooting. *Address:* Fairlie, Ayrshire, NB; 45 Cadogan Place, SW. *T:* Victoria 6170. *Clubs:* Athenæum, Brooks's.

Died 9 May 1920.

PARKER, Edward Harper, MA (Manchester); Professor of Chinese, the Victoria University of Manchester, since 1901; Reader in Chinese, University College, Liverpool, since 1896; *b* 3 Jan. 1849; 2nd *s* of Edward Parker (*d* 1887), surgeon, Liverpool, and Mary (*d* 1860), *d* of William Rushton, Liverpool; *m*; one *d*. *Educ:* Dr Brunner's Preparatory School, Everton; Royal Institution School, Liverpool. Barrister-at-law, Middle Temple; in the cotton-broking, silk, and tea trades, Liverpool and London, 1864–66; studied Chinese under Dr J. Summers, George Yard, EC, 1867; student-interpreter in Peking, 1869–71; served at Tientsin, Taku, Hankow, Kewkiang, and Canton consulates, 1871–75; studied at Middle Temple, 1875–77; served at Foochow, Pagoda Island, Chinkiang, and Canton consulates, 1877–80; consular-agent at Chungking, 1880–81; called to the Bar, 1882; acting-consul at Wênchow, 1883–84; temporary vice-consul at Fusan and Chemulpo, 1885–86; acting consul-general at Söul, 1886–87; served in Shanghai consulate, 1887–88; at Pagoda Island and Hoihow consulates, 1889–94; commissioned HM Consul, Kiungchow, 1892; Adviser on Chinese Affairs in Burma, 1892–93; at Hoihow, 1893–94; retired on a pension, 1895. *Publications:* Comparative Chinese Family Law, 1879; The Opium War, 1887; China's Relations with Foreigners, 1888; Up the Yangtsze, 1892; Burma, 1893; A Thousand Years of the Tartars, 1895, 2nd enlarged edn 1925; China, 1901, enlarged edn 1917; John Chinaman, 1901; China, Past and Present, 1903; China and Religion, 1905; Ancient China Simplified, 1908; Studies in Chinese Religion, 1910, etc. *Recreations:* travelling, walking. *Address:* 14 Gambier Terrace, Liverpool. *Club:* Athenæum, Liverpool.

Died 26 Jan. 1926.

PARKER, Rt. Rev. Edward Melville DD, DCL; Bishop of New Hampshire since 1914; *b* Cambridge, Mass, 11 July 1855; *s* of Henry M. Parker, lawyer, and Fanny C. Stone; *m* 1st, 1885, Grace (*d* 1888), *d* of Prof. J. J. Elmendorf, Racine, Wisconsin; one *s*; 2nd, 1914, Isabella, *d* of Rev. James B. Goodrich of Concord, NH; two *s* one *d*. *Educ:* St Paul's School, Concord, New Hampshire; Keble College, Oxford (2nd class Mathematic Moderations and Theology; MA). A master at St Paul's School, 1879–1905; Bishop Coadjutor of New Hampshire, USA, 1906–14; DD Berkely Divinity School, 1905; DCL Bishop's College, Lennoxville, Canada, 1906; DD Dartmouth College, 1914. *Address:* Concord, New Hampshire, USA.

Died 22 Oct. 1925.

PARKER, Sir (Stephen) Henry, KCMG 1914; Kt 1908; KC; Chief Justice of Western Australia, 1906–13; *b* York, WA, 7 Nov. 1846; *s* of Stephen Stanley Parker; *m* 1872, Amy Katherine, *d* of George Walpole Leake, QC; nine *c*. *Educ:* Bishop's College, Perth, WA. Called to the Bar, WA, 1868; QC 1890; Puisne Judge, 1901; represented Perth, in Legislative Council, 1878–88; Busselton, 1888–90; Member Legislative Assembly for York, 1890–92; Member Legislative Council, 1892–97; Colonial Secretary, WA, 1892–94; Delegate from Legislature to Imperial Parliament to advocate Responsible Government, 1890; represented WA in London on the delegation relative to the Federation of Australia, 1900; Mayor of Perth, 1873, 1880, 1881, 1892, 1901; President Weld Club, 1899–

1906; President of the Arbitration Court, 1904–6. *Address:* Melbourne. *Died 13 Dec. 1927.*

PARKER, Horatio William; organist; Professor of Music, Yale University, since 1894; *b* Auburndale, Mass, 15 Sept. 1863; *m* 1886, Anna Ploessl, Munich. *Educ:* Royal Conservatoire, Munich. Organist Holy Trinity, New York, 1888–93; Trinity Church, Boston, 1893–1901; Hon. AM Yale, 1892; MusD Cambridge, 1902. *Publications:* oratorios: Hora Novissima, 1898; St Christopher, 1898; A Wanderer's Psalm, 1900; cantatas: King Trojan; The Kobolds; operas: Mona, 1912; Fairyland, 1915. *Address:* Yale University, New Haven, Conn, USA. *Died 18 Dec. 1919.*

PARKER, Joseph, CSI 1896; *b* Chislehurst, 12 Aug. 1831; *e s* of late Rev. Joseph Timothy Parker, Vicar of Wyton, Huntingdonshire, and Mary, *d* of Gen. F. Campbell (Melfort), RA; *m* 1st, 1865, Bessie (*d* 1892), *d* of John Moxon Clabon; 2nd, 1894, Eva, *d* of late Col Edmund Campbell (Melfort), Bombay Staff Corps; two *s* three *d*. *Educ:* Cheltenham. Entered HEICS, 1851; senior clerk in Store Dept, 1866; Director-Gen. of Stores at India Office, 1891; retired, 1896. *Recreation:* golf. *Address:* Trelawneys Cottage, Sompting. *Club:* Primrose. *Died 6 July 1924.*

PARKER, Maj.-Gen. Neville Fraser; Bengal Infantry; *b* 30 July 1841; *m*; two *s*. Entered army, 1859; Maj.-Gen. 1897; transferred to unemployed supernumerary list, 1900; served Hazara Campaign, 1868 (medal); Afghan War, 1878–79 (despatches, medal). *Address:* Craymead, Highview Road, Sidcup.
Died Jan. 1916.

PARKER, Percy Livingstone; Editor and Proprietor of Public Opinion; *b* Ipswich, 1867; *s* of M. P. Parker; *m* 1894, Hilda, *d* of late Rev. W. H. Tindall, Weybridge. Private Sec. to late Rev. Hugh Price Hughes, 1889–93; to late Sir John Hutton, as Chairman of the LCC, 1893–94; Sub-editor The New Age, 1894–97; Assistant Editor and Editor of Harmsworth Magazine, 1898–1902; Editor of Daily Mail Year-Book, 1901–12. *Publications:* edited John Wesley's Journal, with introduction by Hugh Price Hughes and Augustine Birrell; George Fox's Journal, with introduction by Sir William R. Nicoll. *Address:* Baston Lodge, St Leonards-on-Sea; 44 Essex Street, Strand, WC. *T:* Central 948. *Died 1 April 1925.*

PARKER, Brig.-Gen. Robert Gabbett, CB 1919; CMG 1918; DSO 1915; late The King's Own (Royal Lancaster Regiment); *b* Dec. 1875; *s* of Robert Gabbett Parker. *Educ:* Clifton College; RMC, Sandhurst. Entered army, 1896; Captain, 1900; Major, 1910; Lt-Col, 1915; Col, 1919; served S African War, 1899–1902 (despatches twice, Queen's medal 6 clasps, King's medal 2 clasps); European War, 1914–18 (despatches six times, DSO, CMG, CB, French Croix de Guerre, Officer of the Order of the Crown of Italy); retired pay, 1926. *Address:* Bally Valley, Killaloe, Co. Clare.
Died 26 June 1927.

PARKER, William Frye, FRAM; Professor Royal Academy of Music; *b* 10 Sept. 1855; *m* 1879; two *s* one *d*. *Educ:* Royal Academy of Music. Principal Violin (Leader) at Philharmonic Society's Concerts, Leeds Musical Festival, etc, 1895–1910. *Address:* 17 Luxemburg Gardens, W6. *T:* Hammersmith 355. *Club:* Arts. *Died 1919.*

PARKER, William Newton, PhD; FZS; Professor of Zoology at the University College of South Wales and Monmouthshire in the University of Wales; 2nd *s* of late Prof. W. Kitchen Parker; *m* Hedwig, 2nd *d* of late Professor August Weismann and Mary Gruber; one *s* two *d*. *Educ:* Royal College of Science, London; Morphological Laboratory, Cambridge; University of Freiburg-in-Baden. Formerly Assistant to late Professor Thomas H. Huxley; Deputy-Prosector to the Zoological Society; Lecturer on Biology at University College, Aberystwyth. *Publications:* On the Structure and Development of Lepidosteus (in conjunction with late Professor F. M. Balfour); On the Anatomy and Physiology of Protopterus; Elementary Course of Practical Zoology (with late Professor T. Jeffery Parker); translations of Wiedersheim's Comparative Anatomy of Vertebrates and Weismann's Germ-Plasm. *Address:* University College, Cardiff.
Died 22 Feb. 1923.

PARKES, Sir Edward Ebenezer, Kt 1917; MP (LU) Birmingham, Central, 1895–1918; ironmaster; Magistrate for Birmingham; *b* 1848; *s* of late Israel Parkes, Edgbaston; *m* Louise, *d* of late Henry H. Hartshorne; two *s* two *d*. *Address:* Oak Grange, Hermitage Road, Edgbaston, Birmingham. *TA:* Edward E. Parkes, Birmingham. *T:* Edgbaston, Birmingham, 53. *Clubs:* Constitutional, Royal Automobile. *Died 29 June 1919.*

PARKIN, Sir George Robert, KCMG 1920 (CMG 1898); LLD, DCL hon. Oxon; Organising Representative of Rhodes Scholarship Trust since 1902; author and lecturer on Imperial Federation; *b* Salisbury, New Brunswick, 8 Feb. 1846; *s* of John Parkin, farmer, and Elizabeth McLean; *m* 1878, Annie Connell, *d* of William Fisher of Fredericton; one *s* four *d*. Principal of Upper Canada College, Toronto, Canada, 1895–1902. *Publications:* Imperial Federation, 1892; Round the Empire, 1892; The Great Dominion, 1895; Life and Letters of Edward Thring, 1898; Life of Sir John A. Macdonald, Prime Minister of Canada, 1906; The Rhodes Scholarships, 1912. *Address:* Seymour House, Waterloo Place, SW; 7 Chelsea Court, SW3. *Club:* Athenæum. *Died 25 June 1922.*

PARKINGTON, Sir John Roper, Kt 1902; DL and JP Co. London; *b* 1845; *s* of late John Weldon Parkington; *m* 1873, Marie Louise (gold medal, 1st Order of Mérite Civile, and Red Cross decoration—both of Montenegro), *d* of late A. Sims Silvester of the Stock Exchange, London; three *d*. *Educ:* private Catholic schools in England and France. Hon. Col 7th VB Essex Regiment; Major 3rd Batt. East Surrey Regiment (Militia), 1891–98; FRGS; FRCI; Vice-President Anglo-Portuguese Chamber of Commerce; one of HM Lieutenants for the City of London; founder l'Entente Cordiale, Anglo-French Association, 1896. Chevalier de la Légion d'honneur; Officier d'Académie Française, 1906; Commandeur Royal Orders of Montenegro and Servia; Red Cross of Spain; Knight Commander of Our Lady of Conception of Villa Viçosa, Portugal. *Address:* Broadwater Lodge, Wimbledon, SW19. *M:* PC 5719. *Clubs:* United Service, Royal Automobile, West Indian, City Carlton.
Died 14 Jan. 1924.

PARKINSON, Rt. Rev. Mgr. Henry, DD, PhD (Gregorian University, Rome); Rector of St Mary's College, Oscott; *b* Cheadle, Staffordshire, 1852. *Educ:* Sedgley Park School, near Wolverhampton; Douai; Olton; English College, Rome. Ordained, 1877; Vice-Rector of Olton Seminary, 1877–87; and Professor of Philosophy, Senior Curate, and Choirmaster at St Chad's Cathedral, Birmingham, 1887–89; Vice-Rector and Professor of Philosophy at Oscott College, 1889; first Rector of the Central Seminary at Oscott, 1897, when he was created a Domestic Prelate; Protonotary Apostolic, 1917; President of the Catholic Social Guild, of the Birmingham Society of St Cecily; Assistant General (for England) of the Apostolic Union of Secular Priests; Canon of Cathedral Chapter of Birmingham since 1913. *Publications:* Definitiones Philosophiæ Universæ; Refectio Spiritualis; A Primer of Social Science. *Address:* Oscott College, Birmingham. *T:* East 890. *Died 22 June 1924.*

PARKINSON, John Wilson Henry; Colonial Civil Service; *b* 13 July 1877; *e s* of W. H. Parkinson, The Hall, East Ravendale, Lincs; *m* 1919, Winifred Mary, *o d* of J. A. Forster, Croslands Park, Barrow-in-Furness; one *s*. *Educ:* Brighton College. Solicitor Supreme Court, 1900; Administrator-General, East African Protectorate, 1909; Currency Commissioner, East Africa, 1909–19; Secretary, Wakf. Commission, East Africa. *Recreations:* cricket, golf. *Address:* Mombasa, Kenya Colony. *Club:* Sports. *Died 17 June 1923.*

PARKINSON, William Edward, ARCA; FSAM; Principal of the School of Arts and Crafts, York; *b* 1 Jan. 1871; *s* of late James Henry Parkinson, Chester; *m* 1899, Rosemary, *d* of late Joseph R. Curnow, Chester; two *s*. *Educ:* School of Art, Chester; Royal College of Art, London. Formerly Art Master at Barnard Castle; Member of the Soc. of Yorkshire Artists. *Recreations:* caravanning, boating. *Address:* 103 High Petergate, York. *Died 26 May 1927.*

PARKS, Sir John, Kt 1914; DL, JP; Mayor of Bury, 1914, and three previous times; *b* 24 Nov. 1844; *m* 1868, Rachel, *d* of Samuel Grundy of Bridge Hall, Bury; three *s* two *d*. Director, Manchester and Liverpool Bank and Burnley Paper Works Co., Ltd; Chairman, Smallman's Ltd, Vulcan Spinning and Manufacturing Co., Ltd, and Liverpool Storage Co., Ltd; contested Bury, 1892. *Address:* Bank House, Bury. *Club:* National Liberal.
Died 9 Jan. 1919.

PARKYNS, Sir Thomas Mansfield Forbes, 7th Bt, *cr* 1681; *b* 30 April 1853; *s* of Sir Thomas George Augustus Parkyns, 5th Bt, and Annie, *d* of W. Jennings; *S* father, 1895; *m* 1886, Beatrice, *d* of late Arthur Travers Crawford, CMG; one *d*. *Educ:* Eton; Brasenose Coll., Oxford. Barrister Inner Temple, 1879. *Recreations:* shooting, golf. *Heir:* none. *Address:* 12 Westminster Palace Gardens, SW1. *T:* Victoria 1495. *Club:* Garrick. *Died 2 Feb. 1926 (ext).*

PARMELEE, William Grannis, ISO 1903; Ex-Deputy-Minister of Trade and Commerce, and Chief Controller of Chinese Immigration,

Canada; *b* 27 Aug. 1833; *s* of Rotus Parmelee, MD, Waterloo, Quebec, and Sarah M., *d* of William Grannis; *m* 1st, 1856, Marcella A. (*d* 1899), *d* of William Whitney of Montpelier, Vermont; 2nd, 1901, Jessie Blackburn, *d* of late Samuel Christie of Ottawa, Ontario. *Educ:* Waterloo. Engaged several years in insurance and railway offices and as bank manager; entered Civil Service, 1876; was Commissioner of Customs; transferred to new Department of Trade and Commerce, which he organised, 1892; served with and on several Commissions; retired, 1908. *Address:* Ottawa, Canada. *TA:* Parmelee. Ottawa. *T:* 408. *Died 15 Jan. 1921.*

PARNELL, John Howard; *b* 1843; *s* of late John Henry Parnell, Avondale, and Delia Tudor (*d* 1898), *d* of Capt. Charles Stewart, US Navy; *brother* of late Charles Stewart Parnell, MP; *m* 1907, Olivia Isabella, *e d* of late Colonel James Smythe, 69th Regt, and *widow* of Archibald Matier, JP, The Grove, Carlingford, Co. Louth; one *s*. Contested Co. Wicklow, 1874, W Wicklow, 1892; MP (N) Co. Meath, S, 1895–1900. *Address:* Lion House, Glenegary, Kingstown; Laragh Castle, Co. Wicklow.

Died 3 May 1923.

PARR, Cecil Francis, JP; *b* 1847; *y s* of late Thomas Parr, of Grappenhall Heyes, Cheshire, and 2nd wife, Alicia, *d* of late Philip Charlton, of Wytheford Hall, Shropshire; *m* 1882, Amy Ursula, 2nd *d* of late Hon. Robert, 7th Baron Dimsdale, of Essendon Place, Hertfordshire; one *s. Educ:* Harrow; Exeter College, Oxford (BA). Called to the Bar, Inner Temple, 1874. *Address:* Kimpton Grange, near Welwyn. *T:* Kimpton 3. *TA:* Kimpton. *Clubs:* United University, Royal Automobile.

Died 13 Jan. 1928.

PARR, Maj.-Gen. Sir Harington Owen, Kt 1926; CB 1922; CMG 1919; Military Secretary, Army Headquarters, India, 1924; retired, 1926; *b* 1867; *s* of Harington Wellford Parr. *Club:* United Service.

Died 1 Oct. 1928.

PARR, Joseph Charlton, JP, DL; *b* 2 June 1837; 3rd and *e* surv. *s* of late Thomas Parr and 2nd wife, Alicia, *d* of Philip Charlton of Wytheford Hall, Co. Salop; *m* 1872, Jessie Maria, *e d* of late Lt-Col George Lister Kaye; one *s* three *d. Address:* Grappenhall Hayes, Warrington; Staunton Park, Staunton-on-Arrow. *Clubs:* Carlton, Junior Carlton, Constitutional.

Died 27 Feb. 1920.

PARRATT, Sir Walter, KCVO 1921 (CVO 1917; MVO 1901); Kt 1892; MA; Hon. RAM; Hon. Fellow of Magdalen College, Oxford; Professor of Music, Oxford, 1903–18; Dean of Faculty of Music, London University, since 1916; late Private Organist to Queen Victoria; Organist St George's Chapel Royal, Windsor; Master of the Music to Queen Victoria, 1893–1901, to King Edward VII, 1901–10, and to King George V, since 1910; Professor at Royal College of Music; *b* 10 Feb. 1841; *s* of Thomas Parratt, Huddersfield, and Sarah Elizabeth, *d* of William Perkins; *m* 1864, Emma, *d* of Luke Gledhill, Huddersfield; one *s* three *d* (and one *d* decd). *Educ:* College School, Huddersfield; privately. Organist of Armitage Bridge Church; afterwards of Great Witley; Wigan Parish Church; Magdalen College, Oxford; St George's Chapel Royal, Windsor; Past Grand Organist of the Freemasons; Member of the Associated Board of the Royal Academy and Royal College of Music; Past Examiner in Music to Universities of Oxford, Cambridge, London, and Wales; Past President, Royal College of Organists; Past President, Union of Graduates in Music; Hon. DMus Oxon, 1908; Hon. MusD Cantab, 1910; Hon. DCL Durham, 1912. *Publications:* the article on Music, in Ward's Reign of Queen Victoria; contributor to Grove's Dictionary of Music and other works; music for the Tale of Troy, etc. *Recreation:* chess (President Oxford University Chess Club; two years Captain of the eight chosen to play against Cambridge). *Address:* Cloisters, Windsor Castle. *Club:* Athenæum.

Died 27 March 1924.

PARROTT, Sir (James) Edward, Kt 1910; Editor to publishing house of Thomas Nelson & Sons since 1898; *b* 1 June 1863; *e s* of Edward B. Parrott, Marple, Cheshire, and Margaret, *d* of John Johns, Carmarthenshire; *m* 1891, Elizabeth Sophia, *y d* of late John Shirley, Derby (Lady Parrott was for seven years Inspectress of Schools in Liverpool); three *d. Educ:* St Paul's College, Cheltenham; Trinity College, Dublin. MA (senior prizeman in English) and LLD (head of examination list, Dec. 1900); FEIS. Had scholastic experience in Sheffield and Liverpool; chairman of S Edinburgh Liberal Association, 1904–17; chairman of Edinburgh United Liberal Committee, 1908–19; MP (L) South Division of Edinburgh, 1917–18; Life Governor of Cheltenham Training College; JP County of City of Edinburgh; Palms in Gold of the Order of the Crown, Belgium; Officer of the Order of St Sava. *Publications:* A Pageant of British History; A Pageant of English Literature, 1914; Children's Story of the War (ten volumes); Allies, Foes, and Neutrals, 1918; Britain Overseas; Editor of Funk and Wagnall's Standard Encyclopædia and of Nelson's New Age Encyclopædia, 1920; numerous school books, including the Highroads Series, etc. *Recreation:* golf. *Address:* 12 Cumin Place, Edinburgh. *Club:* National Liberal.

Died 5 April 1921.

PARRY, Sir (Charles) Hubert (Hastings), 1st Bt, *cr* 1902; Kt 1898; CVO 1905; JP; MA, MusD, DCL, LLD; Director Royal College of Music; Fellow of the University of London; *b* Bournemouth, 27 Feb. 1848; 2nd *s* of Thomas Gambier Parry, Highnam Court, Gloucester, and 1st wife, Anna Maria Isabella, *d* of Henry Fynes Clinton; *m* 1872, Lady Elizabeth Maud Herbert, *d* of 1st Lord Herbert of Lea and sister of 14th Earl of Pembroke; two *d. Educ:* Eton; Exeter Coll., Oxford (Hon. Fellow). Professor of Music, Oxford, 1899–1908. *Publications:* Studies of Great Composers, 1886; Evolution of the Art of Music; Summary of Musical History; Music of the 17th Century; Style in Musical Art, 1912; Life of John Sebastian Bach; many articles in Grove's Dictionary of Music (Assistant Editor). *Works:* Music to the Birds of Aristophanes, 1884; Music to the Frogs of Aristophanes; Music to the Clouds of Aristophanes, 1905; Music to the Agamemnon of Aschylus, 1900; Judith, 1888; Ode for St Cecilia's Day, 1889; The Lotos Eaters; L'Allegro and Penseroso; Blest Pair of Sirens; Invocation to Music; De Profundis, 1891; Job, 1892; King Saul, 1894; Magnificat, 1896; Song of Darkness and Light, 1898; Processional Anthem for the Coronation of King Edward VII; Te Deum, 1900; War and Peace, 1903; Voces Clamantium, 1903; The Love that Casteth out Fear, 1904; The Pied Piper of Hamelin, 1905; The Soul's Ransom, 1906; The Vision of Life, 1907; Beyond these Voices, 1908; Te Deum for the Coronation of King George V; Hymn to the Nativity, 1913; Music to the Acharnians of Aristophanes, 1914. *Heir:* none. *Address:* Highnam Court, Gloucester; 17 Kensington Square, W; Knight's Croft, Rustington, Worthing; Royal College of Music, SW. *TA:* Initiative, London. *M:* A 7338. *Clubs:* Athenæum, Savile, National Liberal, Royal Thames Yacht; Royal Yacht Squadron, Cowes.

Died 7 Oct. 1918 (ext).

PARRY, Admiral Sir John Franklin, KCB 1919 (CB 1916); FRGS; *b* 15 Aug. 1863; *s* of Rt Rev. Edward Parry (*d* 1890), Bishop Suffragan of Dover; *m* 1893, Emily Lemprière, *d* of Hon. Henry Dobson, then Premier of Tasmania; one *d.* Entered Navy, 1877; Sub-Lieut 1883; Lieut 1885; Commander 1899; Captain 1905; Rear-Admiral 1916; Vice-Admiral, retired 1920; Chief Assistant to Hydrographer, 1900–3; Asst Hydrographer, 1910–14; Hydrographer of the Navy, 1914–19; served in Suakin campaign, 1885 (Egyptian medal and star); served on many technical Committees in connection with Hydrography and Navigation; in command of surveys in many parts of the world. *Recreations:* fishing, boating. *Address:* Palais de la Terrasse, Monte Carlo. *Club:* United Service. *Died 21 April 1926.*

PARRY, Alderman William John, CBE 1920; FCA; chartered accountant; *b* 28 Sept. 1842; *s* of John Parry and Elizabeth Jones; *m* 1st, 1864, Jane Roberts (decd); 2nd, 1878, Mary Pughe (decd); 3rd, 1902, Mary Guy; two *s* one *d. Educ:* British and National Schools, Bethesda; Grammar School, Llanrwst. Liberal agent for his district, 1862–79; took an active part in the Penrhyn strikes of 1865 and 1874, and the lockouts at Llanberis and Glynrhonwy; elected on the Bethesda Board of Commissions, 1867; established the North Wales Quarrymen's Union, 1874, and acted as its first Secretary for 2½ years, its President for nine years, and its Umpire for 22 years; took an active part for establishing the North Wales University College at Bangor; edited the Werin and Genedl newspapers for 4½ years; visted Canada and the United States in the interest of quarrymen five times, and South America twice; gave evidence before Government Committees on Towns Holdings, Quarries Bill, Royal Commission on Labour, Bankruptcy and Building Societies and Quarries Bills; a member of first County Council, and filled the chairs of the County Council, and the Standing Joint Police Committee; a frequent contributor to the national and religious periodicals of his native country during the last sixty years, and acted continuously without a break for sixty years on public bodies. *Publications:* Gyfansoddiadan Eisteddfod Cymreigyddion, Bethesda, 1864; Ymdrafodaeth Caebraechycafn, 1875; Helyntion 73 Undewr, 1885; Cofiant Tanymarian, 1886; Review of Evidence before Royal Commission on Labour, 1893, the same in Welsh, 1893; Chwareli and Chwarelwyr, 1896; Cyfrol y Jiwbili Capel Bethesda, 1900; The Penrhyn Lockout, 1901; Telyn Sankey, 1901; The Penrhyn Quarry Dispute, 1902; Ail Argraffiad Tanymarian, 1901; The Cry of the People, 1906; The English Hymnal, 1907; Cofiant Hwfa Mon, 1909; Ail Argraffiad Telyn

Sankey, 1915; Ail Argraffiad o Gofiant Hwfa Mon, 1916. *Recreations:* collecting books, reading and writing, the company of friends. *Address:* Coetmor Hall, Bethesda. *TA:* Coetmor, Bethesda. *T:* 6. *M:* 1530. *Club:* National Liberal. *Died 1 Sept. 1927.*

PARRY-OKEDEN, William Edward, ISO 1903; JP; *b* Monaro, NSW, 13 May 1840; *o s* of late David Parry-Okeden, JP, late RN, last survivor battle Navarino; *m* 1873, (Elizabeth) Gertrude, *e d* of late Rev. John Pilgrim Wall, St Vincent and Barbados, WI; three *s* four *d*. *Educ:* Melbourne Diocesan and St Kilda Grammar Schools. Studied law under articles and had training Victoria Volunteer Rifles, 1857–60; migrated to Queensland; after ten years pioneering and pastoral pursuits, appointed Inspector Police and Customs Border Patrol, 1870; Police Magistrate various towns, 1872–86, when appointed Immigration Agent for Queensland; established Government Labour Bureau; Commission of Inquiry into Gaols Management, 1887; Under Colonial Secretary, 1889; subsequently first Principal Under-Secretary, Queensland; District Magistrate under special Peace Preservation Act, 1894; Commissioner Queensland Police, 1895; retired on pension, 1905; appointed 1906–7, by Commonwealth Government of Australia, Royal Commissioner, to visit and report on Present Conditions and Methods of Government in British New Guinea (Papua), and Best Means for Improvement; first Aboriginal Protector for whole State. *Recreations:* riding, driving, cricket. *Address:* Okewall, Redcliffe, Queensland, Australia. *Club:* Queensland. *Died 30 Aug. 1926.*

PARSONS, Alfred William, RA 1911 (ARA 1897); RWS 1905 (President 1914); landscape painter; *b* Beckington, Somersetshire, 2 Dec. 1847; 2nd *s* of Joshua Parsons. *Educ:* private schools. Clerk in Savings Bank Department of Post Office, 1865–67; since then painting; exhibitor at Royal Academy, Grosvenor, New Gallery, etc; picture, When Nature painted all Things Gay, bought by Chantrey Fund, 1887; special exhibitions of the Warwickshire Avon, Gardens, Japanese Flowers, etc; illustrations for Harper's Magazine and other publications, and for The Genus Rosa, by Ellen Willmott. *Publications:* (author and illustrator) Notes in Japan, 1896; Alone, for Wordsworth's Sonnets; The Warwickshire Avon; illustrated: F. D. Millet's The Danube, from the Black Forest to the Black Sea, 1893; Ellen Willmott's The Genus Rosa, 1910; illustrations with Edwin Austin Abbey, RA: Herrick's Hesperides and Noble Numbers, 1882; She Stoops to Conquer, 1887, Old Songs, 1889; The Quiet Life, 1890. *Recreations:* canoeing, gardening. *Address:* Broadway, Worcestershire. *Clubs:* Athenæum. *Died 16 Jan. 1920.*

PARSONS, Maj.-Gen. Sir Charles (Sim Bremridge), KCMG 1899; CB 1906; FRGS; *b* 9 May 1855; *e s* of late John Parsons, Ringmore, Shaldon; *m* 1898, Margaret, *o d* of late Alfred Christian, CMG; 1898; two *d*. *Educ:* Rugby; Royal Military Academy. Served in Gaika and Zulu Campaigns, including battles of Isandhlwana and Ulundi (despatches, medal with clasps for 1877–78–79); served in Transvaal war, including actions at Laing's Nek and Ingogo (despatches and general orders for gallantry), severely wounded, horse shot; served in Egyptian campaign, 1882, including actions at Mahsama, Kassassin, and Tel-el-Kebir (despatches, horse shot, Brev. Major, medal with clasp, and 5th class Medjidieh and 4th class Osmanieh); served in Dongola campaign in command of Egyptian Artillery, including action at Hafir (despatches, and Brev. Lieut-Colonel, medal with clasp); appointed Governor of Red Sea Littoral, 1896; employed on special mission in Eritrea when Kassala was handed over to Egyptian Government (2nd class Medjidieh); commanded at capture and defence of Gedaref, 1898 (despatches, Brev. Colonel, and KCMG, clasp to medal); Assistant Adjutant-General, Woolwich, 1898–99; Col on Staff RA, Ireland, 1899; Assistant Inspector-General Lines of Communication, South Africa, 1900–1 (despatches); commanded Regular Forces Canada, 1902–6; a Commissioner for the Royal Hospital, Chelsea. *Address:* 28 Onslow Square, SW7. *T:* Kensington 1760. *Club:* Naval and Military. *Died 25 June 1923.*

PARSONS, Lt-Gen. Cunliffe McNeile, CB 1915; *b* India, 15 Feb. 1865; *s* of late Gen. James Edmond Bacon Parsons, ISC, and late Mrs Parsons of Southbourne, Hants; *m* 1903, Christina Jeannette Paton, *d* of late Colonel Edgar Hastings Thomas, ISC; two *d*. *Educ:* Dulwich College. Entered RMLI, 1883; served in China, 1900 (medal); commanded Chatham Battalion Royal Marines in operations round Antwerp, 1914, and on Gallipoli Peninsula from 29 April till wounded, 28th June 1915; Colonel, 2nd Commandant, Royal Marines, 1915 (despatches thrice, CB); commanded 181st Infantry Brigade at home, and with Expeditionary Force, 1916, and 63rd (Royal Naval) Division Reserves, 1917–18; Commandant, Depot, Royal Marines, 1918; Maj.-Gen. RM, 1920. *Address:* c/o Stilwell and

Sons, 42 Pall Mall, SW1. *Club:* Junior Army and Navy. *Died 21 Jan. 1923.*

PARSONS, Maj.-Gen. Sir Harold Daniel Edmund, KCMG 1918 (CMG 1900); CB 1915; late Royal Army Ordnance Corps; *b* London, 3 July 1863; *s* of late Maj.-Gen. James Edmund Bacon Parsons, late ISC; *m* 1892, Julia, *d* of late Thomas Archer, CMG; one *s*. *Educ:* Dulwich College. Lieut The Queen's Regt, 1882; Captain, 1891; Major, 1898; Ordnance Officer, 3rd Class, 1900; Ordance Officer, 2nd Class, 1904; Lieut-Colonel AOD, 1904; Ordnance Officer, 1st Class, and Colonel, 1910; Principal Ordnance Officer, 1920; retired pay, 1923; served Burmese Campaign, 1885–89 (medal with two clasps); South African War, 1899–1902 (despatches, CMG, Queen's medal with 3 clasps, King's medal with 2 clasps); European War, 1914–18: despatches five times; 1914 Star; CB; promoted Maj.-Gen.; KCMG; Commander of Belgian Order of Leopold; Russian Order of St Stanislaus 2nd Class with Swords; American Distinguished Service Medal; Belgian Croix de Guerre; British War Medal; Allied Victory medal. *Club:* United Service. *Died 13 Feb. 1925.*

PARSONS, John Inglis, MD; MRCP, MRCS, etc; Hon. Fellow of two medical societies abroad, and Fellow of several others; Consulting Surgeon to Chelsea Hospital for Women; *b* Melbourne House, Kidbrooke, Kent, 1857; 3rd *s* of late Percival Parsons (the inventor of manganese bronze). *Educ:* private tuition; Guy's Hospital; Durham University. MB 1883; MRCS 1884; MD 1886; MRCP 1892. Entered Guy's Hospital, 1879; House Surgeon, 1884; Assistant Physician to Chelsea Hospital for Women, 1886; Fellow of the Royal Society of Medicine; Hon. Fellow of the American Electro-Therapeutic Association, 1891; Corr. Mem. de la Société Française d'Electro-thérapie, 1893. *Publications:* Evolution Explained, 1925; The Disintegration of Organic Tissue by High Tension Discharges; Changes Produced by the Constant Current in Uterine Fibromata; A New and Bloodless Operation for Prolapsus Uteri. *Recreations:* shooting, golf, music, gardening. *Address:* Azalea Cottage, Howard Road, Bournemouth. *M:* LN 51. *Died 2 July 1928.*

PARSONS, Lt-Gen. Sir Lawrence Worthington, KCB 1912 (CB 1900); *b* 23 March 1850; *o s* of Lawrence Parsons of Parsonstown, King's County; *m* 1880, Florence Anna, *d* of Robert Graves, MD, of Cloghan Castle, King's County; one *d*. *Educ:* Cheltenham. Served South Africa, 1899–1900 (despatches thrice, Queen's medal 6 clasps, CB); Inspector-Gen. Artillery, India, 1903–6; Major-General, 1903; Lt-Gen. 1909; commanded 6th Division, Cork, 1906–9; 16th (Irish) Division, 1914–15; Colonel Comdt RA, 1917. *Club:* Army and Navy. *Died 20 Aug. 1923.*

PARSONS, Philip Harry, LRCP, LRCS, LRFPSG; Anæsthetist University College Hospital; Physician Australian Auxiliary Hospital; Anæsthetist Masonic War Hospital; Anæsthetist Kensington General Hospital; Surg. Major 1st CB London Scottish Regt; *s* of George Parsons; *m* Mary, *d* of T. B. M. Richards. *Educ:* Melbourne University; Royal Coll. of Surgeons of Edinburgh. Resident Medical Officer Manchester Hospital for Consumption and Diseases of Throat; House Surgeon Royal Edinburgh Infirmary; Surgeon in charge Ear, Nose, and Throat Dept Kensington General Hospital; District Medical Officer LCM; Fellow Royal Society of Medicine; Hon. Sec. Assoc. of Med. Dip. Scot.; Sec., Treas., Chairman, Chelsea Division; Vice-President Metropolitan Counties Branch; Member of Council British Medical Association; Member Manchester Pathological and Medical Society. *Publications:* A Simple Inhaler, Lancet, 1902; Case of Recklinghausen's Disease, Medical Press, 1906; New Ethyl Chloride Inhaler, British Medical Journal, 1910. *Address:* 6 Foulis Terrace, Onslow Gardens, SW7. *T:* Kensington 1915. *Club:* Junior Athenæum. *Died 27 April 1920.*

PARSONS, Hon. Richard Clere; *b* 21 Feb. 1851; 3rd surv. *s* of 3rd Earl of Rosse and Mary, *er d* of John Wilmer Field, Yorks; *m* Agnes Elizabeth (*d* 1922), *d* of John Frederick La Trobe Bateman, FRS; five *s* (and one *s* decd). *Educ:* privately; Trinity College, Dublin. Senior Moderator and Gold Medallist in Physical Science and Chemistry, and Engineering degree with honours, 1873. Partner in Kitson & Co., Leeds, and took an active part in the development of the Yorkshire College, subseq. the University of Leeds, 1880–87; partner of J. F. La Trobe Bateman, FRS, 1887–89; amongst other works superintended the design and construction of the water and drainage works of the city of Buenos Aires; Engineer to the Congested Board for Ireland, 1893–95; invited and subsequently prepared complete designs for a drainage system for the city of Petrograd, 1898; Engineer to the Consolidated Waterworks Company of Rosario, Limited, the Montevideo Waterworks Company, Limited, and designed and carried out numerous works abroad; a Director of the Mersey Railway Company; Member of the Institution of Civil Engineers (Millar Scholarship for researches in connection with Centrifugal Pumps; a Telford Gold Medal and a Manby Premium); Member of the Institution of Mechanical Engineers; Membre de la Société des Ingénieurs Civils de France; Treasurer and Deputy Chairman of the Delegacy of King's College University of London; a Governor of the Imperial College of Science and Technology, nominated by the University of London; a Vice-President of the Royal Society of Arts; a Vice-President and a Manager of the Royal Institution of Great Britain; contested Univ. of Dublin, 1887. *Publications:* contributed numerous papers to scientific societies. *Address:* 48 Prince's Gardens, SW7. *T:* Kensington 3410. *Clubs:* Athenæum, Junior Carlton, British Empire. *Died 26 Jan. 1923.*

PASCAL, Rt. Rev. Albert, OMI; RC Bishop of Prince Albert since 1907; *b* Languedoc, 1848. Indian Missionary in the North-West, 1874–91; Bishop of Mosynopolis and Vicar Apostolic of Saskatchewan, 1891. *Address:* Paina Albert, Saskatchewan.
Died July 1920.

PASCAL, Jean Louis; Commander of Legion of Honour; architect; Inspecteur général des Bâtiments civils; Member of the Institute of France and of the Académie des Beaux Arts; Officer of Public Instruction; *b* 4 June 1837. *Educ:* Ecole des Beaux Arts; Villa Medici (Grand Prix de Rome); Atelier Gilbert Questel. King's Gold Medal, 1914; Gold Medal of the Institute of American Architects, 1914. *Works:* (monuments): Colonel d'Argy, at Saint Louis-des-Français, Rome; Michelet, at Père-Lachaise; Carnot, at Bordeaux; Victor Hugo, and Garnier, in Paris; (new buildings): Château du Doux, Corrèze; Château de Maubuisson, Clairefontaine; Villa Renouard, Pau; numerous houses and hotels; (restorations, additions, etc): at Bibliothèque Nationale, Paris; Faculté de Médecine et de Pharmacie, Bordeaux. *Address:* 8 Boulevard Saint-Denis, Paris.
Died 16 May 1920.

PASLEY, Thomas Hamilton Sabine, MVO 1904; Secretary Royal Yacht Squadron; *b* 10 May 1861; *e s* of late Captain Hamilton Sabine Pasley and 1st wife, Catherine Anne, *e d* of Lt-Col Hon. Richard Hare; *m* 1899, Alice Marion Margaret Watson, *d* of Thomas Conolly; one *s* two *d. Educ:* privately. Served in Egyptian War, 1882 and 1884; retired, 1898, as Staff Paymaster, RN. *Address:* Northlands, Cowes, Isle of Wight. *Clubs:* Naval and Military, Beefsteak.
Died 25 Feb. 1927.

PASTURE, 4th Marquis de la; Gerard Gustavus Ducarel; (*g-grandfather* came over from France and settled in England, 1791); *b* 1 March 1836; *S* father, 1840; *m* 1st, 1864, Léontine Standish (*d* 1869); one *d*; 2nd, 1873, Georgiana Mary, *d* of Robert J. Loughnan, an Indian Judge; one *s* one *d* (and one *s* one *d* decd). *Heir: s* Gerard Hubert de la Pasture, *b* 3 May 1886. *Address:* Cefu Ila, Usk, Monmouthshire. *Died 28 Jan. 1916.*

PATCH, Col Robert, CB 1896; HM Indian Army; retired; *b* 25 July 1842; 3rd *s* of late Lieut-Col Henry Revel Patch, HEICS, and Charlotte, *d* of Captain Robert Davies; *m* 1867, Frances Maria, *d* of James Lloyd of Compton, Dundon Rectory, Somerton; four *s. Educ:* Cheltenham College. Ensign 55th Foot (later 2nd Battalion Border Regt), 1863; Capt. BSC (later Indian Army), 1875; Major, 1883; Brevet Lieut-Colonel, 1888; Colonel, 1891; served with Bhootan Expedition, 1865 (medal with clasp); during Afghan war, 1879–80 (despatches, medal); Hazara Expedition, 1888 (despatches, Brevet Lieut-Colonel); Miranzai Expedition, 1891 (mentioned by Government of India and in despatches); Chitral Relief Expedition, 1895 (despatches, medal and clasp); Comy-General, Punjab, 1887–95; granted Good Service Pension, 1902. *Recreations:* hunting, gardening. *Address:* Fersfield, Newton Abbot, Devon.
Died 23 Feb. 1927.

PATERSON, Andrew Melville, MD (Edin.), MB; FRCS, FRAI, FRAM; Assistant Inspector of Military Orthopædics; Major, Royal Army Medical Corps; Professor of Anatomy, University of Liverpool since 1894; *b* 7 March 1862; *s* of late Rev. J. Carruthers Paterson, minister of St Andrew's Presbyterian Church, Manchester; *m* Beatrice, *d* of late Richard Eadson, Manchester; two *s* three *d. Educ:* Manchester Grammar School; Owens College; Edinburgh University (MB and CM with 1st class Hons, 1883; MD, gold medallist, 1886). Demonstrator of Anatomy, Edinburgh University and Owens College; 1st Professor of Anatomy, University College, Dundee, 1888; Dean of Medical Faculty, Liverpool, 1895–1904; Examiner in Anatomy, Universities of Oxford, Cambridge, Durham, London, Wales, Indian Medical Service, Conjoint Board, the College of

Surgeons, etc; Hunterian Professor, the Royal College of Surgeons, 1903; ex-President of the Anatomical Society of Great Britain and Ireland; member of the Association of American Anatomists. *Publications:* Duval's Artistic Anatomy; The Human Sternum; article in Cunningham's Text-Book of Anatomy; The Anatomist's Note Book; Manual of Embryology; numerous articles on anatomical subjects. *Recreation:* golf. *Address:* 21 Abercromby Square, Liverpool. *T:* Royal 918. *Clubs:* Royal Societies; Royal Liverpool Golf, Racquet, Liverpool; Royal and Ancient Golf, St Andrews.
Died 13 Feb. 1919.

PATERSON, Arthur Henry; novelist; *b* Bowdon, Cheshire, 15 Jul 1862; *y s* of late Alexander Henry Paterson, MD; also *b* to late Mrs William Allingham (Helen Allingham); *m* 1894, Mary, *d* of late Lieut Col G. Kellie M'Callum, late 92nd Gordon Highlanders, Gentleman-at-Arms; one *s. Educ:* University Coll. School, London. Sheep rancher, New Mexico, USA, 1877–79; farmer in Western Kansas, 1879–80; clerk and afterwards sub-manager in merchant's office, Birkenhead, 1881–84; District Sec., Charity Organization Society, London, 1885–96; Secretary Social Welfare Association for London since 1910; Secretary, National Alliance of Employers and Employed, 1917; Grand Scribe, Order of Crusaders, 1923. *Publications:* The Better Man, 1890; A Partner from the West, 1892; The Daughter of the Nez Percés, 1894; A Man of his Word, 1894; A Son of the Plains, 1895; For Freedom's Sake, 1896; Father and Son, 1897; The Gospel writ in Steel, 1898; Cromwell's Own, 1899; Oliver Cromwell: a Biography, 1899; Colonel Cromwell, an Historical Drama, 1900; The King's Agent, 1902; The Homes of Tennyson, 1905; John Glynn, 1907; Administration of Charity, 1908; The Metropolitan Police, 1909; Our Prisons, 1911; Public Health and the Insurance Act, 1912; The Weapon of the Strike, 1922; Crusaders, 1925; Man or Beast? 1926. *Recreations:* entomology, cycling. *Address:* 6 Thurlow Road, Hampstead, NW3. *T:* Hampstead 1358. *Club:* Reform.
Died 16 Jan. 1928.

PATERSON, Surg.-Maj.-Gen. Henry Foljambe, MD, FRCS, FRGS; *b* 9 July 1836; *m*; two *d.* Entered army, 1857; Principal Medical Officer, Aldershot, 1894–96; retired, 1896. *Address:* 99 Alexandra Road, South Hampstead, NW.
Died 11 May 1920.

PATERSON, Lt-Col Norman Fitzherbert; Registrar of the Court of Appeal, 1908, and Clerk of the Supreme Court, of Ontario; *b* 3 Sept. 1843; *m* 1872, Sarah Vernon (*d* 1909), 2nd *d* of late George Currie, Port Perry, Ont; one *s* two *d.* Barrister, 1874; KC 1883. *Address:* 48 Rushton Road, Toronto. *T:* Hillcrest 6480.
Died 22 July 1925.

PATERSON, Thomas Wilson; Lieutenant-Governor of British Columbia, 1909–14; *b* Ayrshire, 6 Dec. 1851; *s* of William P. Paterson; *m* 1886, Emma E., *d* of Senator George Riley; no *c. Educ:* Oxford schools. Commenced career in Public Works, Ontario, 1869; went to British Columbia, 1885; elected for North Victoria to British Columbia Legislature in 1902 and 1903. *Recreations:* golf, motoring. *Address:* Victoria, BC. *Clubs:* Union, Pacific, Victoria.

PATERSON, William Bromfield, FRCS, LDS; dental surgeon; of William Paterson of Ridge Stockland, Devon; *m* Agnes Stirling, *d* of late David Gillies, JP, Londonderry; one *s. Educ:* Mercant Taylors' School; St Bartholomew's and Royal Dental Hospitals. Late Senior Dental Surgeon to St Bartholomew's Hospital, and Dental Surgeon and Lecturer on Dental Surgery, Royal Dental Hospital of London; late Examiner in Dental Surgery, Royal College of Surgeons of England; Past President of British Dental Association; Odontological Sect. of Royal Society of Medicine; Representative Board, British Dental Association; Hon. President International Dental Federation; late Examiner in Dentistry, Royal Army Medical Corps, and Dental Expert Advisory Board, RAMC; Fellow Royal Society of Medicine; British Medical Association; Member Dental Tribunal (War) 1916–17. *Publications:* various addresses and contributions to medical and dental societies and journals. *Recreations:* shooting, outdoor sports. *Address:* 7A Manchester Square, W1.
Died 2 Sept. 1924.

PATON, Diarmid Noël, MD, BSc, LLD; FRS 1914; FRCPE; physiologist; *b* Edinburgh, 19 March 1859; *e s* of late Sir Joseph Noël Paton, RSA, and Margaret, *d* of Alexander Ferrier; *m* 1898, Agatha H., *d* of late Alexander Balfour and Mrs Balfour of Dawyck, Peeblesshire; one *s* one *d. Educ:* Edinburgh Academy and University; Paris. Baxter Scholar in Natural Science, Edinburgh Univ. 1882; Biological Fellow of Edinburgh University, 1884; Lecturer in Physiology, School of Medicine of Royal Colleges, Edinburgh, 1886

Superintendent of Research Laboratory, Royal College of Physicians, Edinburgh, 1889; Regius Professor of Physiology, Glasgow University, 1906–28; late Member of Royal Commission on Salmon Fisheries, 1900, and of the Medical Research Council, 1918–23. *Publications:* Nervous and Chemical Regulators of Metabolism, 1913; The Physiology of the Continuity of Life, 1926; large number of papers on physiological (including, with Dr Leonard Findlay, Poverty, Nutrition and Growth), and on fishery subjects. *Recreations:* golf, fishing, sailing. *Address:* The University, Glasgow. *T:* Hillhead 3999. *Club:* Athenæum.   *Died 30 Sept. 1928.*

PATON, Hugh, Hon. ARE; retired; *b* Glasgow, 5 Feb. 1853; *e s* of late Alexander Paton, a Glasgow merchant; *m* Jeannie Black; one *s* one *d. Educ:* Glasgow Academy. A business man; no particular art training beyond a little drawing at school, and some painting lessons after leaving; inspired by Maxine Lalanne's Treatise on Etching; began the practice of that art about 1880; exhibited regularly in Manchester, Liverpool, Leeds, etc, once at the Royal Acad., and many times at the Paris Old Salon, as well as at the Painter Etchers' regularly since election as an Associate, 1887; lectured on etching for the Manchester Art Committee, and gave a series of printing demonstrations, 1914; presented the Manchester City Art Gallery with a case of copper plates and proofs illustrating the art of the etcher. *Publications:* Etching, Drypoint, Mezzotint, 1895; Colour Etching, 1909. *Recreations:* art, golf (art his chief hobby for forty years). *Address:* Ardenadam, Marple by Stockport. *Club:* Athenæum, Manchester.

Died 24 Oct. 1927.

PATON, James; Superintendent of Museums and Art Galleries of Corporation of Glasgow, 1876, retired; *b* Auchtergaven, Perthshire, 15 April 1843; *m* 1866, Mary D. (*d* 1903), *d* of James Kesson, Fordoun, Kincardineshire; three *s* two *d. Educ:* parish school; private tuition; Edinburgh University. Trained for legal profession in Perth; Assistant in Museum of Science and Art, Edinburgh 1861–76; Pres. of Museums Association of United Kingdom, 1896; Hon. Secretary, Fine Art and Historical Section, Glasgow International Exhibition, 1901. *Publications:* The Fine Art Collection of Glasgow, 1906; edited and largely wrote Scottish National Memorials, folio, 1890; wrote Glasgow: its Municipal Organisation and Administration (with Sir James Bell, Bt), Qto, 1896; edited and partly wrote Scottish History and Life, folio, 1902; numerous contributions to Encyclopædia Britannica and Chambers's Encyclopædia; journalistic work. *Recreations:* golf, fishing. *Address:* Camphill House, Glasgow. *T:* Queen's Park 135. *Club:* Art, Glasgow.

Died 26 Feb. 1921.

PATRON, Joseph Armand, CMG 1911; *b* 1856; 3rd *s* of Joseph Patron, MD; *m* 1885, Clemence, *y d* of Chevalier Jerome Saccone. Barrister-at-law, Inner Temple, 1877; Acting Police Magistrate, 1894–95; Sanitary Commissioner since 1895; Chairman Exchange Committee since 1898; deputed by the Chamber of Commerce and Exchange Committee as Representative of the Civil Community at HM's Coronation; JP. *Address:* Gibraltar. *Club:* Mediterranean, Gibraltar.   *Died 25 Feb. 1922.*

PATTERSON, Alexander Blakeley, CIE 1895; *b* Ballymena, Co. Antrim, 17 Feb. 1842; *s* of late Rev. Alexander Patterson, and Emily Gaston, *d* of Rev. Robert Stewart; *m* 1863, Charlotte Maria (*d* 1917), *d* of late John Black, JP, of Annaskea House, Co. Louth; two *s* three *d. Educ:* Royal Belfast Academical Institution; Queen's College, Belfast (two scholarships). Entered Indian Civil Service, 1863; appointed to North-West Provinces as Assistant Magistrate and Collector, 1864; Settlement Officer of Fatehpur, 1870, of Karwi, 1878; Magistrate and Collector of Allahabad, 1882; Magistrate and Collector of Saharanpur, 1887–90; Commissioner of Jhansi, 1890; Commissioner Northern India Salt Revenue, 1891–98. *Publications:* Settlement Reports of Fatehpur and Karwi. *Address:* Buckleigh House, Buckleigh, N Devon. *Club:* East India United Service.

Died 9 Nov. 1919.

PATTERSON, George, KC 1909; MA; Master and Referee of the Court of King's Bench, Manitoba, since 1911; Registrar in Bankruptcy since 1921; *b* Perth, Ont, 20 April 1846; *s* of James and Jane Patterson; *m* 1st, 1870, Annie G. Baker (*d* 1897); 2nd, 1908, Viola G. Geddes; three *s* two *d. Educ:* Perth High School; University of Toronto. Gold Medallist in Mathematics; First-class Military School Certificate, Toronto, 1867. In action at Ridgway, Ont, Fenian Raid; Mathematical Master at Hamilton and Galt Collegiate Institutes, 1867–72; called to the Bar at Toronto, 1874; practised law in Hamilton, Ont, till 1882, when moved to Winnipeg; Deputy Attorney-General of Manitoba, 1898–1911. *Publications:* Editor Manitoba Law Reports, and of Digest of volumes i–xxi of the same reports. *Recreations:* lawn bowling,

canoeing, skating, golf. *Address:* Court House, Winnipeg, Manitoba. *T:* N40–341; F 1879. *Club:* Canadian, Winnipeg.

Died 23 Aug. 1925.

PATTERSON, James Kennedy, AM, PhD, LLD; FRHistS, FSAScot.; President, State University of Kentucky, 1869–1910, subseq. Emeritus; *b* Glasgow, Scotland, 26 March 1833; *e s* of Andrew Patterson and Janet Kennedy, both of Dunbartonshire; *m* 1859, Lucelia W., *d* of Captain Charles F. Wing. *Educ:* Hanover College, Indiana (AB 1856, PhD 1875). LLD Lafayette College, Penn., 1896; LLD Vermont, 1910, Kentucky, 1916. Principal, Greenville Presbyterial Academy, 1856–59; Prof., Stewart College, Tennessee, 1859–61; Principal, Transylvania High School, Lexington, Kentucky, 1861–65; Prof. of Latin and Civil History, Agric. and Mech. College of Kentucky, 1865–69; Delegate to International Congress of Geographical Sciences, Paris, France, 1875, and British Association, Bristol, England, 1875; Delegate to British Association for Advancement of Science, Leeds, England, 1890; obtained from Legislature of Kentucky ½ cent tax on each $100 of taxable property for maintenance of State University, 1880; defended tax when assailed by all the donominational colleges, 1882, before the Legislature and Appellate Court, and won; assisted in obtaining additional endowment from Congress, 1890 and 1907, and from State Legislature, 1900, 1904, and 1903; President, Association of State Colleges and Universities in 1903; Trustee of the University, Hanover Coll., Indiana, and Vice-Pres. of American Civil Alliance; Fellow American Geographical Society, American Historical Society, National Tax Association, and American Academy of Political and Social Science; Member of National Tax Association. *Publications:* numerous newspaper articles, etc. *Recreation:* travelling at home and abroad. *Address:* Lexington, Kentucky State University Grounds, USA. *Clubs:* Authors'; Beta Theta Pi, New York; Filson, Louisville, Ky.

Died 15 Aug. 1922.

PATTERSON, John Edward; littérateur; *b* Deepcar, Yorkshire; *s* of Joseph and Mary Patterson; *m* 1902, Ida Harrylynn Pittendreigh. *Educ:* the village school, Normanton, and at similar houses of correction, till he ran away to sea under the age of 13; was in the deep-sea fishery, merchant service, RNR, and about the world generally for 17 years, during which he had some adventures, and passed through 6½ years of rheumatism that left him a cripple for long afterwards; in 1897 Sir Henry Irving invited him to the Lyceum, where he served in a humble capacity while obtaining a footing in London journalism; he was 2 years on the staff of the Westminster Gazette, and has edited some periodicals. *Publications:* The Mermaid; The Lure of the Sea (poems); Ballads and Addresses; Fishers of the Sea; Watchers by the Shore; Tillers of the Soil; Love Like the Sea; The Story of Stephen Compton; His Father's Wife; Hillary Marrtyn; Bond Slaves (novel); My Vagabondage; Sea Pie; Epistles of the Sea (autobiography); The Sea's Anthology. *Recreations:* gardening, walking, boat sailing, etc. *Address:* c/o Simpkin, Marshall and Co., 4 Stationers' Hall Court, EC.   *Died 4 April 1919.*

PATTI, Madame Adelina, (Baroness Rolf Cederström), prima donna; *b* Madrid, 19 Feb. 1843; *d* of Salvatore Patti of Catania, Sicily, and Caterina Chiesa, a well-known opera singer; naturalized British citizen, 1898; *m* 1st, 1868, Marquis de Caux (marr. diss. 1886); 2nd, 1886, Signor Nicolini Ernesto (*d* 1898); 3rd, 1899, Baron Rolf Cederström. Studied under Ettore Barili; début, Academy of Music, New York, Nov. 1859; Italian Opera House, Covent Garden, in La Sonnambula, May 1861. *Compositions:* song, On Parting; waltz, Fior di Primavera. *Address:* Craig-y-Nos Castle, Penycae, SO, Breconshire, South Wales.   *Died 26 Sept. 1919.*

PATTINSON, Rev. Canon Joseph Alfred, MA; Headmaster King's School, Parra Matta, since 1916; *b* Yorkshire, 24 Dec. 1861; *s* of Thomas Pattinson, engineer and ironfounder; *m* Gertrude Teresa Lucy, *d* of Canon Lysons of Hempstead Court, Gloucester; no *c. Educ:* St John's College, Cambridge. Scholar and Hare Exhibitioner and Wright's Prizeman; First Class Mathematical Honours, BA 1884, MA 1888, Cambridge; MA University of Queensland, 1912. Deacon, 1885; Priest, 1886; Christ Church, Salford, 1885–90; Vicar of St George, Chorley, 1890–1903; Volunteer Chaplain, 1890–1903; Rector of St Bartholomew, Salford, 1903–7; Vicar of St James, Hope, Manchester, 1907–10; Chaplain to the Forces, Australia, 1910; Sub-Dean of Brisbane, 1910–15; Warden of St Paul's College, 1915–16. *Recreations:* tennis, chess. *Address:* King's School, Parra Matta, New South Wales. *T:* U 8064. *M:* 553. *Club:* University, Sydney.

Died 1 May 1919.

PATTISSON, Admiral John Robert Ebenezer; *b* Witham, Essex, 10 Dec. 1844; 4th *s* of Jacob Howell Pattisson, LLM, and Charlotte

Garnham Luard, *d* of William Wright Luard, and *sister* of Admiral Sir William Garnham Luard, KCB; *m* 1874, Emma Agnes Streeten (*d* 1923); one *d*. *Educ:* Royal Naval Academy, Gosport. Entered the navy as a naval cadet, 1859; went to sea first in Donegal, a wooden steam battleship; Sub-Lieutentant, 1864; Acting Lieutenant of the Wasp, 1864, and proceeded from East India Station to East Coast of Africa, where he was actively engaged in the suppression of the slave trade; was carried across a tight-rope on Charles Blondin's back; Lieut 1867; landed from Wasp at taking of Nicobar Islands; served in Hart on coast of Spain during Intransigeant War; Commander, 1879, on Minotaur, flagship of the Channel Squadron; was in the Thalia during the Egyptian War of 1882; Captain, 1886; had command of the Euphrates, an Indian troopship, for three years, and later was in command of the Crocodile, the Amphion, the Edinburgh, the Rodney, and the Sans Pareil; Rear-Admiral, 1899; Vice-Admiral, 1904, in which year he retired; Admiral, 1908; entitled to wear the Egyptian medal, the Khedive's bronze star, and the Jubilee medal; since his retirement, actively interested in municipal work at Tonbridge. *Address:* Rodbourne, Tonbridge.

Died 13 Feb. 1928.

PAUL, Sir George Morison, Kt 1911; *b* 18 Aug. 1839; *s* of Rev. William Paul, DD, Minister of Banchory Devenick; *m* 1872, Mary (*d* 1914), *d* of Alexander John Kinloch of Park, Aberdeenshire; one *d*. *Educ:* Aberdeen and Edinburgh Universities (MA 1858; LLD 1908). Writer to the Signet, 1867; Deputy Keeper of the Signet in Scotland and President of the Society of Writers to His Majesty's Signet, 1905; a Governor of Donaldson's Hospital, Edinburgh; one of the Walker Trustees for the Episcopal Church in Scotland; Chairman of Fettes College Trust; also of the Dick Bequest Trust for Higher Education in the Counties of Aberdeen, Banff, and Moray; and of John Watson's and Miss Mary Murray's Educational Institutions, Edinburgh; a Deputy Governor and Ordinary Manager of the Royal Asylum for the Insane, Edin.; Mem. of Royal Commission on the Civil Service, 1915; a Member of Council of the Scottish History Society, and of the New Spalding Club; an Extraordinary Director of the Royal Bank of Scotland; a Director of the Scottish Provident Institution; a member of the King's Body Guard for Scotland (Royal Company of Archers); DL, JP Edinburgh; knighted on the occasion of the Coronation of King George V. *Recreation:* travelling. *Address:* 9 Eglinton Crescent, Edinburgh. *T:* Central 4609. *M:* S 1382. *Clubs:* Junior Carlton, University, Edinburgh. *Died 4 May 1926.*

PAULTON, James Mellor; MP (L) Bishop Auckland, Durham, 1885–1910; Assistant Paymaster-General, Supreme Court, 1909–21; *b* 1857; *s* of late A. W. Paulton (London Chairman of the Anti-Corn Law League, and 1st editor of Manchester Examiner), Manchester. *Educ:* privately; Trinity Hall, Cambridge. War Correspondent for Manchester Examiner in Soudan Campaign; present at Battle of El Teb, Egypt, 1884; Private Secretary to James Bryce, Hugh Childers, Home Dept, 1886, and Assistant Private Secretary to Herbert Henry Asquith, Home Dept, 1893–95. *Address:* 2 Bolton Street, W1. *T:* Grosvenor 1027. *Clubs:* Brooks's, Turf, Beefsteak.

Died 6 Dec. 1923.

PAYNE, John Bruce, MA; Headmaster, Bishop Stortford School since 1904; *e s* of late Rev. Canon David Bruce Payne, DD, and Elizabeth Woodfull, *d* of R. G. Davey, Walmer; *m*; one *d*. *Educ:* King's School, Canterbury; Rossall School (Capt.); Cambridge. Head Mathematical Master, Ascham School, Bournemouth: Headmaster, St Aubyn's, Lowestoft. *Recreations:* motor-driving only; formerly rowing, fives, cricket. *Address:* The School, Bishop Stortford, Herts. *TA:* Bruce Payne, Bishop Stortford. *M:* NK 7136.

Died 4 Feb. 1928.

PAYNE, John Horne, KC; MA; *b* 12 Nov. 1837; *e s* of Reuben Craven Payne, Bridgwater, Somerset; *m* 1868, Georgiana (*d* 1911), *widow* of G. Sergent Atwood, USA; one *s*. *Educ:* University College, London (double hons). Special Correspondent of Morning Herald and Standard in Hungary, 1861; called to the Bar, Inner Temple, 1863; joined Home Circuit and Sussex Sessions; admitted Jamaica Bar, 1866; QC 1886; Asst Boundary Commissioner, SE District, 1867; for several years acted as Commissioner for Spanish Government to take evidence in England in cases pending in Spanish Courts; contested Mansfield Div. Notts (C), 1885. *Publications:* The Hungarian Diet of 1861; occasional articles to the daily press. *Recreations:* Egyptian and Assyrian archæology, long country walks. *Address:* Westow Lodge, Upper Norwood, SE. *Club:* Junior Carlton.

Died 9 Sept. 1920.

PAYNE, Maj.-Gen. Richard Lloyd, CB 1905; DSO 1886; *b* 24 May 1854; 2nd *s* of late John Selwyn Payne; *m* 1884, Clara Fripp Agnes,

o d of late Brig.-Gen. Henry Bethune Patton; one *s*. Gazetted 13th Light Infantry, 1876; Lieut-Col, 1900; commanded 3rd Division, N Army, India, 1912–13; served Sekuki Campaign, Transvaal, 1878; Zulu War, 1879 (medal with clasp); Burmese Expedition 1885–86 (despatches, DSO, medal with clasp); NW Frontier of India, 1897 (medal with clasp); served South Africa, 1900–2 (despatches twice, Queen's medal with 3 clasps, King's medal 2 clasps, Brevet Col); retired pay, 1917. *Died 20 Dec. 1921.*

PAYTON, Sir Charles Alfred, Kt 1914; MVO 1906; *b* York, 12 Nov. 1843; *s* of late Rev. Charles Payton; *m* 1st, 1880, Eliza Mary (*d* 1909), *d* of late John Olive (six *s* killed in battle, 1915); 2nd, 1913, Mary Stuart, *d* of Joseph J. Elliott, Monken Hadley, Barnet. *Educ:* Scarborough; New College, London; Bonn. Matriculated University College, London, 1860, with Honours in Classics. Consul at Mogador, 1880; passed examination before Civil Service Commissioners; Consul at Genoa, 1893; at Calais, 1897; HBM Consul-General at Calais, 1911; retired on a pension, 1913; angling correspondent, The Field, 1867–1914. *Publications:* The Diamond Diggings of South Africa, 1872; Moss from a Rolling Stone, 1879; Days of a Knight, 1924. *Recreations:* fishing, shooting. *Clubs:* Flyfishers', Authors'.

Died 11 March 1926.

PEACE, Sir Walter, KCMG 1897 (CMG 1893); ISO 1905; *b* 19 Oct. 1840; 2nd *s* of late James Peace, Prof. of Music, Huddersfield; *m* 1869, Caroline, *y d* of William Tilbrook, Woodham Lodge, near Chelmsford; one *d*. *Educ:* Huddersfield; privately. Went to Natal, 1863; in business there as a merchant and shipper till 1879; travelled often to Cape Colony and Mauritius for business purposes; took active interest in public affairs of Natal; became Natal Government Emigration Agent, and Agent for Natal Harbour Board in England, 1880; was Belgian Consul in Natal, 1870–79; Portuguese Vice-Consul, 1870–78; member Tariff Commission, 1904; Agent-General for Natal, 1893–1904; Royal Commissioner for the Paris Exhibition, 1900; an original member of the Advisory Committee of the Board of Trade; member of the Tariff Reform Commission. *Publications:* Our Colony of Natal; Notes on Natal; Emigration Literature. *Address:* 83 Victoria Street, SW; The Yarrows, Camberley. *Clubs:* St Stephen's; Durban. *Died 31 Jan. 1917.*

PEACH, Benjamin Neeve, ARSM; LLD; FRS, FGS, FRSE; *b* Gorran Haven, Cornwall, 1842; *widower*, twice married; two *s* two *d*. *Educ:* Academy, Peterhead; Academy, Wick; Royal School of Mines, London. Retired District Geologist HM Geological Survey; Murchison Medal and Wollaston Medal of Geological Society of London; Neill Medal of Royal Society of Edinburgh. *Publications:* The Silurian Rocks of Britain, vol. i Scotland, 1899; The Geological Structure of the North-West Highlands of Scotland, 1907. *Address:* 33 Comiston Drive, Edinburgh.

Died 29 Jan. 1926.

PEACOCK, Major Frederick William, CB 1919; DL, JP; Chairman, Territorial Force Association; *b* 1859; *m* 1884, Augusta Rose, *d* of Lt-Col Richard Henry FitzHerbert and 2nd wife, Susan, *d* of Michael Hinton Castle. *Address:* Vernons Oak, Somershall Herbert, Derbyshire. *Died 8 May 1924.*

PEACOCK, Sir Robert, Kt 1919; MVO 1913; Chief Constable of Manchester since 1898; *b* 1859; *s* of William Peacock, Guisborough, Yorks. Chief Constable of Canterbury, 1888–92; of Oldham, 1892–98; Order of the Redeemer (Greece). *Address:* Town Hall, Albert Square, Manchester.

Died 18 Nov. 1926.

PEACOCKE, Most Rev. Joseph Ferguson, DD; late Primate of Ireland; *b* Queen's Co., Ireland, 5 Nov. 1835; *y s* of late George Peacocke, MD, Longford, and Catherine Ferguson; *m* 1865, Caroline Sophia, *y d* of late Major John Irvine of Killadeas, Co. Fermanagh; four *s* one *d*. *Educ:* Trinity Coll., Dublin. 1st Senior Moderator in History, English Lit., and Political Economy, 1856; 1st Divinity Prizeman, 1858. Ordained 1858; Rector of St George's, Dublin, 1873–78; Rector of Monkstown, 1878–94; Professor of Pastoral Theology, Dublin Univ., 1893; Bishop of Meath, 1894–97; Archbishop of Dublin, 1897–1915. *Publications:* sermons, and charges, 1895–1901. *Club:* University, Dublin.

Died 26 May 1916.

PEAKE, Hon. Archibald Henry; Premier and Treasurer, South Australia, since 1919; *b* London, 1859; *s* of late Robert and Mary Peake; *m* Annie, *e d* of late Rev. Henry Byron Thomas; three *s* four *d*. *Educ:* public schools and by private tuition. Left England with parents, 1862; for several years was Clerk of District Council of

Narracoorte; entered Parliament, 1897; Treasurer and Attorney-General, 1905; Premier, Treasurer, and Minister of Education, 1909 and 1912–15; Premier, Commissioner of Crown Lands, and Minister of Education, 1909–10; Premier and Chief Secretary, 1917–19. *Recreations:* tennis, golf, bowls. *Address:* Parkside, Adelaide, South Australia. *Club:* Liberal.   *Died April 1920.*

PEAKE, Brig.-Gen. Malcolm, CMG 1900; Assistant Adjutant-General, War Office, since 1914; *b* 27 March 1865; 3rd *s* of Frederic Peake of Burrough, Melton Mowbray, Leicestershire; *m* 1900, Louisa, *e d* of Patrick H. Osborne, NSW. *Educ:* Charterhouse. Entered army, 1884; Capt. 1895; Major, 1900; served Dongola, 1896 (4th class Medjidie, British medal, Khedive's medal with two clasps); in operations, 1897, in command of a battery of Egyptian Artillery (despatches, clasp); Atbara and Khartoum, 1898 (despatches, brevet major, two clasps); operations against Khalifa, 1899 (4th class Osmanieh, clasp); opened the Upper Nile, 1900 (3rd class Medjidie, CMG); Bt-Col 1915; Officer Legion of Honour. *Address:* 17 Thurloe Square, SW. *T:* Kensington 3519. *Club:* Naval and Military.
Died 27 Aug. 1917.

PEARCE, Charles E.; Editor of South London Press, 1878–82; of Funny Folks, 1882–86; serial stories, Answers, 1896–97; novelettes, upwards of seventy, 1896–1910. *Publications:* The Amazing Duchess (biography), 1910; The Beloved Princess, 1911; Polly Peachum and the Beggar's Opera, 1913; The Jolly Duchess (Harriot Mellon), 1915; Marching Songs, 1914; War Up-to-date, 1915; Love's Masquerade; Corinthian Jack; A History of Perfumes and Cosmetics, 1920; Lloyds' Boys' Adventure Stories; A Queen of the Paddock, 1921; Madam Flirt, a Romance of the Beggar's Opera, 1922; Polly Peachum (revised edition); The Beautiful Devil; Madame Vestris and her Times, 1923; Sims Reeves, Fifty Years of Music in England, 1924; Unsolved Murder Mysteries, 1924; novels: Love Besieged, Red Revenge, and A Star of the East (Indian Mutiny Trilogy); The Bungalow under the Lake, 1910; The Eyes of Alicia, 1913; The Crimson Mascot, 1914; criminology series, 1908–13: Unsolved Mysteries; Remarkable Clues; Romances of Crime; The Deadly Hand; Dark Dramas of Life; boys' books: The Ball of Fortune, 1896; Frank the Fisher Boy; The Golden Island; Billy Bos'n; The Boojum Club and Others; Mascot series: Vengeance is Mine; Dragged from the Dark; A Foe in the Shadow, 1918; Stirring Deeds of the Great War: Our Boys's History of British Heroism, 1919. *Address:* 37 Homefield Road, Chiswick, W. *Club:* Whitefriars.   *Died 9 Nov. 1924.*

PEARCE, Charles William, MusD Cantab; MA (Hon.) Dunelm; FRCO, FTCL; Director of Studies, Trinity College of Music, 1916–24 (Director of Examinations, 1902–16); Hon. Treasurer Royal College of Organists, 1909–26, Vice-President, 1926; *b* Salisbury, 5 Dec. 1856; *m* Agnes, 4th *d* of late Frederick Bird, JP, of Norton House, Midsomer Norton, near Bath; one *s* three *d. Educ:* Salisbury; London. MusB Cambridge, 1881; MusD 1884; MA Hon. Organist of St Martin's Church, Salisbury, 1871; St Luke's, Middlesex, 1874–85; St Clement's, Eastcheap, 1885–1919; Professor at Trinity College of Music, 1882; Examiner for musical Degrees at Cambridge University, 1888–91 and 1895–97; London University, 1901–4, and 1921–25; Victoria University, Manchester, 1905–7, and 1921–22; Durham University, 1911–13; Dean of the Faculty of Music in London University, 1908–12; Editor of Organist and Choirmaster, 1893–1917. *Publications:* Trinity College Text-Books of Musical Knowledge; Modern Academic Counterpoint; Students' Counterpoint; Composers' Counterpoint; Voice-Training Exercises and Studies, twelve books; The Art of the Piano-teacher; The Priest's Part in the Anglican Liturgy; Organ Accompaniment to Plainchant; Organ Versets and Descants; The Evolution of the Pedal Organ; Life and Work of E. J. Hopkins; Biographical Sketch of E. H. Turpin; composer of Church cantatas, anthems, organ and piano music, and songs. *Recreations:* archæology, architecture. *Address:* The Paddocks, Ferndown, Wimborne, Dorset. *Club:* Bristol Musical.
Died 2 Dec. 1928.

PEARCE, Sir Edward Charles, Kt 1922; *b* 9 April 1862; *s* of late John Swayne Pearce; *m* 1894, Marion Everett; no *c. Educ:* Charterhouse. Went to China, 1884; merchant; Chairman Shanghai Municipality, 1913–20; Chairman of Shanghai General Chamber of Commerce, 1921 and 1923; Chairman China Association, Shanghai, 1921 and 1923; Chevalier Légion d'Honneur; Chinese Order of Merit; Chinese Decoration of the Chiaho, 4th grade. *Recreations:* golf; in earlier years, riding, rowing. *Club:* Thatched House.
Died 8 Sept. 1928.

PEARCE, Major Francis Barrow, CMG 1904; British Resident, Zanzibar, 1914–22; *b* London, 16 Sept. 1866; *s* of Stephen Pearce.

Educ: Cheltenham; Sandhurst. Appointed Lieutenant 2nd Batt. West Yorkshire Regiment, 1886; Captain, 1893; served Ashanti Campaign, 1895 (star); British Central Africa, 1898 (medal and clasp); commanded British Force ´in combined Anglo-Portuguese operations in East Nyasaland, 1899 (medal, clasp, despatches, Brevet Majority); South Africa, 1900 (medal and clasp); seconded and appointed Assistant Deputy Commissioner, British Central African. Protectorate under Foreign Office, 1897; Deputy Commissioner, 1901; acted as Commissioner, Commander-in-Chief, and Consul-General, British Central African Protectorate, 1903; Deputy Governor, Nyasaland, 1907; acted as Governor and Commander-in-Chief, 1913–14; Acting High Commissioner for Zanzibar, 1917–18-21; Brilliant Star of Zanzibar 1st Class, 1922. *Publications:* Zanzibar: the Island-Metropolis of Eastern Africa; Rambles in Lion-Land, etc. *Address:* Lennox Lodge, Shanklin.   *Died 11 June 1926.*

PEARCE, Henry, JP; *b* 7 Dec. 1869; 2nd *s* of late Frederick Pearce; *m* Lily Blanche, 2nd *d* of late Joseph Gould, CE; two *d.* Prior to the Boer War, was a well-known traveller in South Africa and took an active interest in politics; joined the Intelligence Department as special service officer at the outbreak of hostilities, Boer War; commercial adviser to the Military Governor of the Orange River Colony (Sir George Pretyman); Director of Civil Supplies for the ORC; resigned position in Civil Service, 1902, and travelled extensively; wrote many articles for magazines, reviews, and newspapers; during European War initiated the Superfluity movement. *Address:* The Chaundrye, Eltham, Kent. *Clubs:* Authors'; Royal Wimbledon; Union, Victoria, BC.
Died 10 Jan. 1925.

PEARCE, Sir Robert, Kt 1916; FRAS; solicitor; MP (L) Leek Division, 1906–10, and 1910–18; *b* 15 Jan. 1840; *s* of Joseph Pearce of Ipswich, Suffolk, and Frances Margaret Hayward; *m* 1st, 1880, Elizabeth (*d* 1910), *d* of Edward Deane, Streatham; one *d*; 2nd, 1914, Margaret, *d* of Rev. R. B. Exton. *Educ:* privately; Ipswich Grammar School. Began business life as an accountant; admitted Solicitor, 1865; practised in Ipswich till 1872, then in London in the firm subseq. named Baylis, Pearce and Co., 116 Fore Street, EC; Clerk to the Cripplegate Charities; Vestry Clerk of Cripplegate; Solicitor to the City Parochial Foundation; a member of the Carmen's Company; contested Leek, 1895 and 1900. *Address:* 9 Downside Cresent, Hampstead, NW3. *T:* Hampstead 7359. *Club:* National Liberal.
Died 29 Sept. 1922.

PEARCE, Rev. Robert John, MA, DCL; Rector of Beachampton, Bucks, since 1914; *b* Bury St Edmunds, 22 Sept. 1841; *m* 1870, Lydia Freeman, *d* of Roger Moser, Kendal; two *s* five *d. Educ:* Commercial School, Bury St Edmunds; Caius Coll., Cambridge (3rd Wrangler, 1864; Fellow). Head Mathematical Master at Rossall and Blackheath Proprietary Schools; Professor of Mathematics at Durham University; sub-Warden of Durham University, 1883–95; Vicar of Bedlington, Northumberland, and Rural Dean, 1895–1914; Hon. Canon of Newcastle, 1899–1914. *Recreation:* photography. *Address:* The Rectory, Beachampton, Stony Stratford. *TA:* Rector, Beachampton.
Died 8 Aug. 1920.

PEARCE-SEROCOLD, Brig.-Gen. Eric, CMG 1918; King's Royal Rifle Coprs; *b* 1870; 2nd *s* of late Charles Pearce-Serocold of Taplow, Bucks; *m* 1st, 1901, Beatrix Lucy (*d* 1906), *d* of Admiral Sir Ernest Rice, KCB, and Laura, *d* of Edward York; 2nd, 1912, Hon. Blanche Florence Daphne Stanley, 4th *d* of 4th Baron Sheffield. Served South African War, 1899–1900 (Queen's medal and three clasps); European War, 1914–18 (despatches, CMG, Order of St Maurice and St Lazarus, Italy). *Club:* Brooks's.   *Died 26 June 1926.*

PEARD, Frances Mary, *d* of Captain Peard, RN. *Publications:* One Year; Unawares; The Rose Garden; A Madrigal; Near Neighbours; The Baroness; Mother Molly; Contradictions; Madame's Granddaughter; Alicia Tennant; The Swing of the Pendulum; Paul's Sister; An Interloper; Jacob and the Raven; The Career of Claudia; Donna Teresa; Number One and Number Two; The Ring from Jaipur; The Flying Months; and other novels; also several boys' books: Scapegrace Dick; The Blue Dragon; The Abbot's Bridge, etc. *Address:* St James, Torquay.   *Died 1 Oct. 1923.*

PEARS, Sir Edwin, Kt 1909; *b* York, 18 March 1835; *yr s* of Robert Pears, York, and Elizabeth Barnett; *m* 1857, Mary, *d* of John Ritchie Hall, surgeon, RN; four *s* three *d. Educ:* privately. Graduated LLB London University, first of first class in Honours, Roman Law and Jurisprudence. Called to the Bar, Middle Temple, 1870 (Exhibitioner in Constitutional Law and Legal History); General Secretary, Social Science Association, 1868–73; of International Prison Congress, 1872; Editor of Transactions of Social Science Assoc. and Congress; settled

in Constantinople, 1873; practising in Consular Courts, became President of European Bar in that city, 1881; as correspondent of Daily News sent letters in May and June 1876 on Moslem atrocities in Bulgaria, two of which were published in Blue Books and awakened widespread interest, which was followed by popular demonstrations led by Mr W. E. Gladstone; Editor, Law Magazine, 1872. *Publications:* The Fall of Constantinople, being the Story of the Fourth Crusade, 1885; The Destruction of the Greek Empire, 1903; Turkey and its People, 1911; Forty Years in Constantinople, 1915; Life of Abdul Hamid, 1917; contributions to English Historical Review; and to other periodical literature. *Address:* Pera, Constantinople. *Club:* Reform.
Died 27 Nov. 1919.

PEARS, Major (Temp. Lt-Col) M. L., CMG 1916; Reserve of Officers; commanding 17th Battalion Northumberland Fusiliers. Served NW Frontier, India, 1897–98 (medal, 2 clasps); Tirah, 1897–98 (clasps); S African War, 1899–1902 (despatches, Queen's medal, 2 clasps, King's medal, 2 claps); European War, 1914–16 (CMG). *Died 20 Oct. 1916.*

PEARSE, Col Hugh Wodehouse, DSO 1900; *b* 13 Aug. 1855; *s* of late Rev. Robert W. Pearse; *m* 1889, Ada Gordon, *d* of late Walter Scott, of Goldielea, Kirkcudbrightshire, NB; one *s* one *d*. Entered army, 1875; Col 1904; served Afghan War, 1878–79 (medal); South Africa, 1899–1902 (despatches, Queen's medal four clasps, King's medal two clasps, Brevet of Lieutenant-Colonel, DSO); Assistant Director on Headquarter Staff of the Army, 1907–11; retired, 1911. *Publications:* Memoirs of Colonel Alexander Gardner; The Crimean Diary of Lieutenant-General Sir Charles Windham; The Hearseys, 1905; Life of General Viscount Lake, 1908. *Address:* 58 Elm Park Gardens, Chelsea, SW. *Club:* Army and Navy.
Died 23 Oct. 1919.

PEARSON, Aylmer Cavendish; CMG 1919; Governor of North Borneo, 1915–22, and since 1925; *b* 5 Aug. 1876; 2nd *s* of late Col Hugh Pearson, CB, and Ellen Thomas; *m* 1907, Violet, *d* of Edward Gueritz, late Governor of N Borneo; one *d*. *Educ:* Felsted School; Trinity College, Dublin. Cadet British North Borneo Civil Service, 1897; Resident, 1901; Sessions Judge, 1905; Acting Judicial Commissioner, 1908; Acting Commissioner Lands, 1908; Government Secretary, 1909; Acting Governor, 1910, 1911. *Address:* c/o B. N. Borneo (Chartered) Co. 37 Threadneedle Street, EC.
Died 15 March 1926.

PEARSON, Sir (Cyril) Arthur, 1st Bt, *cr* 1916; GBE 1917; President National Institute for the Blind, and Fresh Air Fund; Vice-President Tariff Reform League, and Vice-Chairman of Tariff Commission, 1903; *b* Wookey, near Wells, 24 Feb. 1866; *o s* of late Rev. Arthur Cyril Pearson, Rector of Springfield, Essex, and Phillippa Maxwell-Lyte; *m* 1st, 1887, Isobel Sarah, *d* of Rev. F. Bennett, Maddington, Wilts; three *d*; 2nd, 1897, Ethel Maude (DBE 1920), 3rd *d* of William John Fraser; one *s*. *Educ:* Winchester. Founded business of C. Arthur Pearson, Ltd, of which Chairman; Proprietor of various newspapers, including the Daily Express, Standard, and Evening Standard, until failure of sight; Joint Hon. Sec. Collecting Committee National Relief Fund, 1914; Chairman Blinded Soldiers and Sailors Care Committee, 1914. *Publications:* Victory over Blindness, 1919; Conquest of Blindness, 1921. *Heir: s* Neville Arthur Pearson, *b* 13 Feb. 1898. *Address:* 15 Devonshire Street, W1. *T:* Langham 2308. *Clubs:* Carlton, Bath; Travellers', Paris. *Died 9 Dec. 1921.*

PEARSON, Sir Edward Ernest, Kt 1917; JP; Director of S. Pearson & Son, Ltd, and S. Pearson & Son (Contracting Department), Ltd, Contractors for Public Works; *b* 10 May 1874; 2nd *s* of late George Pearson (*b* of 1st Viscount Cowdray), and Sarah, *d* of Weetman Dickinson, Yorks; *m* 1904, Susannah Grace, *y d* of late Richard Benyon Croft of Fanhams Hall, Ware, and Anne Elizabeth, *d* of Henry Page; three *s* three *d*. *Educ:* Rugby. Joined the firm of S. Pearson & Son and became a Director, 1900; had charge of numerous works, amongst them Malta Dry Docks and Breakwater for the Admiralty, and Port of Valparaiso for the Chilian Government; during the European war responsible for construction of HM Factory, Gretna; travelled extensively; joined the 1st Middlesex Royal Engineers (Vol.), 1895; retired with rank of Capt. 1911; High Sheriff for Herts, 1909; Mayor of Hertford, 1921–23; interested in agriculture, breeder of Shire Horses, Shorthorns, etc. *Recreation:* shooting. *Address:* 10 Victoria Street, Westminster, SW; Brickendonbury, Hertford, Herts. *Clubs:* Reform, Bachelors'. *Died 19 Nov. 1925.*

PEARSON, Henry Harold Welch, MA; ScD; FLS; Harry Bolus Professor of Botany, South African College, and Hon. Director, National Botanic Gardens, Kirstenbosch, Cape Town; *b* Long Sutton,

Lincolnshire, 28 Jan. 1870; *o s* of Henry Jackson Pearson; *m* 1902, Ethel, *y d* of late William Pratt of Little Bradley, Suffolk. *Educ:* privately; Cambridge. Scholar of Christ's College; visited Ceylon as Wort's Travelling Scholar, 1897–98; Frank Smart Student of Botany at Gonville and Caius College, 1898; Assistant Curator of the Herbarium of the University of Cambridge, 1898–99; Walsingham Medallist, 1899; Assistant for India, Royal Botanic Gardens, Kew 1899–1901; Assistant (Director's Office), Royal Botanic Gardens, Kew, 1901–3. *Publications:* various botanical and geographical papers. *Address:* National Botanic Gardens, Kirstenbosch, Cape Town. *Club:* Savile. *Died 3 Nov. 1916.*

PEARSON, Hugh Drummond; Lieutenant-Colonel Royal Engineers; Director of Surveys, Sudan Government, since 1904; *b* 17 Feb. 1873; *s* of David Ritchie Pearson, MD (*d* 1901), and Jean Rae; *m* 1919, Blanche, *d* of late Colonel E. E. Grigg. *Educ:* St Paul's School; RMA Woolwich. Commissioned 2nd Lieut RE, 1892; Chatham, 1892–94; India, 1894–1902; Tirah Expedition, 1897–98; China Field Force, Relief of Pekin, 1900–2; Beir Expedition, 1912; served European War, 1914 (despatches, DSO, Bt Lt–Col); Murchison Award, RGS, 1913; 4th Class Osmanieh, 1911; 2nd class star of Ethiopia, 1916; 3rd class Order of the Nile, 1916; 2nd class Nadha, 1920. *Recreations:* golf, lawn-tennis. *Address:* Chestnuts, Beckley, Sussex; Khartoum. *Club:* Naval and Military.
Died 28 Dec. 1922.

PEARSON, Col Michael Brown, CB 1902; VD 1892; commanded the 2nd Middlesex Royal Garrison Artillery (Volunteers), 1890–1904; *b* London, 8 April 1840; 2nd *s* of late William Pearson, formerly of Newcastle-on-Tyne and London; *m* 1870, Sarah Jane, *d* of late Henry Thomas Bird of Boulogne-sur-Mer; three *s* one *d*. *Educ:* privately. Served in the Vol. Artillery, 1860–1904; Chairman of Council, London and Middlesex Archæological Society; President of Council National Artillery Association. *Address:* 31 Burnt Ash Road, Lee, Kent. *Club:* Junior Army and Navy.
Died 12 Nov. 1923.

PEARSON, Robert Hooper; *b* 18 July 1866; 3rd *s* of late William Pearson of Brewood, Staffs; *m* Mary, *e d* of late James Evans of Llangattock-Lingoed, Monmouthshire; one *d*. *Educ:* privately, and trained for horticultural career. Joined editorial staff of Gardeners' Chronicle, 1892; Assistant Editor, 1903; Managing Editor, 1908; member of Scientific and Floral Committees of Royal Horticultural Society; of Executive Committee of Royal Gardeners' Orphan Fund; Hon. Secretary of Horticultural Club. *Publications:* Garden Pests and Plant Diseases; general editor of the Present-Day Gardening series, My Garden series, and other works. *Address:* Braewyn, Earlsfield Road, SW. *T:* Gerrard 1543. *Died 11 June 1918.*

PEARSON, Thomas Bailey, CBE 1922; late Director of Audit, Exchequer and Audit Department; *b* Epworth, Lincolnshire, 1864; *s* of late J. R. Pearson, Doncaster; *m* 1891, Gertrude Effie, *d* of late John Nutt, London; three *d*. *Educ:* Doncaster Grammar School. Entered Exchequer and Audit Department, 1883; served in France, 1915–16; in Canada, 1916. *Address:* 48 Tetherdown, Muswell Hill, N10. *Died 11 May 1927.*

PEARY, Robert Edwin; Rear-Admiral United States Navy, retired; Discoverer of North Pole; Chairman United States Aero Coast Patrol Commission; *b* Cresson Springs, Penn, USA, 6 May 1856; *o c* of Charles N. and Mary Wiley Peary; *m* 1888, Josephine C. Diebitsch of Washington, DC; one *s* one *d*. *Educ:* Bowdoin Coll., Brunswick, Maine, USA (class of '77). Entered US Navy, 1881; asst engineer Government Surveys Nicaragua Ship Canal, 1885–86; reconnaissance Greenland Inland Ice, 1886; sub-chief engineer Nicaragua Canal Co., 1887; superintending engineer US Naval Dry Dock, League I, 1888–91; first expedition to North Greenland; determination of insularity of Greenland, 1891–92; second expedition to North Greenland, 1893–95; Arctic summer voyages, 1896, 1897; discovery and securing of the Cape York meteorites, the largest known meteorites in the world; third Arctic expedition for discovery of the North Pole, 1898–1902; rounded northern end of Greenland, the most northerly known land in the world, and reached 84° 17' N latitude, the highest latitude up to that time attained in the Western Hemisphere; expedition in SS Roosevelt, 1905, 1906, attaining 87° 6' N lat., the farthest north; second Roosevelt expedition, 1908–9; reached North Pole, 6 April 1909; promoted Rear Adm. and given thanks of Amer. Congress by special act, 1911; Gold Medallist of the Royal, Royal Scottish, Paris, Marseilles, Berlin, Normandy, Italian, Belgian, Swiss, Hungarian, Austrian, American, National, and Philadelphia Geographical Societies, the City of Paris, and the Explorers Club (President); Ex-President Amer. Geographical

Society; President 8th International Geog. Congress 1904; Hon. Vice-Pres. 9th and 10th Congresses; Hon. and Corr. Member various geog. societies; LLD Edin. University; Bowdoin College; Tufts College; Grand Officier of Légion d'Honneur, 1913. *Publications:* Northward Over the Great Ice, 1898; Nearest the Pole, 1907; The North Pole, 1910; various papers in geographical and other journals. *Recreations:* boating, riding, hunting. *Address:* Navy Department, Washington, DC, USA.   *Died 19 Feb. 1920.*

PEASE, Sir Arthur Francis, 1st Bt, *cr* 1920; DL; JP; coalowner; Chairman, Durham County Council, 1922; a Director of Pease Partners, Limited, Lloyds Bank, Ltd, and the London and North-Eastern Railway Company; *b* 11 March 1866; *e s* of late Arthur Pease, MP, of Hummersknott, Darlington, and Cliff House, Marske-by-Sea, and late Mary Lecky, *d* of Ebenezer Pike, Besborough, Co. Cork; *m* 1889, Laura Matilda Ethelwyn, *d* of late Charles Peter Allix, Swaffham Prior House, Cambridge; one *s* three *d. Educ:* Brighton College; Trinity College, Cambridge (BA (Historical Tripos) 1888; MA 1893). 2nd Civil Lord of the Admiralty, Jan. 1918–March 1919; High Sheriff, Co. Durham, 1920. *Heir: s* Richard Arthur Pease, Capt. Northumberland Hussars Yeomanry [*b* 18 Nov. 1890; *m* 1917, Jeannette Thorn, *d* of late Gustav Edward Kissel, Wheatsheaf House, Morristown, New Jersey, USA; three *s* one *d.* Served European War, 1914–18 (wounded twice)]. *Address:* Middleton Lodge, Middleton Tyas, Yorks; 12 Montagu Square, W1. *T:* Mayfair 6772. *Club:* Brooks's.   *Died 23 Nov. 1927.*

PEASE, Joseph Gerald, CBE 1920; the Umpire under the Unemployment Insurance Act 1923; Reader in Common Law to the Council of Legal Education since 1925 (Assistant Reader, 1903–25); *b* 17 April 1863; 4th *s* of late Thomas Pease of Cote Bank, Westbury-on-Trym; *m* 1904, Winifred, 2nd *d* of late Col Josiah Hudleston, Madras Staff Corps; two *d. Educ:* University College, London (BA). Called to the Bar, Inner Temple, 1887; practised on the Western Circuit; Chairman of Court of Referees (the Unemployment Insurance Act) for Metropolitan District, 1915–22; Chairman of Local Munitions Tribunal for Cambridge District, 1916–19. *Publications:* A Treatise on the Law of Markets and Fairs; A Summary of the Law on Contract; and other legal works. *Address:* 36 Downshire Hill, Hampstead, NW3. *T:* Hampstead 6472. *Clubs:* Athenæum, Royal Cruising.   *Died 3 March 1928.*

PEASE, Col Sir Thales, KCB 1901 (CB 1889); *b* 1835; *s* of late William Pease of Woolwich (late Storekeeper-General Naval Ordnance, Admiralty, Whitehall, retired 1902); *m* 1st, Lavinia (*d* 1902), *d* of Robert Jolly of Woolwich; 2nd, 1904, Flora Louise, *d* of M Hubert; two *s* two *d.* Entered Ordnance Store Department, 1855; Asst Comy-Gen.; 1880; Deputy Comy-Gen., 1885; served Soudan Expedition, 1884–85 (despatches, promoted Colonel, medal with clasp, Khedive's star); was Senior Ordnance Store Officer, S Dist, 1887–91; Storekeeper-General Naval Ordnance, 1891; retired, 1902. *Address:* 53 Drayton Gardens, South Kensington, SW.   *Died 26 Feb. 1919.*

PEASE, William Edwin; JP; MP (C) Darlington since 1923; *b* 3 June 1865; *e s* of Edwin Lucas Pease of Mowden, Darlington, and Frances Helen Edwards, Cascob, Radnorshire. *Educ:* Clifton College; Trinity College, Cambridge. Director of Cleveland Bridge and Engineering Co., Darlington; Consett Iron Co.; and Durham and N Yorks Public House Trust; Mayor of Darlington, 1924–25. *Address:* Mowden, Darlington. *Club:* Boodle's.   *Died 23 Jan. 1926.*

PECK, Sir William, Kt 1917; FRSE; FRAS; Director of City Observatory, Calton Hill, Edinburgh; *b* Castle Douglas, 3 Jan. 1862; *s* of William Peck; *m* 1889, Christina (*d* 1922), *e d* of late James Thomson, Roseburn House, Edin. *Educ:* Edinburgh. Patented inventions in internal combustion engines, propellers, pumps, astronomical instruments, optical instruments, electric ignition devices, etc. *Publications:* Handbook of Astronomy; Constellations and how to find them; Observers' Atlas of the Heavens; an Introduction to the Celestial Sphere, etc. *Recreation:* motoring. *Address:* City Observatory, Calton Hill, Edinburgh; 51 Inverleith Row, Edinburgh. *T:* Edinburgh 1984. *M:* S 1516.

Died 7 March 1925.

PECKOVER, 1st Baron, *cr* 1907, of Wisbech; **Alexander Peckover,** JP; LLD; FSA, FLS, FRGS; President of Essex Hall Asylum, Colchester; Vice-President of Hakluyt Society, Biblical Archæological, British Numismatic Societies, etc; *b* Wisbech, 16 Aug. 1830; *s* of Algernon Peckover, Wisbech, and Priscilla, *y d* of Dykes Alexander, Ipswich; directly descended from Edmund Peckover, who

served in Cromwell's army, and whose landed property he possessed; *m* 1858, Eliza (*d* 1862), *o d* of Joseph Sharples, Hitchin; three *d. Educ:* Grove House School, Tottenham. Partner many years in bank of Gurney, Peckover, and Co., retired; took a special interest in collections of ancient MSS, early Bibles, and maps, also early printed books, especially English; also in meteorology; Lord-Lieut of Cambridgeshire, 1893–1906. Owned about 4,000 acres. *Heir:* none. *Recreations:* chess, cricket, tennis. *Address:* Bank House, Wisbech.

Died 21 Oct. 1919 (ext).

PEDLER, Sir Alexander, Kt 1906; CIE 1901; FRS, FCS, FIC; *b* 21 May 1849; *s* of late George Stanbury Pedler, Dulwich; *m* 1st, 1878, Elizabeth Margaret (*d* 1896), *d* of Christian Karl Schmidt of Frankfurt; 2nd, 1905, Mabel, *y d* of late William Warburton, RN, of Dedham. *Educ:* City of London School; Royal Coll. of Science. Educn Dept, Bengal, 1873; formerly Prof. of Chemistry, Presidency Coll.; Principal, Presidency Coll.; Director of Public Instruction for Bengal; Vice-Chancellor University of Calcutta; additional Member of Legislative Council of Governor-General of India; retired 1906; Member of three Government Total Eclipse Expeditions of 1868, 1875 and 1898. *Publications:* various papers in Proceedings Royal Society, Journal Chemical Society, Journal Asiatic Society, Bengal, Indian Meteorological Memoirs, etc. *Recreations:* lawn-tennis, golf. *Address:* 23 Stanhope Gardens, Queen's Gate, SW. *T:* 3685 Western. *Clubs:* Constitutional, Ranelagh, Royal Automobile.

Died 13 May 1918.

PEEK, Sir Wilfrid, 3rd Bt, *cr* 1874; DSO 1918; Major, late Royal 1st Devon Yeomanry; *b* 9 Oct. 1884; *s* of Sir Cuthbert Edgar Peek, 2nd Bt and Hon. Augusta Louisa Brodrick, *d* of 8th Viscount Midleton; S father, 1901; *m* 1913, Edwine Warner, *d* of late William Henry Thornburgh, St Louis, USA; one *s. Educ:* Eton; Trinity College, Cambridge. Served European War, 1914–18 (DSO). *Heir: s* Francis Henry Grenville Peek, *b* 16 Sept. 1915. *Address:* Rousdon, Devon. *TA:* Rousdon. *Clubs:* Carlton, Cavalry.

Died 12 Oct. 1927.

PEEL, Algernon Robert, MVO 1904; *b* 20 Jan. 1862; 5th *s* of late Sir Charles Lennox Peel, GCB, and Hon. Caroline Georgina, *e d* of 1st Baron Templemore. *Educ:* Marlborough. Private Secretary to 6th Duke of Richmond and Gordon when Secretary for Scotland; Private Secretary to 5th Earl Cadogan, 1885–1904.

Died 26 June 1920.

PEEL, Rev. Hon. Maurice Berkeley, BA; Vicar of Tamworth since 1915; *b* 23 April 1873; *y s* of 1st Viscount Peel and Adelaide, *d* of William Stratford Dugdale, Warwicks; *m* 1909, Emily (*d* 1912), *d* of late Julius Alington; one *s* one *d. Educ:* New College, Oxford; Wells College. Ordained 1899; Curate of St Simon Zelotes, Bethnal Green, 1899–1906; Rector of Wrestlingworth, 1906–9; Vicar of Eyeworth, 1906–9; Vicar of St Paul's, Beckenham, 1909–15; Chaplain to the Forces, 1915 (severely wounded). *Address:* Tamworth Vicarage, Stafford.   *Died May 1917.*

PEEL, Sir Robert, 4th Bt, *cr* 1800; *b* 12 April 1867; *e s* of Sir Robert Peel, 3rd Bt and Lady Emily Hay (*d* 1924), *d* of 8th Marquess of Tweeddale; S father, 1895; *m* 1897, Mercedes, *d* of Baron de Graffenried, Thun, Switzerland; one *s. Educ:* Harrow; Balliol College, Oxford. Formerly Lieut Staffs Yeo. Cavalry. Owned about 10,000 acres. *Publications:* A Bit of a Fool, 1896; An Engagement, 1897. *Heir: s* Robert Peel [*b* 8 April 1898; *m* 1920, Beatrice Gladys Lillie; one *s. Educ:* Harrow]. *Address:* Drayton Manor, Tamworth.

Died 12 Feb. 1925.

PEEL, Col Robert Francis, CMG 1922; Governor and Commander-in-Chief, St Helena, since 1920; *b* 30 April 1874; *s* of Capt. Francis Peel and Caroline Edith Blanche, *y d* of Anthony Brown Story; *m* 1903, Alice Maud, 2nd *d* of late Sir Thomas Charlton-Meyrick, 1st Bt; one *s. Educ:* Harrow. Entered Coldstream Guards, 1898; Captain, 1906; served S Africa, 1899–1902 (Queens' medal, 6 clasps, King's medal, 2 clasps); retired, 1909; Lt-Col and Bt Col 4th Battalion (Special Reserve) East Surrey Regt; served European War, 1914–19. MP (U) Woodbridge Division of Suffolk, 1910–20. *Address:* Government House, St Helena. *Clubs:* Carlton, Guards', Windham.

Died Aug. 1924.

PEEL, Rt. Rev. William George, DD (Hon.); Bishop of Mombasa since 1899; *b* India, 1854; *s* of late Capt. Peel, HM 53rd Regiment; *m* Agneta Jane Bryan, Monkton Combe, Somerset; three *s* four *d. Educ:* Blackheath Proprietary School; CMS Theological Coll., Islington, London. Ordained, 1879; Curate of Trowbridge, Wilts, 1879–80; Rugby Fox Master of CMS Noble Coll., Masulipatam,

1880–87 (acting Principal three years); Sec. CMS Madras, 1888–89 and 1892; Sec. CMS W India, 1892–99. *Address:* Bishop's Court, Mombasa, British East Africa; The Walnuts, Buntingford, Herts. *TA:* Peel, Mombasa. *Died 15 April 1916.*

PEGLER, Louis Hemington, MD, MCh Edin.; MRCS; Consulting Surgeon, Metropolitan Throat, Nose, and Ear Hospital, Fitzroy Square; late Surgeon in charge of Ear and Throat Department, Mile End Military Hospital; *b* 1852; *s* of Daniel Pegler of Colchester, pianist and musical composer; *m* Maude Edith, *y d* of F. W. Palmer of Bedford; no *c. Educ:* Royal Grammar School, Colchester; University College, London; Edinburgh University. Commenced practice in London, 1892; Registrar and Pathologist to Central London Throat Hospital, 1893–95; Hon. Secretary to British Laryngological, Rhinological and Otological Assoc., 1893–96; organised the International meeting of same in 1895; Surgeon Laryngologist and Aurist to the Governesses' Benevolent, Clergy Orphan Corporation, and London College of Music; Fellow of Royal Society of Medicine, and Vice-President of Laryngological Section of same; Member of Council and Curator of Museum, Laryngological Section of International Medical Congress, London, 1913; compelled for health reasons to refuse Presidency of Oto-Laryngological Section, British Medical Association Meeting, 1921; member of several archæological and geological societies, and British Bryological Society; presented his collection of fossil trees and ferns to British Museum of Natural History, South Kensington; had large herbariam and collection of prehistoric flint implements. *Publications:* The Surgical Treatment of some Common Forms of Nasal Insufficiency; The Pathology and Treatment of Discrete Nasal Angioma; Headaches in association with Nasal Obstruction; A Map Scheme of the Fifth Nerve and its connections, 1913, with book; On the Desirability for a More Discriminative Nomenclature for the Nasal Nerves, Transactions, XVII International Congress of Medicine, London, 1913. *Recreations:* botany, geology, music. *Address:* 7 Bartholomew Terrace, Exeter. *M:* TT 1945. *Club:* Edinburgh University. *Died 26 Feb. 1927.*

PELHAM, Rev. Sidney; Hon. Canon of Norwich, 1896–1901 and since 1916; *b* 16 May 1849; 3rd *s* of late Hon. John Thomas Pelham (Bishop of Norwich, 1857–93), and Henrietta, *d* of Thomas William Tatton, Cheshire; *m* 1897, Caroline Elizabeth, *d* of late Canon John Patteson, Rector of Thorpe St Andrew, Norfolk. *Educ:* Harrow; Oxford. Ordained Deacon, 1873; Priest, 1874; Curate at Stalbridge, Dorsetshire, 1873–74; Redenhall, Norfolk, 1874–79; Vicar of S Peter, Mancroft, Norwich, 1879–81; Private Secretary to the Bishop of Norwich, 1890–1901; Rural Dean of Norwich; Chaplain of the Norfolk and Norwich Hospital, 1901–6; Archdeacon of Norfolk 1901–16. *Recreation:* Captain of Harrow Eleven, 1868; played for the University of Oxford, 1871. *Address:* 85 Newmarket Road, Norwich. *Died 14 July 1926.*

PELHAM, Hon. Thomas Henry William, CB 1905; Assistant Secretary (Harbour Department) Board of Trade, 1895–1913; *b* 21 Dec. 1847; *s* of 3rd Earl of Chichester and Mary, *d* of 6th Earl of Cardigan; *m* 1883, Louisa Keith, *d* of William Bruce; one *s* two *d. Educ:* Eton; Trinity College, Cambridge (2nd Class Law Tripos, 1869). Barrister, Inner Temple, 1871; Home and SE Circuits, and Sussex Sessions, 1871–82; legal adviser to Veterinary Department of Privy Council, 1882–89, and to Board of Agriculture, 1889–95; held inquiries for Privy Council, for Local Government Board, and other Departments, 1879–95; Boundary Commissioner for Redistribution of Seats Bill, 1884–85; Glasgow Boundary Commissioner, 1887; Boundary Commissioner under Local Government (Scotland) Act, 1889; appointed by Board of Trade to settle canal rates, 1893, and railway rates, 1895; Treasurer and Hon. Secretary of Homes for Working Boys; a Governor of the Polytechnic, Regent Street. *Recreations:* golf, cycling, lawn-tennis. *Address:* Deene House, Putney Hill, SW. *T:* 823 Putney. *Died 23 Dec. 1916.*

PELL, Major Albert Julian; *b* 19 Nov. 1863; *e s* of Rev. Beauchamp Henry St John Pell (*d* 1907), Rector of Ickenham, Uxbridge, and Julia Caroline (*d* 1902), *d* of late Edward Tyndall, RN; *m* 1897, Catherine Marion, 3rd *d* of Sir (Edward) Walter Greene, 1st Bt, of Nether Hall, Bury St Edmunds; two *d. Educ:* Winchester College; Merton College, Oxford (BA 1886). Barrister, Lincoln's Inn, 1890; DL Cambridgeshire; JP Isle of Ely, and Chairman of Quarter Sessions; Vice-Chairman Isle of Ely County Council; Vice-Chairman of Cambs and Isle of Ely Territorial Forces Association; was Captain (Hon. Major, 1898), 4th Batt. (Militia) Suffolk Regiment, till 1908. *Publication:* article on William Cobbett, in Vol. lxiii (1902), of Journal of Royal Agricultural Society. *Address:* Wilburton Manor, Ely. *TA:* Wilburton. *Club:* Carlton. *Died 28 Aug. 1916.*

PELLETIER, Lt-Col J. M. J. Pantaleon, MD; FRCI; Agent General for the Province of Quebec in London since 1911; *b* River Ouelle, Co. of Kamouraska, 27 July 1860; *s* of Joseph Pelletier and Henriette Martin; *m* 1st, 1888, Alice Hudon (*d* 1910), of Quebec; 2nd, 1912, Cecile Belleau, *widow* of late J. Boivin, Assistant-Secretary of the Province of Quebec. *Educ:* Ste Anne College and Laval University, Quebec. Began to practice at Sherbrooke, 1887; studied in New York, 1897; continued the study in Paris of surgery and gynæcology; belonged to the 9th Battalion of Quebec, 1885; and took part in the quelling of the Reil rebellion; acted as coroner of the district of St François, 1890–1900; elected to represent the county of Sherbrooke at the Quebec Parliament, re-elected in 1904 and 1908; Member of the Provincial Office of Health; unanimously elected Speaker of the Legislative Assembly, Quebec, 1909; President of Trustees of Catholic Schools; Hon. President and Director of the Canadian Agricultural Association; was director of the Sherbrooke Lumber Co.; Liberal; Roman Catholic. *Address:* Quebec Government Offices, 38 Kingsway, WC2. *Clubs:* Royal Automobile, British Empire, Overseas; Canadian, Montreal. *Died 20 Oct. 1924.*

PELLETIER, Hon. Louis Philippe, KC; MP; Judge of the Court of Appeals, Quebec, since 1914; *b* Trois Pistoles, Quebec, 1857; *s* of Hon. Thomas P. Pelletier and Caroline Casault; *m* 1883, Adèle Lelièvre. *Educ:* St Anne Coll.; Laval Univ. Called to the Bar, 1880; Legislative Council of Province of Quebec, 1888; elected County of Dorchester, 1890; Provincial Secretary, 1891; Attorney-General for his native province, 1896; retired from provincial politics, 1904; elected for county of Quebec, 1911; Postmaster-General, 1911–14; an LLD and Professor in Laval University. *Address:* 38 Garden Street, Quebec. *Clubs:* Rideau, Ottawa; Garrison, Quebec.

Died Feb. 1921.

PEMBERTON, Rev. Thomas Percy, JP; MA; Canon and Prebendary of Bilton, York Minister, since 1879; *s* of William Hudson, Ousecliffe, York; surname changed to Pemberton by Royal Warrant, 1900; *m* 1870, Patience Frances Sophia, *d* of Capt. William Huntly Campbell, 20th Regt, and Frances Maria Sophia, *o c* of Colonel Francis C. J. Pemberton, Trumpington Hall, Cambridge; one *d. Educ:* St Peter's School, York (Scholar and Exhibitioner); Trinity College, Cambridge. Scholar; 6th Wrangler and 3rd class Classical Tripos. Fellow of Trinity Coll., Cambridge, 1856–70; Assistant Tutor, 1856–66; Tutor, 1866–70; Rector of Gilling East, Malton, Yorks, 1870–1901; Succentor, York, 1883; Proctor in Convocation, 1874–80; Rural Dean of Helmsley, 1890–1901. *Publications:* works on arithmetic and trigonometry. *Recreation:* music (Founder and conductor of Hovingham Musical Festival, 1887–1905; Conductor of York Musical Society, 1896–1900). *Address:* Trumpington Hall, Cambridge. *TA:* Trumpington. *T:* Trumpington 1. *Died 31 Jan. 1921.*

PEMBERTON, Maj.-Gen. Sir Wykeham Leigh, KCB 1910 (CB 1879); JP; *b* 4 Dec. 1833; *s* of late Edward Leigh Pemberton of Torry Hill, Kent; *m* 1884, Jessie, *d* of late John Graham, Skelmorlie, NB; one *s* two *d. Educ:* Rugby. Served in Royal Navy, 1845–46; joined 60th Rifles, 1852; served in Indian Mutiny, 1857; severely wounded at Cawnpore, 27 Nov. (medal); commanded 3rd Batt. 60th Rifles in Zulu War, 1879, and brigade at Ginghiloro (medal and clasp); AQMG Headquarters, 1880–85; ADC to HRH Duke of Cambridge, 1885–90; promoted Major-General in 1890; Colonel Commandant 60th Rifles, 1906. Decorated for command of brigade in active service. *Recreations:* cricket, shooting, etc. *Address:* Abbots Leigh, Haywards Heath, Sussex. *Club:* Army and Navy. *Died 2 March 1918.*

PEMBREY, John Cripps, Hon. MA; *b* 1831; *m* 1863; three *s* four *d.* Entered service of University Press, Oxford, 1846; with his father was the first to set up Sanskrit in type for first vol. of the Rig-Veda, 1849; from then and until 1916, responsible for the reading of most of the Oriental books printed at Oxford; among others, Rig-Veda (4to and 8vo editions), Sacred Books of the East (50 vols), Anecdota Oxoniensia, Semitic and Aryan series (21 vols); *dictionaries*—Sanskrit (Williams), Syriac (Payne Smith), Compendious Syriac (Mrs Margoliouth), Vernacular Syriac (Maclean), Hebrew (Gesenius, ed Driver and others), Yônâh's Hebrew Roots (Neubauer), Tamil (Pope); *grammars*—Sanskrit by Wilson (1847), by Williams, by M. Müller, by Macdonell (1914), Arabic (Green), Hebrew (Gesenius), Tenses in Hebrew (Driver); *catalogues*—Syriac, Sanskrit, Hebrew, Persian, Japanese and Chinese for the Bodleian Library, Persian for India Office. *Publications:* edited and published Gospel Banner, monthly, 1872–1916; Pastoral Letters of Rev. J. Hobbs; Life, etc, of Joseph Tanner; Life and Ministry of Bernard Gilpin; and several other devotional books. *Address:* 164 Walton Street, Oxford.

Died 1 May 1918.

PENBERTHY, John, JP; late Major Devonshire Regiment; *b* Treruffe, Redruth, Cornwall, 19 April 1858; *e s* of late William Penberthy of Treworgie, Redruth, and Mary, *d* of John Boskean; *m* Eleanor, *e d* of John Rees, JP, Neath, Glamorganshire; one *d*. *Educ:* Fowey School; University College. Member of Hon. Soc., Inner Temple, 1885; Inspector of Privy Council under Contagious Diseases (Animals) Act, 1882; Professor of Pathology, 1888, of Medicine, 1892–1908, Royal Veterinary College; President of Royal College of Veterinary Surgeons, 1897; Fellow Royal Society of Medicine; Member Council Central and Gloucestershire Chambers of Agriculture; Governor Royal Agricultural College, Cirencester; Member Court Universityof Bristol; Advisory Council on Horse Breeding; Departmental Committee on Swine Fever and Foot and Mouth Disease. *Publications:* Text-book of Equine Medicine; Pain, its Indications and Significance in the Lower Animals; Diseases Communicable from the Lower Animals to Man; Protective Inoculation against Anthrax, etc. *Recreation:* gardening. *Address:* Dean Hall, Newnham, Gloucestershire. *T:* Newnham 26. *Clubs:* Royal Societies, Farmers'; Gloucester.
Died 23 May 1927.

PENDAVIS, Ven. Whylock, MA; Rector of Fringford since 1921; *m*; one *s*. *Educ:* Trinity College, Dublin. Curate of St Philip's, Chorley, 1875–77; St James's, Collyhurst, 1877–81; Incumbent of St Augustine, Monsall, 1881–86; Moka, Mauritius, 1886–99; Religious Instructor, Royal College, Mauritius, 1899–1907; Hon. Canon of Mauritius, 1899–1907; Archdeacon, 1903–7; Sub-Dean, 1905–7; Examining Chaplain to Bishop, 1903–7; Chaplain at Havre, 1907–9; Rector of Hethe, 1909–21. *Address:* The Rectory, Fringford, Bicester.
Died 29 Oct. 1924.

PENDER, Sir James, 1st Bt, *cr* 1897; JP; Director of Globe, Telegraph, and Trust Co., and Telegraph Construction and Maintenance Co.; *b* 28 Sept. 1841; *e s* of late Sir John Pender, GCMG, MP Wick, and 1st wife, Marion, *d* of James Cearns, Glasgow; *m* 1867, Mary Rose, 3rd *d* of Edward John Gregge Hopwood, Hopwood Hall, Lancashire. *Educ:* University Coll. London. Formerly Lieut King's Own Borderers; MP (C) Mid Northamptonshire, 1895–1900. *Recreations:* hunting, yachting. *Heir:* none. *Address:* Donhead House, Donhead St Andrew, Wilts. *Clubs:* Turf, Naval and Military; Royal Yacht Squadron, Cowes. *Died 20 May 1921 (ext).*

PENDLETON, Alan O'Bryan George William, CMG 1905; *b* Collon, Co. Louth, Ireland, 17 May 1837; *s* of Henry Latham Pendleton of Lough Derry, Co. Monaghan, Ireland; *m* 1877, Agnes, 2nd *d* of John Edis of Cambs. Entered service of Manchester, Sheffield, and Lincolnshire Railway, 1856; made joint representative in Ireland of the GNR (England) and the Manchester, Sheffield, and Lincolnshire Railway, 1860; Manager and Agent of the Calcutta and South-Eastern Railway, Bengal, 1861; Assistant Superintendent of the GNR England, 1870; General Manager of Railways, South Australia, 1876; Commissioner of Railways, S Australia, 1895–1909. *Address:* Carnagoen, Mount Lofty, Adelaide, South Australia.
Died 18 Nov. 1916.

PENFOLD, Very Rev. John Brookes Vernon, BD; Dean of the Island and Bailiwick of Guernsey and its Dependencies (Alderney, Sark, etc); *b* 1864; *s* of Rev. William Penfold, MA (Rector of Ruardean, Gloucestershire, and Chaplain to the Duke of Beaufort); *m* 1st, Maude Frances, *o d* of Francis Edward Carey, MD (Insp.-Gen. Royal Guernsey Militia, etc), of Villa Carey, Guernsey; one *s*; 2nd, 1918, Janet Lily, 2nd *d* of P. F. Carey, Constable of St Peter Port, etc. *Educ:* St John's School, Leatherhead; Jesus College, Cambridge. Chaplain King William's College, Isle of Man, 1888; Assistant Minister St James', Welbeck Street, W, 1890; Editor Church of England Pulpit, and occasional contributor to various papers and magazines; Vicar of St James', Guernsey, 1893; A/G Chaplain to the Forces, 1895; Chaplain Royal Guernsey Artillery, 1901; Dean of Guernsey (Patron, the Crown), Commissionary-General of the Bishop of Winchester, and Judge of the Ecclesiastical Court, 1917; Rector of St Peter Port, 1918; a Freemason, Past Senior Grand Warden of the Province of Guernsey and Alderney, and Past Grand Chaplain of England; Chairman of the Board of Directors of the Royal College of Queen Elizabeth in Guernsey; Chairman of Ladies' College; President of Intermediate Education Committee, and St Peter Port Education Committee; chiefly interested in Church and Social Reform; a strong supporter of the proposals of the Archbishops' Committee on relations between Church and State; took a prominent part in the development of Trades Unions in Guernsey; principal work outside ecclesiastical duties concerned education, in the advancement of which he actively engaged for twenty years, having at some time or other directed most of the Educational Departments of Guernsey. *Publications:* Inaugural Address to the Decanal Conference of the Deanery of Guernsey;

Memoir of the Very Rev. Thomas Bell, MA, Dean of Guernsey and Canon of Winchester. *Address:* The Deanery, Guernsey.
Died 4 May 1922.

PENFOLD, Lt-Col Sir Stephen, Kt 1915; VD; JP for the Borough of Folkestone and the County of Kent; Mayor of Folkestone twelve times; *b* 17 May 1842; 4th *s* of John Penfold, Folkestone, and Susannah, 2nd *d* of Henry Jeffery, Folkestone; *m* 1874, Margaret Elizabeth, *o d* of Henry Acton Hall, East Hanney, Berks; one *d*. *Educ:* private school. Thirty-five years' volunteering, afterwards municipal work in the Borough of Folkestone and County of Kent; Officer of the Order of the Crown of Belgium; Croix de Chevalier de la Légion d'Honneur, France; Cavalieri of the Order of the Crown of Italy. *Recreation:* gardening. *Address:* Canadian Villa, 70 Cheriton Road, Folkestone. *Clubs:* Constitutional; Radnor, Folkestone.
Died 9 Jan. 1925.

PENNEFATHER, Sir (Alfred) Richard, Kt 1909; CB 1896; Diamond Jubilee Silver Medal, King Edward's Coronation Silver Medal; JP Essex; *b* 10 March 1846; *s* of John Pennefather, QC; paternal grandfather, The Rt Hon. Baron Pennefather; maternal grandfather, The Hon. Edward de Moleyns; *m* 1867, Thomasina (Sina) Cox, *y d* of Thomas Cox Savory. *Educ:* private school. Home Office Clerk, 1868; Receiver Metropolitan Police District, 1883–1909; Visiting Justice of HM Prison, Chelmsford; Member of Essex Standing Joint Committee; Member of House of Layman for Province of Canterbury; Member Central Board of Finance of Church of England. *Decorated* for public services. *Address:* Little Waltham Hall, near Chelmsford. *T:* Little Waltham 8; 30 Westminster Mansions, SW1. *M:* LL 3541. *Club:* Union. *Died 14 Aug. 1918.*

PENNEFATHER, Rev. Preb. Somerset Edward, MA, DD; Vicar of Kensington since 1897; *b* Dublin, 1 March 1848; *y s* of late John Pennefather, QC (*s* of Baron Pennefather), and Elizabeth Jemima, *d* of Hon. Edward De Moleyns, and *g d* of 1st Baron Ventry; *m* 1870, Catherine Emily, *d* of late T. C. Savory; three *s* one *d*. *Educ:* King's College, London; Trinity College, Dublin (MA). MA (*ad eund*) Durham University; DD (Hon.) Aberdeen. Ordained, 1871; Curate, East Claydon, 1871–74; Vicar of Christ Church, Wakefield, 1874–75; Kenilworth, 1875–82; Jesmond, Newcastle-on-Tyne, 1882–88; St George's, Jesmond, 1888–97; Hon. Canon of Newcastle, 1888–1907; Rural Dean of Kensington, 1901; Prebendary of St Paul's Cathedral, 1907; Proctor for Dio. of London, 1909; Hon. Chaplain 4th Middlesex West London Rifles, 1898; Chaplain to HM Troops, Kensington Barracks, 1898; Chaplain (2nd Class) Territorial Forces, Chaplain, Kensington Barracks, 1908; FKC; Alderman, Royal Borough of Kensington, 1898. *Address:* The Vicarage, Kensington, W. *TA:* Pennefar. London. *T:* Park 3519.
Died 29 Aug. 1917.

PENNELL, Arthur; Registrar of Criminals, Home Office; *b* Nov. 1852; *s* of Sir Henry Pennell, of the Admiralty, and Harriet Francis, *g d* of Sir Philip Francis, MP (reputedly author of Junius Letters); *m* 1875, Louisa Erica, 2nd *d* of H. H. Hungerford, DL, of Dingley Park, and Maydwell Hall, Northamptonshire, and *g d* of Lady Louisa Forester, *d* of Duke of Cleveland; one *s*. *Educ:* Jesus College, Cambridge. Entered the Admiralty, and subsequently appointed to the Home Office; contested Elland Div. of Yorkshire, 1900; Rotherhithe Div. of London County Council, 1901. *Recreations:* hunting, shooting, golf, fishing. *Address:* 4 Foulis Terrace, Onslow Square, SW7. *T:* 2542 Kensington. *Clubs:* Wellington, Portland; Sunningdale; Westward Ho!
Died 25 Aug. 1926.

PENNELL, Joseph; artist and author; *b* Philadelphia, Penn, USA, 1860; *m* Elizabeth R. Pennell. *Educ:* School of Industrial Art, Philadelphia; Pennsylvania Academy of Fine Arts. Member American Academy Arts and Letters, National Academy of Designs, NY, and Royal Belgian Academy; Hon. ARIBA, Hon. AAIA; represented in National Art Galleries of Europe and America. *Publications:* A Canterbury Pilgrimage, 1885; An Italian Pilgrimage, 1886; Two Pilgrims' Progress, 1887; Our Sentimental Journey through France and Italy, 1888; Pen Drawing and Pen Draughtsmen, 1889; Our Journey to the Hebrides, 1889; The Stream of Pleasure, 1891; The Jew at Home, 1892; Play in Provence, 1892; To Gipsyland, 1893; Modern Illustration, 1895; The Illustration of Books, 1896; The Alhambra, 1896; The Work of Charles Keene, 1897; Lithography and Lithographers, 1900; The Life of James McNeill Whistler, 1907; Pictures of the Panama Canal, 1912; The Wonder of Work, 1916; Etchers and Etching, 1919; The Whistler Journal, 1921; The Graphic Arts, 1922; Adventures of an Illustrator, 1925. *Address:* Century Club, New York. *Club:* Reform. *Died 23 April 1926.*

PENNINGTON, Brig.-Gen. Arthur Watson, MVO 1907; retired; late 9th Hodson's Horse; *b* 20 March 1867; *s* of late Lieutenant-General Sir Charles Richard Pennington, KCB, and Lydia Harriot, *e d* of Capt. Henry Becher, BSC; *m* Helen Bethea, *d* of late Colonel James Bird Hutchinson, CSI; one *d*. *Educ:* Haileybury; Oxford Military College. Entered Border Regt 1888; Captain, Indian Army, 1899; Major, 1906; Lt-Col 1914; served Chitral, 1895 (medal with clasp); Tirah, 1897–98 (two clasps); DAAG Indian Coronation Contingent at King Edward's Coronation; in charge of King Edward's Indian Orderly Officers, 1907; served European War in Egypt, France, and Mesopotamia, 1914–18 (despatches thrice); retired, 1922. *Address:* Mylncroft, Frimley Green, Surrey.

Died 8 May 1927.

PENNY, Edmund, CIE 1900; Superintendent Engineer and Secretary to Chief Commissioner, Central Provinces Public Works Department, 1899; invalided 1900; retired 1902; *b* 23 April 1852; *s* of Alfred Penny, MICE, and Sarah, *d* of W. A. Weightman; *m* 1881, Ellen Margaret, *d* of Major-Gen. P. S. Cunningham. *Educ:* Cheltenham College; Cooper's Hill. Appointed Public Works Department, India, 1874; executive engineer Central Provinces, 1883; planned and carried out scheme for Nagpur Waterworks, 1890. *Address:* India Office, SW. *Died 13 Aug. 1919.*

PENRHYN, 3rd Baron, *cr* 1866; Edward Sholto Douglas-Pennant, JP, DL; *b* 10 June 1864; *e s* of 2nd Baron Penrhyn and Pamela Blanche, *d* of Sir Charles Rushout-Rushout, 2nd Bt; *S* father, 1907; *m* 1887, Hon. Blanche Georgiana Fitzroy, *d* of 3rd Baron Southampton; one *s* three *d* (and one *s* decd). *Educ:* Eton; Sandhurst. Lieut 1st Life Guards, 1885–91; MP (C) Northamptonshire, S, 1895–1900; Member of Jockey Club. *Heir: s* Hon. Hugh Napier Douglas-Pennant [*b* 6 Aug. 1894; *m* 1922, Hon. Sybil Mary Hardinge, *yr d* of 3rd Viscount Hardinge]. *Address:* Penrhyn Castle, Bangor; Wicken Park, Stony Stratford. *Clubs:* Carlton, Bachelors'; Royal Yacht Squadron, Cowes.

Died 22 Aug. 1927.

PENRHYN, Rev. Oswald Henry Leycester; Rector of Winwick, 1890–1917; Canon of Liverpool since 1880; Proctor in York Convocation since 1880; Chaplain to the Bishop; *b* East Sheen, 6 May 1828; 2nd *s* of Edward Penrhyn, JP, DL, and Lady Charlotte Elizabeth, *e d* of 13th Earl of Derby; *m* Charlotte Louisa Jane, 4th *d* of Edmund G. Hornby, JP, DL of Dalton Hall, Burton, Westmorland; one *s* three *d*. *Educ:* Eton; Balliol Coll., Oxford (BA 3rd class, 1849; MA 1852); Wells Theol Coll. Ordained, 1852; Priest, 1853; Curate of Upton St Leonard's, Gloucestershire, 1852–56; Curate of Winwick, Lancashire, 1856–57; Incumbent of Bickerstaffe, 1857–69; Vicar of Huyton, 1869–90; Proctor Archdeaconry of Warrington, 1887–1908; Rural Dean of Winwick, 1892–1910. *Recreation:* cricket in early life. *Address:* Lymm, Warrington, Lancashire. *Club:* Athenæum, Liverpool.

Died 3 Dec. 1918.

PENROSE, Brig.-Gen. Cooper, CB 1910; CMG 1917; *b* 8 March 1855; 3rd *s* of Rev. J. D. Penrose, of Woodhill, Co. Cork; *m* 1885, Sylvia Alice, 2nd *d* of late Thomas Greene, 49 St Stephen's Green, Dublin; three *d*. *Educ:* Haileybury; Woolwich. Obtained commission in Royal Engineers, 1873; Captain, 1885; Major, 1893; Lt-Col, 1900; Colonel, 1904; Brig.-Gen., 1910; served South African War, 1879; China, 1900; employed with local forces, NSW, 1885–89; Assistant Inspector of Submarine Defences at War Office, 1891–96; Inspector, 1897; employed on Survey of Wei-Hai-Wei, and CRE, 1898–1901; CRE, Gosport, 1901–5; Chief Engineer, Southern Coast Defence, 1906–10; Chief Engineer Southern Command, Salisbury, 1910–12; retired 1912; Temp. Chief Engineer, Scottish Command, 1915–16; employed under Admiralty, 1917–19. *Club:* Junior United Service.

Died 12 April 1927.

PENTECOST, Rev. George F., MA, DD, LLD; *b* Illinois, USA, 23 Sept. 1841; *e s* of Hugh L. Pentecost, Virginia, and Emma, *e d* of George Flower, Herts, England; *m* Ada, *y d* of Augustus Webber, MD, Kentucky; two *s*. *Educ:* Georgetown College, USA. Private Secretary to Governor of State of Kansas, 1857; Clerk US District Court, 1858; Captain 8th Kentucky Cavalry, USA, 1862–64; ordained to Gospel ministry, 1862; Boston, Mass, 1868–71; Brooklyn, 1868–71, 1880–87; evangelical work in Scotland, 1887–88; special mission to English-speaking Brahmins in India, 1888–91; minister Marylebone Presbyterian Church, London, England, 1891–97; 1st Presbyterian Church, Yonkers, NY, 1897–1902; Special Commissioner of American Board and Presbyterian Board of Foreign Missions to China, Japan, and Philippine Islands, 1902–3; since then Bible teaching and evangelistic work; pastor Bethany Presbyterian Church, Philadelphia, Pa, 1914. *Publications:* Bible Studies (10 vols), 1881–91; In the Volume

of the Book, 1884; Out of Egypt, 1885; A South Window, 1886; Birth and Boyhood of Christ, 1896; Forgiveness of Sin, 1896; Systematic Beneficence, 1897; Precious Truth, 1900; Christian Imperialism, 1902; Fighting for Faith. *Recreation:* gardening. *Address:* Bethany Church, Philadelphia, Pa, USA.

Died Aug. 1920.

PENTLAND, 1st Baron, *cr* 1909, of Lyth, Caithness; John Sinclair, GCSI 1918; GCIE 1912; PC 1905; *b* 7 July 1860; *e s* of late Capt. George Sinclair and Agnes, *o d* of John Learmonth, Edinburgh; *g s* of late Sir John Sinclair, 6th Bt, Dunbeath; *m* 1904, Lady Marjorie Adeline Gordon, DBE, *o d* of 7th Earl of Aberdeen; one *s* one *d*. *Educ:* Edinburgh Academy; Wellington; Sandhurst. Entered army, 1879; served in Soudan Expedition, 1885 (medal and clasp); retired as Captain, 1887; ADC to Lord-Lieutenant of Ireland (7th Earl of Aberdeen), 1886; contested (GL) Ayr Burghs, 1886; LCC, 1889–92; MP for Dumbartonshire, 1892–95; Secretary to Governor-General of Canada (7th Earl of Aberdeen), 1895–97; MP (L) Forfarshire, 1897–1909; Secretary for Scotland, 1905–12; Governor of Madras, 1912–19. *Heir: s* Hon. Henry John Sinclair, *b* 6 June 1907. *Address:* Frognal End, Frognal Gardens, Hampstead, NW3. *T:* Hampstead 6184. *Clubs:* Brooks's, Athenæum.

Died 11 Jan. 1925.

PENTON, Maj.-Gen. Arthur Pole, CB 1910; CMG 1917; CVO 1909; Member Executive Council, Malta, since 1909; *b* 6 Oct. 1854. Entered RA 1873; Capt. 1882; Major, 1889; Lieut-Col 1898; Col 1904; served Afghanistan, 1878–80 (despatches, medal); Inspector of Warlike Stores, 1888–91; Assistant to Director of Artillery, 1891–93; Brig.-Major RA 8th District, 1893–96; Commandant Defence Forces, New Zealand, 1896–1901; Commandant Ordnance College, 1904–7; Commander Coast Defences, Scotland, 1907–8; Vice-Pres. Ordnance Board, 1908; commanding RA, Malta, 1908–12; South-West Coast Defences, 1912–16. *Clubs:* Junior United Service, Ranelagh.

Died 28 Aug. 1920.

PEPYS, Rev. Charles Sidney, BD; Vicar of Aylesbury; *b* 1875; *m* 1913, Adelaide Mary Elizabeth, *d* of late Charles Duncan Cutts of Buenos Aires; one *s* four *d*. *Educ:* Winchester; Oriel College, Oxford. English Chaplain at Iquique and Rosario; Hon. Canon of St John's, Buenos Aires; Chaplain to the Forces, European War, 1917–19 (despatches). *Address:* Vicarage, Aylesbury, Bucks.

Died 21 Sept. 1927.

PEPYS, Rev. Herbert George, MA; Hon. Canon of Worcester Cathedral since 1878; *b* 31 Oct. 1830; *y s* of Rt Rev. Henry Pepys, DD, Lord Bishop of Worcester; *m* 1863, Louisa Harriet, *d* of J. Whitmore Isaac of Boughton Park, Worcestershire; two *s* five *d*. *Educ:* Trinity College, Cambridge; Wells Theological College. Curate of Kidderminster, 1853–54; Vicar of Grimley, 1854–77; Vicar of Hallow, 1854–1900. *Address:* Florence Court, Torquay. *TA:* Torquay.

Died 21 Feb. 1918.

PERAK, HH The Sultan of, GCMG (hon.) 1901 (KCMG 1892); GCVO (hon.) 1913. *Address:* Perak, Straits Settlements.

Died March 1916.

PERCEVAL, Sir Westby (Brook), KCMG 1894; *b* Launceston, Tasmania, 11 May 1854; *s* of Westby Hawkshaw Perceval, late of Knightsbrook, Co. Meath, and Carrickmakegan, Co. Leitrim, and Sarah Brook, *d* of John Bailey, MD, Brooklands, Essex; *m* 1880, Jessie, *d* of Hon. John Johnston, MLC, Wellington, New Zealand; two *s* two *d*. *Educ:* Christ's Coll. Grammar School, Christchurch, New Zealand; Stonyhurst Coll. Barrister Middle Temple, 1878; practised in Christchurch; represented Christchurch in Colonial Parliament, 1887–91; Chairman of Committees, 1891; Agent-General in London for New Zealand, 1891–96; Agent-General for Tasmania, 1896–98; created Knight of St Gregory the Great by Pope Leo XIII 1891; Member of Royal Commission for Chicago Exhibition, 1894–95; also Paris Exhibition, 1900; Member of Tariff Commission, 1904. *Publications:* Farming and Labour in New Zealand; Productions of New Zealand; New Zealand Timbers and Forest Products. *Recreations:* golf, motoring. *Address:* Southdown, Wimbledon, SW19. *T:* 196 Wimbledon. *Clubs:* Union, City of London.

Died 23 June 1928.

PERCIVAL, Rt. Rev. John, DD; *b* 27 Sept. 1834; *s* of William Percival, Brough Sowerby, Westmorland, and Jane, *d* of William Longmire, Bolton, Westmorland; *m* 1st, 1862, Louisa (*d* 1896), *d* of James Holland; six *c*; 2nd, 1899, Mary Georgina, 2nd *d* of late Frederick Symonds, FRCS, Oxford. *Educ:* Grammar School, Appleby, Westmorland; Queen's Coll., Oxford (Scholar). Junior Mathematical

University Scholar, 1855; Double First Mods and Finals; MA 1861; Fellow of Queen's Coll., Oxford. Ordained 1860; Assistant Master, Rugby; Headmaster, Clifton Coll., 1862–78; Prebendary of Exeter, 1871–82; President Trin. Coll., Oxford, 1878–87; Canon of Bristol, 1882–87; Headmaster, Rugby, 1887–95; Bishop of Hereford, 1895–1918. *Publications:* The Universities and the Great Towns; Some Helps for School Life (Clifton College Sermons); sermons at Rugby. *Address:* 64 Banbury Road, Oxford. *Club:* Athenæum.

Died 3 Dec. 1918.

PERCY, Sir James Campbell, Kt 1921; DL, JP; Chairman, Sackville Press, Dublin; Managing Director, Mecredy, Percy & Co., Ltd; Director, Central Hotel, Dublin, and Grand Hotel, Greystones; Switzer & Co. Ltd, and Car and General Insurance Co. Ltd (London); *b* 15 Feb. 1869; *s* of James Percy, Belfast; *m* 1898, Harriet Constance, *d* of Richard Topham; one *s* two *d*. *Educ:* St Enochs, Belfast. Associated with journalism and the production of technical papers for over thirty years. *Publications:* Bulls, Ancient and Modern; Bulls and Blunders; More Bulls and Blunders. *Recreations:* played international for Ireland Association, 1889; golf, motoring. *Address:* Failte, Totterage Lane, Herts. *T:* Crossley 27628. *Clubs:* Savage, Engineers; Royal Automobile, Dublin. *Died 26 Oct. 1928.*

PEREIRA, Brig.-Gen. George Edward, CB 1917; CMG 1905; DSO 1900; explorer; late Grenadier Guards; *b* 26 Jan. 1865; *s* of Edward Pereira and Hon. Margaret Anne Stonor, *d* of 3rd Baron Camoys; unmarried. *Educ:* The Oratory School, Edgbaston, Birmingham. Home service, 1884–99; attached to Chinese regiment till 1900; served China, 1900 (slightly wounded, medal with clasp, DSO); South Africa, 1902 (Queen's medal, 3 clasps); Military Attaché, Peking, 1905–10; served European War (despatches, CB, Hon. Brig.-Gen.); explored China and Tibet. *Recreations:* travelling, racing, cricket. *Clubs:* Guards', Travellers', Bachelors'.

Died 20 Oct. 1923.

PEREIRA, Rt. Rev. Henry Horace, DD; Hon. Canon of Canterbury Cathedral; Rector of All Hallows, Lombard Street, since 1904; *b* 16 Jan. 1845; *s* of Dr Pereira; *m* 1874, Adela, *e d* of Col and the Hon. Mrs Stretton; one *s* one *d*. *Educ:* Trinity College, Dublin. Theological Prizeman, and Prizeman in Hebrew and Modern Languages. After serving curacies at Eston, Yorkshire, and Holy Trinity, Southampton, he became the first Warden of the Wilberforce Memorial Mission in South London; then Rector of St Lawrence, Southampton, from whence he was appointed by the Bishop of Winchester, Rector of Chilbolton and Rural Dean of Stockbridge; Vicar and Rural Dean of Croydon, 1894–1903; Bishop of Croydon, 1904–24; Proctor in Convocation for Diocese of Canterbury; formerly Chaplain to Queen Victoria and to King Edward. *Recreation:* reading. *Address:* 18 Collingham Place, SW5. *T:* 314 Western.

Died 1 Jan. 1926.

PERFECT, Captain Herbert Mosley, CBE 1919 (OBE 1918); Royal Navy (retired); *b* 14 October 1867; *s* of late Henry Goodwin Perfect, Pontefract, Yorks; *m* Esther Sophia, *o d* of late Major-General Arthur Rainey, Madras Cavalry, of Rostrevor, Co. Down; one *s*. *Educ:* privately; HMS Conway. Served in Boxer rebellion, 1900; North China (medal and two clasps); served in Naval Transports as acting Captain RN, 1914–19; Divisional Naval Transport Officer at Folkestone, Hull, and Southampton (OBE, CBE); awarded by President of USA Distinguished Service Medal for embarkation of USA troops and service during the War; JP Co. Down. *Address:* Rathturret, Warrenpoint, Co. Down. *Club:* Junior Naval and Military.

Died 27 March 1928.

PERKIN, Frederick Mollwo, CBE 1920; PhD; FIC; consulting and technical chemist; *b* 1869; *y s* of late Sir William Henry Perkin, FRS, and 2nd wife, Alexandrine Caroline, *y d* of Ivan Hermann Mollwo; *m* 1898, Elizabeth Margaret, 4th *d* of late George Mackay of Edinburgh; one *s* two *d*. *Educ:* Amersham Hall School, Reading; Royal College of Science; Edinburgh University; Owens College, Manchester; University of Würzburg (PhD). Specially interested himself in study of electro-chemistry and carbonization of coal, particularly production of smokeless fuel, also peat and its utilization; Head of Chemistry Department Borough Polytechnic Inst., London, 1897–1909; one of Founders of Faraday Society (Treasurer, 1903–17); President, Paint and Varnish Society; President, Oil and Colour Chemists' Association, 1918–20; Hon. Member Institution of Gas Engineers; interested in technology of oils; Technical Adviser to the Committee on the Production of Oil from Cannel Coal and Allied Minerals; Hon. Sec. British Science Guild, 1908–16; Vice-President of Jury, Franco-British Exhibition, 1908; Member of Jury, Brussels International Exhibiton, 1910; Vice-President Jury, Turin

International Exhibition, 1911; and Vice-President Group Jury, Ghent International Exhibition, 1913. *Publications:* Cantor Lectures on Oils, 1915; Qualitative Chemical Analysis; Practical Methods of Electrochemistry; Practical Methods of Inorganic Chemistry; The Metric System; Text-book of Elementary Chemistry; also a number of original papers before Chemical and Faraday Society and Society of Chemical Industry. *Recreations:* gardening, breeding cocker spaniels. *Address:* 91 Talgarth Road, Barons Court, W; Laboratories, Sudbury, Harrow. *T:* Wembley 108; Albion House, 59 New Oxford Street, WC1. *T:* Museum 2854.

Died 24 May 1928.

PERKINS, Lt-Col Alfred Edward, DSO 1900; *b* 21 Feb. 1863; *s* of Lucius Perkins, Eastern Creek, Qld; *m* 1884, Elizabeth, *d* of late Richard Shortlands, Sydney. Served South Africa, NSW Bearer Co., 1900 (despatches, Queen's medal 6 clasps, DSO). *Address:* Wyoming, Macquarie Street, Sydney, NSW, Australia. *T:* 2996.

PERKINS, Brig.-Gen. Arthur Ernest John, CB 1918; Royal Artillery. Served Hazara Expedition, 1891 (clasp); European War, 1914–18 (CB). *Died 20 July 1921.*

PERKINS, George Walbridge; Director International Mercantile Marine Co. and United States Steel Corporation; *b* Chicago, 31 Jan. 1862; *s* of George Walbridge Perkins and Sarah Louise Mills; *m* 1889, Evelyn Ball, Cleveland, Ohio. *Educ:* public schools, Chicago. Partner in J. P. Morgan & Co., 1901–10. *Address:* Riverdale, NY.

Died 18 June 1920.

PERKINS, Harry Innes, ISO 1904; FRGS, FGS; *b* Simla; *s* of late Maj.-Gen. Edward Norman Perkins, BSC; *m* 1889, Josephine Amy, *d* of George Monkhouse; one *s* three *d*. *Educ:* privately; Kings' School, Rochester. Clerk to Director of Public Works and Surveys, Trinidad, 1880–81; Third Assistant Crown Surveyor, Crown Lands Dept, British Guiana, 1881; 2nd, 1884; 1st, 1889; Acting Crown Surveyor, 1890, 1892–93; Commissioner for settlement of East Indian immigrants in Colony in lieu of return passages to India, 1895; Acting Commissioner of Mines, 1895–1901; Acting Crown Surveyor in addition during 1896; Commissioner to delimit boundary between British Guiana and Venezuela, 1900; Senior Commissioner January 1903; completed delimitation, 1904; sometime member of the Institution of Mining and Metallurgy; Surveyor-General British Honduras, 1905; Member of the Executive Council, 1908; Acting Director of Public Works, and Member of the Legislative Council, 1915; retired 1919; made first ascent of Mt Roraima, British Guiana, in 1884 with E. F. im Thurn. *Publications:* (with Professor J. B. Harrison) Geology of the Barima, Barama, Potaro, Essequibo, Demerara, and Mazaruni Rivers, 1897–99; papers on the natural history and mining industries of British Guiana. *Recreations:* photography, natural history, travel. *Address:* c/o Lloyds Bank, Ltd, 9 Pall Mall, SW1. *Died 24 Oct. 1924.*

PERKINS, Lt-Col John Charles Campbell, DSO 1902; Military Accounts Department, India, since 1894; *b* London, 2 April 1866; *s* of late Surgeon-General R. H. Perkins, IMS, HEICS, and Anne Bowden Campbell of Invernield and Ross; a direct descendant in eldest line of John Perkins, senior partner Barclay and Perkins, brewers; *m* 1st, 1895, Emma Victoria Augusta (*d* 1912), *d* of Lt-Gen. Douglas Gordon Seafield St John Grant, ISC; 2nd, 1913, Charlotte Mary, *d* of Harold Beauchamp, Wellington, New Zealand, and Annie Burnell Dyer. *Educ:* Stamford Grammar School; Rossall School. Militia 4th Batt. Shropshire Light Infantry; Commission in 1st Leinster Regt, 1887; joined 1st Batt. in India, 1888; joined Indian Staff Corps, 1890; 44th Gurkha Rifles, also served with 43rd Gurkha Rifles in Assam and Manipur; then short while with 10th Bengal Infantry; Field Service, SA, 1900–3; held conjointly appointments Controller Military Accounts and Field Paymaster Indian Contingent, and Officer Commanding Indian Details, SA Force (despatches, DSO). *Recreations:* cricket, football, racquets, sport of all kinds, reading books of travel. *Address:* Grindlay and Co., 54 Parliament Street, SW. *Clubs:* Caledonian, East India United Service.

Died 28 Feb. 1916.

PERKINS, Joseph John, MA, MB (Cantab); FRCP; Consulting Physician St Thomas' Hospital, Brompton Hospital for Consumption and Diseases of the Chest, and King Edward VII Sanatorium, Midhurst. *Educ:* Owens College, Manchester; Emmanuel College, Cambridge (Scholar; 1st Class Natural Sciences Tripos); St Thomas' Hospital. Late Assistant Physician and Pathologist to the City of London Hospital for Diseases of the Chest, Victoria Park. *Publications:* contributions to various medical journals. *Address:* 57 Harley Street, W1. *Died 13 Sept. 1928.*

PERKINS, Surg.-Capt. Robert Clerk, DSO 1900; MRCS, LRCP; Medical Officer to Swaziland Administration. *Address:* Headquarters, Swaziland. *Died 7 May 1916.*

PERKINS, Robert George; *b* Southampton, 1850. *Educ:* Springfield, Chelmsford. Early training as journalist on Chelmsford Chronicle and Essex Herald; subsequent experience on South Durham Herald, Worcester Herald, and Worcestershire Chronicle; News Editor Worcestershire Echo; District Representative of The Times, Daily Sketch, Central News Agency, etc. *Address:* Verona Villas, Worcester. *T:* Worcester 117. *TA:* 72 High Street, Worcester.
Died 25 Jan. 1922.

PERKINS, Rev. William; *b* Haverfordwest, Pembrokeshire, 21 March 1843; *s* of Thomas Perkins; *m* 1868, Margaret, *o d* of Joseph Whicher of Milford Haven; one *s* five *d*. *Educ:* Grammar School, Haverfordwest. Entered Civil Service as clerk and draughtsman RE Dept; Wesleyan Minister, 1864 (churches almost entirely in Staffordshire, Lancashire, and Gloucestershire); Pres. of Wesleyan Methodist Conference, 1909; Sec. Wesleyan Methodist Missionary Society, 1898-1914. *Publications:* contributions to magazines and journals. *Address:* Nolton, Audley Road, Hendon, NW.
Died 19 Dec. 1922.

PERKINS, William Turner; Editor House of Commons Official Report (Assistant Editor, 1908-16); *e s* of late Henry Johnson and Mary Ann Perkins; *m* 1st, Hannah Maria Spears (*d* 1921), Manchester; four *s* four *d*; 2nd, Edith Helen, *o d* of Alfred Garry, Beckenham, Kent. *Educ:* Dr Halley's School; Manchester Grammar School. Reporter, Manchester Courier, and first Parliamentary representative of that paper, 1881-92; also London correspondent, Manchester Evening Mail; leader writer and special correspondent, Shipping Gazette, 1891-95; joined Times Parliamentary staff, 1892; Secretary, Gallery Committee, Houses of Parliament, 1888-90; Chairman, 1892-94; Sec., Gallery (Masonic) Lodge, 1893-98 (Worshipful Master, 1891-92); editor, Parliamentary Debates, for The Times and Waterlow and Sons, Ltd, 1895-98; special correspondent, Standard, 1900; literary secretary, Channel Tunnel Company, for Bill promoted in Parliament, 1907; editor, Railway Magazine, 1909-13. *Publications:* Popular Illustrated Guide to South-Eastern and Chatham Railway, 1906; local Guides to Dorset, Devon, and Cornwall; contributions to Engineering Wonders of the World. *Address:* House of Commons, SW. *Died 14 May 1927.*

PERRIER, Edmond; Commandeur de la Légion d'Honneur; Membre de l'Institut de France et de l'Académie de Médecine de Paris; Directeur honoraire du Muséum National Français d'Histoire Naturelle; *b* Tulle, Corrèze, 9 mai 1844; *s* of Antoine Perrier (Directeur d'Ecole normale, Chevalier de la Légion d'Honneur), et Jeanne Roche; *m* Cécile Henry-Bertin; two *s*. *Educ:* Collège de Tulle; Lycée Bonaparte, Paris; Ecole normale supérieure. Professeur au Lycée d'Agen; Maître de Conférences à l'Ecole normale supérieure; Assistant, puis Professeur et Directeur du Muséum d'Histoire Naturelle; Directeur et Président du Comité de Patronage de la section des Sciences naturelles de l'Ecole pratique des Hautes Etudes; Membre de l'Institut de France (Académie des Sciences), de l'Academie de médecine et de la Société de Biologie; Président de la Société nationale d'Acclimatation; Membre at ancien Président de la Commission Centrale de la Société de Géographie; Vice-Président de l'Institut général de Psychologie, etc. *Publications:* Les Colonies animales et la Formation des Organismes, 1881; Les Explorations sous-marines, 1884; La Philosophie zoologique avant Darwin, 1886; Le Transformisme, 1888; La Femme dans la nature et l'évolution du sexe féminin, 1908; Traité de zoologie, 1890-1900, La vie dans les Planètes, 1911; France et Allemagne, 1914—à Travers le monde vivant, 1916; La vie en action, 1918; La bene avant l'Histoire, 1919, etc; mémoires nombreux de zoologie sur les echinodermes, sur les vers, sur l'embryogénie générale. *Address:* Jardin des Plantes, 57 rue Cuvier, Paris. *T:* Gobelins 808, 39. *Club:* St Hubert, Paris.
Died 1 Aug. 1921.

PERRING, Rev. Sir Philip, 4th Bt, *cr* 1808; *b* 15 July 1828; 2nd *s* of Sir Phillip Perring, 3rd Bt and Frances Mary, *o d* of late Henry Roe, Ganton, Devon; *S* father, 1866. *Educ:* Trin. Coll., Cambridge (Scholar, Brown Medallist, 4th in Classical Tripos 1852, MA). Late Curate of St James's, Westminster; The National Party; Christian. *Publications:* Churches and their Creeds; Hard Knots in Shakespeare; Work-days of Moses; Spirit and the Muse; *verse*—translation of Florian's Fables; Air Raids from Dreamland. *Heir:* none. *Address:* 7 Lyndhurst Road, Exeter.
Died 8 June 1920 (ext).

PERRIS, George Herbert, CBE 1920; writer and speaker, especially on international affairs; *b* Liverpool, 1866; *s* of Rev. H. W. Perris; *m*; two *d*. Journalist from 1883; Editor Hull Express, 1885; ten years on editorial staff of The Speaker under Wemyss Reid; Editor of Concord, 1898-1906; Foreign Editor of The Tribune, 1906-7; and of Daily News, 1908-10; Originator and Assistant Editor Home University Library, 1912-14; War Correspondent of the Daily Chronicle in France, 1914-18; one of founders and Hon. Sec. of Anglo-German (1905) and Anglo-Russian (1906) Friendship Committees; Secretary Cobden Club, 1903-5; Chevalier of the Legion of Honour, 1918. *Publications:* Eastern Crisis and British Policy, 1897; Leo Tolstoy the Grand Mujik, 1898; Short History of the First Hague Conference, 1899; Further Memoirs of Marie Bashkirtseff, 1901; Life and Teaching of Tolstoy, 1901; Blood and Gold in South Africa, 1902; Protectionist Peril, 1903; Russia in Revolution, 1905; R. W. Emerson, 1910; Short History of War and Peace, 1911; Our Foreign Policy; Germany and the German Emperor, 1912; The Industrial History of Modern Europe, 1914; The Campaign in France and Belgium, 1915; The Battle of the Marne, 1920. *Address:* 5 Ashburn Place, South Kensington, SW. *T:* Western 3655. *Clubs:* National Liberal, Whitefriars. *Died 23 Dec. 1920.*

PERROTT, Sir Herbert Charles, 6th Bt, *cr* 1716; CH 1918; CB 1902; late Lieutenant-Colonel commanding and Hon. Colonel 3rd Battalion The Buffs (East Kent Regiment); *b* Charlton, Kent, 26 Oct. 1849; *e surv. s* of Sir Edward George Lambert Perrott, 5th Bt, Plumstead, and Emma Maria, *d* of Commander Charles Evelyn Houghton, RN; *S* father, 1886; *m* 1901, Ethel Lucy (RRC first-class; Médaille de la Reine Elizabeth; 1911 Coronation Medal; Lady of Justice St John of Jerusalem; Lady-Superintendent-in-Chief of Nursing Divisions, St John Ambulance Brigade; Hon. Secretary Queen's War Committee of Ladies of the Order of St John; late Lady-Commandant-in-Chief of Women's VAD Territorial Branch St John Ambulance Association), *d* of late Capt. Marcus Stanley Hare, RN, of Court Grange, Newton Abbot, and Matilda Jane Tollemache; two *d*. *Educ:* Ipswich Grammar School. Formerly Ensign 21st Kent Rifle Volunteers and Capt. Reserve of Officers; Assistant Secretary Order of St John of Jerusalem, 1875-88; Secretary, 1894-1910; Secretary-General, 1910-15; Knight of Justice St John of Jerusalem since 1876; Chief Secretary of St John Ambulance Association from its formation, 1877 to 1915; Member, late Vice-Chairman, of the Joint War Committee of the Order of St John and British Red Cross Society; Titular Bailiff of Egle since 1915; Member Executive Committee Standing Council of the Baronetage; was Hon. Secretary of the Eastern War Sick and Wounded Relief Fund; Vice President, late Vice-Chairman, of the British College for Physical Education; President or Patron of several cricket, football, and other athletic clubs. *Recreations:* riding, shooting, etc; formerly cricket, football (compiled Regimental Records). *Heir:* none. *Address:* 44 Queen's Gate, SW7. *T:* Kensington 2186. *Club:* United Service.
Died 15 Feb. 1922 (ext).

PERROTT, Maj.-Gen. Sir Thomas, KCB 1914 (CB 1900); Royal Artillery; *b* 5 May 1851; *s* of S. W. Perrott; *m* 1880, Gertrude Louisa Grace, *d* of late W. C. Cornwall of Richmond, Monkstown, Co. Dublin; one *s*.. Entered army, 1870; Captain, 1880; Major, 1886; Lieut-Col 1896; Colonel, 1900; Major-General, 1906; served South Africa, 1899-1900 (despatches, Queen's medal, 4 clasps, CB); China, 1900 (medal); Brig.-Gen. Commanding Scottish Coast Defences, 1906; commanding troops in the Straits Settlements, 1907-10; commanding Royal Artillery, Gibraltar, 1910-13; retired 1913; re-employed Inspector Royal Horse and Field Artillery, Oct. 1914; retired, Oct. 1915. *Club:* United Service.
Died 3 Nov. 1919.

PERRY, Rev. Arthur John; Hon. Canon of Truro, 1918; Vicar of Gwinear. *Address:* St Gwinear Vicarage, Hayle, Cornwall.
Died 13 Jan. 1926.

PERRY, John, DSc, LLD; FRS; ME; Emeritus Professor of Mechanics and Mathematics, Royal College of Science, South Kensington; *b* Ulster, 14 Feb. 1850; 2nd *s* of Samuel Perry, Garvagh; *m* Alice Jowitt (*d* 1904) of Sheffield. *Educ:* Queen's Coll., Belfast. Assistant Master Clifton College, 1870-74; Professor of Engineering, Japan, 1875-79; electrical engineer and inventor, 1879-96; Professor of Engineering and Mathematics, City and Guilds London Technical College, Finsbury, 1881-96; educational reformer, especially in mathematics and physical science; past President of the Institution of Electrical Engineers; past President Physical Society of London; General Treasurer, British Association; Member S African University Commission, 1914. *Publications:* Cantor Lectures, Hydraulics, 1882; The Steam Engine, 1874; Practical Mechanics, 1883; Spinning Tops,

1890; Calculus, 1897; Applied Mechanics, 1897; Steam, 1899; Practical Mathematics, 1899; England's Neglect of Science, 1901; about 100 scientific papers published before the Royal and other societies. *Address:* 25 Stanley Cresent, Notting Hill, W11. *T:* Park 4311. *Club:* Athenæum.   *Died 4 Aug. 1920.*

PERRY, Hon. John; *b* Sydney, July 1845; *m* 1870, Susan M'Auslan, 2nd *d* of late Thomas Alston, Sydney. *Educ:* Fort St Model School. Member Legislative Assembly, Richmond River, NSW, 1889; Minister of Public Instruction, Labour, and Industry, 1899–1904; Chief Secretary, 1904; Minister for Mines, 1907–8; Minister for Agriculture to 1910. *Address:* George Street, Marrickville, Sydney.
Died 1922.

PERRY, Rear-Adm. John Laisné; Royal Navy. Entered Navy, 1852; Commander, 1858; Captain, 1865; retired, 1873; Rear-Adm. 1881.
Died 16 Nov. 1917.

PERTAB SINGHJI, Gen. Sir, GCB 1918 (KCB 1901) GCSI 1886; GCVO 1911; LLD; Hon. Aide-de-camp to HM the King-Emperor; *b* 1845; *m* Maharani Bhatianiji (*d* 1907); four *s* one *d.* Hon. Commandant of the Imperial Cadet Corps; placed at the head of the Jodhpur administration; under the guidance of HH Maharaja Sir Jaswant Singh he introduced far-reaching reforms in every department of the State and suppressed crime and dacoities which were then rife; by introducing railways and constructing large irrigational bunds, substantial additions were made to revenue, and the country was protected against famines to which it was chronically subject; he was one of the Kabul Mission of 1878, an extra ADC to General Ellis in the Muhmand Expedition in 1897, and to General Sir William Lockhart in the Tirah Campaign in 1898 (wounded, and despatches); in 1900 he went with the British Force to China in command of the Jodhpur Imperial Service Troops and saw active service; was made the Ruling Chief of Idar State in Guzerat in 1902, which he abdicated in favour of his son; made Lt-Col and subsequently Lieut-General in the British Army; European War, 1914–15 (despatches); Grand Officer, Legion of Honour. *Address:* Jodhpur, Rajputana.
Died Sept. 1922.

PERTWEE, Rev. Arthur, MA; Vicar of Brightlingsea since 1872; Hon. Canon of Chelmsford, 1917. *Educ:* Pembroke College, Oxford. Ordained, 1861; Curate of Brancepeth, 1861–64; St Margaret's, Leicester, 1865–72. *Address:* Brightlingsea Vicarage, Colchester.
Died 14 Jan. 1919.

PERUGINI, Charles Edward; artist; *b* Naples, 1839; *s* of late Leonardo Perugini; *m* Kate Perugini. *Educ:* in Italy under Giuseppe Bonolis and Giuseppe Mancinelli; in Paris under Ary Scheffer, 1855. *Works:* Hero, Royal Acad., 1914; An Offering to Pan, Royal Acad., 1915. *Address:* 32 Victoria Road, Kensington, W. *Clubs:* Garrick, Arts.
Died 22 Dec. 1918.

PETERKIN, Rt. Rev. George William, DD, LLD; First Bishop of West Virginia since 1878; *b* Clearspring, Maryland, 21 March 1841; *s* of Rev. J. Peterkin, DD, and Elizabeth Howard Hanson; *m* 1st, 1868, Constance Gardner Lee (*d* 1877); 2nd, 1884, Marion M'Intosh Stewart; one *s* three *d. Educ:* Episcopal High School of Virginia; University of Virginia; Theological Seminary of Virginia. Served in Confederate Army, 1861–65; private in Co. F 21 Virginia Infantry; corporal, sergeant, and lieut-adjutant of regiment; 1st lieut and ADC staff of General W. A. Pendleton, Chief Artillery Army, Northern Virginia; assistant to his father at St James's Church, Richmond, Va, 1868; Rector St Stephen's Church, Culpeper, Va, 1869; Memorial Church, Baltimore, Md, 1873; organised Mission in Brazil, 1893; Porto Rico, 1901; founded Sheltering Arms Hospital, 1886; member of Board of Missions since 1886. *Publications:* Records of Protestant Episcopal Church in Western Virginia and West Virginia; addresses at Church conferences and fugitive articles. *Address:* Parkersburg, West Virginia, USA.   *Died 22 Sept. 1916.*

PETERS, Major John Weston Parsons, DSO 1916; OBE 1919; Reserve of Officers, 7th Dragoon Guards; *b* 1864; *s* of W. P. Peters, Somerset; *m* 1897, Mary Bertram Brunton (*d* 1922). *Educ:* Winchester; RMC Sandhurst. Served Chin-Lushai Expedition, 1889–90 (medal with clasp); Hazara Expedition, 1891 (clasp); S African War, 1900–2 (Queen's medal 4 clasps, King's medal 2 clasps); Brigade-Major, 4th Cavalry Brigade; District Comdr Middleburg; Assistant Military Governor, Pretoria; European War, 1914–19 (despatches four times, DSO, OBE, 1915 medal, War medal, Victory medal). *Address:* 5 Palmer Street, Westminster, SW1. *T:* Victoria 2072. *Clubs:* Naval and Military; Royal Southern Yacht.
Died 21 July 1924.

PETERSEN, Sir William, KBE 1920; Chairman of Petersen & Co., Ltd, London, shipowners; *b* 29 May 1856; *m* 1889, Flora McKay (*d* 1918), *e d* of George Sinclair, JP, Aberdeen; three *d. Educ:* Roskilde and Copenhagen, Denmark. Founder and Director of London-American Maritime Trading Co., Ltd, and Director of several other shipping companies; Founder of the Royal and Uraneum Passenger Lines to Canada and USA; Chairman of the British Committee of the International Shipping Registry, Bureau Veritas (nominated by the Board of Trade); Hon. Comdr RNR; proprietor of the Hebridean Island, Eigg; owned over 18,000 acres. *Publications:* The Alien in our Midst; The Kiel Canal Problem; numerous contributions to Standard Shipping and other magazines. *Recreations:* yachting, shooting. *Address:* 80 Portland Place, W1. *T:* Mayfair 6022; Herons G'hyll, Uckfield, Sussex; The Lodge, Eigg, Inverness-shire. *Clubs:* Junior Carlton, Constitutional, Royal Societies, Ranelagh; Royal Clyde Yacht; Royal Highland Yacht.   *Died 12 June 1925.*

PETERSON, Sir Arthur Frederick, Kt 1915; **Hon. Mr Justice Peterson;** Judge of the High Court of Justice, Chancery Division, since 1915; *b* 1859. Called to the Bar Lincoln's Inn and Inner Temple. *Address:* 39 Cheyne Walk, SW3. *T:* Kensington 5195. *Clubs:* Athenæum, Albemarle.   *Died 12 May 1922.*

PETERSON, Brig.-Gen. Frederick Hopewell, CB 1916; DSO 1895; Indian Staff Corps; *b* 1864; *s* of F. V. W. Peterson; *m* 1896, Mary Elizabeth, *d* of H. Howard. Entered army (Yorks Light Infantry), 1885; Capt. 1896; Major 1903; Lt-Col 1909; Col 1914; served Sikkim Expedition, 1888 (medal with clasp); Hazara, 1891 (clasp); relief of Chitral Fort, 1895 (despatches, DSO, medal with clasp); Tibet, 1903–4 (despatches, medal and clasp); Abor Expedition, 1911–12 (despatches, Brevet Col, medal and clasp); retired, 1919.
Died 25 Jan. 1925.

PETERSON, Sir William, KCMG 1915 (CMG 1901); MA; *b* Edinburgh, 29 May 1856; 5th *s* of John Peterson, merchant, Leith, and Grace Mountford Anderson; *m* 1885, Lisa Gibb, *e d* of late William Ross of 12 Hyde Park Gardens, W, and Gleneam, Perthshire; two *s. Educ:* High School and University, Edinburgh; Univ. of Göttingen; Corpus Christi College, Oxford (Scholar). Ferguson scholar in classics, 1876; MA Edin. and Oxford; FRSC. Asst Professor of Humanity in the University of Edinburgh, 1879–82; Principal of University College, Dundee, 1882–95; Principal of McGill University, 1895–1919; Chairman of the Protestant Committee of the Council of Public Instruction, Province of Quebec; one of the Vice-Presidents of the Archæological Institute of America; Hon. LLD St Andrews (1885); Princeton, NJ (1896); University of New Brunswick (1900); Yale (1901); Johns Hopkins (1902); Pennsylvania, Queen's (1903); Aberdeen (1906); Toronto (1907); Harvard (1909); Trinity College, Dublin (1912); Hon. DLitt Oxford and Durham (1912); Doctor Litterarum Classicarum, Groningen, 1914. *Publications:* edited Book X, Quintilian's Institutes of Oratory, 1891; The Dialogus of Tacitus, 1893 (and in the Loeb Classical Library, 1914); The Speech of Cicero for Cluentius, 1895 (critical edn 1899); The Cluni MS of Cicero, 1901; Cicero's Verrine Orations, 1907; Canadian Essays and Addresses, 1915; Longman's School Poetry Books, etc. *Recreations:* golf, billiards, curling, etc. *Address:* Wildwood, North End, Hampstead, NW3. *Clubs:* Athenæum, Savile; Royal and Ancient, St Andrews; University, Mount Royal, Montreal.
Died 4 Jan. 1921.

PETHEBRIDGE, Col Sir Samuel Augustus, KCMG 1917 (CMG 1913); Naval and Military Expeditionary Force; Administrator late German New Guinea and Islands since 1915; Secretary Department of Defence, Australia, since 1910; *b* Brisbane, 3 Aug. 1862; *s* of late Henry Lander Pethebridge and Elizabeth Mary Symons; *m* 1887, Mary Ada Simmonds; two *s* one *d. Educ:* Brisbane and Townsville Public Schools. Entered Public Service, Queensland, 1876; Secretary Marine Board and Dept to 1901; Chief Clerk Commonwealth Defence Dept, 1901; Sub-Lieut, Lieut and Commander, Queensland Navy, 12 years; Commonwealth Commissioner NW Pacific Islands, Nov. 1914–Jan. 1915. *Address:* Defence Department, Melbourne; Rabaul, New Britain. *Clubs:* Athenæum; Naval and Military, Melbourne.
Died 24 Jan. 1918.

PETHERAM, Sir William Comer, Kt 1884; KC; *b* 1835; *s* of William Petheram, Devon; *m* 1863, Isabel Christine (*d* 1907), *d* of Sir William Congreve, 2nd Bt and Isabella Charlotte, *widow* of Henry Nisbett MacEvoy. Special Pleader, 1862; Barrister Middle Temple, 1869; QC 1880; Chief Justice of NW Provinces of India, 1884; of Bengal, 1886–96. *Address:* 49 York Terrace, Regent's Park, NW. *Club:* St Stephen's.   *Died 15 May 1922.*

PETRE, Hon. Albert Henry; *b* 15 March 1832; *y s* of 11th Baron Petre and 2nd wife, Emma Agnes, *d* of Henry Howard, Cumberland; *m* 1883, Elsie, *d* of Rev. Professor William Robinson Clark, DCL; one *s* decd. Member of Stock exchange, 1854; Director of National Bank, Limited; of Argentine Land and Investment Company, Limited. *Address:* 9 Rosary Gardens, SW. *Club:* Reform.

Died 5 April 1917.

PETRE, Francis Loraine, OBE 1920; *b* 22 Feb. 1852; *o s* of late Hon. Edmund George Petre and Mary Anne, *e d* of Loraine M. Kerr; *m* 1887, Maud Ellen, *d* of Rev. W. C. Rawlinson; one *s* two *d. Educ:* Oscott College. Called to the Bar, Lincoln's Inn, 1873; joined Indian Civil Service, 1874; served in NWP and Oudh up to grade of Commissioner of Division; also in Secretariat of Board of Revenue and of Foreign and Revenue Departments of Govt of India; in Political Department (Central India and Hyderabad), 1885–89; retired, 1900; Ministry of Munitions (Finance Dept), 1915–20. *Publications:* Napoleon's Campaign in Poland 1806–1807; Napoleon's Conquest of Prussia 1809; Napoleon and the Archduke Charles 1809; Napoleon's Last Campaign in Germany 1813; Napoleon at Bay 1814; The Republic of Columbia; Simon Bolivar, El Libertador; History of the Norfolk Regiment; numerous articles in The Times and other journals. *Address:* Bekyngton, Farnham Royal, Bucks. *T:* Farnham Common 9. *Club:* East India United Service.

Died 9 May 1925.

PETRE, Francis William; *b* 26 Sept. 1847; *s* of late Hon. Henry William Petre, DL, and 1st wife, Mary Ann Eleanor, *o d* of Richard Walmesley; *g s* of 11th, and *cousin* and *heir-pres.* of 17th Baron Petre; *m* 1881, Margaret, *e d* of Edward Bowes Cargill of Dunedin, NZ; two *s* one *d. Educ:* Mt St Mary's; HMS Britannia; Ushaw. Studied architecture; went to New Zealand and practised engineering. *Works:* Catholic Cathedral, Christchurch, NZ, etc. *Address:* Writtle House, St Clair, Dunedin, New Zealand.

Died 10 Dec. 1918.

PETRIE, Sir Charles, 1st Bt, *cr* 1918; Kt 1903; Member of Liverpool City Council; *b* 23 Feb. 1853; *s* of Alexander Petrie, Co. Sligo, and Margaret, *d* of Charles Lyell, Perthshire; *m* 1880, Hannah Lindsay, *d* of late William Hamilton; two *s. Educ:* Wesley College, Dublin. Lord Mayor of Liverpool, 1901–2; Alderman, JP, DL; President of the Liverpool Constitutional Association. *Recreations:* golf, shooting. *Heir: s* Edward Lindsay Haddon Petrie [*b* 30 Sept. 1881; *m* 1912, Blanche, *d* of C. J. Allen, Berks; two *d*]. *Address:* Oakfield, Grassendale, Liverpool. *T:* Garston Liverpool 396. *M:* K 4030. *Clubs:* Junior Carlton; Conservative, Liverpool.

Died 8 July 1920.

PETRIE, Lt-Col Charles Louis Rowe, DSO 1902; late the Manchester Regiment; *b* 15 Dec. 1866; *s* of George Petrie, London; *m* 1912, Dorothy Frances, *e d* of late Rev. E. P. Dew. *Educ:* Marlborough. Entered army, 1887; Captain, 1896; served with Uganda Rifles, 1902 (despatches, medal with clasp, DSO); Somaliland, 1902–3 (despatches); retired, 1907; Temporary Lt-Col commanding 16th (Service) Batt. Manchester Regiment; European War, 1914–18; France, 1916–18 (despatches); Lt-Col; retired. *Club:* Army and Navy.

Died 24 Oct. 1922.

PETRIE, Sir Edward (Lindsay Haddon), 2nd Bt, *cr* 1918; *b* 30 Sept. 1881; *s* of Sir Charles Petrie, 1st Bt and Hannah Lindsay, *d* of late William Hamilton; *S* father, 1920; *m* 1912, Blanche, *d* of C. J. Allen, Stanbury, Spencer's Wood, Berks; two *d. Heir: brother* Charles Alexander Petrie [*b* 28 Sept. 1895; *m* 1st, 1920, Ursula Gabrielle Borthwick (marr. diss. 1926), *er d* of His Honour Judge (Harold Chaloner) Dowdall; one *s*; 2nd, 1926, Jessie Cecilia, *er d* of Frederick James George Mason, 14 Thurleigh Road, SW]. *Address:* Dorincourt, Leatherhead, Surrey. *Clubs:* Windham, St Stephen's, Royal Automobile.

Died 18 Dec. 1927.

PETRIE, Col Ricardo Dartnel, CB 1915; late Royal Engineers; *b* 15 Sept. 1861; *s* of George Petrie; *m* 1906, Inez, *d* of late B. Horace Wood, Claremont, Natal. Entered army, 1881; Captain, 1889; Major, 1899; Lt-Col 1905; Colonel, 1918; served Burma, 1886–88 (despatches, medal 2 clasps); Chin-Lushai Expedition, 1890 (despatches, clasp); China, 1900 (medal); Chief Engineer, Northern Command, 1912; served European War, 1914–15 (CB). *Club:* Naval and Military.

Died 27 Dec. 1925.

PEYTON, Sir Algernon Francis, 6th Bt, *cr* 1776; JP; Captain 11th Hussars (retired); Hon. Lieutenant-Colonel Imperial Yeomanry; *b* 24 Nov. 1855; *s* of Maj.-Gen. Sir Thomas Peyton, 5th Bt and Lucy, *d* of William Watts; *S* father, 1888; *m* 1888, Ida Fanny, *d* of James

Mason, Eynsham Hall, Oxfordshire; two *s* one *d.* High Sheriff, Co. of Oxford, 1896. Owned about 4,000 acres. *Heir: s* Algernon Thomas Peyton, Lieut 11th Hussars [*b* 4 Jan. 1889. Served European War, 1914–15 (wounded). *Address:* Swift's House, Bicester, Oxfordshire.

Died 11 April 1916.

PEYTON, Rev. Thomas Thornhill, JP; MA; Rector of St Mary's, March, since 1882; Rural Dean of March, 1909–24; Hon. Canon of Ely Cathedral, 1915; *b* 8 Dec. 1856; 2nd *s* of Sir Thomas Peyton, 5th Bt, and Lucy, *d* of William Watts; *m* 1884, Mary Louisa (*d* 1909), *d* of Sir William Henry Marsham Style, 9th Bt, and 1st wife, Hon. Rosamond Marion, *d* of 1st Baron Tredegar; one *d. Educ:* Wellington College; Magdalen College, Oxford. *Address:* St Mary's Rectory, March, Cambridge.

Died 29 Sept. 1927.

PHEAR, Rev. Samuel George, MA, DD; *b* 30 March 1829; 3rd *s* of Rev. John Phear, MA, Rector of Earl Stonham, Suffolk; unmarried. Master of Emmanuel College, Cambridge, 1871–95; Chaplain to Bishop of Winchester, 1873–75; Vice-Chancellor of Cambridge, 1874–75. *Address:* Emmanuel College, Cambridge. *Club:* Athenæum.

Died 26 Nov. 1918.

PHELAN, Major Ernest Cyril, DSO 1918; MC; Royal Army Medical Corps; *m* 1926, *widow* of late MacDonald, Highfield, Southampton. *Educ:* Trinity College, Dublin (MB, CM 1906). Served European War, 1914–18 (despatches, MC, DSO.). *Address:* c/o Glyn, Mills & Co., 3 Whitehall Place, SW1.

PHELAN, Rt. Rev. Patrick; RC Bishop of Sale (Victoria) since 1913; *b* Co. Kilkenny, 1860. *Educ:* Mount Melleray Seminary and St Patrick's College, Carlow. Priest, 1888; Administrator of St Patrick's Cathedral, 1900–13. *Publications:* The Holy Sacrifice of the Mass; The Mission of St Ignatius Loyola; Christian Marriage; The Episcopate; Refutation of Protestant Calumnies; Priesthood of Christ; Martyrdom of Blessed Oliver Plunket; The Twin Evils of Society—Race Suicide and Divorce. *Address:* Sale, Victoria, Australia.

Died 5 Jan. 1925.

PHELIPS, William Robert, JP; DL Somerset; Alderman of Somerset CC since 1894; *b* 30 March 1846; *s* of William Phelips of Montacute and Ellen Harriett, *d* of William Helyar of Coker Court, Somerset; *m* 1st, Cicely Grace Augusta, *d* of Frederick Fane of Moyles Court, Hants; one *d*; 2nd, Constance Louisa, *d* of Rt Hon. Sir Spencer Ponsonby-Fane, GCB, ISO and Hon. Louisa, *d* of 13th Viscount Dillon; two *s* one *d. Educ:* Harrow; Trin. Coll., Cambridge. Lieut in 6th Dragoon Guards, 1866–70; twenty-six years Chairman of Yeovil Board of Guardians; twenty years Chairman of the South Somerset Conservative Association. *Recreations:* golf, shooting. *Address:* 13 Brompton Square, SW3. *T:* Kensington 5133. *Clubs:* Carlton, Naval and Military.

Died 23 Nov. 1919.

PHELPS, Lt-Gen. Arthur; Bombay Infantry; President National Anti-Vaccination League; *b* 24 Nov. 1837; *m* 1868, Caroline Ann (*d* 1904), *d* of late Abel Peyton, Edgbaston; three *s* one *d.* Entered army, 1853; Lt-Gen. 1892; served Indian Mutiny, 1858–60; US list, 1893. *Publication:* Lord Dunchester. *Recreation:* gardening. *Address:* Woodbourne Grange, Edgbaston, Birmingham. *T:* Edgbaston 492. *Clubs:* Union, National Liberal.

Died 4 Oct. 1920.

PHILIPPS, Sir Charles (Edward Gregg), 1st Bt, *cr* 1887; JP for Carmarthenshire and Pembrokeshire (High Sheriff, 1882); Lord-Lieutenant and Custos Rotulorum of Haverfordwest, 1876–1925; Member of the Governing Body of the Church in Wales; *b* Huddersfield, 6 Oct. 1840; *e s* of late Edward Fisher, Spring Dale, Yorkshire, and Jane, *d* of Dominick Gregg, Lisburn, Ireland; assumed name of Philipps by Royal licence, 1876, in compliance with testamentary injunction of his father-in-law; *m* 1868, Mary Philippa, *e d* and *co-heiress* of Rev. James Henry Alexander Philipps, MA, and *niece* of late Baron Milford, Picton Castle; two *s* four *d. Educ:* Cheltenham Coll. Barrister Middle Temple, 1868. Chairman of Pembrokeshire County Council, 1898–1903; three times Mayor of Haverfordwest; Lieut-Col (Hon. Col) commanding Pembroke Yeomanry, 1898–1900; contested Pembrokeshire (C), 1880, 1885, 1886 and 1892; Military Member of Pembrokeshire Territorial Force Association. Owned with Lady Philipps, about 20,000 acres. *Recreation:* shooting. *Heir: s* Capt. Henry Erasmus Edward Philipps, JP, DL [*b* 9 March 1871; *m* 1909, Victoria Gladys Elizabeth, *o c* of late John William Gwynne-Hughes of Tregeyb, Llandilo, Lord Lieutenant of Carmarthenshire; one *s* one *d. Club:* Junior Carlton]. *Address:* Picton Castle, Haverfordwest. *T:* Haverfordwest 42. *Clubs:* Carlton, Junior Carlton, Cavalry; Pembrokeshire County, Haverfordwest.

Died 5 June 1928.

PHILIPS, Lt-Col Burton Henry, CMG 1899; Aide-de-camp to Lt-Gen. Sir Herbert Chermside, GCMG, CB; Reserve of Officers; late Royal Welsh Fusiliers; *b* 1 Oct. 1858; *e s* of late John Capel Philips and Hon. Frances (Fanny) Esther, 2nd *d* of 5th Viscount Ashbrook; *m* 1904, Lucy Madeline, 2nd *d* of Col George B. H. Marton, Capernwray, Lancs; one *s* two *d. Educ:* Eton; Cambridge. Entered army, 1879; Capt. 1887; Major, 1898; served South Africa, 1900; promoted Lt-Col. *Address:* The Heath House, Tean, Stoke-on-Trent. *Club:* Naval and Military.   *Died 30 March 1927.*

PHILIPS, Francis Charles; novelist, dramatist; *b* Brighton, 3 Feb. 1849; *y s* of Rev. George Washington Philips, Ruxley Park, Surrey, and Charlotte, *d* of late Thomas Jesson, Hill Park, Sevenoaks, Kent; *m* 1st, Maria, *d* of Charles Jones of Llanelly, Carmarthenshire; one *s*; 2nd, Eva, *y d* of W. Trevelyan Knevills, Croft Castle, and Wigmore Hall, Herefordshire; one *s* two *d. Educ:* Brighton Coll.; RMC Sandhurst. Gazetted 2nd Queen's Royal Regt 1868; served in Regt three years; Barrister 1884, and shortly afterwards novelist and dramatist, and contributor to many leading London newspapers and magazines; Knight Commander of the Order of St Sava. *Publications:* novels—As in a Looking-Glass, 1885 (adapted for the stage, and played by Mrs Bernard Beere and Madame Sarah Bernhardt, it being the first English production in Paris by the latter); A Lucky Young Woman, 1886; Jack and Three Jills, 1886; The Dean and His Daughter, 1887; A Full Confession; Social Vicissitudes; One Never Knows; Mrs Bouverie; Constance; Young Mr Ainslie's Courtship; The Luckiest of Three; A Doctor in Difficulties; The Worst Woman in London, 1895; A Devil in Nun's Veiling, 1895; An Undeserving Woman, 1896; A Question of Colour, 1896; The Strange Adventures of Lucy Smith; Little Mrs Murray; Poor Little Bella; Men, Women and Things; A Woman of the World's Advice; The Matrimonial Country; My Varied Life (F. C. Philips' Reminiscences); with C. J. Wills—The Fatal Phryne; The Scudamores; A Maiden Fair to see, and others; with Percy Fendall—Margaret Byng; A Daughter's Sacrifice; My Face is My Fortune; Disciples of Plato; A Honeymoon and After; with A. R. T. Philips—Judas the Woman; Life; The Man and the Woman; and others; with Rowland Strong—A White Sin. plays—The Dean's Daughter (with Sydney Grundy); Husband and Wife (with Percy Fendall); Godpapa (with Charles H. E. Brookfield); John Chetwynd's Wife; A Woman's Reason (with Charles H. E. Brookfield); The Fortune of War; A Free Pardon (with Leonard Merrick); Lady Paddington (with Walter Parke); The Burglar and the Judge (with Charles H. E. Brookfield); Papa's Wife (with Seymour Hicks, founded on F. C. Philip's story, In the Third Capacity), and others. *Recreations:* field sports, the theatre. *Address:* 1 Elm Court, Temple, EC. *TA:* Philips, 21 Temple.   *Died 21 April 1921.*

PHILIPSON, Sir George Hare, Kt 1900; JP; MA, MD, DCL, LLD; FRCP; Vice-Chancellor of the University of Durham, 1912 and 1913; President University of Durham College of Medicine, Newcastle; Professor of Medicine, University of Durham, since 1876; a President of and Consulting Physician to Newcastle Royal Victoria Infirmary; *b* Newcastle, 18 May 1836; 3rd *s* of late George Hare Philipson, JP. *Educ:* University Coll. London; Caius College, Cambridge (Mecklenberg Scholar, Thruston Speaker). Hon. Associate of the Grand Priory of the Order of St John of Jerusalem in England; Bradshaw Lecturer, Royal Coll. of Physicians, London, 1884; President British Medical Association, 1893; member of the General Medical Council; Fellow of the Royal Society of Medicine; Member of Association of Physicians; Corr. Mem. Royal Coll. of Physicians, 1901–2–3; Hon. Col RAMC (T), Northumbria, 1908–13. *Publications:* Pathological Relations of the Absorbent System; Investigation of the Prevalent Diseases of the District by a System of Registration; Health and Meteorology of Newcastle and Gateshead. *Recreation:* art. *Address:* 7 Eldon Square, Newcastle-upon-Tyne. *T:* Nat. 1202. *Clubs:* Royal Societies; Northern Counties, Newcastle; Durham County, Durham.   *Died 24 Jan. 1918.*

PHILIPSON, Robert; *b* 1860; *s* of William Philipson, Stocksfield, Northumberland; *m* 1st, Annie, *d* of John Patterson, Alnwick; one *s* one *d*; 2nd, Edith Mary, *d* of Charles Jackson of Newcastle-on-Tyne. *Educ:* privately. Commenced official career in the service of the Tyne Improvement Commissioners at Newcastle-on-Tyne; advanced to the position of Assistant Secretary to that undertaking; Secretary to the Thames Conservancy, 1900; Secretary of the newly constituted Port of London Authority, 1909; General Manager of the Port of London Authority, 1909–13. *Recreations:* golfing, motoring. *Address:* 9 Chelsea Court, Chelsea Embankment, SW. *T:* 6507 Western. *Club:* Bath.   *Died 14 Aug. 1916.*

PHILLIMORE, John Swinnerton, JP; MA, LLD (St Andrews); DLitt (Dublin); Professor of Humanity, Glasgow University, since 1906; *b* 26 Feb. 1873; 4th *s* of late Vice-Admiral Sir Augustus Phillimore,

KCB, DL, and Harriet Eleanor, *d* of Hon. George Matthew Fortescue; *m* 1900, Cecily, *o d* of Rev. Spencer Compton Spencer-Smith; one *s* one *d. Educ:* Westminster; Christ Church, Oxford. 1st Class Classical Moderations; 1st Class Literæ Humaniores; Hertford, Craven, and Ireland Univ. Scholarships; Chancellor's Prize for Latin Verse. Was a Lecturer of Christ Church, 1895, Tutor and Student, 1896–99; Professor of Greek at Glasgow University, 1899–1906; appointed by the University of California to hold the Sather Professorship of Classics there for the year 1914–15. *Publications:* (contrib.) Essays in Liberalism by Six Oxford Men, 1897; (with S. G. Owen) Musa Clauda, or Latin Versions, 1898; Propertius (text), 1901 and (Riccardi Press) 1911; Poems, 1902; Statius' Silvæ (text), 1905, 2nd edn 1917; Propertius, Index Verborum, 1906, translation, 1906; Sophocles (3 plays translated), 1902; Philostratus' Apollonius of Tyana, translated with Introduction and Notes, 2 volumes, 1912; Things New and Old (poems), 1918; (trans.) A Hero of Nowadays, by Mikhail Lermontov, 1921; The Hundred Best Latin Hymns, 1925; The Silver Latin Book, 1925; papers and addresses, including some Remarks on Translation and Translators, 1919, and *Ille Ego,* or Virgil and Professor Richmond, 1920; an occasional contributor to Dublin Review, Classical Review, Mnemosyne and G. K.'s Weekly. *Address:* 5 The University, Glasgow. *T:* Western 167. *Clubs:* Athenæum; Western, Glasgow.   *Died 16 Nov. 1926.*

PHILLIPPS, Maj.-Gen. Henry Pye; JP Suffolk; retired; *b* 6 Nov. 1836; 2nd *s* of Charles Phillipps; *m* Emily Hester St Albyn, *d* of William Savage Wait, Woodborough, Somersetshire. *Educ:* Sandhurst. Entered 2nd Queen's Regt 1854; served in British Kaffraria; as Adjutant throughout China War, 1860 (Medal for Taku Forts and Pekin); in Ionian Islands, Gibraltar, Bermuda, Halifax, Malta; commanded 2nd Batt. in India; retired as Major-General, 1882. *Club:* United Service.   *Died 25 July 1927.*

PHILLIPPS, Lt-Gen. Picton, CB 1924; CMG 1919; MVO 1912; late Royal Marines; late Aide-de-camp to King George V; *b* Aldershot, 3 March 1869; 2nd *s* of late Major Charles Burch Phillipps, Barham Hall, Suffolk, and Mrs Phillipps, Claydon, Suffolk; *m* 1902, Monica Gabrielle, 4th *d* of late Thomas Neale Fonnereau, Christchurch Park, Ipswich; two *s. Educ:* Aldeburgh; Oxford Military College. Joined RMA 1886; Lieut-Gen., 1926; Retired List, 1926. *Recreation:* shooting. *Address:* The Lodge, Claydon, Ipswich.

Died 2 April 1928.

PHILLIPPS-WOLLEY, Sir Clive, Kt 1914; JP; FRGS; *b* England, 1854; *e s* of R. A. L. Phillipps, MA, FRGS, FRSC; assumed name Wolley on succeeding to estates of the Wolleys of Woodhall, Shropshire; *m* 1879, Jane, 2nd *d* of Rear-Admiral Fenwick. *Educ:* Rossall. Was HBM's Vice-Consul at Kertch; Barrister Middle Temple; Oxford Circuit; formerly Captain 4th Batt. South Wales Borderers; explored in the Caucasus; settled in British Columbia; ran unsuccessfully twice for the Commons in the Conservative interest; Vice-President Navy League. *Publications:* Sport in the Crimea and Caucasus; Big Game volumes of Badminton Library; Gold, Gold in Cariboo; The Chicamon Stone; Songs of an English Esau, etc. *Address:* The Grange, Somenos, British Columbia. *Clubs:* Authors', Shikar; Shropshire County, Shrewsbury; Union, BC.

Died 9 July 1918.

PHILLIPS, Sir Claude, Kt 1911; BA; Barrister-at-Law; Art critic of The Daily Telegraph; Keeper of the Wallace Collection, 1897–1911; *b* 29 Jan. 1846; *s* of Robert Abraham Phillips and Helen, *d* of Moses Lionel Levy. Barrister Inner Temple, 1883; Hon. Member Royal Academy of Milan; Chevalier, Order of Leopold, Belgium. *Publications:* Life of Sir Joshua Reynolds, 1894; monographs: Life of Frederick Walker, 1894; Life of Antoine Watteau, 1895; Picture Gallery of Charles I, 1896; The Earlier Work of Titian, 1897; The Later Work of Titian, 1898; contributor to Quarterly, Edinburgh, Nineteenth Century, Fortnightly, and North American Reviews, the Burlington Magazine, and the Gazette des Beaux-Arts of Paris. *Address:* 40 Ashburn Place, SW. *Club:* Beefsteak.

Died 9 Aug. 1924.

PHILLIPS, Rev. Forbes Alexander, *(pseudonym* Athol Forbes); Vicar of Gorleston, Great Yarmouth; Rector of Southtown; novelist, dramatist; *b* 1866; *s* of George Phillips, HM Civil Service; *m* Helena Bell of Blyth, Co. Northumberland; two *d. Educ:* Durham Univ. and private tutors. Ordained to All Saints', Newcastle, 1889; senior curate to Tynemouth Parish Church, 1891–93; vicar and rector, Gorleston, 1893; surrogate for Norfolk and Suffolk, 1894; select speaker Church Congress, 1895; past provincial grand chaplain of Norfolk and Suffolk; prelate of the Order of Knights Templar; Plantagenet preceptory; chaplain to Church Actors' Union; chaplain, V Norfolk Territorial.

Publications: Some Mysteries of the Passion, 1893; Gorleston and its Parish Church, 1894; Cassock and Comedy, 1898; A Son of Rimmon, 1899; Odd Fish, 1901; If Love were All, 1902; The Romance of Smuggling, 1909; What was the Resurrection?; Is Death the End?; *plays:* Her First Proposal, produced in Dublin; Church or Stage?, produced by Mrs Brown-Potter; Lord Danby's Affair; A Maid of France, 1905; When it was Dark, 1906; The Last Toast. *Recreations:* writing for magazines, shooting. *Address:* Gorleston Vicarage, Great Yarmouth. *TA:* Vicar, Gorleston.   *Died 29 May 1917.*

PHILLIPS, Francis, CB 1903; late Assistant Comptroller and Auditor, Exchequer and Audit Department; *b* 8 Sept. 1835; *o surv. s* of late Charles Henry Phillips, FRCS, surgeon to HM's household; *m* 1868, Mary (*d* 1906), *e d* of late George Addison, 2nd partner in the Bank of Messrs Child & Co. *Address:* 5 Porchester Square, Hyde Park, W.   *Died 8 June 1925.*

PHILLIPS, Brig.-Gen. George Fraser, CB 1918; CMG 1916; *b* 14 May 1863; *s* of H. W. Phillips, artist. *Educ:* Uppingham. Joined West Yorkshire Regt 1885; ADC to the Governor, Hong Kong, 1897; commanded 2nd Batt. West Yorkshire Regt; commanded International Force in Scutari, Albania, and Governor of Scutari, 1913 until war broke out, 1914; commanded 2nd Batt. West Yorkshire Regt in France, 1914; Military Attaché, Servia and Montenegro, 1915–16 (CMG); commanded 10th District, 1916; Head of British Military Mission, Greece, and member of Allied Military Control Mission, Athens, 1916–17 (CB); Commandant, Paris Area, 1917–18; Albania, 1918–20; retired 1920. *Clubs:* Junior United Service, Travellers', Beefsteak.   *Died 2 Dec. 1921.*

PHILLIPS, Sir John, Kt 1918; JP Hants; MA, MD (Cantab); FRCP; Hon. Physician to Queen Mary, 1918; Professor Emeritus of Obstetric Medicine, King's College, London, and Consulting Obstetric Physician King's College Hospital; *b* 6 July 1855; *e s* of late L. Phillips of Birchmoor Manor, near Bedford, and Ann, *d* of Robert Ayres of Barford; *m* 1890, Rachel Rattray (*d* 1917), *d* of late Robert Tweedie Middleton, MP and DL, of Hillfoot, Kilpatrick, Dunbartonshire; one *s* three *d*; *m* 1926, Beatrice Margaret, *e d* of Rev. Clement Naish, Vicar of Upnor, Kent. *Educ:* Bedford; St John's College, Cambridge. Fellow, King's College, London. *Publications:* Outlines of Diseases of Women (4th edition); papers in obstetric medicine and gynæcology. *Recreations:* literature, fishing, shooting, gardening. *Address:* 24 Queens' Road, St John's Wood, NW8. *T:* Primrose Hill 4422.   *Died 8 Dec. 1928.*

PHILLIPS, John; JP; MP (N) South Longford since 1907; *b* Corboy, Co. Longford. *Educ:* Tertiary Carmelites School, Clondalkin; Queen's College, Galway. *Address:* House of Commons, SW.   *Died 2 April 1917.*

PHILLIPS, J. S. Ragland; editor of the Yorkshire Post since 1903; Chairman of the Press Association, 1912; President of the Newspaper Society, 1914; magistrate, City of Leeds; *b* Pendleton, Manchester, 1850, of Welsh-Norse descent; *y s* of Richard Ayres Phillips; *m* 1875, S. J. C. More; three *s*. *Educ:* Owens College, Manchester (evening classes). Editor Kendal Mercury, 1878; worked as a journalist in Worcester, Belfast, York, Newcastle-on-Tyne, Edinburgh (leader writer and reviewer on The Scotsman, 1887–89); editor Manchester Examiner, 1889–91; assistant editor Yorkshire Post, 1891–1903; lectured on travel scenes, and on the Elizabethan drama and stage; contributed to the Cambridge History of English Literature chapter dealing with Journalism in the Nineteenth Century, 1916. *Recreations:* reading, music, farming, gardening, bee-keeping, walking; a Cumberland "statesman" at Knot End, Ravenglass, via Carnforth, and spent holidays at that postal address. *Address:* Shaw Lane, Headingley, Leeds. *T:* 160 Headingley. *Clubs:* Authors'; Leeds, Leeds Conservative, Leeds.   *Died 4 Nov. 1919.*

PHILLIPS, Lawrence Barnett, FSA 1885; FRAS 1865; ARE; artist and author; *b* London, 29 Jan. 1842; *s* of late Barnett Phillips, of Bloomsbury Square, diamond merchant; *m* Judith, *d* of M. Cohen, of Clifton Gardens, W; two *s*. *Educ:* Dr Pinches' School; private tuition. Inventor of the rocking bar keyless work for winding watches; patent sketching boxes and palette; simplified mechanism for chronographs; perpetual calendars and calculating machines; from 1882 devoted himself to art, and exhibited at Royal Academy, New Gallery, Institute, Grosvenor, and the principal provincial galleries. *Publications:* Autographic Album, 1866; Horological Rating Tables, 1871; The Dictionary of Biographical Reference, 1873. *Recreation:* travel. *Address:* Chesham House, Sutherland Avenue, W9. *T:* Hampstead 1960. *Club:* Royal Societies.   *Died 14 April 1922.*

PHILLIPS, Llewellyn Powell, MA, MD, BC Cantab; FRCS, FRCP; Emeritus Professor of Medicine, Royal School of Medicine, Cairo; Consulting Physician, Kasr-el Ainy Hospital, Cairo; *b* 28 July 1871; *s* of late James Mathias Phillips, MD, of Cardigan, South Wales; *m* 1904, Edith Helen, *d* of late Alfred Coxon; three *d*. *Educ:* Epsom College; Gonville and Caius College, Cambridge; St Bartholomew's Hospital, London. Formerly house surgeon and extern midwifery assistant St Bartholomew's Hospital, and Demonstrator of Anatomy, Medical School, St Bartholomew's Hospital; house physician, Royal Free Hospital, Gray's Inn Road; resident surgical officer, Kasr-el Ainy Hospital, Cairo; principal medical officer Gresham Life Office for Egypt, Palestine, and Syria; late Hon. Commandant British Red Cross Hospital, Giza, Egypt; Lt-Col RAMC (temp. and honorary); despatches four times, 3rd Class Order of the Nile, 3rd Class Order of Medjidieh. *Publications:* Amœbiasis and the Dysenteries; papers in various medical journals, and hospital reports. *Recreations:* numismatics, motoring. *Address:* Kasr-el-Dubara, Cairo, Egypt. *TA:* Nyllewell, Cairo (Eastern Telegraph Co. only). *T:* en ville 400. *M:* C 21. *Clubs:* Garden; Turf, Cairo.   *Died 1 Jan. 1927.*

PHILLIPS, Reginald William, MA, DSc; FLS; late Professor of Botany, University College, North Wales, 1884–1922; *b* Talgarth, 15 Oct. 1854; *s* of Thomas Phillips, Registrar; *m* Esther, *d* of Henry Lloyd Jones, Solicitor, Bangor; three *d*. *Educ:* Normal Coll., Bangor; St John's Coll., Cambridge. Formerly Tutor at Bangor Normal Coll.; graduated while at St Saviour's College, taking first-class Honours in Natural Science Tripos; Foundation Scholar and Prizeman of the College; appointed Lecturer in Biology in the North Wales University College, Bangor, at its foundation, 1884; DSc degree (London) for a thesis on Algæ; interested in educational questions; formerly Member and Vice-Chairman of the late Bangor School Board; former President of the North Wales Congregational Union; member of the Merionethshire Education Committee; JP County of Carnarvon. *Publications:* memoirs on Algæ. *Recreations:* golf, fond of collecting as a field botanist. *Address:* University College, Bangor. *TA:* Dr Phillips, Bangor.   *Died 2 Dec. 1926.*

PHILLIPS, Rev. Sidney, MA; Hon. Canon of Worcester; *b* 30 June 1840; *s* of Sidney James and Fanny Phillips; *m* 1868, Alice Margaret, *d* of Rev. Edward and Lady Harriet Moore; three *s* five *d*. *Educ:* Radley; Oxford. Deacon, 1864; priest, 1866; Vicar of Castle Hedingham, Essex, 1868–75; Vicar of Monmouth, 1875–79; Rector of Nuneham Courtenay, 1879–87; Vicar of Kidderminster, 1887–1909. *Publications:* The Conflict; A Faithful Servant; The Heavenward Way; Communion of Sick. *Recreations:* travelling abroad, motoring. *Address:* The Blanquettes, Worcester. *TA:* Worcester. *T:* Worcester 324.   *Died 21 March 1917.*

PHILLIPS, Rev. Stephen, DD. *Educ:* St Albans Hall; Merton Coll., Oxford (MA). Curate of St Saviour, S Hampstead, 1870–73; All Saints, Hampstead, 1873–74; St Andrews, Deal, 1874–76; Farnborough, Warwickshire, 1875; Chaplain and Sub-Vicar, Stratford-on-Avon, 1876; Minor Canon of Peterborough, 1876–83; Reader and Chaplain of Gray's Inn, 1884–92; Precentor, Peterborough, 1892–1906; Hon. Canon, 1906–17.   *Died 30 Oct. 1919.*

PHILLIPS, Rear-Adm. Thomas Tyacke; retired; *b* Bermuda, 10 March 1832; *m* 1866, Ellen Annie, *e d* of Thomas Hand, Richmond, Surrey; no *c*. *Educ:* Helston Grammar School. Entered Navy, 1846; served in HMS Fury at the destruction of a large piratical Fleet in China, 1849 (despatches); while serving in HMS Hastings as mate commanded an armed schooner on the Irrawaddy, 1850 (medal and clasp, Pegu); served in Queen's yacht, 1854 (promoted to Lieutenant); served in HMS Esk, Baltic Campaign, 1855 (medal); Gunnery Lieut for 9½ years; arrested at the Havana, Austin Bidwell, the great bank forger, who was evading justice, 1873. *Recreation:* gardening. *Address:* The Hermitage, Paignton, Devon.

     Died 26 Aug. 1920.

PHILLIPS, William Lambert Collyer, OBE 1918; BA; Colonial Treasurer, Barbados, since 1899; *b* Oct. 1858; *s* of late John Randal Phillips and Mary Anne Evelyn of Mt Clapham Plantation, Barbados; *m* Emily Lovell, *d* of Joseph Lovell Canfield of Morris Plains, New Jersey, USA; one *s* one *d*. *Educ:* Lodge School and Codrington College, Barbados; BA (Dunelm), 1877. Deputy Clerk, House of Assembly, Barbados, 1879; Clerk, House of Assembly, 1891; Commissioner of Probates and JP 1882; Acting Colonial Secretary in 1911 and successive years; Acting Governor of Barbados, 1913; Delegate from Barbados to the Canada-West India Conference held in Ottawa, 1920. *Recreations:* various. *Address:* Innismoyle, Barbados. *Clubs:* West Indian; Bridgetown, Savannah (Bridgetown).   *Died 24 March 1924.*

PHILLPOTTS, Arthur Stephens, JP; Captain Royal Navy (retired); *b* Torquay, 13 Oct. 1844; 2nd *s* of late Henry Phillpotts, Torquay; *g s* of late Bishop of Exeter; *m* 1883, Camilla, *d* of Rt Hon. Sir Bernhard Samuelson, 1st Bt. *Educ:* Chudleigh Grammar School; Royal Naval Academy, Gosport. Entered RN 1858; sub-lieut on board HMS "Bombay," in Dec. 1864, when that ship was destroyed by fire off the mouth of the Rio de la Plata, on which occasion 92 officers and men perished; served in Abyssinian Expedition, mentioned in despatches; and also noted for services in connection with the suppression of the slave trade on the East Coast of Africa; MP (C) Torquay Div. of Devon, 1895–1900. *Address:* Phillpottstown, Navan; Chelston Cross, Torquay. *Club:* Carlton.

Died 12 Aug. 1920.

PHILLPOTTS, Lt-Col Louis Murray, DSO 1900; Royal Field Artillery; *b* 3 June 1870; *s* of Rev. Henry John Phillpotts; *m* 1909, Amy Anne Charlotte, *o d* of Stewart James Charles Duckett, Co. Carlow. Entered RA 1890; Capt. 1900; served South Africa, 1899–1901 (despatches, Queen's medal, three clasps, DSO); European War, 1914–15 (despatches). *Died 8 Sept. 1916.*

PHILP, Hon. Sir Robert, KCMG 1914; *b* Glasgow, 28 Dec. 1851; *m* twice; two *s* five *d*. *Educ:* Anderston UP Church School, Glasgow; Normal School, Brisbane. With the firm of Bright Bros & Co., Brisbane, for 11 years; one of the founders of the firm of Burns, Philp, and Co.; first entered Qld Parliament, 1886; joined the Ministry of Hon. Sir Thomas M'Ilwraith, 1893; Minister for Mines and Works; also held portfolios of Education, Railways, and the office of Treasurer; Premier and Secretary for Mines, Queensland, 1899–1903; and Home Secretary, 1900–3; Leader of the Opposition, 1903–8, 1909; Premier and Chief Secretary, 1908–9. *Recreation:* bowls. *Clubs:* Queensland, Brisbane; North Queensland, Townsville.

Died June 1922.

PHILPOT, Frederick Freeman; a Master of the Supreme Court. *Address:* Royal Courts of Justice, Strand, WC.

Died May 1916.

PHIMISTER, Rev. Alexander, MA; Minister of John Knox Church, Newcastle-on-Tyne, 1882–1919. *Educ:* Irvine Academy; Edinburgh University. Minister of the Free Church, Gordon, Berwickshire, 1874; Moderator of the Presbyterian Church of England, 1908. *Address:* 50 Beech Grove Road, Newcastle-on-Tyne.

Died 5 Jan. 1921.

PHIPPS, Rev. Constantine Osborne, MA Oxon; Vicar of The Lee, Buckinghamshire, since 1914; Hon. Canon of Christ Church Cathedral, Oxford; Surrogate for the Diocese of Oxford; Chaplain to the Territorial Forces, 1914; Rural Dean of Wendover, 1919; *b* 28 March 1861; *e s* of Rev. Pownoll William Phipps, MA Oxon; *m* 1886, Jessie Mabel, *d* of Joseph Challinor, Compton House, Leek; two *d*. *Educ:* Marlborough College; Exeter College, Oxford. Deacon, 1885; Priest, 1886; Assistant Curate of All Saints, Fulham, SW, 1885–88; Vicar of Cookham Dean, Berks, 1888–95; Diocesan Inspector of Schools in Religious Knowledge, 1891–95, 1901–9, 1914–17; Vicar of Aylesbury, 1895–1914; Rural Dean of Aylesbury, 1906–11, 1912–14; Commissioner under the Pluralities Act Amendment Act for the Archdeaconry of Buckingham; Assessor under the Clergy Discipline Act for the Archdeaconry of Buckingham; Member of the Bucks County Cricket Club Committee. *Recreations:* golf, fly-fishing. *Address:* The Vicarage, The Lee, Great Missenden, Bucks. *T:* The Lee 5.

Died 7 Nov. 1921.

PHIPPS, Hon. Harriet Lepel, VA; *y d* of late Col Hon. Sir Charles Beaumont Phipps, KCB (*s* of 1st Earl of Musgrave, GCB and *brother* of 1st Marquess of Normanby, KG, GCB) and Margaret Anne, *d* of Ven. Hy Bathurst, sometime Archdeacon of Norwich. Maid of Honour to the Queen, 1862–89; Bedchamber-Woman in Ordinary, 1889–1901. *Address:* Kensington Palace, W8. *T:* Park 4687.

Died 7 March 1922.

PICK, Thomas Pickering, FRCS; HM Inspector of Anatomy in England and Wales; Consulting Surgeon to St George's Hospital and to the Victoria Hospital for Children; *b* 13 June 1841; *m* 1873, Adeline, *d* of late John Lawrence of Liverpool. *Educ:* Royal Institution School, Liverpool. Late Hunterian Professor of Surgery and Pathology; member of the Court of Examiners and Vice-President, Royal College of Surgeons of England; Examiner in Surgery, University of Durham. *Publications:* Treatise on Surgery; Fractures and Dislocations; editor of Gray's Anatomy and Holmes's Principles and Practice of Surgery; author of numerous papers and lectures in the medical journals.

Recreation: photography. *Address:* The Nook, Great Bookham, Surrey.

Died 6 Oct. 1919.

PICKARD-CAMBRIDGE, Rev. Octavius, MA; FRS; Rector of Bloxworth since 1868; *b* 1828; *m* 1866, Rose (*d* 1910), *d* of Rev. James Lloyd Wallace of Sevenoaks, Kent; five *s*. *Educ:* University College, Durham. *Publications:* Specific Descriptions of Trap-Door Spiders, 1873; The Spiders of Dorset, 1879–81; articles: Arachnida, 9th edition Ency. Brit.; Araneidea Biologia Centrali Americana; etc. *Recreation:* general natural history, especially entomology and arachnology. *Address:* Bloxworth, Wareham, Dorset.

Died 9 March 1917.

PICKERING, Edward Charles; Director of the Astronomical Observatory of Harvard College, since 1877; *b* Boston, 19 July 1846; *s* of Edward Pickering and Charlotte Hammond; *m* 1874, Lizzie Wadsworth, *d* of Jared Sparks. *Educ:* Boston Latin School; Lawrence Scientific School, Harvard (AM 1880). Instructor in Mathematics, Lawrence Scientific School, 1865–67; Thayer Professor of Physics, Mass Institute of Technology, 1867–77; established first physical laboratory in US; study of light and spectra of the stars a special feature of his wo ; made nearly a million and a half measures of the ligh of the stars; by establishing an auxiliary station in Arequipa, Peru, southern stars also observed; Founder and first President of the Appalachian Mountain Club; Ex-President Amer. Association; Member National Academy, Amer. Phil. Soc., Amer. Academy; President American Astronomical Society; Foreign Associate of Royal Society, Institut de France, and other societies, academies and institutes (dei Lincei, Royal Prussian, Imperial Petrograd, Royal Institution, Connaissance des temps, Upsala, Royal Irish, Royal Swedish, Lund, Cherbourg, Toronto, Mexico, Edinburgh, etc); Kt German Order of Merit; received the Bruce, Draper, Rumford and two Royal Astronomical Society's gold medals; LLD California, 1886; Michigan, 1887; Chicago, 1901; Harvard, 1903; Pennsylvania, 1906; DSc, Victoria Univ. of Manchester, 1900; PhD Heidelberg, 1903; LHD Pittsburgh, 1912). *Publications:* Elements of Physical Manipulation; and eighty volumes of annals and other publications of Harvard College Observatory. *Recreations:* music; formerly mountain climbing, bicycling. *Address:* Harvard College Observatory, Cambridge, Mass, USA. *TA:* Observatory, Boston. *T:* Cambridge 2286 W. *Club:* Century Association, New York.

Died 3 Feb. 1919.

PICKERING, Percival Spencer Umfreville, MA; FRS 1890; Director of the Woburn Experimental Fruit Farm; Investigator in Chemical Physics; *b* 1858; *s* of Percival A. Pickering, QC, and Anna Maria, *d* of John Spencer Stanhope, Cannon Hall, Barnsley; *m* 1898. *Educ:* Eton, Balliol Coll., Oxford (1st class Honours in Science, 1880). Lecturer on Chemistry at Bedford College, 1881–88. *Publications:* The Pickerings of Barlby, York, and Wetherby; (with the Duke of Bedford) Reports of the Woburn Experimental Fruit Farm; Science and Fruit-growing; edited Memoirs of Anna Maria Pickering, and author of about 150 papers on chemical and physical investigations in the Journals of the London and Berlin Chemical Societies, the Philosophical Magazine, Proceedings of the Royal Society, etc. *Recreation:* horticulture. *Address:* Harpenden, Herts; Woolacombe, N Devon. *Club:* Athenæum.

Died 5 Dec. 1920.

PICKETT, Jacob, MD St Andrews; MRCS, LRCPE; Consulting Surgeon to the Metropolitan Ear, Nose, and Throat Hospital, Fitzroy Square, London; *b* 1835; 2nd *s* of late Samuel Ballard Pickett of Wroughton, Wiltshire; *m* 1879, Maria Ann Hopper, 2nd *d* of late R. J. Chaplin, JP Kent, and DL City of London; no *c*. *Educ:* privately; Saint Bartholomew's Hospital. Late Senior Surgeon to the Metropolitan Ear, Nose, and Throat Hospital, London; Member of British Medical Association; Member and Vice-President of the West London Medical and Chirurgical Society; Member of St Andrew's Graduates Society; Vice-President Medical Sick Insurance Society. *Publications:* articles in the British Medical Journal and Lancet at different times. *Recreations:* travelling, outdoor sports generally. *Address:* 18 Worthing Road, Southsea.

Died 3 March 1922.

PICKETT, Rev. James; President of Primitive Methodist Conference, 1908–9; *b* Berwick Bassett, Wiltshire, 19 Dec. 1853; two *s* four *d*. *Educ:* Wootton Bassett, Wiltshire. Business in London 17 to 23 years of age; entered Primitive Methodist ministry, 1876; minister at Bognor, 1876–78; Southwark, 1879–81; Forest Hill, 1881–85; Leicester, 1885–97; Hull, 1897–1903; Harringay, N, 1908–13; Chesterfield, 1913–16; General Missionary Secretary, 1903–8. *Publications:* The Hartley Lecture, 1913; The Modern Missionary

Crisis; various sermons. *Address:* 17 Morrill Street, Hull.
Died 22 Aug. 1918.

PICKOP, Rev. James, BA; Hon. Canon of Manchester; *b* 26 April 1847; *s* of James Pickop, Solicitor, Blackburn; *m* 1888, Sara T. Greer; two *s* three *d. Educ:* London University. Curate of Walmersley, Bury, 1875–79; St Luke's, Heywood, 1879–88; Rector of Hatcliffe, Lincolnshire, 1888–1903. *Address:* Winston Hall, Blackburn. *T:* 538.
Died 7 March 1919.

PIELOU, Douglas Percival; MP (C) Stourbridge Division since 1922; *b* 17 Oct. 1887; *e s* of Percival Gaberial Pielou, retired Civil Servant; *m* 1914, Nora, *d* of late Joseph Thomas Pitchford, Dudley; two *s. Educ:* Marling School, Gloucestershire. Entered bank, 1903; resigned, 1914; joined Cameron Highlanders (severely wounded Battle of Loos, Sept. 1915); Accountant HM Ministry of Munitions, Whitehall; Registrar for Tipton, Staffs; Member Tipton Council and Education Committee; President Tipton Branch and Club, British Legion; Chairman West Midland Area British Legion; Vice-Chairman British Legion throughout Country; Member of Ministry of Pensions Advisory Committee; Vice-President (elected) British Empire Services League; Hon. Secretary House of Commons Branch British Legion; served in Worcestershire Hussars Yeomanry and Warwickshire Royal Garrison Artillery (Vol.); late Commissioner Baden-Powell Boy Scouts; Governor Birmingham University. *Recreations:* (pre-War) hunting, hockey, swimming, etc (disabled, on crutches). *Address:* 103 Dudley Road, Tipton, Staffs. *T:* Tipton 130.
Died 9 Jan. 1927.

PIERCE, Rev. Francis Dormer, FRHistS; Vicar of Brighton since 1916; 2nd *s* of J. Timbrell Pierce, JP, DL of Frettons, Danbury, Essex; *m* Mabel, *y d* of P. Woolley of the Brokes, Reigate; no *c. Educ:* Bedford Grammar School; Bury St Edmunds; St David's College, Lampeter. Deacon, 1894; Priest, 1895; Curate of St Andrew's, Manchester, 1894–97; St Mark's, Reigate, 1897–99; Rector of Wickford, Essex, 1899–1908; Vicar of St John's, Southend, 1908–14; Chaplain to the Forces (Territorial), 1910; Vicar of Prittlewell, Essex, and Rural Dean of Southend, 1914–16; Hon. Canon of Chelmsford, 1915; Prebendary of Chichester, 1917; Rural Dean of Brighton, 1918; Proctor in Convocation; travelled widely and much interested in the missionary work of the Church. *Publications:* History of Wickford; Problems of Pleasure Towns; magazine articles. *Recreations:* travelling, tennis, croquet. *Address:* Vicarage Lodge, Brighton. *Clubs:* Reform, Royal Societies, Authors'; New, Brighton.
Died 2 Dec. 1923.

PIGGOTT, Sir Francis (Taylor), Kt 1905; *b* 25 April 1852; *s* of Rev. Francis Allen Piggott, of Worthing; *m* 1881, Mabel Waldron, *e d* of Jasper Wilson Johns, JP, DL; two *s. Educ:* Paris; Worthing College; Trinity Coll., Cambridge (MA, LLM). Called to the Bar, 1874; special mission to Italy, 1887; Legal Adviser to Prime Minister of Japan, 1887–91; Secretary to the Attorney-General, Sir Charles Russell, MP, on the Behring Sea Arbitration, 1893; Acting Chief Judge, Mauritius, 1895–97; Procureur and Advocate-General, Mauritius, 1894–1905; Chief-Justice Supreme Court, Hong-Kong, 1905–12. *Publications:* Foreign Judgments, 3rd edn 1908; Principles of Law of Torts, 1885; Exterritoriality and Consular Jurisdiction, 2nd edn 1907; The Garden of Japan, 1892; Music and Musical Instruments of the Japanese, 1893; Behring Sea Letters, 1893; Revised Edition of Laws of Mauritius, 6 vols, 2nd edn 1904; Nationality and Naturalisation and the English Law on the High Seas and beyond the Realm, 1904; Extradition, 1911; Huafeng Lao Jen, Letters on the Chinese Constitution, 1913; The Neutral Merchant; many publications on the rights of belligerents and neutrals and the Freedom of the Sea, 1914–17; The Law of the Sea Series, dealing with the Armed Neutralities, the French Wars, and the Declaration of Paris, 1919; The Freedom of the Seas. *Recreation:* golf. *Address:* 7 Stone Buildings, Lincoln's Inn, WC.
Died 12 March 1925.

PIGOT, His Honour Judge John H., KC 1909; Circuit Judge for the City and County of Dublin; *b* 1863; *s* of Master D. R. Pigot, sometime County Court Judge of West Cork, and *g s* of Right Hon. D. R. Pigot, Chief Baron of the Exchequer in Ireland; *m* Alice Maud Knox (*d* 1914). *Educ:* Trinity College, Dublin. *Address:* Avondale, Blackrock, Co. Dublin. *Died 14 April 1928.*

PIGOT, Rev. William Melville; *b* Cromford, Matlock, 23 March 1842; *s* of Henry Becher Pigot, BCL; *m* 1st, 1867, Eleanor Anne (*d* 1887), *d* of Rev. Arthur Roberts, Rector of Woodrising; 2nd, Ada Mary, *d* of John Woodland, JP, of Taunton; five *c. Educ:* Islington Proprietary School, London; Brasenose College, Oxford. Ordained by the Bishop of Norwich to the curacy of Hardingham, 1865; Vicar

of Eaton, Norwich, 1875–1904; Rural Dean of Humbleyard, 1897–1904; Hon. Canon of Norwich Cathedral, 1901; Vicar of St Mary-le-Tower, Ipswich, 1904; Rural Dean of Ipswich, 1908; editor Norwich Diocesan Gazette and Diocesan Calendar; Diocesan Inspector of Schools in the Deanery; Member of Standing Committee of SPG; Chaplain to Actors' Church Union; Battalion Chaplain to Church Lads' Brigade; retired, Jan. 1915. *Publication:* Service for Children. *Recreations:* rowing and running at Oxford, tennis, golf, etc. *Address:* Garwich Lodge, Felixstowe. *Clubs:* Junior Army and Navy; Ipswich and Suffolk, Ipswich.
Died 25 Oct. 1916.

PIGOTT, John Robert Wilson; *b* 27 Nov. 1850; *y s* of late Rev. John R. Pigott, Rector of Ashwellthorp-with-Wreningham, Norfolk; *m* 1893, Louisa, 2nd *s d* of late Richard Young Bazett, of HEICS, Bombay, and of Highfield, Reading, Berks. *Educ:* King Edward VI School, Norwich. Planting, Ceylon, 1877–85; exploration, Australia, 1886–88; Assistant Administrator, Imperial British E Africa, 1888–89; Acting Administrator, 1891, and from 1 Jan. 1893 to 30 June 1895; Sub-Commissioner, British E Africa, 1895–96; Vice-Consul in Zanzibar, and for British Sphere E Coast of Africa, 1896; HM Consul for Sicily, 1896; for Surinam and Cayenne, 1898–1911. *Address:* Frankfort Manor, Sloley, Norfolk. *T:* Coltishall 31. *TA:* Smallburgh.
Died 6 Feb. 1928.

PIGOTT, Montague Horatio Mostyn Turtle, MA, BCL; Barrister of the Middle Temple; author and journalist; *b* 9 Aug. 1865; *s* of late Robert Turtle Pigott, DCL; unmarried. *Educ:* Westminster School; University College, Oxford. 2nd class honours in classical moderations and in law; scholarship in international and constitutional law at the Middle Temple; for ten years coached pupils for the Bar examination; Founder and first editor of the Isis. *Publications:* contributor to many papers and magazines, particularly The World; author and composer of many songs; author of various lyrics and of a play entitled All Fletcher's Fault, produced at the Avenue Theatre, and of Common Room Carols, Two on a Tour, and Songs of a Session. *Recreations:* anything that comes along. *Clubs:* Savage, Beefsteak.
Died 26 Aug. 1927.

PIGOTT, Sir (Thomas) Digby, Kt 1906; CB 1890; JP Norfolk; *b* 1840; *s* of Rev. John Pigott and Emma, *d* of Abbot Upcher, of Sheringham; *m* 1878, Julia, *d* of the Hon. Augustus Henry Macdonald-Moreton (MP West Gloucestershire), Largie, Argyllshire; one *s* four *d. Educ:* Marlborough; abroad. A clerk in War Office, 1859; Private Secretary to Lord Northbrook, 1871–72; to Marquis of Landsdowne, 1872–74; to Earl of Pembroke, 1874–75; Secretary to Royal Commission on promotion and retirement for the Army, 1874–76; for a short time as private secretary to Mr Gathorne-Hardy (Earl of Cranbrook), Secretary of State for War, 1877; Controller of HM's Stationery Office, 1877–1905; printer to HM of all Acts of Parliament, and held under HM's letters patent the copyright in all Government publications, 1888–95. *Publications:* London Birds, and other Sketches; The Changeling; various magazine articles, chiefly ornithological, etc. *Recreation:* ornithology (member of British Ornithological Union; visited the Shetlands, Holland, Finland, etc, in pursuit of favourite hobby). *Address:* The Lodge, Sheringham, Norfolk. *Club:* Carlton.
Died 26 Jan. 1927.

PIGOTT, Vice-Adm. William Harvey, JP; *b* 8 March 1848; *o s* of George Grenville Wandesford Pigott, MP (*d* 1865), and Charlotte (*d* 1883), *y d* of late William Lloyd of Aston Hall, Shropshire; *m* 1886, Edith, 3rd *d* of late Richard Thomas Lloyd of Aston Hall, Shropshire; one *d.* Vice-Admiral; retired, RN; patron of one living; Order of the Osmanieh, 4th Class. *Address:* Doddershall Park, Aylesbury.
Died 1 Sept. 1924.

PIGOU, Very Rev. Francis, DD; Dean of Bristol since 1891; President of Church Choir Guilds; *b* Baden-Baden, 3 Jan. 1832; *m* 1st, 1859, Mary Somers; two *d;* 2nd, 1869, Harriet Maude, *d* of William and Mrs Gambier. *Educ:* Neuwied; Ripon Grammar School; Cheltenham Coll.; Edinburgh Academy; Trinity Coll., Dublin. Curate of Stoke Talmage, Oxon, 1855–56; Chaplain at Marbœuf Chapel, Paris, 1856–58; Readership, St Peter's, Vere Street, 1858–59; Incumbent of St Philip's, 1862–73; Vicar of Doncaster, 1869–75; Vicar and Rural Dean of Halifax, 1875–88; Hon. Canon of Ripon, 1885–88; Dean of Chichester, 1888–91; Hon. Chaplain-in-Ordinary to Queen Victoria, 1871–74; Chaplain-in-Ordinary, 1874–89. *Publications:* Addresses on Holy Communion; Addresses to my District Visitors, 1895; Addresses to Clergy and Workers; Phases of my Life, 1899; Odds and Ends, 1903; Acts of the Holy Ghost, 1908. *Recreation:* science, especially the microscope. *Address:* Deanery, Bristol.
Died 25 Jan. 1916.

PIKE, Vice-Adm. Frederick Owen, CMG 1918; DSO 1917; Temporary Captain Royal Naval Reserve; *b* 1851; *s* of late Capt. T. W. R. Pike, RN; *m* 1893, *d* of late Judge Pohlman, Melbourne. Vice-Adm., retired, 1911; served European War with RNR (CMG, DSO). *Address:* 2 Clifton Villas, Alverstoke, Gosport.
Died 5 April 1921.

PILCHER, Maj.-Gen. Thomas David, CB 1901; *b* 8 July 1858; *s* of Thomas Webb Pilcher of Harrow; *m* 1st, 1889, Kathleen Mary, *d* of Col Thomas Gonne, 17th Lancers; 2nd, 1913, Mrs J. C. L. Knight-Bruce; two *s* one *d. Educ:* Harrow. Joined 5th Fusiliers, 1879; Major, 1897; served Niger, 1897–98; raised 1st Batt. West African Frontier Force, 1899; commanded expedition to Lapai and Argeyah (despatches, brevet of Lieut-Col, medal with clasp; promoted to command 2nd Beds Regiment; received thanks of HM's Government); South Africa, 1899–1902, in command of a column of mounted men (despatches, promoted Col); ADC to the King, 1901; Major-Gen. 1907; held various commands in India until 1914; commanded 17th Division BEF in England and France, Jan. 1915–July 1916 (wounded, despatches); contested Thornbury Division, Gloucestershire, Dec. 1918. *Publications:* Lessons from the Boer War; The Writing on the Wall; A General's Letters to his Son; A General's Letters on Minor Tactics; War according to Clausewitz; East is East. *Recreations:* hunting, shooting, fishing, polo. *Club:* Naval and Military.
Died 14 Dec. 1928.

PILKINGTON, Sir George Augustus, Kt 1893; JP; DL; *b* Upwell, Cambridgeshire, 7 Oct. 1848; *s* of Robert Gorton Combe, surgeon; *m* 1875, Mary Elizabeth, *d* of James Pilkington; assumed surname of Pilkington, 1882; two *d. Educ:* privately; Guy's Hospital. Practised medicine in Southport, 1870–84; Mayor of Southport, 1884–85, 1892–93; MP (L) Southport Division of Lancashire, 1884–85, 1899–1900; Hon. Lieut RNV; High Sheriff, Lancashire, 1911–12. *Recreations:* shooting, yachting, cycling, athletics generally. *Address:* Bellevue, Southport; Swinithwaite Hall, Yorks. *TA:* Bellevue. *T:* 177. *M:* 698. *Clubs:* Reform, National Liberal, Royal Automobile.
Died 28 Jan. 1916.

PILLANS, Charles Eustace, ISO 1907; JP; Horticultural Assistant, Cape Colony, since 1905; *b* Rosebank, Cape Colony, 26 Feb. 1850; *s* of Charles Stuart Pillans and Alida Dorothea Colyn; *m* 1883, Mary Eliza Siddons Porter; one *s. Educ:* Diocesan College, Rondebosch, Cape. Third-class clerk, Audit Office, Cape, 1873; Resident Magistrate's clerk, Wynberg, 1875; transferred to General Post Office, 1876; served as Lieut and Acting Adjutant to Frontier Light Horse (Maj.-Gen. Sir Frederick Carrington's) during Gaika-Gealeka Kaffir War, 1877–78 (Kaffir War medal) and in the DEOVR during Basuto War, 1880–81 (Basuto War medal); Surveyor, Provincial Post Offices, 1884; Agricultural Assistant, 1899; Director of Information Bureau, 1902; Director of Government Labour Bureau and Immigration Officer, 1902; attached to Excise Branch, Treasury, 1904; Stamping Commissioner, 1904. *Publication:* Manual of Orchard Work at the Cape. *Recreations:* gardening, collecting and growing Cape succulent plants. *Address:* Rosedale, Rosebank, Cape Colony.
Died 15 March 1919.

PIM, Frederick William; Director, and Chairman 1896–1917, Dublin and South-Eastern Railway; *b* Dublin, 1839; *s* of late Jonathan Pim, MP City of Dublin, 1865–74; *m*, 1st, 1865, Hannah (*d* 1876), *d* of late Joshua Beale of Cork; 2nd, 1882, Mary S. (*d* 1884), *d* of late Erasmus C. Pratt of Philadelphia, USA; two *s* three *d. Educ:* Bootham School, York; Grove House, Tottenham. Director of cos. *Publications:* The Health of Dublin (three Presidential addresses to the Dublin Sanitary Association, 1890–92); Private Bill Legislation—Suggestions for Devolution to a Permanent Commission, 1896; The Early Friends and War, 1910; The Railways and the State, 1912; The Sinn Fein Rising, 1916; The Mites in the Cheese (the War and the Struggle for Existence), 1918; Home Rule through Federal Devolution, 1919. *Recreation:* gardening. *Address:* Lonsdale, Blackrock, Co. Dublin. *Club:* Royal Irish Yacht, Kingstown.
Died Jan. 1925.

PINE-COFFIN, Major John Edward, DSO 1900; North Lancashire Regiment; *b* 24 Dec. 1866; *e s* of John Richard Pine-Coffin (*d* 1890), JP and DL, of Portledge, and Matilda, *y d* of William Speke, of Jordans, Somerset; *m* 1894, Louisa Gertrude Douglas, *y d* of John Barre Beresford, JP and DL, of Learmount and Ashbrook, Co. Londonderry; two *s* two *d. Educ:* Eton; Cambridge. Entered army, 1888; Captain, 1898; served South Africa, commanding Mobile Column (despatches, Brevet-Major, Queen's medal, 2 clasps, King's medal, 2 clasps, DSO); appointed to command Mounted Infantry, Egypt, 1904–8; commanded 2nd Batt. Loyalist N Lancashire Regiment, Mauritius, 1908–9; retired 1909. *Address:* Portledge, near Bideford.
Died 22 Aug. 1919.

PINE-COFFIN, General Roger; *b* 22 Feb. 1847; *m* 1876, Flora Isabella, *y d* of late Andrew Wilson, Inspector-General of Hospitals, India; one *s.* Entered Royal Marines, 1864; Capt. 1880; Major, 1886; Lt-Col 1893; Col 1901; Major-Gen. 1903; Lt-Gen. 1910; General, 1911; served Egypt, 1882 (despatches twice, medal with clasp, bronze star, Bt-Major); Soudan, 1885 (two clasps). *Address:* The Old Hall, Brackley, Northants.
Died 25 March 1921.

PINHEY, Lt-Col Sir Alexander Fleetwood, KCSI 1915 (CSI 1911); CIE 1901; Indian Army; Resident in Hyderabad; Political Department; *b* 10 July 1861; *s* of Hon. Mr Justice Pinhey, Bombay CS; *m* 1891, Violet Beatrice, *d* of late Gen. Sir Henry Gordon, KCB; three *s* two *d. Educ:* Clifton Coll.; Sandhurst. Lieutenant, King's Liverpool Regt, 1882; served in Banswara as Assistant Political Agent and as Supt Moghia operations, 1886; Political Agent Baghel Khand, 1895; Resident in Mewar, 1900; Resident in Gwalior, 1907; Officiating Asst AG, Rajputana, 1908–9; Private Secretary to the Viceroy, 1910. *Address:* The Residency, Hyderabad. *Club:* Junior United Service.
Died 7 April 1916.

PINK, Sir Thomas, Kt 1904; *b* London, 5 April 1855; 2nd *s* of Edward Pink, Portobello House, Kingsdown, Sevenoaks; *m* 1st, 1878, Ellen Amelia (*d* 1917), *o d* of Edmund Purssey, Camberwell; two *s* one *d*; 2nd, 1918, Minnie Jane, 2nd *d* of George Brown Davis, AIME, Westminster. *Educ:* London. Head of E. and T. Pink; Pres. Grocers' Benevolent Society; Trustee London Commercial Travellers' Benevolent Society; was interested in political work in West Newington, 1895–98. *Recreations:* shooting, tennis, motoring. *Address:* 4 Whitehall Court, SW1. *T:* Victoria 2122; Hambleden Place, Henley-on-Thames. *T:* Henley 154. *Clubs:* Constitutional, Royal Automobile.
Died 23 Jan. 1926.

PINKHAM, Rt. Rev. William Cyprian, DD, DCL; *b* 1844; *s* of William Pinkham, Teignmouth, Devon, and St John's, Newfoundland; *m* 1868, Jean Anne, 2nd *d* of late William Drever, Winnipeg; four *s* four *d. Educ:* St Augustine's Coll., Canterbury; BD by Archbishop of Canterbury, 1880. Incumbent of St James's, Manitoba, 1868–82; Superintendent of Education for Protestant Public Schools of Manitoba, 1871–83; Archdeacon of Manitoba and Canon of St John's Cathedral, Winnipeg, 1882–87; Acting Rector, All Saints', Winnipeg, 1883–84; Secretary of Synod, 1882–87; Bishop of Saskatchewan, 1887–1903; Bishop of Calgary, 1888–1926; Chairman Board of Education, NWT, from 1887 for several years; Hon. DCL Trinity University, Toronto; University of Alberta; Hon. DD University of Manitoba, 1887. *Address:* 603 13th Avenue, Calgary, Alberta, Canada.
Died July 1928.

PIPON, Maj.-Gen. Henry, CB 1900; late Royal Artillery; Major of the Tower of London, 1909–23; *b* 4 Dec. 1843; 2nd *s* of Colonel James Kennard Pipon of Noirmont Manor, Jersey; *m* 1872, Louisa Anne (*d* 1921), *d* of Admiral Sir William Edmonstone, 4th Bt, CB, of Duntreath, Stirlingshire. *Educ:* RMA, Woolwich. Entered Royal Artillery, 1861; served in Fenian Raid, Canada, 1866 (medal and clasp); in RHA during Afghan Campaign of 1879–81, including actions at Shutagandau, Charasia, and subsequent operations at Kabul; Adjutant RA on march to Kandahar; battle of Kandahar (medal and three clasps and bronze star, despatches thrice); commanded RA, China Field Force, 1900–1 (despatches, medal).
Died 14 Jan. 1924.

PIRIE, Major Arthur Murray, DSO 1898; late serving with Egyptian Army; *b* 3 May 1869; 3rd *s* of Gordon Pirie of Waterton; *m* 1907, Marie Valerie, *d* of Philip Gurdon and *widow* of Claude Loraine Barrow; one *d.* Entered 21st Lancers, 1889; Captain, 1899; served Soudan, 1898, including Khartoum (despatches, DSO, British medal, Khedive's medal with clasp, 4th class Medjidie); retired, 1906. *Club:* Cavalry.
Died 21 Nov. 1917.

PIRRIE, 1st Viscount, *cr* 1921; **William James Pirrie,** KP 1909; PC 1897; JP; Hon. LLD, DSc; Baron 1906; Controller-General of Merchant Shipbuilding, March 1918; HM's Lieutenant County of City of Belfast, 1911; Ex-Comptroller of the Household of the Lord-Lieutenant of Ireland; Pro-Chancellor of Queen's University, Belfast; *b* Quebec, 31 May 1847; *o s* of late James Alexander Pirrie of Little Clandeboye, Co. Down, and Eliza, *d* of Alexander Montgomery of Dundesart, County Antrim; *m* 1879, Margaret Montgomery, *d* of John Carlisle, MA, of Belfast. *Educ:* Belfast Royal Academical Institution. Entered Harland and Wolff's shipbuilding and engineering establishment, 1862; became partner in 1874, subseq. chairman; Lord Mayor of Belfast, 1896–97; High-Sheriff of Co. Antrim, 1898, and Co. Down, 1899; first Hon. Freeman of the City of Belfast, 1898; JP City of Belfast, Co. Antrim and Co. Down. *Heir:* none. *Address:*

24 Belgrave Square, SW1. *T:* Victoria 278; Witley Park, Godalming; Ormiston, Strandtown, Belfast. *Clubs:* Reform; Kildare Street, Dublin; Ulster, Belfast.   *Died 7 June 1924 (ext).*

PITCHER, Colonel Duncan George; *b* 2 Nov. 1839; *e s* of late Lieut and Adjt St Vincent Pitcher, 6th Madras Lt Cavalry, and Rose, *d* of Admiral George Le Geyt, CB; *m* 1867, Rose *d* of Capt. J. C. Evison, RN; one *s* six *d*. *Educ:* Christ's Hospital; Victoria College, Jersey; RN College, Portsmouth joined HMS Excellent as marine cadet, 1856; 2nd Lieut RMLI 1856; qualified for the RM Artillery (1st class certificates in naval gunnery and steam); Ensign 5th Fusiliers, 1858; passed at Sandhurst for a direct Commission in November 1855, but elected to remain with RMA; resigned Commission in RMA on being appointed Cornet Bombay Lt Cavalry, 1859; proceeded to India, 1859, and served successively with 6th Inniskilling Dragoons, 3rd Bombay Lt Cavalry, 3rd Southern Maratha Horse, and 21st Hussars (1862-68); Interpreter, Adjt, and Musketry Instructor, 1865-67; qualified as Military Engineer and Surveyor; transferred to BSC and to 5th Bengal Cavalry, 1868; various revenue, judicial, and magisterial posts in the United Provinces, 1868-90; special thanks from Secretary of State, 1872, for a scheme of Agricultural Banks, and of Govt of India for unravelling a pension fraud at Lucknow, and saving for Govt £5,000 a year, 1872; also thanks from Govt of India and Local Govt on many occasions, particularly for special inquiries and reports on: forest conservancy in Oudh, 1876; famine mortality in Rohilkand, 1878; working of Oudh Rent Acts, 1883; emigration of natives from India to the Colonies, 1882; effecting an economy in printing and stationery of 1 lakh rupees *per annum*, 1889; for work in connection with Indian arts and crafts, carried out on behalf of the UP; for exhibitions held in various years at Amsterdam, Vienna, Paris, Calcutta, Lucknow, and London; in 1890 deputed by Indian Foreign Office to the Maratha State of Gwalior to organise a Dept of Land Records, Cadastral Survey, and Revenue Settlement; remained so employed until departure from India in 1903; famine commissioner for Gwalior through two famines; Kaiser-i-Hind medal, 1st class, for public service in India, 1901; Médaille du Roi Albert, 1921, for services during the war to the Belgian cause; Hon. Secretary Huguenot Society of London; Member Genealogical Society; Fellow Royal Colonial Institute; Member RUSI. *Address:* c/o Child and Co., 1 Fleet Street, EC4.

PITCHER, William J. C., (C. Wilhelm), RI; artist and designer for the stage; *b* Northfleet, Kent, 21 March 1858; *s* of Henry Sotheby Pitcher, ship-builder. Self trained as draughtsman; while still a youth, keenly interested in the art of the theatre; was recommended by J. R. Planché to E. L. Blanchard, to design costumes for Drury Lane Pantomime, resulting in a wide connection for similar work on fantastic and romantic lines, not only in long series with big spectacular scenes at Drury Lane for Sir Augustus Harris, but also the ballets, often entirely invented and produced by him, at the Empire Theatre 1887-1915, including among many others Orféo, Faust, The Press, Les Papillons, Old China, Fête Galante, The Débutante, The Vine, Cinderella; and similar works at the Crystal Palace and the Lyceum for Mr Oscar Barrett; was associated with Mr Seymour Lucas, RA, in the spectacular drama, The Armada, at Drury Lane, 1888; designed the important Olympia productions Nero and Venice for Imre Kiralfy, 1889-91; the Gilbert and Sullivan operas at the Savoy (Iolanthe, Princess Ida, The Mikado, and Ruddigore); Mr Courtneidge's productions of Midsummer Night's Dream and As You Like It; Edward German's opera Tom Jones, 1907; The Arcadians, 1909; The Mousmé, Japanese opera, 1911; Young England, Elizabethan opera, 1917; wrote and decorated historical ballet, La Camargo, for Mlle Adeline Genée, at Coliseum, 1912; elected member of the Royal Institute of Painters in Water Colours, 1919. *Publications:* The art of the theatre, in several articles in The Magazine of Art. *Recreations:* listening to good music, contemplating beauty in Nature, congenial work. *Address:* 122 Coleherne Court, Earls Court, SW5. *T:* Kensington 4187.   *Died 2 March 1925.*

PITMAN, Captain Robert, CMG 1903; Royal Navy; *b* 15 Feb. 1836; *s* of Capt. William Pitman, RN; *m* 1869, Elizabeth (*d* 1917), *d* of Andrew Howard of Ringmore, Devon. Entered Navy, 1849; Lieut 1856; Commander, 1867; Captain retired, 1882; served Baltic, 1854-55 (medal); Chief Superintendent under Board of Trade for carrying out the scheme (originated by him) for transmitting seamen's wages and sending them to their homes from English and Continental ports, 1875-1903. *Address:* 122 Inverness Terrace, W2. *T:* Park 259. *Club:* United Service.   *Died 4 Jan. 1921.*

PITTAR, Sir Thomas John, KCB 1905 (CB 1899); CMG 1903; *b* 29 Oct. 1846; 3rd *s* of late Thomas John Pittar, Hove, Sussex, and Margaret Waring, Waringstown, Ireland; *m* 1870, Annie Frances, 2nd

d of late Thomas Letts of Chale, Isle of Wight; three *s* one *d*. Principal of the Statistical Office, Board of Customs, 1889-1900; Commissioner of Customs, 1900; Chairman, Board of Customs, 1903-8; Principal expert to the British Delegation at the Brussels Sugar Conference, 1901-2; Assistant British Delegate to the Brussels Permanent Commission, 1903; Late Member of Council, Royal Statistical Society; edited the Board of Trade Returns relating to the trade of the United Kingdom, 1889-1900. *Publication:* Law and Practice regulating the Registration of Merchant Shipping, 1881.
                                                       Died 20 July 1924

PITTI, Sir Thyagaraya Chetti Garum, Diwan Bahadur, Kt 1920; President of the Madras Corporation.
                                                       Died 28 April 1925

PITTS, Thomas, CB 1903; Assistant Secretary Local Government Board, 1897-1917; *b* 1857; *s* of late John Pitts, of Inland Revenue Department, London. *Address:* Taplow, Bucks. *Club:* Isthmian.
                                                       Died 5 Sept. 1919

PLANT, Morton F.; *s* of late H. B. Plant. Chairman of Board and Director Southern Express Co.; Vice-President and Director Chicago, Indianapolis, and Louisville Railway Co.; Vice-President and Director Peninsular and Occidental Steamship Co.; Director Atlantic Coast Line RR Co.; Interborough Rapid Transit Co.; Interborough-Metropolitan Co.; Lincoln Trust Co.; Windsor Trust Co.; Bowling Green Trust Co.; National Bank of Commerce of New London; Casualty Company of America. *Address:* 2 East 52nd Street, New York; Groton, Conn, USA.   *Died 5 Nov. 1918*

PLATT, J. Arthur, MA; Professor of Greek in University College, London, since 1894; *b* 11 July 1860; *m* 1885, Mildred Barham, *d* of Sir Edward Augustus Bond, KCB, LLD, and Caroline Frances Barham. *Educ:* Harrow; Trinity College, Cambridge (Fellow). Worked in Wren's, 1886-94. *Publications:* an edition of Homer's Iliad and Odyssey; translations of Aristotle's De Generatione and Historia Animalium, and Aeschylus' Agamemnon; various papers on classical subjects. *Address:* 5 Chester Terrace, NW1. *T:* Museum 5477.
                                                       Died 16 March 1925

PLATTS, Thomas, ISO 1902; *b* Chatham, 24 Oct. 1843; *s* of Thomas Platts, of Chatham, and *g s* of Thomas Platts, RMLI; *m* 1870, Sarah Ann, *d* of William Plumb, Tunbridge Wells. *Educ:* private schools, Chatham. Clerk, Paymaster's Department, 1st Division Royal Engineers, Chatham and Southampton, 1861-64; Writer, Chatham Dockyard, 1864-70; Admiralty, 1870-76; 2nd Division Clerk, 1876-95; Staff Clerk, 1895-1903. *Address:* Claremont Villa, 15 Decimus Burton Road, Thornton Heath, Surrey.
                                                       Died 13 March 1919.

PLAYFAIR, Arthur Wyndham; actor; *b* Elichpoor, India, 20 Oct. 1869; *y s* of late Maj.-Gen. Archibald Lewis Playfair and Isabella, *d* of J. Ord, Manchester; *m* 1912, Laurie (*d* 1917), *d* of Alexander Stevens. *Educ:* The Oratory, Edgbaston; Oxford Military College. Started on stage, August bank holiday, 1887; favourite part—Preserving Mr Panmure. *Recreations:* golf, lawn tennis. *Address:* 109 Park Road, NW.   *Died 28 Aug. 1918.*

PLAYFAIR, George Macdonald Home, MA; HBM Consul, Foochow, 1899; retired, 1910; *b* Shahjehanpore, India, 22 Aug. 1850; *s* of Surg.-Gen. George R. Playfair, MD; *m* 1884, Winifred May Fraser; one *d*. *Educ:* Cheltenham; Trinity College, Dublin. Entered Consular Service in China, 1872; Vice-Consul, Shanghai, 1891; Consul at Pakhoi, 1894; at Ningpo, 1894. *Publication:* Cities and Towns of China. *Address:* c/o Keymer, Son & Co., 1 Whitefriars Street, EC. *Clubs:* Thatched House; Royal and Ancient Golf, St Andrews.   *Died 29 Aug. 1917.*

PLAYFAIR, Rev. Patrick M., TD; MA (Edin.), DD (St Andrews); Minister of the First Charge, St Andrews, since 1899; Chaplain to the 7th Battalion The Black Watch, 1899-1921; Officiating Chaplain to Presbyterians on ships of the Royal Navy at St Andrews; Chaplain to the Royal and Ancient Golf Club since 1899; *b* 5 Nov. 1858; *y s* of Rev. D. Playfair (BA Cantab), Abercorn, Linlithgowshire; *m* 1888, Eliza Anne, *d* of late John Walker, WS; one *s* one *d*. *Educ:* Blair Lodge; Edinburgh University (Neil Arnott Scholar in Physics, Herbarium Gold Medallist). Assistant Minister in St Stephen's Parish, Edinburgh, 1882-86; Minister of Glencairn Parish, Dumfriesshire, 1886-99; occasional preacher to Queen Victoria and King George V in Scotland. *Recreations:* field botany, gardening. *Address:* Wyvern, St Andrews, Fife. *T:* St Andrews 63. *Club:* Royal and Ancient Golf, St Andrews.   *Died 6 Oct. 1924.*

PLEYDELL-BOUVERIE, Rev. Hon. Bertrand, JP Wilts; MA; Hon. Canon of Salisbury; Clerk in Holy Orders, retired; *b* 23 April 1845; 3rd *s* of 4th Earl of Radnor and Mary Augusta Frederica, *d* of 1st Earl of Verulam; *m* 1870, Lady Constance Jane (*d* 1922), 2nd *d* of 3rd Earl Nelson and Lady Mary Jane Diana, *o d* of 2nd Earl of Normanton. *Educ:* Harrow; Trinity Coll., Cambridge. Curate, Halesowen, nr Birmingham, 1869–70; Rector of Stanton St Quentin, nr Chippenham, 1870–80; Rector of Pewsey, Wilts, 1880–1910; held winter chaplaincies at S Raphael, 1910–11; Beaulieu, 1911–12–13; Madeira, 1914–15. *Publication:* A Childrens's Service Book—with Hymns. *Recreations:* water-colour sketching, wood and marble carving, etc. *Address:* 32 Stourcliffe Avenue, West Southbourne, Hants.
Died 7 Nov. 1926.

PLIMMER, Henry George, FRS, FLS, FRMS, MRCS; Professor of Comparative Pathology in the Imperial College of Science and Technology, South Kensington; *b* Melksham, Wilts; *m* 1887, Helena, *d* of Alfred Aders. *Educ:* Guy's Hospital. Late Pathologist and Lecturer on Pathology and Bacteriology, St Mary's Hospital, London; Fellow Royal Society of Medicine; Member Royal Institution; Fellow Philharmonic Society; President of the Royal Microscopical Society, 1911–12; late Prosector Royal College of Surgeons. *Publications:* Reports of Sleeping Sickness Committee of the Royal Society; various papers in Proceedings of the Royal Society; Centralblatt für Bakteriologie; Proceedings of Zoological Society; Lancet; Nature; Revue Scientifique; Science Progress, etc. *Address:* 32 Queens' Road, NW8. *Club:* Savile.
Died 22 June 1918.

PLOWDEN, Sir Henry Meredyth, Kt 1887; *b* 26 Sept. 1840; *s* of George Augustus Chicheley Plowden, Bengal Civil Service; *m* 1887, Helen, *e d* of late Sir Cecil Beadon, KCSI; two *d. Educ:* Harrow; Trinity College, Cambridge (BA 1863). Barrister Lincoln's Inn, 1866; Government Advocate at Lahore, 1870–77; Judge of Chief Court, Punjab, 1877; Senior Judge, 1880–94. *Recreations:* Harrow XI, 1858; Cambridge University XI, 1860–63 (Captain, 1862–63); University Challenge Racquet, 1862; Cambridge and Oxford Racquet, 1863. *Club:* Royal Societies.
Died 8 Jan. 1920.

PLUMMER, Rev. Alfred, DD; *b* Haworth, near Gateshead, 17 Feb. 1841; 3rd *s* of Rev. Matthew Plummer and Louisa, *d* of late J. D. Powles; *m* 29 Dec. 1874, Bertha Katharine, *d* of Rev. W. F. Everest, Canon of Truro; one *s* one *d. Educ:* Lancing Coll.; Exeter Coll., Oxford. Fellow Trinity Coll., Oxford, 1865–75; Tutor and Dean, 1867–74; Master of University College, Durham, 1874–1902; Sub-Warden University of Durham, 1896–1902. *Publications:* translations of several of Dr Döllinger's works, 1870–75; Introduction to Joshua and Nehemiah, 1881; Handbook on the Church of the Early Fathers, 1887; Commentaries on 2 St Peter and St Jude, 1879; St John's Gospel and Epistles, 1880–86; The Pastoral Episodes, 1889; Epistles of St James and St Jude, 1890; St Luke's Gospel, 1896; 2 Corinthians, 1903, enlarged 1914; St Matthew, 1909; St Mark, 1914; Lectures on English Church History: 1575–1649, 1904; 1509–1575, 1905; 1649–1702, 1906; The Church of England in the 18th Century, 1910; The Churches in Britain before AD 1000, 1911; The Humanity of Christ, and other Sermons, 1913; 1 and 2 Thessalonians, 1918; Philippians, 1919. *Address:* Dulany, Bideford, Devon.
Died 17 April 1926.

PLUMMER, Rev. Charles; Fellow since 1873, and Chaplain, since 1875, Corpus Christi College, Oxford; *b* St Leonards-on-Sea, 24 Jan. 1851; 5th *s* of Rev. Matthew and Louisa Plummer. *Educ:* St Michael's College, Tenbury; Magdalen College School, Oxford; Corpus Christi College, Oxford (Scholar). 1st Class Classical Moderations, 1871; 1st Class Final Classics, 1873; BA, SCL 1873; MA 1876. Deacon, CCC, 1875; various College offices at different times; Senior Proctor of University of Oxford, 1890–91; Ford's Lecturer in English History, 1901; Select Preacher, 1918–20; Hon. DD Durham, 1921; Hon. DLitt Dublin, 1923; Fellow of the British Academy, 1924; Hon. Member of the Royal Irish Academy, 1925; Hon. DLitt Celtic National University of Ireland, 1925. *Publications:* Life and Times of Alfred the Great, 1902; editor of Fortescue's Governance of England, 1885; Elizabethan Oxford, 1887; Baedae Venerabilis Opera Historica, 2 vols, 1896; Vitae Sanctorum Hiberniae, 2 vols, 1910; Bethada Naem nÉrenn (Lives of Irish Saints), 2 vols, 1922; Miscellanea Hagiographica Hibernica, 1925; Irish Litanies, 1925; Colophons and Marginalia of Irish Scribes, 1926; Devotions from Ancient and Mediaeval Sources, 1916; Joint Editor two of the Saxon Chronicles Parallel, vol. i, 1892; vol. ii, 1899. *Recreations:* walking, music. *Address:* Corpus Christi College, Oxford; 95 London Road, Salisbury.
Died 8 Sept. 1927.

PLUMMER, Sir Walter Richard, Kt 1904; JP; DCL; Plummer and Co., merchants; Alderman of Newcastle; Director North Eastern

Railway Co., Northern Counties Newspaper Co., Newcastle and Gateshead Gas Co., and of The Wallsend Slipway and Engineering Co., Ltd; *b* Newcastle, 8 Nov. 1858; *s* of Benjamin Plummer. MP (C) Newcastle-on-Tyne, 1900–6; contested same Division, 1906 and 1910. *Address:* 4 Queen Square, Newcastle. *Clubs:* Carlton, Constitutional.
Died 10 Dec. 1917.

PLUMMER, William Edward, FRAS; Director of Liverpool Observatory; Astronomer to the Mersey Docks and Harbour Board; Hon. Reader in Astronomy, University of Liverpool, since 1900; late President of Liverpool Astronomical Society; *b* Deptford, 26 March 1849; *y s* of John Plummer; *m* Sarah (*d* 1927), two *s* one *d. Educ:* privately; Oxford (Hon. MA). Entered Royal Observatory, Greenwich; assistant to Dr J. R. Hind at Mr Bishop's Observatory, Twickenham; senior assistant at Oxford University Observatory; appointed Examiner in Astronomy to the University of Edinburgh, 1895. *Publications:* On the Motion of the Solar System; Researches in Cometary Astronomy; Examination of Anemometer Records, 1896; Great Cluster in Hercules, 1905; Annual Reports from the Liverpool Observatory. *Recreation:* chess. *Address:* Liverpool Observatory, Bidston, Birkenhead. *T:* Neptune, Liverpool. *T:* 455 Birkenhead.
Died 22 May 1928.

PLUNKET, 5th Baron, *cr* 1827; **William Lee Plunket,** GCMG 1910 (KCMG 1905); KCVO; KBE 1918; DL, JP Co. Dublin; JP Co. Wicklow; *b* 19 December 1864; *s* of 4th Baron (Archbishop of Dublin and Primate of Ireland) and Anne Lee (*d* 1889), *o d* of Sir Benjamin Lee Guinness, Bt, and *sister* of Lords Ardilaun and Iveagh; *S* father, 1897; *m* 1894, Victoria Alexandrina, *y d* of 1st Marquess of Dufferin and Ava, KP; three *s* four *d* (and one *d* decd). *Educ:* Harrow; Trin. Coll., Dublin (BA). Honorary Attaché to the Embassy at Rome, 1889–92, Constantinople, 1892; retired 1894; Private Sec. to Lords-Lieut of Ireland, 1900–4; Governor of New Zealand, 1904–10. *Heir:* *s* Hon. Terence Conyngham Plunket, *b* 12 July 1899. *Address:* 40 Elvaston Place, SW7; Old Connaught House, Bray, Co. Wicklow. *Clubs:* Carlton; Kildare Street, Dublin; Royal St George's Yacht, Kingstown.
Died 24 Jan. 1920.

PLUNKET, Hon. Emmeline Mary; *b* 1835; *d* of 3rd Baron Plunket and Charlotte, *d* of Rt Hon. Charles Kendall Bushe. *Publications:* Merry Games in Rhyme from the Olden Time, 1886; Very Short Stories in Very Short Words, 1887; Ancient Calendars and Constellations, 1903; The Judgement of Paris, and some other legends astronomically considered. *Address;* 19 The Grove, Boltons, SW.
Died 6 April 1924.

PLUNKETT, Brig.-Gen. Edward Abadie, CBE 1919; *b* 1870; *s* of late Lt-Col G. T. Plunkett of Belvedere Lodge, Wimbledon; *m* Grace Mary, *d* of Col T. Morgan Martin; one *d.* Served in Nile Expedition, 1898 (despatches); Balkan War, 1912–13, as Military Attaché; Great War, 1914–19 (despatches); employed in Persia under foreign department Govt of India, 1903–4; Military Attaché at Belgrade, Sofia, Athens, and Bucharest, and chief of military missions at Belgrade, Athens, and Sofia, 1913–22; formerly Lincolnshire Regt; retired with hon. rank of Brigadier-General. *Address:* 8 Moore Street, Cadogan Square, SW. *Club:* Naval and Military.
Died 8 June 1926.

PLUNKETT, Lt-Col George Tindall, CB 1901; Royal Engineers, retired; Director of Science and Art Institutions, Dublin, 1895–1907; *b* 8 Aug. 1842; *s* of late Valentine W. Plunkett, Blackheath Park; *m* 1865, Emily Marian (*d* 1912), *d* of late G. B. Richardson, Blackheath; one *s* one *d. Educ:* RMA Woolwich. MRAS, FRGS. Entered army, 1862; Lt-Col 1889; retired, 1894; served Soudan, 1885. *Address:* Belvedere Lodge, Wimbledon. *Club:* Travellers'.
Died 2 May 1922.

PLYMOUTH, 1st Earl of, *cr* 1905; **Robert George Windsor-Clive,** GBE 1918; CB 1905; PC; DL, JP; Viscount Windsor (UK), 1905; 14th Baron Windsor (England), 1529; Lord-Lieutenant of Glamorganshire since 1890; High Steward of Cambridge University, 1919; Hon. Colonel of 2nd Glamorganshire Volunteer Artillery since 1890; of 2nd Battalion Worcestershire Regiment since 1891; of 3rd Battalion Welsh Regiment; *b* 27 Aug. 1857; *s* of late Hon. Robert Windsor Clive, MP Salop, and Lady Mary Selina Louisa, *d* of 2nd Earl of Bradford; *g s* of Baroness Windsor, and of Mary, *d* of 2nd Earl Bradford; *S* grandmother, as 14th Baron Windsor, 1869; *m* 1883, Alberta Victoria Sarah Caroline, *d* of Rt Hon. Sir Augustus Berkeley Paget; one *s* one *d* (and two *s* decd). *Educ:* Eton; St John's Coll., Cambridge (MA, Hon. LLD). Paymaster-General, 1891–92; 1st Commissioner of Works, 1902–5; Mayor of Cardiff, 1895–96; Sub-Prior Order of St John of Jerusalem. Owned about 30,500 acres.

Publication: John Constable, RA, 1903. *Heir: s* Viscount Windsor, *b* 4 Feb. 1889. *Address:* Hewell Grange, Redditch; St Fagan's Castle, Cardiff. *Clubs:* Carlton, Bachelors', Marlborough, St Stephen's.
Died 6 March 1923.

POCOCK, Sir Charles Guy Coventry, 4th Bt, *cr* 1821; *b* 3 Nov. 1863; *s* of Alfred George Drake Pocock (3rd *s* of 2nd Bt), and 1st wife, Mary, *d* of Charles Culverhouse; *S* uncle, 1915. *Heir:* none.
Died 31 March 1921 (ext).

PODMORE, Edward Boyce; *b* 13 June 1860; *s* of Rev. J. Buckley Podmore, BA, Rector of Cowfold, Sussex. Hunted with own hounds, riding nearly 18 stone; won prizes at boxing, rowing, riding, running, and bicycle riding; a pilot certificate of Shoreham Harbour, and Master of his own yacht; and recognised as one of the leading amateur four-in-hand whips of the day; ran his own coach, the "Star," between Kenilworth and Stratford-on-Avon 5 years, without being late, into either place; and late Master of Vine and Cotswold Foxhounds; joint Master, with Earl De La Warr, of Bexhill Harriers. *Address:* Petworth, Sussex. *TA:* Podmore, Petworth. *T:* Petworth 18.
Died 13 Jan. 1928.

POE, Admiral Sir Edmund (Samuel), GCVO 1912 (KCVO 1906; CVO 1903; MVO 1896); KCB 1908; JP for Queen's County; Commander-in-Chief, Mediterranean Station, 1910–12; *b* 11 Sept. 1849; *s* of William Thomas Poe, barrister-at-law, Glen Ban, Abbeyleix, and Curraghmore, Co. Tipperary; *m* 1877, Frances Catherine, *e d* of late Gen. Sir Justin Sheil, KCB; two *s* one *d*. *Educ:* Royal Naval Academy, Gosport. Entered navy, 1862; served in HMS "Bombay" when destroyed by fire off Monte Video, 1864; Captain, 1888; Naval Adviser to Inspector-General of Fortifications, 1889–90; commanded HMS "Imperieuse," "Blenheim," "Victorious", "Active", "Raleigh", and "St George"; in command of the Training Squadron as Commodore, 2nd class, 1897–1900; second in command of the Home Fleet, 1903; Commanding First Cruiser Squadron, 1904–5; Commander-in-Chief, East Indies, 1905–7; Cape of Good Hope, 1907–8; ADC to Queen Victoria, 1899; to King Edward VII, 1901; First and Principal Naval ADC to King George V, 1912–14; retired Sept. 1914; attached to Prince Arthur of Connaught's Funeral and Garter Mission to Japan, 1912 (Grand Cordon of the Rising Sun of Japan with Paulownia Flower); Member, Imperial War Graves Commission, 1917; received Royal Humane Society's bronze medal for saving life in 1875, and the clasp in 1876; Queen's Jubilee medal, 1897; King's Coronation medal, 1911; Grand Cordon of the Osmanieh; Grand Officer of the Legion of Honour. *Recreations:* shooting, fishing, cycling. *Address:* Black Hill, Abbeyleix, Queen's Co. *TA:* Black Hill, Abbeyliex. *T:* Maryborough Area, Abbeyleix II. *Clubs:* United Service; Royal Naval, Portsmouth; Kildare Street, Dublin.
Died 4 April 1921.

POLACK, Rudolph, JP; LLD (St Andrews); ex-President, Dundee Chamber of Commerce; Councillor, Dundee University College; Director, Dundee Orphan Institution; *b* 1842; *m* Franziska, *d* of Gustav Weil, Professor of Oriental Languages; one *s* one *d*. Mercantile education and career. *Address:* Glamis House, Dundee. *TA:* Polack, Dundee. *T:* 2450. *Club:* Eastern, Dundee.
Died 17 Feb. 1917.

POLAND, Sir Harry (Bodkin), Kt 1895; JP, DL; KC; *b* London, 9 July 1829; 6th *s* of late Peter Poland, merchant, London and Highgate, and Sarah Selina, *d* of Edward M. Jackson; unmarried. *Educ:* St Paul's School. Barrister, Inner Temple, 1851; Bencher, 1879; QC 1888; for many years one of the counsel to the Treasury and Home Office; retired from practice, 1895; Recorder of Dover, 1874–1901; for some years Alderman of the LCC; Hon. Freeman of Dover. *Publications:* Trade Marks: the Merchandise Marks Act 1862, 1862; (contrib.) A Century of Law Reform (lectures), 1900; various articles and letters on the reform of the law. *Address:* 28 Sloane Gardens, SW; 5 Paper Buildings, Temple, EC. *Clubs:* Garrick, Junior Carlton.
Died 2 March 1928.

POLAND, Vice-Adm. James Augustus; *b* 1832; *m* 1883, *d* of late W. O. Markham, FRCP; two *d*. Naval Cadet, 1846; served as Lieutenant and Gunnery Officer in the Baltic and Black Sea during the Russian War, 1854–56; in China War, 1857–60; in Naval Brigade at capture of Canton; also against the Taiping rebels around Shanghai, 1860; engaged as Senior Lieutenant in HMS Pearl in the attack and destruction of the forts and batteries of Kagosima, Japan, 1863 (promoted Commander); commanded HMS Plover on West Coast of Africa, 1868–71; Captain, 1871; commanded HMS Juno, China, 1875–79; Valiant, Coast Guard District on West Coast of Ireland, 1880–83; Duncan Flagship at Sheerness, 1883–86; retired, 1886; Rear-

Admiral, 1888; Vice-Admiral, 1893. *Address:* 4 Cresswell Gardens, South Kensington, SW. *T:* 1660 Kensington. *Clubs:* United Service, Junior Carlton.
Died 14 March 1918.

POLE, Sir Frederick Arundell de la, 11th Bt, *cr* 1628; *b* Dec. 1850; *s* of Sir William Edmund Pole, 9th Bt and Margaret Victoriosa, 2nd *d* of Admiral Hon. Sir John Talbot, GCB; *S* brother, 1912. JP Devon, 1916; High Sheriff, Devon, 1917. Owned about 4,600 acres. *Heir: cousin* John Gower Pole-Carew, *b* 4 March 1902. *Address:* Shute House, Kilmington, Devon.
Died 12 Feb. 1926.

POLIGNANO, 6th Duke of; **James Edwin-Cole,** JP; FRHistS; Barrister-at-Law; *b* 1835; 2nd but *o* surv. *s* of John Cole (*de jure,* Duke and Marquis of Polignano) of Easthorpe Court, Co. Lincoln, and Susanna, *d* of Capt. John Bourchier, RN (Lieut-Gov. of Greenwich Hospital) and 2nd wife, Charlotte, *d* of Thomas Corbett of Darnhall, Cheshire, and Elsham, Lincolnshire, and Elizabeth, sole *heiress* of Humphrey Edwin of Lincoln's Inn and St Albans; as sole *heir* and direct lineal representative of Elisabeth (*e d* of Don Gaetano de Leto, who inherited the Marquisate of Polignano (*cr* 1495), confirmed to him 1729 by the Emperor Charles VI of Austria, and who was in 1730 by that monarch created Duke of Polignano, with remainder to his descendants of both sexes in order of primogeniture), established his right in 1905 to these dignities, which had been dormant since the death in 1854, without issue, of Don Camillo de Leot, Duke of Polignano; *m* Mary Barbara (*d* 1910), *d* of G. Huddleston. Called to the Bar, Inner Temple, 1856. JP Lincs. *Publications:* The Genealogy of the Cole Family; A Genealogical Memoir of the Family of Bourchier; Memoir of the Family of Edwin; contributor under pseudonyms to The Herald and Genealogist, The Genealogist, Notes and Queries, etc. *Recreations:* historical and genealogical researches, horticulture, riding, Continental travel. *Address:* Brampton Manor, near Huntingdon.
Died 13 Sept. 1920.

POLLARD, Rear-Adm. George Northmore Arthur; Royal Navy; *b* 17 March 1847; *s* of G. A. Pollard of Castlepollard, Ireland, and A. D. Smith of Leicester; *m* 1880, N. E. Wright, *d* of Rev. G. Garrett of Kilmeague, Co. Kildare, and *widow* of Major Wright, 70th Regiment. *Educ:* Exeter. Entered Royal Navy, 1861; Lieutenant, 1871; Commander, 1885; Captain, 1894; Rear-Adm. 1905; served Canada, 1866 (medal with clasp); Ashantee War, 1873–74 (despatches, medals); Captain in charge, Ascension Island, 1899–1902; held the usual commands to the time of his retirement, 1902, under the age clause; no opportunity for special distinction. *Address:* Parkmount, Kent Road, Southsea.
Died Dec. 1920.

POLLEN, John, CIE 1903; VD; BA, LLD; Lieutenant-Colonel Bombay Volunteer Reserve; Barrister-at-Law; Hon. Fellow Bombay University; Commissioner of Customs, 1898, and additional member of Legislative Council, Bombay, 1902; President of Civil and Military Examination Board in Arabic, Persian, Marathi, etc, 1893; *b* 3 June 1848; *s* of John Pollen, Kingstown, Ireland; *m* 1880, Mary, 3rd *d* of Colonel T. T. Haggard, RA; two *s* two *d*. *Educ:* Stackpooles; Trin. Coll., Dublin. Entered ICS 1871; served as Assistant Collector and Magistrate in Khandesh, 1871; on famine relief duty in Bengal, 1874; on special settlement duty, 1876; Acting Under-Sec. to Govt of Bombay, 1880; Asst-Commissioner and Inspector-General of Registration and Stamps, Sind, 1881; Sindi translator to Government, 1882; Political Supt and Civil Judge, Thar and Parkar; Acting Collector and Magistrate, Hyderabad, 1887, of Broach, Ratnagiri, and Panch Mahals; Interpreter in Russian and Reporter General External Commerce, 1890; Junior Collector and Magistrate, 1892; Political Agent, Rewa Kantha; Senior Collector, 1896; Political Officer in charge of the fifteen Indian representative guests of Crown at Coronation of King Edward VII (thanks from Secretary of State); Special Correspondent Daily Mail, St Petersburg, 1905; President British Esperanto Association, 1904; on special duty with HH the Nawab of Radhanpur, 1906–7; President of Third International Congress of Esperantists, Cambridge, 1907; Hon. Sec. East India Association, 1909–20; Kaiser-i-Hind Gold medal. *Publications:* Rhymes from the Russian; Omar Khayyám; Russian Songs and Lyrics. *Clubs:* National Liberal, Northbrook, Polyglot.
Died June 1923.

POLLEN, Rev. John Hungerford, SJ; writer on English Catholic history; *b* London, 1858; *s* of late J. H. Pollen, MA, artist. *Educ:* Germany; Oratory School; BA Lond. Entered Society of Jesus, 1877; Priest, 1891; made prolonged archive studies at the Vatican, Paris, and elsewhere; a founder of the Catholic Record Society. *Publications:* Acts of English Martyrs, 1891; Papal Negotiations with Queen Mary Stuart, MS and the Babington Plot (Scottish History Society), 1901,

1922; Letter of Queen Mary to the Duke of Guise (*ibid.*), 1904; Unpublished Documents relating to the English Martyrs (Catholic Record Society), 1908, 1919; Institution of Archpriest Blackwell, 1916; English Catholics in the Reign of Queen Elizabeth, 1920; The Counter-Reformation in Scotland, 1921; also many contributions to The Month and the Catholic Encyclopædia. *Recreation:* sketching. *Address:* 31 Farm Street, W1.

Died 28 April 1925.

POLLEN, Sir Richard Hungerford, 4th Bt, *cr* 1795; JP; Hon. Lieutenant-Colonel 4th Battalion Gloucestershire Regiment, 1891; *b* London, 6 Oct. 1846; *s* of Sir Richard Hungerford Pollen, 3rd Bt, and 1st wife, Charlotte Elizabeth, *d* of John Godley, Co. Leitrim; *S* father, 1881; *m* 1875, Frances Anne St Albyn, *e d* of William Savage Wait, Woodborough, Somersetshire; two *s* one *d*. *Educ:* Eton; Christ Church, Oxford. Owned about 1,400 acres. *Heir: s* Richard Hungerford Pollen, late Lieut 4th Batt. Gloucester Regt, *b* 23 June 1878. *Recreations:* hunting, shooting. *Address:* Rodbourne, Malmesbury. *TA:* Rodbourne. *Clubs:* Carlton, New University.

Died 5 May 1918.

POLLOCK, Lt-Col Arthur Williamson Alsager; retired; late Major The Prince Albert's (The Somersetshire Light Infantry); *b* 3 July 1853; *o s* of late Major W. P. Pollock, RA; *m* 1881, Edith Laura, *d* of Copleston Lopes Radcliffe, Derriford, Devon; one *s* two *d*. *Educ:* Shrewsbury; Brasenose Coll., Oxford. Served S African campaigns, 1878–79 (medal with clasp); and Suakin, 1885 (medal with two clasps and bronze star); special correspondent of The Times in the Boer War; editor United Service Magazine, 1898–1920; conducted the training of the Spectator Experimental Company, March to September 1906; appointed to command 10th (Service) Battalion King's Own Yorkshire Light Infantry, 19 Sept. 1914; commanded the battalion at the battle of Loos, 25–26 Sept. 1915; invalided home on account of gas-poisoning; subsequently attached to various units to assist in training; served on the lines of communication in France, June 1917–Jan. 1919 (despatches). *Publications:* With Seven Generals in the Boer War; Simple Lectures for Company Field-Training; Elementary Military Training; Lord Roastem's Campaign in North-Eastern France; In the Cockpit of Europe; contributed to many magazines and newspapers. *Recreations:* (formerly) hunting, shooting, rowing (rowed in Brasenose College's Torpid, 1873 and 1874). *Address:* Eastway, Bishop's Waltham, Hants. *Club:* Junior United Service.

Died 2 July 1923.

POLLOCK, J. Arthur, DSc; FRS 1916; Professor of Physics, Sydney University, since 1899. Major, AE, AIF, France, 1916–18 (despatches). *Address:* The University, Sydney.

Died 24 May 1922.

POLLOCK, Rev. Jeremy Taylor, MA; Vicar of Brigham; Hon. Canon of Carlisle; Rural Dean of Cockermouth and Workington; Chaplain to Bishop of Carlisle; *b* 18 May 1850; *s* of Ven. W. Pollock, Archdeacon of Chester; *m d* of E. Waugh, MP, Cockermouth; two *s* three *d*. *Educ:* Haileybury; St John's College, Cambridge. *Recreations:* fishing, golf, chess. *Address:* Brigham Vicarage, Cockermouth. *TA:* Brigham.

Died 11 Dec. 1916.

POLLOCK, Walter Herries; barrister and author; *b* 21 Feb. 1850; 2nd *s* of late Sir (William) Frederick Pollock, 2nd Bt, and Juliet *d* of Rev. Henry Creed; *m* 1876, Emma Jane (*d* 1922), *d* of late Col James Kennard Pipon, Seigneur de Noirmont of Jersey; one *s*. *Educ:* Eton (King's Scholar); Trinity Coll., Cambridge (MA, Classical Tripos). Called to the Bar, Inner Temple; but taking to journalism, became firstly sub-editor, then (1883) editor, of the Saturday Review, which he left 1894. *Publications:* The Modern French Theatre, 1878; Verse, Old and New; Sealed Orders and Other Poems; Lectures on French Poets, republished from lectures given at the Royal Institution; A Nine Men's Morrice; King Zub; The Paradox of Acting (from Diderot with full annotations); The Charm and Other Drawing-Room Plays (with Sir Walter Besant); Mémoires Inédits du Marquis de—(in French); Jane Austen, her Contemporaries and Herself; The Ballad-Monger (stage version with Sir Walter Besant of Banville's Gringoire); Fencing, in the Badminton Library, with F. C. Grove and Camille Prevost; Animals that have Owned Us; Hay Fever (story with Guy C. Pollock); Impressions of Henry Irving, Alfred de Musset, and William Makepeace Thackeray in Encyclopædia Britannica, etc. *Recreations:* various outdoor sports, fencing and sword-play. *Address:* Chawton Lodge, Alton, Hants; 18 Old Square, Lincoln's Inn, WC. *Club:* Athenæum.

Died 21 Feb. 1926.

POLLOK, Rev. Dr Allan; Hon. Principal Presbyterian College, Halifax, Nova Scotia; *b* 19 Oct. 1829; *s* of late Dr Pollok, minister

of Kingston; *m* 1854; one *d*. *Educ:* Glasgow University. Licensed by Presbytery of Dunoon, 1852; went to Nova Scotia, 1852; in New Glasgow, 1852–73; Prof. of Ecclesiastical History and Practical Theology, 1875. *Publications:* Studies in Practical Theology, 1907; Short Family Prayers, 1916. *Address:* Halifax, NS.

Died 7 July 1918.

POLTIMORE, 3rd Baron, *cr* 1881; **Coplestone Richard George Warwick Bampfylde,** DL, JP; Bt 1641; *b* 29 Nov. 1859; *e s* of 2nd Baron and Florence Sara Wilhelmine, *d* of Richard Brinsley Sheridan, MP, Frampton Court, Dorsetshire; *S* father, 1908; *m* 1881, Hon. Margaret Harriet, *d* of 1st Baron Allendale; three *s* one *d*. Owned about 20,000 acres; possessed some good pictures: Gainsborough, Godfrey Kneller. *Heir: s* Hon. George Wentworth Warwick Bampfylde, *b* 23 Sept. 1882. *Address:* Poltimore Park, Exeter; Court Hall, North Molton, Devonshire; 8 Belgrave Square, SW. *T:* Gerrard 3386. *TA:* Broadclyst. *Club:* Marlborough.

Died 2 Nov. 1918.

POLWARTH, 8th Lord (styled 6th) *cr* 1690 (Scot.); **Walter Hugh Hepburne-Scott,** DL; Representative Peer for Scotland, 1882–1900; Lord-Lieutenant of Selkirkshire since 1878; late Convener of Roxburghshire; *b* Mertoun House, 30 Nov. 1838; *s* of 5th Baron and Georgina, *d* of George Baillie of Jerviswood and Mellerstain, and *sister* of 10th Earl of Haddington; *S* father, 1867; *m* 1st, 1863, Lady Mary Hamilton Gordon (*d* 1914), *e d* of 5th Earl of Aberdeen; five *s* five *d*; 2nd, 1915, Katherine Grisell, *d* of Rev. Hon. John Baillie (*brother* of 10th Earl of Haddington), Canon Residentiary of York Cathedral. *Educ:* Harrow. Owned about 6,000 acres. *Heir: s* Master of Polwarth, *b* 7 Feb. 1864. *Address:* Harden, Hawick, Roxburghshire; Humbie, Upper Keith, Haddingtonshire.

Died 13 July 1920.

POMEROY, F. W., RA 1917 (ARA 1906); sculptor; *m* 1913, Patricia Morrison Coughlan of Douglas, Co. Cork; two *s*. Commenced studying at Lambeth School of Art; entered Royal Acad. Schools, 1881; Gold Medal and Travelling Studentship for Sculpture, 1885; Medallist at Chicago Exhibition and the International Exhibition of Paris, 1900; made many public monuments in Great Britain and the Colonies, notably Robert Burns, centenary statue for Paisley, NB, and for Sydney, NSW; W. E. Gladstone for Houses of Parliament, Westminster; Duke of Westminster for Chester Cathedral; Archbishop Temple for Canterbury Cathedral; Dean Hole for Rochester Cathedral; Bishop Ridding for Southwell; Dr Guthrie for Princes Street, Edinburgh; the monument to Lord Dufferin and Ava, Belfast; Lord Curzon of Kedleston for Calcutta; General John Nicholson for Lisburn; also decorated many important public edifices. *Address:* 15 Kensington Square, W8. *T:* Western 1135. *Club:* Arts.

Died 26 May 1924.

PONSONBY, Noel Edward, MA, BMus (Oxon); Organist of Christ Church Cathedral, Oxford, since 1926; *b* 14 Jan. 1891; *e s* of Stewart Gordon Ponsonby (Rev. Chancellor Ponsonby), and Mary Catherine, *d* of late Sir Thomas Fowell Buxton, 3rd Bt and Lady Victoria Noel, *d* of 1st Earl of Gainsborough; *m* 1925, Mary Adela, *o d* of Rt Rev. Leonard Jauncey White-Thomson, Bishop of Ely; one *s*. *Educ:* St George's, Windsor Castle; Repton; Trinity College, Oxford. Organist, Royal Naval College, Dartmouth, 1912–14; Director of Music, Marlborough College, 1914–18; Organist and Magister Choristarum of Ely Cathedral, 1919–26. *Publications:* Five Short Pianoforte Pieces, 1917; Church Music, etc. *Address:* Christ Church, Oxford.

Died 10 Dec. 1928.

PONSONBY, Capt. William Rundall, DSO 1900; late 3rd Dragoon Guards; retired; *b* Aug. 1874; *e* surv. *s* of Col Justinian Gordon Ponsonby; *m* 1902, Lilian Patteson, *d* of late Sir Patteson Nickalls and Florence, *d* of T. S. Womersley; one *d*. Served South Africa in Thorneycroft's Mounted Infantry and SAC.

Died 18 Jan. 1919.

PONTYPRIDD, 1st Baron, *cr* 1912; **Alfred Thomas,** Kt 1902; JP; DL; LLD; retired merchant; Ex-President of University College of South Wales; *b* 1840; *s* of late Daniel Thomas, Penylan, Cardiff. Was President Baptist Union of Wales; Mayor of Cardiff, 1882; Freedom of Cardiff conferred on him, 1888; MP (GL) Glamorganshire, E, 1885–1910; Chairman of Welsh Members, 1897–1910; First President, National Museum of Wales. *Heir:* none. *Address:* Bronwydd, Cardiff. *Clubs:* Reform, National Liberal.

Died 14 Dec. 1927 (ext).

POOLE, Rev. Frederic John, MA; Rector of St John-sub-Castro, Lewes, since 1910; Rural Dean of Lewes, and Prebendary of Bishop

Hurst in Chichester Cathedral; *b* 15 June 1852; *y s* of Rev. T. Poole, Rector of Letwell, Worksop, and Mary, *e d* of Rev. T. Guy, Vicar of Howden; *m* 1881, Eleanor, *d* of Thomas Charington of Chislehurst; two *s* two *d*. *Educ:* Forest School, Walthamstow; Lincoln College, Oxford. Rector of Telscombe, 1901–10; Chairman, Newhaven Rural District Council, and JP, 1900. *Address:* St John's Rectory, Lewes.

Died 10 Dec. 1923.

POOLE, Henry, ARA 1920; FRBS; sculptor; *b* Westminster, 28 Jan. 1873; *s* of Samuel Poole; *m* Ethel Cogswell. *Educ:* King's College School; Lambeth School of Art; Royal Academy Schools. Studied under the late Harry Bates, ARA, and George Frederick Watts, OM, RA. Works on Public Buildings—Deptford and Cardiff Town Halls; Obach and Colnaghi's Art Gallery, Bond Street; the Wesleyan Hall at Westminster; memorials to Lord de Vesci, Earl Cowper, Sir Daniel Cooper; the statue and fountains of the King Edward VII Memorial, Bristol; the sculpture on the Naval Memorials at Portsmouth, Plymouth and Chatham; the Marble Statue, Giraldus Cambrensis, for the City Hall, Cardiff; Captain Ball, VC, Memorial, Nottingham, and many other works. *Recreations:* lawn tennis, badminton, billiards. *Address:* 1 Wentworth Studios, Manresa Road, Chelsea, SW3. *T:* Kensington 0570. *Clubs:* Arts, Chelsea Arts.

Died 15 Aug. 1928.

POOLE, Hon. Thomas Slaney; Judge of Supreme Court of South Australia since 1919; *b* Strathalbyn, South Australia, 3 July 1873; *e s* of Rev. Canon F. Slaney Poole, MA, of Adelaide; *m* 1903, Dora Frances, 2nd *d* of Rev. Francis Williams, MA; three *d*. *Educ:* St Peter's Collegiate School, Adelaide; Trinity College, University of Melbourne (Prizeman, Exhibitioner and Scholar). Scholarship in Final Honours Classics and Comparative Phil.; BA 1894; MA 1896; LLB 1897. Admitted to Victorian Bar, 1897; SA Bar, 1900; KC 1919; Lectr in Classics, Univ. of Adelaide, 1896; Lecturer in Wrongs, 1909–18; Warden, Senate, 1922; Member Council, 1924; Administrator of the Government and Acting Chief Justice, 1925; Chancellor, dio. of Adelaide, 1916–19. *Address:* Judge's Chambers, Supreme Court, Adelaide, South Australia. *Club:* Adelaide.

Died 2 May 1927.

POOLE-HUGHES, Rev. W. Worthington, MA; Warden of Llandovery College since 1901; Canon of St David's Cathedral, 1923; Rural Dean of Llangadock, Carmarthenshire; *b* Aberayron, 26 Nov. 1865; *s* of late William Poole Hughes; *m* 1914, Bertha Cecil, *y d* of late Richard Rhys; one *s* one *d*. *Educ:* Llandovery College; Balliol College, Oxford (Scholar). 1st Class Mathematical Moderations, 1886; 2nd Class Mathematical Finals, 1888. Master, Uppingham Lower School, 1888–91; Army Class Master, Sherborne School, 1892–1900. *Recreations:* fishing, fives. *Address:* The College, Llandovery.

Died 7 July 1928.

POOLER, Ven. Lewis Arthur, DD; Rector of Down with Hollymount; Archdeacon of Down; Hon. Canon St Patrick's Cathedral, Dublin, since 1916; Examining Chaplain to Bishop of Down; Rural Dean, Lecale East; Member Representative Church Body; Hon. Secretary General Synod; *b* 29 Jan. 1858; *s* of Rev. Canon Pooler, DD (descended from Captain Robert Pooler (*b* 1541), who settled at Tyross, Co. Armagh), and Angelica, *d* of Edward Leslie, BD, and *g d* of Charles Powell Leslie, MP, Glasslough, Co. Monaghan; *m* 1885, Augusta, *d* of Ven. John Charles Wolfe, of Forenaghts and Bishopland, Co. Kildare; one *s* one *d*. *Educ:* Armagh Royal School; Trin. College, Dublin. Classical Scholar, 1879; Double First Prizeman, Classics and Modern Literature; BA 1881; MA 1885; BD 1897; DD 1904. Senior Resident Master, Royal School, Armagh, 1882–84; Curate, St James', Belfast, 1884–89; Incumbent of Hollymount and Residentiary Preacher, Down Cathedral, 1889–99; Select Preacher, Dublin Univ., 1897, 1914, 1915, 1918; Donellan Lectr, 1902–3. *Publications:* History of the Church of Ireland, 2nd edn, 1902; Studies in the Religion of Israel, 1904; Eschatology of the Psalms, 1904; St Patrick in Co. Down, a Reply to Professor Zimmer, 1904; Down and its Parish Church, 1907; Social Questions, 1910; Urgent Social Problems, 1912. *Recreations:* tennis, fishing, sailing. *Address:* The Rectory, Downpatrick, Ireland. *Clubs:* Down County; University, Dublin.

Died June 1924.

POORE, Maj.-Gen. Francis Harwood; Royal Marine Artillery, retired; *b* 10 Nov. 1841; 4th *s* of Commander John Poore, RN; *m* 1885, Harriot Elizabeth (*d* 1888) (Lady-in-Waiting to the Duchess of Edinburgh), *e d* of 2nd Earl of Verulam; one *s* two *d*. *Educ:* Royal Naval School, New Cross. Entered HM service, 1858; served in expedition to Mexico in alliance with French and Spanish Forces, 1861–62; served in HM ships Racoon, Galatea, Sultan, Black Prince, and Minotaur; Equerry to the late Duke of Saxe-Coburg-Gotha (Duke of Edinburgh), 1881–91; Extra Equerry, 1891–1900; Colonel Commandant, Royal Marine Artillery, 1896–99; Retired List, with honorary rank of Maj.-Gen., 1899. *Address:* Priory Lodge, Andover. *Clubs:* United Service; Royal Naval, Portsmouth.

Died 19 Feb. 1928.

POORE, Major Roger Alvin, DSO 1900; Royal Wiltshire Yeomanry; *b* 8 July 1870; 3rd *s* of Major Robert Poore of Old Lodge, Salisbury, and Juliana Benita, *d* of Rear-Adm. Armar Lowry-Corry; *m* 1913, Lorne Margery, *d* of late Major R. F. W. Dennistoun; one *s*. Served S Africa, 1899–1902 (despatches, Queen's medal, 7 clasps, DSO); afterwards Resident Magistrate in the Transvaal; Deputy Commissioner of Police at Pretoria. *Clubs:* Cavalry, Arthur's.

Died 26 Sept. 1917.

POPE, Arthur William Uglow, CIE 1906; VD 1907; *b* 2 Aug. 1858; *s* of Rev. G. U. Pope, DD, MA; *m* 1886, Annie Catherine, *d* of Rev. J. T. Becher of Ballygiblin, Co. Cork. Late General Manager, Imperial Chinese Railways; Lt-Col (retired) Indian Volunteer Service; late of Oudh and Rohilkhand Batt.; Royal Engineer Volunteers (Railways). *Address:* Clyda, Bath Road, Devizes, Wilts.

Died 14 Dec. 1927.

POPE, Lt-Col Edward Alexander, DSO 1917; Commanding 3rd Battalion Welsh Regiment and 12th Service Battalion South Wales Borderers; County Councillor, Dorset, since 1904; *b* 1875; 2nd *s* of Alfred Pope, of South Court and Wrackleford, Dorchester; *m* 1904, Sybil Aline, *d* of Lt-Col C. J. Briggs, JP, DL, of Hilton Castle, Co. Durham; no *c*. *Educ:* Winchester College. Served in S African War, 1900–1 (Queen's medal 2 clasps); Assistant Provost Marshal, Vryburg; European War, 1914–17: France, 1916–17 (despatches, DSO); JP, Dorset, 1915. *Recreations:* golf, fishing, shooting, etc. *Address:* Woodbridge, Branksome Park, Bournemouth. *Clubs:* United Service; Bournemouth and County.

Died 9 April 1919.

POPE, Sir Joseph, KCMG 1912 (CMG 1901); CVO 1908; ISO 1906; Under-Secretary of State for External Affairs, Canada, 1909–25; *b* Charlottetown, Prince Edward Island, 16 Aug. 1854; *e s* of late Hon. William Henry Pope and Helen Des Brisay; *m* 1884, (Marie Louise Josephine) Henriette, *e d* of late Chief-Justice Sir Henri Thomas Taschereau, Montreal, and 1st wife, Marie Louise Sévérine Pacaud; five *s* one *d*. *Educ:* Prince of Wales College, Charlottetown. Entered Civil Service of Canada, 1878; Private Secretary to Rt Hon. Sir John Macdonald, Prime Minister of Canada, 1882–91; Assistant Clerk of the King's Privy Council for Canada, 1889; Under-Secretary of State and Deputy Registrar-General of Canada, 1896; attached to the staff of the British Agent on the Behring Sea Arbitration at Paris, 1893; was Agent of the Canadian Government at the proceedings of the Joint High Commission which met at Quebec and Washington, 1898–99; Associate Secretary to the Alaska Boundary Tribunal, London, 1903; HM Plenipotentiary at the Pelagic Sealing Conference, Washington, 1911; deputed by the Government to make arrangements for the tour of the Prince and Princess of Wales in Canada in 1901 (CMG); for similar services on the occasion of the Quebec Tercentenary Celebrations received CVO, 1908; attended Prince Arthur of Connaught in his tour through Canada in 1906, and Prince Fushimi of Japan, 1907; Grand Cordon of the Rising Sun of Japan, also the 2nd Class of the Japanese Order of the Sacred Treasure. *Publications:* Memoirs of Sir John Macdonald; The Royal Tour in Canada, 1901; The Day of Sir John Macdonald; The Federal Government; The Story of Confederation; Selections from the Correspondence of Sir John Macdonald, 1840–1891, etc. *Address:* 286 Stewart Street, Ottawa, Canada. *Club:* Rideau, Ottawa.

Died 2 Dec. 1926.

POPE, Colonel Philip Edward, JP, DL; *b* 14 Dec. 1842; *m* Alice Mary, 3rd *d* of Charles Taylor of Horton Manor, Bucks. Entered army, 1863; served Egyptian expedition, 1882 (medal, bronze star); Col, retired 1893; Sheriff of Bucks, 1906. *Address:* Churchmead House, Datchet, Windsor. *Clubs:* United Service, Cavalry, Junior United Service; Royal Yacht Squadron, Cowes.

Died 10 May 1916.

POPE, Rev. Richard William Massy, DD; *b* Bangor, 10 Feb. 1849; 2nd *s* of late Rev. Richard Thomas Pembroke Pope, MA; *m* 1878, Cecilia Mary (*d* 1918), *d* of Horatio Tennyson. *Educ:* Friars' School, Bangor; Worcester Coll., Oxford (Scholar). Curate of Marston, 1872–74; of St Giles', Oxford, 1874–86; Lecturer of Worcester College, 1874–87; Chaplain of Balliol Coll., 1879–88; Senior Proctor, 1884–85; Select Preacher, 1890–92; Censor of non-collegiate students, Oxford, 1887–1919; Censor Emeritus by Decree of Convocation, 1920. *Address:* 4 Keble Road, Oxford. *Club:* Oxford and Cambridge.

Died 6 Jan. 1923.

POPE, Lt-Col William Wippell, CMG 1917; *b* 1857; *s* of John Pope, Baring Lodge, Exeter; *m* 1917, Mabel Jennie, *o c* of George Whitwell, Durham. *Educ:* Sherborne School. Joined RAMC 1881; served Egyptian War, 1882 (Tel-el-Kebir medal with clasp, Khedive's star); Bechuanaland Expedition, 1884–85; operations in Zululand, 1888; NW Frontier of India, 1897–98, with Terah Expeditionary Force (medal with clasp); S African War, 1897–1900, operations in Natal, defence of Ladysmith (Queen's medal with clasp); European War, 1914–17 (CMG). *Address:* 93A Warwick Road, SW5. *T:* Western 3317. *Clubs:* Junior United Service; Devon and Exeter, Exeter.

Died 31 Jan. 1926.

PORRAL, Albert, CMG 1912; ISO 1903; Chairman of Chamber of Commerce, Gibralter, since 1910; late Commissioner of Crown Property, Gibraltar; Local Adviser of Anglo-Egyptian Bank, Ltd, Gibraltar; Consul for Russia at Gibraltar, since 1903; *b* 27 Aug. 1846; *s* of Michael Porral, Gibraltar; *m* 1873, Mary, *d* of Chevalier Jerome Saccone; one *d*. *Educ:* privately. *Address:* Gibraltar.

Died 7 Jan. 1918.

PORRITT, Edward; journalist and author; *b* Bury, Lancashire, 8 Dec. 1860; *s* of John Porritt and Elizabeth Longshaw; *m* 1891, Annie Gertrude, *d* of John S. Webb, Darwen, Lancs; two *s* two *d*. *Educ:* People's College, Warrington. Entered journalism on Warrington Guardian; reporter, Liverpool Daily Mail, 1881; chief reporter, London Echo, 1882–84; reporter and special correspondent, Globe-Democrat, St Louis, 1884–85; in gallery of House of Commons, 1886–92; London editor, Manchester Examiner, 1888–92; settled at Farmington, Conn, as history writer and contributor to press, and correspondent, writing on political subjects and giving personal attention and investigation to industrial developments in US and Canada; visited S Africa to investigate trade and economic conditions after the war, 1902; Correspondent with Canadian Tariff Revision Commn, 1905–6; lecturer at Harvard, 1908–9, 1909–10; University of California, summer session, 1910; Johns Hopkins University, Baltimore, 1916; member Society of Friends; Associate Editor Sell's Dictionary of World's Press, 1890–1912. *Publications:* Englishman at Home, 1894; Breakup of English Party System, 1895; The Unreformed House of Commons (2 vols), with Mrs Annie G. Porritt, 1903; Sixty Years of Protection in Canada, 1846–1906, 1907; Revolt against the New Feudalism in Canada, 1911; Barriers against Democracy in the British Electoral System, 1911; The Evolution of the Dominion of Canada: its Government and its Politics, 1918. *Address:* 63 Tremont Street, Hartford, Conn, USA. *TA:* Porritt, Hartford.

Died 8 Oct. 1921.

PORTELLI, Rt. Rev. Angelo, STM; OP; Titular Bishop of Selinonte; Vicar-General of the Archbishop of Malta; *b* Valetta, 1852. Joined Dominican Order, 1869; Priest, 1874. *Address:* The Palace, Valletta, Malta.

PORTER, Surg.-Col Alexander, MD; FRCSI; MRIA; *b* 7 April 1841; *s* of Alexander Porter, Beech-hill, Belfast; *m* Maud Mary D'Arcy, *d* of General M. K. Atherley, Colonel, the Gordon Highlanders; one *s* two *d*. *Educ:* Queen's College, Belfast. Entered Indian Medical Service, 1865; Civil Surgeon, Akola, 1866–74; Sanitary Commissioner, Berar, 1870–71; Surgeon, 4th District, and Professor, Medical College, Madras, 1874–86; Fellow, Madras University, 1883; Principal, Medical College, 1886–90; Deputy Surgeon-General, 1890; retired, 1895. *Publication:* Notes on the Pathology of Famine Diseases. *Address:* 26 Collingham Place, South Kensington, SW. *Club:* East India United Service.

Died 20 May 1918.

PORTER, Sir Alexander, Kt 1912; JP City of Manchester; City Councillor for Manchester; Barrister-at-Law; *b* Manchester, 27 Feb. 1853; *s* of James Porter of Manchester; *m* 1880, Mary Rachel, *d* of Robert Nuttall of Bury; three *s* three *d*. *Educ:* Owens College, Manchester. Called to the Bar, Middle Temple, 1905; Lord Mayor of Manchester, 1916–17. *Address:* 60 King Street, Manchester. *Clubs:* National Liberal; Manchester Reform.

Died 11 Oct. 1926.

PORTER, Rt. Hon. Sir Andrew Marshall, 1st Bt, *cr* 1902; PC (Ireland) 1883; Master of the Rolls, Ireland, 1883–1906; *b* 27 June 1837; *s* of Rev. John Scott Porter, Belfast, and Margaret, *e d* of Andrew Marshall, MD; *m* 1869, Agnes Adinston, *d* of late Col Alexander Horsbrugh, Peeblesshire; two *s* two *d* (and two *s* decd). *Educ:* Queen's Coll., Belfast. Irish Barrister, 1860; QC 1872; MP Co. Londonderry, 1881–83; Solicitor-General for Ireland, 1881–82; Attorney-General, 1882–83. *Heir: s* John Scott Porter, BA [*b* 18 July 1871; *m* 1906, Elaine Maud, *y d* of Thomas Jefferies, JP, of Newbay, Co. Wexford, and

Los Buyos, Buenos Ayres; one *s*. *Educ:* Oxford]. *Address:* Donnycarney House, Dublin. *Club:* Kildare Street, Dublin.

Died 9 Jan. 1919.

PORTER, Gene Stratton-; *b* Wabash Co., Ind., 1868; *d* of Mark Stratton and Mary Shellenbarger; *m* 1886, Charles Darwin Porter. Editor Camera Department of Recreation; on Natural History Staff of Outing; Specialist in Natural History Photography on Photographic Times Annual Almanac. *Publications:* The Song of the Cardinal, 1902; Freckles, 1904; What I have done with Birds, 1907; At the Foot of the Rainbow, 1908; A Girl of the Limberlost, 1909; Birds of the Bible, 1909; Music of the Wild, 1910; The Harvester, 1911; Moths of the Limberlost, 1912; Laddie, 1913; Michael O'Halloran, 1915; Morning Face, 1916; A Daughter of the Land, 1918; Homing with the Birds, 1919; Her Father's Daughter, 1921; narrative lyric poem, The Fire Bird, 1922; Friends in Feathers, 1922; The White Flag, 1923; Jesus of the Emerald, 1924. *Address:* Limberlost Cabin, Rome City, Ind., USA; 356 South Serrano Avenue, Los Angeles, California, USA. *T:* 560223. *M:* 529216.

Died Dec. 1924.

PORTER, John; trainer of racehorses; *b* Rugeley, Staffordshire, 2 March 1838; *s* of John Porter of that place; *m* 1st, Emily Jane (*d* 1902), *d* of Edward Moodie, Findon, Sussex; 2nd, 1903, Isabel, *d* of Herbert Pilsbury, Bedford. *Educ:* Mr Joseph Brittons, Etchinghill, Rugeley. Trainer of 7 Derby winners, and winners of stakes amounting to £794,017, the largest amount ever won by any trainer of racehorses; eight times second for the Derby and twice third. *Publication:* Kingsclere. *Recreations:* all kinds of sport. *Address:* Ormonde House, Newbury, Berks. *Club:* South Berks, Newbury.

Died 21 Feb. 1922.

PORTER, Dr John Fletcher, CBE 1920; JP (County of London); MB (Lond.); *b* 7 Jan. 1873; *e s* of Rev. John Fletcher Porter; *m* 1901, Ida Mary, 2nd *d* of late Rev. T. H. Richards; two *d*. *Educ:* Elmfield College, York; Yorkshire College, Leeds (Victoria University); London Hospital; London University. General practitioner; specialist in medico-legal work; Major, RAMC (1916); on Special Army Board for Functional Nervous Diseases, Neurasthenia, Epilepsy, etc; Acting Chairman of Board; with Sir John Collie formed the Medical Service of Ministry of Pensions, 1917, as a whole-time pensionable Civil Servant; resigned, 1920. *Address:* 206 Upper Clapton Road, E5. *T:* Clissold 1686. *M:* XO 3891.

Died 17 Feb. 1927.

PORTER, Captain John Grey Archdale, DSO 1915; 9th (Queen's Royal) Lancers; *b* 9 June 1886; *e s* of J. Porter Porter, DL, of Belleisle, Lisbellaw; *m* 1915, Enid Mary, *o d* of late G. W. Assheton-Smith, Vaynol, Carnarvon. *Educ:* Harrow; Sandhurst. Entered army, 1906; Captain, 1912; served European War, 1914–15 (twice wounded, DSO). *Address:* Belleisle, Lisbellaw, Ireland. *Clubs:* Cavalry, Bath, Ranelagh.

Died 22 Nov. 1917.

PORTER, Sir Ludovic (Charles), KCSI 1923 (CSI 1916); KCIE 1921 (CIE 1911); OBE 1920; *b* 27 Nov. 1869; *s* of L. Porter. *Educ:* Eton; Trinity College, Cambridge. Entered ICS 1887; City Magistrate, Lucknow, 1895; Magistrate and Collector, 1904; Secretary to Government of India, Department of Education, 1910–15; temporary Member Governor-General's Council, 1915–18; Executive Member of Council, UP Govt, 1921–24; Finance Member UP Govt, 1921–23; OBE for services in Mesopotamia, 1918–19; retired from ICS, 1924. *Address:* 26 Devonshire Place, Wimpole Street, W1. *T:* Paddington 2635. *Clubs:* United University, Oriental.

Died 9 March 1928.

PORTER, Maj.-Gen. Sir Robert, KCB 1921 (CB 1916); CMG 1919; MB; late Director of Medical Services, 2nd Army; *b* Co. Donegal, 31 Jan. 1858; *s* of late Andrew Porter; *m* 1903, Mary Phillipa, *d* of late John Johnstone, Barnard Castle; three *s*. *Educ:* Foyle College, Londonderry; Glasgow University; Paris. Entered RAMC 1881; served Ashanti, 1895–96, including capture of Coomassie (hon. mention, Star); S African War, 1899–1902 (Queen's medal 5 clasps, King's medal 2 claps); European War, 1914–18 (despatches 6 times, promoted Maj.-Gen. for distinguished service); Commander of the Order of the Crown, Belgium; Croix de Guerre, Belgium. *Recreation:* golf. *Club:* Royal Automobile.

Died 27 Feb. 1928.

PORTER, Robert P.; journalist and writer on economic subjects; special correspondent to The Times in South America and the Far East; *b* Norwich, 30 June 1852; *s* of late James Winearls Porter, Marham, Norfolk. *Educ:* King Edward VI School, Norwich; privately in America. Engaged in journalism, Chicago Inter Ocean, 1872;

expert US Census, reporting on wealth, debt, taxation, and on transportation, 1880–81; US Tariff Commissioner, 1882; editorial staff, New York Tribune and Philadelphia Press, 1884–87; founded New York Press, 1887–94; Director of Eleventh US Census; Special Fiscal and Tariff Commissioner of President McKinley to Cuba and Porto Rica, 1898; negotiated the arrangement with the late General Maximo Gomez for the disbandment of the Cuban army in 1899; joined the staff of The Times as editor of the Engineering Supplement, 1904; and as principal correspondent for North America, 1906–9; in charge of the Special Supplement Department of that journal; travelled extensively in North and South America, Mexico, Japan, China, Russia, the Balkans, Roumania, Turkey, and other countries. *Publications:* The West in 1880, 1882; Breadwinners Abroad, 1884; The Free Trade Folly, 1886; Life of William McKinley, 1896; Industrial Cuba, 1899; Dangers of Municipal Trading, 1907; The Full Recognition of Japan, 1911; The Ten Republics, 1911; Japan a World Power, 1915; Editor of Porter's Progress of Nation Series; contributor to numerous reviews, articles, and addresses before various scientific and educational associations in Great Britain and the United States. *Address:* Queen Anne's Mansions, St James's Park, SW. *Club:* Authors'. *Died 26 Feb. 1917.*

PORTER, Rev. Robert Waltham; Rector of Steeple Aston, Oxfordshire, since 1926; Hon. Canon of Chelmsford since 1914; *m* 1917, Monica, 3rd *d* of Rev. C. M. McAnally; one *s* two *d. Educ:* Brasenose College, Oxford. Vicar of East Ham, 1908–26. *Address:* The Rectory, Steeple Aston, Oxon.

Died 30 Sept. 1927.

PORTER, Col Thomas William, CB 1902; Colonel Commanding Canterbury District, New Zealand; *b* 2 Aug. 1844; *s* of late Major J. W. Porter of Demerara; *m* 1st, Herewaka Te Rangi Pala, a Maori chieftainess (*d* 1905); 2nd, 1906, Florence Ellen, *e d* of late J. H. Sheppard. Served NZ War, 1863–72 (medals); South Africa, 1901–2, commanding 7th and 9th NZ Mounted Rifles (despatches, medal and clasps, CB); Under-Secretary for Defence, 1904; Judge of Native Land Court, 1905. *Address:* Heatherlee, Gisborne or Wellington, New Zealand. *Died 12 Nov. 1920.*

PORTER, William Smith, MD; LRCP, MRCS; Consulting Physician, Royal Infirmary, Sheffield, and Sheffield Royal Hospital; Lieutenant-Colonel Royal Medical Corps (Territorial) (retired), 3rd Northern Hospital; *b* 24 Dec. 1855; *s* of late John Taylor Porter, FRCS, and Sarah, *d* of William Smith, JP, Barrister-at-Law, of Sheffield; *m* 1893, Jessie, *d* of late Charles Lockwood of Greno House, Grenoside, near Sheffield; three *d. Educ:* Repton School; Leeds Medical School; King's College Hospital; Durham University. Former House Surgeon, Royal Infirmary, Sheffield; Lecturer on Physiology and Medicine, Sheffield School of Medicine; Examiner 1st MB Examination, Durham University; Hon. Secretary and President of the Sheffield Medico-Chirurgical Society; President of the Sheffield Microscopical Society; of the Sheffield and District Press Club; of Sheffield Literary and Philosophical Society, 1926. *Publications:* Handbook and Guide to Sheffield, 1908; edited same, 1910; Sheffield Literary and Philosophical Society: a Centenary Retrospect, 1922; Notes from a Peakland Parish, 1923; some contributions to medical papers and pamphlets on local archæological subjects. *Address:* 8 Sale Hill, Broomhill, Sheffield. *T:* Broomhill 61489.

Died 5 Oct. 1927.

PORTER, Hon. William Thomas; *b* 21 June 1877; *e s* of William Porter, Preston Park, Sussex; *m* 1908, Edith, *o d* of late J. Johnson, Southport, Lancs; one *s. Educ:* privately; Jesus College, Cambridge. Barrister Inner Temple; went NE Circuit; Stipendiary Magistrate East African Protectorate, 1907; President District Court, Cyprus, 1911; Judge Supreme Court, Gold Coast Colony, 1915–21; Acting Puisne Justice, Cyprus, 1915–16; Justice Supreme Court, Ceylon, 1921; Acting Chief Justice, 1921; retired, 1924. *Recreations:* golf, tennis, yachting. *Address:* 47 Carlisle Road, Eastbourne. *Clubs:* West Lancashire; Corinthian Yacht.

Died 14 Jan. 1928.

PORTMAN, 2nd Viscount, *cr* 1873; **William Henry Berkeley Portman,** GCVO 1918; JP, DL; Baron Portman, 1837; Master of Foxhounds (Portman Hunt); *b* London, 12 July 1829; *e s* of 1st Viscount and Emma, *d* of 2nd Earl of Harewood; *S* father, 1888; *m* 1st, 1855, Hon. Mary Selina Charlotte Wentworth-Fitzwilliam (*d* 1899), *d* of late Viscount Milton (*s* of 5th Earl Fitzwilliam); four *s* three *d* (and two *s* one *d* decd); 2nd, 1908, Frances Maxwell Buchanan, *d* of Boyd Cunninghame and *widow* of Andrew James Livingstone Learmonth. *Educ:* Eton; Merton College, Oxford. Sat in House of Commons as a Whig, 1852–85; followed 8th Duke of Devonshire

in his secession from Home Rule party; 18 years Col West Somerset Yeomanry. *Heir: s* Hon. Henry Berkeley Portman [*b* 16 Feb. 1860; *m* 1901, Emma Andalusia Frere, *o d* of Lord Nigel Kennedy and *widow* of 5th Earl of Portarlington; one *d*]. *Address:* Bryanston, Blandford, Dorset; Wentworth Lodge, Boscombe; 22 Portman Square, W. *Clubs:* Brooks's, Travellers', Hurlingham.

Died 16 Oct. 1919.

PORTMAN, 3rd Viscount, *cr* 1873; **Henry Berkeley Portman;** *b* 16 Feb. 1860; *e s* of 2nd Viscount and Hon. Mary Selina Charlotte Wentworth-Fitzwilliam (*d* 1899), *d* of late Viscount Milton (*s* of 5th Earl Fitzwilliam); *S* father, 1919; *m* 1901, Dowager Countess of Portarlington (Emma Andalusia Frere), *d* of Lord Nigel Kennedy (*s* of Earl of Cassilis, and *g s* of 1st Marquess of Ailsa); one *d. Educ:* Eton; Christ Church, Oxford. *Heir: brother* Hon. Claud Berkeley Portman [*b* 1 Nov. 1864; *m* 1st, 1888, Mary Ada (marr. diss. 1897; she *d* 1900), *o d* of Major Francis Gordon-Cumming; one *d* (and one *d* decd); 2nd, 1898, Harriette Mary, *d* of William Stevenson; one *s* two *d*]. *Address:* Bryanston, Blandford, Dorset; 22 Portman Square, W1. *T:* Mayfair 1711. *Clubs:* Brooks's, Travellers', Bachelors'; Royal Yacht Squadron, Cowes. *Died 18 Jan. 1923.*

PORTMAN, Hon. Edwin Berkeley, BCL; Barrister-at-Law; *b* 3 Aug. 1880; *s* of 1st Viscount Portman and Emma, *d* of 2nd Earl of Harewood; *m* 1887, Caroline Ella, *d* of David Ward Chapman; one *d. Educ:* Rugby; Balliol Coll., Oxford (BA). Called to the Bar, Inner Temple, 1852; MP (L) North Dorset, 1885–92. *Address:* 46 Cadogan Place, SW1. *T:* Victoria 1796. *Clubs:* St James's, Wellington, United University. *Died 27 April 1921.*

PORTSMOUTH, 6th Earl of, *cr* 1743; **Newton Wallop,** DL, JP; FSA; Viscount Lymington, Baron Wallop, 1720; Hereditary Bailiff of Burley, New Forest; *b* 19 Jan. 1856; *s* of 5th Earl and Lady Eveline Alicia Juliana Herbert, *d* of 3rd Earl of Carnarvon; *S* father, 1891; *m* 1885, Beatrice Mary, *d* of Edward Pease, Greencroft, Darlington, and Wribbenhall, Bewdley, and *niece* of Sir Joseph Whitwell Pease, 1st Bt. *Educ:* Eton; Balliol Coll., Oxford (MA 1881). MP (L) Barnstaple, 1880–85; for N Devonshire, 1885–91 ((LU), 1886–91); Parliamentary Under Secretary for War, 1905–8; an Ecclesiastical Commissioner, 1909. Owned about 66,000 acres. *Heir: brother* Hon. John Fellowes Wallop, *b* 27 Dec. 1859. *Address:* 16 Mansfield Street, W. *T:* Paddington 4105; Eggesford House, Wembworthy, N Devonshire; Hurstbourne Park, Hampshire; Guisachan, Beauly, NB. *Clubs:* Brooks's, Garrick, Travellers', MCC, Burlington Fine Arts.

Died 4 Dec. 1917.

PORSMOUTH, 7th Earl of, *cr* 1743; **John Fellowes Wallop,** DL, JP; Viscount Lymington, Baron Wallop, 1720; Hereditary Bailiff of Burley, New Forest; *b* 27 Dec. 1859; *s* of 5th Earl and Lady Eveline Alicia Juliana Herbert, *d* of 3rd Earl of Carnarvon; *S* brother, 1917. *Educ:* Eton; Cambridge (BA). Formerly private secretary to Governor of Tasmania; Vice-Lt Devon. *Heir: brother* Hon. Oliver Henry Wallop [*b* 13 Jan. 1861; *m* 1897, Marguerite, *d* of Samuel Johnson Walker, Ky; two *s*]. *Address:* Morchard Bishop, N Devon. *Clubs:* Brooks's, Wellington. *Died 7 Sept. 1925.*

POSTGATE, John Percival, LittD Cambridge; Hon. LittD Dublin and Manchester; FBA 1907; Fellow Trinity College, Cambridge; *b* 24 Oct. 1853; *s* of late John Postgate, FRCS, and Mary Ann, *d* of late Joshua Horwood, surgeon, RN; *m* 1891, Edith, *d* of late T. B. Allen; four *s* two *d. Educ:* King Edward's School, Birmingham; Trinity College, Cambridge (Scholar; 1st class in Classical Tripos and Chancellor's medallist, 1876). Professor of Comparative Philology, University College London, 1880–1908, Univ. of London, 1908–10; Classical Lecturer, Trin. Coll., Cambridge, 1884–1909 (Senior Lecturer 1903–9); Deputy-Reader in Comparative Philology in Univ. of Cambridge, 1889–90; Prof. of Latin (subseq. Emeritus), Univ. of Liverpool, 1909–20; Corresponding Member of Virgilian Academy of Mantua, 1910; President of the Philological Society, 1922–26, and of the Classical Association, 1924–25; editor of Classical Review, 1899–1907, of Classical Quarterly, 1907–10; hon. editor of Riccardi Classical Texts, 1913. *Publications:* Select Elegies of Propertius, 1881; editor-in-chief of the Corpus Poetarum Latinorum, vol. i 1893–94, vol. ii 1900–5, including critical edns of Catullus, Propertius, Grattius, Columella X, Nemesianus Cynegetica, and (with Mr G. A. Davies) Statius Silvae; Lucan, book vii, 1896; Silva Maniliana, 1897; Preface and Appendix to English trans. of Bréal's Sémantique, 1900; Selections from Tibullus, 1903; critical edn of Tibullus, 1905; How to Pronounce Latin, 1907; Dead Language and Dead Languages, 1910; text and translation of Tibullus in Loeb Library, 1913; Lucan, viii (text and commentary), 1917; editor of New Latin Primer (completely revised edition, 1918); Sermo Latinus (enlarged edition, 1913); critical edition of Phædrus' Fables, 1920; Translation and Translations, 1922; Prosodia Latina, 1923; Guide to Greek Accentuation, 1924; On Ancient Greek Accentuation (Proc. British Academy), 1925; articles on Latin literature, textual criticism, etc, in Encyclopædia Britannica (11th edn); numerous papers in classical and philological journals, English and foreign. *Recreations:* cycling, walking. *Address:* 16 Brookside, Cambridge. *Clubs:* Author's, University of London.

Died 15 July 1926.

POTTER, Frank; General Manager, Great Western Railway, since 1912; *b* 1856. *Educ:* Cranford Hall Sch. Entered service of Company, as jun. clerk in Goods Dept, Paddington, 1869; was engaged for many years in various departments; Chief Assistant to General Manager, 1904–12; Member of Railway Executive Committee since 1914. *Address:* Great Western Railway, Paddington, W.

Died 23 July 1919.

POULETT, 7th Earl, *cr* 1706; **William John Lydston Poulett;** Baron Poulett, 1627; Viscount Hinton of Hinton St George, 1706; late 2nd Lieutenant, 4th Battalion Royal Welsh Fusiliers; 2nd Lieutenant Royal Horse Artillery; *b* 11 Sept. 1883; *s* of 6th Earl and 3rd wife, Rosa, *d* of Alfred Hugh de Melville; *S* father, 1899; *m* 1908, Sylvia Lilian, *d* of Fred Storey; one *s* one *d*. *Educ:* Cheltenham; Trinity Hall, Cambridge. *Heir: s* Viscount Hinton, *b* 23 June 1909. *Address:* Hinton St George, Crewkerne, Somerset.

Died 11 July 1918.

POUNDS, Charles Courtice, FRAM; actor and vocalist; *b* London, 30 May 1862; *e s* of Charles Pounds; mother well-known singer, under name Mary Curtice. *Educ:* St Mark's Coll., Chelsea; Royal Academy of Music. Solo treble at St Stephen's, South Kensington, and Italian Church, Hatton Garden; created parts of Fairfax in Yeomen of the Guard and Marco in The Gondoliers at Savoy Theatre; appeared at that theatre in all subsequent productions till 1892; returned 1894 for Mirette and Chieftain; joined Williamson and Musgrove's Opera Company in Australia, 1895; returned to London, 1896; played The Novice in La Poupée, following with the tenor parts in The Royal Star, The Coquette, The Snowman, and Wilder in a revival of Dorothy; the Clown in Twelfth Night; Ferdinand in the Last of the Dandies; The Minstrel in Ulysses; Sir Hugh in Merry Wives; Touchstone; the name part in a revival of Chilperic; Papillon in London and New York productions of Duchess of Dantzic; The Blue Moon; The Cherry Girl; The Belle of Mayfair; visited Berlin with Herbert Beerbohm Tree; appeared in Lady Tatters in 1907; Charles, his Friend; played Touchstone at His Majesty's, 1908; also in The Two Pins; The Dashing Little Duke; The Merry Peasant; A Modern Othello; The Spring Maid; Orpheus in the Underground; Princess Caprice; Oh! oh! Delphiné; The Laughing Husband; Chez Nous; The Bos'n's Mate; Lady Frayle; Chu Chin Chow; Abu in Cairo; Franz Schubert in Lilac Time; The First Kiss; Spring Time; Just a Kiss; Jed, in Shavings; The Toymaker, on tour. *Recreation:* golfing. *Clubs:* Savage, Green Room.

Died 21 Dec. 1927.

POWEL, Thomas, MA (Oxon); Professor of Celtic in the University College of South Wales and Monmouthshire, 1884–1918, subseq. Emeritus; *b* 1845; *o s* of Thomas Powel of Llanwrtyd, Breconshire, and Elizabeth Rowland of Penybont, Tregaron, Cardiganshire; *m* 1890, Gwenny Elizabeth, *d* of late Rev. Samuel Jones, Penarth, Glam; one *s*. *Educ:* Llandovery College; Jesus College, Oxford (BA (Classical Honours), 1872). Second Master, Independent College, Taunton, 1873–80; Head Master, Bootle College, 1880–83; Editor of Journal and publications of London Cymmrodorion Society, 1880–86; Examiner in Welsh, University of London. *Publications:* edited (with notes) The Gododin of Aneurin, by Thomas Stephens, 1888; edited (with introductions) Collotype facsimile of Bishop Morgan's Welsh Psalter of 1588, 1896; various articles and papers, *inedita,* etc, in Transactions of Cymmrodorion Society, Philological Society, etc. *Recreations:* cycling, golf, gardening. *Address:* University College, Cardiff; Aberystwyth.

Died 16 May 1922.

POWELL, Arthur, OBE 1919; BA, MD, MS; consulting physician; *b* 10 May 1864; *s* of John Donor Powell; unmarried. *Educ:* Trinity College, Dublin; Royal College of Surgeons, Dublin; Queen's College, Belfast. Professor of Medical Jurisprudence, Fellow and Syndic in Science, Bombay University; Prof. of Biology, Medical College, Bombay; Captain Indian Mounted Infantry, S African War; arrested in Germany, outbreak of European war; escaped Switzerland, returned England, Sept. 1914; Lieut-Col Indian Defence Force; Officer commanding Byculla Officers' Hospital, 1915–19; Consulting Physician for Tropical Diseases, Ministry of Pensions; Steward, Western India Turf Club, 1904–16. *Publications:* Practical Biology for Indian Students, four editions; chapters in Lyon's Medical

Jurisprudence, 6th edition. *Address:* 9 Harley Street, W1. *T:* Langham 1777; The Firs, Sutton. *T:* Sutton 1508. *Club:* Oriental.

Died 28 Aug. 1926.

POWELL, Rt. Rev. Edmund Nathanael, DD; Vicar of St Columba, Wanstead Slip, since 1921; Hon. Canon of Chelmsford, 1921; *b* Buckhurst Hill, 2 Sept. 1859; *s* of Nathanael Powell, JP, DL; unmarried. *Educ:* Winchester; Trinity College, Oxford (MA; Hon. DD, 1907). Curate of Chelmsford, 1883–87; Priest-in-Charge, Beckton East, 1887–91; Vicar of St Stephen, Upton Park, 1891–98; Bishop of Mashonaland, 1908–10; Vicar of St Saviour, Poplar, 1910–17; Vicar of Castle Hedingham, Essex, 1917–21. *Address:* The Vicarage, Wanstead Slip, Essex.

Died 11 April 1928.

POWELL, Ellis Thomas, LLB (Lond.), DSc (Lond.); FRHistS, FREconS, FJI, FRCI; Barrister-at-Law; for many years a Member of Council of Newspaper Proprietors' Association and of Empire Press Union; *b* Ludlow, Salop, 1869; *o s* of Thomas Powell and Harriet, *d* of Ellis Stanier Jones; *m* Rose Alberta, *d* of William Badams; one *s* two *d*. *Educ:* Ludlow Grammar School (Langfordian Scholar). Called to the Bar, Inner Temple; gave evidence before Marconi Committee; one of the London delegates to Imperial Press Conference, Ottawa, 1920; Member of London Diocesan Conference; Editor of the Financial News, 1909–20. *Publications:* The Essentials of Self-Government; The Management of Parliamentary Elections; The Mechanism of the City; The Sheaves of Empire; The Evolution of the Money Market; The Practical Affairs of Life; How to Pass your Exam; The Psychic Element in the New Testament; numerous popular manuals on investment and banking; thousands of leading and other articles. *Recreations:* music, public speaking, psychic research, the microscope and telescope, electioneering (chief Unionist agent in the longest election petition on record, and in Thanet, 1904–6). *Address:* Rosedene, Brondesbury Park, NW. *T:* Willesden 489. *Club:* University of London.

Died 1 June 1922.

POWELL, Admiral Sir Francis, KCMG 1902; CB 1894; Royal Navy; *b* 15 Sept. 1849; 4th *s* of late Arthur Powell of Milton Heath, Dorking; *m* 1875, Rebecca Wilson, *d* of late John Warren Glynn of Cape Town, South Africa; three *s* three *d*. *Educ:* St Andrew's Coll., Bradfield. Joined Royal Navy as Cadet, 1862; Midshipman, 1864; Sub-Lieut, 1868; Lieut, 1872; Commander, 1883; Capt., 1889; Rear-Admiral, 1903; Commodore, Hong-Kong, 1899–1902; Vice-Admiral, 1907; retired, 1907; CB for services in Benin River, W Africa; KCMG for services in China. *Address:* Clapton, Shanklin.

Died 5 Oct. 1927.

POWELL, George Herbert; *b* 1856; 2nd *s* of Rev. T. E. Powell, 52 years Vicar of Bisham, Berks; *m* 1904, Beatrice Mary Harding; one *s*. *Educ:* Uppingham; Trinity, then King's College, Cambridge (Classical Exhibitioner and Greek Verse Prizeman; BA 1879). Called to the Bar, Inner Temple, 1885; Associate Toynbee Hall (15 years Anti-socialist Campaign). *Publications:* Rhymes and Reflections, 1892; Excursions in Libravda, 1895; Duelling Stories from French of Brautome; La France Monarchique (40 selections from contemporary memoirs); Burlesques and Parodies (Pelopidæ Papers), 1912; Crown Prince's First Lesson Book (Rhymes on the War); articles in Quarterly, Fortnightly, Contemporary, Englishwoman, and other magazines. *Recreations:* book-hunting, singing, reading aloud, fives, croquet (manual), hockey (on ice), Guidebook Alpine climbing (first ascent of Pitz Albina, Engadine, out in famous and fatal Matterhorn storm (21 hours on Finster Aarhorn and glacier), 1881). *Club:* Savile.

Died 28 July 1924.

POWELL, Col James Leslie Grove, CBE 1918; VD; TD; DL, JP Surrey; retired Territorial Force; *b* 26 April 1853; *e s* of late James Powell, Chichester; *m* 1875, Harriette Charlotte (*d* 1908), *d* of Henry Huish, MD, Surgeon-Major 3rd King's Own Hussars; one *s* one *d*. *Educ:* Prebendal School, Chichester; Cheltenham College. Admitted a solicitor, 1874; CC 1910, and Alderman, 1919, Surrey; Lieut-Colonel and Hon. Col commanding 6th Batt. East Surrey Regiment, 1898–1909; Hon. Colonel of the battalion since 1909; Lieut-Colonel (temp.), 1914; Master of the Coachmakers' and Coach Harness Makers, Livery Company of London, 1922–23; Chairman Richmond Royal Hospital; Director of Richmond Royal Horse Show Society; Member of Board of Thames Conservancy. *Address:* Tapton House, Richmond, Surrey. *T:* Richmond 245. *M:* P 8037. *Clubs:* St Stephen's, Royal Automobile.

Died 28 Feb. 1925.

POWELL, Rt. Hon. Mr Justice John Blake, PC (Ireland) 1920; Judge of the High Court of Justice in Ireland, Chancery Divison, since 1918. KC 1905. *Address:* 41 Fitzwilliam Place, Dublin.

Died 13 Sept. 1923.

POWELL, Sir Richard Douglas, 1st Bt, *cr* 1897; KCVO 1901; MD; FRCP, MRCS; Hon. FRCPI; Physician in Ordinary to King George V, since 1910; Consulting Physician and Emeritus Lecturer on Medicine to Middlesex Hospital; Consulting Physician to Brompton and Ventnor Hospitals; Deputy-Chairman of the Clerical, Medical, and General Life Assurance Society; *b* Walthamstow, 25 Sept. 1842; 2nd and *o* surv. *s* of late Captain Scott Powell, formerly 23rd Royal Welsh Fusiliers, and Eliza, *d* of Richard Meeke; *m* 1st, 1873, Juliet (*d* 1909), 2nd *d* of Sir John Bennett; three *s* one *d* (and one *d* decd); 2nd, 1917, Edith Mary Burke, *d* of late Henry Wood. *Educ:* Streatham; University Coll. Hospital. Graduated in Honours, University of London, 1866. Physician in Ordinary to Queen Victoria, 1899, and King Edward VII, 1907; Hon. Fellow Royal Society of Medicine; Pres. Royal College of Physicians, 1905–10; late President Royal Medical, Chirurgical, Clinical and Medical Societies; Hon. LLD Aberdeen, 1906, Birmingham, 1909; Hon. DSc Oxon 1907; Hon. MD Dublin; KGStJ 1898. *Publications:* On Diseases of the Lungs and Heart; Harveian Oration, 1914, On Advances in Knowledge regarding the Circulation and Attributes of the Blood since Harvey's Time, etc. *Recreation:* outdoor exercise. *Heir: s* Douglas Powell, CBE [*b* 8 July 1874; *m* 1904, Albinia Muriel, *e d* of William Folliott Powell, Ripon; one *s* two *d*]. *Address:* 10 Cleveland Square, W2. *T:* Paddington 20. *Club:* Athenæum.

Died 15 Dec. 1925.

POWER, Sir George, 7th Bt, *cr* 1836; Professor of voice production and singing; *b* Dublin, 24 Dec. 1846; 4th *s* of Sir John Power 2nd Bt, of Kilfane, Co. Kilkenny, Ireland, and Frances Elizabeth, *o d* of William Blaney Wade; *S* brother, 1903; *m* 1915, Eva Gertrude, *d* of Sir Samuel Bagster Boulton, 1st Bt. *Educ:* Cheltenham College; Trinity College, Dublin. First studied singing in Milan and Florence, 1873–76; went on the stage as tenor; sang in Malta and Italy; then in first production of HMS Pinafore at the Opéra Comique. *Recreations:* music, travelling. *Address:* 31 Addison Road, W14.

Died 17 Oct. 1928.

POWER, Hubert; *b* 1860; *s* of late Patrick Joseph Mahon Power and Lady Olivia Jane Nugent, *d* of 9th Earl of Westmeath; *m* 1888, Maria Thérèse Aimée, *y d* of M Alexis Charles Toussaint Bourges; one *d*. High Sheriff of Co. Waterford, 1888. *Address:* Faithlegg House, Waterford.

POWER, Sir James Talbot, 5th Bt, *cr* 1841; DL; *b* 23 June 1851; *s* of Sir James Power, 2nd Bt and Jane Anna Eliza, *d* and *co-heir* of John Hyacinth Talbot, Castle Talbot, Co. Wexford; *S* nephew, 1914; *m* 1877, Gertrude Frances, *d* of Thomas Hayes, Grenville House, Cork; no *c. Educ:* Oscott College, Warwickshire. Chairman of Sir John Power & Son, Distillers, Dublin, established 1791. Owned about 1,300 acres in Co. Wexford. *Heir: b* Thomas Talbot Power. [*b* 3 May 1863; *m* 1884, Margaret, *d* of Thomas Martin, Stillorgan, Co. Dublin]. *Recreation:* coaching. *Address:* Leopardstown Park, Stillorgan, Co. Dublin. *TA:* Power, Dublin. *T:* 100. *Clubs:* St Stephen's Green, United Service, Dublin.

Died 4 July 1916.

POWER, John Danvers, MVO 1906; JP Bucks; Member of Council of the British Red Cross Society and of Malvern College; *b* 4 April 1858; *s* of Samuel Browning Power; *m* 1st, 1891, Ethelston (*d* 1924), *d* of late Thomas Owen Wethered of Seymour Court, Marlow; one *s* one *d*; 2nd, 1925, Mary Gertrude, *d* of late Sir Juland Danvers, KCSI, and Sarah Frances, *d* of Rev. Henry Rochfort. *Educ:* Malvern Coll.; Downing Coll., Cambridge. Barrister, 1887; contested (U) East Leeds, 1895; Chairman of the National Hospital for the Paralysed and Epileptic, 1903–5; Hon. Secretary of Sir Edward Fry's Committee on Medical Schools, 1904–5; of Queen's Unemployed Fund, 1905–6; of King Edward's Hospital Fund, 1904–7; Chairman International Red Cross Conference Committee, 1907; Editor of Red Cross Official Journal, 1914–18, and of the Official Report of the Red Cross and St John on Voluntary Aid during the War, 1921. *Address:* 8 Eccleston Square, SW1. *T:* Victoria 1861. *Club:* Carlton.

Died 3 June 1927.

POWER, Admiral Sir Laurence Eliot, KCB 1921 (CB 1916); CVO 1917 (MVO 1907); Royal Navy; Aide-de-camp to King George V, 1915; Director of Dockyards 1917–23; *b* Bramley, 7 May 1864; *s* of Rev. Henry Bolton Power; *g s* of Maj.-Gen. Sir Manley Power, KCB; *m* 1900, Muriel, *e d* of Sydney A. Want, Sydney, NSW; one *s* two *d. Educ:* East Sheen; Burney's. Entered Royal Navy, 1877; Midshipman, 1879; Lieut 1887; Commander, 1899; Captain, 1905; Rear-Adm., 1916; Vice-Admiral, 1920; retired, 1920; Admiral, retired, 1925; Shadwell testimonial, 1890; commanded HMS Dryad (navigation school), 1907–10; Master of the Fleet, King Edward VII Review of Fleet off Cowes, 1907. *Recreations:* various. *Address:* The

Old Vicarage, Corsham, Wilts. *Club:* United Service.

Died 20 Jan. 1927.

POWER, Hon. Lawrence Geoffrey, PC 1905; KC; LLD; Senator of Canada since 1877; *b* Halifax, Nova Scotia, 9 Aug. 1841; *e c* of late Patrick Power, formerly MP for Halifax County, and Ellen Gaul; *m* 1880, Susan, *d* of M. O'Leary of West Quoddy, Halifax County; two *d. Educ:* St Mary's Coll., Halifax, NS; Carlow Coll.; the Catholic University, Dublin; Harvard Law School. Admitted to the Bar, 1866; an Alderman of Halifax, 1870–76; School Commissioner for thirteen years; Member of Senate of University of Halifax, 1876; Speaker of Senate, 1900; a Director of School for the Blind, of Institution for Deaf and Dumb, of Halifax Visiting Dispensary, of Legislative Library, of Nova Scotia Historical Society, and of Game Society of Nova Scotia, of which last he was for several years president. *Publications:* Canadian Opinion on the Home Rule Question, Dublin Review, July 1886; The Whereabouts of Vinland, New England Magazine, Oct. 1892; The Manitoba School Question from the Point of View of a Catholic Member—a pamphlet, 1896; Richard John Uniacke: a sketch; a frequent contributor to the press. *Recreations:* formerly rowing, fishing, lawn tennis. *Address:* Halifax, Nova Scotia. *T:* 992. *Club:* Halifax.

Died 17 Sept. 1921.

POWER, Sir William Henry, KCB 1908 (CB 1902); FRS 1895; late Principal Medical Officer to Local Government Board; *b* 15 Dec. 1842; *e s* of William Henry Power, MD, Market Bosworth, and Charlotte Smart; *m* 1875, Charlotte Jane (*d* 1882), *d* of Benjamin Charles Godwin; two *d. Educ:* St Bartholomew's. Chairman Royal Commission on Tuberculosis, 1907; Member Royal Commission on Sewage Disposal; Member of the General Council of Medical Education, 1900–8; Buchanan Medal Royal Society for services to Sanitary Science. *Address:* Holly Lodge, East Molesey; 5 Old Palace Yard, SW.

Died 28 July 1916.

POWLETT, Adm. Armund Temple; retired, 1901; *b* 17 March 1841; *s* of Rev. Percy W. Powlett and Isabella, *d* of C. Wheler; *m* 1870, Horatia Frances Janet, *d* of F. A. Powlett; three *s* two *d. Educ:* Southampton. Entered Navy, 1853; in HMS Terrible during Russian War; in HMS Cambrian in China, operations in Canton river, 1858 (wounded dangerously at Taku Forts, 24 June 1859); commanded HMS Champion, 1883–87; commanded HMS Benbow, 1887–89; commanded Training Squadron (Active) as Commodore, 1889–91; Superintendent Sheerness Dockyard, 1892–94; second in command Channel, 1896–97. *Address:* The Manor House, Frankton, near Rugby.

Died 22 Jan. 1925.

POWNALL, George Henry; President of the Institute of Bankers; Member Foreign Trade Debts Committee; Member of the American Dollars Committee; *b* 3 March 1850; 3rd *s* of James Pownall, Manchester; *m* 1877, Margaret Haines Adin; no *c. Educ:* home; Owens College, Manchester. Union Bank of Manchester (Junior); Manager, St Ann Street, and Secretary of Bank, Manchester and Salford Bank; London Manager, Williams Deacons Bank; pupil of Jevons; President Manchester Statistical Society; first Chairman Council Manchester and District Bankers' Institute. *Publications:* Banking Statistics as a Measure of Trade; The Relations of Capital and Labour; Local Taxation and Government; Bank Reserves, the Central Stock of Gold and £1 Notes; The Insufficiency of our Cash Reserves; The Relative Use of Credit Documents and Metallic Money; Savings Banks and their Relation to National Finance; English Banking; Lectures at London School of Economics; numerous occasional articles on economic and social subjects. *Address:* Croham Mount, Selsdon Road, South Croydon. *T:* Croydon 2391. *Club:* Royal Societies.

Died 16 Dec. 1916.

POYNTER, Sir Ambrose Macdonald, 2nd Bt, *cr* 1902; Lieutenant Royal Naval Volunteer Reserve, 1916–19; *b* 26 Sept. 1867; *s* of Sir Edward John Poynter, 1st Bt and Agnes (*d* 1906), *d* of Rev. George Browne Macdonald; *S* father, 1919; *m* 1907, Cherry Margaret, *o c* of Lt-Col Joseph John Burnett, late South Wales Borderers and Army Pay Department; no *c. Heir: brother* Hugh Edward Poynter [*b* 28 Jan. 1882; *m* 1905, Mary Augusta Mason, *d* of Charles Mason Dickinson, USA]. *Address:* Botley, Hants. *Club:* St James's.

Died 31 May 1923.

POYNTER, Sir Edward John, 1st Bt, *cr* 1902; GCVO 1918 (KCVO 1913); Kt 1896; RA 1876 (ARA 1869); DCL, LittD; President Royal Academy since 1896; *b* Paris, 20 March 1836; *s* of Ambrose Poynter, architect; *m* 1866, Agnes (*d* 1906), *d* of Rev. George Browne Macdonald; two *s. Educ:* Westminster; Ipswich Grammar School. Studied art in English schools, 1854–56; Paris under Gleyre, 1856–59; Slade Professor of Art, University Coll. London, 1871–75; Director for Art and Principal of National Art Training School, South Kensington (resigned, 1881); Director of the National Gallery in succession to Sir Frederick Burton, 1894–1905. *Pictures:* Royal Academy—Israel in Egypt, 1867; Perseus and Andromeda, 1872; Atalanta's Race, 1876; The Fortune Teller (diploma picture), 1877; A Visit to Æsculapius, 1880; The Meeting of Solomon and the Queen of Sheba, 1891; Horae Seranae, Idle Fears, 1894; The Ionian Dance, 1899; The Cave of the Storm Nymphs, 1903; The Nymphs' Bathing Place, 1904; The Cup of Tantalus, 1905; Lesbia and her Sparrow, 1907; Brewing a Storm, 1909; A Naval Disaster, 1912; At Low Tide, 1913; The Sea Bath, or The Champion Swimmer, 1914; *portraits:* King Edward VII; The Duke and Duchess of Northumberland; Edward Pember, KC; Sir Edward Maunde Thompson, GCB; Mrs Dubose Taylor; Sir Frederick Eaton (Secretary Royal Acad.), 1913; Miss Doris Peterson, 1915, and others; and numerous watercolours, figure and landscape; two sets of designs for the new coinage, 1894; cartoons for mosaics of St George and St David in Westminster Palace; designed architectural and tile decorations for grill-room at South Kensington; Editor of The National Gallery. *Publication:* Ten Lectures on Art, 1879. *Heir:* s Ambrose Macdonald Poynter [*b* 26 Sept. 1867; *m* 1907, Cherry Margaret, *o c* of Major Joseph John Burnett, late South Wales Borderers and Army Pay Department]. *Clubs:* Athenæum, St James's. *Address:* 70 Addison Road, W. *Clubs:* Athenæum, Burlington Fine Arts.   *Died 26 July 1919.*

POYSER, Arthur Horatio, KC, MA; *b* 21 Jan. 1849; *s* of Charles Poyser of Summer Hill, Gwersyllt; *m* 1872, Alice, *d* of William Whytehead of Clifton, York; one *s* four *d*. *Educ:* Shrewsbury School; Christ Church, Oxford. Second class in Honour School of Jurisprudence; BA 1872; MA 1876. Called to the Bar, 1873. *Recreations:* golf, chess. *Address:* Burneston, Sydenham, SE26. *T:* Sydenham 642; 1 Temple Gardens, Temple, EC4. *TA:* 70 Temple. *T:* Central 9514.   *Died 6 June 1923.*

POYSER, Col Richard, DSO 1896, FRCVS; *b* 1842; *s* of Joseph Poyser, Wirksworth, Derbyshire; *m* 1870, Annie Maria, *d* of John Cruikshank of Ecclefechen, Dumfries; one *s* two *d*. Gazetted 1865; 7th Dragoon Guards, Royal Horse Artillery, and 6th Dragoon Guards (Carabiniers), with which latter regiment he served through the Afghan War, 1879–80 (medal); Principal Veterinary Officer, Chitral Relief Force, 1895 (despatches, DSO, medal and clasp); subsequently, till retirement, 1897, Principal Veterinary Officer, Punjab Army, India; rewarded by promotion from Lieut-Col to Col (1902) for services during operations in South Africa, and received the thanks of Earl Roberts, Commander-in-Chief. *Address:* 155 Victoria Road, Old Charlton, SE.   *Died 4 June 1919.*

POZZI, Prof. Jean Samuel; Professor to the Faculty of Medicine, Paris; Surgeon of Hospital Broca; Member of the Academy of Medicine; *b* Bergerac, Dordogne, 3 Oct. 1849; *m* Thérèse Loth-Cazalis; two *s* one *d*. *Educ:* Lycée of Pau and of Bordeaux; Faculty of Medicine, Paris. Grand Officer Legion of Honour. *Publications:* Clinical and Operative Gynæcology, etc. *Address:* 47 avenue d'Iéna, Paris. *T:* 660-18; La Graulet, near Bergerac.
                    Died 1918.

POZZONI, Mgr Dominico; RC Bishop of Tavia and Vicar Apostolic of Hong-Kong since 1905; *b* Paderno d'Adda, Italy, Dec. 1861. Went as Missionary to Hong-Kong, 1885; engaged in mission work in Kwang-tung, 1885–1905. *Address:* Caine Road, Hong-Kong.
                    Died 1924.

PRAED, Sir Herbert Bulkley Mackworth-, 1st Bt, *cr* 1905; JP, DL; *b* 2 May 1841; *s* of late Bulkley John Mackworth-Praed, and 2nd wife, Elizabeth Colthurst, *e d* of late Patrick Persse FitzPatrick. *Educ:* Harrow. Formerly Lieut King's Own Scottish Borderers; High Sheriff, Suffolk, 1886; Patron of Owsden; late a banker in London; MP(C) Colchester, 1874–80; Treasurer of Charity Organisation Society, and assisted in its formation; Chairman of Victoria Dwellings Association for Working Men; Treasurer and one of Founders of Working Men's Club and Institute Union, and interested in many other philanthropic endeavours; Chairman of Association of Conservative Clubs. *Heir:* none. *Recreations:* hunting, shooting, fishing, deerstalking, yacht-racing, golf, tennis, fencing. *Address:* 29 St James's Place, SW. *T:* Regent 1083; Owsden Hall, Newmarket. *Clubs:* Arthur's, Carlton, Bachelors', Turf, Beefsteak.

                    Died 21 Nov. 1921 (ext).

PRAGNELL, Sir George, Kt 1912; JP London (Newington). Commander Lieutenancy, City of London; Managing Partner, Cook, Son & Co., St Paul's Churchyard; Chairman, National Patriotic Association, Employers' Territorial Association and Wholesale Textile

Association; *b* 1863; *s* of late W. G. Pragnell, Sherborne; *m*; one *s* one *d*. *Recreation:* deep-sea fishing. *Address:* Grove Park, Kent. *T:* Lee Green 1351. *Club:* Royal Automobile.
                    Died 14 Feb. 1916.

PRATT, Edward Roger Murray, JP, DL; County Councillor Norfolk; landowner; *b* 3 Dec. 1847; *e s* of Rev. Jermyn Pratt of Ryston Hall; *m* 1881, Hon. Louisa Frances Mulholland, 2nd *d* of 1st Baron Dunleath; three *s* two *d*. *Educ:* Eton; Trinity Coll., Cambridge; (BA 1869). In boats at Eton; rowed for 3rd Trinity, Cambridge; travelled in N and Central America, N Africa, Caucasus, Armenia; Special Commissioner for Stafford House Ottoman Relief Committee, 1879; Russo-Turkish War (received war medal; 3rd class Osmanie; 3rd class Medjidie); Colonel (retired) PWO Norfolk Artillery; Past President Royal English Arboricultural Society; Order of St John of Jerusalem. *Recreations:* shooting, estate management, forestry. *Address:* Ryston Hall, Downham. *Club:* Brooks's.
                    Died 20 Nov. 1921.

PRATT, Brig.-Gen. (Ernest) St George, CB 1916; DSO 1902; Durham Light Infantry; Inspector of Infantry; *b* 3 Sept. 1863; *y s* of late Spencer Pratt of Stanwick House, Higham Ferrers; *m* 1902, Edith, *d* of late Capt. H. P. Andrew, 8th Hussars; one *d*. Entered army, 1884; Captain, 1894; Major, 1903; Lt-Col 1910; Col 1913; served South Africa, 1899–1902 (despatches three times, DSO, brevet Major). *Address:* 15 Wilton Street, SW1. *Club:* Naval and Military.
                    Died 24 Nov. 1918.

PRATT, Col Henry Marsh, CB 1889; Unemployed Super-numerary list; *b* 24 Oct. 1838; *s* of Rev. William Pratt of Harpley, Norfolk; *m* 1891, Evelyn Margaret, 2nd *d* of Clayton William Feake Glyn, Durrington House, Harlow; two *d*. *Educ:* Marlborough. Arrived in India as Direct Cadet, 1856; present at mutiny of his regt, 51st Bengal Infantry, 1857 (medal); served in campaign, N China, 1860 (medal and 2 clasps, "Taku Forts" and "Pekin"; served in Afghanistan, 1878–79–80 (medal 4 clasps, "Piewar", "Charasiab", "Kabul, 1879", "Kandshar", despatches); Brevet of Lieut-Col, bronze star, for (Earl) Roberts march; commanded column in Black Mountain expedition, 1888 (medal and clasp, despatches). *Decorated* for distinguished service in the field; granted a good service pension for distinguished and meritorious service, 1893. *Recreations:* country sports in general. *Address:* 24 Sussex Mansions, South Kensington, SW. *T:* Kensington 6103. *Club:* United Service.   *Died 16 April 1919.*

PRATT, Surg.-Gen. William Simson, CB 1906; MB; late Principal Medical Officer, Southern Command; *b* 21 Jan. 1849; *s* of Gen. Sir Thomas Simson Pratt, KCB; *m* 1884, Mary Isabel Pollock, Adelaide, SA. Lt-Col RAMC 1893; Col 1902; served Soudan, 1884–85 (despatches, medal with clasp, bronze star, promoted Surgeon-Major); PMO Gibraltar, 1900–2; Administrative Medical Officer, 1902. *Club:* Junior United Service.   *Died 8 Sept. 1917.*

PRATTEN, Herbert Edward; Minister for Trade and Customs, Commonwealth of Australia, since 1924; *b* Downland, near Bristol, 7 May 1865; *m* Agnes, *d* of late J. P. Wright, Sydney; two *s* three *d*. *Educ:* Merchant Venturers School, Bristol. Left England for Australia when 20 years old; had a successful mercantile, manufacturing and mining career there; 7 years in municipal life; 3 times a Mayor; 3 years President of the Manufacturers' Association; member of the British Parliamentary Munitions Committee, 1915–16; elected to the Commonwealth Senate, 1917; resigned; elected to the House of Representatives, 1921. *Publications:* (brochures): Asiatic Impressions; Through Orient to Occident. *Recreation:* fishing. *Address:* Canberra, Australia.   *Died 7 May 1928.*

PREECE, John Richard, CMG 1899; FRGS; *b* 1843; *s* of late R. M. Preece; *m* 1916, Mary, *d* of David Graham-Allardice and *widow* of G. G. Duncan. *Educ:* private school; Imperial College, France. Assistant Traffic Manager, Indo-European Telegraph Department, Teheran, 1868; joined Consular Service, 1891; British Consul at Ispahan, 1891; Consul-General, 1900–6; Member Electrical Engineers Society; read papers in the societies to which he belonged on Persian travel and telegraphs. *Address:* 46 Bullingham Mansions, Kensington, W. *Clubs:* Royal Societies', Junior Constitutional, MCC and Surrey CC.   *Died 25 Feb. 1917.*

PRENDERGAST, Maj.-Gen. Guy Annesley; Indian Army; Colonel, 15th Lancers, since 1904; *b* 11 March 1834; *m* 1858, Catherine (*d* 1902), *d* of late Major Philip Cortlandt Anderson. Entered army, 1850; Maj.-Gen. 1891; unemployed list, 1893; served Indian Mutiny, 1858 (despatches, medal); Afghan War, 1879 (medal). *Address:* 6 Bramham Gardens, SW.   *Died 8 July 1919.*

PRENDERGAST, Hon. Sir James, Kt 1881; *b* 1828; *s* of Michael Prendergast, QC, and Caroline Dance. *Educ:* St Paul's School; Queens' Coll., Cambrige (BA 1850). Barrister Middle Temple, 1856; Chief Justice of New Zealand, 1875-99. *Address:* Bolton Street, Wellington, New Zealand.   *Died 1 Feb. 1921.*

PRENDERVILLE, Arthur de, LLB; MRCS; Anæsthetist to Charing Cross Hospital, the Throat Hospital, Golden Square, W, and the Acheson Military Hospital, NW; *b* St Helena, South Atlantic; *s* of Major J. H. de Prenderville, late of St Helena Regt, and afterwards Inspector-General of Constabulary, Jamaica, WI. *Educ:* Stonyhurst; St Mary's Hospital, London. Formerly Medical Staff Imperial Maritime Customs, Amoy, S China; Port Surgeon, Perim, Red Sea; later on staff of Prince of Wales's Hospital, N, and Teacher of Anæsthetics in North-West London Post-Graduate College; Examiner to the British Red Cross Society, London; Acting Medical Officer to the Marconi Company, Ltd; Fellow Royal Society of Medicine; Member British Medical Association. *Publications:* The Place of Ether in General Practice; Anæsthetic Technique for Operations on Nose and Throat; Anæesthesia and the Nurse's Duties, 1917; Versiculi Medicinæ, etc; A Life Tragedy and Other Verses; Lyrics of the Streets; reports of Chinese Hospital, Amoy, 1892-97; contributions to various professional journals. *Recreations:* music, historical research. *Address:* 54 Wimpole Street, W1. *T:* Mayfair 566.   *Died 4 Jan. 1919.*

PRESCOTT, Ven. John Eustace, DD; Archdeacon and Canon of Carlisle since 1883; Chancellor of Diocese of Carlisle since 1900; *b* Wakefield, Yorkshire; *e s* of George Prescott, Gibraltar, and Phœbe, *d* of Rev. Dr Naylor, Crofton, Yorkshire; *m* Rosalie (*d* 1919). *Educ:* Peterborough; Corpus Christi Coll., Cambridge. 12th Wrangler, 1855; Scholar and Fellow Corpus Christi College. Ordained, 1858; Vicar of St Edward's, Cambridge, 1868-71; Examining Chaplain to Bishop of Carlisle (Goodwin), 1869-91; St Mary's, Carlisle, 1877-79. *Publications:* Statutes of Carlisle Cathedral, 2nd edn 1903; Christian Hymns and Hymn Writers, 2nd edn 1886; Visitations in Ancient Diocese of Carlisle, 1888; Register of Wetherhal, 1897. *Address:* The Abbey, Carlisle.   *Died 17 Feb. 1920.*

PRESGRAVE, Col Edward Robert John, CB 1908; DSO 1895; *b* London, 29 June 1855; *o s* of late Lieut Edward Presgrave, HEICS (retired). *Educ:* Wellington College. Joined 21st Regiment, 1875; admitted to Madras Staff Corps, 1879; Adjt 15th Madras Infantry, 1882-86; Capt. 1886; Brevet Major, 1893; Major, 1895; temporary Lieut-Col, 1895; Lt-Col 1901; Col 1904; employed Rumpa Rebellion, 1879; Afghan Campaign, 1879-80 (medal); Burma, 1886-87-89 (medal and 2 clasps); Manipur Expedition, 1891 (clasp); Chin Hills, 1892-94 (despatches, Bt Major DSO, clasp); Commandant 10th Gurkha Rifles, 1893-1902; Brigade Staff, India, 1900-1; Divisional Staff, India, 1902-6; special appointment, Nov. 1914—graded as GSO 3rd Class, 1917 (despatches). *Club:* East India United Service.   *Died 12 Sept. 1919.*

PRESSLY, David Leith; editor Yorkshire Herald and allied newspapers, York, since 1903; *b* Stuartfield, Aberdeenshire, 14 July 1855; father, carpenter and crofter; *m;* two *s* five *d. Educ:* Old Deer Public School; Aberdeen schools. Reporter in Aberdeen, 1872; connected with Aberdeen Free Press and People's Journal till 1880; went out to Cape Colony; was on staff of Cape Times; 14 years in Ulster as editor Londonderry Sentinel, and leader-writer on Evening Telegraph, Belfast; editor of Aberdeen Daily Journal and Aberdeen Evening Express, 1894-1902; managing editor of East of England Newspaper Company's series of daily and weekly papers, Norwich, 1902-3; organized and edited the King's Book of York Heroes as war memorial, 1920. *Recreations:* painting, sketching, gardening. *Address:* Holgate House, York. *T:* York 452.

Died 11 April 1922.

PRESTON, Henry Edward; JP East and West Riding of Yorks; *b* July 1857; *o s* of Thomas Henry Preston of Moreby, Yorks, and Georgina Geneviève Louisa, 3rd *d* of Sir Guy Campbell, 1st Bt; *m* 1886, Beatrice, 3rd *d* of Archbishop Thomson of York; one *s* one *d. Educ:* Eton. *Publication:* editor of Foxhound Kennel Stud Book. *Address:* Moreby Park, York. *Club:* Yorkshire.

Died 5 June 1924.

PRESTON, Sir Jacob, 4th Bt, *cr* 1815; partner firm of Loewen, Harvey, and Preston, Ltd, Vancouver, British Columbia; *b* 6 May 1887; *s* of Sir Henry Jacob Preston, 3rd Bt and Mary Hope, *d* of late Edmund Lewis Clutterbuck, Hardenhuish Park, Wiltshire; *S* father, 1897. *Educ:* Eton; Trinity College, Cambridge (BA, LLB). Owned about 6,000 acres. *Heir: brother* Edward Hulton Preston, Lieut 2nd

Batt. Royal Sussex Regt, *b* 17 Sept. 1888. *Address:* Barton Hall, Neatishead, Norwich. *Club:* Bath.

Died 12 Feb. 1918.

PRETYMAN, Maj.-Gen. Sir George Tindal, KCMG 1900; CB 1896; *b* 1 March 1845; *e s* of late Rev. John Radclyffe Pretyman, MA, formerly Vicar of Aylesbury, and Amelia, *d* of Thomas Tindal, of Prebendal House, Aylesbury; *m* 1889, Winifred, *d* of late Frederick Locke, JP, DL, Kent, of Dane House, Hartlip, Sittingbourne; two *s. Educ:* Wimbledon School; RMA Woolwich. Joined RA 1865; served Canada during Fenian Raids, 1866 and 1870 (medal and 2 clasps); ADC to Gen. Sir Frederick Roberts (1st Earl Roberts) during Afghan War, 1878-80 (despatches thrice, Afghan medal and threeclasps, bronze star for march from Kabul to Kandahar, brevets of Major and Lieut-Colonel); Military Secretary to Sir Frederick Roberts in Madras, 1881-84; AAG for RA in India, 1887-89; commanded a 2nd class district, Bengal, 1889-94, with rank of Brigadier-General; commanded 1st Infantry Brigade, Isazai Expedition, 1892; Major-Gen. 1897; Commandant at Headquarters, South Africa, 1899-1900 (despatches twice); Military Governor, Bloemfontein, 1900; commanded Kimberley District, 1901 (medal, 4 clasps, KCMG); commanded Secunderabad District, India, 1902-3; Forces in Madras, 1904; Burma Division, 1906; retired 1907; Colonel Commandant, Royal Artillery, 1908; Distinguished Service Reward, 1903. *Recreations:* shooting, riding, sport generally. *Address:* Beech Hurst, Camberley. *Club:* United Service.

Died 3 Aug. 1917.

PRICE, Sir Charles Rugge-, 6th Bt, *cr* 1804; DL, JP; late Hon. Colonel 3rd Battalion East Surrey Regiment; *b* 26 May 1841; *o s* of Sir Arthur James Rugge-Price, 5th Bt and 1st *cousin,* Mary, *d* of Richard Price, South Lambeth; *S* father, 1892; *m* 1867, Antonia Mary (*d* 1918), *d* of William James Harvey, of Carnousie, Co. Banff; one *s* four *d* (and one *s* one *d* decd). *Educ:* Harrow. *Heir: s* Charles Frederick Price, late Lt-Col Royal Field Artillery [*b* 5 Feb. 1868; *m* 1901, Isabella Napier Keith, *e d* of Maj.-Gen. Sir James Keith Trotter, KCB; two *s* two *d*]. *Address:* Spring Grove, Richmond, Surrey.

Died 4 May 1927.

PRICE, Commander George Edward; Royal Navy, retired; *b* France, 1842; *s* of late George Price (*s* of Sir Rose Price, 1st Bt, of Trengwainton), and 1st wife, Hon. Emily Valentine Plunkett, *d* of 14th Lord Dunsany; *m* 1873, Gertrude Laurence, adopted *d* of Phoebe Locke, (*widow* of Joseph Locke, MP); three *d.* MP(C), Devonport, 1874-92. *Address:* Thorpe Place, Chertsey. *Clubs:* Carlton, Wellington.   *Died 29 June 1926.*

PRICE, Sir (John) Frederick, KCSI 1898 (CSI 1893); *b* 3 Oct. 1839; *e s* of late John Price (4th *s* of Sir Rose Price, of Trengwainton, 1st Bt), and Mary, *d* of Major James Franklin; *m* 1863, Alice, *y d* of Hon. H. D. Phillips, Member of Council, Fort St George, Madras; three *s* three *d. Educ:* Melbourne University. Entered Madras Civil Service, 1862; retired, 1897. *Publications:* Ootacamund, a History; editor of the first three volumes of Ananda Ranga Pillais Diary. *Address:* Trengwainton, Exmouth, South Devon.

Died 12 June 1927.

PRICE, Julius Mendes, FRGS; artist, author, war correspondent; Official War Correspondent to Italian Government, 1917; *b* London; *s* of Simon Price, merchant, London. *Educ:* University Coll. School; Brussels; Ecole des Beaux-Arts, Paris. Special war artist-correspondent of the Illustrated London News; was in the Bechuanaland campaign, South Africa, 1884-85, on which occasion enlisted for journalistic purposes as a trooper in Methuen's Horse, and served with the regiment till it was disbanded; with exploration expedition to open up the Nordenskiold route to the interior of Siberia via the Kara Sea, the Arctic coast of Siberia, and up the Yenesei river, afterwards unacccompanied traversing Siberia, Mongolia, the Gobi Desert, and Northern China to Pekin, 1890-91; expedition through the Western Australian Goldfields, 1893; with the Greek Army during the Græco-Turkish War, 1897; Expedition across N-W Territory, Canada, and down the Yukon River to Klondike, 1898; with the Russian Army in Manchuria, Russo-Japanese War, 1904-5, acting in a dual capacity as special artist of the Illustrated London News and war correspondent of the Daily Telegraph; in the Great War, on the French Front in the early months and later with the Italian Army; GHQ Lecturer, British Army of Occupation, Germany, 1919; exhibitor at the Royal Academy and Paris Salon; medal, Paris Exhibition, 1900. Italian Military Medal, 1918; Knight of the Order of the Crown of Italy. *Publications:* From the Arctic Ocean to the Yellow Sea, 1892; The Land of Gold, 1896; From Euston to Klondike, 1898; Dame Fashion, 1913; My Bohemian Days in Paris, 1913; My Bohemian Days in

London, 1914; Six Months on the Italian Front, 1917; On the Path of Adventure, 1919; writer Fortnightly Review and innumerable magazine articles illustrated from his own sketches. *Address:* 21 Golden Square, W1. *TA:* Pricellum, London. *T:* Gerrard 2575. *Club:* Savage.

Died 29 Sept. 1924.

PRICE, Richard John Lloyd, JP, DL Merionethshire; JP Caernarvonshire and Denbighshire; FRA, FAS, FID, FZS; Deputy Chairman of Quarter Sessions for Merionethshire; Member Committee, Dee Conservations at Chester (temporary Deputy Chairman during European War); served on County Advisory Committee, mostly Acting Chairman during strenuous portion of war; *b* 17 April 1843; *m* 1869, Evelyn, *y d* of late Capt. Gregge-Hopwood of Hopwood Hall, Lancs; one *s*. *Educ:* Eton; Christ Church, Oxford. High Sheriff, Merionethshire, 1868. Owned 64,000 acres in Merionethshire and property in Denbighshire. *Publications:* Rabbits for Profit and Rabbits for Powder; Practical Pheasant Rearing; Grouse Driving; Dogs Ancient and Modern; The Valley of the Welsh Dee; Walks in Wales; Dogs' Tales; Whist over a Sandwich; Bridge over a Sandwich. *Recreations:* literature, journalism, judging at field trials and dog shows, shooting, fishing, the study of dogs, animals and birds generally. *Address:* 40 Albemarle Street, W1. *T:* Regent 5299. *TA:* Canis, St James's, London; Rhiwlas, Bala, N Wales. *TA:* Price, Rhiwlas, Bala. *M:* FF46. *Clubs:* Turf, Carlton, Union, Eccentric, MCC, City University; Grosvenor, Chester.

Died 9 Jan. 1923.

PRICE, Sir Robert John, Kt 1908; MP (L) East Norfolk, 1892–1918; *b* 26 April 1854; *y s* of late Edward Price, railway contractor, Highgate, and Elvina Eliza, *d* of S. Mountford; *m* 1881, Eva Montgomery, 2nd *d* of late Jasper Wilson Johns, formerly MP for NE Warwickshire. *Educ:* Cholmeley School, Highgate; University Coll. Hospital. MRCS 1876. Barrister Middle Temple, 1883. *Recreations:* golf, bicycling. *Address:* 6 Sussex Mansions, SW7. *T:* Kensington 3254; The Thatched House, Wroxham, Norfolk; Bank, Lyndhurst, Hants. *Club:* National Liberal. *Died 18 April 1926.*

PRICE, Sir Thomas Rees, KCMG 1908 (CMG 1901); Railway Commissioner South African Railways, Johannesburg, 1902–16; a Public Debt Commissioner for the Union of South Africa; *b* Merthyr Tydvil, 20 Feb. 1848; *o s* of late Rees Price, of Llandovery, Carmarthenshire, South Wales, and Hannah Rhys, of Llandilo, Carmarthenshire; *m* 1872, Mary, *d* of Matthias Howell, of Neath; one *s* one *d*. *Educ:* private school, Ballarat, Victoria; Melbourne; Normal College, Swansea, South Wales. Trained for railway service by late Joshua Williams, General Manager of Vale of Neath Railway, etc; filled various positions on Great Western Railway until 1880; entered service of Cape Government as District Traffic Superintendent at Grahamstown; Acting Assistant Traffic Manager, Cape Town, 1880; Assistant Traffic Manager, Port Elizabeth, 1881; Traffic Manager of the Eastern System, 1882; Traffic Manager, Northern System, 1892; Cape Government Railway Agent in the Transvaal and Orange Free State, 1892; Chief Traffic Manager, 1893; Assistant General Manager of Railways, 1901; General Manager Central South African Railways, 1902, and a Commissioner of Railways and Harbours of the Union of South Africa on the establishment of Union, 1910; acted as railway adviser to Sir James Sivewright in the negotiations with the Transvaal Government, which resulted in the Railway Convention of 1891; Hon. Associate of the Order of St John of Jerusalem; member of Geographical Society of Lisbon; JP Cape Colony and Transvaal. *Address:* Glyn Neath, 19 Union Street, The Gardens, Cape Town. *Clubs:* Royal Societies; Civil Service, Cape Town; Pretoria; East London. *Died 26 Sept. 1916.*

PRICE, Sir William, Kt 1915; President and Managing Director, Price Bros & Co., Ltd, Lumber and Paper Manufacturers; *b* Talca, Chile, 30 Aug. 1867; *s* of Henry Ferrier Price and Florence S. Rogerson; *m* 1904, Amelia Blanche, *e d* of Dr R. H. Smith, President Quebec Bank; four *s* two *d*. *Educ:* Bishop's College School, Lennoxville; St Mark's School, Windsor, England. Entered firm, 1886; sole partner, 1899; MP Quebec West, 1908; Chairman, Quebec Harbour Commission, 1912; Conservative; Anglican. *Recreations:* yachting, fishing. *Address:* 145 Grand Allee, Quebec. *Clubs:* Garrison, Quebec; Rideau, Ottawa; Mt Royal, Montreal; St George's, Sherbrooke. *Died 2 Oct. 1924.*

PRICE, Rev. William James; Hon. Canon, Birmingham, 1905. *Educ:* Jesus College, Oxford (Scholar). Curate of Shelton, Staffs, 1870–72; Mirfield, 1872–75; St Peter's, Wolverhampton, 1875–79; Vicar of Lilleshall, Salop, 1879–91; Vicar and Rural Dean of Harborne, 1891–1915. *Address:* Salterton Road, Exmouth. *Died 11 Feb. 1928.*

PRICHARD, Arthur William, VD; MRCS; Lieutenant-Colonel Royal Army Medical Corps (Territorial Force), retired; late Commanding 3rd South Midland Field Ambulance; Consulting Surgeon to Bristol Royal Infirmary; to the British Eye Dispensary; late Surgeon to Clifton College; *s* of late Augustin Prichard of Clifton, and *g s* of Dr James Cowles Prichard, FRS, the ethnologist; *m* Sarah Anne, *e d* of late Dr William Adye of Bradford-on-Avon; two *s* three *d*. *Educ:* Clifon College; Bristol Medical School; University College, London. Practiced as a surgeon in Clifton; was for 28 years on the active staff of the Bristol Royal Infirmary, and Lecturer on Practical Surgery; Surgeon to the Bristol Rifles for many years, and Brigade Surgeon to the Portland Volunteer Infantry Brigade; when the Territorials came into existence in 1908 he was asked to raise and command a Field Ambulance for Bristol; this unit was one of the first completed to its full establishment of officers and men. *Address;* 6 Rodney Place, Clifton. *T:* Bristol 689.

Died Jan. 1926.

PRICHARD, Major (Hesketh Vernon) Hesketh, DSO 1918; MC; *b* Nov. 1876; *s* of Lieutenant Hesketh Brodrick Prichard and Kate, *d* of Maj.-Gen. B. W. Ryall; *m* 1908, Lady Elizabeth Grimston, 4th *d* of 3rd Earl of Verulam; two *s* one *d*. *Educ:* Fettes. Travelled and shot big game in Patagonia, Labrador, Canada, Sardinia, Spain, Mexico, Newfoundland, Haiti, etc; leader of Patagonian Expedition, 1900–1; played cricket for Hampshire, 1899–1913, and Gentlemen *v* Players, 1903–4–5; ADC to Lord Lieutenant of Ireland, 1907; served European War, 1914–18 (despatches twice, Commander of the Military Order of Avis). *Publications:* Where Black Rules White: a Journey across and about Haiti, 1900; Through the Heart of Patagonia, 1902; Hunting Camps in Wood and Wilderness, 1910; Through Trackless Labrador, 1911; (in collaboration with his mother, Mrs K. Hesketh Prichard) A Modern Mercenary, 1898; Karadac, Count of Gersay, 1900; Tammer's Duel, 1901; Roving Hearts, 1903; Don Q, 1904; New Chronicles of Don Q, 1906; Sniping in France, 1920. *Recreations:* cricket, shooting, natural history, fishing. *Address:* Prae Wood, St Albans. *Clubs:* MCC, Author's.

Died 14 June 1922.

PRICHARD-JONES, Sir John, 1st Bt, *cr* 1910; DL, JP; LLD; *b* 31 May 1845; assumed surname of Prichard-Jones by deed poll, 1917; *m* 2nd, 1911, Marie, *y d* of late Charles Read; two *s*. Chairman of Dickins and Jones, Ltd, Regent St; Sheriff of Anglesey, 1905; Treasurer, Welsh National Museum; Appointments Board of Wales and The Roberts Marine Mansions, Bexhill-on-Sea; Member of the Council of the North Wales University College, Bangor, and Vice-President of the Council, 1909. *Heir: s* John Prichard-Jones, *b* 20 Jan. 1913. *Address:* Maes yr Hâv, Elstree, Herts; Bron Menai, Dwyran, Anglesey. *Club:* Royal Automobile. *Died 17 Oct. 1917.*

PRIDEAUX, Sir Walter Sherburne, Kt 1891, for services on various occasions and especially with the repeal of the gold and silver plate duties; *b* London, 23 Feb. 1846; *e s* of Walter Prideaux, Goldsmiths' Hall, London, and Faircroush, Wadhurst, and Fidlands, *d* of General Sherburne Hodgkinson Williams, RE; *m* 1873, Catharine Mary (*d* 1924), *er d* of Rev. John Vidgen Povah, Minor Canon of St Paul's; three *s* two *d*. *Educ:* Eton. Admitted solicitor (Honours), 1870; Assistant Clerk of the Goldsmiths' Co., 1871–82; Clerk, Company, 1882–1918. *Publications:* Memorials of the Goldsmiths' Company, 2 vols 1896 (printed for private circulation). *Recreations:* shooting, natural history; formerly Captain of Eton Cricket and Football Elevens, and President of Eton Debating Society. *Address:* Goldsmiths' Hall, EC. *Club:* Junior Carlton. *Died 29 Jan. 1928.*

PRIDMORE, Albert Edward, FSI; President of the Society of Architects, 1905–6, 1906–7; *b* Coventry, 1864; 3rd *s* of George Alexander Pridmore; *m* 1893, Edith Maud, 2nd *d* of late Tom Bonsell Shepperson. *Educ:* private schools. Architect of many important buidlings of a public, commercial, and private character; as a surveyor, a recognised authority on rating matters and valuations for parochial assessments; Member of Court of Common Council of City of London, 1894–1907; Chairman of Guildhall School of Music Committee, 1899; Billingsgate and Leadenhall Markets Committee, 1905; Member Hon. Irish Society, 1904–5; Past President Bishopsgate Ward Club; Past Master Painter Stainers' Co.; Chairman Watford Town Council, 1900; First Chairman of Executive Committee Society of Warwickshire Folk in London; late an Estates Governor of Dulwich College. *Publication:* Rating and City Assessments. *Recreation:* fishing. *Address:* 3 Broad Street Buildings, EC2. *T:* London Wall 1374; 35 Ashworth Mansions, Elgin Avenue, W.

Died 1 Nov. 1927.

PRIMROSE, Rt. Hon. Sir Henry William, KCB 1899 (CB 1895); CSI 1885; ISO 1904; PC 1912; *b* 22 August 1846; *s* of late Hon. Bouverie Francis Primrose, CB (2nd *s* of 4th Earl of Rosebery), and Frederica Sophia, *d* of 1st Viscount Anson; *m* 1888, Helen Mary (*d* 1919), *d* of Gilbert McMicking of Miltonise, Wigtownshire; one *s*. *Educ:* Trinity College, Glenalmond; Balliol College, Oxford. Entered Treasury, 1869; Private Secretary to Viceroy of India (Marquis of Ripon), 1880–84; and to Mr Gladstone, 1886; Secretary to HM Office of Works, 1886–95; Chairman Board of Customs, 1895–99; Board of Inland Revenue, 1899–1907; Chairman Pacific Cable Board, 1907–14; Welsh Church Commission, 1914. *Address:* 44 Ennismore Gardens, SW7. *T:* Western 1565.

Died 17 June 1923.

PRIMROSE, Sir John Ure, 1st Bt, *cr* 1903; JP; LLD Glasgow; Lord Provost of Glasgow, 1902, and Lord Lieutenant of the County of the City of Glasgow; Senior Partner William Primrose and Sons, flour millers, Centre Street, Glasgow; *b* 16 Oct. 1847; *e s* of late William Primrose, merchant miller in Glasgow, and Annie (*d* 1913), *d* of John Ure (*s* of late John Ure, LLD, ex-Lord Provost of Glasgow), baker and merchant miller in Glasgow; *m* 1st, 1877, Margaret Jane (*d* 1896), *d* of James Adam, merchant, Glasgow; one *s*; 2nd, 1897, Anna (*d* 1913), *d* of Alexander Spence Wylie, merchant, Glasgow; 3rd, 1915, Muriel, *d* of late Edwin Pilling of Rochdale and Liverpool, and *widow* of James Donald, shipowner, Glasgow. *Educ:* Collegiate School. Entered Town Council of Glasgow 1856; magistrate, 1891; Chairman of the Clyde Navigation Trustees; president of numerous public institutions in the city. *Heir: s* William Louis Primrose [*b* 1 June 1880; *m* 1907, Elizabeth Caroline, *d* of Hugh Dunmuir, Glasgow; two *s*]. *Recreations:* music, photography. *Address:* Redholme, Dumbreck, Glasgow. *Clubs:* Constitutional; Art, Glasgow.

Died 29 June 1924.

PRIMROSE, Rt. Hon. Neil (James Archibald), PC 1917; MP (L) Wisbech Divison, Cambridge, since 1910; *b* 14 Dec. 1882; *yr s* of 5th Earl of Rosebery and Hannah (*d* 1890), *o d* of Baron Mayer Amschel de Rothschild; *m* 1915, Lady Victoria Alice Louise Stanley, *o d* of 17th Earl of Derby; one *d*. *Educ:* Eton; Oxford. Capt. Bucks Yeomanry; Parliamentary Under-Secretary to Foreign Office, Feb–May 1915; Parliamentary Military Sec. to Min. of Munitions, Sept.–Dec. 1916; Parliamentary Secretary to Treasury, Dec. 1916–May 1917. *Address:* 5 Great Stanhope Street, W; The Manor House, Postwick, Norwich. *T:* Mayfair 2560.

Died 17 Nov. 1917.

PRINCE, J.-E., KC; AB, LLD; advocate; retired; *b* St Célestin, district of Three Rivers, 15 May 1851; *m* 1884, Miss Rivard, Quebec; five *d*. *Educ:* Nicolet Seminary; Laval Univ. Admitted at the Quebec Bar, 1879; late teacher of Roman Law and Civil Procedure, later of Economics at Laval University. *Publications:* several writings on divers topics and public lectures. *Recreations:* literature, music, etc. *Address:* 81 Dorchester Street, Quebec, Canada.

Died 6 June 1923.

PRING, Hon. Robert Darlow; Judge of Supreme Court of New South Wales since 1902; *b* NSW, 29 Jan. 1853; *s* of John and Elizabeth Newnham Pring; *m* 1882, Mary Jane King; three *s* one *d*. *Educ:* The King's School; Sydney University (BA 1873; MA 1876). Admitted to Bar, 1874. *Recreations:* reading, walking. *Address:* Supreme Court, Sydney, NSW. *T:* Ashfield 356. *Club:* Australian, Sydney.

Died Aug. 1922.

PRINGLE, Sir John, KCMG 1911 (CMG 1900); Member of Privy and Legislative Councils, Jamaica; landowner; *b* 26 July 1848; *s* of John Pringle of Whaup, Co. Roxburgh; *m* 1876, Amy Zillah, *d* of late Hon. J. Levy of St Jago Park, Spanish Town, Jamaica; four *s* two *d*. *Educ:* University, Aberdeen. *Address:* The Manor House, Conostant Spring, Jamaica. *Clubs:* Constitutional, Empire, West Indian; Jamaica, Kingston.

Died 15 March 1923.

PRINGLE, John James, MB, CM; FRCP; 3rd *s* of late Andrew Pringle of Borgue, Kircudbrightshire, NB. *Educ:* Edinburgh, Dublin, Vienna, Paris, Berlin. Consulting Physician, Skin Department, Middlesex Hospital; late President of Dermatological Section, Royal Society of Medicine; Physician, Royal Scottish Corporation and Royal Caledonian Asylum. *Publications:* numerous articles on diseases of the skin. *Address:* 23 Lower Seymour Street, W1. *T:* Paddington 3205.

Died 18 Dec. 1922.

PRINGLE, Sir Norman Robert, 8th Bt, *cr* 1638; *b* 18 Oct. 1871; *o s* of Sir Norman William Drummond Pringle, 7th Bt and Louisa Clementina, *y d* of Robert Steuart, MP, Alderston; *S* father, 1897;

m 1902, (Florence) Madge, *d* of T. Vaughan; three *s* one *d*. *Heir: s* Norman Hamilton Pringle, *b* 13 May 1903. *Address:* Newhall, Galashiels, NB.

Died 18 April 1919.

PRINGLE, Maj.-Gen. Sir Robert, KCMG 1917; CB 1909; DSO 1902; Veterinary Surgeon, Army Veterinary Department, 1878; Veterinary Lieutenant-Colonel 1901; *b* 25 Aug. 1855; *s* of Gilbert Pringle of Stranraer; *m* 1898, Sophie, *e d* of George Moir Byres of Tonley. Served Afghan War, 1879–80 (medal), Wuzeree Expedition, 1881 (despatches); Zhob Valley Expedition, 1884; South Africa, 1900–1 (despatches, DSO, medal 3 clasps); Director-General Army Vet. Service, 1910–17; served European War (KCMG, medal); Colonel, 1907. *Address:* Fairbourne, Farnham, Surrey.

Died 30 June 1926.

PRINGLE, William Mather Rutherford; MP (L) NW Lanarkshire, 1910–18, and Penistone Division of Yorks, 1922–24; *b* Berwickshire, 22 Jan. 1874; *s* of George Pringle and Elizabeth (née Mather), Berwickshire and Glasgow; *m* 1906, Lilian Patrick, *d* of Joseph Somerville, Glasgow; four *s* one *d*. *Educ:* Glasgow University. Called to the Bar, 1906; contested Camlachie Division, Glasgow, 1906; Springburn Div., Glasgow, 1918; Rusholme Div., Manchester, 1919; Penistone Div., Yorkshire, 1921; Ayr Burghs, 1925. *Address:* 1 Garden Court, Temple, EC; 17 Enmore Road, Putney, SW.

Died 1 April 1928.

PRIOR, Col Hon. Edward Gawler, PC (Victoria City); Lieutenant-Governor of British Columbia since 1919; *b* Dallowgill, near Ripon, Yorkshire, 21 May 1853; 2nd *s* of late Rev. Henry Prior; *m* 1st, 1878, Suzette (*d* 1897), *y d* of Hon. John Work, of Hillside, Victoria; 2nd, 1899, Genevieve, *e d* of Capt. J. Wright; one *s* three *d*. *Educ:* Leeds Grammar School. Mining engineer and surveyor for the Vancouver Coal Mining and Land Company, 1873; Government Inspector of Mines, 1878–80; resigned to commence business as an iron and hardware merchant; Lieut-Col commanding the 5th Regt Canadian Artillery, 1888–96; Hon. ADC to the Governors-General of Canada, 1889, under Lords Stanley and Aberdeen; Member of Legislature, British Columbia, 1886–88, resigned at the request of his constituents, and was elected by acclamation the same day to Dominion House of Commons; re-elected, 1891 and 1896; Controller of Inland Revenue and a member of the Cabinet in the administrations of Sir Mackenzie Bowell and Sir Charles Tupper; Minister of Mines in Local Legislature of British Columbia, 10 March 1902 to 31 May 1903; Premier of BC from 21 Nov. 1902 to 31 May 1903; commanded the Canadian rifle team at Bisley, 1890; twice President of the Dominion Artillery Association; one of the Canadian contingent present at Queen Victoria's Diamond Jubilee, 1897; a Conservative. *Recreations:* riding, driving, fishing. *Address:* Victoria, British Columbia. *Clubs:* Constitutional; Union, Victoria; Vancouver, Vancouver.

Died 12 Dec. 1920.

PRIOR, Maj.-Gen. George Upton; *b* 27 Oct. 1843; *s* of Col Prior of Sydney Place, Bath, and Maria Louisa, *d* of late Colonel Way, Denham Place, Bucks; *m* 1893, Kathleen, Lady of Grace St John of Jerusalem, *d* of Captain Dickinson, Ashton Keynes, Wilts, and *widow* of late Col Sinclair, 38th Staffs Regt. *Educ:* Sandhurst. Joined 100th Royal Canadians, exchanging later to 1st Royals; passed Staff College; served on the staffs of the Western, Southern, and Aldershot Districts; was DAQMG during the Afghan campaign of 1879 on the staffs of Generals Sir Donald Stewart and Sir Michael Biddulph (despatches twice, brevet of Lieut-Col); commanded 2nd Batt. Royal Scots, 1886; AAG Gibraltar, 1891; commanded Curragh District, 1900, and was at intervals Commander of the Forces in Ireland; member of the South African Deportation, 1901; received thanks of Government; retired 1904; Colonel of the Prince of Wales's Leinster Regiment, Royal Canadians, 1910; Knight of Grace of the Order of St John of Jerusalem; FRGS. *Address:* Ethorpe, Gerrard's Cross, Bucks. *TA:* Gerrard's Cross. *T:* Gerrards' Cross 39. *Clubs:* Army and Navy, Turf, etc.

Died 12 Oct. 1919.

PRITCHARD, Robert Albion, DCL; Senior Registrar, Probate Registry. *Address:* 21 Dealtry Road, Putney, SW; Higham St Mary, near Colchester. *Club:* Reform.

Died 13 Jan. 1916.

PRITCHARD, Urban, MD, FRCS; Emeritus Professor of Aural Surgery, King's College, London; *b* 21 March 1845; 5th *s* of Andrew Pritchard, FRSE; *m* 1872, Lottie, *e d* of Blades Pallister; two *s* two *d*. *Educ:* King's College, London; University of Edinburgh. MD Edinburgh (gold medallist and scholar); Fellow, King's College, London. Formerly House Physician King's College Hospital; Surgical Registrar, Demonstrator of Physiology, Pathologist, King's College;

over twenty-five years Aural Surgeon to King's College Hospital, and Consulting Aural Surgeon to the Royal Ear Hospital; ex-President of the Otological Society of the United Kingdom; President of 6th International Congress of Otology, 1899. *Publications:* Handbook of Diseases of the Ear, 3 edns; Cochlea of the Ornithorhynchus Platypus, Royal Society's Philosophical Transactions; co-editor for United Kingom of Archives of Otology. *Address:* St Teresa, Chesham Bois, Bucks. *T:* Amersham 79. *Clubs:* National Liberal; University, Edinburgh. *Died 16 Oct. 1925.*

PROBYN, Rt. Hon. Sir Dighton Macnaghten, VC 1858; GCB 1902 (GCB mil. 1910; KCB 1887; CB 1858); GCSI 1911 (KCSI 1876); GCVO 1896; ISO 1903; PC 1901; General, retired; Comptroller to Queen Alexandra since 1910; Extra Equerry to King George V, since 1910; *b* 21 Jan. 1833; *s* of late Captain George Probyn and Alicia, *d* of the late Sir Francis Workman-Macnaghten, 1st Bt; *m* 1872, Letitia Maria (*d* 1900), *d* of Thomas Robarts Thellusson. Entered army, 1849; Gen. 1888; served Trans-Indus Frontier, 1852–57; Indian Mutiny, 1857–58; China, 1860; Umbeyla Campaign, North-West Frontier, 1863; Col 11th King Edward's Own Lancers (Probyn's Horse); Equerry to King Edward VII when Prince of Wales, 1872–77; Comptroller and Treasurer, 1877–91; Keeper of the Privy Purse and Extra Equerry to King Edward VII, 1901–10; member of Council of Duchy of Lancaster 1901–10; retired from office of Governor of Wellington Coll., 1919. *Address:* Marlborough House, SW; Sandringham, Norfolk. *Clubs:* United Service, Marlborough. *Died 20 June 1924.*

PROBYN, Sir Lesley Charles, KCVO 1906; Director of Great Northern Railway since 1883; Member of Council of Prince of Wales since 1897; *b* 11 Aug. 1834; 4th *s* of late Captain George Probyn; *m* 1859, Victoria Charlotte Isabella (*d* 1911), *d* of late James John Kinloch of Kair, Kincardineshire. *Educ:* Finchley; Haileybury. Entered Bengal Civil Service, 1854; served as Assistant Magistrate in the Ghazeepore district with the military forces during the Indian Mutiny (medal); joined Financial Department Government of India, 1860, serving for ten years at Lahore as Accountant-General of the Punjab; during this time was for five years Lt-Col Commandant of the 1st Punjab Volunteer Rifle Corps; retired from Indian Civil Service, 1879; sent by the Colonial Office on a Special Commission to British Guiana, 1882; Auditor Duchy of Cornwall, 1891–1915. *Publications:* papers read before, and published in, the Journals of, the Institute of Bankers, the Royal Statistical Society, the East India Association, and the Royal Colonial Institute, on financial and monetary questions.*Address:* 79 Onslow Square, SW. *Club:* East India United Service. *Died 20 Oct. 1916.*

PROCTER, Rev. Charles James, MA; Prebendary of St Paul's Cathedral, 1917–23; Chairman of Peache Trustees; *s* of late George Procter, of Wakefield and Ebor House, Cambridge; *m* Emily E., *d* of Rev. Walter Scott Dumergue (godson of Sir Walter Scott), Vicar of Fareham; no *c. Educ:* Owens College, Manchester; Trinity College, Cambridge. Formerly Vicar and Rural Dean of Islington. *Recreations:* gardening, literature. *Address:* 10 Scroope Terrace, Cambridge. *Died 24 Nov. 1925.*

PROCTER, Sir Henry Edward Edleston, Kt 1911; CBE 1918; *b* 30 April 1866; *s* of late Charles Edward Procter, of Macclesfield; *m* 1897, Helen Matilda, CBE, *d* of late Lieut-Col Thomas Arthur Freeman, East Surrey Regiment; one *s* two *d. Educ:* Birkenhead School. Late Commandant of the Bombay Light Horse. *Address:* 36 Princes Gardens, SW7. *Clubs:* Royal Automobile, Oriental. *Died 11 July 1928.*

PROCTER, Henry Richardson, DSc; FRS; FIC; FCS; Emeritus Professor of Applied Chemistry (Leather Industries), University of Leeds; Hon. Member of Leathersellers Company; *b* 6 May 1848; *s* of John Richardson Procter of North Shields; *m* 1874, Emma Lindsay, *d* of late James Watson of Newcastle; two *s* one *d. Educ:* Bootham School, York; Royal College of Chemistry. Late Head of Leather Industries Dept, Univ. of Leeds, 1891; Hon. Editor of Journal of Society of Leather Trades Chemists; Hon. Director of Procter International Research Laboratory, Leeds. *Publications:* joint translator of Kohlrausch's Physical Measurements; Textbook of Tanning; Cantor and Cobb Lectures on Leather Manufacture; Leather Industries Laboratory Book; Principles of Leather Manufacture; Leather Chemists Pocket Book; The Making of Leather, etc; article on Aurora, Encyclopædia Britannica, ninth edition. *Recreations:* gardening, photography, sketching. *Address:* Fragden, Newlyn, Penzance; The University, Leeds. *T:* 20251. *M:* AF 4882. *Club:* Authors'. *Died 17 Aug. 1927.*

PROCTER, Rev. John Mathias, MA; Hon. Canon of St Albans since 1882; *b* 7 Sept. 1835; 2nd *s* of Edward Procter, Solicitor, of Macclesfield; *m* 1864, Marian Marden, *o d* of Samuel Mitchell of Great Newbury, Ilford; two *s* one *d. Educ:* Macclesfield Grammar School; Trinity College, Oxford (Exhibition). 2nd class Mods 1856, 2nd class Lit. Hum. 1858. Fellow of Jesus College, Oxford, 1859–64; Deacon, 1859; Priest, 1860; Curate of Barkingside and Aldborough Hatch, 1862–64, Vicar, 1864–79; Rector of Laindon cum Basildon, 1879–83; of Thorley, 1883–1909; Rural Dean of Bishop's Stortford, 1893–1904; Hon. Secretary of Bishop of Rochester's Fund, 1870–78; Bishop of St Albans Fund, 1878–1910; Proctor in Convocation for the Diocese of St Albans, 1895–1906. *Address:* Thorley Rectory, Bishop's Stortford. *Died 22 Jan. 1917.*

PROCTOR, Capt. Andrew Weatherley Beacuchamp, VC; DSO 1918; MC; DFC; Royal Air Force. Served European War, 1914–18 (despatches, MC with bar, DFC, DSO, VC). *Died 21 June 1921.*

PROE, Thomas, CMG 1901; Mayor of Brisbane, 1901; mechanical engineer; *b* 21 Jan. 1852; *s* of Thomas Proe; *m* 1881, Mary Kurth. Alderman, 1895. *Address:* Merthyr Road, Brisbane. *Died 17 Dec. 1922.*

PROTHERO, Sir George Walter, KBE 1920; MA, LittD (Cambridge); FBA 1903; Vice-President Royal Historical Society; editor of the Quarterly Review, since 1899; *b* Wiltshire, 14 Oct. 1848; *e s* of late Rev. Canon George Prothero, Whippingham, Isle of Wight, and Emma, *d* of Rev. William Money-Kyrle, Homme House, Herefordshire; *m* 1882, Mary Frances, *d* of late Dr Samuel Butcher, Bishop of Meath. *Educ:* Eton; King's Coll., Cambridge (Scholar; MA; Hon. Fellow). Univ. of Bonn; Bell Scholar, 1869; 1st class in the Classical Tripos, 1872. Fellow of King's Coll., Cambridge; Assistant Master at Eton; Lecturer under University Extension Scheme at Nottingham, Leicester, etc; University Lecturer in History and Tutor of King's College, Cambridge, 1876–94; Prof. of History, University of Edinburgh, 1894–99; Rede Lecturer (Cambridge), 1903; Lowell Lecturer (Boston), and Schouler Lecturer (Johns Hopkins), 1910; Chichele Lecturer (Oxford), 1920; Governor of Holloway College, 1916; Member of Royal Commission for Ecclesiastical Discipline, 1904–6; Director of the Historical Section, FO, 1918–19; Member of the British Peace Delegation, 1919; Pres., Royal Historical Society; Corresponding Member of Massachusetts Historical Society; Foreign Honorary Member of the American Academy of Arts and Sciences (Boston); Member of Société d'Histoire Modern (Paris); Hon. LLD Edinburgh and Harvard; Officer of the Crown of Belgium, 1919. *Publications:* Life and Times of Simon de Montfort, 1877; edition of Voltaire's Louis Quatorze, with notes, 1879; translation of vol. i of Ranke's Weltgeschichte, 1883; Memoir of Henry Bradshaw, 1889; Select Statutes and other documents bearing on the reigns of Elizabeth and James I, 1894; editor of Sir J. R. Seeley's Growth of British Policy, 1895; British History Reader, 2 vols 1898; School History of Great Britain and Ireland (to 1910), 1912; German Policy before the War, 1916; editor of the Cambridge Historical Series; co-editor of the Cambridge Modern History, 1901–12; editor of the series of Peace Handbooks issued by the Foreign Office, 1920; contributor to Enyclopædia Britannica and the Dictionary of National Biography. *Recreations:* mountaineering, fishing, cycling. *Address:* 24 Bedford Square, WC1. *T:* Museum 1495. *Clubs:* Athenæum, Alpine; Rye Golf. *Died 10 July 1922.*

PROTHERO, Vice-Adm. Reginald Charles, CB 1900; MVO 1903; Royal Navy; *b* 15 June 1849; *s* of Charles Prothero, Newport, Monmouthshire. *Educ:* Royal Navy. Entered Navy, 1863; Captain, 1895; retired, 1904; Rear-Admiral, 1906; served South Africa, 1900 (CB); commanded Naval Brigade at battles of Belmont and Graspan (wounded). *Died 26 March 1927.*

PROUT, Henry Goslee; formerly Editor of Railroad Gazette, New York; formerly President and General Manager of companies manufacturing engineering products; late Governor of provinces of the Equator, Africa. *Educ:* Univ. of Michigan (CE). Colonel of General Staff and Major of Engineers, army of Khedive; AM (hon.) Yale Univ.; LLD (hon.) Univ. of Michigan; Corresponding Member American Geographical Society. *Publications:* Life of George Westinghouse; numerous fugitive pieces. *Address:* Nutley, New Jersey. *Club:* Century, New York. *Died 26 Jan. 1927.*

PROVIS, Sir Samuel Butler, CH 1918; KCB 1901 (CB 1887); *b* Warminster, 9 Feb. 1845; *e s* of Samuel and Mary Provis, Bath. *Educ:* Queens' Coll., Cambridge. Barrister, Middle Temple, 1866; Junior

Legal Assistant to the Local Government Board, 1872; Assistant Secretary, 1882–89; Permanent Secretary, 1898–1910. *Address:* 2 Whitehall Court, SW. *Clubs:* Union, New Oxford and Cambridge.
Died 11 July 1926.

PROWSE, Arthur Bancks, MD; FRCS; Lieutenant-Colonel Royal Army Medical Corps (T); lately Administrator and Officer Commanding 2nd Southern General Hospital, Bristol; Consulting Physician, Bristol Royal Infirmary, since 1919; County Organiser for Devonshire, English Place-Name Society; *b* Millbrook, Plymouth, 1856; *e s* of Dr William Prowse; *m* 1896, Margaret W. (*d* 1921), *y d* of late G. Mitchell of Glasgow and Helensburgh; two *s* one *d. Educ:* Amersham Grammar School, Bucks; Amersham Hall School, nr Reading; Liverpool Medical School; St Mary's Hospital, London. MB Lond. with Honours in Medicine, Obstetric Medicine and Forensic Medicine, 1878. Assistant Physician, Bristol Royal Infirmary, 1883; Physician, 1888; Dean of the Faculty, 1888–1910; Lecturer in Materia Medica, Pharmacology, and Therapeutics, Bristol Medical School, 1888–1905; Churchwarden, Clifton Parish Church, 1888–1917; President, Bristol Naturalists' Society, 1901–3; President, Bristol Anti-Narcotic League, 1902–4; Pres., British-Israel National Union, 1909—10; abstainer, non-smoker, and spelling reformer. *Publications:* papers on medical and archæological subjects (especially upon Dartmoor). *Recreations:* gardening, family history, prehistoric archæology. *Address:* 5 Lansdown Place, Clifton, Bristol. *T:* 1947 Bristol.
Died 26 April 1925.

PROWSE, Richard Thomas, CB 1897; JP Hertfordshire; *b* Swanage, Dorset, 1835; 2nd *s* of late Captain William Prowse, RN, Weymouth; unmarried. *Educ:* Christ's Hospital, London. Entered the Customs Service, 1853; Surveyor-General of the Customs, 1883–88; Secretary to the Board of Customs, 1888–1900. *Address:* Howton, Bushey Heath, Hertfordshire. *TA:* Bushey Heath. *M:* AR 2273.
Died 17 Dec. 1921.

PRUDDEN, T. Mitchell, MD; LLD; Emeritus Professor of Pathology, College of Physicians and Surgeons, Columbia University, New York; member of Board of Directors of theRockefeller Institute for Medical Research; *b* 7 July 1849. *Publications:* A Text-book on Pathology; various researches in experimental pathology; popular works on sanitation and travel. *Address:* 160 West 59th Street, New York.
Died 10 April 1924.

PRYCE, Rev. R. Vaughan, DD; Principal and Professor of Theology, New College, London University, 1889–1907; subseq.Principal Emeritus; *b* Bristol, Dec. 1834; *s* of late George Pryce, FSA, Librarian of the city of Bristol. *Educ:* Queen Elizabeth's Hospital, Bristol; New College, London. Graduated in the University of London, BA 1859, LLB 1860, MA 1861; DD of the University of Glasgow. Congregational minister in Brighton, 1862–71; Worcester, 1871–77; London (Stamford Hill), 1877–89; Lecturer in Logic and Mental and Moral Science in Cheshunt College, Herts, 1877–85; formerly a member of the Faculty of Theology and of the Senate of the University of London; was elected on the Brighton School Board (1870) to represent the advocates of the view that State-supported education should be free, compulsory, and secular. *Recreation:* foreign travel. *Address:* 68 Bethune Road, Stamford Hill, N.
Died 20 Sept. 1917.

PRYCE-JONES, Sir Pryce, Kt 1887; JP; *b* 16 Oct. 1834; *s* of William Jones, Newtown, Montgomeryshire; assumed additional surname of Pryce, 1887; *m* 1859, Eleanor (*d* 1914), *d* of Edward Rowley Morris, Newtown; four *s* four *d.* Chairman, Pryce-Jones Ltd, cloth manufacturers, Newtown; MP (C) Montgomery, 1885–86 and 1892–95; High Sheriff for Montgomeryshire, 1891. *Address:* Dolerw, Newtown, Wales.
Died 11 Jan. 1920.

PRYCE-JONES, Col Sir (Pryce) Edward, 1st Bt, *cr* 1918; TD; JP; DL; *b* Newtown, N Wales, 6 Feb. 1861; *e s* of late Sir Pryce Pryce-Jones and Eleanor, *d* of Edward Rowley Morris; *m* 1886, Beatrice,*d* of Herbert Hardie of Orford House, Cheshire; one *s* one *d. Educ:* Liverpool College; Jesus College, Cambridge (MA). Barrister, Inner Temple, 1892. Man. Dir, Pryce-Jones Ltd, cloth manufacturers, Newtown; MP(C) Montgomery District, 1895–1906 and 1910–18; Joint Hon. Secretary-General of Commercial Committee of Allied Inter-Parliamentary Groups, 1917–18, and Joint Hon. Treasurer International Parliamentary Union (British Group), 1911–18; Past Master No 1 Grand Masters' Lodge (London); Junior Dep.-Chancellor of Univ. Court of Wales, 1911–13; retired from Montgomeryshire Yeomanry Cavalry as Hon. Major after 15 years, 1895; raised 5th Vol. Batt. South Wales Borderers, becoming its first and last commanding officer, 1897–1908; Hon. Col 7th Royal Welsh

Fusiliers, 1908; CC and DL Montgomeryshire; High Sheriff, 1923. *Heir: s* Capt. Pryce Victor Pryce-Jones, *b* 10 June 1887. *Address:* Dolerw, Newtown, North Wales. *Clubs:* Carlton, 1900; Phyllis Court (Henley-on-Thames).
Died 22 May 1926.

PRYKE, Rev. William Emmanuel, MA; Canon and Chancellor of Exeter Cathedral; *b* 10 March 1843; *m*; one *s. Educ:* St John's College, Cambridge. Foundation Scholar and Naden Divinity Student; 14th Wrangler, 1866; Curate of Stapleford, Cambs, 1867–71; St Andrew the Great, Cambridge, 1871–72; Headmaster, Lancaster School, 1872–93; Select Preacher, Cambridge University, 1873, 1887 and 1912; Rector of Marwood, N Devon, 1893–1900; Vicar of Ottery St Mary, 1900–8; Rural Dean of Ottery, 1900–8; Canon of Exeter Cathedral, 1908; Treasurer, 1910; Chancellor, 1915; Chaplain to Bishop of Exeter, 1903; Examining Chaplain, 1907; Proctor in Convocation of Canterbury, 1906–10; re-elected, 1911; resigned 1918; Member of Devon County Education Committee. *Address:* The Close, Exeter.
Died 1 Feb. 1920.

PRYNNE, Edward A. Fellowes, RBA; painter of portraits and subject pictures, chiefly sacred, church decorations and stained-glass designs and sculpture; *b* 14 Oct. 1854; 3rd *s* of Rev. George Rundle Prynne, MA, and Emily, *d* of Admiral Sir Thomas Fellowes, KCB, DCL; *m* 1888, Emma Mary Joll; two *s* three *d. Educ:* Eastman's Royal Naval Academy, Southsea; London; Antwerp; Florence; Paris. Exhibited at Royal Acad., Royal Soc. of British Artists, New Gallery, Grosvenor Gallery, Brussels International, Liverpool, Birmingham, and at Dusseldorf International Exhibition of Religious Art, etc; command visit to Osborne by Queen Victoria, 1891. *Address:* 1 Woodville Road, Ealing.
Died 28 Dec. 1921.

PRYOR, Arthur Vickris, JP, DL, Leics; *b* 3 Aug. 1846; *e s* of late Arthur Pryor of Hylands and Elizabeth Sophia, *e d* of late Tomkyns Dew of Whitney Court, Herefordshire; *m* 1886, Elizabeth Charlotte Louisa (*d* 1919), *e d* of 2nd Earl of Craven, and *widow* of 3rd Earl of Wilton. *Educ:* Eton; Christ Church, Oxford (BA 1867). *Address:* Egerton Lodge, Melton Mowbray. *Clubs:* Carlton, Travellers', Turf, St James's.
Died 18 June 1927.

PRYOR, S. J.; *b* Clifton, Derbyshire, 8 June 1865; *m* 1894, Laura A. Wells (*b* Clifford, Pa, USA); one *d.* Editor The Gleaner, Kingston, Jamaica, West Indies, 1889; on various newspapers in America, including five years on editorial staff New York Sun; correspondent in London for New York Journal, 1896; Managing Editor and Director of the Daily Mail for four years to Nov. 1900; Managing Editor Daily Express, 1900–4; Editor St James's Gazette, 1904, and Evening Standard and St James's Gazette, 1905; Editor and Managing Director The Tribune, 1907; Day Editor of The Times, 1909, and Director of The Times Publishing Company until 1918; Press Secretary, Buckingham Palace, 1918–20. *Address:* 2 The Grove, Highgate Road, NW5. *T:* Hampstead 1244. *Club:* Whitefriars
Died 25 March 1924.

PRYSE, Sir Edward John Webley-Parry-, 2nd Bt, *cr* 1866; *b* 10 July 1862; *o s* of Sir Pryse Pryse, 1st Bt and Louisa Joan, *d* of Capt. John Lewes, Llanlear, Cardiganshire; *S* father, 1906; assumed additional surnames of Webley-Parry, by Royal Licence, 1892; *m* 1891, Nina Katharine Angharad, *o d* of D. K. W. Webley-Parry, Noyadd Trefawr. Formerly Captain 1st Batt. Welsh Regiment. *Heir: brother* Lewes Thomas Loveden Pryse [*b* 5 Feb. 1864; *m* 1894, Florence Madeline, *d* of Col F. Howell; one *s*]. *Address:* Gogerddan, Bow Street RSO, Cardiganshire. *Club:* Army and Navy.
Died 20 Oct. 1918.

PTOLEMY, William John, ISO 1910; JP; CA; Deputy Treasurer of the Province of Manitoba since 1886; *b* 29 March 1850; *s* of late John Ptolemy and Elizabeth M'Waters, Hamilton, Ontario; *m* 1877, Isabella (*d* 1915), *d* of Charles Muir; three *s* three *d. Educ:* public schools; Smithville Grammar School, Ontario. Great Western Railway Co. of Canada, 1873–75; Canadian Pacific Railway, Dominion Govt, telegraph construction, 1875; in mercantile life, 1876–82; Manitoba Government Service (accountant), 1883–85; Municipal Commissioner, 1886; District Deputy Grand Master (Masonic) District No 1, 1887; Presbyterian; Treasurer of Church Boards, 1880–1914. *Publications:* contributor to the public Press. *Address:* Winnipeg, Manitoba, Canada. *Clubs:* Canadian, Rotary, Winnipeg.
Died 10 Sept. 1920.

PUCCINI, Giacomo; music composer; *b* Lucca, 23 Dec. 1858. *Educ:* Conservatorio di Musica, Milan, under Bazzini, Ponchielli. *Principal works:* Le Villi, 1884; Edgar, 1889; Manon Lescaut, 1893; La Bohème, 1896; La Tosca, 1900; Madame Butterfly, 1904; La Fanciulla del West,

1910; La Rondine, 1916; Il Tabarro, Suor Angelica, Gianni Schicchi (trilogy of one-act operas), 1918; Turandot (performed posthumously, 1926). *Address:* c/o G. Ricordi & Co., Milan; Torre del Lago, Tuscany, Italy. *Died 29 Nov. 1924.*

PUCKLE, Lt-Col John, DSO 1900; Army Service Corps; *b* 6 Oct. 1869; *s* of Col Henry Glover Puckle, late MSC, Worthing; *m* 1896, Mary, *d* of late Hon. James Fellows, Agent-Gen. for NB. *Educ:* Westward Ho!; Bedford; Malvern; St Peter's College, Cambridge; Sandhurst. Entered army, 1893; Capt. 1899; Major, 1906; Lt-Col, 1914; served S Africa, 1899–1902 (despatches, DSO); European War, 1914–15 (despatches). *Address:* Wyndham House, Sloane Gardens, SW. *Clubs:* Naval and Military, Junior Naval and Military. *Died 15 April 1917.*

PUCKLE, Richard Kaye, CIE 1878; *b* 1830; *s* of R. Puckle; *m* 1864, Caroline Victoria, *d* of C. J. F. Combe, Stoke D'Abernon. *Educ:* Tonbridge School; Haileybury. Entered Madras Civil Service, 1851; Collector and Magistrate, Tinnevelly, 1866; Director of Revenue Settlement, 1874; member of Board of Revenue, 1879; retired, 1881. *Address:* Lingmoor, Gratwicke Road, Worthing. *Died 29 July 1917.*

PUDUKOTA, Raja of; HH Raja Martand Bhairava Tondiman Bahadur, GCIE 1913; *b* 1875; *S* grandfather, 1886; *m* 1915, Esmé Mary Sorrett,*y d* of late W. Fink, MA, LLD, Melbourne, Australia; one *s* (Marthanda Sydney, *b* Australia, 1916). The State had an area of 1,170 square miles and population of 426,813, and was ruled by Tondiman dynasty from time immemorial; the Raja granted his people a representative assembly for consulative and legislative purposes; salute of 11 guns. *Address:* La Favorite, Cannes, South of France. *Died 28 May 1928.*

PUGSLEY, Hon. William; Lieutenant-Governor, New Brunswick, 1917–23; *b* Sussex, Kings Co., New Brunswick, 27 Sept. 1850; *s* of William Pugsley, farmer; *m* 1st, 1876, Fannie J. (*d* 1914), *d* of Thomas Parks, merchant, of the City of St John; two *s*; 2nd, 1915, Gertrude Macdonald. *Educ:* public school in Sussex, Kings Co.; University of New Brunswick. Alumni Gold Medallist in Junior Year; graduated at head of class, 1868; second in competition for Gilchrist Scholarship, University of London, 1868 (BCL, DCL). Admitted Attorney at Law, 1871; Barrister, 1872; Reporter of the Supreme Court, 1873–83; QC 1891; elected to Legislative Assembly of New Brunswick 1885; elected Speaker of the House, 1887; resigned 1890, and went into the Government as Solicitor-General; resigned and retired from politics, 1892; again elected to the Legislature for Kings, 1899; entered the Provincial Govt as Attorney-Gen. 1900; Minister of Public Works, Canada, 1907–19. *Address:* Rothesay, New Brunswick, Canada. *Clubs:* Rideau, Country, Ottawa; Union, St John, Riverside, Golf and County. *Died March 1925.*

PULFORD, Col Russell Richard, CIE 1897; retired; *b* 20 Dec. 1845. Entered RE 1866; Col 1895; joined India Dept 1870; served Afghan War, 1878–80; Superintending Engineer, 1892; Officiating Chief Engineer and Secretary to Government NWP and Oudh, 1894; Rajputana and Central India, 1896; Chief Engineer, India Public Works Dept, 1899–1901. *Died 29 March 1920.*

PULLAR, Rufus D., JP; FCS; Chairman of J. Pullar & Sons, Ltd, Cleaners and Dyers, Perth; President Society of Dyers and Colourists, 1914; *b* Perth, 1861; *e s* of late Sir Robert Pullar; *m* 1890, Rose Lindsay, *d* of late Robert Morison, accountant, Perth; two *s*. *Educ:* Sharp's Institution, Perth; Craigmount School, Edinburgh; Universities of Edinburgh and Leeds. Interested in scientific pursuits; devoted special attention to chemistry as applied to cleaning and dyeing; travelled on the Continent, Canada and United States. *Address:* Brahan, Perth. *Clubs:* Royal Automobile, Royal Societies: Royal, Perth; University, Edinburgh. *Died 22 Sept. 1917.*

PULLEN, William le Geyt, CB 1917; Paymaster-Rear-Admiral retired; *b* 1 Sept. 1855; *s* of Captain T. C. Pullen, RN; *m* Harriette, *d* of George E. Fox, of Hillside, Plymouth; one *s* one *d.* Entered Royal Navy, 1872; Paymaster-in-Chief, 1910; served as Secretary to the Admiral commanding Coast of Ireland, 1885, and to the Naval Commanders-in-Chief in Australia 1889, China 1895, and at Plymouth 1900; Secretary to the Admiral commanding Coastguard and Reserves, 1904, and to the Naval Commander-in-Chief, The Nore, 1911–15, including the early part of the European War. *Club:* Royal Western Yacht, Plymouth. *Died 18 Jan. 1922.*

PULLEY, Col Charles, CB 1904; Indian Army, retired; *b* 21 Oct. 1851; *s* of Maj.-Gen. Charles Pulley, Madras Army, and Annie Eliza, *e d* of William Blunt, BCS; *m* 1st, 1880, Edith Marion (*d* 1888), *d* of Maj.-Gen. H. S. Obbard, IA; 2nd, 1896, Rachel, *d* of Rev. J. White, Stevenston, Ayrshire; one *s* one *d.* Served Afghanistan, 1878–80 (medal and clasp); Burma, 1886–87 (wounded, despatches, Bt-Major, medal and clasp); Lushai, 1892–93; NW Frontier, India, 1897–98 (despatches, medal 2 clasps); Tirah, 1897–98 (despatches, Bt-Col, clasp). *Address:* Llanberis, Langton Green, Kent. *Died 30 Oct. 1925.*

PULLING, Rev. Edward Herbert, CBE 1919; *b* Traine House, Modbury, Devon, 23 Jan. 1859; *y s* of Rev. F. W. Pulling, Vicar of Pinhoe, Devon; *m* 1892, Emily Frances, *e d* of Oswald Cornish Arthur of Gascoigne Place, Plymouth; three *s. Educ:* Royal Academy, Gosport (Burneys); Oxford University; Salisbury Theological College. Curate of Melksham, 1883–90; Chaplain to the Forces, 4th class, 1900; 1st class, 1910; served at Aldershot, 1890–93; Cavalry Dept, Canterbury, 1893–98; Sudan Expedition,1898; Alexandria, 1898–1903; Plymouth, 1903–6; Senior Chaplain, Dublin, 1906–12; Portsmouth, 1912–16; Humber Garrison,1916–19; with Lincolnshire Coast Defences,1918–19; brought to notice twice, 1917 and 1919, of Secretary of State for War for valuable services rendered in connection with the war; retired list, 1919; Vicar of Morgan's Vale, Salisbury 1919–23. *Address:* c/o Westminster Bank Ltd, Salisbury. *Club:* Church Imperial. *Died 25 Jan. 1928.*

PULLINGER, Frank, CB 1912; MA (Oxon), BSc (Lond.); HM Chief Inspector of Technical Schools; *b* 19 March 1866; *m* 1896; one *s* one *d. Educ:* Manchester Grammar School; Corpus Christi College, Oxford. Oxford University Extension Lecturer, 1891; Education Secretary to the Devon County Council, 1891–94. *Address:* Board of Education, Whitehall, SW. *Died 23 Dec. 1920.*

PUMPELLY, Raphael; author, geologist; *b* Owego, NY, 8 Sept. 1837; *s* of William Pumpelly and Mary H. Welles Pumpelly; *m* 1869, Eliza Frances Shepard; one *s* two *d. Educ:* Owego Academy; private schools in America; Royal School of Mines, Freiberg, Saxony. Made geological explorations in Corsica; had charge of Mines in Arizona, 1860–61; made scientific explorations for Japanese Govt, 1861–63; private geol expedn through Central, Western and Northern China and Mongolia, 1863–64; explored northern coalfields for Imperial Chinese Govt, 1864; journey of exploration across the Gobi Desert; returned to Europe through Siberia, 1864–65; Professor of Mining, Harvard,1866–73; made the explorations of discovery inaugurating the development of the iron ore industry of most of the iron ore ranges of Michigan and Western Ont, 1867–1901; State Geologist, Mich, 1869–71; Dir Mo Geol Survey and in charge of mineral industries, the Tenth census,1879–81; organised and directed Northern Trancontinental Survey, 1881–84; initiated and directed a physical-geographical and archæological exploration of Central Asia, 1903–4, under auspices of Carnegie Inst. of Washington. *Publications:* Geological Researches in China, Mongolia, Japan, 1866; Across America and Asia, 1870; Geology of the Upper District of Michigan, 1873; Iron Ores and Coal Fields of Missouri, 1873; Bulletins and Maps of the Northern Transcontinental Survey, 1882–83; Mineral Industries of the US, vol. xv, Tenth Census, 1886; Geology of the Green Mountains, 1894; Explorations in Central Asia, 1905; Prehistoric Civilisations of Anau, 1908; Reminiscences, 1918. *Address:* Newport, Rhode Island, USA. *T:* Newport 1541; Dublin, New Hampshire. *Clubs:* Authors, Century, University, New York. *Died 10 Aug. 1923.*

PUNCHARD, Rev. Elgood George, DD Oxon; Hon. Canon of Ely since 1895; *b* Framlingham, Suffolk, 18 April 1844; 2nd *s* of John Elgood Punchard and Elizabeth; *m* 1879, Catherine Mary, *y d* of Joseph and Ann Johnson of Windsor; one *s* one *d. Educ:* New Inn Hall, Oxford, 1868–72; transferred to Balliol Coll., 1887. Second class, Law and History, 1872; BA 1872; MA 1874; BD 1880; DD 1884; *proxime accessit* for the Newdigate, 1871; prize for English Sacred Poem, 1875. Deacon, 1872; priest by Bishop Mackarness of Oxford, 1873; Curate of Wendover, 1872–77; Oriental Fellow of St Augustine's College, Canterbury, 1878; Curate in charge of Shalbourne,1879; Vicar of Linslade, 1880–83; Vicar of Christ Church, Luton, 1883–1902; Rural Dean of Luton, 1897–1902; elected Bishop of Antigua, 1896, but declined; Chaplain to Bishop of Truro, 1906; Vicar of Ely St Mary's, 1902–15. *Publications:* King Saul and other Poems, 1877; Commentary on St James, in the New Testament for English Readers, edited by Bishop Ellicott, 1879; Christ of Contention (three essays), 1885; The Organisation and Work of a Parish, 1889; Records of an Unfortunate Family—Punchard of Heanton-

Puncardon, 1894; editor of Ely Diocesan Remembrancer, 1906–9; reviews and various articles in the Church Quarterly, Asiatic Quarterly, Indian Church Quarterly. *Address:* Ely, Cambs. *TA:* Punchard, Ely. *Died 2 March 1917.*

PURCELL, Rev. Handfield Noel, VD; JP Cornwall; MA; Vicar of Fowey, 1867–1920; Canon of Truro Cathedral; late Chairman of St Austell Board of Guardians; *b* Dundalk, Co. Louth; *s* of late Admiral Edward Purcell; *m* 1st, Annie Ellen Treffry (*d* 1877); 2nd, 1899, Elizabeth Anna Adams; four *s* three *d. Educ:* Bath College; Exeter College, Oxford. Curate of St Kenelms, Halesowen, Worcester; Senior Chaplain, RGA, Cornwall. *Address:* Lisnawilly, Fowey. *Club:* Royal Fowey Yacht. *Died 15 April 1925.*

PURCELL, Sir John Samuel, KCB 1900 (CB 1888); Director of Industrial and General Trust; *b* Carrick-on-Suir, Ireland, 1839; *s* of late Dr Purcell, sometime a Commissioner of Irish Poor Laws; *m* 1868, Alice Fanny, *d* of Captain Charles Leighton Kennett; two *s* four *d. Educ:* private school. Entered secretariat of Inland Revenue Department, 1856; appointed Principal Clerk, 1867; Controller of Stamps and Registrar of Joint-Stock Companies, 1883; retired from public service, 1900; was a member of the Joint Committee on Postage Stamps which sat in 1885–86; and his name much identified with the series of those stamps issued in the Jubilee Year 1887; was one of the six promoters and original members of the London Irish Rifle Volunteers, in which corps he served for some years with the rank of Major. *Decorated* for official service. *Address:* Glebe Lodge, Blackheath, Kent. *TA:* Blackheath. *T:* Lee Green 140. *Club:* Constitutional. *Died 7 Dec. 1924.*

PURCELL, Major Raymond John Hugo, JP; *b* 1885; *s* of late M. J. Purcell, JP, Burton Park, Co. Cork. *Educ:* Beaumont; Christ Church, Oxford (MA). Succeeded 1906; entered King's Royal Rifle Corps from Oxford, 1907; retired as Major, 1921 (owing to severe wounds received in European War). *Recreations:* yachting, hunting, big-game shooting. *Address:* Burton Park, Churchtown, Co. Cork. *Clubs:* Arthur's, Army and Navy; Royal Yacht Squadron, Cowes; Kildare Street, Dublin. *Died 24 July 1928.*

PURCHASE, Edward James, KC 1923; *o s* of late James Purchase; *m* Charlotte, 3rd *d* of late Edwin Guy; one *s. Educ:* Wadham College, Oxford (MA). Formerly in Holy Orders; Rector of Owsden, Newmarket, 1903–5; student of Middle Temple, 1905; called to the Bar, 1908; Western Circuit. *Address:*1 Brick Court, Temple, EC. *T:* Temple 97; Central 1596. *Died 3 Feb. 1924.*

PURCHASE, Sir William Henry, Kt 1921; member of W. H. Purchase & Co.; *b* 19 July 1860; *s* of J. Bentley Purchase, Lymington; *m* 1890, Jane Norman, *d* of Randal George Vogan, Redhill; one *s.* Chairman National Appointments Committee, Ministry of Labour; Chairman London Telephone Advisory Committee; Member of Council and Member of Commercial Education Committee, London Chamber of Commerce; Member Board of Management, Throat Hospital, Golden Square, W; Member of City of London Court of Arbitration. *Address:* The Old Vicarage, Wrotham, Kent. *Clubs:* Royal Automobile, City Carlton. *Died 2 July 1924.*

PURDIE, Thomas, BSc Lond.; PhD Würzburg; LLD Aberdeen and St Andrews; FRS; ARSM; Professor Emeritus, University of St Andrews, since 1909; *b* Biggar, Lanarks, 27 Jan. 1843; *e s* of late James Purdie, writer and banker, Biggar; *m* 1878, Marianne, *d* of late John Rotherham, Coventry. *Educ:* Edinburgh Academy; Royal School of Mines; Universities of St Andrews and Würzburg. Demonstrator in Chemistry, Royal College of Science, 1875–78; Science Master at the High School, Newcastle, Staffs, 1881–83; Professor of Chemistry, United College University of St Andrews, 1884–1909. *Publications:* a series of researches in Journal of Chemical Society 1881–1910. *Recreations:* angling, golfing, cycling. *Address:* University, St Andrews. *Club:* Savile. *Died 14 Dec. 1916.*

PURDOM, Thomas Hunter, KC; Member of legal firm, Purdom & Purdom, Barristers; *b* London, Canada, 25 July 1853; *s* of Alexander Purdom, builder, and Margaret Hunter (who came to Canada from Hawick, Scotland, 1849); *m* 1st, 1886, Isabella (*d* 1897), *d* of John C. Craig; 2nd, 1893, Nellie (*d* 1901), *d* of David Davies; 3rd, 1902, Marion, her sister; one *s* one *d. Educ:* Joint Grammar and Common School, London, Ont. Called to the Bar, 1876; Solicitor, 1875; Bencher, Law Society at Osgoode Hall, Toronto, 1885–90; President—Dominion Savings and Investment Society; Fidelity Trusts Co. of Ontario; The Northern Life Assurance Co. of Canada; The London Advertiser Co., Ltd; The Advertiser Job Printing Co., Ltd; Director—The Masonic Temple Co.; The London and Lake Erie

Railway Transportation Co.; The Purdom Hardware Co., Ltd. *Recreation:* golf. *Address:* 383 King Street, London, Canada. *T:* 387. *Clubs:* London Golf, Rotary, London.
Died 14 Nov. 1923.

PUREFOY, Richard Dancer, MD; Hon. LLD; FRCS; President, Royal Academy of Medicine in Ireland; Consulting Gynaecologist, Rotunda Hospital, Dublin. *Educ:* Trinity College, Dublin. *Address:* 62 Merrion Square, Dublin.
Died 27 June 1919.

PURVES, (William) Laidlaw, MD; Consulting Aural Surgeon, Guy's Hospital; Consulting Ophthalmic and Aural Surgeon, Hospital for Diseases of Nervous System; Aural Surgeon to Royal Normal College and Academy of Music for the Blind; *s* of William Brown Purves, surgeon, Edinburgh; *m* Elizabeth, *d* of Patrick Adie of Worton Hall, Isleworth. *Educ:* Universities of Edinburgh, Berlin, Leipzig, Vienna, Utrecht and Paris. *Publications:* Enlargement of the Thyroid, a Beneficial Physiological Action; Endothelium en Emigratie; Determination of the Anomalies of Refraction of the Human Eye; A Contribution to Ophthalmoscopy; Method of Determining the Focal Distance of Single or Combined Lenses; An Optometer; An International Calculating Scale for Ophthalmological Purposes; Paracentesis of the Tympanic Membrane; Hearing and the Examinations for the Public Services; The True Value of Artificial Tympanic Membranes; The Determination of the Hearing Power; The Authorship of Robinson Crusoe; The "O" Edition of Robeson Cruso; The First English Translation of Gil Blas, etc. *Address:* 20 Stratford Place, W. *Died 29 Dec. 1917.*

PURVIS, Brig.-Gen. Alexander Burridge, JP, DL Fife; *b* 21 Sept. 1854; *e s* of John Purvis of Kinaldy, and Wilhelmina, *d* of William Berry of Tayfield; *m* 1894, Bertha, *d* of Rev. E. R. Pitman. *Educ:* Glenalmond; Marlborough; RMA, Woolwich. Commissioned Royal Artillery, 1874; Col, 1907; commanding Volunteer Infantry Brigade, 1906; retired, 1908; Brigadier-General commanding 17th Divisional Artillery, 1914–15; County Commandant Fifeshire Volunteer Corps, 1916–19. *Clubs:* Junior United Service, MCC; Royal and Ancient, St Andrews; New, Edinburgh. *Died April 1928.*

PURVIS, Sir Robert, Kt 1905; LLD; *b* Roxburghshire, 1844; *s* of Joseph Purvis; *m* 1874, Elizabeth Marion (*d* 1913), *e d* of William Henry Peat, late of Mincing Lane, London. *Educ:* Marlborough School; Downing College, Cambridge (MA). Barrister, Inner Temple, 1873. Contested Abingdon Div. of Berks, 1885; Edinburgh (South), 1886; Peterborough, 1889–92; MP (U) Peterborough, 1895–1906; contested same Division, 1910. *Publication:* Sir William Arrol, a Memorial. *Club:* Oxford and Cambridge.
Died 23 June 1920.

PYE, Joseph Patrick, JP; MD; FRUI; Professor of Anatomy and Physiology, Queen's College, Galway; Hon. Surgeon, Galway Hospital. *Educ:* Queen's Coll., Galway; London; Paris. *Address:* Rusheen-na-curra, Clifton, Co. Galway.
Died 25 March 1920.

PYE-SMITH, Rutherfoord John, JP City of Sheffield; ChM (Sheffield); FRCS; Consulting Surgeon, Sheffield Royal Hospital; Emeritus Professor of Surgery, University of Sheffield; *b* London, 1848; 3rd *s* of Ebenezer Pye-Smith, FRCS; *m* Barbara, 4th *d* of John Edgcumbe Gill. *Educ:* Amersham Hall; Guy's Hospital. Commenced general medical practice at Sheffield, 1876; consulting surgical practice, 1895; retired 1919; formerly President Yorks Branch, British Medical Association; President and Treasurer Sheffield Medico-Chirurgical Society; Member of the Sheffield Education Committee; Medical Referee Workmen's Compensation Act; Member of General Medical Council. *Publications:* address in Surgery, Annual Meeting, British Medical Association, 1908; Arsenic Cancer (Lancet), 1913. *Address:* Clvda, Ampthill, Bedfordshire.
Died 23 March 1921.

PYM, Charles Guy, JP, DL Beds; FGS; Grand Councillor Primrose League; *b* Willian, Herts, 11 Feb. 1841; *y s* of Rev. W. W. Pym, Willian Rectory, and Sophia, *d* of late Samuel Gambier, Commissioner of Navy; *g s* of Francis Pym, MP, Hasells Hall, Beds; *m* 1885, Mildred, *d* of late Henry Sykes Thornton, banker. *Educ:* Rossall School. Naval Service, 1855–58; War Office, 1859–74; mercantile pursuits to 1886; MP(C) Bedford, 1895–1906; High Sheriff for the County of London, 1911. *Recreations:* athletics (founder of Civil Service sports), cricket, yachting, golf (captain of Royal Wimbledon, 1884). *Address:* 35 Cranley Gardens, SW. *T:* Western 4078; Cæsar's Camp, Sandy, Beds. *Clubs:* Carlton, Junior Carlton. *Died 12 Nov. 1918.*

PYM, Francis, JP, DL; *b* 6 Dec. 1849; *e s* of late Francis Leslie Pym and Mary Jemima, *d* of Rev. Henry Palmer of Withcote Hall, Leicester; *m* 1891, Alice, *y d* of Sir George Conway Colthurst, 5th Bt, MP, of Blarney Castle, Cork. *Educ:* Eton; Oxford. Patron of one living; late Sub-Lieut 1st Life Guards; High Sheriff, Beds, 1903. *Address:* Hasells Hall, Sandy, Bedfordshire. *T:* Sandy 12. *Clubs:* Travellers', Carlton; Royal Yacht Squadron, Cowes.

Died 7 June 1927.

PYNE, Sir (Thomas) Salter, Kt 1894; CSI 1894; MInstCE, MInstME; formerly Chief Engineer to Government of Afghanistan; *b* 1860; *s* of John Pyne and Alice, *d* of Thomas Salter, Rochdale. *Educ:* private tutors. Engineer's apprentice, 1875–78; manager of foundry and engineering works, 1879–83; with a mercantile firm in India, 1883–85; introduced into Afghanistan many and various industries, including works for the manufacture of guns, rifles, ammunition, swords, coining, distilling, soap, candles, etc; Ambassador for His Highness the Amir to His Excellency the Viceroy of India in 1893, and at the satisfactory conclusion of the negotiations awarded a Knighthood and CSI and thanked by Her Majesty's Government; awarded an Afghan decoration by His Highness the Amir, with other presents at various periods; granted a commission in the King's Own Yorkshire LI; employed at the Ministry of Munitions, 1915. *Recreations:* riding, fishing, shooting. *Club:* Badminton.

Died Sept. 1921.

Q

QUARRINGTON, Rev. Edwin Fowler; Prebendary of Lincoln. *Address:* Welby Lodge, Woodhall Spa, Lincs.

Died 3 Sept. 1922.

QUEENSBERRY, 10th Marquess of, *cr* 1682; **Percy Sholto Douglas;** Viscount Drumlanrig and Baron Douglas, 1628; Earl of Queensberry, 1633; Bt (Nova Scotia), 1668; *b* 13 Oct. 1868; *s* of 9th Marquess and 1st wife, Sybil, *d* of Alfred Montgomery, and *g d* of Sir Henry Conyngham Montgomery, 1st Bt; *S* father, 1900; *m* 1st, 1893, Anna Maria (*d* 1917), *d* of Rev. Thomas Walters, Vicar of Boyton, Cornwall; two *s* one *d*; 2nd, 1918, Mary Louisa, *d* of late Richard Bickel, Cardiff, and *widow* of Ernest Morgan. Formerly midshipman RN and Lieut 3rd Militia Batt. King's Own Scottish Borderers. *Heir: s* Viscount Drumlanrig, *b* 17 Jan. 1896. *Address:* 14 Brook Green, W.

Died 1 Aug. 1920.

QUENINGTON, Viscount; Michael Hugh Hicks-Beach; MP (U) Tewkesbury Division of Gloucestershire since 1906; *b* 19 Jan. 1877; *o s* of 1st Earl St Aldwyn and 2nd wife, Lady Lucy Catherine, *d* of 3rd Earl Fortescue; *m* 1909, Marjorie (*d* 1916), *d* of Henry Dent Brocklehurst (*brother* of 1st and last Baron Ranksborough), Sudeley Castle, Glos; one *s* one *d*. *Educ:* Eton; Christ Church, Oxford (MA). Was Captain 4th (Militia) Batt. Gloucester Regt; 2nd Lieut Royal Gloucestershire Yeomanry, 1908; served St Helena during South African War; acted as Asst Private Secretary to Chancellor of Exchequer (his father), 1901–2; to Sir Alexander Hood, Chief Unionist Whip, 1904–5; travelled round the world, 1902–3; JP Glos; Member of Northleach Board of Guardians and RDC. *Recreations:* hunting, shooting, fishing. *Address:* Coln St Aldwyns, Fairford, Glos; 81 Eaton Place, SW. *Clubs:* Carlton, Bachelors'.

Died 23 April 1916.

QUERIPEL, Hon. Col Alfred Ernest, CB 1917; retired pay, late Army Veterinary Department; *b* 27 Aug. 1870; *m*. Retired 1901. *Address:* c/o Holt & Co., 8 Whitehall Place, SW.

Died 28 April 1921.

QUIGLEY, Most Rev. James Edward, DD, LLD; Archbishop of Chicago (RC) since 1903; *b* Oshawa, Ontario, 15 Oct. 1854; *s* of James Quigley and Mary Lacey. *Educ:* St Joseph's College, Buffalo, NY; Niagara University, Niagara Falls, NY; University of Innsbruck, Austria; Propaganda Coll., Rome. Ordained, 1879; Rector, St Vincent's Church, RC, Attica, NY, 1879–84; St Joseph's Cathedral, Buffalo, NY, 1884–96; St Bridget's Church, Buffalo, NY, 1896–97;

Bishop of Buffalo, 1897–1903. *Address:* 1555 N State Street, Chicago, Ill, USA. *T:* North 815.

Died July 1916.

QUILL, Maj.-Gen. Richard Henry, CB 1917; Army Medical Staff; *b* 8 June 1848; *e s* of late Jerome Quill, JP of Kilmoily, Co. Kerry; *m* 1886, Marion, *o d* of Deputy Inspector-General W. Gunn, RN; one *s. Educ:* Trinity College, Dublin. BA 1869; MB, MCh 1871. Entered army as Assistant Surgeon 1872; served with RA, Afghanistan, 1879–80 (medal); was Senior Medical Officer, Thames District at Chatham, and subsequently Senior Medical Officer, Ceylon Command, 1898–1902; Administrative Medical Charge of South Eastern District, 1902–5; Principal Medical Officer, Royal Victoria Hospital, Netley, 1905–8; retired, 1908; 2nd Class of the Royal Prussian Order of the Red Eagle with the Star, 1907. *Recreations:* formerly hunting and athletics of various kinds; latterly golf (won Amateur Golf Championship of Ceylon, 1899, besides many subsequent golf trophies). *Address:* Craigleith House, Cheltenham. *T:* Cheltenham 1014. *Clubs:* Junior United Service; Cinque Ports Golf, Deal; New, Cheltenham.

Died 18 Oct. 1924.

QUIN, Maj.-Gen. Thomas James; Bengal Infantry; *b* 1 May 1842; *m* 1870, Mary (deceased), *e d* of late Major James Wemyss. Entered army, 1859; served Bhootan Expedition, 1865 (medal); Officiating Assistant Commissioner and Cantonment Officer, NW Provinces, 1869–89; Deputy Commissioner, 1889; Maj.-Gen. 1898; retired, 1898.

Died 24 Oct. 1919.

QUINLAN, Hon. Timothy Francis, CMG 1913; JP; *b* Tipperary, Ireland, 18 Feb. 1861; *s* of Michael Quinlan; *m* 1883, Teresa, (*d* 1904), *d* of Daniel Connor; four *s* three *d*. Arrived in Australia with his parents, 1863; MLA, West Perth, in first West Australian Parliament, 1890; represented Tooday, 1897–1911; Minister for Works in Morgan's Government, 1901; Chairman of Committees, 1905; Speaker from 1905 (re-elected 1908) until 1911, when he retired; gazetted Honourable, 1912; City Councillor of Perth for 12 years; Director of South British Insurance Co., Southern Cross Life Co., and Chairman Perth Building Society; had extensive landed interests. Created Knight of Order of St Silvester, Holy See, by Leo XIII. *Address:* Avoca, Adelaide Terrace, Perth, Western Australia.

Died 8 July 1927.

QUINN, John; lawyer; head of own law office, since 1906; *b* Tiffin, Ohio, 24 April 1870; *s* of James W. Quinn and Mary Quinlan; unmarried. *Educ:* University of Michigan; Georgetown Univ., Washington, DC (LLB 1893); Harvard Univ. (LLB 1895). Private Secretary to Hon. Charles Foster, Sec. of Treasury in (Benjamin) Harrison Cabinet, 1890–93; associated in practice in NYC with Gen. Benjamin F. Tracy, 1895–1900; mem. law firm, Alexander & Colby, 1900–6; delegate, Democratic National Convention, Denver, 1908; Baltimore, 1912; Member, Amer. Bar Assoc.; NY State Bar Assoc.; Association of Bar, City of New York; New York Co. Lawyers' Assoc.; Contemporary Art Soc.; Société de Cent Bibliophiles, etc; one of organisers of Internat. Exhibition of Modern Art, New York, 1913; Hon. Fellow for life, Metropolitan Mus. of Art, New York (in recognition of services in the cause of free art); an authority on modern Irish literature and drama, and possessor of valuable collection of modern art; conducted campaign which resulted in removal of all duty on modern works of art; Chevalier Legion of Honour, France, for services during 1914–18 War. *Publications:* essays on literature and art. *Address:* 58 Central Park W, New York; 31 Nassau Street, New York. *Clubs:* Harvard, Manhattan, New York.

Died 28 July 1924.

QUIRK, Rev. James Francis, JP, MA; Rector of Great Coates and Vicar of Aylesby; Canon of Lincoln Cathedral; Surrogate; *b* Willoughby, near Rugby, 5 March 1850; *s* of late Rev. J. R. Quirk, MA, Rector of Blandford-Forum, Dorset; *m* 1880, Dora, *o d* of late Rev. W. H. Parson, Vicar of Lynchmere, Surrey; four *s* one *d. Educ:* Atherstone Grammar School; Milton Abbas, Dorset; Queen's College, Oxford (BA and MA 1876). Curate of Haslemere, 1876–79; Vicar of Grasby, near Caistor, Lincolnshire (on the presentation of the late Lord Tennyson, Poet Laureate), 1879–92; Chaplain to High Sheriff of Lincolnshire, 1901–2, 1903–4 and 1920–21; Immigration Board, Grimsby; Chairman of Grimsby County Bench of Magistrates. *Publication:* article on shooting in Victoria History of the Counties of England, vol. ii. *Recreations:* shooting, fishing. *Address:* Great Coates Rectory, Lincolnshire. *TA:* Grimsby. *T:* 2Y3 Healing. *M:* FU 2929.

Died 20 March 1927.

QUIRK, Rt. Rev. Canon John Nathaniel, DD, DLitt; Suffragan Bishop of Jarrow since 1914; Archdeacon of Durham and Canon

Residentiary of Durham Cathedral since 1922; Canon Residentiary of York Minster, 1912–14; of Durham Cathedral since 1914; Proctor in Convocation for Chapter of Durham, 1914; *b* 1849; *s* of Rev. Charles Thomas Quirk, MA, Rector of Golborne, Lancs; *m* 1880, Mary Jane, *d* of Rev. John Clay, MA, Vicar of Stapenhill, Derbyshire; two *s. Educ:* Shrewsbury School; St John's College, Cambridge. 9th Junior Optime and BA 1873; MA 1876; DD *jure dignitatis,* 1902. Trained for Holy Orders by Dean Vaughan, The Temple, 1873–74; ordained, 1874; curate St Leonard's, Bridgnorth, 1874–78; Doncaster, 1878–81; Vicar of St Thomas's, Douglas, 1881–82; Rotherham, 1882–89; St Mary, Beverley, 1889–94; St Paul, Lorrimore Square, SE, 1894–95; Canon and Prebendary of York, 1888; Rector of Bath and Rural Dean, 1895–1901; Proctor in Convocation, 1898–1901; Vicar of Doncaster, 1901–05; Vicar of St Mark's, Sheffield, 1905–11; Bishop-Suffragan of Sheffield, 1901–14; Hon. DLitt Sheffield Univ., 1914. *Address:* Lake End, Greenodd, Ulverston; The College, Durham. *Clubs:* Royal Societies; Durham County, Durham.

Died 26 April 1924.

QUIRK, Col John Owen, CB 1897; DSO 1886; retired; late commanding 41st Regimental District; *b* 13 Aug. 1847; 3rd *s* of late Philip Quirk, Knockaloe House, Bromborough, Cheshire; *m* 1875, Eugénie Marie, *y* of late Octavius O'Brien, Kildare St, Dublin. *Educ:* private school; Trinity College, Dublin (BA, CE). Joined the 41st (The Welsh) Regt, 1869; Colonel, 1897; served in South African War, 1881; Egyptian Expedition, 1884, on transport duties; present at the battles of El Teb and Tamai, and advance on Tamanieb (despatches, medal with clasp, and bronze star); Soudan Expedition, 1884–85, as AAG to Egyptian Army (despatches, clasp, 3rd class Medjidie); Soudan Expedition, 1885–86, as AAG to Egyptian Army, present at action of Geniss (horse shot, despatches, DSO); Soudan with Nile Field Force, 1889, as Commandant Korosko (3rd class Osmanieh). *Recreation:* shooting. *Club:* Army and Navy.

Died 29 Jan. 1928.

R

RABAN, Brig.-Gen. Sir Edward, KCB 1906 (CB 1902); KBE 1919; Royal Engineers; *b* 8 Aug. 1850; *s* of late Maj.-Gen. H. Raban; *m* 1873, Edith, *e d* of Col H. W. P. Welman; two *d. Educ:* Sherborne; RMA, Woolwich. Entered Army, 1871; Capt. 1883; Major, 1889; Lt-Col 1896; Col 1900; retired list, 1900; served expedition against Naga Hill tribes, 1879–80 (despatches, medal with clasp); Director of Works, Admiralty, 1895–1912; recalled to Army, 1914; Brig.-Gen. 1917; served on Staff of Viscount French, 1916–17; Deputy Director at War Office, 1917; reverted to retired list, 1918; Past President The Junior Institution of Engineers; Fellow Society of Engineers. *Address:* 35 Elm Park Gardens, SW10. *T:* Kensington 3040. *Club:* United Service.   *Died 8 Feb. 1927.*

RABY, Joseph Thomas, JP; FJI 1910; Alderman for City of Lichfield; District Manager of the Staffordshire Advertiser at Lichfield; *b* 28 Oct. 1853; *e s* of Samuel Raby, marble mason of Derby; *m* 1872, Hannah Lord, *step-d* of John Newsome, woollen manufacturer, Batley, Yorkshire; five *s* five *d. Educ:* King Street School, Derby; private academies at Leicester. Journalist; engaged on first daily paper published in Leicester, 1870; afterwards in Lancashire, Yorkshire, Berkshire and South Wales; Editor of local paper at Lichfield, 1882; a correspondent of the Press Association since 1871; took an active part in movement which led to formation of National Association of Journalists; Chairman of Birmingham and Midland Counties District (Inst. of Journalists), 1902; Vice-President, 1903; Member of British Press Tour in Sweden, 1906; Member of Lichfield City Council and Lichfield Board of Guardians since 1898; Sheriff, 1903; Mayor, 1915; one of the founders of the Johnson Library and Museum at Lichfield. *Publications:* Lichfield and Dr Johnson; Johnsonian Memorials at Lichfield; numerous pamphlets and papers. *Recreations:* billiards, bowls. *Address:* The Tower House, Lichfield, Staffs. *TA:* Raby, Lichfield. *T:* 126 Lichfield.

Died 30 May 1916.

RADCLIFFE, His Honour Francis Reynolds Yonge, KC 1904; JP; Barrister; Judge of County Courts Circuit 36 (Oxfordshire) since 1914; *b* Westminster, 20 Sept. 1851; *e s* of late John Alexander Radcliffe and Fanny Johnson, *d* of Rev. W. J. Yonge; *m* Helen, *o*

d of Edward Harbord Lushington of Brackenhurst, Cobham, Surrey; three *s* three *d. Educ:* Eton; Corpus Christi Coll., Oxford (Exhibitioner). 1st class Classical Moderations, 1872; 1st class Final Classical School, 1874; Fellow of All Souls Coll., 1874–82. Barrister 1876; Revising Barrister 1894; Recorder of Devizes, 1887–1904; Recorder of Portsmouth, 1904–14; a Chairman of Quarter Sessions. Chevalier de l'Ordre de Léopold, Belgium. *Publications:* The New Politicus; Cases illustrative of the Law of Torts, etc. *Recreations:* rowing, fishing, shooting. *Address:* Headington Rise, Oxford. *T:* Oxford 601. *Club:* Athenæum.   *Died 23 April 1924.*

RADCLIFFE, Henry; Senior Partner in Evan Thomas, Radcliffe & Co., steamship company, Cardiff; director of companies.

Died 16 Dec. 1921.

RADCLIFFE, Major Jasper Fitzgerald, DSO 1900; the Devonshire Regiment; *b* 18 Aug. 1867; *s* of late Walter Copleston Radcliffe, of Warleigh; *m* 1893, Emily Maude, *d* of Rev. Edward Chatterton Orpen, of Exleigh, Starcross, Devon. *Educ:* Cheltenham. Entered army, 1889; Captain, 1898; served South Africa (despatches twice, Queen's medal with clasp, DSO); European War, 1914–15 (despatches, wounded).   *Died 2 Feb. 1916.*

RADCLIFFE, Rev. John Ed.; Christian minister of the United Methodist Church, and President of Conference in the year 1899; *b* Saddleworth, West Riding of Yorkshire, 11 Nov. 1846; *m* 1st, 1875 (she *d* 1892), *d* of late Alderman Garside of Leeds; 2nd, 1898, *o d* of S. Naylor of Adwalton, Yorkshire; two *s* two *d. Educ:* in the fields, by the streams, on the moors, at "an elementary school," with the assistance of evening classes, and at Ranmoor Coll., Sheffield. Upon leaving college in 1870 served four years as a probationary minister; was ordained in 1874; ministered in Hunslet (Leeds), Guernsey, Leicester, Ashton-under-Lyne, Forest Hill (London), Manchester, Hanley, Batley, Leeds, Lindley, Halifax and Bradford; retired, 1917. *Publications:* magazine articles. *Recreation:* choicest, a country walk. *Address:* Batley, Yorkshire.

Died 22 April 1919.

RADCLIFFE, Wyndham Ivor, MA; *s* of late Henry Radcliffe, JP, of Druidstone, Michaelston-y-Vedw, Cardiff. *Educ:* privately; Christ Church, Oxford. Barrister Inner Temple, 1919; formerly Lieut, Special Reserve of Officers and RFA (TF); Sheriff of Glamorgan, 1924. *Address:* 1 Park Lodge, Park Place, Knightsbridge, SW1. *T:* Kensington 8265; Druidstone, Michaelston-y-Vedw, near Cardiff. *T:* St Mellons (Mon) 7. *Clubs:* United University, Royal Automobile, Queen's; Cardiff and County, Cardiff.

Died 15 April 1927.

RADFORD, Sir Charles Horace, Kt 1907; sometime Mayor of Plymouth; *b* 31 May 1854; 3rd *s* of late George David Radford of Plymouth; *m* 1893, Bessie, *d* of late William May of Devonport. *Educ:* Amersham Hall, Caversham, Reading. Member of Plymouth County Borough Council since 1892; Alderman since 1896; Mayor during Diamond Jubilee Year, 1896–97; again elected, 1907; JP Devonshire 1895; and County Borough of Plymouth, 1906. *Address:* 4 The Crescent, Plymouth; Polbream, Mullion, Cornwall. *Club:* National Liberal.   *Died 19 Feb. 1916.*

RADFORD, Edward, ARWS; *b* Devonport, Devon, 22 April 1831; 4th *s* of William Radford, civil engineer, of Irlam, Buglawton, Cheshire; *m* Hester Blunden Helsham (*d* 1877); one *s. Educ:* Stock's School, Poplar; Tredegar Square Grammar School, Bow. Indentured pupil of Thomas Wickstead, civil engineer; in employ of J. and C. Rigby, Government contractors, Holyhead and Portland breakwaters; assistant to his brother William, engineer to Regent's Canal, and under J. M. Rendel, PICE; practised as architect at Toronto, Canada West; afterwards with W. Tinsley, architect, Cincinnati, Ohio; Acting-Lieutenant 11th Ohio Battery, United States Artillery, under Major A. G. A. Constable, Bengal Horse Artillery, early in Secesh War; member of Liverpool Society of Painters in Water Colours; for many years member of Society of Arts. *Recreations:* country walks, a good novel; when young, fond of rowing, yachting, shooting, sparring. *Address:* Morley House, Southwick, Brighton.

Died 9 June 1920.

RADFORD, Sir George Heynes, Kt 1916; JP Surrey; MP (L) East Islington since 1906; Chairman National Liberal Club Buildings Company, Ltd; Senator University of London; solicitor; *b* 1851; *e s* of G. D. Radford of Plymouth, and Catherine Agnes Heynes; *m* 1882, Emma Louisa, *d* of Daniel Radford, JP; three *d. Educ:* London Univ. (LLB). Solicitor; Sen. Partner, Radford and Frankland; Mem. LCC, 1895–1907. *Publications:* Occasional Verses; Shylock and Others.

Address: 27 Chancery Lane, WC. *TA:* Radland, Holborn, London. *T:* Holborn 90. Chiswick House, Ditton Hill, Surrey. *Clubs:* National Liberal, Reform. *Died 5 Oct. 1917.*

RADFORD, Col Oswald Claude, CB 1905; CIE 1900; Indian Army; *b* 4 Nov. 1850; *s* of James Radford; *m* 1st, 1883, Alice Sarah, *d* of J. H. Herdon; 2nd, 1917, Margaret, *d* of Thomas Fleming. Served Jowaki-Afridi Expedition, 1877–78 (despatches, medal with clasp); Afghanistan, 1879–80 (medal); Takht i Suliman, 1883 (despatches); Zhob Valley Expedition, 1884; Black Mountain, 1888 (wounded, despatches, brevet of Major, clasp); Miranzai, 1891 (despatches); Waziristan, 1894 (clasp); China, 1900—commanded force of British, French and Japanese at Tai-Tao-Ting (despatches twice, medal, CIE); Kabul Kheyl Expedition, 1901—commanded a column (despatches); retired, 1910. *Died 23 Sept. 1924.*

RAE, Sir Alexander, Kt 1911; JP Caithness; Hon. Sheriff of Caithness, Orkney, and Shetland; *b* 1849; *s* of late William Rae, publisher, Provost of Wick, 1874–86; *m* Mary, *e d* of late William Crowe, Factor for the British Fisheries Society. *Educ:* Wick; Royal High School, Edinburgh. Was in business as publisher with his father, and, on the latter's death in 1893, conducted the business until 1910, when he retired; Provost of Wick, 1904–6; President of Wick Liberal Association since 1894. *Recreations:* golf, bowls, chess. *Address:* Langhills, Wick, Scotland. *Club:* Scottish Liberal, Edinburgh. *Died 1924.*

RAE, Sir (Henry) Norman, Kt 1922; MP (Coalition L) Shipley Division of Yorks, Dec. 1918–23; wool merchant; *b* 20 Jan. 1860; *s* of Rev. James Rae, Harrogate; *m* 1883, Emily (*d* 1927), *d* of Joshua Cass, Mirfield, Yorks; one *s* one *d.* Contested Ripon Division, 1910. *Address:* Rossett Green, Harrogate. *Club:* Reform. *Died 31 Dec. 1928.*

RAE, Captain Sir James Robert, KBE 1920 (OBE 1918); Master, SS City of Exeter; *b* 1859; *s* of George Rae, Glasgow; *m* 1892, *d* of N. Noble. *Address:* 73 Caledonia Road, Saltcoats, Scotland. *Died 29 Dec. 1928.*

RAEBURN, Sir Ernest Manifold, KBE 1920; late Director-General, British Ministry of Shipping, New York; *b* 13 Dec. 1878; *s* of Sir William H. Raeburn, MP; *m* Greta Mary Alison, *d* of Eng.-Capt. J. H. Watson, RN; one *s* one *d. Educ:* Kelvinside Academy, Glasgow. With his father's firm, Raeburn & Verel, Ltd, Shipowners, Glasgow; a partner for ten years; Commercial Advisor, Transport Dept of Admiralty shortly after outbreak of European war; then Private Secretary to Sir Joseph P. Maday, Bt, PC, Shipping Controller; then assistant to Sir Thomas Royden, Bt, in Washington, DC; then Director of Transport Dept, Ministry of Shipping, New York. *Recreations:* fishing, golf, tennis, badminton, etc. *Address:* 45 West Nile Street, Glasgow. *TA:* Vernay Glasgow. *Clubs:* Caledonian, Royal Societies; Conservative, Glasgow; London and Press, New York. *Died 1 June 1922.*

RAFFAELLI, J. F.; Chevalier de la Légion d'honneur; artiste, peintre; Inventeur des "couleurs solides à l'huile"; *b* Paris, 20 avril 1850; *m* Aglaè Rosine Héran; grand'mère était une de Giuli; les de Giuli étaient alliés à la grande famille des Gonzague. Officier de la Couronne royale d'Italie; Chevalier de l'ordre de Léopold de Belgique; médaille d'or Exposition Universelle de Paris, 1889–1900. *Address:* rue Chardin I, Paris. *Died Feb. 1924.*

RAFFLES, Rev. Thomas Stamford; Rector of Lexden, Essex; *b* 11 July 1853; *m* 1884, Cecil Helen, 2nd *d* of Col Lovett of Henlle, Shropshire; two *s. Educ:* Rugby; Clare College, Cambridge (MA); Cuddesdon Theological College. Curate of Hawarden, 1880; Whittington, Salop, 1880–82; Ashton-on-Mersey, 1882–83; Rector of Owmby, 1883–87; Langham, 1887–1914. *Address:* Lexden Rectory, Colchester. *T:* Colchester 57. *TA:* Lexden. *Died 1 March 1926.*

RAFFLES-FLINT, Ven. Stamford Raffles, FZS; Archdeacon of Cornwall since 1916; Canon Residentiary and Treasurer of Truro Cathedral; *b* 6 Feb. 1847; *s* of Rev. W. C. Raffles Flint (*nephew* of Sir T. Stamford Raffles), and Jenny Rosdew, *d* of Col Mudge of Beechwood, S Devon; *m* 1884, Ethel Maud, *d* of Major Quentin, late 10th Hussars, and *g d* of Col Sir George Quentin, 10th Hussars; two *d. Educ:* Eton; University Coll., Oxon (MA). Curate of Alverstoke, Hants, 1871–79; Ladock, 1879–85; Rector of Ladock, Cornwall, 1885–1920. *Publication:* Memoir of the Mudge Family. *Address:* Nansawsan, Ladock, Cornwall. *TA:* Ladock. *Club:* Athenæum. *Died 15 Aug. 1925.*

RAGHAVA RAU, G. Pantulu; Member of the Legislative Council of Madras, and Vakil of the Madras High Court; *b* 1862; three *s* five *d. Educ:* Presidency College, Madras. Practising as lawyer in Ganjam District; Member of Municipal Council and Talug and District Boards in Ganjam; was Chairman of Berhampore for six years. *Recreations:* tennis, riding. *Address:* Anandabag, Vepery, Madras. *Club:* Cosmopolitan, Madras. *Died 1921.*

RAGHUNATH DAS, Diwan Bahadur Sir Chaube, Kt 1923; CSI 1912; *b* Nov. 1849; *s* of Pande Jagannath Dasji, a Chaturvedi Brahman of Etawah District, UP, India; *m*; three *s. Educ:* Humes High School, Etawah; Government Coll., Agra. Entered Native State Service in Rajputana; was Assistant Superintendent of Revenue, Kotah, 1877–93; Vice-President of the Kotah Municipality, 1885–93; Revenue Superintendent 1894, and soon after a Member of the State Council, Kotah; Diwan (Minister), Kotah State, from 1896; a "Tazimi" Sardar of Kotah State; held landed property in Etawah District, paying annually under 4,000 rupees as revenue to British Government; Rai Bahadur, 1897; Diwan Bahadur, 1906. *Address:* Kotah State, Rajputana, India. *Died 1 Dec. 1923.*

RAGHUNATH RAO DINKAR, Rao Raja, Mashir-i-Khas Bahadur, Madar-ul-Moham, CIE; Political Secretary to HH the Maharaja Scindia; a member of His Highness' Majlis-i-Khas; ranked as a first-class Sardar in Bombay, and above Raja Bahadurs in the United Provinces; *b* 4 Aug. 1858; *s* of Rao Raja Sir Dinkar Rao, KCSI, late Prime Minister to HH the Maharaja Scindia of Gwalior; *m*; two *s. Educ:* privately, under the tuition of Mr K. Deighton, Principal, Agra College. Private Secretary to late Maharaja, and was Additional Accountant-General; Famine Commissioner, 1896; member of the Council of Appeal, and member of the Board of Revenue, Gwalior, 1901. *Recreations:* music, photography. *Heir:* *s* Col Ganpatrao Raghunath Rajwade, Adjutant-General of the Gwalior Army, *b* Jan. 1884. *Address:* Gwalior, Central India. *Club:* Elgin, Gwalior.

RAGLAN, 3rd Baron, *cr* 1852; **George Fitz-Roy Henry Somerset,** GBE 1919; CB 1907; Lieutenant-Governor, Isle of Man, 1902–19; *b* London, 18 Sept. 1857; *s* of 2nd Baron and 1st wife, Lady Georgiana Lygon, *d* of 4th Earl Beauchamp; *S* father, 1884; *m* 1883, Lady Ethel Jemima Ponsonby, *d* of 7th Earl of Bessborough; three *s* three *d. Educ:* Eton; Sandhurst. Page of Honour to Queen Victoria, 1868–74; Sub-Lieut unattached, 1875; joined Grenadier Guards, 1876; Captain, 1886; RE (Militia), Monmouthshire, 1887; Lieut-Colonel and Hon. Colonel till 1908; ADC to Sir James Fergusson, Bt, Governor of Bombay, 1880–83; Orderly Officer to Major-General Sir R. Phayre in 2nd phase of Afghan War (medal, despatches); Under Secretary for War, 1900–2. Tory; owned about 1,100 acres, and Cefntilla Court. *Publications:* various magazine articles, letters, etc, on military and sporting subjects. *Recreation:* shooting. *Heir:* *s* Hon. Fitz-Roy Richard Somerset, *b* 10 June 1885. *Address:* 24 Sloane Gardens, SW1. *T:* Victoria 9435; Cefntilla Court, Usk, Monmouthshire. *Clubs:* Guards', Carlton. *Died 24 Oct. 1921.*

RAIKES, Arthur Stewart; *b* 16 June 1856; 5th *s* of Henry Raikes of Llwynegrin, Flintshire. *Educ:* Winchester; Trinity Coll., Cambridge. 1st class History Tripos, 1877; BA 1878; MA 1882. Entered Diplomatic Service; Attaché at Athens, 1880; 3rd Sec., Copenhagen, 1882; 2nd Sec., Buenos Ayres, 1885; Berlin, 1887; Rome, 1892; 1st Sec., Rio de Janeiro, 1896; Brussels, 1898; Washington, 1901–4; HBM's Minister, Santiago, 1904; retired 1907. *Address:* The Gate House, Ingatestone, Essex. *Club:* Travellers'. *Died 22 March 1925.*

RAIKES, Maj.-Gen. Charles Lewis; Retired List, Indian Staff Corps; *b* 20 July 1837; *s* of late Henry Thomas Raikes, Judge of High Court, Calcutta; *m* 1893, Maude Caroline, *d* of Deputy-Surgeon-General Fowler; one *s. Educ:* Temple Grove, East Sheen; private tutor; Addiscombe College. Entered Madras Army, 1855; transferred to the Indian Staff Corps; retired with hon. rank of Major-General, 1887. *Address:* 18 Albany Road, Bedford. *Club:* Junior Conservative. *Died 25 July 1919.*

RAIKES, Francis Edward, CVO 1922 (MVO 1917); OBE 1918; *b* 7 June 1870; 2nd *s* of late Rt Hon. Henry Cecil Raikes and Charlotte Blanche, 4th *d* of Charles Blayney Trevor-Roper of Plasteg, Flintshire; *m* 1906, Iris Veronica, *d* of late Thomas Sopwith, CE; one *d. Educ:* Haileybury. Held a Commission in 3rd Batt. Cheshire Regt, 1888–91; Private Secretary to Postmaster General, 1890–91; Queen's Foreign Service Messenger, 1892; Senior King's Foreign Service Messenger; resigned, ill-health, 1921; received the Coronation Medals of Kings Edward VII and George V. *Address:* Moy Lodge, Datchet. *T:* Windsor 196. *Club:* Carlton. *Died 11 Sept. 1922.*

RAIKES, Rev. Walter Allan, MA; *b* Madras, 1852; *s* of Major R. W. Raikes, commanding Madras Governor's Bodyguard; *m* 1884, Catherine Amelia, *d* of William Cotton Oswell of Hillside, Groombridge; three *s* three *d*. *Educ:* Wellington College; Trinity College, Cambridge. Master at Wellington College, 1875; Curate at Christ Church, Folkestone, 1879; Vicar of Ide Hill, Sevenoaks, 1880; Hon. Canon of Rochester, 1908–12; Vicar of Goudhurst, 1911–28; Rural Dean of West Charing, 1920–24. *Address:* Goudhurst, Kent.   *Died 25 Nov. 1928.*

RAINSFORD, Col Stephen Dickson, CB 1917; late Royal Artillery; *b* 12 Aug. 1853; *s* of Rev. Marcus Rainsford of Belgrave Chapel, W; *m* 1890, Annie Marion, *widow* of Captain Jourdier, 20th Dragoons, French Army; one *d*. Entered army, 1873; served Afghanistan, 1878–79 (medal and clasp); Lt-Col 1899; Bt Col 1904; retired, 1905. *Address:* Pond House, Boxted, near Colchester, Essex.
                                                    Died 2 Oct. 1920.

RAJAGOPALA, Sir Chariyar, Perungavur, KCSI 1920; CIE 1909; MA, BL; Member of Council of India since Jan. 1924; *b* 1862; *s* of P. Varada Chari. *Educ:* Madras University. Entered Civil Service, 1888; Diwan to Raja of Cochin, 1896–1902; Diwan of Travancore, 1907–14; Secretary to Government, Madras, 1914–17; Member of the Madras Executive Council, 1917–20; President of the Madras Provincial Legislature, 1921. *Address:* c/o India Office, SW1.
                                                    Died 1 Dec. 1927.

RALEIGH, Hon. Sir Thomas, KCSI 1904 (CSI 1902); KC; Fellow of All Souls College, Oxford, since 1876; Member of Council of India, 1909–13; *b* Edinburgh, 2 Dec. 1850; *e s* of Samuel Raleigh, manager Scottish Widows' Fund; unmarried. *Educ:* Edinburgh; Tübingen; Oxford (MA, DCL; Lothian Prize, 1878). Barrister, 1877; Reader in English Law at Oxford, 1884–96; contested South Edinburgh, 1885; and West Edinburgh, 1888; Registrar of the Privy Council 1896–99; Legal Member of Viceroy's Council in India, 1899–1904. *Publications:* Elementary Politics, 1886; Outline of the Law of Property, 1889. *Address:* All Souls College, Oxford. *Clubs:* Athenæum, Savile.
                                                    Died 8 Feb. 1920.

RALEIGH, Sir Walter, Kt 1911; Professor of English Literature, Oxford, since 1904; Fellow of Merton College, 1904; *b* 5 Sept. 1861; *s* of late Dr Alexander Raleigh, Congregationalist minister, and Mary Darling, *o d* of James Gifford, Edinburgh; *m* 1890, Lucie Gertrude, *d* of Mason Jackson; four *s* one *d*. *Educ:* University College, London (BA 1881); King's College, Cambridge. Professor of Modern Literature, University College, Liverpool, 1890–1900; Prof. of English Language and Literature, Glasgow, 1900–4. *Publications:* The English Novel, 1894; Robert Louis Stevenson: an Essay, 1895; Style, 1897; Milton, 1900; Wordsworth, 1903; The English Voyages of the Sixteenth Century, 1906; Shakespeare, 1907; Johnson on Shakespeare, 1908; Six Essays on Johnson, 1910; Romance, 1917; England and the War, 1918; The War in the Air (History of the Great War based on official documents), vol. I, 1922; edited Sir Thomas Hoby's Book of the Courtier, from the Italian of Count Baldassare Castiglione, 1900; Complete Works of George Savile, first Marquess of Halifax, 1912; sundry articles. *Address:* Oxford. *Club:* Athenæum.
                                                    Died 13 May 1922.

RALLI, Pandeli, JP, DL; *b* 28 May 1845; *o s* of late Thomas Ralli of London, and Mary, *d* of Pandeli Argenti of Marseilles. *Educ:* King's College, London. MP (L) Bridport, 1875–80; Wallingford, 1880–85. *Address:* 17 Belgrave Square, SW1. *T:* Victoria 436. *Clubs:* Athenæum, Carlton, Bath.   *Died 21 Aug. 1928.*

RALPH, William, ISO 1903; late Secretary to Registrar-General for Scotland; *b* 1841; *s* of James Ralph, Alyth; *m* 1891. Three times Superintendent of Scottish Census. *Address:* Nethersole, Wymynswold, Canterbury.   *Died 29 June 1928.*

RAM, Abel John, KC; barrister-at-law; Recorder of Wolverhampton, 1900–18; *b* Ilam, Staffs, 21 Sept. 1842; 2nd *s* of late Rev. A. J. Ram of Clonatin, Co. Wexford, and Lady Jane Stopford, *d* of 3rd Earl of Courtown; *m* 1874, Hon. Mary Grace (*d* 1912), *d* of 13th Lord Inchiquin; one *s* two *d*. *Educ:* Repton; Corpus Christi College, Oxford. 2nd class Moderations; 3rd class Natural Science; BA 1865; MA 1867. Barrister 1873; joined the Oxford Circuit, of which he became Leader; Revising Barrister, 1879–96; Bencher of the Inner Temple, 1897; formerly member of the Bar Council; Recorder of Hanley, 1891–1900; Chairman of Royal Commission on Vivisection; member of East Coast Raid Commission; 1915; Knight of Grace of St John of Jerusalem; JP County Herts. *Recreations:* golf, fishing. *Address:* Berkhampstead Place, Great Berkhampstead. *T:*

Berkhampstead 59; (chambers) 3 Paper Buildings, Temple, EC; Palace Chambers, Bridge Street, SW. *T:* Victoria 1040. *Club:* Oxford and Cambridge.   *Died 8 Aug. 1920.*

RAM, Rev. Robert Digby, MA; late Prebendary of St Paul's; *b* 24 Jan. 1844; *s* of Rev. Canon Abel John Ram, Clonatin, County Wexford, Ireland, and Lady Jane Ram, *d* of 3rd Earl of Courtown; *m* 1877, Mary, *o c* of late George Edward Anson, CB, Keeper of Privy Purse to late Queen Victoria; one *s* one *d*. *Educ:* Repton; Corpus Christi College, Cambridge. Deacon, 1867; Priest, 1868; Curate of Dunchurch, Warwickshire, 1867–73; of Rolleston, Staffordshire, 1873–77; Vicar of Teddington, 1878–82; of Hampton, 1882–1911. *Address:* 93 Eaton Terrace, Eaton Square, SW1. *T:* Victoria 6439.
                                                    Died 18 Oct.1925.

RAM, Rev. Stephen Adye Scott; Canon and Prebendary of Fenton in York Cathedral, 1916; *b* London, 16 Aug. 1864; *s* of Stephen Adye and Susan Amelia Ram; *m* Margaret King, *d* of John Woodcock, Oakley, Rawtenstall; three *s* one *d*. *Educ:* Charterhouse; St John's College, Cambridge. 1st class, 3rd division, Classical Tripos, 1886; BA 1886, MA 1890. Deacon, 1887; Priest, 1888; curacies— Haslingden, Bolton-le-Sands, and S Augustine's, Pendlebury; Vicar of S Mary, Hull, 1899–1926. *Address:* 8 St Peter's Grove, York. *T:* 3231. *M:* DN 9298.   *Died 28 Nov. 1928.*

RAMACIOTTI, Maj.-Gen. Gustave, CMG 1917; VD; JP; *b* Leghorn, 13 March 1861; *s* of late A. Ramaciotti; *m* 1882, Ada, *d* of late William George Wilson, of Hawick, Scotland; one *s* one *d*. *Educ:* Italy. Commanded 2nd Australian Infantry Regt, 1909–13; 11th Australian Infantry Brigade, 1914–15; 2nd Military District, NSW, 1915–17; Inspector-General of Administration, 1917–20. *Publications:* Tripoli (Turco-Italo War); various military text-books. *Recreations:* tennis, yachting, motoring. *Address:* Australia House, Strand, WC; 33 Hunter Street, Sydney, NSW. *TA:* Rami. *Club:* Royal Automobile.
                                                    Died 6 Dec. 1927.

RAMAKRISHNA, T., BA; the South Indian poet; *b* 1854. *Educ:* Madras Christian College. Fellow and Chairman of the Board of Studies in Dravidian Languages, Madras University; visited England, 1911. *Publications:* Life in an Indian Village; Tales of Ind and other Poems; Padmini, an Indian Romance; The Dive for Death; My Visit to the West; Early Reminiscences, etc. *Address:* Thottakkadu House, Madras.

RAMBAUT, Arthur Alcock, MA (Dublin and Oxon); DSc; FRS, FRAS; Radcliffe Observer, Oxford, since 1897; *b* Waterford, 21 Sept. 1859; 3rd *s* of Rev. E. F. Rambaut; *m* 1883, Emily Longford; three *s*. *Educ:* Arlington House, Portarlington; Royal School, Armagh; Trinity College, Dublin. 1st Science Scholar, 1880; Senior Moderator and Gold Medallist Mathematics and Mathematical Physics, 1881. Senior Science Master, Royal School, Armagh, 1881; Assistant Astronomer Trinity College, Dublin, at Dunsink, 1882–92; Andrew's Professor of Astronomy in the University of Dublin, and Royal Astronomer of Ireland, 1892–97. *Publications:* biographical notices of astronomers in the Ency. Brit.; four Catalogues of Stars published in Astronomical Observations and Researches, Dunsink, and in the publications of the Radcliffe Observatory, Oxford; papers published in the Philosophical Transactions and Proceedings of the Royal Society, the Monthly Notices of Royal Astronomical Society, the Transactions and Proceedings of the Royal Dublin Society, the Royal Irish Academy, the Publications of the Radcliffe Observatory, Astronomische Nachrichten, etc. *Address:* Radcliffe Observatory, Oxford.   *Died 14 Oct. 1923.*

RAMSAY, Sir George Dalhousie, Kt 1900; CB 1882; retired Civil Service; *b* Montrose, 23 May 1828; 6th *s* of Sir Alexander Ramsay, 2nd Bt, of Balmain, MP Kincardine, and 2nd wife, Elizabeth, *d* of 1st Baron Panmure and *sister* of 11th Earl of Dalhousie; *m* 1864, Eleanor Julia Charteris (*d* 1918), *d* of late John Crawford, FRS, Governor of Singapore; one *d* (one *s* decd). *Educ:* France and Germany. War Office, 1846–93; private secretary to Secretary at War, 1849–52, 1853–55; to President Board of Control, 1852; to Secretary of State for War, 1855; Secretary to Royal Commission on Promotion in the Army, 1854; Assistant Director Army Stores and Clothing, 1855–63; Director Army Clothing, 1863–93. Decorated for services at War Office. *Publication:* The Panmure Papers. *Recreations:* literature, art collector. *Address:* 7 Manson Place, Queen's Gate, SW7. *T:* Kensington 3545. *Club:* Arthur's.

                                                    Died 16 Jan. 1920.

RAMSAY, George Gilbert, LLD Edinburgh, Aberdeen, and Glasgow; LittD Dublin; FRSL; *b* 1839; 3rd *s* of Sir George Ramsay, 9th Bt,

of Bamff, and Emily Eugenia, *d* of Capt. Henry Lennon; *m* 1865, Gertrude Schuyler (*d* 1911), *d* of Robert Graham, Ayrshire; three *s* two *d* (and one *s* decd). *Educ:* Rugby School (Scholar); Trinity College, Oxford (First Class (Classics), 1861; MA 1862). Professor of Humanity Glasgow University, 1863–1906. *Publications:* Selections from Tibullus and Propertius, 1887; Manual of Latin Prose Composition in three volumes: (1) Elementary; (2) Introduction and Selected Passages; (3) Latin Versions by selected scholars (4th edition 1897); The Annals of Tacitus, i-vi, trans. with Introduction, Notes, and Maps, 1904; vol. ii of above, containing Annals, xi-xvi, 1909; The Histories of Tacitus, 1915; Translation of Juvenal and Persius for the Loeb Library, 1918. *Recreations:* shooting, golf, cycling, skating, mountaineering. *Address:* Drumore, Blairgowrie, Perthshire. *TA:* Blackiunans. *Clubs:* Oxford and Cambridge, Alpine; New, Edinburgh; Western, Glasgow.
Died 8 March 1921.

RAMSAY, Sir Herbert, 5th Bt, *cr* 1806, of Balmain; *b* 9 Feb. 1868; *s* of Sir Alexander Entwisle Ramsay, 4th Bt and Octavia, *d* of Thomas Haigh, Elm Hall, Liverpool; *S* father, 1902; *m* 1902, Mabel, *d* of Rev. (William) Joseph Hutchinson, Australia; two *s* two *d*. *Educ:* Cheltenham College. *Heir: s* Alexander Burnett Ramsay, *b* 26 March 1903.
Died 22 March 1924.

RAMSAY, Maj.-Gen. Herbert Maynard; *b* 1843. In Indian Service, 1863, as Assistant Superintendent, District Superintendent, and Personal Assistant to Inspector-General; one of the Commissioners to report on Chaukidari System, 1890–91; Maj.-Gen. 1899; retired, 1903.
Died 13 Sept. 1917.

RAMSAY, Sir James (Henry), 10th Bt, *cr* 1666, of Bamff; DL; *b* 21 May 1832; *s* of Sir George Ramsay, 9th Bt, and Emily Eugenia, *d* of Capt. Henry Lennon; *S* father, 1871; *m* 1st, 1861, (Elizabeth) Mary (Charlotte) (*d* 1868), *d* of William Scott-Kerr; three *d*; 2nd, 1873, Charlotte Fanning (*d* 1904), *d* of William Stewart of Ardvorlich; one *s* three *d* (and one *s* decd). *Educ:* Rugby; Christ Church, Oxford (MA). Barrister Lincoln's Inn, 1863; Hon. LLD Glasgow University, 1906; LittD Cambridge University; Fellow British Academy. Owned about 13,900 acres. *Publications:* Lancaster and York: a Century of English history, 1399–1485, 2 vols, 1892; The Foundations of England, 2 vols, 1898; The Angevin Empire, 1154–1216, 1903; The Dawn of the Constitution, 1216–1307, 1908; The Genesis of Lancaster, 1307–1399, 2 vols, 1914; Bamff Charters and Papers, 1915; A History of the Revenues of the Kings of England, 1066–1399, 1925 (posthumous). *Heir: s* James Douglas Ramsay [*b* 19 April 1878; *m* 1908, Hope Anita Jane, *d* of Lt-Col Alexander Donald MacGregor; two *s*]. *Address:* Bamff, Alyth, Perthshire. *Clubs:* Alpine, London Skating; New, Edinburgh.
Died 17 Feb. 1925.

RAMSAY, Maj.-Gen. Sir John George, KCB 1911 (CB 1900); Indian Army, retired; Colonel 24th Punjabis; *b* 5 Nov. 1856; *s* of Commander J. D. Ramsay, RN; *m* 1878, Ethel, *d* of Major-Gen. George Noble Cave, ISC. *Educ:* Queen Elizabeth's School, Ipswich; Stubbington House, Stubbington, Hants. Joined 14th Foot, 1875; joined 24th Punjab Infantry, 1877; Afghan War, 1878–80; Action of Kandahar, 1 Sept. 1880; Kabul-Kandahar march (medal, clasp, bronze star); Hazara Expedition, 1888 (medal and clasp); North-West Frontier, 1897–98; Malakand (despatches, medal, 2 clasps); served China, 1900; Relief of Pekin, Action at Peitsang, Action at Yangtsun (despatches, medal, clasp, CB); Mohmand Expedition, 1908 (despatches, medal, clasp); commanding 24th Division, 1914–15. *Address:* Twyford House, Dereham, Norfolk.
Died 31 March 1920.

RAMSAY, Sir William, KCB 1902; LLD, DSc, MD, PhD; FRS 1888; FCS; Professor Emeritus, University College London, since 1913; *b* Glasgow, 2 Oct. 1852; *o s* of late William Ramsay, CE, and Catherine Robertson; *m* 1881, Margaret, *d* of late George Stevenson Buchanan; one *s* one *d*. *Educ:* Glasgow Academy and University; Tübingen University. Assistant, Young Laboratory of Technical Chemistry, Glasgow Univ., 1872–74; Tutorial Assistant of Chemistry, Glasgow Univ., 1874–80; Professor of Chemistry, 1880–87, and Principal, 1881–87, University Coll., Bristol; Professor of Chemistry, University Coll. London, 1887–1913; Honorary Member of the Institute of France; of Royal Academies of Ireland, Berlin, Bohemia, Holland, Rome, Petrograd, Turin, Roumania, Vienna, Norway, and Sweden; of Academies of Geneva, Frankfurt, and Mexico; of German Chemical Society; of Royal Medical and Chirurgical Society; of the Académie de médecine of Paris; of Pharmaceutical Society; of Philosophical Societies of Manchester, Philadelphia, and Rotterdam; Nobel Prizeman, 1904; Commander, Crown of Italy; Kt, Order Pour le Mérite, Prussia; Officier de la Légion d'Honneur, France. *Publications:* Essays and Addresses (collection of lectures); numerous

papers, the most important of which perhaps The Molecular Surface-Energy of Liquids; Argon, a New Constituent of the Atmosphere (in conjunction with Lord Rayleigh); and Helium, a Constituent of Certain Minerals; also Neon, Krypton, and Xenon, three new atmospheric gases; also the transmutation of radium into helium (with Mr Frederick Soddy); three text-books of Chemistry, and of The Discovery of the Constituents of the Air. *Recreations:* languages, travelling. *Address:* Beechcroft, Hazlemere, Bucks. *Club:* Athenæum.
Died 23 July 1916.

RAMSDEN, Sir William, Kt 1926; JP; solicitor; Senior Partner in firm of Ramsden, Sykes and Ramsden, Solicitors, Huddersfield; *b* 7 April 1857; *s* of James Ramsden, Dudd House, Meltham, Yorkshire; *m* 1894, Ethel H., *e d* of T. H. Ramsden, Oakwell House, Golcar, Yorkshire; no *c*. *Educ:* Huddersfield College. President of Huddersfield Law Society, 1902–4; Governor from 1906; Director and President of Halifax Building Society; Director of Union Bank of Manchester (Yorkshire Board); Director of Hopkinsons Ltd, Huddersfield; Chairman of Munitions Court for Huddersfield, 1915–20; of Huddersfield Interviewing Board for Officers, 1920–24; of Court of Referees for Huddersfield, from 1912; of Huddersfield Insurance Committee; of Huddersfield Employment Committee; of Huddersfield War Pensions Committee; of Huddersfield King's Roll Committee; and of Huddersfield Juvenile Employment Committee. *Address:* Marshfield, Huddersfield. *T:* Huddersfield 4. *TA:* Ramsden, Marshfield, Huddersfield. *Clubs:* Junior Athenæum; Huddersfield.
Died 22 Oct. 1928.

RAMSEY, Col Colin Worthington Pope, CMG 1916; consulting engineer; *b* Bury, Quebec, Canada, 15 Jan. 1883; *s* of William Allan Ramsey, CE; *m* 1918, Dorothy Elsie, *d* of late Sir John Jackson and Ellen Julia, *y d* of Gregory Myers, London; one *s* one *d*. *Educ:* Dufferin Grammar School; Royal School of Infantry, St Johns; private tuition. Entered service Canadian Pacific Railway Co., 1901; employed in various capacities (chiefly Engineering Dept) until 1911; Chief Engineer of Construction, Montreal, 1911–15; Lt-Col Canadian Expeditionary Force, Feb. 1915–April 1917; promoted Colonel 13 April 1917; Superintendent Canadian Pacific Railway, Montreal, 1919–20; Dominion Construction Co. Ltd, and Ramsey, engineers and contractors, 1921; Consulting Engineer and Director Greyville Crushed Rock Co. Ltd; member Canadian Society of Civil Engineers, American Railway Engineering Association, and Canadian Railway Association. *Recreations:* golf, curling. *Address:* Lancaster, Ontario. *Clubs:* St James's, Canadian, Montreal.
Died Sept. 1926.

RANBIR SINGH, Raja Sir, KCSI 1903; Sahib of Patiala; *uncle* of HH Maharaja Dhiraj of Patiala; *m*; one *s* one *d*. Gave his residence and estates at Kasauli for the use of the Indian Pasteur Institute there; appointed member of the Punjab Legislative Council, 1904, and of the Imperial Council, 1910; title of "Raja" was conferred by the Maharaja of Patiala, Feb. 1915. *Address:* Patiala, Punjab.
Died 18 Jan. 1916.

RANDALL, Rt. Rev. James Leslie, MA, DD; 2nd *s* of Archdeacon James Randall and Rebe, *o d* of Richard Lowndes; *m* Ann Harriet (*d* 1899), *d* of G. A. Bruxner; one *s* three *d*. *Educ:* Winchester; New College, Oxford (Fellow). Rector of Newbury, 1857–78; Hon. Canon of Christ Church, 1878–95; Rector of Sandhurst, Berks, 1878–80; Rector of Mixbury, Oxford, 1882–85; Prebendary of Chichester, 1894–95; Archdeacon of Buckingham, 1880–95; of Oxford, and Canon of Christ Church, 1895–1902; Suffragan Bishop of Reading, 1889–1908. *Address:* Abbey House, Abingdon.
Died 17 Jan. 1922.

RANDOLPH, Rev. Berkeley William, DD; *b* 10 March 1858; *s* of Rev. Cyril Randolph, MA, Rector of Chartham, Kent. *Educ:* Haileybury; Balliol College, Oxford. Hebrew (minor) Exhibitioner; BA, 2nd class Theol. Schools, 1879; Denyer and Johnson Theological Scholar, 1880; MA, 1884; DD, 1901. Ordained deacon, 1881 (Canterbury); priest, 1882; Fellow of St Augustine's Coll., Canterbury, 1880–83; Hon. Fellow, 1884; Principal of St Stephen's House, Oxford, 1884–85; Domestic Chaplain to Bishop of Lincoln (Rt Rev. Edward King), 1885–90; Examining Chaplain, 1890–1910; Vice-Principal of Ely Theological College, 1890–91; Principal, 1891–1911; Canon of Ely, 1910; Warden of the Community of St Mary, Wantage, 1911. *Publications:* The Law of Sinai, 1896; The Threshold of the Sanctuary, 1897; Meditations on the Old Testament for Every Day of the Year, 1899; The Example of the Passion, 1901; The Prayer-Book Psalter with Notes, 1901; Meditations on the New Testament for Every Day of the Year, 1902; The Virgin-Birth of Our Lord, 1903; Ember Thoughts, 1903; The Empty Tomb, 1906; Christ in the Old Testament, 1907; The Precious Blood of Christ, 1909; Confession in the Church of England, 1911; Memoir of Arthur Douglas, 1912; The Seven Sacraments of the Universal Church, 1916; A Communicant's Manual, 1917; (joint) The Mind and Work of Bishop King, 1918; The Plain Man's Book of Religion, 1919; The Coming of the Lord, 1920; The Person of Christ in the First Three Gospels, 1922; Meditations on the Psalms, 1922; Meditations on the Holy Spirit, 1923; Editor of A Revised Liturgy, 1914; Bishop King's Spiritual Letters; Mowbray's Devotional Library; etc. *Address:* The Almonry, Ely. *Died 9 Jan. 1925.*

RANKIN, Guthrie, MD Glasgow; FRCP, FRCPE; Physician to the Dreadnought and Royal Waterloo Hospitals; *b* 1854; a native of Ayrshire; *s* of David Rankin, Kilmarnock, NB; *m* 1883, Janet Hutcheson (*d* 1916), *d* of John Guthrie. *Educ:* Kilmarnock Academy; Neuchâtel; Glasgow University; London. Fellow of several learned societies; was for several years Examiner in Medicine at Glasgow University; Lecturer on Medicine London School of Clinical Medicine. *Publications:* medical lectures and papers contributed to current medical literature. *Recreations:* yachting, fishing. *Address:* 9 Harley Street, Cavendish Square, W. *TA:* Rankigen, London. *T:* Paddington 2949; The Orchard, Helford, Cornwall. *M:* LD 3792. *Clubs:* Union, Royal Automobile; Royal Clyde Yacht.
Died 14 Sept. 1919.

RANKIN, John, JP; LLD; High Sheriff, Westmorland, 1910; *b* New Brunswick, 1845. *Educ:* Dr Ihne's, Liverpool; St Andrews University. Shipowner; Chairman, Rankin Gilmour & Co. Ltd; member Mersey Docks and Harbour Board, 1900–12; Director Bank of Liverpool, 1900, Chairman, 1906–9; Director Royal Insurance Co., 1892, Chairman, 1909–12; Director British and Foreign Marine Insurance Committee, 1909; Pacific Steam Navigation Co., 1898–1910; member of Committee of the Liverpool and London Steamship Protection Association, 1896–1911; Lloyd's Registry of Shipping (Liverpool), 1880–1910, Chairman, 1890–91; member of Liverpool Shipwreck and Humane Society, 1880–96, Chairman, 1891–96; on Council of Liverpool University, 1902–7; Governor of Sedbergh School, 1911; Chairman Soldiers and Sailors' Club, 1915; LLD University of Liverpool, 1920; Hon. Freedom of City conferred, 1921. *Address:* St Michael's Mount, St Michael's Hamlet, Liverpool.
Died 23 Dec. 1928.

RANKINE, Sir John, Kt 1921; JP; KC; LLD; Professor of Scots Law, University of Edinburgh, 1888; *b* Scotland, 18 Feb. 1846; *e s* of Rev. John Rankine, DD, Minister of Sorn, Ayrshire; unmarried. *Educ:* Sorn; Ayr and Edinburgh Academies; Edinburgh (MA) and Heidelberg Universities. Scottish Barrister, 1869; Advocate-Depute, 1885; QC 1897. Owner of 1,000 acres. *Publications:* The Law of Land-ownership in Scotland, 4th edn 1909; The Law of Leases in Scotland, 3rd edn 1916; The Law of Personal Bar in Scotland, 1921; editor of Erskine's Principles of the Law of Scotland, 18th–20th edns, and general editor of 21st edn, 1911; editor of Scots Revised Reports, House of Lords and Court of Session; and joint consulting editor of the Scots Style Book. *Recreations:* travel, shooting. *Address:* 23 Ainslie Place, Edinburgh; Threepwood, Lauder. *Clubs:* Royal Societies; University, Conservative, Edinburgh. *Died 8 Aug. 1922.*

RANKSBOROUGH, 1st Baron, *cr* 1914, of Ranksborough; **Maj.-Gen. John Fielden Brocklehurst,** CB 1900; CVO 1902; Lord-in-Waiting to King George V, 1915; Equerry to Queen Alexandra, since 1901; Lord-Lieutenant, County of Rutland, 1906; *b* 13 May 1852; *s* of late Henry Brocklehurst, of Foden Bank; *m* 1878, Louisa Alice, *d* of Hon. Lawrence Parsons and 2nd wife, Jane, *e d* of 2nd Lord Feversham. *Educ:* Rugby; Trinity College, Cambridge (BA 1873). Entered army 1874; Colonel, 1899; served Egyptian War, 1882 (medal with clasp, Khedive's star); Nile Expedition, 1884–85 (despatches, brevet of Major, clasp); commanded Royal Horse Guards, 1894–99; commanded 3rd Cavalry Brig., Natal (Ladysmith), 1899. Equerry to Queen Victoria, 1899–1901. *Heir:* none. *Address:* Thatched House Lodge, Richmond Park; Ranksborough, Oakham. *Clubs:* Brooks's, Turf, Carlton. *Died 28 Feb. 1921 (ext).*

RANSOME, Arthur, MA; MD; FRCP; FRS; Consulting Physician, Manchester Hospital for Consumption and Diseases of the Chest and Throat; Royal Victoria and West Hampshire Hospital; *b* Manchester, 11 Feb. 1834; *e s* of Joseph Atkinson Ransome (*d* 1868), and Eliza, 3rd *d* of Joseph Brookhouse, Derby; *m* 1862, Lucy Elizabeth Fullarton (*d* 1906); three *s* four *d*. *Educ:* Manchester; Trinity Coll., Dublin; Caius Coll., Cambridge (Hon. Fellow); St. George's Hosp., London; Paris. Caian Scholar in Anatomy; Mecklenberg Scholar in Chemistry; Senior Optime in Mathematical Tripos; 1st Class Nat. Sci. Tripos, 1856. Lecturer in Biology, 1857–61; Lecturer, and afterwards

Professor of Hygiene and Public Health at Owens College, Manchester, 1880–95; Examiner in Sanitary Science, Cambridge Univ. and Victoria Univ. of Manchester; Milroy Lectr to Coll. of Physicians on Causes and Prevention of Phthisis, 1890; Vice-Pres. of Manchester and Salford Sanitary Assoc.; Fellow of Coll. of State Medicine; Weber-Parkes Prize Essayist on Tuberculosis, 1897. *Publications:* Stethometry, 1876; Prognosis in Lung Disease, 1882; Causes of Consumption, 1884; Causes and Prevention of Phthisis, 1890; Treatment of Phthisis, 1896; Researches on Tuberculosis; The Principles of Open-Air Treatment of Phthisis and Sanatorium Construction, 1903; A Campaign against Consumption, 1914. *Recreations:* bacteriology, photography. *Address:* Sunnyhurst, Bournemouth. *T:* Bournemouth 55. *Club:* Bournemouth.
Died 25 July 1922.

RAPHAEL, Sir Herbert Henry, 1st Bt, *cr* 1911; MP (L) South Derbyshire, 1906–18; *b* 23 Dec. 1859; *s* of late Henry Louis Raphael, banker, chief partner in R. Raphael & Sons, and cousin, Henriette (Trustee of National Gallery), *d* of John Raphael; *m* 1884, Rosalie, *o d* of G. F. Coster, Upper Chine, Shanklin, Isle of Wight. *Educ:* Hanover; Vevey; Trinity Hall, Cambridge (Hons in Law, LLB, BA). Called to the Bar, Inner Temple, 1883; practised for some years but gave it up for public work; was a Member of the first London County Council, and for three years a Member of the London School Board; was a Member of the Essex County Council; stood twice for Romford Div. of Essex, once for North St Pancras, and once for South Derbyshire; enlisted in the Royal Fusiliers; afterwards raised the 18th and 23rd KRRC; promoted Major and second in command of each of these Battalions; retired with hon. rank of Major; Trustee of National Portrait Gallery; Governor of Guy's Hospital; JP Essex and Derbyshire. *Heir:* none. *Recreations:* fishing, shooting, golf, motoring. *Address:* Hockley Sole, near Folkestone. *T:* Folkestone 660. *Club:* Reform. *Died 24 Sept. 1924 (ext).*

RAPHAEL, John N. (Percival); Paris correspondent of The Referee, The Bystander, and The Era; *b* 16 May 1868; *s* of Charles and Rosalie Raphael; *m* Eugénie (Aimée) Gobillet. *Educ:* Charterhouse. A false start; then, Paris by Day and Night, for Illustrated Bits; the Dreyfus Case, for the Daily Mail; and journalistic work of all kinds. *Plays:* The Jesters, an adaptation in English alexandrines of Les Bouffons by Zamacoïs, 1908; Cochon d'Enfant (with André de Lorde); Madame X, adaptation of La Femme X by Bisson, 1909; The Uninvited Guest, from the French of Tristan Bernard, 1911; Peter Ibbetson, from the novel by the late George du Maurier, 1915; an adaptation in French of Potash and Perlmutter, 1916; a number of sketches for music halls. *Publications:* Bookland and its Inhabitants; An English Version of the Songs of Yvette Guilbert; Pictures of Paris and some Parisians; Paris in Pen and Picture; Up Above; The Caillaux Drama, 1914; English translations of Marie Claire, and Valserine and Other Stories, by Marguerite Audoux; Jean and Louise, by Antonin Dusserre; etc. *Recreations:* things theatrical in every sense, other people's automobiles, a lazy life. *Address:* 62 boulevard de Clichy, Paris. *T:* Marcadet, 15–16 Paris.
Died 23 Feb. 1917.

RAPIER, *see* Watson, A.E.T.

RASHDALL, Very Rev. Hastings, FBA 1909; Dean of Carlisle since 1917; *b* 24 June 1858; *s* of Rev. John Rashdall, Vicar of Dawlish, and Emily, *d* of Thomas Hankey, banker; *m* 1905, Constance, *d* of late Henry Francis Makins. *Educ:* Harrow; New College, Oxford (Hon. Fellow, 1920). 2nd class in Classical Moderations and in Lit. Hum.; BA 1881; MA 1884; DLitt 1901; DD 1921; Stanhope Prize, 1879; Chancellor's English Essay, 1883. Lecturer in St David's College, Lampeter, 1883; ordained, 1884; Tutor in the University of Durham, 1884–88; Fellow and Lecturer of Hertford Coll., Oxford, 1888–95; Chaplain and Theological Tutor of Balliol Coll., Oxford, 1894–95; Fellow of New College, Oxford, 1895–1917; Tutor, 1895–1910; Lecturer, 1910–17; Select Preacher in Univ. of Oxford, 1895–97; Hon. Fellow, 1920; Public Examiner at Oxford in Lit. Hum., 1896–99; Preacher at Lincoln's Inn, 1898–1903; Bampton Lecturer, 1915; Canon of Hereford, 1910–17; Hon. DCL Durham, 1898; LLD St Andrews, 1911; Hon. DD Glasgow, 1920. *Publications:* The Universities of Europe in the Middle Ages, 3 vols, 1895; Doctrine and Development (university sermons), 1898; (with R. S. Rait) New College (College Histories Series), 1901; Christus in Ecclesia, 1904; The Theory of Good and Evil, 2 vols, 1907; Philosophy and Religion, 1909; Is Conscience an Emotion?, 1914; Conscience and Christ, 1916; The Idea of Atonement in Christian Theology, 1919; contributor to Contentio Veritatis, 1902. *Address:* The Deanery, Carlisle. *Club:* Athenæum. *Died 9 Feb. 1924.*

RASON, Hon. Sir Cornthwaite Hector, Kt 1909; *b* Somerset, 18 June 1858; father medical officer, RN; *m* 1884, Mary Evelyn, *e d* of John Terry, York. *Educ:* Brighton; Reading. Emigrated to Western Australia, 1881; entered local Parliament, 1889, and held seat almost continuously; Minister for Works and Railways, 1902–4; Treasurer, 1904–5; Premier, 1905–6; Agent-Gen. in London for Western Australia, 1906–9; JP for the State. *Address:* Valetta, Palace Park Road, Sydenham, SE. *Died 15 March 1927.*

RASON, Ernest Goldfinch. Entered Navy, 1865; Lieutenant, 1875; Commander, 1890; retired Captain, 1898; First Lieut of HMS Ready during Egyptian War; in command of Ready on the occasion of the capture of the Suez Canal (Egyptian medal and bronze star); First Lieut of Sphinx at Suakin (Suakin clasp); passed interpreter in Russian, first in the Royal Navy, 1887; when in command of HMS Plover received the thanks of the Admiralty three times; brought home the first live specimen of the smaller Orangutan; when in command of Cockatrice was elected Commodore of the Stationaires assembled to do honour to the King of Roumania at the opening of a branch of the Danube; when in command of Royalist received the thanks of the Royal Society for assistance rendered to Science; first British Commissioner to New Hebrides; in conjunction with French Commissioners quieted the natives and obtained the Anglo-French Protectorate; retired on its proclamation; member of Royal United Service Institution and of Royal Colonial Institution; FZS. *Recreation:* languages.

RATCLIFFE-ELLIS, Sir Thomas Ratcliffe, Kt 1911; Law Clerk and Secretary to the Lancashire and Cheshire Coal Association since 1892; *b* 31 Dec. 1842; *s* of Thomas Ellis, late of Wigan, builder and timber merchant, and Elizabeth, *d* of Thomas Ratcliffe, of Haigh, farmer; assumed the additional surname of Ratcliffe, 1911; *m* 1868, Mary Dean (*d* 1917), *d* of late Matthew Barton, of Wigan, merchant; three *s* four *d*. *Educ:* Wigan Grammar School. Solicitor, admitted 1865; Law Clerk and Secretary to the Mining Association of Great Britain, 1892–1921; Member of the Royal Commission on Mines, 1906, and of the Royal Commission on the Railways Conciliation Scheme of 1907, 1911; Member of the Board of Trade Railway Conference, 1909; and Industrial Council, 1911; Secretary to the Lancashire and Cheshire Coal Owners' Defence Association; Member of the Governing Body of the Wigan Mining and Technical College; Clerk to Wigan Borough Justices, 1874–1900; Capt. 21st Lancs Rifle Volunteers, retired 1880. *Address:* The Hollies, Wigan. *TA:* Lex, Wigan. *T:* 22 Wigan. *Died 6 March 1925.*

RATHBONE, William (Gair), BA; FRGS; *b* 1849; *e s* of late William Rathbone, MP, DL, LLD, of Greenbank, Liverpool; *m* 1877, Blanche Marie, *e d* of Charles Luling, New York; one *s* one *d*. *Educ:* Rugby; University College, Oxford (BA 1872). Director of Royal Exchange Assurance Corporation; London County and Westminster Bank; P&OSN Co.; British India Steam Navigation Co.; Hong-Kong and Shanghai Bank (London Committee); Commissioner of Income Tax for the City of London; Hon. Secretary to the Council of Queen Victoria's Jubilee Institute for Nurses; KGStJ. *Address:* 39 Cadogan Gardens, SW. *Clubs:* Athenæum, St James's, Savile. *Died 9 April 1919.*

RATHMORE, 1st Baron, *cr* 1895; **David Robert Plunket,** PC; LLD; *b* 3 Dec. 1838; 3rd *s* of 3rd Baron Plunket and Charlotte, *d* of Rt Hon. Charles Kendal Bushe, Lord Chief Justice of King's Bench, Ireland. *Educ:* Trin. Coll., Dublin (LLD 1875). Barrister King's Inn, Dublin, 1862; QC 1868; Law Adviser to Irish Government, 1868–69; late Professor of Law at King's Inn, Dublin; MP (C) Dublin University, 1870–95; Solicitor-General Ireland, 1875–77; Paymaster-General, 1880; first Commissioner of Works, 1885–92. *Heir:* none. *Address:* Southfield House, Wimbledon Park, SW. *Clubs:* Athenæum, Carlton, Garrick; Kildare Street and University, Dublin. *Died 22 Aug. 1919 (ext).*

RATHOM, John Revelstoke; Editor and General Manager, Providence Journal, Providence, RI, USA since 1912; *b* Melbourne, Australia, 1868; *m* Florence Mildred Campbell of New Cumberland, West Virginia; no *c*. *Educ:* Whinham College, Adelaide, SA; Scotch College, Melbourne, Victoria; English public schools. War Correspondent, Soudan, 1886; Member Bunbury Expedition to New Guinea, 1888; Schwatka's Alaska Expedition, 1890; for several years Staff Correspondent San Francisco Chronicle and Chicago Herald; War Correspondent Cuba, 1898 and South Africa, 1900–2; Managing Editor Providence Journal, 1905–12; Member of Board of Directors and Executive Committee, The Associated Press, 1917–23; an authority on immigration and sociological subjects and on international relations; Commander of the Crown of Italy; Chevalier of the Order of Leopold (Belgium); Trustee American Defence Society, and honorary member of numerous patriotic societies. *Recreation:* an authority on trout-fishing and angling generally. *Address:* 89 Brown Street, Providence, RI, USA. *TA:* Kalyptus, Providence. *M:* 1424, 8000. *Clubs:* Pilgrims, Austral, Authors, Hope, Providence. *Died 11 Dec. 1923.*

RATTIGAN, Sir Henry Adolphus Byden, Kt 1918; **Hon. Mr Justice Rattigan;** Chief Justice, High Court, Punjab, since 1919; *b* 11 Oct. 1864; *s* of late Sir William Henry Rattigan, KC, MP, and 1st wife, Teresa Matilda, *d* of Col A. C. B. Higgins, CIE; *m* 1891, Edith Nellie Maud, *e d* of late Captain C. Thorne, RN; two *d*. *Educ:* Harrow; Balliol College, Oxford (BA 1888). Called to the Bar, Lincoln's Inn, 1888; joined the Bar as an Advocate of the Chief Court, Punjab, 1889; Legal Remembrancer to Punjab Government, 1900; officiated several times as Judge of the Chief Court until 1909; Judge, 1909–19. *Publications:* Law of Divorce in India; joint author of Tribal Law in the Punjab; editor of The Digest of Customary Law of the Punjab (7th edn). *Recreations:* golf, fishing. *Address:* Lawrence Road, Lahore, Punjab. *Club:* East India United Service. *Died 11 Jan. 1920.*

RATTRAY, Lt-Col Haldane Burney, DSO 1898; Indian Civil Service; Wing Officer 45th Bengal Infantry; *b* 27 May 1870; *s* of late Col Thomas Rattray, CB, CSI; *m* 1905, Ethel Marguerite, *d* of late W. Piper of Ackleton Hall, Shropshire; one *s* one *d*. Entered Derbyshire Regt, 1890; served NW Frontier, India, 1897–98 (wounded); Tirah Expeditionary Force (despatches, DSO, medal with three clasps). *Address:* Dera Ismail Khan, Bengal. *Died 1 Feb. 1917.*

RAU, Bhimanakunté Hanumanta, ISO; BA; Fellow and Syndic; Chairman of the Board of Studies and the Board of Examiners in Mathematics in the University of Madras; *b* 1855; *s* of B. Bhima Rau of Tangore; *m* 1873; three *s* three *d*. *Educ:* SPG High School, Tangore; Government College, Kumbakonam (BA 1874). Headmaster London Mission School, Negapatam, 1874–75; Maharajah's College, Mysore, and Central College, Bangalore, 1875–77; Calicut College, 1877–79; Lecturer in Mathematics, Government College, Kumbakonam, 1879–93; Professor of Mathematics, College of Engineering, Madras, 1894–1912. *Publications:* First Lessons in Geometry; Hall and Steven's Elementary Algebra, fully revised, etc. *Address:* Martinivas, Mylapur, Madras, India. *Died 3 Dec. 1922.*

RAVEN-HART, Rev. William Roland; Hon. Canon of St Edmundsbury and Ipswich. *Address:* Fressingfield Vicarage, Harleston, Suffolk. *Died 20 Nov. 1919.*

RAVENSHAW, (temp.) Maj.-Gen. Hurdis Secundus Lalande, CMG 1915; 1st Battalion the Connaught Rangers; *b* 16 June 1869; *m* 1898, Rose Constance, OBE, *d* of Col Sir H. R. Thuillier. Entered army (East Yorks Regt), 1888; Captain Devonshire Regt, 1897; Major, 1907; Lt-Col Connaught Rangers, 1914; served Chitral, 1895 (medal with clasp); Malakand, 1897–98 (clasp); Tirah, 1897–98 (clasp); S African War, 1899–1902 (despatches, five times, Queen's medal, 5 clasps, King's medal, 2 clasps, Bt-Major); DAA&QMG, Straits Settlements, 1910–12; Coast Defences, Southern Command, 1912–14; served European War, 1914–16 (despatches twice, CMG, Bt-Col). *Club:* Naval and Military. *Died 6 June 1920.*

RAVENSWORTH, 5th Baron, *cr* 1821; **Arthur Thomas Liddell;** Bt 1642; *b* 28 Oct. 1837; *s* of Rev. Hon. Robert Liddell (5th *s* of 1st Baron Ravensworth), and Emily Ann Charlotte, *d* of Rev. Hon. Gerald Valerian Wellesley; *S* cousin, 1904; *m* 1866, Sophia Harriet (*d* 1918), *d* of Sir Thomas Wathen Waller, 2nd Bt; three *s* two *d*. *Heir:* *s* Hon. Gerald Wellesley Liddell [*b* 21 March 1869; *m* 1899, Isolda Blanche, *d* of C. G. Prideaux-Brune; one *s* two *d*]. *Address:* Eslington Park, Whittingham, RSO, Northumberland; Ravensworth Castle, Gateshead. *T:* Newcastle 574. *Club:* Junior Carlton. *Died 12 Nov. 1919.*

RAWDON, Rev. J. Hamer, MA; Hon. Canon of Manchester; retired; *s* of late Joshua Rawdon of Larchwood, Cheshire, and Everilda Sarah, *d* of James Hamer of Hamer Hall, Lancashire; *m* 1875, Frances, *d* of George Bramwell; one *s* three *d*. *Educ:* Brasenose College, Oxford (BA 1858; MA 1861). Ordained, 1863; Fellow of St Peter's, Radley, 1861–62; Vicar of Preston, Lancs, 1877–99; Rector of Yelverton, Norfolk, 1900–7. *Address:* The Hermitage, Stockton-on-Forest, York. *Died 19 Jan. 1916.*

RAWLING, Brig.-Gen. Cecil Godfrey, CMG 1916; CIE 1909; DSO 1917; FRGS; Somerset Light Infantry; *b* 16 Feb. 1870; *s* of late

Samuel Bartlett Rawling, Beaumont, Stoke, and Ada Bathe, *d* of S. Withers, Wilts; unmarried. *Educ:* Clifton College. Entered army, 1891; Captain, 1901; Major, 1914; Bt Lieut-Colonel, 1917; served NW Frontier, India, 1897–98 (medal with clasp); Tibet Mission, 1904 (medal with clasp); explored and surveyed 40,000 square miles of Western Tibet, 1903; commanded the Gartok Expedition across Tibet, 1904–5; awarded the Murchison Bequest by the Royal Geographical Society, 1909; received the thanks of the Government of India; Chief Survey Officer and afterwards leader of the British Expedition to Dutch New Guinea, 1909–11; received the thanks of the Netherlands Government; received the Patrons' Gold Medal, Royal Geographical Society, 1917 (for his explorations in Western Tibet and Rudok, 1903, for his journey from Gyantse via Gartok, 1904, and for his New Guinea, 1908). *Publications:* The Great Plateau, 1905; The Land of the New Guinea Pygmies, 1913. *Address:* 16 Montagu Street, Portman Square, W. *T:* Mayfair 1201. *Club:* Army and Navy.   *Died 28 Oct. 1917.*

RAWLINGS, Edmund Charles, JP; Alderman, Hammersmith; *b* Wallingford, 1854; *s* of Rev. Edmund Rawlings. Admitted Solicitor, 1879; one of the four Representatives of the Free Churches selected to be received by King Edward VII at the time of his Coronation; contested North Islington; late Mayor of Hammersmith; took active part in relief of unemployed and assistance of cripples; senior partner in firm of Rawlings, Butt, and Bowyer of Walbrook. *Publications:* The Free Churchman's Legal Handbook; other legal handbooks. *Address:* 6 Gunnersbury Avenue, W. *T:* Ealing 1106; Winkfield, Berks. *Clubs:* The New City, National Liberal.   *Died Dec. 1917.*

RAWLINS, Maj.-Gen. Alexander Macdonell, RA; *b* 29 Aug. 1838. Entered army, 1857; served Indian Mutiny, 1857–58 (medal); Maj.-Gen. 1893; retired, 1894; JP Kirkcudbrightshire. *Address:* Laghall, Dumfries. *Club:* United Service.   *Died 28 July 1916.*

RAWLINS, Francis Hay; Assistant Master at Eton College, 1875–1905; Lower Master of Eton, 1905–16; Vice-Provost of Eton since 1916; *b* Moseley, Worcestershire, 2 Oct. 1850; *s* of late Samuel Rawlins and Catherine Anne, *d* of Stuart Donaldson. *Educ:* Eton (Newcastle Scholar, Tomline Prizeman); King's College, Cambridge (Scholar, 1870; Fellow, 1875). Bracketed Senior Classic and Chancellor's Medallist, 1874; Browne's Medallist, 1871, 1872, 1873; Governor of Radley, Royal Holloway, and Imperial Service Colleges. *Publications:* The Advanced Eton Latin Grammar (with the Dean of St Paul's); editions of portions of Livy. *Address:* The Cloisters, Eton College. *Clubs:* Athenæum, Wellington, Cavendish, Royal Automobile, MCC; Leander, Henley-on-Thames.

Died 13 April 1920.

RAWLINS, Col (temp. Col-Comdt) Stuart William Hughes, CB 1924; CMG 1918; DSO 1915; Director of Artillery at the War Office, 1924–27; commanding Royal Artillery, 2nd Division, Aldershot, since Feb. 1927; *b* 11 May 1880; *s* of late (William) Donaldson Rawlins, KC, and Elizabeth Margaret, *d* of late Charles King; *m* 1910, Dorothy Pepys, *d* of late John Rennie Cockerell, Madras CS; four *s. Educ:* Eton. Entered Army, 1898; Captain, 1910; Major, 1914; served S African War, 1902 (Queen's medal 3 clasps); King's African Rifles, 1903–8; served European War, 1914–18 (despatches ten times, DSO, Bt Lt-Col, Bt Col, Croix de Guerre, CMG, Legion of Honour, Order of Leopold, Belgian Croix de Guerre, 1914 Star). *Address:* White Waltham Grove, near Maidenhead, Berks. *T:* Littlewick Green 75. *TA:* White Waltham; Carwythenack, Downderry, Cornwall. *M:* YN 6603. *Club:* Sports.   *Died 16 Dec. 1927.*

RAWLINS, William Donaldson, KC; MA; *b* Moseley, Worcestershire, 20 July 1846; *e* surv. *s* of late Samuel Rawlins (*d* 1884) and Catherine Anne, *d* of Stuart Donaldson; *m* 1878, Elizabeth Margaret, *o d* of late Charles John King; three *s. Educ:* Eton; Trinity Coll., Cambridge (Scholar, 1866; Fellow, 1869). Third in 1st class Classical Tripos, 1868. Assistant Master at Eton, 1868–69; Barrister Lincoln's Inn, 1872; QC 1896; Bencher, 1900; Commissioner for Income Tax, Lincoln's Inn; Alderman Holborn Borough Council; Mayor of Holborn, 1906–7; JP County of London and County of Berks. *Publications:* Rawlins on Specific Performance; (joint) Rawlins and Macnaghten on Companies; editor of 4th and 5th editions of Fry's Specific Performance of Contracts, and of Treatises on the Law of Landlord and Tenant, and on Receivers. *Recreations:* riding, cycling, rowing, tennis, golf. *Address:* White Waltham Grove, near Maidenhead, Berks; 1 New Square, Lincoln's Inn, WC. *Club:* Athenæum.
Died 21 May 1920.

RAWLINSON, 1st Baron, *cr* 1919, of Trent, Dorset; **Henry Seymour Rawlinson,** GCB 1919 (KCB 1915; CB 1900); GCSI 1924; GCVO

1917; KCMG 1918; Bt, 1891; Commander-in-Chief of the Army in India since 1920; Member of the Executive Council of the Governor-General of India since 1920; General late 60th Rifles and Coldstream Guards; Member of Army Council, 1918; *b* 20 Feb. 1864; *e s* of Maj.-Gen. Sir Henry Creswick Rawlinson, 1st Bt, and Louisa Caroline Harcourt, *d* of Henry Seymour, Knoyle, Wilts; *S* father, as 2nd Bt, 1895; *m* 1890, Meredith Sophia Frances, *o d* of Coleridge John Kennard. *Educ:* Eton; RMC, Sandhurst; Staff College, Camberley (psc). Entered 60th KRR, 1884; ADC to Sir Frederick Roberts (later 1st Earl Roberts), Commander-in-Chief of India, 1887–90; served with Mounted Infantry, Burma campaign (medal and clasp); entered Staff College, 1892; exchanged into Coldstream Guards, 1892; served in Soudan campaign as DAAG to Maj.-Gen. Horatio Herbert Kitchener (later 1st Earl Kitchener of Khartoum), 1898; present at battles Atbara and Khartoum (medal and two clasps, despatches twice); served war in S Africa (two medals and eight clasps); AAG (Ladysmith siege) Natal, 1899; AAG Headquarters, S Africa, 1900; commanded Mobile Column, 1901–2 (despatches three times); Commandant Staff College, 1903–6; commanded 2nd Brigade, Aldershot, 1907–9; commanding 3rd Division, Salisbury Plain, 1910; served European War, 1914–18 (despatches eight times, KCB, GCB, KCVO, GCVO, KCMG; promotion to Gen. and Lt-Gen.); commanded 4th Corps and 4th Army; commanded Forces in N Russia, 1919; GOC Aldershot, 1920; ADC to the King; Grand Officer Legion of Honour; Order of Danilo (Montenegro), 1st Class, 1917; French Croix de Guerre; Belgian Croix de Guerre; Rising Sun of Japan, 2nd Class; Order of St George, Russia. *Publication:* The Officers' Note-book. *Recreations:* hunting, polo, cricket, rackets, drawing. *Heir to Baronetcy:* brother Alfred Rawlinson [*b* 17 Jan. 1867; *m* 1st, 1890, Margarette Kennard (*d* 1907), 5th *d* of William Bunce Greenfield; one *s* one *d* (and two *d* decd); 2nd, 1913, Jean Isabella Griffen Aitken (marr. diss. 1924)]. *Clubs:* Guards', Turf, Travellers', Hurlingham.

Died 28 March 1925 (ext).

RAWLINSON, Lt-Col Charles Brooke, CIE 1905; Revenue Commissioner, North-West Frontier Province, 1910; *b* 10 April 1866; *s* of Rev. George Rawlinson; *m* 1891, Wilhelmina Forrester. *Educ:* Marlborough. Entered Army, 1885; Captain, 1896; Major, 1903; Assistant Commissioner, Punjab, 1889; Deputy Commissioner, 1899; Political Agent, 1906; Additional Revenue Commissioner, 1907.
Died 15 Jan. 1919.

RAWLINSON, Rt. Hon. John Frederick Peel, JP Cambs, 1901; PC 1923; KC; LLD; MP (U) Cambridge University since 1906; Recorder of Cambridge since 1898; Commissary of Cambridge University since 1900; Deputy High Steward Cambridge University since 1918; Fellow of Eton College since 1919; *b* 21 Dec. 1860; *y s* of late Sir C. Rawlinson (Chief Justice of Madras, 1850–59); unmarried. *Educ:* Eton; Trinity Coll., Cambridge. LLB, LLM; 1st class Law Tripos, 1882; Prizeman in Common Law. Barrister Inner Temple, 1884; South-Eastern Circuit; sometime Lecturer and Examiner in Law, Pembroke College, Cambridge (Hon. Fellow); represented the Treasury in Inquiry in South Africa as to circumstances connected with Jameson Raid, 1896; QC 1897; contested Ipswich (C), 1900; Member General Council of Bar from its formation, later Vice-Chairman; Bencher of Inner Temple, 1907; a temporary Chairman of Committees in the House of Commons from 1916; Hon. LLD Cambridge; Member of the Governing Bodies of Eton, Malvern, and Brighton College. *Publication:* Rawlinson's Municipal Corporations' Acts, tenth edition. *Address:* 5 Crown Office Row, Temple, EC4. *T:* Central 731. *Clubs:* Carlton, United University, Travellers', Princes'; Cambridge County.

Died 14 Jan. 1926.

RAWNSLEY, Rev. Hardwicke Drummond; Canon of Carlisle; Proctor in Convocation; Hon. Chaplain to King George V since 1912; *b* Shiplake Vicarage, Henley-on-Thames, 28 Sept. 1851; 2nd *s* of Canon R. D. B. Rawnsley and Catherine Ann, *o d* of Sir Willingham Franklin, and *niece* of Sir John Franklin, the Arctic explorer; *m* 1st, 1878, Edith (*d* 1916), *d* of late John Fletcher, Croft, Ambleside; one *s*; 2nd, Eleanor Foster, *d* of late Frederick W. Simpson, The Wray, Grasmere. *Educ:* Uppingham; Balliol College, Oxford (MA). Ordained, 1875; Curate in charge of Clifton College Mission; Vicar of Wray, Windermere, 1878–83; Vicar of Crosthwaite, Keswick, and Rural Dean, 1883–1917; Hon. Secretary of the National Trust for Places of Historic Interest and Natural Beauty; Hon. Secretary of Secondary Schools Association; Chairman, St George's School, Harpenden; Vice-President of the Holiday Association of National Home Reading Union; Vice-President of the Sunday Imperial Alliance; Chairman, Secondary School Committee, Cumberland Education Authority. *Publications:* Sonnets Round the Coast; Sonnets at the English Lakes; Edward Thring, Teacher and Poet; St Kentigern

of Crosthwaite; Ballads, Lyrics, and Bucolics; Valete and other Poems; Notes for the Nile; Idylls and Lyrics of the Nile; A Coach Drive at the Lakes; Literary Associations of English Lakes (another edn, illus., 1901); Harvey Goodwin, Bishop of Carlisle, a Biographical Memoir; The Darkened West; Ballads of Brave Deeds; The Revival of the Decorative Arts at Lucerne; Editor of revised edition of Jenkinson's Guide to the Lakes; The Sayings of Jesus: Six Village Sermons on a Papyrus Fragment; Henry Whitehead: a Memoir; Life and Nature at the English Lakes, 1899; Sonnets in Switzerland and Italy, 1899; Ballads of the War, 1900 (illus. edn 1901); Memories of the Tennysons, 1900; Ruskin and the English Lakes, 1901; illustrated edition of the Literary Associations of the English Lakes, 1902; A Rambler's Note-book at the Lakes, illustrated, 1902; A Coach Drive at the Lakes and the Buttermere Round, 1902; Sketches at the English Lakes, 1903; Flower-time in the Oberland, 1904; The Sacrum Commercium of St Francis, 1904; Sermons on the Sayings of Jesus, from the Oxyrhyncus Papyri, 1905; Months at the Lakes, 1906; A Sonnet Chronicle, 1900–1905, 1906; Round the Lake Country; Poems at Home and Abroad; By Fell and Dale at the English Lakes, 1911; Memories of the Tennysons, 1912; Chapters at the English Lakes, 1913; The European War: Poems, 1915; Past and Present at the English Lakes, 1916. *Recreations:* chiefly literary and travel; observations of scenery, bird life and habits of animals; local history and traditions. *Address:* Allan Bank, Grasmere. *TA:* Grasmere. *Club:* Royal Societies.
Died 28 May 1920.

RAWORTH, Benjamin Alfred, MIMechE; MIM; Member of the Iron and Steel Institute; Whitworth Scholar; Joint-editor of Engineering; *b* Chesterfield, 1 June 1849; *s* of B. J. Raworth, Sheffield; *m* 1886, Florence May, *d* of Charles Tysoe Harvey, MD; one *s* one *d*. *Educ:* Chesterfield Grammar School; Owens College, Manchester. Professional training at Wren and Hopkinson, Manchester; private assistant to Sir Joseph Whitworth, Manchester; Departmental Works Engineer to Siemens Bros, Woolwich; in practice as an engineer in Manchester; joined staff of Engineering, 1882. *Address:* 36 Bedford Street, Strand, WC; Dorleon, Mayfield Road, Sutton, Surrey. *TA:* Engineering, London. *T:* Gerard 3663. *Club:* St Stephen's.
Died 30 Sept. 1919.

RAWSON, Frank, CMG 1903; was acting Manager on Uganda Railway; *b* 16 Dec. 1856; *s* of late Samuel Rawson. *Club:* Oriental.
Died 30 Sept. 1928.

RAWSON, Col Herbert Edward, CB 1902; JP; Royal Engineers, retired 1909; *b* 3 Sept. 1852; 2nd *s* of late Sir Rawson William Rawson, KCMG, CB, and (Mary-Anne) Sophia, *d* of Hon. Rev. Henry Ward; *m* 1875, Elizabeth Stuart Armstrong (*d* 1885), *d* of late Richard Owen, JP Co. Dublin. *Educ:* Westminster; Royal Military Academy, Woolwich. Royal Engineers, 1872; submarine mining, 1874; Bermuda defence, 1877, Malta, 1885; Treasury, 1880–84; Canada, 1885–89, raising a submarine mining militia; Secretary of RE committee and War Office Ordnance committee, 1890–94; selected to command the Royal Engineers in Natal, 6 Oct. 1899, and served on the staff throughout the Boer War, returning to England, Nov. 1902; was present at the engagements Tugela Heights, Relief of Ladysmith, Laing's Nek; commanded district Natal and Zululand Frontier during operations of 1901, battle of Itala (medals and 4 clasps, brevet-colonelcy, CB, despatches 3 times); Member of Natal Defences Commission, 1902; Natal Native Affairs Commission, 1906–7; Chief Engineer and commanding RE, S Africa, 1905–7; Chief Engineer Northern Command, 1907–9. Pres., Old Westminsters' Cricket Club; Vice-Pres., Meteorol Soc.; Mem. Council, African Royal Aeronautical Soc.; Mem. Council, and Standing Cttee of Emigration, Royal Colonial Inst.; Mem. Diocesan Finance Bd, Herts and Beds; FRGS; FRHortS; Fellow of Linnean, Physical, and Herts Natural History Societies; Fowke Medal, RE. *Publications:* Selective Screening (British Assoc., 1908, 1913; S African Assoc., 1906; Linnean Soc., 1919, and RHortS 1916); Migration of Belts (Journal of Meteorological Soc. 1899–1908–10); contributions to Journals of United Service Club and Royal Aero Society. *Recreations:* played cricket for Kent, 1874; International Football (Association) for England, 1874; in the final matches for the Cup, 1874, 1875. *Address:* Home Close, Heronsgate, Herts. *T:* Chorleywood West. *Clubs:* Junior United Service, MCC, Free Foresters.
Died 18 Oct. 1924.

RAWSON, Col Richard Hamilton, JP, DL Sussex; MP (U) Reigate Division, Surrey, since 1910; Colonel Commanding Sussex Yeomanry since 1908; *b* 21 Feb. 1863; *e s* of Philip Rawson, JP, DL, of Woodhurst, Sussex, and Octavia, *d* of P. Gilmour, JP, Londonderry; *m* 1890, Lady Beatrice Anson, 2nd *d* of 2nd Earl of Lichfield; one *s* two *d*. *Educ:* Eton; BNC, Oxford. Served nine years in the 1st Life

Guards, and retired with the rank of Captain, 1892; afterwards served in the Sussex Yeomanry; High Sheriff of Sussex, 1899; contested (U) Reigate Division of Surrey, 1896. *Recreation:* hunting. *Address:* Gravenhurst, Haywards Heath; 64 Cadogan Square, SW. *T:* Kensington 4169. *Clubs:* Bachelors', Arthur's, Carlton.
Died 18 Oct. 1918.

RAY, Mahendranath, CIE 1914; MA, BL; Vakil, Calcutta High Court; Member, Bengal Legislative Council, since 1911; *b* Oct. 1862; *s* of late Girija Charan Ray of Taxpur, Howrah, India; *m* 1878, Probodhmoyi Dassi; two *s* two *d*. *Educ:* Presidency College, Calcutta. Burdwan, Vizianagram and Ishan Scholarships; BA 1883; Haris Chandra Prize; Gwalior Medal and Gold Medal for Mathematics; MA 1st Class Honours, 1884; BL 1885. Vakil, 1886; Vice-Chairman, Howrah District Board, 1888–96; Professor of Mathematics and Law, Calcutta City College, 1886–98; Fellow, Calcutta University, 1891; Member of the Syndicate, Calcutta University, 1910–18; Hon. Magistrate, Municipal Commissioner, and Member, District Board, Howrah; Chairman Howrah Municipality, 1916–20. *Publication:* Algebra, Parts I and II. *Address:* 8 Khooroot Road, Howrah, and 2 Boloram Bose's 1st Lane, Bhawanipur, Calcutta. *T:* Calcutta 3242. *M:* 777. *Club:* India, Calcutta.
Died Aug. 1925.

RAY, Prithwis Chandra, Editor, Indian World; *b* 1870; *m;* two *s* three *d*. *Educ:* The Mymensingh Zilla School; Presidency College, Calcutta. Editor, Bengalee, 1921–24; Secretary, 21st and 26th sessions of the Indian National Congress, held in Calcutta in 1906 and 1911; Secretary, Bengal Social Reform Association, 1908–14; Founder of the National Liberal League, Bengal, 1918; Member of the Moderate Deputation to England, 1919, and Bengal Landholders' Delegate to England, 1920; Donor of the Gokhale Library to the Indian Association of Calcutta, 1920. *Publications:* Poverty Problem in India, 1896; Indian Famines, 1901; The Map of India, 1904, reprinted 1927; Our Demand for Self-Government, 1917; A Scheme of Indian Constitutional Reforms, 1918; Life and Times of C. R. Das, 1927. *Address:* 5 Rifle Road, Ballygunge, Calcutta. *Club:* National Liberal.
Died Dec. 1927.

RAYLEIGH, 3rd Baron, *cr* 1821; **John William Strutt,** OM 1902; PC 1905; JP; FRS 1873; Chancellor Cambridge University, since 1908; Scientific Adviser to Trinity House since 1896; *b* 12 Nov. 1842; *e s* of 2nd Baron and Clara Elizabeth La Touche, *d* of Captain Vicars, RE; *S* father, 1873; *m* 1871, Evelyn Georgiana Mary, *d* of James Maitland Balfour, Whittingehame, and Blanche, *d* of 2nd Marquis of Salisbury; two *s* (and two *s* decd). *Educ:* Trinity Coll., Cambridge. Senior Wrangler and Smith's Prizeman, 1865; Fellow, 1866; Professor of Experimental Physics, Cambridge, 1879–84; Prof. of Natural Philosophy, Royal Instn, 1887–1905; Secretary to Royal Society, 1887–96; Lord Lieut of Essex, 1892–1901; Pres., Royal Soc., 1905; Hon. DCL Oxon, 1883; Hon. LLD Glasgow, 1884, Dublin, 1885, Edinburgh, 1888, Birmingham, 1909; Hon. DSc Dublin, 1892; Nobel Prize for Physics, 1905; Officer Legion of Honour. Owned about 7,000 acres. *Publications:* Treatise on the Theory of Sound, 1877; numerous scientific papers. *Heir: s* Hon. Robert John Strutt [*b* 28 Aug. 1875; *m* 1905, Lady Mary Hilda Clements, *d* of 4th Earl of Leitrim; three *s* one *d* (and one *d* decd)]. *Address:* Terling Place, Witham, Essex. *TA:* Terling. *Club:* Athenæum.
Died 30 June 1919.

RAYMOND, E.T.; *see* Thompson, Edward Raymond.

RAYNER, Henry, MD, MRCP; *b* Nov. 1841; *s* of W. Rayner, Hythe; *m* Rosa, *d* of A. Field of Leam, Leamington; two *s* one *d*. *Educ:* private schools; St Thomas's Hospital; Aberdeen University (highest Academical honours, with MB). Late Editor of Journal of Mental Science; late Lecturer and Physician for Mental Diseases at St Thomas's Hospital; Assistant Physician Bethlehem Hospital; Medical Superintendent Hanwell; former President of Medical Psychological Assoc.; Lecturer on Mental Diseases, Middlesex Hospital. *Publications:* Melancholia and Hypochondriasis (Allbutt's System of Medicine); Sleep in relation to Narcotics (Journal of Med. Sci.); Early Treatment of Mental Defects in Children (Med. Mag.); Gout and Insanity (Trans Internat. Med. Congress); Moral Insanity (Brain); Temperaments, Journal of Mental Science, 1921. *Recreation:* golf. *Address:* Upper Terrace House, Hampstead, NW3. *T:* Hampstead 378. *Club:* Reform.
Died 8 Feb. 1926.

RAYNOR, Sir William (Pick), Kt 1912; JP; sole proprietor of Thomas Hirst & Co., wool merchants, Huddersfield, Bradford, London and Australia; *b* 25 Oct. 1854; 2nd *s* of late John and Hannah Raynor; *m* 1877, (Sarah) Janet (*d* 1921), *d* of Robert Kirk, Huddersfield; no *c*. Entered the service of Thomas Hirst & Co., 1868; partner, 1888; on the Commission of the Peace for Huddersfield County Borough,

1906; West Riding, Yorks, 1910. *Address:* Rein Wood, Huddersfield. *TA:* Reinwood. *T:* 206. *Clubs:* Huddersfield; Union, Bradford.
Died 26 Aug. 1927.

REA, Rt. Hon. Russell, PC 1909; a Junior Lord of the Treasury since 1915; MP (L) South Shields since 1910; shipowner and merchant; Founder and Head of firm R. & J. H. Rea; *b* 11 Dec. 1846; 3rd *s* of late Daniel K. Rea of Eskdale, Cumberland, and Elizabeth, *d* of late Joseph Russell, shipbuilder, of Liverpool; *m* 1872, Jane Philip, *d* of P. L. MacTaggart of Liverpool; two *s. Educ:* privately. Late Deputy Chairman Taff Vale Railway; Chairman of Departmental Committee appointed to consider the economic effect of an Eight-Hour Day for Miners, 1906; Chairman of the Liberal Publication Department; of the Joint-Committee on the Port of London Bill; of Departmental Committee on Railway Amalgamations, 1909; Member of Royal Commission on Malta, 1911; Chairman of Coal Exports Committee; contested Exchange Division, Liverpool, 1897; MP (L) Gloucester, 1900–10. *Publications:* Insular Free Trade; Free Trade in Being; various articles and pamphlets on economic subjects. *Address:* Dean Stanley Street, SW. *T:* Victoria 4649; Tanhurst, Dorking. *M:* P 6702, P 7033. *Clubs:* Reform, National Liberal; Liberal, Newcastle.
Died 5 Feb. 1916.

READ, Brig.-Gen. Hastings, CB 1904; *b* 19 Aug. 1852; *s* of late Hastings Read, ICS; *m* 1899, Ada Mary, 3rd *d* of Maj.-Gen. H. Tod Stuart. *Educ:* Cheltenham. Entered army, 1873; Captain, 1893; Major, 1899; served Afghanistan, 1879–80 (medal); Burmah, 1887 (medal with clasp); Thibet, 1903–4 (despatches, CB); commanding Belgaum Brigade, 1906–8.
Died 24 Oct. 1928.

READE, Sir George Franklin, 10th Bt, *cr* 1660; *b* 22 Nov. 1869; *s* of Sir George Compton Reade, 9th Bt and Melissa, *d* of Isaac Ray, Michigan; *S* father, 1908; *m* 1893, Carrie, *d* of Nathan Nixon, Michigan; two *s* two *d. Heir: s* John Stanhope Reade [*b* 12 Sept. 1896. Served European War]. *Address:* Howell, Livingstone, County Michigan, USA.
Died 30 May 1923.

READE, John, LLD; FRSC; Associate Editor, Gazette, Montreal, since 1870; *b* Ballyshannon, Co. Donegal, Ireland, 13 Nov. 1837. *Educ:* Enniskillen; Belfast. Arrived in Canada, 1856; mostly engaged in journalism and literature; consistently advocated the conciliation of race and religion in Canada, Canadian Confederation and the unity of the Empire; one of the original Members, Royal Society of Canada (founded by Marquis of Lorne), 1882, and Pres. of Historical and Archæol Section (English). *Publications:* Volumes of Verse, 1870 and 1906; The Making of Canada, 1884; The Half-breed, 1885; The Basques in North America, 1887; etc. *Address:* 340 Laval Avenue, Montreal.
Died 1919.

REAL, Hon. Patrick; Judge of Supreme Court of Queensland, 1890–1922; *b* Limerick, 1847. Went to Australia, 1851; called to the Bar, 1874; was Crown Prosecutor in Central District, and Member of Royal Commission on Establishment of Queensland University. *Address:* Ulalie, M'Ilwraith Avenue, Coorparoo, Brisbane, Queensland.
Died 9 June 1928.

REAY, 11th Lord, *cr* 1628, of Reay, Caithness; **Donald James Mackay,** KT 1911; GCSI 1890; GCIE 1887; PC 1905; DL, JP; Bt 1627; Baron Reay (UK), 1881; Baron Mackay of Ophemert, Holland; Lord-Lieutenant of Roxburghshire, 1892–1918; Chief of Clan Mackay; *b* The Hague, 22 Dec. 1839; *s* of 10th Lord and Maria Catherine Anne Jacoba, *d* of Baron Fagel, PC, The Netherlands; *S* father, 1876; naturalised, 1877; *m* 1877, Fanny Georgiana Jane (*d* 1917), CI, *d* of late Richard Hasler, Aldingbourne, Sussex, and widow of Capt. Alexander Mitchell. Rector of St Andrews University, 1884–86; Governor of Bombay, 1885–90; Under-Secretary for India, 1894–95; Chairman London School Board, 1897–1904; President Royal Asiatic Society and University College, London; 1st President British Academy, 1901–7; Hon. LLD Edin., 1882, Aberdeen, 1905; Hon. DLitt Oxon, 1904; Hon. LittD Cantab, 1905. *Heir:* (to Scottish titles) *cousin* Baron Eric Mackay [*b* 2 April 1870; *s* of Baron Æneas Mackay and Baroness Elizabeth de Lynden; *m* 1901, Baroness Maria Johanna Bertha Christina Van Dedem; three *s* one *d*]. *Address:* 35 Berkeley Square, W1. *Clubs:* Athenæum; New, Edinburgh.
Died 1 Aug. 1921.

REAY, 12th Lord, *cr* 1628, of Reay, Caithness; **Eric Mackay;** Bt 1627; Baron Mackay of Ophemert, Holland; Chief of Clan Mackay; *b* 2 April 1870; *s* of Baron Æneas Mackay and Baroness Elizabeth de Lynden; *S* cousin, 1921; *m* 1901, Baroness Maria Johanna Bertha Christina Van Dedem; three *s* one *d. Heir: s* Aeneas Alexander Mackay, *b* 25 Dec. 1905.
Died 2 Nov. 1921.

RECKITT, Sir James, 1st Bt, *cr* 1894; JP, DL; Chairman of Reckitt and Sons, Ltd; Garden Village Co.; Priestman Bros; and the Hull Royal Infirmary Board; *b* 14 Nov. 1833; *s* of Isaac Reckitt and Ann, *d* of Charles and Elizabeth Coleby, Hempstead, Norfolk; *m* 1865, Kathleen (*d* 1923), *d* of Robert Saunders, Lilling, York; two *s* two *d. Educ:* Ackworth School, the principal public school of the Society of Friends. Chiefly known from his long and prosperous business career, his interest in most philanthropic and educational work, his gifts of free library, orphan home, convalescent home, new wing to Royal Infirmary, and other gifts to Hull; the building of a complete Model Garden Village in Hull of 600 houses. *Recreation:* an art collector (had a fine collection of modern pictures and other works of art). *Heir: s* Harold James Reckitt [*b* 4 May 1868; *m* 1st, 1899, Christine Thomazia (marr. diss. 1907), *d* of Alexander Howden; one *d*; 2nd, 1908, Julia Allen, *e d* of Charles H. Conner, Ind, USA]. *Address:* Swanland Manor, Hull. *TA:* North Ferriby. *T:* Ferriby 19. *M:* BT 695, AT 470. *Club:* National Liberal.
Died 18 March 1924.

REDDY, Michael; MP (N) Birr Division of King's County, 1900–18; farmer. *Address:* Shannon Bridge, King's County.
Died 30 July 1919.

REDESDALE, 1st Baron, *cr* 1902; **Algernon Bertram Freeman-Mitford,** GCVO 1905; KCB 1906; JP, DL; *b* 24 Feb. 1837; 3rd *s* of Henry Reveley Mitford, Exbury, Hants, and Georgina Jemima, *d* of 3rd Earl of Ashburnham; assumed by Royal licence additional surname of Freeman, 1886; *m* 1874, Lady Clementine Gertrude Helen Ogilvy, *d* of 7th Earl of Airlie, KT; four *s* four *d* (and one *s* decd). *Educ:* Eton; Christ Church, Oxford (2nd class Moderations). Entered Foreign Office, 1858; 3rd Secretary of Embassy, St Petersburg, 1863; appointed to Peking, 1865; transferred to Japan, 1866; 2nd Secretary of Legation, 1868; Secretary to HM's Office of Works, 1874–86; accompanied HRH Prince Arthur's Mission to Japan, 1906; MP (C) for South-West Warwickshire, 1892–95; member of Royal Commission on Civil Services, 1887; trustee of Wallace Collection; trustee of National Gallery; governor of Wellington College. Decorated for public services. *Publications:* Tales of Old Japan, 1871; The Bamboo Garden, 1896; The Attaché at Peking, 1900; The Garter Mission to Japan, 1906; A Tragedy in Stone, 1912; Memories (autobiog.), 1915. *Heir: s* Hon. David Bertram Ogilvy Freeman-Mitford, *b* 13 March 1878. *Address:* Batsford Park, Moreton in Marsh, Glos. *Clubs:* Travellers', Carlton, Marlborough; Royal Yacht Squadron, Cowes.
Died 17 Aug. 1916.

REDFERN, Rev. Thomas, MA; Rector and Rural Dean of Denbigh since 1907; Canon of St Asaph; Chaplain of North Wales Asylum; *b* 1853; *s* of Absalom Redfern, Halkyn, Flintshire; *m* 1st, Jane, *d* of John Roberts, Rhyl; 2nd, Henrietta Maria, *d* of Major-General Connolly M'Causland, RE, Bessbrook, Newtown, Limavady, Co. Derry; two *s* three *d. Educ:* Clare College, Cambridge. Deacon, 1879; priest, 1880; Curate of Oswestry, 1879–82; Rector of Trefonen, 1882, 1887; Vicar on Holy Trinity, Oswestry, 1887–1907; Rural Dean of Oswestry, 1903. *Address:* The Rectory, Denbigh.
Died Feb. 1924.

REDFERN, Thomas William, MVO 1908; representative of International Sleeping Car Co. at Paris; *b* 1859; *s* of William Redfern, Derby; *m* 1890. *Address:* 40 rue de l'Arcade, Paris.
Died 2 Sept. 1924.

REDFORD, George Alexander; Examiner of Plays, 1895–1911; *e s* of late George Redford, FRCS. *Educ:* Clewer House School, Windsor. Was a bank manager for many years; became Licenser of Plays, 1875; formerly assistant and deputy to late Mr Pigott, Examiner of Plays, 187 Queen's Gate, SW. *Recreations:* punting, sculling, occasionally golf; formerly cricket. *Address:* 38 Harrington Gardens, SW.
Died 12 Nov. 1916.

REDMAN, Rev. Alfred; Vicar of St James', Heywood, since 1884; Hon. Canon of Manchester. Deacon, 1876; Priest, 1877; Curate of Royton, 1876–78; Vicar of High Crompton, Manchester, 1878–84. *Address:* St James's Vicarage, Heywood, Lancs.
Died 15 Feb. 1927.

REDMOND, John Edward; MP (N) Waterford since 1891; Chairman of Irish Parliamentary Party; *b* 1 Sept. 1856; *s* of late William Archer Redmond, late MP Ballytrent, and Mary, *d* of Major R. Hoey, Co. Wicklow; *m* 1883, Johanna, *d* of late James Dalton, New South Wales; one *s* two *d. Educ:* Clongowes; Trinity College, Dublin. Barrister Gray's Inn, 1886; Irish Barrister, 1887; MP (N) New Ross, 1881–85; N Wexford, 1885–91. *Address:* 18 Wynnstay Gardens, SW.
Died 6 March 1918.

REDMOND, Sir Joseph Michael, Kt 1911; MD NUI (*hon. causa*); FRCP, LRCS; Physician to Mater Misericordiæ Hospital; Physician to the Castle Red Cross Hospital; Consulting Physician to Coombe Hospital, St Michael's Hospital, Kingstown, National Hospital and Cottage Hospital, Drogheda; Consulting Physician to the Royal College of St Patrick, Maynooth; *s* of late Denis Redmond and Bridget Emily Gorman; *m* Oswaldina, *d* of late James Nelson, JP. Vice-President, 1900–2, President, 1906–8, Royal Coll. of Physicians; formerly President, State Medicine Section, Royal Academy of Medicine; formerly Lecturer on the Practice of Medicine and Pathology in the Ledwich School of Medicine, and Pathologist to the Coombe Hospital; late Senior Physician to Fever Hospital, Cork Street, etc; KCHS. *Publications:* Cancer of the Liver; Acromegaly; Ulcer of Stomach; Multiple Small Abscesses of the Liver; Tumour of the Brain, etc. *Address:* 41 Merrion Square, Dublin; Gortmore, Dundrum, Co. Dublin. *T:* 1690. *M:* IK 932. *Club:* Stephen's Green, Dublin.   *Died 25 Nov. 1921.*

REDMOND, Major William Hoey Kearney; MP (P) Clare, E, since 1892; barrister-at-law; *b* 1861; 2nd *s* of late William Archer Redmond, MP, and Mary, *d* of Major R. Hoey, Co. Wicklow; *m* 1886, Eleanor, *d* of James Dalton, Orange, NSW. *Educ:* Clongowes. MP (N) Wexford, 1883–85; Co. Fermanagh, 1885–92. *Publications:* A Shooting Trip in the Australian Bush, 1898; Through the New Commonwealth, 1906. *Address:* Glenbrook, Delgany, Co. Wicklow. *Club:* Leinster, Dublin.
                                                      Died 9 June 1917.

REDWOOD, Sir (Thomas) Boverton, 1st Bt, *cr* 1911; Kt 1905; DSc (hon.); FRSE; FRGS consulting chemist and engineer; Adviser on Petroleum to the Admiralty, the Home Office, the India Office, and the Colonial Office (Consulting); Consulting Adviser to the Corporation of London under the Petroleum Acts; Adviser on Petroleum Transport to the Port of London Authority; Adviser to the Thames Conservancy; *b* London, 26 April 1846; *e s* of late Professor Theophilus Redwood, PhD, of Boverton, Glamorganshire, and Charlotte Elizabeth, *d* of Thomas Newborn Robert Morson; *m* 1873, Mary Elizabeth, *e d* of late Frederick Letchford; two *d* (one *s* decd). *Educ:* University Coll. School; Pharmaceutical Society of Great Britain. Accompanied late Sir Vivian Majendie on visits of inspection to chief centres of petroleum distribution in this country, the principal European countries, the United States and Canada, and gave evidence before Committees of Lords and Commons; was member of several juries at International Inventions and Health Exhibitions; president of International Jury for lighting appliances and materials at Brussels Exhibition, 1897; member of Jury, Paris Exhibition, 1900; Home Office Committee on Acetylene Generators, 1901; Royal Commission St Louis Exhibition, 1904; Chairman Liberal Arts Committee, and member of Superior Jury, Franco-British Exhibition, 1908; Royal Commission Brussels, Rome, and Turin Exhibitions; Chairman Chemical Industries Committee; member of Superior Jury, Brussels, 1910; member of Delegacy, City and Guilds (Engineering) Coll., Imperial College of Science and Technology; Royal Commission on Fuel and Engines, 1912; Director of Technical Investigations, HM Petroleum Executive; Chairman, Gas Traction Committee; Pres., Soc. of Chemical Industry, 1907–8; Jun. Instn of Engineers, 1913; Instn of Petroleum Technologists, 1914–16; Mem. Council and Past Vice-Pres., Royal Soc. of Arts; Associate, Inst. of Civil Engineers; MIME; Mem., Inst. of Chemistry; Hon. Mem., Amer. Phil Soc.; Hon. Corres. Mem., Imperial Russian Technol Soc.; Chevalier, Order of Leopold, Belgium. *Publications:* Cantor Lectures on Petroleum and its Products, 1886; Petroleum: its Production and Use, 1887; Report (with Sir Frederick Abel) on Accidents with Mineral Oil Lamps, 1890; also on the Transport of Petroleum through the Suez Canal, 1892; articles on Petroleum in Professor Thorpe's Dictionary of Applied Chemistry, 1893; The Transport of Petroleum in Bulk (Telford Premium), Inst. of Chemical Engrs, 1894; articles on the Petroleum Industry, and Lamps in Chemical Technology, 1895; A Treatise on Petroleum (2 vols), 1896, 3rd edn (3 vols), 1913; The Detection and Estimation of Inflammable Gases and Vapours in the Air, 1896 (with Prof. Clowes); Handbook on Petroleum (with Captain J. H. Thomson), 1901, 2nd edn 1906, 3rd edn (with Major A. Cooper-Key), 1913; The Petroleum Lamp (with Captain J. H. Thomson), 1902; Petroleum, in Ency. Brit. (supplement), 1902, and Ency. Brit. 11th edn, 1911; Petroleum Technologist's Pocket-Book (with Arthur W. Eastlake), 1915. *Heir: g s* Thomas Boverton Redwood, *b* 15 Oct. 1906. *Address:* The Cloisters, 18 Avenue Road, Regent's Park, NW. *T:* Avenue 5814; Wayside Cottage, Cooden Down, Little Common, Sussex; 4 Bishopsgate, EC. *TA:* Olefiant, London. *T:* Hampstead 1127. *M:* LD 8484. *Clubs:* Savage, Royal Thames Yacht, City of London, Royal Automobile; Royal Motor Yacht.
                                                      Died 4 June 1919.

REECE, Surg.-Col Richard James, CB 1917; MA, MD Cantab; MRCP, MRCS; DPH; Senior Medical Officer, Ministry of Health; *b* 1862; *o s* of late George Reece, Kensington; *m* 1894, Ada Eleanor, *o d* of James Watt Perkins, Edgware; two *s* two *d*. *Educ:* Kensington School; Downing College, Cambridge; St Bartholomew's Hospital. First Assistant Medical Officer of Health, Port Sanitary Authority of London; entered Local Government Board as Medical Inspector, 1893; Surgeon-Colonel, A Battery, Horse Artillery Division, Honourable Artillery Company; late Senior Examiner State Medicine, Cambridge University; President Epidemiological Section Royal Society of Medicine, 1922 and 1923; Vice-Pres. Public Health Section, BMA Meeting, Glasgow, 1922. *Publications:* Reports on Acute Poliomyelitis, Cerebrospinal Fever, Infectious Disease, etc; contributions to the Epidemiological Section of the Royal Society of Medicine. *Address:* Ministry of Health, Whitehall, SW1; 62 Addison Gardens, W14; Basketts, Birchington-on-Sea, Kent. *Clubs:* Savage; Leander, Henley-on-Thames.
                                                      Died 20 April 1924.

REED, Herbert Parker, KC; *b* London; *e s* of Herbert Adolphus Reed, solicitor. *Educ:* Brighton, privately. Solicitor, 1873; never practised; engaged in literature; entered Inner Temple, 1874; called to the Bar, 1877; admitted Gray's Inn, 1887; Bencher, 1896; QC 1892; Treasurer, 1902. *Publication:* The Law of Bills of Sale, etc. *Recreation:* the cares of a garden. *Address:* Watcombe, near Torquay. *T:* Torquay 189.
                                                      Died 30 Jan. 1920.

REED, Rev. Martin; Hon. Canon of St Albans, 1915; Rural Dean of Ware, 1914–22; Proctor in Convocation, 1920–21; *b* Brussels, 10 Dec. 1856; 3rd *s* of B. B. Reed (formerly Managing Director of the Great Luxemburg Railway), The Knowle, Reigate, Surrey; *m* 1888, Annie Elizabeth, *d* of Rev. D. C. Neary, DD, Vicar of South Ossett, Yorks; no *c*. *Educ:* Trinity College, Cambridge. Went nearly blind when entered for public school, and had to prepare for the university under private tuition; was Secretary and a frequent speaker at the Union, and took Honours in Theology, 1879. Ordained to Holy Trinity, Leicester, 1879; Vicar, 1882; Rector of Eastwell, Kent, 1890–94; St Thomas', Nottingham, 1894–1907; Vicar of Ware, Herts, 1907–24; elected Guardian for city and served ten years; Secretary of Housing Committee for Diocese of Southwell; member of Standing Council of Diocese since 1916; member of County Council Education Committee; much interested in housing reform. *Publications:* papers on the housing question in town and country. *Recreation:* golf. *Address:* 18 Cunningham Avenue, St Albans, Herts.
                                                      Died 11 March 1926.

REES, Ven. David John, LTh; Archdeacon in Diocese of Mombasa; Principal of Huron Training College, Church Missionary Society; *b* 16 Dec. 1862; *m* Agnes, *d* of late W. B. Cooper, Aberdeen; one *s*. *Educ:* University College, Durham. *Address:* Huron Training College, Kongwa, Gulwe Station, Dar-es-Salaam, Tanganyika Territory.   *Died 24 March 1924.*

REES, His Honour Griffith Caradoc; County Court Judge for North Wales since 1921; *b* Birkenhead, 1868; *s* of Griffith Rees, Cilgerran, Cardiganshire, and Sarah Rees, Llangynog, Montgomeryshire; unmarried. *Educ:* Liverpool Institute. Solicitor, 1895–1905; Barrister, Middle Temple, 1905–21; contested (L) Denbigh Boroughs, Dec. 1910; MP (L) Carnarvon, 1915–18; Parliamentary Secretary to Home Office, 1916–17. *Recreation:* golf. *Address:* 5 Elm Court, The Temple, EC.   *Died 20 Sept. 1924.*

REES, Rev. Henry, MA; Canon and Precentor, Bangor Cathedral, 1892; *b* 4 March 1844; *s* of David Rees, Llandovery; *m* 1879, Harriet (*d* 1919), *y d* of Andrew Schofield, Tanyrallt, Llandudno; one *s*. *Educ:* Llandovery College; Sidney Sussex College, Cambridge (BA 1866; MA 1883). Ordained, 1867; Surrogate, 1870; licensed to officiate in diocese of Winchester, 1896; Curate of Conway, 1867–70; Vicar, 1870–93; Chaplain to Bishop of Bangor, 1891–98. *Publication:* The Welsh Clergyman's Vade Mecum. *Recreations:* golf, fishing, cycling. *Address:* The White Cottage, Shanklin, IW.
                                                      Died 5 Feb. 1924.

REES, Sir John David, 1st Bt, *cr* 1919; KCIE 1910 (CIE 1890); CVO 1908; JP Middlesex, 1907; Director Prisoners of War Information Bureau, 1915–20; MP (U) East Division of Nottingham since 1912; *b* 16 Dec. 1854; *e s* of the late Lodowick William Rees and Ann, *d* of J. Jones; *m* 1891, Hon. Mary Catherine, *d* of Lt-Gen. Hon. Sir James Charlemagne Dormer, and *sister* of 14th Lord Dormer; one *s* one *d*. *Educ:* Cheltenham Coll. Indian Civil Service, 1875; Under Secretary Madras Government; private secretary, Sir Mountstuart Grant Duff, Lord Connemara, and Lord Wenlock, Governors of

Madras; Government Translator in Tamil, Telugu, Persian and Hindustani; Russian interpreter; HS Arabic; on special duty with Duke of Clarence in Madras Presidency, 1889–90; British Resident in Travancore and Cochin; Additional Member of Governor-General of India's Council, 1895–1900; retired ICS 1901; travelled in Corea, Manchuria, China, Arabia, Persia, Siberia, Asia Minor, Mesopotamia, Japan and America; Chairman British Central Africa Co., Ltd; Director, South India Railway Co., Ltd; Mysore Gold Mining Co., Ltd; Champion Reef Gold Mining Co., Ltd; Port Madryn (Argentina) Co., Ltd; Chubut Railway Co., Ltd; Kolar Power Co., Ltd; Bengal-Dooars Railway Co., Ltd; Oregum Gold Mining Co., Ltd; Consolidated Tea and Lands Co., Ltd; Anglo-American Direct Tea Trading Co., Ltd; Kanan Devan Hills Produce Co., Ltd; Amalgamated Tea Estates Co.; MP (LI) Montgomery Dist, 1906–10; contested Kilmarnock (U), 1911; Parly Cand. (U) Walworth, 1911–12; Cand. (C) LCC Peckham, 1901; Comdr. Imperial Russian Order of St Stanislaus. Decorated: Indian services. *Publications:* Tours in India; Duke of Clarence in S India; The Mahommedans; The Real India; Modern India; Current Political Problems; articles in Ninth Ceneteentury, Fortnightly; and other reviews. *Heir: s* Richard Lodowick Montagu Edward Rees, *b* 4 April 1900. *Address:* 9 Chesham Place, SW1. *T:* Victoria 7831; Thames House, Queen Street Place, EC. *T:* City 3497; 5 Burton Street, Nottingham. *M:* LL 676. *Clubs:* Carlton, Travellers', Bachelors', Hurlingham.

Died 2 June 1922.

REES, Rev. Thomas, MA, PhD (London); BA (Oxon); Principal of Bala Bangor Independent College, Bangor, since 1909; *b* Llanfyrnach, Pembrokeshire, 1869; *m* 1902, Charlotte Elizabeth, *d* of Michael Davies, Bridgend, Glamorganshire; five *s* one *d*. *Educ:* Presbyterian College, Carmarthen; University College, Cardiff; Mansfield College, Oxford. Professor of Theology at the Memorial College, Brecon, 1899–1909. *Publications:* Duw, ei Fodolaeth a'i Natur; Hanes Ymneilltuaeth yng Nghymru; Esboniad ar yr Epistol at yr Hebreaid (2 vols); The Holy Spirit in Thought and Experience; Cenadwri'r Eglwys a Phroblemau'r dydd; Editor of Geiriadur Beiblaidd and of Y Dysgedydd. *Recreation:* mountaineering. *Address:* Independent College, Bangor. *Died 20 May 1926.*

REESE, Frederick Focke, DD (Univ. of Georgia, 1900; Univ. of the South, 1908); Bishop of Georgia Episcopal Church since 1908; *b* Baltimore, Maryland, 23 Oct. 1854; *s* of John S. and Arnoldina O. Focke Reese; *m* 1879, Ella, *d* of I. M. and Mary B. Parr, Baltimore; five *d*. *Educ:* University of Virginia and Berkeley Divinity School. Deacon, 1878; priest, 1879; Priest in Charge, All Saints, Baltimore, 1878–85; Rector, Trinity Church, Portsmouth, Va, 1885–90; Rector, Christ Church, Macon, Ga, 1890–1903; Christ Church, Nashville, Tenn, 1903–8; elected, and declined Missionary Bishop, Wyoming, 1907; Deputy to General Convention from Georgia, 1892–1901; from Tennessee, 1904 and 1907; other positions of trust in the Church; representative of the Province of Sewanee in the Executive Council of the National Church; Trustee, University of the South, Sewanee, Tenn, from 1893; Phi Beta Kappa. *Publications:* occasional sermons. *Recreation:* golf. *Address:* Christ Church, Savannah, Georgia. *Clubs:* Delta Psi College Fraternity; Savannah Golf; Colonade, University of Va. *Died 20 Nov. 1924.*

REEVE, Henry Fenwick, CMG 1900; MICE, FRGS, FSA; *b* Kent, 7 April 1854; *o s* of Allen Reeve and Priscilla (*née* Fenwick). *Educ:* privately; St Peter's College; Melbourne University. Served under Government of New South Wales, Victoria, Fiji, Windward Islands, Gambia, and Lagos, West Africa; Chief Commissioner, Anglo-French Boundary Commission, 1895–96 and 1898–99; Acting Governor, Lagos, 1902. *Publication:* The Gambia, 1912. *Recreations:* general shooting, fishing, yachting. *Clubs:* Royal Societies, St Stephen's.

Died 18 Jan. 1920.

REEVE, Simms, DL, JP Norfolk; JP Norwich; *b* 1826; *e s* of Joseph N. Reeve and Mary, *d* of late Law Simms, Brancaster; *m* 1854, Annie, *d* of late William Browne. Recorder of Great Yarmouth, 1872–1908; High Sheriff for the county of Norfolk, 1898; *Address:* Brancaster Hall, King's Lynn; St Helen's Lodge, Norwich. *Club:* Norfolk County. *Died 29 Oct. 1919.*

REEVE, Rt. Rev. William Day, DD; Assistant Bishop of Toronto since 1907; *b* Harmston, Lincs, 3 Jan. 1844; *e s* of James Reeve; *m* 1st, 1869, Emily (*d* 1906), *e d* of George Parker; three *s* four *d*; 2nd, 1907; Alice Mary, *d* of late R. R. Grindley of Montreal. *Educ:* National School, Harmston; CMS College, Islington. After two years on a farm, followed by a business training, entered CMS College in 1866; deacon, 1869; priest, 1874; CMS Missionary 1869; Fort Simpson, 1869–79, including one year at Fort Rae; Fort Chipewyan, 1879–89,

including one year's furlough, 1880–81; Bishop's Chaplain and Registrar, 1874; Archdeacon of Chipewyan, 1883; consecrated Bishop in Winnipeg, 1891. *Publications:* editor of New Testament, Book of Common Prayer, Hymnal, etc, in Slavi Language, translated by Bishop Bompas. *Recreations:* chess, draughts, shooting. *Address:* Assistant Bishop's Room, Synod Office, and 544 Huron Street, Toronto, Canada. *T:* 0123 Hillcrest. *Died 12 May 1925.*

REFALO, His Honour Sir Michelangelo, Kt 1921; CBE 1918; Chief Justice and President of HM Court of Appeal, Malta; *b* Malta, 1 March 1876; *s* of late Notary Vincenzo Refalo; *m* 1900, Mary (deceased), 2nd *d* of late G. D. Debono, architect; three *s* two *d*. *Educ:* Malta University (BA 1894; LLD 1898). Called to the Malta Bar, 1899; Examiner in Italian Literature, 1902; Prof. of Commercial Law, 1907; Univ. of Malta; Assistant Crown Advocate, 1910; Crown Advocate, Member of the Legislative and Executive Council, Malta, Legal Adviser to the Naval and Military Authorities, and Proper Officer of the Crown in Prize Cases, 1915; Examiner in Faculty of Law, 1915; Member of the Control Board, 1916; Vice-President of the Council of Government of Malta, 1919–21. *Publications:* contributed an account of the Commercial Laws of Malta in a work dealing with the Commercial Laws of the British Possessions and Protectorates, 1912. *Address:* Valletta, Malta. *TA:* Chief Justice, Malta. *Club:* Casino Maltese, Valletta. *Died 20 Dec. 1923.*

REHAN, Ada; actress; *b* Limerick, 22 April 1860. *Educ:* Brooklyn, New York. Début, Newark, New Jersey, 1874; during the seasons of 1875–78 enacted nearly 200 different characters in Philadelphia, Louisville, Albany, Baltimore; played the heroines of Shakespeare with Edwin Booth, Laurence Barrett, John M'Cullough, etc; engaged by Augustin Daly for his New York theatre, 1879; played under Mr Daly's management in London, Berlin, Paris, etc, as well as New York and San Francisco; created a furore with her impersonations of Katherine (Taming of the Shrew), Rosalind (As You Like It), Viola (Twelfth Night), Lady Teazle (School for Scandal), etc. *Recreations:* cycling, travelling, reading (preferences for Balzac and Thackeray). *Address:* 164 West Ninety-third Street, New York City.

Died 9 Jan. 1916.

REIACH, Herbert; publisher, naval architect; Founder and Editor of the Yachting Monthly, since 1906; Joint-Editor of the Badminton Magazine since 1916; Manager of the Saturday Review; Managing Director of Herbert Reiach, Ltd, Publishers; *b* Greenock, 22 Jan. 1873; *y s* of late George Reiach, Edinburgh, HM Inspector of Scottish Fisheries. *Educ:* Royal High School and George Watson's College, Edinburgh. Studied and practised shipbuilding, naval architecture and yacht designing, 1890–1902; Associate Member, Institution of Naval Architects; Business Editor of The Field, 1908–10; writer on naval architecture and yachting under the pseudonym of "Mina." *Recreation:* yachting. *Address:* 9 King Street, Covent Garden, WC2. *T:* Gerrard 8157. *Club:* Royal Thames Yacht. *Died 16 July 1921.*

REICHEL, Rev. Oswald Joseph, MA, BCL; FSA; *b* 2 Feb. 1840; *e s* of late Rev. Samuel Rudolph Reichel of Ockbrook, Co. Derby, and 2nd wife, Matilda, *d* of Joseph Hurlock of Oxted, Co. Surrey; *m* 1887, Julia Maria Harriet Louisa, *d* of F. Ashenden and *g d* of Thomas Lestock Ashenden of Old Barn Court, Nonington, Co. Kent. *Educ:* Queen's College, Oxford. Taylorian Scholar; Ellerton Theological Essayist and Johnson and Denyer Theological Scholar in University of Oxford, and Vice-Principal of Cuddesdon Theological College; Member of St Thomas' Board of Guardians, Devon; Public Preacher in the Diocese of Exeter. *Publications:* The See of Rome in the Middle Ages, 1870; Sparsholt Feast, an antiquarian sermon, 1882; contributor to the Devon Association of articles on Domesday, the Pipe Rolls, the Hundreds, Manors, and Churches of Devon; The Rise of the Parochial System, 1906; The Treasury of God and the Birthright of the Poor, 1907; Domesday Survey, the Feudal Baronage, and Translation of Domesday text for the Victoria History of the County of Devon; A Complete Manual of Canon Law; Editor of Devon Feet of Fines for Devon and Cornwall Record Society, and of Bishop Lacy of Exeter Episcopal Registers. *Address:* A la Ronde House, near Lympstone, Devon.

Died 30 April 1923.

REID, Surg.-Gen. Sir Adam Scott, KCB 1911 (CB 1903); MB, MCh; Indian Medical Service, retired; lately Principal Medical Officer, Punjab Command; *b* 4 April 1848; *s* of John Alexander Reid, Co. Ross; *m* 1875, Sidney Vaughan (*decd*), *d* of Sidney Vaughan Jackson of Ballina, Mayo; one *s* two *d*. Asst-Surg. 1872; Surg.-Gen. 1902; served Afghan War, 1879–80 (medal); Chin Lushai Expedition, 1889–90 (medal with clasp); NW Frontier, India, 1897–98 (despatches, medal with two clasps); formerly Administrative Medical

Officer, Central Provinces, India, and Inspector-General Civil Hospitals, Punjab; initiated and was President of a Malaria Conference held at Nagpur, 1901; granted a Good Service Pension in recognition of his services to the State. *Publications:* Chin Lushai Land; and numerous contributions to the lay and medical Press. *Recreations:* fishing, shooting, golf, billiards, travel, literature. *Address:* 10 Zetland House, Cheniston Gardens, Kensington, W. *T:* Western 1658. *Club:* East India United Service.   *Died 2 Feb. 1918.*

REID, Alexander, ISO 1904; Under Treasurer of Tasmania, 1895-1914; *b* 12 Aug. 1843; *s* of Alexander Reid, Tas; *m* 1871, Blanche Alice Goldsmith. Entered Civil Service, 1857; Accountant, 1882; retired on pension, 1914. *Address:* Mount Nelson Road, Hobart, Tasmania.   *Died 22 July 1919.*

REID, Lt-Col Alexander, DSO 1900; VD; *b* 2 Oct. 1863; *s* of Thomas Reid, Hampstead; *m* 1906, Margaret Frederica, *widow* of late Major Harry Chalmers Hundson, IMS, 16th Bengal Cavalry; one *s. Educ:* Highgate School. Served South Africa, 1900 (despatches, Queen's medal 4 clasps, DSO); served European War, 1914-20, England, France and Flanders (despatches); commanded POW Camp, Queensferry, Chester; 20th Batt. Lancashire Fusiliers; 18th Cheshire; 37 Labour Group. *Address:* 39 St Paul's Avenue, Willesden Green, NW.   *Died 25 Feb. 1927.*

REID, Sir Archibald Douglas, KBE 1919; CMG 1917; MRCS, LRCP; DMR&E (Cambridge); Royal Army Medical Corps; Superintendent Radiological Department, St Thomas' Hospital; *b* 1871; *s* of Dr Douglas A. Reid, JP, of Tenby; *m* Annie Allan, *d* of late John Clapperton of Greenock. *Educ:* Bradfield College; King's College Hospital. Capt. RAMC (TF); temp. Lt-Col RAMC; President of War Office X-Ray Committee, 1914-19; President Electrotherapeutic Section of Royal Society of Medicine, 1911-12. *Address:* 30 Welbeck Street, W1. *T:* Paddington 4501.
                                            Died 15 Jan. 1924.

REID, Clement, FRS, FLS, FGS; late District Geologist on survey of England and Wales; *m* E. M. Wynne Edwards, BSc. Studied tertiary formations in the South of England, pliocene deposits, glacial phenomena of the east and south coasts, pliocene and pleistocene botany, Cornish geology. *Publications:* Geology of the Country around Cromer, 1882; Geology of Holderness, 1885; Pliocene Deposits of Britain, 1890; Origin of the British Flora, 1899; The Island of Ictis, 1905; Geology of Newquay, 1906; Geology of Land's End, 1907; Geology of Mevagissey, 1907; Submerged Forests, 1913; jointly with Mrs Reid—Pre-Glacial Flora of Britain, 1907; Fossil Flora of Tegelen, 1907-10; The Lignite of Bovey Tracey, 1910; The Pliocene Floras of the Dutch-Prussian Border, 1915; reports on the botany of Roman Britain; many contributions to geological journals. *Address:* One Acre, Milford-on-Sea, Hampshire.   *Died 10 Dec. 1916.*

REID, Col Ellis Ramsay, CB 1907; DSO 1902; Chief Paymaster Army Pay Department; *b* 23 Jan. 1850; *s* of Lestock Robert Reid, late Bombay CS; *m* 1901, Helena Kate, *d* of Joseph Risley. *Educ:* Hampstead; Harrow; Sandhurst. Joined 108th Regiment as ensign, 1869; exchanged as captain to 44th Foot, 1878; joined APD 1881; served Bechuanaland campaign, 1884-85 (honourably mentioned); S African War from Nov. 1899 to the end (despatches, DSO). *Address:* Blenheim, Blackheath, Colchester.   *Died 14 Oct. 1918.*

REID, Col Francis Maude, DSO 1917; retired pay; late the Highland Light Infantry; *b* 17 June 1849; 6th *s* of late William Reid, of The Node, Welwyn, Herts; *m* 1874, Katharine Elizabeth Julia, *e d* of late Colonel George Ross, of Cromarty; no *c. Educ:* Harrow. Joined 71st the HLI as Ensign by Purchase, 1868; went as Adjutant Sutherland Highland Rifles, 1884-89; commanded 1st Batt. the HLI, 1894-99; saw service in Cretan rising at Kandia, 6 Sept. 1898 (despatches); joined up for European War, 6 Sept. 1914; commanded 7th SB the Lincolnshire Regt; transferred May 1915 to 13th SB the Worcestershire Regt; again transferred April 1916 to 34th Labour Batt. Royal Fusiliers; went to France with it (despatches twice, DSO); once Master of Pack of Beagles; Master of Harriers, 1885-88 and 1903-7. *Recreations:* sporting generally. *Address:* 45 Earl's Court Square, SW5. *T:* Western 589. *Club:* Naval and Military.
                                            Died 27 Feb. 1922.

REID, George, OBE 1918; MD; DPH; Consulting Medical Officer of Health for Staffordshire; *b* 22 Jan. 1854; *s* of David Reid, Aberdeen; *m* Grace, *d* of J. H. D. Goldie. *Educ:* Aberdeen Grammar Sch.; Aberdeen Univ. Examiner in Public Health to Cambridge Univ. *Address:* County Public Health Offices, Martin Street, Stafford.
                                            Died 6 Nov. 1925.

REID, Rt. Hon. Sir George Houstoun, GCB 1916; GCMG 1911 (KCMG 1909); PC 1897; KC; DCL, LLD Adelaide; MP (U) St George's, Hanover Square, since Jan. 1916; *b* Johnstone, Renfrewshire, 25 Feb. 1845; *s* of Rev. John Reid, Church of Scotland, and Marion, *d* of William Crybbace, Edinburgh; *m* 1891, Flora (GBE 1917), *d* of John Bromby, Thornton, Cressy, Tasmania. Barrister New South Wales, 1879; elected to Legislative Assembly, 1880; Member for East Sydney, with break in 1884-85, until 1901; after Federation, Member for East Sydney, 1901-9; Leader of Federal Opposition during same time, except 1904-5, when Prime Minister of Australia; Prime Minister and Colonial Treasurer of New South Wales, 1894-99, during which period as senior Premier he carried the Federal movement to a successful issue; High Commissioner for Australia, 1910-16; Gold Medal, Cobden Club; Presbyterian. *Publications:* Five Free Trade Essays; New South Wales, The Mother Colony of the Australias; My Reminiscences, etc. *Address:* 1 Melbury Road, Kensington, W. *T:* Park 4265. *Clubs:* Athenæum, British Empire.
                                            Died 12 Sept. 1918.

REID, George Ogilvy, RSA 1898; *b* 1851. *Address:* 11 Carlton Street, Edinburgh. *Club:* Scottish Arts, Edinburgh.
                                            Died 11 April 1928.

REID, Rev. Henry M. B., MA, BD, DD; FEIS; Professor of Divinity, University of Glasgow, since 1903; *b* Glasgow, 22 March 1856; *s* of Rev. A. F. Reid, Chaplain to HM Prison, Dundee, and Elizabeth Jane, *d* of Rev. James Beckwith. *Educ:* High School, Dundee; St Andrews University (First Class in Classics). Assistant to Professor of Humanity in St Andrews, 1878-79; licensed by Presbytery of St Andrews, 1879; appointed Assistant first in Anderston Parish, Glasgow, latterly in Glasgow Cathedral; ordained Minister of the parish of Balmaghie, Kirkcudbrightshire, 1882. *Publications:* Songs for the use of St Andrews Students, 1876; About Galloway Folk, by a Galloway Herd, 1889, 2nd edn 1901; The Kirk Above Dee Water, 1895; Lost Habits of the Religious Life, 1896; Books that Help the Religious Life, 1897; A Cameronian Apostle, 1897; One of King William's Men, 1898; Historic Significance of Episcopacy in Scotland, Lee Lecture, 1899; The Layman's Book, 1900 to 1911; A Country Parish (studies in Pastoral Theology and Church Law), 1908; The Professor's Wallet: essays theological and historical, 1910; The Divinity Principals in the University of Glasgow, 1917; A Text-book of Dogmatics, 1919; The Divinity Professors in the University of Glasgow, 1923; The Holy Spirit and the Mystics (Croall Lectures), 1925. *Address:* 12 The University, Glasgow. *T:* Western 2019. *Clubs:* University, Edinburgh; Western, Glasgow.   *Died 18 Oct. 1927.*

REID, Sir James, 1st Bt, *cr* 1897; GCVO 1901; KCB 1895 (CB 1889); VD; JP; MD, LLD; Physician-in-Ordinary to King George V; *b* Scotland, 23 Oct. 1849; *e s* of late James Reid, MD, Ellon, Aberdeenshire, and Beatrice, *d* of late John Peter, of Canterland, Kincardineshire; *m* 1899, Hon. Susan Baring (formerly Maid of Honour to Queen Victoria), *d* of 1st Baron Revelstoke; two *s* two *d. Educ:* Aberdeen Grammar School (Dux and Gold Medallist, 1865), and Aberdeen Univ. MA Aberdeen (Honours in Natural Science and Gold medallist), 1869; MB and CM (highest Honours), 1872; MD 1875; LLD 1895; Hon. MD RUI, 1900; Hon. LLD Glasgow, 1901; FRCP 1892 (MRCP 1887); Hon. FRCPI 1900; studied in Vienna, 1876-77; practised in Scotland, 1877-81; Resident Physician to Queen Victoria, 1881-1901; Physician Extraordinary, 1887-89; Physician-in-Ordinary, 1889-1901; Physician-in-Ordinary to King Edward VII, 1899-1910; Consulting Physician to Convalescent Home for Officers, Osborne; to King Edward VII Sanatorium, Midhurst; and to the Prince of Wales's General Hospital, Tottenham; Fellow of Royal Society of Medicine; Red Eagle of Prussia (1st Class); Royal Order of the Crown of Prussia (1st Class); Ernestine Order of Coburg; Commander of the Legion of Honour, France. *Publications:* papers to medical journals. *Heir: s* Edward James Reid, Page of Honour to King George V, 1911-17 [*b* 20 April 1901; godson of King Edward VII. *Educ:* King's College, Cambridge (Scholar). Browne Medallist, 1920, 1921 and 1922; First Class Classical Tripos, 1922]. *Address:* 72 Grosvenor Street, W1. *T:* 1147 Mayfair; The Chestnuts, Ellon, Aberdeenshire. *Club:* Athenæum.
                                            Died 28 June 1923.

REID, James Smith, MA, LLM, LittD; FBA 1917; Professor of Ancient History, Cambridge, 1899, Emeritus Professor since 1925; Fellow (1878) and Tutor (1885) of Gonville and Caius College, Cambridge; *b* Scotland, 3 May 1846; *e s* of John Reid, schoolmaster, and Mary Smith; *m* 1872, Ruth, *d* of Thomas Gardner; two *s* one *d* (and one *s* decd). *Educ:* City of London School; Christ's Coll., Cambridge (Browne's Medal, 1868; Chancellor's Medal, 1869; Whewell Scholar, 1870; Hon. Fellow). Classical Medal (London),

1869. Fellow of Christ's Coll., Cambridge, 1869–72; Classical Lecturer of Christ's College, 1870–80; Classical Lecturer of Pembroke College, Cambridge, 1873–78, 1880–85; Hon. LittD Dublin; Hon. LLD St Andrews; late President of the Roman Studies Society. *Publications:* Municipalities of the Roman Empire, 1913; editions of the works of Cicero: Academica, 1874, enlarged edn 1885; Pro Archia, 1877; Pro Balbo, 1878; De Amicitia, 1879; De Senectute, 1879; Pro Sulla, 1882; Pro Milone, 1894; De Finibus, 1925; also translations of De Finibus and Academica; contributions to the Encyclopædia of Religion and Ethics; many scattered papers on classical subjects. *Address:* Gonville and Caius College, and Lysmore, West Road, Cambridge. *T:* Cambridge 56.

Died 1 April 1926.

REID, John Robertson, RI; *b* 1851. *Address:* 62 Parkhill Road, Hampstead, NW; Polperro, Cornwall.

Died 10 Feb. 1926.

REID, Sir Marshall Frederick, Kt 1916; CIE 1902; East India merchant; partner Wyer and Hawke, 4 Crosby Square, EC; Member of Council of India, 1916–20; Director Anglo-Egyptian Bank and National Bank of India; *b* 3 Aug. 1864; *s* of late Daniel Reid, Glasgow; *m* 1912, (Henrietta) Mabel, *d* of James Tait-Burton, Scotstoun, South Queensferry; two *d*. *Educ:* Loretto. Member Indian Currency Committee, 1919; Delegate (India) Financial Conference of League of Nations, Brussels, 1921; Chairman of Bombay Chamber of Commerce, 1914–15; Member of the Imperial Legislative Council of India, 1914–15; Member of Legislative Council, Bombay, 1912–14, and Director Presidency Bank of Bombay. *Recreations:* riding, shooting, golf. *Address:* Woodcote Lodge, Epsom, Surrey. *T:* Epsom 321. *Clubs:* City of London, Oriental, Royal Automobile.

Died 20 March 1925.

REID, Lt-Col Richard; Agent-General for Ontario in London; *b* Millbank, Ontario; *s* of James and Esther Reid; *m* 1st, 1886, Alice Woodsend, Nottingham, England; four *s* one *d*; 2nd, 1913, Alice Mulholland, Toronto; one *s*. *Educ:* St Catherine's Collegiate Institute and Normal College, Ottawa. Career, mainly scholastic and agricultural; initiated many educational reforms and was President of Teachers' Association of Ontario; an authority on agriculture and live-stock; one of the founders of the Canadian Jersey Cattle Club; Fellow Royal Colonial Institute; Hon. Colonel 108th Canadian Battalion. *Recreations:* golf, motoring, riding. *Address:* 163 Strand, WC. *TA:* Burocolon. *T:* Gerrard 5793. *Clubs:* British Empire, Constitutional, Royal Automobile.

Died 21 Oct. 1918.

REID, Robert Lawrence; Assistant Mining Engineer, Memba Minerals, Mozambique, Portuguese East Africa; *b* near Ballarat, Victoria, 1858; father, Scotch, station owner; mother, English; unmarried. *Educ:* Queensland State Schools and private tutors. Brought up to the career of pastoralist on his father's station, Echo Hills, in Queensland; left this and started contracting, then mining, both successfully; went to West Australia when goldfields broke out, and was interested in several successful enterprises; left West Australia, 1900, and came to Africa big game shooting; made map of part of Portuguese East Africa, published by Royal Geographical Society; entered Congo Free State service, 1904; engaged in mining work in the Congo up to 1910; mapped the Aruwimi River, award from Royal Geographical Society; was engaged in mineral research work and survey in the Mozambique country, and later mining work for Nigerian New Territories Syndicate. *Publications:* (by the Royal Geographical Society) Map and Notes of Portuguese East Africa; Map and Notes of the Aruwimi River, Belgian Congo. *Recreations:* big game shooting, travel, exploration. *Address:* c/o Union Bank of Australia, 71 Cornhill, EC. *Died 16 April 1916.*

REID, Samuel, RSW; painter and author; *b* Aberdeen, 4 July 1854; 6th *s* of late George Reid and Esther Tait; *y b* of Sir George Reid (PRSA, 1891–1902); *m* 1883, Agnes, *e d* of late Charles Stewart, Liverpool; one *s* one *d*. *Educ:* Grammar School, Aberdeen. Exhibited at Royal Acad., New Gallery, NEAC, Royal Scottish Acad., Glasgow Inst.; gold medal, Crystal Palace, 1899; member of Royal Scottish Water-Colour Soc. *Publications:* Pansies and Folly-Bells (collected poems), 1892; contributed poems and tales, Blackwood, Chambers's, Cornhill; contributed numerous illustrations to Black and White, Good Words, Magazine of Art, etc. *Recreations:* singing, the Georgi flute. *Address:* Caversham Lodge, Chorley Wood, Herts.

Died 1919.

REID, Stuart J., JP Sussex; DCL (Durham, 1907); 4th *s* of late Rev. Alexander Reid, Newcastle-on-Tyne, and *y b* of late Sir Wemyss Reid;

m 1882, Mary Emily, *d* of late Alfred Fryer, Wilmslow, Cheshire. At the request of the 8th Duke of Marlborough, arranged and catalogued the Blenheim State and Family Manuscripts at Blenheim Palace, and drew up a report which remains unprinted, 1889–90; also created an Historical Library at Blenheim for the 9th Duke of Marlborough, to take the place of the old Sunderland Library, 1896–1900; literary adviser to Cassell's, 1903; literary director and editor-in-chief to Isbister & Company (Sir Isaac Pitman & Sons), 1904–6; joined forces with Duckworth and Co., 1907; retired, 1914; wrote "First Impressions" in the Speaker, 1890–99; between 1887 and 1901 chief literary critic to the Leeds Mercury; and was for thirty years on the literary staff (non-political) of the Standard; a Director of Sampson, Low & Co., 1891–98; of British Equitable Assurance Company from 1914; and of the Kelani Valley Rubber Produce Co. from 1919. *Publications:* Representative Men in the Reign of Queen Victoria, 1878–79; Life and Times of Sydney Smith, 5th edn 1901; Life of Lord John Russell, 4th edn 1905; The Life and Letters of the first Earl of Durham, 1792–1840; Life of Sir Richard Tangye, 1908; An Annotated Catalogue of Historical Tracts from the reign of Queen Elizabeth to that of George III (six hundred pages—being the clue to the Redpath Collection of many thousand pamphlets presented to the McGill Univ., Montreal, 1901; privately printed); John and Sarah, Duke and Duchess of Marlborough (from the Blenheim Archives), 1914; editor of Queen Victoria's Prime Ministers Series; the Essays of Dr Johnson; The Memoirs of Sir Edward Blount, 1815–1902; The Memoirs of Sir Wemyss Reid, 1842–1885, 1905. *Address:* Blackwell Cliff, East Grinstead, Sussex. *TA:* Stuart Reid, East Grinstead. *Clubs:* Athenæum, Royal Societies.

Died 27 Aug. 1927.

REID, Walter; proprietor of Western Daily Press, Bristol Evening News, and Bristol Observer; *m* in Newcastle-on-Tyne, Charlotte, 2nd *d* of William Latimer. Started (with the late P. S. Macliver) Western Daily Press, 1858; Fellow of Journalists' Institute. *Address:* The Woodlands, Woodland Road, Tyndall's Park, Clifton, Bristol. *T:* 3565, 492 and 1217. *Clubs:* National Liberal; Bristol Liberal.

Died 18 Feb. 1917.

REID, Sir William Duff, Kt 1916; a Director of British Empire Steel Co.; *b* NSW, 20 Nov. 1869; *s* of late Sir Robert Gillespie Reid and Harriet Duff; *m* 1894, Minnie, *d* of late John H. Cormack, Ottawa; three *s* one *d*. *Educ:* Galt Collegiate Institute. Went to Newfoundland, 1890. *Recreations:* motoring, fishing. *Address:* Bartra, Circular Road, St John's, Newfoundland. *Clubs:* Royal Automobile; City, St Johns; St James, Royal St Laurence Hunt, Forest and Stream, Montreal.

Died March 1924.

REILLY, Col Charles Cooper, CB 1917; late Army Medical Staff; *b* 18 July 1862. Major, RAMC, 1897; Lt-Col 1905; Col 1914; served Sudan, 1885–86 (medal, bronze star); S Africa, 1900–1 (Queen's medal, 4 clasps); Asst Director of Medical Services, 1915; Deputy Director, 1915. *Address:* The Cottage, Countess Wear, near Exeter.

Died 3 May 1926.

REILLY, Very Rev. Thomas; Dean of Ardagh since 1913. *Educ:* Trinity College, Dublin. Ordained, 1876; Curate of Killashee, 1876–77; Incumbent, 1882–1900; Cashel, 1878–82; Rathaspeck, 1900. *Address:* The Glebe, Rathowen, Co. Westmeath.

Died April 1921.

REINACH, Joseph; contributor to Le Figaro under the name Polybe, and to the Revue de Paris; Vice-President de la Commission supérieur des services de santé; *b* Paris, 30 Sept. 1856; *m* 1st, Henriett Reinach (*d* 1918); one *s* (Adolphe, killed Aug. 1914) one *d*; 2nd, Mme Pierre Goujon, *widow* of P. Goujon, deputy (killed Aug. 1914). *Educ:* Lycée Condorcet, Paris. Lawyer; Secretary to Léon Gambetta, 1881–82; Chief Director of the République Française, after Gambetta's death, till 1893; articles against General Georges Boulanger; Deputy for the Basses-Alpes, 1889–97; promoter of the revision of the Dreyfus case; was not re-elected in 1897 on account of his prominent part in that affair; re-elected in 1906 and 1910; Vice-President of the Army Commission; President of the Commissions against Alcoholism and against Tuberculosis; a considerable number of speeches on the electoral reform, etc; one of the promoters of the law on the three years' military system; during the war, for six months, on the staff of General Gallieni. *Publications:* Voyage en Orient; Les Récidivistes; Le Ministère Gambetta; La Logique parlementaire; La Politique opportuniste; Le Ministère Clemenceau; Le Scrutin de liste; Gambetta orateur; Les Grandes Manœuvres de l'Est; Histoire de l'Affaire Dreyfus; Contre l'alcoolisme; La Réforme électorale; Discours et Plaidoyers politiques de Gambetta; Discours choisis de Gambetta; Discours, Proclamations et Dépêches de Gambetta pendant la Défense

Nationale; Les Commentaires de Polybe (séries 1 à 19); La Guerre sur le front occidental (1914–15); La Serbie et le Monténégro; Les Petites Catilinaires; Pages republicaines; Démagogues et Socialistes; Essais de Littérature et d'Histoire; Essais de Politique et d'Histoire; Diderot; Manuel de l'Enseignement primaire; Le "Conciones" français; La France et l'Italie devant l'Histoire; Histoire d'un Idéal; Raphaël Lévy; Vers la Justice par la Vérité; Le Crépuscule des traitres; Tout le Crime; Les Blés d'hiver; La Réorganisation de l'Artillerie; L'Armée toujours prête; La Fixité des effectifs; Mes Comptes rendus; Récits et Portraits contemporains; Histoire de Douze Jours; Discours de Challemel-Lacour; Les Origines diplomatiques de la Guerre de 1870–71; La Vie politique de Gambetta. *Recreations:* Cavalry Officer in the Reserve; travelled in the West and Russia. *Address:* 6 avenue van Dyck, Paris. *T:* Elysée 09.85. *Club:* Interallié.

Died 18 April 1921.

REINOLD, Arnold William, CB 1911; MA; FRS; late Professor of Physics, Royal Naval College, Greenwich; *b* Hull, June 1843; *s* of John Henry Arnold Reinold, shipbroker; *m* Marion Studdy (*d* 1918). *Educ:* St Peter's School, York; Brasenose Coll., Oxford (MA). Fellow of Merton Coll., Oxford, 1866; Lee's Reader in Physics at Christ Church, 1869; sometime Lecturer in Physics, Guy's Hospital; Past President of the Physical Society; Hon. Member Yorkshire Phil Soc. *Publications:* papers on the properties of thin films in Phil Trans. *Address:* East Cosham House, Cosham, Hants.

Died 11 April 1921.

RÉJANE, Madame, (Gabrielle Réju); actress; *b* Paris, 6 June 1857; *m* M Porel (marr. diss. 1905), Director of the Vaudeville. *Educ:* Conservatoire (under Régnier). Début at Vaudeville in Revue des Deux Mondes, 1875; left the Vaudeville for Théâtre des Variétés, 1882; passed to L'Ambigu in order to create La Glu in 1882; afterwards created Ma Camarade, Palais Royal; Clara Soleil, Vaudeville; Les Demoiselles Clochard, Variétés; Germinie Lacerteux, l'Odéon; Marquise, Vaudeville; Ma Cousine, Variétés; Amoureuse, l'Odéon; Lysistrata, Grand Théâtre; Madame Sans Gêne, Vaudeville, 1893; and Maison de Poupée, 1894; toured in America in 1895, and obtained an enormous success; one of Madame Réjane's later successes at the Vaudeville was La Passerelle. *Address:* avenue d'Antin (VIII), Paris.

Died 14 June 1920.

REMSEN, Ira; President, 1901–13, and Professor of Chemistry, 1876–1913, subseq. President Emeritus and Professor Emeritus, Johns Hopkins University; *b* New York, 10 Feb. 1846; *m* 1875, Elizabeth H. Mallory, New York; two *s*. *Educ:* College City of New York; College of Physicians and Surgeons, New York; Universities of Munich, Göttingen, and Tübingen. Professor, Williams College, Massachusetts, 1872–76. *Publications:* many scientific articles and books—almost wholly in the field of chemistry. *Address:* Johns Hopkins University, Baltimore, Md, USA. *Clubs:* University, Baltimore; Chemists', New York.

Died March 1927.

RENALS, Sir James Herbert, 2nd Bt, *cr* 1895; Lieutenant for City of London; *b* 5 Nov. 1870; *s* of Sir Joseph Renals, 1st Bt, and Mary (*d* 1908), *d* of Alfred Wilson, Nottingham; *S* father, 1907; *m* 1918, Susan Emma, *d* of James William Crafter, Bromley, Kent; three *s* four *d*. Heir: *s* Herbert Renals, *b* 29 Sept. 1919.

Died 27 March 1927.

RENARD, Samuel, ISO 1913; late a Principal Clerk, Supreme Court Pay Office. *Address:* 91 Addison Road, Kensington, W.

Died 29 March 1924.

RENAULT, Louis, GCMG (hon.); Hon. DCL Oxford; Commander of Legion of Honour; Member of the Institute; Fellow of British Academy; Professor of International Law, University of Paris; *b* 21 May 1843. Nobel Peace Prize, 1907. *Publications:* several papers. *Address:* 5 rue de Lille, Paris; Villa des Troenes, Barbizon, Seine-et-Marne. *Died Feb. 1918.*

RENDEL, Sir Alexander Meadows, KCIE 1887; civil engineer; Consulting Engineer to the India Office, the East Indian Railway, and other Indian railways, since 1874; *b* 3 April 1829; *e s* of late James Meadows Rendel, FRS, and Catherine Jane Harris; *m* 1853, Eliza (*d* 1916), *d* of Capt. William Hobson, RN, Governor of New Zealand; five *s* three *d*. *Educ:* King's School, Canterbury; Trinity College, Cambridge (Scholar and Wrangler). Engineer London Dock Co., 1856; visited India, 1857–58; Member of Commission to determine narrow gauge for Indian Railways, 1870. *Principal Works:* Shadwell Basin, Royal Albert Dock; the Albert and Edinburgh Docks at Leith; the Workington Dock and Harbour; the Sukker Bridge over the

Indus, etc. *Address:* Rickettswood, Charlwood, Surrey. *Club:* Athenæum. *Died 23 Jan. 1918.*

RENDELL, Rev. Arthur Medland; Rector of Eydon, Northamptonshire, since 1908; Hon. Canon of Peterborough Cathedral since 1899; *b* Steyning, Sussex, 7 March 1842; *s* of John Rendell, Commander, RN, of Tiverton, and Sophia Medland of Exeter; *m* 1877, Helen Bliss Barrett (*d* 1887), of Shenley, Bucks. *Educ:* Steyning Grammar School; Sir Roger Cholmeley's School, Highgate; Trinity College, Cambridge. Foundation Scholar, Twenty-third Wrangler, 1865; BA 1865; 2nd class in Honours, Theological Examination, Easter 1866; MA 1868. Ordained Deacon, 1866; Priest, 1867; assistant master of Highgate School, 1865–72; Curate of St James', Muswell Hill, 1866–72; Rector of Coston, Leicestershire, 1872–89; Vicar of St Margaret's, Leicester, 1889–1908; Rural Dean of Leicester, 1899–1908; Vice-Chairman of the Coston and Garthorpe School Board, 1874–89; member of the School Board for Leicester, and Chairman of the School Management Committee, 1894–1903; a co-opted member of the Education Committee of the Leicester Borough Council, 1903–8. *Recreation:* gardening. *Address:* Eydon Rectory, Byfield, Northants.

Died 7 May 1918.

RENDELL, Rev. James Robson, BA London; late Minister of New Church (Swedenborgian), Accrington; Editor of New Church Magazine, since 1900; *b* Preston, 1850; *s* of Rev. Elias de la Roche and Elizabeth Rendell; *m* 1877, Anne (*d* 1902), *d* of James Bannister of Tarleton; two *s* two *d*. *Educ:* Preston Grammar School (Scholarship); Owens College, Manchester; University College, London. Minister of the New Church, Bradford, 1875–90; ordained, 1878; became an Ordaining Minister, 1899; Lecturer and Demonstrator in Physics in the Yorkshire College (subseq. Leeds University), 1882–90; went to Accrington, 1890; President of the New Church College (1892, 1893, 1897, 1902, 1904, 1905, 1912); President of the Science Section of the Swedenborg Congress, 1910; President New Church Conference, 1891, 1899, at the Centenary, 1907, and 1917; President of the New Church Sunday School Union, 1917. *Publications:* translator of Swedenborg's Principia, Heaven and Hell, Dicta Probantia, and Arcana Coelestia, vols i and ii; frequent contributor to New Church Journals. *Recreation:* mechanical arts. *Address:* Whinside, Accrington.

Died 8 March 1926.

RENNENKAMPFF, Gen.-Lt Paul Charles von; Commandant of 3rd Corps of Russian Army; *b* Estlande, 17 April 1854; *m*; two *d*. *Educ:* Reval Gymnasium; Military School of Finland; Nicolas Academy, Petrograd. Entered 5th Ulan Regiment; commanded Acktizsky Regiment of Dragoons; Chef d'Etat-Major East Baykal district; commanded First Brigade of Cavalry; 3rd Cossack Division of West Baykal; 7th Siberian Corps; 3rd Siberian Corps; served Macedonia, 1900 (Cross of St George); commanded Siberian Cossack Division, and Chief of the 5th Siberian Corps, Russo-Japanese War (Chevalier, Order of St Stanislas, General-Lieutenant, sabre of gold and diamonds from the Emperor); in command during European War, 1914–15. *Address:* Petrograd, Russia. *Died May 1918.*

RENNIE, Edward Henry, MA, DSc; Professor of Chemistry, Adelaide University, since 1885; *b* Sydney, 19 Aug. 1852; *s* of E. A. Rennie, late Auditor-General, NSW; *m* Agnes, *d* of Dr J. G. Cadell, Sydney; one *s* two *d*. *Educ:* Grammar School and University, Sydney; Royal College of Science, London. Master, Sydney Grammar School, 1870–75; Brisbane Grammar School, 1876–77; went to London, 1877; Assistant in Chemical Dept, St Mary's Hospital Medical School; graduated DSc London, 1882; returned to Australia; twice President of Royal Society, S Australia; Fellow, Institute of Chemistry, Great Britain and Ireland. *Publications:* papers on chemistry of several Australian natural products in the Journal of the Chemical Society. *Address:* 178 Childers Street, North Adelaide.

Died 8 Jan. 1927.

RENNIE, Major John George, DSO 1900; The Black Watch (Royal Highlanders); *b* 25 Feb. 1865; *m*; one *s* one *d*. *Educ:* Cheltenham. Entered army 1896; Captain, 1903; served Soudan, 1898 (despatches, 4th class Medjidie, British medal, Khedive's medal with clasp); South Africa, 1899–1902 (despatches, DSO, two medals with clasps); Adjutant, 5th VB, HLI, 1902. *Address:* 29 Dorset Road, Bexhill.

Died 22 Feb. 1920.

RENNY, Maj.-Gen. Sidney Mercer, CSI 1919; CIE 1914; Director General of Ordnance, India; Director of Ordnance Factories, Woolwich, 1906; *b* 3 June 1861; *s* of late Maj.-Gen. G. A. Renny, VC, RA; *m d* of Rev. W. W. Cazalet; two *s* one *d*. *Educ:* Cheltenham

College; Woolwich. Entered Army, 1880; served Burmese War, 1885–86; Assistant Superintendent gun carriage factory, Fatehgarh, 1888; foundry and shell factory, Cossipore, 1891; Superintendent, 1899; Ordnance Consulting Officer for India, India Office, 1905; Inspector-General of Ordnance Factories in India, 1906. *Club:* United Service. *Died 27 April 1921.*

RENSHAW, Arthur Henry; company director; *b* 18 Feb. 1851; *y s* of Thomas Charles Renshaw, QC (a Bencher of Lincoln's Inn), of Sandrocks, Hayward's Heath, Sussex, and Elizabeth, *d* of George Blaker, Sussex; *m* 1899, Lady Winifred Edith Clements, *e d* of 4th Earl of Leitrim; three *s* two *d*. *Address:* Watlington Park, Oxon; 37 Portman Square, W. *T:* Mayfair 4765. *Club:* Garrick.
Died 25 Dec. 1918.

RENSHAW, Sir Charles Bine, 1st Bt, *cr* 1902; DL; manufacturer; Chairman A. F. Stoddard and Co., Limited, Elderslie, and of Caledonian Railway; Chairman Board of Referees for Excess Profits Tax, since 1916; *b* 9 Dec. 1848; 3rd *s* of Thomas Charles Renshaw, QC, and Elizabeth, *d* of George Blaker, Sussex; *m* 1872, Mary Home, *d* of Arthur Francis Stoddard, Broadfield, Renfrewshire; one *s* four *d*. *Educ:* St Clere, Sevenoaks; Germany. MP (C) W Div. of Renfrewshire, 1892–1906. *Heir: s* Charles Stephen Bine Renshaw [*b* 9 Dec. 1883; *m* 1911, Edith Mary, 4th *d* of late Rear-Adm. Sir Edward Chichester, 9th Bt, of Raleigh, Devonshire; one *s* two *d*]. *Address:* 82 Cadogan Square, SW. *T:* Victoria 2114; Barochan, Houston, Renfrewshire; Garvocks, Greenock. *Clubs:* Carlton, Garrick; Western, Glasgow. *Died 6 March 1918.*

RENSHAW, Walter Charles, KC; LLM; *b* 24 Sept. 1840; *e s* of Thomas Charles Renshaw, QC, and Elizabeth, *d* of George Blaker, Patcham; *m* 1870, Elizabeth, *d* of late John W. Wilson (Officer of the Legion of Honour and Knight of Belgian Order of Leopold), Elsbrock, Holland; one *d* (two *s* decd). *Educ:* King's College, London; Trinity Hall, Cambridge (LLB 1862). Barrister, Lincoln's Inn, 1864; Bencher, 1890; QC 1886; practised at Chancery Bar; for some years member of the Supreme Court Rule Committee and of the Council of Law Reporting; member of the Bar Committee many years; member of Baronetage Committee; Chairman of Councils of Sussex Archæological and Sussex Record Societies, and Mem. Council and late President of Selden Society; JP Sussex. *Publications:* several genealogical works, and many articles in the Sussex Archæological Collection and The Genealogist. *Recreations:* reading; formerly cricket, rowing, shooting. *Address:* Sandrocks, near Hayward's Heath, Sussex. *Club:* New University. *Died 16 July 1922.*

RENTELL, Henry William Sidney, AMIEE; FZS; Editor of Electricity; Managing Director, S. Rentell & Co. Ltd, publishers; *b* 1864; *m* 1899, Sophie, *d* of George Strohmenger; two *s* two *d*. *Educ:* Philological School, London; Neuenheim College, Heidelberg; Finsbury Technical College. After several years of engineering practice, acquired and edited Electricity; subseq. founded the publishing firm bearing his name. *Recreation:* freemasonry. *Address:* Haroldene, 61 Tytherton Road, Tufnell Park, N19. *T:* North 1148. *Died 22 Oct. 1927.*

RENTON, James Crawford, MD; FFPS; Surgeon and Lecturer on Clinical Surgery, Western Infirmary, Glasgow; *b* Auchtermuchty, Fifeshire; *s* of Rev. J. Renton, United Free Church of Scotland Manse, Auchtermuchty; *m* Margaret Annie, *d* of Dr James Mill, Thurso; two *s* one *d*. *Educ:* Abbey Park, St Andrews; Edinburgh University; Paris and Vienna. Resident-Surgeon to Sir Patrick Heron Watson in the Royal Infirmary, Edinburgh; Senior President of Royal Medical Society, Edinburgh University; Assistant to late Professor George Buchanan, Professor of Clinical Surgery, University of Glasgow; Examiner in Surgery and Clinical Surgery in the Universities of Edinburgh and Aberdeen; Surgeon to the Eye Infirmary, Glasgow. *Publications:* contributions to Clinical Surgery, Notes of Surgical Cases, Lancet and British Medical Journal, etc. *Recreations:* sport, fishing, shooting. *Address:* 1 Woodside Terrace, Glasgow, W. *T:* 116 Charing Cross, Glasgow, and 2153 Post Office. *Clubs:* Royal Societies; Western, Glasgow. *Died 1919.*

RENTOUL, His Honour James Alexander, KC, LLD; Judge of City of London Court and Judge of Central Criminal Court since 1901; *b* 1854; *e s* of late Rev. Alexander Rentoul, DD, MD, Manor Cunningham, Co. Donegal, and Erminda, *e d* of James Chittick, Manor Cunningham; *m* 1882, Florence Isabella (*d* 1914), *y d* of late D. W. Young, Wallington Lodge, Surrey, and London; two *s*. *Educ:* Queen's College, Galway; Queen's University, Belfast; University of Berlin; Brussels. BA (Honours); LLB (Honours and first exhibitioner); LLD (first place by examination); first prizeman, Senior

Scholarship in Modern Continental Languages and Literature; Senior and Junior Scholarships in Law. Member first London County Council and member of the Belfast Chamber of Commerce; called to the English Bar, 1884; obtained first place and scholarship of one hundred guineas; QC 1895; MP (C) East Down, 1890–1902. *Recreation:* reading Who's Who. *Address:* 44 Lexham Gardens, Kensington, W. *T:* Western 2332; City of London Court, EC. *Clubs:* Carlton, Royal Temple Yacht.
Died 12 Aug. 1919.

RENTOUL, Rt. Rev. John Laurence, AM, DD; Professor of Biblical Greek, and of Christian Philosophy, and President of Senatus of Ormond College, Melbourne University, since 1888; ex-President Melbourne College of Divinity; ex-Moderator Presbyterian Church of Australia; *b* 1846; *s* of late Rev. James B. Rentoul, DD, Garvagh, Co. Derry, Ireland, and Sara, *y d* of late Rev. W. Wilson, DD, Coleraine; *m* Annie Isobel, 3rd *d* of late D. T. Rattray, The Elms, Southport, and Chile; two *s* two *d*. *Educ:* Queen's College, Belfast; Queen's University, Dublin; Leipzig University. BA 1867, MA 1868; First Honours, Gold Medallist in Literature, History, and Economic Science, Queen's University, Ireland; Early English Text Society's Prizeman, London. Incumbent of St George's Church (Presbyterian), Southport, Lancashire, 1872–79; St George's Church, St Kilda, Melbourne, 1879–84; Professor of Hebrew and Sacred Languages, Ormond College, Melbourne University, 1884; delegate from Australia to General Assemblies and Councils in the three kingdoms and America; took a leading part in vindication of the toiling masses, settlement of strikes, protection of the Australian aborigines; Chaplain-General Commonwealth Military Forces, 1913–19; Australian Imperial Forces at War Front, 1916–17. *Publications:* From Far Lands: Poems of North and South, 1914; Rome and the Early Church (six editions); The Church At Home; Prayers for Australian Households; The Sign of the Sword, 1915; At Vancouver's Well, and Poems, 1917; sermons; and many articles. *Recreations:* angling (in New Zealand, etc), cycling. *Address:* St Oswald's, Ormond College, Melbourne. *Club:* Naval and Military, Melbourne.
Died April 1926.

REPINGTON, Lt-Col Charles A'Court-, CMG 1900; writer on military matters; *b* 29 Jan. 1858; *er s* of Charles Henry Wyndham A'Court, later Repington, Warwicks, and Emily, *e d* of Henry Currie, Surrey; assumed additional surname of Repington, 1903; *m* 1882, Mellony Katherine, *d* of Henry Sales Scobell, Worcs; two *d*. *Educ:* Eton; Sandhurst. Entered army (Rifle Brigade), 1878; Lieut-Col 1898; served in Afghanistan, 1878–79 (medal, 3 clasps); Burma, 1888–89; Soudan, 1898 (despatches twice, Brevet Lieut-Col, British and Khedive's medals, 3 clasps); South Africa, 1899–1900 (despatches twice, medal 3 clasps, CMG); Military Attaché, Brussels, and The Hague, 1899–1902; posts on the Morning Post, The Times, and the Army Review; Comdr. Order of Leopold, Belgium; Officer, Legion of Honour, France. *Publications: autobiography:* Vestigia, 1919, The First World War, 1920, After the War, 1922; Policy and Arms, 1924. *Address:* Amington Hall, Tamworth, Warwickshire. *Club:* Naval and Military. *Died 25 May 1925.*

RESTLER, Sir James William, KBE 1918; Chairman Metropolitan Munitions Committee, and Fire Brigade Co-ordination Committee; Chairman Rickmansworth and Uxbridge Valley Water Co., and St Albans Water Co. *Address:* 17 Queen's Gate, SW7. *T:* Kensington 184. *Died 11 Nov. 1918.*

RESZKE, Jean de, Hon. MVO (4th class); operatic singer; *b* Varsovie, 1853; *m* la Comtesse Maria de Goulaine. Appeared in London, 1875. *Recreations:* riding, shooting, tennis, breeding race horses. *Address:* rue de la Faisanderie 53, Paris; Château Skrzydlom, Poland.
Died 3 April 1925.

RETZIUS, Magnus Gustaf, DM; late Professor of Anatomy; *b* Stockholm, 17 Oct. 1842; *s* of Anders Retzius, Professor of Anatomy and Physiology at the Karolinska Institutet in Stockholm; *m* 1876, Anna Hierta; no *c*. *Educ:* The Medical Schools in Stockholm and Uppsala. Doctor of Medicine in Lund, 1871; Professor of Histology at the Caroline Institute, Stockholm, 1876; Professor of Anatomy, 1889; Member of the Academies of Science of Berlin, Petrograd, Paris, Rome, Washington, Vienna, Munich, Copenhagen, Christiania, Philadelphia, of the Academies of Medicine, Petrograd, Budapest, Brussels, Paris, Turin, etc; Foreign Member of the Royal Societies of London, Edinburgh, Göttingen, etc; Hon. Dr of Medicine and Philosophy and Jurisprudence of Bologna, Würzburg, Uppsala, Harvard, Geneva, etc. *Publications:* Anatomical Researches, 1872; Anatomy of Nervous System, 1875–76; Finnish Craniology, 1878; Hearing Organs of Vertebrates, 1881–84; Biological Researches,

1890–1912; Human Brain, 1896; Ancient Swedish Skulls, 1898; Swedish Anthropology, 1902; Brain of Apes, 1906; various contributions. *Address:* Stockholm, 116 Drottninggatan, Sweden.
Died 21 July 1919.

REVILLE, Rt. Rev. Mgr Stephen; RC Bishop of Sandhurst, Australia, since 1901; *b* Wexford, 9 May 1844. *Educ:* St Peter's College, Wexford. Became a Member of the Order of St Augustine, and proceeded to Belgium to prosecute his studies; after his ordination he was appointed to the Convent of his Order in Dublin; during seven years he had charge of St Laurence O'Toole's Seminary, Usher's Quay; accompanied Most Rev. Dr Crane to Australia, 1875; Coadjutor Bishop of Sandhurst, 1885–1901; Assistant Pontifical Throne, 1910; Knight of Holy Sepulchre, 1910. *Address:* Bendigo, Victoria.
Died 19 Sept. 1916.

REWAH, HH Maharaja Venkat Raman Singh Bahadur, GCSI; Hon. Lieutenant-Colonel in the Army, 1915; *b* 23 July 1876; *s* of His Highness Maharajah Raghuraj Singh Bahadur, GCSI; *m* Princesses of Dumraon and Rutlam, and *daughter* of a Parihar Thakur in Oudh. *Educ:* in his own capital at Rewah. Invested with full powers as Ruling Chief of Rewah State in November 1895, at the age of 19; had to combat three severe famines which strained the resources of the State to the utmost; Rewah a model State from an administrative point of view. Decorated for arrangements for relief of the sufferers in the Indian Famine of 1896–97; gave 5,000 rupees for purchase of vaseline for Indian Troops during European War, 1915; placed all resources of the State at the disposal of the King-Emperor at the commencement of the War; presented a number of horses and two aeroplanes to Government; was one of the Chiefs who fitted up the Hospital Ship Loyalty. *Heir:* Maharajkumar-Prince Gulab-Singhji, *b* 12 March 1903. *Recreations:* an excellent sportsman and shot; took a deep interest in many exercises, and army drill and discipline. *Address:* Rewah, Central India.
Died 3 Nov. 1918.

REYMONT, Wladislaw Stanislaw; Polish novelist; Chairman of the Polish Literary and Press Syndicate; *b* near Piotrkow, 1867. Nobel Literary Prize, 1924. *Publications:* The Promised Land, 1920; The Comedienne, 1920; The Peasants, 1924; The Year 1794 (trilogy), 1913–18; Insurrection; Autumn, 1925. *Address:* Warsaw.
Died 5 Dec. 1925.

REYNARD, Robert Froding, ISO 1904; Secretary and Registrar of the Imperial Service Order since 1904; *b* 22 June 1857; *y s* of late Charles Reynard, Nether Hall, Nafferton, Yorkshire; *m* 1885, Agnes, *e d* of late William Peter of Rockbank, Gisborne, Victoria; one *d*. *Educ:* Uppingham; Germany and France. Entered Civil Service, Class I, Open Competition, 1878; Clerk in Home Office, 1885–1921. *Address:* 54 Cambridge Terrace, Hyde Park, W2. *T:* Paddington 6539. *Clubs:* Boodle's, Hurlingham.
Died 6 Dec. 1926.

REYNARDSON, Col Charles Birch-, JP; *b* 10 Dec. 1845; *e s* of late Charles Thomas Samuel Birch-Reynardson and Anne, *d* of late Simon Yorke of Erddig, Co. Denbigh; *m* 1875, Emma Maria, *d* of Rev. William Stracey of Buxton, Norfolk; two *d*. *Educ:* Eton. Late Grenadier Guards; ADC to Viceroy of India, 1872–74; Egypt, 1882; High Sheriff of Rutland, 1895; patron of one living. *Address:* Holywell Hall, near Stamford. *Clubs:* Carlton, Guards'.
Died 14 Nov. 1919.

REYNOLDS, Major Douglas, VC 1914; 37th Battery Royal Field Artillery; *b* 21 Sept. 1881; 2nd *s* of late Lt-Col H. C. Reynolds, RE; *m* 1915, Doris, *d* of William Petersen, Cherkley Court, Leatherhead. Entered army, 1900; Captain, 1908; served S Africa, 1902 (Queen's medal, 3 clasps); European War, 1914–15 (severely wounded, DSO); Knight of Legion of Honour.
Died 23 Feb. 1916

REYNOLDS, Ernest Septimus, DL Co. Lancaster; BSc (Manchester); MD (London); LSA, MRCS, FRCP; Consulting Physician to the Manchester Royal Infirmary; Emeritus Professor of Clinical Medicine, Manchester University; Lieutenant-Colonel Royal Army Medical Corps (T); *b* 7 April 1861; *s* of John Henry Reynolds, Manchester; *m* Rosa Maud, *d* of Thomas Hooker; one *d*. *Educ:* Owens College, Manchester. Various appointments in teaching of hygiene and medicine; resident medical officer for several years in asylums and general hospitals; late Senior Physician to the Ancoats Hospital, and Visiting Physician for sixteen years to Manchester Workhouse Infirmary; Bradshaw Lectures, 1917; late Member of Council British Medical Association; Past President of the Owens College Union, Pathological Society and Clinical Society of Manchester, the

Manchester Medical Soc., and Neurological Section Royal Soc. of Medicine; Fellow of Royal Society of Medicine; discoverer of arsenic as cause of epidemic beer poisoning in N England in 1901. *Publications:* Hygiene for Beginners; many medical publications, especially relating to nervous diseases; numerous essays and reviews. *Address:* 2 St Peter's Square, Manchester. *T:* Manchester, Central 2893; Platt Cottage, Rusholme, Manchester. *T:* Rusholme 72. *M:* NC 2743 and NC 9783.
Died 22 May 1926.

REYNOLDS, Sir Francis Jubal, Kt 1921; JP of County of Stafford; *b* 22 July 1857; 3rd *s* of late Thomas Reynolds, Birmingham; *m* 1st, 1884, Julia (*deceased*), *d* of Samuel Kirkby, London; 2nd, 1919, Catherine, *d* of James Austin, Abberley, Worcestershire, and *widow* of George Trentham, Birmingham; one *d*. *Educ:* Birmingham. Admitted Solicitor, 1885; Commissioner for Oaths; Perpetual Commissioner for taking acknowledgments of Deeds by Married Women; Notary Public; Organizer and Expert in Transport for Parliamentary and other Elections; Brewery Director, and practised as a Solicitor, principally in brewery matters and licensed trade generally, in which he was engaged throughout professional career, and regarded as having made a speciality therein. *Recreations:* fishing, photography, farming. *Address:* Cow Hayes, Solihull. *T:* 159; 1 Lancaster Gate, W2. *T:* Paddington 3526; Anfield Hey, Douglas, Isle of Man. *T:* 460; Muchall Manor Farm, Wolverhampton; 17 Waterloo Street, Birmingham. *T:* Central 3422; 12 Queen Street, EC4. *T:* City 7550. *Clubs:* Constitutional, Royal Thames Yacht.
Died 22 Oct. 1924.

REYNOLDS, Herbert John, CSI 1885; late Indian Civil Service; *b* 1832; *s* of S. Reynolds; *m* 1856, Margaretta Catherine, *d* of late H. F. Waring of Lyme Regis. *Educ:* King's Coll., Cambridge. Entered ICS, 1855; retired, 1889; sometime Member of Bengal Legislative Council and Board of Revenue. *Address:* Southcliff Tower, Cliff Cottage Road, Bournemouth, W.
Died 30 Nov. 1916.

REYNOLDS, J. H., MSc; late Director of Higher Education and Principal, Municipal School of Technology, Manchester; *b* 8 Feb. 1842; *m* 1868, Ellen Ferguson; one *s* two *d*. Hon. Member Association of Directors of Education; President of the Association of Technical Institutions, 1913–14; Vice-President National Association of Teachers of Manual Training; Vice-President of Union of Lancashire and Cheshire Institutes; Vice-President of the Old Owensian Association of the Victoria University of Manchester; Member of the British Science Guild, and of the Teachers' Guild of Great Britain and Ireland; Member and ex-Governor of the Manchester Whitworth Institute. *Address:* Glyn Malden, Cheadle Hulme, near Manchester.
Died 17 July 1927.

REYNOLDS, (James) Emerson, MD, DSc; FRS 1880; Professor of Chemistry, Trinity College, Dublin, 1875–1903; *b* Booterstown, Co. Dublin, 8 Jan. 1844; *s* of Dr James Reynolds; *m* 1875, Janet Elizabeth, *o c* of Canon John Finlayson, Christ Church Cathedral, Dublin, one *s* one *d*. *Educ:* Dublin University (MD and DSc, *causa honoris*). MCRP Dublin; MRCPE. Became Keeper of Minerals at National Museum, Dublin, 1867; Analyst to Royal Dublin Society, 1868–75; Professor of Chemistry to Royal Coll. of Surgeons, Ireland, 1870–75; President of Society of Chemical Industry, 1891; of Section British Association, 1893; of Chemical Soc., London, 1902–3; Vice-Pres., Royal Soc., 1902; discovered a large number of chemical substances, including the primary thiocarbamide and many of its allies, a new class of colloids, and later, several groups of organic and other derivatives of the element silicon; these were described in a series of papers in Trans Chemical Society and to Royal Society. *Publications:* Lectures on Experimental Chemistry, 1874; Experimental Chemistry for Junior Students, 4 vols, 1882; also papers on the periodic law, spectrum analysis, and electro-chemistry. *Recreation:* horticulture. *Address:* 3 Inverness Gardens, Kensington, W.
Died 19 Feb. 1920.

REYNOLDS, Stephen, BSc; Adviser on Inshore Fisheries to Development Commission since 1913, and Resident Inspector of Fisheries, South-West area, since 1914; Member Fish Food and Motor Loan Committee, 1917; *b* Devizes, Wilts, 16 May 1881. *Educ:* The College, Devizes; All Saints' School, Bloxham; Manchester University. Left Ecole des Mines, Paris, to become sub-editor of an Anglo-French Review, 1902; became associated with the Woolley brothers, fishermen, of Sidmouth, 1903; worked for one of them for several years, but gradually drifted from fishing into fishery affairs and controversies; member Committee of Inquiry into Devon and Cornwall Fisheries, 1912; member Departmental Committee on Inshore Fisheries, 1913. *Publications:* Devizes and Roundabout, 1906; A Poor Man's House, 1908; The Holy Mountain (novel), 1909;

Alongshore, 1910; Seems So!: a Working-Class View of Politics (in collaboration with Bob and Tim Woolley), 1911; How 'Twas: Short Stories and Small Travels, 1912; The Lower Deck, the Navy and the Nation, 1912; contributions, fictional, literary, on social questions from the working-class point of view, and on fisheries. *Address:* Sidmouth, S Devon. *TA:* Stephen Reynolds, Sidmouth. *T:* Sidmouth 95.   *Died 14 Feb. 1919.*

REYNOLDS, Warwick, RSW; black and white artist; working for the Press since 1895; *b* Islington, 1880; *s* of Warwick Reynolds, black and white artist, and Martha A. Dunhill; *m* 1906, Mary F. L. Kincaid; two *d*. *Educ:* private school, Stroud Green; life-drawing, Grosvenor Studio, Vauxhall Bridge Road, and St John's Wood; Julian's, Paris, 1908; studied animals at the Zoological Gardens, Regent's Park, 1895-1901. Contributor to London, Strand, Pearson's, Royal Windsor, Quiver, and other magazines; exhibitor Royal Academy, Royal Scottish Academy, Royal Glasgow Institute of Fine Arts. *Recreations:* walking, reading. *Address:* 26 West Princes Street, Glasgow, C4.   *Died 15 Dec. 1926.*

REYNOLDS, William George Waterhouse, JP; company director; MP (U) Southern Division of Leicester, 1922-23; *b* 1860; *s* of Thomas Leethem Reynolds, late of Southsea, and Ruth Augusta Reynolds, of Australia; *m* 1887, Ida Maud (*d* 1927), *d* of late Joseph Roberts of Leicester; one *d*. *Educ:* Vicary's School, Southsea. A member of many War Committees, including Military Service Tribunal; Vice-Chairman of War Pensions Committee at Leicester until 1921; Income Tax Commissioner for Leicestershire; President of Leicester Central Conservative Association. *Recreations:* shooting, golf, fishing. *Address:* The Gables, St Mary's Road, Leicester. *Clubs:* Junior Carlton, Constitutional, Unionist, 1900.   *Died 3 Sept. 1928.*

REYNOLDS-BALL, Eustace Alfred, BA; FRGS; *b* Bridgwater, Somerset; *e s* of late Rev. A. W. Ball, MA, and Julia Maria, *e d* of late Rev. Anthony Ely, Vicar of Whitminster, Glos; *m* 1893, Mary Hannah, *d* of late Edwin Andrew Chudleigh, Liverpool; three *s* one *d*. *Educ:* Clifton College; St John's College, Oxford (Hons Mod. Hist. 1882). Barrister-at-law, Inner Temple, 1891, but never practised; travelled extensively in Europe, the Western Mediterranean, North Africa, Palestine, Canada, and Australasia; Literary Editor, Court Journal, 1907-8; Editor, Travel and Exploration, 1909-11; employed temporarily by the War Office as Assistant Cable Censor, 1915; transferred to another Dept of the Censorship, 1916; part owner of the Manor of Madeley Wood, Shropshire. *Publications:* Mediterranean Winter Resorts, 7th edn 1914; South Italy and Egypt in the Picturesque Mediterranean, 1891; Cairo: the City of the Caliphs, 1897; Cairo of To-day, 10th edn 1926; Paris in its Splendour, 2 vols, 1900; Jerusalem, 3rd edn 1909; Practical Hints for Travellers in the Near East, 1903; Rome, 3rd edn 1913; The Tourists' India, 1907; The Levantine Riviera (with Dr W. T. Beeby), 1908; Sport on the Rivieras (with Sir C. A. Payton, 'Sarcelle''), 1911; (ed) Outfit and Equipment for the Traveller, Explorer, and Sportsman, 1912; (ed) Bradshaw's Through Routes to the Chief Cities of the World, 1913; Unknown Italy: Piedmont and the Piedmontese, 1927; occasional articles. *Recreations:* cycle-touring, chess, reading novels. *Address:* Villa Osella, Borgo Osella, Carmagnola, N Italy. *Clubs:* Authors'; Turin Chess.   *Died 30 March 1928.*

RHEAD, George Woolliscroft, RE; Hon. ARCA; painter, etcher and illustrator; writer on art educational subjects; *b* 1855; *m* 2nd, 1914, Annie French, artist, Glasgow. *Educ:* studied under Alphonse Legros and Ford Madox Brown. National Art scholar; gold and silver medallist. Member of the Art-Workers' Guild; ex-Member of the Arts and Crafts Society and Royal Society of Arts; Art Examiner to the Board of Education; Honorary Freeman of the Worshipful Company of Fanmakers; designer of HM Queen Mary's Coronation Fan. *Paintings:* O Salutaris Hostia; Vespers; The Wise and Foolish Virgins; A Sacrifice to Neptune; The Sisters; *etchings:* The Foundation of Manchester by the Romans; The Dream of Sardanapalus; and Crabtree, after Ford Madox Brown; also works by George F. Watts, Pettie, Sir Luke Fildes, George Boughton, Marcus Stone, John Philip, and others. *Publications:* A Handbook of Etching; Studies in Plant Form; The Principles of Design; The Treatment of Drapery in Art; Chats on Costume; A History of the Fan; Nature Studies for Schools; British Pottery Marks; Staffordshire Pots and Potters; Modern Practical Design; *illustrated works:* Bunyan's Pilgrim's Progress, and Life of Mr Badman; Tennyson's Idylls of the King. *Recreations:* music, shooting. *Address:* Doune Lodge, Oxford Road, Putney, SW.
                                                        Died 30 April 1920.

RHEAM, Henry Meynell, RI; artist; *b* Birkenhead, 13 Jan. 1859; *m* 1900, Alice Elliott; one *s* one *d*. *Educ:* Cassel; Düsseldorf. Began to

study painting at Heatherleys, 1884; afterwards in Paris under Adolphe William Bouguereau and Tony Robert Fleury; Member Royal Institute Painters in Water Colours, 1893; worked mostly in Cornwall. *Address:* West Lodge, Alverton, Penzance.
                                                         Died Nov. 1920.

RHIND, Lt-Col Sir (Thomas) Duncan, KBE 1919 (CBE 1918); TD; The Royal Scots; Statistical Adviser to Ministry of Pensions; *b* 14 July 1871; *s* of late John Rhind, ARSA, sculptor; *m* 1902, Mary Elizabeth, *d* of late W. Matthews Gilbert, Edinburgh. *Educ:* George Watson's College, Edinburgh. *Address:* 8 Gunsterstone Road, W14. *T:* Western 4497. *Club:* Scottish Artists', Edinburgh.
                                                       Died 24 April 1927.

RHOADES, James; *b* 9 April 1841; *s* of Rev. J. P. Rhoades, Rector of Clonmel, Ireland, and Philadelphia Palmer Tull; *m* 1st, Charlotte Elizabeth, *d* of late Maj.-Gen. F. P. Lester, Bombay Artillery; two *s* two *d*; 2nd, Alice, *d* of late John Hunt, 22 Lancaster Gate, W. *Educ:* Rugby; Trinity College, Cambridge (Scholar). Chancellor's Medallist for English Verse; BA Classical Tripos, 1864; MA 1865. Assistant Classical and House Master, Haileybury College, 1865-73; Sherborne School, 1880-93; Hon. DLitt Durham University. *Publications:* Poems, 1870; Timoleon, a Dramatic Poem, 1875; translated Virgil's Georgics in English verse, 1881; *ditto* Æneid, vol. i 1893, vol. ii 1896; re-issued with Eclogue added as The Poems of Virgil in The World's Classics, 1921; Dux Redux, or a Forest Tangle, a Comedy, 1887; Teresa, and other Poems, 1893; The Little Flowers of St Francis in English Verse, 1904; Out of the Silence, 1906; The Training of the Imagination (essay); O Soul of Mine! (poem), 1912; The City of the Five Gates (poem), 1913; Words by the Wayside (poems), 1915; Narrative Choruses in Pageants of Sherborne, Warwick, Bury St Edmunds, Dover, Colchester, and York; numerous verse contributions to The Times and other journals. *Recreations:* cycling, lawn tennis. *Address:* Kingsthorpe, Kelvedon, Essex. *Club:* Omar Khayyam.
                                                       Died 16 March 1923.

RHODES, George, KC 1909; Recorder of Oldham since 1914; *b* Manchester, 1851; *s* of John Rhodes, Manchester; *m* 1882, Bessie (*d* 1919), *niece* of Dr Lancashire of Stand, near Manchester; three *s*. *Educ:* private school; Owens College, Manchester. In business as a merchant in Manchester up to 1889; Member Manchester City Council, 1890-92; called to the Bar, Gray's Inn, 1892; Bencher, 1909; JP Cheshire and Lancashire; Chairman Shireoaks Colliery Co., Ltd, and Director, Thos Rhodes & Son, Ltd, Hadfield Mills, near Manchester, and Lunderston Rubber Co., Ltd. *Publication:* Manchester Municipal Code. *Recreations:* golf, motoring, etc. *Address:* Allandale, Bowdon, Cheshire. *TA:* Allandale, Altrincham. *T:* 224 Altrincham. *M:* MA 9561. *Clubs:* National Liberal; Manchester Reform.
                                                       Died 23 Sept. 1924.

RHODES, Sir George Wood, 1st Bt, *cr* 1919; JP Cheshire; Chairman Dukinfield Petty Sessions; Chairman and Managing Director Thomas Rhodes, Ltd; *b* 4 Sept. 1860; *o surv. s* of Thomas Rhodes, JP, and Amelia Fletcher; *m* 1st, 1883, Margaret Catherine (*d* 1915), *o d* of John Phillips, Liverpool; two *s* one *d*; 2nd, 1922, Diana, *d* of Daniel Murphy, Calif, and *widow* of H. Morgan Hill, of Washington, DC. *Educ:* Rugby; abroad. Contested (L) Hyde Division of Cheshire, 1895. *Recreations:* travelling, golf. *Heir: s* Lt-Col John Phillips Rhodes [*b* 19 July 1884; *m* 1913, Elsie Constance, *er d* of Lt-Col George Alexander Maclean Buckley, CBE, DSO; one *s*]. *Address:* 37 Pont Street, SW1. *T:* Kensington 1910; Hollingworth, Cheshire. *TA:* Hollingworth, Colossus, Manchester. *T:* Manchester City 1906. *M:* EC 574, LY 5409. *Clubs:* Union, Baldwin, Ranelagh.
                                                         Died Feb. 1924.

RHODES, James Ford; engaged in the study and writing of history, since 1885; Lecturer on the History and Institutions of the United States of America in Oxford University, 1912; *b* Cleveland, Ohio, 1 May 1848; *s* of Daniel P. Rhodes and Sophia Russell; *m* 1872, Ann Card; one *s*. *Educ:* New York Univ.; Univ. of Chicago; School of Mines, Univ. of Berlin. Engaged in coal-mining and the manufacture of pig-iron, 1870-85; Pres., American Historical Association, 1899; Member of Massachusetts Historical Society; American Academy of Arts and Letters; American Philosophical Society; Corresponding Fellow British Academy; LLD Adelbert, 1893; Harvard, and Yale, 1901; Wisconsin, 1904; New York University, 1908; Princeton, 1912; California, 1916; LittD Kenyon, 1903; Brown, 1914; DLitt Oxford, 1909; Loubat prize, American History, Berlin Academy of Science, 1901; Gold medal National Institute Arts and Letters, 1910; Harvard Phi Beta Kappa orator, 1915; Pulitzer prize, Columbia University, 1918. *Publications:* vols i to vii of the History of the United States from the Compromise of 1850, to the Final Restoration of Home

Rule at the South in 1877, 1892–1906; Historical Essays, 1909; Oxford Lectures on the American Civil War, 1913; History of the Civil War, 1917; From Hayes to McKinley, 1877–1896, 1919; The McKinley and Roosevelt Administrations, 1897–1909, 1922. *Recreation:* walking. *Address:* 392 Beacon Street, Boston, Mass. *T:* Back Bay 692. *Clubs:* Tavern, Somerset, Algonquin, Boston; University, Authors', New York.   *Died 22 Feb. 1927.*

RHONDDA, 1st Viscount, *cr* 1918, of Llanwern; **David Alfred Thomas,** DL Glamorganshire; MA; senior in the firm of Thomas and Davey, coal sale agents; Food Controller since 1917; *b* Aberdare, 26 March 1856; *s* of late Samuel Thomas, Yscyborwen, Aberdare, and 2nd wife, Rachel Joseph; *m* 1882, Sybil Margaret, *d* of George Augustus Haig, Penithon, Radnorshire; one *d. Educ:* privately; Caius College, Cambridge (MA). Scholar of Jesus and Caius Colleges. President Cardiff Chamber of Commerce, 1895; President South Wales Liberal Federation, 1893–97; MP (L) for Merthyr Burghs, 1888–1910; for Cardiff, 1910; President of Local Government Board, 1916–17; Managing Director of Cambrian Combine and other colliery companies in South Wales. *Recreation:* farming. *Heir: d* Margaret Haig Thomas [*m* 1908, Sir Humphrey Mackworth, 7th Bt]. *Address:* Llanwern, Newport, Monmouthshire. *T:* PO Newport 512; 122 Ashley Gardens, SW. *T:* PO Victoria 327. *Clubs:* Reform, National Liberal, Argentine.   *Died 3 July 1918.*

RIBBLESDALE, 4th Baron, *cr* 1797; **Thomas Lister,** PC 1892; JP; *b* Fontainebleau, 29 Oct. 1854; *s* of 3rd Baron and Emma, *d* of Col William Mure, Caldwell, Ayrshire; *S* father, 1876; *m* 1st, 1877, Charlotte Monckton (*d* 1911), *d* of Sir Charles Tennant, 1st Bt; three *d* (two *s* decd); 2nd, 1919, Ava, *d* of Mr Willing, Philadelphia, and *widow* of Col J. J. Astor. Sub-Lieut 64th Regt, 1873; Lieut Rifle Brigade, 1874; Major, retired, 1886; Lord-in-Waiting, 1880–85; Master of Buckhounds, 1892–95. Owned about 4,800 acres. *Publications:* The Queen's Hounds and Stag-hunting Recollections, 1897; Charles Lister, 1917. *Heir:* none. *Address:* Gisburne Park, near Clitheroe. *Club:* Brooks's.

       Died 21 Oct. 1925 (ext).

RIBOT, Alexandre F.; Member of Senate; *b* St Omer, 1842; *m* 1877, Minnie Burch of Chicago; one *s. Educ:* Lycée of St Omer. Admitted to Bar, 1864; became substitut du tribunal de la Seine, 1870; appointed by M Dufaure secretary-general of ministère de la Justice, 1878; elected a member of chambre des deputés, 1878; Minister for Foreign Affairs in M C.L. de Freycinet's ministry, 1890–93; during that period the alliance between France and Russia was concluded; President of Cabinet during stormy period of Panama case, and became, for second time, Prime Minister after resignation of M Jean P.P. Casimir-Perier; Minister of Finance, 1914–17; Prime Minister, March–September 1917; during last few years, strongly opposed policy of retaliation against religious orders; his most important speeches were delivered on finance, foreign affairs, and the question of liberté d'enseignement; Member of Académie française et Académie des Sciences Morales et Politiques; Corresponding Fellow British Academy. *Publications:* Life of Lord Erskine, a speech delivered before the conférence des avocats, 1866; Réforme de l'enseignement secondaire, edited 1900; Discours Politiques, edited 1905. *Address:* 11 Quai d'Orsay, Paris.   *Died 13 Jan. 1923.*

RICARDO, Lt-Col Ambrose St Quintin, CMG 1917; CBE 1919; DSO 1900; Royal Inniskilling Fusiliers; retired 1904; *b* 21 Nov. 1866; 4th *s* of late Henry David Ricardo of Gatcombe; *m* 1893, Elizabeth Alice, 2nd *d* of Emerson Tennent Herdman of Sion House, Co. Tyrone. Entered army, 1888; Capt. 1897; served North-West Frontier, India, 1897–98 (medal with 2 clasps); S Africa, 1899–1902 (despatches thrice, Queen's medal 3 clasps, King's medal 2 clasps, DSO); Temp. Lt-Col Commanding 9th Service Batt. Royal Inniskilling Fusiliers in France, Sept. 1914–1918 (despatches, Bt Major, CMG, Bt Lt-Col); Brigadier (despatches seven times, CBE). *Address:* Sion Mills, Co. Tyrone. *M:* JI 57.

       Died 9 July 1923.

RICARDO, Col Francis Cecil, CVO 1902; CBE 1920; JP, DL Berkshire; retired pay, 1909; *b* 3 July 1852; *s* of late Percy Ricardo of Bramley Park, Surrey; *m* Marie Annie (May) (*d* 1907), *d* of T. Littlefield. *Educ:* Eton (Capt. of the Boats and Keeper of the Field, 1870–71). Entered army, 1872; Capt. 1884; Major, 1890; Lieut-Colonel, 1897; Colonel, 1903; Adjutant Grenadier Guards, 1880–85; Brigade-Major, Home District, 1885–90; AAG Home District, 1900–4; High Sheriff of Berkshire, 1913. *Address:* Lullebrook Manor, Cookham, Berks. *T:* 26 Bourne End. *Clubs:* Guards', Vikings'; Leander, I Zingari; Berkshire County.

       Died 17 June 1924.

RICARDO, Halsey Ralph, FRIBA; architect; *b* 6 Aug. 1854; *s* of Harry Ralph Ricardo and Anna (*née* Halsey); *m* 1882; one *s* two *d. Educ:* Rugby. Was articled for two years to Mr John Middleton of Cheltenham; afterwards served as pupil and clerk to Mr Basil Champneys; commenced individual practice in 1878 after some time spent abroad; designed various houses, etc, including the coloured house in Addison Road, Kensington; was also architect of the Terminal Railway Station at Howrah, Calcutta; Past Master Art Workers' Guild; Member of the Arts and Crafts Society. *Publications:* various articles for the Arts and Crafts Exhibition Society, the Magazine of Art, and the Architectural Review. *Recreations:* listening to music, idling in the country. *Address:* 13 Bedford Square, WC1. *T:* Museum 0159; Graffham, Petworth, Sussex.

       Died 15 Feb. 1928.

RICE, (Benjamin) Lewis, CIE 1884; late Director of Archæological Researches, Mysore; *b* 1837; *s* of Rev. B. Rice; *m* 1869, Mary Sophia, *d* of late John Garrett of Chorlton Lodge, New Hampton; six *s* four *d.* Was Director of Public Instruction in Mysore and Coorg; Secretary to the Education Commission under Sir William W. Hunter; Secretary to Government of Mysore in Education and Miscellaneous Departments; Hon. Fellow of University of Madras; Acting Secretary Police Department. *Publications:* Mysore, 2 vols (revised edition); Bibliotheca Carnatica, 6 vols; Epigraphia Carnatica, 12 vols; Mysore and Coorg from the Inscriptions; Mysore and Coorg in the Imperial Gazetteer of India; Coorg Inscriptions (revised edition). *Address:* Greenhalgh, Maxted Park, Harrow-on-the-Hill. *T:* Harrow 0779.   *Died 10 July 1927.*

RICE, Admiral Sir Ernest, KCB 1914; *b* 24 Feb. 1840; *s* of Edward Royds Rice, of Dane Court, Kent; *m* 1st, 1870, Laura (*d* 1899), *d* of Edward York, of Wighill Park, Tadcaster; 2nd, 1903, Fanny Julia (*d* 1923), *d* of Clinton George Dawkins and *widow* of Lt-Col Robert Henry Gunning, KRR; two *d.* Present in HMS Odin, bombardment and taking of Bomarsund, 1855; severe boat action Gamla Carleby; bombardment of Sveaborg (medal); Commander, 1870; Assistant Director of Naval Ordnance at Admiralty, 1870–74; Captain, 1878; Naval Attaché, 1879–83; Rear-Admiral, 1893; Vice-President Ordnance Select Committee, 1894–96; Admiral Supt HM Dockyard, Portsmouth, 1896–99; made all the arrangements in Paris with French Minister of Marine for joint occupation of Egypt, 1882; ordered to Egypt same year; present at battle of Tel-el-Kebir (medal and bronze star); Vice-Admiral, 1899; commanding Coastguard and Naval Reserves, 1904. *Decorated:* Baltic medal, 1854–55; Egyptian medal, 1882; Khedive's star, 1882. *Recreations:* hunting, shooting, golf. *Address:* Dane Court, Dover, Kent; Bramber, Steyning, Sussex. *Club:* United Service.   *Died 15 April 1927.*

RICH, Alfred William; water colour painter, and teacher; *b* at Gravely, Sussex, 4 March 1856; 2nd *s* of Stiles Rich of Tetbury, Glos; *m* 1884, Cassandra Philippa, *e d* of Edward Berney, FRCS, Croydon; no *c.* Brought to London by his parents, 1860; lived in various parts of the North of London till 1874, when removed to Croydon; apprenticed to an heraldic draughtsman, 1871, and practised that work till 1890; entered the Slade School under late Professor Alphonse Legros, and later Professor F. Brown till 1896; Member of the New English Art Club, 1898, and later a Member and on the Council of the International Society of Sculptors, Painters, and Gravers; most of his work executed direct from nature; his paintings exhibited at the Print Room, British Museum, the Victoria and Albert Museum, the Tate Gallery, the Musée du Luxembourg, the Walker Art Gallery, Liverpool, the Corporation Galleries of Birkenhead, Oldham, Dudley, Brighton, the Fitzwilliam Museum, Johannesburg, Pietermaritzburg, and private collections. *Publication:* Water-Colour Painting. *Recreations:* very fond of all sports, and practised them in a casual way; played football (Rugby Union) for Croydon as a young man; devoted to bicycling as a touring rider, but never raced. *Address:* Ovingdene, Carlisle Avenue, St Albans, Herts. *Clubs:* Savile, Chelsea Arts.   *Died Sept. 1922.*

RICH, Rev. Leonard James; Hon. Canon of Liverpool. *Address:* St Margaret's, Anfield, Liverpool.

       Died 30 Aug. 1920.

RICHARD, Timothy, DD, LittD; missionary and mandarin; General Secretary Society for Diffusion of Christian and General Knowledge among the Chinese, subseq. called the Christian Literature Society for China; *b* Carmarthenshire, 1845; parents farmers; *m* 1878, Mary Martin (*d* 1903), Edinburgh. *Educ:* Swansea Normal College; Haverfordwest Baptist College, Pembrokeshire. Missionary in China under Baptist Missionary Society; Public Almoner in the greatest famine in history; Lecturer to Mandarins; Adviser of the Governor of Shansi; Editor of daily, weekly, and monthly organs; Publisher, with his colleagues, of more than three hundred books; Reformer, appointed as one of the Emperor Kuang Hsu's advisers; Arbitrator, chosen by the Chinese plenipotentiaries to settle affairs after the Boxer massacres; Educator, founded the Modern Imperial University in Shansi; Mandarin, appointed religious adviser to the Chinese Government, and given the rank of mandarin of the first grade; Double Dragon Decoration, 2nd order, 2nd grade. *Publications:* in English—Historical Evidences of Christianity; Conversion by the Million, 2 vols; The Awakening of Faith in New Buddhism (a translation); Guide to Buddhahood (a translation); The New Testament of Higher Buddhism, 1910; A Mission to Heaven, being a translation of an ancient Chinese epic and allegory, 1913; in Chinese—books and pamphlets on the forces which make for the rise and progress of nations. *Recreations:* none, if not electricity, petrol engines, flying machines. *Address:* 143 North Szechuen Road, Shanghai. *TA:* Literature, Shanghai. *T:* 303.

Died 17 April 1919.

RICHARDS, Hon. Albert Elswood; Puisne Judge of Court of Appeal, Manitoba, since 1906; *b* Toronto, 10 July 1848; *s* of late Hon. Stephen Richards, QC, of Toronto; *m* 1877, Harriet Edith, *d* of late J. A. Henderson, QC, of Kingston, Ontario. *Educ:* Upper Canada College, Toronto; University College, Toronto. Called to the Bar of Ontario, 1874, and to the Bar of Manitoba, 1882; practised at Brockville, Ontario, 1874–82, and at Winnipeg, Manitoba, 1882–99; Puisne Judge of Court of King's Bench, Manitoba, 1899–1906. *Address:* Winnipeg, Canada. *Club:* Manitoba.

Died 27 May 1918.

RICHARDS, Edward Windsor, JP, DL; Past President Iron and Steel Institute, and of Institution of Mechanical Engineers; High Sheriff of Monmouthshire, 1902. *Address:* Plâs Llecha, Tredunnock, Caerleon, Monmouthshire. *Clubs:* Junior Carlton, Royal Societies, Royal Automobile.   *Died 12 Nov. 1921.*

RICHARDS, Rear-Admiral G. E.; retired; *b* 10 Dec. 1852; *e s* of late Admiral Sir G. H. Richards, KCB; *m* Emily, *y d* of late John de Courcy Bremer of NSW, Australia; two *d*. *Educ:* Stubbington House, Fareham. Employed on Surveying Service in Japan, Australia, N America, and coast of England during career in Navy. *Recreations:* shooting, fishing. *Address:* Silverton Grange, Silverton, Devon.

Died 8 Dec. 1927.

RICHARDS, Sir (Henry) Erle, KCSI 1909; KC 1905; *b* 6 Dec. 1861; *e s* of late Rev. Prebendary William Henry Parry Richards; *m* 1897, (Mary) Isabel, *e d* of late Spencer Butler of Lincoln's Inn; four *d*. *Educ:* Eton; New College, Oxford. Called to the Bar, Inner Temple, 1887; joined Oxford Circuit; was Counsel for Great Britain in Samoa arbitration, 1902, and in Venezuela arbitration at Hague, 1903; legal member of Viceroy of India's Council, 1904–9; Counsel for Newfoundland and Canada in North Atlantic Coast Fisheries Arbitration at The Hague, 1910; Counsel to the India Office, 1911–21; Chichele Professor of International Law and Fellow of All Souls College, Oxford; BCL, MA, 1911. *Publications:* lectures and articles on legal subjects. *Address:* 4 Temple Gardens, EC; Baysworth Corner, Foxcombe Hill, Oxford. *Club:* United University.

Died 23 April 1922.

RICHARDS, Sir Henry George, KBE 1919; Kt 1911; KC; MA; Puisne Judge High Court of Judicature for the North-Western Provinces of India, 1905–11; Chief Justice 1911; retired, 1919; *b* 21 Sept. 1860; *e* surv. *s* of late John Henry Richards, Chairman of Quarter Sessions for County of Mayo, Ireland; *g s* of the late Right Hon. John Richards, Baron of Court of Exchequer in Ireland; *m* 1891, Frances Maud Lyster, OBE, *y d* of late Henry Mathew Smythe of Barbavilla, Co. Westmeath. *Educ:* Trinity College, Dublin. Called to the Irish Bar, 1883; joined Connaught Circuit; extensive and varied practice in Irish Courts; Senior Crown Prosecutor for Counties of Roscommon and Mayo. *Recreations:* riding, hunting, shooting, polo. *Address:* Ballygueni, Hluhluwe, Zululand, S Africa. *Clubs:* East India United Service; University, Dublin.

Died 10 March 1928.

RICHARDS, Herbert Paul; Subwarden, Fellow since 1870, and Lecturer (late Tutor), Wadham College, Oxford; *b* Kensington, 15 Oct. 1848; 2nd *s* of Thomas Richards, printer. *Educ:* Kensington Grammar School; Balliol College, Oxford (Scholar). Examiner at various times in Hons Moderations and Literæ Humaniores, Oxford; Senior Proctor, 1886–87. *Publications:* Notes on Xenophon and Others, 1907; Aristophanes and Others, 1909; Platonica, 1911; Aristotelica, 1915; articles and reviews in Classical Review and Classical Quarterly. *Address:* Wadham College, Oxford.

Died 18 Feb. 1916.

RICHARDS, John Morgan; Chairman, John Morgan Richards & Sons, Ltd, London, EC; *b* Aurora, New York, USA, 16 Feb. 1841; 2nd *s* of Rev. James Richards, DD, late of Charlestown, West Virginia, USA; *m* Laura Hortense (*d* 1914); two *s* one *d*. *Educ:* public schools in USA. Connected with commercial firms in USA until 1867; in 1867 came to England, and continued in residence here; proprietor of The Academy, 1888–1905. *Publications:* With John Bull and Jonathan; Sixty Years of an American's Life in England and the United States, 1905; The Life and Letters of Mrs Craigie (John Oliver Hobbes), 1911; Almost Fairyland, 1914. *Recreations:* walking, driving. *Address:* Steephill Castle, Ventnor, Isle of Wight. *TA:* Steephill, Ventnor. *T:* 53 Ventnor. *Clubs:* Reform; County and Castle, Isle of Wight.   *Died 11 Aug. 1918.*

RICHARDS, Col Samuel Smith Crosland, CB 1897; VD; JP Leics; formerly Lieutenant-Colonel Commanding and Hon. Colonel 19th Middlesex Volunteer Rifles. *b* 1841; 2nd *s* of late Samuel Richards, MD; *m* 1884, Josephine, *d* of late Charles Thomson, New York; two *s*. *Educ:* University Coll. School and Coll. London. Received the Jubilee Decoration, being in command of the North London Vol. Infantry Brigade during Procession of 22 July 1897. *Address:* 3 Brunswick Court, Brunswick Place, Hove. *Clubs:* Constitutional; New, Brighton.   *Died 6 Oct. 1918.*

RICHARDS, Theodore William, PhD; Professor of Chemistry, Harvard University, since 1901; Director of Walcott Gibbs Memorial Laboratory since 1912; *b* 31 Jan. 1868; *s* of late William T. Richards (1833–1905), and Anna Matlack; *m* 1896, Miriam S., *d* of Prof. Joseph Henry Thayer; two *s* one *d*. *Educ:* Haverford College, Pa (SB 1885; Hon. LLD 1908); Harvard University (AB 1886; AM, PhD 1888; Hon. ScD 1910); Göttingen; Dresden; Munich; Leipzig. Hon. ScD Yale, 1905, Princeton, 1923; Hon. DSc Cambridge, Oxford, Manchester, 1911; Hon. ChemD Clark, 1909; Hon. PhD Prague, 1909, Christiania, 1911; Hon. MD Berlin, 1910; Hon. LLD Pittsburgh, 1915, Pennsylvania, 1920. Assistant in Chemistry, Harvard, 1889–91; Instructor, 1891–94 (Member of Faculty of Arts and Sciences of Harvard, 1892); Assistant Professor, 1894–1901; Chairman of Division of Chemistry, 1903–11; Visiting Professor at University of Berlin, 1907; Research Associate, Carnegie Institution of Washington, from 1902; Lecturer, Lowell Institute, 1908; Davy Medallist, Royal Society, 1910; Faraday Lecturer, 1911; Willard Gibbs Medallist, 1912; Nobel Prize for Chemistry, 1914; Franklin Medallist, 1916; Le Blanc and Lavoisier Medallist, 1922; Member of International Commissions on Atomic Weights, Elements, etc; Officier de la Légion d'Honneur, 1925; Member National Academy of Sciences; Foreign Member of the Royal Society of London; Hon. and Foreign Member of Chemical Society of London; Hon. Member of Royal Institution of Great Britain; Hon. Fellow, Royal Society of Edinburgh; Membre d'Honneur de la Soc. Chim. de France; Foreign Member of Royal Swedish Academy, R. Accad. dei Lincei, and Hon. Member Royal Irish Academy; Corresponding Member Royal Bologna Academy, Royal Danish Academy of Science, Royal Prussian Academy of Sciences; Fellow of American Academy of Arts and Sciences (Pres. 1919–21); Member of American Philosophical Society; Fellow of American Association for Advancement of Science (Pres. 1917); Hon. Member of American Chemical Society (Pres. 1914), etc; Member of various committees and advisory boards connected with use of chemistry in the war. *Publications:* about three hundred papers on chemical and physical topics. *Recreations:* sketching, golf, sailing. *Address:* 15 Follen Street, Cambridge, Mass, USA. *TA:* Professor Richards, Cambridge, Mass. *T:* University 8117. *M:* Mass 118286. *Clubs:* Saturday, Colonial, Oakley Country, Harvard Union, Harvard, Tavern (Hon.), Boston; Chemists, New York.

Died 2 April 1928.

RICHARDSON, Sir Alexander, Kt 1922; MP (C) Gravesend, 1918–23; *b* Dumbarton, 27 March 1864; *s* of James Richardson; *m* 1886, Georgina, *d* of Capt. George Fleming, merchant marine; one *s* one *d*. A student of engineering in all its applications; was a member of the editorial Staff of Engineering from 1888, being successively Assistant Editor, Joint Editor, and sole Editor, and a Managing Director of Engineering, Ltd; retired in 1924, and became Consulting Editor of Shipbuilding and Shipping Record, Marine Engineering and Motor Shipbuilder, and other technical journals; Associate of the Institution of Naval Architects; Vice-President of the Junior Institution of Engineers; Companion of the Institute of Marine Engineers. *Publications:* The Evolution of the Parsons Steam Turbine; The Man Power of the Nation; and other works, as well as contributions on engineering, shipbuilding, naval and economic subjects; contributed to the Naval Annual from 1908, principally on machinery of all types for war, including airships and aeroplanes, and in 1921 became Governing Director and Joint-Editor, the title becoming Brassey's

Naval and Shipping Annual. *Address:* 33 Tothill Street, Westminster, SW1. *T:* Victoria 8836; Garshake, Clarence Road, Clapham Park, SW4. *T:* Brixton 1666. *Clubs:* Carlton, Authors.

Died 30 March 1928.

RICHARDSON, Ven. Edward Shaw, MA (Cantab); Vicar and Rural Dean of Blackburn; Archdeacon of Blackburn, since 1920; Proctor in Convocation and Honorary Canon of Manchester, 1919; *b* 1862; *s* of Rev. William Richardson and Mary Anne Shaw; one *s* three *d*. *Educ:* Rossall School; Trinity College, Cambridge. Curate of Corbridge-on-Tyne; St Paul's, Kersal; and St Philip's, Ancoats, Manchester; Rector of St Paul's, Hulme, Manchester; Vicar of St Matthew's, Bolton, 1895–1909; Rector of St George's, Hulme, and Canon Residentiary of Manchester, 1909–19. *Recreations:* games, sports; played football for Northumberland and hockey for Lancashire. *Address:* The Vicarage, Blackburn.

Died 15 Nov. 1921.

RICHARDSON, Major Francis James, DSO 1900; late Argyll and Sutherland Highlanders; Major 4th Battalion; Deputy Assistant Director of Remounts, Eastern Command; *b* 6 March 1866; *s* of late Francis Richardson, Dorking; *m* 1899, Rhoda Dagmar, *d* of Rastell Bevis; one *s* one *d*. *Educ:* Charterhouse; Jesus Coll., Cambridge. Joined 2nd Batt. Argyll and Sutherland Highlanders, 1888; served with 1st Battalion in South Africa, 1899–1901; Modder River, Paardeberg, Driefontein, Johannesburg, and Diamond Hill (despatches, medal six clasps, DSO). *Address:* The Coombes, Marston Trussell, Market Harborough. *Clubs:* Naval and Military; Kildare Street, Dublin.

Died 11 Dec. 1917.

RICHARDSON, Frank; barrister and novelist; *b* 1870. *Educ:* Marlborough; Christ Church, Oxford. Called to the Bar, 1891. *Publications:* King's Counsel, 1902; Semi-Society, 1903; The Man who Lost his Past, 1903; The Bayswater Miracle, 1903; There and Back, 1904; The Secret Kingdom, 1905; 2835 Mayfair, 1907; Love and all about it, 1907; Bunkum, 1907; The Worst Man in the World, 1908; The Other Man's Wife, 1908; More Bunkum, 1909; Whiskers and Soda, 1910; Shavings, 1911; Love and Extras, 1911. *Recreation:* The Whisker Question. *Address:* 4 Albemarle Street, W. *T:* 2835 Mayfair. *Clubs:* Garrick, Devonshire.

Died 31 July 1917.

RICHARDSON, Ven. James Banning, MA, DCL; Rector of St John's, London Township, 1899–1919; retired from parochial service, 30 June 1919; Archdeacon of London since 1903; *b* 23 Nov. 1843; *s* of James Richardson; *m* 1869, Mary Jane, *d* of Laurence Tremain, MD; two *s* four *d*. *Educ:* privately; Collegiate School and University, King's College, Windsor, Nova Scotia. Ordained, 1866; Rector of Dartmouth, NS, 1868–74; St Thomas, Hamilton, Ont, 1874–77; Memorial Church, London, Ont, 1877–99; Hon. Canon, Saskatchewan, 1885; Canon of S Paul's Cathedral, London, Ont, 1889. *Publications:* Concerning the Church, 1901; Diocese of Huron, its past fifty years, 1907. *Address:* 1095 Richmond Street, W, London, Ontario.

Died 3 May 1923.

RICHARDSON, James Nicholson; Chairman of Bessbrook Spinning Co.; member of Armagh Grand Jury; *b* 1846; *e s* of late John G. Richardson; *m* 1st, 1867, Sophia Malcomson, Portlaw, Co. Waterford; 2nd, 1893, Sara Alexandra, *d* of Samuel Alexander Bell, Lurgan, Co. Armagh. *Educ:* Tottenham. Spent earlier years assisting father and uncles in linen business of Ulster, in which the family engaged from father to son for 150 years; Liberal Unionist; MP Co. Armagh, 1880–85. Sold 5,000 acres to tenants under Wyndham Act. *Publications:* The Quakers at Lurgan and Grange; O'Neill of Mourne; Concerning Servants. *Recreations:* riding, golf, water-colour sketching. *Address:* Mount Caulfield, Bessbrook, Co. Armagh. *TA:* Richardson, Bessbrook. *T:* Newry 14. *M:* O 1558. *Club:* Reform.

Died 11 Oct. 1921.

RICHARDSON, Engr-Rear-Adm. John, CB 1916; Royal Navy; *b* 1862; *s* of late John Strachan Richardson; *m* 1896, Elizabeth Maria, *e d* of late A. B. M. C. Chiappini, MLA, Cape Town; three *s*. *Educ:* Peterhead Academy; privately. Joined HMS Marlborough, Training School for Engineer Officers, RN, 1878; RN College, Greenwich, 1884–85; Engineer-Comdr, 1903; Engineer-Capt., 1912; Engineer-Rear-Adm. 1917; served Benin Expedition 1894, landed from HMS Philomel (despatches, promotion, medal and clasp); S African War, 1899–1902 (despatches, promotion, 2 medals 3 clasps); European War, 1914–17, including Jutland Bank (despatches, CB); on staff of Vice-Admirals commanding 4th Battle Squadron, 1912–17; on staff of Vice-Admirals commanding East Coast of England, 1917–19; Coronation Medal, 1911; Order of St Anne (Russia), 2nd class, with crossed

swords; retired, 1919. *Recreations:* cricket, golf, fishing, shooting. *Club:* Caledonian United Service, Edinburgh.

Died 7 July 1928.

RICHARDSON, Maj.-Gen. John Booth; Colonel Commandant Royal Artillery; *b* 1838; *e s* of Sir John Richardson, CB, FRS, etc, Arctic traveller and naturalist; *m* 1878, Annie Leslie, *d* of R. Dalglish; one *s*. *Educ:* Cholmondeley School; RMA, Woolwich. Served in West and East Indies, Burmah, and Mediterranean; commanded RA, Western District; Commandant School of Gunnery; GOC, RA Gibraltar, etc; Silver Medallist RA Institute, etc. *Publications:* many professional pamphlets and works. *Address:* Halton House, Spilsby.

Died 31 Oct. 1923.

RICHARDSON, Ven. John Gray, MA; *b* 1849; *e s* of Samuel Richardson, Sheffield; *m* 1878, Jane Temple (*d* 1923), *d* of Rev. W. H. Perkins, Tunbridge Wells; one *s* one *d*. *Educ:* Trinity Coll., Cambridge (Scholar and Fellow). Vicar of St Michael, Cambridge, 1877–78; of Monk's Kirby, Withybrook, and Copston, Warwickshire, 1878–84; of St John the Evangelist, Darlington, 1884–86; Vicar, St Mary's, Nottingham, 1886–1900; Archdeacon of Nottingham, 1894–1913; Rector of Southwell St Mary's, 1900–13; Select Preacher at Cambridge, 1882–84–85; Chairman Nottingham School Board, 1889–92, 1892–95. *Address:* Combe Fishacre, Newton Abbot.

Died 13 July 1924.

RICHARDSON, Spencer William, DSc, MA; FInstP; *b* 13 Dec. 1869; 2nd *s* of Alfred Spencer Richardson, DD. *Educ:* The School of Malvern Link; The High School, Newcastle, Staffs; University College, Aberystwith; Trinity College, Cambridge. DSc London (First in First Class Honours in Physics at BSc); Research Student of Trinity College, Cambridge; Certificate of Research and MA, Cambridge; late 1851 Exhibition Research Scholar, etc. Formerly Lecturer in Physics and Mathematics at University College, Nottingham; Principal of the University College, Southampton, 1902–12; Professor of Physics at the University College, Southampton, 1902–12; at the request of the Southampton Education Authority, prepared a scheme for the co-ordination of education in Southampton, 1906; for four years a Member of the Council of the Association of Technical Institutions of Great Britain and Ireland; Research Worker in the Davy Faraday Research Laboratory, Royal Institution; Captain (R) TF. *Publications:* contributions to scientific societies and journals on electricity and magnetism. *Recreations:* lawn tennis, rifle-shooting, theatre, etc. *Address:* Royal Institution, 21 Albemarle Street, W.

Died 10 April 1927.

RICHARDSON, Thomas; MP (Lab) Whitehaven, 1910–18; *b* Usworth, Durham, 6 June 1868; *s* of Robert Richardson, miner; *m* 1888, Mary E., *d* of John Purvis. Late member Durham Miners Executive and Durham Coal Conciliation Board; Labour candidate, Federal by-election, 1920, in Yale constituency, British Columbia. *Address:* 10 Denny Crescent, SE11.

Died 22 Oct. 1928.

RICHARDSON-GRIFFITHS, Major Charles Du Plat, DSO 1900; late the Gloucestershire Regiment; *b* 2 June 1855; *s* of Lt-Col T. Richardson-Griffiths, Armagh; *m* 1894, Florence E., *d* of late H. Schwabe, Lymm. Entered army, 1875; Captain, 1885; Major 1896; served Afghan War, 1879–80 (medal); South Africa, 1900–2 (despatches, Queen's medal three clasps, King's medal two clasps); European War, 1914–19.

Died 1 July 1925.

RICHEPIN, Jean; Commandeur de la Légion d'honneur; poet, novelist, lecturer, dramatist; Chancellor of French Academy since 1923; *b* Médéah, Algérie, 1849; *s* of Dr Richepin, army surgeon; *m* 1st, 1879 (marr. diss. 1902); 2nd, 1902; four *s*. *Educ:* Ecole Normale Supérieure. *Publications: poetry*—La Chanson des gueux, 1876; Les Caresses, 1877; Les Blasphèmes, 1884; La Mer, 1886; Mes Paradis, 1894; La Bombarde, 1899; Les Glas, 1922; *theatre*—La Glu, 1883; Nana-Sahib, 1883; Le Chien de garde, 1889; Théâtre Chimérique (27 actes), 1896; Le Chemineau, 1897; Le Mage (opéra, avec Massenet), 1897; Les Truands, 1899; Miarka (opéra-comique, avec Alexandre Georges), 1905; La Belle-au-bois-dormant, 1907; La Route d'émeraude, 1908; Le Tango, 1913; Macbeth, 1914; Monsieur Scapin (Comédie-Française), 1886; Le Flibustier (*idem*), 1888; Par le glaive (*idem*), 1892; Vers la joie (*idem*), 1894; La Martyre (*idem*), 1898; Don Quichotte (*idem*), 1905; *fiction*—Jules Vallès, 1872; Madame André, 1877; Les Morts bizarres, 1877; La Glu, 1881; Le Pavé, 1883; Miarka la fille à l'Ourse, 1884; Braves Gens, 1886; Césarine, 1888; Le Cadet, 1890; Truandailles, 1890; Cauchemars, 1892; La Miseloque, 1893; L'Aimé, 1893; Flamboche, 1895; Les Grandes Amoureuses, 1896; Contes de la décadence romaine, 1898; Lagibasse (roman magique),

1900; Contes espagnols, 1901; L'Aile, 1911; Proses de Guerre, 1916; La Clique, 1917; Le Coin des Fous, 1921; Interludes, 1923. *Recreations:* the chase, fencing, gymnastics, yachting. *Address:* 8 Villa Guibert, 83 rue de la Tour, XVIe Paris; La Carrière au Val-André (Côtes-du-Nord); Palma de Mallorca (Iles Baléares).

Died 11 Dec. 1926.

RICHMOND, 7th Duke of, *cr* 1675; **Charles Henry Gordon-Lennox,** KG 1905; GCVO 1904; CB 1902; Earl of March, Baron of Settrington, Duke of Lennox, Earl of Darnley, Baron Methuen, 1675; Duke of Gordon, Earl of Kinrara, 1876; Duke d'Aubigny (France), 1683–84; Hereditary Constable of Inverness Castle; *b* London, 27 Dec. 1845; *e s* of 6th Duke of Richmond and Frances Harriett, *d* of Algernon Frederick Greville; *S* father, 1903; *m* 1st, 1868, Amy Mary (*d* 1879), *d* of Percy Ricardo; two *s* two *d* (and one *s* decd); 2nd, 1882, Isobel Sophie (*d* 1887), *d* of William George Craven; two *d*. *Educ:* Eton. Entered Grenadier Guards, 1865; Col 3rd Royal Sussex Regt; ADC to Queen Victoria, King Edward VII and King George V; MP West Sussex, 1869–85; SW Sussex, 1885–88; served S Africa, 1901–2 (despatches); Chancellor, Aberdeen University, 1917. Owned about 286,500 acres. *Recreations:* hunting, shooting, fishing, racing. *Heir: s* Earl of March [*b* 30 Dec. 1870; *m* 1893, Hilda Madeleine, *e d* of Henry Arthur Brassey; one *s* two *d* (and two *s* decd)]. *Address:* 67 Cadogan Square, SW1. *T:* Victoria 4360; Goodwood, Chichester; Gordon Castle, Fochabers, Banffshire; Glenfiddich Lodge, Dufftown, Scotland. *Clubs:* Carlton, Turf.

Died 18 Jan. 1928.

RICHMOND, Maurice Wilson; Professor of English Law, Victoria College, Wellington, since 1906; *b* 26 April 1860. *Educ:* Nelson College; University Coll., London; University of New Zealand. Barrister and Solicitor, 1883. *Address:* Wellington, New Zealand.

Died 26 Feb. 1919.

RICHMOND, Sir William Blake, KCB 1897; RA 1895 (ARA 1888); MA; painter; *b* London, 29 Nov. 1842; *s* of George Richmond, DCL, LLD, RA, and Julia, *d* of Charles Heathcote Tatham; *m* 1867, Clara Jane (*d* 1915), *d* of William Richards, Cardiff; four *s* one *d* (and two *s* decd). *Educ:* student Royal Acad. (2 silver medals). Exhibited portrait of his two brothers, Royal Acad., 1860; Slade Professor at Oxford, 1878–83; President of Society of Miniature Painters, 1899; spent much time in Italy, Greece, and Egypt. *Publications:* The Silver Chain, 1917; Assisi, Impressions of Half a Century, 1919. *Address:* Beavor Lodge, Beavor Lane, Hammersmith, W. *T:* Hammersmith 758. *Club:* Athenæum.

Died 11 Feb. 1921.

RICHTER, Dr Hans, MVO 1904; Conductor to the Hallé Concerts Society, 1900–11; *b* Raab, Hungary, 4 April 1843; *m* a Hungarian lady. *Educ:* Lonenburg School, Vienna; studied under Kleinecke (the horn) and Prof. Simon Sechter (organist and composer) at the Conservatorium in Vienna. Assumed direction of the Court Opera Theatre, Vienna, 1875; in 1876 directed Bayreuth Festival; commenced orchestral concerts in London from 1879; created Doctor of Music (*honoris causa*) by the University of Oxford, 1886.

Died 5 Dec. 1916.

RICKARD, Rev. Herbert, MA; Vicar of Amberley with Houghton since 1918; Prebendary of Chichester Cathedral since 1905; *e s* of late John Rickard of Derby and London; *m* 1890, M. R. Spanoghe (*d* 1900). *Educ:* Derby School; King's College School; Jesus College, Oxford. Open Classical Scholar; First Class Mods, 1883; Second Class Greats, 1886. Ordained, 1888, to Curacy of St Paul's, Lozells, Birmingham; Asst Organising Secretary of ACS, 1890; Curate of Christ Church, Epsom, 1892; Vice-Principal of Chichester Theological College, 1897; Principal, 1899–1918. *Recreation:* cycling. *Address:* Amberley Vicarage, Sussex. *TA:* Chichester.

Died 1 Dec. 1926.

RICKARDS, Arthur George, VD; KC; *b* 1848; *o s* of Sir George Kettilby Rickards, KCB; *m* 1882, Elinor Frances, *y d* of Charles Butler of Warren Wood, Herts; two *s* two *d*. *Educ:* Eton; Brasenose College, Oxford (MA). Called to the Bar, Inner Temple, 1875; Member of Midland Circuit; QC 1899; Bencher of Inner Temple, 1909; served 23 years in the Volunteer Forces, retiring as Major, 1896; Vice-Chairman of the Central (Unemployed) Body for London; JP Gloucestershire; a member of Executive Committee of the National Service League; and of the Military Appeal Tribunals for London and Gloucestershire. *Publications:* The Metropolis Water Act, 1902; Social Reform and National Military Training. *Address:* 20 Southwell Gardens, SW7. *T:* Western 2964; Barn's Close, Amberley, Glos. *Clubs:* Athenæum, British Empire.

Died 28 July 1924.

RICKARDS, Rev. Marcus Samuel Cam; poet and naturalist; *b* Exeter, 28 April 1840; *y s* of late Robert Hillier Rickards, JP and DL, of Llantrissant House, Glamorganshire, and Caroline, *d* of late Col Andrew Knox, MP, of Prehen, Co. Londonderry; *m* 1865, Edith Elizabeth (*d* 1927), *d* of late Charles Anson; two *s* one *d*. *Educ:* Merton College, Oxford (BA (Theological Honours), 1875; MA 1878). Admitted a Solicitor (with Honours of the Incorporated Law Society), 1862; practised for many years in Bristol; Deacon, 1875; Priest, 1876; Curate of Holy Trinity, Clifton, until 1889; Vicar of Twigworth, Gloucester, 1889–1913; a Vice-President of the Poetry Society; FLS 1871. *Publications:* Sonnets and Reveries, 1889; Creation's Hope, 1890; Songs of Universal Life, 1891; Lyrical Studies, 1892; Lyrics and Elegiacs, 1893; Poems of Life and Death, 1895; The Exiles: a Romance of Life, 1896; Poems of a Naturalist, 1896; Music from the Maze, 1899; Gleams through the Gloom, 1900; The Clock of Arba: a Romance, 1901; Musings and Melodies, 1902; Soliloquies in Song, 1903; Poems, Old and New, 1905; Lyrics of Life and Beauty, 1906; Musical Imaginings, 1908; Twilight Music, 1909; Echoes of the Infinite, 1909; Garnered Beauty, 1910; Musical Echoes, 1911; Reflected Radiance, 1912; A Soul's Symphony, 1913; Echoes from the Gospels, 1914; Echoes from the Epistles, 1915; Echoes from the Psalms, 1915; Echoes from the Prophets, 1916; Echoes from the Pentateuch, 1918; contributions on ornithological subjects to natural history periodicals. *Recreations:* music, reading, study of nature and art. *Address:* The Retreat, Clevedon. *Club:* Clifton.

Died 26 Feb. 1928.

RICKETTS, Sir Frederick William Rodney, 5th Bt, *cr* 1827; *b* 27 Sept. 1857; *s* of Sir Cornwallis Ricketts, 2nd Bt and 2nd wife, Lady Caroline Augusta Pelham Clinton, *d* of 4th Duke of Newcastle; *S* nephew, Sir Tristram Tempest Tempest, 1909; *m* 1879, Alice Eve Grace, *d* of late Charles Fox Webster; three *s* one *d*. Formerly Lieutenant Scots Guards. *Heir: e s* Claude Albert Frederick Ricketts [*b* 27 April 1880; *m* 1907, Lilian Helen Gwendolen, *d* of Arthur M. Hill, of Silver Birches, Waltham and Goodanevy, South Devon; one *s* two *d*].

Died 18 Sept. 1925.

RICKETTS, George William; Barrister-at-law; Recorder of Portsmouth since 1914; *b* Allahabad, India, 2 June 1864; *e s* of late George Henry Mildmay Ricketts, CB, and 1st wife, Charlotte, *d* of Percy Gough; *m* 1909, Evelyn Annie, *d* of Thomas Watson Parker of Blackheath, and *widow* of Edward Hastings Buckland. *Educ:* Winchester; Oriel College, Oxford (Scholar). Oxford University XI, 1887; Barrister-at-law, Inner Temple, 1889; Bencher, 1920. *Address:* 1 Pelham Crescent, SW7. *T:* Kensington 5796; 2 Hare Court, Temple, EC4. *Clubs:* Oxford and Cambridge; Hampshire, Winchester.

Died 16 June 1927.

RICKMAN, Lt-Col Arthur Wilmot, DSO 1917; *b* Leicester, 25 Sept. 1874; *s* of late Lieut-Gen. William Rickman and Mary Pulsford Rickman; *m* Muriel Joicey Fulton. *Educ:* Winchester College. Served South African War, 1899–1902 (Queen's medal and three clasps, King's medal and two clasps); European War, 1914–18 (wounded twice, despatches four times, DSO and bar). *Address:* The Old House, Coombe Bissett, near Salisbury. *Club:* Junior United Service.

Died 16 Oct. 1925.

RICKMAN, Capt. William Edward, DSO 1900; Imperial Light Horse; *b* 1855; *s* of Philip Rickman, Brighton; *m* 1895, Margaret Menzies Haliburton, S Africa. *Educ:* Haileybury. Served S Africa, 1900–2 (despatches, Queen's medal 3 clasps, King's medal 2 clasps).

Died 1 June 1927.

RIDDEL, James, ARSA, RSW; *b* Glasgow, 1857; parents Scotch; *m* Margaret G. Shepherd, Perthshire; one *s*. *Educ:* Wellington Academy, Glasgow; Glasgow University; Glasgow School of Art; Edinburgh Royal Institution and Royal Scottish Academy. Began life in merchant's office; for 20 years Headmaster of Art Department of Heriot-Watt College, Edinburgh; during these years continued to practise painting, landscapes and portraits; regularly exhibited in the Royal Scottish Academy, Royal Glasgow Institute, and other art centres in Scotland; also from time to time in the Royal Acad., Liverpool, Manchester, and other exhibitions in England; Chairman of the Society of Scottish Artists, 1904; found subjects for landscape work mostly in Scotland and Belgium, and also painted a little in Canada. *Publications:* Handbook on Practical Plane and Solid Geometry; article on The Art of the Forth in A Guide to the Forth; article on Teaching of Drawing in the Teachers' Encyclopedia; articles on perspective, water-colour painting, and drawing. *Recreations:* golf, billiards. *Address:* Balvonie, Balerno, Midlothian. *T:* Balerno 28. *Clubs:* Scottish Arts, Edinburgh; Art, Glasgow; Baberton Golf.

Died 14 March 1928.

RIDDELL, Sir (Alexander) Oliver, Kt 1904; *b* Edinburgh, 1844; 3rd *s* of late Alexander Oliver Riddell, CE, Edinburgh; *m* 1880, Jane Fazackerley, 2nd *d* of late Henry Hornby of Seaforth, near Liverpool. DL of the City and County of the City of Edinburgh; LLD Edinburgh University; JP for the County of Midlothian; a member of the Royal Company of Archers, the King's Body Guard for Scotland; proprietor of the Estate of Bavelaw Castle on the northern slope of the Pentlands, Midlothian, and also of Craiglockhart. *Recreations:* shooting; formerly hunting. *Address:* Craiglockhart, Slateford, Midlothian. *T:* Central 4610. *M:* SY 366. *Clubs:* Caledonian, United Service, Scottish Unionist, Edinburgh.   *Died 10 Oct. 1918.*

RIDDELL, Sir John Walter Buchanan-, 11th Bt, *cr* 1628; JP; *b* 14 March 1849; *S* uncle, 1892; *m* 1874, Sarah Isabella, *d* of Robert Wharton, barrister; one *s* three *d. Educ:* Eton; Christ Church, Oxford (MA). Barrister Inner Temple, 1874. *Heir: s* Walter Robert Buchanan-Riddell [*b* 21 April 1879; *m* 1919, Hon. Rachel Beatrice, *y d* of 8th Viscount Cobham]. *Address:* 8 Elm Park Gardens, SW10. *T:* Kensington 2985; Hepple, Northumberland.
      Died 31 Oct. 1924.

RIDEING, William Henry; associate editor of the Youth's Companion, Boston, Mass, since 1881; *b* Liverpool, 1853, of a line of seafaring men, his great-uncle having been Admiral Sir Edward Walpole Browne, RN, and his father a well-known Cunard officer; *m* Margaret Elinor, *d* of C. E. Bockus, editor Boston Herald. *Educ:* privately. Went to the United States in 1869; at the age of nineteen became an assistant-editor New York Tribune; afterwards special correspondent of New York Times with United States Geographical Surveys for three years; a frequent contributor to Harper's publications, The Century, Scribner's Magazine, etc; appointed managing editor North American Review, 1888; resigned 1899; *Publications:* sixteen volumes of fiction, travel, and criticism, including A Little Upstart; A-saddle in the Wild West; Thackeray's London; In the Land of Lorna Doone; How Tyson came Home, 1904; Many Celebrities, 1912; A Young Folk's Life of George Washington, 1916, etc. *Recreations:* rural walks and drives; ocean steamers (about which he wrote much, and of which his knowledge said to be "extensive and peculiar." *Address:* c/o The Youth's Companion, Boston, Mass; c/o Baring Brothers, Co.. EC. *Club:* Authors'.
      Died 23 Aug. 1919.

RIDER, Thomas Francis, MVO 1918; *b* 12 April 1843; *o surv. s* of Thomas and Mary Rider of Union Street, Southwark; *m* Elizabeth (*d* 1919), *d* of William Low of Southwark; two *s* one *d. Educ:* Clarendon House, Lambeth (Dr Pinches). Member of Corporation of City of London, 1897–99 and from 1902; Chairman of Assessment Committee from 1915 and received special vote of thanks from Common Council; Chairman of Reception Committee on King George V's and Queen Mary's visit to Guildhall on their Silver Wedding Anniversary; Estates Governor of Dulwich College; Trustee of Crystal Palace; Governor of St Olave's and St Saviour's Grammar School; Deputy Chairman of Belgrave Hospital; Corporation Representative on Sunday Hospital Fund; Chairman of Builders Accident Insurance Company; Past-President of National Federation of Builders, Institute of Builders and London Master Builders; also of Builders' Benevolent and Builders Clerks Benevolent; Order of Sacred Iraasm, 4th Class, from Emperor of Japan on occasion of visit of Prince Fushimi. *Recreations:* reading, watching cricket (Member of Surrey County Club from 1870). *Address:* Stanstead House, Durand Gardens, SW9. *T:* Brixton 769. *Clubs:* St Stephen's, City Carlton.
      Died 13 March 1922.

RIDGEWAY, Rt. Rev. Charles John, DD; *b* 14 July 1841; *s* of Rev. Joseph Ridgeway, MA, Vicar of Christ Church, Tunbridge Wells; *m* 1st, 1868, Susan Jane, *o d* of Rev. Gerald S. FitzGerald; one *s* one *d*; 2nd, 1899, Katharine Margaret, *e d* of late Rev. Canon Johnston, Rector of North Cray. *Educ:* St Paul's School; Trinity College, Cambridge. Perry Exhibitioner; BA 1863; Theological Tripos, 2nd Class, 1865. Curate of Christ Church, Tunbridge Wells, 1866; Vicar of North Malvern, 1868; Rector of Buckhurst Hill, 1875–80; Inspector of Schools, St Albans, 1876–80; Incumbent of St Paul's, Edinburgh, 1880; Vicar of Christ Church, Lancaster Gate, 1884–1905; Prebendary of St Paul's Cathedral; Rural Dean of Paddington, 1901; Surrogate Commissary of Archbishop of Cape Town and Bishop of North China; Dean of Carlisle, 1905–8; Bishop of Chichester, 1908–19; retired, 1919; Select Preacher, Cambridge, 1890 and 1907; Golden Lecturer, 1895; Past Chaplain of Grand Lodges of Masons both in England and Scotland. *Publications:* What Think Ye of Christ?; The Mountain of Blessedness; What does the Church of England Say?; Manual on Holy Communion; How to Prepare for Confirmation;

Foundation Truths; In Paradise, etc. *Address:* 169 Queen's Gate, SW5. *T:* Western 4455; Drumsell, Limpsfield. *Club:* Athenæum.
      Died 28 Feb. 1927.

RIDGEWAY, Major Edward William Crawfurd, CIE 1916; 1st Battalion 2nd King Edward's Own Gurkha Rifles; Recruiting Officer for Gurkhas. Served NW Frontier, India, 1897–98 (medal with clasp); S Africa, 1900–2 (Queen's medal, 4 clasps); European War, 1914–16 (CIE).   *Died 23 Feb. 1917.*

RIDGEWAY, Rt. Rev. Frederick Edward; Bishop of Salisbury since 1911; *b* 1848; *m* 1875, Pauline Josephine, *d* of late John Vibart, ICS; four *s. Educ:* Tonbridge School; Clare Coll., Cambridge (MA). Priest, 1872; Incumbent of St Mary Virgin, Glasgow, 1878–90; Dean of Diocese, Glasgow and Galloway, 1888–90; Vicar of St Peter's, S Kensington, 1890–1900; Rector of St Botolph, Bishopsgate, 1900; Bishop of Kensington, 1901–11; Prebendary of St Paul's Cathedral, 1901–3; chaplain HAC, 1900–11; Precentor of the Province of Canterbury; select preacher, Cambridge, 1891 and 1903; select preacher, Oxford, 1913–14; Hon. DD Glasgow, 1890. *Address:* The Palace, Salisbury; Bishop's Cottage, Broadstone, Dorset.
      Died 4 May 1921.

RIDGEWAY, Col Richard Kirby, VC 1879; CB 1905; Indian Army Staff Corps; retired; *b* County Meath, Ireland, 18 August 1848; 2nd *s* of R. Ridgeway, FRCS, and Annette, *d* of R. Adams; *m* 1871, Emily Maria (Amy) (*d* 1917), *d* of S. W. Fallon. *Educ:* private school; RMC, Sandhurst. Joined 96th Regt, 1868; Indian Staff Corps, 1872; Adjt 44th Gurkha Rifles, 1874–80; Naga Hills Expedition, 1875; Naga Hills Expedition, 1879–80 (despatches, medal, VC); passed Staff College, 1883; DAQMG, 1884; AQMG Army Headquarters, India, 1889–90; comd 44th Gurkha Rifles, 1891–95; AQMG Army Headquarters, India, 1895–98; AAG Peshawar, 1898–1900; Manipur, 1891 (clasp); Tirah, as AAG 2nd Division, 1897 (medal, three clasps). *Clubs:* United Service, Sports.
      Died 11 Oct. 1924.

RIDGEWAY, Sir William, Kt 1919; MA, ScD Cambridge; FBA 1904; FZS; Professor of Archæology, Cambridge University, since 1892; Brereton Reader in Classics since 1907; Fellow of Caius College, Cambridge, 1880; *b* Ireland, 6 Aug. 1853; *y s* of Rev. John Henry Ridgeway, MA, Ballydermot, King's Co., and Marian, *d* of Samuel Ridgeway, Aghanvilla, King's Co.; *m* 1880, Lucy, *d* of Arthur Samuels, Kingstown; one *d. Educ:* Portarlington School; Trinity College, Dublin. Berkeley Greek Medal, Vice-Chancellor Latin Medal, Greek Essay, and Greek Verse (with 3 Greek Comedies) Prizes (graduated Sen. Moderator in both Classics and Modern Literature); and Cambridge (5th Classic). Professor of Greek, Queen's College, Cork, 1883–94; Mem. Council, Cambridge Senate, 1900–4; took leading part in founding Cambridge Departments of Anthropology and Architecture, and in reforming Classical Tripos; Gifford Lecturer in Natural Religion, University of Aberdeen, 1909–11; Stokes Lecturer in Irish Archæology, Dublin, 1909; Hermione Lecturer in Art, Dublin, 1911; Pres. of Royal Anthropological Inst., 1908–10; Pres. of Anthropological Section, British Association, 1908; President of Classical Association of England and Wales, 1914; formerly President of Cambridge Philological, Antiquarian, Classical, and Anthropological Societies; Corresponding Member Archæological Society, Athens; French Assoc. pour les Sciences Anthropologiques; Foreign Member of Sociétés d'Anthropologie of Paris and Brussels, 1909; and of the Deutsche Gesellschaft für Anthropologie, 1913; Hon. Mem. Bihar and Orissa Research Society; Hon. DLitt Dublin, 1902; Manchester, 1906; Hon. LLD Aberdeen, 1908; Edinburgh, 1921. *Publications:* Origin of Metallic Currency and Weight Standards, 1892; The Early Age of Greece, 1901; The Origin and Influence of the Thoroughbred Horse, 1905; Homeric Land System; Who were the Romans?, 1907; The Oldest Irish Epic, 1907; The Differentiation of the Chief Species of Zebras, 1909; The Origin of Tragedy, with special reference to Greek Tragedians, 1910; Minos the Destroyer, 1910; The Dramas and Dramatic Dances of Non-European Races in special reference to the origin of Tragedy, 1915; various articles in Encyclopædia Britannica, Encyclopædia Biblica, etc. *Recreations:* boating; collected ancient and mediæval coins, precious stones, Greek, Roman, Anglo-Saxon, and mediæval objects, and prehistoric and savage implements. *Address:* Caius College, Cambridge; Flendyshe, Fen Ditton, Cambridge.   *Died 12 Aug. 1926.*

RIDLEY, 2nd Viscount, *cr* 1900; **Matthew White Ridley,** DL; JP; Baron Wensleydale 1900; Bt 1756; Lieutenant-Colonel Northumberland Yeomanry; *b* 6 Dec 1874; *e s* of 1st Viscount Ridley and Hon. Mary Georgiana Marjoribanks, *d* of 1st Baron Tweedmouth; *S* father, 1904; *m* 1899, Hon. Rosamond Cornelia Gwladys Guest, *y d* of 1st Baron Wimborne; one *s* two *d*. *Educ:* Eton; Balliol Coll., Oxford (BA with honours). MP (C) Stalybridge, 1900–4. Owned about 10,200 acres. *Heir: s* Hon. Matthew White Ridley, *b* 16 Dec. 1902. *Address:* 10 Carlton House Terrace, SW. *T:* Regent 727; Blagdon, Cramlington, Northumberland. *Clubs:* Turf, Carlton.

Died 14 Feb. 1916.

RIDLEY, Rt. Hon. Sir Edward, Kt 1897; PC 1917; Judge of the King's Bench Division of the High Court of Justice, 1897–1917; *b* Blagdon, Northumberland, Aug. 1843; 2nd *s* of Sir Matthew White Ridley, 4th Bt, and Cecilia Ann, *e d* of Sir James Parke, afterwards Baron Wensleydale; *m* 1882, Alice, *d* of William Bromley Davenport, Cheshire; two *s*. *Educ:* Harrow; Corpus Christi College, Oxford. First class Moderations, 1864; First class Final Schools, 1866. Fellow of All Souls Coll., 1866–82; Barrister 1868; went on Northern and North-Eastern Circuits; MP (C) South Northumberland, 1878–80; Official Referee, 1886–97; QC 1892. *Publication:* translation of Lucan's Pharsalia. *Recreations:* shooting, cycling, reading. *Address:* 48 Lennox Gardens, SW1. *T:* Kensington 4968. *Clubs:* Carlton, Oxford and Cambridge, Athenæum. *Died 14 Oct. 1928.*

RIDSDALE, Sir (Edward) Aurelian, GBE 1920; JP Pembrokeshire; FGS; *b* 23 Feb. 1864; *e s* of late Edward Lucas Jenks Ridsdale and Esther Lucy Thacker; *m* 1900, Susan Stirling, 3rd *d* of late John Ritchie Findlay of Aberlour, Banffshire; one *s* one *d*. *Educ:* University Coll. School; Royal School of Mines. MP (L) Brighton, 1906–10; Special Commissioner Salonika and Mesopotamia, 1915–16; Member of Commission of Enquiry into Medical arrangements in Mesopotamia, 1916; Chairman Executive Committee British Red Cross Society, 1912–14; Deputy Chairman, 1914–19; Acting Red Cross Commissioner, France, 1916; High Sheriff Pembrokeshire, 1921. *Publication:* Cosmic Evolution. *Address:* 14 Ennismore Gardens, SW7. *T:* Western 6478; Waterwynch, Tenby, Pembrokeshire. *Clubs:* Reform, Bath, Brooks's. *Died 6 Sept. 1923.*

RIGG, Herbert Addington, JP Sussex; KC 1906; MA; FSA; Deputy Chairman of Quarter Sessions for West Sussex; Alderman West Sussex County Council; 2nd *s* of Jonathan Rigg of Wrotham Hill Park, Kent; *m* Dora, *y d* of late William Chappell, FSA. *Educ:* Tonbridge School; Trinity College, Cambridge. Barrister, Inner Temple, 1871; went Northern Circuit; and practised at Parliamentary Bar. *Recreations:* hunting, shooting, farming. *Address:* Wallhurst Manor, Cowfold, Sussex. *TA:* Cowfold. *T:* Cowfold 11. *Clubs:* New University, Athenæum. *Died 7 March 1924.*

RILEY, James Whitcomb; poet and public reader; *b* Greenfield, Indiana, USA, 1849; *s* of Reuben A. Riley and Elizabeth Marine; unmarried. Began life as a journeyman signwriter; joined a theatrical troupe, rewrote their plays and improvised songs for them; in 1872 began to publish in local papers poems in the Hoosier dialect; for some years travelled about giving entertainments with the late "Bill Nye," and later by himself; connected with the Indianapolis Journal for a number of years; member of American Academy of Arts and Letters, and awarded by them the gold medal for poetry in 1912. *Publications:* The Old Swimmin'-Hole and 'Leven More Poems, 1883; The Boss Girl and other Sketches, 1885; Afterwhiles, 1887; Pipes o' Pan at Zekesbury, 1887; Old-Fashioned Roses (in England), 1888; Rhymes of Childhood, 1890; The Flying Islands of the Night, 1891; Neighborly Poems, on Friendship, Grief, and Farm-Life, 1891; Green Fields and Running Brooks, 1892; Poems Here at Home, 1893; Armazindy, 1894; A Child-World, 1896; Rubaiyat of Doc Sifers, 1897; The Golden Year (in England), 1898; Riley Child Rhymes, 1898; Riley Love Lyrics, 1899; Home-Folks, 1900; Riley Farm Rhymes, 1901; An Old Sweetheart of Mine, 1902; The Book of Joyous Children, 1902; His Pa's Romance, 1903; Out to Old Aunt Mary's, 1904; A Defective Santa Claus, 1904; Riley Songs o' Cheer, 1905; While the Heart beats Young, 1906; Morning, 1907; Home Again with Me, 1908; Riley Song of Summer, 1908; The Orphant Annie Book, 1908; Riley Roses, 1909; Riley Songs of Home, 1910; The Lockerbie Book, 1911; The Complete Works of James Whitcomb Riley, biographical edition, 1913. *Address:* c/o Union Trust Co., Indianapolis, Ind, USA. *Died 22 July 1916.*

RILEY, Engr Rear-Adm. William Henry, CB 1916; retired, 1912. At the Admiralty, 1899–1905; in Engineering Branch of Controller's Dept, 1899–1901; employed on special service, the Admiralty, in connection with watertube boilers, 1902–3; with oil-fuel experiments, 1907–17; Engr Rear-Adm., 1907. *Address:* Beechin Wood, Platt, Borough Green, Kent. *Died March 1926.*

RIMINGTON, Alexander Wallace, ARE, RBA; Hon. FSA; artist; *b* London, 1854; *e s* of Alexander Rimington, descendant of William

de Rimington, of 13th century of Rimington in Yorks; *m* 1st, Charlotte (*d* 1913), *d* of G. A. Haig; 2nd, Evelyn, *d* of Rev. F. Whyley. *Educ:* Clifton Coll.; studied art in London and Paris. Ex-Professor of Art at Queen's Coll., London; frequent exhibitor at Royal Academy, Royal Society of Painter Etchers, and Royal Society of British Artists, and an occasional one at Paris Salon, New Gallery, and international exhibitions of the Continent and America, etc; had seven special exhibitions of his water-colours in the Fine Art Society's Galleries; Hon. Mention at Berlin International; carried out original researches upon the relations between colour and music; inventor of the Colour Organ, an instrument for producing Colour-Music, and other forms of the art of Mobile Colour, which was used in Colour-Music concerts and lectures given in London and elsewhere; his theory adopted and employed by Scriabin the composer in his Prometheus and other works. *Publications:* Architecture seen through the Painter's Glasses, 1891; Colour-Music, 1912. *Recreations:* trout-fishing, chess. *Address:* 11A Pembridge Crescent, W. *T:* 2606 Park. *Clubs:* Arts, Odd Volumes. *Died 14 May 1918.*

RIMINGTON, Maj.-Gen. Sir Michael Frederic, KCB 1921 (CB 1900); CVO 1912; Hon. Colonel 6th Inniskilling Dragoons; *b* 23 May 1858; *s* of Michael Rimington of Tynefield, Penrith; *m* 1888, Agnes, *d* of late Henry Forestal Cunningham of Oakley Park, Co. Galway; one *s*. *Educ:* Oxford University (BA). Entered 6th (Inniskilling) Dragoons, 1881; Major, 1897; served Bechuanaland Expedition, 1884–85; Zululand, 1888; South Africa, 1899–1900 (despatches 5 times, Queen's medal 8 clasps, King's medal 2 clasps, CB, Brevet Col); Inspector of Cavalry in India; Commander Legion of Honour, 1915. *Publications:* Our Cavalry; Hints on Stable Management. *Club:* Naval and Military.

Died 19 Dec. 1928.

RIND, Col Alexander Thomas Seton Abercromby, CMG 1887; late Assistant Commissary-General, 1st class, Naini Tal; Indian Staff Corps, late 102nd Foot; *b* 1847; *s* of Dep. Surg.-Gen. M. MacNeill Rind. Entered army, 1866; Capt. 1878; Major, 1881; Lieut-Col 1892; Col 1898; served Afghan War, 1879–80 (despatches twice, brevet of Major, medal with clasp, bronze decoration); Egyptian War, 1882 (medal, Khedive's Star). *Died 29 Sept. 1925.*

RING, George Alfred; Attorney-General, Isle of Man, 1897–1921; 3rd *s* of late Dr C. P. Ring, Scholar of Trinity College, Dublin; *m* Helena de Guise, *e d* of late Ven. Archdeacon Hughes-Games. *Educ:* privately. Called to the Manx Bar, 1873; Chairman of the Douglas School Board, 1883–97. *Publications:* The Legislature and Judicature of the Isle of Man; Land Tenure in the Isle of Man; The West Riding Judgment; Communicants and the Deceased Wife's Sister's Act 1907; The Legal Aspect of Vestments. *Address:* 8 Palmeira Court, Hove, Sussex. *Died 1 Feb. 1927.*

RIPON, 2nd Marquess of, *cr* 1871; **Frederick Oliver Robinson,** GCVO 1909 (KCVO 1902); Bt 1690; Baron Grantham, 1761; Earl de Grey, 1816; Viscount Goderich, 1827; Earl of Ripon, 1833; Treasurer in the Household of Queen Alexandra since 1901; *b* 29 Jan. 1852; *e s* of 1st Marquess of Ripon and Henrietta Anne Theodosia, CI, *d* of Capt. Henry Vyner, Gautby Hall, Lincolnshire, and *g d* of 2nd Earl de Grey; *S* father, 1909; *m* 1885, Constance Gladys (*d* 1917), *d* of 1st Baron Herbert of Lea, *sister* of 14th Earl of Pembroke, and *widow* of 4th Earl of Lonsdale. MP (L) Ripon, 1874–80; a Trustee of the Wallace Collection. Owned about 21,800 acres. *Heir:* none. *Address:* Studley Royal, Ripon. *Clubs:* Marlborough, White's.

Died 22 Sept. 1923 (ext).

RISSIK, Hon. Johann Friedrich Bernhardt; Member of the South African Railway Board; *m*; two *s*. Formerly Minister for the Lands and Native Affairs, Transvaal; Administrator Province of the Transvaal; Member, Transvaal Legislative Assembly for North Central Pretoria; Member, Executive Council. *Address:* Linschoten, Sunnyside, Pretoria. *Died Aug. 1925.*

RITCHIE, Anne Isabella, (Lady Ritchie); writer of stories and magazine articles; *b* 9 June 1837; *e d* of W. M. Thackeray; *m* 1877, Sir Richmond Ritchie, KCB (*d* 1912); one *s* one *d*. *Educ:* Paris; Kensington. Lived at home in her father's house and with her sister for many years until her marriage; appointed to the Academic Committee of the Royal Society of Literature, 1911. *Publications:* The Story of Elizabeth, 1863; The Village on the Cliff, 1865; To Esther, and other Sketches, 1869; Old Kensington, 1873; Toilers and Spinsters, 1873; Bluebeard's Keys, 1874; Miss Angel, 1875; Anne Evans, 1880; Madame de Sévigné, 1881; A Book of Sibyls, 1883; Mrs Dymond, 1885; Alfred Lord Tennyson and his Friends, Portraits and Reminiscences (folio), 1893; Chapters from some Memoirs, 1894;

an edition of the works of W. M. Thackeray, 1898; Blackstick Papers, 1908; introductions to editions of Mrs Gaskell's Cranford, Our Village, and The Fairy Tales of Madame d'Aulnoy. *Address:* 9 St Leonard's Terrace, Chelsea, SW. *T:* Kensington 4858. *Club:* Sesame.
Died 20 Feb. 1919.

RITCHIE, Sir George, Kt 1910; JP Forfarshire; DL, JP County of City of Dundee; merchant; President of the Dundee Liberal Association; *b* Kingsmuir, 1849; *s* of Alexander Ritchie; *m* 1877, Agnes, *d* of David Scrimgeour. *Educ:* Kingsmuir Parish and Forfar Burgh School. Served on the City Council for nearly 20 years; for the greater part of that time Finance Convener and Hon. City Treasurer; Director of the High School and Technical College; a director of several financial and industrial local companies; took a keen interest in social and religious work, and served on various boards. *Address:* Dundee. *TA:* Mars, Dundee. *T:* 1055 and 873.
Died 3 Dec. 1921.

RITCHIE, Major Hon. Harold, DSO 1918; *b* 30 Oct. 1876; 3rd *s* of 1st Baron Ritchie of Dundee and Margaret, *d* of Thomas Ower, Perth; *m* 1907, Ella, *o d* of R. C. Priestley; two *s* two *d*. *Educ:* Winchester. Partner of Brightwen & Co., Bill Brokers, Nicholas Lane, EC. *Address:* 13 Kensington Court, W8. *T:* Western 3605. *Club:* Union.
Died 28 Oct. 1918.

RITCHIE, James, MA, BSc (Edin. and Oxon), MD (Edin.); FRCPE; Irvine Professor of Bacteriology, University of Edinburgh, since 1913; *b* 1864; *s* of Rev. William Ritchie, DD, Duns; *m* 1898, Lily, *d* of James Souttar, Aberdeen; three *d*. *Educ:* Edinburgh; Oxford. Studied Arts and Medicine in University of Edinburgh; engaged in bacteriological and pathological research in University of Oxford, 1892-1907; successively Lecturer, Reader, and Professor of Pathology there; Hon. Physician, Radcliffe Infirmary, Oxford, 1897-1906; Pathologist to same, 1900-7; Fellow of New College, Oxford, 1902-7; Superintendent, Royal College of Physicians Laboratory, Edinburgh, 1907-20. *Publications:* Joint Author, Muir and Ritchie's Manual of Bacteriology; Joint Editor, Pembrey and Ritchie's General Pathology; papers on bacteriology and pathology in scientific journals. *Address:* 10 Succoth Gardens, Murrayfield, Edinburgh, W. *T:* Central 4942. *Clubs:* Royal Societies; University, Edinburgh.
Died 28 Jan. 1923.

RITCHIE, Maj.-Gen. John; Royal Artillery, retired; *b* 31 Jan. 1834; *y s* of John Ritchie, merchant, Calcutta; *m* 1st, 1859, Jane Craig (*d* 1859); 2nd, 1862, Janet (*d* 1900), *d* of Archibald Sharp; 3rd, 1904, Louisa Mary, *widow* of Alfred Slocock, Montagu House, Southsea; one *s*. *Educ:* Glasgow Academy; Addiscombe. Served in Indian Mutiny, 1857 (despatches). *Recreations:* hunting, golf, yachting. *Address:* Montagu House, 10 Clarence Parade, Southsea. *Club:* Royal Albert Yacht, Southsea.
Died 20 Nov. 1919.

RIVAZ, Hon. Sir Charles Montgomery, KCSI 1901 (CSI 1895); *b* 11 March 1845; *s* of late John Theophilus Rivaz, Bengal Civil Service, and Mary, *d* of late William Lambert, Bengal Civil Service; *m* 1874, Emily, *d* of late Major-General Agnew, Bengal Staff Corps; three *s*. *Educ:* Blackheath Proprietary School. Entered ICS, 1864; served in the Punjab till 1898; Member of Viceroy's Executive Council, 1898-1902; Lieut-Gov. of Punjab, 1902-6. *Address:* 21 Hyde Park Street, W2. *T:* Paddington 1194.
Died 7 Oct. 1926.

RIVAZ, Col Vincent, CB 1900; Indian Staff Corps; *b* 26 June 1842; *s* of (John) Theophilus Rivaz, late Bengal Civil Service, of Watford Place, Watford; *m* 1877, Louisa Caroline, *d* of late Rev. Edward Revell Eardley Wilmot and 2nd wife, Emma Hutchinson, *d* of William Lambert; two *d*. Entered army, 1860; Col 1890; served Hazara Campaign, 1868 (medal with clasp); Dour Valley Expedition, 1872; Afghan War, 1878-79 (despatches, medal); Mahsood Wuzeeree Expedition, 1881 (despatches); Hazara Expedition, 1891 (despatches, clasp). *Address:* Millfield, Leamington Spa.
Died 1 March 1924.

RIVERS, Lady; (Emmeline Laura); *o d* of Captain John Pownall William Bastard; *m* 1st, 1873, 6th and last Baron Rivers (*d* 1880); 2nd, 1881, Montague George Thorold, *s* of Sir John Charles Thorold, 11th Bt, and Elizabeth Frances, *d* of Col T. B. Thoroton-Hildyard. *Address:* 1 Abbot's Court, Kensington Square, W; Honington Hall, Grantham.
Died 1 Oct. 1918.

RIVERS, William Halse R., MA, MD; FRS; FRCP; Fellow and Prælector in Natural Sciences, St John's College, Cambridge; President Royal Anthropological Institute and Folklore Society; *b* 1864; *s* of Rev. H. F. Rivers. *Educ:* Tonbridge; St Bartholomew's Hospital. Formerly Lecturer on Psychology, Guy's Hospital; Lecturer on Physiological and Experimental Psychology, Univ. of Cambridge; Croonian Lecturer, Royal Coll. of Physicians, 1906; FitzPatrick Lecturer, 1915-16; President, Section for Anthropology, British Association, 1911; late temp. Capt., RAMC; MO Craiglockhart War Hosp., and Military Hosp., Maghull; Psychologist, Central Hosp., RAF; Hon. LLD St Andrews; DSc Manchester; Royal Society's Royal Medal, 1915. *Publications:* The History of Meianesian Society; Kinship and Social Organisation; The Todas; The Influence of Alcohol and other Drugs on Fatigue; Dreams and Primitive Culture; Mind and Medicine; Instinct and the Unconscious; various papers in Reports of Cambridge Expedition to Torres Straits, and in scientific journals. *Address:* St John's College, Cambridge.
Died 4 June 1922.

RIVETT-CARNAC, Col John Henry, CIE 1878; VD; JP; Aide-de-camp to King George V; Indian Civil Service (retired); Hon. Commandant Ghazipur Light Horse and Volunteer Rifles; Lord of the Manor of Stanstead Hall, Suffolk; *b* London, 16 Sept. 1838; 2nd *s* of late Admiral John Rivett-Carnac, RN, and Maria Jane, *d* of J. Samuel Davis, FRS, RE, and *sister* of Sir John Francis Davis, 1st Bt, KCB; *m* 1868, Annie Marion, *d* of Gen. Sir Henry Marion Durand, RE. *Educ:* abroad for diplomatic service; HEICS. FSA; Fellow of the University of Bombay, the Royal Academies of Spain and Sweden; Royal Society of Northern Antiquaries, and Honorary Fellow of several Antiquarian Societies; Bengal Civil Service, 1859-94; Sec. to Sir Richard Temple in Central Provinces; Commissioner of Cotton and Commerce with Government of India; Special Commissioner in Bengal Famine of 1874; Opium agent; extra Private Secretary to Lord Lytton at Delhi; ADC to Commander-in-Chief FM Sir Donald Stewart; raised and commanded the Ghazipur Volunteer Light Horse and Rifles; commanded the Volunteer Brigade at the Grand Manœuvres, Delhi, 1888, and Indian Rifle Team at Wimbledon, 1885 and 1887; Vice-Pres. East Anglian Society. Decorated: CIE, as Special Commissioner for Transport in Bengal Famine of 1874. *Publications:* Report on Indian Cotton Supply; Indian Railway Traffic; Indian Antiquities; Archaic Rock Markings in India and Europe; Many Memories, 1910, etc. *Recreations:* sport of all sorts; Winner of the Regimental Silver Cup for Rifle Shooting, 1880. *Club:* United Service.
Died 11 May 1923.

RIVETT-CARNAC, Sir William Percival, 5th Bt, *cr* 1836; *b* 1847; *e s* of William John Rivett-Carnac (2nd *s* of 1st Bt), and Mary Anstruther, *d* of Rev. Percival S. Wilkinson; *g s* of Sir James Rivett-Carnac, 1st Bt; *S* cousin, 1924 on the presumption of latter's death in 1909; *m* 1885, Frances Maria, *d* of late Francis Charles Forbes, BCS; two *d*. Heir: *brother* Rev. George Clennell Rivett-Carnac [*b* 1850; *m* 1st, 1885, Emily Louisa (*d* 1894), *d* of Rev. George Crabbe; two *s* one *d*; 2nd, 1901, Eva Mary Bernard, *d* of James Orr; one *s* one *d*].
Died 21 March 1924.

RIVIERE, Briton, DCL; RA 1880 (ARA 1879); painter; Hon. Fellow of Oriel College, Oxford; *b* London, 14 Aug. 1840; *y c* of William Riviere, London, and Ann, *d* of Joseph Jarvis, Warwickshire; *m* 1867, Mary Alice, *d* of John Dobell of Detmore, Gloucestershire, and *sister* of Sydney Thompson Dobell, the poet; five *s* two *d*. *Educ:* Cheltenham Coll.; St Mary Hall, Oxford (MA). Began work as an artist while still a boy, and exhibited at British Gallery and Royal Academy while at Cheltenham and Oxford; went to live in Kent; there he worked at illustrating for various English and American publications, and exhibited in oils and water-colours at Dudley Gallery and Royal Academy; came to live in London, 1870, and remained there; a constant exhibitor at Royal Academy and various international exhibitions abroad; a great number of his works engraved. *Works:* The Poacher's Nurse, 1866; The Long Sleep, 1868; Prisoners, 1869; Charity, 1870; Circe, 1871; Daniel, 1872; Argus, 1873; War Time, 1875; Pallas Athene and Dogs, 1876; Lazarus, 1877; Sympathy, Persepolis, and An Anxious Moment, 1878; In Manus tuas, 1879; The Last Spoonful and the Night Watch, 1880; The Magician's Doorway, 1881; Miracle of the Gadarene Swine, 1883; Actaeon, The King and his Satellites, The Sheep-Stealer, 1884; Vae Victis, Union is Strength, 1885; Rizpah, 1886; Adonis Wounded, An Old-World Wanderer, 1887; Requiescat, Adonis' Farewell, 1888; Pale Cynthia, A Fool and His Folly, Prometheus, 1889; Daniel's Answer to the King, 1890; A Mighty Hunter before the Lord, 1891; Dead Hector, 1892; King's Libation, 1893; Beyond Man's Footstep and Ganymede, 1894; Apollo, 1895; J. F. H. Read, Esq. and Dogs, Aggravation, and a bronze, The Last Arrow, 1896; Lady Wantage, Mrs F. Methold and her Deerhounds, 1897; The Temptation in the Wilderness, 1898; Lady Tennyson and the Poet's Old Wolf Hound, Karenina, 1899; St George and The Heron, 1900; To the Hills, 1901; Aphrodite, 1902;

The Rt Hon. Lord Tennyson and Hark! hark! the Lark, 1909. *Address:* Flaxley, Finchley Road, NW8. *T:* Hampstead 4966. *Club:* Athenæum.
Died 20 April 1920.

RIVINGTON, Charles Robert, JP and DL Westmorland; *b* 7 Dec. 1846; *s* of late Charles Rivington, solicitor, London, and Emily, *d* of William Chadwell Mylne, FRS, of Great Amwell, Herts; *m* 1st, 1869, Fanny Anne (*d* 1875), *d* of Duncan Campbell of Adpar, Cardiganshire; 2nd, 1881, Amy, *d* of William Chippindale of Dulwich, Surrey; three *s* one *d*. *Educ:* King's College, London. Admitted a Solicitor, 1869; Master of Stationers Co., 1921-22; Governor of St Bartholomew's Hospital, and London Hospital; Treasurer of Eastern Dispensary, Whitechapel; formerly member of Victoria Rifles, and subsequently Captain in 2nd Vol. Batt. Durham Light Infantry; Mayor of Appleby, 1894-95; High Sheriff of Westmorland, 1908; Past Master of Lodge of Antiquity and Vale of Eden Lodge (Freemasons), PGS; Director of the Equity and Law Life Assurance Society. *Publications:* Records of the Stationers Co. *Recreation:* shooting. *Address:* Castle Bank, Appleby, Westmorland; 74 Elm Park Gardens, SW10. *T:* Kensington 1894. *Clubs:* Conservative, Ranelagh. *Died 22 Aug. 1928.*

ROACH, Rt. Rev. Frederick, DD; Assistant Bishop of Natal since 1913; Vicar General of Natal, 1916; *b* 1856. *Educ:* Earl of Ducie's School, Tortworth; Cheltenham Training College. Ordained, 1886; Schoolmaster, Kwamagwaza, Zululand, 1881; Isandhlwana, 1885; missionary at Etalaneni, 1886-1913; Canon of St Peter's Pro-Cathedral, Vryheid, 1904; Archdeacon of Eshowe, 1905-13. *Address:* 15 Burger Street, Maritzburg, Natal.
Died June 1922.

ROBARTS, Abraham John, JP, DL; *b* 1838; *e s* of late Abraham George Robarts, banker, London, and Elizabeth Sarah, *d* of late Col John Henry Smyth, MP, of Heath Hall, Co. York; *m* 1869, Hon. Edith Barrington, *d* of 8th Viscount Barrington and Louisa, *d* of Tully Higgins. *Educ:* Eton; Christ Church, Oxford. Partner, Robarts, Lubbock and Co., bankers; High Sheriff, Bucks, 1869; later Capt. Bucks Yeomanry. *Address:* 29 Hill Street, W1. *T:* Mayfair 1451; Tile House, Buckingham. *Died 24 Jan. 1926.*

ROBBINS, Sir Edmund, KBE 1917; *b* Launceston, 4 April 1847; 2nd *s* of late R. Robbins; *m* 1870, Jeannette, *o d* of William Pearson, Plymouth; three *s* six *d*. *Educ:* Eagle House Academy, Priory House Academy, Launceston. Served apprenticeship (1858-65) with Mr J. Brimmell at office of Launceston Weekly News; joined Central Press Agency, 1865; appointed sub-editor on the Press Association on its formation, 1870, simultaneously with the taking over of the telegraphs by the State; became secretary and assistant manager in 1874; chief of the Staff in 1878; manager, 1880-1917; secretary of the Provincial Newspaper Society from Oct. 1870 to May 1881; was an active member of the Executive of the Liberator Relief Fund, and was Chairman when in 1917 the Fund was transferred to the Public Trustee; Secretary of the Admiralty, War Office, and Press Committee from its formation; a Vice-President of the Newspaper Press Fund, 1917. *Address:* 168 Peckham Rye Common, SE22.
Died 21 Dec. 1922.

ROBERTS, Hon. Charles James, CMG 1882; MLC New South Wales, since 1890; *b* 29 March 1846; *e s* of late Charles Warman Roberts of Sydney; *m* 1867, Lucretia, *d* of late Abraham Abraham of Sydney; one *s* five *d*. *Educ:* Sydney Grammar School. MLA for Hastings and Manchester, NSW, 1882-90; Postmaster-General, NSW, 1887-89; Mayor of Sydney, 1879. *Address:* Rockmore, Elizabeth Bay, Sydney, Australia.
Died 14 Aug. 1925.

ROBERTS, Rev. Charles Philip, MA; Hon. Canon of Manchester; *b* 1842; *s* of Rev. Philip Roberts, MA, of Coleshill, Warwickshire; *m* 1875, Lilias, *d* of J. Scholes Walker, Bury, Lancs; three *s* one *d*. *Educ:* Marlborough; Trinity College, Oxford. Assistant Master, Rossall School, 1864-68; Curate of Walmersley, Lancs, 1868-71; Vicar of Peel, Little Hulton, 1871-87; Rector of Longsight, 1887-1915; Chairman of Urban District Council of Little Hulton; Chairman of Education Committee of Bolton Board of Guardians; Past Provincial Grand Chaplain, East Lancs Freemasons. *Recreations:* angling, golf, rowing (Oxford University eight, 1864). *Address:* 6 Egerton Road, Fallowfield, Manchester. *Club:* Old Rectory, Manchester.
Died 21 Sept. 1918.

ROBERTS, David Lloyd, MD; FRCP; FRSE; Consulting Obstetric Physician, Manchester Royal Infirmary; Physician to St Mary's Hospitals, Manchester; Lecturer on Clinical Obstetrics and Gynæcology in Manchester University; *b* Stockport; *s* of Robert Roberts, cotton spinner; *m* Martha, *d* of W. H. Occleshaw, of Plymouth Grove, Manchester. *Educ:* Rippenden College (formerly Making Place Hall); Royal School of Medicine and Surgery, and Royal Infirmary, Manchester; articled pupil to William Smith, FRCS, the first Prof. of Physiology in Owens College. Fellow of Royal Medico-Chirurgical Society and Medical Society, London; and member of other professional and scientific bodies; late President of North of England Obstetrical and Gynæcological Society; Vice-President of London Obstetrical Society; President of Manchester Medico-Ethical and Medical Societies; President in 1902 of Section of Midwifery, British Medical Association. *Publications:* The Practice of Midwifery, 1876, 4th edn 1896; editor of Sir Thomas Browne's Religio Medici, 1892, rev. edn 1898; The Scientific Knowledge of Dante, 1914; various professional papers. *Recreations:* reading; collecting objects of art, books, bindings, etc. *Address:* Broughton Park, Manchester.
Died 20 Sept. 1920.

ROBERTS, Rev. Edward Dale; Hon. Canon of Birmingham; Vicar of Hill, Four Oaks; *b* 1848; *m*; one *s*. *Educ:* Oxford. Curate of St George's, Birmingham, 1872-77; Vicar of St Paul's, Lozells, forty years. *Died 8 Sept. 1927.*

ROBERTS, Frederick Thomas, MD, FRCP; Hon. DSc University of Wales; Consulting Physician to University College Hospital and to Brompton Hospital. *Educ:* University College, London. Emeritus Professor of Medicine and Clinical Medicine, University College, London; formerly assistant editor of Quain's Dictionary of Medicine. *Publication:* A Handbook of the Theory and Practice of Medicine, 10th edn. *Address:* 95 North Gate, Regent's Park, NW.
Died 28 July 1918.

ROBERTS, Rt. Hon. George Henry, PC 1915; JP; MP (Lab) Norwich, 1906-18, (Ind.) 1918-23; director of companies; *b* Chedgrave, Norfolk, 27 July 1869; *s* of George Henry Roberts and Anne Larkman; *m* 1895, Anne, *d* of Horace Marshall, Norwich; two *s* one *d*. Was Secretary Typographical Association and President Trades Council, Norwich; joined ILP, 1886; Norwich School Board, 1889; a Lord Commissioner of the Treasury, 1915-16; Parliamentary Sec. to Board of Trade, 1916-18; Minister of Labour, 1917-18; Food Controller, Jan. 1919-Feb. 1920; Chairman National Advisory Committee on the Blind, Ministry of Health, 1920; contested (Lab) Norwich, 1904; contested Norwich as Unionist, 1923. *Address:* 56 Abbey House, Victoria Street, Westminster, SW; Westminster House, 104 Earlham Road, Norwich. *Died 25 April 1928.*

ROBERTS, Lt-Col Henry Roger Crompton-, DSO 1902; retired; late Grenadier Guards; *b* 18 May 1863; *e s* of Charles Henry Crompton-Roberts of Drybridge, Monmouthshire, and Mary, *d* and *heiress* of Roger Crompton of Kearsley, Lancs; *m* 1905, Blanche Alexandra, *d* of Lieut-Col E. A. Hannay of Ballylough, Co. Antrim; one *s* two *d*. *Educ:* Eton. Entered Army, 1884; Capt. 1895; Major, 1899; Lieut-Col 1905; served S Africa (despatches twice). *Address:* 10 Park Street, Mayfair, W1. *Club:* Guards'.
Died 16 Sept. 1925.

ROBERTS, Col Sir Howland, 12th Bt, *cr* 1620, and 5th Bt, *cr* 1809; VD; DL and JP for County of London; late commanding London Irish Rifles; *b* 2 Sept. 1845; 2nd *s* of Sir Thomas Howland Roberts, 10th (3rd) Bt and 2nd wife, Anne Elliott, *d* of Hon. Captain William Langdon, MLC, RN; *S* half-brother, 1899; *m* 1895, Elizabeth Marie, *d* of late William Tell La Roche, MD; two *s*. *Educ:* King's College, London. Ensign London Irish Rifles 1868; Colonel, 1896-1906; a Freemason. *Heir:* *s* Thomas Langdon Howland Roberts, *b* 18 June 1898. *Address:* 75A Lexham Gardens, W. *T:* Western 6206. *Clubs:* St Stephen's; Royal Cork Yacht. *Died 19 Dec.1917.*

ROBERTS, James Frederick, CMG 1912; FRGS; *b* 13 Sept. 1847; *o s* of late James Frederick Roberts, barrister-at-law, of Waston, near Bath; *m* 1874, Mary Beatrice, 2nd *d* of Sankey Gardner, JP, of Eaglesbush, Neath; one *d*. *Educ:* Tonbridge School; France and Germany. Deputy Commissioner and Vice-Consul, Oil Rivers Protectorate, 1891; Acting Commissioner and Consul-General for the Niger Coast Protectorate, March to June 1893; Consul, Guatemala, 1894; was also in charge of the British Legation at Guatemala as Chargé d'Affaires, 1895-96; Consul, Barcelona, 1897; Consul-General, 1901-14; Consul-General, Odessa, 1914; retired, 1916; Coronation medal, 1911. *Club:* St James's.
Died 10 March 1927.

ROBERTS, Sir John, Kt 1911; Mayor of Carnarvon, 1910; *b* 9 Jan. 1861; *m* 1887, Evelyn Augusta, *d* of Evan Evans; one *s* one *d*. Solicitor,

1884; Clerk to Carnarvonshire County Council, 1903. *Address:* Plas Llanwnda, Carnarvon. *Died 7 April 1917.*

ROBERTS, Sir John Reynolds, Kt 1911; JP; County Councillor Essex and County borough of West Ham; *b* Camberwell, Surrey, 14 June 1834; *e s* of Thomas Roberts of Dulwich, and Elizabeth, *d* of Thomas Pring of Bradninch, Somerset; unmarried. *Educ:* Dulwich Grammar School. Member of the Worshipful Company of Framework Knitters; Essex Sewer Commissioner; Freedom of City of London; Life-Governor of Cancer Hosp., Brompton, London. *Recreations:* shooting, motoring, golf. *Address:* Salway House, Woodford Green. *T:* 506 Woodford. *M:* F 5296. *Clubs:* National Liberal, Royal Automobile. *Died 25 Sept. 1917.*

ROBERTS, John Varley; Organist and Director of the Choir at Magdalen College, Oxford, 1882-1918; *b* Poplar House, Stanningley, near Leeds, 25 Sept. 1841; *s* of Joseph Varley Roberts; *m* 1866, *e d* of Rev. P. J. Maning, Vicar of Farsley, Leeds; one *d. Educ:* privately. MusB Oxon, 1871; MusD 1876; Hon. MA 1916; FRCO 1876. Organist of St Bartholomew's, Armley, 1862-68; Halifax Parish Church, 1868-82; St Giles', Oxford, 1885-93; Conductor of Oxford Choral and Philharmonic Society, 1885-93; Examiner for Degrees at Oxford in 1883-86, 1889, 1890-99-1900. *Publications:* Practical Method for Training Choristers; *church cantatas:* The Story of the Incarnation; Advent; The Passion, for organ and voices; Jonah, for full orchestra and chorus; very considerable organ voluntaries; about sixty anthems; five morning and evening Church Services; two full Communion Services; part songs, tunes, etc. *Address:* 18 Holywell, Oxford. *Died 9 Feb. 1920.*

ROBERTS, Martin, MInstCE, MIEE; FCS; consulting engineer; *b* Lichfield, 21 Nov. 1853; *s* of late William Roberts of Charlton Kings, Gloucestershire; *m* 1879, Alice, *d* of Jaques Hein of Erfurt; two *s* one *d. Educ:* Bayley Hall, Hertford; King's College, London. Entered Engineering Department, Post Office, 1871; Inspecting Engineer, 1873; Superintendent of Factories, 1880; Assistant Engineer-in-Chief, 1898; retired from Post Office, 1909; designed Post Office Factories, Post Office Power Stations, and engineering work for Post Office London Telephone System; Member of Engineering Standards Committee and of Physical Standards Committee; an authority on telegraph and telephone engineering, and the design of electrical power stations. *Publications:* contributions to journals of Institution Civil Engineers and Institution Electrical Engineers. *Recreations:* yachting, golf, fishing. *Club:* Reform. *Died 22 Feb. 1926*

ROBERTS, Rt. Hon. Sir Samuel, 1st Bt, *cr* 1919; Kt 1917; PC 1922; JP, DL: MA; *b* 30 April 1852; *e s* of late Samuel Roberts, JP, MA, of Queen's Tower, Sheffield, and 2nd wife, Sarah Anne, *o d* of Robert Sorby; *m* 1880, Martha Susan, *o d* of late Archdeacon John Edward Blakeney; four *s* one *d* (and one *s* decd). *Educ:* Repton; Trinity College, Cambridge. Called to the Bar, Inner Temple, 1878; Lord Mayor, Sheffield, 1899-1900; Deputy-Chairman West Riding Quarter Sessions; contested (C) High Peak Division of Derbyshire, 1900; MP (C) Ecclesall Division of Sheffield, 1902-23. *Recreations:* shooting, fishing, golf. *Heir: s* Samuel Roberts [*b* 2 Sept. 1882; *m* 1906, Gladys Mary, *d* of William Ernest Dring, MD; two *s*]. *Address:* Queen's Tower, Sheffield; 4 Whitehall Court, SW. *Clubs:* Carlton, Oxford and Cambridge. *Died 19 June 1926.*

ROBERTS, Sir Thomas Edwards, Kt 1911; JP, DL; High Sheriff of Carnarvonshire; *b* 1851; *s* of Pierce Roberts, Llyndy, Beddgelert; *m* 1888, Emily, *d* of James Taylor, Greenleys, Manchester. Commercial career in Manchester and Director of several large companies in England and Wales. *Address:* Plasybryn, Carnarvon. *T:* 47 Carnarvon. *M:* CC 12, 371 and 116. *Clubs:* Brasenose, Garrick, Manchester. *Died 29 Aug. 1926.*

ROBERTS, Thomas Francis; Principal, University College of Wales, Aberystwyth, since 1891; *b* 25 Sept. 1860; *e s* of Thomas Roberts, Aberdovey, Merioneth; *m* 1893, Mary Elizabeth, *o c* of Robert Davies, Cardiff; one *s. Educ:* Towyn Academy; University Coll. of Wales, Aberystwyth (Scholar and Associate, 1874-79); St John's Coll., Oxford (Scholar, 1879-83). 1st Class Classical Moderations, Oxford, 1881; 1st Class Lit.Hum. 1883; MA 1886; Hon. LLD Victoria Univ., Manchester, 1902. Professor of Greek, University College of South Wales and Monmouthshire, Cardiff, 1883-91; Chairman of the Cardiganshire County Governing Body of Intermediate Schools, 1896-99, 1901-2; Vice-Chancellor of the Univ. of Wales, 1897-98, 1901-3, 1907-9, 1913-15; Fellow of Jesus College, Oxford, 1915-16; Member of Cardiganshire Education Committee; Member of Council of St David's College, Lampeter; President of Baptist Union

of Wales and Monmouthshire, 1907-8; Member of the Council of the National Library of Wales, of the Executive Committee of the Central Welsh Board of Intermediate Education, and of the Joint Board of Legal Education for Wales. *Publications:* addresses and articles in English and Welsh, mainly on education. *Address:* Treathro, Aberystwyth. *TA:* Principal Roberts, Aberystwyth. *T:* Aberystwyth 115. *Died 4 Aug. 1919.*

ROBERTS, Sir Thomas Lee, Kt 1918; *b* Stockport, 8 Aug. 1848; *s* of Thomas Roberts, JP, civil engineer, and Ellen Lee, Bolton, Lancashire; *m* 1st, 1868, Jemima (Mima) (*d* 1920), *d* of Samuel Horten, Warrington; eight *s;* 2nd, 1920, Emily Sarah, *d* of late W. Davis, Odiham, Hants. *Educ:* Grammar School, Stockport. Early in life entered the legal profession; served his articles in a firm of London Solicitors; entered the Inner Temple as a Barrister; called to the Bar, 1879; joined the Northern Circuit. *Recreations:* indoor games, but chiefly the enjoyment of a well-stocked library. *Address:* Doddington Lodge, near Ludlow. *Clubs:* Devonshire, National Liberal. *Died 16 Jan. 1924.*

ROBERTS, His Honour Sir Walworth Howland, Kt 1921; CBE 1920; JP Staffs; formerly Judge of the Marylebone County Court; retired, 1921; was member (Chairman) of Standing County Courts Rules Committee; Standing Arbitrator under Ministry of Transport Act 1922; *b* 30 Aug. 1855; 3rd *s* of Sir Thomas Howland Roberts, 3rd Bt, and 2nd wife, Anne Elliott, *e d* of Comdr William Langdon, RN; *m* 1890, Katherine, *d* of John Gibson Thomson of Aitechuan, Ardrishaig, and Catherine, *d* of John Sinclair of Lochaline, Co. Argyll; one *s* one *d. Educ:* Highgate School; King's College, London. Called to the Bar, Middle Temple, 1878; went Western Circuit and Devon and Exeter Sessions; an Examiner of the Court, and a Revising Barrister for London and Middlesex, 1889-1900; Lieut 3rd Vol. Batt. Rifle Brigade, 1873-78; Judge Circuit 25, 1900-5; Circuit 37, 1905-11; Circuit 41, 1912-19; President Walsall and District Board of Conciliation and Arbitration, 1904-5; served 1918-19 as one of the Chairmen of Committee on Production, and of Court of Arbitration under Wages (Temporary Regulations) Acts. *Publications:* joint author of Roberts' and Wallace's Duty and Liability of Employers; joint editor of Amos' and Ferard's Law of Fixtures. *Address:* Curtesden, Camberley, Surrey. *Died 21 Dec. 1924.*

ROBERTS, Rev. William Henry, DD, LLD; Stated Clerk, General Assembly Presbyterian Church in USA, since 1884; American Secretary of The Alliance of the Reformed Churches throughout the World since 1888; *b* Holyhead, Wales, 31 Jan. 1844; *s* of Rev. William Roberts, DD, and Katherine Parry; *m* 1867, Sarah E. M'Lean, Washington; two *s* two *d. Educ:* College, City of New York, 1863. Statistician US Treasury Dept, 1863-65; Asst Librarian, Congress, Washington, 1866-71; graduated Princeton Theological Seminary, 1873; Pastor, Presbyterian Church, Cranford, NJ, 1873-77; Librarian, Princeton Theological Seminary, 1878-86; Professor of Practical Theology, Lane Theological Seminary, Cincinnati, 1886-93; Acting Pastor, 4th Presbyterian Church, Trenton, NJ, 1895-1900; Treasurer, Centennial Fund, 1888-89; President, Glasgow, Scotland, Pan-Presbyterian Council, 1896; Secretary, American Inter-Church Conference on Marriage and Divorce, 1903-10; President, Inter-Church Conference on Federation, New York City, 1905, and of Federal Council of the Churches of Christ in America, 1908; Moderator, Presbyterian General Assembly, 1907; Treasurer, Sustentation Fund, 1906-12; first Chairman, Executive Committee Federal Council of American Protestant Churches, 1908-12; Chairman, Presbyterian Committee on Church Co-operation and Union since 1903; Member, American Deputation to Great Britain for World Conference of Churches, 1914; Chairman, Armenian Relief Committee, etc, Philadelphia, 1915-19; Secretary, National Service Commission Presbyterian Church, 1917-18; Chairman, Conference of American Churches on Organic Union, 1918-19; DD, Western University of Pennsylvania, 1884; Lafayette College, 1907; LLD, Miami University, 1887. *Publications:* History of the Presbyterian Church, 1888; The Presbyterian System, 1895; Laws Relating to Religious Corporations, 1896; Manual for Ruling Elders, 1897, etc; Editor, Minutes of General Assembly, 34 vols, 1884-1917; Presbyterian Handbook, 1896-1919; Addresses at the 250th Anniversary of the Westminster Assembly, 1898; Proceedings, Presbyterian Inter-Church Conference on Federation, 1905; many magazine articles. *Address:* Witherspoon Building, Philadelphia, Pa. *TA:* Alliance, Philadelphia. *T:* Walnut 44-33. *Club:* City. *Died 26 June 1921.*

ROBERTS, Col William Henry, JP; *b* 1848; *o s* of late Capt. William Henry Roberts, RE, and Anne, *e d* of late William Lee, MP, of

Holborough Court; *m* 1870, Edith, *y d* of John Jerdein, London. *Educ:* Eton. Patron of one living; Major and Hon. Lt-Col Queen's Own West Kent Yeomanry. *Address:* Holborough Court, near Rochester. *Clubs:* United Service; Royal Yacht Squadron, Cowes.

Died 7 April 1926.

ROBERTS, William Lee Henry, JP Kent; *b* 15 Jan. 1871; *e s* of late Col W. H. Roberts; unmarried. *Educ:* Eton College; RMC, Sandhurst. Late Lieut Royal Dragoons; Captain West Kent Yeomanry; High Sheriff, Kent, 1920. *Address:* Holborough Court, Rochester, Kent. *Clubs:* Army and Navy, Carlton.

Died 18 Oct. 1928.

ROBERTS, Rev. William Masfen; Rector of Luddesdown since 1893; Hon. Canon of Rochester, 1895. *Educ:* Jesus College, Cambridge (MA). Curate of St John and Ladywood, Birmingham, 1869; Upton-on-Severn, 1869–74; Fellow of St Augustine's College, Canterbury, 1874–75; Curate of Melton, Hants, 1875–78; St Cross, Winchester, 1878–81; Shoreham, Kent, 1881–89; Hayes, 1889–92; Luddesdown, 1892–93. *Address:* Luddesdown Rectory, Gravesend.

Died 9 Feb. 1927.

ROBERTS, Very Rev. William Page-; Dean of Salisbury, 1907–19; *b* 2 Jan. 1836; *s* of W. Roberts, Brookfield, Lancashire; *m* 1878, Hon. Margaret Grace (*d* 1926), 6th *d* of 4th Baron Rivers and Susan Georgiana, *e d* of 1st Earl Granville; three *d. Educ:* Liverpool College; St John's College, Cambridge (MA). DD Glasgow. Vicar of Eye, Suffolk; Minister of St Peter's, Vere Street, London, 1878–1907; Canon of Canterbury, 1895–1907. *Publications:* Law and God, 5th edn: Reasonable Service, 3rd edn; Liberalism in Religion, 2nd edn; Conformity and Conscience, 1899, 3rd edn. *Address:* Highlands, Shanklin, Isle of Wight. *Club:* Albemarle.

Died 17 Aug. 1928.

ROBERTSON, Rev. Charles; Hon. Canon of Newcastle. *Address:* Belford, Northumberland. *Died Jan. 1921.*

ROBERTSON, Rev. David, MA; Hon. Canon of Worcester, 1905; Hon. Chaplain to King George V; Chaplain to Bishop of Bath and Wells; *b* 1838; *s* of late Hon. Lord Benholme; *m* 1871, Eleanora Charlotte Dalrymple, *y d* of Sir Charles Dalrymple Fergusson, 5th Bt; one *s* two *d. Educ:* Edinburgh Academy; Trinity College, Cambridge (Senior Optime, 1861). Formerly Vicar of Lye, Worcestershire; Rector of Market Deeping, Lincolnshire; Rector of Hartlebury. *Address:* Benholme, Malvern Wells.

Died 11 April 1916.

ROBERTSON, David, ARSA; FRIBA. *Address:* 23 St Roman's Terrace, Edinburgh. *Club:* Scottish Art, Edinburgh.

Died 20 Feb. 1925.

ROBERTSON, Sir Frederick Alexander, KBE 1918; Kt 1913; *b* 28 Feb. 1854; *s* of James R. Robertson and Mary Elizabeth Campbell of Bragleen, Argyllshire; *m* 1st, Beatrice Mary Angelo; 2nd, Dorothy, *d* of Colonel E. R. Bromhead; one *d. Educ:* privately; King's College. Entered Indian Civil Service, 1876; Barrister-at-law; Director of Department of Agriculture, Punjab, 1889–96; Vice-Chancellor of the Punjab University, 1909–10; LLD; Puisne Judge, Chief Court, Punjab, India, 1898–1913; Fellow of King's College, London, 1915; Lecturer on Hindu and Mahomedan Law to the Council of Legal Education; Lecturer on Mahomedan Law at Imperial Institute. *Publications:* Report on the Settlement and Forest Settlement of the Rawal Pindi District; Customary Law and Gazetteer of the Rawal Pindi District; Report on the Tenures of the Maler Kotla State. *Recreations:* cricket, golf, shooting, etc. *Address:* 1 Eaton Terrace, SW. *T:* Victoria 7070. *Clubs:* East India United Service, MCC; Royal and Ancient, St Andrews. *Died 20 Dec. 1918.*

ROBERTSON, Sir George Scott, KCSI 1895 (CSI 1892); MP (L) Central Bradford since 1906; *b* London, 22 Oct. 1852; 2nd *s* of Thomas James Robertson (*o s* of Thomas J. Robertson, Rousay, Orkney), and Robina Corston, 2nd *d* of late Robert Scott, Kirkwall, Orkney; *m* 1st, 1882, Catharine Edith (*d* 1886), *e d* of Colonel Alexander John Edwin Birch, late BSC; one *d*; 2nd, 1894, Mary Gertrude, *d* of Samuel Laurence, the painter. *Educ:* Westminster Hospital Medical School. Entered Indian Medical Service, 1878; served through Afghan campaign, 1879–80, including siege of Sherpur; from June 1888 passed into the employment of the Indian Foreign Office, and was continually employed on Gilgit frontier of Kashmir, and eventually became British Agent of Gilgit; travelled in Kafiristan, 1890–91, living for a year amongst the wild hillmen; chief political officer Hunza-Nagar Expedition, 1891–92; installed

the Mir of Hunza in presence of Chinese envoys, 1892; besieged in Thalpen entrenchment, and present at capture of Chilas, 1892; conducted a political mission to Chitral, 1893; besieged in Chitral, where he was severely wounded, during March and April 1895; installed the ruler of Chitral, Sept. 1895; for services was granted three war medals, etc; retired, 1899; Hon. DCL of Trinity University, Toronto; contested (L) Stirlingshire , 1900. *Publications:* The Kafirs of the Hindu Kush, 1896; Chitral: the Story of a Minor Siege, 1898. *Address:* 14 Cheyne Walk, Chelsea, SW. *T:* Kensington 3695. *Clubs:* Athenæum, Savile, National Liberal, Burlington Fine Arts.

Died 3 Jan. 1916.

ROBERTSON, Sir Helenus Robert, Kt 1913; Chairman Mersey Docks and Harbour Board since 1911 (Member since 1883), and Union Marine Insurance Co.; Director Phœnix Assurance Co. and Bank of Liverpool; *b* Greenock, 1841; *s* of James Hunter Robertson of Bagatelle, Greenock; *m*; one *s* one *d. Educ:* Upper Canada College, Toronto. Formerly partner in the firm of Finlay, Robertson & Co., cotton brokers; President of the Cotton Association, 1882; retired from business, 1883. *Recreation:* golf principally. *Address:* Upton Grange, Chester. *Clubs:* Union, Alpine.

Died 22 March 1919.

ROBERTSON, Henry Robert, RE, RMS; *b* Windsor, 1839; *m* Agnes Lucy Turner; one *s* three *d*. Academy student; exhibitor at Royal Acad. in oil, water-colour, and etching; picture "Winter" in the Sheffield Municipal Gallery. *Publications:* wrote and illustrated Plants We Play With; Life on the Upper Thames, etc; Handbooks on Etching, Pottery-Painting, and Pen-and-Ink Drawing. *Address:* 1 Steele's Studios, Haverstock Hill, NW; 9 Elsworthy Terrace, NW.

Died 6 June 1921.

ROBERTSON, Herbert, JP; Barrister, Lincoln's Inn; *b* 26 April 1849; *s* of late Thomas Storm Robertson, MD, FRCS, and Maria, *d* of Robert Manning; *m* 1880, Helen , *e d* of Alexander Durdin, Huntington Castle, Clonegal, Co. Carlow; three *s* one *d*. MP (C) South Hackney, 1895–1906. *Educ:* Magdalen Coll., Oxford (MA). *Address:* Huntington Castle, Clonegal, Ireland; 36 Bedford Square, WC. *Clubs:* Athenæum, Carlton, Savile.

Died 11 July 1916.

ROBERTSON, Very Rev. James, DD; Parish Minister of Whittinghame, 1865–1918; *b* 1837; *s* of Charles Robertson, Schoolmaster, Lethendy, Perthshire; *m* 1885, Elizabeth Mary, *d* of Robert Scott-Moncrieff of Fossaway. *Educ:* St Andrews. Assistant Minister at Kinghorn, 1861–65; Chaplain to the Lord High Commissioners, 1883–85, 1907–8; Lecturer on Pastoral Theology, 1899–1900, 1902–4; Chairman of Christian Unity Association, 1908–17; Moderator of the General Assembly of the Church of Scotland, 1909. *Publications:* Our Lord's Teaching; The Christian Minister, His Aims and Methods; Lady Blanche Balfour, a Reminiscence; Christian Upbringing; Spiritual Power in the Church (closing address of General Assembly), 1909. *Address:* 36 Queen's Crescent, Newington, Edinburgh.

Died 27 May 1920.

ROBERTSON, Rev. James, DD, LLD; *b* Alyth, Perthshire, 2 March 1840; *m* 1864, Catherine, *d* of John Martin, manufacturer, Dundee; one *s* two *d. Educ:* Alyth Parish School; Grammar School, Aberdeen; Univ. and King's College, Aberdeen (MA 1st Class Hons Philosophy, 1859); St Mary's Coll., St Andrews. Missionary Church of Scotland, Constantinople, 1862–64; Beyrout, Syria, 1864–75; Minister of Mayfield Church, Edinburgh, 1875–77; Professor of Hebrew and Semitic Languages (late Oriental Languages), Glasgow Univ., 1877–1907; Officier d'Académie, 1906. *Publications:* translation of Müller's Outlines of Hebrew Syntax, 1882; The Early Religion of Israel, 1892; The Old Testament and its Contents, 1893, enlarged edn 1896; The Poetry and the Religion of the Psalms, 1898; The First and Second Books of the Kings (Temple Bible), 1902. *Recreations:* gardening, walking. *Address:* 161 Mayfield Road, Edinburgh. *T:* 5559 Central.

Died Dec. 1920.

ROBERTSON, Lt-Col James Currie, CMG 1917; CIE 1914; CBE 1919; MB, MA, BSc, DPH; *b* 1870; *s* of Alexander Robertson; *m* 1903, Catherine Jones. Entered Indian Medical Service, 1896; Captain, 1899; Major, 1907; Lt-Col, 1915; served with Dongola Expedition (Suakin), 1896 (medal, Khedive's medal); South Africa, 1902, on special duty under the Director of Burgher Camps, Transvaal (Queen's medal with two clasps, despatches); Deputy Sanitary Commissioner, United Provinces, 1901; Sanitary Commissioner with the Government of India, 1912. *Address:* Simla, India.

Died 13 May 1923.

ROBERTSON, James Logie, (Hugh Haliburton); first English Master, Edinburgh Ladies' College, 1891; retired 1914; *b* Milnathort, Kinross-shire; 2nd *s* of William Robertson and Mary Logie; *m* 1881, Janet, *d* of P. Simpson, SSC; two *s* three *d. Educ:* Orwell Parish School; Edinburgh University. Medallist in Rhetoric, 1870; Gray prizeman, 1871; MA 1872; Murchison prizeman in Geology, 1873; Glasgow St Andrew's Society prizeman, 1874. Assistant Master Heriot's Hospital, 1871; Asst Master George Watson's College (Boys), 1872; Edin. Ladies' College, 1876; travelled in Norway (Sætersdal) and Sweden (Swedish Lapland). *Publications: poetry*—Poems, 1878; Orellana and other Poems, 1881; Our Holiday Among the Hills (conjointly with his wife), 1882; Horace in Homespun, 1886, new illus. edn 1900; Ochil Idylls, 1891; *prose*—The White Angel, and other Stories, 1886; For Puir Auld Scotland, 1887; In Scottish Fields, 1890; Furth in Field, 1894; A History of English Literature, 1894; Outline of English Literature for Young Scholars, 1897; *editorial work*—Poems of Allan Ramsay, 1887; Burns's Letters, 1888; Selections from Burns, 1889; Thomson's Seasons and The Castle of Indolence, 1891; Scott's Poetical Works, 1894; Burns's Poetical Works, 1896; Milton's Paradise Lost, books i–iv, 1900; The Select Chaucer, 1902; The Select Tennyson, 1903; Excursions in Prose and Verse, 1905; Campbell's Poetical Works, 1907; Thomson's Poems, and The Seasons, a variorum edition, 1908; Nature in Books, 1914; Petition to the De'il and Other War Verses, 1917. *Recreations:* travelling, angling, geologising. *Address:* 1 Braidburn Crescent, Edinburgh.

Died June 1922.

ROBERTSON, Col James Peter, CB 1858; retired; *b* 1822; *s* of Hon. Duncan Robertson and Susan Stewart, of the Royal House of Fincastle; *m* 1862, Louisa (*d* 1910), *y d* of John Churchill, JP, Oakfield, Wimbledon. *Educ:* High School, Edinburgh; Edinburgh Military Academy. Served in 31st Regt throughout Sutloj campaign; also the Crimean campaign; and commanded a regiment of Light Cavalry throughout the Indian Mutiny; retired in 1870, having 11 decorations for active service. Decorated for capture of Lucknow. *Publication:* Personal Adventures and Anecdotes of an Old Officer. *Address:* Callander Lodge, Callander, NB.

Died 11 Feb. 1916.

ROBERTSON, John, MBE 1918; MP (Lab) Bothwell Division of Lanarkshire since 1919; Chairman Scottish Miners' Union; *b* 1867; *m* 1893, Helen, *d* of J. Nimmo. Worked in coal mines as a boy of thirteen; a Lord Commissioner of the Treasury, 1924; contested (Lab) Bothwell, 1918. *Address:* Cadzowbury House, Hamilton, Lanarkshire. *T:* Hamilton 223.

Died 14 Feb. 1926.

ROBERTSON, Rev. John; Hon. Canon of Newcastle. *Address:* The Vicarage, Acklington SO, Northumberland.

Died 17 Dec. 1925.

ROBERTSON, Thomas, ISO 1903; *b* Edinburgh, 17 Aug. 1842; *s* of Alexander Robertson and Eliza Dryden; *m* 1867, Helen Graham (*d* 1912), *d* of James Leask, Kirkwall; three *s* four *d. Educ:* Parish School of Shapinshay, Orkney. Apprenticeship in law office, Kirkwall, 1859–62; entered Inland Revenue Department, 1863; Chief Clerk, Solicitor's Office, Inland Revenue, Edinburgh, 1876–1904. *Address:* Stromberry Villa, Newhaven Road, Edinburgh.

Died 25 Oct. 1925.

ROBERTSON, Sir William, Kt 1910; linen manufacturer; Lord Lieutenant, County of Fife; Vice-Chairman of the Carnegie Trusts, Dunfermline; Member of Extra Parliamentary Panel under Scottish Provisional Orders Bill; *b* 7 Oct. 1856; *s* of William Robertson, manufacturer; *m* 1887, Elizabeth, *e d* of William Berry, Scotston, Aberdeen. *Address:* Benachie, Dunfermline. *Clubs:* Reform; Scottish Liberal, Edinburgh.

Died 27 Feb. 1923.

ROBERTSON, William Chrystal, ISO 1902; Secretary, Fishery Board for Scotland, 1892–1909; *b* 8 April 1850; *s* of James Robertson; *m* 1894, Laura, *d* of William Blackie. *Address:* 47 Colinton Road, Edinburgh.

Died 31 Aug. 1922.

ROBINS, Rev. William Henry, DD; Rural Dean and Hon. Canon of Rochester, 1907; *b* 17 March 1847; *s* of William Robins of The Limes, Buxton, Derbyshire; *m* 1874, Annie Maria Isabella, *e d* of William Rumney, Stubbins House, Lancashire; three *s* one *d. Educ:* College for Blind Sons of Gentlemen, Worcester; Trinity College, Dublin. BA 1872; Divinity Test, 1873; MA 1876; BD and DD 1889. Curate of Tickenhall, Derbyshire, 1875–78; Vicar of Gillingham, 1878–1915. *Recreations:* music, walking, reading. *Address:* The Restoration House, Rochester. *T:* Chatham 373.

Died 27 March 1923.

ROBINSON, Rev. Arthur William, DD (Cantab); Residentiary Canon, Canterbury Cathedral, since 1916; *b* Keynsham Vicarage, Somerset, 19 Jan. 1856; *s* of Rev. George and Henrietta Cecilia Robinson; *m* 1918, Mary Beatrice, *d* of late Rev. Dr Moore, Canon of Canterbury; two *s* one *d. Educ:* Bristol Grammar School; Liverpool College; Jesus College, Cambridge (Carus University prize; 1st class Theological Tripos). Ordained as Curate to his father at St Augustine's, Liverpool, 1879; Rector of East Shefford, Berks, 1881; Vicar of Bilton, Harrogate, 1884; joined the Mission Staff of Allhallows, Barking, 1888; Vicar of Allhallows, Barking, 1895; Rural Dean of the East City, 1908; Six-preacher of Canterbury Cathedral, 1896; Examining Chaplain to the Bishop of London, 1909; Proctor in Convocation for Clergy of London, 1910; for the Chapter of Canterbury, 1919. *Publications:* The Church Catechism Explained; A Commentary on Tennyson's In Memoriam; The Epistle to the Galatians Explained; The Personal Life of the Clergy; Co-operation with God; The Voice of Joy and Health; Spiritual Progress; God and the World, a Survey of Thought; The Trend of Thought in Contemporary Philosophy; The Christ of the Gospels; The Christianity of the Epistles; The New Learning and the Old Faith; etc. *Address:* The Precincts, Canterbury.

Died 7 Dec. 1928.

ROBINSON, Rev. Charles Henry, DD; Hon. Canon of Ripon since 1897; Editorial Secretary to the Society for the Propagation of the Gospel, 1902; Lecturer in Hausa, University of Cambridge, 1896–1906; *b* Keynsham, 1861; *s* of Rev. G. Robinson, Monaghan, Ireland; *m* 1st, 1896, Clare, *d* of Joseph Arnold, Tunbridge Wells; one *d;* 2nd, 1907, Cecily, *d* of Sir Ernest George and Mary Allan, *d* of Robert Burn, Epsom; one *s* one *d. Educ:* Liverpool College; Trinity College, Cambridge. College and University Prizeman; BA 1883; MA 1888; Hon. DD Edinburgh, 1910. Deacon, 1884; Priest, 1885; Fellow and Tutor of St Augustine's College, Canterbury, 1889; Vice-Chancellor of Truro Cathedral, 1890–93; travelled in Armenia in order to report to Archbishop of Canterbury on the condition of Armenian Church, 1892; conducted pioneer expedition to Kano, the commercial centre of the Central Soudan, starting by way of the river Niger, after first making an ineffectual attempt to reach Kano by crossing the Great Sahara from the north, 1893–95. *Publications:* The Church and Her Teaching, 1893; Hausaland, or Fifteen Hundred Miles through the Central Soudan, 1896, 3rd edn 1900; Specimens of Hausa Literature, 1896; Grammar of the Hausa Language, 5th edn 1925; Mohammedanism: Has it any Future?, 1897; The Gospel of St John in Hausa, 1899; Dictionary of the Hausa Language, 4th edn 1924; Studies in the Character of Christ, 8th edn 1920; Nigeria, our latest Protectorate, 1900; Human Nature, a Revelation of the Divine, 3rd edn 1910; Studies in the Resurrection, 3rd edn 1911; Studies in Worship, 3rd edn 1910; The Interpretation of the Character of Christ to Non-Christian Races, 4th edn 1913; Studies in the Passion of Jesus Christ, 3rd edn 1916; Our Bounden Duty, 1912; A Devotional Psalter, 1912; The Missionary Prospect, 2nd edn, 1912; History of Christian Missions, 1915; The Conversion of Europe, 1918; How the Gospel spread through Europe, 1917; Life of Otto, Apostle of Pomerania, 1920; Life of Anskar, the Apostle of the North, 1921. *Address:* SPG House, 15 Tufton Street, SW1. *T:* Victoria 1398; 11 Croham Park Avenue, S Croydon. *T:* Croydon 1721.

Died 23 Nov. 1925.

ROBINSON, Maj.-Gen. Sir Charles Walker, KCB 1923 (CB 1887); retired (late Rifle Brigade); *b* Toronto, Canada, 3 April 1836; *y s* of Sir John Beverley Robinson, 1st Bt, CB, and Emma, *d* of Charles Walker of Harlesden, Middlesex; *m* 1884, Margaret Frances, *d* of Gen. Sir Archibald Alison, 2nd Bt, GCB, and Jane, *o d* of James Black; one *s* two *d. Educ:* Upper Canada Coll.; Trin. Coll., Toronto (BA and Hon. LLD). Joined Rifle Brig., 1857; passed through Staff College, 1865; served in the Indian Mutiny (medal); in Ashanti Expedition, 1873–74; Brigade-Major, European Brigade (despatches, medal with clasp and brev. of Major); Zulu War, 1879 (AAG 2nd Div.) (despatches, medal with clasp, brevet of Lt-Colonel); held appointments of Brigade Major, DAAG and AAG at Aldershot; Assistant Military Secretary Headquarters of the Army, 1890–92; commanding the troops, Mauritius, 1892–95; Lt-Governor and Secretary Royal Hospital, Chelsea, 1895–98; retired 1898. Decorated for military service. *Publications:* Strategy of the Peninsular War; Life of Sir John Beverley Robinson, Bt; Wellington's Campaigns, 1808–15; Canada and Canadian Defence. *Recreations:* riding, cycling. *Address:* 5 Stanford Road, Cottesmore Gardens, Kensington, W8. *Club:* Army and Navy.

Died 20 May 1924.

ROBINSON, Edward Kay; President of the British Empire Naturalists' Association; projector and editor of The Country-side, and Country Queries and Notes (both incorporated, with Science Gossip, in the monthly Country-side); naturalist and author; *b* Naini

Tal, 1857; *s* of late Rev. Julian Robinson, Indian Army Chaplain, and Harriet Woodcocke Sharpe; *m* 1887, Florence Theresa Gordon; two *s*. *Educ:* Cheltenham College. Originator of the "By the Way" column in The Globe; editor of the Civil and Military Gazette, Lahore, 1887-95; on staff of Globe, 1896-98; contributor to the Nineteenth Century, Fortnightly Review, etc. *Publications:* To-day with Nature, 1889; My Nature Notebook, 1901; In the King's County, 1903; The Country Day by Day, 1905; The Religion of Nature, 1906; The Meaning of Life, 1915; At Home with Nature (wireless talks), 1925. *Recreation:* natural history. *Address:* Warham, Hampton Wick.

Died 20 Jan. 1928.

ROBINSON, Sir Ernest William, 5th Bt, *cr* 1823; *b* 22 May 1862; *s* of late Major-General John Innes Robinson, ISC (*g s* of 1st Bt), and Bertha, *d* of Rev. G. A. Biedermann and *widow* of Col E. S. Swyng; *S* uncle, 1895; *m* 1st, 1897, Christina Eleanor (*d* 1916), *d* of Major Grant of Glen Grant, Rothes, NB; one *d*; 2nd, 1920, *widow* of Col Gordon Watson. *Heir: brother* Douglas Innes Robinson [*b* 24 Sept.1863; *m* 1903, cousin Violet, *d* of late Charles Herbert Ames]. *Address:* Jersey. *Died 21 Dec. 1924.*

ROBINSON, Frederic Cayley-, ARA 1921; RWS 1919; RBA 1888; ROI 1906; New English Art Club, 1912; Artistic Adviser, Haymarket Theatre, 1911; *b* Brentford-on-Thames, 18 Aug. 1862; *s* of Frederic Robinson; *m* 1896, Winifred Lucy Dalley; one *d*. *Educ:* Dr Head, Cliftonville; Lycée de Pau; Royal Academy Schools. Lived on a small yacht, 1888-90; painted The Outward Bound, The Ferry, Drifting, and other works; studied at Julian's, 1890-92; painted Souvenir of a Past Age (exhibited Royal Academy 1894, later in the Adelaide permanent collection), The Close of Day (exhibited Paris International Exhibition), 1892-98; The Foundling, Romance, and other works, 1900; studied in Italy, painted Fata Morgana, The Depth of Winter, Twilight, and other works, 1898-1902; worked in Paris, painted The Deep, Midnight, Dawn, and other works, 1902-6; Youth (in Cape Town permanent collection), The Farewell, Reminiscence, Waning Day, and other works, 1906-10; A Winter Evening and The Fisherman (both in Italian National Collections); The Death of Abel (in the Luxembourg Gallery, Paris); illustrated Genesis for the Medeci Society; Mural decorations for the Middlesex Hospital, 1910-14; painted The Word, 1922, purchased for the Canadian National Gallery, 1922; painted Pastoral, 1924, purchased for the nation under the terms of the Chantry Bequest. *Address:* 1 Lansdowne House, Lansdowne Road, W. *Died 4 Jan. 1927.*

ROBINSON, Rev. Henry; Rector of Badsworth, Yorks, since 1910; Canon and Prebendary of Ulleskelf in York Cathedral, 1908; Proctor and Synodal Secretary, York Convocation, 1904; *b* 1849; *s* of Mark A. and Sophia Robinson; *m* 1880, Caroline C. S., *d* of late Archibald Sturrock, VD, JP, Cadogan Place; two *d*. *Educ:* Pembroke College, Oxford (BA 1875; MA 1878). Took Holy Orders, 1875; Curate, St James's, Doncaster, 1875-79; Vicar, Grosmont, 1879-93; Rector, St Maurice, etc, York, 1893-1910; Hon. Chaplain to Archbishop of York, 1904-9. *Recreation:* motoring. *Address:* Badsworth Rectory, Pontefract. *M:* O 4365 and U 2206. *Clubs:* Junior Constitutional; Yorkshire, York. *Died 4 May 1918.*

ROBINSON, Rt. Hon. Sir Henry Augustus, 1st Bt, *cr* 1920; KCB 1900 (CB 1897); PC (Ireland) 1902; Vice-President of the Local Government Board for Ireland, 1898-1920; *b* 20 Nov. 1857; *s* of late Sir Henry Robinson, KCB, and Eva, *d* of Arthur Henry Medora, 10th Viscount Valentia; *m* 1885, Harriet, *d* of Sir Robert Lynch Blosse, 10th Bt, of Athavallie Balla, Co. Mayo, and Harriet, *d* of 2nd Marquis of Sligo; three *s*. *Publications:* Memoirs: Wise and Otherwise, 1923; Further Memories of Irish Life, 1924. *Heir: s* Christopher Henry Robinson, late Resident Magistrate, Co. Louth [*b* 18 Oct. 1884; *m* 1912, Dorothy Mary Augusta, *d* of Henry Charles Jackson Warren, of Carrickmines, Co. Dublin; one *s*. *Educ:* Wellington. *Address:* Highmoor, Parkstone]. *Clubs:* Carlton; Kildare Street, Dublin.

Died 16 Oct. 1927.

ROBINSON, Henry Betham, MD, MS London; FRCS; Surgeon to, and Lecturer on Surgery and Teacher of Operative Surgery at, St Thomas' Hospital; Consulting Surgeon to East London Hospital for Children, Shadwell, and to Children's Hospital, Plaistow; Major Royal Army Medical Corps (Territorial Force); *b* 6 Aug. 1860; *s* of Henry Robinson of West Norwood; *m* Eveline Louise, *y* surv. *d* of John Milling of Harrogate. *Educ:* Dulwich College; St Thomas's Hospital. Graduated as Bachelor of Medicine and Bachelor of Surgery in the University of London, 1885, obtaining the Scholarship and Gold Medal in Medicine and Gold Medal in Surgery; Surgeon for Diseases of the Throat, and Lecturer and Demonstrator of Anatomy at St Thomas's; Hunterian Professor of Surgery and Pathology at the Royal College of Surgeons, England, giving lectures on Diseases of the Breast, 1892; Examiner in Surgery, Universities of London and Manchester. *Publications:* St Thomas' Hospital Surgeons and the Practice of their Art in the Past; papers relating to surgery and diseases of the throat in medical periodicals. *Recreations:* golf, motoring. *Address:* 1 Upper Wimpole Street, W. *T:* Mayfair 5363. *M:* Y 732. *Club:* Sports. *Died 31 July 1918.*

ROBINSON, Captain Henry Harold, DSO 1916; MRCS, LRCP; Royal Army Medical Corps; Hon. Medical Officer Birkenhead Children's Hospital. *Educ:* Owens College, Manchester. Late Senior House Surgeon, Southport Infirmary; House Surgeon, Infirmary, Burton-on-Trent; served European War, 1914-17 (DSO). *Address:* 39 Park Road, South Birkenhead, and 38 Woodchurch Road, Birkenhead. *T:* 318. *Died 1919.*

ROBINSON, Sir John Holdsworth, Kt 1924; JP; a member of Council, Yorkshire Provincial Division, National Unionist Association; *b* 1855; *s* of James Robinson, Bradford. Chevalier, Legion of Honour. *Address:* Greenhill Hall, Bingley, Yorks. *Died 19 April 1927.*

ROBINSON, Rev. John J., DD Dublin; Warden of St John's College, and Head Master of Collegiate School, Winnipeg, since 1913; *b* Dublin; *s* of John Robinson, owner of Daily Express newspaper, and Isabella Boyd of Ballymacool, Co Donegal; *m* (Henrietta) Harriet (*sister* of 1st Baron Avebury), *y d* of Sir John William Lubbock, 3rd Bt, and Harriet, *d* of Lt-Col George Hotham; four *s* two *d*. *Educ:* Blackheath School; Trinity College, Dublin. Ordained, 1875; held curacies in England and Ireland; subsequently rector of Delgany, Co. Wicklow, and other places; Dean and Vicar of Belfast, 1903-11; Incumbent of St Andrew, Edmonton, Alberta, 1911-12; Rector of Christ Church, Edmonton, 1912-13. *Address:* St John's College, Winnipeg, Canada. *Club:* University, Dublin.

Died 14 June 1916.

ROBINSON, Rev. Ludovick Stewart; Vicar of Pershore, Worcestershire; Hon. Canon of Worcester, 1922; *b* 1864; *s* of Rev. Canon Charles Kirkby Robinson, DD (Master of St Catharine's College, Cambridge), and Margaret, *d* of Major Stewart of 24th Regt; *m* Ellen Duval, *d* of E. J. Mortlock, Banker, Cambridge; three *s* two *d*. *Educ:* Haileybury College; St Catharine's College, Cambridge; Clergy Training School. Curate St Andrew's, Haverstock Hill, NW; Chaplain to Bishop of Ripon and Inspector of Schools; Chaplain to Marquis of Zetland; Rector of Richmond, Yorks; Rural Dean of Richmond, W; Vicar of Bingley, Yorks; Rural Dean of South Craven; Rector of Keighley, Yorks; Hon. Canon of Ripon; Rural Dean of Pershore, 1920. *Recreations:* golf, lawn tennis. *Address:* Pershore Vicarage. *T:* Pershore 36. *M:* NP 1454.

Died 12 Oct. 1923.

ROBINSON, Sir Richard Atkinson, Kt 1916; DL, JP; *b* 16 Oct. 1849; *e s* of Henry Robinson, shipowner, Whitby; *m* 1876, Jeanie, *d* of Thomas Thistle, Whitby; two *s* three *d*. *Educ:* Pickering; Manchester. Chairman, London County Council, 1908-9; formerly member Thames Conservancy, Governor Imperial College of Science, London County Territorial Association, Alderman of Kensington, Hon. Treasurer, London Municipal Society; took a prominent part in political and municipal work for many years; was leader of the Municipal Reform Party on LCC, 1907, when it came into power for the first time. *Recreation:* outdoor life. *Address:* 19 Bagdale, Whitby. *Died 28 April 1928.*

ROBINSON, Robert Thomson, KC 1914; *b* Ireland, 1867; *s* of John Robinson of Albany, WA. *Educ:* Prince Alfred College, Adelaide. Barrister, Western Australia, 1889; formerly Attorney-General, Minister for Mines, and Minister for Industries and Woods and Forests, Western Australia. *Address:* Howard Street, Perth, Western Australia.

Died 19 Sept. 1926.

ROBINSON, Col Stapylton Chapman Bates, CB 1917; Officer Commanding Queen Mary's Military Hospital, Whalley, 1914-19; *b* 21 May 1855; *s* of late Maj.-Gen. Stapylton Robinson, RA; *m* 1899, Constance Mary, *e d* of Thomas Haydon Harrison, JP, of Broxbourne, Herts; two *s*. *Educ:* privately; St Thomas' Hospital. Surgeon, Army Medical Department, 1881; retired as Col 1912; was in India, Mediterranean, and South Africa; served South African Campaign (Queen's medal with 7 clasps, King's medal 2 clasps); Hon. County Director Hertfordshire Voluntary Aid Detachments, 1913-14; volunteered and was recalled to the Service, 14 Dec. 1914 (despatches, CB). *Address:* Roden Lodge, Hoddesdon, Herts. *Club:* Army and Navy. *Died 7 March 1927.*

ROBINSON, Sir Thomas, KBE 1917; JP; steam trawler owner, etc; County Councillor for the Parts of Lindsey; *b* 23 Jan. 1855; *s* of John and Betsy Robinson; *m* 1876, Cornelia Agnes (*d* 1921), *d* of George Wheeler; one *s* three *d*. *Educ:* Humberstone Grammar School. Left school 1869; started at sea, followed the sea, fishing fourteen years; commenced business on the Fish Dock, 1883, and continued as owner, salesman, fish-merchant; acted for some considerable time as Technical Adviser to the Board of Agriculture and Fisheries, Fisheries Dept, and the Fish Food Committee. *Recreations:* motoring, cycling, billiards. *Address:* Southlands, Cleethorpes; Fish Docks, Grimsby. *TA:* Reliance, Grimsby. *T:* Grimsby 615.
Died 8 Feb. 1927.

ROBINSON, Tom, MD; consulting physician; *b* East Keal, Spilsby, Lincolnshire; *m;* one *s*. *Educ:* Peterborough; The London Hospital. House Physician, House Surgeon, and Clinical Assistant; Gold Medallist in Medicine, Surgery, and Midwifery. *Publications:* works on eczema, syphilis, acne, baldness and greyness. *Recreation:* country life. *Address:* 9 Princes Street, Cavendish Square, W. *Clubs:* Authors', Green Room.
Died 7 May 1916.

ROBINSON, William Edward; MP (L) Burslem, 1923–24; *b* 1863; *s* of William Robinson, Stoke-on-Trent; *m* 1892, *d* of Thomas Cope. Alderman and former Mayor, Stoke-on-Trent. *Address:* The Mount, Porthill, Stoke-on-Trent.
Died 10 May 1927.

ROBINSON, Maj.-Gen. William Henry Banner, CB 1915; Indian Medical Service; Hon. Surgeon to King George V; *b* 7 Dec. 1863; *m* Elsie Marian, *d* of William Deane Butcher, MRCS. Entered IMS, 1886; served Burma, 1885–87 (despatches, medal, 2 clasps); Waristan Expedition, 1894–95 (clasp); Chitral, 1895 (medal with clasp); Tirah, 1897–98 (two clasps); European War, 1914–16 (CB, despatches twice); served under Foreign Department, Govt of India, as Residentiary Surgeon, Alwar, Bikanir, Jaipur, Marwar, Mount Abu, and as Chief Medical Officer in Rajputana; as Inspector-General Civil Hospitals, Central Provinces; and as Sanitary Commissioner Surgeon-General Govt of Bengal; officiating Dir.-Gen., IMS. *Clubs:* East India United Service; United Service, Calcutta.
Died 7 Feb. 1922.

ROBINSON, William Leefe, VC 1916; Worcestershire Regiment and Royal Flying Corps; *b* Tollidetta, S India, 14 July 1895; *s* of Horace Robinson, coffee planter, and Elizabeth Leefe; *g s* of W. C. Robinson, RN, Chief Naval Constructor, Portsmouth Dockyard. *Educ:* St Bee's School; Sandhurst. Entered army, 1914; joined Royal Flying Corps, March 1915; served European War (France), 1915 (wounded); was night pilot in England for seven months before bringing down first Zeppelin on English soil, at Cuffley, near London, on the morning of Sunday, 3 Sept. 1916 (VC).
Died 31 Dec. 1918.

ROBSON, Baron (Life Peer), *cr* 1910, of Jesmond; **Rt. Hon. William Snowdon Robson,** GCMG 1911; Kt 1905; PC 1910; KC; a Lord of Appeal in Ordinary, 1910–12; *b* 10 Sept. 1852; 3rd surv. *s* of late Robert Robson, JP, Newcastle; *m* 1887, Catherine Emily, *d* of late Charles Burge, of 7 Park Crescent, Portland Place; one *s* three *d*. *Educ:* privately; Caius College, Cambridge (Hon. Fellow; MA). Barrister, 1880; QC 1892; Bencher, Inner Temple, 1899; MP (L) Bow and Bromley, 1885–86; Recorder of Newcastle, 1895–1905; MP (L) South Shields, 1895–1910; Solicitor-General, 1905–8; Attorney-General, 1908–10; Hon. DCL Durham, 1906. *Address:* 26 Eaton Square, SW. *T:* Victoria 1336; 11 King's Bench Walk, Temple, EC. *Clubs:* Brooks's, Reform, Athenæum.
Died 11 Sept. 1918.

ROBSON, Edward Robert, FRIBA, FSA, FSI; in private practice at Westminster as architect and surveyor; *b* 2 March 1835; *e s* of late Robert Robson, JP, of Durham; *m* Marian, *e d* of late Henry Longden, Sheffield. *Educ:* private schools. Three years in shops for practical building construction; pupil, first of John Dobson, Newcastle-on-Tyne, then of G. Gilbert Scott, RA; travelled much in Europe, America and Canada; built Piccadilly Art Galleries, New Gallery, Regent Street, the People's Palace, with its Library and Queen's Hall, several hundred schools in London, also churches and mansions; was architect in charge of Durham Cathedral six years; surveyor to the Corporation of Liverpool seven years; then first architect to the School Board for London, and so continued until offered posts under Government. *Publications:* School Architecture; numerous articles and essays. *Recreations:* golf, bicycling, billiards. *Address:* Palace Chambers, Westminster, SW. *T:* Victoria 4292; Blackheath, SE. *Club:* St Stephen's.
Died 22 Jan. 1917.

ROBSON, Henry Naunton, MRCS, LRCP; Doctor, retired; a Vice-President of the Society for the Prevention of Venereal Disease; *b* Richmond, Surrey, 1861; father and mother English; unmarried. *Educ:* Westminster School; St Thomas's Hospital, London. RMO at Stroud Hospital, Glos; spent several years travelling in Europe, Asia, America and Australia trying to find a preventative remedy for venereal disease; the first doctor on the British Register to publish a book advocating the medical prevention of venereal diseases. *Publication:* Sexual Disease and its Medical Prevention, 1909. *Recreations:* formerly golf, rifle-shooting, rowing. *Address:* 6 Vale Road, Bournemouth. *Club:* Junior Constitutional.
Died 1 July 1925.

ROBSON, Robert, ISO 1906; *b* 15 Feb. 1845; *s* of late Thomas Robson, formerly of Great Ayton in Cleveland; *m* 1st, 1870, Margaret Ann (*d* 1888), *o d* of late James Kelly, Newcastle-on-Tyne; 2nd, 1892, Helen Julia (*d* 1913), *e d* of James J. Hicks, KCSG, Highbury Grove and Hatton Garden; four *s* one *d*. *Educ:* private tuition; BA Honours, 1865. Entered Customs Service as Clerk and Examining Officer at Middlesbrough, 1866; transferred to Secretary's Office of Department, 1867; nominated by Secretary of State to reorganise the Customs Service in the Island of Trinidad, 1876; and on staff of Lord Wolseley to organise Customs and Excise Services in Cyprus, 1878; Private Secretary to Deputy Chairman of Customs, 1883–86; Principal Clerk, 1886–90; Committee Clerk, 1890–1900; Surveyor-General, 1900–6; Collector of the Port of London and Chief Registrar of Shipping, 1906; retired, 1910; President of the Customs Annuity and Benevolent Fund Incorporated, 1916; retired, 1917. *Address:* 56 York Road, Tunbridge Wells.
Died 15 Aug. 1928.

ROCHE, Alexander, RSA; painter; corresponding member of Munich Secession; *b* Glasgow, 17 Aug. 1861; *m* 1906, Jean, *d* of Robert Alexander, RSA. *Educ:* Glasgow; Paris. Started as an architect, but liking painting better, went to Paris and studied there; tried all sorts of subjects, landscape and figure. Best works—Tête-à-tête (Gold Medal, Munich), 1891; Squall on the Clyde (Honourable Mention, Salon), 1892; Idyll (bought by the Auckland Picture Gallery), 1892; Landscape (Gold Medal, Dresden), 1897; The Window-Seat (Medal, Pittsburg, and bought for Permanent Gallery), 1898; Spring (Medal, Paris International), 1900; Margaret (Scottish National Gallery), 1900; frescoes decorating Banqueting Hall, Glasgow Municipal Buildings, 1900; Prue (bought by Munich Gallery), 1902; An Old Song (bought for Stuttgart Public Museum), 1902; Mrs Andrew Carnegie and daughter, 1903; Nancy (bought by Walker Art Gallery, Liverpool), 1904; Portrait of Miss Flora Stevenson, LLD (National Portrait Gallery, Edinburgh), 1905; In Maiden Meditation Fancy Free (Museum, Odessa), 1905; The Building of the Ship (Municipal Gallery of Modern Art, Dublin), 1905; Landscape (bought by the Modern Arts Association, Scotland), 1908; Pittenweem Harbour (presented to the Modern Arts Association, Scotland), 1908; The Prison Gate, Mogador; self-portrait bought by Modern Arts Association, 1916; Here Ouse slow winding thro' a Lonely Plain, bought by Glasgow Corporation, 1918. *Publications:* Finish in Art (Transactions of the National Association for the Advancement of Art), 1889; several essays and lectures on art subjects. *Clubs:* Scottish Arts, Edinburgh; Glasgow Arts.
Died 10 March 1921.

ROCHE, Col Hon. Ulick de Rupe Burke, CB 1900; late commanding South Wales Borderers; retired 1903; *b* 16 Jan. 1856; 4th *s* of 1st Baron Fermoy and Eliza Caroline, *e d* of James R. Boothby; *m* 1st, 1882, Agnes Blair (*d* 1905), *e d* of General Jasper Otway Mayne, RE; 2nd, Dorothea Blanche, *d* of John Jones of Ynysfor, Penrhyndeudraeth, N Wales; one *s*. Entered army, 1876; Capt. 1881; Major, 1891; Lt-Col 1899; served Kaffir War, 1877–78 (medal with clasp); Burmese Expedition, 1886–89 (medal with two clasps); South Africa, 1900–2 (despatches, Queen's medal, 3 clasps, King's medal, 2 clasps, DSO); DAAG Bengal, 1890–95; commanded 11th Service Batt. Royal Welsh Fusiliers, 1914–15. *Address:* Saffronhill, Doneraile, Co. Cork.
Died 13 April 1919.

ROCHE, Hon. William; Senator since 1910; *b* Halifax, NS, 1842. *Educ:* Halifax, NS. MP, 1900–8; Pres., Halifax Fire Insurance Company. *Address:* Halifax, Nova Scotia.
Died 19 Oct. 1925.

ROCHFORT, Maj.-Gen. Sir Alexander Nelson, KCB 1911 (CB 1900); CMG 1904; Royal Artillery; Lieutenant-Governor and Commanding troops, Jersey, 1910–16; *b* 3 June 1850; 5th *s* of late Horace William Noel Rochfort, DL, of Clogrenane, and Hon. Charlotte, *d* of 2nd Baron Bridport. Entered army, 1871; Captain, 1881; Brevet Major, 1885; Lieut-Col, 1886; Colonel, 1900; Maj.-Gen. 1907; served Soudan, 1885 (despatches, Brevet major, medal with clasp, Khedive's star); South Africa, 1899–1902 (severely wounded, despatches twice, Queen's medal, 4 clasps, King's medal, 2 clasps, CB); special service, Somaliland, 1902–4 (despatches, and general service African medal with clasp, CMG); Inspector Horse and Field Artillery, 1904–10. *Address:* Government House, Jersey. *Clubs:* Naval and Military, Arthur's.

Died 5 Dec. 1916.

ROCHFORT-BOYD, Lt-Col Henry Charles, DSO 1915; Royal Horse Artillery; *b* 13 Oct. 1877; *s* of Col C. A. Rochfort-Boyd; *m* 1908, Dorothy, *d* of Arthur Nicholson; one *s*. *Educ:* Charterhouse; RMA Woolwich. Entered army, 1897; Captain, 1904; Major, 1914; served S African War, 1899–1900 (despatches twice, Queen's medal 3 clasps); European War, 1914–17 (despatches thrice, DSO, three times wounded). *Address:* Belvedere House, Farnborough, Hants. *Club:* Army and Navy.   *Died 4 Dec. 1917.*

RODDICK, Sir Thomas George, Kt 1914; MD, CM; Hon. FRCS; *b* Harbour Grace, Newfoundland, 31 July 1846; *s* of John Irving Roddick; *m* 1st, 1880, (Urelia) Marion (*d* 1890), *d* of late Hugh Mackinnon; 2nd, 1906, Amy, *o d* of late J. J. Redpath, Montreal. *Educ:* McGill University. Surgeon, Montreal General Hospital, 1874; Consulting Surgeon to Montreal General and Royal Victoria Hospital; Governor, McGill University; Professor of Surgery, 1890–1907; Dean of Medical Faculty, 1901–8; President, British Medical Association, 1896–98; Hon. President Medical Council, Canada; Hon. President Canadian Medical Association; served NW Rebellion, 1885 (despatches, medal); Fenian Raid, 1870 (medal and clasp); Member for Montreal West, Canadian Parliament, 1896–1904; Hon. LLD Edinburgh, and Queen's Univ. at Kingston. *Address:* 705 Sherbrooke Street West, Montreal. *Clubs:* University, Mount Royal, Montreal.   *Died 20 Feb. 1923.*

RODIN, Auguste, DCL Oxon; sculptor; President International Society of Painters, Sculptors, Engravers; *b* Paris, 1840; *m* Rose Beurre (*d* 1917). A workman in ateliers of Barye and Carrier-Belleuse, 1864–70; Associé de Van Rasbourg (Brussels), 1871–77. *Works:* L'Homme au Nez Cassé, 1864; L'Age d'Airain, 1877; St-Jean prêchant and The Creation of Man, 1882; La Cariatide; La Danaïde; monument to Victor Hugo; Balzac; Le Baiser, 1886; l'Eve; Les Bourgeois de Calais, 1889; Le Penseur, 1905; La Porte de l'Enfer; Le Frère et la Sœur; Le Printemps; L'éternelle Idole; La Guerre; Psyche; Amor Fugit; L'Homme qui s'éveille; Art; busts of Jean Paul Laurens, Carrier-Belleuse, Victor Hugo, Antonin Proust, Dalou, 1882–85, and of Puvis de Chavannes, Falguièr, Henri Rochefort, Becque, Octave Mirbeau, Mme M. V., etc. *Address:* rue de l'Université, No 182, Paris; Meudon-Val-Fleury, Seine-et-Oise.

Died 18 Nov. 1917.

RODWAY, James, FLS; Curator British Guiana Museum; Librarian and Assistant Secretary Royal Agricultural and Commercial Society of British Guiana, 1888–1926; *b* Trowbridge, Wilts, 1848; *m* 1873, Kate Reedon, creole of Demerara; eleven *c*. *Educ:* Trowbridge. Chemist until 1888; naturalist from boyhood; studied British flora before leaving for British Guiana, 1870; made a special study of the Colony from every standpoint, the people, history, geography, fauna and flora, as well as the economic products which may be developed; specially interested in the life histories of plants and animals, and their interdependence. *Publications:* History of British Guiana, 3 vols; Handbook of British Guiana; In the Guiana Forest; Story of Forest and Stream; West Indies and Spanish Main (Story of the Nations Series); In Guiana Wilds (a story); Guiana, British, Dutch, and French; papers in Longman's Magazine, Cornhill, Popular Science Monthly, etc. *Recreations:* change of work, collecting, gardening—from the study to the field and forest. *Address:* Georgetown, British Guiana.

Died 19 Nov. 1926.

ROE, 1st Baron, *cr* 1916; **Thomas Roe,** Kt 1894; *b* 13 July 1832; *s* of Thomas Roe (formerly Mayor of Derby), and Deborah, *d* of Absolam Oakley, Derby; *m* 1903, Emily (*d* 1909), *d* of late Matthew Kirtley. Mayor of Derby, 1867–68, 1896–97, and 1910–11; MP (C) Derby, 1883–95 and 1900–16; JP for Derby and Derbyshire. *Heir:* none. *Address:* Litchurch, Derby. *Club:* National Liberal.

Died 7 June 1923 (ext).

ROE, Sir Charles Arthur, Kt 1897; *b* 24 Sept. 1841; *s* of John Banister Roe, of Blandford, Dorset; *m* 1865, Elizabeth (d 1891), *d* of late Frederick Gaskell; two *s* one *d*. *Educ:* Merton College, Oxford. Entered Bengal Civil Service, 1863; retired 1898; was Chief Judge of Chief Court of the Punjab and Vice-Chancellor of the Punjab University (Hon. LLD 1899); represented the University of Oxford at the opening of the New Law Schools of the University of Pennsylvania, 1900, and received from the latter university the degree of LLD. *Publication:* Tribal Law in the Punjab. *Address:* 1 Holywell Street, Oxford.   *Died 28 Jan. 1927.*

ROE, Brig.-Gen. Cyril Harcourt, CMG 1919; CIE 1916; *b* 15 Oct. 1864. Lieut RE, 1884; Capt. 1892; Major, 1901; Lt-Col 1908; Col 1912; served Burma, 1886–87 (medal, two clasps); Burma, 1893 (clasp); DAAG Bangalore District, 1904–8; served European War, 1914–19 (despatches twice, CMG, CIE); retired on Indian pension. *Address:* Rydal Mount, Kidderminster Road, Bromsgrove, Worcestershire.   *Died 26 Nov. 1928.*

ROE, Rev. Robert Gordon, MA; Rector of Acle since 1923; Hon. Canon of Norwich, 1918; Rural Dean, Walsingham, 1919; *b* 1860; *s* of Robert Roe (artist in miniatures) and Maria, *d* of Rev. W. G. Plees, Vicar of Ash Bocking, Suffolk; *m* 1885, Isabel Alice, *d* of Lt Col John Anthony Kysh, 5th Northumberland Fusiliers; two *s* three *d*. *Educ:* The Perse School, Cambridge; St Catharine's College, Cambridge. Ordained, 1885; Priest, 1886; Curacies at Weaverham, Cheshire; Teddington, Middlesex; Vicar of Badwell Ash, Suffolk, with Hunston, 1888; Priest in charge of St Stephens, Buckhurst Hill, 1890; Rector of Blo' Norton, Norfolk, 1895–99; Vicar of King's Lynn, 1895–1909; Rural Dean of Lynn, Marshland; Rector of Leiston, Suffolk, 1909–15; Rector of Blakeney with Glandford and Cockthorpe, 1915–23. *Publications:* article on Old Stained Glass of St Edmundsbury, etc. *Recreations:* archæological; painting in water-colours. *Address:* The Rectory, Acle, Norfolk.

Died 19 May 1927.

ROE, Rev. Robert James; Hon. Canon of Truro. *Address:* Lanteglos Rectory, Camelford, Cornwall.

Died 29 July 1921.

ROE, Dep. Surg.-Gen. William Carden; *b* 1834; 3rd *s* of late William Roe of Lismore House, Queen's Co.; *m* 1864, Emily Louisa (*d* 1894), 3rd *d* of General William Twistleton Layard. Served in the Crimea and Indian Mutiny Campaigns; retired, 1880. *Address:* Loran Park, Roscrea; Shackenhurst, West Cliff, Bournemouth. *M:* EL 996.   *Died 8 Oct. 1922.*

ROE, Lt-Col William Francis, DSO 1916; LRCSI; late Royal Army Medical Corps (Territorial Force); Surgeon White Star Line since 1923; *b* 4 May 1871; *e s* of late William Roe, MD, Dublin; *m* 1900, Emma Mary Alexandrina, 3rd *d* of late Benjamin Ormsby, Blackrock, Co. Dublin; one *d*. Acted as surgeon on Bibby Line; had practice in Northampton Square, EC, previous to War; Volunteer Bloomsbury Rifles, 1903 (Queen Victoria Rifles (amalgamated), TF); Lecturer and Examiner First Aid, LCC; Major, 1915; Temp. Lt-Col, 1916; served European War, 1914–19 (despatches twice, DSO); resigned commission 1922. *Address:* 35 Ladbroke Road, W11. *Club:* Royal Automobile.   *Died 23 June 1925.*

ROFF, William George, ISO 1911; late Inspector of Dockyard Accounts, Admiralty; retired, 1918; *b* 20 May 1858; *s* of late William Roff, RN. *Educ:* privately; Admiralty School, Portsmouth Dockyard. Entered Admiralty Service, 1872; Yard Accounts Branch of the Admiralty Office, 1882; professional assistant to Inspector of Dockyard Accounts, 1891; officer in charge of accounts of Chatham Dockyard, 1895; Senior Assistant Inspector, Admiralty, 1901–4; Member of the Bournemouth County Borough Council from 1920. *Address:* St Faith, Castlemain Avenue, Bournemouth.

Died 25 Aug. 1926.

ROGER, Captain Archibald, ISO 1913; District Magistrate, St Kitts, Leeward Islands; *b* Tortola, Virgin Islands, 27 Nov. 1842; *s* of late James Dean Roger, St Kitts, West Indies and Bridge of Allan, Scotland; *m* Alicia Julia, *d* of late William Henry Hall, Nassau, Bahamas; two *d*. *Educ:* Collegiate School, Glasgow; College, Brunswick, Germany. Ensign 2nd Royal Lanark Militia, 1859; joined 2nd West India Regiment, 1860; Lieut, 1861; Captain, 1866; exchanged to 1st Batt., 17th Regiment, 1867; sold out, 1870; private secretary to Mr Bayley, Governor of the Bahamas, 1860–63; Fort-Adjutant, Jamaica, 1863–64; Police Magistrate, Rural District, St Christopher, 1873; District Magistrate, 1874; Commissioner of Oaths; Official Member, Legislative Council, 1896–1900; Executive Council, 1914; Acting Administrator, St Kitts-Nevis, in 1912, 1913, 1914, and 1915. *Address:* Romneys, St Kitts, West Indies.

ROGERS, His Honour Benjamin; President of Rogers & Co., Ltd, General Merchants; *b* 7 Aug. 1837; parents immigrants from Caermarthenshire, Wales, about 1831; *m* 1st, 1862, Susannah Abell (*d* 1897), *d* of late Capt. William Hubbard, Tignish, PEI; three *s* three *d*; 2nd, 1898, Annie M., *d* of late James Hunter of Kilmahumaig, Argyllshire. *Educ:* District School Course at Bedeque, PEI. Member Legislative Council, 1878–93; President of Council, 1890–93; Member of Amalgamated Council and Assembly, 1893–97, 1900–4;

Member of several Administrations, and Provincial Secretary, Treasurer, and Minister of Agriculture, 1900–4; Lieut.-Gov. Prince Edward Island, 1910–15. *Address:* Alberton, Prince Edward Island.
Died 16 May 1923.

ROGERS, Rev. Charles Fursdon, MA Oxon; Hon. Canon Truro; retired; licensed preacher and surrogate, Diocese of Truro; *b* 19 June 1848; *s* of John Jope Rogers of Penrose, Co. Cornwall; *m* 1877, Frances Fox (*d* 1926), *d* of Preb. Harvey, Rector of Truro; one *s* three *d*. *Educ:* Winchester College; Trinity College, Oxford (2nd Cl. Mathematics). Assistant Curate, Loughton, Essex, 1872–75; St Mary, Truro, 1875–77; Organising Secretary, National Society, 1877–88; Vicar of Mithian, Cornwall, 1888–91; Sithney, 1891–1901; Penzance, 1901–16; Rural Dean of Kirrier, 1898–1901; Penwith, 1913–16. *Address:* The Manor Cottage, Goldsithney, Marazion, Cornwall. *Club:* Cornwall County, Truro.   *Died 13 Aug. 1928.*

ROGERS, Francis Edward Newman, JP Wilts; Commissioner, Board of Agriculture, 1911; *b* 26 Dec. 1868; *s* of Walter Lacy Rogers of Rainscombe, Pewsey, Wilts, and Hermione Lucy, *d* of John James Edward Hamilton and *sister* of Sir Edward Archibald Hamilton, 4th Bt, Iping House, Midhurst; *m* 1893, Louisa Annie, *d* of Edward Jennings of Gellidég, Carmarthenshire; one *s* one *d*. *Educ:* Eton; Balliol College, Oxford. Contested (L) E Wilts, 1900, S Wilts, Dec. 1910; MP (L) East Wilts, 1906–10; worked on Wilts CC, 1894–1911, and other local bodies; farmer. *Recreations:* shooting, fishing, nature study. *Address:* Rainscombe, Marlborough, Wilts. *Club:* Brooks's.
Died 28 March 1925.

ROGERS, Ven. George Herbert; Archdeacon of Rockhampton and Examining Chaplain since 1907; *s* of Rev. Thomas Percival Rogers, Vicar of Batheaston, and Mary Robinson, *d* of C. E. Broome, of Elmhurst, Batheaston; unmarried. *Educ:* Lancing (Exhibitioner); Magdalen College, Oxford (Demy; MA); Leeds Clergy School. Ordained, 1896; Curate of Holy Trinity, Leeds, 1896–99; St Hugh's Missioner, 1899–1900; Vicar of Hainton, 1900–6; Rector of St Paul's Cathedral, Rockhampton, 1907–16; Organizing Secretary Home Mission Fund, 1917. *Address:* Lis Escop, Rockhampton, Queensland, Australia. *TA:* Archdeacon, Rockhampton.
Died 6 Dec. 1926.

ROGERS, Col George William, DSO 1889; *b* 1843; *m* 1892, Janie Isabella, *d* of Maj.-Gen. J. S. Rawlins. Served Lushai Expedition, 1871–72 (medal with clasp); Afghan War, 1878–80 (despatches, medal, three clasps, bronze star); DAAG, Bengal, 1884–86; served Sikkim Expedition, 1888.   *Died 27 April 1917.*

ROGERS, Henry Wade, AM, LLD; Judge of United States Circuit Court of Appeals, 2nd Judiciary Circuit, since 1913; Emeritus Professor of Law at Yale University, since 1921; *b* Holland Patent, New York, 10 Oct. 1853; *m* 1876, Emma Ferdon Winner (*d* 1922). *Educ:* Univ. of Michigan. Barrister, 1877; Professor in Michigan University Law School, 1883; Dean, 1885–90; President of Northwestern University, Evanston-Chicago, Illinois, 1890–1900; Prof. in Yale Law School, 1900; Dean of Yale University Law School, 1903–16; former President of Association of American Law Schools; former Chairman of American Bar Association's Section on Legal Education; late Chairman of American Bar Association's Committee on Legal Education and Admissions to the Bar; late Chairman of Council on Legal Education; Hon Member of the Bar Associations of Connecticut, Kansas, Illinois, Missouri, New York; President of the Peace Congress of New England States, Hartford, Conn, May 1910; Chairman, World's Congress on Jurisprudence and Law Reform, Chicago, 1893; President of the Layman's Association of the Methodist Episcopal Church in the United States; Methodist Episcopal; President of National Council of Schools of Religion. *Publication:* Treatise on Expert Testimony. *Address:* New Haven, Connecticut, USA. *T:* 691. *Clubs:* Graduates, New Haven; University, Evanston, Illinois; Alpha Delta Phi, Yale, NY.
Died 16 Aug. 1926.

ROGERS, Lt-Col Sir John Godfrey, KCMG 1898 (CMG 1896); DSO 1886; late Director-General Sanitary Department, Egypt; *b* 11 April 1850; *s* of George Frederick Rogers; *m* 1883, Edith Louisa Julie, CBE, Lady of Grace St John of Jerusalem, *d* of late Major W. H. F. Sykes, Bombay Cavalry. *Educ:* Trinity Coll., Dublin (BA, MB, MCh). Entered Army Medical Department, 1871; Surg.-Major, 1882; Surg. Lieut-Col., 1891; retired, 1892; Lt-Col RAMC 1896; served Afghan War, 1878–81 (medal); Egypt, 1882; present at Kassassin and Tel-el-Kebir (despatches, medal with clasp, bronze star, promoted Surg.-Major); Nile Expedition, 1884–85 (despatches, 3rd Cl. Osmanieh); Soudan Frontier Field Force, 1885–86 (despatches,

clasp, DSO); Suakin Field Force, 1888–89, as PMO of Force (despatches, clasp, 2nd Cl. Medjidie); Principal Medical Officer Egyptian Army, 1883–92; Director-General Sanitary Department, 1892–99 (2nd class Osmanieh, Grand Cordon Medjidie); Commissioner of the British Red Cross, Cairo, 1915–18; Bt Col, 1 Jan. 1919; 2nd class Order of the Nile, 1918; Knight of Grace St John of Jerusalem, 1918. *Publication:* Sport in Vancouver and Newfoundland, 1912. *Recreations:* fishing, shooting. *Address:* Whitelands, Edenbridge, Kent. *Clubs:* Junior United Service; Turf, Cairo.   *Died 10 Jan. 1922.*

ROGERS, Sir Robert Hargreaves, Kt 1897; Sheriff of London, 1896–97; Deputy-Alderman; Member of Common Council; Chairman of R. H. & S. Rogers, Ltd, shirt manufacturers of London and Coleraine; Governor of St Thomas' Hospital; *b* 20 Jan. 1850; *s* of Thomas Rogers, Sevenoaks, and Priscilla, *d* of Robert Hargreaves Self, London; *m* 1877, Jane, *d* of William Stark, Croydon. *Educ:* Roxborough House, Liverpool Road, Islington. Entered Common Council, 1886; made Deputy, 1890; Chairman of Finance and Improvement Committee, 1900; Chairman of the Gresham Committee, 1901; Chairman of City School of Music, 1891; Deputy-Governor of Irish Society, 1894; Jubilee Medal, 1897, and Officers' Order of Leopold of Belgium. *Recreation:* gardening. *Address:* Marl House, Bexley, Kent. *TA:* Producing, London. *T:* 97 Bexley Heath. *M:* D 5831. *Clubs:* City Carlton, Royal Automobile; Dartford Conservative.   *Died 30 Nov. 1924.*

ROGERS, Roland, MusD Oxon; Organist, Bangor Cathedral; *b* West Bromwich, Staffordshire, 17 Nov. 1847. *Educ:* privately. Organist, St John's, Wolverhampton, 1862; Tettenhall Parish Church, 1867; Bangor Cathedral, 1872; resigned, 1891; reappointed, 1906; choir trainer and adjudicator. *Publications:* cantatas: Prayer and Praise; The Garden; Floribel; a large number of part songs, including The River Floweth; organ compositions and anthems. *Address:* Cibrhedyn, Bangor, N Wales.   *Died July 1927.*

ROGERSON, Capt. John Edwin, OBE 1919; DL; JP; MP (U) Barnard Castle Division of Durham, 1922–23; *b* 8 Jan. 1865; *e s* of late John Rogerson, CE, Croxdale, Durham; *m* 1892, Frances Mary, *y d* of Pierse Creagh, Mount Elva, Co. Clare; one *s* two *d*. *Educ:* Durham; Trinity College, Cambridge (BA Hist. Tripos, 1886; MA 1892). Associate Institute Civil Engineers; Director of various iron and coal companies on North-East coast; Alderman for County Durham; Sheriff, 1905–6; contested Barnard Castle, 1918; Secretary Durham County Territorial Force Association, 1914–19, Chairman, 1920; Master of North Durham Foxhounds from 1888. *Recreations:* hunting, shooting, racing. *Address:* Mount Oswald, Durham. *T:* Nat. 67. *M:* J 1243. *Clubs:* Carlton, Boodle's; Durham County, Durham; Yorkshire, York.   *Died 23 March 1925.*

ROHAN, Duchesse de, (dowager); Herminie de Verteillac; Chevalier de la Légion d'Honneur; Superintendent of the Nursing Staff of military hospital VG 81 Hôtel-Rohan in Paris; *o c* of Marquis de Verteillac; *widow* of Duke de Rohan, deputy conseiller général major of Jasselin, Morbihan; one *s* (Vicomte de Rohan, lieutenant pilote aviateur) two *d* (Princesse Lucien Murat and Marchioness de Caraman); eleven *g c*, including the Duke de Rohan. Lecturer; painter in water-colours; member of the Société des Gens de Lettres des Poètes français, des Artistes français, de l'Union des Femmes peintres et sculpteurs, de la Société Internationale du Syndicat des Femmes peintres et sculpteurs (médaille de Vernueil à l'exposition de Vichy), de la Société d'Histoire de France, de la Société diplomatique, du Comité de Prix Femina; présidente des gymnastes du cardinal archevêque de Paris, des comités belges et serbes et des cantines anglaises; et du comité France Amérique; et présidente des femmes alliées de la grande guerre; decorated with the Médaille de Vermeil des Épidemies, de l'Insigne Spécial et de la Reconnaissance Italienne; Commandeur de l'Ordre Serbe de St Sava de celui de la Charité Serbe. *Publications:* Le Chant du Cygne; before the War, wrote four books, three of poetry, one in prose. *Address:* 35 boulevard des Invalides, Paris. *Clubs:* Lyceum, Interallié, Paris.
Died April 1926.

ROLFE, Rev. Harry Roger; Vicar of St Michael's, Derby, since 1885; Hon. Canon, Southwell Cathedral; Surrogate; Hon. Secretary Derbyshire DPAS; Chairman, Derby Board of Guardians; Assessor under the Clergy Discipline Act; *b* 1851; *s* of William Rowland Rolfe, Sudbury, Suffolk. Ordained Curate of Beighton and Staveley, Derbyshire, 1874; Vicar of Misson, Notts, 1884; Rural Dean of Derby, 1908–10. *Address:* St Michael's Vicarage, Derby. *TA:* Canon Rolfe, Derby.   *Died 18 Aug. 1924.*

ROLL, Sir James, 1st Bt, *cr* 1921; Lord Mayor of London, 1920–21; *b* 9th Dec. 1846; *s* of Nathaniel Roll; *m* 1867, Emma, *d* of James Gilding; two *s*. Fifty years with Pearl Assurance Company: commenced as a representative and became Chairman (retired, 1916); Common Councilman for Bridge Ward, Sheriff of the City, 1909–10; was Alderman of Billingsgate Ward, Member of the Paviors', Horners', Glovers' and Carmen's Companies; a prominent Freemason, holding the craft rank of Past Grand Treasurer; President of the Pickwick Coaching Club; Chairman of Charles Webster, Ltd, and Chapman & Sons, Eastbourne, Ltd. *Recreation:* coaching. *Heir:* *s* Frederick James Roll [*b* 20 Sept. 1873; *m* 1899, Kate Helen, *d* of John West, Leytonstone; two *d*]. *Address:* The Chestnuts, Wanstead, E11. *T:* Wanstead 134. *Died 30 Jan. 1927.*

ROLLAND, Brig.-Gen. Stewart Erskine; Indian Army; *b* 1846; *s* of Capt. C. W. Rolland, Madras Artillery; *m* E. S. Cammerer; one *s* two *d*. *Educ:* Edinburgh Academy; Bonn; Kensington Grammar School; Sandhurst. Ensign, 2/19th Yorks Regt, 1866; 26th MI, 1868–95; Burmese War, 1885–89, commanding Western Frontiers and Movable Column, Action at Segu (severely wounded, despatches twice, Bt Lt-Col, medal 2 clasps); on Staff, 1887–96; commanding Chin Hills, 1894–95; AQMG, Headquarters, Madras, 1895–96; Brig.-Gen. Southern, Rangoon, and Belgaum Dists, 1896–99; thanks of Government for services during plague while commanding Belgaum District; received thanks of OC Lines of Communications and Chief of Staff, Upper Burma Field Force; Hon. Brig.-Gen. and Col 86th Carnatic Infantry, 1912; Inspector, Ealing Special Constabulary, X Division, 1914–16. *Address:* 8 Woodville Road, Ealing, W5. *Died 11 Jan. 1927.*

ROLLESTON, Sir John Fowke Lancelot, Kt 1897; JP, DL; MP (U) Hertford, 1910–16; *b* 26 March 1848; *e s* of Rev. William Lancelot Rolleston and Mary Sophia, *e d* of late Sir Frederick Gustavus Fowke, 1stBt; *m* 1st, 1874, Catherine (*d* 1891), *d* of Charles Adshead, Brighton; 2nd, 1892, Eliza, *d* of late George Morant, Farnborough, Hants. *Educ:* Repton School; Applied Science Department, King's College, London. President Surveyors' Institution, 1901; Chairman Investment Registry, Ltd; Director Law Union and Rock Assurance Co.; Chairman Leicester Conservative Association, 1889–1909; contested (C) Leicester borough, 1894, 1895, 1900, and twice in 1906; MP (C) Leicester, 1900–6; Liveryman of the City and Master of the Spectacle Makers' Company; Knight of Grace, St John of Jerusalem; member of Grand Council Primrose League from 1896; Senior Deacon, Grand Lodge of Freemasons. *Recreations:* arboriculture, travel; President Fosse Football Club, 1896. *Address:* Glen Parva Grange, Leicester; 54 Curzon Street, W. *T:* Gerrard 8115. *Clubs:* Carlton, Junior Carlton, Royal Automobile. *Died 9 April 1919.*

ROLLESTON, Thomas William; author and journalist; *b* Glasshouse Shinrone, King's Co., 1857; 3rd *s* of Charles Rolleston-Spunner, QC, and Elizabeth, *d* of Rt Hon. John Richards, Chief Baron of the Court of Exchequer, Ireland; *m* 1st, 1879, Edith, *d* of Rev. William de Burgh, DD; 2nd, 1897, Maud, *d* of late Rev. Stopford A. Brooke; five *s* three *d*. *Educ:* St Columba's College, Rathfarnham; Trinity College, Dublin. Lived in Germany, 1879–83; Editor, Dublin University Review, 1885–86; Assistant-Editor, New Irish Library, 1893; Managing Director and Secretary, Irish Industries' Association, 1894–97; Leader-writer, Dublin Daily Express, and Dublin Correspondent, Daily Chronicle, 1898–1900; Organiser of Lectures, etc, to the Department of Agriculture and Technical Instruction, Ireland, 1900–5; Organiser Irish Historic Loan Collection, St Louis Exhibition, 1904; First Hon. Secretary, Irish Literary Society, London, 1892–93; Hon. Secretary, Irish Arts and Crafts Society, 1898–1908; Hon. Secretary India Society, 1910; Taylorian Lecturer, Oxford, 1892. *Publications:* The Encheiridion of Epictetus (translated with introduction and notes), 1881; The Teaching of Epictetus, 1888; Grashalme (German translation of Walt Whitman, with Dr K. Knortz), 1889; Life of Lessing, 1889; Treasury of Irish Poetry (edited with Stopford Brooke), 1900; Imagination and Art in Gaelic Literature, 1900; Parallel Paths: a Study in Biology, Ethics and Art, 1908; Sea Spray (poems), 1909; The High Deeds of Finn, 1910; Myths and Legends of the Celtic Race, 1911. *Address:* 16 Prince Arthur Road, Hampstead, NW3. *T:* Hampstead 6700. *Died 5 Dec. 1920.*

ROLLIT, Sir Albert Kaye, Kt 1885; Consul-General for Roumania in London since 1911; *b* Hull, 1842; *s* of John Rollit, solicitor, of Hull, and Eliza, *d* of Joseph Kaye, JP, architect, of Huddersfield; *m* 1st, 1872, Eleanor Anne (*d* 1885), 2nd *d* of late William Bailey, JP, of Winestead Hall, Holderness; 2nd, 1896, Mary Caroline, Duchess of Sutherland (*d* 1912), *d* of late Rev. Dr Michell, Principal of Hertford College, Oxford. *Educ:* King's College (Fellow); University of London (Fellow

and Member of Senate). BA 1st class honours, 1863; LLB 1st class honours Principles of Legislation, etc, 1864; LLD 1st and University Gold Medallist, 1866. A Solicitor in Mincing Lane and at Hull; a prizeman of the Incorporated Law Society, 1863, and President of the Society; Director National Telephone Co.; also a steamship owner (firm, Bailey and Leetham) at Hull, Newcastle, and London; Sheriff of Hull, 1875–76, and Mayor, 1883–84–85; MP (C) Islington (S), 1886–1906; contested (C) Hull W, 1885; contested (L) Epsom Div., Surrey, 1910; Hon. Freeman of Hull and Huddersfield; Elder Brother, Trinity House, Hull; Ex-President of Associated Chambers of Commerce, UK, and of London and Hull Chambers of Commerce; late a Director of the British Chamber of Commerce, Paris; Member of the Commercial Intelligence Committee of the Board of Trade; President Municipal Corporations Association; Chairman of Savings Bank Inspection Committee; Lieut-Col Engineer Militia (Humber Div. Submarine Miners); JP Co. of London and Co. of Berks, and DL London and Yorks, and Lieut of City of London; DCL Montreal, 1870; Durham, 1891; LLD Victoria, 1902; Officer of the Legion of Honour and of the French Academy; Knight Commander of Leopold (Belgium), of Crown of Italy, of Danebrog (Denmark), of Rising Sun (Japan), etc; Grand Cross of the Order of St Sava, 1907; a "progressive and independent Conservative," and in favour of wide local government for both England and Ireland. *Address:* St Anne's Hill, Chertsey; Manar, Inverurie, NB; 18 Avenue d'Antin, Paris. *Clubs:* Carlton, Junior Naval and Military. *Died 12 Aug. 1922.*

ROLLO, 10th Baron, *cr* 1651; **John Rogerson Rollo,** DL; FRGS, FSA; Baron Dunning (UK), 1869; *b* 24 Oct. 1835; *s* of 9th Baron and Elizabeth, *o d* of John Rogerson, Wamphray and Dumcrieff; *S* father, 1852; *m* 1857, cousin Agnes Bruce (*d* 1906), *d* of late Colonel Robert Knox Trotter and Mary, *d* of 8th Baron Rollo; four *s* three *d*. *Educ:* Trinity College, Cambridge (MA). Representative Peer, Scotland, 1860–68. Owned about 17,400 acres. *Heir:* *s* Master of Rollo [*b* 8 Jan. 1860; *m* 1882, Mary Eleanor, *d* of Beaumont Williams Hotham; one *d*]. *Address:* Duncrub Castle, Dunning, Perthshire; Dumcrieff House, Moffat, NB; Wilmington, Ryde, Isle of Wight. *Clubs:* Athenæum, United University. *Died 3 Oct. 1916.*

ROLT, Very Rev. Cecil Henry, MA; Chaplain of Hornchurch since 1925; *b* 1865; *s* of Rev. H. G. Rolt, Harbledown, Canterbury; *m* 1910, Mary Foxley, *e d* of Very Rev. William Foxley Norris; three *s*. *Educ:* Winchester; New College, Oxford. Deacon, 1888; Priest, 1890; served curacies at St Thomas's, Sunderland, Christ Church, West Hartlepool, St Hilda's, South Shields, St Cuthbert's, Benshaw; Vicar of Holy Trinity, Darlington, 1897; took part in the Mission of Help to S Africa, 1904; Vicar of Batley, Yorkshire, 1905; Vicar of Huddersfield, 1910; Dean of Cape Town, 1917–24; late Hon. Canon of Wakefield. *Address:* The Chaplaincy, Hornchurch. *Died 14 Sept. 1926.*

ROMANES, Ethel, (Mrs G. J. Romanes); *b* Liverpool; *d* and heiress of late Andrew Duncan; *m* 1879, George John Romanes, FRS (*d* 1894); three *c*. *Educ:* privately. Was on several committees of work for women; lectured for some years on theology and on Dante, etc, to educated women; lectured by request in New York, Boston, etc, on the same subjects; entered the Catholic Church, 1919. *Publications:* Life and Letters of George John Romanes, 1896; The Hallowing of Sorrow, 1896; Meditations on the Penitential Psalms, 1902; Meditations on the Epistle of St James, 1903; How to Use the Prayer Book, 1905; Story of Port Royal, 1907; Bible Readings, 1908; Charlotte Yonge, an Appreciation; A Great Mistake, a novel, 1921; Anne Chichester, a novel, 1925; several smaller devotional books, reviews, etc. *Recreations:* reading, music. *Address:* 52 Ashley Gardens, SW1. *T:* Victoria 8984; Pitcalzean, Ross-shire. *Club:* Sesame. *Died 30 March 1927.*

ROMER, Rt. Hon. Sir Robert, GCB 1901; Kt 1890; PC 1899; FRS 1899; a Lord Justice of Appeal, 1899–1906; Judge of the Chancery Division of the High Court of Justice, 1890–99; *b* 23 Dec. 1840; 2nd *s* of late composer Frank Romer and Mary Lydia Cudworth; *m* 1864, cousin Betty (*d* 1916), *d* of Mark Lemon, editor of Punch. *Educ:* private schools; Trinity Hall, Cambridge (Scholar; MA). Senior Wrangler Mathematical Tripos, 1863; Smith's Prizeman, 1863; Professor of Mathematics, Queen's Coll., Cork, 1865–66; Fellow of Trin. Hall, 1867; Barrister, Lincoln's Inn, 1867; QC 1881; Bencher, Lincoln's Inn; contested (L) Brighton, 1884. *Recreations:* shooting, cycling, rowing. *Address:* 21 Queens Gate Gardens, SW. *T:* Western 6486. *Club:* Athenæum. *Died 19 March 1918.*

ROMER, Thomas Ansdell; Senior Master of the Supreme Court, Chancery Division; *b* 16 Dec. 1848; *s* of late Thomas Romer of

Kensington; *m* 1892, Leila Harriette, *d* of late John Harding Robinson, Examiner of Standing Orders, House of Lords; one *d*. *Educ*: Kensington Grammar School; Brighton; Frankfort-on-the-Maine; Paris. Admitted a Solicitor, 1873; Certificate of Honour, Final Examination, 1872. *Publications*: The Judicial Trustees' Guide; paper on Copyright Law Reform read at Meeting of Law Society, 1882; and various articles on these subjects. *Recreations*: music, shooting, fishing. *Address*: 14 Oakwood Court, Kensington, W; Room 292, Royal Courts of Justice, WC. *Died 1 Sept. 1917.*

RONAN, Rt. Hon. Stephen; Lord Justice of Appeal and Privy Councillor in Ireland, latterly for Irish Free State, 1915–24; *b* 13 April 1848; *s* of Walter Ronan, solicitor, of Cork, and Sarah McNamara; unmarried. *Educ*: schools in Cork and France; Queen's College, Cork; MA QUI. Called to the Irish Bar, 1870; QC 1889; Bencher, King's Inns, Dublin, 1892; Queen's Advocate-General for Ireland, 1892; called to the English Bar, Inner Temple, 1888; KC (England), 1909. *Address*: 45 Fitzwilliam Square, Dublin. *Died 3 Oct. 1925.*

RONAYNE, Thomas, ISO 1914; Colonel, Railway Transport Service, 1905–14; *b* Youghal, 1848; father Irish, mother English; three *s* three *d*. *Educ*: Corsham; Wakefield. Served apprenticeship at the Inchicore Works, Great Southern and Western Railway, Ireland; subsequently had experience with Sharpe, Stewart and Co., Manchester; went to New Zealand, 1875; appointed General Manager, Kaipara Railway; General Manager, Greymouth Brunner Railway, 1876; Resident and Locomotive Engineer, Wellington and Masterton Railway, 1886; Locomotive Engineer, Hurunui Bluff Railway, 1888; General Manager, Greymouth Brunner Railway, 1900; a Railway Commissioner, 1904; General Manager, New Zealand Railways, 1905–14. *Recreations*: fishing, shooting, gardening. *Address*: 50 Tinakori Road, Wellington, New Zealand. *Club*: Wellington. *Died 7 Sept. 1925.*

ROOKE, Col Harry William, JP; Royal Artillery, retired; *b* 1842; *e* surv. *s* of late Rev. Canon George Rooke, of Embleton, Northumberland, and Clara Frances, *d* of late William Moffat; *m* 1881, Jane Henrietta, *o d* of late Thomas Rowlandson Dunn, of Hazelwood, Rylands, and Langthwaite, Lancashire. *Educ*: Ordnance School, Carshalton; Woolwich. Commanded the RA in Scotland, 1895–99. *Address*: Haynford Hall, Norwich; Villa Constance, Biarritz. *Clubs*: Army and Navy; Norfolk County, Norwich. *Died 29 Nov. 1921.*

ROOKE, Ven. Henry; *b* 16 Oct. 1829; *s* of Henry Rooke and Elizabeth Warburton; *m* 1859, K. E. Lloyd; three *s* one *d*. *Educ*: Trinity College, Dublin (MA). Ordained 1853; Chancellor's Vicar of St Patrick's Cathedral, Dublin, 1860–1904; Rector of Wicklow, 1878–1906; Rural Dean, 1879; Canon of Christ Church Cathedral, Dublin, 1892–1905; Archdeacon of Glendalough, 1905–14; retired; Chaplain of Troops, Wicklow, 1877; Good Service Pay, 1885. *Address*: 4 Belgrave Square, Monkstown, Dublin. *Died March 1926.*

ROOKE, Maj.-Gen. William, FRGS; Royal Artillery; *b* 29 Dec. 1836. Entered army, 1854; Col, 1885; retired, 1886; served Crimean War, 1855 (medal with clasp; Turkish medal). *Address*: Ellerslie, Ryde, Isle of Wight. *Died 7 Sept. 1919.*

ROONEY, Rt. Rev. John, DD; Bishop of Sergiopolis and Vicar-Apostolic of the Western Districts of the Cape of Good Hope since 1908; Administrator of the Central Prefecture and of the Islands of St Helena and Ascension; *b* Ireland. *Educ*: All Hallows College, Dublin; Propaganda Coll., Rome. Colonial and Naval Chaplain at Simonstown for about twenty years; Coadjutor Bishop, Cape Town, 1886–1908. *Address*: St Mary's, Bouquet Street, Cape Town, South Africa. *Died Feb. 1927.*

ROOS, Gustaf Ehrenreich; Kt Order of Vasa, Sweden; *b* Sweden, 15 Sept. 1838; *s* of O. G. Roos, Director of Ordnance, Stockholm, and Ulrica Euphrosyne von Keppel; *m* Annie (*d* 1926), *d* of George Roffey of Twickenham. *Educ*: Gothenburg. Associated with Thorsten Nordenfelt, 1880–90 (the inventor of the guns), and introduced the Nordenfelt guns in the following countries — Russia, Austria-Hungary, Turkey, Roumania, Servia, Bulgaria, Greece, Montenegro, Italy, Spain and Portugal; travelled a great deal in nearly every country in Europe, Asia Minor, Morocco, United States and Canada; Grand Officer, Order of Military Merit, Spain; Comdr of Order of St Stanislas, Russia; of Order of Medjidie; Kt, of Order of Christ, Portugal. *Publications*: A Travers L'Orient et L'Occident; L'Emploi des Mitraillenses et Canons à Tir Rapide, and several other minor publications connected with artillery and powder. *Address*: 7 Queen's Gate Terrace, SW7. *T*: Western 1339. *Died 7 Dec. 1928.*

ROOSEVELT, Col Theodore; Associate Editor New York Outlook; Vice-President of the United States, 4 March–14 Sept. 1901, President, 1901–8; *b* New York, 27 Oct. 1858; father of New York (Knickerbocker), mother of Georgian (Scotch) family; *m* Edith Kermit Carow. *Educ*: Harvard. Progressive; Member of the New York Legislature, 1882–84; leader of the minority in 1883; leader of House in 1884; US Civil Service Commissioner, 1889–95; President, New York Police Board, 1895–97; appointed Asst Sec. of Navy, April 1897; organised 1st US Cavalry Volunteers (Roosevelt's Rough Riders) and commanded it in Cuba, 1898; Governor of New York State, 1898–1900; went big-game shooting, British East Africa, 1909. *Publications*: War of 1812, 1882; Hunting Trips of a Ranchman, 1885; Life of Thomas Hart Benton, 1886; Life of Gouverneur Morris, 1887; Ranch Life and the Hunting Trail, 1888; The Winning of the West, 1889–95; The Wilderness Hunter, 1893; American Ideals, 1898; The Rough Riders, 1899; The Strenuous Life; Life of Cromwell; The Deer Family (with others); The Outdoor Pastimes of an American Hunter, 1905; African Game Trails, 1910; Theodore Roosevelt: an Autobiography, 1913; History as Literature, 1913; Life Histories of African Big Game, 1914; A Hunter Naturalist in the Brazilian Wilderness, 1914; Life Histories of African Game Animals (with E. Heller), 1915; Fear God and Take Your Own Part, 1916; A Book-Lover's Holidays in the Open, 1916. *Recreations*: ranching and big-game hunting on the great plains and in the Rocky Mountains; much interested in zoology, especially mammalogy, and field natural history generally. *Address*: Sagamore Hill, Oyster Bay, Long Island, New York. *Clubs*: Century, Union League, Boone and Crockett, New York; Metropolitan, Washington. *Died 6 Jan. 1919.*

ROOTH, Henry Goodwin; Metropolitan Police Court Magistrate and JP for the six Home Counties since 1917; *b* London, 1861; *o s* of late Goodwin Rooth (shipowner, West Indian merchant, and proprietor of West Indian plantations), of Weatherall House, Hampstead, NW, and Monyash, Derbyshire, and Augusta Anne, *e d* of Henry Smith (Deputy Past Grand Master, Bristol); *m* 1897, Beatrice Mary, 4th *d* of late Edmund Tattersall of Colherne Court (subseq. demolished), S Kensington; one *s*. *Educ*: Harrow; Trinity College, Cambridge (BA). Called to the Bar, Inner Temple, 1887; joined and practised on the South Eastern Circuit, County Court Circuit, Kent and London Sessions, representing the Director of Public Prosecutions frequently both on Circuit and at Courts Martial; appointed to HQ Staff and Discipline Board of Special Constabulary at Scotland House, Jan. 1915; Junior Treasury Counsel in Appeals at London Sessions, 1916. *Recreations*: travelling, painting, golf, shooting. *Address*: Weatherall House, NW3. *T*: Hampstead 2126. *Clubs*: Garrick, Arts, Royal Automobile. *Died 12 Oct. 1928.*

ROPER, Freeman, MA; *b* 8 Sept. 1862; *e s* of late Freeman Clarke Samuel Roper of Palgrave House, Eastbourne; *m* 1898, Elizabeth Harriot, *o d* of late George Wildman Yates FitzGerald of Maperton, County Somerset, and *heiress* of William Herbert Evans of Forde Abbey, Dorset; one *s* one *d*. *Educ*: Radley College; New College, Oxford. Practised for 15 years as a solicitor in London, and retired 1903; High Sheriff of Dorset, 1917; Alderman Dorset County Council; JP for Dorset and Somerset. *Address*: Forde Abbey, Chard, Somerset. *TA*: Forde Abbey, Winsham. *Clubs*: Oxford and Cambridge, Bath. *Died 17 Feb. 1925.*

ROPER, Henry Basil, ISO 1903; *b* Highgate, 1846; *e s* of Rev. Thomas Henry Roper, late of Puddlehinton Rectory, Dorset, and Mary Emma, *d* of Basil G. Woodd, late of Hillfield, Hampstead, and Oughtershaw Hall, Yorks; *m* 1875, Emilie Bessie Earle, *d* of William Hicks, late of Penryn, Falmouth. *Educ*: Eton. Joined Colonial Service, 1872; at various times Civil Commissioner and Resident Magistrate of Kimberley, Herbert, and Hay; Commissioner of Police and Chief of Criminal Investigation Department; Commandant of Burghers in 1878 war (medal); Member of Treason Court, 1901–2; Chief Inspector of Prisons for Cape Colony, retired, 1907. *Address*: Beechworth, Havant, Hants. *Club*: Royal Albert Yacht, Southsea. *Died 13 March 1918.*

ROPNER, Col Sir (Emil Hugo Oscar) Robert, 1st Bt, *cr* 1904; Kt 1900; VD; MP (C) Stockton, 1900–10; *b* 16 Dec. 1838; *m* 1858, Mary Anne (*d* 1921), *d* of John Craik, of Newton Stewart, NB; five *s* four *d*. Late Colonel 1st Volunteer Batt. Durham LI (VD); Chairman, Ropner and Sons, Ltd, shipbuilders, ship repairers and ship owners, Stockton-on-Tees; Director North-Eastern Banking Co.; Sheriff of Durham, 1896; JP, DL Co. Durham; JP Co. York (North Riding); contested (C) Cleveland, 1895 and 1897. *Heir*: *s* John Henry Ropner [*b* 7 Sept. 1860; *m* 1888, Margaret, *d* of John Macgregor; two *d*.

Address: Ragworth, Norton, Stockton]. *Address:* Preston Hall, Stockton-on-Tees; Skutterskelf, Yarm, Yorks. *Clubs:* Carlton, Constitutional. *Died 26 Feb. 1924.*

ROSE, Frank Herbert; MP (Lab) North Aberdeen since Dec. 1918; author, dramatist, journalist; *b* Lambeth, 5 July 1857; *s* of late Thomas Rose of Lambeth; *m* 1880, Ellen Mary, 2nd *d* of late Noah Bishop of Lambeth; three *s*. *Educ:* British School, George Street, Lambeth; evening classes afterwards. Operative engineer until 1893; Trade Union organizer until 1900; journalism and other literary pursuits from 1900; best known as industrial and labour authority and statistician; contested (Lab) Stockton, 1906; Crewe, 1910. *Publications:* The Coming Force (official history of Labour Party); Our Industrial Jungle; also author of The Whispering Well, Trouble in the House, The Second Mrs Banks, The Young Guv'nor, and other plays; numerous pamphlets and voluminous press work, stories, sketches. *Recreations:* reading, walking. *Address:* House of Commons, SW1. *Club:* Manchester Press. *Died 10 July 1928.*

ROSE, George Pringle, CIE 1892; late Public Works Department, India; *b* 1855; *s* of Rev. Donaldson Rose, MA, of Brechin, Forfarshire. *Educ:* Aberdeen University; Wren's; Cooper's Hill. Entered ICS; assistant engineer, 1877; State Railways, 1878; executive engineer, 1891; Sind Peshni State Railway, 1884–87; Chapper Rift Works and Bridge (thanks of Government of India); Superintendent of Works, Extension Railway and Kojak Tunnel; in executive and afterwards administrative charge, 1888–91; thanks of Secretary of State, Viceroy, Government of India, and Commander-in-Chief (decorated); Deputy Manager NW State Railway, 1892–93; lent to Nizam of Hyderabad's Government to advise as to Railway Policy, 1895; Nizam of Hyderabad's State Railway Co. as Engineer-in-Chief of Hyderabad-Godavery Valley Railway, 1897–1900; Junior Consulting Engineer for Railways, Calcutta, to Government of India, 1902; retired, 1904; Director, Hyderabad (Deccan) Co., etc. *Address:* Tilthams, near Godalming, Surrey. *Died 20 Nov. 1918.*

ROSE, Major Hugh Alexander Leslie, DSO 1917; Royal Artillery; *s* of late Hugh Rose. *Educ:* Wellington College. Entered RFA, 1901; Capt. 1914; Major, 1916; served European War in France since 15 Aug. 1914 (despatches twice, DSO). *Club:* Junior United Service. *Died 18 April 1918.*

ROSE, John; *b* 1841; *s* of J. R. Rose, Stoke-upon-Trent; *m* 1882, Janet, *o d* of late Charles Darling, Langham Hall, Essex. Barrister, Gray's Inn, 1868; Bencher, 1885; Metropolitan Police Magistrate, 1891; resigned, 1912. *Address:* Marlows, Westmonkton, Somersetshire. *Died 5 Feb. 1926.*

ROSE, Sir Philip Frederick, 2nd Bt, *cr* 1874; JP and DL Co. Bucks; High Sheriff of Bucks, 1898–99; *b* London, 4 Nov. 1843; *e s* of Sir Philip Rose, 1st Bt, Rayners, Penn, and Margaretta, *d* of Robert Ranking; *S* father, 1883; *m* 1866, Rose Annie, *d* of Rev. William Wollaston Pym; one *s* three *d* (and two *s* one *d* decd). *Educ:* Harrow. Commenced life as junior partner in well-known firm of Parliamentary solicitors, Baxter, Rose, and Norton; for many years legal adviser to the Brighton Railway Co., but retired from legal practice; director of several large public companies. *Recreations:* farming, country sports, motoring. *Heir: g s* Philip Humphrey Vivian Rose, *b* 16 March 1903. *Address:* Rayners, Penn, Bucks. *T.A:* Penn, Bucks. *T:* High Wycombe 29. *M:* BH 1163 and BH 2891. *Clubs:* Junior Carlton, Royal Automobile.

Died 23 Oct. 1919.

ROSE-INNES, His Honour Sir Patrick, Kt 1918; JP Middlesex, Aberdeenshire, and Kent; KC 1912; barrister; *b* 1853; 2nd surv. *s* of late George Rose-Innes, JP, DL, of Blachrie, Aberdeenshire; *m* 1897, Jane (*d* 1914), *y d* of William Palmer, Cote Hill, Cumberland. *Educ:* University of Aberdeen. Called to the Bar, 1878; member of South Eastern Circuit; Recorder of Sandwich and Ramsgate, 1905–20; Bencher, Lincoln's Inn, 1915; sat as Commissioner of Assize SE Circuit, 1914–15; Judge of County Courts (Circuit 18), 1920–22; contested (U) Elgin Burghs, 1905; West Lothian, 1906; Jarrow, 1907; Middleton Division, Lancs, 1910; Major West London Rifles. *Recreations:* shooting, golf. *Address:* 2 King's Bench Walk, Temple, EC4. *T:* Central 754; Vale Court, W; Blachrie, Aberdeenshire; The Cottage, St Margaret's Bay, Kent. *Clubs:* Carlton, Junior Carlton, Junior Constitutional; University, Aberdeen.

Died 2 Oct. 1924.

ROSEDALE, Capt. Rev. Honyel Gough, MA, DD; FSA, FRSL; Rector of Copford, Colchester, since 1924; Editor of The Blind Record; public lecturer; *b* 17 May 1863; *s* of W. L. Rosedale, LLD,

Vicar of S Saviour's, Brockley Hill, and of Middleton, Norfolk, and Caroline, *d* of R. Gough, JP, of Gorsebrook House, Wolverhampton; *m* Ada, *e d* of Percy Leonard Pelly, JP, of Oakley, Merstham, and *g d* of Sir (John) Henry Pelly, 1st Bt; two *s*. *Educ:* Merchant Taylors' School; Christ Church, Oxford; Guy's Hospital. Curate, S Andrew's, Stockwell, 1886; Spitalfields, 1888; Holy Trinity, Canning Town, 1890; Vicar of Middleton, Norfolk, 1891; S Peter's, Bayswater, 1894; resigned, 1909; Principal, S Peter's, Bayswater, Church School; Brompton Boys' School; Acting Chaplain, Middlesex RE Vol. (resigned); late Hon. Foreign Secretary of Royal Society of Literature; President of CCC, 1913–14; Vice-Pres. Ethological Society; Chaplain to Sheriffs of London; Hon. Treasurer London Association for the Blind; Past Master and Chaplain of the Worshipful Company of Coachmakers; Past Master and Chaplain, Worshipful Company of Horners; late Chaplain City of London National Guard, 5th Batt.; President Sette of Odd Volumes, 1920; Freemason; Past Grand Chaplain of Grand Lodge of England. *Publications:* Life of S Agnes; Book of Verses; Growth of Religious Ideals in the Great Poets, 1902 and 1926; Queen Elizabeth and the Levant Company, 1904; Celano's Lives of S Francis, 1904; With the British Association through South Africa; The Spanish Match, 1908; Milton's Religious Views (Milton Tercentenary Lecture), 1908; Some Notes on the Old Book of the Worshipful Company of Horners, 1910; A Short History of the Horners' Company, 1912; Some Notes on the History of the Worshipful Company of Coach and Coach-Harness Makers; contributor to Ars Quatuor Coronatorum and other Masonic periodicals; and numerous other smaller works. *Recreations:* travel, golf, outdoor games; collector of prints, china, curios, old books, and MSS. *Address:* The Rectory, Copford, near Colchester. *T:* Marks Tey 32; 7 Gloucester Street, Victoria, SW; Rosedale House, Warwick Street, SW1. *T:* Victoria 6720 and 5682; 22 Grafton Road, Worthing.

Died 14 Jan. 1928.

ROSEVEARE, Rev. Richard Polgreen; Vicar of Lewisham since 1917; Hon. Canon of Southwark Cathedral, 1919; Canon residentiary since 1922; *b* 11 Nov. 1865; *m*; four *s* one *d*. *Educ:* Cambridge University. Ordained, 1889. *Address:* The Vicarage, Lewisham. *T:* Lee Green 560. *Died 24 Feb. 1924.*

ROSS, Alexander, MInstCE; Consulting Engineer, Westminster; Lieutenant-Colonel Engineer and Railway Staff Corps; *b* 20 April 1845; married; one *s* one *d*. *Educ:* Aberdeen; Manchester. Pupil, Great North of Scotland Railway, 1862–71; on Engineering Staff, London and North-Western Railway, 1871–75; District Engineer, Liverpool, 1875–84; Asst Engineer, Lancs and Yorks Railway, 1884–90; Chief Engineer, Great Central Railway, 1890–97; Chief Engineer, Great Northern Railway, 1897–1911; President Institution of Civil Engineers, 1915–16. *Address:* 36 Fellows Road, NW3. *T:* Hampstead 4188; 23 Abingdon Street, SW. *T:* Victoria 1004. *Club:* St Stephen's. *Died 3 Feb. 1923.*

ROSS, Andrew; Ross Herald; *b* Rosskeen, Ross-shire, 3 Sept. 1849. *Publications:* Old Scottish Regimental Colours; The Nisbet Plates; The Lyons of Cossins and Wester Ogill, cadets of Glamis. *Address:* 14 Blacket Place, Edinburgh. *Died 21 Feb. 1925.*

ROSS, Rt. Rev. Arthur Edwin, DD; Bishop of Tuam since 1920; *b* 1869; *s* of David Ross, Glenagarey, Co. Dublin; *m* Mary Elizabeth Linzee, *d* of Lieut-Col R. J. Hezlet, Bovagh, Aghadowey, Co. Derry. *Educ:* Trinity College, Dublin. Temp. Chaplain to the Forces, 1916–18 (MC and bar). *Address:* The Palace, Tuam. *Club:* University, Dublin. *Died 24 May 1923.*

ROSS, Rev. David Morison, DD; Minister of Westbourne Church, Glasgow, since 1898; Senior Minister since 1912; *b* 1852; *s* of Peter Ross, Leitfie, Perthshire; *m* 1885, Isabel, *e d* of George Smith, CIE, LLD, Edinburgh. *Educ:* Edinburgh High School and University (MA, with 1st class honours in Philosophy; DD); studied also at Tübingen and Paris. Assistant to Professor of Logic and Metaphysics, Edinburgh University, 1874–77; Minister of St John's Free Church, Dundee, 1878–98; Lecturer on Moral Philosophy in Dundee College in 1887. *Publications:* The Cradle of Christianity: chapters on Modern Palestine; Christ and the Home; The Teaching of Jesus; A Plea for Temperance Legislation; Scottish Minister and Soldier: Rev. Peter Ross Husband; The Christ of Faith and the Jesus of History; The Faith of St Paul: A Study of St Paul as the Interpreter of Jesus; The Spiritual Genius of St Paul. *Recreation:* fishing. *Address:* Ivy Knoll, Crieff. *Club:* Liberal, Edinburgh. *Died 27 Sept. 1927.*

ROSS, Col George, ISO 1909; JP; General Superintendent of Post Service Branch, Dominion of Canada, 1921–23; Officer Administering Canadian Postal Corps; *b* Hamilton, Ontario, 21 Feb.

1853; *e s* of late John and Mary Ross; *m* 1874, Rebecca, 2nd *d* of late John and Letitia Chapman; seven *s* six *d. Educ:* Hamilton, Ontario. After leaving school was engaged in the printing business for about ten years; accepted a position in the Hamilton, Ontario, Post Office in 1875, and was promoted through the various grades to the Chief Clerkship of that office; Assistant Postmaster at Toronto, Ontario, 1900; Past Officer of the Grand Lodge of Masons, GRC, an Oddfellow, a Member of the Ancient Order of United Workmen, and a Past President of the Irish Protestant Benevolent Society of Hamilton. *Address:* PO Box 485, Toronto. *T:* Kenwood 180.
Died July 1926.

ROSS, Major (Temp. Lt-Col) Hugh Alexander, DSO 1915; 2nd Battalion The Gordon Highlanders; *b* 19 Feb. 1880; 2nd *s* of late John MacDonald Ross, of Ledgowan, Ross-shire; *m* 1917, Winifred, *d* of S. Giles, Chatham; one *s. Educ:* Loretto. Captain and played in School XV for five seasons; played in the Scottish Trial Internationals; joined the 3rd Scottish Rifles, 1900; the Gordon Highlanders, 1901; Captain, 1910; Major, 1916; Adjutant of 3rd Batt. and Depot; served South African War (Queen's medal, 5 clasps) and European War (despatches thrice, DSO, and Order of Danilo of Montenegro, 1916); commanded 2nd Battalion in the Battle of Loos. *Recreations:* all sports. *Address:* c/o Holt & Co., 3 Whitehall Place, SW. *Clubs:* United Service, Royal Automobile.
Died Oct. 1918.

ROSS, Hugh Campbell; Director of the McFadden Research Foundation, Lister Institute of Preventive Medicine; *b* 1875; *s* of Sir Campbell C. G. Ross, KCB. *Educ:* Isle of Wight College; St Thomas' Hospital. Qualified as a doctor 1898, and travelled in Egypt and China; served as surgeon in S African War (Queen's medal five clasps); served in Royal Navy as surgeon, 1902–6, when new methods of microscopical study of living human cells were devised; acted as Medical Officer of Health, Cairo, 1906–8, and started mosquito extermination there under Lord Cromer's administration; resumed investigation of cellular pathology at Royal Southern Hospital and School of Tropical Medicine, Liverpool, 1908; Director McFadden Research Fund, Lister Institute, Chelsea, 1910, since when new methods were developed for cancer research; conducted research with and advised Factory Department Home Office on industrial cancer, and on certain miner's diseases, 1910–19; inventor of the molybdeno-tungsten ultra-violet light processes for the prevention of industrial cancer in South Wales; of new medical tests; and of tungsten drugs. *Publications:* Induced Cell-Reproduction and Cancer, Vols I–IV; papers published in Proceedings of Royal Society, Royal Society of Medicine, Physiological Society and Medico-Legal Societies; also read papers before the Pathological Society, Philadelphia, and Rockfeller Institute, New York, and American Association for Cancer Research. *Recreations:* motoring, sailing. *Club:* Bath.
Died 14 Dec. 1926.

ROSS, Janet Anne; *b* London, 24 Feb. 1842; *e c* of Sir Alexander Cornewall Duff Gordon, Bt, and Lucie, *o c* of John and Sarah Austin; *m* 1860, Henry James Ross, banker, Alexandria, Egypt; one *s. Educ:* home. Lived six years in Egypt, during three of which was Times correspondent; from 1867, lived in Italy. *Publications:* Italian Sketches, 1887; Three Generations of English Women, 1888; The Land of Manfred, 1889; Early Days Recalled, 1891; Leaves from our Tuscan Kitchen, 1899; Florentine Villas, 1901; Old Florence and Modern Tuscany, 1904; Florentine Palaces, 1905; Lives of the Early Medici, 1910; The Fourth Generation: Reminiscences, 1912; Letters of Principal J. M. Lindsay to Janet Ross, with Preface by Janet Ross, 1922. *Recreations:* viticulture, music. *Address:* Poggio Gherardo, Settignano, Florence, Italy.
Died 23 Aug. 1927.

ROSS, Sir John, Kt 1922; FRGS; late Chairman of Directors, Ross & Glendining, Ltd, chief towns of New Zealand; *b* Halkirk, Caithness, 24 Nov. 1834; *s* of John Ross; *m* Margaret Watson Cassels; three *s* three *d. Educ:* local schools. Founder of firm, Ross & Glendining (as above); founder of Knox College, Dunedin, NZ; part founder Ross Home for Aged, Dunedin; Member Knox College Council; former Member of University Council, Otago, and High Schools Board, Dunedin. *Address:* Morven, 3 Newington Avenue, Maori Hill, Dunedin, NZ.
Died 5 Jan. 1927.

ROSS, Major John Alexander, DSO 1916; Canadian Infantry; *b* Kenora, Ont, 20 Oct. 1893; *s* of Walter Inkerman Ross; unmarried. *Educ:* Trinity College School, Port Hope, Ont; Royal Military College, Kingston, Ont. Lieut in Victoria Rifles of Canada, 1914; temp. Capt. 1915; temp. Major in Canadian Expeditionary Force, 1915; temp. Major British Expeditionary Force, 1915; served European War, 1914–16 (DSO). *Recreations:* all sports. *Address:* Lethbridge, Alberta, Canada. *Clubs:* Chinook, Lethbridge.
Died 17 Feb. 1917.

ROSS, John M. E., MA; Editor of the British Weekly since 1923; *b* Rothesay, 1870; *s* of Rev. William Ross; *m* 1897, Margaret (*d* 1923), yr *d* of late Rev. Thomas Macadam. *Educ:* Glasgow High School; University and Free Church College. Minister of the Free Church of Scotland, 1896–1900; of the Presbyterian Church of England, 1900–21; Editor Presbyterian Messenger, 1913–21; Editorial Secretary, Scottish Churches Press Bureau, 1922–23. *Publications:* The Self Portraiture of Jesus; William Ross of Cowcaddens; The Christian Standpoint; 3 vols of Devotional Commentary; edited Church Praise; many newspaper and magazine articles. *Recreations:* music, motoring, travel. *Address:* North Hall, Mortimer Crescent, NW6. *T:* Maida Vale 1255. *Clubs:* Royal Societies, National Liberal, Savage, Whitefriars.
Died 3 Aug. 1925.

ROSS, Hon. Mr Justice Reginald James Blair; Judge of the Supreme Court of Nigeria; *b* 19 Sept. 1871; 3rd *s* of late Sir David Palmer Ross, CMG (Surgeon-General of British Guiana), and Mary Eliza, *d* of Hon. Alexander Heslop; unmarried. *Educ:* Ipswich School; Gonville and Caius College, Cambridge. Barrister-at-Law, Inner Temple, 1894; entered Colonial Civil Service as District Commissioner at Lagos, 1898; subsequently Police Magistrate, Solicitor-General. *Address:* Lagos, Nigeria, W Africa. *Clubs:* Royal Societies, Sports.

ROSS, Robert Baldwin; Additional Trustee of the National Gallery; Executor and Administrator for the literary and dramatic Estate of the late Oscar Wilde; Adviser for the purchase of works of art to the Felton Bequest Committee, Melbourne, Australia; *b* Tours, France, 25 May 1869; *s* of Hon. John Ross, QC, Attorney-General for Upper Canada, and Augusta Elizabeth, *d* of Hon. Robert Baldwin, CB, First Premier of Upper Canada under responsible government. *Educ:* private schools; King's College, Cambridge. After leaving university without taking a degree, from 1889 contributed signed and anonymous articles on art, literature, and drama to Scots Observer, Saturday Review, Pall Mall Gazette, Cornhill, Daily Chronicle, and later to Lancet, Burlington Magazine, The Times, Westminster Gazette; assistant editor of The Author, under late Sir Walter Besant, 1891; Director of Carfax and Co. Ltd, picture dealers, 1900–8; staff of Morning Post, 1908–12; Adviser to the Inland Revenue on picture valuations for estate duty, 1912–14. *Publications:* Life of Charles Robert Maturin, in collaboration with More Adey, 1892; Aubrey Beardsley, 1908; edited Oscar Wilde's posthumous work, De Profundis, 1905; Wilde's Complete Works, 1908; Masques and Phases, 1909; Really and Truly, 1915. *Recreation:* editing new editions of Wilde's works. *Clubs:* Reform, Burlington Fine Arts, Royal Automobile.
Died 5 Oct. 1918.

ROSS, Sir Thomas MacKenzie, Kt 1927; late Chairman Madras Chamber of Commerce. *Address:* Best & Co., First Line Beach, Madras, India.
Died 12 Aug. 1927.

ROSS of Cromarty, Brig.-Gen. Sir Walter Charteris, KBE 1919; CB 1900; CMG 1918; (late) Durham Light Infantry; retired pay; *b* 5 Aug. 1857; *s* of Col George William Holmes Ross of Cromarty, and Adelaide, *d* of late Duncan Davidson of Tulloch, MP; *m* 1st, 1887, May (*d* 1891), *d* of FM Sir Donald Martin Stewart, 1st Bt, GCB, GCSI, CIE; 2nd, 1897, Gertrude May Gathorne, *d* of Charles Hill of Clevedon Hall and Hazel Manor, Somerset; two *s* four *d.* Served Afghan War, 1879 (medal); South Africa, 1899–1900 (despatches three times, Queen's medal 5 clasps, CB); European War, 1914–19 (KBE, CMG, despatches four times); JP, DL Ross and Cromarty. *Address:* Cromarty House, Cromarty, Scotland. *T:* Cromarty 2. *Club:* Naval and Military.
Died 9 Feb. 1928.

ROSS, Hon. William, VD; JP; Member Provincial Council, Cape Province; *b* Stranraer, Scotland, 6 May 1850; *m* Jeanette, *d* of late George Page, bank manager, Bloemfontein; three *s* one *d. Educ:* Stranraer Academy. First elected Griqualand West for Legislative Council, 1883; representative for 28 years, never opposed at any election; Chairman Legislative Council Committees, 1904–8; acted as President of Council; Honourable for life conferred for long Parliamentary services; after Union, was returned unopposed for Beaconsfield as Member Provincial Council, selected unopposed as one of the four Executive members; again in 1914 and 1917 and 1920; first Captain in command of Kimberley Highlanders (Volunteers), later amalgamated with Kimberley Regiment, of which he became Hon. Lieut-Colonel. *Recreations:* very keen sportsman all round—athletics, shooting, fishing, boxing, horse-racing, etc. *Address:* Lochinch, The Gardens, Cape Town. *Clubs:* Kimberley, Kimberley; Rand, Johannesburg; Civil Service, Cape Town.
Died Oct. 1925.

ROSS, Hon. William Roderick, MA; KC; *b* Fort Chipewyan, Alberta, 29 March 1869; *s* of Donald Ross and Anna M'Kenzie (both Scotch); father's family employed by Hudson's Bay Company for two or three generations back; *m* 1892, Leila Young; two *s* three *d*. *Educ:* St John's College, Winnipeg, Man; BA, MA. Barrister-at-law; practised in Fernie, BC, for several years; Member (C) Provincial Assembly, 1903, 1907, 1909, 1912–16; Minister of Lands, British Columbia, 1910–16. *Died 4 Feb. 1928.*

ROSS-LEWIN, Ven. Richard S.; Archdeacon of Limerick, 1919; Rector of Kilmurry, Limerick, 1886; Rural Dean of St Mary's, 1900; *b* 1848; *s* of Rev. George Ross-Lewin, JP, Ross-Hill, Co. Clare; *m* 1877; no *c*. *Educ:* Bristol; Durham University. Served in Royal Navy, 1864–73; took Holy Orders, 1877; Rector of Killscully, 1883; Prebend of Croagh, Limerick Cathedral, 1908–12. *Publications:* West Briton (poems), 1907; In Britain's Need, 1917. *Recreations:* cricket, golf, lawn tennis. *Address:* Kilmurry Rectory, Limerick.

Died Nov. 1921.

ROSS-LEWIN, Rev. Robert O'Donelan, MA; retired Chaplain Royal Navy; Hon. Canon of Newcastle Cathedral, 1909; Rural Dean of Bellingham, 1904; Rector of Wark-on-Tyne; *b* 26 March 1850; *s* of late Rev. George Ross-Lewin, Rector of Thorneyburn, and of Ross Hill, Co. Clare, Ireland; *m* 1897, Katherine Mary Beatrice, *d* of J. W. Walton-Wilson, JP, of Shotley Hall, Northumberland; one *s* one *d*. *Educ:* Bristol Grammar School; private tuition; Durham University. Curate of Ponteland, Northumberland, 1874–76; Chaplain in Royal Navy; served in HMS 'London' (at Zanzibar), 1876–77; 'Jumna' (Indian Troop Service), 1878–80; 'Audacious' (Home Station), 1880–81, and in 'Audacious' (China Station), 1886–88; HMS 'Repulse' (Hull), 1881–83; 'Duncan' (Sheerness Flagship of Prince Leiningen), 1883–86; 'Indus' (Devonport), 1888–91; 'Swiftsure' (Flagship of Duke of Edinburgh), 1891–92; Royal Marines, Walmer, 1892. *Publications:* articles in various journals and papers; illustrations in Graphic, Daily Graphic, and Illustrated London News; several military and naval songs. *Recreations:* drawing, painting, golf. *Address:* Achnamara, Oban, Argyllshire.

Died 11 March 1922.

ROSS-OF-BLADENSBURG, Sir John Foster George, KCB 1903 (CB 1892); KCVO 1911; LLD; DL, JP; Lieutenant–Colonel, 1896; *b* Ireland, 27 July 1848; 2nd *s* of David Ross-of-Bladensburg, Rostrevor, Co. Down, and Harriet, *e d* of 2nd Viscount Ferrard and Harriet, 9th Viscountess Massereene in her own right; *g s* of Maj.-Gen. Robert Ross, who defeated the Americans at the battle of Bladensburg, and captured Washington immediately afterwards, 1814; *m* 1870, Hon. Blanche Amelia Skeffington, *d* of 10th Viscount Massereene and Ferrard. *Educ:* Radley; RMA, Woolwich; Gold Medallist (military) Royal United Service Institution, 1876. Joined RA; transferred Lieut to Coldstream Guards, 1873; served in Suakin Campaign, 1885 (medal and clasp, Khedive's star); served on International Boundary Commission as assistant British Commissioner in Turkey, 1878–79; Secretary to Rt Hon. R. Bourke (Lord Connemara), Financial Commission, Constantinople, 1881; Assistant Private Secretary to Rt Hon. W. E. Forster, Chief Secretary for Ireland, 1881–82; served on staff of Earl Spencer and Earl of Carnarvon when Lord-Lieut of Ireland, 1882–85; Secretary to two British Missions to the Holy See (Duke of Norfolk's), 1887, and (Field-Marshal Sir Lintorn Simmons'), 1889–90; Chief Commissioner, Dublin Metropolitan Police, 1901–14. *Publications:* The Marquess of Hastings, KG (Rulers of India Series), 1893; History of the Coldstream Guards from 1815 to 1885, 1896; The Coldstream Guards in the Crimea, 1897. *Recreation:* collector of trees and shrubs. *Address:* Rosstrevor House, Co. Down. *Clubs:* Guards; Kildare Street, Dublin.

Died 10 July 1926.

ROSSE, 5th Earl of, *cr* 1806; **William Edward Parsons;** Bt 1677; Baron Oxmantown, 1792; Major Irish Guards; HM Lieutenant King's County; Representative Peer for Ireland since 1911; *b* 14 June 1873; *s* of 4th Earl and Hon. Frances Cassandra Harvey-Hawke, *o c* of 4th Baron Hawke; *S* father, 1908; *m* 1905, Lois, *d* of Cecil and Lady Beatrice Lister-Kaye; two *s* one *d*. *Educ:* Eton; Oxford University. Late Lieut 1st Batt. Coldstream Guards; served S Africa, 1899–1900 (Queen's medal, three clasps); European War, 1914–15 (wounded). Owned about 26,500 acres. *Heir: s* Lord Oxmantown, *b* 28 Sept. 1906. *Address:* Birr Castle, King's Co.; Womersley Park, Pontefract.

Died 10 June 1918.

ROSSETTI, William Michael; author; Government-pensioner (Assistant Secretary, 1869–94, Board of Inland Revenue); *b* 25 Sept. 1829; *s* of Gabriele Rossetti, author and Prof. of Italian, King's College, London, and Frances Mary Lavinia Rossetti; *m* 1874, Emma Lucy (*d* 1894), *d* of the painter, Ford Madox Brown, herself an author and painter; four *c*. *Educ:* King's College School, London. Entered Excise Office, 1845. *Publications:* blank-verse translation of Dante's Comedy, The Hell, 1865; Fine Art, chiefly Contemporary, 1867; Lives of Famous Poets, 1878; Life of Keats, 1887; Dante G. Rossetti as Designer and Writer, 1889; Memoir of Dante G. Rossetti, 1895; Gabriele Rossetti (translated autobiography), 1901; Some Reminiscences, 1906; various minor publications; editor of The Germ, 1856; of Shelley's Poems, 1870, etc; of Chaucer's Troylus and Cryseyde, 1875, etc; of Moxon's Popular Poets, 1870, etc; of William Blake's Poems (Aldine edition), 1874; of Poems by Dante and Christina Rossetti, 1886, 1896, 1904; of Ruskin, Rossetti, Præraphaelitism, 1898; of Præraphaelite Diaries and Letters, 1900; of Rossetti Papers, 1862–1870, 1903; Dante and his Convito, 1910; art-critiques in Encyclopædia Britannica (lives of Painters, mostly Italian), etc. *Recreation:* chess occasionally. *Address:* 3 St Edmund's Terrace, Regent's Park. *T:* 2085 Post Hampstead.

Died 5 Feb. 1919.

ROSSMORE, 5th Baron, *cr* 1796; **Derrick Warner William Westenra,** JP; HM's Lieutenant of the County of Monaghan since 1897; Lieutenant 1st Life Guards, retired, 1876; *b* 7 Feb. 1853; *s* of 3rd Baron and 2nd wife, his cousin Josephine, *d* of Henry Lloyd, Farrinrory, Co. Tipperary, and Harriet, *d* of Sir John Craven Carden, Bt; *S* brother 1874; *m* 1882, Mittie, *d* of Richard Christopher Naylor, Hooton, Chester; two *s* one *d*. Sub-Lt 9th Lancers, 1872; 1st Life Guards, 1874; Hon. Col Monaghan Militia; 4th Batt. Royal Irish Fusiliers. *Publication:* Things I Can Tell, 1912. *Heir: s* Hon. William Westenra [*b* 12 July 1892. Lieut RNVR, Royal Naval Division, personal Staff]. *Address:* Rossmore Park, Monaghan; The Stud House, Hampton Court, near London. *T:* Kingston 1492. *Clubs:* Carlton; Kildare Street, Dublin. *Died 31 Jan. 1921.*

ROSTAND, Edmond; dramatist; Member Académie Française since 1901; *b* Marseilles, 1 April 1868; *s* of Eugene Rostand (*d* 1915); *m* Rosemonde Gérard; two *s*. *Educ:* Lycée de Marseilles; Collège Stanislas. *Plays:* Les Romanesques, 1894; La Princesse Lointaine, 1896; La Samaritaine, 1897; Cyrano de Bergerac, 1898; L'Aiglon, 1900. *Poems:* Les Musardises, 1890; Pour la Grèce; Un Soir à Hernani; Les Mots; Chantecler, 1910; Le Cantique de l'Aile, 1911; Le Printemps de l'Aile, 1912, etc. *Address:* Arnaga, Cambo, Basses-Pyrénées. *T:* 4. *Died 2 Dec. 1918.*

ROTH, Brig.-Gen. Reuter Emerich, CMG 1917; DSO 1900; *b* 20 March 1858; *s* of Mathias Roth and Anna Maria Collins; *m* 1883, Lily May Hart, Christchurch, New Zealand. *Educ:* University College School, University Coll. and Hospital, London. MRCS. JP for NSW; served South Africa, 1899–1900 (medal and six clasps); European War, 1915–17 (CMG); CO 5th Australian Field Ambulance, Gallipoli; DDMS 1st ANZAC, Egypt, then DDMS 2nd ANZAC, Egypt and France (despatches). Kt of Grace St John of Jerusalem. *Recreation:* country walks. *Club:* Imperial Service, Sydney.

Died 3 Sept. 1924.

ROTHERHAM, 1st Baron, *cr* 1910, of Broughton; **William Henry Holland,** Kt 1902; Bt 1907; *b* 15 Dec. 1849; *y s* of late William Holland, JP, of Manchester; *m* 1874, Mary, *e d* of late James Lund, DL, Malsis Hall, near Leeds; one *s* two *d*. MP North Salford, 1892–95; (L) Rotherham (WR Yorks), 1899–1910; temp. Chairman of Ways and Means; JP Manchester and Cheshire; member of Advisory Committee of the Board of Trade on Commercial Intelligence, 1900, of the Indian Currency Committee, 1898, of the Joint-Stock Companies' Committee, 1905; Chairman of the Regimental Canteens' Committee, 1913; Commissioner, Paris, Milan, and Brussels Exhibitions; Pres. Associated Chambers of Commerce, 1904–7; Past President, Institute of Directors, Machinery Users' Association, and Textile Institute; Officer of the Order of Leopold, Belgium; Hon. Freeman of the Borough of Rotherham; for many years Chairman of the Fine Cotton Spinners and Doublers Association. *Heir: o s* Captain Hon. Stuart Lund Holland, *b* 25 Oct. 1876. *Address:* Lothersdale, Rottingdean, Sussex. *Club:* Royal Automobile.

Died 26 Dec. 1927.

ROTHES, 19th Earl of, *cr* before 1457; **Norman Evelyn Leslie;** Baron Leslie and Ballenbreich, 1457; Lieutenant 4th Battalion Devonshire Regiment, retired; Captain, Fife Royal Garrison Artillery Militia, 1906; formerly a Representative Peer for Scotland; *b* 13 July 1877; *o s* of Martin Leslie (*d* 1882) and Georgina Francis, *d* of H. Studdy of Waddeton Court, Brixham, Devon; *g s* of Countess of Rothes (18th in line); *S* grandmother, 1893; *m* 1900, Noëlle Lucy Martha, *d* of late T. Dyer Edwardes, of Prinknash Park, Gloucester; two *s*. *Educ:* Eton. *Heir: s* Lord Leslie, *b* 8 Feb. 1902. *Address:* 45 Draycott Place, Chelsea, SW3. *T:* Kensington 6617; Leslie Lodge, Iver Heath, Bucks. *Clubs:* Windham; New, Edinburgh. *Died 29 March 1927.*

ROTHSCHILD, Alfred Charles de, CVO 1902; partner in the firm of Messrs N. M. Rothschild and Sons; *b* London, 20 July 1842; 2nd *s* of late Baron and Baroness Lionel de Rothschild. *Educ:* King's College School, London; Trinity Coll., Camb. Engaged in banking business; for some years a director of the Bank of England, and later a trustee of the National Gallery, and of the Wallace Collection, Hertford House. Légion d'honneur of France. *Address:* 1 Seamore Place, Mayfair, W. *T:* Mayfair 2947; Halton House, Tring, Herts. *Clubs:* Turf, Marlborough, St James's, Bachelors, Boodle's, Pratt's.
Died 31 Jan. 1918.

ROTHSCHILD, Leopold de, CVO 1902; DL, JP; *b* 22 Nov. 1845; 3rd *s* of Baron Lionel de Rothschild, MP; *m* 1881, Marie, *d* of A. Perugia, Trieste; three *s*. *Address:* 5 Hamilton Place, W. *T:* 4237 Gerrard; Ascott, Leighton Buzzard; Palace House, Newmarket; Gunnersbury Park, Acton. *T:* 129 Ealing. *Clubs:* Turf, Bachelors, Jockey.
Died 29 May 1917.

ROTHSCHILD, Hon. Nathaniel Charles; partner in N. M. Rothschild & Sons; *b* 9 May 1877; *s* of 1st Lord Rothschild; *m* 1907, Rozsika, 3rd *d* of Captain Alfred Edler von Wertheimstein of Nagy-Varad, Hungary; one *s* three *d*. *Educ:* Harrow; Trinity College, Camb. BA Nat. Science, 1898; MA 1901. Chairman of Alliance Assurance Co., Ltd. *Publications:* several papers on entomology. *Recreations:* shooting, travel, entomology. *Address:* Arundel House, Kensington Palace Gardens, W8; Ashton Wold, Oundle. *TA:* Eightfold, Notting, London, and Rothschild, Oundle. *Clubs:* Bachelors, Savile, Union, Beefsteak.
Died 12 Oct. 1923.

ROTTON, Sir John Francis, Kt 1899; MA, LLB; KC 1891; *b* 1837; *s* of Richard Rotton, London. Called to Bar, Lincoln's Inn, 1860 (certificate of honour); Legal Adviser to Local Govt Board, 1883; Asst-Sec., 1876–83; Legal Asst Medical Dept, 1869–76; Member of Council University Coll., London, 1869; Vice-Pres. of Senate, 1878 and 1882. *Address:* Lockwood, Frith Hill, Godalming.
Died 9 April 1926.

ROUND, Francis Richard, CMG 1887; of East Hill House, Colchester; *b* 22 Jan. 1845; *s* of late Rev. J. T. Round, Colchester; *m* 1881, Frances Emily, *d* of the late J. J. Tufnell, Langleys, Essex; three *s* one *d*. *Educ:* Marlborough; Balliol College, Oxford. Clerk, Office of Secretary of State for Colonies, 1869; accompanied Sir P. Julyan to Mauritius, 1873; Private Secretary to Sir M. Hicks-Beach, 1880; to the late Sir R. Herbert, 1881; First-class Clerk, 1881; on special service to British Bechuanaland and Mauritius, 1886; Acting Colonial Secretary, Mauritius, 1886–87; Principal Clerk, 1896; retired on pension, 1905; JP Essex, 1906. *Address:* Avenue House, Witham, Essex. *Club:* United University.
Died 24 Nov. 1930.

ROUND, Rt. Hon. James, PC 1902; JP; *b* Colchester, 6 April 1842; *s* of late Rev. J. T. Round, BD; *m* 1870, *c* Sybilla (*d* 1912), *d* of late Rev. H. Freeland; one *s* five *d*. *Educ:* Eton; Christ Church, Oxford (MA). Barrister 1868; MP (C) E Essex, 1868–85, NE Essex or Harwich, 1885–1906; owner of 8,000 acres in Essex and Middlesex. *Address:* Birch Hall, near Colchester; 31 De Vere Gardens, W. *T:* Kensington 2748. *Club:* Carlton.
Died 25 Dec. 1916.

ROUND, John Horace, DL; Hon. LLD (Edin.); late Hon. Historical Adviser to the Crown in Peerage Cases; Vice-President Essex Archæological Society (President, 1916–21); Vice-President English Place-Name Society; *b* 22 Feb. 1854; *o s* of John Round, landowner. *Educ:* Balliol College, Oxford; MA, 1st class in Modern History. *Publications:* Geoffrey de Mandeville, 1892; Feudal England, 1895; The Commune of London, 1899; Calendar of documents preserved in France, 1899; Studies in Peerage and Family History, 1900; Peerage and Pedigree, 1910; The King's Serjeants, 1911; and smaller works; contributor to Domesday Studies, Dictionary of National Biography, The Complete Peerage, Victoria County History, etc; also to English Historical Review, Archæological Transactions, etc. *Address:* 15 Brunswick Terrace, Brighton. *Club:* Carlton.
Died 24 June 1928.

ROUNDWAY, 1st Baron, *cr* 1916, of Devizes; **Charles Edward Hungerford Athol Colston,** JP, DL; *b* 16 May 1854; *s* of late E. Colston, Roundway Park; *m* 1879, Rosalind, *d* of Col Gostling-Murray, Whitton Park, Hounslow, Middlesex; one *s*. *Educ:* Eton; Christ Church, Oxford. MP (C) Thornbury Div. Gloucestershire, 1892–1906. *Heir: s* Brig.-Gen. Hon. Edward Murray Colston, CMG, DSO, MVO, *b* 31 Dec. 1880. *Address:* Roundway Park, Devizes. *Clubs:* Carlton, Arthur's.
Died 17 June 1925.

ROUNSEVELL, Hon. William Benjamin; *b* Sept. 1842; *s* of William Rounsevell who went to South Australia in 1839; *m* 1864, Louisa Ann Carvosso. *Educ:* John Whinham's; St Peter's Colleges, SA. Devoted himself to breeding stud stock (merino sheep and shorthorn cattle), Corryton Park, Mt Crawford; carried on Moolooloo Sheep Station, Cowarie Cattle Run; sold out in the early 'eighties and retired; purchased the wine and spirit business of Johnstone & Furness; floated it with the Kent Town and West End Breweries as a public company called SA Brewing Co. (Chairman); Chairman of Directors of Cotton, Palmer & Preston, Ltd; entered Parliament as Member for Burra, 1875; Treasurer, Morgan Ministry, 1882; Treasurer, Cotton Ministry, 1884; Treasurer, Downer Ministry, 1892–93; Commissioner Public Works, Playford Government, 1890–92; Commissioner Public Works, Johnson Government, 1899. *Recreations:* fond of all sports, shooting particularly—all game; coursing—bred scores of greyhounds; racing—Committeeman on South Australia Jockey Club for a number of years. *Address:* Tremere, Glenelg, S Australia. *Club:* Adelaide, Adelaide.
Died 18 July 1923.

ROUTH, Amand J. McC., MD, BS (London); FRCP; Consulting Obstetric Physician to Charing Cross Hospital and Consulting Physician to the Samaritan Free Hospital for Women; Past President Obstetric and Gynæcological Section of Royal Society of Medicine; retired from practice: *b* London, 1853; *e s* of C. H. F. Routh, MD, and Mary Anne, *d* of James McConnel of Ardwick; *m* 1st, 1880, Blanche, *d* of Richard Routh of Constantinople; 2nd, 1917, Mrs Carline E. Tocher. *Educ:* King's College School, London; Holbrook, Ipswich; University College and Hospital, London. Elected to Obstetric staff of Samaritan Free Hospital for Women, 1880, and to Charing Cross Hospital, 1883 (later consulting); Obstetric Physician (later consulting) St Marylebone General Dispensary, 1882; Consulting Obstetric Physician to St John's Hospital, Twickenham; Examiner in Midwifery, Royal Coll. of Surgeons, 1894–99; Royal Coll. of Physicians, 1900–5; Examiner in Obstetric Medicine University of London, 1900–3; University of Cambridge, 1913–17; University of Birmingham, 1906–8; Councillor on Municipal Council, Folkestone, 1923. *Publications:* Cæsarean Section; Ante-natal Hygiene; numerous papers and articles on midwifery and gynæcology. *Address:* Grimston Court, Folkestone. *T:* Folkestone 480. *Club:* Athenæum.
Died 18 Dec. 1927.

ROUTHIER, Hon. Sir Adolphe Basile; President of the Court of Admiralty for the Province of Quebec; *b* St Placide, County of Two Mountains, Province of Quebec, 8 May 1839; *s* of Charles Routhier and Angélique Lafleur; *m* 1862, Marie Clorinde, *o d* of Jean Mondelet, a lawyer of Three Rivers; one *s* two *d*. *Educ:* Ste Therese College; Laval University (LD and LLD), and became a Professor of International Law). Called to Bar, 1861; Queen's Counsel, 1872; a Judge of the Superior Court of the Province of Quebec, 1873; Chief Justice, 1904; was made a Knight Commander of the Order of St Gregory the Great by Pope Pius IX, and Grand Cross of the same order by Leo XIII, and a Knight of St Michael and St George by King George the Fifth; travelled much in Europe and the Eastern countries. *Publications:* many volumes, speeches, critical essays, travels, and poetry; author of the Canadian National Song, O Canada; A travers l'Europe; A travers l'Espagne; Les Echos, poems; Quebec; Conférences et Discours; Le Centurion, a novel of the Messianic times, translated into five languages; De l'Homme à Dieu, an apology of Christianity; Paulina (novel); Montcalm and Levis (drama). *Address:* Quebec, Canada; St Irénie les Bains, County of Charlevoix.
Died June 1919.

ROW, Canchi Sarvothama, ISO; (retired) District Registrar of Assurances; *b* 1856; *m*; one *d*. *Educ:* Saidapet High School; Madras Presidency College. Graduated, 1876; employed as a clerk in the Madras Board of Revenue, 1878–84; in the office of the Inspector-General of Registration, 1884–96; Personal Assistant to the Dewan of Baroda, 1897–1901; District Registrar, Madras Presidency, 1901–14. *Address:* Saidapet, Madras Presidency, India.

ROWBOTHAM, Rev. John Frederick, MA Oxon; poet and historian; *b* Bradford, Yorkshire, 18 April 1859; *s* of Rev. Frederick Rowbotham, MA, Rector of St James's, Edin. *Educ:* Edinburgh Acad.; Rossall; Balliol Coll., Oxford. Captain of Rossall School; Scholar of Balliol College; 1st class Classical Moderations and Finals; Taylorian University Scholar in Italian. Travelled for some years in Spain, Italy, Austria, Germany, and France; collected materials for the History of Music; ordained, 1891; Vicar of Ratley, 1892; Rector of Huntley, 1895; British Chaplain of Buda-Pesth and Hungary, 1896; Vicar of Abbotsley, 1897; Editor and Proprietor of The Bard, 1910; Vicar of Sutton Cheney, 1916. *Publications:* The History of Music (3 vols),

1887; The Death of Roland, an Epic Poem, 1888; The Human Epic, 1890; A Short History of Music, 1891; The Private Life of the Great Composers, 1892; The History of Rossall School, 1894; The History of the Troubadours and the Courts of Love, 1895; The God Horus, a novel of Ancient Egypt, 1898; The Epic of London, 1908; The Epic of God and the Devil, 1911; The Epic of the Swiss Lake Dwellers, 1913; The Epic of the Empire, 1914; The Epic of Semiramis, Queen of Babylon, 1920; Epic of the Globe, 1921. *Recreations:* travelling, driving. *Address:* The Vicarage, Sutton Cheney, Leicestershire. *Died 20 Oct. 1925.*

ROWCROFT, Major Ernest Cave, DSO 1900; Indian Army; 35th Sikhs, retired 1907; *b* 6 Oct. 1866; *s* of Major-Gen. G. C. Rowcroft; unmarried. *Educ:* private school, Eastbourne; Sandhurst. Served China, 1900; present at taking of Tientsin and advance from Tientsin on Pekin, and at the relief of the Legations. *Address:* Srinagar, Kashmir. *Clubs:* United Empire, Junior Conservative.

Died 27 July 1916.

ROWCROFT, Maj.-Gen. George Cleland; Indian Army; *b* 17 Sept. 1831; *s* of late Lt-Gen. F. E. R. Rowcroft, CB; *m* 1860, Oriana Rachel (*d* 1921), *d* of late Hon. P. D. Souper, Registrar-General of Mauritius; one *s* four *d*. *Educ:* private schools. Entered army 1849; Maj.-Gen., 1890; unemployed list, 1889; served Scind Frontier Expedition, 1852; NW Frontier of India Campaign, 1852-53 (medal with clasp); Indian Mutiny, 1857 (medal); NW Frontier of India Campaign, 1858 (despatches). *Recreations:* formerly, shooting, polo, etc. *Address:* Chinnor, Oxon. *Died 5 June 1922.*

ROWDEN, Aldred William, KC; *s* of late Rev. G. Croke Rowden, DCL. *Educ:* Rugby; Balliol College, Oxford. Called to Bar, 1874; QC 1899; Bencher, Lincoln's Inn, 1906. *Publication:* The Primates of the Four Georges, 1915. *Address:* 34 Courtfield Gardens, SW. *T:* Western 3911. *Club:* New University.

Died 12 Feb. 1919.

ROWE, Rev. Alfred William; Principal, Lincoln College, 1892-1912; Canon of Lincoln and Prebendary of Biggleswade since 1896; *m*. *Educ:* Trinity College, Cambridge (MA). Assist Master, Felstead School, 1860-88; Vicar of New Brentford, 1888-92. *Address:* 3 St Giles Avenue, Lincoln. *Died 10 March 1921.*

ROWE, Charles Henry, CMG 1918; Paymaster Captain, Royal Navy (retired); *b* 13 July 1869; *s* of Major W. A. S. Rowe, RMLI; *m* 1898, Margaret, *d* of late Edwin Hills, JP, Deal; one *s* one *d*. *Educ:* Portsmouth Grammar School. Entered Navy, 1885; Secretary to Vice-Admiral, Channel Fleet, 1904-5; to Commander-in-Chief, China, 1906-8; served in HMS Lion, 1912-17; present at actions of Heligoland Bight, 28 Aug. 1914, Dogger Bank, 24 Jan. 1915, and Jutland, 31 May 1916 (despatches); Order of Crown of Italy (Officer), conferred 11 Aug. 1917; specially promoted for distinguished services rendered during the war. *Address:* 11 Victoria Road, Deal.

Died 31 Jan. 1925.

ROWE, S. Grant, ROI; *b* London, 1861; 3rd *s* of late Charles J. Rowe, lyric author. *Educ:* private school, and finished at City Middle Class Schools, City, EC. After leaving school studied from the antique at British Museum and St Martin's School of Art, and, acting on good professional advice, adopted art as a profession; first exhibited at Royal Academy; represented at all the most important art galleries and museums. *Recreations:* walking, cycling. *Address:* 6 The Studios, Camden Street, Oakley Square, NW.

Died 22 July 1928.

ROWE, Chief Engineer William, DSO 1915; RD; RNR. Served European War, 1914-15 (DSO, despatches for services in patrol work). *Died Feb. 1924.*

ROWELL, Sir Herbert Babington, KBE 1918; MInstCE; MINA; *b* 1860; *o* surv. *s* of Robert Rowell, Newcastle-on-Tyne; *m* 1891, Mary Dobree, *d* of John N. Robin, Naples; two *s* two *d*. *Educ:* Mill Hill School; in Switzerland. President Shipbuilding Employers' Federation, 1912-14; President NE Coast Inst. of Engineers and Shipbuilders, 1915-17; Chairman, R. & W. Hawthorn, Leslie & Co., Ltd; JP (1906), Co. Durham; Vice-President Federation of British Industries. *Address:* The Manor House, Jesmond, Newcastle; Redesmouth House, Northumberland; 242 St James' Court, SW1. *Clubs:* Royal Automobile, Royal Societies.

Died 23 June 1921.

ROWELL, John Soulsby, ISO 1907; Agent to the Corporation of Lloyds', the Liverpool and Glasgow Underwriters' Associations for

the port and district of Havre, France; *b* Hexham, 9 Aug. 1846; *s* of Soulsby Rowell. *Educ:* France; Germany. Was Acting-Consul at Havre on various occasions, 1867-83; Vice-Consul, 1870; passed an examination before the Civil Service Commissioners, 1874; HM Vice-Consul for Havre to reside at Havre, 1898; Acting Consul-General on various occasions, 1884-1906; retired on a pension, 1906. *Publications:* French Port Charges; Souvenirs de voyages, in the Harz Mountains. *Recreation:* fishing. *Address:* 23 Place Gambetta, Havre, France. *TA:* Rowell, Havre. *Clubs:* Northern Counties; Association des anciens élèves du Collège et Lycée, at Havre.

Died 3 Oct. 1916.

ROWETT, John Quiller; Managing Director, Rowett Leaky & Co. Ltd, 19 Eastcheap, EC; Chairman, Jude, Hanbury & Co., Ltd, Wateringbury; *b* 19 Sept. 1876; *s* of late John Quiller Rowett, Polperro, Cornwall; *m* Helen Graham, *d* of John Jackson Coats, Glasgow; one *s* two *d*. *Educ:* Mannamead School, Plymouth; Dulwich College. Founded Rowett Institute of Research in Animal Nutrition in connection with Aberdeen University and North of Scotland College of Agriculture; mainly financed Shackleton-Rowett Expedition of the Quest to the South Antarctic, 1921-22; Master of the Worshipful Company of Fruiterers, 1921; Hon. LLD University of Aberdeen, 1922. *Recreations:* farming, shooting, billiards. *Address:* 9 Hyde Park Terrace, W2. *T:* Paddington 1465; Ely Place, Frant, Sussex. *T:* Frant 17. *TA:* Roquille London. *Clubs:* Junior Carlton, Royal Automobile. *Died 2 Oct. 1924.*

ROWLAND, Rev. Alfred, LLB, BA (London); DD, Congregational Church of Canada; Member of Convocation; Minister of the Congregational Church, Park Chapel, Crouch End, 1875-1911; Ancient Merchants Lecturer, Chairman of London Congregational Union, 1892; Chairman of the Congregational Union of England and Wales, 1898; *b* Henley-on-Thames, 1840; *s* of late Rev. James Rowland; *m* 1868, Ellen Mary (*d* 1909), *d* of William Trewent, Pembroke; six *s* two *d*. *Educ:* Crauford College, Maidenhead; New College, London. Pastor of the Congregational Church in Zion Chapel, Frome, 1865. *Publications:* Half-hours with Teachers; Paul's First Letter to Timothy; The Burdens of Life, 1898; Open Windows, 1903; Possibilities of Obscure Lives, 1904; The Exchanged Crowns; After Death—What?, 1910; An Independent Parson, 1923; various sermons and addresses; articles in magazines, Pulpit Commentary, etc. *Recreation:* golf. *Address:* Brightlands, Etchingham Park Road, Church End, Finchley, N. *Died 3 Sept. 1925.*

ROWLAND, John William, CMG 1897; MB, CM; *b* 30 Dec. 1852; *e s* of Colonel John Christian Rowland, and *g s* of Col George Tempest Rowland, RA. *Educ:* Edinburgh University. Served in India, 1877-78; Assistant Colonial Surgeon, Gold Coast and Lagos, 1880; acted also as District Commissioner; Chief Medical Officer, 1896; was on several occasions an extraordinary member of the Council; acted as botanist to the expedition of Sir Gilbert Carter in 1893. Decorated for services in West Africa. *Recreation:* yachting.

Died 18 Oct. 1925.

ROWLANDS, James; MP (L and Lab) NW or Dartford Division of Kent, 1906-Jan. 1910, and since Dec. 1910; *b* 1 Oct. 1851; *s* of William Bull Rowlands; *m* 1879, Kate (*d* 1905), *d* of Joseph Boyden. *Educ:* Working Men's College, and similar institutions. Apprenticed to watch-case making; early took interest in politics; organised registration in old borough of Finsbury; member of London Municipal Reform League, organised Finsbury branch of it, and became its Hon. Secretary; MP East Finsbury, 1886-95; President of the Gas Consumers' Protection League, 1893; Secretary of Leaseholds Enfranchisement Association; took active part in the international arbitration movement; was a member of the last London School Board; Hon. Secretary of Land Law Reform Association; took an active part in Parliament in promoting Bills for reform of the land laws for town and country, and the housing question. *Publications:* pamphlets and articles. *Address:* 119 Mercers Road, Tufnell Park, N19; 8 Buckingham Street, Strand, WC2. *Club:* National Liberal.

Died 1 March 1920.

ROWLEY, Adm. Charles John, JP; Royal Navy, retired 26 Dec. 1897; *b* Weeting Hall, Brandon, Norfolk, 24 Dec. 1832; 2nd *s* of late Capt. Richard F. Rowley, RN, and Elizabeth Julia, *d* of late John Angerstein, Weeting Hall, Brandon; *m* 1867, Alice M. A., 3rd *d* of late George Cary Elwes; one *s* one *d*. *Educ:* at home. Entered Royal Navy, 24 Dec. 1844; served in Black Sea and Sea of Azoff, 1854-55 (medals and clasps and 5th class Medjidie); Naval ADC to the Queen, 1882-84; 2nd in command Channel Squadron, 1887-88; Admiral, 1895; retired, 1897; JP Bucks and Hants. *Address:* Holmesland, Botley,

Hants. *TA:* Botley, Hants. *Clubs:* United Service; Royal Navy, Portsmouth; Royal Southern Yacht, Southampton.

Died 11 Nov. 1919.

ROWLEY, Rev. Sir George Charles Augustus, 4th Bt, *cr* 1836; *b* 18 March 1869; *s* of Sir George Rowley, 3rd Bt and Alicia (*d* 1888), *d* of late Capt. R. Hollis, 1st Dragoon Guards; *S* father, 1922; *m* 1891, Caroline, *o d* of late Rev. John Cuming, MA; one *s* two *d*. *Educ:* Trinity College, Cambridge. Ordained deacon, 1893; priest, 1894; Curate of Scunthorpe, 1893–95; Brabourne, 1895–97; Vicar of Harmston, Lincs, 1897–99; Rector of Eastwick, Herts, 1899–1916. *Heir: s* George William Rowley, Captain Essex Regt, *b* 1896. *Address:* Wrottesley House, Mount Ephraim Road, Streatham, SW16. *T:* Streatham 1153. *Died 7 Sept. 1924.*

ROWLEY, Sir George (Charles Erskine), 3rd Bt, *cr* 1836; Hon. Lieutenant-Colonel in Army, retired 1885; *b* 26 Sept. 1844; *S* uncle, 1884; *m* 1st, 1867, Alicia (*d* 1888), *d* of Capt. Hollis, 1st Dragoon Guards; 2nd, 1890, Amy Isabel, OBE, *d* of William Foster Batt, Cae Kenfy, Abergavenny; two *s*. *Educ:* Cheltenham; Sandhurst. Captain 1st Batt. Royal Welsh Fusiliers, 1879–85; retired. *Heir: s* Rev. George Charles Augustus Rowley [*b* 18 March 1869; *m* 1891, Caroline, *o d* of late Rev. John Cuming; one *s* two *d*]. *Address:* Eastfield Lodge, Epsom Road, Guildford. *T:* Guildford 149. *Club:* Army and Navy. *Died 15 Jan. 1922.*

ROWNTREE, Joseph; *b* 24 May 1836; *s* of Joseph Rowntree; *m* 1867, Emma Antoinette Seebohm; three *s* one *d*. *Educ:* Friends' School, York. Engaged in business, and in social, political, and literary work. *Publications:* (joint) The Temperance Problem and Social Reform; British Gothenburg Experiments; Public Control of the Liquor Traffic, etc. *Recreations:* natural history, gardening. *Address:* Clifton Lodge, York. *T:* 1060 York.

Died 24 Feb. 1925.

ROWSELL, Mary Catharine; novelist; essayist; dramatist; *b* London; *o d* and *y c* of Charles John Rowsell, London. *Educ:* Queen's College, Harley St; Brussels; Bonn. *Publications:* Love Loyal; Traitor or Patriot, 1884; The Silver Dial, 1886; Thorndyke Manor, 1887; Miss Vanbrugh, 1887; Richard's Play, comedietta, collaborated, produced, 1894; The Friend of the People, 1894 (new issue 1908); The Pedlar and his Dog, Honour Bright, Dick of Temple Bar, with other stories for children; History of France (volume of 'Children's Study' Series), 1897; The Heir of Willowcote, 1901; Red House, and many serials and short stories for magazines; The Wild Swans, 1902; joint translator of Murger's Latin Quarter; Life-Story of Charlotte de la Tremoille, Countess of Derby; The Song of Liberty (drama) (translated and produced in Sweden); The Secret of the Ivory Room; Monsieur de Paris, 1907; Ninon de L'Enclos, 1910; Haunted, 1911; Portraits of Robespierre (translation); Robin Hood (drama) (collaborated). *Recreation:* music. *Address:* 11 Clarence Avenue, Bickley, Kent.

ROWSELL, Rev. Walter Frederick, MA; *b* 1837; 2nd *s* of Rev. Evan Edward Rowsell, MA, Rector of Hambledon, Surrey; *m* 1867, Catherine Harriet (*d* 1923), *o d* of Major George Fulljames, late Commander of the Guzerat Horse and Political Agent at Rewa Kanta, India. *Educ:* Elstree; Sedbergh; St John's College, Cambridge (Scholar). BA; Classical Tripos, 1860; MA 1863. Deacon, 1863; priest, 1864; Curate of Hove with Preston, 1863–7; Vicar of Copmanthorpe, Yorkshire, 1867–76; Rural Dean of Bishopthorpe, York, 1874–84; Vicar of St Paul's, Sculcoates, Hull, 1876–91; Vicar of Topcliffe, Yorkshire, 1891–1902; Rural Dean of Thirsk, Yorkshire, 1892–1902; Hon. Secretary of the York Diocesan Conference, 1876–1902; Prebendary of York Cathedral from 1882. *Recreations:* reading, cycling, etc. *Address:* Meadowcroft, St Margarets-on-Thames.

Died 15 March 1924.

ROXBURGHE, Duchess of; (Anne Emily), VA; *d* of 7th Duke of Marlborough; *m* 1874, 7th Duke of Roxburghe (*d* 1892); three *s* three *d*. Late Mistress of the Robes and Lady of the Bedchamber to Queen Victoria. *Address:* Broxmouth Park, Dunbar, Scotland.

Died 20 June 1923.

ROY, Most Rev. Paul Eugene; Archbishop of Quebec since 1925; *b* 9 Nov. 1859; *s* of Benjamin Roy and Desanges Gosselin. *Educ:* Quebec; Paris. Professor at Laval University, 1886–90; Pastor at St Ann's Church, Hartford, Conn, 1890–99; Missionary at Quebec, 1899–1901; Curé of Jacques Cartier à Québec, 1901–7; Directeur de l'Action Sociale Catholique, 1907–8; Bishop of Eleutheropolis, 1908; Archbishop of Séleucie, 1914; Coadjutor cum futura successione, 1920. *Address:* Archbishop's Palace, Quebec.

Died Feb. 1926.

ROY, Commander Robert Stewart, CMG 1918; Royal Navy (retired); *b* 2 March 1878; *s* of late Rev. James Roy, of Appleton Roebuck, Yorkshire; *m* 1912, Marjorie, *d* of late Henry Pigeon of Furzedown, Hythe, Southampton; two *s* one *d*. *Educ:* St Peter's School, York; HMS Britannia. Naval Cadet, 1892; served all over the world; Commander, 1914; served European War (despatches, CMG); invalided and placed on retired list, Aug. 1919. *Recreations:* all kinds of outdoor sport. *Address:* The Mount, Chobham, Surrey. *T:* Chobham 20. *M:* IO 381. *Club:* Junior United Service.

Died 3 Dec. 1924.

ROYCE, William Stapleton; MP (Lab) Holland-with-Boston since Dec. 1918; *b* 1857; *m* 1882, Emma Louisa, *d* of O. L. Broedelet, Rotterdam. *Educ:* Pretty's Preparatory School, Spalding. Twice contested the Spalding Division (U); late President of the Holland-with-Boston Unionist Association. *Address:* Pinchbeck Hall, Spalding, Lincs. *Died 23 June 1924.*

ROYDEN, Sir Thomas Bland, 1st Bt, *cr* 1905; DL, JP, Co. Chester; *b* 20 Feb. 1831; *s* of late Thomas Royden, of Frankby Hall; *m* 1865, Alice Elizabeth, *d* of late Thomas Dowdall; two *s* six *d*. High Sheriff of Cheshire, 1903–4; ex-Chairman of Liverpool Conservative Association; MP (C) West Toxteth, 1885, 1886–92; moved reply to Queen's Speech; was Member of Royal Commission on Tonnage and on Unseaworthy Ships, also represented Liverpool upon the Load Line Committee; head of firm T. B. Royden, steamship owners, 20 Brown's Buildings, Liverpool. *Heir: s* Thomas Royden, JP, Deputy Chairman Cunard Steamship Co., Director, Lancs and Yorks Railway, and the London, City, and Midland Bank, *b* 22 May 1871. *Address:* Frankby Hall, Frankby, Cheshire. *Clubs:* Carlton, Constitutional, Conservative. *Died 29 Aug. 1917.*

ROYDS, Col Sir Clement Molyneux, Kt 1906; CB 1902; TD; DL, Co. Lancashire; FSA; late Colonel Commanding Duke of Lancaster's Own Imperial Yeomanry; Hon. Colonel 2nd Battalion Lancashire Fusiliers; Knight of Justice of the Order of St John of Jerusalem in England; *b* 3 April 1842; *e s* of William Edward Royds, Greenhill, Rochdale, and Danehill Park, Sussex, and Mary Ann, *e d* of Anthony Molyneux, Newsham House, Lancashire; *m* 1882, Annette Nora Jane, 2nd *d* of Thomas Littledale of Highfield, Lancs, Lady of Grace of the Order of St John of Jerusalem in England. *Educ:* on the Continent. Contested Rochdale, 1892; MP (C) Rochdale, 1895–1906. *Address:* 71 Eaton Place, SW. *T:* Victoria 4275; Greenhill, Rochdale. *Clubs:* Carlton, United Service. *Died 28 Jan. 1916.*

ROYLE, Arnold, CB 1884; Gentleman Usher to the King, 1901; *b* 30 Aug. 1887; *s* of W. Royle, solicitor, Lymington; *m* 1880, Cecily Jane Longueville, 2nd *d* of Thomas Snow, Blundellsands, Liverpool; one *s* two *d*. *Educ:* King's Coll., London. Joined army as assistant surgeon on the Staff, 1859; served five years in India; retired half pay, 1871; appointed medical attendant to Duke of Albany, 1875, and remained with him till his death, 1884; appointed temporary Medical Inspector Local Government Board, 1884; confirmed as permanent Inspector, 1893; late Clerk of the Robes and Groom of the Privy Chamber to Her Majesty Queen Victoria. *Recreations:* yachting, golf, etc. *Address:* Albany Lodge, Esher. *M:* Q 281. *Club:* Naval and Military. *Died 16 Feb. 1919.*

ROZE, Madame Marie; Officier de l'Instruction Publique; *b* Paris, 2 March 1846. *Educ:* Paris Conservatoire, under Auber and Mocker; first prize singing, 1865; gold medal, 1866. Made début at Opéra Comique, in Paris at the Grand Opera, 1870; presented with gold medal by M Thiers for her gallant conduct during siege of Paris; Médaille de 1870; first appearance in England, 1872; America, 1877; had a school for singing and lyric declamation. *Address:* Château du Belvédère, 3 rue du Pavillon, Parc des Princes, Boulogne sur Seine, France. *Died 21 June 1926.*

ROZE, Raymond, (J. H. Raymond Roze-Perkins); *b* London, 1875; *m*; one *d*. 1st prize with honours of Brussels Royal Conservatoire of Music. Musical Director to late Sir Henry Irving at Lyceum Theatre; and to Sir Herbert Tree at His Majesty's Theatre; composer of Overture and Incidental Music to Shakespeare's plays: Julius Caesar, King John, Henry IV, Henry V, Much Ado About Nothing, Tempest, Merry Wives of Windsor, Taming of the Shrew, Antony and Cleopatra; also to Trilby, and many other plays; conducted symphonic concerts of his own works at Spa, Dieppe, Aix-les-Bains, Monte Carlo, Paris, etc; Director of the Royal Opera House, Covent Garden, autumn season, 1913, when he produced his own opera, Joan of Arc; wrote and composed the fantastic opera, Arabesque, produced at Coliseum, 1916; conducted his own music, Julius Caesar, at Command Performance, Drury Lane, 1916. Founded July 1914, organised and directed, by the special permission of the Army Council, the first new Volunteer Home Defence Corps, the United Arts' Rifles, recruited entirely from members of the fine Arts, later recognised by the War Office under the title of 1st Central London Regiment; invited by Special Committee of House of Commons to act as Hon. Secretary to the Inter-Parliamentary Commercial Conference, 1918 (official thanks of House of Commons Committee). *Address:* 18 Palace Gardens Terrace, W8. *Club:* Bath.

Died 31 March 1920.

RUBENS, Paul Alfred; dramatic author and composer; *b* 29 April 1875; *s* of Victor Rubens, 8A Kensington Palace Gardens, W. *Educ:* Winchester College; University College, Oxford. Student at Inner Temple, 1898; gave up career of Barrister for Dramatic and Musical Work; at one time an ardent amateur actor, and always a Member of the Oxford University Dramatic Society; wrote some of the incidental music for Mr Tree's revival of Twelfth Night, but chiefly wrote music to his own lyrics and librettos; author of two comedies. *Publications:* Three Little Maids; Lady Madcap; Young Mr Yarde (with Harold Ellis); The Dairymaids (with Frank Tours); The Blue Moon (with Howard Talbot); Mr Popple; Miss Hook of Holland; The Balkan Princess; The Girl from Utah; The Sunshine Girl; author and composer of numerous songs in The Country Girl, The Cingalee, Florodora, The Messenger Boy, The Orchid, The Girl from Kay's, etc; many other songs and ballads. *Recreations:* motoring, golfing, shooting, working, getting up late—anything, in fact, except London and social functions. *Address:* 27 Shaftesbury Avenue, W. *TA:* Sleepy, London. *T:* Gerrard 6700. *Clubs:* Garrick, Royal Automobile, Aero.

Died 5 Feb. 1917.

RUDDOCK, Ven. David; Archdeacon of Hawkes Bay since 1907; *m*; two *s* killed in the War. *Educ:* St Catharine's College, Cambridge; Lichfield College. Ordained 1879; Missionary, Melanesia, 1879–84; Curate of Redmire, NSW, 1885; All Saints', Parramatta, 1886; St Mary's, Kangaroo Point, 1886–87; Priest in charge, Rockhampton, 1887–88; Rector of Holy Trinity, Wooloongabba, 1888–93; SPG, 1894–1900; Curate of Shefford Magna, 1901–3; Vicar of Wairoa, 1904–7. *Address:* Napier, N Zealand.

Died 30 Jan. 1920.

RUFF, Howard; Founder (1894) and Hon. Secretary of the Royal Society of St George; Founder (1908) and Hon. Editor of the English Race. Through his exertions all of the Royal Navy, Army, and Air Force wear their National Emblems on their respective Saints' days; Fellow of Huguenot Society of London; Royal Colonial Institute; Royal Geographical Society and other Associations; visited Australia, Canada, USA. *Recreations:* reading, freemasonry; formerly farming and country sports. *Address:* 5 Bloomsbury Square, WC1. *TA:* Georgical, London. *T:* Museum 5654. *Club:* Royal Societies.

Died 29 Oct. 1928.

RUFFER, Sir Marc Armand, Kt 1916; CMG 1905; MA, MD; FLS; President of Sanitary, Maritime, and Quarantine Council of Egypt, Alexandria; President of the Municipal Delegation, and Vice-President of the Municipality, Alexandria; Commissioner, British Red Cross Society and Order of St John; Egyptian Representative International Bureau of Hygiene, Paris; *b* 1859; *s* of late Baron Alphonse Jacques de Ruffer; *m* Alice Mary, *e d* of late Captain Greenfield, RA; three *d. Educ:* Brasenose College, Oxford; University College, London. Formerly Director of British Inst. of Preventive Medicine; Prof. of Bacteriology at Cairo Medical School; Member of Indian Plague Commission; Egyptian Delegate to Sanitary Conferences, Paris, 1908 and 1911, and Rome, 1907; Grand Cross Medjidieh and Grand Officer Osmanieh; Commander Order of Saviour of Greece, St Anne of Russia, and Cross of Italy. *Publications:* various papers in scientific and medical journals. *Recreation:* billiards. *Address:* Villa Ménival, Ramleh, Egypt. *TA:* Ruffer, Alexandria. *Clubs:* Savile, Royal Societies; Khedivial, Union, Alexandria.

Died 2 May 1917.

RUGGLES, Maj.-Gen. John; Retired List, Indian Army; *b* 21 July 1827; *e s* of late W. H. Ruggles, Lewisham, Kent; *m* 1885, Ellen Sophia, (Nellie), *y d* of late G. F. Johnson, HMCS; no *c. Educ:* Addiscombe Mil. Coll. First Commission Indian Service, 1845; at siege and capture of Fort Kanysu, 1846; Indian Mutiny, 1857, one of the Lucknow garrison; served in China as volunteer in 1860; in Bhootan, 1865, commanded column of attack which resulted in capture of Bula stockades (thanks of Commander-in-Chief, 3 medals, 2 clasps); Colonel 19th Punjabis. *Publication:* Recollections of a Lucknow Veteran. *Address:* Montana, Swanage.

Died 26 July 1919.

RUGGLES-BRISE, Maj.-Gen. Sir Harold Goodeve, KCMG 1919; CB 1915; MVO 1910; *b* 17 March 1864; 5th *s* of late Sir Samuel B. Ruggles-Brise, KCB, and Marianne, *d* of Sir Edward Bowyer-Smyth, 10th Bt; *m* 1895, Lady Dorothea Stewart-Murray, *e d* of 7th Duke of Atholl. *Educ:* Winchester; Balliol College, Oxford. Joined Grenadier Guards, 1885; Captain, 1897; Major, 1902; Lt-Col, 1907; Colonel, 1911; Maj.-Gen., 1917; Brigade-Major, Gibraltar, 1899, S Africa, 1899–1900; Brigade of Guards, 1901–3; Commandant, School of Musketry, 1911; served S African War, 1899–1900 (despatches, five times; Bt Major, Queen's medal 7 clasps); European War, France and Flanders, 1914–18; Brigade Commander, severely wounded, Divisional Commander, and Mil. Sec. GHQ (CB, promotion to Major-General, KCMG, despatches five times). Commander Legion of Honour, Croix de Guerre, Commander Order of Leopold, Belgian Croix de Guerre. *Address:* 5 Bickenhall Mansions, Gloucester Place, W1. *T:* Mayfair 6369. *Club:* Guards.

Died 24 June 1927.

RUMSEY, Robert Murray, ISO 1903; *b* 1849; *m* 1892, Francesca, *d* of W. B. Treacher, Carlisle Mansions, Westminster. Entered Royal Navy, 1862; Lieut 1873; Commander (retired), 1882; served on North America, East India and Pacific and Home Stations; Canadian (Fenian Raid) and Abyssinian medals; Commissioner of Volta District, Gold Coast, 1880; Assistant Colonial Secretary, Lagos, 1883; Deputy Governor, 1884; Assistant Harbour-master, Hong-Kong, 1884; Harbour-master, 1888; Member of Executive and Legislative Councils; pensioned 1904. *Address:* Lavethan, Blisland, Bodmin, Cornwall. *Club:* Naval and Military.

Died 18 Nov. 1922.

RUNTZ, Sir John (Johnson), Kt 1903; *b* 14 March 1842; *s* of late John Runtz of Stoke Newington; *m* 1st, Emma (*d* 1911), *d* of W. Westwood of Ventnor, Isle of Wight; two *s* one *d*; 2nd, 1914, Adeline, *e d* of late William Jenkinson. First Mayor of Stoke Newington; JP Co. London; a prominent figure in the Conservative cause in Stoke Newington and North Hackney, and also an active worker in the municipal and church life of that district for over thirty years; a member of the Corporation of the City of London and City of London Conservative Association; Hon. Treasurer of the Metropolitan Division of National Union of Conservative Associations; President of N Hackney Conservative Association; President (first) of the Corporation of Insurance Brokers of United Kingdom. *Address:* Tunnel Woods, near Watford, Herts. *T:* Watford 175; 33 Nicholas Lane, EC. *TA:* Runtz, London. *T:* 1216 Avenue. *Clubs:* City Carlton, Constitutional.

Died 4 Nov. 1922.

RUSHBROOKE, William George, BA London, LLM Cambridge; FRSL; Senior Classical Master, City of London School, 1872–93; Headmaster of St Olave's Grammar School, 1893–1922; President of the Headmasters' Association, 1918; Dean of the College of Preceptors since 1911; Chairman, Society of Schoolmasters; *b* 21 Jan. 1849. *Educ:* City of London School; St John's College, Cambridge (Scholar and Fellow). First in Classics in London BA; sixth in first class of Classical Tripos, 1872. *Publications:* First Greek Reader; The Common Tradition of the Synoptic Gospels (with Dr Abbott); Synopticon, an attempt to set forth the inter-relations of the three Synoptic Gospels, and occasionally their relation to the Fourth Gospel; Olivetum Olavianum, and the Olavian Hymnal. *Address:* 13 Cathcart Hill, N19. *T:* Hampstead 412. *Club:* Overseas.

Died 30 Jan. 1926.

RUSHTON, William S., ISO 1902; Surveyor, General Post Office, since 1890; *b* 1850; *s* of William Rushton, of Eversley, Southsea; *m* 1891, Gertrude Jurin, 2nd *d* of William Bache Roberts, of Exchequer and Audit Office; one *s* one *d. Recreations:* golf, cycling, boating. *Address:* Landguard, Granada Road, Southsea. *Clubs:* Constitutional; United Service Golf. *Died 20 Feb. 1924.*

RUSSELL, 1st Baron, *cr* 1919; **Edward Richard Russell,** Kt 1893; editor of Liverpool Daily Post (later Daily Post and Mercury), since 1869; *b* London, 9 Aug. 1834; *s* of Edward Haslingden Russell and Mary Ann Crook; *m* 1st, 1858, Eliza Sophia (*d* 1901), *d* of Stephen Bradley and Mary Sophia Ede, Bridge, Canterbury; 2nd, 1902, Jean Stewart, *widow* of Joseph M'Farlane and *d* of late Alexander Macdonald of Campbeltown, Argyllshire. *Educ:* privately. Secretary of Whittington Club, 1858; assistant editor Liverpool Daily Post, 1860; writer of leading articles and dramatic critic, Morning Star, London, 1866; MP (L) Glasgow, Bridgeton Division, 1885–87; Life Member of the Court of Liverpool University and Life Governor of University College, Aberystwith; Treasurer Newspaper Press Fund; was first Chairman of the Liverpool Reform Club. *Publications:* An Editor's Sermons,

1901; Arrested Fugitives, 1912; A Speculation on Hypothesis in Religion, 1915; a volume of reminiscences under the title of That Reminds Me; also many pamphlets on Shakespearian, literary, and philosophical subjects. *Recreations:* theatre, music, travel. *Heir:* none. *Address:* The Gables, Croxteth Road, Liverpool. *TA:* 5 Croxteth Road, Liverpool. *T:* Royal 2171. *Clubs:* Reform, National Liberal; Liverpool Reform, Liverpool Junior Reform, Liverpool University.

Died 20 Feb. 1920 (ext).

RUSSELL, Hon. Sir Charles, 1st Bt, *cr* 1916; KCVO 1921; Solicitor; *b* London, 8 July 1863; 2nd *s* of late Lord Russell of Killowen; *m* 1889, Adah Walmsley Williams, *g d* of Sir Joshua Walmsley; one *d*. *Educ:* Beaumont College, near Windsor; abroad. Contested (L) Hackney and South Salford; in 1893 acted as Solicitor for the British Agent in the Behring Sea Arbitration between Great Britain and the United States; Solicitor for the Government of the Dominion of Canada; Solicitor for the Stewards of the Jockey Club; Director of the Equity and Law Life Assurance Society and the Law Reversionary Society; Chairman of the Board of Management of the Hospital of St John and St Elizabeth; Chairman of the Collections Committee of the British Red Cross Society and the Order of St John; Knight of Grace of the Order of the Hospital of John of Jerusalem in England, 1921. *Recreation:* golf. *Heir:* nephew Alec Charles Russell, RHA, *b* 19 Dec. 1894. *Address:* 37 Norfolk Street, Strand, WC2. *T:* Gerrard 7979; 13 Dean's Yard, Westminster Abbey, SW1. *T:* Victoria 6631; Littleworth Corner, Burnham, Bucks. *T:* Burnham 18. *TA:* Toilful, London. *Clubs:* Turf, Beefsteak, Garrick.

Died 27 March 1928.

RUSSELL, Charles Alfred, KC; *b* 1855; 2nd *s* of late J. A. Russell, QC; *m* 1882, Amy Mary, 4th *d* of late J. S. Westmacott. *Educ:* University College School and University College. Barrister Gray's Inn, 1878; Bencher, 1894; QC, 1896. *Address:* 2 Harcourt Buildings, Temple, EC.

Died 21 June 1926.

RUSSELL, Charles Gilchrist, JP; LLD; *b* Edinburgh, 1840; *s* of late Thomas Russell; *m* 1865, Annie, *e d* of J. Best Davidson, for many years chief sub-editor of Leeds Mercury; two *s* two *d*. *Educ:* Northern District School; Edinburgh Univ. Was for some years teacher in public schools and tutor in private families; studied medicine Edinburgh University, 1860–63; reporter Caledonian Mercury, 1862–64; Leeds Mercury, 1864–66; London correspondent Leeds Mercury, 1866–67; literary editor Sportsman, 1867–75; assistant editor Glasgow Herald, 1875–87; Editor of Glasgow Herald, 1887–1906; President Institute of Journalists, 1892–93. *Address:* 11 Buckingham Terrace, Glasgow. *T:* 203 Western, Glasgow. *Clubs:* Press; New, Glasgow.

Died 22 Dec. 1916.

RUSSELL, Charles Taze, (Pastor Russell); independent minister; *b* Pittsburgh, 16 Feb. 1852; *s* of Joseph L. Russell and Ann Eliza Birney; *m* 1879, Maria Frances, *d* of Mahlen and Salena Ackley. *Educ:* private tutors. Began in independent ministry Pittsburgh, 1878; regularly elected pastor of numerous congregations from Maine to Calif, USA, and also in Great Britain, chiefly serving London and Brooklyn Tabernacles; travelled upward of 50,000 miles each year in his work; disclaimed being the founder of a religious sect; interpreted the punishment of the Bible as eternal death and not eternal torture; President Watch Tower Bible and Tract Society of Pa, People's Pulpit Association of New York, International Bible Students' Association, London. *Publications:* a series of books, Studies in the Scriptures, issued from 1886; Editor of The Watch Tower and Herald of Christ's Presence; his Sunday sermons published by many English, German, French, Swedish, etc, newspapers. *Address:* Brooklyn Tabernacle, 13–17 Hicks Street, Brooklyn, NY; London Tabernacle, Lancaster Gate, W.

Died Nov. 1916.

RUSSELL, Hon. Cyril; *b* 3 March 1866; 3rd *s* of late Lord Russell of Killowen; *m* 1894, Helen Mary, *d* of late Alexander George Pirie of Leckmelm, Ross-shire; four *s* two *d*. *Educ:* Beaumont College; University College, Oxford (BA). Partner in Helbert Wagg and Russell, Bankers; retired 1913. *Publications:* Stilts, 1914; Wren's Wife, 1918. *Address:* Kensington House, Bayswater Hill, W2. *T:* Park 4993. *Club:* Garrick.

Died 14 May 1920.

RUSSELL, Rev. Edward Francis, MA; *b* 1 Jan. 1844; *o s* of late Lord Edward Russell, CB; unmarried. *Educ:* Victoria College, Jersey; Trinity College, Cambridge; Cuddesdon Theological College. Assistant Curate of St Alban's, Holborn, 1867–1917; Chaplain-General to the Guild of St Barnabas for Nurses since 1876; Chaplain to the Sisters of Bethany from 1870–86. *Publication:* Lest We Grow Hard, a volume of Addresses to Trained Nurses. *Recreation:* travel. *Address:* 7 Gray's Inn Square, WC1. *Died 7 Nov. 1925.*

RUSSELL, Senator Hon. Edward John; *b* Warrnambool, Victoria, 1879. Vice-President, Federal Executive Council, Commonwealth of Australia, 1918–21; Minister in Charge of Shipping; President of the Commonwealth Board of Trade; Chairman of the Australian Wheat Board. *Address:* Federal Parliament House, Melbourne.

Died 18 July 1925.

RUSSELL, Rt. Hon. George William Erskine, PC 1907; LLD, St Andrews, 1899; *b* London, 3 Feb. 1853; *y s* of Lord Charles Russell, MP, 6th *s* of 6th Duke of Bedford, KG. *Educ:* Harrow; University College, Oxford (Scholar, Prizeman, MA). MP (L) Aylesbury, 1880–85; North Beds, 1892–95; Parliamentary Secretary to the Local Government Board, 1883–85; Under-Secretary of State for India, 1892–94; for the Home Department, 1894–95; Alderman, County Council of London, 1889–95; Chairman of Churchmen's Liberation League; Lay-Reader in the Diocese of Southwark. *Publications:* A Londoner's Log-Book; The Household of Faith; Collections and Recollections (two series), 1898; St Alban the Martyr, Holborn; Fifteen Chapters of Autobiography; Edward King, 60th Bishop of Lincoln, 1912; The Spirit of England, 1915; A Short History of the Evangelical Movement, 1915; Portraits of the Seventies, 1916; Arthur Stanton, 1917, Politics and Personalities, 1917; Basil Wilberforce; etc. *Address:* 18 Wilton Street, SW. *Clubs:* Reform, Eighty.

Died 17 March 1919.

RUSSELL, Admiral Gerald Walter, JP; *b* 1850; 6th *s* of Lieut-Col A. H. Russell, late 58th Regiment; *m* 1893, Katherine, 2nd *d* of H. G. Gatman, Fernden, Haslemere, Surrey; one *s* two *d*. *Educ:* privately; HMS Britannia. Naval Cadet, 1863; Lieutenant HMS Tourmaline during Egyptian Campaign, 1882; Superintendent, Pembroke Dockyard, 1902–4; Retired List, 1908; Admiral, 1912. *Address:* Hatchfield, near Haslemere, Surrey. *T:* Haslemere 398. *M:* PX 4318. *Club:* United Service.

Died 7 Nov. 1928.

RUSSELL, Harold John Hastings; Recorder of Bedford since 1912; *b* 23 Jan. 1868; *e s* of Lord Arthur Russell and Laura, *d* of Viscount de Peyronnet; *m* 1896, Lady Victoria Alberta Leveson-Gower, *d* of 2nd Earl Granville; one *s* two *d*. *Educ:* Balliol Coll., Oxford. FLS; FZS; MBOU. Called to Bar, Inner Temple, 1894; practised on the Midland Circuit, the Aylesbury, Bedford, and Northampton Sessions, the Railway Commission Court, and as a Parliamentary draughtsman; Admiralty War Staff, Intelligence Division, Feb. 1915; Foreign Office, Political Intelligence Department, 1919; Joint-Secretary to Anglo-German Mixed Arbitral Tribunal under Act 304 of Peace Treaty, 1920. *Publications:* The Law of Railway Rates and Charges Orders, 1906; Chalkstream and Moorland, 1911; The Flea, 1913. *Recreations:* natural history, walking, fishing, fox-hunting. *Address:* 16 Beaufort Gardens, SW3. *T:* Western 4517; 12 King's Bench Walk, Temple, EC4. *T:* Central 2758. *Clubs:* Brooks's, Athenæum.

Died 22 Aug. 1926.

RUSSELL, James, ISO 1903; *b* 15 June 1839; *m* Georgina Waddell (deceased), *d* of late Alexander Waddell; one *s* one *d*. *Educ:* Torphichen Parish School; Edinburgh University. Entered Civil Service (Inland Revenue, Stamps and Taxes); Supernumerary Surveyor of Taxes, 1858; Surveyor of the District of Banff, 1868; Surveyor of the Elgin District, 1871; Aberdeen I Survey, 1883; Aberdeen II Survey, 1891; Surveyor of Edinburgh II Survey, 1893; Inspector of Stamps and Taxes, 1895; Superintending Inspector in Scotland, 1902; retired, 1903. *Address:* 16 Blacket Place, Newington, Edinburgh.

Died 25 March 1923.

RUSSELL, Sir James Alexander, Kt 1894; JP, DL; MA, MB, BSc Pub. Health, LLD; FRSE; FRCPE; Chairman Burgh Committee on Secondary Education, 1893–1902; member of George Heriot's Trust, 1880–1903; and of Corporation of Edinburgh, 1880–1900; *b* 6 April 1846; *m* 1st, Marianne Rae (*d* 1882), *d* of James Wilson, FRS; 2nd, 1897, Mary Ruth, *d* of late Capt. G. B. Prior, RA, and *widow* of Captain Mackenzie, Bombay Cavalry; two *d*. *Educ:* Edinburgh University. Lord Provost of Edinburgh, and Lord-Lieut of Co. of City of Edinburgh, 1891–94. *Address:* Woodville, Edinburgh. *T:* 518 Central. *Clubs:* Reform; Scottish Liberal, Edinburgh.

Died 22 Jan. 1918.

RUSSELL, Rt. Rev. Dr James Curdie; *b* 19 June 1830; *s* of Archibald Russell, proprietor, Ardrossan; *m* 1858, Martha Stevenson (*d* 1916), *d* of William Watson, Banker, Campbeltown; one *d*. *Educ:* Irvine Academy; Glasgow Univ. Licensed by the Presbytery of Kintyre, 1854; presented to the First Charge, Campbeltown, and ordained and inducted, 1854; still minister of the same parish; was member of both School Boards, Burgh and Landward, and for several years,

Chairman of the former; was Chaplain of Argyll and Bute Artillery Vols (medal); Member of Synodal Board of Glasgow University, 1872–1903; Convener of Highland Committee of Church of Scotland from 1893; Clerk of the Presbytery of Kintyre for 41 years, and Clerk of Synod of Argyll from 1880; Member of many Committees of the Church; Member of the Classical Association of Scotland, British Archæological Association, British Astronomical Association, Royal Scottish Geographical Society, and Society of Scottish Artists; FSAScot; Fellow of the Zoological Society of Scotland; Moderator, General Assembly, Church of Scotland, 1902; present at Coronation of Their Majesties, 1902, as Moderator; was special preacher on 21 Sept. 1902, when His Majesty was at Balmoral, and received the coronation medal; presented the address of the Commission of the General Assembly of the Church of Scotland to the King at the Palace of Holyrood House, 12 May 1903; Fellow of the Zoological Society of Scotland; Father of the Church of Scotland. *Address:* 9 Coates Gardens, Edinburgh.   *Died 18 March 1925.*

RUSSELL, James George, ISO 1903; Commissioner of Insolvency and of Taxes for South Australia, and President of the State Board of Conciliation; *b* England, March 1848; *m* 1875, Annie P., *d* of Alfred France, Adelaide. Went to S Australia, 1860; Barrister, 1873; Commissioner of Inland Revenue, 1878–84. *Address:* Park Terrace, Parkside, Adelaide.   *Died 5 Jan. 1918.*

RUSSELL, Captain James Reginald, DSO 1914; Royal West Kent Regiment; *b* 9 Oct. 1893; *m* 1919, Gwendolen Edith, *d* of Rev. G. W. Lawson. Entered army, 1914; served European War, 1914–17 (despatches twice, DSO).   *Died 9 Feb. 1920.*

RUSSELL, Reginald Pemberton, CSI 1915; Secretary to Government of India Public Works Department since 1913; Member of Legislative Council of Governor General; *b* 1 Nov. 1860; *s* of late Rev. S. F. Russell, MA, Rector of Isfield parish, Sussex; *m* 1897, Mary Mason; no *c*. *Educ:* Queen Elizabeth's School, Cranbrook, Kent; RIE College, Egham (passed open competition for entry to Royal Indian Engineering College, Cooper's Hill, 1879). Practical training, St Alban's and Bethesda Sewerage Works, 1882–83; appointed to PWD in India, 1882; posted to Punjab Irrigation Branch, 1883; served on Irrigation Works, Punjab, 1883–1907; Under-Secretary to Punjab Government, 1890–1904; Officiating Superintending Engineer, 1906; transferred to Burma, PWD, 1907; Superintending Engineer, 1908; Chief Engineer and Secretary to Government, Burma, March 1912. *Address:* The Shrubbery, Simla. *Club:* United Service, Simla.
                                                   Died 22 Nov. 1917.

RUSSELL, Rt. Hon. Sir Thomas Wallace, 1st Bt, *cr* 1917; PC (Ire.) 1908; *b* Cupar, Fife, 28 Feb. 1841; *s* of late David Russell and Isabella Wallace; *m* 1st, 1865, Harriet (*d* 1894), *d* of late Thomas Agnew, Dungannon; 2nd, 1896, Martha, *d* of the late Lieut-Col Keown, 15th Hussars. *Educ:* Madras Academy, Cupar, Fife. Settled in Ireland, 1859; secretary to various Temperance organisations, 1864–82; contested (L) Preston, 1885; took an active part in the House and in the country against the early Home Rule movement; principal promoter of the Land Acts Committee in 1894, which resulted in the passing of the Land Act of 1896; founder of the New Land Movement in Ulster; Parliamentary Secretary Local Government Board, 1895–1900; MP (L) S Tyrone, 1886–1910; N Tyrone, 1911–18; Vice-Pres. Dept of Agriculture and Technical Instruction for Ireland, 1907–18. *Publications:* Ireland and the Empire, a Review, 1800–1900; The Irish Land Question Up to Date. *Address:* Olney, Terenure, Co. Dublin. *Club:* National Liberal.   *Died 2 May 1920.*

RUSSELL, Sir William Fleming, Kt 1922; JP 1906; President Glasgow Chamber of Commerce, 1921–22; Member of the Glasgow Town Council for many years; *b* 1851; *s* of James Russell of Glasgow; *m* 1877, Robina Jane Laing. Honorary President of the Scottish Unionist Association and past Chairman of its Western Divisional Council. *Address:* 90 Mitchell Street, Glasgow. *Clubs:* Constitutional, Royal Automobile; London Conservative, Glasgow.
                                                   Died 29 May 1925.

RUSSELL-WELLS, Sir Sydney, Kt 1921; MD, BSc; FRCP, MRCS; MP (U) University of London since 1922; Representative of the University of London on the General Medical Council; Senior Physician Seaman's Hospital, Greenwich; Lecturer on Practice of Medicine, London School of Clinical Medicine; Physician National Hospital for Diseases of the Heart; Hon. Physician to Diocese of Lebombo, Rangoon, and Zululand; Vice-Chancellor University of London, 1919–22; *b* Kensington, 25 Sept. 1869; *s* of late Benjamin Weston Wells; *m* 1895, Harriett, 3rd *d* of late Stephen Smith; one *s* two *d*. Studied science at Royal College of Science, London, and

at University College (BSc 1889); studied medicine at St George's Hospital, University of London; obtained Pollock Prize in Physiology, Treasurer's Prize, Brackenbury Prize in Medicine; William Brown £100 exhibitioner for two years. House surgeon; house physician; Assistant Curator of Museum; Medical Registrar at St George's Hospital; took an active interest in university and scientific education. *Publications:* various contributions to scientific and medical journals. *Recreations:* various scientific and mechanical pursuits. *Address:* 126 Wigmore Street, Portman Square, W1. *T:* Paddington 687; Riverside Cottage, Irstead, Norfolk. *Club:* Athenæum.
                                                   Died 14 July 1924.

RUTHEN, Sir Charles Tamlin, Kt 1919; OBE 1918; FRIBA; Director-General of Housing, Ministry of Health, 1921–26; Consulting Chief Inspector of Government Official Accommodation, HM Office of Works; Architect and Surveyor; *b* 22 Oct. 1871; *s* of late John Ruthen, South Shields; *m* 1894, Matilda Jane, *d* of late William Bondfield Westlake, Swansea; one *d*. *Educ:* public school, South Shields, and privately. Entered office of Matthew Hall, South Shields, as a pupil 1886; served 4 years; Assistant Surveyor, Swansea County Council, 1890–96; began practice in Swansea, 1896; designed Hotel Cameron, Mond Buildings, Carlton Restaurant, New Exchange Buildings, Pantygwydir Baptist Chapel, etc, and many private houses; Inspector War Cabinet Committee on Accommodation, 1917–18; Chief Inspector and Deputy Controller of Accommodation (London Area), 1918–20; President of the Institute of Arbitrators; Pres. of the Institution of Structural Engineers; Mem. of the Council of the London Society; President of the Society of Architects, 1920–21; Member of the Grants Committee of the Ministry of Labour and of the General Advisory Committee of the Empire Timber Exhibition, 1920; Chairman of Government Commission to Belgium to inquire into housing and labour conditions, 1921; Member of Inter-departmental Committee to inquire into the effect of trade combinations upon prices in the Building Industry, 1923; Member of Government Committee to inquire into new methods of house building, 1924; and of Committee appointed by the Board of Education to consider methods of building as applied to schools, 1925; JP Swansea. *Publications:* An Architect's Holiday with a Camera in Northern Italy; The Timber-Frame House—its possibilities; Urban Housing, National Housing, Housing in the Netherlands; and many articles upon housing, town-planning and kindred subjects. *Recreations:* music, foreign travel. *Address:* Bank Chambers, Heathfield Street, Swansea. *T:* Swansea 2594; 44 Bedford Row, WC1. *T:* Holborn 1655; Y Dderwen-Fawr, Blackpyl, Swansea. *T:* Sketty 8118. *M:* CY 405. *Clubs:* National Liberal, 1920; Swansea Liberal; Swiss Alpine.
                                                   Died 19 Sept. 1926.

RUTHERFOORD, Capt. J. B., DSO 1900; Behar Light Horse; Hon. Captain in Army; *b* 11 Oct. 1864; *s* of John Rutherford. Served S Africa with Lumsden's Horse, 1900 (DSO). *Address:* Pepperstone, Ardee, Louth.

RUTHERFORD, Col Charles, CB 1911; CMG 1900; FRCVS 1886; *b* 20 Jan. 1858; *s* of Richard Rutherford, Edinburgh; *m* 1890, Kate, *d* of Thomas Turner, solicitor, Leeds. *Educ:* Watson's College, Edinburgh. Gazetted to Army Vet. Dept 1879; Captain, 1889; Major, 1899; Lt-Col, 1902; Col, 1907; served Transvaal War, 1881; Bechuanaland Expedition, 1884–85; S African War, 1899–1901 (despatches, Queen's medal 6 clasps, CMG); District Veterinary Officer, Natal Command, 1900–1 and 1902–3; Principal Veterinary Officer, India, 1908–13; retired 24 March 1918. *Address:* c/o Holt and Co., 3 Whitehall Place, SW1.
                                                   Died 2 April 1922.

RUTHERFORD, John Gunion, CMG 1910; DVS; HARCVS; Commissioner, Board of Railway Commissioners for Canada; membre correspondant to the Société Centrale de médecine vétérinaire of France, 1922; Superintendent of Agriculture and Animal Industry, Department of Natural Resources, Canadian Pacific Railway, 1912–18; Veterinary Director-General, 1902–12, and Live Stock Commissioner, 1906–12, for the Dominion of Canada; *b* 25 Dec. 1857; *s* of Rev. Robert Rutherford, MA, Mountain Cross, Peeblesshire; *m* 1887, Edith, *d* of Washington Boultbee, Ancaster, Ontario, Canada; three *d*. *Educ:* High School, Glasgow; private tuition; Ontario Agricultural College; Ontario Veterinary College. Practised veterinary medicine, Canada, United States, and Mexico; settled Portage la Prairie, Manitoba, 1884; engaged there in practice and horse-breeding operations; Veterinary Inspector, Manitoba Government, 1887–92; member for Lakeside, Manitoba Legislature, 1892 and 1896; member for Macdonald, Canadian House of Commons, 1897; Delegate for Canada to International Institute of Agriculture at Rome and to International Congress on Tuberculosis at Washington, DC, 1908; President American Veterinary Medical Association, 1908–9; President Civil Service Association of Canada, 1909–11; Chairman International Commission on Control of Bovine Tuberculosis; Pres. Western Canada Live Stock Union, 1914–18; was for many years President of the Horse Breeders' Association of Manitoba and the North-West Territories; served as Veterinary Officer to the North-West Field Force under General Middleton during the Riel Rebellion, 1885. *Publications:* various monographs on veterinary subjects, also on horse-breeding and care of horses. *Recreations:* riding, driving, fly-fishing. *Address:* Ottawa, Canada. *Clubs:* Rideau, Hunt, Country, Ottawa: Ranchmen's, Calgary.

Died 24 July 1923.

RUTHERFORD, Sir (William) Watson, 1st Bt, *cr* 1923; Kt 1918; JP Liverpool; MP (C) Edge Hill Division, Liverpool, 1903–23; head of firm of Rutherfords, formerly Miller, Peel, Hughes & Rutherford, 43 Castle Street, Liverpool, and 48 Cannon Street, EC; *b* Liverpool, 1853; *e s* of late William Rutherford; *m* 1878, Elspeth Rose (*d* 1914), 2nd *d* of Captain Alexander Strachan, Great Crosby; one *s* three *d*. *Educ:* Merchant Taylors' School, Great Crosby. Admitted Solicitor, 1875; elected to Liverpool City Council, 1895; contested Scotland Division, Liverpool, 1900; Lord Mayor, Liverpool, 1902–3. *Heir: s* John Hugo Rutherford, *b* 31 Oct. 1887. *Address:* 49 Stanhope Gardens, SW7. *TA:* Roffrid, Liverpool; Roffrid, London. *T:* City 3116. *Clubs:* Carlton, Constitutional. *Died 3 Dec. 1927.*

RUTHERFURD, James Hunter; Master of Foxhounds, Linlithgow and Stirlingshire Hounds, since 1915; *b* 13 June 1864; *s* of Andrew Rutherfurd, Sheriff of The Lothians and Peebles, and *g s* of Major J. H. Rutherfurd, RE. *Educ:* Edinburgh Academy; Sherborne School; Edinburgh University. WS, 1887; Hon. Secretary to Linlithgow and Stirlingshire Hunt, 1902. *Publications:* The History of the Linlithgow and Stirlingshire Hunt, 1911. *Recreations:* hunting, fishing, etc. *Address:* 17 Great Stuart Street, Edinburgh. *T:* Central Edinburgh 22514. *Clubs:* New, University, Edinburgh. *Died 7 Oct. 1927.*

RUTHERFURD, Maj.-Gen. Thomas Walter; Indian Army; *b* 4 Sept. 1832; 2nd *s* of Thomas Rutherfurd of Fairnington, Roxburgh, NB. Entered army, 1851; Maj.-Gen. 1892; unemployed list, 1891. *Recreations:* reading, travelling. *Address:* 145 Oakwood Court, Kensington, W. *Died 15 Dec. 1918.*

RUTHVEN OF FREELAND, 9th Lord, *cr* 1651 (1st creation 1487); **Walter James Hore-Ruthven,** DL, JP; Lieutenant-Colonel Rifle Brigade, 1916; *b* 14 June 1838; *s* of Hon. William Hore (*s* of Baroness Ruthven (7th in line), 75th Regt, and Dells Honoria, *d* of Lt-Col Pierce Lowen, KH; *S* grandmother, 1864; *m* 1869, Lady Caroline Annesley Gore (*d* 1915), *d* of 4th Earl of Arran, KP; four *s* one *d*. *Educ:* Mr Murray, Wimbledon. Entered Rifle Brigade, 1854; served in Crimea, India, Abyssinia, and S Africa (medals for all); Capt. 1st Batt. Rifle Brigade; Major 9th Batt. Rifle Brigade (London Scottish), 1878–86; Extra King's Messenger during European War, and Assistant Provost-Marshal, London. Grand Officer Crown of Belgium. *Heir: s* Master of Ruthven, DSO, *b* 6 June 1870. *Address:* Newland, Gorebridge, Midlothian; Harperstown, Taghmon, Wexford; 11 Clarges Street, W. *T:* Mayfair 5647. *Clubs:* Carlton; New, Edinburgh. *Died 28 Feb. 1921.*

RUTLAND, 8th Duke of, *cr* 1703; **Henry John Brinsley Manners,** KG 1918; TD; JP Leicestershire; Marquess of Granby, 1703; Earl of Rutland, 1525; Baron Manners of Haddon, 1679; Baron Roos of Belvoir, 1896; Hon. Colonel 3rd and 4th Battalions Leicestershire Regiment, 1897; President Leicestershire Territorial Association since 1908; Lord Lieutenant of Leicestershire since 1900; President of University College, Leicester; *b* London, 16 April 1852; *s* of 7th Duke and Catherine Louisa Georgina, *o d* of Lieut-Col George Marlay, CB, Belvedere, Co. Westmeath; *S* father, 1906; *m* 1882, Marion Margaret Violet, artist, *d* of Col Hon. C. H. Lindsay, CB; one *s* three *d* (and one *s* decd). *Educ:* Eton; Trinity Coll., Camb. 3rd Batt. Leicestershire Regt, 1872–83; Captain, 1878; principal Private Secretary to Marquess of Salisbury, 1885–86, 1886–88; MP (C) Leicestershire (Melton Division), 1888–95. Owned 18,000 acres; minerals in Leicestershire and Derbyshire; picture gallery at Belvoir Castle. *Publications:* various magazine articles on sporting subjects, and a volume on Trout Fishing. *Recreations:* shooting, fishing, golfing; very fond of natural history, especially as regards English wild birds. *Heir: s* Marquis of Granby, *b* 21 Sept. 1886. *Address:* Belvoir Castle, Grantham; 16 Arlington Street, SW1. *T:* Gerrard 2010. *Clubs:* Carlton, Turf, Beefsteak. *Died 8 May 1925.*

RUTLEDGE, Hon. Sir Arthur, Kt 1902; *b* 29 Aug. 1843; *s* of late James Rutledge of Sydney; *m* 1st, 1869, Mary Thomas, 5th *d* of late Rev. Stephen Rabone; three *s* four *d*; 2nd, Rose Ann, *d* of late Robert F. Davey, Victoria. *Educ:* New South Wales. Called to Bar, Queensland, 1878; MP Enoggera, 1878–83, Kennedy, 1883; Attorney-General, 1883–88; MP Charters Towers, 1888–93; MP Maranoa, 1899 and 1902; was one of the delegates for Queensland at the first Federal Convention held in Sydney, 1891; was confirmed in the title of Honourable by despatch, 1889; Attorney-General, Queensland, 1899–1903; QC 1899; District Court Judge, 1906. *Address:* Tamavua, Toowong, Brisbane, Queensland.

Died 8 Feb. 1917.

RUVIGNY and RAINEVAL, 9th Marquis of, (France, 1651); **Melville Amadeus Henry Douglas Heddle de La Caillemotte de Massue de Ruvigny;** Baron of Raineval before 1080; Baron of Ruvigny about 1524; Baron of La Caillemotte about 1598; Marquis of Raineval, 1621; Viscount of Ruvigny, 1637; Count of La Caillemotte, 1651; *b* London, 26 April 1868; *s* of 8th Marquis and Margaret Melville, *o d* of George Moodie, of Cocklaw and Dunbog, Co. Fife; *S* father, 1883; *m* 1893, Rose Amalia (*d* 1915), *d* of Poncrazio Gaminara of Tumaco; one *s*. President of the Legitimist Jacobite League of Great Britain and Ireland, 1893–94 and 1897–99; a member of the Cou il of Catholic Record Society since 1908; Knight of the Royal and Distinguished Order of Charles III of Spain, 1898; member of several learned societies. *Publications:* The Blood Royal of Britain, 1903; The Jacobite Peerage, etc, extracted from the Stuart Papers at Windsor Castle, 1904; The Plantagenet Roll of the Blood Royal: Clarence Vol. 1905; Exeter Vol. 1906; Essex Vol. 1908; Mortimer-Percy Vol., pt i 1911; The Moodie Book, 1906; The Nobilities of Europe, 1908; Compiler and Editor of The Titled Nobility of Europe, an International Peerage, 1914, etc. *Recreation:* genealogical researches. *Clubs:* Wellington, Royal Automobile.

Died 6 Oct. 1921.

RYALL, Sir Charles, Kt 1921; CBE 1918; FRCS; Senior Surgeon to the Cancer Hospital, and Senior Surgeon to the Bolingbroke Hospital; Consulting Surgeon London Lock Hospital and Rescue Home; Consulting Surgeon to the Gordon Hospital for Diseases of the Rectum, and also to the Leatherhead Cottage Hospital; Fellow of the Royal Society of Medicine and of the Medical Society of London; Member of the Société Internationale de Chirurgie; *b* Brading, IW; of Cromwellian Irish descent; *s* of late E. C. Ryall, MRCS, AMD (who served in the Crimean War and Indian Mutiny, surgeon, 18th and 86th Regiments), and Elizabeth, *d* of William Phayer, JP; *m* 1901, Frances Mary, *d* of late Thomas Collier, JP, of Alderley Edge. *Educ:* Dublin, Paris, Westminster and King's College Hospitals. Member of Council of the Royal College of Surgeons of England. During the War, Member of the Special Medical Appeal Board; Assessor in Charge of the Board of Medical Assessors to Appeal Tribunals; Member of the Advisory Medical Board to National Service; Surgeon to the King George V Hospital. *Publications:* various papers on cancer and abdominal diseases. *Recreations:* all field sports, shooting, fishing, golf. *Address:* 62 Harley Street, W1. *T:* Langham 1612, 2708; Aldenham Corner, Radlett, Herts. *Clubs:* Ranelagh, Reform, Pilgrims, etc. *Died 5 Sept. 1922.*

RYAN, Sir Charles Lister, KCB 1887 (CB 1881); JP; late Comptroller and Auditor-General; *b* Worcester, 30 Sept. 1831; 5th *s* of Rt Hon. Sir Edward Ryan and Louisa, *d* of W. Whitmore, Dudmaston Hall; *m* 1862, Jane (*d* 1914), *d* of Sir John Shaw-Lefevre, KCB; two *d*. *Educ:* Eton. Entered Civil Service as a junior examiner in Audit Office, 1851; clerk in the Treasury, 1852–65; private secretary to Mr Disraeli when Chancellor of the Exchequer, to Sir Stafford Northcote, and to Mr Gladstone, 1859–65; secretary to Board of Audit, Assistant Comptroller, and Comptroller and Auditor-General till March 1896; a commissioner of the Exhibition of 1851; Governor of Wellington and Royal Holloway Colleges. *Address:* Burley Bushes, Ascot, Berks. *T:* 271 Ascot. *Club:* Athenæum.

Died 20 Nov. 1920.

RYAN, Maj.-Gen. Sir Charles (Snodgrass), KBE 1919; CB 1916; CMG 1919; Consul-General for Turkey; Consulting Surgeon Melbourne and Children's Hospitals; *b* 20 Sept. 1853; *s* of the late Charles Ryan of Derriwait, Upper Macedon, and *g s* of Henry Ryan, Kilfera, Co. Kilkenny, Ireland; *m* 1884, Alice (*d* 1923), *d* of late Hon. Theo. Sumner; one *s* one *d*. *Educ:* Melbourne Grammar School. Graduated as Surgeon in Edinburgh University, 1875; spent two years in Turkish Army as Surgeon; served through the Servian and Russo-Turkish Wars, through the sieges of Plevna and Erzeroum; also European War, 1914–18 (CB). *Publication:* Under the Red Crescent. *Recreations:* golf, shooting, fishing. *Address:* 37 Collins Street, Melbourne, Australia. *Clubs:* Oriental; Melbourne, Australia.

Died 23 Oct. 1926.

RYAN, Major Denis George Jocelyn, DSO 1915; 6th Gurkha Rifles; *b* 1885; *s* of late Major C. A. Ryan, RA, and Thomasine Caroline, *d* of Maj.-Gen. George Shaw, CB; *m* 1922, Aileen, *d* of Stephen Grehan, Clonmeen, Co. Cork; one *s* one *d. Educ:* Stonyhurst. Entered army, 1905; Major, 1920; served European War (despatches six times, DSO and bar). *Address:* Grindlay & Co., Bombay. *Club:* United Service.
Died 18 July 1927.

RYAN, Edward Joseph, ISO; Civil Servant, Upper Division, retired; *b* 1845; *s* of late Daniel Ryan, Rowan House, Blackrock, Co. Dublin; unmarried. *Educ:* private academies; Dublin University. Appointed, 1866; rewarded, 1870 and 1874, for performing special duties to the satisfaction of the Lords of the Treasury; promoted, 1884; retired, 1910; Queen Victoria's Commemoration Medal, 1900; King Edward the Seventh's Commemoration Medal, 1903. *Recreation:* gardening. *Address:* Rowan House, Blackrock, Co. Dublin.
Died 1 June 1923.

RYAN, Thomas Joseph; Premier, Chief Secretary and Attorney-General of Queensland since 1915; *b* Port Fairy, Victoria, 1 July 1876; *m* 1910, Lily Virgina Cook; one *s* one *d.* Graduated Melbourne University, BA 1897, LLB 1899. Admitted to Queensland Bar, 1900; elected to Queensland Parliament, 1909; leader of Parliamentary Opposition, 1913. *Address:* Auchenflower House, Toowong, Brisbane, Queensland.
Died 1 Aug. 1921.

RYCROFT, Bt Major Julian (Neil Oscar), DSO 1918; MC; Black Watch; *b* 22 Feb. 1892; *o s* of late Maj.-Gen. Sir William Henry Rycroft, KCB, KCMG; *m* 1920, Elizabeth Mildred, *yr d* of Sir Ralph Anstruther, 6th Bt; two *d. Educ:* Eton. 2nd Lieut Royal Highlanders, 1911; Capt. 1915; ADC, 1914–15; commanded 12th Batt. HLI 1918; served European War (DSO, MC, Belgian Croix de Guerre); Brevet Major, June 1919. *Address:* Tinsley House, Musgrave Road, Durban, Natal. *Club:* Naval and Military.
Died 12 Jan. 1928.

RYCROFT, Sir Richard Nelson, 5th Bt, *cr* 1784; JP, DL; *b* 12 Dec. 1859; *e s* of 4th Bt and Juliana, *e d* of Sir John Ogilvy, 9th Bt, of Inverquharity; *S* father, 1894; *m* 1st, 1886, Lady Dorothea Hester Bluett-Wallop (*d* 1906), *d* of 5th Earl of Portsmouth; two *s* (and one *s* decd); 2nd, 1911, Emily Mary, *d* of Col Hon. Henry Corry, Edwardstone Hall, Boxford; two *s* two *d. Educ:* Eton; Trinity Coll., Camb. Major Hampshire Carabiniers Yeo.; Capt. 3rd Batt. Hampshire, 1891–95; late Lieut 2nd Batt. Rifle Brigade; served with Yeomanry Cavalry in South Africa (despatches); High Sheriff of Hampshire, 1899. *Heir: s* Nelson Edward Oliver Rycroft [*b* 19 Dec. 1886; *m* 1912, Ethel Sylvia Nurton; one *s* (and one *s* decd)]. *Address:* Dummer House, Basingstoke. *TA:* Dummer House, Dummer.
Died 25 Oct. 1925.

RYCROFT, Maj.-Gen. Sir William Henry, KCB 1919 (CB 1910); KCMG 1918 (CMG 1915); Governor of British North Borneo, 1922–25; *b* 17 Feb. 1861; 2nd *s* of late Sir Nelson Rycroft, 4th Bt, Kempshott Park, Basingstoke, and Juliana, *e d* of Sir John Ogilvy, 9th Bt; *m* 1887, Grace Ronald, *o c* of late F. N. Menzies of Menzies; one *s* one *d. Educ:* Eton; Sandhurst. Joined 71st HLI 1879; served in Nile Expedition (including desert march to Metemmeh), 1884–85 (medal and clasp and bronze star); with Egyptian Army, 1886–87; action of Sarras (despatches, 4th Class Medjidie); promoted into 7th Dragoon Guards, 1888; Staff College, 1891–92; DAAG, York, 1895–96; promoted into 11th Hussars, 1896; service, North-West Frontier of India, 1897–98 (medal and clasp); DAAG, Cairo, 1898–99; served in S Africa on Staff, 1899–1900 (despatches, medal and 2 clasps); Somaliland, 1902–3 (despatches, medal with clasp); commanded 11th Hussars, 1904–8; Staff, S Africa, 1911–12; AQMG, Southern Command, 1913–14; European War, 1914–18 (despatches 7 times, CMG, promoted Major-General, KCMG, Knight of Grace, St John of Jerusalem, Legion of Honour, Croix de Commandeur, Orders of White Eagle of Serbia, Redeemer of Greece, Star of Roumania, Greek Order of Merit 2nd Class); retired pay, 1921. *Recreation:* shooting. *Address:* Rosebank, Perth. *Clubs:* Naval and Military; New, Edinburgh.
Died 4 Nov. 1925.

RYDER, Rev. Alexander Roderick, DD; Canon of Down Cathedral; formerly Rector of Drumbeg; Prebendary of Durnsford; Donellan Lecturer; *b* 21 Feb. 1852; *s* of Rev. Roderick Ryder, Rector of Errismore, and Sarah M. Bailey; *m* 1917, Beatrice L., *d* of George Bennett, Holland Park, London. *Educ:* Abbey School, Tipperary; Trinity College, Dublin (scholar). Vice-Chancellor's Latin Medal, 1872; Jun. Mod. Classics, 1873; Archbishop's King's Divinity Prize, 1874; Divinity Test, 1877; Downe's Prize (first), Written Composition, 1877; reading of Liturgy, Downe's Prize (first), 1878;

MA 1878; BD 1895; on publication of a volume of lectures, DD 1911; Ennis College. Deacon, 1877; Priest, 1878; Master of Armagh College, 1874–76; Curate of Sea Patrick, 1877–80; Rector of Scarva, 1880–82; Tullylish, 1882–88; Rural Dean of Aghaderg, 1883. *Publications:* Priesthood of the Laity, 1911; The Vision of Christ, 1919. *Recreation:* golf. *Address:* 48 Osborne Park, Belfast.
Died 29 Nov. 1919.

RYDER, Col Francis John, CMG 1916; 3rd Dragoon Guards; Deputy Director of Remounts (temp.); *b* 21 March 1866. Served S African War, 1899–1902 (despatches, Bt Lt-Col; Queen's medal, 3 clasps; King's medal, 2 clasps); European War, 1914–17 (despatches twice, CMG); retired, 1920. *Club:* Army and Navy.
Died 8 Nov. 1920.

RYERSON, Maj.-Gen. George Sterling, MB, MD; LRCPE, LRCSE; Founder, 1896, and President of the Canadian Red Cross Society, 1914–16; *b* 21 Jan. 1854; *s* of late Rev. George Ryerson; *m* 1st, 1882, Mary (lost Lusitania, 1915), *d* of late James Crowther, Toronto; two *s* one *d*; 2nd, 1916, Mrs Elizabeth T. Mann, *d* of E. R. Thomas, Buffalo, NY. *Educ:* Galt Grammar School; Trinity University (MB 1875, MD 1876); Victoria University (MD, CM *ad eund.* 1892). Mem., Coll. of Physicians and Surgeons, Ont, 1878; Senator Toronto University, 1895. Surgeon Royal Grenadiers, Toronto, 1881; served North West Rebellion, 1885 (medal and clasp); Fenian Raid, 1870 (general service medal and clasp); deputy surg.-gen., 1895; Lt-Col, 1900; served S African War, 1900–2; Canadian Red Cross Comr, and British Comr at Lord Roberts' Headquarters (Queen's medal and two clasps); Hon. Col, 1902; Hon. Surg.-Gen., 1915; Hon. Col-in-Chief, Army Medical Corps, 1917; made tour of inspection Red Cross work, European War, 1915; founder St John Ambulance Association in Canada, 1895; General Secretary Canadian St John's Ambulance Association; Pres. United Empire Loyalists, 1896–98; Hon. Associate Order of St John of Jerusalem, 1893, Esquire 1897, Knight of Grace, 1901; Freemason; Anglican. *Publications:* Looking Backwards (an autobiography); articles on professional subjects. *Address:* Peaceacres, Niagara on the Lake, Ontario. *Clubs:* York, Toronto, Royal Canadian Yacht, Toronto.
Died May 1925.

RYLAND, Henry, RI; *b* Biggleswade, Bedfordshire, 1856; *s* of John Benjamin and Elizabeth Ryland; *m* 1901, Mabel Louise Mann; one *s* one *d. Educ:* South Kensington Art Schools; West London and Heatherley's; Paris under Benjamin Constant, and at Julian's Academy under Boulanger and Lefebvre. Spent some time designing stained glass, and was a contributor to the English Illustrated Magazine from its commencement until it changed hands. *Works:* exhibited first at the Grosvenor Gallery; exhibited water-colours fairly regularly at the Royal Academy and New Gallery, and at the Royal Institute of Painters in Water-Colour; a great number of his pictures were engraved, or published in other ways. *Recreations:* chiefly reading, bicycling. *Address:* 32 Fairfax Road, Bedford Park, W.
Died 23 Nov. 1924.

RYLE, Rt. Rev. Herbert Edward, KCVO 1921 (CVO 1911); DD 1895; Hon. DD Oxford, 1908; Glasgow, 1914; FBA; Dean of Westminster since 1911; *b* London, 25 May 1856; 2nd *s* of late Bishop of Liverpool; *m* 1883, Nea, *d* of Maj.-Gen. G. Hewish Adams, late Royal Irish Rifles; one *s* (and two *s* decd). *Educ:* Eton, on foundation; Newcastle Scholar, 1875; Classical Scholar of King's Coll., Cambridge, 1875 (BA *Aegrotat,* 1879); Fellow, 1881; 1st class in Theol. Tripos, 1881; Carus Prize (undergrad.), 1875; Jeremie Prize, 1877; Winchester Reading Prize, 1878; Crosse Scholarship, 1880; Hebrew, Evans, and Scholefield Prizes, 1881. Divinity Lecturer at Emmanuel Coll., Camb., 1881–84; at King's Coll., 1882–86; deacon, 1882; priest, 1883; Principal of St David's Coll., Lampeter, 1886–88; Professorial Fellow of King's Coll., Camb., 1888; examining chaplain to late Bishop of St Asaph, 1887–89, and to Bishop of Ripon, 1889; Hon. Canon of Ripon, 1895; Chaplain to the Queen, 1898–1901; Hulsean Professor of Divinity, Camb. Univ., 1887–1901, and President of Queens' College, Cambridge, 1896–1901; Warburton Lecturer, 1899–1903; Hon. Fellow of King's, and of Queens' College, Cambridge; Bishop of Exeter, 1901–3; Bishop of Winchester, 1903–11; Chaplain of Royal Academy of Arts, 1919; Prolocutor to the Lower House of Convocation of Canterbury, 1919–25; Chairman of the House of Clergy, 1920–25. *Publications:* joint-editor (with Dr M. R. James) The Psalms of Solomon, 1891; author, The Canon of the Old Testament, 1892; The Early Narratives of Genesis, 1892; Commentary on Ezra and Nehemiah, 1893; Philo and Holy Scripture, 1895; On the Church of England, 1904; On Holy Scripture and Criticism, 1904; Commentary on Genesis, 1914; Life after Death, 1916; among other literary work article Apocrypha in Smith's Bible Dictionary, edn 2,

and contributions to Camb. Companion to the Bible, 1893; Hastings' Dictionary of the Bible; Charles' Apocrypha and Pseudepigrapha, 1913. *Address:* The Deanery, Westminster, SW1. *Club:* Athenæum.
Died 20 Aug. 1925.

RYLE, Reginald John, JP County Borough of Brighton; MA, MD Oxon; MRCS; physician; *b* 1854; *s* of J. C. Ryle (Bishop of Liverpool); *m* Catherine, *d* of late S. K. Scott, surgeon, Brighton; five *s* five *d*. *Educ:* Repton School; Oxford University; Guy's Hospital. In medical practice at Barnet (Herts) for 10 years; subsequently in practice at Brighton; President of Medico-Sociological Section at Annual Meeting of the British Medical Association, Brighton, 1913. *Publication:* Origin of Feeble-mindedness, in Report of National Association for the Feeble Minded, 1911. *Recreations:* walking, swimming, etc. *Address:* Tutt's Clump, Bradfield, Berks.
Died 4 Dec. 1922.

RYMER, Sir Joseph Sykes, Kt 1901; *b* 27 Feb. 1841; *s* of Matthew Rymer, merchant, York, and Ann Rymer, *d* of Joseph Sykes, of Huddersfield; *m* 1864, Sarah, *d* of John Leetham, steamship owner, of York; four *s* one *d*. *Educ:* York. Sheriff of York, 1882–83; Lord Mayor of York, 1887–88, 1899–1900, 1907–8, and 1912–13; JP for the City of York and for the North Riding. *Recreations:* bowls, chess, whist, bridge. *Address:* The Mount, York. *T:* York 1192.
Died 18 Feb. 1923.

S

SABATIER, Paul; *b* St-Michel de Chabrillanoux, dans les Cévennes, 3 Aug. 1858. *Educ:* Faculté de Théologie de Paris; devint immédiatement vicaire de l'église St Nicolas de Strasbourg, 1885; en 1889, le gouvernement allemand lui ayant offert une situation supérieure par laquelle il serait devenu citoyen allemand, il demanda à rester simple vicaire; cette demande fut considérée comme une manifestation politique et il fut expulsé; revint dans ses montagnes natales et se fit nommer pasteur à St-Cierge, village qui depuis quinze ans était sans pasteur; mais sa santé était ruinée et après quatre ans d'efforts, il dut renoncer à la parole, et se consacrer entièrement aux études historiques; il a organisé la 'Société Internationale des études Franciscaines' inaugurée solennellement à Assise le 2 juin 1902; en 1898 la Ville d'Assise par un vote unanime de son 'Consiglio Comunale' lui a décerné un titre qu'elle n'avait plus conféré depuis Garibaldi, celui de 'Cittadino d'onore'; en 1899, il a été nommé membre de l'Académie Royale de Rome; nommé professeur d'histoire de l'Eglise à l'Université de Strasbourg, 1919. *Publications:* En 1885 avait déjà publié le texte grec de la 'Didachè' accompagné d'un commentaire qui attira l'attention des spécialistes, mais c'est la 'Vie de St-François' qui a rendu son nom populaire; la première édition française parut en novembre 1893; un an plus tard avaient déjà paru des éditions en presque toutes les langues de l'Europe, même en Suédois et en Polonais (la première avait été la traduction russe faite sous la direction de Tolstoi); quelques érudits allemands ayant contesté certains points de cette œuvre Paul Sabatier commença alors pour les spécialistes une série de travaux destinés à montrer le travail scientifique dont la 'Vie de St-François' n'était que le résultat; delà la 'Collection d'études et de documents sur l'histoire littéraire et religieuse du moyen âge,' pour laquelle il fit appel à la collaboration de ses contradicteurs eux-mêmes; c'est un spectacle nouveau que cette union d'érudits de toutes nations et de tous cultes travaillant sur le même chantier qu'un Huguenot français; le titre i, publié en 1898, a provoqué de tous côtés d'autres travaux qui deviennent chaque jour plus nombreux et plus importants; il est intitulé, 'Speculum Perfectionis seu sancti Francisci Assisiensis Legenda Antiquissima, auctore Fr Leone, Nunc primum edidit Paul Sabatier'; le titre ii est intitulé, 'Fr Francisci Bartholi Tractatus de Indulgentia Portiunculae, Nunc primum integre edidit Paul Sabatier'; le titre iii: 'Fr Elie de Cortone, étude biographique par le Dr Ed. Lempp'; le titre iv: 'Actus b. Francisci et Sociorum eius, edidit Paul Sabatier'; en mai 1901, il découvrit à Capestrano, dans les Abruzzes, la 'Regula Antiqua Tertii Ordinis,' qui depuis des siècles avait échappé à toutes les recherches; il en profita pour commencer les 'Opuscules de Critique Historique' qui paraissent par fascicules trimestriels; enfin vers la même époque il retrouva le texte Latin original du fameux recueil des Fioretti dont il donna deux éditions, une pour les érudits, mentionnée plus haut 'Actus,' etc, l'autre populaire, 'Floretum S Francisci Assisiensis, Liber

aureus qui italice dicitur I Fioretti di San Francesco'; Disestablishment in France, 1907; Lettre ouverte à Son Eminence le cardinal Gibbons, 1907; Modernism: the Jowett Lectures, 1908, translated by C. A. Miles; France To-day: Its Religious Orientation, translated by H. B. Binns, 1913; A Frenchman's Thoughts on the War, 1915. *Address:* 3 Ile Sainte Hélène, Strasbourg.
Died March 1928.

SACHS, Edwin O., FRSE, FRGS, etc; architect; Chairman of British Fire Prevention Committee; *b* London, 5 April 1870; *e s* of late G. Sachs, London. *Educ:* University College School, London. Travelled extensively and studied practical side of fire protection; commenced architectural practice, London, 1892; in 1898 he applied electrical power to the working of the stage for the first time in England, at Drury Lane; technical adviser to Royal Opera, Covent Garden, since 1899; founded British Fire Prevention Committee, 1897, and first fire-testing station established in Europe, 1899; organised the technical side of the Internat. Fire Exhibition at Earl's Court, acting as Vice-Pres.; organised first Internat. Fire Prevention Congress, London, 1903; organised Special Fire Survey Force in connection with the War, acting as its Commissioner; Member Home Office Departmental Committee on Celluloid Dangers; Vice-President of International Fire Service Council; Associate, Inst. of Mechanical Engineers; Hon. Member Imperial Russian Society of Architects; French, Italian, Belgian, and other Fire Service Corporations; Knight of the Swedish Wasa Order (1st class); French Gold Medal of Merit; Officier d'Académie (France); Officer of the Order of the Oaken Crown (Luxemburg); Russian Insignia of St Anne, Gold Medals of St Andrew and of St Valdimir, and Russian Imperial Fire Service Insignia; Coronation Medal, 1911. *Publications:* Modern Opera Houses and Theatres, 1896–1898; Stage Construction, 1898; Fires and Public Entertainments, 1897; Facts on Fire Prevention, 1902; The International Fire Exhibition, 1903; The Iroquois Theatre Fire, 1903; The Baltimore Fire, 1904; The Brussels Exhibition Fire, 1910; Fire-Protection in Paris, 1911; Fire-Protection in Russia, 1913; numerous essays and papers. *Recreations:* attending fires, travel. *Address:* 8 Waterloo Place, SW. *T:* Gerrard 5164.
Died 9 Sept. 1919.

SACKVILLE, 3rd Baron, *cr* 1876; **Lionel Edward Sackville-West,** JP, DL; Vice-Chairman of Kent County Council; Chairman Kent Territorial Army Association; formerly Lieutenant-Colonel West Kent Yeomanry; *b* 15 May 1867; *s* of Col Hon. William Edward Sackville-West, Grenadier Guards, and Georgina, *y d* of George Dodwell, Kevinsfoot, Co. Sligo; *S* uncle, 1908; *m* 1890, *cousin,* (Josephine) Victoria Sackville-West; one *d* [Vita, poet and novelist, *m* 1913, Hon. Harold Nicolson, 3rd *s* of Lord Carnock]. *Educ:* Wellington; Christ Church, Oxford (MA). Served European War, Gallipoli, Egypt, Palestine, France, 1914–18. *Heir: brother* Maj.-Gen. Hon. Sir Charles John Sackville-West, *b* 10 Aug. 1870. *Address:* 9 Bentinck Street, Manchester Square, W1. *T:* Mayfair 5030; Knole, Sevenoaks. *Clubs:* Carlton, White's; Royal Yacht Squadron, Cowes.
Died 28 Jan. 1928.

SACKVILLE, Major Lionel Charles Stopford, DSO 1915; Rifle Brigade; *b* Belfast, 30 April 1891; *s* of late Colonel Lionel Stopford Sackville, the Rifle Brigade. *Educ:* Eton; Sandhurst. 2nd Lieut in Rifle Brigade in 1910; Lieut 1912; Capt. 1915; served European War, France and Flanders, 1914–15, and at Salonika, 1915–18 (despatches, DSO, Bt Major, Croix de Guerre avec Palme). *Recreations:* polo, racing. *Address:* 33 Brunswick Gardens, Kensington, W8. *Clubs:* Travellers', Army and Navy.
Died 31 Dec. 1920.

SACKVILLE, Sackville George Stopford; Hon. Colonel, late Lieutenant-Colonel Commandant, 3rd Battalion Northamptonshire Regiment; late Chairman of Northamptonshire Quarter Sessions; late Chairman County Council; *b* 19 March 1840; *s* of William Bruce Stopford (who assumed by Royal Licence the additional name of Sackville) and Caroline Harriet, *niece* and *heiress* of Charles Sackville, last Duke of Dorset; *m* 1875, Edith Frances (*d* 1905), *o d* of William Rashleigh of Menabilly, Cornwall. *Educ:* Eton; Christ Church, Oxford (MA). JP and DL Northants; MP (C) North Northants, 1867–80, 1900–6. *Address:* Drayton House, Thrapston. *T:* Lowick 2. *Clubs:* Travellers', Carlton, Royal Automobile.
Died 6 Oct. 1926.

SADASIVA AIYAR, Sir Theagaraja Aiyar, Diwan Bahadur, Kt 1921; Judge of High Court, Madras, 1914–21. Entered Madras Civil Service, 1887; Sub-Judge, 1905; Dist and Sessions Judge, 1910; an additional Puisne Judge, 1912; Puisne Judge, 1914. *Address:* c/o High Court, Madras.
Died 1 Dec. 1927.

SADLER, Lt-Col Sir James Hayes, KCMG 1907; CB 1902; HM Governor and Commander-in-Chief Windward Islands, 1909–14; *b* 1851; *s* of late Sir James Hayes Sadler, KCMG; *m* 1875, Rita Annie (*d* 1918), *d* of Col Wemyss Smith, Indian Army; one *s.* Joined 61st Regt 1870; served with 40th Regt and 33rd Bengal Infantry; joined Political Department in 1877, in which held various appointments; Consul, Muscat, 1892–96; Consul-General, Somali Protectorate, 1898; Commissioner, etc, in Uganda, 1901–5; Governor British East Africa Protectorate, 1905–9; Governor of the Windward Islands, 1904–14; received Coronation medals, 1902 and 1911. *Club:* Junior United Service.   *Died 21 April 1922.*

SADLER, Walter Dendy; artist; *b* Dorking, Surrey, 12 May 1854; 5th *s* of John Dendy Sadler, solicitor, Horsham. *Educ:* private school, Horsham. Studied in London and Düsseldorf; exhibited at Royal Academy since 1873. *Pictures:* Thursday; Pegged down Fishing Match; Darby and Joan; The Widow's Birthday; The New Will; London to York; The End of the Skein; Dummy Whist; Toddy at the Cheshire Cheese; For Weal or Woe; Nearly Done. *Recreation:* fishing. *Address:* Hemingford Grey, St Ives, Hunts.

Died 13 Nov. 1923.

SAFONOFF, Wassily; conductor and pianist; *b* Caucasus, 1852; *m* Warwara Yschnegradski. *Educ:* Petrograd Conservatoire. Was four years Professor at the Conservatoire, then Professor, Moscow Conservatoire; Conductor, Moscow Imperial Musical Society for seventeen years; directed the Philharmonic Society, New York, for six years. *Club:* English, Moscow.   *Died 1918.*

SAILANA, Raja of; HH Sir Jeswant Singhji Bahadur, KCIE 1903; *b* 1864; *s* of Maharaj Bhawani Singhji, late Jagirdar of Semlia; adopted by HH Raja Duleh Singhji; *S* 1895; *m* 1st, Ranawatji, *d* of late Rao of Dhariawad; 2nd, Kachhawaiji (*d* 1906), *d* of late Raja of Machhand; 3rd, Sisodniji, *d* of late Rana of Barwani; five *s* three *d. Educ:* Daly (Rajkumar) College, Indore. The State had an area of 450 square miles, and a population of 30,000, the Chief receiving a salute of 11 guns; for his efficient administration of famine relief in 1900, when the State suffered from drought, he received the Kaiser-i-Hind Gold Medal. Gave contribution of 50,000 rupees to British war expenses and various charitable funds pertaining to war. *Recreations:* riding, driving, sauntering, and especially reading. *Address:* Sailana, Malwa.

Died 4 Aug. 1919.

SAINT, Sir Thomas Wakelin, Kt 1927; JP; Alderman of Islington since 1906; Chairman East Islington Conservative Association; member of Metropolitan Water Board; *b* 1861. *Address:* Bank Chambers, Finsbury Park, N4; The Woodlands, Sewardstone, Essex.

Died 1 June 1928.

ST ALBANS, Duchess of; (Grace); *d* of late Ralph Bernal Osborne, MP; *m* 1874 (as his 2nd wife), 10th Duke of St Albans (*d* 1898); two *s* three *d. Address:* Newtownanner, Clonmel, Ireland. *T:* Victoria 3180.   *Died 18 Nov. 1926.*

ST ALDWYN, 1st Earl, *cr* 1915, of Coln St Aldwyn; **Michael Edward Hicks-Beach,** PC 1874; JP, DL; Bt 1619; Viscount St Aldwyn, 1906; Viscount Quenington, 1915; High Steward of Gloucester; Provincial Grand Master, Gloucester, since 1880; an Ecclesiastical Commissioner since 1908; *b* 23 Oct. 1837; *s* of Sir Michael Hicks Beach, 8th Bt and Harriett Vittoria, *d* of John Stratton, Farthinghoe Lodge, Northamptonshire; *S* father as 9th Bt, 1854; *m* 1st, 1864, Caroline Susan (*d* 1865), *d* of John Henry Elwes, Colesbourne Park; 2nd, 1874, Lucy Catherine Fortescue, *d* of 3rd Earl Fortescue; three *d* (one *s* decd). *Educ:* Eton; Christ Church, Oxford (MA). Hon. DCL. MP (C) E Gloucestershire, 1864–85; W Bristol, 1885–1906; Under-Secretary Home Department, and Secretary of Poor Law Board, 1868; Chief Secretary for Ireland, 1874–78, 1886–87; Secretary for the Colonies, 1878–80; Chancellor of the Exchequer, 1885–86 and 1895–1902; President of Board of Trade, 1888–92. *Heir:* *g s* Viscount Quenington, *b* 9 Oct. 1912. *Address:* Coln St Aldwyn's, Fairford, Gloucestershire. *TA:* 81 Eaton Place, SW. *Clubs:* Athenæum, Carlton.

Died 30 April 1916.

ST AUBYN, Alan, (Frances Marshall); novelist; *b* Surrey; *y c* of George Bramstone Bridges, lawyer and dramatist; *m* Matthew Marshall, St Aubyn's, Tiverton, N Devon. *Educ:* Essex; Cambridge. Author and archæologist; member of Cambridge Antiquarian Society, and Somerset Archæological Society. *Publications:* Old English Embroidery, its Technique and Symbolism; *novels:* A Fellow of Trinity, 1890; The Junior Dean, 1891; The Master of St Benedict's; Trollope's Dilemma; With Wind and Tide, 1892; An Old Maid's Sweetheart; Broken Lights, 1893; Orchard Damerel; To His Own

Master; In the Face of the World, 1894; A Tragic Honeymoon, 1894; The Tremlett Diamonds, 1895; Modest Little Sara; To Step Aside is Human; A Proctor's Wooing, 1897; Mary Unwin; Fortune's Gate; A Fair Impostor; Under the Rowan Tree; Gallantry Bower; Bonnie Maggie Lauder; Mrs Dunbar's Secret, 1899; In the Sweet West Country; The Bishop's Delusion; The Wooing of May; The Loyal Hussar; A Prick of Conscience; May Silver, 1901; The Maiden's Creed; The Scarlet Lady; A Coronation Necklace; The Greenstone; The Red Van; Purple Heather; The Ordeal of Sara; The Harp of Life. Juvenile Books: Joseph's Little Coat; The Dean's Little Daughter; With Wind and Tide; Wapping Old Stairs; Lizzy's Shepherd; A Silver Cord; The Squire of Bratton; Little Lady Maria; Jenny Dear; Antonia's Promise; The Squire's Children; The Harvest of the Year; The Trivial Round; Footprints, etc. *Recreation:* gardening. *Address:* c/o Dr Rygate, Hunstanton. *Club:* Lyceum.

Died 22 Oct. 1920.

ST AUBYN, Geoffrey Peter; Judge of Turks and Caicos Islands since 1898; *b* London, 7 June 1858; 2nd *s* of Geoffrey St Aubyn of the Civil Service; *m* 1897, Edith, *e d* of Edgar Sydney of Greenwich. *Educ:* St Charles Coll., Notting Hill. Barrister Middle Temple, 1880; went Western Circuit; appointed Magistrate, Kingstown, St Vincent, WI, 1891; Acting Chief Justice, St Vincent, Nov. 1896 to July 1898. *Recreations:* tennis, reading. *Address:* Grand Turk, Turks Islands, WI.

ST AUDRIES, 1st Baron, *cr* 1911; **Alexander Fuller-Acland-Hood;** Bt 1806 and 1809; PC 1904; BA; Vice-Chamberlain to His Majesty; *b* St Audries, 26 Sept. 1853; *e s* of Sir Alexander Bateman Periam Fuller-Acland-Hood, 3rd Bt and Isabel, *d* of Sir Peregrine Palmer Fuller Palmer Acland, 2nd Bt (ext); *S* father as 4th Bt, 1892; *S* kinsman, Sir Edward Dolman Scott, as 6th Bt, 1905; *m* 1888, Hon. Mildred Rose Eveleigh de Moleyns, 2nd *d* of 4th Baron Ventry; two *s* two *d. Educ:* Eton; Balliol Coll., Oxford (BA). Entered Grenadier Guards, 1875; Adjutant, 1881–86; served in Egyptian campaign, 1882 (medal and clasp); 5th class Medjidieh and bronze star; ADC; Governor, Victoria, 1889–91; retired from army, 1892; MP (C) W Somerset, 1892–1911; Parliamentary Sec. to the Treasury, 1902–6. *Recreations:* cricket, hunting, shooting, fishing, rowing. *Heir:* *s* Hon. Alexander Peregrine Fuller-Acland-Hood [*b* 24 Dec. 1893. *Educ:* Magdalen College, Oxford. Lieut Somerset Light Infantry]. *Address:* St Audries, Bridgwater. *Clubs:* Guards, Carlton, Pratt's.

Died 4 June 1917.

ST CLAIR, Lt-Col William Augustus Edmond, CMG 1918; Royal Engineers; Brevet Colonel (retired); *b* 1854; *y s* of James Louis St Clair of Staverton Court, Gloucester; *m* 1886, Louise, *d* of Walter Crawshay, of Le Chasnay, Fourchambault, Nièvre, France; one *d. Educ:* Private School; RMA, Woolwich. Entered the Royal Engineers, 1873; served in Afghan War, 1880 (medal); Soudan, 1885 (Suakin, medal with clasp and bronze star); South African War, 1902 (Queen's medal with four clasps); retired, 1905; re-employed, 1914–18, as commanding Royal Engineers, Dublin district; JP Surrey. *Address:* The Beacon, Dormansland, Surrey.

Died 12 Sept. 1923.

ST CLAIR, Major William Lockhart, DSO 1918; Royal Horse Artillery; *b* 22 June 1883; *e s* of Hon. Lockhart Matthew St Clair and Ellen Mary Margaret, *d* of Surg.-Maj.-Gen. William Roche Rice. *Educ:* Royal Military Academy, Woolwich. Served Togoland and Cameroons, 1914–16; European War, 1916–18 (despatches, DSO). *Address:* Derriana, Mayfield Road, Sutton, Surrey. *Clubs:* Army and Navy, Cavalry.   *Died 23 Feb. 1920.*

ST CYRES, Viscount; Stafford Harry Northcote; *b* 29 Aug. 1869; *o s* of 2nd Earl of Iddesleigh and Elizabeth Lucy, *e d* of Sir Harry Stephen Meysey Thompson, 1st Bt; *m* 1912, Dorothy (Lady of Grace of St John of Jerusalem; author of The Holy City, 1912), *y d* of late Alfred Morrison of Fonthill Park, Wilts. *Educ:* Eton; Merton College, Oxford; 1st class Modern History; Senior Student of Christ Church (DLitt). Clerical Assistant at Queen Alexandra Military Hospital, Millbank, Nov. 1915–April 1917, when he entered HM Diplomatic Service as Hon. Secretary at Berne; promoted Hon. Counsellor there April 1918; resigned through ill-health, Dec. 1918. *Publications:* François de Fenelon, 1901; Pascal, 1909. *Recreation:* formerly unskilled agricultural labour. *Address:* 54 Prince's Gate, SW7; Walhampton Park, Lymington, Hants. *T:* Kensington 8210.

Died 1 Feb. 1926.

SAINT-GEORGE, Henry; violinist, composer, conductor, and writer on musical subjects; *b* London, 1866; *s* and pupil of George Saint-George, composer of violin music; *m* Lilly, *d* of Capt. F. W. von Kornatzki and *g d* of late Joseph Lilly, the antiquarian; one *s. Educ:*

privately. Known as an expert in the history of ancient instruments, and especially as a performer on the Viola da Gamba and Viola d'Amore; with his father introduced to the British public three hitherto unknown works by J. S. Bach, and was the first to give in England a recital solely of Bach's works; Colonial Examiner to Trinity College. *Publications:* The Bow, its History, Manufacture, and Use, 1895; The Place of Science in Music, 1905; Fiddles, their Selection, Preservation, and Betterment, 1910; The Young Man from Stratford, 1911; A Musical Zoo, 1913; a number of serial articles in the musical press, amongst them being Observations on the Principles of Modulation; the Symphonies of Beethoven; composer of Advanced Studies for the Pianoforte; edited the Strad for 4 years. *Recreations:* painting, photography, debating. *Address:* Eldon House, Walterton Road, W. *Club:* Authors'. *Died 29 Jan. 1917.*

ST GERMANS, 6th Earl of, *cr* 1815; **John Granville Cornwallis Eliot,** DL, JP; Baron Eliot, 1784; Captain Royal Scots Greys; *b* 11 June 1890; *s* of 5th Earl and Hon. Emily Harriet Labouchere, *y d* of 1st and last Baron Taunton; *S* father, 1911; *m* 1918, Lady Blanche Somerset, *d* of Duke of Beaufort; two *d. Educ:* Eton. Served European War, 1914–17 (MC, wounded); owned about 7,000 acres; Church of England. *Heir: cousin* Granville John Eliot, *b* 22 Sept. 1867. *Address:* Port Eliot, St Germans, Cornwall.
Died 31 March 1922.

ST JOHN OF BLETSO, 17th Baron, *cr* 1558; **Henry Beauchamp Oliver St John,** DL, JP Beds; Bt 1660; *b* 24 June 1876; *s* of 16th Baron and Helen Charlotte, *d* of Harry Thornton, Kempston Grange, Beds; *S* father, 1912. *Educ:* Wellington Coll.; Magdalene Coll., Cambridge. Church of England; Conservative; owned about 8,000 acres. *Recreations:* country pursuits, county business. *Heir: brother* Hon. Moubray St Andrew Thornton St John, *b* 5 Nov. 1877. *Address:* Melchbourne Park, Bedford. *Club:* Junior Carlton.
Died 17 Oct. 1920.

ST JOHN, Sir Frederick (Robert), KCMG 1901; *b* 2 March 1831; 4th *s* of late Hon. Ferdinand St John and Selina Charlotte, *d* Col Maurice St Leger Keatinge; *m* 1882, Isabella Annie, 2nd *d* of Hon. James Terence Fitzmaurice; three *s* three *d. Educ:* Cheltenham. Attaché at Florence and at Stuttgart; 2nd Secretary at Peking, Constantinople, and Vienna; Secretary of Legation at Buenos Ayres and Rio de Janeiro; Secretary of Embassy at Constantinople; Minister Resident in Central America, Colombia, and Venezuela; Envoy Extraordinary and Minister Plenipotentiary at Belgrade and at Berne; retired on a pension. *Publication:* Reminiscences of a Retired Diplomat, 1906. *Address:* 9 Elm Park Road, SW3.
Died 27 Feb. 1923.

ST JOHN, Henry Percy; formerly a Clerk in the House of Lords; *b* 23 March 1854; *e s* of late Canon (Maurice William) Ferdinand St John (*g s* of 3rd Viscount Bolingbroke), and late Charlotte Lucy Hamilton, *d* of John Dalyell of Lingo; *heir-pres.* to 6th Viscount Bolingbroke; *m* 1887, Maud Louisa, *d* of Hon. Pascoe Charles Glyn; one *s* two *d. Address:* 64 Eccleston Square, SW1. *T:* Victoria 2725.
Died 9 Sept. 1921.

ST JOHN, Mabel; *see* Cooper, H. St J.

ST LEGER, Col Henry Hungerford, DSO 1886; *b* 26 April 1833; *m* 1860, Florence Stuart (*d* 1892), *d* of late John Moore. Entered army, 1854; Colonel, 1885; served Indian Mutiny, 1858–59 (medal with clasp); Egypt, 1882 (medal with clasp, Khedive's star); Nile Expedition, 1884–85 (clasp); Soudan, 1885–86 (despatches, DSO). *Club:* Junior United Service. *Died 24 Jan. 1925.*

ST MAUR, Lord Ernest; *b* 11 Nov. 1847; *s* of 14th Duke of Somerset and Horatia Isabella Harriet, *d* of John Philip Morier; *brother* and *heir-pres.* to 15th Duke of Somerset; *m* 1907, Dora, *d* of late Rev. John Constable. *Educ:* Harrow; Trinity Hall, Cambridge. *Address:* Wilcot Manor, Marlborough, Wilts. *Clubs:* New University, Wellington.
Died 21 May 1922.

ST OSWALD, 2nd Baron, *cr* 1885; **Rowland Winn,** DL, JP; *b* 1 Aug. 1857; *s* of 1st Baron and Harriet Maria Amelia, *d* of Col Henry Dumaresq and Elizabeth, *sister* of 5th Earl of Lanesborough; *S* father, 1893; *m* 1892, Mabel Susan, *d* of Sir Charles Forbes, 4th Bt; four *s* one *d. Educ:* Eton. Capt. 2nd Batt. Coldstream Guards, 1889; retired 1893; served in Soudan Expedition, 1885; MP (C) Pontefract, 1885–93. *Heir: s* Hon. Rowland George Winn, *b* 29 July 1893. *Address:* 19 Hill Street, Berkeley Square, W. *T:* Mayfair 1384; Nostell Priory, Wakefield; Appleby Hall, Doncaster. *Clubs:* Carlton, Turf, Guards, Bachelors'. *Died 13 April 1919.*

SAINT-SAENS, Camille, LLD Cambridge; DMus Oxford; composer; *b* Paris, 9 Oct. 1835. *Educ:* under Stamaty and Maleden, and at the Conservatoire under Benoist and Halévy. Organist of Church of St Merri, 1853; of the Madeleine, 1858. Elected member of the Institute, 1881; grand croix de la Légion d'Honneur, 1913. *Publications:* Les Noces de Prométhée, 1867; La Princesse Jaune, 1872; Le Timbre d'Argent, 1877; Samson et Dalilah, 1877; Etienne Marcel, 1879; Rouet d'Omphale; Danse Macabre; Jeunesse d'Hercule; Symphonies en *mi*, en *la* et en *ut*; Henry VIII, 1883; Ascanio, 1890; Phryné, 1893; Chœurs d'Antigone, 1893; Javotte, 1896; Déjanire, 1898; Les Barbares, 1901; Parysatis, 1902; Hélène, 1903; L'Ancètre, 1906; concertos de piano, de violon, de violoncelle, sonates, trios, quatuors, quintette, septuor, etc. *Publications littéraires:* Harmonie et Mélodie; Portraits et Souvenirs; Ecole Buissonnière; Au Courant de la vie; Germanophilie, Problèmes et Mystères; Rimes familières; Comédies, etc. *Address:* 83bis Rue de Courcelles, Paris.
Died 16 Dec. 1921.

SALE, George S.; *b* 1831; 3rd *s* of John Shaw Sale of Rugby; *m* Margaret, 2nd *d* of James Bonwell Fortune, of Cobourg, Canada; one *s* two *d. Educ:* Rugby; Trinity College, Cambridge (Scholar, Fellow, and Classical Lecturer). Went to New Zealand, 1860; at the request of the Canterbury Provincial Govt, took charge of the West Coast Goldfields as Commissioner, 1865; Classical Professor, University of Otago, New Zealand, 1870–1908. *Publications:* various contributions to the Classical Review and other magazines.
Died 25 Dec. 1922.

SALE-HILL, Gen. Sir Rowley Sale, KCB 1902 (CB 1881); unemployed Supernumerary List Indian Army; *b* India, 6 Nov. 1839; 2nd *s* of late Capt. Rowley John Hill, HEICS (*d* 1850), and Caroline Catherine, 2nd *d* of Maj.-Gen. Sir Robert Sale, GCB; assumed additional surname of Sale, 1889; *m* 1872, Caroline Sophia, 2nd *d* of Colonel Robert Sale, HEICS; one *s* three *d. Educ:* King William's College, Isle of Man; Dr Behr's, Winchester. Entered Bengal Army, 1856; joined 66th Gurkhas, later 1st Gurkha Rifles, till 1882; Maj.-Gen. 1885; Lieut-Gen. 1890; Gen. 1896; served with Regt during Indian Mutiny, 1857–58–59 (medal); Bhutan Campaign, 1865–66; in Huzara Campaign, 1868 (medal with 2 clasps); with Malay Peninsula Expedition, 1875–76 (despatches, clasp); throughout Afghan Campaigns, 1878–79–80—(1) in command 1st Gurkhas; (2) brigade on Khyber line; (3) line of communications and movable column (medal, CB); commanded Rawal Pindi Brigade, 1882; Eastern Frontier District, 1882–86; and in command of Akka Expedition NE Frontier, 1883–84 (thanked by Government and Comdr-in-Chief), 1889; Distinguished Service Pension for war services. *Recreations:* fishing, riding, rowing. *Address:* Folkestone. *Clubs:* East Indian United Service; Radnor, Folkestone.
Died 23 March 1916.

SALISBURY, Francis, CBE 1918; ISO 1911; JP; late Postmaster Surveyor of Liverpool; *b* Brixton, 1850. *Educ:* Stockwell Grammar School. *Club:* Athenæum. *Died 4 Feb. 1922.*

SALMON, Alfred; Managing Director and Chairman of the Board of J. Lyons & Co. Ltd; Director, Strand Hotel, Ltd; *b* 20 July 1868; *e s* of Barnett and Lena Salmon; *m* 1894, Frances Abrahams; three *s. Educ:* privately. Member of House Committee of London Hospital and of the Board of Management of West London Hospital. *Recreations:* golf, bridge. *Address:* 24 Albert Court, Kensington Gore, SW7. *T:* Western 4536. *Clubs:* Constitutional; Walton Heath Golf.
Died 11 Oct. 1928.

SALMON, Prof. Amédée Victor; Officier de l'Instruction Publique; Lauréat de l'Institut de France; Professor of Romance Philology at the University of London, King's College, and Professor of French Language and Literature at University College, Reading; Examiner at the University of London; former Examiner in the Universities of Liverpool, Manchester, Birmingham, St Andrews, and Glasgow; *b* Drouilly (Seine-et-Marne), France, 1857; *m* C. Huss; one *s* three *d. Educ:* Lycée of Versailles; Univ. of Paris. Editor of Godefroy's Dictionary of Old French; general editor of the Dictionnaire des Dictionnaires, later Encyclopédie du XXe Siècle; co-editor of La Romania, Le Moyen Age, La Grande Encyclopédie, etc; Fellow of the Ecole des Hautes Etudes (Romance Philology and History); President of the Federation of the British Branches of the Alliance Française; Chairman of Committee of the British Bureau of the Office National des Universités et Ecoles Françaises. *Publications:* Remèdes populaires du moyen age (XIIIe Siècle), d'après un MS de Cambrai; Trois Poèmes de Jean Brisebarre, de Douai (XIVe Siècle), d'après un MS de Charleville; critical edn of Philippe de Beaumanoir's Coutumes de Clermont en Beauvaisis; Chevalerie Vivien; Les

Manuscrits de la Bibliothèque du Tribunal de Beauvais; Deux Rédactions abrégées des Coutumes de Beauvais de Philippe de Beaumanoir; Lexique de l'Ancien Français; Grammaire sommaire de l'Ancien Français; Extraits de Montaigne; L'Explication française; Deux mois en France au début de la guerre, etc. *Recreations:* rowing, cycling. *Address:* 54 Western Elms Avenue, Reading. *Clubs:* University of London, Carlyle.   *Died 11 Nov. 1919.*

SALMON, Lt-Col Hon. Charles Carty, JP; MP; LRCPE, LRCSE, LFPS Glasgow; Speaker House of Representatives, 1909–10; Chairman of Committees and Deputy-Speaker, 1904, 1905, 1906; Lieutenant-Colonel Australian Army Medical Corps, attached 9th Light Horse; *b* Daisy Hill, Amherst, Victoria; *s* of Frederick Browne Salmon and Susannah Carty Arnell; *m* 1900, Nancy, *d* of Sir Matthew Harris; three *s*. *Educ:* Scotch Coll., Melbourne; Trinity Coll., University of Melbourne; Medical School, Edinburgh. Elected Member for Talbot and Avoca in Victorian Parliament, 1893, 1894, 1897, and 1900; Minister for Public Instruction, 1899–1900; elected Member for Laanecoorie in Commonwealth Parliament, 1901–13; Vice-President Imperial Federation League, 1905; President Australian Natives' Assoc. 1898; Chairman Platform Committee, Australian Federation, 1898; Member Council Diocese of Melbourne; Lay Canon St Paul's Cathedral, Melbourne; Lay Representative, Church Synod Diocese, Ballarat; Trustee Trinity College, University of Melbourne; Chairman Trinity College Council; Grand Master, Fr AM, 1914. *Recreations:* cricket, rowing, golf. *Address:* Warrane, Walsh Street, South Yarra; Daisy Hill Park, Talbot, Victoria.
                                                                    Died Sept. 1917.

SALMON, John Cuthbert, RCA; landscape painter, oil and water-colour; *b* Colchester, Essex, 28 Feb. 1844; *m* 1869; four *d*. *Educ:* Birkbeck Institution, London. First exhibited at the British Institute, Pall Mall, 1865; Suffolk St Gallery; Royal Scottish Acad., Edinburgh, for many years; at the Royal Academy, London, and nearly all the provincial exhibitions for many years, including the Liverpool Autumn, Walker Art Gallery, for forty-one years; elected full Member of the Liverpool Academy of Arts, 1901; one of the first members of the Royal Cambrian Academy of Art, Conway, and served on its Council from the foundation of that Academy. *Recreations:* walking, cycling. *Address:* Westhope, Deganwy, Llandudno.
                                                                    Died 2 Oct. 1917.

SALMOND, Hon. Sir John William, Kt 1918; MA, LLB; a Judge of the Supreme Court of New Zealand; *b* North Shields, 3 Dec. 1862; *s* of Professor W. Salmond, University of Otago, NZ; *m* 1891, Anne Bryham, *d* of late James Guthrie, Newcastle-on-Tyne, England; one *s* one *d*. *Educ:* University of Otago; University College, London. Barrister of Supreme Court of New Zealand, 1887; Professor of Law in University of Adelaide, 1897–1906; Victoria University College, Wellington, NZ, 1906–7; Counsel to the Law Drafting Office of New Zealand Government, 1907–10; Solicitor-General for New Zealand, 1910–20; Member of British Delegation, Washington Conference on Armaments, 1921. *Publications:* Essays in Jurisprudence and Legal History, 1891; Jurisprudence, 1902, 7th edition, 1923; Law of Torts, 1907, 6th edition, 1923. *Address:* Wellington, NZ.
                                                                    Died Sept. 1924.

SALMOND, Rev. William, DD; Professor of Mental and Moral Philosophy, 1886–1914; Emeritus Professor, 1914; *b* Edinburgh, 9 Feb. 1835; *m* 1861, Jane Panton Young, Dunfermline. *Educ:* Heriot's Hospital, High School, and University, Edinburgh; Berlin. Minister, English Presbyterian Church, North Shields, 1858–75; Professor of Theology to the Presbyterian Church, New Zealand, 1875–86. *Address:* 186 Queen Street, Dunedin.
                                                                    Died 6 March 1917.

SALOMONS, Sir David Lionel Goldsmid-Stern-, 2nd Bt, *cr* 1869; JP, DL; AICE; engineer; past Vice-President and Treasurer Institution of Electrical Engineers; Barrister Middle Temple; Director, South-Eastern Railway; *b* 28 June 1851; *s* of Phillip Salomons, Brighton, and Emma, *d* of Jacob Montefiore; *S* uncle, 1873; assumed additional surnames of Goldsmid and Stern, 1899; *m* 1882, Laura Julia, *d* of Baron de Stern; three *d* (one *s* decd). *Educ:* privately; short time University Coll., Caius Coll., Camb. (MA; Natural Science Honours). Contested (L) Mid Kent, 1874; St George's-in-the-East, 1885; Mayor of Tunbridge Wells, 1895; late Alderman of Tunbridge Wells; County Councillor of Kent for Tonbridge Division, etc; Fellow of Royal Astronomical Soc., Geological Soc., Physical Soc. of London, and many others; served on Jury at International Exhibition, Paris, 1900; Hon. Col Kent (Fortress), RE. *Publications:* Electric Light Installations, 11th edn, 3 vols; Photographic Formulæ; many pamphlets and papers on electrical and other subjects; also on horseless carriages, being one

of the pioneers of the movement in England. *Recreations:* scientific research, four-in-hand driving, designing motor carriages, mechanical work generally. *Heir:* none. *Address:* Broomhill, Tunbridge Wells; 47 Montagu Square, W1. *Clubs:* Carlton, Athenæum, City of London, Grosvenor, Savage, Royal Societies.
                                                                    Died 19 April 1925 (ext).

SALT, Rev. Enoch; Wesleyan Minister; *b* 20 Jan. 1845; *s* of Joseph and Anne Salt, Butterton, Staffordshire; *m* Sabina Chambers, Scarborough; one *s* four *d*. *Educ:* privately; Richmond College. Entered Ministry at age of 20 in City of Manchester, and for 44 years held positions in London, Birmingham, Bradford, Oxford, and Southport; member of Legal Conference, 1896; Chairman of Oxford District, 1893–96; Chairman of Birmingham and District FC Council, 1900; Ministerial Treasurer of Wesleyan Education Fund, Deputy Treasurer of London Mission and Extension Fund, and held the following Secretaryships: Wesleyan Education Committee, Board of Management of Secondary Schools, Connexional Funds Office, Committee of Privileges, and Committee of Aged Ministers' and Widows' Fund; for 11 years Convener of Committee on Memorials, and for 12 years Examiner in Theology in Richmond, Didsbury, and Handsworth Colleges; Member of three Methodist Œcumenical Conferences held at Washington, London, and Toronto. *Recreation:* golf. *Address:* Central Buildings, Westminster, SW. *T:* Victoria 6148; 18 Blenheim Crescent, Croydon. *T:* Croydon 2178. *Clubs:* Croham Hurst, Croydon.   *Died 15 July 1919.*

SALT, Sir Shirley Harris, 3rd Bt, *cr* 1869; JP; *b* 4 May 1857; *o s* of Sir William Henry Salt, 2nd Bt and Emma Dove Octaveana, *o c* of John Dove Harris, of Ratcliffe Hall, Leicestershire; *S* father, 1892; *m* 1880, Charlotte Jane, *d* of Very Rev. John Cotter MacDonnell, DD, Canon of Peterborough, Rector of Misterton; two *s* two *d* (and one *s* decd). *Educ:* Trinity Coll., Camb. (MA). Barrister Inner Temple, 1882. *Heir:* *s* John William Titus Salt, Lieut Commander, RN [*b* 30 Nov. 1884; *m* 1913, Dorothy, *e d* of Col William Baker Brown, late RE]. *Address:* 5 East Pallant, Chichester. *Club:* Junior Carlton.
                                                                    Died 11 Feb. 1920.

SALTER, Sir Arthur Clavell, Kt 1917; Hon. Mr Justice Salter; Judge of the King's Bench Division, High Court, since 1917; *b* 30 Oct. 1859; *s* of late Dr Henry Hyde Salter, FRS, and Henrietta Laura, *e d* of Rev. Edward Powlett Blunt; *m* 1st, 1894, Mary Dorothea (*d* 1917), *d* of late Major John Henry Lloyd, RA; one *s* decd; 2nd, 1920, Nora Constance, *er d* of late Lt-Col Thomas Heathcote Ouchterlony, RA, Guynd, Forfarshire. *Educ:* Wimborne Gram. Sch.; King's Coll., London; BA and LLB Univ. of London. Called to Bar, Middle Temple, 1885; joined the Western Circuit, 1886; MP (U) Basingstoke Div., Hants, 1906–17; KC 1904; Recorder of Poole, 1904–17. *Address:* Queen Anne's Mansions, St James's Park, SW1. *Clubs:* Carlton, Garrick, Bath.   *Died 30 Nov. 1928.*

SALTER, Mortyn de Carle Sowerby, FRMetS; Superintendent, British Rainfall Organization, Meteorological Office, Air Ministry; *b* 17 Nov. 1880; *s* of M. J. Salter, FIC, FCS, of Bank House, Mickleton, Glos; *m* 1908, Leila Margaret, *d* of Edward F. Willoughby, MD, DPH, London; one *s*. *Educ:* Bancroft's School. Assistant to late G. J. Symons, FRS, Founder of the British Rainfall Organization; Chief Assistant to Dr H. R. Mill, 1907; Assistant Director, 1914; Joint Director with Dr Mill, 1918; Superintendent in charge on the transfer of the Organization to Government in 1919; Joint-Editor of British Rainfall, 1913–18; Editor since 1919; Joint Editor of the Meteorological Magazine; Vice-President, Royal Meteorological Society, 1915–17; Associate, Institution of Water Engineers. *Publications:* The Relation of Rainfall to Configuration (President's Premium, Instn of Water Engineers, 1919); The Rainfall of the British Isles, 1921; numerous papers on meteorological subjects. *Address:* 5 Stanhope Gardens, SW7; Meteorological Office, Exhibition Road, SW7. *T:* Kensington 5810. *Club:* Royal Societies.
                                                                    Died 21 May 1923.

SALTMARSH, John, ISO 1902; *b* 9 April 1848; *s* of Henry J. Saltmarsh; *m* 1st, 1868, Harriott Fanny (*d* 1900), *o d* of Captain George Ingram; 2nd, 1902, Emily Mary, *o c* of Charles Prujean Stevens of Surbiton and Las Palmas, Grand Canary; one *s* one *d*. *Educ:* privately in Guernsey. Assistant Royal Commission for the Paris Universal Exhibition, 1867; late of the Board of Education; Member of governing body of Wandsworth Technical Institute. *Recreations:* gardening, educational work. *Address:* The Rowans, Fairdene Road, Coulsdon, Surrey.   *Died 5 Dec. 1916.*

SALTUS, Edgar Evertson; publicist; *b* New York, 8 Oct. 1858. *Publications:* The Philosophy of Disenchantment, 1884; The Anatomy of Negation, 1885; Mr Incoul's Misadventure, 1886; The Truth about Tristrem Varick, 1887; Eden, 1888; A Transaction in Hearts, 1888; The Place that Kills, 1889; Mary Magdalen, 1890; Imperial Purple, 1892; A Transient Guest, 1893; Love and Lore, 1894; Enthralled, 1895; When Dreams come True, 1896; Purple and Fine Women, 1903; The Pomps of Satan, 1903; The Perfume of Eros, 1904; Vanity Square, 1905; Historia Amoris, 1906; The Lords of the Ghostland, 1907; The Monster, 1912; Oscar Wilde, 1917; The Paliser Case, 1919; The Imperial Orgy, 1920. *Recreation:* work. *Address:* 25 Madison Avenue, New York. *Club:* Manhattan, New York.

Died 31 July 1921.

SALVIDGE, Rt. Hon. Sir Archibald Tutton James, KBE 1920; Kt 1916; PC 1922; JP; Managing Director, Bent's Brewery Co. Ltd; Liverpool Alderman; *b* 4 Aug. 1863; 2nd *s* of Archibald Tutton Salvidge and Sarah, *d* of William Croxton; *m* 1885, Alice Margaret, *d* of late Thomas McKernan; two *s* one *d*. *Educ:* Liverpool Institute. Chairman of Council National Unionist Assoc. of Conservative and Liberal Unionist Organisations, 1913; President Liverpool Constitutional Association; declined Lord Mayoralty (Liverpool), 1910; promoted Mersey Road Tunnel Scheme, 1925; Hon. Freeman of Liverpool, 1925; Hon. LLD Liverpool, 1928; Leader of Liverpool City Council. *Recreation:* golf. *Address:* Braxted, Hoylake. *M:* TU 7814. *Clubs:* Constitutional; Conservative, Royal Golf, Liverpool.

Died 11 Dec. 1928.

SALVIN, Gerard Thornton; *b* 16 Sept. 1878; *e s* of late Henry Thomas Thornton Salvin and Agnes Jane, *y d* of Herman Julias Schier, Newcastle-on-Tyne. *Educ:* Beaumont College. Lord of the Manor of Croxdale. *Address:* Croxdale Hall, Durham. *M:* Y 1504. *Club:* Durham County.

Died 15 Sept. 1921.

SALVIN, (Marmaduke) Henry, DL; *b* 1849; 2nd *s* of late Marmaduke Charles Salvin and Caroline, *y d* of Sir Charles Wolseley, 7th Bt; *m* 1897, Annette Mary, 2nd *d* of Sir William Edward Joseph Vavasour, 3rd Bt. *Educ:* Oscott College. *Address:* 21 South Street, Park Lane, W1. *T:* Mayfair 5757; Burn Hall, Durham. *Clubs:* Turf, Arthur's, Jockey, Newmarket.

Died 2 Nov. 1924.

SAMARTH, Narayan Madhav; a Member of the Council of India since 1924; Lawyer, Journalist, and Politician. Was a member of the Royal Commission on the Superior Public Services in India, 1924; Member, Legislative Assembly, 1921-24. *Address:* India Office, Whitehall, SW1.

Died 18 Sept. 1926.

SAMMAN, Sir Henry, 1st Bt, *cr* 1921, of Routh; Chairman of Hull Underwriters Association; Hon. Elder Brother, Trinity House, Hull; *b* 14 July 1849; *s* of late Alban Samman and Sarah Fallover; *m* 1st, 1877, Elizabeth (*d* 1893), *d* of John Sanders; one *s* two *d*; 2nd, 1901, Kate (*d* 1916), *d* of William Southall. *Educ:* Brunswick House, Kelvedon, Essex. Master Mariner, Shipowner, and Underwriter; patron of one living. *Recreations:* hunting, shooting, salmon fishing. *Heir:* *s* Henry Samman, MC, Lieut RFA (TA) [*b* 18 Feb. 1881; *m* 1914, Ellis Watson, *d* of Bryan Boyes of King's Mill, Driffield]. *Address:* Manor House, Willerby, E Yorks. *TA:* Samman Hull. *T:* Kirkella 44 Hull. *Club:* Junior Athenæum.

Died 7 March 1928.

SAMPAYO, Sir Thomas Edward de, Kt 1924; KC 1903; LLB Cantab; Puisne Judge of Supreme Court of Ceylon, 1915-24; *b* 1855; *s* of Gabriel de Sampayo, Mahavidane Mudaliyar, and Philippa Perera Karunaratne, native of Ceylon; Sinhalese by race; unmarried. *Educ:* St Benedict's Institute and Royal College, Colombo; Clare College, Cambridge. Winner of the Government University Scholarship, 1877; proceeded to Cambridge University; graduated in the Law Tripos, 1880; called to Bar, Middle Temple, 1881; Advocate of the Supreme Court of Ceylon, 1881; acted as Commissioner of Assize and Puisne Judge of the Supreme Court; Member of the Council of Legal Education, Ceylon; President of the Catholic Union of Ceylon; Delegate from Ceylon to the Eucharistic Congress at Westminster, 1908, and to the Jubilee celebration of Pope Pius X, 1908; Kt Commander of St Gregory the Great. *Publications:* co-editor of the Ceylon Law Reports; translator of J. Voet's Title on Donations. *Address:* Colombo, Ceylon. *Clubs:* Orient, Catholic, Colombo.

Died 1 Dec. 1927.

SAMPSON, Rev. Gerald Victor, MA; Vicar of New Beckenham, since 1915; *b* Moor Hall, Battle, Sussex, 23 May 1864; *s* of Thomas Sampson, Lt-Col RHV, and Julie de Méric Sampson; *m* 1st, 1887, Evelyn (*d* 1888), *d* of Edward Bonham, HM Consul Calais and Boulogne; 2nd, 1890, Amy Constance Alleyne, *widow* of H. Alleyne and *d* of George Bright, ICS (Bengal Presidency), Clifton, Bristol;

five *s*. *Educ:* Westminster School, Queen's Scholar; Exeter College, Oxford. Graduated BA (Classical Honours), 1887; MA 1896. Deacon, 1887; priest, 1888; Curate of St Barnabas, Pimlico, 1887; Curate-in-Charge of St John's, Pimlico Road, 1893; Vicar of France Lynch, Stroud, Glos, 1895; Rector of Staunton, Coleford, Glos, 1897; Gloucester Diocesan Missioner, 1899; Canon Missioner and Residentiary, Truro Cathedral, 1902; Vicar of St Winnow with St Nectan, 1911-15; late Chaplain of St Faith's House of Mercy, Lostwithiel; Sub-Warden of Truro Diocesan Mission Society, 1911. *Address:* The Vicarage, New Beckenham.

Died 27 Sept. 1928.

SAMPSON, John, CBE 1918; MICE, MINA; Director of John Brown & Co., Ltd, of Sheffield and Clydebank, and other steel production, shipbuilding, engineering, electricity and ordnance companies; *b* London, 1859; *s* of John Sampson of Hayle, Cornwall; *m* 1890, Lucy Elizabeth, *d* of John Pearce Sawyer, of Filham House, Ivybridge, South Devon; one *s*. *Educ:* private school. Was British Representative Anglo-Russian Commission in New York during War, and Member of Financial Facilities Committee. *Recreations:* golf, sketching, travel. *Address:* Queen Anne's Mansions, St James Park, SW1; Granard Lodge, Folkestone, Kent. *Clubs:* Athenæum, Reform.

Died 11 May 1925.

SAMPSON, Major Patrick, DSO 1914; Royal Army Medical Corps; *b* 4 Jan. 1881; *s* of M. Sampson, Knocklong, Limerick; *m* 1917, Dorothea, *e d* of Comdr H. D. Kirwan, RN; one *s* one *d*. Entered army, 1906; Captain, 1909; Major, 1918; served European War, 1914-17 (despatches twice, DSO, wounded). *Address:* Brook House, Cricklade, Wilts.

Died 30 Aug. 1922.

SAMPSON, Hon. Victor, KC; Ex-Attorney-General, Cape Colony; Member of Jameson Ministry; late Acting Judge Eastern Districts Courts. *Club:* Civil Service, Cape Town.

SAMSON, Charles Leopold; solicitor; Senior Partner in the firm of Grundy, Kershaw, Samson & Co., of London and Manchester; *b* Manchester, 1853; *s* of late Leopold Samson; *m* 1881, Margaret Alice, 2nd *d* of late William Rumney of Stubbins House, Lancashire; four *s*. *Educ:* privately. Admitted a Solicitor, 1874; Law Society's Prizeman and Stephen Heelis Gold Medallist. Was President of Manchester Law Society; Vice President, 1911-12; and President of the Law Society, 1912-13; contested (U) Northwich Division of Cheshire, 1900. *Publication:* Treatise on the Law of Bankruptcy. *Recreation:* literature. *Address:* 121 Ashley Gardens, SW1. *T:* Victoria 3517. *Clubs:* Thatched House, Royal Automobile.

Died 8 June 1923.

SAMUEL, Jonathan, JP; MP (L) Stockton-on-Tees, 1895-1900, and since 1910; Alderman of Durham County Council; Member of the Tees Conservancy Board; *b* 1853; *s* of late Thomas Samuel, Tredegar, Monmouth, and Jane Clara, *d* of E. Davies; *m* 1892, Hannah Exley, 5th *d* of late Joshua Mellor, Huddersfield; four *d*. Mayor of Stockton, 1894-95 and 1902; Hon. Freeman, 1904; JP Stockton-on-Tees, 1893. *Address:* Lorne Terrace, Stockton-on-Tees. *Club:* National Liberal.

Died 22 Feb. 1917.

SAMUEL, Sir Stuart Montagu, 1st Bt, *cr* 1912; JP County of London; MP Whitechapel Division of Tower Hamlets, 1900-16; late member of Samuel Montagu and Co., foreign bankers; *b* 24 Oct. 1856; *s* of Edwin Louis Samuel and Clara, *d* of Ellis Samuel Yates, Liverpool; *m* 1893, Ida Bessie Evaline, *d* of Alphonse Mayer of London; two *d*. *Educ:* Liverpool Institute; University College School, London. *Heir:* none. *Address:* 12 Hill Street, Mayfair, W1. *T:* Grosvenor 2122; Chelwood Vetchery, Nutley, Sussex. *T:* Nutley 10. *M:* A 1150; FY 1001.

Died 13 May 1926 (ext).

SAMUELS, Rt. Hon. Arthur Warren, PC 1918; JP; KC (Ireland); LLD; MRIA; Judge of the High Court of Justice in Ireland, King's Bench, since 1919; Bencher, Gray's Inn, 1919; Bencher, King's Inns; *b* 19th May 1852; 2nd *s* of late Arthur Samuels, MA, Langara, Kingstown, and Katharine, *d* of Owen Daly, Mornington, Co. Westmeath; *m* 1881, Emma Margaret (*d* 1904), 2nd *d* of Rev. James William Irwin, MA, Sharon, Co. Donegal, and Florine Griffiths-Lloyd (*o sister* of late Sir Herbert Edwardes, KCB, KCSI); two *d* (one *s* decd). *Educ:* Royal School, Dungannon; Trinity Coll., Dublin. 1st Classical Scholar; Royal Scholar; Sen. Exhibitioner; 1st Honours Classics, Modern Literature, History, and Political Economy; Vice-Chancellor's Prizeman; gold medallist Historical Society. Called to Irish Bar, 1877; Prizeman, King's Inns; Bacon Scholar, Gray's Inn; Professor Personal Property, King's Inns, 1891-94; QC 1894; called to English Bar, 1896; contested Dublin University, 1903; MP (U) Dublin University, 1917-19; Attorney-General, 1918; Solicitor-

General for Ireland, 1917-18; Pres. Social and Statistical Society of Ireland, 1906-8; Member of Senate and Council of Dublin University; Chancellor of Armagh; Chancellor of United Dioceses of Limerick, Ardfert, and Aghadoe; Unionist; took a prominent part in movements for Irish Private Bill Procedure Reform, and on the Irish Political Financial and Social Questions. *Publications:* pamphlets on Irish Financial Questions; The Expenditure Account, The Financial Report, What it Finds; The Fiscal Question; Features of Recent Irish Finance; Home Rule: What is It?, 1910; Home Rule Finance, 1912; articles on Private Bill Procedure and Devolution, and against Home Rule; articles in Quarterly and other Reviews; (ed) Edmund Burke's Early Life and Writings, by Arthur P. I. Samuels, 1923. *Recreations:* sailing, rowing (ex-Captain Dublin University Rowing Club), angling. *Address:* Cloghereen, Howth, Co. Dublin. *T:* Howth 56. *Clubs:* Carlton, Constitutional; University, Dublin.

Died 11 May 1925.

SAMUELSON, Berhard Martin, CIE 1918; MICE; Chief Engineer, Public Works Department, Burma; *b* 1874; *m* Eleanor Mary, *d* of late A. D. Dufty. *Educ:* Rugby; Cooper's Hill. Entered ICS 1894. *Address:* T. Cook & Son, Rangoon, Burma.

Died 20 Feb. 1921.

SAMWELL, Ven. Frederick William, VD; Archdeacon of Adelaide; Senior Chaplain Australian Military Forces; Secretary General of Synod, Church of England in Australia; *b* Leicester, England, 18 Feb. 1861; *s* of Robert Owen Samwell; *m* 1888, Marion, *d* of A. W. Richardson, JP, Mount Barker, SA; one *s* two *d*. *Educ:* St Augustine's College, Canterbury. A founder of the District Trained Nursing Society of South Australia; Past Grand Chaplain of Grand Lodge of Freemasons of South Australia; served in World War as Senior Chaplain Australian Imperial Forces, 1914-15. *Publications:* editor, Adelaide Diocesan Year Book, 1896-1902; editor, Official Report of Adelaide Church Congress, 1902; editor of Adelaide Church Guardian, 1908-15. *Recreation:* tennis. *Address:* Adelaide, South Australia. *Died April 1925.*

SANDARS, John Drysdale, JP, DL; CC; *b* 15 Dec. 1860; *s* of J. E. Sandars, North Sandsfield, Gainsborough; *m* Maud Evelyn, *o d* of 5th Baron Graves; one *s* one *d*. *Educ:* Wellington College; Trinity Hall, Cambridge. Called to the Bar, Inner Temple. Served 12 years in North Lincs Militia, retiring as Captain; served as High Sheriff; on death of father, 1890, gave up the Bar and took up the malting business, which his father had conducted, and extended this considerably; opened maltings on the Manchester Ship Canal in the early days of this enterprise; took great interest in all local County work and politics; member for S Ward, Gainsborough, on County Council, and president of the West Lindsey Conservative Association. *Recreations:* interested in all sports, particularly hunting and shooting, though later the former gave way to golf. *Address:* Gate Burton Hall, Lincs. *TA:* Sandars, Gainsborough. *T:* 7 Gainsborough. *M:* BE 1, BE 303. *Clubs:* Boodle's, Wellington, Hurlingham, Ranelagh.

Died 18 Feb. 1922.

SANDAY, Rev. William, DD, LLD, LittD Cambridge; FBA 1903; Lady Margaret Professor of Divinity and Canon of Christ Church, Oxford, 1895-1919; Chaplain in Ordinary to His Majesty since 1903; *b* Holme Pierrepont, Nottingham, 1 Aug. 1843; *e s* of William Sanday (well known as breeder of Leicester sheep and shorthorns), Holme Pierrepont, and Elizabeth Mann, Scawsby, Doncaster; *m* 1877, Marian C. A. (*d* 1904), *e d* of Warren Hastings Woodman Hastings, JP, Twyning, Tewkesbury (eldest direct descendant of the sister of Warren Hastings). *Educ:* Repton; Balliol Coll., Oxford; Corpus Christi Coll., Oxford (Scholar). 1st class Mods 1863; 1st class Lit. Hum. 1865. Fellow of Trinity Coll., Oxford, 1866; Lecturer, 1866-69; ordained, 1867; in charge of Navestock, Romford, 1869-71; Lecturer at St Nicholas, Abingdon, 1871-72; Vicar of Great Waltham, Chelmsford, 1872-73; Rector of Barton-on-the-Heath, Shipston-on-Stour, 1873-76; Principal of Bishop Hatfield's Hall, Durham, 1876-83; Examining Chaplain to Bishop Lightfoot, 1879-81; Dean Ireland's Professor of Exegesis and Tutorial Fellow of Exeter Coll., Oxford, 1883-95; Hon. Fellow, 1898; last of the Oxford preachers at Whitehall. *Publications:* The Authorship and Historical Character of the Fourth Gospel, 1872; The Gospels in the Second Century, 1876; Romans and Galatians (in Bishop Ellicott's Commentary), 1878; Portions of the Gospels according to St Mark and St Matthew from the Bobbio MS, 1886; Appendices ad Novum Testamentum Stephanicum, 1889; The Oracles of God, 1891; Two Present Day Questions, 1892; Inspiration (the Bampton Lectures), 1893; (with Dr A. C. Headlam) Critical and Exegetical Commentary on the Epistle to the Romans, 1895; Sacred Sites of the Bible, 1903; Outlines of the Life of Christ (repr. from Hastings' Dictionary of the Bible),

1905; Criticism of the Fourth Gospel, 1905; The Life of Christ in Recent Research, 1907; Christologies, Ancient and Modern, 1910; Personality in Christ and in Ourselves, 1911; Oxford Studies in the Synoptic Problem, 1911; The Primitive Church and Reunion, 1913; Bishop Gore's Challenge to Criticism, 1914; Spirit, Matter, and Miracle, 1916; (with Rev. N. P. Williams) Form and Content in Christian Tradition, a friendly discussion, 1916; The New Testament Background, 1918; joint-editor, Variorum Bible, 1880-89; joint-editor with the Bishop of Salisbury, Old Latin Biblical Texts, Part II 1886; articles (God in NT, etc) in Hastings' Dictionary of the Bible, vol. ii, etc. *Address:* Christ Church, Oxford. *Club:* Athenæum.

Died 16 Sept. 1920.

SANDBACH, Maj.-Gen. Arthur Edmund, CB 1910; DSO 1900; *b* 30 July 1859; 3rd *s* of late H. R. Sandbach of Hafodunos, Co. Denbigh, and Elizabeth, *d* and *co-heir* of Martin Williams of Bryn Gwyn, Co. Montgomery; *m* 1902, Hon. Ina Douglas-Pennant, 5th *d* of 2nd Baron Penrhyn; one *d*. *Educ:* Eton; Royal Military Academy, Woolwich. Entered Army, 1879; Colonel, 1904; Brig.-Gen. 1910; Maj.-Gen. 1914; served Egyptian War, 1882, including Tel-el-Kebir (medal with clasp, Khedive's star); Soudan Campaign, 1885 (clasp); Burmese Expedition, 1886-87, horse shot in action (medal with clasp); Sikkim Expedition, 1888 (clasp); Hazara, 1891, as ADC to Maj.-Gen. Elles commanding (despatches, clasp); Nile Expedition, 1898, as AAG, Egyptian Army, including Khartoum (despatches, Brevet Lt-Col, medal with clasp, Khedive's medal with clasp); Military Secretary to Lord Curzon of Kedleston, Viceroy of India, 1898-99; AAG South Africa, 1899-1901 (despatches, medal with six clasps, DSO); Commandant 1st Sappers and Miners, Indian Army, 1904-7; Commanding RE Troops, Aldershot, 1908-10; Chief Engineer in Ireland, 1910-14; European War, 1914-15 and 1917 (despatches thrice, wounded, promoted Major-General for distinguished service in the field); DL, JP Montgomeryshire; High Sheriff, 1919; Chairman of County Territorial Force Association, 1908-20. *Address:* Bryn Gwyn, Bwlch-y-Cibau, Montgomeryshire. *Clubs:* Naval and Military, Athenæum. *Died 25 June 1928.*

SANDEMAN, Albert George, JP for Hertfordshire; Chairman of George G. Sandeman, Sons, and Co., Limited, London; late Director of the Bank of England (Governor, 1895-96); one of HM's Commissioners of Lieutenancy for the City of London; Commissioner of Income Tax for City of London; President of the London Chamber of Commerce, 1898; *b* 21 Oct. 1833; *s* of George Glas Sandeman, merchant of London and Oporto, and Elizabeth, *d* of Albert Forster; *m* 1856, Maria Carlota Perpetua de Moraes Sarmento, *d* of Viscount Moncorvo, Portuguese Ambassador to Court of St James's; two *s* four *d*. High Sheriff of Surrey, 1872; late Major 12th Middlesex (Prince of Wales's Own Civil Service) RV. *Address:* Greylands, Bexhill-on-Sea. *T:* Bexhill 381. *Died 6 Jan. 1923.*

SANDEMAN, Rear-Admiral Henry George Glas, CMG 1918; *b* 18 June 1868; *y s* of late Lt-Col John Glas Sandeman, MVO; *m* 1908, Nina, *d* of late Alfred Evans. *Educ:* Cordwalles, Maidenhead. Joined HMS Britannia as Naval Cadet, 1881; served as Flag-Lieut to Admiral Sir John Ommanney Hopkins, GCB, in N America and West Indies, and in Mediterranean; commanded HMS Britannia, European War; Commodore and Senior Naval Officer at Hong-Kong, 1916-18; retired, 1918. *Address:* Chicksgrove Mill, Tisbury, Wilts.

Died 16 May 1928.

SANDEMAN, John Glas, MVO 1902; FSA; late sub-officer and Senior Member HM Bodyguard, Hon. Corps of Gentlemen-at-Arms; *b* 18 Aug. 1836; 2nd *s* of late George Glas Sandeman of Westfield, Hayling Island; *m* 1862, Eliza Victoire Cormick, *e d* of late Captain Henry Cormick Lynch of Galway, and Leigh Park, Hants; two *s* three *d*. *Educ:* King's College, London. Served in 1st Royal Dragoons, 1853-59; Crimean Campaign, 1854-56, battles of Balaklava, Inkerman, and Tchernaya, and siege of Sebastopol; afterwards Lt-Col commanding Essex Yeomanry Cavalry, and Hon. Lieutenant Royal Naval Reserve; Cavalheiro of the Order of Christ in Portugal. *Publications:* The Spears of Honour and the Gentlemen Pensioners; Compiler of the Sandeman Genealogy; Editor of the Clan Sandeman Family Magazine; a short account of the Select Knot of Friendly Brothers in London. *Recreation:* collector of Greek and Roman objects of art. *Address:* Whin-Hurst, Hayling Island, Havant. *T:* Hayling Island 27. *Clubs:* Junior United Service (Hon. Mem.); Royal St George Yacht, Kingstown; Union, Brighton.

Died 7 Dec. 1921.

SANDERS, Rev. Charles Evatt; Hon. Canon of Southwark Cathedral, 1906; *b* 1846; *s* of Evatt Sallows and Hannah Sanders; *m* Evelyn Augusta Gilliat; one *s* three *d*. *Educ:* Worcester College,

Oxford. Deacon, 1870; priest, 1871; Curate of Kingstone, Herefordshire; Whitchurch, Salop; Englefield Green, Surrey; Vicar of Betchworth, 1880-1910; Rural Dean of Reigate, 1905-10. *Publication:* Necessary to Salvation. *Address:* 33 Argyll Road, Kensington, W. *Died 6 Jan. 1927.*

SANDERS, Rev. Ernest Arthur Blackwell, MA; Vicar of Edmonton, Middlesex, since 1900; Rural Dean of Enfield, 1904; Prebendary of St Paul's Cathedral, 1911; *b* 1858; *s* of Frederick Sanders, Freeman of City of London; *m* 1882, Jane, *d* of John Biggs of Dallington, Sussex; one *d.* *Educ:* Highgate School; Worcester College, Oxford. Curate of St John's, Holloway, 1882-84; Vicar of All Saints', Holloway, 1884-91; Rector of Whitechapel, 1891-96; Vicar of St Mark's, Dalston, 1896-1900. *Publication:* The Record of a Noble Life (a biography of his father), 1901. *Recreations:* walking; in former years rowing, athletics (public school record for 100 yards under 18). *Address:* Edmonton Vicarage, Middlesex. *TA:* Vicar, Edmonton. *T:* 1871 Tottenham. *Clubs:* Primrose, Church Imperial. *Died 24 Sept. 1917.*

SANDERS, Rev. Canon Henry S., MA; Canon of Chelmsford since 1917; *b* 1864; *s* of late Rev. W. S. Sanders, MA; *m* 1906, Elsie Marion Mitchell, Upwood, Bingley, Yorkshire; one *s* one *d.* *Educ:* Selwyn College, Cambridge (BA 1886; MA 1890). Deacon, 1887; priest, 1888; Curate of Portsea, 1887-90; St Mary's, Southampton, 1890-94; St John's, Westminster, 1894-97; Rector of Eastnor and Hereford Diocesan Missioner, 1897-1901; Vicar of Bromley by Bow, E; Rural Dean, 1916-19; Rector of Woodford, 1906-20. *Address:* Chelmsford. *T:* Chelmsford 334. *Died 26 Nov. 1920.*

SANDERS, Thomas W., FLS, FRHS, etc; Editor of Amateur Gardening; lecturer and writer on scientific and practical horticulture, agriculture, etc; *b* Martley, Worcestershire, 6 Nov. 1855; *m* Annie, *d* of late Richard Hoare; one *s* one *d.* *Educ:* village school, and afterwards by self instruction. Had a practical training in gardening and farming, and wrote a great deal on both subjects; chairman of party of experts invited by Swedish Government to inspect agricultural industries of Sweden, 1906; Kt 1st Cl., Order of Vasa (Sweden), 1906. *Publications:* Garden Calendar; An Encyclopædia of Gardening; Garden and Grounds; The Amateur's Greenhouse; Roses and their Cultivation; Vegetables and their Cultivation; Book of the Potato; A Garden of Annuals; Hardy Perennials and Biennials; Alphabet of Gardening; Bulbs and their Cultivation; Lawns and Greens; Window and Indoor Gardening; The Flower Garden; Hardy Fruits and their Cultivation; revised edition of Rustic Adornments; Mushrooms and their Cultivation; Carnations, Picotees, and Pinks; Garden Foes; Popular Hardy Perennials; Salads and their Cultivation; Allotment and Kitchen Gardens, etc; also edited the following handbooks—Chrysanthemums for Garden and Greenhouse; Vegetables for Profit; Ducks, Geese, and Turkeys for Profit; Rabbits for Profit; Pigs for Profit; Horse, its Care and Management; Dairy Cows and Dairying; Incubation; Grape Growing; The Goat; Sheep, their Breeding and Management; Pansies and Violets; Small Holder's Guide; Bees for Profit and Pleasure; Tomatoes, and How to Grow them; Rock Gardens and Alpine Plants; Orchids for Amateurs. *Recreations:* natural history (especially British botany), entomology, geology; also freemasonry (Past Master of Caxton Lodge, 1853, also of Philanthic Lodge, 3032; London rank). *Address:* 124 Embleton Road, Lewisham, SE. *Club:* Horticultural. *Died 13 Oct. 1926.*

SANDERSON, 1st Baron, *cr* 1905, of Armthorpe, York; **Thomas Henry Sanderson,** GCB 1900 (KCB 1893; CB 1880); KCMG 1887; ISO 1902; *b* 11 Jan. 1841; *s* of Richard Sanderson, MP, and Hon. Charlotte Matilda Manners Sutton, *d* of 1st Viscount Canterbury; unmarried. *Educ:* Eton. Passed a competitive examination, and appointed Junior Clerk Foreign Office, 1859; attached to Lord Wodehouse's (Earl of Kimberley) special Mission to King of Denmark, 1863-64; Assistant Protocolist for Conferences on the affairs of Denmark, 1864, and on the Black Sea, 1871; Private Secretary to Parliamentary Under-Secretary of State, Mr (Sir A. H.) Layard, 1866; Assistant Agent of HM Government at Geneva, in the Arbitration on the Alabama Claims, 1871; Private Sec. to late Earl of Derby, Secretary of State for Foreign Affairs, 1866-68, 1874-78; Private Secretary to late Earl Granville, Secretary of State for Foreign Affairs, 1880-85; Senior Clerk, 1885; Assistant Under-Secretary of State for Foreign Affairs, 1889; Permanent Under-Sec. of State for Foreign Affairs, 1894-1906; Chairman of Committee on Indian Emigration to the Crown Colonies, 1909-10; Chairman of Council of Royal Society of Arts, 1911-13; Hon. DCL Oxford, 1907. *Heir:* none. *Address:* 65 Wimpole Street, W1. *T:* Langham 2168. *Clubs:* Athenæum, Travellers', St James's. *Died 21 March 1923 (ext).*

SANDERSON, Frederick William, JP Co. Northants; MA; Headmaster of Oundle School since 1892; *b* 13 May 1857; *y s* of late Thomas Sanderson, Brancepeth, Durham, and Margaret Andrews; *m* Jane, *d* of L. T. (Tom) Hodgson, Broughton Hall; one *s* one *d.* *Educ:* Univ. of Durham (Van Mildert Theological Scholar, 1877; Fellow, 1881); Christ's Coll., Cambridge (bracketed 11th Wrangler, 1882). Lecturer at Girton Coll., 1882-85; Assistant Master at Dulwich College, 1885-92. *Publications:* Elementary Hydrostatics; Elementary Electricity; Introduction to Modern Geometry; Essays on Education; A Synopsis of the Life of Christ. *Recreations:* walking, bicycling, climbing. *Address:* Oundle School, Northants. *Club:* Royal Societies. *Died 15 June 1922.*

SANDERSON, Oswald; Managing Director Ellermans Wilson Line, Hull; Chairman Wilsons and North-Eastern Railway Shipping Co., Hull; Chairman Humber Conservancy, 1915-25; *b* 3 Jan. 1863; *s* of Richard Sanderson, Liverpool; *m* 1888, Beatrice M. F., *d* of E. F. Beddall, New York; three *s* one *d.* *Educ:* King's School, Ely. Director Suez Canal Co.; Lloyds Bank, Ltd; London and North Eastern Railway; North British and Mercantile Insurance Company; Earles Shipbuilding and Engineering Co. Ltd, Hull; United Shipping Co. Ltd, London; Hull Underwriters' Association, Ltd; Hull Mutual SS Protection Society; Hon. Elder Brother Trinity House, Hull; Member Lloyd's Register, Shipping Federation, Chamber of Shipping; President of Chamber of Shipping of United Kingdom, 1906; Member of Royal Commission on Shipping Rings, 1907; Hon. Lt-Col East Yorkshire Regiment; Hon. Colonel 73rd Northumbrian Brigade RFA (T); DL East Riding, Yorkshire. *Address:* 2 Mansfield Street, W1; Hessle Mount, Hessle, East Yorks. *TA:* Hessle *T:* Hessle 15. *M:* BT18. *Clubs:* Carlton, White's; Royal Yacht Squadron, Cowes. *Died 25 Dec. 1926.*

SANDERSON, Sir Percy, KCMG 1899 (CMG 1886); *b* London, 7 July 1842; *s* of late Richard Sanderson and Charlotte Matilda, *d* of 1st Viscount Canterbury. *Educ:* Eton; Addiscombe. Lieut Royal Madras Artillery, 1859; appointed to Royal Horse Artillery, 1864; ADC to Sir William Denison, Governor of Madras, 1865-66; 3rd class Commissary of Ordnance, 1866; acting ADC to Lord Napier, Governor of Madras, 1868; acting 1st class Commissary of Ordnance, Fort St George, 1868; retired on half-pay, 1870; Consul at Galatz, 1876; Consul-General for Roumania, to reside at Galatz, and Commissioner for the navigation of the Danube, 1882; employed on public service in London during the Danube Conference, 1883; acting Chargé d'Affaires at Bucharest at intervals in 1881, 1883, 1884, 1885, 1886; Consul-General, New York, 1894-1907; retired, 1907; JP Oxfordshire, 1908; Reading, 1915. *Address:* Grove Hill, Caversham. *Club:* East India United Service. *Died 11 July 1919.*

SANDFORD, Capt. Francis Hugh, DSO 1915; RN; Assistant-Director of the Plans Division of the Naval Staff; *b* 10 Oct. 1887; 6th *s* of late Ven. E. G. Sandford, Archdeacon of Exeter, and Ethel, *d* of Gabriel Poole, Brent Knoll, Somerset. *Educ:* Clifton College; Balliol College, Oxford; BA. Served Dardanelles, 1915 (severely wounded, despatches, DSO); promoted Comdr, and Croix de Guerre with palm, 1918, for services in raids closing Zeebrugge and Ostend harbours; Capt. 1924. *Club:* United Service. *Died 15 Feb. 1926.*

SANDHURST, 1st Viscount, *cr* 1916, of Bath; **William Mansfield,** GCSI 1900; GCIE 1895; GCVO 1917; PC 1906; JP; Baron 1871; Lieutenant Coldstream Guards, retired 1879; Hon. Colonel Bombay Rifles since 1895; Lord-Chamberlain since 1912; *b* 21 Aug. 1855; *s* of 1st Baron Sandhurst and Margaret, *d* of Robert Fellowes, Shotesham Park, Norfolk; *S* father as 2nd Baron, 1876; *m* 1st, 1881, Lady Victoria Alexandrina Spencer, CI (*d* 1906), *d* of 4th Earl Spencer, KG; one *s* decd one *d* decd; 2nd, 1909, Eleanor Mary Caroline, *d* of Matthew Arnold and *widow* of Hon. Armine Wodehouse. *Educ:* Rugby. Sub-Lieutenant, Coldstream Guards, 1873; Lord-in-Waiting, 1880-85; Under-Secretary for War, 1886, 1892-94; Governor of Bombay, 1895-99; was one of a small committee sent by Government to S Africa in 1906 to report on the subject of Representative Government for S Africa; Treasurer, St Bartholomew's Hospital from 1908; KGStJ 1898; Grand Cross Order of Dannebrog. *Heir* to Barony: *brother* Hon. John William Mansfield, *b* 10 July 1857. *Address:* 60 Eaton Square, SW1. *T:* Gerrard 3280. *Clubs:* Brooks's, Turf, Garrick. *Died 2 Nov. 1921.*

SANDIFORD, Charles Thomas, CB 1903; MICE, MIME; Engineer on Uganda Railway; *b* 1840. Worked on Sind, Punjab, and Delhi Railway; Locomotive Superintendent NW State Railway, 1886; retired, 1899. *Address:* c/o Henry S. King & Co., Pall Mall, SW. *Died 1 March 1919.*

SANDS, Rev. Hubert, MA; Vicar of Burbage, near Marlborough, Wilts, since 1913; Rural Dean of Bordesley, 1905–13; Hon. Canon of Birmingham, 1906–13; *b* Bleasby, Notts, 1855; *s* of T. B. Sands of Liverpool; *m* 1889, Lucy Mary, *e d* of Samuel Blakemore Allport of Moseley; four *s* one *d*. *Educ:* Bedford School; Oriel College, Oxford. Curate of Solihull, 1878–85; Moseley, 1886–89; Vicar of St Oswald's, Bordersley, 1889–1913. *Publications:* The First Miracle; Eucharistic Doctrine. *Recreations:* cycling, fly-fishing. *Address:* Burbage Vicarage, Marlborough, Wilts. *Died 5 Oct. 1922.*

SANDS, Sir James Patrick, Kt 1917; President Legislative Council, 1916–23, Member Executive Council, 1901–23, Bahama Islands; *b* 7 Oct. 1859; *e s* of late Thomas Hilton Sands; *m* 1884, Laura Louisa, 3rd *d* of late John Robert Hall, Bahamas; seven *s* one *d*. *Educ:* private schools. Merchant; Member of the House of Assembly, Bahamas, 1889–1916; Leader of the Government in the House of Assembly, 1909–16. *Recreation:* boating. *Address:* George Street, Nassau, New Providence, Bahamas. *Died 11 March 1925.*

SANDS, William Southgate, MVO 1914; Inspector of Buckingham Palace since 1906; *b* 26 Nov. 1853; *e* surv. *s* of Thomas S. Sands, Slough; *m* Lucy (*decd*), *o d* of J. Crissall, London; no *c*. *Educ:* London; Windsor. Entered the Lord Chamberlain's Dept 1873; Inspector of Holyrood Palace, Edinburgh, 1893–1906; Queen Victoria's Jubilee Medal and bar; King Edward's and King George's Coronation Medals, and various foreign orders. *Recreations:* painting, antiques. *Address:* Buckingham Palace, SW1. *Died 13 Dec. 1924.*

SANDWICH, 8th Earl of, *cr* 1660; **Edward George Henry Montagu,** KCVO 1906; JP; Viscount Hinchingbrooke and Baron Montagu of St Neots, 1660; Lord-Lieutenant of Huntingdonshire since 1891; Colonel, late Grenadier Guards; Hon. Colonel 5th Battalion King's Royal Rifles, 1886; Chairman Huntingdonshire County Council; *b* 13 July 1839; *s* of 7th Earl and Lady Mary Paget, *d* of 1st Marquess of Anglesey; *S* father, 1884. *Educ:* Eton. Entered Grenadier Guards, 1857; Lieut and Capt. 1862; Adj. 2nd Batt. 1864; Capt. and Lieut-Col 1870; Col 1881; attached to special Embassies to Constantinople, 1858; Berlin, 1861; Portugal, 1874; Morocco, 1875; Military Secretary at Gibraltar, 1875–76; Hon. Col 5th KRR, 1884; Brig.-Gen. S Midland Vol. Brigade, 1888–94; MP Huntingdon, 1876–84; Mayor of Huntingdon, 1897–99; KJStJ. Owned about 20,000 acres; Church of England; Unionist. Picture gallery, Hinchingbrooke. *Heir: nephew* George Charles Montagu, *b* 29 Dec. 1874. *Publication:* My Experiences in Spiritual Healing, 1915. *Address:* 18 Buckingham Palace Gate, SW. *T:* Victoria 8439; Hinchingbrooke, Huntingdon; Hooke Court, Beaminster, Dorset. *Clubs:* Travellers', Turf, United Service. *Died 26 June 1916.*

SANDWITH, Fleming Mant, CMG 1916; Temporary Colonel Army Medical Services; Consulting Physician with HM troops in Alexandria; *b* 11 Oct. 1853; 2nd *s* of Col J. W. F. Sandwith; *m* Gladys, *d* of Dr Humphry Sandwith of Kars; two *s* two *d*. *Educ:* Charterhouse; St Thomas' Hosp. MD Durham; FRCP. Gresham Professor of Physic; Lecturer at London School of Tropical Medicine and St Thomas' Hospital; Senior Physician, Albert Dock Hospital; Examiner in Tropical Medicine, London and Liverpool Universities; served as Ambulance Surgeon in the Turco-Servian War, 1876 (Order of Takova and war medal); and Russo-Turkish Campaign, 1877–78; present at the fighting in Shipka Pass, and served on Baker Pasha's staff during his retreat across the Rhodope Mountains (Order of Medjidieh and war medal); proceeded to Egypt for cholera epidemic, 1883; became Vice-Director of the Public Health Department of the Egyptian Government until 1885; and Professor of Medicine, Egyptian Government School of Medicine, till 1903 (3rd Order of Osmanieh); was Senior Physician of the Imperial Yeomanry Hospital at Pretoria during South African War, 1900 (medal and 3 clasps); served European War, 1914–17 (CMG); KGStJ. *Publications:* Egypt as a Winter Resort; Medical Diseases of Egypt, 1905; History of Kasr el Ainy, AD 1466–1901; and various papers, mostly on medical subjects. *Address:* 31 Cavendish Square, W. *T:* 679 Mayfair. *Club:* Athenæum. *Died 17 Feb. 1918.*

SANDWITH, Major Ralph Leslie, CMG 1900; late the Leicestershire Regiment; *b* 19 March 1859; *s* of late Major-General John Pitcairn Sandwith, Bombay Army; *m* 1901, Mabel Ellison Manisty; one *s*. *Educ:* Harrow. Entered army in 17th Foot, 1880; served Boer War at Talana Hill; commanded Base Depot, Natal, with rank of Lieut Col (despatches, CMG, medal with clasp). *Recreations:* genealogical research, croquet. *Address:* Mount Side, Harrow-on-the-Hill. *Died 16 Sept. 1920.*

SANDYS, Sir John (Edwin), Kt 1911; LittD Cambridge, 1886; FBA 1909; FRSL 1914; Fellow of St John's College, Cambridge, since 1867; Public Orator in the University of Cambridge, 1876–1919; Orator Emeritus; *b* 19 May 1844; *s* of late Rev. Timothy Sandys, CMS, and Rebecca, *d* of Joseph Swain; *m* 1880, Mary Grainger, *d* of late Rev. Henry Hall. *Educ:* Repton; St John's Coll., Camb. (Scholar, 1863). Bell Scholar, 1864; Browne's Medallist for Greek Ode, 1865; Porson Prizeman, 1865, 1866; Members' Prizeman for Latin Essay, 1866, 1867; Senior Classic, 1867. Classical Lecturer at Jesus Coll., 1867–77, and at St John's Coll., 1867–1907; Tutor, St John's, 1870–1900; Lane Lecturer at Harvard, 1905; Hon. LittD Dublin, 1892; Hon. DLit Oxford, 1920; Hon. LLD Edinburgh, 1909; Athens, 1912; Cambridge, 1920; Comdr. Order of the Redeemer, Greece, 1914. *Publications:* editor of: Isocrates, Ad Demonicum et Panegyricus, 1868; Demosthenes, Select Private Orations, 1875, 4th edn 1910; Cope's Commentary on Aristotle's Rhetoric, 3 vols 1877; Euripides' Bacchae, 1880, 4th edn 1900; Cicero's Orator, 1885; Leptines, 1890; Philippic Orations, (1) First Philippic and Olynthiacs, 1897, (2) Second and Third Philippics, De Pace, and De Chersoneso, 1900; Euripides, Bacchae (with illustrations from works of ancient art), 1880, 4th edn 1900; Aristotle's Constitution of Athens, 1903, 2nd edn 1912; Jebb's translation of Aristotle's Rhetoric, and the new edn of Jebb's Theophrastus, 1909; translation of Pindar (Loeb Library), 1915, 2nd edn 1919; joint-editor (with Prof. Nettleship) of Seyffert's Dictionary of Classical Mythology, Religion, Literature, Art and Antiquities, 1891; author of: History of Classical Scholarship, in 3 vols, with Chronological Tables, Facsimiles Portraits, and other Illustrations: vol. i, From the Sixth Century, BC, to the End of the Middle Ages, 1903, 3rd edn 1921; vol. ii, From the Revival of Learning to the End of the Eighteenth Century (in Italy, France, England, and the Netherlands), 1908; vol. iii, The Eighteenth Century in Germany and the Nineteenth in Europe and the United States of America, 1908; Harvard Lectures on the Revival of Learning, 1905; Ancient University Ceremonies in Fasciculus J. W. Clark dicatus, 1909; Orationes et Epistolæ Cantabrigienses (1876–1909), 1910; Short History of Classical Scholarship, 1915; Introduction to Latin Epigraphy, 1919; contributor to 'Social England,' 1896–97, and Cambridge Companion to Greek Studies, 1905; editor of (and contributor to) Cambridge Companion to Latin Studies, 1910, 3rd edn 1921; writer of chapter on Latin Literature, from John of Salisbury to Richard of Bury, in Cambridge History of English Literature, vol. i 1907, and on Scholars, Antiquaries, and Bibliographers, vol. xii 1915; also on Education and Scholarship, in Shakespeare's England, 1916; papers: Literary Sources of Milton's Lycidas (Royal Society of Literature), 1914; Roger Bacon (British Academy), 1914; Tincommius (Numismatic Chronicle), 1918; contributor of articles on Pausanias and the elder and younger Plinies, and on Greek Law, and the History of Classical Studies, in the 11th edition of the Encyclopædia Britannica. *Recreation:* travelling. *Address:* St John's House, Grange Road, Cambridge. *Club:* Athenæum.

Died 6 July 1922.

SANFORD, Col Edward Charles Ayshford, CMG 1902; late 3rd Battalion Wiltshire Regiment; *b* 6 June 1859; *s* of William Ayshford Sanford, Nynehead Court, Wellington, Somerset, and Ellen, *d* of Henry Seymour, Knoyle House, Semley, Wilts; *m* 1904, May, *e d* of Lloyd Griffith of Hurst Court, Ore, Hastings; three *s*. *Educ:* Eton. Gazetted 3rd Wilts Regt (Royal Wilts Militia), 1878; Captain, 1881; Hon. Major, 1893; Lieut-Col 1894; Hon. Col 1898; served with Sir Charles Warren's Field Force in Bechuanaland, 1884–85; embodied 17 Jan. 1900, being quartered in Cork command, Ireland; went to St Helena to guard prisoners of war, 20 June 1901; disembodied, 1902; retired, 1903; JP Somerset, Devon, and St Helena. *Club:* Brooks's. *Died 22 March 1923.*

SANKEY, Capt. Matthew Henry Phineas Riall, CB 1916; CBE 1920; Royal Engineers (retired); Director and Consulting Engineer to Marconi's Wireless Telegraph Co., Ltd, the Marconi International Marine Communication Co., Ltd, and other companies; *b* Nenagh, 9 Nov. 1853; *s* of late Gen. W. Sankey, CB; *m* E. M., *d* of General E. L. Pym, RMLI; one *s* three *d*. *Educ:* Morges and Schaffhausen, Switzerland; Mr Rippin's School, Woolwich; RMA, Woolwich; SME, Chatham. First Commission, Royal Engineers, 1873; assisted at Railway Continuous Brake Experiments, 1875; Gibraltar, 1878–79; Instructor in Fortification at the RMC, Kingston, Canada, 1879–82; Ordnance Survey, Southampton, in charge of Trigonometrical Division, Stores and Workshops, 1882–89; retired, and joined the Board of Willans and Robinson, Ltd, 1889–1905; Vice-President, Institution of Civil Engineers; Past President, Institution of Mechanical Engineers; Member of the following Institutions: American Mechanical Engineers, Electrical Engineers, Iron and Steel, Naval Architects, and Gas Engineers; Member of the Governing Board, National Physical Laboratory; Member of several Committees of the Institutions of Civil Engineers and Mechanical Engineers on Steam and Gas Engine Research; Member of several Sub-Committees of the Engineering Standardisation Committee; Member of two Committees of the British Association, Wireless Telegraphy and Gaseous Explosions; Chairman of the Heat Engine Committee of the Institution of Civil Engineers and other institutions. *Publications:* The Energy Chart, Practical Application to Reciprocating Steam Engines; Part IV of Rimington's Construction (anonymously); author of papers read before the Institutions referred to above, and others. *Address:* 57 Castlebar Road, Ealing, W5. *TA:* c/o Expanse Estrand, London. *T:* Ealing 998; City 8710. *Club:* St Stephen's.

Died 3 Oct. 1925.

SANT, James, CVO 1914; RA (1870–1914, when he resigned); late principal Painter-in-Ordinary to Queen Victoria; Corresponding Member of La Regia Accademia Raffaello in Urbino; *b* Croydon, 1820; *m d* (*d* 1907) of R. M. M. Thomson, staff-surgeon, Bengal; one *s* four *d*. *Educ:* pupil of John Varley and Sir Augustus Calcott, RA; studied at Royal Acad. for four years. A collection of his works at Strawberry Hill, painted for the Countess Waldegrave, was exhibited at French Gallery, 1861; frequent contributor to Royal Acad. exhibitions. *Paintings:* Dick Whittington; Little Red Riding Hood; Infant Samuel; Mother's Hope; Infant Timothy; Morning; Evening; Light of the Cross; She Never Told Her Love; Harmony; Young Minstrel; Retrospection; Saxon Women; The Boy Shakespeare; The Walk to Emmaus; The Miller's Daughter; Young Steele; The Soul's Awakening; The Last Phase. *Address:* 43 Lancaster Gate, Hyde Park, W. *T:* Paddington 7210.

Died 12 July 1916.

SANTLEY, Sir Charles, Kt 1907; baritone singer; *b* Liverpool, 28 Feb. 1834; *e* s of William Santley and Margaret Fletcher; *m* 1st, 1859, Gertrude (*d* 1882), *g d* of Charles Kemble; two *s* three *d*; 2nd, 1884, Elizabeth Mary, *d* of George Rose-Innes; one *s*. *Educ:* England (Liverpool Inst.) and Italy. First appeared in London, 1857; his first great success was in the opera Dinorah, at Covent Garden, 1859; first appearance in Italian Opera, Covent Garden, three nights, 1862; remainder of same season engaged with Mapleson at Her Majesty's Theatre (burned, 1867), Italian Opera; Valentine in Faust, first representation in England, 1863; Drury Lane, Mapleson management, 1868; Covent Garden—Gye and Mapleson coalition—Hamlet, in production of Ambrose Thomas' Opera, 1869; Drury Lane, Mapleson management, Vanderdecken, in Flying Dutchman, the first opera of Wagner produced in England, 1870; visited America, 1871, 1891; Australia, 1889–90; the Cape, 1898, 1903; Knight Commander of St Gregory the Great, 1887. *Publications:* Student and Singer, 1892; Art of Singing, 1908; Reminiscences of My Life, 1909. *Address:* 13 Blenheim Road, NW. *Died 22 Sept. 1922.*

SAO, Sir Moung, KCIE 1916 (CIE 1908); Sawbwa of Yawng Hwe, Southern Shan States, Burma; Member of Federated Shan States; *b* 1847; two adopted *s* three adopted *d*. *Address:* Yawng Hwe, Southern Shan States, Burma. *Died 3 Dec. 1926.*

SAPARA-WILLIAMS, Hon. Christopher Alexander, CMG 1914; Barrister-at-law; Member of Legislative Council, Nigeria, since 1901; of Municipal Board of Health, Lagos; Licensing Justice for the Municipal Area, Lagos; Leader of the Nigerian Bar; *b* 19 July 1854; *s* of Alexander Charles and Nancy Sapara-Williams, Lagos; *m* 1886, Anna Sophia (*d* 1904), *d* of Hon. Robert Hutchison of Cape Coast, Gold Coast. *Educ:* Wesleyan School, Buxton Chapel, Freetown, Sierra Leone; CMS Grammar School, Sierra Leone; Wesley College, Sheffield, England. Called to Bar, Inner Temple, 1879; practised on the Gold Coast, Lagos, and Nigeria since 1880; Counsel for the Government in several cases, and as Junior to Attorney-General in several important cases. *Address:* The Nest, Customs Street, Lagos, Nigeria. *TA:* Sapara, Lagos. *Club:* National Liberal.

Died 14 March 1915.

SARAWAK, Rajah of; Sir Charles Anthony Johnson Brooke, GCMG 1888; 2nd 'Rajah' of Sarawak; *b* 1829; *s* of Rev. F. Johnson; *S* uncle, Sir James (Rajah) Brooke, 1868 (and changed surname to Brooke); *m* 1869, Margaret Alice Lilly, *d* of Clayton de Windt, Blunsden Hall, Wilts. Joined HM's Navy 1840; resigned commission to serve under his uncle in Sarawak, 1851; was prominent in helping to restore the country to order and put down piracy and head-hunting; ruled over a population of 500,000 souls and a country 40,000 sq. miles in extent. *Recreations:* hunting, reading. *Heir: s* Charles Vyner Brooke, *b* Sept. 1874. *Address:* The Palace, Sarawak, Borneo; Chesterton House, Cirencester; Villa Raffo, Bogliasco, near Genoa, Italy. *Died 17 May 1917.*

SARGANT, Ethel, FLS 1904; *b* 28 Oct. 1863; 3rd *d* of Henry Sargant of Lincoln's Inn and Emma Beale; unmarried. *Educ:* North London

Collegiate School for Girls; Girton College, Cambridge. Natural Sciences at Cambridge; worked under Dr D. H. Scott, FRS, at the Jodrell Laboratory in Kew Gardens, 1892–93; from 1893, worked at home on various botanical subjects; on Council of Linnean Society, 1906–10; President of Section K (Botany) at British Association Meeting, Birmingham, 1913; Hon. Fellow Girton College, 1913. *Publications:* several papers in the Annals of Botany from 1893 onwards. *Address:* The Old Rectory, Girton, Cambs. *TA:* Girton, Histon. *Clubs:* Ladies' University. *Died 16 Jan. 1918.*

SARGEAUNT, John; Sixth Form Master at Westminster, 1890–1918; *b* Irthlingborough, Northamptonshire, 12 Aug. 1857; *e s* of John Barneby Sargeaunt, Barrister-at-Law, and Elizabeth, *d* of Rev. William Drake. *Educ:* Bedford (head of the school); University College, Oxford. First Class Classical Moderations, 1878; 2nd Class Classical Finals, 1880; President of the Oxford Union Society; Past Prior of the Johnson Club; Member of the Council of Brighton College. *Publications:* Annals of Westminster School, 1898; Virgil's Pastorals in English Verse, 1900; Pope's Essay on Criticism, 1909; Dryden's Poems (the restored text), 1910; Terence in English prose (Loeb Classics), 1912; The Trees, Shrubs, and Plants of Virgil, 1920; several Latin and English schoolbooks and many reviews. *Recreations:* gardening, bridge. *Address:* Arnolds, Fairwarp, Sussex. *Club:* Reform. *Died 20 March 1922.*

SARGENT, Very Rev. John Paine; Dean, St Peter's Pro-Cathedral, Diocese of Qu'Appelle, 1903; *b* Dublin, 16 Jan. 1838; *s* of R. S. Sargent, MD, Fellow of King and Queen's Colleges of Physicians, Ireland; *m* Elizabeth, *d* of Harry King, DCL, Judge of Probate, Windsor, Nova Scotia; two *s* two *d*. *Educ:* King's College University, Windsor, Nova Scotia, 1864; BA. Formerly Ensign in HM 62nd Regiment of Foot, 1855–61; SPG Missionary, Nova Scotia and NW Canada, 1864–1900; Archdeacon of Assiniboia, 1898–1903; Chaplain, No 2 Field Hospital, NW Canadian Field Force, 1885 (medal); Secretary, Synod Diocese of Qu'Appelle, 1892–1911; Deputy-Prolocutor, Provincial Synod of Rupert's Land, 1899–1902; Prolocutor, 1902–5; Chaplain Masonic Grand Lodge of Saskatchewan, 1910–11; Hon. DD University of Manitoba. *Address:* Qu'Appelle, Canada. *Died 11 Dec. 1919.*

SARGENT, John Singer, RA 1897 (ARA 1894); RSW 1908; DCL Hon. Oxon; Hon. LLD Cambridge; portrait painter; *b* Florence, 12 Jan. 1856; American citizen; *s* of FitzWilliam Sargent, physician of Boston, USA, and Mary Newbold Singer. *Educ:* Italy; France. Studied under Carolus Duran; exhibited at the Salon, 1879; since then exhibited continually at the Salon and Academy. Officier de la Légion d'Honneur. *Principal works:* El Jaleo; portraits—Carolus Duran; Ellen Terry; Rt Hon. Joseph Chamberlain; Mrs Carl Meyer and Children; Octavia Hill; Lady Faudel Phillips; and many others. *Address:* 31 Tite Street, Chelsea, SW3. *T:* Western 4849. *Club:* Athenæum. *Died 15 April 1925.*

SARTORIS, Francis Charles; *b* 1857; *e s* of late Alfred Sartoris and Hon. Mary Frances Barrington, 2nd *d* of 6th Viscount Barrington; *m* 1915, Petronel Marion, *widow* of George Turner Phillips. Late Lieutenant Royal Fusiliers. *Address:* 11 Chesham Street, SW1. *T:* Victoria 1771. *Clubs:* Naval and Military, Orleans; Royal Yacht Squadron, Cowes. *Died 7 Feb. 1923.*

SARTORIUS, Maj.-Gen. Euston Henry, VC 1881; CB 1896; *b* Cintra, Portugal, 1844; 3rd *s* of late Admiral of the Fleet Sir George Rose Sartorius, GCB; *m* 1874, Emily (*d* 1915), *d* of Sir Francis Cook, 1st Bt; two *d*. *Educ:* Royal Naval School, New Cross; Woolwich; RMC, Sandhurst. Joined 59th Regt 1862; passed Staff College; Afghan War (twice mentioned in despatches, thanked by Indian Government for work on the Survey; Brevet of Major, and VC); DAAG and DAQMG Aldershot; Egyptian Campaign, 1882 (DAAG, class Osmanieh, Brevet of Lieut-Col, despatches); CSO Portsmouth; Military Attaché, Japan; CB; Humane Society's bronze medal; attached to Crown Prince of Siam at celebration of HM Jubilee and Coronation of King Edward; attached Prince Chakrabhong of Siam, Coronation of HM King George; title of Conde de Penhafirme while in Portugal. Decorated for taking a hill at Shahjui in possession of Ghazis (leading the attack). *Address:* 17 Chelsea Embankment, SW3. *TA:* Penhafirme, Sloane. *T:* Kensington 861; Hurtwood, Holmbury St Mary, Surrey. *T:* Ewhurst 14. *Clubs:* Naval and Military, Royal Automobile. *Died 19 Feb. 1925.*

SARZANO, 11th Marquis of, *cr* 1695; **Frank James Carandini;** Major, retired, 5th Royal Irish Lancers; *b* 20 May 1847; *e s* of 10th Marquis (*d* 1870); *m* 1887, Florence Annie, *y d* of late Lt-Gen. C. D. Clementson, Indian Army; one *d*. Granted His Majesty's Royal

Licence and authority to bear and use in this country the titles of Marquis of Sarzano, Patrician of Modena, and Noble of Bologna, 1910; Captain in 8th Hussars to 1893; served Afghan War, 1879–80 (medal).   *Died 6 Aug. 1920.*

SASSOON, Sir Edward Elias, 2nd Bt, *cr* 1909; chief partner in E. D. Sassoon & Co., merchants and bankers of India, London, and China; *b* 6 Jan. 1853; *s* of Elias David Sassoon and Leah, *d* of Moses Gubbay; *g s* of David Sassoon of Baghdad and Bombay; *S* brother, 1916; *m* 1880, Leontine, *d* of Abraham Levy; one *s* two *d* (and one *s* decd). *Heir: s* (Ellice) Victor Sassoon, late Capt. RAF, *b* 30 Dec. 1881. *Address:* 46 Grosvenor Place, W1. *T:* Victoria 176.
Died 2 Dec. 1924.

SASSOON, Sir Jacob Elias, 1st Bt, *cr* 1909; *b* 1844; *s* of Elias David Sassoon and Leah, *d* of Moses Gubbay; *g s* of David Sassoon of Baghdad and Bombay; *m* 1880, Rachel Simon (*d* 1911), *d* of Simon H. Isaacs of Calcutta. Established a Central College of Science in Bombay; built first mill, 1883, and later constructed several others; chief partner in E. D. Sassoon and Co., merchants and bankers of India, London, and China. *Heir-pres.* (by special remainder), *brother* Edward Elias Sassoon [*b* 6 Jan. 1853; *m* 1880, Leontine, *d* of Abraham Levy; two *s* two *d*. *Address:* 46 Grosvenor Place, W[. *Address:* Braganza Hall, Bombay; Ashley House, Poona; Glen Ogle, Mahableshwar, India. *Clubs:* Bombay Yacht; Poona Gymkhana; Mahableshwar.
Died 23 Oct. 1916.

SASSOON, Joseph S., JP; *b* 31 Dec. 1855; *e s* of late Sassoon David Sassoon, and Flora, *d* of Solomon Reuben, of Baghdad; *m* 1884, Louise, *e d* of Baron Horace de Gunzburg of Petrograd; five *s*. *Educ:* Christ Church, Oxford (MA). *Address:* Ashley Park, Walton-on-Thames.   *Died 4 Jan. 1918.*

SASSOON, Meyer Elias; *b* 7 July 1855; *s* of Elias David Sassoon and Leah, *d* of Moses Gubbay; *brother* of Sir Edward Elias Sassoon, 2nd Bt and *g s* of David Sassoon of Baghdad and Bombay; *m* 1892, Mozelle, *d* of late A. M. Gubbay and *g d* of Sir Albert Sassoon, 1st Bt (*cr* 1890); one *s* one *d*. *Address:* 6 Hamilton Place, W1. *T:* Grosvenor 2624; Port Breton, Dinard, France. *Clubs:* Cavalry, Baldwin.
Died 5 Nov. 1924.

SATOW, Samuel Augustus Mason; late a Master of the Supreme Court; *b* 1847; *s* of Hans David Christopher Satow; *m* 1875, Kathrin Jarvis (*d* 1907), *d* of Joseph Dakin. *Address:* Berkhamsted, Herts.
Died 30 May 1925.

SAUNDBY, Robert, JP Co. Warwick; MD Edin., MSc Birmingham; LLD McGill, LLD St Andrews; FRCP; FRCPI Hon.; Emeritus Professor of Medicine, University of Birmingham; Consulting Physician, General Hospital, Birmingham; Lieutenant-Colonel, Royal Army Medical Corps (T); Physician to 2nd Southern Military Hospital; formerly member of General Medical Council of Education for the United Kingdom; *b* London, 9 Dec. 1849; *m* 1880, Mary Edith Spencer; three *s* one *d*. *Educ:* Edinburgh University. Emeritus Senior President, Royal Medical Society; House Physician, Edinburgh Royal Infirmary, 1874; House Physician to the Royal Hospital for Diseases of the Chest, 1875; Pathologist to the General Hospital, Birmingham, 1876; Assistant Physician, 1877; Physician, 1885; retired, 1912; Examiner in Medicine, English Conjoint Board, 1894–97; President British Medical Association, 1911–12, President of the Council, 1896–99; President, Birmingham Medical Institute, 1895–99, and Birmingham Library, 1904–8; Harveian Orator RCP, 1917. *Publications:* Treatment of Diseases of the Digestive System, 2nd edn 1914; Lectures on Renal and Urinary Diseases, 4th edn 1900; The Common Forms of Dyspepsia in Women, 1894; Medical Ethics, 2nd edn 1907; article Diabetes, in Allbutt's System of Medicine, 1907; Old Age, its Care and Treatment in Health and Disease, 1913; Urgent Symptoms in Medical Practice, 1915; numerous contributions to the medical press. *Address:* 68 Hagley Road, Edgbaston; 140B Great Charles Street, Birmingham. *T:* C 905. *Clubs:* Reform; Union, Birmingham.   *Died 28 Aug. 1918.*

SAUNDERS, Major Frederick John, DSO 1901; Royal Marine Light Infantry; *b* 18 Sept. 1876; *s* of William Saunders, Sydenham; *m* 1902, Muriel, *d* of late Alexander Maxwell Todd, Walmer; one *s*. Entered Royal Marine Light Infantry, 1895; landed from HMS Powerful, and joined Naval Brigade in South Africa, 1899–1900 (medal and 4 clasps, despatches, DSO); Captain, 1901; Major, 1914; served European War in Gallipoli (despatches). *Club:* United Service.
Died Nov. 1916.

SAUNDERS, George, OBE 1920; BA Oxford; LLD Glasgow; *b* Rattray, Perthshire, 1859; *e s* of late David H. Saunders, JP, Dundee

and Craigmill, Blairgowrie, NB; *m* 1893, Gertrude, *d* of late Oscar Hainauer, Berlin; three *s* two *d*. *Educ:* Dundee High School; Universities of Glasgow, Bonn, Göttingen, and Oxford (Snell exhibitioner of Balliol College). Buchanan prizes for Moral Philosophy, English Literature, Rectorial prize for essay on Constantine the Great, Monteath Bursary for German, etc, Glasgow University. First foreign correspondence was contributed to Scotsman; series of letters to Pall Mall Gazette from Paris and Departments during General Boulanger's electoral campaign; Berlin Correspondent, Morning Post, 1888–97; many special missions for that journal to Germany army manœuvres; and in France, Austria, Italy, Greece, Turkey, Bulgaria, Russia; Berlin Times Correspondent, 1897–1908; Paris Times Correspondent, 1908–14; served in Department of Political Information and other War Departments, 1915–18; a temporary Senior Clerk in the Foreign Office, March 1918–Feb. 1920 and Aug. and Nov. 1920. *Recreation:* golf. *Address:* Pontsarn, Woking. *Clubs:* St James's, Athenæum.
Died 10 Sept. 1922.

SAUNDERS, Captain (Temp. Major) Harold Cecil Rich, DSO 1917; East Yorkshire Regiment; *b* Kingston, Jamaica, 28 April 1882; *e s* of A. R. Saunders, MB, FRCS, and Louise, *e d* of Dr J. C. Phillippo; *m* 1915, Dorothy, *e d* of Brig.-General C. P. Triscott, CB. *Educ:* Clifton College. Joined East Yorkshire Regt from Tasmania Militia Infantry, 1905; in Burma and India; seconded 3rd King's African Rifles, 1909–12; served East Africa (medal and clasp, Somaliland); served European War, 1914–17; arrived France, Jan. 1915; wounded, Feb. 1915 (despatches, DSO). *Recreations:* sketching, usual field sports and games. *Club:* Junior Naval and Military.
Died 30 March 1919.

SAUNDERS, Thomas Bailey, MA; author; *b* Alice, Cape Colony, 2 Dec. 1860; 2nd *s* of late Deputy-Inspector-Gen. George Saunders, CB (*s* of Lieut-Colonel Richard Saunders, Co. Kerry), and Isabella, *d* of Thomas Bailey, Co. Fermanagh, Ireland; *m* 1887, late Contessa Elena Alberti di Poja, *o c* of late Conte Gustavo Alberti di Poja, Rovereto, S Tyrol. *Educ:* King's College, London; University College, Oxford. 2nd class Lit. Hum. 1884. After leaving Oxford spent some time in Germany; Barrister Inner Temple, 1886; from Aug. 1898 to June 1900 Sec. of the Statutory Commission for the Reorganisation of the University of London; Fellow and Member of Council of King's College, and of the Senate of the University of London, 1913–21; Chairman of the Trustees of the Sladen Memorial Fund for assisting scientific research, from 1904. *Publications:* several volumes of translation from Schopenhauer's essays, The Wisdom of Life, Studies in Pessimism, The Art of Literature, On Human Nature, etc, 1889–96; Goethe's Maxims and Reflections (selected in part by Huxley and Leighton), 1893; The Life and Letters of James Macpherson, 1894; Notes on Technical Instruction in the German Universities, 1899; The Quest of Faith, 1899; Schopenhauer, 1901; Prof. Harnack and his Oxford Critics, 1902; versions of Prof. Harnack's Christianity and History, 1896, Thoughts on Protestantism, 1899, and What is Christianity?, 1901; contributions to the Quarterly Review, the Athenæum, the Dictionary of National Biography, etc. *Recreation:* music. *Address:* Staveley Corner, Eastbourne. *T:* 1766. *Club:* Athenæum.   *Died 8 Feb. 1928.*

SAUZIER, Anatole; *b* Mauritius, 20 July 1849; *m* 1879; six *s* two *d*. *Educ:* Royal College, Mauritius; Edinburgh Academy. Called to Scottish Bar in Edinburgh, 1873; practised as barrister in Mauritius until 1882; District Magistrate in Mauritius, 1882–88; Judicial Vice-Consul at Tamatave, Madagascar, 1888; Acting Consul, 1889–97; Consul, 1897–1910. *Address:* Curepipe, Mauritius.
Died April 1920.

SAVAGE, Sir George Henry, Kt 1912; MD, FRCP, FRAMI; Consulting Physician Guy's Hospital, and to Earlswood Idiot Asylum; *b* Brighton, 12 Nov. 1842; *m* 1st, Margaret, *d* of Jacob Walton of Greenends, Alston Moor; 2nd, *d* of Dr Sutton, Physician to London Hospital; one *s* one *d*. *Educ:* Brighton Schools; Sussex County Hospital; Guy's Hospital (Treasurer's Gold Medal). Former Physician-Superintendent of Bethlem Royal Hospital; former President of Medico-Psychological Association of Great Britain; and of Neurological Society; Examiner in Mental Physiology, University of London; former Lecturer on Mental Diseases, Guy's Hospital. *Publications:* Manual on Insanity; former Editor of Journal of Mental Science. *Recreations:* mountaineering, fishing, fencing. *Address:* 26 Devonshire Place, W1. *T:* 2075 Paddington; The Island, Hurstbourne Priors, Whitchurch, Hants. *Club:* Athenæum.
Died 5 July 1921.

SAVAGE-ARMSTRONG, Major Francis Savage Nesbitt, DSO 1915; 1st Battalion South Staffordshire Regiment; *b* 5 July 1880.

Entered army, 1900; Captain, 1909; Major, 1915; Lieut-Col (temp.) 1916; served South Africa, 1900–2 (Queen's medal, 3 clasps; King's medal, 2 clasps); European War, 1914–15 (despatches, DSO). *Address:* Strangford House, Strangford, Co. Down, Ireland. *Club:* Army and Navy.   *Died April 1917.*

SAVARY, Alfred William; retired Judge; *b* Plympton, Digby County, Nova Scotia, 10 Oct. 1831; *s* of Sabine Savary and Olive, *d* of Samuel Marshall, MPP, Yarmouth, NS; a lineal descendant from Thomas Savory who went to Plymouth, Mass, 1633, from Hannington or vicinity, Wilts; *m* 1st, 1877, Elizabeth Crookshank (*d* 1887), *d* of H. P. Otty; 2nd, 1892, Eliza T., *d* of late Rev. Abraham Spurr Hunt; two *s*. *Educ:* King's College, Windsor, NS (MA 1857, DCL Hon. 1909). Attorney, New Brunswick, 1857; Barrister, NS, 1860; MP Digby, 1867–73; KC 1872; Judge of County Courts, NS, 1876–1907; a Vice-President NS Historial Society and regular or corresponding member of several other historical, antiquarian, and genealogical societies. *Publications:* Savery and Severy Genealogies, with biography of William Savery, eminent Quaker minister, 1893, Supplement to same, 1905; finished and published Calnek's inchoate History of the County of Annapolis, 1897; Narrative of Colonel David Fanning, Loyalist, American Revolution, 1908; Ancestry of General Sir Fenwick Williams, with sketch of allied historic families of Annapolis Royal, 1911, and other short genealogical compilations; Supplement to History of Annapolis, 1913. *Address:* Annapolis Royal, Nova Scotia. *Club:* Halifax, Halifax.   *Died 23 Feb. 1918.*

SAVILE, Colonel Henry Bourchier Osborne, CB 1902; VD; Hon. Colonel of the Wessex Royal Engineers; *b* 5 May 1819; 3rd *s* of Albany Savile of Oaklands, Devon, and Eleanora Elizabeth, *d* of Sir Bourchier Wrey, 7th Bt; *m* 1st, 1842, Katherine (*d* 1846), *o d* of Rev. Thomas Law; one *s*; 2nd, 1848, Mary (*d* 1870), *e d* of Cornelius O'Callaghan of Ballynahinsh, Co. Clare; two *s*; 3rd, 1872, Ellen Lucy, *o d* of Richard Sisson Darling of the Lothians, Trinidad; one *s*. *Educ:* Royal Military Academy, Woolwich. Received 1st Commission, 1837, in the Royal Artillery, in which he served fifteen years; became Major of the Royal North Gloster Militia, 1853, and served with them till the commencement of the Volunteer Movement, when he raised and commanded the Artillery Corps of Gloster and Somerset; JP for the City and County of Bristol, and High Sheriff of the same, 1883–84. *Address:* Clifton, Bristol. *Club:* National.

Died 17 Aug. 1917.

SAVILE, Brig.-Gen. Walter Clare, CB 1917; DSO 1900; *b* 4 July 1857; *s* of late Col Henry Bourchier O. Savile, CB; *m* 1881, Helen, 4th *d* of William Ruxton, Ardee House, Co. Louth; one *s* one *d*. *Educ:* Clifton College. Entered RA 1877; Captain 1885; Major 1894; Lt-Col 1904; Col 1909; Assistant to Director of Artillery, 1888–92; occupation of Crete, 1898; Boer War, 1899–1901, including defence of Ladysmith (despatches thrice, medal and four clasps, and DSO); Col Commanding Harwich Coast Defences, 1906–9; Assistant Director of Artillery, 1909–12; commanding South Irish Coast Defences, 1912–14; retired, 1914; re-employed War Office, 1914–15; Ministry of Munitions, 1915. *Address:* 35 Cadogan Gardens, SW3. *T:* Kensington 4415. *Club:* Army and Navy.

Died 13 Nov. 1928.

SAVORY, Vice-Admiral Herbert Whitmore, MVO 1906; Royal Navy; *b* 15 July 1857; *s* of Charles Harley Savory; *m* 1890, Kate Worthington, *o d* of Archibald McIntyre Gregory of New York; one *s* one *d*. Entered Navy, 1870; Commander, 1895; Captain, 1901; Rear-Admiral, 1911; Ashanti War, 1873–74 (medal and clasp); Flag Captain in China, HMS Diadem, conveyed Prince Arthur of Connaught and Garter Mission to Japan (MVO and Order of Rising Sun); Flag Capt. in Mediterranean to HSH Prince Louis of Battenberg, 1907; Inspecting Captain of Training Establishments, 1909; Vice-Adm., retired, 1916. *Address:* 10 Eaton Terrace, SW. *T:* Victoria 5763. *Club:* Naval and Military.   *Died 23 Feb. 1918.*

SAVORY, Sir Joseph, 1st Bt, *cr* 1891; DL, JP; Lieutenant and Alderman of City of London, 1883; Chairman of Almoners of Christ's Hospital since 1891; Chairman of Princess Helena College; Governor of Queen Anne's Bounty; Royal Holloway College, St Bartholomew's, and St Thomas' Hospitals; *b* 23 July 1843; *s* of Joseph Savory and Mary Caroline, *d* of Isaac Braithwaite; *m* 1888, Helen Pemberton, *d* of late Col Sir G. A. Leach, KCB, RE. *Educ:* Harrow. Sheriff of London and Middlesex, 1882–83; member of School Board for City, 1885–88; Lord Mayor, 1890–91; MP (C) Westmorland (Appleby), 1892–1900. *Heir:* none. *Address:* Wyndham House, Sloane Gardens, SW; Buckhurst Park, Sunninghill. *Clubs:* Carlton, National.

Died 1 Oct. 1921 (ext).

SAWARD, Maj.-Gen. Michael Henry; *b* London, 22 Dec. 1840; *e s* of late Michael Saward, Croydon, Surrey, and Westbarrow Hall, Essex, and Harriet, *d* of Rev. J. Morbeck Sumner, JP, DL; *m* 1877, Katherine Isabella (*d* 1919), *d* of late Gen. F. C. Maisey; one *s* (Captain Royal Scots, killed in Great War) one *d*. *Educ:* Merchant Taylors' School; Addiscombe Mil. Coll. Lieut Bengal Artillery, 1859; Lieut Royal Artillery, 1861; Col Army, 1889; Major-Gen. 1896; Col Comdt RA, 1905 and RHA, 1926; Hon. Col Royal Guernsey and Alderney Militia, 1914; ADC to Gen. Sir H. Tombs, VC, KCB, 1871–74, and to Gen. Sir Crawfurd Chamberlain, GCIE, CSI, 1875–76; AQMG, 1874; DAAG RA in India, 1877–82; Inspector Gen. School of Gunnery, 1882–87; AAG RA India, 1889–94; Col on Staff CRATD, 1895–96; Lieut-Governor and Comdg Guernsey and Alderney Dist, 1899–1903. *Address:* 29 Brechin Place, SW7. *Club:* United Service.

Died 13 Feb. 1928.

SAWBRIDGE, Rev. John Sikes; Hon. Canon of St Edmundsbury and Ipswich. *Address:* Thelnetham Rectory, Diss, Norfolk.

Died 9 May 1925.

SAWYER, Sir James, Kt 1885; JP; MD, FRCP; FSA, FRSE; consulting physician; Consulting Physician to Queen's Hospital, Birmingham; *b* Carlisle, 11 Aug. 1844; *s* of late James Sawyer, Carlisle, and Ann, *e d* of William George, Ross, Herefordshire; *m* 1873, Adelaide Mary, *d* of Rev. John Harwood Hill, Rector of Cranoe, Leicestershire; two *s* two *d*. *Educ:* Queen's College, Birmingham; London University. Professor of Pathology, Queen's College, Birmingham, 1875–78; Prof. of Materia Medica, 1878–85; Prof. of Medicine, 1885–91; Lumleian Lecturer, RCP, 1908; Chairman of Warwicks Chamber of Agriculture, 1898–99; VP Therapeutics Section International Medical Congress, London, 1913. *Publications:* Diagnosis of Diseases of the Lungs, Heart and Kidneys, 1870; Notes on Medical Education, 1889; Causes and Cure of Insomnia, 1904; Contributions to Practical Medicine, 4th edn 1904; Maladies of the Heart (Lumleian Lectures), 1908; Coprostatis, 1912; many papers in medical periodicals. *Recreations:* literature, archæology, agriculture. *Address:* Haseley Hall, Warwick; 29 Old Burlington Street, W. *TA:* Consultant, Birmingham. *T:* Central 3477. *Clubs:* Junior Conservative; Midland Conservative, Birmingham.

Died 27 Jan. 1919.

SAWYER, Maj.-Gen. Richard Henry Stewart, CB 1918; CMG 1915; MB, FRCSI; *b* 9 Oct. 1857; *m* Flora Murray, *y d* of late Malcolm MacGregor, SSC, Edinburgh. *Educ:* Trinity College, Dublin. Major 1893; Lt-Col 1901; Col 1910; served Nile Expedition, 1898 (Egyptian medal with clasp, medal); South African War, 1899–1902 (despatches, Queen's medal 4 clasps, King's medal 2 clasps); Asst Director of Medical Services, Irish Command, 1910; served European War, 1914–18 (despatches 5 times, CMG, CB); Grand Officer, Military Order of Aviz, Portugal, 1919. *Address:* c/o Lloyds Bank, Ltd, Cox and King's Branch, 6 Pall Mall, SW1. *Clubs:* Junior United Service; University, Dublin.   *Died 23 April 1926.*

SAYER, Dr Ettie; Hon. Medical Officer to the Society for Distressed Gentlefolk; and Consulting Physician to the National Society for the Welfare of the Feeble-minded; *d* of William Sayer, Bacton, Norfolk. *Educ:* Rossell School (Mrs Nall), Paignton, Devon; University College, London; Royal Free Hospital; Queen Charlotte's Hospital. Qualified London University (MB, BS, 1899); Chesterfield Medallist; Fellow of the Royal Society of Medicine; House Surgeon, Tunbridge Wells Eye and Ear Hospital, 1899; Physician to the Cowley Mission to Mohammedan and Kaffer women; Medical Officer for Plague to the Cape Colonial Government in 1901; visited Concentration Camps during the Boer War, and later the Lepers in Robben Island; Assistant Medical Officer, London County Council (Education Department); Lecturer on First Aid to the Injured to LCC and to the Church Army Nurses; Medical Examiner to International Safety Emigration Society; Member of the Council of the Psycho-Medical Society; and the National Society for the Welfare of the Feebleminded; Fellow of the Royal Society of Medicine, and of the American Electro-Therapeutical Society. *Publications:* Effects of Electric Currents upon Blood-Pressure; Deterioration of Vision during School Life; Morally Defective Children; Textbook for Nurses on Medical Electricity and Light. *Address:* 4 Ennismore Gardens, Knightsbridge. *T:* Kensington 39. *M:* PB 6523. *Clubs:* Lyceum, Ladies' Army and Navy.

Died 7 July 1923.

SAYER, Captain Maxwell Barcham, CBE 1918; RD; RNR; Royal Naval Reserve Aide-de-camp 1928; Captain Superintendent, Thames Nautical Training College, HMS Worcester, off Greenhithe, Kent; *b* 1874; *s* of Edmund Barcham Sayer of Thurlton, Norfolk; *m* 1914, Elaine Constance, *d* of Alfred Talbot, Seacroft, Southend-on-Sea;

no c. *Educ:* Mr Lowe's, Stranraer, Bournemouth; HMS Worcester. Served in Mercantile Marine, 1890–95; Colonial Office Service, Southern Nigeria Marine, 1895–1914; served on Kuno Patrol Expedition, 1912; surveyed and charted Lagos Harbour and Bar, S Nigeria, 1912; Royal Naval Reserve, Sub-Lieut, 1903; Lieut, 1906; Lieut-Commander, 1914; Commander, 1916; Captain, 1921; served in Navy, 1914–16, then lent to War Office for Service; Lt-Colonel RE; Marine-Supt War Office in Inland Water section, responsible for despatch of all War Office vessels to Mesopotamia; Younger Brother Trinity House, 1919. *Recreations:* yachting, golf, tennis. *Address:* HMS Worcester, off Greenhithe, Kent. *TA:* Worcester, Greenhithe. *T:* Greenhithe 39. *M:* T 9315. *Club:* Junior Army and Navy. *Died 24 Dec. 1928.*

SCAFE, Gen. Charles; Royal Marines; *b* 1844; *s* of late Capt. W. Scafe, NI, Madras; *m* 1874, Sarah Ann, *e d* of G. Morris. Entered Royal Marines, 1862; Major General, 1900; Lieut-Gen., 1902; General, 1903. *Address:* 2 Clarence Cottages, Auckland Road, West Southsea. *Died 15 July 1918.*

SCALES, Francis Shillington, MA, MD, MB, BCh (Cantab); University Lecturer in Medical Radiology and Electrology; Hon. Physician in charge of X-ray and Electrical Department, Addenbrooke's Hospital, Cambridge; Secretary for the Cambridge Diploma in Medical Radiology and Electrology; *b* London; 3rd *s* of George Johnston Scales, London, and Mary, 2nd *d* of W. R. Carter, Nottingham; *m* 1892, Marion, *y d* of late Thomas Shillington, JP, of Tavanagh House, Portadown, Ireland; two *d. Educ:* privately; Jesus College, Cambridge; Middlesex Hospital, London. Raymond Horton Smith Prize, University of Cambridge, 1912; Fellow of the Royal Microscopical Society (late Curator, Hon. Secretary and Vice-President); Fellow of the Cambridge Philosophical Society; Member of the Council of the British Institute of Radiology; Fellow of the Royal Society of Medicine; Member of the British Medical Association; Examiner for the Cambridge Diploma in Medical Radiology and Electrology since 1920; late Lecturer in Microscopy at Westminster Hospital. *Publications:* Elementary Microscopy, 1905; Practical Microscopy, 1909 and 1926; contributions to various scientific journals dealing with microscopy and radiology. *Recreations:* shooting, fishing, travel, books, music. *Address:* Redcourt, Adams Road, Cambridge. *T:* Cambridge 441. *M:* ER 6. *Clubs:* New University, Royal Automobile; Cambridge Union Society. *Died 28 Feb. 1927.*

SCANNELL, Rev. Canon Thomas Bartholomew, DD; theological and historical writer; *b* London, 8 July 1854. *Educ:* St Edmund's College, Ware (10th in Honours, London University Matriculation, 1873; 1st LLB Honours in Jurisprudence and Roman Law); English College, Rome (BD 1877; DD 1898). Professor of Philosophy, St Edmund's College, 1878–85; appointed by Pope Leo XIII to Commission in Rome on Anglican Orders, 1896. *Publications:* Manual of Catholic Theology, 3rd edn; Priests' Studies in the Westminster Series; articles in Catholic Dictionary, of which he was Editor; numerous articles, including those on Pastor's History of the Popes, Lamennais, Maury, De Maistre, Fénelon, Bossuet, and Rosmini, in the Dublin Review and Irish Ecclesiastical Record, etc. *Address:* St Charles's Cottage, Weybridge. *Died 11 Feb. 1917.*

SCARISBRICK, Sir Charles, Kt 1903; JP; late Mayor of Southport; *b* 20 April 1839; *m* 1860, Bertha Petronella (*d* 1915), *d* of Ernst Marquard Schonfeld, of Hanau-on-Main and Düsseldorf; one *s* two *d. Address:* Scarisbrick Lodge, Southport, Lancs. *Club:* Junior Carlton. *Died 15 Jan. 1923.*

SCARLETT, Lt-Col James Alexander, DSO 1915; Royal Artillery; *b* 16 June 1877; *o s* of late Rev. G. W. Scarlett, Rossington, Yorks; *m* 1922, Muriel, *o d* of Walter Blease, JP, FCA, of Sefton Park, Liverpool; one *s*. Entered army, 1900; Captain, 1908; Adjt, 1913–14; Major, 1914; Lt-Col, 1922; served European War, 1914–18 (despatches, DSO). *Died 29 Dec. 1925.*

SCARSDALE, 4th Baron, *cr* 1761; **Rev. Alfred Nathaniel Holden Curzon,** JP; Bt 1641; Rector of Kedleston, 1856; *b* 12 July 1831; 2nd *s* of Hon. and Rev. Alfred Curzon (*s* of 2nd Baron by 2nd wife), and Sophia, *d* of Robert Holden, Nuttall Temple, Nottinghamshire; *S* uncle, 1856; *m* 1856, Blanche (*d* 1875), *d* of Joseph Pocklington-Senhouse, Netherhall, Cumberland; four *s* six *d* (and one *d* decd). *Educ:* Rugby; Oxford (MA). Owned 11,000 acres. *Heir: s* Earl Curzon of Kedleston, *b* 11 Jan. 1859. *Address:* Kedleston, Derby. *Clubs:* Carlton, Arthur's. *Died 23 March 1916.*

SCARTH, Sir Charles, Kt 1914; Head of the firm of Charles Scarth and Sons, Ltd; *b* Morley, 5 Jan. 1846; *e s* of Henry and Grace Scarth; *m* 1st, 1869, Jane (*d* 1885), *d* of James and Ann Pears of East Cottingwith, Yorks; two *s* seven *d*; 2nd, 1887, Jessie Glendinning Watson; one *s* two *d. Educ:* locally. Always took a deep interest in educational work; Member of School Board for seventeen years, nine years Chairman; a Member of Town Council from its formation, 1885; several times Mayor; Hon. Freeman of the Borough of Morley, 1903; JP for West Riding of Yorkshire, also for Borough of Morley; Liberal. *Address:* Scarthingwell House, Morley, Yorks. *M:* 4078. *Club:* National Liberal. *Died 3 Feb. 1921.*

SCATCHERD, Felicia Rudolphina, (Felix Rudolph); *b* London; *d* of Watson Scatcherd, ICS, and Emily Frances, *o d* of Rev. Augustus Crofton. Some time Editor Asiatic Review and continued association therewith as Hon. Co-Editor; Member of Council, East India Association; Life Member Sociological Society, and British Association for the Advancement of Science; travelled extensively in the Near East, and lectured on social science, psychology, and the oppressed nationalities; was one of late W. T. Stead's helpers in the founding of Julia's Bureau, hailed by him and others as the MP for Humanity; Vice-President of the Stead Bureau, and Member of the Society for Psychical Research; Vice-President Greek Socialist Party and Greek Labour League; Delegate, International Conference of Housing and City-Planning, New York, 1925; International Psychic Congress, Paris, 1926; originator of the Literary Silhouette. *Publications:* Human Radioactivity; Sir William Crookes as Psychical Researcher; articles on the Near East, Armenia, Russia, etc; Friends of India: Wise and Otherwise. *Recreations:* walking in hilly country, psychical research. *Address:* Ringmore House, Hastings; 14 Park Square (East), NW1; 3 Victoria Street, SW1. *T:* Victoria 1201. *Died 12 March 1927.*

SCEBARRAS, Sir Fillipo, Kt 1921; MD; *m* 1881, Teresa Testeferrata Abela. *Address:* 70 Strada Mercato, Floriana, Malta. *Died 28 Aug. 1928.*

SCHELFHAUT, Mgr Philip, CSSR; Fifth Bishop of Roseau, Dominica, since 1902; *b* Belgium, 27 Sept. 1850. *Educ:* The Seminary in his native town, and The Redemptorist House of Studies of Wittem (Holland). Professed, 1873; consecrated priest, 1878; Professor of Poesy at St Trond, Belgium, 1879–80; Superior, St Thomas, West Indies, 1881–94; went to Montreal for 3 years on account of health; Superior at St Croix for 4 years; Superior at St Thomas 1 year. *Publications:* founded The Ecclesiastical Bulletin of Roseau; The Dominica Chronicle. *Address:* Bishop's House, Roseau, Dominica, BWI. *Died 22 May 1921.*

SCHIFF, Sir Ernest Frederick, Kt 1911; *b* 25 Dec. 1840; *s* of Leopold Schiff, Trieste. Founded a Convalescent Home; Knight of Imperial Austrian Order of Iron Crown; Commander Order of Francis Joseph, with the Star; Knight of Grace of the Order of St John of Jerusalem. *Address:* 1 Carlos Place, W. *T:* Gerrard 3354. *Club:* Devonshire. *Died 5 Nov. 1918.*

SCHINDLER, Gen. Albert Houtum, Hon. CIE 1900; General in the Persian Army. *Publication:* Eastern Persian Irak. *Address:* Teheran, Persia. *Died 15 June 1916.*

SCHLESWIG-HOLSTEIN, HRH Gen. Prince Frederick Christian Charles Augustus of, KG 1866; GCVO; PC 1894; High Steward of Windsor; *b* 22 Jan. 1831; *m* 1866, HRH Princess Helena, 3rd *d* of Queen Victoria. ADC to the King; Colonel 3rd Batt. Royal Berkshire Regiment; DCL, Oxford, 1910; Ranger of Windsor Great Park. *Address:* Cumberland Lodge, Windsor Park; Schomberg House, Pall Mall, SW. *Died 28 Oct. 1917.*

SCHLETTER, Colonel Percy, CB 1902; late the King's Liverpool Regiment; *b* 4 Aug. 1855; *s* of M. C. Schletter; *m* 1896, Edith Mary, *d* of late William Ellis; one *d*. Entered army, 1874; Captain, 1882; Major, 1891; Lieutenant-Colonel, 1900; Colonel, 1904; served Afghan War, 1878–80 (medal); South Africa (medal, clasps, despatches, and CB), 1900–2; European War, France and Italy, 1917–19 (despatches twice). *Club:* Junior United Service. *Died 26 Aug. 1922.*

SCHLICH, Sir William, KCIE 1909 (CIE 1891); MA Oxon 1905; PhD 1867; FRS 1901; Professor of Forestry, University of Oxford, 1905; retired, 1919; *b* Germany, 28 Feb. 1840; *s* of late Kirchenrat Daniel Schlich, Hesse-Darmstadt, and Charlotte Frank; naturalised in England, 1886; *m* 1st, 1874, Mary Margaret (*d* 1878), *d* of William Smith, CE; one *d* (one *s* decd); 2nd, 1886, (Adèle Emilie) Mathilde, *d* of late Herman Marsily, Antwerp; one *s* three *d*. *Educ:* Darmstadt; University of Giessen. Appointed to the Indian Forest Department, 1866; Conservator of Forests of Bengal, 1872; of Punjab, 1880; Inspector-General of Forests to the Government of India, 1881; organised the first School of Forestry in England at the Royal Indian Engrg Coll., Coopers Hill, 1885; transferred to Oxford University, 1905. *Publications:* A Manual of Forestry, in 5 volumes, 1889–96; The Outlook of the World's Timber Supply; Afforestation in Great Britain and Ireland; Forestry in the United Kingdom, 1904 (three editions). *Address:* 29 Banbury Road, Oxford.

Died 28 Sept. 1925.

SCHOLDER, Dr Charles Albert; Directeur-propriétaire de l'Institut médico-mécanique et orthopédique de Lausanne (Suisse); né à Zürich le 26 mai 1861. *Educ:* aux universités de Zürich, Berne, Vienne, Berlin. Docteur et médecin diplômé de l'université de Zürich; Assistant d'anatomie, de médecine interne et de chirurgie à Zürich; fait deux voyages aux Indes; au retour assistant de la clinique chirurgicale universitaire de Berne; pratiqué la médecine générale pendant 6 ans, puis fondé l'Institut médico-mécanique et orthopédique de Lausanne après études spéciales faites en Suède; inventé l'Arthromoteur, machine pour déraidir les articulations ankylosées et une machine pour traitement de la scoliose. *Publications:* Dissertation inaugurale; La traitement médico-méchanique; L'Arthromoteur; Les Déviations de la colonne vertébrale dans les Ecoles de Lausanne (avec les Drs Weith et Combe). *Address:* Boulevard de Graucy No 39, Lausanne (Suisse). *TA:* Scholder, Lausanne. *T:* 751. *Died Aug. 1918.*

SCHOOLING, John Holt; actuary, statistician, and author; *b* London, 25 March 1859; *s* of late Henry Schooling and Harriet Maria Holt; *g s* of Captain John Schooling, HAC; *g g s* of James Schooling, London; *m* Jessie Ellen Sanders; one *s* one *d*. *Educ:* Elizabeth College, Guernsey. Fellow of the Royal Statistical Society; Associate of the Institute of Actuaries; Consulting Actuary to various assurance bodies; formerly Chairman of the Richmond Surrey Division of the National Service League; strongly in favour of Tariff Reform. *Publications:* The British Trade Book; Mr Chamberlain's Proposal; Local Rates and Taxes; London County Council Finance; A Peep into Punch; contributed to Nineteenth Century, Fortnightly Review, Monthly Review, National Review, Morning Post, Pall Mall Gazette, etc, mainly on economic subjects, and to Pall Mall Magazine, Strand Magazine, etc, on miscellaneous subjects; short stories in English Illustrated Magazine, The Sketch, etc. *Recreations:* fishing, music, chess, lathe and bench work. *Address:* 19 Linton Road, Hastings.

Died 14 July 1927.

SCHREIBER, Sir Collingwood, KCMG 1916 (CMG 1893); CE; General Consulting Engineer to the Government of Canada, and Chief Engineer of the Western Division of the National Transcontinental Railway since 1905; *b* Essex, 14 Dec. 1831; *s* of late Rev. Thomas Schreiber of Bradwell Lodge, Essex, and Sarah, *d* of Adm. Bingham; *m* 1st, Caroline (*d* 1892), *d* of late Col Allan Maclean, 41st Foot; four *d*; 2nd, 1898, Julia Maud, *d* of late Hon. John Wellington Gwynne, Puisne Judge of Supreme Court of Canada. Went to Canada 1852; Assistant Engineer, Hamilton & Toronto Railway, 1852–55; in private practice in the firm of Flemming, Ridout, and Schreiber, Civil Engineers, Toronto, 1855–60; Supt Engineer Northern Railway, 1860–62; Chief Engineer of Govt Railways in operation, 1873; Chief Engineer of Canadian Pacific Railway, 1880; Deputy Minister and Chief Engineer, Railways and Canals, Canada, 1893–1905. *Address:* 192 Argyle Avenue, Ottawa. *Clubs:* Rideau, Golf and Country, Ottawa. *Died 20 March 1918.*

SCHREINER, Olive Emilie Albertina, (Mrs S. C. Cronwright Schreiner), (*pseudonym* Ralph Iron); author; *b* in Basutoland, 24 March 1855; *d* of late Rev. Gottlob Schreiner, who was a missionary sent out by the London Missionary Society; her mother was Rebecca Lyndall of London; *m* 1894, Samuel Cron Cronwright (amended his name to Cronwright Schreiner); one *d* decd. *Publications:* The Story of an African Farm, 1883; Dreams, 1890; Dream Life and Real Life; Trooper Peter Halket of Mashonaland, 1897; An English South African's View of the Situation, 1899; Women and Labour, 1911; also (jointly with her husband) The Political Situation, 1895; From Man to Man (posthumous, with introduction by husband), 1926. *Address:* De Aar, Cape Colony.

Died 11 Dec. 1920.

SCHREINER, Rt. Hon. William Philip, CMG 1891; PC 1917; KC; politician and barrister; High Commissioner for Union of South Africa in England, 1914; *b* Cape Colony, 1857; *s* of Rev. Gottlob Schreiner and Rebecca Lyndall; *brother* to Olive Schreiner; *m* 1884, Frances

Hester, *sister* of ex-Pres. Francis William Reitz of Orange Free State; two *s* three *d*. *Educ:* Cape Univ. (University and Porter Scholarships, 1877); London Univ.; Downing Coll., Cambridge (Fellow). Senior in Law Tripos and Chancellor's Legal Medal, 1881; Senior Studentship Inns of Court, 1880; called to the Bar, Inner Temple, 1882; Parliamentary Draftsman, 1885–91; Legal Adviser to High Commissioner, Cape, 1887–93; Member of Mr Cecil Rhodes's second ministry, 1893; twice Attorney-General; delegate at various conferences between Cape and other SA states and colonies regarding railways and customs; witness before British South Africa Committee of House of Commons, 1897; sat in Cape Legislative Assembly for Kimberley, 1893; Barkly West, 1894–98; Malmesbury, 1898–1900; Queenstown, 1908–10; Prime Minister of Cape Colony, 1898–1900; Senator South African Union, 1910–14. *Recreation:* golf. *Address:* 32 Victoria Street, SW. *Clubs:* Civil Service, Cape Town; Kimberley.

Died 28 June 1919.

SCHÜDDEKOPF, Albert Wilhelm, MA, PhD (Göttingen); Professor of German Language and Literature at the University of Leeds; Examiner in German in various universities; *b* Göttingen, 19 Nov. 1861; *m d* of late Wilhelm Blau, Berlin; one *s*. *Educ:* Gymnasium and University of Göttingen. Staatsexamen, 1887; Professor of German at Bedford College, London, 1888; Lecturer in German at Yorkshire College, Leeds (later Univ. of Leeds), 1890; Professor of German at Yorkshire College, 1897; Dean of the Faculty of Arts and Member of the University of Leeds Council, 1912–14. *Publications:* Sprache und Dialekt des me. Gedichtes William of Palerne, 1886; Ancient German Glass in Wragby Church (Yorkshire Arch. Journal); many literary articles in the Literarische Echo, etc. *Recreations:* music, foreign travel. *Address:* 32 Springfield Mount, Leeds. *T:* Central 180.

Died 11 Sept. 1916.

SCHULER, Gottlieb Frederick Henry; Editor, The Age, Melbourne, since 1900; *b* Stuttgart, Germany, 26 Feb. 1854; *m* Sarah, *d* of Richard Strahan, of Dublin, Ireland; two *d*. *Educ:* privately. Arrived with parents in Melbourne, 1860; joined Age literary staff, 1877; remained continuously on active service of that journal. *Recreations:* painting, music. *Address:* Age Office, Melbourne.

Died 11 Dec. 1926.

SCHUSTER, Ernest Joseph, KC 1922; Barrister-at-Law since 1890; *b* 7 July 1850; *e s* of Francis Joseph Schuster, London; *m* 1876, Hilda, *e d* of Sir Hermann Weber, MD; two *s*. *Educ:* Frankfort; Geneva; Doctor of Laws in the University of Munich. A managing partner in firm of Schuster, Son & Co. of Cannon Street, EC, 1873–88; Member of Executive of Society of Comparative Legislation; Member of Council of International Law Association; lectured for Institute of Bankers and for School of Economics and Political Science. *Publications:* The Principles of German Civil Law; The Wife in Ancient and Modern Times; The Effect of War on Commercial Transactions; numerous contributions to legal and other periodicals, and to Palgrave's Dictionary of Political Economy. *Recreations:* formerly cycling and rowing; later walking. *Address:* 33 Albert Court, SW7. *T:* Western 515. *Club:* Savile.

Died 16 Dec. 1924.

SCHWAB, John Christopher; Professor of Political Economy, Yale, 1898–1905; Librarian, Yale, 1905; *b* New York, 1865; *s* of Gustav Schwab and Catherine Elizabeth von Post; *m* 1893, Edith A. Fisher. *Educ:* Yale; Berlin University; Göttingen University (PhD). Editor of Yale Review, 1892–1911. *Publications:* History of New York Property Tax, 1890; The Confederate States of America, 1901; various articles in historical reviews and magazines. *Address:* 310 Prospect Street, New Haven, Conn. *Clubs:* Century, New York; Graduates', New Haven.

Died 12 Jan. 1916.

SCHWARZ, Ernest H. L., ARCS; FGS; Professor of Geology, Rhodes University College, Grahamstown, since 1905; *b* 27 Feb. 1873; *s* of F. M. Schwarz, South American merchant, Basinghall Street; *m* Daisy Murray Bowen, *d* of J. C. O'Halloran, late of the Colonial Service; no *c*. *Educ:* Westminster; Royal College of Science, London. Went to Johannesburg, 1895; editor Scientific African; joined Geological Survey of Cape Colony, 1896; with Dr A. W. Rogers, carried out first Systematic Geological Survey of South Africa. *Publications:* Causal Geology; Handbook of South African Geology; South African Geography; The Kalahari, or Thirstland Redemption; Brendavale; articles in Geographical Journal, Geological Magazine, Quarterly Journal Geological Society, Science Progress, Annals and Mag. Natural History, Journal of Geology, American Journal of Science, Records Albany Museum, etc. *Recreations:* tennis, driving. *Club:* Authors'.

Died 19 Dec. 1928.

SCLATER, Edith Harriet, (Lady Sclater), DBE 1918; *d* of late Rt Hon. Sir Walter Barttelot-Barttelot, 1st Bt, CB, PC, and Harriet, *d* of Sir Christopher John Musgrave, 9th Bt; *m* 1884, General Sir Henry Crichton Sclater, GCB, GBE (*d* 1923), *s* of James Henry Sclater. *Address:* 2 Ovington Gardens, SW3.

Died 29 March 1927.

SCLATER, General Sir Henry Crichton, GCB 1916 (KCB 1913; CB 1902); GBE 1919; Colonel Commandant, Royal Artillery; *b* 5 Nov. 1855; *s* of late James Henry Sclater of Newick Park, Sussex; *m* 1884, Edith Harriet, DBE, *d* of late Sir Walter Barttelot-Barttelot, 1st Bt. *Educ:* Cheltenham. Entered army, 1875; Captain, 1883; Brevet Major, 1885; Lieut-Col, 1900; General, 1919; served Nile Expedition, 1884–85, as Staff Officer, and afterwards as DAAG at headquarters (despatches, brevet of Major, medal with clasp, Khedive's star); Egyptian Frontier Field Force, 1885–86; DAAG, Cairo, 1885–90; South Africa, 1899–1902, as AAG for RA, and Col on Staff for RA (despatches thrice, Brevet Colonel, Queen's medal 6 clasps, King's medal 2 clasps, CB); Director of Artillery, War Office, 1903–4; Quarter-Master General in India, 1904–8; commanded Quetta Division, 1908–12; GOC-in-Chief Southern Command, 1916–19; Adjutant-General to the Forces and Member of HM's Army Council, 1914–16; retired pay, 1922. *Address:* Holmwood, Edenbridge, Kent.

Died 26 Sept. 1923.

SCOBELL, Ven. Edward Chessall, MA; Archdeacon of Gloucester since 1903; Residentiary Canon of Gloucester since 1912; Examining Chaplain to the Bishops of Gloucester since 1883; *b* 27 Jan. 1850; *s* of Rev. S. G. Scobell, Vicar of Market Rasen; *m* 1879, Dora M., *d* of C. Sumner, Judge of County Court. *Educ:* Marlborough; Pembroke Coll., Oxford (second class, Theology). Deacon, 1873; Curate, Horsham, 1873–77; Curate, St Luke's, Gloucester; Lecturer Gloucester Theological Coll., 1877–81; Vicar, St Luke's, Gloucester, 1881–89; Rector of Upton St Leonards, 1889–1912; Rural Dean of Gloucester, 1890–1903; Hon. Canon, 1895–1912; Governor Gloucester Endowed Schools, 1901; member of Gloucestershire Education Committee; Sec. Gloucester Diocesan Conference, 1890–92. *Publications:* sermons, addresses, etc. *Recreations:* travel, Swiss mountain climbing, cycling. *Address:* 7 College Green, Gloucester. *Clubs:* New Oxford and Cambridge; Gloucester.

Died 8 Feb. 1917.

SCOBLE, Rt. Hon. Sir Andrew Richard, KCSI 1890 (CSI 1889); PC 1901; KC; *b* London, 25 Sept. 1831; 2nd *s* of John Scoble, Kingsbridge, Devon, sometime member Provincial Parliament of Canada; *m* 1863, Augusta Harriette (*d* 1904), *o d* of Joseph Nicholson. *Educ:* City of London School. Barrister Lincoln's Inn, 1856; Advocate-General, and Member of Legislative Council, Bombay, 1872–77; QC 1876; Member Council of the Gov.-Gen. of India, 1886–91; Treasurer of Hon. Society of Lincoln's Inn, 1899; MP (C) Hackney, Central Div., 1892–1900; Member of Judicial Committee of Privy Council, 1901. *Publications:* translations of Mignet's History of Mary Queen of Scots, Guizot's History of the English Revolution, and other works. *Address:* Chivelston, Wimbledon Common. *Clubs:* Athenæum, Carlton. *Died 17 Jan. 1916.*

SCOTT, Alexander MacCallum, MA; Barrister-at-Law; *b* Boathouse, Blantyre, 16 June 1874; 3rd *s* of late John Scott, of Millhill, Polmont, and Rebecca MacCallum; *m* 1910, Jessie, *e d* of Dr John Hutchison, ex-Rector of the Glasgow High School; one *s*. *Educ:* Polmont Public School; Falkirk High School; Glasgow University. President of the Union, Glasgow University, 1896–97; graduated, 1897; engaged in journalistic and political work in London; Secretary, League of Liberals against Aggression and Militarism, 1900–3; Sec. New Reform Club, 1903–6; Member of Lewisham Borough Council, 1903–6; called to the Bar, Middle Temple, 1908; Private Sec. to Lord Pentland, 1910–22; Secretary for Scotland, 1909–10; MP (L) Glasgow (Bridgeton), 1910–22; Member of the Speaker's Committee on Electoral Reform, 1916–17; Parliamentary Private Secretary to Mr Churchill, Minister of Munitions, 1917–19; to Mr Churchill, Secretary of State for War, 1919; Member of Interim Forest Authority, 1918; Coalition Liberal Whip for Scotland, 1922; joined Labour party, 1924; made frequent visits to Russia and Finland. *Publications:* Winston Spencer Churchill, a Biography, 1905; The Truth about Tibet, 1905; Through Finland to St Petersburg, 1908; Licensing in Scandinavia, 1908; Winston Churchill in Peace and War, 1916; Barbary, 1921; Bits of Chelsea, 1922; Clydesdale, 1924; Beyond the Baltic, 1925; Suomi, the Land of the Finns, 1926. *Recreations:* walking, cycling, Northern travel. *Address:* 13 Wellington Square, Chelsea, SW3. *Clubs:* Devonshire, Savage, Whitefriars.

Died 25 Aug. 1928.

SCOTT, Arthur William, MA; Phillips Professor (Science), St David's College, Lampeter, since 1872; *b* Dublin, 1846; *s* of late David Scott, Dublin. *Educ:* Trinity College, Dublin. BA 1868; Senior Moderator and Gold Medallist in Mathematics, and Senior Moderator and Gold Medallist in Experimental and Natural Science; MA 1872; Fellow of the Physical Society of London; Fellow of the American Association for the Advancement of Science; Fellow of the Institute of Physics; Mayor of Lampeter, 1910–11. *Recreation:* travelling. *Address:* St David's College, Lampeter. *Club:* St Stephen's.

Died 7 March 1927.

SCOTT, Ven. Avison Terry; Archdeacon of Tonbridge since 1906; Vicar of St James', Tunbridge Wells, since 1886; *b* 18 July 1848; *s* of late Rev. Canon Scott, Vicar of Wisbech, Cambs; *m* 1874, Dora, *d* of late Rev. R. H. Tillard, Rector of Blakeney, Norfolk; four *s* two *d*. *Educ:* Trinity College, Cambridge; MA. Curate of Swaffham, 1871–73; Wimbledon, 1873–79; Vicar of Christ Church, Bootle, 1879–86; Hon. Canon of Canterbury Cathedral, 1904; Rural Dean of Tunbridge Wells, 1894. *Address:* St James' Vicarage, Tunbridge Wells. *T:* Tunbridge Wells 518. *Died 18 June 1925.*

SCOTT, Sir Basil, Kt 1909; MA; *b* June 1859; 2nd *s* of late Henry Scott of Bombay; *m* 1914, Gertrude Gwendoline, *d* of late Henry W. Villiers-Stuart, JP, DL, Dromana, Co. Waterford; two *s*. *Educ:* Haileybury; Balliol College, Oxford. Called to the Bar, 1883; admitted Advocate of High Court, Bombay, 1885; Acting Advocate-General of Bombay, 1899; Advocate-General of Bombay, 1900–8; Chief Justice of Bombay, 1908–19. *Club:* New University.

Died 1 May 1926.

SCOTT, Sir Benjamin, Kt 1904; JP City of Carlisle and County of Cumberland; *b* Carlisle, 1841; *e s* of late Hudson Scott of Carlisle; *m* 1874, Sarah, *d* of late Joseph Hope of Whooff House, Cumberland; one *d*. *Educ:* Society of Friends' School, Wigton. Mayor of Carlisle, 1885, 1891, 1892, 1902, 1911, and 1912. *Address:* Linden House, Stanwix, Carlisle. *TA:* Stanwix, Carlisle. *T:* Carlisle 24.

Died 10 July 1927.

SCOTT, Col Bertal Hopton, CMG 1917; late Army Medical Staff; *b* 12 Aug. 1863; *s* of late Rev. G. H. Scott and Frances S. Armstrong; *m* 1898, Hilda A., *d* of late C. Hamilton Jackson, formerly Administrator-General, Jamaica; two *s*. *Educ:* Cholmeley School, Highgate; Trinity College, Toronto; London Hospital. Surgeon, MS, 1887; Major 1889; Lt-Col 1911; Col 1915; Dep. Asst Dir Gen., AMS, 1910–14; Asst Director of Medical Services, 1915; served Chitral, 1895 (medal with clasp); Sierra Leone, 1898–99 (severely wounded, medal with clasp); European War, 1914–17 (despatches thrice, CMG). *Address:* 29 Amherst Road, Ealing, W.

Died 24 Oct. 1926.

SCOTT, Charles Clare, KC 1910; Bencher of the Middle Temple, 1898; Treasurer, 1920; *b* 2 Sept. 1850; *e s* of late John Scott, Inspector-General of Hospitals, Bombay; unmarried. *Educ:* Rugby; King's College, London; Wren's; Student of the Middle Temple, 1871. Called to the Bar, 1874; joined the Home (later South-Eastern) Circuit. *Address:* 69 Inverness Terrace, W2. *T:* Central 1240.

Died 4 May 1925.

SCOTT, Maj.-Gen. Sir Charles Henry, KCB 1909 (CB 1898); Colonel-Commandant Royal Artillery; *b* 15 June 1848; *s* of late Edward John Scott of Portland Lodge, Southsea; *m* 1872, Frances (*d* 1889), *d* of Gen. John Gustavus Halliday; two *s* two *d*. *Educ:* privately; Woolwich. Entered RA 1868; became Captain, 1879; Major, 1885; Lieutenant-Colonel, 1892; Col 1896; Maj.-Gen. 1902; served with Tirah Expedition, 1897–98, including capture of Sampagha and Arhunga Passes, and Bazar Valley Expedition (despatches, CB, medal, 2 clasps); was Superintendent, Gunpowder Factory Bengal, 1881–92; Ordnance Consulting Officer for India, 1892–95; Dep. Director-Gen. of Ordnance, 1895; Inspector-Gen. of Ordnance, India, 1895–1900; Ordnance Consulting Officer for India (2nd time), April 1900–1902; Director-General of Ordnance in India, 1902–5; Member of Council of Governor-General of India, 1905–9; retired RA, 1910. Decorated for service with the Tirah Expeditionary Force. *Address:* Colleens, Cousley Wood, Wadhurst. *Club:* United Service. *Died 6 Oct. 1919.*

SCOTT, Rt. Rev. Charles Perry, DD; *b* 1847; *s* of Rev. John Scott, Hull; *m* 1889, Frances (*d* 1900), *d* of late Capt. Montagu Burrows, MA, Chichele Professor of Modern History, Oxford. *Educ:* Charterhouse; Jesus College, Cambridge (BA). Ordained, 1870; Missionary at Chefoo, 1874–80; Bishop in North China, 1880–1913. *Address:* Chung Te School, Pekin, N China.

Died 13 Feb. 1927.

SCOTT, Rt. Hon. Sir Charles (Stewart), GCB 1899 (CB 1886); GCMG 1899 (KCMG 1896); PC 1898; *b* Ireland, 17 March 1838; 4th *s* of late Major Thomas Scott, Willsborough, Co. Londonderry, and second wife Ann, *d* of Rev. Edward Lucas, Coote Hill, Co. Monaghan; *m* 1875, Christian Crauford (*d* 1922), *d* of James Macknight, WS, Edinburgh; one *s* four *d*. *Educ:* Cheltenham College; Trinity College, Dublin. Entered Diplomatic Service, Dec. 1858; employed as Attaché at Paris, Dresden, and Copenhagen; 3rd Secretary, Madrid, 1865; 2nd Secretary, Mexico, 1866; subsequently at Lisbon, Stuttgart, Munich, Vienna, St Petersburg, and Darmstadt, until 1879; appointed Secretary of Legation and Chargé d'Affaires, Coburg, 1879, also accredited to Prince of Waldeck, 1883; Secretary of Embassy, Berlin, where he was repeatedly acting Chargé d'Affaires; appointed Envoy Extraordinary and Minister Plenipotentiary to Swiss Confederation, 1888; 2nd Plenipotentiary to Samoan and Labour Conferences, Berlin, 1889, 1890; Envoy Extraordinary at Copenhagen, 1893–98; Ambassador to the Court of Russia, St Petersburg, 1898–1904; Hon. LLD Trinity College, Dublin, 1898. *Address:* Glengair, Roseneath, Scotland.

Died 26 April 1924.

SCOTT, Hon. David Lynch, KC; Chief Justice of the Appellate Division, Supreme Court of Alberta, and Chief Justice of Alberta since 1921; *b* 21 Aug. 1845; *m* 1883, Mary, *d* of Thomas M'Vittie; two *s* two *d*. *Educ:* Brampton Grammar School. Barrister, 1870; Mayor of Regina, 1883; QC 1885; raised to Bench, NWT, 1894. *Address:* 9825 106th Street, Edmonton, Alberta, Canada. *T:* 1979. *Club:* Edmonton. *Died 26 July 1924.*

SCOTT, Maj.-Gen. Douglas Alexander, CB 1897; CVO 1901; DSO 1886; FGS; *b* 14 Dec. 1848; *s* of late John Scott, MD, and Alicia Lucy, *d* of George St Vincent Thomas Nelson Murray; *m* 1894, Mary (*d* 1918), *d* of late Capt. Christopher Baldock Cardew, 74th Highlanders, and late Hon. Mrs (Eliza Jane) Cardew (*d* of 1st Baron Westbury), East Hill, Liss; one *s* two *d*. *Educ:* Milton Abbas Grammar School; RMA, Woolwich. Deputy Consulting Engineer to Government of India for Guaranteed Railways, 1876–77; in charge of Royal train on Govt Railways on occasion of Prince of Wales's visit to India, 1876 (received thanks of Govt of India); Afghan War, 1878–80 (medal); Egyptian Campaign, 1882 (despatches, medal, bronze star, brevet of Major); Director of Railways Soudan Expedition, 1884–85 (despatches, clasp, brevet Lieut-Colonel); Soudan, 1885–86, DAA&QMG (despatches, DSO); Colonel, 1889; AAG RE Headquarters, 1894–99; CRE Southern District, 1899–1902; Maj.-Gen. on the Staff, CRE, II Army Corps, 1902–4; Chief Engineer, Southern Command, 1904–5; Hon. Col Engineer and Railway Staff Corps; Commanded Eastern Coast Defences, 1906–9; Colonel Commandant Royal Engineers, 1921. *Recreations:* golf, music, cycling. *Club:* Army and Navy.

Died 4 Feb. 1924.

SCOTT, Edward John Long, MA, DLitt Oxon; MRAS; Keeper of Muniments at Westminster Abbey; late Keeper of Manuscripts and Egerton Librarian, British Museum; *b* Bridgwater, 11 April 1840; 2nd *s* of late George H. C. Scott, Rector of Rhôs-Crowther, Co. Pembroke, and Mary Favell Dehany, Jamaica; *m* 1869, Anna F. K., *o d* of Edward T. Donoghue; three *s* two *d*. *Educ:* Marlborough; Lincoln Coll., Oxford. Classical Scholar, 1859; Senior Exhibitioner, Goldsmiths Company, 1861; Boden Sanskrit Scholar, 1862; in College eight and eleven; BA 1862; MA 1866; DLitt 1902. Assistant MSS Department, British Museum, 1868; Assistant Keeper, 1879; Keeper, 1888. *Publications:* Introduction to Reprint of Eikon Basilike, 1880; The Eclogues of Virgil, translated into English verse, 1884; Letter-Book of Gabriel Harvey, edited for Camden Society, 1884; Private Diary of Shakespeare's Cousin, Thomas Greene, Town-Clerk of Stratford-upon-Avon, 1885; Records of Harrow School, 1886; William Harvey's Original Lectures on the Circulation of the Blood, 1886; The Eclogues of Calpurnius, translated into Engish verse, 1890. *Recreations:* bridge, golf. *Address:* 37 Culverden Road, Balham, SW. *Club:* United Sports. *Died 19 May 1918.*

SCOTT, Lt-Col George John, DSO 1900; *b* 7 May 1858; *m* 1886, Mary Ethel (*d* 1906), *d* of J. F. Christy, JP, of Upton, Alresford, Hants. *Educ:* Marlborough. Joined Shropshire Militia, 1875; Sub-Lt 2nd Dragoon Guards, 1879; served with 7th Dragoon Guards in Egypt, 1882 (medal with clasp, Tel-el-Kebir, and Khedive's star); exchanged to 18th Hussars, 1885; retired, 1889; served with 19th Batt. Imperial Yeomanry in South Africa, 1900–1 (medal 2 clasps, despatches, DSO); City of London Yeomanry, 1901–13; 3rd Middlesex Yeomanry, 1915–16. *Recreations:* shooting, fishing. *Clubs:* Cavalry, Marlborough.

Died 4 May 1925.

SCOTT, Sir James, Kt 1911; engineer; *b* Broughty Ferry, 11 Nov. 1838; *s* of David Scott; *m* 1862, Jeannie, *d* of Robert Brough; five *s* one *d*. *Educ:* Broughty Ferry. Trained as mechanical engineer at Monifieth; six years in Royal Gun Factories, Woolwich; ten years Manager of the Paragon Works, S Queensferry, and for forty years Prospector of the Tayport Engine Works; a member of the Engineers' and Shipbuilders' Association in Scotland; a Fellow of the Society of Antiquaries of Scotland; twice elected Provost of Tayport; a JP for the county, and member of the St Andrews Licensing Bench. *Address:* Rock Knowe, Tayport, Scotland. *TA:* Scott, Tayport. *M:* SP 194. *Club:* Liberal, Dundee.

Died 12 May 1925.

SCOTT, James, ISO 1905; *b* 11 Oct. 1850. Student Interpreter, China, 1872; 1st Class Assistant, 1886; Vice-Consul in charge of shipping business, Shanghai, 1892; Senior Vice-Consul, 1893; Consul, Chin Kiang, 1898; Swatow, 1899; Consul-General, Canton, 1902–6. *Publications:* English-Corean Vocabulary; Corean Manual for Students. *Address:* 54 Birch Grove, West Acton, W3.

Died 10 May 1920.

SCOTT, Sir John, 2nd Bt, *cr* 1907; Proprietor of Tyne Brass and Tube Manufacturing Co., Jarrow; Member Walter Scott and Middleton, Ltd, Contractors, and of the Walter Scott Publishing Co., Ltd; *b* 23 Aug. 1854; *s* of Sir Walter Scott, 1st Bt and Ann, *d* of John Brough of Branfield, Cumberland; S father, 1910; *m* 1st, 1882, Elizabeth (*d* 1911), *d* of Mark Garbutt, of Saltburn; no *c*; 2nd, 1919, Emily, *d* of late Thomas Cotes, Benwell, Darlington. *Heir: nephew* Walter Scott, Lieut ASC [*b* 31 March 1895; *m* 1915, Nancie Margaret (Margot), *d* of Samuel Herbert March, Châlet du Parc, Cannes]. *Address:* Danby Lodge, Darlington. *Died 29 April 1922.*

SCOTT, John, RI. *Address:* 47A Stanley Gardens, Belsize Grove, Haverstock Hill, NW. *Died 1919.*

SCOTT, John Healey; Chief Magistrate, East Griqualand, South Africa; *b* Gravesend, Kent, 23 May 1843; *s* of Rev. George Scott, Wesleyan Minister; *m* 1870, Elizabeth Ann, *d* of Rev. George H. Green, Wesleyan Minister. *Educ:* Grammar School, Preston, Lancashire. With Messrs H. Pooley & Sons, weighing-machine makers, 1857; emigrated to South Africa, 1859; engaged as farm tutor and teacher of Wesleyan Mission schools; Wesleyan Minister, 1867–76; entered Government Service as Magistrate with Bacela, 1876; served in Gealeka War and Northern Border War, 1878–80; retired on pension, 1902. *Recreation:* mechanics. *Address:* Kokstad, East Griqualand. *Club:* Kokstad.

Died Jan. 1925.

SCOTT, Commander John Wilfred, DSO 1919; Royal Navy, retired; *b* 1881; *s* of late Ven. Avison Terry Scott; *m* Primrose Helen, *d* of late Robert Turner; one *s*. *Educ:* HMS Britannia. Served European War, 1914–19 (despatches, DSO); retired list, 1924. *Address:* St James' Vicarage, Tunbridge Wells. *T:* 518. *M:* KK 5963.

Died 8 Aug. 1926.

SCOTT, Dr Kenneth, MD, CM; FRCSE, MRCS; Consulting Ophthalmic Surgeon, St Mary's Hospital for Women and Children, London, E; Medical Officer, City of London Branch, British Red Cross Society; *b* Morton, Bingley, Yorkshire; *s* of Thomas Graham Scott, Edinburgh, and Ann, *d* of James Whitley, Morton, Bingley; widower; no *c*. *Educ:* Edinburgh Academy; University of Edinburgh; King's College, London. Graduated Edinburgh University, with Honours in Final, 1887; Lecturer, and later Professor of Ophthalmology, Egyptian Government Medical School, Cairo; and Ophthalmic Surgeon, Kasr-el-Aïni Hospital, Cairo, Egypt, 1889–99; Organiser and Hon. Secretary, Cairo Blind School, 1900–6; Lecturer on Ophthalmology, West London Post-graduate College, 1907–9; Membre de l'Association Valentin Haüy pour le Bien des Aveugles, Paris. *Publications:* Refraction and Visual Acuity; numerous articles and contributions on ophthalmic work. *Recreations:* water-colour painting, gardening. *Address:* 7 Manchester Square, W. *T:* Mayfair 487. *Died 19 Feb. 1918.*

SCOTT, Lt-Col Lothian Kerr, CB 1897; late Royal Engineers; *b* 24 May 1841; *s* of George Scott, formerly of Glendowran, Lanarkshire, and of *d* of General Graham, Governor of Arcot; *m* A. H., *d* of G. A. Anstey; two *s*. *Educ:* Winchester for seven years, which he joined at the age of 9½ years. Entered the Royal Mil. Academy by competition and obtained commn in the RE; joined at Chatham, 1862; served at the Curragh till 1868; volunteered for service in India, and was employed in the public works, railways, and irrigation; was invalided in 1869; returned, 1871; invalided again; joined at Dover;

musketry instructor Chatham till 1877; instructor in fortifications, Sandhurst, till 1882; Prof. of fortifications and artillery, 1882–89; inspector of telescopic sights, and instructor to the RA in artillery sights, 1889–91; made many inventions relating to improvement in the shooting of artillery; in 1872 invented telescopic sight which was adopted for all our guns; invented automatic sights in 1878; took out several patents for various improvements relating to the service; retired from the service on account of ill-health. Decorated for services regarding telescopic sights. *Recreations:* cricket (captain of cricket at the RMC); represented his Corps for years in racquet matches *v* RA; boating, skating, hunting, shooting. *Address:* Forest Lodge, Farnborough, Hants. *Club:* Junior United Service.

Died 7 July 1919.

SCOTT, Margaret; *b* 1841; maiden name, Colquhoun; *m* Colonel Courtenay Scott. *Publications:* Every Inch a Soldier; Invasion of India from Central Asia; Under Orders; Primus in India. *Address:* Pennant Hall, Abermule, RSO, Montgomeryshire.

Died 14 Sept. 1917.

SCOTT, Hon. Mrs Maxwell, (Mary Monica); *b* 2 Oct. 1852; *d* of late James Robert Hope Scott, QC, and Charlotte Harriet Jane Lockhart, *d* of John Gibson Lockhart; *g g d* of Sir Walter Scott; *m* 1874, Hon. Joseph Constable-Maxwell, 3rd *s* of 10th Baron Herries, of Terregles; took additional surname of Scott; four *s* two *d* (and two *d* decd). *Publications:* Abbotsford and its Treasures, 1893; The Tragedy of Fotheringay, 1895; The Making of Abbotsford, and Incidents in Scottish History, 1897; Henry Schomberg Kerr, Sailor and Jesuit, 1901; Joan of Arc, 1905; Garcia Moreno; Madame Elizabeth de France, 1908; Madame de La Roche-jacquelin, 1911; St Francis de Sales and his Friends, 1913. *Address:* Abbotsford, Melrose, Roxburghshire. *Died 15 March 1920.*

SCOTT, Owen Stanley; Curator and Secretary of the Bowes Museum, Barnard Castle, since 1884; *b* Devonport, Sept. 1852; *m* 1878, Isabella Christy, *d* of late James Collins; one *s* four *d*. *Educ:* Ardingly. Technical Assistant in South Kensington Museum, 1872; Assistant Secretary, Fine Art Section, Glasgow International Exhibition, 1901; Past Master Barnard Lodge of Freemasons; PPSGD, Durham. *Publications:* Raby, its Castle and its Lords, etc. *Recreations:* photography, golf. *Address:* Bowes Museum, Barnard Castle. *T:* 35 PO. *Died 22 Jan. 1922.*

SCOTT, Admiral Sir Percy, 1st Bt, *cr* 1913; KCB 1910 (CB 1900); KCVO 1906 (CVO 1902); Hon. LLD Cambridge; in charge of gunnery defences of London against aircraft attacks, 1915–16; late Inspector of Target Practice; *b* 10 July 1853; *s* of Montagu Scott and Laura Kezia Snelling; *m* 1st, 1894, (Teresa) Roma (whom he divorced 1911), *e d* of Sir Frederic Dixon Hartland, 1st and last Bt; one *s* one *d* (and one *s* decd); 2nd, 1914, Fanny Vaughan Johnston, *d* of Thomas Ramsay Dennis and former wife of Col Arthur Pole Welman. Entered Navy 1866; Captain, 1893; Admiral, 1913; served Ashanti War, 1873–74 (medal); Congo Expedition, 1875 (despatches, special promotion); Egyptian War, 1882 (despatches, medal); South Africa, 1899–1900 (CB, despatches, medal); China War, 1900 (despatches, medal); served on Ordnance Committee, on Committee on Naval Uniforms, and Naval Exhibition Committee; inventor of night signalling apparatus adopted by RN and of various appliances for improving heavy gun shooting; also invented the gun carriages which enabled 6-inch and 4.7-inch guns to be used in South Africa; retired, 1913; Medjidie 3rd class, Khedive's Bronze Star. *Publication:* Fifty Years in the Royal Navy, 1919. *Heir:* *s* Douglas Winchester Scott, *b* 4 Feb. 1907. *Address:* 52 South Audley Street, W1. *T:* Grosvenor 1043; The Warren, Ascot. *Clubs:* United Service; Royal Yacht Squadron, Cowes. *Died 18 Oct. 1924.*

SCOTT, Robert George, VC 1879; DSO 1900; Lieutenant-Colonel Cape Colonial Forces; late Cape Mounted Rifles; *b* 1857; *s* of Fleet-Surg. Robert Charles Scott, RN; *m* Constance, *d* of Lt-Col C. A. Daniell. Served Kaffir Wars, 1877–79; with Kimberley Light Horse, Scott's Railway Guards, and Cape Railway Sharpshooters, S Africa, 1900–2 (despatches, Queen's medal, 3 clasps, King's medal, 2 clasps, DSO). *Address:* Kimberley, South Africa.

Died 3 Oct. 1918.

SCOTT, Robert Henry, MA, DSc; FRS; *b* Dublin, 28 Jan. 1833; *y s* of James Smyth Scott, QC, and Louisa, *d* of Hon. Charles Brodrick, DD, Archbishop of Cashel; *m* 1865, Louisa (*d* 1901), *d* of Hon. W. Stewart, Island Secretary, Jamaica. *Educ:* Rugby, Trinity College, Dublin; studied also at Berlin and Munich, 1856–58. Classical Scholar Trinity Coll., Dublin, 1853; 1st Senior Mod. Experimental Physics, 1855; MA 1859; DSc 1898; Keeper of Minerals Royal Dublin Society,

1862–67; superintended Meteorological Office, 1867–1900; Officer Legion of Honour. *Publications:* Weather Charts and Storm Warnings, 1876, 2nd edn 1887; Elementary Meteorology, 1883; numerous papers in the Proceedings Royal Society, Quarterly Journal Royal Meteorological Society, etc. *Recreations:* cricket and football up to 1860. *Address:* 6 Elm Park Gardens, SW. *Club:* Athenæum.

Died 18 June 1916.

SCOTT, Sir Robert Townley, Kt 1909; ISO 1903; *b* Dawney, Berks, 30 Dec. 1841; *m* 1868, Ellen, *d* of George Parkinson Wright, Brisbane; four *s* one *d*. *Educ:* private schools, Brisbane. Went to Australia, 1848; entered General Post Office, Brisbane, 1862; Under Secretary and Superintendent of Telegraphs, Queensland, 1899–1901; Secretary, Postmaster-General's Dept and Permanent Head of Commonwealth Telegraph Service, 1901–10. *Address:* Brisbane, Queensland.

Died Aug. 1922.

SCOTT, Rev. Samuel Cooper, MA; Vicar of St John Baptist, Chester, 1875–1915; Hon. Canon of Chester, 1896; Rural Dean, 1905; *b* Kingston-upon-Hull, 12 March 1838; *s* of Rev. John Scott, Vicar of St Mary's, Kingston-upon-Hull, and *g g s* of Thomas Scott the Commentator; *m* 1875, Susannah Jane, *d* of Dr Leggett, HEICS, and *g d* of General Bell; two *s* two *d*. *Educ:* private school; Trinity College, Cambridge. Clerk in Smith's Bank, Derby, 1854–63; Trinity College, Cambridge, 1863–66; deacon, 1866; priest, 1867; Curate of Wisbech; in charge of St James', Derby, 1869–70; Curate of St George's, Bloomsbury, 1870–74; Minister of St Peter's, Battersea, 1874. *Publications:* Lectures on the History of the Parish and Church of St John Baptist, Chester; Guide-book to ditto. *Recreation:* carpentry. *Address:* 19 Clifton Dale, York.

Died 12 Aug. 1923.

SCOTT, Rev. Samuel Gilbert; Rector of Havant, 1892–1916, and Rural Dean, 1900–16; Hon. Canon of Winchester, 1905; *b* 1847; *s* of Samuel King and Georgina Scott; *m* 1874, Louisa, *d* of late William Aldwin Soames, Tramore Lodge, Brighton; three *s* four *d*. *Educ:* Brighton College; Magdalen College, Oxford. Curate of Battersea, 1873; Vicar of S Saviour's, Battersea, 1877–83; Rector of Woolwich, 1883; Rural Dean of Woolwich, 1885; Rural Dean of Landport, 1896–1900; Hon. Secretary, Portsmouth Church Extension Fund, 1897–1904; Bishop of Winchester's Fund, 1904–11; Grand Chaplain of England for Freemasons, 1916; Director Hants Friendly Society, 1916; Surrogate. *Publication:* History of S Faith's Church, Havant. *Recreations:* walking, cycling, angling; member of British Ornithological Union. *Address:* Belmore House, Upham, Hants.

Died 5 Nov. 1916.

SCOTT, Thomas Bodley, JP Bournemouth; MRCS, LRCPE; physician; Member of Bournemouth Borough Council; 3rd *s* of late S. K. Scott, MRCS, Brighton; *m* Adeline, *d* of Albert Savory, Potters Park, Chertsey; eight *s* two *d*. *Educ:* Brighton College. House Physician St Bartholomews, 1873; in practice at Bournemouth. *Publications:* The Religion of a Doctor; The Road to a Healthy Old Age; Why do we Die?; Modern Medicine; Endocrine Therapeutics. *Address:* 7 Poole Road, Bournemouth. *T:* 37. *Club:* Junior Constitutional; Bournemouth.

Died 2 Feb. 1924.

SCOTT, Tom, RSA, hon. retired list; water-colour painter; *b* Selkirk, 12 Oct. 1854; *e s* of T. Scott, clothier, Selkirk. *Educ:* Selkirk Grammar School. Commenced studying at the Royal Institution, Edinburgh, 1877; afterwards in Royal Scottish Academy life classes; had sketching trips to the following places:—Grez, near Paris; Florence, Rome, Naples, and Capri; Naples, Ravello, and Salerno; Tunis; Holland. *Paintings:* The Otter Hunt; Meet of Foxhounds at Riddell; Mosstroopers returning from a Raid; Return to Selkirk after Flodden; The Legend of Ladywood; Return to Hawick from Hornshole, 1514; Newark Castle; St Mary's Loch; The Trysting Tree; Daybreak; Reparabit Cornua Phæbe; A Stronghold of the Scots; A Hayfield in Ettrick; A Witch lived here in days gone by; Canal Scene near Dordrecht; After the Battle of Philiphaugh; Ettrick Pen, Selkirkshire; Goldielands Tower near Hawick; Whin-burning, Gordon, Berwickshire; The Warrior's Rest, Yarrow; November in Liddesdale; Carnoustie; Tweed at Abbotsford; Auld Wat O'Harden; The Crofter's Mare; Sir Walter's Gate; Bemersyde Hall. *Recreation:* collecting stone and flint implements; possessed a good collection of Border antiquities. *Address:* Leslie Cottage, Selkirk. *Club:* Scottish Arts, Edinburgh. *Died July 1927.*

SCOTT, Walter Montagu, JP Glos 1906; MA Cantab; *b* 1867; *y s* of late John Scott, MD, of 8 Chandos Street, Cavendish Square, W. *Educ:* Harrow; Jesus College, Cambridge. *Recreations:* hunting, shooting, fishing. *Address:* Nether Swell Manor, Stow on the Wold. *T:* 17 Stow on the Wold. *Clubs:* Carlton, Junior Carlton, Royal Automobile. *Died 14 Aug. 1920.*

SCOTT, William A., ARHA, ARIBA, MSA, FRIAI; architect in private practice; Professor of Architecture, National University of Ireland, since 1911; *b* Dublin, 1 Sept. 1871; *s* of Anthony Scott, MSA, FRSAI, architect, and Catherine Hayes; *m* 1900, Catherine, *d* of Patrick Crumley, JP, DL, MP, Fermanagh; no *c. Educ:* Classical School, Manorhamilton; St Finian's Seminary, Navan; Metropolitan School of Art, Dublin. Apprenticed to Sir Thomas Newenham Deane and Son, 1891; engaged on reparation of National Monuments; design selected, and executed Enniskillen Town Hall, open competition; 3 years various London offices, and staff appointment in London CC; returned Dublin, 1902; late Hon. Examiner Planning and Design, London Society of Architects; Member of Council and Past Hon. Treas., Royal Inst. of Architects of Ireland; Past President, Architectural Association of Ireland; designed and carried out Spiddal Church; O'Growney Mausoleum, Maynooth; Garden Village, Kilkenny; Town Hall, Cavan; Spiddal House for Lord Killanin; Convent Chapel and Schools, Enniskillen; Church and Convent, Edenderry; Irvinstown Church; St Mary's College, Galway; designed Cathedral for Galway; studied and sketched in British Isles, Belgium, France, Germany, Austria, Italy, Constantinople, Asia Minor. *Publications:* papers and lectures at various Architectural Society's meetings. *Recreations:* fishing, yachting, motoring, nature study. *Address:* 45 Mountjoy Square, Dublin. *TA:* Scott, Mountjoy Square, Dublin. *T:* Dublin 2380. *Died 20 April 1918.*

SCOTT, Ven. William Edward; Chaplain of Holy Trinity, Geneva, 1915-18; Rector of Bradwell-by-Braintree, 1909-14. *Educ:* Keble College, Oxford (MA). Fellow of Bombay University; Curate of Merton, Surrey, 1875-77; Headmaster Northallerton Grammar School, 1877-80; Curate of Yafforth, 1879-80; Rector of Hawthorn, Durham, 1880-85; chaplain Nasir-abad, 1885-87; Deolali, 1888; Christ Church, Byculla, 1888-91; chaplain to Bishop of Bombay, 1894-95; at Colaba, 1895-97; Archdeacon of Bombay, 1897-1907; chaplain of Kirkee, 1901; Rector of Tolleshunt Knights, Essex, 1907-9; Chairman, Committee of Women's Work, SPG, 1910. *Address:* Hotel Beau Séjour, Vevey. *Clubs:* New Oxford and Cambridge; Alpin Suisse. *Died 29 Dec. 1918.*

SCOTT-GATTY, Sir Alfred Scott, KCVO 1911 (CVO 1906); Kt 1904; FSA; Garter Principal King-of-Arms since 1904; *b* Ecclesfield Vicarage, Co. York, 26 April 1847; 2nd *s* of Rev. Alfred Gatty, DD, Sub-Dean of York Cathedral and Vicar of Ecclesfield, and Margaret, *d* and *heir* of Rev. Alexander John Scott, DD, sometime Private Secretary to Horatio, Viscount Nelson; assumed by Royal Licence, 1892, the additional surname and arms of Scott; *m* 1874, Elizabeth, *d* of John Foster, Newhall Grange, Laughton-en-le-Morthen, Co. York; one *s. Educ:* Marlborough; Christ's Coll., Cambridge. Rouge-Dragon Pursuivant of Arms, 1880; York Herald of the College of Arms, London 1886-1904; Acting Registrar of the same, 1899-1904; Knight of Justice of the Order of St John of Jerusalem and Genealogist of that Order; Commander, Royal Norwegian Order of St Olaf; at an early age showed a great love for music, and commenced musical compositions in mother's magazine, entitled Aunt Judy's Magazine, 1868. *Publications:* Little Songs for Little Voices, 3 vols; Musical Plays for Children; Rumpelstiltskin; The Goose Girl; The Three Bears; Plantation Songs, 4 vols; and hundreds of songs sentimental and humorous; in many instances both words and music. *Address:* Wendover Lodge, Welwyn, Herts; The College of Arms, Queen Victoria Street, EC. *Clubs:* Athenæum, Garrick. *Died 18 Dec. 1918.*

SCOTT-MONCRIEFF, Sir Colin Campbell, KCSI 1903 (CSI 1878); KCMG 1887; *b* Scotland, 3 Aug. 1836; 6th *s* of late Robert Scott-Moncrieff, Fossaway, and Susan, *d* of A. Pringle, Whytbank; *m* 1st, 1860, Lucy (*d* 1874), *d* of late John Sturge; 2nd, 1879, Margaret (*d* 1885), *widow* of Lewis J. Sturge, barrister; 3rd, 1890, Mary Deborah, *d* of Arthur Albright, Mariemont, Birmingham; two *d. Educ:* Edinburgh Academy; HEIC Military College, Addiscombe. 2nd Lieut Bengal Engineers, 1856; retired with rank of Col, 1883; engaged in suppression of Indian Mutiny (medal); Irrigation Depart NW Provinces; Chief Engineer Burmah; Under-Secretary of State Public Works, Cairo, 1883-92; Under-Sec. for Scotland, 1892-1902; President of Indian Irrigation Commn, 1901-3; Hon. LLD Edinburgh. *Publication:* Irrigation in Southern Europe, 1868. *Address:* 11 Cheyne Walk, Chelsea, SW. *Club:* Athenæum. *Died 6 April 1916.*

SCOTT-MONCRIEFF, Maj.-Gen. Sir George Kenneth, KCB 1915 (CB 1907); KCMG 1918; CIE 1900; Royal Engineers; *b* 3 Oct.

1855; *s* of Major Alexander Pringle Scott-Moncrieff, ISC; *m* 1886, Helen Morin (*d* 1916), *d* of Robert Moubray, of Cambus, NB; six *d. Educ:* Edinburgh Academy; RMA Woolwich. Served Afghanistan, 1878-80 (despatches, medal with clasp); Instructor School of Military Engineering, 1893-98; commanded RE China Expeditionary Force, 1900-1 (despatches, medal and clasp); served Waziristan Expedition, 1901 (medal and clasp); Chief Engineer, Aldershot, 1909-11; Director of Fortifications and Works, War Office, 1911-18; medal for European War; retired, 1918; Vice-Pres., CMS; Hon. MICE. *Address:* 31 Ladbroke Square, W11. *T:* Park 5177. *Club:* National.
Died 4 June 1924.

SCOTT-MONCRIEFF, William George, MA; FSAScot, FZSScot; advocate; Sheriff-Substitute of Lanarkshire at Lanark, 1900-17, Hon. Sheriff, 1917; *b* 15 April 1846; *s* of late Rev. William Scott-Moncrieff; *m* 1878, Jessie Margaret, *d* of Robert Scott-Moncrieff, Edinburgh; three *s. Educ:* privately; Edinburgh University. MA 1866; called to Scottish Bar, 1870; appointed Sheriff-Substitute of Banffshire, 1877; Stirlingshire, 1887; Inverness-shire, 1897; served on Scottish Departmental Commission relating to the Inebriate Laws, 1908. *Publications:* contributor to legal journals, and editor of Nimmo's Narrative and Justiciary Proceedings for the Scottish History Society. *Address:* Whitchurch Rectory, Edgware, Middlesex. *Club:* University, Edinburgh. *Died 2 Jan. 1927.*

SCOUGAL, Andrew E.; *b* 1846; *s* of late James Scougal, one of HM Inspectors of Schools in Scotland. *Educ:* Cheltenham Grammar School; Edinburgh Academy, Institution, and University; Aberdeen Free Church College. MA Edin. 1865; LLD Edin. 1908; FRSE. Acting Inspector of Schools, 1868-69; HM Inspector, 1869; Chief Inspector, Western Division of Scotland, 1899; Senior Chief Inspector and Inspector of Training Colleges, 1904; HM Chief Inspector for the Training of Teachers in Scotland, 1910-11; retired, 1911. *Address:* 1 Wester Coates Avenue, Edinburgh. *Club:* Northern, Edinburgh.
Died Nov. 1916.

SCOURFIELD, Sir Owen Henry Philipps, 2nd Bt, *cr* 1876; DL, JP; *b* 10 Oct. 1847; *e s* of Sir John Henry Scourfield, 1st Bt and Augusta Lort, 2nd *d* of J. Lort Phillips of Lawrenny Park, Pembrokeshire; *S* father, 1876; *m* 1st, 1877, Gertrude Katharine (*d* 1894), *o d* of Seymour Phillips Allen of Cresselly, Pembrokeshire; 2nd, 1896, Frances Katharina Harriet (*d* 1914), *d* of late Rev. Josiah Turner Lea, of Orchardlea, Droitwich, and Vicar of Far Forest, Bewdley. *Educ:* Harrow; Christ Church, Oxford. Owned about 8,000 acres. *Heir:* none. *Address:* Williamston, Neyland, RSO, Pembrokeshire. *TA:* Houghton, Pembrokeshire. *Clubs:* Carlton, Boodle's, United University. *Died 5 Feb. 1921 (ext).*

SCOVELL, Sir Augustus Charles, Kt 1907; JP Co. of London; *b* 1840; *s* of George Scovell, JP, DL, Grosvenor Place, London; *m* 1865, Arabella Barrington (*d* 1916), *y d* of Captain Vincent Frederick Kennett of the Manor House, Dorchester-on-Thame, Oxfordshire; one *s* four *d. Educ:* Harrow; Christ Church, Oxford (BA 1862). A manager of the Metropolitan Asylums Board from 1882; Chairman, 1904-7; took an active part in Poor Law and other public work, metropolitan and local; for many years chairman of the Guarantee Society, Birchin Lane, London. *Address:* 8 Primrose Mansions, Battersea Park, SW. *Club:* Oxford and Cambridge.
Died 28 May 1924.

SCRATCHLEY, Herbert Arthur, MVO 1905; British Vice-Consul and Lloyd's Agent at Bona, Algeria, since 1906; proprietor of corkwood forests near Bona; *b* 10 Aug. 1855; 3rd *s* of late Arthur Scratchley, MA (Cantab), Barrister-at-Law, and Marian Beaumont, *d* of T. Beaumont, RN, of Bath; *m* 1887, Maria Matilde Elena Prax y Prax, *e* late Señor Don Victoriano Prax y Roca of La Junquera, Catalonia, Spain, and Philippeville, Algeria; one *s. Educ:* Brighton College; University College School, London. Went to Algeria as mining engineer to an English company established near Bona; AMICE 1884; British Vice-Consul at Philippeville, 1892-1906; Vice-Consul for Portugal at Philippeville, 1898-1906; for Norway, 1906; Lloyd's Agent at Philippeville, 1898-1903; acting Vice-Consul for Norway, June 1916-18; for Portugal, 31 May 1919. *Publications:* newspaper articles; consular reports; guide-book of Algeria. *Recreations:* reading, walking. *Address:* Bona, Algeria. *TA:* Scratchley, Bona. *Club:* Cercle de l'Union, Bona. *Died 22 April 1920.*

SCRIVEN, Ven. Augustine; Archdeacon of Vancouver since 1884. *Educ:* St Mary Hall, Oxford (MA). Ordained 1875; Curate of Kirkham, 1875-78; Frindsbury, 1879-80; Martinhoe, 1880-81; St Peter, Rochester, 1882-84. *Address:* Victoria, British Columbia.
Died 21 July 1916.

SCULLARD, Rev. Herbert Hayes, MA, DD; Professor of Church History, Christian Ethics, and History of Religions, Hackney and New Colleges, London University; *b* 1862; *s* of Rev. H. H. Scullard, who for more than 50 years was a Congregational Minister; *m* 1901, Barbara Louisa, *e d* of G. W. Dodds, Sydenham, and *g d* of Ebenezer Viney, for many years Treasurer of Hackney College; one *s. Educ:* Pembroke House School, Lytham; Lancashire Independent and Owens Colleges; St John's College, Cambridge. At Owens College distinctions in Modern Philosophy, Ethics, Political Economy, Psychology, Logic, and other subjects; at London University, MA in Mental and Moral Science, 1885; BD (first division), 1903; DD 1907 (the first Nonconformist to obtain a DD degree from any English University); at St John's Coll., Cambridge, Foundation Scholar, Hughes Exhibitioner, Naden Divinity Student, and Greek Testament prizeman; also honours in 1st and 2nd parts of Theological Tripos, Cambridge, and Hulsean prizeman, Cambridge; BA 1888; MA 1891. Pastor of Congregational Churches at York Street, Dublin, and Howard Church, Bedford, the latter of which John Howard the Philanthropist was a founder. *Publications:* St Martin: Apostle of Gaul; John Howard; Christian Ethics in the West; Essays in Christ and Civilization, and London Theological Essays; articles in Contemporary Review, Hibbert Journal, London Quarterly Review, etc. *Address:* 10 Wessex Gardens, Golders Green, NW.

Died 21 March 1926.

SEAFORTH, 1st Baron, *cr* 1921 of Brahan; **James Alexander Francis Humberston Stewart-Mackenzie,** JP; FRGS, FZS; *b* 1847; *o s* of late Keith William Stewart-Mackenzie, JP, and 1st wife, Hannah Charlotte (*d* 1868), *e d* of late James Joseph Hope-Vere of Craigie Hall, Midlothian; *m* 1899, Mary. Was Military Secretary to Governor of Madras; served Afghan War, 1878–80 (wounded, despatches twice, Bt-Major, medal with two clasps, and bronze star); Vice-Lieut of Ross and Cromarty; Col retired, late commanding 9th Lancers; Hon. Col 4th Batt. Seaforth Highlanders. *Heir:* none. *Address:* Brahan Castle, Cononbridge, Ross-shire; 47 Berkeley Square, W1. *T:* Mayfair 3358; Lydhurst, Hayward's Heath. *Clubs:* Carlton, Army and Navy, Turf.

Died 3 March 1923 (ext).

SEAGER, Philip Samuel, ISO 1906; Registrar of Supreme Court, Tasmania; Registrar of Deeds and Commissioner of Stamp Duties since 1894; *b* 1845; *s* of late Charles Seager, of Tasmanian Civil Service; *m* 1869, Emma Elizabeth, *d* of late J. T. Smales, Hobart. *Educ:* privately. Entered public service Tasmania, 1863; a member of several Public Boards; was associated with the experiment of introducing Salmonidæ into Tasmanian waters; a Commissioner of Fisheries; Chairman of Tasmanian Tourist Association; and a Justice of the Peace for Tasmania. *Address:* Hobart, Tasmania.

Died Jan. 1924.

SEAMAN, Colonel Edwin Charles, CMG 1917; Royal Engineers; *b* 4 Nov. 1867. Entered RE 1886; Capt. 1896; Major, 1904; Lt-Col 1912; Col 1916; Asst Instructor, School of Military Engineering, 1890–92; School of Submarine Mining, 1892–97; Supt Brennan Torpedo Factory, 1902–4; Inspector of Electric Lights, HQ of Army and War Office, 1904–12; Assistant Director of Fortifications and Works War Office, 1916; served European War, 1914–17 (CMG); White Eagle (Servia), 4th Class.

Died 10 May 1919.

SEARLE, Maj.-Gen. Arthur Thaddeus; Indian Army; *b* 29 Dec. 1830. Entered army, 1849; Maj.-Gen., 1890; unemployed list, 1888.

Died 15 Aug. 1925.

SEARLE, Sir Malcolm William, Kt 1923; **Hon. Mr Justice Searle;** Judge President of Cape Provincial Division of Supreme Court of South Africa. *Address:* Highlands, Wynberg, Cape Province.

Died 9 June 1926.

SEATON, Rev. Douglas; Vicar of Goodrich since 1875; Prebendary of Bartonsham, Hereford Cathedral, since 1893; Rural Dean of Archenfield since 1902; *b* 1 May 1839; 2nd *s* of George and Eleanor Seaton, of the Yorkshire branch of the Seaton family; *m* 1866, Catherine Mary (*d* 1920), *d* of late Frederick Hale Thomson; one *s* three *d. Educ:* Hyde Abbey School, Winchester; Brighton; Trinity Coll., Camb. BA 1861, and MA 1875. Deacon, 1862; Priest, 1863; Curate, Bishop's Hatfield, Herts, 1862–64; Chertsey, 1864–66; All Saints, Hereford, 1866; Goodrich, 1866–75; Vicar of Breinton, 1875; Secretary and Treasurer of the Hereford Archidiaconal Board of Education, 1875; Secretary of the Archdeaconry of Hereford Voluntary Schools Assoc.; Member of the Herefordshire County Council Committee on Education; Past Provincial Grand Chaplain and Senior Grand Warden of Herefordshire; Past M. W. Scr. Rouge

Croix Chapter (St Thomas); prelate of Rouge Croix Chapter 18 St Thomas, Gloucester. *Publications:* Handicraft or Manual Training; Guide to Goodrich Castle; History of Goodrich Castle; History of the Deanery of Archenfield. *Address:* Goodrich Vicarage, Ross, Herefordshire. *TA:* Goodrich.

Died 25 Feb. 1923.

SEAVERNS, Joel Herbert; foreign and colonial merchant; partner of the firm of Henry W. Peabody & Co. of London; *b* Boston, USA, 13 Nov. 1860; *o s* of Joel Seaverns, MD, and Jane M. Seaverns; *m* 1892, Helen, *d* of H. B. Brown of Portland, Me, USA. *Educ:* Harvard University (BA, with honours, 1881). A resident of London from 1884; MP (L) Brixton Division of Lambeth, 1906–10; Member of Territorial Force Association of the County of London, and Joint Committee of County and City Associations; ex-President Harvard Club of London; DL, JP County of London. *Recreation:* golf. *Address:* 25 Grosvenor Road, SW1. *T:* Victoria 2172; 16 Eastcheap, EC. *Club:* Reform.

Died 11 Nov. 1923.

SEBRIGHT, Sir Edgar Reginald Saunders, 11th Bt, *cr* 1626; JP Herts; Major and Hon. Lieutenant-Colonel (retired) 4th Battalion (Militia) Bedfordshire Regiment; *b* 8 Nov. 1854; 3rd *s* of Sir Thomas Gage Saunders Sebright, 8th Bt and 2nd wife, Olivia, *y d* of John Joseph Henry, of Straffan; *brother* of Sir John Gage Sebright, 9th Bt; *S* nephew, 1897. *Educ:* Eton; Magdalen College, Oxford. Equerry to late Duchess of Teck, 1885–97; Aide-de-Camp to Governor of Victoria, Earl of Hopetoun, 1892–94; Private Secretary to Governor of South Australia, Earl of Kintore, 1894–95; High Sheriff, Herts, 1902. *Heir: brother* Guy Thomas Saunders Sebright [*b* 19 Aug. 1856; *m* 1882, Olive Emily, *d* of Arthur Frederick. *Address:* 82 Eaton Place, SW. *Clubs:* Travellers', Bachelors']. *Address:* Cheverells, Dunstable; 14 Arlington Street, SW. *Clubs:* Carlton, Marlborough, Bachelors', United Service, Beefsteak, Pratt's.

Died 25 Dec. 1917.

SECCOMBE, Thomas; Professor of English Literature, Queen's University, Kingston, Ontario, 1921–23; *b* Terrington, 18 June 1866; *s* of Dr John Thomas Seccombe and Elizabeth Margaret, *d* of Thomas Clout; *g s* of Sir Thomas Lawrence Seccombe, GCIE; *m* 1896, Elizabeth Jane, *d* of Henry Goddard; one *s* two *d. Educ:* Felsted; Balliol Coll., Oxford (Stanhope prize, 1887). BA 1889; MA 1895. Assistant editor Dictionary of National Biography, 1891–1901; Lecturer, Owens Coll., 1901; East London College, 1907–12; Professor in English, RMC, Sandhurst, 1912–19; Lectr, Oxford Univ., 1919–21. *Publications:* The Lives of Twelve Bad Men, 1894; The Age of Johnson, 1900; The Age of Shakespeare (with J. W. Allen), 1903; Bookman History of English Literature (with William Robertson Nicoll), 1905–6; George Meredith, 1913, etc; editor of Smollett's Miscellanies, and Travels through France and Italy; Constable's English Garner and Religions Ancient and Modern; George Borrow's Isopel Berners and Lavengro; George Gissing, an Introductory Survey; Mrs Gaskell's novels; Florio's Montaigne; Boswell's Letters; Dr Johnson and Mrs Thrale; Goldsmith's Plays and Poems; Adlington's Golden Ass; works by Francis Parkman and W. H. Prescott; In Praise of Oxford. *Address:* Queen's University, Kingston, Ontario. *Club:* Athenæum.

Died 20 June 1923.

SECKHAM, Lt-Col Bassett Thorne, DSO 1900; JP Staffordshire; late Lieutenant-Colonel Commanding 4th Battalion South Staffordshire Regiment; *b* 22 Nov. 1863; *e s* of late Samuel Lipscomb Seckham, JP, DL; *m* 1888, Alice Dorothy, *d* of W. F. Moore of Cronkbourne, Douglas; one *s* two *d.* Served South Africa, 1900–1 (despatches, Queen's medal, 3 clasps, DSO). *Address:* Whittington Old Hall, Staffs. *Club:* Junior United Service.

Died 29 June 1925.

SEDGWICK, Rev. Gordon; Hon. Canon of Coventry; Vicar of Sherborne, Warwickshire, since 1898; *b* 1840; *m;* four *s* five *d. Educ:* Brighton College; Gonville and Caius College, Cambridge (Scholar); 6th Senior Optime, 1863, BA, MA. Ordained, 1866; Assistant Curate, Holy Trinity, Coventry, 1866–70; Monks Kirby, Warwickshire, 1871–77; Vicar of St Mark's, Coventry, 1877–98. *Address:* Barford, Warwickshire. *M:* AC 2662.

Died 11 Oct. 1921.

SEDGWICK, William Thompson, PhD, ScD; Professor of Biology, Massachusetts Institute of Technology, since 1883; Curator, Lowell Institute, since 1897; *b* West Hartford, Conn, 29 Dec. 1855; *s* of William Sedgwick and Anne (*née* Thompson); *m* 1881, Mary Katrine Rice. *Educ:* Yale (PhB 1877); Johns Hopkins Univ. (PhD 1881). Instructor Yale Univ., 1878–79; Fellow, Assistant, Associate, Johns Hopkins University, 1879–83; Biologist State Board of Health, Mass,

1888–96; President, Soc. of American Bacteriologists, 1900; American Soc. of Naturalists, 1901; New England Water Works Association, 1906, and American Public Health Association, 1915; Member Advisory Board, US Public Health Service; Public Health Council, Mass State Dept of Health; International Health Board, Rockefeller Foundation. *Publications:* General Biology (with E. B. Wilson), 1896; Principles of Sanitary Science and Public Health, 1902; The Human Mechanism (with T. Hough), 1907; A Short History of Science (with H. W. Tyler), 1917; and numerous special papers. *Address:* Massachusetts Institute of Technology, or Lowell Institute, Boston.

Died 25 Jan. 1921.

SEELY, Sir Charles Hilton, 2nd Bt, *cr* 1896; JP; MP (L) Mansfield Division of Nottinghamshire, 1916–18; colliery owner; *b* 7 July 1859; *e s* of Sir Charles Seely, 1st Bt, and Emily, *d* of William Evans and *sister* of Sir Francis Henry Evans, 1st Bt; *S* father, 1915; *m* 1891, Hilda Lucy, *d* of Richard Tassell Anthony Grant; four *s* two *d* (and one *s* decd). *Educ:* Harrow; Trinity Coll., Camb. Contested Mid-Derbyshire, 1886; Rushcliffe Division, Nottinghamshire, 1892; MP (UL) Lincoln, 1895–1906; Lt-Col and Hon. Col 5th Volunteers Batt. Hants Regt (Isle of Wight Rifles, Princess Beatrice's), 1900–8. *Heir:* s Hugh Michael Seely, *b* 2 Oct. 1898. *Address:* Sherwood Lodge, Arnold, Notts; Gatcombe House, Newport, Isle of Wight; 25 Belgrave Square, SW1. *T:* Victoria 20. *Clubs:* Brooks's, Athenæum; Royal Yacht Squadron, Cowes.

Died 26 Feb. 1926.

SEGUR, Marquis de Pierre Marie Maurice Henri; Membre de l'Académie Française; *b* Paris, 13 Feb. 1853; *m* Thérèse Hely d'Oissel; one *s*. *Educ:* Collège Stanislas. *Publications:* Le Maréchal de Segur, 1895; Le Royaume de la rue St-Honoré, 1897; La Dernière des Condé, 1899; Gens d'autrefois, 1900; Le Maréchal de Luxembourg, 1904; Le Tapissier de Notre Dame, 1906; Julie de Lespinasse, 1906; Au Couchant de la Monarchie (2 vols), 1913. *Address:* 45 avenue d'Iéna, Paris. *T:* 1662–09; Château de Villiers par Poissy, Seine-et-Oise.

Died 14 Aug. 1916.

SEIGNE, John Thomas, MVO 1904; Agent to Marquess of Ormonde and other landowners in Ireland; *b* 14 Dec. 1844; *o s* of late Thomas Seigne; *m* 1877, Elizabeth, *d* of Richard Barter, St Ann's Hill, Co. Cork; two *s* one *d*. High Sheriff of the County of Kilkenny, 1912. *Address:* Grenane House, Thomastown, Co. Kilkenny. *TA:* Seigne, Kilkenny.

Died 7 Jan. 1922.

SELBY, 2nd Viscount, *cr* 1905; **James William Herschell Gully;** *b* 4 Oct. 1867; *e s* of 1st Viscount and Elizabeth Ann Walford, *e d* of Thomas Selby; *S* father, 1909; *m* 1st, 1893, Ada Isabel (who obtained a divorce, 1909), *d* of late Alexander George Pirie of Stoneywood House, Aberdeen; one *d*; 2nd, 1909, Dorothy Evelyn, *y d* of late Sir William Grey, KCSI; one *s* three *d*. *Educ:* Winchester; Balliol Coll., Oxford. Called to the Bar, Inner Temple, 1892; practised at Parliamentary Bar. *Heir:* s Hon. Thomas Sutton Evelyn Gully, *b* 16 Feb. 1911. *Address:* 18 Brunswick Square, Brighton. *Club:* Oxford and Cambridge.

Died 2 Feb. 1923.

SELBY, Francis Guy, CIE 1908; MA; Hon. LLD, Bombay, 1908; *b* 8 Dec. 1852; *s* of F. T. Selby. *Educ:* Durham School; Wadham College, Oxford (Scholar and Hody Greek Exhibition; 1st Class Mods and 1st Class Lit. Hum., 1875). Formerly Director of Public Instruction, Bombay Presidency; Fellow of the University of Bombay; Vice-Chancellor of the University of Bombay, 1906. *Publications:* The Metaphysic of Aristotle; An Introduction to the Study of Kant; edited Bacon's Advancement of Learning, and Essays; Burke's Reflections on the French Revolution; American Speeches and Letters to the Sheriff of Bristol; Thoughts on the Cause of the Present Discontent. *Recreations:* gardening, bicycling. *Address:* Bridstow, Worcester Park, Surrey.

Died 7 May 1927.

SELBY, Lt-Col William, DSO 1898; Indian Medical Service (Bengal); Hon. Surgeon to the Viceroy; Principal King George's Medical College, Lucknow; Dean of the Faculty of Medicine, and Member of the Syndicate, Allahabad University; *b* Dunedin, New Zealand, 16 June 1869; *y s* of late Prideaux Selby, Koroit, Park Hill, Croydon, and Rose Anne, *d* of late John Wise; *m* 1896, Eliza Kinsman, *d* of late Frederick Benjamin, Wood Lane, Falmouth. *Educ:* Whitgift Grammar School; St Bartholomew's Hospital. MRCS, LRCP 1892; FRCS 1905. Joined Indian Medical Service, 1894; served in Chitral Relief Force, 1895 (medal with clasp); North-West Frontier and Tirah Expeditionary Force, 1897–98 (three clasps, despatches, DSO). Decorated as above. *Address:* Lucknow, UP, India. *Club:* East India United Service.

Died 8 Sept. 1916.

SELFE, Sir Robert Carr, Kt 1910; *b* 4 Dec. 1840; *s* of late John Selfe of Stockwell; *m* 1864, Rosetta (*d* 1917), *d* of late Benjamin Priest. Entered office of Ecclesiastical Commission, 1860; Accountant and Assistant Financial Adviser, 1891; Assistant Secretary, 1897; Secretary and Financial Adviser, 1908; retired, 1909. *Address:* Cedarlea, Parklands, Surbiton Hill.

Died 28 Sept. 1926.

SELFE, His Honour Sir William Lucius, Kt 1897; *b* London, 11 June 1845; 3rd *s* of Henry James Selfe Selfe (*d* 1870), Metropolitan Police Magistrate, and Anna Maria, *e d* of Venerable William Spooner, Archdeacon of Coventry; *m* 1876, Ellen, 2nd *d* of late Henry Sanford Bicknell. *Educ:* Rugby; Corpus Christi Coll., Oxford. Scholar, 1863; 1st class Moderations, 1865; Final Classics, 1867; BA 1868. Barrister Inner Temple, June 1870; practised as conveyancer and equity draftsman; engaged in the preparation of Statute Law Revision Bills, the publication of the Revised Edition of the Statutes, the Chronological Table and Index to the Statutes, and in the office of the Parliamentary Draftsman; Principal Secretary to Lord Chancellor, Earl Cairns, 1880; Judge of County Courts, Monmouthshire and Cardiff, 1882–84; East Kent, 1884–1905; Chairman East Kent Quarter Sessions, 1893–1905; Marylebone and West London, 1905–19; retired, 1919; member of County Courts Rules Committee, 1894–1919. *Address:* 13 Connaught Square, W2. *Club:* Athenæum.

Died 19 March 1924.

SELINCOURT, Agnes de; Principal of Westfield College (University of London) since 1913; *b* Streatham, 1872; *d* of Charles Alexander de Sélincourt and Theodora Bruce Bendall. *Educ:* Notting Hill High School; Girton College, Cambridge; Somerville College, Oxford. First Class in Mediæval and Modern Languages Tripos, Cambridge, 1894; engaged in educational missionary work in India, 1896–1909; Principal of the Lady Muir Memorial Training College, Allahabad, 1901–9; Central Volunteer Secretary of the Student Christian Movement, 1910–12; Member of the Board of Oriental Studies of the University of London. *Address:* Westfield College, Hampstead, NW. *TA:* Discipula, Kilfort, London. *T:* Hampstead 734. *Club:* University of London.

Died 31 Aug. 1917.

SELKIRK, Countess of; (Cecely Louisa); *d* of Sir Philip de Malpas Grey-Egerton, 10th Bt; *m* 1878, Dunbar James, 6th Earl of Selkirk (*d* 1885). *Address:* Balmae, Kirkcudbright, Scotland; 50 Berkeley Square, W1. *T:* Mayfair 507.

Died 10 Jan. 1920.

SELLAR, Lt-Col Thomas Byrne, CMG 1916; DSO 1918; commanded 8th Battalion King's Own Scottish Borderers; *b* 2 March 1865; *s* of late Thomas Sellar, Hall Grove, Bagshot; *m* 1902, Evelyn, *d* of late L. P. Pugh, JP, DL, Abermaed, Cardiganshire. *Educ:* Fettes. Served Chitral, 1895 (medal with clasp); NW Frontier, India, 1897–98 (clasp); Tirah, 1897–98 (clasp); South Africa, 1899–1900 (Queen's medal, 4 clasps); European War, 1914–17 (despatches, CMG, DSO); Order of St Michael and St Lazarus (Chevalier). *Address:* Eirianfa, Aberdovey, N Wales. *Club:* Army and Navy.

Died 11 April 1924.

SELLHEIM, Maj.-Gen. Victor Conradsdorf Morisset, CB 1900; CMG 1916; Administrator of Norfolk Island since 1926; Permanent Staff Australian Military Forces; *b* Sydney, New South Wales, 12 May 1866; *s* of late P. F. Sellheim, Permanent Under-Secretary for Mines, Queensland, and Laura Theresa, *d* of late Lt-Col Morisset, His Majesty's 48th Regiment; *m* 1890, Susan Henrietta, *d* of late Rev. Edward Meredith and Harriett Howell-Griffiths, Clocaenog Rectory, North Wales. *Educ:* Brisbane Grammar School Adjutant Kennedy Regiment, 1896; extra ADC to Right Hon. Baron Lamington, GCMG, 1896; Staff Officer Northern Military District (Queensland), 1897; officiating DAAG, Queensland, 1900; DAAG and DQMG Queensland Mil. Dist, 1902; attended special courses of military instruction in England during 1899; special service in South Africa, 1899–1900; served with 2nd Batt. Northampton Regiment, Queensland Mounted Infantry, staff of Pilcher's Mounted Infantry Brigade, staff of Chauvel's Mounted Infantry (despatches, medal and 6 clasps); Staff Officer Central Military District (Queensland), 1900; DAAG and DAQMG District Headquarters, Queensland, 1902–7; attached Headquarters, 3rd Infantry Brigade, Aldershot, 1906; Headquarters, Aldershot Army Corps, 1906–7; 4th Division Indian Army at Quetta, 1907; AAG Victoria, 1907–11; AAG, NSW, 1911–12; Quartermaster-General and 3rd Military Member Military Board, 1912–14; Adjutant-General and 2nd Military Member Military Board, Australian Military Forces, 1914–16; AA&QMG 1st Division AIF, 1914–15; GOC AIF Troops in Egypt, Jan. 1915–May 1916; Commandant Administrative Headquarters, London, and GOC Australians in England, 1916 (despatches, CMG, 1914–15 Star, British

War Medal and Victory Medal); commanding 3rd Military District, 1917; re-appointed Adjt-General Australian Military Forces, 1917–24; ADC to the Governor-General, 1917–20. *Address:* Norfolk Island. *Clubs:* Melbourne; Australasian Pioneers', Sydney.

Died 25 Jan. 1928.

SELOUS, Frederick Courteney, DSO 1916; Captain Royal Fusiliers; *b* London, 31 Dec. 1851; *s* of Frederick Lokes Selous and Ann Sherborn (mixed French and English parentage on father's side, and Scotch and English on mother's); *m* 1894, Marie Catherine Gladys, *d* of Canon Henry William Maddy, Down Hatherley Parish, Gloucestershire; two *s. Educ:* Bruce Castle Sch., Tottenham; Rugby; Neuchâtel, Switzerland; Wiesbaden, Germany. Left England for South Africa on 25 July 1871; proceeded to Matabeleland in the following year, and from that time until 1890 travelled continually all over South Central Africa, making a living by elephant hunting and the collection of specimens of natural history; in 1890 took service under the BSA Company, and acted as guide to the Pioneer Expedition to Mashonaland; returned to England in Dec. 1892, but went back the following year in order to take part in the first Matabele war; after another visit to England, again got back to Matabeleland just in time to witness the outbreak of the rinderpest and the native insurrection in that country; served European War with Legion of Frontiersmen, East Africa (DSO); awarded by the Royal Geographical Society the Cuthbert Peek grant, the Back Premium, and the Founder's Gold medal; also elected a Corresponding Member by the Zoological Society. *Publications:* A Hunter's Wanderings in Africa, 1881; Travel and Adventure in South-East Africa, 1893; Sunshine and Storm in Rhodesia, 1896; Sport and Travel, East and West, 1900; Recent Hunting Trips in British North America, 1907; African Nature Notes and Reminiscences, 1908. *Recreations:* football and birds'-nesting when young; later hunting big game, shooting, cricket, lawn tennis, cycling, collecting specimens of natural history. *Address:* Heatherside, Worplesdon, Surrey, England.

Died 4 Jan. 1917.

SELWYN, Rev. Edward Carus, DD; Hon. Canon of Peterborough Cathedral, 1905; *b* Blackheath, 25 Nov. 1853; *o s* of Rev. E. J. Selwyn, Principal of Blackheath Proprietary School; *m* 1st, Lucy Arnold, adopted *d* of J. W. Cropper, Dingle Bank, Liverpool, and *g d* of Dr Arnold of Rugby; 2nd, Maud Stuart Dunn, *d* of James A. Dunn; four *s* two *d. Educ:* Eton; King's Coll., Camb. Newcastle Scholar; King's Scholar; Bell Scholar; Carus Prizeman; Browne's Medallist twice; Fellow of King's Coll.; Lecturer there, 1876–78; Curate of St Paul's, Jarrow-on-Tyne, 1879; Dean of King's Coll., Cambridge, 1880–82; Lecturer there and at Emmanuel Coll.; Principal of Liverpool Coll., 1882–87; Headmaster of Uppingham School, 1887–1907; Select Preacher, Cambridge, 1881, etc. *Publications:* The Christian Prophets; St Luke the Prophet; The Oracles in the New Testament; contributions to The Expositor, JTS, etc. *Address:* Undershaw, Hindhead. *Clubs:* Alpine, Athenæum.

Died 8 Nov. 1918.

SEMON, Sir Felix, KCVO 1905 (CVO 1902); Kt 1897; MD; FRCP; late Physician Extraordinary to King Edward VII; Consulting Laryngologist and Vice-President National Hospital for Epilepsy and Paralysis; *b* Dantzic, 8 December 1849; *s* of Simon Joseph Semon, stockbroker, and Henrietta Aschenheim; *m* 1879, Augusta Dorothea, *d* of late Heinrich Redeker; three *s. Educ:* Berlin, Heidelberg, Vienna, Paris, London (St Thomas's). Studied medicine in Germany, 1868–73; having finished his studies at home, travelled to Vienna, Paris, London; became attached first to Throat Hospital (Golden Square), later to St Thomas' Hospital, and held the post as Physician for Diseases of the Throat at that hospital from 1882–97; one of the founders and (3 years) President of the Laryngological Society of London; had on his retirement the Semon Lectureship in Laryngology founded in his honour at the University of London; Hon. and Corresponding Member of many learned societies; Commander, Order of Isabel the Catholic (Spain); Grand Officer, Order of Medjidie (Egypt); Grand Cordon of Star of Zanzibar. *Publications:* Forschungen und Erfahrungen, 1880–1910, 2 vols 1912 (collection of contributions to scientific medicine); also numerous physiological and clinical contributions to Phil. Trans, Proc. of Royal Soc. *Recreations:* music, gardening, travelling, shooting, fishing. *Address:* Rignalls, Great Missenden, Bucks. *TA:* Semon, Great Missenden. *T:* Great Missenden 33. *Died 1 March 1921.*

SENIER, Alfred, MD, PhD, DSc; Professor of Chemistry, University College (formerly Queen's College), Galway, since 1891; Member of Council, 1893–1908, and of Governing Body since 1908; Dean of the Faculty of Science since 1912; Member of Senate, National University of Ireland, since 1908; *b* Burnley, 24 Jan. 1853; *e s* of late

Alfred Senier and Jane, *e d* of Donald Sutherland; *m* Elsbeth Ida, *e d* of late Justizrath Heinrich Friedrich Wagner, of Berlin; two *d. Educ:* privately; Universities of Wisconsin, Michigan, and Berlin. FIC 1878; Demonstrator and Asst in Chemistry, Pharmaceutical Society, 1874–82; Lecturer on Chemistry, St John's College, Battersea, 1881–84; Research Student with the late Professor von Hofmann, Berlin, 1884–87; in charge of Chemistry, Queen's College, Cork, 1890–91; President of the Chemical Section of the British Association, 1912; Fellow of Chemical Societies of London, 1875, Berlin, 1885; Hon. Secretary and Treasurer Aristotelian Society, from foundation till 1884; Hon. Member, 1902; MRIA 1907; Treasurer, from its foundation, 1893–94 till 1910, University, formerly Queen's, College Athletic Union; Conservator of Fisheries, Galway, from 1900. *Publications:* scientific memoirs, mainly devoted to organic chemistry, in Transactions of London and Berlin Chemical Societies and in other journals; essays, notably A Visit to Giessen, 1898, Bonn on the Rhine, 1901, and The University and Technical Training, 1910; address, Section B, British Association, 1912; article on Cyanic Acids in Watt's Dictionary of Chemistry, and articles on Chemistry of Drugs in Thorpe's Dictionary of Applied Chemistry. *Address:* 28 Herbert Park, Donnybrook, Co. Dublin; University College, Galway. *Clubs:* Galway County; United Service, Dublin.

Died 29 June 1918.

SENIOR, Mark; Member of the National Portrait Society; *b* Hanging Heaton, Yorkshire, 1863. *Address:* 15 Park Row, Leeds.

Died Jan. 1927.

SENIOR, William; author. Adopted journalism as a profession, 1858; was a regular lecturer at literary and mechanics' institutions in the South and Western counties; joined staff of Daily News, 1866, and became a contributor to serial literature; in 1875 went to Queensland to establish and edit a Parliamentary Hansard for that colony; resumed connection with Daily News as special correspondent on returning home, 1881–99; succeeded Francis Francis as angling editor of The Field, 1883; editor-in-chief of The Field, 1900–9; Fellow of Institute of Journalists; ex-President of Fly-fishers' Club. *Publications:* Notable Shipwrecks, 1873; Waterside Sketches, 1875; By Stream and Sea, 1877; Anderton's Angling, 1878; Travel and Trout in the Antipodes, 1880; Angling in Great Britain, 1883; Near and Far, 1888; The Thames from Oxford to the Tower, 1889; A Mixed Bag, 1895; new edition of Blakey's Angling, 1898; Pike and Perch volume of Fur, Feather, and Fin series, 1900. *Recreations:* angling, cycling, golf. *Clubs:* Authors', Savage, Fly-fishers'.

Died 7 Oct. 1920.

SERAO, Matilde; *b* Patras, Greece, 1856; *m* Edouardo Scarfoglio. Founded with her husband Il Corriere di Roma, Il Corriere di Napoli, and Il Mattino; founded and directed Il Giorno in Naples. *Publications:* La Conquista di Roma; Il Paese di Cuccagna (The Land of Cockayne); The Ballet Dancer, and On Guard Sentinel, 1901; In the Country of Jesus, 1905; Farewell Love; Castigo; Sister John of the Cross; After the Pardon; Fantasy; Evvivia la Vita; Ella non respose, and others. *Address:* Il Giorno, Naples. *Died 25 July 1927.*

SERENA, Arthur, JP; FRGS; Knight Grand Cross of the Crown of Italy; Commendatore of the Order of San Maurizio and Lazzaro; Senior Partner in the Firm of Galbraith, Pembroke & Co., Shipowners, Underwriters at Lloyd's, Ship and Insurance Brokers; *s* of late Chevalier Leon Serena, the Venetian Patriot of 1848–49; unmarried. *Educ:* London University School; Bonn. Visiting Justice of Holloway Prison; Past Vice-Chairman and Treasurer of the London Chamber of Commerce, Member of the Council; Member of Council of Association of British Chambers of Commerce; Member of the Military Appeal Tribunal, County of London; of Council of the Chamber of Shipping of United Kingdom; Hon. Vice-President Italian Chamber of Commerce; on Executive Committee London Savings Bank; on the Committee of Management Royal Academy of Music; on the Committee of the London Hospital; Consul-General for the Republic of San Marino; Envoy Extraordinary and Minister Plenipotentiary at the Coronation of King George; founded Chairs of Italian at the Universities of Oxford, Cambridge, Manchester, and Birmingham; established an annual Gold Medal for Italian Studies in the gift of the British Academy; founded Chairs in English in Italy; Representative on Commerce Degrees Committee, University of London; contested (L) Penryn and Falmouth, 1892. *Address:* 36 York Terrace, Regent's Park, NW1. *TA:* Serena, London. *T:* Paddington 1755, Avenue 5014. *Clubs:* Reform, City of London, Arts, Bath, Ranelagh. *Died 31 March 1922.*

SETH, Arathoon, ISO 1905; JP; Registrar of the Supreme Court of Hong-Kong, 1903; formerly Official Administrator, Official Trustee, and Registrar of Companies; *b* 1852; *s* of late Seth Aviet Seth, merchant, Hong-Kong; *m* 1878, Katherine, *d* of late Peter Aviet Seth, merchant, Singapore; three *s* two *d*. *Educ*: St Paul's College, Hong-Kong. Called to the Bar, Lincoln's Inn, 1893; entered Magistracy, Hong-Kong, 1868–69; Third Clerk, 1872; Second Clerk, 1873; First Clerk, 1875; Clerk of Councils, and Chief Clerk Colonial Secretary's Office, 1881; Valuer under Rating Ordinance 1875, 1881–83; Superintendent of Opium Revenue, 1883–85; Imports and Exports, 1887; Secretary to Board under Taiping-shan Resumption Ordinance, 1894–95 (thanks of Government); Secretary to Sanitary Properties Commission, 1896; Acting Deputy Land Officer, 1894–95 and 1895–96; Deputy Registrar and Appraiser Supreme Court, and Commissioner for Oaths, 1895; Commissioner for taking Acknowledgments of Married Women, 1896; Secretary to Squatter's Board, Official Receiver in Bankruptcy, 1895–96; Acting Assistant Registrar-General, 1897; Acting Registrar, Supreme Court, Acting Land Officer, Acting Registrar of Companies, Official Administrator and Official Trustee, 1898–1900; Member of Board of Examiners, 1902; retired, 1909. *Address*: 1 Upper Addison Gardens, Kensington, W; Common Room, Lincoln's Inn, WC; Norman Cottage, Peak Road, Hong-Kong. *TA*: Adash, London; Cottager, Hong-Kong. *Club*: Hong-Kong, Hong-Kong.

Died 30 Dec. 1918.

SETH, James, MA, LLD; Professor of Moral Philosophy in the University of Edinburgh since 1898; *b* Edinburgh, 1860; *brother* of Prof. Andrew Seth. *Educ*: George Watson's College; University of Edinburgh (MA 1881); Leipzig, Jena, Berlin. Asst to Prof. Campbell Fraser (Logic and Metaphysics), 1883–85; Prof. of Philosophy, Dalhousie Coll., Halifax, Nova Scotia, 1886–92; Brown University, USA, 1892–96; Sage Professor of Moral Philosophy in Cornell University, USA, 1896–98; co-editor of the Philosophical Review. *Publications*: A Study of Ethical Principles, 1894, 14th edn 1918; English Philosophers and Schools of Philosophy, 1912. *Address*: 3 Queen's Crescent, Edinburgh. *Club*: University, Edinburgh.

Died 24 July 1924.

SETH-SMITH, W. H., FRIBA; architect; *b* London, 1852; *e s* of late William Seth-Smith; *m* 1887, Beatrice, 3rd *d* of Colonel H. Brabazon, Urmston. President Society of Architects, 1888–91; President Architectural Association, 1900–2; Fellow and late member of Board of Examiners, RIBA. *Address*: 46 Lincoln's Inn Fields, WC2. *T*: Holborn 4924. *Died 30 Aug. 1928.*

SETON, Miles Charles Cariston, CB 1915; MB, CM Edin.; FRCSE; Hon. Anæsthetist, Alfred Hospital, Melbourne; *b* 1874; *e s* of late William Carden Seton of Cariston and Treskerby, Capt. 82nd Regiment, and Amy Isobel, 3rd *d* of James Forsyth of Dunach and Glengorm, Argyllshire; in line male, the representative of the Setons of Cariston, and of the family of Cocke of Treskerby, Cornwall. Served South Africa, 1901–2; late Captain Cape Medical Staff Corps. *Recreations*: walking, shooting, bridge. *Address*: Hotham Street, East St Kilda, Melbourne, Australia; 24 Collins Street, Melbourne. *Club*: Savage, Melbourne. *Died 13 Jan. 1919.*

SETON, Walter Warren, MA, DLit London; DJur Padua; PhD Prague; FSA, FRHistS; Fellow of University College, London; Secretary of University College, London, since 1903; Lecturer in Scottish History, University College, London, since 1923; *b* 4 Oct. 1882; 4th *s* (3rd surv.) of late Col Alexander Reginald Seton, RE; *brother* of Sir Bruce Gordon Seton, 9th Bt, of Abercorn, Co. Linlithgow; unmarried. *Educ*: privately miseducated; subsequently educated at University College, London, 1899–1903. Assisted in foundation of University College Hall, Ealing, 1908; Warden of University College Hall, 1912–23; Political Secretary to Ministry of Information, with charge of propaganda in Balkans, 1918; Knight Gold Cross, Order of the Redeemer, Greece, 1919; Knight Officer of the Order of the Crown of Italy, 1921; represented University of London at celebrations of seventh centenary of Padua University, 1922, and at similar celebrations at Naples University, 1924; Secretary of the Ramsay Memorial Fund, 1917–23, and later Secretary to the Ramsay Fellowship Trust; responsible for securing for Scotland the Penicuik Jewels of Mary Queen of Scots, 1923; Secretary and Treasurer British Society of Franciscan Studies, since 1923. *Publications*: Two Fifteenth-Century Franciscan Rules, 1914; Blessed Agnes of Bohemia, 1915; Blessed Giles of Assisi, 1918; Vita di S Chiara Vergine, 1921; Nicholas Glassberger and his Works, 1923; Penicuik Jewels of Mary Queen of Scots, 1923; numerous articles in Archivum Franciscanum Historicum, Scottish Historical Review, Antiquaries' Journal. *Recreation*: collecting books and MSS. *Address*: 20 Stafford Place, Buckingham Gate, SW1. *T*: Victoria 9333. *Clubs*: Athenæum, Union. *Died 26 Jan. 1927.*

SETTLE, Lt-Gen. Sir Henry Hamilton, KCB 1900 (CB 1898); DSO 1891; Royal Engineers; *b* 27 Jan. 1847; *s* of Captain Henry T. Settle; *m* 1875, Edith, *o d* of late John Rigg of Wrotham Hill Park, Kent; one *d*. *Educ*: Cheltenham College. Entered army, 1867; Col 1893; psc; served Nile Expedition, 1884–85 (despatches, brevet of Major, medal with clasp, Khedive's star); as Senior Staff Officer, operations, Suakim, 1888 (despatches, brevet of Lieut-Col and clasp); Toski, 1889 (despatches, clasp, 2nd class Medjidieh); Tokar, 1891 (despatches, clasp); South Africa Field Force, 1899–1902 (despatches twice, KCB, promoted Maj.-Gen. for distinguished service in the field); Surveyor-General and Quartermaster-Sergeant, Egyptian Army, 1886–92; Inspector-General of Police of Egypt, 1892–94; Assistant Inspector-General of Fortifications, War Office, 1895; GOC Cape Colony, 1902–4; Portsmouth Defences, 1905–8; retired, 1911; Colonel Commandant RE, 1921; rank of Pacha, 2nd class Osmanieh, 1st class Medjidieh. *Address*: 7 Park Street, Bath. *Club*: United Service.

Died 22 April 1923.

SETTRINGTON, Lord; Charles Henry Gordon-Lennox; *b* 26 Jan. 1899; *s* and *heir* of Earl of March, Darnley, and Kinrara, and Hilda Madeleine, *e d* of Henry Arthur Brassey; *g s* of 7th Duke of Richmond. *Address*: Molecomb, Chichester. *Died 24 Aug. 1919.*

SEWALL, Mrs May Wright; Founder and Hon. President International Council of Women; a Director of the National Conservation League of Childhood; Hon. President International New Thought Alliance; *b* Milwaukee, Wisconsin; *née* Montague Wright; *m* 1880, Theodore Lovett Sewall. *Educ*: by private tutors; at Bloomington Academy; and the North-Western University. ML and MA. Member of National Historical Association and of the National Geographical Society, USA; of the Union Universelle de Lettres et Sciences (Paris); Founder of Propylæum Association, and Art Association, Indianapolis; Chairman of Committee to organise a World's Conference of Internationalists for 1915. *Publications*: Higher Education of Women in the Western States; Historical Resumé of the World's Congress of Representative Women, 2 vols; The Open Mind; The New Internationalism, etc; editor of The Genesis of the International Council of Women, 1888–93; Transactions of the Third Quinquennial International Council of Women, Berlin, 2 vols, 1904; Women, World War and Permanent Peace; many monographs on subjects of education and reform. *Recreations*: walking, rowing, the theatre. *Address*: Indianapolis, Indiana, USA. *TA*: Maydore, Indianapolis, USA. *Clubs*: Lyceum; Sorosis, Artists, New York; Women's, Contemporary, Art Association, Indianapolis.

Died 22 July 1920.

SEWARD, Edwin, FRIBA, RCA; *b* Yeovil, Somerset, 1853; *s* of William Seward of Hendford Hill, Yeovil; *m* 1884, Edith Jessie, *e d* of late Thomas Maddox, Surveyor, Hereford; two *d*. *Educ*: Aldridge's Grammar School, Yeovil. Articled as Architect at Yeovil, 1867; Cardiff, 1870; winner of various medals, National Competitions, South Kensington; Architect of the Cardiff Original Municipal Buildings; the Wye Bridge, Monmouth; Cardiff Coal and Shipping Exchange; Glamorgan and Monmouth Infirmary; Cardiff Workhouses and Hospitals; Library, Museum, Art Schools of Cardiff; Harbour Trust Offices and Council Chamber, Swansea; Exhibitor Royal Academy, etc; First President South Wales Architects' Society; Founder South Wales Art Society; Past-President Naturalists' Society of Cardiff. *Publications*: pamphlets on antiquarian, artistic, and scientific subjects connected with professional matters and archæology, and as delegate to and Hon. Secretary of Sections of the British Association. *Recreations*: landscape gardening, collector of works of art and antiquities. *Address*: 12 Victoria Esplanade, Weymouth. *Club*: Royal Dorset Yacht. *Died 21 June 1924.*

SEWELL, Col Thomas Davies, FRAS; senior proprietor of the Broad Arrow; the Naval and Military Gazette; clerk of the Spectacle-makers' Company, and Secretary of its diploma scheme; *b* London, 21 Sept. 1832; *s* of late Henry William Sewell, sword-bearer of the City of London, and late Mary Davies; two *s* one *d*. *Educ*: City of London School. Formerly: clerk of the Fanmakers', Shipwrights', and Loriners' Companies; Master of the Loriners' and Pattenmakers' Companies in the City of London; clerk of the Chamberlains Court, Guildhall, London; Past Grand Sword-bearer of England; Major and Lt-Col Royal London Militia (4th Batt. Royal Fusiliers); Col Commanding 4th Batt. Essex Regiment, RV; Major and Lt-Col Tower Hamlets Volunteers, RE; Senior Captain London Rifle Volunteer Brigade; Member National Reserve, City of London Section; Senior Churchwarden of St John the Evangelist, Westminster, from 1894. *Address*: 9/11 Temple House, Temple Avenue, EC. *TA*: Sagittaria, London. *T*: 4883 Holborn; 29 Grosvenor Road, SW. *Club*: Junior Army and Navy. *Died 13 April 1916.*

SEXTON, Col Michael John, CB 1916; LLD, MD; late Army Medical Staff; *b* 1860; *s* of John Sexton, Cork; *m* Katherine, *e d* of Capt. J. Conway, Duke of Cornwall's LI; one *d*. *Educ:* Queen's College, Cork. Served Burma, 1889 (medal with clasp); Chin Lushai Expedition, 1888–90 (clasp); S Africa, 1901–2 (Queen's medal 3 clasps); European War, 1914–18 (despatches twice, CB). *Address:* Holt & Co., 3 Whitehall Place, SW1. *Died 29 April 1922.*

SEYMOUR, Dr Edgar William, MVO 1912; MA, MB, BC (Cantab); MRCS; late Surgeon in Ordinary to Princess Beatrice, *b* 1868; *s* of late Dr William Hoffmeister, MVO; changed name to Seymour by deed poll dated 6 June 1918; *m* 1896. *Educ:* Cambridge; St Bartholomew's. Late Consulting Physician, Royal Convalescent Home for Officers, Osborne, and Surgeon Royal Yacht Squadron; retired. *Address:* Debourne, Cowes, Isle of Wight. *Died 24 July 1926.*

SEYMOUR, Lord Edward Beauchamp; 2nd Lieutenant, 4th Battalion Royal Warwickshire Regiment; *b* 22 Nov. 1879; 3rd *s* of 6th Marquess of Hertford and Hon. Mary Hood, *d* of 1st Viscount Bridport; *m* 1914, Elfrida Adelaide, 2nd *d* of Sigismund Cathcart de Trafford. Served South African War, 1900–1 (wounded), and 1914 War. *Died 5 Dec. 1917.*

SEYMOUR, Sir Michael Culme-, 3rd Bt, *cr* 1809; GCB, GCVO; Admiral of the Royal Navy, 1893 (retired 1901); Vice-Admiral of the United Kingdom, 1901–20; *b* Northchurch, Berkhampstead, 13 March 1836; *s* of Sir John Hobart Culme-Seymour, 2nd Bt, and Elizabeth, *er d* of Rev. Thomas Culme; *S* father, 1880; *m* 1866, Mary Georgiana (*d* 1912), *d* of Hon. Richard Watson, MP, Rockingham Castle, and *g d* of 2nd Baron Sondes; three *s* one *d* (and one *d* decd). *Educ:* Harrow. Entered Navy, 1850; served Burmah War, 1852; Baltic, 1854; Black Sea, 1854–55, including Naval Brigade in Crimea; China War, including Fatshan, Canton, and Peiho, 1858; Naval ADC to the Queen, 1869; Private Secretary to First Lord of Admiralty, Rt Hon. G. Ward Hunt, 1874–76; Rear-Admiral, 1882; Vice-Admiral, 1888; in command of Pacific Squadron, 1885–87; Channel Squadron, 1890–92; Mediterranean Squadron, 1893–97; Commander-in-Chief, Portsmouth, 1897–1900; First and Principal ADC to the Queen, 1899–1901; Grand Commander, Order of the Redeemer (Greece), 1920. *Heir: s* Rear-Adm. Sir Michael Culme-Seymour, *b* 29 Aug. 1867. *Recreations:* shooting, hunting, fishing, golf. *Address:* Wadenhoe House, Oundle. *TA:* Wadenhoe. *Club:* United Service. *Died 11 Oct. 1920.*

SEYMOUR, Vice-Admiral Sir Michael Culme-, 4th Bt, *cr* 1809; KCB 1920 (CB 1916); MVO 1912; Second Sea Lord and Chief of Naval Personnel since 1924; *b* 29 Aug. 1867; *e s* of Sir Michael Culme-Seymour, 3rd Bt and Mary (*d* 1912), *d* of Hon. Richard Watson, MP, Rockingham Castle, and *g d* of 2nd Baron Sondes; *S* father, 1920; *m* 1896, Florence Agnes Louisa, *y d* of late Albert Llewellyn Nugent; one *s* one *d*. Lieut 1889; Captain, 1905; Rear-Adm. 1916; Vice-Adm. 1920; served Battle of Jutland, 1916 (despatches, CB); Rear-Admiral Commanding Black Sea and Caspian Squadron, 1919; Second-in-Command in the Mediterranean, 1920; Commander-in-Chief North America and West Indies Station, 1923–24. *Heir: s* Michael Culme-Seymour, naval cadet, *b* 26 April 1909. *Address:* Tothill, Christchurch, Hants. *Clubs:* Naval and Military, Carlton. *Died 2 April 1925.*

SEYMOUR, Comdr Ralph Frederick, CMG 1919; DSO 1916; Royal Navy; *b* 6 Jan. 1886; *e s* of late Sir Horace (Alfred Damer) Seymour, KCB, and Elizabeth Mary, *d* of Col Frederick Romilly. Served European War, 1914–19, on personal staff of Admiral Sir David Beatty including battles of Heligoland, Dogger Bank, and Jutland Bank (despatches, DSO); promoted Commander, 1917; Commander HM Yacht Victoria and Albert, 1920. *Address:* 19 Chesham Road, Brighton. *Clubs:* Turf, United Service. *Died 5 Oct. 1922.*

SEYMOUR, Gen. Sir William Henry, KCB 1904 (CB 1859); Colonel Queen's Bays; *b* 1829; *s* of Sir William Seymour and Sarah Lydia, *e d* of Lieut-Gen. Sir Henry Oakes, 2nd Bt; *m* 1875, Anne Charlotte, *d* of Ven. Archdeacon John Wright Bowles. Entered army, 1847; served in the Crimea, 1854–55 (medal 4 clasps, Turkish medal); Indian mutiny, 1857–59 (despatches three times, brevet major, medal with clasp, CB). *Died 20 June 1921.*

SHACKLETON, Major Sir Ernest (Henry), Kt 1909; CVO 1909 (MVO 1909); OBE 1919; explorer; *b* Kilkee, 15 Feb. 1874; *e s* late Henry Shackleton, MD, and Henrietta Letitia Sophia, *d* of Henry John Gavan; *m* 1904, Emily Mary, 2nd *d* of late Charles Dorman;

two *s* one *d*. *Educ:* Dulwich Coll. 3rd Lieut National Antarctic Expedition, 1901; Commander British Antarctic Expedition, 1907; Antarctic Expedition, 1914; Director Equipment and Transport Mobile Forces North Russia Winter Campaign, 1918–19; Commander British Oceanographical and Sub-Antarctic Expedition, 1921. *Publications:* The Heart of the Antarctic, 1909; South, 1919; The Diary of a Troopship. *Address:* 14 Milnthorpe Road, Eastbourne. *Clubs:* Marlborough; Royal Yacht Squadron, Cowes. *Died 5 Jan. 1922.*

SHADWELL, Dr Charles Lancelot; Provost of Oriel College, 1905–14; late Fellow of Winchester College; *b* London, 16 Dec. 1840; *e surv. s* of Lancelot Shadwell, barrister-at-law, and *g s* of Sir Lancelot Shadwell, late Vice-Chancellor of England. *Educ:* Westminster School (Queen's Scholar); Christ Church, Oxford. 1st class Moderations, 1861; 1st class Final Classical School, 1863; BA 1863; MA 1866; DCL 1898. Fellow of Oriel College, Oxford, 1864–98; Senior Proctor, 1875–76; called to the Bar, Lincoln's Inn, 1872. *Publications:* The Laudian Statutes, 1888; History of Oriel College, in A. Clark's Colleges of Oxford, 1891; The Purgatory of Dante, translated into English verse, 1892; Registrum Orielense, 1500–1900, vol i 1893, vol. ii 1902; The University and College Estates Acts, 1898; The Earthly Paradise, 1899; Quaestio de Aqua et Terra, 1909; The Paradise, 1915; edited Walter H. Pater's Greek Studies, 1895; Miscellaneous Studies, 1895; Gaston de Latour, 1896. *Recreations:* punting, billiards, chess problems, chronograms. *Address:* 103 Banbury Road, Oxford. *Club:* Athenæum. *Died 13 Feb. 1919.*

SHADWELL, Lionel Lancelot, MA; Commissioner of the Board of Control, 1913–20; *b* 1845; *e surv. s* of Lancelot Shadwell, barrister-at-law, and *g s* of late Vice-Chancellor of England. *Educ:* Winchester; New College, Oxford. 1st class Moderations, 1866; 1st class Final Classical School, 1868; Barrister, Lincoln's Inn, 1873; Secretary to Commissioners in Lunacy, 1901–4; Commissioner in Lunacy, 1904–14. *Publications:* Enactments in Parliament specially concerning the Universities of Oxford and Cambridge, the Colleges and Halls therein, and the Colleges of Winchester, Eton, and Westminster, 1912; Odes of Horace translated into English Verse, 1920. *Recreation:* golf. *Address:* La Pastorelle, Icart, Guernsey. *Clubs:* Union, Albemarle. *Died 2 Dec. 1925.*

SHAH, Hon. Sir Lallubhai Asharam, Kt 1920; MA, LLB; a Judge of High Court of Judicature, Bombay, since 1913; acted as Chief-Justice in 1922, 1923 and 1924; *b* 4 Feb. 1873; *s* of Asharam Dalichand Shah of Ahmedabad, late Karbhari of several Native States in Kathiawar. *Educ:* The Gujerat College, Ahmedabad; Government Law School, Bombay. Practised as Pleader of the Bombay High Court since 1895; Fellow of the Bombay University, 1904–11, and since 1915; officiated as Government Pleader, 1910, 1911, and 1912–13. *Recreations:* billiards, tennis. *Address:* Malabar Hill, Bombay. *Clubs:* Orient, Hindu Union, Willingdon, Bombay. *Died Nov. 1926.*

SHAH, Khan Bahadur Sir Sayyid Mehdi, KCIE 1924 (CIE 1921); OBE 1910; Honorary Magistrate and Pres., Municipal Committee, Gojra; Senior Vice-Chairman District Board; Member Sanitary Board, Punjab; Member NW Railway Advisory Board; Member Provincial Cotton Committee. *Address:* Gojra, Lyallpur District, Punjab. *Died 5 Oct. 1927.*

SHAKESPEAR, Maj.-Gen. George Robert James; Indian Army; *b* 14 Oct. 1842; *m* 1873, Lily Alice, *e d* of Maj.-Gen. Charles Stuart Lane. Entered army, 1860; Maj.-Gen. 1899; served Soudan, 1885 (despatches, medal with clasp, bronze star, brevet Lieut-Col); Hazara Expedition, 1891 (despatches, medal with clasp). *Address:* South View, Denville, Havant. *Died 2 Sept. 1926.*

SHAKESPEARE, Rev. John Howard, MA (London); DD (Glasgow); LLD (McMaster, Toronto); Secretary of the Baptist Union of Great Britain and Ireland, 1898–1924; European Secretary of the Baptist World Alliance; Moderator of the Federal Council of the Evangelical Free Churches of England, 1919–21; Joint Secretary of the Federal Council of the Evangelical Free Churches of England; *b* Malton, Yorkshire, 1857; *m* Amy, *d* of late Rev. William Goodman, BA. *Educ:* University Coll., London; Regent's Park Baptist College. BA (Honours), 1881; MA 1882. Minister, St Mary's Baptist Church, Norwich, 1883–98. President of the National Council of Evangelical Free Churches, 1916; ex-Chairman of United Navy, Army, and Air Force Board. *Publications:* Baptist and Congregational Pioneers; The Churches at the Cross-Roads, 1918. *Recreation:* golf. *Address:* Fallowhurst, Finchley, N. *T:* Finchley 1527. *Died 12 March 1928.*

SHAMS-UL-HUDA, Nawab Sir Syed, KCIE 1916; MA, BL; **Hon. Mr Justice Shams-ul-Huda;** President of the Bengal Provincial Legislature since 1921; *b* 1864; belonged to well-known family of Syeds in Tippera, East Bengal; grandfather was Judicial Officer in Chittagong, and father was a distinguished Arabic and Persian scholar, and for some time editor of the Persian newspaper Doorbeen. *Educ:* The Presidency College, Calcutta; Calcutta University (MA; Fellow 1894). Commenced practice as a Vakil in the High Court at Calcutta; Member of Eastern Bengal Legislative Council, 1908; elected to represent the Mahomedans of Eastern Bengal in the Imperial Legislative Council, 1909; Member Bengal Executive Council, 1912–17; Vice-President Bengal Executive Council, April—June 1917; Judge, Calcutta High Court, 1917–21; held the office of Secretary of the Bengal Provincial Moslem League and that of Bengal Landholders' Association; President-Elect of the All-India Moslem League, 1912; received the title of Nawab as a personal distinction, 1913. *Recreations:* gardening, Persian poetry. *Address:* 220–2 Lower Circular Road, Calcutta. *Clubs:* Calcutta, India, Calcutta.

Died Oct. 1922.

SHAMSHER SINGH, Sir Sardar, Sardar Bahadur, KCIE 1917 (CIE 1911); Chief Minister Jind State since 1903; *b* 1860; *s* of Sardar Jaimal Singh of Raipur, Ludhiana District, Punjab. *Educ:* Jullundur and Hoshiarpur High Schools, and at Government College, Lahore. Served during Afghan War, 1879–80, with march from Kabul to Kandahar (medal, bronze star); Secretary to the Maharaja of Jind, 1885–87; Postmaster-General and Secretary to Council of Regency, Jind State, 1887–99, and Chief Judge of State, High Court, 1899–1903; received personal title of Sardar Bahadur, 1906; Coronation medals, 1903 and 1911. *Address:* Sangrur, Jind State, Punjab. *Died 8 March 1920.*

SHAND, His Honour Sir Charles Lister, Kt 1922; JP County of Lancaster; *b* Liverpool, 2 Dec. 1846; *o s* of late Alexander Shand, Warmsworth, Doncaster, and Mary Anne, *d* of James Lister, Ousefleet Grange, Goole; *m* 1892, Isabel Eleanor Louisa, *d* of Rev. John Richardson, Knowsley, Prescot; one *s* two *d. Educ:* Harrow; Trinity College, Oxford. Barrister Inner Temple, 1870, and joined the Northern Circuit; Revising Barrister, 1884–89; Judge of County Courts, Circuit No 6 (Liverpool), 1889–1921. *Recreations:* shooting, fishing. *Address:* Stand House, Childwall, Liverpool. *TA:* Stand House, Broadgreen. *T:* 170 Wavertree. *Club:* Junior Carlton.

Died 4 April 1925.

SHANN, Sir Thomas Thornhill, Kt 1905; JP; Lord Mayor of Manchester, 1903–4, 1904–5; *b* 1846; *m* Hannah (*decd*), *d* of late William Sutcliffe, Stansfield Hall, Todmorden. Alderman of Manchester City Council; Chairman Manchester Education Committee; Trustee and Treasurer of the John Rylands Library; Treasurer of the Manchester Industrial Schools; Chairman of Mayes Charity. *Address:* Lincluden, Formby, Lancs. *T:* Formby 169. *TA:* Bundles, Manchester. *T:* Manchester 1291 and 1132. *Clubs:* Constitutional; Constitutional, Manchester.

Died 14 July 1923.

SHANNON, 7th Earl of, *cr* 1756; **Richard Bernard Boyle;** Viscount Boyle, Baron of Castle-Martyr, 1756; Baron Carleton (UK), 1786; *b* 6 Dec. 1897; *s* of 6th Earl and Nellie, *d* of late Charles Thompson, 14 Park Square, NW; *S* father, 1906. *Heir: brother* Hon. Robert Henry Boyle, *b* 1 Feb. 1900. *Died 13 April 1917.*

SHANNON, Sir James Jebusa, Kt 1922; RA 1909 (ARA 1897); RBC 1920; RHA; portrait painter; *b* Auburn, New York, 1862; *s* of Patrick Shannon; *m* 1886, Florence Mary Cartwright; one *d*. Came to England in 1878; worked 3 years at South Kensington School, where he took gold medal for painting the figure; first important picture at Royal Acad., portrait of Hon. Horatia Stopford, 1881; full length of Henry Vigne, Esq., Royal Acad., 1887 (a picture which later gained 1st class medals at Paris, Berlin, and Vienna Exhibitions); medal at Chicago Exhibition for full length of Mrs Charlesworth; painted a large number of portraits and a few subject pictures; was an original member of the New English Art Club, and remained a member for some years; a member of Chelsea Arts Club; President Society of Portrait Painters. *Address:* 3 Holland Park Road, Kensington, W14. *T:* Park 4670. *Club:* Athenæum. *Died 6 March 1923.*

SHANSFIELD, William Newton; partner in The Press Agency; *b* Mistley; *s* of late William Jarrold Shansfield. Trained on the East Anglian Daily Times; Parliamentary Sketch Writer; contributor to British Medical Journal, and to leading provincial dailies; Hon. Secretary, Whitefriars Club; Editor, National Press Agency, 1905–9. *Recreations:* chess, sidelights on psychology. *Address:* Albany Chambers,

Queen Anne's Gate, SW. *T:* Victoria 484. *Clubs:* National Liberal, Savage, Whitefriars. *Died 27 July 1925.*

SHAPCOTT, John Dufour, ISO 1913; *b* 6 Nov. 1857; *s* of late George Guy Shapcott, Perth, NB. *Educ:* St Xavier's College, Calcutta. Entered Government of India Service, 1877; Department of Revenue and Agriculture, 1881; Registrar, Department of Revenue and Agriculture, 1910–17. *Address:* Simla, India.

Died 1923.

SHAPURJI, Sir Burjorji Broacha, Kt 1911; Sheriff of Bombay. *Address:* Bombay. *Died 24 June 1920.*

SHARFUDDIN, Hon. Mr Justice Syed; one of the Puisne Judges of the Patna High Court since 1915; Member of Executive Council, Governor-General of Behar; *b* Neora (Dist of Patna), 10 Sept. 1856; *y s* of Syed Farzand Ali, Pleader of Chupra; *m* 1882; one *s* one *d. Educ:* Patna College. Called to the Bar in 1880; practised at Patna, Behar; Puisne Judge, Calcutta, 1907–15; Member of the Senate of Calcutta University, 1904; Bengal Legislative Council, 1905, for Behar Landholders' Association; President of All India Mahomedan Educational Conference, 1906. *Address:* High Court, Patna. *Club:* Calcutta.

SHARP, Cecil James, BA; musician, writer, and lecturer; *b* 22 Nov. 1859; *e s* of John James Sharp and Jane Bloyd; *m* 1893, Constance Dorothea, *d* of Priestley Birch; *m* 1893; one *s* three *d. Educ:* Uppingham; Clare College, Cambridge. MusM (hon.) Cambridge, 1923. Associate to the Chief Justice of South Australia, 1883–89; Co-Dir, Adelaide Coll. of Music, 1889–91; Music teacher, Ludgrove Sch., 1893–1910; Principal of the Hampstead Conservatoire of Music, 1896–1905; Director of English Folk-Dance Society, 1911; Occasional Inspector, Board of Education, 1919–23. *Publications:* A Book of British Song, 1902; Folk-Songs from Somerset, series 1–5 (with Rev. C. L. Marson), 1904–9; English Folk-Song, Some Conclusions, 1907; English Folk-Carols; English Folk-Chanteys; Songs, Dances, and Incidental Music to A Midsummer Night's Dream; The Country Dance Book, parts 1–6 (with George Butterworth); The Morris Book, parts 1–5 (with Herbet MacIlwaine and George Butterworth); The Sword Dances of Northern England, parts 1–3; English Folk-Songs from the Southern Appalachians; Folk-Songs collected in the Appalachian Mountains, parts 1 and 2, etc. *Address:* 4 Maresfield Gardens, Hampstead, NW3. *T:* Hampstead 5791. *Club:* Savile. *Died 23 June 1924.*

SHARP, David, MB, CM, MA; FRS, FZS; Past President of Entomological Society of London; Editor Zoological Record; *b* 1840; *s* of W. Sharp. *Educ:* privately. Curator of Museum of Zoology, Cambridge, to 1909; Hon. Member of Institute of NZ, and of the Entomological Societies of France, Germany, The Netherlands, Russia, Washington, and Hawaii. *Publications:* Aquatic Carnivorous Coleoptera, 1882; Cambridge Natural History, 'Insects', 1895 and 1899; Insects and Termites (Ency. Brit.), 1902; A Scheme for a National System of Rest-Funds (or Pensions) for Working People, 1892. *Address:* Lawnside, Brockenhurst.

Died 27 Aug. 1922.

SHARP, Ernest Hamilton, OBE 1918; KC; BCL, MA; *s* of Edmund Hamilton Sharp; *m* 1900, Sarah, *d* of Roger Cunliffe, of Tunbridge Wells. *Educ:* Lincoln College, Oxford. Called to the Bar, Inner Temple, 1891; Midland Circuit; Acting Attorney-General, Hong-Kong, 1902 and 1904–5; Member of Executive Council, Hong-Kong; Chairman of War Charities Executive Committee, Hong-Kong, 1915–18; of Military Service Commission, Hong-Kong, 1917; of General Military Service Tribunal, Hong-Kong, 1918; of Hong-Kong University Commission, 1920. *Address:* The Peak, Hong-Kong; Great Bookham, Surrey; 5 Stone Buildings, Lincoln's Inn, WC. *Clubs:* Junior Carlton, New Oxford and Cambridge; Hong-Kong.

Died 8 Feb. 1922.

SHARP, Lt-Col Frederick Leonard, CMG 1915; Royal Artillery; *b* 18 May 1867. Entered army, 1886; Captain, 1896; Major, 1901; Lieut-Col, 1913; served European War, 1914–15 (CMG). *Died 13 Aug. 1916.*

SHARP, Rev. John, MA; *b* Bradford, Yorkshire, 13 March 1837; *e s* of late William Sharp, MD, FRS; *m* 1864, Elizabeth (*d* 1906), *d* of late Dr Lachlan M'Lean of Oban; one *s* one *d. Educ:* Rugby; (Taberdar) Queen's College, Oxford (graduated in honours, BA 1860, MA 1863). Deacon, 1861; priest, 1864; Missionary, CMS, in S India, 1861–70, and 1872–78; Rugby Fox Master, 1861–65, and Principal of the Noble College at Masulipatam, 1865–78; curate in charge of Langton, by

Partney, Lincs, 1870–72; first University Lecturer in Telugu and Tamil at Cambridge, 1878–80; Sec. British and Foreign Bible Society, London, 1880–1900; Sunday Evening Lecturer, St Catherine Cree, Leadenhall Street, 1881–89; Editorial Superintendent of Translations and Editions of the Holy Scriptures, and Consulting Secretary of the British and Foreign Bible Society, 1901–8; Vice-President, 1908. *Publications:* detached sermons on some special occasions; reports and pamphlets for the British and Foreign Bible Society. *Address:* 82 Harold Road, Upper Norwood, SE.

Died 20 May 1917.

SHARP, Major John Reuben Philip, ISO 1903; VD; Chief Clerk of the Ordnance Survey (Board of Agriculture), 1873–1907; *b* 2 Feb. 1842; 2nd *s* of William Sharp of Freemantle, Southampton. *Educ:* privately. Commanded the Civil Service Company 2nd VB Hampshire Regt from its formation in 1882 until 1904. *Address:* Red Hill House, Bassett, Southampton. *Clubs:* Overseas; Royal Southampton Yacht.

Died 8 Oct. 1922.

SHARP, Sir Milton Sheridan, 1st Bt, *cr* 1920; Chairman of Bradford Dyers' Association; *b* 30 Jan. 1856; *s* of James Sharp and Hannah, *d* of Joseph Gaunt; *m* 1879, Annie (*d* 1919), *d* of James Turner; six *s* (one *d* decd). *Heir: s* Milton Sharp, *b* 22 April 1880. *Address:* Spring House, Norristhorp, Heckmondwike, Yorks.

Died 22 May 1924.

SHARP, Thomas Herbert, ISO 1902; Deputy Assistant Paymaster-General for Supreme Court business, retired; *b* 4 June 1840; *s* of Thomas Sharp, sculptor (Royal Academy Silver Medallist, 1830); *m* 1st, Katharine Frances (marr. diss. 1893), 2nd *d* of Edmund Jones of Mirzapore, India; three *d;* 2nd, 1895, Florence, 3rd *d* of Chester Cheston, FSI, of Upper Clapton; one *s* one *d. Educ:* Hurstpierpoint; King's Coll. Evening School. Appointed Clerk in Accountant-General's Office in Chancery by Lord Chancellor on nomination of William Russell, Accountant-General, 1857; transferred to Paymaster-General under Chancery Funds Act, 1872; Civil Service Volunteer Corps, 1860–80; Captain, 1877–80; received Long Service Medal, 1894; late Member of Committee, Civil Service Benevolent Fund; People's Warden, Holy Trinity, Lamorbey, Bexley, 1895–1903; Hon. Treasurer and Correspondent, Lamorbey National Schools, 1893–1905; late Member Council Sidcup Conservative Polling Association, Dartford Division of Kent. *Address:* Chaumont, Prospect Road, Tunbridge Wells. *Club:* Junior Constitutional.

Died 12 Nov. 1918.

SHARP, Rev. Canon William Hey, MA; Canon of St Andrew's Cathedral, Sydney, since 1884; *b* Hull, Yorkshire, 21 Sept. 1845; *s* of William Sharp, MD, FRS; *m* 1876, Mary E. P., *d* of late Archdeacon Farr, LLD, of Adelaide, South Australia; two *s. Educ:* Rugby School (Exhibitioner); Lincoln College, Oxford (Scholar). Deacon, 1869; Priest, 1870; Warden of St Paul's College within the University of Sydney, 1878–1908; examining Chaplain to Bishop Barry at Sydney, 1884–89; Chaplain to Archbishop of Sydney, 1893–1909; Fellow and Registrar of Australian College of Theology, 1896–1927. *Publications:* sermons at St Paul's College; papers at Australian Church Congresses, etc. *Address:* Horton, Gordon, Sydney, Australia.

Died 6 Feb. 1928.

SHARPE, Reginald Robinson, DCL; Records Clerk to the Corporation of the City of London, 1876–1914; Barrister-at-Law of the Inner Temple; *b* 1848; *s* of Rev. Lancelot Arthur Sharpe, BD, late Rector of Tackley, Oxon, and Ellen Elizabeth, *d* of William Robinson, LLD; *g s* of Rev. Lancelot Sharpe, MA, FSA, sometime Rector of All Hallows, Staining, in the City of London. *Educ:* Merchant Taylors' School, London; St John's Coll., Oxford. Appointed Dr Andrew's Civil Law Scholar, St John's Coll., Oxford, 1866; a senior assistant in the Department of MSS in the British Museum, 1871–76; Barrister 1888. *Publications:* London and the Kingdom (3 vols); editor of Calendar of Letters, City of London, 1350–70; Calendar of Wills, Court of Husting, London, 1258–1688 (2 vols); Calendar of Letter Books (A–L) of the Corporation of London from AD 1275–1497; Calendar of City Coroners' Rolls, AD 1300–1378. *Recreation:* golf. *Address:* Tresco, York Road, Sutton, Surrey. *Club:* Constitutional.

Died 3 Feb. 1925.

SHARPE, Major Wilfred Stanley, CMG 1900; Resident, Northern Nigeria; 4th Battalion Royal Irish Rifles, 1893; *b* Richmond, Surrey, 29 April 1860; *s* of John Charles Sharpe (*d* 1913), of Gosling & Sharpe, 19 Fleet Street, EC; unmarried. *Educ:* Radley; Oxford University. Served with the 9th Lancers in India, 1883; promoted into 19th Hussars, and transferred to Inniskilling Dragoons, 1890; District Commissioner Sierra Leone, 1894–1900; served Sierra Leone

rebellion, 1898–99 (medal and clasp, CMG); Dakkakari Expedition, 1903 (medal and clasp). *Recreations:* shooting, yachting. *Address:* Sutton Court, Chiswick, W. *Clubs:* Sports, Junior Naval and Military.

Died 20 April 1917.

SHARPIN, Ven. Frederick Lloyd, MA; *b* Blofield; 4th *s* of late Henry Sharpin of Blofield, Norfolk, formerly of the 4th Light Dragoons; *m* 1868, Helen Georgiana, *d* of General Sealy, RA; three *s* three *d. Educ:* Bedford School; Exeter College, Oxford. Graduated 1860; ordained, 1862, to the Curacy of Northill, Beds; Chaplain on Bombay Ecclesiastical Establishment, 1865; after serving a few years at Nasirabad and elsewhere, was appointed to the Cathedral as Junior Chaplain and afterwards as Senior Chaplain, until in 1886 he became Archdeacon of Bombay, having previously acted in that office for several years on different occasions; on resigning the Archdeaconry in 1888, was appointed to the living of Millbrook, Beds, which he held for 21 years. *Address:* 37 Eversley Road, Bexhill-on-Sea. *Club:* New, Bexhill-on-Sea.

Died 2 June 1921.

SHATTOCK, Prof. Samuel George, FRS 1917; FRCS; Fellow of University College, London, 1910; Pathological Curator, Royal College of Surgeons, London; joint-teacher in Pathology, St Thomas's Medical School, London; *b* 3 Nov. 1852; *s* of Samuel Chapman Betty and Jane Brown; changed surname from Betty to Shattock; *m* Emily Lucy Wood; three *s* one *d. Educ:* University College, London. External Examiner in Pathology, Victoria University of Manchester, 1898–1901; External Examiner in Pathology, University of London, 1900–8; Editor and General Secretary Pathological Society of London, 1900–7; Hunterian Lecturer, Royal College of Surgeons, 1908–9; Member of Committee for the Revision of the Nomenclature of Diseases, Royal College of Physicians, 1902–13; President, Pathological Section, Royal Society of Medicine, 1907; President, Pathological Section, British Medical Association Meeting, London, 1910; President, Section of General Pathology and Morbid Anatomy, International Congress of Medicine, London, 1913; formerly editor of and contributor to Trans and Proc. of Pathological Section, Royal Soc. of Medicine. *Publication:* (posthumous) Thoughts on Religion, 1926. *Address:* Royal College of Surgeons, Lincoln's Inn Fields, WC2.

Died 11 May 1924.

SHAUGHNESSY, 1st Baron, *cr* 1916, of Montreal; **Thomas George Shaughnessy,** KCVO 1907; Kt 1901; President, Canadian Pacific Railway, 1899–1918; *b* Milwaukee, 6 Oct. 1853; *s* of Thomas Shaughnessy; both parents Irish; *m* 1880, Elizabeth Bridget, *d* of M. Nagle, Wisconsin; one *s* three *d* (and one *s* decd). General purchasing agent CPR, 1882; subsequently Assistant General Manager, President, and Chairman of board of directors; President and Director of a number of railway companies, all of which directly or indirectly connected with the CPR. *Heir: s* Hon. William James Shaughnessy, *b* 1883. *Address:* 905 Dorchester Street, W, Montreal.

Died 10 Dec. 1923.

SHAW, Sir Alexander (William), Kt 1906; Head of firm W. J. Shaw and Sons, Limerick; *b* 27 Oct. 1847; *s* of late William John Shaw; *m* Eleanor R. Gubbins, *d* of late William Gough-Gubbins; three *s* four *d. Educ:* St Mary's College, Limerick. Pres., Limerick Chamber of Commerce. *Publications:* Irish Trade; Irish Canals and Waterways. *Recreations:* golf, motoring, fishing. *Address:* Derravoher, Limerick. *TA:* Limerick. *T:* Limerick 246. *M:* TI 393. *Club:* Limerick County.

Died 28 Nov. 1923.

SHAW, Rev. Sir Charles (John Monson), 8th Bt, *cr* 1665; Rector of Wrotham, Kent, 1913–21; *b* 24 Nov. 1860; *s* of Rev. Charles John Kenward Shaw (brother of 7th Bt), and Julia Elizabeth, *d* of Captain John Harvey Boteler, RN; *S* uncle, 1909; *m* 1893, (Elizabeth) Louisa Whatman Best, *d* of James Whatman Bosanquet; one *s. Educ:* Haileybury; Hertford College, Oxford. Ordained, 1884; Curate, Bexley, 1884–89; Swanley, 1890–92; Vicar, 1892–1902; Vicar of Margate, 1902–12. *Heir: s* John James Kenward Best-Shaw, Lieut RN [*b* 11 June 1895; *m* 1921, Elizabeth Mary Theodora, *e d* of Robert Hughes, Stowford Lodge, Ivybridge, S Devon]. *Address:* Wrotham, Kent.

Died 11 Sept. 1922.

SHAW, Sir Doyle Money, KCB 1911 (CB 1882); Inspector-General of Hospitals, Royal Navy, retired 1892; *b* 1830; 5th *s* of late Dr David Shaw, HEICS; *m* 1883, Jessie Martin, *d* of John Graham. *Educ:* Edinburgh Academy and University. Entered Navy as Asst-Surgeon, 1854; served during Crimean War in HMS 'Spiteful' (medal, with clasp for Sebastopol, and Turkish medal); with battalion of Marines in China, 1857–61 (mentioned in despatches, promoted to Staff Surgeon, medal with 3 clasps); on board 'Octavia,' flagship during Abyssinian War (medal); Senior Medical Officer on board flagship

'Alexandra' at bombardment of forts of Alexandria, 1882 (medal with clasp, CB, and promoted to Deputy-Insp.-Gen.); in charge of RN Hospitals at Plymouth, Malta, and Haslar between 1884 and 1892.
Died 30 Sept. 1918.

SHAW, Edward Wingfield, DSO 1915; 1st Battalion The Duke of Cambridge's Own (Middlesex Regiment); *b* 19 Feb. 1895; *s* of Col G. J. Shaw; unmarried. *Educ:* Lancing and Dulwich College. Served European War, 1914–15 (despatches, DSO). *Address:* 14 Richmond Bridge Mansions, East Twickenham, Middlesex. *Club:* Junior United Service.
Died Dec. 1916.

SHAW, Sir Frederick William, 5th Bt, *cr* 1821; DSO 1900; DL, JP; *b* Dublin, 15 March 1858; *e s* of Sir Robert Shaw, 4th Bt and Catherine (Kate) Grace, *d* of William Barton, Grove, Co. Tipperary; *S* father, 1895; *m* 1885, Eleanor Hester, *d* of Major Horace de Vere, RE, of Curragh Chase; two *s* four *d. Educ:* Harrow; Oriel College, Oxford. Lieut Royal Dragoons, 1879–85; Lieut-Col 5th Batt. Royal Dublin Fusiliers; served South Africa, 1900–2 (despatches); commanded 8th (S) Batt. Royal Dublin Fusiliers. *Recreations:* hunting, shooting, fishing, golf, cycling. *Heir: s* Robert de Vere Shaw, MC, Capt. RFA [*b* 24 Feb. 1890. Served European War, 1914–18 (despatches, MC)]. *Address:* Bushy Park, Terenure, Co. Dublin. *Club:* Kildare Street, Dublin.
Died 15 July 1927.

SHAW, Sir James Dods, Kt 1913; Manager of House of Commons Official Staff for recording the Parliamentary proceedings since 1908, and Editor of the Commons Debates; *s* of late Andrew Shaw of Garliestown and Glasgow; *m* Kate Mary, *d* of late Francis Wood. Was on literary staffs of Liverpool Daily Post, Leeds Mercury, and Manchester Guardian; Managing Editor of Nottingham Daily Express; acted for many years as political representative of Press Association in Parliamentary Lobbies; life member of the Imperial Society of Knights Bachelor; wrote on holiday travels in Canada, Egypt, Siberia, Japan, China, Malaya, Ceylon, as well as on social, political and antiquarian subjects. *Recreation:* golf. *Address:* House of Commons, SW.
Died 14 Nov. 1916.

SHAW, John Byam Lister, ARWS 1913; Partner with Rex Vicat Cole in School of Art, Campden Hill, W; *b* Madras, 13 Nov. 1872; *s* of John Shaw, Registrar High Court, Madras, and Sophia Alicia Byam Gunthorpe; *m* 1899, Evelyn Pyke-Nott; four *s* one *d. Educ:* privately. Came to England, 1878, and London, 1879; went to St John's Wood School of Art; entered Royal Academy Schools, 1889; first picture, Rose Mary, Royal Academy, 1893; other pictures include: Whither?, 1896; Love's Baubles, 1897; The Comforter, 1897; Love, the Conqueror, 1899; The Flag, 1919 (for Canadian War Records). *Publications:* illustrated Browning's Poems, 1898; Tales from Boccaccio, 1899; The Chiswick Shakespeare, 1900; Old King Cole's Book of Nursery Rhymes, 1901; Coronation Book, 1902; Pilgrim's Progress, 1904; Cloister and the Hearth, 1909; Tales of Mystery and Imagination, Edgar Allan Poe, 1909; The Garden of Kama, Laurence Hope, 1914. *Recreation:* boating. *Address:* 62 Addison Road, W. *T:* Park 4198. *Club:* National Sporting.
Died 26 Jan. 1919.

SHAW, Lauriston Elgie, MD, FRCP; Consulting Physician to Guy's Hospital, and to the Royal Buckinghamshire Hospital; *b* London, 1859; *s* of Archibald Shaw, of St Leonards; *m* May, *d* of late Howard Spalding; one *s. Educ:* City of London School; University College, London; Guy's Hospital. *Publications:* contributions to medical literature. *Address:* Oatlands Chase, Weybridge. *T:* Walton-on-Thames 293.
Died 25 Dec. 1923.

SHAW, Thomas Claye, BA, MD (London); FRCP; consulting practitioner; *b* 1841; *m* Hannah Gratrix (*d* 1925), *d* of late J. Ridgway of Kytes, Leavesden, Herts; two *d. Educ:* King's College, London (Senior Warneford Scholar). Formerly Medical Director of the London County Asylum at Banstead; Examiner in Mental Physiology at the University of London, and to the Board of Studies, Army Medical Service; Emeritus Professor of Psychological Medicine at St Bartholomew's Hospital, and on Clinical Insanity at St Luke's Hospital; Ex-President of the Society for the Study of Inebriety; Member of the Medico-Legal, Harveian Society; was one of the earliest co-operators (with Rev. H. Hawkins) in foundation of After-Care Association; medical journalist. *Publications:* Ex Cathedra—Essays on Insanity, 1905; articles in St Bartholomew's Hospital Reports and in Tuke's Dictionary of Insanity, etc. *Recreations:* fishing, bicycling, music. *Address:* 29 Queen Anne Street, W1. *T:* Langham 2137. *Club:* Garrick.
Died 14 Jan. 1927.

SHAW, Captain Walter William; MP (C) Westbury Division since 1924; *b* 1868; *y s* of late Edward Dethick Shaw of Oaklands,

Wolverhampton; *m* 1893, Mary Louise, *y d* of William Webb Wakeman, New York; one *s* one *d. Educ:* private school; Jesus College, Cambridge. Served European War; sent on Special Mission to the United States by the War Office, 1917; Captain in the 3rd Queen's; Sheriff for county and town of Poole, 1913; CC for Dorset; contested the Houghton-le-Spring Division, Durham, 1922, and the Westbury Division, 1923. *Address:* Rood Ashton, Trowbridge, Wilts. *Clubs:* Carlton, Ranelagh, Royal Automobile, Pilgrims.
Died 10 May 1927.

SHAYLOR, Joseph; one of the directors of Simpkin, Marshall, Hamilton, Kent & Co., Ltd, since 1894; also a director of other companies; *b* Thrupp, near Stroud, Gloucestershire, 1844; *s* of Charles and Hepzebah Shaylor; *m* 1870, Emily Lark; two *s* two *d. Educ:* privately. Was apprenticed to a bookseller at Stroud, 1857; entered the firm of Simpkin, Marshall & Co., 1864; Liveryman of the City of London and a member of the Stationers' Company; a vice-president of the Booksellers' Provident Institution, and also of the Gloucestershire Society in London. *Publications:* The Fascination of Books, and other Essays; The Pleasures of Bookland, with Introduction by Andrew Lang; In Friendship's Garden; In Nature's Garden; Some Favourite Books and their Authors; Saunterings in Bookland. *Recreations:* books, gardening. *Address:* Gloucester House, Holden Road, Woodside Park, N12. *T:* Finchley 803. *Club:* Whitefriars.
Died 22 Dec. 1923.

SHEARD, Thomas Frederick Mason, MA; RBA 1896; Professor of Art, Queen's College, London, since 1915; *b* 16 Dec. 1866; *s* of T. J. W. Sheard, Oxford; *m* 1901, Mabel, *o d* of late T. G. Harrison, of St George's East; one *s* one *d. Educ:* Magdalen College School, and Keble College, Oxford. Grove Exhibitioner, 1888; Second Class in Modern History, 1889. Went to Paris, 1889; studied painting under Courtois, Rixens, Lefebvre and Rigolot; began exhibiting at Royal Academy, the Salon, Royal Inst. of Painters in Water Colours, etc, in 1891; Hon. Sec. Royal Soc. of British Artists, 1899–1904; represented in British section at Brussels International Exhibition, 1896; at Paris Exhibition, 1900 (bronze medal); at St Louis International Exhibition, 1905; New Zealand International Exhibition, 1907, and International Exhibition, Rome, 1911; pictures often of Oriental subjects, with effects of strong sunlight, as in A Market Morning in a City of the Sahara, An Arab Blacksmith, An Arab Fete, Desert Tribesmen returning from a Raid, etc; also Birds of a Feather, The Outcast, Parted, The Price of Victory, Hull Docks, End of the Day, and many portraits; member of the Pastel Society. *Recreations:* the garden and motor bike. *Address:* Ye Monk's Orchard, East Hendred, Berks; 49 Hugh Street, SW1.
Died 4 Oct. 1921.

SHEARER, Colonel Johnston, CB 1908; DSO 1898; MB; Indian Medical Service, retired; *b* Aberdeen, 22 Oct. 1852; *s* of Johnston Shearer; *m* 1890, Elizabeth Smith, *d* of late James Kinghorn, JP, Aberdeen; two *s. Educ:* Grammar School and University, Aberdeen. MA (honours in Nat. Sci.), 1873; MB and CM (honours), 1877; Maclaine Prizeman in Military Surgery, Army Medical School, Netley, 1881; DPH Aberdeen, 1897. Joined IMS, 1880; Egyptian Expedition, 1882 (medal and bronze star); Burmese Expedition, 1887–88 (medal and 2 clasps); Hazara Expedition, 1891 (clasp); Miranzai (2nd) Expedition, 1891 (clasp); Waziristan Expedition, 1894–95 (clasp, despatches); Tirah Expeditionary Force, 1897–98 (medal and 2 clasps, DSO, despatches); retired, 1910. Decorated for Tirah Expedition. *Recreations:* shooting, reading. *Address:* c/o H. S. King & Co., 9 Pall Mall, SW. *Clubs:* East India United Service; United Service, Simla.
Died 6 Feb. 1917.

SHEARME, Edward, JP; FSA; late Master of the Supreme Court of Judicature; *e s* of late Edward Shearme, Stratton, Cornwall; *m* Caroline, *d* of W. Major Cooke, late Metropolitan Police Magistrate. *Educ:* Marlborough College. JP Cornwall, 1879. *Address:* West Cliff, Bude, Cornwall.
Died 11 Sept. 1920.

SHEARME, Paymaster-Captain Edward Haweis, CBE 1920 (OBE 1917); Royal Navy, retired; Anglo-Persian Oil Company, Ltd, London, since 1920; *b* Dublin, 21 June 1876; *s* of John Shearme, Bude, Cornwall; *m* 1913, Angela Mallaby, *d* of Rev. Prebendary R. H. Barnes, Exeter; no *c. Educ:* Plymouth College. Joined Navy, 1893; retired, 1912; served as Secretary to the late Admiral Lord Milford-Haven, 1904–11; served at Admiralty during World War as Assistant Chief Naval Censor; specially promoted to Paymaster-Captain (retired list), Nov. 1918, for services; Ministry of Labour, 1919. *Recreations:* golf, tennis, sailing. *Address:* Campden House Chambers, W8. *TA:* Pulmonary, London. *T:* Park 2641. *Clubs:* Junior United Service, Roehampton.
Died 11 Nov. 1925.

SHEARME, Rev. John, MA; Hon. Canon of Winchester since 1903; *b* 1842; 2nd *s* of Edward Shearme, of Stratton, N Cornwall; *m* 1881, Mary Stewart, 3rd surv. *d* of Henry Fowler Broadwood of Lyne, Surrey; one *s. Educ:* Exeter; Pembroke College, Oxford. Ordained to Toddington, Bedfordshire, 1866–68; Curate of Linslade, Bucks, 1868–71; Curate of Cranleigh, Surrey, 1871–79; Rector of Holmbury St Mary, Surrey, 1879–91; Vicar of Ryde, IW, 1891–1905; Vicar of Oakwood, Surrey, 1905–18. *Publication:* Lively Recollections, 1917. *Address:* Upwood, Ryde, Isle of Wight.
Died 7 Jan. 1925.

SHEDLOCK, John South; *b* Reading, 29 Sept. 1843; *s* of Rev. John Shedlock. *Educ:* studied at Paris, the piano under Ernst Lübeck, and composition under Edouard Lalo; BA at London University, 1864. Many years teacher of the pianoforte and of harmony; musical critic of the Academy; and of the Athenæum, 1900–15. *Publications:* The Pianoforte Sonata, 1895; A Translation of Beethoven's Letters, 1909; Beethoven-Cramer Studies; two of Kuhnau's Bible Sonatas; pieces by Pasquini, etc. *Address:* 36 Brondesbury Road, NW6.
Died Jan. 1919.

SHEEPSHANKS, William, JP; Chairman of Aire & Calder Navigation; *b* 1851; *s* of Rev. T. Sheepshanks of Arthington Hall, Leeds; *m* 1876, Emily Florence, *d* of Rev. Henry Blunt; one *s* one *d. Educ:* Cheam School; Eton College; Trinity College, Cambridge. Called to the Bar, 1874; West Riding County Council, 1888–1907; Chairman of Petty Sessions, 1895–1913; Director and Chairman of Yorkshire Penny Bank, 1894–1911; Chairman of Pateley Bridge District Council and Board of Guardians, 1904–7; Chairman of Quarter Sessions (West Riding of Yorkshire), 1915–24; represented Ripon Diocese in the Church National Assembly. *Recreation:* shooting. *Address:* Arthington Hall, Leeds. *Clubs:* Carlton, Oxford and Cambridge; Yorkshire, York.
Died 21 July 1928.

SHEFFIELD, 4th Baron, *cr* 1783, of Roscommon; **(Edward) Lyulph Stanley;** Bt 1660; Baron Eddisbury, 1848; Baron Stanley of Alderley (UK), 1839; PC 1910; member School Board for London (Marylebone Division), 1888–1902; *b* London, 16 May 1839; *s* of 2nd Baron and Henrietta, *d* of 13th Viscount Dillon; *S* brother, 1903; *m* 1873, Mary Katharine, CBE, *d* of Sir Lowthian Bell, 1st Bt, of Washington Hall, Durham; two *s* four *d* (and one *s* one *d* decd). *Educ:* Eton; Balliol Coll., Oxford (2nd in Classical Mods; 1st in Final Classical School, Oxford, 1861). Fellow of Balliol Coll., 1862; Barrister Inner Temple, 1865; Assistant Commissioner, Friendly Societies Commission, 1872; MP (L) Oldham, 1880–85; Member Royal Commission Housing of Poor, 1884; on Elementary Education, 1887; Commissioner to investigate Royal Liver Friendly Society and Cardiff Savings Bank; Member of Departmental Committee on London Poor Law Schools, 1895; Member of London School Board, 1876–85, 1888–96. *Publication:* Our National Education, 1899. *Heir:* *s* Hon. Sir Arthur Lyulph Stanley, *b* 14 Sept. 1875. *Address:* Alderley Park, Chelford, Cheshire. *Clubs:* Reform, National Liberal; Manchester Reform.
Died 18 March 1925.

SHEHYN, Hon. Joseph; *b* Quebec, 10 Nov. 1829, of Irish and French parentage; *m* 1st, 1858, Marie Zoé Virginie (*d* 1892), *e d* of late Ambroise Verret, coachmaker, of Quebec; 2nd, Josephine Beliveau, *widow* of N. Leduc; four *s* two *d. Educ:* Quebec Seminary and privately. Sole proprietor of the firm M'Call Shehyn & Co., later converted into M'Call, Shehyn & Son, Ltd, wholesale dry goods merchants; in business for 50 years; several years President of the Quebec Board of Trade, and a member of the Harbour Commission; elected to Legislature, 1875, and re-elected up to 1900; called to Senate, 1900; Provincial Treasurer, 1887–91; Minister without portfolio, 1897–1900; a Liberal; Knight Commander, Order of St Gregory the Great (Holy See); Officer of the Order of Leopold II (Belgium). *Publication:* Railways *versus* Canals (pamphlet). *Recreations:* reading, outdoor exercise. *Address:* Quebec, Canada.
Died 15 July 1918.

SHEILD, Arthur Marmaduke, MB, BC, Cantab; FRCS; consulting surgeon to St George's Hospital, London; late surgeon in charge of Throat Department; consulting surgeon Hospitals of St John and St Elizabeth; and to Hospital for Women and Children, Waterloo Bridge Road; *b* 1858; *s* of William Henry Sheild, Gilfach, Pembrokeshire. *Educ:* privately; Downing College, Cambridge; Bachelor of Medicine. Was House Surgeon to St George's Hospital, London and Addenbrooke's Hospital, Cambridge; Assistant Surgeon and Aural Surgeon to Charing Cross Hospital, and Lecturer on Operative Surgery; Surgeon and Lecturer on Practical Surgery to St George's Hospital; late additional Examiner in Surgery to University of

Cambridge; late Examiner to Apothecaries Company; late Secretary Medical Society of London, and of Dermatological Society; Surgical Secretary British Medical Association; late Member of Council of Royal Medico-Chirurgical Society; retired from London practice through ill-health. *Publications:* A treatise on diseases of the breast; diseases of the ear; nasal obstruction and its treatment; articles—diseases of breast, Quain's Dictionary of Medicine; dislocations and joint injuries, Treves' System of Surgery; many other papers on surgical subjects. *Club:* New University.
Died 4 Aug. 1922.

SHEPHARD, Sir Horatio Hale, Kt 1908; MA, LLD Glasgow; late Legal Adviser and Solicitor to Secretary of State for India; *s* of John Shephard of Doctors' Commons; *m* 1876, Agnes, *d* of Maj.-Gen. J. W. Rideout; two *s. Educ:* Eton; Balliol College, Oxford. Called to the Bar at Inner Temple, 1867; went to Madras, 1872, and there held various legal appointments, including that of Advocate-General, until appointed Judge of the High Court; resigned office of Judge, 1901, and returned to England. *Publications:* Commentary on the Indian Contract Act; Commentary on the Transfer of Property Act; Commentary on Limitation. *Address:* 58 Montagu Square, W1. *T:* Paddington 4028. *Club:* Athenæum.
Died 19 April 1921.

SHEPHARD, Rev. John, MA; Hon. Canon of Christ Church, Oxford, since 1902; *b* 8 Dec. 1837; *s* of John Shephard of Castlehill, Englefield Green; *m* 1867, Caroline Emily (*d* 1895), *d* of Captain Brownlow Layard of Windsor; one *s* six *d. Educ:* Eton, 1850–56; Balliol College, Oxford, 1856–60. 2nd class Mods; 2nd class Lit. Hum. 1860. Private Tutor at Eton, 1860–62; ordained, 1862; acted as voluntary Curate to Canon T. T. Carter at Clewer; Curate of Rev. Charles Wellington Furse (afterwards Archdeacon) at Staines, 1863; Conduct of Eton College, 1863–75; Vicar of Eton, 1875–1905; Member of Oxford Diocesan Conference, 1876–1905; Member of Whitelands College Council, 1903–24. *Publication:* Old Days of Eton Parish, 1908. *Address:* 33 Craven Hill Gardens, Hyde Park, W2. *T:* Paddington 6189.
Died 13 March 1926.

SHEPHERD, Col Charles Herbert, CBE 1918; DSO 1889; 1st Garrison Battalion Lincolnshire Regiment; late commanding 9th Regiment District; *b* 4 April 1846; 2nd *s* of late Thomas Shepherd, Beverley, Yorkshire; married. *Educ:* Rugby. Gazetted Ensign 9th Foot, 1865; Lieutenant, 1871; Captain, 1880; Major, 1883; Lieut-Colonel, 1893; Colonel, 1897; served Burmese Expedition, 1887–89; operations in Chin Hill (despatches, medal with clasp, DSO); Chin-Lushai Expedition, 1889–90 (clasps). *Club:* Naval and Military.
Died 2 Jan. 1920.

SHEPHERD-CROSS, Herbert; *b* Bolton, 1 Jan. 1847; 2nd *s* of Thomas Cross, Ruddington Hall, Nottinghamshire; *m* 1st, 1870, Lucy Mary Shepherd (*d* 1891), *o d* and *heir* of late Rev. John Shepherd Birley, MA; 2nd, 1895, Penelope, *d* of James Hortor. *Educ:* Harrow; Exeter College, Oxford (MA). Late Major, Duke of Lancaster's Own Yeomanry; MP (C) Bolton, 1885–1906. *Address:* Hamels Park, Buntingford. *Club:* Junior Carlton.
Died 9 Jan. 1916.

SHEPPARD, Rev. Canon Edgar, KCVO 1914 (CVO 1902); DD Oxon; Canon and Precentor of St George's Chapel, Windsor Castle, since 1907; Sub-Dean of Chapels Royal since 1884; Deputy Clerk of the Closet to King Edward VII; Sub-Almoner to the King, since 1901, and Domestic Chaplain since 1910; Domestic Chaplain to Queen Alexandra, 1910; *b* 10 August 1845; *s* of Edgar Sheppard, MD, DCL (Professor of Psychology at King's College); *m* 1874, Mary, *e d* of Richard White, of Instow; two *s* one *d*. Formerly Curate of Marlow and Hornsey; Minor Canon of St George's, Windsor, and Priest-in-Ordinary to Queen Victoria, 1878–84; Chaplain to late Duchess of Cambridge; Sub-Almoner and Chaplain-in-Ordinary to Queen Victoria, and Duke of Cambridge; Chaplain-in-Ordinary to King Edward VII, 1901–9; Domestic Chaplain, 1908–10; Chaplain of Order of St John of Jerusalem; Hon. Chaplain to Royal Society of Musicians; Hon. Chaplain to Royal Academy of Music; Hon. Chaplain 4th Batt. VB Royal Fusiliers (Brigade Chaplain); Knight of the Order of Dannebrog (Denmark). *Publications:* Memorials of St James's Palace; The old Royal Palace of Whitehall; Life of the Duke of Cambridge; various sermons and addresses. *Address:* St James's Palace, SW. *TA:* Subdean, St James's Palace, SW; The Cloisters, Windsor Castle. *Club:* Oxford and Cambridge.
Died 30 Aug. 1921.

SHEPPERSON, Claude Allin, ARA 1919; ARWS; painter and illustrator; *b* Beckenham, Kent, 25 Oct. 1867; 2nd surv. *s* of late Allin

Thomas Shepperson of Winsland Harberton, S Devon, and Florence Mary, *e d* of late William Hinkes Cox, JP; *m* Mary Isabel, *o d* of Arthur W. G. Adey of the Indian Medical Service; one *s* one *d. Educ:* privately. First studied Law, and afterwards studied Art in Paris and London, 1891. *Address:* 5 Mulberry Walk, Chelsea, SW3. *T:* Kensington 6472. *Club:* Arts.

Died 30 Dec. 1921.

SHEPSTONE, John Wesley, CMG 1888; JP Colony of Natal; late Judge of the Native High Court of Natal, 1884–95; *b* Grahamstown, Cape Colony, 29 March 1827; 3rd *s* of late Rev. William Shepstone; *m* Mary Maria, 2nd *d* of late Capt. James Geary, RN. *Educ:* Salem, Cape Colony. Entered Civil Service of Natal, 1846; proceeded 1847 and 1850 on Mission of Zulu King and Chief of Pondo Nation, 1850; Asst Magistrate, Pietermaritzburg, 1851; commanded native forces against native chiefs, 1857; on two occasions carried out vaccination of 60,000 natives, 1863; acted as Secretary for Native (and Judicial Assessor) Affairs for the Colony in 1861, 1874, 1876–83; member Zulu-Transvaal Boundary Commission, 1878; delivered High Commissioner's Ultimatum to the Zulu Delegates, 1878; accompanied Sir Garnet (later Lord) Wolseley as adviser to arrange settlement of Zululand after Zulu War, 1879 (mentioned in despatches); British Commissioner Native Reserve, Zululand, 1882. *Decorated* for long service. *Recreations:* shooting, riding. *Address:* Cliff House, Pietermaritzburg, Natal.

Died 23 Jan. 1916.

SHERARD, 11th Baron, *cr* 1627; **Philip Halton Sherard;** *b* 2 May 1851; *s* of Rev. Simon Haughton Sherard and Mary Halton, *d* of Sir Simon Haughton Clarke, 9th Bt; *S* brother, 1902. *Heir: cousin* Robert Castell Sherard [*b* 1858. *Address:* South Perth, Western Australia]. *Address:* Roscrea, Paignton, Devon.

Died 1 May 1924.

SHERARD, Colonel Ralph Woodchurch; Indian Army (retired); *b* 11 Nov. 1860; *s* of late Rev. Simon Haughton Sherard (*b* of 9th Lord Sherard), and Mary Halton, *d* of Sir Simon Haughton Clarke, 9th Bt, of Shirland; *heir* to brother, 11th Baron Sherard; *m* 1895, Juliet Valentine, *y d* of late Robert Raynsford Jackson, 31 Harrington Gardens, SW; one *d.* Entered 15th Foot, 1879; served Afghan War, 1880 (medal); transferred to Indian Staff Corps, 1881; commanded 36th Jacob's Horse, 1901–8; retired 1911; employed under War Office, 1917–19. *Address:* 3 Douro Terrace, Jersey, CI.

Died 14 March 1922.

SHERBORNE, 4th Baron, *cr* 1784; **Edward Lenox Dutton,** JP; *b* Bilbury, Co. Gloucester, 23 April 1831; *s* of 3rd Baron and Elizabeth, *d* of 16th Earl of Suffolk; *S* father, 1883; *m* 1894, Emily (*d* 1905), *d* of late Baron de Stern. *Educ:* Harrow; Balliol College, Oxford (BA). Diplomatic Service; Church of England; sat on cross benches. Owned about 15,773 acres. *Recreations:* gardening, estate management. *Heir: brother* Rev. Hon. Canon Frederick George Dutton, *b* 28 May 1840. *Address:* Sherborne House, near Northleach. *TA:* Sherborne, Glos; 9 St James's Square, SW; Bibury Court, Fairford, and Standish House, Stonehouse, Gloucester. *Clubs:* Bachelors', Boodle's, Travellers', Athenæum, Portland; Union, Brighton.

Died 20 July 1919.

SHERBORNE, 5th Baron, *cr* 1784; **Frederick George Dutton,** *b* 28 May 1840; *s* of 3rd Baron and Elizabeth, *d* of 16th Earl of Suffolk; *S* brother, 1919. *Educ:* Christ Church, Oxford (MA). Ordained 1869; Vicar of Sherborne, 1870–74; Hon. Canon of Gloucester, 1901; Vicar of Bibury, 1874–1916. Owned about 15,775 acres. *Heir: nephew* Major James Huntly Dutton, DSO, *b* 5 March 1873. *Address:* Mosborough, Cheltenham. *Club:* Athenæum.

Died 3 Jan. 1920.

SHERBROOKE, Rev. Henry Nevile; *b* 1846; 2nd *s* of late Henry P. Sherbrooke, of Oxton Hall, Notts; *m* 1st, 1871, Lady Harriet Alice Curzon (*d* 1875), *o d* of 2nd Earl Howe; 2nd, 1878, Lady Lilias Charlotte (*d* 1889), *e d* of 1st Earl Cairns; 3rd, 1892, Alice, 4th *d* of late Henry Abel Smith, of Wilford House, Nottingham; two *s* five *d.* Was Captain 43rd Foot; incumbent of Portman Chapel, 1877–91; Vicar of Clifton, Bristol, 1891–97. *Address:* 15 Paragon, Clifton.

Died 2 Oct. 1916.

SHERBURN, Sir John, Kt 1902; VD; MB, CM (Edin.); MRCS; JP East Riding of Yorks and City of Hull; *b* 3 March 1851; *s* of late John Sherburn of Howden; *m* 1884, Louisa Ainley, *y d* of late William Bailey, JP, Winestead Hall, Holderness; two *s* three *d. Educ:* Edin. Univ. Hon. Consulting Surgeon, Hull Royal Infirmary and Victoria Hospital for Children, Hull; Sheriff of Hull, 1886–87; entered Hull

Council, 1887; Mayor, 1888–89, 1889–90; Alderman since 1889; contested Gateshead (U), 1900; West Hull, 1906 and 1910; Lt-Col Northumbria Brigade, RFA (retired); Representative Member ER Yorks Territorial Force Association. *Address:* Brantingham Thorpe, East Yorks. *TA:* Brough. *T:* Brough 11.

Died 7 July 1926.

SHERIFF, Rev. Thomas Holmes, MA; Hon. Canon of Chester, 1911; Rural Dean of Mottram since 1921. *Address:* St Paul's Vicarage, Stalybridge. *Died 20 Nov. 1923.*

SHERLOCK, Ven. William; Member of the Senate of Trinity College, Dublin; Member of General Synod; *b* Canada; *s* of Richard T. Sherlock of Sherlockstown, Co. Kildare; *m* Adelaide, *d* of Col Francis Sherlock, KH, of Southwell, Notts. *Educ:* privately; Trinity Coll., Dublin. Senior Moderator and Gold Medallist, Ethics and Logic; Junior Moderator and Silver Medallist in History, Law, and Political Economy; MA. Formerly Canon of Christ Church Cathedral, Dublin; of St Brigid's Cathedral, Kildare, and Archdeacon of Kildare. *Publications:* The Constitutions of the American and Colonial Churches; articles in County Kildare Archæological Society's Journal; The Bible and the Young; The Vindictive Psalms, etc. *Address:* Sherlockstown, Sallins, Ireland.

Died 17 March 1919.

SHERRARD, Col James William, CBE 1924; Indian Army (retired); *s* of Col C. W. Sherrard, RE (retired); *m* 1905, Margaret Craig; one *s* two *d. Educ:* Monkton Combe School; Sandhurst. Served North-West Frontier, India, Mohmand and Buner operations, 1915–16; Mesopotamia, 1916–18; Palestine, 1918–19; Razmak operations (NWF), India, 1922–23 (despatches thrice, Bt Lt-Col, CBE); Order of the Nile, 3rd Class (Egypt). *Address:* 65 Dorset Road, Bexhill-on-Sea. *Died 9 Feb. 1926.*

SHERSTON, Colonel William Maxwell, DSO 1901; JP for Somerset; *b* 14 April 1859; *s* of late John Davis Sherston, JP Somerset, of Evercreech, near Bath; *m* 1894, Evelyn Maude Maitland, *e d* of late John Maitland Spencer, of Oakhill, near Bath. *Educ:* Marlborough; Pembroke College, Cambridge. Enlisted 7th Dragoon Guards, 1877; promoted Lieut Rifle Brigade, 1882; Captain 18th Hussars, 1888; served Boer War, 1881; Egypt, 1884–85 (medal 2 clasps); Burmah, 1887 (medal 1 clasp, despatches); S Africa, 1900–1 (medal 5 clasps, despatches, DSO); ADC to Commander-in-Chief, 1901–4; commanded North Somerset Yeomanry, 1904–9; served European War, Egypt and France, 1914–18. *Address:* Shore Lodge, Lilliput, Dorset. *M:* FX 1554. *Clubs:* Army and Navy; Royal Dorset Yacht. *Died 18 Aug. 1925.*

SHERWOOD, William Albert, ARCA, CNA; Life Member Canadian Institute; President Anglo-Saxon Union; *b* Omemee, Canada, 1 Aug. 1855; father English, mother Irish; unmarried. *Educ:* Omemee Grammar School. Began the study of portrait painting at an early period of life; painted many Canadian genre pictures, amongst which are The Gold Prospector (Ontario Government); The Negotiation (Dominion Government); The Canadian Rancher; The Canadian Backwoodsman; exhibited at The International Exhibition, Chicago, 1893; San Francisco, 1894; International, Paris, 1900; Pan-American, Buffalo, 1902; World's Fair, St Louis, 1905; the British Colonial Art Exhibition, London, England, 1902; chief portraits— Hon. Sir George William Ross, Rev. Canon Scadding, Lt-Col Sir Henry Pellatt, Rev. George F. Sherwood, Dr Samuel Passmore May, Col Gunsaulus, John G. Griffin, Lt-Col A. E. Belcher, Abraham Levy, O. B. Sheppard, Capt. George H. Capron Brooke, T. Arthur Kirvan, John W. McCullough, KC, Flight Sub-Lieut C. L. Calvert, RN. *Publications:* articles in leading magazines of Canada and in Encyclopædia of Canada; lectures upon the National Spirit in Art. *Recreations:* walking, swimming, canoeing. *Address:* 31 Queen Street, W, Toronto. *Died 5 Dec. 1919.*

SHERWOOD, Rev. William Edward; Hon. DCL Oxon, 1915; *b* Cumberland, April 1851; *e s* of Thomas Sherwood; widower. *Educ:* Magdalen Coll. School; Christ Church, Oxford (MA); 1st class Math.-Mods; 3rd Math. Final Schools. Mathematical Master, Magdalen School, 1875; Vice-Principal Sidney College, Bath, 1878; remaining after that school was absorbed by Bath College; Chaplain of the School, 1881; Headmaster Magdalen College School, Oxford, 1888–1900; Vicar of Sandford-on-Thames, 1901–10; Divinity Lecturer and Assistant Chaplain, CCC, Oxford, 1912–20; Mayor of Oxford, 1913–15. *Publications:* Oxford Rowing; Oxford Yesterday. *Recreations:* rowing (Putney, 1873–74), cycling. *Address:* 260 Iffley Road, Oxford. *Died 23 Sept. 1927.*

SHIFFNER, Sir John Bridger, 6th Bt, *cr* 1818; *b* 5 Aug. 1899; *e s* of Sir John Shiffner, 5th Bt and Elsie, *d* of Ogden Hoffman Burrows, of Rhode Island, USA; *S* father, 1914; *m* 1918, Sybil Helen, *y d* of Sills Clifford Gibbons, Staynes Hill, Sussex. *Heir:* brother Henry Burrows Shiffner, *b* 29 July 1902. *Address:* Coombe Place, Lewes, Sussex.   *Died 24 Sept. 1918.*

SHIPLEY, Sir Arthur Everett, GBE 1920; FRS 1904; MA, ScD; FZS, FLS; Vice-Chancellor of Cambridge University, 1917–19; Master, Christ's College, Cambridge, since 1910; Reader in Zoology in the University, 1908; *b* 10 March 1861; 2nd *s* of late Alexander Shipley, of the Hall, Datchet, Bucks. *Educ:* University College School; Bartholomew's Hospital; Christ's College, Cambridge, 1st class Natural Sciences Tripos, Part I, 1882; 1st class, Part II, 1884; Demonstrator of Comparative Anatomy in the University of Cambridge, 1885–94; Lecturer on Advanced Morphology of the Invertebrata, 1894–1908; Fellow of Christ's College, 1887; sent on a mission by Colonial Office to investigate plant disease in the Bermudas, 1887; appointed Secretary of the Museums and Lecture Rooms Syndicate, 1891; Member of the Council of the Senate, 1896–1908, 1917–19; late Vice-President Linnean Society; Vice President of the Research Defence Society; Chairman of Council of Marine Biological Association; Chairman of the Governing Body of the West Indian Agricultural College; Member of the Central Medical War Committee; Foreign Member American Association of Economic Entomologists and of the Helminthological Society of Washington; Hon. Mem. of the Société Royale Zoologique et Malacologique, Belgium, and of the Yorkshire Phil. Soc.; Hunterian Trustee; Tancred Trustee; Beit Trustee; Member of the Royal Commissions on the Civil Service, Trinity College, Dublin, and the Importation of Store Cattle, and the Departmental Enquiry into Grouse Disease; and other Colonial Office Commissions; Hon. DSc Princeton; Hon. LLD Michigan; Hon. MSc Drexel Institute, Philadelphia. *Publications:* The Zoology of the Invertebrata, 1893; (editor with S. F. Harmer and contributor) Cambridge Natural History, 10 vols, 1895–1909; (with Prof. E. W. MacBride) Textbook of Zoology, 1901, 4th edn 1920; Pearls and Parasites (essays), 1908; 'J', a Memoir of John Willis Clark, 1913; The Minor Horrors of War, 1915; More Minor Horrors, 1916; Studies in Insect Life, 1916; (with A. Schuster) Britain's Heritage of Science, 1917; The Voyage of a Vice-Chancellor, 1919; Cambridge Cameos, 1924; Islands—West Indian and Aegean, 1924; Grouse in Health and in Disease; part translator of Weismann on Heredity, 2 vols, 1889–92; part author and editor of Handbook to Natural History of Cambridgeshire; editor of the Pitt Press Natural Science Manuals, Biological Series; and of the Fauna of British India Series; author of articles in the Encyclopædia Britannica, the Encyclopædia of Sport, Allbutt and Rolleston's System of Medicine, and the Ency. Biblica; co-editor (with Prof. G. H. F. Nuttall) of Parasitology, 1908–14; asst editor of Journal of Economic Biology, 1905–13; author of numerous zoological papers in various scientific journals; Hunting under the Microscope, 1928 (posthumous). *Address:* Christ's College Lodge, Cambridge. *T:* Cambridge 894. *Clubs:* Athenæum; Pitt, Cambridge.
                                                                    Died 22 Sept. 1927.

SHIPLEY, Orby; *b* 1 July 1832; *y s* of Rev. Charles Shipley, Twyford House, Hampshire; *m* 1868, Zoë, 4th *d* of Rt Hon. James Wilson. *Educ:* Jesus College, Cambridge (Rustat Scholar). BA 1854; MA 1857. Worked as a clergyman of the Church of England for 23 years, and was received into the Catholic Church in 1878; as an Anglican, wrote articles, reviews, and essays in contemporary periodicals, and published lectures and sermons; as a Catholic, contributed to Catholic and other papers and reviews; reprinted Old English ascetical books. *Publications* include: Four Cardinal Virtues, 1871; Theory about Sin, 1872; Principles of the Faith, 1878; edited 3 vols of Sacred Lyræ, 1863–65; 3 yearly vols of Church and the World, 1867–69; Tracts for the Day, 1867; Glossary of Ecclesiastical Terms, 1871; Essays on Ecclesiastical Reform, 1873; 2 vols of Studies in Modern Problems, 1874; adapted foreign and Catholic devotional works, *eg* 4 vols of Ascetic Library, 1868–70; Quesnel on St Matthew, 1869; Spiritual Exercises of St Ignatius, 1870; also reprinted Anthony Stafford's Female Glory (Life of the Blessed Virgin Mary 1635), 1860; and published in 1870 and in 1878 Ritual of the Altar, an edition of the Anglican Communion Service, supplemented from the Roman Missal; Truthfulness and Ritualism, 1879–80; Annus Sanctus, Hymns of the Church, 1884; Carmina Mariana, anthologies in honour of the Blessed Virgin Mary, 1893 and 1902 (a third and final volume in preparation); also in preparation a reprint of Lyra Eucharistica (1863), revised, with additions. *Address:* Colway, Lyme Regis, Dorset.   *Died 12 July 1916.*

SHIPLEY, Lt-Col Reginald Burge, CMG 1915; TD; late 9th London Regiment (Queen Victoria's Rifles) (Territorial Force); *b*

1867; *y s* of late Alexander Shipley, The Hall, Datchet; *m* 1907, Flora Marion, *d* of D. F. Wallace, Kansas City, USA; one *s* one *d*. Served South Africa, 1900 (despatches); European War, 1914–15 (despatches, CMG). *Address:* The Manor Cottage, Englefield Green, Surrey.
                                                                    Died 11 March 1924.

SHIPLEY, Sir William Alexander, Kt 1905; Mayor of Windsor, 1902; County Councillor for Berkshire, 1905; *b* 15 April 1857; *s* of the late Alexander Shipley, of The Hall, Datchet, Bucks; *m* 1882, Edith, *d* of Thomas Hirst. *Recreation:* golf. *Address:* Riverbank, Datchet, Windsor. *T:* 71 Windsor. *M:* 352 BL. *Clubs:* Constitutional, Royal Thames Yacht; Berkshire, Reading.
                                                                    Died 6 Oct. 1922.

SHOLL, Richard Adolphus, ISO 1903; *b* 18 Dec. 1846; *s* of Robert John (late Govt Resident, NW Territory) and Mary Sholl; *m* 1887, Mary Howard, *er d* of Lt-Col Gilbert Howard Sanders. *Educ:* Bishop Hale's College, Perth, WA. Entered General Post Office, Perth, 1863; Chief Clerk, 1873; Chief Clerk and Accountant, Treasury, 1879; Postmaster-General and General Superintendent of Telegraphs, 1889; Deputy Postmaster-General under Commonwealth of Australia, 1901; retired, 1904; Lieutenant of Local Forces, 1875; Captain, 1883; Capt. Commandant, 1888; Major, 1893. *Recreations:* amateur sport of every kind, horse-racing especially. *Address:* 156 Aberdeen Street, Perth, Western Australia. *T:* 4333. *Clubs:* Weld, Masonic, Civil Service, Perth.   *Died May 1919.*

SHOOLBRED, Frederick Thomas, CB 1911; *b* 1841. *Address:* Thames Bank, Goring.   *Died 30 April 1922.*

SHORE, Brig.-Gen. Offley Bohun Stovin Fairless, CB 1914; CIE 1916; DSO 1901; Indian Army, retired; *b* 9 Aug. 1863; *o s* of Offley Bohun Shore; *m* 1908, Caroline Perry, *d* of Charles P. Sinnickson, Philadelphia, USA. Entered West Yorks Regt 1882; transferred to Bengal Cavalry, 1884; Capt. 1893; Bt-Maj. 1898; Major, 1901; Lt-Col 1906; Bt-Col 1910; Col 1911; DAAG, India, 1895–1900; passed Staff Coll.; served North-West Frontier, India, 1897–98 (despatches, brevet of Major, medal with two clasps); S Africa, 1900–2; DAAG Army, Brig.-Major Mounted Infantry, Yeomanry and Mounted Troops; actions Poplar Grove, Driefontein, entry into Bloemfontein; operations in Orange River Colony, Western Transvaal, and Griqualand West; District Commandant, Cape Colony; Staff Officer to cavalry column, operations Eastern Transvaal and Orange River Colony (despatches, DSO, Queen's medal, three clasps, King's medal, 2 clasps); Director of Staff Duties and Military Training, Army Headquarters, India, 1913–15; Head of British Military Mission to the Caucasus, 1917–18; retired 1919. *Club:* United Service.
                                                                    Died 26 Oct. 1922.

SHORT, Richard, RCA; marine artist; *b* St Ives, Cornwall, 29 Dec. 1841; *s* of Richard Short (Master Mariner), and Grace Ninnes Short; *m* Charlotte Martin Noall; three *s* three *d*. *Educ:* Navigation School, St Ives. Went to sea for about twelve years; served through various grades in the merchant service, including Master in Steam; gave up sea life and turned to art; exhibited at many of the leading exhibitions, including about twelve years at the Royal Academy. *Publication:* after visiting the ruins of Ephesus, wrote and published a book entitled Saronia: a Romance of Ancient Ephesus. *Recreations:* a voyage at sea or acting as a nautical assessor (Admiralty jurisdiction). *Address:* 22 The Walk, Cardiff.   *Died 8 Dec. 1916.*

SHORT, Thomas Sydney, MD (London), DPH (Cambridge); MRCP; Senior Physician to the General Hospital, Birmingham; Consulting Physician to the General Dispensary, Birmingham,: *b* Sheffield; *s* of William Short of Sheffield and Birmingham. *Educ:* Sheffield Royal Grammar School; King's College School and King's College, London. House Physician to King's College Hospital; Resident Medical Censor, King's College; Resident Medical and Surgical Officer, Jaffray Hospital; Resident Medical Officer, General Hospital, Birmingham; Chairman of William Dudley Charity Trust, Birmingham; Major RAMC (T); President Birmingham Branch of British Medical Association, 1921–22. *Publications:* On a Special Form of Dilatation of the Stomach; On some of the Characteristics of George Meredith's Prose Writing, 1907; papers and articles on medical subjects in the medical press. *Recreations:* cycling, motoring. *Address:* 85 Edmund Street, Birmingham. *T:* Central 6969. *Clubs:* Union, University Graduates', Birmingham.
                                                                    Died 27 Aug. 1924.

SHORT, Lt-Col William Ambrose, CMG 1916; Royal Artillery. Served European War, 1914–16 (despatches twice, CMG). *Address:* 12 Inglis Road, Colchester.   *Died 21 June 1917.*

SHORTALL, Sir Patrick, Kt 1916; High Sheriff of Dublin, 1915; *b* 1872; *e s of* late James Shortall, Kilkenny; *m* Mary, *e d of* late P. Coyle, Dublin; four *s.* Member Municipal Council, Dublin, and Royal Institute Public Health; building contractor. *Address:* Wilford, St Lawrence Road, Clontarf, Dublin.   *Died 27 June 1925.*

SHORTER, Clement King; editor of The Sphere, 1900–26, and a Director of The Sphere and Tatler Company since 1900, and of The Illustrated London News and Sketch Company since 1922; *b* London, 19 July 1857; *y s* of Richard Shorter and Elizabeth Clemenson; of Hunts and Norfolk ancestry; *m* 1st, 1896, Dora (*d* 1918), poet, *d* of late George Sigerson, MD; 2nd, 1920, (Annie) Doris, *y d* of late John Banfield and Mrs Banfield, of Alverton Vean, Penzance; one *d. Educ:* Downham Market. Civil servant, Exchequer and Audit Department, Somerset House, 1877–90; Assistant Editor Penny Illustrated Paper, 1890; Editor Illustrated London News, 1891–1900; founded The Sketch for Illustrated London News Company, 1893, and edited it for seven years; also, Illustrated London News and English Illustrated Magazine; founded The Sphere, 1900, and The Tatler, 1903; one of the founders of the Omar Khayyam Club, and an ex-President of the Johnson Club. *Publications:* Charlotte Brontë and her Circle, 1896 (re-issued as The Brontës and Their Circle, 1914); Victorian Literature: Sixty Years of Victorian Literature, 1897; edited Mrs Gaskell's Life of Charlotte Brontë, with many new letters, 1899 and 1919; Charlotte Brontë and her Sisters, 1905; The Brontës: Life and Letters, 2 vols, 1907; Immortal Memories: Essays and Addresses, 1907; Napoleon and his Fellow Travellers, 1909; Highways and Byways of Buckinghamshire, 1910; Napoleon in his Own Defence, 1910; edited The Complete Poems of Emily Brontë, and Wuthering Heights, 1910–11; George Borrow and his Circle, 1913; an edition of Boswell's Life of Johnson, 1922; an edition of the Complete Works of George Borrow, 16 vols, 1923; also editions of the novels of Henry Kingsley and of Mrs Gaskell; C.K.S., an Autobiography, 1926. *Address:* Knockmoroon, Great Missenden, Bucks. *T:* 9.
          Died 19 Nov. 1926.

SHORTER, Dora, (Dora Sigerson); poet; *b* Dublin, 1866; *d* of George Sigerson, MD; *m* 1896, Clement Shorter. *Publications:* Verses, 1894; The Fairy Changeling and other Poems, 1897; My Lady's Slipper and other Poems, 1898; Ballads and Poems, 1899; The Father Confessor (stories), 1900; The Woman who went to Hell, 1902; As the Sparks Fly Upward, 1904; The Country House Party, 1905; The Story and Song of Earl Roderick, 1906; Through Wintry Terrors, a Novel, 1907; Collected Poems, 1909; The Troubadour, 1910; New Poems, 1912; Madge Lindsey and other Poems, 1913; Do-Well and Do-Little, a Fairy Story, 1914; Love of Ireland: Poems and Ballads, 1916. *Address:* 16 Marlborough Place, NW. *T:* Paddington 1386; Knockmoroon, Great Missenden, Bucks. *T:* 9 PO. *Club:* Lyceum.
          Died 6 Jan. 1918.

SHOUBRIDGE, Maj.-Gen. (Thomas) Herbert, CB 1918; CMG 1916; DSO 1898; *b* 15 June 1871; *s* of late Lieut-Colonel H. W. Shoubridge, Indian Army; *m* 1910, Gladys Constance, *e d of* late Major H. Dugdale, 16th Lancers; one *s* one *d. Educ:* Blundell's School, Tiverton. Entered Dorset Regiment, 1893; Captain Northumberland Fusiliers, 1900; Brevet Lieut-Colonel, 1914; Brevet Colonel, 1917; served Tirah Expedition, 1897–98 (despatches, DSO, medal with two clasps); served South Africa as Staff Captain and DAAG with the Natal army, 1899–1902 (despatches twice, Bt Major, Queen's medal four clasps, King's medal two clasps); European War, 1914–18 (despatches six times, CMG, Bt Col, CB, 1914 Star); DAQMG Headquarters SA Command, 1902–5; Brigade Major 13th Inf. Brigade, 1906–10; commanded East Lancs Div. (TF), 1919–23; Commandant, Royal Military College, Sandhurst, 1923; resigned Oct., 1923. *Club:* United Service.   *Died 27 Oct. 1923.*

SHOWERS, Lt-Col Herbert Lionel, CSI 1911; CIE 1902; Indian Staff Corps; British Commissioner, Mewar Enquiry Committee; *b* London, 16 June 1861; *s* of General C. L. Showers, ISC; *m* 1903, Christian, 2nd *d* of James Stirling of Garden, Port of Menteith, NB; one *s* one *d. Educ:* private schools. Entered army, 1883; joined the Welsh Regiment in Natal; transferred to Norfolk Regiment and arrived in India, 1884; entered Staff Corps, 1885, and served with 17th Bengal Infantry, 4th Gurkhas, Meywar Bhil Corps, and Erinpura Irregular Force; served Soudan Campaign, 1885 (medal with two clasps, Khedive's star); entered the Political Department, 1890; served during the assault and capture of Nodiz Fort, Mekran, 1901. *Address:* Udaipur, India. *Clubs:* East India United Service, Ranelagh.
          Died 2 Feb. 1916.

SHREWSBURY, 20th Earl of, *cr* 1442; **Charles Henry John Chetwynd-Talbot,** KCVO 1907; Earl of Waterford, 1446; Baron

Talbot, 1733; Earl Talbot, Viscount Ingestre, 1784; Premier Earl of England; Hereditary Great Seneschal or Lord High Steward of Ireland; Lord High Steward of Stafford since 1892; *b* London, 13 Nov. 1860; *o s* of 19th Earl and Anna Theresa, *d* of Commander Richard Howe Cockerell, RN, and Theresa, afterwards Countess of Eglinton; *S* father, 1877; *m* 1882, Ellen Mary, *d* of Charles Rowland Palmer-Morewood, Ladbroke Hall, Warwick, and Alfreton Hall, Derbyshire; one *d* (one *s* decd). *Educ:* Eton. Protestant. Conservative. Very fond of coaching; ran the Greyhound Coach from Buxton to Alton Towers daily for several seasons; first person to start cabs fitted with noiseless tyres in London and Paris. *Heir: g s* Viscount Ingestre, *b* 1 Dec. 1914. *Address:* Ingestre, Stafford; 67 Portland Place, W1. *T:* Mayfair 6018. *TA:* Wexford, London. *Club:* White's.
          Died 17 May 1921.

SHUCKBURGH, Sir Stewkley Frederick Draycott, 10th Bt, *cr* 1660; *b* Shuckburgh, 20 June 1880; *e s* of Sir George Thomas Francis Shuckburgh, 9th Bt and Ida Florence Geraldine, *o d* of Rev. Frederick W. Robertson of Brighton; *S* father, 1884. *Heir: brother* Gerald Francis Stewkley Shuckburgh [*b* 28 Feb. 1882; *m* 1909, Honor Zoë, *d* of Neville Thursby, of Harlestone, Northamptonshire; two *s* one *d*]. *Address:* Shuckburgh, Daventry. *TA:* Daventry. *T:* 23 Daventry.
          Died 17 Nov. 1917.

SHUTTLEWORTH, Alfred, JP, DL; *b* 1843; *e s* of late Joseph Shuttleworth, Hartsholme Hall, and Old Warden Park, Beds; *m* 1869, Mary (*d* 1880), *y d* of Nathaniel Clayton, East Cliff, Lincoln. High Sheriff, Lincoln, 1889. *Address:* Eastgate House, Lincoln. *Clubs:* Wellington; Royal Yacht Squadron, Cowes.
          Died 22 Nov. 1925.

SHUTTLEWORTH, George Edward, MRCS; Fellow and Hon. Associate of King's College, London; Licentiate and Member of Society of Apothecaries, London; *b* Edgbaston, Warwickshire, 16 Nov. 1842; *s* of Charles Edward Shuttleworth; *m* Edith Mary, *d* of Henry Hadwen, Lancaster; one *s* one *d. Educ:* Philological and City of London Schools; King's College, London (BA Honours in Physiology); Heidelberg University (MD). Medical Superintendent, Royal Albert Asylum, Lancaster, 1870–93; Medical Examiner of Defective Children, School Board for London, 1899–1901; Medical Expert (Metropolitan Asylums Board), Rochester House Institution for Improvable Imbeciles, 1901–5; Consulting Medical Officer, National Association for Feeble-minded, 1900–10; Hon. Consulting Physician, Royal Albert Institution for the Feeble-minded of the Northern Counties, Lancaster; late Medical Officer for Schools for Mentally Defective Children, Willesden Education Committee; Member of Royal Medico-Psychological Association of Great Britain and Ireland; Vice-President of the National Association for the Feeble-minded; of the Central Association for Mental Welfare; of the Child Study Society, London; formerly Hon. Secretary of Asylum Workers' Association and instrumental in obtaining the Asylum Officers' Superannuation Act of 1909; Member of Departmental Committee, Board of Education, on Report of which Elementary Education (Defective and Epileptic Children) Act 1899 was framed; Examiner, St John Ambulance Assoc.; Hon. Associate, Order of St John of Jerusalem. *Specialty:* psychological medicine (specially in respect of mentally deficient children). *Publications:* Mentally Deficient Children: their Treatment and Training, 1895, 5th edn 1922; articles: Mental Deficiency, Encyclopædia Medica, vol. viii; Idiocy (joint author), Allbutt's New System of Medicine; Educational Training of Idiots and Imbeciles, Hack Tuke's Dictionary of Psychological Medicine; Aetiology of Idiocy and Imbecility (joint author), *ibid.;* Education of Exceptional Children, Teachers' Encyclopædia, and Encyclopædia of Education, etc. *Recreations:* travel, literature. *Address:* 36 Lambolle Road, Hampstead, NW3. *T:* Primrose Hill 2578.
          Died 28 May 1928.

SIAM, HM King of, Rama VI, GCVO 1902; Hon. General British Army; *b* 1 Jan. 1881; *S* father, 1910. *Educ:* private tutor; Royal Mil. Coll., Sandhurst; Christ Church, Oxford. Came to England, 1893; proclaimed heir to the throne of Siam on the death of elder brother, 1895; represented the King of Siam at the Jubilee of Queen Victoria, 1897; joined RMC, 1898; attached to 1st Battalion Durham LI, 1899; during same year was attached to No 6 Mountain Battery during training at Okehampton; in November and December 1899 joined School of Musketry at Hythe, and obtained officer's extra certificate; went up to Oxford, January 1900, and remained till end of 1901; represented the King of Siam at the funeral of Queen Victoria; represented King of Siam at King of Spain's Coronation in May and King Edward's Coronation in June 1902. *Publications:* The War of the Polish Succession, 1901; and others on history, archæology, and the drama; also some 30 plays in Siamese and English. *Recreations:*

riding, driving. *Address:* Bangkok, Siam. *Clubs:* United Service, Army and Navy, Junior United Service, Travellers', Bachelors'.
Died 26 Nov. 1925.

SIDDALL, Joseph Bower, MD, CM (Aberdeen); MRCS, LSA; DPH (Cantab); retired; *b* 4 March 1840; 4th *s* of late George Siddall and Mary Oldham of Matlock; *m* 1870, Mary Elizabeth (*d* 1906), 2nd *d* of late Charles Binns, JP, of Clay Cross Hall, Chesterfield; no *c*. *Educ:* Chesterfield Grammar School; St Thomas's Hospital, London; University of Aberdeen. Graduated with highest academical honours. House Surgeon, St Thomas's Hospital, 1864; Prosector, Royal College of Surgeons, 1864; House Surgeon to Bristol General Hospital, 1867–68; Medical Officer to HM Legation, Japan, 1868; was in charge, till the conclusion of the War of Restoration in Japan, of the first Military Hospital at Tokio, where he attended large numbers of the wounded soldiers; subsequently founded the Dai-Biyoin (Great Hospital), the first civil hospital, and generally assisted in the earliest development of modern medical science in Japan (Order of the Rising Sun); returned to England, 1874; Physician to the Bristol General Hospital, 1876. *Publications:* Surgical Experiences in Military Hospitals in Japan; St Thomas's Hospital Reports, 1875. *Recreations:* formerly cricket, later golf. *Address:* Oriel House, Malvern. *Clubs:* Malvern; Royal North Devon; Royal Eastbourne; Worcestershire Golf.
Died 4 July 1925.

SIDEBOTHAM, Joseph Watson; *b* 1857; *s* of late Joseph Sidebotham, Erlesdene, Bowdon, Cheshire, and Anne, *o d* of Edward Coward; *m* 1886, Marian, *d* of late Rev. Edward Dowling; two *s* two *d*. *Educ:* Owens Coll., Manchester. MP (C) Hyde Div. of Cheshire, 1886–1900; JP County of Chester. *Address:* Merlewood, Bowdon, Cheshire.
Died 10 June 1925.

SIDGREAVES, Rev. Walter, SJ; Director of Observatory, Stonyhurst College; *b* Preston, 1837; *s* of Edward Sidgreaves of Grimsargh. *Educ:* Stonyhurst College. Professor of Physics in same College 25 years; served on the expeditions for observing the Transits of Venus across the sun's disc—1874, Kerguelen Land, and 1882, Madagascar; awarded Gold Medal at the St Louis Exposition, 1904, and Grand Prix at the Franco-British Exhibition, 1908, for photographic work on stellar spectra. *Publications:* in the Memoirs and Monthly Notices of the Royal Astronomical Society and other scientific periodicals. *Address:* Observatory, Stonyhurst College, Blackburn. *TA:* Stonyhurst. *T:* 23 Whalley.
Died 12 June 1919.

SIDGWICK, Arthur; Fellow of Corpus Christi College, Oxford, 1882–1902 and since 1903; *b* 9 April 1840; *m*. *Educ:* Rugby; Trinity College, Cambridge (Fellow). Bell Scholar, 1860; Porson Scholar, 1861; Member's Prizeman, 1862, 1863, 1864; 2nd Classic and Senior Chancellor's Medallist, 1863; Hon. LLD Glasgow, 1898; Hon. LittD Leeds, 1910; Reader in Greek, Oxford University, 1894–1906. *Publications:* Greek Prose Composition, 1876; edition of Æschylus (text and five annotated plays), 1880–1903; Greek Verse Composition, 1882; edition of Virgil, 1890; other school-books, and a few educational essays. *Address:* Woodstock Road, Oxford.
Died 25 Sept. 1920.

SIDNEY, Herbert, (Sidney Herbert Adams), FSA; portrait and historical painter; *s* of Frederick W. Adams, art dealer, Piccadilly, London; assumed surname of Sidney by deed-poll; unmarried. *Educ:* Royal Academy, London; Royal Academy, Antwerp, under de Keyser and Van Lérius; Beaux Arts, Paris, under Gérôme. Exhibitor, Royal Acad., London, and Salons, Paris, Brussels, etc; commanded by the late King Edward, and by King George and Queen Mary, to submit some of his works for inspection at Buckingham Palace in 1909, 1911, and 1919; painted portrait of Crown Prince Olav of Norway, Royal Academy, 1913, and memorial portrait of late Prince Francis of Teck; portraits of Mayors of Westminster, 1914 (R. W. Granville-Smith) and 1915 (G. Booth-Heming), for the City Hall, Westminster; painted 'The Sorrow of the Mothers' for War Relief Fund Exhibition, Royal Academy, 1915. *Recreations:* music, literature, historical research. *Address:* 4 St Paul's Studios, W14.
Died 30 March 1923.

SIDNEY, Thomas Stafford, KC 1911; Attorney-General, Leeward Islands, since 1909; *b* 1863; *e s* of late Thomas Sidney (Lord Mayor of London, 1853–54; and sometime MP for Stafford). *Educ:* Harrow; Trinity Hall, Cambridge (MA 1888). Barrister Middle Temple, 1885; SE Circuit, Surrey and South London Sessions; for some years practised in India and engaged in journalism; Advocate of the High Court of Madras, 1894; was a District Commissioner, Lagos 1901–3. *Recreations:* walking, golf. *Address:* St John's, Antigua, BWI. *Clubs:* MCC, British Empire.
Died 16 Nov. 1917.

SIEMENS, Alexander; *b* Hanover, 22 Jan. 1847; *s* of Gustav Siemens and Sophie Heise; was released formally from German citizenship and became a naturalised British subject, 1878; *m* 1881, Frances Dodwell, of Campden, Glos; three *d*. *Educ:* Hanover; Berlin. Came to England to work in the shops of Siemens Brothers at Woolwich, 1867; went to Persia to assist in building Indo-European Telegraph Line, 1868; assisted in laying cable in the Black Sea for same co., 1869; went through the Franco-Prussian War as a private in an infantry regiment, and received the Iron Cross, 1870–71; after the war returned to England and worked as a pupil of the late Sir William Siemens, assisting in building regenerative gas furnaces for various purposes, and in laying submarine cables from 1875 onwards; built furnaces for Sir William Siemens in Canada and the USA in 1876–77; took over the management of the Electric Light Dept of Siemens Bros, 1879; Pres. Institute of Electrical Engineers, 1894 and 1904; Pres. Institute of Civil Engineers, 1910–11. *Publications:* papers read before the British Association, the Society of Arts, and the Institution of Electrical Engineers, and some other societies. *Address:* Westover, Milford-on-Sea, Hants. *Clubs:* Athenæum, Royal Automobile.
Died 16 Feb. 1928.

SIENKIEWICZ, Henryk; Polish novelist; *b* Okreya, Podlasia; family originally Lithuanian; removed to Poland in consequence of Russian War. *Educ:* Warsaw Gymnasium and University. Travelled in USA, 1877; Central Africa, 1891; Hon. Member, Russian Academy of Sciences. Nobel prize for literature, 1905. *Publications:* Hania, 1874; Sketches in Charcoal, 1877; Fire and Sword, 1884; The Deluge, 1885–87; Pan Michael, 1888; Without Dogma, 1891; Children of the Soil, 1894; Quo Vadis, 1896; The Knights of the Cross, 1900; Monte Carlo; Through the Desert, etc.
Died 16 Nov. 1916.

SIFTON, Rt. Hon. Arthur Lewis, PC 1920; KC; MA, LLB, DCL; Secretary of State, Canada, since 1920; *b* 26 Oct. 1858; *s* of late Hon. John W. Sifton, formerly Speaker of Manitoba Assembly, and Kate Sifton; *m* 1882, Mary H. Deering; one *s* one *d*. *Educ:* various public schools; Wesley College, Winnipeg; Victoria University, Cobourg. Called to the Bar, Manitoba, 1883; practised law; first elected North-West Assembly, 1898; Treasurer and Commissioner Public Works, NWT, 1901; Chief Justice, NWT, 1903–5; Chief Justice, Alberta, 1905–10; portfolios of Public Works and Treasury, 1910–12; Premier of Alberta; Minister of Railways and Telephones, 1912–18; Minister of Customs and Inland Revenue, Canada, 1917–20; Minister of Public Works, 1919. *Address:* Château Laurier, Ottawa, Canada. *Clubs:* Rideau, Country, Ottawa; Ranchmen's, Calgary; Edmonton, Edmonton.
Died 21 Jan. 1921.

SIGERSON, George, MD, MCh; Professor of Biology, Dublin University College, Dublin; Senator, National University, Ireland; *m*; one *s* two *d*. *Educ:* Queen's Coll., Cork; Dublin; Paris. Hon. FRCPI. Member of Senate, Irish Free State, 1922–23. *Publications:* Microscopical Researches on the Atmosphere; Heat as a Factor in (so-called) Vital Action; Cause of Buoyancy of Bodies of Greater Density than Water; Changes in the Physical Geography of Ireland; Additions to the Flora of 10th Botanical District; Relationship of the Inflorescences; trans. with notes, Prof. Charcot's Lectures on Diseases of the Nervous System; On Alternate Paralyses; History of Land Tenures and Land Classes; Modern Ireland; Bards of the Gael and Gall; The Last Independent Parliament of Ireland. *Recreation:* collecting miniatures, pastels, etc. *Address:* 3 Clare Street, Merrion Square, Dublin.
Died 17 Feb. 1925.

SIGSBEE, Rear-Adm. Charles Dwight; United States Navy; *b* Albany, New York, 16 January 1845; *s* of Nicholas Sigsbee and Agnes Orr Sigsbee; *m* 1870, Eliza Rogers Lockwood, *d* of General Henry H. Lockwood. *Educ:* United States Naval Academy. Entered the Naval Academy, 1859; served in the Civil War, 1863–65; China Station, 1865–69; head of several departments of the Naval Academy; commanded the 'Kearsage', 'Dale' (twice), 'Constellation', 'Portsmouth', 'Maine', 'St Paul', and 'Texas'; commanded the 'Maine' when she was destroyed in Havana, 15 Feb. 1898; from 1874–78 engaged in deep sea exploration in command of US Coast Survey Steamer, 'Blake' (gold medal and two diplomas of honour for deep sea inventions at the International Fisheries Exhibition, London; Red Eagle of Prussia, 1880); in charge of the US Hydrographic Office, 1893–97; commanded 'St Paul' in war with Spain, 1898; advanced for extraordinary heroism, 11 Feb. 1901; retired 1907. *Publications:* Deep Sea Sounding and Dredging, US Coast and Geodetic Survey, 1880; The Story of the 'Maine,' 1898; Graphical Method for Navigators, US Hydrographic Office. *Address:* 539 W 112th Street, New York.
Died July 1923.

SILCOCK, Thomas Ball; architect and surveyor; *b* Bradford-on-Avon, 19 Sept. 1854; *s* of T. B. and Amelia Silcock; *m* 1881, Mary Frances, *d* of Rev. H. Tarrant of Bath; three *s* two *d*. *Educ:* Bristol Grammar School. BSc of London University; Mayor of Bath, 1900–1 and 1910–11; MP (L) Wells Division of Somerset, 1906–10; JP. *Address:* Walden, Bath. *T:* Bath 1090.

Died 1 April 1924.

SIM, Henry Alexander, CIE 1901; FRGS; *b* 1856; *s* of James Duncan Sim, CSI, of Moxley, Surrey; unmarried. *Educ:* Cheltenham. ICS 1876; went to India, 1878; served in Revenue, Judicial, Forest, and Account branches; Private Sec. to Governor, 1897–1901; Mem. Board of Revenue, Madras, 1901; Mem. of Governor-General's Legislative Council, 1904–8; retired, 1908. *Address:* c/o Lloyds Bank, 6 Pall Mall, SW. *Club:* East India United Service.

Died 21 April 1928.

SIM, Hon. Sir William Alexander, Kt 1924; Judge of Supreme Court of New Zealand since 1911; *b* Wanganui, NZ, 13 Sept. 1858; *e s* of late P. L. Sim; *m* 1886, Frances Mary, *d* of late Joseph Walters, of Victoria; three *s* one *d*. *Educ:* Wanganui Grammar School; Otago University. Admitted as barrister and solicitor, November 1879; Judge of Arbitration Court, 1907–14; temporary Judge of Supreme Court, 1909. *Publications:* Divorce Act and Rules (New Zealand); (with Sir Robert Stout) The Practice of the Supreme Court and Court of Appeal of New Zealand. *Address:* Dunedin, New Zealand. *Clubs:* Authors'; Dunedin, Dunedin; Christchurch, Christchurch; Wellington, Wellington. *Died Aug. 1928.*

SIMM, Matthew Turnbull; MP (Coalition Lab) Wallsend Division of Northumberland, Dec. 1918–22; *b* 4 Jan. 1869; *s* of Frank Simm, miner; *m* 1895, Elizabeth Emma, *d* of George Dodds; one *s*. *Educ:* colliery school. Merchant taylor. *Recreation:* walking. *Address:* 29 Otterburn Avenue, Gosforth, Newcastle.

Died 8 Oct. 1928.

SIMMONDS, Frederick, MVO 1906; VD; late Crown Receiver of Windsor Parks; *b* 4 Dec. 1845; *s* of J. C. Simmonds. *Address:* 16 Abingdon Court, Kensington, W8. *T:* Western 3106. *Club:* Junior Army and Navy. *Died 14 July 1921.*

SIMMONS, Sir (William) Anker, KBE 1920 (CBE 1918); JP Berkshire; *b* 5 Oct. 1857; *e s* of late Charles Simmons, JP, of Crandem Gate, Henley-on-Thames; *m* 1883, Edith Nora, *o d* of Edward Smith Beddome, of Lloyd's; one *s* three *d*. *Educ:* privately; Henley Old Grammar School. Fellow of Surveyors' Institution and Auctioneers' and Estate Agents' Institute; Vice-President of Auctioneers' Institute; formerly senior partner and later Adviser and Consultant to Simmons & Sons, chartered surveyors, of Henley-on-Thames, Reading, and Basingstoke; an authority on agricultural and land questions; Agricultural Adviser, from its formation, to the Ministry of Food; Official Arbitrator under the Acquisition of Land (Assessment of Compensation) Act 1919, 1924–26; Past Chairman of the Farmers' Club; took an active part in political, masonic, and local government matters; Alderman and senior member of Henley Town Council (39 years); four times Mayor of Henley; five times Past Master; read several papers at the Farmers' Club, and spoke all over England on land questions; was invited to stand as agricultural candidate for S Oxon, 1918. *Recreations:* an old athlete; rowing, swimming, cycling, running; winner of many races. *Address:* Bird Place, Henley-on-Thames. *T:* 146. *M:* BW 6696. *Clubs:* Constitutional, Farmers'.

Died 20 Oct. 1927.

SIMMONS, Arthur Thomas, BSc (London); ARCS; author; joint editor of The Journal of Education and School World; Inspector of Secondary Schools for University of London; Examiner in Science for various public examinations; *b* Devonport, 26 June 1865; 2nd *s* of Thomas Simmons of Southampton; *m* 1909, Winifred Mabel, *y d* of late Thomas Mortimer Jacombs; two *s*. *Educ:* Hartley University Coll., Southampton; Royal College of Science, London. 1st class Honours BSc in Physical Geography and Geology, London University, 1890; 1st class Associateship in Physical Division of Royal College of Science, London, 1886. Lecturer in Physics, Chemistry, etc, at Southport Science and Art Institute, 1887–90; Science Master and Second Master of Tettenhall College, Staffs, 1891–97; contributor to educational and other periodicals since 1889. *Publications:* Physiography for Beginners; Physiography for Advanced Students; joint author of the following among other text-books: Elementary General Science; Exercises in Practical Physics; Science of Common Life; Introduction to Physical Geography; Class-Book of Physical Geography. *Address:* Passaic, Kew, Surrey. *T:* Richmond 1873. *Club:* University of London. *Died 19 Aug. 1921.*

SIMMS, Ven. Arthur Hennell; Archdeacon of Totnes since 1910; Canon Residentiary of Exeter Cathedral, 1920; *b* 1853; *s* of William Simms, FRS; *m* 1896, Jenny, *d* of John Marks, of Newton Abbot. *Educ:* Trinity College, Cambridge. Ordained, 1878; Curate of Lifton, 1878–81; St John, Clifton, 1881–82; Vicar of Churchstow, 1882–88; Rector of Wolborough, 1888–96; Vicar of St Michael, Cambridge, 1896–1902; Holy Trinity, Ely, 1902–3; St Luke, Torquay, 1903–20; Select Preacher, Cambridge, 1897 and 1898. *Address:* The Close, Exeter. *Died 13 Jan. 1921.*

SIMONS, Admiral Ernest Alfred; *b* Lucknow, 3 Sept. 1856; *s* of Capt. A. Parmenter Simons, Bengal Artillery (killed defending Lucknow Residency, 1857); *m* 1881, Florence Isabella (*d* 1922), 2nd *d* of late Philip George, Redland Bank House, near Bristol; one *d*. Entered Navy, 1870; specially promoted to Lieut for proficiency in examinations, and as Lieut was a Gunnery Staff-Officer; as Commander was Senior Naval Officer, Suakim, during the Dongola Expedition, 1896 (Khedive's medal and thanks of Govt of India); Captain, 1896; sometime Assistant to Director of Naval Ordnance at the Admiralty, 1901; received the acknowledgments of the Govt of India for Service as Senior Naval Officer at Koweit; Admiral Superintendent Malta Dockyard, 1910–12; ADC to the King, 1906–7; Rear-Adm. 1907; Vice-Adm. 1911; Admiral, 1914; retired, 1915; Officer Legion of Honour; Order of Redeemer of Greece. *Address:* 50 Charlwood Street, SW1.

Died 30 Aug. 1928.

SIMONS, Very Rev. William Charles; 3rd *s* of Rev. John Simons, Vicar of Dymock, Gloucestershire; *m* Emily Martha, *d* of Thomas Harding, Wick House, Brislington, Bristol; one *s*. *Educ:* private schools; Oxford (MA 1866). Deacon, 1867; Priest, 1868; Curate Kirby Underdale, Yorks, 1867; Priest-in-Charge Knowle, Bristol, 1870; Chaplain to Lord Kinnaird, Rossie Priory, Scotland, 1873; Chaplain to Frances, Lady Kinnaird, and Knapp Chapel, 1878; Rector of All Souls, Invergowrie, Dundee, 1883; Canon, St Paul's, Dundee, 1905; Examining Chaplain to Bishop of Brechin, 1906; Dean of Brechin, 1913; retired. *Publication:* Some Things Hard to be Understood. *Address:* Lynchmere, Petersfield, Hants.

Died 7 Jan. 1921.

SIMPSON, Sir Alexander Russell, Kt 1906; MD; DSc (*hc*); Hon. LLD; *b* Bathgate, West Lothian, 30 April 1835; 2nd *s* of Alexander Simpson, bank agent; *m* 1872, Margaret Stewart (*d* 1911), *d* of George Freeland Barbour, Bonskeid and Gryffe Castle; four *s* one *d*. *Educ:* Bathgate Academy; Edinburgh Univ.; apprenticed to Prof. John Goodsir. Whilst still a student elected one of the Presidents Royal Medical Society; studied at Univ. of Montpellier and Berlin; Assistant seven years to his uncle, Sir James Young Simpson, 1st Bt; five years in private practice in Glasgow; formerly Dean of the Faculty of Medicine and Emeritus Professor of Midwifery and the Diseases of Women and Children, Univ. of Edinburgh, 1870–1905. *Publications:* editor of Sir James Young Simpson's Lectures on Diseases of Women; author of Contributions to Obstetrics and Gynecology; and of an Atlas of the Frozen Section of a Cadaver in the Genu-pectoral Position (along with Dr Berry Hart); and many memoirs. *Recreations:* travel; interested in Evangelistic work in Edinburgh, and especially in the mission movement among students. *Address:* 52 Queen Street, Edinburgh. *TA:* Chloroform, Edinburgh. *T:* 2580.

Died 6 April 1916.

SIMPSON, Alfred Muller; Australian manufacturer; *b* London, 4 April 1843; *s* of Alfred Simpson (*d* 1891), afterwards of Adelaide, SA; *m* 1st, 1871, Catherine, *e d* of James Allen, Unley, SA; 2nd, 1888, Violet Laura, *d* of John Sheridan, MD, Edinburgh, NB; two *s* three *d*. Arrived in Colony, 1849; introduced six or more different industries into the Colony from 1869; Member of Legislative Council for metropolitan district, 1887–93; Member of the State Board of Conciliation, 1895; President of the Royal Agricultural Society of SA, 1898, 1899; Governor of Botanic Gardens, 1899; one of the equippers of the Bushmen's Contingent in the South African War, 1900; Trustee of the State Bank of South Australia, 1902; Associate of Order of St John of Jerusalem for services in connection with ambulance work, 1910. *Address:* Young House, Parkside, South Australia.

Died 20 Sept. 1918.

SIMPSON, Hon. Archibald Henry; Chief Judge in Equity, New South Wales, since 1896; Barrister of Lincoln's Inn; *b* 1843; *s* of George Simpson, Barrister. *Educ:* Tonbridge School; Christ's Coll., Cambridge (Fellow). Went to Australia, 1881; Fellow of the University of Sydney, 1897; Vice-Chancellor, 1902–4. *Address:* Chancery Square, Sydney, New South Wales. *Clubs:* Savile; Australian, Sydney. *Died 1918.*

SIMPSON, Sir Benjamin, KCIE 1887; *b* 1831; *s* of Robert Simpson; *m* 1859, (Agnes) Jane (Sarah), *d* of Brigadier Hugh Sibbald, CB; one *s* one *d. Educ:* Dublin University (BA, MD). Late Surgeon-Gen. and Sanitary Commissioner with Govt of India, 1885–90. *Address:* 77 Ashley Gardens, SW1. *T:* Victoria 5582.

Died 27 June 1923.

SIMPSON, Miss Evelyn Blantyre; *b* Edinburgh, Dec. 1856; *d* of Sir James Young Simpson, 1st Bt (discoverer of chloroform). *Publications:* Dogs of Other Days; Sir James Young Simpson's Biography in Famous Scot Series; R. L. Stevenson's Edinburgh Days, 1898; R. L. S., 1905; R. L. S.'s Originals. *Recreations:* cycling, walking, gardening. *Address:* 15 Inverleith Row, Edinburgh.

Died 23 Jan. 1920.

SIMPSON, Frederick Moore, FRIBA; Emeritus Professor of Architecture in the University of London; *s* of James Moore Simpson; *m* 1894, Maud Mary Sandilands (*d* 1914). Articled to George Frederick Bodley, RA, 1876; was admitted a student of the Royal Academy, 1880; gained the Royal Acad. Travelling Studentship, 1884; first Prof. of Architecture, University Coll., Liverpool, 1894–1903; started School of Architecture there, 1894; elected a member of the Art Workers' Guild, 1887; President of the Liverpool Architectural Society 1900–1 and 1901–2; Member Council, RIBA, 1917–20; Member of Commission appointed by Norwegian Government on Trondhjem Cathedral, 1922; *buildings:* Laboratories at University College, London, for Physiology, Pharmacology, Chemistry, Eugenics, Applied Statistics, Anatomy (Rockefeller gift), Engineering, and School of Architecture, etc; Queen Victoria Memorial, Liverpool (in collaboration); School of Oriental Studies, Finsbury Circus, London Univ.; various country houses, etc. *Publication:* A History of Architectural Development (3 vols); editor The Architect's Library. *Address:* 10 Campden Grove, W8. *T:* Park 7910; Chelwood Gate, Sussex. *Club:* Athenæum. *Died 13 June 1928.*

SIMPSON, Henry Fife Morland, JP; MA, LLD; Rector of Aberdeen Grammar School, since 1893; *b* Newcastle-on-Tyne, 25 Nov. 1859; *s* of late William Graham Simpson; *m* 1893, Jenny F. Dohm, Eutin, Holstein; two *s* two *d. Educ:* Oundle; Pembroke Coll., Cambridge (1st class Classical Tripos), 1882). Private Tutor in Germany; Assistant Master, Marlborough College, and at Fettes College, Edinburgh, 1883–93. *Publications:* Prehistory of the North (trans. from Worsaae); Southesk and other Rune Prime Staves (Proc. Soc. Antiquaries Scotland, etc); Wishart's Deeds of Montrose (joint-editor); Scott's Legend of Montrose; Selections from Ovid; Bon Record, Records and Reminiscences of Aberdeen Grammar School, 1256–1906, etc. *Address:* Amatola, Aberdeen. *Died 15 May 1920.*

SIMPSON, Sir James Hope, Kt 1917; Director and formerly General Manager, Bank of Liverpool, and Martin's, Ltd; *b* 4 Nov. 1864; *s* of John Hope Simpson; *m* 1895, Mary, *y d* of late Isaac Whitwell Wilson, JP, Kendal; two *s* one *d. Educ:* Liverpool College; the Continent. Banking—in the service of Williams Deacons Bank, Ltd, Bank of Egypt, Bank of Liverpool, Ltd. *Address:* The Firs, London Road, Guildford. *T:* Guildford 972.

Died 6 Oct. 1924.

SIMPSON, Sir James Walter Mackay, 3rd Bt, *cr* 1866; *b* 6 Sept. 1882; *e s* of Sir Walter Grindlay Simpson, 2nd Bt and Anne Fitzgerald, *d* of late Alexander Mackay; *S* father, 1898. *Educ:* Eton; Balliol College, Oxford. An ardent supporter of temperance; interested in social problems; COS, Finsbury Industrial Improvement Committee, City Council, etc; travelled extensively in Europe and America. *Publication:* work on Training for Games. *Recreations:* walking, gardening (specially interested in trees), deep-sea fishing. *Heir:* none. *Address:* Ballabraes of Ayton, Berwickshire; Strathavon, Linlithgowshire, Scotland; Oxford House, Bethnal Green Road, E. *TA:* Candour, London. *T:* Kensington 2484. *Club:* Sports.

Died 16 March 1924 (ext).

SIMPSON, Sir Robert Russell, Kt 1918; WS; *b* 1840; *y s* of Alexander Simpson, banker, Bathgate, and *nephew* of Sir James Young Simpson, Bart, MD, etc; *m* 1877, Helen Dymock (*d* 1923), *d* of Samuel Raleigh, Manager of the Scottish Widows' Fund Life Assurance Society; four *s* one *d. Educ:* Bathgate Academy; Edinburgh University. Admitted a member of HM Society of Writers to the Signet, 1869; a JP for the City of Edinburgh; Deputy (Lay) Clerk (Emeritus) of the General Assembly of the United Free Church of Scotland; Chairman of Dr Guthrie's Industrial Schools; Vice-President of the Edinburgh Industrial Brigade; Vice-President of the National Bible Society of Scotland, and Director of various philanthropic and other institutions in Edinburgh. *Recreations:* golf, travelling. *Address:* 23 Douglas

Crescent, Edinburgh. *TA:* Simla, Edinburgh. *T:* 2636. *Club:* University, Edinburgh. *Died 14 Dec. 1923.*

SIMPSON, Col Thomas Thomson, CB 1893; *b* 1 June 1836; *s* of late John Simpson of Findermore, Co. Tyrone; *m* 1879, Margaret, *y d* of late Robert Batt of Pundy's Burn, Co. Down; no *c. Educ:* Nutgrove School, Dublin; privately. Entered army, 1857; Captain, 1864; Major, 1873; Lt-Col N Staffordshire Regt, 1880; Col 1884; served Indian Mutiny, 1858; against Cabul Kal Wazeerees, 1860 (medal with clasp); commanded 98th Regiment, 1880–85; Zhob Valley Field Force, 1884 (despatches, CB); commanded Regimental District 33, 1886–91; JP for Cos of Waterford and Kerry. *Recreation:* salmon-fishing. *Address:* Glenmore, Glencairn, SO, Co. Waterford. *Club:* Army and Navy. *Died 30 Dec. 1916.*

SIMS, Charles; RA 1916 (ARA 1900); RWS; Keeper and Trustee of Royal Academy, 1920–26; Trustee of National Gallery of British Art, 1920 (Tate Gallery); *b* Islington, 1873; *m* 1896, Agnes Helen, *d* of late John MacWhirter, RA; two *s. Educ:* private schools. Entered commission agent's office in Paris, 1887, and three other offices subsequently; began to study art at South Kensington (National Art Training School), 1890; Académie Julian, under J. Le Febvre and Benjamin Constant, 1891; Royal Academy Schools, 1893; exhibited RA 1894; exhibited The Vine and a portrait at Royal Academy, 1895; Childhood, 1896, purchased in 1900 for the Musée du Luxembourg, Paris, and obtained medal at Salon; Gold medal (International Exhibition), Amsterdam, 1912; Gold medal (International Exhibition), Pittsburg, 1912; The Fountain and The Wood Beyond the World, Tate Gallery (Chantrey Bequest); pictures in the Permanent Municipal Collections of Leeds, Christchurch, New Zealand; Bristol, Durban, and Pietermaritzburg (SA), and NSW. *Recreations:* chamber music for strings, golf. *Clubs:* Athenæum, Garrick. *Died 13 April 1928.*

SIMS, George Robert, journalist and dramatic author; *b* 2 Sep. 1847; *m* 1901, Florence Wykes. *Educ:* Hanwell College and Bonn. Journalist and playwright since 1874; writer of Mustard and Cress columns in the Referee, under the pen-name of Dagonet, from the birth of the paper in 1877. Knight of the Roy. Norwegian Order of St Olaf, 1st class, 1905. *Publications:* How the Poor Live, 1883; The Dagonet Ballads; Rogues and Vagabonds; Three Brass Balls; Memoirs of Mary Jane; Mary Jane Married, 1888; Tales of Today, 1889; Dramas of Life, 1890; Memoirs of a Landlady; Social Kaleidoscope; Ten Commandments, 1896; As it was in the Beginning, 1896; Dorcas Dene, Detective, 1897; In London's Heart; Once upon a Christmas Time, 1898; Without the Limelight; A Blind Marriage; Living London; The Cry of The Children; The Black Stain; The Death Gamble; Young Mrs Caudle; Among my Autographs; The Life we Live; For Life—and After; Joyce Pleasantry; His Wife's Revenge; Anna of the Underworld; My Life; Glances Back, etc; author or part-author of following plays—Lights of London; In the Ranks; Harbour Lights; Master and Man; Mother-in-Law; Faust up to Date; Member for Slocum; Merry Duchess; Golden Ring; Little Christopher Columbus; Grey Mare; Guardsman; The Trumpet Call; The English Rose; Two Little Vagabonds; In Gay Piccadilly; The Elixir of Youth; Romany Rye; My Innocent Boy; Dandy Fifth; Gipsy Earl; Gay City; Golden Ladder; For Life and After; Hop o' my Thumb; Sleeping Beauty; Puss in Boots; Ever-Open Door, etc. *Recreations:* battledore and shuttlecock, bull-dogs, and motoring. *Address:* 12 Clarence Terrace, Regent's Park, NW1. *TA:* Hybiscus, London. *T:* Padd. 70. *Clubs:* Devonshire, etc. *Died 4 Sept. 1922.*

SIMSON, Colonel William Amor, CMG 1919; DSO 1916; *b* 1872; *m* 1911, Louise, *d* of late E. L. Du Barry, Norfolk, Virginia. Served European War, 1st Divisional Train, Canadian Force, 1914–18 (despatches, CMG, DSO). *Died 17 Nov. 1925.*

SINCLAIR, 15th Baron, *cr* 1449; **Charles William St Clair;** Representative Peer for Scotland since 1885; *b* 8 Sept. 1831; *e s* of 14th Baron and Jane, *d* of Archibald Little, Shabden Park, Surrey; *S* father, 1880; *m* 1870, Margaret, *d* of James Murray, Ancoats Hall; one *s* three *d* (and one *s* decd). *Educ:* RMC Sandhurst. Entered army, 1848; served in 57th Regt in Crimean War, Indian Mutiny, and New Zealand War; retired with rank of Col, 1878; JP, DL, Berwickshire. Conservative; *Heir:* s Master of Sinclair, *b* 16 Feb. 1875. *Address:* Herdmanston, Pencaitland; Nisbet House, Duns, NB; 55 Onslow Square, SW7. *TA:* Stonedge, London. *T:* Western 4163. *Clubs:* Carlton, United Service; New, Edinburgh.

Died 25 April 1922.

SINCLAIR, Archibald; journalist and author; *b* 11 Jan. 1866; *e s* of Archibald Sinclair, Lanark; *m* 1888, Helen Elizabeth Miller. *Educ:*

St Mark's College, Chelsea. Vice-President, Royal Life-Saving Society, and joint Hon.-Secretary, 1891–96; sub-editor The Referee since 1897; was sporting editor of The Morning, and on the staff of The Sportsman for several years. Hon. Assoc. Order of St John of Jerusalem in England. *Publications:* (joint) Swimming, Badminton Library; various publications dealing with swimming and amateur sport. *Recreations:* angling, shooting, swimming, and trotting; for many years an official of the Amateur Athletic and Amateur Swimming Associations. *Address:* Twickenham, Middlesex.
Died 24 March 1922.

SINCLAIR, Surg.-Gen. David, MB, CM (Aberdeen); CSI 1899; Indian Medical Service, retired; *b* 26 Jan. 1847; 2nd *s* of William Sinclair, Milltimber, Peterculter; *m* 1876, Jane Birnie, 2nd *d* of late John Ferguson, advocate, Aberdeen; one *s* five *d. Educ:* Aberdeen Grammar School and University (MB, CM). *Decorated* for services in Burma. *Address:* 11 Mortonhall Road, Edinburgh. *Club:* Caledonian United Service, Edinburgh. *Died 11 Oct. 1919.*

SINCLAIR, Deputy Surgeon-General Edward Malcolm, CB 1907; MD St Andrews, 1853; MRCS 1853; *b* 1832; *s* of Martin Sinclair, MD, FRCSE, of Edinburgh; *m* 1870, Annie Catherine, 2nd *d* of Andrew Hamilton, Co. Donegal; one *d.* Entered Army Medical Service, 1854; retired 1888; served Crimea, 1854–56, Fall of Sebastopol; Indian Mutiny, 1857–59, several actions in Oude with Gen. Frank's force, Capture of Lucknow, operations in Bundelcund; South Africa, Transvaal Campaign, 1881 (despatches). *Address:* 30 Nevern Square, SW. *Club:* Junior United Service.
Died 14 June 1916.

SINCLAIR, George Robertson, MusDoc Cantuar; Hon. FRCO, Hon. RAM, LRAM; Hon. Fellow of St Michael's College, Tenbury; Organist and Master of the Choristers, Succentor and Sub-Canon at Hereford Cathedral since 1889; *b* Croydon, 28 Oct. 1863. *Educ:* St Michael's College, Tenbury. Studied music under Rev. Sir Fred. Ouseley, Sir Robert Stewart, and Dr C. H. Lloyd, 1879. Assistant organist of Gloucester Cathedral, and organist and choirmaster of St Mary de Crypt Church, Gloucester, 1880; appointed at 17 years of age organist and choirmaster of Truro Cathedral; conducted the Festivals of the Three Choirs at Hereford in 1891, 1894, 1897, 1900, 1903, 1906, 1909, and 1912; Conductor Birmingham Festival Choral Society, Hereford Choral Society, Herefordshire Orchestral Society, and Diocesan Choral Union, and Ross Musical Society; Grand Organist to the Grand Lodge of England, 1902; Grand Organist to the Grand Lodge of Mark Master Masons, 1903; Grand organist in the Supreme Grand Chapter of the Royal Arch, 1909. *Recreations:* motor cycling, photography. *Address:* The Close, Hereford. *TA:* Hereford. *T:* 1370. *Clubs:* Junior Constitutional; Herefordshire County. *Died 7 Feb. 1917.*

SINCLAIR, Col Hugh Montgomerie, CB 1910; CMG 1917; CBE 1919; FRGS; *b* 23 Feb. 1855; *s* of Rev. Canon W. Sinclair, Rector of Pulborough, and *g s* of Rt Hon. Sir John Sinclair, 1st Bt, PC; *m* 1905, Rosalie Sybil, *d* of late Sir John Jackson, MP; two *s* two *d. Educ:* Malvern; Repton; Woolwich (Pollock medallist). Private Secretary to High Commissioner, Cyprus, 1881–86; passed Staff College with honours, 1890; served Ashanti Campaign, 1895–96 (despatches); Military Secretary to GOC-in-C, Bengal, 1899; AAG in India, 1899–1901; S Africa, 1900 (despatches); AQMG Western District and Southern Command, 1903–7; Chief Engineer Scottish Command, 1908–12; retired, 1912; Commandant Railway Troops, RE, Longmoor, 1914–19 (despatches, CMG, CBE). *Recreations:* hunting, painting, music. *Address:* Barming House, Maidstone. *Club:* Junior United Service. *Died 10 July 1924.*

SINCLAIR, Sir John Rose George, 7th Bt, *cr* 1704; DSO 1901; JP, DL; *b* Slough, 10 Aug. 1864; *e s* of Col A. Y. Sinclair, 26th BNI; *S* grandfather, 1873; *m* 1885, Edith, *o d* of Lieut-Col W. M. Dunbar. *Educ:* Military College, Oxford. Lieut 4th Batt. Cheshire Regt, 1881–85; Lieut-Col Commandant, 1892–1900; Hon. Colonel, 1900, 1st Caithness Volunteer Artillery; President Caithness Territorial Force Association, 1908–20; farmed from 1885; served South Africa (Imp. Yeo.), 1900–1 (despatches); European War, 1914–19, with 14th Batt. King's Liverpool Regt. Owner of 6,300 acres; Vice Lieut of Caithness. *Recreations:* cycling, horses, turning. *Heir: nephew* Ronald Norman John Charles Udny Sinclair, *b* 30 June 1899. *Address:* Barrock House, Wick. *TA:* Lyth. *M:* SK 838. *Club:* Constitutional. *Died 3 Nov. 1926.*

SINCLAIR, Ven. John Stewart; Archdeacon of Cirencester; Hon. Canon of Gloucester; *b* 15 May 1853; *s* of Prebendary Wm Sinclair, Rector of Pulborough, Sussex; *g s* of Rt Hon. Sir John Sinclair, 1st

Bt, PC, of Ulbster; *m* 1893, Clara Sophia, *d* of John Dearman Birchall of Bowden Hall, Gloucestershire; two *s* two *d. Educ:* Repton School; Oriel College, Oxford. 2nd class Mod. History (rowed in the Oxford boat, 1874). Curate of Pulborough; Curate of All Saints', Fulham; Vicar of St Dionis, Fulham; elected Chairman of the Fulham Vestry, 6 years; Vicar of Cirencester, 1898–1908; Past Grand Chaplain of England. *Publications:* Civic Duties, and other sermons. *Recreations:* archæology, riding, fishing. *Address:* The Greenway, Shurdington, near Cheltenham. *Club:* Oxford and Cambridge.
Died 30 April 1919.

SINCLAIR, Louis; *b* Paris, 1861, of English parents, who returned to England in 1864; *m* 1886, Nina, *d* of Daniel de Pass, of Natal and London; three *s* one *d. Educ:* University Coll., London; Continental Colleges. Went to Australia, 1878, and started life on the staff of the Argus, Melbourne; subsequently engaged in commercial pursuits, and retired from business at twenty-five years of age; deeply interested in commercial questions, and was entirely instrumental in forming the Commercial Committee of the House of Commons, 1899, of which he was Hon. Sec.; initiated the Anglo-French Interparliamentary visits; MP (C) Romford Div. Essex, 1897–1906; was the appellant in the Birkbeck Bank disaster, and secured equal and proper treatment to the depositors; reformed the Commercial Committee of the House of Commons, 1913; was entirely responsible for the formation of Commercial Committees in the Parliaments of Europe; appointed Permanent Hon. Sec. General of the Commercial Inter-Parliamentary Congress, in recognition of his services; during the War served in the RAC War Transport Service, in which he was Emergency Officer; visited the Australasian Dominions and formed Commercial Committees in the Federal Parliament, and also in the Queensland, New South Wales and South Australian Parliaments, 1920. *Publications:* Our Commercial Disabilities; Ministry of Justice instead of Home Office; Our Poor Laws and their Degrading Operation. *Address:* Daydawn, 7 Netherhall Gardens, NW3. *T:* Hampstead 145; 28 Castle Hill Avenue, Folkestone. *Clubs:* Carlton, Royal Automobile. *Died 4 Jan. 1928.*

SINCLAIR, Ven. William Macdonald, Hon. DD Glasgow; FRSL, FRGS, FRHS; examining chaplain to Bishop of London; honorary chaplain to HM the King; *b* Leeds, 3 June 1850; *e* surv. *s* of late Rev. William Sinclair, Prebendary of Chichester (5th *s* of Rt Hon. Sir John Sinclair, 1st Bt, and Diana, *d* of Alexander, 1st Lord Macdonald). *Educ:* Repton; Balliol Coll., Oxford (Scholar); 2nd class Moderations and Classics. President Oxford Union Society, 1873. Assistant minister of Quebec Chapel, 1876; resident chaplain to Bishop of London, 1877; Vicar of St Stephen's, Westminster, 1880; member London School Board, 1885; Grand Chaplain of England, 1894; Chaplain to Order of St John of Jerusalem, 1900; chaplain-in-ordinary to Queen Victoria; Hon. Chaplain to King Edward VII; Archdeacon of London and Canon of St Paul's, 1889–1911; Rector of Shermanbury, Henfield, Sussex, 1911–15. *Publications:* The Psalms in the original Rhythm, 1879; Commentary on the Epistles of St John, 1880; Lessons on the Gospel of St John, 1882; The Servant of Christ, 1891; The Christian's Influence, 1892; Christ and our Times, 1894; Words to the Laity, 1895; Leaders of Thought in the English Church, 1896; Simplicity in Christ, 1896; The New Law, 1897; The Happy Life, 1897; Unto You, Young Men, 1900; Words from St Paul's (first series), 1900; Likewise the Younger Women, 1901; Words from St Paul's (second series), 1902; John MacWhirter, RA, 1903; Difficulties of our Day, 1905; Memorials of St Paul's Cathedral; The Chapels Royal, 1912; Joseph Farquharson, ARA, 1912; short edition of Memorials, 1913; charges—Condition of the People; The Church, Visible, Invisible, Catholic, National; Sacred Studies; The English Church and the Canon Law; Points at Issue between the Church of England and the Church of Rome; The Ancient British Churches; The Churches of the East, 1898; Church Courts, 1899; The Duties of Archdeacons, 1901; The Church and the Non-conformists, 1902; The Authority of Sunday, 1903; Catholic and Protestant, 1906; The Catholic Faith and the New Theology, 1907; The Part of Faith in the Healing of the Sick, 1910. *Recreations:* riding, cycling, and swimming. *Clubs:* Athenæum, Authors'. *Died 4 Dec. 1917.*

SINCLAIR-LOCKHART, Sir Robert Duncan, 11th Bt, *cr* 1636, of Castle Hill, Co. Lanark; held Sinclair of Stevenson Baronetcy; *b* 12 Nov. 1856; *s* of late George Duncan and Elizabeth Amanda Lockhart; *S* uncle, 1904; *m* 1895, Flora Louisa Jane Beresford, *d* of Captain Edward Power; five *s* one *d. Heir: s* Graeme Duncan Power Sinclair-Lockhart, *b* 29 Jan. 1897. *Address:* Kanoulla, Remuera, Auckland, NZ. *Died 8 Nov. 1919.*

SINDING, Stephan; sculptor; *b* 1846; *brother* of Christian Sinding, composer, and late Otto Sinding, painter; *b* Drontheim, 1846. Studied and worked in Berlin, Paris, Rome, and Copenhagen. *Works:* May; Mother Earth; The Joy of Life; The Barbarian Mother; Man and Woman; Walküre; The Eldest of Her Kin; Grave Monument of the Isenberg Family. *Died 24 Jan. 1922.*

SINGLETON, Rev. John J., MA; Hon. Canon of Southwell since 1885; *b* 1838; *s* of Rev. W. Singleton, MA; *m e d* of Rev. W. Calder, MA, Headmaster of the Chesterfield Grammar School, and afterwards Rector of Wingerworth, Derbyshire. *Educ:* Ipswich Grammar School; Pembroke College, Cambridge. Ordained Deacon, 1861; Priest, 1862; Assistant Curate of Chesterfield, 1861–70; Vicar of Ogley Hay, 1870–73; Rector of Brimington, 1873–88; Vicar of Melbourne, Derbyshire, 1888–1908. *Address:* Southwell, Notts.
Died 27 Dec. 1917.

SINHA, 1st Baron, *cr* 1919 of Raipur; **Rt. Hon. Sir Satyendra Prassano Sinha,** KCSI 1921; Kt 1914; PC 1919; KC 1918; Member of Judicial Committee of Privy Council since 1926; late Member of Viceroy's Executive Council, India (1st native); *b* 1864; *s* of Babu Siti Kantha Sinha; four *s* three *d. Educ:* Birbhoom Zilla School; Presidency College, Calcutta (Scholar). Came to England, 1881; Lincoln's Inn; called to Bar, 1886; Barrister, Calcutta High Court; Standing Counsel, Government of India, 1903; Advocate-General, Bengal, 1907–9, 1915–17; a Representative of India in Imperial War Conference, 1917; Member Imperial War Cabinet, 1918; Freeman of City of London, 1917; Under-Secretary of State for India, 1919–20; Governor of Bihar and Orissa, Dec. 1920–21. *Address:* Queen Anne's Mansions, SW1. *Clubs:* Reform, Marlborough, National Liberal.
Died 6 March 1928.

SINNETT, Alfred Percy; *b* 18 Jan. 1840; *s* of E. W. P. Sinnett, journalist (*d* 1845), and Mrs Percy Sinnett, author of Byways of History, etc; *m* 1870, Patience (*d* 1908), *d* of Richard Edensor of Shaw Wood, Derbyshire. *Educ:* London University School. Asst sub-editor of the Globe, 1859; afterwards sub-editor and leader-writer on various London papers; appointed editor of the Hong-Kong Daily Press, 1865; returned London, 1868; leader-writer on Standard; appointed editor of the Pioneer of India, 1872; became interested in theosophical movement, 1879; wrote The Occult World, 1881; Esoteric Buddhism, 1883; Vice-President of the Theosophical Society; author of two novels founded on occult ideas, Karma and United; in 1896 published The Growth of the Soul. Brought out new monthly review called Broad Views, 1904; ceased publication, 1907; author of play, Married by Degrees, produced London, 1911. *Club:* Junior Carlton.
Died 26 June 1921.

SIVEWRIGHT, Hon. Sir James, KCMG 1892 (CMG 1880); *b* 1848; *s* of William Sivewright, Fochabers, NB; *m* 1880, Jennie, *d* of George Page, Bloemfontein. *Educ:* Aberdeen University (MA 1866; LLD 1893). General Manager South African Telegraphs, 1877–85; Commissioner of Crown Lands and Public Works, Cape Colony, 1890–92; Commissioner of Public Works, 1896–98. *Address:* Tulliallan Castle, Kincardine-on-Forth; Lourensford, Somerset West, Cape Colony. *Died 9 Sept. 1916.*

SKEGGS, Rev. Thomas Charles, MA; Chaplain at Palermo, 1900–26; Canon of Gibraltar, 1899–1926. *Educ:* Hertford College, Oxford. Deacon, 1879; Priest, 1880; Curate of St Thomas, Pendleton, 1879–81; St Ambrose, Pendleton, 1881–85; Chaplain of Marseilles, 1885–1900. *Address:* Homes of St Barnabas, Dormans, Surrey.
Died 25 Sept. 1927.

SKEMP, Arthur Rowland, MA, PhD; Winterstoke Professor of English, University of Bristol, since 1911; Lecturer on Military Training; *b* Eccles, 1882; 2nd *s* of Thomas Rowland Skemp, cotton manufacturer, and later, Unitarian minister; *m* 1909, Jessie, *d* of J. Clarkson, JP, of Barrow-in-Furness; one *s* one *d. Educ:* Universities of Manchester (1st class English, 1904, MA 1907, Univ. Scholar, Falconer Fellow in Arts), Berlin, Strassburg i/E (PhD summa cum laude, 1908). Editor (joint), Manchester University Magazine, 1902–5; President, SRC, 1904; Lektor of English in University of Strassburg, 1906; Lecturer, University of Sheffield, 1909. Acting Capt. unattached list TF, attached No 3 Officer Cadet Batt. *Publications:* (creative): Guenevere, tragedy in three acts, produced by Miss Muriel Pratt at the Theatre Royal, Bristol, 1914; (critical): Tragedy of Messallina (Bang's Materialen), 1910; Francis Bacon, 1912; Robert Browning, 1916; articles and reviews, chiefly on Old English poetry or on subjects connected with the drama, in Modern Philology, Jahrbuch der deutschen Shakespeare-gesellschaft, Modern Language Review, Essays and Studies by members of the English Association, etc. *Recreations:* boxing, lacrosse, the theatre. *Address:* 8 Cavendish Road, Westbury-on-Trym. *Died 1 Nov. 1918.*

SKERRINGTON, Hon. Lord; William Campbell, of Skerrington, Ayrshire; one of the Senators of the College of Justice in Scotland, 1908–25; *b* 27 June 1855; *o s* of the late Robert Campbell of Skerrington, and Anne, *d* of late John Carr of Dunston Hill, County Durham; *m* 1880, Alice Mary, 2nd *d* of late Patrick Fraser, one of the Senators of the College of Justice in Scotland; two *s* one *d.* QC 1898; Dean of the Faculty of Advocates, 1905–8; Knight Commander of Gregory the Great. *Address:* 12 Randolph Crescent, Edinburgh.
Died 21 July 1927.

SKETCHLEY, Major Ernest Frederick Powys, DSO 1915; General Staff Officer 2nd Grade, Royal Naval Division, since 1914; *b* 6 Aug. 1881; *s* of Rev. E. Powys Sketchley; *m* Phyllis, *d* of J. F. Campbell, Deputy Master of the Mint, W Australia; one *s* one *d. Educ:* Dulwich College. 2nd Lieut RMLI 1900; Lieut 1901; Capt. 1911; ADC and private secretary to Governor of Western Australia, 1905–8; Adjutant, Portsmouth Division RMLI, 1910–14; served European War in France and Antwerp with RM Brigade as Brigade Major; through whole of Gallipoli campaign as GSO 2nd grade, including landing and final evacuation of Cape Helles (despatches, DSO). *Recreations:* riding, golf, tennis, etc. *Address:* Forton Barracks, Gosport, Hants. *TA:* Marine Gosport. *Died Oct. 1916.*

SKILBECK, William Wray; Editor of the Nineteenth Century and After since 1908; *b* 12 July 1864; *s* of William Skilbeck, solicitor, Bedford Row, and Janet, *d* of Stuart Donaldson; *m* 1894, Beatrice Isabel, *y d* of Sir James Knowles, KCVO; two *d. Educ:* Harrow; Trinity College, Cambridge (BA, LLB 1886). Solicitor, 1890; called to Bar, Inner Temple, 1898; Private Secretary to Sir James Knowles, founder and editor of the Nineteenth Century, from 1893 until his father-in-law's death in 1908. *Recreations:* boating, lawn tennis, bicycling (formerly captain of the Clapham Rovers and East Sheen Rugby Football Teams, and member of the Surrey Fifteen). *Address:* Queen Anne's Mansions, SW. *Club:* Oxford and Cambridge.
Died 17 July 1919.

SKINNER, Col Edmund Grey, CB 1891; *b* 29 Jan. 1850; *s* of Russell Morland Skinner, BCS, sometime Judge of Kishnagur; *m* 1st, 1878, Alice Augusta (*d* 1902), *d* of F. Gilliat Smith of The Oaks, Surrey; five *d*; 2nd, 1904, Amy, *d* of T. H. Foreman, Breadsell, Battle; two *s. Educ:* Wimbledon School; RMC Sandhurst. Joined Army Ordnance Department, 1867; Perak Exhibition, 1875–76 (medal); Egypt, 1882–85; including actions Kassassin, Tel-el-Kebir, and Suakin, 1885, when he was CO Ordnance of the expedition (medal and clasps, 4th class Medjidie, bronze star); Major, 1882; Bt Lt-Col 1885; Col 1894; retired, 1901. *Died 18 Nov. 1917.*

SKINNER, Rev. John, DD; Emeritus Principal; Professor of Old Testament Language and Literature and Apologetics, Theological College of Presbyterian Church of England, 1890–1922; Principal, 1908–22; *b* 18 July 1851; *e s* of James Skinner, Inverurie, Aberdeenshire; *m* 1885, Jessie Elizabeth, *d* of James Niven, Mills of Echt. *Educ:* Gymnasium, Old Aberdeen; Aberdeen University and Free Church College, Aberdeen; New College, Edinburgh; Leipzig; Göttingen. MA and DD Aberdeen; DD St Andrews; Hon. MA Cambridge; Hon. DD Oxford. Minister of Free Church of Scotland: St Fergus, 1880–86; Kelso, 1886–90. *Publications:* Historical Connection between the Old and New Testaments; The Book of Ezekiel (Expositor's Bible); The Book of the Prophet Isaiah, 2 vols; articles in Hastings Dictionary of the Bible; I and II Kings (Century Bible); A Critical and Exegetical Commentary on the Book of Genesis, 1910; The Divine Names in Genesis, 1914; Prophecy and Religion, 1922. *Address:* 55 Hartington Grove, Cambridge.
Died 20 March 1925.

SKINNER, Sir Thomas, 1st Bt, *cr* 1912; JP Middlesex; *b* 23 Nov. 1840; *m* 1st, 1866, Sara Margaret (*d* 1902), *d* of Jonas D. Hewitt; three *s* three *d* (and one *s* one *d* decd); 2nd, 1903, Martha Lauretta (*d* 1924), *d* of Job Long, and widow of C. J. Williamson. Founder and editor of the Stock Exchange Year-Book, The Stock Exchange Gazette, The Directory of Directors, The Bankers Almanac and Year Book, The Canadian Gazette, etc; a Director of the Canadian Pacific Railway, the Canadian Pacific Ocean Services, the Bank of Montreal, and the Commercial Cable Company. *Heir: s* Thomas Hewitt Skinner [*b* 12 June 1875; *m* 1899, Ellen Constance, *d* of James Hay Hall; two *s* two *d. Address:* Falconhurst, Wimbledon, SW]. *Address:* 330 Gresham House, EC2. *T:* 2886 Central; 22 Pont Street, SW1. *T:* 506 Victoria; The Gables, Worthing. *T:* 394 Worthing. *TA:* Desollar, London. *M:* LF 6206. *Clubs:* City of London, Junior Athenæum.
Died 11 May 1926.

SKINNER, Walter Robert; journalist; Editor and Proprietor of The Mining Manual, and Mining Year-Book, established 1887; Oil and Petroleum Manual, established 1910; The Capitalist, established 1885; *b* 1851; *s* of James Skinner, Bristol; *m* 1876; two *s* one *d. Educ:* privately. *Address:* 15 Dowgate Hill, Cannon Street, EC4. *T:* Central 1929; 29 Palmeira Square, Hove, Sussex.

Died 12 May 1924.

SKOTTOWE, Britiffe Constable, 4th Baron Skottowe in the peerage of France (creation by Louis XVIII 1814); *b* 1857; *o s* of Thomas Britiffe Skottowe of Harrow Weald House, 3rd Baron, and Lœtitia Mourgue, *d* of John Constable of Wassand; *m* 1899, Jane Margaret Phillips (*d* 1923), *o c* of John Orwell Phillips, Lieutenant of City of London, of 44 Grosvenor Street, W, and The Common, Weybridge. *Educ:* Harrow; New College, Oxford (MA); 1st class Modern History, 2nd class Jurisprudence; FRGS. *Publications:* Our Hanoverian Kings; A Short History of Parliament; Sudden Death, etc. *Recreations:* many. *Address:* 64 Prince's Gate, SW7. *T:* Kensington 5545. *Clubs:* Carlton, Wellington, Hurlingham; Mid-Surrey Golf.

Died 22 Feb. 1925

SKRINE, Rev. John Huntley, DD; Vicar of St Peter in the East, Oxford, since 1908; *b* Somerset, 3 April 1848; 3rd *s* of Henry Duncan Skrine, Warleigh, Somerset, and Susanna C. Mills, *d* of Thomas Mills, Saxham House, Suffolk; *m* 1878, Mary, *d* of Rev. T. H. Tooke; one *d. Educ:* Uppingham; Corpus Christi College, Oxford (Scholar, MA); DD 1912. 1st class (Classics) in Mods and in Final Schools; Newdigate Prize Poem, 1870. Fellow of Merton Coll., Oxford, 1871–79; ordained, 1874; assistant master, Uppingham, 1873–87; canon of Perth Cathedral, 1897–1902; Warden of Trinity College, Glenalmond, 1888–1902; Vicar of Itchenstoke, 1903–7; select preacher to University of Oxford, 1907; Bampton Lecturer for 1911. *Publications:* Margaret of Anjou (Newdigate Prize Poem), 1870; Uppingham by the Sea, 1878; Under Two Queens (Lyrics), 1884; The Ocean Throne (a Jubilee Masque), 1887; A Memory of Edward Thring, 1890; Columba (a Poem), 1892; Joan the Maid (a Dramatic Poem), 1895; Songs of the Maid, and other Ballads and Lyrics, 1896; A Goodly Heritage (School Sermons), 1897; The Heart's Counsel (General Sermons); Thirty Hymns for Public School Singing, 1899; The Queen's Highway, lyrics of the war, 1900; Saints and Worthies (General Sermons), 1901; Pastor Agnorum, a Schoolmaster's Afterthoughts; The Mountain-Mother (Glenalmond Sermons), 1902; The Christ in the Teacher (Addresses), 1905; What is Faith? (Theology), 1907; Pastor Ovium, 1909; Problems of Hope and Love; Village Hymns and Litanies; Sermons to Pastors and Masters, 1910; Creed and the Creeds, Bampton Lectures, 1911; Miracle and History, 1912; Pastor Futurus (Dramatic Idyll); Eucharist and Bishop, 1914; The Survival of Jesus (study in telepathy), 1917; The Gospel of the Manhood, 1922. *Address:* 1 Church Road, Oxford.

Died 8 May 1923.

SLACK, Captain Charles, FRGS, FRCI, MRUSI; served for sixteen years as Commissioned Officer in Lancashire and Middlesex Artillery, retaining rank on retirement; Captain in National Reserve. *Educ:* privately. Travelled through all the countries of Europe, also in Algeria, Tunis, Egypt, United States, Canada, Siberia, China, and Japan; Councillor for borough of Lambeth in the Conservative interest since 1906; Chairman of Education Committee, 1911, and of Libraries Committee, 1916; on staff of Army and Navy Gazette and Brixton Free Press. *Publications:* Handbook of Company Drill, 48 editions; Handbook of Infantry Drill; Handbook of Artillery Drill; Attack Formations; Military Models for Instruction in Drill and Tactics; Military Essays; Manual of Languages (22) for Tourists and Students; also Manual of Burmese; Introduction to Swahili; My Tour in the Far East; Federation of the British Empire; The New Europe; Ireland and its Traditions; contributions to the public press on naval, military, political, and social subjects, etc. *Recreation:* foreign travel. *Address:* 45 Medora Road, Brixton Hill, SW2.

Died Dec. 1925.

SLADDEN, Sir Julius, Kt 1926; Chairman of Conservative and Unionist Association, Evesham Division; County Councillor, Worcestershire; Chairman of Governors, Prince Henry's Grammar School, Evesham; Commissioner of Income Tax; *b* 25 June 1847; *y s* of late John Sladden, MRCS, of Ash-next-Sandwich; *m* 1877, Eugénie Narcisse, *d* of John Mourilyan of Paris, and formerly of Sandwich, Kent; four *s* four *d. Educ:* Epsom College. *Address:* Seward House, Badsey, Evesham. *TA:* Sladden, Badsey. *T:* Badsey 11. *M:* UY 70. *Died 21 Dec. 1928.*

SLADE, Admiral Sir Edmond John Warre, KCIE 1911; KCVO 1911 (MVO 1903); RN; Vice-Chairman Anglo-Persian Oil Company, Ltd; *b* 20 March 1859; *s* of Rev. George Fitzclarence and Eleanor Frances Slade; *m* 1887, Florence Madeleine, *e d* of late James Carr Saunders; two *d. Educ:* Eton. Entered Navy, 1872; Lieut 1879; Commander, 1894; Captain 1899; served in HMS Hecla during the Egyptian War, 1882; Commander-in-Chief, East Indies, 1909–12; retired, 1917. *Address:* 63 Bedford Gardens, Campden Hill, W8. *T:* Park 4959. *Clubs:* United Service, Royal Automobile, City of London.

Died 20 Jan. 1928.

SLADEN, Brig.-Gen. David Ramsay, CMG 1915; DSO 1898; 1st Battalion King's Own Scottish Borderers; *b* 7 Feb. 1869; *s* of late Major-General John Ramsay Sladen; *m* 1911, Isabel, *d* of late John Blakiston-Houston of Orangefield, Co. Down; two *s* one *d.* Entered army, 1888; Capt. 1897; Major, 1907; Lt-Col 1914; served Suakim Field Force, 1888 (medal with clasp, Khedive's star); Soudan Frontier, 1889; North-West Frontier of India, 1897–98 (slightly wounded, despatches, DSO, medal with two clasps); South Africa, 1899–1902 (despatches, Queen's medal, 3 clasps, King's medal, 2 clasps); European War, 1914–18 (wounded twice, despatches, CMG); Commanded 2/KOSB France, 1915–17; Brig.-Gen. France, 1917. JP, DL, Radnorshire. *Address:* Rhydoldog, Rhayader. *Club:* Naval and Military.

Died 21 June 1923.

SLATER, John, BA; FRIBA; architect; surveyor to the Berners Estate, London; *b* Bishop's Stortford, 28 July 1847; *e s* of late John Slater, JP; *m;* one *s* two *d. Educ:* Collegiate School, Bishop's Stortford; Univ. Coll., London. Articled to Professor T. Roger Smith, 1868; President Architectural Association, 1887; Vice-President Royal Institute of British Architects, 1900–4; Member of Tribunal of Appeal London Building Acts. *Publications:* A Short History of the Berners Estate; (with Professor Roger Smith) Classic and Early Christian Architecture. *Address:* 46 Berners Street, W1; 13 Welbeck Mansions, West Hampstead, NW6. *T:* Museum 1433. *Club:* Athenæum.

Died 1 Dec. 1924.

SLATER, Rev. William Fletcher, MA; late Professor of Biblical Literature, Didsbury College; *b* Uttoxeter, Staffordshire, 25 Aug. 1831; *m* 1860, Mary, *d* of W. C. Aruison, MRCS, Allendale; three *s* four *d. Educ:* Wesleyan College, Didsbury; Cambridge University. Wesleyan Minister at Allendale, Newcastle upon Tyne, Sunderland, Harrogate, Cambridge, Leeds, Edinburgh, Liverpool, London. *Publications:* Methodism in the Light of the Early Church (Fernley Lecture, 1885); The Faith and Life of the Early Church, 1892; Manual of Modern Church History, 1895; St Matthew (Century Bible), 1901. *Address:* 49 Redbourne Avenue, Finchley, N.

Died 30 March 1924.

SLAUGHTER, Sir William Capel, Kt 1915; partner in the firm of Slaughter and May, Solicitors, 18 Austin Friars, EC; *b* 1857, *y s* of late Mihill Slaughter; *m* 1st, Ida (*d* 1890), 3rd *d* of Loraine Weaver; 2nd, Hester Mary, *e d* of William Duff Bruce; three *s* one *d. Educ:* privately. *Address:* 3 Berkeley House, Berkeley Square, W. *T:* Gerrard 8420; White Ness, Kingsgate, Thanet. *Club:* Bath.

Died 10 March 1917.

SLEIGHT, Sir George Frederick, 1st Bt, *cr* 1920; Kt 1918; JP Lincolnshire; steam trawler owner, general wholesale merchant and gentleman farmer; *b* Cleethorpes, 26 March 1853; 3rd *s* of Joseph Sleight, wholesale merchant, Grimsby and Cleethorpes; *m* 1872, Rebecca, *d* of John Longden; four *s* three *d. Educ:* Cleethorpes School. Owner of the largest private steam trawler fishing business in the world; formerly the principal fishing-smack owner; saw possibilities of steam; became a pioneer in effecting a change from the old to the new order; was the first merchant to finance a privately-owned steam trawler in Grimsby; during the war lent the Government between fifty and sixty steam ships; lost over thirty boats by enemy action; purchased a number of obsolete ships, altered these, and refitted and equipped them on modern lines to keep up the fishing fleet; so contributed to the nation's food supply; an extensive farmer, cattle breeder, and rearer of pigs and sheep; bred a herd of the noted Lincolnshire red shorthorns; believed in applying the most modern methods to farming as to other businesses, and considerably increased food crops on land brought under his control. *Recreations:* farming, motoring, outdoor country life. *Heir: e s* Major Ernest Sleight, OBE, *b* 14 Oct. 1873. *Address:* Weelsby Hall, near Grimsby, Lincs. *TA:* Sleight, Grimsby. *T:* Grimsby 830. *Club:* County, Grimsby.

Died 19 March 1921.

SLOAN, John MacGavin; *b* Scotland; *m* 1880, Mary Jane, *d* of late Thomas Helme, wood merchant; one *d. Educ:* privately; University of Glasgow. Withdrew from ministry to become a *littérateur;* Editor of Dumfries and Galloway Courier and Herald, 1897–1900; thereafter settled in London. *Publications:* Quintin Doonrise, a Study in Human Nature, 1892; Fallacies of State Socialism, 1894; The Carlyle Country, with a Study of Carlyle's Life, 1903; edited Lockhart's Lives of Burns and Scott in Library of Standard Biographies, 1904; Galloway, in Black's Colour-book Series, 1908; Studies in Burns contributed to TP's Weekly; Our Referee on many Matters in Yorkshire Weekly Post since 1907; contributor to Saturday Review, Fortnightly Review, Chambers's Journal, Landmark, John o'London's Weekly. *Recreation:* bowling. *Address:* 9 Bonham Road, Brixton Hill, SW.

Died 13 Nov. 1926.

SLOANE, William Milligan, AM, PhD, LHD, LLD; Seth Low Professor of History, Columbia Univ. New York City; *b* Richmond, Ohio, USA, 12 Nov. 1850; *e s* of Rev. James Renwick Sloane of New York (*d* 1886), and Margaret Milligan (*d* 1854); *m* 1877, Mary Espy Johnston; two *s* two *d*. *Educ:* Columbia Coll., New York; Berlin and Leipzic Univs. Classical Master of the Newell School, Pittsburgh, 1868–72; Secretary to George Bancroft, US Ambassador in Berlin, 1872–75; Professor of Latin 1876–84, and of History, 1884–96, Princeton University; Director of Historical Studies, Columbia University, 1896–1916; Member of International Olympic Committee, 1894; Chancellor of the American Academy of Arts and Letters, 1908–20, President 1920; ex-Vice-President NY Historical Society; Member American Historical Society and ex-President; Officier de la Légion d'Honneur, 1910; Commander of the North Star, Sweden, 1912. *Publications:* The Poet Labid, 1876; The Life and Work of J. R. W. Sloane, 1887; The French War and the Revolution, 1892; The Life of James M'Cosh, 1895; The Life of Napoleon Bonaparte, 1897; The French Revolution and Religious Reform, 1901; Parteiherrschaft in Amerika, 1913; The Balkans, 1914; Party Government in the United States, 1914; The Powers and Aims of Western Democracy, 1919; Greater France in Africa, 1924. *Recreations:* golf, walking. *Address:* Columbia Univ., New York. *Clubs:* Century, University, New York; Nassau, Princeton, NJ.

Died 12 Sept. 1928.

SLOMAN, Rev. Arthur, MA; Hon. Canon of Ely, 1907–14; Hon. Canon of St Albans, 1914; Rural Dean of Huntingdon, 1908–14; Rector of Sandy; *b* Farnham, Surrey, 18 Oct. 1851; 2nd *s* of S. G. Sloman, Surgeon, and *d* of Dr W. Newnham; *m* 1884, Bessie, *d* of late Wm Penrose of Glenmore, Queenstown; two *s*. *Educ:* Epsom College; Pembroke College, Oxford (Scholar). 1st Class Honours in Classical Moderations; 2nd Class in Final Classical School; President of Union Society, 1875; Assistant Master, Rossall, 1876–77; Westminster, 1877–86, and Master of the King's Scholars 1881–86; Headmaster of Birkenhead School, 1886–97. *Publications:* Trinummus of Plautus, and the Andria, Adelphi, and Phormio of Terence (two former with C. E. Freeman); St Matthew, Greek text with notes; A Grammar of Classical Latin; An Elementary Latin Grammar; Latin Prose for Middle Forms (with W. H. Spragge). *Recreations:* keen mountaineer, member of Alpine Club since 1879, cricket, tennis. *Address:* Sandy Rectory, Beds. *TA:* Sandy. *Club:* Alpine.

Died 20 Dec. 1919.

SLOMAN, Very Rev. Ernest; Dean of Georgetown, 1910; Rector of St George's Cathedral, Georgetown, since 1910; Archdeacon of Demerara, 1914; Vicar-General, 1910–14. *Educ:* St Edmund Hall, Oxford (MA); Leeds Clergy School. Ordained 1878; Curate of S Hackney, 1878–83; Christ Church, Georgetown, 1883–84; Principal of Belair Training Institute, 1884–89; Rector of St Patrick's, Berbice, 1889–1910. *Address:* The Deanery, Georgetown, British Guiana. *Club:* New Oxford and Cambridge.

Died 8 July 1918.

SLY, Sir Frank George, KCSI 1918 (CSI 1911); Hon. DLitt (Nagpur), 1924; Chief Commissioner, Central Provinces and Berar, 1920; Governor of Central Provinces, 1921–25; *b* 1866. *Educ:* Balliol College, Oxford. Entered ICS 1885; Under-Secretary, Government of India, 1895–98; Political Agent, Chattisgarh Feudatories, 1899; Commissioner of Settlements and Agriculture, 1901; Inspector-General of Agriculture, 1904–5; Commissioner of Berar, 1908–12; Member of Royal Commission on Indian Services, 1912–14; Chairman of PWD Reorganisation Committee, 1916–17; Chairman of Champaran Enquiry, 1917; Vice-Chairman, Lord Southborough's Committee on Franchise, 1918–19. *Address:* c/o Lloyds Bank, 6 Pall Mall, SW1. *Club:* East India United Service.

Died 16 July 1928.

SLYNE, Denis, CBE 1919; Barrister-at-law; Lord O'Hagan medallist and David Lynch medallist, King's Inns, Ireland; *b* 1859; *m*; two *d*. Entered Imperial Inland Rev. Dept, 1880; Treas. and Receiver-General, Trinidad, 1903; Member of Legislative and Executive Councils, Trinidad; Commissioner of Currency; Member of Port of Spain Sewerage Board and Water Authority, and Member of Port of Spain Town Board, 1904–7; Chairman of Committee for Liquidation of Enemy Businesses, 1914; Custodian of Enemy Property, 1916; Chairman of Public Officer's Guarantee Fund and of Board of Management of Agricultural Banks, Trinidad; Controller of Enemy Debts Clearing House, 1920; Commissioner of Income Tax, 1922; retired from public service, 1923. *Address:* 19 Collingham Place, Earl's Court, SW5.

Died 27 Feb. 1928.

SMALE, Morton Alfred, MRCS, LSA, LDS; Hon. Dental Surgeon, King George's Hospital; Consulting Dental Surgeon, Royal Dental Hospital and St Mary's Hospital; Dental Surgeon to St Mary's Hospital, 1891–1907; *b* London, 1847; *m* 1897, Madeline, *widow* of Dr Andrew Miller, Hampstead. *Educ:* Philological School, London; St Mary's Hospital; Royal Dental Hospital. First appointment was Dental Surgeon to West London Hospital, subsequently to Westminster Hospital, and St Mary's Hospital; was Dean of the School Royal Dental Hospital for 20 years, and instrumental in causing the new hospital to be erected; was a member of Dental Board of Examiners at Royal College of Surgeons for 12 years; President Stomatological Section International Medical Congress, 1913; was Hon. Secretary of the British Dental Association; refused the office of president both of that Association and of the Odontological Society; was President of Dental Section of British Medical Association for 1905; a member of many of the medical and dental societies. *Publications:* joint-author of Injuries and Diseases of the Teeth; and of many communications to Lancet, British Medical Journal, etc. *Recreations:* boating, swimming. *Address:* 22a Cavendish Square, W. *T:* Gerrard 2696; Henley-on-Thames. *T:* Henley 55.

Died 4 Aug. 1916.

SMALLEY, George Washburn, MA; American correspondent of The Times, 1895–1906; retired from active journalism, but contributor to the New York Tribune and Reviews; *b* Franklin, Norfolk Co., Mass, 2 June 1833; *s* of Rev. E. Smalley and Louisa, *d* of Hon. A. Washburn. *Educ:* Yale University (BA and MA) and Harvard Law School. Barrister, Boston, Mass, 1856–61; JP and Commissioner of Insolvency; war correspondent, Nov. 1861–Oct. 1862 (Civil War), for New York Tribune; then on editorial staff till 1867; organised its European Bureau in London, 1866–67; in charge European correspondence during Franco-German War, and till 1895; special Commissioner for US at Paris Exposition, 1878. *Publications:* Bright's Speeches, 1868; London Letters, 1890; Studies of Men, 1895; Life of Sir Sydney Waterlow, Bart, 1909; Anglo-American Memories, 1st series 1911, 2nd series 1912. *Address:* 4 Down Street, W. *T:* 3634 Mayfair. *Clubs:* Garrick, Beefsteak.

Died 4 April 1916.

SMALLMAN, Sir (Henry) George, Kt 1906; one of HM Lieutenants of the City of London; Commander of the Order of the Redeemer of Greece; Knighthood (First Class) of the Royal Order of Saint Olaf of Norway; a Governor of St Bartholomew's Hospital; Past Master of the Fanmakers' Company; *b* 1854; *s* of late Henry Smallman; *m* 1880, Louisa, *e d* of Richard Strong, JP; four *s*. *Educ:* Thanet College, Margate, Kent. Articled to Messrs Nash and Field, solicitors, 12 Queen Street, EC, and admitted a Solicitor, 1879; practised for several years at Queen Street, EC; retired, 1893; entered Corporation of London as representative of the ward of Cheap, 1888; Alderman and JP for the City of London, 1898–1909; Sheriff of the City of London, 1905–6; retired, 1909. *Address:* Eliot Lodge, Beckenham, Kent. *T:* Bromley 866. *Club:* Constitutional.

Died 2 April 1923.

SMALLWOOD, Lt-Col Frank Graham, CVO 1911 (MVO 1905); Ordnance Officer, Rawalpindi; *b* 10 Feb. 1867; *m* 1900, Isobel, *d* of Sir James Thomson; one *s*. Entered RA 1886; Capt. 1897; Major, 1905; Lt-Col 1914; served Sikkim Expedition, 1888 (medal with clasp); Chitral, 1895. *Club:* Army and Navy.

Died 30 Dec. 1919.

SMEATON, Lt-Col (Charles) Oswald, CB 1915; FZS 1909; FRSA 1909; retired; held Pilot-Aviator's Certificate No 115, 1911; *b* 3 Aug. 1862; *s* of David James Smeaton of Letham and Abbey Park, NB, and great-grand-nephew of John Smeaton, CE; *m* 1913, Evelyn Marion Rashleigh, *o c* of Rev. Francis R. Burnside, Rector of Great Stambridge, Essex. *Educ:* Royal Military Academy, Woolwich. Entered RA, 1882; Lieut-Col 1911; in conjunction with Captain Fred Harvey, solved the problem of the cure of Trypanosomiasis in animals, 1907–12; served Bechuanaland Expedition, 1884–85; Zululand, 1888; Crete, 1897; Nile Expedition, 1898 (despatches, medal); European War, 1914–17 (despatches, CB). *M:* LB 5955. *Clubs:* Royal Aero; Royal and Ancient Golf, St Andrews.

Died 23 April 1923.

SMEETON, Captain Samuel Page, ISO 1903; late Registrar-General and Deputy-Keeper of Records, Jamaica; *b* 25 Jan. 1842; *s* of Thomas Smeeton; *m* 1st, 1863, Emma (*decd*), *d* of Edward Moore; 2nd, 1899, Jean, *d* of John Henderson; two *s* four *d. Educ:* private tuition. Extra Clerk, Colonial Office, 1862-70; First-Class Clerk, Colonial Secretary's Office, Jamaica, 1870; Registrar-Gen. Jamaica, 1878-1908; Lieutenant, Jamaica Militia Garrison Artillery, 1885; Captain, 1887; retired. *Publications:* Reports on Jamaica Census, 1881 and 1891; Annual Reports Jamaica Vital Statistics, 1878-1908. *Recreations:* principal, rifle-shooting. *Address:* Edmonton, Alberta, Canada.
Died 19 July 1916.

SMELLIE, Alexander, MA, DD; Minister, Original Secession Church; *b* 1857; *m* 1897; two *s. Educ:* Edinburgh Royal High School; George Watson's College, Edinburgh; Edinburgh University. Ordained minister at Stranraer, 1880; edited Sunday School Chronicle, 1896; ordained at Carluke, 1900; received DD from Senatus of Edinburgh University, 1908. *Publications:* Men of the Covenant; In the Hour of Silence; In the Secret Place; Out of the Desert, a Gift; The Well by the Way; Lift up your Heart; Torch-Bearers of the Faith; Talks about Jesus; Service and Inspiration; Robert Murray McCheyne; Evan H. Hopkins, a Memoir. *Address:* Original Secession Manse, Carluke, Lanarkshire.
Died 23 May 1923.

SMIJTH, Sir William Bowyer-, 12th Bt, *cr* 1661; *b* 1 Sept. 1840; *e s* of Sir William Bowyer-Smijth, 11th Bt and Marianne Frances, 2nd *d* of Sir Henry Meux, 1st Bt; *S* father, 1883. *Educ:* Eton. Entered Diplomatic Service, 1858; Secretary of Legation at Yeddo, 1881. Owner of about 9,300 acres. *Heir:* cousin Alfred John Bowyer-Smijth, late Major and Hon. Lt-Col, 3rd Batt. Hampshire Regiment, *b* 12 Sept. 1850. *Address:* Hill Hall, Theydon Mount, Epping. *Club:* Carlton.
Died 22 July 1916.

SMITH, Adam, CMG 1916; Unofficial Member of Legislative Council, Trinidad; *b* Scotland, 1854; *e s* of Adam Smith, MA; *m;* two *s* two *d. Educ:* private school. Hon. Secretary Chamber of Commerce, Trinidad, since 1902; Commissioner of Currency since 1908; Chief Commissioner, Port of Spain, 1907-14; Mayor of Port of Spain, 1919-20. *Recreations:* reading, billiards. *Address:* St Clair, Port of Spain, Trinidad. *Club:* Trinidad Union, Port of Spain.
Died 3 Oct. 1920.

SMITH, Alfred John, MB, MCh, MAO, RUI; FRCSI; late Vice-President, British Gynæcological Society; late President Obstetric Section, Royal Academy of Medicine; ex-Assistant Master, Rotunda Hospital; Professor of Midwifery and Gynæcology, National University; Consultant Gynæcologist, St Vincent's Hospital, Dublin; *b* Kevit Castle, Nov. 1865; *s* of late Philip Smith, JP, of Kevit Castle, Crossdoney, Cavan; unmarried. *Educ:* St Patrick's College, Cavan; Dublin; Leipsic; Vienna. *Publications:* large contributor to various societies and journals on questions of interest to gynæcologists and laparotomists. *Recreations:* golf, fishing, shooting, motoring. *Address:* 30 Merrion Square, Dublin. *T:* 1295 Dublin. *M:* RI 839. *Club:* Stephen's Green, Dublin.
Died 20 Feb. 1925.

SMITH, Hon. Alfred Lee; Member of Legislative Council of New Zealand; *b* Sutton-on-Hull, Yorkshire, England, 1838; *y s* of late John Lee Smith, of Sutton, near Hull, Yorkshire; *m* 1864, Elizabeth, *d* of John Sharp, of Hedon, Yorkshire; one *s. Educ:* privately; Beverley. Was for some years in business in London; emigrated to New Zealand, 1868; interested in various commercial and industrial undertakings; represented New Zealand at the Colonial Conference held at Ottawa, Canada, 1894; chairman of three companies. *Recreation:* farming. *Address:* Anderson's Bay, near Dunedin, NZ. *TA:* Dunedin.

SMITH, Allan Ramsay, MA; Headmaster, Loretto School, Musselburgh, since 1908; *b* 10 Jan. 1875; *s* of James Smith of Craigielands, Beattock, and Merle Dene, Bidston, Birkenhead, Cotton Broker; *m* Violet, 4th *d* of Champion Russell; one *s* one *d. Educ:* Loretto School; Trinity Coll., Oxford. Graduated with second-class honours Lit. Hum.; Captain of Oxford University Rugby Football team; also captained Scottish International Football team. Travelled round the world; and after two years as House Tutor at the Borough Road Training College, became one of HM's Inspectors of Schools. *Recreations:* shooting, fishing, outdoor games. *Address:* Loretto School, Musselburgh, NB. *T:* 100 Musselburgh. *Clubs:* Bath; Liverpool University; Edinburgh University.
Died 31 March 1926.

SMITH, Arthur Lionel, MA; LLD St Andrew's; successively Jowett Fellow, and Tutor and Dean, and Master since 1916, of Balliol College, Oxford; *b* 4 Dec. 1850; *s* of W. H. Smith, civil engineer;

m 1879, Mary Florence, *e d* of John Forster Baird of Bowmont Hill, Northumberland; two *s* seven *d. Educ:* Christ's Hospital; Balliol College; 1st cl. Classical Mods and Lit. Hum. Lothian Prizeman. Fellow of Trinity College, Oxford, 1874-79; Examiner in Modern History in Universities of Oxford, Cambridge, Manchester, Liverpool, Birmingham, Bristol, Glasgow, and Wales; Ford's Lecturer in English History, 1905; Curator of Bodleian Library; Trustee of Oxford University Endowment Fund; Delegate for University Extension; Member of Hebdomadal Council, 1920. *Publications:* Notes on Stubbs' Charters; Life and Bibliography of F. W. Maitland, 1908; Church and State in the Middle Ages, 1913; contributor to Dictionary of English History, Dictionary of Political Economy, Cambridge Modern History, Social England (ed. Traill). *Address:* Balliol College, Oxford. *T:* Oxford 354.
Died 12 April 1924.

SMITH, Ven. Augustus Elder; Rector of Holy Trinity, Port of Spain, since 1888; Archdeacon of Trinidad since 1902. *Educ:* Codrington College, Barbados. Ordained, 1868; Curate of St Silas, Barbados, 1870-71; Checkleigh, Staffs., 1877-79; Holy Trinity Cathedral, 1871-88. *Address:* Deanery, Port of Spain, Trinidad.
Died 8 Jan. 1916.

SMITH, Basil Guy Oswald, MA; *b* 28 Sept. 1861; *e s* of late Oswald Augustus Smith of Hammerwood Lodge, Sussex, and Rose Sophia, *d* of late Arthur Vansittart of Foots Cray, Kent, and Shotesbrooke Park, Berkshire; *m* 1893, Rose Marguerite, 3rd *d* of late Charles Bruce Henry Somerset and Victoria Alice Anne, *d* of late William FitzGibbon of Sydney House, Cork; one *d. Educ:* Eton; Trinity College, Cambridge. *Address:* Shottesbrooke Park, Berkshire; 19 Hill Street, W1. *Clubs:* Travellers', Windham.
Died 13 July 1928.

SMITH, Rt. Hon. Sir Cecil Clementi, GCMG 1892 (KCMG 1886; CMG 1880); PC 1906; retired 1893; *b* London, 23 Dec. 1840; *s* of Rev. John Smith, MA, and Cecilia, *d* of Muzio Clementi, the composer; *m* 1869, Teresa, *d* of A. Newcomen, Kirkleatham Hall, Redcar; three *s* four *d. Educ:* St Paul's School; Corpus Christi Coll. Camb. (MA). After competitive examination 1862, was elected one of the first student interpreters, Hong-Kong; served in various offices; promoted from Colonial Treasurer, Hong-Kong, to Colonial Secretary, Straits Settlements, 1878; administered Government, 1884-85; and then appointed Lieutenant-Governor and Colonial Secretary, Ceylon; Governor and Commander-in-Chief of the Straits Settlements, 1887; HM High Commissioner and Consul-General for Borneo and Sarawak, 1889; British Commissioner under the FO to settle certain marine claims at Manila, and received the thanks of HM Government, 1878; as also for the 'Nisero' case, 1884; revived the Volunteer Corps in Singapore under the style of the Singapore Volunteer Artillery, and Hon. Col of the Corps; Master of the Mercers' Company, 1897-98; one of the Royal Commissioners for the Paris Exhibition, 1900; Member of the Advisory Committee, Imperial Institute, 1902; Member of Tariff Commission, 1904; Head of the British Delegation to the International Opium Commission, Shanghai, 1909 (received the thanks of HM Government); Chief British Delegate to the International Opium Conference at The Hague, 1911 (received the thanks of HM Government); Hon. Fellow Corpus Christi College, Cambridge, 1912. *Address:* The Grange, Welwyn, Herts. *Clubs:* National, Sports.
Died 6 Feb. 1916.

SMITH, Charles, MA; Master of Sidney Sussex College, Cambridge, 1890; Vice-Chancellor University of Cambridge, 1895-96, 1896-97; *b* Huntingdon, 11 May 1844; *m* 1882, Annie, *o d* of late Lt D. B. Hopkins, RN; four *s. Educ:* Sidney Sussex Coll. Camb., (BA). 3rd Wrangler, 1868; Fellow of Sidney Sussex Coll. 1868; tutor, 1875; Governor of Eton Coll., 1896-1909. *Publications:* An Elementary Treatise on Conic Sections, 1882; An Elementary Treatise on Solid Geometry, 1884; Elementary Algebra, 1886; Treatise on Algebra, 1887; Arithmetic, 1891; Geometrical Conics, 1894; Euclid (Smith and Bryant), 1901. *Address:* The Lodge, Sidney Sussex College, Cambridge.
Died 13 Nov. 1916.

SMITH, Hon. Sir (Charles) Abercrombie, Kt 1903; *b* 12 May 1834; *y s* of Andrew Smith; *m* 1897, Christina Caroline, *y d* of H. Remington Horne. *Educ:* Glasgow Univ. (MA and Breadalbane Scholar); Cambridge (MA, 2nd Wrangler and 2nd Smith's Prizeman, 1858). Fellow of St Peter's College, 1860-97, Hon. Fellow since 1897; LLD Cape University, 1917. Member of Legislative Assembly, Cape of Good Hope, 1866-75; Member of Executive Council since 1872; Minister of Crown Lands and Public Works, 1872-75; Controller and Auditor-General, 1875-1903; Commissioner for reduction of

Public Debt, 1872–74, and 1897–1903; Member of University Council since 1873; Vice-Chancellor Cape University, 1877–79, 1905–11; Science Examiner for 25 years; Chairman of Meteorological Commission, 1874–1911; Chairman of Tender Board, 1875–1903; Chairman War Expenditure Commission, 1881; Chairman of Civil Service Examining Commission, 1887–1910; served also on a number of important Commissions, such as Federation Commission 1871, Civil Service Enquiry Commission 1882–3 and 1904–6, etc. *Publications:* Schemes of Account-books and Accounts for the several departments of the Civil Service; a number of Blue-books every year, 1875–1911; Financial, Public Debt, and other Regulations, etc. *Recreations:* rambles to the habitats of the magnificent Cape flora. *Address:* St Cyrus, Wynberg, near Cape Town. *Club:* Civil Service, Cape Town.   *Died May 1919.*

SMITH, Captain Charles Appleton, CBE 1919; RD; RNR (retired); *b* Liverpool, 3 March 1864; *s* of William Charles Smith, Master Mariner, and Caroline Smith; *m* 1885, Edith Strawbridge, Liverpool, three *s* two *d*. *Educ:* Southport Grammar School. Served European War, Commander of Caronia and Captain of Aquitania (despatches). *Address:* 106 Mortlake Road, Kew Gardens, Surrey.
                                                 Died 17 Nov. 1928.

SMITH, Capt. Charles Futcher, DSO 1902; *b* 1876. Served South Africa with Driscoll's Scouts, 1900–2 (despatches, Queen's medal 4 claps, King's medal 2 clasps, DSO).
                                                 Died 17 Aug. 1925.

SMITH, Maj.-Gen. Sir Charles Holled, KCMG 1892; CB 1891; retired; *b* 12 Sept. 1846; *s* of Charles Sergison Smith, late of Consall Hall, Leek, and Georgiana, *d* of Hon. Herbert Gardner; *m* 1883, Maud Mary (*d* 1917), *d* of Major Fearnley Whittingstall; one *s*. *Educ:* Shrewsbury. Entered army, 1865; Captain, 1877; Brevet Major, 1882; Brevet Lt-Col, 1885; Brevet Colonel, 1888; Major-Gen. 1900; served Zulu and Boer Wars, 1879–81 (despatches, medal with clasp); Egyptian War, 1882 (despatches, brevet of Major, medal with clasp, Khedive's star); Nile Expedition, 1884–1885 (despatches, Brevet Lieut-Col, clasp); Soudan, 1885–86; Suakin, 1888 (despatches, Brevet Col, clasp); Tokar, 1891 (clasp, Khedive's star, 2nd class Medjidie); Governor of Red Sea Littoral (2nd class Osmanieh); Commandant at Suakim, 1888–92; Commandant of Forces in Victoria, 1894. *Club:* Naval and Military.   *Died 18 March 1925.*

SMITH, Charles Michie, CIE 1910; BSc; FRAS, FRSE; Director of the Kodaikánal and Madras Observatories, 1899–1911; *b* Keig, Aberdeenshire, 13 July 1854; *s* of Rev. Dr W. Pirie Smith; unmarried. *Educ:* home; Aberdeen and Edinburgh Universities. On Electrical Staff, Thomson & Jenkin, 1874–75; Professor of Physical Science, Madras Christian College, 1877; Government Astronomer, Madras, 1891. *Publications:* Publications of the Madras and Kodaikánal Observatories and various scientific papers. *Recreations:* golf, fishing, gardening. *Address:* Winsford, Kodaikánal, S India. *Clubs:* Savile, Royal Societies; Madras.   *Died 27 Sept. 1922.*

SMITH, Rev. Clement, MVO 1901; MA; Chaplain-in-Ordinary to the King; Canon of Windsor; *b* 1845; 3rd *s* of late Henry Smith, Accountant-General of the War Office; *m* 1871, Mary Eliza, *d* of late Stephen Spurling. *Educ:* St Paul's School; Christ Church, Oxford. *Address:* Whippingham Rectory, East Cowes, Isle of Wight; The Cloisters, Windsor.   *Died 22 May 1921.*

SMITH, Brig.-Gen. Clement Leslie, VC 1904. Entered Army, 1900; Captain, 1911; Maj. 1916; with Egyptian Army 1905–15; served S Africa, 1901–2 (medal with 3 clasps); Somaliland, 1904 (despatches, medal with two clasps); Soudan, 1910 (medal with clasp); European War, 1914–17 (Bt Lt-Col); Brig.-General, Dec. 1916–Jan. 1921; Colonel Comdt Jan.–Oct. 1921; commanded 2nd Duke of Wellington's Regt, 1921–25; retired pay, 1925. *Club:* United Service.
                                                 Died 14 Dec. 1927.

SMITH, Lt-Col Douglas Kirke, DSO 1917; *b* 24 May 1883; 2nd *s* of Rev. A. Kirke Smith, Boxworth Rectory, Cambridge; *m* 1906, Mary Ellen Beadle; one *s* two *d*. *Educ:* Haileybury College. Joined Territorial RA 1908; served European War in France, 1914–17 (despatches, DSO). *Recreations:* hunting, shooting, fishing. *Address:* Knowle House, Westcombe Park Road, Blackheath, SE3. *T:* Greenwich 479. *Club:* Devonshire.

                                                 Died 21 May 1923.

SMITH, Edgar Albert, ISO 1903; *b* 1847. Late Assistant Keeper, The Natural History Museum, Cromwell Road, SW; retired, 1913. *Address:* Mill Hill Park, Acton, W.   *Died 22 July 1916.*

SMITH, Maj.-Gen. E. Davidson-, on retired pay; *s* of late S. Smith of 23 Westbourne Terrace Road, Hyde Park; *m* 1863, Mary Matilda, *d* of late Wm Cooke-Collis of Castle Cooke, Co. Cork, and *niece* of late John Hyde of Castle Hyde, Co. Cork; two *s* three *d*. Served in Bulgaria, 1854; with the 95th Regt in Crimea, present at battles of Alma and Inkerman, at the affair of 26th October, and at the siege of Sevastopol (dangerously wounded in the trenches before Sevastopol; medal with 3 clasps and Turkish war medal); served Indian Mutiny, 1857–58; present at capture of the fortress of Awah, Rajpootanah, siege and capture of Kotah, battle of Kotah-Ke-Serai, siege and capture of city and fortress of Gwalior, capture of Chindaree, and other minor affairs, Central India (medal with clasp); served on the staff in Jersey; was Assistant Adjutant-General, West Indies, and Assistant Quarter-Master-General, Dublin district; reward for distinguished and meritorious services, 1903. *Address:* Allen House, Allen Street, Kensington, W. *Clubs:* Carlton, United Service, Junior United Service, Constitutional, Albemarle.

                                                 Died 8 Sept. 1916.

SMITH, Sir Edward, Kt 1916; JP; Vice-President, National Liberal Club and Crystal Palace Trustees; Chairman Tower Bench of Magistrates; Standing Joint Committee of London; *b* 20 Oct. 1857; *s* of William and Sophia Smith; *m*. *Educ:* private school. Member Lord Chancellor's Advisory Committee JP's, London. *Recreations:* golf, driving. *Address:* 75 Gore Road, NE; Ganbrook, Frinton-on-Sea, Essex. *Club:* National Liberal.

                                                 Died 20 Sept. 1926.

SMITH, Edward; *b* Dunstable, 1889. Official life in London; leisure almost entirely given to historical studies. *Publications:* The Peasant's Home, 1875 (first Howard medal of Statistical Society); William Cobbett, a Biography, 1878; The Story of the English Jacobins, 1881; Foreign Visitors in England, 1889; England and America after Independence, 1900; a Life of Sir Joseph Banks, PRS, 1911; An Index Locorum to Birch's Cartularium Saxonicum; items in bibliography, English topography and antiquities. *Recreations:* pedestrian touring, chess-play. *Address:* 42 Rosehill Road, Wandsworth Common, SW.
                                                 Died Nov. 1919.

SMITH, Hon. Sir Edwin Thomas, KCMG 1888; *b* 6 April 1830; *s* of late Edwin Smith of Walsall; *m* 1st, 1857, Florence (*d* 1862), *d* of late Robert Stock of Clifton; 2nd, 1869, Elizabeth, *d* of Edward Spicer of Adelaide. *Educ:* Queen Mary's Grammar School. Mayor of Kensington and Norwood, 1868, 1869, 1870, 1872 and 1873; of Adelaide, 1880, 1881, 1882, 1887, and 1888; Minister of Education, 1884; Commissioner of International Exhibitions at Philadelphia, 1876; Paris, 1878; Sydney 1880; Melbourne, 1881; Colonial and Indian Exhibition, 1886; Melbourne Centennial Exhibition, 1888; Vice-President and Promoter of Adelaide Jubilee Exhibition, 1887; Member of House of Assembly of South Australia, 1872–93; MLC of South Australia since 1894; JP of the Colony; Chairman of Trustees of Savings Bank of South Australia, of National Park Commissioners, and of Old Colonists' Association; Member of numerous Institutions. *Address:* The Acacias, Marryatville, S Australia. *Clubs:* Adelaide, Commercial Travellers.   *Died 25 Dec. 1919.*

SMITH, Frederick Bonham, ISO 1903; *b* Codrington College, Barbados, West Indies, 31 March 1837; *s* of Rev. E. P. Smith, MA of Pembroke College, Oxford, who was Tutor of Codrington College; *m* 1869; a widower; two *s* one *d*. *Educ:* Lodge School, Barbados, and subsequently completed education at Codrington College, having obtained an Island Scholarship there. Entered the Public Service of Barbados, 1859; Senior Police Magistrate of Bridgetown and St Michael, 1873; Acting Judge Assistant Court of Appeal, 1878–80; Acting Colonial Secretary, Barbados, in 1879; Provost-Marshal, 1882; and Inspector of Prisons in Island of Barbados, West Indies, 1878; retired on pension, 1917. *Recreations:* captained the Barbados team in first intercolonial cricket match, Barbados *v* Demerara, played in Barbados about 1865; also acted as captain in return match played in Demerara about 1868. *Address:* Bridgetown, Barbados, WI.

SMITH, Fred John, MA, MD Oxon 1891; FRCP Lond. 1895; Consulting Physician; *b* Castle Donington, Leicestershire, 17 Aug. 1857; *m* 1889. *Educ:* Christ's Hosp.; Balliol Coll., Oxford. Scholar, 1876; BA 1880; Radcliffe Trav. Scholar, 1885–88; MB 1886. Asst Physician, Lond. Hosp., 1891; full Physician, 1902; Lectr on Forensic Medicine since 1895; Referee under the Workmen's Compensation Act; Examiner University of Leeds and Society of Apothecaries; Hunterian Society's Orator, 1901; Pres. 1904. *Publications:* Differential Diagnosis of Diseases; Lectures on Forensic Medicine; Domestic Hygiene for Nurses; editor of Taylor's Principles and Practice of

Medical Jurisprudence, 6th edn 1910, and many contributions to Hunterian Society's Transactions, etc; article on the Treatment of Typhoid Fever, etc. *Recreations:* botanising, billiards, cycling, rowing, and golf. *Address:* 138 Harley Street, W. *T:* Paddington 1168.

Died 30 April 1919.

SMITH, Sir Frederick William, Kt 1910; JP; Mayor of Capetown, 1908–12; merchant; sole partner, Smith, Webster & Co., Capetown; *b* 30 Oct. 1861; 7th *s* of William James Smith of London and Capetown; *m* 1890, Lillie Edith, OBE, *d* of John A. Mathew; two *d.* Educ: S African College, Capetown. Chairman, S African Association, and Southern Life Association; Director, Atlas Fire Company; SGIG 33rd Degree of Scottish Freemasonry in Western Province of the Cape; President United Municipal Associations of S Africa and Municipal Association of Cape Province, 1909–10, 1910–11, and 1911–12. *Recreations:* tennis, mountain-climbing. *Address:* c/o Smith, Webster & Co., St George's Street, Capetown. *TA:* Dorodith. *T:* 177. *Club:* City, Capetown.

Died June 1926.

SMITH, George, CIE 1878; LLD; FRGS, FSS; Foreign Secretary, United Free Church of Scotland, 1878–1910; *b* Leith, 28 April 1833; *s* of Adam Smith, Fillyside; *m* 1st, 1855, Janet C. (*d* 1888), *d* of Robert Adam, Edinburgh; 2nd, 1890, Mary Agnes, *d* of William Mackintosh, Inshes house, Inverness-shire; five *s* five *d.* Educ: High School; Univ. Edinburgh. Principal of Doveton College, Calcutta, 1854–59; Fellow and Examiner Univ. of Calcutta, 1856–77; editor of Calcutta Review, 1857–64; editor of The Friend of India (weekly newspaper), Serampore, Bengal, and of the Annals of Indian Administration (19 vols); India correspondent of The Times, 1860–75; JP of Bengal-Behar, and Orissa; a Vice-President of the Royal Scottish Geographical Society. *Publications:* Student's Geography of British India; The Conversion of India; Short History of Christian Missions (8th edn); Bishop Heber, Poet and Missionary; Henry Martyn, Saint and Scholar; Twelve Indian Statemen (2nd edn); Twelve Pioneer Missionaries; Life of William Carey, DD (4th edn); Life of John Wilson, DD, FRS (2nd edn); Life of Alexander Duff, DD, LLD (4th edn); Stephen Hislop, Missionary and Naturalist (2nd edn); A Modern Apostle (2nd edn); Physician and Friend; articles in Encyclopaedia Britannica, Dict. of Nat. Biography, and Quarterly Review, etc. *Recreation:* travel. *Address:* 10 South Learmonth Gardens, Edinburgh. *T:* 2809.

Died 24 Dec. 1919.

SMITH, Brig.-Gen. George Barton, CB 1918; CMG 1915; Army Pay Department; *b* 10 Aug. 1860; *m* 1899, Kathleen, *d* of Col F. Haynes, APD; one *d.* Educ: Tonbridge School; private tutor; Caius College, Cambridge. Entered army (North Staffs Regt), 1884; Captain, 1893; Major, 1900; Lt-Col 1901; Colonel, 1910; Paymaster, 1892–1901; Chief Paymaster, 1910; served European War, 1914–18 (despatches thrice, CMG, CB); placed on retired pay with hon. rank of Brigadier-General. *Club:* Army and Navy.

Died 15 Nov. 1921.

SMITH, Rev. George Herbert, MA Oxon; late Principal of the SPG Theological College, Madras; Secretary of the Madras Diocesan Committee of SPG, 1901–20; Hon. Canon of St George's Cathedral, Madras, 1910; late Incumbent of St Thomas' Church, San Thome, Madras; *b* Bishopthorpe, York, 31 Aug. 1851; *s* of Rev. Charles Francis Smith of Beeford, Yorks, and Ellen Smith; *m* 1879, Mary Elinor, 2nd *d* of Edward Donkin of Sleights Old Hall, Yorks; one *s* two *d.* Educ: Richmond School, Yorks; Queen's College, Oxford (Lady Elizabeth Hastings Exhibition 1870, first-class Classical Mods., fourth-class Lit. Hum.). Senior Classical Master, Forest School, Walthamstow, 1875; Curate of Leytonstone, Essex, 1878; Vice-Principal of Theological School, Ambatoharanana, Madagascar, 1879; founded new Mission at Mahanoro, Madagascar, 1884; Organising Secretary SPG for Dioceses of Lichfield and Chester, 1887; Pioneer Missionary on West Coast of Madagascar, 1891; returned to Mahanoro as Missionary-in-charge, 1893; Principal SPG College, Trichinopoly, 1897; Examiner University of Madras, 1900–4; Examining Chaplain to the Bishop of Madras, 1902. *Publications:* Among the Menabe (thirteen months on the West Coast of Madagascar). *Recreations:* golf, cricket, tennis, boating. *Address:* Chesmead, Belmont Park Avenue, Maidenhead, Berks.

Died 1 July 1923.

SMITH, George Hill; Barrister-at-Law; Father of Bar of Northern Ireland, 1922; Crown Prosecutor on Northern Circuit for Down, Antrim, and Belfast; *b* 7 July 1833; 7th *c* of George Smith and Elizabeth Lee; *m* 1858, Eliza Graham (*d* 1895); three *s* three *d.* Educ: private schools, Dublin; matriculated at Queen's College, Belfast, 1874. For some years managing assistant in solicitor's office, Dublin; acting registrar, Probate Court, Dublin, 1867; district registrar, Armagh,

1873–86; called to Bar, 1877; joined NE Circuit, 1878; KC 1914. *Publications:* Torrens Registration Scheme; Rambling Reminiscences; Concise Guide to Probate Practice; Concise Guide to Matrimonial Court Practice. Forms of Indictments; Sketch of the North-East Bar, etc. *Address:* Glenmona, Cregagh Road, Belfast.

Died 1 April 1926.

SMITH, Sir George John, Kt 1897; JP, CA, DL; Managing Director, Bickford, Smith and Co., Ltd, etc; *b* 24 June 1845; *s* of Geo. Smith, JP, LLD, Trevu, Camborne, and Elizabeth Burrall, *d* of William Bickford; *m* 1871, Jane Symons, *e d* of Edward Burgess, Mountroy, Wells; seven *s* four *d.* Educ: privately; University, London. Succeeded to management of his father's business in 1870; a Conservative (younger brother of late William Bickford-Smith, Trevarno, Helston, formerly MP Truro-Helston Div.); Hon. Col 4th Batt. Duke of Cornwall's LI, formerly commanding 1st Vol. Batt. DCLI. *Recreations:* formerly cricket; music. *Address:* Treliske, Truro. *T:* 75 Truro and 65 Camborne. *M:* AF 709. *Club:* Constitutional.

Died 9 Oct. 1921.

SMITH, Rt. Rev. George John; RC Bishop of Argyll and the Isles since 1893; *b* Cuttlebrae, Banffshire, 1840. Ordained 1864. *Address:* Bishop's House, Oban.

Died 18 Jan. 1918.

SMITH, Rev. George Maberly, MA; *b* 5 June 1831; *m* 1863, Emily Harriet, *d* of Maxwell Macartney, MD, of Rosebrook, Armagh; one *s.* Educ: Tonbridge School; Gonville and Caius College, Cambridge. Curate of Penshurst, 1856–69; engaged in tuition at Tunbridge Wells, 1869–78; Hon. Canon of Canterbury; Rural Dean of Tonbridge, 1884–1912; Rector of Penshurst, Kent, 1878–1916. *Address:* Grenville Lodge, Henley on Thames. *T:* 166.

Died 7 Nov. 1917.

SMITH, George Munro, MD (Br.), LRCP Lond., MRCS; Hon. Consulting Surgeon Bristol Royal Infirmary since 1909; *b* 17 June, 1856; *s* of William Smith, MRCS, LSA; *m* 1889, Amy Elizabeth Hassell; one *s* one *d.* Educ: Clifton College; Bristol Medical School; University College, London. Suple Gold Medals, Medicine and Surgery; Bristol Royal Infirmary; Clarke Scholarship; 2nd and 3rd years Prizeman, Bristol Medical School. Medical Tutor, Bristol Med. School, 1879; Demonstrator of Physiology, 1881–87; Lecturer on Physiology, 1887–93; Professor of Physiology, University College, Bristol, 1893–99; Acting Surgeon, 2nd Gloucestershire Engineer Vol., 1886–87; Hon. Surgeon, Clifton Dispensary, 1896; Assistant Surgeon Bristol Royal Infirmary, 1889; Hon. Surgeon, 1897–1909; Hon. Secretary Bristol Med. Chirurgical Society, 1888; President, 1902; President Bath and Bristol Branch British Med. Assoc., 1909; President Association of Alumni, Bristol University, 1909; President Bristol Naturalists' Society, 1910; Lieut-Colonel 'à la suite' 2nd Southern General Hospital Royal Army Corps, 1910. *Publications:* The Medical Life; The Vis Medicatrix Naturae; various articles in British Medical Journal, Bristol Medico-Chirurgical Journal, and other periodicals. *Address:* 18 Aspley Road, Clifton, Bristol. *T:* 616.

Died 13 Jan. 1917.

SMITH, George Murray; Chairman Midland Railway since 1911; Alderman Leicestershire County Council; DL and JP Leicestershire; *b* 4 Feb. 1859; *e s* of George M. Smith, publisher and founder of Dictionary of National Biography, and Elizabeth, *d* of J. Blakeway; *m* 1885, Hon. Ellen Strutt, *y d* of 1st Baron Belper; one *s* one *d.* Educ: Harrow; Jesus College, Cambridge. Was associated with his father's publishing firm, Smith, Elder & Co., for 10 years; Captain in South Notts Yeomanry Cavalry; Member of the Leicestershire County Council; was Vice-Chairman of Leicester Infirmary and Member of Market Harborough Board of Guardians for many years; contested (U) Rushcliffe Division of Notts, 1895. *Recreations:* shooting, fishing, hunting. *Address:* Gumley Hall, Market Harborough. *TA:* Gems, Leicester. *T:* 1 Kilworth. *Clubs:* Brooks's, Athenæum.

Died 18 April 1919.

SMITH, Lieut-Col Sir Gerard, KCMG 1895; JP; Scots Fusilier Guards (retired); *b* 12 Dec. 1839; *s* of late M. T. Smith, MP; *m* 1871, Isabella Chatelaine (*d* 1915), *d* of Canon Hamilton; two *s* three *d.* Groom-in-Waiting to Queen Victoria, 1883–85; MP High Wycombe, 1883–85; Governor of West Australia, 1895–1900. *Address:* 237 Cromwell Road, SW5. *Club:* Brooks's.

Died 28 Oct. 1920.

SMITH, Granville; a Master of the Supreme Court; *b* Dartmouth, 17 May 1859; *s* of late William Smith, Solicitor, Dartmouth; *m* 1900, Nellie Claire, *d* of Alfred Mead, London. Educ: Blundell's School, Tiverton. Member of the Law Society; a Member of the Court of the Worshipful Company of Woolmen; a Vice-President of the London Devonian Association. *Address:* 288 Royal Courts of Justice, WC. *Club:* Royal Automobile.

Died 13 April 1925.

SMITH, Col Granville Roland Francis, CB 1911; CVO 1911; late AAG and QMG, London District; half-pay; *e s* of late Roland Smith and Constance Henrietta Sophia Louisa, *d* of late Lord Granville Charles Henry Somerset; *b* 1860; *m* 1883, Lady Blanche Catherine, 2nd *d* of 8th Earl of Kintore; two *s* (and one *s* decd). *Educ:* Eton; Sandhurst. Late Coldstream Guards; Patron of one living. *Address:* Duffield Hall, near Derby; 6 Grosvenor Square, W. *Clubs:* Carlton, Guards'. *Died 4 March 1917.*

SMITH, Sir Harold, Kt 1921; KC 1923; JP Co. Northants; barrister-at-law, Gray's Inn; Recorder of Blackburn since 1922; MP (C) Warrington (Lancs) Division, 1910–22, Wavertree Division of Liverpool since 1922; *b* 18 April 1876; *s* of Frederick Smith, Birkenhead, Cheshire, barrister-at-law, Middle Temple; *m* 1914, Joan, *y d* of late Rev. and Mrs Furneaux; one *s. Educ:* Birkenhead School, Cheshire. Until the end of 1908 a partner in firm of surveyors and valuers in Liverpool and Birkenhead; entered Gray's Inn, 1908; called to bar, 1911; Bencher, 1920; contested (C) Huddersfield, 1910. *Recreations:* golf, lawn tennis. *Address:* 4 Elm Court, Temple, EC4; *T:* Central 3110; 68 St James's Court, SW1; Middleton House, Middleton Cheney, near Banbury. *Clubs:* Carlton, Constitutional.

Died 10 Sept. 1924.

SMITH, Sir Henry, Kt 1916; JP Norfolk; one of HM's Lieutenants for City of London; Adviser to Quartermaster-General's Department, Equipment and Stores, 1914. *Address:* Luxor Lodge, Elsworthy Road, NW3; Uplands, Sheringham.

Died 1 Nov. 1919.

SMITH, Lt-Col Sir Henry, KCB 1897 (CB 1896); *b* 15 Dec. 1835; *s* of Rev. George Smith, DD, Edinburgh; *m* 1909, Annie, *d* of late John Graham. Chief Superintendent of Police in City of London, 1885–90; Commissioner of Police, 1890–1901; resigned 1901. *Publication:* From Constable to Commissioner, 1910. *Club:* New, Edinburgh. *Died 2 March 1921.*

SMITH, Sir Henry Babington, GBE 1920; CH 1917; KCB 1908 (CB 1905); CSI 1897; *b* 29 Jan. 1863; *s* of late Archibald Smith, FRS, of Jordanhill, Renfrewshire; *m* 1898, Lady Elisabeth Bruce, *d* of 9th Earl of Elgin; four *s* five *d. Educ:* Eton; Trinity Coll., Cambridge. Fellow; 1st class in Classical Tripos (Parts I and II); Chancellor's Medallist (MA); Examiner in the Education Dept, 1887; Principal private sec. to the Chancellor of the Exchequer (Mr Goschen), 1891; clerk in the Treasury, 1892; sec. to the British delegates at the Brussels Monetary Conference, 1892; private secretary to Earl of Elgin, Viceroy of India, 1894–99; Represented Treasury in Natal, 1899; British Representative on Council of Administration of Ottoman Public Debt, 1900; President, 1901; British Delegate at Postal Congress, Rome, 1906; at Radio-Telegraph Conference, Berlin, 1906; at Telegraph Conference, Lisbon, 1908; at Radio-Telegraph Conference, London, 1912; Secretary to Post Office, 1903–9; President, National Bank of Turkey, 1909; Member of Financial Mission to United States, 1915; Chairman, Royal Commission on Civil Service, 1915; Fellow of Eton; Assistant Commissioner for Great Britain in United States, 1918–19; Chairman, Committee on Indian Currency, 1919; Chairman, Railways Amalgamation Tribunal, 1921–23; Deputy-Governor British Trade Corporation; Director of the Bank of England. *Address:* 121 St James' Court, SW; Vineyards, Saffron Walden. *T:* Saffron Walden 61. *Clubs:* Brooks's, Athenæum.

Died 29 Sept. 1923.

SMITH, Col Henry Robert, CMG 1911; ISO 1903; JP; Sergeant-at-Arms, House of Commons, Ottawa, since 1892; *b* 30 Dec. 1843; *e s* of the Hon. Sir Henry Smith, of Roselawn, Kingston, Canada; *m* 1887, Mary Gurley, *widow* of Major Barrow, Royal Canadian Rifles. *Educ:* Kingston Grammar School. Entered Civil Service, 1859; Deputy Sergeant-at-Arms, 1872; Extra ADC to the Earl of Derby, Governor-General; served on Canadian Frontier 1866 and 1870 (medal and 2 clasps); North-West Campaign, 1885 (despatches, medal); was ADC to Lt-Gen. Sir E. Selby-Smyth, and Lt-Gen. Luard, CB; Hon. ADC to Earl of Minto, Governer-General, 1899–1903; was Extra ADC to Earl Grey, Governor-General; Extra ADC to HRH the Duke of Connaught; President Frontenac Loan and Investment Society, Kingston, and a Commissioner of Parliament. *Recreations:* shooting, fishing. *Address:* House of Commons, Ottawa, Canada. *Clubs:* Rideau, Canadian, Country, Ottawa.

Died 20 Sept. 1917.

SMITH, Horace, JP; Metropolitan Magistrate, Westminster, 1888–1917; *b* 18 Nov. 1836; 5th *s* of Robert Smith, merchant, Westbourne Terrace, and Hannah, *d* of John Boden, Ednaston, Derbyshire; *m* 1870, Susan, *d* of Rev. C. Watkins; three *s* three *d. Educ:* private schools; Highgate Grammar School; King's College, London; Trinity Hall, Cambridge (BA in Mathematical Honours; prize essays each year at Trinity Hall). Barrister, 1862; counsel to the Mint; revising barrister on Midland Circuit; secretary to Oxford Bribery Commission; Recorder of Lincoln, 1881; Bencher of the Inner Temple, 1886. *Publications:* Treatises on Landlord and Tenant, and Negligence; editor of Addison on Contracts, Addison on Torts; Roscoe's Criminal Evidence; Russell on Crimes; Poems, 1860; Poems, 1890; Interludes, 1892; Interludes (2nd series), 1894; Poems, 1897; Interludes (3rd series), 1899; Hymns and Psalms, 1903; Interludes (4th series), 1905; Collected Poems, 1908; Interludes (5th series), 1910; Interludes (6th series), 1913. *Recreations:* literature, painting, gardening, golf. *Address:* Keston, The Avenue, Sherborne, Dorset.

Died 25 Nov. 1922.

SMITH, Hugh Bellingham; Member, New English Art Club since 1894; *b* London, 1866; *m* 1915; one *d. Educ:* Slade School under A. Legros; Paris under Benjamin Constant. *Works:* The Viaduct, Hampstead; On the Arun; Romance; Teesdale; Barnard Castle; The Dream Fan; The Downs, Lewes; The Crinoline, etc.

Died 3 April 1922.

SMITH, Rev. Dr Isaac Gregory, MA Oxford, Hon. LLD Edinburgh; Rector of Great Shefford to 1906; *b* Manchester, 21 Nov. 1826; *s* of Rev. Jeremiah Smith, DD, High Master of the Free Grammar School, Manchester; *m d* of Rev. Canon G. W. Murray. *Educ:* Rugby; Trinity Coll. Oxford (Scholar). Hertford University Scholar; Ireland University Scholar; Fellow of Brasenose Coll. Rector of Tedstone Delamere, Herefordshire; afterwards Vicar of Gt Malvern; successively Prebendary of Hereford Cathedral, and Honorary Canon of Worcester, and while in Worcestershire Rural Dean of Powick; in Herefordshire he was Diocesan Inspector of Schools; Bampton Lecturer, 1873; Examining Chaplain to Bp of St David's, 1880–1900. *Publications:* Faith and Philosophy; Fra Angelico and other Lyrics (3rd edn); Aristotelianism (Ethic) and Modern Thought (3rd edn); History of Worcester Diocese (with Rev. Phipps Onslow); History of Christian Monasticism; The Silver Bells (2nd edn); The Holy Days (Vignettes in verse); The Athanasian Creed; What is Truth? Practical Psychology, 1908; Riullera (In Memoriam); On Assent to Creeds; Thoughts on Education, etc. *Address:* The Howdah, Horsell, Woking.

Died 17 Jan. 1920.

SMITH, Most Rev. James A., DD, PhD; RC Archbishop of St Andrews and Edinburgh since 1900; *b* Edinburgh, 18 Oct. 1841. *Educ:* St Mary's Coll, Blairs, Aberdeen, and Gregorian Univ., Rome. Ordained priest, 1866; Prof. at Blairs, 1867–90; cons. Bishop of Dunkeld, 1890. *Address:* St Bennet's, 42 Greenhill Gardens, Edinburgh. *Died 25 Nov. 1928.*

SMITH, Very Rev. James Allan, DD; Dean of St David's since 1903; and Chaplain to Bishop of St David's; Surrogate for granting marriage licences; *b* Pyecombe, Sussex, 2 Aug. 1841; *s* of late Rev. James Allan Smith, Rector of Pyecombe, and *d* of late William Catt of Bishopston; *m* 1st, 1865, Charlotte Isabella (decd), *d* of late Rev. Henry Linton, MA, of Stirtloe, Huntingdon, and Hon. Canon of Christ Church, Oxford; 2nd, 1902, Annie (*d* 1916), *d* of late Thomas Hawksley, Surgeon, of Nottingham; two *s* one *d. Educ:* as pupil of late Rev. Charles Shorting, Rector of Stonham Aspall, Suffolk, and Hon. Canon of Norwich; Wadham College, Oxford, 1860–63; BA 1863; MA 1867; BD and DD 1898. Curate, Trinity Church, St Marylebone, 1864–66; Lecturer of Boston, Lincs, 1866–71; Vicar of Holy Trinity, Nottingham, 1871–84; Prebendary of Sanctæ Crucis, Lincoln Cathedral, 1875; Vicar of Swansea and Rural Dean of E Gower, 1884–92; Vicar of Hay, 1902–3; Chancellor of St David's Cathedral and Canon Residentiary, 1898–1903. *Publications:* several sermons. *Address:* The Deanery, St David's, RSO.

Died Nov. 1918.

SMITH, Lieut-Col Sir James Robert Dunlop, KCSI 1910 (CSI 1909); KCVO 1916; CIE 1901; Knight of Grace of the Order of St John of Jerusalem; Knight Commander of the North Star of Sweden; Political ADC to Secretary of State for India; *b* 24 Aug. 1858; *s* of late George Smith, CIE; *m* 1887, Beatrice Clementina (*d* 1902) *e d* of Sir Charles Umpherston Aitchison, KCSI; two *d. Educ:* Edinburgh University (MA); Royal Military College, Sandhurst. 2nd Lieut 22nd Regiment, 1879; Lieut Indian Staff Corps, 1882; Private Sec. to Lt-Governor, Punjab, 1883; Settlement Officer, Sialkot, 1887; Deputy-Commissioner, Hissar, 1896; Director of Land Records and

Agriculture, Punjab, 1897; Famine Commissioner, Rajputana, 1899; member of Horse and Mule-Breeding Commission, India, 1900; Political Agent, Phulkian States and Bhawalpur, 1901; Private Secretary to Earl of Minto, Viceroy of India, 1905–10. *Address:* 25 Ovington Square, SW3. *T:* Western 170. *Clubs:* Bath, Brooks's.
Died 24 April 1921.

SMITH, John, CB 1895; *b* 9 July 1837; *s* of late David Smith of Edinburgh; *m* 1867, Annie Grant, 5th *d* of late Peter Nicolson of Adelphi, Berbice, British Guiana; one *s* five *d. Educ:* High School and University, Edinburgh. Admitted a Member of the Society of Chartered Accountants in Edinburgh, 1861; engaged in banking in Bombay, 1862–67; a merchant in Hull, Yorkshire, 1868–72; General Manager and Director of the London and Yorkshire Bank Ltd (later incorporated with the Union of London and Smith's Bank, Ltd), 1872–83; first Inspector-General in Bankruptcy, 1883; Inspector-General in Companies Liquidation, 1890; retired 1904. *Publications:* Official Reports to Board of Trade for presentation to Parliament, on the working of the Bankruptcy and Companies (Winding-up) Acts from 1884 to 1903. *Address:* Dunedin, Chichester Road, Croydon. *T:* Croydon 720.   *Died 25 Feb. 1922.*

SMITH, Very Rev. John, TD; JP; MA; BD, DD; Hon. FEIS; Minister of Partick Parish, Church of Scotland; Moderator, General Assembly of Church of Scotland, 1922; *b* Tollcross, Lanarkshire, 14 Oct. 1854; *s* of Robert Smith, iron merchant, and Jean Wright; *m* Helen, *d* of late Rev. Gilbert Johnston of Shettleston; three *s* one *d. Educ:* Annfield Academy, High School, and University of Glasgow. Studied in Germany; ordained, 1881; after a brief ministry in North Parish, Stirling, called to Partick Parish; formerly Covener of the Business Committee of Glasgow University Council, and Member of the University Court; Vice-Chairman of Glasgow Education Authority; formerly Chairman of Govan Parish School Board, and President of the Scottish School Boards Association since its inception; Chairman of National Committee and Chairman of Glasgow Provincial Committee for Training of Teachers; Convener of the Church of Scotland Education Committee; formerly Convener of Committee on Sabbath Schools; Convener of Examining Board; formerly Convener of Committee on Education for the Ministry; Chaplain, 6th HLI (Territorials); Member of Advisory Board in Scotland for the Blind. *Publications:* Broken Links in Scottish Education; Andrew Melville; George Heriot; Short Studies in the Gospels; one of the authors of Scottish Sabbath School Teachers' Books; The Hebrew Psalmist and the Scottish Bard; articles on education; frequent contributor of expositions and reviews to journals and magazines. *Recreations:* travelled on the Continent, France, Germany, Denmark and Sweden, and South Africa; golf. *Address:* The Manse, Partick, Glasgow. *T:* Western 1502.   *Died 9 June 1927.*

SMITH, Maj.-Gen. John Blackburne, CB 1918; CIE 1922; BA, MB, MCh (RUI), DPH, DTM&H(Camb); Indian Medical Service, retired; President, Medical Board, India Office, and Medical Adviser to the Secretary of State for India; *b* 21 Jan. 1865; *s* of Rev. J. A. Smith, MA, Cork; *m* 1896, Leta Mayne, *d* of late W. R. Nelson, Belfast; three *s* one *d. Educ:* Queen's College, Cork. Civil Surgeon various stations Bombay Presidency; ADMS Poona Division; DDMS Eastern Command, India; served European War (despatches, CB). *Address:* 51 Gordon Road, Ealing, W5. *T:* Ealing 2727. *Club:* East India United Service.   *Died 2 Nov. 1928.*

SMITH, Lt-Col John Manners, VC 1891; CIE 1894; CVO 1911; Political Department, Government of India; a Political Resident, 1st class; *b* Lahore, 30 Aug. 1864; 5th *s* of late Charles Manners Smith, FRCS (Surg.-Gen. IMS); *m* 1896, Bertha Mabel, *e d* of late Philip Arderne Latham. *Educ:* Trinity Coll. Stratford-on-Avon; King Edward VI School, Norwich; RMC Sandhurst. Lieut Norfolk Regt, 1883–85; joined Indian Staff Corps, and served with 3rd Sikhs (infantry) and 5th Gurkha Rifles, 1885–87; appointed Military Attaché, Foreign Office, Govt of India, and admitted Political Department, 1887; accompanied Sir Mortimer Durand on his Missions to Sikkim, 1888, and Kabul, 1893; held Political appointments in Kashmir, Bundhelkand, Baluchistan, Rajputana, Central India and Nepal, 1889–1918; served in NW Frontier Expeditions—capture of Nilt Position (medal with clasp, VC); Hunza-Nagur, 1891; Isazai, 1892; Punjab Frontier and Tirah, 1897–98 (medal with 3 clasps). *Address:* The Residency, Mount Abu, Rajputana, India. *Clubs:* Junior United Service, MCC.   *Died 6 Jan. 1920.*

SMITH, Rev. John Reader; Vicar of Edgbaston since 1916; Hon. Canon of Birmingham Cathedral since 1906; Rural Dean of Edgbaston, 1913; unmarried. *Educ:* Bishop Hatfield's Hall, Durham; MA. Curacies at Bangor and St Hilda's, Darlington; clerical secretary

of the Church Lads' Brigade, 1900–2; Chaplain to Rt Rev. Dr Gore when appointed Bishop of Worcester, 1902; Chaplain to Bishop of Birmingham, 1905–10; Hon. Chaplain to present Bishop of Birmingham, 1911; Vicar of St James's, Edgbaston, 1910–16; Chaplain (2nd Class) 3rd S Midland Brigade, RFA. *Address:* The Vicarage, Edgbaston. *T:* Edgbaston 368.   *Died 13 Jan. 1923.*

SMITH, John William, TD; DL Lancashire; MCh, MB; FRCS; Emeritus Professor of Surgery, University of Manchester, 1922; Consulting Surgeon, Manchester Royal Infirmary; *b* 1864; *e s* of Thomas Davidson Smith and Mary Gorrill; *m* Irène Maud, *o d* of H. J. Mason, Holland Park, W; one *s* one *d. Educ:* Lancaster School; Edinburgh Univ.; Vienna. MB Edinburgh (with first-class honours), 1886. Resident Surgeon, Edinburgh Royal Infirmary, 1887; Demonstrator of Anatomy, University of Edinburgh and Victoria University of Manchester, 1888–91; Resident Surgical Officer, Manchester Royal Infirmary, 1891–94; Visiting Surgeon, Withington Hospital, and Assistant Surgeon, Cancer Hospital, Manchester; served South Africa, 1900 (Hon. Lieut in the Army, Queen's medal two clasps); commanded 3rd East Lancashire Field Ambulance, Territorial Force, 1908–12; Lieut-Col (Bt Col) RAMC, TF, retired;Lecturer in Operative Surgery, 1904–11. *Publications:* various surgical and anatomical papers. *Address:* Richmond Road House, Ingleton (via Carnforth); *T:* Ingleton 16; Gamblesholme, Tatham, Lancaster.
Died 13 April 1926.

SMITH, Maj.-Gen. Joseph Barnard, Indian Army; *b* 12 June 1839; *m* 1871, Edith Olivia (*d* 1920), *d* of late Joseph Mansfield, MA. Entered army, 1856; Maj.-Gen. 1895; retired list, 1898; served NW Frontier of India, 1863 (medal with clasp); Tooshai Expedition, 1871–72 (clasp); Afghan War, 1878–80 (medal, brevet Lieut-Col).
Died 2 Jan. 1925.

SMITH, Rt. Rev. Joseph Oswald, OSB; first Abbot of Ampleforth since 1900; *b* St Helens, 1854. *Educ:* Ampleforth; Belmont; Rome. Was Prefect of Studies at Ampleforth, Professor of Philosophy at Belmont, and Canon of the Cathedral Chapter of St Michael's Priory, Hereford; Prior of Ampleforth, 1898. *Publications:*An Easy Way to use the Psalms; The Ordinary of the Mass the Food of Prayer; The Spirit of Our Lady's Litany; Our Lord's Own Words in the Gospel of St John; Meditations on the Passion; Meditations on the Litany of the Holy Name; Meditations on the Litany of the Sacred Heart. *Address:* Ampleforth Abbey, York.   *Died 4 Nov. 1924.*

SMITH, Sir Lumley, Kt 1914; JP Sussex; KC; MA; Chairman of Quarter Sessions for West Sussex, 1904–14; Vice-Chairman Sussex Territorial Force Association, 1908–10; a Lieutenant for City of London since 1877; *b* 1834; *y b* of Richard Horton-Smith, KC; *m* 1874, Jessie (*d* 1879), 2nd *d* of late Sir Thomas Gabriel, 1st and last Bt. *Educ:* University College School; University College, London; Trinity Hall, Cambridge. Ninth Wrangler, 1857; Le Bas Prize, 1858; and late Fellow of Trinity Hall, Camb. Called to Bar, 1860; Bencher (since 1881) and late Treasurer (1906) of Inner Temple; QC 1880; Recorder of Sandwich, 1883–94; Judge of Shoreditch and Bow County Courts, 1892–93; Judge of the Westminster County Court, 1893–1901; Judge of City of London Court, and a Judge of Central Criminal Court, 1901–13. *Publications:* The Koran in India, 1858; Editor of Mayne on Damages. *Address:* 25 Cadogan Square, SW; 4 Paper Buildings, Temple, EC. *Clubs:* Athenæum, Oxford and Cambridge.   *Died 7 June 1918.*

SMITH, Maynard, CB 1918; MB, BS (Lond); FRCS (Eng.); Knight of Grace of the Order of St John of Jerusalem; Surgeon to St Mary's Hospital; Surgeon to London Fever Hospital; Consulting Surgeon, St Luke's House; Hon. Surgeon Royal Masonic Institute for Girls; Consulting Surgeon, King Edward VII Memorial Hospital, Ealing; formerly Senior Assistant Surgeon, Victoria Hospital for Children, and Surgeon in charge of the Orthopædic Department, St Mary's Hospital; Fellow of the Association of Surgeons of Great Britain and of the Société Internationale de Chirurgie; *b* 20 Sept. 1875; *s* of W. H. Smith, Admiralty; *m* 1917, Isabel, *d* of F. I. Pitman; one *s* one *d. Educ:* Epsom College. Civil Surgeon, South African Field Force (medal and two clasps); went to France 1915 as Surgeon-in-Chief to the St John Ambulance Brigade Hospital (Hon. Major, RAMC); Colonel, AMS, and appointed Consulting Surgeon to the Fifth Army, 1916 (despatches thrice, CB, Croix de Guerre). *Publications:* Fractures of Lower Extremity, Official History of War; articles, Head Injuries and Dislocations, Index of Treatment; Surgical Infective Diseases, etc, System of Treatment; Inflammation, Choyce's System of Surgery; and papers in medical journals and Transactions of societies. *Address:* 49 Wimpole Street, W1. *T:* Langham 2030.
Died 18 March 1928.

SMITH, Morton William; Barrister-at-law; Recorder of Rochester since 1897; *b* 29 March 1851; *e s* of late F. J. Smith, Recorder of Margate; *m* Adrienne Ernestine Blanche, *d* of M. A. Blonet of Paris. *Educ:* Cowbridge Grammar School. Recorder of Gravesend, 1889–97; JP Cornwall; Chancellor Diocese of Sierra Leone; Member of the Diocesan Conference for Rochester. *Address:* Sunset House, Atlantic Road, Newquay, Cornwall; 4 Essex Court, Temple, EC.
Died 5 Feb. 1925.

SMITH, Lt-Gen. Octavius Ludlow, Indian Army; *b* 31 July 1828; *m* Mary Harriett Mackenzie Eyre; two *s*. Entered army, 1847; Lt-Gen. 1892; unemployed list, 1886; served Indian Mutiny, 1857–59 (twice severely wounded, thanked by Govt of India, medal with 2 clasps). *Address:* 7 Manson Place, SW7. *T:* Kensington 3828.
Died 7 May 1927.

SMITH, Peter Caldwell, CBE 1919; Medical Officer of Health, Metropolitan Borough of Wandsworth, since 1901; *b* Uddingston, Lanarkshire, 1858; *s* of James Smith, LLD, JP; *m* 1883, Ina, *d* of A. S. Macdonald, JP, Sutherlandshire; two *s* one *d*. *Educ:* Glasgow University; MA 1878; MB, CM 1881; MD 1884; DPH, Cambridge, 1888. Lecturer on Public Health, Anderson's College, Glasgow, 1890–93; Medical Officer of Health, Parish of Wandsworth, 1894–1901; Major and OC 2nd London Sanitary Co., RAMC, TF, 1909–13; Sanitary Officer 2nd London Division, 1913–15; Lt-Col 1915; President Travelling Medical Board, London District, 1916–18 (despatches, CBE). *Publications:* numerous papers on Public Health in Lancet, British Medical Journal, Glasgow Medical Journal, and The Hospital, etc. *Address:* 79 East Hill, Wandsworth, SW18. *T:* Battersea 290. *Clubs:* Caledonian, Yorick.
Died 21 Feb. 1923.

SMITH, Philip; Principal Clerk of the Vote Office, and Sub-Accountant, House of Commons; retired 1918; *b* 1853; *s* of late J. G. Smith, Clerk to the Librarian of House of Commons; *m* 1878, Catherine Laslett Dane; one *s* three *d*. Assistant Clerk in Vote Office, 1875; made a special study of Parliamentary customs and the interesting features of the old and new Palaces of Westminster. *Publications:* part author of Parliament Past and Present, a popular and picturesque history of 1000 years in the home of the Mother of Parliaments. *Address:* Hillfield, Broadway, Dorset.
Died 29 Aug. 1922.

SMITH, His Honour (Philip) Howard; Judge of County Courts, Circuit 25, since 1905; *e* surv. *s* of late Sir Wm Smith, DCL, LLD; *b* 27 Dec. 1845; *m* 1879, Mary Beaumont, 3rd *d* of late Richard O'Shaughnessy, one *s*. *Educ:* St Paul's School; Trinity College, Cambridge, MA. Called to Bar, 1867; member of the Oxford Circuit; a revising barrister; Recorder of Bridgnorth, 1900–5. *Address:* The Ford House, Wolverhampton. *Clubs:* New University, Savile.
Died 13 May 1919.

SMITH, His Honour Philip H. Law, KC 1906; MA, LLD; County Court Judge of City and County of Limerick since 1908; *b* 1866; 2nd *s* of late Philip Smith, JP, Kevit Castle, Co. Cavan; *m* 1914, Ellen, *o d* of Col Sir Wm Henry Dunn, 1st Bt. *Educ:* St Patrick's College, Cavan; Trinity College, Dublin. Called to Irish Bar, 1887; Senior Crown Prosecutor, North-West Circuit. *Publications:* (joint) Practice of Supreme Court of Judicature in Ireland. *Address:* 22 Ailesbury Road, Dublin. *Clubs:* Reform; County Limerick.
Died 6 Jan. 1920.

SMITH, Sir Prince, 1st Bt, *cr* 1911; JP West and East Ridings of Yorkshire; Chairman of Bradford District Bank; worsted machinery maker; *b* Keighley, Yorks, 3 Sept. 1840; *s* of late Prince Smith, of Holly House, Keighley, worsted machinery maker, and Martha, *d* of John Edmondson, of Keighley, contractor; *m* 1864, Martha Ann (*d* 1913), *d* of John Greenwood, of Skipton-in-Craven, Yorks; one *s* two *d*. *Educ:* Wesley College, Sheffield. Engaged in business as worsted machinery maker all his life. *Heir:* *s* Prince Smith, jun. [*b* 13 Oct. 1869; *m* 1894, Maud Mary, *d* of Henry Wright, of Mayfield, Keighley; one *s* two *d*. *Address:* Whinburn, Keighley]. *Address:* Hillbrook, Keighley; Southburn, Driffield. *TA:* Prince, Keighley. *T:* 236 Keighley.
Died 20 Oct. 1922.

SMITH, Reginald, RBA, RWS, ARCA. *Educ:* Manchester Branch of Royal College of Art; afterwards abroad. Has exhibited pictures at Royal Academy for many years; also an exhibitor at Paris Salon. *Address:* 92 Pembroke Road, Clifton, Bristol.

SMITH, Reginald John, KC; principal of Smith, Elder, and Co., publishers; editor Cornhill Magazine since 1897; President Publishers'

Association, 1904–5 and 1915–16; Member of Council, Royal Geographical Society; Member of Executive Committee of Royal Literary Fund, and Chairman of Anniversary Committee; on Employers' Panel of Board of Trade Conciliation; Treasurer and Member of Management Committee Poplar Hospital for Accidents; *b* 30 May 1857; *s* of late John Smith, Britwell House, Oxfordshire; *m* 1893, Isabel Marion, *d* of late George Murray Smith, 40 Park Lane, W. *Educ:* Eton; King's College, Cambridge (1st class Classics; distinguished in examination for Chancellor's Medals, BA, LLM). Barrister, 1883; assisted late Lord Russell of Killowen in his work at the Bar, 1886–94; QC 1894. *Address:* 11 Green Street, W. *T:* Mayfair 1395; 15 Waterloo Place, SW. *Clubs:* Athenæum, Brooks's, New University, Burlington Fine Arts.
Died 26 Dec. 1916.

SMITH, Robert Addison, CVO 1917 (MVO 1908); Senior partner of the firm of R. Addison Smith & Co., WS, Edinburgh; Hon. Treasurer, Queen Victoria School, Dunblane, NB, the Scottish National Memorial to the late Queen; Solicitor to Edinburgh Parish Council and Board of Control; Clerk and Treasurer Midlothian and Peebles Board of Control, etc; *b* 1869, Mary, *d* of David Lind, Edinburgh, who built the Scott Monument, Edinburgh; four *s* three *d*. *Educ:* private schools; Edinburgh University (honours Logic and Law). Took a prominent part in the movement for the Secretary for Scotland (1885) Bill, and the Private Legislation (Scotland) Bill 1889. *Recreations:* cricket, golf. *Address:* 3 Belgrave Crescent, Edinburgh.
Died 2 April 1925.

SMITH, Robert Cooper, KC; DCL; LLD; Professor of Commercial Law, McGill University, since 1899; *b* Montreal, 1859; *s* of Robert Smith; *m* 1890, Charlotte Florence Elizabeth, *d* of Milton Pennington. *Educ:* Montreal High School; McGill University. Called to Bar, 1882; QC 1897; Ex-Batonnier of the Bar; Officier d'Académie, France, 1917; practising as senior member of legal firm of Smith, Markey, Skinner, Pugsley and Hyde. *Address:* 112 St James Street, Montreal. *TA:* Smar, Montreal. *Clubs:* National Liberal; St James, Forest and Stream, Mount Royal; University, Royal St Lawrence Yacht, Montreal; Quebec Garrison, Quebec; Rideau, Ottawa.
Died 22 Sept. 1917.

SMITH, Robert Macaulay, MA, LLB; Advocate; Sheriff-Substitute of Berwickshire since 1908; *b* Dalry, Ayrshire, 1859; *s* of David Smith, merchant, Dalry; *m* 1898, Jean, *d* of John Wylie, merchant, Largs, Ayrshire; no *c*. *Educ:* Public School, Ayrshire; Edinburgh University. Called to Scottish Bar, 1889; Advocate-Depute in Sheriff Court, 1895; held position of Prosecutor for Public Interest for City of Edinburgh, 1899–1908; known during period at Bar as platform speaker and worker in Liberal interest in politics. *Publications:* edited The Liberal Platform, 1895. *Recreations:* golf, cycling. *Address:* Duns, Berwickshire. *Club:* Scottish Liberal, Edinburgh.
Died 13 Jan. 1927.

SMITH, Robert Murray, CMG 1884; MA; one of the leaders of Constitutional Party in Victoria; a Trustee of the Melbourne Argus; Trustee of Public Library; *b* 29 Oct. 1831; *s* of late Alexander Smith, Liverpool; *m* 1858, Jane (*d* 1913), *d* of Hon. J. F. Strachan, MLC; three *d*. *Educ:* Repton; Oriel College, Oxford (Scholar). Hon. MA Oxford, 1883. Emigrated to Victoria, 1854; elected MLA for St Kilda, 1873; for Boroondara, 1877; as joint leader of the Conservative opposition in 1881, he helped to carry Sir B. O'Loghlen's vote of want of confidence in the Berry Ministry—but did not take office; appointed Agent-General for Victoria in London, 1882; renewed in 1885; returned to Victoria, 1896; elected member for Hawthorn, 1894–97. *Recreation:* literature. *Address:* Repton, Toorak, Australia. *Club:* Melbourne, Victoria.
Died 31 Aug. 1921.

SMITH, Robert Shingleton, MD (Lond. and Bristol), BSc; FRCP; FRHS; Consulting Physician Bristol Royal Infirmary, 1905; *b* 1845; *m* Eliza Mary Dowson; one *s*. *Educ:* Queen's College, Taunton; King's College, London. Physician Bristol Royal Infirmary, 1873–1905; Consulting Physician Bristol Dispensary and Hospital; Fellow Royal Society of Medicine; Fellow and Associate King's College, London. *Publications:* late Editor, Bristol Medico-Chirurgical Journal; many contributions to various medical journals. *Address:* Deepholm, Clifton Park, Clifton, Bristol. *T:*553.
Died 15 April 1922.

SMITH, Sir Ross Macpherson, KBE 1919; MC, DFC, AFC; Aviator; *b* Adelaide, Australia, 4 Dec. 1892; unmarried. *Educ:* Queen's School, Adelaide; Warriston School, Moffat, Scotland. Served on Gallipoli and Sinai with Australian Light Horse; two years with Australian

Flying Corps in Palestine (MC and bar, DFC and 2 bars, Order of el Nahda); first flight from Cairo to Calcutta, 1918 (AFC); first flight England to Australia, 1919 (KBE). *Recreations:* golf, tennis, etc. *Address:* Gilberton, South Australia. *Club:* Junior Naval and Military.

Died 13 April 1922.

SMITH, Samuel, FRHistS, FLA; Consultant Librarian, Sheffield Public Libraries, since 1921; *b* Harrogate, 14 Aug. 1855; *e s* of Thomas Smith; *m* 1st, Jane Hustler; 2nd, Olivia Flint; one *s. Educ:* privately; Yorkshire College. Assistant Librarian, Leeds Public Libraries, 1872; City Librarian, Worcester, 1880; City Librarian, Sheffield Public Libraries, 1894–1920; Ex-President of the Sheffield Branch of the Dickens Fellowship; President of the North Midland Library Association; member of many of the leading literary societies, and lecturer on literary and social subjects. *Publications:* History of the Parish and Church of Leigh, in Transactions of Worcester Diocesan Architectural and Archæological Society; papers contributed to the Library Association, various magazines, and the press. *Recreations:* raconteur, photography, reading. *Address:* Allendale, Barnsley Road, Sheffield.

Died Aug. 1921.

SMITH, Sir Swire, Kt 1898; JP; MP (L) Keighley Division, Yorks, since 1915; *b* Keighley, 4 March 1842; *e s* of George Smith, Keighley, and Mary, *d* of Thomas Swire, Keighley. *Educ:* Keighley; Wesley College, Sheffield. Member of Royal Commission on Technical Instruction, 1881–84; Vice-Chairman Royal Commission on International Exhibitions, 1909; LLD University of Leeds, 1912. *Publications:* pamphlets and magazine articles on technical education. *Address:* Steeton Manor, near Keighley.

Died 16 March 1918.

SMITH, Rev. Sydney Fenn, SJ; on the staff of writers attached to the Jesuit Residence at Farm Street, Berkeley Square, W, since 1891; *b* Margate, 11 March 1843; *e s* of Rev. Sydney Smith, MA Cantab, Vicar of Worth, Sandwich, and Frances Mary, *d* of James Mallcott Richardson. *Educ:* private school. Received into the Catholic Church, 1864; entered the Society of Jesus, 1866; Priest, 1877; Professor of Ethics at Stonyhurst College, 1878–9; of Dogmatic Theology and Holy Scripture at the St Beuno's College, 1883–9; editor of the Month, 1897–1901. *Publications:* many articles in exposition and defence of Catholic doctrine and history in the Month and other periodicals, also for the Catholic Encyclopædia; the article on Ordinations Anglicanes in the Dictionnaire apologetique de la foi Catholique; numerous tracts for the Catholic Truth Society; editor of Scripture Manuals for Catholic Youth. *Address:* 31 Farm Street, Berkeley Square, W. *Died 1921.*

SMITH, Vernon Russell, KC; *b* 7 April 1849; *s* of Thomas Smith, Highgate; *m* 1879, E. Gertrude, *d* of Charles H. Lovell, Highgate; one *s. Educ:* Highgate School; St Peter's College, Cambridge (MA). Barrister, Inner Temple, 1872; QC 1894; retired, 1904. *Club:* Oxford and Cambridge. *Died 5 Dec. 1921.*

SMITH, Vincent Arthur, CIE 1919; LittD Dublin; MA Dublin and Oxford; MRAS; Indian Civil Service, retired; *b* Dublin, 1848; *s* of Aquilla Smith, MD; *m* 1871, *d* of W. C. Tute; three *s* one *d. Educ:* Trinity College, Dublin. Classical Scholar; 1st Senior Moderator in English Literature and Mod. History; 2nd Senior Moderator in Classics; University Student. Some time Lecturer in Indian History and Hindustani at TCD, and in Indian History at Oxford; Fellow of the Allahabad University; Gold Medallist of the Royal Asiatic Society, 1918; served in ICS 1871–1900 as Assistant Magistrate, etc; Settlement Officer; Magistrate and Collector; District and Sessions Judge; Commissioner of Division; and Chief Secretary to Govt of UP and Oudh; retired, 1900; then devoted life to work on Indian history, numismatics, art, and archaeology. *Publications:* Asoka, 2nd edn, 1909; Early History of India, 3rd edn, 1914; History of Fine Art in India and Ceylon, 1911; Akbar, the Great Mogul, 1917; Oxford History of India, 1919; many minor books and editions and innumerable papers in Quarterly Review and various journals. *Recreation:* reading. *Address:* 6 Fyfield Road, Oxford. *Clubs:* Oxford and County. *Died 6 Feb. 1920.*

SMITH, W. Harding, RBA; Hon. Secretary Japan Society. *Address:* White Lodge, 209 Brixton Hill, SW.

Died 9 Jan. 1922.

SMITH, Rev. Walter Percy, MA; Hon. Canon of Winchester Cathedral since 1910; *b* 1848; 2nd *s* of Nathaniel Smith of Cheltenham; *m* 1874, Annie Maria, *d* of H. D. Martin of Cheltenham. *Educ:* Marlborough; New College, Oxford. 1st Class Classical Moderations, 1869; 1st Class Law and Modern History, 1871; Assistant

Master at Marlborough, 1872; Winchester, 1873–1901; Chaplain to Winchester College, 1883–1901; Secretary to Winchester Diocesan Conference, 1903–20; to Winchester Clergy Sustentation Fund, 1904–13; Gen. Sec. to Church Congress, Southampton, 1913; Chairman of the Council of the University College, Southampton, 1917. *Publications:*Sir Thomas Browne's Religio Medici; pamphlet on Father Henry Garnet, SJ; papers in Winchester College, 1393–1893; and Memorials of Old Hampshire. *Address:* Wychbury, Winchester.

Died 11 Sept. 1922.

SMITH, Rev. Walter R.; *b* Parsonage, King's Cove, Bonavista Bay, Newfoundland, 5 July 1845; *s* of Rev. Benjamin Smith, Rural Dean, and SPG Missionary, Newfoundland; *m* 1871, Mary (*d* 1910), 2nd *d* of George H. Le Messurier, Deputy Postmaster-General, Newfoundland; two *s* one *d. Educ:* Queen's College, St John's, Newfoundland. Matriculated, 1865; Deacon, 1869; Priest 1871; Incumbent of Greenspond, 1869–70; SPG Missionary at Exploits, 1870–73; Rector of Tilt Cove, great mining centre, Notre Dame Bay, Newfoundland, 1874–79; Assistant Priest to his father at Trinity East, 1880–85; Clerical Member, Executive Committee Diocesan Synod, 1894, and re-elected to same office at every biennial session of Synod thereafter; Vice-President, Newfoundland Historical Society, 1905; Canon of the Cathedral and Rural Dean of Avalon, 1905; Incumbent of Portugal Cove, 1886; Clerical Member Executive Committee Diocesan Synod; Member of Council of Queen's College (Theological), 1906; also of Corresponding Committee Colonial and Continental Church Society; Episcopal Commissary, 1912; retired 1914. *Publications:* many articles on both religious and secular subjects for Newfoundland newspapers and magazines. *Address:* Episcopal Commissary, 44 Angel Place, S John's, Newfoundland.

Died 24 April 1921.

SMITH, Watson, FCS, FIC; Editor, Journal of Society of Chemical Industry, 1881–1915; *b* Stroud, Gloucestershire, 16 June 1845; *s* of late Rev. Watson Smith; *m* 1st, 1880, Susanne Felber of Zürich; five *s* two *d*; 2nd 1915, Dorothy Getrude Orchard. *Educ:* Owens College, Manchester; Heidelberg University; Polytechnikum, Zürich. Chemist and manager in works and factories, 10 years; Examiner, Institute of Chemistry; Lecturer in Technical Chemistry, Owens College, Victoria University, Manchester, and Professor of Applied Chemistry in University College, London; on first staff of abstractors for Journal of Chemical Society. Discoverer of true cause of flour-mill explosions, 1876; also of dinaphthyls and phenylnaphthalene; Discoverer of arseniate of Eucalyptol and glycerol phthalate; Investigator of Miike coal and its high resinoid constituents. *Publications:* contributions to Journal of Chemical Society, etc on the Destructive Distillation of Wood; Resinoid Coals, Ammonium Salts, Bye-products of Coke Ovens, also of Blast Furnace Gases and Tars, etc to the Journal of Society of Chemical Industry. *Recreation:* musical composition. *Address:* 34 Upper Park Road, Haverstock Hill, NW.

Died 1 May 1920.

SMITH, Sir William, Kt 1913; JP, Co. Derby; in business as corn miller since 1859; senior partner in Smith and Son, Ltd, Langley Mill, Derbyshire; Smith Brothers, Ltd, Walsall, Staffordshire; Smith Brothers, Ltd, Worksop, Notts; *b* 1843; *s* of Wm and Hannah Smith, of Milnhay House, Langley Mill; married; six *s* three *d. Educ:* Wesley College, Sheffield; Mansfield Grammar School. Visited Australia in old sailing-ship days, 1868; America, 1893; New Zealand, 1903 and 1911; Wesleyan local preacher; temperance and political speaker. *Recreations:* horse-riding, historical reading. *Address:* Dunstead House, Langley Mill. *TA:* Smith, Langley Mill. *T:*13.

Died 12 Jan. 1916.

SMITH, Maj.-Gen. William; Royal Artillery, retired; *b* 1835; 5th *s* of late William Smith of Carbeth-Guthrie, Stirlingshire; *m* 1869, Emma Corrie, *d* of Francis Henry Crozier, HEICS; three *s* two *d. Educ:* Edinburgh and Glasgow Universities. Joined Royal Artillery and appointed to a field battery at Ipswich, 1855; served Indian Mutiny, 1857–59; relief of Lucknow (horse shot), battle of Cawnpore, actions of Serai Ghat, Chanda, Umeerpore and Sultanpore, siege and capture of Lucknow, attack of the Moosabagh and action of Baree, Trans-Gogra campaign (despatches, medal with two clasps); served in the Horse Artillery, 1859–63; New Zealand War, 1864; campaigns on the Waikato and at Te Ranga, and attack on the Gate Pah (medal); Garrison Artillery, 1865–71; Gunnery-Instructor at the School of Gunnery at Shoeburyness, 1871–74; Garrison Instructor at Lucknow and Rawal Pindi, 1875–79; commanding a Field Battery in India, 1879–82; commanding Auxiliary Artillery in Dublin district, 1882–87; retired, with rank of Maj.-Gen. 1887. *Address:* Balcarras House, Charlton Kings, Cheltenham.

Died 25 Dec. 1922.

SMITH, Col William Apsley, CB 1900; CMG 1918; retired; late Royal Artillery; *b* 11 March 1856; *e s* of late John Smith, Britwell House, Oxfordshire; *m* 1885, Mary, 2nd *d* of late Gen. Sir John Adye; one *d. Educ:* Eton; RMA, Woolwich. Passed Staff College, 1886, Honours, etc. Staff Captain SE District, 1886–88; Brig. Major, Aldershot, 1888–91; Assistant Military Secretary to GOC Canada, 1894–96; Special Services Officer at Headquarters, 1896–98; Ordnance Committee, 1906–8; Brig. General, Commanding RA 3rd division, 1908–9; AQMG Eastern Command, 1914–18; served Afghan War, 1880 (medal); Egyptian War, 1882 (medal, star, and despatches, 5th class Medjidie); S African War, 1899–1900 (despatches, medal, and four clasps, CB); Military Attaché Russo-Japanese War, 1904–5; Japanese War medal; 3rd Class Rising Sun. *Address:* Ashdown House, Danehill, Sussex. *T:* Chelwood Gate 11. *Club:* United Service.
Died 1 May 1927.

SMITH, Sir William Frederick Haynes, KCMG 1890 (CMG 1897); *b* 1839; *m* 1867, Ellen Parkinson (*d* 1923), *d* of J. T. White. Barrister Middle Temple; Solicitor-Gen. of Brit. Guiana, 1865; Attorney-Gen. 1874; Governor of British Guiana, 1884–87; Leeward Isles, 1888–95; the Bahamas, 1895–97; High Comr and Comdr-in-Chief of the Island of Cyprus, 1897–1904. *Address:* 26 Chester Terrace, Regent's Park, NW. *Clubs:* Athenæum, Garrick.
Died 17 Dec. 1928.

SMITH-DORRIEN, Rev. Walter Montgomery, BD, MA; Prebendary of Exeter; Vicar of Crediton since 1901. *Educ:* Harrow School; Magdalen, Oxford (President OUAC 1874). Curate, Parish Church, Leeds, 1876–79; St Martin's, Brighton, 1881–85; Minor Canon of Durham, 1885–93; Precentor, 1886–7; Chaplain, St Mary's Chapel, Dalkeith, NB, 1893–99. *Address:* The Vicarage, Crediton.
Died 17 Dec. 1924.

SMITH-MARRIOTT, Sir William Henry, 5th Bt, *cr* 1774; JP; *b* Horsemonden, 7 Aug. 1835; *S* father, 1864; *m* 1868, Eliza (*d* 1904), *d* of Hon. Richard Cavendish, Thornton Hall, Buckinghamshire; two *s* two *d. Educ:* Harrow; Balliol Coll., Oxford. Owner of about 3,900 acres. *Heir: s* William John Smith-Marriott, *b* 6 Nov. 1870. *Address:* The Down House, Blandford, Dorsetshire. *Club:* Windham.
Died 30 Nov. 1924.

SMITHERS, Sir Alfred Waldron, Kt 1919; JP; MP (Co. U) Chislehurst division of Kent, Dec. 1918–22; late Deputy Chairman South-Eastern and Chatham Railway; Chairman of the English Association of American Share and Bondholders; *b* 4 Oct. 1850; *s* of late William Henry Smithers of the Bank of England; *m* 1880, Emma Roberta, *d* of R. M. Theobald, MA, MRCS. *Address:* Knockholt, Sevenoaks, Kent. *Clubs:* Devonshire, City of London.
Died 22 Aug. 1924.

SMYLY, William Cecil, JP; KC; LLB; *b* Dublin, 2 Jan. 1840; *y s* of John George Smyly, QC, DL, Castlederg and Camus, and Eliza, *d* of Sir Andrew Ferguson, Bt, MP Londonderry; *m* 1884, Alice, *o d* of Samuel Wm Brooks, Watford; two *s* two *d. Educ:* Harrow; Trinity Coll., Camb. Judge of County Courts, Derbyshire and part of Staffordshire, 1895–1902; Judge of CC Bow and Shoreditch, 1902–15. *Publications:* late editor of County Court Practice. *Recreations:* rowing; Captain Cambridge University Boat Club, 1862–63; Capt. 1st Trinity Boat Club, 1861–62. *Address:* Heathfield, Windlesham, Surrey. *Clubs:* New University, Alpine.
Died 4 March 1921.

SMYTH, Sir Alfred John Bowyer-, 13th Bt, *cr* 1661; late Major and Hon. Lieutenant-Colonel, 3rd Battalion Hampshire Regiment; *b* 12 Sept. 1850; *s* of late Rev. A. J. E. Smyth, Rector of Attleborough, and Mary *d* of late Major-Gen. Sir J. Rolt; *S* cousin, 1916. *Heir: n* Lieut-Comdr Philip Weyland Bowyer-Smyth, RN, *b* 4 Feb. 1894. *Address:* 4 The Crescent, Winchester. *Clubs:* Junior United Service; Hampshire, Winchester.
Died 4 Aug. 1927.

SMYTH, Col Charles Coghlan, CB 1891; retired, 1896; *b* 1842. Entered army, 1860; Col 1889; served Red River Expedition, Canada, 1870; Jowaki Campaign, 1877 (medal with clasp); Afghan War, 1877–80 (despatches, medal with clasp); Nile, 1884–85 (despatches, brevet of Lieut Col, medal with clasp, Khedive's star); Suakin, 1888 (despatches, clasp, 3rd class Medjidie).
Died 3 March 1920.

SMYTH, Capt. Gerald Brice Ferguson, DSO 1914; RE; *b* 7 Sept. 1885. Entered army, 1905; Captain, 1914; served European War, 1914–17 (severely wounded, despatches four times, DSO and bar).
Died July 1920.

SMYTH, Rear-Adm. Harry Hesketh, CMG 1917; DSO 1917; Royal Navy (retired); *b* 23 April 1872; *s* of late Charles Robert Knox Smyth, Commander Royal Navy (retd); *m* 1923, Helen Irene Carlyle, *widow* of late Captain S. J. Lovegrove, KAR. Joined HMS Britannia, 1885; Captain 1914; Commanded HM Ships Intrepid, Orvieto, Wahine, Ariadne, Amphitrite, Princess Margaret, during the European War (despatches twice, DSO, CMG, Officier Légion d'honneur); Rear-Admiral, 1925. *Recreations:* golf, lawn-tennis. *Address:* Pitmore Cottage, Sway, Hants. *T:* Sway 33. *Club:* Naval and Military.
Died 9 July 1926.

SMYTH, Major Humphrey Etwall, DSO 1917; OBE 1919; RAOC; *b* Sialkot, India, 1884; 2nd surv. *s* of Col E. W. Smyth, CB; *m* 1908, Kathleen, *e d* of Aubrey Robinson; one *s. Educ:* Royal Military Academy, Woolwich. First commissioned in the RGA 1902; transferred to RAOC 1918; served European War, 1915–19 (despatches four times, DSO, OBE). *Address:* Lloyds Bank Ltd (Cox's Branch), 6 Pall Mall, SW1.
Died 1 Nov. 1927.

SMYTH, John, MA, DPhil; Professor of Education, University of Melbourne, since 1918; Principal of the Teachers' College, State of Victoria, since 1902; *b* Lanarkshire, Scotland, 1864; *m*, 1891; one *s. Educ:* Otago University; Edinburgh University; Heidelberg and Jena Universities. Educated and trained to be a teacher in the National Schools, Ireland; commenced teaching career N Zealand, 1882; gained the MA degree with scholarship in Mental Science, 1892; Rector district High School, Waimate, NZ; relieved Prof. Salmond, Mental Science classes, Otago University, NZ 1897; studied Edinburgh, Heidelberg, Jena, 1898–1900, gaining Doctor of Phil. degree, Edinburgh; Chief Inspector of Schools, Wanganui district, NZ, 1900–2; Principal of Teachers' College, Melbourne, and Lecturer in Education, University of Melbourne, 1902–18. *Publications:* Truth and Reality; Guide to a Modern Infant Room; The Rural School in Australasia. *Recreation:* golf. *Address:* 632 St Kilda Road, Melbourne. *T:* Windsor 6731.
Died 20 Aug. 1927.

SMYTH, Col Owen Stuart, DSO 1886; late commanding mountain batteries Jutogh; *b* 1853; *m. Educ:* RMA Woolwich. Entered Royal Garrison Artillery, 1873; Lieut-Col 1898; served Afghan War, 1878–80 (despatches); Candahar (medal, two clasps, bronze decoration); Burmah, 1885–86 (despatches, DSO, medal with clasp); Wuntho Expedition, 1891 (despatches, clasp); Manipur (despatches, clasp).
Died 30 Jan. 1923.

SMYTHE, His Honour Charles John; *b* 21 April 1852; 2nd *s* of late W. Smythe, Methven Castle, Perthshire, MB 1876, Margaret, *y d* of late J. King of Lynedoch, Natal; seven *s* five *d. Educ:* Glenalmond College, Perthshire. Came to Natal 1872; began stock farming in Nottingham Road district, 1876; JP for colony, 1887; elected Member of Legislative Assembly for Lion's River Division on the introduction of Responsible Government, 1893; Speaker, 1897–99; Colonial Secretary Natal 1899–1903; Prime Minister, Natal, and Colonial Secretary, 1905–6; one of the delegates for Natal to S Africa National Convention, 1908–9; Administrator, Natal, 1910. *Address:* Strathearn, Nottingham Road, Natal. *Club:* Victoria, Maritzburg.
Died May 1918.

SMYTHE, Col David Murray; retired Colonel; *b* 17 Nov. 1850; *e s* of William Smythe of Methven, and Emily, *d* of Sir John Oswald of Dunnikier; *m* 1898, Hon. Katherine, *d* of 3rd Lord Bagot and Lucia, *d* of Lord Dover; one *d. Educ:* Trinity College, Cambridge; Sandhurst. Joined Royal Perth Rifles (Militia), 1870; joined Cameron Highlanders, 1872; joined 3rd Batt. Royal Highlanders (Militia), 1880; commanded 3rd Royal Highlanders 1893–97; served in the Zulu War in the Natal Native Contingent, 1879. DL and JP Perthshire. *Address:* Moulin Almond, near Perth. *TA:* Almondbank. *T:* Methven 6. *Club:* New, Edinburgh.
Died 10 Feb. 1928.

SMYTHE, Sir (John) Walter, 8th Bt, *cr* 1660; JP, Shropshire; DL, Monmouthshire; late Captain Louth Rifles; *b* 7 Nov. 1827; 4th *s* of Sir Edward Joseph Smythe, 6th Bt, and Bridget Frances, *d* of Sir Edward Bellew, 6th Bt; *S* brother, 1898; *m* 1864, Marie Louise, 2nd *d* of William Herbert, Clytha Park, Monmouth; one *s* two *d.* Owner of about 8,700 acres. *Heir: s* Edward Walter Joseph Patrick Herbert Smythe [*b* 20 March 1869. *Educ:* Downside]. *Address:* Acton Burnell Park, Shropshire; Eshe Hall, Durham. *Clubs:* Hurlingham, Wellington.
Died 5 March 1919.

SMYTHE, Lionel Percy, RA 1911 (ARA 1898); RWS; *b* 1840. Germinal, painted 1890, in the Chantrey Collection. *Address:* 40 Dover Street, W; Château d'Honvault, Wimereux, Pas de Calais, France.
Died 10 July 1918.

SNEYD, Maj.-Gen. Thomas William; *b* 14 Jan. 1837; *s* of Thomas Sneyd, 2nd *s* of William Sneyd of Ashcombe, and Emma, *d* of George Whitley of Norley Hall, Cheshire; *m* 1879, Charlotte Marion, *d* of late Capt. W. W. Repton; one *s* two *d*. *Educ:* Harrow. Served in the Queen's Bays in the Indian Mutiny; commanded the Regiment, 1877–82. *Address:* Ashcombe Park, near Leek, Staffs. *TA:* Cheddleton.
Died 1 May 1918.

SNOWDEN, Sir Arthur, Kt 1895; *b* Dartford, 1829; *m* 1856, Elizabeth (*d* 1900), *d* of Benjamin Jarvis. Went to Australia, 1852; Mayor of Melbourne, 1892–93, 1893–94, 1894–95; MLC Victoria, 1895–1904. *Address:* St Heliers, Abbotsford, Melbourne, Victoria.
Died 18 June 1918.

SOARES, Sir Ernest Joseph, Kt 1911; MA, LLD; *b* 20 Oct. 1864; *m* 1893, Kate Carolyn, *d* of late Samuel Lord; one *d*. *Educ:* St John's Coll., Camb. Formerly Solicitor in Manchester; Parliamentary Private Secretary to the Home Secretary, 1906–7; Charity Commissioner, 1908–10; Junior Lord of the Treasury, 1910–11; Assistant Comptroller Reduction of National Debt and Life Annuity Office, 1911–16; MP (L) North-West or Barnstaple Division of Devonshire, 1900–11. *Address:* Corriemoillie, Garve, Ross-shire. *Club:* Oxford and Cambridge.
Died 15 March 1926.

SODEN, Thomas Spooner; Barrister-at-Law; *b* Bath, 15 May 1837; *y s* of late John Smith Soden, FRCS; *m* 1873, Isabella Clavering (*d* 1911), *y d* of late Edward Cator Seaton, FRCP of Local Government Board. *Educ:* privately; Exeter Coll. Oxford (MA). Called to Bar, Middle Temple, 1862; Midland Circuit; was a Revising Barrister in 1868, and 1875–1901; Assistant Recorder at Birmingham, 1882–1912; Recorder of Grantham, 1897–1914; formerly Counsel for Mint at Warwick Assizes and Sessions. *Publications:* joint author of Smith and Soden's Landlord and Tenant. *Address:* 1 Courthope Road, Wimbledon. *Club:* Athenæum.
Died 5 Aug. 1920.

SOLOGUB, Feodor, (Feodor Kuzmich Teternikov); *b* 1864. *Educ:* Petrograd. Formerly schoolteacher. *Publications:* Bad Dreams, 1896; The Little Demon, 1907; The Created Legend, 1907–13; The Old House, 1915; The Sweet Scented Name, 1915.
Died 5 Dec. 1927.

SOLOMON, Solomon Joseph, PRBA, RA; painter; *b* London, 16 Sept. 1860; *s* of Joseph Solomon; *m* 1897, *d* of late Hyman Montague, FSA; one *s* two *d*. *Educ:* school of Mr Thomas Whitford; privately by Rev. Mr Singer. Studied Art at Heatherly's, the RA schools, Munich Academy, and the Beaux Arts, Paris; worked in Italy, Spain, and Morocco; Vice President of the Maccabæans Society; and President RBA, 1918; at the beginning of the War drew attention to the need for camouflage in modern warfare, and initiated it in the British Army; was a Lieut-Col, RE; introduced fishing net, the base of our effective camouflage during the War, 1916. *Paintings:* Cassandra, 1886; Samson, 1887; Niobe, 1888; The Judgment of Paris, 1890; Portrait of Mrs Patrick Campbell, 1893; I. Zangwill; Echo and Narcissus, 1894; Birth of Love, 1895; decoration for Royal Exchange; Laus Deo; and the Houses of Parliament. *Publications:* Strategic Camouflage, 1920; The Practice of Painting. *Recreation:* horse-riding. *Address:* 18 Hyde Park Gate, SW7. *T:* Western 3869; Whitecliffe, Birchington. *Clubs:* Athenæum, Arts, Omar Khayyam.
Died 27 July 1927.

SOLTAU-SYMONS, George William Culme, JP, DL; *b* 29 May 1831; *e s* of George William Soltau (*d* 1884) and Frances, *d* of late Rev. Thomas Culme, of Tothill, Devon; *m* 1st, 1859, Hon. Adèle Isabella (*d* 1869), 2nd *d* of 3rd Lord Graves; 2nd, 1875, Mary Elizabeth, *d* of Lt-Col Frederick William Todd, and *widow* of St John Coventry. *Educ:* Winchester; Christ Church, Oxford. High Sheriff, Devon, 1875. *Address:* Chaddlewood, Plympton, Devon.
Died 24 Oct. 1916.

SOLVAY, Ernest; Grand Officer Order of Leopold; Ministre d'Etat de Belgique; Inventor of Soda; *b* 1839; *m*. President of the Bureau of International Institute of Bibliography, Brussels; hon. member Royal Institute of Great Britain; holds Lavoisier Medal, Institute of France; Grand Medal, University of Paris; established Solvay Society of Brussels; founded International Institutes of Physic, of Chemistry and of Sociology; was a member of Belgian Senate. *Address:* 43 rue des Champs Elyseés, Brussels.
Died 26 May 1922.

SOMERSET, 15th Duke of, *cr* 1547; **Algernon St Maur,** JP; Baron Seymour, 1547; Bt, 1611; Lieutenant 60th Rifles (retired); Lieutenant-Colonel 1st Wiltshire Rifle Volunteers; *b* 22 July 1846; *s* of 14th Duke and Horatia, *d* of John Philip Morier, minister, Dresden; *S* father, 1894; *m* 1877, Susan, *d* of Charles Mackinnon. Owner of about 25,400 acres. *Heir:* cousin Brig.-Gen. Sir Edward Hamilton Seymour, KBE, CB, CMG, *b* 19 May 1860. *Address:* 35 Grosvenor Square, W1; *T:* Mayfair 6872; Maiden Bradley, Bath; Berry Pomeroy, Totnes, Devon. *Clubs:* Carlton, Army and Navy; Royal Yacht Squadron, Cowes.
Died 22 Oct. 1923.

SOMERSET, Lady Henry, (Isabella Caroline); late President National British Women's Temperance Association and World's Women's Christian Temperance Union; *b* 3 Aug. 1851; *e d* of 3rd Earl Somers; *m* 1873, Rt Hon. Lord Henry Somerset, PC, 2nd *s* of 8th Duke of Beaufort; one *s*. Established the Woman's Signal, and edited that paper in the interest of woman's work; founded in 1895 the industrial farm colony for inebriate women at Duxhurst, Surrey (the first institution opened in England for women on those lines); had for 15 years a home for training workhouse children; also The Children's Village, Duxhurst, for saving child-life. Formerly owned properties in Surrey, and in Herefordshire and Worcestershire, but made them over to her heirs. *Publications:* edited the Woman's Signal; leaflets on different phases of woman's work; a book of stories; Studies in Black and White; Under the Arch of Life; magazine articles; A Book for Children, illustrated and written by her; Our Village Life; and a book on reform for women, Beauty for Ashes. *Recreations:* modelling, painting. *Address:* 4 Gray's Inn Square, WC1. *T:* Holborn 5646; The Homes of the Holy Redeemer, Duxhurst, Reigate.
Died 12 March 1921.

SOMERSET, John Henry William; late Principal Clerk of the Private Bill Office, House of Commons; *b* 29 Jan. 1848; *y s* of late Rev. Villiers Henry Plantagenet Somerset (*s* of late Lord Charles Somerset); *m* 1st, 1889, Mary de Chair (*d* 1892), *d* of Rev. W. C. Denshire, of Thetford House, Lincoln; one *s* decd; 2nd, 1893, Isabel Maud, *d* of Frederick Courtney; one *d*. *Educ:* Marlborough. *Address:* Westfield, Cheltenham.
Died 2 March 1928.

SOMERSET, R(ichard) Gay, Member of Society of Oil Painters; Member Manchester Academy; RCA; *b* 1848. *Address:* Pengwern, Bettws-y-Coed.
Died 1928.

SOMERVELL, James, JP, DL; *b* 19 Sept. 1845; *e s* of late Graham Somervell and Henrietta Jane, *d* of William Stirling; *m* 1892, Kathleen Emile, *e d* of Maclaine of Lochbuie; one *s* two *d*. *Educ:* Harrow. Called to Bar, Inner Temple, 1870; Major and Hon. Lieut-Col late Ayrshire Yeomanry; MP (C) Ayr Burghs, 1890–92.
Died 10 Feb. 1924.

SOMERVILLE, David Hughes, ISO 1902; retired Civil servant; *b* 20 June 1840; *y s* of late William Somerville of Castlecomer, Co. Kilkenny, Ireland; *m* Anne Elizabeth (*d* 1914). *Educ:* private schools. Appointed Clerk in General Post Office, London, 1860; held appointment of Head-Postmaster of several London districts in succession, 1885–1905. *Recreations:* country walks and sketching. *Address:* 18 Queenswood Road, Forest Hill, SE.
Died 5 Feb. 1918.

SOMERVILLE, William Dennistoun; *b* 8 June 1842; *s* of late Tenison Alan Somerville and Cecilia, *d* of Daniel O'Connor of Shoreham, Sussex; *heir-pres.* to Baronetcy held by his cousin, 2nd Baron Athlumney. *Address:* Clermont, Rathnew, Co. Wicklow.
Died 10 March 1917.

SONNINO, Baron Sidney; *b* Pisa, 11 March 1847 (mother English); single. LLD Univ. of Pisa, 1865. Diplomacy, 1867–72; entered Parliament, 1880; Minister of Finance, 1893–94; Minister of the Treasury, 1894–96; Premier and Minister of Interior, Italy, during 1906, and 1909–10; Minister for Foreign Affairs, 1914–19; Member of Parliament (Italy), 1880–1919; Senator, 1920. *Publications:* Contadini in Sicilia, 1876; editor of the Rassegna Settimanale, 1878–82; several articles in the Nuova Antologia of Rome on Politics and Economics. *Address:* 1 A. Via delle Tre Cannelle, Rome. *T:* 13-63.
Died 24 Nov. 1922.

SOOTHILL, Alfred, BA (Lond.); Headmaster of Ashville College, Harrogate, since 1905; *b* 25 July 1863; *s* of William Soothill, Halifax; *m* Emma, *y d* of late Rev. Richard Gray, Darlington; one *s* one *d*. *Educ:* private School, Halifax; London University; United Methodist College, Victoria Park, Manchester. United Methodist Minister, 1885–1905, having Pastorates at Bow, Sunderland, Leeds, Newcastle upon Tyne. *Recreations:* music, tennis. *Address:* Ashville College, Harrogate. *T:* Harrogate 234.
Died 12 Sept. 1926.

SOUTHAM, Frederick Armitage, MB (Oxon); FRCS; late Examiner in Surgery, Victoria University; late Examiner in Surgery, University of Oxford; Consulting Surgeon, Manchester Christie Hospital; Consulting Surgeon, Manchester Royal Infirmary; Consulting Surgeon, Northern Hospital for Women and Children; Consulting Surgeon, Victoria Jewish Hospital, Manchester; Emeritus Professor of Surgery, Victoria University, Manchester. *Educ:* Oxford; Owens College, Manchester. *Publications:* Regional Surgery, including Surgical Diagnosis; A Manual for Students. *Address:* 13 St John Street, and 10 Kinnaird Road, Withington, Manchester. *T:* Manchester 1480. *M:*ND 5871.   *Died 9 March 1927.*

SOUTHEY, Senator Hon. Charles William, CMG 1902; JP; *b* 1832; *s* of late Sir Richard Southey, KCMG, of Southfield, Plumstead, Cape Colony; *m* 1864, Georgina Greaves; two *s* three d. Educ: Diocesan College, Cape Town. Entered Cape Civil Service, 1855; Commissioner and Resident Magistrate, Richmond, 1865; Alexandria, 1866; Middelburg, 1868; retired, 1870; farmer—thorough-bred horses, shorthorn cattle and ostriches; served South Africa, 1900–2 (CMG); nominated to the Senate 1910; received King's Medal on Act of Union. *Address:* Culmstock, Schoombie, Cape Province, South Africa. *Clubs:* Rand, Johannesburg; Civil Service, Cape Town; Port Elizabeth.   *Died 30 July 1924.*

SOUTHWARD, Rev. Walter Thomas, MA, MusB Camb; Fellow, Tutor, Chaplain of St Catharine's College, Cambridge; Inter-Collegiate Lecturer in Theology; *b* Liverpool, 1851; *s* of Jackson Southward, printer; *m* 1st, 1889, Ellen Bartlett (*d* 1898); 2nd, 1904, Ellen Banks; one *s*. *Educ:* Liverpool Coll. 1862–71; St Catharine's Coll. Cambridge, 1871–75 (First Class in Classics and highly distinguished in Chancellor's Medals, 1875). Master at Dulwich, 1875; private tutor in Liverpool, 1876; ordained, 1876; curate of Fairfield, St Michael, Liverpool; Huyton, 1879; returned to Cambridge, 1884; Examiner for Bell Scholarships, local examinations, previous examinations; took charge of choir of St Catharine's Coll., 1887; Senior Proctor and Select Preacher, 1889 and 1898; Tutor of St Catharine's, 1892; travelled in Germany, Italy, France. *Publications:* Commentary on Acts of the Apostles in Greek; Analysis of History of Church of England; Musical Setting of Evening Service; songs; musical essays. *Recreations:* amateur photography, chamber music. *Address:* St Catharine's College, Cambridge; Brookfield, Newnham, Cambridge.   *Died 4 July 1919.*

SOUTHWELL, Rev. Herbert Burrows; Canon of Worcester Cathedral since 1912; married. *Educ:* Charterhouse; Pembroke Coll. Oxford (2nd class Lit. Hum.; 2nd class Theology; Denyer and Johnson Theological Scholar, 1881). Ordained 1881; Curate of St Mary the Virgin, Oxford; Chaplain to the late Bishop Lightfoot, 1881; Principal of Lichfield Theological College, 1885, and Prebendary of Lichfield Cathedral, 1887; Principal of Bishop Jacob Hostel, and Canon of the Cathedral, Newcastle upon Tyne, 1901–12. *Address:* The College, Worcester.   *Died 9 April 1922.*

SOWTER, Ven. Francis Briggs; Prebendary of Highworth Sarum, 1903–27; Canon Residentiary of Sarum, 1910–16; Bishop's Chaplain, 1903; *m* 1877. *Educ:* Corpus Christi Coll., Camb. (Scholar). Rector of Corscombe, Dorset, 1877–84; Vicar of Holy Trinity, Weymouth, 1884–90; Vicar of Fleet, Dorset, 1886–90; Archdeacon of Dorset, 1889–1901; Rector of Holy Trinity, Dorchester, 1895–98; Rural Dean, 1895–98. *Address:* 17 The Close, Salisbury.
                                               Died 10 Sept. 1928.

SPALDING, Colonel Warner, CMG 1885; *b* Portsmouth, 1 May 1844; *e s* of late Col R. C. Spalding, Royal Marines; *m* 1st, 1868; 2nd, 1884, La Valette, *d* of late James Keele of Sydney; three *s* four d. *Educ:* Royal Naval School, New Cross. Royal Marine Cadet, HMS Excellent, 1860–61; Lieutenant Royal Marines, 1862–69; Captain New South Wales Permanent Artillery, 1871, and Adjutant Volunteer Artillery, Colonel commanding New South Wales Artillery Forces, 1892–96; Acting Commandant New South Wales Force, 1892; Chief Magistrate Norfolk Island, 1896–98; present at bombardment of batteries by English and French fleets at Simonoseiki, Japan; carried colours—Royal Marines—during assault and capture of batteries, etc, 1864; Soudan Expedition (Suakim), 1885, second in command New South Wales contingent (despatches, brevet of Colonel, CMG, medal with clasp, Khedive's star). *Recreations:* motoring, shooting. *Address:* Valetta, Macksville, Nambucca River, NS Wales, Australia.
                                               Died 22 Aug. 1920.

SPEAR, Sir John Ward, Kt 1911; JP; MP (LU) West or Tavistock Division of Devonshire, 1900–6 and 1910–18; Alderman of Devon County Council; *b* 1848; *m* 1877, *d* of John Willcock of Kingsbridge;

one *s* two d. *Educ:* Duke of Bedford's School, Milton Abbott; Bodmin. President of Poor Law Union Association for England and Wales; Trustee of Tavistock Hospital; Member of Tavistock Board of Guardians; Nonconformist; Income Tax Commissioner. *Address:* Venu, Tavistock. *Club:* St Stephen's.
                                               Died 27 April 1921.

SPEARMAN, Edmund Robert, CMG 1901; Acting 1st Secretary in Diplomatic Service; Vice-Counsul at Chantilly since 1901; *b* 10 May 1837; 2nd *s* of Rt Hon. Sir Alexander Young Spearman, 1st Bt, PC; *m* 1859, Lady Maria Louisa Fitzmaurice, 3rd *d* of 5th Earl of Orkney; two *d* (two *s* decd). *Educ:* Eton; France, Germany. Entered Public Service, 1854; Asst Secretary Public Works Loan Board and West Indian Islands Relief Board, 1860; Secretary, 1880–85; Asst Delegate, International Penitentiary Congress, Paris, 1895; Representative in Paris of the Royal Commission for Paris Exhibition, 1898–1901; late Capt. Middlesex Yeomanry; JP Middlesex, 1863. *Publications:* articles in most of leading English and American Reviews. *Recreations:* gardening, shooting. *Address:* Chantilly, France. *Club:* Sports.   *Died 6 Oct. 1918.*

SPEARMAN, Sir Joseph Layton Elmes, 2nd Bt, *cr* 1840; JP, DL; *b* Holmer, near Hereford, 22 Sept. 1857; *s* of late Alexander Young Spearman and Betha, *d* of late Sir Joseph Bailey, 1st Bt; S grandfather, 1874; *m* 1st, 1878, Ethel (*d* 1909), *d* of William Leask, 48 Queen's Gate; three *s* five d; 2nd, 1914, Carrie, *d* of late F. Eastwood and *widow* of Richard Sykes, Denver, USA. *Educ:* Eton; Brasenose Coll., Oxford. *Recreations:* hunting, shooting, golf. *Heir:* s Joseph William Spearman, *b* 22 Aug. 1879. *Address:* Grove House, Bexhill. *Club:* Junior Carlton.   *Died 11 Feb. 1922.*

SPECK, Rev. Jocelyn Henry; Hon. Canon of St Alban's; Vicar of St Paul's, Bedford and Hon. Warden of Diocesan Deaconesses Home; Chaplain at Depôt, Kempton Barracks; *s* of Rev. Edward J. Speck and Anna Katherine Lally; *m* Rosalie Dalrymple; one *s* two d. *Educ:* Marlborough; Worcester College, Oxford (MA). Formerly Proctor in Convocation; resigned, 1919. *Address:* St Paul's Vicarage, Bedford.
                                               Died 9 July 1922.

SPEER, Rear-Adm. F. Shirley Litchfield-, CMG 1917; DSO 1916; RN; Superintendent of Sheerness Dockyard since 1919; *b* 24 March 1874; *e s* of Frederick Litchfield; assumed additional name of Speer by Royal Licence, 1915; *m* 1902, Marianne Frances Cecilia, *e d* of late Edward F. Sandys; five *s*. *Educ:* Stubbington House, Fareham; HMS Britannia. Entered RN 1887; Commander, 1905; Capt. 1911; in Command of Mine-layer Squadron, 1915–17 (despatches); Deputy Director of Mining, Admiralty, 1918–19. *Address:* Wateringbury Place, Wateringbury, Kent. *Club:* United Service.
                                               Died 31 May 1922.

SPEIR, Robert Thomas Napier, of Culdees, Co. Perth, and Blackstone and Burnbrae, Co. Renfrew; JP, DL Renfrewshire and Perthshire; *b* 15 Oct. 1841; *o s* of Robert Speir of Culdees and Burnbrae, and Mary, *d* of Sir William Milliken Napier of Milliken; *m* 1868, Hon. Emily Gifford, 3rd *d* of 2nd Baron Gifford; four *s* two d. *Educ:* Eton; Christ Church, Oxford. For forty years Chairman of the Executive Committee and Home Mission Board of the Scottish Episcopal Church; was Captain in 4th Batt. Argyll and Sutherland Highlanders. *Publication:* one of the Essays on Church Reform, edited by the Bishop of Birmingham. *Address:* Culdees, Muthill, Perthshire.
                                               Died 3 April 1922.

SPENCE, Col Gilbert Ormerod, CB 1921; DSO 1917; TD; JP NR Yorks, 1914; DL County of Durham; Vice-Chairman Durham Territorial Association; *b* 1879; *o s* of Henry Grant Spence, JP, of Elmwood, Hartburn, Stockton-on-Tees; unmarried. *Educ:* Uppingham. Col-Commandant commanding the Durham LI Brigade, TA; Hon. Col 5th Batt. Durham LI; served European War, 1914–18 (wounded, despatches thrice, DSO); formerly Director of Richardson, Duck & Co., shipbuilders. *Recreations:* agricultural and county pursuits. *Address:* Far End, Kirklevington, Yarm-on-Tees. *T:* Eaglescliffe 50. *Clubs:* Junior Army and Navy, Kennel.
                                               Died 28 Nov. 1925.

SPENCE, James Knox, CSI 1898; *b* 10 Dec. 1844; *s* of Gen. J. K. Spence, ISC; *m* 1882, Emma, *d* of G. W. Hemming, KC. *Educ:* Cheltenham. Bombay Civil Service, 1865–1900; was in Postal Department, 1878–80; Political Agent, Koluba, 1885; Senior Collector, Bombay, 1888; Commissioner, 1891; Member, Legislative Council, 1895, 1897, and 1898; Member of Gov.-Gen.'s Legislative Council, 1899–1900. *Address:* 6 Connaught Square, W.
                                               Died 15 Feb. 1919.

SPENCE, John Bowring; HBM's Consul-General, Tripoli of Barbary, since 1914; *b* 26 Feb. 1861; *s* of late B. E. Spence, sculptor, Rome, and Rosina Gower; *m* 1895, Costanza (*d* 1912), *d* of Count Bentivoglio Middleton of Rome; two *s*. *Educ:* Dulwich College. Pro-Consul, Leghorn, 1887–90; International Customs Tariffs Bureau, Brussels, 1891–95; Vice-Consul, Madrid, 1895–97; Consul, Madeira, 1897–1905; Consul and Consul-General, Trieste, 1905–14. *Address:* British Consulate-General, Tripoli, N Africa. *Club:* Constitutional.
Died 26 Feb. 1918.

SPENCE, Thomas William Leisk, CB 1912; JP; *b* 1845; *s* of late Basil Spence, Raefirth, Shetland; *m* 1876, Henrietta Fanny, 3rd *d* of R. J. Hebden, of Eday, Orkney, and Ely Grange, Sussex. Was Secretary to General Board of Lunacy for Scotland, 1888–1911. *Address:* 30 Comely Bank, Edinburgh; Uyea, Uyeasound, Shetland.
Died 9 Nov. 1923.

SPENCE-JONES, Very Rev. Henry Donald Maurice, DD; Dean of Gloucester since 1886; Professor of Ancient History in the Royal Academy, 1906; *b* Pall Mall, 14 Jan. 1836; *e s* of late George Spence, QC, MP; *m* 1871, Louise, *d* of David Jones, MP Pantglâs, Carmarthenshire; one *s*. *Educ:* Westminster School; Cambridge (MA); DD honoris causa. 1st class Theological Tripos, 1865; Carus University Prizeman, 1862; Carus and Scholefield University Prizeman, 1865; Professor Eng. Lit. and Hebrew Lecturer, St David's Coll. Lampeter, 1865–70; Rector of St Mary de Crypt, Gloucester, 1870–77; Principal Gloucester Theol Coll., 1875–77; Hon. Canon Gloucester, 1875; Examining Chaplain to Bishop of Gloucester and Bristol, 1871–86; Vicar and Rural Dean of St Pancras, London, 1877–86; Select Preacher Camb. 1883, 1887, 1901, 1905; Oxford, 1892, 1903. JP Cardiganshire. *Publications:* editor of Pulpit Commentary (47 vols), author of Commentary on St Luke (2 vols, Pulpit Commentary); on 1 Samuel, and Pastoral Epistles in Bishop Ellicott's Commentary; on Acts, in Anglo-American Commentary; The Teaching of the Apostles, Greek Text, with Translation and Notes; Introduction to Talmudical Commentary on Genesis; Dreamland and History, the Chronicle of the Norman Dukes; Cloister Life in Days of Cœur de Lion; The Church of England: a History for the People—vol. i. British or Saxon Church; vol. ii. The Mediæval Church; vol. iii. The Reformation; vol. iv. The Anglican Church; The White Robe of Churches of the Eleventh Century; Early Christianity and Paganism: a History, AD 64–320; The Golden Age of the Church (studies in the 4th century), The Early Christians in Rome, 1910; contributor to Quarterly Review, Contemporary, Good Words, Quiver, English Illustrated Magazine, etc. *Recreation:* favourite amusement—working at mediæval ecclesiastical architecture, in his leisure moments. *Address:* The Deanery, Gloucester; Pantglâs, Caermarthenshire. *Club:* Athenæum.
Died 2 Nov. 1917.

SPENCER, 6th Earl *cr* 1765; **Rt. Hon. Charles Robert Spencer,** KG 1913; GCVO 1911; PC 1892; MA; Baron and Viscount Spencer, 1761; Viscount Althorp, 1765; Viscount Althorp (UK), 1905; Lord Chamberlain to the King, 1905–12; Lord-Lieutenant of Northants, 1908; *b* 30 Oct. 1857; *o s* of 4th Earl by his second wife, Adelaide, *o d* of late Sir Horace Beauchamp Seymour; *S* half-brother, 1910; *m* 1887, Hon. Margaret Baring (*d* 1906), *d* of 1st Baron Revelstoke; three *s* three *d*. *Educ:* Harrow; Trinity Coll. Cambridge (MA). MP (L) N Northants, 1880–85; Mid Northants, 1885–95; contested East Herts, 1898; Parliamentary Groom-in-Waiting to the Queen, 1886; Vice-Chamberlain, 1892–95; MP (L) Mid Northants, 1900–5. Grand Cross, Danebrog, 1906. Owner of about 20,000 acres. *Heir: s* Viscount Althorp, *b* 23 May 1892. *Address:* Althorp, Northampton; North Creake, Fakenham, Norfolk; 28 St James's Place, SW1. *T:* Regent 1089. *Clubs:* Brooks's. Turf.
Died 26 Sept. 1922.

SPENCER, Rev. Arthur John, TD; MA; FRGS; Rector of Drayton with Hellesdon, Norwich, since 1904; Rural Dean of Taverham; Hon. Canon of Norwich; Chaplain 1st Class, Territorials; Surrogate; *b* 18 June 1850; *s* of John Spencer, barrister-at-law and afterwards Vicar of Eastwood, Essex, and Margaret, *d* of Rev. E. Penny, Master at Charterhouse, and afterwards Rector of Great Stambridge, Essex; *m* 1st, Jane Anne (*d* 1914), *d* of John Hugh Bainbridge of Frankfield, Co. Cork; 2nd, Agnes Elizabeth, *widow* of Rev. Thomas Carpenter, Rector of Thwaite. *Educ:* Uppingham; Trinity Coll. Camb.; Wells Theological College. Curate in Charge of St John's, Great Yarmouth; Vicar of Hinckley; Vicar of Christ Church, Chelsea; Vicar of Eye, Suffolk. *Recreations:* golf, etc. *Address:* Drayton Rectory, Norwich. *TA:* Rectory, Drayton, Norfolk. *T:* Drayton 4. *M:* 714. *Club:* Norfolk, Norwich.
Died 24 Aug. 1922.

SPENCER, Augustus, ARCA London; Principal and Headmaster of the Royal College of Art, Board of Education, South Kensington,

1900–20; *b* Silsden, Yorkshire, 18 April 1860; 7th *s* of John Spencer; unmarried. *Educ:* Keighley Grammar School and School of Art. Entered Royal College of Art with a Scholarship, 1881; Headmaster of the School of Art, Coalbrookdale, Shropshire, 1885; Headmaster of the School of Art, Leicester, 1888; New School of Art erected 1897, when the School became municipalized; same year all Board Schools in Leicester affiliated to School of Art, from which a new Drawing Syllabus was issued for them. *Club:* Arts.
Died 3 Oct. 1924.

SPENCER, Ven. George; Incumbent of North Goulburn, 1908–12; Archdeacon of Young, 1903. *Educ:* Moore College, NSW. Ordained, 1867; Curate of St Stephen's Ballarat, 1867–69; Incumbent of St Stephen's, 1869–72; of St Saviour, Tarnagulla, 1872–75; Adelong, 1875–77; Tumut, 1877–85; Bega, 1885–94; St Nicholas, Goulburn, 1894–97; St Matthew, Albury, 1897–1903; Canon of Goulburn, 1894–1912. *Address:* Neath, 315 Miller Street, North Sydney, New South Wales.
Died 1926.

SPENCER, Hugh, CIE 1909; FRGS, FZS; ICS, retired; *b* 1867; *s* of late Charles Innes Spencer, MICE; *m* 1911, Mowbray, *d* of late William Smith, JP, Sundon House, Clifton, Glos. *Educ:* Bristol Grammar School; Magdalen College, Oxford. Entered ICS 1888; Magistrate and Collector, retired 1915; Hindustani and Hindi Censor, Cairo, 1915–19. *Address:* 5 Clifton Gardens, W9. *T:*Paddington 718. *Club:* East India United Service.
Died 14 Jan. 1926.

SPENCER-SMITH, Michael Seymour, DSO 1919; MC; partner in H. S. Lefevre & Co., 16 Bishopsgate, EC; a Director of the Bank of England since 1920; *b* 1881; *y s* of late Rev. Spencer Compton Spencer-Smith, Kingston Vicarage, Dorset; *m* 1907, Evelyn Penelope, *y d* of Rev. Arthur Delmé-Radcliffe; two *s* one *d*. *Educ:* Eton; New College, Oxford. Started in business, 1903; spent nine years in Japan; joined Army, Aug. 1914; served in King's Royal Rifle Corps and on staff of Canadian Corps Heavy Artillery; promoted Lt-Colonel and employed as AA and QMG Murmansk 1918 (despatches, DSO, MC). *Address:* Norman House, Stansted, Essex. *Club:* Bath.
Died 20 Jan. 1928.

SPENDER, Arthur Edmund; Editor of the Shrewsbury Chronicle since 1922; *b* London, 26 Oct. 1871; surv. *s* of late Edward Spender (known as the Prince of the Lobby, founder of the first London Letter for the provincial newspapers, co-founder of the Western Morning News), and Mrs Ellen Spender, *d* of late Dr Edmund E. Rendle, Plymouth; *m* 1905, Helen Frances, *d* of late Arthur Champernowne, Dartington Hall, Devon; four *s* three *d*. *Educ:* Radley; Christ Church, Oxford (Honours in History finals, 1894). Called to Bar, Inner Temple, 1895; tour round the world, 1896; Managing Director Western Morning News, 1900–22; Member of the Moseley Education Commission to the United States, 1903; Special Correspondent for the Winter Sports in Norway, 1902; Mayor of Plymouth, 1908–9; Magistrate of Plymouth, 1911; President Port of Plymouth Chamber of Commerce, 1912; Captain Territorial Reserve Force, Devon Regiment, 1915; President of the Newspaper Society, 1916; Chairman of the Press Association, 1917. *Publications:* Two Winters in Norway; Random Notes on the Moseley Education Commission; Impressions on Finland (pamphlet), 1920. *Recreation:* gardening. *Address:* The Limes, Shrewsbury. *T:* Shrewsbury 162.
Died 6 July 1923.

SPENDER, E. Harold, LLD (Athens); FRGS; author, journalist and lecturer; *b* Bath, 22 June 1864; *s* of late Dr and Mrs J. K. Spender, novelist; *m* 1904, Violet Hilda (*d* 1921), *d* of late Ernest Schuster, KC; three *s* one *d*. *Educ:* Bath College (Head Boy, 1882–83); Exhibitioner of University College, Oxford. 1st in Mods. 1884; 1st. in Lit. Hum. 1887; MA. On staff of the Echo, 1887–89; Lecturer for Oxford Univ. Extension Delegacy, 1889–92; on staff of the Pall Mall Gazette, 1891–93; Westminster Gazette, 1893–95; Daily Chronicle, 1895–99; Manchester Guardian, 1899–1900; Daily News, 1900–14. During the war gave himself up to war savings propaganda, volunteering, and other war activities, 1914–18; contested Bath as United Liberal candidate, General Election, Nov. 1922; Chairman of Social Welfare Council, Hampstead. Commander Greek Order of the Redeemer; *Publications:* Story of the Home Rule Session, 1893; At the Sign of the Guillotine, 1895; Through the High Pyrenees, 1898; The Arena, 1906; Home Rule, 1912; In Praise of Switzerland, 1912; The Call of the Siren, 1913; One Man Returns, 1914; The Flame of Daring, 1915; The Dividing Sword, 1916; The Man Who Went, 1919; three biographies—Herbert Henry Asquith, 1915; General Botha, 1916; David Lloyd George, 1920; A Briton in America, 1921; Byron and Greece, 1924; Men and Mansions, 1924;

The Cauldron of Europe, 1925; numerous short stories and magazine articles. *Recreations:* mountaineering, travelling, golfing. *Address:* 10 Frognal, Hampstead, NW3. *T:* Hampstead 3137. *Clubs:* National Liberal, Alpine, Whitefriars; Wimbledon Park Golf.

Died 15 April 1926.

SPICER, Sir Howard, KBE 1918; papermaker and wholesale stationer; Vice-Chairman and Joint Managing Director of Spicers, Limited; Director of United Newspapers, Ltd, and Edinburgh Evening News; *b* 1872; *e s* of late James Spicer of Eltham; *m* 1st, 1896, Muriel, *d* of Rev. S. B. Handley; 2nd, 1923, Ethel Anne, *o d* of Frederick Marsh. *Educ:* Leys School, Cambridge; privately on the Continent. Co-founder, Boys Empire League. *Publications:* editor, Sandow's magazine, 1899–1901; resigned to edit Boys of Our Empire, 1901; editor, Sports Library, The Girls' Empire; author of Sports for Boys, Sports for Girls; general articles. *Recreations:* riding, travelling. *Address:* 12 Elm Tree Road, St John's Wood, NW8. *Clubs:* Reform, Kennel, Royal Automobile, 1920.   *Died 16 Aug. 1926.*

SPICER, John Edmund Philip, JP; *b* 1850; *e s* of late John William Gooch Spicer and Juliana Hannah Webb, *d* of late Rev. Edmund Probyn, of Longhope, Co. Gloucester; *m* 1888, Lady Margaret Mary Fane, *y d* of 12th Earl of Westmorland; five *s*. *Educ:* Wellington. High Sheriff, Wilts, 1889; Patron of one living; late Captain, 1st Life Guards. *Address:* Spye Park, Chippenham. *TA:* Spye Park, Bromham. *Club:* Arthur's.   *Died 31 March 1928.*

SPICER, Rev. Canon John Maurice; Vicar of Kirk-Malew since 1895; Canon of St Columba since 1912. Ordained 1885; Curate of Kirk-Michael, 1885–87; Chaplain, Laxey, 1887–95. *Address:* Malew Vicarage, Ballasalla, Isle of Man.

Died 12 Aug. 1920.

SPICER, Robert Henry Scanes, MD London; specialist for nose, throat, and ear affections; Consulting Surgeon Diseases of the Throat, St Mary's Hospital; *e s* of late Robert H. S. Spicer, MD, of North Molton, Devon, and *g s* of late Robert Spicer of Exeter; *m* Mary Wilhelmina Huelin; one *s* two *d*. Won Open Natural Science Scholarship at St Mary's Hospital; Anatomical Scholar and Demonstrator; Gold Medal Society of Apothecaries; graduated MB and BSc in honours; afterwards visited leading throat clinics in Vienna, Berlin, and Paris; MRCS; Fellow Royal Society of Medicine. Hon. Phys. Royal Soc. of Musicians of Great Britain; President Sect. of Laryng. and Otol. British Med. Assoc. 1900; one of the founders, jointly first Secretary, and later Vice-Pres. Laryng. Soc. of Lond.; one of founders of Otolog. Society of Great Britain. *Publications:* numerous technical pamphlets and contributions to medical press on diseases of throat, nose and ear, cancer, and physical education. *Recreations:* country life, travel, literature, music, and theatre. *Address:* 26 Graham Street, Eaton Square, SW1. *T:* Victoria 9309.

Died 18 June 1925.

SPIELMANN, Sir Isidore, Kt 1905; CMG 1907; FSA; Commander of Order of the Crown of Belgium; Grand Cordon of Order of the Crown of Italy; Officer of Order of Leopold; *b* London, 21 July 1854; *e* surv. *s* of Adam Spielmann; *m* 1879, Emily, *d* of Sir J. Sebag-Montefiore; one *s* three *d*. *Educ:* privately in England. Director for Art, Board of Trade (Exhibitions Branch); Executive Committee National Art Collections Fund; Member of Advisory Council, Victoria and Albert Museum; a Governor, British Institute Industrial Art, Boards of Trade and Education; assisted the promotion of the Stuart, Tudor, Guelph, Early Italian, Venetian, Spanish, and other Art Exhibitions; Hon. Sec. and Delegate of the British Commission Fine Art Section, Brussels Internat. Exhibition, 1897; Sec. and Delegate of the British Fine Art Section Royal Commission, Paris Internat. Exhibition, 1900, and British Juror for Decoration; Hon. Sec. (London) Fine Art Section, Glasgow Internat. Exhibition, 1901; Representative in Great Britain for the Belgian Govt Exhibitions of Early Flemish Art, Bruges, 1902; the Toison d'Or, Bruges; Early Belgian Art, Brussels, 1910; International Miniature Exhibition, Brussels, 1912; Hon. Sec. and Member Art Committee, and Hon. Asst Sec. Royal Commission St Louis Internat. Exhibition, 1904; Member British Government Committee and Director for Art, British Government Exhibit and an Executive Commissioner New Zealand International Exhibition, 1906–7; Member Departmental Committee to inquire and report to Government upon British participation in International Exhibitions, 1907; Commissioner for Art, Franco-British Exhibition, 1908; Member of Royal Commission for the Brussels International Exhibition, 1910, and Turin International Exhibition, 1911; Commissioner-General for Great Britain, Rome International Fine Arts Exhibition, 1911; Director, Exhibition of British Arts and Crafts, Louvre, Paris, 1914; Member Spanish Art Exhibition,

Burlington House, 1920; Council British Empire Exhibition, 1924; an Executive Commissioner New Zealand Exhibition, 1926; Member of Council of Imperial Society of Knights Bachelor. *Publications:* The Royal Pavilion (illustrated), Paris International Exhibition, 1900; The British Section at the St Louis Exhibition, 1904, at the New Zealand International Exhibition, and International Fine Art Exhibition, Rome, 1911 (all illustrated); The Fine Art Section, Franco-British Exhibition (illustrated); The Germans, as others see them; Open letters to Herr Max Harden, 1917 and 1918; Germany's Impending Doom, 1918. *Recreation:* interest in Art Exhibitions, especially for the furtherance of British Art. *Address:* 56 Westbourne Terrace, Hyde Park, W2. *T:* Paddington 1931. *Club:* Arts.

Died 10 May 1925.

SPIERS, R. Phene, FSA, FRIBA; architect; Corresponding mem. of the Institute of France; Associate and Fellow of King's Coll. London; Past President of Architectural Association; Hon. and Corresponding member of the Société centrale des Architectes, Paris; Sociedad de los Arquitectos, Madrid, and Hon. Associate American Institute of Architects. *Educ:* King's Coll. London; Ecole des Beaux Arts, Paris. Gold Medallist; Scholar and Travelling Student of the Royal Academy; Soane Medallist and Travelling Student of the Royal Institute of British Architects; architect of two Board Schools, London—Lord Monkswell's house on Chelsea Embankment—Locke Park, Barnsley—and of painters' studios in various parts of London. *Publications:* re-edited Pugin's Normandy in 1870; Fergusson's History of Architecture, 1893; author of works on Architectural Drawing, 1887; The Orders of Architecture, 1902; The Architecture of Greece and Rome, 1907; Architectural Essays on Sassanian Architecture; Domed Churches in Périgord; Mosque at Damascus; Architecture, East and West; and other subjects. *Recreations:* archælogy, chiefly of eastern lands; delineation in pencil and colour of ancient architecture; study of Japanese art. *Address:* 21 Bernard Street, Russell Square, WC. *Club:* Arts.   *Died 3 Oct. 1916.*

SPINNEY, George Franklin; President and manager Daily and Sunday Globe, St Paul, Minnesota, USA; *b* Great Falls, New Hampshire, 9 July 1852; *m*. *Educ:* Public Schools, Lawrence, Massachusetts. Printer; proof-reader; foreman; reporter; political correspondent; managing editor and publisher of The New York Times, New York City. *Recreation:* newspaper business. *Clubs:* Press, New York; Minnesota, Commercial, St Paul.

Died 26 Sept. 1926.

SPITTA, Edmund Johnson, LRCP (Lond.), MRCS (Eng.), 1874; President of Quekett Microscopical Club, 1904–8; Past Pres. Brighton and Hove Natural History and Philosophical Society; Past Vice-President Royal Astronomical Society, and of Royal Microscopical Society; Chairman of the Sussex County Survey; *b* Clapham, 1853; *s* of R. J. Spitta, MD (London); *m* 1876, Francis Catherine Dacre; one *s* two *d*. *Educ:* Clapham Grammar School; privately. Entered St George's Hospital, 1870; Senior Demonstrator of Anatomy, 1873–74; four years prizeman, St George's Hospital Medical School; Ophthalmic Assistant, St George's Hospital, 1874; made hon. perpetual pupil, St Thomas's Hospital, 1874; also studied at Middlesex Hospital and Children's Hospital, Great Ormond Street; commenced practice at Clapham, 1875; retired from Clapham, 1905. *Publications:* article Kidney, Gray's Anatomy, 1874; (joint-author) An Atlas of Bacteriology, 1898; Photomicrography, 1899; Microscopy, 1907, 1909 and 1920; silver medal for contributions to Photomicrography, Paris Exhibition, 1900; and gold medal, St Louis Exhibition, 1903. *Address:* 41 Ventnor Villas, Hove, Sussex. *T:* Hove 8876.

Died 21 Jan. 1921.

SPITTLELER, Carl Friedrich Georg; author; *b* Liestal, Baselland, Switzerland, 24 April 1845; *m* Marie Op den Hooff of The Hague; two *d*. *Educ:* Basel, Zürich and Heidelberg Universities. Hon. PhD Zürich and Lausanne Universities; Hon. Member of Société des gens de lettres, Paris; Officer of Order of Leopold II, Belgium, Commandeur de la Légion d'Honneur, France, etc; tutor in Russia, 1871–79, afterwards contributor to various leading Swiss newspapers. Nobel prize for literature, 1919. *Publications:* Prometheus and Epimetheus, 2 vols, 1881; Schmetterlinge (Butterflies, lyrics); Conrad der Leutnant (French trans.); Imago (a novel, French trans.); Literarische Gleichnisse (Literary Parallels); Balladen (poems); Die Mädchenfeinde (French trans., Les Misogynes); Glockenlieder; Der Olympische Frühling, (1st edn 1900–3), several times revised; Lachende Wahrheiten, 1898; Meine frühesten Erlebnisse (autobiography), 1914; Unser Schweizer Standpunkt (Our Swiss Standpoint, a warning to Swiss against the influence of the foreign press), 1914. *Recreation:* pinaoforte playing. *Address:* 12 Gesegnetmatt Strasse, Lucerne, Switzerland.   *Died 29 Dec. 1924.*

SPOKES, Arthur Hewett; Recorder of Reading since 1894; *b* 28 June 1854; 2nd *s* of late Sir Peter Spokes; *m* 1892, Ethel Mary, *d* of Arthur Gurney, Russell House, Balham. *Educ:* University College, London (Fellow); BA, BSc, LLB, London. Matriculated 3rd in Honours, University of Lond., 1870; Gilchrist Scholarship, Univ. Hall, 1870; Andrews Entrance Scholarship, Univ. Coll. 1870; 1st year, 1871; Jews' Commemoration Scholarship, Univ. Coll. 1870; Studentship Jurisprudence and International Law, Inns of Court, 1875. Called to the Bar, 1875; Recorder of Newbury, 1893. *Address:* 6 St Andrew's Place, Park Square, NW1. *T:* Museum 574; 5 Pump Court, Temple, EC4. *T:* Central 2532. *Died 7 Dec. 1922.*

SPONG, Major Charles Stuart, DSO 1898; *b* Faversham, Kent, 12 June 1859; *s* of W. Nash Spong, FRCS; *m* 1900, Mary Barnsley, *o d* of late Henry Y. Pickering of Titusville, Penn; one *d. Educ:* Epsom College; Guy's Hospital. FRCS Eng.; BSc London. Joined army as surgeon, 1887; seconded to Egyptian Army, 1890; served through Soudan Campaign as SMO to 1st Egyptian Brigade (despatches four times, DSO, English Soudan medal, 4th class Medjidie and Egyptian Soudan medal wih 6 clasps); World War, 1916 (despatches). *Address:* Saugata, Clarens, Vaud, Switzerland. *Club:* Army and Navy. *Died 12 July 1925.*

SPOOR, Rt. Hon. Benjamin Charles, OBE 1918; PC 1924; MP (Lab) Bishop Auckland Division of Durham since Dec. 1918; a Member of the Executive Council of the Labour Party, 1919; *b* 2 June 1978; *m* 1st, 1900, Annie Louisa (*d* 1920), *d* of William Leyburn, Bishop Auckland; 2nd, 1923, Ann Mary, *d* of James Fraser, Wrexham. Parliamentary Secretary to Treasury, 1924; Chief Whip of Labour Party, 1924–25. *Died 22 Dec. 1928.*

SPRAGGE, Lt-Col Basil Edward, DSO 1887; JP County of Suffolk; Gentleman-at-arms; *b* 9 Oct. 1852; *s* of late F. H. Spragge, JP, of Paignton, Devon; *m* 1892, Anne Ingham, *d* of late Edward Brook of Hoddom, Dumfriesshire; three *s* one *d. Educ:* Cheltenham College; Trinity College, Cambridge. Joined 51st Light Infantry, 1872; Major, 1889; retired, 1894; adjutant of regiment, 1879–85; on staff Quartermaster-General's Department, India, 1885–89; served in Jowaki Expedition, 1877, as orderly officer to Brig.-Gen. Doran (medal with clasp); in 1st Afghan War, 1878–79, as Supt. Army Signalling (despatches); 2nd Afghan War, 1879–80, as adjutant to regiment (despatches, medal with clasp); Burmah War, 1885–89, as DAAG (despatches twice, medal with two clasps, Brevet Major, and DSO); served with Yeomanry Cav. in S Africa, 1900, in command of a regiment (medal 3 clasps); raised and commanded 2/1 Loyal Suffolk Hussars, 1914–16; served on the Staff IV Army Corps BEF, 1917–18. *Address:* Denbie, Lockerbie, Dumfriesshire. *Clubs:* Naval and Military, Royal Cruising, Garden. *Died 12 Feb. 1926.*

SPRAGGE, Brig-Gen. Charles Henry, CB 1898; JP; *b* 8 March 1842; *s* of F. H. Spragge, JP Co. Devon; *m* 1st, 1869, Esther E. (*d* 1903), *d* of Hon. George Moss; two *s* two *d*; 2nd, F. J., *widow* of W. H. Rawson of Bramhope. *Educ:* Cheltenham College. Entered Royal Artillery, 1860; retired, 1899; was General commanding the Royal Artillery during the Tirah Campaign, 1897–98; present at the actions of Chagra Kotal, Sampagha, and Ahungha Passes, occupation of Maidan, operations in Bazaar Valley and Khyber Pass (medal and two clasps; despatches, CB). Special award for distinguished and meritorious service; Hon. Col 4th Wessex Brigade RFA since 1909. *Address:* The Quinta, Babbacombe, South Devon; 8 Pont Street, SW. *T:* Victoria 5897. *Club:* Wellington. *Died 9 Jan. 1920.*

SPRAGUE, Thomas Bond, MA Camb.; LLD St Andrews; FIA, Hon. FFA; *b* 29 March 1830; *s* of Thomas Sprague, wholesale stationer, London; *m* 1st, Margaret Vaughan, *y d* of James Steains, Liverpool, tea merchant; four *s* four *d*; 2nd, Jean Elizabeth, 3rd *d* of Morris Forsyth Stuart, Edinburgh, army and navy contractor. *Educ:* private schools; St John's College, Cambridge. Senior Wrangler and First Smith's prizeman, 1853; Fellow and Assistant Tutor at St John's; formerly Actuary Liverpool and London Insurance Company; Actuary and Sec. Equity and Law Life Assurance Society, 1861–73; Manager of the Scottish Equitable Life Assurance Society, Edinburgh, 1873–1900. He invented a new form of Mortality Tables, applicable to lives selected for Insurance or otherwise, and showing the gradual disappearance of the benefit of Selection. *Publications:* A Treatise on Life Insurance Accounts, and many papers in the Journal of the Institute of Actuaries; also papers in the Transactions of other Societies — the Edinburgh Mathematical, the Philological, Naturalists' Field Club, Edinburgh, Scottish Natural History Society. *Recreations:* the microscope, especially in connection with the study of the Entomostraca, novel-reading, mathematics. *Address:* West Holme, Woldingham, Surrey. *Club:* Scottish Unionist. *Died 29 Nov. 1920.*

SPRECKLES, John Diedrich; *b* Charleston, SC, 16 Aug. 1853; *s* of late Claus Spreckles. *Educ:* Oakland College, California; Polytechnic School, Hanover, Germany. Founded J. D. Spreckles and Bros Co., shipping and commission merchants, owning large fleet of tugs and vessels trading with Hawaii, 1880; President of the Oceanic Steamship Co., mail and passenger line to Hawaii, Australia, and New Zealand; the Beaver Hill Coal Co.; Western Sugar Refining Co.; proprietor San Francisco Morning Call, etc. *Address:* 327 Market Street, San Francisco. *Died June 1926.*

SPRIGG, Alfred Gordon; editor and manager of the Leicester Mail; *b* 1861; *y s* of late James Sprigg, Coventry; *m* Laura, *e d* of late William Smith, Coventry, a journalist and writer of stories for young people. *Educ:* privately. Articled on the Coventry Herald; for some years on the reporting, and afterwards on the editorial staff of daily newspapers in Sheffield and Leeds, and took a prominent part in exposing false marking of foreign cutlery as of Sheffield origin; managing editor of the Scarborough Post, 1898–1909; Vice-President, The Newspaper Society, 1919–21. *Address:* Eversley, Stoneygate, Leicester. *T:* Leicester 1745. *Died 7 March 1921.*

SPRING-RICE, Rt. Hon. Sir Cecil Arthur, GCMG 1916 (KCMG 1906); GCVO 1908; PC 1913; British Ambassador to the United States since 1912; *b* 27 Feb. 1859; 2nd *s* of Hon. C. Spring-Rice; *m* 1904, Florence, *d* of Rt Hon. Sir Frank Lascelles; one *s* one *d. Educ:* Eton; Balliol Coll., Oxford. Exhibitioner; 1st class moderations and final classical school; clerk in War Office, and Foreign Office; Asst Priv. Secretary to Earl Granville, précis writer to Earl of Rosebery; Secretary at Brussels, Washington, Tokio, Berlin, and Constantinople; Chargé d'Affaires, Teheran, 1900; British Commmissioner of Public Debt, Cairo, 1901; 1st Secretary of Embassy at Petrograd, 1903–5; Minister and Consul-General, Persia, 1906–8; Minister to Sweden, 1908–12; Hon. LLD McGill University, Montreal, Princeton University, Harvard University, 1917. *Decorated:* 1st class Medjidie; 1st class Polar Star. *Address:* British Embassy, Washington, USA. *Clubs:* Travellers', St James', Savile, Beefsteak. *Died 14 Feb. 1918.*

SPRINGETT, Rev. William Douglas, DD Oxon; Hon. Canon of Canterbury, 1919; Diocesan Preacher, 1924; Rural Dean of East Charing, 1914; *b* 14 Sept. 1850; *e s* of late Rev. W. J. Springett, MA; *m* 1887, Katharine Henrietta, 2nd *d* of late Sir Edwyn Sandys Dawes, KCMG, and Lucy, *d* of William Bagnall, Staffs; no *c. Educ:* Queen's College, Oxford. Deacon, 1873; Priest, 1874; Curate of St Mary, Nottingham, 1873; St Stephen-at-Hackington, Canterbury, 1876; Vicar of Hernhill, Kent, 1883; West Tarring, Sussex, 1892; Brixton, Surrey, 1898; Rector of Pluckley-cum-Pevington, 1905–24; Lecturer at St Margaret Lothbury, 1912; Member of Diocesan Conference; and Diocesan Finance, Education, Building and Missionary Committees; formerly Member of Committee for forming the diocese of Southwark; Hon. Fellow of the GCMus, 1896. *Publications:* Statistical Tables on British Church History, 1886; Prize Essay on the Sabbath, 1891; Apocalyptic Prophecies, 1912; assisted editing Murray's Guides (Kent, 1890; Sussex, 1892); papers in Chambers's Journal; and Literary Churchman and Archæologia, 1887–97; *music:* part song, The Sunbeams; Tunes to Hymns with unusual Metres; Easter hymn, By the Grave, 1922; Easter Chorale; Good Old Kent (county song), 1925. *Recreations:* music (organ, piano); foreign travel; formerly rowing, rifle corps, mountain climbing, walking tours. *Address:* 7 Ethelbert Road, Canterbury. *Died 21 Sept. 1928.*

SPROULE, Thomas Simpson, MD; MP East Grey since 1878; Speaker of the House of Commons, Canada, since 1911; *b* township of King, County of York, Ontario, 25 Oct. 1843; parents both Irish from Tyrone; *m* 1881, Mary Allice, *d* of W. K. Flesher, MP; one *d. Educ:* common schools, Co. Grey; University of Michigan; Victoria University, Toronto. Graduated in Medicine, 1868. Was engaged in commercial life for about 4 years, before study in medicine; practised medicine and surgery for 40 years; carried on farming for 30 years; also in drug and stationery business for 12 years, and in flour and saw-milling for some time; served in Municipal Council, and connected with agricultural societies for 30 years; 5 years Chairman of Standing Committee on Agriculture and Immigration, and for some years Chairman of Committee, Miscellaneous Private Bills; was MG Master of the LO Association of British America for 10 years; and President, Triennial Orange Council of the World, for 3 years; a

Methodist, a Conservative. *Address:* Markdale, Ontario, Canada; Speaker's Chambers, House of Commons, Ottawa, Canada.

Died 10 Nov. 1917.

SPURGEON, Rev. Thomas; President of Pastors' College and of Stockwell Orphanage; *b* London, 20 Sept. 1856; twin *s* of C. H. Spurgeon (*d* 1892); *m* 1888, Lila M'Leod, *e d* of Gideon Rutherford, Dunedin, New Zealand; one *s* one *d*. *Educ:* Pastors' Coll.; Metropolitan Tabernacle. Studied art at South Kensington, and wood-engraving at Fetter Lane; visited Australia and Tasmania, 1877; second visit to Australasia, 1879; accepted pastorate of Baptist Church, Auckland, New Zealand, 1881; evangelist of New Zealand Baptist Union, 1889–93; commenced ministry at Metropolitan Tabernacle, 1893; resigned through ill-health, 1908. *Publications:* The Gospel of the Grace of God (sermons), 1884; Scarlet Threads and Bits of Blue (poems), 1892; Down to the Sea (sea sermons), 1895; Light and Love (sermons), 1897; God save the King (sermons), 1902; My Gospel (sermons), 1902. *Recreation:* sketching. *Address:* San Remo, 40 Prentis Road, Streatham, SW. *T:* Streatham 1384.

Died 20 Oct. 1917.

SPY; *see* Ward, Sir Leslie.

SQUAIR, John; *b* Bowmanville, Ont, 1850; Scotch parents; *m* 1886, Laura Prout; one *d*. *Educ:* public and high schools in Clarke, Newcastle, and Bowmanville; Univ. of Toronto. Began to teach at public school in Darlington, Ontario, 1874; matriculated into University of Toronto, 1879; graduated from University of Toronto, 1883, with gold medal in Modern Languages; was Fellow, Lecturer, Associate Professor and Professor of French in University College, Toronto; Emeritus, 1916; was Lecturer in School of Pedagogy, Toronto, and Examiner in French and German for the Education Department; late Secretary of the Modern Language Association of Ontario; Chairman of College and High School Dept of Ontario Educational Association; President of Higher Education Section of the Dominion Educational Association; Officier de l'Instruction Publique, 1914; Chevalier de la Légion d'Honneur, 1924. *Publications:* joint author, with Prof. William H. Fraser, of High School French Grammar, 1891; revised edns of same, 1900 and 1921; joint author with same of High School French Reader, 1891, and of Shorter French Course, 1913; joint author with J. H. Cameron of Exercises in French Prose, 1895; editor of several French texts for high schools; En Temps de Guerre, 1916; John Seath, and the School System of Ontario, 1920; Alumni Associations in the University of Toronto, 1922; Admission of Women to the University of Toronto, 1924; The Townships of Darlington and Clarke, including Bowmanville and Newcastle, Province of Ontario, Canada, 1927. *Address:* 368 Palmerston Avenue, Toronto, Canada. *Club:* York, Toronto.

Died 15 Feb. 1928.

SQUIRE, John Edward, CB 1904; VD; MD (Lond.); DPH (Cantab); FRCP, MRCS; Consulting Physician, Mount Vernon Consumption Hospital; National Sanatorium for Workers, Benenden; Medical Adviser (Sanatorium Benefits), London Insurance Committee; Consulting Medical Officer, Pearl Life Assurance Company; *b* 20 Dec. 1855; *s* of William Squire, MD, FRCP; *m* 1894, Mary Lilian, *d* of John Youngman; two *d*. *Educ:* University College, London. House Physician, University College, London; Senior Medical Officer to Red Cross in Soudan Campaign, 1885 (Egypt medal, clasp Suakin, 1885, Khedive's Bronze Star); commanded London Companies RAMC Vol. 1898–1904 (CB (civil), VD); Member of Council, National Association for Prevention of Consumption; Member of Sanitary Inspectors' Examination Board; Corresponding Member, International Association for the Prevention of Tuberculosis, Berlin; Knight of Grace Order of St John of Jerusalem; Queen Victoria Jubilee medal; King Edward VII Coronation medal; King George V Coronation medal. *Publications:* Essays in Consumption; The Hygienic Prevention of Consumption; Medical Hints for Medical Officers with Troops. *Address:* 2 Bentinck Terrace, North Gate, Regent's Park, NW. *T:* Paddington 2824. *Club:* Savage.

Died 2 May 1917.

SQUIRE, Sir Peter Wyatt, Kt 1918; *b* 6 Feb. 1947; *s* of late Peter Squire; *m* Mabel Jane, *d* of late Alexander Bramwell Bremner; two *d*. *Educ:* King's College School. Chemist on the Medical Staff of the Royal Household since 1867; Hon. Secretary Thames Punting Club since 1894. *Publications:* Squire's Companion to the British Pharmacopœia; Squire's London Hospital Pharmacopœias; Methods used in the Preparation of Tissues for Microscopical Examination; Punting section of the Badminton Library. *Recreations:* punting, golf. *Address:* The Ryepeck, Shepperton. *TA:* Squire, Shepperton. *T:* Weybridge 65. *M:* A 8161.

Died 16 Sept. 1919.

SQUIRE, William Barclay, MVO 1926; MA; FSA, FRCM, FRGS; Hon. Curator of the Royal Music Library; Librarian Royal College of Music; *b* 16 Oct. 1855; *o s* of late William Squire of Feltham Hill, Middlesex, and Elizabeth Ogden. *Educ:* privately; Germany; Pembroke College, Cambridge (Honours (History) Tripos, 1878; Hon. Fellow, 1925). Admitted a Solicitor, 1883, but not in practice from 1885; awarded Silver Medal for assistance at Musical Historical Exhibition, South Kensington, 1885; in charge of Printed Music in British Museum; Deputy Keeper, Department of Printed Books, British Museum, 1912–20; Musical Critic of the Saturday Review, 1888–94; Westminster Gazette, 1893; Globe, 1894–1901; and Pilot, 1900–4; worked for the War Intelligence Department of the Admiralty, 1916–18; on Editorial Staff of the Historical Section of the Foreign Office, 1918–20; KGStJ. *Publications:* Catalogue of Music in Chapter Library, Westminster, 1903; Catalogue of Printed Music in Royal College of Music, 1909; Catalogue of Pictures in the Collection of the Earl of Radnor (with Helen, Countess of Radnor), 2 vols, 1909; Catalogue of old Printed Music in the British Museum, 2 vols, 1912; The Tribes of Tunisia, 1916; librettos of The Veiled Prophet of Khorassan (opera by Sir Charles V. Stanford), 1881 and Callirhoe (cantata by Sir F. Bridge), 1888; edited Palestrina's Stabat Mater; Purcell's Harpsichord Music, 4 vols, 1918; Byrd's Masses; R. Jones's Muses' Garden for Delights, 1901; the Fitzwilliam Virginal Book (1894–90), Fourteen Pieces by William Byrd, Twenty-five Pieces from Cosyn's Virginal Book (all with J. A. Fuller Maitland); articles in Grove's Dictionary of Music, Dictionary of National Biography, Archæologia, Encyclopædia Britannica, Music and Letters, etc and many old madrigals and motets. *Address:* 14 Albert Place, Kensington, W8. *Club:* Athenæum.

Died 13 Jan. 1927.

STACEY, Major Gerald Arthur, DSO 1916; 2nd in Command, 2nd Battalion London Regiment; *b* 26 Dec. 1881; *s* of late Arthur Stacey of Leigh Place, Surrey; *m* 1907, Annette Hope Neild; two *s* two *d*. *Educ:* privately. Passed final exam. of Institute of Chartered Accountants, 1906; practised as Chartered Accountant in London, 1907, until outbreak of war; obtained Commission in 2nd VB Royal Fusiliers, 1902; Capt. 1905; Major, 1915; served European War, 1914–15 (despatches, DSO); Légion d'Honneur, 1915. *Recreations:* soldiering, golf, sailing. *Address:* The Haven, Rottingdean, Sussex.

Died 11 Oct. 1916.

STACK, Maj.-Gen. Sir Lee Oliver Fitzmaurice, GBE 1923 (KBE 1918); CMG 1914; Governor-General of Sudan, and Sirdar of the Egyptian Army, since 1919 (Acting Governor-General and Sirdar, 1917–19); *b* 15 May 1868; *s* of Oliver Stokes Stack, Inspector-Gen. of Police, Bengal, and Emily Dickson; *m* 1902, Flora Center, *d* of Edwin Ramsay Moodie; one *d*. *Educ:* Clifton; Sandhurst. Joined the Border Regt 1888; Major, 1909; temp. Lieut-Col 1914; temp. Major-Gen. 1917; Staff Officer to the British Military Commissioner and General Officer commanding HM troops in Crete, 1899; joined Egyptian Army, 1899; retired, 1910; commanded Shambe Field Force, 1902 (despatches, medal and clasp, 4th class Osmanieh); Sudan Agent and Director of Military Intelligence, 1908; Civil Secretary, Sudan Government, 1913–16; 1st Class Orders of the Nile, 1917, the Hahda, 1920, and 3rd Class Medjidieh. *Address:* The Palace, Khartoum. *Clubs:* United Service, Travellers'.

Died 20 Nov. 1924.

STACPOLE, Col John, CMG 1902; CVO 1901; JP Hants; *b* 27 Dec. 1849; 2nd *s* of late Thomas Stacpole, of Ballinahow, Co. Tipperary; *m* 1st, 1876, Leila (*d* 1906), 3rd *d* of late George Smith, Iping, Sussex; 2nd, 1907, Isabella, 2nd *d* of late Michael Phillips Grazebrook, Holly Grove, Hagley, Worcester. Entered army 1874; Captain, 1884; Major, 1891; Lieut-Col 1895; Colonel, 1900; retired, 1904; served Soudan, 1885 (medal with clasp, bronze star). *Address:* Sharvells, Milford-on-Sea, Hants. *Club:* United Service.

Died 30 Dec. 1916.

STAGNI, Most Rev. Pellegrino Francesco, DD; OSM; Titular Archbishop of Ancyra, and Apostolic Delegate to Canada and Newfoundland since 1910; *b* Budrio, Italy, 1859. *Educ:* Italy; England (where he spent youth as a member of the English Province of the Servite Order). Professed, 1875; Priest, 1881; for some years Parish Priest at Fulham; Professor of Philosophy at the College of Propaganda, 1893; Prior-General of the Order, 1901–7; Archbishop of Aquila, in the Abruzzi, 1907; Apostolic Delegation, Ottawa.

Died 23 Sept. 1918.

STAINFORTH, Lt-Col Herbert Graham, CMG 1915; Indian Army; Commandant 4th Cavalry; *b* 18 May 1865; *s* of late Maj.-Gen. C. R. Stainforth, Madras Cavalry; *m* Georgina Helen, 3rd *d* of Maj.-

Gen. Pipon, Major of Tower of London; two *s* one *d*. *Educ:* Tonbridge; RMC Sandhurst. Entered army, 1885; Captain Indian Army, 1896; Major, 1903; Lt-Col 1911; served European War, 1914–15 (CMG). *Address:* c/o H. S. King & Co., 9 Pall Mall, SW. *Club:* Cavalry. *Died 11 May 1916.*

STALKER, Rev. James, MA, DD; Professor of Church History in the United Free Church College, Aberdeen, 1902; Emeritus since 1924; *b* Crieff, 21 Feb. 1848; *m* 1884, Charlotte Melville (*d* 1920), *d* of Francis Brown-Douglas, Edinburgh; one *s* four *d*. *Educ:* Univs of Edinburgh, Halle, and Berlin; New College, Edinburgh. Minister of St Brycedale Church, Kirkcaldy, 1874; St Matthew's, Glasgow, 1887; delivered the Lyman Beecher Lectures on Preaching at Yale Univ., USA, 1891; was Cunningham Lecturer at Edinburgh in 1899; Gay Lecturer at Louisville, Kentucky, 1904; James Sprunt Lecturer at Richmond, Virginia, 1914. *Publications:* The Life of Jesus Christ; The Life of St Paul; Imago Christi; The Preacher and his Models; The Trial and Death of Jesus; The Two St Johns; The Four Men; Christ's Teaching about Himself; The Seven Deadly Sins; The Seven Cardinal Virtues; John Knox, His Ideas and Ideals; Three Lectures on the Atonement; The Ethic of Jesus; How to read Shakespeare; Christian Psychology; The Beauty of the Bible, etc. *Recreations:* reading publishers' catalogues, cutting open new books. *Address:* Balbegno, Crieff, Perthshire. *T:* 201. *Club:* Liberal, Edinburgh. *Died 5 Feb. 1927.*

STANDAGE, Lt-Col Robert Fraser, CIE 1922; FRCS, MRCP; Indian Medical Service, retired; *b* 5 April 1868; *s* of late Alfred Standage of Hurcott House, Worcestershire; *m* 1902, Gwendolen, *d* of late William Lonsdale of Hutton Roof, Eastbourne, and Mysore State; one *s*. *Educ:* St Bartholomew's Hospital. Bentley Surgical Prize, 1890; House Surgeon and Physician, 1891–93; Lieutenant IMS 1894; Capt. 1898; Major, 1906; Lieut-Colonel, 1915; MO 2nd Bombay Lancers (subseq. 32nd Lancers), 1895–97; famine duty, Bombay, 1897 (thanks of Government); Uganda Mutiny, 1897–99 (despatches, medal and clasp); East Africa Field Force, 1917–19 (despatches); Consulting Surgeon, East Africa Field Force, 1918–19; under Foreign and Political Dept, India, 1903–26 as Residency Surgeon in Mysore; retired 1926; Esquire of Order of Hospital of St John of Jerusalem, 1926. *Publications:* contributions on surgical and gynæcological subjects to Lancet, British Medical Journal, Journal of RAMC, Journal of Gynæcology, Indian Medical Gazette. *Recreations:* cricket, tennis, big and small game shooting. *Clubs:* East India United Service, MCC. *Died 16 Jan. 1927.*

STANDEN, Edward James, CB 1891; *b* 1836; *s* of late Edward Standen; *m*. *Educ:* King's College, London. Served Crimea with Turkish Contingent Engineers, 1855–56 (medal); Secretary to British Commissioner on European Commission of the Danube, 1857–72; Resident Director in Paris to represent HM's Government on Council of Suez Canal Company, 1876–91; made Member of Managing Committee, 1888. *Address:* 37 Queen's Gate Gardens, South Kensington, SW. *Died 1 Nov. 1921.*

STANDFORD, Col William, DSO 1902; MVO 1911. Served South Africa, 1877–78 (medal with clasp); Transkei, 1880–81 (medal with clasp); South Africa and Cape Town Highlanders, 1899–1902 (despatches, Queen's medal with clasp, King's medal two clasps, DSO). *Address:* Cape Town. *Died 7 April 1926.*

STANDISH, Henry Noailles Widdrington; *b* 2 Nov. 1847; *e s* of late Lionel C. H. Standish and Sabine de Noailles, *d* of le Duc de Foix, France; *m* 1870, Helène de Perusse, *d* of le Comte des Cars, France. *Address:* Standish Hall, Wigan. *Clubs:* Marlborough; Royal Yacht Squadron, Cowes. *Died 31 July 1920.*

STANDISH, Major William Pery; OBE 1919; JP Hants and Cumberland; Major, Army Remount Service, 1915–19; *b* 3 Aug. 1860; *o s* of late William Cecil Standish, and *nephew* of late Rowland E. W. Pery Standish of Marwell, Hants, and Scaleby, Cumberland; *m* 1901, Evelyn Cecilia, *d* of late C. N. P. Phipps of Chalcot, Wilts; two *s* four *d*. *Educ:* Eton. Joined 15th Regt 1881; Capt. E Yorks Regt, 1888–93; Capt. Royal Reserve Regt, 1900–1; High Sheriff of Cumberland, 1902; Master Hambledon Foxhounds, 1900–21. *Recreations:* all country pursuits. *Address:* Marwell Hall, Owslebury, Winchester; Scaleby Castle, Carlisle. *Clubs:* Naval and Military, Boodle's. *Died 11 Nov. 1922.*

STANFORD, Sir Charles Villiers, Kt 1902; MA, MusD, DCL, LLD; Professor of Music, Cambridge University; Professor of Composition and Orchestral Playing in the Royal Coll. of Music; *b* Dublin, 30 Sept. 1852; *o s* of late John Stanford, Examiner to Court of Chancery in Ireland, and Mary, 3rd *d* of William Henn, Master of High Court of Chancery in Ireland; *m* 1878, Jane Anna Maria (Jennie), 4th *d* of late Henry Champion Wetton, Joldwynds, Surrey; one *s* one *d*. *Educ:* privately; Cambridge (Queens' Coll., 1870–72 and Trin. Coll. after 1872); afterwards studied at Leipzig under Karl Reinecke, and at Berlin under Friedrich Kiel. BA Cambridge Classical Tripos, 1874. Organ and Classical Scholar at Queens' College, Cambridge, 1870–72; Organist of Trinity College, Cambridge, 1872–93; Conductor of Cambridge University Musical Society, 1872–93; Conductor of Bach Choir, 1885–1902; of the Leeds Philharmonic Society; Conductor of the Leeds Festival, 1901–10; produced operas in Germany (Hanover, Hamburg, Breslau and Leipzig), and conducted concerts in Berlin, Amsterdam, Brussels and Paris; Maatschappij der Toonkunst, Amsterdam, 1906; many works produced at the Festivals of Birmingham, Leeds, etc, and on the London stage, and at the Albert Hall, Richter concerts Crystal Palace, etc. *Compositions* include: Cushendall, a Fire of Turf (song-cycles); Symphony No 7 in D minor; Irish Rhapsody, No 4 and 5; Pianforte Quartet and Trio; 5 organ sonatas; Verdun, for orchestra, etc; Capriccios, Fairy Day Cantata for Women's Voices, etc. *Publications:* Studies and Memories, 1908; Musical Composition, 1911; Pages from an Unwritten Diary, 1914; (with Cecil Forsyth) A History of Music, 1916; Interludes, 1922. *Address:* 9 Lower Berkeley Street, Portman Square, W1. *T:* Mayfair 2696. *Clubs:* Athenæum, Savile. *Died 29 March 1924.*

STANHOPE, Ven. Hon. Berkeley Lionel Scudamore, MA; *b* 1824; 3rd *s* of Sir Edwyn Francis Scudamore Stanhope, 2nd Bt (*brother* of 9th Earl of Chesterfield), and Mary, *d* of Thomas Dowell; *m* 1858, Caroline Sarah, *e d* of John Arkwright, of Hampton Court, Herefordshire; one *d* (one *s* decd). *Educ:* Balliol Coll., Oxford. Fellow of All Souls' College, Oxford, 1846–58; Vicar of Bosbury, Herefordshire, 1856–66; Rector of Byford, 1866–1908; Archdeacon of Hereford, 1887–1910. *Address:* The Grange, Much Wenlock. *Died 21 March 1919.*

STANHOPE, Hon. Evelyn Theodore Scudamore, DL; Chief Constable of Herefordshire, 1895–1923; *b* 9 Jan. 1862; 5th *s* of 9th Earl of Chesterfield and Dorothea, *e d* of Sir Adam Hey, 7th Bt; *m* 1888, Julia, *y d* of J. Gerald Potter; one *s* one *d*. Late Lieut King's Royal Rifle Corps, and Captain Army Service Corps. *Club:* Naval and Military. *Died 9 Nov. 1925.*

STANHOPE, Hon. Richard Philip, JP; County Councillor, Lindsey Division of Lincolnshire; Lieutenant Lincolnshire Yeomanry; *b* 16 Jan. 1885; *y s* of 6th Earl Stanhope and Evelyn Henrietta, *o d* of Richard Pennefather; *m* 1914, Lady Beryl Le Poer Trench, *o d* of 5th Earl of Clancarty. *Educ:* Eton; Magdalen College, Oxford (BA 1907; MA 1910). *Recreations:* rowing, shooting, hunting, fishing. *Address:* Revesby Abbey, Boston, Lincolnshire. *TA:* Revesby. *M:* BE 912. *Clubs:* Bachelors', Cavendish; Leander, Henley-on-Thames. *Died Sept. 1916.*

STANIER, Sir Beville, 1st Bt, *cr* 1917; DL, JP Shropshire; MP (U) North Shropshire, 1908–18, and Ludlow since Dec. 1918; Deputy Chairman of North Staffordshire Railway; Deputy Chairman Trent and Mersey Canal; Director Home Grown Sugar; *b* 12 June 1867; *s* of Francis Stanier, Staffs, and Caroline Judith, *d* of Gen. William Justice; *m* 1894, (Sarah) Constance, *d* of late Rev. Benjamin Gibbons; three *s* one *d*. *Educ:* privately; Royal Agricultural Coll., Cirencester (Member, RAC). CC, 1902–12; Governor Harper Adams Agricultural College; Captain in Territorial Reserve; Hon. Secretary Shropshire Territorial Association, 1914–18; Chairman of British Sugar Beet Growers' Society; Director Farmers' Land Purchase Co. *Heir:* *s* Alexander Beville Gibbons Stanier; *b* 31 Jan. 1899. *Address:* The Citadel, Weston, Preston Brockhurst, near Shrewsbury; 21 Buckingham Gate, SW1. *Club:* Carlton. *Died 15 Dec. 1921.*

STANIFORTH, Joseph Morewood; Artist, Western Mail, Cardiff; *b* 16 May 1863; 4th *s* of Joseph and Mary Staniforth, Cardiff; *m* 1891, Emily, *d* of J. Chidgey, Somerset. *Educ:* St John's School, Cardiff. Apprenticed to the Lithographic Department of the Western Mail, Ltd, 1878; after about ten years' experience of this trade, joined the Editorial Staff of the paper and was engaged in illustrating current events; during some years contributed daily cartoons to the Evening Express, and in 1893 commenced the daily cartoon in the Western Mail, which continued from that time; practised painting in oil and water-colours; and a Member of the South Wales Art Society since its inception, 1888, exhibiting regularly at its annual exhibitions. *Recreations:* sketching, gardening. *Address:* The Bungalow, Lynton, Devon. *Died 17 Dec. 1921.*

STANLEY, Rt Rev. Mgr the Hon. Algernon Charles; Bishop of Emmaus; a Canon of St Peter's, Rome, 1919; *b* 16 Sept. 1843. 4th *s* of 2nd Baron Stanley of Alderley and Henrietta Maria, *d* of 13th Viscount Dillon; *Educ:* Harrow; Rugby; Trinity College, Cambridge (BA 1865; MA 1868). Formerly curate of Kidderminster, West Bromwich, and St Mary's, Soho; incumbent of Holy Cross, St Pancras; in holy orders of the Church of Rome; Bishop Assistant at Pontifical Throne; was at St James's, Spanish Place, 1883–93; resident in Rome; consecrated in Rome, 1903; appointed Auxiliary Bishop to Cardinal Vaughan, Archbishop of Westminster. *Address:* 1 Via Giulia, Rome. *Club:* Athenæum. *Died 23 April 1928.*

STANLEY, Dorothy, (Lady Stanley); *d* of late C. Tennant of Cadoxton Lodge, Vale of Neath, Glamorganshire; *m* 1st, 1890, Sir Henry Morton Stanley, (*d* 1904), African explorer; 2nd, 1907, Henry Curtis, FRCS. *Publications:* London Street Arabs, 1890; Autobiography of Henry M. Stanley (edited), 1909. *Address:* 2 Richmond Terrace, Whitehall, SW1. *Died 5 Oct. 1926.*

STANNARD, Henry, RBA; landscape and sporting painter; married; two *s* two *d*. *Educ:* South Kensington. Exhibitor of the Royal Academy and of the Royal Institute of Painters in Water Colours for several years; established the Academy of Arts, Bedford, 1887, where he received a number of students. *Publications:* illustrated his own manuscripts of Outdoor Common Birds, Master Bob Robin, and other books; artist for The Encyclopædia of Sport; The Badminton Magazine; Baily's Magazine; The Illustrated London News; Sporting and Dramatic News. *Recreation:* shooting. *Address:* Harpur Place, Bedford. *Died 15 Nov. 1920.*

STANSFELD, Capt. John, JP; *b* 16 Jan. 1840; *o* surv. *s* of late Robert Stansfeld, of Field House, and Hannah Lætitia (*d* 1864), *o c* and heiress of late Lewis Farley Clogstoun Johnston; *m* 1871, Eliza (*d* 1916), *y d* and co-heiress of late Patrick Arkley, of Dunninald Castle; no *c*. Late Capt. Royal Scots Greys. *Address:* Dunninald Castle, Montrose. *Clubs:* Junior United Service; New, Edinburgh. *Died 22 Jan. 1928.*

STANSFIELD, Sir Charles Henry Renn, Kt 1922; CB 1911; *b* 8 Feb. 1856; *s* of late Henry Renn Stansfield; *m* 1881, Agnes Helen, *d* of James Sargent; three *s*. Entered Admiralty, 1876; was Private Secretary to Admirals Sir Richard Vesey Hamilton, Sir Henry Fairfax, Sir Frederick Richards, and Lord Walter Kerr; Director of Greenwich Hospital, 1903–21; Member of the Royal Patriotic Fund Corporation; of Executive Committee of Royal Naval Fund; and Committee of Seamen's Hospital Society. *Address:* The Hollies, Bromley Common, Kent. *Club:* Union. *Died 29 May 1926.*

STANTON, Major Harold James Clifford, MVO 1919; *b* 1859; *s* of late James Thomas Stanton and Louisa Loveday Stanton of The Leaze, Eastington, Gloucestershire; *m* Henrietta, 3rd *d* of late Sir Alexander Jardine of Applegarth, 8th Bt, and Henrietta, *d* of William Younger, Dumfriesshire; one *s*. *Educ:* Harrow; Christ's College, Cambridge. Joined King's Own Scottish Borderers, 1881; Chaplain, 1890; Adjutant, 1st Roxburgh and Selkirk Rifle Volunteers, 1895–1901; retired, 1901; joined the War Office Staff in the Department of the Military Secretary, 1902; gazetted a Staff Captain at Headquarters on the outbreak of the War, 1914; resigned that appointment, 1917; promoted Brevet Major on the retired list, 1918; finally retired, 1919. *Club:* Naval and Military. *Died 22 Feb. 1927.*

STANTON, Lionel William, ISO; JP; *b* England, 1843; *e s* of late Rev. L. W. Stanton, MA, Incumbent of S Mary's, Kooringa, SA; *m* 1st, 1873, Catherine, *e d* of Edward William Hitchin, Auditor-General of South Australia; four *s* three *d*; 2nd, 1892, Alice Mary, *y d* of late William Giles, Melbourne; no *c*. *Educ:* S John's Foundation School, Kilburn, London; City of London School, Cheapside. Second Master of Lichfield Grammar School of King Edward VI; went to South Australia, 1868; Head Master of Clare Grammar School, 1870–75; Inspector of Schools, 1876; Assistant Inspector-General of Schools, 1892; Chairman of the Board of Inspectors of Schools, 1896; Inspector-General of Schools, 1902; Secretary to the Minister Controlling Education, South Australia, 1906; retired, 1916. *Recreation:* gardening. *Address:* Adelaide, S Australia. *T:* 1732. *Died 15 Aug. 1925.*

STANTON, Rev. Vincent Henry, DD; Regius Professor of Divinity, University of Cambridge, 1916–22; *b* Victoria, Hong-Kong, 1 June 1846; *s* of Rev. V. J. Stanton, late Rector of Halesworth, Suffolk, and formerly Colonial Chaplain of Victoria, Hong-Kong; descended, on mother's side, from Robert Barclay of Ury. *Educ:* Kensington

Grammar School; Trinity Coll., Cambridge. Minor Scholar, 1866; Major Scholar, 1868; BA 1870 (20th Wrangler and 2nd class Classical Tripos); MA 1873; BD 1890; DD 1891. Fellow of Trinity College, 1872; Deacon, 1872; Priest, 1874; University Extension Lecturer, 1873; Junior Dean of Trinity College, 1874–76; Senior Dean, 1876–84; Tutor, 1884–89; Divinity Lecturer, 1882–89; Select Preacher before the University of Cambridge, 1874, 1878, etc; and before University of Oxford, 1896–98; Hulsean Lecturer, 1879; Cambridge Whitehall Preacher, 1880–81; Examining Chaplain to Bishop of Ely, Dr Woodford, 1875–85; and to Bishop of Ely, Lord Alwyne Compton, 1885–1905; Ely Professor of Divinity, Cambridge Univ., and Canon of Ely, 1889–1916. *Publications:* The Jewish and the Christian Messiah, a Study in the Earliest History of Christianity, 1887; The Place of Authority in Matters of Religious Belief, 1891; The Gospels as Historical Documents, Part I 1903, Part II 1909, Part III 1920; articles in Hastings' Dictionary of the Bible; the Encyclopædia Britannica; the Dictionary of National Biography (Supplement). *Address:* Selwyn Croft, Cambridge. *Died 8 June 1924.*

STAPLETON-BRETHERTON, Frederick, JP, DL; *b* 1841; *o* surv. *s* of late Bartholomew Bretherton and Martha, *d* of late Charles Annesley; assumed additional surname of Stapleton by Royal Licence, 1884; *m* 1869, Hon. Isabella Mary, 2nd *d* of 12th Baron Petre and Mary Theresa, *e d* of Hon. Charles Thomas Clifford, Lincs. *Address:* The Hall, Rainhill, near Prescot; Heathfield House, Fareham, Hampshire. *Club:* Windham. *Died 13 April 1919.*

STAPLETON-COTTON, Col Hon. Richard Southwell George; *b* 9 Oct. 1849; 2nd *s* of 2nd Viscount Combermere and Susan Alice, *e d* of Sir George Sitwell, 2nd Bt; *uncle* and *heir-pres.* to 4th Viscount Combermere; *m* 1870, Hon. Jane Charlotte Methuen (*d* 1924), *d* of 2nd Baron Methuen; two *s* three *d* (and one *s* decd). Entered army, 1868; served Zulu War, 1879 (despatches) including Ulundi (despatches, medal with clasp); Bechuanaland Expedition, 1884–85. *Address:* Gambles House, Antigua, BWI. *Club:* Carlton. *Died 24 Nov. 1925.*

STAPLEY, Sir Richard, Kt 1908; JP; Member of Council City of London; *b* 23 Oct. 1842; *s* of Robert Stapley, Twineham, Sussex; *m* 1866, Annie (*d* 1917), *d* of Henry Jenner, Brighton. Contested (L) Brixton Division, Lambeth, 1892, and Holborn Division, Finsbury, 1910. *Address:* 33 Bloomsbury Square, WC1. *T:* Central 8556; Horeham Road, Sussex. *Died 20 May 1920.*

STARK, Rev. James, DD Aberdeen; *b* Glasgow, 24 Dec. 1838; *m* 1st, 1865, Jean (*d* 1905), *d* of George Aimer, St Andrews; one *s*; 2nd, 1908, Amelia, 2nd *d* of late Alexander G. Burnett of Kemnay. *Educ:* Edinburgh University; Scottish Congregational Theological Hall. Called to Elgin, 1864; Edinburgh, 1872; Aberdeen, 1877; retired from pastoral work, 1908; Hon DD Aberdeen University, 1895; Editor of Scottish Congregational Mag., 1872–77; Chairman of Scottish Congregational Union, 1888; represented Union at International Council of Congregationalists in London, 1891, and in Boston, USA, 1899. *Publications:* John Murker of Banff; Dr Kidd of Aberdeen; The Lights of the North; Comradeship in Sorrow; Priest Gordon of Aberdeen; Lord Cullen, the first of the Monymusk Grants; Spiritualism, a Review; Met by the Way; The Lord is my Strength and Song, and other Sermons. *Address:* Braes o'Benachie, Kemnay, Scotland. *Died 15 Nov. 1922.*

STARKIE, Rt. Hon. William Joseph Myles, PC (Ireland) 1914; BA (Cambridge), MA; Resident Commissioner of National Education, Ireland, since 1899; Chairman of the Board of Intermediate Education since 1911; *b* Sligo, 10 Dec. 1860; 5th *s* of late William Robert Starkie, JP, RM, Cregaue Manor, Rosscarbery; *m* 1893, May, *e d* of C. Walsh; one *s* four *d*. *Educ:* Shrewsbury (head boy); Trinity College, Cambridge; Trinity College, Dublin. Foundation Scholar, Trinity College, Cambridge; 1st class Classical Tripos; 1st Scholar, 1st Senior Moderator and Fellow, Trinity College, Dublin; President of Queen's Coll., Galway, 1897–99; late Fellow and Tutor of Trinity College, Dublin; Member of the following Boards—Academic Council Dublin University; National Education; Intermediate Education; President of the British Empire Shakespeare Society (Dublin Branch); President of the Classical Association (Ireland), 1911; Member of Royal Commission on University Education in Ireland, 1901–1902; Hon. LittD Dublin; Hon. LLD Royal Univ. *Publications:* The Vespæ of Aristophanes, edited, with Introduction, Critical Notes, Commentary, and Appendices, 1897; Recent Reforms in Irish Education, 1902; The Acharnians of Aristophanes, edited, with Translation, etc, 1909; also the Clouds of Aristophanes, 1911; A

History of Irish Primary and Secondary Education during the last Decade, 1911; Continuation Schools, 1912; contributions to Sabrinæ Corolla, Kottabos, Hermathena, Classical Review, Quarterly Review, etc. *Recreations:* at one time rowing, Alpine climbing, cycling, lawn tennis, golf. *Address:* Tyrone House, Dublin; Melfort, Shrewsbury Road, Dublin. *Clubs:* Athenæum; Dublin University, Royal Irish Yacht, Fellows' (Trinity College), Dublin. *T:* Ballsbridge 134.

Died 21 July 1920.

STARLING, Ernest Henry, CMG 1918; FRS 1899; Foulerton Research Professor of Royal Society; late Jodrell Professor of Royal Society; Jodrell Professor of Physiology, University College, London, 1899–23; Lieutenant-Colonel Royal Army Medical Corps, 1916; *b* 17 April 1866; *e s* of late Matthew Henry Starling (Barrister-at-law and Clerk to the Crown, Bombay), and Ellen Mathilda, *d* of Henry George Watkins, Islington; *m* 1891, Florence Amelia, *e d* of Sir Edward Henry Sieveking, MD and Jane, *d* of John Ray, Finchley, and *widow* of Leonard Charles Wooldridge; one *s* three *d*. *Educ:* King's Coll. School; Guy's Hospital; Heidelberg. MD, BS London; FRCP. Entered Guy's Hospital as student, 1882; Demonstrator of Physiology, 1889; Joint Lecturer on Physiology, 1890–99; Lecturer on Physiology at School of Medicine for Women, 1898–99; Croonian Lecturer Royal Society, 1904; Croonian Lecturer, Royal College of Physicians, 1905; Baly Medallist, 1907; Herter Lecturer, New York, 1908; Royal Medal of Royal Society, 1913; Linacre Lecturer, Cambridge, 1915; Oliver Sharpey Lecturer, RCP, 1919; Harveian Orator, RCP, 1923; served European War, 1915–17 (CMG); Chemical Adviser, Salonica Force, 1916–17; Scientific Adviser Ministry of Food, 1918; British Delegate Inter-Allied Food Commission, 1918; with W. M. (later Sir William) Bayliss, discovered secretin, 1902; Hon. DSc Dublin and Sheffield; Hon. ScD Cantab; Hon. MD Breslau; Hon. Dr Strasbourg; Officier l'Ordre de la Couronne de Belgique. *Publications:* Elements of Human Physiology, 8th edn, 1908; Primer of Physiology, 1904; Lectures on the Physiology of Digestion, 1906; The Fluids of the Body, 1909; Principles of Human Physiology, 1912, 4th edn, 1925; Monographs on Physiology, 1918; The Feeding of Nations, 1919; The Action of Alcohol on Man, 1923; editor of Metchnikoff's Lectures on Inflammation; numerous papers on various physiological subjects, published chiefly in the Journal of Physiology. *Address:* Physiological Institute, University College, WC1. *Club:* Athenæum.

Died 2 May 1927.

STARR, Clarence L., MB Toronto, MD New York, LLD; FACS; Professor of Surgery, University of Toronto; Surgeon-in-Chief, Toronto General Hospital; Consulting Surgeon, Hospital for Sick Children, Toronto; Lieutenant-Colonel, Canadian Army Medical Corps; Consultant Orthopedic Surgeon, Canadian Army Medical Corps in Canada; *b* 1 July 1868; *s* of M. H. Starr, MD, Brooklin, Ont, and Sabra Wilcox; *m* Annie Louise, *d* of Hon. John Dryden, late Minister of Agriculture for Province of Ontario; four *d*. *Educ:* University of Toronto; Bellevue, NY. Graduated Toronto, 1890; Resident House Surgeon, Hospital for Ruptured and Crippled, New York; Assistant, Out-Patient Department, New York Hospital; Postgraduate work in Germany, France and England; commenced practice in Toronto, 1896; Demonstrator in Anatomy, University of Toronto, 1897; subsequently Demonstrator in Surgery. *Publications:* Deformities of the Spine; American Practice of Surgery; various contributions to medical journals. *Recreations:* motoring, golf. *Address:* 182 Bloor Street West, Toronto. *T:* Kingsdale 2481. *M:* 12582–12583. *Clubs:* York, Rosedale Golf, Toronto. *Died 25 Dec. 1928.*

STATHAM, Rev. Prebendary George Herbert; Rector of Torwood, Torquay, since 1884; Prebendary of Exeter, 1903; *b* Liverpool, 3 Sept. 1842; *s* of H. H. Statham, solicitor; *m* 1877, Emily Florence, *d* of Rev. Alldersey Dicken, DD; one *s*. *Educ:* Liverpool Coll.; Christ's Coll., Cambridge. Second Master, Bury St Edmund's Grammar School, 1865–75; Tutor at St Columba's College, Ireland, 1875–77; Head Master, Crediton Grammar School, 1877–84; Rural Dean, 1889–94; Chairman, Torquay Schools Union, 1887–1904; Vice-Chairman, Torquay Education Committee, 1902–4, and since 1909. *Recreations:* cricket, golf. *Address:* Torwood Rectory, Torquay. *T:* Torquay 575. *Died 23 March 1922.*

STATHAM, Henry Heathcote, FRIBA; architect; for twenty-five years editor of The Builder; *b* 11 Jan. 1839; *s* of H. Heathcote Statham, solicitor, Liverpool; *m* 1887, Florence Elizabeth, *y d* of W. Stephens Dicken, Deputy General Inspector of Hospitals, East India Co.'s Service; two *s* two *d*. *Educ:* Liverpool Collegiate Institution, under Dr Howson. Articled to an architect in Liverpool, where he subsequently practised for a time; at about the age of thirty took up residence in London; in 1883 appointed editor of The Builder; an amateur musician and writer on music, and for many years musical

critic to the Edinburgh Review; for several successive years gave classical organ recitals at the Albert Hall on Sunday afternoons during the London season; author of many papers read before the Institute of Architects and the Architectural Association; Hon. Member the Architectural Association and the Musical Association, and Fellow of the Royal Philharmonic Society. *Publications:* Architecture for General Readers; Modern Architecture; Architecture among the Poets; My Thoughts on Music and Musicians; Form and Design in Music; Winged Words, published anonymously, 1907; The Organ and its place in Musical Art, 1909; Design for remodelling the front of the National Gallery and laying out Trafalgar Square, 1912; A Short Critical History of Architecture, 1912; What is Music?, a short analysis for the general reader, 1913; a contributor to Grove's Dictionary of Music, and author of many essays on artistic, musical, and literary subjects, more especially in the Edinburgh and Fortnightly Reviews and the Nineteenth Century.

Died 29 May 1924.

STAUNTON, Lt-Col Reginald Kirkpatrick Lynch, DSO 1915; Royal Artillery; *b* 9 April 1880; *s* of Capt. G. S. Lynch Staunton, Purbrook House, Hants. Entered army, 1899; Captain, 1907; Adjutant, 1913–14; Major, 1914; Bt Lt-Col 1916; served South Africa, 1900 (Queen's medal 3 clasps); employed with Egyptian army, 1907–11; Brigade-Major, 1914; served Soudan 1910 (medal with clasp); European War, 1914–15 (despatches, DSO, wounded); Mesopotamia, 1915–17; Russian decoration, Order of St Anne and Cross Swords. *Club:* Naval and Military.

Died 7 Nov. 1918.

STEAD, Francis Herbert, MA; Warden of Robert Browning Settlement, Walworth, 1894–1921; *b* Howdon-on-Tyne, 20 Oct. 1857; *s* of Rev. William and Isabella Stead (Independent Church); *m* 1887, Bessie, *d* of Rev. G. D. Macgregor (Paddington Chapel); one *s* three *d*. *Educ:* at home; Owens Coll., Manchester; Airedale College, Bradford; Glasgow Univ.; at Halle, Göttingen, Giessen, Berlin Universities. Buchanan Medallist in Logic and in English Literature; graduated with honours in Classics and Philosophy at Glasgow; Dr Williams' Divinity Scholar. Reporter on Northern Daily Express, 1874; on Northern Echo, 1875–76; studied for Congregational Ministry, 1876–84; was pastor of Gallowtreegate Church, Leicester, 1884–90; member of the Leicester School Board, 1888–90; editor of the Independent and Nonconformist, 1890–92; Assistant Editor of the Review of Reviews, 1894–1912; initiated the series of conferences with Mr (later Rt Hon.) Charles Booth which resulted in National Committee on Old Age Pensions, 1898; initiated Labour Weeks, 1910; convener of Browning Hall Conferences on Housing and Locomotion, 1901; of the League to Abolish War, 1916; of International Conference on Labour and Religion, 1919. *Publications:* Handbook on Young People's Guilds, 1889; The Kingdom of God, a Plan of Study, 1894; How Old Age Pensions Began to Be, 1909; Eighteen Years in the Central City Swarm, 1913; No More War, A Novel, 1917; The Proletarian Gospel of Galilee, 1922; The Unseen Leadership, 1922; Story of Social Christianity, 1924; The Deed and the Doom of Jesus, 1927. *Address:* 29 Humber Road, Blackheath, SE3. *Died 14 Jan. 1928.*

STEAD, John Edward, FRS, FIC, FCS; JP 1903; President of the Iron and Steel Institute, 1920–21; metallurgical chemist; Borough Analyst, and Senior Partner of the firm of Pattinson and Stead, Middlesbrough; *b* 17 Oct. 1851; *s* of Rev. W. Stead; *m* 1887, L.M. Livens (*d* 1907); one *s*. President of the Iron and Steel Institute, 1921; Hon. DSc Manchester, 1914; Leeds, 1912; Hon. Dr of Metallurgy, Sheffield, 1910; Bessemer medallist. *Address:* Everdon, Redcar, Yorkshire; 11 Queen's Terrace, Middlesbrough. *TA:* Stead, Middlesbrough. *M:* NT 7 AJ 12.

Died 31 Oct. 1923.

STEAVENSON, David Fenwick, JP; BA, LLB; *b* 10 Sept. 1844; *y s* of John Carpenter Steavenson of Fortrose and Berwick-on-Tweed, and Elizabeth, *d* of John Fenwick, Campville, Northumberland; *m* 1st, 1873, Eleanor Matilda, *d* of J. G. Bennett, Isle of Man; 2nd, Gertrude, *d* of T. Hughes, Caermarthen; two *d*. *Educ:* private tuition; King William's College; Trinity Hall, Cambridge. Barrister, North-Eastern Circuit; County Court Judge, Cumberland and Westmorland, 1891–1912. *Recreations:* rowed in the Cambridge University Eight, 1864–65–66; golf, cycling. *Address:* Dunvegan, Carbis Bay, Cornwall. *T:* St Ives 52. *Club:* New University.

Died 12 March 1920.

STEBBING, Rev. Thomas Roscoe Rede, MA; FRS, FLS, FZS; Fellow of King's College, London; a serf to Natural History, principally employed about crustacea; *b* London, 6 Feb. 1835; 4th *s* of late Rev. Henry Stebbing, DD, FRS; *m* 1867, Mary Anne (FLS), 3rd *d* of late W. Wilson Saunders, FRS. *Educ:* King's Coll. School and King's Coll., London. Scholar of London; Scholar of Lincoln College; Scholar and Fellow of Worcester College, Oxford (Hon. Fellow, 1908). Engaged in tuition, 1858–84; at the same time and in literary and scientific pursuits; ordained deacon, 1858, priest, 1859; tutor of Worcester College, 1865–67; spent several years in preparing Report on the Amphipoda of the 'Challenger' Expedition; Chairman of Conference of Delegates, corresponding societies of British Association, 1899; Zoological Secretary of Linnean Society, 1903–7; gold medallist, 1908; President of South-Eastern Union of Scientific Societies, 1896, 1897 and 1916. *Publications:* Eventide, a Book of Prayer for the Schoolroom, 1864; Translation of Longinus On The Sublimes, 1867; Essays on Darwinism, 1871; The Naturalist of Cumbrae, a true Story, being the Life of David Robertson by his Friend, 1891; A History of Crustacea, 1893; Amphipoda Gammaridea of Das Tierreich, 1906; Australian Amphipoda, 'Thetis' Expedition, 1910; Cumacea (Sympoda) of Das Tierreich, 1913; Marine Investigations in South Africa, parts, 1900–1924; On Crustacea brought by Dr Willey from the South Seas, etc.; Faith in Fetters, 1919; 'Challenger' Reports, Zoology, vol. xxix 1888; Isopoda and Amphipoda from Angola and South Africa, in Göteborgs K. Vet. Handlingar, 1922; an Autobiographic Sketch, with Portrait, in the Torquay Natural History Society's Transactions, vol. iv, 1923; contributions to magazines, etc. *Recreations:* novels with a 'good' ending, the morning paper, humorous writings in general. *Address:* Ephraim Lodge, The Common, Tunbridge Wells.

Died 8 July 1926.

STEBBING, William, MA; Barrister-at-law; author; 3rd *s* of late Rev. Henry Stebbing, DD, FRS; *m* 1870, Anne Pinckard (*d* 1925), 3rd *d* of late J. S. Pidgeon of Warley Elms, Essex; three *s* one *d*. *Educ:* Westminster School (Queen's Scholar); King's College, London (Fellow); University of Oxford. Scholar, Lincoln College; Scholar, Fellow and Hon. Fellow, Worcester College, Oxford; 1st class Moderations, double 1st class in Final Classical and Law and Modern History Schools. Conveyancer and Equity Draftsman, Lincoln's Inn; Evening Lecturer in History at King's College; Examiner for India Civil Service, and for admission to Sandhurst and Woolwich; contributor to Saturday and Edinburgh Reviews, etc; for nearly thirty years on the staff of The Times as leader-writer, and as second to the late Mr J. T. Delane in the editorship. *Publications:* Some Verdicts of History Reviewed; Biographies of Sir Walter Ralegh and Earl of Peterborough; Memorials of Charles Henry Pearson; Probable Tales; Rachel Wulfstan; Borderland Tales; The Poets; Impressions (new revised edition, Five Centuries of English Verse: Impressions); Truths or Truisms, Parts I, II, and III; passages translated from Virgil and Lucretius; Some Greek Masterpieces thought into English (verse); Some Latin Masterpieces; Greek and Latin Anthology, 3 vols. *Recreations:* novel-reading, gardening. *Address:* Frith Park, Walton on the Hill, Surrey. *M:* XE 2578. *Clubs:* Athenæum, Reform.

Died 27 May 1926.

STEEL, Charles; General Manager of the Great Northern Railway, 1898–1902; formerly Manager of Highland Railway; *b* 1847; *m* 1st, 1879 (*d* 1887), 2nd, 1903. *Club:* St Stephen's.

Died 4 Nov. 1925.

STEEL, Major Edward Anthony, DSO 1915; Royal Field Artillery; *b* 12 Dec. 1880; *s* of Colonel J. P. Steel, RE. Entered army, 1900; Captain, 1908; Major, 1914; employed with W African Frontier Force, 1904–8; served W Africa, 1904–5 (despatches, medal with clasp); 1905–6 (despatches, clasp); with Anglo-Belgian Boundary Commission, N Rhodesia, 1911–14; European War, 1914–16 (despatches twice, DSO, wounded); Mesopotamia, 1918; Siberia, 1919. *Address:* 17a Longridge Road, SW5. *Club:* Royal Automobile.

Died 19 Oct. 1919.

STEEL, Col Richard Alexander, CMG 1919; CIE 1916; late 17th Cavalry, Indian Army; *b* 1873; *e s* of late Col E. H. Steel, ISC; *m* 1st, 1902, Adine (*d* 1923), *d* of W. Acton-Adams, JP, of Tipapa, Canterbury, NZ; two *s*; 2nd, 1925, Rosalind, *y d* of late Dr Saumarez Smith, Archbishop of Sydney. *Educ:* Rugby; Sandhurst. Entered army (7th Dragoon Guards), 1892; 87th Royal Irish Fusiliers, 1893; Capt., 1901; Major, 1910; served Indian Frontier, 1897 (medal); China, 1900; Relief of Peking (despatches, medal); France, 1914 (despatches, Bt Lt-Col, CMG, Bt Col, CIE; Legion of Honour; Orders of White Eagle, Serbia, Rising Sun, Japan, Crown, Belgium, St Maurice and St Lazarus, Italy, St Anne and St Stanislas, Russia); retired, 1921. *Club:*United Service. *Died 13 July 1928.*

STEELE, John, CB 1899; JP; *b* Drumour, Perthshire, 30 Sept. 1837; *s* of John Steele, Perthshire; *m* 1862, Janet, *e d* of James Henderson Forrester of Mayfield, Kennoway, Fifeshire. Late Chief Inspector in Excise Department of Inland Revenue. *Recreations:* scientific pursuits (mainly chemical), reading, gardening; special fondness for ornithology. *Address:* Laurel Bank, Holders Hill, Hendon, NW.

Died 7 March 1922.

STEELE, Maj.-Gen. Julian McCarty, CB 1918; CMG 1916; DSO 1918; *b* 1870; *e* surv. *s* of late General Sir Thomas Montagu Steele, GCB; *m* 1903, Sybil, *d* of late William John Mure, CB, and Emily May, MBE, *d* of J. B. Innes, WS, Edinburgh; two *s* one *d*. *Educ:* Eton; Sandhurst. Entered Coldsteam Guards, 1890; Lt-Col 1915; Col 1919; Maj.-Gen. 1925; Adjutant 2nd Batt., 1896–1900, during S African War (despatches, Bt Major, Queen's medal 7 clasps); Commandant Guards Depot, 1903–5; Brigade Major (Brigade of Guards), 1905–9; DAA & QMG 1st Territorial London Division, 1912; commanded 22nd Infantry Brigade, 1915–19; served European War, 1914–19 (despatches seven times, CMG, Bt-Col, CB, DSO and bar, Croix de Guerre, Croce di Guerra); Commanding 1st Guards Brigade, Aldershot, 1920–24; Commendatore St Maurice and St Lazarus, Italy. *Address:* 58 Pont Street, SW. *T:* Kensington 4928. *Club:* Guards'.

Died 13 March 1926.

STEELE, Maj.-Gen. Sir Samuel Benfield, KCMG 1918; CB 1900; MVO 1901; Major-General Canadian Permanent Staff; *b* Purbrook, Canada, 5 Jan. 1849; 4th *s* of Capt. Elmes Steele, RN, of Coleford, Gloucestershire, and 2nd wife, Anne, *y d* of Neil Maclan Macdonald, of Islay; *m* 1890, Marie Elizabeth, *e d* of Robert W. Harwood, a Seigneur of Vaudreuil, PQ, Canada; one *s* two *d*. *Educ:* Orillia, County Simcoe; British American Commercial School, Toronto. 35th Batt. Simcoe Foresters, 1866; served Red River Expedition, 1870 (medal with clasp); joined Canadian Permanent Artillery, 1871; North-West Mounted Police, 1873; Inspector, 1878; Superintendent, 1885; served campaign of 1885 in North-West Canada, and was present at action of Frenchman's Butte; commanded the Mounted Forces in pursuit of Big Bear's Band and the Wood Crees (despatches, medal with clasp); commanded an expedition into Kootenay, British Columbia, 1887 (thanked in General Orders); commanded the North-West Mounted Police posts, White and Chilkoot passes, 1898; was magistrate and had charge of the Customs (thanked by the Governor-General in Council); promoted Lt-Col; member of Council Yukon Territory; Commandant of Lord Strathcona's Corps in Boer War, 1899–1901 (despatches twice, Bt Col, MVO, CB, Queen's medal three clasps); commanded B or Northern Transvaal Division SAC, Boer War, 1901–6 (despatches, King's medal two clasps); commanded Boer cordon round the Rand to suppress the Chinese outrages; (thanked by Lord Milner and Lord Selborne for services in S Africa); Inspector General of Forces, Western Canada, 1914; organised, commanded, and trained 2nd Canadian Division, 1915; commanded Imperial and Canadian Troops, Shorncliffe, 1915–18. *Recreations:* interested in all sports. *Publication:* Forty Years in Canada, 1915. *Address:* c/o C. A. Harewood, Quebec Bank Building, Place D'Armes, Montreal, Canada; 38 Kingsway, WC2. *Clubs:* Constitutional, Services, Junior Army and Navy. *Died 30 Jan. 1919.*

STEEN, Robert Hunter, MD London; FRCP; Emeritus Professor of Psychological Medicine, King's College, London; Medical Superintendent of the City of London Mental Hospital, Dartford, Kent, 1904–25; *b* Belfast, 1870; *m* Alice, *d* of Lawrence Barnes; one *d*. *Educ:* Royal Belfast Academical Institute; Queen's College, Belfast; St Mary's Hospital. Late Out-patient Physician in Psychological Medicine, King's College Hospital. *Address:* 51 Sutherland Avenue, Bexhill. *Died 12 July 1926.*

STEER, Henry Reynolds, RI 1884; artist; *b* London, 25 Aug. 1858; *m*. *Educ:* The Priory, Highbury; art education at Heatherley's, 1879–88. Society of Miniature Painters, 1896; Leicester Society of Artists, 1895. *Recreation:* hunting for curios, costumes, etc, necessary to art. *Address:* 60 Clarendon Park Road, Leicester.

Died 28 Feb. 1928.

STEEVENS, Maj.-Gen. Sir John, KCB 1902 (CB 1897); KCMG 1917; Colonel Commandant, Royal Army Ordnance Corps, since 1921; *b* London, 9 June 1855; *s* of late John Steevens, Henley-on-Thames; *m* 1st, 1891, Alice Kate (*d* 1922), *d* of late Herbert Cautley Blackburn; two *s*; 2nd, 1922, Louise Marguerite Strang, *d* of late Henry Alphonse Rossel, Eltham, Kent. *Educ:* St John's College, Hurstpierpoint; private tuition in Germany. Joined Control Department of Army, 1874, and transferred to Army Ordnance Department, 1880; served Zulu War, 1879, as Senior Ordnance Officer 2nd division (specially promoted, medal with clasp); Egyptian

Expedition, 1882 (present at battle of Tel-el-Kebir, despatches, special promotion, medal with clasp, bronze star, 3rd class Order of the Medjidie); Assistant Director-General of Ordnance at Headquarters, 1893-98 (CB); Principal Ordnance Officer, Royal Arsenal, in connection with the South African War, 1899-1902 (KCB); Inspector General, Ordnance Stores Headquarters, 1903-5; Inspector of Equipment, India Office, 1905-14 and 1919-23; Director of Equipment and Ordnance Stores, 1914-18; Controller of Salvage, 1918-19; Commander of the Crown of Italy. *Address:* Chieflowman, Tiverton, Devon. *Club:* Junior United Service.

Died 12 June 1925.

STEINAECKER, Lt-Col Francis Christian Ludwig, Baron von, DSO 1902; late commanding the Regiment of Steinaecker's Horse; *b* Berlin, 28 Sept. 1854; mother *née* Baroness von Thumen; father was colonel German Army (Guards); *m* 1881, *d* of Geheimer Ober Regierungs Rath Kegler of Berlin. *Educ:* Royal Cadet Corps at Wahlstatt and Berlin. Entered German Army (Leib Grenadiers) in the early seventies; resigned commission, 1879, going to Bulgaria with Prince Alexander of Battenberg; during Bulgarian revolution commanded at Plevna; resigned about 1885; led expedition to interior of German South-West Africa; returned, 1888; came out to Pondoland, 1889; settled in Natal, 1890, Port Shepstone district; British subject; was president political association of this district; joined Colonial Scouts at outbreak of war; left Maritzburg beginning of March 1900, to break enemy's communication on Delagoa line; blew up Malalene Bridge, 17 June; took the commandant of that line, Van Dam, prisoner; raised Steinaecker's Horse in the enemy's country without base to draw from, without transport or provisions (despatches, Queen's medal, 3 clasps, King's medal, 2 clasps, DSO). *Publications:* different articles on agriculture, politics and phylloxera. *Recreations:* fond of books and horse-flesh. *Address:* Bushbank Ridge, near Pilgrim's Rest, Transvaal.

STEINLEN, Theophile Alexander, Hon. ARE; artist, painter and illustrator; *b* Lausanne, 20 Nov. 1859; *m;* one *d. Educ:* College and Academy, Lausanne. *Works:* illustrations for numerous books, periodicals, posters, etc. *Address:* 21 rue Caulaincourt, Paris; Jouy la Fontaine, Seine-et-Oise, France.

Died 14 Dec. 1923.

STENNING, Sir Alexander Rose, Kt 1910; JP; *b* 9 Feb. 1846; 5th *s* of William Stenning of Godstone Court, Surrey; *m* 1st, 1869, Theresa Marcia (*d* 1913), *d* of Rev. Charles Hensley Maberly, Vicar of Owlesbury, Hants; two *s;* 2nd, 1914, Emmeline Augusta, *d* of Rev. G. O. Vandeleur, Ballinamora, Limerick. With Alexander R. Stenning and Partners, architects and surveyors, London, EC; was President of the Surveyors' Institution.

Died 22 April 1928.

STENTIFORD, Charles Douglas, JP; late Editor and Managing Director of the South Wales Argus. For some years sub-editor of the Western Morning News; subsequently, as editor of the Hampshire Independent, established the Southern Echo, an evening daily, but resigned the editorship of those papers on a change of proprietorship; in 1892 undertook the establishment of the South Wales Argus (daily) and the South Wales Weekly Argus, with the position of Managing Editor; later, appointed Managing Director of the proprietary company, but resigned owing to ill-health, 1917; Life Governor of the Royal Gwent Hospital. *Address:* 5 Meadfoot Terrace, Plymouth.

Died 1920.

STEPHEN, Katharine; Principal of Newnham College, 1911-20; *b* 26 Feb. 1856; *e d* of late Sir James Fitzjames Stephen, 1st Bt, formerly Judge of the High Court, and Mary Richenda, *d* of the Rev. John William Cunningham, formerly Vicar of Harrow; unmarried. *Educ:* private school, Brighton; Bedford College, London. Vice-Principal of Newnham College, 1892-1911; Librarian, 1887-1910; Member of the Managing Committee of Stormont House Tubercular School, and of Carlyle School, Chelsea; a Governor of the Horticultural College, Swanley. *Publications:* French History for English Children; Three Sixteenth-Century Sketches. *Address:* 4 Rosary Gardens, SW7. *Club:* University Women's. *Died July 1924.*

STEPHEN, Sir (Matthew) Henry, Kt 1904; *b* 5 Dec. 1828; 3rd and *e* surv. *s* of late Rt Hon. Sir Alfred Stephen, GCMG; *m* 1st, 1854, Caroline Sibella (*d* 1897), *d* of Henry Tudor Shadforth; 2nd, Florence Sophia *d* of late Augustus George Dunstan Huthwaite, sometime Lieut RN. Barrister New South Wales, 1850; QC 1879; member of Legislative Assembly, 1869-71; Puisne Judge, 1887; appointed acting Chief Justice during Sir Frederick Darley's absence, 1902; late Senior Puisne Judge of Supreme Court of New South Wales; retired, 1904. *Address:* Woollahra, Sydney. *Club:* Australian, Sydney.

Died 1 April 1920.

STEPHENS, Maj.-Gen. Adolphus Haggerston, CB 1887; *b* 14 June 1835; *s* of Gen. Stephens. Entered army, 1851; Maj.-Gen. 1889; served with Rifle Brigade, Crimea, 1855 (medal with clasp, Turkish medal); Indian Mutiny, 1857-58 (medal with clasp); Ashanti, 1874 (slightly wounded, despatches, Brevet Lt-Col, medal with clasp). *Address:* 2 Carlisle Place, Victoria Street, SW.

Died 24 Oct. 1916.

STEPHENS, George Henry, CMG 1902; *b* 1855; *e s* of late Samuel Henry Stephens of Clifton, Bristol; *m* 1901, Dorothy, 3rd *d* of late Thomas Woolner, RA; one *s.* Engaged on construction of railway, harbour, and irrigation works, India, 1879-86; England, America, West Africa, and West Indies, 1887-97; Egypt Superintending Engineer, Assiout Barrage, 1898-1903; Medjidie, 2nd class, 1902. *Address:* 13 Campden Hill Road, W8. *T:* Park 5233. *Club:* Junior Carlton. *Died 13 Dec. 1927.*

STEPHENS, Henry Morse; Professor of History, University of California, since 1902; Director of University Extension, 1902-10; *b* Edinburgh, Scotland, 3 Oct. 1857. *Educ:* Haileybury; Balliol College, Oxford. Lecturer on Indian History, Cambridge, 1892-94; Professor of Modern European and English History, Cornell University, 1894-1902; Editor of American Historical Review, 1895-1905; President American Historical Association, 1915; Commander of the Order of Isabel the Catholic of Spain, 1916. *Publications:* History of French Revolution, 1886; Portugal, 1891; Albuquerque, 1892; Speeches of Statesmen and Orators of the French Revolution, 1892; Revolutionary Europe (1789-1815), 1893; Modern European History (1600-1890), 1899; Select Documents of English Constitutional History, 1901; St Patrick at Tara (a forest play), 1909; editor, The Pacific Ocean in History, 1916; contributor to Ency. Brit. and Dictionary of National Biography. *Address:* Berkeley, Calif, USA. *Clubs:* Savage; Century, New York; Tavern, Boston; Bohemian, University, San Francisco. *Died 16 April 1919.*

STEPHENS, Rev. John Otter; Hon. Canon of Southwark Cathedral, 1914; *b* 1832; *m* 1887, Emma Charlotte, *d* of Alexander Samuel Leslie-Melville of Branton Hall, Lincoln, and Hon. Mrs (Albinia Frances) Leslie-Meville, *d* of 6th Viscount Midleton; two *d. Educ:* Winchester College; Brasenose College, Oxford. Deacon, 1854; Priest, 1856; Curate at Steeple Aston, 1857; Belgrave, 1858-61; Vicar of Savernake, 1861-79; founded, with the Marquis and Marchioness of Ailesbury, Savernake Hospital; Rector of Blackney, 1879-1903; founded with others the Alexandra Hospital, Woodhall Spa; left co-trustee with Mr Nicholl under the will of the late Lady Charles Brudenell-Bruce for £140,000 to found a Parish and erect the necessary buildings in the County of London to the memory of his friend Lord Charles Brudenell-Bruce, 1903; built and endowed All Saints, Tooting-Graveney, and became first Vicar, 1903-12; Chaplain for several seasons at Beaulieu sur Mer, and built the Church of St Michael and All Angels there; Chaplain at Sorrento, 1912-13, and at Marienbad, 1908-10. *Address:* 25 Chester Terrace, Chester Square, SW1. *T:* Victoria 4729. *Club:* Wellington.

Died 14 Aug. 1925.

STEPHENSON, Sir (Albert) Edward, KCMG 1921 (CMG 1914); VD 1910; Major (retired) 4th Volunteer Battalion East Surrey Regiment; Director of Colonial Audit since 1910; *b* 1 Feb. 1864; *s* of Alfred Stephenson, Bradford; *m* 1901. Entered Exchequer and Audit Dept, 1884; Local Auditor, Lagos, 1888; appointed to Colonial Audit Service in London, 1891; undertook local official investigations in several colonies. *Address:* Colonial Audit Department, 58 Victoria Street, SW. *Club:* Junior Army and Navy.

Died 17 April 1928.

STEPHENSON, Francis Lawrance, CB 1907; VD; MB; Hon. Colonel Royal Army Medical Corps; a Territorial, 2nd London Division; *b* 18 Feb. 1845; *s* of Col John Stephenson, late 17th Lancers; *m* 1872, Grace A., *d* of late Rev. C. I. Furlong.

Died 28 April 1920.

STEPHENSON, Admiral Sir Henry Frederick, GCVO 1902; KCB 1897 (CB 1876); Gentleman Usher of the Black Rod since 1904; *b* 7 June 1842; *s* of late Henry Frederick Stephenson and Lady Mary Stephenson, *d* of 4th Earl of Albemarle; *m* 1903, Hon. Charlotte Elizabeth Eleanor Fraser, *e d* of 17th Baron Saltoun, and *widow* of William H. A. Keppel. Entered RN 1855; Vice-Adm. 1896; served Crimean War, 1855; China Expedition, 1857; Indian Mutiny,

1857–58; Canada, 1866; Arctic Expedition, 1875–76; Egyptian Campaign, 1882; Naval ADC to Queen Victoria, 1888–90; Equerry to HRH the Prince of Wales, 1878–93; Commander-in-Chief, Pacific Station, 1893–96; commanding Channel Squadron, 1897–98; First and Principal ADC to King Edward VII, 1902–4; retired list, 1904. *Address:* 18 Lowndes Street, SW1. *T:* Kensington 497.

Died 16 Dec. 1919.

STEPHENSON, Rev. Jacob; Hon. Canon of Winchester, 1903; *b* 21 May 1844; *e s* of Jacob Stephenson of Newton Kyme, Yorkshire; *m* 1871, Martha Elizabeth (*d* 1926), *d* of James Greenwood of Melmerby, Yorkshire; three *s* four *d*. *Educ:* private school; Richmond College. Graduated BA, London Univ., 1867; MA (in mental and moral science, fifth in list), 1882; prizeman in Hebrew and New Testament Greek. A Wesleyan minister in London, Waterloo, and Southport, 1867–83; ordained Deacon by Bishop Lightfoot of Durham, 1883; Priest by Bishop Harold Browne of Winchester, 1884; Curate of St Augustine, Southampton, 1883–85; of Alverstoke, with charge of Christ Church, 1885–88; Vicar of Forton, and Sub-Warden of St Thomas Home, 1888–1910; Rector of Droxford, 1910–26; Rural Dean of Alverstoke, 1901–10; of Bishop's Waltham, 1912–22; member of the Councils of The Rescue Union, Board of Education, also of the Consultative Committee of the National Society, London. *Publications:* The Prophecies, the Gift, the Warfare, an Ordination Sermon; The Chief Truths of the Christian Faith, 1902. *Address:* 2 Clifton Road, Winchester. *TA:* Winchester.

Died 1 Feb. 1927.

STEPHENSON, Sydney, MB, ChM; FRCSE; late Ophthalmic Surgeon to Queen's Hospital for Children, the Evelina Hospital, Queen Charlotte's Hospital, etc; *b* 1862; *s* of Appleby Stephenson, MD, and Annie Manlove; *m* Jane Finch, *d* of J. H. Peck, JP; one *s* one *d*. *Educ:* privately; Nottingham High School; Epsom College; University of Edinburgh. Diploma in Ophthalmology, Oxon. Inspector of the Local Government Board for ophthalmic purposes, 1896–97; Visiting Surgeon to the Ophthalmic School, Hanwell, VA, 1889–1903; co-founder of the Society for the Study of Disease in Children; Ophthalmic Referee under Workmen's Compensation Act for London and its environs; late Vice-President of the Ophthalmological Society of the United Kingdom; Master of the Oxford Ophthalmological Congress; Middlemore Prizeman, 1907; editor British Journal of Ophthalmology. *Publications:* Epidemic Ophthalmia, 1895; Contagious Ophthalmia, 1899; Ophthalmic Nursing (2nd edn); translations of Dr Feuer's Die Beziehungen zwischen Zahn und Augen-Affectionen, and of Dr Darier's Leçons de Therapeutique Oculaire, 1903; Report upon the Opthalmic State of Poor-Law Children in the Metropolis, 1897 (Blue Book). *Address:* 33 Welbeck Street, Cavendish Square, W1. *T:* Mayfair 403. *M:* LR 6861. *Died 15 Dec. 1923.*

STEPHENSON, Maj.-Gen. Theodore Edward, CB 1900; *b* 28 March 1856; *s* of Rev. Canon J. Stephenson of Weymouth; *m* 1889, Philippa Anna Frederica, OBE, *d* of Col Gordon Watson; one *d*. *Educ:* Marlborough College. psc. Joined 56th Regt, 1874; promoted Captain Essex Regt, 1881; Major, 1883; Lieut-Col, commanding 1st Battalion Essex Regiment, 1895; Brevet Col, 1899; was DAAG Gilbraltar, 1883–86; for N Dist, 1883–89; NE Dist, 1889–90; served in SA; gazetted 18 Feb. 1900, as Major-Gen. on Staff Commanding 18th Brigade; commanded at Barberton with charge of the Portuguese frontier, Oct. 1900; commanded mobile columns in Cape Colony, Oct. 1901 (CB, despatches four times, 8 clasps); Major-General commanding Bloemfontein District and troops in Orange River Colony, 1902–4; Major-General Commanding Transvaal, 1904–6; acted GOC-in-C S Africa, 1904; rank of Major-General confirmed, 1906; Accredited Agent of Lord Selborne in Zululand to report progress of the rebellion and military operations for its suppression, 1906 (medal); commanded 6th Division, Colchester, 1906; Distinguished Service Reward, 1906; 2nd Division, Aldershot, 1907–10; commanded troops in Straits Settlements and Malay Peninsula, at Singapore, 1910–14; commanded 65th Division, 1916; served on London Pensions Committee and on Children's Welfare Committee (Foundling Hospital). *Address:* 75 Carlisle Mansions, Westminster, SW1. *T:* Victoria 0224. *Club:* United Service.

Died 19 Jan. 1928.

STEPHENSON, William, MD, LLD; FRCS; Professor of Midwifery, University of Aberdeen, 1875–1912; *b* Edinburgh, 2 July 1837; *m* 1909, Alice Irene, 3rd *d* of late James Lawrance, Melbourne; one *s*. *Educ:* High School and University, Edinburgh. Practised in Edinburgh; was Physician to the Royal Hospital for Sick Children; Obstetric Physician, Maternity Hospital, Aberdeen; Council Obstetrical Society, London, 1881–83; Vice-President, 1887–89;

President Obstetrical Society, Edinburgh, 1908. *Publications:* numerous papers on professional subjects to medical journals. *Address:* 11 Bonaccord Crescent, Aberdeen. *M:* TN 1555.

Died Feb. 1919.

STEPHENSON, Sir William Haswell, Kt 1900; DL; DCL; Alderman and Magistrate, Newcastle-upon-Tyne; *b* 15 May 1836; *s* of William Stephenson, of Throckley House, Northumberland; *m* 1862, Eliza Mary (*d* 1901), *d* of James Bond; one *d*. *Educ:* Wesley College, Sheffield. Formerly Sheriff, four times Mayor of Newcastle, and Lord Mayor, 1909-10, 1910–11, and 1911–12; Chairman of Tyne Commission, and director of several public companies; Chairman of Newcastle Commercial Exchange Co.; presented with the Freedom of Newcastle-upon-Tyne for public service to the community. *Address:* Elswick House, Newcastle-upon-Tyne. *TA:* Throckley, Newcastle Tyne. *T:* PO 549 and 37 Nat. *M:* BB 1059.

Died 7 May 1918.

STERLING, Maj.-Gen. John Barton; *b* 12 Oct. 1840; *o* surv. *s* of late Rev. John Sterling, and *g s* of late Edward Sterling; *m* Caroline (*d* 1917), *e d* of Sir John Salusbury Trelawny, 9th Bt. After a short service in the Navy, gazetted to 8th Foot, 1861; transferred to Coldstream Guards in same year; served in that regiment till 1896, and commanded the 2nd Battalion for four and the regiment and North London Volunteer Brigade for five years; present with 2nd Battalion in Egypt, 1882; 2nd in command of 1st Battalion in the Soudan and in Cyprus, 1885; Major-General 1896; retired 1901. *Clubs:* Athenæum; Royal Yacht Squadron, Cowes.

Died 5 Dec. 1926.

STERNBERG, Hon. Joseph; MLC Victoria, for Bendigo Province, since 1904; *b* 1855; *s* of late Alexander Sternberg, JP, a Victorian pioneer landowner; *m* Selina, *o d* of late B. Lazarus of Bendigo. *Educ:* private college. Member for Northern Province Legislative Council of Victoria, 1891; was member of the Royal Commission on Old Age Pensions and Shops and Factories Acts; on Royal Commission to inquire into the Electrification of the Victorian Railways; and on Royal Commission inquiring into the Housing Conditions in the Principal Cities of Victoria, Australia; first Commssioner of the Campaspe Irrigation Trust; and member of the first Council of Education in Victoria; Past Grand Warden in the Grand Lodge of Freemasons of Victoria; Past Grand Master of MUIOOF of Victoria; largely interested in Bendigo mining; Director of the following goldmining companies:-Clarence, New Prince of Wales, Suffolk, United Moon, and New Moon Consolidated, and others. *Recreations:* athletic sports, cycling, reading. *Address:* State Parliament House, Melbourne; Kalumna, Bendigo, Australia.

Died 13 Jan. 1928.

STERNDALE, 1st Baron, *cr* 1918, of King Sterndale; **William Pickford,** Kt 1907; PC 1914; QC 1893; Master of the Rolls since 1919; *b* 1 Oct. 1848; 2nd *s* of Thomas Edward Pickford, Manchester, and Georgina, *d* of Jeremiah Todd-Naylor, Liverpool; *m* 1880, Alice Mary (*d* 1884), 2nd *d* of John William Brooke, Sibton Park, Yoxford, Suffolk; two *d*. *Educ:* Liverpool College; Exeter College, Oxford (MA; Hon. Fellow). Joined Northern Circuit, 1875; Recorder of Oldham, 1901–4; of Liverpool, 1904–7; Commissioner of Assize, NE Circuit, 1906; Judge of the High Court, King's Bench Division, 1907–14; a Lord Justice of Appeal, 1914–18; President of the Probate Division, Admiralty Court, 1918–19. *Heir:* none. *Address:* Queen's House, Cheyne Walk, Chelsea, SW; King Sterndale, near Buxton. *Clubs:* Athenæum, United University, Alpine.

Died 7 Aug. 1923 (ext).

STEVEN, Temp. Capt. (John) Fraser, DSO 1916; MA, BSc, MB, ChB; Royal Army Medical Corps; 2nd *s* of late Roderick Steven, Glasgow; *m* 1916, Gladys, *o d* of late Major Fraser; one *s*. Served European War, 1914–17 (despatches, DSO). *Address:* 43 Lansdowne Crescent, Glasgow. *T:* W 3575.

Died 4 July 1920.

STEVENS, Bertram; joint-editor, Art in Australia (quarterly magazine); *b* Inverell, NSW; *s* of W. Matheson Stevens, formerly of London; *m* Edith Wogaman; two *s* one *d*. *Educ:* NSW public schools. Editor Red Page (Literary) of Sydney Bulletin, 1909–11; The Lone Head (magazine) 1911–18. *Publications:* edited Poetical Works of John Farrell, with memoir, 1904; Wine and Roses, verses by Victor Daley, with memoir, 1911; Golden Treasury of Australian Verse, 1908 (an enlarged and revised edition of An Anthology of Australian Verse, 1906); Australian Birthday Book, 1907; Bush Ballads; The Charm of Sydney; Poems of Henry Kendall, 1920; The Bulletin Book of Humorous Verse, 1902; and several other books; joint-editor—Pen

Drawings of Norman Lindsay, 1918; Art of J. J. Hilder, 1918; Art of Arthur Streeton, 1919; and other art publications. *Address:* 24 Bond Street, Sydney, NSW.

Died 14 Feb. 1922.

STEVENS, Lt-Col Cecil Robert, MD, BS London; FRCS; Indian Medical Service; Professor of Clinical and Operative Surgery, Medical College, Calcutta; *b* 14 March 1867; *s* of Sir Charles Cecil Stevens, KCSI, and Mary Anne Caroline, *d* of late Captain Turner, HEICS; *m* 1892, Katharine, *d* of Lt-Col James Duff of Knockleith; one *s* one *d*. *Educ:* Malvern; University College, London; St Bartholomew's. Served in Chitral Expedition, 1895; operations in Samana, Tirah, and NW Frontier, 1897; late Professor of Anatomy, Medical College, Calcutta; Surgeon to Medical College Hospital; Member of Governing Body of State Medical Faculty, Bengal; Member of Council of State Medical Registration, Bengal. *Publications:* Notes on Appendicitis, etc. *Recreations:* shooting, fishing, tennis, golf. *Address:* 6 Middleton Street, Calcutta. *T:* Calcutta 1059. *M:* 1421. *Clubs:* Bengal, Bengal United Service, Calcutta.

Died 1919.

STEVENS, Charles John, JP; Associate Editor of the Register, Adelaide, 1899-1910; *b* London, 16 Aug. 1857; *e s* of late John Stevens, formerly of Marlborough, Wilts; *m* 1st, 1878, Elizabeth, *e d* of Henry Brandwood, Walsall; 2nd, 1884, *Julia, 3rd d* of W. R. Rashleigh of St Keverne, Cornwall; six *s* one d. Educ: Herrold's School, Bermondsey. Spent five years in Law Offices, London; arrived in Adelaide, 1875; connected with the Register; Manager of Port Adelaide Office, 1876-86; sub-Editor, 1886-92; leader of Reporting Staff, 1892-99; Associate Editor, 1899; Acting Editor, 1905-6; regular contributor to Provincial Press; Worshipful Master of Commercial Lodge No 39 SAC of Freemasons, 1914; President of Masters and Wardens Association, 1915. *Publications:* The Barrier Silver and Tin Fields, 1888—the first work published describing the leading Broken Hill and Euriswie Mines; Spirit of History; Masonic Mysteries; and other addresses. *Recreations:* farming, gardening. *Address:* Glengowan, Enfield, Adelaide, S Australia.

Died 10 Feb. 1917.

STEVENS, Hon. Ernest James, FRGS, FRS, FRCI; MLC (Queensland); late Chairman Brisbane Newspaper Company, Limited; Local Deputy Chairman Australian Mutual Provident Society; *b* Melbourne, Victoria, 10 July 1845; *s* of F. P. Stevens of Melbourne; *m* 1877, Ada C., *d* of J. H. Jackson, Sanford Downs, Victoria; two *s* six *d*. *Educ:* Church of England Grammar School, Melbourne. Went to Queensland to manage Yarronvale for a Victorian company, 1886; took up country on Bulloo River for himself, 1868; his nearest neighbour was 80 miles distant, the blacks were very treacherous, revolvers being carried for about four years; elected Legislative Assembly for Warrago, 1878; Logna, 1883, 1888, and 1893, retiring in 1899, when he was called to the Legislative Council; founded four schools of arts and established several rifle clubs; patron or president of many athletic clubs. *Publications:* twenty-two serial stories of life in the Never-Never bush (Bulloo). *Recreations:* shooting, fishing. *Address:* Myninn, Southport, Queensland. *Clubs:* Queensland, Johnsonian, Brisbane.

Died 3 March 1922.

STEVENS, Frederick, ISO 1902; *b* Aug. 1840; *s* of late T. J. Stevens, Cheshunt; *m* 1867, Agnes, *d* of late John Dennett Potter; one *d*. Formerly Principal of Statistical Department of Local Government Board. *Address:* The Poplars, Mill Road, West Worthing.

Died 18 Sept. 1917.

STEVENS, Rev. Henry Bingham, MA; Hon. Canon of Rochester, 1906; *b* Wilmington Vicarage, Kent, 1835; *s* of Rev. Henry Stevens, Vicar of Wateringbury (*s* of Very Rev. Robert Stevens, Dean of Rochester), and Mary Frances Stevens, *d* of late Colonel Charles Cox Bingham, RA; *m* 1885, Catherine E., *d* of Rev. Henry Charles Bartlett, Vicar of Westerham; two *d*. *Educ:* Tonbridge School (Foundation Exhibitioner, 1853); Emmanuel College, Cambridge (Senior Optime Math. Tripos and BA, 1857; MA 1860). Curate of Thatcham, Berks, 1858-61; Curridge, Berks, 1861-67; St Lawrence, Reading, 1867-68; Rector of Chatham, 1868-83; Rural Dean of Gravesend, 1901-9; Vicar of Darenth, Kent, 1883-1911. *Recreations:* captain of the Tonbridge School CC, 1853; captain of Second Emmanuel Boat, 1856. *Address:* The Beck, Wateringbury, Kent.

Died 14 Jan. 1924.

STEVENS, Sir John (Foster), Kt 1905; *b* 9 July 1845; *s* of late Charles Green Stevens; *m* 1868, Frances Louisa (*d* 1904), *d* of late Capt. W. H. Jeremie, Indian Army; one *s* three *d*. *Educ:* King Edward's School, Birmingham; Lycée of Versailles; and other foreign schools; King's

College, London. Entered ICS (Bengal), 1865; joint-Magistrate, 1876; Acting District and Sessions Judge, 1876, 1878, and 1879-1884; District and Sessions Judge, 1884; Acting Judicial Commissioner, Central Provinces, 1891; Judicial Commissioner, 1894; Acting Judge, High Court, Calcutta, 1895; Judge, High Court, 1897; retired, 1904. *Address:* 2 Lansdown Place West, Bath. *Club:* Bath and County, Bath.

Died 19 Sept. 1925.

STEVENS, Rt. Rev. Thomas, DD; FSA; Archdeacon of Essex since 1894; *b* 1841; *m* 1866, Anne Elisabeth (*d* 1918), *d* of George Bertram, and *sister* of Sir George Clement Bertram, late Bailiff of Jersey; one *d*. *Educ:* Shrewsbury School; Magdalene Coll., Cambridge (Scholar and Exhibitioner). Assistant Master, Charterhouse, 1863-66; Vicar of St Luke, Victoria Docks, 1875-82; Vicar of Saffron Walden, 1882-89; Vicar of St John's, Stratford, 1889-1901; Bishop of Barking (Suffragan), 1901-19; Chaplain of St Mary's Hospital, Ilford, 1901-4; Grand Chaplain of English Freemasons, 1896-97; Hon. Canon of St Albans, 1891-94; President, Essex Archæological Society, 1911-16. *Address:* Orsett. *Club:* Royal Societies.

Died 22 Aug. 1920.

STEVENSON, 1st Baron, *cr* 1924, Holmbury; **James Stevenson,** GCMG 1922; Bt 1917; Chairman of Standing Committee of British Empire Exhibition; *b* Kilmarnock, 2 April 1873; *e s* of Archibald Stewart Stevenson; *m* 1st, 1897, Jessie Baird Hogarth (*d* 1917), Ardrossan; 2nd 1918, Stella Johnstone, *widow*. *Educ:* Kilmarnock Academy; privately. Managing Director of John Walker & Sons, Ltd., Distillers, Kilmarnock; Director of Area Organisation, Ministry of Munitions, 1915-17; Vice-Chm. of Ministry of Munitions Advisory Committee, 1917; Member of Central Reconstruction Committee; Member of Munitions Council for Ordnance 1918, and Chm. of Council Committee on Demobilisation and Reconstruction; Surveyor-Gen. of Supply, WO, 1919-21; Member of the Army Council, 1919; Member of the Air Council, 1919-21; Vice-Chairman of Advisory Committee on Civil Aviation; Chairman of Rubber Investigation Committee; appointed by Secretary of State for Colonies personal Commercial Adviser, 1921; all the above appointments in an honorary capacity; travelled extensively. Commander, Legion of Honour. *Recreations:* golf, motoring. *Heir:* none. *Address:* Holmbury House, Holmbury St Mary, Surrey; *T:* Ewhurst 3; 22 Old Queen Street, SW1; *T:* Victoria 371. *Clubs:* Reform, Royal Automobile.

Died 10 June 1926 (ext).

STEVENSON, Sir Edmond Sinclair, Kt 1905; JP; MD, FRCS (Edin.), etc; *b* Geneva, 10 July 1850; *s* of late William Ford Stevenson and Æneas, *e d* of Col Sinclair of Forse, Caithness; *m* 1880, Emily Anna d'Urban Musgrave, *d* of J. Eaton. *Educ:* Geneva; Edinburgh; London; Paris; Berlin. Served as Medical Officer during Kaffir War, 1879 (medal); in Natal in last Boer War; late President British Medical Association, Cape Town; late President South African Congress; late President Council for the Colony; Physician-in-Ordinary to the late High Commissioner (Lord Milner); Lieut-Col SAMC. *Address:* Strathallan and St Clair, Rondebosch, Cape Colony. *TA:* Rondebosch. *T:* Central 12, Cape Town. *Club:* Civil Service, Cape Town.

Died April 1927.

STEVENSON, Edward Snead Boyd, CIE 1905; *b* 1849; *m* 1876, Constance, *d* of Rev. Thomas Ffoulkes. Entered Service, 1870. Deputy Inspector-General, Madras Police Department, 1895-1904. *Address:* Salem, Madras Presidency, India.

Died 14 Dec. 1917.

STEVENSON, Colonel Francis, CB 1906; *b* 8 March 1851. Entered army, 1870; Capt. Bombay Staff Corps, 1882; Major, ISC 1890; Lieut-Col, Indian Army, 1896; brevet Col 1900; AAG Bombay, 1891-94; served Afghan War, 1879-80 (despatches, medal with 2 clasps, bronze star); Soudan, 1885. Awarded the Royal Humane Society's Bronze Medal for saving the lives of two lascars who fell overboard the transport Asia, Porebunder, India, 22 Jan. 1874.

Died 30 May 1922.

STEVENSON, Colonel James, CB 1905; VD, TD; JP, DL; *b* Braidwood, Carluke, NB, 6 Nov. 1838; *e s* of late Nathaniel Stevenson, JP, of Braidwood, and Margaret Jane, *e d* of Thomas Rennie Scott, DL, JP; *m* 1st, 1866, Eliza Hamilton (*d* 1875) of Fairholm, *e d* of late Jas Hamilton; 2nd, 1879, Frances (*d* 1880), *e d* of late Frederick Richards Leyland of Woolton Hall, Lancashire; 3rd, 1885, Florence, *o d* of Samuel Mountford Gibbs; three *s* three *d*. *Educ:* Rugby. Cornet 12th Royal Lancers, 1860; Lieut 1862; Capt. 1866; commanded a squadron in Kerry during Fenian disturbances, 1867; Major commanding 3rd Ad. Batt. Lanark Rifle Vols. 1872; Lieut-Col commanding 9th Lanark Rifle Vols. 1875; Colonel in

Volunteer forces, 1896; Brig.-Gen. commanding HLI Vol. Brigade, 1905; retired; ADC to the Queen, 1896–1901; ADC to King Edward VII 1901, and to King George V 1910; retired, 1920. *Recreations:* racing (won Grand Military Steeplechase, 1865), hunting, shooting, fishing, cycling, skating, curling. *Address:* Braidwood, Carluke, Lanarkshire. *TA:* Braidwood, Carluke. *T:* Carluke 34. *Club:* Army and Navy.
Died 6 Nov. 1926.

STEVENSON, Sir Malcolm, KCMG 1923 (CMG 1920); Governor and Commander-in-Chief, Seychelles, since 1927; *b* 25 March 1878; *s* of late Alexander Stevenson, Lisburn; *m* 1914, Mabel, *d* of 1st Baron Chalmers; one *s* one *d. Educ:* Trinity College, Dublin; BA 1901; MA 1907. Entered Ceylon Civil Service, 1901; Second Assistant Colonial Secy., 1911; Private Secy. to the Governor, 1913; Principal Assistant Colonial Secy., 1915; Chief Secy. to Government, Cyprus, 1917; Administered the Government of Cyprus, 21 November 1918–July 1920; High Commissioner and Commander-in-Chief, Cyprus, July 1920; Governor and Commander-in-Chief, Cyprus, 1925–26. *Recreations:* tennis, golf, billiards. *Address:* Government House, Mahé, Seychelles. *TA:* Mahé-Seychelles. *Club:* Badminton.
Died 27 Nov. 1927.

STEVENSON, Maj.-Gen. Thomas Rennie, CB 1882; *b* Braidwood House, Lanarkshire, 26 Oct. 1841; 3rd *s* of N. Stevenson of Braidwood; *m* 1870, Isabella, *d* of J. Banks Friend of Ripple Vale, Kent, and 30 Sussex Square; one *s* one *d. Educ:* private. Joined 67th Regiment, 1861; 87th RI Fusiliers 1863; commanded RI Fusiliers, 1882–86; commanded 26th and 71st Regt Dists, 1887–92; retired as Maj.-Gen. 1898; Colonel Royal Irish Fusiliers, 1899; served during Egyptian Campaign, 1882, including battle of Tel-el-Kebir (despatches, CB, medal and clasp, and Khedive's star); DL, JP Lanarkshire. *Recreations:* fishing, shooting. *Address:* Sunnyside, Lanark. *TA:* Sunnyside, Lanark. *T:* Lanark 18. *M:* V 682. *Clubs:* Army and Navy, United Service; New, Edinburgh.
Died 19 Nov. 1923.

STEVENSON, Maj.-Gen. William Flack, CB 1900; King's Hon. Surgeon, 1905; late Professor of Military Surgery, Royal Army Medical College, London; *b* 29 May 1844; *s* of John Stevenson, Strawberry Hill, Dalkey, Co. Dublin; *m* 1871, Marie Teresa, *d* of G. Riddick, Monkstown, Co. Dublin. *Educ:* Dublin University. BA, MB, MCh. Entered Medical Service, 1866; Asst-Surgeon Royal Artillery; served in West Indies and in India; Army Med. School, 1892; PMO Lines of Communication, SA, Nov. 1899; PMO Lord Roberts' Headquarter Staff, 6 Feb. 1900 (despatches, CB, medal and 5 clasps). *Publication:* Wounds in War, the Mechanism of their Production and their Treatment (3rd edn), 1910. *Clubs:* Junior United Services; Bournemouth.
Died 7 July 1922.

STEVENSON, William Grant, RSA 1896 (ARSA 1885); sculptor; *b* Ratho, 7 March 1849; *m* 1885, Jeanie, *d* of late John Dickson, Edinburgh. *Educ:* parish school, Ratho. Student Royal Institution, Edinburgh; Royal Scottish Academy Life School. Public statues: Burns, Kilmarnock; Burns, Denver; Burns, Chicago; Wallace, Aberdeen. *Publications:* Wee Johnnie Paterson; Puddin'; The M'Crankys, etc. *Recreations:* golf, shooting. *Address:* 8 Osborne Terrace, Edinburgh. *Club:* Scottish Arts, Edinburgh.
Died 6 May 1919.

STEWARD, Maj.-Gen. Edward Harding, CMG 1887; late Inspector of warlike stores for Crown Colonies, colony of New Zealand, and Egypt; late RE; *b* 13 July 1835; *e s* of late Samuel Steward; *m* 1862, Jessie, 2nd *d* of late Henry Baskerville of Crowsley Park, Oxon; four *s* two *d. Educ:* Weybridge; RMA Woolwich. Served in Royal Engineers, 1854–83; quartered in Malta, the Ionian Islands, Halifax NS, Bermuda, and at home; employed in the Defence Department, War Office, 1865–78; served with South African Field Force as commanding RE, 1879; Commandant of Colony of Natal, 1880; commanding RE at Manchester, 1880–82–83, and commanded the Garrison. Decorated for services rendered to the Colonies and Dependencies. *Publication:* Notes on Submarine Mines. *Address:* Newton Lodge, Nailsworth, Glos.
Died 15 March 1918.

STEWARD, Lt-Col Sir George, KBE 1918; CMG 1909; VD; JP; FFIA; Chief Commissioner of Police, Victoria, since 1919; Commanding Officer, 50th Battalion Infantry; *b* Portree, NB, 17 March 1866; *m* 1908, Anna Lucas Synnot. *Educ:* Ipswich; Durham. English Civil Service and Royal Engineers, 1882–92; entered Tasmanian Civil Service, 1892; Chief Clerk and Accountant, Education Department; Chief Inspector of Explosives and Magazines; Secretary to the Premier; Under Secretary for the State; transferred

to Commonwealth Service, 1901; Secretary to Federal Executive Council, and Official Secretary to Governor-General, Commonwealth of Australia, 1902–19. *Recreation:* farming. *Address:* Federal Government House, Melbourne; St Kilda, Victoria, Australia. *Clubs:* Naval and Military, Athenæum, Melbourne.
Died 10 May 1920.

STEWART, Lt-Col Albert Fortescue, CMG 1918; OBE 1919; retired pay, Regular Army; *b* 30 March 1868; *s* of late Sir John Marcus Stewart, 3rd Bt, DL, JP; *m* 1902, Margarita Minnie Eva, *d* of late Rt Hon. J. Christian, Lord Justice of Appeal, Ireland; no *c. Educ:* Victoria College, Jersey. Joined Regular Army, 1887; retired on completing command 1st Batt. Suffolk Regiment, 1920; served Aro Expedition, Nigeria, 1901–2 (despatches); Great War (despatches four times, Brevet Lieut-Colonel, CMG, OBE, Chevalier de l'ordre de Léopold des Belges). *Recreations:* cricket, tennis, racquets, golf, etc. *Address:* Eastleigh, Greenham, Newbury, Berkshire.
Died 25 Nov. 1925.

STEWART, Rev. Alexander, MA; Rector of Liverpool since 1870; Hon. Canon, Liverpool, since 1880; Chaplain to Bishop of Liverpool, 1900. *Educ:* Clare College, Cambridge. Ordained, 1849; Curate of Smalley, Derby, 1849–55; South Cadbury, 1855–58; Chilton-Cantelo, Somerset, 1858–68; Vicar of Cogges, Oxford, 1868–70; Chaplain to Bishop Ryle of Liverpool, 1888–1900. *Address:* 29 Sandon Street, Liverpool.
Died 30 March 1916.

STEWART, Maj.-Gen. Alexander Charles Hector, DL, JP; *b* 15 Nov. 1838; *e s* of late John Vandeleur Stewart of Rockhill, Co. Donegal, and Lady Helen Graham-Toler, 4th *d* of 2nd Earl of Norbury; *m* 1872, Gertrude Mary, *e d* of E. Carrington Smith of Ashfold, Sussex; one *d. Educ:* Harrow. Entered army, 1856; Lieut-Col 1870; retired 1878 as Colonel 2nd Life Guards; High Sheriff, Donegal, 1881. *Address:* 23 Lennox Gardens, SW. *T:* Kensington 5050; Rockhill, Letterkenny, Co. Donegal. *Clubs:* Carlton, Bachelors'.
Died 8 March 1917.

STEWART, Major Algernon Bingham Anstruther, DSO 1900; Seaforth Highlanders; *b* 6 Dec. 1869; *e s* of Colonel C. E. Stewart, CB; *m* 1911, Edith Evelyn, *d* of Sir Arthur Vivian; twin *d.* Entered army, 1890; Capt 1899; Maj. 1908; served Chitral Relief Force (medal with clasp); South Africa, 1899–1902 (despatches, Queen's medal, 5 clasps, King's medal, 2 clasps); European War, 1914–15 (despatches); Adjt 3rd Batt. Seaforth Highlanders, 1903–8; India, 1908. *Address:* 51 Redcliffe Square, SW; Ornockenoch, Gatehouse, NB. *Club:* Naval and Military.
Died 23 May 1916.

STEWART, Charles; *b* 1840; 4th *s* of late Duncan John Stewart, and Harriet (*d* 1884), 3rd *d* of late Major Anthony Gore (*brother* of Sir Ralph Gore, 7th Bt); *m* 1st, 1870, Eva (*d* 1872), 4th *d* of late Henry Robert Kingscote; 2nd, 1874, Alice Louisa, 2nd *d* of late Robert Johnstone-Douglas of Lockerbie, Dumfriesshire. *Educ:* Rugby; Edinburgh University. Admitted a Member of the Scottish Faculty of Advocates, 1862; a Solicitor in London, 1872; a retired Member of the Council of the Law Society; proprietor of Castle Stalker (or Stalcaire), Strath Appin, Loch Linnhe; contested (U) Argyllshire, 1903. *Publications:* Reminiscences of Fifty Years of Legal Life in Edinburgh and London, 1903; In the Evening (Essays), 1910. *Address:* Achara, Duror of Appin, Argyllshire; 38 Eaton Place, SW. *Clubs:* Carlton; New, Edinburgh.
Died 2 Aug. 1916.

STEWART, Lt-Col Charles Edward, CMG 1915; 1st Battalion Royal Highlanders; *b* 27 Sept. 1868. Entered army, 1889; Captain, 1898; Major, 1908; Lt-Col 1914; Brig.-Major, S Africa, 1900–2; Adjutant, Volunteers, 1903–8; served S Africa, 1899–1902 (despatches; Queen's medal, 4 clasps; King's medal, 2 clasps); European War, 1914–15 (CMG). *Club:* Army and Navy.
Died 14 Sept. 1916.

STEWART, Rev. Charles Henry Hylton, VD 1905; MA; Hon. Canon of Chester, 1916; Warden of Special Service Clergy; *m* Florence Hope, *d* of Thos Dixon, Banker, Chester; four *s* one *d. Educ:* St Catharine's College, Cambridge (choral scholar). Deacon, 1875; priest, 1876; organist of Chichester Cathedral, 1874–75; curate of Pebmarsh, Essex, 1875–77; minor canon, precentor, and sacrist of Chester, 1877–89; vicar of New Brighton, 1889–1905; rector of Bathwick, 1905–16. Assistant County Director BRCS for City Division, Chester. *Recreations:* cricket, tennis, rowing. *Address:* 10 Abbey Square, Chester. *Clubs:* Junior Army and Navy; Grosvenor, Chester.
Died 7 April 1922.

STEWART, Charles Hunter, MB, DSc; FRSE; Professor of Public Health, and Director of the John Usher Institute of Public Health, University of Edinburgh; *b* Edinburgh, 29 Sept. 1854; *m* 1st, 1888, Ann Maria (*d* 1905), *e d* of late George Gordon Gibson, civil engineer, Edinburgh; 2nd, 1912, Agnes Millar MacGibbon, *y d* of late Robert Somers, Thrushville, Stirling. *Educ:* Edinburgh. After graduation studied in various foreign laboratories; Assistant to the Professor of Medical Jurisprudence and Public Health, 1884–97; elected first occupant of the Bruce and John Usher Chair of Public Health, 1898. *Publications:* various contributions to the Transactions and Proceedings of Royal Society of Edinburgh, etc. *Recreation:* walking. *Address:* University, Edinburgh. *Club:* Royal Societies.

Died 30 June 1924.

STEWART, Charlotte, *(pen name* Allan McAulay); *b* Cachar, Assam, 30 Sept. 1863; *d* of late Colonel Robert Stewart of Ardvorlich. *Educ:* home. *Publications:* The Honourable Stanbury and Others, 1894; The Rhymer, 1900; Black Mary, 1901; Poor Sons of a Day, 1903; The Eagle's Nest, 1910; collaborated with Kate Douglas Wiggin and the Misses Findlater in The Affair at the Inn, 1904; The Safety of the Honours, 1906; Beggars and Sorners, 1912. *Occupation:* knitting socks. *Address:* Ardvorlich Cottage, Balquhidder, Perthshire.

Died 18 April 1918.

STEWART, Sir David, Kt 1896; MA, LLD; DL, JP; *b* 29 July 1835; *s* of late John Stewart, JP, Banchory-Devenick and Leggart, and of Mary Irvine; *m* 1860, Margaret Dyce, *d* of Rev. David Brown, DD, LLD; three *s* five *d. Educ:* King's College, Aberdeen (MA). Chairman Great North of Scotland Railway Company, and Director of Northern Assurance Company and Aberdeen Comb Works Company; six years Lord Provost of Aberdeen, and nine years in University Court, during which he greatly extended the Aberdeen University buildings and the City of Aberdeen, so as to incude Old Aberdeen, Woodside, and Torry. *Address:* Banchory House, Banchory-Devenick, Kincardineshire. *TA:* Banchory House, Aberdeen. *T:* 1865 Aberdeen. *Clubs:* Carlton, Caledonian; Royal Northern, Aberdeen.

Died 11 Oct. 1919.

STEWART, David Mitchell, ISO 1915; Superintending Engineer, General Post Office, 1895–1918; *b* 7 Nov. 1853; *s* of Andrew Stewart, Woodend, Coupar Angus, Perthshire; *m* Annie Torrance, *d* of J. T. Weir of Blantyre Park, Lanarkshire; one *s* one *d.* Entered Post Office Service, 1870; Assistant Superintending Engineer, 1892. *Recreations:* farming, Shetland pony breeding. *Address:* Blantyre Park, Blantyre, Lanarkshire. *T:* 60. *M:* 989. *Club:* Scottish Automobile, Glasgow.

Died 25 Jan. 1924.

STEWART, Sir Francis (Hugh), Kt 1916; CIE 1911; MA (Oxon); partner in Gladstone, Wyllie & Company, Merchants, London and Calcutta; *b* Nov. 1869; *s* of late Robert Stewart of London and Calcutta; *m* 1906, Frances Henrietta, *e d* of A. G. Rickards, KC; three *s* four *d. Educ:* Harrow; Magdalen College, Oxford. Captain Oxford University Golf Club, 1894; Amateur Golf Champion of India, 1897; President Bengal Chamber of Commerce, 1915; Member of Bengal Legislative Council, 1911–12, 1914; Imperial Legislative Council, 1915; a Commissioner for the port of Calcutta, 1909–12, 1914–15; Sheriff of Calcutta, 1914. *Recreations:* cricket, golf. *Address:* 5 Council House Street, Calcutta. *Clubs:* Union; Bengal, Calcutta.

Died 29 Dec. 1921.

STEWART, Maj.-Gen. George, CB 1887; Colonel Queen's Own Corps of Guides; *b* 20 July 1839; *s* of late Major W. Murray Stewart, HEICS, of Ardvorlich, NB; *m* 1881, Mary (*d* 1924), *d* of J. Monteath Douglas. *Educ:* St Andrews; London. Entered Bengal Army, 1856; Capt. Bengal Staff Corps, 1868; Major, 1876; Lieut-Col 1879; Colonel, 1883; Major-General (retired), 1887, served throughout Indian Mutiny, 1857–59; present at Havelock's relief of Cawnpore and Lucknow, and its final capture (despatches, medal with two clasps); in China War, 1860 (despatches, medal with twice clasps); in Ambeyla Campaign (medal and clasp); with Jawaki Expedition, 1878 (despatches, clasp); in Afghan War, 1878–80; present at Ali Masjid; actions about Kabul; siege of Sherpur and Charasiab (despatches, medal and two clasps. *Address:* Baldorran, College Road, SE19. *T:* Sydenham 764.

Died 2 Feb. 1927.

STEWART, Rt Hon. George Francis, PC (Ireland) 1921; JP, DL; FSI; *b* 1 Nov. 1851; 8th *s* of James Robert Stewart of Gortleitragh, Co. Dublin, DL, and Martha, *e d* of Richard Benson Warren, Serjeant-at-law; *m* 1881, Georgiana Lavinia, 2nd *d* of Admiral R. R. Quin; two *s* one *d. Educ:* Marlborough College; Trinity College, Dublin. Senior Moderator and Gold Medallist, 1872; Member of University Senate; had very extensive agencies in Co. Leitrim, of which county

he was twice High Sheriff, 1893 and 1913; Director of Bank of Ireland, 1902; Governor of the Bank, 1914 and 1915; Chairman of Irish Branch of Surveyors' Institution, 1899; President of the Surveyors' Institution, 1916–17; senior partner in the firm of J. R. Stewart & Sons, Dublin, and member of boards of public companies and hospitals; elected as a Representative of the Southern Unionists to Irish Convention, 1917. *Recreations:* travelling, yachting. *Address:* Summerhill, Killiney, Co. Dublin. *M:* IK 51. *Clubs:* Kildare Street, Dublin; Royal St George Yacht, Kingstown.

Died 12 Aug. 1928.

STEWART, Sir James Watson, 1st Bt, *cr* 1920, of Balgownie; Chartered Accountant; Member of the Chartered Institute of Accountants and Actuaries; Fellow of the Chartered Insurance Institute, and Senior Partner of J. W. Stewart & Co., CA, Glasgow; *b* Rome, 1852; *s* of late Alexander Stewart, JP, Springhill, Muirkirk, and late Marion Watson; *m* 1883, Marion Symington, *e d* of late Rev. Alexander Young, of Darvel, Ayrshire; three *s* five *d. Educ:* Irvine Academy; privately. Member of County Council of Dumbartonshire, 1890–1910; Chairman of Eastern District Committee of the County for seventeen years; Chairman of Dumbartonshire Secondary Education Committee for twenty-seven years; Vice-Chairman of the County of Dumbarton for twelve years, and thereafter Convener of the County and Chairman of the County Council, 1908–10; Member of Glasgow Provincial Committee for the Training of Teachers, and Chairman of Finance Committee, 1905–18; Member of Corporation of Glasgow, 1904–20; acted as Magistrate of the City, and as Convener of the Electricity Committee, and of the Health Committee; Lord Provost of Glasgow, and Lord-Lieutenant of the County of the City of Glasgow, 1917–20; a Governor of the West of Scotland Agricultural College since 1899, and a Member of the Clyde Navigation Trust since 1905; JP, DL, City of Glasgow; DL, County of Lanark; JP, County of Dumbarton; LLD, Glasgow University; a Commander of the Legion of Honour, and of the Order of the Crown of Belgium. *Heir: s* Alexander Stewart, *b* 5 Nov. 1886. *Address:* Balgownie, Bearsden, Dumbartonshire. *Clubs:* New, Art, Conservative, Royal Scottish Automobile, Glasgow; Royal Clyde Yacht.

Died 3 Nov. 1922.

STEWART, Sir John Henderson, 1st Bt, *cr* 1920, of Fingask; DL, JP; partner of Messrs Alex. Stewart & Son, of Dundee; *b* 1877; *s* of Alexander Stewart; *m* Ethel Bailey, *d* of John Fraser, Arbroath; one *s.* Freeman of the City of London. *Heir: s* Bruce Fraser Stewart, *b* 6 Sept. 1904. *Address:* Fingask Castle, Errol, Perthshire.

Died 6 Feb. 1924.

STEWART, John Graham, KC (Scot.) 1906. *Educ:* Edinburgh University, MA, LLB; Forensic Prizeman, 1885; Vans Dunlop Scholar in Scots Law and Conveyancing, 1887–1890; admitted to Faculty of Advocates, 1887; Advocate Depute, 1905; contested (C) East Perthshire, 1900. *Publication:* A Treatise on the Law of Diligence in Scotland. *Address:* 17 Abercromby Place, Edinburgh. *Clubs:* Conservative, Barnton, Edinburgh.

Died 21 May 1917.

STEWART, Sir Mark John MacTaggart, 1st Bt, *cr* 1892, of Southwick, Ardwell; DL, JP Wigtownshire; DL, JP Stewartry of Kirkcudbright; *b* Stevenson House, East Lothian, 12 October 1834; *e s* of late Mark Hathorn Stewart of Southwick (*s* of Robert Hathorn Stewart of Physgill) and Janet, *d* of John Sprot of Riddell; *m* 1866, Marianne Susanna (*d* 1914), *o d* of late John Orde Ommanney and Susanna, *d* and *heiress* of Sir John MacTaggart, Bt, of Ardwell, in accordance with whose will the surname of MacTaggart prior to that of Stewart was assumed, 1895; one *s* five *d* (and three *s* decd). *Educ:* Winchester Coll.; Christ Church, Oxford (MA). Barrister, Inner Temple, 1862; Hon. Col 1st Administrative Bde Ayr and Galloway Artillery Volunteers (medal); MP (C) Wigtown Burghs, 1874–80; Stewartry of Kirkcudbright, 1885–1906 and 1910; Chairman of School Board since 1874; travelled in East and West. The landed properties extended over 18,000 acres. *Recreations:* travelling, possessed celebrated herd of pedigreed Ayrshire cattle. *Heir: s* Edward Orde Stewart [*b* 31 Jan. 1883; *m* 1917, Hon. Margaret, *e d* of 3rd Lord Donnington. *Educ:* Eton; Christ Church, Oxford. Lieut Gren. Guards]. *Address:* Southwick, Dumfries, NB. *Clubs:* Carlton, Athenæum; New, Scottish Conservative, Edinburgh.

Died 26 Sept. 1923.

STEWART, Sir Norman (Robert), 2nd Bt, *cr* 1881; CB 1901; *b* 27 Sept. 1851; *s* of Sir Donald Stewart, 1st Bt, GCB, GCSI, CIE and Marina, *d* of Comdr Thomas Dymock Dabine, RN; *S* father, 1900; *m* 1875, Ada, *d* of P. Hewitt of Bombay; one *s* two *d.* Entered Army, 1871; Capt. 1879; Col 1890; served Afghan War, 1878–80 (despatches, Brevet Major, medal with clasp); Nile Expedition, 1884–85 (despatches, Brevet Lieut-Col, medal with two clasps, Khedive's star); commanding 1st Infantry Brigade, China, 1900 (despatches); retired; late commanding 2nd class District, India. *Publication:* My Service Days, 1909. Heir: *s* Douglas Law Stewart [*b* 1 July 1878; *m* 1903, Lilian Dorothea, *d* of F. W. Quarry].

Died 9 Nov. 1926.

STEWART, Rev. Ravenscroft; Archdeacon of N Wiltshire, 1910–19; *b* 23 June 1845; *s* of James Stewart, JP, DL, of Cairnsmore, Newton Stewart, NB; *m* 1871, Lucy Penelope, *d* of R. W. M. Nesfield, Castle Hill, Bakewell; six *s* one *d*. *Educ:* Loretto; Uppingham; Trinity College, Cambridge, BA 1869; MA 1879. Deacon, 1869; Priest, 1870; Curate of Bakewell, 1869–71; Rector of Pleasley, Derbyshire, 1871–83; Vicar of All Saints Ennismore Gardens, SW, 1882–1904; Canon of Bristol, 1903; Archdeacon, 1904–10. *Club:* Athenæum.

Died 16 Aug. 1921.

STEWART, Gen. Sir Robert Macgregor, GCB 1911 (KCB 1902, CB 1881); Colonel-Commandant, RA; *b* 1842; *s* of late John Stewart; *m* 1st, 1868, Caroline, *o c* of late Rev. A. Glasse; one *d*; 2nd, 1889, Jessie, *d* of 1st Baron Playfair (*widow* of Capt. Peel). Served in Hazara Campaign, 1868; Afghan War, 1878–79; Soudan, 1885; ADC to the Queen, 1887–97; late GOC Royal Artillery, Southern District, Portsmouth; Governor of Bermuda, 1904–7; Lieutenant of the Tower, 1907–09. *Address:* 41 Egerton Crescent, SW.

Died 22 Oct. 1919.

STEWART, Major William, of Ardvorlich, Lochearnhead, Perthshire; Governor, HM Prison, Edinburgh; *b* 8 Oct. 1859; *m* 1891, Lily, *d* of Dr A. C. MacLaren, 60 Harley Street, W; one *s* two *d*. *Educ:* Cheltenham; Sherborne. Joined the York and Lancaster Regt. 1879, and the 10th Lancers, Hodson's Horse, 1882; served through the Malakand Campaign, 1897 (medal); retired to join the Scottish Prison Dept, 1899. *Recreations:* shooting, golf. *Address:* The Governor's House, The Calton, Edinburgh. *T:* Central 4961. *Clubs:* New, Caledonian United Service, Edinburgh; Royal and Ancient Golf, St Andrews.

Died 8 June 1918.

STEWART, William, DD, LLD; Dean of Faculties in Glasgow University since 1911; *b* Annan, 15 Aug. 1835; *e s* of William Stewart, Registrar of Births, etc, district of Dalbeattie, Kirkcudbrightshire; *m* 1868; three *s*. *Educ:* Dalbeattie Parish School and Glasgow University; BA 1861; MA 1862; BD 1867; DD 1874; LLD 1911. Examiner in Mental Philosophy for Degrees in Arts, Univ. of Glas., 1867–70; Minister of Church and Parish *quoad sacra* of St George's-in-the-Fields, Glasgow, 1868–75; Professor of Divinity and Biblical Criticism in University of Glasgow, 1873–1910; Clerk of Senate in University of Glasgow, 1876–1911; one of the Governors of the Glasgow City Educational Endowments Board since 1885; one of the Governors of the Glasgow General Educational Endowments Board since 1885; Member of the University Court, 1889–1909; Dean of the Faculty of Theology, 1895–1910; one of the Governors of the Glasgow and West of Scotland Agricultural College, 1899–1908; Representative of Glasgow University on Carnegie Trust, 1901–11. *Publications:* The Plan of St Luke's Gospel, 1873; Editor of The University of Glasgow, Old and New, 1891. *Address:* 3 Annfield Road, Partickhill, Glasgow. *T:* 182 Partick.

Died 18 Sept. 1919.

STEWART-BAM of Ards, Lt-Col Sir Pieter Canzius van Blommestein, Kt 1907; OBE 1918; JP; MLA Cape Town, 1904–10; *b* Cape Town, 29 July 1869; *e* surv. *s* of late J. A. Bam, MLA; *m* 1910, Ena Dingwall Tasca, *d* and *co-heir* of late Alexander G. J. Stewart of Ards, Co. Donegal; by Royal consent added name of Stewart, 1910; two *s* three *d*. *Educ:* Cheltenham; Normal College and South African College, Cape Town; Diocesan College, Rondebosch; Cheltenham College. Entered Cape Garrison Artillery, 1892; retired with rank 1901; served South African War (medal); contested Cape Town, 1904; Victoria West, 1904; Chairman of the General Executive of South African Exhibition, 1907; originator in 1910 of the British Empire Exhibition; raised in 1915, and in command of, the 3/7th Batt. the London Regt; Chief Recruiting Officer City London Territorials, May–Sept. 1915; Founder and first Chairman and present Vice-President of the South African National Union; special medal granted in 1910 by King Edward for services rendered in connection with formation of the Union of South Africa; Originator and Chairman of the Executive of the British National Union; connected with many imperial organisations in England and S Africa; JP Co. Donegal. *Recreations:* all sorts of sport. *Address:* Laurencetown House, Ducks Hill, Northwood. *T:* Northwood 210; Ards, Cashelmore, Co. Donegal; Sea Point, Cape Town. *Clubs:* Sports, Royal Automobile; City, Civil Service, Cape Town.

Died 20 Dec. 1928.

STEWART-CLARK, Sir John, 1st Bt, *cr* 1918; JP and DL Linlithgowshire; Director Clark & Co., Ltd, and Scottish Provident Institution; a member of the Royal Company of Archers, King's Body Guard for Scotland; *b* 14 Sept. 1864; *o s* of late Stewart Clark of Dundas and Cairndhu, and Annie, *d* of John Smiley, Larne, Co. Antrim; *m* 1903, Marie Gertrude, *d* of Major Marcell Conran of Brondyffryn, Denbigh; four *s* two *d*. *Educ:* Merchiston Castle School, Edinburgh; Jesus College, Cambridge. On the Boards of the Queen Victoria Institute for Jubilee Nurses, Edinburgh; Governesses Benevolent Society (Scotland); Royal Victoria Eye Infirmary, Paisley; Edinburgh Agricultural and Fat Stock Societies. *Recreations:* shooting, fishing, golf, motoring. Heir: *s* Stewart Stewart-Clark, *b* 4 July 1904. *Address:* Dundas Castle, South Queensferry, NB. *TA:* Chateau, Corstorphine. *T:* 21 Corstorphine. *Clubs:* Royal Automobile, Caledonian, Royal Thames Yacht; Western, Glasgow; New, Edinburgh; Royal Northern and Royal Clyde Yacht; Royal and Ancient, Prestwick, and Hon. Company of Edinburgh Golfers.

Died 3 March 1924.

STEWART-SMITH, Sir Dudley, Kt 1917; KC 1902; Vice-Chancellor of the County Palatine of Lancaster, 1912; *b* 3 Feb. 1857; *s* of Alexander Stewart-Smith, of London and Hong-Kong; *m* Katherine, *d* of Henry Cautley, of Burton Pidsea; two *s* three *d*. *Educ:* University College, London; LLB London University. Called to the Bar, 1886; Bencher Middle Temple; Chairman Lancaster Quarter Sessions (Salford Hundred); on the Council of the Victoria and Liverpool Universities; Royal Commissioner (Land Transfer); JP Westmorland, Lancashire, and Cheshire; MP (L) Kendal Division, Westmorland, 1906–10; contested Kendal and East Nottingham, 1910. *Publication:* Law of Winding-up and Reconstruction of Joint-Stock Companies. *Address:* Assize Courts, Manchester; 42 Albert Court, Kensington Gore, SW7. *T:* Western 2280. *M:* EC 186. *Clubs:* Reform; Westmorland County; Union, Manchester; Athenæum, Liverpool.

Died 9 May 1919.

STEYN, Martinus Theunis; Barrister-at-law, Inner Temple, London; *b* Winburg, ORC, 2 Oct. 1857; 3rd *s* of Martinus Steyn, Bloemfontein, ORC, and Cecilia Johanna Wessels, *d* of Commandant Wessels, Winburg, ORC; *m e d* of Rev. Colin J. Fraser of Philippolis, ORC. *Educ:* Grey Coll. Bloemfontein; Wevente, Holland; Inner Temple, London. Advocate, Bloemfontein, 1883–89; State Attorney, 1889; Second Puisne Judge, 1889–93; First, 1893–96; State President, Orange Free State, 1896–1900. *Recreations:* shooting, riding. *Address:* Bloemfontein, ORC.

Died 28 Nov. 1916.

STIGAND, Major Chauncey Hugh, FRGS; FZS; Fellow Royal Anthropological Institute; *s* of William and Agnes Catherine Stigand; *m* 1913, Nancy Yulee, *d* of Major Wallace Neff, Washington, DC; one *d*. *Educ:* Radley; Army tutors. Entered The Queen's Own Royal West Kent Regiment, 1899; served Burmah and Aden; Special Service Officer, Somaliland, 1900; served with King's African Rifles in Nyasaland, British East Africa and Zanzibar, 1902–7; Captain Royal W Kent Regt, 1904; attached East Africa Survey, 1907; Egyptian Army, 1910; Major, 1915; Governor, Upper Nile, 1916. *Publications:* The Game of British East Africa; The Land of Zinj; To Abyssinia through an Unknown Land; Scouting and Reconnaissance in Savage Countries; Hunting the Elephant in Africa; Administration in Tropical Africa; A Comparative Grammar of Swahili Dialects, etc. *Address:* c/o Cox and Co., Charing Cross, SW1. *Club:* Naval and Military.

Died 20 Dec. 1919.

STIKEMAN, William Rucker, CIE 1911; retired merchant; *b* Lee, Kent, 2 March 1854; *s* of Henry Frederic Stikeman; unmarried. *Educ:* Uppingham School. Merchant in Calcutta and Rangoon; recently additional Member of the Burma Legislative Council; Chairman of the Burma Chamber of Commerce. *Recreations:* riding, golf. *Address:* 61 Onslow Gardens, SW. *Club:* Oriental.

Died 3 June 1927.

STILEMAN, Rt. Rev. Charles Harvey; Secretary, Church Pastoral Aid Society since 1918; Vicar of Emmanuel Church, Clifton, Bristol, 1916–18; *b* 1863; *s* of late Major-General W. C. Stileman; *m* 1887, Frances Dale Fenwick; two *s* one *d*. *Educ:* Repton; Trinity College, Cambridge. Ordained 1887; Curate, North Shields, 1887–89; CMS Missionary, Baghdad, 1889–91; Julfa (Persia), 1891–93; Secretary CMS Persia Mission, 1895–1900, 1901–6; Clerical Secretary, CEZMS, 1908–12; Bishop in Persia, 1912–16. *Publication:* The Subjects of the Shah. *Address:* Falcon Court, 32 Fleet Street, EC4; 37 Lingfield Road, Wimbledon, SW19.

Died 23 Feb. 1925.

STILL, William Chester, CBE 1918; Managing Director of W. M. Still & Sons, Ltd, since 1914; *b* 17 June 1878; *s* of late William Mudd

Still; *m* Maud Ellen, *d* of late Edward Bullock, Civil Servant; one *s*. *Educ*: Cowper Street Schools. Apprenticed in works of W. M. Still & Sons, Ltd, and became works manager; became a Director, 1907. *Address*: Aberfoyle, Broad Walk, Winchmore Hill, N21. *T*: Palmers Green 283. *Died 12 Aug. 1928*.

STIRLING, Archibald William, BCL; senior partner in the firm of Maddison, Stirling, and Humm, 13 Old Jewry Chambers, EC2, solicitors; *s* of Charles Stirling of Hamden, S Australia, and Edith, *e d* of John Whitnash of Taunton, Somerset; *m* 1887, Laura Bidduplh, *d* of John H. Biddulph Pinchard of Taunton; two *s* one *d*. *Educ*: Taunton, Lincoln Coll., Oxford. 2nd class in Law Honour School, 1878; and 1st class in Civil Law School, 1881; called to Bar but became a solicitor, 1893; visited Australia, 1884, and returned to this country permanently, 1888. *Publication*: The Never Never Land, 1884. *Recreations*: breeding, judging, and showing Dandie Dinmont terriers, and growing sweet peas for exhibition; some journalism. *Address*: Holmesea, Goring-on-Thames. *Died 13 March 1923*.

STIRLING, Sir Edward Charles, Kt 1917; CMG 1893; MA, MD, ScD Cantab; FRS, FRCS, CMZS; Hon. Fellow Anthropological Institute of Great Britain; Professor of Physiology, Adelaide University; director, South Australian Museum; *b* South Australia, 8 Sept. 1848; *e s* of late Hon. E. Stirling, MLC; *m* 1877, Jane, *d* of late Joseph Gilbert, Pewsey Vale, SA; five *d*. *Educ*: St Peter's College, SA; Trinity College, Cambridge; St George's Hospital, London. House surgeon, assistant surgeon, lecturer on Physiology, St George's Hospital; returning to SA in 1881 became Lecturer and subsequently Professor of Phys., Adelaide Univ.; consulting surgeon, Adelaide Hospital; late director, SA Museum; member, House of Assembly, 1883–86; member, Council Adelaide Univ.; Pres. Australasian Medical Congress, Adelaide, 1905. *Publications*: contributions to medical journals; joint author of article Hydatids in Allbutt's System of Medicine; Notoryctes typhlops, a New Genus and Species of Marsupial (Trans RS of SA); Genyoris newtoni, a Fossil Struthious Bird from Lake Callabonna (Trans RS of SA); manus and pes of Diprotodon australis (Mem. RS of SA); Report on the Anthropology of Central Australia, Report Horn Scientific Expedition; and other contributions to Trans RS of SA, R. Zool. Soc., etc. *Recreations*: shooting, horticulture. *Address*: St Vigeans, Mt Lofty, South Australia. *TA*: Adelaide. *Clubs*: Athenæum, New University; Adelaide.
Died 20 March 1919.

STIRLING, Rt. Hon. Sir James, Kt 1886; PC 1900; LLD; FRS; *b* Aberdeen 3 May 1836; *e s* of Rev. James Stirling, George Street UP Church, Aberdeen, and Sara Irvine; *m* 1868, Aby, *e d* of John Thomson Renton, Bradstone Brook, Shalford, Surrey; *one s* two *d*. *Educ*: Grammar School and University, Aberdeen; Trinity Coll. Camb. (BA) Cambridge (Senior Wrangler and First Smith's prizeman), 1860; MA Cambridge, 1863. Barrister, Lincoln's Inn, 1862, Bencher, 1886; practised as conveyancer and equity draftsman; Junior (equity) Counsel to the Treasury, 1881; Judge of the Chancery Division of the High Court of Justice, 1886–1900; Lord Justice of Appeal, 1900–6. *Recreation*: interested in physical and natural science. *Address*: Finchcocks, Goudhurst, Kent. *Club*: Athenæum.
Died 27 June 1916.

STIRLING, James Heron; *b* Cookstown, Co. Tyrone, 7 Sept. 1867; *s* of James Stirling, Ayrshire, and Elizabeth Heron, Co. Tyrone; *m* 1901, Lisette C. Adami, Ashton-on-Mersey; two *d*. Educ: Royal Belfast Academical Institution. Entered York Street Flax Spinning Co. Ltd, Belfast, 1882; remained there since, subseq. Senior Managing Director; Hon. Treasurer, Queen's University and Member of Senate; Chairman, Board of Governors R. B. Academical Institution; Vice-Chairman Ulster Hospital; Past President Belfast Chamber of Commerce; Danish Consul for Ireland, Knight of the Dannebrog; Prov. GM, AF and AM, Antrim. *Recreations*: golf, gardening. *Address*: Mount Randal, Belfast. *T*: Malone 26. *M*: XI2527, OI7497. *Clubs*: Constitutional; Ulster Reform, Belfast; Royal County Down Golf.
Died 23 Nov. 1928.

STIRLING, Hon. Brig.-Gen. James Wilfred, CB 1918; CMG 1917; *b* 1855; *o s* of late J. Stirling, of Ballawley Park, Dundrum; *m* 1881, Cecilia Mary, *d* of late Maj.-Gen. D. E. Hoste, CB. *Educ*: Wellington College. Lieut-Col and Brevet Col RFA (retired), and an Hon. Brig.-Gen.; served European War 1914–18 (despatches five times, CB, CMG, Croix de Guerre); DL, JP Devon. *Address*: Hensleigh House, Exeter. *Club*: Army and Navy. *Died 4 June 1926*.

STIRLING, John W., MB (Edin.); MD, McGill, 1913; Professor of Ophthalmology, McGill University; Consulting Surgeon Oculist to Royal Victoria Hospital; *b* Halifax, NS, 2 July 1859; *s* of W. S. Stirling, Manager Union Bank of Halifax; *m* 1898, Annie, *e d* of Howard Primrose, Picton, NS; no *c*. *Educ*: Halifax; Galt, Ont; Edinburgh; Vienna; Berlin. After school career in Halifax, short business course, then entered Edinburgh University; graduated 1884; House Surgeon Royal Infirmary; studied in Vienna and Berlin; attached to Royal Moorfields Ophthalmic Hospital; settled in Montreal, 1887. *Publications*: numerous short articles on Ocular Diseases, etc. *Recreation*: golf. *Address*: 388 Sherbrooke Street West, Montreal; Keewaydin, Pointe Claire, PQ. *T*: up 1489. *Clubs*: Mount Royal, University, Forest and Stream, Royal Montreal Golf, Beaconsfield Golf.
Died 11 Dec. 1923.

STIRLING, Rt. Rev. Waite Hockin, DD; *b* 1829; *s* of Captain T. Stirling, RN. Curate of St Mary's Church, Nottingham, 1852–56; Secretary to South American Mission, 1857–62; Superintendent of English Church Mission in Tierra del Fuego and Patagonia, 1862–69; 1st Bishop of Falkland Isles, 1869–1901; Assistant to Bishop of Bath and Wells, 1901–12; Canon Residentiary, of Wells Cathedral, 1901–20; Precentor, 1903–20. *Publication*: (jointly) The Story of Commander A. Gardiner, RN, 1867. *Address*: 24 Holland Park, W11. *T*: Park 428. *Died 19 Nov. 1923*.

STOCK, Eugene; Secretary of Church Missionary Society, 1873–1906; *b* 26 Feb. 1836; *m* 1st, 1862, Eliza Mann (*d* 1882); 2nd, 1902, Hon. Mrs Isabella Emily Fiennes. *Educ*: private schools. In mercantile life till 1873; also Editor to Church of England Sunday School Institute, 1867–75; Editor of Church Missionary Society's Publications, 1873–1902; visited the Colonies, 1892 and 1895; India, 1892–93; United States, 1900; Member of London Diocesan Conference from its establishment, 1883; Member of House of Laymen from its establishment, 1885; Member of National Church Assembly from its establishment to 1925; Diocesan Lay Reader for the Diocese of London from 1891, also for Diocese Rochester and Winchester; Hon. DCL Durham, 1908. *Publications*: Lessons on the Life of our Lord, 1871; Steps to Truth, 1878; for nine years, 1873–81, contributed the English Teachers' Notes to the Sunday School Journal, America; Lesson Studies on Genesis, 1880; planned the Church Missionary Gleaner, 1874; author of History of Church Missionary Soc. (4 vols), 1899–1916; Short Handbook of Missions, 1904; and several other works on Missions; also Story of the Bible, 1906; Talks on St Luke, 1907; My Recollections, 1909; English Church in 19th century, 1910; The Servant, 1912; An Heroic Bishop (Valpy French), 1913; Plain Talks on the Pastoral Epistles, 1914; Beginnings in India, 1917. *Address*: Melita, Bournemouth West. *T*: Bournemouth 1846. *Club*: National. *Died 7 Sept. 1928*.

STOCKENSTRÖM, Sir Andries, 3rd Bt, *cr* 1840; Member of the Railway Board; *b* 22 Sept. 1868; *s* of late Hon. Andries Stockenström; *S* uncle, 1912; *m* 1897, Mabel, *d* of J. H. Booysen of Klip Drift, Graaf Reinet, S Africa; one *s* two *d* (and one *s* decd). *Educ*: Pembroke College, Cambridge. Called to Bar, Middle Temple, 1891; was MLA Transvaal and Union of S Africa. Heir: *s* Anders Johan Booysen Stockenström, *b* 13 March 1908. *Address*: Maaström, Bedford, Cape Province, S. Africa. *Died 1 Dec. 1922*.

STOCKER, Ven. Harry; Vicar of St John, Invercargill, 1882; Archdeacon of Invercargill 1885, retired; *m*; one *s*. *Educ*: Trinity College, Dublin (BA). Ordained, 1868; Curate of Kingsclere, Hants, 1868–74; Vicar of Lincoln, NZ, 1874–79; Incumbent of Akaroa, 1879–82. *Address*: 111 Springfield Road, Christchurch, New Zealand.
Died 1 Sept. 1922.

STOCKLEY, Colonel Charles More, CB 1894; *b* 1845; 2nd *s* of Captain W. S. Stockley, HEICS; *m* 1st, 1874, Margaret, *d* of Stephen Creagh Sandes; 2nd, 1890, Eleanor, *d* of F. Fryer, and *widow* of Capt. H. Thornton, RN. Entered army, 1862; Colonel, 1888; retired, 1897; served NW Frontier, India, 1863 (medal with clasp); Jowaki, 1877–78 (clasp); Afghan Campaign, 1880–81 (despatches, medal, Brevet Major); Commanded Regimental District 27, 1892–97. *Address*: Round Oak, Newbury, Berks.
Died 18 Oct. 1923.

STOCKMAN, Sir Stewart, Kt 1913; MRCVS; Chief Veterinary Officer and Director of Veterinary Research Ministry of Agriculture and Fisheries since 1905; *b* Edinburgh, 27 Sept. 1869; 4th *s* of W. J. Stockman, merchant; *m* 1908, Ethel, *e d* of Sir John M'Fadyean; two *d*. *Educ*: Royal High School, Edinburgh; Royal Veterinary College, Edinburgh; Paris and Brussels. Professor of Pathology and Bacteriology, Royal Veterinary College, Edinburgh, 1892–99; served S African War, 1900 (medal and four clasps); served in Indian Civil Veterinary Department, 1902–3; appointed Principal Veterinary

Officer, Transvaal Department of Agriculture, 1903–5. *Publications:* A Text-book of Meat Inspection; various scientific articles and reports. *Recreations:* riding, golf. *Address:* 4 Whitehall Place, SW1. *TA:* Agrifi, London.

Died 2 June 1926.

STOCKS, Rev. John Edward; Residentiary Canon of Peterborough since 1920; Examining Chaplain to Bishop of Peterborough, 1915; *b* 28 Aug. 1843; *s* of Samuel Stocks, Leeds; *m* 1871, Emily Jane, 3rd *d* of Thomas Mallam, solicitor, Oxford; six *s* four *d. Educ:* Christ Church, Oxford (Chaplain, 1867–71). Vicar of Market Harborough, 1871–84; Vicar of St Saviour's, Leicester, 1884–1902; Rural Dean of Gartree, 1884; of Leicester, 1891–99; Archdeacon of Leicester, 1899–1920; Hon. Canon of Peterborough, 1893–99; Rector of Misterton, Lutterworth, 1903–14; Prolocutor, Lower House of Convocation, Canterbury, 1913–18. *Address:* Precincts, Peterborough. *Club:* Church Imperial.

Died 29 Aug. 1926.

STOCKTON, Rear-Adm. Charles Herbert; *b* Philadelphia, Penn, US, 13 Oct. 1845; *s* of Rev. W. R. Stockton, DD, and Emma T. Stockton; *m* 1st, 1875, Cornelia Carter; 2nd, 1880, Pauline Lentilhon, *d* of Peter V. King of New York; one *s* two *d. Educ:* US Naval Acad. Graduated from the Naval Acad. 1865 and went into active service at once as a midshipman, making various cruises, and being promoted to the rank of Commander, 1892; while Lt-Comdr in command of the USS 'Thetis', cruised in the Arctic Ocean from mouth of the Mackenzie to Wrangel land, 1889; in command 'Yorktown', Asiatic Station, 1895–97; President US Naval War Coll., 1898–1900; promoted Capt. 1899; in command battleship 'Kentucky', Asiatic Station, 1901–3; Naval Attaché to American Embassy, London, 1903–6; promoted Rear-Admiral, 1906; on duty Navy Department, Washington DC, 1906–7; in command Special Service Squadron, 1907; retired, 1907; first representative of the United States at International (Naval) Conference which met in London, 1908; LLD George Washington Univ., 1909; Pres. of George Washington Univ., 1910–18. *Publications:* History of the United States Naval Asylum; The Laws and Usages of War, a Naval War Code; editor of a Manual of International Law (2nd edn); Manual of International Law for Naval Officers, 3rd edn 1921; Outlines of International Law, 1915. *Address:* 2017 O Street NW, Washington. *T:* North 6959, Washington. *Clubs:* University, New York; University, Providence; Metropolitan, Washington, etc.

Died 31 May 1924.

STOKER, George, CMG 1901; LMCSI; MRCPI and MRCS England; JP for Co. Kerry; Physician, London Throat Hospital; Medical Officer, Oxygen Hospital; *b* 20 July 1855; 5th *s* of late Abraham Stoker of Dublin Castle; *m* 1882, Agnes, *e d* of Richard The M'Gillycuddy of The Reeks, Co. Kerry. *Educ:* Dublin. Hon. Associate of Order of St John of Jerusalem in England; Vice-President (formerly President) of British Laryngological Association; Fellow of Medical Society of London; Member of Pathological and Clinical Societies; Physician to London Throat Hospital, and Hon. Medical Officer of Actors' Benevolent Fund; formerly Surgeon to Hospital for Diseases of the Throat (Golden Sq.); Surgeon in Imperial Ottoman Army; was Medical Officer of Bulgarian Relief Fund, 1877; acted as Chef de l'ambulance du Croissant Rouge during Turko-Russian War, 1876–78 (special medal for Champcharee, 4th class Medjidie); was through the sieges of Shipka, Plevna, and Erzeroum, and as Stafford House Commissioner during Zulu War, 1879–80 (medal); initiated and organised Civil Hospital in S Africa, 1899–1900; and served as 2nd Surg., Irish Hosp. (despatches, medal with three clasps). *Publication:* With the Unspeakables. *Recreation:* golf. *Address:* 14 Hertford Street, Mayfair, W1. *Club:* Princes Golf, Mitcham.

Died 23 April 1920.

STOKER, Robert Burdon; MP (C) S Manchester since 1918; Shipowner; Chairman and Managing Director of Manchester Liners, Ltd, 108 Deansgate, Manchester; Director of Manchester Ship Canal Co.; Chairman of SS Knutsford, Ltd, of Ocean Dry Docks Co., Ltd, Swansea, and Director of other Companies—Insurance, Shipping, and Engineering; JP County Palatine of Chester; President (1916, 1917, and 1918) of Manchester Chamber of Commerce; *b* 1859; *m*; two *s* two *d. Educ:* Liverpool College, Liverpool. *Address:* Heather Lea, Green Walk, Bowdon, Cheshire. *Clubs:* Carlton; Constitutional, Clarendon, Manchester.

Died 4 Sept. 1919.

STOKER, Thomas, CSI 1898; BA; ICS; *b* 20 Aug. 1849; 3rd *s* of late Abraham Stoker; *m* 1891, Enid, *d* of late William Robert Bruce; one *d. Educ:* Trinity Coll., Dublin. Entered ICS 1872; held various appointments, including District and Settlement Officer, Commissioner, Special Famine Secretary, and Chief Secretary to Government, North-Western Provinces and Oudh, 1897–98; retired,

1899; served throughout in NWP and Oudh. Decorated for services in 1897 famine. *Publications:* A Gold Standard for India; Settlement Report, Bulandshahr District, etc. *Address:* 42 Egerton Crescent, SW3. *T:* Western 6697. *Club:* East India United Service.

Died 14 June 1925.

STOKES, Adrian, DSO 1918; OBE 1919; MD, FRCSI; Sir William Dunn Professor of Pathology, in the London University since 1922; *b* Lausanne, 1887; *s* of Henry John Stokes, ICS, and Mary Anne MacDougal; unmarried. *Educ:* private school; Trinity College, Dublin. Medical School, honours in Anatomy; Demonstrator in Anatomy; MB 1910; MD 1911; Medical Travelling Prize. Assistant to Professor of Pathology; Professor of Bacteriology and Preventive Medicine, Dublin University, 1919–22; Pathologist Royal City of Dublin Hospital; Pathologist Adelaide Hospital; Lt RAMC 11 Aug. 1914 (despatches, DSO, OBE, Chevalier Ordre de la Couronne Belgium, 1918); Member Rockefeller Commission on Yellow Fever, West Africa, 1920. *Publications:* Infectious Jaundice, Typhoid Carriers, Dysentery, etc. *Recreation:* cricket. *Address:* Guy's Hospital, St Thomas's Street, SE1; 602 Clive Court, Maida Vale, W9. *M:* MI 30. *Clubs:* Athenæum, MCC; University, Dublin.

Died 19 Sept. 1927.

STOKES, Sir Arthur Romney, 2nd Bt, *cr* 1889; *b* 27 Sept. 1858; *s* of Sir George Gabriel Stokes, 1st Bt, Master of Pembroke College, Cambridge, at one time MP for Cambridge University; *S* father, 1903; *m* 1897, Mary Winifred, *d* of late Hubert Garbett, of Rushen House, Castletown, Isle of Man; two *d. Educ:* Charterhouse; King's College, Cambridge. *Heir:* none. *Recreations:* sailing, shooting, skating, travelling, cycling. *Address:* Kingsland, Shrewsbury.

Died 12 June 1916 (ext).

STOKES, Rev. Augustus Sidney; Hon. Canon, Ely, 1891; *m* 1879, Alice, *d* of John Hill of Wombourn, Staffs; four *s* four *d. Educ:* St John's College, Cambridge (MA). Curate of St John Baptist, Kidderminster, 1872–75; St Anne's, Soho, 1875; St Lawrence, Jewry, 1876–77; Diocesan Inspector, Ely, 1877–96; Vicar of Elm, 1896–1920; Rural Dean of Wisbech, 1916. *Address:* 87 Cheriton Road, Folkestone.

Died 24 Sept. 1922.

STOKES, Sir (Frederick) Wilfrid Scott, KBE 1917; MInstCE; Past President of British Engineers' Association, and of the Ipswich and District Engineers Employers' Assoc.; Chairman of Ransomes & Rapier Ltd; *b* 9 April 1860; 5th *s* of late Scott Nasmyth Stokes, BA, Barrister, and Emma Louisa, *y d* of late Benjamin Walsh, Worcestershire; *m* 1900, Irene Theodora, 2nd *d* of Luke Ionides. *Educ:* Kensington Catholic Public School; Catholic University College, Kensington. Inventor of Stokes' gun, shell, etc; Order of the Osmanieh, 2nd class, and Medjidie, 2nd class. *Address:* Millwater, Ripley, Surrey; 7 Park Lane, W1. *T:* Gerrard 3472.

Died 7 Feb. 1927.

STOKES, Sir Gabriel, KCSI 1909 (CSI 1903); *b* 7 July 1849; *s* of Henry Stokes, for many years county surveyor of Kerry; *m* 1st, 1885, Rebecca (*d* 1886), *d* of Alfred Horsfall of Formby, Liverpool; one *s*; 2nd, 1889, May Florence (*d* 1897), *d* of James Fuller of Glashuachrse, Kenmare, Co. Kerry; three *s. Educ:* Kilkenny College; Armagh Royal School; Trinity College, Dublin, Graduated TCD 1871; entered Indian Civil Service, 1871; superintended the census of the Madras Presidency, 1881; Revenue Secretary to Madras Govt, 1896; acting member of Council, 1902; Chief Sec. Government of Madras, 1898–1903; Member of Council, 1903–8; acted as Governor of Madras, 1906. *Club:* University, Dublin.

Died 22 Oct. 1920.

STOKES, Sir Henry Edward, KCSI 1892 (CSI 1889); *b* 23 July 1841; *m* 1st, 1865, Janet (*d* 1870), *d* of William Stokes, MD; 2nd, 1872, Helena Amy (*d* 1874), *d* of Surg.-Gen. Currie; two *s. Educ:* Trinity College, Dublin. Entered Madras CS 1863; Secretary to Govt of Madras, 1883; Member of Council of Governor of Madras, 1888–93. *Address:* 32 Brunswick Gardens, Campden Hill, W8. *T:* Park 3451.

Died 20 Oct. 1926.

STOKES, Leonard (Aloysius Scott), FRIBA; *b* 1858; 2nd surv. *s* of Scott Nasmyth Stokes; *m* 1898, Edith Nellie, *d* of William Edward Louis Gaine; two *s* two *d.* Vice-President of the Architectural Association, 1887–88; President, 1889; President of the Royal Institute of British Architects for 1910 and 1911; Royal Gold Medalist, 1919; médaille d'argent (Architecture) at Paris Exhibition, 1900; buildings include the Chelsea Town Hall; Lincoln Grammar School; several Exchange Buildings for the National Telephone Co. Ltd, at Birmingham, Glasgow, Aberdeen, etc, and in London; Minterne

House (for Lord Digby); additions to Downside School; All Saints Convent, Colney, near St Albans; churches at Maidenhead, Folkestone, Southampton, Exeter; St Begbroke and St Clare's, Sefton Park; Nazareth House, Southsea; and Nazareth House, Bexhill; new quadrangle at Emmanuel College, Cambridge; RC Cathedral, Georgetown, Demerara, etc; member, Royal Commission on Historical Monuments (England), appointed 1908, and a member of the Committee for the King Edward Memorial for London. *Address:* 3 Mulberry Walk, Chelsea, SW3. *T:* Gerrard 672. *Clubs:* Arts, Chelsea, Arts.   *Died 25 Dec. 1925.*

STONE, Ven. Arthure Edward, *b* 1852; *s* of Rev. Meade Nisbett Stone, HEICS; *m* 1897, Elinor Mabel, *e d* of Innes Rogers. *Educ:* St Peter's, York; Trinity College, Dublin; Gloucester Theological College. Chaplain, Bengal Ecclesiastical Establishment, 1877–1902; Chaplain, Upper Burma Field Force, 1886–88 (despatches, medal, clasp); Commissary-in-Charge of the Diocese of Calcutta; Fellow Calcutta University, 1898; Chaplain, Calcutta Light Horse, 1892–1902; Archdeacon of Calcutta, 1898–1903; Rector of Islip, Oxon, 1902–10; Vicar of Burcombe, 1910–17. *Recreation:* fishing. *Address:* 3 Horace Road, Boscombe, Bournemouth.
          Died 11 Jan. 1927.

STONE, Hon. Sir Edward Albert, KCMG 1912; Kt 1902; Lieutenant-Governor of Western Australia since 1906; *b* 9 March 1844; 2nd *s* of late Hon. G. F. Stone, Attorney-Gen.; *m* 1867, Susan, *d* of late G. Shenton. *Educ:* Chigwell, Essex, England. Called to WA Bar, 1865; Clerk to Legislative Council, 1870–74; Acting Attorney-General, 1879; Nominee Member of Legislative Council, 1880; Acting Chief Justice, 1881, 1887, 1889, 1890; Crown Solicitor, 1881; Puisne Judge, 1884; Chief Justice, Perth, WA, 1901–6. *Address:* Rose Hill, Perth, WA.   *Died 30 April 1920.*

STONE, George Frederick; Managing Editor and Chief Leader Writer, Western Daily Press, Bristol, since 1921; Director of Walter Reid & Son, Ltd, the company publishing that and other papers; *b* Bath, 25 Sept. 1855; *s* of late Frederick Stone, Bristol; *m* Selina, *e d* of late Richard Upham Rossiter, Bristol; one *s* three *d*. *Educ:* Bristol Trade and Mining School (later Merchant Venturers' Technical College). Apprenticed newspaper reporting, Bristol Times and Mirror, 1870; transferred to Western Daily Press, 1877; did much special work for that paper; became chief reporter and deputised for editors; President Bristol Press Fund 1907, 1908, 1922; member Bristol Rotary Club; Bristol Committee of London Press Fund; Bristol Officers' Association Committee; Council of Bristol Chamber of Commerce and Shipping; Colston Research Society Committee; Bristol and Gloucestershire Archæological Soc. *Publications:* Bristol as it Was and as it Is; with Mr C. Wells edited Bristol and Great War. *Recreations:* cycling, gardening, photography, etc. *Address:* 18 Logan Road, Bristol. *T:* Bristol 5634. *Club:* Bristol Liberal.
          Died 8 Dec. 1928.

STONE, Marcus, RA 1887 (ARA 1877); *b* 4 July 1840; 2nd *s* of late Frank Stone, ARA. *Educ:* home. Exhibited in 63 consecutive exhibitions of the RA, rarely elsewhere; received medals at the international exhibitions of Paris, Berlin, Vienna, Philadelphia, Chicago, Melbourne, and others; when young illustrated books, Dickens, Trollope, Cornhill Magazine, etc; painter of subjects of human interest and historical genre. *Publications:* the greater number of his works published as engravings. *Recreations:* omnivorous reader of books; a player of billiards. *Address:* 8 Melbury Road, Kensington, W. *Clubs:* Athenæum, Arts.
          Died 24 March 1921.

STONE, Rev. W. H., MA; Rector of Sevenoaks since 1920; *b* 1860; *s* of W. Stone, JP; *m* Helena Jane, *d* of late Colonel G. Grant Gordon, CB, CVO, Controller to Prince Christian; three *d*. *Educ:* Rugby; Trinity College, Cambridge. Rector of Charleton, Devon, 1888–91; Vicar of St James's, Hatcham, 1891–96; St Mary, Kilburn, 1896–1907; Prebendary in Wells Cathedral, 1911; Rector of Walcot, Bath, 1907–13; Chipstead, Surrey, 1913–20. *Recreation:* golf. *Address:* Sevenoaks Rectory, Kent. *Club:* New Oxford and Cambridge.
          Died 17 Nov. 1920.

STONE-WIGG, Rt. Rev. Montagu John, DD; Commissary in Australia to Bishop of New Guinea, 1910; *b* 1861; *m* 1907, Elfie Marcia, *d* of late James Mort; two *d*. *Educ:* Winchester; University College, Oxford; Ely. Deacon, 1884; Priest, 1885; 1st Canon Residentiary and Subdean of St John's Cathedral, Brisbane, 1892–98; 1st Bishop of New Guinea, 1898–1908; resigned, 1908; Ramsden Preacher at Oxford, 1908; Fellow, St Paul's College, Sydney

University, 1914. *Address:* Colonna, Burwood, New South Wales, Australia.   *Died 16 Oct. 1918.*

STONECLINK; *see* Dale, Rev. T. F.

STONEX, Rev. Francis Tilney; Hon. Canon of Chester Cathedral; Vicar of Bowdon since 1919; *b* Gt Yarmouth, 28 Sept. 1857; *s* of late Henry Stonex, Gt Yarmouth; *m* Alice Mary Rowe, *d* of late Dr Pring, of Elmfield, Taunton, Somerset; three *s* one *d*. *Educ:* Gt Yarmouth Grammar School; Trinity College, Dublin. Curate of St Mary's, Taunton, 1880–83; Curate in charge of St Michael's, Claughton, Birkenhead, 1883–87; Vicar of Holy Trinity, Birkenhead, 1887–91; Surrogate, 1888; Vicar of Bredbury, Stockport, 1891–93; Rector of St Peter's, Chester, 1893–1905; Vicar of St James, New Brighton, 1905; Rural Dean of Wallasey, 1914–19. *Address:* The Vicarage, Bowdon, Cheshire. *TA:* Bowdon.
          Died Jan. 1920.

STONHAM, Charles, CMG 1901; FRCS, FZS; Senior Surgeon, Lecturer on Surgery, Teacher of Operative Surgery, Westminister Hospital, London; Examiner in Surgery, Society of Apothecaries, and Royal University, Ireland; Hon. Major in the army, and Lieutenant Colonel in command of London Mounted Brigade Field Ambulance; *b* 27 March 1858; 3rd *s* of T. G. Stonham, of Maidstone, Kent. *Educ:* King's School, Canterbury; Univ. Coll., London; Aitchison Scholarship, Univ. Coll., London.; Gold Medallist in Surgery, in Medicine, and in Gynæcology; Member of British Ornithologists' Union; Fellow of Royal Soc. of Medicine. Professional education at University College, London, where held all house posts, and for some years was Senior Demonstrator of Anatomy and Curator of the Pathological Museum; made Assistant Surgeon, Westminster Hospital, 1887, then resigning other surgical posts, promoted to full staff, 1895, and became Senior Surgeon, 1897. Decorated for services in South Africa as Chief Surgeon and officer commanding Imperial Yeomanry Field Hospital (medal and 4 clasps). *Publications:* The Birds of the British Islands; A Manual of Surgery, and various other surgical and pathological works; Report of Field Hospital and Bearer Company in South Africa. *Recreations:* mountaineering; natural history, especially ornithology. *Address:* 4 Harley Street, W. *T:* 1466 Paddington. *M:* A 1011. *Clubs:* Conservative, Alpine.
          Died 31 Jan. 1916.

STOODLEY, Edwin Edward, CB 1906; Joint Secretary to Board of Inland Revenue, Stamps and Taxes, 1902–9; *b* 1844; *m* 1885, Ada Mary, *d* of late Francis Ballard, Leominster. Served in Secretaries Dept, Inland Revenue, 1868–1902. *Address:* Oketon, Hampton Road, Teddington.   *Died 13 Feb. 1922.*

STOPFORD, Hon. Horatia Charlotte Frances; a Woman of the Bedchamber to late Queen Victoria; *b* 1835; *d* of Lieut-Col Hon. Edward Stopford; *g d* of 3rd Earl of Courtown. *Address:* 6 St Katherine's, Regent's Park, NW.
          Died 6 Feb. 1920.

STORER, Bellamy; *b* Cincinnati, Ohio, 28 Aug. 1847; *m* Mrs Maria Longworth. *Educ:* Harvard University. Bar, 1869; Representative 1st Dist, Ohio, to US Congress, 1890–95; Minister to Belgium, 1897–99; to Spain, 1899–1902; Ambassador of the United States at Vienna, 1902–6. *Recreations:* engravings, books, golf. *Address:* Cincinnati, USA. *Clubs:* Metropolitan, Washington; Queen City, Cincinnati; Jockey, Vienna.   *Died 12 Nov. 1922.*

STOREY, Hon. Sir David, Kt 1923; Member Legislative Council, New South Wales, since 1920; Governing Director, David Storey & Co., Ltd; Chairman of Directors, Insurance of Australia, Ltd; *b* 18 Aug. 1856; *s* of late Robert Storey, Monaghan, Ireland; *m* Rachel Agnes, *o c* of late Capt. Andrew Doig, Edinburgh; four *s* one *d*. *Educ:* Wattsbridge Academy. Arrived in Australia, 1879, at age of 23; founded firm of David Storey & Co., Ltd, 1880; first elected to NS Wales Parliament, as Member for Randwick, in 1894; represented that electorate till resignation, 1920; Hon. Minister in the National Ministry of NS Wales, 1916–19; Minister for Public Health, 1919–20. *Recreation:* bowls. *Address:* Sherbrooke, Randwick, Sydney, NSW, Australia. *TA:* Yerots, Sydney. *T:* Randwick 12. *Clubs:* New South Wales, Masonic, Randwick Bowling, Sydney.
          Died July 1924.

STOREY, George Adolphus, RA 1914 (ARA 1876); Professor of Perspective, Royal Academy, since 1914; *b* London, 7 Jan. 1834; 2nd *s* of James Payne Storey and Emily Fitch; *m* Emily, *y d* of late James Hayward, London; one *d*. *Educ:* in Paris, under M Morand, Prof. of Mathematics. Reurned to England, 1850; studied at J. M. Leigh's

Art School in Newman Street; became a student at Royal Academy; exhibited first picture RA, 1852; visited Spain, 1862–63; Teacher of Perspective at the Royal Academy, 1900; Examiner in Drawing, Board of Education, 1913. *Pictures:* The Widowed Bride, 1858; The Bride's Burial, 1859; The Annunciation, 1860; War Time, 1862; The Closed House, 1862; The Danaides, 1864; Lady Godiva, 1865; A Royal Challenge; After You, 1867; The Shy Pupil, 1868; The Old Soldier, 1869; Only a Rabbit, 1870; Scandal, 1872; Blue Girls of Canterbury; Little Swansdown; Christmas Visitors, 1874; Dame Octavia Beaumont, 1874; Mrs Finch, 1875; Caught; Mistress Dorothy; The Pump-Room, Bath; The Connoisseur; The Young Prodigal, etc; First Practice, 1894; Double Dummy; Coming Events; Rival Minstrels, 1895; A Love Stratagem, and the Town Gossip, 1896; Summer Days, 1897; In Evening Shade, 1898; The Lost Labour of the Danaides; Philomel, 1900; The Love Letter, 1901; A Love Sonnet; Miss Reynolds, 1902; Pluto's Messenger, 1904; Venus Lamenting the Death of Adonis; Griselda, 1905; Leda, Pamela, etc, 1906; Phryne, 1908; Circe, Pan and Syrinx, and Phillis Meyerstein, 1909; My Mother's Portrait, purchased by the Committee of National Arts Collections Fund, 1912, for the National Gallery of British Art; My Father's Portrait, 1874, in the National Gallery of British Art, purchased by the Contemporary Art Society and subscriptions in 1914; Lady in Furs; Miss Gladys Storey, 1912; Her First Letter, 1913; A Young Painter, Edward Cressy; Armida in the Enchanted Wood, 1914; Viola (diploma work), Diana, 1915; Girl in White; A Kentish Garden, 1916; The Mill Stream; Chevening, 1917; Cupid Fishing, 1918. *Publications:* Sketches from Memory, 1899; Theory and Practice of Perspective, 1910. *Recreations:* reading, etc. *Address:* 39 Broadhurst Gardens, Hampstead, NW. *T:* Hampstead 7033.

Died 20 July 1919.

STOREY, Samuel, DL, JP Durham County and Berwickshire; *b* 13 Jan. 1840; *s* of Robert Storey, of Whitburn; *m* 1st, 1864, Mary Ann (*d* 1877), *e d* of J. Addison; 2nd, 1898, Sarah (*d* 1908), *widow* of John Newton; one *s* two *d.* Mayor of Sunderland, 1876, 1877, and 1880; MP (R) Sunderland, 1881–95, and Jan. 1910 as Ind. TR; retired Dec. 1910; Chairman of Durham County Council, 1894–1905. *Recreations:* motoring, salmon-fishing. *Address:* Southill, Chester-le-Street, Co. Durham. *M:* J 8500. *Club:* Royal Automobile.

Died 18 Jan. 1925.

STORMONTH-DARLING, Major John Collier, DSO 1915; 1st Battalion the Cameronians (Scottish Rifles); temporary Lieutenant-Colonel commanding 9th Highland Light Infantry (Glasgow Highlanders); *b* 9 Feb. 1878. Entered army 1900; Captain, 1912; Major, 1915; served S African War, 1899–1902 (despatches, Queen's medal 3 clasps, King's medal 2 clasps); European War, 1914–15 (despatches, DSO). *Address:* Edenbank, Kelso; Lednathie, Kirriemuir. *Club:* Caledonian.   *Died 1 Nov. 1916.*

STORR, Francis, BA; Officier d'Académie; late editor of Journal of Education; *b* Suffolk, 28 Feb. 1839; *e s* of late Rev. Francis Storr and Caroline, *d* of Colonel Holland; *m* Rose, *d* of late Francis Lloyd; one *s* three *d. Educ:* Harrow; Trinity Coll., Camb. (Scholar). Bell University Scholar; 6th in Classical Tripos, 1861. Master at Marlborough College, 1864–75; Merchant Taylors', 1875–1901; Authors' Society, College of Preceptors (Fellow). Teachers Guild, Froebel Society, Modern Language Association (Vice-President), Women's Training and Registration Society (Vice-Chairman of Council), University of London Board of Pedagogy. *Publications:* Heine's Travel Pictures; Lermontoff's Demon; Canterbury Chimes; Bacon's Essays; Life and Remains of R. H. Quick; Sophocles, verse translation; and various school-books. *Recreations:* fishing, billiards. *Address:* 40 Mecklenburgh Square, WC. *Club:* Athenæum.

Died 8 April 1919.

STORRS, Very Rev. John, MA; Dean of Rochester since 1913; *b* Canada; *m* Lucy (*d* 1923), *d* of late Major Cust of Ellesmere, Salop; three *s* two *d. Educ:* Pembroke College, Cambridge (Scholar). Curate of St Mary's, Bury St Edmunds, 1871–73; St Peter's, Eaton Square, 1873–80; Vicar of St James', Bury St Edmunds, 1880–83; Rural Dean of St George's, Hanover Square, 1891–1902; Rural Dean of Westminster, 1902–13; Prebendary of Brownswood in St Paul's Cathedral, 1900–13; Vicar of St Peter's, Eaton Square, with St John's, Wilton Road, and St Peter's Chapel, Buckingham Gate, 1883–1913; Hon. Chaplain to Bishop of Salisbury, 1911–13; Hon. Chaplain to HM the King, 1912–13; Surrogate, Diocese of London, 1904–13; Select Preacher at Cambridge, 1914; took part in the Mission of Help to South Africa, organised by the late Bishop of St Andrews, 1904; visited Egypt and Cyprus as Archbishop's messenger, Jan.–May 1917. *Recreations:* golf, music, chess. *Address:* The Deanery, Rochester. *Clubs:* Athenæum, New University; County, Rochester.

Died 29 Feb. 1928.

STORY, Douglas, CBE 1920; author and journalist; Captain 5th (Reserve) Battalion Middlesex Regiment; *b* Edinburgh, 31 Dec. 1872; *e s* of Dan. F. Story, JP, Peebleshire. *Educ:* George Watson's College, and University, Edinburgh. Daily Mail war correspondent with the Boers, South African War 1899–1900; Daily Express war correspondent with the Russians, Russo-Japanese War, 1904–5; New York Herald special correspondent with the present King through Canada, 1901; Tribune special correspondent, Egypt, Siam, China, Japan, Russia, and South Africa, 1905–8; special correspondent for various syndicated newspapers, Russia, Siberia, and India; editor of various journals in London, New York, Johannesburg, and Hong Kong; DAQMG Army Headquarters, India, 1916–18; Shipping Controller in India, 1918–20 (thanks of the Ministry of Shipping, thanks of the Government of India, C-in-C's despatches, CBE); Director of Bureau of Information, Government of Bengal, 1920. *Publications:* Ten Miles from Anywhere, 1895; The Drift of the Day, 1902; The Campaign with Kuropatkin, 1904; To-Morrow in the East, 1907.   *Died 8 July 1921.*

STORY, Mrs Janet Leith; *b* Bombay, 19 Jan. 1828; *d* of Captain Philip Maughan, HEICS, and Elizabeth Arnott; *m* 1863, Rev. Robert Herbert Story, Minister of Rosneath, Dumbartonshire; afterwards Principal of Glasgow University; two *d. Educ:* Edinburgh; Hampstead. *Publications:* Charley Nugent, or Passages in the Life of a Sub., 1860; St Aubyns of St Aubyn; The Co-Heiress, 1863; Early Reminiscences, 1911; Later Reminiscences, 1913; contributions to magazines, etc. *Recreations:* reading, whist, music. *Address:* 30 Lilybank Gardens, Glasgow.   *Died 11 Sept. 1926.*

STORY, John Benjamin, MB Dublin; Hon. Surgeon Oculist to HM in Ireland; President, Royal College of Surgeons in Ireland, 1918–20; President of Ophthalmological Society of the United Kingdom, 1918–20; Professor of Ophthalmic Surgery Royal College of Surgeons; President and Hon. Consultant Surgeon, Royal Victoria Eye and Ear Hospital; *s* of Rev. William Story of Corick, Clogher, Tyrone, and Sara Bernard, *d* of John Black, Sligo; *m* 1892, Blanche Christabel, *d* of Rev. J. Hallowell; two *d. Educ:* Winchester; Trinity Coll., Dublin; Zürich, Vienna. High Sheriff of Co. Tyrone, 1911; Pres. of the Irish Med. Association, 1913; Hon. Surg. Oculist to Earls Cadogan and Dudley, Lord-Lieuts of Ireland, during their tenure of this office; Hon. Secretary Dublin Branch of National Service League from foundation till it closed down during the War. *Publications:* papers in the various ophthalmological journals. *Address:* 4 Carlisle Terrace, Malahide, Dublin; Corick, Clogher, County Tryone. *T:* 1271. *Club:* Tyrone County, Omagh.   *Died 18 Feb. 1926.*

STORY, Lt.-Gen. Philip, Bengal Infantry; *b* 17 Jan. 1840; *s* of late Gen. P. F. Story, CB, Bengal Cavalry; *m* 1879, Elisabeth Louisa, *d* of Rev. C. J. Waterhouse; two *s* two *d.* Entered army, 1857; Lt-Gen. 1893; retired list, 1893; served Indian Mutiny, 1858–59 (medal); Bhootan Expedition, 1865–66 (medal with clasp); Perak Expedition, 1875–76 (clasp); Afghan War, 1878–1880 (despatches, medal). *Address:* The Hill, Stowmarket.   *Died 26 Sept. 1916.*

STOTT, Edward, ARA 1906; *b* Rochdale, Lancashire, 1859; unmarried. *Educ:* Rochdale Grammar School; King's School, Ely, Cambridgeshire. In Paris (where he remained some three years), worked for a short time under Carolus Duran, but his studies were conducted chiefly at the Ecole des Beaux Arts under Cabanel. *Recreations:* in winter time, a regular evening walk or horse-ride. *Address:* Amberley, Sussex. *Club:* Arts.

Died 19 March 1918.

STOURTON, Rt. Rev. Monsignor Joseph; Pastor of Oldcotes since 1885; Domestic Prelate to the Pope, 1918; *b* 23 March 1845; *y s* of late Hon. William Stourton. *Educ:* Jesuit College, Namur; St Cuthbert's College, Ushaw. Priest, 1868. *Address:* St Helen's, Oldcotes, Rotherham.   *Died March 1921.*

STOWE, Leonard, CMG 1913; Clerk of Parliaments since 1889; Clerk of the Legislative Council since 1865; Examiner of Standing Orders relative to Private Bills since 1888; *b* 11 March 1837; *s* of Dr W. Stowe, Trolly Hall, Buckingham; *m* 1871, Jane, *d* of Dr Greenwood, late Sergeant at Arms to the House of Representatives; two *s* two *d. Educ:* Rugby. Went to New Zealand, 1858; Clerk to the Provincial Council, 1864; invented Stowe's Patent Calculating Machine, exhibited at the Melbourne Exhibition of 1881, and received honourable mention. *Address:* Tiakiwai, Tinakori Road, Wellington.

Died 25 April 1920.

STOWELL, Rev. Thomas Alfred, MA; Rector of Chorley, 1890–1907; Hon. Canon of Manchester since 1879; *b* Salford, 15 July

1831; 2nd s of Rev. Hugh Stowell, MA, Rector of Christ Church, Salford, and Hon. Canon of Chester; *m* 1861, Emma, 2nd *d* of Richard Tatham of Lowfields, Burton in Lonsdale; eight *s* five *d*. *Educ:* Manchester Grammar School; Queen's College, Oxford. Bridgeman Exhibitioner; 2nd class in Classical Moderations, 1853; BA (3rd class Lit. Hum. and hon. 4th Law and Modern History), 1855; MA, 1858. Ordained, 1857; Priest, 1858; Curate of Calverley, near Leeds (in sole charge of Bolton); Perpetual Curate of St Stephen's, Bradford, 1860–65; Rector of Christ Church, Salford, 1865; Rural Dean of Salford, 1876–90; Rural Dean of Leyland, 1890–1901; Proctor in Convocation for Achdeaconry of Blackburn, 1900–6; Hon. Sec. of Manchester Diocesan Bd of Education, 1870–81; Representative on Central Council of Diocesan Conferences, 1882; Assessor for Chapter of Manchester Cathedral under Clergy Discipline Act, 1892–1907. *Publications:* The Church Catechism Simply and Clearly Explained, 1882; The Church Catechism for the use of Teachers and Students, 1894; Hymns chiefly for Children and Sunday Schools, 1898; papers in The Churchman. *Address:* Danehurst, 10 Morley Road, Southport.
Died 10 Feb. 1916.

STRACHAN, James, CIE 1897; late Engineer and Secretary to the Karachi Municipality; *b* 10 Feb. 1841; *s* of late James Strachan, Aberdeen. *Address:* 47 Kirkdale, Sydenham, SE. *Club:* Constitutional.
Died 7 Feb. 1917.

STRACHAN, John, KC; *b* South Shields, 18 June 1838; 3rd *s* of John Strachan, JP; *m* 1859, Sarah Matilda, *y d* of Charles Hayward, Orono, Ontario; one *d*. *Educ:* privately. Journalist and dramatic author up to 1876, when called to the Bar; practised since in London and on North-Eastern circuit; QC 1896; Bencher of Middle Temple, 1904; Chairman and Umpire Conciliation Board, Northumberland Coal Trade up to termination in 1911; District Probate Registrar, Lincoln, 1914. *Publications:* numerous dramatic works up to 1876; Northumbrian Masonry, 1898. *Address:* White Hart Hotel, Lincoln.
Died 3 June 1918.

STRACHAN, William Henry Williams, CMG 1902; LRCP (Lond.); MRCS Eng.; FLS; FZS; FRAI; Member Royal Sanitary Institute; Member Royal Society of Arts; *e s* of late Col W. H. P. FitzM. Strachan. *Educ:* private schools and private tuition; Guy's Hospital. Junior resident Medical Officer Public Hospital, Kingston, Jamaica, 1882; senior resident, 1885; senior medical officer, 1892; PMO Lagos, 1897; acted as Colonial Secretary, Lagos, 1899–1900; PMO of Amalgamated South Nigeria, 1906–11. *Publications:* in various scientific journals. *Address:* c/o Cox & Co., 16 Charing Cross, SW1.
Died 13 June 1921.

STRACHAN-DAVIDSON, James Leigh, MA Oxford; Hon. LLD St Andrews and Glasgow; Master of Balliol College, Oxford, since 1907; *b* 22 Oct. 1843; *s* of James Strachan, merchant, Manila and Madras (afterwards James Strachan-Davidson of Ardgaith, Perthshire), and Mary Ann Richardson, Penrith, Cumberland; unmarried. *Educ:* Leamington College; Balliol College, Oxford. Exhibitioner (Warner and Jenkyns); first-class in Moderations and in Lit. Hum. Fellow of Balliol, 1866; Tutor and Dean, 1882; Jowett Fellow, 1906. *Publications:* Selections from Polybius; Appian Civil Wars, Book I.; articles on Roman Constitution in Smith's Dictionary of Antiquities; Life of Cicero in Heroes of the Nations series; Problems of the Roman Criminal Law. *Address:* Balliol College, Oxford. *Club:* New University.
Died 28 March 1916.

STRACHEY, Jane Maria, (Lady Strachey); *d* of Sir John Peter Grant of Rothiemurchus, GCMG, KCB, and Henrietta Chichele Plowden; *m* late Lt-Gen. Sir Richard Strachey, GCSI, FRS; four *s* five *d*. *Publications:* Lay Texts; Poets on Poets; Nursery Lyrics; Memoirs of a Highland Lady. *Address:* 51 Gordon Square, WC1. *T:*Museum 0987. *Club:* Lyceum.
Died 14 Dec. 1928.

STRACHEY, John St Loe; journalist; late Editor and proprietor of the Spectator till Dec. 1925, when he retired; he continued to be a weekly contributor; *b* 9 Feb. 1860; 2nd *s* of Sir Edward Strachey, 3rd Bt, and Mary Isabella, 2nd *d* of John Addington Symonds, MD; *m* 1887, Amy, *d* of late C. T. Simpson; one *s* one *d*. *Educ:* Balliol Coll. (1st class History), Oxford. Barrister; journalist in London since 1884; editor of Cornhill Magazine, 1896–97. *Publications:* From Grave to Gay; The Manufacture of Paupers, 1907; Problems and Perils of Socialism; The Practical Wisdom of the Bible, 1908; A New Way of Life, 1909; The Adventure of Living, 1922; Economics of the Hour, 1923; The Referendum, 1923; The River of Life, 1924; The Madonna of the Barricades, 1925; American Soundings, 1926. *Recreations:* riding, motoring, and cycling. *Address:* 76 Chester Square, SW; *T:* Victoria 9767; Newland's Corner, Merrow, Guildford. *Clubs:* Brooks's, Athenæum.
Died 26 Aug. 1927.

STRAFFORD, 5th Earl of, *cr* 1847; **Rev. Francis Edmund Cecil Byng;** Baron Strafford (UK) 1835; Viscount Enfield, 1847; *b* 15 Jan. 1835; 3rd *s* of 2nd Earl of Strafford; *S* brother, 1899; *m* 1st, 1859, Florence, (*d* 1862), *d* of late Sir W. Miles, 1st Bt; one *s* (and one *s* decd); 2nd, 1866, Emily, *d* of late Lord F. Kerr; two *s* two *d* (and one *s* three *d* decd). *Educ:* Eton (Prince Albert Prizeman for Modern Languages, 1850–51); Christ Church, Oxford (3rd class Law and Modern History). Rector of Little Casterton, Rutland, 1859–62; Vicar of Holy Trinity, Twickenham; Chaplain at Hampton Court, 1862–67; Hon. Chaplain to Queen Victoria, 1867; Chaplain-in-Ordinary, 1872; Chaplain to the Speaker, 1874–89; Vicar of St Peter, Cranley Gardens, 1867–89; Grand Chaplain of Freemasonry in England, 1889. *Heir: e* surv. *s* Viscount Enfield, *b* 27 Jan. 1862. *Address:* 5 St James's Square, SW; Wrotham Park, Barnet, Herts. *T:* Barnet 34. *Club:* Oxford and Cambridge.
Died 18 Jan. 1918.

STRAFFORD, Countess of; (Alice); *b* 1830; *e d* of 1st Earl of Ellesmere, KG; *m* 1854, 3rd Earl of Strafford (*d* 1898). *Publications:* edited Personal Reminiscences of the Duke of Wellington, by 1st Earl of Ellesmere; Leaves from the Diary of Henry Greville. *Address:* 51 South Street, Park Lane, W1.
Died 22 Dec. 1928.

STRAHAN, Sir Aubrey, KBE 1919; ScD, MA; Hon. LLD (Toronto); FRS 1903; FGS, FRGS; Director Geological Survey of Great Britain and Museum of Practical Geology, 1913–20; *b* London, 20 April 1852; *s* of William Strahan and Anne, *d* of Gen. Sir George Fisher; *m* 1886, Fanny Evelyn Margaret (*d* 1926), *d* of Edward H. Roscoe; one *s*. *Educ:* Eton; St John's College, Cambridge. President Geological Society, 1913–14; Wollaston Medallist, 1913–14; President Section C British Association, 1904; Member of Royal Commission on Coal Supplies, 1903; Vice-Pres. International Geological Congress, 1913; Vice-President Berkshire Archæological Society; Hon. Member RE Inst., North of England Inst. Engin., Institute Mining and Metallurgy, Institute Petroleum Technologists, and Chester Soc. Nat. Sci., Corresp. Member Geological Society of Belgium. *Publications:* Geological Survey Memoirs on Chester, Rhyl, Flint, Isle of Purbeck, and Weymouth, South Wales Coal Field, etc; and contributions to scientific journals. *Address:* Fairfield House, Goring, Reading. *Club:* Athenæum.
Died 4 March 1928.

STRAHAN, Rev. Prof. James, MA, DD; Professor of Hebrew and Biblical Criticism in the Magee College, Londonderry, since 1915; *b* Cardenwell, Fyvie, Aberdeenshire, 1 May 1863; *m* 1909, Catherine Evangeline Booth-Clibborn, *g d* of General Booth; two *s* one *d*. *Educ:* Grammar School, Old Aberdeen; King's College, Aberdeen; New College, Edinburgh; Universities of Tübingen and Berlin; Hebrew Tutor, New College, Edinburgh, 1885; Minister of Fergus Free Church, 1890–1903; Belgrave Presbyterian Church, London, 1903–10; Cunningham Lecturer, Edinburgh, 1915; Smyth Lecturer, Londonderry, 1916; Carey Lecturer, 1925. *Publications:* Hebrew Ideals (2 vols), 1903–6; The Captivity and Pastoral Epistles, 1910; The Book of Job, 1913; The Maréchale, 1914; Life of Professor A. B. Davidson, 1917; Judges and Ruth, 1919; Memoir of Mary Crawford Brown, 1920; God in History, 1923; contributions to Theological Review, Critical Review, Expository Times, and Hastings' Dictionaries. *Recreations:* travel, mountain-climbing. *Address:* 7 College Avenue, Londonderry.
Died 24 March 1926.

STRANG, Alexander Ronald, CBE 1920; JP; *b* 23 Nov. 1848; *e s* of Robert Strang, Alloa; *m* 1884, Agnes, *e d* of Alex. Begg, Paisley; one *s* two d. Educ: The Academy, Alloa. Late Captain Argyll and Sutherland Highlanders; Provost of Alloa at outbreak of war; Chairman of Tribunal and Recruiting Committees; engaged in initiating and organising the various War Schemes and Relief Committees; travelled for a year in China, Japan, and Canada. *Recreations:* golf, curling, bowling. *Address:* North Park, Alloa, Scotland. *T:* 83.
Died 19 Aug. 1926.

STRANG, William, ARA 1906; LLD Glasgow, 1909; painter, etcher; President of the International Society of Sculptors, Painters, and Gravers since 1918; *b* Dumbarton, 18 Feb. 1859; *m* 1885, Agnes M'Symon, *d* of David Rogerson, JP; four *s* one d. Educ: Dumbarton Academy; Slade School; Univ. College, London. Studied and worked in London since 1875; Silver Medal for Etching, Paris International Exhibition, 1889; First Class Gold Medal for Painting, Dresden International Exhibition, 1897. *Publications:* The Earth Fiend, a ballad; Death and the Ploughman's Wife; Etchings illustrating Kipling's Short Stories, 1901; Thirty Etchings of Don Quixote, 1903. *Address:* 7 Hamilton Terrace, NW8. *T:* Paddington 4946. Club: Art Workers' Guild.
Died 12 April 1921.

STRANG-WATKINS, Watkin, FZS; *b* 4 June 1869; *o s* of late George Strang-Watkins and Helen Watkins, heiress of Shotton Hall and Tilley Park, Shropshire, and Calderbank, Lanarkshire; *m* 1896, Lady Muriel Lindsay, *o d* of 11th Earl of Lindsay; one *s. Educ:* Eton; Cambridge. BA 1890; called to the Bar (Inner Temple), 1893; Member British Ornithologists' Union; Lieut Royal Defence Corps, 1914. *Publications:* Birds of Tennyson; Editor of the Wild Birds' Protection Acts, etc. *Recreations:* shooting, all natural history pursuits. *Clubs:* Wellington; County, Salop. *Died 25 Nov. 1921.*

STRANGE, Maj.-Gen. Thomas Bland, late Royal Artillery; JP Kerry; Member of Council, National Service League; President Local Branch Tariff Reform League; *b* Meerut, 1831; 2nd *s* of Col H. F. Strange, KOSB, and Letitia, *d* of Major N. Bland, 47th Regt; *m* 1st, Elinor Maria (*d* 1917), *d* of Capt. Robert Taylor, HEICS; two *s* three *d*; 2nd, 1918, Janet, *d* of late Rev. J. A. Fell, and *widow* of Col. F. C. Ruxton, Worcs Regt. *Educ:* Edinburgh Academy; RMA, Woolwich. Served Indian Mutiny, siege and capture of Lucknow (despatches four times, captured two guns of the Black Horse Sepoy Battery by leading a charge of artillery); Commandant RM Repository, Woolwich, 1865; Inspector Canadian Artillery, 1871; Commandant Fortress of Quebec; commanded Alberta Field Force, 1885; fought action of Frenchman's Butte, defeating the Cree Indian Chief, Big Bear (received thanks of Canadian Government). *Publications:* Artillery Retrospect of the War, 1870-1871; Military Aspect of Canada; Gunner Jingo's Jubilee, an Autobiography. *Recreations:* artistic and literary. *Address:* Geraghmeen, Camberley, Surrey. *T:* Camberley 165. *Died 9 July 1925.*

STRATHCLYDE, 1st Baron, *cr* 1914; **Alexander Ure,** GBE 1917; PC 1909; KC; LLD; Lord President Court of Session and Lord Justice-General for Scotland, 1913-20; *b* Glasgow, 24 Feb. 1853; 2nd *s* of John Ure, Cairndhu, Helensburgh, ex-Lord Provost of Glasgow; *m* 1879, Margaret Macdowall, *d* of Thomas Steven; one *d. Educ:* Glasgow (MA) and Edinburgh Universities. Scotch Bar, 1878; Lecturer on Constitutional Law and History, Glasgow University, 1878-88; contested West Perthshire, 1892, and Linlithgowshire, 1893; Solicitor-General, Scotland, 1905-9; Lord-Advocate, 1909-13; MP (L) for Linlithgowshire, 1895-1913. *Address:* Cairndhu, Helensburgh. *M:* 4213. *Clubs:* Reform, Royal Automobile; Western, Scottish Automobile, Glasgow; University, Edinburgh; Royal Northern Yacht, Royal Clyde Yacht. *Died 2 Oct. 1928.*

STRATHCONA AND MOUNT ROYAL, Baroness (2nd in line), *cr* 1897; **Margaret Charlotte Smith Howard;** *b* 17 Jan. 1854; *d* of 1st Baron and late Isabella Sophia, *d* of late Richard Hardisty, Canada; *S* father, 1914; *m* 1888, R. J. Bliss Howard, FRCS (*d* 1921); two *s* two *d* (and one *s* decd). *Heir: s* Hon. Donald Sterling Palmer Howard, *b* 14 June 1891. *Address:* 46 Green Street, Park Lane, W1; *T:* Mayfair 4300; Glencoe, NB; Colonsay, NB; 911 Dorchester Street, Montreal. *Died 18 Aug. 1926.*

STRATHEDEN, 3rd Baron, *cr* 1836, **AND CAMPBELL, 3rd Baron,** *cr* 1841; **Hallyburton George Campbell,** JP; Bengal Civil Service, retired 1855; *b* 18 Oct. 1829; *s* of 1st Baron Campbell and Mary, Baroness Stratheden (1st in line), *d* of 1st Lord Abinger; *S* brother, 1893; *m* 1865, Louisa, *d* of Rt Hon. A. J. B. Beresford Hope, MP and Lady Mildred Beresford Hope, Bedgebury Park, Kent; two *s* one *d* (and two *s* decd). Entered Bengal CS, 1849; Associate to Lord Chief Justice, 1853; Secretary of Commissions in Court of Chancery, 1860-73; Master of Supreme Court of Judicature; Col 40th Middlesex Rifles, 1866-72. *Heir: g s* Alastair Campbell, *b* 21 Nov. 1899. *Address:* 17 Bruton Street, W; Hartrigge, Jedburgh. *Clubs:* Brooks's, Bachelors'. *Died 26 Dec. 1918.*

STRATON, Rt. Rev. Norman Dumenil John, DD; *b* 4 Nov. 1840; *e* surv. *s* of late Rev. George W. Straton, Rector of Aylestone; *m* 1873, Emily (*d* 1916), *d* of J. R. Pease, Hesslewood, Hull. *Educ:* Trinity College, Cambridge (BA 1862; MA 1869; DD 1892); DD Durham 1908. Curate of Market Drayton, 1865-66; Vicar of Kirkby Wharfe, Yorkshire, 1866-75; Vicar and Rural Dean of Wakefield, 1875-92; Proctor for Archdeaconry of Craven, 1880-85; Hon. Canon of Ripon, 1883; Hon. Canon of Wakefield and Archdeacon of Huddersfield, 1888; Bishop of Sodor and Man, 1892-1907; Dean of Sodor and Man, 1895; Bishop of Newcastle, 1907-15 (when he resigned). *Address:* Bishopscourt, Broadwater Down, Tunbridge Wells. *Club:* National. *Died 5 April 1918.*

STRATTON, Rev. Joseph, MA; Master of Lucas' Hospital, Wokingham, since 1889; *b* 1 May 1839; 2nd *s* of John Stratton, of Clifton Campville, Staffordshire, and Anne *d* of Edward Mousley, of Haunton, near Tamworth; *m* 1892, Louise Cecilia Bazalgette Lucas

Lucas, *d* of St John Welles Lucas, MRCS, and *niece* of Sir Joseph W. Bazalgette, CB, CE. *Educ:* Appleby Grammar School; Worcester College, Oxford. Engaged for some years in tuition; ordained, 1870; held Curacies in Swansea, Burton-on-Trent, New Barnet, etc; retired from the Church on theological grounds, 1878; returned in 1886, and became Curate of Winchfield, Hants; interested in social questions, education, housing of the people, putting labourers on the land, management of prisons and workhouses, etc; of late years an active humanitarian, one of his aims being the abolition of the Royal Buckhounds (presented with a public testimonial in connection with this event, 1 July 1901). *Publications:* Vivisection and Anti-Vivisection, which Side must I Take, 1898; Sports Legitimate and Illegitimate, 1898; The Decline and Fall of the Royal Buckhounds, 1901; Fireside Poems, 1901; Ethelfleda and other Poems, 1915; Letter to a Friend on Theology; A Defence of the Broad Churchman's Position in the Establishment, 1902; innumerable Press letters dealing with the rights of men and animals; The Attitude, Past and Present, of the RSPCA towards such Spurious Sports as Tame Deer Hunting, Pigeon Shooting, and Coursing Rabbits, 1906. *Recreations:* reflective walks, and, when sympathetic companions are at hand, philosophical talks; fond of music, vocal and instrumental. *Address:* Wokingham, Berks. *Died 14 Jan. 1917.*

STRATTON, Hon. J. R.; publisher; *b* 3 May 1858; *s* of James Stratton and Rosanna Armstrong; *m* 1881, Eliza J. Ormond; no *c. Educ:* Peterborough Collegiate Institute. Elected to the Ontario Legislature as a Liberal for West Peterborough, 1886, 1890, 1894, 1898, 1900, 1902 and 1908; Provincial Secretary, 1900; President of the Peterborough Examiner, Ltd, publishers of the Daily and Weekly Examiner. *Address:* 751 George Street, Peterborough, Ont. *TA:* Peterborough, Ontario. *T:* 178. *M:* 34010. *Clubs:* National, Toronto, Toronto; Peterborough, Peterborough. *Died 19 April 1916.*

STRAUS, Oscar S., AM, LLD, LittD, Member of the Permanent Court of Arbitration at The Hague; Chairman of the Paris Committee of The League to Enforce Peace; *b* 23 Dec. 1850; *s* of Lazarus and Sara Straus; *m*; one *s* two *d. Educ:* Columbia University, New York City. Attorney and Counsellor-at-law, 1873-81; afterwards a member of the commercial firm of L. Straus & Sons; Envoy and Minister Plenipotentiary to Turkey, 1887; reappointed to the same position on a special mission to adjust differences between the US and Turkey, 1897; Secretary of Commerce and Labour, 1906; Ambassador to Turkey, 1909; one of the founders of the National Civic Federation, and its Vice-President for a number of years; acted as arbitrator in a number of labor controversies, and in 1912 was chosen as Chairman of the Board to arbitrate the differences between the fifty-two Railroads east of the Mississippi and their locomotive engineers; late Chairman of the Public Service Commission of the State of New York; Member of President Wilson's Industrial Commission, 1919-20; Member of President's Advisory Committee of the Commission for Relief in Belgium; Member of the Permanent Court of Arbitration at The Hague; Member of Board of Trustees, Carnegie Peace Foundation; late President American Social Science Association and NY Board of Trade and Transportation; one of the founders and Vice-President of the American International Law Association; trustee of the New York Life Insurance Co. *Publications:* The Origin of Republican Form of Government in the US; The Development of Religious Liberty in the US; Roger Williams, the Pioneer of Religious Liberty; The American Spirit, 1913; Under Four Administrations from Cleveland to Taft, 1922. *Recreations:* fishing, reading. *Address:* 5 West 76th Street, New York City. *Clubs:* Authors', City, Bankers', New York. *Died 3 May 1926.*

STRAUSS, Arthur; MP (U) North Paddington, 1910-18; partner in A. Strauss and Co., tin merchants; *b* 1847; *s* of A. Strauss, Mayence; *m* 1893, Minna Cohen. MP (LU) Camborne Div. Cornwall, 1895-1900. *Address:* 1 Kensington Palace Gardens, Bayswater, W8. *T:* Park 4520; 16 Rood Lane, City, EC3. *Club:* Carlton. *Died 30 Nov. 1920.*

STREATFEILD, Frank Newton, CMG 1879; *b* 2 Feb. 1848; 3rd *s* of late W. C. Streatfeild of Chart's Edge, Kent; *m* 1864, Agatha, *d* of R. Fry; two *s* one *d.* Commandant of Levies, South African War, 1877-79; Resident Magistrate Transkei, 1878-84; Civil Commissioner British Bechuanaland, 1887-89. *Publications:* Kafirland, a Ten Months' Campaign; The Da chick; Reminiscences of an Old'un, 1910; Sporting Recollections of an Old'un. *Address:* Hever Cottage, Edenbridge, Kent. *Died 23 Jan. 1916.*

STREATFEILD, Rev. Henry Bertram, MA; Vicar of St Mark's, Milverton, Leamington, 1901-20; Hon. Canon of St Michael's,

Coventry; *b* 1852; *y s* of Rev. William Streatfeild, Vicar of East Ham, Essex; *m* 1st, 1880, Agnes Blount, *d* of late Dr Mercer-Adam, Boston, Lincs; 2nd, 1905, Eleanor Mary, *d* of late Henry Smith Lawford, Solicitor to India Office; one *d*. *Educ:* Charterhouse; Exeter College, Oxford. Curate of All Saints, Woodford Wells, 1875–76; Holy Trinity, Louth, Lincs, 1876–80; Vicar of Holy Trinity, Skirbeck, Lincs, 1880–83; Holy Trinity, Louth, Lincs, 1883–1901. *Address:* 42 Hamilton Road, Boscombe, Hants.

Died 25 April 1922.

STREATFEILD, Richard Alexander, BA; Assistant, Department of Printed Books, British Museum, since 1889; Musical Critic of The Daily Graphic, 1898–1912; *b* Carshalton, 1866; *e* surv. *s* of late Frank Newton Streatfeild, CMG, and Agatha Maria Fry. *Educ:* Oundle School, 1877–83; Senior Classical Scholar, Pembroke College, Cambridge, 1883; 2nd class, Classical Tripos, 1886. *Publications:* Masters of Italian Music, 1895; The Opera 1897, 2nd edn 1902, 3rd edn 1907; Modern Music and Musicians, 1906 (translated into French by Louis Pennequin as Musique et Musiciens modernes, Paris, 1910); Handel, 1909; Musiciens Anglais Contemporains (translated by L. Pennequin), 1913; and numerous articles and pamphlets on the history of music; edited George Darley's Nepenthe, 1897; Christopher Smart's Song to David, 1901; Darley's Selected Poems, 1903; T. J. Hogg's Shelley at Oxford, 1904; translated Henrik Ibsen's Lyrical Poems, 1902; literary executor of Samuel Butler, author of Erewhon, whose posthumous Way of all Flesh, 1903, Essays on Life, Art, and Science, 1904, Sonnets, 1904, and God the Known and Unknown, 1909, he prepared for publication, and of whose Life and Habit, Evolution Old and New, Unconscious Memory, Alps and Sanctuaries, Humour of Home, Fair Haven, and First Year in Canterbury Settlement, he brought out new editions. *Recreation:* golf. *Address:* 26 Great Ormond Street, WC. *Club:* Sports.

Died 6 Feb. 1919.

STREET, Captain Edmund Rochfort, DSO 1915; 3rd Battalion the Sherwood Foresters (Nottinghamshire and Derbyshire Regiment). Served European War, 1914–15 (wounded, DSO).

Died 15 Oct. 1916.

STREET, Colonel Harold Edward, CMG 1916; RA; *s* of late Joseph Edward Street of Lloyd's; *m* 1916, Gladys Mary, *d* of G. Fenwick Harrison, and *widow* of Major W. Sholto Douglas, RE. Served S Africa, 1899–1902 (despatches thrice, Queen's medal, 6 clasps, King's medals, 2 clasps); European War (Dardanelles), 1914–15 (despatches thrice, CMG, Bts of Lt-Col and Col). *Address:* Woodside, Caterham.

Died 25 Aug. 1917.

STRETCH, Rt. Rev. John Francis, BA, LLB (Melbourne); DD (Oxon); Bishop of Newcastle (New South Wales) since 1906; *b* Geelong, Jan. 1855; *m* 1885, Amelia Margaret, *y d* of R. H. Weekes, of Chevy, Geelong; four *s* two *d*. *Educ:* Trinity College, Melbourne (BA). Ordained, 1878; Assistant Curate, All Saints, Geelong, 1879–80; All Saints, St Kilda, 1880–81; St Andrew's, Brighton, 1881–2; LT, Little Brighton, 1883; Vicar, Holy Trinity, Maldon, 1883; Vicar, St Mark's, Fitzroy, 1885; Vicar, St Andrew's, Brighton, 1892; Dean of Ballarat and Vicar of Christ Church Cathedral, Ballarat, 1894–95; Bishop Coadjutor of Brisbane, Queensland, 1895–1900; Dean of Newcastle and Vicar of Christ Church Cathedral, Newcastle, 1900–6. *Address:* Bishop's Court, Newcastle, New South Wales.

Died 19 April 1919.

STRETTEN, Charles James Derrickson, MVO 1903; JP Cambridgeshire; late Chief Constable of Cambridgeshire; *b* 1830; *s* of late Thomas Stretten, Assistant Chief Constable of Wiltshire; *m* Catherine Wisbey (*d* 1910). *Address:* 71 Chesterton Road, Cambridge.

Died 23 Aug. 1919.

STRICKLAND, Algernon Henry Peter; a partner in the banking firm of Hoare & Co.; *b* 19 Dec. 1863; *e s* of late Algernon Augustine de Lille Strickland and late Charlotte Anne, *y d* of late Peter Richard Hoare, of Luscombe, Devonshire; *m* 1890, Mary Selina, *y d* of Walter Drummond; one *s* one *d*. *Educ:* Eton; Christ Church, Oxford, BA. *Address:* Apperley Court, near Tewkesbury; 90 Eaton Place, SW1. *T:* Sloane 4948. *Club:* Carlton.

Died 22 Feb. 1928.

STRICKLAND, Walter G.; Director, National Gallery of Ireland, retired, 1916; late Hon. Secretary, Royal Society of Antiquaries of Ireland; Vice-President, Royal Irish Academy; *b* 3 June 1850; *s* of Thomas Strickland, of the family of Sizergh, Westmorland; *m* Margaret, *d* of P. Ryan of Sevenhills, South Australia; one *s* one *d*. *Educ:* Ushaw College, Durham; King's College, London. *Publications:*

A Dictionary of Irish Artists, 1914; Georgian Society, vols i and ii; Catalogue of National Portrait Gallery, Dublin; Catalogue of Pictures in Trinity College, Dublin, 1916; various historical and archæological papers, etc. *Address:* 63 Merrion Square, Dublin.

Died 16 Oct. 1928.

STRONG, Herbert A., MA, LLD; formerly President of Liverpool Royal Institution and Liverpool Guild of Education; Professor of Latin, University of Liverpool, 1882–1909; Emeritus Professor since 1910; *b* at St Mary's Clyst Rectory, near Exeter; *s* of Rev. Edmond Strong; *m* 1st, Miss Edmiston; 2nd, Miss Isabel White, artist; two *s*. *Educ:* Blackheath, Eliot Place School; Winchester Commoners and College; Corpus Christi Coll., Oxford. Was Assistant-Professor of Humanity at Glasgow University for six years under Professor Ramsay; then appointed to the Chair of Classics at the University, Melbourne, Australia; was for twenty years employed by the Scottish Education Department as Examiner of Secondary Schools; elected as Hon. President of the French Society of Liverpool; Vice-Pres., Liverpool Devonian Society; for twenty years, Pres. of Liverpool Univ. Athletic Club; Officier de l'Instruction publique. *Publications:* an edition of Catullus and Juvenal; (with Professors Logeman and Wheeler) The History of Language; many articles contributed to literary journals. *Address:* Clyst, Farnham, Slough. *Clubs:* Albemarle; Stoke Poges; University, Liverpool.

Died 13 Jan. 1918.

STRONG, Hugh W., FJI; author and journalist; contributor on antiquarian, literary, industrial, economic, and sociological subjects to reviews and periodicals; joined Upper Staff, Census of Production (Board of Trade), on its formation, 1907, as Investigator and Examiner; *b* 1861; native of Liskeard, Cornwall; *m* 1891, Agnes Ward, *d* of William King, Maidstone. Editor, Daily Argus, Birmingham, 1891–98; editor-manager, Oxford Chronicle, 1899–1901; editor Newcastle Daily Leader, Evening Leader, Weekly Leader, 1901–3; President Birmingham Press Club, 1895; Vice-President Institute of Journalists, 1895–1900; President Birmingham and Midland Cornish Association, 1899–1900. *Recreations:* field botany, gardening, cricket, football, the play. *Address:* 59 Marine Avenue, Whitley Bay, Northumberland. *Club:* National Liberal.

Died 21 July 1920.

STRONG, John Alexander, ISO 1903; Superintending Clerk, Admiralty; *b* 12 March 1844; *s* of Rev. Clement Dawsonne Strong, MA Oxon, late vicar of All Saints, Bristol; *m* 1878, Lucebella, *d* of Lieut Marcus Theodore Hare, RN, and Hon. Lucy Anne Stanley, *d* of 1st Baron Stanley; two *s*. *Educ:* Marlborough College. Entered Admiralty, 1861; Examiner of Indian Accounts at Portsmouth Dockyard, 1885–92; Head of Finance Branch Transport Department of Admiralty through Boer War. *Address:* Moorhill, Westend, Hants. *Club:* National.

Died 20 March 1917.

STRONG, Rt. Hon. Sir (Thomas) Vezey, KCVO 1911; KBE 1918; Kt 1905; PC 1911; Lieutenant of City of London; Lord Mayor of City of London, 1910–11; Senior Sheriff of London, 1904–5; an Hon. Colonel 1st London Brigade, Royal Field Artillery; *b* 5 Oct. 1857; 3rd and *y s* of late John Strong; *m* 1900, Lillie (Lady of Grace), *d* of late James Hartnoll of Ganwic, Barnet. *Educ:* privately. Chairman Hospital Saturday Fund; of HM Prison, Holloway; Licensing Magistrates, City of London; and of London Temperance Hospital; Director of the United Kingdom Temperance and General Provident Institution; Officer of the Legion of Honour, France; Commander of the Order of Isabella the Catholic of Spain; of the Order of Our Lady of Villa Vicosa of Portugal; of the Order of the Crown, Belgium. *Recreation:* rowing. *Address:* 197 Upper Thames Street, EC. *Clubs:* Reform, Bath.

Died 3 Oct. 1920.

STRONGE, Sir Francis (William), KCMG 1915; Envoy Extraordinary and Minister Plenipotentiary, Chile, 1913–19; *b* 22 Nov. 1856; *y s* of Sir John Calvert Stronge, 4th Bt, and Margaret Zoe, *o d* of Hon. Henry Caulfield, and *sister* of 3rd Earl of Charlemont; *m* 1909, Mary Elizabeth Florence, *e d* of late Gen. Hon. Sir David Macdowall Fraser, GCB, and Mary, *d* of Edward Gonne Bell, Streamstown. *Educ:* Dublin University. Attaché, 1878; Secretary of Legation, Mexico, 1894; Athens, 1899; Secretary of Embassy, 1903; Consul-Gen. Buda-Pesth, 1903–5; Councillor of Embassy, Constantinople, 1905–6; Minister Resident, Columbia, 1906–11; Minister Plenipotentiary, Mexico, 1911–13. *Address:* Kilbroney House, Rostrevon, Co. Down. *Club:* Travellers'.

Died 20 Aug. 1924.

STRONGE, Rt Hon. Sir James (Henry), 5th Bt, *cr* 1803; PC (NI) 1924; *b* 8 Dec. 1849; *s* of Sir John Calvert Stronge, 4th Bt and Margaret Zoe, *o d* of Hon. Henry Caulfield, and *sister* of 3rd Earl of Charlemont;

S father, 1899; *m* 1885, Ethel Margaret (*d* 1926), *d* of Colonel Ynyr Henry Burges; five *d* (one *s* decd). *Educ:* Eton; Brasenose College, Oxford. 2nd class in Law and Modern History; MA 1875. Barrister Lincoln's Inn, 1874; Past Grand Master of the Orangemen of Ireland; served 15 years in 4th Royal Inniskilling Fusiliers (Tyrone Militia); retired as Hon. Major, 1885; High Sheriff of Tyrone, 1880; High Sheriff of Armagh, 1885; Sec. to Ulster Defence Union, 1894; Chairman of Armagh Dist Council, 1899–1900. *Publications:* article in National Review on Irish politics, in reply to Sir Charles Gavan Duffy, 1885; article in Nineteenth Century, Sep. 1907, on Ireland and the Transvaal; article in Irish Church Quarterly, 1912, A Plea for Charity in Irish History. *Recreation:* football till thirty years of age (played in Old Etonian eleven in semi-final for Association Cup). *Heir: cousin* Walter Lockhart Stronge, *b* 5 Sept. 1860. *Address:* Tynan Abbey, Tynan, Co. Armagh.

Died 20 May 1928.

STRUBEN, William Charles Marinus, CMG 1900; Natal Guides; *b* 12 May 1856; *s* of Capt. J. H. M. Struben, of Pretoria; *m* 1882, Helen, *d* of Archibald Keir Murray. Served Zulu War, 1879–80; Boer War, 1880–81; South Africa (despatches, medal). *Address:* Glen Athol, near Charlestown, Natal.

STRUTHERS, Sir John, KCB 1910 (CB 1902); Secretary, Scotch Education Department, 1904–21; *b* 19 Jan. 1857; *s* of Robert Struthers, Oban, and Agnes Muir; *m* 1912, Gertrude, *d* of Julian Hill of Dean's Yard, Westminster. *Educ:* Glasgow and Oxford Universities. 1st class hons Lit.Hum. Oxford, 1885. Inspector of Schools, Scotland, 1886–98; Assistant, then Principal Assistant Secretary, Scotch Education Dept, 1898–1904; Member of Royal Commission on Manual and Practical Instruction (Ireland), 1898; Committee on Physical Deterioration, 1904; Committee on Local and Imperial Taxation, 1912; Joint Board of Insurance Commissioners, 1912; LLD Aberdeen, 1905. *Address:* 31 Sloane Gardens, SW1. *T:* Victoria 2716. *Clubs:* Athenæum, Caledonian; Northern, Edinburgh.

Died 25 Oct. 1925.

STRUTT, Alfred William, ARE, RCA, RBC, FRGS, etc; animal-figure and landscape painter; also painter of many portraits; an etcher and painter in oil, water-colour, and pastel; *b* Taranaki, New Zealand, 1856; *s* of late William Strutt, RBC, FZS; fourth generation of artists of same name; *m* Nellie Maria, *d* of B. R. Ketchlee; two *s* two *d*. *Educ:* Sutton Valence; pupil of William Strutt, and at a Kensington school where he was a medallist and prize-winner. Spent early years in Australia; exhibitor of fifty-one pictures at Royal Acad. since 1877; exhibitor at all principal galleries of this country, and at Paris Salon and in the Colonies; painter of In a Fix, They'll want us again, Any Port in a Storm, The Run of the Season, At his Wits' End, Head over Ears in Love, Ilka Lassie has her Laddie, See how they Run, Three Offers, Thanks Awfully, Never too Late to Mend, Where's the Field, The Cold Shoulder, Getting it Hot, First Aid to the Wounded, Cavalier and Roundhead, and many others. *Publications:* all the above pictures were engraved, and a great many more. *Recreations:* driving, gardening. *Address:* Afterglow, Wadhurst, Sussex. *TA:* Wadhurst. *Club:* Savage.

Died 8 May 1924.

STRUTT, Hon. Charles Hedley, JP; BA; Chairman of Essex Quarter Sessions, 1904–21; County Alderman, 1888–1925; *b* 18 April 1949; 4th *s* of 2nd Baron Rayleigh and of Clara Elizabeth La Touche, *d* of Captain Richard Vicars, Royal Engineers; *m* 1919, Evangeline Bernard, *d* of Henry Hoare of Staplehurst, and *widow* of Percy Brodrick Bernard of Castle Hacket, Ireland. *Educ:* Winchester; Trinity College, Cambridge (BA). 1st class Moral Science Tripos, 1871; English Essay and old masters' prize, Trinity College, 1871. MP (C) for East Essex, 1883–85; MP (C) Maldon Div. of Essex, 1895–1906; contested Saffron Walden Div. of Essex, 1885; Chairman of Anglo-Dutch Plantations, and of other companies; travelled to North Borneo and Sumatra, etc; an agriculturist. *Recreation:* golf. *Address:* Wevaham, St Tudy, Cornwall; St Ermins, Caxton Street, Westminster, SW1. *Club:* Carlton.

Died 19 Dec. 1926.

STRUTT, George Herbert, JP; DL; VD; *b* 21 April 1854; *e s* of late George Henry Strutt of Bridgehill, and Agnes Ann, *d* of Edward Ashton of Prescot; *m* 1st, 1876, Edith Adela (*d* 1897), *e d* of Major Charles Yelverton Balguy; one *s* five *d*; 2nd, 1898, Emily, 2nd *d* of Rev. Robert Hind, RN, of Crosby-on-Eden, Cumberland; one *s* four *d*. *Educ:* Harrow; Magdalen College, Oxford. High Sheriff, Derbyshire, 1903; Patron of one Living; Capt. and Hon. Major 1st Vol. Batt. Sherwood Foresters, 1877–97. *Address:* Bridge Hill, Belper. *T:* 15; Kingairloch, Argyllshire, NB.

Died 17 May 1928.

STRUTT, Hon. Richard; *b* 29 Feb. 1848; 2nd surv. *s* of 2nd Baron Rayleigh and Clara Elizabeth La Touche, *d* of Capt. Richard Vicars, RE; *m* 1879, Augusta, *o c* of 5th Baron Braybrooke, of Audley End, Essex, and Billingbear, Berks; one *s* one *d* (and one *s* decd). *Educ:* Winchester; Magdalen College, Oxford (MA 1876). Entered business in an American Bank in London, and afterwards joined the Stock Exchange; for over thirty years Warden and Choirmaster of St John's Church, Wilton Road, London; member of the London Diocesan Conference; on the Councils of the Corporation of the Church House, Whitelands Training College, Chelsea, the North China and Shantung Mission, the Gregorian Association, and the Church Music Society; Fellow of the Philharmonic, Horticultural, and Zoological Societies; Honorary Member of the London Society of Organists. *Address:* 39 Tite Street, Chelsea, SW; The Court, St Catharine, Bath. *TA:* Strutt, Batheaston. *T:* Batheaston 59.

Died 14 Oct. 1927.

STUART OF WORTLEY, 1st Baron, *cr* 1916, of the City of Sheffield; **Charles Beilby Stuart-Wortley,** PC 1896; KC; MA; *b* Escrick Park, York, 15 Sep. 1851; *s* of Rt Hon. James Archibald Stuart-Wortley, QC (3rd *s* of 1st Baron Wharncliffe), and Jane, *d* of Paul Beilby, 1st Baron Lord Wenlock; *m* 1st, 1880, Beatrice (*d* 1881), *d* of Thomas Adolphus Trollope, the historian of Florence; one *d*; 2nd, 1886, Alice Sophia Caroline, 3rd *d* of late Sir John Everett Millais, 1st Bt, PRA; one *d*. *Educ:* Rugby; Balliol Coll., Oxford (MA 1879). Barrister 1876; practised North-Eastern Circuit, 1876–85; QC 1892; Parliamentary Under-Secretary of State for Home Department, 1885, and again, 1886–92; added to Chairman's Panel for Standing Committees, 1895; nominated by Mr Speaker a Deputy Chairman of Committee of the whole House, 1895; appointed by Archbishop Benson to the office of Ecclesiastical Commissioner and Church Estates Commissioner, 1895; attended as principal Delegate of HBM Government the International Conference at Madrid on the Protection of Industrial Property and the Repression of False Trade Descriptions, 1890; and again at Brussels, December 1897, and December 1900; contested Sheffield, 1879; MP (C) undivided borough of Sheffield, 1880–85; Hallam Division, Sheffield, 1885–1916; director of the Underground Electric Railways Co., Ltd. *Heir:* none. *Address:* 7 Cheyne Walk, Chelsea, SW3. *T:* Kensington 313. *Clubs:* Carlton, Beefsteak, St Stephen's.

Died 24 April 1926 (ext).

STUART, Hon. Charles Allan; Puisne Judge of the Supreme Court of Alberta, Canada, since 1907; *b* Caradoc, Middlesex Co., Ontario, 3 Aug. 1864; *s* of Charles Stuart, emigrant from Blair Atholl, Perthshire, Scotland, and Hannah Campbell, emigrant from Morpeth, England; *m* 1901, Beatrice Roxburgh, Norwood, Ontario; three *s*. *Educ:* University of Toronto (Gold Medal in Classics, 1891); Columbia College, New York; Osgoode Hall, Toronto. Called to the Bar of Ontario, 1896; North-West Territories of Canada, 1898; practised Law at Calgary, Alberta, 1898–1906; Member of First Legislature of Province of Alberta for Gleichen, 1905; Puisne Judge of Supreme Court of North-West Territories, 1906; Chancellor of University of Alberta, 1908. *Recreations:* riding, canoeing, fishing. *Address:* 718 7th Avenue, West Calgary, Alberta. *TA:* Casjus, Calgary. *M:* 2563.

Died March 1926.

STUART, Rev. Edward Alexander; Canon of Canterbury since 1907; Mid-day Lecturer at St Mary le Bow since 1888; *b* Calcutta, 17 April 1853; *s* of James Stuart of Sudbury Hill, Harrow; *m* Emily Ada, *d* of John Guy of Catton House, Norwich; four *s* four *d*. *Educ:* Harrow, 1866–72 (Capt. of Cricket Eleven, 1872); St John's Coll., Cambridge. Capt. of Lady Margaret Boat Club, 1875; Foundation Scholar; 2nd class Classical Tripos, 1876. Ordained, 1876; Curate of St Andrew's, Thorpe, 1876–77; St Giles's, Norwich, 1877–79; Vicar of St James's, Holloway, 1879–93; Vicar of St Matthew's, Bayswater, 1893–1907; Prebendary of St Paul's, 1905–7; Select Preacher, Cambridge, 1892, 1899; Jones's Lecturer, St Margaret's, Lothbury, 1897–98, 1906–7. *Publication:* Children of God, 1892. *Address:* The Precincts, Canterbury.

Died 26 Feb. 1917.

STUART, Sir Harold (Arthur), GCMG 1922 (KCMG 1921); KCSI 1914 (CSI 1903); KCVO 1906; Indian Civil Service; British Commissioner in Allied Administration for the Plebiscite of Upper Silesia, 1921–22 (GCMG); *b* York, 29 July 1860; *s* of late Peter Stuart; *m* 1885, Alice Catharine, *d* of late Rev. Frederick William Whitehead, of Cambridge; one *s* one *d*. *Educ:* Bishop's Stortford; King's College, Cambridge. Entered Indian Civil Service, 1881, and was posted to Madras, where he filled from time to time the usual administrative posts, and also served as Under Secretary to Government under Sir Mountstuart Grant Duff and Lord Connemara, as Secretary under Lord Ampthill, and as Private Secretary to Sir Arthur Havelock;

directed the Census operations, 1891, and wrote the report; Inspector-General of Police in Madras, 1898; after officiating as Deputy Secretary to the Government of India, became Secretary to the Police Commission appointed by Lord Curzon, 1902; First Director of Central Criminal Intelligence Department, India, 1904; Home Secretary to the Government of India, 1908–11; Member of Executive Council, Madras, 1912–16; retired Oct. 1916; served in the Ministry of Food, 1916–18; HM's High Commissioner on the Inter-Allied Rhineland High Commission, 1920–21. *Address:* Oppeln, Germany; 10 Cleveland Gardens, W2. *Club:* East India United Service. *Died 1 March 1923.*

STUART, John, CBE 1918; Managing Director of Ross, Ltd, opticians, Clapham Common, SW4; proprietor of the British Journal of Photography; *b* Grantown, 19 July 1836; *s* of William and Mary Stuart; *m* Mary Annie, *d* of George Bacon, St Albans, Herts; two *d.* *Educ:* Grantown; Inverness; Aberdeen. Entered business in Edinburgh, 1853; professional photographer, 1860; travelled extensively on the Continent and in America, producing large series of landscapes and architectural photographs; joined Ross and Co. in the management of Photographic Lenses Dept, 1870; associated with Francis Herbert Wenham (the inventor of binocular microscopes); during the following fifteen years introduced several series of new types of photographic lenses, such as the portable and rapid symmetricals, universal lenses, etc; also several forms of new and improved microscopes, objectives, and apparatus; on the introduction of the new Jena optical glasses, a series of concentric lenses were brought out, being the first anastigmat lenses invented; followed by a number of more rapid anastigmat lenses, such as the homocentric, telecentric, xpres, and combinable lenses; a new form of variable power gun sighting telescope was introduced, 1889 (awarded the Grand Prix and the Gold Medal, Paris Exhibition); this variable power gun sighting telescope was the forerunner of many types of naval gun sighting instruments and periscopes, and became the standard type in the British, Italian, Japanese, and many other foreign navies; on the outbreak of the European War, the entire output of Ross, Ltd was requisitioned by the Government, necessitating the stoppage of all general trade; special machinery was installed, old buildings were extended, and new buildings erected. *Recreations:* landscape and rock gardening, farming, etc. *Address:* Stonehurst, Ardingly, Sussex. *TA:* Stuart, Stonehurst, Ardingly. *T:* Ardingly 8; Battersea 376 and 702. *M:* AP 965 and LM 4384. *Club:* Royal Automobile.
Died 28 April 1926.

STUART, Leslie; composer; *b* Southport, 15 March 1866; *m.* Organist to St John's RC Cathedral, Salford, at age of fifteen, where he remained 7 years; organist to Church of the Holy Name, Manchester, for 7 years; composer of Florodora; The Silver Slipper; The School Girl; The Belle of Mayfair; Havana; The Slim Princess; Peggy; *songs:* Soldiers of the Queen; Little Dolly Day-dream; Louisiana Lou; The Bandolero; Rip Van Winkle; The Vales of Arklow; Is Your Mammie always wid Ye?; The Lily of Laguna; The Little Octoroon; I May Be Crazy; Sweetheart May; Sheelah Magee; The Willow Pattern Plate; Trilby will be True; The Dandy Fifth; My Little Black Pearl; On the Road to Tipperary; The Old Shield; Mighty Mother England. *Recreation:* billiards. *Died 27 March 1928.*

STUART, Ruth M'Enery; author; *b* Louisiana, USA; *d* of James M'Enery and Mary Routh Stirling; *m* 1879, Alfred O. Stuart (decd), cotton planter. *Educ:* New Orleans. Writer since 1888. *Publications:* A Golden Wedding and other Tales; Carlotta's Intended; Solomon Crow's Christmas Pockets; In Simpkinsville; The Story of Babette; Moriah's Mourning; Sonny; Holly and Pizen; Napoleon Jackson, The Gentleman of the Plush Rocker; George Washington Jones, A Christmas Gift that went A-begging; The Rivers' Children; The Second Wooing of Salina Sue; Aunt Amity's Silver Wedding, and other Tales; Sonny's Father; The Haunted Photograph; Daddy Do-funny's Wisdom-Jingles. *Recreations:* mycology, collecting aboriginal baskets, out-doorings, etc. *Address:* 220 Central Park, South, NY; summer, Columbine Cottage, Onteora Park, via Tannersville, NY, USA. *Clubs:* Barnard, Wednesday Afternoon, Onteora; Cosmopolitan, New York. *Died 6 May 1917.*

STUART, Sir Thomas Anderson, Kt 1914; MD; LLD Hon. Edinburgh; DSc Hon. Dunelm; Professor of Physiology, University of Sydney; Dean of the Faculty of Medicine; Fellow of the Senate since 1883; Chairman of Board of Directors of Royal Prince Alfred Hospital; Member of Board of Health; *b* Dumfries, Scotland, 20 June 1856; *s* of Alexander Stuart, Dean of Guild, and Jane Anderson; *m* 1893, Dorothy Primrose, *g-d* of late Hon. Bouverie Francis Primrose, Edinburgh; four *s.* *Educ:* Dumfries Academy; Gymnasium, Wolfenbüttel; Universities of Edinburgh and Strassburg. MB and

ChM Edinburgh University, First-Class Honours, First of Year and Ettles Scholarship, 1880; MD, with Gold Medal, 1882. Hon. Fellow Royal Academy Medicine in Ireland; President Royal Medical Society, Edinburgh, 1882; twice President of Royal Society of NSW; Member of Medical Board of NSW; Physician Children's Hospital; President Board of Health; Medical Adviser to Govt and Health Officer for Port Jackson; Trustee Australian Museum; Councillor of Women's College; President of Highland Society; of United Dental Hospital; of Industrial Blind Institution; of Civil Ambulance Brigade; of Zoological Society; of Health Society of New South Wales; held many other offices, and member of many learned societies; organised Royal Society (London) Expedition to Funafuti, which bored coral reef, proving Darwin's theory of reef formation correct; took principal part in promoting main existing Public Health Legislation of NSW; promoted and planned Medical School, Offices, and Laboratories of Board of Health, Queen Victoria Memorial and extensions of Royal Prince Alfred Hospital; initiated the movement which led to the foundation of the Australian Institute of Tropical Medicine at Townsville, N Queensland, 1906. *Publications:* principally papers in scientific journals on anatomical and physiological subjects. *Recreation:* golf. *Address:* 2 Lincluden Gardens, Fairfax Road, Double Bay, Sydney, NSW. *Club:* Union, Sydney.
Died 28 Feb. 1920.

STUCK, Ven. Hudson, DD; FRGS; Archdeacon of the Yukon since 1904; *b* England, 11 Nov. 1863; *s* of James Stuck and Jane Hudson; unmarried. *Educ:* private schools, London; classes at King's College, London, for two years; University of the South, Sewanee, Tenn; (graduated in Theology, 1892). Left England for Texas, 1885; schoolmaster in Texas for three years; ordained, 1892; Rector, Gracechurch, Cuero, Texas, 1892–94; Dean of St Matthew's Cathedral, Dallas, 1894–1904. *Publications:* Ascent of Denali (Mt McKinley), 1914; Ten Thousand Miles with a Dog-Sled, 1914; Voyages on the Yukon and its Tributaries, 1917. *Address:* Fort Yukon, Alaska, USA; 281 4th Avenue, New York.
Died Oct. 1920.

STUCLEY, Sir Edward Arthur George, 3rd Bt, *cr* 1859; Major, 1st South Australian Regiment; retired; *b* 12 Feb. 1852; *s* of Sir George Stucley, 1st Bt and 1st wife, Elisabeth, *d* of 2nd Marquis of Thomond, KP; *S* brother, 1911; *m* 1892, May (*d* 1922), *e d* of late Hon. Thomas King, formerly Minister of Educn, S Australia. *Educ:* private; Jesus College, Cambridge. *Recreations:* hunting, fishing, reading. Heir: half-brother Hugh Nicholas Granville Stucley [*b* 22 June 1873; *m* 1902, Gladys, *d* of Wynne Albert Bankes of Wolfeton House, Dorchester; three *s* two *d* (and one *s* decd). *Address:* Pillhead, Bideford. *Club:* Travellers']. *Address:* 41 Gwydyr Mansions, Hove. *Club:* Wellington.
Died 7 Dec. 1927.

STUDER, Paul, MA (Oxon); DLit (London); Taylorian Professor of the Romance Languages in the University of Oxford since 1913; *b* Biel, Switzerland, 1879; *m* 1908, Julie Adèle Knoll of Le Locle, Neuchâtel; two *s* one *d.* *Educ:* Le Locle, Neuchâtel; Univ. of Berlin MA (London), with special distinction, 1904; DLit (London), 1912. Professor of French and German in the Hartley University Coll., Southampton, 1907–13; Admiralty War Staff, 1916–18. *Publications:* Studies in Anglo-Norman; The Oak Book of Southampton (3 vols), 1910–11; The Port Books of Southampton, 1913; Le Mystère d'Adam, 1918; The Study of Anglo-Norman, 1920; An Anglo-Norman Poem by Edward II, King of England, 1921; The Franco-Provençal Dialects of Upper Valais, with Texts, 1924; Anglo-Norman Lapidaries (in collaboration), 1924; A Historical French Reader, Medieval Period (in collaboration), 1924; St Joan of Orleans, scenes from the 15th Century Mystère du Siège d'Orléans (in collaboration), 1926. *Address:* Exeter College, Oxford; Beech House, Headington Hill, Oxford. *Died 23 Jan. 1927.*

STURDEE, Admiral of the Fleet Sir (Frederick Charles) Doveton, 1st Bt, *cr* 1916, of the Falkland Isles; GCB 1921 (KCB 1913); KCMG 1916 (CMG 1900); CVO 1906 (MVO 1903); LLD Cambridge; *b* 9 June 1859; *s* of Frederick Rannie Sturdee, Capt. RN, and Anna France, *d* of Col Charles Hodson; *m* 1882, Marion Adela, *d* of William John Andrews; one *s* one *d.* *Educ:* Royal Naval School, New Cross. Entered Navy, 1871; Captain, 1899; Rear-Admiral, 1908; served Egyptian War, 1882 (Egyptian medal, Alexandra clasp, Khedive's bronze star); Assistant to Director of Naval Ordnance, 1893–97; commanded British Force in Samoa, 1899 (CMG); Assistant Director of Naval Intelligence, 1900–2; Chief of the Staff, Mediterranean Fleet, 1905–7; and Chief of the Staff, Channel Fleet, 1907; ADC to King Edward VII, 1907–8; Rear Admiral 1st Battle Squadron, 1910; commanded 2nd Cruiser Squadron, 1912–13; Chief of War Staff, 1914–15; Commander-in-Chief HMS Invincible in action off the Falkland Isles, 1914 (despatches, Bart, Parliamentary grant £10,000); battle of Jutland Bank, 1916 (despatches, KCMG); Admiral, 1917; Commander in Chief The Nore, 1918–21; Admiral of the Fleet, 1921; received gold medal of Royal United Service Institution, 1886 and 1894; Commander, Legion of Honour; St Anne of Russia, 1st class with swords; Grand Officer of St Maurice and St Lazarus, Italy; Grand Cordon of Rising Sun, Japan; Croix de Guerre with palm, France; Striped Tiger, 1st class, China. *Heir: s* Commander Lionel Arthur Doveton Sturdee, RN [*b* 3 Sept. 1884; *m* 1910, Dorothy Mary Mowbray, *d* of William Feetham, Sayer; one *d*]. *Address:* Wargrave House, Camberley, Surrey. *T:* Camberley 110. *Club:* United Service.   *Died 7 May 1925.*

STURGE, William Allen, MVO (4th class) 1897; MD London; FRCP; *b* Bristol, 1850; *s* of William Sturge; *m* 1886, Julia, *d* of late A. C. Sheriff, MP for Worcester. *Educ:* privately. Formerly Physician Royal Free Hospital, London, and to Hospital for Epilepsy and Paralysis, Regent's Park, London; practised at Nice, 1881–1907. *Publications;* various papers on medical subjects to different medical societies and publications. *Recreation:* possessor of a large collection of prehistoric implements and weapons in stone and bronze, also of objects (vases, etc) connected with classical archælogy. *Address:* Icklingham Hall, Mildenhall, Suffolk

Died 27 March 1919.

STURLEY, Major Albert Avern; Professor of Physics, University of King's College, Windsor, NS; *b* Harbury, Warwickshire, 9 Aug. 1887; *s* of late W. B. Sturley; *m* V. W. E. Hill of Dibden, Hants; two *s*. *Educ:* Banbury, Oxon; Lennoxville, Quebec; Christ Church, Oxford. 193rd Nova Scotia Regt Canadian Expeditionary Force; seconded to Imperial Forces; OC King's Coll. COTC. *Recreations:* tennis, cricket. *Address:* Windsor, Nova Scotia.

Died 22 Oct. 1922.

STURROCK, John, CIE 1900; late Indian Civil Service; *b* 17 Feb. 1845; *s* of John Sturrock; *m* 1871, Regina Mary, *d* of late Major-Gen. George Staple Dobbie, Madras Army; three *s* one *d*. *Educ:* High School, Dundee. Entered ICS, 1863; served Madras as Asst Collector and Magistrate; Acting Secretary of Govt Revenue Department, 1873; Under Secretary to Government in Chief Secretary's Department, 1875; additional Sub-Secretary Board of Revenue, 1878; Sub-Secretary, 1879; Collector and Magistrate, 1883; Member, Legislative Council, 1894; Member, Revenue Board and Commission Land Tax, 1894; Commissioner, Land Revenue, 1898; Member, Legislative Council, Madras, 1896 and 1898; retired, 1899. *Address:* 12 Greenhill, Weymouth. *Club:* Royal Dorset Yacht.

Died 12 Feb. 1926.

STURT, George, (George Bourne); author; *b* 18 June 1863. *Educ:* Farnham GS. *Publications:* The Bettesworth Book, 1901; Memoirs of a Surrey Labourer, 1907; The Ascending Effort, 1910; Change in the Village, 1912; Lucy Bettesworth, 1913; William Smith, 1920; A Farmer's Life, 1922; The Wheelwright's Shop, 1923; A Small Boy in The Sixties, 1927. *Address:* Vine Cottage, The Bourne, Farnham, Surrey.   *Died 4 Feb. 1927.*

STURT, Hon. Gerard Philip Montagu Napier; Captain Coldstream Guards; *b* 9 April 1893; *e s* of 2nd Baron Alington and Lady Feodorowna Yorke, *d* of 5th Earl of Hardwicke. Entered army, 1912; Lieut 1914; Capt. 1915; served European War, 1914–18 (wounded). *Address:* 38 Portman Square, W. *Clubs:* Guards, Bath, Pratt's.

Died 11 Nov. 1918.

STYLE, Rev. George; Rector of Chalbury since 1905. *Educ:* Queens' College, Cambridge. Fellow of Queens' College, 1864–77; Assistant Master Clifton College, 1868–69; Headmaster Giggleswick School, Yorkshire, 1869–1904. *Address.* Chalbury Rectory, Wimborne.

Died 16 Jan. 1922.

SUART, Brig.-Gen. William Hodgson, CMG 1918; JP; *b* 17 Dec. 1850; *s* of late Major William Swainson Suart, of Bowles, Chigwell, Essex; *m* Mary Catharine, *d* of late Maj.-Gen. W. C. Lester of Battwick Lodge, Boscombe, Hants; one *d*. *Educ:* privately; RMA, Woolwich. Entered Royal Artillery, 1871; served Afghanistan, 1880 (medal); retired, 1907; commanding Home Counties Divisional Artillery Territorials, April 1909–Nov. 1913; re-employed Nov. 1914; commanded Training Divisional Artillery at home, ending up with a Field Artillery Reserve Brigade, Dec. 1917. *Address:* Rusthall Cottage, Tunbridge Wells. *Club:* United Service.

Died 23 June 1923.

SUCKLING, Rev. Robert Alfred J.; Vicar of St Alban's, Holborn, since 1882; Superior-General of the Confraternity of the Blessed

Sacrament, 1895–1915. *Educ:* St Edmund Hall, Oxford. Ordained, 1865; Curate of Rowde, 1865–68; Rector of Barsham, Suffolk, 1868–80; Vicar of St Peter's, London Docks, 1880–82; Patron and Lord of the Manors of Barsham and Shipmeadow. *Address:* St Albans Clergy House, Brooke Street, Holborn, EC.

Died 24 Sept. 1917.

SUDELEY, 4th Baron, *cr* 1888; **Charles Douglas Richard Hanbury-Tracy,** PC; DL, JP; FRS; Lieutenant, Royal Navy, retired 1863; *b* Brighton, 3 July 1840; 2nd *s* of 2nd Baron and Emma Elizabeth Alicia, *d* of George Hay Dawkins Pennant of Penrhyn Castle, Carnarvon, and Sophia, *d* of 1st Viscount Hawarden; *S* brother, 1877; *m* 1868, Ada Maria Katharine, *d* of Hon. Frederick James Tollemache (*nephew* of 7th Earl of Dysart); one *s* four *d*. Entered Navy, 1854; Lieut 1860; served in Russian War, 1854, and was present at siege of Bomarsund, of Fatshan in China and at San Blas in Mexico; was gunnery Lieut in Mediterranean, 1862; Barrister Inner Temple, 1866; Commissioner Electrical Exhibition, Vienna, 1883; MP (L) for Montgomery, 1863–77; Lord-in-Waiting, 1880–85; Captain of Hon. Corps of Gentlemen-at-Arms, 1886. *Publications:* lectures, and various pamphlets and articles in magazines on the public utility of museums. *Heir: s* Hon. William Charles Frederick Hanbury-Tracy [*b* 19 April 1870; *m* 1905, Edith Celandine, *y d* of Lord Francis Cecil]. *Address:* Beston Lodge, Petersham, Surrey. *TA:* Petersham. *T:* Richmond 2365.   *Died 9 Dec. 1922.*

SUDERMANN, Hermann; dramatist and novelist; *b* Matzicken, Heydekrug, East Prussia, 30 Sept. 1857. *Educ:* Elbing and Tilsit; Universities of Königsberg and Berlin. Journalist from 1881 (editor of the Deutsches Reichsblatt); afterwards man of letters; first play put upon the stage, 1889. *Publications:* Im Zwielicht (stories), 1887; Frau Sorge (novel), 1887; Geschwister (stories), 1888; Katzensteg (novel), 1889; Die Ehre (drama), 1890; Sodoms Ende (drama), 1891; Iolanthes Hochzeit (tale), 1892; Heimat (drama), 1893; Es War (novel), 1894; Die Schmetterlingsschlacht (comedy), 1896; Das Glück im Winkel (drama), 1896; Morituri: Teja, Fritzschen, Das Ewigmännliche (three dramas), 1896; Johannes (tragedy), 1898; Die drei Reiherfedern (drama), 1899; Johannisfeuer (drama), 1900; Es lebe das Leben (drama), 1901; Der Sturmgeselle Sokrates, 1903; Stein unter Steinen (drama), 1905; Das Blumenbost (drama), 1905; The Undying Past, 1906; Das Hohe Lied, 1908; Strandkinder, 1909; Der Bettler von Syrakus (tragedy), 1911; The Indian Lily (stories), 1911; Der gute Ruf (comedy), 1913. *Address:* (winter) Grunewald Bettinastrasse 3, Berlin; (summer) Schloss Blankensee bei Trebbin (Kreis Teltow). *Clubs:* Berliner Presse Verein, Litterarische Gesellschaft.

Died 21 Nov. 1928.

SUFFIELD, 6th Baron, *cr* 1786; **Charles Harbord,** CB 1900; MVO 1902; Bt 1745; Scots Guards, Colonel retired; Captain of Yeomen of the Guard, 1915–18; *b* 14 June 1855; *e s* of 5th Baron and 1st wife, Cecilia Annetta (Lady of Bedchamber to Queen Alexandra) (*d* 1911), *d* of Henry Baring, and *sister* of 1st Baron Revelstoke; *S* father, 1914; *m* 1896, Evelyn Louisa, *d* of Capt. Eustace Wilson-Patten and Emily Constantia (later Marchioness of Headfort); two *s* two d. *Educ:* Eton. Served on the staff of Lord Lorne in Canada, staffs of Lords Ripon, Dufferin, and Lansdowne, 1881–94; served in S Africa 1900 to end of war; Groom-in-Waiting to the late Queen. *Heir: s* Hon. Victor Alexander Charles Harbord, Capt. Scots Guards [*b* 12 Sept. 1897. Page of Honour to King George, 1910–15]. *Address:* Gunton Park, Norwich. *Clubs* Guards', Turf.

Died 10 Feb. 1924.

SUFFOLK, 19th Earl of, *cr* 1603, **AND BERKSHIRE,** 12th Earl of, *cr* 1626; **Henry Molyneux Paget Howard;** Viscount Andover and Baron Howard, 1622; commanded Wiltshire Battery 3rd Wessex Brigade (Territorial); *b* 13 Sept. 1877 *e s* of 18th Earl and Mary Eleanor Lauderdale, 4th *d* of Hon. Henry Coventry; *S* father, 1898; *m* 1904, Margaret Hyde, *y d* of late Levi Zeigler, Washington, USA; three *s*. *Educ:* Winchester. Liberal Unionist; owned 10,000 acres; celebrated picture-gallery and wellknown collection of Old Masters. *Recreations:* hunting, fishing. *Heir: s* Viscount Andover, *b* 2 March 1906. *Address:* Charlton Park, Malmesbury. *Clubs:* Turf, Orleans, Carlton.

Died 21 April 1917.

SUGDEN, Charles; actor; *b* Cambridge, 24 Dec. 1850; *o s* of Charles Langworthy Sugden and Mary, *o d* of James Camper Wright, Fellow of Eton and King's Coll., Cambridge; *m* Helen de la Feuillade, a descendant of an old Bourbon family, herself a well-known actress, known to the playgoing public as Miss Vane. *Educ:* Beccles Grammar School; and at Rev. Henry Mackaness, Ash, nr Sandwich, Kent. Theatre Royal, Brighton, 1867; Theatres Royal, Dublin and Edinburgh, 1868–69 and 1870; first appeared in London at Globe

Theatre 1871, under management of H. J. Montague, in Partners for Life; afterwards created the parts of King William in Clancarty, Chevalier in Two Orphans, Charles in Our Boys, which he played 600 nights; Captain Bradford in Peril, at the old Prince of Wales's Theatre; Allen Villiers in Red Lamp; Judge Brack in Hedda Gabler; and Paillard in A Night Out, at Vaudeville Theatre; was Touchstone in a revival of As You Like it at St James's Theatre in 1890. *Publications:* The Kite Flyer, comedy, 1894; The Limit of the Law, 1912; Forty Years of Turf and Stage, 1912. *Recreations:* shooting, fishing, racing (owned racehorses, 1879–1910); had wonderful collection of birds' eggs, all gathered by himself; famous sprint runner in 1870 (won LAC hundred yards challenge cup and beat Roland Upcher in 200 and 100 yards races, winning the former in 21 seconds, the latter in $10^{1}/_{5}$ seconds). *Address:* 5A Hyde Park Mansions, Marylebone Road, W.

Died 3 Aug. 1921.

SUDGEN, Frank; *b* 28 Oct. 1852; *e s* of late Rev. Hon. Frank Sugden and Henrietta Maria, *d* of Philip Saltmarshe; *g s* of 1st and *c* and *heir pres.* to 3rd Baron St Leonards; *m* 1st, 1894, Edyth Mary (*d* 1904), *d* of late General Sir Arthur Becher, KCB; 2nd, 1909, Alice (*d* 1921), *d* of late Rev. C. J. Phipps Eyre, formerly Rector of St Marylebone. *Address:* 2 Ryder Street, St James's, SW1. *Club:* Conservative.

Died 19 Aug. 1927.

SULIVAN, Col Ernest Frederic, CBE 1919; a Director of the Pacific and Papua Produce, Ltd; *b* 1860; *s* of late Rev. Filmer Sulivan; *m* 1885, Florence Mary, *d* of James Houldsworth, of Coltness. Served Afghan War, 1879–80 (medal with clasp); S Africa, 1902 (Queen's medal with two clasps); European War, 1914–19 (despatches, CBE). *Address:* Wilmington, Woking.

Died 14 Oct. 1928.

SULLIVAN, Sir Edward, 2nd Bt, *cr* 1881; *b* Ireland, 27 Sept. 1852; *s* of Rt Hon. Sir Edward Sullivan, 1st Bt (Lord Chancellor of Ireland), and Bessie Josephine, *d* of Robert Bailey, Cork; *S* father, 1885; unmarried. *Educ:* Portora Royal School, Enniskillen; Trinity Coll., Dublin. First Honourman in Classics; Classical Scholar and Moderator; Vice-Chancellor's Prizeman in Latin Verse. Barrister, King's Inns, Dublin, 1879; Middle Temple, 1888; contested (LU) St Stephen's Green Div. of Dublin, 1886; Chester le Street Div. of Durham, 1892; ex-Trustee of National Library of Ireland; ex-President of Ye Sette of Odd Volumes. *Publications:* Dante's Comedy, in English Prose, part i Hell, 1893; Tales from Scott, 1894; Buck Whaley's Memoirs; The Book of Kells, 1914; The Introduction to Guazzo's Civile Conversation of 1581 (translated by George Pettie) (Tudor Translations); contributor to Quarterly Review, Nineteenth Century, etc. *Recreations:* literature, book-cover decoration. *Heir:* brother William Sullivan, Barrister, King's Inn, Dublin, Resident Magistrate, Co. Meath [*b* 21 Feb. 1860; *m* 1866, Charlotte Anna, *d* of late Right Hon. Richard Dowse, a Baron of the Exchequer; one *d*]. *Address:* 26 Queensberry Place, South Kensington, SW7. *Clubs:* Reform; Royal Irish Yacht.

Died 19 April 1928.

SULLIVAN, William Charles, MD; Superintendent, Broadmoor Criminal Lunatic Asylum, Crowthorne, Berks; *y s* of late W. K. Sullivan, PhD (Giessen), President of Queen's College, Cork; *m* Mary (authoress of The One Outside and other Irish stories), *d* of late John Fitzpatrick; one *s*. *Educ:* Cork; Dublin; Paris. Formerly in prison medical service; was Scientific Adviser to Central Control Board (Liquor Traffic), 1915–19; Lecturer on Criminology and Forensic Psychiatry at the Maudsley Hospital. *Publications:* Alcoholism, 1896; Crime and Insanity, 1924; various contributions to scientific journals on criminology, psychiatry, and alcoholism. *Address:* Broadmoor, Crowthorne, Berks.

Died 26 Feb. 1926.

SULLIVAN, Hon. Sir (William) Wilfred, Kt 1914; Chief Justice, and Judge of Vice-Admiralty Court, Prince Edward Island, since 1889; *b* 6 Dec. 1843; *m* 1872, Alice Maud Mary, *d* of John Fenton Newbery. *Educ:* Central Academy; St Dunstan's College, Charlottetown. Called to the Bar, PEI, 1867; QC 1876; Attorney-General of Province and Premier, 1879–89; Roman Catholic. *Address:* Brighton Villa, Charlottetown, Prince Edward Island.

Died 1923.

SULLY, James, LLD; Emeritus Professor of Philosophy, University College, London, and late Lecturer on Education to the University of Cambridge, the College of Preceptors, etc; writer on psychology; *b* Bridgwater, 3 March 1842; *e s* of J. W. Sully, merchant and colliery proprietor; *m*; one *d* one *s*. *Educ:* Independent College, Taunton; Regent's Park College, London (MA and gold medallist of the University of London); Universities of Göttingen and Berlin. *Publications:* Sensation and Intuition, 1874; Pessimism, 1877; Illusions,

1881; Outlines of Psychology, 1884; Teacher's Handbook of Psychology, 1886; The Human Mind, 1892; Studies of Childhood, 1895; Children's Ways, 1897; An Essay on Laughter, 1902; Italian Travel Sketches, 1912; My Life and Friends, 1918. *Address:* 30 Arlington Park Mansions, Chiswick, W.

Died 1 Nov. 1923.

SULTE, Benjamin, FRSC; retired Civil Servant; *b* Three Rivers, PQ, 17 Sep. 1841; *s* of Benjamin Sulte, navigator, and Marie Antoinette Lefebvre; *m* 1871, Augustine (*d* 1918), *d* of Etienne Parent, Under Sec. of State. *Educ:* Friars' School, Three Rivers. Engaged in commerce and lumbering business; served as a volunteer at the frontier, 1865; Military School certificate, 1865; served at the frontier, 1866 (medal); Translator in Parliament, 1867; Private Secretary to Minister of Militia and Defence, 1870–73; Clerk in same department, 1870; Chief Clerk and Acting Deputy Minister, 1889; retired on superannuation, 1903; President, Institut Canadien, Ottawa, 1874; President, St John the Baptist Society, Ottawa, 1883; President of St Joseph Society, 1877; President of the Royal Society of Canada; 1904; LLD University of Toronto, 1916; Corresponding Member of several historical societies; translated the National Anthem into French, and delivered many lectures on historical subjects. *Publications:* Les Laurentiennes (poems), 1870; Les Chants Nouveaux (poems), 1876; Mélanges d'Histoire, 1876; Histoire des Canadiens-Français (8 vols), 1882–84; Pages d'Histoire, 1891; Histoire de la Milice Canadienne, 1897; La Langue Française en Canada, 1898; La Bataille de Châteauguay, 1899; History of Quebec, 1908; Historiettes et Fantaisies, 1910; Cinquante-six ans de vie littéraire, 1916; Mélanges Historiques, 10 vols, 1918–22; besides many small publications. *Address:* 43 Fairmont Street, Ottawa.

Died 6 Aug. 1923.

SULZBERGER, Mayer; Resident Lecturer on Jewish Jurisprudence and Institutes of Government, Dropsie College, Philadelphia; *b* Heidelsheim, Baden, 22 June 1843. *Educ:* Central High School, Philadelphia. Admitted to the Bar, 1865; Judge, Court of Common Pleas, 1895–1915; Presiding Judge, 1902–15; Member of Constitutional Commission of the State of Pennsylvania, 1919–21. *Publications:* An-ha-Aretz, 1909; The Polity of the Ancient Hebrews, 1912; The Ancient Hebrew Law of Homicide, 1915; The Status of Labor in Ancient Israel, 1922. *Recreations:* walking, reading. *Address:* 1303 Girard Avenue, Philadelphia. *T* Poplar 4516.

Died 1923.

SUMMERS, Bt-Lt-Col and Temp. Col Sir Gerald Henry, KCMG 1925 (CMG 1920); FRGS; Governor and Commander-in-Chief, Somaliland, since 1922; 8th King George's Own Light Cavalry (Indian Army); *b* 12 Oct. 1885; *s* of late Rev. Walter Summers, Danehill, Sussex; *m* 1916, Margaret Frances Troath, *d* of late Lt-Col T. R. Swinburne, of Pontop Hall, Durham; one *s* one d. Educ: Ashdown House; Bradfield; Sandhurst. Entered Army, 1904; attached 1st Royal Sussex Regt, 1904; 93rd Burma Infantry, Burma, 1905–6; 26th Cavalry, 1907; Capt. 1913; Major, 1919; attached Somaliland Indian Contingent King's African Rifles, 1912; action of Dul Madoba with Somaliland Camel Corps, 1913 (severely wounded three times; Brevet Major); Staff Officer to troops, Somaliland and Intelligence Officer, 1914; Operations at Shimber Berris, 1914–15 (despatches, medal and clasp); Officer commanding troops and Deputy Commissioner Somaliland (despatches, temp. Lt-Col), 1916; temp. Col, 1919; commanded Military Force in operations against the Dervishes in Somaliland, Jan.–March 1920 (despatches, clasp, Brevet Lt-Col); Acting-Governor Somaliland Protectorate, March–Dec. 1921. *Address:* Government House, Berbera, Somaliland; Slough House, Danbury, Essex. *Club:* Cavalry.

Died 29 Nov. 1925.

SUNDARLAL, Hon. Pandit, Rai Bahadur, CIE 1907; Advocate, High Court North-West Province, Allahabad; member Legislative Council, United Provinces of Agra and Oudh, since 1895; Fellow of the University of Allahabad since 1889; *b* May 1857; *s* of Pandit Gobiud Ram Davè of Allahabad. *Educ:* Muir Central College, Allahabad; University of Calcutta. Graduated, 1881; enrolled as a Vakil of Allahabad High Court, 1880; enrolled as an Advocate, 1895; member of Council of Law Reporting, 1888; Vice-Chancellor, University of Allahabad, 1906–8 and 1912–16; reappointed 1916; Judicial Commissioner of Oudh, UP, 1909; Vice-Chairman, United Provinces Exhibition, 1910–11; Judge, High Court, NWP, 1914; reappointed 1916; member Legislative Council of Viceroy and Governor-General of India, 1915; first Vice-Chancellor, Benares Hindu University, 1916. *Recreations:* tennis, cycling, etc. *Address:* 9 Elgin Road, Allahabad. *T:* No 25. *Club:* Indian, Allahabad.

Died April 1918.

SUPPLE, Col James Francis, CB 1900; Royal Army Medical Corps; *b* 14 Nov. 1843; *e s* of J. Supple, St Anne's, Glenageary, Co. Dublin, and Feltrim, Cork; *m* Julia Mary, *e d* of Robert Lambkin, JP. Entered army, 1867, Asst Surgeon 1st Royal Scots; served in Ashanti War, 1873–74 (thanked by Director-Gen., medal with clasp); Afghanistan, 1878–79 (medal); Burmah, 1886–87 as PMO 6th Brigade under Sir Robert Low (despatches, medal with clasp); South Africa, 1899–1901 (despatches, Queen's medal with clasp, CB); PMO Durbar Troops, India, 1903 (medal); awarded Distinguished Service Pension. *Recreations:* music, painting, cricket, tennis, boating. *Address:* c/o Messrs Holt & Co., 3 Whitehall Place, SW1.
Died 8 Aug. 1922.

SUTHER, Gen. Cuthbert Collingwood; Royal Marine Artillery; *b* 1 Aug. 1839; *m* 1868, Louise Adelaide (*d* 1899), *e d* of J. W. Jennings. Entered Royal Marines, 1855; General, 1899; retired, 1904. *Address:* Eastney, Heene Road, Worthing.
Died 29 Sept. 1927.

SUTHERLAND, Angus, CB 1907; *b* 1848; 3rd *s* of late William Sutherland, Helmsdale, Sutherland; unmarried. *Educ:* parish school; Edinburgh Training College; Glasgow University. Contested Sutherlandshire, 1885; MP (L) Sutherlandshire, 1886–96; Member of Royal Commission on Highlands and Islands of Scotland, 1892; Chairman of Fishery Board for Scotland, 1896; Member of Congested Districts Board for Scotland, 1892; Member of Royal Commission on Congestion in Ireland, 1906. *Address:* 101 George Street, Edinburgh; Helmsdale, Sutherland. *Club:* Scottish Liberal, Edinburgh.
Died 16 Jan. 1922.

SUTHERLAND, Edward Davenport, ISO 1906; Auditor-General of Canada, Ottawa; *b* 19 Nov. 1853; *s* of Edward Buckner Sutherland, Sydney, NS; *m* 1877, Kate, *d* of William Joseph Goodeve. *Address:* Ottawa, Canada.
Died 8 Jan. 1923.

SUTHERLAND, John Ebenezer; MP (L) Elgin Burghs since 1905; *b* 1854. *Educ:* Aberdeen Univ. Partner, P. and J. Sutherland; Chm., Cttee on Scottish Sea Fisheries, 1917. *Address:* Durn House, Portsoy, SO, Banffshire, NB. *Clubs:* Reform, National Liberal.
Died 17 Aug. 1918.

SUTHERLAND, Rt. Hon. Robert Franklin, PC; KC 1899; BA; a Puisne Judge of the Exchequer Division of the High Court of Justice for Ontario since 1909; *b* Newmarket, Ont, 5 April 1859; *s* of Donald Sutherland (Scotch) and Jane Boddy (Irish); *m* 1888, Mary Bartlet; two *d. Educ:* Public and High Schools, Newmarket; High School, Windsor; Toronto University; Western University. Called to the Bar, 1886; Liberal; MP Essex N, 1900–9; Speaker of House of Commons, 1905–9. Alderman of City of Windsor; President Windsor St Andrew's Society; President Windsor Library Board; a Presbyterian, and Elder of St Andrew's Church, Windsor. *Address:* Toronto, Canada. *Clubs:* York, Toronto Golf, Toronto; Rosedale Golf.
Died 17 June 1922.

SUTHERLAND, Sir Thomas, GCMG 1897 (KCMG 1891); LLD; Vice-President, and late Chairman of London Board, Suez Canal Co.; Chairman Peninsular and Oriental Steamship Co., 1881–1914, retired; Director London City and Midland Bank; Chairman Marine and General Assurance Society; *b* Aberdeen, 16 Aug. 1834; *s* of Robert Sutherland and Christian, *d* of Thomas Webster; *m* 1880, Alice (*d* 1920), *y d* of late Rev. John Macnaught, MA Oxon, Vicar St Chrysostom's, Liverpool; one *d* (two *s* decd). Educ: Aberdeen Grammar School and University. Entered service of P&O Steamship Company, and was in China for some years, where represented that Company; was one of founders Hong-Kong Docks and of Hong-Kong and Shanghai Bank; Member of Legislative Council of that Colony; MP (L, later LU) Greenock, 1884–1900; Kt of St John of Jerusalem, and of Legion of Honour, France. *Recreations:* motoring, golf. *Address:* 7 Buckingham Gate, SW1. *T:* Victoria 5821. *Clubs:* Reform, Brooks's.
Died 1 Jan. 1922.

SUTTON, Sir Abraham, Kt 1903; JP, Co. Cork; *b* Aug. 1849; *s* of late Abraham Sutton of Monkstown, Co. Cork. *Educ:* Clongowes. High Sheriff of Cork, 1903. *Address:* Windsor, Douglas, Co. Cork. *TA:* Sutton, Douglas, Cork. *T:* 8 Douglas, Cork. *Clubs:* Cork, Cork; RCYC, Queenstown. *M:* IF 469.
Died 27 Nov. 1921.

SUTTON, Col Alfred, CB 1918; CMG; Australian Army Medical Corps; *Address:* 29 Wickham Terrace, Brisbane.
Died 15 April 1922.

SUTTON, Rev. Arthur Frederick, FSA; Prebendary of Lincoln; Rural Dean of Loveden; *s* of Canon Augustus Sutton, Rector of West Tofts, Norfolk. *Educ:* Uppingham School; Jesus College, Cambridge. Secretary of Lincolnshire Architectural Society; Member of Agricultural Institute. *Address:* The Vicarage, Earls Colne, Essex.
Died 18 Nov. 1925.

SUTTON, Arthur Warwick, JP; FLS, VMH, FRHS; *b* Reading, 1854; *s* of Martin Hope Sutton; *m* 1881, Arabella Constance, *d* of Rev. E. Gambier Pym, late Rector of Washington; one *s* two *d. Educ:* Malvern College; Royal Agricultural College, Cirencester. Became partner in the firm of Sutton & Sons, Reading, 1876; senior partner, 1913; retired owing to illness, 1921. *Publications:* My Camel Ride from Suez to Mount Sinai; several bulletins on horticultural research, and papers read before the Linnean Society, Farmers' Club, Royal Horticultural Society, Royal Agricultural Society, Genetical Society, and Victoria Institute. *Recreations:* Eastern travel, golf, shooting, fishing; special hobby, lecturing on Eastern travels, with original lantern slides. *Address:* 8 Clifton Road, Southbourne, Bournemouth. *TA:* Sutton, Southbourne. *T:* Southbourne 112. *M:* EL 7056. *Clubs:* Royal Automobile; Berkshire, Reading; Royal and Ancient, St Andrews.
Died 15 April 1925.

SUTTON, Charles William, MA; Librarian of the Manchester Public Free Libraries; *b* Manchester, 14 April 1848; *s* of late Thomas Sutton; *m* 1st, Sarah H. Evans; 2nd, Marie Pocklington; five *s*. Sub-librarian of Manchester Public Libraries, 1874; chief librarian, 1879; vice-president of Library Association; late treasurer, Manchester Literary Club; hon. librarian, Manchester Statistical Society; hon. secretary of Spenser Society (later defunct); hon. secretary of Chetham Society; past president of Lancashire and Cheshire Antiquarian Society and Manchester Association for Masonic Research; Hon. MA of Victoria University, 1902; editor of Transactions of Lancashire and Cheshire Antiquarian Society since 1885. *Publications:* List of Lancashire Authors, 1876; Special Collections of Books in Lancashire and Cheshire, 1899; contributions to Chetham Soc., including Life of Humphrey Chetham; many articles in the Dictionary of National Biography, etc. *Address:* 323 Great Clowes Street, Higher Broughton, Manchester.
Died 24 April 1920.

SUTTON, Sir Henry, Kt 1906; BA; *b* 10 Jan. 1845; 2nd surv. *s* of James Sutton of Shardlow Hall, Derby; *m* 1872, Caroline Blanch (*d* 1916), *e d* of late John Nanson, Knells, Carlisle; one *s* four *d. Educ:* Rugby; Cambridge (Scholar of Christ's Coll., and Senior Optime). Called to the Bar, Lincoln's Inn, 1870; Bencher; formerly Junior Counsel to Treasury; Judge of King's Bench Division of High Court of Justice, 1905–10. *Publication:* Law of Tramways. *Recreation:* fishing. *Address:* 49 Lexham Gardens, SW. *T:* Western 3125. *Clubs:* Athenæum, New University.
Died 30 May 1920.

SUTTON, Rev. Henry; Hon. Canon, Birmingham; *b* 28 Sept. 1833; 2nd *s* of Rev. Thomas Sutton, Vicar of Marton, Gainsborough. *Educ:* Louth Grammar School, Lincolnshire; Trinity College, Dublin. Curate of Tealby and Legsby, Lincolnshire, under his uncle, Rev. Field Flowers, 1858–61; Association Secretary, Church Missionary Society, 1861–64; Vicar of St Augustine's, Everton, Liverpool, 1864–70; St Barnabas', Douglas, Isle of Man, 1870–72; St Cleopas', Liverpool, 1872–79; Central or Home Secretary, CMS, 1879–87; Vicar of Holy Trinity, Bordesley, Birmingham, 1887–95; Proctor in Convocation for Diocese of Birmingham, May 1905; Vicar of Aston-juxta-Birmingham, 1895–1917. *Publications:* The Christian's Recreations; articles in National Review on church patronage, and the children of literature; and many unsigned articles in Church papers. *Recreations:* cricket, cycling. *Address:* 65 Locking Road, Weston-super-Mare.
Died 18 April 1921.

SUTTON, Maj.-Gen. Hugh Clement, CB 1916; CMG 1919; Lieutenant-Governor Royal Hospital, Chelsea, since 1923; *b* 20 Jan. 1867; *s* of late Henry George Sutton and 1st wife, Matilda Harriet, *e d* of G. H. Walker Heneage, Wilts; *g s* of Sir Richard Sutton, 2nd Bt; *m* 1st, (Mabel) Ida, *d* of Sir Campbell Munro, 3rd Bt, of Lindertis, and Henrietta, *d* of John Drummond; one *s*; 2nd, Hon. Alexandra Mary Elizabeth Wood, *d* of Viscount Halifax; three *d. Educ:* Eton; RMC, Sandhurst. Joined Coldstream Guards, 1887; Adjutant, 1894–98; served South African War with 2nd Batt. Coldstream Guards (despatches, Brevet of Major), and afterwards was Deputy Assistant Director of Railways; after the war was DAAG at Cape Town till 1906; Commanded 1st Batt. Coldstream Guards, 1910–13; AAG War Office, 1913–16; DAQMG with Army in France, 1916; Inspector-General of Communication, Home Forces, 1917; Deputy IGC Mesopotamia, 1918; IGC, 1919 (despatches four times, CMG,

Order of St Anne of Russia, 2nd class); Colonel i/c Administration, London District, 1920; Deputy Director Personal Services, War Office, 1921; Order of the Rising Sun, Japan, 3rd Class, 1921. *Address:* Royal Hospital, Chelsea, SW3. *T:* Victoria 7619. *Clubs:* Guards', Arthur's. *Died 15 April 1928.*

SUTTON, Sir Richard (Vincent), 6th Bt, *cr* 1772; Captain 1st Life Guards; *b* posthumously, 26 April 1891; *o c* of Sir Richard Francis Sutton, 5th Bt and Constance Edith, *d* of Sir Vincent Corbet, 3rd Bt (she *m* 2nd, 1895, Hubert Delaval Astley); *S* father, 1891. *Educ:* Eton. Served European War, 1914–17. Owned about 13,000 acres, exclusive of London estates. *Heir: uncle* Arthur Edwin Sutton [*b* 24 Sept. 1857; *m* 1885, Cecile Blanche, *d* of Walter Douglas Dumbleton, Cape Colony; one *s* one *d. Address:* Shanks, Wincanton, Somerset. *Club:* Junior Conservative]. *Address:* Benham-Valence, Newbury, Berks. *T:* Newbury 227; 41 South Audley Street, W. *T:* Mayfair 2992. *Clubs:* Naval and Military, Arthur's, St James's, Pratt's. *Died 29 Nov. 1918.*

SUYEMATSU, Viscount Kencho; Privy Councillor, Japan; BA, LLM Cantab; DLitt, LLD Tokyo Imperial Univ.; *b* Buzen, Kiusiu, Aug. 1855; *m e d* of Prince Ito. Was a civilian staff officer to Commander-in-Chief of the Imperial Force during Satsuina Rebellion, 1877; a Member of House of Commons, elected at the first formation of the Diet, 1890; created Baron, 1895, for distinguished service rendered in connection with the China War, since which time elected to the House of Peers by the Barons; Minister of Communications; Minister of Interior; Viscount, 1907. *Publications:* The Risen Sun; A Fantasy of Far Japan, 1905; English translation of Genji Monogatari; translation of Anderson's Pictorial Japan; translations and annotations of Justinian, of Gaius, of Ulpian, etc. *Address:* Shiba, Tokyo. *Died 5 Oct. 1920.*

SWABY, Rt. Rev. William Proctor, DD; FRGS; Bishop of Barbados and the Windward Islands since 1900; *b* 1844. *Educ:* Durham University (Exhibitioner and Barry Scholar). Vicar of Castletown, Durham, 1874–84; St Mark, Millfield, Durham, 1884–93; Bishop of Guiana, 1893–1900; Fellow, Royal Microscopical Society; Fellow, Colonial Institute. *Publication:* History of Hylton Castle, 1883. *Address:* Bishop's Court, Barbados, West Indies. *Club:* Royal Societies. *Died 16 Nov. 1916.*

SWAIN, Hon. Col George Llewellyn Douglas, CMG 1914; VD; *b* Corfu, Ionian Islands, 8 June 1858; 2nd *s* of late Assistant Commissary-General Charles Olton Swain, and Elisa Dominga Sanchez de Piña of Gibraltar; *m* 1899, Charlotte Elizabeth Mary (*d* 1921), *d* of Robert Patten, of Clone, Co. Wicklow; four *d. Educ:* schools in England and Ireland and Colonies; Harrison's College, Barbados. Clerk, Colonial Banks, Barbados and British Guiana, 1878–82; Paymaster Police Force, British Guiana, 1882–84; District Inspector of Police, 1884; training with Royal Irish Constabulary, 1890; County Inspector, British Guiana, 1892; Chief County Inspector and Second in Command, 1899; acted Inspector-General and Colonel Commandant Militia, British Guiana, 1902; Deputy Inspector-General, Constabulary, Trinidad, 1903; Inspector-General of Trinidad Constabulary, and Commandant Local Forces, 1907–16; Member of Executive and Legislative Councils, Trinidad and Tobago; Member of Commission to inquire into working of Poor Law Board, British Guiana; Member of Medical Inquiry Commission, Trinidad, 1911; served with Ashanti Expedition, 1895–96 (Star, special mention); Colonial Forces Decoration, VD, 1911; commanded Trinidad Coronation Contingent, 1911 (Coronation medal); Hythe Certificate Musketry, 1887. *Recreations:* shooting, fishing, etc. *Address:* c/o Capital and Counties Bank, Southsea. *Club:* Royal Albert Yacht, Southsea. *Died 1 May 1924.*

SWAIN, Joseph; Emeritus President Swarthmore College since 1921; *b* Pendleton, Ind, 16 June 1857; *s* of Mary A. and Woolston Swain; *m* Frances Morgan, Knightstown, Ind. *Educ:* Indiana University; University of Edinburgh. Professor of Mathematics, Indiana University, 1886–91; Leland Stanford University, 1891–93; President Indiana University, 1893–1902; Swarthmore College, 1902–21; Member National Councils of Education and of Religious Education; President Indiana State Teachers' Association, 1894; President Higher Education Section of National Education Association, 1897, President of Assoc., 1913–14; President National Council, 1907–10; LLD Wabash College, 1893, Lafayette College, 1912, University of Penn, 1912, Indiana University, 1920, Swarthmore College, 1921. *Publications:* numerous scientific and educational papers. *Recreation:* golf. *Address:* Swarthmore, Pennsylvania. *TA:* Swarthmore. *T:* Swarthmore 200. *Died 19 May 1927.*

SWAIN, Percival Francis, CBE 1919 (OBE 1918); Principal Clerk Public Trustee Office since 1917; *b* 1888; *s* of William A. Swain of Wynchcroft, Reading; *m* Winifred, 2nd *d* of late F. W. Balding, of Padworth, Berks. *Educ:* Reading School and University College, Reading. Qualified as Chartered Accountant, 1909; entered the office of the Public Trustee, 1910; Assistant Principal Clerk, 1915. *Address:* Dingley, Tilehurst-on-Thames, Berks. *Died 19 July 1924.*

SWAINE, Col Charles Edward, CB 1897; Assistant Adjutant-General for Cavalry, Headquarters, 1900–1; retired; *b* Hamburg, 20 Sept. 1844; *y s* of Robert Victor Swaine, sometime Consul-General for Belgium in Hamburg; unmarried. *Educ:* Louth Grammar School, Lincolnshire; private tutor; and Trin. Coll., Cambridge (MA). Joined 17th Lancers, 1868; Lieut 1870; Zulu Campaign, 1879; battle of Ulundi (medal and clasp); Adjutant 17th Lancers, July to Dec. 1879; Captain 11th Hussars, 1880; ADC to GOC Cavalry, Transvaal Campaign, 1881; ADC to GOC Cavalry, Egyptian Expedition, 1882; present at action of Mahuta; capture of Mahsameh; both actions of Kassassin; battle of Tel-el Kebir; pursuit to Belbeis; surrender and occupation of Cairo (medal with clasp, bronze star, 4th class Medjidie, Brev. of Major, despatches, 1882); Major, 1883; served with Light Camel Corps in Nile Expedition, 1884–85 (clasp); ADC and Mil. Private Sec. to Viceroy of Ireland, 1886–88; Lieut-Col 1891; commanded 11th Hussars, 1891–96; Colonel, 1895; 2nd Class Red Eagle of Prussia, 1901; 2nd Class Redeemer of Greece, 1910. *Address:* 88 St James's Street, SW1. *T:* Regent 2894. *Clubs:* Army and Navy, Turf. *Died 2 May 1928.*

SWAMIKANNU PILLAI, Louis Dominic, MA, LLB; Diwan Bahadur; CIE 1924; ISO 1917; President, Madras Legislative Council, Fort St George, since 1924; *b* 4 Feb. 1865; *m;* three *s* ten *d. Educ:* St Joseph's College, Negapatam. Assistant and Lecturer, St Joseph's College, Trichinopoly, 1883–87; Clerk to the Legislative Council and French Translator, Chief Secretariat, Fort St George, 1888–90; Latin Master, Presidency College, Madras, 1890–91; Deputy Collector and Magistrate, 1892–95; Assistant Secretary, Board of Revenue, Madras, 1895–1906; Secretary, Board of Revenue, Revenue Settlement, Madras, 1906–11; Registrar of Co-operative Societies, 1911–17; Collector and District Magistrate, 1917–19; Secretary to Government and Director of Agriculture, 1920; Secretary, Legislative Council, 1920–23; deputed to England to study House of Commons Procedure, April to July 1922; Fellow of Madras University, 1900; Chairman, Board of Examiners to Madras University in Greek, Latin, French, and German, 1903–17. *Publications:* Indian Chronology, 1911, 2nd edn 1922; Indian Ephemeris, AD 1800–2000, 1915, 2nd edn 1922; Indian Ephemeris, AD 700–1800, 6 vols, 1922 (Madras Government publication); various articles in Indian Antiquary and Epigraphia Indica on: Indian Chronology; Secret of Memory, 1909; Credibility of Indian Astrology, 1922; Maximum Age of Dhruva Nadi, 1923; Panchang and Horoscope, 1925. *Address:* Roseville, Royapuram, Madras, India. *Club:* Cosmopolitan, Madras. *Died Oct. 1925.*

SWANN, Frederick Samuel Philip, CIE 1915; Magistrate and Collector, United Provinces, 1911. *Educ:* Berkhampstead School; Magdalen College, Oxford. Entered ICS, 1893; Joint-Magistrate, 1903; Commissioner, 1909. *Died 30 Nov. 1921.*

SWANN, Harry Kirke, FZS; MBOU; Managing Director, Wheldon & Wesley, Ltd; *b* 18 March 1871. *Educ:* privately. Made ornithological researches in Spain, Roumania, and other parts of Europe, as well as in N America; Corr. Fell., Amer. Ornithol Union; Member, Internat. Ornithol Cttee; Vice-Pres., Barnet Boy Scouts Assoc.; formerly Editor of The Naturalist's Journal, The Ornithologist, The Naturalist's Directory, etc, and Editor and Literary Adviser to W. C. Nimmo. *Publications:* A Monograph of the Birds of Prey; Two Ornithologists on the Lower Danube; A Dictionary of English and Folk-names of British Birds; A Synopsis of the Accipitres; The Birds of London; A Concise Handbook of British Birds; Nature in Acadie; H. Kirke White (Canterbury Poets), etc; (with W. H. Mullens) A Bibliography of British Ornithology. *Recreations:* ornithology, zoology, foreign travel. *Address:* Thorncombe, Lyonsdown Road, New Barnet, Herts; 2, 3 and 4 Arthur Street, New Oxford Street, WC2. *Club:* Authors. *Died 14 April 1926.*

SWANSEA, 2nd Baron, *cr* 1893; **Ernest Ambrose Vivian,** DL, JP; Bt 1882; *b* 11 Feb. 1848; *s* of 1st Baron and 1st wife, Jessie Dalrymple, *d* of Ambrose Goddard, MP, The Lawn, Swindon; *S* father, 1894. *Educ:* Eton; Magdalen Coll., Oxford. *Heir: half-brother* Hon. Odo Richard Vivian [*b* 22 April 1875; *m* 1906, Hon. Winifred Hamilton, *d* of 1st Baron Holm-Patrick; one *d*]. *Address:* Singleton, Swansea. *Clubs:* Carlton, Athenæum, Bachelors'.

Died 17 July 1922.

SWANSON, Sir John Warren, Kt 1923; *b* 13 May 1865; *s* of late William Swanson, Caithness. *Educ:* Walker's School, Melbourne. Was President of Master Builders' Association, Melbourne, and of Federated Master Builders' Association; Lord Mayor of Melbourne, 1920. *Address:* Town Hall, Melbourne.

Died 4 Feb. 1924.

SWAYNE, Col Charles Henry, DSO 1898; late Royal Army Medical Corps; *b* Carrick-on-Shannon, Ireland, 18 Sept. 1848; 2nd *s* of late A. C. Swayne, JP, MD, Carrick-on-Shannon, and Anne, *d* of D. Brown; *m* 1896, Margaret Blakeney, *d* of late David Gillies, Londonderry; two *d. Educ:* private school; Ledwich School of Medicine, Dublin (prizeman in Medicine, Surgery, Midwifery). Appointed Staff Asst-Surg., 1872; Surg. 1973; Surg. Major 1886; Surgeon Lt-Col 1894; Brigade Surgeon Lt-Col 1897; Lt-Col Royal Army Medical Corps, 1898; Col 1902; retired Sept. 1905; served with distinction during the yellow fever in Trinidad, WI, 1881; in the Nile campaign, 1884–85, and thanked for services (medal, clasp, and Khedive's star); Burmese campaign, 1886–89 (specially reported for services, medal and two clasps), in charge No 6 Burmah Field Hosp.; Senior Medical Officer, 1st Brigade, Tirah Expeditionary Force, NWP, 1897–98 (medal and two clasps, despatches, DSO). *Recreations:* golfing, fishing, tennis. *Address:* 7 Palmerston Park, Dublin. *T:* Rathmines 670.

Died Aug. 1925.

SWAYNE, Charles Richard, CMG 1906; *b* 26 Aug. 1843; *s* of Rev. C. B. Swayne; *m* 1898, Frances Edith, *d* of Thomas Richard Pace. Stipendiary Magistrate, Colony of Fiji, 1878; had various administrative and executive offices in Fiji; Deputy Commissioner and First British Resident of Gilbert and Ellice Islands, 1896; retired, 1906. *Address:* Lifton House, St Marychurch, South Devon.

Died 11 June 1921.

SWAYNE, Maj.-Gen. James Dowell; Retired List, Indian Army; *b* Delhi, 9 Nov. 1827; *s* of Major Stephen Swayne, HEIC; *m* 1877, Mary Morris Cormack; one *s* one *d. Educ:* Blackheath New Proprietary School; Addiscombe HEIC Military College. Joined 11th Bengal Native Infantry; after eight years with the 11th Native Infantry obtained an appointment in the Public Works Department, in which he remained until he retired from the service, 1878. *Recreations:* cricket chiefly. *Address:* 4 Vanbrugh Park, Blackheath, SE.

Died 6 Dec. 1916.

SWAYNE, Prof. Walter Carless, VD; MD, BS (London); MD, ChB (Bristol); MRCS, LRCP; Professor of Obstetrics, and Director of Clinical Obstetrics, Bristol University, since 1909; Consulting Obstetric Physician, Bristol Royal Infirmary; *b* 1862; *e s* of R. A. Swayne, JP, Tillington Court, Hereford; *m* Louisa Margaret, *d* of late Rev. R. F. Heath; one *s* three *d. Educ:* King Edward's School, Birmingham; University College, Bristol; Guy's Hospital. Fellow Royal Society of Medicine. Major TF Reserve, late Comdg 1st Battery Glos RFA (TF); Bristol Univ. Contingent, OTC (SD); 3/1st SM Glos Brig. and NZ Reserve Field Ambulance (attached). *Recreations:* fly-fishing, riding, shooting. *Address:* Clarence House, 2 Clifton Park, Clifton. *T:* Bristol 2620. *Club:* Clifton.

Died 14 Aug. 1925.

SWAYTHLING, 2nd Baron, *cr* 1907; **Louis Samuel Montagu,** JP; 2nd Bt 1894; *b* 10 Dec. 1869; *e s* of 1st Baron Swaythling and Ellen, *y d* of late Louis Cohen, of the Stock Exchange; 1st Baron assumed name of Montagu by Royal Licence; *S* father, 1911; *m* 1898, Gladys Helen Rachel, *d* of late Col Albert Edward Williamson Goldsmid, MVO; three *s* one *d*. Head of the banking firm of Samuel Montagu & Co., London; owned about 1,200 acres. *Heir: s* Hon. Stuart Albert Samuel Montagu [*b* 19 Dec. 1898; *m* 1925, Mary Violet, *e d* of Major Walter Henry Levy, DSO, and Nellie, *d* of 1st Viscount Bearsted]. *Address:* 28 Kensington Court, W8. *T:* Western 800; Townhill Park, Bitterne, near Southampton. *Clubs:* Reform, Bath; Royal Southern Yacht.

Died 11 June 1927.

SWEENEY, Hon. Francis J.; KC; *b* 1862. *Educ:* St Joseph's College, New Brunswick. Was for some years a school teacher; called to the Bar, 1902; Member for Westmorland, New Brunswick, 1903; Member Provincial Government, 1903–4; Member, Exec. Council, NB, 1905; Solicitor-General, 1904–5; Surveyor-General, 1905–8. *Address:* Moncton, New Brunswick, Canada.

Died 2 May 1921.

SWEENY, Lt-Col Roger Lewis Campbell, DSO 1916; OBE 1922; MC; Indian Army Service Corps; *b* 21 Nov. 1878; *s* of Col James Fielding Sweeny, British Service; *m* 1902, Hilda, *d* of late G. Lumgair, Collector of Customs, Mauritius; one *s* two *d. Educ:* Montreal, Quebec, and Royal Military College, Kingston, Ontario, Canada. 2nd Lieut Unattached List for Indian Army, 1899; Lieut 1901; Captain, 1908; Major, 1915; Lt-Col, 1924; on field service in Jubaland, BEA, March–July 1914; in East Africa, Oct. 1914–May 1917 (despatches twice, DSO, MC); Egyptian Expeditionary Force, June–Dec. 1918; operations against Afghanistan, May–Nov. 1919; operations in Waziristan, 1919–20 (despatches, OBE). *Address:* c/o Grindlay & Co., 54 Parliament Street, SW1.

Died Oct. 1926.

SWETE, Henry Barclay, DD (Cambridge and Glasgow), LittD (Dublin and Oxford); FBA 1902; Regius Professor of Divinity, University of Cambridge, 1890–1915; Emeritus Professor, 1915; *b* Redlands, Bristol, 14 March 1835; *s* of Rev. John Swete, DD, and 2nd wife, Caroline Ann Skinner Barclay; unmarried. *Educ:* King's College, London; Gonville and Caius College, Cambridge. Deacon, 1858; Priest, 1859; Fellow of Caius College, 1858–77; Hon. Fellow, 1886–90; re-elected Fellow, 1890; Dean, Tutor and Theological Lecturer, Caius College, 1869–77; Rector of Ashdon, Essex, 1877–90; Professor of Pastoral Theology, King's College, London, 1882–90; Fellow of King's College, London, 1891; Examining Chaplain to Bishop of St Albans, 1881–90; Hon. Canon of Ely, 1906; Hon. Chaplain to King George V, 1911. *Publications:* two essays on History of the Doctrine of the Holy Spirit, 1873, 1876; Theodore of Mopsuestia's Commentary on the Epistles of St Paul, 1880–82; contributions to Smith and Wace's Dictionary of Christian Biography (vols iii and iv), 1882–87; and to Hastings' Dictionary of the Bible (vols ii and iii), 1899–1900; The Old Testament in Greek according to the Septuagint, 3 vols, 1887–94 (3rd edn 1901-7); The Akhmim Fragment of the Gospel of Peter, 1893; The Apostles' Creed in relation to Primitive Christianity, 1894 (3rd edn 1899); Faith in Relation to Creed, Thought, and Life, 1895; Church Services and Service Books before the Reformation, 1896; The Gospel according to St Mark: the Greek Text, with Introduction, Notes, and Indices, 1898 (2nd edn 1902); An Introduction to the Old Testament in Greek, 1900 (2nd edn 1902); Patristic Study, 1902; Studies in the Teaching of our Lord, 1903; The Apocalypse of St John: the Greek Text with Introduction, Notes, and Indices, 1906 (2nd edn 1907); The Appearances of our Lord after the Passion, 1907 (2nd edn 1908); The Holy Spirit in the New Testament, 1909; The Ascended Christ, 1910; The Holy Spirit in the Ancient Church, 1912; The Last Discourse and Prayer of our Lord, 1913; The Holy Catholic Church; The Communion of Saints, 1915; Editor of Cambridge Theological Essays, 1905; and Cambridge Biblical Essays, 1909. *Recreation:* reading works of fiction. *Address:* 23 Old Park Road, Hitchin.

Died 10 May 1917.

SWETENHAM, Clement William; retired Lieutenant-Commander Royal Navy, 1882; Chairman of Congleton Petty Sessional Division; *b* 1852; *e s* of Clement Swetenham of Somerford Booths, Cheshire; *m* Louisa, *y d* of Ralph Creyke of Marton and Rawcliffe Halls, Yorkshire. *Educ:* HMS Britannia. *Address:* Somerford Booths, Congleton. *TA:* Lower-Withington. *M:* 5712. *Club:* Naval and Military.

Died 12 Dec. 1927.

SWIFTE, Sir Ernest Godwin, Kt 1921; Chief Metropolitan Police Magistrate, Dublin, 1910–21; *b* 3 June 1839; *o s* of late William Richard Swifte, of Whitechurch Lodge, Co. Dublin, and Elizabeth Catherine (*d* 1887), *d* and *co-heiress* of Rev. Daniel Kelly, of Dawson's Grove, Co. Armagh; *m* 1869, Frances (*d* 1925), *d* of late Robert Coddington, of Kilmoon, Co. Meath; three *s* one *d. Educ:* private school in England; Trinity College, Dublin. MA University of Dublin. Called to the Irish Bar, 1863; KC 1911; appointed a Metropolitan Police Magistrate of Dublin, 1890. *Address:* 18 Fitzwilliam Square, Dublin. *T:* Dublin 61776.

Died 7 May 1927.

SWINBURNE, Hon. George, MICE, MIMechE; *b* Newcastle-on-Tyne, 1861; *s* of M. W. Swinburne; *m* 1890, Ethel, *d* of Rev. D. Jones Hamer, Wolverhampton and Melbourne; four *d. Educ:* Royal Grammar School, Newcastle-on-Tyne. Arrived in Australia, 1886; practised as engineer; initiated several large hydraulic and gas undertakings; Member of Parliament for Hawthorn, Vic, 1902–13; Minister of Water Supply and Agriculture, Vic, 1904–8; author of Water Acts on which Government Irrigation policy was founded, and which nationalised all the waters in the rivers and streams of the State; Member of four Interstate Conferences of State and Federal Ministries to consider financial and other questions; Member of the Interstate Commission for the Commonwealth, 1913–17; Controlled issue of Capital and Companies, and Chairman Business Board

Defence Department during War of 1914–18; Member State of Victoria Electricity Commission; Chairman Mount Lyell Railway and Mining Co.; Director National Mutual Life Association, Electrolytic Zinc Co. of Australia, etc. *Address:* Shenton, Kinkora Road, Hawthorn, Melbourne. *Clubs:* Melbourne, Australian, Melbourne.

Died 4 Sept. 1928.

SWINBURNE, Lt-Col Thomas Robert, of Pontop Hall, Durham; *b* 4 Oct. 1853; *e s* of late Capt. T. A. Swinburne, RN, of Pontop Hall, and Eilean Shona, Inverness-shire; *m* 1886, Louise Gertrude, *e d* of late Robert Stewart of Kinlochmoidart; one *d.* Entered the Royal Marine Artillery, 1872; served in Egypt, 1882 (despatches); Sudan, 1884–85 (medal and clasp). Address; Reeds, Liss, Hants; 23 Eaton Place, SW1. *T:* Victoria 2557. *Club:* United Service.

Died 8 Oct. 1921.

SWINDLEY, Maj.-Gen. John Edward, CB 1907; *b* 21 March 1831. Entered army, 1847; Lt-Col 1874; retired, 1884; served Kaffir War, 1852–53 (medal); Crimea, 1855–56 (medal with clasp, Turkish medal); Indian Mutiny, 1858–59 (medal); Afghan War, 1879 (despatches). *Address:* Raleigh House, Raleigh Drive, Esher, Surrey. *Club:* Army and Navy. *Died 11 March 1919.*

SWINEY, Maj.-Gen. John; Indian Army; *b* 9 Feb. 1832; *m* 1871, Rosa, *d* of Major J. Biggs, 4th Dragoon Guards. Entered army, 1849; Maj.-Gen. 1890; unemployed list, 1890; served Indian Mutiny, 1857–59. *Address:* Sandford Lawn, Bath Road, Cheltenham. *Clubs:* Primrose, New, Cheltenham.

Died 17 May 1918

SWINFEN, 1st Baron, *cr* 1919, of Chertsey; **Charles Swinfen Eady,** Kt 1901; PC 1913; *b* 31 July 1851; 2nd *s* of George John Eady, surgeon, Chertsey, and Laura Maria, *d* of Richard Smith, physician; *m* 1894, Blanche Maude, *yr d* of Sydney Williams Lee, Putney Hill; one *s* two *d. Educ:* privately; London Univ. Called to the Bar, Inner Temple, 1879; Bencher, 1901; QC 1893; Judge of the Chancery Division, High Court of Justice, 1901–13; Lord Justice of Appeal, 1913–18; Chairman of the Council of Legal Education; Member of the Senate of the University of London. *Address:* 23 Hyde Park Gardens W. *T:* Padd. 2078; Wood Norton, Evesham, Worcester. *Clubs:* Athenæum, St Stephen's.

Died 15 Nov. 1919.

SWINLEY, Maj.-Gen. George, CB 1893; late Royal Bengal Artillery; *b* 24 April 1842; *s* of late Maj.-Gen. George Henry Swinley, RA; *m* 1873, Alice (*d* 1922), *d* of W. G. Probyn; three *d. Educ:* Harrow; HEIC Coll., Addiscombe. Entered army, 1860; Maj.-Gen. 1895; served Bhootan Field Force, 1865–66 (medal with clasp); Black Mountain Expedition, 1868 (clasp); Jowaki Afreedee Expedition, 1877–78 (despatches, clasp); Afghan War, 1878–80 (despatches several times, brevets of Major and Lt-Col, medal with three clasps, bronze decoration). *Address:* 2 Fauconberg Villas, Bayshill Road, Cheltenham. *T:* Cheltenham 736. *Club:* New, Cheltenham.

Died 26 July 1924.

SWINNY, Shapland Hugh; editor of the Positivist Review; President of the London Positivist Society since 1901, and of the English Positivist Committee since 1904; *b* Dublin, 30 Dec. 1857. *Educ:* St John's College, Cambridge (MA 1884). Member of the Council of the Sociological Society from its foundation (Chairman, 1907–9); Secretary of the South Africa Conciliation Committee, 1900–2; Treasurer of the Nationalities and Subject Races Committee, 1908–13; Vice-President, Irish Literary Society, London; visited India, America, the Near East, Portugal, etc, and wrote on India and in defence of the Portuguese Republic; a life-long advocate of the Anglo-French alliance. *Publications:* The History of Ireland, 1890; The Day of All the Dead, 1892; joint-editor of the New Calendar of Great Men, 1902; a frequent contributor to periodicals. *Recreation:* travel. *Club:* National Liberal. *Died 31 Aug. 1923.*

SWINSTEAD, George Hillyard, RI; RCA; artist painter; Vice-President Hampstead Society of Artists; *b* 1860; 4th *s* of Charles Swinstead, artist, and Jane Hillyard of Ipswich; *m* 1887, Rosalie, 3rd *d* of late John Sheppard Edmonds of Highgate, two *d. Educ:* Royal Academy Schools, 1881. Chorister in Queen Victoria's Private Chapel Choir, Windsor, from 11 to 16 years of age; exhibited first picture at 17 years of age; first picture exhibited at Royal Academy in 1882; member of The Worshipful Company of Painter Stainers; *works:* By Appointment; When Trumpets Call; When the Heart is Young; The First Step; Baby's Own; Wild Flowers and Thorns; Across the Bridge of Time; Lilies; Reunited; Song of the Sailors on a Nile Dahabeah; The Road from Gizeh to Cairo; A Wild-Flower; First on the Antarctic

Continent; The Early Days of Golf; A Church Window; Poppy Land; Violets; Pomona's Blossom; The Angel's Message; The White Horse; Home from the Meadows; Wanderers; Steady; Blossoms; My Little Bird; Haven under the Hill; Black and Ivory; The Wounded Wanderer; The White Cliff; Hardanger Fjord; The Pathway of Light; Pandora; A Summer Reverie; Polperro Harbour; Francis Belsey; The White Comrade; The Boy Scouts; Boy Scouts Stalking; The Bay of Villefranche; many portraits. *Publication:* My Old World Garden, and how I made it in a London Suburb. *Recreations:* cricket, golf, etc. *Address:* 14 Kidderpore Avenue, Hampstead, NW3. *T:* Hampstead 5214. *Clubs:* MCC; Northwood Golf.

Died 16 Jan. 1926.

SWINSTEAD, Rev. John Howard, MA, DD; Vicar, St Peter's, Bayswater, and Surrogate; *b* 14 July 1864; *s* of Charles Swinstead, artist; *m* 1st, Agnes Marion Thomas, *d* of Elias Squarey, Downton; 2nd, Hannah Sclater, *d* of George Humphrey, West Dene; two *d. Educ:* City of London School (Saddlers' Company Scholar); St Catharine's College, Cambridge (Classical Scholar and librarian; BA 1886, MA 1890). Assistant Master, NECS, Barnard Castle, and Dover College; Head of Cathedral Choir School, Oxford; Curate St Mary's, Dover, Marylebone, and Cathedral and Close of Salisbury; St Andrew's Missioner, Sarum; Chaplain, Christ Church, Oxford (MA and DD); Vicar of Chalgrove-cum-Berrick, Oxon; Chaplain to HBM's Legation, Sweden; Fellow of Royal Botanic Society; Liveryman of Guild of Saddlers; Chaplain to the Guild of Showmen; Chaplain to St Luke's Hospital, W2; Lecturer, Christian Evidence Society. *Publications:* A Parish on Wheels; Chalgrove Field and John Hampden; In a Wonderful Order; Brought to the Bishop; History of English Church, Stockholm; Through English Eyes; The Cradle of the Swedish Church; The Swedish Church and Ours; After Fifty Years. *Recreations:* cricket, golf, lawn tennis. *Address:* 13 Ladbroke Gardens, W11. *T:* Park 1980.

Died 28 Aug. 1924.

SWINTON, Lt-Col Francis Edward, CIE 1919; Indian Medical Service, retired; *b* 1866; *e surv. s* of late Robert Blair Swinton, Madras Civil Service (late HEICS); unmarried. *Educ:* St Bartholomew's Hospital. Medical Officer, 28th Bombay Pioneers; Personal Asst to PMO Bombay Command; Med. Store Keeper to Government, Bombay; Deputy Director-General IMS; Med. Store Keeper to Government, Madras; retired, 1922. *Recreation:* navigation. *Clubs:* United Service, Simla; Byculla, Royal Bombay Yacht, Bombay; Madras; Western India, Poona.

Died 23 Dec. 1927.

SWINTON, Captain George Herbert Tayler; retired; *b* 25 Dec. 1852; *o s* of Archibald Adam Swinton, Bengal Civil Service; *m* 1885, Mary M'Chlery, *d* of S. Becher, BCS; one *s* one *d. Educ:* Cheltenham College. Joined Royal Brecknock Rifle Militia, 1871; transferred as Lieutenant to 2nd Batt. 16th Bedfordshire Regt, 1874; Captain, 1884; retired, 1893; JP Berwickshire. *Recreations:* shooting, fishing. *Address:* Swinton, Berwickshire. *M:* SH 327.

Died 19 Sept. 1923.

SWINTON, John Liulf Campbell, VD; JP and DL Berwickshire; *b* 3 March 1858; *e s* of late Archibald Campbell Swinton, LLD, of Kimmerghame, and 2nd wife, Georgiana Caroline, 3rd *d* of Sir George Sitwell, 2nd Bt; *m* 1893, Agnes Cecil, *y d* of late George Towry White, barrister-at-law; one *d.* Late Major 2nd (Berwickshire) Vol. Batt. King's Own Scottish Borderers; Member Royal Company of Archers, King's Body Guard for Scotland. *Recreations:* salmon-fishing, shooting, bridge. *Address:* Kimmerghame, near Duns, NB. *Clubs:* Carlton; New, Edinburgh; Royal Highland Yacht, Oban.

Died 6 Sept. 1920.

SWITHINBANK, Harold William, FRSE; FRGS; *b* 1858; *s* of late George Edwin Swithinbank, LLD, FSA; *m* 1883, Amy, *d* of James Crossley Eno of Wood Hall, Dulwich, Kent; one *s* two *d.* Late Lieutenant and Adjutant, 11th Hussars; Captain, Middlesex Yeomanry, and Reserve of Officers; Commander RNR for Special War Service, 1914; DL, JP Bucks; High Sheriff, 1891; member of first Buckinghamshire County Council; Governor of Royal Agricultural Society of England; Vice-President of Royal Veterinary College. *Publications:* Bacteriology of Milk; various papers to Royal Society and other kindred bodies. *Address:* Denham Court, Denham, Bucks; 2 Sussex Gardens, W2. *T:* Paddington 2829. *Clubs:* Naval and Military, Cavalry; Royal Yacht Squadron, Cowes; Royal Thames Yacht.

Died 9 Feb. 1928.

SYKES, Sir Henry, 6th Bt, *cr* 1781; *b* 9 Dec. 1828; 3rd *s* of Sir Francis William Sykes, 3rd Bt and Henrietta, *d* of Henry Villebois, of Marham

Hall, Norfolk; S brother, 1899; m Mary Winifred, d of Henry Tuck. Joined RN; late Capt. Royal Dragoons; served in Crimean War (medal). Heir: kinsman Arthur Sykes, b 2 Sept. 1871. Address: 2 Greenhill Terrace, Weymouth, Dorset.

Died 10 April 1916.

SYKES, Lt-Col Sir Mark, 6th Bt, cr 1783; JP; FRGS; MP (U) Central Hull since 1911; b 16 March 1879; o s of Sir Tatton Sykes, 5th Bt and Christina Anne Jessica, e d of Rt Hon. George Augustus Cavendish-Bentinck, MP; S father, 1913; m 1903, Edith Violet, 3rd d of late Rt Hon. Sir John E. Gorst; three s three d. Educ: Beaumont; Ecole des Jesuites, Monaco; Institut St Louis, Brussels; Jesus College, Cambridge. Served South Africa, 1902; Hon. Captain in the Army, 1902; Captain 3rd Battalion Yorkshire Regiment, 1902–7; Major 5th Batt. Yorkshire Regt, 1908; Lt-Col 1911; Member NR Territorial Force Association; CC ER Yorks; contested Buckrose Div. of ER, Jan. and Dec. 1910; traveller and diplomat in Middle East. Publications: Through Five Turkish Provinces, 1900; (with Edmund T. Sandars) Tactics and Military Training by Maj.-Gen. D'Ordel, 1902; Pantechnicon (ditto), 1904; Dar-ul-Islam, 1904; Five Mansions of the House of Othman, 1909; The Caliphs' Last Heritage, 1915; contributions to journals and reviews. Heir: s Mark Tatton Richard Sykes, b 24 Aug. 1905. Address: Sledmere, Malton, Yorks. Clubs: Carlton, Marlborough, Beefsteak, Prince's, 1900; Yorkshire, York.

Died 16 Feb. 1919.

SYLVA, Carmen, (nom de plume of Queen Elizabeth (Pauline Elizabeth Ottilie Louise) of Roumania); b Neuwied, Germany, 29 December 1843; d of late Prince Hermann of Wied and the Princess Maria of Nassau; m 1869, Prince Charles, later King of Roumania, 2nd s of Prince Anthony of Hohenzollern (d 1914); one d (b 1870; d 1874). Travelled, 1863–68; Roumania declared a kingdom, 1881, and on 22 May of same year she was crowned Queen; member Academy of Sciences of Bucharest, 1882; visited England, 1890. Publications: Thoughts of a Queen, 1890; Edleen Vaughan, 1892; Shadows on Life's Dial, 1895; A Real Queen's Fairy Book, 1901; In Memory's Shrine; Sweet Hours; and many poems, novelettes, fairy-tales, and dramas. Address: Bucharest, Roumania.

Died 2 May 1916.

SYLVESTER, Asst Surgeon Henry Thomas, VC 1857; MD, LRCSE, LSA; b 16 April 1831. Served at siege and fall of Sebastopol, 1855 (despatches, medal with clasp, VC, Kt of Legion of Honour); Indian Campaign, 1857–58, including relief of Lucknow (medal with two clasps); retired, 1861. Decorated for dressing wounds of an officer under heavy fire.

Died March 1920.

SYLVESTER, Rev. Samuel Augustus Kirwan; Vicar of Roby, near Liverpool, since 1885; Rural Dean of Prescot; Hon. Canon of Liverpool; Hon. Chaplain to the Bishop of Liverpool; b 1852; 4th s of George Mairis Sylvester of Trowbridge, Wiltshire; m 1880, Harriet Eliza (d 1917), e d of Henry H. Hornby of Beechwood, Aigburth, Liverpool. Educ: Epsom College; New College, Oxford. Curate of Huyton, 1875; Priest, 1876; Curate of Windermere Parish Church, 1879. Address: The Vicarage, Roby, Liverpool. TA: Roby. Club: Athenæum, Liverpool.

Died 22 Nov. 1928.

SYM, Maj.-Gen. Sir John Munro, KCB 1908 (CB 1889); b Edinburgh, 15 Feb. 1839; o s of Rev. John Sym of Free Greyfriars Church, Edinburgh, and Catharine Glassfurd, o d of Lieut-Col John Munro, HEICS; m 1870, Eliza d'Oyley Vincent, o d of Major Hugh Rees James, CB, Indian Staff Corps; one s. Educ: High School and University, Edinburgh. 58th Bengal Infantry, 1858; 5th Gurkha Rifles, 1863; Capt. 1870; Major, 1878; Brev. Lieut-Col 1881; Lieut-Col 1884; Col 1885; Major-Gen. 1896; Hon. Col 5th Gurkha Rifles, 1916. Field Services: NW Frontier of India; Umbeyla, 1863 (medal with clasp); Hazara, 1868 (clasp); Afghanistan, 1879–80 (three times in despatches, medal with 3 clasps, bronze star and Brevet of Lieut-Col); NW Frontier of India, Hazara, 1883; commanded 1st, Col 1st Brigade (despatches, clasp and CB); 2nd, Miranzai, 1891; commanded 1st Brigade (despatches, clasp) in Hazara. Decorated for services in Hazara. Recreations: shooting, fishing, golf. Address: 4 Belgrave Place, Edinburgh. Club: New, Edinburgh.

Died 5 Oct. 1919.

SYMES, Rev. John Elliotson; b London, 31 Dec. 1847; 2nd s of E. S. Symes, MD. Educ: University Coll. School, London; Downing Coll., Cambridge (MA). Cambridge University Extension Lecturer, 1875–80; Second Master Royal Grammar School, Newcastle-on-Tyne, 1880–81; Professor of English Literature, etc, University Coll., Nottingham, 1881–96; Principal of University College, Nottingham, 1890–1912. Publications: Newcastle Sermons, 1882; Political Economy, 12th edn 1920; The Prelude to Modern History, 1890;

The French Revolution, 2nd edn 1904; Broad Church, 1913. Address: 78 Elsham Road, W14.

Died 31 March 1921.

SYMINGTON, Johnson, MD (Edin.); LLD Belfast, FRCSE; FRS 1903; late Professor of Anatomy, Registrar and Member of Senate and of Statutory Commission, Queen's University, of Belfast; b 1851. Educ: Taunton; Edin. Univ. Ex-Fellow and Examiner in Anatomy, Royal Univ. of Ireland; President of Section of Anthropology, British Association, Southport, 1903; of Anatomical Society of Great Britain and Ireland, 1904–5–6. Publications: The Topographical Anatomy of the Child; An Atlas of Skiagrams of the Teeth (with Dr Rankin); An Atlas on the Topography of the Head and Neck, Thorax and Abdomen; one of the editors of Quain's Anatomy; numerous papers on human and comparative anatomy. Address: 4 Montague Street, WC1.

Died 24 Feb. 1924.

SYMMONS, Israel Alexander, LLB; Police Magistrate, Greenwich and Woolwich, 1911; Clerkenwell, 1916; Marylebone since 1922; b 1862; m 1895, d of Jonas Drucquer. Barrister, Middle Temple, 1885. Address: 31 Sheriff Road, Kilburn, NW. Clubs: Garrick, British Empire.

Died 31 July 1923.

SYMONDS, Captain Frederick Cleave Loder-, JP; Chairman of Faringdon Petty Sessional Division; Alderman Berkshire County Council; late Royal Artillery; b 1846; e s of late James Frederick Symonds, JP, of Okeleigh, Hereford; succeeded cousin, John Loder-Symonds, of Hinton Manor, and assumed the additional name of Loder by Royal Licence; m 1873, Isabel Emily Annette, d of late Captain John Parland, Russian Imperial Guard; one s two d. Educ: Royal Military College, Woolwich. Publication: A History of the Old Berkshire Hunt. Recreations: shooting, motoring (took part in 1912 in the motor contest between the Royal Auto Club and Imperial German Club organised by Prince Henry of Prussia). Address: Hinton Manor, Faringdon. TA: Longworth. T: Kingston Bagpuize 7. M: BL 1, BL 115, and BL 215. Club: Army and Navy.

Died 27 Dec. 1923.

SYMONDS, Rev. William, MA; Rector and Patron of the Advowson of Stockport Parish Church since 1875; b 2 April 1832; s of Stephen Symonds of Handforth, Cheshire; m 1867, Maria (d 1905), d of Charles Sainsbury of Court Hill, Potterne, Wilts; three s four d. Educ: privately; Gonville and Caius College, Cambridge (Junior Optime). Deacon, 1856; Curacies, St Simon's, Salford, St Stephen's, Camden Town, Parish Church, Croydon; Priest, 1859; Rector of Greystoke, 1871–75; Hon. Canon Chester Cathedral, 1886; Rural Dean of Stockport, 1889–1905; Assessor Surrogate; during incumbency Parish Church restored, Almshouses rebuilt, Offerton Schools built, St Albans's, Offerton, built and endowed, Mission Churches built, St Stephen's and St Andrew's National Schools rebuilt. Publications: Forty Rectors of Stockport; Six Weeks in Ægean Sea. Address: Stockport.

Died 15 March 1919.

SYMONS, Lt-Col Frank Albert, DSO 1915; MB; Royal Army Medical Corps; b 28 April 1869. Educ: Edinburgh. Captain, 1896; Major, 1904; Lt-Col, 1915; served S African War, 1899–1900 (Queen's medal, 3 clasps); European War, 1914–15 (despatches, DSO).

Died 30 April 1917.

SYMONS, Capt. Thomas Raymond, JP, DL; b 30 March 1866; o s of Thomas George Symonds (d 1868), and 2nd wife, Mary Hayley, y d of late Rev. Thomas Edward Allen; m 1888, Margaret Ethel, 2nd d of Sir James Rankin, 1st Bt; one s. Educ: Eton. High Sheriff, Herefordshire, 1894; Patron of Much Birch; late Captain Imperial Yeomanry in S Africa, and Lieut N Somerset Imperial Yeomanry; previously Lieut Royal Monmouthshire Engineer Militia. Address: The Mynde Park, Hereford. Club: Badminton.

Died 26 July 1922.

SYMPSON, Edward Mansel, JP City of Lincoln; MA, MD Cantab; FSA; Hon. Lieutenant-Colonel Royal Army Medical Corps (Territorial Forces); Surgeon Lincoln County Hospital; Consulting Surgeon, General Dispensary; President, Midland Branch, British Medical Association, 1906–7; b 22 March 1860; o c of Thomas Sympson, FRCS, of Lincoln, and Caroline, d of Rev. E. Peacock, MA, Fifehead Magdalene, Dorset; m 1888, Florence Mabel, y d of Joseph Knight, FSA, Barrister-at-law, of 27 Camden Square, NW; one s. Educ: Lincoln Grammar School; Shrewsbury School; Gonville and Caius College, Cambridge; St Bartholomew's Hospital. Edited Cambridge Review; was House Physician and House Surgeon at St Bartholomew's Hospital; in practice in Lincoln since 1888; Fellow, Medical Society of London; associate editor Quarterly Medical Journal; Hon. Local Secretary Society of Antiquaries; editor

Lincolnshire Notes and Queries; co-Editor Associated Architectural Societies' Reports and Papers; Hon. Treasurer Lincolnshire Architectural Society; Governor Christ's Hospital and Girls' High School, Lincoln; ex-Chairman of the Lincoln Conservative and Liberal Unionist Association; Member of Council National Union Conservative Association; Vice-President, Royal Archæological Institute (Lincoln Meeting). *Publications:* Lincoln, a Historical and Topographical History of; Lincolnshire (Cambridge County Geographies); editor of Memorials of Old Lincolnshire; many articles and papers in professional and archæological journals. *Recreation:* archæology. *Address:* Deloraine Court, Lincoln. *TA:* Sympson, Lincoln. *T:* Lincoln 32.   *Died 15 Jan. 1922.*

SYNGE, Sir Francis Robert Millington, 6th Bt, *cr* 1801; *b* 27 May 1851; *s* of Sir Robert Synge, 5th Bt and 2nd wife, Laura, *d* of John Hart; *S* father, 1894; *m* 1st, 1876, Frances (*d* 1911), *d* of Robert Evans, Rock Ferry, Cheshire; three *s* three *d*; 2nd, 1912, Fanny Cecil, *d* of late Charles Robert Wade-Gery, Wornditch Hall, Kimbolton; one *d*. Major South Lancashire Regt, 1898–99; Adjutant 4th Batt. Liverpool Regt, 1890–95. *Heir: s* Robert Millington Synge, *b* 17 Nov. 1877. *Address:* 101 Eaton Terrace, SW1. *T:* Victoria 7451. *Address:* Syngefield, Birr, King's Co.

Died 1 March 1924.

SYNGE, Major Mark, (Powell Millington), CIE 1919; DSO 1917; Indian Army Supply and Transport Corps; *b* 25 April 1871; *y s* of late Joshua Sing, Aigburth, near Liverpool, JP; *m* 1899, Beatrice Ellen, *d* of late Sir William White Cooper; one *s* three *d*. *Educ:* Shrewsbury; Christ Church, Oxford. Entered Army, 1894; medals Punjab Frontier, 1897–98; Abor, 1911–12; served European war, 1914–17 (despatches twice, DSO). *Publications:* (1) unofficial, under the *nom de plume* Powell Millington: In Cantonments, 1898; In and Beyond Cantonments, 1904; To Lhassa at Last, 1905; A Homeward Mail, 1907; On the Track of the Abor, 1912; (2) official (as a publication of the Government of India): Certain Subjects taught to Officers at the London School of Economics, 1909; Elementary Economics as an aid to the Supply and Transport Office, 1918. *Recreations:* golfing, climbing, riding. *Club:* Rawal Pindi.   *Died 11 July 1921.*

SYNGE, Sir Robert Follett, KCMG 1919 (CMG 1897); HM Deputy Marshal of the Ceremonies, Foreign Office, since 1902; *b* 8 Dec. 1858; *e s* of late William Webb Follett Synge; *m* 1881, Laura Mary, *d* of late John C. Fletcher, Dale Park, Arundel. *Educ:* Charterhouse. Lieut in Royal Surrey Militia; appointed to the Treaty Department of Foreign Office, 1884; appointed to assist the Master of the Ceremonies, 1894; Assistant Marshal of the Ceremonies, 1899; Secretary to Lord Wolseley's Special Mission to announce the accession of King Edward VII, 1901; to Lord Roberts' Special Mission to announce the acccession of King George V, 1910; received the Jubilee Medal for 1887, and clasp for 1897; Coronation Medal, 1902, and several foreign decorations; Officer Legion of Honour. *Decorated for services in connection with the Queen's Diamond Jubilee. Address:* 7 Chester Square, SW1. *T:* Victoria 7899. *Clubs:* St James's, London Fencing, Princes' Golf.   *Died 22 Jan. 1920.*

SYNNOTT, Nicholas Joseph; JP Co. Kildare; *b* 1856; *e s* of late Thomas Synnott, JP, of Innismore, Co. Dublin, and Catherine, *d* of J. Dunne; *m* 1891, Barbara, *d* of J. MacEvoy Netterville, and Hon. Mary Netterville, *d* and *heiress* of 7th Viscount Netterville of Dowth, Co. Meath; two *s* four *d*. *Educ:* Stonyhurst College; University of London (BA 1877). Called to the Bar, Middle Temple, 1879; joined the Northern Circuit; contested seat at the London County Council, 1895; High Sheriff of Co. Kildare, 1906; Governor of the Bank of Ireland and director of the Great Southern and Western Railway; chairman of the Naas Board of Guardians, 1899–1905; member of Royal Commission on Income Tax, 1919; gave evidence before the Royal Commission on University Education in Ireland and on the Local Taxation Commission. *Publications:* pamphlets and articles on the Irish University question, on the valuation of land, on Irish financial questions. *Address:* Furness, Naas, Co. Kildare. *T:* Naas 3X. *Clubs:* Garrick; Stephen's Green, Dublin.

Died 13 Aug. 1920.

SZCZEPANSKI, Maj.-Gen. Henry Charles Antony; Indian Army; *b* 21 Jan. 1841. Entered army, 1857; Maj.-Gen. 1897; retired list 1897; served Indian Mutiny, 1857–58 (medal); Assistant Commissioner, Punjab, 1860; Hyderabad, 1864; in turns Cantonment Magistrate and Small Cause Court Judge and Deputy Commissioner; Judicial Commissioner, 1894–95; Officiating Commissioner, 1888–89; reverted to military department, 1895.

Died 2 June 1923.

SZLUMPER, Sir James Weeks, Kt 1894; JP Surrey and JP and DL, Cardiganshire; MInstCE; *b* 29 Jan. 1834; *m* 1867, Mary (*d* 1914), *d* of James Culliford, Bristol; one *s* two *d*. *Educ:* privately. Extensively constructed English and Welsh railways; Mayor of Richmond, Surrey, 1894, when Prince Edward was born in that borough, and on two occasions that year received Her late Majesty Queen Victoria when visiting Richmond; again Mayor, 1900–1 and 1904–5; High Sheriff, Surrey, 1898–99; Co-opted Member Surrey Territorial Force Association. *Address:* 17 Victoria Street, Westminster, SW1. *T:* Victoria 5076; Glanteif, Kew Gardens. *T:* 1433 Richmond.

Died 26 Oct. 1926.

T

TAAFFE, George Joseph; DL, JP Co. Louth; JP Co. Meath; Captain 3rd Battalion Queen's Own Royal West Kent Regiment; *b* 29 April 1866; *o s* of Stephen Taaffe of Glenkeiran and *g s* of George Taaffe, JP, DL of Smarmore Castle, Co. Louth; *m* 1895, Alice Catherine Trevor, *d* of late Capt. B. T. Griffith-Boscawen, JP, DL, Trevalyn Hall, Denbighshire, N Wales, and *sister* of Right Hon. Sir A. Griffith-Boscawen, MP; two *s* one *d*. *Educ:* Stonyhurst College. Formerly Capt. 4th Batt. King's Own Royal Lancaster Regt; served as ADC to GOC 26th Division in Salonica during European War; took an active part in the formation of the Irish Land Conference Committee, and also of the Committee for the Settlement of the Irish question along the lines of Devolution; Smarmore Castle has been in possession of the family since the 10th century. *Recreations:* hunting, shooting, golf, tennis. *Address:* Smarmore Castle, Ardee, Co. Louth, Ireland. *Club:* Royal Automobile.   *Died 7 June 1923.*

TACON, Sir Thomas Henry, Kt 1900; Alderman of the East Suffolk County Council since its formation; JP for counties of Suffolk and Norfolk and borough of Eye; High Sheriff, 1898, and DL of Suffolk; Deputy-Chairman of the County Finance Committee; Governor of Eye Grammar School; President of Eye Volunteers; Mayor of Eye, 1892–93, 1893–94, 1905–6, 1906–7, 1907–8, 1913–14, 1914–15, 1915–16; Unionist; *b* Eye, 14 March 1838; *s* of Charles Tacon of Eye, Suffolk; *m* 1868, Catherine Elizabeth, *e d* of R. B. Orford of Occold Hall; one *d*. Alderman, Eye Town Council. *Address:* Red House, Eye, Suffolk.   *Died 19 Feb. 1922.*

TAFLIA, 4th Marquis of (Malta); **Lt-Col Frederick Sedley;** *b* 1837; *s* of F. Sedley (*d* 1885), Superintendent of Police at Malta, and Catherine (*d* 1866), *d* of 2nd Marquis of Taflia; *m* 1871, Edith (*d* 1899), *d* of late Rev. G. H. Langdon, Vicar of Oving, Sussex, and *g d* of late Admiral Sir John Acworth Ommanney, KCB; one *d*. Served in China War, 1860 (medal and three clasps); formerly Captain 5th Lancers and 48th Regt; retired 1880; granted hon. rank of Lieut-Colonel, 1881. *Address:* Badgergate, Rye, Sussex. *Club:* Constitutional.

Died 13 March 1921.

TAILLON, Hon. Sir Louis Olivier, Kt 1916; *b* 26 Sept. 1840; *s* of Aimé Taillon and Marie Josephte Daunais; *m* 1875, Marie Louise Georgina (*d* 1876), *d* of late Hon. P. U. Archambault. *Educ:* Masson College. Called to Bar, 1865; commenced practice in Montreal; QC 1882; Batonnier, 1882; Member for Montreal East, 1875–86; Speaker of Assembly, 1882–84; Attorney-General, 1884–87; formed an Administration, Jan. 1887, but resigned in two days; Leader of Opposition to 1890; Minister without Portfolio, Dec. 1891; Member for Chambly, 1892; Prime Minister, 1892–96; Postmaster-General, 1896; defeated in General Elections, 1896 and 1900; declined seat on Bench, 1888. Hon. DCL, Bishop's College, 1895, and Laval, 1900. Retired into private life. Roman Catholic. *Address:* 595 St Denis Street, Montreal. *T:* 1537.   *Died April 1923.*

TAIT, Hon. Sir Melbourne McTaggart, Kt 1897; DCL; LLD M'Gill University, 1912; *b* 20 May 1842; *s* of Thomas Tait, merchant, Melbourne, Canada; *m* 1st, 1863, Monica (*d* 1876), *d* of James Holmes, Montreal; one *s* two *d*; 2nd, 1878, Lydia, *d* of H. B. Kaighn, Newport, RI; three *s*. *Educ:* St Francis Coll. School, Richmond, Province of Quebec; University M'Gill Coll. Montreal. Barrister, Montreal, 1863; QC 1882; Judge Superior Court, 1887; Acting Chief Justice, Montreal, 1894; Chief Justice of Superior Court for the Province of Quebec, 1906–12. *Address:* 1004 Dorchester Street, W Montreal, Quebec. *Club:* St James's, Montreal.

Died 19 Feb. 1917.

TAKAMINE, Jokichi; chemist; *b* Takaoka, Japan, 1854; *m* 1887, Caroline Hitch, New Orleans; two *s. Educ:* Imperial University of Japan, 1879, as chemical engineer; University of Glasgow, 1879–81. Head chemist, Japanese Department of Agriculture and Commerce, 1881–84; Imperial Japanese Commissioner to Cotton Centennial Exposition at New Orleans, 1884–85; organised first superphosphate works erected in Japan, 1887; removed to United States, 1890, and has since resided there; discovered diastatic enzyme known as takadiastase, used as starch digestant; isolated the active principle of suprarenal glands in product known as adrenalin; consulting chemist, Parke, Davis & Co., Detroit, Michigan; President, Takamine Laboratory, Inc., Takamine Ferment Company, International Takamine Ferment Company, and Sankyo Company (Tokio). Doctor of Chemical Engineering, 1899; and Doctor of Pharmacy, 1906, Imperial University of Japan; Fourth Order of Rising Sun, 1915; Members of Imperial Academy of Science in Japan, 1913; Fellow of Chemical Society, London; Member, Society of Chemical Industry, England; American Chemical Society, Institute of Chemical Engineers, and Electro-Chemical Society, USA; President Nippon Club, New York; Vice-President Japan Society, New York. *Address:* 334 Riverside Drive, New York City. *Clubs:* Lotus; Chemists; Drug and Chemical; Athletic; Bankers, New York.

Died 22 July 1923.

TALBOT DE MALAHIDE, 5th Baron *cr* 1831; **Richard Wogan Talbot,** DL; Baron Talbot of Malahide (Ire), Baron Malahide of Malahide (Ire), 1831; Baron Talbot de Malahide (UK), 1856; Hereditary Lord Admiral of Malahide and adjacent seas (15 Edward IV); late Lieutenant 9th Lancers; *b* London, 28 Feb. 1846; *s* of 4th Baron and Maria, *d* of Patrick Murray, Simprim, Forfarshire; *S* father, 1883; *m* 1st, 1873, Emily (*d* 1898), *d* of Sir James Boswell, 2nd and last Bt; one *s*; 2nd, 1901, Isabel Charlotte, DBE, *d* of late R. B. Humfrey, of Wrexham House, Norwich, and *widow* of John Gurney of Sprowston Hall, Norwich. *Educ:* Eton. Owned 3,600 acres. *Heir: s* Hon. James Boswell Talbot, *b* 18 May 1874. *Address:* Malahide Castle, Co. Dublin; Auchinleck House, Ayrshire. *Clubs:* Army and Navy, Carlton; Kildare Street, Dublin.

Died 4 March 1921.

TALBOT, Lieut-Col Sir Adelbert (Cecil), KCIE 1895 (CIE 1885); *b* 3 June 1845; *s* of Rev. Hon. William Whitworth Chetwynd Talbot, and *g s* of 2nd Earl Talbot, KG; *m* 1870, Agnes Mary (*d* 1894), *d* of Rev. W. Clarke; one *s* three *d. Educ:* Eton. Lt RA, 1867; ISC 1869; Capt. 1879; Major, 1887; Lieut-Col, 1891; Resident, Persian Gulf, 1891–94; Deputy Secretary, Indian Dept, Govt of India, 1894–96; accompanied Shahzadah Nasrullah Khan of Afghanistan to England, 1895; Resident in Kashmir, 1896–1900; Unemployed Super. list, 1900. *Address:* High Barn, Effingham. *Club:* United Service.

Died 28 Dec. 1920.

TALBOT, Rev. Arthur Henry; Rector of Edgmond; Prebendary of Wellington in Lichfield Cathedral; Provost of Denstone College since 1896; *b* 27 Sept. 1855; *s* of Rev. Hon. Arthur Chetwynd Talbot, 2nd *s* of 2nd Earl Talbot, KG; *m* 1903, Eveline Mary, *co-heiress* of Lieut-Col Charles Ashton of Little Onn Hall, Stafford; four *s* two *d. Educ:* privately; Keble College, Oxford, MA, 3rd class Theological School. Curate of Stoke-on-Trent; Vicar of Lapley; Rector of Church Eaton; Rural Dean of Stafford; Rural Dean of Edgmond; Chaplain to the late Bishop of Lichfield. *Address:* Edgmond Rectory, Newport, Salop. *T:* Newport 38. *M:* AY 8796. *Clubs:* Oxford and Cambridge, Royal Automobile.

Died 26 Nov. 1927.

TALBOT, Charles Henry, JP; *b* 2 Feb. 1842; *o s* of late William Henry Fox Talbot, MP, and Constance, *y d* of late Francis Mundy, of Markeaton, Co. Derby. *Educ:* Harrow; Trinity College, Cambridge (BA). *Address:* Lacock Abbey, Chippenham. *Club:* National Liberal.

Died Dec. 1916.

TALBOT, Emily Charlotte; *e d* of late Christopher Rice Mansel Talbot, Lord-Lieutenant of Glamorganshire, and Lady Charlotte Butler, *d* of 1st Earl of Glengall. Patron of five livings. *Address:* Margam Park, Port Talbot; Penrice Castle, Reynoldstone, RSO, Glamorganshire; 3 Cavendish Square, W.

Died Sept. 1918.

TALBOT, Rt. Rev. Ethelbert, DD, LLD; DD Oxon, 1924; Presiding Bishop of the Protestant Episcopal Church, Feb. 1924–Jan. 1926; Bishop of Bethlehem since 1909; *b* Fayette, Missouri, USA, 9 Oct. 1848; *s* of John A. and Alice W. Talbot; *m* 1873, Dora Harvey; one *d. Educ:* Dartmouth College, Hanover, New Hampshire; General Theological Seminary, New York. Deacon, 1873; Priest, 1873; Rector St James's Church, Macon, Mo, and Headmaster of St James's

Military Academy, Macon, Missouri, 1873–87; Bishop of Wyoming and Idaho, 1887; Central Pennsylvania, 1898. *Publications:* My People of the Plains; A Bishop among his Flock; Tim: the Autobiography of a Dog; A Bishop's Message: What the Episcopal Church Stands For; various addresses and magazine articles. *Recreations:* golf, horseback riding. *Address:* Bishop's House, Bethlehem, Penna. *Club:* University, Philadelphia.

Died Feb. 1928.

TALBOT, Gustavus Arthur; MP (Co. U) Hemel Hempstead Division of Herts since Dec. 1918; *b* 24 Dec. 1848; *s* of Rev. Hon. George Gustavus Chetwynd-Talbot and Emily Sarah, 2nd *d* of Henry Elwes; *m* 1880, Susan Frances, *d* of Robert Elwes; two *s* two *d* (and one *s* one *d* decd). *Educ:* Wellington. JP; Mayor of Hemel Hempstead; late MLC Ceylon. *Address:* Marchmount House, Hemel Hempstead. *Clubs:* Carlton, City of London.

Died 16 Oct. 1920.

TALBOT, Howard; composer and conductor; *b* New York, 1865; *s* of Lillie and Alexander Munkittrick; *m* Dorothy Maud, *d* of late Arthur H. Cross of Sandringham; four *d. Educ:* King's College, London. Received musical education at the Royal College of Music under Sir Hubert Parry, Sir Frederick Bridge, and Dr F. E. Gladstone; first opera Wapping Old Stairs, 1894; subsequent works include Monte Carlo, 1896; A Chinese Honeymoon, 1899, 1901; Kitty Grey (part composer), 1901; Three Little Maids (part composer), 1902; The Blue Moon (part composer), 1905; The White Chrysanthemum, 1905; The Girl behind the Counter, 1906; The Three Kisses, 1907; The Belle of Brittany, 1908; The Arcadians (part composer) 1909; The Mousmé (part composer), 1911; A Narrow Squeak (operetta), 1913; Simple-hearted Bill (sketch), 1913; The Pearl Girl (part composer), 1913; A Mixed Grill (revue), 1914; A Lucky Miss (musical comedietta), 1914; The Light Blues (part composer), My Lady Frayle (part composer), 1915–16; Mr Manhattan, 1916; High Jinks (part composer), 1916; Houpla (part composer), 1916; The Boy (part composer), 1917; Who's Hooper (part composer), 1919; My Nieces, 1921; conducted at Daly's, The Adelphi, The Prince of Wales' and other theatres since 1900. *Recreations:* motoring, yachting. *Address:* 35 Croydon Road, Reigate, Surrey. *T:* Reigate 339. *Club:* Green Room.

Died 12 Sept. 1928.

TALBOT, Sir William Henry, Kt 1906; *b* Leeds, 1831; *s* of John Talbot and *g s* of Matthew Talbot, both of Leeds; *m* 1861, Maria Emma (*d* 1915), *o d* of James Winser, Jr, of Ratsbury, Tenterden, Kent; two *s. Educ:* privately; University College School, London. Articled to Mr Joseph Munn, Town-Clerk of Tenterden, Kent, and admitted a solicitor, 1853; Town-Clerk of Manchester, 1890–1910. *Address:* Woodlands Road, Cheetham Hill, Manchester.

Died 9 May 1919.

TALBOT, William John, JP, DL; *b* 1859; *o s* of late John Talbot and 2nd wife, Gertrude Caroline, *d* of Lt–Col Bayly of Ballyarthur; *m* 1897, Julia Elizabeth Mary (*d* 1922), *o c* of Sir Capel Molyneux, 7th Bt. *Educ:* Eton; Magdalene College, Cambridge. High Sheriff, Co. Roscommon, 1886, Armagh, 1903; HM Lieut of Co. Roscommon; late Capt. Wicklow Artillery, S Division, RA. *Address:* Mount Talbot, Roscommon; Castle Dillon, Co. Armagh. *TA:* Ballygar, Ireland. *M:* DI 5, DI 112. *Clubs:* White's; Kildare Street, Dublin; Royal St George Yacht. *Died 7 June 1923.*

TALLBERG, Prof. Axel, ARE 1891; Hon. RE 1911; Professor and Principal of the School of Etching and Engraving, Royal Academy of Arts, Stockholm, Sweden, retired, with a state pension, 1926; *b* Gefle, Sweden, 23 Sept. 1860; *s* of Carl Erik Tallberg and Christina Johanson, the former owner of an iron foundry and machine works in Falun, Dalecarlia; *m* 1900, Greta Santesson; one *s* one *d. Educ:* Grammar School, Falun; Royal Academy of Arts, Stockholm; Royal Academy of Arts, Dusseldorf; Rome, Paris, and other capitals. Started as draughtsman to the Royal Academy of Science, Stockholm (entomological section); illustrator and correspondent to several Swedish and foreign newspapers and magazines; aquarelliste and finally etcher; Member of the Royal Archæological Institute, London, 1892, and of Royal Society of Arts, London, 1907; lived exclusively in England, near Windsor, 1886–95; many travels in Africa, Asia, and the Continent; after many years' endeavours and hard work succeeded in getting the Swedish Parliament to found and maintain a School of Etching and Engraving at the Royal Academy, Stockholm; appointed its first head, 1909; principal study has been the technical ways and means relating to all forms of painting, etching, and engraving, old and new. Gold medal Literis et Artibus, 1896. *Publications:* About Etching and Engraving, 1911; Chemistry of Paints and Painting, 1912; Etchings and Engravings, A Handbook for Print Collectors, 1917; The Etcher, his Ways and Means, 1917; Swedish

Etchers and Engravers, 1895–1918, 2 vols, 1918; Zorn: his childhood and youth, 1920; The Etcher, a Practical Handbook for Art Students, 1924; a great number of articles regarding the Arts in The Studio and other magazines. *Recreations:* scientific experiments, chemical and physical, reading, angling, and fishing, but above all, study. *Address:* Royal Academy of Arts, Stockholm, Sweden. *Club:* Artists', Stockholm.   *Died Feb. 1928.*

TALLENTS, George William, JP; Barrister-at-Law; Alderman of the Westminster City Council; a Governor of Harrow School; a Director of the London Assurance; *b* 26 Sept. 1856; *s* of late Godfrey Tallents, Newark-on-Trent, and Mary Anne Frances, *d* of late George William Brande, of HM Treasury; *m* 1883, Hon. Mildred Sophia, *d* of 1st Baron Ashcombe; three *s* two *d*. *Educ:* Harrow (entrance scholar, Head, 1874–75; Lyon Scholar); Balliol College, Oxford (Exhibitioner); 1st class Mods, 2nd class Lit. Hum. Called to Bar, Lincoln's Inn, 1882; Mayor of the City of Westminster, 1906–7 and 1918–19. Knight of the Order of Dannebrog, 1907; Officier de la Légion d'Honneur, 1919. *Address:* 49 Warwick Square, SW1. *T:* Victoria 6051. *Clubs:* Athenæum, Carlton.
      Died 17 Dec. 1924.

TAMPLIN, Herbert Travers, KC; Crown Prosecutor since 1903; *b* 1853; *s* of R. W. Tamplin, FRCS; *m d* of late John Cooper Forster, FRCS. President Royal College of Surgeons, London; called to Bar, Middle Temple, 1875; Advocate Supreme Court, Cape Colony, 1880; QC 1898; High Court, 1908; edited Cape Law Journal, 1885–99; MLA Victoria East, 1891–1902; Lieut 1st City Grahamstown Volunteers, 1883; commanding officer, 1896; served Langeberg Campaign, 1897; Boer War, 1899 (VD, Colonial Aux. Forces Officers Decoration; Colonial Forces Field Service medals). *Clubs:* Royal Societies; Grahamstown; Kimberley; Civil Service, Cape Town.   *Died 24 April 1925.*

TANCOCK, Rev. Charles Coverdale, DD 1899 Oxford; *b* 1 Dec. 1851; *s* of Rev. O. J. Tancock, DCL Oxford, late Vicar of Tavistock, *s* of Rear-Admiral John Tancock, RN, and Emma, *d* of W. Davey Sole, Devonport; *m* 1886, Marion Alma Smith, *d* of Robert Smith of Killcott, Godalming; two *d*. *Educ:* Sherborne School; Exeter Coll. Oxford; scholar; 1st class Classical Moderations, 1872; 1st class Literæ Humaniores, 1874; BA, 1874; MA, 1877; BD, 1899. Ordained, 1880; Assistant Master at Charterhouse, 1875–86; Headmaster of Rossall, 1886–96; Vicar of Leck, Kirkby Lonsdale, 1896–98; Headmaster of Tonbridge School, 1899–1907; Hon. Canon of Rochester Cathedral, 1905–8; Rural Dean of Rutland Second Deanery, 1909–12; Member of Rutland Education Committee, 1909–12; Trustee of Oakham School, 1911–12; Warden of Peterborough Diocese Lay Readers' Association, 1910–12; Rector of Little Casterton, 1907–12. *Address:* Sussex House, Winchester.   *Died 16 April 1922.*

TANNER, Maj.-Gen. Edward, CB 1881; retired full pay; *b* 1839; *s* of Joseph Bouverie Hussey Tanner, Wexcombe, Wilts; *m* 1867, Georgina Wyndham (*d* 1910), *d* of Gen. George William Powlett Bingham, CB, The Vines, Rochester. Entered Army, 1855; Captain, 1860; Major 1869; Lieut-Col 1877; Col 1881; Maj.-Gen. (retired) 1886; served Afghan Campaign, 1878–80 (despatches, medal with clasp); formerly Lieut-Colonel Commandant 1st Batt. The King's (Liverpool) Regt; commanded regiment at the storming of Peiwar Khotal, Afghan Campaign, 1878–80. *Recreations:* golf, cricket, boating, tennis, shooting. *Address:* Woodside, Old Shirley, Southampton. *Clubs:* Junior Conservative, Royal Southern Yacht.
      Died 8 March 1916.

TANNER, Brig.-Gen. John Arthur, CB 1911; CMG 1916; DSO 1888; retired; *b* Tidcombe, Wilts, 27 Feb. 1858; *e s* of late John Tanner, Poulton, Marlboro'; *m* 1916, Gladys Helen, *d* of late Charles Townshend Murdoch, MP. *Educ:* Cheltenham College; RMA Woolwich. Lieut RE 1877; Captain, 1888; Major, 1895; Lt-Col, 1903; Col, 1906; served Waziristan, 1881; Suakin, 1885; Burma, 1885–88; Chitral, 1895; Punjab Frontier, 1897. Decorated for services in Burma. *Address:* South View, Aldbourne, Wilts. *Club:* Junior United Service.   *Died 23 July 1917.*

TANNER, John Arthur Charles, MA; Taxing Master of the Supreme Court (Bankruptcy) since 1887; *b* 6 Aug. 1854; *s* of late John Tanner, of Yatesbury, Calne, Wilts; *m* Grace Mann, *d* of late W. W. Aldridge, 31 Bedford Row, WC, Solicitor; two *s* one *d*. *Educ:* Marlborough; St John's College, Oxford. Assistant Solicitor to the Official Receiver in Bankruptcy, 1885–87. *Recreations:* shooting, golf. *Address:* 31 Orsett Terrace, Hyde Park, W2. *T:* Paddington 2582; Bankruptcy Buildings, Carey Street, WC. *T:* Holborn 6700, Bankruptcy Extension, 126.
      Died 12 March 1928.

TARLETON, Captain Alfred Henry, MVO 1904; *b* 16 May 1862; *o s* of late Admiral Sir Walter Tarleton, KCB, ADC, and late Lady Tarleton, *d* of 4th Baron Dimsdale; *m* 1888, Henrietta, *o c* of late Admiral E. C. Tennyson d'Eyncourt, CB, of Bayons Manor, Lincs, and late Lady Henrietta Tennyson d'Eyncourt, *y d* of 4th Duke of Newcastle; three *d*. Served on Admiralty War Staff, 1914–19; specially promoted to Captain for War Service; Captain, RN; JP, DL, Middlesex; Sheriff, 1903; Hon. Equerry to Duchess of Albany. Order of Mercy; Knight of Grace, St John of Jerusalem. *Address:* Breakspears, Uxbridge. *TA:* Tarleton Harefield. *T:* Harefield 17. *Clubs:* Marlborough, Carlton, Travellers', Constitutional.
      Died 7 June 1921.

TARLETON, Francis Alexander, LLD, ScD; Fellow of Trinity College, Dublin, 1866; Professor of Natural Philosophy, University of Dublin, 1890; co-opted a Senior Fellow, 1901; Commissioner of Intermediate Education for Ireland, 1901; President, Royal Irish Academy, 1906; *b* Co. Monaghan, 28 April 1841; *y s* of late Rev. J. R. Tarleton, Rector of Tyholland, and Judith, *d* of F. Falkiner, Congar House, Tipperary; *m* Gertrude, *d* of late Rev. Charles Fleury, DD. *Educ:* by his father; Trinity Coll. Dublin (Scholar). Senior Moderator in Mathematics, Junior Moderator in Logics and Ethics, 1861. Assistant to Professor of Applied Chemistry, 1876; Church of Ireland; Unionist. *Publications:* An Introduction to the Mathematical Theory of Attraction, 1899, vol. ii, 1913; A Treatise on Dynamics (in conjunction with Dr Williamson), 3rd edn 1900. *Address:* 24 Upper Leeson Street, Dublin. *Clubs:* Royal Societies; University; Dublin.   *Died 19 June 1920.*

TARRANT, Rev. William George, BA (Lond.); Unitarian Minister and Journalist; Editor of The Inquirer 1887–97, and since 1918; *b* 1853; *s* of Matthew Tarrant, Worcestershire; *m* Alice, *d* of Henry Stanley, Manchester; one *d* two *s*. *Educ:* Birmingham; Owens College, Manchester; Manchester New College, London; University College, London. Minister at Wandsworth, 1883–1920; Member of Executive of British and Foreign Unitarian Association since 1887; Lecturer and Representative in Canada, United States, South Africa, and several European Congresses; Examiner and Visitor to Carmarthen College and Unitarian Home Missionary College; Elementary Education Manager to LCC and LSB since 1886. *Publications:* hymns, in various hymnals; several volumes on Early Christianity and Modern Religion, including The Story and Significance of the Unitarian Movement (Essex Hall Lecture), 1910; Unitarianism, 1912; also Bee Songs, 1906; Songs Devout, 1912; John Milton, 1908, etc. *Recreations:* walking, cycling, verse. *Address:* 53 Westover Road, SW18.
      Died 15 Jan. 1928.

TARRING, Sir Charles James, Kt 1906; *b* London, 17 Sept. 1845; *s* of John Tarring, architect; *m* 1883, Edith, *d* of J. B. Carlill, MD Lond.; one *s* one *d*. *Educ:* City of London School; Trinity College, Cambridge (BA 1868; MA 1881). Called to Bar (Inner Temple), 1871; Professor of Law in Imperial University of Japan, 1878–80; Assistant Judge and subsequently Judge of HBM Supreme Consular Court at Constantinople, 1883–97; Chief Justice of Grenada, West Indies, 1897–1905; JP, County of London. *Publications:* Chapters on the Law relating to the Colonies; Analytical Tables of the Laws of Real Property; British Consular Jurisdiction in the East; A Practical Turkish Grammar; article on Dependencies and Colonies (other than India) in Lord Halsbury's Laws of England. *Address:* S. Godric, 18 Arkwright Road, Hampstead, NW3. *Club:* National Liberal.
      Died 31 March 1923.

TARVER, J. C.; *b* Filgrave, Bucks. *Educ:* Eton; Cambridge; Heidelberg. Was a master at King's School, Canterbury; Clifton College. Headmaster of High School at Gateshead. *Publications:* Tiberius the Tyrant; Observations of a Foster Parent; Life and Letters of Gustave Flaubert; Muggleton College. *Address:* Brookside, Woburn Sands.
      Died 6 Nov. 1926.

TASADDUK RASUL KHAN, Raja Sir, KCSI 1898; Taluqdar of Jahangirabad, Bara Banki, Oudh; member of Legislative Council of United Provinces; title of Raja, conferred in 1893, made hereditary in 1897; member British India Association, Oudh; Hon. Magistrate, 1st class; Chairman Municipal Board, Bara Banki, till 1917; President Hockey Club, Bara Banki, Oudh; awarded a Sword of Honour for services during the war, 1919. *Address:* Bara Banki. *T:* 65. *Club:* United Service, Lucknow.   *Died Sept. 1928.*

TATA, Sir Ratanji Jamsetji, Kt 1916; *b* Bombay, 20 Jan. 1871; *y s* of Jamshedji Nusserwanji Tata; *m* 1892, Naja, *y d* of Ardesir Merwanji Sett, Bombay. *Educ:* St Xavier's College, Bombay. Partner of Tata, Sons, and Co., Bombay; Director of Indian Hotels Co., Ltd, Bombay;

Director of Tata Limited, London; Tata Iron and Steel Works, Sakchi; the Tata Hydro-Electric Power Supply Co., Ltd, India; besides various cotton spinning and weaving mills, and other industrial concerns in India. *Recreations:* travelling, gardening, riding, tennis. *Address:* York House, Twickenham, Middlesex. *T:* Richmond 1665; Tata House, Bombay, India. *Clubs:* Carlton, Queen's; Automobile of France, Paris; Western India Turf, Bombay.

Died 5 Sept. 1918.

TATE, James William, ("That"); Composer and Partner on the Variety Theatres and Music Halls with Clarice Mayne; *b* July 1875; *s* of Jacob Tate, Wolverhampton; *m* 1912, Clarice Mayne. *Educ:* St Wilfred's College, Gatton, Cheadle, Staffs. Musical Director of Carl Rosa Opera Company; composer of many successful and popular songs, including A Broken Doll, Every Little While, etc. *Recreations:* golf, horse-riding, tennis, river, flying. *Address:* 65 Gordon Mansions, Francis Street, WC1. *T:* Museum 3298; Clarijin Bungalow, The Lammas, Staines; 5 Lisle Street, WC2. *TA:*Funniosity, Westrand, London. *M:* LU 5680, KN 7191. *Clubs:* Eccentric; Burnham Yacht.

Died 5 Feb. 1922.

TATE, Walter William Hunt, MD, FRCP; Obstetric Physician to St Thomas' Hospital; Gynæcologist to the National Hospital, Queen's Square; Consulting Gynæcologist to the Radium Institute; *b* 18 Dec. 1865; *s* of late Dr George Tate; *m* Flora Dalzell, *widow* of Dr Anthony Dalzell. *Educ:* University College School and Hospital. *Publications:* various contributions to scientific societies. *Recreations:* motoring, archery. *Address:* 1 Queen Anne Street, Cavendish Square, W. *TA:* Tatendish, London. *T:* Paddington 1085. *Club:* British Empire.

Died 5 July 1916.

TATE, Sir William Henry, 2nd Bt, *cr* 1898; Sheriff of Co. Palatine of Lancaster, 1907; DL, JP Lancs; *b* 23 Jan. 1842; *e s* of Sir Henry Tate, 1st Bt and Jane, *d* of John Wignall, Aughton, Lancs; *S* father, 1899; *m* 1863, Caroline H. R. Glasgow, adopted *d* of late John Glasgow, Old Trafford, Manchester; two *s* seven *d* (and one *s* decd). *Educ:* privately. Director of Henry Tate and Sons, Ltd, Sugar Refiners, Liverpool and London. *Heir: s* Ernest William Tate [*b* 7 Jan. 1867; *m* 1892, Mildred Mary, 2nd *d* of F. H. Gossage of Camp Hill, Woolton, Liverpool; one *s* two *d*]. *Address:* Highfield, Woolton, Lancashire; Bodrhyddan Rhuddlan, Flintshire.

Died 21 Dec. 1921.

TAVEGGIA, Rt. Rev. Santino; Bishop of Dinajpur since 1927; Bishop of Krishnagar, 1906–27; *b* Italy, 1855. Went to India, 1879. *Address:* Dinajpur, North Central Bengal.

Died 2 June 1928.

TAVERNER, Hon. Sir John William, KCMG 1913; Kt 1909; *b* 20 Nov. 1852; *m* 1879, Elizabeth A. Bassett, *d* of James and Mary Luxton. *Educ:* Melbourne. Member of Swan Hill Shire Council, Victoria, 1879; twice President and resigned 1889; Member of Legislative Assembly for Donald and Swan Hill, 1889–1904; Member of first Railway Standing Committee, 1890–94; Minister of Agriculture, Commissioner of Public Works, and Vice-President of Board of Lands and Works, 1894–99; Minister of Lands and Agriculture and President of Board of Lands and Works, 1902–4; President of Royal Commission for Victoria, Greater Britain Exhibition, 1899; Agent-General for Victoria, 1904–13. *Recreations:* cricket, cycling, boating. *Address:* General Buildings, Aldwych, WC2. *TA:* Jerukian, Estrand. *T:* City 1968. *Clubs:* Empire, Overseas, Royal Automobile.

Died 17 Dec. 1923.

TAWNEY, Charles Henry, CIE 1888; MA; retired, 1903; *b* 1837; *s* of Rev. Richard Tawney, Vicar of Willoughby, and Susan James, *d* of Dr Bernard, Clifton; *m* 1867, Constance Catharine (*d* 1920), *d* of Charles Fox, MD. *Educ:* Rugby; Trinity College, Cambridge. Bell University Scholar, 1857; Davies University Scholar, 1858; Scholar of Trinity, 1858; bracketed Senior Classic, 1860; Fellow of Trinity, 1860. Appointed Asst Professor in the Presidency Coll., Calcutta, 1864; served for many years as Prof. in and Prin. of the Presidency College, and as Registrar of the Calcutta University; officiated three times as Director of Public Instruction, Bengal; late Librarian, India Office. *Publications:* translated from the Sanskrit the Kathā Sarit Sāgara; the Kathā Kośa; the Mālavikāgnimitra; the Uttara Rāma Charita; the Prabandha Chintāmani; and two Centuries of Bhartrihari; edited Richard III. *Address:* Chartley, Camberley, Surrey.

Died 29 July 1922.

TAY, Waren, FRCS, LSA; late Consulting Surgeon, Queen's Hospital for Children, Hackney Road, Bethnal Green; also London Hospital, Royal London Ophthalmic Hospital, and Hospital for Diseases of the Skin, Blackfriars. *Educ:* London Hospital. *Address:* 61 Oakfield Road, West Croydon.

Died 15 May 1927.

TAYLER, Albert Chevallier, RBC; *b* 5 April 1862; 7th *s* of late William M. Tayler, solicitor; *m* 1896, Mrs Cotes, *d* of Mr Allingham, surgeon. *Educ:* Bloxham; Slade School; Paris. Spent twelve years in Cornwall, awarded medal of the 2nd Class, Paris Salon, 1891; Hors concours, etc. *Principal works:* The Last Blessing; La vie Boulounaise; Gentlemen, the Queen; Honi soit qui mal y pense; Royal Exchange panel, The Vintners' Company entertaining the five Kings; since painter for the permanent Collection of the Corporation of London; Guildhall Art Gallery portraits of Admiral Earl Beatty and Field-Marshal Earl Haig; represented in the Corporation Galleries of Liverpool, Birmingham, Hartlepool, Preston, Bristol, Kettering, Durban, Adelaide, Bendigo, etc. *Address:* 23 Orsett Terrace, Hyde Park, W2. *T:* Paddington 1198. *Club:* Devonshire.

Died 20 Dec. 1925.

TAYLOR, Alexander; Sheriff-Substitute of Forfarshire at Forfar since 1912; Captain 9th Battalion (Highlanders) The Royal Scots; *b* Carrickfergus, Co. Antrim, 1872; *s* of James Taylor, of James Taylor & Sons, Limited, Barn Mills, Carrickfergus, Flax Spinners; *m* 1905, Rhoda, *d* of James Macintyre of J. & J. Macintyre, Glasgow, Manufacturers; no *c*. *Educ:* Glasgow Academy and University. Called to the Scottish Bar, 1896; 2nd Lieut 9th Battalion (Highlanders) The Royal Scots, 1900; retired as Captain, 1912; Re-gazetted, 1914; wounded near Ypres, 23 April 1915. *Recreations:* shooting, walking, cycling. *Address:* Rosehill, Brechin. *T:* Brechin 10. *Clubs:* New, Brechin; Scottish Liberal, Edinburgh.

Died 21 April 1917.

TAYLOR, Charles Edward, JP; MFH Sedbergh; *b* 1853; *s* of Robert Taylor, Lancaster; *m* 1880, Alice, *e d* of James Turner, Lancaster. *Address:* Akay, Sedbergh SO, Yorks.

Died 5 Nov. 1924.

TAYLOR, Lt-Col Edward Harrison Clough, JP, York ER; *b* 1849; *m* 1st, 1880, Lady Elizabeth Campbell (*d* 1896), *d* of 8th Duke of Argyll; 2nd, 1898, Lady Mary Stuart, *y d* of 5th Earl of Castlestuart; three *s* one *d*. *Educ:* Harrow. Formerly Royal Welsh Fusiliers; retired 1886; ADC to Viceroy of India (Marquis of Ripon), 1880–84; re-employed and commanded Details Royal Welsh Fusiliers, 1900–1. *Address:* Firby Hall, York. *TA:* Firby, Kirkham-Abbey. *Clubs:* Naval and Military; Yorkshire.

Died 1 April 1921.

TAYLOR, Edward Henry, MD, DSc; Professor of Surgery, Dublin. *Educ:* Trinity College, Dublin; Vienna. *Address:* 77 Merrion Square South, Dublin. *T:* Dublin 1953.

Died April 1922.

TAYLOR, Col Francis Pitt Stewart, CMG 1915; late RASC; *b* 15 June 1869; *m* 1903, Anne Isabel, *d* of late Capt. Frederick Allhusen and *widow* of C. P. Hall. Entered army (South Lancs Regt), 1889; Captain ASC, 1898; Major, 1903; Lt-Col, 1912; Deputy Asst Director of Supplies and Transport, Eastern Command, 1905–6; Brig.-General commanding British Adriatic Mission, 1915–16; served Nile expedition, 1898 (Egyptian medal; medal); S African War, 1900–2 (Queen's medal 3 clasps, King's medal 2 clasps); European War, 1914–17 (Bt Col, despatches twice, CMG); retired pay, 1919; Grand Cordon White Eagle of Serbia, 1916; Officer Crown of Italy.

Died 22 Dec. 1924.

TAYLOR, Franklin; pianist and teacher of pianoforte; Professor at Royal College of Music; *b* Birmingham, 5 Feb. 1843. *Educ:* Leipzig Conservatoire. Professor at National Training School, 1876; member of Associated Board of RAM and RCM. *Publications:* Primer of Pianoforte Playing, 1877; Technique and Expression in Pianoforte Playing, 1897; articles in Grove's Dictionary, etc. *Address:* 49 Iverna Court, Kensington, W.

Died 19 March 1919.

TAYLOR, Sir Frederick, 1st Bt, *cr* 1917; MD, FRCP; Consulting Physician to Guy's Hospital; Physician to Seamen's Hospital, Greenwich; Member of Senate of University of London; late Representative of University of London on General Medical Council; *b* 6 April 1847; *s* of David Taylor, MRCS, of Kennington; *m* 1884, Helen Mary (*d* 1917), *d* of Frederick Manby of East Rudham, Norfolk; two *s* one *d*. *Educ:* Epsom College; Guy's Hospital. MD University of London; University Scholar in Obstetric and in Forensic Medicine; late President, Royal College Physicians (1915–18), Royal Society of Medicine; Examiner in Medicine, Universities of London, Durham, Birmingham, Cambridge, and Belfast; Harveian Orator, 1907. *Publications:* The Practice of Medicine, 11th edn; Lumleian Lectures;

On some Disorders of the Spleen; contributions to medical societies and journals. *Heir: s* Eric Stuart Taylor, MD Cantab; *b* 28 June 1889. *Club:* Athenæum.   *Died 2 Dec. 1920.*

TAYLOR, Hon. George; Senator since 1911; President and Manager of the Ontario Wheel Co., also President of the Pease River Land and Investments Co.; *b* 31 March 1840; 2nd *s* of William Taylor and Ann Graham, both of the north of Ireland; *m* 1863, Margaret Ann Latimer; no *c. Educ:* common school at Lansdown in county of Leeds. Began life in mercantile business as clerk in country general store when eleven years of age; continued with same firm afterwards as partner over twenty-five years; first elected as Reeve of Gananoque, 1872; held office for seven years, then elected Warden of united counties of Leeds and Grenville; Member of House of Commons, 1882, 1887, 1891, 1896, 1900, 1904, 1908, and 1911; Chief Whip of the Conservative Party in House of Commons for over twenty-five years. *Address:* Gananoque, Ontario. *T:* 37.   *Died March 1919.*

TAYLOR, George Paul; metropolitan police magistrate, Marylebone, since 1905; *b* 1860; *m* 1900, Rosa, *d* of Henry Williamson, Chasetown, Staffordshire. *Educ:* Downside Coll.; Catholic University College, Kensington. Barrister, Middle Temple, 1885; contested (L) Ince Div., Lancs, 1886; Metropolitan Police Magistrate, N London, 1895-97; Greenwich, 1897-98; Southwark, 1898-1905. *Address:* 7 Lancaster Gate Terrace, W. *Club:* Reform.   *Died 4 May 1917.*

TAYLOR, Harry Mead, CB 1923; Assistant Secretary for Finance, Board of Trade, 1920-27; *b* 1872; *e s* of late Henry Taylor; *m* 1896, Katie, *y d* of late Alfred Maynard; no *c. Educ:* privately. Entered Board of Trade Department of the Official Receivers in Companies Liquidation, 1891; resigned on joining S. Allsopp & Sons of Burton-on-Trent, 1900; Manager, 1901-7; associated with commercial and financial undertakings until 1914, and travelled in Canada and USA; on outbreak of war appointed Secretary of Foreign Trade Debts Committeee, and in 1916 of Enemy Debts Committee; Controller of Trading Accounts, Board of Trade, 1918. *Club:* Royal Societies.   *Died 19 July 1928.*

TAYLOR, Henry Martyn, JP; FRS 1898; FRAS; Barrister-at-law; Fellow of Trinity College, Cambridge, 1866; *b* Bristol, 6 June 1842; 2nd *s* of Rev. James Taylor, DD. *Educ:* Wakefield Grammar School; Trinity Coll. Camb.; 3rd Wrangler and 2nd Smith's Prizeman, 1865; BA 1865; MA 1868. Vice-Principal of the Royal School of Naval Architecture and Marine Engineering, 1865-69; assistant tutor, Trinity Coll. Camb. 1869-74; tutor, 1874-84; lecturer, 1884-94; Mayor of Cambridge, 1900-1. *Publications:* editor of Pitt Press Euclid. *Recreations:* formerly cricket, tennis, shooting, fishing. *Address:* The Yews, Cambridge. *T:* 118.   *Died 26 Oct. 1927.*

TAYLOR, Colonel H. Brooke, CBE 1919; VD; DL; Senior Partner in the firm of Brooke Taylor & Co., Solicitors, Bakewell, Derbyshire; *b* 6 Oct. 1855; *s* of John and Catherine Ann Taylor, of Darley-in-the-Dale, Derbyshire; *m* 1884, Mary Taitt, *o d* of Rev. W. Mallalieu of Ockbrook, Derbyshire; four *s* one *d. Educ:* Ockbrook; Lausanne. Admitted a Solicitor, 1878; has taken part in public duties of various kinds; Colonel Commanding 2nd VB Sherwood Foresters (retired 1904); Member Derbyshire Territorial Force Association from commencement; Hon. Secretary and Organiser, Derbyshire Branch of British Red Cross Society prior to war; served on Recruiting Staff 45th Recruiting Area and No 6 District, 1914-17; Assistant Director of National Service, Derbyshire, 1917-18; Hon. Secretary Derbyshire Volunteer Training Corps (eight Battalions) and CSO, 1914-15. *Recreations:* cricket, golf. *Address:* The Close, Bakewell, Derbyshire. *T:* Bakewell 9. *Club:* County, Derby.   *Died 20 Feb. 1923.*

TAYLOR, James Henry, ISO; late Deputy Commissioner, Angul District, Orissa, Bihar and Orissa, India; *b* 20 Aug. 1861; *s* of William Colebrooke Taylor; *m* 1884, Hélene Berthe, *d* of late Henry Augustus Cowper, HM Consular Service; two *s. Educ:* Western Coll., Brighton; Rev. C. Jenkins, Brussels. Studied medicine, Charing Cross Hospital; gave up this profession; proceeded to India; obtained post in Forest Department of Baramba and Narsingpur Feudatory States; appointed to Government post, Tahsildar, Kondmals, Orissa, 1887; promoted Sub-Deputy Collector, Deputy Collector, Assistant Settlement Officer, Orissa; Settlement Officer of Darpan, Porahat, Midnapur and Revision Settlement of Orissa; held listed appointment of Magistrate and Collector in Indian Civil Service; retired, 1919. *Recreations:* a keen shikari and fisherman; interested in natural history, pisciculture, agriculture, gardening. *Address:* c/o The National Bank of India, 26 Bishopsgate, EC. *Club:* Overseas.   *Died 14 Jan. 1926.*

TAYLOR, James Monroe, AB, DD, LLD; President of Vassar College, 1886-1913; *b* Brooklyn, 5 Aug. 1848; 3rd *s* of E. E. L. Taylor, DD, and Mary Jane Perkins; *m* 1873, Kate Huntington; three *s* one *d. Educ:* Rochester, NY; Germany. Pastor, South Norwalk Ct, 1873-82; pastor, Providence, RI, 1882-86. *Publications:* various essays; privately printed for classes, a volume on Psychology; also, for classes, a Syllabus of Ethics, 1907; printed address on A New World and and Old Gospel; Practical or Ideal; Before Vassar opened. *Address:* c/o Brown, Shipley and Co. *Clubs:* University, AΔΦ, Century, New York; Adirondack League.   *Died 19 Dec. 1916.*

TAYLOR, John, MVO 1909; British Vice-Consul, Cannes, since 1884; *b* 20 Oct. 1834; *s* of William Taylor, of Coddenham, Suffolk; *m* Harriett Taylor (*d* 1908); one *d. Educ:* Coddenham village school. *Recreation:* gardening. *Address:* 43 rue de Frejus, Cannes. *TA:* Taylor, Cannes. *T:* 1,32.   *Died 21 April 1922.*

TAYLOR, Luke, RE 1910; Fellow of the Royal Society of Painter-Etchers and Engravers; *b* 20 Sept. 1876; unmarried. *Educ:* Royal College of Art, South Kensington. *Address:* Hawley Grange, Dartford.   *Died 3 June 1916.*

TAYLOR, Rev. Malcolm Campbell, DD, LLD; Extra Chaplain-in-Ordinary to the King in Scotland since 1901; Professor of Ecclesiastical History, Edinburgh University, 1876-1908; Ex-Secretary of University Court. *Address:* 6 Greenhill Park, Edinburgh.   *Died 10 March 1922.*

TAYLOR, Rev. Richard; Hon. Canon of Carlisle, 1906. *Address:* Bromfield Vicarage, Carlisle.   *Died 10 Feb. 1922.*

TAYLOR, Sir Richard Stephens, Kt 1919; JP Bucks; Solicitor, Gray's Inn; senior partner, R. S. Taylor, Son & Humbert; Chairman Equity and Law Life Assurance Society; President of the Law Society, 1915-16; *b* 19 July 1842; *s* of R. S. Taylor, of Gray's Inn, Solicitor; *m* 1st, Clara (*d* 1877), *d* of Charles Humbert; 2nd, 1885, Anna Gordon (*d* 1923), *d* of J. Geddes, Orbliston, Morayshire; three *s* three *d. Educ:* Merchant Taylors' School. *Address:* 38 Lennox Gardens, SW1. *T:* Kensington 151. *Clubs:* Garrick, Conservative.   *Died 30 March 1928.*

TAYLOR, Sir Robert, Kt 1920; Partner in the Firm of John Taylor & Sons, Civil and Mining Engineers; *b* 1855; *s* of John Taylor, Great Cumberland Place, W; *m* Blanche G., *d* of Thomas Borrow Myers, Porters Park, Shenley, Herts; one *s* two *d. Address:* 28 Lennox Gardens, SW. *Club:* Windham.   *Died 4 April 1921.*

TAYLOR, Thomas, JP; MP (L) Bolton since 1912; *b* Bolton, 1851; *s* of late William Taylor, corn merchant; *m* 1874, Mary E., 3rd *d* of late Robert Lomax, manufacturer, of Bolton; two *d. Educ:* Bolton Church Institute. Apprenticed at age of 15 to Barlow and Jones, Ltd, cotton manufacturers; retired and founded a business of his own at the Saville Mill, 1894; Examiner in Cotton Weaving to the City and Guilds of London Institute, 1888-94; formerly Member Bolton School Board. *Address:* Saville Mill, Bolton.   *Died 17 Dec. 1916.*

TAYLOR, Hon. Sir Thomas Wardlaw, Kt 1897; MA; *b* Auchtermuchty, Fife, 25 March 1833; *o s* of late Rev. John Taylor, MD, DD, and Marion Antill, *d* of late John Wardlaw, Banker, Dalkeith; *m* 1st, 1858, Jessie (*d* 1863), *d* of late John Cameron, MD, Wilmington, USA; 2nd, 1864, Margaret, *d* of late Hugh Vallance. *Educ:* privately; Edinburgh University. Barrister, Upper Canada, 1858; QC 1876; Master in Chancery, 1872-83; Puisne Judge, Court of Queen's Bench for Manitoba, 1883-87; Chief Justice, 1887-99; Administrator of the Government of the Province in 1890, and again in 1893. *Publications:* Chancery Statutes and Orders; Commentaries on Equity Jurisprudence; Investigation of Titles; Public Statutes relating to the Presbyterian Church in Canada. *Recreations:* fishing, golf. *Address:* 67 Victoria Avenue, Hamilton, Canada.   *Died 1 March 1917.*

TAYLOR, Surg.-General Sir William, KCB 1902 (CB 1898); retired 1904; *b* Moorfield, Ayrshire, 5 April 1848; 3rd *s* of late James Taylor, Etruria, Staffordshire, and Moorfield, Ayrshire, and Mary Hamilton, *d* of the late William Hamilton, Purroch. *Educ:* Carmichael, Lanarkshire; Glasgow University. Joined Army Medical Staff, 1864; served in Canada, 1865-69, and took part in the operations against the Fenian raiders on the Vermont frontier (medal); in India, 1870-80, and again, 1882-98; was in the Jowaki Expedition (medal); served on the staff of the Commander-in-Chief in India, and was with him during the Burman Campaign, 1886–87 (despatches, clasp); sent as Militaro-Medical Attaché to the Japanese army during the war with China (Japanese war medal); PMO of the Ashanti Expedition, 1895–96 (Queen's star and specially promoted to Surgeon-General); PMO of expedition to Khartoum, 1898; and was present at the battle of Omdurman (despatches, CB, 2nd class of the Medjidie, English and Egyptian medals); PMO HM forces in India, 1898–1901; King's Hon. Physician, 1901; Director-General Army Medical Service, 1901–4. Knight of Grace of the Order of St John of Jerusalem in England; Hon. LLD, Glasgow. *Club:* Conservative.

Died 10 April 1917.

TEALE, Major Joseph William, DSO 1916; RE; *b* 1876; *s* of Goodman Teale of Allendale, Toorak, Melbourne; *m*; one *s* one *d*. *Educ:* Elizabeth College, Guernsey; Crystal Palace School of Engineering; Camborne School of Mines. Member of Institution of Mining and Metallurgy, and American Institute of Mining Engineers; served European War, 1914–19 (despatches three times, DSO); has visited the following countries professionally—Africa, Australia, Brazil, Burma, Canada, Ceylon, France, Mexico, Spain, Turkey, United States. *Recreations:* shooting, fishing, golf. *Clubs:* Royal Automobile, Mining. *Died 11 April 1926.*

TEALE, Thomas Pridgin, MA, MB; Hon. DSc University of Leeds; FRS 1888; Consulting Surgeon, General Infirmary, Leeds; *b* Leeds, 28 June 1831; *s* of Thomas Pridgin Teale, FRS, and Frances, *d* of Rev. Charles Isherwood, sometime Fellow of Magdalene Coll., Camb.; *m* 1st, Alice (*d* 1891), *d* of Rev. W. H. Teale; 2nd, Jeanie, 2nd *d* of late D. C. Jones of Tamworth; four *s* four *d*. *Educ:* Leeds Grammar School; Winchester; Brasenose Coll. Oxford; King's Coll., London. Lecturer on Anatomy and Surgery, Leeds School of Medicine, 1858–76; Surgeon, General Infirmary, Leeds, 1864–84; Crown Member General Medical Council, 1876–1901; Hon. Fellow Royal Society of Medicine. *Publications:* Dangers to Health: a Pictorial Guide to Domestic Sanitary Defects, 1879 (translated into German by HRH the Princess Christian); Economy of Coal in House Fires; The Principles of Domestic Fireplace Construction; Hurry, Worry, and Money, the Bane of Modern Education; Dust and Fresh Air: how to keep out the one, and let in the other; besides publications on surgical subjects. *Recreation:* trout-fishing. *Address:* North Grange, Headingley, Leeds. *TA:* Teale, Headingley 92. *T:* Headingley 92.

Died 13 Nov. 1923.

TEALL, Sir Jethro Justinian Harris, Kt 1916; MA, DSc (Oxon, Camb., and Dublin); LLD (St Andrews); FRS 1890; FGS; *b* Northleach, Gloucestershire, 5 Jan. 1849; *o c* of Jethro and Mary Teall (*née* Hathaway); *m* 1879, Harriet, *d* of G. R. Cowen; two *s*. *Educ:* Berkeley Villa School, Cheltenham; St John's College, Camb. Sedgwick Prizeman; Fellow, St John's College, 1875–79. Sometime Lecturer on the Cambridge University Extension Scheme; Director HM's Geological Survey and Museum of Practical Geology, 1901–13; Bigsby Medallist, 1889, and Wollaston Medallist, 1905, of the Geological Society of London; President Section C, British Association, 1893; President Geological Society of London, 1900–2; Vice-President Royal Society of London, 1900–1; Delesse Prizeman, Academy of Science, Paris, 1907; Member of Royal Commission on Coal Supplies, 1901–5. *Publications:* British Petrography, a Description of the Rocks of the British Isles, 1888; scientific papers on Geology and Petrology. *Recreations:* cycling, golf. *Address:* 174 Rosendale Road, Dulwich, SE21. *T:* Brixton 1306. *Club:* Athenæum.

Died 2 July 1924.

TEBB, William, FRGS; *b* Manchester, 22 Oct. 1830; *m* 1856, Mary Elizabeth Scott of Hopedale, Massachusetts, US; one *s* three *d*. *Educ:* private school. Chairman, Burstow Parish Council, 1894–1903. *Publications:* Compulsory Vaccination in England, 1884; The Recrudescence of Leprosy and its Causation, 1893; Premature Burial and How it may be Prevented (with late Col E. P. Vollum), 1896, 2nd edition, 1905 (edited by Dr Walter Hadwin). *Recreations:* travel and change of occupation. *Address:* Rede Hall, Burstow, Horley, Surrey. *TA:* Shipleybridge. *Died 23 Jan. 1918.*

TEDDER, Henry Richard, FSA; late Secretary since 1889, and Librarian since 1874, of the Athenæum Club; retired 1922; *b* South Kensington, 25 June 1850; *e s* of late William Henry Tedder and Elizabeth, *d* of Richard Ferris; *m* 1st, Alice (*d* 1915), *d* of D. Callan; two *d*; 2nd, 1916, Violet, *d* of late Frederick H. Anns. *Educ:* privately, and in France. From early life devoted himself to librarianship; librarian to 1st Lord Acton, 1873–74; one of the organisers and joint-sec. of 1st International Conference of Librarians, 1877; joint hon. sec. of Library Association, 1878–80; hon. treas. of the same, 1889–97, and

from 1898; President, 1897–98; treas. and sec. Metropolitan Free Libraries Committee, 1878–80; organising sec. of Pope Commemoration Committee, Twickenham, 1888; hon. treas. second International Conference of Librarians, 1897; hon. treas. and hon. sec. Advanced Historical Teaching Fund from 1902; hon. treasurer Royal Historical Society from 1904; VP, 1923; Secretary to Herbert Spencer's Trustees; Member of Royal Commission on Public Records, 1910–19. *Publications:* joint-editor of first three volumes of Transactions of Library Association, and of Reports of 1st and 2nd International Library Conference; editor of continuation of Descriptive Sociology (Herbert Spencer Trust); author of many papers in publications of Library Association, some printed separately, articles in reviews, and contributions to Encyclopædia Britannica, Dictionary of National Biography, and Palgrave's Dictionary of Political Economy. *Club:* Athenæum.

Died 1 Aug. 1924.

TEELING, Bartholomew, KCP; Private Chamberlain to the Pope; head of family of Syddon and Mullagha; *b* 27 June 1848; *e* surv. *s* of Charles George Teeling; *m* 1st, 1879, (*d* 1906) *d* of Rev. Thomas Clarke, Rector of Woodeaton, Oxford; three *s* two *d*; 2nd, 1911, Florence, *y d* of late T. R. Auld. Served in the Pontifical Zouaves during the Campaign of 1867 (Cross Fidei et Virtuti); received a medal for special service in 1870 from Pope Pius the Ninth, and the Bene Merenti medal from Pope Leo XIII; served as Captain in 8th Batt. Rifle Brigade and 3rd Batt. Royal Irish Rifles; retired as Hon. Captain in the Army; in conjunction with Cardinal Cullen and the Earl of Granard organised The Catholic Union of Ireland in 1872, of which Association he was Secretary; possesses historical family relics of 1798, and the bureau which stood in the Irish House of Lords. *Publications:* Military Maxims and Apophthegms of Commanders Ancient and Modern; My Weatherwise Companion; My First Prisoner; contributes to literary magazines. *Recreations:* riding on horseback, making genealogical research.

Died 4 Jan. 1921.

TEELING, Charles Hamilton, KC, Ireland. Called to Bar, 1868; QC 1894. *Died 1921.*

TEETZEL, Hon. James Vernal; retired Justice of the Supreme Court of Judicature for Ontario, Common Pleas Division; *b* 6 March 1853; *m* 1880, Priscilla, *d* of late John Darling; no *c*. *Educ:* Woodstock, Galt, Toronto. Called to Bar, 1877; QC 1889; Bencher Law Society, Upper Canada, 1891, 1896, and 1901; Mayor of Hamilton, 1899–1900; contested Hamilton for Dominion Parliament, 1900; LLD MacMaster University, 1907. *Recreations:* golf, riding. *Address:* The Alexandra Apartments, Toronto. *TA:* Teetzel, Toronto. *T:* Main 4991. *Clubs:* Toronto; York; Hamilton.

Died 24 Aug. 1926.

TEIGNMOUTH, 4th Baron, *cr* 1797; **Frederick William John Shore,** Bt 1792; *b* 27 Aug. 1844; *s* of 2nd Baron and Caroline, *d* of William Browne, Tallantire Hall, Cumberland; *S* brother, 1915; *m* 1894, Anne Louisa, *d* of late Peter Connellan. *Educ:* Harrow. Joined RA 1867; Lieut-Col 1894. *Heir: b* Henry Noel Shore, *b* 29 Aug. 1847. *Address:* Ballyduff, Thomastown, Co. Kilkenny.

Died 11 Dec. 1916.

TEIGNMOUTH, 5th Baron, *cr* 1797; **Commander Henry Noel Shore,** RN; Bt 1792; *b* 29 Aug. 1847; *s* of 2nd Baron and Caroline, *d* of William Browne, Tallantire Hall, Cumberland; *S* brother, 1916; *m* 1880, Mary Aglionby, *d* of Rev. Canon Porteus; two *s*. *Educ:* Edinburgh Academy. HMS Britannia as naval cadet, 1861; served in several ships; Inspecting Officer of Coastguard, 1881–89; retired on account of ill-health, 1891; studied art under Professor Legros at University College, 1879–80; exhibited pictures at Royal Institute of Painters in Water Colours, Royal Scottish Academy, Royal Irish Academy, and other galleries. *Publications:* read paper on China and Japan by request of Council of Society of Arts, Commerce, and Manufactures, 1882; The Flight of the Lapwing in China, Japan, and Formosa; Smuggling Ways and Smuggling Days; Old Foye Days; Three Pleasant Springs in Portugal; (with Charles G. Harper) The Smugglers (2 vols); many magazine and newspaper articles, and contributions to professional journals. *Recreations:* painting, motoring, magic. *Heir: s* Hon. Hugh Aglionby Shore, late India, PWD [*b* 12 July 1881; *m* 1915, Caroline, *d* of Col Marsh, RE; two *s* one *d*]. *Address:* Mount Elton, Clevedon, Somerset.

Died 15 Feb. 1926.

TEIXEIRA DE MATTOS, Alexander Louis; Chevalier of the Order of Leopold II, 1920; FZS; author and translator; *b* Amsterdam, 9 April 1865; *s* of late Jacques Teixeira de Mattos and Bertha, *d* of

Augustus Mendes; *m* 1900, Lily, *d* of late William Armit Lees and *widow* of W. C. K. Wilde. *Educ:* Kensington Catholic Public School; Beaumont; private tuition under Monsignor Capel. Settled in England, 1874; editor of Dramatic Opinions, 1891; assistant-editor and afterwards editor of the Candid Friend, 1901–2; Head of Intelligence Section, War Trade Intelligence Dept, 1915–18; Secretary of the Dept, 1918–19; represented the Dept on Main Licensing Committee, 1917–19; translated many books and plays from the French, Flemish, German, Danish and Dutch; a liberal and a Catholic. *Publications:* Tyltyl; translations of Melati van Java's Resident's Daughter, Couperus' Ecstasy (with John Gray), Majesty (with the late Ernest Dowson), Books of the Small Souls and all later works, Zola's Curée, van Hoytema's Happy Owls, Arthur Byl's Yvette Guilbert, Israëls' Spain, the Souvenirs of Léonard, Memoirs of Marshal Oudinot, the Recollections of Alexis de Tocqueville, the Memoirs of Chateaubriand, the Memoirs of President Kruger, Rompel's Heroes of the Boer War, Maeterlinck's Double Garden and all later works, Georgette Leblanc-Maeterlinck's Choice of Life and children's Blue Bird, Grenard's Tibet, Vicomte R. d'Humières' Through Isle and Empire, Stijn Streuvels' Path of Life, Ewald's My Little Boy, the Old Room and all the fairytales, Marius' Dutch Painting in the Nineteenth Century, Leblanc's Exploits of Arsène Lupin and all later works, Leroux's Phantom of the Opera and Balaoo, Fabre's Life of the Spider and all later works, Weissl's Mystery of the Green Car, Paoli's Their Majesties, etc. *Plays:* Zola's Thérèse Raquin and Heirs of Rabourdin, Van Nouhuijs' Goldfish, Josine Holland's Leida, Maeterlinck's Joyzelle, Blue Bird and all later plays, the Cradle (from the Flemish), etc. *Recreation:* bridge. *Address:* 9 Cheltenham Terrace, Chelsea, SW3. *TA:* Teixeira, Sloane, London. *T:* Victoria 643. *Clubs:* Reform, Cleveland, Pilgrims.   *Died 5 Dec. 1921.*

TEMPERLEY, Rev. Canon Arthur, MA; late Rector of South Willingham, Lincolnshire; Hon. Secretary, Lincoln Diocesan Board of Education; Canon and Prebendary of Lafford in Lincoln Cathedral; *b* 1850; *m* 1880, Frances G. Howard Tripp; two *s* five *d. Educ:* Sidney Sussex College, Cambridge. Mathematical master at Hereford Cathedral School; Headmaster of De Aston School, Market Rasen; Examiner for Cambridge Local Examination Syndicate; Member of the Education Committee of the Lindsey County Council. *Recreations:* cycling, woodcarving, tennis. *Address:* Heighington, Lincoln. *TA:* Branston. *M:* FU 947.   *Died 21 Feb. 1927.*

TEMPEST, Sir Percy Crosland, KBE 1923 (CBE 1918); MInstCE; General Manager, Southern Railway, since 1923; *b* 1861; *s* of Charles Tempest, solicitor, Leeds; *m* 1897, Evelyn, *d* of Alfred Willis, DL, JP; two *d. Educ:* Grammar School and University, Leeds. Joined the SE and Chatham Railway Engineers Department, 1882; Assistant Engineer, 1896; Chief Engineer, 1899; General Manager and Chief Engineer SE and Chatham Railway, 1920–23; Engineer to the English Channel Tunnel Co. since 1916. Belgian Croix d'Officier de l'Ordre de Leopold; Chevalier of the Legion of Honour; Member of the Order of Dannebrog, Denmark. *Address:* 77 Carlisle Mansions, SW1. *T:* Victoria 896.   *Died 3 Nov. 1924.*

TEMPEST-HICKS, Brig.-Gen. Henry, CB 1900; JP Herts and Middlesex; *b* 25 November 1852; *s* of late George Henry Tempest-Hicks of Hillgrove, Wells, Somerset; *m* 1885, Anne Clara Georgiana, *d* of late Charles Hemery of Gladsmuir, Monken Hadley, Herts; one *s* one *d. Educ:* Harrow; Trinity College, Cambridge. Joined 2nd Royal Dublin Fusiliers, 1872; commanded his regiment in Boer War, 1899–1902 (despatches, Queen's medal, 5 clasps, King's medal, 2 clasps, CB); served in the Aden Hinterland; Brevet Col 1904; retired, 1904; commanded Coast Defences and 2nd South Wales Infantry Brigade, 1915. *Recreations:* won Freshman's 100 yards and hurdles at Cambridge. *Address:* Gladsmuir, Monken Hadley, Herts; Hillgrove, Wells, Somerset. *Clubs:* Arthur's, Army and Navy.
                     Died 10 Nov. 1922.

TEMPLE, Sir Alfred (George), Kt 1920; FSA; Director of the Guildhall Gallery; *b* 27 Oct. 1848; *m* 1880, Elizabeth Mary Harriot (*d* 1926), *e d* of late Edwin Undecimus Crosley, CE; one *s.* Knight Commander of Order of the Dannebrog, Denmark; Knight Commander of Order of Alfonso XII of Spain; Officier de l'Instruction Publique de France, Chevalier of the Order of Leopold of Belgium, Officier of Order of the Crown of Belgium; Commander of the Royal Order of Isabel the Catholic of Spain, and of the Inca of Peru; corresponding Member of the Royal Academy of San Fernando, Madrid; Member of Executive Committee of the National Trust, and of Council of Royal Drawing Society; Chairman of Fine Art Section Irish International Exhibition, 1907; Member of British Art Committee Franco-British Exhibition, 1908, of International Exhibition, Rome, 1911, of Exhibition of Miniatures, Brussels, 1912,

and of the Exhibition of Spanish Painting at the Royal Academy, 1920, etc. Has organised at the Guildhall since 1890 special exhibitions, which have embraced the works of British artists, including a separate exhibition of the works of J. M. W. Turner, and of those of France, Spain, Holland, Belgium, and Denmark. The sixteenth exhibition was of naval and military works by painters of the allied nations—Great Britain, France, Russia, and Belgium. *Publications:* contributor to various Art periodicals, and author of the Art of Painting in the Queen's Reign, 1897; Sacred Art, 1898; The Nation's Pictures, 1901; Great Pictures in Private Galleries, 1905; the Wallace Collection, 1903; Modern Spanish Painting, 1908; By Rochford Town, and other Poems, 1926; Guildhall Memories, 1918, etc. *Address:* The Guildhall, EC. *T:* London Wall 6400; 31 College Road, Dulwich Village, SE21. *T:* Sydenham 4530. *Club:* Conservative.
                     Died 8 Jan. 1928.

TEMPLE, John, CB 1917; Chairman, Warrington Wire Rope Works, Ltd; Director, Horden Collieries Ltd, North Brancepeth Coal Co., Ltd; Trustee for Debenture Holders, United Alkali Co., Ltd; *b* 18 April 1839; *s* of Robert Temple, Banker, Colne, Lancashire; *m* 1st, 1867, Mary Anne (*d* 1917), *d* of late Humphrey Roberts, Queen's Gate Place, SW; three *s* one *d*; 2nd, Katherine Mary, *d* of Walter Hull of Staley, near Manchester. *Educ:* privately. Entered the telegraph service in Leeds, Manchester, and London, 1852; joined the Atlantic Telegraph Company upon its formation, 1856, and worked on the staff of Sir Charles Bright, Engineer-in-Chief, subsequently obtaining a post on the Agamemnon during the laying of the first cable across the Atlantic; engaged by Glass, Elliot and Co. 1859; afterwards the Telegraph Construction and Maintenance Company, and acted over four years as Engineer for the Malta and Alexandria Cable and other Mediterranean Cable Companies, having his Headquarters at Malta; returned to England in time for the laying, in the summers of 1865–66, of the Second Atlantic Cable, and was Third Engineer-in-Charge in these expeditions on the Great Eastern, under Sir Samuel Canning; was in charge of the grappling ship Albany, which picked up the first piece of the lost 1865 cable; Managing Director of the Warrington Wire Rope Works, 1867; for some years a Director of the West India Pacific Company, and acted as liquidator on its final sale; has large interests in coal, particularly in Durham. *Address:* Mossley Bank, Aigburth, Liverpool. *TA:* Temple, Aigburth. *T:* Mossley Hill 158. *M:* K7003. *Clubs:* Constitutional; Exchange, Liverpool.
                     Died 17 May 1922.

TEMPLE, Lieut-Col William, VC 1864; BA, MB, LRCSI; Army Medical Staff, retired pay; *b* 7 Nov. 1833; *o s* of late William Temple, MD, of Monaghan, and Anne, *d* of Hugh Hamill of Rooskey; *m* 4th *d* (*d* 1918) of late Maj.-Gen. T. R. Mould, CB, RE; three *s* five *d. Educ:* private school; Trinity College, Dublin. Entered the service, 1858; served in Royal Artillery in New Zealand Wars, Taranaki Campaign, 1860–61, and Waikato Campaign, 1863–65; present in actions of Teairei, Rangiriri, Rangiawhia, etc. (despatches, VC 'for gallant conduct during the assault on the enemy's position at Rangiriri, in exposing his life to imminent danger in crossing the entrance to the Maori keep at a point on which the enemy had concentrated their fire, with a view to render assistance to the wounded, more especially the late Capt. Mercer, RA'); Hon. Surgeon to Viceroy, in recognition of services in that country. *Recreations:* takes an interest in photography, mechanical work, field sports, etc. *Address:* c/o Cox and Co., Charing Cross, SW.
                     Died 13 Feb. 1919.

TEMPLE-GORE-LANGTON, Hon. Chandos Graham; *b* 8 Sept. 1873; *brother* and *heir-pres.* 5th Earl Temple; *m* 1907, Frances Ethel, *y d* of late Rev. A. L. Gore; two *s* one *d. Educ:* Eton. Was Captain 1st Dragoon Guards, North Somerset Imperial Yeomanry. *Address:* The Mount, Newton St Loe, Bristol.
                     Died 19 Aug. 1921.

TEMPLEMORE, 3rd Baron, *cr* 1831; **Arthur Henry Chichester,** late Major (Mil.) Irish Regiment; *b* 1854; *e s* of 2nd Baron and Laura, *d* of Rt Hon. Sir Arthur Paget, GCB, *brother* of 1st Marquis of Anglesey, KG; *S father*, 1906; *m* 1st, 1879, Evelyn (*d* 1883), *d* of late Rev. W. J. Stracey-Clitherow; one *s*; 2nd, 1885, Alice, *d* of C. J. Augustus Dawkins, DL and JP for Co. Wexford; one *s. Educ:* Eton. Private secretary to Rt Hon. R. A. Cross, Home Secretary, 1875–78. Owned about 26,700 acres. High Sheriff, Co. Wexford, 1890. *Heir:* *s* Hon. Arthur Claud Spencer Chichester, *b* 12 Sept. 1880. *Address:* 4 Portman Square, W1. *T:* Paddington 2698; Dunbrody Park, Arthurstown, Co. Wexford.   *Died 28 Sept. 1924.*

TEMPLER, His Honour Judge Frederic Gordon; County Court Judge, York Circuit, since 1898; *b* Greenwich, 12 June 1849; 3rd s of late John Charles Templer, Master of the Court of Exchequer, and Hannah Frances, *e d* of Admiral of the Fleet Sir James Alexander Gordon, GCB; *m* 1876, Alice Blanche (*d* 1914), 5th *d* of late Rev. W. C. Templer, Rector of Burton Bradstock. *Educ:* Harrow; Trinity Coll. Camb., BA, 1870. Barrister, 1872; Inner Temple, Western Circuit, Dorset Sessions; appointed District Judge, Cyprus, 1882; Queen's Advocate, 1893. *Publications:* Summary Jurisdiction Act, 1878. *Recreations:* cricket, golf, shooting, fishing, skating, astronomy, chess. *Address:* The Hall, Eaglescliffe, Yorks. *Club:* The Yorkshire.

Died 28 Aug. 1918.

TEMPLER, Col J. L. B.; formerly Adviser in Ballooning to the Government, and Superintendent Balloon Factory at Aldershot; *b* 1846; *s* of John Templer, Master in HM Court of Exchequer; *m* 1889, Florence Gilliat, of Chorleywood Cedars, Herts; one *d. Educ:* Harrow; Trinity College, Cambridge. Director of Steam Road Transport in South Africa, 1900; in command of Balloon Detachment, Egypt, 1885; organiser of steam road transport for the army. *Address:* Laughton Grange, Lewes, Sussex.

Died 2 Jan. 1924.

TENNANT, Charles Coombe, JP; *b* 30 July 1852; *o s* of late Charles Tennant, MP, and the late Gertrude Barbara Rich, *e d* of Adm. Henry Theodosius Brown Collier, RN; *m* 1895, Winifred Margaret, *y d* of George Pearce-Serocold of Cherry Hinton, Cambridgeshire; two *s. Educ:* Harrow; Balliol College, Oxford (BA). Called to Bar, Inner Temple, 1882. *Address:* Cadoxton Lodge, Vale of Neath, South Wales. *Club:* Brooks's. *Died 5 Nov. 1928.*

TENNANT, Hercules, CMG 1906; Secretary to the Law Department of the Transvaal Government, 1901–8; JP for the Transvaal; of the Inner Temple, Barrister-at-Law, 1871; *b* Cape Town, 3 March 1850; *e s* of the Hon. Sir David Tennant, KCMG; *m* 1874, Mary Cathcart, *d* of Robert Graham, 14th of Fintry. Member of Cape House of Assembly, for several years representing the division of Caledon; Advocate of the Supreme Courts of Cape Colony and Transvaal; was Lieutenant in the Duke of Edinburgh's Own Volunteer Rifles, Cape Town; Extra ADC to Governor of Cape Colony (The Rt Hon. Sir Bartle Frere); served Basuto War, 1880–81 (medal), with rank of Captain as ASO to GOC; held various positions in Cape Civil Service since 1882, such as Registrar and Taxing Officer of Cape Supreme Court, Acting Master of Supreme Court, and High Sheriff of Cape Colony, from which latter position he was transferred to his post in the Transvaal. *Publications:* editor and compiler of a number of legal text-books. *Address:* Royal Colonial Institute, Northumberland Avenue, WC. *Club:* British Empire.

Died 21 May 1925.

TENNYSON, 2nd Baron, *cr* 1884; **Hallam Tennyson,** GCMG 1903 (KCMG 1899); PC 1905; DL and JP, Hants; Hon. Colonel South Australian Artillery, and 7th Victorian Light Horse; Deputy-Governor of the Isle of Wight since 1913; *b* 11 Aug. 1852; *s* of Alfred, 1st Lord Tennyson, DCL, FRS; *S* father, 1892; *m* 1st, 1884, Audrey (*d* 1916), *d* of Charles Boyle, and *g d* of Admiral the Hon. Sir Courtenay Boyle; one *s* (and two *s* decd); 2nd, 1918, Mary Emily, *widow* of Andrew Hichens, Monks Hatch, Compton, Guildford, and *d* of Charles Prinsep (Advocate-General, India). *Educ:* Marlborough; Trinity College Cambridge; Inner Temple. After that he lived with his father as his private secretary; Governor and Commander-in-Chief of South Australia, 1899–1902; first Acting Governor-General of the Commonwealth of Australia, 1902, and Governor-General of Australia, 1902–04. Member Marlborough Coll. Executive Council; President of the Folk Song Society; Gordon Boys' Home Executive Council, etc. Grand Cross of the Japanese Order of the Rising Sun, 1905; LittD Camb., Melbourne, and Adelaide; DCL Oxford; Unionist. Owned important modern pictures by G. F. Watts, RA, Briton Riviere, RA, Hubert Herkomer, RA, Holman Hunt, R. Doyle, E. Lear. *Publications:* Jack and the Beanstalk, illustrated by R. Caldecott; Alfred, Lord Tennyson: a Memoir, 1897; edited Charles Turner's Collected Sonnets (with preface); Poems by Two Brothers (with preface); In Memoriam (with Notes); Eversley Edition of complete works of Tennyson (with own and father's notes), 1908; contributed articles and poems to magazines; Tennyson and his Friends. *Heir: s* Hon. Lionel Hallam Tennyson, *b* 7 Nov. 1889. *Address:* Farringford, Freshwater, Isle of Wight. *Club:* Athenæum.

Died 2 Dec. 1928.

TENNYSON-d'EYNCOURT, Edmund Charles; Metropolitan Police Magistrate, 1897–1924; Marylebone, 1916–22; Marlborough Street, 1922–24; *b* 11 Feb. 1855; *e s* of late Louis Chas Tennyson d'Eyncourt, Metropolitan Police Magistrate of Bayons Manor, Market Rasen; *m* 1892, Ruth (JP Lindsey, Lincs), *o c* of Sir Augustus Godson,

MP; three *s* three *d. Educ:* Eton; University College, Oxford (MA). Barrister, Inner Temple, 1881; formerly Hon. Sec., United Club; Captain Lincs Imperial Yeomanry; Chairman Lincs Lindsey Quarter Sessions. *Recreations:* riding, shooting, golf. *Address:* Bayons Manor, Tealby, Lincoln. *TA:* Tealby; *T:* Tealby 2; 57 Lowndes Square, SW1; 4 Lyall Street, SW1. *T:* Victoria 6342 and 6476. *Club:* United University. *Died 29 Oct. 1924.*

TERRELL, Thomas, KC. Called to Bar, Gray's Inn and Middle Temple, 1879; Bencher; Treasurer of the Gray's Inn, 1904; QC 1895. *Address:* 1 New Court, Temple, EC4. *T:* Central 1724.

Died 27 April 1928.

TERRINGTON, 1st Baron, *cr* 1918, of Huddersfield; **James Thomas Woodhouse,** Kt 1895; JP, DL; one of HM Railway Commissioners, 1906; MP (L) Huddersfield, 1895–1906; *b* 16 July 1852; *e s* of James Woodhouse; *m* 1876, Jessy, *d* of W. J. Reed, of Skidby, Yorks; two *s* two *d. Educ:* Hull College; Univ. College, London. LLB (Lond.). Mayor of Hull, 1891; JP and DL East Riding, Yorkshire; JP Co. Buckingham; Ex-President of Association of Municipal Corporations; Director of London City and Midland Bank, of the Hull and Barnsley Railway Company; Chairman of Governors of Hymers College, and late Chairman of Grand Committee on Law, House of Commons, Chairman of Royal Commission under Defence of the Realm Acts. *Heir: s* Hon. Harold James Selborne Woodhouse, *b* 8 May 1877. *Address:* 42 North Gate, Regent's Park, NW8. *T:* Hampstead 3620; 105 Pall Mall, SW1. *Clubs:* Reform, Bath, Ranelagh, Royal Automobile. *Died 8 Feb. 1921.*

TERRY, Dame Ellen (Alice), GBE 1925; *b* 27 Feb. 1848; *d* of Benjamin Terry, actor and Sarah Ballard; *m* 1st, 1864, G. F Watts (div.); one *s* one *d* by E. W. Godwin, FSA; 2nd, 1877, C. C. Wardell (Charles Kelly); 3rd 1907, J. Usselmann (James Carew). Made first appearance at Princess's, under Charles Kean; played first with Sir Henry Irving in The Taming of the Shrew, Queen's Theatre, Long Acre; joined Mr Bancroft at Prince of Wales's, 1875; joined Mr John Hare at the Court in Lord Lytton's The House of Darnley, 1876; on 30 Dec. 1878 made her first appearance at the Lyceum (as Ophelia); visited America with Sir H. Irving, etc. *Recreations:* reading, driving, motoring. *Address:* 35 Burleigh Mansions, WC2; The Farm, Small Hythe, Tenterden, Kent. *Died 21 July 1928.*

TERRY, Rev. Canon George Frederick, FSA 1898; FRSL 1890; FRHistS 1892; Rector of St John's Church, Princes Street, since 1909, and Canon of St Mary's Cathedral, Edinburgh; *b* 1864; *e s* of late C. F. Terry; *m* 1901, Alice Taylor, *e d* of John Musker, Shadwell Court, Thetford; two *s* three *d. Educ:* University College, Durham; LTh 1891. Educated as an architect; Deacon, 1892; Priest, 1893; Curate St Saviour, Nottingham, 1892–94; Senior Curate St Peter, Kensington, W, 1894–1901; Vicar All Souls, South Hampstead, NW, 1901–9. *Publications:* Religion in Modern Thought, 1899; The Old Theology in the New Age, 1904; Memorials of the Church of St John the Evangelist, Edinburgh, 1911, 2nd edition, 1918; Essays in Constructive Theology, 1914, etc. *Address:* 10 Learmonth Terrace, Edinburgh. *T:* Central, Edinburgh, 6286. *Club:* University, Edinburgh. *Died 7 Feb. 1919.*

TERRY, Stephen Harding, MICE; Member Inst. Mech. Engineers; *b* Dummer, Hants, 15 April 1853; *e s* of late Stephen Terry of Dummer and Anne Margaret, *d* of late Rev. Charles Shrubsole Bonnett, Rector of Avington, Hants. *Educ:* King's College, London. Apprenticed to Aveling and Porter, engineers, Rochester; employed by them and by Clayton and Shuttleworth at Lincoln and Vienna; Engineering Inspector to the Local Govt Board, 1878–89; made the Type Drawings adopted by the Board, and conducted some 800 Inquiries and reported on Water Supply, Sewerage, and other matters under the Public Health Act; equipped the First National Vaccine Station; managing partner in Engineering Works in the Midlands, 1890–93; for some 20 years in practice as Consulting Engineer, advising in numerous Engineering Works connected with Gas, Water and Electricity, Heating and Warming, Steam Cars, Cranes, Petroleum Storage and Transport, Refuse Destructors, Forced Draught and Ventilation of Ships, Rating Valuations; with Sir Fortescue Flannery, MP, devised and patented the system universally adopted of Petroleum Ship Ventilation; wrote the pioneer letter in The Lancet, 10 June 1882, which eventually led to The Standard Bread Movement. *Publications:* The Foundering of Steam-ships, 1882; many papers read before Societies; Monograph; The Crime of Docking Horses. *Recreations:* sailing, swimming, photography, carpentry. *Address:* Upcott, Seaton, Devon. *M:* T 27. *Club:* Royal Automobile (Founder Member). *Died 15 Dec. 1924.*

TETLEY, Rev. James George; Canon of Bristol, 1891–1922; Examining Chaplain to Bishop of Bristol, 1900; *b* Torquay, 6 July 1843; *o* surv. *s* of late James Tetley, MD, FRCP, and Sarah Anne, *d* of William Langmead, Elfordleigh, Devon; *m* 1868, Mary Anne Grace (*d* 1918), *d* of late George Milward, Barrister-at-Law, of Lechlade Manor, Gloucestershire. *Educ:* Magdalen Coll., Oxford (DD); DLitt Bristol 1919. Curate of Caldicot, Monmouthshire, 1867; Badminton, 1868–75; Henley-on-Thames, 1875–76; Vicar of Highnam, 1876–92; Rural Dean of North Forest, 1888–92; Proctor in Convocation for Chapter of Bristol, 1894–1910; Archdeacon of Bristol, 1910–21. *Publications:* Old Times and New, 1904; Forty Years Ago and After, 1910. *Address:* Belmont, Torre, Torquay. *Club:* United University. *Died 10 March 1924.*

TEUNON, Sir William, Kt 1921; *b* 23 May 1863; *s* of William Teunon, Aberdeen; *m* 1888, Alice Charlotte Lovell (*d* 1922); one *s* one *d. Educ:* King's College, Aberdeen; King's College, Cambridge. Entered the Indian Civil Service and posted to Bengal (Lower Provinces), 1883; to Assam, 1887; reposted to Bengal, 1895; to Eastern Bengal and Assam, 1905; again to Bengal, 1912. Appointments held: Assistant and Joint-Magistrate, Bengal; Asst Deputy-Commissioner, Assam; District and Sessions Judge, Bengal and Eastern Bengal; Legal Remembrancer and Secretary to Lieut Governor's Legislative Council, Eastern Bengal and Assam; Puisne Judge of the High Court, Calcutta; retired, 1922. *Publication:* Report on Civil Judicial Offices, Eastern Bengal and Assam. *Recreation:* golf. *Clubs:* East India United Service; United Service, Calcutta. *Died 29 April 1926.*

TEW, Percy, JP, DL, West Riding of York; *b* Heath, near Wakefield, 3 July 1840; *y s* of late Edward Tew, JP, DL, Wakefield; *m* 1868, Madeline Elizabeth, *o d* of Rev. Canon Thomas Lowe, Vicar of Willingdon, Sussex, and Canon of Chichester; one *s* five *d. Educ:* Exeter College, Oxford (BA 1862; MA 1865). Became a Member of the Firm of Leatham, Tew & Company, Bankers of Wakefield, Pontefract, and elsewhere, 1862; upon the amalgamation of the above firm with Barclay's Bank of 58 Lombard Street, EC, became a Director of the latter Company, 1906; a Director of the Aire and Calder Navigation; Chairman of the Justices of the Petty Sessions at Division of Lower Agbrigg in the West Riding of Yorkshire. *Address:* Heath, Wakefield, Yorkshire; Brightling Park, Sussex. *M:* C 4300. *Club:* Carlton. *Died 24 March 1921.*

THACKERAY, Col Sir Edward Talbot, VC 1857; KCB 1897 (CB 1886); *b* 19 Oct. 1836; *s* of Rev. Francis Thackeray of Broxbourne, Herts, and Mary Anne, *d* of John Shakespear, Singleton, Sussex; *m* 1st, 1862, Amy Mary Anne (*d* 1865), *d* of Eyre Evans Crowe; 2nd, 1869, Elizabeth, Lady of Grace, Order of St John of Jerusalem, *d* of Major T. B. Pleydell; four *s* two *d. Educ:* Marlborough; HEIC Military Coll., Addiscombe. Entered RE 1854; Capt. 1865; Major, 1872; Lt-Col 1880; Col 1884; retired, 1888; served throughout Indian Mutiny, 1857–58 (medal two clasps, VC at siege of Delhi); Afghan War, 1879–80 (severely wounded, despatches, medal); held various posts in PWD, 1858–71; commanded Bengal Sappers and Miners, 1879–85; Chief Commissioner Order of St John of Jerusalem, 1893–98, and Knight of Grace of the Order; Commissioner, Bordighera branch British Red Cross Society, Italy, 1917–19 (despatches, War and Victory Medals). *Publications:* Two Indian Campaigns; Biographies of Officers of the Bengal Engineers; Reminiscences of the Indian Mutiny and Afghanistan, 1916; History of Sieges in the XIXth Century; etc. *Address:* c/o H. S. King & Co., Pall Mall, SW1. *Club:* Athenæum. *Died 3 Sept. 1927.*

THACKERAY, Rev. Francis St John, FSA; FGS; MA; Vicar of Mapledurham since 1883; *b* 13 Dec. 1832; *s* of Rev. Francis Thackeray, author of Life of Chatham, and Mary Anne, *d* of John Shakespear, of Singleton, Sussex; *m* 1860, Louisa Katharine, *d* of Rev. A. Irvine, Vicar of St Margaret's, Leicester; one *s* three *d. Educ:* Eton; Merton College, Oxford. First Class (Classics), 1854, Moderations; First Class, 1856, Lit. Hum. Fellow and Tutor of Lincoln College, 1857; Assistant Master of Eton College, 1858–83. *Publications:* Anthologia Latina, 8th edn, 1900; Anthologia Græca, 9th edn, 1900; Eton College Library, 1881; Guide to the Roman Coins at Eton, 1882; Translations from Prudentius into English verse, with Introduction and Notes, 1890; Memoir of Provost Hawtrey, 1896; Sermons preached in Eton College Chapel, 1897; Christian Biographies through Eighteen Centuries, 1908; Joint Editor with Rev. E. D. Stone of Florilegium Latinum, vol. i, 1899, vol. ii, 1902; Three Lectures on the Psalms, 1917. *Recreation:* fossilising in England and France, 1890–1906. *Address:* Mapledurham Vicarage, Reading. *Clubs:* Athenæum, Authors'. *Died 14 July 1919.*

THACKERAY, Lance; painter and illustrator. Held one-man exhibitions at the Leicester Galleries, 1908; Fine Art Society, 1910; Walker's Galleries, 1913. *Publications:* The Light Side of Egypt, 1908; The People of Egypt, 1910. *Clubs:* Savage, Arts; Turf, Cairo. *Died 11 Aug. 1916.*

THACKERSEY, Sir Vithaldas Damodher, Kt 1908; JP; millowner; *b* 1 Dec. 1873; *s* of late Damodher Thackersey Mooljee, a Bhattia millowner in Bombay. *Educ:* Elphinstone College, Bombay. Caste Bhattia Hindu; controls five of the largest cotton mills in Bombay; Member of Corporation, 1898–1910, Non-official Member of the Bombay Legislative Council, 1903–10; Chairman of Standing Committee and President of Corporation, 1907; was Chairman of Millowners' Association; Chairman, National Congress Exhibition Committee, 1904; President of the Second Industrial Conference held at Calcutta, 1906; takes deep interest in Indian mining and railways promotion; Chairman Bombay Central Co-operative Bank, Ltd; Director of many Joint-Stock Companies; representative Bombay Chamber of Commerce and Bombay Millowners' Association on the Indian Factory Commission, 1907–8; Member of Bombay Improvement Trust, 1909–15; Member of Imperial Legislative Council, Calcutta, 1910–13; Trustee the Grant Medical College since 1908; Trustee of the Sir Sassoon David Trust for Agricultural and Educational Fund, 1912; millowners' representative on Bombay Port Trust, 1913–17; Chairman of Committee on proposed Reclamation of the foreshore of Bombay, 1912; Chairman Indian Merchants' Chamber and Bureau, 1917–18. *Address:* Damodher Bhuvan, Warden Road, Mahaluxmi. *TA:* Dragonnade. *T:* 811 and 811A. *M:* 1003, 1115, 1665, and 2209. *Died 12 Aug. 1922.*

THARP, Arthur Keane; Deputy Chairman National Mutual Life Assurance Society; Chairman of Bullers, Limited; *b* Chippenham, 1848; *s* of Rev. Augustus James Tharp, of Chippenham, Cambridgeshire; *m y d* of Rev. H. Jodrell. *Educ:* Haileybury College; Gonville and Caius College, Cambridge (BA). Served in the Derbyshire Yeomanry Cavalry. *Recreations:* shooting, yachting, golf, etc. *Address:* Midanbury, Bitterne Park, Hants. *T:* Southampton 2893. *Clubs:* Marlborough, Naval and Military, MCC, Beefsteak; Royal Motor Yacht; Royal Yacht Squadron, Cowes. *Died 17 Nov. 1928.*

That, *see* Tate, James William.

THESIGER, Hon. Sir Edward (Peirson), KCB 1911 (CB 1886); Clerk Assistant of House of Lords, 1890–1916; *b* London, 19 Dec. 1842; *y s* of 1st Baron Chelmsford, Lord Chancellor of Great Britain, and Anna, *d* of William Tinling, Southampton, *neice* of Maj. Peirson the defender of Jersey; *m* 1869, Georgina (*d* 1906), *d* of William Bruce Stopford Sackville; three *s* one *d. Educ:* Eton. A clerk in Parliament Office, 1862; sec. of Presentations to successive Lord Chancellors, 1866–90; Clerk Assistant of the Parliaments, 1890; Chairman of the United Westminster Schools; Member of the London Diocesan Conference; Treasurer of the Queen Victoria Clergy Fund and Church House. *Recreations:* member I Zingari Cricket Club; for twelve years secretary Civil Service Cricket Club; golf, cycling; plays the violin; late member of the orchestra of the Wandering Minstrels, Imperial Institute; member of Handel Society. *Address:* 142 Sloane Street, SW1. *T:* Victoria 1349. *Club:* Junior Carlton. *Died 11 Nov. 1928.*

THESIGER, Capt. Hon. Wilfred (Gilbert), DSO 1900; Consul-General, New York, since 1919; *b* 25 March 1871; 3rd *s* of 2nd Baron Chelmsford; *m* 1909, Kathleen, *d* of T. M. C. Vigors, Burgage, Co. Carlow; four *s. Educ:* Cheltenham. Nominated Vice-Consul, Algiers, but did not proceed; transferred to Taranto, Italy, 1897; Vice-Consul at Belgrade, Servia, 1901–6; given local rank of 2nd Secretary in Diplomatic Service since 1902, and was in charge of Legation, 1903–6; served 15th Batt. Imperial Yeomanry, South Africa, 1900–1 (despatches, DSO); European War, 1914–15 (despatches); Consul for N and NE Russia, 1906–7; HBM's Consul for Congo, 1907–9; Consul-General Abyssinia, 1909–14, with local rank of Envoy Extraordinary and Minister Plenipotentiary; General Staff, War Office, 1914–19. *Address:* British Consulate-General, New York. *Club:* St James's. *Died 31 Jan. 1920.*

THIBAUDEAU, Hon. Alfred Arthur; Senator since 1896; head of Thibaudeau Frères et Cie, Montreal; *b* 1 Dec. 1860; *m* 1894, Marie Thérèse Irene Eva, *d* of late Hon. E. Rodier, Montreal. *Educ:* Quebec High School. *Club:* St James's, Montreal. *Died Aug. 1926.*

THIBAULT, Jacques Anatole François; *see* France, Anatole.

THICKNESSE, Rt. Rev. Francis Henry, DD; Canon of Peterborough, 1875–1920; Rector of Oxendon, Northamptonshire, 1892–1914; *b* 14 May 1829; 2nd *s* of Rev. W. E. Coldwell, Prebendary of Lichfield, and Mary, *d* of E. Norman; *m* 1st, Anne, *d* of Ralph Thicknesse, MP; two *s* two *d*; 2nd, Beatrice, *d* of Marsham Argles, DD, Dean of Peterborough. *Educ:* Brasenose College, Oxford. Hon. Canon of Manchester, 1863–75; Bishop of Leicester, 1888–1902; Archdeacon of Northampton, 1875–1911. *Address:* South Luffenham Hall, Rutland. *Club:* United University.

Died 2 Nov. 1921.

THISELTON-DYER, Sir William Turner, KCMG 1899 (CMG 1882); CIE 1892; MA, BSc, LLD, ScD, PhD; FRS 1880; JP Glos; Director Royal Botanic Gardens, Kew, 1885–1905; *b* Westminster, 28 July 1843; *s* of late William George Thiselton-Dyer, MD; *m* 1877, Harriet Ann, *d* of late Sir Joseph Dalton Hooker, OM, GCSI; one *s* one *d*. *Educ:* King's College School; Christ Church, Oxford (Hon. Student, 1899). Professor of Natural History at RAC Cirencester, 1868; Professor of Botany, Royal College of Science for Ireland, 1870; Assistant Director Royal Gardens, Kew, 1875–85; Fellow University of London, 1887–90; VPRS, 1896–97; Royal Commissioner Melbourne Centennial Exhibition, 1888; Paris International Exhibition, 1900; St Louis Exhibition, 1904; Botanical Adviser to Secretary of State for Colonies, 1902–6; Representative of University of Oxford on Gloucestershire Education Committee, 1908–16; Member of Court of University of Bristol since 1909. *Publications:* joint author of Flora of Middlesex, 1869; edited English edition of Sachs's Text-book of Botany, 1875; editor of Flora Capensis and Flora of Tropical Africa. *Address:* The Ferns, Witcombe, Gloucester. *Died 23 Dec. 1928.*

THOM, Donaldson Rose, MA; Secretary of the University of Aberdeen; advocate; *b* and *educ* in Aberdeen. *Recreation:* golf. *Address:* 42 Albyn Place, Aberdeen; Hazlehead House, near Aberdeen. *Clubs:* Royal Northern, University, Aberdeen.

Died 23 Jan. 1920.

THOMAS, Rev. Alexander; Canon of Killaloe, 1913; Incumbent of Nenagh since 1888. Ordained, 1875; Curate of Castleconnor, 1875–79; Rector of Kilcollmin Erris, 1879–82; Tubbercurry, 1882–88. *Address:* Nenagh, Co. Tipperary.

Died 9 June 1918.

THOMAS, Annie, (Mrs Pender Cudlip); novelist; *b* Aldborough, Suffolk, 1838; *o d* of Lieut George Thomas, RN; and *widow* of the Rev. Pender Cudlip. *Educ:* at home. *Publications:* beginning with Sir Victor's Choice, and Denis Doune, in 1862, has since written upwards of 100 novels and innumerable stories, sketches, etc; Blotted Out, 1876; Our Set, 1881; That Other Woman, 1889; Comrades True, 1900; The Diva, 1901; The Cleavers of Cleaver, 1902; Social Ghosts, 1903; Penholders of the Past, 1913.

Died 24 Nov. 1918.

THOMAS, Colonel Arthur Havilland, CB 1902; DSO 1900; retired 1910; *b* India, 31 July 1860; 3rd *s* of Henry S. Thomas, retired, Indian Civil Service; *m* 1903, Louie Marion, *d* of Edward Druce, Dover. *Educ:* Cheltenham Coll.; Royal Military Coll., Sandhurst. Joined 31st Regt, 1880; promoted Captain, 1887; joined Army Service Corps, 1887; promoted Major, 1895; Lt-Col, 1900; Colonel 1904; DAAG China and Hong Kong, 1893–96; in charge of supply and transport Sierra Leone Rebellion, 1898, and Sierra Leone Protectorate Expedition, 1898–99 (despatches, medal with clasp, and DSO); DAAG Field Army, South Africa, 1899–1900; AAG and Director of Supplies, 1901–2 (despatches, SA medal, 3 clasps, King's medal, 2 clasps, CB); served European War as ADST. *Recreations:* fishing, golf. *Address:* Dunmow, Fleet, Hants. *Club:* Army and Navy.

Died 8 Nov. 1919.

THOMAS, Maj.-Gen. Charles Frederick, Indian Army; *m* Edith Eliza (*d* 1917), *e d* of late Rev. Weston Joseph Sparkes. Maj.-Gen. 1899. *Address:* Oakcliff, Dawlish.

Died March 1922.

THOMAS, Ven. David Richard, MA; FSA; Hon. Fellow RSA Ireland; Archdeacon of Montgomery and Canon of St Asaph since 1886; Rector of Llandrinio since 1892; *m* Louisa, *e d* of Wm Goodenough Bayly, DCL, Vicar of Fittleworth; two *s* two *d*. *Educ:* Ruthin School; Jesus College, Oxford (Scholar). Rector of St M. Cefn, 1864–77; Vicar of Meifod, Montgomeryshire, 1877–92. *Publications:* History of the Diocese of St Asaph, 1874, new enlarged and illustrated edition, 1906–13; A History of the Church in Wales (in Welsh), 1874; The Life and Work of Bishop Davies and William Salesbury, 1902,

etc. *Recreations:* the archæology and history of Wales. *Address:* Llandrinio Rectory, Oswestry; The Canonry, St Asaph. *T:* Llandrinio.

Died 4 Oct. 1916.

THOMAS, General Sir Francis William, KCB 1911; *b* 10 May 1832; *o s* of late Capt. J. W. Thomas, RM; *m* 1857, Virginia (*d* 1905), *e d* of late A. Stodart; two *s* three *d*. *Educ:* privately. Entered RM 1849; Gen. 1889; retired, 1897; served Crimea, 1854–55, at Eupatoria, Balaklava, and Kinburn (despatches, medal with clasp, 5th class Medjidie, Turkish medal); Col Commandant, RMLI, Plymouth, 1885–86. *Recreations:* photography, music. *Address:* 14 New Road, Rochester. *Died 25 June 1925.*

THOMAS, Sir George Sidney Meade, 6th Bt, *cr* 1766; *b* 12 Feb. 1847; *s* of Sir William Sidney Thomas, 5th Bt, Captain RN, and Thomasin, *d* of Capt. Henry Haynes, RN; *S* father, 1867; *m* 1874, Edith Margaret, *d* of Morgan Hugh Foster, CB, Brickhill, Bedfordshire; one *s* two *d* (and one *s* decd). *Educ:* Caius College, Cambridge. *Heir: s* George Alan Thomas, *b* 14 June 1881. *Address:* 11 Kenilworth Court, Putney, SW.

Died 9 March 1918.

THOMAS, Brig.-Gen. Sir Godfrey Vignoles, 9th Bt, *cr* 1694; CB 1904; DSO 1900; DL; late Brig.-General, RA 3rd Division; *b* Hafod, Cardiganshire, 27 March 1856; *e s* of Sir Godfrey John Thomas, 8th Bt and Emily, *d* of late W. Chambers, Hafod; *S* father, 1861; *m* 1887, Isabelle, *e d* of late C. Oppenheim, 40 Great Cumberland Place, W; one *s*. *Educ:* Brighton Coll.; Woolwich. Served Afghan War (medal), 1878–80; Egypt (medal with clasps, Khedive's star), 1882; Soudan (medal with clasps), 1884; 4th class Order of Medjidie; South Africa, 1899–1901 (despatches, medal 7 clasps, DSO); European War as Brig.-Gen. RA, 1914–17. *Recreations:* field sports generally. *Heir: s* Godfrey John Vignoles Thomas [*b* 14 April 1889. *Educ:* Harrow. Third Secretary, Diplomatic Service, 1914. *Clubs:* Marlborough, Bachelors']. *Address:* Wynters, Harlow, Essex. *T:* Potters Street 5. *M:* OA 39. *Clubs:* Junior United Service, Royal Automobile.

Died 17 Feb. 1919.

THOMAS, Sir Griffith, Kt 1904; JP Glamorgan; *b* 24 Nov. 1847; *s* of late John Thomas, of Court Herbert, Neath, and Mary, *d* of late Griffith Griffiths. *Educ:* Swansea Grammar School; Cheltenham College; King's College, London. High Sheriff, Glamorgan, 1901; Mayor of Swansea, 1901, 1902, 1903; Mayor of Neath, 1908. *Address:* Court Herbert, Neath, Glamorgans.

Died 9 Feb. 1923.

THOMAS, Grosvenor, RSW; landscape painter; Associate of International Society of Sculptors, Painters, and Gravers; Royal Scottish Society of Painters in Water Colours; Corresponding Member Royal Society des Beaux-Arts, Brussels; Pastel Society; *b* Sydney, Australia, 1856; *m* 1884; one *s* one *d*. *Educ:* Warminster Grammar School, England. Adopted art as a profession about 1892; self-taught; gold medal, Munich, 1901; gold medal, Dresden, 1901; served on Jury at International Art Exhibition, Amsterdam, 1912. Chevalier of the Order Crown of Italy, 1910; Gold Medal of Honour for Art and Science, Holland, 1912 (Order of the House of Orange). Represented in following Museums: Oldham Corporation Art Gallery; Municipal Gallery of Modern Art, Venice; Hungarian National Gallery, Buda-Pest; Bohemian National Gallery, Prague; Permanent Gallery, Weimar; Fine Arts Academy, Buffalo, USA; in private collections of King of Italy, late Prince Regent Luitpold of Bavaria, late Herr Krupp, late James Staats Forbes, etc. *Recreations:* collecting old stained glass, billiards. *Address:* St Anne's, 13 Leonard Place, W8. *T:* Western 226. *M:* LB 4638.

Died 5 Feb. 1923.

THOMAS, Harold; Recorder of Hull since 1904; *b* 1847; *s* of Henry Thomas of Sheffield, surgeon. Called to the Bar, Lincoln's Inn, 1874; Recorder of Rotherham, 1901–4. *Address:* 9 Bank Street, Sheffield.

Died 1 April 1917.

THOMAS, Henry Arnold, MA (Camb. and London); Minister of Highbury Congregational Church, Bristol, 1876–1923; Chairman of the Congregational Union, 1899; *b* 13 June 1848; *s* of Rev. David Thomas, thirty-one years minister of Highbury Church; *m* Emily Georgina, 2nd *d* of late G. H. Newall, formerly of Dundee. *Educ:* Mill Hill School; Univ. Coll., London; Trinity Coll., Cambridge. 1st class in Moral Science Tripos, Camb. Formerly minister at Ealing. *Publications:* Memorials of Rev. David Thomas, 1876; Three Questions, 1892; The Way of Life, 1899. *Address:* Seafield Lodge, Stoke Bishop, Bristol. *Died 28 June 1924.*

THOMAS, Major Sir Hugh James Protheroe, Kt 1922; OBE 1919; DL, JP; *b* 22 April 1879; *s* of James Thomas, JP, Haverfordwest; *m* 1904, Charlotte Eveline, *d* of late Bayly Matthews; two *s* two *d*. *Educ*: Haverfordwest Grammar School. Sole surviving partner of James Thomas & Son, land and estate agents, Haverfordwest; Mayor of Haverfordwest, 1909–10, 1918–19; Alderman of Pembrokeshire County Council, and a trustee of the Haverfordwest charities for many years; a Governor of the Pembrokeshire County Hospital; a member of the Pembrokeshire Territorial Force Association. *Address*: Castle Hall, Milford Haven. *TA*: Sir Hugh Thomas, Milford Haven. *T*: Milford Haven 75. *M*: DE 2. *Clubs*: Junior Carlton, Royal Automobile. *Died 30 Dec. 1924.*

THOMAS, James Jonathan, CMG 1908; Legislative Council, Sierra Leone; *b* 1850; *m* 1st, Patience, *d* of Thomas Joe; 2nd, Rhoda, *d* of Abram Hebron. *Address*: Wilberforce House, Gloucester Street, Freetown, Sierra Leone. *Died 4 Nov. 1919.*

THOMAS, Sir John, Kt 1907; JP; CA; paper manufacturer; *b* 1834; *s* of late William Thomas of The Elms, Wooburn; *m* 1st, 1857, Sarah Eleanor Elizabeth (*d* 1878), *d* of Benjamin George of West Malling; 2nd, 1879, Ada (*d* 1915), *e d* of late William Stimson, of Marston Morteyne, Beds; 3rd, 1916, Helen Mary, *d* of late J. W. B. Cattle, Norbury, Surrey. *Address*: Brook House, Wooburn, Bucks. *Club*: National Liberal. *Died 15 March 1920.*

THOMAS, J. Havard, MA; RBS, RWA; sculptor and draughtsman; Member of the International Society of Sculptors, Painters, and Gravers; *b* 22 Dec. 1854; *m* Sofia, *d* of Sig. Milano Gennaro; three *s* three *d*. *Educ*: National School, South Kensington; Ecole des Beaux-Arts, Paris. Worked for many years in the South of Italy. *Public statues*: Samuel Morley, Bristol; Rt Hon. W. E. Forster, Bradford; Edmund Burke, Bristol; S. Morley, Nottingham; many portrait-busts, poetical statues and bas-reliefs and drawings, including bronze statues Lycidas, Tate Gallery, and Thyrsis, Johannesburg; Manchester City Gallery by wax models, and Bradford Corporation Gallery by bas-reliefs and drawings; teacher of sculpture, Slade Schools, University College. *Address*: 21A Upper Cheyne Row, Chelsea, SW. *Club*: Chelsea Arts. *Died June 1921.*

THOMAS, John Owen, MA, DD; Acting Principal and Professor of New Testament at the United Theological College, Aberystwyth, 1922–26; *b* Bangor, 18 Sept. 1862; *e s* of Rev. Josiah Thomas, MA; unmarried. *Educ*: Liverpool Coll.; Glasgow University (MA 1885; Hon. DD 1924); New College, Oxford; Berlin and Strassburg Universities; 2nd class Honours Classical Mods and 2nd Class Honours Lit. Hum., Oxford; BA 1887; MA 1890. Minister of Presbyterian Church of Wales successively at Everton Brow, Liverpool, 1887–91, Aberdovey, 1892–99, and Menai Bridge, 1899–1907; Secretary of North Wales Quarterly Association (or Synod), 1902–7; Moderator, 1921; Secretary of General Assembly, 1907; served with the YMCA, in France, 1916–18; Professor of New Testament at the Theological College, Bala, North Wales, 1907–22; Member of the University Court and of the Faculty of Theology (Wales); and of the Council and of the Court of Governors of Aberystwyth University College. *Publications*: occasional contributions to periodicals. *Address*: Bronygraig, Bala, North Wales. *Died 15 Feb. 1928.*

THOMAS, Percy, RE (an original Member); painter and etcher; *b* London; 3rd *s* of Ralph Thomas, Serjeant at Law; *m* Alice Tree; two *s* four *d*. *Educ*: Schools—Oxford, London, Paris; Royal Academy of Arts. One of the earliest friends and first pupil of J. A. M. Whistler, from whom he learnt etching, and learnt printing of Auguste Delatre; exhibited at the RA since 1876; picture entitled Relics exhibited in the RA 1886, was reproduced in the only illustrated catalogue issued by the Royal Academy. *Publications*: etched the portrait of Whistler for Ralph Thomas's catalogue of Whistler's Etchings, 1874; for the Art Union of London, Windmill by John Crome; a series of The Temple, London, the text written by Canon Alinger. *Recreations*: boating, swimming, walking. *Address*: 16 Seafield Road, Hove, Sussex. *Died July 1922.*

THOMAS, (Philip) Edward; Corporal in Artists' Rifles; *b* 1878. *Educ*: St Paul's School; Lincoln College, Oxford. Always a writer. *Publications*: Horæ Solitariæ; Beautiful Wales; The Heart of England; The South Country; Life of Richard Jefferies; Maurice Maeterlinck; George Borrow; Lafcadio Hearn; Swinburne; Pater; Keats; The Icknield Way; In Pursuit of Spring; Rest and Unrest; Light and Twilight; The Happy-go-lucky Morgans; Four and Twenty Blackbirds; The Duke of Marlborough. *Address*: Steep, Petersfield. *Died April 1917.*

THOMAS, Philip Henry, ISO 1902; *b* Tredegar, Monmouthshire, 1854; *s* of Henry Eastaway Thomas; *m* 1877, Mary Elizabeth, *d* of Edward Thos Townsend of Newport, Monmouthshire; five *s* (and one *s*, the poet, Edward Thomas, killed in action). *Educ*: Sirhowy and Swindon. Entered Board of Trade, by open competition, 1873; promoted to Tramway, Gas, and Water business, 1879; special allowance for services in connection with Provisional Orders, 1885; Secretary of a Committee appointed by the President of the Board of Trade to advise on further Light Railway legislation, 1901; Staff Clerk for Light Railways, 1904; retired, 1914; secretary of a Special Committee of HM Treasury dealing with Naval and Munition matters, 1917; Liberal Candidate for Clapham, 1918; Leader of Church of Humanity, Chapel St, Holborn, 1909–19. *Publications*: A Religion of this World, with numerous articles and lectures on questions of political, social, and religious reform. *Recreation*: a day at the Oval. *Address*: Rusham Gate, Rusham Road, SW12. *Died 18 Dec. 1920.*

THOMAS, Rev. William Henry Griffith, MA, DD (Oxon); AKC; Fellow of the College and Member of the Corporation, King's College, London, since 1913; *b* 1861; *o s* of late William Thomas, *s* of Thomas Thomas, Coton, Ruyton XI Towns, Salop, and Annie, *o d* of late William Griffith, MD, Oswestry, Salop; *m* Alice, *d* of late Alfred Monk; one *d*. *Educ*: King's College, London; Christ Church, Oxford. Ordained, 1885; Curate of St Peter's, Clerkenwell, 1885–88; St Aldate, Oxford, 1888–96; Vicar of St Paul, Portman Square (formerly Portman Chapel), 1896–1905; Principal of Wycliffe Hall, Oxford, 1905–10; Professor, Wycliffe College, Toronto, 1910–19. *Publications*: The Catholic Faith; The Apostle Peter; A Sacrament of Our Redemption; Methods of Bible Study; Handbook to The Acts; Commentary on Genesis (3 vols); Life Abiding and Abounding; Christianity is Christ; Commentary on Romans (3 vols); The Work of the Ministry; The Holy Spirit of God; The Prayers of St Paul; The Power of Peace; Grace and Power; The Christian Life; Christ Pre-eminent (Studies in Colossians); The Apostle John; 'Let us go on' (Studies in Hebrews). *Address*: 129 Maplewood Avenue, Philadelphia, USA. *Club*: City, Philadelphia. *Died 2 June 1924.*

THOMAS, William Thelwall, MBE 1920; ChM (Liverpool); FRCS (Eng.); Consulting Surgeon, Royal Infirmary, Liverpool; Emeritus Professor of Regional Surgery, and Clinical Lecturer in Surgery, University of Liverpool; Consulting Surgeon King Edward VII Memorial Hospital for Wales; Fellow Royal Society of Medicine; Member of Council, Royal College of Surgeons; Member of General Medical Council; Member of University Council, Liverpool; *b* Liverpool, 1865; *s* of late John and Eliz. Thomas; *m* 1892, Anabel, *d* of late Alexander Spence, Huntly, Aberdeen. *Educ*: Liverpool Institute; Glasgow Royal Infirmary; University College, Liverpool. House Surgeon and House Physician, Royal Infirmary, Liverpool; Holt Scholar at Anatomy, University of Liverpool, 1887; Assistant Surgeon, Royal Infirmary; late Assistant Lecturer on Anatomy and Lecturer in Operative Surgery; President of Surgery Section BMA, 1913; President, Liverpool Medical Institution, 1918–19. *Publications*: many articles on surgical subjects in medical journals and Encyclopædia Medica. *Address*: 84 Rodney Street, Liverpool; Verdala Tower, Allerton. *T*: Royal 2501; Mossley Hill 39. *M*: K 998. *Clubs*: Royal Automobile; University, Reform, Athenæum, Liverpool. *Died 10 Sept. 1927.*

THOMPSON, Alfred Corderoy; Chairman The Prudential Assurance Company, Ltd; Director since 1918. *Address*: Chetnole, Oatlands Avenue, Weybridge. *Died 9 Nov. 1928.*

THOMPSON, Lt-Gen. Arnold Bunbury; *b* 15 June 1822; *m* Charlotte Wilkinson (*d* 1910), *o d* of Robert Dent, Flass House, Crosby, Ravensworth. Entered army, 1839; Maj.-Gen. 1870; retired 1880; served Crimea, 1855–56. *Address*: Northfield, Maidenhead. *Clubs*: United Service, Army and Navy. *Died 7 Feb. 1917.*

THOMPSON, Lt-Col Cyril Powney, CBE 1919; *b* 21 Aug. 1864; *e s* of late Fendall Thompson, BCS; *m* 1892, Mary (MBE), *e d* of Lt-Gen. R. C. R. Clifford, CB. *Educ*: Charterhouse; RMC, Sandhurst. Joined Wiltshire Regt, 1885; 3rd Sikhs PFF, 1888; Panjab Commission, 1889; Commissioner Multan Division, 1915–19; retired, 1919. *Club*: East India United Service. *Died 27 Oct. 1924.*

THOMPSON, Edward Raymond, (E. T. Raymond); journalist; Editor of the Evening Standard since 1923; *b* 1872; *y s* of late Ephraim

Thompson, solicitor; *m* Elsie Mabel, *d* of George Watts; one *s* one *d*. *Educ:* privately. Received training of a journalist at Brighton, Leeds and elsewhere; joined staff of Star, 1897; associated with late Captain Brinkley, RA, of Tokyo, on Japan Mail, 1898–1900; Editor Japan Gazette, Yokohama, 1900–2; Night Editor, Daily Mirror, 1904–7; on staff of the Standard, first as Night Editor, afterwards as News Editor, and finally as leader-writer, 1907–16; edited the Outlook, 1919–20; chief leader-writer of Evening Standard since 1916. *Publications:* Uncensored Celebrities, All and Sundry, 1919; Mr Balfour, 1920; Portraits of the Nineties, 1921; Mr Lloyd George, 1922; The Man of Promise (Lord Rosebery), 1923; Disraeli: The Alien Patriot, 1925; Portraits of the New Century, 1927; numerous contributions, chiefly on political subjects, to British and American periodicals. *Address:* 44 Clarges Street, W1. *T:* Grosvenor 2197; Waltham St Lawrence, Twyford, Berks. *T:* Shurlock Row 13.

Died 9 April 1928.

THOMPSON, Frederick Charles; Secretary, Public Works Department, India Office, 1901–11. *Club:* Reform.

Died 11 July 1919.

THOMPSON, Gibson. *Educ:* privately; King's College, London. Engaged in municipal government work before journalism; now part proprietor and editor of Surveyor and Municipal and County Engineer. *Publications:* Wolfe-Land; Westerham and District, 4th edn 1911; Picturesque Kent, 1900; Picturesque Surrey, 1902. *Recreations:* archæology, philately, and lawn tennis; in Upton Park FC team that won London Cup in two consecutive years; played for Surrey and for London. *Address:* St Bride's House, 24 Bride Lane, Fleet Street, EC. *T:* City 1046; Thames Ditton, Surrey. *TA:* Municipium, London. *Died 12 March 1917.*

THOMPSON, Captain Harold, DSO 1916; 21st Royal Scots Fusiliers; *b* 17 Nov. 1881; *m* 1912, Sophia Hepburn; one *d*. *Educ:* Ardvreck, Crieff; Fettes College, Edinburgh. Joined 3rd Royal Scots Fusiliers (Militia), 1900; 2nd (Line), 1901; served S Africa, 1902 (Queen's medal, 3 clasps); European War, 1914–16, Cape Helles, Egypt (DSO). *Recreations:* shooting, fishing, golf. *Club:* Army and Navy. *Died 22 April 1917.*

THOMPSON, Major-Gen. Sir Harry Neville, KCMG 1919 (CMG 1916); CB 1918; DSO 1902; BA, MB, BCh; AMS; *b* 15 March 1861; *s* of late Rev. Mungo Neville Thompson, Rector of Clonmany, Donegal. *Educ:* Trinity College, Dublin; BA, MB, BCh, 1883; MD (Hon.) 1919. Surgeon, 1884; Surgeon-Major, 1896; Major RAMC, 1898; Lt-Col, 1904; Colonel Army Medical Service, 1913; Maj.-Gen. 1917; retired pay, 1920; served Nile Expedition, 1898 (medal and Khedive's medal); South Africa, 1900–2 (despatches, Queen's medal 5 clasps, King's medal 2 clasps, DSO); European War, 1914–18—as ADMS 2nd and 48th Div.; DDMS 6th Corps, 29 May 1915; DMS First Army, July 1917; British Army of the Rhine, 1918 (despatches seven times, CB, CMG, KCMG, French Croix de Guerre with two palms; American Distinguished Service Medal; Portuguese Grand Officer of the Order of St Aviz); Coronation and Delhi Durbar medals, 1903; King George's Coronation medal, 1911. *Club:* Army and Navy. *Died 21 June 1925.*

THOMPSON, Rev. Henry; Hon. Canon, Norwich. *Educ:* Corpus Christi College, Cambridge. Mawson Scholar; BA 1863; Curate, Christ Church, Lee, 1865–67; Perpetual Curate, Farnham, Suffolk, 1869–74; Vicar of Aldeburgh, 1874–1904; Rural Dean of Orford, 1891; Select Preacher, University of Cambridge, 1901; Proc. for Convocation, 1903; Bishop's Commissary for Suffolk, 1904; Vicar of Eaton in Norwich, 1904–10. *Address:* 68 Mill Hill Road, Norwich.

Died 6 Aug. 1916.

THOMPSON, Henry Yates, JP; Officer of the Legion of Honour, 1907; *b* 1838; *e s* of late S. H. Thompson of Thingwall Hall, Lancs. *Educ:* Harrow; Trinity College, Cambridge (BA). Barrister Lincoln's Inn, 1867; formerly proprietor of Pall Mall Gazette. *Address:* 19 Portman Square, W1. *Died 8 July 1928.*

THOMPSON, Rt. Rev. James Denton, MA; Bishop of Sodor and Man since 1912; Rural Dean of Birmingham (Central) and Hon. Canon of Birmingham Cathedral; *b* Liverpool, 20 July 1856; *s* of John Roper Thompson and Jane Denton; *m* Isabella Susannah, *d* of Alfred Roberts Arnold of Bournemouth; two *s* three *d*. *Educ:* Liverpool Inst. and Coll.; Corpus Christi Coll., Camb. BA (aeg.) Greek Test, Prize, 1882; MA, 1886. Deacon, 1882; Priest, 1883; Hon. Canon of Liverpool, 1895; Curate of Didsbury, Manchester, 1882–84; St Saviour's, Liverpool, 1884–86; Clerical Supt of Church of England Scripture Readers' Soc., 1886–89; Vicar of St Leonard's, Bootle,

1889–94; Member of Bootle School Board, 1891–94; Rector of North Meols (Southport), 1894–1905; Rector of Birmingham 1905–12. *Publications:* God and the Sinner; Church and the People; Problems of Church Work; Central Churchmanship; Missions, Parochial and General; Revived Churchmanship; Vision and Vocation; The Holy Communion; Peace, Perfect Peace, etc. *Recreation:* golf. *Address:* Bishop's Court, Isle of Man.

Died 31 Oct. 1924.

THOMPSON, Rev. Sir Peile, 2nd Bt, *cr* 1890; Barrister, Inner Temple; *b* 19 July 1844; *e s* of Sir Matthew William Thompson, 1st Bt (Mayor of Bradford and MP), and *c* Mary Ann, *d* of Benjamin Thompson, of Parkgate, Guiseley; *S* father, 1891; *m* 1871, Jessie, *d* of Joseph Beaumont, Huddersfield; three *s* one *d*. *Educ:* Rugby; Trinity College, Cambridge (MA). Ordained 1877; Curate of Monken Hadley, 1877–81; Christ Church, Marylebone, 1881–85. *Heir: s* Matthew William Thompson [*b* 28 June 1872; *m* 1909, Harriet Kathleen, *o d* of Colonel S. Hamilton-Grace. *Educ:* Trinity College, Cambridge. *Address:* Salters Hall, Sudbury, Suffolk. *Club:* Oxford and Cambridge]. *Address:* Howard Square, Eastbourne; Great Yeldham, Sussex. *Died 8 April 1918.*

THOMPSON, Peter, MD (Vict.); Professor of Anatomy, Birmingham University since 1909; and Dean of the Faculty of Medicine, 1912–19; *b* Earlestown, Lancs, 13 Feb. 1871; *o s* of late Peter Thompson; *m* 1906, Nessy, *d* of late G. L. Davies, The Old Hall, Helsby, Cheshire; two *s*. *Educ:* Upholland Grammar School; Owens College, Manchester. MB, ChB (Honours) in 1894; MD (Gold Medallist), 1899; formerly Senior Demonstrator of Anatomy in the Owens College, Lecturer on Anatomy in the Victoria University, Manchester, and Lecturer on Anatomy at the Middlesex Hospital, London; Hon. Secretary of the Anatomical Society of Great Britain and Ireland, 1901–4; Professor of Anatomy, and Dean of the Faculty of Medicine, King's College, London, 1905–9; Fellow of King's College, London. *Publications:* The Myology of the Pelvic Floor, 1900, and other papers dealing with Human Anatomy, Morphology, and Embryology in the Journal of Anatomy and Physiology. *Address:* Tai Bach, Penmænmawr, N Wales.

Died 16 Nov. 1921.

THOMPSON, Rev. Ralph Wardlaw; Foreign Secretary, London Missionary Society, 1881–1914, subseq. Secretary Emeritus; Chairman Congregational Union of England and Wales, 1908; *b* Bellary, South India; *s* of Rev. William Thompson and Jessie Crawford, *d* of late Rev. Ralph Wardlaw, DD, of Glasgow; *m* Mary Stewart, *d* of late John Brown, jun., JP, of Glasgow. *Educ:* South African College, Cape Town; Cheshunt College. BA of the Univ. of the Cape of Good Hope; DD Glas. and Edin. Universities; Minister of Ewing Place Congregational Church, Glasgow, 1865–70; Norwood Congregational Church, Liverpool, 1871–80; at various times visited the missions of the Society in India, China, South Africa, Madagascar, New Guinea, and the South Seas. *Publications:* My Trip in the 'John Williams'; joint author of British Foreign Missions; The Life of Griffith John, Fifty Years in China; and various articles in magazines and reviews. *Recreation:* fishing, especially trout-fishing. *Address:* 16 New Bridge Street, EC. *TA:* Missionary, London. *T:* 13737 Central.

Died 10 June 1916.

THOMPSON, Rt. Hon. Robert, PC Ire. 1916; JP, DL; MP (C) North Belfast since 1910; Chairman of Lindsay, Thompson & Company, Limited, flax spinners and linen thread manufacturers; *b* Ballylesson, near Belfast, 1839. *Educ:* Purdysburn Preparatory School and Wellington Academy, Belfast. President Ulster Flax Spinners' Association, 1903–10; Chairman Belfast Harbour Commissioners; Ex-President Belfast Chamber of Commerce; President Board of Governors, Campbell College, Belfast. *Address:* Drum House, Co. Down; Bertha House, Malone Road, Belfast. *Clubs:* Carlton, Constitutional, St Stephen's; Ulster, Union, Belfast.

Died 3 Aug. 1918.

THOMPSON, Sir Robert James, Kt 1908; JP Kent; *b* Northallerton, 29 May 1845. RE Dept, Chatham, 1866–71; HM Office of Works, 1871–98; Treasury Valuer and Inspector of Rates, 1898–1909; Chief Valuer, Inland Revenue, Somerset House, 1909–11. *Address:* 5 Homefield Road, Bromley, Kent.

Died 11 April 1926.

THOMPSON, Silvanus Phillips, DSc, BA Lond, Hon. MD, LLD; FRS 1891; Principal and Professor of Physics in the City and Guilds Technical College, Finsbury, since 1885; Professor of Applied Physics, University of London; *b* York, 19 June 1851; *s* of Silvanus Thompson, York; *m* 1881, Jane, *e d* of late James Henderson, Pollokshields; four *d. Educ:* Bootham School, York; Flounders' Institute, Pontefract; Royal School of Mines. Science Master, York; Professor of Experimental Physics, Univ. Coll. Bristol, 1876–85. Past President of Physical Society; of Institution of Electrical Engineers; of Röntgen Society; of Optical Society; of Illuminating Engineering Society; of the Optical Conference, 1912; of the Sette of Odd Volumes. *Publications:* Michael Faraday, 1898; sundry technical works on electricity, including treatises on Dynamo-electric Machinery, and the Electromagnet; The Life of Lord Kelvin, 1910; Lectures on Light, and other optical works. *Recreations:* walking, water-colour sketching. *Address:* City and Guilds Technical College, Finsbury. *Clubs:* Sette of Odd Volumes, Athenæum.

Died 12 June 1916.

THOMPSON, Hon. Thomas; MLC since 1903; MP Auckland City North, 1884–99; Minister for Justice and Defence, 1900. *Address:* Mount Eden, Auckland, NZ.

THOMPSON, Sir William Henry, KBE 1918; MD, MCh; FRCS Eng.; resigned, 1914; FRCPI; King's Professor of Institutes of Medicine; School of Physic, Trinity College, Dublin, since 1902; Scientific Adviser, Ministry of Food; *b* Co. Longford, Ireland; 3rd *s* of William Thompson, Ballynulty House, near Granard, and *g s* of Robert Thompson, formerly of Cloncoose, Co. Longford; *m* 1894, Isabel, *e d* of Peter Redfern, MD, 4 Lower Crescent, Belfast, and Templepatrick House, Donaghadee; one *s* four *d*. *Educ:* Dundalk Institution; Queen's Coll. Galway; medical study, Galway, Dublin, London, Leipsic, Paris, Marburg, Heidelberg. Peel Prize Mathematics, QUI; 1st Science Sch. (Math.), 1879, 1st Med. Scholar for four years, 1880–83, and Senior Schol. Anat. and Physiol. 1884, Queen's Coll., Galway; 1st of 1st Honours and 1st class Exhibition at Graduation, 1883; Special Prize and Diploma in Mental Diseases, 1885. Demonstrator of Anatomy, Trinity Coll., Dublin, 1887–91; Foreign Study and Research, 1892–93, also 1896, 1900, 1901, 1904, 1905; Dunville Professor of Physiology, Queen's College, Belfast, 1893–1902; Hon. Member Imperial Military Academy of Medicine; Petrograd, 1899; ScD Hon. Causa, Univ. Dublin, 1904. *Publications:* Translation of The Work of the Digestive Glands (Pavlov); Foods and their Relative Nourishing Value; The Food Value of Great Britain's Food Supply; Collected Papers from Physiological Laboratory, Queen's College, Belfast, and Trinity College, Dublin; papers in reports, British Association, Journal of Physiology, Archives de Physiologie Normale et Pathologique, British Medical Journal, and elsewhere. *Recreations:* tennis, golf, cycling. *Address:* 14 Hatch Street, Dublin. *T:* Dublin 3564.

Died 11 Oct. 1918.

THOMPSON, Col William Oliver, DSO 1895; ISC; retired; *b* 14 Nov. 1844. Entered army, 1863; Col 1895; served Afghan War, 1878–79 (medal); Mahsood-Wuzeeree Expedition, 1881; Hazara Expedition, 1888 (medal with clasp); Miranzai, 1891 (despatches, clasp); Waziristan (despatches twice, DSO, clasp). *Club:* East India United Service.

Died 10 Sept. 1917.

THOMPSON, William Whitaker, MA, LLB; JP London; Chairman London County Council, 1910–11; Mayor of Kensington, 1911–12; *b* 27 Feb. 1857; 3rd *s* of Sir Matthew William Thompson, 1st Bt; *m* 1889, Isabella, *d* of Spencer Robert Lewin, of The Bourne, Widford, Herts; one *s* one *d*. Contested (C) Otley Division, WR Yorks, three times. *Address:* 24 Argyll Road, W8. *T:* Park 4132. *Clubs:* Oxford and Cambridge, Carlton.

Died 2 March 1920.

THOMSON, Hon. Alex. Macdonald; *b* Turriff, Scotland, 27 Sept. 1863; 2nd *s* of J. W. Thomson, MA, schoolmaster, and Isabella, *e d* of late Alex. Macdonald of Kindrought, Portsoy, NB. *Educ:* Aberdeen University (MA, with 1st class in Mathematics, 1883). Lecturer in Mathematics, Naini Tal College, NWP, India, 1884–85; Assistant Professor of Mathematics, Aberdeen, 1887; entered Hong Kong Civil Service, and attached for one year to the Colonial Office, 1887; Bacon Scholar, Gray's Inn, 1888; passed examination in Chinese, 1890; served in following offices in the Colony— Superintendent, Victoria Gaol, Assistant Colonial Secretary, Registrar-General Postmaster-General, Colonial Secretary, and Treasurer; confirmed in last appointment, 1898, with seat *ex officio* on Executive and Legislative Councils; retired, 1918. *Recreations:* reading, gardening, golf. *Address:* Crescent Avenue, San Mateo, California, USA.

Died 28 July 1924.

THOMSON, Alexander Stuart Duff, BA, LLB; Advocate; Sheriff-Substitute of Lanarkshire, 1903–26; *b* New York, 1 May 1854; *s* of Rev. John Thomson, DD; *m* 1905, Mary Agnes (*d* 1924), *d* of Rev. James Brown, DD, Paisley. *Educ:* New York and Edinburgh

Universities. Admitted to Scottish Bar, 1883. *Address:* Averley, Great Western Road, Glasgow. *Clubs:* Western, Glasgow; Conservative, Edinburgh.

Died 9 Sept. 1927.

THOMSON, Brig.-Gen. Andrew Graham, CB 1911; CMG 1916; RE; retired, 1919; *b* 8 Feb. 1858; *s* of late Surgeon-Maj.-Gen. W. A. Thomson, Honorary Physician to Queen Victoria and King Edward VII; *m* Anne, *d* of late Rev. W. Yalden Thomson. *Educ:* privately; Woolwich. Joined Royal Engineers, 1877; served Egypt, 1882; Suakin, 1885; South Africa, 1899–1902; European War, 1914–17 (despatches, CMG); specially employed Holland, 1918–19; on Ordnance Survey, United Kingdom, 1885–90; in office of Inspector-General of Fortifications, 1897–99; commanded Training Battalion RE, 1903–8; Commandant Royal Military Academy, Woolwich, 1908–12. *Address:* 72 St George's Square, SW1. *T:* Victoria 2128. *Club:* Junior United Service.

Died 14 Feb. 1926.

THOMSON, Captain Anthony Standidge, CB 1897; CBE 1919; FRGS; Commander (retired) Royal Naval Reserve, 1899; Elder Brother of Trinity House, 1898–1922; *b* Blackpool, Lancashire, 1 Aug. 1851; *e s* of Rev. Anthony F. Thomson, BA Oxon, and Betsy Sowter Richardson; *m* 1888, Alethea Isabella Evans Davis (*d* 1912); three *d*. *Educ:* St John's Foundation School, Kilburn. First went to sea 1868; Mercantile Marine, Royal Mail Steam Packet Co. 1872–79; Orient Steam Navigation Co. 1880–83; commanded the 'Silvertown' and other telegraph steamships, 1883–95; served in the Royal Navy on several occasions as Lieut RNR; elected Younger Brother of Trinity House, 1892; Lieutenant RNR, 1887. Takes much practical interest in the science of oceanography and current surveying; contributed a paper on Ocean Currents to the Sixth International Geographical Congress, held in London, 1895; served on the Departmental Committee of BoT on ship's side lights, 1895. *Address:* Northwood Court, near Ramsgate.

Died 16 April 1925.

THOMSON, David Alexander, CIE 1920; Conservator of Forest Utilization Circle, Bombay, since 1920; *b* 4 July 1872; *s* of late James Balfour Thomson; *m* Mary Fulton, *d* of James Mill; one *s* two *d*. *Educ:* High School, Dundee; RIEC, Cooper's Hill. Joined Indian Forest Service as Assistant Conservator of Forests, 1894; Deputy Conservator of Forests, 1898. *Recreations:* shooting, golf. *Clubs:* Club of Western India, Poona; Royal Bombay Yacht.

Died 17 May 1922.

THOMSON, Lieut-Col David George, CBE 1919; MD; late Medical Superintendent, County Mental Hospital, Thorpe, Norwich; *b* Edinburgh, 1856; *s* of Thomas Thomson, of Princes Street, Edinburgh; *m* 1887, Melina Louisa Stromeyer; one *s* one *d*. *Educ:* Edinburgh University; Dresden; Dunkirk. MD with honours, 1881; commanded the Norfolk War Hospital during European War (despatches, CBE); President of Medico-Psychological Association, 1914–18. *Publications:* articles on Medico-Psychological subjects in Journal of Mental Science; The Evolution of the Nervous System, Trans of Norfolk and Norwich Naturalists, etc. *Recreations:* music, boating, camping, natural history of the Norfolk Broads. *Address:* 16 Mount Pleasant, Norwich. *T:* Norwich 1387. *M:* S 1319. *Club:* Norfolk, Norwich.

Died 4 Jan. 1923.

THOMSON, Hon. Dugald; Member of the House of Representatives, Parliament of the Commonwealth of Australia; *b* London, 1848; *s* of John Thomson, Shipbroker. *Educ:* private schools in Australia and in Liverpool, England. Left England with parents for South Australia, 1850; returned to relatives in Liverpool, 1854; after leaving school was for a short time in the service, ashore and afloat, of Balfour, Williamson & Co., Liverpool; left England for Melbourne, Australia, and there entered mercantile pursuits, 1867; removed to Sydney, New South Wales, opening as managing partner business for a firm of manufacturers and importers, 1877; retired from the firm, 1892; Member for Warringah, New South Wales Legislative Assembly, 1894; Hon. Treas. and one of the platform speakers of the Federal Association until the accomplishment of Australian union; Member for North Sydney, Federal House of Representatives, 1900, 1903, and 1906; Commonwealth Minister for Home Affairs, 1904–5; a Representative of the Commonwealth at the Imperial Conference on Merchant Shipping Legislation, London, 1907; Member of Australian Royal Commission on Food Supplies, Trade and Industry during the war. *Publications:* Federal and Political pamphlets. *Address:* Wyreepi, Kirribilli Point, Sydney. *T:* 213 North Sydney. *Club:* Royal Sydney Yacht Squadron.

Died 27 Nov. 1922.

THOMSON, Edward William, FRSL, FRS (Can.); *b* near Toronto, Canada, 12 Feb. 1849; *s* of William Thomson, banker and littérateur, and Margaret Hamilton Foley; *m* A. L. G. St Denis (*d* 1921); one *s. Educ:* public schools; Trinity Coll. Grammar School. Served under Grant, 3rd and 5th Pa Volunteer cavalry regiments, last year of American Civil War; served in Queen's Own Rifles, Toronto, and Fenian Raid of 1866; civil engineer until 1878; since then political writer, story writer, versifier, and general journalist. *Publications:* Old Man Savarin; sundry other collections of short stories; versifier in M. S. Henry's translation of Aucassin and Nicolette; When Lincoln Died, The Many-Mansioned House, and other poems. *Recreations:* walking and talking. *Address:* 52 Hereford Street, Boston, Mass, USA. *T:* Queen 2565.   *Died March 1924.*

THOMSON, George William, JP; retired banker; *b* Aberdeen, 11 March 1845; *s* of George Thomson and Elizabeth S., *o d* of Peter Duguid, Bourtie, Aberdeenshire, and Auchlumies, Kincardineshire; *m* 1st, 1878, Ellen Augusta, *d* of A. W. Gadesden, DL, JP, Ewell Castle, Surrey; 2nd, 1888, Coralie Louise, *d* of Edward John Woollett, of Paris and Brussels; three *s* two *d. Educ:* Aberdeen University. Lieutenant Volunteer Artillery, 1860–62; Oriental Bank, China and Japan, 1870–83; Volunteer Artillery, Shanghai, 1870; wrecked at Cape Gardafui, published account, 1877; founded first European bank in Persia, 1888 (Order of Lion and Sun); founded African Banking Corporation, 1891; Chief Manager for 18 and a Director for 11 years; President Caledonian Society of London, 1906–7; Member Council Japan Society; Fellow Institute of Bankers; travelled in America, Africa, Persia, India, China, and Japan, and in every country in Europe except Greece; during war equipped and commanded Volunteer Corps; retired from active life, 1920. *Publications:* Verses from Japan, 1884; contributions to Chambers's Journal, etc, The Japan of Forty Years Ago, Persia and its People, and other lectures and speeches. *Recreations:* reading, motoring, wireless. *Address:* St Valery, Beaconsfield, Bucks. *T:* Beaconsfield 80. *Club:* Savile.
Died 6 Sept. 1928.

THOMSON, Harry Redmond, MA; Barrister-at-Law; late Headmaster, Eastbourne College; *b* St Leonard's, Sussex, 24 Oct. 1860; *y s* of late H. P. Thomson, Monkton House, Taunton; *m* Alice Elizabeth, *d* of late Clement Cazalet of Petrograd. *Educ:* Marlborough; Univ. Coll. Oxford (Scholar). 1st class Classical Moderations, 1881; 2nd class Lit. Hum., 1883. Equity Scholarship, Inner Temple, 1887; Barrister, 1887. Assistant master at Sherborne School. *Address:* Beechwood, Lake Road, Wimbledon, SW. *T:* Wimbledon 520.
Died 29 Aug. 1917.

THOMSOM, Henry, JP; *b* 1840; 2nd *s* of late Henry Thomson of Newry, Co. Down, and Anne, *d* of late Rev. William Henry, of Tassagh, Co. Armagh; *m* 1866, Alice Cecilia, *y d* of late Henry Corbet-Singleton of Aclare, Co. Meath. *Educ:* Trinity College, Dublin. MP Newry, 1880–85. *Address:* Scarvagle House, Scarva, Co. Newry. *Club:* Carlton.   *Died 30 Dec. 1916.*

THOMSON, Henry Alexis, CMG 1916; MD, FRCS; Professor of Surgery, University of Edinburgh since 1909; and Surgeon to the Royal Infirmary; *b* Edinburgh, 1863; *m* Ethel Kate, 4th *d* of C. Grey Wotherspoon, barrister-at-law, of 18 Great Stuart Street, Edinburgh, and Hillside, Aberdour, Fife. *Educ:* High School, Edinburgh; Realschule, Hanover; Edinburgh University; London Hospital. Graduated with Honours, Bachelor of Medicine and Master of Surgery; Thesis Gold Medallist, Edin.; Bachelor of Science in Public Health, 1888. Served European War, 1914–16 (CMG); Consulting Surgeon to III Army in France. *Publications:* Neuroma and Neurofibromatosis, 1900; Manual of Surgery (joint author), 1904, etc; joint editor of Edinburgh Medical Journal. *Address:* 39 Drumsheugh Gardens, Edinburgh. *TA:* Deltoid, Edinburgh. *T:* Edinburgh 2168; Moredun, Gilmerton, Midlothian. *T:* Central 4237, Edinburgh. *Club:* University, Edinburgh.
Died 5 March 1924.

THOMSON, Hugh; artist; *b* 1 June 1860; *m* 1884; one *s. Publications:* illustrated—Cranford; Jane Austen's novels; Peg Woffington; St Ronan's Well; A Kentucky Cardinal and Aftermath; The Great Hoggarty Diamond; Highways and Byways of London; Evelina; Scenes from Clerical Life; The Fair Hills of Ireland; Highways and Byways in Donegal and Antrim; Esmond; As You Like It; Merry Wives of Windsor; School for Scandal; Highways and Byways of Kent, Surrey, and Middlesex, and the Border; The Vicar of Wakefield; Silas Marner; She Stoops to Conquer; Quality Street; The Famous Cities of Ireland; Tom Brown's School Days. *Recreations:* golf, out-door sketching. *Address:* 8 Patten Road, Wandsworth Common, SW.
Died 7 May 1920.

THOMSON, John, MD, FRCP, Edinburgh; Hon. LLD, Edinburgh; Consulting Physician to the Royal Edinburgh Hospital for Sick Children, and to the Royal Scottish National Institution, Larbert; formerly University Lecturer on the Diseases of Children; *b* Edinburgh, 23 Nov. 1856; *s* of Thomas Thomson, WS, and Elizabeth Cleghorn; *m* 1887, Isobel F., *d* of Rev. John S. McPhail, UFC, Benbecula; three *s* two *d. Educ:* Edinburgh Academy and University; Vienna; Berlin. Elected Hon. Member of American Pediatric Society, 1903; Member of Association of Physicians. *Publications:* Guide to Clinical Study and Treatment of Sick Children (translated into French and Spanish), 4th edn; articles on Diseases of Children in various textbooks and medical journals. *Address:* 14 Coates Crescent, Edinburgh. *T:* Central 2271.   *Died 2 July 1926.*

THOMSON, John Ebenezer Honeyman, MA, BD, DD; *b* Glasgow, Aug. 1841; *s* of Ebenezer Thomson and Catherine Ferguson Honeyman; left Glasgow for reasons of health, 1856; *m* 1893, Margaret Dalgleish, *d* of Provost James Gray, JP, Dalkeith; no *c. Educ:* private schools and private tutor; Glasgow University; United Presbyterian Divinity Hall, and Divinity Hall of Glasgow University. Licentiate of UP Church, 1867; Missionary to Palestine, 1895; retired for reasons of health, 1899; Alexander Robertson Lecturer to University of Glasgow, 1916; stayed in Dennyloanhead, Stirlingshire, 1856–69; Blairlogie, Perthshire, 1869–74; Stirling, 1874–1906, with the exception of stay in Palestine; in Edinburgh from that date. *Publications:* A Short Treatise on New Testament Psychology, 1876; Upland Tarn, poem, 1881; Memoir of George Thomson, 1881; Books which influenced our Lord and His Apostles, 1891; Modern Criticism Examined, 1902; Commentary on Daniel in the Pulpit Commentary Series, 1897; edited with Dr Ewing Temple Dictionary of the Bible, 1910; Memoirs of Rev. Thomas Dunlop, 1919; The Samaritans, 1919; The Pentateuch of the Samaritans, when they got it and whence; The Readers for whom Matthew wrote his Hebrew Gospel, 1922. *Recreation:* light reading. *Address:* 170 Mayfield Road, Edinburgh. *T:* Edinburgh 1885.   *Died 9 June 1923.*

THOMSON, General Sir Mowbray, KCIE 1911; Bengal Infantry; *b* April 1832; *m* Mary Ironside (*d* 1903), *d* of late Rev. William Money. Entered army, 1853; General, 1894; retired list, 1885; served Indian Mutiny, 1857–58 (wounded four times, medal with clasp, brevet Maj., one year's service). *Address:* 19 Victoria Square, Reading.
Died 25 Feb. 1917.

THOMSON, Theodore, CMG 1905; MA (Aberdeen); MD (Lond.); Barrister-at-Law; Inspector HM Local Government Board, 1891–1911; Assistant Medical Officer since 1911; *b* 30 Dec. 1857; *s* of Rev. Wm Thomson, Belhelvie, Aberdeen. *Educ:* Aberdeen and Edinburgh Universities. Member of Committee of Inquiry into the Public Health of the City of Dublin, 1900; a British Delegate to the International Sanitary Conferences of Paris, 1903, and Rome, 1906; Plenipotentiary to sign the International Sanitary Conventions of 1903 and 1906; Imperial Delegate to the West Indian Intercolonial Sanitary Conference of Barbados, 1904, sent on Special Mission of Inquiry into the Sanitary Defence of the Persian Gulf, 1906; British representative on the Committee of the Office International d'hygiène publique. *Publications:* numerous official reports on public health subjects. *Address:* Local Government Board, Whitehall, SW.
Died 6 March 1916.

THOMSON, Trevelyan; MP (Ind. L) Middlesbro' West since Dec. 1918; JP County Boro' of Middlesbro'; *b* Stockton-on-Tees, 30 April 1875; *s* of late T. James Thomson, iron founder and merchant; *m* 1907, Hilda Mary, *d* of late Rev. J. G. Tolley, London; one *s* one *d. Educ:* Friends' Schools, Ackworth and Bootham, York. Joined his father in business as iron and steel merchants, which he still continues at 17 Albert Road, Middlesbro'; a Member of Middlesbro' County Boro' Council since 1904; served overseas in the ranks of the RE, 1917–18. *Address:* The Corner, Old Battersby, near Great Ayton; 17 Albert Road, Middlesbro'. *TA:* Merchant, Middlesbro'. *T:* Middlesbro' 218. *Clubs:* National Liberal; Cleveland, Middlesbro'.
Died 8 Feb. 1928.

THOMSON, Walter Henry, ISO; BA; JP; Municipal Commissioner, Dumka (Sontal Pergunnahs); *b* 21 August 1856; *m* 1892; one *s. Educ:* Hooghly College, Chinsurah; Presidency College, Calcutta. Graduated in 1877 with Honours in Mathematics. Three years Professor of Mathematics and Chemistry at the Doveton College, Calcutta; entered the Executive Branch of the Provincial Civil Service, 1880; rose to its top, 1910; retired 1913. *Recreations:* a practical gardener and builder. *Address:* Sontal Pergunnahs (Bihar), Dumka, India. *Club:* Dumka.   *Died 26 May 1917.*

THORBURN, Septimus Smet, FRGS, FRAS; Indian Civil Service (retired); *b* 12 Aug. 1844; *s* of late D. Thorburn of Dumfries and Edinburgh; *m* 1881, Mary Melise (*d* 1917), *d* of F. Leeston Smith of Leeston, Weston-super-Mare, and New Zealand; two *s*. *Educ:* Cheltenham College. Passed thence direct into the ICS; posted to Punjab, 1865; served trans-Indus until 1890, when appointed Commissioner of Rawalpindi; afterwards appointed Financial Commissioner of the Punjab until retirement, 24 Nov. 1899; a member of the Council of the EI Association. *Publications:* Bannu, or our Afghan Frontier, 1876; David Leslie, a Story of the Afghan Frontier, 1879; Musalmans and Moneylenders, 1886; Asiatic Neighbours, 1894; His Majesty's Greatest Subject, 1897; Transgression, 1898; The Punjab in Peace and War, 1904; India's Saint and the Viceroy, 1908; Sir John's Conversion, 1913. *Address:* Old Bracknell House, Bracknell, Berks. *TA:* Thorburn, Bracknell. *T:* Bracknell 34. *Died 26 April 1924.*

THORBURN, Thomas, MVO 1912; RD, RNR; Chief Engineer, P&O Steam Navigation Co. *Address:* Eildon Bank, Melrose, NB. *Died 1927.*

THORBURN, Rev. Thomas James, DD, LLD; *b* 24 Feb. 1858; *s* of late Thomas Charles Thorburn, CE (formerly RE) of Claughton, Birkenhead, and Charlotte, *d* of James Evans of Kentchurch, Herefordshire; *m* 1887, Emilie J., *d* of late Edward Hailstone; one *s* one *d*. *Educ:* Birkenhead; Christ's College, Cambridge; Trinity College, Dublin. Curate of St Leonard's, Colchester, 1881; 2nd Master, Chesterfield Grammar School, 1882–85; Senior Science Master, Royal Grammar School, and Curate of Sheffield, 1885–93; Headmaster of Caistor School, 1893–97; Odiham School, 1897–1903; Acting Headmaster of Hastings Grammar School (War Service), 1915–19. *Publications:* A Critical Examination of the Evidences for the Doctrine of the Virgin Birth; The Resurrection Narratives and Modern Criticism; Jesus the Christ: Historical or Mythical?; The Historical Jesus; The Mythical Interpretation of the Gospels (Bross Prize, 1915, Lake Forest University, Ill, USA). *Recreations:* most active games, but especially walking. *Address:* 21 St Helen's Road, Hastings. *Died 11 Jan. 1923.*

THORBURN, Sir William, KBE 1919; CB 1916; CMG 1919; DL Co. Lancaster; MD, BS, BSc London; FRCS England; BSc (Manchester); (hon.) MD, Malta; Emeritus Professor of Clinical Surgery, University of Manchester, 1910–21; Member of Council and of Court of Examiners, Royal College of Surgeons; Honorary Consulting Surgeon, Manchester Royal Infirmary; *s* of John Thorburn, MD, FRCP, Professor of Obstetric Medicine, Owens Coll., Manchester, and Annie Pollok Anderson; *m* Augusta (*d* 1922), *d* of W. E. Melland; three *d*. *Educ:* Owens College; Manchester Royal Infirmary; various London Hospitals. Medical Referee under Workmen's Compensation Act, etc; Col late RAMC (T), 2nd Western General Hospital, and Colonel AMS, Consulting Surgeon in Malta, Salonika, etc (despatches); Consulting Surgeon to the Forces in France since Sept. 1917 (despatches). Member of Court and Council of Victoria University of Manchester; Past President of Owens College Union, Owens College Associates, Pathological Society of Manchester, and Manchester Med. Society, and Neurological Section of Royal Soc. of Medicine; Jacksonian Essayist and Hunterian Professor of Royal College of Surgeons of England. *Publications:* Surgery of the Spinal Cord; many surgical publications, papers, essays, lectures. *Address:* 8 York Gate, Regent's Park, NW1. *Clubs:* Athenæum, Oriental; Union, Brasenose, Manchester. *Died 18 March 1923.*

THORNE, Edward Henry, MusD; Organist and Choirmaster of St Anne's, Soho, since 1891; *b* Cranborne, Dorset, 9 May 1834; *m* 1861, Elise Payn, Jersey; two *s* one *d*. *Educ:* St George's Chapel, Windsor. Organist and Choirmaster, Henley-on-Thames, 1853; Chichester Cathedral, 1863; St Patrick's, Brighton, 1870; St Peter's Cranley Gardens, 1873; St Michael's, Cornhill, 1875. *Publications:* organ music; church music; pianoforte music; songs and part-songs; A Short Life of Johan Sebastian Bach. *Recreation:* reading. *Address:* 19 Clarendon Gardens, Maida Vale, W. *Died 26 Dec. 1916.*

THORNE, Guy; *see* Gull, C. A. E. R.

THORNE, Sir William, Kt 1904; MLA; *b* Llanstedwell, Pembrokeshire, 27 Jan. 1839; *m* 1863, Ellen, *d* of Thomas Lane, Chichester; two *s* three *d*. *Educ:* privately. Went to Cape Town, 1859; thrice Mayor of Cape Town; Director Stuttaford & Co., Merchants, Cape Town and Johannesburg. *Address:* Rusdon, Rondebosch, Cape Town. *Clubs:* Junior Civil Service, City, Cape Town. *Died 28 May 1917.*

THORNELY, P. Wilfrid, MA, LLD (Cantab.); LLD, TCD, etc; Judge of the International Court of Appeal and Adviser to the Ministry of Justice, Bangkok, Siam, since 1911; *b* 1879; *o s* of late John and Helen Thornely, of Southbourne; *m* 1911, Doreen Hammersley, *y d* of late Lt-Col Beech Johnston, MD; one *s* two *d*. Member of Trinity Hall, Cambridge, and of the Inner Temple, Barrister-at-Law; practised in London (Fountain Court, Temple) and on the South-Eastern Circuit, 1901–11. Siam Coronation Medal 1st Class, 1911; Knight Comm. Order of the Crown of Siam; Commander Order of the White Elephant. *Publications:* History of Negotiability; The History of a Transition; Angelus (libretto of the winning opera in Ricordi Competition, first produced at Royal Opera House, Covent Garden, in 1909); Torrington Towers; translation with lyrics of Siamese Opera; various short stories, etc. *Recreations:* writing, motoring. *Address:* Ministry of Justice, Bangkok, Siam. *TA:* Thornely, Bangkok. *Club:* Royal Sports, Bangkok. *Died 9 March 1926.*

THORNTON, Rev. Canon Herbert Parry, MA; Hon. Secretary Winchester Diocesan Clerical Registry since 1913; 3rd *s* of late Canon Francis Vansittart Thornton and Mary Louisa, *e d* of Rev. Horace George Cholmondeley; *m* 1890, Alice Mary (*d* 1913), *y d* of late General Edward Darvall; no *c*. *Educ:* Sherborne; Trinity College, Cambridge, Jun. opt. Math. Tripos, 1878. Vicar of Normanton, Yorks, 1889–97; Curate, 1897–1900; Diocesan Missioner, Grafton and Armidale, NSW, 1901; Vicar of Market Weighton, 1902–8; Chaplain of Taormina, 1906–7, 1911–12; Chaplain of Patras, 1908–9; Hon. Canon, Winchester Cathedral, 1921. *Address:* Wonersh, Guildford. *TA:* Wonersh. *T:* Bramley 44. *Died 9 Oct. 1923.*

THORNTON, Sir James Howard, KCB 1904 (CB 1885); Deputy Surgeon-General, Indian Medical Service (retired); *b* 1834; *y s* of late Major John Thornton, 78th Regt; *m* 1861, Mary (*d* 1918), *y d* of late J. Astor of Jersey; three *s* two *d*. *Educ:* Chatham House, Ramsgate; King's Coll., London. BA, University of London, 1854; MB 1855; MRCS 1855; Associate of King's Coll., London, 1855; Fellow of King's Coll., Lond. 1898. Entered Indian Medical Service, 1856; served throughout Indian Mutiny Campaigns, 1857–59; China War, 1860; Khasia and Jyntia Hills Campaign, 1862–63 (wounded in action); Bhootan War, 1865–66; Egyptian Expedition, 1882; Suakin Expedition, 1885 (as Principal Medical Officer); Hazara Expedition, 1888 (as Principal Medical Officer); was five times mentioned in despatches, and received four war medals with seven clasps, the Khedive's star, and the CB; retired in 1891. Decorated for services in the Suakin Expedition, 1885. *Publication:* Memories of Seven Campaigns. *Recreations:* cricket, lawn-tennis, chess. *Died 6 Jan. 1919.*

THORNTON, Percy Melville, LLM (Camb.); *b* 12 Upper Gloucester Place, London, 29 Dec. 1841; *e s* of late Rear-Admiral Samuel Thornton and Emily Elizabeth, *d* of Rev. J. Rice; *m* 1877, Florence, 3rd *d* of late Henry Sykes Thornton. *Educ:* Harrow; Jesus Coll., Camb. At Cambridge was first secretary of the inter-University sports, and afterwards in London; during 1866, first amateur champion half mile; since 1880 has pursued a literary career, which has only been interrupted by parliamentary duties; MP (C) Clapham and Battersea, 1892–1910; one of the Registrars of the Royal Literary Fund; a Vice-President 1917; when war broke out was elected Hon. Commandant of the Veteran Athlete Volunteers. *Publications:* Recovered Thread of England's Foreign Policy, 1880 (5 editions); Foreign Secretaries of the Nineteenth Century, 3 vols, 1881 (2 editions); Harrow School and its Surroundings, 1883; The Brunswick Accession, 1887; The Stuart Dynasty, 1890; Continental Rulers of the Nineteenth Century; Some Things we have Remembered, 1912. *Recreations:* a lover of cricket, rowing, and athletics for years; hon. sec. Middlesex County Cricket Club until 1898. *Address:* 30 Evelyn Gardens, South Kensington, SW. *T:* Kensington 3050; Ryders Wells House, Lewes, Sussex. *Clubs:* Carlton, United University. *Died 8 Jan. 1918.*

THORNTON, Rt. Rev. Samuel, DD Oxon; MA Melbourne; Assistant Bishop, Diocese of London, and Hon. Diocesan Visitor of the Church Army since 1911; *b* London, 1835; 3rd *s* of Thomas Thornton, FRAS, and Elizabeth, *d* of H. Robinson, Bagshot, Surrey; *m* 1st, 1866 (she *d* 1909), *d* of H. Thornton; one *s*; 2nd, 1913, Caroline Wakefield, *widow* of Rev. Dr Rice. *Educ:* Merchant Taylors' School; Queen's College, Oxford (late Michel Fellow). Open Exhibition, 1851; Scholarship, 1853; 1st class Classics, mods; 2nd class in Classics and in Nat. Science, finals. Graduated at 19; educational work on leaving Oxford; ordained Deacon to Fellowship, 1858; Priest, 1859; London Diocesan Home Mission, 1858; Incumbent of St Jude's, Whitechapel, 1859; Rector of St George's, Birmingham, 1864–75;

first Bishop of Ballarat, 1875-1900; Assistant Bishop to Bishop of Manchester, and Vicar of Blackburn, 1901-10; Proctor, York Convocation, 1906-10; Chaplain, Langho Female Inebriates Asylum, 1907-10; Rural Dean, 1907-10. *Recreations:* boating, tennis, and horseback days are over; now reading in all departments: 'Humani nihil alienum puto'. *Address:* 80 Elsham Road, Kensington, W. *Club:* Church Imperial.   *Died 25 Nov. 1917.*

THORNTON-DUESBURY, Rt. Rev. Charles Leonard, MA; DD 1925; Bishop of Sodor and Man since 1925; *b* Glen Helen, Isle of Man, 3 Feb. 1867; *s* of Capt. W. H. Thornton-Duesbery, BA, JP, late of Durham Light Infantry, and Catherine Wilkinson, of East Riding, Yorkshire; *m* 1896, Ethel Nixon, *d* of General Baumgartner, CB, of Island Hall, Godmanchester; one *s* one *d*. *Educ:* Shattallan Hall, Isle of Man; Trinity College, Dublin; BA 1890; MA 1893; BD and DD 1925; Catech. Prize 1889. Deacon, 1890; Priest 1891; Hon. Canon of Chelmsford, 1914; Rural Dean of Leyton, 1915; Curate of St George-in-the-East, 1890-94; Vicar of St Mark's, Barrow-in-Furness, 1894-1905; Vicar of St Peter's, Islington, 1905-7; Vicar of Leyton, 1907-18; Rector of Holy Trinity, St Marylebone, W, 1919-25; Chairman of Church of England Sunday School Institute, 1917-25; Vice-Chairman, CETS, 1920-25; Chairman of CMS Home Committee, 1920-25. *Address:* Bishop's Court, Kirkmichael, Isle of Man.   *Died 11 March 1928.*

THORNYCROFT, Sir John Isaac, Kt 1902; LLD; FRS 1893; naval architect and engineer; Vice-President of Institute of Naval Architects; *b* Rome, 1 Feb. 1843; *e s* of Thomas and Mary Thornycroft, both sculptors; *m* 1870, Blanche, *d* of Frederick Coules, Gloucester; two *s* five *d*. *Educ:* private school; Glasgow University. Diploma, Glasgow Univ. Founded shipbuilding works at Chiswick, 1866; introduced improvements in naval architecture and marine engineering, which have promoted the development of high speeds at sea. *Publications:* papers in the Trans of British Assoc.; Institution of Naval Architects and Civil Engineers. *Recreations:* small boat sailing and racing, skating, photography, motoring. *Address:* Steyne, Bembridge, Isle of Wight. *M:* H 99. *Clubs:* Royal Automobile; Bembridge Sailing.
                                Died 28 June 1928.

THORNYCROFT, Sir (William) Hamo, Kt 1917; RA 1888 (ARA 1881); sculptor; Hon. Member of Royal Academy of Munich; *b* London, 9 March 1850; 2nd *s* of Thomas and Mary Thornycroft; *m* 1884, Agatha, 2nd *d* of Homersham Cox, Tonbridge. *Educ:* Macclesfield Grammar School; University College School, London. Gold medallist Royal Academy of Arts, 1875; hon. member Royal Academy of Munich, 1889; médaille d'Honneur, Paris, 1900. *Statues:* National Monument to General Gordon in Trafalgar Square and in Melbourne; John Bright in Rochdale; Sir Steuart Bayley in Calcutta; Lord Granville in Houses of Parliament; Her Majesty the Queen in the Royal Exchange; Archbishop Thomson in York; Bishop Goodwin in Carlisle; Teucer in Chantrey Collection; Artemis at Eaton Hall; The Mower, Liverpool Gallery; Lot's Wife; Edward I; The Sower; Summer; Joy of Life; Cromwell Statue at Westminster; National Memorial to Gladstone, Strand, London; Queen Victoria Memorial at Karachi; War Memorial at Durban; Armstrong Memorial at Newcastle; Lord Curzon Memorial, Calcutta; King Edward Memorial at Karachi, 1915; The Kiss, marble group, Tate Gallery, 1916; Bronze Statue of Courage as War Memorial at Luton, 1923; Bishop Yeatman-Biggs Statue in Coventry Cathedral, 1925. *Recreations:* gardening, bicycling, trout fishing. *Address:* 2A Melbury Road, Kensington, W; The Old Farmhouse, Coombe, Handborough, Oxford. *Club:* Athenæum.   *Died 18 Dec. 1925.*

THORODDSEN, Prof. Dr Thorvald; *b* Flatey, Breidifjord, W Iceland, 6 June 1855; *s* of Jon Thoroddsen, poet and author; *m* 1887, Thora (*d* 1917), *d* of Dr P. Pjetursson, DD, Bishop of Iceland. *Educ:* Coll. in Reykjavik, Iceland. Studied zoology and geology at the Univ. of Copenhagen, 1875-80; and geology and physical geography in Germany, 1884-85; teacher at the Technical School in Mödruvellir, N Iceland, 1880-84; teacher at the College in Reykjavik, 1885-95. Lived from 1895 in Copenhagen, occupied with scientific work, but stayed during the summer mostly in Iceland; travelled in Iceland to explore the geology and geography of that country, 1881-99, and made a geological survey of the entire island, and for first time mapped parts of the little known deserts and high plateaus in the interior. Hon. PhD, Univ. of Copenhagen, 1894; Hon. Prof. 1902; Member of the R Acad. Science, Copenhagen, 1909; gold medallist of Geographical Societies of Paris, New York, and Copenhagen and of Royal Academies in Copenhagen and Stockholm; Cuthbert Peek Grant, RGS, London, 1897; Hon. Corresponding Member and Hon. Member of Geographical Societies of London, Berlin, Berne, Copenhagen, Stockholm, of Geological Societies of London, Brussels,

and Copenhagen; formerly President of Icelandic Liter. Society; Knight of Dannebrog, 1899. *Publications:* History of Icelandic Geography, 1892-1904; Geological Map of Iceland, 1901; Description of Iceland, 1881, 1900, 1919; Description of Iceland, 1908-21; Travels in Iceland, 1913-15; Climate Conditions in Iceland During One Thousand Years, 1916-17; History of Icelandic Volcanoes, 1882; Volcanoes and Earthquakes in Iceland, 1896; Earthquakes in Iceland, 1899; Iceland, Geography and Geology, 1905-6, etc; many papers on the geology and geography of Iceland in Icelandic, Danish, Swedish, German, and English scientific journals. *Recreations:* has travelled in Sweden, Germany, England, Switzerland, and Italy for recreation and scientific purposes. *Address:* Reykjavik, Iceland.   *Died Nov 1921.*

THOROLD, Sir John Henry, 12th Bt, *cr* 1642; DL, JP; landowner; *b* 9 March 1842; *e s* of Sir John Charles Thorold, 11th Bt and Elizabeth Frances, *d* of Colonel Hildyard, Flintham Hall, Notts; *S* father, 1866; *m* 1869, Hon. Henrietta Alexandrina Willoughby, *e d* of 8th Baron Middleton; two *s* two *d* (and one *s* decd). *Educ:* Eton; Hon. LLD (Camb.). Late Lieut Leicestershire Regt, 1888; Hon. Col 2nd Vol. Lincs Regt, 1868-88; MP (C) Grantham, 1865-68. Owned about 9,000 acres. *Heir:* *s* Major John George Thorold, *b* 2 Oct. 1870. *Address:* Syston Old Hall, Grantham. *Club:* Carlton.
                                Died 4 Oct 1922.

THOROLD, Montague George, JP; late RN; *b* 22 Aug. 1844; 2nd *s* of Sir John C. Thorold, 11th Bt; *m* 1881, Emmeline Laura Thorold (*d* 1918), *d* of Captain John Bastard, and *widow* of 6th Baron Rivers. *Address:* Harston House, Grantham. *Club:* Royal Yacht Squadron, Cowes.   *Died 19 Dec. 1920.*

THORP, Austin, DSO 1917; Lieutenant-Colonel Royal Garrison Artillery, Commanding 82nd Brigade, Royal Field Artillery, since Dec. 1915; *b* Todmorden, 23 Oct. 1873; *s* of late Charles William Thorp, MD, Dobroyd, Todmorden, and Mrs Thorp, Foxleigh, Wem; *m* 1911, Edith May, *e d* of late William Henry Petrie, Rochdale; one *s* one *d*. *Educ:* Elstow School, Bedford; Royal Military Academy, Woolwich. 2nd Lieut Royal Artillery, 1893; served in India and Burma in the Royal Field Artillery, Royal Garrison Artillery, and Indian Mountain Artillery, 1893-1901; passed through the Gunnery Staff Course, 1902; served in Royal Garrison Artillery in Malta, 1903-7, and in Indian Mountain Artillery in India and Burma, 1908-14; at the outbreak of the War was commanding the RGA Depot, Plymouth; joined BEF France July 1915 in command of a 4.5 Howitzer Battery with the 18th Division (despatches four times, DSO). *Recreations:* golf, motoring. *Address:* 7 Dorset Road, Bexhill-on-Sea.   *Died 30 Oct. 1918.*

THORPE, Sir (Thomas) Edward, Kt 1909; CB 1900; PhD, DSc, ScD, LLD; FRS 1876; Emeritus Professor of General Chemistry in the Imperial College of Science and Technology, S Kensington; *b* near Manchester, 8 Dec. 1845; *s* of George Thorpe, Trafford Bank, near Manchester; *m* 1870, Caroline Emma, *d* of John Watts, Manchester. *Educ:* Owens Coll., Manchester; Universities of Heidelberg and Bonn. Professor of Chemistry in the Andersonian Institution, 1870; Yorkshire Coll. Leeds, 1874; Royal Coll. of Science, London, 1885; formerly treasurer and president Chemical Society; president Chemical Section, British Association, 1890; vice-president, 1900; vice-president Royal Society, 1894-95; president Society of Chemical Industry, 1895; a Fellow of the Univ. of Lond.; Hon. or Corres. Memb. of the Royal Soc. of Edinburgh, Literary and Phil. Societies of Glasgow, Manchester, Leeds, Haarlem, Berlin, Petrograd, Chemists' Club of New York, etc; late Director of the Government Laboratories, London; Foreign Secretary Royal Society to 1908; President of the British Association for the Advancement of Science, 1921. *Publications:* Chemical Problems, 1870; Inorganic Chemistry, 2 vols, 1874; Quantitative Analysis, 1874; Qualitative Analysis, 1873; A Dictionary of Applied Chemistry, 7 vols; Essays in Historical Chemistry; Humphry Davy, Poet and Philosopher; Joseph Priestley; A History of Chemistry, 2 vols; The Scientific Papers of Henry Cavendish; A Yachtsman's Guide to the Dutch Waterways; The Seine from Havre to Paris, 1913; Alcoholometric Tables, 1915; Life of Sir Henry Roscoe, 1916; Editor of Monographs on Industrial Chemistry; numerous memoirs in the Philosophical Transactions of the Royal Society, and of the Chemical Society. *Address:* Whinfield, Salcombe, S Devon. *Clubs:* Athenæum; Salcombe Yacht.
                                Died 23 Feb. 1925.

THRIFT, Sir John Edward, Kt 1909; *b* 30 Jan. 1845; *s* of late William Thrift; *m* 1872, Fanny Selina, *d* of late James Hart, Nottingham; one *s* one *d*. *Educ:* privately. Entered Inland Revenue Department, 1866; Superintendent Inspector Stamps and Taxes for the City of London,

1903; knighted for special services in connection with the Finance Act 1907; Chief Inspector of Inland Revenue, 1907–10. *Address:* The Whare, Woodcote Road, Wallington, Surrey.

Died 15 March 1926.

THROCKMORTON, Sir Nicholas William George, 9th Bt, *cr* 1642; DL, JP; *b* 25 April 1838; 2nd *s* of Sir Robert George Throckmorton, 8th Bt and Elizabeth, *o d* of Sir John Acton, 6th Bt; *S* father, 1862. Owned about 22,400 acres. *Heir: b* Capt. Richard Charles Acton [*b* 26 April 1839; late Captain 87th Foot; *m* 1866, Frances Stewart (*d* 1895), *d* of Maj. John A. Moore; four *s* three *d*]. *Address:* 17 Clifford Street, W; Coughton Court, Coughton, SO, Warwickshire. *Clubs:* Travellers', Boodle's.

Died 21 Dec. 1919.

THROCKMORTON, Sir Richard (Charles Acton), 10th Bt, *cr* 1642; *b* 26 April 1839; *s* of Sir Robert George Throckmorton, 8th Bt and Elizabeth, *o d* of Sir John Acton, 6th Bt; *S* brother, 1919; *m* 1st, 1866, Frances Stewart (*d* 1895), *d* of Maj. John A. Moore; four *s* three *d* (and one *s* decd); 2nd, 1921, Florence (*d* 1924), *widow* of Major Charles Allix Lavington Yate, VC, and formerly wife of late Col G. Burroughs, 3rd Bombay Cavalry. Late Captain 87th Foot. Owned about 22,400 acres. *Heir: g s* Robert George Maxwell Throckmorton [*b* 15 Feb. 1908; *s* of late Lt-Col Courtenay Throckmorton and Lilian, *o d* of Col Langford Brooke, Mere Hall, Cheshire. *Address:* Coughton Court, Coughton, SO, Warwickshire]. *Address:* 18 Milner Street, Lennox Gardens, SW.

Died 28 April 1927.

THUILLIER, Sir Henry Ravenshaw, KCIE 1895 (CIE 1893); Colonel RE, retired 1895; *b* India, 26 March 1838; *e s* of late Gen. Sir Henry Landor Thuillier, CSI; *m* 1867, Emmeline, 3rd *d* of Fleetwood Williams, CSI; two *s* two *d*. *Educ:* Wimbledon School; Military Coll. Addiscombe. Entered Bengal Engineers, 1857; Survey of India Department, 1859; Surveyor-General of India, 1886–95. *Address:* 10 Philbeach Gardens, South Kensington, SW.

Died 4 March 1922.

THULRAI, Taluqdar of, Rana Sir Sheoraj Singh Bahadur of Khajurgaon, KCIE 1911; Rai Bareli District; *b* 1865; *s* of Hon. Rana Sir Shankur Bux Singh Bahadur, KCIE; *S* father, 1897; *m* 1st, *d* of Bahu Amarjit Singh (*y brother* of the Raja of Majhonli); 2nd, *d* of Raja Somesurdutt Singh, a Raja of Kundwar; 3rd, *d* of the Raja of Bijaipur District, Mirzapur; two *s* five *d*. *Educ:* Government High School, Rai Bareli. Hon. Magistrate and a Munsif; held about 150 villages, and maintained a dispensary, an upper Primary Village School and Coronation Anglo-Sanskrit Pathshalaat Khajurgaon; the house descended from King Sahvahan, whose Sumvat Era was current in India during the Rana's time and so he was a Bais Rajput. *Recreations:* hunting, sports, etc. *Heir:* Kunwar Lal Eima Natti Singh Bahadur. *Address:* Thulrai, Khajurgaon, India. *TA:* Dalman District, Rai Bareli.

Died 14 April 1920.

THURLOW, 5th Baron, *cr* 1792; **Thomas John Hovell-Thurlow-Cumming-Bruce,** PC; FRS; DL, JP; *b* 5 Dec. 1838; *s* of 3rd Baron and Sarah, *o d* of Peter Hodgson; *S* brother, 1874; *m* 1864, Lady Elma Bruce, *o d* of 8th Earl of Elgin and Kincardine, KT, and 1st wife, Elizabeth, *d* of Major C. L. Cumming-Bruce; two *s* (and two *s* two *d* decd). Entered Diplomatic Service, 1858; at Embassies at Stockholm; at Paris, 1859–60; on Earl of Elgin's Mission to China, 1860–61; present at capture of Taku Forts and of Pekin; Private Secretary to Viceroy of India (Earl of Elgin), 1862–63; 3rd Secretary at Vienna, 1864; Private Secretary to Minister at Washington, 1865–66; 2nd Secretary at the Hague, 1866–70; Lord-in-Waiting, 1880–86; Paymaster-Gen. 1886; Lord High Commissioner of General Assembly of Church of Scotland, 1886; Chairman of Salt Union. Owned about 13,900 acres. *Publications:* The Company and the Crown; Trades Unions Abroad, etc. *Heir: s* Rev. Hon. Charles Edward Hovell-Thurlow-Cumming-Bruce, *b* 6 Oct. 1869. *Address:* Dunphail, NB.

Died 12 March 1916.

THURSBY, Sir John (Ormerod Scarlett), 2nd Bt, *cr* 1887; DL, JP; *b* 27 April 1861; *s* of Sir John Hardy Thursby, 1st Bt and Clara, *d* of Col Williams, RE; *S* father, 1901; *m* 1888, Ella Beatrice (*d* 1915), *d* of T. Richard Crosse; one *d*. *Educ:* Eton; Trinity College, Cambridge (BA). Barrister-at-Law; High Sheriff of Lancashire, 1905; President of British Chess Federation; President of Burnley Chamber of Commerce; Steward of Jockey Club, 1915–18. *Heir: half-b* George James Thursby [*b* 17 Nov. 1869; *m* 1894, Mary Augusta, *e d* of Thomas Hardcastle of Bradshaw Hall, Bolton-le-Moors. *Address:* Fountain Court, Brook, Lyndhurst. *Club:* Arthur's]. *Address:* Ormerod House, Burnley. *Clubs:* Carlton, Garrick, Turf, Savile.

Died 26 Dec. 1920.

THURSFIELD, Sir James Richard, Kt 1920; MA; *b* Kidderminster, 16 Nov. 1840; *y s* of late Thomas Thursfield, MRCS; *m* 1880, Emily, *d* of late Rev. S. A. Herbert; one *s* one *d*. *Educ:* Merchant Taylors' School; Corpus Christi College, Oxford (scholar, 1859); 1st class Moderations (classical), 1861; 1st class Lit. Hum., 1863. Fellow of Jesus College, 1864–81, Tutor, Dean, Librarian, and Lecturer; Classical Moderator (pass), 1870; Public Examiner (classical honours), 1873; Junior Proctor, 1875; Hon. Fellow of Jesus College, 1908. A writer on The Times, and a frequent contributor to the Naval Annual, and an occasional contributor to the Quarterly, Westminster, and National Reviews, the Athenæum, Academy, and Literature; acted as correspondent to The Times during naval manœuvres from 1887; an Hon. Member of the RUSI and a JP for Co. Herts. *Publications:* Peel, in the series of English Statesmen; The Navy and the Nation, conjointly with Sir George S. Clarke (later Lord Sydenham); Nelson and other Naval Studies; Naval Warfare. *Recreation:* walking, fishing, golf. *Address:* 57 Rotherwick Road, NW4. *T:* Finchley 1055.

Died 22 Nov. 1923.

THURSTON, Col Hugh Champneys, CB 1918; CMG 1900; AMS; *b* 14 March 1862; *s* of late O. E. Thurston of Kington, near Thornbury; *m* 1896, Susie, *d* of Charles Steele, Clifton; one *s* one *d*. Entered Army, 1887; Major, 1899; served Wuntho Expedition, 1891, under Lt-Gen. Sir G. Wolseley, KCB (medal with clasp); South Africa, 1899–1902 (despatches, Queen's medal, five clasps, King's medal, 2 clasps, CMG); European War, 1914–18 (despatches, CB). *Address:* Thornbury, Co. Gloucester.

Died 17 Aug. 1919.

THYNNE, Lord Alexander George, DSO 1917; Major Royal Wilts Yeomanry; MP (U) Bath since 1910; LCC (MR) East Marylebone since 1910; *b* 17 Sep. 1873; *s* of 4th Marquess of Bath. *Educ:* Eton; Balliol Coll., Oxford. Contested (U) Frome Division of Somerset, 1896; City of Bath, 1905; represented the City of London on the London County Council, 1899–1900; Greenwich, 1907–10; Chairman of Improvements Committee, 1909–12; served South Africa with 1st Batt. Imperial Yeomanry, and on the Staff, 1900–2 (Queen's medal, 3 clasps, King's medal, two clasps); Sec. to the Lieut-Gov. Orange River Colony, 1902–5; accompanied Somaliland Field Force, 1903–4, as Reuter's Special Correspondent (medal and clasp); European War, 1914–17 (DSO). *Address:* 15 Manchester Square, W. *T:* Mayfair 2471. *Clubs:* White's, Turf, Carlton.

Died 16 Sept. 1918.

THYNNE, Major Algernon Carteret, DSO 1902; Major Royal North Devon Hussars Yeomanry; *b* 9 April 1868; 2nd *s* of late Francis John Thynne of Haynes Park, Bedford, and Edith Marcia Caroline, *e d* of Richard Brinsley Sheridan of Frampton Court, Dorset; *m* 1904, Constance, *d* of late Edward William Bonham, and *widow* of Francis Philips. Served S Africa, 1900–2 (despatches, Queen's medal with four clasps, King's medal with two clasps, DSO). *Address:* Penstowe, Kilkhampton, N Cornwall. *Club:* Travellers'.

Died 6 Nov. 1917.

THYNNE, Col Hon. Andrew Joseph; VD; MLC, Queensland, 1882–1922; *b* Ireland, 30 Oct. 1847; *m* 1st, 1869, Mary, *d* of late William Cairncross; three *s* five *d*; 2nd, 1922, Christiana J., *widow* of Leslie Gordon Corrie. *Educ:* private tuition; Queen's College, Galway. Went to Queensland, 1864; Solicitor, 1873; Minister of Justice and Attorney-General, 1888–90; Delegate to First Federal Convention, Sydney, 1891, and to Colonial Conference, Ottawa, 1894; Postmaster-General, 1894–97; Secretary for Agriculture, 1896–98; President Queensland Ambulance Brigade; Chairman Queensland Law Society for thirty-five years; Vice-Chancellor Univ. of Queensland; Chairman Queensland Recruiting Committee during War; Vice-Chairman Australian Council of St John's Ambulance Association. *Recreations:* agriculture, horticulture. *Address:* Thoonbah, S Brisbane. *Clubs:* Queensland, Johnsonian, Brisbane.

Died 28 Feb. 1927.

THYNNE, Rev. Arthur Barugh; Vicar of Seend, 1873–1916; Rural Dean of Bradford since 1896; Prebendary of Salisbury since 1899; *b* 29 May 1840; *m*; seven *c*. *Educ:* King's College School; Trinity College, Cambridge. Curate of Northam, Southampton, 1865; Thames Ditton, 1865–69; Wilsford, Marlborough, 1869–73. *Address:* Seend Vicarage, Melksham.

Died 2 Nov. 1917.

THYNNE, Maj.-Gen. Sir Reginald Thomas, KCB 1902 (CB 1885); *b* 23 Dec. 1843; *s* of late Rev. Lord John Thynne, DD, 3rd *s* of 2nd Marquess of Bath; *m* 1890, Louise, *widow* of Major William Ewing, and *d* of Douglas Du Bois; *two d*. *Educ:* Radley. Entered army,

Grenadier Guards, 1862; Maj.-Gen. 1893; served Zulu War, 1879 (medal with clasp); Egypt, 1882 (medal, 4th class Osmanieh, Khedive's star); Soudan, 1885 (despatches, CB, clasp); commanding NE District, 1894–1902. *Address:* 24 Park Square, Regent's Park, NW1. *T:* Museum 6262. *Clubs:* Guards, Travellers'.

Died 30 Dec. 1926.

TIBBLES, William, DCL (Washington), LLD, MD (Chicago); LRCP (Edin.), MRCS (Eng.), LSA (Lond.); *b* Leicester, 10 April 1859; *s* of William Tibbles, MD; *m* Selina, *d* of Thos Pearson, Goxhill, Lincs; one *s* one *d. Educ:* Charing Cross (London University). Speciality: Dietetics and the Diseases of Nutrition and Metabolism. Acting Asst Physician Nottingham General Hospital, 1915–19; Member of Pensions Medical Board, Nottingham; MOH Melton Mowbray R District; MO 4th District Nottingham Parochial Union; Fellow Royal Institute of Public Health; Member British Medical Association; Member American Association Physicians and Surgeons, and Nottingham Medico-Chirurgical Society; late Pathological Assistant, Charing Cross Hospital. *Publications:* Life and Evolution, 1927; Food and Hygiene; Dietetics: or Food in Health and Disease; Foods: their Origin, Manufacture and Composition; The Theory of Ions: a Consideration of its Place in Biology and Therapeutics; Diet in Dyspepsia; articles on Diet in various medical papers; works on Diet were largely used by Ministry of Food and by USA Government in European War. *Recreations:* motoring, travel. *Address:* 119 Derby Road, Parkside, Nottingham. *Died 26 Feb. 1928.*

TICKELL, Rear-Adm. Frederick, CMG 1900; Director of Naval Reserves, Australia, since 1911; *b* 7 March 1857; *m* 1886, Mary Elizabeth, *d* of Edward G. Figg, MD. Torpedo-Lieut, 1892–97; Commander 1897; Captain 1900; Naval Commandant, Victoria, 1897–1904, and 1907–10. Served with Victorian Naval Contingent, China, 1900–1; Naval Commandant, Queensland, 1904–7. *Address:* Delmira, Kew, Victoria, Australia.

Died 20 Sept. 1919.

TIGHE, Edward Kenrick Banbury, JP and DL, Co. Kilkenny; Director, Dublin and South-Eastern Railway; *b* 24 Aug. 1862; *s* of Lieut-Col F. E. B. Tighe and Lady K. Ponsonby, *d* of 4th Earl of Bessborough; *m* 1894, Viola, *d* of E. Skeffington Smyth, DL, Queen's Co. *Educ:* Harrow; Trinity College, Cambridge. Lieut Rifle Brigade, 1884–87; served in Burmese War, 1886–88 (medal, two clasps); Grenadier Guards, 1887–93; contested NW Norfolk, 1895; High Sheriff, Kilkenny, 1895; Westmeath, 1903; Director Dublin, Wicklow, and Wexford Railway since 1894; The Hibernian Bank, Ltd, since 1912. *Recreation:* country life. *Address:* Woodstock, Inistioge, Co. Kilkenny. *Clubs:* Guards, Brooks's, Turf; Kildare Street, Dublin.

Died 17 Nov. 1917.

TIGHE, Lt-Gen. Sir Michael Joseph, KCB 1922 (CB 1911); KCMG 1916; CIE 1912; DSO 1889; Colonel-in-Chief 2nd Frontier Force Rifles (IA); *b* 21 May 1864; *e s* of late Captain M. J. Tighe, 70th Regiment; *m* 1900, Katharine Helen Mackay-Scott, *d* of late Hugh Baillie Scott; one *s. Educ:* Sandhurst. Joined Leinster Regiment, 1883; served in Burmese War, 1886–88 (medal and clasp); Red Karen Expedition, 1889 (clasp and DSO); Chin-Lushai Expedition, 1889–90 (clasp); Chin Hills Expedition, 1890–91 (clasp); E African Expedition, 1895 (medal and Brilliant Star of Zanzibar, 2nd class); Uganda, Aukole, and Unyoro Expeditions 1898–99; commanded Aukole operations (medal, clasp, and Bt Maj.); operations in Mukran and SE Persia; capture of Nodiz fort (Bt Lieut-Col); served European War (East Africa), in chief command, 1914–16 (despatches, 1914 Star, Victory Medal, Allies Medal); 3rd Afghan War, 1919–20 (medal); Colonel, 1907; Major-Gen. 1915; Lieut-Gen. 1920; retired, 1921. *Recreations:* big-game hunting, shooting, fishing, hunting, etc. *Address:* Kensington Palace Mansions, W8. *Club:* Naval and Military.

Died 5 Sept. 1925.

TIGHE, Major Vincent John, DSO 1899; late West India Regiment and Manchester Regiment; *b* 1865; *s* of late M. J. Tighe, Major 70th East Surrey Regt; *m* 1906, Angela Lucy, 4th *d* of Osmond Seager; four *d.* Employed with Royal Niger Co.; operations on the Niger, 1897–98; expeditions to Egbon, Bida, Ilorin (medal and clasp); expedition to Eboussa, Benin Hinterland, 1898 (clasp); to Siama, 1898 (wounded); employed West African Regt, 1899–1908; Ashanti Expedition, 1900; relief of Kumasi (medal and clasp). *Address:* 12 Leyburn Road, Dover. *Died 7 June 1919.*

TILDEN, Sir William Augustus, Kt 1909; DSc Lond., ScD Dublin, DSc Victoria; LLD Birm.; FRS; *b* London, 15 Aug. 1842; *e s* of late Augustus Tilden; *m* 1st, 1869, Charlotte (*d* 1905), *d* of late Robert Bush; one *s*; 2nd, 1907, Julia Mary, *y d* of late C. W. Ramié. *Educ:*

various private schools; two years at Bedford school; Pharmaceutical Society; Royal College of Chemistry. Demonstrator at Pharmaceutical Society, 1864–72; Science Master, Clifton College, 1872–80; Professor of Chemistry, Mason College, Birmingham, 1880–94; President Institute of Chemistry, 1891–94; Treas. Chemical Soc. 1899–1903, President, 1903–5; Professor of Chemistry, Royal College of Science, London, 1894–1909, and Dean of the College, 1905; Davy Medal, Royal Society, 1908; Emeritus Professor in the Imperial College of Science and Technology, 1909. *Publications:* Introduction to Chemical Philosophy, 1876; Practical Chemistry, 1880; Hints on Teaching Chemistry, 1895; A Manual of Chemistry, 1896; A Short History of the Progress of Scientific Chemistry, 1899; The Elements, 1910; Chemical Discovery and Invention in the Twentieth Century, 1917; Life of Sir William Ramsay, 1918; Famous Chemists, 1921; and many scientific papers. *Address:* The Oaks, Northwood, Middlesex. *Died 11 Dec. 1926.*

TILLARD, Maj.-Gen. John Arthur, CB 1887; RA; retired; *b* 13 Sept. 1837; *s* of Philip Tillard of Stukeley Hall, county Huntingdon; *m* 1st, 1859, Eliza Scott (*d* 1895), *d* of Gen. G. P. Whish, BSC; three *s* two *d* (and one *s* decd); 2nd, 1917, Annie Jane, *d* of G. J. Scott, and *widow* of H. Buckland, of Kiatoa, Otago, New Zealand. *Educ:* Brighton College; Trinity College, Cambridge. 1st commission in the Royal (late Bengal) Artillery, 1857; Major-General, 1891; placed on retired list, 1895; served Afghan War, 1878–80; action of Ahmed Khel; march from Kabul to relief of Kandahar, and battle of 1st Sept. 1880 (despatches thrice, medal with 2 clasps, bronze star, brevet of Lt-Col); Burmese Expedition, 1886–87 (despatches, medal, CB). *Address:* c/o Barclay & Co., 54 Lombard Street, EC.

Died 9 July 1928.

TINLEY, Col Gervase Francis Newport, CB 1909; CMG 1916; Indian Army; *b* 4 Nov. 1857; *s* of Maj.-Gen. Robert Newport Tinley; *m* 1st, 1891, Elsie Benton (*d* 1907), *d* of Col W. B. Hughes, DQMG US Army; 2nd, Beryl R., *d* of Francis Tytherleigh-Easton of Heatherwood House, Farnham; three *s* two *d. Educ:* Victoria College, Jersey; St James's Collegiate School, Jersey; Sandhurst. Entered Army, 1875; Captain Indian Staff Corps, 1887; Major, 1896; Lt-Col Indian Army, 1902; Col, 1905; AAG India, 1905–8; served Zhob Valley Expedition, 1884; Burmah, 1885–89 (wounded, horse shot, despatches, medal with two clasps); Egypt, 1896 (medal, Egyptian medal); European War, 1914–17 (despatches three times; CMG); Commandant lines of communication, 1914–17. *Address:* Tower Hill House, Kingsclere, Hants. *TA:* Tinley, Kingsclere.

Died 18 Feb. 1918.

TIRARD, Prof. Sir Nestor (Isidore Charles), Kt 1916; MD, FRCP; Emeritus Professor of Medicine at King's College; Consulting Physician at King's College Hospital; Consulting Physician to Evelina Hospital for Children, etc; Crown Nominee on General Medical Council until 1927; Lt-Col commanding 4th London General Hospital, RAMC (T); *b* 23 Sept. 1853; *m* 1885, Helen Mary, *d* of Rev. R. S. Beloe; one *s* two *d. Educ:* King's College Hospital. Scholarship and gold medal in Forensic and Obstetric Medicine, and Honours in Medicine at London University. Order of St Sava of Serbia, 2nd Class. *Publications:* Diphtheria and Anti-Toxin, 1896; Albuminuria and Bright's Disease, 1899; Medical Treatment (Diseases and Symptoms), 1900; senior editor, British Pharmacopœia, 1914; editor of King's College Hospital Reports. *Recreations:* sketching, fishing. *Address:* 74 Harley Street, W1. *T:* Langham 2646. *Club:* Athenæum. *Died 10 Nov. 1928.*

TISDALL, Colonel Arthur Lance, CMG 1914; late Royal Artillery; *b* 25 Nov. 1860; *s* of Major-General Archibald Tisdall, 85th Royal Sussex Regt; *m* 1898, Katherine Maud, *widow* of Major Alexander Gzowski, Welsh Regt, and *d* of John Gordon Bowen, Burt House, Co. Donegal. *Educ:* Clifton College; Woolwich. Lt RA, 1880; retired as Lieut-Colonel, 1914; re-employed in Remount Service, 1915–19; Bt Col, 1919. *Address:* Athgaine, Budleigh Salterton. *T:* Budleigh Salterton 28. *Died 18 May 1927.*

TISDALL, Rev. William St Clair, DD; *b* 19 Feb. 1859; *e s* of Major William St Clair Tisdall; *m* Marian L., *d* of Rev. W. Gray, MA, Sec. CMS; four *s* (two killed in the War, one of whom gained the VC at the landing from River Clyde, Gallipoli, April 1915) four *d.* BA (1st class Classical Honours) and MA, University of New Zealand; Hon. DD of Edinburgh University, 1903. Deacon, 1882; priest, 1883; Vicar of Wakefield, Nelson, NZ, 1882; Hebrew and Classical Lecturer, Bishopsdale Theological College, Nelson, 1883; Vice-Principal, St John's College, Lahore, Panjab, 1885; Principal, Training College, Amritsar, Panjab, 1886; in charge CMS Muhammadan Mission, Bombay, 1887; head of CMS Persia and Baghdad Mission,

1892; James Long Lecturer in Islâm, Hindûism, Buddhism, and Comparative Religion, 1900-5; Hebrew Lecturer, CMS Coll., Islington, 1910; Vicar of St George-the-Martyr Corporation Church, Deal, Kent, 1913-26; Surrogate for Deal; Hon. CF, 1916-19. *Publications:* Christianity and Other Faiths; Comparative Religion; The Noble Eightfold Path; Religion of the Crescent; Religio Critici; Original Sources of the Qur'ân; Mythic Christs and the True; numerous pamphlets against Higher Criticism, etc; translator of Four Gospels into Kirmanshâhî Kurdish; author of numerous works in the Persian language; contributor to Bible Encyclopædias, Victoria Institute Journal, etc; author of Grammars of Gujarâtî, Panjâbî, Urdû, and Persian languages. *Recreation:* literary work. *Address:* Ferahabad, Warwick Road, Walmer, Kent.

Died 1 Dec. 1928.

TITHERIDGE, Lieut Benjamin, MVO 1909. Was chief gunner on Royal yacht Alexandra. *Address:* Woolston, Southampton.

Died Feb. 1918.

TIZARD, Capt. Thomas Henry, CB 1899; RN; FRS 1891; Assistant Hydrographer of the Admiralty, 1891-1907; *b* 13 March 1839; *s* of late Joseph Tizard; *m* 1881, Mary Elizabeth, *d* of W. H. Churchward, CE; one *s* four *d.* Joined the Navy as Master's Asst, 1854; served in the Baltic during the Russian War, 1854-56; present at the attack on Hango forts and the bombardment of Sveaborg (Baltic medal); joined the Surveying Service, 1861; was Navigating Officer of the 'Challenger' in her expedition, 1872-76; contributed the Hydrographical part of the official narrative of that expedition; was in charge of Surveys in England, 1879-91. *Publications:* contributed papers on the Exploration of the Faroe Channel to the Royal Society and to the Royal Society of Edinburgh. *Address:* 23 Geneva Road, Kingston-on-Thames. *Died 17 Feb. 1923.*

TOD, Hunter F., MA, MD, FRCS; Senior Surgeon, the Ear, Nose and Throat Department, London Hospital; Lecturer in Aural Surgery at London Hospital Medical College; late Surgeon, Throat and Ear Department, Paddington Green Children's Hospital; 2nd *s* of late David Tod, JP, of Eastwood Park and Hartfield, Renfrewshire, NB; *m* Yvonne Grace, *e d* of Stanley Rendall, of Chantmerle, Aix-les-Bains, France; one *s* three *d. Educ:* Clifton College; Trinity College, Cambridge; London Hospital; Leipzig, Vienna, Halle, Berlin. *Publications:* Diseases of the Ear, Oxford Medical Manuals; Operations on the Ear, Burghard's System of Operative Surgery; Diseases of the External Auditory Canal and Tympanic Membrane, in Allbutt and Rolleston's System of Medicine. *Address:* 11 Upper Wimpole Street, W1. *T:* 4750 Paddington. *M:* LD 19; LH 3265. *Clubs:* Oxford and Cambridge, Royal Automobile.

Died 23 Jan. 1923.

TODD, Howard, CB 1911; Hon. Surgeon to the King; *b* 20 Sept. 1855; *s* of M. G. Todd, Hove, Brighton, and M. A., *d* of Capt. Pryce, RN; *m* 1893, Florence Agnes, *d* of E. Haynes, Thimbleby, Yorks; one *s* two *d. Educ:* Dr Seaver's, Brighton; St Thomas' Hospital (Prizeman). Served Niger Expedition, 1879; yellow fever epidemic, Jamaica, 1885-86 (received thanks of Admiralty); thanked by Foreign Office for services rendered at Mapanda's Kraal, acting Consular Surgeon, 1891; Surgeon-General Royal Navy; JP Hampshire. *Recreations:* golf, tennis, fishing. *Address:* Anglesey House, Anglesey, near Gosport, Hants. *Died 6 Nov. 1925.*

TODD, (John) Spencer Brydges, CMG 1878; ISO 1905; *b* Dresden, 28 Aug. 1840; *y s* of late Col George Todd and Mary, *d* of Sir Egerton Brydges, Bt; *m* 1865, Susan Margaret, *e d* of late Baron Goert van Reede van Oudtshoorn; two *s* two *d. Educ:* Blochmann's Gymnasium, Dresden; and the Imperial Lyceum, St Omer. Civil Service, Cape of Good Hope, 1860-1904; Sec., Department of Agent-Gen. in London, 1882-1904; Executive Commissioner for the Cape, and an International Juror, Paris Universal Exhibition, 1878; CMG for services as such; ISO on retirement. *Publications:* The Resident Magistrate at the Cape of Good Hope, 1882; Handy Guide to Laws and Regulations at the Cape of Good Hope, 1887. *Address:* Hotel Roland, 3 and 4 Roland Houses, South Kensington, SW7.

Died 15 April 1921.

TODD, Sir Joseph White, 1st Bt, *cr* 1913; Chairman of Central Argentine Railway and Director Buenos Ayres Western Railway; Deputy-Chairman Callander and Oban Railway; Member of the Royal Commission on Sugar Supply, 1917-21; Member International Sugar Committee, New York and Washington, 1917-18; *b* Stirlingshire, 23 June 1846; *m* 1st, 1879, Aline Fannie (*d* 1924), *d* of Louis Lefebvre of New York, and *widow* of T. Orihuela; no *c*; 2nd, 1925, Euphemia, *widow* of Charles Day Halsey, of New York, *o d*

of Ed. Burot Grubb, formerly US Minister to Spain. *Educ:* privately. Resided in Havana, Cuba, several years, Merchant Banker, and retired in 1885. Grand Cross of Spanish Order of Merit. *Recreations:* shooting, fishing, etc. *Heir:* none. *Address:* 33 Eaton Place, SW1. *T:* Victoria 508; Morenish Lodge, Killin, Perthshire. *Clubs:* Reform, City of London. *Died 19 Feb. 1926 (ext).*

TODD, Dr Margaret; *see* Travers, Graham.

TODHUNTER, John, MD; author; *b* Dublin, 30 Dec. 1839; *e s* of late Thomas Harvey Todhunter, merchant; *m* 1st, 1870, Katharine, *d* of late Robert Ball, LLD, Dublin; 2nd, 1879, Dora Louisa, *d* of late William A. Digby, Dublin; one *s* two *d. Educ:* York School; Trinity College, Dublin. MD and MCh, Dublin; Vice-Chancellor's Prize for English Verse, 1864, 1865, 1866; Gold Medallist Philosophical Society (for Prose Essay), 1866. Studied in Vienna and Paris, and practised medicine for some years in Dublin; Professor of English Literature, Alexandra Coll., Dublin, 1870-74; travelled on the Continent and in Egypt, and finally settled in London. *Publications:* The Theory of the Beautiful (a lecture delivered in Trinity Coll.), 1872; Laurella and other Poems, 1876; Alcestis, 1879; A Study of Shelley, 1880; True Tragedy of Rienzi, and Forest Songs, 1881; Helena in Troas, 1885 (performed 1886); The Banshee, and other Poems, 1888; A Sicilian Idyll (several times performed), 1890; The Poison Flower (performed 1891); The Black Cat (performed 8 Dec. 1893), pub. 1895; A Comedy of Sighs (performed 1894); Life of Sarsfield, 1895; Three Irish Bardic Tales, 1896; Sounds and Sweet Airs, 1905; translation of Heine's Book of Songs, 1907. *Recreation:* sketching. *Address:* Orchardcroft, Bedford Park, W. *Clubs:* Savile, Sette of Odd Volumes, Poets', Authors', Pepys, Omar Khayyam.

Died 25 Oct. 1916.

TOLE, Hon. Joseph Augustus, KC; BA, LLB; Crown Solicitor and Crown Prosecutor, Auckland, NZ; *b* Wakefield, England; 5th and *y s* of late John Tole, land surveyor; *m* Eleanor, *d* of Edward Lewis; one *s* three *d. Educ:* St John's College, Sydney; University of Sydney. Admitted Bar, NSW, 1871, and NZ Bar, 1872; MP 1876-87; Minister of Justice, 1884-87; drafted and carried through Parliament, First Offenders' Probation Act, 1886 (the first in the Empire); Member of Board, Governors of Grammar School, and of University College, and also a Fellow of University of NZ. *Recreations:* music, reading, walking, billiards. *Address:* Remuera, near Auckland, NZ. *T:* 722. *Clubs:* Northern, Pacific, Auckland.

Died 13 Dec. 1920.

TOLLEMACHE, Arthur Frederick Churchill; *b* 1 Aug. 1860; heir to baronetcy of 9th Earl of Dysart; *m* 1888, Susan Eleanor (*d* 1919), *e d* of Capt. J. C. Campbell, RN, of Ardpatrick, Argyllshire, NB; two *d* (and one *s* decd). *Educ:* Eton; Christ Church, Oxford (BA 1883). JP King's Co.; High Sheriff 1888. *Clubs:* Arthur's; Kildare Street, Dublin; St George Yacht. *Died 18 Aug. 1923.*

TOLLEMACHE, David, FRSL; author and journalist; *m* 1913, Grace, *d* of late W. H. Dodd. *Educ:* Larchfield, Helensburgh; Andersonian University, Glasgow. Member of Council Royal Society of Literature, 1904-7; Freeman of City of London and of the Worshipful Company of Spectacle-Makers; Assistant Literary Secretary, Tariff Reform League, since 1907. Formerly editor Court Circular, Commercial Traveller, Trade and Industy, Home and Export Trade Review, and Insurance Agents' News; editor, Cassell's Newspaper Press Agency, 1905; contributed short stories under the pen-name of Mark Lovell, and political and social articles, to many periodicals; leader-writer and London Correspondent of many provincial newspapers. *Publications:* English Coronations; The Story of the English Boroughs; Bible Stories for Young Readers; Cassell's New Dictionary of Cookery, 1904; Wayside Warblings. *Recreations:* the drama, Freemasonry (PM, PZ, LR). *Address:* 7 Grand Parade Mansions, Muswell Hill, N. *Club:* Constitutional. *Died Nov. 1918.*

TOLLEMACHE, Hon. Lionel Arthur; author; *b* 28 May 1838; 2nd *s* of 1st Baron Tollemache and Georgina Best; *m* 1870, Hon. Beatrix Lucia Catherine Egerton, 4th *d* of 1st Baron Egerton of Tatton (author of Russian Sketches). *Educ:* Harrow; Balliol College, Oxford; Balliol Scholar, 1856; 1st class Classics and honorary class in Mathematics, 1860. *Publications:* Safe Studies and Stones of Stumbling, 1891; Benjamin Jowett, a Personal Memoir, 1895; Talks with Mr Gladstone, 1898; Old and Odd Memories, 1908; Nuts and Chestnuts, 1911. *Recreations:* debarred by extreme near-sightedness from ordinary amusements; hearing poetry and novels read aloud, and studying human nature. *Address:* Dunrozel, Haslemere, Surrey. *Club:* Athenæum. *Died 29 Jan. 1919.*

TOLLNER, Col Barrett Lennard, CB 1902; RA; *b* 25 Nov. 1839. Entered army, 1861; Captain, 1875; Major, 1881; Lieut-Col 1889; Col 1894; Assistant Inspector of Remounts, Woolwich, 1899–1905; Inspector since 1905. *Address:* 42 Half Moon Street, W.
Died 25 Nov. 1918.

TOMASSON, Capt. Sir William Hugh, KBE 1920 (CBE 1918); MVO 1906; Chief Constable of Notts since 1892; Assistant Inspector of Constabulary; *b* 1858; *m* 1882, Eliza, *d* of late George Lees. *Educ:* Clifton. *Address:* Woodthorpe, Nottingham. *Clubs:* Boodle's, Pratt's.
Died 12 Oct. 1922.

TOMBS, Robert Charles, ISO 1902; *b* 11 Nov. 1842; *s* of officer in Bengal Horse Artillery, Hon. East India Company's Service; of Gloucestershire family; *m* Annie Maria, *d* of William Brown Rooff, of Highgate, London; four *s* one *d. Educ:* Stratford-on-Avon. Appointed Clerk, Foreign Branch, General Post Office, under competitive system, 1861; Principal Clerk, Circulation Department, 1868; Assistant Controller, London Postal Service, 1884; Controller, 1887; retired through ill health, 1892; Special Postal Mission to Ireland, 1870–73; served on many Departmental Committees. *Publications:* London Postal Service of To-Day; Visitors' Guide to the General Post Office; Bristol Royal Mail; Service Instruction Books; The King's Post; The Tombs Families of the Cotswolds, etc. *Recreations:* genealogy, archæology, literature. *Address:* Henleaze, near Bristol.
Died 18 Sept. 1923.

TOMES, Sir Charles Sissmore, Kt 1919; MA, LLD; FRS, FRCS; *b* London, 6 June 1846; *s* of late Sir John Tomes, FRS, and Jane Sibley. *Educ:* Radley; Christ Church, Oxford; Middlesex Hospital. 1st class, Natural Science. Was examiner in dental surgery at Royal College of Surgeons for fourteen years; Inspector of dental examinations in United Kingdom on behalf of General Medical Council, 1895–96; Crown nominee on and Treasurer of General Medical Council; late Vice-President Zoological Society. *Publications:* papers relating to Odontology, in Phil. Trans of Royal Society, etc; A Manual of Dental Anatomy, Human and Comparative, 6th edn 1904. *Recreations:* shooting, fishing, motoring. *Address:* Welbeck House, Wigmore Street, W; Mannington Hall, Aylsham. *M:* H 1621. *Clubs:* Savile, Norfolk, Norwich.
Died 24 Oct. 1928.

TOMKINS, Ernest William, CIE 1920; OBE 1919; Inspector-General of Police, North-West Frontier Province, since 1920; *b* 19 May 1872; *s* of late Rev. G. W. Tomkins, MA. *Educ:* privately. Entered the Indian Police, 1893; officiating Inspector-General of Police, North-West Frontier Province, 1919; mentioned in London Gazette for valuable services in connection with the War, 1919; 1914–15 Star and 3rd Afghan War medal, British War medal, 1914–18 Victory medal. *Address:* Peshawar, North-West Frontier Province, India.
Died 20 Nov. 1925.

TOMKINS, Lieut-Col Harry Leith, CMG 1916; DSO 1898; late 28th Punjabis, Indian Army; *b* 1870; *s* of late Samuel Leith Tomkins. Entered 4th King's Own (Royal Lancashire) Regt 1890; Lieut, 1893; joined Indian Army, 19th Punjabis, 1894; 28th Punjabis, 1895; Capt. 1901; Major, 1908; served NW Frontier, India, 1894–95, Waziristan (medal and clasp); as Railway Staff Officer, Line of Communications, 1897–98 (despatches, DSO); NW Frontier, India, Mahsud Waziri, 1901–2 (medal and clasp); Somaliland, with 27th Punjabis, 1903–4 (medal and clasp); NW Frontier, India, 1908; operations in the Zakkha Khel country (medal and clasp); European War, 1914–17 (despatches twice, Bt. Lt-Col, CMG); Assistant Military Secretary and ADC to GOC Northern Army, India; retired 1920. *Club:* Junior United Service.
Died 20 Feb. 1926.

TOMKINS, Gen. William Percival, CIE 1890; Colonel Commandant RE; *b* 11 June 1841; *s* of late Samuel Tomkins; *m* 1864, Annie, *d* of late Robert Thurburn. Entered army, 1860; General, 1898; served Zhob Valley Expedition, 1884. *Address:* 120 Lexham Gardens, SW. *Club:* East India United Service.
Died 19 Nov. 1922.

TOMKINSON, Michael, JP, DL, Alderman, CC Worcestershire; JP Shropshire; *b* 1841; 2nd *s* of Michael Tomkinson, of Leamington; *m* 1871, Annie, *d* of M. P. Stonehouse, of Wakefield, Yorks; seven *s* five *d. Educ:* privately. Mayor of Kidderminster, 1887, 1893, 1894, 1895, 1905, 1912; High Sheriff for Worcestershire, 1892; Governor of Birmingham University and Member of Council. *Publication:* A Japanese Collection, 2 vols, 1898. *Recreations:* shooting, fishing, interested in Japanese art, early printed books and manuscripts,

member of Roxburghe Club. *Address:* Franche Hall, near Kidderminster, Worcestershire; Chilton, Cleobury Mortimer, Shropshire. *Club:* Burlington Fine Arts.
Died 28 June 1921.

TOMPKINS, Engineer Captain Albert Edward, CBE 1919; Royal Navy (retired); Director, Tangential Dryers, Limited; *b* 30 May 1863; *s* of late John Tompkins, of Aveley Hall, Essex; *m* Dorothea Frances, *e d* of late Edmund G. Reader, Genoa; one *d. Educ:* private schools. Appointed to HMS Marlborough, Portsmouth, as RN Engineer Student, 1878; Engineer Commander, 1901; Engineer Captain (retired), 1913; China, 1885–86; Mediterranean, 1886–88 and 1890–94; Australia, 1897–1900, including warlike operations in Samoa, HMS Porpoise under Commander (later Admiral) Sturdee, Annexation of Savage Island and Protectorate of Tonga Islands; Engineer Commander of Flagship of Second Cruiser Squadron, 1906–7; Flagship of East Indies Squadron (Admiral Sir E. Slade), 1909–11, during Persian Gulf Blockade (NGS medal, Persian Gulf clasp, and East African medal, Somaliland clasp); Instructor in Marine Engineering at RN College, Greenwich, and Lecturer to the RN War Colleges, 1902–6; on War service; appointed to Clyde District to supervise Emergency Repairs; transferred to Italy in 1917 in charge of repairs to HM ships and vessels by Italian private firms (despatches, CBE). *Publications:* Marine Engineering (a Text-Book), 5th edition; Turbines (Romance of Science Series), 3rd edition. *Address:* Tiptoe, Sway, Hants.
Died 10 Sept. 1927.

TOMPSON, Maj.-Gen. William Dalrymple, CB 1879; Colonel of the Leicestershire Regiment, 1912; *b* 1833; *m* 1884, Ellen Mary, *d* of late William Carroll. *Educ:* Cheltenham. Entered army, 1852; Maj.-Gen. 1884; served Crimea, 1855 (dangerously wounded, despatches, medal with clasp, Turkish medal, Kt of Legion of Honour); Afghan War, 1878–79 (despatches, CB, medal with clasp). *Address:* Iver House, Iver, Bucks. *Club:* Army and Navy.
Died 7 Dec. 1916.

TOMSON, Rev. John, MA; Prebendary of Hereford since 1913. *Educ:* Magdalene College, Cambridge, MA. Deacon, 1878; priest, 1879; Rector of Rochford, Worcester, 1892–1919. *Address:* Engleton, Tenbury.
Died 28 Jan. 1926.

TOOTH, Howard Henry, CB 1918; CMG 1901; Hon. MD, Malta Univ.; MA, MD, Cantab; FRCP; Consulting Physician to St Bartholomew's, the National Hospital for the Paralysed and Epileptic, and the Metropolitan Hospitals; late Examiner in Medicine, Cambridge and Durham Universities; late Censor, Royal College of Physicians; *b* 22 April 1856; *s* of late Frederick Tooth of Hove, Sussex; *m* 1st, 1881, Mary Beatrice (*d* 1905), *d* of late Edward Price; one *d*; 2nd, 1908, Helen Katharine, OBE 1920, 2nd *d* of Rev. C. S. Chilver; one *s* two *d. Educ:* Rugby School; St John's Coll., Cambridge. Temp. Col AMS Consulting Physician to troops in Malta and Italy (despatches twice); Col AMS (TF, Res.) retired; late OC 1st London General Hospital, and Medical Unit Officers' Training Corps, London University Contingent. Decorated for service in South Africa as Physician to the Portland Hospital, and as Physician to troops in Malta. *Publications:* many contributions to scientific and medical societies and journals. *Address:* The Moat, Hadleigh, Suffolk. *T:* Hadleigh 20; 90 Harley Street, W1. *T:* Mayfair 3311.
Died 13 May 1925.

TOOVEY, Rev. Henry, MA Oxon 1868; Canon and Prebendary of Botevant in York Minster since 1898; Master of Lord Leycester's Hospital, Warwick, since 1901; Chaplain to Lord De L'Isle and Dudley since 1880; *b* 1843; *s* of John and Marianna Toovey; *m* Jane, *e d* of Robert Hubie of Barlby Grove, Yorkshire; one *d. Educ:* France; Worcester College, Oxford. Private Sec. and Domestic Chaplain to the Earl of Feversham, 1867–70; Vicar of Ingleby Greenhow, Yorks, 1870–80; Inspector of Schools for the Diocese of York, 1880–1902; Rector of Newton Kyme, Yorks, 1894–1902. *Address:* The Master's Lodge, Lord Leycester's Hospital, Warwick. *Club:* Warwick and County, Warwick.
Died 17 July 1922.

TOPHAM, Frank W. W., RI; *b* London, 1838; *s* of late F. W. Topham, RWS; *m* 1870, Helen, *d* of Mark Lemon, editor of Punch; three *s* five *d. Educ:* private schools in England and France; in art Royal Academy Schools and Atelier Gleyre, Paris. Since 1863 constant exhibitor at the Royal Academy and other exhibitions throughout the country; among other pictures, the following are in permanent Public Galleries; Burning the Vanities by order of Savonarola, Sydney, NSW, Australia; A Roman Triumph, Leicester; A Prize in the Lottery, Leeds; The Fall of Rienzi, Liverpool; Drawing for the Conscription, Modern Italy, Manchester; The Emigrant's Letter, Reading; Rescued from the Plague, London, 1665. *Recreation:* gardening. *Address:* Coneyhurst, Ewhurst, Guildford.

Died 25 May 1924.

TOPPING, Colonel (Hon. Brig.-Gen.) Thomas Edward, CB 1919; CMG 1917; DSO 1900; ADC to the King, 1920; West Lancashire Territorial Artillery; (retired); *b* 1871. Served 1st Brigade Imperial Yeomanry, South Africa (despatches, Queen's medal four clasps, DSO); European War, 1914–18 (CMG, CB); Brig., 1915; Brig.-Gen., 1918; Col, 1919. *Address:* Whitehall Court, SW. *Club:* White's. *Died 8 July 1926.*

TORR, Cecil; *b* 1857; *s* of late T. S. Torr, and *g s* of late John Torr of Wreyland; unmarried. *Educ:* Harrow, Trinity College, Cambridge. Called to the Bar, 1882. *Publications:* Ancient Ships, and other antiquarian works; also Small Talk at Wreyland. *Address:* Wreyland, near Lustleigh, Devon. *Died 17 Dec. 1928.*

TORR, Rev. William Edward, MA; Vicar of Eastham, 1880–1917; Hon. Canon of Chester Cathedral; *b* 18 July 1851; *e* surv. *s* of late John Torr, MP; *m* Julia Elizabeth (*d* 1920), *d* of John Holmes of Somerfield, Maidstone; two *s* three *d*. *Educ:* Harrow; Trinity College, Cambridge. Vicar of Flamstead, Herts, 1878–80; succeeded to Carlett Park, 1880; Proctor in York Convocation, 1895–1910. *Address:* Carlett Park, Eastham, Cheshire. *TA:* Eastham. *T:* 86 Bromborough (Birkenhead). *M:* K 4337. *Died 17 Sept. 1924.*

TORRE-DIAZ, Count de, Brodie Manuel de Zulueta; GCSG; GCIC; retired Banker; *b* 1842; *s* of 2nd Count de Torre-Diaz and Sophia Anne, *d* of Brodie M'Ghie Willcox, MP; *m* 1st, 1873, Constance, *d* of Hon. Federick Petre; one *s* three *d*; 2nd, 1892, Hon. Bertha Clifford, *d* of 8th Lord Clifford of Chudleigh. Conservative; Roman Catholic. *Address:* 21 Devonshire Place, W. *Died 20 Sept. 1918.*

TORREY, Reuben Archer; Special Lecturer, Moody Bible Institute, Chicago; *b* Hoboken, New Jersey, 28 Jan. 1856; *s* of R. S. Torrey and Elizabeth A. Swift; *m* 1879, Clara B. Smith, Garrettsville, Ohio; one *s* two *d*. *Educ:* Yale; Leipsic; Erlangen. Entered Congregational Ministry, 1878; was Superintendent of the Minneapolis City Mission Society; joined late D. L. Moody at Chicago, 1889; Superintendent Moody Bible Institute, Chicago, 1889–1906; pastor of Chicago Avenue Church, 1894–1906; conducted Torrey-Alexander Mission in Australia, New Zealand, India, and Great Britain, 1902–5; conducted Torrey Missions in United States and Canada, 1906–11; Torrey Missions in England, Scotland, and Ireland, 1911; Dean of the Bible Institute of Los Angeles, 1912–24; Pastor, Church of the Open Door, Los Angeles, 1914–24; Missions in China and Japan, 1902, 1919, 1921; Torrey Missions in US, Canada, and other lands since 1924. *Publications:* How to bring Men to Christ; How to obtain Fulness of Power; The Baptism with the Holy Spirit; What the Bible Teaches; Divine Origin and Authority of the Bible; How to Work for Christ; How to Promote and Conduct a Successful Revival; Revival Addresses; How to Study the Bible for Greatest Profit; Real Salvation; How to Pray; How to Succeed in the Christian Life; The Bible and its Christ; The Gist of the Lessons; Anecdotes and Illustrations; Difficulties and Alleged Contradictions in the Bible; Practical and Perplexing Questions Answered; Studies in the Life and Teachings of our Lord; The Person and Work of the Holy Spirit; The Return of the Lord Jesus; The Joy of Soul Winning; The Fundamental Doctrines of the Christian Faith; The Voice of God in the Present Hour; The Real Christ; Jesus the Prophet, the Priest, the King, the Wonder; The Importance and Value of Proper Bible Study; Is the Bible the Inerrant Word of God?; The Gospel for To-day; New Evangelistic Sermons for a New Age; The God of the Bible; How to be Saved and How to be Lost; The Christ of the Bible; Soul Winning Sermons; The Power of Prayer and the Prayer of Power; Divine Healing; Why God used Dr L. Moody; The Bible the Peerless Book, God's Own Book, and God's Only Book; How to get the Gold out of the Word of God; The Holy Spirit: Who He Is and What He Does; The Conversion and Christian Training of Children; Exposition Lectures on the First Epistle of John. Some of these books have been translated into thirty-four different languages. *Address:* Asheville, North Carolina, USA; Chicago, Illinois, USA; Montrose, Pennsylvania, USA. *TA:* Bible, Chicago. *Died Oct. 1928.*

TOSTI, Sir (Francesco) Paolo, KCVO 1908 (Hon. CVO 1906); composer; *b* Abruzzi, 1847. *Educ:* Conservatoire, Naples. Came to England, 1876; Singing Master to the Royal Family, 1880; Prof. of Singing, RAM, 1894. *Songs:* Come to my Heart, For ever and for ever, Good-bye, That Day, Let it be soon, Ask me no more, Help me to pray, Yesterday, At the Convent Gate, We have loved, Tell them! *Died 2 Dec. 1916.*

TOTHILL, Admiral Sir Hugh Henry Darby, KCB 1923 (CB 1916); KCMG 1918; KCVO 1921; ADC; Admiral commanding Reserves, 1923–25; *b* 14 March 1865; *m* 1892, Hilda Montgomerie, *d* of late John Beddoe, FRS. Served Egyptian War, 1882, including bombardment of Alexandria (medal, star); European War, 1914–18, including Battle of Jutland Bank, 1916 (despatches, CB); 4th Sea Lord of the Admiralty, 1917–19; Commander-in-Chief, East Indies, 1919–21; Vice-Adm. 1921; Admiral, 1926. *Address:* The Chantry, Bradford-on-Avon, Wilts. *Clubs:* Army and Navy, Wellington. *Died 25 Sept. 1927.*

TOTTENHAM, Col Charles George, DL Co. Wicklow; JP Cos Wexford and Wicklow; *b* 11 April 1835; *s* of Charles Tottenham of Ballycurry and Isabella Catherine, *d* of Gen. Sir George Airey; *m* 1859, Catherine Elizabeth (*d* 1905), *d* of Rev. Hon. Sir Francis Stapleton, 7th Bt; four *d*. *Educ:* Eton. Served in Scots Fusilier Guards; gained 5th class of Medjidie and British and Turkish medals; MP (C) New Ross, 1863–68, and 1878–80; Hon. Col Wicklow Militia Artillery. *Address:* Ballycurry, Ashford, Co. Wicklow. *TA:* Ashford, Wicklow. *Clubs:* Carlton; Kildare Street, Dublin; Irish Automobile. *Died 10 May 1918.*

TOULMIN, Sir George, Kt 1911; *b* Bolton, 17 March 1857; *m* 1882, Mary Elizabeth, *e d* of late Alderman Thomas Edelston, Preston; two *s* two *d*. *Educ:* Preston Grammar School. Newspaper proprietor; managing director of the Lancashire Daily Post and Preston Guardian; Chairman Press Association, 1919–20; Hon. Treasurer, Newspaper Society; JP Co. Lancaster, 1906, and County Borough of Preston, 1897; Fellow Institute of Journalists; contested Bury (L), 1900; MP (L) Bury, 1902–18. *Address:* 127 Fishergate, Preston. *Clubs:* Reform, National Liberal, Eighty; Ninety-five, Manchester. *Died 21 Jan. 1923.*

TOWER, Charlemagne; American Ambassador to Germany, 1902–8; *b* Philadelphia, 17 April 1848; *s* of Charlemagne and Amelia Bartle Tower, 8th in descent from John Tower who emigrated from Hingham, in Norfolk, to Massachusetts, in 1637; *m* 1888, Helen, *d* of G. Frank Smith of San Francisco, California; three *s* two *d*. *Educ:* Exeter Academy, New Hampshire, 1868; graduated Harvard Univ. 1872. Called to the Bar at Philadelphia, 1878; LLD Glasgow and St Andrews, Chicago, 1903, Hamilton, 1909, Lafayette, 1897; attaché, US Legation, Madrid, 1872–73; studied history and literature in Spain, France, and Germany, 1873–76; President, Duluth and Iron Range Railway; Managing Director, Minnesota Iron Company, 1882–87; President, Finance Company of Penna, 1887; Member of the Board of City Trusts of Philadelphia, 1915; President of the Historical Society of Pennsylvania, 1917; Minister to Austria-Hungary, 1897; Ambassador to Russia, 1899–1902; Member Board of Trustees, Carnegie Endowment for International Peace. Grand Officer of the Legion of Honour of France; Grand Cordon of St Alexander Nevsky of Russia. *Publications:* The Marquis de La Fayette in the American Revolution, 1895; Essays Political and Historical, 1914; The Origin, Meaning, and International Force of the Monroe Doctrine, 1921. *Address:* 228 South Seventh Street, Philadelphia, Pennsylvania, USA. *Clubs:* Metropolitan, University, New York; Rittenhouse, Union League, Philadelphia. *Died 25 Feb. 1923.*

TOWER, Christopher John Hume, JP, DL; *b* 20 Jan. 1841; *e s* of Christopher Tower Huntsmoor, and Lady Sophia Frances Cust, *d* of 1st Earl Brownlow; *m* 1st, 1865, Mary (*d* 1865), 2nd *d* of Rev. Delves Broughton, Broughton Hall; 2nd 1883, Cecilia, *o d* of Rev. R. B. Tower and *widow* of Osgood Hanbury. *Educ:* Harrow; Christ Church, Oxford. High Sheriff of Essex, 1876. *Address:* Wealdside, Brentwood. *TA:* South Weald.

Died 11 July 1924.

TOWERS-CLARK, James; *b* 1852; *e s* of late William Towers-Clark of Wester Moffat and 2nd wife, Isabella, 3rd *d* of James Curle of Evelaw, Berwick; *m* 1880, Annie, 4th *d* of late Thomas Lever Rushton. Major North Somerset Imperial Yeomanry; late Captain 1st Royal Dragoons. *Address:* The Hooke, Chailey, Sussex. *Clubs:* Army and Navy; New, Edinburgh; Western, Glasgow; Royal Yacht Squadron, Cowes. *Died 19 Nov. 1926.*

TOWNSEND, Surg.-Gen. Sir Edmond, KCB 1904 (CB 1898); CMG 1900; RAMC; MA, MD, MCh; retired; *b* 1845; *s* of late W. C. Townsend, MD of Cork; *m* 1884, Frances Josephine, *d* of late J. W. MacMullen, JP Clontymon, Cork; one *s* two *d*. Entered army, 1867; Surg.-Gen. 1901; served Abyssinian Campaign, 1867–68 (medal); Malay Peninsula, 1875–76 (severely wounded; medal with clasp); Zulu War, battle of Ulundi, 1879 (despatches); operations against Sekukuni (medal with clasp); Egyptian War, 1882, including Kassassin, Tel-el-Kebir (medal with clasp, Khedive's star); Burmese Expedition, 1885–86 (medal with clasp); Ashanti Expedition, 1885–86 (despatches, star); North-West Frontier of India, 1897–98; PMO Mohmund Field Force (despatches); PMO 1st Div. Tirah Expeditionary Force (despatches, CB, medal with two clasps); South Africa, 1899–1902; PMO 1st Div., and afterwards PMO Western District, Belmont, Enslin, Modder River, Magersfontein, Paardeberg (despatches, dangerously wounded, CMG, Queen's medal four clasps, King's medal two clasps). *Address:* Clontymon, Cork, Ireland.

Died 3 Jan. 1917.

TOWNSEND, Frederick Henry, ARE; artist; Art Editor, Punch, since 1905; *b* 25 Feb. 1868; *m*; one *s.* Studied at Lambeth School of Art. *Publications:* Illustrated Kipling's They and Brushwood Boy; contributed drawings to Lady's Pictorial; Illustrated London News, Graphic, Sphere, Tatler, Queen, etc. *Recreations:* cricket, golf, fencing. *Address:* 89 Hampstead Way, NW4. *T:* 994 Finchley. *Clubs:* Arts, Chelsea Arts; Hampstead Golf.

Died 11 Dec. 1920.

TOWNSEND, Thomas Sutton, JP and CC for Warwickshire; Lord of the Manor, and Lay Rector of Clifton-upon-Dunsmore, near Rugby; *b* 1847; *e s* of late William Townsend of Clifton Manor, Warwickshire; *m* 1st, 1877, Mary Alice (*d* 1896), *d* of late Thomas Ainsworth, DL, The Flosh, Cumberland; 2nd, 1904, Ursula Verelst, 3rd *d* of Lord Justice Farwell; one *s* one *d. Educ:* Rugby. Medical practitioner in London; landowner in Warwickshire; a member of many public bodies in the county, Chairman of Income Tax Commissioners for the Rugby and Monk's Kirby Divisions, and has been Chairman of Parish Council since its commencement; restored the chancel of the Parish Church of Clifton-upon-Dunsmore, and built a Working Men's Club and Village Hall. *Address:* Clifton Manor, near Rugby; 68 Queen's Gate, SW. *T:* 276 Kensington, 85 Rugby. *Clubs:* Athenæum, Reform. *Died 4 Dec. 1918.*

TOWNSHEND, 6th Marquess, *cr* 1786; **John James Dudley Stuart Townshend,** DL; Bt 1617; Baron Townshend, 1661; Viscount Townshend, 1682; High Steward of Tamworth; *b* 17 Oct. 1866; *s* of 5th Marquess and Lady Anne Elizabeth Clementina Duff, *d* of 5th Earl of Fife, KT; *S* father, 1899; *m* 1905, Gladys Ethel Gwendolen Eugenie (author of In the King's Garden (verse), Maxims and Musings, and several other literary works), *e d* of late Thomas Sutherst, Barrister; one *s* one *d.* Owned about 20,000 acres. Heir: *s* Viscount Raynham, *b* 13 May 1916. *Address:* 78 Avenue Road, Regent's Park, NW8. *T:* Hampstead 4535. *Died 17 Nov. 1921.*

TOWNSHEND, Hon. Sir Charles James, Kt 1911; DCL King's College University, Windsor, Nova Scotia, 1908; *b* 22 March 1844; *s* of Rev. Canon Townshend, Rector of Christ Church, Amherst, Nova Scotia; *m* 1st, 1867, Laura, *d* of J. D. Kinnear; 2nd, 1887, Margaret, *d* of John M'Farlane; three *s* two *d. Educ:* Collegiate School and King's College, Windsor, Nova Scotia (BA 1862, BCL 1872). Barrister, Canada, 1866; QC 1881; MLA Cumberland, 1878 and 1882; to House of Commons of Canada, 1884; MEC 1878–82; Judge of Supreme Court of Nova Scotia, 1887–1907; Chief Justice of the Supreme Court of Nova Scotia, 1907–15; Chancellor of King's College, Windsor, Nova Scotia, 1912. *Address:* Halifax, Nova Scotia. *Club:* Halifax, Halifax. *Died June 1924.*

TOWNSHEND, Maj.-Gen. Sir Charles (Vere Ferrers), KCB 1916 (CB 1895); DSO 1898; MP (Ind.) Wrekin Division of Salop, 1920–22; *b* 21 Feb. 1861; *g s* of late Lord George Townshend; *cousin* and *heir-pres.* of 7th Marquess Townshend; *m* 1898, Alice, *d* of Comte Cahen d'Anvers; one *d.* Entered Royal Marines, 1881; ISC 1886; Capt. 1892; Major, 1895; Lt-Col, 1896; Col 1904; Brig.-Gen. 1909; Maj.-Gen. 1911; Royal Fusiliers, 1900; Shropshire Light Infantry, 1908; served Soudan Expedition, at Suakim with Mounted Infantry, and in Nile Expedition with the Guards' Camel Regiment in Desert Column actions of Abu Klea and Cubat, 1884–85 (despatches, medal with two clasps, bronze star); Hunza Naga Expedition, 1891–92 (despatches, medal with clasp); commanded garrison of Chitral Fort during siege (thanked by Government of India, despatches, medal with clasp, Brevet Major, CB); Dongola Expedition, 1898 (despatches, medal with two clasps, Brevet Lt-Col); Atbara, 1898 (despatches, clasp); Nile Expedition, 1898 (despatches, DSO); South Africa, 1899–1900; European War (Mesopotamia), 1914–16 (despatches, KCB); commanded 6th Division and Force in Mesopotamia battles of Kurna, Kut-el Amara, Ctesiphon, and Defence of Kut; commanding a Division Territorial Force, 1912–13; resigned, 1920. *Publications:* Life

of Field-Marshal 1st Marquis Townshend; My Mesopotamia Campaign, 1920. *Address:* Vere Lodge, Raynham, Norfolk. *Clubs:* Bachelors', Brooks's, White's, Naval and Military; Union, Paris.

Died 18 May 1924.

TOWNSHEND, Colonel Frederick Trench; *b* 1838; *y s* of late Richard Townshend of Myross Wood, Co. Cork, and Helen, *d* of Very Rev. T. Trench, Dean of Kildare, *brother* of Lord Ashtown. *Educ:* Harrow; Oxford. BA 1860; FRGS. Entered 2nd Life Guards, 1861; Capt. 1865; Major, 1877; Lieut-Col, 1882; Colonel, 1886; commanded 2nd Life Guards, 1888; retired from army, 1895; served Egyptian Campaign, 1882 (wounded, medal, Khedive's star, Brevet Lieut-Col, Order of Osmanieh); with United States troops on staff of General Augur in Sioux Indian War, 1868. *Publications:* three books of travel. *Address:* 6 William Street, Lowndes Square, SW. *Clubs:* Arthur's, Bachelors', Carlton.

Died 3 June 1924.

TOWNSHEND, Captain Harry Leigh, JP Warwickshire; *b* 27 June 1842; *s* of Henry Townshend; *m* 1880, Hon. Annie Ellen, *d* of 1st Lord Crawshaw; one *s. Educ:* Westminster. Served in Royal Dragoons and in the 12th Suffolk Regiment; Sheriff for Warwickshire, 1901. *Address:* Caldecote Hall, Nuneaton. *Club:* Arthur's.

Died 30 April 1924.

TOY, Crawford Howell, AM (University of Virginia); Professor of Hebrew in Harvard University since 1880; Professor Emeritus since 1909; *b* Norfolk, Virginia, 23 March 1836; *e s* of late Thomas Dallam Toy and Amelia, *d* of James Rogers; *m* 1888, Nancy, *d* of Rev. R. M. Saunders. *Educ:* University of Virginia. Instructor in Albemarle Institute, 1856–59; attached to the Confederate Army, 1861–64; Professor in University of Alabama, 1864–65; studied at University of Berlin, 1866–68; Professor of Hebrew in Southern Baptist Theological Seminary, 1869–79. *Publications:* Religion of Israel, 1882; Quotations in the New Testament, 1884; Judaism and Christianity, 1890; Ezekiel (revised Hebrew text and translation), 1899; Proverbs (revised translation and commentary), 1899; Introduction to the History of Religions, 1913. *Recreations:* walking, rowing. *Address:* 7 Lowell Street, Cambridge, Massachusetts, USA. *TA:* Cambridge, Mass. *Died 12 May 1919.*

TOYNE, Rev. Frederick Elijah; Hon. Canon of Winchester, 1905. Ordained, 1877; Curate of Mudeford, Hants, 1877–81; Vicar of St Michael's, Bournemouth, 1881–1915. *Address:* 4 Drury Road, Bournemouth. *Died 9 Sept. 1927.*

TOZER, Rev. Henry Fanshawe, MA; FRGS; Hon. Fellow of Exeter College, Oxford since 1893; *b* 18 May 1829; *o s* of Aaron Tozer, Captain Royal Navy, of Plymouth, and Mary Hutton of Lincoln; *m* 1868, Augusta Henrietta, *d* of H. D. C. Satow of Upper Clapton. *Educ:* Winchester; Exeter Coll., Univ. of Oxford (2nd cl. Lit. Hum. 1850). Fellow Exeter Coll., 1850; Tutor, 1855–93; Classical Moderator in Honours, 1866–68, 1873, 1878–79, 1882–84; Curator of the Taylor Institute, 1869–93; Fellow of the British Academy; Corresponding Member of Historical Society of Greece, and of the United Armenian Educational Societies; Hon. Member of the Parnassus Philological Society of Athens. Travelled extensively in Greece, and in European and Asiatic Turkey. *Publications:* The Highlands of Turkey, 2 vols, 1869; Lectures on the Geography of Greece, 1873; Primer of Classical Geography, 1877; Turkish Armenia and Eastern Asia Minor, 1881; The Church and the Eastern Empire, 1888; The Islands of the Aegean, 1890; History of Ancient Geography, 1897; An English Commentary on Dante's Divina Commedia, 1901; English Prose Translation of Dante's Divina Commedia, 1904. *Edited:* Finlay's History of Greece, 1877; Wordsworth's Greece, 1882; Byron's Childe Harold, with introduction and notes, 1885; Selections from Strabo, with introduction and notes, 1893; various contributions to Ency. Brit., Journal of Hellenic Studies, Classical Review, the Academy, and other literary periodicals. *Address:* 18 Norham Gardens, Oxford. *Died 2 June 1916.*

TOZER, Hon. Sir Horace, KCMG 1897; Solicitor in Brisbane; *b* NSW, April 1844; *m* 1st, 1868, Mary Hoyles Wilson; 2nd, 1880, Louisa Lord (*d* 1908). *Educ:* Collegiate School, Newcastle, and Sydney, NSW. Member of Gympie Social Mining Court, 1868; elected Alderman 1st Municipal Council, Gympie, 1880; Secretary for Public Works, 1890–93; Colonial and afterwards Home Secretary, 1890–98; Acting Prime Minister, Queensland, Mar. to Nov. 1897; Official Representative Queensland Government in London, 1898–1909; under his direction Free Public Library and National Art Gallery were started in 1896. *Address:* Brisbane, Queensland.

Died 21 Aug. 1916.

TRACY, Louis, CBE 1920; author; *b* Liverpool, 18 March 1863; *m*; one *s. Educ:* privately in Yorkshire, and in France. Began journalism on the Northern Echo, Darlington, 1884; thence went to Cardiff, 1886; and to Allahabad, India, 1889; returned to England, 1893, and acquired an interest with others in The Evening News, 1894; went to United States, 1895; revisited States and Delhi, Punjab, 1896–1900; Sub-commandant, Whitby District North Riding Regt of Volunteers, Oct. 1915; went to United States, Mar. 1916, and lectured and wrote extensively on the war; joined the Headquarters Staff of the British War Mission in the USA, 13 Sept. 1917; liquidator of British Bureau of Information; temporarily attached to Foreign Office, July 1919; later, while on Editorial Staff of The Times and Daily Mail, became Member of Westminster Abbey Restoration Fund, and collected many thousands of pounds for the Fund in USA during 1921. *Publications:* The Final War, 1896; The Pillar of Light, 1905; Waifs of Circumstance, 1906; The Wheel o' Fortune, 1907; The Red Year, 1908; The Message, 1909; The Stowaway, A Son of the Immortals, 1910; The Silent Barrier, The Silent House, Sylvia's Chauffeur, 1911; Mirabel's Island, 1912; The Only Way, One Wonderful Night, The Terms of Surrender, 1913; Diana of the Moors, 1914; His Unknown Wife and Number 17, 1915; Flower of the Gorse, The Day of Wrath, 1916; The Postmaster's Daughter, The Revellers, 1917; The Second Baronet, The Park Lane Mystery, 1923; The Turning Point, The Token, 1924; The Passing of Charles Lanson, The Black Cat, The Gleave Mystery, 1925; The Law of the Talon, 1926; The Third Miracle, The Woman in the Case, 1927. *Address:* c/o Barclays Bank, Ltd, Whitby, Yorkshire. *Clubs:* Authors', Savage; Lotos, New York.
Died 13 Aug. 1928.

TRAIL, James William Helenus, MA, MD; FLS, FRS; Regius Professor of Botany, University of Aberdeen, since 1877; *b* Birsay, Orkney, 4 March 1851; *y s* of late Very Rev. Samuel Trail, DD, LLD, Professor of Systematic Theology in the University of Aberdeen, 1867–87; Moderator of the Church of Scotland, 1874; *m* Katherine, *e d* of late Very Rev. Wm Milligan, Professor of Biblical Criticism in the University of Aberdeen, 1860–93; Moderator of the Church of Scotland, 1882. *Educ:* home; Grammar School, Old Aberdeen; University of Aberdeen. MA with Highest Honours in the Natural Sciences; MB and CM with Highest Honours. Travelled in North Brazil as Naturalist of an Exploring Expedition, 1873–75. *Publications:* numerous papers on botanical and zoological subjects in scientific journals. *Recreations:* field botany, zoology, and the mutual relations of plants and animals. *Address:* University, Aberdeen.
Died 18 Sept. 1919.

TRAILL, Major Thomas Balfour, DSO 1914; 1st Battalion Royal Scots Fusiliers; *b* 21 Nov. 1881; *o s* of late Major-General George Traill, CB; *m* 1918, Winifred Jean Bertha, *d* of Major W. A. Warren. Entered army, 1900; Indian army, 1902; Captain, 1909; served European War, 1914–17 (wounded, despatches, DSO, Bt Major). *Club:* Cavalry.
Died 7 July 1920.

TRAIN, Rev. John Gilkison; Moderator of the Synod of the Presbyterian Church of England, 1907–8; *b* 1847. *Educ:* Collegiate School and University of Glasgow; Theological Hall, Edinburgh; Universities of Leipsic and Tübingen. Ordained, St David's Church, Buckhaven, 1874; Inducted, Prospect Street Church, Hull, 1886; Inducted, St Andrew's Church, Norwood, 1892, Re-inducted, Prospect Street Church, Hull, 1905; Inducted, United Free Church of Scotland, Southend, Presbytery of Kintyre, 1914. *Address:* UFC Manse, Southend, Argyll.
Died 17 Nov. 1920.

TRAPANI, Lt-Col Alfred, MVO 1912; late Royal Malta Artillery; *b* Malta, Jan. 1859; *s* of G. B. Trapani, LLD, CMG; *m* Mary, *e d* of Professor A. Mifsud, MD; three *d. Educ:* private school. Commissioned as 2nd Lieutenant, 1877; Lieutenant, 1880; Captain, 1885; Major, 1896; Lt-Col 1909; served Egyptian Campaign, 1882 (Queen's Medal, Khedive's bronze star); retired, 1915. *Address:* 314 SS Paolo, Valletta, Malta.
Died 9 Dec. 1928.

TRASK, Katrina; living in retirement on her estate since the death of her husband; *d* of George L. Nichols, English descent, and Christina Cole, Dutch descent; *m* 1874, Spencer Trask, banker; no *c. Educ:* private schools and tutors. The life of the home and of society, and the education of her children; later, after her children were taken, devoted herself to literary work; owns the estate of Yaddo, to be left to literary and other artists. *Publications:* Sonnets and Lyrics; Night and Morning; The Mighty and the Lowly, 1915, and various stories, etc, under her own name; Mors et Victoria and King Alfred's Jewel, published anonymously in England; the third edition of King Alfred's

Jewel published in her own name; and In the Vanguard, etc. *Recreations:* walking, improvising on the piano. *Address:* Yaddo, Saratoga Springs, NY, USA.
Died 7 Jan. 1922.

TRAVANCORE, HH Sir Bala Rama Varma, Maharajah of; GCSI 1888; GCIE 1903; MRAS; Officier de l'Instruction Publique; Hon. Colonel of 10th Battalion 3rd Madras Regiment, 1923; *b* 25 Sept. 1857; *S* 1885. The State has an area of 6,730 square miles and a population of 3,000,000. *Address:* The Palace, Trivendrum, Travancore, South India.
Died 7 Aug. 1924.

TRAVERS, Graham, (*nom de guerre* of Dr Margaret Todd); novelist, and late assistant physician to Edinburgh Hospital for Women and Children; *b* 1859; *d* of James Cameron Todd of Glasgow and Rangoon. *Educ:* Edinburgh and Glasgow University Classes for Women, and in Berlin. Engaged in teaching; studied at Edinburgh School of Medicine for Women; LRCP&SE; MD Brux. 1894. *Publications:* Mona Maclean, 1892; Fellow Travellers, 1896; Windyhaugh, 1898; The Way of Escape, 1902; Growth, 1906. *Address:* 18 Challoner Mansions, W. *Club:* Lyceum.
Died 3 Sept. 1918.

TRAVIS, Harry, CBE 1920; ISO 1911; MIME, MINA; Advising Officer on Boats and Vessels to HM Customs; late Superintending Engineer and Constructor of Shipping, Royal Arsenal; *b* 18 July 1858; *s* of John Travis, of Devonport; *m* 1881, Emmeline, *d* of G. Hamlyn, late of Roborough, South Devon; one *s* one *d. Educ:* Devonport. Was a pupil for five years with the firm of Robert Napier and Sons, engineers, etc, Glasgow, and student at Glasgow Univ.; joined the War Dept, 1881; Asst Superintending Engineer and Constructor of Shipping, 1891; invented the means for improving the speed of targets used in Royal Artillery practice from fortresses. *Address:* Custom House, EC.
Died 5 Nov. 1927.

TRAVIS, Rev. James; *b* Summit, Littleborough, 6 March 1840; *m* Jane Killip, Lonan, Isle of Man; one *d. Educ:* privately. Entered ministry, 1858; President of National Council of Evangelical Free Churches, 1903–04; President of Primitive Methodist Conference, Norwich, 1892; formerly General Missionary Secretary and Superintendent Home Missions; an Examiner of Candidates for the Ministry for 13 years; superannuated, 1906. *Publication:* 75 Years. *Address:* 3 Waterloo Road, Chester.
Died 5 Dec. 1919.

TRAVIS, Rev. William Travis; Hon. Canon of Ripon. *Address:* The Rectory, Ripley, Yorks.
Died 2 May 1924.

TREACHER, Sir William Hood, KCMG 1904 (CMG 1890); MA Oxford; *b* Wellington, Somerset, 1 Dec. 1849; *y s* of late Rev. J. S. Treacher; *m* 1881, Cornelia, *d* of Rev. J. Rumsey; two *d.* Colonial Secretary, Labuan; Acting Consul-General, Brunei; employed on a mission to the Sulu Islands and North Borneo, in connection with Spanish claims; first Governor of British North Borneo, 1881–87; Secretary to Government, Perak, 1888; British Resident, Selangor, 1892; British Resident, Perak, 1896; acted as Resident-General, Federated Malay States, 1897–98, 1900–01; Resident-General, Federated Malay States, 1902–1904 (retired). *Publication:* British Borneo. *Address:* 97 Cadogan Gardens, SW. *T:* Kensington 4959; St Stephen's Cottage, St Albans. *T:* St Albans 418. *M:* LO 6494. *Clubs:* Oriental, Sports, City Carlton.
Died 3 May 1919.

TREANOR, Ven. James; Archdeacon of Tuam since 1898; Rector of Ballinrobe since 1882. *Educ:* Trinity College, Dublin (MA). Ordained, 1870; Curate of Tuam, 1870–74; Rector of Athenry, 1874–77; Kiltullagh, 1877–82; Canon of Tuam, 1887–90; Provost, 1890–98. *Address:* Ballinrobe, Co. Mayo.
Died 15 May 1926.

TREASURE, William Houston, ISO 1914; Clerk to Legal Adviser to Secretary of State for India, 1887; to Solicitor of the Supreme Court, 1887; Asst to the Legal Adviser, 1892; Asst Solicitor, 1900; Commissioner for Oaths, 1908; retired, 1913. *Address:* India Office, SW.
Died 3 March 1916.

TREBLE, Rev. Edmund John; Rector of Morningthorpe, Norfolk, since 1908. *Educ:* King's Coll., London (Theological Associate, 1st in first class, 1885; Hebrew Prizeman, 1884; Prayer-Book Prize, 1885; Universities' Preliminary Theological Examination, 1st in first class, 1885; Gospeller at Ordination); and Freiburg University (Canon Law and History of Art). Appointed to Board of Trade, Whitehall Gardens,

1873; retired 1884; deacon, 1885; priest, 1886; served curacies in Marylebone and Hackney; chaplain at Freiburg in Black Forest, 1891–1900; travelled in Greece and Egypt, 1899; acted as chaplain at Assouan, winter 1899–1900; English Chaplain, Wiesbaden, 1900–6; Curate, Hunstanton, 1906–8. *Publications:* Plain Teaching about the Church of England, 1893; Sermons on Sunday Observance, 1893; Anglican Jurisdiction on the Continent, 1898; Notes on Morning and Evening Prayer, 1912; articles in journals and magazines; contributor to the Encyclopædia Britannic (10th edn), 1902; editor of The Chaplaincy Quarterly Magazine, 1900–6. *Recreations:* older novels, walking. *Address:* The Rectory, Morningthorpe, Norfolk.

Died 19 June 1924.

TREDCROFT, Lieut-Col Charles Lennox, JP, Surrey; Hon. Lieutenant-Colonel Royal West Surrey Regiment (2nd Volunteer Battalion); *b* 24 Oct. 1832; *o s* of Rev. R. Tredcroft of Tangmere, Sussex, and *d* of Sir T. Brooke Pechell, 2nd Bt; *m* 1st, 1863, Harriette Sophia Louisa (*d* 1869), *e d* of J. H. Woodward; 2nd, 1871, Elizabeth (*d* 1886), *e d* of Sir William Scott, 6th Bt of Ancrum; 3rd, 1889, Hon. Constance Mary Fitz-Alan Howard, *d* of 1st Lord Howard of Glossop; two *s* four *d*. *Educ:* Woolwich. Late Capt. RHA; served Crimea, 1855–56 (medal and clasp, and Turkish medal and order of Medjidie); County Alderman, 1889–1904. *Address:* Glen Ancrum, Guildford. *TA:* Guildford. *Club:* Army and Navy.

Died 20 Dec. 1917.

TREE, Sir Herbert Beerbohm, Kt 1909; actor; *b* London, 17 Dec. 1853; 2nd *s* of Julius Beerbohm and Constantia Draper; *m* 1882, Maud Holt; three *d*. *Educ:* Schnepfeuthal College, Germany. Made his first appearance on the stage in 1877; became manager of the Haymarket Theatre in 1887; relinquished its management in 1896; subseq. proprietor and manager of His Majesty's Theatre. Order of St John of Jerusalem; Crown of Italy. *Publications:* lectures on The Imaginative Faculty, and on Hamlet from an Actor's Prompt Book, Henry VIII and His Court; Thoughts and Afterthoughts, 1913, etc. *Address:* 1 All Souls' Place, Portland Place, W. *T:* Gerrard 2135. *Clubs:* Garrick, Beefsteak, Green Room, Royal Automobile.

Died 2 July 1917.

TREFFRY, Charles Ebenezer, JP; *b* 1 May 1842; *m* 1st, 1866, Udney Maria Blakeley, *d* of Baron von Bretton; one *s* two *d*; 2nd, 1905, Henrietta, 2nd *d* of late John Kingsley, Manchester. High Sheriff of Cornwall, 1886; late Captain 2nd Brigade Western Division RA, first Mayor of Fowey under new Charter. *Address:* Place, Fowey, Cornwall.

Died 27 Feb. 1924.

TREFUSIS, Lady Mary; Woman of the Bedchamber to HM the Queen since 1895; *b* 26 Feb. 1869; *d* of 6th Earl Beauchamp and Lady Mary Catherine, *d* of 5th Earl Stanhope; *m* 1905, Lieut-Col Hon. Henry Walter Hepburn-Stuart-Forbes-Trefusis, *yr s* of 20th Baron Clinton; one *s*. Hon. Secretary Church Music Society since 1906; President English Folk Dance Society since 1912; Member Church Assembly and Missionary Council. *Recreation:* music. *Address:* Trefusis, Falmouth.

Died 12 Sept. 1927.

TREGEAR, Maj.-Gen. Sir Vincent William, KCB 1909 (CB 1890); US list, Indian Army; *b* 25 June 1842; *e s* of Vincent Tregear, Educational Department, Government of India; *m* 1867, Jane Charlotte (*d* 1899), *e d* of William Oswald Bell; *three s* one *d*. *Educ:* private school. Entered Bengal Army, 1859; served in the 19th PI, 41st BI, 29th PI, and commanded the 9th BI Regiment; Colonel on the Staff at Mooltan, Punjab, 1895–97, when vacated on promotion to Maj.-Gen.; served Afghanistan, 1879–80, with Khyber Field Force (medal); NE Frontier of India, Lushai, 1889, commanded the Force (thanks of Government, despatches); Chin-Lushai, 1889–90, commanded the Chittagong Column (mentioned by Government of India, medal with 2 clasps, CB). *Address:* c/o Henry S. King and Co., 9 Pall Mall, SW1. *Club:* Royal Albert Yacht, Southsea.

Died 17 July 1925.

TREHERNE, Rev. Charles Albert, MA; Vicar of Tintagel, N Cornwall, since 1919; *b* 25 July 1856; *m* 1886, Mabel, *d* of late Richard Dodd, Calcutta; one *s*. *Educ:* Godolphin School; Sheffield Collegiate; Gonville and Caius College, Cambridge (scholar). Curate of St John the Evangelist, Newbury, 1880; Dilbury Vicar in Hereford Cathedral, 1882; Curate of Tupsley, 1883; Minor Canon, St George's Chapel, Windsor, 1884; Curate, Eton, 1885; Curate, Clewer, 1892; Divinity Lecturer at St George's Chapel, 1884; Vicar of All Saints, Hereford, 1895; Chaplain, HM Prison, Hereford, 1902; Prebendary of Moreton and Whaddon in Hereford Cathedral, 1918. *Recreations:* music, painting. *Address:* The Vicarage, Tintagel.

Died 16 Nov. 1919.

TRELAWNY, Sir William Lewis Salusbury-, 10th Bt, *cr* 1628; DL, JP; *b* 26 Aug. 1844; *s* of Sir John Salusbury-Trelawny, 9th Bt and Harriet, *e d* of J. H. Tremayne, Heligan, Cornwall; *S* father, 1885; *m* 1st, 1868, Jessy (*d* 1871), *o d* of Sir John Murray, 6th Bt; one *s* one *d*; 2nd, 1872, Harriet, *d* of Rev. James Buller Kitson, Vicar of Morval, Cornwall; two *s* two *d*. *Educ:* Eton; Trinity Coll., Camb. Late Capt. 3rd Batt. Duke of Cornwall's Light Infantry. Owned about 8,000 acres. *Heir: s* John William Salusbury-Trelawny [*b* 6 May 1869; *m* 1st, 1891, Agnes Hedewig Helga (who divorced him), *e d* of W. B. Braddick; one *d*; 2nd, 1905, Catherine Penelope (Mrs W. C. Howard), *d* of late A. S. Cave-Browne-Cave; one *s*]. *Address:* Trelawne, Duloe, Cornwall. *Club:* Brooks's.

Died 30 Nov. 1917.

TRELOAR, Sir William Purdie, 1st Bt, *cr* 1907; Kt 1900; Alderman (Ward of Farringdon Without) since 1892; Principal of firm of Treloar and Sons, Ludgate Hill; Director and Trustee of T. Cook and Son, Egypt, Ltd; one of Sheriffs of London, 1899–1900; Lord Mayor, 1906–7; Founder of the Lord Mayor Treloar Cripples Hospital and College, Alton and Hayling Island, Hants; Hon. Fellow of the British Orthopædic Assoc.; JP Kent, Surrey, and London; *b* London, 13 Jan. 1843; 2nd *s* of late Thomas Treloar, of Helston, Cornwall; *m* 1865, Annie (*d* 1909), *d* of G. Blake. *Educ:* King's College School. Member of the Corporation of the City of London since 1880; Chairman of the Commissioners of Sewers, 1891; Deputy Chairman Commissioners of Income Tax for City of London; Presented with the honorary freedom of the City of Truro, the Boroughs of Bury St Edmunds, Croydon, Helston, and Okehampton; Knight of several foreign Orders. *Publications:* Ludgate Hill, Past and Present; Prince of Palms; Wilkes and the City, 1917; A Lord Mayor's Diary, 1920. *Recreation:* reading. *Heir:* none. *Address:* Grange Mount, Upper Norwood, SE19. *TA:* Treloar, London. *T:* Sydenham 238. *Clubs:* Carlton, Savage, Press, Whitefriars, Authors'.

Died 6 Sept. 1923 (ext).

TREMATON, Viscount; Rupert Alexander George Augustus Cambridge; *b* 24 Aug. 1907; *er s* of 1st Earl of Athlone, KG, GCB, GCMG, GCVO, DSO, FRS and Princess Alice of Albany. *Educ:* Eton.

Died 15 April 1928.

TRENCH, Hon. Cosby Godolphin, JP, DL; *b* 6 Jan. 1844; *y s* of 2nd Lord Ashtown and Henrietta, *d* of Thomas Phillips Cosby; *m* 1873, Maria, *e d* of Sir Richard Musgrave, 4th Bt; three *s* (and one *s* decd). *Educ:* Eton; Sandhurst; Corpus Christi College, Oxford. High Sheriff, Tipperary, 1886; formerly Capt. 1st Royal Dragoons; contested North Tipperary (LU), 1892. *Recreations:* shooting, riding, motoring. *Address:* Sopwell Hall, Cloughjordan, Co. Tipperary. *TA:* Ballingary Roscrea. *Clubs:* Naval and Military; Kildare Street, Dublin.

Died 9 Dec. 1925.

TRENCH, Hon. Frederic Sydney; 2nd Lieutenant 3rd Battalion KRRC; *b* 9 Dec. 1894; *e s* of 3rd Baron Ashtown. *Educ:* Eton; Sandhurst; Magdalen Coll. Oxford. Entered army, 1914. Served European War, 1914–16 (wounded).

Died 24 Nov. 1916.

TRENCH, Herbert; writer of poems and plays; late Senior Examiner and Assistant Director of Special Enquiries at Board of Education; *b* Avoncore, Co. Cork, Nov. 1865; *m* 1891, Lilian Isabel, *d* of Robert Fox, of Grove Hill, Falmouth, and Penjerrick, Cornwall; two *s* three *d*. *Educ:* Haileybury; Oxford. Fellow of All Souls College; Examiner at the Board of Education, 1891; went up the Nile, 1888, and has travelled in Syria, Russia, Austria, Spain, Morocco, Algeria, and rural Italy; retired 1908. While Director of the Haymarket Theatre staged Shakespeare's King Lear, Maeterlinck's The Blue Bird, Bunty Pulls the Strings, etc; Hon. Vice-Chairman of the Istituto Britannico, Florence, for which he drew up the scheme that obtained the first grant from the British Government for the promotion, by means of a public library and lectures, of better mutual understanding between Great Britain and Italy, 1918. *Publications:* Deidre Wedded and nineteen other poems, 1901: also New Poems; Apollo and the Seaman, Stanzas to Tolstoy, the Questioners, 1907; Lyrics and Narrative Poems, 1911; Ode from Italy in time of War, 1915; Poems with Fables in Prose (including Bitter Serenade, Battle of the Marne, etc), 1917; Napoleon (a play), 1918. *Address:* Villa Viviani, Settignano, Florence. *Clubs:* Athenæum, United University.

Died 11 June 1923.

TRENHOLME, Hon. Norman William; Judge, Court of King's Bench, Quebec, since 1904; *b* 18 Aug. 1837; *m* 1st, 1868, Lucy Wilkes (*d* 1885), *d* of late Samuel Hedge, Montreal; 2nd, 1886, Grace Low, *d* of late Robert Shaw, Quebec. *Educ:* McGill University. Advocate,

1865; KC 1889; Professor of Roman and Public Law, McGill University, 1868–88; Puisne Judge, Superior Court, 1901. *Address:* 65 Rosemount Avenue, Montreal. *Club:* University, Montreal.

Died 25 June 1919.

TREVELYAN, Sir Ernest John, Kt 1909; DCL; Assessor, Chancellor's Court, Oxford, since 1910; Fellow and Subwarden, All Souls College, Oxford; Member Oxford University Hebdomadal Council, 1914–20; Chairman Court of Referees under National Insurance Act (Unemployment Insurance), Oxford; Chairman Local Munitions Tribunal, Oxford and Reading, 1914–19; *b* 7 Dec. 1850; 2nd *s* of late Maj.-Gen. H. W. Trevelyan, CB, RA; *m* 1st, 1880, Mary Katherine (*d* 1885), *d* of late Patrick Black, MD; one *s*; 2nd, 1890, Julia Isabel (*d* 1903), *d* of E. W. Mark; four *d*; 3rd, 1909, Winifred Helen, *d* of late Sir C. U. Aitchison, KCSI. Barrister, Middle Temple, 1873; Judge, High Court, Calcutta, 1885–98; Vice-Chancellor, Calcutta University, 1897–98; Reader in Indian Law, Oxford Univ., 1900–23; Lecturer in Hindu and Mahomedan Law to the Council of Legal Education, 1910–14; Councillor Oxford Town Council, 1905–15. *Publications:* Works on Indian Law. *Address:* 1 Marston Ferry Road, Oxford. *T:* Oxford 399. *Club:* Oriental.

Died 29 July 1924.

TREVELYAN, Rt. Hon. Sir George Otto, 2nd Bt, *cr* 1874; OM 1911; PC; LLD, DCL; DL; resigned as MP, 30 Jan. 1897; *b* Rothley Temple, Leicestershire, 20 July 1838; *o s* of Sir Charles Edward Trevelyan, 1st Bt, KCB and Hannah More, *d* of Zachary Macaulay, Secretary of the Anti-Slavery Society, and *sister* of the historian Lord Macaulay; *S* father, 1886; *m* 1869, Caroline, *d* of R. N. Philips, formerly MP for Bury, Lancashire, of The Park, Manchester, and Welcombe, Stratford-on-Avon; three *s*. *Educ:* Harrow; Trinity Coll. Camb. 2nd in 1st class of the Classical Tripos, Camb., 1861; Scholar and Honorary Fellow of Trinity Coll. Camb.; Honorary Fellow of Oriel College, Oxford; MP (L) Tynemouth, 1865; Hawick Burghs, 1868; Bridgeton Division of Glasgow, 1887–97; Civil Lord of the Admiralty, 1868; Secretary of the Admiralty, 1880; Chief Secretary for Ireland, 1882; Chancellor of the Duchy of Lancaster, with a seat in the Cabinet, 1884; Secretary for Scotland, 1886; again Secretary for Scotland, 1892; took an active part in furthering the abolition of purchase in the Army, and the extension of Household Suffrage to the counties. Owned about 14,000 acres. *Publications:* The Competition Wallah, 1864; Cawnpore, 1865; The Ladies in Parliament, Horace at the University of Athens, and other pieces, collected and published in 1868; The Life and Letters of Lord Macaulay, 1876; Selections from the Writings of Lord Macaulay, 1876; The Early History of Charles James Fox, 1880; Interludes in Prose and Verse, 1905; The American Revolution (four vols), 1909; George III and Charles Fox, vol. i 1912, vol. ii 1914. *Recreations:* shooting, country pursuits generally, touring in Italy. *Heir: s* Charles Philips Trevelyan, *b* 28 Oct. 1870. *Address:* Wallington, Cambo, Northumberland; Welcombe, Stratford-on-Avon.

Died 17 Aug. 1928.

TREVES, Sir Frederick, 1st Bt, *cr* 1902; GCVO 1905 (KCVO 1901); CB 1901; LLD, MD, FRCS; Serjeant Surgeon to the King; Surgeon in Ordinary to Queen Alexandra; consulting surgeon to the London Hospital; Lord Rector of Aberdeen University, 1905–8; *b* Dorchester, 15 Feb. 1853; *m* 1877, Annie, *y d* of A. S. Mason of Dorchester; one *d*. *Educ:* Merchant Taylors' School. Hunterian Prof. of Anatomy and Wilson Prof. of Pathology, Royal College of Surgeons, 1881–6; Examiner in Surgery, Univ. of Cambridge, 1891–96; Col AMS; late President of Headquarters Medical Board at War Office; Member of the Army Sanitary Committee, War Office; late Member of the Advisory Board of the Army Medical Service; one of the Founders of the British Red Cross Society, and First Chairman of Executive Committee; Chairman of the Radium Institute; Consulting Surgeon to Forces in South Africa, 1900; was with the Ladysmith relief column (medal and three clasps); performed the operation for appendicitis upon HM King Edward VII on 24 June 1902; Sergeant Surgeon to King Edward VII; Surgeon Extraordinary to Queen Victoria, 1900–1. Knight of Grace of the Order of St John of Jerusalem. *Publications:* Physical Education; System of Surgery; Manual of Operative Surgery: Surgical Applied Anatomy; treatises on Intestinal Obstruction, Peritonitis, and Appendicitis; German-English Dictionary of Medical Terms; Tale of a Field Hospital, 1900; The Other Side of the Lantern, 1905; Highways and Byways in Dorset, 1906; Cradle of the Deep, 1908; Uganda for a Holiday, 1910; The Land that is Desolate, 1912; The Country of the Ring and the Book, 1913; The Riviera of the Corniche Road, 1921; The Lake of Geneva, 1922. *Recreations:* boatsailing, sea-fishing. *Heir:* none. *Club:* Marlborough.

Died 7 Dec. 1923 (ext).

TREVOR, 2nd Baron, *cr* 1830; **Arthur William Hill-Trevor,** JP; Lieutenant-Colonel 1st Life Guards, retired 1895; *b* 19 Nov. 1852; *s* of 1st Baron and 1st wife Mary, *d* of Sir Richard Sutton, 2nd Bt; *S* father, 1894; *m* 1st, 1893, Hon. Anne Mary Eleanor Fraser (*d* 1895), *d* of 17th Baron Saltoun; 2nd, 1897, Rosamond C., MBE, *g d* of 11th Baron Petre and *widow* of 4th and last Earl of Bantry. Owned about 23,700 acres. *Heir: half-b* Hon. Charles Edward Hill-Trevor, *b* 22 Dec. 1863. *Address:* Brynkinalt, Chirk, Denbigh. *Club:* Carlton.

Died 19 May 1923.

TREVOR, Sir Arthur Charles, KCSI 1898 (CSI 1894); ICS (Bombay); *b* Jellalabad, Afghanistan, 6 April 1841; 5th *s* of late Capt. R. S. Trevor (killed at Cabul, Dec. 1841), 3rd Bengal Cavalry; *m* 1867, Florence Mary (*d* 1918), 2nd *d* of Colonel C. J. Prescott, Bombay Staff Corps; two *s* four *d*. *Educ:* St John's Foundation School and Trinity and Lincoln Colls, Oxford; Scholar of Lincoln. Appointed after examination of 1860; arrived, 1861; served in Bombay as Assistant Collector and Magistrate, and Deputy Commissioner of Customs and Opium; Collector of Customs, Bombay, 1879; Senior Collector, 1884; Collector of Salt Revenue, 1885; Commissioner of Customs, Salt, Opium, and Abkari, and Reporter-General of External Commerce, 1888; also British Delegate for the Portuguese Treaty; Commissioner in Sind, 1890; member of Bombay Council, 1892; temporary member of Governor-General's Council in charge Railways and Public Works, April to Oct. 1895; confirmed April 1896–1901. *Address:* 16 Harcourt Terrace, West Brompton, SW.

Died 22 Sept. 1920.

TREVOR, Arthur Hill, BA Oxon; Barrister-at-Law; Commissioner, Board of Control, since 1914; *b* 1858; *o s* of Charles Binny Trevor, late ICS. *Educ:* Winchester, Corpus Christi College, Oxford. Called to Bar, Inner Temple, 1884; South-Eastern Circuit; Sussex Sessions; Secretary to Commissioners in Lunacy, 1904–7; Commissioner in Lunacy, 1907–14. *Recreations:* golf and shooting; Winchester XI, 1877; Oxford XI, 1880, 1881; played for Sussex, 1880–84. *Address:* 4 Albemarle Street, W1. *T:* Regent 443. *Clubs:* Arthur's, Brooks's, Royal Automobile.

Died 27 Sept. 1924.

TREVOR, Sir (Charles) Cecil, Kt 1896; CB 1882; *b* July 1830; *e s* of Charles Trevor, Somerset House; *m* 1863, Mary (*d* 1892), *d* of James Weston. *Educ:* Rugby; St Catharine's College, Cambridge; Hon. Fellow (MA). Barrister Lincoln's Inn, 1855; Assistant Secretary to Board of Trade, 1867–95; a Conservator of the River Thames, 1895–1906; delegate to North Sea Fishery Conference at Hague, 1881–82; to Submarine Cables Conference at Paris, 1882–83 and 1886; to North Sea Liquor Traffic Conference at Hague, 1886; to Channel Fisheries negotiations at Paris, 1886. *Address:* 28 Bramham Gardens, South Kensington, SW. *Clubs:* Athenæum, Oxford and Cambridge.

Died 18 Sept. 1921.

TREVOR, Surg.-Gen. Sir Francis (Woollaston), KCSI 1911; CB 1907; Hon. Surgeon to His Majesty; *b* 11 Dec. 1851; *s* of E. S. R. Trevor, Trowscoed, Welshpool; *m* Mary H. Mytton, *d* of R. H. Mytton, Garth, Welshpool; two *s* one *d*. *Educ:* Guy's Hospital; Aberdeen University. Lieut-Col RAMC, 1894; Col, 1903; PMO Scottish District, 1903–4; Administrative Medical Officer, India, 1904; PMO 6th Div., India; Principal Medical Officer of HM's Forces in India, 1908; served Afghanistan, 1878–80 (medal two clasps, bronze star); Soudan, 1884–85 (medal with clasp, bronze star); South Africa, 1901–2 (despatches, Queen's medal, five clasps); Colonel Commandant, RAMC, 1921–22. *Address:* Oerley Hall, Oswestry, Salop. *Club:* Naval and Military.

Died 16 Nov. 1922.

TREVOR, Frederick George Brunton, CIE 1900; JP Surrey; late Director of Funds, India Office; *b* India, 28 Oct. 1838; 2nd *s* of late Rev. George Trevor, DD, Canon of York, and Elizabeth Louisa Garrick; *m* 1860, Rose (*d* 1902), 3rd *d* of William Hudson, of York; four *s*. *Educ:* Marlborough. Entered India Office, 1858; retired, 1903. *Recreation:* cricket. *Address:* Redholme, Richmond, Surrey.

Died 20 Feb. 1924.

TREVOR, Hon. George Edwyn Hill-; Major, Reserve of Officers; *b* 15 Nov. 1859 at Norwood Park, Notts; 2nd *s* of 1st Baron Trevor, of Brynkinalt, N Wales, and Mary C., *d* of 3rd Baron Scarsdale, of Kedleston Hall, Derby; *heir-pres.* to 2nd Baron Trevor; *m* 1st, 1893, Ethel G. M. (div. 1910), *d* of H. Chapman and Ethel, *d* of Sir Francis Dugdale Astley, 2nd Bt; one *s* decd; 2nd, 1910, Helen (*d* 1919); *d* of Thomas Stuart, Edinburgh. Lieut Shropshire Yeomanry Cavalry, 1882–88; Commanded 4/8th Middlesex Regt (Duke of Cambridge's Own), June–Dec. 1915. *Recreations:* shooting, foreign travel, numismatics, fire brigade work, soldiering. *Address:* 15 Duke Street, St James, SW1.   *Died 19 July 1922.*

TREVOR, Col George Herbert, CSI 1891; Supernumerary List, Indian Army; *b* 29 Jan. 1840; *s* of Rev. George Trevor, DD, Canon of York; *m* 1870, *d* of Col E. K. Elliot, BSC; two *s* one *d. Educ:* Marlborough College. Served in RA, 1858–62, when transferred to Indian Staff Corps consequent on entering civil employ; held various posts in the Political Department, 1867–95, ending with that of Agent to Governor-General for Rajputana, and Chief Commissioner of Ajmere and Merwara. *Club:* Union, Brighton.

Died 10 July 1927.

TREVOR, Rev. Thomas Warren, MA; Rector of Llanfaelog since 1902; Prebendary and Senior Canon of Bangor Cathedral; *b* 1839; *s* of Rev. I. W. Trevor, MA, Chancellor of the Diocese of Bangor, Canon Residentiary, and Rector of Llanfaelog; *m* Caroline Maria, *d* of C. H. Evans of Plas-gwyn and Henblas, Anglesey; two *s* three *d. Educ:* Marlborough College; Jesus College, Oxford. Curate of Beaumaris, 1862–65; Dolgelley, 1867–68; Vicar of Penmon and Llanfaes, 1868–89; Rural Dean of Tyndaethwy, 1874–89; Rector of Machynlleth, 1889–1902; Prebendary of Penmynydd and Canon of Bangor Cathedral, 1891; Proctor in Convocation for the Clergy, 1892–95; Proctor for the Chapter, 1895–1919; Hon. Secretary Diocesan Clergy Charity, 1877; Clergy Life Insurance Society, 1882. *Publication:* Church Finance and Aided Life Insurance, 1882. *Address:* c/o Llanfaelog Rectory, Ty-Croes, Anglesey.

Died 12 April 1924.

TREVOR-BATTYE, Aubyn Bernard Rochfort, MA; FLS, FZS, FRGS; *b* Hever, Kent; 2nd *s* of late Rev. William Wilberforce Battye of Tingrith Manor, Beds, and Little Hampton, Bucks [in right of Ruth, *d* of John Hampden the patriot, who *m* Sir John Trevor], Rector of Hever, and Harriet Dorothea, *o d* of Edmund Wakefield Meade-Waldo, of Stonewall Park and Hever Castle; *m* 1901, Margaret Amy (*d* 1906), *y d* of late C. North Graham; two *d. Educ:* St Edward's School, Oxford; Christ Church, Oxford; studied Natural Science under Professor H. N. Moseley of the 'Challenger'. Has for several years travelled in various countries: N-W America, Africa, Arctic Russia, Spitsbergen, Nepal, etc, for exploration and natural history; was first explorer of Kolguev in Barent's Sea; Zoologist to the Conway Arctic Expedition, 1896; Editor and proprietor of The Artist, 1897; Editor-in-Chief of Natural History in the Victoria History of the Counties of England, and Hon. Sec. to Advisory Council, 1899. *Publications:* Pictures in Prose, 1893; Icebound on Kolguev, 1895; A Northern Highway of the Tsar, 1897; editor of Lord Lilford on Birds, 1903; Camping in Crete, 1913; and many scattered papers. *Address:* Ashford Chace, Petersfield, Hants. *M:* AA 1639.

Died 20 Dec. 1922.

TRICKETT, William, AM, DCL, LLD; Dean of Dickinson School of Law since 1890; *b* Leicester, 9 June 1840. *Educ:* Dickinson College, Carlisle, Pennsylvania. For five years Professor, Dickinson College; Member of Bar of Pennsylvania, 1875. *Publications:* The Law of Boroughs; Law of Highways; Law of Liens; Law of Limitations; Law of Witnesses; Guardians; Landlord and Tenant; Criminal Law; Partition; also many articles in Law Reviews. *Address:* Carlisle, Pennsylvania.   *Died 1 Aug. 1928.*

TRICKETT, Hon. William Joseph, JP; MLC; Deputy Chairman of Committees of the Legislative Council, New South Wales; *b* 2 Sept. 1844; married; two *s* four *d. Educ:* Sydney Grammar School. Went to Australia, 1854; MLA Paddington, 1880–89; has been Postmaster-General, Minister for Public Instruction, chairman of Committees of the Legislative Assembly, chairman of Committees of Legislative Council, and Acting President, is Vice-President and Parliamentary Founder of the National Art Gallery, member and chairman of the Parliamentary Public Works Committee; Local Alderman for 33 years; Member of State Children's Relief Board. *Publication:* Trip to China and Japan. *Recreations:* yachting, touring. *Address:* Shorwell, 121 Queen Street, Woollahra, Sydney, New South Wales. *Club:* Australian, Sydney.

Died July 1916.

TRIGGS, H. Inigo, ARIBA; architect and garden designer; *b* Chiswick, 28 Feb. 1876; *m* 1907, Gladys Claire, *y d* of late Sir Edward Hill, KCB, of Rookwood, Llandaff. *Educ:* Godolphin School; Schools of Royal Academy. Devoted special attention to the study of garden planning. *Publications:* Some Architectural Works of Inigo Jones, written in conjunction with Henry Tanner, Jun., 1900; Formal Gardens in England and Scotland, 1902; The Art of Garden Design in Italy, 1906; Town Planning, Past, Present, and Possible, 1909;

Garden Craft in Europe, 1913. *Address:* Little Boarhunt, Liphook, Hants. *T:* Liphook 13; 38 Sackville Street, Piccadilly, W1. *Club:* Arts.

Died 8 April 1923.

TRIMEN, Roland, FRS 1888; FLS, FZS, FES; Hon. MA Oxon 1899; *b* London, 1840; 3rd *s* of Richard and Mary Ann Trimen; *m* 1883, Henrietta Blanche, *d* of H. E. Boyes Bull of Calcutta, and originator of the League of the Empire, 1901. *Educ:* private school; King's Coll. School. Entered Cape Civil Service, 1860; served in offices of Auditor-Gen., Colonial Sec., Commissioner of Lands and Public Works, Governor, etc; Curator of South-African Museum, Cape Town, 1873–95; President of South-African Philosophical Society, 1883–84; retired from Cape Civil Service 1895. President of the Entomological Society of London, 1897–98; awarded Darwin Medal by Royal Society, 1910; Corr. Mem. American Entom. Soc. *Publications:* Rhopalocera Africae Australis: a Catalogue of South-African Butterflies, 1862–66; South-African Butterflies: a Monograph of the Extra-tropical Species, 1887–89; various memoirs and papers on entomology and other branches of zoology, etc, in the Transactions of the Linnean, Zoological and Entomological Societies, and other publications. *Address:* Glaslyn, Waterden Road, Guildford. *Club:* Royal Societies.   *Died 25 July 1916.*

TRIPP, George Henry, CB 1913; *b* 28 May 1860; *s* of George Lewis Tripp; *m* 1881, Sophia Caroline, *d* of G. A. F. Freeman; three *s* one *d. Educ:* Mercers' School. Clerk in Home Office, 1878; Secretary to Home Office Committee on Metropolitan Police Superannuation, 1889; Auditor of Royal Patriotic Fund, 1893–98; Member of Home Office Committee on Housing of Metropolitan Police, 1903, and Metropolitan Police Finances, 1909; Member of Treasury Committee on Education Rates, 1905; Receiver for the Metropolitan Police District and Courts, 1910–18; Coronation Medal, 1911. *Address:* Pymlicoe House, Hadley Green, Herts.

Died 18 Feb. 1922.

TRISCOTT, Col Charles Prideaux, CB 1910; CMG 1917; DSO 1888; RA; *b* 2 Sept. 1857; *y s* of late Joseph Blake Triscott of Plymouth and Helston; *m* 1884, Catherine May, 2nd *d* of Maj.-Gen. M. M. Prendergast; two *d. Educ:* Royal Military Academy. Lieut RA, 1876; served in Afghanistan, including action at Charasiab and march from Kabul to Kandahar (medal and bronze star); Burma Campaign, 1885–88; commanded expedition against Salay Hill Kachins, and also to Lake Endawgyee and Jade Mines (despatches, DSO, medal with two clasps); served as AQMG 2nd Division, Tirah Expeditionary Force (despatches, medal with 2 clasps); Officer Comdg Western Coast Defences, 1912–16; retired pay, 1916. *Recreation:* fishing. *Club:* Naval and Military.   *Died 17 Aug. 1926.*

TRISTRAM, Rev. John William, DD; Canon of St Patrick's, Dublin, 1908–22; Chaplain to the Lord Lieutenant; Lord Lieutenant's Inspector of Education; *s* of Thomas Everard Tristram of Farmley, Wexford, and Alice, *d* of Major Bolton of the Wexford Yeomanry; *m* 1st, C. S. Cavanagh; 2nd, Gertrude, *d* of late F. Brock-Hollinshead, 12th Lancers; one *s* two *d. Educ:* Tipperary Grammar School; Trinity College, Dublin. Curate and afterwards Rector in Ossory Diocese; Organising Secretary of Dublin Board of Education, 1880; to him is largely due the present system of Religious Instruction in Protestant Schools in Ireland; took a prominent part in resisting Home Rule, 1893–95; spoke in over 400 meetings in 28 English counties and boroughs; largely engaged in journalistic work, and for many years a leader-writer in Irish Times. *Publication:* A False Alarm: a Plea for Toleration in Irish Education. *Recreation:* golf. *Address:* Ardoyne, Bramshott Chase, Hindhead, Surrey. *T:* Grayshott 121. *Club:* University, Dublin.   *Died 8 Oct. 1926.*

TRITTON, Sir (Charles) Ernest, 1st Bt, *cr* 1905; senior partner in firm of Brightwen and Co., bill-brokers and banking agents, London; Director of the UK Temperance and General Provident Institution, 1897; *b* 4 Sept. 1845; *s* of late Joseph Tritton, Lombard Street; *m* 1872, Edith, 2nd *d* of late Frederick Green; one *s* two *d. Educ:* Rugby; Trinity Hall, Camb. (BA 1868). MP (C) for Norwood Division of Lambeth, 1892–1906; Vice-Chairman Hospital Sunday Fund and Chairman of Finance Committee; Vice-Chairman London City Mission; Chairman Princess Christian's Hospital for British Wounded, South Norwood; President Norwood Cottage Hospital; Member of Board of Management British Home for Incurables; a Vice-President of British and Foreign Bible Society and of Church Missionary Soc. *Heir: s* Alfred Ernest Tritton [*b* 8 June 1873; *m* 1898, Agneta Elspeth, *d* of W. M. Campbell; one *s* three *d*]. *Address:* 5 Cadogan Square, SW; Bloomfield, Norwood. *Clubs:* Carlton, New University.

Died 28 Dec. 1918.

TRITTON, Joseph Herbert; one of HM Lieutenants for the City of London; *b* 1844; *e s* of late Joseph Tritton; *m* 1869, Lucy Jane (*d* 1919), *e d* of late Henry Abel Smith of Wilford, Notts; four *s* four *d. Educ:* Rugby. Formerly partner in Barclay, Bevan, Tritton & Co., bankers, and Director of Barclay's Bank, Ltd; Chairman of Indo-European Telegraph Co., Ltd; member of the Council of Foreign Bondholders, of The Shipwrights' Company, and of the Fellowship of the Russia Company; Hon. Secretary, London Clearing Bankers, 1888–1906; Vice-President of the Committee of English Country Bankers; ex-President Institute of Bankers, and of London Chamber of Commerce. Order of The Lion and the Sun, Persia. *Publications:* Tritton, the Place and the Family; The Assault on the Standard; many presidential addresses and articles on banking, financial, and economic subjects; volume of Religious Poetry—privately printed; various religious addresses and articles. *Address:* 6 Sloane Court, SW3; Lyons Hall, Great Leighs, Chelmsford. *Clubs:* Athenæum, National Liberal.
Died 11 Sept. 1923.

TROLLOPE, Sir Thomas Ernest, 11th Bt, *cr* 1641; Barrister; *b* 14 Sept. 1858; 3rd *s* of late General Sir Charles Trollope, KCB, and Frances, *o c* of John Lord; *S* twin brother, 1921. *Educ:* Eton; Magdalene College, Cambridge (MA). *Heir: cousin* Henry Cracroft Trollope, *b* 5 June 1860. *Address:* 18 Montpelier Square, SW7. *T:* Kensington 2573. *Clubs:* Junior Carlton, Wellington.
Died 23 Sept. 1927.

TROLLOPE, Sir William (Henry), 10th Bt, *cr* 1641; Barrister; *b* 14 Sept. 1858; 2nd *s* of late General Sir Charles Trollope, KCB, and Frances, *o c* of John Lord; *S* to baronetcy on death of his cousin, 3rd and last Baron Kesteven, 1915; *m* 1894, Louisa Charlotte Campbell, *d* of Capt. Frederick Johnston, RN; two *d. Educ:* Eton; Trinity College, Cambridge (MA). *Heir: twin b* Thomas Ernest Trollope, *b* 14 Sept. 1858. *Address:* 5 Montagu Square, W1. *Club:* Junior Carlton.
Died 24 Aug. 1921.

TROTTER, Rev. Canon Edward Bush, VD; MA; Commissary to Bishop of Trinidad, 1918; *b* 10 Dec. 1842; 4th *s* of late Alexander Trotter, and Jaqueline, *d* of Bishop Otter (of Chichester); *m* 1870, Gertrude Mary, 2nd *d* of late Rev. F. Fitch, Rector of Cromer, Norfolk; no *c. Educ:* Harrow; King's College, London; and Christ's College, Cambridge. BA 1865; MA 1869; Junior Optime and 3rd Cl. Theol. Tripos. Deacon, 1866; Priest, 1867; Curate of Holy Trinity, Habergham Eaves, Lancs, 1866–69; Vicar of Alnwick, Northumberland, and Domestic Chaplain to Duke of Northumberland; Chaplain to 3rd Artillery Volunteers, and to the Light Infantry Militia, 1869–90; Hon. Canon of Newcastle upon Tyne, 1884–90; Rector of St Stephen's Savanna Grande, Trinidad, BWI, 1890–1901; Canon of Holy Trinity Cathedral, Trinidad, 1896–1903, and since 1908; Archdeacon and Vicar-General of Trinidad, 1896–1903; Archdeacon of Western Downs and Canon of Brisbane Cathedral, Queensland, 1903–8; Canon of Port of Spain, Trinidad; Chaplain to HBM Legation, Carácas, Venezuela, and in charge of the Anglican congregations throughout Venezuela, 1908–16. *Publications:* The Church of England: Early History, Property, and Mission, Reformation Period; The Three Days of Grace; The Church Catechism and Bible Story (3 vols); Two Historical Charts of Church of England; Royal Progress of Our Lord. *Recreations:* walking and climbing, when younger. *Address:* 105 Alumhurst Road, Bournemouth. *Club:* Church Imperial.
Died 14 July 1920.

TROTTER, Major Edward Henry, DSO 1900; Grenadier Guards; *b* 1 Dec. 1872; *s* of late Maj.-Gen. Sir Henry Trotter, GCVO and Hon. Eva, *d* of 2nd Baron Gifford. Entered army, 1893; Captain, 1900; served Soudan, 1898 (British medal, Khedive's medal with clasp); South Africa, 1900–2 (despatches, medal and 4 clasps, DSO). *Club:* Guards.
Died 8 July 1916.

TROTTER, Lieut-Colonel Sir Henry, KCMG 1906; CB 1880; *b* Cowfold, Sussex, 30 Aug. 1841; 3rd *s* of late Alexander Trotter and Jaqueline, *d* of late Rt Rev. William Otter, Bishop of Chichester; *m* 1890, Olivia Georgina, *o d* of late Adm. Sir George Wellesley, GCB; two *d. Educ:* Cheltenham College; EI Military Coll. Addiscombe. Lieut RE (late Bengal), 1860; retired as Lieut-Col, 1890; served 1863–75 on great Trigonometrical Survey of India; accompanied Sir Douglas Forsyth's mission to Yarkand and Kashgar, 1873–74, as geographer; employed on special service in China, 1876; was awarded, 1878, the Victoria medal of Royal Geog. Soc. for explorations in Turkestan; appointed additional military attaché at Constantinople during Turko-Russian War, 1877–78; accompanied the Turkish armies throughout the campaign in Asia (siege and relief of Kars, battles of Yeshek Ilias, and Deveh Boyoun, etc), Turkish war medal; Consul

for Kurdistan, 1878–82; superintended International relief operations at Scio after the great earthquake of 1881; military attaché, Constantinople, 1882–89, during which time he was frequently employed on special missions; Consul-General in Syria, 1890–94; frequently acted as HM Chargé d'Affaires at Bucharest; British Delegate on the European Commission of the Danube, and HBM Consul-Gen. for Roumania, 1894–1906; Jubilee medal 1897. *Publications:* various papers contributed to the Royal Geog. Soc. *Recreation:* shooting, was the first European to shoot the *Ovis Poli* or wild sheep of the Pamirs, 5 May 1874. *Address:* 18 Eaton Place, SW. *Clubs:* Athenæum, United Service.
Died 25 Sept. 1919.

TROTTER, Rev. Henry Eden, MA; Hon. Canon of Christ Church, Oxford, since 1898; *b* 2 June 1844; 3rd *s* of William and Mary Elizabeth Trotter of Horton Manor, Surrey; *m* 1877, Mary Hodgson, *d* of William S. Gillett, Harefield, Southampton. *Educ:* Radley; Christ Church, Oxford. Ordained deacon, 1869; priest, 1870; Curate of St John, Bedminster, 1869–72; Cobham, Surrey, 1872–73; Vicar of Northam, Hants, 1873–83; Ardington, Berks, 1884–99; Rector of Whitchurch, 1899–1914; Rural Dean of Henley, 1913–17. *Address:* Horton Lodge, Reading.
Died 4 July 1922.

TROTTER, Rev. John George; Vicar of Polesworth since 1882; Hon. Canon of Birmingham; Rural Dean, Surrogate; *b* 4 Feb. 1848; *s* of Rev. Thomas L. Trotter; *m* 1880, Elizabeth Case; one *s* one *d. Educ:* St John's College, Oxford (MA). Curate of Burghfield, Berks, 1872–75; Northden, 1875–78; Ashburn, 1878–82; Assistant Diocesan Inspector of Schools, 1891–93; Hon. Canon of Worcester, 1901–5. *Address:* Polesworth Vicarage, Tamworth.
Died 16 Feb. 1917.

TROTTER, Lieut-Col John Moubray, DL, JP, and Convenor of Midlothian; *b* 6 Sept. 1842; 4th *s* of Archibald Trotter of Dreghorn, Midlothian (*d* 1844), and Louisa Jane, *y d* of late James Strange of Madras Civil Service; *m* 1876, Hon. Mary Catherine Elizabeth (*d* 1908), *o c* of Ralph, 2nd Lord Dunfermline, KCB; two *s* two *d. Educ:* Harrow; Addiscombe. Served for many years on the Staff of the Army in India. *Address:* Colinton House, Midlothian, Scotland. *Clubs:* Naval and Military; New, Edinburgh.
Died 15 Feb. 1924.

TROTTER, Col Sir Philip, Kt 1908; JP, DL; Colonel commanding troops, Stirling Castle; *b* 13 June 1844; 4th surv. *s* of A. Trotter of Dreghorn, JP, Midlothian, and Louisa, *d* of J. Strange and Hon. Anne Strange, *d* of 1st Viscount Melville; *m* 1886, Eliza, *d* of C. Scott Plummer of Middlestead, and Sunderland Hall, Selkirk; one *s* one *d. Educ:* Harrow. Joined 93rd Highlanders, 1866; served Nile Campaign, 1884–6 (medal, clasp, bronze star, Bt Lt-Col, despatches, 3rd class Medjidie); commanded 93rd Highlanders, 1891–94; 91st Regimental District, 1898–1902; 34th Field Army Brigade Scots Border Brigade, etc. Received freedom of Royal Burgh of Stirling, 1902; Chairman Ex-Committee QV School, Dunblane. *Publication:* Our Mission to the Court of Morocco. *Address:* Mainhouse, Kelso. *Clubs:* Naval and Military; New, Edinburgh.
Died 26 Oct. 1918.

TROUBRIDGE, Adm. Sir Ernest Charles Thomas, KCMG 1919 (CMG 1904); CB 1911; MVO 1904; *b* 15 July 1862; 3rd *s* of Col. Sir Thomas St Vincent H. C. Troubridge, 3rd Bt; *m* 1st, 1891, Edith (*d* 1900), *y d* of William Duffus, Halifax, NS; one *s* two *d*; 2nd, 1908, Una (authoress of Guests and Memories, 1925), *y d* of late Capt. Harry Taylor, MVO; one *d*. Naval Attaché, Vienna, Madrid, and Tokio, 1901–4; Captain and Chief of Staff Mediterranean, 1907–8; Chief of the War Staff, Admiralty, 1911–12; commanding Mediterranean Cruiser Squadron, 1912; Head of the British Naval Mission to Serbia, 1915; Admiral Commanding on the Danube, 1918; Admiral, 1919; retired list, 1921; President of the International Commission of the Danube, 1919–24. Grand Officer of the Rising Sun; Officer of Legion of Honour; Grand Cordon of Star of Roumania, with Swords, 1919; Grand Officer of SS Maurice and Lazarus, 1917; Grand Officer of Redeemer of Greece, 1918; Croix de Guerre with Palms, 1918; 2nd Class of Red Eagle; 2nd Class of Spanish Naval Merit; Gold Medal of Order of Imtiaz; Grand Officer of Kara George with Swords, 1915; First Class Order of White Eagle, 1916. *Address:* 6 Cheltenham Terrace, SW3. *T:* Kensington 3346. *Clubs:* Travellers', Beefsteak.
Died 28 Jan. 1926.

TROUP, James; Consul-General, retired; *b* 15 April 1840; *s* of late Alexander Troup, grain merchant, Aberdeen; *m* 1st, Hannah (*d* 1903), *d* of late Robert Scott, Gilston, Herts; 2nd, Catherine, *d* of late Donald Macpherson, Inverness; three *s* one *d. Educ:* Gymnasium, Old

Aberdeen; Aberdeen University, MA. Entered HM Consular Service, Japan Establishment, 1863; Vice-Consul, 1873; Consul, 1877; Consul-General at Yokohama, and Assistant Judge of HM Court for Japan, 1896; retired, 1898. Jubilee Medal. *Publications:* Trade Reports; Papers on Buddhistic and other subjects in Transactions Asiatic Society of Japan, Japan Society, and Royal Asiatic Society, London, etc. *Recreations:* travelling, fishing, studies. *Address:* Wollescote, Springhill, Ventnor, Isle of Wight. *Died 26 July 1925.*

TROUTON, Frederick Thomas, FRS; *b* Dublin, 24 Nov. 1863; *y s* of Thomas Trouton, of that city; *m* Annie, *d* of George Fowler, Liverpool; two *s* three *d*. *Educ:* Dungannon Royal School; Trinity Coll. Dublin; and also Engineering School, Trinity College, Dublin; MA, DSc (Dublin); assistant to the Professor of Physics, Trinity Coll. Dublin, 1884–1901; Lecturer in Experimental Physics, Trinity College, Dublin, 1901–2; Quain Professor of Physics, University College, London, 1902–14. *Publications:* On Molecular Latent Heat (Phil. Mag. vol. xviii), commonly referred to as 'Trouton's Law'; Repetition of Hertz's Experiments and Determination of the direction of the vibrations of Light (Nature, vol. xxxix); Experiments on Electromagnetic Radiations, including some of the phases of secondary waves (Nature, vol. xl), and the various other papers. *Address:* The Rookery, Downe, Kent. *T:* Bromley 1812.
Died 21 Sept. 1922.

TROWBRIDGE, John Townsend; *b* Ogden, NY, 18 Sept. 1827; *s* of Windsor Stone and Rebecca Willey Trowbridge, parents of English stock; *m* 1st, 1860, Cornelia Warren, of Lowell, Mass; 2nd, 1873, Sarah Adelaide Newton, of Arlington, Mass; one *s* two *d*. Attended common country school in boyhood, but mostly self-taught, in intervals of leisure, while working on father's farm; began to write verses at an early age; one term at a classical school in Lockport, New York, 1844–45; went to prairie country of Illinois, 1845, and spent one year there, farming, hunting, school-teaching, and pursuing private studies; to New York City in spring of 1847, and began writing for the press; to Boston 1848, wrote for the press, edited newspapers, and published first of a series of small books, Father Brighthopes, 1853; spent one year abroad, mostly in Paris, 1855–56; contributor to Atlantic Monthly, 1857; edited Our Young Folk's Magazine, 1870–73; visited Europe, 1888–91, and again, 1908–9. *Publications:* The Vagabonds, and other Poems; The Book of Gold, and other Poems; The Emigrant's Story, and other Poems; A Home Idyl, and other Poems; The Lost Earl, and other Poems; books for the young: The Little Master; The Tinkham Brothers' Tide Mill; His One Fault; His Own Master; The Pocket Rifle; The Prize Cup; Two Biddicut Boys; The Silver Medal; The Kelp Gatherers; Jack Hazard stories (five vols); The Fortunes of Toby Trafford; A Pair of Madcaps, 1909; novels and tales: Neighbors' Wives; Coupon Bonds; Cudjo's Cave; Neighbor Jackwood; My Own Story (autobiography), and Poetical Works (complete), 1903. *Address:* Arlington, Mass, USA.
Died 12 Feb. 1916.

TROWER, Rt. Rev. Gerard, DD; Rector of Chale, Isle of Wight, since 1927; *b* 1860; *s* of Rev. Arthur Trower, Rector of St Mary-at-Hill, Eastcheap, EC. *Educ:* Keble College, Oxford (3rd Class Theological Schools); Ely College. Ordained 1888; Curate of St Alban the Martyr, Birmingham, 1888–93; St Mary Redcliffe, Bristol, 1893–95; Rector of Christ Church, Sydney, 1895–1901; Bishop of Nyasaland, 1901–10; Bishop of North-West Australia, 1910–27. *Address:* Chale Rectory, Isle of Wight. *Club:* New Oxford and Cambridge. *Died 25 Aug. 1928.*

TROWER, Sir Walter, Kt 1915; senior partner in the firm of Trower, Still, Parkin & Keeling, of Lincoln's Inn; *b* 14 Feb. 1853; *y s* of late Captain Edward Spencer Trower, 9th Lancers, of Stansteadbury, Herts, and Emma, *d* of Admiral Gosselin of Bengeo Hall, Herts; *m* 1884, Mabel, *d* of late Capt. Phelips, RA, of Oaten Hill, Canterbury; one *s* one *d*. *Educ:* Haileybury. Admitted a Solicitor, 1876; Member of Council of the Law Society, 1902; Vice-President, 1912–13; Chairman of Finance Committee, 1902–20; President, 1913–14; Member of the Council of King Edward's Hospital Fund for London; of the Committee on the Transfer of Land in England and Wales, 1918; of the Royal Commission on Income Tax, 1920; of the Council of Law Reporting; of the Committee to enquire into Civil Litigation between the Subject and the Crown, 1921–22. *Address:* 8 Westbourne Terrace, Hyde Park, W2. *Clubs:* Travellers'; Stoke Poges and Woking Golf. *Died 5 April 1924.*

TUBB, Captain Frederick Harold, VC 1915; 7th Battalion Australian Imperial Force; *y s* of Harry Tubb, of Longwood East, Victoria. Was some years in Australian Light Horse; Captain, 1915; served European War, 1914–15 (wounded, VC for Lone Pine Trenches, Gallipoli). *Died 22 Sept. 1917.*

TUCK, Sir Adolph, 1st Bt, *cr* 1910; Chairman and Managing Director Raphael Tuck and Sons, Ltd, Art Publishers to their Majesties the King and Queen; Extraordinary Director, Scottish Equitable Life Assurance Society; President of the Association of Publishers of Christmas Cards and Calendars; President of the Association of Publishers of Picture Postcards; Treasurer of Jews' College; *b* 30 Jan. 1854; 2nd *s* of late Raphael Tuck of Highbury, N, and Ernestine (*d* 1895), *d* of David Lissner, of Schrimm, Poland; *m* 1882, Jeanetta, *d* of late William Flatau of Lusan House, Highbury; two *s* three *d*. *Educ:* Elizabeth Gymnasium (College), Breslau. Entered his father's art business in London, 1869; inaugurated the first of a series of Original Christmas Card Designs Exhibitions at the Dudley Gallery with Sir Coutts Lindsay, John Everett Millais, RA, and Marcus Stone, RA, as judges, 1879; introduced Picture Postcards into the British Empire, 1894. *Heir: s* William Reginald Tuck, Major 3rd County of London Yeomanry (Sharpshooters) [*b* 8 July 1883; *m* 1917, Gladys, 2nd *d* of N. Alfred Nathan of Wickford, Auckland, NZ, and *widow* of Desmond Fosberry Kettle, Lieut, Auckland Mounted Rifles, two *d*]. *Recreations:* riding, walking. *Address:* 29 Park Crescent, Portland Place, W1. *T:* Langham 1854. *M:* F 4431. *Clubs:* National Liberal, City Reform, Empire. *Died 3 July 1926.*

TUCK, William Henry, MA; author and writer for press; *b* Great Moulton, Norfolk, 3 Oct. 1840; *e s* of late Rev. William Gilbert Tuck, Tostock House, and Anne Elizabeth, *o c* of Edward Smyth, West Bradenham Hall, Norfolk; *m* 1866, Jane St John, *o d* of late J. W. Budd, MD, of Plymouth. *Educ:* Ipswich; Emmanuel Coll. Cambridge (MA 1866). *Publications:* The Avi-Fauna of a Suffolk Village; The Aculeate Hymenoptera of Bury St Edmunds District. *Recreations:* reading, fishing, general entomology. *Address:* 5 Southgate Green, Bury St Edmunds. *Died 29 Nov. 1922.*

TUCKER, Francis Ellis, ISO 1909; retired Civil Servant; *b* 29 May 1844; *e* surv. *s* of late Rev. Francis Tucker, Baptist Minister of Manchester and London; unmarried. *Educ:* private schools in Manchester and Leatherhead, Surrey; matriculated at London University, 1860. After a short commercial engagement, obtained an appointment on the staff of the British Museum (Director's Office), 1862; Assistant Secretary, 1903; retired, 1908, after a total service of 46½ years; visited Egypt and Palestine, 1871; America, 1878; South Africa, 1909–10. *Publications:* Tourist Notes in Egypt, 1872; Fairy's Rainbow, and other addresses to Sunday Schools. *Recreations:* music, literary study. *Address:* 7 Purbeck Road, West Cliff, Bournemouth. *Died 28 Oct. 1921.*

TUCKER, Maj.-Gen. Louis Henry Emile, CIE 1891; *b* 1843; *s* of Robert Tudor Tucker, formerly BCS; *m* 1877, Annie Lætitia, *d* of Sir Robert Henry Davies, KCSI, CIE. *Educ:* Wimbledon School; Addiscombe. Entered Bengal army, 1860; Capt. 1869; Major, 1880; Lieut-Colonel, 1886; Colonel, 1890; Major-General, 1899; served NW Frontier of India Campaign, 1863 (despatches, medal with clasp); Jowaki Expedition, 1877–78 (despatches, and clasp); Afghan War, 1878–80 (despatches, medal with two clasps); formerly Inspector-Gen. of Police, Punjab. *Address:* Winhaven, The Undercliffe, Sandgate, Kent. *Died 15 Oct. 1925.*

TUCKWELL, Rev. W.; Unbeneficed Clerk in Orders; *b* Oxford, 1829; *s* of William Tuckwell, Surgeon, and Margaret Wood; *m* 1858, Rosa, *d* of Captain Stron, HEICS; one *s* three *d*. *Educ:* Winchester; New College, Oxford (Fellow). Master at St Columba's College, Ireland, 1853–54; Curate, St Mary Magdalen, Oxford, 1856; Master of New College School, 1857–63; Headmaster of Taunton College School, 1864–77; Rector of Stockton, Warwickshire, 1878–93; Rector of Waltham, Lincolnshire, 1893–1905. *Publications:* Tongues in Trees, 1891; Winchester Fifty Years Ago, 1898; A. W. Kinglake: a Biographical Study, 1902; Reminiscences of Oxford, 1st edition, 1900, 2nd edition, 1907; Reminiscences of a Radical Parson, 1905; Life of Chaucer, 1904, Horace, 1905, Spenser, 1906; Pre-Tractarian Oxford, 1909; Monograph of Lycidas, 1911; Nuggets from the Bible Mine, 1913. *Address:* Pyrford Rough, Woking. *TA:* Pyrford Maybury. *Died 1 Feb. 1919.*

TUDOR, Sir Daniel (Thomas), Kt 1917; KC; Chief Justice of Gibraltar since 1922; *b* Lampeter, South Wales, 21 July 1866; *m* 1896, Hettie Josephine (*d* 1924), 2nd *d* of Gustavus Thompson, Cadogan Gardens, London; three *d*. Called to Bar, Gray's Inn, 1890; went Western Circuit and various local Sessions, 1893–1903; Attorney-General of the Colonies of Grenada and St Vincent, British West Indies, 1903–11, during which time he acted on several occasions as Chief Justice, also as Colonial Secretary of Grenada, and administered the Government both for Grenada and St Vincent; Commissioner to revise the laws of Grenada, 1911; acted as Legal

Assistant, Colonial Office, London, 1911; Chief Justice of Supreme Court of Bahama Islands, 1911-22; President of the Discharged Soldiers' Commission, 1918-19. *Publication:* The Revised Laws of Grenada, 1911. *Recreations:* swimming, riding. *Address:* The Haven, Gibraltar. *Club:* Boodle's.   *Died 23 Nov. 1928.*

TUDOR, Hon. Frank Gwynne, MP; Minister of Trade and Customs, Australia, 1908-13, and 1914-16; *b* 27 Jan. 1866; 3rd *s* of John L. and Ellen C. Tudor; two *s* three *d. Educ:* State Schools, Williamstown and Richmond, Victoria. Worked in England and America at Felt Hat trade, 1889-94; introduced Trade Union Label into England and Felt Hatters Society, 1892; returned to Victoria, 1894; President Melbourne Trades Hall Council, 1900-1; elected to first Commonwealth Parliament; Whip for (Watson) Labour Ministry; Leader of Australian Labour Party since 1916. *Recreations:* cycling, rowing, lover of football and cricket. *Address:* Aberfoil, Rowena Parade, Richmond, Melbourne.

Died Jan. 1922.

TUFNELL, Col Arthur Wyndham, CMG 1916; *o s* of late Rt Rev. Edward Wyndham Tufnell, DD, Bishop of Brisbane; *m* 1897, Frances Mary Adelaide, *d* of late Capt. John Campion Wells, RN; one *d. Educ:* Eton; Sandhurst. Joined The Queen's Regiment, 1891; Lieut, 1896; Captain, 1900; Major, 1914; Bt Lt-Colonel, 1916; passed Staff College, 1904; attached General Staff, War Office, 1904-6; General Staff, Scottish Command, 1906-10; General Staff Officer, East Lancashire Division, 1912-14; served with 1st Batt. The Queen's Regt, NW Frontier of India and in The Tirah Campaign, 1897-98 (medal with 2 clasps); S African War with the Natal Field Force, including the Relief of Ladysmith, and afterwards in the Transvaal and Orange River Colony, 1899-1902, with 2nd Batt. The Queen's Regt, and afterwards as ADC to Brig.-General E. O. F. Hamilton, CB (despatches, severely wounded, Queen's medal with 6 clasps, King's medal with 2 clasps); European War, 1914-16, as General Staff Officer, Brigade-Commander and Brigadier-General General Staff (despatches thrice, wounded, Brevet of Lt-Col and Col, CMG, Chevalier of the Legion of Honour). *Clubs:* Army and Navy, Royal Automobile.   *Died 17 May 1920.*

TUFNELL, Col William Nevill, DL and JP; Local Director of Barclay's Bank; *b* 1838; 2nd surv. *s* of late J. J. Tufnell, DL, JP, of Langleys; *m* 1861, Eleanor Frances (*d* 1919), *d* of late Maj.-Gen. C. Gostling, RA; four *s* one *d. Educ:* Cheam. Entered Royal Navy on board HMS Britannia, Flagship of Admiral Sir D. Dundas, 1852; served through the Russian War in that ship and HMS Niger, and in the batteries at Balaclava; served also in the Boxer Gunboat in Sea of Azof; present at loss of HM Steam frigate Tiger, off Odessa; engaged in suppression of slave trade on East Coast of Africa; retired, 1863; commanded 2nd VB Essex Regt for eighteen years, retiring in 1897. *Publication:* Tour in Palestine with Duke of Edinburgh in 1859. *Recreations:* country sports, carving in wood, painting. *Address:* Langleys, Chelmsford. *T:* Little Waltham 4.

Died 3 Nov. 1922.

TUFTON, Hon. Charles Henry, CMG 1917; Secretary, Foreign Office; *b* 16 May 1879; 3rd *s* of 1st Baron Hothfield; *m* 1903, Stella Josephine, *y d* of Sir G. Faudel Phillip, 1st Bt; two *s* one *d. Address:* 33 Albert Road, NW8. *T:* Hampstead 8491.

Died 23 Sept. 1923.

TUFTS, J. F., BA, MA, DCL; Professor of History in Acadia University since 1874, and Dean of the Faculty of Arts and Science; *b* New Albany, Annapolis County, Nova Scotia; *s* of Samuel Tufts and Lorisa Kniffin; *m* 1878, Marie Woodworth (*d* 1900); two *s* two *d. Educ:* Acadia University; Harvard University. Principal of Horton Collegiate Academy, a preparatory school affiliated with Acadia College, 1874-89; Professor of History and Political Economy, 1892-1912. *Recreations:* gardening and care of lawn and grounds. *Address:* Wolfville, Nova Scotia. *T:* 78.   *Died 7 Feb. 1921.*

TUITE, James, JP; Chairman of Mullingar Town Commissioners; *b* 1849; *s* of late J. Tuite, Mullingar. MP (N) Westmeath, N, 1885-1900. *Address:* Greville Street, Mullingar, Co. Westmeath.

Died 6 Oct. 1916.

TULLOCH, Maj.-Gen. Sir Alexander Bruce, KCB 1902 (CB 1882); CMG 1893; retired; *b* Edinburgh, 2 Sept. 1838; 2nd *s* of late Lieut-Col J. G. D. Tulloch and Anne, *d* of late S. Staunton; *m* 1st, 1865, Arabella (*d* 1904), *d* of late Stephen Heelis; five *s*; 2nd, 1907, *d* of late Canon Brandreth, and *widow* of Mr Attwood of Glaslyn Court, Brecknocks. *Educ:* private school; Royal Military Coll. Sandhurst (cadet 13 to 16 years of age). Joined 1st Royals 1855; passed

Staff College 1869; served as acting engineer, gunboat expeditions, and DAQMG South China; DAAG for instruction; DAQMG Southern District. Intelligence Dept War Office; several confidential missions for War and Foreign Offices; special service officer to Commander-in-Chief, Mediterranean Fleet, 1882; in charge Intelligence Dept, Egypt; commanded Welsh Regt, South Africa and Egypt; Brigadier-General, Cairo; Major-General commanding Victorian military forces, and general military adviser to Australian colonies; President, Royal Commission on Defence Organisation, Sydney, 1892; served Crimea, 1855-56; India, 1857-58; China Campaign, 1859-60; Egyptian Campaign, 1882; also for Intelligence Dept, with Spanish army during Carlist War in Pyrenees, 1874; requested by King of Belgians to undertake Gordon's work in Central Africa when that officer was shut up in Khartoum (not sanctioned); several times mentioned in despatches by both naval and military Commanders-in-Chief, 1882. *Decorated:* CB for Intelligence Dept work, and arrangements made in Egypt for the expected naval and military operations; promoted Lieut-Colonel on recommendation of Admiralty to War Office; also recommended for Victoria Cross; CMG for arrangements made in Australia whereby the different Colonies at last agreed to furnish the necessary funds to build fortifications and barracks at the important coaling ports of King George's Sound and Thursday Island; president of a joint Naval and Military Committee which decided on the positions of the batteries; Times War Correspondent, Manchuria, 1904; awarded Good Service Pension; Hon. Colonel 5th Federal Regiment, Australia. *Publications:* Elementary Lectures on Military Law, 1871; Possible Battlefields in the next European War, 1890; The Highland Rising of the 45, 1901; Recollection of Forty Years' Service, 1903; Recollection of Four Years' Farming, 1905; The Argentine Republic and its Neighbours, 1907; A Soldier's Sailoring, 1912; and many professional papers. *Recreations:* farming, salmon and trout fishing, keeping bees, antiquarian research. *Address:* Glaslyn Court, Crickhowell. *Club:* United Service.   *Died 25 May 1920.*

TULLOCH, Major Hector, CB 1893; late Royal Engineers; late Chief Engineering Inspector, Local Government Board; *b* 16 April 1835; *s* of General John Tulloch, CB; *m* 1st, 1855, Sophia Jane (*d* 1858), *d* of George Smith, one *s* one *d*; 2nd, 1860, Ada (*d* 1907), *d* of Edward Morton of Kensington Gate; one *s* three *d. Educ:* Kensington Grammar School; Addiscombe. Got his commission in 1855; served in India in Public Works Department up to 1868; appointed Municipal Engineer of Bombay in 1868, and an engineering inspector under the Local Government Board in 1873; made Chief Engineering Inspector in 1888; retired on 31st Dec. 1897. *Address:* 33 Half Moon Lane, Herne Hill, SE24. *T:* Brixton 1197.

Died 11 July 1922.

TULLOCH, Rev. W. W., MA, BD, DD; *b* Dundee, 22 Sept. 1846; *e s* of Very Rev. Principal Tulloch, DD, LLD, Principal of St Andrews University, and Jane Anne Sophia Hindmarsh, Alnwick; *m* 1st, 1872, Margaret Mather Crawford Hill (*d* 1879); four *s*; 2nd, 1884, Esther Proctor Hamilton Adamson; one *s* two *d. Educ:* Madras College; St Andrews University. For twelve years contributor of Tangled Talk by Orion to Glasgow Citizen; Editor of Scots Magazine for four years and of Sunday Talk for five years. Gained Rector's Prize (Mr J. A. Froude) at University for Essay on the Gowrie Conspiracy. Ordained Minister, Old West Kirk, Greenock, 1871; assistant and successor to Parish of Kelso, 1874; Past Grand Chaplain of Freemasons of Scotland; Minister of Maxwell Parish, Glasgow, 1877-1901; Chaplain to Lord High Commissioner, 1891. *Publications:* Biographer of Leyden and editor of his Scenes of Infancy; one of the St Giles' Lectures on the Creeds of Christendom—The Society of Friends and the Congregational Church; The Story of the Life of Queen Victoria (revised by the Queen); The Story of the Life of the Prince Consort (revised by the Queen; translated into Urdu); The Story of the Life of Emperor William; For the Sorrowful; Life of Tom Morris, 1907; Biographer of A.K.H.B. in Stray Sermons and Essays; Church Union in Scotland. *Recreations:* golf, reading novels and light literature of all kinds, writing *causeries* for newspapers and magazine articles. *Club:* Royal and Ancient, St Andrews.

Died Jan. 1920.

TUNNICLIFFE, Francis Whittaker, MD; physician; *b* Eccleshall, Staffs; Physician, King's College Hospital, London; Member of the Departmental Committee on Food Preservatives; formerly Professor of Pharmacology, King's College, London. *Publications:* scientific papers upon the physiology and pathology of the respiratory, circulatory, and digestive organs. *Address:* 129 Harley Street, W1. *T:* Langham 2538. *Clubs:* Arts, Royal Automobile.

Died 15 Dec. 1928.

TUOHY, James M.; b Cork, 1859; y s of late Patrick Tuohy, manager, Cork Examiner; m 1885, Florence, d of late Jerome Donovan, Cork; two s two d. *Educ:* privately. London correspondent, Dublin Freeman's Journal, 1881–1912; European Manager, New York World, since 1897. *Recreation:* golf. *Address:* 23 Warwick Gardens, Kensington, W14. *TA:* Promulgate, Westrand, London. *T:* Western 411. *Clubs:* National Liberal, Savage, Pilgrims'.
Died 7 Sept. 1923.

TUPPER, Hon. Sir Charles Hibbert, KCMG 1893; KC; LLB Harvard; b 3 Aug. 1855; 2nd s of late Sir Charles Tupper, 1st Bt; m 1879, Janet, d of Hon. James Macdonald, CJ, of Nova Scotia; three s three d. *Educ:* McGill Coll., Montreal (Gov.-Gen. Scholarship); Harvard Law School. Barrister, Nova Scotia, 1877; Ontario, 1895; British Columbia, 1898; Bencher of BC Law Society; elected to House of Commons, 1882, 1887, 1888, 1891, 1896–1900; Member of Canadian House of Commons for Pictou, Nova Scotia, 1882–1904; Minister of Marine and Fisheries, 1888–95; Minister of Justice and Attorney-General for Canada, 1895–96; Agent of HBM Paris Tribunal of Arbitration, 1892 (KCMG); senior member of legal firm Tupper, Bull & Tupper, Vancouver, BC. *Address:* Vancouver, BC. *Clubs:* Union, Victoria; Vancouver, Country, Jericho, Vancouver.
Died 30 March 1927.

TUPPER, Sir Daniel Alfred Anley, Kt 1909; MVO 1901; Serjeant-at-Arms in Ordinary to HM; b 1849; m 1st, 1882, Mary, d of late Lieut-Col C. E. Dering; 2nd, 1894, Rose, e d of Sir E. J. Reed, KCB, MP, FRS. Entered Lord Chamberlain's Office, 1869; Chief Clerk, 1894–1901; Assistant-Controller, 1901–10. *Address:* Doric House, Bath. *T:* 854. *Clubs:* Athenæum; Bath and County, Bath.
Died 29 April 1922.

TURING, Henry, ISO 1913; Coronation Medal, 1911; b 1 Aug. 1843; 5th s of late Sir James Henry Turing, 7th Bt; m Jeanne Marie Catherine (d 1917), d of late S. A. Chabot, banker, of Rotterdam; one s three d. *Educ:* in Holland; Queen Elizabeth's Grammar School, Sevenoaks. Was Acting British Consul at Rotterdam at different times, 1862–74; Vice-Consul, 1874; Consul for the provinces of South Holland, Zealand, and Limburg, 1882; retired on a pension, 1913. *Address:* Rotterdam. *Clubs:* Amicitia, Royal Rowing and Sailing, De Maas, Rotterdam.
Died March 1922.

TURING, Sir James Walter, 9th Bt, cr 1638; b 3 Jan. 1862; s of Sir Robert Fraser Turing, 8th Bt and Catherine, d of Walter S. Davidson; S father, 1913; m 1891, Mabel Rose, d of Andrew Caldecott, of Pishiobury, Sawbridgeworth; two s. *Heir:* er twin s Robert Andrew Henry Turing [b 13 Sept. 1895. Capt. The Rifle Brigade (Prince Consort's Own). *Club:* Naval and Military]. *Address:* Crocker Hill House, Chichester. *Club:* Junior Carlton.
Died 21 Feb. 1928.

TURNBULL, Major Dudley Ralph, DSO 1914; Gordon Highlanders; b 15 Oct. 1891. Entered army, 1912; Adjutant 1st Batt., June–Sept. 1915; Staff Captain 91st Infantry Brigade, June 1916; served European War, 1914–17 (wounded, despatches, DSO, Bt-Major). *Club:* United Service.
Died 1 Oct. 1917.

TURNBULL, Maj.-Gen. Peter Stephenson, MD; KHS; HM Indian Army (retired); b 1836; m 1870, Mary, 2nd d of George Oliver, Hawick; three s four d. Joined Indian Medical Service, 1860; served in Abyssinia under Lord Napier of Magdala, 1867–68 (medal); Secretary to the PMO, HM Forces, Bombay, 1882–88; Acting Inspector-General of Prisons, Bombay Presidency, 1883–85; PMO Sind District, 1888–93; Surgeon-General with the Government of Bombay, 1893–96; retired 1896; Fellow of the University of Bombay, 1893; awarded Good Service Pension, 1896; Hon. Surgeon to King, 1902. *Recreations:* golf, etc. *Address:* 4 Church Hill, Edinburgh.
Died 7 Oct. 1921.

TURNBULL, Sir Robert, Kt 1913; MVO 1910; b 21 Feb. 1852; s of Rev. Robert Turnbull, Vicar of Wybunbury, Cheshire, and Louisa Phillippina; m 1889, Kate, 2nd d of late James Morten and widow of Sidney Humbert; one s. *Educ:* Whitechurch Grammar School, Salop. Joined the London and North-Western Railway, 1868; Assistant to Superintendent of the Line, 1889; Superintendent of the Line, 1893–1914; General Manager, 1914; joined the Board, 1915; Lt-Col in Railway Engineer and Staff Corps. *Address:* Gallowshill, Kings Langley, Herts.
Died 22 Feb. 1925.

TURNER, Alfred; b Bootham, York, 27 March 1874; s of Charles Turner; m 1897, Annie Elizabeth Davies; no c. *Educ:* Grove School, York; privately. Trained in journalism from the age of seventeen;

Dramatic Critic and Special Correspondent on the staff of The Yorkshire Post; Editor Yorkshire Evening Post for seven years; became associated with Carmelite House, 1911. *Publications:* In Faëry Lands Forlorn; Grey Days; Songs of the Sunset (Verse); On Falling in Love (Essays); two short plays produced in London and the Provinces; several short stories. *Recreations:* tramping anywhere in the open country, swimming, trying to play golf, reading. *Clubs:* Authors', Savage.
Died 13 Dec. 1922.

TURNER, Maj.-Gen. Sir Alfred Edward, KCB 1902 (CB (mil.) 1897; CB (civ.) 1891); Director of British North Borneo Company; of Manchester North Borneo Rubber Co.; Chairman of North Borneo State Rubber, Ltd; b London, 3 March 1842; e s of late Richard E. Turner, BL, Bencher, Inner Temple, and Frances d of Charles Johnstone; m 1st, 1865, Blanche (d 1899), d of Charles Hopkinson of Wotton Court, Gloucester; 2nd, 1902, Juliette Elizabeth Marie, o d of late Henry Whiting; two s one d. *Educ:* Westminster School; Addiscombe. Joined RA, 1860; ADC and military private secretary to Viceroy of Ireland, 1882–84; DAAG Nile Expedition, 1884–85 (despatches, medal and clasp, bronze star); assistant military secretary, Commander-in-Chief in Ireland, 1885–86; private secretary, Viceroy of Ireland, 1886; Commissioner of Police, Cork Kerry, Clare, Limerick, 1886–92; Asst Adjt-Gen. RA Army Headquarters, 1895–98; Inspector-General of Auxiliary Forces, 1900–4. President of Salon; Member of Japanese Society; Chairman of the Alliance Franco-Britannique. Decorated for civil services in Ireland (civil CB), for military services and being mentioned in despatches (mil. CB). *Publications:* The Retreat from Moscow and Passage of the Beresina; From Weissenburg to Sedan; Sixty Years of a Soldier's Life, 1912. *Recreations:* reading, riding, and Alpine climbing. *Address:* Carlyle House, Chelsea Embankment, SW. *T:* 1222 Western. *M:* LA 8797. *Clubs:* Savage, Junior United Service, Sesame, Royal Automobile, Swiss Alpine, Polyglot.
Died 20 Nov. 1918.

TURNER, Engineer Rear-Admiral Arthur William, CB 1918; RN; b 29 Aug. 1859; 3rd s of late Rev. George Turner; m 1st, Lily Seymour; one d; 2nd, Sarah Faulconer. *Educ:* Kingswood School, Bath; Royal Naval Colleges, Devonport and Greenwich. Entered Navy as Assistant Engineer, 1880; Engineer, 1886; Chief Engineer, 1893; Engineer Commander, 1902; Engineer Captain, 1909; Engineer Rear-Admiral, 1912; served in Amethyst, Thames, Colossus, Renard, Sharpshooter, on introduction of Belleville boilers, Argonaut, Terrible, Nile, Vengeance, King Edward VII; and on the staffs of Admirals Sir A. B. Milne, Sir G. A. Callaghan, Sir J. Jellicoe, all 2nd Division Home Fleet; Sir G. A. Callaghan, Commander-in-Chief Home Fleet; retired, 1917. *Recreation:* motoring. *Address:* The Mount, Mannamead Avenue, Mannamead, Plymouth. *M:* CO 723. *Clubs:* Royal Automobile; Royal Western Yacht, Plymouth.
Died 30 Oct. 1928.

TURNER, Col Augustus Henry, CB 1897; Unemployed Supernumerary List Indian Army; b 12 Oct. 1842; s of George Turner, Beacon Downs, Devon. *Educ:* Marlborough. Entered army, 1861; Brev. Col 1891; served Hazara Campaign, 1868 (medal with clasp); Afghan War, 1878–80 (despatches, medal with two clasps); Mahsood-Wuzeeree Expedition, 1881; Zhob Field Force, 1890 (despatches); in command of column, Miranzai Expedition, 1891 (despatches, brevet of Col, clasp); in command of brigade, Waziristan, 1894–95 (thanks of Government of India, despatches, clasp). *Address:* Sunnyside, Dulverton, Somerset. *Club:* East India United Service.
Died 3 April 1925.

TURNER, Rt. Rev. Charles Henry, DD; Suffragan to Bishop of London; Bishop of Islington since 1898; b 14 Jan. 1842; s of Thomas Turner (barrister-at-law and treasurer of Guy's Hospital, formerly Fellow of Trinity College, Camb.); m 1877, Edith Emma, 2nd d of Bishop McDougall, late Bishop of Labuan and Sarawak; four s four d. *Educ:* Cholmeley School, Highgate; Trinity Coll. Camb.; Scholar, 10th Wrangler, 1864; MA 1867; DD 1898; read for orders with Dr Vaughan. Ordained deacon, 1868, priest, 1869, Ely; curate of Godmanchester, Hunts, 1868–73; resident chaplain to Bishop Jackson of London, 1873–77; Vicar of St Saviour's, Fitzroy Square, 1877–82; Rector of St George in the East, 1882–97; Rural Dean of Stepney, 1893–97; Prebendary of St Paul's 1893–1912; Examining Chaplain to Bishop of London, 1884–98; Hon. Chaplain to the Queen, 1895–98; Chaplain in ordinary, 1898; Rector of St Andrew Undershaft, 1898–1912. *Address:* Stainforth House, Clapton Common, E5. *T:* Dalston 1526. *M:* 4747. *Club:* Athenæum.
Died 13 July 1923.

TURNER, Dawson, BA, MD; FRCPE, MRCP Lond.; FRSE; Lecturer on Medical Physics, Surgeons Hall; Additional Examiner to the University of Edinburgh, and to the Royal Colleges of London and Edinburgh; in charge of radium treatment at the Royal Infirmary; late President of the Royal Scottish Society of Arts; Lieutenant Army Motor Reserve; *b* Liverpool, 1857; *s* of Rev. Dawson Turner, DCL; *m* Emily, *d* of William Barry, of Romford. *Educ:* Shrewsbury; Oxford; Dalhousie; Edinburgh; Vienna. After graduating with honours in Edinburgh University, devoted particular attention to medical physics and to electricity, the X-rays and radium; for thirty years medical electrician to the Royal Infirmary, Edinburgh. *Publications:* A Manual of Practical Medical Electricity, 4th edition; Radium, its Physics and Therapeutics, 2nd edition; A Student's Handbook of Diseases of the Skin; many original papers to scientific societies. *Recreations:* a motor pioneer of Scotland, and a founder member of the Royal Automobile Club; golf, motoring. *Address:* Belton, Hydon Heath, Godalming. *T:* Hascombe 31X. *M:* S 11. *Club:* Athenæum.

Died 25 Dec. 1928.

TURNER, Rt. Hon. Sir George, KCMG 1897; PC 1897; Premier and Treasurer of Victoria; MP for St Kilda, Victoria; Councillor and ex-Mayor of St Kilda; JP for Victoria; member of Executive Council of Victoria; *b* Melbourne, Victoria, 8 Aug. 1851; *s* of Alfred Turner; *m* 1872, Rose, *d* of John Morgan, Bovey, Devon. *Educ:* Central School, Melbourne. LLD Cambridge; Under-graduate, Melbourne. Practising as solicitor and barrister in Victoria; entered St Kilda Council in 1887; and still a member; elected to Parliament for St Kilda in 1889; has held office in two previous Governments as Minister of Customs, Minister of Health, and Solicitor-General; has also been Minister of Defence; became Premier in Sept. 1894; Treas. Australian Federal Government, 1901–4, and 1904–5; also Pres. of the Federal Council of Australasia, and Chairman of the Standing Committee of such Council; a member of the Australian National Federation Convention. *Recreation:* bowls. *Address:* 341 Collins Street, Melbourne; Summerlee, Riversdale Road, Hawthorn.

Died 14 Aug. 1916.

TURNER, Rev. Herbert William, MA; Rector of Sutton, Surrey, since 1886; *b* 25 Nov. 1846; *s* of Richard Edward Turner, barrister. *Educ:* Merchant Taylors' Sch.; St John's College, Oxford. Asst Master, Archbp Whitgift's Sch., Croydon, 1871–86; ordained deacon, 1872, priest, 1875; Curate, St Michael's, Croydon, 1872–75; St Saviour, Croydon, 1875–76; Christ Church, Sutton, 1876–86; Hon. Canon in Southwark Cathedral, 1918. *Address:* The Rectory, Sutton, Surrey.

Died 14 June 1922.

TURNER, John Andrew, CIE 1916; JP; MD Edin.; MB, CM, DPH Camb.; Executive Health Officer, Bombay, 1901–16; *b* 1858; *m* 1881, Vera Marguerite Lambert. *Educ:* Edinburgh, London, Paris, Bonn. *Publications:* Sanitation in India; Water Supply for Rural Districts, etc. *Address:* 34a Pembroke Square, W8.

Died 21 Aug. 1922.

TURNER, John Herbert; *b* 7 May 1833; *s* of John and Martha Turner, Ipswich, Suffolk; *m* 1860, Elizabeth Eilbeck, of Whitehaven, Cumberland; one *s*. *Educ:* Whitstable, near Canterbury. Mercantile; went to Nova Scotia in 1856; subsequently to Charlottetown, Prince Edward Island; left for British Columbia, 1862; commenced in Victoria, 1863; elected to the City Council, 1877; Mayor of Victoria, 1879, 1880, 1881; elected Legislative Assembly of province, 1886 (city of Victoria); Minister of Finance and Agriculture, 1887–98 and 1899–1901; Premier, 1895–98; introduced the Budget for thirteen years, and Acts for encouragement of fruit growing, dairying, and formation of Farmers' Institutes and Farmers' Banks, etc; changed the financial system of province, 1888, by issue of 3 per cent inscribed stock in London. Joined the first company of Volunteers, 1864; retired into Canadian Reserve Militia, 1881, as Lieutenant-Colonel; Agent-General for British Columbia in London, 1901 until retirement, 1916; whilst in office he arranged the purchase of lease for 99 years of Nos 1 and 3 Regent Street, and had erected the new British Columbia building thereon; Fellow of Royal Colonial and Royal Horticultural Societies. *Recreations:* riding, fishing, cricket, etc. *Address:* Bingham House, Richmond, Surrey. *Clubs:* Junior Constitutional, Royal Automobile; Union, Victoria.

Died 9 Dec. 1923.

TURNER, John Sidney, MRCS Eng.; FLS; Fellow Royal Society of Medicine; JP (Kent); Chairman, Petty Sessions, Penge Division; Consulting Surgeon, Norwood Cottage Hospital; Member of Council (a Founder) of Lister Institute of Preventive Medicine; Member of Board of Management, British Home and Hospital for Incurables; General Editor of The Kennel Encyclopædia; Chairman of The Kennel Club; Chairman of the Society for the Prevention of Hydrophobia; Vice-President Battersea Home for Lost and Starving

Dogs; Chairman of Penge and Upper Norwood Conservative Association (Dulwich); Vice-Chairman, Conservative and Unionist Association, Bromley Division of Kent; Member of Executive and Organization Committees of National Unionist Association; *b* Old Shoreham, 12 Feb. 1843; *s* of Jas S. Turner of Chyngton, Seaford, Sussex; *m* 1st, Isabella (*d* 1893), *d* of Arthur Scott of India Office; two *s* one *d*; 2nd, 1898, Emily Jane, *d* of late Dr John Boyle Barry of Calcutta and Dilkhoosh, Sydenham Hill; one *d*. *Educ:* Merchant Taylors' School; Guy's Hospital. Late President South-Eastern Branch British Medical Association; late President of Sydenham District Medical Society; Fellow Obstetrical Society of London (Member of Council, 1893–94). *Publications:* articles in International Journal of Microscopy and Natural Science, Hazell's Annual; contributions to medical societies and journals. *Recreations:* shooting, fishing. *Address:* Stanton, Anerley, SE20. *T:* Sydenham 1071. *M:* LT 7394. *Clubs:* Royal Societies, Kennel, Omar Khayyam.

Died 16 Jan. 1920.

TURNER, Percy Frederick, CBE 1920; Partner in the firm of Turner, Brightman & Co.; *b* July 1878; 4th *s* of late W. H. Turner; *m* 1918; two *s*. Private Secretary and Personal Assistant to Shipping Controller during European War; represented the Shipping Controller on British Allied Mission to Germany in connection with the interned British steamers in German ports in December 1918. *Address:* 28 Bolton Gardens, SW5. *T:* Kensington 2229. *Club:* Devonshire.

Died 5 April 1926.

TURNER, Sir Samuel, Kt 1914; JP; twice Mayor of Rochdale; Senior Partner in cotton mills of S. Turner & Co., Ltd, the Asbestos works of Turner Bros, Ltd, and Chairman of Turner's and Newall, Ltd; *b* Rochdale 25 Feb. 1840; *s* of Samuel Turner of Rochdale and Jane, *d* of Robert Nuttall of Rochdale; *m* 1st, 1864, Sarah Jane (*d* 1896), *d* of Thomas Fielding of Clitheroe; 2nd, 1900, Arabella (*d* 1911), *d* of late William Sothern Bellamy, of Gedney, Lincs; 3rd, 1916, Lavinia Heath, *d* of William Wilson of Knaresborough, Yorkshire. Mayor of Rochdale, 1901–03; received Hon. Freedom of Borough, 1906. *Address:* Chaseley, Rochdale.

Died 11 Aug. 1924.

TURNER, Sir William, KCB 1901; Kt 1886; VD; DSc, LLD, DCL; FRS; Principal and Vice-Chancellor of Edinburgh University since 1903; late President Royal Society, Edinburgh; *b* Lancaster, 7 Jan. 1832; *s* of William Turner, Lancaster; *m* 1863, Agnes (*d* 1908), *e d* of Abraham Logan of Burnhouses, Berwickshire; three *s* two *d*. *Educ:* private schools; St Bartholomew's Hospital. MB University of London; Hon. LLD Glasgow, St Andrews, Aberdeen, Montreal, and Western University, Pennsylvania; Hon. DCL Oxford, Durham, and Toronto; Hon. DSc Dublin and Camb.; FRS London and Edinburgh; FRCS London and Edinburgh; Hon. Member Royal Irish Academy, and of learned societies in Paris, Berlin, Rome, St Petersburg, Brussels, New South Wales, etc; Demonstrator of Anatomy, University of Edinburgh, 1854–67; Professor of Anatomy, University of Edinburgh, 1867–1903; Member of General Medical Council, 1873–1905; President 1898–1904; Member of the Medical Acts Commission, 1881; President British Association for Advancement of Science, 1900; Hon. Lieut-Col Queen's Royal Vol. Brig. (VD); DL and Hon. Burgess, City of Edinburgh. *Publications:* numerous memoirs on human and comparative anatomy, anthropology; several reports in the publications of HMS Challenger; editor of Journal of Anatomy and Physiology. *Recreation:* travel. *Address:* 6 Eton Terrace, Edinburgh. *Club:* Athenæum.   Died 15 Feb. 1916.

TURNER, Sir William Henry, KBE 1921; Senior Partner, Turner, Brightman & Co., Shipowners, London; *b* 6 Dec. 1868; *s* of William Henry Turner and Sarah Jane Paul; *m* 1895, Eleanor, *er d* of E. L. Ashworth, JP, Knutsford, Cheshire; one *d*. *Educ:* privately; abroad. Entered City in service of Turner, Brightman & Co., 1885; Partner, 1892; Vice-Chairman, Baltic Exchange; President, Institute of Chartered Shipbrokers; Member Committee, Lloyd's Register; Ex-Chairman, London General Shipowners' Society; Governor, London Orphan School, Merchant Seamen's Orphan Asylum; Member of Council, Chamber of Shipping, Committee Lifeboats Institution, etc. *Recreations:* golf, tennis. *Address:* Cranford, Weybridge. *T:* Weybridge 121. *M:* PB 8749, LY 5641, PA 6562. *Clubs:* Conservative, Devonshire, Royal Automobile, City.

Died 19 Oct. 1923.

TURNEY, Sir John, Kt 1889; JP for the City, and for the County of the City of Nottingham; MIME; *b* 2 Jan. 1839; *m* 1st, 1866, Mary Eleanor (*d* 1867), *d* of Edward Nicholson, Manchester; 2nd, 1870, Juliette Emma (*d* 1891), *d* of A. Topham, of Calais. Mayor of Nottingham, 1887–89; Member of Chamberlain Tariff Commission;

Managing Director and Chairman of Turney Brothers, Ltd; Chairman of Murray Brothers Ltd, and of the Walsall Glue Co. Ltd. *Address:* Gedling House, Gedling, Notts. *Died 17 March 1927.*

TURNOR, Algernon, CB 1887; MA; JP; *b* London, 14 Nov. 1845; 4th *s* of Christopher Turnor of Stoke Rochford, and Caroline, *d* of 9th Earl of Winchilsea; *m* 1880, Lady Henrietta Caroline Stewart, *d* of 9th Earl of Galloway; one *s* three *d. Educ:* Eton; Christ Church, Oxford. Entered the Treasury, 1867; appointed private secretary to the Permanent Secretary, and in 1874 private secretary to the Prime Minister, Earl of Beaconsfield; attached to the special embassy at Congress of Berlin, 1878; appointed Financial Sec. of HM Post Office, 1880; resigned, 1896. *Address:* 9 Clarges Street, Mayfair, W1. *T:* 4598 Gerrard. *Clubs:* Carlton, St James'.
Died 11 Dec. 1921.

TURPIN, Ven. William Homan; Canon of Grahamstown, 1903; Archdeacon of Craddock, 1911. Ordained 1859; SPG Missionary St Philip's, Grahamstown, 1864–1905. *Address:* Grahamstown, Cape.
Died 30 Nov. 1920.

TURQUAN, Joseph; homme de lettres; appartient à une vieille famille parisienne, originaire du Poitou, anoblie en 1413 par le roi Charles VI; noblesse confirmée en 1777; *m* 1883, Marie de la Motte de la Motte-Rouge, *nièce* du général de ce nom qui s'illustra dans la guerre de Crimée (1854–55) et celle d'Italie (1859). Paralysé des deux jambes depuis 1885; s'est adonné à la littérature. *Publications:* L'Impératrice Joséphine; Les sœurs de Napoléon; La reine Hortense; La citoyenne Tallien; La duchesse d'Abrantès; La duchesse d'Angoulême; Les femmes de l'Emigration; Madame Récamier; Le roi Jérôme; Napoléon amoureux; Le monde et le demi-monde sous Napoléon; Lady Hamilton; La belle Paméla (Lady Edward Fitz-Gerald); Madame de Stäel, etc. *Recreations:* ne quitte jamais sa chaise longue. *Address:* Rue Mignet 1, Paris (16e). *Died Sept. 1928.*

TUSON, Sir Henry Brasnell, KCB 1895 (CB 1882); *b* 30 April 1836; *m* 1864, Ann Frances, *d* of the late Major J. Bates, 40th Madras NI; one *s* three *d. Educ:* Christ's Hospital; King's College, London. Entered army, 1854; Lieut-Gen. 1893; General, 1899; served China, 1858–60 (despatches, medal with 2 clasps); Egyptian Campaign, 1882 (despatches twice, 2 clasps, 3rd class Osmanieh, 3rd class Medjidie); Soudan Campaign, 1884; holds 1st class Saxe-Ernestine Order. *Address:* 16 Walpole Road, Surbiton, Surrey. *T:* 315 PO Kingston.
Died 21 Dec. 1916.

TUTTIETT, Mary Gleed; *see* Gray, Maxwell.

TUTTLE, Rt. Rev. Daniel Sylvester, STD, LLD; Bishop of Missouri since 1886; Presiding Bishop of the Protestant Episcopal Church, USA, since 1903; *b* Windham, NY, 1837; *m* 1865; three *s* one *d. Educ:* Columbia University; General Theological Seminary, New York City. Deacon, 1862; Priest, 1863; Missionary Bishop of Montana, Utah, and Idaho, 1867. *Publication:* Reminiscences of a Missionary Bishop, 1905. *Address:* St Louis, Missouri, USA.
Died 17 April 1923.

TWEEDIE, Colonel John Lannoy, DSO 1886; *b* 6 May 1842; 5th *s* of late Capt. M. Tweedie of Quarter, Peeblesshire, and Frances, *d* of late R. W. Forbes of Rawlinson, Kent; *m* 1891, Emma Constance, 3rd *d* of late W. G. Murray of Avonmore, Ballybrack, Co. Dublin; two *d. Educ:* privately. Served in Royal West Kent Regt (97th and 50th); joined the 97th Regt, 1860; Transvaal Campaign; served with the Natal Field Force; Soudan Expedition 1884–85 (Nile medal with clasp, bronze star); Soudan Field Force; action at Giniss (despatches, DSO). *Recreations:* shooting, riding, skating, etc. *Address:* Calder, Dorchester, Dorset. *Died 28 Aug. 1920.*

TWEEDIE, Hon. Lemuel John, KC; LLD; *b* Chatham, NB, 30 Nov. 1849; descended from the Tweedies of Drummelzier, Peeblesshire, Scotland; *m d* of the late Alexander Loudoun of Chatham; four *s* two *d. Educ:* At a Presbyterian College. Admitted to the Bar of NB, 1871; elected to the House of Assembly of NB for Northumberland, 1874, and has represented that County ever since, except 1878–1882; Surveyor-General, 1890; Provincial Secretary, 1896; Premier, 1900–7; represented New Brunswick at the King's Coronation in 1901–2; Lieutenant-Governor of New Brunswick, 1907–12; holds long service medal in Militia of Canada. *Recreations:* yachting, shooting, fishing, curling. *Address:* Elmhurst, Chatham, New Brunswick, Canada. *Club:* Union, St John. *Died Sept. 1917.*

TWEEDIE, Maj.-Gen. Michael, FRGS (retired); *b* 1836; *s* of Capt. M. Tweedie, RA, of Rawlinson, Rolvenden, Kent; *m* 1872, Louisa

Bateson Hammond. *Educ:* Royal Military College, Woolwich. Crimea; siege of Sebastopol; battle of Tchernaya, 1855–56; Indian Mutiny, 1858; mutiny at Mooltan; served in India, Ceylon, Canada, Australia, Mediterranean, etc. *Recreations:* riding, boating, shooting, etc. *Address:* Boveney, Folkestone. *Club:* Army and Navy.
Died 8 Aug. 1917.

TWEEDY, Sir John, Kt 1906; Past President of the Royal College of Surgeons, the Ophthalmological Society of the United Kingdom, The Medico-Legal Society, the Medical Defence Union and Royal Medical Benevolent Fund; a Trustee of the Hunterian Collection, Royal College of Surgeons; Member of Council and formerly of the Distribution Committee of King Edward's Hospital Fund; Emeritus Professor of Ophthalmic Medicine and Surgery in University College London; Consulting Ophthalmic Surgeon to University College Hospital; Consulting Surgeon to the Royal London Ophthalmic Hospital (Moorfields); LLD Edinburgh; *b* Stockton-on-Tees, 1849; *m* 1885, Mary *y d* of Richard Hilhouse, Finsbury Place; two *s* one *d. Educ:* Elmfield College, York; University College, London. *Publications:* various articles and papers on ophthalmological subjects, medical history, education, and politics; Hunterian Oration, Royal College of Surgeons, 1905; The Thomas Vicary Lecture on the History of Anatomy and Surgery, Royal College of Surgeons, 1919; The Annual Oration Medical Society of London, 1919, etc. *Address:* 100 Harley Street, W1. *T:* Mayfair 4036. *Club:* Reform.
Died 4 Jan. 1924.

TWEMLOW, Colonel Francis Randle, DSO 1900; commanded 4th Battalion North Staffs Regiment; retired, 1908; *b* 20 Dec. 1852; *m* 1st, 1878, Evelyn Harriet (*d* 1880), *d* of Sir John Thomas Buller Duckworth, 2nd Bt; 2nd, 1882, Annie Mary Gertrude, *o c* of Rev. Edward Lewis; one *d. Educ:* Winchester; Christ Church, Oxford. MA (first-class honours in Modern History), 1875; Barrister of Inner Temple, 1879; served South Africa, 1900–2. *Address:* Peatswood, Market Drayton. *Club:* United University.
Died 21 Jan. 1927.

TWIGG, John James, KC; *b* 1825; *s* of late Rev. Thomas Twigg, MA, Rector of the parish of Pomeroy, Co. Tyrone, and Sarah Macausland of Streeve, Co. Londonderry; *m* 1868, Eliza, *d* of late James Corry Lowry, QC, of Rockdale, Co. Tyrone. *Educ:* Armagh Royal School; Trinity College, Dublin. Called to the Bar, 1851; Inner Bar, 1877; QC 1877; Bencher of King's Inns, 1889. *Club:* University, Dublin.
Died June 1920.

TWINING, Maj.-Gen. Sir Philip Geoffrey, KCMG 1919 (CMG 1915); CB 1918; MVO 1911; late RE; Director of Fortifications and Works, War Office; *b* Halifax, Nova Scotia, 7 Sept. 1862; *s* of late Edmund Crawley Twining, *s* of Chas Twining, QC, barrister-at-law, of Halifax, NS, and Elizabeth Lee Whitman, *d* of John Whitman of Annapolis, Nova Scotia; *m* 1897, Louise Mary, *d* of George and Mary Daly of Napanee, Ontario. *Educ:* Kingston, Canada. Gazetted Lt Royal Engineers, 1886; served in England, Canada, East Africa, India, and China; Regimental Employment, Staff and Special Service; Col, 1915; Maj.-Gen. 1 Jan. 1917; served European War, 1914–18 (despatches seven times, CMG, CB, Order of St Stanislaus). *Publications:* contributions to reviews and periodicals upon military and general subjects. *Recreations:* travel, riding, golf. *Clubs:* Ranelagh; United Service, Simla. *Died 15 Jan. 1920.*

TWISADAY, Major C. E. J., ISO; VD 1892; *b* 9 May 1850; *s* of Rev. J. Twisaday; *m* 1886, Jose E. S., *d* of late General Sir A. J. Cloete, KCB; one *s. Educ:* Lewes Grammar School; private tuition. Indo-European Telegraph Dept; India Office, 1869–1915; accompanied Director-in-Chief to India, Persian Gulf, Persia, and Constantinople; 30 years commissioned service in Queen's Westminster RV; retired as Major. *Publications:* joint-author of official translations of three International Telegraph Conventions. *Recreations:* shooting, golf, woodcarving, clockmaking, etc. *Address:* Chichester House, Upper Westbourne Terrace, W2. *T:* Paddington 2924. *Clubs:* St Stephen's, Neasden Golf. *Died 6 Feb. 1925.*

TWISS, Lt-Col George Edward, CMG 1917; RAMC; MD, MK, and QCPI, FRCSI; Hon. Sec. Southampton Centre St John Ambulance Association; member chapter General Order of St John and Ambulance Committee; *b* Dublin, 5 Nov. 1856; *s* of John Twiss and Ann Willis; *m* 1912, Ethel Madeline Sprague; no *c. Educ:* Columbia University, New York (MD). Graduated 1876; Demonstrator of Anatomy, RCSI, 1878–79; Civil Surgeon Zulu War, 1879–80; Surgeon AMD, 1881; Lt-Col RAMC, 1901; retired, 1907; re-employed 5 Aug. 1914; relegated to retired pay 8 June, 1919. Knight of Grace, Order of St John of Jerusalem, 1908; medals: Zulu with clasp, Egyptian and Khedive's Star, Queen's medal with 3 clasps, King's medal with 2 clasps, despatches twice; European War, 1914–19 (despatches, CMG; GS medal); St John Ambulance Bde Coronation medal. *Publication:* Manual for Voluntary Aid Detachments. *Recreations:* masonry, work. *Address:* Mayfield, Oakley Road, Southampton. *Club:* Royal Southampton Yacht.

Died 27 June 1921.

TWISS, Vice-Admiral Guy Ouchterlony; *b* 19 Oct. 1834; *m* 1880; three *s* two *d. Educ:* Launceston, VD Laud. Joined the Navy as Cadet, 1848; served in the Channel, West Indies, China; as Lieut present at capture of Taku Forts in HMS Pique; served in Excellent and in Royal Oak in Mediterranean; as Commander in Warrior and in Eagle, drill ship RNR; Serapis 3 years, and in Belleisle at Kingstown. *Address:* Lindfield, Hayward's Heath.

Died 7 Oct. 1918.

TWYFORD, Thomas William, JP, DL; *b* 1849; *e s* of Thomas Twyford (*d* 1872), of Shelton, Staffordshire, and Sarah (*d* 1874), *d* of late Robert Jones, of Bordeaux; *m* 1872, Susannah, *d* of Edward Whittingham; one *s* one *d.* High Sheriff, Staffordshire, 1906; has the Order of St Ann of Russia; Conservative Candidate for NW Staffordshire, 1907; Chairman, Twyfords, Ltd, Hanly, Staffordshire Sentinel Newspaper, and North-Western Electricity and Power Gas Co. *Address:* Whitmore Hall, Newcastle, Staffordshire. *Clubs:* Carlton, Junior Carlton. *Died 21 March 1921.*

TWYNAM, Col Philip Alexander Anstruther, CB 1882; *b* Ceylon, 5 May 1832; 5th *s* of late Thomas Holloway Twynam, RN, and Mary, *d* of late Major Somerville, 83rd Regt; *m* 1862, Elizabeth Annie, *e d* of late Captain Horrocks Whitehead, HEICS. *Educ:* private school. Joined 15th East Yorks Regt, 1851; Captain, 1858; Major, 1868; Lieut-Col, 1876; Col, 1881; retired on age clause, 1890. Commanded 15th Regt, 1876–81; passed Staff Coll. 1859; Brig.-Maj. Aldershot, 1860; DAQMG Aldershot, 1861–66; and DAQMG Ireland, 1869; AAG and AQMG Egypt, 1882 (medal and clasp, despatches, CB, 3rd class Osmanieh); commanded 15th Regimental District, 1883–84; AAG and Chief Staff Officer S District, 1884–89. *Address:* 55 Elsham Road, Kensington, W. *Club:* Army and Navy.

Died 27 Dec. 1920.

TWYNAM, Sir William Crofton, KCMG 1896 (CMG 1884); *m* Elizabeth (*d* 1897). Entered Government Service, Ceylon, 1845; Asst Agent, Jaffa, 1848; Hanbantota, 1854; Manaar, 1858; NW Provinces, 1868; Government Agent, Northern Province, Ceylon, 1869–95; retired 1896. *Address:* Jaffna, Ceylon.

Died 14 March 1922.

TYLER, Maj.-Gen. Trevor Bruce, CB 1917; CSI 1903; DL; JP Co Glamorgan; Colonel Commandant RA; *b* 7 Jan. 1841; *s* of Rev. Roper Trevor Tyler, of Llantrithyd, Glamorgan; *m* 1873, Ada, *d* of Edward Perkins, Birtley Hall, Durham; one *d. Educ:* RMA Woolwich. Entered army, 1859; served Fenian Raid, Canada, 1866 (medal and clasp); commanded B Battery, RHA, 1881–86; Commandant Okehampton Camp, 1891–93; Colonel on the Staff, Poona, 1893–95; Brigadier-Gen. RA Punjab, 1895–97; Maj.-Gen. 1900; Inspector-General of Artillery, India, 1897–1903; retired, 1903; Chairman Glamorgan County Terr. Association. *Address:* Llantrithyd, Glamorgan. *TA:* Bouvilston. *Club:* Naval and Military.

Died 12 Feb. 1923.

TYLOR, Sir Edward Burnett, Kt 1912; JP; DCL, LLD; FRS; Hon. Fellow of Balliol College; Emeritus Professor of Anthropology, University of Oxford; *b* London, 2 Oct. 1832; *m* 1858, Anna, *d* of late Sylvanus Fox, Willington, Somerset. *Educ:* Grove House School, Tottenham. Author and anthropologist; Keeper, University Museum, Oxford, 1883; Reader in Anthropology, 1884; first Professor of Anthropology, 1896–1909. *Publications:* Anahuac, Mexico and the Mexicans, 1859; Researches into the Early History of Mankind, 1865; Primitive Culture, 1871; Anthropology, 1881. *Address:* Linden, Wellington, Somerset. *Club:* Athenæum.

Died 2 Jan. 1917.

TYMMS, Rev. T. Vincent, DD; *b* London, 1842; *s* of Ebenezer Tymms; *m* 1st, 1869, Agnes, *d* of Ralph Dodds of Berwick-on-Tweed; 2nd, 1888, Louisa I., *d* of James Doré of Clapton; three *s* three *d. Educ:* private school and Regent's Park College, London. Became pastor of the Baptist Church at Berwick-on-Tweed, 1865; removed to Accrington, 1868; first minister of the Downs Chapel, Clapton, London, 1869–91; President, and Professor of Theology, Baptist College, Rawdon, Leeds, 1891–1904; President of the London Baptist Association, 1881, and while in that office built Woodberry Down

Chapel, London, N; Vice-President of the Baptist Union of Great Britain, 1895; President, 1896; DD St Andrews, 1897; Angus Lecturer Regent's Park College, 1903. *Publications:* The Mystery of God, 5th edition; The Christian Idea of Atonement, 1904; The Private Relationships of Christ, 1907; The Evolution of Infant Baptism and Related Ideas, 1912; wrote the first essay in The Ancient Faith in Modern Light. *Recreations:* cricket in earlier years, later golf. *Address:* 82 Marina, St Leonards-on-Sea.

Died 25 May 1921.

TYNDALL, Lt-Col William Ernest Marriott, DSO 1900; West Riding Regiment; DAAG, Western Command; *b* 2 Feb. 1875; *m* 1908, Alice Lorna, *d* of late Mr Sedgwick, Byfleet, Surrey. Entered army, 1895. Served South Africa, 1899–1902 (despatches thrice, Queen's medal, 4 clasps, King's medal, 2 clasps, DSO); European War, 1914–15 (wounded). *Address:* 17 Castellain Road, Maida Vale, W; Chester. *Died 1 Aug. 1916.*

TYRRELL, Lt-Col Gerald Ernest, DSO 1915; Royal Garrison Artillery; *b* 31 Oct. 1871. Entered army, 1892; Captain, 1900; Major, 1912; with Macedonian Gendarmerie, 1907–9; Military Attaché, Constantinople and Athens, 1909–13; served NW Frontier, India, 1897–8 (medal, 3 clasps); European War, 1914–15 (despatches twice, DSO, Bt Lt-Col). *Died 17 May 1917.*

TYRWHITT, Rev. Hon. Leonard Francis, OBE 1919; MVO 1906; Rector of Rolleston, Burton-on-Trent, since 1907; Canon of St George's Chapel, Windsor, since 1910; chaplain-in-ordinary to the King; *b* 29 Oct. 1863; *s* of Sir Henry Tyrwhitt, 3rd Bt, and Baroness Berners. *Educ:* Marlborough Coll.; Magdalene College, Cambridge (MA); Wells Theological Coll. Curate at Henley-on-Thames, 4½ years; Hendon, Middlesex, 2½ years; Chaplain to HMS Renown for tour of TRH's the Prince and Princess of Wales to India, 1905–6; Vicar of Fenton, 1895–1907; Vice-Provost of Denstone since 1906; Acting-Chaplain to the Forces since 1914 (wounded, despatches); Deputy Assistant Chaplain-General, 1918. *Address:* Rolleston Rectory, Burton-on-Trent; The Cloisters, Windsor Castle. *Club:* Wellington.

Died 7 July 1921.

TYSER, Sir Charles Robert, Kt 1909; *b* 24 Dec. 1848; 4th *s* of George Dorman Tyser; *m* 1893, Lilian Adelaide, *d* of Rev. Charles John Kennard Shaw. *Educ:* Rugby; Trinity College, Cambridge. Called to Bar, Inner Temple, 1873; Attorney-General Leewards, 1886–89; President, District Court, Kyrenia, Cyprus, 1895; Puisne Judge, Cyprus, 1902; Chief Justice Cyprus, 1906–19. *Publications:* Marine Insurance Losses, 1894; translated Omar Hilmi Effendi's Evkaf Law, 1899, and the Mejelle, 1901. *Club:* United University.

Died 23 Aug. 1926.

TYSON, William Joseph, MD, FRCP Lond.; FRCS Eng.; JP Kent; Chairman of the Elham Division; Hon. Physician, Royal Victoria Hospital, Folkestone; *b* 9 Sept. 1851; *s* of W. Taylor Tyson, MRCS; *m* Lola Houssemayne, *d* of Julius Houssemayne du Boulay, of West Lawn, Sandgate; three *d. Educ:* Guy's Hospital. Fellow of the Royal Society of Medicine, etc; practised as a Physician; Member of the Church Assembly of the Church of England. *Publications:* several contributions to medical literature, addresses, etc. *Address:* Kimberley, Jointon Road, Folkestone. *T:* 361. *M:* KL 3105.

Died 5 Sept. 1927.

TYTLER, Maj.-Gen. Robert Francis Christopher Alexander, Indian Army. Major-General, 1895; served Afghan War, 1878–80 (despatches, medal with clasp, Brevet Lt-Colonel). *Address:* 62 Bedford Gardens, Campden Hill, W.

Died 19 Oct. 1916.

U

UDNY, Sir Richard, KCSI 1897 (CSI 1894); *b* 1847; *s* of George Udny, Bengal Civil Service; *m* 1st, 1883, Alicia (*d* 1904), *d* of Samuel Tomkins, banker, London; 2nd, 1917, Edith Phyllis, 4th *d* of late William Davies, Liverpool, and of Mrs Davies, Prestatyn; one *d. Educ:* Aberdeen Univ. MA 1866; 1st class Honours Mathematics; 2nd class Classics; Fullerton Mathematical Scholar, 1867; Hon. LLD 1898. Entered Bengal Civil Service, 1869, retired 1899; served as a political officer with following frontier expeditions, viz.: Jowaki, 1877–78; Mahsud Waziri, 1881; Samana (Miranzai), 1891 (medal and two clasps); and Isazai (Black Mountain), 1892; also as chief of the political staff with the Tirah Expedition against the Afridis and Orakzais, 1897–98 (medal and two clasps); was appointed on a special mission to the Kurram Valley, 1888; Commissioner of the Peshawar Division, 1891; Commissioner for Delimitation of parts of the Indo-Afghan Boundary, 1894–95 and 1896–97. *Address:* 5 Clarendon Road, St Helier, Jersey. *Died 24 April 1923.*

UHTHOFF, John Caldwell, MD, FRCS; *b* 1856; *s* of Edward Uhthoff; *m* 1st, 1884, Ellen Aston, *d* of late Charles King, formerly of North Lodge, Enfield; one *s* three *d*; 2nd, 1913, Ida, *d* of late Francis Goode Cuningham, of Bentley House, Hants. *Educ:* Brighton College; Guy's Hospital. Knight of Grace St John of Jerusalem. *Recreations:* golf, travel. *Address:* 7 Branksome Wood Road, Bournemouth. *T:* 2747. *Club:* Bournemouth.
Died 19 Jan. 1927.

UMFREVILLE, Colonel Percy, CMG 1915; CBE 1919; Royal West Kent Regiment; *b* 29 Feb. 1868; *s* of late S. C. Umfreville, Ingress Abbey, Greenhithe, Kent; *m* Edith Margaret, *d* of late J. B. Tracey, ICS; one *d*. Entered army, 1887; Bt Lieut-Colonel, 1917; Lt-Col, 1919; Col, 1920; Adjutant, 1894–7; Captain, 1896; Major, 1905; Adjutant Volunteers, 1897–1902; Governor Military Prison, 1902–12; Commandant Detention Barracks, 1912–14; Governor Military Prisons in Field, France, 1914–16; Director Military Prisons in Field, British Army in France, Aug. 1916–Oct. 1919; Temp. Brig.-Gen. Aug. 1916–Oct. 1919; Half Pay, Oct. 1919–March 1920; Assistant Adjutant General Scottish Command, March 1920; served European War, 1914–19 (CMG, Bt Lt-Col). *Died 11 July 1922.*

UMNEY, John Charles; a Managing Director of Wright, Layman, and Umney, Ltd, wholesale druggists, Southwark; Joint-Managing Director of W. Woodward, Ltd, Nottingham and London; Managing Director of Thomas Wilkinson, Ltd, London; Director of R. Carter & Sons, Ltd, London; *b* London, 1868; 2nd *s* of late Charles Umney, FIC, FCS; *m* Constance, *d* of late John Sloane Carter; one *s* one *d*. *Educ:* Dulwich College (Scholar); Pharmaceutical Society's School (bronze and silver medallist). Member of the Pharmaceutical Society; Past President British Pharmaceutical Conference; Past President of the Wholesale Druggists' Club; Ex-Chairman of the Chemical Trades Section of the London Chamber of Commerce, also of the Proprietary Articles Section of the London Chamber of Commerce, also Toilet Soap Trades Section; Past Pres. of Proprietary Articles Trade Association; a Member of the Council of the Advertisers' Protection Society; Member of the Pharmaceutical Committee of Reference for the British Pharmacopoeia; Silver Medallist of the Royal Society of Arts; Fellow of the Chemical Society, of the Royal Botanical Society, the Royal Horticultural Society, and of the Society of Public Analysts; Juror at Franco-British and Imperial International Exhibitions, 1908–9; *Publications:* A Short Guide to the British Pharmacopoeia, 1898; Essential Oils in their relation to the British Pharmacopoeia and Trade; Standards for Medicines; Editor of Perfumery and Essential Oil Record; etc. *Address:* 27A Sloane Square, SW1. *T:* Victoria 2478; Berea Court, Yapton, Arundel, Sussex.
Died 9 Oct. 1919.

UNDERHILL, Admiral Edwin Veale, CB 1918; RN; *b* 27 March 1868; *m*; three *s*. Served Tokar, Eastern Sudan, 1891 (Bronze Star); present at bombardment of Sultan of Zanzibar Palace, 1896; served in Punitive Naval Expedition against King of Benin, 1897 (medal and clasp); European War, 1914–18 (CB); Admiral Superintendent, HM Dockyard, Devonport, 1919–22; retired list, 1924. *Address:* Bellair House, Havant, Hants. *M:* PT 3251.
Died 22 July 1928.

UNDERWOOD, Arthur Swayne, LDS, MRCS; late Professor of Dental Surgery, King's College, London, Dental Surgeon, King's College Hospital, and Examiner in Dental Surgery, Royal College of Surgeons, 1900–10; Inspector of Dental Examinations in the United Kingdom on behalf of the General Medical Council, 1911; Hon. Dental Surgeon to King George Hospital for wounded; Tomes prize for research, Royal College of Surgeons, 1906–8. *Educ:* King's College, London. *Publications:* Surgery for Dental Students, 1881; Aids to Dental Surgery, 1906 (2nd edn); Notes on Anæsthetics, 1893; Aids to Dental Anatomy and Physiology, 1914 (3rd edn); Studies in Comparative Odontology, 1903. *Address:* 38 Harley Street, W. *T:* Mayfair 6848. *Died 2 Dec. 1916.*

UNWIN, Francis Sydney; *b* Stalbridge, Dorset, 11 Feb. 1885; *s* of Rev. C. E. Unwin; *m* 1917, Clara Miyadera, *d* of R. S. Schwabe,

pianist, of Yokohama. *Educ:* DCMS Cheltenham; Slade School, London; Paris; Italy. Draughtsman, etcher, lithographer, painter; Member New English Art Club, 1912; work in National Gallery of British Art, Millbank, Print Room, British Museum, New York Public Library and Metropolitan Museum; Sydney National Gallery, etc. *Publications:* Decorative Arts of the Church; critical articles; Maloja, Portfolio of Etchings, 1921. *Recreation:* travelling. *Address:* 61 High Street, Hampstead, NW3. *Died 26 Nov. 1925.*

UNWIN, Colonel Garton Bouverie, DSO 1908; Indian Army; late 21st Cavalry; *b* 9 July 1859; *m* 1898, Katharine, *e d* of Sir Arthur Fanshawe, KCIE; two *d*. *Educ:* Wellington. Entered Army, Somerset Light Infantry, 1878; Captain, 1889; Major, 1898; Lieut-Col, 1904; Bt-Col, 1907; served Zhob Valley expedition, 1890; Waziristan, 1894–5 (medal with clasp); NW Frontier, 1897–98 (medal with clasp); Waziristan, 1901–2 (clasp); Mohmund expedition, 1908 (medal with clasp, DSO); European War, Remount Dept, and QMG's Dept. *Address:* Pin Close, Budleigh Salterton, Devon.
Died 4 July 1928.

UPCHER, Henry Morris, JP, DL; BOU; *b* 15 Dec. 1839; *e s* of late Henry Ramey Upcher and Caroline, *d* of Joseph Morris of Ampthill; *m* 1869, Maria Hester, *o c* of Rev. Edward Bowyer Sparke, of Feltwell, Norfolk; two *s* two *d*. *Educ:* Harrow; Trinity College, Cambridge. *Address:* Sheringham Hall, Norfolk; East Hall, Feltwell, Norfolk. *Club:* Conservative. *Died 6 April 1921.*

UPCOTT, Ven. Arthur William, DD Oxon; Rector of Brightling and Archdeacon of Hastings since 1920; *b* Manor House, Cullompton, Devon, 6 Jan. 1857; 4th *s* of John Samuel Upcott, of Manor House, Cullompton; *m* 1888, Sophia Madeline, 3rd *d* of late Charles Anderson Dalgairns, MD, FRCS; one *s* one *d*. *Educ:* Sherborne School; Exeter Coll., Oxford. Scholar, 1875; Goldsmiths' Exhibitioner, 1877; 1st class Class. Mods, 1876; 2nd class Lit. Hum., 1879; BA, 1879; MA, 1882; BD and DD 1906; Deacon, 1884, Priest, 1886; Assistant Master, St Mark's School, Windsor, 1880–82, 1884–86; Head Master, 1886–91; Assistant Master, Westminster School, 1882–84; Head Master, St Edmund's School, Canterbury, 1891–1902; Head Master, Christ's Hospital, 1902–19. *Publications:* Caesar, De Bello Gallico, Book iv; Euripides, Hecuba. *Address:* The Rectory, Brightling, Sussex.
Died 22 May 1922.

UPCOTT, Sir Frederick Robert, KCVO 1906; CSI 1900; MICE; *b* 28 Aug. 1847; 2nd *s* of J. S. Upcott, Cullompton, Devon; *m* 1878, Jessie, *d* of late Harold Turner; one *s*. *Educ:* Sherborne School; King's College, London. Appointed by examination to the Public Works Dept India, 1868; was engaged on the construction of Indian railways; appointed consulting engineer to Madras Government for railways, 1892; Director-General of Railways in India, 1896; Secretary in the Public Works, India, 1898–1901; Govt Director of Indian Railways, 1901–4; Chairman Board of Indian Railways, 1904–8. Decorated for services in the Railway Department of India. *Recreation:* a Lieut-Colonel in the Indian volunteer forces. *Address:* c/o Cocks, Biddulph, Bankers, Charing Cross, SW1. *Died 15 Oct. 1918.*

UPPERTON, Maj.-Gen. John, CB 1882; ISC; *b* 10 June 1838; *s* of late Robert Upperton, of Westburton, Sussex. Entered Bengal army, 1854; Maj.-Gen. 1894; served Indian Mutiny, 1857–59 (medal with clasp); China, 1860 (thanked by Commander-in-Chief of French forces, medal with two clasps); NW Frontier of India (medal with clasp); in 1869 accompanied the Ameer Sher Ali, of Cabul, to Umballa, on the occasion of his visit to the Viceroy (thanked by Government); appointed to political charge of the Envoy, from the Ameer of Kabul, to India, 1873; specially employed in a mission to Beluchistan, 1876; Egyptian War, 1882 (despatches, CB, 3rd class Medjidie, Khedive's star). *Address:* 7 Sloane Street, SW1. *T:* Kensington 1110. *Club:* Naval and Military.
Died 2 July 1924.

UPTON, Prof. Charles B.; Professor of Philosophy in Manchester College, Oxford, 1875, later Professor Emeritus; *b* Portsea, Hampshire, 19 Nov. 1831; *m* 1863. *Educ:* Dr J. R. Beard's School at Higher Broughton, Manchester; Manchester New College; University College, London. Graduated in the University of London; BA, 1857; BSc, 1862. Minister of Toxteth Park Chapel, Liverpool, 1867–75. *Publications:* many philosophical articles in various Reviews; delivered the Hibbert Lectures on the Bases of Religious Belief, 1893, published 1894; author of the philosophical portion of the Life and Letters of Dr James Martineau, later published separately as Dr Martineau's Philosophy. *Recreation:* cultivation of fruit-trees. *Address:* St George's, Littlemore, near Oxford.
Died 21 Nov. 1920.

UPTON, Florence; Associate Société Nationale des Beaux Arts, Paris; portrait painter; *b* New York, of English parents, Thomas Harborough Upton and Bertha, *d* of John W. Hudson, architect. *Educ:* New York and Paris; Art Education—New York, Paris, and Holland. Exhibitor at Salon, Royal Academy, Continental and American Exhibitions; Médaille d'honneur Inter. Exp. Nantes, 1905. *Publications:* The Golliwogg Series; The Vegemen's Revenge; Borbee and the Wisp, etc. 1895–1909. *Address:* 21 Great College Street, Westminster, SW1. *T:* Victoria 2423. *Died 17 Oct. 1922.*

UPTON, Rev. William Clement, Prebendary of Lincoln. *Address:* 4 Queensway, Lincoln. *Died 6 Aug. 1922.*

UPWARD, Allen; Barrister-at-law; *b* Worcester, 1863; *s* of George Upward, JP; unmarried. *Educ:* Great Yarmouth Grammar School; Royal University of Ireland. Brook Scholarship; O'Hagan Gold Medal for Oratory; Silver Medal, Dublin; Inns of Court Studentship; two 1st class Scholarships, Middle Temple; Corr. Member Parnassos Philolog. Soc. Athens; Hon. Bard National Gorsedd (Maenhir); FRAI. Barrister, Ireland, 1887; Barrister, England, 1889; South Wales Circuit; contested Merthyr-Tydvil, 1895; fought as volunteer in Greco-Turkish War, 1897; British Resident, Northern Nigeria, 1901; Mission to Macedonia, 1907–8; volunteered as Scoutmaster at the Front, thanked by General Commanding, 1914; Head Master of Inverness College, 1916. *Publications:* Secrets of the Courts of Europe, and International Spy (AV) series in Pearson's Magazine, 1895–1905; A Flash in the Pan (play), 1896; A Day's Tragedy, 1897; Treason, 1903; The New Word (Geneva), 1907; The East End of Europe, 1908; Secrets of the Past, 1909; The Divine Mystery, 1913; Some Personalities, 1921; and numerous romances, etc. *Recreation:* bridge. *Address:* c/o A. Wallace, 162 Bath Street, Glasgow. *Club:* Royal Societies. *Died 12 Nov. 1926.*

URMSON, Rev. Thomas; Hon. Canon of Durham; Rector of Willington, Co. Durham, 1890–1920; Special Service Clergy, Chester, 1921. *Educ:* Trinity College, Cambridge, MA. *Address:* Riverside, Boughton, Chester. *Clubs:* Grosvenor, Chester; Durham County. *Died 28 Sept. 1926.*

URMSTON, Colonel Edward Brabazon, CB 1902; JP Co. Argyll; *b* 13 Feb. 1858; *m* 1903, Christina Beatrice, *d* of late Rev. A. Burn-Murdoch. Entered army, 1878; Capt. 1886; Major, 1896; served South Africa, 1899–1902 (despatches twice, Queen's medal, 4 clasps, King's medal, 2 clasps, brevet Lieut-Colonel, CB); late 1st Battalion Argyll and Sutherland Highlanders; Commanding Highland District, 1908–12; retired 1914. *Address:* Glenmorven, Argyllshire. *Died 6 Dec. 1920.*

URQUHART, Colonel Robert, MVO 1905; DL; VD; 6th Battalion Seaforth Highlanders (retired); Town Clerk of Forres, Morayshire; *b* 10 Dec. 1845; *s* of Alexander Urquhart, Banker, Forres, and Margaret Milne; *m* 1874, Finella Hoyes, *d* of Andrew Smith, Cluny, Forres; no *c. Educ:* Forres Academy; Edinburgh University. Served forty-six years in the Regiment. *Address:* Cluny, Forres, Morayshire. *TA:* Urquhart, Cluny, Forres. *T:* Forres 6. *Died 24 Nov. 1922.*

USHER, James Ward; art jeweller and silversmith; *b* Lincoln; *s* of James Usher; unmarried. *Educ:* Lincoln Grammar School; Totteridge Park, Herts. Has been engaged in the jewellery and plate business during the greater part of his life; a connoisseur of works of art; has formed private collection of miniatures, antique gold watches (generally admitted to be the finest known), old English silver, china, and Battersea enamels, all from famous collections dispersed during the above term at Christie's Rooms, of which he has been a constant habitué; Sheriff of the City of Lincoln, 1916–17. *Publications:* Objects of Art, forming the private collection of James Ward Usher of Lincoln; An Art-Collector's Treasures, illustrated and described by himself, in water colour. *Recreations:* water-colour painting, motoring. *Address:* Lincoln. *M:* FE 738. *Died 20 Sept. 1921.*

UTTING, Sir John, Kt 1924; JP; DL Lancashire; Lord Mayor of Liverpool, 1917–18; Alderman; *b* Rackheath, Norfolk; *s* of H. A. Utting; *m* twice; two *s* one *d. Educ:* King Edward VI School, Norwich; Guy's Hospital. General medical practitioner in Liverpool for fifty years; Major, RAMC (T); eighteen years Chairman of the Port Sanitary and Hospitals Committee of Liverpool; President of School of Hygiene, Liverpool; Chairman of Finance Committee, Liverpool, for six years. *Recreations:* shooting, fishing. *Address:* St Anne's Hill, Anfield, Liverpool. *TA:* Anfield 70, Liverpool. *T:* Anfield 70. *M:* KB 254 and KB 177. *Clubs:* Conservative, University, Liverpool. *Died 17 Feb. 1927.*

V

VAIZEY, Mrs G. de Horne. *Publications:* About Peggy Saville; More about Peggy; Pixie O'Shaughnessy; More about Pixie; The Love Affairs of Pixie; The Fortunes of the Farrells; A Houseful of Girls; The Independence of Claire; Betty Trevor; Big Game; A College Girl; The Lady of the Basement Flat. *Address:* 4 Bouverie Street, EC4. *Died 23 Jan. 1927.*

VALENTIA, *(de jure)* 11th Viscount, *cr* 1621; **Arthur Annesley,** KCVO 1923 (MVO 1901); CB 1900; JP; Bt 1620; Baron Mountnorris (Ire), 1628; Baron Annesley (UK), 1917; Premier Baronet of Ireland; *b* 23 Aug. 1843; *e s* of Hon. Arthur Annesley and Flora, *d* of Lieut-Col James Macdonald; *S* grandfather, 1863; *m* 1878, Laura Sarah, *y d* of Daniel Hale Webb, Wykham Park, Oxfordshire, and *widow* of Sir Algernon William Peyton, 4th Bt; two *s* (elder killed in action, 16 Nov. 1914) six *d. Educ:* Royal Mil. Academy, Woolwich. Entered 10th Hussars, 1864; Lieut, 1868; served with Yeomanry Cavalry, AAG, South Africa (despatches); MP (C) Oxford since 1895; Comptroller of HM Household, 1898–1905; Lieut 10th Hussars, retired 1872; formerly a Lord-in-Waiting to HM. Owned about 7,000 acres. *Heir: s* Hon. Caryl Arthur James Annesley, *b* 3 July 1883. *Recreations:* fox-hunting, Master of Fox-hounds, 1872–84; shooting, deer-stalking. *Address:* Bletchington Park, Oxford. *Clubs:* Carlton, Cavalry. *Died 20 Jan. 1927.*

VAN BUREN, Rt. Rev. James Heartt, DD; Bishop of Porto Rico, 1902–12; *b* 7 July 1850; *s* of James S. and Harriet A. Van Buren; one *s. Educ:* Yale University; Berkeley Divinity Schools. Deacon, 1876; Priest, 1877; Rector in St Peter's Church, Milford, Ct; Trinity Church, Seymour, Ct; St Paul's Church, Englewood, NJ; St Paul's Church, Newburyport, Mass; St Stephen's Church, Lynn, Mass; Archdeacon in Massachusetts; Examining Chaplain; went as a Missionary to Porto Rico, 1901. *Publications:* Short History of the Christian Church; Confirmation or the Laying on of Hands; Latin Hymns in English Verse; Himnario Provisional; Sermons That Have Helped; Sermon in Commemoration of King Edward VII; Pagans, a Missionary Play. *Address:* 9 Trumbull Street, New Haven, Conn. *Died 28 July 1917.*

VANDERBILT, William Kissam; *b* Staten Island, 12 Dec. 1849; *s* of William Henry Vanderbilt and Maria Louisa Kissam; *m* 1st, Alva Smith, Mobile, Ala.; 2nd, 1903, Mrs L. M. Rutherford. Director of many companies. *Address:* 660 Fifth Avenue, New York. *Died 22 July 1920.*

VAN DER VEER, John Conrad; London Editor of De Telegraaf Amsterdam, 1903–25; President of the Foreign Press Association in London; during the War Voluntary Secretary of the Foreigners Section of National Service; *b* Friesland, Holland, 5 Feb. 1869; *g s* of a Dutch medical man who died in America after being shipwrecked on accompanying as doctor a party of Dutch emigrants to New Orleans; *m*; no *c. Educ:* Sneek, Holland, at a public school, further self-educated. Worked as youth in a printing office; took leading part in the early Dutch labour movement as speaker, organiser, writer; edited some years a weekly paper at Middelburg; organised afterwards a Tolstoyan movement in Holland; corresponded with the late Count Leo Tolstoy; came to England in 1899; lived for a time with a Russian colony in Essex; settled two years later in London; studied the life of homeless people; was appointed in 1903 London correspondent of De Telegraaf; at the outbreak of the Great War openly took the side of the Allies in sympathy with their fight for justice and national freedom; gave over 150 voluntary lectures supporting Britain's cause, chiefly under auspices of Navy League; elected Life Vice-President, Navy League. *Recreations:* book collecting, reading, diligent writer. *Address:* 15 Rondu Road, Cricklewood, NW2. *T:* Hampstead 4663. *Club:* Savage. *Died 30 Aug. 1928.*

VAN DER VLUGT, W.; Emeritus Professor of the Philosophy and the Encyclopædia of Jurisprudence at Leyden University (Professor, 1880–1923); *b* 12 March 1853; *s* of Jan Van der Vlugt, banker at Haarlem, and J. H. M. Hinlópen; *m* 1882, Anna, *d* of late Dr L. W. E. Rauwenhoff, Professor of Theology at Leyden, and of F. F. Tobias; two *s* two *d. Educ:* Haarlem; Leyden Univ. Doctor utriusque iuris, 1879. Member of the 2nd Chamber of the States-General, 1902–06. *Publications:* De rechtstaat volgens de leer van Rudolf Gneist (Dissertation), 1879; various papers in the Dutch monthly De Gids, amongst others, in den stryd om het recht, 1889, and Toynbee werk, 1892; In memoriam Dr Abraham Kuenen in biographies of deceased members of the Maatschappy v. Letterkunde, 1890; idem Dr James

Martineau in Theologisch Tydschrift; article on De Geestelyke wetenschappen in Eene halve eeuw. Historisch gedenkboek, 1898; Transvaal versus Great Britain, 1899; Finland, de rechtsvraag (translated into French), and other papers on the same subject; Les vrais coupables: lettre à M. Tallichet, 1900. A series of papers on Crime and the Criminal; articles on Two Varieties of Parliamentary Government: The British Atmosphere and The British School of Political Self-discipline, besides several studies on Dutch politics in the Dutch monthly, Onze Eeuw, since 1901; a paper on the methods of the study of international law in Rechtsgeleerd Magazyn, 1913; a contribution to the American publication: The Church, The People, and the Age, 1914; a rectorial address on Two Dutch Masters of Jurisprudence (Huber and Noodt), delivered 8 Feb. 1916; two presidial addresses to meetings of the Dutch Lawyers Association, 1919–20; a study of Samuel von Pufendorf, in the farewell book, dedicated to Professor Greven; Papers read in the Royal Dutch Academy on the Codex iuris canonici and on Christian Thomasius; a study on La question des îles d'Aland, 1921; an answer to the Swedish Livre Bleu concerning the same matter, 1921; two papers on East Carelia in De Gids, 1923; a farewell address to the Leyden students of law, 1923; a selection of the author's principal works was published by his colleagues at the end of his active professorship, 1923; since then appeared *inter alia:* a necrology of late Mr C. Krantz, a remarkable captain of Leyden industry; a couple of papers in De Gids on the history of diplomacy between the end of the Middle Ages and Frederick the Great; an aperçu (in the same monthly) of Rüdolph Stammler's philosophy of law, a study of Dr D. S. Lohman and the law of nations (1926); lastly, an unfinished introductory volume to the text of his own lectures on the Encyclopædia of Jurisprudence, to be followed by a series of lectures on l'œuvre de Grotius et son influence sur le développement du droit des gens, in the publications of the Académie du droit des gens de La Haye (1925). *Address:* 28 Oegstgeest, Wilhelmina Park, Leyden. *T:* 941.

Died 5 Nov. 1928.

VAN DER WAALS, Prof. Johannes Diederik; Professor of Theoretical Physics, Amsterdam University; *b* 1837. Nobel Prize for Physics, 1910. *Address:* The University, Amsterdam.

Died 8 March 1923.

VAN DEVENTER, Hon. Lt-Gen. Sir Louis Jacob, KCB 1917 (CB 1917). Served S African War as second in command to Gen. Smuts, 1899–1902; Commander-in-Chief East Africa, 1917–19 (CB, KCB). *Address:* c/o High Commissioner for South Africa, 32 Victoria Street, SW. *Died 27 Aug. 1922.*

VAN DYCK, Ernest Marie Hubert; operatic tenor; Professor for Dramatic Art at the Conservatoires of Brussels and Antwerp; Officier Order of Leopold, Chevalier Légion d'Honneur, etc; *b* Antwerp, 2 April 1861; *m* 1886, Augusta, *d* of F. Servais. *Educ:* Jesuits' College, Antwerp; Universities of Louvain and Brussels. Originally journalist; sang at Bayreuth, 1886; Mem., Vienna Court Opera, 1888. *Address:* Chateau de Berulaer, near Antwerp, Belgium.

Died Sept. 1923.

VANE, Captain Hon. Henry Cecil; Captain Royal Field Artillery; *b* 19 Sept. 1882; *e s* and *heir* of 9th Baron Barnard; *m* 1914, Lady Enid Victoria Rachel Fane, *e d* of 13th Earl of Westmorland. *Educ:* Eton; Christ Church, Oxford. Late Major Yorkshire Hussars Yeo.; ADC to Governor of Madras, 1903–7. *Address:* Raby Castle, Darlington. *Clubs:* Marlborough; Yorkshire, York.

Died 9 Oct. 1917.

VANE, Hon. Ralph Frederick; *b* 8 June 1891; 3rd *s* of 9th Baron Barnard and Lady Catherine Sarah Cecil (*d* 1918), *d* of 3rd Marquess of Exeter; *m* 1917, Kathleen Airini, *o c* of late Capt. Gilbert Mair, NZC, formerly Judge of Native Land Court, Tauranga, NZ. *Educ:* Eton; Trinity College, Cambridge, BA. Formerly Captain Durham Light Infantry; served European War, 1914–18. *Clubs:* Travellers'; Devon and Exeter, Exeter. *Died 6 June 1928.*

VANE, Hon. William Lyonel, DL; *b* 30 Aug. 1859; 4th *s* of late Sir Henry Morgan Vane and Louisa, *y d* of Rev. Richard Farrer of Ashley, Northamptonshire; *brother* of 9th Baron Barnard; *m* 1904, Lady Katharine L. Pakenham, *d* of 4th Earl of Longford; one *s* two *d.* Late Major 1st Batt. Durham Light Infantry; Lt-Col and Hon. Col commanding 6th batt. Durham Light Infantry, 1903–11; Vice-Chairman Durham Territorial Force Association. *Address:* Haughton Hall, Darlington. *Club:* Carlton. *Died 23 Jan. 1920.*

VANE-TEMPEST, Lord (Herbert Lionel) Henry, KCVO 1911; *b* 6 July 1862; *s* of 5th Marquess of Londonderry, KP and Mary

Cornelia, *o d* of Sir John Edwards, 1st and last Bt. Late Major, 8th Vol. Brigade, N Division, RA. *Address:* Plas Machynlleth, Montgomeryshire. *Clubs:* Turf, Bachelors'.

Died 26 Jan. 1921.

VANOC; *see* White, Arnold.

VAN REETH, Rt. Rev. Joseph, SJ; Bishop of Galle since 1895; *b* Antwerp, 1843. *Educ:* Collège Notre Dame, Antwerp. Entered the Society of Jesus, 1860; Priest, 1875; Secretary of the Provincial Belgian Province, 1877–82; Provincial Belgian Province, 1882–88; Rector and Master of Novices at Tronchiennes, 1888–95. *Address:* Galle, Ceylon. *Died 11 Sept. 1923.*

VANSITTART, Spencer Charles Patrick, JP Co. Limerick; *b* 1860; *s* of Captain Spencer Vansittart and Emily Teresa, *d* of Admiral Warde, KH, of Squerryes Court, Kent; *m* 1889, Hon. Matilda Isabella Massy, 2nd *d* of 6th Lord Massy; three *d. Club:* Junior United Service.

Died 9 Aug. 1928.

VANSTON, Sir George Thomas Barrett, Kt 1917; KC 1908; LLD, MA (stip. con.); Legal Adviser to the Local Government Board for Ireland 1900–22; *b* 31 May 1853; 2nd *s* of John David Vanston, Solicitor, Hildon Park, Terenure, Co. Dublin, and Hacketstown, Co. Carlow, and Catherine *d* of George Washington Biggs, Bellevue, Borrisokane, Co. Tipperary; *m* 1899, Clementina Mary, *e* surv. *d* of Marcus Clement Sullivan, 26 Highfield Road, Rathgar, Co. Dublin; two *s* two *d. Educ:* Kingstown School; Trinity College, Dublin (Classical Scholar; First Senior Moderator and Gold Medallist in History, Law, and Political Economy; Senior Moderator and Gold Medallist in Classics; Vice-Chancellor's Latin Gold Medallist; Gold Medallist in History, College Historical Society). Called to Irish Bar, 1878. *Publications:* The Grand Jury Laws of Ireland, 1883; The Law of Public Health in Ireland, 1892; Supplement, 1897, 2nd edn 1913; The Law relating to Local Government in Ireland, 2 vols, 1899, 1905, 2nd edn vol. i, 1916; Supplement to vol. ii, 1919; The Law relating to Municipal Towns in Ireland, 1900; The Law relating to Municipal Boroughs in Ireland, 1905. *Recreations:* travel, cycling, gardening. *Address:* Hildon Park, Terenure, Co. Dublin.

Died 6 July 1923.

VAN STRAUBENZEE, Maj.-Gen. Turner, CB 1882; late RA; *b* 9 Aug. 1838; *e s* of late Col Henry van Straubenzee, JP, DL, of Spennithorne, Yorkshire, and Henrietta, *d* of 1st Baron Wrottesley; *m* 1877, Florinda, *e d* of late W. J. Hamilton; one *s* one *d. Educ:* RMA, Woolwich. Entered Royal Artillery, 1855; ADC to Maj.-Gen. Sir C. T. van Straubenzee, commanding a division in India, 1862–66; to Governor of Bombay, 1869–72; Instr in Gunnery, Shoeburyness, 1874–79; in command of Cadet Co. RMA, 1879, until promoted Lieut-Col in India, 1882; commanded RA Indian contingent Egyptian Campaign, 1882; served in RHA in India until 1887; Col on the Staff RA in India, 1888–91; commanded the Madras District as Brig.-Gen., 1891–95, when retired with the honorary rank of Major-General. Decorated for Egyptian Campaign, 1882 (medal and clasp for Tel-el-Kebir, 3rd class Medjidie, Khedive's star, and CB). *Address:* Spennithorne, RSO, Yorkshire. *Club:* Army and Navy.

Died 27 Feb. 1920.

VAN WYCK, Robert Anderson; Democrat; lawyer; Mayor of New York, 1898–1902; *b* New York, 20 July 1849; descended from Cornelius Barento Van Wyck, who settled in the New Netherlands in 1650; unmarried. *Educ:* Columbia Law School. Judge, City Court of New York, 1889–97. *Address:* 135 East 46th Street, New York.

Died Nov. 1918.

VASSAR-SMITH, Sir Richard Vassar, 1st Bt, *cr* 1917; DL, JP; *b* 11 July 1843; *e s* of Richard Tew Smith, of Wotton, Gloucester, assumed by Royal Licence additional name of Vassar; *m* 1866, Mary, *d* of John Partridge, Malvern; one *s* three *d* (and one *s* decd). *Educ:* College School, Gloucester. Chairman, Lloyds Bank, Ltd, Lloyds and National Provincial Foreign Bank, Ltd, Gloucester Railway Carriage and Wagon Co., Ltd, and Gloucester Gas Light Co.; Director, Baldwin's Ltd, Port Talbot Steel Co., Ltd; Brymbo Steel Co., Ltd; British Mannersman Tube Co., Ltd; Yorkshire Penny Bank, Ltd; London and River Plate Bank, Limited; and the P&O Bank Corporation, Ltd; Member of Council, Cheltenham College; Chairman of Council, Cheltenham Ladies' Coll.; Chairman of Council, St Hilda's Incorporated Colleges, Oxford and Cheltenham; late Chairman, Committee of London Clearing Bankers, and of Central Association of Bankers, 1916–17; late President and Chairman of the Council of the Institute of Bankers; Alderman, County Council of Gloucestershire; Provincial Grand Master, Freemasons,

Gloucestershire; Grand Superintendent, Royal Arch Freemasons, Gloucestershire and Herefordshire; Deputy Grand Master and Provincial Grand Master, Mark Freemasons, Glos and Herefordshire. *Recreations:* fishing, shooting, walking, archæology. *Heir:* s John George Lawley Vassar-Smith, *b* 10 Dec. 1868. *Address:* Spiel, Charlton Kings, Glos; 16 St James's Street, SW1. *T:* Regent 1293. *Clubs:* Carlton, Boodle's, British Empire.

Died 2 Aug. 1922.

VAUDIN, William Marshall, ISO 1914; Superintendent of Public Works and Surveys since 1901, and Chairman of the Local Board of Health since 1902; Chairman of the Agricultural Board, 1915, Seychelles; *b* 13 Dec. 1866; *s* of late Rev. A. Vaudin of Sark, Channel Islands, and Isabella, *d* of George Spain Marshall of Northumberland, England; *m* Bertha, *e d* of Rev. J. Larzen, Vicar of Methwold, Norfolk; one *d. Educ:* Royal College, Mauritius. Entered service, 1888; Acting-Assistant, Government Surveyor, Mauritius, 1890, 1891–92 and 1897–1900; Assistant Surveyor, Seychelles, 1900; has been Acting Auditor, Acting Police Magistrate, and Acting Treasurer and Collector of Customs, Seychelles; Director of Labour Bureau, 1917; Controller of Food Stuffs, 1918; Member of Executive and Legislative Councils, Seychelles, since 1912. *Address:* Mahe, Seychelles. *Club:* Seychelles.

Died 21 March 1919.

VAUDREY, Sir William Henry, Kt 1905; Solicitor and Notary; *b* 26 Feb. 1855; *s* of late Henry Vaudrey of Bayswater, London; *m* 1880, Florence Eleanor, *d* of Septimus Campbell Slade. *Educ:* City of London School. Has practised in Manchester as a Solicitor since 1878; Lord Mayor of Manchester, 1898–99; contested (C) North-east Manchester, 1910. *Recreation:* golf. *Address:* Devon Cottage, Mount Avenue, Ealing, W5. *T:* Ealing 0663. *Clubs:* Constitutional, Conservative, Manchester.

Died 11 Oct. 1926.

VAUDREY-BARKER-MILL, William Claude Frederick, JP; *b* 1874; *e s* of late William Vaudrey, of Langley Manor, Hants, and Marianne, *d* and *heir* of Frederick Ibbotson, of Colbury Manor, Hants; *m* 1905, Hon. Mary Brenda Collins, 3rd *d* of late Lord Collins; one *s* one *d. Educ:* Oxford University, BA. *Address:* Mottisfont Abbey, Romsey, Hants.

Died 16 Sept. 1916.

VAUGHAN, Rev. Bernard, SJ; *b* 20 Aug. 1847; *s* of late Col Vaughan of Courtfield, Herefordshire, and *brother* of late Cardinal B. Vaughan. *Educ:* Stonyhurst. As a professed Father of the Society of Jesus for 18 years, took an active and conspicuous part in the religious and civic life of Manchester; after which he came to London (1901) to Farm Street, W; worker among the poor at Westminster and in the East End; organised concerts and bazaars for erection of clubs for working class; his sermons on The Sins of Society in 1906 drew large audiences; so too his Lenten course, The Sins of Society gauged by the Passion of Christ, 1907, and the course entitled, Why believe in Christ and Christianity? 1907; Cathedral preacher at Eucharistic Congress, Montreal, 1910; toured through the United States and parts of Canada and Alaska; lectured before Wasada and Imperial Universities of Tokyo, and addressed the House of Peers, and ladies of Society in Japan; also lectured in China, and in Italy and France; preached the Lent of 1914 in Dublin on Jesus Christ as Guest and Host; received letter from Pope Benedict XV, 1916 congratulating him on his religious Jubilee, and giving privilege of Portable Altar. *Publications:* The Roman Claims; Faith and Reason; The Triple Alliance; The Demon of Drink in the Temple of God; Her Golden Reign; The Sins of Society, 1906; Society, Sin and the Saviour, 1907; Life Lessons from Joan of Arc, the Matchless Maid; Socialism, 1910; The Our Father, Our Country's Need To-day, 1911; Socialism from the Christian Standpoint, 1913; What of To-day? 1914; The Menace of the Empty Cradle, 1917; The Worker's Right to Live, 1918. *Address:* 114 Mount Street, W.

Died 31 Oct. 1922.

VAUGHAN, Charles Edwyn, MA; LittD; *b* 10 Feb. 1854; *o s* of the late Rev. E. T. Vaughan, Rector of Harpenden, Herts; unmarried. *Educ:* Marlborough; Balliol Coll., Oxford. Assistant Master at Clifton College, 1878–88; Professor of English Literature, University College, Cardiff, 1889–98; Professor of English Literature, Armstrong College, Newcastle upon Tyne, 1899–1904; Professor of English Literature, University of Leeds, 1904–13. *Publications:* edited Burke's Reflections on the French Revolution, 1892, and American Speeches, 1893; Webster's Duchess of Malfi, 1896; English Literary Criticism, 1896; Milton's Areopagitica and other Tracts (Temple Classics), 1900; The Romantic Revolt, 1907; Types of Tragic Drama, 1908; The Political Writings of Rousseau, with Introductions and Notes, 2 vols, 1915; Rousseau's Essay on A Lasting Peace, translated with Introduction, 1917; Rousseau's *Contrat Social,* edited with Introduction and Notes,

1918. *Recreation:* gardening. *Address:* 9 St Aldwyn's Road, Withington, Manchester.

Died 8 Oct. 1922.

VAUGHAN, Francis Baynham, JP, DL; *b* 18 March 1844; 5th *s* of late Col John Francis Vaughan, and 1st wife, Louisa Elizabeth, *d* of late John Rolls of The Hendre, Co. Monmouth; *m* 1871, Caroline Ruth, *d* of Charles Alexander Pope, of St Louis, USA; three *s* three *d.* Late Col Commanding Royal Monmouthshire Engineer Militia; Chamberlain to the Pope. *Address:* Court-Field, Ross.

Died 9 Aug. 1919.

VAUGHAN, Prebendary Henry; Rector of Wraxall, near Bristol, since 1891; Prebendary of Combe II, Wells Cathedral, 1904; Rural Dean of Chew, 1900–20; Deanery Inspector of Schools, 1892–1912; Surrogate; *b* 1848; *s* of Rev. E. P. Vaughan; *m* 1874, Ellen Christine Crake, *d* of late John Crake, of The Lawn, Datchet; two *s. Educ:* Westminster; Clifton; University College, Oxford. Curate of Mere, Wilts, 1871–72; Datchet, 1872–74; Curate in Charge, Savernake, Wilts, 1874–75; Vicar of Easton Royal, 1875–77; Curate of Wraxall, Bristol, 1877–91. *Address:* Wraxall, near Bristol.

Died 31 Dec. 1920.

VAUGHAN, Rev. Canon John; Rector of St Andrew's, Summer Hill, Sydney, since 1881; Canon of St Andrew's Cathedral, Sydney, 1902; *b* Hereford, Eng., 28 Oct. 1841; *m* 1863, Annie Graham; three *s* one *d. Educ:* Moore Theological College, Liverpool, NSW. Licensed as Lay Reader by Bishop of Sydney, 1860; conducted the first Church of England service held at Botany Bay, 1861; Deacon, 1865; Priest, 1866; Rector, St Thomas', O'Connell, 1866; Rector, St Stephen's, Penrith, 1868; started to form parish of St Andrew's, Summer Hill, 1881; Synod Nominator, Member of Standing Com., Provincial and General Synods; Trustee of Moore College and Church Missionary Association; first in NSW to start the principle of direct giving in the Lord's House on the Lord's Day. *Publications:* Sermons, Priest and Priesthood, etc; Lectures, Palestine, Egypt, America, France. *Recreations:* walking, riding. *Address:* The Rectory, Summer Hill, Sydney, NSW.

Died 13 Dec. 1918.

VAUGHAN, Rev. Canon John, MA; Canon Residentiary of Winchester Cathedral since 1909; *b* 22 Jan. 1855; 2nd *s* of Rev. Matthew Vaughan, late Vicar of Finchingfield; *m* 1891, Gertrude Blomfield, *e d* of Rev. F. Whyley; two *d. Educ:* Felstead; Corpus Christi College, Cambridge. Vicar of Porchester, 1890; Vicar of Langrish, 1897; Rector of Droxford, Hants, 1902–10; Hon. Canon of Winchester, 1903–9. *Publications:* contributed to the Nineteenth Century, Cornhill, Saturday Review, and other publications; articles on the Isle of Wight, and the Botany of Hampshire in Dent's County Guides; The Wildflowers of Selborne and other Papers, 1906; Lighter Studies of a Country Rector, 1909; A Mirror of the Soul, 1913; Winchester Cathedral Close, 1914; Winchester Cathedral, its Monuments and Memorials, 1919; The Music of Wild Flowers, 1920. *Recreations:* botany, archæology. *Address:* The Close, Winchester.

Died 10 July 1922.

VAUGHAN, Rt. Rev. John Stephen, DD; Bishop of Sebastopolis and Auxiliary to Bishop of Salford since 1909; Domestic Prelate of the Papal Court since 1896; Rector of St Bede's College, Manchester, 1912–15; *b* Courtfield, Ross, 24 Jan. 1853; *y s* of late Colonel John Vaughan of Courtfield. *Educ:* St Gregory's College, Downside, Bath; Monte Cassino, Italy; Ecclesiastical Studies at Collegio Inglese, Rome, and at Grand Séminaire, Bruges. Priest, 1876; professor of mathematics at St Bede's College, Manchester; sailed to Australia, and for three years travelled about that colony, preaching and lecturing and doing missionary work; returned and settled down in London, where he undertook parochial work, first under Cardinal Manning, and then under his brother, Cardinal Vaughan; Canon of Westminster, 1898; he organised a series of Free Catholic Evidence Lectures delivered in all the Public Halls in London, 1890–1903; in addition to preaching in all the chief Catholic churches throughout the Diocese, he gave spiritual retreats to seminarists and to clergy, both in England and Ireland and United States of America; resided in Rome, 1904–7, when he again went to United States and Canada on a preaching and lecturing tour, visiting the chief Catholic institutions and places of interest; in 1909 went, as Bishop, to live in Manchester; a writer to papers and periodicals. *Publications:* Life After Death; Thoughts for All Times; Earth to Heaven; Faith and Folly; Concerning the Holy Bible; Dangers of the Day; The Purpose of the Papacy; Happiness and Beauty; Time or Eternity; Sermons for All the Sundays and for the Chief Feasts throughout the Year; Life Everlasting; Venial Sin; some of these books have been translated into several foreign languages, one of them into Japanese. *Address:* Mission House, Brondesbury Park, NW6.

Died 4 Dec. 1925.

VAUGHAN, Mrs William Wyamar, (Margaret Vaughan); b 15 Jan. 1869; 3rd d of late John Addington Symonds, Clifton, Bristol, and Janet Catherine, 2nd d of Frederick North, Rougham Hall, Norfolk; m 1898, W. Wyamar Vaughan; two s one d. Educ: home. Publications: Our Life in the Swiss Highlands (in conjunction with her father); Days Spent on a Doge's Farm; Melting Snows (translated from the German of Prince Carolath); The Story of Perugia (in conjunction with Lina Duff Gordon) 1898; A Child of the Alps, 1920; Out of the Past, 1925. Address: The School House, Rugby.
Died 4 Nov. 1925.

VAUGHAN-LEE, Admiral Sir Charles Lionel, KBE 1919; CB 1917; b 27 Feb. 1867; 3rd s of late Vaughan H. Vaughan-Lee of Dillington Park, Somerset; m Rose, d of Llewellyn Llewellyn of Nethway, Devon; one s one d. Entered RN as Naval Cadet, 1880; served in Egyptian War; European War, 1914–17 (KBE, CB, Legion of Honour; Order of St Maurice and Lazarus of Italy; Order of Rising Sun, Japan, 2nd Class); Lieut, 1887; Commander, 1899; Captain, 1904; Rear-Adm., 1915; Admiral, 1925; Naval ADC to the King, 1914; Admiral Superintendent of Portsmouth Dockyard; retired list, 1920. Address: Bepton, Midhurst. Club: Naval and Military.
Died 16 March 1928.

VAUGHAN-WILLIAMS, Major Francis, JP, Cos Denbigh and Staffs; b 28 Jan. 1856; e s of late Judge R. Vaughan-Williams, Bodlonfa, Flintshire, North Wales; m Laura, y d of late Peter Walker, JP, of Coed-y-glyn, Wrexham, and Auchenflower, Ayrshire. Educ: Shrewsbury. MFH The Tedworth, 1885–88; MFH North Hereford, 1893–95; MFH Co. Galway, 1895–97; late Major Oxford and Bucks LI and Hampshire Carabiniers. Address: Donnington Lodge, Newbury. Club: Carlton.
Died 24 Nov. 1920.

VAUX, Lt-Col Ernest, CMG 1916; DSO 1900; late 7th Durham Light Infantry; b 1865; s of J. S. Vaux, Sunderland; m 1906, Emily L., d of H. Moon-Ord; two s two d. Served S Africa, 5th Imperial Yeomanry, 1900 (despatches, medal 3 clasps, DSO); European War, 1914–18 (CMG, despatches twice). Address: Brettanby Manor, Barton, RSO, Yorks.
Died 21 Nov. 1925.

VEDDER, Elihu; artist, painter, and modeller; b New York, 26 Feb. 1836; m 1869, Caroline, d of Hon. E. H. Rosekrans of Glen's Falls, NY; one d. Educ: Brinkerhoff School, Brooklyn. Painted with Mattison at Sherburne, NY, and in atelier of Picot, Paris, 1856; worked in Italy, 1856–61; returned to US until 1865; then after one winter in Paris went in 1867 to Rome, where he has since had his studio, making frequent visits to the US. His subjects are principally imaginative; in 1884 he illustrated the Rubaiyat of Omar Khayyám; five decorative panels and the mosaic Minerva in the New Congressional Library at Washington, large panels in Bowdoin College, Maine, also decorative ceiling in the Huntington house, New York City, are his work; other works are in the Boston Art Museum, Brooklyn Art Museum, Metropolitan Museum, NY, and Pittsburg Art Gallery; Academician Nat. Acad. of Design since 1865; member Soc. of American Artists; American Soc. of Mural Decorators; Century Assoc. of New York; Academician American Institute of Arts and Letters; Gold Medal Columbian Exhibition, Chicago. Publications: The Digressions of V., 1910; Miscellaneous Moods in Verse, 1914. Address: 4 Via Porta Pinciana, Rome; Torre Quattuo Venti, Capri. TA: Vedder, Rome.
Died 29 Jan. 1923.

VEITCH, Sir Harry James, Kt 1912; VMH; FLS; b Exeter, 29 June 1840; s of James Veitch, horticulturist; m 1867, Louisa Mary (d 1921), d of late Frederick W. Johnston. Educ: Exeter Grammar School; France; Germany. Came to London, 1853; Vice-Pres. of Royal Horticultural Society; late head of James Veitch & Sons, Ltd; Chevalier of the Legion of Honour; Cross of Officer of the Belgian Order of the Crown. Publications: Veitch's Orchidaceous Plants and Manual Coniferæ. Address: 34 Redcliffe Gardens, SW; East Burnham Park, Slough.
Died 6 July 1924.

VELLA, Hon. Tom; retired; b 15 Sept. 1849; s of late Paul Lewis Vella, LLD, and Irene Magri; m Dolores Borg; one s. Educ: Malta. Clerk (Civil Service), 1865–93; Deputy Collector of Customs, 1893–95 and 1897–1902; Deputy Postmaster-General, 1895–97; Collector of Customs, 1902–3; Postmaster-General, 1903–11; Treasurer and Director of Contracts, 1911; Member of the Executive and Legislative Councils; retired, 1916. Address: 161 Strada Stretta, Valetta. Club: Casino Maltese, Valetta.

VENIS, Arthur, CIE 1911; MA, DLitt; b 4 Oct. 1857. Educ: Edinburgh University; Balliol College, Oxford; Boden Sanskrit Scholar; Fellow

of the Asiatic Society of Bengal and of the University of Allahabad. Entered Indian Educational Service, 1881; Professor of English Literature, Queen's College, Benares, 1885; Professor of Philosophy, and Principal, Sanskrit College, Benares, 1888; Principal, Queen's College, Benares, 1897; Professor of Post-Vedic Sanskrit, University of Allahabad, 1914. Address: Government Sanskrit Library, Benares, India.
Died 5 June 1918.

VENKATAGIRI, Rajah of, Unde Rajaha Raje Sri Maharaja Velugoti Sree Rajagopala Krishna yachendra Bahadur, GCIE 1915 (KCIE 1888); Panchahazar, Munsubdar, Zamindar; b 25 Nov. 1857; s of Unde Rajaha Raje Sri Rajah Velugoti Kumara yachama Naidu Bahadur, CSI, Panchahazar, Mansubdar, Rajah of Venkatagiri; m 1875, a Zamindar's daughter in Godavery District; one s one d. Educ: private study at his palace. Belongs to an ancient family of historical renown; now a leading Rajah amongst the Zamindars; succeeded to the estate in 1878; twice Member of Council of Fort St George; President of Madras Landholders' Association. Publications: none in English, but several in vernaculars. Recreations: outdoor sports, such as tennis, riding, shooting, etc. Address: Venkatagiri Nellore, Madras Presidency. Clubs: Madras Cosmopolitan, Racing, Gymkhana, etc.
Died 23 July 1916.

VENKATASWETA CHALAPATI RUNGA-RAO BAHADUR, Maharajah Sir Ravu, Maharajah of Bobbili, GCIE 1911 (KCIE 1895); CBE 1917; Maharajah, 1900; Ancient Zemindar of Bobbili; b Venkatagiri, 28 Aug. 1862; adopted s of 10th Rajah Seetaramakrishna Rayadappa Runga-Rao Bahadur; m 1st, 1878; 2nd, 1881; 3rd, 1888; two s. Educ: Bobbili, privately, under Dr J. Marsh. Ascended Gaddi in 1881; President of Madras Landholders' Association; Life-member Royal Asiatic Society; Member Northbrook Society and East Indian Association; visited England, 1893, when he was presented to Her Majesty the late Queen-Empress; represented the Madras Presidency at Coronation of King Edward; Member of Madras Legislative Council, 1896, 1898, 1900, and 1902; First Native Member of the Madras Executive Council, 1910–11; on 6 November 1916 abdicated his Zemindary, together with the Incorporated Estates, in favour of his elder son, and gave away by a Deed of Settlement his landed property in Godavari District to his second son. Decorated for the prudent management of his zemindary, for the charitable institutions he founded, and for his attention to his public duties. Owned about 300 square miles of land. Publications: The Rajah of Bobbili's Diary in Europe in 1893; The History of Bobbili Zemindary, 1900; The Maharajah of Bobbili's Diary in Europe, with an Account of the Delhi Durbar, 1902; Advice to the Indian Aristocracy; revised and enlarged History of the Bobbili Zemindary. Recreations: shooting, riding, and other manly sports. Address: Bobbili, Vizagapatam, Madras Presidency, India. M: 13643. Clubs: Waltair, Madras Race, Madras.
Died 12 Sept. 1920.

VENN, Albert John, MB MCh, MD Aberdeen; MRCP London; Graduate University of Chicago; Life Governor of St Bartholomew's Hospital, the Metropolitan Free Hospital, the West London Hospital; Vice-Patron of the Victoria Hospital for Children, Chelsea; b Colombo, Oct. 1840; 2nd s of John Whatley Venn, the first Municipal Magistrate of Colombo, and Ann Tripp Venn; m Emma, o d of William and Ellen Maria Stevens of Tulse Hill; two s one d. Educ: Bath Rectory School; City of London College; University of Aberdeen; St Bartholomew's Hospital; University of Chicago. Fellow Royal Society of Medicine; last Midwifery Assistant, St Bartholomew's Hospital; House Physician, Soho Hospital for Women; Obstetric Assistant, St Bartholomew's Hospital; Assistant Physician, Metropolitan Hospital; Senior Physician, Out-Patients, Victoria Hospital for Children; Obstetrical Physician, Metropolitan Free Hospital, and Physician for Diseases of Women, West London Hospital; Research Student, Marcus Beck Laboratory, Royal Society of Medicine, London. Publications: Editor of 5th, 6th and 7th editions of Beasley's Book of Prescriptions, of 11th edn of Chavasse's Advice to a Mother, of 13th edn of Chavasse's Advice to a Wife, and of 6th edn of Chavasse's Counsel to a Mother; Co-Editor of 3rd edn of Drs Tanner and Meadows' Diseases of Infancy and Childhood; 4th edn of Dr Meadows' Manual of Midwifery, and 5th edn The Prescribers' Companion. Recreations: riding, golf, fishing. Clubs: Junior Carlton; The Phi-Chi Fraternity of America, Rho Chapter.
Died 13 Nov. 1919.

VENN, Rev. Henry; Hon. Canon of Canterbury, 1900; b 27 July 1838; s of Rev. Prebendary Henry Venn; m 1st, Isabel Louisa d of Capt. W. M. De Butts; 2nd, Louisa Jane, d of R. B. and Lady Louisa Wardlaw-Ramsay; three s four d. Educ: Gonville and Caius College, Cambridge. Rector of Clare Portion, Tiverton, Devon; Rural Dean of Tiverton, 1870–85; Vicar of Sittingbourne, Kent, 1885–92; Vicar of Walmer, 1893–1908. *Address:* Precincts, Canterbury.

Died 17 May 1923.

VENN, John, ScD; FRS 1883; FSA; Fellow of Caius College, Cambridge; President, 1903; *b* Hull, Yorkshire, 4 Aug. 1834; *s* of Rev. Henry Venn, BD, and Martha, *d* of Nicholas Sykes, Swanland, Yorkshire; *m* 1867, Susanna C., *d* of Rev. C. W. Edmonstone; one *s. Educ:* Caius Coll., Camb. Lecturer in Logic and Moral Philosophy for many years at Cambridge; Examiner, etc. *Publications:* Logic of Chance, 1866, 3rd edn 1888; Hulsean Lectures, 1869; Symbolic Logic, 1881, 2nd edn 1894; Empirical Logic, 1889, 2nd edn 1907; Biographical History of Gonville and Caius College, 3 vols 1901; Venn Family Annals, 1904. *Address:* Vicarsbrook and Caius College, Cambridge. *Died 4 April 1923.*

VENNING, Alfred Reid, ISO 1907; *b* 18 May 1846; *m* 1879, Katherine Henrietta, *d* of Henry Wilson Reeves, ICS. Member of Council, Bombay; four *s* two *d. Educ:* St Andrews; University College School, London; Germany. Late Federal Secretary, Federated Malay States, previously State Treasurer of Selangor; Secretary to Government of Perak. *Address:* The Homestead, Bracknell, Berks. *Died 22 Aug. 1927.*

VENNING, Sir Edgcombe, Kt 1905; FRCS; *b* 24 April 1837; *s* of J. Meybohm Venning; *m* 1873, Francis Edith (*d* 1916), *o d* of Capt. Aylmer Pearson, late 43rd Light Infantry; one *s* one *d. Educ:* privately. Late House Surgeon and Surgical Registrar, St George's Hospital; Surgeon, 1st Life Guards for 15 years. *Address:* Lamorva, Falmouth. *Club:* Athenæum. *Died 17 Nov. 1920.*

VENTRY, 5th Baron, *cr* 1800; **Lt-Col Frederick Rossmore Wauchope Eveleigh-de-Moleyns;** Bt 1797; DSO 1897; late Commissioner of Police, Mashonaland; *b* 11 Dec 1861; *e s* of 4th Baron and Harriet (*d* 1906), *d* of Andrew Wauchope, Niddrie Marischal, Midlothian; *S* father, 1914. *Educ:* Harrow. Entered army, 1882; Captain, 1890; served South Africa, 1896–7 (despatches twice, DSO, Bt Lieut-Col); acted as Extra Staff Officer; in general command of the troops, 1897; retired 1901. Owned about 93,700 acres. *Heir: b* Hon. Arthur William Eveleigh-de-Moleyns, *b* 6 April 1864. *Address:* Burnham, Dingle, Co. Kerry.

Died 24 Sept. 1923.

VERDIN, Sir Joseph, 1st Bt, *cr* 1896; DL, JP Cheshire; JP Herefordshire; *b* 4 Jan. 1838; *e surv. s* of Joseph Verdin of Highfield House, Cheshire, and Margaret, *d* of Wharton Sadler. *Educ:* privately. Life Trustee of River Weaver; County Alderman for Cheshire; High Sheriff, Herefords, 1903; Lord of the Manor of Dilwyn. *Heir:* none. *Address:* Garnstone Castle, Weobley, Herefordshire. *Club:* Constitutional. *Died 28 Dec. 1920 (ext).*

VERDON, Rt. Rev. Michael; RC Bishop of Dunedin since 1896; *b* Liverpool, 1838. Was Student and Vice-Rector of the Irish College, Rome; President Holy Cross College, Clonliffe, Dublin; and of St Patrick's College, Manly, Sydney. *Address:* Dunedin, New Zealand. *Died 22 Nov. 1918.*

VERE, Very Rev. Canon Langton George; Rector of St Patrick's, Soho, since 1885; Member of Westminster Chapter; President of Westminster Diocesan Schools Association; on Council of Catholic Federated Associations; *b* 1844. *Educ:* English College, Lisbon; St Edmund's, Ware. Ordained 1868; Rector of Homerton Mission, 1877–85; sat on the Vestry and old Strand Board of Works; member of the Westminster City Council. *Publications:* For Better, not for Worse; several volumes of Poems, Essays, Recollections and Short Stories. *Address:* St Patrick's Presbytery, Soho Square, W1.

Died 29 March 1924.

VEREY, Sir Henry William, Kt 1920; *b* 1836; *e s* of late Henry Verey of Bridge House, Twyford, Berkshire; *m* Henrietta Maria, *d* of late Edward Williams Hasell of Dalemain, Cumberland; one *s* one *d. Educ:* Trinity College, Cambridge; Mathematical Tripos, 1859. Bar (Inner Temple), 1865; Revising Barrister Mid-Kent, 1875; ICRV (Devil's Own), Long Service Medal; Official Referee of Supreme Court of Judicature, 1876–1920; JP Berkshire. *Recreations:* shooting, boating, yachting. *Address:* Bridge House, Twyford, Berkshire. *T:* Twyford 7; Royal Courts of Justice, WC. *Clubs:* New University; Berkshire.

Died 4 Dec. 1920.

VERHAEREN, Emil; *b* St Amand, Belgium, 1855, of Flemish parentage. *Educ:* Brussels; Ghent; University of Louvain. *Publications:* Les Flamandes, 1883; Les Moines, 1886; Soirs, 1887; Debacles, 1888;

Flambeaux Noirs, 1890; Les Villages Illusoires, 1894; Les Villes Tentaculaires, 1895; Les Visages de la Vie, 1899; Les Forces Tumultueuses, 1902; Les Aubes; Tendresses Premières, 1904; Heures d'Apres Midi, 1905; La Multiple Splendeur, 1907; Toute la Flandre; Deux Drames, 1915; La Belgique Sanglante, 1915.

Died 28 Nov. 1916.

VERNER, Colonel William Willoughby Cole; *b* 1852; *m* 1881, Hon. Elizabeth Mary Emily Parnell, *d* of 3rd Baron Congleton; one *d.* Joined Rifle Brigade, 1873; passed Staff College, taking 1st place and Honours, 1881. Colonel, 1904; served Nile Expedition, 1884–85; actions of Abu Klea and El Gubat, where guided the fighting square in its march to the Nile (despatches), and subsequent fighting on Gordon's steamers near Metemmeh (medal with two clasps, Khedive's star); awarded bronze medal of Royal Humane Society, 1882; Professor of Military Topography, RMC Sandhurst, 1896–99; served South African campaign, 1899–1900, on the Staff; present at battles of Belmont and Graspan (severely injured, medal and clasps). *Inventions:* inventor and patentee of the Luminous Magnetic and Prismatic Compasses adopted into Service, and of the pattern of Cavalry Sketching Case and Plane Tables likewise adopted, and various other Military Sketching and Surveying Instruments. *Publications:* Sketches in the Soudan, 1885; Rapid Field Sketching and Reconnaissance, 1887; Military Topography and Range Finding, 1889; The First British Rifle Corps, 1890; A British Rifle Man, 1899; Map Reading and Field Sketching, 1891, 4th edn 1906; The Military Life of Field-Marshal HRH the Duke of Cambridge (2 vols), 1905 (by command of HRH); My Life among the Wild Birds in Spain, 1909; Editor of The Rifle Brigade Chronicle (thirty volumes issued), 1890–1919; History and Campaigns of the Rifle Brigade, Part i (1800–1809), 1912; Part ii (1809–1813), 1919; (with the Abbé H. Breuil of the Institut de paléontologie humaine, Paris) La Pileta Cavern (Palæolithic rock drawings in Andalucia), 1915; Cave Exploration (Pre-historic man) in Southern Spain; Battle Cruisers at Falklands Action by late Commander Rudolf Verner, RN (edited), 1920. *Recreations:* wild-fowl shooting, boat sailing, ornithology, zoology, natural history—photography, sketching. *Address:* Hartford Bridge, Hartley-Wintney, Winchfield; El Aguila, Algeciras, Spain. *TA:* Colonel Verner, Hartley-Wintney. *Club:* United Service.

Died 25 Jan. 1922.

VERNHAM, John Edward; Organist and Choirmaster of St Paul's, Knightsbridge, since 1879; Professor of Music, King's College, London, since 1889; *b* Lewes, Sussex, 1854; *m* Julia Augarde, pianiste, and pupil of Scharwenka in Berlin. *Educ:* under late George Cooper and the late Dr Steggall. Played for the first time in Church, Full Choral Evensong, at the age of 13, at St Paul's, Walworth; appointed Organist of All Saints, Lambeth, at the age of 15. *Publications:* Novello's Primers, Nos 49 and 58; Boys' Voices; Communion Service in B Flat; Evening Service in A; Xmas Carols, etc. *Recreation:* country walks. *Address:* 5 Warrington Crescent, Maid Hill, W.

Died 2 March 1921.

VERNON, Sir Harry Foley, 1st Bt, *cr* 1885; JP County of Worcester and DL and County Alderman; *b* Worcestershire, 11 April 1834; 2nd *s* of T. T. Vernon, Hanbury Hall, Worcestershire, and Jessie Anna Laetitia, *d* of Herbert Foley, Ridgeway, Pembrokeshire; *m* 1861, Lady Georgina Sophia Baillie-Hamilton, *d* of 10th Earl of Haddington; one *s* one *d. Educ:* Harrow; Magdalen Coll., Oxford (MA). MP East Worcestershire, 1861–66; Master of Worcestershire Foxhounds, 1862–68; Col of 2nd Vol. Batt. Worcestershire Regt, 1873–85; Hon. Col (retired) of Worcestershire Hussars. *Heir: s* Bowater George Hamilton Vernon [*b* 12 Sept. 1865; *m* 1905, Doris, *d* of James H. Allan, Wood House, Shrawley. Late Capt. Worcestershire Yeomanry; served S Africa, 1900–1. *Address:* Bramfield Hall, Suffolk. *Club:* Cavalry]. *Recreations:* hunting, shooting, cycling, skating. *Address:* Hanbury Hall, Droitwich, Worcestershire. *TA:* Vernon, Stoke Works. *Died 31 Jan. 1920.*

VERNON, Rev. James Edmund, MA Oxon; Vicar of Olveston, Glos, 1885–1918; Rural Dean of Stapleton, 1911–13; Hon. Canon of Bristol, 1912; *b* 13 April 1837; *s* of Rev. W. H. Vernon; *m* 1864, Lavinia (*d* 1922), *d* of Martin Hunnybun, Godmanchester; three *s* two *d. Educ:* private schools; private tutor; Wadham College, Oxford. BA 1859. Mathematical Master, Temple Grove School, 1859–60; Assistant Master, Cheam School, 1860–63. Deacon, 1863; Priest, 1864; Assistant Curate of Leyton, Essex, 1863–67; Vicar of Withiel Florey, Somerset, 1867–69; Bicknoller, Somerset, 1869–77; Assistant Curate of St Paul's, Clifton, 1877–85. *Publications:* Addresses to Children; Bible Truths in Simple Words. *Recreations:* cricket, rowing, mountaineering, golf, chess. *Address:* Lynmouth, Reigate, Surrey.

Died 1 Feb. 1928.

VERNON, Sir William, 1st Bt, cr 1914; head of W. Vernon & Sons, millers, Liverpool and London; b 1835; m 1857, Jane Margaret (d 1910), d of Thomas Cooper, Fulford Hall, Staffs; four s one d. Heir: s John Herbert Vernon [b 12 July 1858; m 1889, Elizabeth, d of J. Bagnall; four s one d. Address: Eastham House, Cheshire]. Address: Shotwick Park, Chester. Club: Constitutional.

Died 24 June 1919.

VERNON HARCOURT, Augustus George, MA, DSc, DCL, LLD; FRS; Vice-President of the Chemical Society; Metropolitan Gas Referee; b London, 24 Dec. 1834; e s of Admiral Frederick E. Vernon Harcourt, and Marcia, sister of 1st Lord Tollemache; m 1872, Hon. Rachel Mary, d of 1st Lord Aberdare; two s eight d. Educ: Harrow; Balliol College, Oxford. First Class in Natural Science, 1858; studentship at Christ Church, 1859. Publications: Exercises in Practical Chemistry (in conjunction with H. G. Madan, Fellow of Queen's College, Oxford); numerous communications to the Royal Society, the Chemical Society, and the British Association. Inventions: two standards of light, of the values one candle and ten candles; an inhaler, for administering chloroform mixed with air in any proportion up to the limit of safety. Address: St Clare, Ryde, Isle of Wight. T: Ryde 16. Club: Athenæum.   Died 23 Aug. 1919.

VERONESE, Senator Giuseppe; Professor of Mathematics, Royal University, Padua; b Chioggia, Venice, 7 May 1854; s of Anthony and Octavia Duse; two s two d. Educ: Venice, Zürich, Rome, Leipzig. Drawer at Vienna, 1873; Assistant of Mathematics at Rome, 1877–80; Professor at Padua, 1881; Deputy, 1897–1900; Senator of the Kingdom of Italy since 1904; Fellow, Royal Academy di Lincei; Ital. Soc. of the XL; Royal Lombard Institute of Sciences; Royal Venetian Inst. of Sciences; Royal Academy of Turin, of Padua; Hungarian Acad. of Sciences of Budapest; Doctor of Laws of Aberdeen; Vice-President of the Superior Counsel of Waters and Forests; President of the Hydra Technical Institute in Stra (Venice), and Royal Technical Institute and Royal School of Decoration and Industrial Arts (Padua), etc. Publications: Nuovi teoremi sull' Hexagrammum mysticum, 1877; Behandlung der proiectivischen Verhältnisse der Räume von mehreren Dimensionen, 1881; Interprétations géométriqués de la théorie des substitutions de n lettres, 1883; La geometria descrittiva a quattro dimensioni, 1882; Superficie omaloide normale del 4° ordine a due dimensioni dello spazio a cinque dimensioni, 1884; Fondamenti di geometria (trans. into German), 1891; Elementi di geometria, 1897–1913; Notions of Intuitive Geometry, 1900–15; Complements of Algebra and Geometry, 1915; Il Vero nella Matematica (lecture), 1906; La geometria non-archimedea (lecture), 1908; Publications on Hydraulics; Parliamentary speeches and reports. Recreation: amateur in painting. Clubs: Mathematical, Palermo; International Artistic, Rome, etc.

VERRETT, Lt-Col Hector Bacon, DSO 1916; Assistant Deputy Postmaster General, Ottawa, Canada, since 1911; b Loretteville, Quebec, 9 Feb. 1874; s of J. A. Verrett and E. Bacon; m 1905, Irene Forbes, Ottawa, Ontario; no c. Educ: Levis College, Laval University, Quebec. Private Secretary to Sir Charles Fitzpatrick, 1896–1902; to Hon. G. H. Carroll, 1902–4; to Hon. Rudolphe Lemieux, 1904–6; successive Solicitors-General of Canada; to Hon. Rodolphe Lemieux, Postmaster General of Canada, 1906–11; Lieutenant in The Governor General's Foot Guards, Ottawa, 1906–8; Capt. 1908; Major, 1915; came to England with 2nd Battalion, 1st Canadian Contingent, as Captain, 1914; promoted Major in the field, 1915, and Lt-Col as above, 1916 (DSO, despatches). Address: Ottawa, Canada. Clubs: Laurentian, Royal Golf, Hunt, Connaught Park, Ottawa; Garrison, Laurentides, Quebec; St Denis, Montreal.

Died Oct. 1926.

VERULAM, 3rd Earl of, James Walter Grimston; Bt 1628; Baron Forrester (Scotland), 1633; Baron Dunboyne and Viscount Grimston (Ireland), 1719; Baron Verulam (Great Britain), 1790; Viscount Grimston and Earl of Verulam (United Kingdom), 1815; b 11 May 1852; s of 2nd Earl and Elizabeth, d of Major Richard Weyland, Wood Eaton, Oxfordshire; S father 1895; m 1878, Margaret Frances, d of Sir Frederic Ulric Graham, 3rd Bt, and Hermione, d of 12th Duke of Somerset; one s five d. Educ: Harrow. Served in 1st Life Guards, 1870–78; Hon. Major, Herts Yeomanry; MP (C) Mid Hertfordshire, 1885–92; County Councillor, Herts; County Alderman, 1912; late Chairman of Quarter Sessions, Liberty of St Albans, Herts. Owned about 40 acres. Heir: s Viscount Grimston. Address: Gorhambury, St Albans. T: St Albans 5. Clubs: Carlton, Bachelors'.

Died 11 Nov. 1924.

VETCH, Col Robert Hamilton, CB 1900; JP; RE; Retired List; b Birmingham, 6 Jan. 1841; e surv. s of Capt. James Vetch, RE, FRS,

of Haddington, NB, Conservator of Harbours at Admiralty, and Alexandrina Ogilvie, d of Robert Auld of Edinburgh; m 1863, Mary Ann, d of Commissary-General George Darley Lardner, and g d of Dr Dionysius Lardner. Educ: Grammar School, Henley-on-Thames; private schools; Royal Military Academy, Woolwich. Lieut Royal Engineers, 1857; Capt., 1869; Maj., 1878; Lieut-Col, 1884; Col, 1888; employed on defences of Bermuda, Bristol Channel, Plymouth Harbour, and Malta, 1861–76; Secretary of RE Institute, Chatham, 1877–83; commanded RE Submarine Mining Batt., 1884; Assistant Inspector-General of Fortifications at War Office, 1884–89; Deputy-Inspector-General of Fortifications and Secretary of the Defence Committee, and of the Joint Naval and Military Committee on Defence, War Office, 1889–94; Chief Engineer in Ireland and Colonel on Staff, 1894–98. Sent by Government in 'Great Eastern' to report on laying of French Atlantic Cable from Brest to St Pierre, and thence to Duxbury, Mass, 1869. Distinguished Service Pension. Decorated for services at War Office in connection with the defences of Empire. Publications: Gordon's Campaign in China; Life of Lieut-Gen. Sir Gerald Graham, VC, GCB; Life of Lt-Gen. Sir Andrew Clarke, GCMG, CB, CIE; edited, The Professional Papers of the Corps of RE, from 1877 to 1884 inclusive; also the RE Journal, during same period; contributor to The Dictionary of National Biography, Encyclopædia Britannica, etc. Address: c/o Messrs Cox & Co., 16 Charing Cross, SW. Club: Constitutional.

Died 28 Jan. 1916.

VIALLS, Lt-Col Harry George, CB 1900; West Australian's Bushmen's Corps; b 7 Nov. 1859. Educ: Cheltenham. Served Afghan War, 1880 (medal); South Africa, 1899–1902 (despatches twice, King's medal, 2 clasps, CB). Address: Kalharrup Ford, Warren River, via Balbanup, West Australia.   Died 16 May 1918.

VIAUD, Louis Marie Julien; see Loti, Pierre.

VIBART, Colonel Henry Meredith, RE (retired); b Taunton, 2 March 1839; 2nd s of Henry Vibart, Madras Civil Service; m 1884, Louisa E., e surv. d of Col Charles F. Le Hardy, Madras Army, 1st Commissioner of Coorg; one s. Educ: private school at Streatham; Addiscombe College. Obtained commission of HEIC Engineers, 1857; served at Chatham till 1859; arrived in India, 1859; appointed to PWD, 1861; served in Tinnevelly and Kistna on Irrigation Works, 1861–68; furlough, 1868–71; Kistna Irrigation Works till 1872; Executive Engineer, Bangalore Military Works, 1872–78; special duty to Madura, 1878, and to Trichinopoly, 1878–79; Under Secretary for Irrigation, 1879; Supt Engineer, 1879–80; Supt of Works, Madras and Bangalore, 1881; furlough, 1881–84; Supt Engineer, Bellary, 1884–87; Madras, 1887–88; 6 months' special leave to England, 1888–89; Supt Engineer, 1889; left Bombay on leave, 1889; retired from the service, 1891. Publications: Military History of Madras Engineers and Pioneers, 2 vols, 1883; Addiscombe, its Heroes and Men of Note, 1894; Richard Baird Smith, the Leader of Delhi Heroes of 1857, 1897; Life of General Sir Harry Prendergast, VC, GCB, RE, 1914. Address: Woodlands, Remenham, Henley-on-Thames. Clubs: East India United Service; MCC.

Died 1 Nov. 1917.

VICARS, Sir Arthur Edward, KCVO 1903 (CVO 1900); Kt 1896; FSA; b Leamington, 27 July 1864; y s of late Col. W. H. Vicars, HM's 61st Regt and Jane, 3rd d of R. Gun-Cuninghame, DL, Mount Kennedy, Co. Wicklow, and widow of P. K. Mahony, of Kilmorna, Co. Kerry; m 1917, Gertrude, e d of late J. J. Wright, MD, of Campfield House, Malton, Yorkshire. Educ: Magdalen College School, Oxford; Bromsgrove School. Ulster King-of-Arms and Registrar and Kt Attendant on Order of St Patrick, 1893–1908; a Govt Trustee, Nat. Library of Ireland; Hon. Sec. Kildare Archaeological Soc. since its foundation, 1891; besides heraldry and genealogy generally interested in matters of art, archaeology, Ex Libris, old plate, etc. Publications: Index to the Prerogative Wills of Ireland 1536–1810, 1897; papers in several archaeological serials. Recreation: hunting. Address: Kilmorna, Co. Kerry. Club: Kildare Street, Dublin.

Died 14 April 1921.

VICKERS, Albert; late Chairman of Vickers Ltd; b 16 Sept. 1838; 3rd s of Edward Vickers, late of Tapton Hall, Sheffield, and of Thenford, Banbury; m 1st, 1862, Helen Gage of Boston, USA; 2nd, 1875, Edith, d of John Foster of Newhall Grange, Maltby, Co. York. Educ: privately. Knight Grand Cross of the Order of Naval Merit of Spain; Order of the Rising Sun, Japan. Recreations: shooting, fishing. Address: 14 Cadogan Square, SW. T: Kensington 400; Meallmore, Daviot, Inverness. Clubs: Junior Carlton, Arts, Royal Automobile.

Died 12 July 1919.

VIDAL, Rt. Rev. Julian, SM; Vicar Apostolic of the Fiji Islands, and Titular Bishop of Abydus since 1887; *b* 1846. *Educ:* Rodez. Went to Fiji Islands, 1873. *Address:* Suva, Fiji Islands.

Died 2 April 1922.

VIGORS, Captain Philip Urban, MVO 1903; late Royal Irish Regiment; *b* 7 July 1875; 3rd *s* of Rev. R. W. Vigors, MA; *m* 1912, Gladys Ingledew, *y d* of T. J. Jones-Williams. Laughern Hill, Wichenford, Worcester; one *s* (posthumous) one *d*. *Educ:* Marlborough College. Entered Army, 1897; Captain, 1904; served S Africa, 1899–1902 (despatches, Queen's medal five clasps, King's medal two clasps); resigned commission, 1907.

Died 2 April 1917.

VILJOEN, Hon. Sir Antonie Gysbert, Kt 1916; MB, CM; MRCS; *b* 1858; *s* of Jacobus Johannes Viljoen; *m* 1887, Margaretha, *d* of H. P. Beyers. *Educ:* S African College; Edinburgh University. Served S African War, 1899–1901; in German SW Africa, 1915; MLA; Director National Bank of S Africa and several Insurance Companies. *Address:* Oak Valley, Elgin Station, Cape Province, S Africa.

Died 25 Oct. 1918.

VILLALOBAR, Marquis of, and Marquis of Guimarey, Hon. KCVO; Spanish Ambassador in Brussels; *b* 1866; *g s* of Duke of Rivas, poet, politician, and General during the Peninsular War; *m* 1921, Marquise de Guimarey. *Educ:* Madrid; England. Has served in the Diplomatic service at the Foreign Office in Madrid, in the United States Spanish Legation, the Embassy in Paris, in London, and as Plenipotentiary Minister in Washington and in Lisbon; Lord Chamberlain to the King of Spain; Maestrante of the Royal Cavalry Order of Saragossa; Grand Cross of Charles III, and of Isabel of Spain; Medal of Alphonse XIII; Medal of the Regency of Maria Christina; Grand Cross of Leopold from Belgium; Grand Cross of St Gregory the Great of Rome; Grand Cross of St Maurice of Italy; Grand Cross of the Rising Sun of Japan; Grand Cross of the Star of Roumania; Grand Cross of St Savas of Servia; Grand Cross of the Order of Honour and Merit of Cuba; Grand Officer of the Legion of Honour, France; Commander of the Orders of Christ and Villaviçosa, Portugal; Medal of the Coronation of King Edward of Great Britain; Gold Medal of Zaragoza, of the Puente de San Payo, of Liège, of Ghent, of the Universal Exhibition of Paris, 1900; Star of the Red Cross from Spain; Civique Belgian Order, 1914–18; Correspondent of the Royal Academy of History from Madrid; Honorary Citizen of Brussels, of Ghent, of Antwerp, of Liège; Doctor (Hon.) of the University of Liège and of Bruges; Minister Protector of the National Committee of Belgium during the war; in charge during the war in Belgium of the interests of France, Russia, Italy, Portugal, the United States, Japan, Brazil, Cuba, Costa Rica, Bolivia, Roumania, Denmark, Servia, etc. *Recreations:* literature, history, political studies, painting. *Address:* Calle del Duque de Rivas 1, Madrid; Rue Montoyer 26, Brussels. *T:* 2340. *Clubs:* Marlborough, Turf, Travellers', United Service, Junior United Service; Cercle du Parc, Cercle Gaulois, Brussels; Nuevo, Madrid.

Died 9 July 1926.

VILLIERS, Colonel Ernest; ADC to the King; Hon. Colonel of First Surrey Rifles; *b* 18 July 1838; *s* of late Hon. Edward Ernest Villiers, *brother* of 4th Earl of Clarendon, and Hon. Elizabeth Charlotte Villiers, *d* of 1st Lord Ravensworth; *m* 1st, 1865, Elizabeth, *d* of late Sir Alexander Wood; 2nd, 1869, Adela, *d* of late Col and Lady Adela Ibbetson. *Educ:* Harrow. Served for seventeen years in 43rd Light Infantry, later 1st Batt. Oxfordshire Light Infantry; served as ADC to Sir William Denison when Governor of Madras; served as ADC to Lord Strathnairn when Commander of the Forces in Ireland; served as ADC to the Earl Spencer when Lord Lieutenant of Ireland; Adjutant of 1st VB East Kent Regiment; served in 18th Middlesex Rifle Volunteers and in command of 1st Surrey Rifles. *Recreations:* stalking, shooting, fishing. *Address:* 50 Thurloe Square, SW7. *T:* Kensington 4182. *Clubs:* Travellers', Wellington, Junior Army and Navy.

Died 23 April 1921.

VILLIERS, Ernest Amherst; *b* 14 Nov. 1863; *s* of Rev. Charles Villiers, late Rector of Croft, Yorkshire, and Florence Amherst, *sister* of 1st Lord Amherst of Hackney; *m* 1898, Hon. Elaine Guest, *d* of 1st Lord Wimborne; two *s* two *d*. *Educ:* Uppingham; Cambridge. MP (L) Brighton, 1905–10. *Address:* 111 Gloucester Place, W1. *T:* Mayfair 1729; Speen Court, Newbury.

Died 26 Sept. 1923.

VILLIERS, Rt. Hon. Sir Francis Hyde, GCMG 1918 (KCMG 1906); GCVO 1909; CB 1894; PC 1919; Grand Cross of Orders of Christ of Portugal and Leopold of Belgium; *b* London, 13 Aug. 1852; 4th *s* of 4th Earl of Clarendon, KG; *m* 1876, Virginia Katharine, *d*

of Eric Carrington Smith of Ashfold, Handcross; two *s* two *d*. *Educ:* Harrow. Entered Foreign Office, 1870; Private Sec. to Lord Tenterden, Sir J. Pauncefote, and Sir P. Currie, Permanent Under-Secretaries for Foreign Affairs; Acting Secretary in Diplomatic Service, 1885; Private Secretary to Earl of Rosebery, Secretary of State for Foreign Affairs, 1886, and 1892–94; Acting Private Secretary to Marquess of Salisbury, 1887; Assistant Under-Secretary of State for Foreign Affairs, 1896–1905; Envoy Extraordinary and Minister Plenipotentiary to Portugal, 1905–11; Envoy Extraordinary and Minister Plenipotentiary to Belgium, 1911–19; Ambassador to Belgium, 1919–20. *Address:* Elm Lodge, Englefield Green, Surrey. *T:* Egham 45. *Club:* Travellers'.

Died 18 Nov. 1925.

VILLIERS, Francis John, CMG 1880; JP Herts; *b* 1851; 2nd *s* of late John F. Villiers, barrister. *Educ:* Aldenham School, Elstree, Herts. Private Secretary to Col Sir W. Owen Lanyon, KCMG, CB, Administrator of Griqualand West, S Africa 1875, and Clerk of Legislative Council; acted as Colonial Secretary, 1877–80; Auditor-Gen. British Guiana, 1882–98. Decorated for services in S Africa. *Address:* Stevenage, Herts. *Died 7 Feb. 1925.*

VILLIERS, Frederic; war artist, correspondent; *b* London, 23 April 1852; 2nd *s* of Henry Villiers and Caroline, *d* of Thomas Bradley; *m* Louise (*d* 1916), *d* of George Lister-Bohne; one *s* one *d*. *Educ:* Guines, Pas-de-Calais, France. Studied art at the British Museum and the South Kensington Schools, 1869–70; admitted as student at the Royal Academy, 1871; exhibitor of war pictures at the Royal Academy and the Institute of Painters in Oil Colours, Piccadilly; recipient of twelve English and foreign war medals, clasps, and decorations. War artist for the Graphic; in Servia, 1876; with the Russians in Turkey, 1877; with the Russians at Passage of the Danube, Biela, Plevna, Shipka; Afghanistan—Gadamuck and the Bazaar Valley, 1878; then round the World; with Lord Beresford on the Condor, El Magfa, Tel-el-Kebir, 1882; invited by the Tzar Alexander III to his coronation in Moscow, 1883; the Eastern Soudan—at Tokar, in the Broken Square at Tamai, 1884; with Admiral Sir William Hewitt on his Mission to King John of Abyssinia; up the Nile for the Relief of Khartoum, twice wrecked, 1884; with Stewart across the Desert— the Battles of Abu Klea and Gubat, 1885; with the Servians invading Bulgaria, 1886; Burma, 1887; across Canada with the Governor-General; then on a lecture tour through America, Canada, and British Isles, Chicago Exhibition, 1892; with the Japanese army, Battles of Ping Yang and the march on and taking of Port Arthur, 1894; a tour round the world lecturing, 1895; Coronation of Nicholas II at Moscow, 1896; in April 1897 joined Green army campaign against Turkey. During armistice visited Crete. Used the cinematograph camera for first time in history of campaigning during the war; also introduced bicycle for first time in any European campaign; joined Sirdar's army on its march to Omdurman, 1898; present at battle which finally crushed the Khalifa; lectured on that campaign throughout the United Kingdom and the Antipodes; left Australia for South African War, 1899; after occupation of Pretoria returned and then for fourth time started for Antipodes; left for Far East beginning of 1904; with Jap forces; only war artist present at the siege of Port Arthur; joined the Spanish army operating in Morocco, 1909; the Italian army on the invasion of Tripoli, 1911; the Bulgarian army in the war with the Balkan Allies and the Turks in 1912–13, and was at the siege of Adrianople; joined the French armies, 1914; was in the retreat in Flanders, Ypres, Neuve Chapelle, La Boiselle, Rheims, the river Aisne, Argonne and Verdun; after two years and a half with both British and French armies left France for a lecture tour and visits to other fronts; lectured through Australia, South Africa, Ceylon, India, failing to get into Mesopotamia, visited NW frontier, saw fighting on Mohmund territory, then continued lecture tour through the FMS, Straits Settlements, China, Japan, Canada, and the USA. Painted 20 feet battle picture of siege, called Sap and Shell. *Publications:* Pictures of Many Wars (illustrated by himself), 1902; Port Arthur (with original sketches), 1905; Peaceful Personalities and Warriors Bold (illustrated by himself), 1907; Villiers: His Five Decades of Adventure, 1921. *Recreations:* cycling, golf, motoring. *Club:* Arts.

Died 3 April 1922.

VINCENT, Marvin Richardson, DD; Professor of New Testament Exegesis and Literature, Union Theological Seminary, New York City, since 1888; *b* Po'keepsie, New York, 11 Sept. 1834; father a clergyman; *m* 1858. Graduated with first honours from Columbia College, New York, 1854; Instructor in the Grammar School of Columbia College, 1854–58; Principal Instructor, 1856–58; Professor of Latin and Greek, Troy University, 1858–61; licensed to preach, 1859; Pastor of the First Presbyterian Church, Troy, New York,

1863-73; Pastor of Church of the Covenant, New York City, 1873-88; Trustee of Columbia University, New York; member Society of Biblical Literature and Exegesis, New York Historical Society, and Religious Education Association; Director of New York College of Dentistry. *Publications:* translation of Bengel's Gnomon of the New Testament, 1860; Amusement a Force in Christian Training, 1867; The Two Prodigals, 1876; Gates into the Psalm-Country, 1879; Stranger and Guest, 1879; Faith and Character, 1880; The Minister's Handbook, 1882, new revised edition, 1900; In the Shadow of the Pyrenees, 1883; The Expositor in the Pulpit, 1884; God and Bread, 1884; Christ as a Teacher, 1886; The Covenant of Peace, 1887; Word Studies in the New Testament, 4 vols, 1887-1900; Student's New Testament Handbook, 1893; Biblical Inspiration and Christ, 1894; That Monster the Higher Critic, 1894; The Age of Hildebrand, 1896; International Commentary on Philippians and Philemon, 1897; A History of the Textual Criticism of the New Testament, 1899; fourth and last vol. of Word Studies in the New Testament, 1900; The Gospel according to Luke, in Temple Bible, 1902; Metrical Translation of Dante's Inferno with commentary; numerous review articles, essays, and addresses. *Address:* No 20 East Ninety-second Street, New York City. *Club:* Century, New York.
Died 15 Aug. 1922.

VINCENT, Ralph, MD, BS; MRCP; Senior Physician and Director of the Research Laboratory, the Infants' Hospital, London; Hon. Fellow of the Glasgow Obstetrical and Gynæcological Soc.; Consulting Physician to the Board of Control, Combe Bank Farm; *b* 20 Dec. 1870; *e s* of Ralph Vincent, solicitor. *Educ:* privately; Universities of Oxford, Durham, and Vienna; St Bartholomew's Hospital, London. Hon. Capt. RAMC (1914-15 medal). *Publications:* Evidence on Infant-Feeding, Milk-Supply, etc, before Privy Council Committee on Physical Deterioration (Minutes of Evidence, 1904); The Milk Laboratory and its relation to Medicine, 1906; Clinical Studies in the Treatment of the Nutritional Disorders of Infancy, 1906; Lectures on Babies, 1908; On Acute Intestinal Toxæmia in Infants: An Experimental Investigation of Etiology and Pathology of Epidemic or Summer Diarrhœa, 1910; The Nutrition of the Infant, 4th edn 1913; and various contributions on scientific subjects. *Address:* 32 Seymour Street, Portman Square, W1. *T:* Paddington 1568. *M:* E 1394.
Died 21 July 1922.

VINCENT, Sir William Wilkins, Kt 1912; JP Leicester and Leicestershire; *b* Bristol, 1843; *e s* of Rev. John Vincent; *m* 1866, Anne Susannah, *d* of Wm Stark of Chard, Somerset; one *s* two *d.* Chairman of Roberts & Roberts, Ltd, and J. Johnson & Co., Ltd; member of local advisory Board of London City and Midland Bank; Member of Leicester Town Council since 1891; Alderman since 1898; Mayor, 1902-3 and 1910-11; Chairman of the Derwent Valley Water Board; Governor of the Leicester Royal Infirmary and of the Wyggeston Hospital. *Recreations:* walking, travelling. *Address:* Knighton Hall, Leicester. *Club:* Leicestershire.
Died 27 Oct. 1916.

VINCENT-JACKSON, Rev. William; 3rd *s* of John Jackson, of London; *m* Annie (*d* 1917), *d* of Thomas Mitchell of West Arthurlie, NB; one *d. Educ:* King's College, London; Exeter and Hertford Colleges, Oxford. Scholar of Hertford College. Curate of Holy Trinity, Nottingham, 1863-69; Vicar of St Stephen's, Nottingham, 1869-95; Rector of Bottesford, Leicestershire, and of Kilvington, 1895-1918; resigned 1918; Hon. Canon of Southwell; JP Leicestershire. *Address:* 49 Campden House Court, W8.
Died 8 June 1919.

VINE, Rev. Marshall George; Warden and Chaplain of Philanthropic Society's Farm School, Redhill, since 1887; *b* Deal, Kent, 24 Aug. 1850; *s* of Rev. Marshall Hall Vine, MA, late Rector of St Mary le Bow, Cheapside; unmarried. *Educ:* Christ's Hospital; Islington Proprietary School; Hertford College, Oxford. BA 1873; Curate of Steyning, Sussex, 1874-81; Far Headingley, Leeds, 1881-86; Incumbent of Micklefield, Yorks, 1886-87; Hon. Diocesan Inspector of Schools, Rochester Diocese; Member of Diocesan Board of Education and of Council of National Association of Reformatory and Industrial Schools; Hon. Canon of Southwark Cathedral, 1906. *Publications:* In Loco Parentis; 23 Annual Reports of the Farm School, Redhill; numerous papers of Reformatory work. *Recreations:* inventions, music, drama. *Address:* Warden's House, Redhill, Surrey.
Died 5 Sept. 1918.

VINES, Rev. Thomas Hotchkin; Prebendary of Lincoln; Rector of Fiskerton, since 1876; *m* Catherine Maria (*d* 1921). *Address:* Fiskerton Rectory, Lincoln.
Died 12 June 1928.

VINOGRADOFF, Prof. Sir Paul Gavrilovitch, Kt 1917; FBA; Corpus Professor of Jurisprudence, Oxford University, since 1903; Member of International Academy of Comparative Law, Geneva; Acting President of Union of Academies, Brussels, 1925; *b* Kostroma, Russia, 1854; *m* 1897, Louise, *d* of Judge A. Strang, of Arendal, Norway; one *s* one *d.* Dr of History, MA, Hon. DCL (Oxford and Durham); LLD (Cambridge, Harvard, Liverpool, Calcutta and Michigan); Dr juris, Berlin; Dr *hc* Paris. While Professor in Moscow he exerted himself for the spread of instruction in Russia, founded the Moscow Pedagogical Society, and acted as Chairman of the Educational Committee in the City of Moscow; resigned his chair in consequence of a conflict with bureaucratic authorities and came to England, where he resumed his interrupted studies in English social and legal history. Lectured in Harvard and other American universities in 1907, and in the University of Leiden in 1921; lectured in the University of Calcutta, 1913-14; lectured in the Universities of Columbia, Johns Hopkins, Yale, Michigan, and California in 1923; conducted a Round Table Conference at the Institute of Politics, Williamstown, Mass, 1924; delivered 10 lectures at the Institute for the Comparative Study of Culture, Oslo, 1924; Director of Publications of the British Academy (Series of Records of Social and Economic History); Editor of the Russian Section of the Social and Economic History of the War (1914-17) published by the Carnegie Endowment Fund. Fellow of the Russian Academy, Petrograd; Foreign Member of Royal Danish, Royal Belgian and Norwegian Academies; Corresponding Member of Prussian Academy, Berlin; of Royal Academy, Bologna; the Academy dei Lincei in Rome; and the Society of Sciences, Livóv, Poland. *Publications:* Villainage in England, Russian edn 1887, English edn 1892; The Growth of the Manor, 1905; English Society in the Eleventh Century, 1908; Roman Law in Mediæval Europe, 1909; Common Sense in Law (Home University Series, 1914); Self-Government in Russia, 1915; edited (with Mr F. Morgan) the Survey of the Honour of Denbigh (1st volume of Records of Social and Economic History, published for the British Academy, 1914); Outlines of Historical Jurisprudence, vol. i 1920, and vol ii 1922; articles on Russia in the 12th edition of the Encyclopædia Britannica; edited (with Dr L. Ehrlich) for the Selden Society the 13th and 14th volumes of their Year Book Series; edited eight volumes of Oxford Studies in Social and Legal History, and the Essays in Legal History contributed by the members of Section VIA of the International Congress of Historical Studies held in London, 1913; The Rise of Feudalism in Lombard Italy (Russ.); Inquiries in the Social History of England (Russ.); Historical Types of International Law in Bibliotheca Wisseriana, Leiden, 1923; Custom and Right in the Series of the Institute of Comparative Study of Culture, Oslo. *Recreations:* chess, music, travelling, motoring. *Address:* 36 Beaumont Street, Oxford. *Clubs:* Athenæum, Reform.
Died 19 Dec. 1925.

VIPAN, Major Charles, DSO 1900; 3rd Battalion The Buffs; Hon. Captain in the Army; *b* 1849; 2nd *s* of late Thomas Curtis Vipan of The Mansells, Harlington, Beds; *m* Mary Frances, 2nd *d* of late Alfred Jones of Needingworth, Hunts, *sister* and *co-heiress* to late John Vipan Jones, also of Needingworth. Fellow of the Linnean Society. Served South Africa, 1900 (despatches, medal with clasps); retired, 1904; JP Hastings. *Address:* Ford Bank, St Leonards-on-Sea. *Club:* United Service.
Died 15 Aug. 1921.

VISETTI, Albert, FRCM; Member of Board of Royal College of Music and Professor of Singing; Examiner for Associated Board of RCM and RAM; *b* Dalmatia, 1846; *m* an American; naturalised British subject for the last 40 years. *Educ:* Royal Conservatoire of Milan. Gained scholarships from Governments both of Austria and Italy; at Milan his diploma exercise was a cantata written by his fellow-student Arrigo Boito; later received appointment as Conductor at Nice; went to Paris, was introduced by Auber to Court of Napoleon; wrote an opera 'Les trois Mousquetaires' to a libretto by Dumas père; came to England, 1870; was musical adviser to Adelina Patti for five years; wrote specially for her 'La Diva', which has been sung in all countries; on its formation was the first to be placed on the Staff of Professors at the National Training School, later merged into the Royal College; for several years held the post of Director and Conductor of the Bath Philharmonic Society, for which society he wrote two successful cantatas; knighted by the King of Italy for his literary attainments; Member of Worshipful Company of Musicians; Freeman of City of London. *Publications:* Italian translation of Hullah's History of Modern Music; Dr Hueffer's Musical Studies; Life of Palestrina, from the Italian into English; an Essay on Musical Culture; Life of Verdi, 1905. *Recreations:* leisure hours are devoted to lecturing and to contributing to musical publications both foreign and English. *Address:* 12 Phillimore Terrace, W8. *T:* Western 611. *Clubs:* Arts, Old Playgoers'.
Died 10 July 1928.

VIVIAN, Sir Arthur Pendarves, KCB 1902 (CB 1894); JP, DL; Hon. Colonel 6th Battalion (Territorial) The Welsh Regiment; *b* London, 4 June 1834; 3rd *s* of late John Henry Vivian, MP for Swansea; *m* 1st, 1867, Lady Augusta Emily (*d* 1877), 2nd *d* of 3rd Earl of Dunraven; one *s* two *d*; 2nd, 1880, Lady Jane Georgina (*d* 1914), *e d* of 10th Earl of Stair; two *d*. *Educ:* Eton; Mining Academy at Freiberg in Saxony; Trinity Coll., Camb. MP (L) West Cornwall, 1868–85; joined the Volunteers, 1859; Col commanding 2nd Vol. Batt. Welsh Regiment, 1872–95; Colonel commanding South Wales Volunteer Infantry Brigade, 1895–1901, when given command of South Wales Border Brigade; retired 1903; Hon. Colonel 7th Batt. (Cyclist) Welsh Regiment. Member of Glamorgan County Council, 1892–98, since which Alderman of Cornwall County Council. Decorated for services in connection with the Volunteers. *Publication:* Wanderings in the Western Land, 1879. *Address:* Bosahan, St Martin SO, Cornwall. *T:* St Keverne 12. *Clubs:* Brooks's; Royal Yacht Squadron, Cowes.

Died 18 Aug. 1926.

VIVIAN, Captain Gerald William, CMG 1918; RN; *b* 11 June 1869; *s* of Sir Arthur Vivian; unmarried. *Educ:* Farnborough; HMS Britannia. Entered Royal Navy, 1882; Midshipman, 1885; Sub-Lieut, 1889; Lieutenant, 1892; Commander, 1904; Captain, 1912; qualified in flying, 1913; commanded Naval Flying Base ship Hermes; commanded, during the War, Europa, 1914, Patia, 1915, Liverpool, 1915–17, Roxburgh, 1917–18; then commanding HMS Glorious. *Recreations:* cricket, shooting, fishing. *Address:* HMS Glorious, Devonport. *Clubs:* Brooks's, United Service, MCC; Royal Western Yacht.

Died 14 Aug. 1921.

VIVIAN, Lieut-Col Ralph, FRGS; *b* 25 May 1845; *s* of late George and Elizabeth Anne Vivian of Claverton Manor, Bath; *m* Susan Lawrence, *d* of John Endicott of Salem, Massachusetts, and *widow* of Marshall Owen Roberts of New York. *Educ:* Eton. Entered Scots Guards, 1864; served Egyptian Campaign, 1882 (medal and clasp and Khedive's star); retired 1883. *Address:* 15 Grosvenor Square, W1. *T:* Mayfair 3135. *Clubs:* Marlborough, Travellers'.

Died 15 Aug. 1924.

VIZETELLY, Ernest Alfred, author, etc; Chevalier of the Legion of Honour; French medal of the War of 1870–71; *b* 29 Nov. 1853; *e surv. s* of late Henry Richard Vizetelly, and Ellen Elizabeth, *d* of John Pollard, MD; *m* 1881, Marie Tissot of Albens, Savoy; one *s* three *d*. *Educ:* Lycée impérial Bonaparte, later Condorcet, Paris. During the Franco-German war (1870) he became a newspaper correspondent (youngest on record) and artist for Daily News, Pall Mall Gazette, and Illustrated London News; was in Paris during part of the German siege; passed out, joined the Army of the Loire, attached to Staff of 3rd Division 21st Army Corps; was in Paris throughout the Commune; continued acting in a journalistic capacity on the Continent until (*circa* 1886) he became an editor and reader to Vizetelly & Co., publishers. After the liquidation of that business, consequent upon a prosecution for publishing translations of some of Zola's novels, Mr Vizetelly reverted to journalism; but in later years prepared or edited English versions of most of Zola's works, besides producing: The Heptameron, English Bibliophilists' edition, 5 vols, 1894; The True Story of the Chevalier d'Eon, 1895; With Zola in England 1899; Bluebeard, Comorre the Cursed and Gilles de Rais, 1902; Émile Zola, Novelist and Reformer, 1904; The Anarchists, their Creed and Record, 1911; also three novels: The Scorpion, a romance of Spain, 1894; A Path of Thorns, a story of French Life, 1901; The Lover's Progress, 1902; further, as Le Petit Homme Rouge: The Court of the Tuileries, 1907; The Favourites of Henry of Navarre, 1910; The Favourites of Louis XIV, 1912; Republican France (1870–1912), 1912; My Days of Adventure, 1914; My Adventures in the Commune of Paris, 1914; In Seven Lands, 1916; The True Story of Alsace-Lorraine, 1918; Paris and her People, 1919. *Address:* c/o Victor Vizetelly, 27 Mount Road, New Malden, Surrey.

Died 26 March 1922.

VOGUÉ, Marquis Charles Jean Melchior de; Commandeur de la Légion d'Honneur; Membre de l'Académie Française et de l'Académie des Inscriptions et Belles-Lettres; Président de la Société Agriculteurs de France; Président de la Croix-Rouge Française; *b* Paris, 18 Oct. 1829; *m*; three *s* three *d*. Ambassadeur à Constantinople, 1871; à Vienne, 1875. *Publications:* Les Eglises de la Terre Sainte, 1860; Le Temple de Jérusalem, 1864; La Syrie Centrale, architecture et inscriptions sémitiques, 1865–77; Mémoires sur l'archéologie, l'épigraphie et la numismatique de l'orient, Villars, 1888; Le Duc de Bourgogne et le Duc de Beauvilliers, 1900; Jérusalem, 1911; Une Famille vivaroise, 1912; Discours agricoles et académiques. *Address:* 2 rue Fabert, Paris. *T:* 700–59; Château de Peseau, à Boulleret, Cher. *M:* 1661–U2. *Clubs:* Union, Jockey, Union artistique.

Died Nov. 1916.

VON DONOP, Lieut-Colonel Pelham George; Chief Inspecting Officer of Railways, Board of Trade, 1913–16; *b* 28 April 1851; *s* of Vice-Admiral E. P. von Donop; *m* 1890, Ethel Farran, *d* of J. Orr, the High Court, Bombay. *Educ:* Somerset College, Bath. Entered Royal Engineers, 1871; Captain, 1883; Major, 1890; Lt-Col, 1897; Inspector Submarine Defences, India, 1889–94; Inspecting Officer of Railways, Board of Trade, 1899–1913. *Address:* Heatherdale Lodge, Camberley. *T:* Camberley 178. *Club:* Junior United Service.

Died 7 Nov. 1921.

VOULES, Sir Gordon Blennerhassett, Kt 1906; late of the Admiralty; *b* 8 Sept. 1839; *s* of late Rev. F. P. Voules; *m* 1866, Frances Cotton (*d* 1912), *d* of James Minchin, Judge in India; two *s* three *d*. *Educ:* Marlborough College. *Address:* Hamslade, Portchester Road, Bournemouth. *Clubs:* Sports, MCC; Surrey Cricket; Bournemouth; Hampshire Cricket.

Died 24 March 1924.

VYVYAN, Rev. Sir Vyell Donnithorne, 9th Bt, *cr* 1644; JP; *b* 16 Aug. 1826; *s* of Rev. Vyell Francis Vyvyan, Rector of Withiel; *S* uncle, 1879; *m* 1857, Mary Frederica Louisa Bourchier (*d* 1907); three *s* one *d*. *Educ:* St John's College, Camb.; St Aidan's College, Birkenhead. Ordained, 1854; Curate of Churchstoke, Montgomeryshire, 1854–55; Rector of Winterbourne-Monkton, Dorset, 1856–66; Vicar of Broad Hinton, Wilts, and Diocesan Inspector, 1866–77; Rector of Withiel, Cornwall, 1877–79. Owned about 13,400 acres. *Heir:* *s* Courtenay Bourchier Vyvyan, *b* 5 June 1858. *Address:* Trelowarren, Mawgan; Trewan, St Columb, Cornwall. *TA:* St Martin, Cornwall. *Club:* Junior Carlton.

Died 27 May 1917.

W

WACE, Colonel Ernest Charles, DSO 1886; late RA; *b* Goring, 19 March 1850; *s* of Rev. R. H. Wace of Wadhurst, Sussex; *m* 1891, Gertrude Mary Hay, *d* of Charles Nathan, FRCS, of Sydney, NSW; one *s* two *d*. *Educ:* Marlborough. Joined Royal Artillery, 1871; served in Jowaki Expedition, NW Frontier, 1877 (medal with clasp); Afghanistan, 1878–80 (despatches, medal with two clasps); Burmah Campaign, 1885–86 (wounded, despatches, clasp for Burmah, and DSO); retired pay, 1926.

Died 29 June 1927.

WACE, Very Rev. Henry, DD; Dean of Canterbury since 1903; *b* London, 10 Dec. 1836. *Educ:* Marlborough; Rugby; King's College, London; Brasenose College, Oxford (BA). 2nd class Hon. Classics and Mathematics; Hon. Fellow of Brasenose, 1911. Ordained Curate, St Luke's, Berwick Street, 1861–63; St James's, Piccadilly, 1863–69; Grosvenor Chapel, 1870–72; delivered Boyle Lectures, 1874, 1875; Bampton Lectures at Oxford, 1879; Warburton Lecturer at Lincoln's Inn, 1896; Select Preacher at Oxford, 1880–81, 1907; at Cambridge, 1876, 1891, 1903, and 1910; Prof. of Ecclesiastical History in King's College, London, 1875; Prebendary of St Paul's, 1881; Principal of King's College, London, 1883–97; Chaplain of Lincoln's Inn, 1872–80; Preacher of Lincoln's Inn, 1880–96; Rector of St Michael's, Cornhill, 1896–1903; Chaplain to Inns of Court RV, 1880–1908; received honorary freedom of the City of Canterbury, 1921. *Publications:* editor, in conjunction with late Sir William Smith, of Dictionary of Christian Biography, Literature, Sects, and Doctrines, during the First Eight Centuries, 4 vols, 1877–87; and, with the Rev. E. Piercy, of Dictionary of Christian Biography during the First Six Centuries, 1 vol, 1911; also of The Speaker's Commentary on the Apocrypha; Boyle and Bampton Lectures; Lectures on the Gospel and its Witnesses, and on our Lord's Ministry; editor of Luther's Primary Works; Sermons on the Sacrifice of Christ, 1898; The Bible and Modern Investigations, 1903; The Principles of the Reformation, 1910; Prophecy: Jewish and Christian, 1911; Some Questions of the Day, 1912, and 1914; The War and the Gospel, 1917; The Story of the Passion, 1922; The Story of the Resurrection, 1923. *Address:* The Deanery, Canterbury. *Clubs:* Athenæum, National.

Died 9 Jan. 1924.

WACE, Maj.-Gen. Richard, CB 1897; retired, 1904; *b* 16 July 1842; *s* of late Rev. R. H. Wace, Wadhurst, Sussex; *m* 1875, Gertrude Mary, *d* of late Major Candy, CSI; one *s* one *d*. *Educ:* Marlborough. Joined the Royal Artillery, 1864; Capt. 1876; Major, 1879; Lieut-Col, 1890; Col, 1894; Maj.-Gen. 1902; served in the Afghan Campaign, 1878–81 (despatches twice, brevet of Major); Director-General of Ordnance in India, 1897–1902; Col Comdt RA, 1913. *Address:* 16 Court Road, Tunbridge Wells.   *Died 25 May 1920.*

WADDELL, Alexander Peddie–; Convener of Stirlingshire; *b* 1832; *s* of James Peddie, WS, of Edinburgh; *m* 1864, Georgina Catherine, *e d* of late Geo. Waddell, of Balquhatstone, whose name he assumed. DL for Co. Stirling. *Address:* Balquhatstone, Falkirk, NB; 4 Great Stuart Street, Edinburgh. *Club:* University, Edinburgh.
Died 26 Jan. 1917.

WADDELL, John; Professor of Chemistry and Librarian of the Science Department, Queen's University, Kingston, Canada; *b* Pictou County, Nova Scotia; *s* of Rev. Jas Waddell and Elizabeth Blanchard; *m* Annie Maud Burrows; two *d*. *Educ:* Pictou Academy, Nova Scotia. BA Dalhousie University, Halifax; BSc London; PhD Heidelberg; DSc Edinburgh; Hope Prizeman and Vans Dunlop Scholar, Edinburgh University; Professor's Assistant in Chemistry, Edinburgh; Professor of Science, Royal Military College of Canada; Member of the American Chemical Society and of the American Association for Advancement of Science; Fellow of the Canadian Institute of Chemistry. *Publications:* The Arithmetic of Chemistry; A School Chemistry; Quantitative Analysis in Practice; articles in a number of chemical and physical periodicals. *Address:* Queen's University, Kingston, Canada. *Club:* Frontenac, Kingston.
Died 4 June 1923.

WADDILOVE, Sir Joshua Kelley, Kt 1919; Wesleyan leader and philanthropist.   *Died 14 Feb. 1920.*

WADDINGTON, Mary King; widow of late W. H. Waddington, French Ambassador to England. *Publications:* Italian Letters of a Diplomatist's Wife, 1905; Letters of a Diplomatist's Wife, 1906; Château and Country Life in France, 1908; My War Diary, 1917. *Address:* rue Auguste Vacquerie 29, Paris.
Died 30 June 1923.

WADDINGTON, Samuel, BA Oxford; late of Board of Trade (retired 1906), poet and littérateur; *b* Boston Spa, Yorkshire, 9 Nov. 1844; *y s* of late Thomas Waddington. *Educ:* St Peter's School, York; St John's, Huntingdon; Brasenose College, Oxford; a Fellow of the Anthropological Institute; Private Secretary to Lord Balfour of Burleigh, and afterwards to Mr Thomas Burt, 1892; has travelled on foot through Norway, Holland, the Ardennes, Savoy, Black Forest, etc. *Publications:* English Sonnets by Living Writers, 1881; English Sonnets by Poets of the Past, 1882; Arthur Hugh Clough, a Monograph, 1883; Sonnets and other Verse, 1884; Sonnets of Europe, 1886; Sacred Song, a Volume of Religious Verse, 1888; A Century of Sonnets, 1889; Poems, 1896; Collected Poems, 1902; Chapters of My Life, 1909; Some Views respecting a Future Life, 1917; contributions to Nineteenth Century, Athenæum, Academy, Literature, Westminster Gazette, Pall Mall Gazette, etc. *Recreations:* rowing, mineralogy, literature. *Address:* 50 Brondesbury Villas, NW6. *Club:* Junior Constitutional.
Died 7 Nov. 1923.

WADDINGTON, Maj.-Gen. Thomas, JP; *b* 1827; *m* 1862, Emilie Helena (*d* 1909), *d* of Major-General Michael Willoughby, CB. *Address:* The Chestnuts, Pangbourne, Berks.
Died 31 Jan. 1921.

WADDY, Henry Turner; Metropolitan Police Magistrate, since 1917, Tower Bridge Police Court; *b* 12 Feb. 1863; 2nd *s* of late Judge Waddy, KC; *m* 1890, Alice Maud, *o d* of late William Dingley; one *s* four *d*. *Educ:* Leys School, Cambridge. Called to Bar, Inner Temple, 1885; Member North Eastern Circuit; late a Member of the General Council of the Bar; Recorder of Scarborough, 1913–17. *Address:* 206 Ashley Gardens, SW1. *T:* Victoria 4084. *Clubs:* Garrick, Devonshire.
Died 4 Nov. 1926.

WADE, Hon. Sir Charles Gregory, KCMG 1920; Kt 1918; KC 1905; KC (Eng.) 1920; Justice of Supreme Court, Sydney, since 1920; *b* Singleton, NSW, 26 Jan. 1863; *s* of W. Burton-Wade, MICE; *m* Ella Louise, *d* of Francis Bell, MICE; two *s* two *d*. *Educ:* All Saints, Bathurst; King's School, Parramatta (Broughton and Forrest Exhibitions); Merton College, Oxford (BA Hons Classics, Hon. Fellow). Called to Bar, Inner Temple, 1886; Crown Prosecutor, NSW, 1891; Prosecutor for Western Circuit and Central Criminal Court, 1894–1902; MLA, 1903–17; Premier, NSW, 1907–10; Attorney-General and Minister for Justice, 1904–10; Leader of Liberal Party in NSW, 1907–16; Fellow of Royal Historical Society, 1918; Chairman of Australian Canteens for Serbians, 1918–19; Agent-General for NSW, 1917–20. L'Ordre de la Couronne (Belgium). *Publications:* Married Women's Property Act and Employer's Liability

Act; Australia: Problems and Prospects. *Recreation:* Oxford University XV 1882–86; English XV 1883–86. *Address:* Supreme Court, Sydney, NSW. *Club:* Australian, Sydney.
Died 22 Sept. 1922.

WADE, Hon. Frederick Coate, KC; BA; Agent-General for British Columbia in Great Britain since 1918; *b* Bowmanville, Ont., 26 Feb. 1860; *s* of William Wade; *m* 1886, Edith Mabel, *d* of late D. B. Read, QC, Toronto; one *s* one *d*. *Educ:* Toronto University. Editorial Writer Toronto Daily Globe, 1882; called to Manitoba Bar, 1886; editorial writer, Manitoba Free Press, 1886–87; represented Department of Justice of United States in inquiry into claims of compensation made by Jean Louis Legare for surrender of Sitting Bull after Custer Massacre, 1887; first President of the Young Liberal Association, Winnipeg, 1886; re-elected, 1887; Member of the Provincial Board of Education, 1889; Member Council of Manitoba University and Winnipeg Public School Board; appointed by Lord Aberdeen Commissioner to inquire into the management of the Manitoba Penitentiary, 1897; Crown Prosecutor, Legal Adviser, and Member of the Yukon Council, 1897–98; one of British Counsel, Alaska Boundary Commission, 1903; first President Canadian Club, Vancouver, 1906–7; Senator of University of British Columbia, 1912; present by invitation at the Coronation of King George and Queen Mary, Westminster Abbey, June 1911. *Publications:* National Schools for Manitoba; The Klondyke: a Four Years' Retrospect; The Alaska-Yukon Boundary Dispute: its Practical Side; Some Comments on the Alaska Award; Canada at the Grave of General Wolfe; The Early Navigators of the Pacific; The Canadian Flag; A Short History of Liberalism in Canada; The Awakening of the Pacific, etc. *Recreations:* reading, travel, camping. *Address:* British Columbia House, Nos 1 and 3 Regent Street, SW. *Clubs:* Canadian (Vice-Pres.), Overseas; Vancouver, Jericho Country, Vancouver.
Died 9 Nov. 1924.

WADESON, Maj.-Gen. Frederick William George, CB 1915; Indian Army; *b* 12 July 1860. Entered army, 1880; Captain, ISC, 1891; Major, Indian Army, 1900; Lt-Col, 1906; Col, 1907; Maj.-Gen. 1916; Brig.-Commander, India, 1913; served European War, 1914–17 (despatches twice, CB).   *Died 10 Dec. 1920.*

WADHAM, Arthur; Founder and Editor of the Machinery Market, established 1879; writer on trade economics; *b* Barnstaple, 7 Sept. 1852; *m* 1st, 1876, Sarah Marina, *d* of Wm Swann of Bradford, Yorks; 2nd, 1916, Eliza Annie, *d* of late Thomas Summerson, Haughton le Skerne, Darlington. *Educ:* Society of Friends' Schools. Associate, Institution of Mechanical Engineers, 1893, Companion, 1922; commenced press agitation in 1879 for cheaper patents, ultimately secured by Act of 1883; contributed articles to Manchester Guardian series, Aug. 1903, in defence of Free Trade for Machinery and Engineering interests (reprinted in book form and published under title, 'Protection and Industry'); article on the Rise and Progress of the Machinery and Engineering trades for 'British Industries under Free Trade', 1903. *Recreations:* water-colour painting, music, golf, tennis. *Address:* Wardrobe Chambers, 146A Queen Victoria Street, EC; 11 Ridge Road, N; Scalebeck, Keswick. *TA:* Wadham, London. *T:* PO Central 730. *Clubs:* Highgate and Keswick Golf.
Died 3 July 1923.

WADIA, Sir Hormasji Ardeshir, Kt 1918; Barrister; Advocate, High Court, Bombay. *Address:* Bombay.
Died 10 Nov. 1928.

WADSON, Hon. Sir Thomas John, Kt 1911; *s* of John James Wadson and Sarah Perot, *d* of Forster Cooper; *b* 22 May 1844; *m* 1874, Eva Bonnell, *d* of John Samuel Darrell; one *s*. *Educ:* Warwick Academy, Bermuda. Member Board of Public Works, 1888–95; Member House of Assembly since 1875; Speaker since 1895; Chairman of Audit Board since 1898; President Chamber of Commerce, 1907–13; represented the general community of Bermuda at the Coronation, 1911. *Address:* Hamilton, Bermuda. *Club:* Royal Bermuda Yacht.
Died 4 Feb. 1921.

WADSWORTH, John; MP (Lab) Hallamshire Division, WR Yorks, 1906–18; *b* West Melton Fields, near Rotherham, 4 Feb. 1850; *m* 1872, Annie Eliza Bell of Newbigin, near Sheffield. *Educ:* Brampton School. Removed to Newbigin, near Sheffield, in the early sixties; was employed at Newton Chambers Co's Thorncliffe pit until the great lockout, 1869; worked at Wombwell Main Colliery, Wombwell, during the period of the Thorncliffe dispute; obtained employment at the Wharncliffe Silkstone Colliery, Tankersley, near Barnsley, as a coal miner, 1870; elected by the Wharncliffe Silkstone miners as their checkweighman, 1883–1904; was Secretary, President, and Delegate for the Wharncliffe Silkstone Branch of the Yorkshire Miners' Association for twenty years; Vice-President of the Yorks Miners' Association for fifteen years; President of the YMA, 1904; General and Corresponding Secretary to the YMA, 1905. *Address:* 2 Huddersfield Road, Barnsley.

Died 10 July 1921.

WAECHTER, Sir Max Leonard, Kt 1902; DL; JP; High Sheriff of Surrey, 1902; *b* Stettin, Germany, 1837; *m* 1st, Harriet Shallcrass (*d* 1910), *e d* of late Thomas Cave, JP, MP; 2nd, 1912, Armatrude, *d* of late Colonel Bertie Hobart, RA, and Mrs Hobart Grimston, of Grimston Garth, Holderness, East Yorkshire, and *g d* of the late Hon. and Very Rev. Henry Lewis Hobart, Dean of Windsor. *Educ:* Stettin. Came to England, 1859; naturalized 1865; published pamphlet on the Federation of the States of Europe (lecture delivered at the London Institution, February 1909), and personally submitted this scheme to the sovereigns and governments of Europe for approval and support; presented Petersham Ait (formerly Glover's Island), and the freehold of Petersham Lodge and grounds, to the town of Richmond as free gifts, for the preservation of the view from Richmond Hill; founded the Victorian Convalescent Home for Surrey Women, also the Princess Mary Memorial Home of Rest, and the King Edward VII Memorial Home for Surrey Children, all at Bognor; founded the Queen Mary's Holiday Home for Governesses at Petersham; founder of the European Unity League. *Recreations:* yachting, motoring, boating. *Address:* The Terrace House, Richmond, Surrey. *T:* Richmond 387. *Clubs:* Liberal Unionist, United Empire, Surrey Magistrates'.   *Died 3 Oct. 1924.*

WAGSTAFF, William George, CMG 1898; *b* Pembroke, 3 Nov. 1837; *e s* of late William Wagstaff, and Elizabeth, *d* of John Vaughan; *m* 1st, 1874, Marie Louise (*d* 1883), *d* of Georges Nein of Fribourg, Switzerland; 2nd, 1886, Sarah Amelia, *widow* of Wm Brenan of Odessa, *e d* of Richard Webster of Jersey, formerly of Leeds, Yorks; three *d. Educ:* Greenwich Hospital School. Was present first bombardment of Sebastopol, 17 Oct. 1854 (Crimean medal and clasp, and Turkish medal); appointed clerk to Consulate, Berdiansk, 1861; Vice-Consul, 1874; Vice-Consul, Nicolaïeff, 1876; Consul at Taganrog for province of Ekaterinoslav, 1884; and ports of the Sea of Azoff; Consul for Governments of Voronetz, Saratof, Samara, Ufa, Orenburg, Astrakhan, Stavropol, the Don Cossack country, and the Kuban and Ter districts, 1887; Consul at Riga for provinces of Livonia and Courland, 1889; Consul-General at Rio de Janeiro, 1895; received the Jubilee Medal, 1897; Consul-Gen. for the States of Rio de Janeiro, Espirito Santo, Minas Geraes and Matto Grosso, 1899; retired on a pension, Aug. 1900. *Address:* Belmont, De Roos Road, Eastbourne.

Died 12 May 1918.

WAHLSTATT, HSH Blucher von, 3rd Prince, *cr* 1814, **Gebhard Gustaw Lebrecht;** Hereditary Member of the House of Lords in Prussia [family old nobility of the German Empire, first mentioned 1214; first Prince was famous Field-marshal, hero of the Katzbach and conqueror of Napoleon]; *b* 18 March 1836; *e s* of 2nd Prince and Mary, Countess Larisch Moennich; *S* father, 1875; *m* 1st, 1860, Marie, Princess Lobkowitz, Duchess of Raudnitz (*d* 1870); two *s* two *d*; 2nd, 1889, Elisabeth, Countess Perponcher Sedinitzky (*d* 1894); one *s* one *d*; 3rd, 1895, Wanda, Princess Radziwill, *g g d* of HRH Princess Louise of Prussia; two *s* two *d. Educ:* at home. Joined 1st Regiment of Dragoons of the Guard, 1855; Military Attaché to the Prussian Legation, Vienna, 1857–59; served as First Lieut Cuirassiers of the Guard during the Austro-German War, 1866 (battles of Skalitz and Königgratz). Owned estates of Krieblowitz and Wahlstatt in Prussia, and of Radun, Stauding, Stiebnik, Brosdorf, and Polanka in Austrian Silesia. *Recreations:* shooting, swimming.

Died 12 July 1916.

WAINWRIGHT, Rev. Frederick; Hon. Canon of Chester, 1908. *Address:* Ballington Vicarage, Altrincham.

Died 12 Nov. 1921.

WAITHMAN, William Sharp; JP and DL County Galway; JP Cheshire; served as High Sheriff; *b* 1853; *s* of late R. W. Waithman, DL, of Moyne Park, County Galway, and *d* of William Sharp, JP, Linden Hall, Lancashire; *m* 1st, 1883, Lady Philippa Stanhope (*d* 1920), *d* of 7th Earl of Harrington; one *s* one *d*; 2nd, 1921, Lydia Frances Elizabeth, *widow* of H. Lyon-Smith, MD, of Harley Street. Served in army as temp. Capt. 1915–16. *Educ:* Eton. *Address:* Merlin Park, Galway; Gawsworth Old Hall, Macclesfield. *Club:* Kildare Street, Dublin.   *Died 8 Nov. 1922.*

WAKE, Sir Herewald, 12th Bt, *cr* 1621; JP; *b* 19 July 1852; *S* father, 1865; *m* 1874, Catherine, *d* of Sir Edward St Aubyn, 1st Bt, St

Michael's Mount, Cornwall, and *sister* of 1st Lord St Levan; three *s* three *d. Educ:* Eton. Capt. 4th Batt. Northamptonshire Regt, 1882–88. Owned about 3,200 acres. *Heir: s* Hereward Wake, *b* 11 Feb. 1876. *Address:* Courteenhall, Northampton. *Club:* Arthur's.

Died 5 Jan. 1916.

WAKERLEY, Rev. John E.; President Wesleyan Methodist Conference, 1922–23; Chairman of Wesleyan Methodist Church, East Anglia District; *b* 12 Nov. 1858; *s* of John and Mary Wakerley, Melton Mowbray; *m* Essie, *y d* of James Illingworth; no *c. Educ:* Melton Public School; Didsbury and Handsworth Colleges. Entered Wesleyan Ministry, 1882; first appointment to Nottingham; Member of Finsbury Borough Council, and of Holborn Board of Guardians; 2nd President National Brotherhood Federation; Secretary of First London District, Wesleyan Methodist Church, for twelve years; Member of the Legal Conference of the Wesleyan Methodist Church, Chairman Western Section of Methodist Œcumenical Conference; Secretary of Wesleyan Conference, 1917–22. *Publications:* Christianity and Business; Christianity and Amusements; The Making of Moral Manhood. *Recreation:* agriculture. *Address:* Tostock, Bury St Edmunds. *TA:* Drinkstone, Suffolk.   *Died 4 Sept. 1923.*

WALCOT, Lt-Col Basil, DSO 1915; RE; *b* 3 Dec. 1880; *m*; two *s*. Entered army, 1900; Capt. 1909; special employ Headquarters, 1906–9; Staff Capt., 1909–11; General Staff Officer, 3rd Grade, 1913; 2nd Grade, 1915; served South Africa, 1902 (Queen's medal 4 clasps); European War, 1914–15 (despatches four times, DSO). *Club:* Army and Navy.   *Died 14 Sept. 1918.*

WALCOTT, Charles Doolittle, LLD, ScD, PhD; Secretary, Smithsonian Institution, Washington, DC, since 1907; *b* 31 March 1850; *s* of Charles D. Walcott and Mary Lane; *m* 1st, 1888, Helena B. Stevens (*decd*); one *s* one *d*; 2nd, 1914, Mary Morris Vaux. *Educ:* Public Schools, Utica, NY. Director, United States Geological Survey, 1894–1907; Secretary, Carnegie Institution of Washington, 1902–5; on National Advisory Committee for Aeronautics (Chairman); Member National Academy of Sciences (President, 1917–23); Mary Clark Thompson medal; National Research Council (1st Vice-Chairman); American Association for Advancement of Science; American Academy of Arts and Sciences (President, 1923); Academy of Natural Sciences, Philadelphia (Hayden Medal); American Philosophical Society (President, 1925); Academy of Sciences of Paris; London Geological Society (Bigsby and Wollaston Medals); Royal Geographical Society of London; Gaudry Medal (1917), Société géologique de France; Royal Academy, Stockholm; Christiania Scientific Society; Academy of Sciences, Institute of Bologna; Imperial Society Naturalists (Moscow); Alpine Club of Canada, etc. *Publications:* The Trilobite; Paleontology of the Eureka District; Cambrian Faunas of North America; Fauna of the Lower Cambrian or Olenellus Zone; Fossil Medusae; Pre-Cambrian Fossiliferous Formations; Cambrian Brachiopoda; The Cambrian Faunas of China; Cambrian Geology and Palæontology; The Cambrian and its Problems in the Cordilleran Region; Pre-Cambrian Algonkian Algal Flora; Discovery of Algonkian Bacteria; Cambrian Trilobites; Evidences of Primitive Life; The Albertella Fauna in British Columbia and Montana; Fauna of the Mount Whyte Formation; Appendages of Trilobites; Middle Cambrian Algae; Middle Cambrian Spongiae; Notes on Structure of Neolenus, etc. *Clubs:* Cosmos, University, Aero of America, New York.

Died Feb. 1927.

WALCOTT, Col Edmund Scopoli, CB 1885; TD; JP, DL, High Sheriff for Devon, 1902; County Alderman for County of Devon; Hon. Colonel 6th Devon Regiment; *b* Castle Caldwell, Co. Fermanagh, 1842; *e s* of John Minchim Walcott; *m* 1900, Mrs Vicary, *widow* of J. Vicary, and *d* of late Lieutenant-Colonel Cox of Manor House, Beaminster. *Educ:* at home and abroad. Entered Bombay Army, 1860; Captain, 1869; Major, 1880; Bt Lieut-Colonel, 1881; Bt Colonel, 1885; served in the China War, 1860–63 (medal); Afghan War, 1879–80 (medal with clasp, mentioned in despatches); Soudan Expedition, 1885 (mentioned in despatches, medal, clasp, star, CB); member of the Geographical, Royal Agricultural, and Horticultural Societies, and the Japanese Society. *Recreations:* on most of the local bodies of the district; his garden. *Address:* Aylwood, Heavitree, Exeter.

Died 11 Oct. 1923.

WALDRON, Rev. Arthur John; Vicar of Brixton, 1906–15; Surrogate for Southwark; Lecturer in City Churches; *b* 30 Sept. 1868; *s* of W. Waldron, RN; *m* Lily J. Wilson, *d* of J. E. Wilson, CE; one *s. Educ:* Plymouth; Handsworth College; Oxford. London and Provincial Lecturer for the Christian Evidence Society from 1892–99; ordained, 1899; Curate, St Luke's, Camberwell, 1899–1901; a well-known lecturer against secularism in London parks, etc. *Publications:* Problems of Life; Ethics of War; Resurrection of Christ; Modern Spiritualism; contributor to several volumes of sermons. *Plays:* Should a Woman Tell?; The Carpenter, etc. *Recreation:* golf. *Address:* 31 Prince of Wales Mansions, Battersea Park, SW11. *T:* Battersea 1738.

Died 1 Sept. 1925.

WALDRON, Rt. Hon. Laurence Ambrose, PC Ireland, 1911; *b* Ballybrack, Co. Dublin, 14 Nov. 1858; 4th *s* of late Laurence Waldron, DL, MP for Co. Tipperary; unmarried. *Educ:* The Oratory School, Birmingham. Member of the Dublin Stock Exchange since 1881; Director of Grand Canal Co. (Chairman); Director Dublin and Kingstown Railway (Chairman); Director Dublin United Tramways (1896) Co. (Chairman); Director Gt South. and West. Rly of Ireland; Director Alliance and Dublin Consumers Gas Co.; one of the Governors and Guardians of National Gallery, Ireland; a Commissioner of National Education, Ireland; of charitable donations and bequests, Ireland; a Trustee of the National Library of (Ireland); Member of Senate of National University; MP (Ind. L) St Stephen's Green, Dublin, 1904–10. *Address:* Marino, Ballybrack, Co. Dublin; 10 Anglesea Street, Dublin. *Clubs:* Reform, National Liberal, Burlington Fine Arts; Sackville Street, St Stephen's Green, Dublin; Royal St George Yacht, Royal Irish Yacht, Kingstown.

Died 27 Dec. 1923.

WALERAN, 1st Baron, *cr* 1905, of Uffculme; **William Hood Walrond,** Bt 1876; PC 1899; DL, JP; *b* 26 Feb. 1849; *s* of Sir John Walrond, 1st Bt and Hon. Frances Caroline Hood, *y d* of 2nd Baron Bridport; *S* father, 1889; *m* 1st, 1871, Elizabeth Katherine (*d* 1911), *heiress* of late James Pitman, Dunchideock House, Devonshire; two *d* (and two *s* two *d* decd); 2nd, 1913, Helena Margaret, *d* of late F. Morrison and *widow* of Wilfred Grant. Capt. Grenadier Guards, retired 1872; MP (C) E Devonshire, 1880–85, Tiverton Div. Devon, 1885–1906; Junior Lord of the Treasury, 1885–86, 1886–92; late Chief Govt Whip; Chancellor of Duchy of Lancaster, 1902–5; Patronage Secretary to Treasury, 1895–1902. *Heir: g s* William George Hood Walrond, *b* 30 March 1905. *Address:* Casa Picciola, Roquebrune, Cap Martin, France. *Clubs:* Carlton, Garrick.

Died 17 May 1925.

WALKER, Maj.-Gen. Albert Lancelot; retired; *b* 23 Sept. 1839; 5th *s* of Edwin Walker of The Chase Cottage, Enfield; unmarried. *Educ:* RMC Sandhurst; received commission, 1857; passed Staff College, 1868. Entered 99th (subsequently Wiltshire) Regiment; served China War, 1860 (medal and clasp); Zulu War, 1879 (Brevet Lt-Col, medal and clasp). *Address:* 24 Marlborough Buildings, Bath.

Died 12 Feb. 1918.

WALKER, Rev. Arthur, MA; Prebendary of Wells Cathedral, 1903–11; 3rd *s* of William Walker of Bolling Hall, Yorkshire; *m* 1st, 1866, Adelaide, *d* of Archdeacon Sandford; one *d*; 2nd, 1881, Harriet, *d* of Rev. E. P. Vaughan of Wraxall. *Educ:* Westminster; Trinity College, Cambridge. Curate of Alvechurch and afterwards of Hammersmith; Rector of Easton in Gordano, and afterwards Rector of Dinder. *Address:* 13 Albert Road, Regent's Park, NW. *Clubs:* Junior Conservative, New Oxford and Cambridge.

Died 30 Dec. 1918.

WALKER, Sir (Byron) Edmund, Kt 1910; CVO 1908; LLD (Toronto), DCL (Trinity University, Toronto); FGS, FRSC, FRCI; President, Canadian Bank of Commerce since 1907; Chairman, Board of Governors, University of Toronto; Member of the National Battlefields Commission of Canada; President of Board of Trustees of the National Gallery of Canada; President and Founder of the Champlain Society for publishing rare works on Canadian History; *b* Township of Seneca, Co. Haldimand, Ont, 14 Oct. 1848; *m* 1874, Mary (*d* 1923), *d* of Alex. Alexander, Hamilton, Ont; four *s* three *d*. *Educ:* public schools. Commenced business career in banking office of his uncle, J. W. Murton, Hamilton; he entered service of The Canadian Bank of Commerce, 1868; General Manager, 1886; has filled the offices of Chairman of the Bankers Section of the Toronto Board of Trade; President and Vice-President of the Canadian Bankers' Association. *Publications:* many papers and addresses on banking and other subjects. *Address:* Long Garth, Toronto; Broadeaves, De Grassi Point, Lake Simcoe. *Clubs:* Toronto, York, Toronto; Rideau, Ottawa. *Died 27 March 1924.*

WALKER, Rear-Adm. Charles Francis, JP; 3rd *s* of Sir James Walker, 1st Bt; *b* 6 Feb. 1836; *m* 1873, Edith Frances (*d* 1906), *d* of Adm. Hon. Arthur Duncombe; one *s* (and one *s* decd). Served Crimea (2 medals and clasp); Silver Medal Royal Humane Society. *Address:* The Hall, Beverley, Yorks. *Died 8 Aug. 1925.*

WALKER, Edmund W.; a Master of the Supreme Court, 1873–1908; *b* 1832; *e s* of late M. H. Walker, solicitor; *m* 1859, Mary, *d* of Samuel Field, of Thame. *Address:* Vale Cottage, Esher, Surrey.

Died 18 Oct. 1919.

WALKER, Sir Edward Daniel, Kt 1908; JP; head of firm of E. D. Walker and Wilson, Wholesale Newsagents and Railway Bookstall Lessees; *b* Brighton, 12 April 1840; ancestor, Sir Henneker Walker, admiral in time of Charles II; *m* 1868, *cousin*, Rosalie, *d* of E. D. Walker, solicitor, Sheffield. *Educ:* privately. After establishing on a firm foundation his wholesale newsagency and many other commercial undertakings, directed his energies to public affairs; a member of the Board of Guardians, Durham County Council, a JP of the Boro', and for nearly twenty years sat on the Town Council; thrice called to the Mayoralty; two of these occasions were the Jubilee year of the late Queen, and the Coronation year of King Edward VII. Twice stood in the forefront of municipal battles: on the question of Gas management he saved the town £3000 a year, and on that of Water, whilst safeguarding on modern lines a wholesome supply was chiefly instrumental in preventing the adoption of a costly scheme (£80,000 to £100,000), afterwards admitted to be unnecessary. *Recreations:* cricketing, gardening, latterly a little golf. *Address:* North Rise, Darlington. *T:* 91 Darlington. *Club:* National Liberal.

Died 21 May 1919.

WALKER, Ernest Octavius, CIE 1891; MIEE; *b* Teignmouth, 16 July 1850; *s* of G. J. Walker, late 18th Light Dragoons, and Anna, *d* of Bishop Corrie of Madras; *m* 1881, Rosa, *d* of Rev. H. C. Deshon, Vicar of East Teignmouth; one *s*. *Educ:* Thorn Park School, Teignmouth; Regent's Park College, London; Hartley Institute, Southampton. Entered Indian Telegraph Department in 1871; in charge telegraph in Lushai Expedition, 1889–90 (mentioned in despatches, CIE); retired, 1892; Superintendent of Telegraphs in Ceylon, 1895–98. Decorated for services in Chin Lushai Expedition, 1889–90. *Publications:* papers upon Earth Currents in Journal of Electrical Engineers; A Romance of Ceylon, 1899. *Recreations:* science, antiquities, travel in wild countries. *Address:* 77 Iverna Court, Kensington, W. *Died 12 Feb. 1919.*

WALKER, Sir Francis (Elliot), 3rd Bt, *cr* 1856; *b* 9 March 1851; *s* of Adm. Sir Baldwin Wake Walker, 1st Bt, KCB and Mary Catherine Sinclair, *o d* of Captain John Worth, RN, of Duren; *S* brother, 1905; *m* 1883, Helen Constance (*d* 1901), *d* of late Rev. A. Paris; one *d* (and one *s* decd). Retired Lieut RN. *Heir: g s* Baldwin Patrick Walker, *b* 10 Sept. 1924. *Address:* Swansfield House, Alnwick.

Died 27 July 1928.

WALKER, Francis S., RHA; RE; painter and etcher; *b* 1848; *e s* of Thomas Walker, Dunshaughlin, Co. Meath. *Educ:* Catholic University, Royal Dublin Society; Royal Hibernian Academy. Was awarded Taylor Scholarship, and came to London 1868, where for some years was engaged in illustrating books, journals, The Graphic, Illustrated London News, etc, until he began to exhibit in the Royal Academy and other galleries; then turned his attention to etching and mezzotinting his own pictures. *Publications:* over seventy original plates, mostly of places of interest; some of these in book form, viz. The Thames from Oxford to the Tower; Rivers of the West of England; Killarney; and colour books—Ireland and Poet's Country. *Recreation:* walking. *Address:* The Firs, Highwood Hill, Mill Hill, NW.

Died 17 April 1916.

WALKER, Sir George Casson, KCSI 1911 (CSI 1906); *b* 9 July 1854; *s* of Rev. Joseph Walker and Catherine Mary, *d* of Admiral Sir William F. Carroll, KCB; *m* 1883, Fanny (Kaiser-i-Hind 1910), *d* of Samuel Coates, MD; one *s* three *d*. *Educ:* Winchester College (scholar); New College, Oxford. Mathematical Honours (Moderation). Entered ICS, 1877; served in various capacities in the Punjab, up to 1901, when he was deputed to the Native State of Hyderabad (Deccan) as Financial Adviser to the Nizam, in which capacity he served continuously until his retirement on pension in 1911; JP Borough of Hove. *Address:* 55 Wilbury Road, Hove, Sussex.

Died 27 April 1925.

WALKER, George Walker, ARCS, MA; FRS; Chief Scientist RN Mining School, HM Gunwharf, Portsmouth; *b* Aberdeen, 24 Feb. 1874; *s* of John Walker, accountant to Messrs Chalmers, advocates; *m* 1904, Agnes Elizabeth, *d* of James Gifford, art dealer, Aberdeen; one *s*. *Educ:* Gordon's College, Aberdeen (Foundationer); Royal College of Science, London (1st National Scholar, Mechanics); ARCS 1894; Trinity College, Cambridge (Major Scholar); 4th Wrangler, Mathematical Tripos, 1897; 'One One', Part II, 1898; Smith's Prize, 1899; Isaac Newton Student, 1899; Fellow of Trinity, 1900; Studied

at Göttingen, 1901; Lecturer on Physics, Glasgow University, 1903–8; Superintendent of Eskdalemuir Observatory, 1908–12; magnetic re-survey of the British Isles for 1915. *Publications:* papers to scientific journals and societies; Modern Seismology. *Recreations:* fishing, walking. *Address:* 17 Anglesey Crescent, Alverstoke, Hants.
Died 6 Sept. 1921.

WALKER, General George Warren, RE; Colonel Commandant, RE since 1899; *b* 6 April 1823; *s* of Major-Gen. George Warren Walker, commanding 21st Royal North British Fusiliers, formerly of the 8th Royal Irish Light Dragoons; *m* 1st, 1858, Margaret (*d* 1904), *d* of late John Anderson, Inverness; 2nd, 1905, Augusta (*d* 1918), *widow* of John Turner, Backwell, Bristol; one *s* two *d*. Entered Army, 1842; General, 1885; unemployed list, 1882; Assistant Civil Engineer, 1847; District Engineer, Kanara, 1859; Superintending Engineer, Coimbatore, 1863; Chief Engineer and Public Works Secretary, Govt of Madras, 1872–76. *Address:* 4 Forester Road, Bath.
Died 4 July 1920.

WALKER, Henry de Rosenbach, BA; *b* 30 May 1867; *s* of late R. F. Walker, Shooter's Hill, Kent, and Marie von Rosenbach, of Karritz, Esthonia, Russia; *m* 1900, Maud Eleanor, *d* of Rev. D. W. Chute, Rector of Sherborne St John, nr Basingstoke; three *d*. *Educ:* Winchester; Trinity Coll., Camb. Clerk in the Foreign Office, 1889–92; contested (L) NW Suffolk, 1895; Plymouth, 1900; MP (L) Melton Div. Leicestershire, 1906–10; elected to the London County Council for East St Pancras, 1913; Alderman of the County of London, 1919; Member of London War Pensions Committee, 1916; travelled extensively in Russia, Central Asia, the Far East, North America, the West Indies, and the Antipodes. *Publications:* Australasian Democracy, 1897; The West Indies and the Empire, 1901; reviews and newspaper articles. *Recreations:* music, travel, shooting. *Address:* 20 Stafford Terrace, W8. *Club:* Reform. *Died 31 July 1923.*

WALKER, James Douglas, KC; *b* 1841; *e s* of Jas Ouchterlony Walker, of London and Blairton, Aberdeenshire, and Jane Charlotte, *d* of Richard Holden Webb; *m* 1871, Susan Matilda, *d* of John Forster of Malverleys, Hants; three *s* one *d*. *Educ:* Rugby; University Coll., Oxford (MA). Barrister, Lincoln's Inn, 1866; Bencher, 1887; QC 1891; Treasurer of Lincoln's Inn, 1913; contested Bridgwater Division of Somersetshire, 1892; Writer of Prefaces to the Black Books of Lincoln's Inn. *Recreations:* golf, travel. *Address:* 20 Queen's Gate Gardens, SW7. *T:* 406 Western. *Club:* Reform.
Died 24 June 1920.

WALKER, Maj.-Gen. James Grant Duff, Madras Cavalry; *b* 4 Sept. 1842. Entered army, 1858; Maj.-Gen. 1897; retired, 1898; served Indian Mutiny, 1859; Burmese Expedition, 1887–89 (medal with clasp). *Died 23 Jan. 1921.*

WALKER, Sir James (Lewis), Kt 1903; CIE 1888; VD 1911; *b* 1845; *s* of late John Walker, Punjab Police; *m* 1st, 1866, Lizzie Marion (*d* 1892), *d* of late W. Hogan, of Simla; 2nd, 1893, Catherine Featherston, *d* of Charles Davey, of Canonbury, N. Lieut-Col Comdt 2nd Punjab Vol. Rifles, 1884–91; a Proprietor of The Pioneer and Civil and Military Gazette newspaper, India. *Address:* Worplesdon Place, Worplesdon, Surrey. *T:* Mayfair 3115. *Clubs:* Oriental, Junior Carlton; Bengal, Calcutta. *Died 13 April 1927.*

WALKER, Hon. James Thomas, JP (Queensland); FRCI; Fellow, Institute of Bankers, London; Senator of NSW in Commonwealth Parliament, 1901–13; Director of Bank, NSW (President, 1898–1901), Australian Mutual Provident Society (1887–1921), etc; Chairman, Women's College Council, and Councillor, St Andrew's College (both in University of Sydney); Chairman, Thomas Walker Convalescent Hospital; Chairman, Finance Committee, Presbyterian Church, 1889–1919; Director of the Burnside Orphans' Home; Trustee, Infants' Home, Ashfield, since 1888; President of Australian Golf Club, 1903–19; *b* Springfield Place, Leith Walk, Midlothian, 1841; *s* of John William Walker, who emigrated 1844, taking up Castlesteads Station, NSW; *m* Janette Isabella, *d* of Thomas Palmer, JP, Summer Hill, Mayo; three *s* two *d*. *Educ:* Circus Place School; Edinburgh Institution; King's College, London. On staff Bank of NSW, London, Sydney, and Queensland, 1860–85; first General Manager Royal Bank of Queensland, 1885–87; Executor of Thomas Walker of Yaralla, NSW; Member of People's Federal Convention at Bathurst, 1896, and Australian Federal Convention, 1897–98; owner of Mount Ubi estate, Wide Bay, Queensland. *Publications:* pamphlets on Australian Banking and Federal Finance. *Recreations:* golf, walking, reading. *Address:* Wallaroy, Woollahra, Sydney. *T:* City 6153. *Clubs:* Queensland, Brisbane; Union, Sydney; Tasmanian, Hobart; Melbourne, Melbourne. *Died 18 Jan. 1923.*

WALKER, John Bayldon; *b* 16 Jan. 1854; *e s* of late Charles Walker, Dewsbury, and Elizabeth Wood, *d* of late John Bayldon, Royston; *m* 1889, Mary Ann Ella, *e d* of late Wm Bayldon, Batley, Yorks. Barrister, Inner Temple, 1875; went NE Circuit and WR Yorks Sessions; Police Magistrate and Coroner, Freetown, Sierra Leone, 1890; Judge Supreme Court, Turks and Caicos Islands, 1895; Chief Justice, St Vincent, 1898; SJP, Port-of-Spain, Trinidad, 1902; Chief Justice, St Lucia, 1903; of Grenada, 1906–9. *Address:* 53 Breakspears Road, Brockley, SE4. *T:* New Cross 1223.
Died 19 April 1927.

WALKER, Maj. Reginald Selby, DSO 1916; RE; *b* 16 April 1871. 2nd Lieut, 1890; Capt. 1901; Major, 1910; Lt-Col, 1916; Chief Instructor RMC, 1904–9. Served S African War, 1900–2 (despatches, Queen's medal 4 clasps); European War, 1914–18 (despatches, DSO).
Died 30 Sept. 1918.

WALKER, Robert, MA (Aberd. et Cantab.), LLD (Aberd.); Registrar Emeritus of the University of Aberdeen; *b* 18 Feb. 1842; *y* of six sons of late Wm Walker; unmarried. *Educ:* Grammar School and University, Aberdeen; Clare College, Cambridge. Fellow, 1866–78; Examiner in Mathematics in Universities of Edinburgh, 1872–75, and Aberdeen, 1877–80; Librarian, University of Aberdeen, 1877–93; and Secretary of University Court, Registrar and Clerk of the General Council, 1877–1907. *Recreations:* gardening, fishing. *Address:* Tillydrone House, Old Aberdeen. *Club:* University, Aberdeen.
Died 27 Oct. 1920.

WALKER, Lt-Col Robert Sandilands Frowd, CMG 1891; FRGS; FZS; Commandant Malay States Guides; *b* 1850; *m* 1896, Beatrice, *d* of late T. J. Ireland, MP, and *widow* of Colonel Bolton. *Educ:* RMC Sandhurst. Ensign, 28th Foot, 1872; Captain, 1881; Hon. Lt-Col, 1889; ADC to Governor, Straits Settlements, 1878–79; attached to Perak Armed Police, 1879; Deputy Commissioner, 1880; Commissioner, 1881; in command of Pahang Expeditionary Force, 1892–94; organised Regt Malay States Guides, 1896; Acting Asst Resident, Perak, 1882; Acting Sec. to Govt, Perak, 1894–95; Acting Resident, Selangor, 1899; Acting British Resident, Perak, 1900–1. *Address:* Scott's Lodge, Knockholt, Kent. *Clubs:* Naval and Military, Ranelagh, Wellington, Sports.
Died 16 May 1917.

WALKER, Sir Thomas Gordon, KCIE 1908; CSI 1903; Hon. LLD Aberdeen; Lieutenant-Governor of the Punjab; *b* 14 Sept. 1849; *s* of late Rev. Henry Walker of Urquhart, Moray; *m* 1879, Adela, *d* of Rev. A. Irwin, Rector of Napton, Warwicks; two *s*. *Educ:* Gymnasium and University, Aberdeen. Entered ICS, 1872; Settlement Officer, Ludhiana, 1878–84; Registrar, Chief Court, 1884–88; Commissioner of Excise and Inspector-General of Registration, 1888; Deputy Commissioner, 1896; Divisional Judge, 1898; Judge, Chief Court, 1898; Commissioner, Delhi Division, 1901–5; Financial Commissioner, Punjab, 1905–7; member of Viceroy's and Provincial Legislative Councils, 1903–7; Lieutenant-Governor, May–Aug. 1907; Jan.–May, 1908. *Address:* Puckaster, W Worthing. *Club:* Junior Carlton. *Died 25 Nov. 1917.*

WALKER, Very Rev. Thomas Gordon; Dean of Achonry since 1907. Ordained, 1880; Curate of Emlaghfad, 1880–82; Rector, 1882–1907; Canon of Achonry, 1896–1907. *Address:* The Deanery, Ballymote, Ireland. *Died 9 May 1916.*

WALKER, William James Dickson, CB 1911; *b* 1854; *s* of late William Walker of Dungannon, Co. Tyrone; *m* 1884, Barbara Paterson; one *s* one *d*. *Educ:* Royal School, Dungannon; private tuition. Industrial Inspector and Adviser to Congested Districts Board, Ireland, 1897–1910; Member of the Congested Districts Board, Ireland, 1910. *Address:* Firbeck, Inverary Avenue, Belfast. *Club:* Ulster Reform, Belfast. *Died 10 May 1926.*

WALKER, William Sylvester, (*pseudonym* Coo-ee); FRCI; FIBP; author; *b* Australia, 16 May 1846; *e s* of late Hon. W. B. Walker, MLC, first Commodore and Founder of the Royal Sydney Yacht Squadron; *m* twice; three *s* two *d*. *Educ:* two English schools; Sydney Grammar School, NSW; Worcester College, Oxford. Sometimes in England, sometimes in Australia, etc; fifteen years in New Zealand; was three years a pastoralist in interior of Queensland; learned station life at Merungle on the Lachlan after leaving Oxford; was amongst the wild natives in Australia at Humeburne on the Paroo River, with the late Mr Sylvester John Browne; volunteered for Parihaka in New Zealand; was in South Africa, amongst the first for Diamond Fields, Klipdrift, Puiel. *Publications:* When the Mopoke Calls; From the Land

of the Wombat; Native-Born; Virgin Gold; In the Blood; Zealandia's Guerdon; The Silver Queen; What Lay Beneath; Blair's Ken; At Possom Creek; Finished; Koi, or The Thing without any Bones. *Recreation:* boating. *Address:* Soroba House, Oban, Argyllshire.
Died 6 April 1926.

WALKLEY, Arthur Bingham; dramatic critic of The Times; *b* Bristol, 17 Dec. 1855; *o s* of late Arthur H. Walkley of that city; *m* Frances Eldridge; one *d. Educ:* Warminster; Balliol and Corpus Christi, Oxford (BA). FRSL 1907. Entered Secretary's Office, GPO, 1877; Assistant Secretary, 1911–19; Sec. to British Delegation, Washington Congress, 1897; Sec. to Imperial Penny Postage Conference, 1898; a British Delegate, Rome Congress, 1906. *Publications:* Playhouse Impressions, 1892; Frames of Mind, 1899; Dramatic Criticism, 1903; Drama and Life, 1907; Pastiche and Prejudice, 1921; More Prejudice, 1923; Still More Prejudice, 1925. *Recreation:* gardening. *Address:* Bristol House, Southampton Row, WC; Brightlingsea, Essex. *Clubs:* Athenæum, Garrick.
Died 7 Oct. 1926.

WALL, Arthur Joseph, CBE 1924 (OBE 1918); late Secretary to the Prison Commissioners for England and Wales; *b* 27 Aug. 1861; *s* of late Capt. Michael Wall; *m* 1st, Jessie Elizabeth Pratt (*d* 1907); 2nd, 1924, Eleanor Annie, *widow* of late Albert Rutherford; two *s* one *d. Educ:* Battersea Grammar School. Entered Prison Commission, 1880; Assistant Secretary, 1910; Secretary and Inspector, 1917. *Recreations:* gardening, sketching in water colours. *Address:* 2 West Parade, Horsham, Sussex.
Died 7 Dec. 1927.

WALLACE, Maj.-Gen. Sir Alexander, KCB 1922 (CB 1908); retired, Indian army; *b* 22 Aug. 1858; *s* of late Alexander Wallace, merchant, Calcutta; *m* 1889, Ethel, *d* of Colonel G. C. Ross, late Indian Army; three *s* one *d. Educ:* Framlingham College, Suffolk (governor, 1916). Entered Army, 1876; Capt. ISC, 1887; Maj. 1896, Lt-Col Indian Army, 1902; Brevet-Col, 1904; Maj.-Gen. 1911; served Afghan War, 1879–80 (medal); Burmah, 1886–88 (medal); Hazara, 1891 (clasp); 2nd Miranzai, 1891 (clasp); in command of Kashmir Imperial Service Troops at occupation of Chilas, 1892 (twice wounded); NW Frontier, India, 1897–98 (medal with clasp); Waziristan, 1901–2 (clasp); East Africa, 1903–4 (despatches, Brevet-Col); AAG Peshawar Division, 1907; commanded Jubbelpore Brigade, 1908–13; in command 15th Scottish Division on formation, 1914; Suez Canal, 11th Indian Division, 1914–15 (despatches); Mediterranean Force, 1915; Egypt, in command Western Frontier Force, 1915–16 (despatches, Order of the Nile, 2nd class, 1916); Council of the British and Foreign Unitarian Association, 1902. *Publications:* occasional papers in Journal of US Institution of India. *Address:* Fleetwood, Wellington College Station, Berks.
Died 25 Dec. 1922.

WALLACE, Alexander Falconer, OBE; partner in Wallace & Co., Bombay; Director of Wallace Brothers & Co., Ltd, London; *b* Edinburgh, 30 June 1836; 6th *s* of late L. A. Wallace, Edinburgh; *m* 1868, Katherine Louisa, 4th *d* of late Wm Harter, Hope Hall, Eccles; one *s* one *d. Educ:* Edinburgh High School and University. *Address:* 20 Hyde Park Gardens, W2. *T:* Paddington 143. *Clubs:* Reform, Oriental.
Died 24 Jan. 1925.

WALLACE, Sir Donald Mackenzie, KCIE 1887; KCVO 1901; *b* 11 Nov. 1841; *o surv. s* of Robert Wallace, Boghead, Dumbartonshire; unmarried. *Educ:* private schools; Universities of Glasgow, Edinburgh, Berlin, Heidelberg; Ecole de Droit, Paris. Resided and travelled in various foreign countries, chiefly in France, Germany, Russia, and Turkey, 1863–84; Private Sec. to Marquess of Dufferin and Marquess of Landsdowne as Viceroys of India, 1884–89; attached to the Czarewitch as political officer during his tour in India and Ceylon, 1890–91; Director of the Foreign Department of the Times, 1891–99; Asst Private Sec. to HRH the Duke of Cornwall and York during his colonial tour, 1901; Extra Groom-in-waiting to King Edward VII, 1909, and to King George V, 1910; attached to Emperor of Russia during his visit to England, 1909; member of Institut de Droit International and Officier de l'Instruction Publique of France; edited 10th edn Ency. Brit. *Publications:* Russia, 1877; Egypt and the Egyptian Question, 1883; The Web of Empire, 1902; New editions of Russia, rearranged and brought up to date, 1905 and 1912. *Recreation:* change of occupation. *Address:* 26 Park Mansions, Knightsbridge, SW1. *Clubs:* Athenæum, Marlborough, St James', Reform, Polyglot.
Died 10 Jan. 1919.

WALLACE, George, KC 1910; MA (Cantab.); *b* 1854; *e s* of late Rev. T. S. Wallace, MA, Incumbent of St Paul's, Bolton, Lancs; *m* 1884, Nicolina Maud (*d* 1904), *e d* of late R. G. Deverell of Tullamore, King's Co.; four *d. Educ:* Clergy Orphan (later St Edmund's) School,

Canterbury; Jesus College, Cambridge. Called to Bar, Lincoln's Inn, 1879; then Middle Temple, Bencher, 1918, retiring, 1926. *Publication:* joint author of Roberts and Wallace on the Duty and Liability of Employers, 4th edn, 1908. *Address:* 26 Ladbroke Gardens, W11. *T:* Park 3272.
Died 24 Nov. 1927.

WALLACE, Lt-Col Hugh Robert, of Busbie; DSO 1916; JP, DL; late commanding Reserve Garrison Battalion Suffolk Regiment; 10th Gordon Highlanders; *b* 31 Aug. 1861; *s* of late Capt. Henry Ritchie Wallace, Gordon Highlanders; *m* 1st, 1886, Matilda Marion Christie (*d* 1905), *d* and *heiress* of late Archibald Campbell of Cammo, Midlothian; 2nd, 1908, Isobel M., *widow* of Charles Ralph Dubs, Glasgow, and *d* of late William Rae Arthur; three *s* one *d. Educ:* Cheltenham College. Vice-Lieutenant of Ayrshire; ex-Convener of County of Ayr; Hon. Sheriff-Substitute for the County; served European War, 1914–18 (despatches twice, DSO); retired Lt-Col, 1918. *Address:* Cloncaird Castle, Maybole, Ayrshire. *Clubs:* Carlton, Orleans; New, Edinburgh.
Died 2 May 1924.

WALLACE, Col Sir Johnstone, KBE 1917; iron and coal merchant; *b* 20 Oct. 1861; *s* of T. Wallace, Magherafelt; *m* 1889, Norah, *d* of John B. Bowes, Newcastle; two *s* one *d.* Sheriff, Newcastle, 1905–6; Lord Mayor, 1913–14; Alderman, DL, JP, Northumberland; Chairman of British Federation of Iron, Steel and Metal Merchants. *Address:* Parkholm, Newcastle. *T:* Central 400 and 4780. *Club:* Junior Constitutional.
Died 14 Nov. 1922.

WALLACE, Roger William, KC; Barrister-at-law; *b* Glasgow, 28 April 1854; *e s* of Hugh Wallace, JP, Dorset Hall, Merton, Surrey; *m* 1877, Sarah, *d* of John Thornton; one *s* one *d. Educ:* London University. Besides legal pursuits, took great interest in chemical, electric, and engineering work; member of Council of Electrical Engineers, 1891, 1899, 1900, 1901, and an Associate; first Chairman of Royal Automobile Club, 1897–1904; Chairman of Motor Union, 1901–4; Chairman of Royal Aero Club, 1901–12, then a Vice-President; Director Westminster Electric Supply Corporation, Ltd, and other electric light companies, from their inception. *Publications:* The Law of Letters Patent for Invention; numerous articles on motoring and chemistry. *Recreations:* shooting, golf, etc. *Clubs:* Reform, Bath, Ranelagh, Royal Automobile, Royal Aero, Hurlingham.
Died 13 Dec. 1926.

WALLACE, Sir William, KCMG 1907 (CMG 1897); FRGS; *b* 12 Sept. 1856; *s* of late James Wallace of Aberbrothock; *m* 1891, Christine Baillie, *d* of late Joseph Rickard, Dundee; one *d. Educ:* Arbroath High School. Late administrator of the Niger Company's Territories; chiefly occupied during thirty-two years acquiring and consolidating British interests and gaining political influence; concluded numerous treaties with the native potentates and Fulani Emirs; one with the Sultan of Sokoto, 1894; commanded or served with over thirty military expeditions. This work in a great measure led to the subjugation of the Fulani nation and native races, and so to the acquisition of Nigeria for the British Empire; three West African medals, five clasps, coronation medal; at the transfer of the Territories to the Crown in 1900 joined Government Service as Resident General; Deputy High Commissioner and acting Governor, Northern Nigeria, 1900–10; retired from Government Service, 1910; received Murchison grant from Royal Geog. Society for explorations in Nigeria. *Address:* Weycroft Manor, Axminster, Devon. *Clubs:* Devonshire, City Liberal.
Died 10 July 1916.

WALLACE, William, MA, LLD; Barrister-at-Law; *b* 17 Nov. 1843; *s* of Jasper Wallace, Culross, Perthshire; *m* 1869, Rebecca, *d* of Peter White, Edinburgh; two *s* one *d. Educ:* Geddes School, Culross; Grammar School and University, Aberdeen; MA; Hon. LLD of St Andrews. After college was Classical Master in Ayr Academy for two years; joined journalism in Edinburgh; edited Dumfries Herald, 1870–78; on staff of Echo and other papers in London, 1878–89; Assistant Editor, Glasgow Herald, 1889–1906; Editor of Glasgow Herald, 1906–9. *Publications:* New Edition of Chambers's Life and Works of Robert Burns, 1896; Burns and Mrs Dunlop, 1898; Scotland Yesterday, 1891; After the Revolution, and other fantasies, 1891; Life and Last Leaves of Robert Wallace, 1903; articles in various magazines. *Recreation:* golf. *Address:* 106 University Avenue, Glasgow.
Died 17 July 1921.

WALLACE, William, CBE 1920; Sheriff-Substitute of Argyll, at Oban since 1910; JP, Argyll; *b* Glasgow, 1860; *o s* of Dr William Wallace, public analyst for Glasgow and Lanarkshire; *m* Barbara, *d* of Alexander Munro; two *s* two *d. Educ:* Glasgow Academy and University (MA 1880). Admitted member of Scots Bar, 1888; Advocate-Depute in Sheriff Courts, 1901; Advocate-Depute on Glasgow Circuit, 1902;

Counsel for the Crown as *Ultimus Haeres*, 1903; Sheriff-Substitute at Campbeltown, 1904–10; late Captain 1st Vol. Battalion Highland Light Infantry. *Publications:* Banking Law, with Forms (with A. M'Neill), 4th edn 1913; The Trial of the City of Glasgow Bank Directors (Notable Scots Trials), 1906; The Scots Law of Bankruptcy, 2nd edn 1914; The Practice of the Sheriff Court of Scotland, 1909; The Sheriff Court Style Book, 1911; many articles in legal encyclopædias and journals, including Green's Encyclopædia of Scots Law and the articles on Scots Law in Modern Business Practice, The Encyclopædia of Accounting, etc. *Recreations:* golf, yachting. *Address:* Glenlee, Oban, NB. *Clubs:* Scottish Conservative, Edinburgh; Royal Highland Yacht, Oban.   *Died July 1922.*

WALLER, Alfred Rayney, MA, of Peterhouse, Cambridge; Secretary to the Syndics of the University Press, Cambridge; *b* York, 1867; *m* 1890, Emily Mary Hudson, Cherry Hill House, York. Engaged in literary work and journalism in London, 1888–1902. *Publications:* edited Florio's Montaigne, 6 vols, 1897; edited, with Arnold Glover, the collected edition of Hazlitt's writings, 13 vols, 1902–6; translated Molière's plays, 8 vols, 1902–7; edited the works of Butler, Cowley, Crashaw and Prior for the University Press, Cambridge, 1904–8; joint-editor with the Master of Peterhouse of The Cambridge History of English Literature, 14 vols. *Address:* 1 Cavendish Avenue, Cambridge. *T:* 543 Cambridge.   *Died 19 July 1922.*

WALLER, Augustus Désiré, MD, LLD; DSc Perth, WA; FRS; Director of Physiological Laboratory, University of London; *b* Paris, 12 July 1856; *s* of Augustus Volney Waller, MD, FRS; *m* Alice Mary, *d* of late George Palmer, formerly MP, Reading; three *s* one *d*. *Educ:* Collège de Genève; Universities of Aberdeen and Edinburgh. Corresponding Member and Mem. Associé of Société de Biologie, Paris, of Physiological Society, Moscow, of Royal Academies of Medicine, Rome and Belgium; Hon. Member Council of University of Tomsk; Lauréat de l'Institut de France, 1889 (discovery of electromotive action of Human Heart, and record by electrocardiogram); Premio Aldini sul Galvanismo R. Acad. d. Scienze d. Instituto di Bologna, 1892. *Publications:* Introduction to Human Physiology; Animal Electricity, 1897; Signs of Life, 1903; Physiology, the Servant of Medicine, 1910; The Psychology of Logic, 1912; scientific papers in Royal Society and Journal of Physiology. *Recreations:* billiards, motoring. *Address:* Weston Lodge, 32 Grove End Road, NW8. *T:* Hampstead 788. *M:* A 220. *Club:* Savile.
                          Died 11 March 1922.

WALLERSTON, Brig.-Gen. Francis Edward, CB 1916; *b* 14 Oct. 1856; *s* of late Edward Francis Wallerston, HM Diplomatic Service; *m* 1913, Phoebe Adeline, *o d* of late Henry Simpson of Bowstead, Cumberland, and Sparken, Notts, and *widow* of Thomas Bright Matthews. *Educ:* Rugby. Entered York and Lancaster Regt, 1876; exchanged to 1st Batt. King's Own Scottish Borderers, which he commanded; commanded No 6 District Lichfield, 1908–12; retired, 1912; served South African War (Queen's medal 3 clasps); European War, Commanding Infantry Brigade, 1914–17 (despatches, CB). *Address:* Sparken, Bournemouth. *Clubs:* Naval and Military, Bath.
                          Died 3 March 1926.

WALLIS, Charles Edward, MRCS, LRCP, LDS Eng.; Principal Assistant Medical Officer (Public Health Department) LCC; Lecturer and Senior Dental Surgeon King's College Hospital; *b* London; *e s* of Augustus and Fanny Margaret Wallis. *Educ:* Bedford; King's College; King's College Hospital. On becoming qualified went for a voyage as ship's surgeon in RMS Garth Castle; then in various vacations, ship's surgeon to Arctic regions, the Tropics, Canada, Cape Colony, United States; spent short time in Buffalo, USA. Late Dental Surgeon, King George Hospital; late Hon. Dental Consultant, London Military Hospitals; late Dental Surgeon, Victoria Hospital for Children, Chelsea; also under London County Council and Metropolitan Asylums Board; Fellow of Royal Society of Medicine; late Vice-President Chelsea Clinical Society and President of School Dentists' Society; Vice-President, Medical Officer of Schools Association; late Member of Representative Board of the British Dental Association; Chairman Marylebone Division, British Medical Association; late Chairman, Editorial Committee, British Dental Association. *Publications:* King's College Hospital Dental Reports (with Professor Underwood); The Care of the Teeth in Public Elementary Schools; School Dental Clinics; Dentistry in Ancient Times; T. R. Malthus; Marat, The French Revolutionary; Cagliostro and Dr Graham; Dog and Duck Water; Richard Partridge and Garibaldi; Why Harley Street, etc. *Recreations:* foreign travel, archæology of London, French history. *Address:* 26 Welbeck Street, Cavendish Square, W1. *T:* Mayfair 6657.   *Died 4 Jan. 1927.*

WALLIS, Rt. Rev. Frederic, MA, DD; Fellow of Caius College, Cambridge, since 1878; Canon of Salisbury since 1913; *b* 1853; *s* of Rev. Joseph Wallis, MA; *m* 1894, Margaret, *d* of Col Sir R. Williams, Bt, MP. *Educ:* St Paul's School; Caius College, Cambridge (Scholar). Carus Prize, 1874, 1877; Scholefield and Evans Prize, 1878; 1st cl. Classical and 1st cl. Theol. Tripos. Dean of Caius Coll., 1878–91; Divinity Lecturer, 1878–94; Examining Chaplain to Bishop of Sarum, 1886–94; Senior Proctor, Camb., 1892–93; Examiner for Theological Tripos, 1883, 1884, 1887, 1889, 1890; Select Preacher to the University, 1897, 1903, 1908; Bishop of Wellington, NZ, 1895–1911; Archdeacon of Wilts, 1911–12; of Sherborne, 1916–19. *Address:* 3 Studland Road, Bournemouth.
                          Died 24 June 1928.

WALLIS, Henry Aubrey Beaumont; *b* 4 July 1861; *s* of John Richard Smith Wallis of Drishane Castle, Co. Cork, and Octavia Willoughby, *d* of 7th Lord Middleton; *m* 1st, 1883, Elizabeth Caroline (marr. diss. 1906), *e d* of Hon. Albert Yelverton Bingham; one *s* one *d*; 2nd, Julia Mary Catherine (*d* 1922), *widow* of Capt. E. W. Curtiss and *o d* and *heiress* of Mrs Wright of Mottram Hall, Cheshire; one *d*; 3rd, Annie Christine Cecil, 2nd *d* of late Acheson ffrench, Monivea Castle, Co. Galway. *Educ:* Eton. Travelled on the Continent, India, Australia, New Zealand; farmed extensively in Ireland until the Irish property was sold in the 'nineties; frequently successful in the showyard with light horses; kept hounds in Ireland; Master of the Four Burrow Hounds in Cornwall, 1910–13; Master of the Woodland Pytchley, 1913–20; successful breeder of hounds, black and tans; temporary Major in command of a squadron in the Remount Service; assumed the name of Wright by royal licence on wife succeeding to the Mottram estates, 1916; resumed surname of Wallis, by deed poll, 1923; well known as a judge of hunters and horses. *Publications:* hunting editor of Land and Water for 2 seasons; polo editor for 3 seasons; wrote numerous articles on coaching, also on hunting and sport generally. *Recreations:* hunting, coaching, shooting; breeder of Polled Aberdeen-Angus cattle. *Address:* Keythorpe, Leicester. *Club:* Carlton.
                          Died 20 April 1926.

WALLIS, Mrs Ransome, Founder and Hon. Directress, the Mission of Hope Incorporated; *b* Walthamstow, 1858; *d* of John McCall; *m* 1883; two *s* three *d*. *Educ:* private schools; Lausanne. Devoted over thirty years to the practical study of the needs of the illegitimate child and the unmarried mother. *Publications:* various articles and pamphlets treating on the care of the unmarried mother. *Address:* Roseneath, South Croydon. *T:* 0817 Croydon.
                          Died 14 Feb. 1928.

WALLIS, Sir Whitworth, Kt 1912; JP; FSA; Director, Corporation Museum and Art Gallery, Birmingham; *b* Handsworth, 23 June 1855; *y s* of George Wallis, FSA, Senior Keeper, South Kensington Museum. *Educ:* privately in London, Paris, Hanover, and Berlin. Royal British Commission, Paris Exhibition, 1878; in charge of Bethnal Green Museum, 1879–81; in charge Indian collections HM Queen Victoria, Prince of Wales (Edward VII), Duke of Edinburgh, S Kensington Museum, 1881–84; at India Museum and at Berlin Exhibition, Stockholm, Copenhagen, Amsterdam; and appointed director Birmingham Art Gallery, 1885; well known as lecturer on Pompeii, Sicily, and English pre-Raphaelite art, etc; delivered special lectures to troops in France, 1917; Hon. Sec. Birmingham and Midland Institute; Trustee National Art Congress Studentship Fund; Member of Council, National Art Collections Fund; Life Trustee of Shakespeare's Birthplace; Governor, Memorial Theatre, Stratford-on-Avon, etc. Knight of several Continental Orders. *Publications:* contributor to many art and other magazines on above and other subjects; edited special catalogues, works of David Cox, 1890; pre-Raphaelite Painters, 1891; William Muller, 1896; English masterpieces by Gainsborough, Reynolds, Romney, etc, 1900; masterpieces by Raeburn-Hoppner, etc, 1903. *Recreations:* travel, photography, painting, golf. *Address:* Red Walls, Stratford-on-Avon. *T:* Central, Birmingham 7003; Stratford 41. *Clubs:* Garrick, Royal Automobile; Clef, Birmingham.   *Died 16 Jan. 1927.*

WALLS, Rev. John W.; Secretary, United Methodist Stationing Committee; *b* Low Norwood, near Gateshead, 7 Oct. 1858; *s* of John Walls; *m* Bertha Whitworth, Ashton-under-Lyne; two *d*. *Educ:* Whickham, Durham. Entered ministry, 1880; Member of the Uniting Conference held in City Road Chapel, 1907; President of the United Methodist Church, 1918. *Address:* The Avenue, Stone, Staffs.
                          Died 1924.

WALLSCOURT, 4th Baron (*cr* 1800), **Erroll Augustus Joseph Henry Blake**, DL, JP; Captain Coldstream Guards, retired 1867; *b* 22 Aug. 1841; *s* of 3rd Baron and Elizabeth, *d* of William Lock,

Norbury, Surrey; *S* father, 1849; *m* 1st, 1874, Lady Jane Harriet Charlotte Stanhope (*d* 1889), *d* of 7th Earl of Harrington; one *s* one *d* (and one *s* two *d* decd); 2nd, 1896, May, *d* of Sir William Palliser, MP. Gentleman Usher to Viceroy of Ireland, Duke of Marlborough, 1876–80; Lieut in Regt, 1866. *Heir: s* Hon. Charles William Joseph Blake, *b* 12 Jan. 1876. *Address:* Ardfry, Oranmore, Co. Galway. *Clubs:* Guards', Marlborough.   *Died 22 July 1918.*

WALLSCOURT, 5th Baron (*cr* 1800), **Charles William Joseph Blake;** *b* 12 Jan. 1876; *o* surv. *s* of 4th Baron and 1st wife, Lady Jane Harriet Charlotte Stanhope, *d* of 7th Earl of Harrington; *S* father, 1918; *m* 1897, Ellen, *d* of Joseph Mayo and *widow* of M. Boisset. *Heir:* none.   *Died 27 May 1920 (ext).*

WALMSLEY, Rt. Rev. John, MA, DD; Bishop of Sierra Leone since 1910; Vicar of St Ann's, Nottingham, 1904–10; late Hon. Canon of Southwell; *s* of late George Walmsley, of Hereford; unmarried. *Educ:* Hereford; Brasenose, Oxford (Somerset Scholar; 2nd Class Mods; 3rd Lit. Hum. 1885; 2nd Theol.; Senior Hall Greek Testament Prize). Ordained 1890; Vice-Principal Wycliffe Hall, Oxford, 1894–98; Vicar of Normanton-by-Derby and Acting Chaplain to the Forces, Normanton Barracks, 1898–1904; Member of Diocesan Committees for Central Society of Sacred Study; Higher Religious Education; Sunday School work; Diocesan Mission. *Recreations:* cycling, walking, climbing, etc. *Address:* Bishop's Court, Sierra Leone.
Died 9 Dec. 1922.

WALMSLEY, Robert Mullineux, DSc (Lond.); FRSE; MIEE, FInstP, FCS, AFRAeS; Chairman of Convocation and, since 1905, Senator of the University of London; Principal since 1896, and Head of the Electrical Engineering Department of the Northampton Polytechnic Institute, EC1; *b* near Liverpool; *s* of Robert Walmsley, jun.; *m* 1896, Emily Victoria, *yr d* of Captain Hicks, Chester; two *s* two *d. Educ:* private school; Queen's College, Liverpool. Matriculated at the University of London, 1879; BSc 1882; DSc 1886. Engaged in secondary school work, and later as a Technical Assistant to Professors Ayrton and Perry; First Senior Demonstrator in Electrical Engineering in the Finsbury Technical College, 1883; Principal of the Sindh Arts College, 1887; Staff of the City and Guilds (Engineering) College, 1888; First Professor of Electrical Engineering and Applied Physics at the Heriot-Watt College, Edinburgh, 1890–95; Chairman of numerous Senatorial Committees, and for 15 years Chairman of the University Extension Board; Chairman of the Council of the Association of Technical Institutions, 1909; Chairman of the Executive Committee of the Optical Convention, 1912; sometime Member of the Council of the Royal Aeronautical Society of Great Britain; Liveryman of the Worshipful Company of Spectacle Makers. *Publications:* The Electric Current, 1894; partly revised and extended the second edition of Dr Urbanitzsky's Electricity in the Service of Man, and in 1904 entirely re-wrote and extended the book, which has since passed through a much larger edition in four volumes, three dealing with the technology of electricity, the last being published in 1921; read Papers before the Institution of Electrical Engineers and the Institution of Mechanical Engineers. *Address:* 23 Hilldrop Road, N7; Northampton Polytechnic Institute, St John Street, EC1. *Club:* University of London.   *Died 15 June 1924.*

WALPOLE, Sir Charles (George), Kt 1897; MA; FRGS; *b* 7 Sept. 1848; *s* of Charles Vade Walpole, CB (*d* 1891), and Annette (*d* 1885), *d* of late Rear-Admiral James Prevost; *m* 1st, 1877, Maria Elizabeth (*d* 1914), *d* of late Henry Forde of Abbeyfield, Cheshire; one *s* (and one *s* two *d* decd); 2nd, 1922, Marie Bowles, *d* of late Percy Hale Wallace, and *widow* of Major H. J. Seton. *Educ:* Eton; Trinity Coll., Camb. (Classical Honours). Barrister, Inner Temple, 1873; President of the District Court of Larnaka, Cyprus, 1882; Attorney-General, Leeward Islands, 1889, and Member of the Executive and Legislative Councils; acting Chief Justice, 1890 and 1891; Chief Justice, Gibraltar, 1892; Chief Justice, Bahamas, 1893; retired, 1897; JP and Deputy-Chairman of Quarter Sessions for Surrey, 1903–14; Chairman of Quarter Sessions for Surrey, 1914–25; Chairman for Surrey Standing Joint-Committee; County Councillor for Chobham and Windlesham, 1912–22; Chairman Chertsey Bench, 1906–22; Chairman Chertsey Division Conservative Association, 1906–22; Chairman of the Surrey Provincial Division of the National Unionist Association, 1912–23; Member of the Surrey Central Defence Committee, Aug. 1914–Dec. 1918; Chairman of the Guildford Appeal Tribunal, 1916, 1917, 1918. *Publications:* A Rubric of the Common Law; A Short History of the Kingdom of Ireland; A Translation of the Ottoman Penal Code; The Leeward Islands Magistrates Acts. *Address:* 4 Kensington Court, W8. *T:* Western 2169. *Clubs:* New University, Surrey Magistrates.
Died 24 May 1926.

WALPOLE, Sir Horatio George, KCB 1892 (CB 1880); Assistant Under-Secretary for India, 1883–1907; *b* 9 Sept. 1843; 2nd *s* of Rt Hon. Spencer H. Walpole, QC, and Isabella, *d* of Rt Hon. Spencer Perceval, MP; *m* 1870, Selina, *d* of Capt. John T. Perceval; two *s* one *d. Educ:* Eton. *Address:* Danegate, Eridge Green, Sussex. *Clubs:* Carlton, Athenæum.   *Died 29 June 1923.*

WALPOLE, Ralph Charles; Librarian, House of Commons, 1887–1908; *b* 1844; 3rd *s* of late Rev. Thomas Walpole, of Stagbury, Surrey. *Educ:* Radley. *Recreation:* golf. *Club:* Union.
Died 20 Feb. 1928.

WALROND, Col Henry, JP; Marquis de Vallado (*cr* 1633), etc, in Spain; *b* Paris, 9 Nov. 1841; *e s* of late Bethell Walrond, Dulford House, Collumpton, and Lady Janet St Clair Erskine, *d* of 2nd Earl of Rosslyn; *co-heir* to the Barony of Welles (*cr* 1254); *m* 1861, Caroline Maud (*d* 1915), *d* of late W. J. Clark, Buckland Tout Saints, Devon; five *s* four *d. Educ:* Christ Church, Oxford. Joined 4th Batt. Devon Regiment, 1863; Capt. 1872; Major, 1882; Lieut-Col and Hon. Col, 1893; retired with hon. rank of Colonel, 1897. *Publications:* Historical Records of 1st Devon Militia (4th Batt. Devon Regt); joint author of the Archery volume of the Badminton Library; editor, Archers' Register. *Recreations:* shooting, yachting, archery. *Address:* 21 Blomfield Street, W. *Club:* Royal Toxophilite Society.
Died 19 June 1917.

WALROND, Main Swete Osmond, CMG 1901; *b* 22 Feb. 1870; *s* of late Rev. Main S. A. Walrond, MA. *Educ:* Harrow; Balliol, Oxford. Companion and Tutor to Prince Kemal el dine, *o s* of Sultan Hussein, 1892–94; Land Tax Adjustment Commission, Ministry of Finance, Egypt, 1894–97; Private Secretary to High Commissioner, South Africa, 1897–1905; appointed District Commissioner, Cyprus, 1905, but did not proceed; employed in Arab Bureau, Cairo, under High Commissioner for Egypt, 1917–18; resided in Cairo, studying Arabic, advised in private capacity Lord Milner's Mission to Egypt, 1919–21. *Club:* St James'.   *Died 14 Nov. 1927.*

WALSH, Hon. Gerald; a General Inspector, Ministry of Health; *b* 16 Dec. 1864; *s* of 2nd Baron Ormathwaite; *m* 1916, Averil Constance Antonette Janetta, *d* of late Col W. T. Markham, Becca Hall, Yorks. *Address:* Charnwood, Melton Mowbray. *Clubs:* Boodle's, White's.
Died 18 May 1925.

WALSH, Colonel Henry Alfred, CB 1905; JP, Somersets.; *b* 18 Aug. 1853; *e s* of late Theobald Walsh; *m* 1880, Ann Pollexfen, *d* of late Benjamin Sparrow, of Cleeve, Ivybridge, Devon; one *s* one *d.* Joined 1st Somerset Militia, 1870; 1st Battalion 13th Light Infantry, 1874; Adjutant, 1880–84; Adjutant 3rd Battalion Somerset Light Infantry, 1885–90; commanded 1st Battalion, 1898–1902; commanded 20th Regimental District, 1902–4; Chief Recruiting Staff Officer, London, 1904; served in the Mounted Infantry in the Sekukuni Campaign, 1877; Zulu War, 1878–79, present at the re-occupation of Isandlwana, and battles of Zlobane, Kambula, and Ulundi (medal with clasp); Nile Campaign, 1884–85, in the Mounted Infantry of the Camel Corps, present reconnaissance to Gakdul Wells, at the battles of Abu Klea and Gubat, and the second Abu Klea (dangerously wounded, despatches, medal with two clasps, bronze star, brevet of Major). *Address:* Hillmore, Bishops Hull, Taunton. *Club:* Army and Navy.
Died 25 Nov. 1918.

WALSH, Very Rev. James Hornidge, DD; Dean of Dublin, commonly called Dean of Christ Church Cathedral, Dublin, 1908–18; *m* 1875, Jane Mary, *y d* of late Francis Alex. Fitzgerald, LLD, Baron of the Court of Exchequer. *Educ:* Trinity College, Dublin; Scholar, BA, Senior Moderator Classical (First), 1858; Archbishop King's Prizeman (First), 1859; Theological Exhibitioner (First), entitling to Divinity Testimonium, 1861. Deacon, 1860; Priest, 1861; Curate of Dundrum, Dublin; Adare, Limerick; Rector of Chapel Russell, Limerick; Curate of St Stephen's, Dublin; Rector of St Stephen's, 1883–1908; Assistant to Archbishop King, Lecturer, TCD, 1877–83; to Regius Professor, 1883–1903; Canon of Christ Church, Dublin, 1893–1905; Chancellor of Christ Church, Dublin, 1905–8; Examining Chaplain to late Lord Plunket, Lord Archbishop of Dublin, 1893–97; to Lord Archbishop of Dublin (Peacocke), 1897; Private and Examining Chaplain to late Bishops of Limerick (Graves and Bunbury); Chaplain to the Lord-Lieutenant; member of General Synod and of Representative Church Body. *Address:* 47 Upper Mount Street, Dublin. *Clubs:* University, Stephen's Green, Dublin.
Died 4 Sept. 1919.

WALSH, John, JP; MP (IN) Cork County South, 1911–18; *b* 1856. Chairman of Beamish & Crawford Bottling Co., Bandon; extensive farming; member of Cork County Council. *Recreations:* fox-hunting, golfing, fishing. *Address:* Eversleigh, Bandon, Co. Cork. *T:* Bandon 30. *TA:* Walsh, Bandon. *Died 25 Aug. 1925.*

WALSH, Langton Prendergast, CIE 1890; JP; *b* 29 Feb. 1856; *e s* of late Col T. Prendergast B. Walsh of Laragh, Co. Cavan, and Ealing, Middlesex; *m* 1st, 1891, Annie Clementina, *d* of late Major R. G. Macgregor, RA (*d* 1894); 2nd, 1902, Laura (*d* 1918), *o c* of late John Forbes, KC; one *s* two *d*. *Educ:* France; Cowley, Oxford. Entered Marine Postal Service, 1873; transferred to Bombay Political Service, 1879; attached to Staff of Indian Div. in Egypt, 1882; present at Kassassin and Tel-el-Kebir (medal, clasp, and bronze star, despatches); services lent to British Foreign Office, 1884; in Consular and administrative charge Berbera and Zeila, NE Africa, 1884–92; raised Somali Coast Protectorate Police; operations against Jibril Abuker tribes, 1886 (thanked by Govt of Bombay); Esa Expedition, 1890; present at Hussein Zareeba (services commended by Governments of India and Bombay); served as Political Assistant in Kathiawar, Aden, and Southern Maratha country; Political Agent at Sawant Wadi and Commandant Sawant Wadi Local Infantry Corps, 1896–1903; retired 1903. *Publications:* for many years a contributor to the Indian press. *Recreations:* big-game shooting, travel, billiards, whist. *Address:* Plas Idwal, Gunnersbury Avenue, W5. *T:* Ealing 1865. *Clubs:* Carlton, Conservative. *Died 17 March 1927.*

WALSH, Ven. Robert, DD; Archdeacon of Dublin, 1909; Rector of Donnybrook, 1889, Chaplain to the Lord-Lieutenant; Examining Chaplain to the Archbishop of Dublin; *e s* of Rt Hon. John Edward Walsh, LLD (*d* 1869), Master of the Rolls in Ireland and formerly MP for the University of Dublin, and Blair Belinda, *o d* of late Captain Gordon John M'Neill, 77th Regiment; *m* 1st, 1873, Elizabeth Sophia (*d* 1893), *d* of Rev. Joseph Carson, DD, Vice-Provost, Trinity College, Dublin; 2nd, 1898, Amy Elinor, *o d* of late Most Rev. Robert Samuel Gregg, DD, Archbishop of Armagh and Primate of all Ireland; three *s* one *d*. *Educ:* Trinity College, Dublin (BA). Auditor College Historical Society and Gold Medallist, Oratory, 1864; Vice-Pres. 1900; Div. Test., MA; DD 1889; Member of Senate, 1889. Ordained curate of Tamlaght Finlagan, Dio. Derry, 1865; Curate of St Mary, Dublin, 1867; Rector, Malahide, 1874; Member General Synod, Representative Church Body, and Standing Committee, 1888; Prebendary, St John, Christ Church Cathedral, 1906. *Publications:* Fingal and its Churches, 1888; sermons. *Address:* St Mary's Rectory, Donnybrook, Dublin. *Club:* University, Dublin. *Died 24 Feb. 1917.*

WALSH, Valentine John Hussey-; *b* 17 Feb. 1862; *e s* of Walter Hussey Walsh, JP, of Mulhassey, Co. Roscommon, and 81 Onslow Gardens, SW; *m* 1907, Elizabeth Duchesse de La Mothe Houdancourt, grandee of Spain, 1st class, *d* of Count Artus de Cossé Brissac (*s* of 10th Duc de Brissac) and Alix, *d* of Louis, Marquis de Walsh-Serrant, Duc de La Mothe Houdancourt, grandee of Spain. *Educ:* Oratory School, Birmingham; Kalksburg, Austria; Edinburgh University. Called to Bar, Middle Temple, 1885; went the Western Circuit and Wiltshire Sessions, 1886–1907; Private Secretary to Lord Londonderry, Postmaster-General, 1900–2; contested (C) Carlisle, Jan. 1910; wrote for the Quarterly Review, Fortnightly Review, Blackwood's Magazine, and Revue Hebdomadaire, and many papers. *Recreations:* golf, cycling. *Address:* 24 Ennismore Gardens, SW. *T:* Western 4025; 7 Rue Galilée, Paris. *TA:* Passy 68.68; Mulhussey, Athlone; Le Fayel Canly (Oise), France; Anglesqueville, St-Valery-en-Caux (Seine Inférieure), France. *Clubs:* Athenæum; Union, Interallié, Paris. *Died 20 April 1925.*

WALSH, Rt. Rev. William, MA, Hon DD; Archdeacon and Canon of Canterbury since 1897; Chaplain of the Cinque Ports, 1901–16; *b* 1836; *m* 1865, Catharine Banchory, *d* of General Pickering, RA; two *s*. *Educ:* St Alban's Hall (transferred to Merton Coll.), Oxford. Prebendary of St Paul's, 1889–91; Bishop of Mauritius, 1891–97; Bishop (Suffragan) of Dover, 1898–1916. *Publication:* Progress of the Church in London, 1887, second edition, 1908. *Address:* The Precincts, Canterbury. *Club:* Athenæum. *Died 17 Oct. 1918.*

WALSH, Most Rev. William J., DD; Archbishop of Dublin (Roman Catholic) and Primate of Ireland since 1885; *b* Dublin, 30 Jan. 1841. *Educ:* St Laurence O'Toole's Seminary, Dublin; Catholic Univ. of Ireland; St Patrick's Coll. Maynooth. Professor of Dogmatic and Moral Theology, Maynooth, 1867; Vice-President, Maynooth Coll. 1878; Canon in Diocesan Chapter of Dublin, 1879; President, Maynooth Coll. 1881; Member of Senate of Royal Univ. of Ireland, 1883 (resigned 1884); Vicar-Capitular of Dublin, 1885; Commissioner of Education in Ireland, 1891 (resigned 1917); Commissioner of

Intermediate Education in Ireland, 1892 (resigned 1919); Commissioner of Charitable Donations and Bequests, Ireland, 1893; Commissioner of National Education in Ireland, 1895 (resigned 1901); member of Consultative Committee on Education in connection with Department of Agriculture and Technical Instruction for Ireland, 1900–4; member of Commission on Manual and Practical Instruction in Primary Schools in Ireland, 1897–98; of Commission on Intermediate Education in Ireland, 1898–99; of the Dublin Statutory Commission appointed by the Irish University Act 1908; of the Senate of the National University of Ireland, 1908; First Chancellor of the National University of Ireland, 1908. *Publications:* Tractatus de Actibus Humanis, 1880, 1891; A Plain Exposition of the Irish Land Act of 1881, 1881; The Queen's Colleges and the Royal University of Ireland, 1883, 1884; Ordo Exsequiarum, 1884, 1890, 1900; Harmony of the Gospel Narratives of the Passion, etc, 1885; Grammar of Gregorian Music, 1885; Addresses on Various Subjects, 1886; Two Addresses on the Irish University Question, 1890; Statement of the Chief Grievances of Irish Catholics in the Matter of Education, Primary, Intermediate, and University, 1890; Bimetallism and Monometallism, 1893, 1894, 1895, 1896; The Irish University Question, 1897; Trinity College and the University of Dublin, 1902; The Irish University Question; Trinity College and its Medical School, 1906; The Motu Proprio Quantavis Diligentia, and its Critics, 1912; O'Connell, Archbishop Murray, and the Board of Charitable Donations and Bequests. *Address:* Archbishop's House, Dublin. *Died 9 April 1921.*

WALSHAM, Hugh, MA, MD (Cantab.); FRCP; FRAS; Consulting Physician to the City of London Hospital for Diseases of the Chest, Consulting Radiologist to St Bartholomew's Hospital; Consulting Radiologist to King Edward VII Sanatorium, Midhurst; late Medical Officer in Charge of the X-ray Department, St Bartholomew's Hospital, and Lecturer of Radiology to the Medical School; *b* London; 2nd *s* of William Walker Walsham, Wisbech, Cambs; *m* 1916, Amy, *d* of Stephen Bannister, Coventry. *Educ:* King's College School, London; Caius College, Cambridge; St Bartholomew's Hospital, and Hospital for Sick Children, Great Ormond Street. Pathologist for some years to the Victoria Park Chest Hospital; Medical Referee to the National Sanatorium, Benenden, Kent, and Consulting Physician, X-ray Department, Eltham Cottage Hospital; awarded by the Royal College of Physicians the Weber Parkes Prize and First Medal for research work on Tuberculosis, 1903; President of the Radiology Section of British Medical Association, Birmingham, 1911; Vice-President, Sec. Radiol. 17th Internat. Cong. Med. Lond., 1913; Fellow, Royal Society of Medicine. *Publications:* The Channels of Infection in Tuberculosis, 1904; The Röntgen Rays in the diagnosis of Diseases of the Chest, 1906; numerous papers to medical societies and journals. *Recreation:* astronomy, especially solar physics. *Address:* 114 Harley Street, W1. *T:* Langham 2157. *Died 13 April 1924.*

WALSINGHAM, 6th Baron (*cr* 1780), **Thomas de Grey,** DL; JP; MA; LLD (Cambridge), 1891; FRS, FLS, FZS, FES (President, 1889–90); High Steward of University of Cambridge since 1891, and of the Borough of King's Lynn since 1894; Trustee of British Museum, the Hunterian Museum (Royal College of Surgeons); *b* 29 July 1843; *s* of 5th Baron and Augusta, *d* of Sir Robert Frankland Russell, 7th Bt of Thirkleby; *S* father, 1870; *m* 1st, 1877, Augusta Selina Elizabeth (Leila) (*d* 1906), *o c* of Capt. William Locke, *widow* of Lord Burghersh (2nd *s* of 11th Earl of Westmorland), and former wife of Duc de Santo Teodoro; 2nd, 1909, Marion Gwytherne-Williams (*d* 1913), FRHS, *d* of late Thomas Rhys Withers; 3rd, 1914, Agnes, *d* of late Frederick Shand Hemming, and *widow* of Richard Dawson. *Educ:* Eton; Trinity College, Cambridge (MA). MP (C) West Norfolk, 1865–70; Lord-in-Waiting, 1874–75. Memb. Soc. Ent. de France; Ent. Ver. zu Berlin; Nederlandsche Ent. Ver.; Soc. Ent. de Russie; Linn. Soc. NSW; Am. Ent. Soc. Philadelphia; Br. Ornith. Union, etc. The Walsingham collection of Micro-lepidoptera is the largest and most important— with it is incorporated the famous Zeller Collection, the Hofmann, Christoph, and others; the Walsingham collections were conveyed by Deed of Gift, dated 23 Nov. 1901, to the Trustees of the British Museum, to which they were transferred in 1910, together with his valuable entomological library. Owner of about 19,200 acres. *Publications:* numerous monographs and papers on the Micro-lepidoptera of the world. *Recreations:* a famous shot—his bag of 1070 grouse to his own gun never surpassed; contributed the articles on the grouse, the pheasant, and the partridge to the Badminton Library; visited California and Oregon (1870–71) on a sporting and collecting tour, and made extensive collections there and subsequently in S France, Corsica, Andalusia, Morocco, Algeria, Jamaica, etc; played in Eton and Cambridge cricket elevens, and in Gentlemen *v* Players, IZ, MCC, etc. *Heir:* half-*b* Hon. John Augustus de Grey, *b* 21 March

1849. *Address:* 6 Montagu Place, Portman Square, W. *T:* Mayfair 4577; Merton Hall, Thetford. *Clubs:* Carlton, Isthmian.

Died 3 Dec. 1919.

WALSTON, Sir Charles, (*né* Waldstein), Kt 1912; LittD (Cantab.); PhD (Heidelb.); Hon. LittD (Columbia Univ., New York); Hon. LittD TCD; Knight Commander of the Greek Order of the Redeemer; Knight of the Danebrog; Hon. ARIBA; High Sheriff of Cambs and Hunts, 1922–23; Member of Standing Committee of Advice on Art to Board of Education; Fellow (since 1894) and Lecturer of King's College, Cambridge; Vice-President Hellenic Society and member of Council of British Archæological School, Athens, Rome, etc; a Vice-President of the English-Speaking Union; *b* New York, 30 March 1856; 3rd surv. *s* of late Henry Waldstein, merchant of New York; *m* 1909, Florence, *e d* of late D. L. Einstein, of New York, and *widow* of Theodore Seligman, New York; one *s* one *d. Educ:* Columbia College, New York; Heidelberg University, Germany. Lecturer in Classical Archæology in Univ. of Camb., 1880–83; Director of Fitzwilliam Museum, Camb., 1883–89; Reader in Classical Archæology, 1883–1907; Slade Prof. of Fine Art, 1895–1901, and 1904–11; Director, American Archæological School, Athens (retaining Readership at Camb.), 1889–93, retaining Professorship there till 1896; excavated site of ancient Platæa, 1889–90; Eretria (tomb of Aristotle), 1891; the Heraion of Argos, 1892–95. *Publications:* Balance of Emotion and Intellect, 1878; Essays on the Art of Phidias, 1885; The Work of John Ruskin, 1894; The Study of Art in Universities, 1895; The Expansion of Western Ideals and the World's Peace, 1899; The Jewish Question and the Mission of the Jews, 1899; The Argive Heræum, 1902; Art in the Nineteenth Century, 1903; (with L. Shoobridge) Herculaneum, Past, Present, and Future, 1908; What may we Read?, 1912; Greek Sculpture and Modern Art, 1914; Aristodemocracy, 1916, new editions 1917 and 1920; What Germany is Fighting For, 1917; Patriotism, National and International, 1917; The Next War, Wilsonism and Anti-Wilsonism, 1918; Truth, etc, 1919; The English-Speaking Brotherhood and the League of Nations, 1919, 2nd edn 1920; Eugenics, Civics, Ethics, 1920; Harmonism and Conscious Evolution, 1922; Alcamenes and the Establishment of the Classical Type in Greek Art, 1926. *Recreations:* hunting, shooting, golf. *Address:* Newton Hall, Newton, Cambridge. *TA:* Harston, Cambs. *T:* Harston 8; Mayfair House, Carlos Place, W. *T:* Grosvenor 2452. *Clubs:* Athenæum, Marlborough, Bath.

Died 21 March 1927.

WALTER, Arthur; Editor, Parliamentary Debates, House of Lords, since 1898; *b* Ditcheat, Somersetshire, 20 June 1874; *e s* of Benjamin Walter; *m* 1899, Mabel Mary, *d* of Richard T. Wooff, of London. *Educ:* Monmouthshire and South Wales University. Was for several years member of editorial staff South London Press; acted for two Sessions as Parliamentary Correspondent of Echo de Paris; travelled through Europe as Private Secretary to late A. Pulitzer, founder of New York Journal; was one of the representatives of British journalism at International Congress of the World's Press, Antwerp, 1894, and Berlin, 1908; admitted a Freeman of City of London, 1903; Hon. Sec. and Fellow Institute of Journalists; President, British International Association of Journalists, 1918–19; Past Master of Duchy of Cornwall Lodge of Freemasons, and Life Governor of the three Royal Masonic Benevolent Institutions; contributed largely to magazines and weeklies on parliamentary and cognate matters. *Recreation:* touring. *Address:* 12 Calais Gate, Myatts Park, SE5. *TA:* Sirdar, Phone, London. *T:* Brixton 2290. *Clubs:* Press, New Oxford and Cambridge, London, Royal Automobile.

Died 27 Jan. 1921.

WALTER, Arthur James, LLB; KC 1906; *m* 1891, Florence Maud, 3rd *d* of Rev. Canon Carver, DD. Equity Scholar of Inner Temple, 1885; called to Bar, Inner Temple, 1885; chiefly engaged in Patent Trade Mark and technical litigation; one of the Governors of Dulwich College; a founder member of Automobile Club; a trustee of James Peek charity. *Address:* 5 Fig Tree Court, Temple, EC; 6 Rutland Gate, SW. *T:* Kensington 3908; Bryn Goleu, Dolwyddelen, North Wales. *Clubs:* Garrick, Savage, Royal Automobile.

Died 9 April 1919.

WALTER, Louis Heathcote, MA; Editor of Science Abstracts since 1903; *b* London; *y s* of late D. Henry Walter; *m* 1900, Rose Mabel, *y d* of late Capt. Edward Williams, late 69th Regt. *Educ:* privately in England; Hanover; Trinity College, Cambridge (Natural Sciences Tripos). An Associate Member of the Institution of Electrical Engineers; sometime Associate Member of the Institution of Civil Engineers; for some years was experimental assistant to Sir Hiram S. Maxim; in 1907 became associated with the inventors of the Bellini-Tosi system of directive wireless telegraphy, and introduced it into England; later the patents were acquired by the Marconi Company,

1912. *Publications:* Directive Wireless Telegraphy, 1921; acted as reviser of the volumes Electrical Engineering, Steam Engines, and Internal Combustion Engines of the Deinhardt-Schlomann Technical Dictionaries; hon. indexer in Physics for the International Catalogue of Scientific Literature; author of some twenty papers on electrical subjects communicated to the Royal Society, the Institution of Electrical Engineers, and other societies and the technical press. *Discoveries:* increase of hysteresis loss due to oscillations superposed on rotating field; self-restoring detector action of a tantalum-mercury contact; valve effect of tungsten electrodes; valve action of zirconium anodes. *Inventions:* a selective system of wireless control, 1898; various forms of coherers, magnetic detectors, etc; for his oscillation galvanometer was awarded the John Scott Medal, 1907. *Address:* Institution of Electrical Engineers, Victoria Embankment, WC2.

Died Sept. 1922.

WALTERS, W. C. Flamstead, MA; Professor of Classical Literature, King's College, London, 1901–24, and in the University of London, 1911–24; Fellow of King's College, London; *s* of Rev. A. V. Walters, BA Oxon, of Winchester; *m* 1st, Ethel (*d* 1902), *y d* of Maj.-Gen. Skyring, RE; one *s*; 2nd, 1912, Fanny, *e d* of late Rev. T. Walters, MA, Vicar of Boyton, Cornwall, and *sister* of late Marchioness of Queensberry. *Educ:* Christ's Hospital; Pembroke College, Oxford. Formerly House and Composition Master at Christ's College, New Zealand; late Lecturer in Classics, University College, Cardiff; Professor of Classics in Queen's College, London, 1901–9; Dean of the Faculty of Arts, King's College, 1904–8, 1911–12; formerly Member of Council of the Roman Society; of the Board of Classical Journals, and of the Council of the Hellenic Society; Treasurer of the Classical Association; formerly Examiner in the Universities of New Zealand, Wales and Manchester. *Publications:* various school-books and editions of authors; occasional papers and notes in Classical Quarterly, Classical Review, etc; co-Editor with Prof. Conway of Livy, i–x. *Recreations:* boating, tennis, golf, etc. *Address:* Limen, Miton Park, Gerrard's Cross.

Died 19 March 1927.

WALTERS, William Melmoth; solicitor; senior partner in firm of Walters, Wood & Co., 9 New Square, Lincoln's Inn (founded about 1780); *b* 28 Jan. 1835; *s* of John Eldad Walters of Batheaston, Somersetshire, and late of Lincoln's Inn and Ewell, Surrey, and Eleanor, *d* of late Alexander Radclyffe Sidebottom of the Middle Temple; *m* 1860, Marian Eleanor, *e c* of late Alfred Leggatt, 13 William Street, Lowndes Square, SW; two *s* six *d. Educ:* tutor, and private school, Bayswater, and King's College, London. Articled with the then firm of Roumieu, Walters & Co., 1852; read in the Chambers of Joshua Williams and of T. K. Kingdon; passed Final Examination (taking 2nd prize), and was admitted Solicitor, 1857; member of firm, 1859; elected to the Council of the Law Society, 1878; President, 1891–92, and late Senior Member of the Council, Director of the Law Fire Insurance Society, the Law Debenture Corporation, the Law Accident Insurance Society, and the Solicitors' Benevolent Association; late Member of the Solicitors' Discipline Committee; a Member of the Committee of Inspection of Trustee Savings Banks from its formation; Member of the Committee of Proprietors of Lincoln's Inn; Member of the Council of Law Reporting; late Member of the Rule-making Committee; late Chairman of the Ewell, Cuddington, and Malden Conservative Association; Governor of St Thomas' Hospital, King's College Hospital, Consumption Hospital, and various other hospitals and philanthropic institutions. *Recreations:* shooting, salmon-fishing, cruising; in earlier life, rowing, swimming, skating, cricket, lawn-tennis, etc. *Address:* 9 New Square, Lincoln's Inn, WC. *T:* Holborn 157; Purberry Shot, Ewell, Surrey. *TA:* Various, Holborn, London. *T:* Epsom 599. *Clubs:* Constitutional; Golf, Conservative, Epsom.

Died 20 Nov. 1925.

WALTON, Edward Arthur, RSA 1905; Hon. RWS; Hon RI; President of the Royal Scottish Society of Painters in Water Colours; Vice-President of the Imperial Arts League; artist painter; *b* Glanderston House, Renfrewshire, 15 April 1860; 6th *s* of late Jackson Walton. *Educ:* Glasgow. Studied drawing and painting, Glasgow and Düsseldorf; medallist Paris, Munich, and Chicago; works in the following permanent galleries: Munich, Carlsruhe, Budapest, Ghent, Venice, Pittsburg, Leeds, Glasgow, Edinburgh, Melbourne, and Auckland; Member of International Society of Sculptors, Painters, and Gravers, London; Associate Société Nationale des Beaux-Arts, France. *Address:* 7 Belford Park, Edinburgh. *Clubs:* Glasgow Art; Scottish-Arts, Scottish Liberal, Edinburgh.

Died March 1922.

WALTON, Frank, RI; ROI; Hon. Member, retired, Royal Institute of Oil Painters, and Royal Institute of Painters in Water Colours; *b*

London, 10 July 1840; *s* of James Walton, publisher; *m* Sophia (*d* 1921), *d* of John Wichham Flower; one *d*. *Educ:* private schools. *Address:* Holmbury St Mary, Dorking. *TA:* Holmbury St Mary. *Club:* Arts.

Died 23 Jan. 1928.

WALTON, Frederick Thomas Granville, CIE 1888; MInstCE; *b* 1840; *s* of William Walton of Hampton, Middlesex; *m* 1877, Charlotte Eliza (*d* 1922), 2nd *d* of Sir Cusack Roney; two *s*. *Educ:* privately. Began his professional career as a pupil of R. Johnson, chief engineer GN Rly, 1861; served on that railway until 1868, when he went out to India in the service of the Oudh and Rohilkhund Rly Co., and was employed on the construction of that line until it was purchased by Govt in 1889; he then entered Govt service as Engineer-in-Chief of the same railway until 1896, when he was sent to construct the railway brige over the Godavari River on the East Coast Rly; among other bridges he constructed the following: Ramgunga, Bareilly; Ramgunga, Moradabad; Kosi, Rampur; Dufferin Bridge, Benares; Godavari, Rajamundry. *Address:* 34 St George's Court, Gloucester Road, SW7.

Died 21 Dec. 1925.

WALTON, James, MP (Lab) Don Valley Division, Yorks, 1918–22; miner; *b* 7 Sept. 1867; *m* 1889, *d* of William Jackson. *Educ:* Broomhill Board Schools. Late Secretary of Mexborough Trades Council and Delegate Yorkshire Miners' Association. *Address:* 101 Avenue Road, Wath-on-Dearne, near Mexborough.

Died Jan. 1924.

WALTON, Sir Joseph, 1st Bt, *cr* 1910; JP Middlesbrough, JP and DL, NR Yorks; MP (L) Barnsley Division, WR Yorks, 1897–1918; (Co. L) Borough of Barnsley since 1918; FRGS; *b* Bollihope, Co. Durham, 19 March 1849; 2nd *s* of late Joseph Walton, Frosterley; *m* 1880, Faith Gill, *d* of late Robert Gill, Middlesbrough; two *d*. *Educ:* privately. Commenced commercial career in Middlesbrough, coal and allied trades, 1870; contested (L) Doncaster Division, 1895; travelled extensively in India, Burma, Africa, America, Canada, Australia, New Zealand, and British Protectorates, also in China, Japan, Persia, Mesopotamia, Russia, Balkans, etc. *Publication:* China and the Present Crisis, 1900. *Recreation:* Alpine climbing. *Heir:* none. *Address:* Rushpool, Saltburn-by-the-Sea. *Clubs:* Reform, Ranelagh, Royal Automobile.

Died 8 Feb. 1923 (ext).

WANAMAKER, John; *b* Philadelphia, 11 July 1838. Started business, April 1861; founder and owner of the largest new kind of Store in the United States, at Philadelphia and New York; Republican; Postmaster-General, 1889–93; founded Bethany School, 1858. *Address:* City Hall Square, Philadelphia.

Died 12 Dec. 1922.

WANAMAKER, Rodman, Hon. CVO; President, John Wanamaker, New York; John Wanamaker, Philadelphia; *b* Philadelphia; *s* of John Wanamaker and Mary B. Brown. *Educ:* Princeton. *Address:* Broadway, 8th, 9th and 10th Streets, New York; City Hall Square, Philadelphia.

Died 9 March 1928.

WANLISS, Captain Harold Boyd, DSO 1916; 14th Infantry Battalion, Australian Imperial Force; *b* Ballarat, 11 Dec. 1891; *s* of Newton Wanliss, MA, LLB, formerly solicitor, Ballarat, and Margaret Boyd; unmarried. *Educ:* Ballarat College (dux, 1908); Hawkesbury Agricultural College, New South Wales. Belonged to one of the oldest pioneer families in the State of Victoria; purchased a landed property in Otway Ranges, Victoria, and was the discoverer of falls on the Upper Erskine River; enlisted in the Australian Imperial Force, April 1915, and left Australia the same year in charge of reinforcements; attached to the 14th Australian Infantry Battalion in Egypt, and accompanied it to France, June 1916, as first lieutenant; led a battalion raid on the German trenches on the night of 2 July 1916; conducted the raid successfully (three times severely wounded, and had to be carried in, DSO); Capt. 1917. *Address:* Little Scotland, Lorne, Victoria, Australia.

Died 20 Sept. 1917.

WANSTALL, Rev. Walter; Non-Residentiary Canon of Lincoln since 1899; Prebendary of Aylesbury in Lincoln Cathedral; Vicar of All Saints, Lincoln, since 1904; *b* Rochester, 13 Aug. 1847; *o s* of Walter Wanstall, LRCP; unmarried. *Educ:* Rome House, Rochester; Bromsgrove School; Exeter Coll. Oxford. Ordained by Christopher Wordsworth, Bishop of Lincoln, 1870; Curate at Sneinton, Notts, 1870–81; Vicar of St Peter at Gowts, Lincoln, 1882–84; Vicar of St Andrew's, Lincoln, 1884–96; Chaplain to the High Sheriff of Lincolnshire, 1894; Vicar of St Swithin's, 1896–1904. *Recreations:* music, reading good novels. *Address:* All Saints, Lincoln.

Died 4 Dec. 1918.

WANTAGE, Lady, Harriet Sarah Loyd-Lindsay, RRC; *b* 1837; *o d* and heir of 1st and only Baron Overstone, and Harriet, *d* of Ichabod Wright of Mapperly Hall, Notts; *m* 1858, 1st and only Baron Wantage, VC, KCB (*d* 1901). *Publication:* Lord Wantage, VC, KCB: a Memoir. *Address:* Lockinge, Wantage, Berks; Overstone Park, Northampton.

Died 7 Aug. 1920.

WARBURTON, John Paul, CIE 1911; *b* 28 Aug. 1840; *s* of Sirdar Faiz Talab Khan, and step *s* of late Col R. Warburton; *m* 1863, Mary Whayman. Joined Police Department, Punjab, 1864; District Superintendent, 1873; Assistant Inspector-General, Railway Police, 1894; retired, 1900. *Address:* Gilbert House, Kasauli, Punjab; Warburton, Gujranwalla District, Punjab.

Died 21 Oct. 1919.

WARD, Sir Adolphus William, Kt 1913; LittD; Hon. LLD; Hon. PhD; FBA 1902; Master of Peterhouse, Cambridge, since 1900; *b* Hampstead, 2 Dec. 1837; 2nd *s* of late John Ward, CB, HM Minister Resident to the Hanse Towns; *m* 1879, Adelaide Laura, *d* of Rev. T. B. Lancaster, Rector of Grittleton, Wiltshire; one *d*. *Educ:* King Edward VI's School, Bury St Edmunds; Peterhouse, Camb. Fellow of Peterhouse, 1861; held Assistant Lectureships at Peterhouse and in Glasgow University, and a temporary Examinership in the Education Office; Professor of History and English Literature, Owens College, Manchester, 1866; Principal, Owens College, Manchester, 1890–97; Honorary Fellow of Peterhouse, 1891; Vice-Chancellor of the Victoria Univ. 1886–90 and 1894–96; Ford Lecturer at Oxford, 1898; received Freedom of the City of Manchester, 1897; Governor of Royal Holloway Coll. 1899–1909; President of Royal Historical Society, 1899–1901; President of the Chetham Society, 1901; Vice-Chancellor of the University of Cambridge, 1901; Governor of St Paul's School, 1902; of Bury St Edmunds School, 1903; President of the British Academy, 1911–13, and of English Goethe Society, 1911–22; one of the Editors of the Cambridge Modern History, 1902; of the Cambridge History of English Literature, 1907; Knight of the Prussian Order of the Crown, 2nd class, 1911. *Publications:* E. Curtius' History of Greece, English translation, 5 vols, 1868–73; Globe edn of Pope's Poetical Works, 1869; The House of Austria in the Thirty Years War, 1869; A History of English Dramatic Literature to the Death of Queen Anne, 2 vols, 1875, 2nd edn 1899; Marlowe's Doctor Faustus and Greene's Friar Bacon, 1878 (and later editions); Chaucer (1880) and Dickens (1882), in English Men of Letters; The Counter-Reformation (1888); The Poems of John Byrom, 2 vols, Chetham Society, 1894–95; Sir Henry Wotton, 1897; Great Britain and Hanover (Ford Lectures), 1899; contributions to vols i, iii–vi, of the Cambridge Modern History, 1902–7, and vols v–x of the Cambridge History of English Literature; The Electress Sophia and the Hanoverian Succession, 1903, 2nd edition, 1909; The Poems of Crabbe (Cambridge English Classics), 1905–6; Lillo's London Merchant and Fatal Curiosity (Belles Lettres Series), 1906; Knutsford edition of the works of Mrs Gaskell, 1906; Germany, 1815–1890 (Cambridge Historical Series), vol. i, 1916, vol. ii, 1917, vol. iii, 1918; Collected Papers, Historical, Literary, and Miscellaneous, 1921; five vols, 1921–22; Introduction and contributions to vols i and ii of Cambridge History of British Foreign Policy from 1783, 1922–23; contributions to the Dictionary of National Biography, Encyclopædia Britannica, Edinburgh and Quarterly Reviews, etc. *Address:* Peterhouse Lodge, Cambridge. *Club:* Athenæum.

Died 19 June 1924.

WARD, Arthur William, MA; Professor of Physics, Canning College, Lucknow, since 1889; *b* Waterloo, 1 Aug. 1858; *y s* of late James Ward, and *b* of Prof. James Ward; *m* 1st, Edith, *d* of late J. A. Houston, RSA; 2nd, Annie, *d* of late Surg.-Maj. Bond; one *s*. *Educ:* Liverpool College; Liverpool Institute; St John's College, Cambridge (Scholar, 1880; BA 1882). Lecturer at Borough Road Training College, 1882; worked in Cavendish Laboratory, 1883–84; Lecturer on Physical Science, Kumbakonam College, S India, 1885–87; invalided home; Fellow and Member of Syndicate, Allahabad University; Member of Senate of Benares Hindu University, 1916. *Publications:* scientific papers in Proceedings Royal Society and Philosophical Magazine; many articles in Indian Press on educational questions; Evidence before Indian University Commission, 1902; Public Service Commission, 1913. *Recreations:* music, gardening, bridge. *Address:* Badshah Bagh, Lucknow, India.

Died July 1919.

WARD, Rt. Rev. Mgr. Bernard, RC; Bishop of Brentwood since 1917; *b* Old Hall, Herts, 4 Feb. 1857; 3rd *s* of W. G. Ward of Northwood, Isle of Wight, known at Oxford as 'Ideal' Ward, one of the leaders of the Oxford Movement. *Educ:* St Edmund's Coll., Old Hall, 1868–75; Oscott Coll., Birmingham, 1879–82. Ordained priest by Cardinal Manning, 1882; a master at St Edmund's Coll. 1882–85; established new mission, Willesden, 1885–88; a master at Oscott, 1888–90; Vice-President, St Edmund's Coll., Old Hall, 1890; President, 1893–1916; the centenary of the Coll. celebrated July 1893; domestic prelate to the Pope, 1895; RC Canon of Westminster, 1903; FRHistS 1907; Rector of Holy Trinity, Brook Green, 1916–17. *Publications:* History of St Edmund's College, 1893; Commentary on St Luke's Gospel, 1899; Life of St Edmund of Canterbury, 1903; St Edmund's College Cl.. el, 1903; Catholic London a Century Ago, 1905; The Dawn of the Catholic Revival, 1909; The Eve of Catholic Emancipation, 1912; The Sequel to Catholic Emancipation, 1915; The Priestly Vocation. 1918. *Address:* Bishop's House, Brentwood.

Died 21 Jan. 1920.

WARD, Lieut-Gen Hon. Bernard Matthew, CB 1905; retired; *b* 26 Aug. 1831; *s* of 3rd Viscount Bangor; *m* 1st, 1865, Emily Maria (*d* 1868), *e d* of John La Touche of Harristown, Co. Kildare; one *s* one *d*; 2nd, 1873, Laura, *d* of Maj.-Gen. E. Maberly, CB; three *s* five *d* (and one *s* decd). Served Crimea, including Inkerman and Sebastopol, 1854–55 (medal with two clasps, Sardinian and Turkish medals); Col of Suffolk Regt. Decorated: Jubilee of Crimean War. *Address:* Staplecross, Christchurch, Hants. *Club:* United Service.

Died 27 June 1918.

WARD, Rev. Charles Triffitt; Hon. Canon of Chelmsford, 1918–25. Deacon, 1886; Priest, 1887; late Vicar of St Peter's, Colchester. *Address:* St Peter's, 36 Montalt Road, Woodford, Essex.

Died 30 Sept. 1925.

WARD, Edward, MA, MB, Cantab.; FRCS; late Professor of Surgery, University of Leeds; Hon. Consulting Surgeon, Leeds General Infirmary; formerly Examiner, Universities of Cambridge and Victoria. *Educ:* Trinity College, Cambridge. *Address:* 30 Park Square, Leeds. *Club:* Leeds. *Died 30 April 1921.*

WARD, Col Sir Edward (Willis Duncan), 1st Bt, *cr* 1914; GBE 1919; KCB 1900 (CB 1886); KCVO 1907; late President Union Jack Club; late President Union Jack Hostel; Director-General of Voluntary Organisations; Hon. Commandant in Chief Metropolitan Special Constabulary; Chairman of Camps Library; Chairman of Royal Society for the Prevention of Cruelty to Animals; *b* Oban, 17 Dec. 1853; *o s* of late Captain John Ward, RN, and Mary Hope, *d* of late John Bowie; *m* 1880, Florence Caroline, *d* of H. M. Simons; two *s*. *Educ:* private school. Entered Army, 1874; Major Army Service Corps, 1885; Lieut-Col, 1890; Brevet Col, 1898; served with Soudan Expedition, 1885 (despatches, medal with two clasps, bronze star); Major; on special service with Ashanti Expedition, 1895–96, as AAG (star, CB); DAAG Headquarters Staff, Ireland, 1892–95; DAAG Home District Staff, 1895–99; AAG Ladyship, 1899–1900 (despatches thrice, KCB); Director of Supplies S African Field Force, 1900 (Queen's medal 3 clasps); AQMG Headquarters, Feb.–April 1901; Permanent Under-Secretary of State, War Office, 1901–14. Hon. Sec. Royal Military Tournament, 1895–99. Knight of Grace, Order of St John of Jerusalem, 1920. *Publication:* Army Service Corps Duties in Peace and in War. *Recreations:* riding, rowing, fishing. *Heir:* s Edward Simons Ward, late Grenadier Guards [*b* 11 July 1882. Served European War, 1914–19 (wounded). *Club:* White's]. *Address:* Wilbraham Place, Sloane Street, SW1. *T:* Victoria 2984; Furnace Mill, Cowden, Kent; *T:* Edenbridge 78. *Clubs:* Carlton, United Service, Ranelagh, Orleans.

Died 11 Sept. 1928.

WARD, Enoch, RBA 1898; MJI; *b* Parkgate, near Rotherham, Yorks, 1859; went with parents to Chicago at age of eleven, and spent boyhood there; returned to England 1880, and studied Art at South Kensington; after which he spent six months in Paris; *m* 1890, Elizabeth, *d* of John Horsfield of Manchester. Upon the staff of Black and White from the inception of that paper; illustrated books for most of the leading publishers, and contributed drawings occasionally to The Illustrated London News and The Queen newspapers. *Recreations:* his spare time spent in his garden or upon his bicycle; essentially a lover of the country, and cared not overmuch for London. *Address:* 20 Lower Teddington Road, Hampton Wick, Middlesex.

Died Feb. 1922.

WARD, Maj.-Gen. Francis William, CB 1904; Colonel Commandant Royal (late Bengal) Artillery; *b* 6 April 1840; *s* of late John Ward, JP, of Bodmin; *m* 1862, Alice (*d* 1916), *d* of Major Macmullen, Bengal Cavalry. Entered Bengal Artillery, 1857; Maj.-Gen. 1895; served Indian Mutiny, 1857 (medal); NW Frontier, 1863–64 (medal with clasp); Afghan War, 1878–80 (medal). *Club:* Army and Navy. *Died 27 March 1919.*

WARD, Rev. Frederick Hubert, MA; Hon. Canon of Birmingham Cathedral; Vicar of Sparkhill, Birmingham; *b* 1858; *s* of late Rev. Thomas Ward, Vicar of Rowley Regis, Staffs, and formerly of Macclesfield, and Agnes Hannah, *d* of Benjamin Shorthouse, Managing Director of Collieries; *m* 1884, Mary St Maurice, *d* of late Rev. F. L. Potter, Vicar of St Leonards; one *s* two *d*. *Educ:* King Edward's Grammar School, Birmingham; Oxford. After two years' curacy at Cullompton, Devon, settled down to work up the district of Sparkhill. *Address:* Sparkhill, Birmingham.

Died 17 July 1918.

WARD, Rev. Frederick William Orde, (*pseudonym* F. Harald Williams); *b* Blendworth, 9 April 1843; 2nd *s* of Rev. E. L. Ward, Rector of Blendworth, Hants.; *m* 1878, Clara Mary (*d* 1920), *o* surv. *c* of Samuel Parker, and *niece* of Rt Hon. John Parker, 1st MP for Sheffield; three *d*. *Educ:* Tonbridge School (Exhibitioner); Wadham College, Oxford (Exhibitioner, 2nd in Classics Moderations), BA 1865. Private tutor at Oxford for some years, and ordained 1868 to Curacy of St Giles', Oxford; Vicar of Pishill, 1883–88; Rector of Nuffield, 1888–97. *Publications:* Women must Weep (4th edn), 1887; 'Twixt Kiss and Lip, 1890; Confessions of a Poet, 1894; Baby Pilgrims (2nd edn), 1895; Matin Bells (2nd edn), 1897; English Roses, 1899; New Century Hymns for the Church Seasons, 1900; The Prisoner of Love, 1904; The Keeper of the Keys, 1905; Lux Hominum, 1907; The World's Quest, 1908; Falling Upwards, 1909; Songs of Sussex; Christ and Woman; Last Crusade; Songs for Sufferers; contributor to Hibbert Journal, etc. *Address:* Nunnykirk, Milnthorpe Road, Eastbourne. *TA:* Orde Ward, Eastbourne.

Died 14 March 1922.

WARD, Genevieve, Countess de Guerbel, DBE 1921; tragedienne; *b* New York, USA, 27 March 1837; *m* Count de Guerbel in Warsaw, 10 Nov. 1855. *Educ:* France, Italy, America. Commenced operatic career under the name of Ginevra Guerrabella, as Lucrezia Borgia at La Scala, Milan, 1856; thence to Paris, London, America, and Cuba; injured voice by over-exertion; taught singing in New York for some years; later on studied dramatic art, making first appearance as Lady Macbeth, Theatre Royal, Manchester, 1873; then starred through Great Britain; in 1879 first produced the play Forget-me-not at Lyceum Theatre, London, and after a long run at Prince of Wales' Theatre, toured every part of the English-speaking world, acting the same play about 2000 times; afterwards acting at Lyceum Theatre with Sir Henry Irving in Becket, King Arthur, Richard III, etc; played in Coriolanus and Richard III with Benson at various times; played Duchess in Basker at St James's, 1916; played Duchesse of Hauteveille in The Aristocrat at St James's, 1917. *Publication:* (with Richard Whiteing) Before and Behind the Curtain, 1918. *Recreations:* riding, swimming, rowing, painting, modelling. *Address:* 22 Avenue Road, NW8. *T:* Hampstead 5272. *Died 18 Aug. 1922.*

WARD, Henrietta Mary Ada; *b* 1832; *o c* of George Raphael Ward and Mary Webb, and *g d* of James Ward, RA, Animal Painter to the King, *niece* of John Jackson, RA, portrait painter, *great-niece* of George Morland, also of William Ward, ARA; *m* 1848, E. M. Ward, RA, at the age of 16; two *d*. *Educ:* at home; Cary's Academy, Bloomsbury Street. Exhibited at the Royal Academy consecutively 1849–79, and constantly thereafter, there and other galleries—chiefly historic works. Worked much for Queen Victoria from time to time. *Works:*—The May Queen, God Save the Queen, Joan of Arc, Palissy the Potter, Art Gallery, Leicester; Mrs Fry visiting the prisoners in Newgate (dedicated by permission to Queen Victoria); Chatterton, Art Gallery, Bristol; The Princes in the Tower, Museum and Art Gallery, Rochdale, and others; painted several portraits for Queen Victoria and Royal Family; exhibited at the Royal Academy, 1903, 1904, 1905, 1906, 1913, and 1921. *Publication:* Reminiscences of Mrs E. M. Ward, 1918. *Recreations:* sketching, collecting curios and antiquities. *Address:* 59 Sydney Street, Chelsea, SW3. *T:* Westminster 6010.

Died 12 July 1924.

WARD, Herbert, sculptor; Knight of Legion of Honour; Member of Society of British Sculptors; *m* 1890, Sarita, *d* of Charles H. Sanford; two *s* two *d*. Survivor of Stanley's Emin Pacha Relief Expedition; awarded the Croix de Guerre for work with the British Ambulance and for succouring French wounded in Les Vosges. *Publications:* Five Years with the Congo Cannibals; My Life with Stanley's Rear Guard, 1891; A Voice from the Congo, 1912; Mr Poilu, 1916. *Address:* 102 Eaton Square, SW; 59 Boulevard Berthier, Paris; Rolleboise, Seine et Oise, France. *Clubs:* St James'; Union Artistique, Paris.

Died 7 Aug. 1919.

WARD, Mrs Humphry, (Mary Augusta); *b* Hobart, Tasmania, 11 June 1851; *e d* of Thomas Arnold, MA, 2nd *s* of Dr Arnold, Rugby;

m 1872, Thomas Humphry Ward, MA; one *s* two *d*. In 1890 founded University Hall (later known as Passmore Edwards Settlement, then Mary Ward Centre); pioneered establishment of nurseries for working women. *Publications:* Milly and Olly, 1881; Miss Bretherton, 1884; Amiel's Journal (translated), 1885; Robert Elsmere, 1888; The History of David Grieve, 1892; Marcella, 1894; Sir George Tressady, 1896; Helbeck of Bannisdale, 1898; Eleanor (played at Court Theatre, 1902 and 1905), 1900; Lady Rose's Daughter, 1903; The Marriage of William Ashe, 1905; Agatha, a play (produced at His Majesty's Theatre), 1905; Fenwick's Career, 1906; Diana Mallory, 1908; Daphne, 1909; Canadian Born, 1910; The Case of Richard Meynell, 1911; The Mating of Lydia, 1913; The Coryston Family, 1913; Delia Blanchflower, 1914; Eltham House, 1915; A Great Success, 1916; Lady Connie, 1916; England's Effort, 1916; Towards the Goal, 1917; Missing, 1917; A Writer's Recollections, 1918; The War and Elizabeth, 1918; Fields of Victory, 1919; Harvest, 1920; numerous articles on West-Gothic Kings and Bishops in vols ii and iii of Smith's Dictionary of Christian Biography; articles in Macmillan's Magazine, Nineteenth Century, Quarterly Review, etc; founded the Passmore Edwards Settlement and the Play Centres for London (1897), and Chairman of the Committee. *Address:* Stocks House, Tring.

Died 24 March 1920.

WARD, James, FBA 1902; Fellow of Trinity College, and Professor of Mental Philosophy, Cambridge; *b* Hull, 27 Jan. 1843; *e s* of James Ward, Great Crosby, Liverpool; *m d* of Rev. H. Martin, Congregational Minister; one *s* two *d*. *Educ:* Liverpool Institute; Spring Hill College (Congregationalist); Universities of Berlin and Göttingen; Trinity Coll., Camb. MA London (gold medal), 1874; Senior Moralist, Cambridge, 1875; ScD Cambridge, 1887; Hon. LLD Edinburgh, 1891; Hon. DSc Oxford, 1908; Hon. LLD Cambridge, 1920; Foreign Member, New York Academy of Sciences, 1908; Foreign Member of the Royal Danish Society, 1913; Corresponding Member of French Institute, 1913. Left school early; articled to a firm of architects, Liverpool; afterwards prepared for the Congregationalist Ministry; pastor for a year of Emmanuel Church, Cambridge; resigned because of change in theological opinions and entered the University; elected scholar of Trinity College, 1872; Fellow, 1875; Lecturer, 1881; Professor in the University, 1897; Gifford Lecturer, University of Aberdeen, 1895–97; University of St Andrews, 1908. *Publications:* various articles in Mind, Journal of Physiology, Encyclopædia Britannica, etc; Naturalism and Agnosticism, 1899, 4th edn 1915; The Realm of Ends or Pluralism and Theism, 1911, 3rd edn 1920; Heredity and Memory, 1913; Psychological Principles, 1918, 2nd edn 1920; A Study of Kant, 1922. *Recreations:* angling, gardening, field natural history, chess. *Address:* 6 Selwyn Gardens, Cambridge.

Died 4 March 1925.

WARD, James, Hon. ARCA; Headmaster, Dublin Metropolitan School of Art, 1907–18; artist, author, lecturer; *b* Belfast, 17 Nov. 1851; *e s* of James Ward, decorative artist; *m* Elizabeth Ham of London; four *s* four *d*. *Educ:* Belfast; at various schools, and private classes. National Scholar at Royal College of Art, 1873–76; assistant to Lord Leighton, PRA, 1878–86; Lecturer on art subjects, exhibitor at the Royal Academy; Membre Correspondant Société Archéologique de France. *Publications:* Elementary Principles of Ornament, 1890; Principles of Ornament, 1892; Report on the Art and Technical Schools of Crefeld, Zürich, and Lyons, 1895; Historic Ornament, in 2 vols, 1897; Progressive Design; Floral Studies for Decorative Design, 1901; Colour Harmony and Contrast, 1902; translated into Japanese, 1917; Fresco Painting, Its Art and Technique, 1909; Relation of Schools of Art to Museums, 1912; History and Methods of Ancient and Modern Painting, 1913; Colour Decoration of Architecture, 1913; painted a series of eight frescoes in the City Hall of Dublin, representing important events in the history of the city, 1915–18. *Recreations:* reading, walking, sketching. *Address:* Upland, Newtown Road, Newbury, Berks.

Died 18 May 1924.

WARD, Sir Leslie, Kt 1918; Member of the Royal Society of Portrait Painters; portrait painter and caricaturist; 'Spy' of Vanity Fair, 1873–1909, but subsequently devoted a large proportion of his time to portraiture; *b* London, 21 Nov. 1851; *e s* of late E. M. Ward, RA, and Henrietta M. A. Ward; *g s* of James Ward, RA; *m* 1899, Judith Mary Topham-Watney, *o d* of Maj. R. Topham, 4th Hussars; one *d*. *Educ:* Eton; Barnes. Studied architecture under Sydney Smirke, RA; entered Royal Academy Schools as architectural student and art student; exhibited bust in sculpture-room RA when at school; from time to time exhibited architectural drawings, oil-colour and water-colour portraits in Royal Academy and elsewhere; drew for the Graphic. *Publication:* Forty Years of Spy, 1915. *Recreation:* resting when

possible. *Address:* 247 Knightsbridge, SW; 16 Wellington Square, SW. *T:* Western 4899. *Club:* Beefsteak.

Died 15 May 1922.

WARD, Philip, JP; Commissioner of National Education, Ireland, since 1910; *b* near Carrickmacross, Co. Monaghan, 1845; *m*; one *s* one *d*. *Educ:* National School, Carrickmacross; privately. Was teacher of a National school for over forty years, ranking before 1900 as first division of first class, and under the new regulations of the National Board as first division of first grade; the teaching of French, Irish, and mathematics was a feature of his school; was member for many years of the Central Executive of the Irish National Teachers' Organization, and three times President; contributed a good deal to literary and educational journals. *Recreations:* fond of outdoor exercise, especially walking and cycling. *Address:* Farney Glen Road, Belfast. *Club:* National, Belfast.

Died 5 Nov. 1916.

WARD, Thomas Humphry, MA; journalist and author; *b* Hull, 9 Nov. 1845; *s* of late Rev. Henry Ward, MA; *m* 1872, Mary Augusta (*d* 1920), *e d* of Thomas Arnold, MA, and *g d* of Dr Arnold of Rugby; one *s* two *d*. *Educ:* Merchant Taylors' School; Brasenose College, Oxford. 1st class Lit. Hum., 1868. Fellow of Brasenose, 1869; Tutor, 1870–81; a writer on The Times. *Publications:* joint author of The Oxford Spectator, 1868, and of Romney, 1904; editor of—The English Poets, 1881–1918; English Art in the Public Galleries of London, 1888; The Reign of Queen Victoria, 1887; Men of the Reign, 1885; Men of the Time (12th edn); author of Humphry Sandwith, a Memoir; engaged on the authorized History of the Athenæum. *Address:* 2 Eccleston Square, SW1. *T:* Victoria 3950. *Club:* Athenæum.

Died 6 May 1926.

WARD, Wilfrid Philip, FSA; *b* Old Hall, Ware, 2 Jan. 1856; 2nd *s* of William George Ward, Northwood Park, Isle of Wight ('Ideal' Ward of the Oxford Movement), and Frances Mary (*d* 1898), *y d* of Rev. John Wingfield, DD, Headmaster of Westminster, Prebendary of Worcester, and Canon of York; *m* 1887, Josephine Mary, 2nd *d* of late James Robert Hope-Scott, QC, Abbotsford, and Lady Victoria Howard, *d* of 14th Duke of Norfolk; two *s* two *d*. *Educ:* St Edmund's Coll., Ware; Ushaw Coll., Durham; Gregorian Univ., Rome. Select Lectr in Philosophy at Ushaw Coll., 1890; Examiner in Mental and Moral Science in the Royal Univ. of Ireland, 1891–92; member of the Council of the Catholic Union of Great Britain since 1886; Chairman of Conservative Committee, Freshwater Division, 1887–88; editor of the Dublin Review; member of the Royal Commission on Irish University Education, 1901; Lecturer at the Lowell Institute, Boston, 1915. *Publications:* The Wish to Believe, 1884; The Clothes of Religion, 1886; William George Ward and the Oxford Movement, 1889; William George Ward and the Catholic Revival, 1893; Witnesses to the Unseen, 1894; The Life and Times of Cardinal Wiseman, 1897; Problems and Persons, 1903; Aubrey de Vere, a Memoir, 1904; Ten Personal Studies, 1908; Life of John Henry, Cardinal Newman, 1912; Men and Matters, 1914; also Essays in the Quarterly, Edinburgh, Dublin, Contemporary, National, and New Reviews, and in the Nineteenth Century. *Recreations:* golf, cycling, music. *Address:* Lotus, Dorking. *Clubs:* Athenæum (under Rule II), Junior Carlton.

Died 9 April 1916.

WARD, Sir William, KCMG 1910; Kt 1900; CVO 1904; *b* 2 June 1841; *y s* of late John Ward, CB, HM Minister Resident at Hamburg; *m* 1872, Jenny Maria (*d* 1910), *d* of late Henry Fowler. *Educ:* partly in Germany and partly in England; British Vice-Consul at Memel, East Prussia, 1866–70; HM Consul at Bremen, 1871–80; at Portland (Maine), US, 1881–83; at Bordeaux, France, 1884–96; HM Consul-General at Hamburg, 1897–1911. *Address:* Glen May, Amhurst Road, Withington, Manchester.

Died 28 Dec. 1927.

WARD, Sir William Erskine, KCSI 1896 (CSI 1888); *b* 4 Feb. 1838; *s* of Hon. J. P. Ward (brother of 3rd Viscount Bangor); *m* 1866, Alicia, *d* of Edward Palmer, Calcutta; four *s* one *d*. *Educ:* Trinity Coll., Camb.; Senior Optime, MA. Entered BCS, 1861; Judicial Commissioner of Lower Burmah, 1889–91; Chief Commissioner of Assam, 1891–96. *Address:* 8 Kent Gardens, Ealing, W. *T:* 329 PO Ealing. *Clubs:* Oriental; Royal Victoria Yacht, Ryde.

Died 24 Dec. 1916.

WARD, Rev. William Hayes, DD, LLD; Editor of the Independent, 1868–1914; Hon. Editor since 1914; *b* Abington, Mass, 25 June 1835; *s* of Rev. James W. Ward and Hetta Lord (Hayes) Ward; *m* Ellen Maria Dickinson; one *s*. *Educ:* Amherst Coll. (AB, AM, LLD); Andover Theological Seminary. DD Rutgers College and University of New York. Pastor, Oskaloosa, Kansas; teacher, Utica, NY, Free Academy; tutor, Natural Sciences, Beloit College, Wis; Prof. of Latin,

Ripon College, Wis; President of American Oriental Society, 1909–10; associate editor of the Independent, 1868; superintending editor, 1873; editor, 1897. *Publications:* Cylinders and other Ancient Oriental Seals, 1909; The Seal Cylinders of Western Asia, 1910; What I Believe, and Why, 1915; articles in reviews, mainly on Oriental archæology; biographical introduction to Poems of Sidney Lanier. *Recreations:* botany, Assyrian archæology. *Address:* South Berwick, Maine, USA. *Club:* Authors'.

Died 28 Aug. 1916.

WARFIELD, Benjamin Breckinridge, DD, LLD, LittD; Professor of Didactic Theology in Princeton Theological Seminary since 1887; *b* near Lexington, Kentucky, 5 Nov. 1851; *s* of William Warfield and Mary Cabell Breckinridge; *m* 1876, Annie Pearce, *d* of George Blackburn Kinkead, Lexington, Kentucky; no *c*. *Educ:* private schools; Princeton University, AB 1871, AM 1874; Princeton Theological Seminary; University of Leipzig. DD Princeton, 1880; LLD Princeton and Davidson, 1892; LittD Lafayette, 1911; STD University of Utrecht, 1913. Ordained to the Presbyterian Ministry, 1879; Instructor in New Testament Language and Literature, 1878–79; Professor of same at the Western Theological Seminary, Pittsburgh, 1879–87; Acting President, Princeton Theological Seminary, 1901, 1914; Joint-Editor of The Presbyterian Review, 1888–89; Editor of The Presbyterian and Reformed Review, 1890–1902. *Publications:* Introduction to the Textual Criticism of the New Testament, 1886; Augustine's Anti-Pelagian Treatises, 1887; Two Studies in the History of Doctrine, 1893; The Right of Systematic Theology, 1897; The Significance of the Westminster Confession as a Creed, 1898; Acts and the Pastoral Epistles (in the Temple Bible), 1902; The Power of God unto Salvation, 1903; The Lord of Glory, 1907; Calvin as a Theologian and Calvinism To-day, 1909; Hymns and Religious Verses, 1910; The Saviour of the World, 1914; The Plan of Salvation, 1915; Faith and Life, 1916; Counterfeit Miracles, 1918. *Address:* 74 Mercer Street, Princeton, New Jersey, USA.

Died 16 Feb. 1921.

WARING, Francis John, CMG 1893; FRGS; MInstCE; Fellow of King's College, London; one of the consulting engineers to the Crown Agents for the Colonies, 1898–1921; *b* Southsea, 25 Oct. 1843; *e s* of Francis Waring and Frances Margaret, *d* of Captain H. Waring, RN; *m* 1883, Mary Elizabeth Maud, 4th *d* of late W. M. Harries of Tenby; four *d*. *Educ:* King's College School, London (Fellow, 1908). Served in India professionally, 1863–72; Brazil, 1873–75; entered service of Government of Ceylon as a civil engineer, 1875; Chief Resident Engineer of Government Railway Extensions in that Colony, 1882–96. *Address:* Uva Lodge, 49 Mount Avenue, Ealing, W5. *T:* Ealing 437. *Club:* St Stephen's.

Died 6 Feb. 1924.

WARNE, George Henry; MP (Lab) Wansbeck since 1922; Trustee of Northumberland Miners' Association; President of Northumberland and Durham Miners Approved Society; a Junior Lord of the Treasury, 1924; *b* Cramlington, Northumberland, 15 Dec. 1881; *s* of William Warne, Ashington; *m* 1904, Dorothy Isabel, *d* of George Fenwick, Ashington. Entered the mines at age of 12. Mem. of Ashington UDC, 1907–22, Chm., 1919–21; Mem., Northumberland CC, 1919–24. *Address:* 18 The Drive, Gosforth, Newcastle upon Tyne. *Died 24 Dec. 1928.*

WARNER, Edward Handley, JP, DL; *b* 1850; *o* surv. *s* of Edward Warner of Quorn Hall (*d* 1894), and Marianne (*d* 1892), 4th *d* of late Rev. J. W. R. Boyer of Swepstone, Leicestershire; *m* 1877, Jessie Nancy, *d* of Thomas Brooks, late of Barkby Hall, Leicestershire. *Educ:* Rugby; Trinity College, Oxford (BA). High Sheriff, Leicestershire, 1897; late Capt., Leicestershire Yeomanry Cavalry. *Address:* Bragbury End, Knebworth, Herts. *Died 16 Aug. 1925.*

WARNER, Francis, MD Lond.; FRCP, FRCS Eng; Consulting Physician London Hospital since 1913; late Lecturer on the Neuroses and Psychoses of Children; Lieutenant-Colonel, Territorial Forces; *b* 10 July 1847; *s* of James Neatby Warner; *m* 1880, Louisa Loder, *d* of William Howard of Hampstead; one *s* one *d*. *Educ:* private school; King's College, London. Honours, MB London, 1872; MD 1873; FRCS 1873; FRCP 1883; Medical Registrar, London Hospital, 1877; Asst Physician, 1879; Asst Physician, East London Hospital for Children, 1878–84; Hunterian Prof. of Comparative Anatomy and Physiology, RCS, 1887; Milroy Lectr, RCP London, 1892; Fellow Royal Medical Society; Hon. Member Society Public Health, Budapest; in residence at London Hospital for war work from Feb. 1916. *Publications:* Mental Faculty Lectures (Cambridge University); The Study of Children; The Nervous System of the Child: its Health and Training; Physical and Mental Condition of Children in 106

Schools, Journal Royal Stat. Soc. 1893–96; other articles on Nervous and Defective Children. *Recreations:* literary and scientific. *Address:* Whitbourne, Warlingham, Surrey. *T:* Upper Warlingham 30.

Died 26 Oct. 1926.

WARRACK, Sir James Howard, KBE 1919; *b* Montrose, 1855; *s* of James Warrack, shipowner, Montrose; *m* 1886, Dorothy Cooper, *d* of George Todd, CA, Edinburgh. *Educ:* Montrose Academy. Received business training in Montrose and Liverpool; became a partner in John Warrack & Co., Leith, 1880; sometime member of Leith Dock Commission, Leith Chamber of Commerce (Chairman), Leith Nautical College (Chairman); Ex-President Edinburgh Chamber of Commerce, Director British Imperial Council of Commerce, Committee of Lloyd's Register of Shipping, Council of Chamber of Shipping of the United Kingdom (President, 1914–15), Council of the Shipping Federation; during the war served on various Government Advisory Committees; Vice-President Admiralty Transport Arbitration Board; Director of the Bank of Scotland, Caledonian Insurance Company, and the North British Rubber Co., Ltd. *Address:* 38 Palmerston Place, Edinburgh. *Clubs:* Junior Constitutional; University, Edinburgh.

Died 30 Oct. 1926.

WARRE, Rev. Edmond, CB 1905; CVO 1910 (MVO 1901); DD; Hon. Chaplain to the King; Prebendary of Wells since 1899; *b* London, 12 Feb. 1837; 2nd *s* of late Henry Warre, Bindon, Somerset, and Mary Caroline, 3rd *d* of Nicolson Calvert, Hunsdon, Herts; *m* 1861, Florence Dora, 2nd *d* of Lieut-Colonel C. Malet, Fontinell Parva, Dorset; five *s* two *d*. *Educ:* Eton; Newcastle Scholar, 1854; Balliol Coll., Oxford; Scholar, 1855; 1st Class Mods, 1856; 1st class Lit. Hum., 1859. Fellow of All Souls, 1859; Hon. Fellow of Balliol, 1896; Hon. DCL Oxford, 1907; Assistant Master Eton, 1860; Headmaster, 1884–1905; Provost, 1909–18; Hon. Col 2nd Bucks (Eton Coll.) RV, 1884; OTC 1910; VD. *Recreation:* rowing (was in Oxford boat, 1857–58–59; President OUBC, 1859). *Address:* The Lodge, Eton College. *Club:* Athenæum.

Died 22 Jan. 1920.

WARRE, Rev. Francis, Rector of Bemerton since 1890; Canon of Salisbury Cathedral; *s* of Henry Warre of Bindon House, Wellington, Somerset, and *d* of Nicholson Calvert, late MP for Hertfordshire, Hunsdon House, Ware; *m* 1860, Ellin Jane (*d* 1914), *d* of Rev. James J. Peach; four *d*. *Educ:* Eton College; Balliol College, Oxford. Vicar of Bere-Regis, Dorset, 1864–76; Vicar of Melksham, Wilts, 1876–90. *Address:* Bemerton Rectory, Salisbury. *T:* 166 Southampton Area.

Died 15 Sept. 1917.

WARREN, Sir Alfred Haman, Kt 1918; OBE 1918; MP (Co. U) Edmonton, 1918–22; *b* Poplar, 6 Feb. 1856; *m* 1896, Jenny Macey (*d* 1926), *d* of George W. Castle, HM Customs; one *s* one *d*. *Educ:* Wesleyan School, Poplar. Mayor of Poplar, 1913–18; Past Grand Master, Manchester Unity of Oddfellows; Past President National Conference of Friendly Societies, and Parliamentary Agent. *Address:* Mountain Ash, Wanstead. *T:* Wanstead 410.

Died 1 Aug. 1927.

WARREN, Arthur; author and journalist; *b* Boston, Mass, 18 May 1860; *y s* of late Capt. M. H. Warren, USA; *m* 1887, Abbie N., *d* of late James Gunnison, Scarborough, Maine, USA. Journalist in London, 1878–82; a special and editorial writer and critic Boston Herald, 1883–88; London correspondent, 1888–97; editorial and special correspondent, 1897–1907; Editor, 1907–9; Dramatic Critic, New York Tribune, 1909–12; also connected actively, 1897–1903, with the affairs of the late George Westinghouse, and again from 1909 till the latter's death in March 1914. *Publications:* London Days, a Book of Reminiscences, 1920; The Charles Whittinghams, a biography, with an account of English printing from 1789 to 1860, 1896; many short stories and articles, etc. *Club:* Royal Automobile.

Died 16 April 1924.

WARREN, Gen. Sir Charles, GCMG 1885 (KCMG 1883; CMG 1878); KCB 1888; RE; FRS 1884; Knight of Justice of the Order of St John of Jerusalem; *b* Bangor, North Wales, 7 Feb. 1840; 2nd *s* of late Maj.-Gen. Sir Charles Warren, KCB; Col 96th Regt; *m* 1864, Fanny Margaretta (*d* 1919), *d* of Samuel Haydon, Guildford; two *s* two *d*. *Educ:* Bridgnorth; Cheltenham Coll.; RMC Sandhurst; RMA Woolwich. Entered RE, 1857; Survey of Gibraltar, 1861–65; Asst Instructor Survey, School of Military Engineering, 1866; conducted Excavations at Jerusalem and Reconnaissance of Palestine for Palestine Exploration Fund, 1867–70; School of Gunnery, Shoeburyness, 1871–73; HM Commissioner for laying down boundary line, Griqualand West and Orange Free State, 1876–77 (CMG);

Commissioner, Land Claims, Griqualand West, 1877; commanded Diamond Fields Horse, Kaffir War, and Rebellion in Griqualand West, 1878; commanded troops against Bechuanas, 1878; Administrator and Comdr-in-Chief, Griqualand West; commanded troops Northern Border Expedition, 1879; Instructor in Surveying, SME, 1880–84; special officer attached to Admiralty, Egyptian Campaign, 1882 (KCMG); engaged in Arabia Petræa; HM Special Comdr and Maj.-Gen. comdg Bechuanaland Expedition, 1884–85, (GCMG); contested Hallamshire, Sheffield, 1885; commanded troops Suakim, 1886; Commissioner Metropolitan Police, 1886–88 (KCB); commanded troops Straits Settlements, 1889–94; Thames District, 1895–98; Lt-Gen. in command of 5th Div. S Africa Field Force, 1899–1900 (despatches). *Publications:* Enlarged General Frome's Outlines of a Trigonometrical Survey, 1873; author of part of the Recovery of Jerusalem; Underground Jerusalem, 1874; The Temple or the Tomb, 1880; Jerusalem, vol. of Survey of Palestine, with Portfolio of Plates and Excavations, 1884; On the Veldt in the Seventies, 1902; The Ancient Cubit and our Weights and Measures, 1903; The Early Weights and Measures of Mankind, 1914. *Address:* 3 Trinity Mansions, Weston-super-Mare. *Club:* Athenæum.
Died 21 Jan. 1927.

WARREN, Admiral Herbert Augustus, MVO 1903; *b* 24 July 1855. Entered Navy, 1869; Commander, 1892; Capt. 1898; Rear-Adm. 1907; served Burmah, 1885–87 (medal with clasp); retired Admiral, 1916. *Address:* The Manor House, East Preston, near Littlehampton. *Club:* United Service. *Died 30 Oct. 1926.*

WARREN, John; Member Legislative Council and JP South Australia; *b* 3 Sept. 1830; *m* 1863; eight *s* four *d*. *Educ:* New Spynie, Morayshire, Scotland. Engaged in agriculture, pastoral, and horticultural, also mining work; pastoral on a large scale in the far north; held office Chairman District Council of Mount Crawford for many years; Captain in military force for twenty-two years (long service medal). *Address:* Mount Crawford, South Australia. *Clubs:* Naval and Military, Adelaide. *Died 13 Sept. 1919.*

WARREN, Vice-Admiral John Borlase; *b* 27 March 1838; 2nd *s* of Sir John Borlase Warren, 4th Bt, and *heir-pres.* to 7th Bt; *m* 1874, Mary Elizabeth St Leger, 2nd *d* of St Leger Atkins of Water Park, Co. Cork, Ireland; three *d*. *Educ:* private tutor. Entered Royal Navy as Cadet, 1850; Midshipman, 1852; Sub-Lieutenant, 1857; Lieutenant, 1859; Commander, 1871; Captain, 1880; Rear-Admiral, 1896; Vice-Admiral, 1901; served in Russian and Chinese Wars of 1855 and 1861; granted a Good Service Pension of £150, 1892. *Address:* Carbery, Salcombe, South Devon. *Club:* United Service.
Died 29 Jan. 1919.

WARREN, Rev. John Shrapnel, MA; Rector of Willoughby, 1875–1922; Rural Dean for Calcewaith, 1889; *b* Beverley, Yorks; *s* of Rev. Z. S. Warren, Vicar of Ancaster, Lincs; *m* 1st, Caroline (*d* 1919), *d* of J. E. Brooke, Hotham House, Yorks; no *c*; 2nd, 1920, Ethel Adelaide, *d* of late Rev. H. A. Marsh, Vicar of Luxford. *Educ:* Rugby; Cambridge. Vicar of Langtoft, Lincs, 1858–75; JP Lincs, 1865; Prebendary of Lincoln Cathedral, 1895.
Died 2 May 1925.

WARREN, Sir Pelham Laird, KCMG 1902 (CMG 1901); HM Consul-General, Shanghai, 1901–11; *b* 22 Aug. 1845; *s* of Admiral Richard Laird Warren; *m* 1875, Mary Donnithorne Humfridge. Student Interpreter, China, 1867; Vice-Consul, Pagoda Island, 1883; Acting Consul, Taiwan, 1883–84, and 1886; Consul, Taiwan (later Tainan), 1886; Consul, Hankow, 1893; Consul-General, Hankow 1899–1901. *Club:* Oriental.
Died 21 Nov. 1923.

WARREN, Philip David, CMG 1908; AICE, FRGS, FRMetS; *b* 7 Feb. 1851; *s* of late John Neville Warren, AMICE; *m* 1881, Julia A. M. (*d* 1915), *d* of late John Graham, Enniskillen; one *s* two *d*. *Educ:* Norwich Grammar School; etc. Served articles to borough engineer, Margate; six years on engineering and survey work in South Wales; joined Survey Department, Ceylon, as Assistant Surveyor, 1878; District Surveyor, 1879; Assistant Surveyor-General, 1897; Surveyor-General of Ceylon, 1904–10; retired; Fellow Royal Colonial Institute. *Address:* St Catherine's, West Hill Road, Woking, Surrey. *Club:* Engineers'. *Died 28 Jan. 1928.*

WARREN, William Henry, Hon LLD Glasgow, WhSc, MInstCE, MAmSocCE; Member of Council of International Society for Testing Materials; Challis Professor of Engineering since 1883, and Dean of Faculty of Science since 1908, Dean of the Faculty of Engineering and President of the Professorial Board since 1919, University of

Sydney; *b* Bristol, 1852; *m* 1875; one *s*. *Educ:* Royal College of Science, Dublin; Owens College, Manchester. Locomotive Works at the L and NW Railway Co., England, 1866–72; studied at the Royal College of Science, Dublin, and Owens College, Manchester, 1872–75; occupied various positions in Manchester and London, including chief of drawing office to firm of E. T. Bellhouse and Co., and supervising and designing engineer to Magnall and Littlewoods, Manchester, 1875–80; specially engaged by L&NWR Co., Euston, to design bridges and roofs for the Victoria Station extensions, Manchester; occupied in Public Works Dept of NSW on roads, bridges, and sewerage, and at the same time organised and directed the Mechanical Engineering Dept, Sydney Technical College, 1881–83; some consulting work as an engineer in every State of Australia, and acted on numerous Boards of Inquiry and Royal Commissions; twice President of the Royal Society of NSW. *Publications:* Engineering Construction, Part I, in Steel and Timber; Part II, Masonry and Concrete; Australian Timbers Testing Materials, Stresses in Structures, and the Physical Properties of Materials used in Engineering Construction; about fifty pamphlets read before the Royal Society, Sydney, and other scientific societies, on materials used in engineering constructions, including four papers on Reinforced Concrete Constructions; bridge work, etc. *Recreations:* golf, billiards, music. *Address:* University of Sydney. *Clubs:* Union, Sydney; Australian Golf.
Died 9 Jan. 1926.

WARREN, Hon. William Robertson, LLD Edin. 1923; KC; a Judge of Supreme Court, Newfoundland, since 1926; *b* 9 Oct. 1879; *s* of late William H. Warren; *m* 1st, Ethel Alice, *e d* of late James Gordon; one *s* two *d*; 2nd, Emilie Jackson, *d* of late R. L. Mare; one *d*. *Educ:* Bishop Field College, St John's, Newfoundland; Framlingham College, Suffolk. MP for Trinity District, 1902; for Port de Grave, 1908 and 1909; for Fortune Bay, 1919–24; Speaker of House of Assembly, 1909–13; represented House of Assembly at Coronation of His Majesty King George V, 1911; Attorney-General, 1919–23; retained by Government of Newfoundland in Labrador Boundary Dispute with Canada before Privy Council; Prime Minister, 1923–24; attended Imperial Conference, London, 1923, representing Newfoundland. *Recreations:* golf, curling, salmon-fishing. *Address:* Balsam Annex, St John's, Newfoundland. *TA:* Warren. *Clubs:* City, St John's; Bally Haly Golf and Country.
Died 31 Dec. 1927.

WARRENDER, Vice-Admiral Sir George John Scott, 7th Bt, *cr* 1715, of Lochend, East Lothian; KCB 1913 (CB 1902); KCVO 1911 (CVO 1907; MVO 1904); Commander-in-Chief, Plymouth, since 1916; *b* Scotland, 31 July 1860; 2nd *s* of Sir George Warrender, 6th Bt and Helen, *o c* of Sir Hugh Hume Campbell, 7th Bt; *S* father, 1901; *m* 1894, Lady Maud Ashley, *y d* of 8th Earl of Shaftesbury; two *s* one *d*. *Educ:* Rev. John Hawtrey's, Slough. Entered RN, Naval Cadet, 1873; Commander, 1893; Capt 1899; with Naval Brigade, Zulu War, 1879; present at battle of Ginghilovo (medal, clasp); C-in-C East Indian Station, 1907–9; Rear-Adm. 1908; Vice-Adm. 1913; commanded 2nd Cruiser Squadron, 1910–12; 2nd Battle Squadron, 1912–16; served European War, 1914–15. *Recreations:* golf, cricket. *Heir: s* Victor Alexander Anthony George Warrender, *b* 23 June 1899. *Address:* 23 Great Cumberland Place, W. *TA:* Ecosse, London. *T:* 1398 Paddington; Bruntsfield House, Edinburgh; Leasam, Rye, Sussex. *Clubs:* Carlton, Turf, Naval and Military; New, Edinburgh; Royal Navy, Portsmouth; Hon. Member Royal Yacht Squadron, Cowes. *Died 8 Jan. 1917.*

WARRENDER, Lt-Col Hugh Valdave, DSO 1916; *b* 14 Sept. 1868; *y s* of late Sir George Warrender, 6th Bt, of Lochend, and Helen, *o c* of Sir H. Hume Campbell, 7th Bt of Marchmont. *Educ:* Eton; Sandhurst. Joined Grenadier Guards, 1889; retired, 1897; joined Civil Service Rifles, TF, on outbreak of European War; served in France, 1914–18 (DSO); commanded 1st Batt. Civil Service Rifles; resigned commission, 1920. *Recreations:* fishing, gardening, shooting, golf. *Address:* Berkeley House, Hay Hill, W1. *T:* Gerrard 6114; High Grove, Pinner, Middlesex. *Clubs:* Turf, Garrick, Beefsteak.
Died 8 March 1926.

WARWICK, 5th Earl of, *cr* 1759, **Francis Richard Charles Guy Greville,** Baron Brooke, 1621; Earl Brooke 1746; DL, JP Warwicks, Somerset, and Essex; CC Warwicks; a Trustee of Rugby School; Past Deputy Grand Master, Freemasons of England; Past Provincial Grand Master of Essex since 1882; Lord Lieutenant of Essex; Hon. Colonel Warwickshire Yeomanry; Hon. Colonel Essex Imperial Yeomanry; Hon. Colonel Essex Militia; *b* 9 Feb. 1853; *s* of 4th Earl and Anne, *d* of 8th Earl of Wemyss and March; *S* father, 1893; *m* 1881, Frances Evelyn, *d* of Col Hon. Charles Henry Maynard, *s* of last Viscount Maynard, and Blanche, afterwards Countess of Rosslyn; two *s* two *d. Educ:* Christ Church, Oxford. MP (C) E Somersetshire, 1879–85; Colchester, 1888–92; Mayor of Warwick, 1894–95, 1895–96, 1915–16; Alderman, Warwick Town Council. Owner of about 10,200 acres. *Publication:* Memories of Sixty Years, 1917. *Heir: s* Lord Brooke, *b* 10 Sept. 1882. *Address:* Warwick Castle, Warwickshire; Easton Lodge, Dunmow, Essex. *Club:* Carlton.

Died 15 Jan. 1924.

WARWICK, 6th Earl of (*cr* 1759), **Leopold Guy Francis Maynard Greville;** Baron Brooke, 1621; Earl Brooke, 1746; CMG 1915; MVO 1905; DL; JP Warwick and Essex; late Captain, 3rd Battalion Essex Regiment; ADC to Inspector-General of Forces; raised and commanded Warwickshire Horse Artillery Territorial; Brevet Lieut-Colonel; Hon. Colonel Essex and Suffolk Cyclist Battalion; Life Governor Birmingham University; *b* 10 Sept. 1882; *e s* of 5th Earl and Frances, Countess of Warwick; *S* father, 1924; *m* 1909, Marjorie, *d* of Sir Wm Eden, 7th Bt; three *s. Educ:* Eton. Late Capt. 1st Life Guards; served South Africa, 1900; extra ADC to Lord Milner, 1901–2; acted as Reuter's Special Correspondent during Russo-Japanese War, 1904–5; Private Secretary to the Chief of the Imperial General Staff, 1913–14; Order Rising Sun, Japan, and Russian war medal; Prussian Order Red Eagle; commanded 2nd Canadian Cavalry Brigade, 1913; Territorial Force Reserve; commanded Manœuvres, Canada, 1914; Brig.-Gen., Canadian Forces, 1914; ADC to Commander-in-Chief, British Army in France, 1914–15 (despatches twice, CMG, Legion of Honour, Order of St Stanislas, Russia, wounded, Croix de Guerre with palm); commanded 4th Canadian Infantry Brigade Expeditionary Force as Brig.-Gen.; commanded 12th Canadian Infantry Brigade. Owner of about 10,200 acres. *Heir: s* Lord Brooke, *b* 4 March 1911. *Address:* Warwick Castle, Warwickshire. *Clubs:* Marlborough, Guards.

Died 31 Jan. 1928.

WASON, Rt. Hon. Eugene, PC 1907; *b* 26 Jan. 1846; *s* of Rigby Wason, MP, Ipswich; *m* 1870, Eleanor Mary, *d* of C. R. Williams, DL Merionethshire of Dolmelyullyn, Dolgelly; three *s* two *d. Educ:* Rugby; Wadham Coll., Oxford (BA 1868, MA 1870). Formerly Lieut in the Rugby School Rifle Corps and 8th Ayrshire Rifle Volunteers; Clubs: rowed in Trial Eights Oxford, 1865 and 1866; Captain of Wadham College Boat Club, and winner of the University foils, 1868. Called to the Bar, Middle Temple, 1870, and went Northern Circuit; disbarred, 1872; admitted solicitor, 1876, a partner in Williams, James & Wason, 1876–85; struck off the Rolls in 1886, and readmitted a member of the Bar the following week, a unique experience, Mr Wason having been both disbarred and struck off the Rolls, but each time at his own request; Chairman of the Scottish Liberal Members, 1908–18; Chairman of Departmental Committee on Food Production, 1915; Member of Committee on Scottish National War Memorial; Assistant Examiner to Incorporated Law Society in Common Law, 1878–82; MP (L) S Ayrshire, 1885–86, 1892–95; Clackmannan and Kinross, 1899–1918. Twice went round the world, in 1886–87 by India, China, Japan, San Francisco, and America, and in 1896–97 by Australia, New Zealand, Fiji, Hawaii, Vancouver, and Canada; a Past Master of the University Lodge, a DL and JP Ayrshire. *Recreations:* formerly football, shooting, rowing, and fishing; later reading, bridge, backgammon, and picquet. *Address:* 8 Sussex Gardens, Hyde Park, W2. *T:* Paddington 4120; Blair, Dailly SO, NB. *TA:* Blair Killochan. *Club:* Reform.

Died 19 April 1927.

WASON, John Cathcart, MP (LU) Orkney and Shetland, 1900; resigned 1902; re-elected as Liberal 1902, 1906, and 1910; *b* 1848; *y s* of Rigby Wason, MP, and Euphemia Mactier; *m* 1874, Alice Seymour, *d* of Edward Bell, CE; *bro.* of Rt Hon. Eugene Wason. *Educ:* Laleham; Rugby. Barrister, Middle Temple; for many years a farmer in New Zealand; and also member New Zealand Parliament. *Address:* 40 Grosvenor Road, SW1. *T:* Victoria 3104; Craig, Pinlan, Ayrshire. *Clubs:* Reform, Royal Automobile.

Died 19 April 1921.

WATERHOUSE, Charles Owen, ISO 1910; FES; *b* 1843; *s* of G. R. Waterhouse of the British Museum; *m*; one *d. Educ:* University College School. Entered Entomological Department of the British Museum, 1866; Assistant Keeper, 1905; retired, 1910; President of the Entomological Society of London, 1908–9. *Publications:* Index Zoologicus; over 200 papers on entomological subjects. *Address:* 22 Avenue Gardens, Acton, W.

Died 4 Feb. 1917.

WATERHOUSE, Edwin, BA London; MA (*honoris causa*) Oxon; FCA; JP; Chartered Accountant; *b* Aigburth, Liverpool, 1841; 4th *s* of late Alfred Waterhouse of Whiteknights, Reading, formerly of Liverpool; *m* 1st, 1869, Georgina (*d* 1896), *d* of John Philipp Thöl; three *d* one *s*; 2nd, 1898, Helen C., *d* of Frederick Weber, MD; one *s. Educ:* University College, London. Commenced practice as a public

accountant, 1864; joined the firm of Price, Holyland and Waterhouse, 1865; head of the firm of Price, Waterhouse & Co., 1887–1906, when he retired from active business as a partner; president of the Institute of Chartered Accountants of England and Wales, 1892–94; assisted in various government and public inquiries. *Address:* 3 Frederick's Place, EC; Feldemore, Holmbury St Mary, Surrey. *Club:* City of London.

Died 17 Sept. 1917.

WATERHOUSE, Maj.-Gen. James; Unemployed Supernumerary List, Indian Army (retired); *b* 24 July 1842; *s* of late J. W. Waterhouse; unmarried. *Educ:* University Coll. School; King's College, London; Addiscombe. Royal (Bengal) Artillery, 1859–66; Indian Ordnance Department, 1866; Asst Surveyor-General in charge of photographic operations in the Surveyor-General's Office, Calcutta, 1866–97; took part in the observation of total eclipses, 1871 and 1875, and of transit of Venus, 1874; President of the Asiatic Society of Bengal, 1888–90; Trustee of the Indian Museum, Calcutta, 1875–97; Chairman, 1888–89 and 1895–97; Hon. Sec. Zoological Gardens, Calcutta, 1894–97; awarded Roy. Phot. Soc. Progress Medal, 1890, also Vienna Phot. Soc. Voigtländer Medal, 1895, for researches in scientific photography; Hon. Member Phot. Soc. India, 1897; President, 1894–97; Hon. Member Vienna Photographic Society, 1901; Hon. Fellow Royal Phot. Society; President, 1905–6. *Publications:* The Preparation of Drawings for Photographic reproduction; Report on the United States Government Surveys, 1906; and numerous papers in the Bengal Asiatic Society's Journal and various photographic journals and publications. *Address:* Hurstmead, Eltham.

Died 28 Sept. 1922.

WATERHOUSE, John William, RA 1895 (ARA 1885); *b* 1849. *Address:* 10 Hall Road, St John's Wood, NW. *Club:* Athenæum.

Died 10 Feb. 1917.

WATERHOUSE, Paul, MA; FSA, architect; *b* Manchester, 1861; *e s* of late Alfred Waterhouse, RA, LLD, of Yattendon, Berks; *m* 1887, Lucy Grace, *d* of Sir Reginald Palgrave, KCB; one *s* two *d. Educ:* Balliol College, Oxford. Past President of Royal Institute of British Architects; formerly Chairman of Board of Architectural Education; Life Trustee of the Soane Museum; designed buildings for the universities of Oxford, Manchester, and Leeds, the Prudential Assurance Co., the Refuge Assurance Co., the Atlas Assurance Co., the London Salvage Corps, the Royal National Pension Fund for Nurses, the National Provincial and Union Bank of England, and (in Paris and Brussels) for Lloyds and National Provincial Foreign Bank; various houses, and work for churches, banks, schools, and hospitals, including the University College Hospital Medical School. *Publications:* articles on architecture in the Edinburgh and many other Reviews and Journals; articles on town-planning; several lives for the Dictionary of National Biography. *Address:* Staple Inn Buildings, High Holborn, WC1. *TA:* Aedilis London. *T:* Holborn 2399; Yattendon Court, Berkshire. *Clubs:* Athenæum, Arts.

Died 19 Dec. 1924.

WATERLOW, David Sydney; *b* Highgate, 18 Dec. 1857; 4th *s* of Sir Sydney Waterlow, 1st Bt; *m* 1883, Edith Emma, *e d* of Mrs F. Maitland; three *d. Educ:* Northampton; Lausanne. Travelled round world, 1879; joined the firm of Waterlow & Sons, Ltd, printers, 1880; retired, 1898 but subseq. Chairman, 1922; Director, Improved Industrial Dwellings Co., Ltd, since 1885; LCC, North St Pancras, 1898–1910; MP (L) North Islington, 1906–10; Chairman Governors, United Westminster Schools, 1914; JP London, 1916. *Address:* Wrydelands, Leatherhead, Surrey. *Clubs:* National Liberal, Reform, Royal Automobile.

Died 25 Aug. 1924.

WATERLOW, Sir Ernest Albert, Kt 1902; RA 1903 (ARA 1890); RWS 1880; late President Royal Society of Painters in Water Colours; landscape painter; *b* London, 24 May 1850; *o s* of late A. C. Waterlow, lithographer; *m* 1876, Mary Margaret Sophia (*d* 1899), *d* of late Prof. Carl Hofman; two *s* two *d*; 2nd, 1909, Eleanor Marion, *widow* of Dr G. Sealy. *Educ:* Eltham Collegiate School; Heidelberg. Entered Royal Academy Schools, 1872; obtained Turner gold medal, 1873. *Address:* 1 Maresfield Gardens, Fitzjohn's Avenue, NW. *Clubs:* Athenæum, Arts.

Died 25 Oct. 1919.

WATERS, James; a dramatic critic on the Daily Mail; also the dramatic critic of the Weekly Dispatch. *Address:* Carmelite House, Carmelite Street, EC. *Club:* Royal Automobile.

Died 14 Jan. 1923.

WATERS, Lt-Col Robert, CB 1891; MD; JP; Army Medical Staff, retired; *b* 1835; *y s* of late James Waters, Tobermore. *Educ:* Royal Academical Institution; Queen's Coll., Belfast (Senior scholar);

Exhibitioner, Queen's Univ. in Ireland. Entered Army Medical Dept, 1860; for special services in the Gambia in 1869 received the thanks of the Colonial Government and of the Sec. of State for the Colonies; promoted Staff-Surgeon (Surgeon-Major); PMO West African Settlements, 1873; served in the Ashanti War of 1873–74 (mentioned in despatches, medal with clasp); served with the Nile Expedition, 1884–85, as chief sanitary officer; for a time officiating PMO on the lines of communication (mentioned in despatches; promoted Brigade-Surgeon; medal with clasp, and Khedive's star); PMO, Quetta District, India, 1888; and of Sirhind District, 1889–90. *Recreation:* travelling and visiting every division of the world and places of interest. *Address:* White Fort, Tobermore, Co. Londonderry.

Died 5 Aug. 1927.

WATERS, Rev. Thomas Brocas, Vicar of Christ Church, Hampstead, since 1917; *y s* of Edwin Hughes Waters and Sarah Maria Deborah Waters of Chilverton Elms, Dover; *m* 1902, Alice Mary, *d* of James Young and Louisa Anderson of Bunker Hill, Co. Durham; one *s. Educ:* Tonbridge School; Trinity College, Cambridge. Deacon, 1888; Priest, 1889; Curate of Southborough, 1888–95; Curate of Holy Trinity, Marylebone, 1895–97; Vicar of Jesmond, Newcastle upon Tyne, 1897–1907; Hon. Canon of Newcastle upon Tyne, 1904–7; Vicar of St Mary's, Bury St Edmunds; Officiating Clergyman to the Depot of the Suffolk Regiment, also Chaplain to West-Suffolk General Hospital and Thingoe Union, Bury St Edmunds, 1907–17; Hon. Canon of St Edmundsbury and Ipswich, 1914–17. *Address:* Christ Church Vicarage, Hampstead, NW3. *T:* Hampstead 5222.

Died 16 Sept. 1922.

WATKINS, Frederick Henry, ISO 1904; OBE 1925; *b* Edgbaston, Birmingham, 1859; *m* Marion Charlotte, *d* of late Rev. Canon Connell of St Vincent; one *d. Educ:* St Olave's, Southwark; Switzerland, Italy, and Germany. Private Secretary to Sir Roger Goldsworthy, Administrator of St Lucia, 1882; Inspector of Schools, St Vincent, 1883–89; Inspector of Schools of the Leeward Islands, 1889–99; Adjutant of St Christopher Nevis Defence Force, 1897–99; Commissioner of Montserrat, 1900–6; Commissioner and Acting Judge of Turks and Caicos Islands, 1906–14; Colonial Secretary of Grenada, 1914; retired, 1915; in Foreign Censorship Department, War Office, 1915; Acting Scientific Asst Imperial Dept of Agriculture, West Indies, 1917; Acting Colonial Secretary of the Leeward Islands, 1917–20; Magistrate, Nevis, 1920–25; retired 1925. *Publications:* educational works; Lives of Comenius Pestalozzi, Froebel, and Locke; Daily Thoughts from Horace; Handbook of the Leeward Islands, 1924. *Address:* Antigua, West Indies.   *Died 8 July 1928.*

WATKINS, Ven. Henry William, MA, DD; Archdeacon and Canon of Durham; Emeritus Professor of Hebrew, University of Durham; Examining Chaplain to Bishop of Durham; *b* 19 Jan. 1844; 4th *s* of late William Watkins, Wern-y-cwm, Abergavenny, and Sarah, *o d* of T. Dew, Llanvetherine Court; *m* 1883, Kate Mary Margaret, *e d* of Sir Henry Thompson, 1st Bt; three *d. Educ:* King's Coll. London; Balliol Coll. Oxford (Scholar, MA); Fellow of King's Coll. London; Hon. Fellow of St Augustine's Coll. Canterbury. Ordained 1870; Vicar of Much Wenlock, 1873; Censor, Tutor and Lecturer in Greek Testament in King's Coll., London, 1875; Professor of Logic and Moral Philosophy, 1877; Warden of St Augustine's Coll. Canterbury, 1879; Bampton Lecturer at Oxford, 1890. *Publications:* Charges addressed to the Clergy; articles in Smith's Dictionary of the Bible, etc; Commentary on the Gospel according to St John; Modern Criticism considered in its Relation to the Fourth Gospel (the Bampton Lectures for 1890). *Recreation:* reading. *Address:* The Archdeaconry, Durham. *Club:* Athenæum.

Died 31 Aug. 1922.

WATKINS, Ven. Oscar Daniel, MA; *b* 29 June 1848; *s* of late Daniel Watkins; *m* 1876, Elizabeth Martha, *d* of Rev. T. B. Ferris; two *s* one *d. Educ:* North London College School; King's College, London; Merton College, Oxford (Postmaster, 1869–73). Curate of St Michael and All Angels, Croydon, 1873; Chaplain, All Saints, Allahabad, 1876; later at Meerut, Mussoorie, Bareilly, Naini Tal; St Martin's, Colchester; Holywell, Oxford; Archdeacon of Lucknow, 1897–1902; Examining Chaplain to Bishop of Lucknow; Chaplain on HM's Bengal Establishment, 1881–1903; Vicar of Holywell, Oxford, 1907–21; Commissary to Bishop of Lucknow, 1902–9; retired, 1921. *Publications:* Holy Matrimony, a Treatise on the Divine Laws of Marriage, 1895; The Divine Providence, 1904; A History of Penance (2 vols), 1920; Holy Marriage, 1925. *Address:* 14 Winchester Road, Oxford.   *Died 19 Feb. 1926.*

WATKINSON, Rev. William L., DD, LLD; Wesleyan Minister; *b* Hull, 30 Aug. 1838; *m* Phoebe (*d* 1911), *d* of Samuel Swindley,

Oldbury; four *s* two *d. Educ:* privately. DD Wesleyan Univ. Middletown, Conn; LLD North-Western Univ. Chicago; Pres. of Wesleyan Conference, 1897–98; Editor of Wesleyan Church, 1893–1904. *Publications:* The Blind Spot and other Sermons, 1899; Studies in Christian Character, Work, and Experience, 1901; The Bane and the Antidote, and other Sermons, 1902; The Education of the Heart, 1904; The Supreme Conquest, 1907; The Fatal Barter, 1910; The Moral Paradoxes of St Paul, 1913; The Shepherd of the Sea, 1920; The Fairness of Trial, 1923. *Address:* 29 Exeter Road, Brondesbury, NW.   *Died 14 Feb. 1925.*

WATNEY, Sir John, Kt 1900; *b* 27 Jan. 1834; *s* of John Watney; *m* 1864, Elizabeth (*d* 1896), *y d* of Stephen Dendy of Leigh Place, Surrey; two *s* one *d. Educ:* Harrow. Hon. Sec. on foundation in 1876, then Chairman of Council of City and Guilds of London Institute for Advancement of Technical Education; FSA; JP, Surrey; one of HM's Lieutenants for the City of London. *Publications:* History of the Hospital of St Thomas of Acon and an account of the Plate of the Mercers' Company; and a short history of the Mercers' Company. *Address:* Shermanbury House, Reigate. *T:* Reigate 171.

Died 25 March 1923.

WATNEY, Vernon James, MA; FSA; DL; JP; Vice-Chairman, Oxfordshire County Council, 1927; *b* 14 Oct. 1860; *s* of late James Watney, MP; *m* 1891, Lady (Gwendolen) Margaret Wallop, *d* of 5th Earl of Portsmouth; one *s* two *d. Educ:* Eton; New College, Oxford. County Councillor for Westminster Division of London, 1889–91; Chairman of Watney & Co's Brewery, 1887–98; Master of the Brewers' Company, 1893–94; High Sheriff of Oxfordshire, 1908; Alderman, Oxfordshire CC, 1905; Chairman of Education Committee, 1908–14; Chairman of Oxfordshire Finance Committee since 1918; Member of the Rubber and Tin Exports Committee, 1915–19; Member of the Council of Oxford Territorial Force Association, 1907–27; Member of the Advisory Council of the Institute on Research in Agricultural Economics, Oxford, since 1912; a Radcliffe Trustee, Oxford, since 1922. *Publications:* Littlecote, 1900; Cornbury, 1910. *Address:* 11 Berkeley Square, W1. *T:* Mayfair 3347; Cornbury Park, Charlbury, Oxfordshire; Fannich, Loch Luichart, Ross-shire. *Clubs:* Brooks's, Garrick.

Died 27 Aug. 1928.

WATSON, Aaron, JP; author and journalist; *b* Fritchley, Derbyshire, 14 Dec. 1850; *m* 1871, Phebe, *d* of late John Gibling, Norwich. Editor Newcastle Critic, 1873; assistant editor Newcastle Weekly Chronicle, 1874–78; leader-writer Newcastle Daily Chronicle, 1878–80; editor Echo, London, 1883; editor Shields Daily Gazette, 1885–93; London correspondent Newcastle Daily Leader, 1893–95; editor Newcastle Leader, 1895–1902. Member Northumberland County Council, 1889; Vice-Chairman Northumberland Sea Fisheries Committee; Vice-President Institute of Journalists, 1885; Hon. Secretary, 1894–95; Vice-President, World's Press Parliament, St Louis, 1904; English Representative, World's Press Congress, San Francisco, 1915. *Publications:* Brown Studies, a book of essays, 1885; Waifs and Strays, with Verses Grave and Gay, 1886; For Lust of Gold, a romance, 1890; Papers on Fishery Questions; More Waifs and Strays; F. C. G., a Sketch; The Savage Club; A Medley of History, Anecdote, and Reminiscence, 1907; Tennyson (The People's Books), 1912; A Great Labour Leader, 1908; A Newspaper Man's Memories, 1925. Part-author of The Royal River, Rivers of Great Britain, etc; in collaboration, The Marquis of Carabas, a novel. *Recreation:* sketching. *Address:* Bewley House, Lacock, Wilts. *Clubs:* Savage, London Sketch, Wigwam; Pen and Palette, Newcastle upon Tyne.

Died 26 June 1926.

WATSON, Alfred Edward Thomas; editor of the Badminton Library and Badminton Magazine; for more than 30 years musical and dramatic critic of the Standard; thereafter on staff of The Times; *b* 10 March 1849; *s* of Capt. B. L. Watson. After having contributed verse and prose to various magazines, joined the staff of the Standard in 1872; contributed much to the Saturday Review, 1885–94; wrote occasionally for Punch, and edited the Illustrated Sporting and Dramatic News, writing under the signature 'Rapier', 1880–95. *Publications:* Sketches in the Hunting Field, 1880; Race Course and Covert Side, 1883; Types of the Turf, 1885; Steeplechasing, 1886; chapters in the Badminton volumes on Hunting, Riding and Driving, Racing and Chasing, 1897; The Turf, 1898, etc; The Racing World and its Inhabitants, 1904; King Edward VII as a Sportsman, 1911; A Sporting and Dramatic Career, 1918; sectional editor (Sports and Pastimes) Ency. Brit., and contributor of various articles to the work. *Recreations:* riding, shooting, racing. *Address:* 29 Catherine Street, Westminster, SW1. *T:* Victoria 29. *Clubs:* Junior Carlton, Beefsteak, Bath, Ranelagh.   *Died 8 Nov. 1922.*

WATSON, Arthur George, DCL; JP; *b* London, 30 Nov. 1829; 3rd *s* of Henry Watson, Barnes, Surrey; *m* 1864, Caroline Jane, *e d* of Hon. and Rev. K. H. Digby; two *s* four *d. Educ:* Rugby; Balliol College, Oxford. First Class in Classics, 1852; Johnson Theological Scholar. Fellow of All Souls College, Oxford, 1853–64; Assistant Master at Harrow, 1854–91. *Address:* Uplands, Wadhurst, Sussex. *TA:* Wadhurst. *T:* 66 Wadhurst. *M:* AP 3361. *Clubs:* New Universty, National Liberal. *Died 21 Oct. 1916.*

WATSON, Arthur William, CB 1923; CBE 1920 (OBE 1918); Principal Assistant Secretary and Director of Establishments, Ministry of Labour; *b* Nieuchwang, China, 16 Nov. 1874; *s* of J. Watson, MD, of Dormans House, Dormans Park, Surrey; *m* 1902, Marion, *d* of W. H. Ashwin, JP, DL, of Bretforten Manor, Worcestershire; one *s* one *d. Educ:* Cheltenham College; Uppingham School; Magdalene College, Cambridge. Entered Indian Civil Service, 1897; served in Bihar, Chota Nagpur and Bengal in various executive and judicial capacities, 1899–1909; acting Registrar, Calcutta High Court, 1909–10; Sessions Judge, Calcutta, 1910–12; Secretary to Bengal Legislative Council, 1912; Secretary to Bengal Government in Legislative Department and Secretary to Bengal Legislative Council, 1913; Deputy Assistant Secretary, Ministry of Munitions (England), 1916; Assistant Secretary, Ministry of Labour (temp.), 1918; transferred permanently to Home Civil Service, 1919. *Address:* Dormans House, Dormans Park, Surrey. *T:* Dormans Park 12. *Club:* Travellers'. *Died 9 Oct. 1925.*

WATSON, Colonel Sir Charles Moore, KCMG 1905 (CMG 1887); CB 1902; MA; *b* Dublin, 10 July 1844; *s* of late Wm Watson, Dublin; *m* 1880, Genevieve, Lady of Grace of Order of St John of Jerusalem in England, *d* of late Rev. Russell Cook. *Educ:* Trinity Coll., Dublin; RMA Woolwich. Lieut RE, 1866; served in Soudan under late Gen. C. G. Gordon, CB, 1874–75; ADC to Field-Marshal Sir Lintorn Simmons, GCB, 1878–80; employed in India Office, 1880–82; special service, Egyptian War, 1882 (Brevet Major and 4th class Medjidie); employed in Egyptian Army, 1882–86, with rank of Pasha (3rd class Osmanieh); Assistant Inspector-General of Fortifications, 1891–96; Deputy Inspector-General, 1896–1902; Sec. to Royal Commission for St Louis Exhibition and Commissioner-General, 1904; British Government Delegate to International Navigation Congresses at Düsseldorf, 1902, Milan, 1905, and Petrograd, 1908; Knight of Grace of Order of St John of Jerusalem in England; Chairman of Committee of Palestine Exploration Fund since 1905. *Publications:* Life of Maj.-Gen. Sir C. M. Wilson, 1909; British Weights and Measures, 1910; The Story of Jerusalem, 1912; Fifty Years' Work in the Holy Land, 1915. *Recreation:* travelling. *Address:* 16 Wilton Crescent, SW. *Clubs:* Athenæum, Junior United Services. *Died 15 March 1916.*

WATSON, Sir Charles Rushworth, 3rd Bt, *cr* 1866; *b* 21 Sept. 1865; *s* of Sir Arthur Townley Watson, 2nd Bt and Rosamond (*d* 1904), *d* of C. P. Rushworth, Queen Anne Street, Marylebone; *S* father, 1907; *m* 1910, Evelyn, *d* of late Aubrey Cartwright, of Edgcote; two *s* one *d. Educ:* Eton. *Heir: s* Thomas Aubrey Watson, *b* 7 Nov. 1911. *Address:* 15 Eaton Place, SW1. *Club:* Travellers', Windham. *Died 27 March 1922.*

WATSON, Maj.-Gen. Sir David, KCB 1918 (CB 1916); CMG 1917; Commanding 4th Canadian Division since 1916; *b* 7 Feb. 1871; *m* Mary Browning; two *d. Educ:* Public School, Quebec. In active journalism all his life; owner of Quebec Chronicle; in military associations for over 20 years; took command of 2nd Batt. 1st Canadian Division, Aug. 1914; commanded 5th Bde 2nd Division, Aug. 1915; European War, 1914–18 (despatches seven times, CB, CMG, KCB, etc); Croix de Commander of the Legion of Honour, France; Commander of the Order of Leopold; Croix de Guerre, Belgium and France. DCL, Bishops' College, Lennoxville. *Address:* Quebec, Canada. *Clubs:* Junior Carlton, Royal Automobile; Garrison, Quebec; St James's, Montreal. *Died 19 Feb. 1922.*

WATSON, George, MA; *b* Edinburgh, 24 Sept. 1845; *e s* of James Watson, Manager of the Scottish Provident Institution for Insurances on Lives; *m* 1874, Margaret Campbell (*d* 1914), *o c* of Patrick Campbell MacDougall, Professor of Moral Philosophy in the University of Edinburgh; two *s* three *d. Educ:* Edinburgh Academy and University. Graduated with first-class honours in Classics, 1867; called to Scottish Bar, 1871; English Bar, Inner Temple, 1884; Sheriff-Substitute of Dumfries and Galloway, 1890–1925. *Publication:* edited Bell's Dictionary and Digest of the Law of Scotland. *Recreations:* music, fly-fishing, travel. *Address:* Corsbie West, Newton Stewart. *Club:* University, Edinburgh. *Died 2 Feb. 1927.*

WATSON, Gilbert; Political Correspondent of the Yorkshire Post; *s* of Edwin Watson, late senior clerk at the Admiralty; *m* Lilian, *d* of C. F. Pearson, late of Clare, Suffolk; one *s. Educ:* St Joseph's College, Clapham; graduate in arts of London University. Had considerable experience of parliamentary and organisation work; entered parliamentary journalism, 1904; acted at times as political correspondent of the Manchester Courier, the Standard, the Times, and the Yorkshire Post; Hon. Sec. of the Parliamentary Press Gallery, 1908–10; Chairman, 1911–12; Chairman, Parliamentary Lobby Journalists, 1913. *Recreations:* rowing, sailing, walking. *Address:* 29 Ellesmere Road, Chiswick, W4. *T:* 794 Chiswick. *Clubs:* Constitutional, University of London, Thames Rowing. *Died 5 April 1920.*

WATSON, Henry Brereton Marriott, BA; author; *b* Caulfield, Melbourne, 20 Dec. 1863; *e s* of Rev. H. C. M. Watson, incumbent of St John's, Christchurch, NZ; at age of nine taken to New Zealand; *m* Rosamund (*d* 1911), *y c* of Benjamin Williams Ball. *Educ:* Grammar School, Christchurch, New Zealand; Canterbury College. Came to England, 1885; took up journalism, 1887; assistant-editor of Black and White and Pall Mall Gazette; was on the National Observer staff under W. E. Henley. *Publications:* Marahuna, 1888; Lady Faintheart, 1890; The Web of the Spider, 1891; Diogenes of London, 1893; At the First Corner, 1895; Galloping Dick, 1896; The Heart of Miranda, 1897; The Adventurers, 1898; The Princess Xeuia, 1899; The Rebel; Chloris of the Island, 1900; The Skirts of Happy Chance; The House Divided, 1901; Godfrey Merivale, 1902; Alarums and Excursions, 1903; Captain Fortune; Hurricane Island, 1904; Twisted Eglantine, 1905; The High Toby, 1906; A Midsummer Day's Dream; The Privateers, 1907; A Poppy Show; The Golden Precipice, 1908; The Flower of the Heart, 1909; The Castle by the Sea, 1909; The King's Highway; Alise of Astra, 1910; At a Venture, 1911; Couch Fires and Primrose Ways; The Tomboy and Others; The Big Fish, 1912; Ifs and Ans, 1913; Rosalind in Arden, 1913; Once Upon a Time; The House in the Downs, 1914; Chapman's Wares, 1915; As it Chanced, 1916; The Affair on the Island, 1916; Mulberry Wharf, 1917; The Excelsior, 1918; The Pester Finger; Aftermath, 1919; joint-author with J. M. Barrie of Richard Savage, play. *Club:* Savile. *Died 30 Oct. 1921.*

WATSON, Sir John, 3rd Bt, *cr* 1895; Lieutenant, 16th Lancers; *b* 24 Feb. 1898; *s* of Sir John Watson, 2nd Bt and Edith Jane, *e d* of W. H. Nott, Liverpool; *S* father, 1903. *Educ:* Eton; RMC Sandhurst. *Heir: b* Derrick William Inglefield Watson, *b* 7 Oct. 1901. *Address:* Earnock, Hamilton, Lanarkshire. *Died 23 March 1918.*

WATSON, Gen. Sir John, VC 1858; GCB 1902 (KCB 1886; CB 1863); *b* 6 Sept. 1829; *m* 1860, Eliza Jesser (*d* 1892), *d* of John Davies of Cranbrook Park, Essex. Entered Bombay Army, 1848; Gen. 1891; served Punjab, 1848–49; Bozdar, 1857; Indian Mutiny, 1857–59; in command of Cavalry of Bombay Field Force despatched to Malta, 1878; in command of Punjab Chief Contingent in Afghan War, 1879–80; Governor-Gen's Agent at Baroda, 1881–88. *Address:* Northcourt, Finchampstead, Berks. *Club:* United Service. *Died 23 Jan. 1919.*

WATSON, John; founder and principal proprietor of the Northern Newspaper Syndicate; JP Westmorland; Alderman, Westmorland County Council; Member Lake District Fishery Board, Lune Conservancy Board, Eden Fisher Board; *b* Kendal; *s* of late William Watson; *m* Emily, *d* of late Isaac Farrer. *Publications:* Sylvan Folk; Nature and Woodcraft; British Sporting Fishes; The English Lake District Fisheries; Poachers and Poaching; Annals of a Quiet Valley; Woodlanders and Field Folk, etc; contributor to the Victorian History of England. *Recreations:* shooting, fishing, hound-breeding. *Address:* Eden Mount, Kendal. *T:* Kendal 122. *Died 30 Sept. 1928.*

WATSON, Reginald George, CMG 1911; *b* 2 June 1862; *s* of late Gen. E. D. Watson, Bengal Army; *m* 1905, Sydney Frances Vivien, *o d* of Duncan Presgrave; three *d. Educ:* Haileybury. Entered Civil Service, Straits Settlements, 1883; Protector of Chinese Perak, 1891; Senior Magistrate, Selangor, 1896; Secretary to Government, 1899; Senior Magistrate, Perak, 1901; Commissioner of Lands and Mines, Federated Malay States, 1903; Commissioner of Lands and Surveys, 1906; Federal Secretary, 1909; British Resident, Selangor, 1911; Perak, 1912–19; retired, 1919. *Address:* 71 Bickenhall Mansions, Gloucester Place, W1. *T:* Mayfair 6845. *Died 20 March 1926.*

WATSON, Rev. Robert A., MA, DD; Minister of United Free Church; *b* Aberdeen, 1845; *e s* of Patrick Watson, merchant; *m* 1874,

Elizabeth Sophia (*d* 1918), *d* of Rev. John Fletcher, London. *Educ:* Grammar School; University, Aberdeen. DD 1891. *Publications:* Gospels of Yesterday, 1888; in Expositor's Bible: Judges and Ruth, 1889; The Book of Job, 1892; The Book of Numbers, 1894; In the Apostolic Age, 1804 (new edn 1912); contributor to the British Weekly, Sunday at Home, etc; in co-operation with Mrs Watson, *nom de plume* 'Deas Cromarty', edited George Gilfillan: Letters, Journals, and Memoir, 1892, and The Christian Leader, 1900–1. *Recreations:* travel, country life, chess. *Address:* Broomlee, Cults, Aberdeen.   *Died 3 Feb. 1921.*

WATSON, Lt-Col Thomas Colclough, VC 1898; RE; Military Works Department, India; *b* 1867; *m* 1892, Edythe, RRC, *y d* of late Major-General John Whately Welchman, CB, Indian Army; one *s*. Entered army, 1888; Capt. 1899; Major, 1906; Lt-Col, 1914; served North-West Frontier, 1897–98 (wounded, despatches, medal with clasp, VC). *Club:* Junior United Service.
                Died 15 June 1917.

WATSON, Sir Thomas Edward, 1st Bt, *cr* 1918; JP; colliery owner, shipowner, and coal exporter; *b* 1 Jan. 1851; *e s* of late Edward Watson, West Hartlepool; *m* 1874, Mary Elizabeth, *e d* of late Thomas Harrison and Sarah Jane Lewen, Scarborough; two *s* one *d.* High Sheriff, Monmouthshire, 1911; Newport Harbour Commissioner and Chairman of River Usk Dredging Committee, 1893–1917; Newport Pilotage Commissioner, 1896–1917; President of the Cardiff Chamber of Commerce, 1914–18; Chairman of the Board of Trade Coal and Coke Supplies Committee for South Wales and Monmouthshire; Chairman of the Cardiff Committee for the Supply of Coal to France and Italy during the War; a Member of the Glamorgan Appeal Tribunal on Recruiting; a Member of the Severn Commission, and of the Committee of Lloyd's Register; a Vice-President of the King Edward Hospital, Cardiff, and of the Royal Gwent Hospital, Newport; a Governor of the Welsh National Memorial to the late King Edward; owner of the Somerton garden suburb for the better housing of the working-classes; entered the office of George Pyman & Company, West Hartlepool, 1865; built his first steamer the SS Spray of West Hartlepool, 1873, which the following year effected the salvage of the derelict French Transatlantic steamer Amerique and her cargo, the most valuable salvage which had ever been effected up to that date; commenced business at Cardiff and Newport in partnership with John William Pyman as steamship owner and coal exporter, 1874; purchased the Ffaldau Collieries, 1883; established Patent Fuel Works in France, 1902; purchased the Fleet of the London and Northern Steamship Company, 1916. *Recreations:* collection of early printed books and MSS, hunting, breeding pedigree shorthorns. *Heir: s* Wilfrid Hood Watson, *b* 23 July 1875. *Address:* St Mary's Lodge, Newport, Mon; Merthyr House, Cardiff; Catsash Farm and Kemeys Folly, Mon. *Clubs:* Devonshire; Cardiff County; Newport County.
                Died 1 May 1921.

WATSON, Ven. W. C., MA (Durham); Rector of All Saints', St Thomas, Danish West Indies, since 1916; Canon of St John's Cathedral, Antigua, BWI, since 1911; Archdeacon of the Virgin Islands, 1916; *b* Barbados, 26 May 1867; *s* of Rev. W. C. and Mrs C. M. S. Watson; *m* 1891, Edith Hutson, *e d* of H. J. Inniss, owner of Welches Plantation, St Thomas, Barbados; three *s* two *d. Educ:* Harrison College and Codrington College, Barbados. Acting Headmaster of the Grammar School and Inspector of Schools in St Vincent, BWI, 1890; ordained, 1890; Curate of St George's, Grenada, BWI, 1890; Priest-in-charge of St Paul's, St Croix, DWI, 1893; Curate of St John's Cathedral, Antigua, 1894. *Recreations:* boating, fishing, motoring; also proof-reading. *Address:* All Saints' Rectory, St Thomas, Danish West Indies. *TA:* Watson, St Thomas.
                Died 1916.

WATSON, Rev. Wentworth; *b* 1 March 1848; *o* surv. *s* of late Hon. Richard Watson, JP, Northants; *m* 1903, Eveleen Frances, *d* of Rev. F. M. Stopford. *Educ:* Eton; Christ Church, Oxford; MA. Formerly Vicar of Monmouth, of St Thomas, Oxford, and Abingdon, Berks. *Address:* Rockingham Castle, Northants. *TA:* Rockingham. *T:*Rockingham 3. *Club:* Travellers'.   *Died 5 July 1925.*

WATSON, Sir Wilfrid Hood, 2nd Bt, *cr* 1918; *b* 23 July 1875; *s* of Sir Thomas Edward Watson, 1st Bt and Mary Elizabeth, *e d* of late Thomas Harrison and Sarah Jane Lewen, Scarborough; *S* father, 1921. *Heir: b* Geoffrey Lewin Watson, *b* 19 July 1879. *Address:* St Mary's Lodge, Newport, Mon.; Merthyr House, Cardiff; Catsash Farm and Kemeys Folly, Mon.   *Died 31 Jan. 1922.*

WATSON, Sir William, Kt 1897; MA Dublin; JP, DL City of Dublin; Chairman and Managing Director, City of Dublin Steam Packet Co.;

b 28 April 1842; *s* of late William Watson, JP; *m* 1868, Janet (*d* 1876), *d* of Very Rev. H. B. Macartney, Dean of Melbourne. *Address:* 25 Fitzwilliam Place, Dublin. *TA:* Watson, Dublin. *T:* 1239. *Clubs:* National; St George's Yacht, Kingstown; Sackville Street, Dublin.
                Died 9 March 1918.

WATSON, William, CMG 1916; DSc; FRS 1901; Associate and Professor of Physics, Royal College of Science, London; *b* 1868. *Educ:* King's College School; Royal College of Science. Served European War (CMG); Temp. Lt-Col. *Publications:* Manual of Elementary Practical Physics; A Text Book of Physics; A Text Book of Practical Physics. *Address:* 7 Upper Cheyne Row, SW; Royal College of Science, South Kensington, SW. *Clubs:* Savile, Royal Automobile.
                Died 3 March 1919.

WATSON, Lt-Col William Walter Russell, CB 1916; CMG 1919; VD; late 24th Battalion, Australian Imperial Force; *b* 19 May 1875; *m* 1904, Minnie Sarah, *d* of late Samuel Hordern, Sydney. Served S Africa, 1900–1 (despatches, Queen's medal 6 clasps); European War, 1914–16 (despatches, CB).   *Died 30 June 1924.*

WATT, Francis; *b* Haddington, 20 Sept. 1849; *e s* of late James Watt, JP, sometime Provost of Haddington; *m* 1895, Edith Mary, *d* of H. Willis, Sittingbourne; one *d. Educ:* Edinburgh University (MA with honours); Heidelberg. Barrister-at-law (Gray's Inn, 1886, Middle Temple, 1898); one of the Examiners of the High Court since 1914; Deputy Librarian, Middle Temple, 1916–19 (War time work). *Publications:* Life and Opinions of the Rt Hon. John Bright, 1885; History of Scotland from Robert the Bruce to the Union, 1885; Picturesque Scotland, 1887; The Laws Lumber Room, 1895, 2nd edn 1896, 2nd series, 1898; Terrors of the Law, 1902; Scotland of To-day (with T. F. Henderson), 3rd edn 1913; Edinburgh and the Lothians, 2nd edn 1912; Book of Edinburgh Anecdote, 1912; RLS, 2nd edn 1913, cheap edition, 1918; Canterbury Pilgrims and their Ways, 1917; Our Inns of Court (with Sir D. Plunket Barton and Charles Benham), 1924, etc; various articles. *Recreations:* Latin, walking. *Address:* 1A Middle Temple Lane, EC4. *TA:* 102 Temple.
                Died 4 Oct. 1927.

WATT, Henry J., DPhil; Reader in Psychology in the University of Glasgow; *b* Aberdeen, 18 July 1879; *m* 1909, Nellie Smith (*d* 1922), pianist, *g d* of Rear-Admiral Townsend Dance. *Educ:* Aberdeen; Berlin; Würzburg; Leipzig. Lecturer on Psychophysiology in the University of Liverpool, 1907; Lecturer in Glasgow since 1908; Principal Lecturer in the Faculty of Arts, 1922; civil prisoner of war in Germany till 6 May 1915. *Publications:* Experimentelle Beiträge zu einer Theorie des Denkens, 1904; various papers in German Psychological Journals till 1907; numerous papers in the British Journal of Psychology, Proceedings of the Royal Society, Mind, Music and Letters, Psyche, etc; article Psychology in Hastings' Encyclopedia of Religion and Ethics, 1918; The Psychology of Sound, 1917; The Foundations of Music, 1919; The Functions of Intervals in Songs, British Journal of Psychology; Melody, Music and Letters; The Dimensions of the Labyrinth Correlated, Proceedings of the Royal Society, 1924. *Address:* Hillhead House, The University, Glasgow.
                Died 1925.

WATT, James Crabb, KC Scotland 1903; Advocate; *b* Muchalls, 1853; *e s* of David Watt, Kinneff; *m* Mary, *e d* of Alexander Mackenzie, Elgin; one *s* one *d. Educ:* Stonehaven; Edinburgh University. Advocate-Depute under the Coalition Government; Honorary Sheriff Substitute of Lanark, and Kincardineshire; Member of General Assembly for many years; began life as journalist, and was youngest editor in this country, at 18; held record for sustained speed in phonography; Member of Nexus Committee of International Shorthand Congress, London, 1887, and contributed largely to its printed proceedings; left journalism for law in youth, and had large practice in teinds, church law, criminal cases, and jury work generally; reporter for 15 years for Scotland for Board of Trade RPC; politician (C) for forty years; contested Rossshire, 1900, in absence of the candidate; selected candidate, 1906, when he contested this county; Banffshire, January 1910. *Publications:* Great Novelists; John Inglis, a Memoir; The Mearns of Old; Place-Names of Kincardine, 1914; editor of series of biographies; wrote one of the first articles on Criminal Appeal Courts (National Review, 1890), and many contributions to newspapers and magazines. *Recreations:* antiquities, archæology, golf. *Address:* 2 Heriot Row, Edinburgh. *T:* 6268. *Clubs:* Scottish Conservative; Burgess Golfing Society.
                Died 15 July 1917.

WATT, Samuel, CB 1920; CBE 1923; retired; *b* 6 April 1876; *s* of W. D. Watt, Newry, Co. Down; *m* Jessie Maud, *e d* of Joseph

Cochrane, Coleraine, Co. Derry; one *s* two *d*. *Educ:* Trinity College, Dublin. Entered Civil Service by Class 1 Exam.; served in Public Record Office, Dublin; Local Government Board of Ireland; Chief Secretary's Office, Dublin, and Admiralty, Whitehall; Private Secretary to Rt Hon. Edward Shortt, KC, when Chief Secretary for Ireland, 1918, also to Rt Hon. Ian Macpherson, KC, MP, Chief Secretary for Ireland, 1918–20. *Address:* Ballinavalley, Sandown Road, Knock, Belfast. *T:* Knock 533. *Club:* Ulster, Belfast.

Died 18 Nov. 1927.

WATTERSON, Hon. Henry, LLD, DCL; Vice-President, Inter-State Perry Commission; fifty years Editor Louisville Courier Journal; retired; *b* Washington City, DC, 16 Feb. 1840; *o s* of Hon. Harvey Watterson; *m* 1865, Rebecca, *e d* of Hon. Andrew Ewing; three *s* two *d*. *Educ:* chiefly by private tutors. Confederate Staff Officer and Chief of Scouts, 1861–65; member of Congress, 1875–77; member Democratic National Conventions, 1872–92; President of the Convention of 1876; Chairman of Platform Committee, 1880 and 1888; repeatedly declined office; Chevalier Légion d'Honneur, France, and de la Couronne, Belgium. *Publications:* Oddities of Southern Life, 1881; History of War with Spain, 1898; The Compromises of Life, 1903; Marse Henry, Memoirs, 1919. *Recreations:* music, yachting, outdoor sports. *Address:* Jeffersontown, Kentucky, USA. *Died 22 Dec. 1921.*

WATTS, Sir (Fenwick) Shadforth, Kt 1919; Chairman of the Shipping Federation; *b* 1858; *s* of Edmund H. Watts; *m* Julia Hamilton, *d* of late A. T. Macgowan. Late President of the Chamber of Shipping of the United Kingdom; principal Representative of Shipowners on the National Maritime Board. *Address:* 7 Whittington Avenue, EC.

Died 25 April 1926.

WATTS, Col Sir Philip, KCB 1905; LLD, DSc; FRS 1900; *b* 30 May 1846; *s* of John Watts of Southsea; *m* 1875, Elise Isabelle, *d* of Chevalier Gustave Simonau of Brussels; two *d*. *Educ:* Kensington School of Naval Architecture. In the Constructive Department of the Admiralty until 1885; Chairman of the Federation of Shipbuilders; Naval Architect and Director of War Shipbuilding Department of Sir W. G. Armstrong, Whitworth & Co., Ltd, 1885–1901. CO of 1st Northumberland RGA Volunteers; later 1st Northumberland Brigade RFA (T); equipped and sent out the Elswick Battery to the Boer War, 1900–1; Director of Naval Construction, Admiralty, 1901–12, constructing from own designs new and more-powerful type of battleship, 1904–5; afterwards Adviser on Naval Construction to the Board of the Admiralty; responsible for construction of series of new ship-types, incl. Dreadnought battleship and Indomitable battle cruiser. Freemason. *Address:* 4 Hans Crescent, SW. *T:* 1210 Kensington. *Clubs:* Athenæum, United Service.

Died 15 March 1926.

WATTS, Col Sir William, KCB 1910 (CB 1900); VD 1912; FSA; DL, JP; late Lieutenant-Colonel and Colonel commanding 3rd Battalion Welsh Regiment; raised and commanded the Cape Volunteer Rifles; Hon. Colonel 1st Cadet Battalion King's Royal Rifle Corps; Colonel Commandant City of London Brigade of Military Cadets; *b* 6 Feb. 1858; *s* of late V. B. Watts, Melcombe Horsey, Dorchester; *m* 1883, Emily Annie, *o d* of C. H. P. Flower. *Educ:* Sherborne School. 3rd Batt. The Welsh Regt; served South Africa, 1900–2 (despatches twice, Queen's and King's medals, CB); Commandant of Kenhardt-Prieska and Wynberg districts; Hon. Col in Army; raised and commanded in 1914 the 13th Batt. the Welsh Regt; and in 1915 the 20th Batt. the Welsh Regt. Deputy Provincial Grand Master of Dorsetshire Freemasons; Grand Superintendent of Royal Arch Masons of Dorset; Provincial Grand Master of Mark Masons of Dorset; Governor, Sherborne School; Vice-President, Society of Dorset Men in London; Governor, United Service College, Windsor; Chairman, Militia Club, 1907–10. Knight of Grace Order of St John of Jerusalem, 1900; Order of Mercy, 1918. *Address:* The Priory, Branksome Wood, Bournemouth, W. *Clubs:* Junior Army and Navy, Public Schools, Royal Automobile, Bournemouth.

Died 4 Aug. 1922.

WATTS, William Marshall, DSc (Lond.), BSc (Vict.); *b* 1844; *y s* of Rev. Isaac Watts; *m* 1877, Ida, *y d* of D. Massey, founder of the Massey-Harris Co. of Toronto; one *d*. *Educ:* Owens College, Manchester; University of Heidelberg. Assistant to Prof. Roscoe at Owens College, 1864–66; Asst Prof. of Chemistry, Univ. of Glasgow, 1866–68; First Science Master, Manchester Grammar School, 1868–72; First Science Master, Giggleswick School, 1872–1904. *Publications:* A School Flora; Introduction to the Study of Spectrum Analysis; The Index of Spectra. *Recreation:* spectroscopic research. *Address:* Shirley, Venner Road, Sydenham, SE.

Died 13 Jan. 1919.

WATTS-DITCHFIELD, Rt. Rev. John Edwin, Hon. MA Durham; DD Lambeth; Victoria University, Manchester, and London College of Divinity; first Bishop of Chelmsford since 1914; *b* 17 Sept. 1861; *m* 1892, Jennie, *d* of late Thomas Lax Wardell; one *d*. Ordained, 1891. Curate of St Peter, Highgate, 1891–97; Founder of St Peter's Men's Service, 1892; Vicar of St James the Less, Bethnal Green, 1897–1914; Member of Bethnal Green Board of Guardians since 1899; Select Preacher Cambridge University, 1909 and 1913; Lecturer in Pastoral Theology, Cambridge University, 1912–13; President Council of St John's Hall, Durham; CEMS delegate to Australia, 1912; Chairman, CEMS. *Publications:* Fishers of Men, 1899; Liturgies for Men's Services, 1901; Here and Hereafter, 1911; The Church in Action, 1913; Reservation, 1917; The Church and Her Problems, 1920. *Address:* Bishopscourt, Chelmsford. *Clubs:* Athenæum, National.

Died 14 July 1923.

WAUGH, Ven. Arthur Thornhill; Canon Residentiary of Ripon Cathedral since 1891; Master of the Ripon Hospitals since 1895; *b* 23 Nov. 1842; *s* of Rev. D. J. Waugh, Principal of the Winchester Diocesan Training College; *m* 1st, Harriette Margaret, *d* of Thomas Butcher, of Hampstead; 2nd, Ethel Maud, *d* of Rev. W. Gibbon, Canon Residentiary of Ripon; one *d*. *Educ:* Christ's Hospital; Jesus College, Cambridge (Scholar; Wrangler and 3rd Class Classics). Head of Modern Department, Rossall; Vicar of Elmstead, Essex, 1869–73; St Mary's, Brighton, 1873–95; Chaplain to Bishop Carpenter, 1884–1910; Archdeacon of Ripon, 1895–1905. *Publications:* occasional sermons and papers. *Recreations:* miscellaneous, active and sedentary. *Address:* Ripon. *M:* AJ 1731.

Died 20 Nov. 1922.

WAUHOPE, Col Robert Alexander, CB 1905; CMG 1905; CIE 1897; retired 1905; *b* 14 April 1855; *s* of Lieut-Col H. J. Wahab, formerly 94th Regiment; in 1911 resumed family name of Wauhope. Entered army, 1873; Major, 1892; Col, 1899; served Afghan War, 1878–80 (medal); Mahsood-Wuzeeree Expedition, 1881; Zhob Valley Expedition, 1884; Hazara Expedition, 1888 (despatches, medal with clasp); Hazara Expedition, 1891 (despatches, clasp); Izazai Field Force, 1892; Waziristan, 1894–95 (despatches twice, brevet of Lieut-Col, clasp); Anglo-Russian Boundary Commission, Pamirs, 1895; Tirah Expeditionary Force, 1897–98 (medal with two clasps); HM Commissioner, Aden Boundary Delimitation, 1902–4. *Address:* The Crescent, Alverstoke, Hants. *Club:* East India United Service.

Died 23 Jan. 1921.

WAY, Maj.-Gen. Nowell FitzUpton Sampson-, CB 1885; late Colonel commanding Royal Marines; *b* 1838; *s* of late Holroyd Fitzwilliam Way; assumed additional surname of Sampson by deed poll, 1897; *m* 1st, 1871, Mary Anne Louisa (*d* 1902), *d* of late Lieut-Colonel G. N. Prior; 2nd, 1903, Lucy Emily (*d* 1921), *widow* of G. L. Matthews. Entered Army, 1855; Maj.-Gen. 1895; served Soudan, 1885 (despatches, CB, medal with two clasps, Khedive's star). *Address:* Henbury, Bristol. *Club:* Junior United Service.

Died 16 May 1926.

WAY, Rt. Hon. Sir Samuel James, 1st Bt, *cr* 1899; PC 1897; QC (Aust.) 1871; Chief Justice of South Australia since 1876; *b* Portsmouth, 11 April 1836; *m* 1898, Katharine Gollan (*d* 1914), *widow* of W. A. S. Blue of Strathalbyn and Hahndorf, SA. Attorney-General, 1875; Vice-Chancellor of Adelaide University, 1876–83; Chancellor since 1883; appointed first Lieut-Governor of South Australia, 1891; administered the government of South Australia ten times, besides frequent short periods of office during absences of the Governor; became first Representative of Australasian Colonies on the Judicial Committee of Privy Council, 1897. Hon. DCL Oxon 1891; LLD Adelaide; Queen's Univ., Kingston, Canada, 1895; Hon LLD Cantab. 1897; Melbourne, 1901. *Heir:* none. *Address:* Montefiore, North Adelaide, S Australia. *Clubs:* Athenæum; Melbourne; Adelaide.

Died 10 Jan. 1916 (ext).

WAY, Captain William, MVO 1903; RN; *b* 16 May 1847; *s* of late William Way of Scheirstein, Nassau, Germany; *m* 1st, 1889, Maria Chattock, *d* of Doctor Shaw, Sutton Coldfield (*d* 1891); one *d*; 2nd, 1898, Florence P. D., *o c* of late J. W. Foulkes of Sutton Lodge, West Molesley, Surrey. *Educ:* Ryde Naval School, Isle of Wight; Ormonde House. Entered Navy, 1862; served as navigating sub-Lieut in Ashanti War, 1873–4 (medal); as navigating Lieut in Egyptian War, 1888 (medal and Khedive's bronze star); operations in Eastern Soudan, 1884 (medal and clasp); Harbour Master at Bermuda Is, 1891–96; Staff Captain, 1900; retired as Captain, 1906. *Address:* 9 Nettlecombe Avenue, Southsea, Hants. *T:* Post Office 3898. *Club:* Royal Albert Yacht, Southsea.

Died 3 April 1927.

WAYMOUTH, Paymaster-Captain Frederick Richard, CMG 1918; RN; *b* 1862; *s* of Henry Waymouth, Plymouth; *m* 1890, Beatrice Lily, *d* of Capt. Edwin Wise, RN; two *d. Educ:* privately. Served European War, 1914–19 (despatches); Legion of Honour; Retired List, 1920. *Died 9 Oct. 1927.*

WAYNFORTH, Harry Morton, AMICe, MIME; Professor of Engineering, University of London, King's College; *b* 19 Dec. 1867; *o s* of late Henry Waynforth; *m* 1898, Florence Julia, *d* of late J. Hutchings of Ramsgate; three *s. Educ:* Haberdashers' Schools; Finsbury Technical College. Served apprenticeship with Messrs Bennett and Son, Engineers, London; Assistant at Finsbury Technical College, 1889; Demonstrator in Engineering, Mason College, Birmingham, 1891; Demonstrator in Engineering, 1896; Sub-Dean of the Faculty of Engineering at King's College. *Address:* 127 Rosendale Road, West Dulwich, SE. *Club:* St Stephen's. *Died 5 Nov. 1916.*

WEAKLEY, Ernest, CMG 1908; Commercial Attaché, Constantinople, 1897–1914; *b* 7 Jan. 1861; *o s* of late Rev. R. H. Weakley of Alexandria. *Address:* Foreign Office, SW. *Died 23 Dec. 1923.*

WEALE, W. H. James; Keeper of the National Art Library, South Kensington, 1890–97; Hon. Member of Royal Flemish Academy, 1887; Associate of the Royal Academy of Belgium, 1896; Hon. Member of Royal Academy of Fine Arts, Antwerp, 1901; Officer of Order of Leopold; *b* Marylebone, 8 March 1832; *e s* of late James Weale and Susan Caroline Ellis Vesien; *m* Helena A. Walton; four *s* five *d. Educ:* King's College, London. *Publications:* Belgium, Aix-la-Chapelle, and Cologne, an Archæological Guide-Book, 1859; Bruges et ses Environs, 1862 (4th edn 1884); Mémoire sur la Restauration des Monuments publics en Belgique, 1862; Le Beffroi: Arts, Héraldique, Archéologie, 1863–76; Hans Memlinc: a Notice of his Life and Works, 1865; La Flandre: Revue des Monuments d'Histoire et d'Antiquités, 1867–73; Chronica monasterii S Andreae iuxta Brugas Ordinis S Benedicti, 1868; Les Eglises du Diocese de Bruges: Doyenné de Dixmude, 1874; Descriptive Catalogue of Manuscripts and Printed Books exhibited at Albert Hall, 1885; Bibliographia liturgica, 1886; Some Account of an Illuminated Psalter for the Use of the Convent of S Mary of the Virgins at Venice, 1887; Analecta liturgica, 1889; Gerard David, Painter and Illuminator: a Monograph, 1895; Hans Memiinc: Biography; Pictures at Bruges, 1901; Catalogue de Tableaux des XIVe, XVe, et XVIe siècles exposés à Bruges, 1902; Hubert and John van Eyck, their life and work, 1907; Peintres Brugeois; L. Blondeel; Les Christus; Les Rycx; Les Claeissins; Les Prevost, 1907–12. *Address:* 29 Crescent Grove, Clapham Common, SW. *Died 26 April 1917.*

WEARDALE, 1st Baron, *cr* 1905, of Stanhope, Co. Durham; **Philip James Stanhope;** *b* 8 Dec. 1847; *y s* of 5th Earl Stanhope and Emily Harriet, *d* of Sir E. Kerrison, Bt; *m* 1877, Alexandra, *d* of Count von Cancrine of the Baltic Provinces, *widow* of Count Tolstoy of Petrograd. Trustee of National Portrait Gallery; President of Inter-Parliamentary Union, 1906; formerly Lieut RN; MP (L) Wednesbury, 1886–92; Burnley, 1893–1900; Harboro' Div. of Leicestershire, 1904–5. *Heir:* none. *Address:* 3 Carlton Gardens, SW1. *T:* Regent 3833; Weardale Manor, Brasted Chart, Kent. *Clubs:* St James', Turf, National Liberal. *Died 1 March 1923 (ext).*

WEATHERALL, Col Henry Burgess, CB 1902; 5th Battalion Royal Fusiliers. *Educ:* Harrow. Served South Africa, 1901–02 (despatches, Queen's medal, 5 clasps, CB). *Club:* Junior United Service. *Died 13 May 1917.*

WEAVER, Mrs Baillie, (Gertrude Weaver), (G. Colmore); novelist; 6th *d* of late John Thomson Renton, Bradstone Brook; *m 1st,* 1882, Henry Arthur Colmore Dunn (*decd*), BA, Barrister-at-law and author of Fencing in the All England Series; 2nd, 1901, Harold Baillie Weaver (*d* 1926), Barrister. *Educ:* school in Frankfort-on-Main; private teaching in Paris and London. *Publications:* Concerning Oliver Knox, 1888; A Conspiracy of Silence, 1889; A Living Epitaph, 1890; A Valley of Shadows, 1892; A Daughter of Music, 1894; Poems of Love and Life, 1896; Love for a Key, 1897; Points of View, 1898; The Strange Story of Hester Wynne, 1899; The Marble Face, 1900; A Ladder of Tears, 1904; The Angel and the Outcast, 1907; Priests of Progress, 1908; The Crimson Gate, 1910; Suffragette Sally, 1911; Mr Jones and the Governess; The Life of Emily Davison: an Outline, 1913; Whispers, 1914; The Guest, 1917; The Thunderbolt, 1919; The Guardian, 1923; A Brother of the Shadow, 1926. *Address:* Eastward House, Wimbledon Common, SW19. *T:* Wimbledon 2122. *M:* PE 6604. *Clubs:* Writers', Pioneer. *Died 26 Nov. 1926.*

WEB-GILBERT, Charles; sculptor; *b* Talbot, Victoria, Australia, 1869; *m*; twin *s. Educ:* Melbourne. Exhibitor at Royal Academy, Liverpool, etc; work bought by the Felton Bequest for Melbourne National Gallery, and many private memorials in bronze and marble; Lieut Australian Imperial Forces Commissioned by Australian Government to execute models of battlefields fought over by the Australian Forces; also executed the memorial to the 2nd Division of Mont St Quentin, France, replica of which went to Australian War Museum. *Works:* The Vintage Offering, 1897; The Wheel of Life; busts of Sir Thomas Gibson-Carmichael, Sir Edward Holroyd, L. A. Adamson, L. Abrahams, Sir Samuel Gillott Memorial at Melbourne, The Critic, bought by the President and Council of the Royal Academy out of funds of the Chantrey bequest for the Tate Gallery, 1917, etc. *Recreation:* sculpture. *Died 3 Oct. 1925.*

WEBB, Sir Arthur Lewis, KCMG 1912 (CMG 1902); MICE; *b* 27 Oct. 1860. *Educ:* Royal Engineering College, Cooper's Hill. Public Works Department, India: Irrigation Branch, 1881–94; Irrigation Department, Egypt, 1894; Inspector-General of Irrigation, 1899; Director-General of Reservoirs, Egypt; Under-Secretary for Irrigation, 1906; Adviser to the Public Works Ministry, Egyptian Government, 1908. *Decorated* for services on Nile Reservoir; 1st Class Medjidieh (Grand Cordon); 2nd Class Osmanieh. *Address:* 143 Maida Vale, W9. *T:* Hampstead 7127. *Clubs:* Oriental; Turf, Cairo. *Died 15 March 1921.*

WEBB, Frederick William, CMG 1894; JP; FRS (NSW) 1897; Clerk of the Legislative Assembly of New South Wales, 1888–1904; *b* Sydney, NSW, 20 Feb. 1837; *o s* of late John Webb of HM Commissariat and Mary, *e d* of late Captain William Bell of the NSW Royal Veteran Corps; *m* 1st, 1866, Charlotte Elizabeth, *e d* of Stephen R. Hickson of Cork; 2nd, 1872, Emily, *y d* of late John Piper Mackenzie, official Assignee, Sydney; one *s* one *d.* Clerk in Legislative Council Dept (NSW), 1851–53 (before responsible government); clerk, General Post Office, 1854–60; clerk in Legislative Assembly Department, 1860–87; elected by the National Australasian Federal Convention (Sydney) its secretary, 1891; assistant clerk, 1897; decorated for public services as Clerk of the Legislative Assembly, and as Secretary to Australasian Federation Convention in 1891; retired, 1904. *Recreations:* boating, fishing, shooting. *Address:* Livadia, Balgowlah, near Manly, New South Wales. *Died 17 July 1919.*

WEBB, Mary Gladys, (Mrs Henry Bertram Law Webb); authoress; *b* Leighton, Cressage, Shropshire, 25 March 1881; *d* of George Edward Meredith, schoolmaster, of Welsh ancestry, and Sarah Alice Scott, *d* of an Edinburgh doctor of the clan of Sir Walter Scott; *m* 1912, Henry Bertram Law Webb, BA Cantab, schoolmaster; no *c. Educ:* chiefly at home; two years at 1 Albert Road, Southport. Began verse writing at ten; afterwards wrote fairy tales and stories; brought up in Shropshire; published verse and prose in various papers and magazines in England and America before coming to London in 1921; subseq. reviewer for The Bookman, and occasionally for The Spectator, English Review, Nation, and New Statesman; contrib. articles to the Daily News and TP's Weekly; poems included in various anthologies, and the authoress hoped to publish a collection of them; awarded the Femina Vie Heureuse Prize for the best English novel of 1924–25; no literary agent, representative, or secretary. *Publications:* The Golden Arrow, 1916; The Spring of Joy (essays), 1917; Gone to Earth, 1917; The House in Dormer Forest, 1920; Seven for a Secret, 1922; Precious Bane, 1924; *posthumous publications:* Armour Wherein he Trusted, 1928; Fifty-One Poems, 1929. *Recreations:* nature study, play-going, social life. *Address:* c/o Society of Authors, 11 Gower Street, WC1. *Died 8 Oct. 1927.*

WEBB, Col Walter George, CB 1898; *b* 1838; *s* of Rev. W. Webb, late Rector of Tixall, Staffs; *m* 1st, 1864, Mary Anne, *d* of late W. D. Webb of Elford, Staffs; 2nd, Jane Ann, *e d* of John Cheesman of Fence, Yorkshire. Late Lieut-Col Commandant and Hon. Col 3rd and 4th Battalions South Stafford Regts (retired 1898); JP Co. Stafford. *Address:* The Grange, Malvern. *Died 7 March 1919.*

WEBB, William Seward; President, Rutland Railroad Co., St Lawrence and Adirondack Railway Co., etc; *b* New York, 31 Jan. 1851; *s* of Gen. J. W. Webb; *m* Leila Osgood, *d* of late W. H. Vanderbilt. *Educ:* private tutors; military school; Columbia Coll. Studied medicine in Vienna, Paris, and Berlin, Coll. of Physicians and Surgeons, New York; practised medicine for some time; became member of W. S. Webb & Co., stockbrokers, but retired 1883; was

President of various companies; Republican Member of Protestant Episcopal Church. *Recreations:* travel, yachting, horse-breeding. *Address:* 680 Fifth Avenue, New York; Shelburne Farms, Shelburne, Vermont, USA.   *Died 29 Oct. 1926.*

WEBB-PEPLOE, Rev. Hanmer William; Prebendary of St Paul's Cathedral since 1893; Vicar of St Paul's, Onslow Square, 1876; resigned March 1919; *b* 1837; *y s* of Rev. J. B. Webb (afterwards Peploe) of Garnstone Castle, Herefordshire, and Mrs J. B. Webb (afterwards Peploe), authoress of Naomi, etc; *m* 1863, Frances Emily, *e d* of late Lord Justice Lush; two *s* one *d*. *Educ:* Marlborough; Cheltenham College; Pembroke College, Camb. (1st class Poll Degree, 1859). As champion gymnast had a heavy fall at opening of second session in Camb., which compelled three years to be spent on his back; all examinations had to be passed (both for degree and ordination) in a recumbent position; reading was practically forbidden. Select Preacher before the University, Cambridge, 1896. *Publications:* I Follow After; All One in Christ Jesus; The Life of Privilege; The Victorious Life; Calls to Holiness; Christ and His Church; Within and Without; Titles of Jehovah; Remarkable Letters of St Paul. *Recreations:* travelling, study. *Address:* 1 Evelyn Gardens, SW7. *Club:* National.   *Died 19 July 1923.*

WEBBER, William Downes, JP Queen's and Cork Counties; AB; resident Irish landowner; *b* 19 July 1834; *e s* of Rev. T. Webber, Rector of Castlemacadam, Co. Wicklow, owner of Leckfield and other estates in Co. Sligo, and Frances, *e d* and *heiress* of the Rev. Thomas Kelly of Kellavil, Queen's Co.; *m* 1873, Anna (*d* 1909), *widow* of 5th Earl of Kingston. *Educ:* Trinity College, Dublin. Engaged in agriculture, estate management. *Recreations:* foreign travel, country pursuits. *Address:* Mitchelstown Castle, Co. Cork. *Clubs:* Kildare Street, Dublin; Cork County.   *Died 22 Feb. 1924.*

WEBER, Sir Herman, Kt 1899; FRCP London; Consulting Physician to the German Hospital, Dalston, and Royal National Hospital for Consumption, Ventnor; *b* 1823; *s* of L. Weber, landed proprietor, and Maria Ruperti; *m* 1854, Matilda (*d* 1911), *d* of J. F. Gruning of Highbury Grove, N; two *s* three *d*. *Educ:* Marburg; Bonn (MD 1848); Guy's Hospital. Fellow of the Royal Society of Medicine, and an Hon. or Corresp. Member of several societies on the Continent and in North America. *Publications:* various works on the treatment by climate and mineral waters, on the prevention and treatment of tuberculosis, prolongation of life, and on other medical and scientific subjects. *Recreation:* Greek numismatics. *Address:* 10 Grosvenor Street, W. *T:* Mayfair 5165.   *Died 11 Nov. 1918.*

WEBSTER, Col Arthur George, CB 1884; *b* Cheltenham, 9 Feb. 1837; 3rd *s* of late James Webster, JP, DL, Hatherley Court, Cheltenham; *m* 1889, Mona, 3rd *d* of late Col Wyatt, CB, 65th Regt. *Educ:* Cheltenham Coll. Cavalry cornet, 1856; Indian Mutiny (mentioned in despatches, 1857–59, medal); Egypt, 1882, Tel-el-Kebir (4th class Osmanieh, despatches, medal with clasp); commanded 19th Queen Alexandra's Own Royal Hussars, 1884, Soudan, Suakin, El-Teb, Tamai, Tokar (2 clasps, CB). *Recreations:* shooting, cycling. *Address:* Ravenswell, Banister's Park, Southampton. *Club:* Junior United Service.   *Died 17 May 1916.*

WEBSTER, Sir Augustus Frederick Walpole Edward, 8th Bt, *cr* 1703; Captain, 2nd Battalion Grenadier Guards (retired); *b* 10 Feb. 1864; *e s* of Sir Augustus Webster, 7th Bt and Amelia Sophia, 2nd *d* of C. F. A. Prosser-Hastings; *S* father, 1886; *m* 1895, Mabel (*d* 1917), *o d* of late Henry Crossley, Aldborough Hall, Bedale, two *d* (one *s* decd). *Educ:* Eton. Lieut of Regt, 1884. Prov. Grand Master Prov. Hants and Isle of Wight. *Heir:* none. *Address:* Battle Abbey, Sussex; Hildon, Broughton, Stockbridge. *Clubs:* Guards, Bachelors.
                    Died 13 Aug. 1923 (ext).

WEBSTER, Sir Francis, Kt 1911; partner in firm of Francis Webster & Sons, Linen Manufacturers and Merchants, Arbroath and London; *b* 1 Sept. 1850; *e s* of Francis Webster, Manufacturer, Arbroath; *m* 1889, Annie (*d* 1918), *d* of Joseph Fairn, MD, of South Shields; three *s* one *d*. *Educ:* Arbroath High School; Edinburgh High School and University. *Address:* Ashbrook, Arbroath.
                    Died 6 Feb. 1924.

WEBSTER, Rev. Francis Scott; Rector of All Souls', Langham Place, W, since 1898; Prebendary of Brownswood in St Paul's Cathedral since 1913; *s* of late Rev. William Webster, MA; *m e d* of late Charles Handfield Jones, MD, FRS, St Mary's Hospital; no *c*. *Educ:* City of London School; Pembroke College, Oxford (Open Mathematical Scholarship). First Class Mathematical Moderations, 1879; First Class Mathematical Greats, 1881. Curate of St Aldate's, Oxford, 1882; Head

of the Church Army Training Homes in Oxford and London, 1882–88; Rector of St Thomas's, Birmingham, 1888–98; Hon. Secretary of the Religious Tract Society, 1909; Chairman of the Young Helpers' League of Dr Barnardo's Homes, 1910; Chairman of the Candidates Committee of the Church Missionary Society, 1916. *Publications:* Spiritual Churchmanship; Christians and Christians; The Beauty of the Saviour; The Secret of Holiness; Elijah the Man of Prayer; Jonah, Patriot and Revivalist; Saving Truths of the Gospel; Trusting and Triumphing; Enemies Reconciled; The Second Gospel. *Recreations:* mountaineering, golf. *Address:* All Souls' Rectory, 12 Weymouth Street, Portland Place, W1. *T:* Paddington 3420. *Clubs:* Chorley Wood Golf; Woodhall Spa Golf.
                    Died 2 Jan. 1920.

WEBSTER, Herbert Cayley, FZS; explorer, naturalist, author, composer; Captain late 7th Brigade, South Irish Division RA; *b* Waltham Abbey; *s* of late William Cayley Webster, JP; *g g s* of Sir William Cayley, Bt, RN; *m* 1901, *e d* of late Major Charles Fred. Campbell-Renton, JP, DL, 87th Royal Irish Fusiliers, of Mordington, Berwick-on-Tweed and Lamberton, Berwickshire. Served in Egypt, Medal and Star, Order of Medjidie (3rd class); travelled several years through the South Pacific in a yacht; also many times round the world; made two expeditions to New Guinea; the first white man to penetrate through German New Guinea to the British boundary; discovered the source of the River Minjim; serious fights with natives; discovered also the non-existence of the Bismark Range, 1896–99; discoverer of numerous new ornithological and entomological species, etc, later named after the discoverer in Natural History Museum; late Master of Foxhounds; founder of the Soldiers' and Sailors' Labour Brigade. *Publications:* Through New Guinea; A Quick Riddance; Melanesia; Other Cannibal Countries; The Bay Tree, etc; contributor to Wide World, Strand, Black and White, Animal Life, The Living Races of Mankind; and other magazines; also composer of several waltzes, songs, etc, the most prominent being The Rose of Memories, The Angel's Dream, Love's Desire, Why should we Part?, March of the King's Colonials, etc. *Address:* 7 Sloane Street, Knightsbridge, SW. *Club:* Junior Naval and Military.
                    Died 29 July 1917.

WEBSTER, Captain John Alexander, CBE 1919; MVO 1908; RN (retired); *b* 23 Nov. 1874; *s* of late John Webster, Barrister, and Jessie, *d* of late John Miller of Leithen, Peeblesshire; *m* 1903, Lalia, *d* of late Sir Wallace Graham, Halifax, NS, Canada; three *s* one *d*. *Educ:* HMS Britannia. Midshipman, 1889; Sub-Lieut, 1893; Lieut, 1895; Commander, 1907; Captain, 1914; navigating officer of HMS Indomitable during HRH the Prince of Wales' voyage to Canada on the occasion of the Quebec Tercentenary (MVO); served European War, 1914–16 (prom. Capt.); Director of Nav., Admiralty, 1917–19; retired list, 1922. *Address:* Braehead, Berkhamsted. *Clubs:* Caledonian, Royal Cruising.
                    Died 24 June 1924.

WEBSTER, Robert Grant, LLB; JP; Captain RFA, 1915–17; *b* 1845; *s* of late R. Webster, Montrose; *m* Emily, *d* of B. M. Jalland, Holderness House, East Yorks; one *s*. *Educ:* Radley; Trinity Coll., Camb. Barrister, Inner Temple, 1869; MP (C) St Pancras, E, 1886–99. *Publications:* Shoulder to Shoulder, 1873; The Trade of the World, 1880; The Law relating to Canals; Japan, from the Old to the New, 1905; The Awakening of an Empire, 1917. *Address:* 18 Eccleston Square, SW1. *T:* Victoria 2796. *Clubs:* Carlton, Hurlingham.
                    Died 14 Jan. 1925.

WEDDERBURN, Lt-Col Henry Scrymgeour, JP, DL; Hereditary Standard-Bearer of Scotland; *b* 28 June 1872; *s* of late H. Scrymgeour Wedderburn and Juliana, *y d* of Thomas Bradell of Coolmelagh, Co. Wexford; *m* 1901, Edith, *o d* of J. Moffat; two *s* one *d*. *Address:* Birkhill, Cupar, Fife, NB.   *Died 12 May 1924.*

WEDDERBURN, Sir William, 10th and 4th Bt, *cr* 1704 and 1803; JP, DL, and CC Gloucestershire; *b* Edinburgh, 25 March 1838; 3rd *s* of Sir John Wedderburn, 8th and 2nd Bt, HEICS and Henrietta, *d* of William Millburn; *S* brother, 1882; *m* 1878, Mary Blanche, *o d* of H. W. Hoskyns, North Perrott Manor, Somerset; two *d*. *Educ:* Loretto School; Edinburgh Univ. Took 3rd place in open competition for Indian Civil Service, 1859; served in Bombay CS, 1860–87; acted as Judge of High Court, Bombay, and retired when acting Chief Secretary to the Government of Bombay; president of Indian National Congress, 1889 and 1910; contested N Ayrshire, 1892; member of Royal Commission on Indian Expenditure, 1895; chairman of Indian Parliamentary Committee; MP (L) Banffshire, 1893–1900. *Publications:* pamphlets on Criminal Procedure, Arbitration Courts, Agricultural Banks, Village Communities, and other matters affecting the condition of the Indian people; Memoir of Allan Octavian Hume, CB. *Recreations:* gardening, golf, travelling. *Heir: kinsman* John Andrew Wedderburn-Ogilvy, Major Scottish Horse Yeomanry [*b* 16 Sept. 1866; *m* 1909, Meta Aileen Odette, *e d* of Col E. G. Grogan; three *d*. *Address:* Ruthven, Meigle, NB]. *Address:* 84 Palace Chambers, Westminster, SW; Meredith, Gloucester. *M:* 4B 8517. *Clubs:* Reform, National Liberal.   *Died 25 Jan. 1918.*

WEDDERBURN-MAXWELL, Major James Andrew Colvile, JP; *b* 5 Feb. 1849; *e s* of late Andrew Wedderburn-Maxwell and Joanna, *y d* of James Keir, MD, Moscow; *m* 1891, Helen Mary Godfrey, *d* of late Rev. Henry Godfrey Godfrey-Faussett-Osborne, of Hartlip Place, Kent; three *s* two *d*. *Educ:* Trinity College, Glenalmond. Major, late 54th Regt, 3rd Punjab Infantry, Punjab Frontier Force, 2nd Queen's Own Bengal, and 38th Bengal Infantry; retired 1889; served Jandola Expedition, 1880 (despatches), Burmese Campaign, 1886–87 (medal and clasp). *Address:* Glenlair, Dalbeattie.
                                        Died 28 Dec. 1917.

WEDGWOOD, Major Cecil, DSO 1902; Director Josiah Wedgwood & Sons, Ltd; first Mayor of Stoke-on-Trent; *s* of late Godfrey Wedgwood. Late 4th Batt. N Staffs Regt; Hon. Major in army. Served South Africa, 1900–2 (despatches twice, medal with clasp, King's medal, 2 clasps, DSO). *Address:* Hanley. Staffs.
                                          Died July 1916.

WEDMORE, Sir Frederick, Kt 1912; author; *b* Richmond Hill, Clifton, 9 July 1844; *e s* of late Thomas Wedmore, JP, Druid Stoke, near Bristol; *m* Martha, *y d* of late John Peele Clapham, JP, of Burley Grange, Wharfedale, Treasurer of County Courts; one *d*. *Educ:* Weston-super-Mare, Lausanne, and Paris. Hon. Fellow, Royal Society of Painter-Etchers; lectured or given readings of verse and his own stories in the chief English cities, and at Harvard and Baltimore, and, as a writer, specially an exponent in England of the art of France, from Nattier, Chardin and Latour, to Méryon, Boudin, Fantin, Ribot. Held the post of chief art critic of the Standard for about thirty years. *Publications:* his work in fiction—Pastorals of France (1877), Renunciations, English Episodes, Orgeas and Miradou, and other short stories and imaginative pieces, and the novels, The Collapse of the Penitent and Brenda Walks On,—the latter of which—a study of the life of the Theatre—was written as lately as 1916; critical writing includes the Life of Balzac (Great Writers Series); Studies in English Art; Méryon; Etching in England; Whistler's Etchings; Fine Prints; On Books and Arts; Whistler and Others; Some of the Moderns, 1909; Etchings, 1911; Memories—a book of reminiscence, social and literary—1912; a contributor to the Nineteenth Century; edited the English edition of Michel's Rembrandt, 2 vols; Turner and Ruskin, 2 vols; with his daughter Millicent—the author of the volumes of poems, A Minstrel in the South and Chiefly of Heroes—he edited the Poems of the Love and Pride of England. *Recreations:* the theatre, collecting. *Address:* White Mill End, Sevenoaks. *Clubs:* Burlington, Fine Arts.   *Died 25 Feb. 1921.*

WEEDON, Hon. Sir Henry, Kt 1908; JP; Member, Legislative Council of Victoria; *b* 16 March 1859; *m*; one *s*. *Educ:* Melbourne. Elected City Corporation, 1899; Lord Mayor, 1905–8; MP Melbourne East 1906–12; appointed and visited England as Commissioner for Franco-British Exhibition, 1908; Chairman of Victorian Commissioners, New Zealand Exhibition, 1906; Life Governor all leading Hospitals and Charitable Institutions; Trustee and Treasurer, Victoria Public Library, Museums and Art Gallery; Member of Faculty, Melbourne University, and of Australian Commonwealth National War Museum; President Royal Life Saving Society, etc. *Address:* Yarallah, South Yarra, Victoria, Australia.
                                        Died 27 March 1921.

WEGUELIN, John Reinhard, RWS; painter; *b* Sussex, 23 June 1849; *s* of Rev. William Andrew Weguelin, Rector of South Stoke; unmarried. *Educ:* Cardinal Newman's Oratory School, Edgbaston, Birmingham. Underwriter at Lloyd's, 1870–73; in which year entered the Slade School under Professor Poynter, and afterwards Professor Legros. *Pictures:* The Labours of the Danaids; Herodias's Daughter; Roman Acrobat; Bacchus and the Choir of Nymphs; Cupid Bound; and many water-colours, etc. *Address:* Cleveland, Fairlight Road, Hastings.   *Died 28 April 1927.*

WEI YUK, Sir Boshan, Kt 1919; CMG 1908; JP; Member of Legislative Council, Hong-Kong; *b* 1849; *s* of late Wei Kwong, banker; *m* 1872, Yuk Hing, *e d* of Hon. Wong Shing, MLC, JP, one of the founders of the Tung Wah Hospital, Hong-Kong. *Educ:* Government Central School, Hong-Kong; Stonygate School, England; Dollar Institution, Scotland. Toured Europe, 1872; entered

service of Chartered Mercantile Bank of India, London, and China (later the Mercantile Bank of India, Ltd), Hong-Kong, of which his father was Compradore, 1872; Compradore since 1882; left the Bank in 1910, and thereafter carried on own business as exporter and importer; Permanent Committee-man, District Watch Committee, Hong-Kong, 1880; Chairman of the Tung Wah Hospital, 1881–83, 1888–90; originator of Railway Scheme in China, which failed on account of opposition of Chinese officials, 1890; one of the Founders, and permanent Committee-man, of the Po Leung Kuk (Home for Destitute Women and Children, and Women's Protection Society), 1893; unofficial Member of Legislative Council, Hong-Kong, representing the Chinese Community, since 1896; Member Standing Law Committee, 1896–1917; Member of Public Works Committee; Member of Hong-Kong Univ. Court; Member of Prize Court; rendered much service in negotiations between Chinese and Hong-Kong Governments on various matters; decorated by Chinese Govt with 3rd class Order of Chas-ho, in recognition of services rendered to Chinese people, 1912; decorated by King Gustav V of Sweden with 1st class Order of Wasa, 1918; also received several gold medals from Chinese Govt from time to time. *Address:* Atack & Co's Building, Des Vœux Road, Hong-Kong. *TA:* Weiyuk, Hong-Kong. *T:* 666.   *Died 16 Dec. 1921.*

WEIGALL, Henry, DL, JP; artist; *b* 1829; *m* 1866, Lady Rose (Sophia Mary) Fane (*d* 1921), 2nd *d* of 11th Earl of Westmorland; six *s* one *d*. *Address:* Southwood, St Lawrence, Ramsgate. *Club:* Athenæum.
                                          Died 4 Jan. 1925.

WEIGALL, Lady Rose (Sophia Mary); *b* 1834; 2nd *d* of 11th Earl of Westmorland; *m* 1866, Henry Weigall; six *s* one *d*. *Publications:* Correspondence of Lady Burghersh with the Duke of Wellington; Correspondence of Priscilla, Countess of Westmorland. *Address:* Southwood, St Lawrence, Ramsgate.

                                        Died 14 Feb. 1921.

WEIGALL, Theyre à Beckett, LLM; Acting Judge of Supreme Court, Victoria since 1923; *b* Melbourne, 1860; *s* of Theyre Weigall and Marian à Beckett, both of England; *m* 1890, Anne S. H., *e d* of late Sir R. G. C. Hamilton, KCB, then Governor of Tasmania; one *s* three *d*. *Educ:* Church of England Grammar School, Melbourne; Trinity College, University of Melbourne. Barrister, Victoria, 1881; KC 1907. *Recreations:* tennis, cycling, golf (President of Lawn Tennis Association of Victoria). *Address:* Supreme Court, Melbourne, Victoria. *T:* Windsor, Victoria 244. *Clubs:* Melbourne, Bohemians, Royal Melbourne Golf.   *Died June 1926.*

WEIGHT, Rev. Thomas Joseph; Rector of Christian Malford, 1912–20; Hon. Canon of Bristol, 1901; *b* 19 Oct. 1845; *s* of Rev. George Weight, Vicar of St George's, Wolverton; unmarried. *Educ:* Elstree Hill; King's College, London; Hertford College, Oxford. BA and MA 1874. Deacon and Priest, 1875; Curate of Blakeney, 1875; Curate in Charge of Newnham-on-Severn, 1875; Vicar, 1881; Vicar of St Barnabas', Bristol, 1890; Rural Dean of Bristol East, 1905; Senior Rural Dean of Bristol, 1909; Chief Secretary of Church Congress, 1903. *Address:* Highworth, Wilts.
                                          Died 1 Dec. 1922.

WEIR, Lt-Col Donald Lord, DSO 1916; MC; Leicestershire Regiment; *b* 21 Sept. 1885. Served European War, 1914–18 (despatches twice, MC, DSO and bar, Serbian Order of Karageorge). *Address:* Deane House, Parkstone, Dorset.
                                        Died 21 April 1921.

WEIR, Rt. Rev. Mgr Peter John; Prelate of the Household of the Pope and Canon of Aberdeen (RC) Cathedral; *b* Nether-Buckie, Banffs, 1831. *Educ:* Blairs College, Aberdeen; Institution Poiloup, affiliated to Sorbonne (University); Vaugirard, Paris, and at Grand Séminaire de St Sulpice, Paris. Incumbent of Fochabers, 1867. *Address:* Fochabers, NB.   *Died 10 Dec. 1917.*

WEIR, Robert Fulton, MD; Professor of Surgery, College of Physicians and Surgeons, Columbia University; Senior Surgeon, Roosevelt Hospital, New York; *b* 16 Feb. 1838; *s* of James Weir and Mary Anne Shapter; *m* 1st, 1863, Maria Washington M'Pherson; one *d*; 2nd, 1895, Mary Badgley Alden. *Educ:* College of the City of New York. AB 1854; AM 1857; Corresponding Fellow Société de Chirurgie, Paris, 1892; Honorary FRCS 1900. Asst Surg. US Army, 1861–65; Surg. in Charge, USA General Hospital, Frederick, Md (thanked in general orders); Surg. St Luke's Hosp. NY, 1865–75; Surg. NY Hosp. 1876–1900; Surgeon, Roosevelt Hospital, 1900–8; President American Surgical Association, 1900; President NY Academy of Medicine, 1900; Chevalier Order of Bolivar. *Publications:*

numerous (over one hundred) surgical papers in medical journals, principally on brain, appendical and gastric lesions. *Recreations:* travel, horticulture. *Address:* 16 E 96th Street, New York; Bar Harbor, Maine. *Clubs:* University, Century, New York.

Died 6 Aug. 1927.

WEIR, Robert Stanley, DCL; FRSC; KC; Recorder of Montreal, 1899–1915; Licence Commissioner; *b* Hamilton, Ontario, Nov. 1856; *s* of late William Park Weir, Surveyor of Customs, Montreal; *m* Margaret, *d* of Alexander Douglas, Montreal. *Educ:* McGill University, Montreal; called to Bar of PQ, 1881; revised Charter of Montreal, 1899; Professor Jurisprudence and Liturgics, Congregational Coll. of British N America, 1890–1904; Representative Fellow in Law, McGill University, since 1909; resumed practice of law, 1915; Elected Fellow Royal Society of Canada, 1923. *Publications:* Administration of the Old Régime; An Insolvency Manual; Bills of Exchange Act, 1890; The Civil Code of Lower Canada; The Code of Civil Procedure; The Education Act; The Municipal Code, and several Municipal Studies in University of Toronto series; author of O Canada, Canadian National Song; After Ypres and Other Verse, 1917; Poems, Early and Late, 1923. *Recreations:* music, golf (President Outremont Golf Club, 1901–7). *Address:* 96 The Boulevard, Westmount; Cedarhurst, Lake Memphremagog. *Clubs:* Outremont Kanawaki Golf; Reform, Montreal; Newport, Vt. *Died Aug. 1926.*

WELBY, Edward Montague Earle; Police and Stipendiary Magistrate for Sheffield, 1874–1915; *b* 12 Nov. 1836; 4th *s* of late Sir G. E. Welby-Gregory of Denton Hall, near Grantham; *m* 1870, Sarah Elizabeth (*d* 1909), *d* of R. Everard, Fulney House, near Spalding; two *s* two *d*. *Educ:* Eton; CCC, Oxford. *Address:* Yew Lodge, Spalding, Lincolnshire. *Died 25 Jan. 1926.*

WELCH, Charles, FSA; late Librarian, Guildhall Library; *b* 21 July 1848; *s* of Charles Welch, physician, of Hackney; *m* 1872, Rose, *y d* of late John Jupp; four *s* six *d*. *Educ:* City of London School, under Rev. Dr Mortimer. Fellow of Library Association; Member of Council of the Bibliographical Society; late Member of Council of the Society of Antiquaries and of the Hakluyt Society; Vice-President and late hon. sec. and hon. editor of London and Middlesex Archæological Society; late Lecturer for London University Board for Extension of University Teaching; formerly licensed Lay Reader, Diocese of London; Lecturer for LCC to London teachers; Past Master of Cutlers' Company; member of Court of Paviors' Company; Liveryman of Clockmakers' and Gardeners' Companies. *Publications:* Civic Lives in Dictionary of National Biography; History of the Tower Bridge; Numismata Londinensia; Modern History of the City of London; Mediæval London (jointly with Rev. Canon Benham); contributor to Victoria County Histories; History of the Pewterers' Company; History of the Paviors' Company; Coat-armour of London Livery Companies; History of the Cutlers' Company; Illustrated Guide to Royal Exchange; Catalogue of the Guildhall Museum; editor of facsimile reproduction of Ogilby and Morgan's Map of London, 1677; Register of Freemen of City of London, temp. Henry VIII; Churchwardens' Accounts of Allhallows, London Wall, 15th to 16th cent; various contributions to learned societies, etc. *Recreations:* vocal music, especially choir and part singing, archæological investigations. *Address:* Montrose, 158 Bethune Road, Stamford Hill, N16. *T:* Dalston 2574. *Clubs:* John Carpenter, Colophon.

Died 14 Jan. 1924.

WELCH, James; actor; *b* Liverpool, 6 Nov. 1865; *y s* of John Robert Welch, chartered accountant; *m* Audrey Ford. *Educ:* Liverpool. Served articles to chartered accountant; joined dramatic profession with Mr Wilson Barrett at Globe Theatre, Dec. 1887; since then played in most London theatres. *Club:* Eccentric.

Died 11 April 1917.

WELD, Reginald Joseph; *b* 24 May 1842; 2nd *s* of late Edward Joseph Weld and Ellen Caroline, *e d* of Sir Bourchier-Palk Wrey, 8th Bt. Lord of the Manors of Lulworth, Coombe Keynes, Winfrith Newburgh and Sutton Pointz; Patron of two livings. *Educ:* Stonyhurst. *Address:* Lulworth Castle, Wareham, Dorset.

Died 13 Aug. 1923.

WELD-BLUNDELL, Charles Joseph; *b* 1845; *s* of Thomas Weld, who succeeded to the Ince Blundell Estates in Lancashire in 1840, and assumed additional name of Blundell; *m* 1884, Charlotte Catherine Marcia (*d* 1926), *e d* of Col Hon. Charles Pierrepoint Lane-Fox, *b* of Lord Conyers; two *d*. *Educ:* Stonyhurst College, Lancashire; Christ Church, Oxford. Travelled widely with especial view to Natural History and Botany. After 3 years in Spanish America, where he made a special study of the question Scent *v* Vision in Birds of Prey, he

published a compendium of his arguments in favour of the latter view in the Times, Oct. 1872. In Bolivia he was entrusted with a special mission to report to Lord Clarendon as to the advisability of renewing diplomatic intercourse with that Republic, and held a commission to report upon and examine the country between the Vermejo and Pilcomayo Rivers, and the country of the Abas, from the Government of Melgarejo. At 40 marrying, and soon after succeeding to the Lancashire estates, he abandoned travel for art, politics, and journalism, lecturing on Tithes, writing for Dublin Review, Tablet, Liverpool Mercury, and Catholic Times, for which paper he wrote a series of Polemical Articles, afterwards published in book form, The Church of the Tithe. Contested Preston, 1885. Defeated at Preston, he was offered Chatham as a solatium by the Liberal Caucus; but through his holding strong views against the then Liberal crusade against the Peers, and in general against the Newcastle programme, was tabooed by the Liberal Caucus. Since when mainly employed in developing his Lancashire estates, and after a protracted study of the foreign methods of forestry, succeeded in clothing the bare sandhills of his coast between Southport and Formby Point with pines. He received his late Majesty in Coronation year at Lulworth Castle, the splendid home of his ancestors in Dorset. His Lancashire seat had a European reputation for its art treasures, which comprised by far the largest private collection of antique marbles in the country. *Address:* Ince Blundell Hall, near Liverpool. *Club:* Travellers'.

Died 5 Aug. 1927.

WELDON, Col Sir Anthony Arthur, 6th Bt, *cr* 1728; CVO 1911; DSO 1900; HM Lieutenant, Co. Kildare; DL Queen's County and JP Queen's County and County Kildare; State Steward and Chamberlain to Lord Lieutenant of Ireland since 1908; Lieutenant-Colonel Commanding the 4th Battalion Leinster Regiment (Royal Canadians); *b* London, 1 March 1863; *e s* of Sir Anthony Weldon, 5th Bt and Elizabeth, *d* of late Col Arthur Kennedy; *S* father, 1900; *m* 1902, Winifred, *d* of late Col Varty Rogers of Broxmore Park, Romsey, and late of the Royal Dublin Fusiliers and HM Bodyguard of Gentlemen-at-Arms; three *s*. *Educ:* Charterhouse; Trinity Coll. Camb. (BA 1884). Vice-Chamberlain to Lord Lieutenant of Ireland (the Earl of Aberdeen), 1906. Joined 4th Batt. Leinster Regiment, 1885; served as special service officer with the Natal Field Force under Sir Redvers Buller, Boer War, 1899–1900 (despatches); ADC to F-M Viscount Wolseley, Commander-in-Chief, 1895–1900. Owner of 2,800 acres. *Recreations:* shooting, fishing, hunting. *Heir:* s Anthony Edward Wolseley Weldon, *b* 1 Dec. 1902. *Address:* Kilmorony, Athy, Co. Kildare; Rahinderry, Ballylinan, Queen's County, Ireland. *Clubs:* Bachelors; Kildare Street, Dublin.

Died 29 June 1917.

WELDON, Major Francis Harry, DSO 1900; the Derbyshire Regiment; retired 1906; *b* 24 April 1869; *e s* of Col Thomas Weldon; *m* 1902, Eveleen Campbell of Rivermount House, Pangbourne; one *s* one *d*. *Educ:* Cheltenham. Entered army, 1890; Captain, 1896; served South Africa, 1899–1902 (despatches, Queen's medal, 3 clasps, King's medal, 2 clasps, DSO). *Address:* Herondean, Pummersdale, Chichester. *Clubs:* Naval and Military, Sports.

Died 8 April 1920.

WELDON, Sir William Henry, Kt 1919; CVO 1902; FSA; Clarenceux King-of-Arms since 1911; *b* 1837; *s* of William Weldon of Bramley Hall, Yorks; *m* 1st, Georgina (*d* 1914), *e d* of Morgan Treherne of Gate House, Sussex; 2nd, 1914, Annie, *widow* of Major Stanley Lowe, Whitehall, Churchstow, Devon. *Educ:* Harrow. Late 18th Hussars; Rouge Dragon, 1869; Windsor Herald, 1880; Norroy King of Arms, 1894; Registrar of the College of Arms, 1886–94; Secretary to Earl Marshal, 1904–11; acted as Deputy Garter at Coronation of King Edward VII. *Recreations:* boat-sailing and motor-boating. *Address:* College of Arms, Queen Victoria Street, EC; Orchard, Shiplake, Oxon. *Clubs:* Army and Navy, Garrick.

Died 25 Aug. 1919.

WELFORD, Richard, MA; JP; *b* Upper Holloway, Middlesex, 29 May 1836; *m* Minnie (*d* 1903), *d* of late Thos Deverell of Hackney; two *s* one *d*. Journalist, 1854–61; Secretary and Managing Director, Tyne Steam Shipping Company, Limited, 1864–1904; Foreign Office Passport Agent, 1872–1909; Vice-Chairman of Tyne-Tees Shipping Co; Director of Free Trade Wharf Co.; Hon. MA Dunelm, 1897; a Vice-President of the Surtees Society, and Newcastle Society of Antiquaries; Member of the Northumb. History Committee; a Governor of the Armstrong College, and of the Newcastle School for the Blind; one of the Visiting Justices for Co. Northumb. *Publications:* History of Gosforth, 1879; History of St Nicholas' Cathedral, Newcastle, 1880; Pictures of Tyneside Sixty Years Ago, 1881; History of Newcastle and Gateshead, 3 vols 1885; Men of Mark

'Twixt Tyne and Tweed, 3 vols, 1895; Royalist Compositions in Durham and Northumb. (Surtees Society, vol. cxi), 1905; Newcastle Typography and Bibliography, from 1639 to 1800; Local Muniments, 5 Series in Archæologia Æliana. *Recreation:* gardening. *Address:* Thornfield, Gosforth, Newcastle. *TA:* Welford, Newcastle. *T:* 54 Gosforth, Nat. *Club:* Newcastle Liberal.

Died 20 June 1919.

WELLER-POLEY, Thomas; JP, Sussex; *b* 8 Nov. 1850; 2nd *s* of J. G. Weller-Poley of Boxted Hall, Suffolk; *m* 1878, Eleanor Mary, *o* surv. *c* of late J. J. Johnson, QC, of West Broyle, Chichester; one *s*. *Educ:* Eton; Merton College, Oxford, MA. Called to Bar, Lincoln's Inn, 1878. *Recreations:* shooting, fishing. *Address:* West Broyle, Chichester. *T:* Lavant 11. *Club:* United University.

Died 29 Dec. 1924.

WELLS, Arthur Collings; JP, CC Hertfordshire; *b* 1857; 6th *s* of late Joseph Wells of Broomfield, Essex; *m*; two *s* two *d*. *Educ:* Repton. *Recreations:* hunting, shooting. *Address:* Caddington Hall, Hertfordshire. *Club:* Junior Carlton.

Died 11 May 1922.

WELLS, Prof. Charles, MA Oxon; PhD Leipzig; Oriental Translator to the Foreign Office since 1892; Professor of Turkish, King's College, London, 1889–1916; formerly Lecturer on Turkish at the University of Oxford; *b* London; *s* of J. W. Wells; *m* Emma Chardon, *d* of Imperial 'Rentmeister' Louis Chardon; two *d*. *Educ:* King's Coll. London (Oriental Dept); Turkish Prizeman, King's Coll. London, 1860. Special correspondent of Daily Telegraph in the Schleswig-Holstein War, 1864; Professor of English at Imperial Naval Coll. Constantinople, 1870–74; Private Secretary to General Kemball on Turco-Persian Frontier Commission, 1875, and in Turco-Servian War, 1876. *Publications:* 'Ilm Tedbir-i-Mulk', an essay on Political Economy in Turkish, 1860; Mehemet the Kurd, and other Tales from Eastern Sources, 1865; A Practical Grammar of the Turkish Language, 1880; a revised and enlarged edition of Redhouse's Turkish Dictionary, 1880; The Literature of the Turks, 1890. *Recreation:* philology. *Address:* Emmaburg, Portslade Station, Brighton; King's College, London.   *Died 5 Oct. 1917.*

WELLS, Eugene; JP for Suffolk; 3rd *s* of Joseph Wells, Broomfield, Essex; *m* Gertrude, *d* of Duncan Campbell of Toronto, Canada. *Recreations:* hunting, shooting, golf; MFH Suffolk, 1898–1903; Master Suffolk Staghounds, 1904–6. *Address:* Buxhall Vale, near Stowmarket, Suffolk. *TA:* Great Finborough. *Club:* Junior Carlton.

Died 21 June 1925.

WELLS, Rev. James, MA, DD; sometime Moderator of United Free Church of Scotland; *b* 11 June 1838; *s* of David Wells, farmer, Dumfriesshire; *m* 1867, Janet Finlay Simpson, Bathgate; two *s* two *d*. *Educ:* Torthorwald School; Dumfries Academy; Edinburgh and Erlangen Universities. Minister in Glasgow of Wynd Church, Barony Free Church, and Pollokshields West Church; deputy to the Presbyterian Churches in United States and Canada, and to missions in India, Africa, and Palestine. *Publications:* Life of Dr Stewart, of Lovedale; Life of Dr Hood Wilson; Travel-Pictures from Palestine; Rescuers and Rescued; Christ in the Present Age; Christ and the Heroes of Heathendom; Bible Echoes; The Parables of Jesus; Bible Images; Bible Children; The Child's Prayer, etc. *Recreations:* travel, mountaineering. *Address:* Pollokshields, Glasgow. *T:* Queen's Park 1226.   *Died Feb. 1924.*

WELLS, Captain John Stanhope Collings, DSO 1917; Acting Lieutenant-Colonel 4th Battalion Bedfordshire Regiment; *b* 1880; *e s* of A. Collings Wells, JP, Caddington Hall, Herts; unmarried. Served European War, 1914–17 (DSO). *Address:* Caddington Hall, Herts. *Club:* Junior United Service.   *Died 27 March 1918.*

WELLS, Sidney Herbert, CBE 1919; AMICE; Director-General of Department of Technical, Industrial, and Commercial Education, Egypt, since 1907; *b* Cottenham, Cambs, 10 Aug. 1865; 2nd *s* of late Rev. J. C. Wells, Baptist Minister; *m* 1st, 1890, Mary Elizabeth (*d* 1907), *d* of late George Mathew, Worsted Lodge, Camb; two *d*; 2nd, 1908, Florence Amelia, *y d* of late George Mathew. *Educ:* private schools; Birkbeck and King's Colleges, London. Educated for Engineering; Whitworth Scholarship, 1885; founded and for five sessions Chairman of Institution of Junior Engineers, 1889; Assistant and Form Master, Dulwich College, Engineering and Science Side, 1889; Senior Assistant, Engineering Dept of Leeds University, 1891; First Principal of Battersea Polytechnic, 1893; original member of Faculty of Engineering of London University; Secretary of Board of Studies, 1903–5, of Faculty, 1905; Member of Incorporated Association of Headmasters and Member of Council, 1904–6; Member of Council of Association of Technical Institutions, 1894; Hon. Secretary, 1903–7; Member of Examinations Board of City and Guilds Inst., 1903, of Teachers' Registration Council, 1904, and of Consultative Committee of Board of Education, 1904; visited Egypt to report on technical education, 1906. 2nd class Medjidieh and 2nd class Nile Orders; mentioned in General Allenby's despatches; Vice-Chairman of Egyptian Commission of Commerce and Industry, 1916–18; Director of Civilian Employment for EEF, 1917–19. *Publications:* textbooks on Engineering, Drawing, and Design, 2 vols, and on Practical Mechanics. *Recreations:* riding, golf, and gardening. *Address:* Department of Technical Education, Cairo. *TA:* Techedu, Cairo. *Clubs:* Royal Societies; Turf, Cairo.

Died 28 March 1923.

WELLS, William Page Atkinson; landscape painter; *b* Glasgow, 1872; *s* of Andrew Wells, decorator and poet; *m* 1897; two *s*. *Educ:* Glasgow High School. Lived in Glasgow until 1885; travelled with parents to Australia; lived both in Sydney and Melbourne for five years; returned to England, studied at the Slade School under Professor Legros, also under Messrs Bongereau and Ferrier at Paris for a number of years; returned again to England and exhibited first pictures at the Institute of Painters in Oil, Piccadilly; worked for some years in North Lancashire; then for ten years settled in the Isle of Man; after the war migrated to Devonshire; then living and working in Appledore, North Devon; exhibited in most of the important British and Continental Galleries; pictures acquired by the Scottish Modern Arts Society and Oldham, Glasgow, and Belfast Corporations and Birkenhead. *Recreations:* various. *Address:* 29 Irsha Street, Appledore, N Devon. *Clubs:* Glasgow Art, Scottish Automobile, Glasgow; Ellen Vannin, Douglas.   *Died 1923.*

WELSH, Elizabeth; Mistress of Girton College, Cambridge, 1885–1903; *b* 1843. *Educ:* Girton Coll., Camb. Taught at Manchester High Sch., 1875–76; Tutor in Classics, 1876–84 and Vice-Mistress, 1880–85, Girton Coll. *Address:* 55 Morningside Park, Edinburgh. *Club:* University Women's.

Died 13 Feb. 1921.

WELSH, Rt. Rev. John Francis, DD; Bishop of Trinidad since 1904; *b* Huddersfield; *y s* of Robert Welsh of Tweedsmuir, Peeblesshire, and Huddersfield; *m* 1882, Jane, *e d* of Matthew Brown of Scaurbank, Arthuret, JP for County of Cumberland. *Educ:* Christ Church, Oxford (BA 1881; MA 1886); DD (hon. causa) 1904. Deacon, 1881; Priest, 1882; Curate of St James, Whitehaven, 1881–83; Lecturer of St Bees' Theological Coll. 1883–86; Principal of Warminster Missionary Coll. 1887–1904. *Recreations:* music, well-known chess-player; was Pres. of Oxford Univ. Club. *Address:* Port-of-Spain, Trinidad, WI. *TA:* Bishop, Port-of-Spain. *T:* 499. *Club:* West Indian.

Died 21 July 1916.

WELSH, Rev. Thomas; Professor St Mary's College, Blairs, Aberdeen; Editor of Catholic Directory for Scotland. *Address:* St Mary's College, Blairs, Aberdeen.   *Died 1920.*

WENDELL, Barrett, LittD Columbia and Harvard; Hon. Dr, Strasbourg; Professor of English at Harvard College, 1898, Professor Emeritus, 1917; Clark Lecturer, Trinity College, Cambridge, 1902; Lecturer at the Sorbonne and other French universities, 1904; Fellow American Academy of Arts and Letters, 1916; *b* Boston, 23 Aug. 1855; *s* of Jacob and Mary Bertodi (Barrett) Wendell; *m* 1880, Edith, *d* of W. W. Greenough of Boston; two *s* two *d*. *Educ:* Harvard Coll. AB 1877; Student of law, 1877–80; Instructor in English, Harvard Coll., 1880–88; Asst Prof., 1888–98. *Publications:* The Duchess Emilia, 1885; Rankell's Remains, 1887; English Composition, 1891; Cotton Mather, 1891; Stelligeri, and other Essays concerning America, 1893; William Shakspere, 1894; A Literary History of America, 1900; Ralegh in Guiana, etc, 1902; The Temper of the Seventeenth Century in English Literature, 1904; Liberty, Union, and Democracy; the National Ideals of America, 1906; The France of To-Day, 1907; The Privileged Classes, 1908; The Mystery of Education, 1909; The Traditions of European Literature (from Homer to Dante), 1920. *Address:* 358 Marlborough Street, Boston. *TA:* Bwendle, Boston. *T:* 305 Back Bay. *Clubs:* Somerset and Tavern, Boston; Century, New York.   *Died 8 Feb. 1921.*

WENDEN, Henry Charles Edward, CIE 1903; MInstCE; *b* 11 April 1841; *e s* of late Henry Wenden, of Barnes, Surrey; *m* 1881, Ada Henrietta, *y d* of late Major Edward Simpson, 2nd Bombay Cavalry. Engaged on Indian railways, 1859–1906, when he retired. *Address:* Summerhill, Horsell, near Woking, Surrey. *Club:* East India United Service.   *Died 31 Jan. 1919.*

WENLOCK, 4th Baron, *cr* 1839; **Richard Thompson Lawley,** Bt 1641; CB 1902; *b* 21 Aug. 1856; *s* of 2nd Baron and Elizabeth, *d* of 2nd Marquis of Westminster; *S* brother, 1912; *m* 1909, Rhoda Edith, 2nd *d* of Rev. Canon Knox-Little, Worcester. Entered army, 1876; Lieut-Col, 1899; Col, 1903; served Nile Expedition, 1884–85 (medal with clasp and Khedive's star); South Africa, 1901–2 (despatches, medal with five clasps). Owner of about 3,500 acres. *Heir: b* Rev. Hon. Algernon G. Lawley, *b* 25 Dec. 1857. *Address:* Monkhopton, Bridgnorth.   *Died 25 July 1918.*

WENTWORTH, Baroness, 14th in line, *cr* 1529; **Ada Mary Milbanke,** *b* 26 Feb. 1871; *o d* of 2nd Earl of Lovelace, and Fannie, 3rd *d* of late Rev. George Heriot, of Fellow Hills, Berwick; *S* father, 1906. *Heir-pres.:* aunt Lady Anne Blunt, *b* 1837. *Address:* White Heather, Sunninghill, Ascot.

Died 18 June 1917.

WENTWORTH, Baroness, 15th in line, *cr* 1529; **Anne Isabella Noel Blunt;** *b* 1837; *d* of 1st Earl of Lovelace; *S* niece, 1917; *m* 1869, Wilfred S. Blunt, author and poet; one *d*. *Heir: o d* Hon. Judith Anne Dorothea Blunt [*b* 1879; *m* 1899, Major Hon. Neville Lytton; one *s* two *d*]. *Address:* Crabbet Park, Three Bridges, Sussex.

Died 15 Dec. 1917.

WERE, Major Harry Harris, DSO 1917; late East Lancs Regiment; *b* 1865; *y s* of Nicholas Were of Wellington, Somerset; *m* 1890, Kathleen, *y d* of late Stephen Creagh Sandes of Sallow Glen, Tarbert, Co. Kerry; no *c*. *Educ:* Kelly College, Tavistock; Sandhurst. Joined E Lancashire Regt, 1885; retired, 1913; served European War, 1916–17 (despatches twice). *Recreations:* shooting, golf. *Address:* c/o Lloyds Bank Ltd, 6 Pall Mall, SW1. *Club:* United Service.

Died 26 Dec. 1925.

WERNER, Prof. Alfred; Professor of Chemistry at Zürich University; *b* Mulhausen, 12 Dec. 1866; *m* 1894, Emma Giesker; one *s* one *d*. Nobel Prize for Chemistry, 1913. *Address:* Freie Strasse 111, Zürich, V, Switzerland.   *Died 1919.*

WERTHEIMER, Prof. Julius, DSc, BA; FIC, FCS; Principal of the Merchant Venturers' Technical College, Bristol, since 1890; also Professor of Applied Chemistry and Dean of the Faculty of Engineering in the University of Bristol since 1909; *b* Birmingham; *e s* of late Maurice Wertheimer; *m* Katharine Eastwood, *o d* of late John Eastwood, of Newlaithes Hall, Yorks. *Educ:* High School of the Liverpool Institute; University College, Liverpool; Owens College, Manchester. Late Exhibitioner of the University of London; Fellow of the Physical Society; Head Master of the Leeds School of Science and Technology, 1887–90; Hon. Secretary of the Association of Technical Institutions, 1893–1903; Chairman of Council, 1904; Président d'honneur du Cercle français de Bristol, 1905–16; Officier d'Académie (de France), 1906; Member of the Council and Senate of the University of Bristol, 1909; DSc honoris causa, Bristol, 1911; Member of the Court, University of Sheffield, 1912; Member of the Teachers' Registration Council, 1912; Chairman of the Experience Committee of the TRC, 1914; Major, Merchant Venturers' Cadet Corps, 1915–19; organised W of England Industrial Reserve for the production of munitions, 1915; Member of Council of Engineering Training Organisation and of W of England (Joint) Disablement Committee, 1917; Member Education Committees of the Gloucestershire County Council, Bristol City Council, and British Science Guild; late Member of Standing Committee of Convocation of University of London; late Examiner for London County Council Scholarships; Chairman of Conference of British Navigation Schools, 1918; Chairman, Fairfield Secondary School Committee, 1919. *Publications:* articles in the Nineteenth Century, The Times, Nature, etc; Text-Books on Chemistry; editor of Series of Text-books of Technology; Experiments with Waterfinders, etc. *Recreations:* golf, motoring. *Address:* 11 The Paragon, Clifton, Bristol. *TA:* Merchants' College, Bristol. *T:* Bristol 407 and 1682. *Clubs:* University of London; Clifton, Constitutional, Bristol and Clifton Golf, Bristol Rotary.

Died 9 Aug. 1924.

WESBROOK, F. F.; President of the University of British Columbia, 1913; of American Public Health Association, 1905; *b* 12 July 1868; *s* of Henry Shaver Wesbrook; *m* 1896, Annie, *d* of late Chief Justice Sir Thomas W. Taylor, Winnipeg; one *d*. *Educ:* University of Manitoba (BA 1887; MA 1890; MD, CM 1890; LLD 1913); LLD Toronto, 1913; Alberta, 1915; University of California, 1918. John Lucan Walker student in Pathology, Univ. of Camb., 1893–95; late Professor of Pathology, University of Manitoba; Dean, College of Medicine and Surgery, 1906, and Professor of Public Health and Bacteriology, University of Minnesota; Director of Minnesota State

Board of Health Laboratories, 1896–1911; Member of Minnesota State Board of Health, 1896–99 and 1911–12; President Section on State and Municipal Hygiene, International Congress of Hygiene and Demography, 1912; Member Advisory Board, Hygienic Laboratory, US Public Health Service, 1904–13. Member Association of American Physicians; Fellow Royal Sanitary Institute; Fellow of Royal Society of Canada; of American Association for Advancement of Science; Canadian Public Health Association; American Physiological Society; Society of American Bacteriologists; Pathological Society of Great Britain and Ireland; Pathological Section of Royal Society of Medicine, London; American Medical Association; National Association for the Prevention and Relief of Tuberculosis, and others. *Publications:* numerous technical and educational papers and reports. *Address:* The University of British Columbia, Vancouver, BC. *Clubs:* Vancouver, University, Jericho Country, Union of BC, American, Vancouver.   *Died Oct. 1918.*

WESSELS, Hon. Sir Cornelius Hermanus, Kt 1920; Commissioner of Public Works, Lands, etc, Orange River Colony, since 1907; *b* Wynberg, 26 April 1851; *s* of John H. Wessels. *Educ:* privately. Member of Volksraad for Boshof, 1885; Chairman for 2 years; represented Orange Free State in England as one of the Peace Commissioners. *Address:* 52 Aliwal Street, Bloemfontein, ORC. *Club:* Bloemfontein.   *Died March 1924.*

WEST, Rt. Hon. Sir Algernon Edward, GCB 1902 (KCB 1886); PC 1894; late Alderman LCC; Director of Northern Assurance, and Member of the Council of Foreign Bond-holders; *b* 4 April 1832; 3rd *s* of M. J. West and Maria, 3rd *d* of 2nd Earl of Orford; *m* 1858, Mary (*d* 1894), *d* of Capt. Hon. George Barrington; three *s* one *d*. *Educ:* Eton; Christ Church, Oxford. Was a clerk in the Admiralty; assistant secretary to Sir C. Wood and Duke of Somerset; secretary to Sir C. Wood at India Office, and Mr Gladstone when Prime Minister; Chairman of Board of Inland Revenue; served on Prison Commission, and was Vice-Chairman of the Licensing Commission. *Publications:* Recollections, 1899; Memoir of Sir Henry Keppel, 1905; One City and Many Men, 1908; Contemporary Portraits: Men of My Day in Public Life, 1920. *Address:* 14 Manchester Square, W1. *T:* 3623 Paddington. *Club:* Brooks's.

Died 21 March 1921.

WEST, Charles Henry, CIE 1903; *b* 20 April 1859; *s* of late Charles Henry West, Merchant in the Punjab; *m* 1888, Agnes Lingard, *d* of late Charles Murphy, Survey of India Department; one *s* one *d*. Joined the service in 1876; served in Civil Departments of Punjab until 1880; became Personal Assistant to AG India, 1890, and Assistant Secretary to Government of India, Army Dept, 1906; served during the Burmah War, 1886–87 (medal with clasp). *Address:* 79 Harcourt Terrace, SW.

Died 15 May 1923.

WEST, Prof. George Stephen, MA, DSc; FLS, ARCS; Mason Professor of Botany, Birmingham University, since 1909; *b* Bradford, 1876; *m* 1906. *Educ:* Bradford Technical College; Royal College of Science, London; St John's Coll. Cambridge (Scholar; Hutchinson Research Student). 1st class in Natural Science Tripos, Part I, 1897; 1st class, Part II, 1898; obtained the Forbes medal and prize at RC Science, London, 1894. Demonstrating in Biology at Cambridge, 1899; Prof. of Natural History, Royal Agricultural Coll. Cirencester, 1899–1906; Lecturer in Botany, Birmingham University, 1906–9. *Publications:* various papers on the Anatomical and Historical Characters of Poisonous Snakes, 1895–1900; Freshwater Rhizopods and Heliozoa, 1901–4, etc; A Treatise on the British Freshwater Algæ, 1904; various systematic and œcological papers on Algæ dating from 1899; joint-author (with late W. West, FLS) of over twenty publications on Freshwater Algæ and Plankton from all parts of the world; and A Monograph of the British Desmidiaceæ, vol. i 1904, vol. ii 1906, vol. iii 1908, vol. iv 1911; Cambridge Botanical Handbooks: Algæ, vol. i 1916. *Recreations:* golf, gardening. *Address:* 13 Pakenham Road, Edgbaston, Birmingham.

Died 7 Aug. 1919.

WEST, John Henry Rickard, ISO 1908; *b* 1846. Late Assistant-Controller, Savings Bank Department, GPO. *Address:* Carlyle, Calton Road, Dulwich Village, SE. *Club:* Constitutional.

Died 27 March 1920.

WEST, Samuel, MA, MD, Oxon; FRCP, London; Consulting Physician St Bartholomew's Hospital; King George Hospital; Consulting Physician, Royal Free Hospital and New Hospital for Women; Member of the Governing Body of Westminster School and a Busby Trustee; *b* 1848; *s* of John West, Deputy Insp.-General of Mails, GPO; *m* Margaret Nanny, *d* of Sir Edward Frankland, KCB,

FRS, DCL; three *s* three *d*. *Educ:* Westminster School (Queen's Scholar); Christ Church, Oxford (Jun. Student); St Bartholomew's Hospital; Berlin; Vienna. At Oxford: 1st class Natural Science Demonstrator of Anatomy, Radcliffe Travelling Fellow, Examiner, Member of Board of Faculty of Medicine; at Royal College of Physicians, London: Bradshaw Lecturer, Examiner, Member of Council, Senior Censor; Examiner in Medicine at Universities of Oxford, Cambridge, Birmingham, and London, and for Conjoint Board; at Royal Society of Medicine: President of Medical Section, and President of Clinical Section; at Medical Society: Lettsomian Lecturer and President; President, Royal Medical Benevolent Fund; Physician, Provident Mutual and Phœnix Life Assoc.; Hon. Phys. to Metropol. Convalescent Inst., and to British Orphan Asylum, Slough; Fellow of Roy. Soc. Med., of Medical, and other Socs; formerly Physician and Lecturer on Medicine, St Bartholomew's Hospital, Physician to City of London Hospital for Diseases of Chest, Victoria Park, and to Royal Free Hospital. *Publications:* Diseases of the Organs of Respiration, 2nd edn 1909; How to Examine the Chest, 3rd edn; Lettsomian Lectures on Granular Kidney and Physiological Albuminuria, 1899; contributions to the various learned societies upon diseases of the heart, lungs, kidneys, diabetes. *Recreations:* country pursuits and sports, music. *Address:* 15 Wimpole Street, W1; Frankland, St Leonards, Bucks. *T:* Paddington 987. *Club:* Athenæum.
Died 2 March 1920.

WEST, William Cornwallis Cornwallis-; Lord Lieutenant of Denbighshire since 1872; Hon. Colonel 4th Battalion Royal Welsh Fusiliers; JP Hampshire; *b* 20 March 1835; 2nd *s* of late F. R. West, *g s* of 2nd Earl De la Warr, and Theresa, *d* of Capt. Whitby, RN; *m* 1872, Mary, *d* of Rev. Frederick and Lady Olivia Fitz-Patrick, and *g d* of 2nd Marquis of Headfort; one *s* two *d*. *Educ:* Eton. Barrister, Lincoln's Inn, 1862; contested Lymington, 1874; W Cheshire (L), 1880; MP W Division, Denbighshire, 1885–92, when he joined the Liberal Unionist party, but subseq. acted with the Conservatives. Owner of about 10,000 acres. *Recreations:* painting, shooting, fishing. *Address:* Ruthin Castle, North Wales. *T:* 21 Ruthin; Newlands Manor, Lymington, Hants. *T:* 5 Milford-on-Sea; 55 Jermyn Street, W. *Clubs:* Brooks's, Windham, Hurlingham.
Died 4 July 1917.

WESTCOTT, Ven. Frederick Brooke, DD; Canon of Norwich since 1909; Hon. Canon, Salisbury Cathedral, 1900; Archdeacon of Norwich since 1910; Chaplain-in-Ordinary to HM; *b* Harrow, 16 Dec. 1857; *s* of Rev. B. F. Westcott, afterwards Bishop of Durham, at the time Assistant Master in Harrow School. *Educ:* Cheltenham College; Trinity College, Cambridge. Scholar of Trinity College, Cambridge, 1879; Bell (University) Scholar, 1878; Senior Classic, 1881; Fellow of Trinity Coll., Camb. 1882; Assistant Master at Rugby, 1884–92; Headmaster of Sherborne School, 1892–1908. *Publications:* St Paul and Justification, 1913; A Letter to Asia. *Recreations:* none. *Address:* The Close, Norwich. *T:* 522 Norwich. *M:* CL984. *Club:* Athenæum.
Died 24 Feb. 1918.

WESTCOTT, Rt. Rev. George Herbert, DD; Bishop of Lucknow since 1910; *s* of late Bishop Westcott of Durham. *Educ:* Marlborough; Peterhouse, Cambridge (MA). Ordained, 1886; Assistant Master of Marlborough, 1886–89; Missionary at Cawnpore, 1889–1910; Examining Chaplain to Bishop of Lucknow, 1898; Member of Syndicate, Allahabad University, 1896; Secretary, Diocesan Board of Missions and SPG Diocesan Representative Canon, Allahabad Cathedral, 1906. *Publication:* Kabir and Kabir Panth. *Address:* Bishop's Lodge, Allahabad.
Died Jan. 1916.

WESTCOTT, Col Sinclair, CB 1915; CMG 1900; DPH 1899; Knight of Grace, St John of Jerusalem; Colonel, AMS, retired pay, 1918; *b* 23 Feb. 1859; *m* 1898, Ethel Constance, *d* of Col Hon. Robert Bradshaw, and *widow* of D. Gifford Ottley; one *d*. Served as PMO South Africa, 1899–1902; present in Ladysmith during siege (despatches 3 times, Queen's and King's medals 5 clasps, CMG); European War, 1914–18; ADMS 1st Division; DDMS First Corps (despatches six times, CB); Med. Officer of Health, Hong Kong, 1895; during plague epidemic; Hon. Surgeon to the Viceroy of India, 1910; DCMS, Ministry of Pensions, 1818–20; Director Metropolitan Association for the Improvement of the Dwellings of the Industrious Classes. *Address:* 59 Cadogan Square, SW1. *T:* Kensington 2530. *Clubs:* New Oxford and Cambridge, Ranelagh.
Died 6 Nov. 1923.

WESTCOTT, William Wynn, JP; *b* 1848; *s* of Dr Peter Westcott of Oundle; *m* Lizzie (*d* 1921), *d* of Edmund Crawford Burnett; three *d*. *Educ:* University Coll., London. MB Univ. London; DPH; MRCS. For ten years in medical practice at Martock, Somersetshire; removed

to London, and was appointed Deputy Coroner for Central Middlesex and Central London; HM's Coroner for North-East London, 1894–1920; was for a short time Medical Officer of Health for Islington; Past President of the Society for the Study of Inebriety; Vice-Pres. of the Medico-Legal Society and National Sunday League; Past President of Coroners' Society; Divisional Director for Islington of the Red Cross Society. *Publications:* joint-author of sixteen editions of the Extra Pharmacopœia; author of Suicide, its History and Causation; Numbers; The Isiac Tablet of Cardinal Bembo; seven volumes of the Collectanea Hermetica. *Recreations:* Freemasonry (Past Master of Quatuor Coronati Lodge, PGD of England); study of Egyptian and Hebrew antiquities; authority on mediæval Rosicrucian, magical and alchemical books; chief of Rosicrucian Society of England. *Address:* 39 Rapson Road, Durban, Natal.
Died July 1925.

WESTERN, Lt-Col James Halifax, CMG 1888; late RE, and Indian Public Works Department; *b* 17 May 1842; *m* 1869, Caroline Sophia, 3rd *d* of G. N. Atkinson of Cangort. Assistant Engineer, NW Provinces, 1863; Executive Engineer, 1868; Punjab, 1882; Superintending Engineer, 1882; Officiating Chief Engineer and Joint Secretary for Irrigation, 1884; served Egypt, 1885–87; retired, 1887. *Address:* Halifax Lodge, Hurstpierpoint, Sussex. *Club:* East India United Service.
Died 2 April 1917.

WESTERN, Sir Thomas Charles Callis, 3rd Bt of Rivenhall, Essex; JP, DL; *b* 29 Aug. 1850; *o c* of Sir Thomas Sutton Western, 2nd Bt and Ginietta Romana, *e d* of Sir Edward Manningham Buller, 1st Bt; *S* father, 1877; *m* 1883, Elizabeth Ellen, *d* of late Isaac Newton. *Educ:* Eton; Christ Church, Oxford. Late Lieutenant 2nd Life Guards. *Heir:* none. *Address:* 82 St George's Square, SW; Rivenhall Place, Essex.
Died 1 Feb. 1917 (ext).

WESTLAKE, Colonel Almond Paul, DSO 1887; *b* 1858; *m* 1884, Alice Agnes, *o* surv. *d* of General W. D'Oyly Kerrich, late RHA; one *d*. Entered army, 1877; served Afghan War, 1879–80 (medal); Burmah, 1886–89 (despatches, DSO, medal with two clasps); late commanding 26th (KGO) Lt Cav., IA; Commandant Remount Dept, 1914.
Died 22 Aug. 1927.

WESTLAKE, Rev. Herbert Francis, MVO 1921; FSA 1917; MA 1908; Custodian since 1910, and Minor Canon since 1909, of Westminster Abbey; *b* 3 Aug. 1879; *s* of late Alfred Westlake, Gloucester; *m* 1913, Edith Mary, *d* of Rev. A. G. S. Raynor, late Master of King's Scholars, Westminster School; one *s* three *d*. *Educ:* Christ's Hospital; Pembroke College, Oxford. Chaplain of Hazelwood School, Limpsfield, 1902–3; Senior Mathematical Master, Lancing College, 1903–9. *Publications:* New Guide to Westminster Abbey; The Palace of Westminster; Westminster: A Historical Sketch; The Parish Guilds of Mediæval England—St Margaret's, Westminster; Westminster Abbey: The Last Days of the Monastery; The Church, Convent, Cathedral, and College of St Peter, Westminster; Hornchurch Priory; articles in encyclopædias, archæological journals, and press generally. *Recreation:* golf. *Address:* 2 The Cloisters, Westminster Abbey, SW1.
Died 27 Nov. 1925.

WESTLAKE, Nathaniel Hubert John, FSA; painter, designer, and writer in Art; *b* Romsey, 1833; *s* of John Westlake and Elizabeth Hinves; *m* 1858, Frances Lloyd; two *s* four *d*. Intended for sea; scheme fell through; was a few years with well-known publishers; studied at Lees's, Newman Street, later called Heatherley's, at Somerset House under Dyce and Herbert, at the British Museum, South Kensington, Antwerp, and Paris for Art; at the suggestion of late W. Burges, RA, went to a firm of glass painters to design, afterwards became Art manager and partner about 1880; subseq. the proprietor of the establishment; designed side windows in St Martin le Grand, and windows in St Paul's, Worcester, and Peterborough Cathedrals, and other prominent churches, also the glass for the Gate of Heaven Church, South Boston, USA; painted the roof and 14 stations of the chapel of Maynooth College; did the Mosaics for Newman Memorial, Birmingham; painted St Thomas of Canterbury Church, St Leonard's-on-Sea, and many other churches, besides various altarpieces, etc; frequently exhibited at RA; Hon. Member of the British and American Archæological Society of Rome. *Publications:* History and Design in Painted Glass, 4 vols; History and Design in Mural Painting; edited parts of the MS 2 B VII, British Museum, with translations; Stations of Cross (the first done by an Englishman, with Preface by Cardinal Manning); Sketches at the Great Malines Ecclesiastical Exhibition; Portraiture of St Francis; Dancing; and contributions to various publications. *Recreations:* various. *Address:* 20 Clifton Gardens, Maida Hill, W.
Died 9 May 1921.

WESTMACOTT, Percy Graham Buchanan; JP Northumberland; MICE, past President, Institute Mechanical Engineers, and member of other institutions; *b* Edinburgh, 11 Sept. 1830; *y s* of Henry Westmacott, Whetstone, Middlesex; *m* Annette Beatrice, 2nd *d* of Rev. Ralph Berners, Erwarton Rectory, Suffolk; seven *s* three *d. Educ:* Edinburgh; Dresden; Chester. Served Millar, Ravenhill, and Co., Marine Engineers, in offices, works, and afloat; joined W. G. Armstrong and Co., Elswick Works, Newcastle upon Tyne, as draughtsman, 1851; manager of works, 1853; partner, 1863; managing director, upon the formation of the concern into a company; raised and commanded for some years the 1st Newcastle upon Tyne Engineer Volunteers. *Recreations:* art, golf. *Address:* Rose Mount, Ascot; Benwell Hill, Newcastle upon Tyne, *TA:* Ascot. *T:* 18 Ascot. *Clubs:* Athenæum, Constitutional.

Died 10 Sept. 1917.

WESTMACOTT, Maj.-Gen. Sir Richard, KCB 1898 (CB 1891); DSO 1890; Indian Staff Corps; *b* 16 March 1841; 2nd *s* of Rev. Horatio Westmacott; *m* 1889, Rose Margaret, *d* of Maj.-Gen. F. J. Caldecott, CB; one *s. Educ:* Rossall. Entered Bombay Army, 1859; served Indian Mutiny, against rebel Bheels, 1860; Naikras, 1868; Afghan War, 1879–80; Soudan Expedition, 1885; Col, 1889; Maj.-Gen. 1899; commanded Advance Column Chin-Lushai Expedition, 1889–90 (DSO, despatches); commanded 28th Bombay Pioneers, 1887–94; Manipur, 1893–94; AAG Poona, 1894–95; Colonel on Staff, 1895–96; commanded Nagpur District, 1896–99; 1st Brigade Mohmund Field Force, 1897; commanded 4th Brigade Tirah Expedition Force, 1897–98 (KCB, despatches); 1st class District Mhow, 1900–3; Unemployed List. *Recreations:* hunting, shooting, fishing. *Address:* Bishop's Caundle, Sherborne, Dorset. *Club:* United Service.

Died 27 Feb. 1925.

WESTMORLAND, 13th Earl of, *cr* 1624; **Anthony Mildmay Julian Fane,** Baron Burghersh, 1624; CBE 1919; JP; *b* 16 Aug. 1859; *s* of 12th Earl and Lady Adelaide Ida Curzon, *d* of 1st Earl Howe; *S* father, 1891; *m* 1st, 1892, Lady Sybil Mary St Claire Erskine (*d* 1910), *d* of 4th Earl of Rosslyn; two *s* two *d;* 2nd, 1916, Catherine Louise, *d* of late Rev. G. Geale. Col 3rd Batt. Northamptonshire Regt, 1900; ADC to King George V. *Recreations:* very fond of hunting and shooting, and all sports. *Heir: s* Lord Burghersh, *b* 15 March 1893. *Address:* Wolverton, Enfield. *Club:* Marlborough.

Died 9 June 1922.

WESTMORLAND, Brig.-Gen. Charles Henry, CB 1908; *b* 30 June 1856; widower. Entered Army, 1874; Captain ISC, 1885; Bt-Major, 1889; Lt-Col, Indian Army, 1900; Col, 1904; AAG Hyderabad Contingent, 1902–5; India, 1904–7; commanded Karachi Brigade, 1907–10; retired 1912 with honorary rank of Brig.-Gen.; served Afghan War, 1878–79 (medal with clasp); Burma, 1887–89 (despatches, medal with clasp, Brevet Major); NW Frontier, India, 1897–98 (medal with clasp); China, 1900 (despatches, medal). *Club:* United Service.

Died 9 Feb. 1916.

WESTON, Dame Agnes (Elizabeth), GBE 1918; Hon. Doctor of Law, Glasgow University; *b* London, 26 March 1840; father a barrister. Founder of Royal Sailors' Rests at Portsmouth and Devonport. *Publications:* My Life Among the Blue Jackets; Ashore and Afloat. *Address:* Royal Sailors' Rest, Portsmouth.

Died 23 Oct. 1918.

WESTON, Rt. Rev. Frank, OBE 1918; Bishop of Zanzibar since 1908; *b* 13 Sept. 1871; 4th *s* of R. W. G. Weston; unmarried. *Educ:* Dulwich College; Trinity College, Oxford (1st class Theology; MA, BD, DD). Curate of Trinity College (Oxon) Mission, 1894–96; St Matthew's, Westminster, 1896–98; Chaplain of St Andrew's Coll., Zanzibar, 1898–99; Warden, St Mark's Theological Coll., Zanzibar, 1899, 1901; Principal, St Andrew's Training College, Kiungani, Zanzibar, 1901–8; Chancellor of Zanzibar Cathedral, 1904–8; Major commanding Zanzibar Carrier Corps, 1916 (despatches 1917, OBE). *Publications:* The One Christ; Ecclesia Anglicana, An Open Letter; God with Us: The Fulness of Christ; Christ and His Critics; Conquering and to Conquer; The Revelation of Eternal Love; and some books in Swahili. *Address:* Universities' Mission, Zanzibar. *TA:* Ulema, Zanzibar; Zanzilik, London.

Died 2 Nov. 1924.

WESTON, Jessie Laidlay, DLitt. *Educ:* Brighton; Paris; Hildesheim; studied Art, Crystal Palace Schools. *Publications:* Parzival, by Wolfram von Eschenbach, trans. into English Verse, 1894; Legends of the Wagner Drama, 1896; The Legend of Sir Gawain, 1897; The Legend of Sir Lancelot du Lac, 1901; The Three Days' Tournament, 1902; The Legend of Sir Perceval, (vol. i) 1906, (vol. ii) 1909 (all published

in the Grimm Library); Arthurian Romances unrepresented in Malory (7 vols); The Soul of the Countess; Romance, Vision and Satire, 1912; Chief Middle-English Poets, 1914; From Ritual to Romance, 1920 (awarded Crawshay Prize for 1920); contributor to the Encyclopædia Britannica, Athenæum, Folk-lore, and Romania (French). *Address:* 85 Biddulph Mansions, Elgin Avenue, W9. *Club:* Lyceum.

Died 29 Sept. 1928.

WESTON, Sir John Wakefield, 1st Bt, *cr* 1926; MP (Ind. U) South Westmorland, 1913–18; (U) Westmorland, 1918–24; Chairman of County Council for Westmorland; Chairman Territorial Association, Cumberland and Westmorland; *b* 13 June 1852; *s* of Rev. G. F. Weston, Vicar of Crosby-Ravensworth, Westmorland; *m* 1890, Kate, *d* of J. R. Brougham; two *d. Educ:* Rugby; University College, Oxford. *Recreations:* golf, hunting, cricket, tennis. *Address:* Enyeat, Endmoor, Kendal. *T:* 27 Sedgwick. *Club:* Carlton.

Died 19 Sept. 1926 (ext).

WESTON-STEVENS, Sir Joseph, Kt 1913; JP, DL; *b* 1861; *s* of W. J. Y. Stevens; *m* 1888, Victoria Alice, *d* of Arthur Keen, Edgbaston; one *s* one *d. Educ:* Clifton College. Entered business in the firm of T. and J. Weston, 1881; later sole proprietor of that business and the Bristol Foundry Co.; Chairman of the Taff Vale Railway Co.; Chairman of the Bristol Wagon and Carriage Works Co.; Director of Guest, Keen and Nettlefolds, Ltd, and the London City and Midland, Ltd; Sheriff of Bristol, 1902–3; President of the Anchor Society, 1897; President of the Bristol Liberal Federation; Chairman of the Executive Committee of the Western Counties Liberal Federation; Chairman of the Bristol Citizens Recruiting Committee; joined Gloucestershire Vol. Artillery, 1883, retiring with rank of Major, 1900. *Address:* Worcester Lodge, Clifton, Bristol. *T:* Bristol 695. *M:* AE 1612, AE 2929, AE 4107. *Clubs:* Reform, Royal Automobile; Clifton and Bristol Liberal.

Died 7 Feb. 1917.

WETHERBEE, George, RI; artist; painter; *b* Cincinnati, USA, Dec. 1851; *s* of J. Q. Wetherbee, Boston, USA. *Educ:* Boston, USA; Royal Academy of Arts, Antwerp; and London. Travelled and resided in West Indies, France, Germany, Italy, Belgium, etc. *Recreations:* golf, cycling. *Address:* 18 Redington Road, NW3. *Clubs:* Arts, St John's Wood Arts. *T:* Hampstead 885.

Died 23 July 1920.

WETHERED, Lt-Col Francis Owen, CMG 1916; VD; Chairman, Thomas Wethered & Sons, Ltd, The Brewery, Marlow; *b* 13 Dec. 1864; *e s* of late Col Owen Peel and Mrs Wethered of El Robado, Puerto Orotava, Teneriffe; *m* 1st, 1899, Adeline Harris (*d* 1900), *e d* of late W. F. MacTier, MD, of Kinnessburn, St Andrews; one *s* one *d;* 2nd, 1917, Margaret, *o d* of J. M. Dyer, MA, Farnham Common, Bucks; one *s. Educ:* Eton; Christ Church, Oxford; MA. JP, DL, Bucks; 2nd Bucks RVC (Eton College), 1878–82; 1st Bucks RVC 1883–1908; Bucks Batt., Oxford and Bucks Light Infantry, 1908–15; Lt-Col 1914–15; Lt-Col 1/6 Royal Warwickshire Regt 1915–16 (VD, CMG); Bucks CC 1910; Thames Conservancy, 1916. *Recreations:* rowed for Oxford, 1885–6–7; Pres. OUBC 1887. *Address:* Measdie, Marlow, Bucks. *T:* 26.

Died 3 Aug. 1922.

WETHERED, Frank Joseph, MD (Lond.) 1888; FRCP (Lond.) 1895; MRCS (Eng.) and LSA, 1885; Consulting Physician to Hospital for Consumption and Diseases of Chest, Brompton, and to the National Hospital for Consumption, Ventnor; Consulting Physician, Royal Cornwall Infirmary, Truro; late Physician to Middlesex Hospital; Consulting Physician to St Saviour's Hospital; late Physician to the Equity and Law Life Assurance Society; Examiner in Medicine, Royal College of Physicians; Captain RAMC (TF), 3rd London General Hospital; *b* 1860; *s* of late Joseph Wethered, Clifton; *m* 1889, Rose, *d* of late Edward How, Devonshire. *Educ:* Clifton College. Studied at Bristol Medical School, London Hospital, Berlin, and Vienna. *Publications:* essay on A Sanatorium for Consumption, 2nd Prize HM the King's competition; two works on the use of the microscope in medicine; various communications to medical journals. *Recreations:* out-door sports, especially sea-fishing. *Address:* Pencaer, Falmouth. *T:* Falmouth 63.

Died 28 Oct. 1928.

WETHERED, Thomas Owen; JP for Bucks; *b* 26 Nov. 1832; *e s* of Owen Wethered, JP, of Remnantz, Marlow, Bucks, and Anne, *d* of late Rev. Giles Haworth Peel of The Grotto, Basildon; *m* 1856, Edith Grace, *d* of Rev. Hart Ethelston, Rector of St Mark's, Cheetham Hill, Manchester; three *d. Educ:* Eton; Christ Church, Oxford. MP (C) Great Marlow, 1868–81; Church of England; was Captain, Bucks RV. *Address:* Seymour Court, Marlow, Bucks. *T:* 21. *Clubs:* Carlton, Oxford and Cambridge.

Died 22 Feb. 1921.

WETMORE, Hon. Edward Ludlow, LLD; Chief Justice, Supreme Court, Saskatchewan, 1907–12; *b* 24 March 1841; *s* of Charles P. and Sarah B. Wetmore; *m* 1872, Eliza J., *d* of Charles Dickson; two *s* one *d. Educ:* Grammar Schools in Fredericton and Gage Town, New Brunswick; King's College, Fredericton, later the University of New Brunswick, Fredericton. Graduated with honours, 1859. Barrister of the Province of New Brunswick, 1864; Mayor of Fredericton, 1874–76; a Commissioner for Consolidating the Statutes of New Brunswick, 1877; QC 1881; President of the Barristers Society, 1886–87; Representative of Alumni Association in Senate of University, 1886–87; a Member of the Local Legislature of the Province, 1883–86, and Leader of the Opposition during that time; defeated at the General Election for Provincial Legislature, 1887; Judge of Supreme Court of the North-West Territories, 1887–1907; a Commissioner for Consolidating the Ordinances of the North-West Territories, 1898; Chancellor, University of Saskatchewan, 1907; Chairman of Commission for Consolidating Laws of Saskatchewan, 1908; Hon. LLD University of New Brunswick, 1908; Hon. DCL University of Saskatchewan, 1919. *Address:* 604 Linden Avenue, Victoria, British Columbia. *Died 1922.*

WETTON, Henry Davan, MusD Univ. Coll., Dunelm; Fellow of the Royal College of Organists; Fellow of the Guildhall School of Music; Organist and Director of the Choir at Christ Church, Lancaster Gate, W, since 1926; Professor of the Organ, Harmony, Counterpoint, and Composition at the Guildhall School of Music; Head of Music Department, Battersea Polytechnic; retired, 1927; Prof. of Sight Singing, Ear Training, and Examiner, Royal College of Music; Member of the Faculty of Music, University of London; Fellow Incorporated Staff Sight-Singing College; Examiner to the Associated Board of the Royal Academy of Music and the Royal College of Music; *b* 1862; *e s* of late Henry Davan and Sarah Wetton, of Hazel-groves, Hayward's Heath, Sussex. *Educ:* The Islington Proprietary School; private tuition. Organist and Choirmaster, All Saints, Stoke Newington, 1877–84; Assistant Organist to Sir Frederick Bridge, Westminster Abbey, 1881–96; Organist and Choirmaster, Christ Church, Woburn Square, 1884–86; St Gabriel's, Pimlico, 1886–89 and 1890–93; Sub-Organist, Wells Cathedral, 1890; Organist and Director of the Music at the Foundling Hospital, 1892–1926; Organist and Chorus-master, Queen's Hall Choral Soc. (season 1893–94); Head of the Musical Department, Northampton Institute, 1896–1906; Organist (retired), Alexandra Palace, 1901; Conductor of the Choir, People's Palace, E, 1902–3; London University Musical Society, 1905–8; etc. *Publications:* Cantata, The Fulfilment; Church services, anthems, carols, part songs, pieces for organ and pianoforte and songs. *Address:* 19 Pembridge Mansions, W2. *Club:* University of London. *Died 2 Dec. 1928.*

WEYMAN, Stanley John, novelist; *b* Ludlow, 7 Aug. 1855; 2nd *s* of late Thomas Weyman, solicitor; *m* 1895, Charlotte, *d* of late Rev. Richard Panting, HEICS. *Educ:* Shrewsbury; Christ Church, Oxford; BA Oxford; 2nd class Modern History. Barrister at Law, 1881. *Publications:* The House of the Wolf, 1890; The New Rector, 1891; The Story of Francis Cludde, 1891; A Gentleman of France, 1893; Under the Red Robe, 1894; My Lady Rotha, 1894; Memoirs of a Minister of France; The Red Cockade, 1895; The Man in Black, 1896; Shrewsbury, 1897; The Castle Inn, 1898; Sophia, 1900; Count Hannibal, 1901; In King's Byways, 1902; The Long Night, 1903; Chippinge, 1906; The Abbess of Vlaye, 1904; Starvecrow Farm, 1905; Laid up in Lavender, 1907; The Wild Geese, 1908; The Great House, 1919; Ovington's Bank, 1922; The Traveller in the Fur Cloak, 1925; Queen's Folly, 1925. *Recreations:* riding, cycling. *Address:* Llanrhydd, Ruthin. *Club:* Athenæum. *Died 10 April 1928.*

WEYMOUTH, Viscount; John Alexander Thynne; 2nd Lieutenant, 2nd Dragoons; *b* 29 Nov. 1895; *e s* of 5th Marquess of Bath. *Died 13 Feb. 1916.*

WHALE, George; solicitor; *b* Woolwich, 25 Nov. 1849; *s* of George and Ellen Whale; *m* 1st, 1874, Matilda Lawson (*d* 1922); one *s* two *d*; 2nd, 1923, Winifred Stephens. *Educ:* Huntingdon; Woolwich. Solicitor, 1872; retired from practice, 1913; contested Marylebone 1892; Oxford City, 1906 and 1910. FRHistS; on Council Folk Lore Society; Hon. Chairman Rationalist Press Association; Chairman of Woolwich Polytechnic, 1918–21; Mayor of Woolwich, 1908–9; held various professional and local government appointments at Lee, Eltham, etc, and member of several local bodies; one of the Founders of the Omar Khayyam and Pepys Clubs. *Publications:* Greater London and its Government, 1888; Essays in Johnson Club Papers, 1899; magazine articles. *Address:* 49 York Terrace, Regent's Park, NW1. *T:* Langham 2884. *Club:* Reform. *Died 4 May 1925.*

WHARNCLIFFE, 2nd Earl of, *cr* 1876; **Francis John Montagu-Stuart-Wortley;** Viscount Carlton, 1876; Baron Wharncliffe, 1826; Commander RN, retired; JP and DL for W Riding, Yorkshire; *b* 9 June 1856; *e s* of Hon. F. D. Montagu-Stuart-Wortley, 2nd *s* of 2nd Baron Wharncliffe; *S* uncle, 1899; *m* 1886, Ellen (*d* 1922), 2nd *d* of late Lt-Gen. Sir T. L. Gallwey, RE; one *s* three *d* (and two *s* decd). *Educ:* Eton; Royal Naval College. Naval cadet, 1869; Lieutenant, 1879; retired, 1889; Commander on Retired List, 1896. *Heir: e* surv. *s* Viscount Carlton, *b* 17 April 1892. *Address:* Wortley Hall, Sheffield. *Clubs:* Carlton; Yorkshire, York. *Died 8 May 1926.*

WHATES, Harry Richard; journalist; Parliamentary Correspondent Birmingham Post (London office); an assistant editor of The Standard, 1896–1905, retired on the change of proprietorship in 1905. Acted as Special Correspondent. *Publications:* The Politican's Handbook: a Review and Digest of the State Papers, 1899, 1900, 1901, 1902; The Third Salisbury Administration, 1895–1900; Dissolution Dialogues, 1900; His Majesty Edward VII, 1901; Canada, the New Nation, 1906; The Life and Times of Edward VII, 1841–1910 (5 vols); Midland Regiments in France, 1917; Disaffected Ireland, 1920. *Address:* Cranford, Middlesex. *Club:* Press. *Died 25 March 1923.*

WHATMAN, George Dunbar; one of HM Lieutenants for the City of London; JP Middlesex and London; Director of Lloyds Bank, Bank of British North America, Liverpool, London, and Globe Insurance Co., etc; *b* 21 Feb. 1846; *e s* of late W. G. Whatman, banker, partner in firm of Bosanquet, Salt & Co., then absorbed in Lloyds Bank; *m* 1872, Frances, *e d* of late G. A. Fuller of Rookery, Dorking, and 77 Lombard Street, Banker; one *s*. *Educ:* Eton; Exeter College, Oxford; BA. *Address:* 2 Cranley Gardens, SW7. *T:* Western 2544. *TA:* Humdrum, London. *Clubs:* Windham, Hurlingham. *Died 26 Dec. 1923.*

WHEATLEY, Henry Benjamin, Hon. DCL (Durham); FSA; *m* 1872, Louisa Louise (*d* 1899), *d* of late Dr George Robins; two *s* three *d. Educ:* privately. Clerk to Royal Society, 1861–79; Assistant Secretary, Society of Arts, 1879–1908; Assistant Secretary Brit. Royal Commission, Section of Chicago Exhibition, 1893; Hon. Sec. Early English Text Society, 1864–72; Treasurer, 1872–1916; President, Samuel Pepys Club, 1903–16; Prior, Johnson Club, 1906–7; President, Hampstead Antiquarian and Historical Society, 1906–16; President of the Sette of Odd Volumes, 1909; President of the Bibliographical Society, 1911–16; Vice-President of the London Topographical Society, 1900–16; Chairman of Council, Shakespeare Association, 1914–16. *Publications:* Anagrams, 1862; Round about Piccadilly and Pall Mall, 1870; What is an Index? 1878; Samuel Pepys and the World he lived in, 1880; How to form a Library, 1886; How to Catalogue a Library, 1889; How to make an Index, 1902; Remarkable Bindings in the British Museum, 1889; London, Past and Present, 1891; Literary Blunders, 1893; new edition Pepys's Diary, 1894–99; Pepysiana, 1899; Historical Portraits, 1897; Prices of Books, 1898; The Story of London, 1904 (Mediæval Towns); Hogarth's London, 1909; Edited The Romance of Merlin, 1865–99; Levins' Manipulus Vocabularum, 1867; Ben Jonson's Every Man in his Humour, 1877; Wraxall's Historical and Posthumous Memoirs, 1884; Shakespeare's Merry Wives of Windsor, 1886. *Address:* 96 King Henry's Road, NW. *Club:* Garrick. *Died 30 April 1917.*

WHEATLEY, Col Moreton John, CB 1901; RE; *b* 2 March 1837; *e s* of late T. R. Wheatley of Gwersyllt Park, Denbighshire; *m* 1864, Edith Frances, *y d* of late Charles Millett of Maiden Erleigh, Berks; three *s* one *d*. Entered army, 1854; Captain 1861; Major, 1872; Lieut-Col 1879; Colonel, 1883; Bailiff of the Royal Parks, 1879–1902. *Address:* 314 St James's Court, SW; Gwersyllt Park, Denbighshire. *TA:* Escorted, London. *T:* 1981 Victoria. *Clubs:* Junior United Service, Union. *Died 13 May 1916.*

WHEATLEY, Major William Prescott Ross, DSO 1917; IASC; *b* 1878; *s* of George Wheatley, 2 Priory Parade, Cheltenham; *m* 1923, Una, *widow* of Major E. W. Worrall, Somerset Light Infantry. Served Somaliland, 1903 (medal with two clasps); France and Mesopotamia, 1914–17 (despatches, DSO). *Club:* Naval and Military. *Died 6 Sept. 1925.*

WHEELER, Major Henry Littleton, CB 1918; DSO 1900; late Hampshire Regiment; Secretary Territorial Association, Staffordshire, since 1908; *b* 8 May 1868; *e s* of late Rev. T. Littelton Wheeler; *m* 1903, Vera, *y d* of Col Gillum Webb, of Walton House, Ashchurch; one *s* one *d*. Joined Militia (Worcestershire), 1887; entered army, 1892; Captain, 1900; served South Africa, 1900–2 (despatches thrice,

Queen's and King's medals, four clasps, DSO). *Address:* The Woodlands, Stafford.

Died 14 Dec. 1924.

WHEELER, His Honour Thomas Whittenbury, MA; JP; KC; late County Court Judge; resigned 1918; *s* of late Serjeant Wheeler, LLD, JP, County Court Judge, and Fanny, *d* of John Whittenbury, Green Heys, Ardwick; *m* Henrietta Brooksbank (*d* 1920), *y d* of Edward Lodge Ogle, MD. *Educ:* Westminster School; Trinity Hall, Cambridge. Barrister, 1865; revising barrister, 1868; junior counsel to the Post Office, 1873–86; Queen's Counsel, 1886; Bencher Inner Temple, 1894; Chairman, Law and Parliamentary Committee, Vestry of Kensington, 1894–97; Chairman of Vestry, 1897; Chairman of Liberal Unionist Association, S Kensington, 1892–98; Alderman, Borough Council; Hon. Member Surveyors' Institution. *Publications:* The Law of Dilapidation, 1887; Betterment; Transactions of Surveyors' Institution; The Good Old Times, 1888; Contracts Implied by Law, 1897, etc.

Died 3 April 1923.

WHEELER, William, CMG 1904; OBE 1918; Treasurer, British Central Africa Protectorate, 1892–1920. Acting Chief Secretary, 1912 and 1916–19; retired, 1920; mentioned in Gen. Van Deventer's Despatch, 1919. *Address:* Edingale, Tamworth, Staffs.

Died 23 Feb. 1926.

WHEELER-BENNETT, John Wheeler, CBE 1921; JP; Director of Metropolitan Railway and other Companies; High Sheriff of Kent, 1922–24; *m* 1882, Christine Hill McNutt of Truro, Nova Scotia, Canada; two *s* one *d*. *Educ:* at Vickery's, Hope House, Southsea, Portsmouth. Carried on business at Hibernia Chambers, London Bridge, SE, for forty years as an import merchant, having large interests in Canada, America, Argentine, and Denmark; was Chairman of the London Home and Foreign Exchange, 1913; retired from active commerce, 1912; engaged in war activities, 1914–19; Chairman Bromley (Kent) Rural Tribunal; an original member of Major Rothschild's City of London Military Advisory Committee; Chairman of Finance, Kent County War Fund, administering nearly 100 VAD hospitals (CBE). *Recreations:* shooting, golf, etc. *Address:* Ravensbourne, Keston, Kent. *Clubs:* City Carlton, Royal Automobile; Bromley and Bickley Golf.

Died 25 June 1926.

WHELER, Sir Granville (Charles Hastings), 1st Bt, *cr* 1925; CBE 1920; MP (C) North-East Kent, subseq. Faversham Division, since 1910; *b* 2 Oct. 1872; *s* of late Charles Wheler Wheler, JP, DL, and Elizabeth, *d* of William Hall of Syndale Park, Faversham; *m* 1905, Florence Faith, *d* of late Captain Clarke of Alcombe Cote, Somerset. *Educ:* Eton; Christ Church, Oxford. Called to Bar, Middle Temple, 1898; Member of West Riding County Council, 1907–10; contested (U) Osgoldcross Division, West Riding, Yorks, 1906; Colne Valley, 1907; Major on Headquarters Staff Western Command, 1915–18; Lt-Col, 1918; JP, DL. *Recreations:* cricket, shooting, hunting. *Address:* Ledston Hall, Yorks; Otterden Place, Faversham, Kent. *Clubs:* Carlton, Royal Automobile.

Died 14 Dec. 1927 (ext).

WHERRY, George Edward, FRCS; University Lecturer in Surgery; Consulting Surgeon to Addenbrooke's Hospital, Cambridge; Lieutenant-Colonel RAMC (T), 1st Eastern General Hospital; Examiner in Surgery, University of Cambridge; Supervisor of Examinations in Surgery; *b* Bourne, Lincolnshire, 1852; *m* 1881, Albinia Lucy Cust; one *d*. *Educ:* St Thomas's Hospital, London; Downing College, Cambridge; MA, MCh. *Publications:* Clinical Notes on Nerve Disorders; Alpine Notes, and the Climbing Foot; Notes from a Knapsack; Cambridge and Charles Lamb, 1925. *Recreations:* walking, climbing, cycling. *Address:* 5 St Peter's Terrace, Cambridge. *TA:* Cambridge. *T:* 98. *M:* CE 1484. *Clubs:* Alpine, Junior Constitutional.

Died 12 Aug. 1928.

WHINNEY, Sir Arthur, KBE 1919; JP; chartered accountant; senior partner in firm of Whinney, Smith & Whinney, London, Paris, Antwerp, Berlin, etc; *b* 16 Dec. 1865; *s* of Frederick Whinney; *m* 1892, Amy Elizabeth (*d* 1923), *d* of William Golden, late of HM Treasury (Solicitor); two *s* one *d*. Late Adviser on Costs of Production to the Admiralty; late Assistant Accountant-Gen. of the Navy, and Adviser and Consultant to the Admiralty in Accountancy; President, Institute of Chartered Accountants; Chairman of Board of Trade Committees *re* Superphosphates and Worsteds under Safeguarding of Industries Enquiry. *Address:* 80 Gloucester Terrace, W2; Lee Place, Charlbury, Oxon. *T:* Paddington 4975. *Clubs:* Marlborough, Reform, Bath, Arts, British Empire, Gresham, Ranelagh.

Died 30 May 1927.

WHIPHAM, Thomas Tillyer, MA, MD Oxon; FRCP; JP Co. Devon; Consulting Physician to St George's Hospital; member Court of Assistants (late Prime Warden) Goldsmiths' Company; *s* of Thomas Henry Whipham of Lincoln's Inn, Barrister-at-Law; *m* Florence, *d* of Charles Tanqueray; one *s*. *Educ:* Rugby, Oriel Coll. Oxford. Was Demonstrator of Anatomy, Curator of the Museum, Lecturer on Botany, Pathology, and Medicine; Assistant-Physician and Physician at St George's Hospital; Examiner in Medicine for the University of Oxford, and for the Conjoint Board of the Royal Colleges of Physicians and Surgeons in England; Censor and Senior Censor of the Royal College of Physicians; Physician to the Legal and General Life Assurance Society; Junior Physician at the West London Hospital. *Publications:* contributions to the Lancet and other medical publications on various subjects. *Address:* Fishleigh House, Hatherleigh, N Devon. *Club:* Oxford and Cambridge.

Died 3 Nov. 1917.

WHITAKER, William, BA; FRS, FGS; AICE; FRSanI; Associate Soc. MOH; hon. member of many societies (English and Foreign); Consulting Geologist; Past President of Geological Society (Wollaston, Murchison and Prestwich medals); Past President of Geologists' Association; retired Civil Service (Geological Survey); *b* London, 4 May 1836; one *s* one *d*. *Educ:* St Albans Grammar School; University Coll. London. Geological Survey of England, 1857–96. Much work in Geology, especially in South-Eastern England, and in Applied Geology (Water-Supply and other sanitary questions). *Publications:* many Geological Survey Maps and Memoirs; many papers and addresses to Geological Society, to several other societies, etc. *Recreations:* walking, cards. *Address:* Wellesley Court, Wellesley Road, Croydon. *T:* Croydon 922.

Died 15 Jan. 1925.

WHITBY, Rev. Thomas, MA; *b* Liverpool, 12 May 1835; *s* of Thos Whitby and Mary Bateson; *m* 1870, Mary Louisa Titley Beverley; three *s* two *d*. *Educ:* Liverpool Coll.; St John's Coll. Camb.; BA 1859; MA 1866. Vicar of St Simon's, Leeds, 1865–77; Christ Church, Plymouth, 1877–81; Member of the Plymouth School Board; Vicar of Parish Church, Dewsbury, 1881–90; Member and Chairman of the Dewsbury School Board; Hon. Canon of Wakefield, 1888–1909; Proctor in Convocation for the Archdeaconry of Halifax, 1889–91; Rural Dean of Dewsbury, 1889–90; Vicar of St John's, Sandown, Isle of Wight, 1891–1905. FRGS 1868. *Publication:* The Church of England, its Property and its Work. *Recreations:* at Cambridge, boating; then foreign travel and rubbing monumental brasses. *Address:* 145 Brondesbury Park, NW.

Died 13 Aug. 1918.

WHITCOMBE, Rt. Rev. Robert Henry; Bishop of Colchester since 1909; Archdeacon of Colchester; *b* 18 July 1862; *s* of Philip Whitcombe, Gravesend; *m* 1892, Annie, 2nd *d* of S. T. G. Evans, of Eton College; six *s* two *d*. *Educ:* Winchester; New Coll., Oxford. Assistant Master, Wellington College, 1886–89; Eton College, 1889–99; Rector of Hardwicke, Aylesbury, 1899–1904; Vicar of Romford, 1904–9; CF in France, 1918; *Address:* Derby House, Colchester.

Died 19 March 1922.

WHITE, Andrew Dickson, BA and MA, Yale; PhD Jena; LLD Yale, St Andrews, Michigan, Cornell, Johns Hopkins, Dartmouth, and Hobart; LHD Columbia; DCL Oxon; *b* Homer, Cortland County, New York State, 7 Nov. 1832; *s* of Horace White and Clara Dickson; *m* 1st, 1857, Mary A. Outwater (*d* 1887); 2nd, 1890, Helen, *d* of Edward Hicks Magill; two *d*. Graduated Yale University, 1853; De Forest Gold Medallist, also Yale Literary Gold Medal; First Clarke Prizeman at Yale; travelled in Europe; studied at Sorbonne and Collège de France, 1853–54; attaché to Legation of the United States, Petrograd, 1854–55; studied University of Berlin, 1855–56; Professor of History and English Literature University of Michigan, 1857–63; returned to Syracuse and elected State Senator, in which capacity (1863–67) he introduced reports and bills codifying the school laws, creating a new system of normal schools, establishing new Health Board in the City of New York, and incorporating Cornell University at Ithaca, all of which became laws; chosen first president of that University, 1866–85; visited Europe to purchase books and apparatus therefor, and make special study of European educational methods; in addition to the presidency filled the chair of Modern History; commissioner to Santo Domingo to study and report on question of annexation, 1871; Commissioner to the Paris Exposition, 1878; minister to Berlin, 1879–81; minister to Petrograd, 1892–94; member of the Venezuelan Commission, 1895–96; Ambassador to Berlin, 1897–1903; President of American Delegation at Peace Conference of The Hague, 1899; a Regent of the Smithsonian Institution, a Trustee, Carnegie Institution for Research and Peace Foundation, Washington, and of Cornell University; ex-president American Social Science Association, and American Historical Society. Officer of the Legion of Honour of France; Member of the Royal Academy of

Sciences of Berlin; Recipient of the Gold Medal in Science and Literature from the Prussian Government, 1902. *Publications:* various essays, papers, addresses, and speeches on historical, educational, and political subjects; also Paper Money Inflation in France; how it came, what it brought, and how it ended—various editions; The Warfare of Science, 1876 (Swedish abridged translation, 1877); History of the Warfare of Science with Theology in Christendom, 1897 (Italian, 1902; French, 1907; German, 1910; Portuguese, 1911; Spanish, 1911, 1912); Autobiography, 1905 (German translation of the chapters on Diplomatic Life, 1906); Seven Great Statesmen in the Warfare of Humanity with Unreason, 1910 (German, 1912); The Work of Benjamin Hale, 1911; Lecture on The Problem of High Crime in the United States. *Address:* Cornell University, Ithaca, New York. *Clubs:* Union League, Century, New York City; Cosmos, Washington.   *Died 4 Nov. 1918.*

WHITE, Arnold; author; *b* 1 Feb. 1848; *m* 1879, Helen Constance (*d* 1918), *o d* of late Lowell Price of Farnham Royal, Bucks. Devoted himself to social problems; in connection with colonization visited South Africa six times and made repeated visits to Canada, the United States, and Russia; acted for Baron de Hirsch in negotiating with Russian Government for Jewish colonization of land in Argentine Republic; contested Mile End, 1886, Tyneside Division, Northumberland, 1892 and 1895, and North Londonderry, 1906; interested in a strong navy, and especially in gunnery; wrote as Vanoc, of the Referee. *Publications:* Letters of SGO to The Times; The Modern Jew, 1899; Problems of a Great City; Tries at Truth; English Democracy; Efficiency and Empire; For Efficiency; The Great Idea; The Navy and its Story; Is the Kaiser Insane?; The Hidden Hand. *Recreations:* climbing, travel, shooting, golf, chess, gardening. *Address:* Windmill Cottage, Farnham Common, Bucks. *T:* Farnham Common 2. *Club:* 1900.   *Died 5 Feb. 1925.*

WHITE, Charles Frederick; MP (L) Western Division of Derbyshire, since 1918; *b* Tetbury, Gloucestershire, 11 March 1863; 2nd *s* of Frederick and Ruth White; *m* 1881, Alice, 2nd *d* of Wm Charlesworth of Bonsall, near Matlock; one *s* five *d. Educ:* private school, Tetbury, Gloucestershire. Registration and Political Agent and Secretary; five years Magistrate by virtue of being Chairman of Local Authority; four years Member of Derbyshire County Council; contested West Derbyshire, Dec. 1910; Liberal; Member of Executive, League of Nations, and of Agricultural Committee, House of Commons. *Recreation:* work. *Address:* The Woodlands, Matlock.
                                    Died 4 Dec. 1923.

WHITE, Charles Percival, MVO 1918; MA, MB, BCh (Cantab.); *s* of late Robert Owen White of Gestingthorpe Hall, Essex; *m* 1892, Marian Irene, *d* of Charles Verrall Willett, Brighton; three *d. Educ:* privately; Clare College, Cambridge; St Bartholomew's Hospital. In practice in London for thirty years. *Address:* 7 Albany Villas, Hove, Sussex. *Clubs:* Garrick, Union, Brighton.
                                    Died 11 Dec. 1928.

WHITE, Lieut-Col Frederick, CMG 1902; Comptroller-General of the North-West Mounted Police in the Dominion of Canada; *b* Birmingham, 16 Feb. 1847; *m* Clara Olivia, *e d* of late R. W. Cruise of Ottawa; one *d. Educ:* Birmingham. 3rd Class Clerk, Dept of Justice, Canada, 1869; Chief Clerk, 1876; on organisation of North-West Mounted Police took charge under Sir John Macdonald of Police Bureau at Ottawa; for some years a Captain in the Governor-General's Foot Guards. *Address:* 368 Besserer Street, Ottawa. *Club:* Rideau.
                                    Died 27 Sept. 1918.

WHITE, Colonel Frederick, DSO 1900; Royal Marine Light Infantry; *b* 14 Oct. 1861; *s* of late Major George White, RMLI. Entered army, 1879; Captain, 1888; Major, 1896; Lieut-Colonel, 1902; Colonel (Brevet), 1906; DCO, 1915–19 (Victory Medal, British War Medal, 1914–15 Star); served Egyptian War, 1882 (medal with clasp, Khedive's Star); Soudan, 1884 (5th class Medjidie, two clasps); South Africa, 1900–3 (despatches, two medals four clasps, DSO); retired, 1909. *Address:* St John's Park, Blackheath, SE.
                                    Died 8 Dec. 1924.

WHITE, Major Frederick Alexander, DSO 1900; Suffolk Regiment; temp. Lieutenant-Colonel; *b* 6 Aug. 1872. Entered army, 1894; Lieut 1897; Capt. 1901; Major, 1914; served S Africa, 1899–1902 (despatches, Queen's medal, 3 clasps, King's medal, 2 clasps, DSO); European War, 1914–17.   *Died 26 Jan. 1919.*

WHITE, Sir George, 1st Bt, *cr* 1904; Hon. LLD Bristol; JP; *b* 28 March 1854; *s* of late Henry White of Bristol and Eliza, *d* of John Tippetts; *m* 1876, Caroline Rosena (*d* 1915), *d* of William Thomas, Bristol;

one *s* one *d.* Established first manufactory of aeroplanes in England, and introduced the Bristol Biplanes and monoplanes in 1910. A pioneer of electric street traction, first to introduce it into London, Dublin, Bristol, Middlesbrough, etc; head of the firm of George White and Company of Bristol; Past President of the Bristol Stock Exchange and of the Council of Associated Stock Exchanges of the United Kingdom; President and Treasurer of the Bristol Royal Infirmary; one of the Charity Trustees, and a Governor of the British Grammar and other Schools; President of the Queen Victoria Memorial Hospital at Nice; Past President of the Dolphin Society; chairman of several important undertakings, and interested in or controlling railway and other industrial concerns in Bristol and South Wales. *Heir: s* George Stanley White [*b* 31 July 1882; *m* 1908, Kate Muriel, *d* of late Thomas Baker of Bristol; one *s*]. *Address:* Old Sneed Park, Bristol. *TA:* White, Bristol. *T:* Stoke Bishop 121. *M:* AE 3348, AE 3349. *Club:* Carlton.
                                    Died 22 Nov. 1916.

WHITE, George Gilbert, CSI 1911; *b* Grayingham, Kirton Lindsey, Lincs, Jan. 1857; *s* of late Rev. John White, and of Emily White, Bydews, Lincoln; *m* 1896, Ethel Maude, *d* of late Arthur John Hughes, CIE, MInstCE; two *d. Educ:* Malvern College; Royal Indian Engineering College, Cooper's Hill. Appointed to PWD, 1877; Assistant and Executive Engineer Central Provinces, 1878–1901; Superintending Engineer and Secretary to Agent of Governor-General, Rajputana and Central India, 1901–5; Chief Engineer Burma, 1905–6; Chief Engineer and Secretary to Local Government of Burma, 1906–12; Member of Legislative Council, Burma, 1908–12. *Address:* Fontenay, Belvedere, St Helier, Jersey.
                                    Died 9 Dec. 1916.

WHITE, Henry, Hon. LLD St Andrews; LLD Johns Hopkins and Harvard Universities; *b* Baltimore, 29 March 1850; *s* of John Campbell White and Miss Ridgely, of Hampton; *m* 1st, 1879, Margaret Stuyvesant Rutherford (*d* 1916); one *s* one *d*; 2nd, 1921, Mrs Emily Vanderbilt Sloane. *Educ:* tutors and private schools in America and France. Secretary of the American Legation at Vienna, 1883–84; transferred to London as Second Secretary of Legation, 1884; Secretary of Legation, 1886, and American Delegate to the International Conference on Sugar Bounties, London, 1888; recalled by President Cleveland, 1893; Secretary of Embassy at London, 1897–1905; American Ambassador to Italy, 1905–7; Senior Delegate from the US to the International Agricultural Conference at Rome, 1905, which resulted in the foundation of the International Institute of Agriculture there; Senior Delegate from the US to the Algeciras Conference, 1906; American Ambassador to France, 1907–9; Chairman of the American Delegation to the fourth Pan-American Conference at Buenos Aires, 1910; Special Ambassador to Chile for the celebration of the centenary of that country's independence, 1910; Regent of Smithsonian Institution, Washington; Commissioner Plenipotentiary to Peace Conference, Paris, 1919. *Recreations:* hunting, shooting, golf. *Address:* 1624 Crescent Place, Washington. *Clubs:* Athenæum, Marlborough, Bachelors, Beefsteak, Royal Automobile; Knickerbocker, Metropolitan, New York; Metropolitan, Washington; Cercles de l'Union and de la Rue Royale, Paris.
                                    Died 15 July 1927.

WHITE, Sir Henry Arthur, Kt 1897; CVO 1907; Private Solicitor to the King and other members of Royal Family; *b* 18 June 1849; *s* of late Henry White, and *nephew* of late Sir Arnold Wm White, with whom he lived as his adopted son from 1856 to the date of his death in 1893; *m* 1st, 1896, Isabel Mary (*d* 1905), *e d* of late Charles Courtenay Colley; one *d*; 2nd, Katie, *d* of late Samuel Seldon, CB; one *d. Educ:* Harrow. Practised as a solicitor from 1873. *Recreations:* fishing, cycling. *Address:* 14 Great Marlborough Street, W1. *T:* Gerrard 1310.   *Died 5 Jan. 1922.*

WHITE, Horace, MA, LLD; *b* Colebrook, NH, 10 Aug. 1834; *s* of Horace White, physician, and Elizabeth Moore; *m* 1st, 1859, Martha H. Root (*d* 1873), 2nd, 1875, Amelia J. MacDougall; three *d. Educ:* Beloit College, Beloit, Wisconsin. Graduated, 1853; went to Chicago, and became city editor of the Chicago Evening Journal, 1854; assistant editor of the Chicago Tribune, 1857; chief editor, 1865–74; removed to New York, 1877; joined others in purchasing the New York Evening Post, 1882; Editor, 1899–1903. Chairman of Committee to Investigate Speculation in Securities and Commodities in NY City, 1908–9. *Publications:* took an active part in supporting the Gold Standard in the monetary struggle following the Civil War, published numerous pamphlets, and also a book entitled Money and Banking in 1895 (5th edition in 1914); translated from the Greek the Roman History of Appian of Alexandria, 1899; Life of Lyman Trumbull, 1913. *Address:* 18 West 69th Street, New York. *T:* 948 Columbus. *M:* 12292 NY. *Club:* Century.   *Died 6 Sept. 1916.*

WHITE, James; Managing Director of the Beecham Trust, Ltd; Chairman, George Edwardes (Daly's Theatre), Ltd; *b* Rochdale, 1878. *Address:* 21 Park Street, Mayfair, W1.

Died 29 June 1927.

WHITE, James; FRGS, FRSC, MEng.Inst.Can.; Technical Adviser to Minister of Justice since 1922; *b* 3 Feb. 1863; *e s* of David White and Christina, *d* of George Hendry; *m* 1888, Rachel, *d* of Thomas Waddell; two *d*. *Educ:* Royal Military College, Kingston, Ont. Topographer on the staff of the Geological Survey of Canada, January 1884; made surveys in the Rocky Mountains, 1884 and 1885; in the Madoc, Ont. gold district, 1886; in the Ottawa County, Que, phosphate district, 1887–90; in the Kingston and Pembroke, Ont, district, 1891–93; Geographer and Chief Draughtsman to the Geological Survey, 1894; Member, Geographic Board of Canada, 1898; Chief Geographer of the Department of the Interior, 1899; organized map-work in this branch; employed on the Alaska Boundary Commission 1903, made investigations respecting fast trans-Atlantic passenger steamships (the All-Red Line), 1907; Secretary, Commission of Conservation, 1909; Assistant Chairman and Deputy Minister, 1913; Chairman, Advisory Board on Wild Life Protection since 1917; Chairman Geographic Board since 1925; Prix Alexandre Roquette, 1917; employed on the Labrador Boundary Case, 1921; Vice-President Section C and Section E British Association for Advancement of Science, 1924; President, Section IV Royal Society of Canada, 1924. *Publications:* Topographical Work of the Geological Survey; Atlas of Canada, 1906; Altitudes in Canada, 1901 and 1915; Dictionary of Altitudes, 1903 and 1916; Maps and Map-making in Canada; Derivation of Place-names in Canada; Treaties and Boundaries affecting Canada; Fuels of Western Canada; Power in Alberta; Senator Lodge and the Alaska Boundary; various articles, etc. *Recreation:* travel. *Address:* 450 Wilbrod Street, Ottawa, Ont. *TA:* Conservation. *T:* Rideau 388. *Clubs:* Authors; Rideau, Ottawa.

Died 26 Feb. 1928.

WHITE, James Charles Napoleon; Chairman of the Governing Body and Treasurer of Birkbeck College; Governor of Northampton Polytechnic Institute; Liveryman of Worshipful Company of Basketmakers; *m* Constance, *d* of late Captain Douglas Charles Kinnaird Dana; no *c*. *Educ:* privately; Birkbeck College; student at St Martin's School of Art. For fifty years actively engaged in honorary work at Birkbeck College. *Recreations:* drama, music, travel. *Address:* 43 Gordon Square, WC. *Club:* British Empire.

Died 16 Nov. 1923.

WHITE, James Cobb, JP; MLC; General Manager for White Brothers, Graziers; *b* Belltrees, Scone, NSW, 29 Nov. 1855; *s* of Francis White, MLA; *m* 1882, Emmeline Ebsworth; three *s* two *d*. *Educ:* Grammar School, Newcastle, etc. Twelve months in a bank; thereafter employed in pastoral pursuits, having interests in stations in the Northern Territory, in the Gulf, in Central Queensland, and in New South Wales; a member of the firm of White Brothers, White & Co., The Gulf Cattle Co., and Lorraine and Talawanta Pastoral Co. *Address:* Edinglassie, Muswellbrook, New South Wales. *Club:* Australian, Sydney.

Died 18 Jan. 1927.

WHITE, James Martin, JP; FRSE; *b* 1857; *s* of J. F. White, Balruddery; MP (GL) Forfarshire, 1895–96; *m* 1st, 1898, Mary MacRae; one *s* one *d*; 2nd, Priscilla A. M. Leigh, Bristol and New York. *Educ:* Edinburgh University; Germany; France. Chairman, Governor, Member of Committee on Boards of many Educational Institutions, Elementary to University. Owner of 1,100 acres. *Recreations:* shooting, golf, touring by motor. *Address:* 1 Cumberland Place, Regent's Park, NW1; Balruddery, Dundee. *T:* Museum 854. *Clubs:* Royal Societies, Authors'.

Died 7 July 1928.

WHITE, James William, MD, PhD, LLD (Aberdeen); *b* Philadelphia, 2 Nov. 1850; *s* of Dr James W. White of Philadelphia; *m* 1888, Letitia, *d* of Benj. H. Brown of Philadelphia. *Educ:* The University of Pennsylvania. Graduated 1871; on staff of Prof. Louis Agassiz during Hassler Expedition to West Indies, Straits of Magellan, both coasts of South America, Juan Fernandez, the Galapagos Archipelago, the Isthmus of Panama, etc, 1871–72; Resident Physician, Philadelphia Hospital, 1873; Surgeon to Eastern Penitentiary, 1874–77; Surgeon, First Troop Philadelphia City Cavalry, 1878–88; taught and wrote on Surgery during whole professional life; was Professor of Genito-Urinary Surgery, Professor of Clinical Surgery, John Rhea Barton Professor of Surgery, University of Pennsylvania, successively; Emeritus Professor of Surgery; Surgeon to the University Hospital; Consulting Surgeon, Philadelphia and Jewish Hospitals; Member, American Surgical Association, American Genito-Urinary Association, College of Physicians of Philadelphia, American Medical

Association, British Medical Association, etc; one of the Editors of the Annals of Surgery; Trustee, University of Pennsylvania; Advisory Surgeon Pennsylvania Railroad; Commissioner of Fairmount Park. *Publications:* American Text-Book of Surgery; Genito-Urinary Surgery; Human Anatomy; numerous surgical articles in text-books and systems of surgery, and in medical journals. *Recreations:* bicycling, swimming, walking, climbing, rowing, automobiling. *Address:* 1810 South Rittenhouse Square, Philadelphia, Pa, USA. *Clubs:* Reform, Royal Automobile; The Kinsmen; Swiss Alpine; American Alpine; Rittenhouse, Pa; Corinthian Yacht; Pa Country.

Died 24 April 1916.

WHITE, Hon. John; Minister for Agriculture and Stock; Member for Musgrave in Parliament of Queensland, 1903–4, and since 1907; *b* Dumbartonshire, 1852; arrived in Queensland, 1883; Managing Director, Bundaberg Foundry Ltd; Chairman of Harbour Board; Chairman of Bundaberg Co-operative Insurance Association and of the Mercantile Association. *Address:* Bundaberg, Queensland. *Clubs:* Johnsonian, Brisbane; Bundaberg.

Died 13 July 1922.

WHITE, John Claude, CIE 1904; FRGS; *b* 18 Oct. 1853; *e s* of Dr John White, IMS; *m* Nina, *d* of Lt-Col Geo. Ranken, HEICS. *Educ:* Rugby; Bonn; Cooper's Hill. Joined PWD Bengal, 1876; Executive Engineer, 1887; Political Officer, Sikhim, 1889; accompanied Tibet Mission, 1904; Political Agent for Sikhim, Bhutan, and Tibetan affairs, 1905–8. *Publication:* Sikhim and Bhutan, Experiences of Twenty Years on the North-East Frontier of India, 1909. *Address:* Newland, Glos; 65 Redcliffe Gardens, SW.

Died 19 Feb. 1918.

WHITE, John Williams, PhD, LLD, LittD; Emeritus Professor of Greek in Harvard University; *b* Cincinnati, Ohio, 5 March 1849; *s* of Rev. John Whitney White and Anna Catharine, *d* of Judge Hosea Williams; *m* 1871, Alice, *d* of Picton Drayton Hillyer; one *s* three *d*. *Educ:* Ohio; Germany; Harvard University; PhD 1877; LLD Wesleyan University 1896; Ohio Wesleyan Univ. 1905; LittD Cambridge, England, 1900; Harvard, 1913; Princeton, 1914. Fellow of the American Academy of Arts and Sciences; Hon. Member of the Society for the Promotion of Hellenic Studies, and member of the Kaiserlich Deutsches Archäologisches Institut; Hon. President of the Archæological Institute of America; first Chairman of the Managing Committee of the American School of Classical Studies at Athens, 1881–87; former Editor of the Harvard Studies in Classical Philology; Associate-Editor of Classical Philology, and the Classical Review and Classical Quarterly. *Publications:* School and College Text-Books; senior editor of the College Series of Greek Authors (thirty volumes); Monographs on Philological and Archæological Subjects; The Verse of Greek Comedy, 1912; The Old Greek Commentary on Aristophanes; Scholia on the Aves, 1914. *Address:* 18 Concord Avenue, Cambridge, Mass. *Clubs:* Royal Societies, Authors'.

Died 9 June 1917.

WHITE, John W.; *m*; two *s* two *d*. Past President of The National Federation of Building Trade Employers of Great Britain and Ireland; Member of the Industrial Council; Member of the Sunderland Town Council; Member of Committee on Production. *Address:* High Barnes Works, Sunderland. *T:* 695 and 696. *TA:* Whibild, Sunderland. *M:* 6BR. *Club:* Sunderland.

Died 24 Sept. 1919.

WHITE, Lt-Col Joshua Chaytor, CMG 1916; Indian Medical Service, retired; late Director of Public Health, United Provinces of India; *b* 21 Oct. 1864; *s* of Albert White, Tower Hill, Waterford; *m* Helen Eliza, *d* of G. C. Bright, Cannes; no *c*. *Educ:* University of Edinburgh (MD, MCh); Heidelberg; Bonn. Diplomate in State Medicine (DPH), University of Cambridge. Entered Indian Medical Service, 1889; served with Chitral Relief Force, 1895 (medal and clasp); in charge Camps, Delhi Durbar, 1903; retired, 1912; served European War as Commandant Convalescent Depot for Indian Troops, Barton, Hants, and as Commandant Convalescent Depot for British Troops, Barton, Hants. *Publications:* Two Monographs on Plague in India. *Recreations:* shooting, fishing, golf, tennis. *Address:* Chewton Farm, near Christchurch. *Club:* East India United Service.

Died 20 Jan. 1924.

WHITE, Sir Luke, Kt 1908; DL, JP; *b* Deighton, Yorks, 1 March 1845; *m* 1869, *d* of A. Wood, of York (she *d* 1916). MP (R) Buckrose Division of East Riding of Yorkshire, 1900–18; solicitor, coroner for East Riding District, Yorks. *Address:* Driffield. *TA:* Driffield. *T:* Nat. 185. *Club:* National Liberal.

Died 17 Aug. 1920.

WHITE, Montagu; barrister; *e s* of late Henry Fancourt White, of Blanco, near George, Cape Colony; married. *Educ:* Diocesan College,

Cape Town. Entered the Cape Colonial Civil Service, 1874; resigned, 1878; sometime secretary of the Divisional Council, Komgha, Kaffraria; took part in the Gaika war at Draaibosch; left for the Transvaal, 1886; entered Mining Department; Mining Commissioner of Boksburg till 1892; Consul-General in London for South African Republc, 1892–1900. *Recreation:* music. *Address:* The Lodge, Haslemere. *Club:* Wellington.

Died 18 April 1916.

WHITE, Sir Richard, Kt 1924; Chief Master of the Supreme Court, Chancery Division. *Educ:* privately; King's Coll. Sch. *Address:* Room 173, Royal Courts of Justice, Strand, WC.

Died 21 Jan. 1925.

WHITE, Vice-Admiral Richard William; *b* 20 Feb. 1849; *s* of Admiral R. D. White, CB. Entered Navy, 1862; Captain, 1891; served Straits of Malacca, 1874 (Perak medal and clasp); Assistant to Director of Naval Ordnance, 1884–88; commanded HMS Porpoise, 1889–91; commanded Naval Forces of Colony of Victoria, 1892–95; Assistant Director of Naval Intelligence, 1895–97; commanded HMS Vulcan, 1897–1900; District Captain at Queensferry in HMS Rodney, Anson, 1900–1; commanded HMS Ocean on China Station, 1901–3; Admiral Superintendent Contract-built ships, Tyne and Thames, 1903–6; retired, 1904; Rear-Admiral, 1904; Vice-Admiral, 1908. *Recreations:* photography, bicycling, golf. *Address:* 3 Manston Terrace, Heavitree, Exeter. *Club:* Devon and Exeter.

Died 4 Dec. 1924.

WHITE, Lt-Col Samuel Robert Llewellyn, DSO 1900; late Leinster Regiment; *b* 4 June 1863; *o s* of Robert White of Scotch Rath, Dalkey, Co. Dublin; *m* 1st, 1895, Dorothy Hey (*d* 1903), *d* of late Rev. B. F. Carlyle, Vicar of Cam, Gloucestershire; one *s*; 2nd, 1913, Louise Mary, *y d* of Charles Hughes, Bryndedwydd, Dolgelly. Entered army, 1885; Major, 1901; served South Africa, 1900–2 (despatches, King's and Queen's medals and 5 clasps, DSO); European War, 1914–15 (1914–15 Star, medals). *Address:* Scotch Rath, Dalkey, Co. Dublin. *Clubs:* United Service, Royal Societies.

Died 2 Sept. 1925.

WHITE, Sinclair, CBE 1919; Senior Surgeon, Sheffield Royal Infirmary; Professor of Surgery, University, Sheffield, since 1911; President British Medical Association, 1909; *b* 1858; *m* 1887, Evelyn, *d* of late Frederick Chalmer, Sheffield. *Educ:* Queen's College, Galway. MD (gold medallist), MCh Royal University; FRCS England; DPH Camb. Graduated, 1879; medical tutor; then House Surgeon; then Medical Officer of Health for the city of Sheffield; subseq. in practice as a Consulting-Surgeon. Lt-Col RAMC(T); Administrator 3rd Northern General Hospital (T). *Publications:* The Solvent Action of Moorland Waters on Lead Piping, 1886; Trade Diseases of Cutlers and File-makers, 1894; various articles on surgical diseases in the Lancet, British Medical Journal, and Quarterly Medical Journal. *Recreation:* golf. *Address:* Ranmoor, Sheffield. *T:* 58 Broomhill. *M:* W 569. *Club:* Sheffield.

Died 8 Aug. 1920.

WHITE, T. Charters, MRCS, LDS, FRMS; *b* Chichester, 11 Nov. 1828; *s* of a solicitor. *Educ:* home, privately. Qualified as Member of the College of Surgeons at King's College, London, and obtained his diploma, 1863; Licentiate in Dental Surgery, 1863; President of the Odontological Society of Great Britain, 1886; President of the Quekett Microscopical Club, 1880–81. *Publications:* An Elementary Manual of Microscopical Manipulation; The Microscope and How to Use it; various papers on Dental Histology, Microscopy, Photography, and Photo-micrography in publications; A Microscopical Analysis of the Dental Tartar or Salivary Calculus on the Teeth of the Stone Age, describing the particles of food found in it. *Recreations:* microscopical investigation, photography, photo-micrography. *Address:* Woodland Villa, 59 Victoria Road South, Southsea.

Died 5 March 1916.

WHITE, Col William Westropp, CB 1916; CMG 1919; BA, MD, MCh, MAO; Indian Medical Service retired; *b* 10 June 1862; *e s* of late John Carpenter White, Cork. Capt. IMS 1887; 4th Indian Cavalry, 1891; Major, 1899; Lt-Col 1907; Col 1915. Served Hazara Expedition, 1891 (medal with clasp); Chitral, 1895 (medal with clasp); NW Frontier, India, 1897–98 (2 clasps); Tirah, 1897–98 (2 clasps); China, 1900 (despatches, medal with clasp); Relief of Pekin; European War, 1914–18 (despatches four times, 1914 Star (France, Mesopotamia, Palestine; Bt Col, CB, CMG); retired, 1921. *Club:* Junior Naval and Military.

Died 21 March 1927.

WHITE-THOMSON, Colonel Sir Hugh Davie, KBE 1919; CB 1915; CMG 1917; DSO 1900; RHA; *b* 6 Sept. 1866; *y s* of late Col

Sir R. T. White-Thomson, KCB; *m* 1893, Ela Louisa Agatha (*d* 1894), *d* of late Rev. J. S. Ruddach. *Educ:* Eton. Served South Africa (wounded, despatches thrice, Queen's medal, 5 clasps, DSO); European War, France and Balkans, 1914–18 (wounded, despatches six times, CB, CMG, KBE, White Eagle, Serbia, 2nd class, Officer of the Légion d'Honneur, France). *Address:* Broomford Manor, Exbourne, Devon. *Club:* Naval and Military.

Died 24 Feb. 1922.

WHITE-THOMSON, Col Sir Robert Thomas, KCB 1897 (CB 1892); DL and JP; Alderman, Devon CC; *b* Glasgow, 21 February 1831; *e s* of Robert Thomson, Camphill, Renfrew; *m* 1857, Fanny Julia, *d* of Gen. Sir H. Ferguson Davie, 1st Bt; two *s* two *d*. *Educ:* Eton. Major late King's Dragoon Guards; Lieut-Col Commandant and Hon. Col 4th Batt. Devon Regt 1867–93; contested Tavistock Division, 1892 and 1895. *Address:* Broomford, Jacobstowe, Exbourne, Devon. *TA:* Exbourne.

Died 13 March 1918.

WHITE-WINTON, Meryon, MA; late Editor of Weekly Notes (The Law Reports); *s* of late Thomas White of 53 Portland Place, W, and of late Louisa Frances, *d* of late William Winton of Halland Park, Sussex; assumed mother's maiden name as additional surname, 1905. *Educ:* St Paul's School; Christ Church, Oxford (MA 1880). Barrister, 1877, Inner Temple and South-Eastern Circuit; Hon. Sec. of Jurisprudence Department of Association for Promotion of Social Science; was formerly Captain 3rd Battalion KOYLI, and Major 4th Middlesex (West Middlesex) Volunteers. *Publications:* The Conveyancing Acts, 1881–82 (two editions); joint-author of White and Blackburn's Married Women's Property Act, 1882; The Law of Primogeniture; The Lunacy Laws; Law Reports: Ten Years' Digest, 1891–1900; Law Reports: Ten Years' Digest, 1901–10; Law Reports; Current Indexes (annually) 1896–1913; also contributed to The Laws of England, vols vi and vii (subject, Constitutional Law), 1909. *Recreations:* shooting, golf. *Address:* 97 Cadogan Gardens, SW; 1 Stone Buildings, Lincoln's Inn, WC. *Clubs:* Athenæum, Authors', Ranelagh.

Died 10 July 1921.

WHITEHEAD, Rt. Rev. Cortlandt, STD; Bishop of Pittsburgh since 1882; *b* New York City, 30 Oct. 1842; *s* of William Adee Whitehead and Margaret Elizabeth Parker; *m* 1868, Charlotte Burgoyne King; one *s* four *d*. *Educ:* Phillip's Academy, Andover; Yale University; Philadelphia Divinity School. Deacon, 1867; Priest, 1868; three years in Colorado as Missionary Priest; Rector of the Church of the Nativity, South Bethlehem, Penn, 1870; Secretary of the Diocesan Convention, Central Pennsylvania; Deputy to General Convention, 1877 and 1880; DD Union College, 1880; DD Hobart College, 1887; STD St Stephen's College, New York, 1890; LLD Pittsburgh, 1912. *Publications:* sermons and addresses, missionary reports and papers; Revision of Bishop Coxe's Thoughts on the Services. *Recreations:* foreign travel, boating, fishing. *Address:* 4868 Ellsworth Avenue, Pittsburgh, Pennsylvania, USA. *T:* Schenly 4869.

Died 18 Sept. 1922.

WHITEHEAD, Maj.-Gen. Sir Hayward Reader, KCB 1917 (CB 1909); FRCS; Colonel Commandant RAMC since 1922; *b* 14 July 1855; 2nd *s* of late Rev. T. C. Whitehead; *m* 1893, Evelyn Wynne, 2nd *d* of late Colonel Cayley, CMG, IMS; no *c*. Entered the medical profession, 1873, and the Army Medical Department, 1882; Asst Professor of Military Surgery, Medical School, Netley, 1891–96; served Tirah Campaign, 1897–98; present at the actions of Dargai, and the taking of Sampagha and Arhanga Passes; expedition against the Chamkanni Khel Afridis; operations in the Bazar Valley, 1897 (despatches, medal 2 clasps, promoted Lieut-Colonel); Colonel, 1905, and Administrative Medical Officer in India; Principal Med. Officer, Mohmand Expedition, 1908 (despatches, medal and clasp); Surgeon-General, 1909; deputy Director, Medical Service, Southern Command, 1909–12; Eastern Command, 1912–15; Director Medical Services, Malta, July 1915–March 1916; British Salonika Force, March 1916–Sept. 1917; Knight of Grace of the Order of St John of Jerusalem, 1912; Commandant of the Legion of Honour, 2nd Class Order of St Sava, Grand Commander of the Order of the Redeemer, Médaille d'or des Epidémies, Serbian Red Cross. *Publications:* various articles in medical journals. *Address:* Whinfield, Cobham, Surrey, *T:* Oxshott 17. *Club:* Junior United Service.

Died 28 Sept. 1925.

WHITEHEAD, Sir Henry, Kt 1922; *b* 12 Jan. 1859; *m* 1887, Alice Mawson, Wath on Dearne; one *d*. Worsted spinner and manufacturer; proprietor of Henry Whitehead, Young Street Mills, Bradford and Crystal Mills, Heckmondwike; Chairman Salts (Saltaire), Ltd; Chairman J. & J. Crombie, Ltd, Aberdeen; Director Yarra Falls Ltd, Melbourne; partner in Robert Archibald & Sons, Tillicoultry,

Scotland; President Bradford Chamber of Commerce, 1921–24; Pres. Worsted Spinners' Federation; President Bradford Masonic Association and Permanent Committee; Chairman Bradford Freemasons Hall Co. Ltd; during the War was one of the three representatives of the Worsted Spinners Federation on the Wool Board of Control; was Deputy Chairman of the Board and Chairman of the Spinners Sectional Committee; served on every advisory committee on wool and its products which the Government set up. *Recreation:* motoring. *Address:* Stagenhoe Park, near Welwyn; Hawkswood, Baildon, Yorks. *TA:* Rampant, Bradford. *T:* Shipley 565. *Club:* Union, Bradford.

Died 29 Feb. 1928.

WHITEHEAD, Henry, MVO 1909; DL, JP; *b* 1842; *e* surv. *s* of John Whitehead (*d* 1898) and Eliza Ellen, *d* of late Robert Allanson of Birtle, Lancashire; *m* Louisa (*d* 1918), *d* of late Peter Priestley of Euxton; five *s* two *d*. *Educ:* Shrewsbury; Uppingham. Director Sir W. G. Armstrong Whitworth and Co.; Vice-Chairman Lancashire and Yorkshire Bank; Director Bleachers' Association; Chairman Liverpool Storage Co.; Director, Whitehead Torpedo, Weymouth and Fiume. *Recreation:* shooting. *Address:* Haslem Hey, Bury, Lancashire. *TA:* Lowercroft. *T:* Bury 390. *Clubs:* Carlton, Constitutional; Constitutional, Union, Manchester.

Died 14 March 1921.

WHITEHEAD, Sir James, 1st Bt, *cr* 1889; DL, JP; FSA, FRHistS, FRSS; Lord of the Manor of Wilmington or Grandison, Kent; *b* 2 March 1834; *y s* of James Whitehead, Appleby, Westmorland; *m* 1860, Mercy (*d* 1911), 4th *d* of Thomas Hinds, Bank House, Hunts; three *s* two *d*. *Educ:* Appleby Grammar School. A Bradford merchant in London, 1860–81. Alderman of City of London, 1882–96; Sheriff of London and Middlesex, 1884; Lord Mayor of London, 1889; High Sheriff of County of London, 1890; contested North Westmorland, 1885 and 1886; MP (L) Leicester without contest, 1892; retired through illness, 1894; one of HM Lieutenants for the City of London; for many years Chairman of the Board of Visitors to Borstal convict prison; also for some years a visitor to HM Prison, Holloway, and the City of London Asylum, Stone, Kent; for several years Governor of Christ's Hospital, St Bartholomew's Hospital, and Queen Anne's Bounty; Commander of the Legion of Honour, France; Knight Commander of Servian Order of Takovo; and Grand Cordon of Royal Order of St Sava; Knight Officer of Belgian Order of Leopold; Lion and Sun of Persia; Chinese Tablet of Honour; Founder of Volunteer Equipment Fund; Gold Medallist Royal Agricultural Society; first Honorary Freeman of the Borough of Appleby, also of Kendal; Honorary Freeman Framework Knitters' Company; Master of the Fruiterers' Company, 1889–90; Master Fanmakers' Company, 1885; Pres. Brit. Section French Exhibition, 1889; for many years President Mansion House Association on Railway Rates, which he founded; 1st Hon. Member of the Institute of Journalists; mediated in and settled Great Dock Strike, 1889; Founder of the Penny a Week Collection for the Metropolitan Hospitals; Founder of the Rowland Hill (Post Office) Benevolent Fund; raised a fund to recompense Pasteur for his gratuitous services to 234 British patients, the surplus from which was devoted to the establishment of the British (now Lister) Institute of Preventive Medicine; founder of several entrance and leaving scholarships at Appleby Grammar School; founder of the Self Help Society, the Village Institute, and the Boy Scouts Troop and Club House, Wilmington. *Publications:* pamphlets on Fruit Culture, Technical Education, and Volunteer Equipment. *Recreations:* travel, fruit and flower culture, farming. *Heir: s* George Hugh Whitehead, *b* 30 Oct. 1861. *Address:* Wilmington Manor, near Dartford, Kent. *T:* Dartford 30. *M:* LM 4991. *Club:* Reform.

Died 20 Oct. 1917.

WHITEHEAD, Sir James Beethom, KCMG 1909; *b* 31 July 1858; 2nd *s* of late Robert Whitehead of Fiume; *m* 1896, Hon. Marian Cecilia Brodrick, *y d* of 8th Viscount Midleton; five *s* two *d*. *Educ:* Austria; St John's College, Cambridge. Graduated in honours, 1880; MA. Entered the diplomatic service, 1881; served at Petrograd, Rio de Janeiro, and Berlin; First Secretary at Tokio, Brussels, and Constantinople; Councillor of Embassy, Berlin, 1903–6; HM's Envoy Extraordinary and Minister Plenipotentiary at Belgrade, 1906–10; JP Hampshire. *Address:* Efford Park, Lymington, Hants. *TA:* Everton, Hants. *T:* Lymington 103. *Club:* Travellers'.

Died 19 Sept. 1928.

WHITEHEAD, Colonel John Herbert, DSO 1917; Hon. Colonel RAMC; Lieutenant-Colonel SAMC; *b* 1 Oct. 1869; *y s* of Walter Whitehead, Shrubbery House, Upper Addiscombe, Surrey, founder of Whitehead, Morris & Co., wholesale stationers, printers, etc; *m* Maude, *d* of Francis Newton Lowe, of Sleaford, Lincs; two *d*. *Educ:*

St Peter's Grammar School, Thanet; Upper Canada College, Toronto; University of London (Charing Cross Hospital). MRCS 1893; LRCP 1893. House Surgeon and House Physician, Charing Cross Hospital; Member British Medical Association; passed into Army Medical Service, 1894; resigned, 1896; rejoined, 1899; served through Siege of Ladysmith and operations Natal and Free State (King's and Queen's medals and 4 clasps); transferred to SA Constabulary (Baden-Powell's Police) in 1901 with rank Capt.; retired, 1904, and took up private practice; served through SA Rebellion, 1914, as Capt. SAMC; assisted to raise and train 8th Mounted Brigade Field Ambulance, and commanded it in German West Africa Campaign; SMO Line of Communication, Northern Force, German South-West Africa (despatches); in 1915 was SMO Polchefstroom with rank of Lt-Col; went to SE Africa in command 4th Field Ambulance and SMO 3rd Brigade; ADMS 2nd Div. (Gen. Van Deventers), 1916, (Colonel, 1916, despatches); returned to South Africa, 1917; ADMS, Durban; retired, 1919. *Address:* The Oaks, Plains, Natal, SA. *T:* Plains 2. *Club:* Royal Natal Yacht.

Died 11 July 1928.

WHITEHEAD, Rev. Silvester; late Governor, Handsworth College, Birmingham; *b* 11 May 1841; *m* 1st, Isabella, *d* of Francis Foster, Markenfield Hall, Ripon; 2nd, Frances, *d* of Benjamin Craven, Hazel Head, Penistone; two *s* two *d*. *Educ:* National School, and Wesleyan Coll., Richmond, Surrey. Ordained, 1866; Missionary in Canton, China, 1867–77; Circuit Minister in England, 1877–1905; President of the Wesleyan Methodist Conference, 1904. *Address:* 3 St Paul's Road, Manningham, Bradford.

Died 3 Jan. 1917.

WHITEHEAD, Spencer; *b* 1845; *s* of Edward Bickerton Whitehead of Bristnall, Worcestershire; *m* 1st, Catherine Ellen, *d* of Dr Birt Davies of Birmingham; 2nd, 1881, Gertrude Fanny, *d* of Austin Piper of The Wilderness, Norwich; one *d*. *Educ:* King Edward the Sixth School, Birmingham. A solicitor, 1868–97; a Master of the Supreme Court, 1897–1921; Deputy-Chairman of the Surrey Quarter Sessions; JP; an Income-tax Commissioner. *Address:* Imber Grove, Esher, Surrey. *T:* Esher 316. *Died 10 Jan. 1922.*

WHITEHOUSE, Rev. Owen Charles, MA (London); Hon. DD Aber.; MA (Camb. Christ's College); Principal and Prof. of Biblical Exegesis and Theology in the Countess of Huntingdon's College, Cheshunt, 1895–1905; Senior Theological tutor after its removal to Cambridge; *b* Palamcottah, S India, 15 Nov. 1849; *s* of Rev. J. O. Whitehouse, formerly missionary in Travancore; *m* 1877, Anne Margaret, *y d* of late Robert Maynard, Tottenham; two *d*. *Educ:* Amersham Hall School, near Reading; Univ. Coll. London (1866–70); Cheshunt Coll. (1872–74); Univ. of Bonn (1876–77). Matriculated London University, 1866, with Gilchrist Scholarship; MA Branch 1 (Classics), 1876. Tutor in Hebrew and Classics in Cheshunt Coll. 1877–95; member of Faculty of Theology, Board of Theological and of Oriental Studies, Univ. of London, 1901–6; Examiner in Hebrew. *Publications:* translated, with additions, Schrader's Cuneiform Inscriptions and the Old Testament (2 vols); Primer of Hebrew Antiquities, 1895; contributions to Dr Hastings' Bible Dict., Dict. of Christ and Gospels, Encycl. of Religion and Ethics, to Encyclopædia Biblica, to Ency. Brit. (11th edn), and to Dr Charles' Apocrypha; also to Critical Review, Expository Times, Interpreter, and Expositor; Temple Bible (Ezekiel); Commentary on Isaiah in Century Bible; Old Testament Books. *Address:* Morley Lodge, Brooklands Avenue, Cambridge.

Died 10 April 1916.

WHITEING, Richard; author and journalist; *b* London, 27 July 1840; father was in Inland Revenue Department, Somerset House; *m* 1869, Helen, *niece* of Townsend Harris, first United States Minister to Japan. *Educ:* privately. First a pupil of the late Benjamin Wyon, Medallist and Chief Engraver of Her Majesty's Seals; in 1866, first essay in journalism—series of satirical papers, political and social, in Evening Star, afterwards republished as 'Mr Sprouts—his Opinions'; leader-writer and correspondent, Morning Star; editorial department, Press Association; editorial staff, Manchester Guardian; Paris Correspondent, Manchester Guardian, World (London), World (New York), etc; returned to London to join editorial staff Daily News; resigned, 1899. *Publications:* The Democracy, 1876; The Island, 1888; No 5 John Street, 1899; The Life of Paris, 1900; The Yellow Van, 1903; Ring in the New, 1906; All Moonshine, 1907; Little People, 1908; My Harvest, 1915; Both Sides of the Curtain (with Dame Geneviève Ward), 1918; Film, No 5 John Street, 1921. *Address:* Burford Close, 35A High Street, Hampstead, NW3.

Died 29 June 1928.

WHITELAW, Græme Alexander Lockhart; *b* 1863; *m* 1st, 1885, Bessie (*d* 1900), *d* of James Reid Stewart; one *s*; 2nd, 1902, Laura, *d* of late James Montagu, Melton Park, Doncaster; three *d. Educ:* Harrow; Trinity College, Cambridge. Late Capt. 3rd Batt. Argyll and Sutherland Highlanders; MP (C) Lanarkshire, NW, 1892–95. *Address:* Brockham Park, Betchworth, Surrey. *Club:* Carlton.

Died 23 July 1928.

WHITELAW, Thomas, MA, DD; Senior Minister of King Street United Free Church, Kilmarnock; Moderator of the United Free Church of Scotland, 1912–13; *b* Perth, 1840; *s* of Thomas Whitelaw, Grain Merchant there, and Barbara Dron; *m* 1867, Alice, *d* of Rev. Thomas M'Creath of Mile-End Road United Presbyterian Church, South Shields; four *s* two *d. Educ:* Perth Grammar School; St Andrews University; United Presbyterian Theological Hall, Edinburgh. Ordained at South Shields, 1864; minister Cathedral Street UP Church, Glasgow, 1867; Kilmarnock, 1877; called to Ballarat, Australia, but declined, 1885; special commissioner UF Church of Scotland for Union of Presbyterian Churches of Australia, Sydney, 1901; visited churches in Queensland, NS Wales, Victoria, W Australia, New Zealand, and Tasmania; also travelled extensively on the Continent, in the United States, Canada, and Egypt; served on principal committees of United Presbyterian and United Free Churches; a member of the United Free Committee conferring with the Established Church Committee with regard to Union. Celebrated his jubilee as an ordained minister in March 1914. *Publications:* The Pulpit Commentary on Genesis; Exegetical and Homiletical Commentary on St John; Preacher's Commentary on the Acts; Patriarchal Times; How is the Divinity of Jesus depicted in the NT?; Old Testment Critics; The Old Lamp, being short studies on the Bible; Jehovah—Jesus; numerous contributions to the Pulpit Commentary on Numbers, Job, 2nd Chronicles, Ecclesiastes, Ezekiel, with various articles in magazines. *Recreation:* change of work. *Address:* 59 Corrour Road, Newlands, Glasgow.

Died 9 Aug. 1917.

WHITELOCKE, R. Henry Anglin, MD, MCh; FRCS; MA Oxon (Hon.), Surgeon; Hon. Surgeon Radcliffe Infirmary and County Hospital, Oxford; Litchfield Lecturer on Surgery, University of Oxford; Examiner in Surgery in the Universities of Aberdeen and Liverpool; a Consulting Surgeon to the Great Western and London and North-Western Railway Companies; Fellow Royal Society of Medicine, President Section Children's Diseases; *b* 1861; 4th *s* of late Rt Hon. Hugh Anthony Whitelocke of Bulstrode Park, Westmorland; *m* Barbara Henry, *e d* of late George Lowe Reid, MICE, Brighton; two *s* three *d. Educ:* Owens Coll., Manchester; University of Edinburgh. After graduating and before settling in practice held various resident hospital appointments in Edinburgh, Glasgow, London, and the provinces; was for a time engaged in teaching anatomy. Late Lt-Col RAMC (T), 3rd Southern General Hospital. *Publications:* Sprains and Allied Injuries of Joints, Football Injuries; Athletics in Relation to Disease; The Substitution of Temporary and Absorbable for Permanent and Unabsorbable Sutures in the Operations on Bone; articles, Injuries of Joints, Injuries in Region of Knee and Leg, in Practitioners' Surgery, 1912, 1916, 1919; Treatment of Sprains, System of Treatment, by Hutchinson and Collier, 1914–20; Loose Bodies in the Knee, British Journal of Surgery, 1914; Operation of Outward Dislocation of the Knee-Cap, *ibid.* 1914; Movements of the Isolated Human Appendix Vermiformi (with Dr Gunn), *ibid.* 1914; Appendicutomy by a New Route, Proceedings Royal Society of Medicine, and BMJ, 1920; many papers in medical journals. *Recreations:* collecting antiques, shooting. *Address:* St Giles' Gate, Oxford. *TA:* Whitelocke, Oxford. *T:* Oxford 389; 11 Upper Wimpole Street, W1. *T:* Langham 1124. *M:* FC 4940. *Clubs:* West Indian; Oxford and County, Vincent's, Oxford.

Died 19 Nov. 1927.

WHITESIDE, Most Rev. Thomas; RC Archbishop of Liverpool (Bishop since 1894); *b* 17 April 1857. *Educ:* St Edward's College, Liverpool; Ushaw; English College, Rome. Professor, Vice-President, President, St Joseph's College, Upholland; Canon of Liverpool, 1893. *Address:* Archbishop's House, Belvidere Road, Liverpool, S.

Died 28 Jan. 1921.

WHITING, William Henry, CB 1914; MICE; Vice-President, Institution of Naval Architects; *b* 1854; *s* of William Whiting, Porchester and Gosport; *m* 1880, Marian, *d* of Robert Little, JP, Slough, Buckinghamshire; three *s* three *d. Educ:* Royal Naval College, Greenwich. Entered Portsmouth Dockyard as apprentice, 1869; student of naval construction, Royal Naval College, 1873–76; draughtsman and assistant constructor, Admiralty, 1877–90; Instructor in Naval Architecture, RN College, 1885–90; Constructor at Chatham and Devonport, 1890–95; Chief Constructor, Hong-Kong Yard, 1895–97; served on Admiralty Committees on Submerged

Torpedo Discharge and on Floating Docks; Chief Constructor and Assistant Director of Naval Construction, Admiralty, 1897–1912; Superintendent of Construction Accounts and Contract Work, Admiralty, 1912–17. *Publications:* Influence of Modern Accessories on the Design of War Ships (Gold Medal of Institution of Naval Architects). *Address:* South Corner, Duncton, Petworth. *TA:* Whiting Petworth. *T:* Sutton (Sussex) 10. *M:* YO 3223.

Died 22 Aug. 1927.

WHITLEY, John Robinson; *b* Leeds, 13 Dec. 1843; *m* Ellen Naylor, Manchester; one *s* three *d. Educ:* France, Germany, and Italy. Associated with Lincrusta (to which he gave name) in Europe and America; creator of Earl's Court as a 25-acre exhibition area, and organiser of a series of National Exhibitions—first of their kind— held there; America 1887, Italy 1888, France 1890, Germany 1891; founder and organiser of Le Touquet (Paris-Plage) as an Anglo-French pleasure resort, and then of Hardelot as a sister Pleasaunce, near Boulogne, as nucleus of which he acquired the historic castle of Hardelot; thanked by M Clémenceau for placing all resources of Hardelot at disposal of Allies. *Address:* Château de Condette, Pont-de-Briques, Pas-de-Calais. *Club:* Constitutional.

Died 21 March 1922.

WHITLEY, Kate Mary, RI 1889; artist; *b* London; *d* of late Rev. J. L. Whitley, Leicester. *Educ:* Manchester. Began to exhibit in London and provinces, 1884; exhibited at RA several times; also at Dresden, Chicago and Brussels. *Address:* Leopold House, South Wigston, near Leiester.

Died 24 Aug. 1920.

WHITLEY-THOMSON, Sir Frederick Whitley, Kt 1916; *b* 2 Sept. 1851; *s* of Jonathan Thomson of Glasgow, and Emma Whitley of Halifax; received grant by Royal Licence to use surname Whitley-Thomson, 1914; *m* 1888, Bertha Florence, 3rd *d* of late Alderman Matthew Smith, Halifax; one *d. Educ:* Glasgow Academy and Andersonian Univ., Glasgow. MP (L) Skipton Div. of West Riding of Yorks, 1900–6; contested South Herefordshire, 1908; Colchester, 1910; Director of English Card-clothing Co., Ltd; JP, County Borough, Halifax; Mayor of Halifax, 1908–11; Alderman, 1908; was instrumental in raising a fund of £10,000 for Royal Halifax Infirmary and Halifax District Nursing Association in memory of King Edward VII; Chairman, Finance Committee of Halifax County Borough Council, 1913–19; Chairman, Halifax War Refugees Committee, and received from King Albert the Medaille du Roi in recognition of services to Belgian refugees resident in Halifax and district during the War; President, Halifax Chamber of Commerce, 1912–14. *Address:* 19 Addison Road, W14. *T:* Park 1838; 40 Prescott Road, Halifax, Yorks. *T:* Halifax 1750. *M:* CP 179 and XF 7171. *Clubs:* Reform, Eighty, Ranelagh; Halifax.

Died 21 June 1925.

WHITMAN, Sidney, FRGS; political writer; *b* London; *m* 1st, 1888, Frances Charlotte (*d* 1907), *e d* of late Captain Edmund Francis Austey, 20th Regiment; 2nd, 1910, Annia Henrietta, *widow* of late Edward Derenberg of Evelyn Gardens, SW. *Educ:* King's College School, London; Germany, and Brussels. Represented New York Herald at Constantinople during outbreak of Armenian conspiracy, 1896, and at Moscow during revolution, 1905–6; visited Edhem Pacha in same capacity at Turkish headquarters, Elassona, 1897; accompanied Turkish mission through Kurdistan, Anatolia, and Syria from Black Sea to Mediterranean, 1897–98; Austrian Grand Gold Medal for Arts and Sciences, Viribus Unitis; Grand Officer's Cross and Star of the Royal Order of the Crown of Roumania; the King of Roumania's Jubilee Medal, etc. *Publications:* Metrical translation of Grillparzer's Medea, 1878; Fetish Worship in the Fine Arts, 1885; Conventional Cant, 1887; Imperial Germany, 1888; Realm of the Habsburgs, 1893; Teuton Studies, 1895; English version (for America) of Bruno Garlepp's illustrated work, Germany's Iron Chancellor, 1897; Story of Austria, 1898; Reminiscences of the King of Roumania, 1899; Conversations with Prince Bismarck; Life of the Emperor Frederick, 1900; My Reminiscences of Prince Bismarck, 1902; German Memories, 1912; Turkish Memories, 1914; Things I Remember, 1916; ed English version of Moltke's Letters, 2 vols; and various contributions to English, German, and American magazines. *Address:* 25 Gledhow Gardens, SW. *Club:* Junior Athenæum.

Died 30 Oct. 1925.

WHITMARSH, Rev. Robert Thomas; Hon. Canon of Norwich. *Address:* Ashby St Mary Rectory, Norwich.

Died 19 July 1921.

WHITNEY, Sir Benjamin, Kt 1897; Clerk of the Crown, Clerk of the Peace and Local Registrar of Titles, Co. Mayo; *b* 23 Dec. 1833;

m 1860, Annabella (*d* 1899), *d* of late Isaac North-Bomford; two *d*. *Address:* 29 Upper Fitzwilliam Street, Dublin; Brayfort, Bray. *Clubs:* Constitutional; Friendly Brothers, Dublin.

Died 21 Dec. 1916.

WHITTAKER, Rt. Hon. Sir Thomas Palmer, Kt 1906; PC 1908; MP (L) Spen Valley Division, Yorks, WR, since 1892; *b* Scarborough, 7 Jan. 1850; *s* of Thomas Whittaker, JP, Scarborough; *m* 1874, Emma Mary, *d* of Capt. Charles Theedham, Scarborough. *Educ:* Huddersfield Coll. In the hardware and iron trade, 1866–82; editor of newspapers, 1882–92; Chairman and Managing Director of Life Assurance Institution; active in Temperance movement; a member of Royal Commission on Licensing, 1896–99; Chairman of Select Committee on Parliamentary Procedure, 1914; Chairman of Royal Commission on Importation of Paper, 1916. *Publications:* The Ownership, Tenure, and Taxation of Land, 1914; wrote much in reviews and newspapers on economical, financial, commercial, statistical, and social questions. *Address:* 2 Wetherby Gardens, Kensington, SW5. *T:* Western 2900. *Club:* Reform.   *Died 9 Nov. 1919.*

WHITTINGTON, Col George John Charles, CB 1900; Army Pay Department; *b* 1836; *s* of George Whittington of Bath. Entered Royal North Gloucestershire Militia, 1856; Royal Canadian Rifles, 1858; Royal Welsh Fusiliers, 1875; and APD, 1878; Hon. Maj. 1882, and Col 1892; served Canada (Fenian Raids), 1866–70 (medal); Egypt, 1882 (medal, Khedive's star); South Africa, 1900–1 (despatches, Queen's medal, 4 clasps, CB). *Address:* Codham Hall, Great Warley, Brentwood.   *Died 5 April 1916.*

WHITTON, James Reid, DLitt University of South Africa; *b* Perthshire. Three years a Resident Master in one of the London Training Colleges; served as an Assistant Inspector of Schools in the South-Eastern District of Scotland; Headmaster of the Public School at Melrose; Rector of the Normal College, Cape Town, 1878–1915; Member of Cape School Board since 1906; Member of the Council of the University of the Cape of Good Hope. *Address:* The University, Cape Town.   *Died 14 Dec. 1919.*

WHITWELL, Edward Robson, JP, DL; *b* Sunderland, 1843; *m* Mary Janet, *d* of late E. Aldam Leatham, DL, of Misarden Park, Gloucestershire; two *s* three *d*. *Educ:* Grove House, Tottenham. Chairman and Managing Director of the North Brancepeth Coal Co., Ltd; Vice-Chairman and Managing Director of the Horden Collieries, Ltd; senior partner Greveson and Whitwell, Darlington. *Address:* The Friarage, Yarm-on-Tees, Yorks. *Clubs:* Wellington, Alpine; Royal Yacht Squadron, Cowes.   *Died 14 Oct. 1922.*

WHYHAM, William Henry, ISO 1906; District Magistrate, Antigua, Leeward Islands; *b* 1848; *s* of late W. Whyham, RN; *m* 1876, Charlotte, *d* of C. M. Eldridge. *Educ:* Royal Naval School, New Cross. Entered RN 1864; retired, 1873; entered Colonial Civil Service; District Magistrate, Dominica, 1874; District Magistrate and Inspector of Prisons, Antigua, 1878; President Legislative Council, 1895–98; Member Executive Council, Antigua, 1895; Member Legislative Council, 1898; Member Executive Council Leeward Islands, 1902. *Recreation:* golf. *Address:* St John's, Antigua, Leeward Islands, WI.

WHYTE, Rev. Alexander, DD, LLD; Principal, New College, Edinburgh, 1909–18; *b* Kirriemuir (Thrums), Forfarshire, 13 Jan. 1836; *m* Jane Elizabeth, *d* of late George Freeland Barbour of Bonskeid, Perthshire, NB; three *s* three *d*. *Educ:* Aberdeen University; New College, Edinburgh. Ordained as colleague in Free St John's, Glasgow, 1866; translated to Free St George's, Edinburgh, as colleague and successor to Dr Candlish, 1870; retired as senior minister, 1916; freedom of the City of Edinburgh, 1909. *Publications:* Commentary on Shorter Catechism, 1882; Characters and Characteristics of William Law, 1893; Appreciation of Jacob Behmen, 1895; Bunyan Characters, vols i–iv; Samuel Rutherford and some of his Correspondents, 1894; Lancelot Andrewes and his Private Devotions, 1895; Bible Characters, 1897, vols i–vi; Santa Teresa, 1897; Father John, 1898; An Appreciation of Browne's Réligio Medici, 1898; Newman, An Appreciation; Bishop Butler, An Appreciation; The Apostle Paul; The Walk, Conversation, and Character of Jesus Christ, Our Lord; Thomas Shepard; James Fraser, Laird of Brea; Thirteen Appreciations. *Recreation:* walking. *Address:* 22 Church Row, Hampstead, NW.

Died 6 Jan. 1921.

WHYTE, James Wilkinson, ISO 1915; JP; Senior Associate of Arts 1870; Recorder of Titles; Registrar of Public Trusts; Collector of Stamp Duties, 1884; Commissioner of the Public Debts Sinking Fund (State), 1893; of Hobart Corporation, 1910; a Trustee of the Agricultural Bank (State Advances), 1910; retired from Public Service,

1921; *b* Hobart, Tasmania, 1852; *s* of late Hon. James Whyte, born on Scottish Border; *m* 1st, Julia Helen Coverdale; 2nd, Annie Coverdale; three *s*. *Educ:* High School, Hobart. Admitted practitioner of Supreme Court, 1876; solicitor to the Lands Titles Commissioners, 1883. *Address:* New-Town Park, New Town, near Hobart, Tasmania. *T:* 1368. *Club:* Tasmanian, Hobart.

Died 29 May 1923.

WHYTE, Ven. Richard Athenry; Canon of Grafton and Armidale, 1911. *Educ:* Pembroke Coll., Cambridge (BA). Ordained 1883, Curate of St James', Plumstead, 1883–86; St Stephen, Ballarat, 1886–88; Vicar of St John, Horsham, Victoria, 1889–92; Rokewood, 1892–99; Coleraine, 1899–1903; Vicar and Archdeacon of Lismore, 1903–11. *Address:* Lismore, NSW.

Died 29 Dec. 1917.

WICKHAM, Rev. Gordon Bolles; Vicar, Bradford Abbas, since 1886; Canon of Salisbury; *b* 1850; *s* of Rev. Frederic Wickham, Winchester College; *m* 1887, Sidney Katherine, *d* of Admiral Lord Frederic Kerr. *Educ:* New College, Oxford; MA. Curate of Newton Ferrers, Devon, 1873–75; Vicar, Church Crookham, 1875–82; Assistant Priest, Winchester College Mission, 1882–86; temp. Chaplain to the Forces, Gibraltar, 1886. *Address:* Bradford Abbas Vicarage, Sherborne, Dorset.

Died 19 Dec. 1920.

WICKHAM, Sir Henry, Kt 1920; *b* 29 May 1846; *e s* of late Henry Wickham, of Corbet Court, Capel Court, City of London, and Rose Cottage, Haverstock Hill; *m* 1871, Violet Cave Carter. Sometime Commissioner for the introduction of the Parà (Hevea) Indian Rubber for the Government of India; also Inspector of Forests, Commissioner of Crown-lands; Acting District Commissioner and JP Colonial Service; explorer and pioneer planter for half a century in equatorial belt (east and west), Central America, Orinoco, Amazon Valley, Australia, New Guinea, Pacific Islands, etc. *Publications:* Journey through the Wilderness, 1872; Introduction, Plantation and Cultivation of Parà (Hevea) Indian Rubber, 1908. *Recreation:* speciality—pioneer planting. *Address:* 32 Newton Road, W2. *T:* Park 8423.   *Died 27 Sept. 1928.*

WICKHAM, Major Thomas Edmund Palmer, DSO 1900; RFA; *b* 30 Jan. 1879; *e s* of R. W. Wickham of Ebley Court, Stroud; *m* 1908, Elsie, *y d* of N. W. Grieve of Coyleigh, Groombridge; two *s*. *Educ:* Marlborough. Entered RA, 1898; served South Africa, 1900–2 (wounded, despatches, Queen's medal, 6 clasps, King's medal, 2 clasps, DSO); European War, 1914–15 (despatches, wounded, Bt Major).

Died July 1917.

WICKSTEED, Joseph Hartley, JP; MInstCE; Past-President IMechE; late Chairman J. Buckton and Co., Ltd, Leeds; *b* 1842; *e s* of Rev. C. Wicksteed; *m* Mary, *d* of John Hancock, JP, of Lurgan; four *d*. *Educ:* Ruthin Grammar School. Inventor of several patents; Member of the Court and Council of Leeds University; late President Leeds Chamber of Commerce; late President of Leeds Philosophical Society. *Publications:* various papers. *Recreation:* golf. *Address:* Weetwood, Leeds. *T:* Headingley 183. *Club:* Leeds.

Died 16 Dec. 1919.

WICKSTEED, Rev. Philip Henry, MA (Lond. Classics); LittD (Leeds and Manchester); lecturer and writer; *b* 25 Oct. 1844; 2nd *s* of Rev. Charles Wicksteed of Leeds; *m* 1868, Emily Rebecca (*d* 1924), *e d* of Rev. Henry Solly; eight *c*. *Educ:* Ruthin Grammar School; University College School; University College; Manchester New Coll., Lond. Entered the Unitarian ministry, 1867; settled first at Taunton; removed, 1870, to Dukinfield, near Manchester; Little Portland Street Chapel, London, 1874–97; Univ. Extension Lecturer, 1887–1918, subjects—Dante, Political Economy, Wordsworth, Greek Tragedy, etc. *Publications:* Translation of Bible for Young People (six vols); Dante, Six Sermons; Alphabet of Economic Science; Co-ordination of the Laws of Distribution; Henrik Ibsen (lectures); Religion of Time and Religion of Eternity, 1899; Translation and Notes to Paradiso; Translation and Notes to Dante's Convivio; (with Ferrers Howell, MA) Translation of Dante's Latin Works, with notes; (with Edmund Gardner, MA) Dante and Del Virgilio; The Common Sense of Political Economy; Dante and Aquinas, 1913; Dogma and Philosophy (a study of Aquinas), 1920; From Vita Nuova to Paradiso, 1922; sermons, translations, etc. *Address:* Childrey, Berks. *Club:* University of London.   *Died 18 March 1927.*

WIDDICOMBE, Rev. John; Canon Emeritus of Bloemfontein; *b* Brixham, 28 March 1839; *s* of John and Louisa Widdicombe; *m* 1877, Matilda Anne Sibley (*d* 1878); one *d*. Ordained, 1863; Curate of George, Cape Colony, 1863–70; Rector of Malmesbury, 1870–71;

Master, St Andrew's School, Bloemfontein, 1872–74; Vicar of Thaba N'Chu, 1875–77; RD Basutoland, 1885–99; SPG Director, St Saviour's Mission, Hlotse Heights, 1876–1906; Canon of Bloemfontein, 1884–1906. *Publications:* Fourteen Years in Basutoland; In the Lesuto, 1907; Distant Brethren of Low Degree; Memories and Musings, 1915. *Recreation:* gardening, especially rose-growing. *Address:* St Raphael's, Faure, Cape, South Africa.

Died 27 June 1927.

WIDDRINGTON, Major Shallcross Fitzherbert, JP, DL; *b* 9 Feb. 1826; 3rd *s* of late Shallcross Jacson, Capt. 3rd Light Dragoons, and Frances, *e d* of late Rev. Joseph Cook; assumed name Widdrington, 1856, on *S* his maternal uncle, Capt. Samuel Widdrington, RN; *m* 1864, Cecilia, *e d* of late Edward John Gregge-Hopwood, of Hopwood Hall, Co. Lancaster; two *s* two *d*. *Educ:* Rugby. High Sheriff, Northumberland, 1874; late Major Northumberland Light Infantry Militia. *Address:* Newton Hall, Felton, Northumberland.

Died Dec. 1917.

WIGGIN, Sir Henry Arthur, 2nd Bt, *cr* 1892; JP, DL; *b* 3 May 1852; *s* of Sir Henry Samuel Wiggin, 1st Bt and Mary, *d* of David Malins, Edgbaston, Birmingham; *S* father, 1905; *m* 1878, Annie Sarah, *d* of C. R. Cope of Kinnerton Court, Radnors; one *s* two *d*. High Sheriff, Co. Stafford, 1896. *Heir: s* Charles Richard Henry Wiggin, Captain Staffordshire Yeomanry [*b* 21 March 1885; *m* 1916, Mabel Violet Mary, *d* of late Sir William Jaffray, 2nd Bt. *Educ:* Eton; Trinity College, Cambridge; BA 1906]. *Address:* Walton Hall, Eccleshall. *Clubs:* Reform, Union.

Died 2 May 1917.

WIGGIN, Kate Douglas, (Mrs George Christopher Riggs), DLitt Bowdoin, 1904; American authoress; *b* 1856. Trained as a teacher; organised the first free kindergartens for the poor on the Pacific coast, and for several years devoted herself to that work. *Publications:* Timothy's Quest; A Cathedral Courtship; Polly Oliver's Problem; A Summer in a Cañon; The Birds' Christmas Carol; The Story of Patsy; Marm Lisa; Nine Love Songs and a Carol; A Village Watch Tower; Penelope's Experiences: 3 vols: England, 1900, Scotland, Ireland, 1901; The Diary of a Goose Girl; in collaboration with her sister, Nora Archibald Smith, The Story Hour; Children's Rights; The Republic of Childhood, 3 vols; The Posy Ring Golden Numbers; Rebecca of Sunnybrook Farm, 1903; The Affair at the Inn; New Chronicles of Rebecca, 1907; Waitstill Baxter, 1913; two books of verse and five of fairy and folk tales collated for children and youth (with her sister Nora A. Smith); Rose o' the River; The Old Peabody Pew; Susanna and Sue; Robinetta; Mother Carey; The Romance of a Christmas Card, 1916; My Garden of Memory (autobiog.), 1923. *Address:* 145 West 58th Street, New York; 12 Henrietta Street, WC.

Died 24 Aug. 1923.

WIGHT-BOYCOTT, Lt-Col Thomas Andrew, DSO 1902; Hon. Lieutenant-Colonel in Army; Major Staffs Yeomanry (QOR Regt); *b* 5 Aug. 1872; *e s* of late C. B. Wight-Boycott of Rudge Hall, Shropshire; *m* 1894, Anne Catherine, *d* of late Rev. J. Morgan, Rector of Llandudno, N Wales; one *d*. *Educ:* Eton. Served with Imperial Yeomanry in South Africa, 1900–2 (despatches twice, Queen's and King's mdals, DSO). *Address:* Rudge Hall, Pattingham, Wolverhampton. *Clubs:* Boodle's, Wellington.

Died 30 March 1916.

WIGLEY, Frederick George, CIE 1912; of the Inner Temple, Barrister-at-Law; Secretary to the Bengal Legislative Council, 1896–1913; attached to India Office, 1913–17; *b* 1855; *s* of late John Gwyn Middleton Wigley, solicitor; *m* Grace Agnes, *d* of late George Davidson Mackay; three *s* three *d*. *Educ:* Melbourne, Victoria. Called to Bar, 1889; Parliamentary Draftsman; practised at the Calcutta Bar, 1895–98; Secretary to the Calcutta Building Commission, 1897–98; Coroner of Calcutta, 1898–99. *Publications:* several works on Indian law. *Recreations:* walking, music. *Club:* Constitutional.

Died 22 March 1918.

WIGLEY, Sir George, Kt 1923; JP; Chairman, George Wigley & Sons, Ltd, silk merchants, Nottingham; *b* 1837; *s* of Robert Wigley; *m* 1870, Clara, *d* of Jos. Clarke; two *s* five *d*. President of Savings Bank, Nottingham; President Nottingham Eastern Division Conservative Association; Director of Eagle, Star, and British Dominion Insurance Co.; Chairman of Directors of Nottingham Manufactory Company. *Recreation:* shooting. *Address:* Redcliffe, Mapperley Road, Nottingham. *T:* 1689. *M:* 1074. *Clubs:* Conservative, Boro', Nottingham.

Died 5 Jan. 1925.

WIGNALL, James; National Organiser, Dock, Wharf, Riverside and General Workers' Union; MP (Lab) Forest of Dean, Gloucester, since

Dec. 1918; *b* 21 July 1856; *m* 1876, *d* of George Rees, Carmarthen; three *s* one *d*. *Educ:* National School. Thirty years Trade Unions organiser; JP Borough of Swansea; Member of old School Board; Vice-Chairman four years; Member of Overseas Settlement Delegation, 1923. *Recreations:* no time for anything but work. *Address:* Newnham, 17 Fawnbrake Avenue, Herne Hill, SE24.

Died 10 June 1925.

WILBERFORCE, Ven. Albert Basil Orme, DD; Archdeacon of Westminster since 1900; Rector of St John's, Westminster; Chaplain of the House of Commons since 1896; *b* Winchester, 14 Feb. 1841; *y s* of Samuel Wilberforce, Bishop of Oxford, subsequently of Winchester; *m* Charlotte (*d* 1909), *e d* of Capt. Netherton Langford, RN, and Caroline St Leger. *Educ:* Eton; Exeter Coll., Oxford (DD). Ordained 1866 as Chaplain to the Bishop of Oxford; subsequently Curate of Cuddesdon, Oxfordshire; of Seaton, Devonshire; of St Jude's, Southsea; appointed Rector of St Mary's, Southampton, 1871; Canon of Westminster, 1894–1900. *Publications:* The Trinity of Evil, 1885; Sermons preached in Westminster Abbey, 1898, second series 1902; Following on to Know, 1904; Speaking Good of His Name, 1905; Sanctification by the Truth, 1906; New Theology, 1908; The Hope that is in me, 1909; The Power that Worketh in us, 1910. *Address:* 20 Dean's Yard, Westminster Abbey, SW. *T:* Victoria 1800.

Died 13 May 1916.

WILCOX, Ella Wheeler; poet; *b* (Wheeler) Johnstown Centre, Wisconsin, 1855; *m* 1884, Robert M. Wilcox (*d* 1916) of New York. *Educ:* University of Wisconsin. Editorial writer and contributor New York Journal and Chicago American. *Publications:* Poems of Passion; Three Women, 1898; An Ambitious Man; Everyday Thoughts in Prose and Verse; Maurine; Poems of Pleasure; Kingdom of Love and other Poems; An Erring Woman's Love; Men, Women, and Emotions; The Beautiful Land of Nod; Poems of Power; The Heart of the New Thought; Sonnets of Abelard and Héloïse; An Ambitious Man, 1908; The Diary of a Faithless Husband, 1910; Poems of Experience; Yesterday; Poems of Progress, 1911; Picked Poems; A Woman's Letters; Cameos, 1912; Poems of Problems, 1914; The Art of being Alive; Historical Mother Goose, 1914. *Address:* Granite Bay, Short Beach, Conn; Hotel Belmont, New York.

Died 28 Oct. 1919.

WILD, James Anstey; JP; Registrar, City of London Court, 1889–1921; Barrister-at-Law, Gray's Inn; *b* 2 July 1853; *e s* of late James Anstey Wild, 104 Westbourne Terrace, W; *m* Beatrice Dorothy Margaret, *e d* and *co-heiress* of late Rev. W. S. Preston, of Warcop Hall, Westmorland, Lord of Manor of Warcop, and patron of that living; two *s* one *d*. *Educ:* privately. *Address:* Warcop Hall, Westmorland; St James's Court, SW; City of London Court, EC. *Club:* Arts.

Died 19 March 1922.

WILD, Rev. Marshall, MA (Oxon); Hon. Canon of Southwell since 1906; *b* 1834; *s* of Thomas Martyr Wild of Strettit Place, East Peckham, Kent. *Educ:* The King's School, Canterbury; Queen's College, Oxford. Deacon, 1858; Priest, 1858; Assistant Curate successively at Talk-on-the-Hill, Alton, Staffs, St Mary's, Wolverhampton, and Newark, Notts, 1860–64; Incumbent of Poynton, Cheshire, 1864–80; Vicar of Newark and Rural Dean, 1880–1907. *Address:* St Werburgh's Vicarage, Derby.

Died 6 Jan. 1916.

WILDE, Henry, DSc, DCL; FRS; *b* Manchester, 1833. *Educ:* private schools. Engaged in scientific pursuits from early age. *Discoveries:* indefinite increase of the magnetic and electric forces from quantities indefinitely small, 1864; the synchronising property of alternating currents to control the rotations of a number of dynamos, an essential feature in the great installation at Niagara and other electro-generating stations, 1868; new multiple relations among the atomic weights by which the existence of undiscovered elements and their properties have been predicted, 1878; that the moving force of celestial bodies is as the square of the velocity, and inversely proportional to the square of the distance, 1909. *Inventions:* the dynamo-electric machine, 1864–65; generated powerful electric light for the first time therefrom, 1865; applied the dynamo, with other of his inventions, to the production of the search-light in the Royal Navy, and to the electro-deposition of metals from their solutions, 1868–80; magnetarium for reproducing the phenomena of terrestrial magnetism and the secular variation of the mariner's compass, 1890. Interested himself in the advancement of science and higher education, and gave substantial aid to institutions for the promotion of these objects. *Publications:* original papers in the Phil. Trans and Proc. of the Roy. Soc., Philosophical Magazine, Memoirs of the Manchester Literary and Philosophical Society, Comptes Rendue de l'Académie des Sciences.

Address: The Hurst, Alderley Edge, Cheshire.

Died 29 March 1919.

WILKIE, Alexander, CH 1917; JP; MP (Lab) Dundee, 1906–22; Alderman of Newcastle City Council; was on Education Committee; *b* 30 Sept. 1850; *s* of William Wilkie; *m* 1872, Mary Smillie (*d* 1921); one *s. Educ:* Public School, Fife. Served his apprenticeship to be a ship-constructor, after some sea-going experiences settled in Glasgow; became Secretary of the Glasgow Shipwrights Society, and for seventeen years represented it on the Glasgow Trades Council, of which Council he was President for some considerable time; took an active interest in Glasgow Parliamentary representation; reconstituted, 1882, the then self-contained local Societies into a National and International Association, subseq. the Ship-constructors' and Shipwrights' Assoc. (was appointed Gen. Sec.); represented the Association thereafter and never missed a single meeting on the Trades Union Congress; Member for years of the Parliamentary Committee; topped the Poll at the Edinburgh Congress and was Chairman for the year; member of the Congress Committee which instituted the Labour Representative Committee, now the Labour Party; acted on the Committee for several years; one of the Committee who framed the Rules and Regulations of the General Federation, and one of its Trustees on the Management Committee all along; represented the British Congress at the Detroit Convention of the American Federation of Labour, 1899; Member of the Mosely Industrial Commission to America, 1902; contested Sunderland, 1900. *Address:* Wilkie Chambers, Eldon Square, Newcastle; Leven House, Lesbury Road, Heaton, Newcastle. *Died 2 Sept. 1928.*

WILKIN, Sir Walter (Henry), KCMG 1896; Kt 1893; DL; *b* 1 April 1842; *s* of D. Wilkin, of Kelvedon Hatch, Essex, and City of London; *m* 1870, Margot, *d* of H. R. Dale; two *s* one *d.* Barrister Middle Temple, 1875; Sheriff of London, 1893; Lord Mayor of London, 1895; late Colonel 3rd Middlesex Artillery Volunteers, VD; a Knight Commander of several foreign orders. *Address:* 43 Gloucester Square, Hyde Park, W2. *T:* Paddington 6742; Linton, Cambridgeshire. *Clubs:* City of London, Oriental. *Died 13 Nov. 1922.*

WILKINS, Rev. George, BD; Fellow and Tutor, Trinity College, Dublin. *Educ:* Trinity College, Dublin. BA 1880; MA 1884. Ordained 1891; Fellow, 1891; Junior Dean, 1892; Tutor and Junior Proctor, 1893; Classical Lecturer and Examiner, 1892; Div. Lecturer, 1893; Univ. Select Preacher, 1895; Professor of Hebrew, 1900. *Publications:* The Growth of the Homeric Poems, 1880; Deuteronomy, 1902. *Address:* Trinity College, Dublin.

Died 11 Feb. 1920.

WILKINS, Rev. Henry Russell; Vicar of St John's, Clifton; Hon. Canon of Bristol; late Rural Dean of Clifton; *b* London, Dec. 1859; *s* of George Dashwood Wilkins, Bengal Civil Service; *m* 1887, Mary Christabel (*d* 1922), *d* of Rev. E. G. Penny, MA, Vicar of St Mary-de-Lode, Gloucester; two *s. Educ:* London; Gloucester Theological College. Deacon, 1885; Priest, 1886; worked in or near Bristol all his life. *Address:* St John's Vicarage, Clifton, Bristol.

Died 15 March 1924.

WILKINS, Col James Sutherland, DSO 1891; LRCP, MRCS; Principal Medical Officer, Aden District; *b* 1851; *m* 1905, Dora Sophia Lee (*d* 1906), 2nd *d* of Rev. F. French of Worlingworth Rectory, Suffolk; one *s.* Entered IMS 1874; served Afghan War, 1880–82 (medal); Burmah, 1886–87 (despatches, medal with two clasps, DSO); Kaiser-i-Hind gold medal for public service in India, and silver cross of the Order of the Hospital St John of Jerusalem in England for four years' plague work in India; in charge Concentration Camps, Orange River Colony, 1902–3 (medal, three clasps); Coronation Medal when Mayor of Eye, 1910. *Address:* Stayer House, Eye, Suffolk.

Died 27 Oct. 1916.

WILKINSON, Maj.-Gen. George Allix, RA (retired); *b* 1828; *s* of Robert Wilkinson, Montague Square, W; *m* 1858, Eliza, *d* of Francis Gosling, Sutton, Surrey; two *s* two *d. Educ:* Royal Military Academy, Woolwich. Entered Royal Artillery, 1847; served in Canada, India, and Mediterranean Stations; Passed Staff College; retired as Colonel with honorary rank Major-General, 1880. *Address:* Edenholme, Thorpe Chertsey. *Died 22 Nov. 1919.*

WILKINSON, Sir Hiram Shaw, Kt 1903; Pro-Chancellor, Queen's University, Belfast; *b* Belfast, 13 June 1840; *s* of late John Wilkinson, Belfast, and Annabella, *d* of late William Shaw of Holden's Valley, Waringstown, Co. Down; *m* 1864, Prudie (*d* 1870), *d* of late Thomas Gaffikin; one *s. Educ:* Queen's College, Belfast (BA, LLD); holder of Studentship award by Four Inns of Court, 1871; Barrister, 1872.

Entered Consular Service in Japan as Student Interpreter, 1864; Vice-Consul, 1877; Acting Assistant Judge, Shanghai, 1879–80; Crown Advocate, 1881; British Commissioner for Settlement of Claims after Canton Riots, 1883; Judge of HM Court for Japan, 1897–1900; Chief Justice HM Supreme Court for China and Corea, 1900–5; retired; DL, JP Co. Londonderry; High Sheriff, 1921. *Address:* Moneyshanere, Tobermore, Co. Derry. *TA:* Wilkinson, Tobermore. *Clubs:* Athenæum, Wellington; Ulster, Belfast.

Died 27 Sept. 1926.

WILKINSON, Vice-Adm. Julian Charles Allix; *b* 1859; *s* of late Capt. James Allix Wilkinson, 15th Regt (later East Yorkshire); *m* Frances, *o d* of late J. W. Welby, late of Cromwell Road, SW. *Educ:* Rev. Arthur Watson's, Egypt House, Cowes. Joined HMS Britannia as Naval Cadet, 1872; Midshipman, 1874; Sub-Lieut, 1878; Lieut, 1882; Comr, 1895; Capt., 1900; commanded HMS Iris, Hawkes, Thetis, London; Inspecting Captain, Western District of Coastguards; Good Service Pension, 1907; Rear-Admiral, 1909; retired 1911. *Club:* United Service. *Died 13 Nov. 1917.*

WILKINSON, Lancelot Craven, FRGS; Adviser to Russian Government on Oriental matters; *s* of Edward Wilkinson, MA, PhD. *Educ:* Harrow; Cheltenham; St Bartholomew's Hospital; abroad. ADC to HSM the Sultan of Morocco, 1908–10; served South African Campaign, 1899–1902, Warwickshire Imperial Yeomanry; Lieut Intelligence Department HQS, and later attached to 7th Dragoon Guards (Queen's medal, 3 bars, King's medal, 2 bars); Hispano-Moorish Campaign, 1910, War Correspondent to New York Herald and Daily Mail (medal and clasp); Moorish Civil War, 1908, attached to HSM Sultan (Moulai Hafid) Personal Staff; Belgrade, 1904, present at assassination of King Alexander with British Consul; MRCS (Eng.), LRCP (Lond.); Chief personal adviser to Secretary of State for War on Foreign Political Matters, 1914–15; senior resident surgeon to the Saideih Hospital, Cairo, 1916. Inventor and patentee of Mehamo process for economising and rendering fuel smokeless, 1907. *Publications:* several works on preventive inoculation and autogenous vaccines as applied to surgery on the field of battle. *Recreations:* Oriental literature and travel. *Club:* Sports.

Died 28 July 1923.

WILKINSON, Rev. Michael Marlow Umfreville; Rector of Reepham St Mary since 1864; Hon. Canon, Norwich, 1902; *b* 10 Dec. 1831; *m* 1866; three *d. Educ:* Trinity College, Cambridge (Scholar, 5th Wrangler). Fellow and Assistant Tutor, Trinity College, 1855–65; Diocesan Inspector, Norwich, 1875–88. *Address:* Reepham Rectory, Norwich. *Died 22 March 1916.*

WILKINSON, Major Thomas Henry Desvœux, DSO 1887; retired pay; *b* London, 11 June 1858; *e s* of Rt Rev. the Bishop of St Andrews, and Caroline, *d* of Lieut-Col Benfield Desvœux, late Scots Guards. *Educ:* Royal Military Coll., Sandhurst. Joined Rifle Brigade, 1879; served in Mahsood Waziri Expedition, 1881; Burmese Expedition, 1886–88 (despatches, DSO, India medal and two clasps); received the Jubilee Decoration of 22 June 1897. *Club:* Naval and Military. *Died 27 Jan. 1928.*

WILKS, Rev. William, MA; VMH, FRHS; *b* Ashford, Kent, 19 Oct. 1843; *s* of Dr G. F. Wilks, of Ashford. *Educ:* under the great scientist, Prof. Charles Pritchard; Pembroke College, Cambridge. After 2 years accepted the Curacy of Croydon; about 1880 became a member of the Floral Committee of RHS, and was elected to a seat on the Council and appointed Hon. Sec. 1888; resigned, 1919; Vicar of Shirley, Surrey, 1879–1912. *Publications:* many papers in the Journal of the Society. *Recreation:* growth and study of plants of all kinds. *Address:* The Wilderness, Shirley, Croydon.

Died 2 March 1923.

WILLANS, Lt-Col Thomas James, DSO 1915; late 57th Wilde's Rifles, Frontier Force; *b* 2 Sept. 1872. Entered army, 1893; Capt. Indian Army, 1902; Major, 1911; served NW Frontier, India, 1897–8 (medal with clasp); European War, 1914–17 (despatches, DSO); retired 1921. *Died 11 Dec. 1922.*

WILLCOCKS, G. Waller, CB 1911; MICE; Chief Engineering Inspector, Local Government Board, 1902–13; *m* 1884, Mary, *e d* of late Rowland Escombe; two *s* one *d. Address:* Redthorn, Rodway Road, Roehampton, SW. *Died 7 July 1918.*

WILLCOCKS, General Sir James, GCB 1921 (KCB 1914; CB 1907); GCMG 1915 (KCMG 1900; CMG 1899); KCSI 1913; DSO 1887; Colonel Loyal Regiment; *b* 1 April 1857; 4th *s* of late Capt. W. Willcocks, HEICS; *m* 1889, Winifred, 2nd *d* of Colonal G. A.

Way, CB; one s. Educ: Tutors; Easton, Somersetshire. Entered Army, 1878; Captain Leinster Regt 1884; Major, 1893; Lieut-Col, 1899; Colonel, 1902; Maj.-Gen., 1906; Lt-Gen., 1908; General, 1916; served in Afghan Campaign, 1879–80 (medal); Waziri Expedition, 1881 (despatches); Soudan Campaign, 1885 (medal with clasp and bronze star); Burma Expedition, 1886–89 (medal with 2 clasps, despatches, DSO); Chin Lushai Expedition, 1889–90 (clasp); Munipoor Expedition, 1891 (despatches, clasp); as AAG with Tochi Field Force, 1897 (despatches, medal with clasp, Brevet of Lieut-Col); as 2nd in command West African Frontier Force, 1898; Borgu, 1898 (medal with clasp); received the special thanks of HM Government; temporary Lieut-Col, Nov. 1897; Commanded West African Frontier Force, 1899–1900; local Colonel Sept. 1898; in command of Ashanti Field Force; Relief of Kumasi, 1900 (Brevet of Colonel); KCMG; received the freedom of the City of London, and a sword of honour; mentioned in King's Speech at opening of his first Parliament; joined Field Force in South Africa, 1902 (medal and clasp); commanding Nowshera Brigade, India, 1902–7; Zakka Khel Expedition, 1908; served European War, 1914–15 (despatches twice, GCMG); Governor of Bermuda, 1917–22; retired pay, 1922; Grand Officer Legion of Honour; LLD of Amherst College, United States, 1918. Publications: From Cabul to Kumassi, 1904; With the Indians in France, 1920; The Romance of Soldiering and Sport, 1925. Recreations: big game shooting, riding, polo. Club: Naval and Military.

Died 18 Dec. 1926.

WILLES, William, MRCS; LRCPE; Consulting Physician to the Miller General Hospital for South-East London; late Additional Medical Officer to the Royal Naval College and Royal Hospital School, Greenwich; b 1855; s of late William P. Willes, solicitor, Weymouth, Dorset; m Emily Kate, d of W. W. Rawes, late Deputy Inspector of Hospitals, Madras Army; two s. Educ: Bath College; St Bartholomew's Hospital. Resident Medical Officer at Royal Free Hospital, Royal United Hospital, Bath, and Royal Sea Bathing Infirmary, Margate; in practice at Greenwich since 1883. Address: Thornleigh, Bodorgan Road, Bournemouth. T: 2815. Club: Bournemouth.

Died 7 May 1924.

WILLIAMS, Capt. Albert, MVO 1908 and 1922; Mus. Doc. Oxon, 1906; late Director of Music, Grenadier Guards; b Newport, Monmouth, 1864. Bandmaster, Grenadier Guards, 1897; Liveryman, Musicians' Company; Conductor, National Welsh Festival; Member Musical Association and Madrigal Society; retired pay, 1921. Club: Savage.

Died 10 Feb. 1926.

WILLIAMS, Maj.-Gen. Sir Albert Henry Wilmot, KCVO 1904; Colonel Commandant RHA; b 7 Feb. 1832; s of late J. W. Williams, of Herringston, Dorset. Entered army, 1849; Captain, 1856; Major, 1872; Lieut-Colonel, 1875; Colonel, 1880. Served Crimea, 1885 (medal with clasp, Turkish medal); Indian Mutiny, 1858 (despatches); Central India (medal). Address: 22 Chesham Place, SW. Clubs: United Service, Turf, Marlborough.

Died 29 Oct. 1919.

WILLIAMS, Aneurin, JP; MP (L) Plymouth, 1910; North-West Durham, 1914; Consett Division, 1918–22; Chairman of House of Commons Committee on Public Accounts, 1921 and 1922; Director, First Garden City, Ltd. Joint Hon. Sec., Labour Copartnership Assoc.; Member of Executive, League of Nations Union; Treasurer, Proportional Representation Society; b Dowlais, Glamorganshire, 11 Oct. 1859; 2nd s of late Edward Williams, CE, JP, ironmaster, of Cleveland Lodge, Middlesbrough; m 1888, Helen Elizabeth (d 1922), d of John Pattinson, JP, of Shipcote House, Gateshead; one s one d. Educ: private school; St John's College, Cambridge (MA Classical Tripos, 1880). Called to Bar, Inner Temple, 1884; one of acting partners, Linthorpe Ironworks, Middlesbrough, 1886–90; contested Mid-Kent (L), 1906. Publications: Copartnership and Profitsharing; Twenty-eight Years of Copartnership at Guise; article on Co-operative Societies in the Encyclopædia Britannica, etc. Address: Hindhead, Surrey. TA: Hindhead. Clubs: Reform, National Liberal, Eighty.

Died 20 Jan. 1924.

WILLIAMS, Anna; Professor of Singing; b 3 Campden Hill Terrace, W, of English parents; m 1910, R. J. Fennessy. Educ: Queen's College; Bedford College. Commenced in 1874 in concerts, oratorios, ballads, also in opera; retired 13 Oct. 1897. Recreations: rowing, walking, gymnastics, fencing, cycling. Address: 72 Comeragh Road, Baron's Court, W.

Died 3 Sept. 1924.

WILLIAMS, Brig.-Gen. Arthur Blount Cuthbert, CB 1913; Director of Supplies and Transport, India, since 1912; b 1 Dec. 1860. Entered army, 1881; Captain, ISC, 1892; Major Indian army, 1901;

Lieut-Col, 1907; served Relief of Chitral (medal with clasp); China, 1900 (despatches, medal); NW Frontier, India, 1908 (despatches, medal with clasp). Address: QMG's Branch, Simla, India.

Died 20 June 1918.

WILLIAMS, Rt. Rev. Arthur Llewellyn, DD; Bishop of Nebraska since 1908; b Canada, 30 Jan. 1856; s of Richard Jones Williams, and Elizabeth Johnstone; m 1880, Adelaide M'Kinstry; one d. Educ: Greenwich Academy; Western Theological Seminary. Deacon, 1888; Priest, 1889; Missionary, White River, Colorado, 1888–92; Rector, Christ Church, Chicago, 1892–99; Bishop Coadjutor of Nebraska, 1899. Publications: occasional sermons and current articles. Address: 1716 Dodge Street, Omaha, Neb., USA.

Died 29 Jan. 1919.

WILLIAMS, Sir (Arthur) Osmond, 1st Bt, cr 1909; JP, DL Carnarvonshire and Merionethshire; Chairman Quarter Sessions; Lord-Lieutenant of Merionethshire; Constable of Harlech Castle, 1909; b 17 March 1849; s of David Williams, first Liberal Member (1868) for Merionethshire since the Commonwealth; m 1880, Frances Evelyn (d 1926), 4th d of J. W. Greaves of Berricote, Warwickshire; one s two d (and two s decd). Was Chairman of Merioneth County Council for three years; MP (R) Merionethshire, 1900–10. Heir: g s (Michael) Osmond Williams, b 22 April 1914. Address: Castle Deudraeth, Penrhyn Deudraeth, N Wales. Clubs: Boodle's, Ranelagh, Brooks's.

Died 28 Jan. 1927.

WILLIAMS, Sir Burton Robert, 6th Bt, cr 1866; b 7 July 1889; 3rd s of Sir William Williams, 3rd Bt and Matilda Frances, d of E. B. Beauchamp of Trevince, Redruth; S brother, 1913. late Lieut 3rd Batt. Devon Regiment; rejoined Aug. 1914; served European War, 1914–17. Owner of about 4,500 acres. Heir: u Captain Frederick Law Williams, b 10 May 1862. Club: Naval and Military.

Died 3 Oct. 1917.

WILLIAMS, Rt. Rev. Charles David, DD, LHD, LLD; Bishop of Michigan, USA, since 1906; b 30 July 1860; s of David and Eliza Williams; m 1886, Lucy Victoria, d of Rev. Samuel Benedict, Rector of St Paul's Church, Cincinnatti, Ohio; four s five d. Educ: Kenyon College; Bexley Theological Seminary, Gambier, Ohio. Tutor, Kenyon College, 1880–84; Assistant at Trinity Church, Columbus, Ohio, 1884; Rector, Church of the Resurrection, Fern Bank, Ohio, 1884–89; St Paul's Church, Steubenville, Ohio, 1889–93; Dean of Trinity Cathedral, Cleveland, Ohio, 1893–1906. Publications: various sermons and sociological pamphlets; A Valid Chistianity for To-day; The Christian Ministry and Social Problems. Address: 24 Eliot Street, Detroit, Michigan, USA. TA: Woodward 2326 and Detroit, Michigan. T: Glendale 196, Main 9583. M: Mich. 23140. Clubs: Cobden; City, New York.

Died 14 Feb. 1923.

WILLIAMS, Charles Riby, CMG 1902; b 1857; m 1892; one d. Member of the Legislative and Executive Councils, Gold Coast; Supervisor of Customs, Gold Coast Colony, 1884; District Commissioner, 1887; Comptroller of Customs, 1890; Chief British Commissioner Anglo-German Boundary Commission, 1892; Treasurer of the Gold Coast Colony, 1895–1909; Acting Colonial Secretary various periods; retired 1909.

Died 13 Dec. 1924.

WILLIAMS, Chisholm, FRCS 1891; Electro-Therapeutist, London Homœopathic Hospital; b London, 10 April 1866; 2nd s of late D. C. Williams, HMC; m 1893, Amy Hannah, d of late W. Woodward, Camberwell; two d. Educ: privately; King's College, London; St Thomas' Hospital. Member Royal College of Surgeons, England, 1892; Past President W Kent Medical-Chirurgical Society; Past President British Electro-Therapeutic Society; Member, British Medical Association, British Orthopædic Society, etc; late Lecturer London School Board; late Electro-Therapeutist and Surgeon late City Orthopædic Hospital; Lecturer on Electro-Therapeutics, West London Hospital Post-Graduate College; St John's Hospital for Skin Diseases. Publications: High Frequency Electrical Currents in the Treatment of some Diseases, 1901; X-Rays in the Treatment of Cancer, Lancet, 1905; and in Archives of Röntgen Rays, 1906; many other papers on X-Rays and Cancer. Recreations: electrical and mechanical experiments, photography. Address: Heriot House, Hendon; Breakers, Shoreham, Sussex. T: Mayfair 3815; 295 PO Finchley. Club: Royal Automobile.

Died 10 April 1928.

WILLIAMS, C. F. Abdy; engaged in musical literary work; b 1855; s of Charles Abdy Williams and Eliza Ellen Windsor; m 1881, Ellen Margaret, d of Frederick Bayard Elton of Whitestaunton Manor,

Somerset. *Educ:* Sherborne; Trinity Hall, Cambridge. Composed music in the Greek modes for the Greek plays at Bradfield College, 1895, 1898, 1900. *Publications:* Historical Account of Degrees in Music at Oxford and Cambridge; Life of J. S. Bach; Life of Handel; Story of Musical Notation; Story of the Organ; Story of Organ Music; The Rhythm of Modern Music; The Aristoxenian Theory of Rhythm; articles and lectures on Ancient Greek Music, Plainsong, etc. *Recreation:* yachting. *Address:* South Mead, Milford-on-Sea, Hants. *Club:* Royal Cruising. *Died 27 Feb. 1923.*

WILLIAMS, David, BA (Wales), MA (Oxon); Professor in Pastoral Theology at the United Theological College, Bala, since 1922; *b* Holyhead, 4 May 1877; *s* of Eliezer and Elizabeth Williams; *m* 1905, Margaret Catherine Owen, Holyhead; no *c. Educ:* Park Board School, Holyhead; High School, Oswestry; University College of Wales, Aberystwyth; Jesus College, Oxford. Pastor of Clifton Street Church (Presbyterian Church of Wales), 1903–5; Professor of Church History at Trevecca College, 1905–6; Professor of New Testament Exegesis at the Theological College, Aberystwyth, 1906–22; Chaplain to HM Forces, 1916–18. *Publications:* Commentaries (in Welsh) on Galatians and 2 Corinthians; assistant editor of and contributor to Welsh Bible Dictionary; articles in religious and theological magazines. *Recreations:* golf, tennis, walking. *Address:* Theological College, Bala, North Wales. *Died 11 July 1927.*

WILLIAMS, Ven. David Edward, MA; Archdeacon of St Davids since 1900; Rector of Bosherston, Pembroke, since 1912; *b* 1847; *y s* of Matthew Davies Williams, JP, DL of Cwmcynfelin, Cardiganshire; *m* 1879, Rose (*d* 1909), *d* of Joshua Paynter, CB; two *d. Educ:* Exeter Coll., Oxford (MA). Formerly curate of St David's, Carmarthen; Vicar of St Michael's, Pembroke, 1877–83; All Saints, Glasbury, 1883; Llanfrynach, 1883–89; Llawhaden, 1889–97; Lampeter Velfrey, 1897–1901; Chaplain to late Bishop of St Davids, 1893–97; Rector of Johnston with Steynton, 1901–12. *Address:* Bosherston Rectory, Pembroke. *Club:* Junior Constitutional. *Died 23 March 1920.*

WILLIAMS, Sir Dawson, Kt 1921; CBE 1919; MD; FRCP; editor of the British Medical Journal since 1898; consulting physician to East London Hospital for Children, Shadwell; *b* Ulleskelf, Yorkshire, 17 July 1854; *e s* of Rev. John Mack Williams, formerly Rector of Burnby, Yorks, and Ellen, *d* of Nicolas Monsarrat; *m* 1882, Catherine (*d* 1917), *d* of Robert Kirkpatrick-Howat, DL, of Mabie, Kirkcudbrightshire. *Educ:* Pocklington; University Coll. London. MB (honours), BS, 1879; MD 1881, University of London; FRCP London, 1895; Hon. DSc Sheffield, 1908; Hon. DLitt Durham, 1921; Hon. LLD Glasgow; Fellow of University College, London. *Publication:* Medical Diseases of Infancy and Childhood, 1898. *Address:* British Medical Association House, Tavistock Square, WC1. *TA:* Aitiology, Westcent, London. *T:* Museum 9864. *Clubs:* Garrick, Bath. *Died 27 Feb. 1928.*

WILLIAMS, Edith; Professor of English, Ecole Normale, Fontenay aux Roses. Chevalier, Legion of Honour. *Address:* International Guild, 6 Rue de la Sorbonne, Paris. *Died 16 Feb. 1919.*

WILLIAMS, Maj.-Gen. Edward Charles Ingouville, CB 1910; DSO 1900; Lieutenant-Colonel, The Buffs; Commanding 16th Infantry Brigade since 1912; *b* 13 Dec. 1861; *s* of late Gen. Sir J. W. C. Williams, KCB. Served Soudan, 1884–85 (medal with clasp, bronze star); Nile, 1898 (despatches twice, Brevet Major, Egyptian medal with 2 clasps, medal); Nile, 1899 (clasp); S Africa, 1899–1902 (despatches five times, Brevet Lieut-Colonel, Queen's medal, 6 clasps, King's medal, 2 clasps, DSO); European War, 1914–15 (despatches twice); Maj.-Gen., 1915. *Club:* Naval and Military. *Died 22 July 1916.*

WILLIAMS, Sir Frederick Law, 7th Bt, *cr* 1866; Captain, late Dorset Regiment; *b* 10 May 1862; *s* of Sir Frederick Williams, 2nd Bt and Mary Christian (*d* 1892), *d* of Rev. V. Law, Rector of Christian Malford, Wilts; *S* nephew, 1917; *m* 1899, Emily, *d* of William Reid, Downpatrick; one *s* two *d.* Heir: *s* William Law Williams, *b* 1 May 1907. *Club:* Naval and Military. *Died 20 Dec. 1921.*

WILLIAMS, Rev. George H.; Rector of Remenham, Henley-on-Thames; *b* Bangor, North Wales, 23 May 1859; *s* of late T. Williams, Caederwen, Upper Bangor; *m* 1887, Florence Marion, *d* of late A. Ogle, Burnley; one *s* one *d. Educ:* Friars School, Bangor; Christ Coll., Brecon; Jesus Coll., Oxford; (Classical Scholar) 2nd Class Classical Mods. 1881; 2nd Class Greats, 1883; BA 1883; MA 1887. Second

Master of Loughborough Grammar School, 1884–89; Curate of Loughborough, 1887–89; Head Master of Kingsbridge Grammar School, 1889–91; Kendal Grammar School, 1891–1901; Carlisle Grammar School, 1901–12; Chief Examiner in Latin for Central Welsh Board, 1913, 1914, 1915, 1916, 1917. *Publication:* Careers for our Sons. *Address:* Remenham Rectory, Henley-on-Thames. *T:* Henley 191. *Club:* Authors'. *Died 9 Sept. 1926.*

WILLIAMS, Rt. Rev. Gershom Mott, AM, DD; Bishop in charge of American Episcopal Churches in Europe since 1913; *b* Fort Hamilton, NY, 11 Feb. 1857; *s* of Gen. Thomas Williams and Mary Neosho Bailey; *m* Eliza, *d* of Wm S. Biddle; four *s* three *d. Educ:* Newburgh (NY) Academy; Cornell University. Admitted to Michigan Bar, 1879. Deacon, 1880; Priest, 1882; Rector of Messiah Church, Detroit, 1882–84; St George's, Detroit, 1884–89; Dean of Milwaukee Cathedral, 1889–91; Archdeacon of Northern Michigan, 1891–96; Editor American Church Times, 1888–89; Chaplain Michigan State Troops, 1884–88; Member of the Psi Upsilon Fraternity, the Military Order of the Loyal Legion, the American Historical Association, the Lambeth Conferences, 1897 and 1908; Member of Lambeth Commission of Conference with the Church of Sweden; Bishop of the Diocese of Marquette (the Northern Peninsula of Michigan, USA), 1896–1919. *Publications:* Sacramental Teachings, 1884; Between Two Christmas Days, Poems, 1888; The Church of Sweden and the Anglican Communion, 1910; Human Questions and Divine Answers, 1913; editor of the Hymnal of the Protestant Episcopal Church as adopted 1916; Sermons, Addresses, and Charges; contributor to The Churchman, The Living Church, The Church Eclectic, etc. *Recreations:* travel, woodcraft. *Address:* 12 Southgate Avenue, Annapolis, USA. *T:* 351. *M:* 31760. *Clubs:* Annapolitan; Knickerbocker Yacht, New York. *Died 14 April 1923.*

WILLIAMS, Col Henry David, CMG 1918; JP, DL, Staffordshire; retired pay; *b* 1854; *m* 1888, Ethel Louisa (*d* 1921), *d* of late Rev. Canon Montagu Hankey. Served Zhob Valley Expedition, 1884. *Address:* Lambert House, Dorchester. *Club:* Naval and Military. *Died 21 July 1924.*

WILLIAMS, Herbert; Medical Officer of Health for the Port of London since 1901; *b* Weymouth, 1862; *s* of Alderman T. H. Williams, JP; unmarried. *Educ:* privately; London University, St Bartholomew's Hospital. Graduated MB Lond. with honours in Medicine and Physiology, 1888; appointed Medical Officer to the Metropolitan Hospital, and subsequently became House Physician to Dr Gee at St Bart's Hosp. for one year; then Resident House Surgeon in charge of the ward for diseases, etc, of the eyes; MD 1890; entered service of Corporation of City of London, 1892, as Assistant Port Medical Officer, took Diploma of Public Health at Cambridge University, and again graduated as MD in State Medicine at London University. *Recreations:* golf, rowing; late Major in 1st Kent Royal Garrison Artillery Volunteers, passed the School of Instruction, Woolwich, and obtained the Artillery certificate; acted as Adjutant of the Corps during the South African War, 1902. *Address:* 51 King William Street, Greenwich. *TA:* Medoff Green, London. *T:* 36 New Cross. *Clubs:* Junior Army and Navy; Walton Heath Golf, Sundridge Park Golf. *Died 16 Jan. 1916.*

WILLIAMS, Hugh Neol; author; *b* Newport, Monmouthshire, 20 Jan. 1870; *s* of late William Williams of Clifton Down, Bristol; *m* 1st, Florence Lulu Holdom; one *s*; 2nd, Eva Kathleen Deane; two *d. Educ:* Clifton College; St John's Coll., Oxford. BA (honours in Modern History), 1892. *Publications:* Madame Récamier, 1901; Madame de Pompadour, 1902; Madame de Montespan, 1903; The Hand of Léonore, 1904; Madame du Barry, 1904; Queens of the French Stage, 1905; Later Queens of the French Stage, 1906; Five Fair Sisters, 1906; Queen Margot, 1906; A Princess of Intrigue, 1907; The Women Bonapartes, 1908; A Rose of Savoy, 1909; The Fascinating Duc de Richelieu, 1910; Henri II: his Court and Times, 1910; A Princess of Adventure, 1911; The Love Affairs of the Condes, 1912; Unruly Daughters, 1913; A Fair Conspirator, 1913; Rival Sultanas, 1915; Tainted Gold, 1915; The Pearl of Princesses, 1916; The Independence of Belgium, 1916; Sir Douglas Haig's Great Push: the Battle of the Somme, 1917; Life and Letters of Admiral Sir Charles Napier, KCB, 1917; The Brood of False Lorraine, 1919; The Grasshampton Stable, 1921; A Gallant of Lorraine, 1921; The Moneylender Intervenes, 1923; Last Loves of Henri of Navarre, 1925. *Address:* c/o Cree & Turner, 109 Jermyn Street, SW1. *Died 13 Oct. 1925.*

WILLIAMS, James Alexander, ISO 1903; District Commissioner, Gold Coast, 1889–1907; *b* 18 June 1856; *s* of George Shotan and Maria

Williams; *m* 1st, 1881, Rebecca Elizabeth, 5th *d* of Rev. Peter William Bernasko, WMS, Gold Coast; 2nd, 1913, Kate Otema, *d* of Joseph Kwaku-Adjaye of Akwapim, Gold Coast Colony. *Educ:* Grammar School, Lagos. Entered public service at Lagos as Messenger and Copyist, Secretariat and Treasury, 1871; Clerk and Keeper Debtors' Prison, 1875; 2nd Clerk Governor's Office, Gold Coast, 1876; Chief Clerk, 1877; Special Interpreter to Benin with the late Governor Young, 1884; Clerk of Legislative Council, 1886–87; retired 1907. *Address:* 11 Oke Olowogbowo, Lagos; Williamsville, Dodowah, via Accra, Gold Coast Colony. *Died 19 Jan. 1937.*

WILLIAMS, Hon. James Rowland, MA Oxon; Director of Education, Jamaica, since 1909; *b* Jamaica, 1860; *m* 1888, Margaret Emily Caroline, 3rd *d* of Maj.-Gen. W. T. Freke Farewell, retired Indian Army, of Bath; three *s* three *d*. *Educ:* Somersetshire College, Bath; Trinity College, Oxford (Scholar). Inspector of Schools, Jamaica, 1884–1909; Acting Assistant Colonial Secretary, Jamaica, 1906–7; attended as Government delegate at Conference on Trade Relations between West Indies and Canada, at Barbados, 1908, and at West Indian Agricultural Conferences at Barbados and Trinidad as representative of the Jamaica Agricultural Society; member Legislative Council, Jamaica, 1910; acted as Member of Privy Council, Jamaica, 1913. *Publication:* School Gardens, for elementary schools in Jamaica, 1907. *Recreations:* anything that is going. *Address:* Education Office, Kingston, Jamaica; Kew Park, Westmoreland, Jamaica. *Died 23 April 1916.*

WILLIAMS, Sir John, 1st Bt, *cr* 1894; GCVO 1911 (KCVO 1902); MD; FRCP; President of the University College of Wales; President of the National Library of Wales; Emeritus Professor of Midwifery at University College, London, and Consulting Obstetric Physician to the Hospital; Hon. Fellow of the Royal Society of Medicine; *b* Carmarthenshire, 6 Nov. 1840; 3rd *s* of Rev. David Williams, Blaenllynant; *m* 1872, Mary (*d* 1915), *d* of Richard Hughes, Ynistawe. *Educ:* Normal Coll., Swansea; University College, London (Fellow). Member, Gen. Council of Med. Education and Registration, 1901; lately physician accoucheur to HRH The Princess of Wales and physician to HRH Princess Beatrice. High Sheriff, Carmarthenshire, 1904. Hon. LLD Edin., Glas., and Aber.; DSc (Hon.) Wales. Grand Cross of Dannebrog. *Publications:* papers in Obstetric Medicine. *Heir:* none. *Address:* Blaenllynant, Aberystwyth. *Died 24 May 1926 (ext).*

WILLIAMS, John, JP County Glamorgan; MP (Lab) Gower Division of Glamorganshire since 1906; Advisory Agent for the Western Miners Association; Lecturer in Economics; Welsh Poet; Baptist Minister; *b* 1861. General Secretary, Amalgamated Society of S Wales Colliery Workers, 1890; on Mountain Ash District Council. A Governor of the Univ. Colls of Wales. *Address:* 36 Charlwood Street, SW; Swansea. *Died 20 June 1922.*

WILLIAMS, John David, JP; farmer; *b* Blaenclydach Farm, Clydach Vale, Rhondda, 12 July 1853; *s* of late John and Mary Williams, Flynon Dwyn Farm, Clydach Vale; *m* 1882, Ann Llewellyn; two *s* six *d*. *Educ:* British School, Trecherburt; Christ College, Cardiff. Devoted his time and attention chiefly to farming; a Director of the Rhondda Valley Brewery Co. upwards of 40 years; a Director of the Cardiff Malting Co. Ltd for upwards of 23 years, also Director of the Town Hall Co. Ltd, Ton-y-Pandy, for 15 years; ex-Chairman and member of Rhondda District Council for over 25 years, and member of the Pontypridd Board of Guardians for 6 years; was Master of the Ystrad and Pentyrch Foxhounds for 12 years up to 1902; then master of the Ystrad Foxhounds. *Recreations:* hunting, shooting. *Address:* Clydach Court, Trealaw, Rhondda Valley. *T:* Porth 126. *Died 19 Sept. 1923.*

WILLIAMS, Joseph Grout, JP; *b* 1848; *e s* of late Rev. James Williams, of Pendley, and Elizabeth, *d* of late James Grout; *m* 1878, Catharine Mary, *d* of late Robert Tidswell. *Educ:* Harrow; Trinity College, Cambridge. High Sheriff, Herts, 1889; JP Herts and Bucks. *Address:* Pendley Manor, Tring, Hertfordshire. *Died 9 Oct. 1923.*

WILLIAMS, Maj.-Gen. Lawrence Henry; Indian Army; *b* 14 Oct. 1834. Entered army, 1850; Maj.-Gen. 1891; retired list, 1891; served Indian Mutiny, 1857 (medal); Cossyah and Jyntiah Hills Campaign, 1862–63; NW Frontier of India, 1863 (medal with clasp); Afghan War, 1878 (medal with clasp); Mahsud Waziri Expedition, 1881 (despatches). *Address:* 46 Castle Hill Avenue, Folkestone. *Died 13 July 1916.*

WILLIAMS, Col Leslie Gwatkin, CMG 1919; DSO 1916; late 5th Cavalry, Indian Army; *b* 1878; *m* 1921, Helen Mary (*née* Landale), *widow* of Dr W. B. Grandage; one *d*. Served South African War, 1900–1 (Queen's medal and five clasps); European War, 1914–18 (despatches, CMG, DSO, Bt Lt-Col, Legion of Honour); retired, 1922. *Address:* 74 Gloucester Road, SW7. *Club:* Cavalry. *Died 28 Jan. 1926.*

WILLIAMS, Sir Ralph (Champneys), KCMG 1907 (CMG 1901); *b* 9 March 1848; *s* of Rev. T. N. Williams, of Treffos, Anglesey; *m* 1875, Jessie (*d* 1917), *y d* of Samuel Dean; one *s*. *Educ:* Rossall. Explored in Patagonia, 1873–74; in Central Africa, 1883–84; head of the Civil Intelligence Department, Bechuanaland Expedition, 1884–85; was also special correspondent of the Standard, 1884–85; appointed British Consular Officer, South African Republic, 1887; appointed 1st British Agent, South African Republic, with letter of credence, 1888; appointed Colonial Treasurer of Gibraltar, 1890; and also to the associated office of Captain of the Port of Gibraltar, 1895; received silver medal and vellum certificate from the Italian Government for services in connection with the wreck of the 'Utopia,' 1891; Colonial Secretary of Barbados, with dormant commission of Governor, 1897–1901; Resident Commissioner Bechuanaland Protectorate, 1901–6; Governor, Windward Islands, 1906–9; Governor of Newfoundland, 1909–13; President of the 2nd Line of Defence for the War in British East Africa, Aug. 1914; invalided home, April 1915, and received the thanks of the Governor and the General Officer commanding; a Governor of Rossall School. *Publications:* The British Lion in Bechuanaland; How I became a Governor, 1913. *Recreation:* ceaseless travelling to far-away countries. *Clubs:* St James', MCC, Royal Thames Yacht. *Died 22 June 1927.*

WILLIAMS, Rt. Hon. Sir Roland Lomax Bowdler Vaughan, Kt 1890; PC 1897; Lord Justice of the Court of Appeal, 1897–1914; *b* 1838; *m* 1865, Laura Susannah, *d* of Edmund Lomax of Netley and Tanhurst, Surrey; one *s*. *Educ:* Christ Church, Oxford (BA 1860). Barrister, Lincoln's Inn, 1861; QC 1889; Judge Supreme Court, Queen's Bench Division, 1890–97. *Address:* 6 Trebovir Road, SW; High Ashe's Farm, Abinger, Dorking. *Club:* Athenæum. *Died 8 Dec. 1916.*

WILLIAMS, Samuel Charles Evans, JP; *b* 20 May 1842; *o s* of late Rev. John Williams, of Bryntirion, and Jane, *widow* of John Patterson, of Devon; *m* 1867, Mary Caroline, *d* of Rev. Henry William Robinson Luttman-Johnson, of Binderton House, Sussex; five *d*. *Educ:* Westminster; Christ Church, Oxford, MA. High Sheriff, Radnor, 1880; MP (L) Radnor, 1880–84. *Address:* 69 Knightsbridge, SW1. *Club:* National Liberal. *Died 2 March 1926.*

WILLIAMS, Rev. Thomas Charles, MA; Minister of the Welsh Presbyterian Church, Menai Bridge, North Wales; *s* of Rev. Hugh Williams, and *g s* of late Rev. John Charles, Gwalchmai, Anglesey; the family served as ministers, from father to son, for over a hundred years; *m* 1911, Evelyn, *d* of David Jones, Manager, Metropolitan Bank, Conway. *Educ:* Oswestry High School; Bala College; Abersytwyth University College; Jesus College, Oxford, graduated in Honours, 1898. Brought up to the ministry; settled in Menai Bridge when he left Oxford, and in spite of calls to English and Welsh churches in the big towns remained there but travelled extensively, both in this country and in America; preached often in London in Welsh and in the leading English churches; late Chaplain 6th Batt. RWF; Secretary General Assembly, 1913–14, and Member Welsh Theological Board; Moderator North Wales Presbyterian Synod, 1918–19; Moderator of the General Assembly for 1921–22; DD Edinburgh University, 1923; preached the Council Sermon at the Pan-Presbyterian Alliance in Cardiff, 1925; in Liverpool Cathedral, 28 Feb. 1926. *Address:* Menai Bridge, Anglesey. *Died 2 Oct. 1927.*

WILLIAMS, Thomas Jeremiah, JP Glamorganshire; MP (L) Swansea District, since 1915; Director of various firms; Barrister-at-law; *b* 1872; *e s* of late William Williams, former MP Swansea District, JP Glamorganshire, and Margret Jeremiah; *m* 1912, Laura Alice, *y d* of late Thomas Marlow, Southport; one *d*. *Educ:* University College School, London; Technical College, Sheffield; Firth College. Technical and commercial training; practised at the Bar, South Wales and Chester Circuit, etc; travelled Canada, America, Japan, China, India, Egypt, the whole of Europe; contested West Glamorgan, 1905. *Recreations:* shooting, motoring. *Address:* Maes-y-Gwernen Hall, near Swansea. *T:* Morriston 90. *M:* CT 1580. *Clubs:* Royal Automobile; Bristol Channel Yacht; Swansea and Counties. *Died 12 June 1919.*

WILLIAMS, Lt-Col Thomas Samuel Beauchamp; MP (Lab) Kennington Division of Lambeth, 1923–24; IMS, retired; *b* Bangor, 1877; *s* of late Ven. Thomas Williams, Archdeacon of Merioneth. *Educ:* Edinburgh University, MB, ChB. Served European War, 1914–19 (despatches, Bt Lt-Col). Contested Bridgwater Division of Somerset, 1922; Kennington, 1924; Eastbourne, 1925; Parliamentary Private Secretary to President of Board of Trade, 1924. *Address:* Imperial Chambers, 3 Cursitor Street, WC.

Died July 1927.

WILLIAMS, W. Phillpotts; late Master East Cornwall Foxhounds; *b* 1860; *m d* of Canon Simpson of Bexhill; one *d.* Master of Netton Harriers, South Molton Harriers, Hursley Foxhounds, and subseq. pack; always interested in the question of the National Horse Supply; founded the Brood Mare Society, which resulted in present government grant of £45,000 a year; worked also at the building up of a genuine reserve of horses within the country; supported Mr Tilling when obtaining the additional grant of £40,000 a year for subsidising 10,000 transport horses; strong advocate of the retaining principle. *Publications:* Poems in Pink; Over the Open. *Recreations:* horses and hounds, Imperial Federation work for the Colonies. *Address:* Barnfield House, Liskeard, Cornwall.

Died 31 Aug. 1916.

WILLIAMS, Surg.-Gen. Sir William Daniel Campbell, KCMG 1916; CB 1900; Knight of Grace of the Order of St John of Jerusalem; Director-General Army Medical Services, Commonwealth Defence, 1902; *b* Sydney, New South Wales, 30 July 1856; *s* of late William James Williams, MD; *m* 1881, Florence, *d* of late Henry A. Severn; one *s* one *d. Educ:* The New School, Sydney; Sydney Grammar School; University College, London. Gold Medallist, Surgery, University College Hospital, London. Staff Surgeon New South Wales Artillery; Surgeon-Major and PMO Soudan Contingent, 1885; PMO Australian and New Zealand Forces, South Africa, and PMO Hamilton's Force and Hunter's Force, South Africa, 1900; Surgeon-General (local), South Africa; European War, 1914–16 (KCMG); Consulting Surgeon St Vincent's Hospital, Sydney, New South Wales. Decorated for South African services. *Address:* Headquarters, Melbourne. *T:* Melbourne 551. *Clubs:* Melbourne, Melbourne; Union, Sydney. *Died 10 May 1919.*

WILLIAMS, Rt. Rev. William Leonard, BA, DD; *b* 1829; *m* 1853, Sarah, *d* of John Bradshaw Wanklyn of Witherslack, Westmorland; five *s* four *d. Educ:* Magdalen Coll., Oxford; BA, 1852; 3rd Class Lit. Hum.; Hon. DD, 1897. Archdeacon of Waiapu, 1862–94; Principal of Maori Theological College, Gisborne, 1883–94; Bishop of Waiapu, 1894–1909. *Publications:* Enlarged Dictionary of the New Zealand Language; First Lessons in Maori. *Address:* Taumata, Napier, NZ.

Died 1 Sept. 1916.

WILLIAMS, William Llewelyn, KC 1912; MP (L) Carmarthen District, 1906–18; Barrister; Recorder of Cardiff since 1915; Bencher of Lincoln's Inn; *b* Brownhill, Co. Carmarthen, 10 March 1867; *m* Elinor Jenkins, Glansawdde, Co. Carmarthen. *Educ:* Foundation Scholar, Llandovery College; Open Hulme Exhibitioner (Modern History) and BCL; BNC Oxford. Recorder, Swansea, 1912–15. *Publications:* The Making of Modern Wales, 1919; numerous essays dealing with Welsh History; editor of Giraldus Cambrensis and Froude's History of England in the Everyman series. *Recreations:* fishing, golf. *Address:* 111 Ashley Gardens, SW1. *T:* Victoria 5849; 3 King's Bench Walk, Temple, EC4. *T:* City 1948. *Clubs:* National Liberal, Reform. *Died 22 April 1922.*

WILLIAMS, Hon. William Micah, OBE 1920; MLC for Hobart since 1916; *b* New Norfolk, Tasmania; *m* 1st, Elizabeth, *d* of John Hoggins; two *d*; 2nd, Grace M., *d* of John Smith, Wellington, Surrey; 3rd, Annie Ellen Winspear, *d* of Rev. Henry Bath, Melbourne. *Educ:* Clifton College, New Norfolk. Magistrate for the city of Hobart and the Municipality of New Town, 1908; Alderman of city of Hobart; Mayor, 1915; Fellow of the Royal Colonial Institute; Chairman of Chamber of Commerce, 1911–13; Deputy Chairman of State War Council; Chairman of State Recruitment Committee; Member Red Cross Executive during War; Chairman General Hospital; Chairman Public Library; Trustee of Public Cemetery; President of National Rose Society; Trustee, State Savings Bank; Ex-officio member of Methodist Conference; Representative English Conference, 1905, 1909; also Ecumenical Conference, Toronto, 1911, 1919. *Address:* Papanui, Augusta Road, New Town, Hobart. *T:* 636. *M:* 1631. *Club:* Commonwealth, Hobart (President).

Died 11 Aug. 1924.

WILLIAMSON, Captain Adolphus Huddleston, CMG 1917; MVO 1909; RN; Captain HMS Africa, Portsmouth; *b* 5 July 1869; 2nd *s* of Sir Hedworth Williamson, 8th Bt, and *heir-pres.* to 9th Bt. Entered Navy, 1882; Lieut 1891; Commander, 1902; Naval Attaché, Rome, 1908; Officer Legion of Honour. *Clubs:* Brooks's, Naval and Military. *Died 14 July 1918.*

WILLIAMSON, Rt. Rev. Andrew Wallace, KCVO 1926 (CVO 1919); MA, DD; HRSA; DL Midlothian; *b* Thornhill, Dumfriesshire, 29 Dec. 1856; *y s* of James Williamson and Margaret Wallace; *m* 1st, 1883, Agnes, 2nd *d* of Walter Blackstock, Edinburgh; 2nd, 1888, Elizabeth Mary Phoebe, *d* of Robert Croall, Craigcrook, Mid-Lothian. *Educ:* Morton School and Wallace Hall; University, Edinburgh. Thomson Scholar, 1878; Hepburn Prizeman, 1881; Assistant, North Leith, 1881; Minister, North Leith, 1882; St Cuthbert's, Edinburgh, 1883–1909; Univ. Lecturer in Pastoral Theology, 1897–98; Croall Lecturer; Moderator of the Church of Scotland, 1913–14; Dean of the Order of the Thistle and the Chapel Royal in Scotland; Minister, St Giles's, Edinburgh, 1910–25; Chaplain-in-Ordinary to the King in Scotland. *Publications:* Macleod Lecture; Ideals of Ministry; The Person of Christ. *Address:* 44 Palmerston Place, Edinburgh. *Club:* University, Edinburgh. *Died 10 July 1926.*

WILLIAMSON, Benjamin, DSc, DCL; FRS 1879; Vice-Provost, Trinity College, Dublin; *b* Cork, 1827; *m* Agnes (*d* 1899), *d* of Rev. W. Wright, Vicar of Selston, Nottingham. *Educ:* Kilkenny College; Trinity College, Dublin. DSc Dublin, 1890; DCL Oxford, 1892. Fellow of Trinity College, Dublin, 1852; Professor of Natural Philosophy, 1884; Senior Fellow, 1897. *Publications:* Treatise on the Differential Calculus, 1872; Integral Calculus, 1874; Dynamics, in conjunction with Professor Tarleton, 1884; Mathematical Theory of Stress and Strain, 1893; author of the articles 'Infinitesimal Calculus,' 'MacLaurin,' 'Variations, Calculus of,' etc, in 9th edn of the Encyclopædia Britannica, etc. *Address:* Trinity College Dublin; 1 Dartmouth Road, Dublin. *Clubs:* Royal Societies; University, Dublin.

Died 3 Jan. 1916.

WILLIAMSON, Charles Norris; journalist and author; *b* Exeter 1859; *s* of Rev. Stewart Williamson; *m* Alice Muriel Livingston. *Educ:* University College, London. Studied science and practical engineering until twenty-two; for eight years on the editorial staff of the Graphic; in 1891 started weekly periodical, Black and White. *Publications:* Life of Thomas Carlyle, 2 vols, 1881; newspaper articles (many on travel and automobilism); with Mrs Williamson: The Lightning Conductor, 1902; The Princess Passes; My Friend the Chauffeur; Lady Betty Across the Water; The Car of Destiny; Rosemary in Search of a Father; The Botor Chaperon; Scarlet Runner, 1908; Set in Silver; The Motor Maid; Lord Loveland Discovers America; The Golden Silence; The Princess Virginia; The Guests of Hercules; The Heather Moon; The Demon; The Love Pirate; It Happened in Egypt; Secret History; The Shop Girl; The Lightning Conductress; The War Wedding, 1916; Crucifix Corner, 1918; The Lion's Mouse, 1919. *Recreations:* travel, walking, autocaring. *Address:* St Christopher, Combe Down, Bath. *Clubs:* Savage, Whitefriars, Royal Automobile.

Died 3 Oct. 1920.

WILLIAMSON, Francis John; sculptor; *b* Hampstead, 17 July 1833; *e s* of Francis Edward Williamson; *m* 1857, Elizabeth Patman Smith; two *s* two *d. Educ:* private school, Hampstead. Articled pupil of late J. H. Foley, RA; assistant to him for some years; after which started practising at Esher, where he resided thereafter. *Works:* statues of Queen Victoria, Australia, India, London, etc; the first statue of Queen Victoria in Ireland; Dean Milman in St Paul's Cathedral; various public statues in various parts of the British Isles; numerous portraits of many of the Royal Family executed for Queen Victoria, etc; many ideal and private commissions. *Recreations:* various. *Address:* Fareholme, Esher, Surrey. *TA:* Esher.

Died 12 March 1920.

WILLIAMSON, Rev. Henry Drummond, MA; Rector of Brent Eleigh since 1922; Hon. Canon of St Edmundsbury and Ipswich, 1914; *b* 17 Dec. 1854; *s* of late Rev. George Frederick Williamson, MA; *m* 1877, Alice Jane, *d* of late Rev. Matthew Collisson, MA; two *s* two *d. Educ:* Rossall; Corpus Christi College, Cambridge (Scholar); 3rd Class Theological Tripos. Went to India under Church Missionary Society, 1878; at Calcutta Cathedral Mission College, 1878; Mandla, Central Provinces, 1878–93; Secretary Bengal Mission, 1893–97; Associate Secretary CMS for Dioceses of Bristol, Gloucester, and Worcester, 1899–1901; Organising Secretary CEZMS, 1901–5; Vicar of St Margaret's, Ipswich, 1905–22. *Publications:* Gondi Grammar; Hindi Church Hymn-book. *Recreations:* golf, cycling. *Address:* Brent Eleigh Rectory, Lavenham. *Died 21 March 1926.*

WILLIAMSON, Herbert; Physician Accoucheur, St Bartholomew's Hospital; Obstetric Physician, Royal Hospital for Women; *b* 1872; *s* of S. L. Williamson, JP, of Grantham, Lincs; *m* 1915, Mrs Edith Lockwood. *Educ:* Cambridge University (MA, MB, BChir); St Bartholomew's Hospital. FRCP London; Brackenbury Scholar in Surgery, 1897; Surgeon to Imperial Yeomanry Hospital, Pretoria, during Boer War. *Publications:* contributions on obstetric and gynæcological subjects to Journal of Obstetrics, Transactions of the Obstetrical Society, St Bartholomew's Hospital Reports, Clifford Allbutt's System of Medicine, etc. *Recreation:* riding. *Address:* 8 Queen Anne Street, Cavendish Square, W1. *T:* Langham 2288. *M:* H 4199. *Club:* Reform.   *Died 16 Dec. 1924.*

WILLIAMSON, Victor Alexander, CMG 1882; *b* 28 June 1838; 4th *s* of Sir Hedworth Williamson, 7th Bt of Whitburn Hall, Sunderland, and Hon. Anne Elizabeth, *d* of 1st Baron Ravensworth; unmarried. *Educ:* Westminster; sometime student of Christ Church, Oxford; 2nd class in Moderations, 1859. Barrister, Inner Temple, 1865; went Northern and, after division of that Circuit, the North-Eastern Circuit; a Royal Commissioner appointed to inquire into the Treatment of Indian Immigrants in Mauritius, 1872–73; chairman of the Lands Commission in Fiji, 1879–82; also MLC and MEC of that colony. *Decorated* for Colonial services. *Address:* Southend House, Whitburn, near Sunderland. *T:* Whitburn 16. *Club:* Brooks's.
                                                        Died 16 Sept. 1924.

WILLINK, Very Rev. John Wakefield, DD; Dean of Norwich since 1919; *b* 24 Oct. 1858; *s* of Rev. Arthur Willink, MA, Vicar of St Paul's, Tranmere, Cheshire, and Sarah Wakefield, *d* of John Cropper, of Liverpool; *m* 1887, Ruth Agnes, *d* of J. D. Sim, CSI, for over thirty years in the Indian Civil Service; two *s* two *d*. *Educ:* Clifton College; Pembroke College, Cambridge. Theological Tripos; Winchester Reading Prize; a year of special training was spent with Bishop Lightfoot, Bishop of Durham, at Auckland Castle; Curate of Bishop Auckland, 1881; Vicar of St John's, Sunderland, 1885–91; St Helen's Lancashire, 1891–1900; Hon. Canon of Liverpool, 1898–1905; Hon. Secretary for Liverpool Cathedral, 1901–5; Acting Chaplain 2nd Norfolk RA Volunteers, 1904; Vicar of Great Yarmouth, 1903–12; Rural Dean of the Flegg Deanery, 1905–12; Hon. Canon of Norwich, 1905–12; Select Preacher Cambridge University, 1912; Rector of Birmingham and Hon. Canon of Birmingham, 1912–19; Proctor in Convocation, 1917–19. *Publication:* History of the Parish Church of Great Yarmouth. *Recreations:* motoring, formerly rifle shooting, bicycling, tennis. *Address:* The Deanery, Norwich. *T:* Norwich 1090. *Club:* Norfolk, Norwich.   *Died 22 Sept. 1927.*

WILLIS, Rt. Rev. Alfred, DD; Assistant Bishop for Tonga since 1902; *b* 3 Feb. 1836; 2nd *s* of late Francis Willis, MD; *m* 1883, Emma Mary, *y d* of late Capt. Charles Simeon, and *g d* of late Sir Richard Godin Simeon, 2nd Bt. *Educ:* Uppingham; St John's Coll. Oxford; Wells Theological Coll. Curate of Strood, Kent, 1856–62; Perpetual Curate of St Mark, New Brompton, Kent, 1863–72; Bishop of Honolulu, 1872–1902. *Publications:* Hawaiian Hymn Book, 1880; Revision of Hawaiian Prayer Book, 1883; Honolulu Diocesan Magazine, 1890–1902; The Unity of the Bible, 1916. *Address:* Nukualofa, Tonga, South Seas.   *Died 14 Nov. 1920.*

WILLIS, Col Charles Fancourt, CB 1911; MD; IMS (retired); *b* 22 May 1854. Major, Indian Medical Service, 1891; Lt-Col 1899; Col 1908; served Egypt, 1882 (medal with clasp, bronze star); NW Frontier, India, 1897–8 (medal, two clasps); Tirah, 1897–8 (despatches, clasp). *Address:* Frith Manor, East Grinstead.
                                                        Died 28 April 1918.

WILLIS, Joseph George, CB 1911; Inspector-General in Bankruptcy, 1908–21; *b* Sept. 1861; unmarried. *Educ:* Christ Church, Oxford; 1st class in (Classical) Moderations, 1882; 1st class in Lit. Hum. 1884. Gained 1st place at Civil Service Competitive Examination (Class 1) 1885, and appointed to clerkship in Board of Trade; Private Secretary to Parliamentary Secretary Board of Trade, 1893–1900; Junior Assistant Secretary (Railway Department), 1907. *Address:* 123 Pall Mall, SW. *Club:* Reform.   *Died 17 May 1924.*

WILLIS, Ven. William Newcombe de Laval; Vicar of Cambridge, NZ, 1878–1912; Archdeacon of Waikato, 1882–1913 (retired); *b* 14 Feb. 1846; 3rd *s* of late Rev. W. N. Willis, sometime Rector of Kilpeacon and Prebendary of St Mary's Cathedral, Limerick, Ireland; *m* 1875, Mary Agnes, *e d* of late G. H. Clarke, sometime of Micheldever, Hampshire; three *s* four *d*. *Educ:* privately, in Ireland; St John's College, Auckland. Deacon, 1874; Priest, 1875; Curate of Holy Sepulchre, Auckland, 1875–78. *Publications:* The Battle for the Bible, 1902; Bible Teaching in State Schools, 1911; Hon. Editor of

Digest of Ecclesiastical Law of the Church of Province of New Zealand, Diocese of Auckland, and of Statistics and Accounts of the said Diocese. *Recreations:* mechanics, gardening, etc. *Address:* Kilpeacon, Cambridge, Auckland, NZ.
                                                        Died 10 Feb. 1916.

WILLIS-BUND, John William, CBE 1918; FSA; JP, DL; *b* 1843; *o s* of late John Walpole Willis, and 2nd wife, Ann Susannah Kent, *d* of late Col Thos Henry Bund, of Wick Episcopi; assumed name of Bund, 1864; *m* 1st, 1872, Harriette Penelope (*d* 1895), *sister* of Sir Richard Temple, 1st Bt; one *s* two *d*; 2nd, 1896, Mary Elizabeth (*d* 1919), *y d* of Gen. Frederick Reynell Thackeray, CB, and *widow* of Col Alexander E. F. Holcombe, 1st Royal Scots. *Educ:* Eton; Caius College, Cambridge (BA, LLB; 1st class Law, MA). Barrister, Lincoln's Inn; late Chairman Worcestershire Quarter Sessions and County Council. *Address:* Wick Episcopi, Worcester. *Clubs:* Oxford and Cambridge, Constitutional.   *Died 7 June 1928.*

WILLISON, Sir John (Stephen), Kt 1913; LLD; FRSC; *b* 9 Nov. 1856; *s* of Stephen Willison, Yorkshire, of Scottish descent; *m* 1st, 1885, Rachel Wood (*d* 1925), *d* of William Turner of Tiverton, Ontario; one *s*; 2nd, 1926, Marjory, *d* of Archibald MacMurdy, MA, Toronto. *Educ:* Canadian schools. Became Member of London Advertiser Staff, 1881; Editor Toronto, Globe, 1890–1902; Toronto Daily News, 1903–17; for years in Parliamentary Press Gallery for Toronto Globe (before 1890). *Publications:* The Railway Question in Canada; The American Spirit; Sir Wilfrid Laurier and the Liberal Party; The New Canada; Personal and Political Reminiscences. *Recreation:* bowling on the green. *Address:* Toronto. *Clubs:* York, Toronto Hunt, Toronto.   *Died 27 May 1927.*

WILLMORE, Henry Horace Albert, MVO 1910; Chief Gunner, RN; officer attending the gun-carriage at funeral of King Edward VII; *b* 19 April 1871; *s* of late Edward Thomas Willmore, Bexley Heath, Kent; *m* 1900, Mabel, *d* of late Edward Wilkinson, Portsmouth. *Address:* Laburnum House, 312 Laburnum Grove, Portsmouth.   *Died 29 Sept. 1919.*

WILLOUGHBY, Maj.-Gen. James Fortnom; Indian army (retired); *b* 1844; 2nd *s* of late Admiral J. B. Willoughby; *m* 1882, Mary Ann (*d* 1915), *d* of late Rev. H. R. Harrison, Rector of Elston, Notts; one *s* (killed in action in Mesopotamia, 1915). *Educ:* Royal Naval School, New Cross. Entered Bombay Army, 1861; Colonel of the 33rd QVO Light Cavalry, 1908; served Abyssinian Expedition, 1867 and 1868 (medal); Afghan War, 1880 (medal and clasp); Maj.-Gen. 1899; retired, 1899; JP Gloucestershire. *Address:* Gabari, Cheltenham; Springfield, Bourton-on-the-Water, Glos. *Clubs:* United Service; New, Cheltenham.   *Died 30 May 1922.*

WILLOUGHBY, Major Sir John Christopher, 5th Bt, *cr* 1794; DSO 1917; JP Oxon; Major Royal Horse Guards (retired); Director of Willoughby's Consolidated Co.; *b* 20 Feb. 1859; *e s* of Sir John Willoughby, 4th Bt, MP and 2nd wife, Maria Elizabeth, 4th *d* of Thomas Fawkes of Hemley House, Staffs; *S* father, 1866. *Educ:* Eton; Trinity Coll. Camb. Lieut 3rd Batt. Oxford Light Infantry, 1879; 2nd Lieut 6th Dragoon Guards, and entered Royal Horse Guards, 1880; Major, 1895; served in Egyptian Campaign, 1882, and Nile Campaign, 1884–85 (medals and clasps, despatches); second in command of forces of Imperial British South Africa Co. Matabeleland, 1890–91; Matabeleland Conquest, 1893; accompanied Dr Jameson, CB, into the Transvaal, 1896; served South Africa, 1899–1900; was in Ladysmith with Cavalry Headquarter Staff during the siege, and appointed Major under General Hunter, in charge of the transport of the Flying Column for the relief of Mafeking, also employed on the Intelligence Department (medal and clasps, despatches); European War, 1914–17 (DSO). Owner of properties in Oxfordshire and Buckinghamshire. *Heir:* none. *Address:* 2 Down Street, W. *T:* Mayfair 5797; Fulmer Hall, Slough, Buckinghamshire. *Clubs:* Carlton, Hurlingham, Marlborough, Turf.
                                                  Died 16 April 1918 (ext).

WILLOUGHBY, Lt-Gen. Michael Weekes, CSI 1885; Indian Army; *b* 18 March 1833; *s* of Maj.-Gen. M. F. Willoughby, Bombay Artillery; *m* 1855, Louisa Frances (*d* 1921), *d* of Robert Anderson; one *s*. *Educ:* Cheltenham. Entered army, 1849; Lt-Gen., 1893; served Persia, 1856–59 (medal with clasp); Abyssinia, 1868 (despatches, medal). *Address:* 17 Lansdown Place, Cheltenham.
                                                        Died 17 March 1925.

WILLOUGHBY DE BROKE, 19th Baron, *cr* 1492; **Richard Greville Verney,** TD; DL; JP; Lieutenant-Colonel in the Warwickshire Yeomanry 2nd Line Regiment, which he commanded during the War; MFH Warwickshire since 1900; *b* 29 March 1869; *e s* of 18th Lord Willoughby de Broke and Geraldine, *d* of late J. H. Smith-Barry: *S* father, 1902; *m* 1895, Marie Frances Lisette, OBE, *y d* of C. A. Hanbury, Strathgarve, Ross-shire; one *s*. *Educ:* Mr Rawnsley's, near Winchester; Eton; New College, Oxford (BA). MP (C) Rugby, Warwickshire, 1895–1900. Owner of about 6,000 acres. *Publications:* Hunting the Fox, 1920; The Sport of Our Ancestors, 1921. *Heir:* *s* Hon. John Henry Peyto Verney, *b* 21 May 1896. *Address:* 23 Gilbert Street, Grosvenor Square, W1; Woodley House, Kineton, Warwickshire. *Clubs:* Carlton, Turf, Beefsteak, Garrick.

Died 16 Dec. 1923.

WILLS, Sir Edward Chaning, 2nd Bt, *cr* 1904; MA; FCS; *b* 25 April 1861; *s* of Sir Edward Payson Wills, 1st Bt, KCB and Mary Ann, *e d* of late J. Chaning Pearce, FGS, Montague House, Bath; *S* father, 1910; *m* 1891, Isabella Sommerville, *d* of P. F. Sparke Evans, JP, of Trinmore, Clifton Down; no *c*. *Educ:* Emmanuel College, Cambridge. A Director Imperial Tobacco Company, Ltd. *Heir:* *b* Ernest Salter Wills, JP [*b* 30 Nov. 1869; *m* 1894, Caroline Fanny Maude, *d* of late William Augustine de Winton, Westbury Lodge, Durdham Down, Bristol; two *s* three *d*. *Address:* Ramsbury Manor, Wilts]. *Address:* Harcombe, Chudleigh, Devon.

Died 14 Oct. 1921.

WILLS, Sir George Alfred, 1st Bt, *cr* 1923; JP Somerset; Hon. DCL Oxford University; Hon. LLD University of Bristol; President of the Imperial Tobacco Co. (of Great Britain and Ireland), Ltd; Director of the Great Western Railway; Chairman of the Council and Pro-Chancellor University of Bristol; President, Bristol General Hospital; Director, British-American Tobacco Co., Ltd; Chairman, Leigh Woods Land Co., Ltd; Sheriff of Bristol, 1899–1900; *b* 3 June 1854; *e s* of late Henry Overton Wills, JP (first Chancellor of the University of Bristol), of Kelston Knoll, near Bath; *m* 1878, Susan Britton, *e* surv. *d* of late Robert Proctor of Clifton, Bristol; one *s* four *d*. *Educ:* private school, Clifton; Mill Hill School, Middlesex. A past President of the Grateful (Colston Society), also a past President of the Colston Research Society. *Recreations:* fishing, shooting. *Heir:* *s* George Vernon Proctor Wills, *b* 21 March 1887. *Address:* Coombe Lodge, Blagdon, Somerset; Burwalls, Leigh Woods, near Bristol. *T:* Bristol 551. *M:* YA 5435, HU 9350, AE 4909. *Clubs:* Reform, University and Literary, Bristol.

Died 11 July 1928.

WILLS, Henry Herbert, JP; Director of the Imperial Tobacco Co. of Great Britain and Ireland, Ltd; President of Bristol Royal Infirmary; Pro-Chancellor of Bristol University; Member of the Council of Clifton College; *b* 20 March 1856; 2nd *s* of late Henry Overton Wills, JP (first Chancellor of University of Bristol), of Kelston Knoll, near Bath; *m* 1886, Mary Monica, *d* of late Sir Philip Cunliffe Owen, KCB, KCMG, CIE; no *c*. *Educ:* Clifton College and University College, Bristol. High Sheriff of Somerset, 1910; a past President of the University Colston Society; formerly an Alderman of the County Council of Somerset; trained as a mechanical engineer. *Recreations:* shooting, fishing, deer-stalking, motoring, bicycling, riding, rowing, lawn tennis, foreign travel, music. *Address:* St Vincent's, Clifton Park, Bristol. *T:* Bristol 2699. *M:* FB 350, Y 1958.

Died 11 May 1922.

WILLSHIRE, Sir Arthur Reginald Thomas Maxwell-, 2nd Bt, *cr* 1840; Lieutenant-Colonel Scots Guards, retired 1885; *b* 23 Nov. 1850; *S* father, 1862; *m* 1891, Frederica (*d* 1912), *d* of late Sir Sanford Freeling, KCMG; one *s*. *Educ:* Wellington College. Served in Egyptian campaign, 1882. *Recreations:* fishing, shooting. *Heir:* *s* Gerard Arthur Maxwell-Willshire [*b* 21 Aug. 1892; *m* 1912, Lilian, *d* of Henry Birtles]. *Address:* 61 Elm Park Gardens, SW. *T:* 4530 Ken. *Clubs:* Guards, Wellington.

Died 26 April 1919.

WILLSON, Leslie; writer on diet and hygiene; *s* of William Rivers Willson; *m* Jessie Mary Guy. *Educ:* Huish's School, Taunton. Studied at Chiswick School of Art; started work as a book illustrator, 1881; engaged subsequently in journalism in USA and in London; contributed drawings to various English and American papers, 1883–98; art editor Ladies' Field, 1899–1907; General Editor of the Book Department, George Newnes, Ltd, 1901–7; editor of the Thin Paper Classics and Newnes' Art Library; Editor Amalgamated Press Novels Department, 1907–9. *Publications:* Songs and Lyrics from the Dramatists; Poems of Michael Drayton; Plays and Poems of Ben Jonson, and numerous articles, mainly on health matters. *Address:* 9A Gloucester Place, W1. *T:* Langham 1771.

Died 8 Dec. 1924.

WILLYAMS, Arthur Champion Phillips, JP, DL; *b* 1837; *y s* of late Humphry Willyams, MP, JP, DL, of Carnanton, Cornwall, and Ellen

Frances (*d* 1885), *y d* of late Gen. William Bridges Neynoe, of Castle Neynoe, Co. Sligo; *m* 1861, Charlotte Elizabeth (*d* 1887), 2nd *d* and co-heiress of late Rev. Harry Longueville-Jones, of Ty-Maen; two *s* one *d*. *Educ:* New College, Oxford. A Deputy Warden of the Stannaries of Cornwall and Devon; late Capt. Duke of Cornwall's Rifle Vols. *Address:* Tolcarne, St Columb. *Club:* Isthmian.

Died 9 Jan. 1917.

WILLYAMS, Edward Brydges, JP and DL Cornwall; Deputy Warden of the Stannaries, Devon and Cornwall; *b* 1836; *m* 1st, 1858, Jane (*d* 1877), *d* and co-heiress of Sir Trevor Whelton, 9th Bt, of Leamington, Hastings, Warwickshire; 2nd, 1882, Emily (*d* 1901), *sister* of 1st Lord Burnham. *Educ:* Merton College, Oxford. High Sheriff for Cornwall; MP (L) Truro, 1857–60, 1880–85; East Cornwall, 1868–73. *Recreation:* Master of Hounds for 15 years. *Address:* Carnanton, St Columb.

Died 10 Oct. 1916.

WILMER, Rev. Canon John Kidd; *b* Portsmouth, England; *e s* of late George Wilmer; *m* Georgina, 2nd *d* of late Thomas Gorringe; two *d*. *Educ:* private school, England; Christ's College, Canterbury, New Zealand. Ordained 1872; Curate of Ellesmere, 1872–75, Fernside, 1876–78, both in New Zealand; Incumbent of Green Ponds, 1879–81; Rector of Brighton, 1881–98; of Devonport, 1898–1904; of Kingston, 1904–11; of Carrick, 1911–19; Rural Dean, 1895–1905, all in Tasmania; Canon of St David's Cathedral, Hobart, Tasmania; Chaplain Australian Commonwealth Military Forces (Capt.). *Address:* 218 Charles Street, Launceston, Tasmania.

Died 1928.

WILMOT, Hon. (John) Alexander, FRGS; Member 'Progressive' (Rhodes) party; Gazetted Honourable after 21 years' service; retired from S Africa Parliament; created a Papal Count for services to the Church: *b* Edinburgh, 9 April 1836; *m* 1860, Alice Mary Slater (*d* 1922); six *s* seven *d* (and three *d* decd). *Educ:* Univs of Glasgow and Edinburgh; Prizeman Univ. of Edin. Passed Civil Service Examination head of list in Cape Colony, and served in various offices until 1886, when retired on a pension; Member of Legislative Council, Cape Colony, 1889; successful in passing several bills through Legislature connected principally with social and temperance subjects; elected by the Loyal Congress of South Africa, 1900, one of their delegates to proceed to Europe, and in England and Scotland addressed various meetings; wrote articles for and worked in common with the Imperial SA Association. KSG, KHS. *Publications:* The History of the Cape Colony; The History of the Zulu War; The Story of the Expansion of Southern Africa; Monomotapa (Rhodesia) Map; The History of our own Times in South Africa; The Life of Sir Richard Southey; The Life and Times of Bishop Ricards; The Climate of S Africa—the Best in the World. *Address:* Wynberg, Cape Province.

Died 3 April 1923.

WILMOT, Sir Ralph Henry Sacheverel, 6th Bt, *cr* 1759; *b* 8 June 1875; *s* of Rev. A. A. Wilmot, 4th *s* of 4th Bt, and Harriet Cecilia, *d* of Rev. A. Fitzherbert; *S* uncle, 1901; *m* 1905, Lady Ada Marian Maitland, *d* of 13th Earl of Lauderdale; two *s* one *d*. Joined Coldstream Guards, 1896; Lieut 1898; Capt. 1903; Capt. Reserve of Officers, 1906. *Heir:* *s* Arthur Ralph Wilmot, *b* 2 Feb. 1909. *Address:* Chaddesden Hall, Derby. *Clubs:* Guards, Arthur's.

Died 14 Jan. 1918.

WILSHERE, Alfred Henry, CMG 1913; *b* 23 Aug. 1854; *s* of Rev. H. M. M. Wilshere; *m* 1882, Annie Florence Isabelle, *d* of Captain A. H. Richetts, late of 2nd Somersetshire Light Infantry Militia; three *s* five *d*. *Educ:* Diocesan College, Rondebosch. Clerk, Colonial Secretary's Office, 1872; Clerk, Customs, East London, 1873; Sub-Collector, Customs, East London, 1900; Controller of Customs, Capetown, and Registrar of Shipping, 1901–14; Chairman of Table Bay Harbour Board, 1902–9; JP Cape Colony; Member, Game Protection Association.

Died 28 Feb. 1927.

WILSON, Alexander Johnstone; proprietor and editor of Investor's Review since 1892; *b* Forglen, Banffshire, 20 Oct. 1841; *s* of late George W. Wilson, HM Photographer for Scotland, Aberdeen; *m* 1862; one *s* two *d*. *Educ:* Dr George Ogilvie's school, Turriff; privately. Junior sub-editor of the Economist, 1872–78; assistant city editor of The Times, 1874–81; city editor of Pall Mall Gazette, 1881–83; city editor of the Standard, 1883–99. *Publications:* The Resources of Modern Countries, 1878; Banking Reform, 1879; Reciprocity, Bimetallism, and Land Tenure Reform, 1880; The National Budget, 1882; edited Supplement to M'Culloch's Dictionary of Commerce, 1882; numerous essays in the Spectator, Fraser, Macmillan, the Fortnightly. *Recreation:* gardening. *Address:* Annandale, Atkins Road, SW12. *TA:* Unveiling. *T:* Streatham 671. *Club:* Reform.

Died 22 July 1921.

WILSON, Alpheus Waters; Bishop in the Methodist Episcopal Church of the South since 1882; *b* Baltimore, 5 Feb. 1834; *m*; three *d*. *Educ:* schools in Md and Virginia; Columbian College, Washington, DC. Secretary Board of Missions, 1878–82; delegate to Ecumenical Methodist Conference in London, 1881 and 1901; took episcopal tours round the world, 1886, 1888, 1890, 1898, 1900; went to Brazil on Episcopal duty, 1892 and 1902; to China, 1907–8. *Publications:* Missions; Lecturers—Witnesses to Christ, etc. *Address:* 1601 Park Place, Baltimore.   *Died Nov. 1916.*

WILSON, Adm. Sir Arthur Knyvet, 3rd Bt, *cr* 1857; VC 1884; GCB 1906 (KCB 1902; CB 1887); OM 1912; GCVO 1905 (KCVO 1903); First Sea-Lord, Admiralty, 1909–12; retired, 1912; *b* 4 March 1842; *s* of late Rear-Admiral George Knyvet Wilson and Agnes Mary, *y d* of Rev. William Yonge, Vicar of Swaffham; *S* brother, 1919. Capt. 1880; Rear-Adm. 1895; Vice-Adm. 1901; served Crimean War, 1854; Chinese War, 1865; Egyptian Campaign, 1882; Soudan Campaign, 1884; ADC to the Queen, 1892–95; a Lord Commissioner of the Admiralty and Comptroller of the Navy, 1897–1901; commanded Channel Squadron, 1901–3; Commander-in-Chief of Home and Channel Fleets, 1903–7; Admiral of the Fleet, 1907. *Heir:* none. *Address:* Swaffham, Norfolk. *Clubs:* United Service, Royal Societies.
                                    Died 25 May 1921 (ext).

WILSON, Rev. Barton Worsley; Hon. Canon of Carlisle, 1898. *Address:* The Rectory, Lazonby, Cumberland.
                                    Died 30 Dec. 1920.

WILSON, Sir Charles Rivers, GCMG 1895 (KCMG 1880); CB 1876; President Grand Trunk Railway, Canada, since 1895; on Council Suez Canal Co., 1876–95; *b* 1831; *s* of Melvil Wilson and Louisa, *d* of Maj.-Gen. Sir Benjamin Stephenson, GCH; *m* 1st, 1860, Caroline (*d* 1888), *d* of R. Cook; 2nd, 1895, Hon. Beatrice Violet Mary Mostyn, *sister* of 7th Lord Vaux. *Educ:* Eton; Balliol Coll., Oxford (BA 1853). Entered Treasury, 1856; Comptroller-Gen. of National Debt Office, 1874–94; Finance Minister, Egypt, 1877–79; Medjidie, 1st class. *Address:* 9 Berkeley Square, W. *T:* Mayfair 5696; Foxhills, Chertsey. *Clubs:* Arthur's, St James', Marlborough, Garrick.
                                    Died 9 Feb. 1916.

WILSON, Col Christopher Wyndham, JP, DL; *b* 1844; *e s* of late William Wilson and 1st wife, Maria Lætitia, *d* of late Richard Parrott Hulme, of Maisonnette, Devon; *m* 1st, 1874, Mildred Eyre (*d* 1878), *y d* of late T. S. Spedding, of Mirehouse, Cumberland; 2nd, 1879, Edith (*d* 1913), *y d* of Sir Walter Minto Townsend Farquhar, 2nd Bt. High Sheriff, Westmorland, 1884; Col late commanding Westmorland and Cumberland Yeomanry. *Address:* Rigmaden Park, Kirkby Lonsdale. *Clubs:* Carlton, Royal Automobile.
                                    Died 8 Dec. 1918.

WILSON, Clive Henry Adolphus, DSO 1900; 12th Battalion Imperial Yeomanry; *b* 1876; 3rd *s* of late Arthur Wilson of Tranby Croft; *m* 1907, Elvira, *d* of late Signor Magherini of Florence. Served South Africa, 1900–2 (severely wounded, despatches twice, Queen's medal 4 clasps, King's medal 2 clasps, DSO). Chairman Lambert Parkers Gaines Ltd; Master of Holderness Hounds. *Address:* Little Tranby, Beverley, ER Yorks. *TA:* Foxes Beverley. *Clubs:* Bachelors', White's.   *Died 18 Jan. 1921.*

WILSON, Rev. Daniel Frederic, MA (Oxon); Hon. Canon of Southwark Cathedral; Vicar of Mitcham, Surrogate; *b* 10 Nov. 1830; *s* of Rev. Prebendary Wilson, Prebendary of St Paul's, Vicar of Islington; *m* 1st, Katherine, *d* of Edward Leathes, Lowestoft; 2nd, Sarah Maria, *d* of Andrew Johnston, MP St Andrews; two *s* three *d*. *Educ:* King's College, London; Oxford, MA 1854. Chaplain at Serampore, Calcutta; Curate at Calne, Wiltshire, and St Mary's, Islington. *Address:* Vicarage, Mitcham. *T:* Mitcham 820. *Clubs:* Primrose; Mitcham Conservative.
                                    Died 17 Feb. 1918.

WILSON, Sir David, KCMG 1899 (CMG 1890); Hon. Colonel (VD) Trinidad Light Infantry Volunteers; *b* 1838; *s* of late Very Rev. Dean Wilson, Fyvie, Aberdeen; *m* 1st, 1870, Jane (*d* 1874), *d* of late Alexander Milne; 2nd, 1881, Nora, *d* of Norval Clyne, Aberdeen; two *s* two *d*. Private Sec. to Gov. of N Brunswick and Trinidad, 1861–69; Stip. Magistrate, Trinidad, 1870–78; Commissioner of Northern Province and Sub-Intendant of Crown Lands, Trinidad, 1878–97; Acting Colonial Sec. Trinidad on several occasions, 1875–96; Capt. New Brunswick Vol. Militia, 1863; Major St John Vol. Batt. on frontier service, 1866 (Canadian medal, one clasp); Officer commanding Trinidad Vol. Force, 1879–90; Col commanding Light Infantry Vols, 1890–97; Governor of British Honduras, 1897–1903. *Address:* Clovelly Cottage, Rydens Avenue, Walton-on-Thames, Surrey.
                                    Died 15 March 1924.

WILSON, Lt-Col Edmond Munkhouse, CB 1902; CMG 1896; DSO 1898; Knight of Grace of the Order of St John of Jerusalem, 1903; retired pay; *b* Oundle, Northamptonshire, 4 Oct. 1855; *y s* of late C. T. Wilson. *Educ:* Sherborne; St George's Hospital; MRCS England; LRCP London; DPH Camb. Served as Civil Surgeon Zulu War, 1879 (medal and clasp); joined Army Med. Dept, 1881; served in Nile Expedition, Egypt, 1884–85 (medal and clasp, Khedive's star); Nile Expedition, 1885–86; Expedition Gambia, West Africa, 1891–92 (medal and clasp); Ashanti Expedition, 1895–96, in command of Base Hospital (honourably mentioned, CMG, star); Soudan Expedition to Khartoum, 1898, as Secretary to Surg.-Gen. (despatches, DSO, English medal, and Soudan medal and clasp); RAMC; Dep. Asst Director-Gen. of AMS at headquarters, 1899–1904; RAMC Record Office, 1905–13, 1914–16; President West London Medico-Chirurgical Society, 1918–19; Secretary RAMC Fund and Benevolent Society. *Publications:* Notes on Malarial Fever in connection with Meteorological Conditions at Sierra Leone, 1896–98. *Address:* 15 Gilston Road, South Kensington, SW. *T:* Victoria 2722. *Club:* Junior United Service.   *Died 9 Oct. 1921.*

WILSON, Col Edward Hales, CB 1896; *b* 1845; *m*. Entered army, 1865; Col 1895; served Hazara, 1888 (medal with clasp); Chitral Relief Force (despatches, CB, medal with clasp).
                                    Died 28 Aug. 1917.

WILSON, Maj.-Gen. Erastus William, CMG 1917; Canadian Forces; Provincial Manager, Canada Life Assurance Co., Montreal; *b* 1860; *m* 1887, Sara E. L. Bricker; two *s*. *Clubs:* Mount Royal, St James', Forest and Stream, Montreal.
                                    Died 15 May 1922.

WILSON, Hon. Frank, CMG 1911; JP; Premier and Colonial Treasurer, Australia, since 1916; *b* Sunderland, 1859; father a member of the firm of J. and W. Wilson and Sons, of Sunderland; *m* Annie, *e d* of Robert Hall Phillips, Sunderland. *Educ:* Moravian School, Neuwied on the Rhine; Wesley College, Sheffield. With his brother founded the firm of J. W. and F. Wilson and Co., marine engineers and boiler manufacturers, at Sunderland in 1878; arrived in Queensland, Australia, 1887; was manager of the firm of A. Overend and Co., railway contractors, engineers, and machinery merchants, Brisbane, until he left for Western Australia, to take up the position of Managing Director of the Canning Jarrah Timber Company, Ltd, 1891; was for four years in succession President of the Perth Chamber of Commerce; President of the Timber Merchants' and Saw Millers' Association for many years; presided over the Coal Owners' Association of Western Australia; sat in Perth City Council, 1895–97; elected member of the Legislative Assembly for Canning, 1897, and for Perth, 1901; Minister for Railways and Mines, 1901; employers' representative on Arbitration Court Bench till June 1904, when he was elected Member of the Legislative Assembly for Sussex, which seat he has won on four successive occasions; Minister for Works, 1905–6 and 1909–10; Colonial Treasurer, Minister for Education and Agriculture, 1906–9; Premier and Colonial Treasurer of Western Australia, 1910–11; member of Senate of University of WA since 1912; Leader of the Opposition, 1911–16. *Address:* Viking House, Perth, Western Australia.   *Died 12 Dec. 1918.*

WILSON, Frederick James, CIE 1910; MInstCE; *b* Edinburgh, 1858; 2nd *s* of late William Wilson of Pilton, Darling Downs, Queensland, Australia, and Edinburgh; *m* 1888, Mary Phoebe, *d* of Col E. A. Birch, MD, late IMS; two *s* one *d*. *Educ:* Royal Indian Engineering Coll., Coopers Hill. A year's practical course on dock works in England; joined the PWD Madras as Assistant Engineer, 1880; services lent to Madras Harbour Trust, 1892; Assistant to Chief Engineer for Irrigation and Under-Sec. to Government, 1896; Local Consulting Engineer to the Madras Harbour Trust; Superintending Engineer PWD, 1902; Chief Engineer Madras Port Trust, 1903–6; Chief Engineer for Irrigation and Joint Secretary of Government, 1905; Chief Engineer and Secretary to Government of Madras Public Works Department, 1906–11; Member of the Legislative Council; President Sanitary Board; retired 1911. *Address:* Meadhurst, Sidmouth, Devon. *Clubs:* East India United Service; Madras; Ootacamund.
                                    Died 1 Oct. 1926.

WILSON, Sir Frederick William, Kt 1907; DL; proprietor East Anglian Daily Times; farmer of own land in Norfolk; *b* Scarning, Norfolk, 26 March 1844; 2nd *s* of William Wilson, Manor House, Scarning, a Liberal tenant farmer, and one of the founders and directors of the Norfolk News, which for many years led the Reform party in Norfolk; *m* 1870, Mary Elizabeth, *d* of Edward Cappes of Forest Hill, an early currency reformer, and winner of the 300-guinea prize offered by the Society of Arts for the best essay on the National Debt. *Educ:* Wymondham Grammar School. Called up as a volunteer to defend Chester Castle against the Fenians in 1866; 29 years after, meeting one of the attacking party as a colleague in the House of Commons; indentured to Mr J. H. Tillett, editor of Norfolk News and MP for Norwich, 1868–80; subsequently assistant to Sir Edward Russell on Liverpool Daily Post; founded the East Anglian Daily Times, 1874; president Newspaper Society of the United Kingdom, 1894, and Institute of Journalists, 1907; JP for Suffolk, 1894; DL for Norfolk; member of the Suffolk Territorial Association; MP (L) Mid Norfolk, 1895–1906; in 1897 session rode in Parliamentary steeplechase, and played chess for the House of Commons against the American House of Representatives; one of the founders of the Norfolk Small Holdings Association, and took great interest in all movements calculated to keep the villager in the village. *Publications:* articles in his own newspaper. *Recreations:* presided at formation of Felixstowe Golf Club, the 5th club established in England, 1880; scored 100 at Queen's ranges with Martini rifle, all bulls' eyes at 500 and 600 yards. *Address:* The Dale, Scarning, Norfolk. *Club:* Reform.

Died 26 May 1924.

WILSON, Harry; *b* 1852; married. *Educ:* Brighton College; Jesus College, Cambridge (Scholar, MA); Ely Theological Coll. Assistant Curate, St Andrew's, Rugby, 1877–81; Rector of Over Worton and Vicar of Nether Worton, 1881–83; Vicar of St Augustine's, Stepney, 1883–1902; received into the Catholic Church, 1917; was Editor of The American Catholic. *Publications:* Why and Wherefore; A Good Communion; Our Dead: Where are They?; A Holy Lent: The Third Day; Follow to Calvary, etc. *Address:* 330 South Vendome Street, Los Angeles, California, USA.

Died 21 Sept. 1928.

WILSON, Helen Russell, RBA 1911; 6th *c* of late James Leonard Wilson and Adelaide Anne, *d* of E. B. Fripp. *Educ:* Slade School; London School, under Frank Brangwyn, ARA; studied Japanese painting in Tokyo. Exhibitor at Royal Academy, Royal Institute of Painters in Oil-Colours, International Society of Sculptors, Painters, and Gravers. Société Nationale des Beaux-Arts, Paris, Liverpool, Leeds, etc. *Recreations:* swimming, reading. *Address:* (studio) The Mountain, Tangier, Morocco.

Died 22 Oct. 1924.

WILSON, Rev. Henry Austin; Fellow of Magdalen College, Oxford, since 1876; *b* Ayr, 7 Dec. 1854; 3rd *s* of Rt Rev. William Scott Wilson, Bishop of Glasgow and Galloway. *Educ:* Glenalmond; Wadham College, Oxford. 1st cl. Classical Moderations, 1874; 2nd cl. Lit. Hum. 1876. Examiner in Hons Sch. of Theol., 1893–95, 1908–10; Curator of the Bodleian Library, 1894–19; Perpetual Curator, 1919; Delegate of the University Press, 1900–19; Hon. Sec. of the Henry Bradshaw Society, 1895–1926; editor of the Journal of Theological Studies, 1902–3. *Publications:* Index to the Roman Sacramentaries of Muratori, 1892; The Gelasian Sacramentary, 1894; History of Magdalen College, in series of Oxford College Histories, 1899; edited for the Henry Bradshaw Society Liber Eveshamensis, 1893; The Missal of Robert of Jumièges, 1896; The Benedictional of Abp Robert, 1903; The Order of the Communion of 1548, 1908; The Pontifical of Magdalen College, 1910; The Gregorian Sacramentary under Charles the Great, 1915; The Calendar of St Willibrord, 1918. *Address:* Magdalen College, Oxford; 55 Dundonald Road, Kilmarnock, Ayrshire.

Died 18 June 1927.

WILSON, Field-Marshal Sir Henry Hughes, 1st Bt, *cr* 1919; GCB 1918 (KCB 1915; CB 1908); DSO 1901; Rifle Brigade; Chief of Imperial General Staff and Member of War Cabinet since 1918; *b* 5 May 1864; *s* of James Wilson, DL, JP, Currygrane, Edgeworthstown, Ireland; *m* 1891, Cecil Mary, *y d* of late George Cecil Gore Wray, JP, Ardnamona, Donegal. *Educ:* Marlborough Coll.; Graduate at Staff College. Entered Royal Irish Regt, 1884; transferred to the Rifle Brigade, 1884; served Burma campaign, 1885–87 (wounded); served again, 1887–89 (medal with 2 clasps); Staff College, 1892–94; Staff Captain, Intelligence Division, 1894–97; Brigade-Major 2nd Brigade, Aldershot, 1897–99; Brigade-Major Light Brigade, South Africa, 1899–1900; DAAG Army Headquarters, South Africa, 1900–1 (despatches 4 times, medal with 5 clasps, and Brevet Lieut-Colonel on promotion to Major, DSO); served European War, 1914–15 (Lt-Gen., KCB); commanded 9th Provisional Batt., 1902–3; DAAG Army Headquarters, 1903; AAG Army Headquarters, 1903–6; Assistant Director Staff Duties, War Office, 1904–6; Commandant Staff College, 1907–10; Director of Military Operations at Army

Headquarters, 1910–14; Assistant Chief of General Staff to Lord French, 1914; Corps Commander; Liaison Officer with the French; Commanded Eastern District; British Military Representative, Versailles, 1917; Field Marshal, 1919; Grand Cross, Legion of Honour; Grand Cross of the Russian White Eagle. *Recreations:* hunting, shooting, polo, lawn tennis. *Heir:* none. *Address:* Currygrane, Edgeworthstown, Ireland; Grove End, Bagshot, Surrey; 36 Eaton Place, SW1. *T:* Victoria 5348. *Clubs:* White's, Travellers'; Royal Yacht Squadron, Cowes.

Died 22 June 1922 (ext).

WILSON, Herbert, KC (Ireland) 1902; *b* Trinidad, West Indies, 8 July 1862; *o s* of Robert Wilson, Thorndale, Milltown, Co. Dublin, and Trinidad; *m* 1891, Emily, *d* of William Dunne, Larch Hill, Co. Kildare. *Educ:* Malvern College; Trinity College, Dublin. Scholar; First Senior Moderator in Classics, 1884; Berkley Gold Medallist, Greek; Vice-Chancellor's Gold Medallist, Latin. Called to the Irish Bar, 1887; Bencher of the King's Inns, Dublin, 1908. *Address:* Holmhurst, Greystones, Co. Wicklow.

Died 22 Jan. 1927.

WILSON, Captain Herbert Haydon, DSO 1901; *b* 14 Feb. 1875; *y s* of late Sir Samuel Wilson of Ercildoune, Victoria. Hon. Captain in Army, 1901; Major, Notts (Sherwood Rangers) Imp. Yeo., 1904; served South Africa, 1900–1 (despatches twice, Queen's medal, 4 clasps, DSO). *Decorated* for defending posts in Boer attack on Lichtenburg. *Clubs:* White's, Bachelors', Carlton.

Died 11 April 1917.

WILSON, Sir James, KCSI 1909 (CSI 1901); *b* 1853; *m* 1888, Anne Campbell (*d* 1921), *d* of late Very Rev. Norman Macleod, DD, Dean of the Thistle. *Educ:* Perth Academy; Univ. of Edinburgh; Balliol Coll., Oxford. Entered ICS 1875; served in the Punjab; Secretary to the Government of India in the Dept of Revenue and Agriculture; Financial Commissioner of Punjab; retired, 1910; Superintending Inspector under the Board of Agriculture and Fisheries, London, 1911–15; a Governor of the Agricultural Organisation Society, 1912–14; Delegate to International Institute of Agriculture, Rome, 1914–17; Chairman of Central Agricultural Wages Committee for Scotland, 1917–21. *Publications:* Gazetteer of Shahpur District; Settlement Report of Sirsa District; Code of Tribal Custom in Shahpur and in Sirsa; Grammar of Western Panjabi; Lowland Scotch; Farmworkers in Scotland; The Dialect of Robert Burns; Scottish Poems of Robert Burns; Dialects of Central Scotland. *Address:* Annieslea, Crieff, Scotland. *T:* Crieff 194. *Club:* Caledonian.

Died 22 Dec. 1926.

WILSON, Rev. James, MA, BD, LittD; Vicar of Dalston since 1888; Hon. Canon of Carlisle; Hon Chaplain to the Bishop; *b* 28 Aug. 1856; 3rd *s* of late James Wilson of Drumgoland and Billis Grove, Co. Cavan; *m* 1886, Laura, *y d* of late T. King Atkinson, JP, of Cardew Lodge, Dalston, and Reston Hall, Westmorland; one *s* one *d*. *Educ:* privately; Trinity College, Dublin. Deacon, 1879; Priest, 1880; Curate of St Paul's, Carlisle; during his incumbency the two churches were restored and beautified at a cost of £5000, and the two church schools added to and kept in line with educational requirements, one of which was recovered for church usage. *Publications:* Editor of the Victoria History of Cumberland, vol. i 1901, vol. ii 1905; Register of the Priory of St Bees, for the Surtees Society; Rose Castle, the Residential Seat of the Bishop of Carlisle; and several local publications; contributor to the Scottish Historical Review. *Address:* Dalston Vicarage, Cumberland.

Died 26 March 1923.

WILSON, James, ISO 1907; *b* Ayr, 27 May 1847; *e s* of late William Wilson, mineral water manufacturer, Dumfries; *m* 1875, Grace M'Candlish, *d* of late Capt. Black, Isle of Whithorn; three *s*. *Educ:* Gemmel's Private School, Dumfries; Dumfries Academy. Forty-one years in the Post Office Service; retired from position of Postmaster and Surveyor of Leeds, 1907; was previously Postmaster at Hull, Derby, Exeter, and Preston; and Chief Superintendent (Postal) at Liverpool. *Address:* 4 Edgerton Road, West Park, Leeds.

Died 5 March 1924.

WILSON, Lt-Col (James) Alban, DSO 1912; late 8th Gurkha Rifles; *b* 12 Feb. 1865; *s* of late James Buck Wilson, JP, of Firbank; *m* 1898, Carrie, *d* of late Gen. F. J. Priestley. *Educ:* Uppingham. Joined 3rd Seaforth Highlanders, 1885; 2nd Seaforth Highlanders, 1887; 44th LI (subseq. 8th Gurkhas), 1889; Capt., 1898; Major, 1905; served Manipur, 1891 (medal with clasp); NE Frontier, Assam (Abor), 1894; Burma, 1895–96; Waziristan, 1901–2 (despatches, medal with clasp); DAAG Bengal, 1901–6; served Abor Expedition, 1912 (medal and clasp, despatches, DSO); commanded Naga Hills Expedition, 1913 (Brevet of Lieut-Col); commanded 1/8th Gurkhas in Mesopotamia,

1916–17; raised and commanded 3/8th Gurkhas, 1917 and 1918; retired, 1920; Knight of the Order of the Red Eagle of Prussia; Knight of the Order of Merit of Pyrmont-Waldeck. *Publication:* Sport and Service in Assam and Elsewhere, 1924. *Recreations:* shooting, fishing. *Address:* West Burton, Aysgarth, Yorks.

Died 27 April 1928.

WILSON, Rev. James Allen, JP, MA; Rector of Bolton-by Bowland, 1859–1915; Hon. Canon of Ripon Cathedral; *b* 3 June 1827; *s* of James Wilson of Brinkcliffe Tower, Sheffield; *m* 1860, Catherine (*d* 1914), *y d* of Henry Remington of Aynsome, Grange-over-Sands, and Crow Trees, Melling, Co. Lancaster; six *s* three *d. Educ:* Sheffield Collegiate School; Trinity College, Cambridge (Foundation Scholar; 22nd Wrangler). Curate of Hornby, Yorkshire, 1854–56; Stanwix, Cumberland, 1857–59; Rural Dean of West Craven, 1881–1904; was Chairman of Clitheroe Board of Guardians. *Address:* Taitlands, Stainforth, Settle. *M:* C 1874. *Club:* New Oxford and Cambridge.

Died 14 Dec. 1917.

WILSON, Sir John, 1st Bt, *cr* 1906, of Airdrie; JP and DL Lanarkshire, Glasgow, Fifeshire; Chairman of Wilson and Clyde Coal Company, Ltd, employing 5,000 men; proprietor of mineral estates in Lanarkshire and Fifeshire, etc; connected with extensive steel and iron works and other industrial undertakings in Lanarkshire; *b* 26 June 1844; *s* of late James Wilson, coalowner, Airdrie, and 1st wife, Agnes, *d* of William Motherwell, Airdrie; *m* 1st, 1878, Margaret Bell (*d* 1885), *d* of James Robertson, Glasgow; two *s* (one *d* decd); 2nd, 1889, Emma Alexandrina, *d* of David Binnie, Glasgow; two *d* (one *s* decd). *Educ:* Airdrie and Glasgow Academies. MP (LU) Falkirk District of Burghs, 1895–1906. Owned about 7,000 acres in Lanarkshire, Fifeshire, Perthshire, and Kinross-shire. *Recreations:* shooting, golfing (in final in parliamentary golf match, 1904). *Heir: s* James Robertson Wilson [*b* 5 May 1883; *m* 1908, Helen Rae Fife, *e d* of Archibald Bulloch Graham, Park Gardens, Glasgow; one *s. Educ:* Oxford (BA)]. *Address:* Airdrie House, Airdrie, NB; Kippen Tower, Dunning, Perthshire. *T:* Dunning 6. *Clubs:* Reform, Bath, Royal Automobile.

Died 28 July 1918.

WILSON, John; *b* 1837; *s* of James Wilson, merchant, Glasgow, and Margaret Gibbs; *m* 1883, Margaret (*d* 1917), *d* of late John Hewetson of Ellergil, Westmorland. MP (LU) St Rollox Div. of Glasgow, 1900–6; DL and JP Stirlingshire. *Address:* Finnich Malise, Drymen, Stirlingshire. *Club:* New, Glasgow. *Died 5 Jan. 1928.*

WILSON, Very Rev. John Skinner; *b* 1849; *y s* of late Very Rev. David Wilson, Dean of Aberdeen; *m* L. Mary, *d* of Norval Clyne, advocate, Aberdeen; five *s* two *d. Educ:* Trin. College, Glenalmond; St Catharine's Coll., Cambridge (MA). Ordained, 1871; Priest, 1873; Rector of St George's, Edinburgh, 1885–96; Synod Clerk, 1890; Canon of Edinburgh, 1890–97; Dean of the Diocese and of St Mary's Cathedral, 1897; retired, 1919; took a prominent part in the administrative and financial work of the Episcopal Church in Scotland from 1880; Hon. DD Edin. *Publications:* editor, Seabury Centenary Report, 1885; Scottish Guardian, 1886–88. *Address:* Aros, Strathtay, Perthshire. *Died 13 Nov. 1926.*

WILSON, Matthew, KC; DCL 1917; Head of law firm of Wilson, Pike, & Stewart, in Chatham, Ontario; a Municipal and Corporation Counsel; *b* Harwich, Ontario, Canada, 28 Aug. 1854; *s* of Robert Wilson and Isabella Waugh; *m* Anna Marsden, *e d* of Charles R. Atkinson, KC; one *s* two *d. Educ:* Chatham, Whitby, and Toronto. Practised before all the higher Courts of Canada and in the Privy Council of England; QC 1889; Hon. Treasurer of the Provincial Synod of Ontario and a member of the highest Court of Appeal for the Church of England in Canada; a Bencher of the Law Society; Past President of the Western Bar Association, and Past President of the Kent Law Association; Member of the Council of Huron Divinity College, and a Past Senator of the Western University of London; Director of the Northern Life Assurance Co. of London, and of the Trusts and Guarantee Co. of Toronto, and President of the Great West Land Co. of Canada; member of the Board of Management and of the Executive Committee of the Missionary Society for all Canada and for Foreign Missions; in 1918 appointed by Government of Ontario Representative of that Province to attend Inter-Provincial Meetings to promote Uniformity of Legislation throughout Canada. *Publications:* articles advocating various law reforms. *Recreations:* horseback riding, tennis. *Address:* 325 Wellington Street, Chatham, Ontario. *TA:* Wilson, Chatham, Ontario. *T:* 508. *M:* 63872.

Died 1 May 1920.

WILSON, P. Macgregor; RSW; artist; *b* Glasgow; *m;* one *d. Educ:* University Glasgow and London. Travelled extensively America, all

Europe, Egypt, India, Arabia, Russia, etc; rode 1000 miles through Persia; painted the late Shah's portrait at Teheran; exhibited in Antwerp, Munich, Berlin, Copenhagen, Edinburgh, and Glasgow; upon two occasions President Glasgow Art Club; member of Committee, International Exhibition, Glasgow. *Publications:* various articles on the East; Autotypes; The North Sea, etc. *Recreations:* travel, patentee of engine for steam launches.

Died 25 Sept. 1928.

WILSON, Reginald Henry Rimington Rimington-, JP; *b* 3 Nov. 1852; *e s* of late James Wilson Rimington-Wilson and Jane, *d* of Robert Wallas. *Educ:* Eton; Trinity College, Cambridge. Patron of one living; late Lieut Inniskilling Dragoons. *Address:* Broomhead Hall, Sheffield. *TA:* Broomhead, Deepear. *T:* 11 Stocksbridge. *Clubs:* Naval and Military, Army and Navy.

Died 31 March 1927.

WILSON, Robert; Director (Chairman) and Editor, Edinburgh Evening News, Ltd; *b* Manchester, 1871; *s* of late Hugh Wilson (editor of the Manchester Evening News); unmarried. *Educ:* George Watson's College, Edinburgh; Monmouth Grammar School; Edinburgh University (MA); Berlin University. On staff of Edinburgh Evening News, of which he was the largest shareholder, for 26 years; Member of the Consultative Board of the Press Association. *Recreations:* shooting, golf, billiards. *T:* 718 Central, Edinburgh. *M:* S 3738. *Clubs:* National Liberal, Savage, Press; Scottish Liberal, Edinburgh.

Died Nov. 1920.

WILSON, Sir Roland Knyvet, 2nd Bt, *cr* 1857; JP Richmond, Surrey; MA, LLM Cantab; *b* Swaffham, Norfolk, 27 August 1840; 2nd *s* of late Rear-Admiral George Knyvet Wilson and Agnes Mary, *y d* of Rev. William Yonge, vicar of Swaffham; *S* uncle 1874; *m* 1873, Christiana Whiting (*d* 1917), *d* of late Richard Phillips, FRS. *Educ:* Eton (King's Scholar and Newcastle Scholar); King's College, Cambridge (Craven University Scholar, 1861; Senior Classic, 1863; late Fellow). Barrister, 1867; reporter for the Weekly Reporter and Law Journal, 1867–71; classical and historical lecturer for Mr Walter Wren (afterwards Wren and Gurney), 1871–78; Reader in Indian Law to the University of Cambridge, 1878–92; Pres. of the National Dwellings Soc. Ltd, 1905. *Publications:* A Short History of Modern English Law (Rivington's Historical Handbooks), 1874; an annotated edition of Sir G. C. Lewis's Use and Abuse of Political Terms, 1877; An Introduction to the Study of Anglo-Muhammadan Law, 1894; A Digest of Anglo-Muhammadan Law, 1895, 4th edn 1912; The Province of the State, 1911; The First and Last Fight for the Voluntary Principle in Education, 1915; articles, etc. *Heir: brother* Admiral Sir Arthur Knyvet Wilson, *b* 4 March 1842. *Address:* 86 Church Road, Richmond, Surrey.

Died 29 Oct. 1919.

WILSON, (Thomas) Woodrow, PhD, LittD, LLD; President of the United States, 1913–20; *b* Staunton, Virginia, 28 December 1856, of Scots-Irish parents; *m* 1st, 1885, Ellen Louise Axson (*d* 1914), Savannah, Georgia; three *d;* 2nd, 1915, Mrs Norman Galt. *Educ:* private schools; Princeton University; University of Virginia; Johns Hopkins Univ. Practised law, Atlanta, Georgia; but, finding study more congenial, gave up practice to enter academic life; Professor of History and Political Economy, Bryn Mawr College, 1885–88; Wesleyan University, 1888–90; Professor of Jurisprudence and Politics, Princeton University, 1890–1910; President of the University, 1902–10; Governor of New Jersey, 1911–13; writer and public lecturer. *Publications:* Congressional Government: a Study in American Politics, 1885; The State: Elements of Historical and Practical Politics, 1889; Division and Reunion, 1829–89, 1893; An Old Master, and other Political Essays, 1893; Mere Literature, and other Essays, 1896; George Washington, 1896; A History of the American People, 1902; The New Freedom, 1916. *Recreations:* bicycling, rowing, golf. *Address:* 2340 S Street, Washington, USA.

Died 3 Feb. 1924.

WILSON, Surg.-Gen. Sir William Deane, KCMG 1900; MB; LRCSI; *b* 27 Aug. 1843; *s* of Joseph Deane Wilson, Rathdowney, Queen's County; *m* 1880, Anna Wilhelmina Elizabeth, *e d* of late Rev. Henry Smythe; five *s.* Entered army, 1867; served Afghan War, 1878–80 (medal); Egyptian Expedition, 1882–84 (medal, bronze star); Soudan, 1884, battles Teb and Tamai (despatches, 2 clasps, promoted Surgeon-Major, ranking Lt-Colonel); S African War, 1899–1902; PMO, S Africa; advance on Kimberley; operations in Orange Free State, April and May 1900; operations in Transvaal, June 1900; operations in Transvaal, east and west Pretoria, July to 29 Nov. 1900; operations in Orange River Colony, May to 29 Nov. 1900; operations in Cape Colony, south Orange River, 1899–1900; operations in Transvaal, Orange River Colony, Cape Colony, 30 Nov. 1900 to

31 May 1902 (despatches thrice, Queen's medal 3 clasps, King's medal 2 clasps). *Address:* Moorside, Westfield, Sussex.

Died 19 Oct. 1921.

WILSON, Very Rev. William Hay; Dean of the United Diocese of Moray, Ross, and Caithness; Rector of St James' Church, Dingwall, and Chaplain of St Anne's Memorial Church, Strathpeffer Spa, NB, 1889; retired; *m* 1889, Lucy, *e d* of William Rhodes, MICE. *Educ:* Edinburgh and Durham Universities; Edinburgh Theological College. BA 1885; MA 1889, of Durham Univ.; FSAScot 1887. Deacon, 1884; Priest, 1885; Chaplain, Diocese of Moray, 1884; Senior Chaplain Inverness Cathedral, 1885; with charge of Holy Spirit Mission, 1887; Chaplain to late Primus Kelly, 1901–4; Synod Clerk of the Diocese and Canon of Inverness Cathedral, 1902; Chaplain to Bishop of Moray, 1904; Grand Chaplain of Scotland (Masonic), 1903–5; JP. *Publications:* After the Change called Death; several Masonic writings. *Address:* Kinnoull, Bridge of Allan, Stirlingshire.

Died 7 Oct. 1925.

WILSON, Major William Herbert, DSO 1917; Royal Field Artillery; *b* 1866; *s* of late Colonel Thomas Wilson, CB, of Liverpool and Gadlys, Cemaes, Anglesey, and Jane, *e d* of Thomas Kirkpatrick, Tyldesley, near Manchester; *m* Florence Kerr, *y d* of late David Fernie, of Blundellsands, Lancs, shipowner; no *c. Educ:* Wellington College. Formerly in business; R. S. Clare & Co. Ltd; Gunner's Venture, Ltd, Kenya Colony; held commission in Auxiliary Forces, 1885–1902, retiring with rank of Major; rejoined Royal Field Artillery shortly after outbreak of war, with temporary rank of Major (DSO, despatches). *Recreations:* hunting, shooting, travelling. *Address:* Runnymede, Nanyuki, Kenya Colony. *Club:* Bath.

Died 19 Nov. 1928.

WILSON, William Robert, ISO 1903; *b* 26 July 1844; *s* of late Henry Charles Wilson, Superintendent Registrar of Births, Deaths, and Marriages for Marylebone; *m* 1873, Mary, *d* of late John G. Barrow, MRCS, of Davies Street, W; one *s* four *d. Educ:* The Philological School, Marylebone. Entered the British Museum, 1863; Superintendent of Reading Room, 1896; Assistant-Keeper of Printed Books in the British Museum, 1899–1909; retired, 1909. *Recreations:* whist, angling. *Address:* 28 Steele's Road, Hampstead, NW.

Died 21 June 1928.

WILSON, William Tyson, JP; MP (Lab) West Houghton Division of Lancashire, since 1906; one of the founders of Bolton Building Trades Federation; *b* 1855; *s* of Edward Wilson, master tailor; *m* 1882, Frances, *d* of George Tyrrell, Lancaster. Whip to Labour Party, 1915; Chief Labour Whip, Jan. 1919. *Address:* 98 Mornington Road, Bolton, Lancs.

Died 14 Aug. 1921.

WILSON, William Wright, JP; FRSE; FRCSE, MRCS; Consulting Surgeon to the Birmingham and Midland Ear and Throat Hospital; *b* Aston juxta Birmingham, 1843; *e s* of Joseph and Ann Wilson; *m* 1st, 1873, Emily Sarah Whitfield (*d* 1902); 2nd, 1909, Amy Hurlston; no *c. Educ:* King Edward's Grammar School; Edgbaston Proprietary School and Queen's College, Birmingham. Consulting Surgeon to the Hospital for Diseases of the Ear, Throat, and Nose; wrote on botany, archæology, heraldry, physics, natural history, anatomy, and Freemasonry; was a Fellow of the Linnean Society; Hon. Secretary and Editor of the Midland Record Society; Hon. Secretary to the Birmingham Naturalist and Microscopical Society; Hon. Librarian to the Birmingham Archæological Society, etc; was a representative of Birmingham University on the Yardley Charity Estates, of which he was chairman, 1911; Deputy Provincial Grand Mark Master for Warwickshire, 1902; Grand Mark Overseer, 1914; a Knight of the 30', etc; JP Co. Warwick. *Publications:* The Physical Education of Girls; Fashions and Habits, especially with Regard to Children; Notes on Bordesley Manor; Notes on Maxstoke; Life of George Dawson; History of Christ Church, Birmingham; The Ancient Deeds of the Yardley Charity Estates; The Creation and other verses, etc. *Recreations:* angling, horticulture, antiquarian pursuits, numismatics, bibliophile, a reader of old deeds. *Address:* Cottesbrook, Acocks Green, Birmingham. *Died 26 Feb. 1919.*

WILSON-TODD, Captain Sir William Pierrepoint, 2nd Bt, *cr* 1903; *b* 3 May 1857; *s* of Sir William Henry Wilson-Todd, 1st Bt and Jane Marian Rutherford, *o c* and *heiress* of late John Todd, Halnaby (whose name 1st Bt took in addition to his own, 1855); *S* father, 1910; *m* 1887, Catharine James Crawford, *d* of late James Russel; one *s* decd. Late Capt. 4th Queen's Own Hussars. *Heir:* none. *Address:* Halnaby Hall, Croft, Darlington. *Clubs:* Naval and Military, Arthur's, Turf, Boodle's. *Died 13 Feb. 1925(ext)*.

WILTON, 6th Earl of, *cr* 1801; **Seymour Edward Frederic Egerton; Viscount Grey de Wilton,** 1801; late Lieutenant Royal Navy; *b* 1 Aug. 1896; *s* of 5th Earl and Hon. Mariota Thellusson, *d* of 5th Baron Rendlesham; *S* father, 1915; *m* 1917, Brenda, *d* of late Sir William Petersen, KBE; one *s* one *d* (and one *d* decd). Served European War. Conservative; owned about 9,900 acres. *Heir: s* Viscount Grey de Wilton, *b* 29 May 1921. *Address:* 43 Park Street, W1. *T:* Mayfair 7047.

Died 12 Oct. 1927.

WIMBLE, Sir John (Bowring), KBE 1919; Director of C. T. Bowring & Co., Ltd, of Liverpool, London, Cardiff, New York, and St John's, Newfoundland; Hon. Treasurer King George's Fund for Sailors; *b* 24 Aug. 1868; *s* of John Wimble and Harriet, *d* of late C. T. Bowring, Liverpool; *m* 1893, Anne Mason, *d* of late William Fothergill Batho; two *s* two *d. Educ:* Clifton College. Chairman London Shipowners' and Transport Workers' Military Service Committee; Chairman London Port Labour Committee; Chairman London General Shipowners' Society, 1916–17; Member of the Port of London Authority; Member of Committee of Lloyd's Register; Chairman Metropolitan Life Assurance Society; Member of the Port and Transit Executive Committee, 1917–19; JP Oxfordshire. *Recreations:* shooting, golf. *Address:* 23 Cambridge Square, Hyde Park, W2. *T:* Paddington 4748; Huntercombe, near Henley-on-Thames. *T:* Nettlebed 14. *Clubs:* Union, Bath, City of London, Ranelagh.

Died 25 Nov. 1927.

WINANS, Walter; *s* of William L. Winans of Ferry Bar Estate, Baltimore, Maryland, USA. *Educ:* Petrograd, Russia. Chevalier of the Imperial Order of St Stanislas of Russia; Commander of the Royal Spanish Order of Isabel the Catholic, and of the Crown of Roumania; Officer of the Star of Roumania. *Publications:* The Modern Pistol; Hints on Revolver Shooting; Automatic Pistol Shooting; The Sporting Rifle; Practical Rifle Shooting; The Art of Revolver Shooting; Shooting for Ladies; Deer Breeding; Animal Sculpture. *Address:* Carlton Hotel, 17 Avenue de Tervueren, Brussels.

Died 12 Aug. 1920.

WINCHILSEA, 13th Earl of, *cr* 1628, **AND NOTTINGHAM,** 8th Earl of, *cr* 1675; **Henry Stormont Finch-Hatton;** Bt 1611; Viscount Maidstone, 1623; Bt English, 1660; Baron Finch, 1674; Hereditary Lord of Royal Manor of Wye; *b* 3 Nov. 1852; *s* of 10th Earl of Winchilsea and 3rd wife, Fanny Margaretta (*d* 1909), *e d* of Edward Royd Rice; *S* brother, 1898; *m* 1882, Anne Jane (*d* 1924), *d* of late Admiral of the Fleet Sir Henry John Codrington, KCB; two *s* one *d. Educ:* Eton; Balliol Coll., Oxford. Owned about 5,000 acres. *Heir: s* Viscount Maidstone, *b* 28 May 1885. *Address:* Haverholme Priory, Sleaford. *TA:* Haverholme, Ruskington. *T:* Ruskington 10. *M:* FF 135. *Clubs:* White's, Carlton.

Died 14 Aug. 1927.

WINDER, Captain Robert Cecil, CB 1918; VD: DL; Secretary East Lancashire Territorial Force Association. *Address:* Wenderholme, Bolton-le-Moors, Lancs. *Died 15 Jan. 1920.*

WINDER, Very Rev. Thomas Edward; Rector of Ulcombe, Maidstone. *Educ:* Trinity College, Dublin (MA). Ordained, 1889; Curate Great Sankey, Lancs, 1889–92; Succenter, St Patrick's Cathedral, 1892–99; Rector, Aghade, 1899–1902; Incumbent, Fiddown, 1902–8; Canon of Kilkenny, 1907–8; Incumbent of Kilkenny, 1908; Dean of Ossory, 1908–23. *Address:* Ulcombe Rectory, Maidstone. *Club:* University, Dublin.

Died 12 June 1926.

WINDHAM, Vice-Adm. Charles, CVO 1901; Royal Navy; Gentleman Usher to King George V, since 1907; *b* 1 March 1851; *e* surv. *s* of General Sir Charles Ashe Windham, KCB, and *g s* of Admiral William Windham, of Felbrigg Hall, Norfolk. Educ: Lee's School, Brighton, and HMS Britannia. Entered Navy, 1865; served in Abyssinian Expedition, 1868; Ashanti, 1874; Egypt, 1882; Captain of Royal Yacht Osborne, 1896–1901; HMS Isis, 1901–2; Amphitrite, 1902; Rear-Admiral, 1905. *Clubs:* Marlborough, Naval and Military, Sports. *Died 20 May 1916.*

WINDSOR-CLIVE, Lt-Col Hon. George Herbert Windsor, DL; Retired List; *b* 12 March 1835; 2nd *s* of Hon. Robert Henry Clive (*s* of 1st Earl of Powis), and late Baroness Windsor; *m* 1876, Hon. Gertrude Albertina Trefusis (*d* 1878), *d* of 19th Baron Clinton and Lady Elizabeth Georgiana Kerr, *d* of 6th Marquess of Lothian; one *s. Educ:* Eton. MP (C) Ludlow, 1860–85; served in 52nd Light Infantry, 1852–60; Coldstream Guards, 1860–70. *Address:* 12 Stratford Place, W. *Clubs:* Carlton, Travellers'.

Died 26 April 1918.

WINGATE, Sir (James) Lawton, Kt 1920; PRSA 1919 (RSA 1887; ARSA 1878); *b* 1846; father, manufacturing chemist; *m*; one *s* five *d*. Attended Glasgow School of Art, Edinburgh School of Art, and Academy Life School. *Address:* 39 Mansionhouse Road, Edinburgh.
Died 22 April 1924.

WINGATE, Captain Malcolm Roy, DSO 1915; MC; 26th Field Company, Royal Engineers; Staff Captain, General Headquarters, British Expeditionary Force; *b* 28 Aug. 1893; 2nd *s* of Gen. Sir (Francis) Reginald Wingate (Bt 1920), GCB, GCVO, GBE, KCMG, DSO, and Catherine Leslie, *o d* of Capt. Joseph Sparkhall Rundle, RN. Entered army, 1912; served European War, 1914–15 (DSO, MC, and Croix de Guerre). *Address:* Knockenhair, Dunbar, Scotland. *Club:* Caledonian. *Died 21 March 1918.*

WINGFIELD, Rev. Lt-Col William Edward, DSO 1916; Rector of Broome, Norfolk, since 1920, and of Thwaite, Norfolk since 1922; *b* 1867; *s* of late Captain Richard Wingfield, 52nd Light Infantry, of Abbeyleix, Queen's Co.; *m* 1896, Elizabeth Mary, *d* of late George J. Trench of Ardfert, Co. Kerry; two *s* two *d. Educ:* Wellington; RMA, Woolwich; Ridley Hall, Cambridge. Received commission in RA, 1886; retired, 1907. Deacon, 1909; Priest, 1911; Curate St Paul, Portman Square, 1911–13; recalled from Reserve of Officers, 1914; served 3½ years overseas in European War (promoted Lt-Col in Gallipoli; wounded in France, 1918; DSO, despatches 3 times). *Recreations:* mountaineering, skiing, yachting. *Address:* Rectory, Broome, Norfolk. *Died 25 Jan. 1927.*

WINKS, William Edward; Baptist minister, retired; *b* Leicester, 1842; *y s* of late J. Foulkes Winks; *m* Annie, *d* of Lewis Whitehead, Chatham; one *s* four *d. Educ:* Rev. T. Carrier's Private School, New Walk, Leicester; Chilwell College, Notts. Minister Allerton, Bradford, 1865–67; Wisbech, 1867–76; Cardiff, 1876–1914; Hon. Curator Cardiff Museum, 1876–1913; Member Public Library Committee since 1876; erstwhile Governor and Councillor of S Wales University College, Cardiff. *Publications:* Thoughts on Prayer, 1879; Lives of Illustrious Shoemakers, 1883; A Pastoral Medley; Prayer in the Four Gospels, 1897; The Gospel of Prayer in St Luke, 1897; Christian Hymns and Songs, 1897, 2nd edn 1906; History of Bethany Baptist Church, Cardiff; An Attempt to solve the School Library Problem, Library Association Record, Pt I, 1900; Danish Place-Names in South Wales; Proceedings of Cardiff Naturalist Society; Sketch of History of the English Bible, 1911. *Address:* Eaton Cottage, Llanishen, Cardiff.
Died 21 Dec. 1926.

WINN, Lt-Comdr Sydney Thornhill, DSO 1914; retired; *b* 1888; *o s* of late Dr Winn, RN; *m* 1919, Mary, *e d* of A. H. A. Knox-Little, Garth House, Dorking. Served European War, 1914–15 (DSO); was in Submarine B11 in her dash into the Dardanelles. *Address:* 23 Lyndale Avenue, Finchley Road, NW2.
Died 16 May 1924.

WINNINGTON, Lt-Col John Francis Sartorius, DSO 1915; 4th Battalion Worcestershire Regiment; AIR Headquarters Western Command, Chester; *b* 17 Sept. 1876; *m* Joyce Mary, *d* of D. Marriage, JP, Boughton Park, Worcester; two *d*. Entered army, 1897; Captain, 1901; Major, 1914; served South Africa with 2nd Batt. Dublin Fusiliers and 2nd Worcestershire Regt, 1899–1900 (Queen's medal, 4 clasps); Adjutant 5th Worcestershire Regt, 1906–10; Adjutant 1st Batt. 1912; European War, 1914–15 (despatches twice, Bt Lt-Col, DSO). *Recreations:* cricket (played for County), shooting, hunting, fishing. *Address:* Boughton Park, Worcester.
Died 22 Sept. 1918.

WINSLOE, Lt-Col Herbert Edward, CMG 1920; DSO 1917; Royal Engineers; *b* 1873; *s* of late Col Richard William Charles Winsloe, CB; *m* 1921, Aileen Marie Constance Venables. *Educ:* University College School; Dover College; RM Academy, Woolwich. Joined RE as 2nd Lieut, 1892; served in India, 1894–1914; Tirah Campaign, 1898 (medal with clasp); Zakka Khel Campaign, 1908 (medal with clasp); Mesopotamia Expeditionary Force, 1914–16, including Siege of Kut (despatches thrice, DSO, promoted Bt Lt-Col). *Recreations:* shooting, riding. *Club:* Naval and Military.
Died 1 Dec. 1921.

WINSLOE, Col Richard William Charles, CB 1889; retired pay; *b* Innerleithen, 20 April 1835; 2nd *s* of Richard Winsloe (*d* 1878), Mount Nebo, Wilton, Somerset, and Isabella Wyld, *d* of late Captain Richard Dawson, The Buffs; *m* 1861, Constance Edwards, 2nd *d* of late F. M. Cromartie, Supt of Stores, Ordnance Department; four *s* five *d. Educ:* Edinburgh Academy. Joined 15th Regt, 1853; volunteered to the Royal Scots Fusiliers, 1854; served with them during the latter part of the Crimean Campaign, 1855–56; present siege and fall of Sebastopol and Expedition to Kinburu (medal and clasp and Turkish medal); Zulu Campaign, 1879; present at Battle of Ulundi (severely wounded, mentioned in despatches, medal and clasp, brevet of Lieut-Col); Transvaal Campaign, 1880–81; commanded troops at siege of Potschefstrom, being thanked in district orders (wounded, mentioned in despatches, ADC to Queen Victoria); Burmese Expedition, 1886–87; in command of the Royal Scots Fusiliers and Thayetmyo District; commanded the troops at the relief of Thabybin in Upper Burmah (mentioned in despatches, medal); ADC to Queen Victoria, 1882–90; Jubilee Medal 1887, and clasp 1897; reward for distinguished service. *Publication:* Siege of Potschefstrom. *Recreations:* gardening, cricket, carpentering. *Address:* 20 Guilford Terrace, Dover. *Club:* Union, Malta.
Died 5 June 1917.

WINSLOW, Rev. William Copley, DD, STD, PhD, ScD, LittD, DCL, LLD; founder of American branch of Egypt Exploration Fund in 1883; its Hon. Secretary, and Vice-President for America till 1902; archæologist-historical writer, and journalist; assisting work of Egyptian Research Account under Petrie, and raising funds in the United States (as Vice President of Research in the United States), and writing articles for journals on the discoveries; *b* Boston, 13 Jan. 1840; *s* of Rev. Hubbard Winslow, DD, author; *m* 1st, Harriet S. (*decd*), *d* of Hon. Joseph Hayward; one *d*; 2nd, Elizabeth Bruce Roclofson, author. *Educ:* Hamilton Coll.; General Theol Seminary (Episcopal), New York City. On executive committees of various leading societies; executive secretary Free Church Association, Massachusetts, since 1883; VP Hamilton College Alumni Association of the USA at its centennial, 1912; ex-President New England Alumni Association; hon. member of leading Canadian and 23 of the State historical societies, including five of the six New England States; Hon. Fellow of Oriental Research Society (USA); university lecturer, etc; formerly: editor of Christian Times; associate editor of World, The Hamiltonian, University Quarterly, American Antiquarian, American Historical Register; on staff of Biblia. *Publications:* A Greek City in Egypt; Pithom and Zoan; Pilgrim Fathers in Holland; Governor Edward Winslow of Plymouth; Egyptian Antiquities in American Museums; Egypt at Home; Distribution of Papyri in the United States; published papers before Amer. Oriental Soc., Amer. Hist. Assoc., Arch. Inst., New Eng. Hist. Soc., NY Biog. Soc., American Statistical Assoc., etc. *Recreation:* summers in the woods of Maine and New York, which he explored, and also on Cape Cod by the sea. *Address:* 525 Beacon Street, Boston, USA. *Clubs:* University, Clerical, Boston.
Died 2 Feb. 1925.

WINTER, Lt-Col Ernest Arthur, DSO 1918; MC; Surveyor of HM Customs and Excise, Grimsby; *b* 1874; 3rd *s* of late James Winter, civil servant, The Lodge, Torrington; *m* 1914, Mary Madeline Jung, Bewdley, Worcs; two *d. Educ:* privately. Entered Civil Service, 1895; served in Cumberland, Devonshire, Ireland, and Worcestershire; joined HM Forces, 1914; served with 23rd Batt. Royal Fusiliers, 1914–19; commanded the Batt., 1917–19; commanded British Base Camp, Antwerp, 26 May–Oct. 1919 (MC, DSO and bar, despatches thrice); demobilised, 1919. *Recreations:* hunting, fishing, shooting. *Address:* Brooklands Avenue, Cleethorpes, Lincs. *TA:* Winter, Brooklands Avenue, Cleethorpes. *M:* EE 4666.
Died April 1925.

WINTER, Hon. Sir Francis Pratt, Kt 1900; CMG 1892; *b* Colony of Victoria, Australia, 23 Feb. 1848; *e s* of George Winter, King's County, Ireland, and Elizabeth, *d* of James Cox of Tasmania; *m* 1903, Edith, *d* of Hon. George Moore of Fiji. *Educ:* private school, London. A solicitor, Colony of Queensland; barrister and solicitor, Colony of Fiji; acting Attorney-General, Colony of Fiji, 1887–88; First Chief Judicial Officer, British New Guinea, 1888–1903. *Decorated for* services in British New Guinea.
Died 29 March 1919.

WINTER, Hon. Henry Daniel, JP; *b* 26 Oct. 1851; *s* of J. E. F. Winter of Pietermaritzburg, Natal; *m* Janet, *d* of William Leslie of Campsie Glen, Estcourt. *Educ:* Pietermaritzburg, Natal. Began farming in Weenen County, Natal, 1875; Member of the Legislative Assembly, 1893; Minister of Agriculture, Natal, under Binns Ministry, 1899; under (Lt-Col Rt. Hon. Sir Albert Henry) Hime Ministry, 1899–1903; under (Hon. Charles John) Smythe Coalition Ministry, 1905–6. *Address:* Loch Sloy, Estcourt, Natal.
Died 4 Nov. 1927.

WINTER, William; author; *b* Gloucester, Massachusetts, USA, 15 July 1836; 2nd *s* of Captain Charles Winter and Louisa Wharff; *m* 1860, Elizabeth Campbell, of the Campbells, formerly of Ederline, Loch

Awe, NB; two s one d. *Educ:* Boston and Cambridge Schools; Dane Law School; Harvard Coll. BL 1857; LittD from Brown Univ., 1895. Lecturer, political speaker, 1856; writer for the press, poet, essayist, traveller, editor, biographer, etc; first visited England in 1877; founded the Arthur Winter Memorial Library in 1886; dramatic editor and reviewer for NY Tribune, 1865-1909; President of Staten Island Academy, 1891-1907. *Publications:* Shakespeare's England; Gray Days and Gold; Old Shrines and Ivy; Brown Heath and Blue Bells; Wanderers (poems); Shadows of the Stage (three series); Life and Art of Edwin Booth; Life and Art of Joseph Jefferson; Orations; Life of John Gilbert; Brief Chronicles; The Actor and other Speeches; The Press and the Stage; The Stage Life of Mary Anderson; Henry Irving; A Wreath of Laurel; George William Curtis; Life of John McCullough; Life of Ada Rehan; Life and Letters of William Law Symonds; Other Days, being Chronicles and Memories of the Stage; Old Friends, being Literary Recollections; Poems, definitive edn; Life and Art of Richard Mansfield; Over the Border; Shakespeare on the Stage; Lives of the Players—1, Tyrone Power; The Wallet of Time; Shakespeare on the Stage (second series); Vagrant Memories, 1915. *Recreations:* study of Shakespeare, antiquarian research, travel. *Address:* 46 Third Avenue, New Brighton, Staten Island, NY; Ederline Cottage, Mentone, California. *T:* Tompkinsville 62 J. *Clubs:* Lotos, New York; Bohemian, San Francisco.

Died 30 June 1917.

WINTER, W. Tatton, RBA; *b* Ashton-under-Lyne. *Educ:* various elementary and private schools. Entered business at an early age in Manchester; studied art at the Board School classes, in evening, and Manchester Academy of Fine Arts; gave up business later; toured through Belgium and Holland; studied under Verlat at Antwerp; exhibitor at Royal Academy since 1889; at New Gallery, Royal Institute of Painters on Water Colours, The Salon, and Munich, etc; elected to London Sketch Club, 1902. *Recreations:* gardening, walking, literature. *Address:* Avondale, South Park, Reigate.

Died 22 March 1928.

WINTERBOTHAM, Rev. Canon Raynor. *Educ:* University of London (BSc, MA, LLB); Wells College. Ordained 1865; Chaplain to Bishop of Grafton, 1867-68; Incumbent of Christ Church, Grafton, NSW, 1867-72; of St Peter's, Fraserburgh, NB, 1878-86; Rector of Holy Trinity, Dean Bridge, Edinburgh, 1886-99; Synod Clerk of the Diocese of Edinburgh and Canon of St Mary's Cathedral, 1897-1900; Hon. Canon of St Mary's Cathedral, 1900. *Address:* Melmoth, Zululand, Natal, S Africa.

Died 7 May 1924.

WINTERBOTHAM, Sir William (Howard), Kt 1919; Official Solicitor to the Supreme Court, 1895-1919; *b* 13 Dec. 1843; *y s* of Lindsey Winterbotham, Stroud, Gloucestershire; *m* 1875, Elizabeth, *d* of Thomas Micklem, Hoddesdon, Herts; four *s* one *d*. *Educ:* Amersham School, Buckinghamshire; University College, London; Pembroke College, Cambridge. Graduated BA (1st class with honours) at London University, 1862; BA (1st class Mathematical Tripos) at Cambridge, 1866; admitted a Solicitor, 1869; senior partner in the firm of Waterhouse & Co., 1 New Court, Lincoln's Inn, until his retirement in 1919; Member of the Council of the Law Society, 1895; President, 1909. *Recreations:* yachting, gardening. *Address:* 51 Ladbroke Grove, Notting Hill, W11. *T:* Park 62; Craig-y-Môr, Abersoch, Carnarvonshire. *Club:* National Liberal.

Died 24 Jan. 1926.

WINTRINGHAM, Thomas; MP (Ind. L) Louth since 1920; *b* 22 Aug. 1867; *s* of John and Mary Wintringham; *m* 1903, Margaret, *d* of David Longbottom, Yorks. Contested (L) Grimsby, 1898. *Address:* House of Commons, SW1.   *Died 8 Aug. 1921.*

WIRGMAN, Ven. Augustus Theodore, VD 1896; DD, DCL; Archdeacon of Port Elizabeth; Hon. Chaplain to King George V; Canon of Grahamstown Cathedral since 1899; Vice-Provost of St Mary's Collegiate Church, Port Elizabeth, since 1888; Senior Chaplain and Hon. Lieutenant-Colonel Colonial Forces, Cape Colony; *b* Bradbourne, Derbyshire, 22 Sept. 1846; *e s* of Rev. Augustus Wirgman, MA, Vicar of Hartington, Co. Derby, and Jane, *d* of Thomas Pearson of Wingfield; *m* 1874, Rose, *d* of A. J. Worthington of Ball Haye Hall, Leek, Co. Stafford. *Educ:* Rossall; Magdalene College, Cambridge (Scholar, 1866). BA Classical Tripos, 1870; 2nd class Theological Tripos, 1871; MA 1873; MA University of the Cape, 1875; Hon. DCL University of the South, USA, 1877; BD Cambridge, 1893; DD Cambridge, 1899. Deacon, 1870; Priest, 1871; Curate of Hartington, Alton, and St Michael's, Handsworth, Birmingham, 1870-73; Vice-Principal of St Andrew's College, Grahamstown, Cape Colony, 1873-75; Rector of St Mary's, Port

Elizabeth, 1875; Rural Dean of Port Elizabeth, 1884-96; Examining Chaplain to Bishop of Grahamstown, 1883-92; to Bishop of Mashonaland, 1899; Secretary of Theological Faculty of Church in South Africa, 1898; Prov. Secretary for South Africa of the Church House, Westminster, 1892; on active service during Boer War, 1899-1900 (medal and clasp). Select Preacher at Cambridge, 1911; S African General Service Medal, 1880; Coronation medal, 1911. *Publications:* The Prayer Book with Historical Notes and Scripture Proofs, 1873; The Beatitudes and the Lord's Prayer, 1877; The Sevenfold Gifts, 1889; The English Reformation, etc, 1890; The Church and the Civil Power, 1893; The Spirit of Liberty, 1893; The History of the English Church and People in South Africa, 1894; The Doctrine of Confirmation, 1896; The Constitutional Authority of Bishops, 1899; The Blessed Virgin and all the Company of Heaven (an eirenicon), 1905; The Life of James Green, DD, Dean of Maritzburg, 1909; History of Protestantism, 1911; articles in Nineteenth Century on Boer War, 1900. *Recreations:* rowing, cricket, football, golf, sketching, painting. *Address:* St Mary's Rectory, Port Elizabeth, South Africa. *Club:* Authors'.

Died 16 Oct. 1917.

WIRGMAN, Theodore Blake, RP; *b* 1848. *Address:* 24 Dawson Place, W2. *T:* Park 2112.   *Died 16 Jan. 1925*

WISE, Alfred Gascoyne, LLB; *b* Colombo, Ceylon, 15 August 1854; *s* of late Alfred Wise; *m* Augusta Frances (*d* 1911), *d* of A. N. C. R. Nugent; two *s*. *Educ:* Repton; Trinity College, Cambridge. Called to the Bar, Lincoln's Inn, 1878; Police Magistrate, Hong-Kong, 1884; Registrar of the Supreme Court, etc, 1892; Puisne Judge of the Supreme Court, Hong-Kong, 1895-1909. *Address:* Valroy, Camberley. *Club:* Conservative.

Died 25 June 1923.

WISE, Hon. Bernhard Ringrose; Agent-General for New South Wales in London since 1915; *b* Sydney, NSW, 10 Feb. 1858; 2nd *s* of Mr Justice Wise of Sydney; *m* 1884, Lilian Margaret, *d* of John Forster Baird of Beaumont Hill, Northumberland. *Educ:* Rugby; Queen's Coll., Oxford (Scholar). Cobden Prize, 1878; *Proxime* for the Lothian Historical Essay, 1880; 1st class in Law, 1880. President of the Oxford Union and OUAC, 1880; one of the founders and first Vice-President Amateur Athletic Association of Great Britain; amateur mile champion, 1879-81; called to the Bar by the Middle Temple, 1883; Attorney-General of New South Wales, 1887-88; QC 1898; Attorney-General of New South Wales, 1899-1904; one of the delegates from New South Wales to the Australian Federal Convention; King Edward VII approved of his retention for life of the title of Honourable, 1907. *Clubs:* Garrick; Australian, Sydney.

Died 19 Sept. 1916.

WISE, Francis Hubert; Master County of Limerick Hounds, 1899-1908; *b* 6 Feb. 1869; *s* of late Charles W. Wise of Rochestown, Cahir, Co. Tipperary; *m* 1898, Jean Orme, *y d* of late General Sir Archibald Little, GCB, of Upton House, Tetbury, Gloucestershire. *Educ:* Harrow. Served as lieutenant in 3rd Durham LI, 1888-90; gazetted to 2nd lieutenancy, 13th Hussars, July 1890; Lieutenant, 1891; served with 13th Hussars during South African War, and was present at all engagements up to Relief of Ladysmith (despatches), awarded Humane Society's Bronze Medal for saving life of trooper, 13th Hussars, in River Tugela, Jan. 1900; hunted 13th Hussars Harriers when regiment quartered at Dundalk, 1895-96; retired, 1901; Major, South of Ireland Imperial Yeomanry, 1903. *Recreations:* hunting, shooting, fishing. *Address:* Rochestown, Cahir. *Clubs:* Naval and Military; Kildare Street, Dublin.

Died 5 June 1917.

WISE, Sir Fredric, Kt 1924; DL, JP; MP (U) for Ilford since 1920; *b* 16 Aug. 1871; *e s* of Alexander Josiah Patrick Wise, of Belleville Park, Cappoquin, Waterford, and Julia, *d* of John Anthony Woods, of Benton Hall, Newcastle-on-Tyne; *m* 1904, Lucy Elizabeth, *d* of late Sir Thomas Wrightson, 1st Bt, and Elizabeth, *e d* of Samuel Wise, Ripon; one *s* one *d*. *Educ:* Marlborough College; abroad. Started life in a bank, and in 1903 founded present stockbroking firm of Wise, Speke & Co., of Newcastle-on-Tyne; travelled a great deal all over the world in interests of his business; during war gave his services voluntarily—in County as Chairman of Volunteers and Military Representative, and in London to National Service, Food Ministry, Treasury; sent to France to lecture to troops on food position; sent to Berlin in March 1919 by Peace Conference to report on Financial Position of Germany; Financial Adviser to Lord Byng's Committee of United Service Fund; Director of Daily Express, Director of Sudan Plantation Syndicate, Ltd. *Address:* Holwell Court, Hatfield. *Clubs:* Carlton, Oriental.   *Died 26 Jan. 1928.*

WISEMAN, Very Rev. Dr James; Dean of Aberdeen and Orkney since 1910; Rector of St Machar since 1874. *Educ:* University of Aberdeen (MA, Hon. DD). Ordained, 1870; Incumbent of Alford, 1870-74. *Address:* The Rectory, Bucksburn, Aberdeen.
Died 20 Nov. 1925.

WITHAM, Philip; *b* 1842; *y s* of Sir Charles Witham, RN; *m* 1878, Louisa, 2nd *d* of Marmaduke Charles Salvin of Burn Hall, County Durham; two *d. Educ:* Mount St Mary's College, Derbyshire; abroad. Admitted solicitor, 1866; Head of firm of solicitors, 1 Gray's Inn Square, WC. *Recreations:* shooting, fishing, golf. *Address:* Whitmoor House, Sutton Park, near Guildford. *TA:* Sutton Green. *T:* Worplesdon 34.
Died 4 May 1921.

WODEHOUSE, Edmond Henry, CB 1897; *b* Norton, Kent, 17 Feb. 1837; 7th *s* of Rev. Thomas Wodehouse, Canon of Wells, and Anne, *d* of Walker King, Bishop of Rochester; *m* 1864, Louisa Clara, *d* of Rev. Nathaniel Wodehouse, Vicar of Worle, Somerset. *Educ:* Westminster; Christ Church, Oxford (Student). 1st class Classical Mods 1857; 2nd class Final School Lit. Hum. 1859; MA. Inspector of Poor Law Schools, 1863-71; Poor Law and Local Govt Board Inspector, 1871-86; Chief General Inspector and Asst Sec. Local Govt Board, 1886-91; Commissioner of Inland Revenue, 1891-1902. *Recreations:* cricket (as a spectator), bicycling. *Address:* Plomer Hill House, West Wycombe, Bucks. *Club:* Oxford and Cambridge.
Died 27 March 1923.

WODEHOUSE, Rev. Preb. Philip John, MA; Rector of Bratton Fleming, Devon, 1875-1913; Rural Dean of Shirwell, 1887-1908; Prebendary of Exeter Cathedral since 1903; *b* Malvern, 6 Oct. 1836; *s* of late Col Philip Wodehouse, of Wribbenhall, Bewdley, Worcestershire; *m* 1st, 1876, Constance Helen (*d* 1877), 3rd *d* of Wade Brown, of Monkton Farleigh, Wilts; 2nd, 1879, Marion Bryan, *d* of Rev. Gilbert I. Wallas, Rector of Shobrooke; two *s* two *d. Educ:* Harrow; Caius College, Cambridge (Eighth Wrangler). Deacon, 1859; Priest, 1860; Curate of Halesowen, Worcestershire, 1859-60; St John, Ladywood, Birmingham, 1860-65; St Mary, Nottingham, 1865-66; Vicar of St Margaret's, Lynn Regis, 1866-71; Diocesan Inspector, Manchester, 1871-75. *Address:* Wheatridge, Chelston, Torquay.
Died 8 Dec. 1917.

WOLFE-MURRAY, Lt-Col Arthur Alexander, CB 1915; Highland Light Infantry; *b* 22 May 1866; *s* of late James Wolfe-Murray and Louisa Grace, *d* of Sir Adam Hay, 7th Bt, and Henrietta Callender, *e d* of William Grant; *m* 1904, Evelyn Mary Hay, *e d* of late Colin Mackenzie, Lord Lieutenant for Peeblesshire; one *s. Educ:* Harrow. Entered army, 1886; Captain, 1893; Major, 1904, Lt-Col, 1912; served S African War, 1899-1900 and 1902 (despatches twice; Queen's medal, 2 clasps; King's medal with clasp); European War, 1914-15 (CB). *Recreations:* shooting, fishing, golf. *Address:* 20 George Square, Edinburgh. *Clubs:* Naval and Military; New, Edinburgh.
Died 7 Dec. 1918.

WOLLASTON, Sir Arthur Naylor, KCIE 1908 (CIE 1886); JP Kent and Cinque Ports; *b* Norwood, 14 Oct. 1842; *y* surv. *s* of late Henry Francis Wollaston, Southsea; *m* 1873, Caroline Marianne (*d* 1902), *o d* of late Sir Albert William Woods, GCVO, KCB, KCMG, and Caroline, *d* of Robert Cole, Rotherfield, Sussex; one *s. Educ:* Stockwell Grammar School. Entered India Office by open competition, 1859; junior clerk, 1860; senior clerk, 1873; assistant secretary, 1884; succeeded Sir Frederic John Goldsmid as examiner in Persian at Royal Staff College, Sandhurst, 1880; selected in 1881 by the Science and Art Department to superintend the translation of Oriental inscriptions in S Kensington Museum; Registrar and Superintendent of Records, India Office, 1898-1907. *Decorated* for Oriental scholarship. *Publications:* (trans.) Anvar-i-Suhaili, or Fables of Bidpai, 1877; Sir Lewis Pelly's Miracle Play of Hasan and Husain, 1879; English-Persian Dictionary, 1882, a larger work of the same kind, 1889; Half-Hours with Muhammad, 1886; Sword of Islam, 1905; The Religion of the Koran, 1905; The Scroll of Wisdom, 1906; Tales within Tales, 1909; (with Sir Roper Lethbridge) Gazetteer of the Territories under the Government of India. *Recreations:* literature, music. *Address:* Glen Hill, Walmer, Kent. *TA:* Walmer. *Club:* Northbrook.
Died 8 Feb. 1922.

WOLLASTON, Sir Harry Newton Phillips, KCMG 1912 (CMG 1907); ISO 1903; JP; Barrister-at-Law; late Permanent Head of Department of Trade and Customs, Commonwealth of Australia, and Comptroller-General of Customs, retired 1911; *b* W Australia, 17 Jan. 1846; *s* of Rev. Henry Newton Wollaston, Trinity Church, E Melbourne; *m* 1st, 1868, Mary Annie (*d* 1902), *d* of John Harker, Yorks; one *s* three *d*; 2nd, 1914, Mary, *d* of late Maj.-Gen. Price-

Dent, Hallaton Manor, Leics. *Educ:* St John's College, Auckland; Nelson College, NZ; Melbourne University. Entered Civil Service of Victoria after examination as a junior, 1863; matriculated at university and completed university course after entering the Civil Service; graduated with honours in Law, 1884; called to the Bar, 1885; admitted as Master of Laws, 1886; Doctor of Laws, 1891; rose through all grades of Civil Service of Victoria and became Secretary for Trade and Customs in that state, 1891; Standing Counsel to Marine Board, 1886-1901; transferred to Commonwealth service, 1901; attended Imperial Conference on Shipping Laws in London in 1907 as an official delegate from Australia. *Publications:* Trade Customs and Marine Law of Victoria; Customs Law of Australia; Marine Board Act of Victoria with Notes; Customs Handbook, etc. *Recreations:* riding, cycling, reading. *Address:* Toorak, Melbourne, Victoria. *Club:* Melbourne.
Died 14 Feb. 1921.

WOLRIGE-GORDON, Col John Gordon, of Hallhead and Esslemont, Aberdeenshire; CMG 1918; retired pay; Lieutenant-Colonel commanding 3rd Battalion Argyll and Sutherland Highlanders, 1914-19; *b* 20 Dec. 1859; *s* of Henry Wolrige-Gordon, Aberdeenshire; *m* 1889, Isabel Hervey (*d* 1911), *o c* of William Hervey Woodhouse of Irnham Hall, Lincolnshire; one *s* two *d. Educ:* Eton; Royal Military Coll., Sandhurst. Entered Army, 1879; served NW Frontier India, 1897-98 (medal and clasp); S Africa, 1899-1902 (despatches twice, Bt Lt-Col, Queen's and King's medals 6 clasps). *Address:* Esslemont, Ellon, Aberdeenshire; 53 Queen's Gate, SW7. *Clubs:* Carlton; New, Edinburgh.
Died 30 Sept. 1925.

WOLSELEY, Sir Capel Charles, 9th Bt, *cr* 1744; FRGS; *b* 24 Aug. 1870; *s* of late Major William Charles Wolseley and Annie, *d* of Rev. Capel Wolseley; *S* kinsman, 1890; *m* 1907, Beatrice Sophia, *d* of late Col W. Knollys. Lieut Royal West Surrey Regiment, 1891-93; Vice-Consul at Archangel, 1900-9; joined 3rd Batt. East Surrey Regt, Dec. 1914; Captain, Feb. 1915; served European War, 1914-18; with the British Expeditionary Force in North Russia, 1919. *Heir: cousin* Reginald Beatty Wolseley, *b* 31 Jan. 1872. *Address:* 32 Knightsbridge, SW.
Died 27 Aug. 1923.

WOLSELEY, Gen. Sir George Benjamin, GCB 1907 (KCB 1891; CB 1885); Colonel York and Lancaster Regiment; *b* 11 July 1839; 4th *s* of late Major Garnet Joseph Wolseley, King's Own Borderers, and Frances Anne, *d* of William Smith, Co. Dublin; *brother* of 1st Viscount Wolseley; *m* 1867, Esther Louise (*d* 1902), *d* of William Andrews; one *s* decd. *Educ:* private tuition. Ensign Cheshire Regiment, 1857; Lieut York and Lancaster Regiment, 1858; by purchase Capt. North Staffordshire Regiment, 1868; Major York and Lancaster Regiment, 1878; Lt-Col 1879; Maj.-Gen. by selection, 1892; served with 84th Foot in Indian Mutiny (medal); AAG in Afghan campaign (medal and Brevet Lieut-Col); AA&QMG Egyptian campaign, including Tel-el-Kebir (medal and bronze star); Col and ADC to Queen Victoria for Egyptian War, 1882; AA&QMG Nile campaign, and subsequently as Col on the Staff commanding troops at Abu Gus (clasp and CB); Brig.-Gen. in Burmese campaign, and commanded expedition which annexed Wunthoo (thanked by Government of India, medal, and KCB); commanded the Forces, Punjab, India, with rank of Lieut-Gen., 1897-98; Madras Forces, 1898-1903; retired, 1906. *Publications:* magazine articles. *Recreations:* shooting, cycling, tennis. *Address:* Thatched Cottage, Wateringbury, Kent. *TA:* Wateringbury. *Club:* United Service.
Died 10 May 1921.

WOMBWELL, Capt. Sir Henry (Herbert), 5th Bt, *cr* 1778; *b* 24 Sept. 1840; 3rd *s* of Sir George Wombwell, 3rd Bt and Georgiana, *d* of Thomas Orby Hunter, Crowland Abbey, Co. Lincoln; *S* brother, 1913; *m* 1902, Hon. Myrtle Mabel Muriel Mostyn, *d* of Hon. George Charles Mostyn and *sister* of 7th Baron Vaux of Harrowden; no *c. Educ:* Harrow. Late 7th Hussars and Royal Horse Guards. *Heir: great-nephew* (Frederick) Philip (Alfred William) Wombwell, *b* 6 July 1910. *Address:* 85 Vincent Square, SW1. *T:* Victoria 5402. *Clubs:* Boodle's, Orleans.
Died 1 Feb. 1926.

WOOD, Sir Alexander, Kt 1922; JP; *b* Partick, 1849; *s* of Alexander Wood; *m* 1878, Mary, *d* of late Alexander Mathers; one *s* one *d. Educ:* Partick Academy; Glasgow University. Was a partner in Alexander Wood & Sons, weighing machine makers; Provost of Partick, 1898-1902; during SA War acted as Chairman to the Advisory Committee on recruiting for the Partick Division of Lanarkshire. *Address:* Woodlands, Partickhill, Glasgow. *TA:* Exprownd, Glasgow. *T:* Western Glasgow 501. *Club:* Conservative, Glasgow.
Died 19 April 1924.

WOOD, Ven. Alfred Maitland; Archdeacon of Macclesfield since 1904; Vicar of Bowdon since 1911; *b* 1840; *s* of Alfred Wood, Basinghall Street, EC; *m* Sarah (*d* 1913), *d* of W. Topham, The Limes, Tarvin, Cheshire; one *s*. *Educ:* Christ's Hospital (Times' scholar, 1859); Trinity Coll., Cambridge (BA, 31st Wrangler, 1863). Mathematical Master, Furness's Rugby, 1863–65; Curate of Tarvin, 1865–71; Wallasey, 1871–78; Vicar of St Mary's, Liscard, 1878–87; Runcorn, 1887–1911; Hon. Canon of Chester, 1890–1904; Rural Dean of Frodsham, 1891–1905; Proctor in Convocation, 1892–1904; Member of Archbishops' Committee upon Elementary Education, 1894–95; Examining Chaplain to Bishop of Chester, 1895. *Address:* The Vicarage, Bowdon. *M:* M 6257.   *Died 28 Dec. 1918.*

WOOD, Rev. Andrew, MA; Rector of Great Ponton; Prebendary of Lincoln; *b* India, 1833; *s* of Andrew and Caroline Wood; *m* 1858, Caroline Colpoys; six *s* four *d*. *Educ:* Blackheath; Trinity College, Cambridge. Assistant Master, Blackheath, 1855 and 1858–62; Curate, Droxford, Hants, 1856–58; Ruddington, Notts, 1862–66; Vicar, Skillington, Lincs, 1866–82; Diocesan Inspector of Schools, 1874–1909; Association Secretary, CMS, 1878; a VP of Midland Evangelical Association. *Publications:* The Hebrew Monarchy; Sermons to Children, and Wedding Leaflet; Promise and Performance, etc. *Recreations:* school inspection and pupil teacher examinations.   *Died 30 Sept. 1917.*

WOOD, Lt-Col David Edward, CB 1917; retired pay; Inspector of Remounts, 1903–21; *b* 22 Aug. 1853; *m*. *Educ:* Harrow; Cambridge. Entered Army, 1874; Lt-Col, 1900; served Afghanistan, 1879–80 (medal); S Africa, 1900–1 (slightly wounded, despatches, Queen's medal 4 clasps); retired, 1903. Protestant. *Address:* Kibworth, Leicester. *Clubs:* Cavalry; Kildare Street, Dublin.   *Died 29 July 1927.*

WOOD, Sir Edward, Kt 1906; JP; *b* 16 Jan. 1839; *s* of William Wood, Leicester; *m* 1862, Annie (*d* 1907), *d* of Thomas Sewell, Uppingham; three *d*. Founded firm of Freeman, Hardy, and Willis, Ltd, Boot and Shoe Manufacturers, Leicester. *Address:* Shirley Lodge, Knighton, Leicester. *Clubs:* City Liberal, National Liberal.

Died 22 Sept. 1917.

WOOD, Francis Derwent, RA 1920 (ARA 1910); sculptor; Professor of Sculpture at Royal College of Art, South Kensington, 1918–23; *b* Keswick, 15th Oct. 1871; *s* of Alpheus Bayliss Wood and Anne Mary, *d* of John Hornby Maw; *father* American, *mother* English; *m* 1903, Florence Schmidt, Australian singer; one *s*. *Educ:* Switzerland, Germany. Began his artistic career at Karlsruhe, returned to England, 1889; National Scholar under Prof. Edward Lanteri at Royal Coll. of Art, South Kensington; Assistant to Professor Alphonse Legros at Slade School for two years; Royal Academy Student, Gold Medallist and Travelling Studentship, 1895; Assistant to Thomas Brock, RA, 1894–95; exhibitor at Royal Acad. of ideal works, since 1894; Award at Paris Salon, 1897; appointed Modelling Master at Glasgow Art Schools; returned to London, where took up residence; enlisted RAMC(T), March 1915; commission, March 1916; general services—in charge of Masks for Facial Wounds Dept; Cavaliere, Order of Crown of Italy, 1911; *principal works:* Queen Victoria for Patiala, India; statue Sir Titus Salt, Saltaire; statue Rev. C. H. Spurgeon, Baptist Church House; four statues of the Arts in Glasgow Art Galleries; Chamberlain bust in the Guildhall; Pitt statue for Washington, to celebrate 100 years' peace; bust of Henry James, bought for the Tate Gallery (Chantry Bequest), 1914; also statue Atalanta; Machine Gun Corps War Memorial, Hyde Park Corner. *Address:* 27 Glebe Place, SW3; 18 Carlyle Square, SW3. *T:* Kensington 530. *Clubs:* Chelsea Arts, Garrick.

Died 19 Feb. 1926.

WOOD, Frederick Benjamin, OBE 1920; ISO 1910; *b* 1849; *s* of Thomas Wood, British Consul for Morea; *m* Mary (*d* 1926), *d* of late A. L. Crowe, British Consul, Zante; two *s* four *d*. *Educ:* abroad. Entered Consular Service, 1874; late HM's Consul for the Morea and Provinces of Etolia and Acarnania; retired from Consular Service, 1922; Gold Cross of the Redeemer, Greece. *Recreations:* shooting, yachting. *Address:* Aroe, Patras, Greece.

Died 25 Dec. 1928.

WOOD, George Arnold, MA; Professor of History in the University of Sydney since 1891; *b* Salford, 1865; *s* of G. Stanley Wood, Manchester; *m* Eleanor Madeline Whitfeld, Sydney; three *s* one *d*. *Educ:* Owens College, Manchester; Balliol College, Oxford. Brackenbury History Scholarship, 1886; Stanhope Essays, 1889. *Publications:* The Discovery of Australia, 1922; The Voyage of the Endeavour, 1926. *Address:* Sydney University.

Died 14 Oct. 1928.

WOOD, Col Henry, CB 1889; *b* 26 March 1835; *s* of R. H. Wood, Richmond, Surrey; *m* 1st, 1866, Charlotte Frances (*d* 1869), *d* of Maj.-Gen. Smith; 2nd, 1871, Helen Mary, *d* of Rev. Henry Brown; five *d*. Entered army, 1853; Colonel, 1884; served in Crimea, 1855; North-West Frontier, 1862; Afghan War, 1878–79; Expedition against Mahsood Wuzeerees, 1881 (despatches); commanded 9th Regimental District, 1887; retired, 1890. *Address:* 71 Thorpe Road, Norwich. *Club:* United Service.

Died 17 March 1919.

WOOD, Field-Marshal Sir (Henry) Evelyn, VC 1859; GCB 1891 (KCB 1879; CB 1874); GCMG 1882; DL; DCL Oxon; Constable of the Tower since 1911; *b* Cressing, Braintree, Essex, 9 Feb. 1838; *y s* of late Rev. Sir John Page Wood, 2nd Bt, and Caroline, *y d* of Admiral Sampson Michell, Croft West, Cornwall; *m* 1867, Hon. Mary Paulina Southwell (*d* 1891), *d* of Arthur Francis Southwell and *sister* of 4th Viscount Southwell. *Educ:* Marlborough Coll. Barrister Middle Temple, 1874; passed Staff Coll.; entered Navy, 1852; served in Crimea with Naval Brigade, 1 Oct. 1854 to 18 June 1855, when he was severely wounded while carrying a scaling ladder to the Redan; mentioned in Lord Raglan's despatches; medal and 2 clasps; Knight of Legion of Honour, Medjidie, Turkish medal; joined 13th Light Dragoons, 1855; served in 17th Lancers in India campaign, 1858; mentioned in despatches twice; granted Victoria Cross, December 1859; Ashantee, Kaffir, Zulu, and Transvaal Wars, 1879–81; commanded Chatham District, 1882–83; 2nd Brigade (2nd Division) Expedition to Egypt, 1882; raised the Egyptian Army, 1883; commanded Eastern District, 1886–88; Aldershot Division, 1889–93; Quartermaster-Gen. to the Forces, 1893–97; served in Nile Expedition, 1894–95; Adjutant-General to Forces, 1897–1901; 2nd Army Corps District, 1901–5. *Publications:* The Crimea in 1854 and in 1894, 1895; Cavalry in the Waterloo Campaign, 1896; Achievements of Cavalry, 1897; From Midshipman to Field Marshal, 1906; The Revolt in Hindustan, 1908; Our Fighting Services and How they Made the Empire, 1916; Winnowed Memories, 1917. *Recreations:* hunting, shooting, cycling, lawn-tennis. *Address:* Millhurst, Harlow. *T:* Harlow 35. *Clubs:* United Service, Army and Navy.

Died 2 Dec. 1919.

WOOD, Rev. Henry Thellusson, MA; Rector of Aldbury since 1890; Hon. Canon St Albans, 1904; Chaplain to Bishop of St Albans since 1913. *Educ:* St John's College, Cambridge. Curate of Baldock, 1874–77; Vicar of Great Chishall, Essex, 1877–84; Biggleswade, 1884–90; Rural Dean, Berkhampstead, 1902–22; Surrogate, 1904. *Address:* Aldbury Rectory, Tring.

Died 21 July 1928.

WOOD, Lt-Col John Bruce, DSO 1918; MC; late 4th Battalion Royal Scots; solicitor and bank agent; *b* 1886. *Educ:* Fayette Academy; Edinburgh University. Served European War with Gordon Highlanders, 1914–18 (despatches thrice, DSO, MC, Croix de Guerre). *Address:* National Bank House, Bathgate.

Died 20 Oct. 1927.

WOOD, Lt-Col John William Massey, MVO 1907; *b* 3 Sept. 1855; *s* of late John Henry Wood; *m* 1895, Ethel Maria, *d* of Capt. H. L. Webb. *Educ:* King's College, London; Caius College, Cambridge. Served in the Royal Dragoons, 1878–98; Provost Marshal and Commandant Military Police Corps, 1898; retired 1910. *Club:* Junior Constitutional.   *Died 9 Dec. 1916.*

WOOD, Rev. Joseph, MVO 1905; DD; Canon Residentiary of Rochester Cathedral since 1914, and Vice-Dean since 1914; *b* 23 Nov. 1842; *s* of John Wood, Cheadle Hulme, Cheshire; *m* 1868, Caroline S., *d* of W. S. Pryce-Hughes, Northwick Hall, Worcester. *Educ:* Balliol College, Oxford. 1st class Classical Mods; 1st class Final Classical School. Deacon, 1865; Priest, 1873; Fereday Fellow of St John's Coll., Cambridge, 1865–68; Headmaster of Leamington College, 1870–90; Headmaster Tonbridge School, 1890–98; Headmaster of Harrow School, 1898–1910; Classical Examiner at Oxford, 1876–77; collated to the Prebend of Mapesbury in St Paul's Cathedral, 1907–11. *Address:* The Precincts, Rochester.   *Died 13 July 1921.*

WOOD, Hon. Josiah; *b* 18 April 1843; *e s* of Mariner and Louisa C. Wood; *m* 1874, Laura S. Trueman; two *s* three *d*. *Educ:* Mount Allison University, Sackville, NB (MA). Merchant; Mayor of Sackville, 1903–8; Treasurer Mount Allison University Board of Regents, 1875; represented Westmorland County, New Brunswick, in Dominion House of Commons, 1882–96; Senator of the Dominion of Canada, 1896–1912; Lieut-Governor of New Brunswick, 1912–17; resigned, 1922. *Address:* Sackville, New Brunswick.

Died May 1927.

WOOD, J. S.; Co-proprietor, Chairman and Managing Director of The Gentlewoman and other newspapers; Chairman of The Press Printers, Ltd; *b* 4 Jan. 1853; *m* Elena Maria Umilta, *d* of late Torello Ambuchi of Florence; one *s* three *d*. Initiated and organised, as a voluntary worker, charitable schemes which raised nearly half a million of money for hospitals and various philanthropic institutions; Member of Council, Chelsea Hospital for Women, 1886–1920; Hon. Sec. for five years at Foundation of Bolingbroke Hospital (the first pay hospital); late Member Council, Hospitals Association; founder two political associations; founder The Children's Salon, 1890 (which endowed 11 cots in children's hospitals); founder The Society of Women Journalists, 1893; for 14 years Member of Grand Council of Primrose League; Deputy Chairman, The Royal Irish Industries Association, 1888–1916, by which means £300,000 was sent to cottage workers in Ireland; Member of Visiting Committee of King Edward's Hospital Fund. *Recreations:* shooting, golfing. *Address:* 29 Kensington Court, W8. *TA:* Jayswood, London. *T:* Western 3684 and Gerrard 9026. *Clubs:* Carlton, Cecil, Savage.

Died 20 Dec. 1920.

WOOD, Sir Lindsay, 1st Bt, *cr* 1897; JP, DL Co. Durham; High Sheriff, 1889; *b* 21 June 1834; 4th *s* of Nicholas Wood (*d* 1865) and Maria Foster Lindsay, *d* of Collingwood Foster Lindsay; *m* 1873, Emma, 4th *d* of Samuel Gooden Barrett, Heighington House, Co. Durham; three *s* two *d* (and one *s* decd). *Educ:* Royal Kepier Grammar School, Houghton-le-Spring; King's Coll., London. Made several elaborate and exhaustive experiments in respect of the pressure of gas in coal; member of the Royal Commission on Accidents in Mines, 1879–86. *Publications:* contributions to Institute of Mining Engineers, of which he was President, 1875–78. *Heir: s* Arthur Nicholas Lindsay Wood, Captain Northumberland Artillery, *b* 29 March 1875. *Address:* The Hermitage, Chester-le-Street, N Durham. *Clubs:* Carlton, Junior Carlton. *Died 22 Sept. 1920.*

WOOD, Rev. Theodore; Vicar of St Mary Magdalene, Wandsworth Common, since 1902; Hon. Canon of Southwark, 1920; Rural Dean of Wandsworth; *b* 6 Aug. 1862; *s* of Rev. J. G. Wood, MA, author of many works on natural history; *m* 1898, Helen Louisa, *e d* of late Commander E. F. Clarke, RN, of St Peter's, Kent. Deacon, 1889; Priest, 1890; Curate of Baldock, 1889–93; Curate of St Mary Magdalene, Wandsworth Common, 1893–1902. *Publications:* Our Insect Allies, 1884; Our Insect Enemies, 1885; Our Bird Allies, 1886; Nature and her Servants, 1886; The Farmer's Friends and Foes, 1887; Life and Work of the late Rev. J. G. Wood, 1890; Out-of-the-way Pets, 1896; Young People's Natural History, 1905; The Zoo, Past and Present (with A. T. Elwes), 1905; The Sea-Shore, 1907; Dwellers in the Garden, Wood, etc, 1908; Butterflies and Moths, 1909; The Second Adam (theological), 1911; Birds One Should Know, 1921. *Recreation:* collecting British beetles. *Address:* The Vicarage, Lyford Road, Wandsworth Common.

Died 13 Dec. 1923.

WOOD, Rt. Hon. Thomas McKinnon, PC 1911; DL; LLD (St Andrews); MP (L) St Rollox Division, Glasgow, 1906–18; *b* London, 26 Jan. 1855; *o s* of the late Hugh Wood and 2nd wife, Jessie, *d* of Rev. Thomas McKinnon; *m* 1883, Isabella, *d* of Alexander Sandison, JP; four *s* one *d* (and two *s* one *d* decd). *Educ:* Mill Hill School; University College, London (BA). Member LCC Central Hackney, 1892–1907; Alderman LCC, 1907; chairman, 1898–99; Chairman Parliamentary Committee, 1895–98; leader of progressive party; Parliamentary Sec. to Board of Education, 1908; Parliamentary Under-Secretary, Foreign Office, 1908–11; Financial Secretary to the Treasury, 1911–12; Secretary for Scotland, 1912–16; Chancellor to the Duchy of Lancaster and Financial Secretary to the Treasury, 1916; contested E Islington, 1895; St Rollox Div. of Glasgow, 1900; Orkney and Shetland, 1902; Hackney Central, 1922. *Publications:* articles in Ency. Brit. and reviews. *Address:* 24 Queen's Gate, SW7. *T:* Western 3016; Starfield, Crowborough. *Clubs:* Reform, National Liberal; Liberal, Glasgow; Scottish Liberal, Edinburgh.

Died 26 March 1927.

WOOD, Rev. William, DD; Rector of Rotherfield Greys, Henley, since 1901; Hon. Canon, Christ Church, Oxford; *b* 1829; *s* of A. Wood, FRCS; *m* 1862, Emma, *e d* of Col R. Moorsom, Scots Guards; five *s* three *d*. *Educ:* Trinity Coll., Oxford. Matriculated at Brasenose Coll., Oxford, 1847; elected Scholar of Trinity Coll.; Second for Hertford (University) Scholarship, 1848; 2nd class Lit. Hum., 1851; BA 1851, MA 1853; elected Fellow of Trin. Coll., 1851; Lecturer, 1852; ordained Deacon, 1852; Priest, 1853; Sub-Warden of Radley Coll., 1853–63; Perpetual Curate of Prestwood, Bucks, 1864; Warden of Radley, 1866; BD and DD 1868; Vicar of Radley, 1868; Vicar of Cropredy, 1870; Diocesan Inspector of Schools, 1877–88; Rural Dean

of Deddington, 1881–98; Rector of Monks Risborough, 1898; Examiner of Training Colleges for National Society, 1895–1906; travelled in Egypt and Palestine in 1861, and visited Ceylon in 1888. *Publications:* various papers and reviews in Cornhill Magazine, Temple Bar, Newberry House, Ludgate, 19th Century, Quarterly, etc. *Address:* Rotherfield Greys Rectory, Henley-on-Thames.

Died 28 Oct. 1919.

WOOD-MARTIN, William Gregory, JP, DL; High Sheriff, County Sligo, 1877; Aide-de-camp to late Queen Victoria, to late King Edward VII, and to King George V(Militia); Colonel Commanding the Duke of Connaught's Own Sligo Artillery, Royal Garrison Artillery, 1883–1902; *b* Woodville, Co. Sligo, 16 July 1847; *o* surv. *s* of late James Wood of Woodville and Anne, *e d* of Abraham Martin of Cleveragh, Sligo; *m* 1873, Frances Dora (*d* 1905), *e d* of Roger Dodwell Robinson of Wellmont, Co. Sligo; two *s* one *d*. *Educ:* private schools, Switzerland and Belgium; RMC Sandhurst. MRIA. Owned 7,062 acres. *Publications:* Sligo and Enniskilleners, 1880 (2nd edn 1881); History of Sligo County and Town (3 vols), 1882–92; The Lake Dwellings of Ireland, 1886; The Rude Stone Monuments of Ireland (Co. Sligo), 1888; Pagan Ireland, 1895; Traces of the Elder Faiths of Ireland, 1902; sometime editor of the Journal of the Society of Antiquaries of Ireland. *Recreations:* archæological pursuits. *Address:* Cleveragh, Sligo. *TA:* Sligo. *Club:* Army and Navy.

Died 1917.

WOOD-SEYS, Roland Alexander; novelist; *b* Stourbridge, Worcestershire, 5 Nov. 1854; *m y d* of John Hebden, The Hollies, Bolton, Lancs, and Woodlands, Siverdale, *via* Carnforth. *Educ:* privately. Abroad in 1876; literary work at home in 1884–96, reading (publishers), reviewing, and contributing to most of the leading London journals; travelling; California, olive-growing, 1903. *Publications:* The Blacksmith of Voe; Woman with a Secret; Bull i' th' Thorn; Cut with His Own Diamond; The Shepherdess of Treva; God's Lad; The Hon. Derek; The Device of the Black Fox, etc. *Recreations:* golf, shooting. *Address:* The Hermitage, Oceanside, San Diego Co., California. *Club:* Authors'.

Died Dec. 1919.

WOODALL, Sir Corbet, Kt 1913; JP; DSc; MInstCE; Governor of the Gas Light and Coke Company; President twice of Institute of Gas Engineers; Hon. Colonel 12th Battalion, County of London Regiment; *b* 1841; *m* 1865, Anne, *d* of W. H. Whiteman, Croydon; five *s* five *d*. Head of firm of Corbet Woodall and Son, civil engineers. *Address:* Walden, Chislehurst. *T:* Bromley 942; Palace Chambers, Westminster, SW. *Clubs:* Reform, National Liberal.

Died 17 May 1916.

WOODARD, Rev. Lambert, MA; Hon. Canon of Ely; *b* 26 Aug. 1848; *s* of Canon Woodard, DCL, Founder and Provost of Lancing College; *m* 1879, Emily, *d* of Henry Perkins, JP, of Thriplow Place, Cambs; three *s* three *d*. *Educ:* Lancing; Jesus College, Cambridge. Vicar of Thriplow, 1878–86; St Paul's, Bedford, 1886–1913; Heath, 1916–19; St Stephen's, Shepherd's Bush, 1919–21. *Recreations:* cricket, football, lawn tennis, bowls. *Address:* 91 Warwick Road, Thornton Heath.

Died 1 Nov. 1924.

WOODFALL, His Honour Judge Robert; Judge of County Courts Circuit 58, 1898; transferred to Westminster County Court, 1902; *b* 1855; 4th *s* of late Henry Woodfall of Stanmore; *m* 1887, Mary Helena, *d* of Lt-Col E. Galt, JP, of Southsea; one *s* one *d*. Called to the Bar, Inner Temple, 1883; Revising Barrister, 1891–97; Secretary to President, Probate Division and Admiralty Div. High Court of Justice, 1892–98. *Publication:* Law of Railway and Canal Traffic, 1889. *Address:* Nutfield, Weybridge. *Club:* Junior Carlton.

Died 6 Feb. 1920.

WOODFORD, Charles Morris, CMG 1912; *b* Gravesend, 1852; *s* of late Henry Pack Woodford; *m* 1889, Florence Margaret, *d* of late John Palmer of Bathurst, NSW; two *s* (second son, Harold Vivian, 2nd Lieut 8th Royal Berkshire Regt, killed in France, 13 Oct. 1915). *Educ:* Tonbridge School. Travelled and explored in Western Pacific, particularly in Solomon Islands, 1882–89; Acting Consul and Deputy Commissioner at Samoa, 1895; Resident Commissioner, British Solomon Islands, 1896–1914; Fellow of Royal Geographical Society, and was awarded the Gill Memorial in 1890 for travels and exploration in Solomon Islands; Fellow of Royal Anthropological Institute; member of Hakluyt Society; Member of British Ornithologists' Union. *Publications:* Naturalist among the Head Hunters; various papers in Geographical Journal, and Journal of Royal Anthropological Institute. *Address:* Bramley, Steyning, Sussex.

Died 4 Oct. 1927.

WOODGATE, Walter Bradford, (Wat Bradford); barrister, journalist, oarsman; *b* 20 Sept. 1840; *e s* of late Canon Henry Arthur Woodgate, Rector of Belbroughton (Bampton Lecturer, 1838), and Maria Bradford. *Educ:* Radley; Brasenose College, Oxford. Rowed first race, Radley *v* Eton, 1858; amateur (aquatic) champion, 1862, *et sequens;* Oxford (winning) Eight, 1862 and 1863; won university pairs three times, sculls twice; Henley Regatta, won Grand Stewards' Cup, 1862, Grand Challenge Cup, 1865, Diamond Sculls, 1864, Goblets, 1861, 1862, 1863, 1866 and 1868, Wingfield Sculls, 1862, 1864 and 1867. *Publications:* Oars and Sculls, and how to use them, 1875; (Badminton Library) Boating; A Modern Layman's Faith, 1893; Reminiscences of an Old Sportsman, 1909; (as Wat Bradford) novels, including O.V.H.; Ensemble; Tandem. *Recreations:* aquatics, hunting, shooting. *Address:* Clovelly, Henley-on-Thames. *Clubs:* Isthmian; Leander (Henley-on-Thames).

Died 1 Nov. 1920.

WOODHEAD, Sir German Sims, KBE 1919; MD Edinburgh; FRCPE, FRSE; Fellow of Trinity Hall, Cambridge; Professor of Pathology, Cambridge University, since 1899; *b* Woodland Mount, Huddersfield, 29 April 1855; *e s* of late Joseph Woodhead (editor Huddersfield Examiner, formerly MP for Spen Valley), and Catherine, *e d* of James Booth Woodhead, The Ridings, Holmfirth; *m* 1881, Harriett Elizabeth St Clair Erskine, 2nd *d* of James Yates, Edinburgh. *Educ:* Huddersfield Coll.; Edin. Univ.; Berlin and Vienna. Superintendent of the Laboratory of the Royal Coll. of Physicians, Edinburgh, 1887–90; Director of the Laboratories of the Conjoint Board of the Royal Colleges of Physicians (London) and Surgeons (England); President of the Royal Microscopical Society, 1890–99; President Royal Medical Society, 1878; Assist Comr to the Royal Commission on Tuberculosis, 1892–95; Member of the Royal Commission on Tuberculosis, 1902; Member of Executive Committee Imperial Cancer Research Fund; Member Scottish Universities Committee (Treasury); Hon. Fellow Henry Phipp's Inst., Philadelphia, 1902; Hon. Fellow Institute of Sanitary Engineers; Captain VMSC, 1886; Major 1902; Lt-Col RAMC (T); Bt Col AMS, 1917; Inspector of Labs in Mil. Hosps in UK; formerly: Adviser in Pathology (UK) to War Office; MO i/c Irish Command Depot, Tipperary (twice mentioned for special war services). *Publications:* Practical Pathology, 1883; Pathological Mycology (with Arthur W. Hare, MB), 1885; Bacteria and their Products, 1891; Report to the Royal Commission on Tuberculosis, 1895; Report on Diphtheria to the Metropolitan Asylums Board; Village Settlements for the Tuberculous (with P. C. Jones Varrier); contributions to medical journals; formerly editor of the Journal of Pathology and Bacteriology. *Recreations:* golf; for many years President of the Edinburgh University Athletic Club; Pres. British Medical Temperance Association and President British Temperance League. *Address:* Dysart House, Luard Road, Cambridge. *T:* 174 and 639. *Clubs:* Athenæum, Savage, National Liberal.   *Died 29 Dec. 1921.*

WOODHOUSE, Sir Stewart, Kt 1908; MD (Dublin); Medical Member of General Prisons Board (Ireland), 1890, retired; *b* 25 Feb. 1846; *s* of late George Woodhouse of Dublin (retired Bank Manager) and Margaret, *d* of John Cochrane of Londonderry; *m* 1879, Charlotte, 4th *d* of Isaac Corry, DL, of Newry, Co. Down; one *d. Educ:* Royal School, Dungannon; Trinity College, Dublin. Classical Scholar and first Senior Moderator in Ethics and Logic in University of Dublin; became Lecturer on Pathology to Carmichael School of Medicine, and Assistant Physician to House of Industry Hospitals, Dublin; a Local Government Board Inspector, 1880; Member of Vice-Regal Commission on Irish Milk Supply, 1911. *Publications:* Hints on Improvement of the Working Man's Life, etc; various reviews, official reports, etc. *Address:* 67 Ailesbury Road, Dublin. *Clubs:* University, Dublin; Royal St George Yacht, Kingstown.

Died 2 Nov. 1921.

WOODLAND, Col Arthur Law, CB 1900; Commanded an Infantry Regimental District to 1905; Officer in charge of Records, Newcastle, 1905–6; *b* 24 June 1849; *s* of Richard Reynolds Woodland. Served South Africa, 1899–1900; action at Colenso; operations Vaal Krantz, Tugela, Pieters Hill, and in Transvaal; relief of Ladysmith (despatches thrice, Queen's medal, 4 clasps, CB). *Address:* 59 Eaton Terrace, Eaton Square, SW. *Club:* Naval and Military.

Died 26 May 1921.

WOODS, Henry, RA 1893 (ARA 1882); *b* Warrington, 22 April 1846; *e s* of late William Woods of that town; *s* of George Woods. *Educ:* The Grammar School, Warrington. Began art education in the School of Art, Warrington; afterwards at South Kensington. Worked afterwards for illustrated periodicals; one of original members of the Graphic staff; exhibited pictures at Royal Academy for the first

exhibition at Burlington House; worked principally in Venice since 1876; Member of College of Academicians, Royal Academy, Venice, 1908. *Address:* Calcina, Zattere, Venice, Italy. *Clubs:* Athenæum, Arts.

Died 27 Oct. 1921.

WOODS, Hon. Henry John Bacon; Postmaster-General of Newfoundland since 1902; *b* 20 Oct. 1842; *s* of John Woods and Anne Lang; *m* 1870, Hannie L., *d* of late John Bemister, Sheriff of Newfoundland; seven *d. Educ:* General Protestant Academy, St John's, Newfoundland. Entered his father's office, and in 1880 became partner under the firm of John Woods and Son, shipowners; elected Liberal for Bay de Verde district and appointed a member of Cabinet with the portfolio of Surveyor-General, 1889; re-elected and took a seat in the Cabinet without portfolio, 1899; resigned 1902; title of Honourable, 1902; was identified with the educational interests of Newfoundland for many years; President Newfoundland Auxiliary British and Foreign Bible Society. *Address:* St John's, Newfoundland.

Died Aug. 1916.

WOODS, Joseph Andrews; Member of Senate, Northern Ireland, 1921; Secretary National Health Insurance Society, Belfast. *Address:* 161 Templemore Avenue, Belfast.

Died 6 Oct. 1925.

WOODS, Matthew Snooke Grosvenor, KC; Bencher of Lincoln's Inn; *b* 14 March 1838; *o s* of Matthew Snooke, Chichester, and Elizabeth, *d* of Francis Smith, MD, Maidstone; adopted name of Woods in 1863, in compliance with directions in father's will; *m* 1877, Mary Amabel (*d* 1915), *d* of John Vincent Thompson, Serjeant-at-Law. *Educ:* Prebendal School, Chichester; Trinity College, Cambridge (Fellow, 1860. Assistant tutor for three years, Trinity Coll., Cambridge. Barrister (Chancery Bar), 1865; QC 1894.

Died 5 April 1925.

WOODS, Percy, CB 1902; *b* 5 July 1842; *s* of late Charles John Woods, Godalming; *m* 1881, Helen Maria (*d* 1888), *d* of late Rev. R. Trimmer; two *d. Educ:* Cheltenham. Entered Admiralty, 1863; transferred to Treasury, 1880; retired, 1902.

Died 7 April 1922.

WOODS, Richard Lennox, ISO 1903; retired Civil Servant; *b* 1838; *s* of late William Whitfield Woods, late of Colonial Office; *m* Emily (*d* 1910), *e d* of J. B. Ellis. *Educ:* Dublin. In the Exchequer and Audit Department, 1857–1903; late Captain Civil Service Volunteers. *Address:* Grove House, Falmouth.

Died 10 June 1918.

WOODVILLE, Richard Caton; artist (battle-painter); *b* Stanhope Gardens, London, 7 Jan. 1856; father, artist, was born in Baltimore and died in London; English extraction. *Educ:* Düsseldorf, Germany. Went through Turkish War, 1878; Egyptian War, 1882; as well as minor warlike operations in Albania and the East generally; Grand Cross of the Red Cross of Spain; Commander of the Medjidie of Turkey; the Daniello of Montenegro; and the Academy Palms of France; exhibited first picture Royal Academy, 1879, and afterwards annually; painted several large pictures in Windsor Castle for Queen Victoria: Wedding at Whippingham Church, Death of Gen. Sir Herbert Stewart, The Guards at Tel-el-Kebir. *Publications:* Random Recollections, 1913; magazine articles on sport and travel. *Recreations:* shooting, big-game hunting, travel. *Address:* Dudley Mansions, 29B Abbey Road, NW8. *T:* Maida Vale 3840. *Club:* Junior Army and Navy.   *Died 17 Aug. 1927.*

WOODWARD, Col Francis Willoughby, DSO 1900; late 1st Loyal Regiment (North Lancashire); *b* Bombay, 5 Dec. 1872; *s* of Willoughby Woodward, late ICS. *Educ:* Shrewsbury School; RMC, Sandhurst. Entered Army, 1893; Lieut, 1896; Capt. 1901; served South Africa, 1899–1902 (despatches twice, SA medal 3 clasps); defence of Kimberley, Orange Free State, Transvaal (King's medal, 1901 and 1902; clasps); Adjutant, 1st Loyal North Lancashire Regiment, 1901–4; served Egyptian Army, 1906–16 (3rd class Mejidieh, 3rd class Order of the Nile); European War (Bt Lt-Col, Croix de Guerre and Croce di Guerra; Officer of St Maurice and St Lazarus); Col, 1924; retired on retired pay, 1924. *Club:* United Service.   *Died 27 Dec. 1926.*

WOODWARD, Henry, LLD; FRS, FGS; President Palæontographica-Society since 1896; Geological Society, 1894–96; Past-President of the Royal Microscopical Society; *b* Norwich, 24 Nov. 1832; *y s* of Samuel Woodward, Norwich, antiquary and geologist; *m* Ellen Sophia (*d* 1913), *o d* of Fountain Page, Norwich; five *d. Educ:* Norwich Grammar School; Rev. George Haddock's,

Botesdale, Suffolk; Royal Agric. College, Cirencester. Entered bank, Norwich, 1850–57; British Museum, 1858; Keeper of Geology, 1880–1901; Pres. Geologists' Assoc., 1873–74; Murchison medallist, 1884; Wollaston medallist, 1906; Pres. Geological Section British Assoc., 1887; Pres. and Founder Malacological Soc., 1893–95; Pres. Museums Association, 1900; editor of the Geological Magazine, a monthly journal of geology and palæontology, since 1864. *Publications:* 300 contributions to scientific journals; a monograph on the Merostomata, 1866–78; on Carboniferous Trilobites, 1883–84; article Crustacea, Ency. Brit. (9th edn vol. vi, 1877); articles Mollusca and Crustacea (Cassell's Nat. Hist.); numerous addresses and lectures. *Address:* Tudor Cottage, Clay Hill, Bushey, Herts.

Died 6 Sept. 1921.

WOODWARD, Col John Henry, CB 1911; VD; Treasurer Society of Merchant Venturers, Bristol; *b* 10 Aug. 1849; 4th *s* of George Rocke and Ellen Woodward, of Clifton, Bristol; *m* 1876, Mary Alice Hamilton, 2nd *d* of Admiral and Mrs Thomas Fisher, of Clifton, Bristol; one *s* four *d. Educ:* Windermere College, Westmorland. Enrolled in Bristol Rifle Volunteer Corps, 1869; commanded 4th Batt. Gloucestershire Regiment, 1905–11; Master of the Society of Merchant Venturers, Bristol, 1886; JP Bristol, 1894; Director of Bristol Wagon Works Co., Limited; Director Bristol and South Wales Building Society and Portishead Gas Co., Ltd. *Address:* Upton Lea, Bitton, N Bristol. *Club:* Constitutional, Bristol.

Died 18 May 1918.

WOODWARD, Sir Lionel Mabbott, Kt 1922; Chief Justice Federated Malay States since 1921; *b* 9 Sept. 1864; *s* of Lionel Mabbott Woodward, of Harrow; *m* 1897, Kathleen Tarifa (marr. diss. 1912), *d* of Col Frederick Fitzroy Gibbons, late of Devonshire Regt; three *s. Educ:* Harrow; Trinity College, Cambridge. BA 1st Class Honours Classical Tripos, 1886; MA 1892. Called to the Bar, Inner Temple, 1897; Cadet Straits Settlements, 1888; Magistrate and JP Singapore, 1890; Sheriff and Deputy Registrar Supreme Court, 1896; Magistrate and JP Penang, 1898; Assistant Registrar Supreme Court, 1902; Deputy Public Prosecutor, 1904; Judicial Commissioner, Federated Malay States, 1906; Senior Puisne Judge Straits Settlements, 1915, acting Chief Justice, 1914–15 and 1919. *Recreations:* tennis, golf, riding. *Address:* Kwala Lumpor, Federated Malay States. *TA:* Kwala Lumpor. *Club:* Constitutional.

Died 5 Sept. 1925.

WOODWARD, Robert Simpson; ex-President of the Carnegie Institution of Washington, Washington, DC; *b* Rochester, Michigan, 1849; of New England ancestry; *m* 1876, Martha Gretton Bond; three *s. Educ:* Rochester Academy; Univ. of Michigan (CE 1872; PhD 1892). Assistant engineer, US Lake Survey, 1871–82; astronomer, US Transit Venus Commission, 1882–84; astronomer, US Geological Survey, 1884–90; assistant, US Coast and Geodetic Survey, 1890–93; Professor of Mechanics and Mathematical Physics, Columbia Univ., 1893–1905; Dean School Pure Science, Columbia Univ., 1895–1905; Hon. LLD Wisconsin, 1904; Michigan, 1912; Johns Hopkins, 1915; Hon. ScD Pennsylvania, and Columbia, 1905. *Publications:* Administrative Reports in Year-Books of Carnegie Institution of Washington, 1905–20; editor (with Mansfield Merriman) of Mathematical Monographs; numerous papers and addresses on subjects in astronomy, geodesy, mathematics, mechanics, and geophysics. *Recreations:* boating, motoring, farming. *Address:* Carnegie Institution of Washington, Washington, DC. *Clubs:* Century Association, New York; Cosmos, Washington.

Died 29 June 1924.

WOOLDRIDGE, Harry Ellis, MA (Trinity College, Oxford); Slade Professor of Fine Art, Oxford University, 1895–1904; *b* 28 March 1845; *m* 1894, Julia Mary, *d* of late Stephen Olding. *Educ:* privately. Student of the Royal Academy, 1865, and about the same time commenced the study of music, chiefly antiquarian; *principal artistic works:* large reredos in the Church of St Martin, Brighton, and frescoes in parish Church of St John, Hampstead; *principal works on music:* new edition of Chappell's Popular Music of the Olden Time with new title—Old English Popular Music, 1893; The Polyphonic Period, Parts I and II (vols I and II of the Oxford History of Music); (ed with Robert Bridges) The Yattendon Hymnal, 1895–99. *Address:* 90 Oakwood Court, Kensington, W. *Club:* Savile.

Died 13 Feb. 1917.

WOOLLEN, James; journalist and editor; *b* Westminster, 3 March 1854; 3rd *s* of Frederick Woollen of NW Somerset, and Damaris, *e d* of John Booth of North Lincolnshire; *m* 1879, Alice Eugenie (*d* 1915), *y d* of Thomas Carpenter, Westminster; one *s. Educ:* St Michael's Schools, Chester Square, SW; privately. Was for three and a half years in Civil Service (Inland Revenue); became a clerk in

weekly newspaper office, and, taking interest in journalism generally, contributed constantly to various publications; becoming early in life associated with some of the earliest temperance reformers and many leading politicians, took prominent part in temperance and political movements from 1874; was Hon. Sec. of Labour Representation Union, founded 1884, and of the Gladstone Election Fund (1886) at National Liberal Club, and acted as Hon. Election Agent for several candidates returned to Parliament and to the LCC; contested LCC in 1888; City of Perth (Advanced Radical), 1892; was one of the originators and founders of the Burlington Magazine (1903); edited Metropolitan Temperance Advocate, Lady's Gazette, etc, etc, and the Crown, the Court, and County Families newspaper, 1906–8; Vanity Fair, Favourite Home Journal, Glass Section Pottery and Glass Record, etc. *Publications:* contributed extensively to periodical literature on political, social, and art subjects. *Recreations:* gardening, walking, cycling, collecting.

Died Nov. 1921.

WOOLLEY, Charles, FRGS; *b* 30 Nov. 1846; *s* of late Nathaniel Woolley of Ecton, Northamptonshire, and Piccadilly, W; *m* Elizabeth, 2nd *d* of late Henry Bone of 5 Pall Mall East, and Clapham, SW; one *s* two *d. Educ:* privately; King's Coll., London. Sec. National Discount Company, Ltd, 1890–1910; Director Consolidated Electrical Company, Ltd, and Anglo-Portuguese Telephone Company, Ltd; Fellow Incorporated Society of Accountants and Auditors, and Institute of Bankers; past President and Fellow Chartered Institute of Secretaries; Fellow Chartered Institute of Directors; an expert in Company Law Procedure, and appeared before Select Committee of House of Lords to give evidence in respect of Company Law Amendment, in connection with Lord Dudley's Bill, which came into operation 1 Jan. 1901; a patentee of pneumatic tyres for cycles and vehicles; Member London Press Club, and Chartered Institute of Journalists; Conservative. *Publications:* Phases of Panics; A Cruise round the British Isles; A Voyage to Viking Land; a contributor to the Press and to magazines. *Recreations:* fond of sport and art, being a book collector and numismatologist. *Address:* Verulam, Dulwich Road, Herne Hill, SE. *Club:* Savage.

Died 5 Aug. 1922.

WOOLLEY, Samuel Walter, FCS; Editor of The Chemist and Druggist, 1917–27; *b* Stamford, Lincs, 1865; unmarried. *Educ:* Stamford Grammar School. Pharmaceutical chemist, 1887; Assistant Editor of The Chemist and Druggist, 1898; Fellow of the Spectacle-makers Company; Corresponding Member of the Société Royale de Pharmacie de Bruxelles. *Publications:* The Chemist-Optician; Pharmaceutical Formulas, etc. *Recreations:* archæology, photography. *Address:* Tresham Lodge, Barnack, Stamford. *Club:* National Liberal.

Died 25 Nov. 1927.

WOOLRYCH, H. R., MA; Headmaster, Blackheath School, 1895–1905; *b* 1858; *s* of Rev. W. H. Woolrych, Vicar of Crowle, Worcester; *m* 1885, Elizabeth Beatrice, *d* of George Owen of Copenhagen; five *s* two *d. Educ:* Rossall School; Pembroke Coll., Oxford (Classical Scholar). 1st Class Moderations, 1879; 2nd Class Lit.Hum., 1882; BA 1882; MA 1884. Asst Master, Rossall School, 1883–84; 2nd Master, Blackheath School, 1884–94. *Publication:* Ovid's Tristia, Book iii. *Recreations:* tennis, golf. *Address:* 31 Redcliffe Gardens, SW. *T:* Western 2076.

Died 30 Aug. 1917.

WOOLS-SAMPSON, Col Sir Aubrey, KCB 1902 (CB 1900); MP Braamfontein; partner in Wools-Sampson and Mullins, financial and estate agents. Founded Imperial Light Horse; Hon. Col in Army; served S Africa, 1899–1902 (severely wounded, despatches four times, Queen's medal 4 clasps, King's medal 2 clasps, KCB). *Address:* Cape Town.

Died May 1924.

WOOLSTON, Thomas Henry, CBE 1918; DL; JP; *b* 10 March 1855; *s* of late Samuel Hames Woolston, Wellingborough; *m* 1910, Florence Katherine, *d* of William Moxon, JP, MRCS, Northampton. *Educ:* St Paul's, Stony Stratford. Knight of Grace of Order of St John of Jerusalem in England; was County Controller Voluntary Aid Detachments, Northamptonshire, and County Director Northants Auxiliary Hospitals and Voluntary Aid Detachments during War, 1914–19; Member of Northamptonshire Territorial Army Association; Member of Board of Management and Vice-Chairman of Finance Committee of the Northampton General Hospital; Member of Board of Management and Chairman of House Committee, Manfield Orthopædic Hospital, Northampton; Chairman of the Northampton and County Crippled Children's Fund; Commissioner (Reserve) St John's Ambulance Brigade. *Address:* 53 East Park Parade, Northampton; The White Cottage, Caister-on-Sea, Norfolk. *T:* Northampton 794.

Died 19 March 1927.

WOOTTEN, Aubrey Francis Wootten, OBE 1921; KC 1921; *b* Headington House, Oxford, 19 Sept. 1866; *s* of William Wootten Wootten, banker, Oxford, and Sarah Wootten Wootten; *m* 1893, Gertrude, 2nd *d* of D. Tremewen, solicitor, Falmouth; one *s* two *d. Educ:* Rugby; Oriel College, Oxford. Captain of School XV and shooting VIII, Rugby; BA Oxford, 2nd Class Honours Jurisprudence, 1889. Called to the Bar, Inner Temple, 1892; Chief Inspector V Division, Special Constabulary, 1914–19; Assistant Commander, 1920; Medal of OBE for Police Work during war, 1921; Chairman Epsom Division Constitutional Association, 1921. *Recreations:* horticulture, bowls. *Address:* 1 Temple Gardens, Temple, EC4. *T:* Central 851; Sunningdale, Downs Road, Epsom. *TA:* Aubrey Wootten, Epsom. *T:* Epsom 576. *Clubs:* New University, Royal Automobile; Surrey County Cricket.

Died 4 Aug. 1923.

WORDINGHAM, Charles Henry, CBE 1918; consulting engineer; engaged in advising on large electric power supply schemes for London, East Midlands and elsewhere, and electrical work generally; *b* Twickenham, Middlesex, 1866; *s* of William Hales Wordingham and Madeline West; *m* 1912, Emily Anne, *e d* of late Charles John West, JP, of Goodwood, Maryborough, Queensland; one *s* four *d. Educ:* King's Coll. School, London; King's College, London. Articled to Dr John Hopkinson, FRS, as civil engineer, 1885–87; United Telephone Co., 1887–89; on engineering staff of the London Electric Supply Corporation, 1889–92; Assistant to Dr J. Hopkinson, 1892–94; City Electrical Engineer to Manchester Corporation, 1894–1901; consulting engineer, advising numerous local authorities and private clients on electrical questions, giving Parliamentary and law court evidence, and acting generally as electrical expert, 1901–3; Director of Electrical Engineering, Admiralty, responsible for the entire electrical equipment of all HM ships and for advising on electric light and power questions in HM dockyards and shore establishments, 1903–18; Member of Institution of Civil Engineers, Institution of Mechanical Engineers, and Institution of Electrical Engineers (Past President of the Institution and Past Chairman of Manchester Section); FSA; Associate of Institution of Naval Architects; Past President and Hon. Member Incorporated Municipal Electrical Association; Past President of Junior Institution of Engineers; President of Illuminating Society; Fellow of King's College, London, 1912, and Member of Council and of Delegacy; Membre de la Société des Ingénieurs Civils de France; Member of Main and Chairman of Electrical Sectional Committee of the British Engineering Standards Association; one of the British representatives on the International Electro-technical Commission; President and Past Chairman of the British Electrical and Allied Industries Research Association, and one of the founders of the Electrical Development Association and of the Society of Radiographers. *Publications:* Central Electrical Stations; numerous papers on engineering subjects presented to engineering institutions of which a member; also articles and reviews in technical journals. *Recreations:* photography, cycling, travelling abroad. *Address:* 7 Victoria Street, Westminster, SW1. *T:* Victoria 7292; 33 Brazennose Street, Manchester. *T:* Central 828; Beechgrove, Ridgeway Road, Redhill, Surrey. *T:* Redhill 453. *TA:* Outguards, Sowest London, and Outguards Manchester. *Clubs:* St Stephen's, Engineers'; Engineers', Old Rectory, Manchester. *Died 28 Jan. 1925.*

WORDSWORTH, William, CIE 1887; *b* 1835; *s* of late Rev. J. Wordsworth; *m* 1st, 1862, Mary Emma (*d* 1898), *d* of late Morris Reynolds, Ambleside; 2nd, 1900, Maria Schonnard (*d* 1903), *e d* of late Gen. W. Hayes, US Army, and *widow* of Lieut-Col J. H. Bille, US Army Medical Corps. Entered ICS, 1861; was Principal of Elphinstone College, Bombay; retired, 1890. *Address:* Villa Wordsworth, Capri. *Died 7 March 1917.*

WORKMAN, Fanny Bullock, FRGS, FRSGS; authoress and lecturer; *b* Worcester, Mass, 8 Jan. 1859; *d* of ex-Governor Bullock of Massachusetts; *m* Dr William Hunter Workman; one *d. Educ:* New York and Germany. Travelled extensively in Spain, North Africa, Palestine, Asia Minor, Egypt, Greece, India, Ceylon, Java, Sumatra, and Cochin China; in 1899 made three first record ascents for women in the Karakoram Mountains, the highest of which was Mount Koser Gunge, 21,000 feet; explored Choge Lungma glacier, Baltistan, 1902; made another expedition to Himalayas, 1903; made two first ascents of 21,500 feet and 22,568 feet; made expedition to Himalayas, 1906; climbed one of Nun Kun peaks, 23,300 feet—a first ascent, which gave her the world record for mountaineering for women; explored and surveyed Hispar glacier and branches, 1908; first ascent of Biafo Watershed Peak, 21,350 ft; crossed Hispar Pass and descended Biafo glacier to Baltistan; in 1911, explored and mapped seven glaciers of the Hushe and Kondus systems, Karakoram, and made first ascent of peak 21,000 feet; 1912, explored and surveyed 50 mile long Siachen glacier and affluents; made seven new ascents of peaks and cols of from 19,000 to over 21,000 feet; discovered the water-parting between the Indus and Chinese-Turkestan regions; lectured before geographical and scientific societies and Alpine clubs in America, Scotland, France, Germany, and Italy; Member Royal Asiatic Society; Corres. Member Amer. Geographical Society; Hon. Member American Alpine Club; Officier de l'Instruction Publique, 1904. *Publications:* (all with her husband) Two Summers in the Ice-Wilds of Eastern Karakoram, 1917; The Call of the Snowy Hispar; Peaks and Glaciers of Nun Kun; Ice-Bound Heights of The Mustagh; Through Town and Jungle; In the Ice World of Himalaya; Algerian Memories; Sketches Awheel in Fin de Siècle; Iberia; contributor to magazines and papers. *Recreations:* mountaineering, cycling. *Address:* c/o The American Express Company, 6 Haymarket, SW1. *Clubs:* Lyceum French, German-Austrian, Italian Alpine, Appalachian.

Died 22 Jan. 1925.

WORKMAN, Walter Percy, MA, BSc; Headmaster of Kingswood School, Bath, since 1889; *b* Peckham, SE, 2 Nov. 1863; *s* of Rev. John-Sansom Workman, Wesleyan minister; *m* 1897, Amelia, *d* of Rev. Edward Workman; one *d. Educ:* Kingswood School, Bath; Trin. Coll., Cambridge (MA). Second Wrangler in Math. Tripos, 1884; 1st Smith's prizeman, 1886. Fellow of Trin. Coll., Cambridge, 1887; Assistant Master, Leys School, 1888. *Publications:* History of Kingswood School, 1898; Tutorial Arithmetic, 1902; Geometry, Theoretical and Practical, 1905; Register of Kingswood School, 1910; Memoranda Mathematica, 1912; Kingswood Sermons, 1917. *Recreations:* golf, motoring. *Address:* Kingswood School, Bath. *TA:* Kingswood, Bath. *T:* Bath 440.

Died Sept. 1918.

WORLLEDGE, Rev. Arthur John,, MA; Canon and Chancellor of Truro Cathedral; Principal of Divinity School, 1887–1901; Acting Treasurer of Cathedral since 1904; *b* London, 29 May 1848; *e s* of late John Worlledge, Judge of the County Courts (Circuit 33), and Mary, *d* of Rev. J. D. Wastell, Risby, Bury St Edmunds; unmarried. *Educ:* Queen Elizabeth's Grammar School, Ipswich; Caius Coll., Cambridge (Scholar). 2nd class Classical Tripos; 1st class Theol. Hons.; Carus Greek Testament prizeman. Curate of St Andrew's, Enfield, 1872–76; Prebendary in Lincoln Cathedral, 1878–87; tutor in the Schol. Cancell. Lincoln, 1876–83; principal of the Leeds Clergy School, and lecturer in Leeds Parish Church, 1883–87; Proctor in Convocation for Truro Chapter since 1892; examining chaplain to Bishop Wilkinson, Truro, 1890; to Bishop Gott, 1891; Bishop Stubbs, 1906; Bishop Burrows, 1912; select preacher at Cambridge, 1879, 1885, 1892, 1899, 1900, 1906, and 1909; Commissary to Bishop of Brisbane, 1885–1903, to Bishop of Natal, 1901–15; Hon. Sec. Conferences on Training of Candidates for Holy Orders, 1881–1912; Member Central Advisory Council of Training for the Ministry, 1918; Editor Truro Diocesan Magazine, since 1904. *Publications:* vol. on Prayer (Oxford Library of Practical Theology); section on Romanism, Dissent, and Unbelief, in SPCK Manual of Parochial Work; edited sermons preached at the Benediction of the Nave of Truro Cathedral; Editor (assistant) The Letters of Bishop Gott. *Recreations:* study of architecture (specially ecclesiastical), antiquities. *Address:* 4 Strangways Terrace, Truro, Cornwall. *Died 20 Feb. 1919.*

WORRELL, John Austin, KC; DCL; barrister and solicitor; head of firm of Worrell, Gwynne & Beatty; *b* Smith's Falls, Ont, 1852; *s* of Rev. Canon Worrell, late Rector of Oakville, Ont. *Educ:* Smith's Falls Grammar School; Trinity College School, Weston; Rev. W. Stennett's Private School, Keswick; Trinity University, Toronto. BA and Prince of Wales Prizeman and Wellington Scholar, 1871; MA 1875; BCL 1880; DCL (*hc*) 1898. Called to the Bar, 1878; QC 1889; President of York Law Association, 1895; Solicitor to Bank of Montreal, etc; Member of Church of England; Delegate Assessor to Prolocutor and formerly Lay Secretary of General Synod of Canada; Hon. Treasurer, Missionary Society, Church of England, in Canada Chancellor of Diocese of Toronto, 1897; member of Corporation of Trinity University, Toronto, of Council of St Hilda's College, and of Governing Body of Trinity College School, Port Hope; Member of Senate of University of Toronto; Chancellor, Trinity University, 1914; Liberal Conservative; President of Young Men's Liberal-Conservative Association of Toronto and of Ontario; member of British Empire League and formerly Secretary of Imperial Federation League of Canada. *Address:* 39 Prince Arthur Avenue, Toronto. *T:* Kingsdale 3347. *Clubs:* Toronto, University, Toronto.

Died 27 Feb. 1927.

WORSLEY, Rev. Edward, MA; Hon. Canon of Peterborough, 1913; *b* 4 Jan. 1844; *s* of late Rev. Charles Worsley, MA; *m* 1880, Ethel Adela, *d* of late Edward Knight, of Chawton House, Alton, Hants;